THE EERDMANS ANALYTICAL CONCORDANCE

to the

REVISED STANDARD VERSION OF THE BIBLE

compiled by

Richard E. Whitaker

Project Director and Programmer

with

James E. Goehring

Data Entry Supervisor

and Research Personnel of the

Institute for Antiquity and Christianity

Claremont Graduate School

Claremont, California

WILLIAM B. EERDMANS PUBLISHING COMPANY

GRAND RAPIDS, MICHIGAN

255 Jefferson Ave. S.E., Grand Rapids, MI 49503

Printed in the United States of America

Printed and Bound at Eerdmans Printing Company, Grand Rapids

TABLE OF CONTENTS

PREFACE

The concept for the present volume originated with Dr. Edgar W. Smith, Senior Editor at Eerdmans Publishing Company. In 1981 he asked the compiler to do a feasibility study on creating an analytical concordance of the Revised Standard Version of the Bible with the assistance of the computer. It was estimated that it would take around eighteen months to enter the RSV text and align the English words with the Greek, Latin, and Hebrew words being translated. Beyond that, the forms would need to be parsed to arrive at a "dictionary" form for each of the words in each of the languages. No estimate was made of the time that this task would take. Eerdmans then asked the compiler to head up a project to produce such a concordance, relying heavily on students at the Claremont Graduate School to do the actual alignment.

The creation of the Concordance, while depending heavily on the computer, involved a large number of people at many stages. The original alignment and checking was done, with computer assistance, by Arvel Eicher, Peter Pettit, William Yarkin, Henry Sun, and Lief Vaage on the Ibycus system at the Institute for Antiquity and Christianity in Claremont, California. The on-site director of that portion of the project was Dr. James E. Goehring, then on the staff of the IAC. Proofreading and checking of the English context was done by Sara Meyer, Tami Van Voorst, Deborah Sonner, and Ellen Stolzfuss, students at Central College in Pella, Iowa.

Those doing original alignment simply marked problem words in order to save time. Later the problem words were checked, using research tools, by Henry Sun and Peter Pettit, along with Dr. Thomas Boogaard and Dr. Philip McMillian of Central College, on the Hebrew, and Dr. Goehring and Lief Vaage on the Greek and Latin.

Because other projects to parse the RSV and the biblical text in the various languages were not yet completed, this project used a partially parsed text of the Hebrew Bible and the Greek of the Apocrphya to get the dictionary forms for the texts. Dr. David Timmer of Central College and Michael Davis, a graduate student at Princeton Theological Seminary, carried the major load in correcting the Hebrew, and Dr. Chad Ray of Central worked with the Greek of the Apocrypha. Using the Apocrypha as a base, Clayton Jefford of the IAC helped to produce a parsing of the Greek of the New Testament. The compiler produced the parsing for the English and Latin.

One of the major problems for the project was to obtain electronic texts. The Greek texts were secured from the Thesaurus Linguae Graecae Project at the University of California in Irvine, with the New Testament text being checked against the partially parsed text of Timothy Frieberg. The Latin text was supplied by Bonifatius Fischer in Bonn, Germany. The Hebrew text used was the Michigan –Claremont text produced under a grant from the David and Lucille Packard Foundation. The RSV text was entered by the project workers in Claremont.

The project is indebted to CATTS personnel at the University of Pennsylvania for the parsing of the Apocrypha. Dr. Robert Kraft, the director, was kind enough to allow the project to use their parsed Apocrypha even though it was not yet at a stage for public release. They also gave partial financial support for the compiler's writing of software to parse the Hebrew. Though the parsing of the Frieberg text of the New Testament was done for other purposes and did not include everything the project needed, it was helpful in the work on the New Testament.

When the first pages of the final concordance had been produced, Dr. Robert Funk of Polebridge Press, Dr. Loren Mack-Fisher, and Dr. Smith at Eerdmans did a final check and offered many helpful corrections and suggestions. Needless to say, the compiler has been involved in checking and correction at every stage and remains responsible for whatever errors may remain. Since the volume has over 400,000 entries, realism says that even after repeated checks, not all errors have been found. We trust that those remaining are few enough that they will not detract from the usefulness of the volume.

The typesetting of this volume was done on an Ibycus system at Polebridge Press in Sonoma, California. The patience and assistance of Charlene Matejovsky, the production manager, has been much appreciated.

While it was clear from the beginning that the time required for the final stages of the project was uncertain because of the lack of parsed texts, the project has taken far longer than anyone had anticipated. The encouragement and understanding of Dr. Smith of Eerdmans has been very welcome.

INTRODUCTION

The whole design of this volume, and all decisions in its development, have been aimed at making this an easy-to-use aid, not just a scholarly reference tool. It was designed primarily for the person with a lively interest in the Bible but limited knowledge of the original languages. It will also prove useful to those who are conversant with the biblical languages, particularly pastors and serious students. Scholars, too, will find it helpful for some types of study.

The Bible, as treated in the present volume, includes the Old Testament, the New Testament, and the Apocrypha of the Revised Standard Version of the Bible. Those who are not concerned with the original languages can use the English concordance without interference from the "analysis." Apart from the exceptions noted below, all words in the English text are included. The words are listed by dictionary form in alphabetical order followed by every context in which any form of the word is found. A citation giving the book, chapter, and verse for the context is provided at the left margin of each context line.

The "analytical" feature of the concordance is that it provides information about what word in an original language is being translated in each context. Following the dictionary form of the English word is a listing in alphabetical order of all of the Hebrew, Aramaic, Greek, and Latin words that the RSV translators have translated by any form of the English word, with a reference number for each of the original language words. At the right end of each context line is the reference number for the original language word that is translated in that particular context.

In order to keep the volume down to a useable size, certain very frequent words have been omitted. These include the prepositions "at," "by," "for," "from," "in," "into," "of," "on," "to," and "with"; the conjunctions "and," "as," "but," "or," "so," and "that"; all personal pronouns, including the personal reflexive pronouns, "one," and "own"; most subordinating and demonstrative pronouns, such as "who," "which," "what," etc.; all forms of the verbs "have" and "be" except "being" when it is a noun and "am" in the phrase "I am" spoken by God; all auxiliary verbs when used with a main verb, such as "shall," "may," and "do"; all articles; and the adverbs "too," "also," and "not." In addition, the conjunctions "after," "now," "then," "when," and "while" are omitted when they translate a grammatical construction or the Hebrew particle "וְ." "What," "which," and "when" are retained when they translate words or phrases that carry the specific meaning "what," "which," or "when."

Other very frequent words are given with citations but no context when they represent words translated hundreds of times. These include "upon," "all," "what," etc. These will present no problem to the user, since they are found in the alphabetic position where they would be expected in the concordance.

In order to group English words into a more helpful arrangement, the various occurrences of a word are listed under a heading word that corresponds to the dictionary form of the word, e.g., all contexts in which "fills," "filling," and "filled" occur will be found under "fill." All of the -ing and -ed forms, e.g., "filling" and "filled," are listed under the verb even if they function in their particular contexts as adjectives or nouns. When, however, forms have become so fixed in English as nouns that they have lost their original verbal force, they are listed as separate nouns, e.g., "building" when it means "a structure" is a separate noun, but "[their] singing" would be under "sing." Nouns are listed under their singular form. Proper names in the contexts have the same form as they have in the RSV. In the heading words, however, the accents and hyphens of the RSV have been omitted. If the proper name in the original language has two or more words, the English names are hyphenated in the headings to indicate the word division of the original language.

Ideally a concordance of this type would list each English word in the Bible with each context referenced to a single corresponding word in one of the original biblical languages. This, however, is not possible, since many times an original language word is translated by an English phrase, or an original language phrase is translated by a single English word. Whenever possible, single English words are used in the headings, but it has often been necessary to include headings that are phrases. If a heading phrase is found, it indicates either that the phrase translates a single original word, or that the phrase translates a phrase in which there is no correspondence between the single words of the original phrase and the single words of the English. It may be that the same English phrase will in one context be listed under each of its component words, while in another context it will be listed as a phrase. In the first case the original language had separate words while in the second it had a single word. For example, in 2Ch 22:6 the

Features explained in Introduction

heading word — **abide** 1. גור 2. דון 3. היה 4. ישב 5. לון 6. מִקְוֶה 7. נוה 8. נוח 9. עמד 10. שׁכן 11. *ἐμμένω* 12. *μένω* 13. *προσμένω* 14. maneo — numbered original language words

Gen 6: 3 the LORD said, "My spirit shall not abide in man 2
Exd 40:35 not able to enter . . because the cloud abode upon it, 10
Lev 16:16 the tent of meeting, which abides with them 10
Num 9:22 continued over the tabernacle, abiding there 10
— various forms combined under heading word
Jdg 5:17 and Dan, why did he abide with the ships? Asher sat 1
20:47 and abode at the rock of Rimmon four months. 4
1Sm 1:22 presence of the LORD, and abide there for ever. 4
1Ch 29:15 are like a shadow, and there is no abiding. 6
Job 41:22 In his neck abides strength 5
Ps 25:13 He himself shall abide in prosperity 5
37:18 their heritage will abide for ever; 3
27 do good; so shall you abide for ever. 10
context — 49:12 Man cannot abide in his pomp, he is like the beasts 5
20 Man cannot abide in his pomp, he is like the beasts 5
91: 1 who abides in the shadow of the Almighty 5
125: 1 Zion, which cannot be moved, but abides for ever. 4
Prv 14:33 Wisdom abides in the mind of . . understanding 8
15:31 He whose ear heeds . . will abide among the wise. 5
citation — Isa 32:16 and righteousness abide in the fruitful field. 4
18 My people will abide in a peaceful habitation 4 — number referring to original language word
Hab 2: 5 the arrogant man shall not abide. 7
Hag 2: 5 My Spirit abides among you; fear not. 9
Zec 5: 4 it shall abide in his house and consume it 5
... abiding in you 12
9 he who abides ...
2Es 7:112 the full glory does not abide in it
Wis 3: 9 the faithful will abide with him in love 13

heading phrase — **ever abide** 1. כון

Ps 89:21 so that my hand shall ever abide with him 1

ability 1. חַיִל 2. חָכָם 3. חָכְמָה 4. חֲכַם לֵב 5. כֹּחַ 6. נשׂא יָד 7. *δύναμις* 8. *εὐπορέω*

Exd 28: 3 you shall speak to all who have ability 4
31: 3 filled him with . . ability and intelligence 3
6 I have given to all able men ability 3
35:25 all women who had ability spun with their hands 4
26 women whose hearts were moved with ability spun 3
31 filled . . with ability, with intelligence 3
35 He has filled them with ability to do every sort 3
36: 1 LORD has put ability and intelligence to know 3
2 man in whose mind the LORD had put ability 2
Lev 27: 8 according to the ability of him who vowed 6
1Ch 26:30 Hashabi'ah and his brethren, 1,700 men of ability 1
32 2,700 men of ability, heads of fathers' houses 1
Ezr 2:69 according to their ability they gave 5
Mat 25:15 to each according to his ability 7
Act 11:29 every one according to his ability 8
1Es 5:44 to the best of their ability. 7
Sir 29:20 Assist your neighbor according to your ability 7

heading phrase — **great ability** 1. חַיִל

1Ch 26: 6 rulers . . for they were men of great ability. 1
31 men of great ability . . were found at Jazer 1

heading phrase — **ability to distinguish** 1. *διάκρισις*

1Co 12:10 to another the ability to distinguish . . spirits 1

Hebrew says literally "THE WOUNDS WHICH HE-HAD-BEEN-WOUNDED." This is translated, "the wounds which he had received." This phrase is listed in the concordance under "wound" and "receive" (translating "HE-HAD-BEEN-WOUNDED"). In Zec 13:6 the Hebrew says "I-WAS-WOUNDED IN THE HOUSE." The English translation is "The wounds I received in the house..." This is listed under a phrase heading "receive a wound" (translating "I-WAS-WOUNDED").

Since phrases contain more than one word, and the order of words in the same basic English phrase may vary from one context to another, e.g., "firmly fixed" versus "fixed firmly," some decisions had to be made about where the phrases would be listed in the concordance. On the assumption that users of the concordance would look up phrases by the word carrying the major meaning of the phrase, a system was developed to list by major or primary meaning. If a phrase contains a verb, it is usually listed after the verb in the concordance. If there are two verbs, it is listed after the verb carrying the primary meaning. Thus, "cause to run," "make run," "keep running," "come running," and "begin to run" are all listed after "run." If the phrase contains a linking verb and an adjective or noun, the phrase will be listed following the adjective or noun, since it carries the primary meaning of the phrase. A phrase containing the verbs "act" or "do" followed by an adverb will be listed after the adverb. Phrases containing nouns with prepositions or modifiers will normally be listed after the noun. Certain rather neutral nouns in English are regularly used with an adjective to translate adjectives in the original language that are used as nouns (as we use adjectives as nouns in expressions like "the poor," "the rich," etc.). Phrases containing a neutral noun plus an adjective will be listed following the adjective. These nouns include "fellow," "man," "woman," "deed," "act," "thing," "person," "people," "one," "sort," "place," "kind," "part," "stuff," and "manner." Names of plants and animals are treated as units even though following the principles listed above they might be listed otherwise. "Cedar tree," for example, will be found following "cedar," not "tree." There is a generous system of cross-references, so if a word is not found where expected, there should be a note there indicating where it is found. The cross references are to the heading word after which the heading phrase will follow, e.g., "**darkness** *See also* full." means that after the heading "full" there is a phrase heading that contains the word "darkness."

Normally words that are omitted in the concordance as a whole are not included as part of a phrase. Exceptions are made when the word is within the phrase or when the omission of the word would cause serious confusion. This means that "he did not believe" will simply be listed under believe, even though the Greek word it translates means "to not—believe," since "not," as well as "he" and "did," is normally omitted.

Often English words or phrases that are spelled the same will have different meanings (e.g., "charge" meaning "attack," "take to court," or "set a price,") or they will be in the same field of meaning but represent different parts of speech (e.g., "hammer" as either a noun or a verb). When the field of meaning varies, there will be separate headings, e.g., "fine" (the condition or quality) and "fine (2)" (monetary punsishment), etc. But words representing the same field of meaning but different parts of speech will be listed under the same heading. Thus "they shall fine him" and "either fine or imprisonment" are both under "fine (2)." Sometimes it is difficult to determine whether a distinction in usage really constitutes a difference in field of meaning. The real test, of course, is whether the distinctions help the user see together the passages with related meaning.

The concordance has separate sections for proper names and numbers. All phrases containing proper names are in the proper names sections. All numbers over twenty are printed in the contexts in this concordance in digits and are listed in the numbers sections. The exception to this is a number used as a name of a group or as a general rather than a specific number, e.g. "thousands." In these cases the numbers are spelled out and are included in the main body of the concordance. Phrases containing cardinal numbers (e.g., twenty-three) are listed after the numbers, but ordinal numbers (e.g., twenty-third) are treated as adjectives in deciding where phrases would be listed.

Each context has to its right either a number, which refers to an original language word or phrase (see next paragraph), or one of the signs "*," "†," or "‡." The "*" indicates that the word in question was supplied by the translator. The translator may have supplied the word to give a more specific meaning to a term on the basis of its context, the translator may have believed this to be the meaning that was originally intended by a text that now contains an error, or the translator may have conjectured a meaning that makes sense in the context even though the original language is not readable at this point. If the original language form, as it is read by the translator, appears in any ancient manuscript or as a marginal note for the Hebrew text, it is referenced to the original language word, not treated as translator supplied. A "†" means that the word or phrase translates a grammatical structure or idiom that cannot conveniently be shown in the concordance. A "‡" indicates that the word translated here is in a language that is not included in this concordance, usually Armenian, Syriac, Ethiopic, or Arabic.

Each heading is followed by a list of one or more words or phrases in Hebrew, Aramaic, Greek, or Latin. Single words will be in their dictionary forms. All verbs will be in their dictionary forms, even in phrases, but other words will have a form appropriate for the phrase in which they occur and as close to the dictionary form as possible. There are rare exceptions to these rules when the results would be intolerable. The goal is to make it possible for the person who knows the alphabets but not the languages to find the words from the original languages in the appropriate dictionaries. The scholar may be somewhat bothered by seeing two finite first person Greek verbs together when the idiom requires that one be a participle or an infinitive, but dictionaries do not list Greek verbs under infinitives or participles. The forms listed are the forms used in the following dictionaries:

Hebrew and Aramaic: Brown, Driver and Briggs, *Hebrew and English Lexicon with an Appendix Containing Biblical Aramaic*

New Testament: Bauer, Arndt, Gingrich, and Danker, A Greek–English *Lexicon of the New Testament and Early Christian Literature*

Apocryphal Greek: Liddell and Scott, *A Greek–English Lexicon*

Latin: Lewis and Short, *A Latin Dictionary*

Whenever Greek words in the Apocrypha are listed in Bauer, they are given the form found there. Since not all *Septuagint* Greek is included in Bauer or Liddell and Scott, the forms found in Hatch and Redpath, *A Concordance to the Septuagint and the Other Greek Versions of the Old Testament*, are also used. Unfortunately, there is no standard dictionary of Old Testament and Apocryphal Greek to which the user may be referred.

In numerous places the translators of the RSV disagree with the dictionaries on how a word in an original language should be analyzed. In those cases, the form listed is the form under which it should be listed if one accepts the translator's analysis.

The fact that a word or phrase in English is referenced to a word or phrase in one of the original languages does not mean that they have the same meaning. Ways of expression vary from language to language. The focus of the concordance is on the English text of the RSV and the words and expressions in the original languages that are behind the words in the RSV. Two examples must suffice here. In Hebrew one would say, "He returns, he speaks" to express what is meant by the English "He speaks again." "Return" does not mean "again," but it is what is behind the English "again" in this phrase. The form for adjectives that is used in the Hebrew dictionary is the unmarked form, which can be lengthened by suffixes to indicate plural, feminine singular or plural, etc. The form translated by a phrase "a [adjective] woman" is the feminine singular form. The unmarked form does not mean "a [adjective] woman," but it is the dictionary form under which one will find the marked form translated "a [adjective] woman." The original language words are not to be seen as having the exact meaning of the English, but as the dictionary form of the word that is behind the English.

The citations of book, chapter, and verse for each context in which a word or phrase is found use the numbering of the RSV. This may vary greatly from the numbering of texts in the original language, particularly in the Apocrypha. Tables of abbreviations for the biblical books are found in the next section of the concordance. Note that Psalm 151 is cited as "151" rather than "Ps 151." This is done because this psalm is not printed in the RSV among the Psalms, but is included as a separate composition, like a separate book, in the Apocrypha.

Wherever possible, the proper names listed in the second concordance section have been standardized in both their Greek and Hebrew forms to make them easier to find in the dictionaries. The variations in spelling in the original languages will be noted there. Greek names in the Apocrypha that are listed in Bauer are given in the same form Bauer uses. Otherwise they are listed without accents or breathing marks, even when they are Greek names.

The indexes at the end of the book include all of the original language words that are cited in the main concordance and in the concordance of proper names, followed in each case by all of the headings to which they are referenced. These indexes are not dictionaries of the languages and do not include any words that are not referenced in the concordances. No attempt is made to indicate the full translation of a word or phrase. Entries in the concordance of numbers are not included in the indexes.

ABBREVIATIONS

Canonical Order

Gen	Genesis	Jol	Joel	Phm	Philemon
Exd	Exodus	Ams	Amos	Heb	Hebrews
Lev	Leviticus	Obd	Obadiah	Jas	James
Num	Numbers	Jon	Jonah	1Pe	1 Peter
Deu	Deuteronomy	Mic	Micah	2Pe	2 Peter
Jos	Joshua	Nah	Nahum	1Jn	1 John
Jdg	Judges	Hab	Habakkuk	2Jn	2 John
Rut	Ruth	Zep	Zephaniah	3Jn	3 John
1Sm	1 Samuel	Hag	Haggai	Jde	Jude
2Sm	2 Samuel	Zec	Zechariah	Rev	Revelation
1Kg	1 Kings	Mal	Malachi	1Es	1 Esdras
2Kg	2 Kings	Mat	Matthew	2Es	2 Esdras
1Ch	1 Chronicles	Mrk	Mark	Tob	Tobit
2Ch	2 Chronicles	Lke	Luke	Jdt	Judith
Ezr	Ezra	Joh	John	AdE	Additions to Esther
Neh	Nehemiah	Act	Acts	Wis	Wisdom of Solomon
Est	Esther	Rom	Romans	Sir	Sirach
Job	Job	1Co	1 Corinthians	Bar	Baruch
Ps	Psalms	2Co	2 Corinthians	LtJ	Letter of Jeremiah
Prv	Proverbs	Gal	Galatians	Aza	Azariah
Ecc	Ecclesiastes	Eph	Ephesians	Sus	Susanna
Sng	Song of Solomon	Php	Philippians	Bel	Bel and the Dragon
Isa	Isaiah	Col	Colossians	Man	Prayer of Manasseh
Jer	Jeremiah	1Th	1 Thessalonians	1Mc	1 Maccabees
Lam	Lamentations	2Th	2 Thessalonians	2Mc	2 Maccabees
Ezk	Ezekiel	1Ti	1 Timothy	3Mc	3 Maccabees
Dan	Daniel	2Ti	2 Timothy	4Mc	4 Maccabees
Hos	Hosea	Tit	Titus	151	Psalm 151

Alphabetical Order

Act	Acts	Jas	James	Nah	Nahum
AdE	Additions to Esther	Jde	Jude	Neh	Nehemiah
Ams	Amos	Jdg	Judges	Num	Numbers
Aza	Azariah	Jdt	Judith	Obd	Obadiah
Bar	Baruch	Jer	Jeremiah	1Pe	1 Peter
Bel	Bel and the Dragon	1Jn	1 John	2Pe	2 Peter
1Ch	1 Chronicles	2Jn	2 John	Phm	Philemon
2Ch	2 Chronicles	3Jn	3 John	Php	Philippians
1Co	1 Corinthians	Job	Job	Prv	Proverbs
2Co	2 Corinthians	Joh	John	Ps	Psalms
Col	Colossians	Jol	Joel	Rev	Revelation
Dan	Daniel	Jon	Jonah	Rom	Romans
Deu	Deuteronomy	Jos	Joshua	Rut	Ruth
Ecc	Ecclesiastes	1Kg	1 Kings	Sir	Sirach
Eph	Ephesians	2Kg	2 Kings	1Sm	1 Samuel
1Es	1 Esdras	Lam	Lamentations	2Sm	2 Samuel
2Es	2 Esdras	Lev	Leviticus	Sng	Song of Solomon
Est	Esther	Lke	Luke	Sus	Susanna
Exd	Exodus	LtJ	Letter of Jeremiah	1Th	1 Thessalonians
Ezk	Ezekiel	Mal	Malachi	2Th	2 Thessalonians
Ezr	Ezra	Man	Prayer of Manasseh	1Ti	1 Timothy
Gal	Galatians	Mat	Matthew	2Ti	2 Timothy
Gen	Genesis	1Mc	1 Maccabees	Tit	Titus
Hab	Habakkuk	2Mc	2 Maccabees	Tob	Tobit
Hag	Haggai	3Mc	3 Maccabees	Wis	Wisdom of Solomon
Heb	Hebrews	4Mc	4 Maccabees	Zep	Zephaniah
Hos	Hosea	Mic	Micah	Zec	Zechariah
Isa	Isaiah	Mrk	Mark	151	Psalm 151

THE EERDMANS

ANALYTICAL CONCORDANCE

to the

REVISED STANDARD VERSION

OF THE BIBLE

A

abandon 1. נוח 2. נטשׁ 3. עזב 4. *ἀφίημι* 5. *ἀφίστημι* 6. *ἐγκαταλείπω* 7. *ἐκδιαιτέω* 8. *ἐκλείπω* 9. *ἐκχέω* 10. *καταλείπω* 11. *καταλύω* 12. *καταπροδίδωμι* 13. *παραλείπω* 14. *περιαιρέω* 15. *περιλύω*

Num32:15 he will again abandon them in the wilderness; 1
2Ch 12: 5 Thus says the LORD, 'You abandoned me 3
5 you abandoned me, so I have abandoned you 3
Neh 9:28 abandon them to the hand of their enemies 3
Job 20:19 For he has crushed and abandoned the poor 3
Ps 37:33 The LORD will not abandon him to his power 3
94:14 For the LORD . . will not abandon his heritage; 3
Jer 12: 7 I have abandoned my heritage; 2
Act 2:27 thou wilt not abandon my soul to Hades 6
31 he was not abandoned to Hades 6
27:20 hope of our being saved was at last abandoned. 14
Jde 1:11 and abandon themselves for the sake of gain 9
Rev 2: 4 you have abandoned the love you had at first. 4
Sir 23: 1 do not abandon me to their counsel 6
29:17 will abandon his rescuer. 6
LJr 1:42 cannot perceive this and abandon them 10
1Mc 1:15 abandoned the holy covenant 5
2Mc 10:13 because he had abandoned Cyprus 8
3Mc 1:19 Those women . . abandoned the bridal chambers 13
20 nurses abandoned even newborn children 13
4Mc 2:10 virtue is not abandoned for their sakes. 12
7: 9 did not abandon the holiness which you praised 11
10: 7 they abandoned the instruments and scalped him 15
18: 5 to abandon their ancestral customs 7

abase 1. כלם 2. שׁפל 3. שָׁפָל 4. שׁפל (A) 5. *ταπεινόω*

2Sm 6:22 and I will be abased in your eyes; 3
Job 22:29 For God abases the proud, but he saves the lowly. 2
40:11 look on every one that is proud, and abase him. 2
Ps 44: 9 Yet thou hast cast us off and abased us 1
Ezk 21:26 which is low, and abase that which is high. 2
Dan 4:37 those who walk in pride he is able to abase. 4
Mal 2: 9 and so I make you despised and abased before all 3
2Co 11: 7 Did I commit a sin in abasing myself 5
Php 4:12 I know how to be abased, and I know how to abound 5
Sir 7:11 there is One who abases and exalts. 5

abate 1. חסר 2. נוס 3. רפה 4. שׁכך 5. שׁקע 6. *λήγω*

Gen 8: 3 At the end of 150 days the waters had abated; 1
5 the waters continued to abate 1
Num11: 2 Moses prayed to the LORD, and the fire abated. 5
Deu 34: 7 his eye was not dim, nor his natural force abated. 2
Jdg 8: 3 Then their anger against him was abated 3
Est 2: 1 when the anger of King Ahasu-e'rus had abated 4
7:10 Then the anger of the king abated. 4
2Mc 9:18 when his sufferings did not in any way abate 6

abbreviate 1. *ἐπιτομή*

2Mc 2:26 who have undertaken the toil of abbreviating 1

abet 1. *διά*

3Mc 2:25 abetted by . . drinking companions and comrades 1

abhor 1. גָּעַל 2. געל 3. זעם 4. קוץ 5. שׁקץ 6. תאב 7. תעב 8. *βδελύσσομαι* 9. zelo

Lev 20:23 all these things, and therefore I abhorred them 4
26:11 my soul shall not abhor you 2
15 if your soul abhors my ordinances 2
30 and my soul will abhor you 2
43 and their soul abhorred my statutes 2
44 I will not spurn them, neither will I abhor them 2
Deu 7:26 you shall utterly detest and abhor it; 7
23: 7 shall not abhor an E'domite, for he is your brother; 7
7 you shall not abhor an Egyptian 7
1Kg 11:25 and he abhorred Israel, and reigned over Syria. 4
Job 9:31 into a pit, and my own clothes will abhor me. 7
19:19 All my intimate friends abhor me 7
30:10 They abhor me, they keep aloof from me; 7
Ps 5: 6 LORD abhors bloodthirsty and deceitful men. 7
22:24 he has not despised or abhorred the affliction 5
106:40 LORD . . abhorred his heritage; 7
119:163 I hate and abhor falsehood, but I love thy law. 7
Prv 24:24 will be cursed by peoples, abhorred by nations; 3
Isa 49: 7 to one deeply despised, abhorred by the nations 7
Ezk 16: 5 you were abhorred, on the day that you were born. 1
Ams 5:10 and they abhor him who speaks the truth. 7
6: 8 I abhor the pride of Jacob, and hate his 6
Mic 3: 9 Israel, who abhor justice and pervert all equity 7
Rom 2:22 You who abhor idols, do you rob temples? 8
2Es 16:49 a . . virtuous woman abhors a harlot 9
50 righteousness shall abhor iniquity 9
Jdt 9: 4 abhorred the pollution of their blood 8
AEs 14:15 abhor the bed of the uncircumcised 8
16 I abhor the sign of my proud position 8
16 I abhor it like a menstruous rag 8
2Mc 5: 8 abhorred as the executioner of his country 8
3Mc 2:33 they abhorred those who separated themselves 8
4Mc 5: 8 Why . . should you abhor eating . . excellent meat 8

make abhor 1. באשׁ

1Sm 27:12 He has made himself utterly abhorred 1

abhorrence 1. דֵּרָאוֹן 2. *στυγέω*

Isa 66:24 they shall be an abhorrence to all flesh. 1
3Mc 2:31 an obvious abhorrence of the price to be exacted 2

abhorrent 1. תעב

1Ch 21: 6 for the king's command was abhorrent to Jo'ab. 1

abide 1. גור 2. דון 3. היה 4. ישׁב 5. לון 6. מִקְוֶה 7. נוה 8. נוח 9. עמד 10. שׁכן 11. *ἐμμένω* 12. *μένω* 13. *προσμένω* 14. maneo

Gen 6: 3 the LORD said, "My spirit shall not abide in man 2
Exd 40:35 not able to enter . . because the cloud abode upon it, 10
Lev 16:16 the tent of meeting, which abides with them 10
Num 9:22 continued over the tabernacle, abiding there 10
Jdg 5:17 and Dan, why did he abide with the ships? Asher sat 1
20:47 and abode at the rock of Rimmon four months. 4
1Sm 1:22 presence of the LORD, and abide there for ever. 4
1Ch 29:15 are like a shadow, and there is no abiding. 6
Job 41:22 In his neck abides strength 5
Ps 25:13 He himself shall abide in prosperity 5
37:18 their heritage will abide for ever; 3
27 do good; so shall you abide for ever. 10
49:12 Man cannot abide in his pomp, he is like the beasts 5
20 Man cannot abide in his pomp, he is like the beasts 5
91: 1 who abides in the shadow of the Almighty 5
125: 1 Zion, which cannot be moved, but abides for ever. 4
Prv 14:33 Wisdom abides in the mind of . . understanding 8
15:31 He whose ear heeds . . will abide among the wise. 5
Isa 32:16 and righteousness abide in the fruitful field. 4
18 My people will abide in a peaceful habitation 4
Hab 2: 5 the arrogant man shall not abide. 7
Hag 2: 5 My Spirit abides among you; fear not. 9
Zec 5: 4 it shall abide in his house and consume it 5
Joh 5:38 do not have his word abiding in you 12
6:56 who eats my flesh and drinks my blood abides in me 12
15: 4 Abide in me, and I in you. 12
4 unless it abides in the vine 12
4 neither can you, unless you abide in me. 12
5 He who abides in me, and I in him 12
6 If a man does not abide in me 12
7 If you abide in me, and my words abide in you 12
7 If you abide in me, and my words abide in you 12
9 so have I loved you; abide in my love. 12
10 you will abide in my love 12
10 just as I . . abide in his love. 12
16 that your fruit should abide 12
1Co 13:13 So faith, hope, love abide, these three 12
Gal 3:10 who does not abide by all things written 11
Heb 10:34 a better possession and an abiding one. 12
1Pe 1:23 through the living and abiding word of God; 12
25 but the word of the Lord abides for ever. 12
1Jn 2: 6 he who says he abides in him ought to walk 12
10 He who loves his brother abides in the light 12
14 and the word of God abides in you 12
17 but he who does the will of God abides for ever. 12
24 Let what you heard from the beginning abide 12
24 what you heard from the beginning abides in you 12
24 then you will abide in the Son and in the Father. 12
27 the anointing . . abides in you 12
27 just as it has been taught you, abide in him. 12
28 now, little children, abide in him 12
3: 6 No one who abides in him sins; 12
9 for God's nature abides in him, and he cannot sin 12
14 He who does not love abides in death. 12
15 no murderer has eternal life abiding in him. 12
17 how does God's love abide in him? 12
24 All who keep his commandments abide in him 12
24 And by this we know that he abides in us 12
4:12 if we love one another, God abides in us 12
13 By this we know that we abide in him and he in us 12
15 God abides in him, and he in God. 12
16 God is love, and he who abides in love abides in God 12
16 God is love, and he who abides in love abides in God 12
16 and God abides in him. 12
2Jn 1: 2 because of the truth which abides in us 12
9 and does not abide in the doctrine of Christ 12
9 he who abides in the doctrine has both the Father 12
2Es 7:112 the full glory does not abide in it 14
Wis 3: 9 the faithful will abide with him in love 13

ever abide 1. כון

Ps 89:21 so that my hand shall ever abide with him 1

ability 1. חַיִל 2. חָכָם 3. חָכְמָה 4. חֲכַם לֵב 5. כֹּחַ 6. נשׂג יָד 7. *δύναμις* 8. *εὐπορέω*

Exd 28: 3 you shall speak to all who have ability 4
31: 3 filled him with . . ability and intelligence 3
6 I have given to all able men ability 3
35:25 all women who had ability spun with their hands 4
26 women whose hearts were moved with ability spun 3
31 filled . . with ability, with intelligence 3
35 He has filled them with ability to do every sort 3
36: 1 LORD has put ability and intelligence to know 3
2 man in whose mind the LORD had put ability 2
Lev 27: 8 according to the ability of him who vowed 6
1Ch 26:30 Hashabi'ah and his brethren, 1,700 men of ability 1
32 2,700 men of ability, heads of fathers' houses 1
Ezr 2:69 according to their ability they gave 5
Mat 25:15 to each according to his ability 7
Act 11:29 every one according to his ability 8
1Es 5:44 to the best of their ability. 7
Sir 29:20 Assist your neighbor according to your ability 7

great ability 1. חַיִל

1Ch 26: 6 rulers . . for they were men of great ability. 1
31 men of great ability . . were found at Jazer 1

ability to distinguish 1. *διάκρισις*

1Co 12:10 to another the ability to distinguish . . spirits 1

ablaze 1. חָרוֹן 2. *στίλβω*

Ps 58: 9 feel the heat of thorns, whether green or ablaze 1
1Mc 6:39 the hills were ablaze with them 2

set ablaze 1. להט 2. *ἀνάπτω*

Ps 83:14 as the flame sets the mountains ablaze 1
Jas 3: 5 How great a forest is set ablaze by a small fire! 2

able 1. בֶּן חַיִל 2. חַיִל 3. חָכָם 4. חָכְמָה 5. חֲכַם לֵב 6. יכל 7. כֹּחַ 8. מַתְּנַת יָד 9. עצר 10. יכל (A) 11. כהל (A) 12. *δύναμαι* 13. *δυνατέω* 14. *δυνατός* 15. *ἔχω* 16. *ἱκανός* 17. *ἰσχύω* 18. *κατισχύω* 19. *ὀδυνάω* 20. *οὐ μή* 21. capio 22. possum

Gen 15: 5 number the stars, if you are able to number them. 6
47: 6 and if you know any able men among them, 2
Exd 18:18 you are not able to perform it alone. 6
21 Moreover choose able men from all the people 2
23 then you will be able to endure, and all this 6
25 Moses chose able men out of all Israel 2
28: 3 whom I have endowed with an able mind 4
31: 6 I have given to all able men ability 5
36: 1 Bez'alel and Oho'liab and every able man in whom 3

2 called . . every able man in whose mind the LORD 5
40:35 Moses was not able to enter the tent of meeting 6
Num 1: 3 all in Israel who are able to go forth to war •
20 old and upward, all who were able to go forth to war •
22 all who were able to go forth to war •
24 people . . all who were able to go forth to war •
26 every man able to go forth to war •
28 every man able to go forth to war •
30 every man able to go forth to war •
32 every man able to go forth to war •
34 every man able to go forth to war •
36 every man able to go forth to war •
38 every man able to go forth to war •
40 every man able to go forth to war •
42 every man able to go forth to war •
45 every man able to go forth to war in Israel– •
11:14 I am not able to carry all this people alone 6
13:30 occupy it; for we are well able to overcome it. 6
31 We are not able to go up against the people; 6
14:16 'Because the LORD was not able to bring 6
22: 6 I shall be able to defeat them and drive them 6
11 curse them for me; perhaps I shall be able to fight 6
37 did you not come to me? Am I not able to honor you? 6
24:13 I would not be able to go beyond the word of the LORD 6
26: 2 all in Israel who are able to go forth to war. •
Deu 1: 9 I said to you, 'I am not able alone to bear you; 6
7:24 not a man shall be able to stand against you •
9:28 Because the LORD was not able to bring them 6
11:25 No man shall be able to stand against you; •
14:24 so that you are not able to bring the tithe 6
16:17 every man shall give as he is able, according 8
31: 2 I am no longer able to go out and come in. 6
Jos 1: 5 No man shall be able to stand before you •
23: 9 no man has been able to withstand you to this day. •
Jdg 8: 3 what have I been able to do in comparison with you? 6
18: 2 the Danites sent five able men from the whole 1
1Sm 6:20 Who is able to stand before the LORD, this holy God? 6
17: 9 If he is able to fight with me and kill me 6
33 You are not able to go against this Philistine 6
1Kg 3: 9 for who is able to govern this thy great people? 6
2Kg 3:21 all who were able to put on armor . . were called •
18:23 I will give . . horses, if you are able on your part 6
29 he will not be able to deliver you out of my hand. 6
1Ch 9:13 very able men for . . the service of the house 2
26: 7 brethren were able men, Eli'hu and Semachi'ah. 2
8 able men qualified for the service; 62 of O'bed-e'dom 2
9 Meshelemi'ah had sons and brethren, able men 2
29: 2 I have provided . . so far as I was able 7
14 that we should be able thus to offer willingly? 9
2Ch 2: 6 But who is able to build him a house •
20: 6 so that none is able to withstand thee. •
37 ships . . were not able to go to Tarshish. 9
22: 9 had no one able to rule the kingdom. 9
25: 5 fit for war, able to handle spear and shield. •
9 The LORD is able to give you much more than this. •
32:13 gods . . at all able to deliver their lands 6
14 Who among all the gods . . was able to deliver 6
14 God should be able to deliver you from my hand? 6
15 no god . . has been able to deliver his people 6
Neh 4:10 we are not able to work on the wall. 6
5: 8 We, as far as we are able, have bought back †
Ps 18:38 they were not able to rise; they fell under my 6
Ecc 6:10 he is not able to dispute with one stronger 6
Isa 36: 8 horses, if you are able on your part to set riders 6
14 for he will not be able to deliver you. 6
47:11 which you will not be able to expiate; 6
12 perhaps you may be able to succeed 6
Jer 49:10 he is not able to conceal himself. 6
Ezk 7:19 silver and gold are not able to deliver them 6
33:12 the righteous shall not be able to live 6
46: 7 and with the lambs as much as he is able †
11 with the lambs as much as one is able to give †
Dan 2:26 Are you able to make known to me the dream 11
47 for you have been able to reveal this mystery. 10
3:17 God . . is able to deliver us from the . . furnace 10
29 no other god who is able to deliver in this way. 10
4:18 not able to make known to me the interpretation 10
18 known to me the interpretation, but you are able 11
37 those who walk in pride he is able to abase. 10
6:20 has your God . . able to deliver you from the lions 10
Hos 5:13 But he is not able to cure you or heal your wound. 6
Ams 7:10 the land is not able to bear all his words. 6
Zep 1:18 nor their gold shall be able to deliver them 6
Mat 3: 9 I tell you, God is able from these stones to raise 12
9:28 Do you believe that I am able to do this? 12
19:12 He who is able to receive this 12
20:22 Are you able to drink the cup that I am to drink? 12
22 They said to him, "We are able. 12
22:46 no one was able to answer him a word 12
26:61 I am able to destroy the temple of God 12
Mrk 3:25 that house will not be able to stand. 12
4:33 as they were able to hear it; 12
9:18 they were not able. 17
39 will be able soon after to speak evil of me. 12
10:38 Are you able to drink the cup that I drink 12
39 they said to him, "We are able. 12
Lke 3: 8 God is able from these stones to raise up children 12
12:26 you are not able to do as small a thing as that 12
13:24 many . . will seek to enter and will not be able. 17
14:29 is not able to finish 17
30 began to build, and was not able to finish.' 17
31 whether he is able with 10,000 to meet him 14
16:26 in order that those . . may not be able 12
20:26 they were not able in the presence of the people 17
21:15 none of your adversaries will be able 12
Joh 10:29 is able to snatch them out of the Father's hand. 12
21: 6 now they were not able to haul it 17
Act 5:39 you will not be able to overthrow them 12
15:10 neither our fathers nor we have been able to bear? 17
20:32 which is able to build you up 12
24: 8 will be able to learn from him about everything 12
Rom 4:21 that God was able to do what he had promised. 14
8:39 will be able to separate us from the love of God 12
14: 4 for the Master is able to make him stand. 13
15:14 and able to instruct one another. 12
16:25 Now to him who is able to strengthen you 12
1Co 2:14 he is not able to understand them 12
10:13 that you may be able to endure it. 12
2Co 1: 4 so that we may be able to comfort 12
5:12 so that you may be able to answer 15
9: 8 God is able to provide you with every blessing 13
Eph 3:20 is able to do far more abundantly 12
4:28 that he may be able to give to those in need. 15
6:11 able to stand against the wiles of the devil. 12
13 that you may be able to withstand in the evil day 12
2Ti 1:12 I am sure that he is able to guard until that Day 14
2: 2 who will be able to teach others also. 16
3:15 which are able to instruct you for salvation 12
Tit 1: 9 be able to give instruction in sound doctrine 14
Heb 2:18 he is able to help those who are tempted. 12
5: 7 to him who was able to save him from death 12
7:25 Consequently he is able for all time to save 12
11:19 God was able to raise men even from the dead 14
Jas 1:21 implanted word, which is able to save your souls. 12
3: 2 a perfect man, able to bridle the whole body also. 14
4:12 he who is able to save and to destroy 12
2Pe 1:15 you may be able at any time to recall these things. 15
Jde 1:24 Now to him who is able to keep you from falling 12
Rev 3: 8 an open door, which no one is able to shut; 12
5: 3 no one . . was able to open the scroll or to look 12
1Es 9:11 we are not able to stand in the open air 17
2Es 2:28 they shall not be able to do anything against you 22
4:27 it will not be able to bring the things 21
5:38 I said, "O sovereign Lord, who is able to know 22
45 it might even now be able to support all of them 22
7:102 the righteous will be able to intercede 22
115 no one will then be able to have mercy on him 22
8: 6 by which every mortal . . may be able to live. 22
47 being able to love my creation more than I 22
9: 7 and will be able to escape on account of his works 22
12:38 whose hearts you know are able to comprehend 22
13:47 that they may be able to pass over 22
14:22 that men may be able to find the path 22
15:17 to go into a city, and shall not be able. 22
Jdt 10:19 they will be able to ensnare the whole world! 12
Wis 17: 5 no power of fire was able to give light 18
Sir 0: 1 those who love learning should be able to help 12
8:17 for he will not be able to keep a secret. 12
LJr 1:34 they will not be able to repay it 12
35 they are not able to give either wealth or money; 12
41 as though Bel were able to understand. 14
57 Gods made of wood . . are not able to save themselves •
58 they will not be able to help themselves. 20
64 they are not able either to decide a case 14
1Mc 3:53 How will we be able to withstand them 12
5:40 we will not be able to resist him 12
6:27 you will not be able to stop them. 12
9: 8 We may be able to fight them 12
9 We are not able. Let us rather save our own lives 12
10:73 now you will not be able to withstand my cavalry 12
2Mc 8:18 is able with a single nod to strike down 12
9:10 no one was able to carry the man 12
3Mc 4:16 are not able even to communicate 12
17 were no longer able to take the census of the Jews 17
4Mc 1:33 because reason is able to rule over appetites 12
2: 6 reason is able to control desires. 12
18 is able to get the better of the emotions 14
4:24 When . . he had not been able in any way 17
7:18 are able to control the passions of the flesh 12
22 would not be able to overcome the emotions •
8: 6 Just as I am able to punish those who disobey 12
10: 7 they were not able in any way to break his spirit 17
11:25 not been able to persuade us to change our mind 19
14:17 If they are not able to keep him away 12
18: 5 Since in no way whatever was he able 17

able *See also* much.

able man 1. חָכָם 2. חֲכַם לֵב
Exd 35:10 let every able man among you come and make all 2
36: 4 so that all the able men who were doing every sort 1
8 able men among the workmen made the tabernacle 2

very able 1. חַיִל
1Kg 11:28 The man Jerobo'am was very able 1

able-bodied 1. חַיִל
Jdg 3:29 of the Moabites, all strong, able-bodied men; 1

ablution 1. *βαπτισμός*
Heb 6: 2 instruction about ablutions 1
9:10 food and drink and various ablutions 1

aboard *See* go, take.

abode 1. חָצִיר 2. ישׁב 3. מִשְׁכָּן 4. נָוֶה 5. סֹךְ 6. *τόπος*
Exd 15:13 guided them by thy strength to thy holy abode. 4
17 which thou has made for thy abode, the sanctuary 2
Lev 26:11 I will make my abode among you 3
Ps 68:16 at the mount which God desired for his abode 2
76: 2 His abode has been established in Salem 5
Prv 3:33 but he blesses the abode of the righteous. 4
Isa 34:13 the haunt of jackals, an abode for ostriches. 1
Tob 3: 6 to go to the eternal abode 6

lofty abode 1. עֲלִיָּה
Ps 104:13 From thy lofty abode . . waterest the mountains; 1

abolish 1. שׁבר 2. *αἴρω* 3. *ἀναιρέω* 4. *διασκεδάννυμι* 5. *ἐξαίρω* 6. *καταλύω* 7. *καταργέω* 8. extermino
Hos 2:18 and I will abolish the bow, the sword, and war 1
Mat 5:17 Think not that I have come to abolish the law 6
17 have come not to abolish them but to fulfil them. 6
Eph 2:15 by abolishing in his flesh the law 7
2Ti 1:10 who abolished death 7
Heb 10: 9 He abolishes the first 3
2Es 15:60 and abolish a portion of your glory 8
63 and abolish the glory of your countenance. 8
AEs 14: 9 to abolish what thy mouth has ordained 5
1Mc 3:29 caused in the land by abolishing the laws 2
6:59 on account of their laws which we abolished 4
2Mc 2:22 the laws that were about to be abolished 6
4Mc 4:20 also the temple service was abolished. 6

abominable 1. תּוֹעֵבָה 2. תעב 3. *βδέλυγμα* 4. *βδελυρός* 5. *βδελύσσομαι* 6. *μιαρός* 7. *σχέτλιος*
Exd 8:26 shall sacrifice . . offerings abominable 1
26 offerings abominable to the Egyptians. 1
Lev 18:30 to practice any of these abominable customs 1
Job 15:16 how much less one who is abominable and corrupt 2
Jer 44: 4 Oh, do not do this abominable thing that I hate! 1
Ezk 7:20 they made their abominable images 1
Sir 19:23 There is a cleverness which is abominable 3
41: 5 children of sinners are abominable children 4
2Mc 9:13 Then the abominable fellow made a vow to the Lord 6
15: 5 in carrying out his abominable design. 7
3Mc 6: 9 the abominable and lawless Gentiles. 5
4Mc 9:17 he replied, "You abominable lackeys 6

abominable *See also* idol, image, make, offering, practice.

abominable deed 1. תּוֹעֵבָה
Ezk 22: 2 Then declare to her all her abominable deeds. 1
23:36 Then declare to them their abominable deeds. 1
36:31 for your iniquities and your abominable deeds. 1

do abominable 1. תעב
Ps 14: 1 They are corrupt, they do abominable deeds 1
53: 1 They are corrupt, doing abominable iniquity; 1

most abominable 1. *μιαρός*
4Mc 9:15 Most abominable tyrant 1
32 You will not escape, most abominable tyrant 1
10:10 We, most abominable tyrant, are suffering 1

abominable thing 1. פִּגּוּל 2. תּוֹעֵבָה
Deu 7:26 not bring an abominable thing into your house 2
12:31 for every abominable thing which the LORD hates 2
13:14 such an abominable thing has been done among you 2
14: 3 You shall not eat any abominable thing. 2
17: 4 true . . such an abominable thing has been done 2
Isa 65: 4 broth of abominable things is in their vessels; 1
Ezk 16:50 They were haughty, and did abominable things 2
18:13 He has done all these abominable things; 2
24 the same abominable things that the wicked man 2

utterly abominable 1. *παμμιαρός*
4Mc 10:17 the bloodthirsty . . and utterly abominable Antiochus 1

act abominably 1. תעב
Ezk 16:52 in which you acted more abominably than they 1

do abominably 1. תעב
1Kg 21:26 He did very abominably in going after idols 1

abominate 1. *βδελύσσομαι*
3Mc 3:23 they abominate those few among them 1

abomination 1. זִמָּה 2. פִּגּוּל 3. שִׁקּוּץ 4. שקץ 5. שֶׁקֶץ 6. תּוֹעֵבָה 7. *βδέλυγμα*
Gen 43:32 for that is an abomination to the Egyptians. 6
46:34 shepherd is an abomination to the Egyptians. 6
Lev 7:18 it shall be an abomination, and he who eats of it 2
21 or an unclean beast or any unclean abomination 5
11:10 are in the waters, is an abomination to you 5
11 They shall remain an abomination to you 5
11 their carcasses you shall have in abomination 4
12 Everything . . is an abomination to you 5

13 you shall have in abomination among the birds 4
13 they shall not be eaten, they are an abomination 5
20 winged insects . . are an abomination to you 5
23 other insects . . are an abomination to you 5
41 swarming thing . . is an abomination 5
42 you shall not eat; for they are an abomination 5
18:22 lie with a male as with a woman; it is an abomination 6
26 and do none of these abominations 6
27 all of these abominations the men of the land did 6
29 For whoever shall do any of these abominations 6
19: 7 it is an abomination; it will not be accepted 2
20:13 both of them have committed an abomination 6
Deu 7:25 for it is an abomination to the LORD your God. 6
17: 1 for that is an abomination to the LORD your God. 6
18:12 does these things is an abomination to the LORD; 6
22: 5 whoever does these things is an abomination 6
23:18 both . . are an abomination to the LORD your God. 6
24: 4 for that is an abomination before the LORD 6
25:16 act dishonestly, are an abomination to the LORD 6
27:15 graven . . image, an abomination to the LORD 6
Jdg 20: 6 have committed abomination and wantonness 1
1Kg 11: 5 after Milcom the abomination of the Ammonites. 3
7 a high place for Chemosh the abomination of Moab 3
7 for Molech the abomination of the Ammonites 3
14:24 all the abominations of the nations 6
2Kg 21:11 Manas'seh . . has committed these abominations 6
23:13 for Ash'toreth the abomination of the Sido'nians 3
13 for . . and for Chemosh the abomination of Moab 3
13 for Milcom the abomination of the Ammonites. 6
24 all the abominations that were seen in the land 3
2Ch 34:33 Josi'ah took away all the abominations 6
36: 8 acts of Jehoi'akim, and the abominations 6
14 following all the abominations of the nations; 6
Ezr 9: 1 peoples of the lands with their abominations 6
11 peoples of the lands, with their abominations 6
14 peoples who practice these abominations? 6
Prv 3:32 perverse man is an abomination to the LORD 6
6:16 seven which are an abomination to him 6
8: 7 wickedness is an abomination to my lips. 6
11: 1 A false balance is an abomination to the LORD 6
20 perverse mind are an abomination to the LORD 6
12:22 Lying lips are an abomination to the LORD 6
13:19 turn away from evil is an abomination to fools. 6
15: 8 sacrifice of . . is an abomination to the LORD 6
9 way of the wicked is an abomination to the LORD 6
26 thoughts of . . are an abomination to the LORD 6
16: 5 who is arrogant is an abomination to the LORD; 6
12 It is an abomination to kings to do evil 6
17:15 both alike an abomination to the LORD. 6
20:10 both alike an abomination to the LORD. 6
23 Diverse weights are an abomination to the LORD 6
21:27 The sacrifice of the wicked is an abomination; 6
24: 9 scoffer is an abomination to men. 6
26:25 for there are seven abominations in his heart; 6
28: 9 even his prayer is an abomination. 6
29:27 An unjust man is an abomination to the righteous 6
27 way is straight is an abomination to the wicked. 6
Isa 1:13 incense is an abomination to me. 6
41:24 an abomination is he who chooses you. 6
44:19 and shall I make the residue of it an abomination? 6
66: 3 and their soul delights in their abominations; 3
17 eating swine's flesh and the abomination 5
Jer 2: 7 and made my heritage an abomination. 6
4: 1 If you remove your abominations 3
6:15 ashamed when they committed abomination? 6
7:10 only to go on doing all these abominations? 6
30 they have set their abominations in the house 3
8:12 ashamed when they committed abomination? 6
13:27 I have seen your abominations, your adulteries 3
16:18 my inheritance with their abominations. 6
32:34 They set up their abominations in the house 3
35 that they should do this abomination 6
44:22 and the abominations which you committed; 6
Ezk 5: 9 because of all your abominations I will do 6
11 defiled . . with all your abominations 6
6: 9 for the evils . . for all their abominations. 6
11 say, Alas! because of all the evil abominations 6
7: 3 I will punish you for all your abominations. 6
4 while your abominations are in your midst. 6
8 I will punish you for all your abominations. 6
9 while your abominations are in your midst. 6
8: 6 see what they are doing, the great abominations 6
6 you will see still greater abominations. 6
9 he said to me, "Go in, and see the vile abominations 6
13 You will see still greater abominations 6
15 You will see still greater abominations 6
17 to commit the abominations which they commit 6
9: 4 men who sigh and groan over all the abominations 6
11:18 detestable things and all its abominations. 6
21 detestable things and their abominations 6
12:16 that they may confess all their abominations 6
14: 6 turn away . . from all your abominations. 6
16: 2 make known to Jerusalem her abominations 6
22 in all your abominations and your harlotries 6
43 lewdness in addition to all your abominations? 6
47 or do according to their abominations; 6
51 you have committed more abominations than they 6
51 the abominations which you have committed. 6
58 penalty of your lewdness and your abominations 6
18:12 his eyes to the idols, commits abomination 6
20: 4 let them know the abominations of their fathers 6
22:11 commits abomination with his neighbor's wife; 6
33:26 You resort to the sword, you commit abominations 6
29 their abominations which they have committed. 6
43: 8 their abominations which they have committed 6
44: 6 let there be an end to all your abominations 6
7 in addition to all your abominations. 6
13 the abominations which they have committed. 6
Dan 9:27 upon the wing of abominations shall come one 3
11:31 set up the abomination that makes desolate. 3
12:11 time . . the abomination that makes desolate 3
Zec 9: 7 and its abominations from between its teeth; 3
Mal 2:11 abomination has been committed in Israel 6
Lke 16:15 an abomination in the sight of God. 7
Rev 17: 4 holding . . a golden cup full of abominations 7
5 mother . . of the earth's abominations. 7
21:27 nor any one who practices abomination 7
1Es 7:13 separated themselves from the abominations 7
Wis 12:23 torment through their own abominations. 7
14:11 because . . they became an abomination 7
Sir 1:25 godliness is an abomination to a sinner. 7
10:13 the man who clings to it pours out abominations. 7
13:20 Humility is an abomination to a proud man; 7
20 a poor man is an abomination to a rich one. 7
15:13 The Lord hates all abominations 7
17:26 hate abominations intensely. 7
27:30 Anger and wrath, these also are abominations 7
49: 2 took away the abominations of iniquity. 7
Man 1:10 setting up abominations and multiplying offenses 7
1Mc 6: 7 the abomination which he had erected 7

abound 1. גָּדוֹל 2. כבד 3. רֹב 4. רַב 5. רבה 6. *περισσεύω* 7. *πλεονάζω* 8. abundo 9. multiplico

Exd 34: 6 slow to anger, and abounding in steadfast love 4
Num14:18 The LORD is . . abounding in steadfast love 4
Neh 9:17 thou art a God . . abounding in steadfast love 4
Ps 4: 7 than they have when their grain and wine abound. 5
72: 7 may righteousness flourish, and peace abound 3
86: 5 abounding in steadfast love to all who call 4
15 abounding in steadfast love and faithfulness. 4
103: 8 slow to anger and abounding in steadfast love. 4
145: 8 slow to anger and abounding in steadfast love. 1
Prv 8:24 when . . no springs abounding with water. 2
28:20 A faithful man will abound with blessings 4
Jol 2:13 slow to anger, and abounding in steadfast love 4
Jon 4: 2 slow to anger, and abounding in steadfast love 4
Rom 3: 7 if . . God's truthfulness abounds to his glory 6
5:15 the grace of God . . abounded for many. 6
6: 1 Are we to continue in sin that grace may abound? 7
15:13 of the Holy Spirit you may abound in hope. 6
1Co 15:58 always abounding in the work of the Lord 6
Php 1: 9 my prayer that your love may abound more and more 6
4:12 I know how to be abased, and I know how to abound 6
Col 2: 7 abounding in thanksgiving. 6
1Th 3:12 may the Lord make you increase and abound in love 6
2Pe 1: 8 For if these things are yours and abound 7
2Es 3:33 and have seen that they abound in wealth 8
7:51 while the ungodly abound 9
Sir 11:12 who lacks strength and abounds in poverty 6
23: 3 in order that . . my sins may not abound 7

abound all the more 1. *ὑπερπερισσεύω*

Rom 5:20 where sin increased, grace abounded all the more 1

make abound 1. יתר 2. multiplico

Deu 28:11 LORD will make you abound in prosperity 1
2Es 7:136 because he makes his compassions abound 2
137 for if he did not make them abound 2

about 1. אֶל 2. בְּ 3. בָּ 4. לְ 5. מִן 6. עַל 7. עַל אֹדוֹת 8. עַל (A) 9. *εἰς* 10. *ἐν* 11. *ἐν τίνι* 12. *ἐπί* 13. *εὑρίσκω* 14. *κατά* 15. *κύκλος* 16. *περί* 17. *περιβολή* 18. *ποιέω* 19. *πρός* 20. *ὑπέρ* 21. ante 22. de 23. super

Gen 21:25 Abraham complained to Abim'elech about a well 6
24:28 told her mother's household about these things. 3
26: 7 When the men of the place asked him about his wife 4
32 came and told him about the well which they had dug 7
39: 8 my master has no concern about anything *
43: 7 man questioned us carefully about ourselves 4
27 he inquired about their welfare, and said 4
Exd 6:27 spoke to Pharaoh . . about bringing out 4
Lev 6: 3 or has found what was lost and lied about it 2
5 or anything about which he has sworn falsely 6
Num11: 1 people complained . . about their misfortunes; *
Deu 12:30 that you do not inquire about their gods, saying 4
Jdg 8:15 Zebah and Zalmun'na, about whom you taunted me *
17: 2 silver . . about which you uttered a curse *
1Sm 9: 5 lest my father cease to care about the asses 5
5 cease to care . . and become anxious about us. 4
6 he can tell us about the journey on which we have *
10: 2 your father . . is anxious about you, saying 4
2 What shall I do about my son? 4
19: 3 and I will speak to my father about you; 2
21: 2 no one know . . of the matter about which I send you *
27:11 Lest they should tell about us 6
2Sm 3:26 they brought . . but David did not know about it. *
4: 4 news about Saul and Jonathan came from Jezreel; *
11: 3 And David sent and inquired about the woman. 4
18 and told David all the news about the fighting; *
19 all the news about the fighting to the king *
13:39 he was comforted about Amnon, seeing he was dead. 6
18: 3 For if we flee, they will not care about us. 1
3 If half of us die, they will not care about us. 1
5 the king gave orders to all . . about Ab'salom. 6
19:10 why . . say nothing about bringing the king back? 4
2Kg 19:20 prayer to me about Sennach'erib king of Assyria 1
2Ch 25: 9 But what shall we do about the 100 talents 4
31: 9 Hezeki'ah questioned . . about the heaps. 6
Ezr 7:14 to make inquiries about Judah and Jerusalem 8
Est 6: 2 how Mor'decai had told about Bigthana and Teresh 6
4 speak to the king about having Mor'decai hanged 4
9:29 confirming this second letter about Purim. *
Ps 41: 7 All who hate me whisper together about me; 6
69:12 the drunkards make songs about me. *
Prv 27: 1 Do not boast about tomorrow, for you do not know 2
Isa 23: 5 Egypt . . in anguish over the report about Tyre. *
45:11 Will you question me about my children 6
Jer 15: 5 Who will turn aside to ask about your welfare? 4
36: 8 ordered him about reading from the scroll 4
46: 2 About Egypt. Concerning the army of Pharaoh 4
13 spoke to Jeremiah the prophet about the coming 4
Lam 3:39 man complain . . about the punishment of his sins? 6
Ezk 12:22 proverb that you have about the land of Israel 6
16:44 proverb about you, 'Like mother, like daughter. 6
33:30 people who talk together about you by the walls 2
38: 7 all the hosts that are assembled about you 6
Nah 1:14 The LORD has given commandment about you 6
Mat 6:25 I tell you, do not be anxious about your life *
25 do not be anxious . . about your body *
28 And why are you anxious about clothing? Consider 16
34 Therefore do not be anxious about tomorrow 9
11: 2 about the deeds of the Christ *
14: 1 the tetrarch heard about the fame of Jesus; *
16:11 that I did not speak about bread 16
18:19 agree on earth about anything they ask 16
19:17 he said . . "Why do you ask me about what is good? 16
21:45 they perceived that he was speaking about them. 16
Mrk 1:45 he went out and began to talk freely about it *
4: 1 a very large crowd gathered about him 19
5:27 She had heard the reports about Jesus 16
6:52 for they did not understand about the loaves 12
7:17 his disciples asked him about the parable. *
8:30 he charged them to tell no one about him. 16
10:10 the disciples asked him again about this matter. 16
12:26 in the passage about the bush 12
Lke 2:33 marveled at what was said about him; 16
9: 9 who is this about whom I hear such things? 16
45 they were afraid to ask him about this saying. 16
10:41 you are anxious and troubled about many things; 16
12:22 do not be anxious about your life *
22 nor about your body, what you shall put on. *
26 why are you anxious about the rest? 16
16: 2 What is this that I hear about you? 16
20:37 even Moses showed, in the passage about the bush 12
22:37 what is written about me has its fulfilment. 16
23: 8 desired to see him, because he had heard about him 16
24: 4 While they were perplexed about this 16
14 talking with each other about all these things 16
44 everything written about me in the law of Moses 16
Joh 1:22 What do you say about yourself? 16
7:12 much muttering about him among the people 16
32 heard the crowd thus muttering about him 16
39 Now this he said about the Spirit 16
8: 5 What do you say about her? *
26 I have much to say about you and much to judge 16
9:17 What do you say about him 16
10:41 everything . . John said about this man was true 16
18:19 about his disciples and his teaching. 16
34 did others say it to you about me? 16
Act 5:24 they were much perplexed about them 16
8:12 as he preached good news about the kingdom of God 16
34 About whom, pray, does the prophet say this 16
34 about himself or about some one else? 16
34 about himself or about some one else? 16
9:13 I have heard from many about this man 16
15: 2 to go up to Jerusalem . . about this question. 16
17:32 others said, "We will hear you again about this. 16
18:15 a matter of questions about words and names 16
19: 8 arguing and pleading about the kingdom of God; 16
21:21 they have been told about you 16
24 is nothing in what they have been told about you 16
22:18 will not accept your testimony about me.' 16
23:11 as you have testified about me at Jerusalem 16
20 to inquire somewhat more closely about him. 16
29 he was accused about questions of their law 16
24: 8 will be able to learn from him about everything 16
25 as he argued about justice and self-control 16
25: 5 if there is anything wrong about the man 10
15 the chief priests . . gave information about him 16
19 dispute . . about their own superstition 16
19 dispute . . about one Jesus, who was dead 16
24 about whom the whole Jewish people petitioned 16
26 nothing definite to write to my lord about him 16
26:26 the king knows about these things 16
28:21 We have received no letters from Judea about you 16
21 reported or spoken any evil about you. 16

23 trying to convince them about Jesus 16
31 teaching about the Lord Jesus Christ 16
Rom 1:19 For what can be known about God is plain to them *
25 they exchanged the truth about God for a lie *
4: 1 What then shall we say about Abraham 13
15:14 I myself am satisfied about you, my brethren 16
1Co 7: 1 concerning the matters about which you wrote. 16
32 is anxious about the affairs of the Lord *
11:34 About the other things I will give directions *
2Co 8: 1 We want you to know, brethren, about the grace *
20 no one should blame us about this liberal gift 10
24 our boasting about you to these men. 20
9: 1 to write to you about the offering for the saints 16
2 of which I boast about you 20
3 so that our boasting about you may not prove vain 20
12: 8 Three times I besought the Lord about this 20
Gal 2:14 straightforward about the truth of the gospel 19
4:20 I am perplexed about you. 10
Eph 4:21 assuming that you have heard about him *
Php 1: 7 It is right for me to feel thus about you all 20
4: 6 Have no anxiety about anything *
1Th 3: 7 comforted about you through your faith; 12
2Th 3: 4 we have confidence in the Lord about you 12
1Ti 1: 7 the things about which they make assertions. 16
Heb 5:11 About this we have much to say 16
6: 2 instruction about ablutions *
7:14 Moses said nothing about priests. 16
Jas 4:14 whereas you do not know about tomorrow. *
1Pe 1:10 searched and inquired about this salvation 16
5: 7 Cast . . anxieties on him, for he cares about you 16
2Pe 3: 9 The Lord is not slow about his promise *
1Jn 2:26 I write this to you about those who would deceive 16
27 as his anointing teaches you about everything 16
Jde 1: 9 Michael . . disputed about the body of Moses 16
Rev 10:11 prophesy about many peoples and nations 12
1Es 1:42 the things that are reported about Jehoiakim 16
2:22 will find . . what has been written about them 16
8:53 again we prayed to our Lord about these things 14
93 Let us take an oath to the Lord about this 10
2Es 4: 9 now I have asked you only about fire and wind 22
9 and you have given me no answer about them! 22
23 For I did not wish to inquire about the ways above 22
23 about those things which we daily experience 22
25 It is about these things that I have asked. 22
28 For the evil about which you ask me has been sown 22
35 in their chambers ask about these matters 22
52 Concerning the signs about which you ask me 22
8:15 About all mankind thou knowest best 22
15 I will speak about thy people 22
16 about thy inheritance, for whom I lament 22
16 and about Israel, for whom I am sad 22
16 about the seed of Jacob, for whom I am troubled. 22
38 concern myself about the fashioning of those 23
38 or about their death, their judgment 21
55 questions about the multitude . . who perish. 22
10:38 and tell you about the things which you fear 22
43 her telling you about the misfortune of her son 22
13:22 As for what you said about those who are left 22
53 And you alone have been enlightened about this *
15:53 and talking about their death when you were drunk? 23
Tob 1:19 went and informed the king about me 16
4: 2 explain to him about the money before I die? *
20 explain to you about the ten talents of silver *
6:15 do not worry about the demon *
7: 8 speak of those things which you talked about 20
8:12 let us bury him without any one knowing about it. *
14: 4 what Jonah the prophet said about Nineveh 16
Jdt 1: 2 he is the king who built walls about Ecbatana 15
2: 1 there was talk . . about carrying out his revenge *
13 do not delay about it. 18
5: 5 I will tell you the truth about this people 16
8: 1 At that time Judith heard about these things *
10: 9 accomplish the things about which you spoke *
18 she waited . . while they told him about her. 16
11:16 as many as shall hear about them. *
Wis 12:14 about those whom thou hast punished. 16
13:17 When he prays about possessions 16
14:22 to err about the knowledge of God 16
Sir 9:15 your discussion be about the law of the Most High. 10
11: 4 Do not boast about wearing fine clothes 17
9 argue about a matter which does not concern you 16
21: 1 Do so no more, but pray about your former sins. 16
29:28 scolding about lodging *
31: 1 anxiety about it removes sleep. *
33: 2 he who is hypocritical about it 10
37:11 Do not consult with a woman about her rival 16
11 with a coward about war 16
11 with a merchant about barter 16
11 with a buyer about selling 16
11 with a grudging man about gratitude 16
11 with a merciless man about kindness 16
11 with an idler about any work 16
11 about completing his work 16
11 with a lazy servant about a big task 16
38:25 whose talk is about bulls? 10
26 he is careful about fodder for the heifers. 9
41: 4 there is no inquiry about it in Hades. *
11 The mourning of men is about their bodies 10
Bar 3:31 No one . . is concerned about the path to her. *

Sus 1:27 nothing like this had ever been said about Susanna. 16
Bel 1:12 who is telling lies about us. 14
35 I know nothing about the den. *
1Mc 3:34 and gave him orders about all that he wanted done 16
48 about which the Gentiles were consulting 16
4:44 what to do about the altar of burnt offering 16
10:19 We have heard about you 16
35 annoy any of them about any matter. 16
63 bring charges against him about any matter 16
11:29 a letter to Jonathan about all these things 16
53 he broke his word about all that he had promised; *
14:21 told us about your glory and honor 16
16:18 Then Ptolemy wrote a report about these things *
2Mc 2:13 collected the books about the kings 16
13 letters of kings about votive offerings. 16
3: 4 about the administration of the city market; 16
7 the money about which he had been informed 16
9 he told about the disclosure that had been made 16
15 who had given the law about deposits 16
38 certainly is about the place some power of God. 16
4: 1 who had informed about the money *
43 Charges were brought . . about this incident. 16
7:42 about the eating of sacrifices 16
11:17 and have asked about the matters indicated therein. 16
12: 1 the Jews went about their farming. 16
14: 5 was asked about the disposition . . of the Jews. 11
3Mc 3: 7 they gossiped about the differences in worship 16
4:19 he was clearly convinced about the matter 16
5:10 to report to the king about these preparations. 16
37 must I give you orders about these things? 16
4Mc 4:13 otherwise he had scruples about doing so *
18:11 He read to you about Abel slain by Cain *
12 he taught you about Hananiah, Azariah, and Mishael *

about (2) 1. הלך 2. נגע 3. קרב 4. *ἕτοιμος* 5. *μέλλω* 6. *πρός* 7. coepio 8. incipio 9. sum

Gen 12:11 When he was about to enter Egypt, he said 3
18:17 Shall I hide from Abraham what I am about to do *
19:13 for we are about to destroy this place *
14 for the LORD is about to destroy the city. *
25:32 Esau said, "I am about to die; 1
41:25 has revealed to Pharaoh what he is about to do. *
28 God has shown to Pharaoh what he is about to do. *
48:21 Behold, I am about to die, but God will be with you *
50: 5 I am about to die; in my tomb which I hewed out *
24 Joseph said to his brothers, "I am about to die; *
Deu 2: 4 You are about to pass through the territory *
18:14 these nations, which you are about to dispossess *
31:16 Behold, you are about to sleep with your fathers; *
1Sm 3:11 I am about to do a thing in Israel *
13 And I tell him that I am about to punish his house *
4:19 was with child, about to give birth. *
2Sm 19:18 Shim'e-i . . as he was about to cross the Jordan *
1Kg 2: 2 I am about to go the way of all the earth. Be strong *
11:31 I am about to tear the kingdom from the hand *
2Kg 2: 1 the LORD was about to take Eli'jah up to heaven *
11: 2 among the king's sons who were about to be slain *
1Ch 21:15 when he was about to destroy it, the LORD saw *
2Ch 2: 4 I am about to build a house for the name of the LORD *
22:11 king's sons who were about to be slain *
Est 9: 1 command and edict were about to be executed 2
Job 29:13 blessing of him who was about to perish came upon *
Isa 30:13 a high wall, bulging out, and about to collapse *
Jer 26:19 we are about to bring great evil upon ourselves. *
37: 7 is about to return to Egypt, to its own land. *
Ezk 24:16 I am about to take the delight of your eyes away *
36:22 I am about to act, but for the sake of my holy name *
37:19 Behold, I am about to take the stick of Joseph *
Hag 2:21 I am about to shake the heavens and the earth *
22 am about to destroy the strength of the kingdoms *
Zec 12: 2 Lo, I am about to make Jerusalem a cup of reeling *
Mat 2:13 Herod is about to search for the child, to destroy 5
Lke 10: 1 where he himself was about to come. 5
21: 7 the sign when this is about to take place? 5
Joh 6:15 they were about to come and take him by force 5
Act 3: 3 Seeing Peter and John about to go into the temple 5
12: 6 when Herod was about to bring him out 5
16:27 he drew his sword and was about to kill himself 5
18:14 when Paul was about to open his mouth 5
20: 3 as he was about to set sail for Syria 5
21:37 As Paul was about to be brought into the barracks 5
22:26 What are you about to do? 5
29 those who were about to examine him withdrew 5
23:27 and was about to be killed by them 5
27: 2 which was about to sail to the ports 5
33 As day was about to dawn 5
Heb 8: 5 when Moses was about to erect the tent 5
Rev 2:10 Do not fear what you are about to suffer. 5
10 devil is about to throw some of you into prison 5
8:13 trumpets which the . . angels are about to blow! 5
10: 4 I was about to write, but I heard a voice 5
12: 4 the woman who was about to bear a child 5
2Es 6:20 the age which is about to pass away 8
46 to serve man, who was about to be formed. 9
9: 2 when the Most High is about to visit the world 8
13:46 and now, when they are about to come again 7
14:25 until what you are about to write is finished. 8
Tob 14: 3 I have grown old and am about to depart this life. 6

Jdt 8:32 I am about to do a thing *
34 until I have finished what I am about to do. *
10:12 are about to be handed over to you to be devoured. 5
11:11 they are about to provoke their God to anger *
Wis 14: 1 and about to voyage over raging waves 5
Sir 51: 3 from the gnashings of teeth about to devour me 4
1Mc 13:14 he was about to join battle with him 5
2Mc 2:16 we are about to celebrate the purification 5
22 the laws that were about to be abolished 5
3:18 the holy place was about to be brought into contempt. 5
6:30 When he was about to die under the blows 5
7:18 when he was about to die, he said 5
8: 3 and about to be leveled to the ground 5
11 the judgment . . that was about to overtake him. 5
14:41 When the troops were about to capture the tower 5
4Mc 1: 1 The subject that I am about to discuss 5
6:26 burned to his very bones and about to expire 5
8:27 though about to be tortured 5
10: 9 When he was about to die, he said 5
12:15 Then because he too was about to die, he said 5
17: 1 when she also was about to be seized 5

about (3) 1. אֶל 2. בְּ 3. לְ 4. בְּ (A) 5. *εἰς* 6. *ἤδη* 7. *κατά* 8. *μέχρι* 9. *περί* 10. *ποῦ* 11. *πρός* 12. *ὡς* 13. *ὡσεί* 14. *ὡσεὶ περί* 15. sicut

Gen 21:16 a good way off, about the distance of a bowshot; 2
38:24 About three months later Judah was told 2
Exd 32:28 there fell of the people that day about 3,000 men. 2
Num 11:31 about a day's journey on this side 2
31 let them fall . . about two cubits above the face 2
Jos 3: 4 shall be a space . . a distance of about 2,000 cubits; 2
4:13 about 40,000 ready armed for war passed over 2
7: 3 but let about 2,000 or 3,000 men go up 2
4 about 3,000 went up there from the people; 2
5 the men of Ai killed about 36 men of them 2
8:12 he took about 5,000 men, and set them in ambush 2
10:13 did not hasten to go down for about a whole day. 2
Jdg 3:29 killed at that time about 10,000 of the Moabites 2
8:10 were in Karkor with their army, about 15,000 men 2
9:49 of Shechem also died, about 1,000 men and women. 2
16:27 on the roof there were about 3,000 men and women 2
20:31 and kill some . . about 30 men of Israel. 2
39 had begun to smite and kill about 30 men 2
Rut 1: 4 They lived there about ten years; 2
2:17 and it was about an ephah of barley. 2
1Sm 4: 2 Philistines, who slew about 4,000 men 2
20 about the time of her death the women . . said 2
9:16 Tomorrow about this time I will send to you a man 2
22 those . . invited, who were about 30 persons. 2
13:15 people who were present with him, about 600 men. 2
14: 2 the people who were with him were about 600 men 2
14 that first slaughter . . was of about twenty men 2
20:12 When I . . about this time tomorrow, or the third 2
22: 2 And there were with him about 400 men. 2
23:13 David and his men, who were about 600 2
25:13 and about 400 men went up after David 2
38 And about ten days later the LORD smote Nabal; 2
2Sm 4: 5 about the heat of the day they came to the house 2
23:13 And three . . came about harvest time to David 1
1Kg 20: 6 send my servants to you tomorrow about this time 2
22: 6 king . . gathered the prophets . . , about 400 men 2
36 about sunset a cry went through the army 2
2Kg 3:20 about the time of offering the sacrifice, behold 2
4:17 bore a son about that time the following spring 3
7: 1 Tomorrow about this time . . meal shall be sold 2
18 barley shall be sold . . about this time tomorrow 2
Ezk 8:16 behold, at the door . . were about 25 men 2
Dan 5:31 Darius . . being about 62 years old. 4
Mat 14:21 those who ate were about 5,000 men 13
20: 3 going out about the third hour he saw others 9
5 Going out again about the sixth hour 9
6 about the eleventh hour he went out 9
9 when those hired about the eleventh hour came 9
27:46 about the ninth hour Jesus cried 9
Mrk 5:13 and the herd, numbering about 2,000 12
6:48 about the fourth watch of the night he came 9
8: 9 there were about 4,000 people 12
Lke 1:56 Mary remained with her about three months 12
3:23 Jesus . . was about 30 years of age 13
8:42 he had an only daughter, about twelve years of age 12
9:14 For there were about 5,000 men. 13
14 Make them sit down in companies, about 50 each. 13
28 Now about eight days after these sayings 13
22:41 he withdrew from them about a stone's throw 13
59 after an interval of about an hour 13
23:44 It was now about the sixth hour 13
24:13 Emma'us, about seven miles from Jerusalem *
Joh 6:19 When they had rowed about three or four miles 12
7:14 About the middle of the feast 6
11:18 Bethany was near Jerusalem, about two miles off 12
19:14 it was about the sixth hour 12
39 about a 100 pounds' weight. 12
21: 8 about 100 yards off. 12
Act 1:15 in all about 120 13
2:41 there were added that day about 3,000 souls. 13
4: 4 the number of the men came to about 5,000 12
5: 7 After an interval of about three hours 12
36 a number of men, about 400, joined him 12

10: 3 About the ninth hour of the day 14
9 about the sixth hour. 9
30 Cornelius said, "Four days ago, about this hour 8
12: 1 About that time 7
13:18 for about 40 years he bore with them 12
19 for about 450 years 12
16:25 about midnight Paul and Silas were praying 7
19: 7 There were about twelve of them in all. 13
23 About that time there arose no little stir 7
34 for about two hours they all . . cried out 12
22: 6 about noon a great light from heaven 9
27:27 about midnight the sailors suspected 7
Rom 4:19 because he was about a 100 years old 10
9: 9 the promise said, "About this time I will return 7
Rev 8: 1 silence in heaven for about half an hour. 12
2Es 7:43 For it will last for about a week of years. 15
1Mc 5:13 and have destroyed about 1,000 men there. 13
7:32 About 500 men of the army of Nicanor fell 13
9:49 about 1,000 of Bacchides' men fell that day. 5
61 Jonathan's men seized about 50 of the men 5
16:10 about 2,000 of them fell 5
2Mc 4:40 Lysimachus armed about 3,000 men 11
5: 1 About this time 9
27 Judas Maccabeus, with about nine others, got away 10
8: 1 so they gathered about 6,000 men. 5
9: 1 About that time, as it happened 9
11: 2 gathered about 80,000 men and all his cavalry 9
5 about five leagues from Jerusalem 13
14: 4 went to King Demetrius in about the 151st year 12
3Mc 5:46 entered at about dawn into the courtyard 9

about (4) 1. אֶל 2. בְּ 3. בְּעַד 4. בַּעַד 5. כְּ 6. לְ 7. סָבִיב 8. עַל 9. עִם 10. עַל (A) 11. *ἔξωθεν* 12. *ἐπί* 13. *κυκλόθεν* 14. *περί* 15. *περιβάλλω* 16. *περικυκλόω* 17. *περιτίθημι* 18. *περίχωρος* 19. *πρός* 20. *ὡς* 21. ad 22. circuitus 23. circum

Gen 41:42 fine linen, and put a gold chain about his neck; 8
Exd 9:18 Behold, tomorrow about this time I will cause 5
11: 4 says the LORD: About midnight I will go forth 5
12:37 about 600,000 men on foot, besides women 5
18:13 stood about Moses from morning till evening. 8
14 you sit alone, and all the people stand about you 8
19:23 Set bounds about the mountain, and consecrate *
Num16:24 Get away from about the dwelling of Korah, Dathan 7
27 got away from about the dwelling of Korah, Dathan 7
Jdg 8:26 collars that were about the necks of their camels. 2
1Sm 22: 6 and all his servants were standing about him. 8
7 Saul said to his servants who stood about him 8
17 the king said to the guard who stood about him 8
1Kg 2: 5 innocent blood upon the girdle about my loins 2
11:24 he gathered men about him and became leader 8
18:26 they limped about the altar which they had made. 8
32 And he made a trench about the altar 7
2Kg 1: 8 with a girdle of leather about his loins. 2
2Ch 13: 7 scoundrels gathered about him and defied 8
Ezr 1: 6 all who were about them aided them 7
Neh 5:17 came to us from the nations which were about us. 7
Job 1:10 Hast thou not put a hedge about him and his house 4
8:17 His roots twine about the stoneheap; 8
17: 2 Surely there are mockers about me 9
19: 6 put me in the wrong, and closed his net about me. 8
29: 5 when my children were about me; 7
36:30 Behold, he scatters his lightning about him 8
Ps 3: 3 But thou, O LORD, art a shield about me 4
44:13 the derision and scorn of those about us. 7
139:11 darkness cover me, and the light about me be night 4
Prv 3: 3 bind them about your neck 8
6:21 tie them about your neck. 8
Sng 3: 7 litter of Solomon! About it are 60 mighty men 7
Jer 26: 9 And all the people gathered about Jeremiah 1
32:44 in the places about Jerusalem, and in the cities 7
40:15 all the Jews who are gathered about you 1
Lam 3: 7 He has walled me about so that I cannot escape; 3
Ezk 32:24 Elam . . and all her multitude about her grave; 7
Dan 5: 7 purple, and have a chain of gold about his neck 10
16 purple, and have a chain of gold about your neck 10
29 purple, a chain of gold was put about his neck 10
Jon 2: 5 round about me; weeds were wrapped about my head 6
Mic 5: 1 Now you are walled about with a wall; *
Zec 12: 8 the LORD will put a shield about the inhabitants 4
Mat 3: 5 Judea and all the region about the Jordan 18
13: 2 great crowds gathered about him 19
Mrk 1:33 gathered together about the door. 19
2: 2 not even about the door 19
13 and all the crowd gathered about him 19
3: 8 from beyond the Jordan and from about Tyre 14
32 a crowd was sitting about him; and they said to him 14
34 looking around on those who sat about him 14
4:10 those who were about him with the twelve 14
5:21 a great crowd gathered about him 12
9:14 they saw a great crowd about them 14
14:51 with nothing but a linen cloth about his body 15
Lke 13: 8 till I dig about it and put on manure. 14
19:43 when your enemies will cast up a bank about you 16
22:49 when those who were about him saw 14
Joh 1:39 they stayed . . for it was about the tenth hour. 20
4: 6 It was about the sixth hour. 20
6:10 the men sat down, in number about 5,000. 20

1Es 3: 6 a necklace about his neck; 14
4:33 he began to speak about truth 14
8:91 there gathered about him a very great throng 19
2Es 11: 2 and the clouds were gathered about him. 21
15:44 all who are about her shall wail over her. 22
16:38 Just as a woman . . has great pains about her womb 23
Jdt 7:23 gathered about Uzziah and the rulers of the city 12
8: 5 girded sackcloth about her loins 12
Sir 12:11 he humbles himself and goes about cringing *
Bar 2:23 to cease . . from the region about Jerusalem 11
LJr 1:43 the women, with cords about them 17
Aza 1:25 the Chaldeans whom it caught about the furnace. 14
1Mc 2:67 You shall rally about you all who observe the law 19
11:47 they all rallied about him 19
4Mc 5: 1 with his armed soldiers standing about him 13

about *See* anxious, beset, bind, boast, bring, carry, cease, come, country, erect, face, feel, flash, gad, gather, go, group, inquire, lead, lie, move, parade, place, prowl, rally, region, rein, roam, roll, round, run, shine, stand, strew, talk, tell, think, throng, toss, turn, walk, wander, what.

about to go 1. הלך

Jos 23:14 And now I am about to go the way of all the earth 1

above 1. לְ 2. לְמַעְלָה 3. מִלְמַעְלָה 4. מִמַּעַל 5. מִמַּעְלָה 6. מִן 7. מַעַל 8. מֵעַל 9. מָעְלָה 10. עַל 11. עַל (A) 12. *ἄνω* 13. *ἄνωθεν* 14. *ἀνώτερος* 15. *ἐπάνω* 16. *ἐπί* 17. *ὅπου* 18. *οὗτος* 19. *παρά* 20. *πρό* 21. *πρός* 22. *ὑπέρ* 23. *ὑπεράνω* 24. propter 25. super 26. superus

Gen 1: 7 from the waters which were above the firmament 8
20 and let birds fly above the earth 10
3:14 done this, cursed are you above all cattle 6
14 cursed are you . . above all wild animals; 6
6:16 for the ark, and finish it to a cubit above; 5
7:17 the ark, and it rose high above the earth. 8
20 the waters prevailed above the mountains 3
28:13 behold, the LORD stood above it and said 10
49:25 will bless you with blessings of heaven above 8
Exd 20: 4 likeness of anything that is in heaven above 7
25:20 shall spread out their wings above 2
22 from above the mercy seat, from between 10
28:27 at its joining above the skilfully woven band 7
37: 9 The cherubim spread out their wings above 2
39:20 its joining above the skilfully woven band 7
31 a lace of blue, to fasten it on the turban above; 2
40:20 and set the mercy seat above on the ark; 2
Lev 11:21 may eat those which have legs above their feet 7
Num 7:89 voice speaking to him from above the mercy seat 10
11:31 about two cubits above the face of the earth. 10
16: 3 do you exalt yourselves above the assembly 10
Deu 4:39 know . . that the LORD is God in heaven above 7
5: 8 any likeness of anything that is in heaven above 7
7:14 You shall be blessed above all peoples; 6
10:15 LORD . . chose . . , you above all peoples 6
11:21 as long as the heavens are above the earth. 10
17:20 his heart may not be lifted up above his brethren 6
26:19 that he will set you high above all nations 10
28: 1 LORD . . will set you high above all the nations 10
43 sojourner . . mount above you higher and higher; 10
33:13 with the choicest gifts of heaven above 8
24 of Asher he said, "Blessed above sons be Asher; 6
Jos 2:11 is God in heaven above and on earth beneath. 4
3:13 the waters coming down from above shall stand 2
16 waters coming down from above stood and rose up 2
1Sm 2:29 and honor your sons above me by fattening 6
2Sm 6:21 before the LORD, who chose me above your father 6
21 who chose me . . above all his house 6
22:49 thou didst exalt me above my adversaries 6
1Kg 7: 3 it was covered with cedar above the chambers 7
11 And above were costly stones, hewn 3
20 capitals were . . above the rounded projection 7
29 both above and below the lions and oxen 2
8: 7 cherubim made a covering above the ark and its 3
23 God like thee, in heaven above or on earth beneath 4
14: 9 you have done evil above all that were before you 6
2Kg 19:15 O LORD . . who art enthroned above the cherubim *
25:28 and gave him a seat above the seats of the kings 8
1Ch 13: 6 the LORD who sits enthroned above the cherubim. *
16:25 he is to be held in awe above all gods. 10
29:11 O LORD, and thou art exalted as head above all. 1
2Ch 5: 8 cherubim made a covering above the ark and its 9
11:21 Rehobo'am loved Ma'acah . . above all his wives 6
24:20 Zechari'ah . . he stood above the people, and said 8
34: 4 incense altars which stood above them; 2
Neh 3:28 Above the Horse Gate the priests repaired 8
8: 5 for he was above all the people; and when he opened 10
9: 5 name . . exalted above all blessing and praise. 10
12:37 above the house of David, to the Water Gate 8
38 upon the wall, above the Tower of the Ovens 8
39 above the Gate of E'phraim, and by the Old Gate 8
Est 3: 1 set his seat above all the princes . . with him. 8
5:11 advanced him above the princes and the servants 10
Job 3: 4 Let that day be darkness! May God above not seek it 4
18: 6 dark in his tent, and his lamp above him is put out. 10
16 roots dry up . . and his branches wither above. 7
28:18 the price of wisdom is above pearls. 6
31: 2 What would be my portion from God above 7

28 for I should have been false to God above. 4
Ps 8: 1 Thou whose glory above the heavens is chanted 10
18:48 yea, thou didst exalt me above my adversaries; 6
27: 6 now my head shall be lifted up above my enemies 10
45: 7 with the oil of gladness above your fellows; 6
50: 4 He calls to the heavens above and to the earth 8
57: 5 Be exalted, O God, above the heavens! 10
11 Be exalted, O God, above the heavens! 10
78:23 Yet he commanded the skies above 7
89: 7 great . . above all that are round about him? 10
95: 3 For the LORD is . . a great King above all gods. 10
96: 4 he is to be feared above all gods. 10
97: 9 O LORD . . thou art exalted far above all gods. 10
103:11 For as the heavens are high above the earth 10
104: 6 waters stood above the mountains. 10
108: 4 thy steadfast love is great above the heavens 8
5 Be exalted, O God, above the heavens! 10
113: 4 The LORD is high above all nations 10
4 his glory above the heavens. 10
119:127 Therefore I love thy commandments above gold 6
127 thy commandments above gold, above fine gold. *
135: 5 For I know . . that our Lord is above all gods. 6
137: 6 if I do not set Jerusalem above my highest joy! 10
138: 2 exalted above everything thy name and thy word. 10
148: 4 Praise him, you . . waters above the heavens! 8
13 his glory is above earth and heaven. 10
Prv 8:28 when he made firm the skies above 4
Isa 2: 2 mountains, and shall be raised above the hills; 6
6: 2 Above him stood the seraphim; each had six wings 7
14:13 above the stars of God I will set my throne on high; 7
14 I will ascend above the heights of the clouds 10
37:16 O LORD . . who art enthroned above the cherubim *
40:22 It is he who sits above the circle of the earth 10
45: 8 Shower, O heavens, from above, and let the skies 7
Jer 4:28 earth shall mourn, and the heavens above be black; 4
17: 9 The heart is deceitful above all things 6
31:37 If the heavens above can be measured 3
35: 4 above the chamber of Ma-asei'ah the son of Shallum 7
43:10 he will set his throne above these stones 7
52:32 and gave him a seat above the seats of the kings 7
Ezk 1:11 And their wings were spread out above; 9
22 firmament . . spread out above their heads. 9
25 voice from above the firmament over their heads; 10
26 above the firmament over their heads there was 7
26 and seated above the likeness of a throne 10
8: 2 above his loins it was like the appearance 2
10: 1 appeared above them something like a sapphire 10
29:15 and never again exalt itself above the nations; 10
31: 5 it towered high above all the trees of the forest; 6
41:17 to the space above the door, even to the inner room 10
20 from the floor to above the door 8
Dan 6: 3 distinguished above all the other presidents 11
11:36 magnify himself above every god, 10
37 for he shall magnify himself above all. 10
12: 6 man . . who was above the waters of the stream 4
7 man . . who was above the waters of the stream 4
Ams 2: 9 I destroyed his fruit above, and his roots 4
Mic 4: 1 and shall be raised up above the hills; 6
Hag 1:10 the heavens above you have withheld the dew 10
Mat 10:24 A disciple is not above his teacher 22
24 nor a servant above his master; 22
Mrk 2: 4 they removed the roof above him 17
Lke 6:40 A disciple is not above his teacher 22
Joh 3:31 He who comes from above is above all; 13
31 He who comes from above is above all; 15
31 he who comes from heaven is above all. 15
8:23 said to them, "You are from below, I am from above; 12
19:11 unless it had been given you from above 13
Act 2:19 I will show wonders in the heaven above 12
Gal 4:26 Jerusalem above is free, and she is our mother. 12
Eph 1:21 and above every name that is named *
4: 6 who is above all and through all and in all. 16
Php 2: 9 the name which is above every name 22
Col 3: 1 seek the things that are above, where Christ is 12
2 Set your minds on things that are above 12
14 above all these put on love 16
Heb 9: 5 above it were the cherubim of glory 23
10: 8 When he said above 14
Jas 1:17 and every perfect gift is from above 13
3:15 This wisdom is not such as comes down from above 13
17 wisdom from above is first pure, then peaceable 13
5:12 above all, my brethren, do not swear 20
1Pe 4: 8 Above all hold unfailing your love 20
2Es 4: 7 or how many streams are above the firmament 25
21 he who is above the heavens 25
21 can understand what is above . . the heavens. 25
23 For I did not wish to inquire about the ways above 26
15:59 Unhappy above all others 24
Tob 1: 2 in Galilee above Asher. 23
Jdt 13: 6 above Holofernes' head 21
18 blessed . . above all women on earth 19
Sir 3: 2 the Lord honored the father above the children 16
15: 5 She will exalt him above his neighbors 19
30:16 there is no gladness above joy of heart. 22
49: 8 above the chariot of the cherubim. 16
16 Adam above every living being in the creation. 22
LJr 1:63 the fire sent from above to consume mountains 13
Aza 1:24 the flame streamed out above the furnace 15

38 Bless the Lord, all waters above the heaven 15
3Mc 7: 1 The letter was written in the above form. 18

above *See also* all, exalt, far, over, reproach, set.

abroad 1. חוץ 2. חוּצָה 3. לַחוּץ

Lev 18: 9 whether born at home or born abroad 1
Est 3: 8 people scattered abroad and dispersed •
Ps 41: 6 mischief; when he goes out, he tells it abroad. 3
Prv 5:16 Should your springs be scattered abroad 2
Sng 4:16 my garden, let its fragrance be wafted abroad. •
Ezk 34:12 some of his sheep have been scattered abroad •
21 till you have scattered them abroad 2

abroad *See also* go, live, scatter, send, shed, spread, walk, wander.

absence 1. ἀπουσία 2. ἄτερ 3. ὑστέρημα

Lke 22: 6 an opportunity . . in the absence of the multitude. 2
1Co 16:17 because they have made up for your absence; 3
Php 2:12 as in my presence but much more in my absence 1

absent 1. סתר 2. ἄπειμι 3. σκορπίζω

Gen 31:49 when we are absent one from the other. 1
1Co 5: 3 For though absent in body I am present in spirit 2
2Co 10:11 what we say by letter when absent 2
13: 2 I warn them now while absent 2
Php 1:27 so that whether I come and see you or am absent 2
Col 2: 5 though I am absent in body 2
Wis 11:11 Whether absent or present 2
1Mc 4: 4 the division was still absent from the camp. 3

absent one 1. ἄπειμι

Wis 14:17 they might flatter the absent one as though present. 1

abstain 1. ἀπέχω 2. ἀποστρέφω 3. μὴ ἐσθίω 4. οὐκ ἐσθίω 5. φυλάσσω

Act 15:20 write to them to abstain from . . idols 1
29 you abstain from what has been sacrificed to idols 1
21:25 should abstain from what has been sacrificed to idols 5
Rom 14: 3 Let not him who eats despise him who abstains 3
3 let not him who abstains pass judgment 3
6 he who abstains, abstains in honor of the Lord 3
6 he who abstains, abstains in honor of the Lord 4
1Th 4: 3 you abstain from unchastity; 1
5:22 abstain from every form of evil. 1
1Pe 2:11 to abstain from the passions of the flesh 1
4Mc 1:33 we abstain from the pleasure to be had from them 2
34 we abstain because of domination by reason. 1

abstinence 1. ἀπέχω

1Ti 4: 3 and enjoin abstinence from foods which God created 1

abundance 1. דֶּשֶׁן 2. הָמוֹן 3. הַרְבֵּה 4. זִיז 5. חֹסֶן 6. יִתְרָה 7. כבר 8. לָרֹב 9. מֶגֶד 10. מוֹתָר 11. מַרְבֶּה 12. עֲתֶרֶת 13. פִּסָּה 14. רֹב 15. רבה 16. שֹׂבַע 17. שׂבע 18. περισσεία 19. περίσσευμα 20. περισσεύω 21. πλῆθος 22. πληθύνω 23. πλησμονή 24. πολύς 25. ὑπερβολή 26. χορηγία 27. abundantia 28. copiosus 29. multitudo 30. plenitudo 31. satietas 32. saturitas

Gen 41:49 stored up grain in great abundance, like the sand 15
Deu 28:47 by reason of the abundance of all things 14
33:15 with the . . abundance of the everlasting hills 9
1Kg 1:19 He has sacrificed . . and sheep in abundance 14
25 and has sacrificed . . and sheep in abundance 14
10:10 never again came such an abundance of spices 14
1Ch 22:15 You have an abundance of workmen 8
29:16 all this abundance that we have provided 2
21 sacrifices in abundance for all Israel; 14
2Ch 2: 9 to prepare timber for me in abundance 14
14:15 and carried away sheep in abundance and camels. 14
18: 2 Ahab killed an abundance of sheep and oxen 14
24:11 and collected money in abundance. 14
32: 5 He also made weapons and shields in abundance. 14
29 provided . . flocks and herds in abundance; 14
Neh 5:18 every ten days skins of wine in abundance; 3
9:25 possession of . . and fruit trees in abundance; 14
Job 36:31 he judges peoples; he gives food in abundance. 7
Ps 5: 7 I through the abundance of thy steadfast love 14
36: 8 They feast on the abundance of thy house 1
37:16 Better . . than the abundance of many wicked. 2
19 in the days of famine they have abundance. 17
49: 6 boast of the abundance of their riches? 14
52: 7 but trusted in the abundance of his riches 14
69:13 in the abundance of thy steadfast love answer me. 14
72:16 May there be abundance of grain in the land; 13
78:25 he sent them food in abundance. 16
106: 7 not remember the abundance of thy steadfast love 14
45 to the abundance of his steadfast love. 14
Prv 11:14 in an abundance of counselors there is safety. 14
20:15 There is gold, and abundance of costly stones; 14
21: 5 plans of the diligent lead surely to abundance 10
24: 6 abundance of counselors there is victory. 14
Isa 7:22 because of the abundance of milk which they give 14
15: 7 Therefore the abundance they have gained 6
30:33 deep and wide, with fire and wood in abundance; 15
33: 6 abundance of salvation, wisdom, and knowledge; 5
23 Then prey and spoil in abundance will be divided; 11
60: 5 the abundance of the sea shall be turned to you 2
63: 7 the abundance of his steadfast love. 14
66:11 with delight from the abundance of her glory. 4
Jer 31:14 feast the soul of the priests with abundance 1
33: 6 and reveal to them abundance of prosperity 12
40:12 wine and summer fruits in great abundance. 15
Lam 3:32 according to the abundance of his steadfast love; 14
Ezk 7:11 none of them shall remain, nor their abundance 2
28:16 In the abundance of your trade you were filled 14
Zec 14:14 gold, silver, and garments in great abundance. 14
Mat 12:34 For out of the abundance of the heart 19
13:12 he will have abundance 20
25:29 he will have abundance 20
Mrk 12:44 For they all contributed out of their abundance; 20
Lke 6:45 out of the abundance of the heart 19
12:15 not consist in the abundance of his possessions 20
21: 4 for they all contributed out of their abundance 20
Rom 5:17 those who receive the abundance of grace 18
2Co 8: 2 their abundance of joy 18
14 your abundance at the present time 19
14 so that their abundance may supply your want 19
12: 7 too elated by the abundance of revelations 25
Php 4:12 facing plenty and hunger, abundance and want. 20
1Es 8:20 100 baths of wine, and salt in abundance. 21
2Es 1:20 so that waters flowed in abundance 31
2:27 you shall rejoice and have abundance. 28
6:44 fruit came forth in endless abundance 29
56 thou hast compared their abundance to a drop 27
7:123 in which are abundance and healing 32
15:41 be filled with the abundance of those waters. 30
Tob 2: 2 Upon seeing the abundance of food I said to my son 24
Sir 10:27 has an abundance of everything 20
13:11 nor trust his abundance of words 24
45:20 he prepared bread of first fruits in abundance; 23
1Mc 10:21 and equipped them with arms in abundance. 24
3Mc 5:10 been filled with a great abundance of wine 26
6: 4 Pharaoh with his abundance of chariots 22

abundance *See also* give, grant, provide.

abundant 1. לָרֹב 2. רַב 3. רֹב 4. שָׂבְעָה 5. שַׂגִּיא (A) 6. δαψιλής 7. περισσοτέρως 8. πλῆθος 9. πληθύνω 10. πλοῦτος 11. πολύς 12. multiplico 13. multus

1Ch 12:40 abundant provisions of meal, cakes of figs 1
2Ch 11:23 he gave them abundant provisions 3
Job 37:23 power and justice, and abundant righteousness 3
Ps 31:19 O how abundant is thy goodness, which thou hast 2
37:11 delight themselves in abundant prosperity. 3
51: 1 according to thy abundant mercy blot out my 3
69:16 according to thy abundant mercy, turn to me. 3
145: 7 pour forth the fame of thy abundant goodness 2
147: 5 Great is our LORD, and abundant in power; 2
Prv 3: 2 abundant welfare will they give you. •
14: 4 abundant crops come by the strength of the ox. 3
Isa 23:18 her merchandise will supply abundant food 4
Ezk 17: 5 he placed it beside abundant waters. 2
8 transplanted it to good soil by abundant waters 2
19:10 full of branches by reason of abundant water. 2
27:16 trafficked . . because of your abundant goods; 3
18 trafficked with you for your abundant goods 3
33 with your abundant wealth and merchandise 3
31: 5 long, from abundant water in its shoots. 2
7 for its roots went down to abundant waters. 2
Dan 4:12 Its leaves were fair and its fruit abundant 5
21 whose leaves were fair and its fruit abundant 5
11:13 come on with a great army and abundant supplies. 3
2Co 2: 4 to let you know the abundant love that I have 7
2Es 7:56 silver is more abundant than gold 12
57 those that are abundant or those that are rare? 12
136 abundant in compassion 13
AEs 10: 6 there was light and the sun and abundant water 11
11:10 there came a great river, with abundant water; 11
Wis 11: 7 thou gavest them abundant water unexpectedly 6
Sir 24:17 blossoms became glorious and abundant fruit. 10
29 for her thought is more abundant than the sea 9
Aza 1:19 in thy forbearance and in thy abundant mercy. 8
1Mc 6: 6 the arms, supplies, and abundant spoils 11

abundant *See also* make, rain.

abundantly 1. לְטוֹבָה 2. לִקְמָצִים 3. לָרֹב 4. עַל יֶתֶר 5. רַב 6. רֹב 7. רבה 8. περισσεύω 9. περισσός 10. ὑπερεκπερισσοῦ

Gen 30:30 you had little . . it has increased abundantly; 6
41:47 years the earth brought forth abundantly 2
Num 20:11 water came forth abundantly 5
Deu 30: 9 LORD . . will make you abundantly prosperous 1
2Ch 31: 5 brought in abundantly the tithe of everything. 3
Job 36:28 skies pour down, and drop upon man abundantly. 6
Ps 31:23 but abundantly requites him who acts haughtily. 4
78:15 and gave them drink abundantly as from the deep. 5
132:15 I will abundantly bless her provisions; †
Isa 35: 2 it shall blossom abundantly, and rejoice †
55: 7 and to our God, for he will abundantly pardon. 7
Joh 10:10 they may have life, and have it abundantly. 9
2Co 1: 5 as we share abundantly in Christ's sufferings 8
5 through Christ we share abundantly in comfort 8
Eph 3:20 is able to do far more abundantly 10

abundantly *See also* breed, bring, grow, water.

abuse 1. עלל 2. קָלוֹן 3. βλασφημέω 4. διαλοιδόρησις 5. ἐπηρεάζω 6. κακόω 7. καταλαλέω 8. λοιδορία 9. ὀνειδισμός 10. abutor 11. contumelia

Jdg 19:25 they knew her, and abused her all night 1
Prv 9: 7 He who corrects a scoffer gets himself abuse 2
22:10 quarreling and abuse will cease. 2
Jer 38:19 lest I be handed over to them and they abuse me. 1
Lke 6:28 pray for those who abuse you. 5
Heb 10:33 being publicly exposed to abuse and affliction 9
11:26 He considered abuse suffered for the Christ 9
13:13 and bear the abuse he endured. 9
1Pe 3:16 so that, when you are abused 7
4: 4 They are surprised . . and they abuse you; 3
2Es 9: 9 those who have now abused my ways shall be amazed 10
10:22 our free men have suffered abuse 11
Sir 7:20 Do not abuse a servant who performs his work 6
27:15 their abuse is grievous to hear. 4
21 there is reconciliation after abuse 8
28 Mockery and abuse issue from the proud man 9

abusive 1. βλάσφημος 2. ὀνειδίζω

2Ti 3: 2 lovers of money, proud, arrogant, abusive 1
Sir 18:18 A fool is ungracious and abusive 2

abusive *See also* word.

abyss 1. ἄβυσσος

Lke 8:31 not to command them to depart into the abyss. 1
Rom 10: 7 or "Who will descend into the abyss? 1
Sir 1: 3 the abyss, and wisdom–who can search them out? 1
16:18 the abyss and the earth 1
24: 5 have walked in the depths of the abyss. 1
29 and her counsel deeper than the great abyss. 1
42:18 He searches out the abyss, and the hearts of men 1

acacia 1. שִׁטָּה

Exd 25: 5 tanned rams' skins, goatskins, acacia wood 1
10 They shall make an ark of acacia wood; 1
13 You shall make poles of acacia wood, and overlay 1
23 you shall make a table of acacia wood; 1
28 You shall make the poles of acacia wood 1
26:15 frames for the tabernacle of acacia wood. 1
26 you shall make bars of acacia wood 1
32 you shall hang it upon four pillars of acacia 1
37 shall make for the screen five pillars of acacia 1
27: 1 You shall make the altar of acacia wood 1
6 make . . poles of acacia wood, and overlay them 1
30: 1 of acacia wood shall you make it. 1
5 You shall make the poles of acacia wood 1
35: 7 tanned rams' skins, and goatskins; acacia wood 1
24 man with whom was found acacia wood of any use 1
36:20 frames for the tabernacle of acacia wood. 1
31 he made bars of acacia wood, five for the frames 1
36 for it he made four pillars of acacia 1
37: 1 Bez'alel made the ark of acacia wood; 1
4 And he made poles of acacia wood 1
10 He also made the table of acacia wood; 1
15 He made the poles of acacia wood to carry 1
25 He made the altar of incense of acacia wood; 1
28 he made the poles of acacia wood, and overlaid 1
38: 1 altar of burnt offering also of acacia wood; 1
6 he made the poles of acacia wood, and overlaid 1
Deu 10: 3 I made an ark of acacia wood, and hewed two tables 1
Isa 41:19 the cedar, the acacia, the myrtle, and the olive; 1

accent 1. λαλιά

Mat 26:73 for your accent betrays you. 1

accept 1. למד 2. לקח 3. נכר 4. נשא 5. נשא פָּנִים 6. קבל 7. ריח 8. רצה 9. רָצוֹן 10. ἀποδέχομαι 11. δέχομαι 12. δόκιμος 13. ἐκδέχομαι 14. ἐπί 15. ἐπιδέχομαι 16. θέλω 17. λαμβάνω 18. παραδέχομαι 19. προσδέχομαι 20. ὑπολαμβάνω

Gen 4: 7 If you do well, will you not be accepted? 4
23:13 accept it from me, that I may bury my dead there. 2
32:20 shall see his face; perhaps he will accept me. 5
33:10 in your sight, then accept my present from my hand; 2
11 Accept, I pray you, my gift that is brought to you 2
Exd 22:11 the owner shall accept the oath, and he shall not 2
28:38 that they may be accepted before the LORD. 9
Lev 1: 3 that he may be accepted before the LORD 9
4 it shall be accepted for him to make atonement 8
7:18 he who offers it shall not be accepted 8
19: 5 you shall offer it so that you may be accepted 9
7 it is an abomination; it will not be accepted 8
22:19 to be accepted you shall offer a male 9
21 to be accepted it must be perfect 9
23 but for a votive offering it cannot be accepted 8
25 they will not be accepted for you 8
29 sacrifice it so that you may be accepted 9
Num 7: 5 Accept these from them, that they may be used 2
35:31 shall accept no ransom for the life of a murderer 2
32 you shall accept no ransom for him who has fled 2
Deu 33:11 Bless, O LORD . . and accept the work of his hands; 8
Jdg 13:23 he would not have accepted a burnt offering 2
1Sm 2:15 he will not accept boiled meat from you, but raw. 2
10: 4 bread, which you shall accept from their hand. 2
26:19 If it is the LORD . . may he accept an offering; 7

2Sm 24:23 And Arau'nah said . . "The LORD your God accept you. 8
2Kg 5:15 accept now a present from your servant. 2
20 in not accepting from his hand what he brought. 2
23 Na'aman said, "Be pleased to accept two talents. 2
26 Was it a time to accept money and garments 2
Est 4: 4 sent garments . . but he would not accept them. 6
Job 21:29 do you not accept their testimony 3
33:26 then man prays to God, and he accepts him 8
42: 8 I will accept his prayer not to deal with you 5
9 the LORD accepted Job's prayer. 5
Ps 6: 9 The LORD has heard . . the LORD accepts my prayer. 2
50: 9 I will accept no bull from your house 2
119:108 Accept my offerings of praise, O LORD, and teach me 8
Prv 4:10 Hear, my son, and accept my words 2
6:35 He will accept no compensation 4
17:23 A wicked man accepts a bribe from the bosom 2
19:20 Listen to advice and accept instruction 6
Ecc 5:19 to accept his lot and find enjoyment in his toil– 4
Isa 29:24 those who murmur will accept instruction. 1
56: 7 their sacrifices will be accepted on my altar; 9
Jer 7:28 and did not accept discipline; 2
14:10 therefore the LORD does not accept them 8
12 and cereal offering, I will not accept them; 8
25:28 if they refuse to accept the cup from your hand 2
Ezk 20:40 there I will accept them, and there I will require 8
41 As a pleasing odor I will accept you 8
43:27 I will accept you, says the Lord GOD. 8
Hos 14: 2 Take away all iniquity; accept that which is good 2
Ams 5:22 and cereal offerings, I will not accept them 8
Zep 3: 2 listens to no voice, she accepts no correction. 2
7 she will fear me, she will accept correction; 2
Mal 1:10 I will not accept an offering from your hand. 8
13 Shall I accept that from your hand? says the LORD. 8
2:13 or accepts it with favor at your hand. 2
Mat 11:14 if you are willing to accept it, he is Eli'jah 11
Mrk 4:20 hear the word and accept it and bear fruit 18
Act 16:21 not lawful for us Romans to accept or practice. 18
22:18 because they will not accept your testimony 18
24: 3 we accept this with all gratitude. 10
15 having a hope in God which these . . accept 19
2Co 6: 1 entreat you not to accept the grace of God 11
8:17 For he not only accepted our appeal 11
10:18 not the man who commends himself that is accepted 12
11: 4 if you accept a different gospel *
4 a different gospel from the one you accepted 11
8 I robbed other churches by accepting support 17
16 even if you do, accept me as a fool 11
1Th 2:13 you accepted it not as the word of men 11
Heb 10:34 you joyfully accepted the plundering 19
11: 4 God bearing witness by accepting his gifts *
35 Some were tortured, refusing to accept release 19
3Jn 1: 7 they . . have accepted nothing from the heathen 17
Tob 13: 6 if he will accept you and have mercy on you? 16
Jdt 11: 5 Accept the words of your servant 11
Wis 3: 6 he accepted them. 19
12:24 accepting as gods 20
Sir 2: 4 Accept whatever is brought upon you 11
6:23 Listen, my son, and accept my judgment 13
7: 9 he will accept it. 19
18:14 compassion on those who accept his discipline 13
32:14 He who fears the Lord will accept his discipline 13
35:12 for he will not accept it 19
16 will be accepted 11
36:21 A woman will accept any man 15
Aza 1:16 Yet with a contrite heart . . may we be accepted 19
1Mc 1:43 the Gentiles accepted the command of the king. 15
6:60 they accepted it. 15
9:31 Jonathan at that time accepted the leadership 15
10:46 they did not believe or accept them 15
14:47 So Simon accepted and agreed to be high priest 15
15:20 it has seemed good to us to accept the shield 11
2Mc 1:26 accept this sacrifice 19
7:29 Accept death 15
12: 4 when they accepted 15
3Mc 3:17 They accepted our presence by word 10
4Mc 8:17 to accept kind treatment if we obey him 14

accept willingly 1. ἐπιδέχομαι
3Mc 6:26 and often have accepted willingly the worst 1

acceptable 1. בחר 2. יטב 3. רצה 4. רָצוֹן 5. שׁפר (A) 6. ἀπόδεκτος 7. δεκτός 8. εὐάρεστος 9. εὐδοκία 10. εὐπρόσδεκτος 11. προσδεκτός
Lev 10:19 would it have been acceptable in he sight 2
22:20 for it will not be acceptable for you 4
27 from the eighth day on it shall be acceptable 3
Ps 19:14 my heart be acceptable in thy sight, O LORD, my rock 4
51:17 sacrifice acceptable to God is a broken spirit; *
69:13 At an acceptable time, O God, in the abundance 4
Prv 10:32 lips of the righteous know what is acceptable 4
21: 3 do . . justice is more acceptable to the LORD 1
Isa 58: 5 call this a fast, and a day acceptable to the LORD? 4
Jer 6:20 Your burnt offerings are not acceptable 4
Dan 4:27 Therefore, O king, let my counsel be acceptable 5
Lke 4:19 to proclaim the acceptable year of the Lord. 7
24 no prophet is acceptable in his own country. 7
Act 10:35 any one who fears him . . is acceptable to him. 7
Rom 12: 1 as a living sacrifice, holy and acceptable to God 8
2 what is good and acceptable and perfect. 8
14:18 he who thus serves Christ is acceptable to God 8
15:16 the offering of the Gentiles may be acceptable 10
31 my service . . be acceptable to the saints 10
2Co 6: 2 At the acceptable time I have listened to you 7
2 Behold, now is the acceptable time 10
8:12 it is acceptable according to what a man has 10
Php 4:18 a sacrifice acceptable and pleasing to God. 7
1Ti 2: 3 it is acceptable in the sight of God our Savior 6
5: 4 for this is acceptable in the sight of God. 6
Heb 12:28 thus let us offer to God acceptable worship 8
1Pe 2: 5 offer spiritual sacrifices acceptable to God 10
Wis 9:12 Then my works will be acceptable 11
Sir 2: 5 acceptable men in the furnace of humiliation. 7
34:18 the gifts of the lawless are not acceptable. 9
35: 7 The sacrifice of a righteous man is acceptable 7

more acceptable 1. πολύς
Heb 11: 4 a more acceptable sacrifice than Cain 1

acceptance 1. רָצוֹן 2. ἀποδέχομαι 3. πρόσλημψις
Isa 60: 7 they shall come up with acceptance on my altar 1
Rom 11:15 what will their acceptance mean but life 3
1Ti 1:15 The saying is sure and worthy of full acceptance 2
4: 9 is sure and worthy of full acceptance. 2

acceptance *See also* find.

access 1. מַהֲלָךְ 2. κάθοδος 3. προσαγωγή 4. πρόσοδος
Zec 3: 7 I will give you the right of access 1
Rom 5: 2 we have obtained access to this grace 3
Eph 2:18 for through him we both have access in one Spirit 3
3:12 confidence of access through our faith in him. 3
1Es 2:24 no longer have access to Coelesyria 2
2Mc 14: 3 to have access again to the holy altar 4

access *See also* difficult.

accessory 1. כְּלִי 2. עֲבֹדָה
Num 3:36 appointed charge . . and all their accessories; 1
4:32 all their equipment and all their accessories; 2

accommodate 1. συμπεριφέρω
3Mc 3:20 But we . . accommodated ourselves to their folly 1

accompaniment 1. ἐν
3Mc 6:35 to the accompaniment of joyous thanksgiving 1

accompany 1. עַל יָד 2. ἔρχομαι σύν 3. μετά 4. παραζεύγνυμι 5. παρακολουθέω 6. περιάγω 7. πορεύω σύν 8. συμπορεύομαι 9. σὺν εἰμί 10. σὺν ἐξέρχομαι 11. συνέπομαι 12. συνέρχομαι
2Ch 29:27 trumpets, accompanied by the instruments 1
Mrk 16:17 these signs will accompany those who believe 5
Lke 14:25 Now great multitudes accompanied him 8
Act 1:21 one of the men who have accompanied us 12
10:20 go down, and accompany them without hesitation; 7
23 some of the brethren from Joppa accompanied him. 12
11:12 These six brethren also accompanied me 2
16: 3 Paul wanted Timothy to accompany him 10
20: 4 Sop'ater of Beroe'a . . accompanied him 11
27: 2 we put to sea, accompanied by Aristar'chus 9
1Co 9: 5 we not have the right to be accompanied by a wife 6
16: 4 they will accompany me. 7
Tob 12: 8 Prayer is good when accompanied by fasting 3
Jdt 10:17 100 men to accompany her and her maid 4
1Mc 12:47 while 1,000 accompanied him. 12
2Mc 3:24 who had been so bold as to accompany him 12
4Mc 4: 5 he proceeded . . accompanied by the accursed Simon 3

accomplish 1. היה 2. כון 3. כָּלָה 4. כלה 5. עשה 6. פעל 7. קום 8. תמם 9. ἄγω ἐπὶ πέρας 10. ἀνύω 11. γίνομαι 12. διαπράσσω 13. ἐνεργέω 14. ἐπιτελέω 15. πληροφορέω 16. πληρόω 17. ποιέω 18. συντέλεια 19. συντελέω 20. τελειόω 21. τελείωσις 22. τελείως ποιέω 23. τελέω 24. χαρίεις 25. perficio
2Sm 3: 9 if I do not accomplish . . what the LORD has sworn 5
2Ch 8:16 Thus was accomplished all the work of Solomon 2
36:22 the word of the LORD . . might be accomplished 4
Ezr 1: 1 word of the LORD . . might be accomplished 4
Neh 6:16 perceived that this work had been accomplished 5
Job 35: 6 have sinned, what do you accomplish against him? 6
37:12 to accomplish all that he commands them 6
Isa 37:32 zeal of the LORD of hosts will accomplish this. 5
46:10 and I will accomplish all my purpose,' 5
55:11 but it shall accomplish that which I purpose 5
Jer 23:20 and accomplished the intents of his mind. 7
30:24 until he has executed and accomplished 7
39:16 shall be accomplished before you on that day. 1
Lam 4:22 punishment of your iniquity . . is accomplished 8
Dan 11:36 prosper till the indignation is accomplished; 3
12: 7 all these things would be accomplished. 4
Mat 5:18 pass from the law until all is accomplished. 11
Mrk 13: 4 when these things are all to be accomplished? 19
Lke 1: 1 which have been accomplished among us 15
9:31 which he was to accomplish at Jerusalem. 16
12:50 how I am constrained until it is accomplished! 23
18:31 everything . . will be accomplished. 23
Joh 4:34 and to accomplish his work. 20
5:36 which the Father has granted me to accomplish 20
17: 4 having accomplished the work 20
Act 20:24 if only I may accomplish my course 20
Eph 1:11 the purpose of him who accomplishes all things 13
20 which he accomplished in Christ 13
1Es 1:17 the sacrifices to the Lord were accomplished 19
2: 1 that the word of the Lord . . be accomplished 18
2Es 6:38 and thy word accomplished the work. 25
Tob 14:11 consider what almsgiving accomplishes 17
Jdt 10: 9 accomplish the things about which you spoke 21
11: 6 God will accomplish something through you 22
16 God has sent me to accomplish with you things 17
AEs 13: 3 how this might be accomplished 9
16: 7 What has been wickedly accomplished 19
2Mc 10:38 When they had accomplished these things 12
14:29 watched for an opportunity to accomplish this 14
3Mc 6:15 so accomplish it, O Lord. 14
7: 4 until this was accomplished 19
4Mc 8: 3 modest, noble, and accomplished in every way 24
9:12 without accomplishing anything 10

successfully accomplish 1. צלח
2Ch 7:11 all he planned . . he successfully accomplished 1

without accomplishing anything 1. ἄπρακτος
2Mc 12:18 without accomplishing anything 1

accord 1. לֵב 2. פֶּה 3. שְׁכֶם 4. ἀπό 5. αὐθαίρετος 6. αὐθαιρέτως 7. αὐτόματος 8. κατά 9. ποιέω 10. συμφώνησις
Num 16:28 that it has not been of my own accord. 1
Jos 9: 2 they gathered together with one accord to fight 2
1Kg 22:13 the words of the prophets with one accord are 2
2Ch 18:12 Behold, the words of the prophets with one accord 2
Ps 83: 5 Yea, they conspire with one accord; 1
Jer 9:13 not obeyed my voice, or walked in accord with it *
Zep 3: 9 and serve him with one accord. 3
Joh 5:19 the Son can do nothing of his own accord 4
7:28 I have not come of my own accord 4
8:42 I came not of my own accord, but he sent me. 4
10:18 I lay it down of my own accord 4
11:51 He did not say this of his own accord 4
18:34 Jesus answered, "Do you say this of your own accord 4
Act 12:10 It opened to them of its own accord 7
Rom 15: 5 in such harmony . . in accord with Christ Jesus 8
2Co 6:15 What accord has Christ with Be'lial? 10
8:17 he is going to you of his own accord. 5
2Th 3: 6 not in accord with the tradition 8
1Ti 6: 3 the teaching which accords with godliness 8
Tit 1: 1 the truth which accords with godliness 8
Sir 37:12 whose soul is in accord with your soul 8
1Mc 14:46 the right to act in accord with these decisions. 9
2Mc 6:19 he . . went up to the rack of his own accord 6
3Mc 7:17 in accord with the common desire 8
4Mc 11: 3 I have come of my own accord 4

full accord 1. σύμψυχος
Php 2: 2 having the same love, being in full accord 1

one accord 1. ὁμοθυμαδόν 2. ὁμόνοια 3. ὁμοῦ
Act 1:14 these with one accord devoted themselves to prayer 1
8: 6 the multitudes with one accord gave heed 1
15:25 it has seemed good to us, having come to one accord 1
1Es 9:38 the whole multitude gathered with one accord 1
Jdt 13:17 and said with one accord, "Blessed art thou, our God 1
15: 5 with one accord they fell upon the enemy 1
9 all blessed her with one accord and said to her 1
Wis 10:20 and praised with one accord thy defending hand 1
18: 9 and with one accord agreed to the divine law 2
3Mc 5:21 all . . joyfully with one accord gave their approval 3
50 they prostrated themselves with one accord 1

accordance 1. בְּ 2. כְּ 3. כְּפִי 4. לְ 5. עַל 6. עַל פִּי 7. ἀκολούθως 8. ἐκ 9. καθά 10. καθώς 11. κατά 12. μετά 13. πρός
Exd 24: 8 in accordance with all these words. 5
34:27 in accordance with these words I have made 6
36: 1 in accordance with all . . the LORD has commanded. 4
Num 6:21 in accordance with the vow which he takes 3
35:24 judge . . in accordance with these ordinances; 5
Deu 29:21 calamity, in accordance with all the curses 2
2Sm 7:17 In accordance with all these words 2
17 in accordance with all this vision, Nathan spoke 2
2Kg 6:18 he struck them . . in accordance with the prayer 2
9:26 take him up and . . in accordance with the word 2
16:11 in accordance with all that King Ahaz had sent 2
17:13 keep . . my statutes, in accordance with all the law 2
1Ch 17:15 In accordance with all these words 2
15 and in accordance with all this vision 2
2Ch 31:21 in accordance with the law and the commandments 1
Jer 32: 8 came . . in accordance with the word of the LORD 2
Ezk 36:19 in accordance with their conduct 2
1Co 15: 3 Christ died . . in accordance with the scriptures 11
4 he was raised . . in accordance with the scriptures 11
1Ti 1:11 in accordance with the glorious gospel 11
18 in accordance with the prophetic utterances 11

1Es 1: 5 in accordance with the directions of David 11
4:52 in accordance with the commandment 9
5:49 in accordance with the directions in the book 7
7: 9 in accordance with the book of Moses 7
8:10 In accordance with my gracious decision •
12 in accordance with what is in the law of the Lord 7
16 perform it in accordance with the will of your God; 11
9: 4 in accordance with the decision 11
15 acted in accordance with all this. 11
Tob 7:12 Take her right now, in accordance with the law 11
Sir 16:14 will receive in accordance with his deeds. 11
46: 1 in accordance with his name 11
Bar 2: 2 in accordance with what is written in the law 11
Aza 1:20 Deliver us in accordance with thy marvelous works 11
Sus 1:62 acting in accordance with the law of Moses 11
1Mc 7:16 in accordance with the word which was written 11
10:64 in accordance with the proclamation 10
3Mc 3:23 in accordance with their infamous way of life 12
7: 6 in accordance with the clemency which we have 11
22 in accordance with the registration 8
4Mc 2: 8 adopts a way of life in accordance with the law •
6:18 who have lived in accordance with truth to old age 13
8: 1 in accordance with devout reason •

accordance with law 1. *νομίμως*

4Mc 6:18 have maintained in accordance with law 1

according 1. אֶל 2. אֵת 3. בְּ 4. כְּ 5. כַּאֲשֶׁר 6. כְּמוֹ 7. כְּעַל 8. כְּפֶה 9. כְּפִי 10. לְ 11. לְפִי 12. מִן 13. עַל 14. עַל פִּי 15. בְּ (A) 16. כְּ (A) 17. לְ (A) 18. *ἀκολούθως* 19. *ἐκ* 20. *ἐν* 21. *καθώς* 22. *κατά* 23. *πρός* 24. *ὡς* 25. ad 26. iuxta 27. secundum

Gen 1:11 each according to its kind, upon the earth 10
12 yielding seed according to their own kinds 10
12 their seed, each according to its kind 10
21 creature . . according to their kinds 10
21 every winged bird according to its kind 10
24 living creatures according to their kinds 10
24 beasts of the earth according to their kinds 10
25 beasts of the earth according to their kinds 10
25 the cattle according to their kinds 10
25 creeps upon the ground according to its kind 10
6:20 Of the birds according to their kinds 10
20 and of the animals according to their kinds 1
20 every creeping thing . . according to its kind 10
7:14 they and every beast according to its kind 10
14 all the cattle according to their kinds 10
14 that creeps on the earth according to its kind 10
14 and every bird according to its kind 1
10:32 the families . . according to their genealogies 10
18:21 have done altogether according to the outcry 4
23:16 according to the weights current •
25:16 twelve princes according to their tribes. 10
33:14 I will lead on slowly, according to the pace 10
14 lead on . . according to the pace of the children 10
34:12 and I will give according as you say to me; 5
36:30 chiefs of the Horites, according to their clans 10
40 the chiefs of Esau, according to their families 10
43 chiefs of Edom . . according to their dwelling 10
41:12 to each man according to his dream. 4
43:33 the first-born according to his birthright 4
33 and the youngest according to his youth; 4
45:21 Joseph gave . . according to the command 14
47:12 provided . . food, according to the number 11
Exd 6:16 the sons of Levi according to their generations 10
19 Levites according to their generations. 10
8:13 the LORD did according to the word of Moses; 4
12: 3 a lamb according to their fathers' houses 10
4 shall take according to the number of persons; 3
4 according to what each can eat you shall make 11
21 Select lambs . . according to your families 10
16:16 take an omer apiece, according to the number •
18 each gathered according to what he could eat. 11
17: 1 moved on . . according to the commandment 13
21:22 shall be fined, according as the woman's 5
31 shall be dealt with according to this same rule. 4
23:24 nor serve them, nor do according to their works 4
24: 4 twelve pillars, according to the twelve tribes 10
25: 9 According to all that I show you concerning 4
26:30 erect the tabernacle according to the plan 4
28:21 stones with their names according to the names 13
29:35 according to all that I have commanded you; 4
30:13 half a shekel according to the shekel 3
24 according to the shekel of the sanctuary 3
37 you shall make according to its composition 3
31:11 According to all that I have commanded you 4
32:28 the sons of Levi did according to the word of Moses; 4
39: 6 engraved . . according to the names of the sons 13
14 stones with their names according to the names 13
32 the people of Israel had done according to all 4
42 According to all that the LORD had commanded 4
40:16 according to all that the LORD commanded him 4
Lev 5:10 for a burnt offering according to the ordinance 4
15 silver, according to the shekel of the sanctuary 3
9:16 and offered it according to the ordinance 4
10: 7 And they did according to the word of Moses 4
11:14 the kite, the falcon according to its kind 10
15 every raven according to its kind 10
16 the sea gull, the hawk according to its kind 10
19 the stork, the heron according to its kind 10
22 you may eat: the locust according to its kind 10
22 may eat . . the bald locust according to its kind 10
22 may eat . . the cricket according to its kind 10
22 may eat . . the grasshopper according to its kind 10
29 the mouse, the great lizard according to its kind 10
25:15 According to the number of years after 3
15 and according to the number of years for crops 3
50 price . . shall be according to the number of his 3
51 according to them he shall refund out 11
52 according to the years of service due from him 8
27: 3 50 shekels of silver, according to the shekel 3
8 according to the ability of him who vowed 14
16 your valuation shall be according to the seed 11
18 the money-value for it according to the years 14
25 Every valuation shall be according 3
Num 1: 2 census . . according to the number of names 3
18 registered . . according to the number of names 3
20 according to the number of names, head by head 3
22 according to the number of names, head by head 3
24 according to the number of the names 3
26 according to the number of names 3
28 according to the number of names 3
30 according to the number of names 3
32 according to the number of names 3
34 according to the number of names 3
36 according to the number of names 3
38 according to the number of names, from twenty 3
40 according to the number of names, from twenty 3
42 according to the number of names, from twenty 3
54 they did according to all that the LORD 4
2:34 According to all that the LORD commanded Moses 4
34 they set out . . according to his fathers' house. 13
3:16 numbered them according to the word of the LORD 13
22 Their number according to the number of all 3
28 According to the number of all the males 3
34 number according to the number of all the males 3
43 first-born . . according to the number of names 3
51 according to the word of the LORD, as the LORD 13
4:37 numbered according to the commandment 13
41 according to the commandment of the LORD. 13
45 numbered according to the commandment 13
49 According to the commandment of the LORD 13
6:21 His offering . . shall be according to his vow 13
21 so shall he do according to the law 13
7: 5 give . . to each man according to his service. 9
7 sons of Gershon, according to their service; 9
8 to the sons of Merar'i, according to their service 8
13 70 shekels, according to the shekel of the sanctuary 3
19 70 shekels, according to the shekel of the sanctuary 3
25 130 shekels, according to the shekel of the sanctuary 3
31 70 shekels, according to the shekel of the sanctuary 3
37 70 shekels, according to the shekel of the sanctuary 3
43 70 shekels, according to the shekel of the sanctuary 3
49 70 shekels, according to the shekel of the sanctuary 3
55 70 shekels, according to the shekel of the sanctuary 3
61 70 shekels, according to the shekel of the sanctuary 3
67 70 shekels, according to the shekel of the sanctuary 3
73 70 shekels, according to the shekel of the sanctuary 3
79 70 shekels, according to the shekel of the sanctuary 3
85 according to the shekel of the sanctuary 3
86 according to the shekel of the sanctuary 3
8: 4 according to the pattern which the LORD had shown 4
20 according to all that the LORD commanded Moses 4
9: 3 according to all its statutes 4
5 according to all that the LORD commanded Moses 4
12 according to all the statute for the passover 4
14 according to the statute of the passover 4
14 passover and according to its ordinance 4
20 then according to the command of the LORD 13
20 according to the command of the LORD they set out. 13
10:28 the people of Israel according to their hosts 10
13: 3 sent . . according to the command of the LORD 13
14:19 according to the greatness of thy steadfast love 4
19 according as thou hast forgiven this people 5
20 LORD said, "I have pardoned, according to your word; 4
34 According to the number of the days in which you 3
15:12 According to the number that you prepare 4
12 do with every one according to their number. 4
24 its drink offering, according to the ordinance 4
17: 2 leaders according to their fathers' houses 10
6 according to their fathers' houses, twelve rods; 10
18:16 according to the shekel of the sanctuary 3
26:12 The sons of Simeon according to their families 10
15 The sons of Gad according to their families 10
18 sons of Gad according to their number, 40,500. 10
20 sons of Judah according to their families were 10
22 families of Judah according to their number 10
23 sons of Is'sachar according to their families 10
25 families of Is'sachar according to their number 10
26 The sons of Zeb'ulun, according to their families 10
27 Zeb'ulunites according to their number, 60,500. 10
28 The sons of Joseph according to their families 10
35 sons of E'phraim according to their families 10
37 E'phraim according to their number, 32,500. 10
37 sons of Joseph according to their families. 10
38 sons of Benjamin according to their families 10
41 sons of Benjamin according to their families; 10
42 sons of Dan according to their families 10
42 families of Dan according to their families. 10
43 Shu'hamites, according to their number 10
44 The sons of Asher according to their families 10
47 sons of Asher according to their number, 53,400. 10
48 sons of Naph'tali according to their families 10
50 Naph'tali according to their families; 10
53 inheritance according to the number of names. 3
54 inheritance according to its numbers. 11
55 according to the names of the tribes 10
56 inheritance shall be divided according to lot 14
57 numbered according to their families 10
29: 6 according to the ordinance for them 4
18 by number, according to the ordinance; 4
21 by number, according to the ordinance; 4
24 by number, according to the ordinance; 4
27 by number, according to the ordinance; 4
30 by number, according to the ordinance; 4
33 by number, according to the ordinance; 4
37 by number, according to the ordinance; 4
30: 2 according to all that proceeds out of his mouth. 4
33: 2 their stages according to their starting places. 10
54 inherit . . by lot according to your families; 10
54 according to the tribes of your fathers 10
36: 5 Israel according to the word of the LORD, saying 13
Deu 1: 3 according to all that the LORD had given him 4
13 Choose . . men, according to your tribes 10
3:11 its breadth, according to the common cubit 3
4:34 according to all that the LORD your God did 4
12: 8 not do according to all that we are doing here 4
15 according to the blessing of the LORD your God 4
16:17 according to the blessing of the LORD your God 4
18 in all your towns . . according to your tribes; 10
17:10 Then . . do according to what they declare to you 14
10 careful to do according to all that they direct 4
11 according to the instructions which they give 14
11 according to the decision which they pronounce 13
20:18 not teach you to do according to all their 4
24: 8 very careful to do according to all that 4
26:13 according to all thy commandments which thou 4
14 done according to all that thou hast commanded 4
31: 5 do to them according to all the commandment 4
32: 8 according to the number of the sons of God. 10
34: 5 died there . . according to the word of the LORD 13
Jos 1: 7 being careful to do according to all the law 4
8 to do according to all that is written in it; 4
2:21 And she said, "According to your words, so be it. 4
4: 5 take up . . according to the number of the tribes 10
8 twelve . . according to the number of the tribes 10
10 according to all that Moses had commanded 4
8:27 Israel took . . according to the word of the LORD 4
34 according to all that is written in the book 4
11:23 according to all that the LORD had spoken to Moses 4
23 gave . . according to their tribal allotments. 10
12: 7 as a possession according to their allotments 4
13:15 Moses gave . . according to their families. 10
23 the inheritance . . according to their families 10
24 Moses gave . . according to their families. 10
28 the inheritance . . according to their families 10
29 it was allotted . . according to their families. 10
31 were allotted . . according to their families. 10
15: 1 The lot for . . Judah according to their families 10
12 is the boundary . . according to their families. 10
13 According to the commandment . . he gave to Caleb 1
20 inheritance . . according to their families. 10
17: 4 according to the commandment of the LORD he gave 1
18:11 The lot . . of Benjamin according to its families 10
20 the inheritance . . according to its families 10
21 the cities . . according to their families 10
28 the inheritance . . according to its families. 10
19: 1 the tribe of Simeon, according to its families; 10
8 inheritance . . according to its families. 10
10 The third lot came . . according to its families. 10
16 the tribe of Zeb'ulun, according to its families 10
17 tribe of Is'sachar, according to its families. 10
23 the tribe of Is'sachar, according to its families 10
24 the tribe of Asher according to its families. 10
31 of the tribe of Asher according to its families 10
32 tribe of Naph'tali, according to its families. 10
39 the tribe of Naph'tali according to its families 10
40 for the tribe of Dan, according to its families. 10
48 of the tribe of Dan, according to their families 10
21: 7 The Merar'ites according to their families 10
Jdg 11:36 do to me according to what has gone forth 4
39 father, who did with her according to his vow •
21:23 and took their wives, according to their number 10
1Sm 2:35 do according to what is in my heart and in my mind; 4
6: 4 Five . . according to the number of the lords •
18 mice, according to the number of all the cities •
8: 8 According to all the deeds which they have done 4
23:20 according to all your heart's desire to come down 10
25:30 LORD has done to my lord according to all the good 4
2Sm 3:39 The LORD requite . . according to his wickedness! 4
7:21 of thy promise, and according to thy own heart 4
22 no God . . according to all that we have heard 3
9:11 According to all that my lord the king commands 4
22:21 LORD rewarded me according to my righteousness; 4
21 according to the cleanness of . . he recompensed 4
25 recompensed me according to my righteousness 4

25 to my righteousness, according to my cleanness 4
1Kg 2: 6 Act therefore according to your wisdom, but do 4
3:12 I now do according to your word. Behold, I give you 4
4:28 they brought . . each according to his charge. 4
6:38 and according to all its specifications. 10
7: 9 made of costly stones, hewn according to measure 4
11 costly stones, hewn according to measurement 4
36 he carved . . according to the space of each 4
8:32 rewarding him according to his righteousness. 4
39 and render to each . . according to all his ways 4
43 according to all for which the foreigner calls 4
56 given rest . . according to all that he promised; 4
9: 4 doing according to all that I have commanded you 4
12:14 he spoke to them according to the counsel 4
24 went home . . according to the word of the LORD. 4
13: 5 altar also was torn down . . according to the sign 4
26 has torn him and slain him, according to the word 4
14:18 mourned for him, according to the word of the LORD 4
24 They did according to all the abominations 4
15:29 destroyed it, according to the word of the LORD 4
16:12 Thus Zimri destroyed . . according to the word 4
34 laid its foundation . . according to the word 4
17: 5 he went and did according to the word of the LORD; 4
16 neither did the . . oil fail, according to the word 4
18:31 stones, according to the number of the tribes 4
22:38 harlots washed . . in it, according to the word 4
2Kg 1:17 So he died according to the word of the LORD 4
2:22 according to the word which Eli'sha spoke. 4
4:44 had some left, according to the word of the LORD. 4
5:14 dipped . . according to the word of the man of God; 4
7:16 two measures . . for a shekel, according to the word 4
8: 2 So the woman arose, and did according to the word 4
10:17 he slew all . . according to the word of the LORD 4
30 have done . . according to all that was in my heart 4
11: 9 captains did according to all that . . commanded 4
14 standing by the pillar, according to the custom 4
14: 6 he did not . . according to what is written 4
25 He restored the border . . according to the word 4
15: 3 he did . . according to all that his father . . had done 4
34 he did . . according to all that his father Uzzi'ah 4
16: 3 He even . . according to the abominable 4
17:34 they do according to the former manner. 4
40 but they did according to their former manner. 4
18: 3 he did . . according to all that David his father 4
21: 2 he did . . according to the abominable practices 4
8 to do according to all that I have commanded them 4
8 to do . . and according to all the law 10
22:13 according to all that is written concerning us. 4
23:16 and defiled it, according to the word of the LORD 4
19 he did to them according to all that he had done 4
25 who turned . . according to all the law of Moses; 4
32 did . . according to all that his fathers had done. 4
35 he . . according to the command of Pharaoh. 13
35 from every one according to his assessment 4
37 he . . according to all that his fathers had done. 4
24: 2 to destroy it, according to the word of the LORD 4
3 sins of Manas'seh, according to all . . he had done 4
9 he did . . according to all that his father had 4
19 he did . . according to all that Jehoi'akim had 4
1Ch 5: 1 in the genealogy according to the birthright; 10
13 kinsmen according to their fathers' houses 10
6:19 the families . . according to their fathers. 10
49 according to all that Moses . . had commanded. 4
54 dwelling places according to their settlements 10
62 To the Gershomites according to their families 10
63 To the Merar'ites according to their families 10
7: 4 with them . . according to their fathers' houses 10
9 according to their generations 10
11 according to the heads of their fathers' houses 10
8:28 according to their generations, chief men. 10
9: 9 their kinsmen according to their generations 10
9 according to their fathers' houses. 10
34 according to their generations, leaders 10
11: 3 according to the word of the LORD by Samuel. 4
10 to make him king, according to the word of the LORD 4
12:23 according to the word of the LORD. 4
15:15 commanded according to the word of the LORD. 4
20 were to play harps according to Al'amoth; 13
21 lead with lyres according to the Shem'inith. 13
16:40 according to all that is written in the law 10
17:19 O LORD, and according to thy own heart 4
20 according to all that we have heard 3
23:24 as they were registered according to the number 3
31 according to the number required of them 3
24: 3 according to the appointed duties 10
19 according to the procedure established 4
30 the Levites according to their fathers' houses. 10
25: 5 according to the promise of God to exalt him; 3
28:15 according to the use of each lampstand 4
19 all the work to be done according to the plan. •
2Ch 6:23 rewarding him according to his righteousness. 4
30 render to each . . according to all his ways 4
33 hear . . and do according to all 4
7:17 doing according to all that I have commanded you 4
8:13 offering according to the commandment of Moses 4
14 According to the ordinance of David his father 4
10:14 Rehobo'am spoke to them according to the counsel 4
17: 4 walked . . not according to the ways of Israel. 4
23: 8 did according to all that Jehoi'ada the priest 4

18 according to the order of David. 13
25: 4 according to what is written in the law 4
26: 4 according to all that . . Amazi'ah had done. 4
11 army . . in divisions according to the numbers 3
27: 2 according to all that . . Uzzi'ah had done 4
28: 3 according to the abominable practices 4
29: 2 according to all that David his father had done. 4
25 according to the commandment of David and of Gad 3
30:16 accustomed posts according to the law of Moses 4
19 even though not according to the sanctuary's rules 4
31: 2 by division, each according to his service 9
16 for their service according to their offices 3
17 priests was according to their fathers' houses; 10
17 Levites . . was according to their offices 3
32:25 according to the benefit done to him 4
33: 2 according to the abominable practices 4
34:21 do according to all that is written in this book. 4
32 Jerusalem did according to the covenant of God 4
35: 4 Prepare . . according to your fathers' houses 10
5 according to the groupings of the fathers' 10
6 to do according to the word of the LORD by Moses. 4
10 according to the king's command. 4
12 distribute them according to the groupings 10
13 with fire according to the ordinance; 4
15 in their place according to the command of David 4
16 according to the command of King Josi'ah. 4
26 his good deeds according to what is written 4
Ezr 2:69 according to their ability they gave 4
3: 4 offerings by number according to the ordinance 4
7 according to the grant which they had from Cyrus 4
10 praise the LORD, according to the directions 13
6:13 according to the word sent by Darius the king •
17 according to the number of the tribes of Israel. 17
7:14 according to the law of your God 15
18 you may do, according to the will of your God. 16
25 you, Ezra, according to the wisdom of your God 16
10: 3 according to the counsel of my lord 3
3 let it be done according to the law. 4
16 according to their fathers' houses 10
Neh 4:13 people according to their families 10
6: 6 become their king, according to this report. 4
7 reported to the king according to these words. 4
14 according to these things that they did 4
8:18 solemn assembly, according to the ordinance. 4
9:27 according to thy great mercies thou didst give 4
28 deliver them according to thy mercies. 4
10:34 according to our fathers' houses, at times 10
12:24 according to the commandment of David 3
44 gather . . according to the fields of the towns; 10
45 according to the command of David and . . Solomon. 4
13:22 spare me according to the greatness 4
Est 1: 7 wine was lavished according to the bounty 4
8 And drinking was according to the law 4
15 According to the law, what is to be done 4
22 speak according to the language of his people. 4
3:12 an edict, according to all that Haman commanded 4
8: 9 according to all that Mor'decai commanded 4
9:13 allowed . . to do according to this day's edict. 4
27 keep these . . days according to what was written 4
Job 1: 5 offer burnt offerings according to the number 22
34:11 according to the work of a man he will requite him •
11 according to his ways he will make it befall him. 4
42: 8 not to deal with you according to your folly; •
Ps 6: 0 according to The Sheminith. A Psalm of David. 13
7: 8 judge me, O LORD, according to my righteousness 4
8 according to the integrity that is in me. 4
8: 0 To the choirmaster: according to The Gittith. 13
9: 0 To the choirmaster: according to Muth-labben. 13
12: 0 To the choirmaster: according to The Sheminith. 13
18:20 LORD rewarded me according to my righteousness; 4
20 according to the cleanness of my hands 4
24 recompensed me according to my righteousness 4
24 according to the cleanness of my hands 4
22: 0 according to The Hind of the Dawn. A Psalm 13
25: 7 according to thy steadfast love remember me 4
28: 4 Requite them according to their work 4
4 according to the evil of their deeds; 4
4 requite . . according to the work of their hands; 4
35:24 O LORD, my God, according to thy righteousness; 4
45: 0 To the choirmaster: according to Lilies. 13
46: 0 A Psalm . . According to Alamoth. A Song. 13
51: 1 Have mercy on me, O God, according to thy steadfast 4
1 according to thy abundant mercy blot out my 4
53: 0 To the choirmaster: according to Mahalath. 13
56: 0 according to The Dove on Far-off Terebinths. 13
57: 0 To the choirmaster: according to Do Not Destroy. •
58: 0 To the choirmaster: according to Do Not Destroy. •
59: 0 To the choirmaster: according to Do Not Destroy. •
60: 0 To the choirmaster: according to Shushan Eduth. 13
62: 0 To the choirmaster: according to Jeduthun. 13
12 For thou dost requite a man according to his work. 4
69: 0 To the choirmaster: according to Lilies. 13
16 according to thy abundant mercy, turn to me. 4
75: 0 To the choirmaster: according to Do Not Destroy. •
77: 0 To the choirmaster: according to Jeduthun. 13
78:10 but refused to walk according to his law. 3
79:11 according to thy great power preserve 4
80: 0 To the choirmaster: according to Lilies. 1
81: 0 To the choirmaster: according to The Gittith. 13

84: 0 To the choirmaster: according to The Gittith. 13
88: 0 choirmaster: according to Mahalath Leannoth. 13
89:30 If . . do not walk according to my ordinances 3
90:11 thy wrath according to the fear of thee? 4
103:10 He does not deal with us according to our sins 4
10 nor requite us according to our iniquities. 4
106:45 relented according to the abundance of his 4
109:26 Save me according to thy steadfast love! 4
119: 9 way pure? By guarding it according to thy word. 4
25 revive me according to thy word! 4
28 strengthen me according to thy word! 4
41 O LORD, thy salvation according to thy promise; 4
58 be gracious to me according to thy promise. 4
65 with thy servant, O LORD, according to thy word. 4
76 according to thy promise to thy servant. 4
107 give me life, O LORD, according to thy word! 4
116 Uphold me according to thy promise 4
124 Deal . . according to thy steadfast love 4
133 Keep steady my steps according to thy promise 3
154 redeem me; give me life according to thy promise! 10
156 O LORD; give me life according to thy justice. 4
159 Preserve . . according to thy steadfast love. 4
169 give me understanding according to thy word! 4
170 deliver me according to thy word. 4
150: 2 praise him according to his exceeding greatness! 4
Prv 12: 8 A man is commended according to his good sense 10
24:12 will he not requite man according to his work? 4
26: 4 Answer not a fool according to his folly 4
5 Answer a fool according to his folly 4
Ecc 8:14 it happens according to the deeds of the wicked 4
14 men to whom it happens according to the deeds 4
Isa 21:16 a year, according to the years of a hireling 4
59:18 According to their deeds, so will he repay 7
63: 7 according to all that the LORD has granted us 7
7 which he has granted them according to his mercy 4
7 according to the abundance of his steadfast love 4
Jer 13: 2 a waistcloth according to the word of the LORD 4
17:10 to give to every man according to his ways 4
10 according to the fruit of his doings. 4
18:12 according to the stubbornness of his evil heart. •
21: 2 according to all his wonderful deeds 4
14 punish you according to the fruit of your doings 4
25:14 I will recompense them according to their deeds 4
32:19 rewarding every man according to his ways 4
19 and according to the fruit of his doings; 4
34:16 whom you had set free according to their desire 10
42: 4 behold, I will pray . . according to your request 4
5 if we do not act according to all the word 4
50:29 Requite her according to her deeds 4
29 do to her according to all that she has done; 4
52: 2 according to all that Jehoi'akim had done. 4
34 given him by the king according to his daily need •
Lam 3:32 have compassion according to the abundance 4
64 requite . . according to the work of their hands. 4
Ezk 5: 7 but have acted according to the ordinances 4
7: 3 and will judge you according to your ways; 4
8 and judge you according to your ways; 4
9 I will punish you according to your ways 4
27 According to their way I will do to them 12
27 according to their own judgments I will judge 3
11:12 according to the ordinances of the nations 4
16:47 or do according to their abominations; 3
18:30 O house of Israel, every one according to his ways 4
20:44 not according to your evil ways, nor according 4
44 nor according to your corrupt doings 4
22: 6 every one according to his power, have been bent 10
23:24 shall judge you according to their judgments. 3
24:14 according to your ways . . I will judge you 4
24 according to all that he has done you shall do. 4
25:14 they shall do in Edom according to my anger 4
14 according to my anger and according to my wrath; 4
33:20 I will judge each of you according to his ways. 4
35:11 I will deal with you according to the anger 4
39:24 I dealt with them according to their uncleanness 4
44:24 they shall judge it according to my judgments. 3
45: 8 Israel have the land according to their tribes. 10
47:21 among you according to the tribes of Israel. 10
Dan 1:13 according to what you see deal with your servants. 4
4:35 does according to his will in the host of heaven 16
6: 8 according to the law of the Medes 16
12 according to the law of the Medes and Persians 16
9: 2 in the books . . according to the word of the LORD •
16 O Lord, according to all thy righteous acts 4
10:15 When he had spoken to me according to these words 4
11: 3 great dominion and do according to his will. 4
4 nor according to the dominion with which he ruled 4
16 who comes . . shall do according to his own will 4
36 king shall do according to his will; 4
Hos 12: 2 and will punish Jacob according to his ways 4
2 and requite him according to his deeds. 4
Jon 3: 3 Jonah arose . . according to the word of the LORD. 4
Hab 3: 1 prayer of Habak'kuk . . according to Shigion'oth. 13
Hag 2: 5 according to the promise that I made you 2
Zec 5: 3 shall be cut off henceforth according to it. 6
3 shall be cut off henceforth according to it. 6
Mat 2:16 two years old or under, according to the time 22
9:29 According to your faith be it done to you. 22
25:15 to each according to his ability 22
Mrk 7: 5 according to the tradition of the elders 22

Lke 1: 9 according to the custom of the priesthood 22
38 let it be to me according to your word 22
2:22 purification according to the law of Moses 22
24 according to what is said in the law of the Lord 22
27 to do for him according to the custom of the law 22
29 according to thy word; 22
39 according to the law of the Lord 22
42 they went up according to custom; 22
12:47 but did not make ready or act according to his will 23
23:56 they rested according to the commandment. 22
Joh 8:15 You judge according to the flesh, I judge no one. 22
44 When he lies, he speaks according to his own nature 19
Act 2:23 delivered up according to the definite plan . . of God *
7:44 according to the pattern that he had seen. 22
11:29 every one according to his ability 21
15: 1 you are circumcised according to the custom of Moses *
22: 3 educated according to . . the law of our fathers 22
12 one Anani'as, a devout man according to the law 22
23: 3 Are you sitting to judge me according to the law 22
31 according to their instructions, took Paul 22
24:14 according to the Way, which they call a sect 22
26: 5 according to the strictest party 22
Rom 1: 3 descended from David according to the flesh 22
4 in power according to the Spirit of holiness 22
2: 6 will render to every man according to his works 22
16 when, according to my gospel, God judges 22
4: 1 Abraham, our forefather according to the flesh? 22
8: 4 in us, who walk not according to the flesh 22
4 us, who walk . . according to the Spirit. 22
5 For those who live according to the flesh 22
5 but those who live according to the Spirit 22
12 not to the flesh, to live according to the flesh– 22
13 if you live according to the flesh you will die 22
27 the Spirit intercedes . . according to the will of God. 22
28 who are called according to his purpose. 22
9: 5 and of their race, according to the flesh 22
12: 3 each according to the measure of faith 24
6 gifts that differ according to the grace given 22
16:25 to strengthen you according to my gospel 22
25 according to the revelation of the mystery 22
26 according to the command of the eternal God 22
1Co 1:26 wise according to worldly standards 22
3: 8 shall receive his wages according to his labor. 22
10 According to the grace of God given to me 22
12: 8 according to the same Spirit 22
2Co 5:10 according to what he has done in the body. 23
8: 3 they gave according to their means, as I can testify 22
12 it is acceptable according to what a man has 22
12 not according to what he has not. 22
Gal 1: 4 according to the will of our God and Father; 22
3:29 Abraham's offspring, heirs according to promise. 22
4:23 the son of the slave was born according to the flesh 22
29 who was born according to the flesh persecuted 22
29 who was born according to the Spirit 22
Eph 1: 5 according to the purpose of his will. 22
7 according to the riches of his grace 22
9 according to his purpose 22
11 according to the purpose of him 22
11 according to the counsel of his will 22
19 according to the working of his great might 22
3: 7 according to the gift of God's grace 22
11 This was according to the eternal purpose 22
16 according to the riches of his glory 22
4: 7 us according to the measure of Christ's gift. 22
Php 4:19 according to his riches in glory in Christ 22
Col 1:11 with all power, according to his glorious might 22
25 according to the divine office 22
2: 8 according to human tradition 22
8 according to the elemental spirits 22
8 not according to Christ. 22
22 according to human precepts and doctrines 22
2Th 1:12 according to the grace of our God 22
2Ti 1: 1 God according to the promise 22
Heb 2: 4 distributed according to his own will. 22
7:16 not according to a legal requirement 22
8: 4 priests who offer gifts according to the law. 22
5 make everything according to the pattern 22
9: 9 According to this arrangement 22
10: 8 these are offered according to the law) 22
Jas 2: 8 fulfill the . . law, according to the scripture 22
1Pe 1:17 judges each one . . according to his deeds 22
4:19 let those who suffer according to God's will 22
2Pe 2:22 It has happened to them according to the true proverb *
3:13 according to his promise we wait for new heavens 22
15 Paul wrote . . according to the wisdom given him 22
1Jn 1: 6 we lie and do not live according to the truth; *
5:14 if we ask anything according to his will he hears 22
1Es 1: 2 according to their divisions 22
5 according to the groupings of . . houses 22
6 according to the commandment of the Lord 22
10 stood according to kindred 22
15 according to the arrangement made by David 22
18 according to the command of King Josiah. 22
3: 9 shall be given according to what is written. 21
5: 1 according to their tribes 22
4 according to their fathers' houses in the tribes 22
55 according to the decree which they had 22
60 according to the directions of David 22
7: 6 according to what was written in the book 18
8 according to the number of . . leaders 23
9 the priests . . stood . . according to kindred 22
8:23 according to the wisdom of God 22
28 according to their fathers' houses 22
2Es 2:18 According to their counsel I have consecrated 25
8:37 it will come to pass according to your words. 26
10:13 with the earth according to the way of the earth 27
Tob 3: 6 now deal with me according to thy pleasure; 22
4: 8 afraid to give according to the little you have. 22
19 according to his will he humbles whomever he wishes 21
6:12 according to the law of Moses 22
7:13 Here she is; take her according to the law of Moses 22
8:16 thou hast treated us according to thy great mercy. 22
Jdt 7:28 who punishes us according to our sins 22
Wis 2:20 according to what he says, he will be protected. 19
6: 4 nor walk according to the purpose of God 22
9: 9 what is right according to thy commandments. 20
16:25 according to the desire of those who had need 23
Sir 1:10 She dwells with all flesh according to his gift 22
5: 2 walking according to the desires of your heart. 20
10:28 honor according to your worth. 22
11:26 to reward a man . . according to his conduct. 22
14:11 treat yourself well, according to your means 21
16:12 he judges a man according to his deeds. 22
29:11 according to the commandments of the Most High 22
20 Assist your neighbor according to your ability 22
32:17 will find a decision according to his liking. 22
35:19 till he repays the man according to his deeds 22
19 repays . . according to their devices 22
36:17 according to the blessing of Aaron 22
38: 1 according to your need of him 23
17 observe the mourning according to his merit 22
45:11 according to the number of the tribes of Israel; 22
49: 6 according to the word of Jeremiah. 20
50:22 deals with us according to his mercy. 22
Sus 1: 3 taught . . according to the law of Moses. 22
Man 1: 7 Thou, O Lord, according to thy great goodness 22
1Mc 1:14 a gymnasium . . according to Gentile custom 22
60 According to the decree 22
2:23 according to the king's command. 22
3:56 return to his home, according to the law. 22
7:42 judge him according to this wickedness. 22
13:46 Do not treat us according to our wicked acts 22
46 according to your mercy. 22
15:21 punish them according to their law. 22
2Mc 6:23 moreover according to the holy God-given law 18
11:25 according to the customs of their ancestors. 22
12:38 they purified themselves according to the custom 22
3Mc 3:14 it was brought to conclusion, according to plan 22
5:29 O king, according to your eager purpose. 22
7: 2 God guiding our affairs according to our desire. 21
4Mc 5:11 philosophize according to the truth *
11: 5 and live according to his virtuous law? 22
15: 3 for eternal life according to God's promise. 22

according *See also* live.

according to the rules 1. *νομίμως*

2Ti 2: 5 unless he competes according to the rules. 1

according to the law 1. *ἐννομέω* 2. *ἐννόμως*

Sir 0: 1 make . . progress in living according to the law 1
3 prepared . . to live according to the law. 2

accordingly 1. *ἄρα οὖν* 2. *διό* 3. *εἰς* 4. *κατὰ ταῦτα* 5. *οὖν* 6. *οὗτος* 7. *τοίνυν* 8. *τότε*

Rom 7: 3 Accordingly, she will be called an adulteress 1
2Co 8: 6 Accordingly we have urged Titus 3
Phm 1: 8 Accordingly, though I am bold enough in Christ 2
AEs 16:24 Every city . . which does not act accordingly 4
Sir 3: 1 act accordingly, that you may be kept in safety. 6
1Mc 12:23 report to you accordingly. 4
2Mc 11:25 Accordingly, since we choose that . . 5
3Mc 6:31 Accordingly those . . arranged for a banquet 8
4Mc 1:13 Our inquiry, accordingly, is . . 7

account 1. אֹדוֹת 2. אוֹדָה 3. אֲשֶׁר 4. בִּגְלַל 5. בַּעֲבוּר 6. דָּבָר 7. כֵּן 8. לְ 9. לְמַעַן 10. מִן 11. מִפְּנֵי 12. עַל 13. שֶׁל 14. *ἀπό* 15. *διά* 16. *ἕνεκα* 17. *ἐπί* 18. *ὑπέρ* 19. *χάρις* 20. per 21. pro 22. propter

Gen 12:13 that my life may be spared on your account. 4
21:11 displeasing to Abraham on account of his son. 2
Lev 7:24 any other use, but on no account shall you eat it *
19:28 cuttings in your flesh on account of the dead 8
Num25:18 slain on the day of the plague on account of Pe'or. 12
Deu 1:37 The LORD was angry with me also on your account 4
3:26 LORD was angry with me on your account 9
4:21 LORD was angry with me on your account 6
28:20 on account of all the evil of your doings 11
31:18 on account of all the evil which they have done 12
Jdg 6: 7 cried to the LORD on account of the Mid'ianites 1
18:12 On this account that place is called Ma'haneh-dan 7
1Sm 23:10 Saul seeks . . to destroy the city on my account. 5
1Ch 16:21 he rebuked kings on their account 12
Neh 13:26 Did not Solomon . . sin on account of such women? 12
Ps 65: 3 To thee shall all flesh come on account of sins. 6
105:14 he rebuked kings on their account 12
106:32 it went ill with Moses on their account; 5
Ezk 12:19 on account of the violence of all those who dwell 10
16:61 but not on account of the covenant with you. 10
Jol 3: 2 on account of my people and my heritage Israel 12
Jon 1: 7 know on whose account this evil has come upon us. 13
8 on whose account this evil has come upon us? 3
Mat 5:11 evil against you falsely on my account. 16
13:21 persecution arises on account of the word 15
Mrk 4:17 persecution arises on account of the word 15
Lke 6:22 revile you . . on account of the Son of man! 16
19: 3 but could not, on account of the crowd 14
Joh 11:42 I have said this on account of the people 15
12: 9 they came, not only on account of Jesus 15
11 on account of him many of the Jews were going away 15
15:21 all this they will do to you on my account 15
2Co 7:12 not on account of the one who did the wrong 16
12 nor on account of the one who suffered the wrong 16
Php 1:24 is more necessary on your account. 15
Col 3: 6 On account of these the wrath of God is coming. 15
4: 3 on account of which I am in prison 15
Heb 6: 6 they crucify the Son of God on their own account *
Rev 1: 7 tribes of the earth will wail on account of him. 17
9 on account of the word of God 15
2Es 4:39 it is perhaps on account of us 22
39 on account of the sins of those who dwell on earth. 22
9: 7 and will be able to escape on account of his works 20
7 on account of the faith by which he has believed 20
12:48 to pray on account of the desolation of Zion 21
48 on account of the humiliation of our sanctuary. 21
Tob 6:14 and bring . . to the grave in sorrow on my account 17
Wis 6:15 he who is vigilant on her account 15
Sir 0: 1 on account of which we should praise Israel 18
10: 8 on account of injustice and insolence 15
16: 8 whom he loathed on account of their insolence. 15
23:14 be deemed a fool on account of your habits *
32: 2 that you may be merry on their account 15
40:10 on their account the flood came. 15
1Mc 6:59 it was on account of their laws 19
2Mc 2:14 the books that had been lost on account of the war 15
4:28 on account of this issue. 15
6:22 on account of his old friendship with them. 15
7:18 we are suffering these things on our own account 15

account (2) 1. דָּבָר 2. חשׁב 3. מִסְפָּר 4. חשׁב (A) 5. טְעֵם (A) 6. *ἐκλογιστής* 7. *ἐκλογιστία* 8. *ἡγέομαι* 9. *λογίζομαι* 10. *λόγος* 11. *λόγου ποιέω* 12. *περί*

1Kg 9:15 this is the account of the forced labor 1
1Ch 11:11 This is an account of David's mighty men 3
29:30 with accounts of all his rule and his might *
2Ch 24:27 Accounts of his sons, and of the many oracles *
Job 31:37 I would give him an account of all my steps; 3
Ps 44:22 and accounted as sheep for the slaughter. 2
Isa 2:22 an . . for of what account is he? 2
40:15 and are accounted as the dust on the scales; 2
17 they are accounted by him as less than nothing 2
Dan 4:35 inhabitants . . are accounted as nothing; 4
6: 2 to whom these satraps should give account 5
Mat 18:23 to settle accounts with his servants. 10
25:19 settled accounts with them. 10
Lke 1: 3 to write an orderly account for you *
16: 2 Turn in the account of your stewardship 10
Act 20:24 I do not account my life of any value 11
Rom 14:12 each of us shall give account of himself to God. 10
Heb 13:17 as men who will have to give account 10
1Pe 3:15 make a defense to any one who calls you to account 10
4: 5 give account to him who is ready to judge 10
Tob 1:21 over all the accounts of his kingdom 7
22 and in charge of administration of the accounts 6
AEs 12: 4 Mordecai wrote an account of them. 12
Wis 7: 8 I accounted wealth as nothing 8
9 silver will be accounted as clay before her. 9
15: 2 because we know that we are accounted thine. 9
Sir 40:19 a blameless wife is accounted better than both. 9
42: 3 of keeping accounts with a partner 10
2Mc 3: 6 did not belong to the account of the sacrifices 10
8:35 he regarded as of the least account *
3Mc 5:15 he gave him an account of the situation. 10

account *See* call, charge, hold, take.

full account 1. פָּרָשָׁה

Est 10: 2 the acts . . and the full account of the high honor 1

little account 1. מְעַט

1Ch 16:19 they were few in number, and of little account 1
Ps 105:12 When they were few in number, of little account 1

no account 1. *ἐξουθενέω*

2Co 10:10 His letters are weighty . . his speech of no account. 1

render account 1. *ἀποδίδωμι*

Mat 12:36 on the day of judgment men will render account 1

account righteous 1. iustifico

2Es 12: 7 if I have been accounted righteous before thee 1

make account righteous 1. צדק

Isa 53:11 my servant, make many to be accounted righteous; 1

small account 1. קלל

Job 40: 4 I am of small account; what shall I answer thee? 1

account worthy 1. καταξιόω
Lke 20:35 who are accounted worthy to attain to that age 1

accountable 1. ὑπόδικος
Rom 3:19 the whole world may be held accountable to God. 1
accounting *See* ask.

accredit 1. δοκιμάζω
1Co 16: 3 I will send those whom you accredit by letter 1

accumulate 1. ἐπισωρεύω 2. συνάγω 3. συναγωγή
2Ti 4: 3 will accumulate for themselves teachers 1
Sir 14: 4 Whoever accumulates by depriving himself 2
4 accumulates for others 2
31: 3 The rich man toils as his wealth accumulates 3

accuracy 1. ἀκρίβεια
Sir 42: 4 of accuracy with scales and weights 1

accurate 1. ἀκριβής
Sir 31:24 testimony to his niggardliness is accurate. 1
32: 3 with accurate knowledge 1

rather accurate 1. ἀκριβῶς
Act 24:22 having a rather accurate knowledge of the Way 1

accurately 1. ἀκριβῶς
Act 18:25 and taught accurately the things concerning Jesus 1

more accurately 1. ἀκριβῶς
Act 18:26 expounded to him the way of God more accurately. 1

accursed 1. ארר 2. זעם 3. חֵרֶם 4. קלל 5. קְלָלָה 6. ἀλάστωρ 7. ἀνάθεμα 8. ἐπάρατος 9. ἐπικατάρατος 10. κατάθεμα 11. κατάρα 12. καταράομαι 13. κατάρατος
Deu 7:26 bring an abominable thing . . become accursed like it 3
21:23 hanged man is accursed by God; 5
Ps 119:21 Thou dost rebuke the insolent, accursed ones 1
Isa 65:20 sinner 100 years old shall be accursed. 4
Mic 6:10 and the scant measure that is accursed? 2
Joh 7:49 this crowd, who do not know the law, are accursed. 8
Rom 9: 3 For I could wish that I myself were accursed 7
1Co 16:22 let him be accursed 7
Gal 1: 8 let him be accursed. 7
9 let him be accursed. 7
2Pe 2:14 hearts trained in greed. Accursed children! 11
Rev 22: 3 There shall no more be anything accursed 10
Wis 3:13 their offspring are accursed 9
12:11 they were an accursed race from the beginning 12
14: 8 the idol made with hands is accursed 9
4Mc 4: 5 he proceeded . . accompanied by the accursed Simon 13
9:24 and take vengeance on the accursed tyrant. 6
18:22 justice . . will pursue the accursed tyrant. 6
accursed *See also* wretch.

accursed man 1. κατάρατος
2Mc 12:35 wishing to take the accursed man alive 1

accursed thing 1. חֵרֶם
Deu 7:26 detest and abhor it; for it is an accursed thing. 1

accusation 1. שִׂטְנָה 2. ἐγκαλέω 3. κατηγορέω 4. κατηγορία
Ezr 4: 6 wrote an accusation against the inhabitants 1
Lke 6: 7 watched him . . so that they might find an accusation 3
Joh 18:29 What accusation do you bring against this man? 4
Act 26: 2 against all the accusations of the Jews 2
accusation *See also* make.

false accusation 1. διαβολή 2. καταψευσμός 3. συκοφαντέω
Lke 3:14 Rob no one by violence or by false accusation 3
Sir 26: 5 the gathering of a mob, and false accusation 2
2Mc 14:27 provoked by the false accusations 1

accuse 1. יכח 2. ענה 3. שׂטן 4. אכל קֶרֶץ (A) 5. γίνομαι κατήγορος 6. ἐγκαλέω 7. ἐντυγχάνω κατά 8. ἐπιφημίζω 9. κατηγορέω 10. κρίσιν εἰσφέρω 11. μωμάομαι 12. accuso
Deu 19:16 malicious witness . . accuse him of wrongdoing 2
18 if the witness . . accused his brother falsely 2
Ps 109: 4 In return for my love they accuse me 3
Dan 6:24 men who had accused Daniel were brought and cast 4
Hos 4: 4 Yet let no one contend, and let none accuse 1
Zec 3: 1 Satan standing at his right hand to accuse him. 3
Mat 12:10 so that they might accuse him. 9
27:12 when he was accused by the chief priests 9
Mrk 3: 2 so that they might accuse him. 9
15: 3 the chief priests accused him of many things. 9
Lke 23: 2 they began to accuse him, saying, "We found this man 9
10 the scribes stood by, vehemently accusing him. 9
Joh 5:45 Do not think that I shall accuse you to the Father 9
45 it is Moses who accuses you 9
Act 22:30 to know the real reason why the Jews accused him 9
23:28 the charge on which they accused him 6
29 he was accused about questions of their law 6
24: 2 Tertul'lus began to accuse him, saying 9
8 everything of which we accuse him. 9
25: 5 let them accuse him. 9
16 before the accused met the accusers face to face 9
26: 7 for this hope I am accused by Jews, O king! 6
Rom 2:15 their conflicting thoughts accuse . . them 9
Rev 12:10 who accuses them day and night before our God. 9
2Es 16:50 and shall accuse her to her face 12
Wis 2:12 and accuses us of sins against our training. 8
10:14 Those who accused him she showed to be false 11
12:12 accuse thee for the destruction of nations 6
Sir 46:19 no man accused him. 6
1Mc 10:61 A group . . gathered together against him to accuse him 7
2Mc 4: 5 not accusing his fellow citizens 5
5: 8 Accused before Aretas the ruler of the Arabs 6
10:13 As a result he was accused before Eupator 9
21 and accused these men of having sold their brethren 9
14:38 he had been accused of Judaism 10

maliciously accuse 1. אכל קֶרֶץ (A)
Dan 3: 8 Chalde'ans . . maliciously accused the Jews. 1

accuser 1. שָׂטָן 2. שׂטן 3. שׁפט 4. ἀντίδικος 5. ἐντυγχάνω 6. κατήγορος 7. κατήγωρ 8. accusator
Job 9:15 I must appeal for mercy to my accuser. 3
Ps 71:13 May my accusers be put to shame and consumed; 2
109: 6 let an accuser bring him to trial. 1
20 this be the reward of my accusers from the LORD 2
25 I am an object of scorn to my accusers; •
29 May my accusers be clothed with dishonor; 2
Mat 5:25 Make friends quickly with your accuser 4
25 with him to court, lest your accuser hand you over 4
Lke 12:58 you go with your accuser before the magistrate 4
Act 23:30 ordering his accusers also to state before you 6
35 I will hear you when your accusers arrive. 6
25:16 before the accused met the accusers face to face 6
18 When the accusers stood up 6
Rev 12:10 the accuser of our brethren has been thrown down 7
2Es 16:65 shall stand as your accusers in that day. 8
1Mc 10:64 when his accusers saw the honor that was paid him 5

accustom 1. לָמֵד 2. מִשְׁפָּט 3. סכן 4. ἐθίζω 5. ἐθισμός 6. ἔθος 7. εἴωθα 8. οἶδα 9. συνεθίζω 10. συνήθεια
Exd 21:29 if the ox has been accustomed to gore in the past •
36 the ox has been accustomed to gore in the past •
Num22:30 I ever accustomed to do so to you?" And he said, "No. 3
2Ch 30:16 They took their accustomed posts 2
Jer 13:23 you can do good who are accustomed to do evil. 1
Mat 27:15 the governor was accustomed to release 7
1Co 8: 7 through being hitherto accustomed to idols 10
Jdt 13:10 as they were accustomed to go for prayer 5
Sir 23: 9 Do not accustom your mouth to oaths 4
13 Do not accustom your mouth to lewd vulgarity 9
15 A man accustomed to use insulting words 9
Bel 1:15 as they were accustomed to do 6
21 through which they were accustomed to enter •
1Mc 6:30 32 elephants accustomed to war. 8

achieve 1. עשׂה
Job 5:12 that their hands achieve no success. 1
achieve *See also* fail.

achievement 1. πρᾶξις
1Mc 16:23 the walls which he built, and his achievements 1

acknowledge 1. זכר 2. ידה 3. ידע 4. נכר 5. ἐξομολογέω 6. ἐπιγινώσκω 7. ἐπιδέχομαι 8. ἔχω ἐν ἐπιγνώσει 9. ὁμολογέω 10. ὁμολογία 11. cognosco
Gen 38:26 Judah acknowledged them and said, "She is more 4
Deu 21:17 acknowledge the first-born . . of the disliked 4
1Kg 8:33 turn again to thee, and acknowledge thy name 2
35 if they pray . . and acknowledge thy name 2
2Ch 6:24 when they turn again and acknowledge thy name 2
26 if they pray . . and acknowledge thy name 2
Job 40:14 Then will I also acknowledge to you 2
Ps 32: 5 I acknowledged my sin to thee, and I did not hide 3
Prv 3: 6 In all your ways acknowledge him 3
Isa 26:13 ruled over us, but thy name alone we acknowledge. 1
33:13 and you who are near, acknowledge my might. 3
61: 9 all who see them shall acknowledge them 4
63:16 not know us and Israel does not acknowledge us; 4
Jer 3:13 Only acknowledge your guilt, that you rebelled 3
14:20 We acknowledge our wickedness, O LORD 3
Dan 11:39 acknowledge him he shall magnify with honor. 4
Mat 10:32 So every one who acknowledges me before men 9
32 I also will acknowledge before my Father 9
Lke 12: 8 every one who acknowledges me before men 9
8 the Son of man also will acknowledge 9
Act 23: 8 the Pharisees acknowledge them all. 9
Rom 1:28 since they did not see fit to acknowledge God 8
1Co 14:37 acknowledge that what I am writing to you 6
2Co 9:13 obedience in acknowledging the gospel 10
Heb 11:13 having acknowledged that they were strangers 9
13:15 the fruit of lips that acknowledge his name. 9
2Jn 1: 7 men who will not acknowledge the coming of Jesus 9
3Jn 1: 9 Diot'rephes . . does not acknowledge my authority. 7
2Es 8:28 those who have willingly acknowledged 11
9:10 as many as did not acknowledge me 11
12 these must in torment acknowledge it 11
Tob 12:22 and acknowledged that the angel . . had appeared •
13: 3 Acknowledge him before the nations 5
Wis 18:13 they acknowledged thy people to be God's son. 9
Sir 44:23 he acknowledged him with his blessings 6
4Mc 6:34 to acknowledge the dominance of reason 9

acknowledge guilt 1. אשׁם
Hos 5:15 until they acknowledge their guilt 1

acknowledge to be just 1. iustifico
2Es 10:16 if you acknowledge the decree of God to be just 1

acquaint 1. ידע 2. נכר 3. סכן 4. ἔμπειρος 5. ἐπιγινώσκω 6. οἶδα
Job 24:13 who are not acquainted with its ways 2
Ps 139: 3 Thou . . art acquainted with all my ways. 3
Isa 53: 3 a man of sorrows, and acquainted with grief; 1
2Ti 3:15 have been acquainted with the sacred writings 6
Tob 5: 5 Are you acquainted with that region? 4
2Mc 14: 9 Since you are acquainted, O king, with the details 5

acquaintance 1. ידע 2. מַכָּר 3. γνώριμος 4. γνῶσις 5. γνωστός 6. συνήθεια
2Kg 12: 5 let the priests take, each from his acquaintance; 2
7 take no more money from your acquaintances 2
Job 19:13 my acquaintances are wholly estranged from me. 1
Ps 31:11 an object of dread to my acquaintances; 1
Lke 2:44 among their kinsfolk and acquaintances; 5
23:49 all his acquaintances and the women 5
Sir 30: 2 will boast of him among acquaintances. 3
2Mc 6:21 because of their long acquaintance with him 4
4Mc 6:13 sympathy from their acquaintance with him 6

acquire 1. יסף 2. נחל 3. קנה 4. רכשׁ 5. γίνομαι 6. κατακληρονομέω 7. κτάομαι 8. κτῆσις 9. μανθάνω 10. περιποιέω
Gen 31:18 cattle in his possession which he had acquired 4
36: 6 property which he had acquired in the land 4
Neh 5:16 held to the work . . and acquired no land; 3
Prv 1: 5 man of understanding acquire skill 3
14:18 The simple acquire folly, but the prudent 2
18:15 An intelligent mind acquires knowledge 3
Ecc 1:16 I have acquired great wisdom, surpassing all 1
Eph 1:14 until we acquire possession of it †
Jdt 8:22 and a reproach in the eyes of those who acquire us. 7
Sir 0: 1 the readers . . should acquire understanding 5
1 acquiring considerable proficiency in them, 10
14:15 what you acquired by toil to be divided by lot? •
15: 6 will acquire an everlasting name. 6
16:24 Listen to me, my son, and acquire knowledge 9
36:24 He who acquires a wife gets his best possession 7
42: 4 of acquiring much or little; 8

acquire much 1. πληθύνω
Sir 34:10 he that has traveled acquires much cleverness. 1

acquire wealth 1. עשׁר
Prv 23: 4 Do not toil to acquire wealth; 1

acquit 1. היה 2. זכה 3. נקה 4. פלט 5. צדק 6. ἀπολύω 7. δικαιόω
Exd 23: 7 for I will not acquit the wicked. 5
Deu 25: 1 acquitting the innocent and condemning 5
1Sm 4: 9 Take courage, and acquit yourselves like men 1
9 to you; acquit yourselves like men and fight. 1
Job 10:14 mark me, and dost not acquit me of my iniquity. 3
23: 7 I should be acquitted for ever by my judge. 4
Isa 5:23 who acquit the guilty for a bribe 5
Mic 6:11 Shall I acquit the man with wicked scales 2
1Co 4: 4 I am not thereby acquitted 7
Sir 42: 2 of rendering judgment to acquit the ungodly; 7
2Mc 4:47 Menelaus . . he acquitted of the charges against him 6
3Mc 7: 7 we justly have acquitted them 6

acquittal 1. בוא בִּצְדָקָה 2. δικαίωσις
Ps 69:27 may they have no acquittal from thee. 1
Rom 5:18 one man's act . . leads to acquittal and life 2

acre 1. צֶמֶד
1Sm 14:14 half a furrow's length in an acre of land. 1
Isa 5:10 ten acres of vineyard shall yield but one bath 1

across 1. בְּעֵבֶר 2. מֵעֵבֶר 3. עַל 4. עַל פְּנֵי 5. διά 6. ἐν 7. πέραν 8. trans
Gen 1:20 the earth across the firmament of the heavens 4
1Kg 6:21 he drew chains of gold across, in front •
Job 1:19 behold, a great wind came across the wilderness 2
Jer 25:22 and the kings of the coastland across the sea; 1
Dan 8: 5 he-goat came . . across the face of the whole earth 3
Mat 4:15 Naph'tali, toward the sea, across the Jordan 7
Joh 6:17 started across the sea to Caper'na-um 7
10:40 He went away again across the Jordan 7
18: 1 he went forth . . across the Kidron valley 7

Act 27:27 as we were drifting across the sea of A'dria 6
2Es 13:40 he took them across the river 8
Jdt 15: 2 fled by every path across the plain *
1Mc 5:39 they are encamped across the stream 7
2Mc 8:35 made his way . . across the country 5

across *See also* go, sail, send, swim, take.

act 1. דָּבָר 2. מסר 3. מעל 4. מַעֲלָל 5. מַעֲשֶׂה 6. מִפְעָל 7. עֲלִילָה 8. עמד 9. עשה 10. ἄγω 11. ἀναστρέφω 12. αὐτόφωρος 13. γίνομαι 14. διεξάγω 15. δράω 16. δύναμαι 17. ἐνέργεια 18. ἐργάζομαι 19. ἔργον 20. ἴδιος 21. λόγος 22. περιπατέω 23. ποιέω 24. πρâγμα 25. πρâξις 26. πράσσω 27. ago 28. gero

Num 5:12 If any man's wife . . acts unfaithfully against 3
13 no witness . . since she was not taken in the act; *
10:25 Dan, acting as the rear guard of all the camps *
31:16 caused . . Israel . . to act treacherously 2
Deu 17:12 The man who acts presumptuously, by not obeying 9
25:16 all who do such things, all who act dishonestly 9
Jos 9: 4 they on their part acted with cunning 9
Jdg 9:16 if you acted in good faith and honor when you made 9
19 if you then have acted in good faith and honor 9
1Kg 2: 6 Act therefore according to your wisdom, but do 9
8:32 hear . . and act, and judge thy servants 9
39 hear . . and forgive, and act, and render to each 9
11:41 the rest of the acts of Solomon, and all that he did 1
41 not written in the book of the acts of Solomon? 1
14:19 the rest of the acts of Jerobo'am . . are written 1
29 rest of the acts of Rehobo'am, and all that he did 1
15: 7 The rest of the acts of Abi'jam, and all that he did 1
23 the rest of all the acts of Asa, all his might 1
31 the rest of the acts of Nadab, and all that he did 1
16: 5 the rest of the acts of Ba'asha, and what he did 1
14 the rest of the acts of Elah, and all that he did 1
20 the rest of the acts of Zimri, and the conspiracy 1
27 the rest of the acts of Omri which he did 1
22:39 the rest of the acts of Ahab, and all that he did 1
45 the rest of the acts of Jehosh'aphat, and his might 1
2Kg 1:18 Now the rest of the acts of Ahazi'ah which he did 1
8:23 the rest of the acts of Joram, and all that he did 1
10:34 Now the rest of the acts of Jehu, and all that he did 1
12:19 the rest of the acts of Jo'ash, and all that he did 1
13: 8 the rest of the acts of Jeho'ahaz and all . . he did 1
12 the rest of the acts of Jo'ash, and all that he did 1
14:15 Now the rest of the acts of Jeho'ash which he did 1
28 the rest of the acts of Jerobo'am and all . . he did 1
15: 6 the rest of the acts of Azari'ah, and all that he did 1
31 the rest of the acts of Pekah, and all that he did 1
36 the rest of the acts of Jotham, and all that he did 1
16:19 Now the rest of the acts of Ahaz which he did 1
21:17 the rest of the acts of Manas'seh . . all that he did 1
25 Now the rest of the acts of Amon which he did 1
23:28 the rest of the acts of Josi'ah, and all that he did 1
1Ch 29:29 acts of King David, from first to last, are written 1
2Ch 6:23 hear thou . . and act, and judge thy servants 9
9:29 Now the rest of the acts of Solomon 1
12:15 Now the acts of Rehobo'am, from first to last 1
13:22 The rest of the acts of Abi'jah 1
16:11 The acts of Asa, from first to last, are written 1
20:34 Now the rest of the acts of Jehosh'aphat 1
26:22 the rest of the acts of Uzzi'ah, from first to last 1
27: 7 Now the rest of the acts of Jotham, and all his wars 1
28:26 Now the rest of his acts and all his ways 1
32:32 rest of the acts of Hezeki'ah, and his good deeds 1
33:18 the rest of the acts of Manas'seh, and his prayer 1
35:26 the rest of the acts of Josi'ah, and his good deeds 1
27 his acts, first and last, behold, they are written 1
36: 8 Now the rest of the acts of Jehoi'akim 1
Neh 6:13 that I should be afraid and act in this way and sin 9
13:18 Did not your fathers act in this way 9
Est 10: 2 all the acts . . are they not written in the Book 5
Ps 31:23 but abundantly requites him who acts haughtily. 9
37: 5 your way to the LORD; trust in him, and he will act. 9
103: 7 made known his . . acts to the people of Israel. 7
106:39 Thus they became unclean by their acts 5
119:126 It is time for the LORD to act 9
Prv 8:22 LORD created me . . the first of his acts of old. 6
12:22 but those who act faithfully are his delight. 9
13:16 In everything a prudent man acts with knowledge 9
14:17 A man of quick temper acts foolishly 9
20:11 Even a child makes himself known by his acts 4
21:24 proud, haughty man who acts with arrogant pride. 9
Jer 14: 7 act, O LORD, for thy name's sake; 9
18:12 act according to the stubbornness of his evil 9
42: 5 if we do not act according to all the word 9
Ezk 5: 7 but have acted according to the ordinances 9
11:12 but have acted according to the ordinances 9
14:21 upon Jerusalem my four sore acts of judgment *
20: 9 I acted for the sake of my name 9
14 But I acted for the sake of my name 9
22 withheld my hand, and acted for the sake of my name 9
24:19 what these . . mean for us, that you are acting thus? 9
25:12 Because Edom acted revengefully 9
15 Because the Philistines acted revengefully 9
30:14 and will execute acts of judgment upon Thebes. *
19 Thus I will execute acts of judgment upon Egypt. *
36:22 I am about to act, but for the sake of my holy name 9
32 It is not for your sake that I will act 9
44:24 In a controversy they shall act as judges 8
Dan 8:12 horn acted and prospered. 9
9:19 O LORD, give heed and act 9
11:23 alliance is made . . he shall act deceitfully; 9
Mal 3:17 my special possession on the day when I act 9
4: 3 on the day when I act, says the LORD of hosts. 9
Lke 12:47 but did not make ready or act according to his will 23
Joh 8: 4 this woman has been caught in the act of adultery 12
Act 3:17 now, brethren, I know that you acted in ignorance 26
17: 7 are all acting against the decrees of Caesar 26
Rom 14:23 because he does not act from faith; *
2Co 10: 2 who suspect us of acting in worldly fashion. 22
12:18 Did we not act in the same spirit? 22
1Ti 1:13 I received mercy because I had acted ignorantly 23
Heb 5: 1 high priest . . is appointed to act on behalf of men *
13:18 desiring to act honorably in all things. 11
Jas 1:25 being no hearer that forgets but a doer that acts 19
2:12 So speak and so act as those who are to be judged 23
1Es 1:25 After all these acts of Josiah 25
33 every one of the acts of Josiah 25
52 his anger . . because of their ungodly acts *
9:15 acted in accordance with all this. 23
2Es 3:30 and hast spared those who act wickedly 27
8:27 not the endeavors of those who act wickedly 27
35 no one . . who has not acted wickedly 28
Tob 1: 1 The book of the acts of Tobit the son of Tobiel 21
AEs 13: 2 always acting reasonably and with kindness 14
16:24 Every city . . which does not act accordingly 23
Wis 12:18 hast power to act whenever thou dost choose. 16
19:13 they justly suffered because of their wicked acts; 20
Sir 3: 1 act accordingly, that you may be kept in safety. 23
8:15 he will act as he pleases 23
10: 6 do not attempt anything by acts of insolence. 19
15:15 to act faithfully is a matter of your own choice. 23
16:22 Who will announce his acts of justice? 19
32:19 when you have acted, do not regret it. 23
23 Guard yourself in every act 19
Sus 1:62 acting in accordance with the law of Moses 23
1Mc 7: 3 when this act became known to him, he said 24
9:22 Now the rest of the acts of Judas 21
14:45 Whoever acts contrary to these decisions 23
46 the right to act in accord with these decisions. 23
16:23 The rest of the acts of John and his wars 21
2Mc 4:33 When Onias became fully aware of these acts *
6:29 who . . had acted toward him with good will 10
7: 2 One of them, acting as their spokesman, said 13
12:43 In doing this he acted very well and honorably 26
3Mc 2: 5 who acted arrogantly 18
4:21 an act of the invincible providence of him 17
5:28 This was the act of God who rules over all things 17
6:24 secretly devising acts of no advantage to the kingdom. *
7: 6 we very severely threatened them for these acts *
9 as an antagonist to avenge such acts. Farewell. 24
4Mc 2: 8 he is forced to act contrary to his natural ways *
4:21 The divine justice was angered by these acts *
5:33 to break the ancestral law by my own act. *
11: 4 for what act of ours are you destroying us 15

act *See also* abominably, amiss, corruptly, disgracefully, faithlessly, firmly, first, immoderately, immorally, impartially, impiously, insincerely, insolently, marvelously, mighty, perversely, presumptuously, quick, righteous, saving, shamefully, shameless, terrible, treacherously, unfaithfully, wicked, wickedly, wisely.

act as a champion 1. προμαχέω

Wis 18:21 a blameless man was quick to act as their champion 1

act as a deputy 1. διαδέχομαι

2Mc 4:31 leaving Andronicus . . to act as his deputy. 1

act as an ally 1. συμμαχέω

1Mc 8:25 the nation of the Jews shall act as their allies 1
27 the Romans shall willingly act as their allies 1

act as an equal 1. ἐξισάζω

Sir 32: 9 Among the great do not act as their equal 1

act of charity 1. ἐλεημοσύνη

Act 9:36 She was full of good works and acts of charity. 1
Tob 1: 3 I performed many acts of charity to my brethren 1
16 I performed many acts of charity to my brethren. 1
Sir 31:11 the assembly will relate his acts of charity. 1

act of daring 1. τόλμα

2Mc 8:18 For they trust to arms and acts of daring," he said 1

act of faithfulness 1. אֱמֶת

2Ch 32: 1 things and these acts of faithfulness 1

act of judgment 1. שֶׁפֶט

Exd 6: 6 redeem you . . with great acts of judgment 1
7: 4 out of . . Egypt by great acts of judgment. 1

act of mercy 1. ἐλεημοσύνη

Sir 16:14 He will make room for every act of mercy 1

act of righteousness 1. δικαίωμα

Rom 5:18 one man's act of righteousness leads 1

act of sacrilege 1. ἱεροσύλημα

2Mc 4:39 When many acts of sacrilege had been committed 1

act of sin 1. ἁμάρτημα

Jdt 13:16 yet he committed no act of sin with me 1

act of treachery 1. ἀθεσία

1Mc 16:17 So he committed an act of great treachery 1

rash act 1. θράσος

2Mc 5:18 and turned back from his rash act 1

action 1. עֲלִילָה 2. ἐνέργεια 3. ἔργον 4. κεῖμαι 5. ὁ κατεργάζομαι 6. πρâξις 7. χειροτονία 8. χρεία

1Sm 2: 3 the LORD is . . and by him actions are weighed. 1
Rom 7:15 I do not understand my own actions. 5
2Es 12:25 and perform his last actions. *
Wis 2:12 he is inconvenient to us and opposes our actions; 3
9:11 she will guide me wisely in my actions 6
19: 1 God knew in advance even their future actions *
Sir 11:31 to worthy actions he will attach blame. *
1Mc 4:34 they fell in action. †
2Mc 15:28 When the action was over 8
3Mc 1: 5 the enemy was routed in the action 7
3:19 and are unwilling to regard any action as sincere. *
5:12 by the action of the Lord 2
26 what the king desired was ready for action. 4

action *See also* take.

former action 1. προπράσσω

3Mc 6:27 begging pardon for your former actions! 1

active 1. ἐνεργέω 2. ἐνεργής

Heb 4:12 For the word of God is living and active 2
Wis 15:11 formed him and inspired him with an active soul 1

active along with 1. συνεργέω

Jas 2:22 faith was active along with his works 1

activity 1. ἐνέργεια

2Th 2: 9 the activity of Satan 1
Wis 7:17 the activity of the elements; 1
Sir 11:10 if you multiply activities *

actually 1. ὅλως 2. συμβαίνω

Act 21:35 he was actually carried by the soldiers 2
1Co 5: 1 It is actually reported 1

adamant 1. שָׁמִיר

Ezk 3: 9 Like adamant harder than flint have I made 1
Zec 7:12 They made their hearts like adamant 1

like adamant 1. ἀδαμάντινος

4Mc 16:13 as though having a mind like adamant 1

add 1. אמר 2. יסף 3. נתן 4. ספה 5. עוֹד 6. קרב 7. יסף (A) 8. εἶπον 9. ἐπί 10. ἐπιδιατάσσομαι 11. ἐπιζεύγνυμι 12. ἐπιτίθημι 13. πληθύνω 14. προσανατίθημι 15. προσποιέω 16. προσταράσσω 17. προστίθημι 18. φθάνω

Gen 24:25 She added, "We have both straw and provender 1
30:24 saying, "May the LORD add to me another son! 2
Lev 5:16 shall add a fifth to it and give it to the priest 2
6: 5 he shall restore it in full, and shall add a fifth 2
22:14 he shall add the fifth of its value to it 2
27:13 he shall add a fifth to the valuation 2
15 he shall add a fifth of the valuation in money 2
19 he shall add a fifth of the valuation in money 2
27 shall buy it back . . and add a fifth to it 2
31 redeem any of his tithe, he shall add a fifth to it 2
Num 5: 7 make full restitution . . adding a fifth to it 2
19:17 running water shall be added in a vessel; 3
36: 3 added to the inheritance of the tribe 2
4 inheritance will be added to the inheritance 2
Deu 4: 2 You shall not add to the word which I command you 2
5:22 words the LORD spoke . . and he added no more. 2
12:32 to do; you shall not add to it or take from it. 2
19: 9 then you shall add three other cities 2
1Sm 12:19 we have added to all our sins this evil 2
2Sm 12: 8 I would add to you as much more. 2
19:35 should your servant be an added burden to my lord 5
24: 3 May the LORD . . add to the people 100 times 2
1Kg 12:11 laid upon you a heavy yoke, I will add to your yoke. 2
14 made your yoke heavy, but I will add to your yoke; 2
2Kg 20: 6 And I will add fifteen years to your life. 2
1Ch 21: 3 May the LORD add to his people 100 times 2
22:14 timber and stone . . To these you must add. 2
2Ch 10:11 laid . . a heavy yoke, I will add to your yoke. 2
14 My father made your yoke heavy, but I will add to it; 2
Est 5:12 Haman added, "Even Queen Esther let no one come 1
Job 34:37 For he adds rebellion to his sin; 2
Ps 69:27 Add to them punishment upon punishment; 3
Prv 9:11 For by me . . years will be added to your life. 2
10:22 makes rich, and he adds no sorrow with it. 2

16:23 adds persuasiveness to his lips. 2
30: 6 Do not add to his words, lest he rebuke you 2
Ecc 3:14 nothing can be added to it, nor anything taken 2
7:27 adding one thing to another to find the sum •
Isa 5: 8 who join house to house, who add field to field 6
29: 1 Add year to year; let the feasts run their round. 2
30: 1 but not of my spirit, that they may add sin to sin; 4
38: 5 behold, I will add fifteen years to your life. 2
Jer 7:21 Add your burnt offerings to your sacrifices 2
36:32 and many similar words were added to them. 2
45: 3 Woe is me! for the LORD has added sorrow to my pain; 2
Dan 4:36 still more greatness was added to me. 7
Mat 6:27 by being anxious can add one cubit to his span 17
Lke 3:20 added this to them all 17
12:25 which of you . . can add a cubit to his span of life? 17
Act 2:41 there were added that day about 3,000 souls. 17
47 the Lord added to their number day by day 17
5:14 more than ever believers were added to the Lord 17
11:24 a large company was added to the Lord. 17
Gal 2: 6 those, I say, who were of repute added nothing to me; 14
3:15 no one annuls even a man's will, or adds to it 10
19 It was added because of transgressions 17
Heb 10: 9 he added, "Lo, I have come to do thy will. 8
17 then he adds, "I will remember their sins •
Rev 22:18 if any one adds to them, God will add to him 12
18 God will add to him the plagues 12
1Es 2: 7 the other things added as votive offerings 17
2Es 7:52 will you add to them lead and clay? ‡
Tob 5:15 besides, I will add to your wages 17
18 Do not add money to money 18
Sir 4: 3 Do not add to the troubles of an angry mind 16
5: 5 so confident . . that you add sin to sin. 17
21:15 he will praise it and add to it 17
26:15 A modest wife adds charm to charm 9
31:30 reducing his strength and adding wounds. 15
42:21 Nothing can be added or taken away 17
45:20 He added glory to Aaron and gave him a heritage 17
1Mc 8:30 both . . shall determine to add or delete anything 17
10:30 the three districts added to it from Samaria 17
38 three districts that have been added to Judea 17
11: 1 and add it to his own kingdom. 17
34 the latter . . were added to Judea from Samaria. 17
14:15 added to the vessels of the sanctuary. 13
2Mc 2:32 adding only so much to what has already been said; 11
3Mc 5:20 he added, "tomorrow . . prepare the elephants •

add an apology 1. προσδέω
Sir 13: 3 he must add apologies. 1

add reproach 1. προσεμβριμάομαι
Sir 13: 3 A rich man does wrong, and he even adds reproaches; 1

adder 1. פֶּתֶן 2. צֶפַע 3. צִפְעוֹנִי
Ps 58: 4 a serpent, like the deaf adder that stops its ear 1
91:13 You will tread on the lion and the adder 1
Prv 23:32 At the last it . . stings like an adder. 3
Isa 11: 8 weaned child . . put his hand on the adder's den. 3
14:29 from the serpent's root will come forth an adder 2
59: 5 They watch adders' eggs, they weave 3
Jer 8:17 serpents, adders which cannot be charmed 3

addict 1. προσέχω
1Ti 3: 8 not double-tongued, not addicted to much wine 1

addition 1. אֶל 2. יסף 3. לְבַד 4. מִלְּבַד 5. עַל 6. עלה 7. ἄλλως 8. ἐπί 9. ἔτι 10. πρός 11. προστίθημι 12. σύν 13. super
Exd 29:25 on the altar in addition to the burnt offering 5
Num 5: 8 in addition to the ram of atonement 4
29:39 offer . . in addition to your votive offerings 3
35: 6 in addition to them you shall give 42 cities 5
1Ch 29: 3 Moreover, in addition to all that I have provided 6
2Ch 28:13 in addition to our present sins and guilt. 2
Ezk 16:43 lewdness in addition to all your abominations? 5
44: 7 in addition to all your abominations. 1
2Es 2: 5 in addition to the mother of the children 13
Tob 2:14 It was given to me as a gift in addition to my wages 8
1Mc 8:30 any addition or deletion that they may make 11
2Mc 4: 9 In addition to this 10
9:17 in addition to all this 10
12: 2 in addition to these 10
3Mc 1:22 In addition . . the citizens would not tolerate 12
4:10 in addition they were confined 9
4Mc 1: 2 and in addition it includes 7

additional 1. ἄλλος 2. πλεονάζω
1Es 4:52 an additional ten talents a year 1
1Mc 10:41 all the additional funds 2

address 1. אמר 2. דבר 3. ἀποκρίνομαι 4. ἀποφθέγγομαι 5. διαλέγομαι 6. λαλέω 7. λέγω πρός 8. προσαγορεύω 9. προσλαλέω 10. προσφωνέω
Ezr 10: 2 Shecani'ah . . addressed Ezra: "We have broken 1
Ps 18: 0 David . . who addressed the words of this song 2
45: 1 I address my verses to the king; 1
Lke 23:20 Pilate addressed them once more 10
Act 2:14 Peter . . lifted up his voice and addressed them 4
3:12 when Peter saw it he addressed the people 3
22: 2 he addressed them in the Hebrew language 10
1Co 3: 1 I, brethren, could not address you as spiritual 6
Eph 5:19 addressing one another in psalms and hymns 6
Heb 7:21 this one was addressed with an oath 7
12: 5 the exhortation which addresses you as sons 5
Rev 7:13 Then one of the elders addressed me, saying 3
Wis 13:17 he is not ashamed to address a lifeless thing. 9
1Mc 14:40 the Jews were addressed by the Romans as friends 8
2Mc 15:15 as he gave it he addressed him thus 10

address the people 1. δημηγορέω
4Mc 5:15 he began to address the people as follows 1

adhere 1. συνευδοκέω
1Mc 1:57 if any one adhered to the law 1

adherent 1. ἐκ 2. περιπατέω
Rom 4:14 If it is the adherents of the law who are . . heirs 1
16 not only to the adherents of the law 1
Heb 13: 9 which have not benefited their adherents. 2

adjoin 1. אֶל 2. נֶגֶד 3. עַל 4. γειτνιάω 5. παράκειμαι 6. προσκυρόω
Ezk 42: 3 Adjoining the twenty cubits which belonged 2
48: 2 Adjoining the territory of Dan, from the east 3
3 Adjoining the territory of Asher, from the east 3
4 Adjoining the territory of Naph'tali 3
5 Adjoining the territory of Manas'seh 3
6 Adjoining the territory of E'phraim 3
7 Adjoining the territory of Reuben, from the east 3
8 Adjoining the territory of Judah, from the east 3
12 adjoining the territory of the Levites. 1
24 Adjoining the territory of Benjamin 3
25 Adjoining the territory of Simeon, from the east 3
26 Adjoining the territory of Is'sachar 3
27 Adjoining the territory of Zeb'ulun 3
28 And adjoining the territory of Gad to the south 3
Sus 1: 4 and had a spacious garden adjoining his house; 4
1Mc 10:39 Ptolemais and the land adjoining it 6
2Mc 12:16 the adjoining lake, a quarter of a mile wide 5

public adjuration 1. קוֹל
Lev 5: 1 he hears a public adjuration to testify 1

adjure 1. שׁבע 2. ἐνορκίζω 3. ἐξορκίζω 4. ὁρκίζω
2Sm 21:17 David's men adjured him, "You shall no more go out 1
1Kg 22:16 How many times shall I adjure you that you speak 1
2Ch 18:15 king said to him, "How many times shall I adjure you 1
Sng 2: 7 I adjure you, O daughters . . that you stir not up 1
3: 5 I adjure you, O daughters . . that you stir not up 1
5: 8 I adjure you, O daughters . . that you tell him I am 1
9 What is your beloved . . that you thus adjure us? 1
8: 4 I adjure . . that you stir not up nor awaken love 1
Mat 26:63 I adjure you by the living God 3
Mrk 5: 7 I adjure you by God, do not torment me. 4
Act 19:13 I adjure you by the Jesus whom Paul preaches. 4
1Th 5:27 I adjure you by the Lord that this letter be read 2

administer 1. עשׂה 2. διακονέω
2Sm 8:15 David administered justice and equity to all 1
1Ch 18:14 David . . administered justice and equity 1
2Co 8:20 this liberal gift which we are administering 2

administer justice 1. שׁפט
1Sm 7:17 there also he administered justice to Israel. 1

administration 1. διοίκησις 2. διοικητής 3. χειρίζω
Tob 1:21 over the entire administration. 1
22 and in charge of administration of the accounts 2
AEs 16: 5 with the administration of public affairs 3

administration of market 1. ἀγορανομία
2Mc 3: 4 about the administration of the city market; 1

administrator 1. δημιουργέω 2. κυβέρνησις
1Co 12:28 helpers, administrators, speakers 2
4Mc 7: 8 those who are administrators of the law 1

admirable 1. θαυμαστός
2Mc 7:20 The mother was especially admirable 1

admiration 1. θαυμασμός
4Mc 6:13 partly out of admiration for his endurance 1

admire 1. ἐκθαυμάζω 2. ζηλόω 3. θαυμάζω
Jdt 10: 7 they greatly admired her beauty, and said to her 3
19 they . . admired the Israelites 3
Wis 8:11 in the sight of rulers I shall be admired. 3
Sir 27:23 he admires your words 1
38: 3 in the presence of great men he is admired. 3
2Mc 4:16 those whose ways of living they admired 2
4Mc 8: 5 Young men, I admire each and every one of you 3
17:16 admire the athletes of the divine legislation? 3
18: 3 were not only admired by men 3

admit 1. בוא 2. מָבוֹא 3. ὁμολογέω 4. ὁμολογουμένως 5. παραδέχομαι 6. ὑποδέχομαι
Exd 40:15 anointing shall admit them to . . priesthood †
Ezk 44: 5 mark well those who may be admitted to the temple 2
7 in admitting foreigners, uncircumcised 1
Act 24:14 I admit to you . . I worship the God of our fathers 3
1Ti 5:19 Never admit any charge against an elder 5
Jdt 13:13 they opened the gate and admitted them 6
3Mc 7:12 admitting . . the truth of what they said 5
4Mc 16: 1 it must be admitted 4

must admit 1. ἐκδεκτέον
LJr 1:56 Why . . must any one admit . . that they are gods? 1

admittedly 1. ὁμολογουμένως
4Mc 6:31 Admittedly, then, devout reason is sovereign 1

admonish 1. עוד 2. νουθεσία 3. νουθετέω 4. νουθέτησις 5. corripio
1Kg 2:42 Did I not . . and solemnly admonish you 1
Ps 81: 8 Hear, O my people, while I admonish you! 1
Act 20:31 not cease . . to admonish every one with tears. 3
1Co 4:14 to admonish you as my beloved children. 3
Col 3:16 teach and admonish one another in all wisdom 3
1Th 5:12 are over you in the Lord and admonish you 3
14 we exhort you, brethren, admonish the idlers 3
Tit 3:10 after admonishing him once or twice 2
2Es 7:49 and will admonish you yet again. 5
Jdt 8:27 scourges . . in order to admonish them. 4

admonition 1. מוֹעֵצָה 2. תּוֹכַחַת
Prv 15: 5 but he who heeds admonition is prudent. 2
31 He whose ear heeds wholesome admonition 2
32 he who heeds admonition gains understanding. 2
22:20 30 sayings of admonition and knowledge 1

adopt 1. לקח 2. ἄγω 3. ἀναιρέω 4. ἀναλαμβάνω 5. μεταλαμβάνω
Est 2: 7 Mor'decai adopted her as his own daughter. 1
15 Mor'decai, who had adopted her as his own daughter 1
Act 7:21 Pharaoh's daughter adopted him 3
2Mc 6: 8 should adopt the same policy toward the Jews 2
4Mc 5:11 adopt a mind appropriate to your years 4
8: 8 by adopting the Greek way of life 5

adopt a way of life 1. πολιτεύω
4Mc 2: 8 as soon as a man adopts a way of life 1

gladly adopt 1. εὐδοκέω
1Mc 1:43 Many . . gladly adopted his religion 1

adoption as a son 1. υἱοθεσία
Rom 8:23 groan inwardly as we wait for adoption as sons 1
Gal 4: 5 so that we might receive adoption as sons. 1

adoption of foreign ways 1. ἀλλοφυλισμός
2Mc 4:13 and increase in the adoption of foreign ways 1

adore 1. adoro
2Es 7:78 first of all it adores the glory of the Most High. 1

adorn 1. יטב 2. עדה 3. פאר 4. צפה 5. κοιμάω 6. κοσμέω 7. κόσμος 8. exorno
2Kg 9:30 she painted her eyes, and adorned her head 1
2Ch 3: 6 He adorned the house with . . precious stones. 4
Ps 149: 4 pleasure . . adorns the humble with victory. 3
Isa 61:10 and as a bride adorns herself with her jewels. 2
Jer 31: 4 Again you shall adorn yourself with timbrels 2
Mat 23:29 adorn the monuments of the righteous 6
Lke 21: 5 how it was adorned with noble stones 6
1Ti 2: 9 women should adorn themselves modestly 6
Tit 2:10 in everything they may adorn the doctrine of God 6
1Pe 3: 3 Let not yours be the outward adorning 7
5 women who hoped in God used to adorn themselves 6
Rev 21: 2 prepared as a bride adorned for her husband; 6
19 foundations . . were adorned with every jewel; 6
2Es 16:47 the more they adorn their cities, their houses 8
AEs 14: 2 every part that she loved to adorn 7
Sir 45:12 the delight of the eyes, richly adorned. 6
48:11 those who have been adorned in love 5
50: 9 adorned with all kinds of precious stones; 6
2Mc 9:16 he would adorn with the finest offerings 6
3Mc 3: 5 they adorned their style of life with the good deeds 6
6: 1 had been adorned with every virtue 6

majestically adorn 1. ἐπιφανής
AEs 15: 2 majestically adorned . . she took her two maids 1

remain adorned 1. ἐγκοσμέω
4Mc 6: 2 who remained adorned with . . his piety. 1

adornment 1. חֵן 2. διακόσμησις 3. κόσμος
Prv 3:22 life for your soul and adornment for your neck. 1
1Mc 2:11 All her adornment has been taken away 3
2Mc 2: 2 gold and silver statues and their adornment. 3
29 only what is suitable for its adornment 2

adrift 1. ποιέω
2Co 11:25 a night and a day I have been adrift at sea; 1

adulterer 1. נאף 2. *μοιχός*

Lev 20:10 both the adulterer and the adulteress shall be 1
Job 24:15 the adulterer also waits for the twilight 1
Ps 50:18 you keep company with adulterers. 1
Isa 57: 3 offspring of the adulterer and the harlot. 1
Jer 9: 2 For they are all adulterers 1
23:10 For the land is full of adulterers; 1
Hos 7: 4 They are all adulterers; 1
Mal 3: 5 against the sorcerers, against the adulterers 1
Lke 18:11 extortioners, unjust, adulterers 2
1Co 6: 9 nor adulterers, nor sexual perverts 2
Wis 3:16 children of adulterers will not come to maturity 2

adulteress 1. אִשָּׁה נאף 2. אֵשֶׁת אִישׁ 3. נאף 4. *μοιχαλίς* 5. *μοιχεύω*

Lev 20:10 adulterer and the adulteress shall be put 3
Prv 6:26 but an adulteress stalks a man's very life. 2
30:20 This is the way of an adulteress: she eats 1
Ezk 23:45 on them with the sentence of adulteresses 3
45 because they are adulteresses 3
Hos 3: 1 is beloved of a paramour and is an adulteress; 3
Mat 5:32 unchastity, makes her an adulteress; and whoever 5
Rom 7: 3 Accordingly, she will be called an adulteress 4
3 marries another man she is not an adulteress. 4

adulterous 1. נאף 2. *μοιχαλίς* 3. *μοιχός*

Ezk 16:32 Adulterous wife, who receives strangers 1
Mat 12:39 An evil and adulterous generation 2
16: 4 An evil and adulterous generation 2
Mrk 8:38 in this adulterous and sinful generation 2
Heb 13: 4 God will judge the immoral and adulterous. 3
Sir 25: 2 an adulterous old man who lacks good sense. 3

adultery 1. נאף 2. נאף 3. נַאֲפוּף 4. *μοιχαλίς* 5. *μοιχεία* 6. *μοιχεύω* 7. *νοθεύω*

Jer 3: 8 for all the adulteries of that faithless one 2
13:27 I have seen your abominations, your adulteries 1
Hos 2: 2 put away . . adultery from between her breasts; 3
Mat 15:19 evil thoughts, murder, adultery, fornication 5
Mrk 7:21 fornication, theft, murder, adultery 5
Joh 8: 3 a woman who had been caught in adultery 5
4 this woman has been caught in the act of adultery 6
2Pe 2:14 They have eyes full of adultery 4
Wis 14:24 or grieve one another by adultery 7
26 sex perversion, disorder in marriage, adultery 5

adultery *See also* commit.

advance 1. בוא 2. גדל 3. נגשׁ 4. נשׂא 5. עלה 6. שׁנה 7. *ἄρχω* 8. *διέρχομαι* 9. *ἐγγίζω* 10. *προάγω* 11. *προηκέω* 12. *προβαίνω* 13. *προκοπή* 14. *προκόπτω* 15. *προσάγω*

Gen 18:11 Now Abraham and Sarah were old, advanced in age; 1
Jos 13: 1 Now Joshua was old and advanced in years; 1
1 You are old and advanced in years 1
23: 1 and Joshua was old and well advanced in years 1
2 I am now old and well advanced in years; 1
1Sm 17:12 the man was already old and advanced in years. 1
1Kg 1: 1 King David was old and advanced in years; 1
Est 2: 9 and advanced her and her maids to the best place 6
3: 1 Ahasu-e'rus promoted Haman . . and advanced him 4
5:11 and how he had advanced him above the princes 4
10: 2 the high honor . . to which the king advanced him 2
Jer 46: 3 Prepare . . shield, and advance for battle! 3
9 Advance, O horses, and rage, O chariots! 5
49:28 says the LORD: "Rise up, advance against Kedar! 5
31 Rise up, advance against a nation at ease 5
Ezk 38: 9 You will advance, coming on like a storm 5
Lke 1: 7 both were advanced in years. 12
18 I am an old man, and my wife is advanced in years. 12
Gal 1:14 I advanced in Judaism beyond many of my own age 14
Php 1:12 really served to advance the gospel 13
Jdt 9: 6 all they ways are prepared in advance •
Sir 20:27 He who speaks wisely will advance himself 10
1Mc 1: 3 He advanced to the ends of the earth 8
6:40 they advanced steadily and in good order. 7
42 Judas and his army advanced to the battle 9
9:12 phalanx advanced to the sound of the trumpets 9
10:77 At the same time he advanced into the plain 10
2Mc 4:40 a man advanced in years 12
40 advanced in years and no less advanced in folly. •
6:18 a man now advanced in age and of noble presence 12
10:27 and advanced a considerable distance 10
11:10 They advanced in battle order 10
13:19 He advanced against Beth-zur . . was turned back 15
15:25 Nicanor and his men advanced with trumpets 15
4Mc 5: 4 advanced in age 11

advance *See also* arrange, know, seize.

advanced in years 1. *γεραιός*

4Mc 16: 1 a woman, advanced in years and mother of seven 1

well advanced 1. בוא

Gen 24: 1 Abraham was old, well advanced in years; 1

advantage 1. יתר 2. יִתְרוֹן 3. מוֹתָר 4. סכן 5. *περισσός* 6. *συμφερόντως* 7. *συμφέρω* 8. *σύμφορος* 9. *ψυχή* 10. *ὠφέλεια* 11. *ὠφελέω*

Job 35: 3 That you ask, 'What advantage have I? 4
Ecc 3:19 and man has no advantage over the beasts; 3
5: 9 a king is an advantage to a land with . . fields. 2
6: 8 For what advantage has the wise man over the fool 1
7:11 Wisdom . . an advantage to those who see the sun. 1
12 the advantage of knowledge is that 2
10:11 there is no advantage in a charmer. 2
Dan 11:17 it shall not stand or be to his advantage. •
Joh 16: 7 it is to your advantage that I go away 7
Rom 3: 1 Then what advantage has the Jew? 5
1Co 10:33 not seeking my own advantage, but that of many 8
2Co 11:20 if a man . . preys upon you, or takes advantage of you •
Gal 5: 2 Christ will be of no advantage to you. 11
Jde 1:16 boasters, flattering people to gain advantage. 10
Sir 20:30 what advantage is there in either of them? 10
37:22 A man may be wise to his own advantage 9
41:14 what advantage is there in either of them? 10
Bar 4: 3 Do not give . . advantages to an alien people. 7
3Mc 6:24 secretly devising acts of no advantage to the kingdom. 7
4Mc 1:17 we learn . . human affairs to our advantage. 6

advantage *See also* gain, take.

no advantage 1. *ἀλυσιτελής*

Heb 13:17 for that would be of no advantage to you. 1

advantageous 1. *συνεργός*

2Mc 8: 7 the nights most advantageous for such attacks. 1

adventuress 1. נָכְרִי

Prv 2:16 saved from . . adventuress with her smooth words 1
5:20 Why . . embrace the bosom of an adventuress? 1
6:24 from the smooth tongue of the adventuress. 1
7: 5 from the adventuress with her smooth words. 1
23:27 an adventuress is a narrow well. 1

adversary 1. אִישׁ רִיב 2. בַּעַל מִשְׁפָּט 3. צור 4. צַר 5. צרר 6. קום 7. קִים 8. ריב 9. שׂטן 10. שָׂטָן 11. שׂנא 12. *ἀνθίστημι* 13. *ἀντίδικος* 14. *ἀντίκειμαι* 15. *διάβολον* 16. *ἐναντιόομαι* 17. *ἐπεγείρω* 18. *σατανᾶς* 19. *ὑπεναντίος* 20. hostis

Exd 15: 7 thou overthrowest thy adversaries; 6
23:22 an enemy to your enemies and an adversary 3
22 an adversary to your adversaries. 5
Num10: 9 go to war in your land against the adversary 4
22:22 took his stand in the way as his adversary. 10
24: 8 he shall eat up the nations his adversaries 4
Deu 32:27 lest their adversaries should judge amiss, lest 4
41 I will take vengeance on my adversaries 4
43 for he . . takes vengeance on his adversaries 4
33: 7 be a help against his adversaries. 4
11 crush the loins of his adversaries •
Jos 5:13 Are you for us, or for our adversaries? 4
Jdg 2: 3 they shall become adversaries to you 20
1Sm 2:10 The adversaries of the LORD shall be broken 8
29: 4 lest in the battle he become an adversary to us. 10
2Sm 19:22 that you should this day be as an adversary to me? 10
22:49 thou didst exalt me above my adversaries 6
1Kg 5: 4 there is neither adversary nor misfortune. 10
11:14 the LORD raised up an adversary against Solomon 10
23 God also raised up as an adversary to him, Rezon 10
25 He was an adversary of Israel 10
1Ch 12:17 but if to betray me to my adversaries 4
Ezr 4: 1 Now when the adversaries of Judah and Benjamin 4
Job 6:23 Or, 'Deliver me from the adversary's hand'? 4
16: 9 my adversary sharpens his eyes against me. 4
19:11 wrath against me, and counts me as his adversary. 4
22:20 saying, 'Surely our adversaries are cut off 7
31:35 I had the indictment written by my adversary! 1
Ps 17: 7 those who seek refuge from their adversaries 6
18:48 yea, thou didst exalt me above my adversaries 6
27: 2 my adversaries and foes, they shall stumble 4
12 Give me not up to the will of my adversaries; 4
31:11 I am the scorn of all my adversaries, a horror 5
38:20 are my adversaries because I follow after good. 9
42:10 my adversaries taunt me, while they say to me 5
55:12 is not an adversary who deals insolently with me- 11
74:23 the uproar of thy adversaries which goes up 6
78:66 he put his adversaries to rout; 4
97: 3 Fire . . burns up his adversaries round about. 4
106:11 waters covered their adversaries; 4
112: 8 until he sees his desire on his adversaries. 4
119:157 Many are my persecutors and my adversaries 4
143:12 steadfast love . . destroy all my adversaries 5
Isa 9:11 So the LORD raises adversaries against them 4
26:11 Let the fire for thy adversaries consume them. 4
50: 8 Who is my adversary? Let him come near to me. 2
59:18 wrath to his adversaries, requital to his 4
63:18 our adversaries have trodden it down. 4
64: 2 to make thy name known to thy adversaries 4
Ezk 39:23 and gave them into the hand of their adversaries 4
Ams 3:11 An adversary shall surround the land 4
Mic 5: 9 hand shall be lifted up over your adversaries 4
Nah 1: 2 the LORD takes vengeance on his adversaries 4
8 he will make a full end of his adversaries 17
Lke 13:17 all his adversaries were put to shame 14
18: 3 saying, 'Vindicate me against my adversary.' 13
21:15 none of your adversaries will be able 14
1Co 16: 9 there are many adversaries. 14
Heb 10:27 fire which will consume the adversaries. 19
1Pe 5: 8 Your adversary the devil prowls around 13
1Es 8:51 to keep us safe from our adversaries; 16
Wis 2:18 deliver him from the hand of his adversaries. 12
Sir 21:27 When an ungodly man curses his adversary 18
23: 3 then I will not fall before my adversaries 19
36: 7 destroy the adversary and wipe out the enemy. 13
47: 7 annihilated his adversaries the Philistines 19
1Mc 1:36 an evil adversary of Israel continually. 15
2Mc 10:26 to be . . an adversary to their adversaries 14
26 to be . . an adversary to their adversaries 14
15:16 you will strike down your adversaries. 19

adversity 1. לַחַץ 2. צַר 3. צָרָה 4. רַע 5. רָעָה 6. תְּלָאָה 7. *κακός* 8. malus

Num20:14 You know all the adversity that has befallen us 6
2Sm 4: 9 who has redeemed my life out of every adversity 3
1Kg 1:29 who has redeemed my soul out of every adversity 3
Job 36:15 opens their ear by adversity. 1
Ps 10: 6 I shall not meet adversity. 4
31: 7 thou hast taken heed of my adversities 3
Prv 17:17 brother is born for adversity. 3
24:10 in the day of adversity, your strength is small. 3
Ecc 7:14 and in the day of adversity consider; 5
Isa 30:20 though the Lord give you the bread of adversity 2
2Es 15:56 and will hand you over to adversities. 8
Sir 11:25 In the day of prosperity, adversity is forgotten 7
25 and in the day of adversity 7
12: 8 nor will an enemy be hidden in adversity. 7
9 in his adversity even his friend will separate 7
20: 9 There may be good fortune for a man in adversity 7

advice 1. דָּבָר 2. עֵצָה 3. *γνώμη* 4. *παρηγορία* 5. *συμβουλία*

Jdg 20: 7 Israel, all of you, give your advice and counsel 1
2Sm 17: 4 the advice pleased Ab'salom and all the elders 1
Est 1:21 This advice pleased the king and the princes 1
Prv 12:15 but a wise man listens to advice. 2
19:20 Listen to advice and accept instruction 2
2Co 8:10 in this matter I give my advice 3
Tob 4:18 Seek advice from every wise man 5
4Mc 5:12 honoring my humane advice? 4

advice *See also* take.

advisable 1. *ἄξιος*

1Co 16: 4 If it seems advisable that I should go also 1

advise 1. אמר 2. דָּבָר 3. יעץ 4. *παραινέω* 5. *συμβουλεύω* 6. *σύμβουλος* 7. *τίθημι βουλήν*

2Sm 17: 6 Thus has Ahith'ophel . . shall we do as he advises? 2
1Kg 12: 6 How do you advise me to answer this people? 3
9 What do you advise that we answer this people 3
2Ch 10: 6 How do you advise me to answer this people? 3
9 What do you advise that we answer this people 3
Est 2:15 asked for nothing except what Hegai . . advised. 1
Act 27: 9 Paul advised them 4
12 the majority advised to put to sea from there 7
2Mc 7:25 urged her to advise the youth to save himself. 6
4Mc 1: 1 it is right for me to advise you 5
5: 6 I would advise you to save yourself by eating pork 5
8: 5 Not only do I advise you 5

adviser 1. יעץ 2. מֵרֵעַ 3. *σύμβουλος*

Gen 26:26 to him from Gerar with Ahuz'zath his adviser 2
Prv 15:22 but with many advisers they succeed. 1
Sir 6: 6 let your advisers be one in 1,000 3

advocate 1. *ἔκδικος* 2. *καταγγέλλω* 3. *παράκλητος* 4. *σύμβουλος*

Act 16:21 advocate customs which it is not lawful for us 2
1Jn 2: 1 we have an advocate with the Father, Jesus Christ 3
Wis 12:12 to plead as an advocate for unrighteous men? 1
4Mc 15:25 she saw mighty advocates 4

afar 1. מֶרְחָק 2. מֵרָחוֹק 3. עַד לְמֵרָחוֹק 4. רחק 5. רָחֹק 6. *ἕως εἰς μακράν* 7. *μακρόθεν* 8. *πόρρωθεν*

Exd 20:18 and they stood afar off 2
Num24: 6 Like valleys that stretch afar •
Deu 28:49 LORD will bring a nation against you from afar 5
Ezr 3:13 with a great shout, and the sound was heard afar. 3
Job 2:12 when they saw him from afar, they did not recognize 2
28: 4 they hang afar from men, they swing to and fro. •
36: 3 I will fetch my knowledge from afar 5
25 men have looked on it; man beholds it from afar. 5
39:25 he says 'Aha!' He smells the battle from afar 5
Ps 55: 7 yea, I would wander afar 4
138: 6 but the haughty he knows from afar. 1
139: 2 thou discernest my thoughts from afar. 5
Prv 31:14 she brings her food from afar. 1
Isa 10: 3 in the storm which will come from afar? 1
23: 7 city . . whose feet carried her to settle afar? 2
43: 6 bring my sons from afar and my daughters 5
49: 1 O coastlands, and hearken, you peoples from afar. 5
12 Lo, these shall come from afar 5
Jer 5:15 Behold, I am bringing upon you a nation from afar 1
30:10 O Israel; for lo, I will save you from afar 5
31: 3 the LORD appeared to him from afar. 5
46:27 for lo, I will save you from afar 5

51:50 go, stand not still! Remember the LORD from afar 5
Hab 1: 8 Yea, their horsemen come from afar; 5
Mat 27:55 also many women there, looking on from afar 7
Mrk 5: 6 when he saw Jesus from afar, he ran and worshiped 7
15:40 There were also women looking on from afar 7
Heb 11:13 having seen it and greeted it from afar 8
1Es 5:65 the sound was heard afar; 7
Tob 13:11 Many nations will come from afar 7
Jdt 13:11 Judith called out from afar to the watchmen 7
Sir 21: 7 He who is mighty in speech is known from afar 7
24:32 I will make it shine afar; 6
Bar 4:15 For he brought against them a nation from afar 7

afar *See also* scatter, stretch.

afar off 1. בְּרָחֹק 2. מִמֶּרְחָק 3. מֵרָחֹק 4. עַד רָחֹק 5. רָחֹק

Gen 22: 4 lifted up his eyes and saw the place afar off. 3
37:18 They saw him afar off, and before he came near 3
Exd 20:18 and they stood afar off 3
21 the people stood afar off, while Moses drew near 3
24: 1 Come up to the LORD . . and worship afar off. 3
Num 9:10 If any man of you . . is afar off on a journey 5
1Sm 26:13 and stood afar off on the top of the mountain 3
Neh 12:43 joy of Jerusalem was heard afar off. 5
Job 39:29 he spies out the prey; his eyes behold it afar off. 3
Ps 10: 1 Why dost thou stand afar off, O LORD? 1
38:11 my kinsmen stand afar off. 3
Isa 5:26 He will raise a signal for a nation afar off 3
59:14 and righteousness stands afar off; 3
66:19 to Tubal and Javan, to the coastlands afar off 5
Jer 23:23 a God at hand, says the LORD, and not a God afar off? 3
31:10 and declare it in the coastlands afar off; 2
Mic 4: 3 and shall decide for strong nations afar off; 4

affair 1. דָּבָר 2. עֲבִידָה (A) 3. ἔργον 4. ἴδιος 5. πρᾶγμα 6. τὸ κατά 7. χρεία

Num16:49 besides those who died in the affair of Korah. 1
2Sm 14:20 to change the course of affairs . . Jo'ab did 1
19:29 Why speak any more of your affairs? I have decided 1
1Kg 10: 6 The report . . of your affairs and of your wisdom 1
1Ch 26:32 oversight . . for the affairs of the king. 1
2Ch 9: 5 The report was true . . of your affairs 1
Est 2:23 the affair was investigated and found to be 1
Ps 112: 5 who conducts his affairs with justice. 1
Dan 2:49 over the affairs of the province of Babylon; 2
3:12 over the affairs of the province of Babylon 2
1Co 7:32 is anxious about the affairs of the Lord •
33 the married man is anxious about worldly affairs •
34 is anxious about the affairs of the Lord •
34 the married woman is anxious about worldly affairs •
Col 4: 7 Tych'icus will tell you all about my affairs 6
1Th 4:11 to mind your own affairs 4
1Es 4:11 no one may go away to attend to his own affairs 3
AEs 13: 6 the letters of Haman, who is in charge of affairs 5
1Mc 3:32 He left Lysias . . in charge of the king's affairs 5
6:57 affairs of the kingdom press urgently upon us. •
2Mc 3: 7 who was in charge of his affairs 5
8:20 when 8,000 in all went into the affair 7
9:20 If . . your affairs are as you wish 4
11:23 be undisturbed in caring for their own affairs. •
26 and go on happily in the conduct of their own affairs. •
29 and look after your own affairs. •
3Mc 3:21 the myriad affairs liberally entrusted to them 5
7: 2 the great God guiding our affairs 5
4Mc 1:17 we learn . . human affairs to our advantage. •

affair *See also* state, turn.

personal affair 1. ὁ αὐτοῦ

Jdt 12:11 the eunuch who had charge of his personal affairs 1
14:13 the steward in charge of all his personal affairs 1

public affair 1. πρᾶγμα 2. χρεία

AEs 16: 5 with the administration of public affairs 1
2Mc 4: 6 affairs could not again reach a peaceful settlement 1
7:24 and entrust him with public affairs. 2

affect 1. efficio

2Es 8:50 For many miseries will affect those 1

affection 1. דּוֹד 2. εὔνοια 3. σπλάγχνον 4. στοργή 5. φιλοστόργως 6. φίλτρον

Prv 5:19 her affection fill you at all times with delight 1
2Co 6:12 you are restricted in your own affections. 3
Php 1: 8 with the affection of Christ Jesus. 3
2: 1 any affection and sympathy 3
2Mc 9:21 I remember with affection your esteem 5
3Mc 5:32 an affection arising from our nurture in common 4
4Mc 2:10 the law prevails even over affection for parents 2
13:19 not ignorant of the affection of brotherhood 6
27 habits had augmented the affection of brotherhood 6

brotherly affection 1. φιλαδελφία

Rom 12:10 love one another with brotherly affection; 1
2Pe 1: 7 and godliness with brotherly affection 1
7 and brotherly affection with love. 1
4Mc 13:23 brotherly affection had been so established 1

affection of love 1. φίλτρον

4Mc 15:13 O sacred nature and affection of parental love 1

affectionately *See* desirous.

affirm 1. λέγω 2. φάσκω

Act 24: 9 affirming that all this was so. 2
Eph 4:17 Now this I affirm and testify in the Lord 1

afflict 1. בֶּן עֳנִי 2. לחץ 3. נֶגַע 4. נגע 5. נגף 6. נכה 7. ענה 8. עָנָו 9. עָנִי 10. צוק 11. צור 12. צרר 13. רעע 14. βασανίζω 15. ἐκδιώκω 16. θλίβω 17. θλῖψιν ἐγείρω 18. θλῖψις 19. κακόω 20. μαστιγόω 21. ὀχλέω 22. πατάσσω 23. προστίθημι 24. συνέχω 25. ταπεινόω 26. humilio 27. tribulo

Gen 12:17 the LORD afflicted Pharaoh and his house 4
Exd 1:11 they set taskmasters over them to afflict them 7
22:22 You shall not afflict any widow or orphan. 7
23 If you do afflict them, and they cry out to me, I will 7
Lev 13: 9 When a man is afflicted with leprosy 3
16:29 you shall afflict yourselves 7
31 you shall afflict yourselves; it is a statute 7
23:27 you shall afflict yourselves and present 7
29 For whoever is not afflicted on this same day 7
32 solemn rest, and you shall afflict yourselves 7
Num24:24 ships . . shall afflict Asshur and Eber; 7
29: 7 have a holy convocation, and afflict yourselves 7
30:13 Any vow and any binding oath to afflict herself 7
Deu 26: 6 Egyptians treated us harshly, and afflicted us 7
Jdg 2:18 those who afflicted and oppressed them. 2
Rut 1:21 Why call me Na'omi, when the LORD has afflicted me 25
1Sm 5: 6 and he terrified and afflicted them with tumors 6
9 and he afflicted the men of the city 6
2Sm 7:10 and violent men shall afflict them no more 7
1Kg 8:35 turn from their sin, when thou dost afflict them 7
11:39 I will for this afflict the descendants of David 7
2Kg 17:20 LORD rejected . . Israel, and afflicted them 7
2Ch 6:26 turn from their sin, when thou dost afflict them 7
15: 5 great disturbances afflicted •
28:20 afflicted him instead of strengthening him. 12
Job 2: 7 Satan . . afflicted Job with loathsome sores 6
34:28 he heard the cry of the afflicted- 9
36: 6 but gives the afflicted their right. 9
15 He delivers the afflicted by their affliction 9
Ps 9:12 he does not forget the cry of the afflicted. 9
10:12 O God, lift up thy hand; forget not the afflicted. 9
22:24 or abhorred the affliction of the afflicted; 9
26 The afflicted shall eat and be satisfied; 8
25:16 be gracious to me; for I am lonely and afflicted. 9
34: 2 let the afflicted hear and be glad. 8
35:13 I afflicted myself with fasting. 7
44: 2 thou didst afflict the peoples 13
69:26 whom thou hast wounded, they afflict still more. 23
29 I am afflicted and in pain; 9
82: 3 maintain the right of the afflicted 9
88:15 Afflicted and close to death from my youth up 9
90:15 Make us glad as many days as thou hast afflicted 7
94: 5 O LORD, and afflict thy heritage. 7
102: 0 A prayer of one afflicted, when he is faint 9
116:10 even when I said, "I am greatly afflicted"; 7
119:67 Before I was afflicted I went astray; 7
71 It is good for me that I was afflicted 7
75 that in faithfulness thou hast afflicted me. 7
107 I am sorely afflicted; give me life, O LORD 7
129: 1 Sorely have they afflicted me from my youth 12
2 Sorely have they afflicted me from my youth 12
140:12 LORD maintains the cause of the afflicted 9
Prv 15:15 All the days of the afflicted are evil 9
22:22 Do not . . crush the afflicted at the gate; 9
31: 5 pervert the rights of all the afflicted. 1
Isa 14:32 in her the afflicted of his people find refuge. 9
49:13 and will have compassion on his afflicted. 9
51:21 Therefore hear this, you who are afflicted 9
53: 4 him stricken, smitten by God, and afflicted. 7
7 He was oppressed, and he was afflicted 7
58:10 and satisfy the desire of the afflicted 7
61: 1 anointed me to bring good tidings to the afflicted; 8
63: 9 In all their affliction he was afflicted 11
64:12 Wilt thou keep silent, and afflict us sorely? 7
Jer 19: 9 and those who seek their life afflict them. 10
Lam 3:33 he does not willingly afflict or grieve . . men. 7
Ams 5:12 you who afflict the righteous, who take a bribe 12
Mic 4: 6 and those whom I have afflicted; 13
Nah 1:12 I have afflicted you, I will afflict you no more. 7
12 I have afflicted you, I will afflict you no more. 7
Zec 10: 2 they are afflicted for want of a shepherd. 7
14:18 plague with which the LORD afflicts the nations 5
Mat 4:24 the sick, those afflicted with various diseases 24
Act 5:16 those afflicted with unclean spirits 21
2Co 1: 6 If we are afflicted, it is for your comfort 16
4: 8 We are afflicted in every way 16
7: 5 we were afflicted at every turn 16
Php 1:17 not sincerely but thinking to afflict me 17
2Th 1: 6 to repay with affliction those who afflict you 16
7 to grant rest with us to you who are afflicted 16
1Ti 5:10 relieved the afflicted 16
Heb 11:37 destitute, afflicted, ill-treated- 16
2Es 9:41 embittered in spirit and deeply afflicted. 26
11:42 for you have afflicted the meek 27
Tob 11:15 For thou hast afflicted me 20
13: 2 For he afflicts, and he shows mercy 20
5 He will afflict us for our iniquities 20
9 he will afflict you for the deeds of your sons 20
Jdt 5:12 he afflicted the whole land of Egypt 22
Wis 5: 1 in the presence of those who have afflicted him 16
19:16 afflicted with terrible sufferings 19
Sir 3:26 A stubborn mind will be afflicted at the end 19
4: 4 Do not reject an afflicted suppliant 16
30:19 So is he who is afflicted by the Lord; 15
21 do not afflict yourself deliberately. 16
31:31 do not afflict him by making demands of him. 16
35:20 Mercy is as welcome when he afflicts them 18
49: 7 For they had afflicted him 19
7 to pluck up and afflict and destroy 19
Bar 4:31 Wretched will be those who afflicted you 19
2Mc 1:28 Afflict those who oppress 14
5:22 he left governors to afflict the people 19

afflict previously 1. προκακόω

4Mc 17:22 that previously had been afflicted. 1

severely afflict 1. μαστιγόω

Sir 30:14 a rich man who is severely afflicted in body. 1

afflicted *See* soul.

afflicted one 1. עָנִי

Isa 54:11 O afflicted one, storm-tossed, and not comforted 1

affliction 1. אָוֶן 2. חֳלִי 3. לַחַץ 4. מוּעָקָה 5. מַכָּה 6. נֶגַע 7. עֱנוּת 8. עֳנִי 9. צַר 10. צָרָה 11. רָעָה 12. תַּעֲלוּלִים 13. ἀνάγκη 14. ἐπαγωγή 15. ἐτασμός 16. θλῖψις 17. κάκωσις 18. μάστιξ 19. σύντριμμα 20. ταπείνωσις 21. dolor 22. malus

Gen 16:11 the LORD has given heed to your affliction. 8
29:32 Because the LORD has looked upon my affliction; 8
31:42 God saw my affliction and the labor of my hands 8
41:52 made me fruitful in the land of my affliction. 8
Exd 3: 7 I have seen the affliction of my people 8
17 I will bring you up out of the affliction of Egypt 8
4:31 heard . . that he had seen their affliction 8
Deu 16: 3 unleavened bread, the bread of affliction 8
26: 7 saw our affliction, our toil, and our oppression; 8
28:59 LORD will bring . . extraordinary afflictions 5
59 afflictions severe and lasting, and sicknesses 5
61 Every sickness also, and every affliction 5
29:22 they see the affliction of the land 5
1Sm 1:11 look on the affliction of thy maidservant 8
9:16 I have seen the affliction of my people 20
2Sm 16:12 may be that the LORD will look upon my affliction 20
1Kg 8:38 each knowing the affliction of his own heart 6
2Kg 14:26 the LORD saw that the affliction of Israel was 8
2Ch 6:29 each knowing his own affliction, and . . sorrow 6
20: 9 cry to thee in our affliction 10
Neh 9: 9 didst see the affliction of our fathers in Egypt 8
Est 7: 4 for our affliction is not to be compared 9
Job 5: 6 For affliction does not come from the dust 1
10:15 with disgrace and look upon my affliction. 8
30:16 days of affliction have taken hold of me. 8
27 days of affliction come to meet me. 8
36: 8 in fetters and caught in the cords of affliction 8
15 He delivers the afflicted by their affliction 8
21 this you have chosen rather than affliction. 8
Ps 22:24 or abhorred the affliction of the afflicted; 7
25:18 Consider my affliction and my trouble 8
31: 7 because thou hast seen my affliction 8
34:19 Many are the afflictions of the righteous; 11
44:24 dost thou forget our affliction and oppression? 8
66:11 thou didst lay affliction on our loins; 4
107:10 prisoners in affliction and in irons 8
41 he raises up the needy out of affliction 8
119:50 This is my comfort in my affliction 8
92 I should have perished in my affliction. 8
153 Look on my affliction and deliver me 8
Ecc 6: 2 this is vanity; it is a sore affliction. 2
Isa 30:20 bread of adversity and the water of affliction 3
48:10 I have tried you in the furnace of affliction. 8
63: 9 In all their affliction he was afflicted 10
66: 4 I also will choose affliction for them 12
Jer 10:19 But I said, "Truly this is an affliction 2
48:16 and his affliction hastens apace. 11
Lam 1: 3 exile because of affliction and hard servitude; 8
7 remembers in the days of her affliction 8
9 O LORD, behold my affliction 8
3: 1 I am the man who has seen affliction under the rod 8
19 Remember my affliction and my bitterness 8
Hab 3: 7 I saw the tents of Cushan in affliction; 1
Act 7:10 rescued him out of all his afflictions 16
11 there came a famine . . and great affliction 16
20:23 imprisonment and afflictions await me. 16
2Co 1: 4 who comforts us in all our affliction 16
4 able to comfort those who are in any affliction 16
8 the affliction we experienced in Asia 16
2: 4 I wrote you out of much affliction and anguish 16
4:17 this slight momentary affliction 16
6: 4 through great endurance, in afflictions 16
7: 4 With all our affliction, I am overjoyed. 16

8: 2 for in a severe test of affliction 16
Col 1:24 what is lacking in Christ's afflictions 16
1Th 1: 6 received the word in much affliction 16
3: 3 that no one be moved by these afflictions 16
7 in all our distress and affliction 16
2Th 1: 4 in the afflictions which you are enduring. 16
6 to repay with affliction those who afflict you 16
Heb 10:33 being publicly exposed to abuse and affliction 16
Jas 1:27 to visit orphans and widows in their affliction 16
2Es 8:27 who have kept thy covenants amid afflictions. 21
15:59 you shall come and suffer fresh afflictions 22
Tob 13:14 those who grieved over all your afflictions 18
Jdt 4:13 the Lord . . looked upon their affliction 16
AEs 11: 8 affliction and great tumult upon the earth! 17
14:12 in this time of our affliction 16
16:20 who attack them at the time of their affliction. 16
Wis 3: 2 their departure was thought to be an affliction 17
Sir 2:11 he forgives sins and saves in time of affliction. 16
3:15 in the day of your affliction 16
28 The affliction of the proud has no healing 14
10:13 brought upon them extraordinary afflictions 14
22:23 stand by him in time of affliction 16
29:12 it will rescue you from all affliction; 17
40: 9 calamities, famine and affliction and plague. 19
51: 3 from the many afflictions that I endured 16
10 not to forsake me in the days of affliction 16
Bar 5: 1 the garment of your sorrow and affliction 17
1Mc 12:13 many afflictions . . have encircled us 16
2Mc 7:37 by afflictions and plagues 15
4Mc 6:24 he was so courageous in the face of the afflictions 13
18:15 'Many are the afflictions of the righteous.' 16
affliction *See also* share, suffer.

great affliction 1. humilio
2Es 10: 7 is in deep grief and great affliction. 1

affluence 1. שֶׁפַע
Deu 33:19 for they suck the affluence of the seas 1

afford 1. הוֹן 2. מצא יָד דֵּי 3. נגע יָד דֵּי 4. נשׂג יָד
5. facio
Lev 5: 7 if he cannot afford a lamb, then he shall bring 3
11 if he cannot afford two turtledoves or two young 4
12: 8 if she cannot afford a lamb, then she shall take 2
14:21 But if he is poor and cannot afford so much 4
22 or two young pigeons, such as he can afford 4
30 offer . . young pigeons such as he can afford 4
32 cannot afford the offerings for his cleansing 4
Num 6:21 apart from what else he can afford; 4
2Es 9:26 the nourishment they afforded satisfied me. 5
Sir 38:11 as much as you can afford. 1

aflame 1. לָהַב 2. πυρόω
Isa 13: 8 look aghast . . their faces will be aflame. 1
1Co 7: 9 it is better to marry than to be aflame with passion. 2
2Mc 14:45 Still alive and aflame with anger, he rose 2

set aflame 1. פוח
Prv 29: 8 Scoffers set a city aflame 1

aforementioned 1. προεῖπον 2. προσημαίνω
3Mc 5:47 destruction of the aforementioned people. 2
6:35 they had arranged the aforementioned choral group 1

aforesaid 1. προεῖπον 2. praedico
2Es 7:99 and the aforesaid are the ways of torment 2
2Mc 3: 7 to effect the removal of the aforesaid money. 1
28 had just entered the aforesaid treasury 1
3Mc 1:26 to bring the aforesaid plan to a conclusion. 1
6:36 observance of the aforesaid days as a festival 1

afraid 1. בעת 2. גור 3. דאג 4. חול 5. חרד 6. יָגוֹר
7. יגר 8. ירא 9. ירא מִפְּנֵי 10. כאה 11. פחד 12. שׂער
13. δειλιάω 14. δειλόομαι 15. δειλός 16. εὐλαβέομαι
17. πτοέω 18. τρέμω 19. φοβέομαι 20. φοβέω
21. metuo 22. timeo
Gen 3:10 and I was afraid, because I was naked; and I hid 8
18:15 I did not laugh"; for she was afraid. 8
19:30 for he was afraid to dwell in Zo'ar; 8
20: 8 and the men were very much afraid. 8
28:17 was afraid, and said, "How awesome is this place! 8
31:31 Jacob answered Laban, "Because I was afraid 8
32: 7 Then Jacob was greatly afraid and distressed; 8
43:18 the men were afraid because they were brought 8
23 He replied, "Rest assured, do not be afraid; 8
46: 3 do not be afraid to go down to Egypt; 8
Exd 2:14 Then Moses was afraid, and thought, "Surely 8
3: 6 hid his face, for he was afraid to look at God. 8
20:18 the people were afraid and trembled; 8
34:30 and they were afraid to come near him. 8
Num 12: 8 Why then were you not afraid to speak against 8
Deu 1:17 you shall not be afraid of the face of man 2
29 I said to you, 'Do not be in dread or afraid of them. 8
2: 4 they will be afraid of you. So take good heed; 8
5: 5 for you were afraid because of the fire 8
7:18 not be afraid of them, but you shall remember 8
19 do to all the peoples of whom you are afraid. 8
9:19 For I was afraid of the anger and hot displeasure 7
18:22 you need not be afraid of him. 2
20: 1 not be afraid of them; for the LORD your God is 8
28:10 peoples of the earth . . shall be afraid of you. 8
60 diseases of Egypt, which you were afraid of; 7
Jos 10:25 Do not be afraid or dismayed; be strong 8
11: 6 Do not be afraid of them, for . . I will give over all 8
Jdg 6:27 but because he was too afraid of his family 8
8:20 the youth did not draw his sword; for he was afraid 8
1Sm 3:15 And Samuel was afraid to tell the vision to Eli. 8
4: 7 the Philistines were afraid; for they said 8
7: 7 when . . Israel heard of it they were afraid 8
17:11 they were dismayed and greatly afraid. 8
24 Israel . . fled from him, and were much afraid. 8
18:12 Saul was afraid of David 8
29 Saul was still more afraid of David. 9
21:12 and was much afraid of A'chish the king of Gath. 8
23: 3 we are afraid here in Judah; how much more 8
15 David was afraid because Saul had come out 8
28: 5 he was afraid, and his heart trembled greatly. 8
2Sm 1:14 How is it you were not afraid to put forth 8
6: 9 And David was afraid of the LORD that day; 8
1Kg 19: 3 he was afraid, and he arose and went for his life 8
2Kg 1:15 Go down with him; do not be afraid of him. 8
10: 4 they were exceedingly afraid, and said, "Behold 8
19: 6 Do not be afraid because of the words 8
25:24 Do not be afraid because of the . . officials; 8
26 for they were afraid of the Chalde'ans. 8
1Ch 13:12 David was afraid of God that day; 8
21:30 afraid of the sword of the angel of the LORD. 1
2Ch 32: 7 Do not be afraid or dismayed before the king 8
Neh 2: 2 Then I was very much afraid. 8
4:14 Do not be afraid of them. Remember the Lord 8
6:13 that I should be afraid and act in this way and sin 8
16 all the nations round about us were afraid 8
Job 6:21 you see my calamity, and are afraid. 8
19:29 be afraid of the sword 2
32: 6 I was timid and afraid to declare my opinion 8
41:25 When he raises himself up the mighty are afraid; 2
Ps 3: 6 I am not afraid of ten thousands of people 8
27: 1 stronghold of my life; of whom shall I be afraid? 11
49:16 Be not afraid when one becomes rich 8
56: 3 When I am afraid, I put my trust in thee. 8
65: 8 earth's farthest bounds are afraid at thy signs; 8
77:16 O God, when the waters saw thee, they were afraid 4
78:53 He led them in safety, so that they were not afraid; 11
112: 7 He is not afraid of evil tidings; his heart is firm 8
8 His heart is steady, he will not be afraid 8
119:120 I am afraid of thy judgments. 8
Prv 3:24 If you sit down, you will not be afraid; 11
25 Do not be afraid of sudden panic 8
31:21 She is not afraid of snow for her household. 8
Ecc 12: 5 they are afraid also of what is high 8
Isa 10:24 my people . . be not afraid of the Assyrians 8
12: 2 I will trust, and will not be afraid; 11
33:14 The sinners in Zion are afraid; 11
37: 6 Do not be afraid because of the words 8
41: 5 The coastlands have seen and are afraid 8
44: 8 Fear not, nor be afraid; 8
51:12 who are you that you are afraid of man who dies 8
Jer 1: 8 Be not afraid of them, for I am with you to deliver 8
10: 5 Be not afraid of them, for they cannot do evil 8
22:25 into the hand of those of whom you are afraid 6
26:21 but when Uri'ah heard of it, he was afraid and fled 8
36:24 was afraid, nor did they rend their garments. 11
38:19 I am afraid of the Jews who have deserted 3
39:17 the hand of the men of whom you are afraid. 6
40: 9 saying, "Do not be afraid to serve the Chalde'ans. 8
41:18 Chalde'ans; for they were afraid of them 8
42:11 the king of Babylon, of whom you are afraid; 8
16 the famine of which you are afraid shall follow 3
Ezk 2: 6 And you, son of man, be not afraid of them 8
6 not afraid of them, nor be afraid of their words 8
6 be not afraid of their words 8
27:35 their kings are horribly afraid 12
Dan 11:30 shall be afraid and withdraw, and shall turn back 10
Ams 3: 6 a trumpet blown . . and the people are not afraid? 5
Jon 1: 5 Then the mariners were afraid, and each cried 8
10 Then the men were exceedingly afraid 8
Zec 9: 5 Ash'kelon shall see it, and be afraid; 8
Mat 2:22 in place of his father Herod, he was afraid to go 19
8:26 he said to them, "Why are you afraid 15
9: 8 When the crowds saw it, they were afraid 20
14:30 when he saw the wind, he was afraid 19
21:26 if we say, 'From men,' we are afraid of the multitude; 20
25:25 so I was afraid, and I went and hid your talent 20
28: 5 Do not be afraid; for I know that you seek Jesus 20
10 Then Jesus said to them, "Do not be afraid 20
Mrk 4:40 Why are you afraid? Have you no faith? 15
5:15 they were afraid. 20
9:32 they were afraid to ask him. 20
10:32 those who followed were afraid 20
11:32 they were afraid of the people 20
16: 8 they said nothing to any one, for they were afraid. 20
Lke 1:13 the angel said to him, "Do not be afraid, Zechari'ah 20
30 the angel said to her, "Do not be afraid, Mary 20
2:10 the angel said to them, "Be not afraid 20
5:10 Jesus said to Simon, "Do not be afraid 20
8:25 they were afraid, and they marveled 20
35 they were afraid. 20
9:34 they were afraid as they entered the cloud. 20
45 they were afraid to ask him about this saying. 20
19:21 I was afraid of you, because you are a severe man; 19
Joh 6:20 he said to them, "It is I; do not be afraid. 20
14:27 neither let them be afraid. 13
19: 8 he was the more afraid; 19
Act 5:26 they were afraid of being stoned by the people. 20
9:26 they were all afraid of him 20
16:38 were afraid when they heard 20
18: 9 Do not be afraid, but speak and do not be silent; 20
22:29 the tribune also was afraid 19
23:10 afraid that Paul would be torn in pieces by them 20
27:24 he said, 'Do not be afraid, Paul 20
Rom 13: 4 But if you do wrong, be afraid 20
2Co 11: 3 I am afraid that as the serpent deceived Eve 20
Gal 4:11 I am afraid I have labored over you in vain. 20
Heb 11:23 they were not afraid of the king's edict. 20
27 not being afraid of the anger of the king 20
13: 6 The Lord is my helper, I will not be afraid 20
2Pe 2:10 they are not afraid to revile the glorious ones 18
2Es 6:33 and to say to you: 'Believe and do not be afraid! 22
10:27 Then I was afraid, and cried with a loud voice 22
55 Therefore do not be afraid 22
13: 8 all . . were much afraid, yet dared to fight. 22
15:18 and people shall be afraid. 21
16:10 who will not be afraid? 22
Tob 2: 8 He is no longer afraid that he will be put to death 20
4: 8 afraid to give according to the little you have. 20
21 Do not be afraid, my son 20
6:14 I am afraid that if I go in I will die 20
17 Do not be afraid, for she was destined for you 20
12:16 they fell upon their faces, for they were afraid. 20
17 he said to them, "Do not be afraid; you will be safe. 20
Jdt 1:11 for they were not afraid of him 20
5:23 they said, "we will not be afraid of the Israelites; 20
10:16 do not be afraid in your heart 20
11: 1 do not be afraid in your heart 20
Wis 8:15 dread monarchs will be afraid of me 20
Sir 22:16 will not be afraid in a crisis. 13
26: 5 Of three things my heart is afraid 16
29: 7 afraid of being defrauded needlessly. 16
1Mc 3:22 as for you, do not be afraid of them. 20
4: 8 Do not . . be afraid when they charge. 14
7:30 he was afraid of him and would not meet him again. 17
12:28 they were afraid and were terrified at heart 20
42 he was afraid to raise his hand against him. 16
16: 6 the soldiers were afraid to cross the stream 14
4Mc 8:14 Be afraid, young fellows 20
15 not only were they not afraid 20
afraid *See also* make.

become afraid 1. יגר 2. φοβέω
Job 9:28 I become afraid of all my suffering 1
1Mc 10:76 the men of the city became afraid 2

exceedingly afraid 1. ἔκφοβος
Mrk 9: 6 for they were exceedingly afraid. 1
afresh *See* break.

after 1. אָז 2. אַחַר 3. אֶל 4. בְּ 5. בְּרֶגֶל 6. וְ 7. כְּ
8. כַּאֲשֶׁר 9. לְ 10. לָאַחֲרוֹנָה 11. לְקֵץ 12. מֵאַחֲרֵי
13. מִדָּה 14. מִן 15. מִקֵּץ 16. עַל 17. שֵׁנִי 18. אַחֲרֵי (A)
19. בָּאתַר (A) 20. כְּ (A) 21. ἀπό 22. ἀφ' ἧς ἡμέρας
23. ἀφ' οὗ 24. διά 25. ἐκ 26. ἐν 27. ἐπειδή 28. ἔπειτα
29. ἐπί 30. ἔχω 31. ἡμέτερος 32. καί 33. κατά
34. κατόπισθεν 35. μεταγενής 36. μετέχω
37. ὄπισθεν 38. ὀπίσω 39. ὅταν 40. ὅτι 41. ὀψέ
42. πᾶς καί 43. ὕστερος 44. ὡς 45. cum 46. ex 47. in
48. post 49. postquam
Gen 1:26 Let us make man in our image, after our likeness 7
4:17 name of the city after the name of his son, Enoch. 7
5: 3 son in his own likeness, after his image 7
7:10 after seven days the waters of the flood came 9
9:28 After the flood Noah lived 350 years; 2
10: 1 Japheth; sons were born to them after the flood. 2
32 spread abroad on the earth after the flood. 2
11:10 father of Arpach'shad two years after the flood; 2
15: 1 After these things the word of the LORD came 2
16: 3 after Abram had dwelt ten years in the land 15
18: 5 after that you may pass on– 2
11 to be with Sarah after the manner of women. •
19:31 to come in to us after the manner of all the earth. 7
22: 1 After these things God tested Abraham 2
24:55 at least ten days; after that she may go. 2
37:17 Joseph went after his brothers, and found them 2
39: 7 after a time his master's wife cast her eyes upon 2
10 although she spoke to Joseph day after day •
40: 1 Some time after this, the butler of the king 2
41: 1 After two whole years, Pharaoh dreamed 15
Exd 10: 5 they shall eat what is left to you after the hail 14
12:44 may eat of it after you have circumcised him. 1
16: 1 second month after they had departed 9
18: 2 had taken Zippo'rah . . after he had sent her away 2
19: 1 On the third new moon after the people of Israel 9
25:40 see that you make them after the pattern for them 4
Lev 14: 8 he shall be clean; and after that he shall come 2
43 after he has taken out the stones and scraped 2

15:28 seven days, and after that she shall be clean 2
19: 9 gather the gleanings after your harvest •
23:11 on the morrow after the sabbath the priest shall •
15 after the sabbath, from the day that you brought •
16 50 days to the morrow after the seventh sabbath •
22 nor . . gather the gleanings after your harvest •
25:15 years after the jubilee, you shall buy 2
29 redeem it within a whole year after its sale •
27:18 if he dedicates his field after the jubilee 2
Num 1: 1 in the second year after they had come out 9
6:19 after he has shaven the hair of his consecration 2
20 after that the Nazirite may drink wine. 2
9: 1 after they had come out of the land of Egypt, saying 9
12:14 days, and after that she may be brought in again. 2
16 After that the people set out from Haze'roth 2
25: 8 went after the man of Israel into the inner room 2
32:22 then after that you shall return and be free 2
42 took Kenath . . called it Nobah, after his own name. 4
33:38 40th year after the people of Israel had come out 9
Deu 3:14 Ja'ir . . called the villages after his own name 16
14:13 buzzard, the kite, after their kinds; 9
14 every raven after its kind; 9
15 ostrich . . the hawk, after their kinds; 9
18 stork, the heron, after their kinds; 9
21:13 after that you may go in to her, and be her husband 2
Jos 5:11 on the morrow after the passover, on that very day •
19:47 calling Leshem, Dan, after the name of Dan 7
Jdg 3:22 the hilt also went in after the blade, and the fat 2
28 he said to them, "Follow after me; for the LORD has 2
11: 4 After a time the Ammonites made war 14
14: 8 And after a while he returned to take her; 14
15: 1 After a while, at the time of wheat harvest, Samson 14
7 be avenged upon you, and after that I will quit. 2
18: 7 in security, after the manner of the Sido'nians 7
29 named the city Dan, after the name of Dan their 4
19: 5 with a morsel of bread, and after that you may go. 2
Rut 2: 2 and glean . . after him in whose sight I shall find 2
18 food she had left over after being satisfied. 14
1Sm 6: 6 After he had made sport of them, did not they let 8
10: 5 After that you shall come to Gib'e-ath-elo'him 2
11: 7 Whoever does not come out after Saul and Samuel 2
13:14 the LORD has sought out a man after his own heart; 7
14:12 Come up after me; for the LORD has given them 2
20:27 on the second day, the morrow after the new moon •
24:21 you will not cut off my descendants after me 2
2Sm 13: 4 why are you so haggard morning after morning? •
23 After two full years Ab'salom had sheepshearers 9
15: 1 After this Ab'salom got himself a chariot 12
16 king went forth, and all his household after him. 5
17 the king went forth, and all the people after him; 5
18:18 he called the pillar after his own name 16
1Kg 1:13 Solomon . . shall reign after me, and he shall sit 2
17 Solomon . . shall reign after me, and he shall sit 2
24 Adoni'jah shall reign after me, and he shall sit 2
30 Solomon . . shall reign after me, and he shall sit 2
3:18 on the third day after I was delivered, this woman 9
6: 1 after the people of Israel came out of . . Egypt 9
7:37 After this manner he made the ten stands; 7
11:24 he gathered men . . after the slaughter by David; 4
13:33 After this thing Jerobo'am did not turn 2
16:24 Sama'ria, after the name of Shemer, the owner 16
17: 7 after a while the brook dried up 15
17 After this the son of the woman . . became ill; 2
18: 1 After many days the word of the LORD came •
28 and cut themselves after their custom 7
19:11 and after the wind an earthquake 2
12 and after the earthquake a fire 2
12 and after the fire a still small voice. 2
21: 2 And after this Ahab said to Naboth •
2Kg 17:33 So they . . after the manner of the nation 7
23: 3 a covenant . . to walk after the LORD and to keep 2
1Ch 2:24 After the death of Hezron, Caleb went 2
6:31 the house of the LORD, after the ark rested there. 14
8: 8 after he had sent away Hushim and Ba'ara 14
27: 1 and went, month after month throughout the year 4
2Ch 18: 2 After some years he went down to Ahab in Sama'ria. 11
24:11 Thus they did day after day, and collected money †
32: 9 After this Sennach'erib king of Assyria 2
Ezr 7: 1 Now after this, in the reign of Ar-ta-xerx'es king 2
Neh 3:30 After him Meshul'lam the son of Berechi'ah 13
9:28 after they had rest they did evil again 7
13: 6 after some time I asked leave of the king 9
19 should not be opened until after the sabbath. 2
Est 2: 1 After these things . . he remembered Vashti 2
12 when the turn came . . after being twelve months 15
3: 1 After these things . . Ahasu-e'rus promoted Haman 2
4 spoke to him day after day and he would not listen 6
7 they cast Pur . . before Haman day after day; †
7 cast it month after month till the twelfth month †
9:26 they called these days Purim, after the term Pur. 16
Job 19:26 after my skin has been thus destroyed 2
20:21 There was nothing left after he had eaten; 9
21: 3 I will speak, and after I have spoken, mock on. 2
30: 5 they shout after them as after a thief. 16
5 they shout after them as after a thief. •
31: 7 from the way, and my heart has gone after my eyes 2
39: 8 he searches after every green thing. 2
42: 7 After the LORD had spoken these words to Job 2
Ps 40: 4 to those who go astray after false gods! •
51: 0 came to him, after he had gone in to Bathsheba. 8
61: 8 praises to thy name, as I pay my vows day after day. •
110: 4 priest for ever after the order of Melchiz'edek. 16
Prv 20:25 snare . . to reflect only after making his vows. 2
24:27 after that build your house. 2
28:22 A miserly man hastens after wealth 9
Ecc 1:11 things yet to happen among those who come after. 10
2:18 I must leave it to the man who will come after me; 2
10:14 and who can tell him what will be after him? 12
11: 1 for you will find it after many days. 4
12: 2 and the clouds return after the rain; 2
Isa 24:22 and after many days they will be punished. 14
43:10 no god was formed, nor shall there be any after me. 2
48: 2 For they call themselves after the holy city 14
Jer 3:15 I will give you shepherds after my own heart 7
7:25 sent . . the prophets to them, day after day; •
13: 6 And after many days the LORD said to me 15
25:12 Then after 70 years are completed 7
26 kings of the north, far and near, one after another 3
40: 1 after Nebu'zarad'an . . had let him go from Ramah 2
4 come, and I will look after you well; 16
41: 4 On the day after the murder of Gedali'ah 17
16 after he had slain Gedali'ah the son of Ahi'kam 2
Ezk 7: 5 Thus says the Lord GOD: Disaster after disaster! 2
11:21 whose heart goes after their detestable things •
20:30 after the manner of your fathers and go astray 4
24: 6 Take out of it piece after piece •
38: 8 After many days you will be mustered; 14
40: 1 fourteenth year after the city was conquered 2
48:31 gates . . being named after the tribes of Israel. 16
Dan 2:39 After you shall arise another kingdom inferior 19
4: 8 named Belteshaz'zar after the name of my god 20
7: 6 After this I looked, and lo, another, like a leopard 19
7 After this I saw in the night visions, 19
24 arise, and another shall arise after them; 18
11: 6 After some years they shall make an alliance 11
13 after some years he shall come on with a great 11
Hos 6: 2 After two days he will revive us; 14
Ams 4:10 among you a pestilence after the manner of Egypt; 4
7: 1 was the latter growth after the king's mowings. 2
Zec 2: 8 after his glory sent me to the nations 2
6: 5 after presenting themselves before the LORD 14
14:16 shall go up year after year to worship the King 4
Mat 3:11 he who is coming after me is mightier than I 38
15:23 Send her away, for she is crying after us. 37
16:24 If any man would come after me 38
22:27 After them all, the woman died. 43
26:22 and began to say to him one after another •
55 Day after day I sat in the temple teaching 33
28: 1 Now after the sabbath 41
Mrk 1: 7 After me comes he who is mightier than I 38
2: 1 when he returned to Caper'na-um after some days 24
8:34 said to them, "If any man would come after me 38
14:19 to say to him one after another, "Is it I? 33
Lke 7: 1 After he had ended all his sayings 27
9:23 he said to all, "If any man would come after me 38
14:27 does not bear his own cross and come after me 38
15: 4 go after the one which is lost, until he finds it? 29
19:14 sent an embassy after him, saying, 'We do not want 38
21: 8 'The time is at hand!' Do not go after them. 38
22:59 after an interval of about an hour •
Joh 1:15 'He who comes after me ranks before me 38
27 even he who comes after me 38
30 'After me comes a man who ranks before me 38
6:66 After this many of his disciples drew back 25
7:10 after his brothers had gone up to the feast 44
12:19 look, the world has gone after him. 38
21:19 after this he said to him, "Follow me. •
Act 5:37 and drew away some of the people after him 38
13:22 a man after my heart, who will do all my will.' 33
18:18 After this Paul stayed many days longer •
19:21 Now after these events 44
20:15 the day after that we came to Mile'tus. 30
30 to draw away the disciples after them. 38
24:17 after some years I came to bring to my nation alms 24
1Co 15:24 after destroying every rule 39
16: 5 visit you after passing through Macedo'nia 39
Gal 2: 1 Then after fourteen years I went up again 24
Col 3:10 after the image of its creator. 33
1Ti 5:15 For some have already strayed after Satan. 38
Heb 5: 6 a priest for ever, after the order of Melchiz'edek. 33
10 a high priest after the order of Melchiz'edek. 33
6:20 after the order of Melchiz'edek. 33
7:11 after the order of Melchiz'edek 33
11 rather than one named after the order of Aaron? 33
17 a priest for ever, after the order of Melchiz'edek. 33
2Pe 2: 8 he was vexed in his righteous soul day after day 25
Rev 12:15 The serpent poured water . . after the woman 38
1Es 5:57 after they came to Judea and Jerusalem. 26
7:10 after the priests and the Levites were purified 40
8: 1 After these things 35
2Es 3: 1 the 30th year after the destruction of our city •
8 every nation walked after its own will 47
4:49 after this a cloud full of water passed before me 48
5: 4 thrown into confusion after the third period; 48
21 after seven days the thoughts of my heart 48
41 or we, or those who come after us? 48
55 those who come after you will be smaller than you 48
6:25 whoever remains after all that I have foretold 46
35 Now after this I wept again and fasted seven days 48
7:29 after these years my son the Messiah shall die 48
31 after seven days the world, which is not yet awake 48
66 salvation promised to them after death. 48
69 if we were not to come into judgment after death 48
75 whether after death . . we shall be kept in rest 48
100 after they have been separated from the bodies 49
107 Joshua after him for Israel in the days of Achan 48
126 consider what we should suffer after death. 48
130 did not believe him, or the prophets after him 48
9:12 must in torment acknowledge it after death. 48
27 after seven days, as I lay on the grass 48
45 after 30 years God heard your handmaid 48
10:46 after 3,000 years Solomon built the city 48
11:17 After you no one shall rule as long as you 48
22 after this I looked, and behold, the twelve wings 48
33 after this I looked, and behold, the middle head 48
12:14 12 kings shall reign in it, one after another. 48
49 and after these days I will come to you. 48
13: 1 After seven days I dreamed a dream in the night; 48
5 After this I looked, and behold, an . . multitude 48
8 After this I looked, and behold, all 48
12 After this I saw the same man come down 48
56 after three more days I will tell you 48
14:30 which you also have transgressed after them. 48
34 and after death you shall obtain mercy. 48
35 For after death the judgment will come 48
15:38 after that, heavy storm clouds shall be stirred 48
47 who have always lusted after you. 45
Tob 8:19 After this he gave a wedding feast for them 32
Jdt 4: 3 had been consecrated after their profanation. 25
16:22 after Manasseh her husband died 22
Sir 27:17 if you betray his secrets, do not run after him. 38
21 there is reconciliation after abuse •
31: 8 who does not go after gold. 38
33:16 like one who gleans after the grape-gatherers 38
34:25 If a man washes after touching a dead body 21
1Mc 1: 9 so did their sons after them for many years; 38
58 those found month after month in the cities. 42
16: 6 when his men saw him, they crossed over after him. 34
2Mc 1: 7 after Jason and his company revolted 23
4:14 after the call to the discus 36
7:36 after enduring a brief suffering 31
41 Last of all, the mother died, after her sons. •
12:11 After a hard fight •
20 hastened after Timothy 29
3Mc 2:24 After a while he recovered 43
4:15 though uncompleted it stopped after 40 days. 29
4Mc 4:23 after he had plundered them he issued a decree 44
6: 3 after they had tied his arms on each side 28
13:21 they were born after an equal time of gestation 24
18: 5 and is being chastised after his death •

after אַחֲרֵי

Gen 5:4, 7, 10, 13, 16, 19, 22, 26, 30; 9:9; 11:11, 13, 15, 17, 19, 21, 23, 25; 13:14; 14:17; 16:13; 17:7^{2}, 8, 9, 10, 19; 18:12, 19; 19:6; 22:20; 23:19; 24:67; 25:11; 26:18; 35:12; 41:3, 6, 19, 23, 27, 30; 44:4; 45:15; 48:1, 4, 6; 50:14, Exd 3:20; 7:25; 11:8; 14:10, 17, 23; 15:20; 23:2; 28:43; 29:29; 33:8; 34:15, 16, Lev 13:7, 35, 55, 56; 14:48; 16:1; 17:7; 20:5, 6; 25:46, 48; 26:33, Num 4:15; 7:88; 8:15, 22; 9:17; 15:39^{2}; 25:13; 26:1; 30:15; 35:28, Deu 1:4, 8; 4:37, 40; 6:14; 8:19; 10:15; 11:4, 28; 12:25, 28, 30; 13:2, 4; 24:4; 28:14; 29:22; 31:16, 27, 29, Jos 1:1; 2:7; 6:9, 13; 8:6, 17; 9:16; 22:27; 24:20, 29, Jdg 1:1; 2:10, 12, 17, 19; 3:28, 31; 7:23; 8:5, 27, 33; 10:1, 3; 12:8, 11, 13; 13:11; 16:4; 19:3, Rut 1:15; 2:3, 7, 9; 3:10; 4:4, 1Sm 1:9; 5:9; 6:12; 7:2; 8:3; 12:21; 14:13^{2}, 22, 36, 37; 15:31; 17:35; 20:37, 38; 22:20; 23:25, 28; 24:8, 14^{4}; 25:13, 19, 42; 26:3, 18; 30:8, 2Sm 1:1, 10; 2:1; 3:16, 26; 5:13; 7:12; 8:1; 10:1; 13:1, 17, 18; 15:13; 17:21; 18:22; 20:7, 13; 21:1, 14, 18; 23:10; 24:10, 1Kg 1:6, 14, 20, 27, 35, 40; 3:12; 9:21; 11:2, 4, 5^{2}, 10; 13:14, 23, 31; 15:4; 19:20, 21; 20:15; 21:26, 2Kg 1:1; 5:20, 21; 7:14, 15; 14:17, 19, 22; 17:15; 18:5; 23:25, 1Ch 5:25; 14:14; 17:11; 18:1; 19:1; 20:4; 27:7; 28:8, 2Ch 1:12; 2:17; 8:8; 11:16, 20; 20:1, 35; 21:18; 22:4; 24:4, 17; 25:14, 25, 27; 26:2, 17; 32:1; 34:31; 35:20, Ezr 3:5; 9:10, 13, Neh 3:16, 17, 18, 20, 21, 22, 23^{2}, 24, 25, 27, 29^{2}, 30, 31; 11:8; 12:32, Job 3:1; 21:21, 33; 29:22; 37:4; 39:10; 42:16, Ps 49:17, Prv 20:7, Ecc 2:12; 3:22; 6:12; 7:14; 9:3, Sng 1:4, Jer 2:5, 8, 23, 25; 3:7; 7:6, 9; 8:2; 9:14, 16, 22; 11:10; 12:6, 15; 13:10; 16:11; 24:1; 25:6, 26; 28:12; 29:2; 31:19^{2}, 33; 32:16, 18, 39; 34:8; 35:15; 36:27; 42:16; 49:37; 50:21, Ezk 5:2, 12; 6:9; 9:5; 12:14; 16:23; 20:16, 30; 44:10, 26; 46:12, Dan 8:1; 9:26, Hos 2:5, 13; 5:11; 11:10, Jol 2:2, 3, Ams 2:4

after μετά

Mat 1:12; 17:1; 20:2; 24:29; 25:19; 26:2, 32, 73; 27:53, 62, 63, Mrk 1:14; 8:31; 9:2, 31; 10:34; 13:24; 14:28, 70; 16:12, 19, Lke 1:24; 2:46; 5:27; 9:28; 10:1; 12:4, 5; 22:20, Joh 2:12; 3:22; 4:43; 5:1; 6:1; 7:1; 11:7; 13:27; 19:28, 38; 21:1, Act 1:3; 5:37; 7:4, 5, 7; 10:37, 41; 12:4; 13:15, 20, 25; 15:13, 16, 36; 18:1; 19:4, 21; 20:1, 6, 29; 21:15; 24:1, 24; 25:1; 28:11, 13, 17, 1Co 11:25, Gal 1:18, Tit 3:10, Heb 8:10; 9:27; 10:15, 16, 26, 2Pe 1:15, Rev 4:1^{2}; 7:1, 9; 11:11; 15:5; 18:1; 19:1; 20:3, 1Es 1:25, 45; 5:1, Tob 11:1; 14:2, 5, Jdt 8:9, 33; 13:9; 16:21, 25, Wis 4:18; 8:13; 15:8; 19:16, Sir 16:29; 23:20; 41:22; 44:9; 46:20; 47:1, 12, Bar 1:9, LJr 1:3, 1Mc 1:1, 5, 9, 20; 3:55; 5:37; 7:33; 8:7, 30; 9:23, 37; 10:34; 11:54; 13:20; 14:24; 16:24, 2Mc 4:23; 6:1; 7:10, 18; 8:28; 10:3; 11:1; 12:27, 32, 3Mc 4:17; 5:37, 4Mc 1:23

after *See also* any, come, day, feel, follow, go, look, lust, pant, run, search, seek, soon, strive.

afterbirth 1. שִׁלְיָה

Deu 28:57 afterbirth that comes out from between her feet 1

afternoon 1. עֶרֶב

2Sm 11: 2 It happened, late one afternoon . . that he saw 1

late afternoon 1. δειλός
1Mc 10:80 men from early morning till late afternoon. 1

afterward 1. אַחַר 2. אַחֲרוֹן 3. אַחֲרֵי 4. אַחֲרֵי כֵן
5. בָּאַחֲרֹנָה 6. וְ 7. מֵאַחֲרֵי כֵן 8. ἀπ' ἐκείνου
9. δεύτερος 10. εἶτα 11. μετά 12. μετὰ δὲ τοῦτο
13. μετὰ τοῦτο 14. μετά χρόνον 15. μετέπειτα
16. ὕστερον 17. post
Gen 6: 4 in those days, and also afterward 4
10:18 Afterward the families of the Canaanites 1
15:14 and afterward they shall come out 3
25:26 Afterward his brother came forth 4
38:30 Afterward his brother came out with the scarlet 1
Exd 5: 1 Afterward Moses and Aaron went to Pharaoh 1
34:32 afterward all the people of Israel came near 4
Lev 14:19 And afterward he shall kill the burnt offering 1
36 afterward the priest shall go in to see the house 1
16:26 and afterward he may come into the camp 4
28 and afterward he may come into the camp 4
22: 7 afterward he may eat of the holy things 1
Num 5:26 afterward shall make the woman drink the water. 1
31: 2 afterward you shall be gathered to your people. 1
24 afterward you shall come into the camp. 1
Deu 17: 7 death, and afterward the hand of all the people. 2
24:21 gather . . you shall not glean it afterward; 3
Jos 2:16 then afterward you may go your way. 1
8:34 And afterward he read all the words of the law 4
10:26 And afterward Joshua smote them 4
23: 1 A long time afterward, when the LORD had given 3
Jdg 1: 9 afterward the men of Judah went down to fight 1
7:11 and afterward your hands shall be strengthened 1
1Sm 9:13 afterward those eat who are invited. 4
24: 5 And afterward David's heart smote him 4
8 Afterward David . . arose, and went out of the cave 4
2Sm 3:28 Afterward, when David heard of it, he said 7
1Kg 17:13 and afterward make for yourself and your son. 5
2Kg 6:24 Afterward Ben-ha'dad . . mustered his entire army 4
1Ch 2:21 Afterward Hezron went in to the daughter 1
2Ch 35:14 afterward they prepared for themselves 1
Ps 73:24 afterward thou wilt receive me to glory. 1
Prv 20:17 but afterward his mouth will be full of gravel. 1
28:23 who rebukes a man will afterward find more favor 3
Isa 1:26 Afterward you shall be called the city 4
Jer 21: 7 Afterward, says the LORD, I will give Zedeki'ah 4
34:11 But afterward they turned around and took back 4
46:26 Afterward Egypt shall be inhabited 4
49: 6 But afterward I will restore the fortunes 4
51:46 one year and afterward a report in another year 3
Ezk 43: 1 Afterward he brought me to the gate 6
Dan 11:18 Afterward he shall turn his face 4
Hos 3: 5 Afterward the children of Israel shall return 1
Jol 2:28 And it shall come to pass afterward 3
Mat 4: 2 and 40 nights, and afterward he was hungry. 16
21:29 he answered, 'I will not'; but afterward he repented 16
32 you did not afterward repent and believe him. 16
37 Afterward he sent his son to them, saying 16
25:11 Afterward the other maidens came also, saying 16
Mrk 16:14 Afterward he appeared to the eleven themselves 16
Lke 17: 8 afterward you shall eat and drink'? 13
18: 4 afterward he said to himself 13
20:32 Afterward the woman also died. 16
Joh 5:14 Afterward, Jesus found him in the temple, and said 13
13: 7 afterward you will understand. 13
36 you shall follow afterward. 16
Gal 3:17 the law, which came 430 years afterward 11
Heb 4: 7 saying through David so long afterward 14
12:17 you know that afterward . . he was rejected 15
Jde 1: 5 afterward destroyed those who did not believe. 9
1Es 1:13 Afterward they prepared the passover 12
2Es 10:56 afterward you will hear as much as your ears 17
Wis 5:11 afterward no sign of its coming is found there; 13
14:22 Afterward it was not enough for them to err 10
Sir 17:23 Afterward he will arise and requite them 13
40: 6 afterward in his sleep, as though he were on watch 8
Bar 3:37 Afterward she appeared upon earth and lived 13
LJr 1:50 it will afterward be known that they are false. 13
1Mc 4:18 afterward seize the plunder boldly. 13
2Mc 5:20 afterward participated in its benefits 16
6:15 take vengeance on us afterward 16

afterward *See also* come, soon.

afterwards 1. אַחַר 2. אַחֲרוֹן 3. אַחֲרֵי כֵן
4. μετὰ ταῦτα 5. postea
Gen 30:21 Afterwards she bore a daughter 1
32:20 and afterwards I shall see his face; 3
Exd 11: 1 one plague more . . afterwards he will let you go 3
Num19: 7 afterwards he shall come into the camp; 1
Deu 13: 9 afterwards the hand of all the people. 2
Jos 24: 5 I sent Moses . . and afterwards I brought you out. 1
2Ch 33:14 Afterwards he built an outer wall for the city 3
Jer 16:16 and afterwards I will send for many hunters 3
2Es 7:101 and afterwards they shall be gathered 5
8:11 and afterwards thou wilt guide him in thy mercy. 5
Sir 13: 7 Should he see you afterwards, he will forsake you 4

afterwards *See also* come.

again 1. אַחֲרֵי 2. גַּם 3. הלך 4. וְ 5. יוֹסֵף עוֹד 6. יסף
7. יסף עוֹד 8. לְעוֹלָם 9. סבב 10. עוֹד 11. עוֹלָם
12. שָׁבִים לְ 13. שוב 14. שנה 15. שֵׁנִי 16. ἀλλά
17. ἀπ' ἄρτι 18. ἀποκρίνω 19. δίς 20. ἔτι 21. μηκέτι
22. οὐκέτι 23. πάλιν 24. ποτέ 25. προστίθημι
26. adhuc 27. iam 28. iterato 29. iterum 30. postea
Gen 4: 2 again, she bore his brother Abel. 6
25 Adam knew his wife again, and she bore a son 10
8:10 again he sent forth the dove out of the ark; 6
21 I will never again curse the ground 6
21 neither will I ever again destroy every living 6
9:15 the waters shall never again become a flood 10
18:29 Again he spoke to him, and said 7
32 be angry, and I will speak again but this once. 7
24:20 she . . ran again to the well to draw 10
26:18 Isaac dug again the wells of water 13
29:33 She conceived again and bore a son 10
34 Again she conceived and bore a son, and said 10
35 she conceived again and bore a son, and said 10
30: 7 conceived again and bore Jacob a second son. 10
19 Leah conceived again, and she bore Jacob a sixth 10
31 if you will do this for me, I will again feed 13
35: 9 God appeared to Jacob again, when he came 10
38: 4 Again she conceived and bore a son 10
5 Yet again she bore a son 10
26 And he did not lie with her again. 10
46: 4 Egypt, and I will also bring you up again; •
Exd 4: 6 Again, the LORD said to him, "Put your hand 10
8:29 only let not Pharaoh deal falsely again by not 6
9:34 he sinned yet again, and hardened his heart 6
10:28 never see my face again; for in the day you see my 6
29 I will not see your face again. 6
11: 6 there has never been, nor ever shall be again. 6
14:13 Egyptians . . you shall never see again. 6
21:19 rises again and walks abroad with his staff •
Lev 13: 6 the priest shall examine him again 15
7 he shall appear again before the priest 15
57 then if it appears again in the garment, in warp 10
14:43 If the disease breaks out again in the house 13
26:18 I will chastise you again . . for your sins 6
Num11: 4 people of Israel also wept again 2
12:14 days, and after that she may be brought in again. •
15 till Miriam was brought in again. •
22:15 Once again Balak sent princes, more in number 6
25 so he struck her again. 6
34 if it is evil in thy sight, I will go back again. •
32:15 he will again abandon them in the wilderness; 6
Deu 13:11 shall . . never again do any such wickedness 6
16 heap of ruins for ever . . not be built again. 10
17:13 people shall . . not act presumptuously again. 10
16 You shall never return that way again.' 10
18:16 'Let me not hear again the voice of the LORD my God 6
19:20 rest . . shall never again commit any such evil 6
22: 4 you shall help him to lift them up again. •
24: 4 husband . . may not take her again to be his wife 13
20 you shall not go over the boughs again; 1
28:68 promised that you should never make again; 10
30: 3 gather you again from all the peoples 13
8 again obey the voice of the LORD, and keep all 13
9 LORD will again take delight in prospering you 13
33:11 crush the loins . . that they rise not again. •
Jos 5: 2 and circumcise . . Israel again the second time. 13
Jdg 3:12 the people of Israel again did what was evil 6
4: 1 the people of Israel again did what was evil 6
8:33 Israel turned again and played the harlot after •
9:37 Ga'al spoke again and said, "Look, men are coming 7
10: 6 Israel again did what was evil in the sight 6
11:14 Jephthah sent messengers again to the king 5
13: 1 the people of Israel again did what was evil 6
8 let the man of God . . come again to us, and teach us 10
9 the angel of God came again to the woman as she sat 10
16:22 the hair of his head began to grow again •
19: 7 urged him, till he lodged there again. 13
20:22 took courage, and again formed the battle line 6
23 Shall we again draw near to battle against our 6
28 Shall we yet again go out to battle against our 6
Rut 1:14 Then they lifted up their voices and wept again; 10
1Sm 3: 5 But he said, "I did not call; lie down again. 13
6 the LORD called again, "Samuel!" And Samuel arose 7
6 But he said, "I did not call, my son; lie down again. 13
8 And the LORD called Samuel again the third time. 6
21 And the LORD appeared again at Shiloh 6
7:13 and did not again enter the territory of Israel. 7
9: 8 The servant answered Saul again, "Here, I have 6
10:22 they inquired again of the LORD, "Did the man come 10
15:35 Samuel did not see Saul again until . . his death 6
17:30 and the people answered him again as before. •
19: 8 there was war again; and David went out and fought 6
21 And Saul sent messengers again the third time 6
20:17 Jonathan made David swear again by his love 6
23: 4 Then David inquired of the LORD again. 5
2Sm 2:22 And Abner said again to As'ahel, "Turn aside 6
3:34 And all the people wept again over him. 6
5:22 the Philistines came up yet again 6
6: 1 David again gathered all the chosen . . of Israel 10
12:23 why should I fast? Can I bring him back again? 10
14:10 bring him . . and he shall never touch you again. 6
13 king does not bring his banished one home again. •
14 like water . . which cannot be gathered up again; •
16:19 And again, whom should I serve? Should it not be his 15
18:22 Then Ahi'ma-az the son of Zadok said again to Jo'ab 6
21:15 The Philistines had war again with Israel 10
18 there was again war with the Philistines at Gob; 10
19 there was again war with the Philistines at Gob; 10
20 And there was again war at Gath 10
24: 1 Again the anger of the LORD was kindled 6
1Kg 10:10 never again came such an abundance of spices 10
12:24 they hearkened to . . the LORD, and went home again 13
13:33 made priests for the high places again 13
19: 6 And he ate and drank, and lay down again. 13
20 Go back again; for what have I done to you? 13
2Kg 1:11 Again the king sent to him another captain 13
13 Again the king sent the captain of a third 50 13
4:22 quickly go to the man of God, and come back again. •
9:20 Again the watchman reported, "He reached them 4
13:25 Jeho'ash . . took again from Ben-ha'dad the son 13
19: 9 he sent messengers again to Hezeki'ah, saying 13
30 the surviving remnant . . shall again take root 6
24: 7 king of Egypt did not come again out of his land 7
1Ch 9: 2 the first to dwell again in their possessions •
14:13 Philistines yet again made a raid in the valley. 10
14 when David again inquired of God, God said to him 10
20: 5 there was again war with the Philistines; 10
6 there was again war at Gath 10
2Ch 10: 5 He said to them, "Come to me again in three days. 10
19: 4 Jehosh'aphat . . went out again among the people 13
25:10 discharged the army . . to go home again. •
28:17 E'domites had again invaded and defeated Judah 10
Ezr 9:14 break thy commandments again and intermarry 13
Neh 9:28 rest they did evil again before thee 13
Est 2:14 she did not go in to the king again, 10
7: 2 king again said to Esther, "What is your petition 2
8: 3 Then Esther spoke again to the king; 6
Job 2: 1 Again there was a day when the sons of God came 4
7: 7 my eye will never again see good. 13
10: 9 wilt thou turn me to dust again? 23
16 like a lion, and again work wonders against me; 13
14: 7 tree, if it be cut down, that it will sprout again 10
12 man lies down and rises not again; •
14 If a man die, shall he live again? •
17:10 come on again, all of you 13
20:15 He swallows down riches and vomits them up again; •
27: 1 Job again took up his discourse, and said 6
29: 1 Job again took up his discourse, and said 6
22 After I spoke they did not speak again 14
Ps 3: 5 I wake again, for the LORD sustains me. •
37:36 Again I passed by, and, lo, he was no more; 4
41: 8 he will not rise again from where he lies. 6
42: 5 Hope in God; for I shall again praise him, my help 10
11 Hope in God; for I shall again praise him 10
43: 5 for I shall again praise him, my help and my God. 10
71:20 me see many sore troubles wilt revive me again; 13
20 from the depths . . thou wilt bring me up again. 13
21 wilt increase my honor, and comfort me again. 9
77: 7 spurn for ever, and never again be favorable? 10
85: 6 Wilt thou not revive us again 13
104: 9 so that they might not again cover the earth. 13
Prv 24:16 righteous man falls seven times, and rises again; •
Ecc 1: 7 where the streams flow, there they flow again. 12
4: 1 Again I saw all the oppressions 13
7 Again, I saw vanity under the sun 13
11 Again, if two lie together, they are warm; 2
5:15 As he came from his mother's womb he shall go again 13
9:11 Again I saw that . . the race is not to the swift 13
Isa 6:13 it will be burned again, like a terebinth or an oak 13
7:10 Again the LORD spoke to Ahaz 6
8: 5 The LORD spoke to me again 10
14: 1 The LORD . . will again choose Israel 10
24:20 and it falls, and will not rise again. 6
29:14 I will again do marvelous things with this 6
37:31 house of Judah shall again take root downward 6
62: 8 I will not again give your grain to be food 10
Jer 3:16 it shall not be made again. 10
8: 4 says the LORD: When men fall, do they not rise again? •
10:20 there is no one to spread my tent again 10
11: 9 Again the LORD said to me 4
12:15 I will again have compassion on them 13
22:12 and he shall never see this land again. 10
30 on the throne of David, and ruling again in Judah. 10
31: 4 Again I will build you, and you shall be built 10
4 Again you shall adorn yourself with timbrels 10
5 Again you shall plant vineyards 10
32:15 vineyards shall again be bought in this land. 10
33:10 there shall be heard again 10
12 there shall again be habitations of shepherds 10
13 flocks shall again pass under the hands 10
34:10 so that they would not be enslaved again; 10
Ezk 3:20 Again, if a righteous man turns 4
5: 4 And of these again you shall take some 10
9 and the like of which I will never do again. 10
12:26 Again the word of the LORD came to me •
16: 1 Again the word of the LORD came to me 4
6 When I passed by you again and looked upon you •
63 confounded, and never open your mouth again 10
18: 1 The word of the LORD came to me again •
27 Again, when a wicked man turns away 4

20:27 In this again your fathers blasphemed me 10
21: 5 out of its sheath; it shall not be sheathed again. 10
18 The word of the LORD came to me again •
26:21 you will never be found again, says the Lord GOD. 10
29:15 and never again exalt itself above the nations; 10
15 they will never again rule over the nations. •
16 it shall never again be the reliance of the house 10
33:14 Again, though I say to the wicked, 'You shall surely 4
36:30 may never again suffer the disgrace of famine 10
37: 4 Again he said to me, "Prophesy to these bones, 4
47: 4 Again he measured 1,000, and led me through 4
4 Again he measured 1,000, and led me through 4
5 Again he measured 1,000, and it was a river 4
Dan 9:25 Then for 62 weeks it shall be built again 13
10:18 Again one having the appearance of a man touched 6
11:10 again shall carry the war as far as his fortress. 13
13 king of the north shall again raise a multitude 13
Hos 1: 6 She conceived again and bore a daughter. 10
3: 1 Go again, love a woman who is beloved of a paramour 10
5:15 I will return again to my place 3
11: 9 I will not again destroy E'phraim; 13
12: 9 I will again make you dwell in tents 10
Jol 2: 2 never been from of old, nor will be again after 6
26 And my people shall never again be put to shame. 11
27 And my people shall never again be put to shame. 8
3:17 and strangers shall never again pass through it. 10
Ams 7: 8 my people Israel; I will never again pass by them; 6
13 but never again prophesy at Bethel 6
8: 2 my people Israel; I will never again pass by them. 6
8 and be tossed about and sink again, like the Nile •
14 they shall fall, and never rise again. 10
9:15 they shall never again be plucked up 10
Jon 2: 4 how shall I again look upon thy holy temple? 6
Mic 1:15 I will again bring a conqueror upon you 10
7:19 He will again have compassion upon us 13
Nah 1:15 never again shall the wicked come against you 10
Hag 2: 6 Once again, in a little while, I will shake 10
Zec 1:17 Cry again, Thus says the LORD of hosts 10
17 My cities shall again overflow with prosperity 10
17 the LORD will again comfort Zion 10
17 again comfort Zion and again choose Jerusalem. 10
2:12 and will again choose Jerusalem. 10
5: 1 Again I lifted my eyes and saw 13
6: 1 again I lifted my eyes and saw 13
8: 4 old women shall again sit in the streets 10
15 so again have I purposed in these days to do good 13
9: 8 no oppressor shall again overrun them 10
13: 3 if any one again appears as a prophet 10
Mal 2:13 And this again you do. You cover the LORD'S altar 15
Mat 4: 7 Jesus said to him, "Again it is written, 'You shall 23
8 Again, the devil took him to a very high mountain 23
5:33 Again you have heard that it was said to the men 23
13:45 Again, the kingdom of heaven is like a merchant 23
47 Again, the kingdom of heaven is like a net 23
18:19 Again I say to you, if two of you agree on earth 23
19:24 Again I tell you, it is easier for a camel 23
20: 5 Going out again about the sixth hour 23
21:36 Again he sent other servants, more than the first; 23
22: 1 again Jesus spoke to them in parables, saying 23
4 Again he sent other servants, saying 23
23:39 I tell you, you will not see me again, until you say 17
26:29 I shall not drink again of this fruit of the vine 17
42 Again, for the second time, he went away and prayed 23
43 again he came and found them sleeping 23
44 So, leaving them again, he went away 23
72 again he denied it with an oath 23
27:21 The governor again said to them 18
50 Jesus cried again with a loud voice 23
63 'After three days I will rise again.' •
Mrk 2:13 He went out again beside the sea 23
3: 1 Again he entered the synagogue 23
20 and the crowd came together again 23
4: 1 Again he began to teach beside the sea 23
5:21 Jesus had crossed again in the boat to the other side 23
7:14 he called the people to him again, and said 23
8: 1 when again a great crowd had gathered 23
13 he left them, and getting into the boat again 23
25 Then again he laid his hands upon his eyes 23
10: 1 crowds gathered to him again 23
1 again, as his custom was, he taught them. 23
10 in the house the disciples asked him again 23
24 Jesus said to them again 23
32 taking the twelve again, he began to tell them 23
11:14 May no one ever eat fruit from you again. 21
27 they came again to Jerusalem 23
12: 4 Again he sent to them another servant 23
14:25 I shall not drink again of the fruit of the vine 22
39 again he went away and prayed 23
40 again he came and found them sleeping 23
61 Again the high priest asked him 23
69 began again to say to the bystanders 23
70 again he denied it 23
70 after a little while again the bystanders said 23
15: 4 Pilate again asked him, "Have you no answer 23
12 Pilate again said to them, "Then what shall I do 23
13 they cried out again, "Crucify him. 23
Lke 6:43 nor again does a bad tree bear good fruit; 23
13:20 again he said, "To what shall I compare the kingdom 23
22:32 when you have turned again 24

Joh 1:35 The next day again John was standing 23
4: 3 he left Judea and departed again to Galilee. 23
13 who drinks of this water will thirst again 23
46 So he came again to Cana in Galilee 23
6:15 Jesus withdrew again to the mountain by himself. 23
8: 2 Early in the morning he came again to the temple 23
11 go, and do not sin again. 21
12 Again Jesus spoke to them, saying, "I am the light 23
21 Again he said to them, "I go away, 23
9:15 The Pharisees again asked him 23
17 they again said to the blind man 23
27 Why do you want to hear it again? 23
10: 7 Jesus again said to them, "Truly, truly, I say to you 23
17 I lay down my life, that I may take it again. 23
18 I have power to take it again 23
19 There was again a division among the Jews 23
31 The Jews took up stones again to stone him. 23
39 Again they tried to arrest him 23
40 He went away again across the Jordan 23
11: 7 Let us go into Judea again. 23
8 are you going there again? 23
38 Then Jesus, deeply moved again, came to the tomb 23
12:28 I have glorified it, and I will glorify it again. 23
39 For Isaiah again said 23
14: 3 I will come again and will take you to myself 23
16:16 again a little while, and you will see me. 23
17 again a little while, and you will see me 23
19 again a little while, and you will see me'? 23
22 you have sorrow now, but I will see you again 23
28 again, I am leaving the world 23
18: 7 Again he asked them, "Whom do you seek? 23
27 Peter again denied it 23
33 Pilate entered the praetorium again 23
38 went out to the Jews again, and told them 23
40 They cried out again, "Not this man, but Barab'bas! 23
19: 4 Pilate went out again, and said to them 23
9 he entered the praetorium again and said 23
37 again another scripture says 23
20:21 Jesus said to them again, "Peace be with you 23
26 his disciples were again in the house 23
21: 1 After this Jesus revealed himself again 23
Act 10:15 the voice came to him again a second time 23
11:10 all was drawn up again into heaven. 23
17:32 others said, "We will hear you again about this. 23
27:28 a little farther on they sounded again 23
Rom 10:19 Again I ask, did Israel not understand? 16
11:23 for God has the power to graft them in again. 23
14: 9 For to this end Christ died and lived again •
15:10 and again it is said, "Rejoice, O Gentiles 23
11 and again, "Praise the Lord, all Gentiles 23
1Co 3:20 again, "The Lord knows 23
7: 5 then come together again, lest Satan tempt you 23
12:21 nor again the head to the feet 23
2Co 1:10 set our hope that he will deliver us again. 20
3: 1 Are we beginning to commend ourselves again? 23
5:12 We are not commending ourselves to you again 23
12:21 I fear that when I come again my God may humble me 23
13: 2 if I come again I will not spare them– 23
Gal 1: 9 As we have said before, so now I say again 23
17 again I returned to Damascus. 23
2: 1 I went up again to Jerusalem with Barnabas 23
18 if I build up again those things which I tore down 23
4: 9 can you turn back again to the weak and beggarly 23
19 little children, with whom I am again in travail 23
5: 1 do not submit again to a yoke of slavery. 23
3 I testify again to every man 23
Php 1:26 because of my coming to you again. 23
2:28 you may rejoice at seeing him again 23
4: 4 again I will say, Rejoice. 23
16 you sent me help once and again. 19
Heb 1: 5 Or again, "I will be to him a father 23
6 again . . he says 23
2:13 again, "I will put my trust in him. 23
13 again, "Here am I, and the children God has given me. 23
4: 5 again in this place he said 23
7 again he sets a certain day, "Today 23
5:12 some one to teach you again the first principles 23
6: 1 not laying again a foundation of repentance 23
10:30 And again, "The Lord will judge his people. 23
Jas 5:18 Then he prayed again and the heaven gave rain 23
2Pe 2:20 again entangled in them and overpowered 23
Rev 10: 8 the voice . . from heaven spoke to me again 23
11 You must again prophesy about many peoples 23
18:14 lost to thee, never to be found again! 22
1Es 6:18 these Cyrus the king took out again 23
8:53 again we prayed to our Lord about these things 23
87 we turned back again to transgress thy law 23
2Es 3: 9 again, in its time thou didst bring the flood 29
12 and again they began to be more ungodly 28
5:13 and if you pray again, and weep as you do now 29
21 the thoughts . . were very grievous to me again. 29
6:31 If therefore you will pray again 29
31 will pray again and fast again for seven days 29
31 I will again declare to you greater things 29
35 Now after this I wept again and fasted seven days 29
36 my heart was troubled within me again 28
41 Again, on the second day, thou didst create 29
7: 1 the angel . . was sent to me again •
78 leaves the body to return again to him who gave it 29

8: 9 when the womb gives up again 29
9:15 I said before, and I say now, and will say it again 30
27 my heart was troubled again as it was before. 29
10:19 I spoke again to her, and said 26
11:19 and then were never seen again. 29
13:46 and now, when they are about to come again 29
47 will stop the channels of the river again 29
14:35 the judgment will come, when we shall live again; 29
16:67 your iniquities, never to commit them again 27
Tob 2: 8 here he is burying the dead again! 23
10: 7 have given up hope of ever seeing me again. •
13: 2 he leads down to Hades, and brings up again •
5 again he will show mercy 23
9 again he will show mercy 23
10 his tent may be raised for you again with joy. 23
14: 5 God will again have mercy on them 23
Jdt 6: 5 you shall not see my face again from this day 20
Wis 10: 4 wisdom again saved it 23
13: 8 Yet again, not even they are to be excused; 23
14: 1 Again, one preparing to sail 23
Sir 17: 1 turned him back to it again. 23
24:32 again make instruction shine forth like the dawn 20
33 I will again pour out teaching like prophecy 20
27:19 will not catch him again. •
34:25 touches it again 23
26 goes again and does the same things 23
Bar 2:35 I will never again remove my people Israel 20
1Mc 3:15 again a strong army of ungodly men went up 25
4:35 enlisted mercenaries, to invade Judea again 23
7:30 he was afraid of him and would not meet him again. 20
8:32 If now they appeal again for help against you 20
2Mc 3:33 the same young men appeared again to Heliodorus 23
4: 6 affairs could not again reach a peaceful settlement 20
5: 7 and fled again into the country of the Ammonites. 23
20 was restored again in all its glory 23
7:11 from him I hope to get them back again. 23
14 the hope . . of being raised again by him 23
23 will . . give life and breath back to you again 23
29 I may get you back again with your brothers. •
33 again be reconciled with his own servants. 23
12: 7 intending to come again 23
14: 3 to have access again to the holy altar 20
46 to give them back to him again 23
15:39 again, to drink water alone 23
3Mc 5:13 again begged him . . to show . . his . . hand 23
25 implored . . God to help them again at once. 23
40 again revoking your decree in the matter? 23
4Mc 18:20 to the catapult and back again to more tortures 23

again *See also* alive, ask, attack, back, bloom, bring, come, deliver, gather, get, go, live, meet, merciful, never, no, pass, put, receive, restore, rise, say, take, turn, young.

again and again 1. שׁוּב 2. *ἅπαξ καὶ δίς* 3. *καὶ πάλιν*

Ps 78:41 They tested him again and again 1
Lam 3: 3 turns his hand again and again the whole day 1
1Th 2:18 I, Paul, again and again 2
Sir 33: 1 in trial he will deliver him again and again. 3

do again 1. יסף 2. שׁנה

Neh 13:21 If you do so again I will lay hands on you. 2
Job 41: 8 think of the battle; you will not do it again! 1
Prv 19:19 deliver him, you will only have to do it again. 1

ever again 1. אַחֲרֵי 2. *ἔτι*

Exd 10:14 as had never been before, nor ever shall be again. 1
Jdt 16:25 no one ever again spread terror among the people 2

yet again 1. sequor

2Es 7:49 and will admonish you yet again. 1

against 1. אֶל פָּנִים 2. אֵת 3. לְ 4. לֹא כְּ 5. לְעֻמַּת 6. לִפְנֵי 7. לִקְרָאת 8. מִן 9. מִנֶּגֶד 10. מִפְּנֵי 11. נֶגֶד 12. עִם 13. לְ (A) 14. לְצַד (A) 15. עַל (A) 16. *ἀντί* 17. *ἀπέναντι* 18. *ἀπό* 19. *διά* 20. *εἰς* 21. *εἰς ἀπάντησιν* 22. *εἰς συνάντησιν* 23. *ἐκ* 24. *ἑκατόν* 25. *ἑκατοστός* 26. *ἔμπροσθεν* 27. *ἐν* 28. *ἐναντίον* 29. *ἐναντίος* 30. *ἐνώπιον* 31. *ἐξ ἐναντίας* 32. *ἐπί* 33. *καί* 34. *καταλαμβάνω* 35. *καταλείπω* 36. *κατὰ πρόσωπον* 37. *κατέναντι* 38. *κατηγορέω* 39. *κατισχύω* 40. *μετά* 41. *μή* 42. *ὁ* 43. *ὀπίσω* 44. *περί* 45. *πρός* 46. *ὑπεναντίος* 47. ad 48. adversum 49. adverto 50. contra 51. de 52. in 53. super

Gen 13:13 were wicked, great sinners against the LORD. 3
14: 9 Ar'ioch king of Ella'sar, four kings against five. 2
18:20 Because the outcry against Sodom and Gomor'rah •
19:13 the outcry against its people has become great •
20: 9 how have I sinned against you 3
32:25 saw that he did not prevail against Jacob 3
39: 9 I do this great wickedness, and sin against God? 3
41:36 a reserve for the land against the seven years 3
Exd 10:16 Pharaoh . . said, "I have sinned against the LORD 3
16 I have sinned . . against you. 3
11: 7 against any of the people of Israel 3
23:33 lest they make you sin against me; 3
Num 17:10 may make an end of their murmurings against me 8
20:18 lest I come out with the sword against you. 7
20 Edom came out against them with many men 7

21:23 went out against Israel to the wilderness 7
33 Og the king of Bashan came out against them 7
22:34 that thou didst stand in the road against me. 7
27:14 rebelled against my word in the wilderness •
32:23 behold, you have sinned against the LORD; 3
Deu 1:41 'We have sinned against the LORD; we will go up 3
44 Amorites . . came out against you and chased you 7
2:32 Sihon came out against us . . to battle at Jahaz. 7
3: 1 Og the king of Bashan came out against us 7
9: 7 you have been rebellious against the LORD. 12
16 behold, you had sinned against the LORD your God; 3
24 rebellious against the LORD from the day 12
15: 7 not . . shut your hand against your poor brother 8
20: 4 LORD . . fight for you against your enemies 12
12 if it makes no peace . . but makes war against you 12
18 so to sin against the LORD your God. 3
22:17 he has made shameful charges against her, saying •
29: 7 Sihon . . and Og . . came out against us to battle 7
31:27 today you have been rebellious against the LORD; 12
33: 7 be a help against his adversaries. 8
Jos 1:18 Whoever rebels against your commandment •
7:20 I have sinned against the LORD God of Israel 3
8: 2 lay an ambush against the city, behind it. 3
4 lie in ambush against the city, behind it; 3
5 And when they come out against us, as before 7
14 there was an ambush against him behind the city. 3
22 others came forth from the city against them; 7
10:21 moved his tongue against any of . . Israel. 3
25 do to all your enemies against whom you fight. •
29 Joshua passed on . . and fought against Libnah 12
19:47 the Danites went up and fought against Leshem 12
20: 5 having had no enmity against him in times past. 3
Jdg 1:22 The house of Joseph also went up against Bethel; •
3:28 fords of the Jordan against the Moabites 3
5:20 from their courses they fought against Sis'era. 12
7:24 Come down against the Mid'ianites and seize 7
24 Mid'ianites and seize the waters against them 3
9:56 crime . . which he committed against his father 3
11: 4 a time the Ammonites made war against Israel. 12
5 when the Ammonites made war against Israel 12
12 What have you against me, that you have come to me 3
25 Did he ever strive against Israel, or did he ever 12
27 have not sinned against you, and you do me wrong 3
12: 5 took the fords . . against the E'phraimites. 3
14: 4 seeking an occasion against the Philistines. 8
5 And behold, a young lion roared against him; 7
19:24 but against this man do not do so vile a thing. 3
20:14 to go out to battle against the people of Israel 12
18 go up first to battle against the Benjaminites? 12
20 Israel went out to battle against Benjamin; 12
23 battle against our brethren the Benjaminites? 12
25 Benjamin went against them out of Gib'e-ah 7
28 yet again go out to battle against our brethren 12
31 the Benjaminites went out against the people 7
34 there came against Gib'e-ah 10,000 picked men 9
1Sm 2:25 If a man sins against a man, God will mediate 3
25 if a man sins against the LORD, who can intercede 3
4: 1 went out to battle against the Philistines; 7
2 The Philistines drew up in line against Israel 7
7: 6 and said there, "We have sinned against the LORD. 3
12:23 far be it . . that I should sin against the LORD 3
14:33 the people are sinning against the LORD 3
17: 2 drew up in . . battle against the Philistines. 7
9 but if I prevail against him and kill him 3
21 the Philistines drew up . . army against army. 7
55 Saul saw David go forth against the Philistine 7
19: 4 because he has not sinned against you 3
23:28 Saul . . went against the Philistines; 7
24:11 I have not sinned against you 3
2Sm 10: 9 he chose . . and arrayed them against the Syrians; 7
10 and he arrayed them against the Ammonites. 7
17 the Syrians arrayed themselves against David 7
12:13 David said . . "I have sinned against the LORD. 3
18: 6 the army went out into the field against Israel 7
1Kg 8:31 If a man sins against his neighbor and is 3
33 the enemy because they have sinned against thee 3
35 no rain because they have sinned against thee 3
46 If they sin against thee . . and thou art angry 3
50 forgive thy people who have sinned against thee 3
11:14 the LORD raised up an adversary against Solomon 3
12:21 to fight against the house of Israel 12
24 You shall not go up or fight against your kinsmen 12
20:26 and went up to Aphek, to fight against Israel. 12
27 the people of Israel . . went against them; 7
21:10 let them bring a charge against him, saying •
13 base fellows brought a charge against Naboth •
2Kg 6:32 shut the door, and hold the door fast against him. •
7:12 what the Syrians have prepared against us. 3
8:28 He went with Joram . . to make war against Haz'ael 12
9:14 been on guard at Ramoth-gilead against Haz'ael 10
13:12 the might with which he fought against Amazi'ah 12
17: 7 the people of Israel had sinned against the LORD 3
1Ch 14: 8 David heard of it and went out against them. 6
19:10 and arrayed them against the Syrians; 7
11 and they were arrayed against the Ammonites. 7
17 David set the battle in array against the Syrians 7
2Ch 6:22 If a man sins against his neighbor and is made 3
24 because they have sinned against thee 3
36 If they sin against thee . . and thou art angry 3
39 thy people who have sinned against thee. 3
11: 1 180,000 chosen warriors, to fight against Israel 12
4 shall not go up or fight against your brethren. 12
13: 3 Jerobo'am drew up his line of battle against him 12
12 O sons of Israel, do not fight against the LORD 12
14:11 O LORD . . let not man prevail against thee. 12
17:10 they made no war against Jehosh'aphat. 12
20:12 we are powerless against this great multitude 6
17 tomorrow go out against them 6
22 had come against Judah, so that they were routed. 3
29 LORD had fought against the enemies of Israel. 12
22: 6 when he fought against Haz'ael king of Syria. 2
26: 7 God helped him . . against the Me-u'nites. •
28:10 Have you not sins of your own against the LORD 3
13 propose to bring upon us guilt against the LORD •
29:22 blood and threw it against the altar; •
22 their blood was thrown against the altar; •
22 their blood was thrown against the altar. •
Ezr 7:23 lest his wrath be against the realm of the king 15
8:22 protect us against the enemy on our way; 8
Neh 1: 6 confessing the sins . . we have sinned against thee. 3
7 We have acted very corruptly against thee 3
5: 7 charges against the nobles and the officials. 2
Est 4:16 though it is against the law; 4
6:13 you will not prevail against him but will . . fall 3
9: 2 And no one could make a stand against them 6
Job 6: 4 the terrors of God are arrayed against me. •
8: 4 If your children have sinned against him 3
10: 2 let me know why thou dost contend against me. •
17 thou dost renew thy witnesses against me 11
17 thou dost bring fresh hosts against me. •
16: 8 has shriveled me up, which is a witness against me; •
9 my adversary sharpens his eyes against me. 3
17: 5 He who informs against his friends to get a share •
20:27 the earth will rise up against him. 3
21: 4 As for me, is my complaint against man? 3
24:13 There are those who rebel against the light •
31:13 when they brought a complaint against me; 12
34:37 among us, and multiplies his words against God. 3
Ps 27: 2 assail me, uttering slanders against me †
35: 1 fight against those who fight against me! 2
3 Draw the spear and javelin against my pursuers! 7
4 confounded who devise evil against me! •
37:12 The wicked plots against the righteous 3
41: 4 heal me, for I have sinned against thee! 3
43: 1 defend my cause against an ungodly people; 8
51: 4 Against thee, thee only, have I sinned 3
52: 1 you boast . . of mischief done against the godly? •
55:18 many are arrayed against me. 12
56: 2 for many fight against me proudly. 3
60:11 O grant us help against the foe 8
61: 3 art my refuge, a strong tower against the enemy. 10
78:17 Yet they sinned still more against him 3
17 rebelling against the Most High in the desert. •
79: 8 not remember against us the iniquities 3
89:38 thou art full of wrath against thy anointed. 12
94:16 Who rises up for me against the wicked? 12
16 Who stands up for me against evildoers? 12
105:28 they rebelled against his words. 2
108:12 O grant us help against the foe 8
109: 2 speaking against me with lying tongues. 2
119:11 in my heart, that I might not sin against thee. 3
129: 2 yet they have not prevailed against me. 3
137: 7 O LORD, against the E'domites the day of Jerusalem 3
139:20 who lift themselves up against thee for evil! •
Prv 21:30 No . . counsel, can avail against the LORD. 11
23:11 Redeemer . . will plead their cause against you. 2
24:15 wicked man against the dwelling of the righteous; 3
Ecc 8:11 sentence against an evil deed is not executed •
Isa 11:14 shall put forth their hand against Edom and Moab •
25: 4 the ruthless is like a storm against a wall •
29: 7 all that fight against her and her stronghold •
37: 9 He has set out to fight against you. 2
42:24 Was it not the LORD, against whom we have sinned 3
48:14 and his arm shall be against the Chalde'ans. •
54:17 tongue that rises against you in judgment. 2
66:14 and his indignation is against his enemies. 2
Jer 1:16 And I will utter my judgments against them, •
18 against the kings of Judah, its princes 3
19 shall not prevail against you, for I am with you 3
3:25 for we have sinned against the LORD our God 3
4:17 she has rebelled against me, says the LORD. 2
8:14 because we have sinned against the LORD. 3
14: 7 we have sinned against thee. 3
20 for we have sinned against thee. 3
16:10 the sin that we have committed against the LORD 3
21: 4 you are fighting against the king of Babylon 2
4 and against the Chalde'ans who are besieging you 2
5 I myself will fight against you 2
32: 5 though you fight against the Chalde'ans 2
33: 8 from all the guilt of their sin against me 3
37:10 army of Chalde'ans who are fighting against you 2
38: 5 for the king can do nothing against you. 2
22 have deceived you and prevailed against you; 3
40: 3 you sinned against the LORD, and did not obey 3
41: 9 made for defense against Ba'asha king of Israel; 10
12 and went to fight against Ish'mael 12
44:23 and because you sinned against the LORD 3
46:22 march in force, and come against her with axes 3
50: 7 for they have sinned against the LORD 3
9 and they shall array themselves against her; 3
14 for she has sinned against the LORD. 3
26 Come against her from every quarter; 3
51: 5 is full of guilt against the Holy One of Israel. 8
48 for the destroyers shall come against them 3
Lam 1:17 the LORD has commanded against Jacob that 3
18 in the right, for I have rebelled against his word; •
3:60 Thou hast seen . . all their devices against me. 3
Ezk 3: 8 I have made your face hard against their faces 5
8 your forehead hard against their foreheads. 5
14:13 a land sins against me by acting faithlessly 3
18:22 None . . shall be remembered against him; 3
25:12 acted revengefully against the house of Judah 3
33:16 has committed shall be remembered against him; 3
42: 3 gallery against gallery in three stories. 1
Dan 3:19 his face was changed against Shadrach 15
29 speaks anything against the God of Shadrach 15
5:23 lifted up yourself against the Lord of heaven 15
6: 4 against Daniel with regard to the kingdom; 13
5 not find any . . complaint against this Daniel 13
7:25 He shall speak words against the Most High 14
9: 8 because we have sinned against thee. 3
11 because we have sinned against him. 3
10:20 return to fight against the prince of Persia; 12
11: 2 shall stir up all against the kingdom of Greece. 2
Hos 2: 6 and I will build a wall against her •
4: 7 the more they sinned against me; 3
12: 2 The LORD has an indictment against Judah 12
Obd 1: 7 your confederates have prevailed against you; 3
Mic 2: 8 But you rise against my people as an enemy; •
7: 9 of the LORD because I have sinned against him 3
Zep 1:17 because they have sinned against the LORD; 3
3:15 LORD has taken away the judgments against you •
Zec 1:12 against which thou hast had indignation •
7:10 none of you devise evil against his brother •
8:17 devise evil in your hearts against one another •
Mal 3: 5 against those who thrust aside the sojourner •
Mat 4: 6 lest you strike your foot against a stone.' 45
10:21 children will rise against parents 32
12:26 he is divided against himself 32
31 the blasphemy against the Spirit •
14:24 for the wind was against them. 29
16:18 powers of death shall not prevail against it. 39
18:15 If your brother sins against you, go and tell him 20
21 Lord, how often shall my brother sin against me 20
23:13 you shut the kingdom of heaven against men 26
31 Thus you witness against yourselves •
24: 7 For nation will rise against nation 32
7 kingdom against kingdom 32
26:55 Have you come out as against a robber 32
27:37 they put the charge against him, which read •
Mrk 3:24 If a kingdom is divided against itself 32
25 if a house is divided against itself 32
26 if Satan has risen up against himself 32
29 whoever blasphemes against the Holy Spirit 20
6:11 for a testimony against them. •
19 Hero'di-as had a grudge against him •
48 the wind was against them 29
10:11 and marries another, commits adultery against her; 32
12:12 he had told the parable against them 45
13: 8 For nation will rise against nation 32
8 kingdom against kingdom 32
12 children will rise against parents 32
14:48 Have you come out as against a robber 32
15:26 the inscription of the charge against him read •
46 he rolled a stone against the door of the tomb. 32
Lke 4:11 lest you strike your foot against a stone.' 45
5:30 their scribes murmured against his disciples 45
6: 7 that they might find an accusation against him. •
9: 5 dust from your feet as a testimony against them. 32
10:11 'Even the dust . . we wipe off against you •
11:17 Every kingdom divided against itself is laid waste 32
18 if Satan also is divided against himself 32
12:10 every one who speaks a word against the Son of man 20
10 he who blasphemes against the Holy Spirit 20
52 three against two and two against three; 32
52 three against two and two against three; 32
53 father against son and son against father 32
53 father against son and son against father 32
53 mother against daughter 32
53 daughter against her mother 32
53 mother-in-law against her daughter-in-law 32
53 daughter-in-law against her mother-in-law. 32
14:31 who comes against him with 20,000? 32
15:18 I have sinned against heaven and before you; 20
21 I have sinned against heaven and before you 20
17: 4 if he sins against you seven times in the day 20
18: 3 saying, 'Vindicate me against my adversary.' 18
20:19 he had told this parable against them. 45
21:10 he said to them, "Nation will rise against nation 32
10 kingdom against kingdom; 32
22:52 who had come out against him 32
52 Have you come out as against a robber, with swords 32
65 they spoke many other words against him 20
23:14 guilty of any of your charges against him; 38
Joh 13:18 who ate my bread has lifted his heel against me.' 32
Act 4:27 gathered together against thy holy servant 32
6: 1 the Hellenists murmured against the Hebrews 45

11 blasphemous words against Moses and God. 20
7:54 they ground their teeth against him. 32
8: 1 a great persecution arose against the church 32
9: 1 against the disciples of the Lord 20
29 he spoke and disputed against the Hellenists; 45
13:50 and stirred up persecution against Paul 42
51 they shook off the dust from their feet against them 32
17: 7 are all acting against the decrees of Caesar 17
19:38 If . . craftsmen . . have a complaint against any one 45
20: 3 when a plot was made against him by the Jews *
23:30 there would be a plot against the man 20
30 to state before you what they have against him. 45
24:19 if they have anything against me. 38
25: 8 Neither against the law . . nor . . the temple 20
8 nor against the temple, nor against Caesar 20
8 nor against the temple, nor against Caesar 20
26: 2 against all the accusations of the Jews 44
11 in raging fury against them *
14 It hurts you to kick against the goads.' 45
27: 4 because the winds were against us. 29
28:17 though I had done nothing against the people 28
Rom 1:18 against all ungodliness and wickedness of men 32
2:21 While you preach against stealing, do you steal? 41
4: 8 the man against whom the Lord will not reckon *
18 In hope he believed against hope 32
1Co 4: 4 I am not aware of anything against myself *
6: 1 When one of you has a grievance against a brother 45
6 brother goes to law against brother 40
18 the immoral man sins against his own body. 20
8:12 Thus, sinning against your brethren 20
12 you sin against Christ. 20
2Co 1:23 I call God to witness against me 32
5:19 not counting their trespasses against them *
10: 2 as I count on showing against some who suspect us 32
Eph 6:11 able to stand against the wiles of the devil. 45
12 we are not contending against flesh and blood 45
12 against the principalities, against the powers 45
12 against the principalities, against the powers 45
12 against the world rulers of this present darkness 45
12 against the spiritual hosts of wickedness 45
Col 2:14 having canceled the bond which stood against us 46
3:13 if one has a complaint against another 45
2Th 2: 4 exalts himself against every so-called god 32
Heb 12: 3 who endured . . such hostility against himself 20
4 In your struggle against sin 45
Jas 4:11 Do not speak evil against one another, brethren. *
11 He that speaks evil against a brother *
11 speaks evil against the law and judges the law. *
5: 3 and their rust will be evidence against you *
1Pe 3:12 the face of the Lord is against those that do evil 32
1Jn 3:17 sees . . in need, yet closes his heart against him 18
Rev 2:16 and war against them with the sword of my mouth. 40
7: 1 blow on earth or sea or against any tree. 32
12: 7 Michael . . angels fighting against the dragon; 40
13: 4 Who is like the beast, and who can fight against it? 40
6 to utter blasphemies against God, blaspheming 45
18:20 for God has given judgment for you against her! 23
19:19 to make war against him who sits upon the horse 40
19 to make war against him . . and against his army. 40
1Es 1:24 the words of the Lord rose up against Israel. 32
25 Josiah went out against him. 21
27 I was not sent against you by the Lord God 45
29 the commanders came down against King Josiah. 45
40 Nebuchadnezzar . . came up against him 32
52 in his anger against his people 32
52 he gave command to bring against them the kings 32
4: 4 if he sends them out against the enemy, they go 45
6:15 when our fathers sinned against the Lord 20
8:92 We have sinned against the Lord 20
2Es 1: 5 iniquities which they have committed against me 52
2:28 they shall not be able to do anything against you 48
4:14 Come, let us go and make war against the sea 47
8:34 that thou art so bitter against it? 51
13: 8 all who had gathered together against him 47
31 they shall plan to make war against one another 52
31 city against city, place against place *
31 city against city, place against place *
31 people against people 47
31 and kingdom against kingdom. 49
33 the warfare that they have against one another; 52
15: 3 Do not fear the plots against you 48
15 and nation shall rise up to fight against nation 50
26 the Lord knows all who transgress against him; 52
27 because you have sinned against him. 52
16:70 insurrection against those who fear the Lord. 53
Tob 4: 9 against the day of necessity. 20
Jdt 1: 5 Nebuchadnezzar made war against King Arphaxad 45
13 he led his forces against King Arphaxad 45
2: 7 I am coming against them in my anger 32
5:17 As long as they did not sin against their God 30
20 they sin against their God 20
6: 2 not to make war against the people of Israel *
17 said so boastfully against the house of Israel. 20
7: 1 to break camp and move against Bethulia 32
11 do not fight against them in battle array 45
28 We call to witness against you heaven and earth *
8: 9 words spoken by the people against the ruler 32
9:13 they have planned . . against thy consecrated house *
13 they have planned . . against the top of Zion *
13 they have planned . . against the house *
11: 2 I would never have lifted my spear against them; 32
10 nor can the sword prevail against them 32
10 unless they sin against their God. 20
14: 2 going down . . against the Assyrian outpost 20
13 to come down against us to give battle 32
AEs 11: 7 to fight against the nation of the righteous *
14:11 turn their plan against themselves 32
11 the man who began this against us. 32
16:20 defend themselves against those who attack *
Wis 2:12 he reproaches us for sins against the law *
12 and accuses us of sins against our training. *
3:10 and rebelled against the Lord; *
5:20 join with him to fight against the madmen. 32
16:18 consume the creatures sent against the ungodly 32
Sir 3:14 against your sins it will be credited to you; 16
7: 7 Do not offend against the public 20
12 Do not devise a lie against your brother 32
8:11 lest he lie in ambush against your words. *
14 Do not go to law against a judge 40
10:29 will justify the man that sins against himself? 20
12:11 watch yourself, and be on your guard against him; 18
18:27 in days of sin he guards against wrongdoing. 18
22:18 high place will not stand firm against the wind; 37
18 will not stand firm against any fear. 37
21 have drawn your sword against a friend 32
22 have opened your mouth against your friend 32
23:23 committed an offense against her husband 20
26:11 Be on guard against her impudent eye 43
11 do not wonder if she sins against you. 20
28: 3 Does a man harbor anger against another *
29:13 will fight on your behalf against your enemy. 37
30: 6 left behind him an avenger against his enemies, 35
34:16 a guard against stumbling 18
16 a defense against falling. 18
35:15 cries out against him who has caused them to fall? 32
36: 3 Lift up thy hand against foreign nations 32
37: 4 in time of trouble are against him. 17
8 lest he cast the lot against you 32
40:29 guards against that. *
45:19 he wrought wonders against them *
46: 2 stretched out his sword against the cities! 32
48:18 he lifted up his hand against Zion 32
51:10 the time when there is no help against the proud. *
Bar 1:13 for we have sinned against the Lord our God *
2: 1 confirmed his word, which he spoke against us 32
1 against our judges who judged Israel 32
1 against our kings and against our princes 32
1 against our kings and against our princes 32
1 princes and against the men of Israel and Judah. 32
5 because we sinned against the Lord our God *
12 O Lord our God, against all thy ordinances. 32
4:15 For he brought against them a nation from afar 32
Sus 1:24 and the two elders shouted against her. 37
55 Very well! You have lied against your own head 20
59 You also have lied against your own head 20
61 And they rose against the two elders 32
Bel 1: 9 because he blasphemed against Bel 20
28 conspired against the king, saying 32
Man 1: 7 those who have sinned against thee *
8 Isaac and Jacob, who did not sin against thee *
1Mc 1:20 He went up against Israel and came to Jerusalem 32
36 It became an ambush against the sanctuary *
58 They kept using violence against Israel *
58 against those found month after month *
2:26 as Phinehas did against Zimri the son of Salu. *
32 prepared for battle against them 45
41 fight against every man who comes to attack us 37
66 and fight the battle against the peoples. *
3:10 a large force . . to fight against Israel. 45
17 fight against so great and strong a multitude 45
20 They come against us in great pride 32
23 he rushed suddenly against Seron and his army 20
35 Lysias was to send a force against them 32
52 Gentiles are assembled against us to destroy us; 32
52 thou knowest what they plot against us. 32
58 who have assembled against us to destroy us 32
4:12 saw them coming against them 31
18 stand now against our enemies and fight them 28
41 to fight against those in the citadel *
5: 5 he encamped against them 32
9 Gentiles . . gathered together against the Israelites 32
10 gathered together against us to destroy us. 32
15 against them had gathered together men 32
21 fought many battles against the Gentiles 45
35 fought against it and took it 34
39 ready to come and fight against you 32
43 Then he crossed over against them first 32
50 he fought against the city *
58 they marched against Jamnia. 32
6:25 not against us alone 32
25 but also against all the lands on their borders. 32
26 today they have encamped against the citadel 32
31 encamped against Beth-zur 32
48 the king's army went up to Jerusalem against them 22
63 he fought against him 34
7:42 has spoken wickedly against the sanctuary 32
8: 4 They also subdued the kings who came against them 32
5 the others who rose up against them 32
6 who went to fight against them 24
10 they sent a general against the Greeks 32
9: 2 encamped against Mesaloth in Arbela 32
3 they encamped against Jerusalem; 25
8 Let us rise and go up against our enemies 35
29 like him to go against our enemies and Bacchides 45
64 Then he came and encamped against Bethbasi 32
64 he fought against it for many days *
10:61 gathered together against him to accuse him 32
69 encamped against Jamnia 32
70 You are the only one to rise up against us 32
70 you assume authority against us in the hill country? 32
76 So they fought against it *
86 encamped against Askalon 32
11: 8 he kept devising evil designs against Alexander. 44
15 came against him in battle 32
20 he built many engines of war to use against it. 32
41 they kept fighting against Israel. *
50 and make the Jews stop fighting against us *
55 they fought against Demetrius 45
65 and fought against it for many days and hemmed it in. *
68 set an ambush against him in the mountains 32
72 he turned back to the battle against the enemy 45
12:13 the kings round about us have waged war against us. *
24 to wage war against him. 45
31 So Jonathan turned aside against the Arabs 32
39 to raise his hand against Antiochus the king. 32
42 he was afraid to raise his hand against him. 32
13:16 he will not revolt against us 18
43 In those days Simon encamped against Gazara 32
14: 1 so that he could make war against Trypho. *
15:13 So Antiochus encamped against Dor 32
19 should not seek their harm or make war against them *
19 or make alliance with those who war against them. 45
39 He commanded him to encamp against Judea 36
16: 4 they marched against Cendebeus 32
2Mc 1:11 for taking our side against the king. 45
12 those who fought against the holy city. 27
2:20 further the wars against Antiochus Epiphanes 45
4: 1 who had informed . . against his own country 33
38 he had committed the outrage against Onias *
39 the populace gathered against Lysimachus 32
43 Charges were brought against Menelaus 45
5: 8 hated as a rebel against the laws *
7:18 because of our sins against our own God. 20
31 contrived all sorts of evil against the Hebrews 20
34 raise your hand against the children of heaven. 32
8: 4 the blasphemies committed against his name 20
16 who were wickedly coming against them 32
17 against the holy place 20
18 to strike down those who are coming against us 32
9: 7 breathing fire in his rage against the Jews 32
10:14 and at every turn kept on warring against the Jews. 45
36 Others . . wheeled around against the defenders 45
11: 2 came against the Jews 32
11 They hurled themselves like lions against the enemy 20
12:10 on their march against Timothy 32
26 Then Judas marched against Carnaim 32
27 he marched also against Ephron 32
32 they hastened against Gorgias 32
13: 1 was coming with a great army against Judea 32
4 the anger of Antiochus against the scoundrel; 32
8 he had committed many sins against the altar 44
19 He advanced against Beth-zur . . was turned back 32
15:24 blasphemers who come against thy holy people 32
32 had been . . stretched out against the holy house 32
3Mc 3: 1 not only was he enraged against those Jews *
24 a sudden disorder should later arise against us *
4:16 improper words against the supreme God. 20
5:43 and would also march against Judea 32
6: 5 Sennacherib . . was lifted up against your holy city 32
6 turning the flame against all their enemies. *
7:10 who had willfully transgressed against the holy God *
4Mc 3:21 a revolution against the public harmony 45
4:22 He speedily marched against them 32
17: 3 against the earthquake of the tortures. 19
18: 5 marched against the Persians. 32

against אֶל

Gen 4:8, Exd 19:24; 32:33, Num 13:31; 16:19; 21:7; 22:25^{2}; 24:10, Deu 20:10; 24:15; 28:7, 25, Jos 10:6, 18; 15:15, Jdg 1:1, 10, 11; 6:39; 9:33; 10:10; 12:3; 20:11, 20, 23, 24, 30^{2}, 36, 48, 1Sm 3:12; 7:7; 14:34; 17:33; 22:13; 23:3; 25:17; 27:10, 2Sm 5:6, 19; 10:9; 11:23; 18:12; 20:15; 24:4, 1Kg 16:7, 12; 17:18, 2Kg 3:7; 6:8, 18; 7:6; 9:14; 16:9; 19:27, 28, 1Ch 19:10, 17, 2Ch 6:26; 11:4; 14:9; 16:4; 18:2, 5; 24:19; 35:21; 36:13, Neh 5:1, Est 7:7, Job 9:4; 15:13, 25, 26; 32:14; 33:13; 40:23, Ps 137:9, Ecc 9:14, Isa 2:4; 3:8; 36:10; 37:23, 28, 29, Jer 1:19; 2:29; 6:3; 13:14; 15:20; 21:13; 25:30^{2}; 26:11, 12, 13, 19; 28:8, 16; 33:4; 35:11; 36:7, 31; 39:1, 16; 40:2; 44:7; 47:7^{2}; 48:40; 49:2, 4, 19, 20^{2}, 28, 31; 50:21, 29, 31, 44, 45^{2}; 51:1, 12, 25, Ezk 6:2; 7:6; 13:2, 8, 9, 17, 20; 19:4; 20:46^{2}; 21:2^{2}, 3, 4; 25:6; 29:10^{2}, 18; 30:22, 25; 34:10; 35:3; 38:3, 8; 39:1, Dan 8:7; 11:7, 16, Hos 7:15, Mic 4:3, Nah 1:9; 2:13; 3:5, Zec 1:21; 14:2

against בְּ

Gen 16:12; 19:9; 30:2; 42:22; 44:18, Exd 1:10; 4:14; 9:17; 14:25, 31; 20:16; 23:21, 27; 32:10, 11, Lev 6:2; 17:10; 20:3, 5^{2}, 6; 26:17, 40, Num 5:12, 13, 27; 11:33; 12:1, 8, 9; 14:9; 21:1, 5^{2}, 7, 23, 26; 22:11; 23:23^{2}; 25:3; 31:16; 32:13, Deu 2:15; 4:26; 5:20; 6:15, 22^{2}; 7:4, 24; 11:17, 25; 13:9; 17:7; 19:15, 16; 28:48; 29:20, 27; 30:19; 31:17, 19, 26, 28; 32:24, Jos 7:1; 22:16^{2}, 18, 19, 29, 31; 23:16; 24:9, 11, 22, 27, Jdg 1:1, 3, 5, 8, 9; 2:14, 15, 20; 3:8; 5:13, 23; 6:32;

7:9, 11, 22[2]; 9:45, 50, 52; 10:7, 9[3], 18; 11:12, 32; 12:1, 3, Rut 1:13, 1Sm 5:9; 7:13; 12:3[2], 5, 9, 15; 14:20, 47[6]; 15:18; 17:28; 18:21; 19:4, 5; 20:30; 23:1; 24:6, 10, 12, 13; 26:9, 11, 19, 23; 28:1, 15, 18; 29:8; 31:1, 2Sm 1:16; 6:7; 8:10; 10:13; 12:5, 26, 27, 29; 18:13, 28; 20:15, 21; 24:1[2], 17, 1Kg 8:50; 11:26, 27; 12:19; 20:1, 2Kg 1:1; 3:5, 7, 21; 13:3; 15:37; 18:7, 20; 22:17; 24:1, 2, 1Ch 5:25; 10:1; 13:10; 21:17, 2Ch 10:19; 15:6[2]; 21:17; 26:6; 36:13, 16, Neh 4:8; 9:10, 26, 29; 13:27, Job 2:3; 10:16; 15:6; 16:8; 19:18, 19; 35:6; 42:7, Ps 5:10; :6; 7:12; 4:16; 0:7, 20; 5:20; 3:9; 4:1; 8:19, 21[2], 31; 1:12; 06:40; 19:23; 24:3; 35:9; 41:5, Prv 17:11; 18:1; 24:28; 25:18; 28:4, Isa 1:2; 3:9; 7:6; 9:8; 10:6; 19:2[5]; 20:1; 27:4; 36:5; 41:11; 43:27; 45:24; 59:12; 63:10; 66:24, Jer 2:8, 29; 3:13; 6:21; 14:7; 21:10; 25:31; 31:20; 33:8; 42:5; 43:3; 44:11; 46:12; 48:18; 50:24; 52:3, Lam 3:3, Ezk 2:3[2]; 5:16; 7:8; 14:8; 15:7[2]; 17:15, 20; 18:31; 20:8[2], 13, 21[2], 38; 21:12[2]; 23:25; 26:9; 35:11; 38:21; 39:26, Dan 9:7, 9, 12; 11:30, 42, Hos 7:10, 13, 14; 8:5; 11:6; 13:16, Ams 3:13, Mic 1:2; 7:6, Nah 1:15, Hab 3:8, Zep 3:11, Zec 8:10; 9:1; 14:3, 14, Mal 3:5

against עַל

Gen 14:15; 16:12; 20:6; 34:30; 43:18; 50:20, Exd 15:24; 16:2, 7[2], 8[3]; 17:3; 23:29; 24:6; 29:16, 20; 32:12, Lev 1:5, 11; 3:2, 8, 13; 19:16, Num 10:9; 14:2, 27[2], 29, 35, 36[2]; 16:3[2], 11[2], 41[2], 42[2]; 17:5; 20:2[2], 24; 26:9[2]; 27:3; 30:9; 31:3, 7; 32:14, Deu 9:19; 13:5; 15:9; 20:1, 3, 19[2], 20; 21:10; 23:4, 9; 28:7, 49, Jos 9:18; 10:5[2], 27; 22:12, 33, Jdg 3:12; 6:4, 31; 7:2; 8:3; 9:18, 25, 31, 34, 43, 49; 15:10; 16:26; 18:9; 20:5, 9, 19, 1Sm 2:10; 7:10; 12:12; 14:52; 17:35; 22:8[2], 13; 23:9; 25:17; 27:10[3]; 30:23, 2Sm 10:14; 12:11, 28; 14:7, 13; 17:21; 18:31, 32; 23:8, 18, 1Kg 6:5, 10; 8:44; 13:2, 4[2], 32[2]; 14:25; 15:17, 20, 27; 16:1, 9, 15; 20:12, 22; 22:6, 32, 2Kg 9:25; 10:9; 12:17[2]; 14:19; 15:10, 19, 25, 30; 17:3, 9; 18:9, 13, 25[2]; 19:8, 22[2], 32; 21:23, 24; 22:13, 19[2]; 23:17, 26; 24:20; 25:1, 1Ch 5:20; 11:11, 20; 12:19, 21; 14:10; 18:10; 21:1, 4, 2Ch 6:34; 12:2, 9; 13:6, 12; 14:11; 16:1; 17:1; 18:31; 19:2; 20:1, 2, 12, 16, 22, 23, 37; 21:16; 22:5; 24:21, 23, 25, 26, 27; 25:27; 26:7[2], 13; 27:5; 28:12, 13, 20; 32:1, 2, 16[2], 17; 33:24, 25; 34:27; 35:20, 21; 36:6, 8, 17, Ezr 4:5, 6, 8, 19; 8:22, Neh 2:19; 4:9, 12; 5:7; 6:12; 9:10; 13:2, Est 2:1; 5:9; 8:3; 9:24, 25, Job 8:15; 13:26; 16:4, 10; 17:8; 19:5[2], 11, 12; 30:12; 31:21, 38; 33:10; 36:33, Ps 2:2; :1, 6; 5:3, 5; 1:11; 7:3[2]; 1:13, 18; 5:15, 20, 21, 26; 8:16; 1:9; 4:3; 6:5; 9:3; 1:14; 3:3[2], 5; 6:14; 4:21; 06:7; 09:2, 6, 20; 24:2; 38:7, Prv 3:29; 19:3, Ecc 9:14; 10:4, Sng 3:8, Isa 1:25; 2:12[2], 13[2], 14[2], 15[2], 16[2]; 5:25[2]; 7:1, 5; 8:7; 9:11, 21; 10:6, 15, 24, 26; 13:17; 14:4, 8, 22; 19:12, 17; 20:3; 23:8; 29:3[2], 7, 8; 31:2[2], 4; 34:2[2]; 36:1, 10; 37:8, 23, 33; 42:13; 54:17; 57:4, Jer 1:15[2], 18; 2:15; 4:16, 17; 5:6; 6:4, 6, 12, 23; 11:17, 19; 12:8, 9; 15:6, 8; 16:10; 18:11[2], 18; 19:15; 21:2, 13; 22:7; 23:30, 31, 32; 25:9[2], 13[2], 29, 30; 26:20[2]; 29:32; 32:24, 29; 34:1, 7[2], 22; 35:17; 36:2; 37:8, 19[2]; 44:29; 48:2, 26, 42; 49:14, 22, 30[2]; 50:3, 9, 14, 15, 21, 42; 51:1, 2, 25, 27[3], 28, 29, 46; 52:4, Lam 1:15; 2:16; 3:46, 61, 62, Ezk 4:2[5], 3, 7; 5:8, 17; 6:14; 11:4; 13:17; 14:9, 13; 16:27, 37, 40; 19:8; 21:22; 23:22[2], 24[2], 46; 25:2, 7, 13, 16; 26:3[2], 8[3]; 28:7, 21, 22, 23; 29:2[3], 3, 18; 30:11; 34:2; 35:2[2], 3, 12, 13[2]; 36:5[2]; 38:2, 11, 16[2], 17, 18, 21; 39:1, 2; 43:18, Dan 8:25; 9:12[2]; 10:21; 11:14, 24, 25[2], 28, 30, 36, Hos 7:13; 10:10, Jol 1:6, Ams 1:8; 3:1[2]; 5:9, 19; 6:14; 7:9, 10, 16, Obd 1:1, Jon 1:2, 13, Mic 2:3, 4; 3:5; 4:11; 5:1, 5, Nah 1:11; 2:1, Hab 2:6, Zep 1:4[2], 16[2]; 2:5, 8, 10, 11, 13, Zec 10:3; 12:2[2], 3, 9; 13:7[3]; 14:12, 13, 16, Mal 3:13

against κατά

Mat 5:11, 23; 10:35[3]; 12:14, 25[2], 30, 32[2]; 26:59; 27:1, Mrk 3:6; 9:40; 11:25; 14:55, 56, 57, Lke 9:50; 11:23, Joh 18:29, Act 4:26[2]; 6:13; 14:2; 21:28; 24:1; 25:2, 15, 27, Rom 8:31, 33; 11:2, 1Co 4:6, 2Co 13:8, Gal 3:21; 5:17[2], 23, 1Ti 5:19, Jas 5:9, 1Pe 2:11, Jde 1:15, Rev 2:4, 14, 20, 1Es 2:16, Jdt 9:13; 13:11, Wis 3:14; 4:6; 5:22, Sir 6:12; 34:3, Sus 1:43, 1Mc 8:32; 10:4, 63; 11:25, 39; 16:6, 13, 2Mc 10:21, 3Mc 3:2, 11; 5:8; 7:9, 4Mc 2:17; 4:22

against *See also* battle, bear, beat, break, bring, cast, charge, cherish, come, conspirator, conspire, dash, defend, fight, gather, go, grow, hold, lay, lift, make, march, murmur, over, plot, plotter, prate, prevail, proceed, rebel, rise, rush, scheme, send, sentence, set, shout, speak, strike, strive, struggle, testify, throw, war, will.

agape 1. *χάσκω*

1Es 4:31 the king would gaze at her with mouth agape 1

agate 1. כַּדְכֹּד 2. שְׁבוֹ 3. *χαλκηδών*

Exd 28:19 the third row a jacinth, an agate, and an amethyst; 2
39:12 the third row, a jacinth, an agate, and an amethyst; 2
Isa 54:12 I will make your pinnacles of agate 1
Ezk 27:16 embroidered work, fine linen, coral, and agate. 1
Rev 21:19 every jewel . . the third agate 3

age 1. בֵּן 2. גִּיל 3. זָקֵן 4. זֹקֶן 5. יוֹם 6. יָשִׁישׁ 7. יָשֵׁשׁ 8. עֵת 9. שֵׂיב 10. *γεραιός* 11. *γέρων* 12. *γῆρας* 13. *γήρως* 14. *ἐν ἡμέραις πολλαῖς* 15. *ἡλικία* 16. *καιρὸς ἡλικίας* 17. *παλαιόω* 18. *πρέσβυς* 19. *πρεσβύτερος* 20. *πρεσβύτης πολυχρόνιος* 21. *συνηλικιώτης* 22. senesco

Gen 18:11 Now Abraham and Sarah were old, advanced in age; 5
48:10 Now the eyes of Israel were dim with age 4
Num 8:25 from the age of 50 years they shall withdraw 1
Jdg 2: 8 Joshua . . died at the age of 110 years. 1
1Kg 14: 4 his eyes were dim because of his age. 9
15:23 But in his old age he was diseased in his feet. 8
1Ch 27:23 did not number those below twenty years of age 1
2Ch 36:17 had no compassion on . . old man or aged; 7
Job 12:12 Wisdom is with the aged 6
15:10 Both the gray-haired and the aged are among us 6
29: 8 the aged rose and stood; 6
32: 6 I am young in years, and you are aged; 6
9 nor the aged that understand what is right. 3
Ps 119:100 I understand more than the aged 3
Prv 17: 6 Grandchildren are the crown of the aged 3
Isa 47: 6 on the aged you made your yoke exceedingly heavy. 3
Ezk 16: 8 behold, you were at the age for love; 8
Dan 1:10 poorer condition than the youths . . of your own age. 2
Zec 8: 4 each with staff in hand for very age. 5
Mrk 5:42 she was twelve years of age •
Lke 2:36 she was of a great age 14
3:23 Jesus . . was about 30 years of age •
8:42 he had an only daughter, about twelve years of age •
Joh 9:21 Ask him; he is of age, he will speak for himself. 15
23 Therefore his parents said, "He is of age, ask him. 15
Gal 1:14 many of my own age among my people 21
1Ti 5: 9 if she is not less than 60 years of age •
Heb 11:11 even when she was past the age 16
1Es 5:41 All those of Israel, twelve or more years of age •
58 the Levites who were twenty or more years of age •
2Es 5:55 as born of a creation which already is aging 22
Tob 14:14 at the age of a 127 years. •
Wis 2:10 nor regard the gray hairs of the aged. 20
Sir 8: 9 Do not disregard the discourse of the aged 11
9:10 when it has aged you will drink it with pleasure. 17
25: 4 for the aged to possess good counsel! 18
5 How attractive is wisdom in the aged 11
6 Rich experience is the crown of the aged 11
20 A sandy ascent for the feet of the aged 18
2Mc 6:18 a man now advanced in age and of noble presence 15
8:30 to the orphans and widows, and also to the aged 19
3Mc 4: 5 sluggish and bent with age 13
4Mc 5: 4 advanced in age 15
7 for I respect your age and your gray hairs. 15
7:16 because of piety an aged man despised tortures 11
8: 3 seven brothers . . along with their aged mother 10
20 have compassion on our mother's age; 12
9: 6 which our aged instructor also overcame. 11
11:14 I am younger in age than my brothers 15
17: 9 Here lie buried an aged priest and an aged woman 11
9 aged priest and an aged woman and seven sons 10

age (2) 1. דּוֹר 2. עוֹלָם 3. *αἰών* 4. *αἰώνιος* 5. *καιρός* 6. *χρόνος* 7. saeculum 8. tempus

Job 8: 8 For inquire, I pray you, of bygone ages 1
Ps 135:13 thy renown, O LORD, throughout all ages. 1
Prv 8:23 Ages ago I was set up, at the first 2
Ecc 1:10 It has been already, in the ages before us. 2
Isa 60:15 make you majestic for ever, a joy from age to age. 1
15 make you majestic for ever, a joy from age to age. 1
Mat 12:32 either in this age or in the age to come. 3
32 either in this age or in the age to come. •
13:39 the harvest is the close of the age 3
40 so will it be at the close of the age. 3
49 So it will be at the close of the age 3
24: 3 the close of the age? 3
28:20 I am with you always, to the close of the age. 3
Mrk 10:30 in the age to come eternal life. 3
Lke 18:30 in the age to come eternal life. 3
20:34 Jesus said to them, "The sons of this age marry 3
35 who are accounted worthy to attain to that age 3
Rom 16:25 the mystery which was kept secret for long ages 6
1Co 1:20 Where is the debater of this age? 3
2: 6 although it is not a wisdom of this age 3
6 rulers of this age, who are doomed to pass away. 3
7 which God decreed before the ages 3
8 None of the rulers of this age understood this; 3
3:18 he is wise in this age 3
10:11 upon whom the end of the ages has come. 3
Gal 1: 4 to deliver us from the present evil age 3
Eph 1:21 not only in this age 3
2: 7 in the coming ages 3
3: 9 plan of the mystery hidden for ages in God 3
Col 1:26 the mystery hidden for ages and generations 3
1Ti 1:17 the King of ages, immortal, invisible, the only God 3
2Ti 1: 9 the grace which he gave us in Christ Jesus ages ago 4
Tit 1: 2 which God, who never lies, promised ages ago 4
Heb 6: 5 the powers of the age to come 3
9: 9 (which is symbolic for the present age). 5
26 he has appeared once for all at the end of the age 3
Rev 15: 3 Just and true are thy ways, O King of the ages! 3
1Es 4:40 the power and the majesty of all the ages. 3
2Es 2:34 because he who will come at the end of the age 7
36 Flee from the shadow of this age 7
39 who have departed from the shadow of this age 7
4:26 because the age is hastening swiftly to its end. 7
27 because this age is full of sadness 7
36 for he has weighed the age in the balance 7
6: 7 when will be the end of the first age •
7 and the beginning of the age that follows? •
9 For Esau is the end of this age 7
9 Jacob is the beginning of the age that follows. •
20 when the seal is placed upon the age 7
7:113 the day of judgment will be the end of this age 8
113 and the beginning of the immortal age to come 8
119 if an eternal age has been promised to us 8
8:52 the age to come is prepared, plenty is provided 8
9:13 those to whom the age belongs ‡
13 and for whose sake the age was made. ‡
18 For there was a time in this age 7
11:44 behold, they are ended, and his ages are completed! 7
13:26 whom the Most High has been keeping for many ages 8
14:10 For the age has lost its youth 7
11 For the age is divided into twelve parts 7
Tob 13: 6 exalt the King of the ages. 3
10 praise the King of the ages 3
14: 5 until the times of the age are completed. 3
Sir 36:17 thou art the Lord, the God of the ages. 3
42:18 he looks into the signs of the age. 3

age *See* man, reach.

old age 1. זִקְנָה 2. זְקֻנִים 3. שֵׂיבָה 4. *γῆρας* 5. *γηράω* 6. *γῆρος* 7. senectus

Gen 15:15 you shall be buried in a good old age. 3
21: 2 Sarah . . bore Abraham a son in his old age 2
7 Yet I have borne him a son in his old age. 2
25: 8 Abraham . . died in a good old age, an old man 3
37: 3 because he was the son of his old age; 2
44:20 a young brother, the child of his old age; 2
Jdg 8:32 Gideon the son of Jo'ash died in a good old age 3
Rut 4:15 a restorer of life and a nourisher of your old age; 3
1Ch 29:28 he died in a good old age, full of days, riches 3
Ps 71: 9 Do not cast me off in the time of old age; 1
18 to old age and gray hairs, O God, do not forsake me 1
92:14 They still bring forth fruit in old age 3
Isa 46: 4 even to your old age I am He, and to gray hairs 1
Lke 1:36 Elizabeth in her old age has also conceived a son; 4
2Es 5:50 Or is she now approaching old age? 7
53 those born during the time of old age 7
14:17 For the weaker the world becomes through old age 7
Tob 3:10 I shall bring his old age down in sorrow to the grave. 4
Wis 3:17 finally their old age will be without honor. 4
4: 8 For old age is not honored for length of time 4
9 a blameless life is ripe old age. 4
16 the prolonged old age of the unrighteous man. 4
Sir 3:12 O son, help your father in his old age 5
25: 3 how then can you find anything in your old age? 4
30:24 anxiety brings on old age too soon. 4
46: 9 which remained with him to old age 6
2Mc 6:23 worthy of his years and the dignity of his old age 4
25 while I defile and disgrace my old age. 4
27 I will show myself worthy of my old age 4
4Mc 5:12 and have compassion on your old age 4
33 I do not so pity my old age 4
36 shall not stain the honorable mouth of my old age 4
6:12 At that point, partly out of pity for his old age 4
18 who have lived in accordance with truth to old age 4

ripe old age 1. כֶּלַח

Job 5:26 You shall come to your grave in ripe old age 1

aged man 1. זָקֵן 2. *γέρων* 3. *ἐσχατογήρως*

2Sm 19:32 Barzil'lai was a very aged man, 80 years old; 1
Jol 1: 2 Hear this, you aged men 1
Sir 42: 8 the aged man who quarrels with the young 3
4Mc 7:10 O aged man, more powerful than tortures 2
8: 2 to compel an aged man to eat defiling foods 2
9: 6 if the aged men of the Hebrews . . lived piously 2
16:17 while an aged man endures such agonies 2

very aged 1. מְלֵא יָמִים

Jer 6:11 shall be taken, the old folk and the very aged. 1

agent 1. *διάκονος*

Gal 2:17 is Christ then an agent of sin? Certainly not! 1
2Mc 4: 3 one of Simon's approved agents •

aghast *See* look.

agile *See* make.

agitate 1. *ταράσσω* 2. ventilo

2Es 3: 3 My spirit was greatly agitated 2
AEs 15:16 the king was agitated 1
3Mc 1:17 those . . were agitated and hurried out 1

agitator 1. *κινέω στάσεις*

Act 24: 5 an agitator among all the Jews 1

aglow 1. *ζέω*

Rom 12:11 Never flag in zeal, be aglow with the Spirit 1

ago 1. מִקַּדְמַת דְּנָה (A) 2. *ἀπό* 3. *ἔμπροσθεν* 4. *πρὸ* 5. *πρὸ χρόνων* 6. ante

1Sm 9:20 As for your asses that were lost three days ago •
30:13 left me . . because I fell sick three days ago. •
Ezr 5:11 rebuilding the house . . built many years ago 1
Prv 8:23 Ages ago I was set up, at the first •
Act 10:30 Cornelius said, "Four days ago, about this hour 2
2Co 12: 2 who fourteen years ago was caught up 4
2Ti 1: 9 the grace which he gave us in Christ Jesus ages ago 5
Tit 1: 2 which God, who never lies, promised ages ago 5
1Es 6:14 the house was built many years ago 3
2Es 10:41 The woman who appeared to you a little while ago 6

ago *See also* time, year.

long ago 1. לְמֵרָחוֹק 2. מֵאָז 3. מִימֵי קֶדֶם 4. מֵעוֹלָם 5. מִקֶּדֶם 6. מֵרָחוֹק 7. עוֹלָם 8. *ἔκπαλαι* 9. *πάλαι*

2Kg 19:25 Have you not heard that I determined it long ago? 6
Ps 77: 5 the days of old, I remember the years long ago. 7
Isa 22:11 or have regard for him who planned it long ago. 6
37:26 Have you not heard that I determined it long ago? 1
45:21 Who told this long ago? Who declared it of old? 5
48: 7 They are created now, not long ago; 2
51: 9 as in days of old, the generations of long ago. 7
Jer 2:20 For long ago you broke your yoke 4

Lam 2:17 as he ordained long ago, he has demolished 3
3: 6 dwell in darkness like the dead of long ago. 7
Mat 11:21 they would have repented long ago in sackcloth 9
Lke 10:13 they would have repented long ago 9
2Pe 3: 5 by the word of God heavens existed long ago 8
Jde 1: 4 some who long ago were designated 9
3Mc 4: 1 which had long ago been in their minds 9

agony 1. חֵבֶל 2. חול 3. תַּחֲלֻאִים 4. αἰκισμός 5. ἀλγηδών 6. βάσανος 7. ὀδύνη 8. tormentum
2Ch 21:19 bowels came out . . and he died in great agony. 3
Isa 13: 8 Pangs and agony will seize them; 1
Ezk 30:16 fire to Egypt; Pelusium shall be in great agony; 2
2Es 12:26 shall die in his bed, but in agonies. 8
1Mc 9:56 Alcimus died at that time in great agony. 6
4Mc 3:18 it can overthrow bodily agonies 5
6: 7 because his body could not endure the agonies 5
34 when it masters even external agonies 5
35 not only that reason has mastered agonies 5
8:28 they were . . sovereign over agonies 5
9:28 he steadfastly endured this agony and said 5
13: 5 who were not turned back by fiery agonies? 5
14: 1 they not only despised their agonies 5
9 in agonies of fire at that. 7
11 mind of woman despised even more diverse agonies 5
15:19 gazing boldly at the same agonies 4
16:17 while an aged man endures such agonies 5
agony *See also* suffer.

agree 1. אות 2. אמר 3. סכן 4. שׂום 5. שׁמע 6. זמן (A) 7. יעט (A) 8. διατίθημι 9. εἰς τὸ ἕν 10. ἐξωμολογέω 11. ἐπιδέχομαι 12. ἐπινεύω 13. ἐπιχωρέω 14. εὐδοκέω 15. ἴσος 16. ὁμολογέω 17. ὁμονοέω 18. προσέρχομαι 19. συγχωρέω 20. σύμφημι 21. συμφωνέω 22. συντίθημι 23. τὸ αὐτὸ λέγω 24. τὸ αὐτὸ φρονέω
Gen 23:16 Abraham agreed with Ephron; 5
34:22 condition will the men agree to dwell with us 1
23 Only let us agree with them 1
Exd 8:12 Moses cried to . . as he had agreed with Pharaoh. 4
2Kg 12: 8 the priests agreed that they should take no more 1
1Ch 13: 4 All the assembly agreed to do 2
Job 22:21 Agree with God, and be at peace; 3
Dan 2: 9 agreed to speak lying and corrupt words 6
6: 7 presidents . . and the governors are agreed 7
Mat 18:19 Again I say to you, if two of you agree on earth 21
20: 2 After agreeing with the laborers 21
13 did you not agree with me for a denarius? 21
Mrk 14:56 their witness did not agree. 15
59 Yet not even so did their testimony agree. 15
Lke 22: 6 So he agreed 10
Joh 9:22 the Jews had already agreed 22
Act 15:15 the words of the prophets agree, as it is written 21
23:20 The Jews have agreed to ask you to bring Paul down 22
Rom 7:16 I agree that the law is good. 20
1Co 1:10 all of you agree 23
Php 4: 2 I entreat Syn'tyche to agree in the Lord. 24
1Ti 6: 3 does not agree with the sound words of our Lord 18
1Jn 5: 8 and these three agree. 9
Tob 5:15 So they agreed to these terms. 14
AEs 14:13 an end of him and those who agree with him. 17
Wis 18: 9 and with one accord agreed to the divine law 8
1Mc 9:71 He agreed, and did as he said 11
14:46 all the people agreed 14
47 So Simon accepted and agreed to be high priest 14
2Mc 11:15 Maccabeus . . agreed to all that Lysias urged. 12
18 he has agreed to what was possible. 19
12:12 agreed to make peace with them 13
14:20 they agreed to the covenant. 12
4Mc 4:17 Jason agreed 22
9:16 Agree to eat so that you may be released 16
14: 6 agreed to go to death for its sake. 21

agree to let 1. ἵστημι
1Mc 6:59 and agree to let them live by their laws 1

agree together 1. יעד 2. συμφωνέω
2Ch 30:23 the whole assembly agreed together to keep 1
Act 5: 9 you have agreed together to tempt the Spirit 2

agree with one another 1. τὸ αὐτὸ φρονέω
2Co 13:11 agree with one another, live in peace 1

agreement 1. חֹזֶה 2. חָזוּת 3. διαστέλλω 4. ὁμόνοια 5. στάσις 6. συγκατάθεσις 7. σύμφωνος 8. συνθήκη
Isa 28:15 with death, and with Sheol we have an agreement; 1
18 and your agreement with Sheol will not stand; 2
1Co 7: 5 except perhaps by agreement 7
2Co 6:16 What agreement has the temple of God with idols? 6
Wis 10: 5 the nations in wicked agreement 4
Sir 25: 1 agreement between brothers 4
1Mc 7:18 they have violated the agreement 5
10:26 Since you have kept your agreement with us 8
15:27 the agreements he formerly had made with Simon •
2Mc 12: 1 When this agreement had been reached 8
14:28 he had to annul their agreement 3
agreement *See also* come, make, reach.
aground *See* run.

ah 1. אֲהָהּ 2. אָח 3. אַךְ 4. הוֹי 5. ἔα 6. ὁράω
Isa 1: 4 Ah, sinful nation, a people laden with iniquity 4
24 Lord says . . "Ah, I will vent my wrath on my enemies 4
10: 5 Ah, Assyria, the rod of my anger, the staff of my fury! 4
17:12 Ah, the thunder of many peoples 4
12 Ah, the roar of nations, they roar like the roaring 4
18: 1 Ah, land of whirring wings . . beyond the rivers 4
Jer 1: 6 Ah, Lord GOD! Behold, I do not know how to speak 1
4:10 Then I said, "Ah, Lord GOD 1
14:13 I said: "Ah, Lord GOD, behold, the prophets say 1
22:18 shall not lament for him, saying, 'Ah my brother!' 4
18 lament . . saying, 'Ah my brother!' or 'Ah sister!' 4
18 They shall not lament for him, saying, 'Ah lord!' 4
18 lament for him, saying, 'Ah lord!' or 'Ah his majesty!' 4
32:17 'Ah Lord GOD! It is thou who hast made the heavens 1
47: 6 Ah, sword of the LORD! How long till you are quiet? 4
Lam 2:16 Ah, this is the day we longed for; now we have it; 3
Ezk 4:14 Then I said, "Ah Lord GOD! 1
9: 8 I fell upon my face, and cried, "Ah Lord GOD! 1
11:13 and said, "Ah Lord GOD! wilt thou make a full end 1
20:49 Then I said, "Ah Lord GOD! 1
21:15 glittering sword; ah! it is made like lightning 2
Hos 12: 8 E'phraim has said, "Ah, but I am rich 3
Lke 4:34 Ah! What have you to do with us, Jesus of Nazareth? 5
Joh 16:29 Ah, now you are speaking plainly, not in any figure! 6

aha 1. הֶאָח 2. οὐά
Job 39:25 When the trumpet sounds, he says 'Aha!' 1
Ps 35:21 they say, "Aha, Aha! our eyes have seen it! 1
21 they say, "Aha, Aha! our eyes have seen it! 1
25 Let them not say to themselves, "Aha 1
40:15 because of their shame who say to me, "Aha, Aha! 1
15 because of their shame who say to me, "Aha, Aha! 1
70: 3 appalled because of their shame who say, "Aha, Aha! 1
3 appalled because of their shame who say, "Aha, Aha! 1
Isa 44:16 and says, "Aha, I am warm, I have seen the fire! 1
Ezk 25: 3 Because you said, 'Aha!' over my sanctuary 1
26: 2 Aha, the gate of the peoples is broken 1
36: 2 Because the enemy said of you, 'Aha!' 1
Mrk 15:29 wagging their heads, and saying, "Aha! 2

ahead 1. לִפְנֵי 2. εἰς τὸ ἔμπροσθεν 3. ἔμπροσθεν 4. πρὸ προσώπου 5. πρῶτος
1Sm 9:12 He is; behold, he is just ahead of you. 1
23:24 And they arose, and went to Ziph ahead of Saul. 1
2Kg 4:31 Geha'zi went on ahead and laid the staff 1
Ps 105:17 he had sent a man ahead of them, Joseph 1
Lke 9:52 he sent messengers ahead of him 4
10: 1 sent them on ahead of him, two by two 4
19: 4 So he ran on ahead 2
28 when he had said this, he went on ahead 3
Tob 11: 3 Let us run ahead of your wife 3
Sir 12:17 you will find him there ahead of you 5
ahead *See also* get, go, lie, push, run, straight, walk.

aid 1. חזק 2. חזק יָד 3. נשׂא 4. עֶזְרָה 5. βοήθεια 6. βοηθέω 7. διακονέω 8. ἐπιβοηθέω 9. ἐπικουρία 10. σκέπης
Ezr 1: 6 about them aided them with vessels of silver 1
6:22 aided them in the work of the house of God 2
8:36 aided the people and the house of God. 3
Ps 22:19 be not far off! O thou my help, hasten to my aid! 4
Ezk 16:49 but did not aid the poor and needy. 2
29:16 their iniquity, when they turn to them for aid. •
Rom 15:25 I am going to Jerusalem with aid for the saints. 7
Wis 13:18 for aid he entreats 9
1Mc 11:47 So the king called the Jews to his aid 5
12:15 have the help which comes from Heaven for our aid 6
16:18 asking him to send troops to aid him 5
2Mc 8: 8 for aid to the king's government. 8
11: 7 to aid their brethren 8
3Mc 1:16 to aid in the present situation 6
4:21 who was aiding the Jews from heaven. 6
5: 6 the Jews were left without any aid 10
35 this also was his aid which they had received. 5
4Mc 13:26 with the aid of their religion •
aid *See also* bring, come, give, invoke.

aide 1. שָׁלִישׁ
2Kg 9:25 Jehu said to Bidkar his aide, "Take him up 1

ail
Jdg 18:23 What ails you that you come with such a company? •
24 have I left? How then do you ask me, 'What ails you?' •
1Sm 11: 5 What ails the people, that they are weeping? •
Ps 114: 5 What ails you, O sea, that you flee? •

ailment 1. ἀσθένεια
Gal 4:13 you know it was because of a bodily ailment 1
1Ti 5:23 your stomach and your frequent ailments. 1

aim 1. דרך 2. כון 3. διώκω 4. προνοέω 5. στοχάζομαι 6. τέλος 7. φροντίζω
Ps 21:12 you will aim at their faces with your bows. 2
64: 3 who aim bitter words like arrows 1
2Co 8:21 we aim at what is honorable 4
1Ti 1: 5 whereas the aim of our charge is love 6
6:11 aim at righteousness, godliness, faith, love 3
2Ti 2:22 aim at righteousness, faith, love, and peace 3
Sir 9:14 As much as you can, aim to know your neighbors 5
31:25 Do not aim to be valiant over wine •
2Mc 2:25 we have aimed to please those who wish to read 7
aim *See also* make, since.

aim in life 1. πρόθεσις
2Ti 3:10 my aim in life, my faith, my patience, my love 1

aim to know 1. στοχάζομαι
Sir 9:14 As much as you can, aim to know your neighbors 1

true aim 1. εὔστοχος
Wis 5:21 Shafts of lightning will fly with true aim 1

aimlessly 1. ἀδήλως
1Co 9:26 Well, I do not run aimlessly 1

air 1. רוּחַ 2. שָׁמַיִם 3. שְׁמַיִן (A) 4. ἀήρ 5. οὐρανός 6. πνεῦμα 7. πρόσωπον 8. aer
Gen 1:26 have dominion . . over the birds of the air 2
28 the birds of the air and over every living thing 2
30 beast of the earth, and to every bird of the air 2
2:19 every beast of the field and every bird of the air 2
20 names . . to the birds of the air 2
6: 7 creeping things and birds of the air 2
7: 3 seven pairs of the birds of the air also 2
23 creeping things and birds of the air; 2
9: 2 of the earth, and upon every bird of the air 2
Deu 4:17 likeness of any winged bird that flies in the air 2
28:26 dead body shall be food for all birds of the air 2
1Sm 17:44 I will give your flesh to the birds of the air 2
46 give the dead bodies . . to the birds of the air 2
2Sm 21:10 allow the birds of the air to come upon them by day 2
1Kg 14:11 one who dies in . . the birds of the air shall eat; 2
16: 4 dies in the field the birds of the air shall eat. 2
21:24 who dies . . the birds of the air shall eat. 2
Job 12: 7 the birds of the air, and they will tell you; 2
28:21 concealed from the birds of the air. 2
35:11 makes us wiser than the birds of the air? 2
41:16 near to another that no air can come between 1
Ps 8: 8 the birds of the air, and the fish of the sea 2
50:11 I know all the birds of the air 5
79: 2 thy servants to the birds of the air for food 2
104:12 birds of the air have their habitation; 2
Ecc 10:20 a bird of the air will carry your voice 2
Jer 4:25 and all the birds of the air had fled. 2
7:33 this people will be food for the birds of the air 2
9:10 both the birds of the air and the beasts have fled 2
14: 6 they pant for air like jackals; 1
15: 3 the birds of the air and the beasts of the earth 2
16: 4 birds of the air and for the beasts of the earth. 2
19: 7 their dead bodies for food to the birds of the air 2
34:20 dead bodies shall be food for the birds of the air 2
Ezk 29: 5 to the birds of the air I have given you as food. 2
31: 6 birds of the air made their nests in its boughs; 2
13 Upon its ruin will dwell all the birds of the air 2
32: 4 cause all the birds of the air to settle on you 2
38:20 the fish of the sea, and the birds of the air 2
Dan 2:38 given . . the beasts . . and the birds of the air 3
4:12 birds of the air dwelt in its branches 3
21 in whose branches the birds of the air dwelt- 3
Hos 2:18 with the beasts of the field, the birds of the air 2
4: 3 languish . . and the birds of the air; 2
7:12 I will bring them down like birds of the air; 2
Zep 1: 3 I will sweep away the birds of the air 2
Mat 6:26 Look at the birds of the air: they neither sow 5
8:20 Foxes have holes, and birds of the air have nests; 5
13:32 so that the birds of the air come and make nests 5
Mrk 4:32 the birds of the air can make nests in its shade. 5
Lke 8: 5 the birds of the air devoured it. 5
9:58 Foxes have holes, and birds of the air have nests; 5
13:19 the birds of the air made nests in its branches. 5
Act 10:12 animals and reptiles and birds of the air. 5
11: 6 beasts of prey and reptiles and birds of the air. 5
22:23 waved their garments and threw dust into the air 4
1Co 9:26 I do not box as one beating the air; 4
14: 9 For you will be speaking into the air. 4
Eph 2: 2 following the prince of the power of the air 4
1Th 4:17 in the clouds to meet the Lord in the air 4
Rev 9: 2 the sun and the air were darkened with the smoke 4
16:17 The seventh angel poured his bowl into the air 4
2Es 6: 4 before the heights of the air were lifted up 8
7:40 water or air, or darkness or evening or morning 8
8:20 and whose upper chambers are in the air 8
Jdt 11: 7 the cattle and the birds of the air 5
Wis 2: 3 the spirit will dissolve like empty air. 4
5:11 when a bird flies through the air 4
11 the light air 6
12 the air, thus divided, comes together at once 4
7: 3 when I was born, I began to breathe the common air 4
13: 2 either fire or wind or swift air 4
17:10 refusing to look even at the air 4
Bar 3:17 those who have sport with the birds of the air 5

Aza 1:58 Bless the Lord, all birds of the air 5
2Mc 4:24 extolled him with an air of authority 7
5: 2 golden-clad horsemen charging through the air 4

open air 1. αἴθριος
1Es 9:11 we are not able to stand in the open air 1
airs *See* put.

alabaster 1. שֵׁשׁ 2. ἀλάβαστρον
Sng 5:15 His legs are alabaster columns, set upon bases 1
Mat 26: 7 with an alabaster flask 2
alabaster *See also* flask.

alacrity 1. ἀσμένως
2Mc 4:12 with alacrity he founded a gymnasium 1

alarm 1. בהל 2. חפז 3. פַּחַד 4. תְּרוּעָה 5. בהל (A) 6. ἀγωνιάω 7. ἔμφοβος 8. θαμβέω 9. θορυβέω 10. θροέω 11. ταράσσω 12. φοβέομαι 13. φόβος
Num10: 5 When you blow an alarm, the camps that are 4
6 when you blow an alarm the second time, the camps 4
6 alarm is to be blown whenever they are to set out. 4
31: 6 with . . the trumpets for the alarm in his hand. 4
Ps 31:22 I had said in my alarm, "I am driven far 2
Sng 3: 8 each with his sword . . against alarms by night. 3
Jer 4:19 I hear the sound of the trumpet, the alarm of war. 4
20:16 a cry in the morning and an alarm at noon 4
Ezk 19: 4 The nations sounded an alarm against him; •
Dan 4: 5 fancies and the visions of my head alarmed me. 5
19 dismayed for a moment, and his thoughts alarmed 5
19 not the dream or the interpretation alarm you. 5
5: 6 color changed, and his thoughts alarmed him 5
9 Then King Belshaz'zar was greatly alarmed 5
10 Let not your thoughts alarm you 5
7:15 visions of my head alarmed me. 5
28 As for me, Daniel, my thoughts greatly alarmed me 5
11:44 tidings from the east and the north shall alarm 1
Mat 24: 6 see that you are not alarmed 10
Mrk 13: 7 do not be alarmed; this must take place 10
Act 20:10 embracing him said, "Do not be alarmed 9
24:25 Felix was alarmed and said 7
2Co 7:11 what indignation, what alarm, what longing 13
Tob 12:16 They were both alarmed 11
Jdt 4: 2 alarmed both for Jerusalem and for the temple 11
14: 7 those who hear your name will be alarmed. 11
AEs 15: 8 in alarm he sprang from his throne 6
Wis 17: 3 they were scattered, terribly alarmed 8
1Mc 10: 8 They were greatly alarmed when they heard 12
alarm *See also* sound.

alas 1. אֲבָל 2. אֲהָהּ 3. אוֹי 4. אָח 5. אָנָּא 6. הָהּ 7. הוֹ 8. הוֹי 9. οἴμμοι 10. οὐαί 11. ὦ 12. vae
Exd 32:31 said, "Alas, this people have sinned a great sin; 5
Num24:23 Alas, who shall live when God does this? 3
Jos 7: 7 And Joshua said, "Alas, O Lord GOD, why hast thou 2
Jdg 6:22 "Alas, O Lord GOD! For now I have seen the angel 2
11:35 Alas, my daughter! you have brought me very low 2
2Sm 14: 5 "Alas, I am a widow; my husband is dead. 1
1Kg 13:30 they mourned over him, saying, "Alas, my brother! 8
2Kg 3:10 the king of Israel said, "Alas! The LORD has called 2
6: 5 he cried out, "Alas, my master! It was borrowed. 2
15 the servant said, "Alas, my master! What shall we do? 2
Jer 30: 7 Alas! that day is so great there is none like it; 8
34: 5 and lament for you, saying, "Alas, lord! 8
Ezk 6:11 Clap your hands, and stamp your foot, and say, Alas! 4
30: 2 Thus says the Lord GOD: "Wail, 'Alas for the day! 6
Jol 1:15 Alas for the day! For the day of the LORD is near 2
Ams 5:16 and in all the streets they shall say, 'Alas! Alas!' 7
16 and in all the streets they shall say, 'Alas! Alas!' 7
Mat 24:19 alas for those who are with child 10
Mrk 13:17 alas for those who are with child 10
Lke 21:23 Alas for those who are with child 10
Rev 18:10 Alas! alas! thou great city . . Babylon! 10
10 Alas! alas! thou great city . . Babylon! 10
16 Alas, alas, for the great city 10
16 Alas, alas, for the great city 10
19 Alas, alas, for the great city 10
19 Alas, alas, for the great city 10
2Es 13:16 alas for those who will be left in those days! 12
16 And still more, alas for those who are not left! 12
19 alas for those also who are left 12
15:14 Alas for the world and for those who live in it! 12
16:17 Alas for me! Alas for me! 12
17 Alas for me! Alas for me! 12
1Mc 2: 7 said, "Alas! Why was I born to see this 9
4Mc 16: 9 Alas for my children 11
10 Alas, I . . am a widow and alone 11

alert 1. γρηγορέω
Act 20:31 Therefore be alert 1
1Mc 12:27 Jonathan commanded his men to be alert 1
alert *See also* keep.

algum 1. אַלְגּוּמִּים
2Ch 2: 8 cedar, cypress, and algum timber from Lebanon 1
9:10 brought algum wood and precious stones. 1
11 king made of the algum wood steps for the house 1

alien 1. אַחֵר 2. בֶּן נֵכָר 3. גֵּר 4. זור 5. נָכְרִי 6. ἀλλογενής 7. ἀλλότριος 8. ἀλλοφυλισμός 9. πάροικος 10. υἱὸς ἀλλογενής
Exd 23:12 your bondmaid, and the alien, may be refreshed. 3
Deu 1:16 man and his brother or the alien that is with him. 3
14:21 may give it to the alien who is within your towns 3
1Ch 22: 2 David commanded to gather together the aliens 3
2Ch 2:17 Solomon took a census of all the aliens who were 3
Job 19:15 I have become an alien in their eyes. 5
Ps 69: 8 I have become . . an alien to my mother's sons. 5
144: 7 rescue me and deliver me from . . hand of aliens 2
11 deliver me from the hand of aliens 2
Prv 5:10 lest . . your labors go to the house of an alien; 5
Isa 1: 7 in your very presence aliens devour your land; 4
7 it is desolate, as overthrown by aliens. 4
14: 1 aliens will join them and will cleave 3
17:10 you plant . . and set out slips of an alien god 4
25: 2 the palace of aliens is a city no more 4
5 Thou dost subdue the noise of the aliens; 4
28:11 by men of strange lips and with an alien tongue 1
21 and to work his work–alien is his work! 5
61: 5 Aliens shall stand and feed your flocks 4
Jer 7: 6 if you do not oppress the alien 3
22: 3 And do no wrong or violence to the alien 3
51:51 aliens have come into the holy places 4
Lam 5: 2 turned over to strangers, our homes to aliens. 5
Ezk 47:22 for the aliens who reside among you 3
23 In whatever tribe the alien resides 3
Hos 5: 7 for they have borne alien children. 4
7: 9 Aliens devour his strength, and he knows it not; 4
8: 7 if it were to yield, aliens would devour it. 4
Act 7: 6 aliens in a land belonging to others 9
1Pe 2:11 I beseech you as aliens and exiles to abstain 9
1Es 8:69 the alien peoples of the land 6
70 mixed with the alien peoples of the land 6
83 the pollution of the aliens of the land 6
AEs 14:15 I . . abhor the bed . . of any alien. 7
16:10 really an alien to the Persian blood 7
Wis 12:15 deeming it alien to thy power 7
19:15 their hostile reception of the aliens; 7
Bar 4: 3 Do not give . . advantages to an alien people. 7
1Mc 2: 7 the sanctuary given over to aliens? 7
3:36 settle aliens in all their territory 10
45 the sons of aliens held the citadel 6
2Mc 6:24 Eleazar . . has gone over to an alien religion 8
alien *See also* dwell.

resident alien 1. πάροικος
Jdt 4:10 every resident alien and hired laborer 1

alienate 1. יקע 2. עבר 3. פרד 4. ἀπαλλοτριόω 5. abalieno
Prv 17: 9 but he who repeats a matter alienates a friend. 3
Jer 6: 8 warned, O Jerusalem, lest I be alienated from you; 1
Ezk 48:14 they shall not alienate this choice portion 2
Eph 2:12 alienated from the commonwealth of Israel 4
4:18 alienated from the life of God 4
2Es 7:48 which has alienated us from God 5

alight 1. בוא 2. ירד 3. נפל 4. צנח 5. רגע 6. ἔρχομαι 7. καταλύω
Gen 24:64 when she saw Isaac, she alighted from the camel 3
Jos 15:18 she alighted from her ass, and Caleb said to her 4
Jdg 1:14 and she alighted from her ass, and Caleb said 4
4:15 and Sis'era alighted from his chariot and fled 2
1Sm 25:23 Ab'igail . . made haste, and alighted from the ass 2
2Kg 5:21 when Na'aman saw . . he alighted from the chariot 3
Prv 26: 2 curse that is causeless does not alight. 1
Isa 34:14 yea, there shall the night hag alight 5
50:11 all you who kindle a fire, who set brands alight! ‡
Mat 3:16 saw the Spirit of God . . alighting on him; 6
Sir 43:17 its descent is like locusts alighting. 7

alike 1. גַּם 2. דמה 3. יַחַד 4. יַחְדָּו 5. כְּ 6. כְּאֶחָד 7. כְּ כְּ 8. לְעֻמַּת 9. עִם 10. שוה 11. ἀπὸ μιᾶς 12. αὐτός 13. ὁμοίως
Deu 1:17 you shall hear the small and the great alike; •
12:22 unclean and the clean alike may eat of it. 4
15:22 unclean and the clean alike may eat it, as though 4
29:19 lead to the sweeping away of moist and dry alike. •
1Sm 30:24 they shall share alike. 4
1Kg 7:37 all of them were cast alike, of the same measure •
1Ch 24:31 head . . and his younger brother alike, cast lots 8
25: 8 they cast lots . . teacher and pupil alike. 9
26:13 they cast lots . . small and great alike 7
2Ch 31:15 portions to their brethren, old and young alike 7
Est 4:11 there is . . one law; all alike are to be put to death •
Job 21:26 They lie down alike in the dust 3
Ps 49:10 the fool and the stupid alike must perish 3
87: 7 Singers and dancers alike say, "All my springs 5
Prv 17:15 both alike an abomination to the LORD. 1
20:10 both alike an abomination to the LORD. 1
27:15 continual dripping . . contentious woman are alike; 10
Ecc 11: 6 do not know . . or whether both alike will be good. 6
Isa 46: 5 equal, and compare me, that we may be alike? 2
Jer 5: 5 But they all alike had broken the yoke 4
Ezk 14:10 and the punishment of the inquirer shall be alike 7
Lke 14:18 they all alike began to make excuses 11
Rom 14: 5 while another man esteems all days alike. •
1Co 15:39 For not all flesh is alike 12
Wis 6: 7 he takes thought for all alike. 13
18: 9 the saints would share alike the same things 13

all alike 1. אֵלֶּה עִם אֵלֶּה 2. יַחְדָּו
1Ch 24: 5 They organized them by lot, all alike 1
Ps 14: 3 have all gone astray, they are all alike corrupt; 2
53: 3 they are all alike depraved; 2

alive 1. חַי 2. חַיִּים 3. נֶפֶשׁ 4. εἰμί 5. ἔμπνους 6. ζάω 7. ζωγρία 8. ζωή 9. μένω 10. περίειμι 11. praesens 12. sum 13. vivo 14. vivus
Gen 43: 7 Is your father still alive? 1
27 Is your father well . . Is he still alive? 1
28 our father is well, he is still alive. 1
45: 3 I am Joseph; is my father still alive? 1
26 they told him, "Joseph is still alive 1
28 It is enough; Joseph my son is still alive; 1
46:30 seen your face and know that you are still alive. 1
Exd 4:18 Let me . . see whether they are still alive. 1
22: 4 stolen beast is found alive in his possession 1
Lev 16:10 goat . . shall be presented alive before the LORD 1
18:18 while her sister is yet alive 1
Num16:30 they go down alive into Sheol, then you shall know 1
33 they . . went down alive into Sheol; 1
Deu 4: 4 held fast to the LORD . . are all alive this day. 1
5: 3 but with us, who are all of us here alive this day. 1
6:24 that he might preserve us alive, as at this day. 1
31:27 behold, while I am yet alive with you, today 1
Jos 8:23 But the king of Ai they took alive, and brought him 1
1Sm 15: 8 And he took Agag the king of the Amal'ekites alive 1
20:14 If I am still alive, show me the . . love of the LORD 1
2Sm 12:18 while the child was yet alive, we spoke to him 1
21 fasted and wept for the child while it was alive; 1
22 While the child was still alive, I fasted and wept; 1
18:14 of Ab'salom, while he was still alive in the oak. 1
19: 6 if Ab'salom were alive and all of us . . dead today 1
1Kg 3:23 'This is my son that is alive, and your son is dead'; 1
26 the woman whose son was alive said to the king 1
12: 6 before Solomon his father while he was yet alive 1
20:18 If they have come out for peace, take them alive; 1
18 if they have come out for war, take them alive. 1
21:15 Arise, take . . for Naboth is not alive, but dead. 1
2Kg 7:12 we shall take them alive and get into the city.' 1
10:14 they took them alive, and slew them at the pit 1
14 they took them alive, and slew them at the pit 1
1Ch 5:21 They carried off . . 100,000 men alive. 3
2Ch 10: 6 before Solomon his father while he was yet alive 1
25:12 The men of Judah captured another 10,000 alive 1
Ps 55:15 let them go down to Sheol alive; 1
124: 3 then they would have swallowed us up alive 1
Prv 1:12 like Sheol let us swallow them alive and whole 1
Ecc 4: 2 more . . than the living who are still alive; 1
Lam 3:53 they flung me alive into the pit and cast stones 2
Ezk 6: 8 Yet I will leave some of you alive. •
Zec 13: 8 and perish, and one third shall be left alive. •
Mat 6:30 which today is alive and tomorrow is thrown 4
27:63 how that impostor said, while he was still alive 6
Mrk 16:11 heard that he was alive and had been seen by her 6
Lke 12:28 the grass which is alive in the field today 4
15:32 your brother was dead, and is alive 6
24:23 a vision of angels, who said that he was alive. 6
Act 1: 3 he presented himself alive after his passion 6
9:41 he presented her alive. 6
20:12 they took the lad away alive 6
25:19 who was dead, but whom Paul asserted to be alive. 6
Rom 6:11 dead to sin and alive to God in Christ Jesus. 6
7: 3 with another man while her husband is alive. 6
9 I was once alive apart from the law 6
8:10 spirits are alive because of righteousness 8
1Co 15: 6 most of whom are still alive 9
1Th 4:15 we who are alive 6
17 then we who are alive, who are left 6
Heb 9:17 as long as the one who made it is alive. 6
Rev 1:18 I died, and behold I am alive for evermore 6
3: 1 you have the name of being alive, and you are dead. 6
19:20 These two were thrown alive into the lake of fire 6
2Es 3: 5 and he was made alive in thy presence. 13
4:26 If you are alive, you will see, and if you live long 12
51 Or who will be alive in those days? 12
5:41 dost have charge of those who are alive at the end 12
7:45 Blessed are those who are alive 11
87 before whom they sinned while they were alive 13
94 that while they were alive they kept the law 13
129of which Moses, while he was alive, spoke 13
14:34 you shall be kept alive 14
Tob 7: 5 They replied, "He is alive and in good health. 6
8:12 Send one of the maids to see whether he is alive 6
14 she came out and told them that he was alive. 6
Sir 17:27 as do those who are alive and give thanks? 6
28 he who is alive and well sings the Lord's praises. 6
30: 5 while alive he saw and rejoiced 8
33:20 While you are still alive and have breath in you 6
1Mc 1: 6 while he was still alive. 6
8: 7 they took him alive 6
10:85 with those burned alive •

14: 2 he sent one of his commanders to take him alive. 6
2Mc 7:24 The youngest brother being still alive 10
10:36 burned the blasphemers alive 6
12:35 wishing to take the accursed man alive 7
14:45 Still alive and aflame with anger, he rose 5
4Mc 18:19 'I kill and I make alive 6

alive *See also* keep, leave, make, preserve, save.

alive again 1. ἀναζάω

Lke 15:24 this my son was dead, and is alive again 1

remain alive 1. חיה 2. מִחְיָה 3. περιβιόω

Gen 16:13 seen God and remained alive after seeing him? *
Num14:38 Joshua . . and Caleb . . remained alive 1
2Ch 14:13 the Ethiopians fell until none remained alive; 2
3Mc 5:18 why the Jews had been allowed to remain alive 3

all 1. אַךְ 2. יַחַד 3. יַחְדָּו 4. כָּלִיל 5. מְאֹד 6. מְלֹא 7. קָטֹן וְגָדוֹל 8. רֹב 9. רַק 10. תמם 11. ἀεί 12. αἰών 13. ἀμφότερος 14. εἷς 15. ἕκαστος 16. ἐν οὐδενί 17. ἐπάνω 18. ἐπὶ τὸ αὐτό 19. καθόλου 20. κακός 21. κατά 22. κατὰ τὰ ῥήματα 23. μέν 24. ὅλος 25. ὅλως 26. ὁμοῦ 27. ὃς ἄν 28. ὅσος 29. οὐ μή 30. πανταχοῦ 31. πάντοτε 32. πάντως 33. πᾶς 34. πολύς 35. σύνολον 36. τίς 37. τοσοῦτος 38. ὡς 39. totus

Gen 20:11 There is no fear of God at all in this place 9
Exd 3:15 to be remembered throughout all generations. †
5:23 and thou hast not delivered thy people at all. †
28:31 you shall make the robe of the ephod all of blue. 4
39:22 the robe of the ephod woven all of blue; 4
Lev 20: 4 if the people of the land do at all hide their eyes †
Num 4: 6 spread over that a cloth all of blue 4
23:25 Neither curse them at all, nor bless them †
25 Neither curse them at all, nor bless them at all. †
Deu 33:17 with them he shall push the peoples, all of them 3
Jos 7: 7 brought this people over the Jordan at all †
1Sm 16:11 And Samuel said to Jesse, "Are all your sons here? 10
20: 6 If your father misses me at all, then say †
25:36 she told him nothing at all until the morning 7
2Sm 19:42 Have we eaten at all at the king's expense? †
2Ch 32:13 gods . . at all able to deliver their lands †
Est 3:12 and to the governors over all the provinces †
Job 4:14 trembling, which made all my bones shake. 8
6: 2 all my calamity laid in the balances! 2
24: 4 the poor of the earth all hide themselves. 2
17 For deep darkness is morning to all of them; 3
Ps 10: 6 I shall not be moved; throughout all generations †
33:11 the thoughts of his heart to all generations. †
15 he who fashions the hearts of them all, 2
49:11 their dwelling places to all generations †
50:12 for the world and all that is in it is mine. 6
61: 6 the king; may his years endure to all generations! †
72: 5 as long as the moon, throughout all generations! †
73:13 All in vain have I kept my heart clean 1
74: 6 then all its carved wood they broke down 2
77: 8 Are his promises at an end for all time? †
85: 5 Wilt thou prolong thy anger to all generations? †
89: 1 proclaim thy faithfulness to all generations. †
4 build your throne for all generations.'" Selah †
11 world and all that is in it, thou hast founded them. 6
90: 1 Lord . . our dwelling place in all generations. †
100: 5 his faithfulness to all generations. †
102:12 thy name endures to all generations. †
24 whose years endure throughout all generations! †
119:90 Thy faithfulness endures to all generations; †
138in righteousness and in all faithfulness. 5
135:13 thy renown, O LORD, throughout all ages. †
146:10 reign for ever, thy God, O Zion, to all generations. †
Isa 10: 8 for he says: "Are not my commanders all kings? 3
13:20 inhabited or dwelt in for all generations; †
18: 6 They shall all of them be left to the birds 3
51: 8 for ever, and my salvation to all generations. †
Ezk 12:19 their land will be stripped of all it contains 6
14: 3 should I let myself be inquired of at all by them? †
19: 7 the land was appalled and all who were in it 6
Mic 1: 2 hearken, O earth, and all that is in it; 6
Nah 2: 1 gird your loins; collect all your strength. 5
Mat 1:22 All this took place to fulfil what the Lord had 24
4:23 And he went about all Galilee teaching 24
24 So his fame spread throughout all Syria 24
5:34 I say to you, Do not swear at all, either by heaven 25
9:26 report of this went through all that district. 24
31 spread his fame through all that district. 24
13:33 till it was all leavened. 24
14:35 they sent round to all that region 24
20: 6 he said to them, 'Why do you stand here idle all day? 24
22:37 love the Lord your God with all your heart 24
37 with all your heart, and with all your soul 24
37 with all your soul, and with all your mind. 24
40 On these two commandments depend all the law 24
26:56 But all this has taken place 24
Mrk 1:28 throughout all the surrounding region 30
39 he went throughout all Galilee 24
3: 8 a great multitude, hearing all that he did, came 28
10 so that all who had diseases pressed upon him 28
10:48 he cried out all the more, "Son of David, have mercy 34
12:30 shall love the Lord your God with all your heart 24
30 with all your soul, and with all your mind 24
30 with all your soul, and with all your mind 24
30 with all your mind, and with all your strength.' 24
33 and to love him with all the heart, 24
33 and to love him . . with all the understanding 24
33 and to love him . . with all the strength 24
Lke 1:65 through all the hill country of Judea; 24
4:14 went out through all the surrounding country. 24
5: 5 Master, we toiled all night and took nothing! 24
10:19 authority . . over all the power of the enemy 17
27 shall love the Lord your God with all your heart 24
27 with all your soul, and with all your strength 24
27 with all your soul, and with all your strength 24
27 with all your strength, and with all your mind; 24
13:21 till it was all leavened. 24
18:39 he cried out all the more 34
22:70 they all said, "Are you the Son of God, then? 33
23: 5 teaching throughout all Judea 24
Joh 1:12 to all who received him, who believed in his name 28
3:31 He who comes from above is above all; 17
31 he who comes from heaven is above all. 17
4:53 and he himself believed, and all his household. 24
Act 1:15 the company of persons was in all about 100 18
2: 2 it filled all the house where they were sitting. 24
47 having favor with all the people 24
4: 6 and all who were of the high-priestly family. 28
18 not to speak or teach at all in the name of Jesus. 19
7:10 governor over Egypt and over all his household. 24
11 came a famine throughout all Egypt and Canaan 24
9:31 throughout all Judea and Galilee and Sama'ria 24
42 it became known throughout all Joppa 24
10:37 word which was proclaimed throughout all Judea 24
11:28 there would be a great famine over all the world; 24
13:49 spread throughout all the region. 24
14:27 declared all that God had done with them 28
15: 4 they declared all that God had done with them. 28
18: 8 Crispus . . together with all his household 24
19:16 mastered all of them, and overpowered them 13
27 she whom all Asia and the world worship. 24
21:30 Then all the city was aroused 24
31 all Jerusalem was in confusion. 24
23: 8 the Pharisees acknowledge them all. 13
25: 8 nor against Caesar have I offended at all. 36
Rom 1: 8 your faith is proclaimed in all the world. 24
2:12 All who have sinned without the law 28
12 and all who have sinned under the law 28
3: 9 What then? Are we Jews any better off? No, not at all; 32
6: 3 all of us who have been baptized into Christ 28
8:14 all who are led by the Spirit of God are sons of God 28
36 we are being killed all the day long; 24
10:21 All day long I have held out my hands 24
1Co 5:10 not at all meaning the immoral of this world 32
6: 7 To have lawsuits at all with one another 25
15:29 If the dead are not raised at all 25
16:12 it was not at all his will to come now 32
2Co 1:20 For all the promises of God find their Yes in him. 28
4:17 weight of glory beyond all comparison †
Gal 3:10 all who rely on works of the law are under a curse; 28
Php 1:20 my . . hope that I shall not be at all ashamed 16
Col 1:29 striving with all the energy 21
2: 1 for all who have not seen my face 28
1Th 1: 2 We give thanks to God always for you all 31
1Ti 6: 1 all who are under the yoke of slavery 28
2Ti 1:18 you well know all the service he rendered 28
Phm 1:18 If he has wronged you at all, or owes you anything 36
Heb 2:15 all those who . . were subject to . . bondage. 28
3: 5 Now Moses was faithful in all God's house 24
10:25 all the more as you see the Day drawing near. 37
Rev 18:17 sailors and all whose trade is on the sea 28
20:13 and all were judged by what they had done. 15
1Es 1:32 in all Judea they mourned for Josiah 24
2: 2 made a proclamation throughout all his kingdom 24
5:53 all who had made any vow to God 28
8:23 throughout all Syria and Phoenicia 24
72 all who were ever moved at the word of the Lord 28
94 to you and to all who obey the law of the Lord. 28
2Es 11:16 Hear me, you who have ruled the earth all this time; 39
Tob 1:12 because I remembered God with all my heart. 24
13: 6 If you turn to him with all your heart 24
6 with all your heart and with all your soul 24
Jdt 3: 5 The men came to Holofernes and told him all this. 22
6:17 all that Holofernes had said so boastfully 28
21 all that night they called on the God of Israel 24
7: 5 they remained on guard all that night. 24
10: 4 to entice the eyes of all men who might see her. 28
AEs 13: 5 doing all the harm they can 20
5 didst do for them all that thou didst promise. 28
15: 6 all covered with gold and precious stones 24
Sir 6:26 keep her ways with all your might. 24
7:27 With all your heart honor your father 24
29 With all your soul fear the Lord 24
30 With all your might love your Maker 24
12: 5 evil for all the good which you do to him. 27
19: 7 you will lose nothing at all. 29
23:23 first of all, she has disobeyed the law of the Most High 23
Bar 3:32 He who prepared the earth for all time filled it 12
Aza 1:18 now with all our heart we follow thee 24
27 the fire did not touch them at all . . or trouble them. 19
Bel 1:18 and with you there is no deceit, none at all. 14
1Mc 2:28 left all that they had in the city. 28
46 circumcised all the uncircumcised boys 28
5:50 all that day and all the night 24
50 all that day and all the night 24
10:15 all the promises which Demetrius had sent 28
12:27 so as to be ready all night for battle 24
13:38 All the grants that we have made to you 28
15: 5 and release from all the other payments 28
2Mc 4:47 Menelaus, the cause of all the evil, he acquitted 24
5: 2 over all the city, for almost 40 days 24
14:35 O Lord of all, who hast need of nothing 24
3Mc 2: 3 the creator of all things and the governor of all 24
3:12 soldiers in Egypt and all its districts 21
26 when these all have been punished 26
29 shall become useless for all time 11
4: 3 or what habitable place at all 35
6: 9 all-merciful and protector of all 24
7: 8 with no one in any place doing them harm at all 35
9 or cause them any grief at all 35
16 praise and all kinds of melodious songs. †
21 they were not subject at all to confiscation 35
23 through all times! Amen. 11
4Mc 3: 7 had been attacking the Philistines all day long 24
4: 7 did all that they could to prevent it. 38
12:12 these throughout all time will never let you go. 24
13:13 Let us with all our hearts consecrate ourselves 24
17:17 The tyrant himself and all his council marveled 24

all כֹּל

Gen 1:26, 29; 2:1, 2, 3, 20; 3:14^{3}, 17, 20; 4:21, 22; 5:5, 8, 11, 14, 17, 20, 23, 27, 31; 6:12, 13, 17, 19, 22; 7:1, 2, 3, 5, 11, 14, 15, 16, 19, 21^{2}; 8:1^{2}, 17; 9:2, 11, 12, 15^{2}, 16, 17, 29; 10:21, 29; 11:6, 8, 9^{2}; 12:3, 5, 20; 13:1, 11, 15; 14:3, 7, 11^{2}, 16; 15:10; 16:12; 17:8, 23, 27; 18:18, 25; 19:4, 25^{2}, 28, 31; 20:7, 8^{2}, 16, 18; 21:22; 22:18; 23:10, 17, 18; 24:2, 20, 36, 66; 25:4, 5, 18, 25; 26:3, 4^{2}, 11, 15; 27:33, 37; 28:14, 22; 29:3, 8, 13, 22; 30:32, 35, 40; 31:1, 6, 8^{2}, 12^{2}, 16, 18^{2}, 21, 34, 37^{2}, 43; 32:10^{2}, 19; 33:8, 13; 34:19, 23, 24^{2}, 25, 29^{3}; 35:2, 4, 6; 36:6^{3}; 37:4, 35^{2}; 39:3, 4, 5^{2}, 6, 22; 40:20; 41:8^{2}, 19, 29, 30, 35, 37, 39, 40, 41, 43, 44, 46, 48, 51^{2}, 54^{2}, 55^{2}, 56^{2}, 57^{2}; 42:6, 11, 29, 36; 44:32; 45:1, 8^{2}, 9, 10, 11, 13^{2}, 15, 20, 22, 26, 27; 46:1, 6, 7, 22, 25, 26^{2}, 27, 32; 47:1, 12, 13, 14, 15, 17, 20; 48:16; 49:28; 50:7^{2}, 8, 14, 15, Exd 1:5, 6^{2}, 14, 22; 3:20; 4:19, 21, 28^{2}, 29, 30; 5:12; 6:29; 7:2, 19^{2}, 20, 21, 24; 8:2, 4, 16, 17^{2}, 24; 9:4, 6, 9^{2}, 11, 14^{2}, 16, 19, 22, 24, 25; 10:6^{2}, 12, 13^{2}, 14, 15^{3}, 19, 22, 23; 11:5^{2}, 6, 8^{2}, 10; 12:3, 12^{2}, 20, 21, 29^{2}, 30^{2}, 33, 41, 42, 47, 48, 50; 13:2, 7, 12^{2}, 15^{3}; 14:4, 7^{2}, 9, 17, 20, 21, 23, 28; 15:15, 20, 26; 16:1, 6, 22, 23; 17:1; 18:1, 8^{2}, 9, 11, 12, 14^{2}, 21, 22, 23, 24, 25, 26; 19:5^{2}, 7, 8^{2}, 11, 16; 20:1, 9, 11, 18; 23:13, 17, 22, 27^{2}; 24:3^{4}, 4, 7, 8; 25:9^{2}, 22, 39; 26:2, 17; 27:3, 17, 19^{3}; 28:3; 29:13, 24, 35; 30:27, 28; 31:3, 6^{2}, 7, 8, 9, 11; 32:3, 13, 26; 33:8, 10^{2}, 16, 19; 34:3, 10^{3}, 19^{2}, 20, 23, 30, 31, 32^{2}; 35:1, 3, 4, 10, 13, 16, 20, 21, 22^{2}, 25, 26, 29, 31; 36:1, 3, 4, 7, 8, 9, 22; 37:24; 38:3^{2}, 16, 17, 20, 22, 24^{2}, 30, 31^{2}; 39:32^{2}, 33, 36, 37, 39, 40, 42^{2}, 43; 40:9^{2}, 10, 16, 36, 38, Lev 2:2, 13^{2}, 16; 3:3, 9, 14, 16, 17; 4:8^{2}, 11, 19, 22, 26, 31, 35; 6:3, 9, 15; 7:3, 9, 10, 19; 8:3, 10, 11, 16, 25, 27, 36; 9:5, 23, 24; 10:3, 6, 11; 11:2, 9, 20, 23, 27, 31, 33, 34, 42^{2}; 13:12, 13^{2}; 14:8, 9^{2}, 36, 45; 15:25, 26; 16:2, 16, 17, 21^{3}, 22, 30, 33, 34; 17:2; 18:24, 27; 19:2, 23, 24, 37^{2}; 20:5, 22^{2}, 23; 21:24; 22:3, 18; 23:3, 14, 21, 31, 38^{2}, 42; 24:14^{2}, 16; 25:7, 9, 10, 24; 26:14, 15; 27:9, 30, 32, Num 1:2, 3, 20, 22, 24, 50^{3}, 54; 2:32, 34; 3:8, 13^{3}, 22, 26, 28, 31, 34, 36^{2}, 39^{2}, 40, 41^{2}, 42, 43, 45; 4:3, 9, 10, 12, 14^{2}, 15, 16^{2}, 23, 26^{2}, 27^{4}, 32^{2}, 37, 41, 46; 5:9, 30; 6:4, 5, 6, 8; 7:1^{2}, 85, 86, 87, 88; 8:7, 16^{2}, 17^{2}, 18, 20^{2}; 9:3^{2}, 5, 12; 10:3, 25; 11:6, 12, 13, 14, 22, 29, 32^{3}; 12:3, 7; 13:3, 26^{2}, 32; 14:1, 2, 5, 7, 10^{2}, 11, 21, 29, 35, 36, 39; 15:13, 22, 23, 24, 25, 26, 33, 35, 36, 39, 40; 16:3, 5, 6, 10, 11, 16, 19^{2}, 22^{2}, 26, 28, 29^{2}, 30, 31, 32^{2}, 33, 34, 41; 17:2, 6, 9^{2}, 12; 18:3, 4, 7, 8, 11, 12^{2}, 13, 15, 19, 28, 29^{2}; 19:18; 20:14, 27, 29^{2}; 21:23, 25^{3}, 26, 33, 34, 35; 22:2, 4; 23:6, 13, 26; 24:17; 25:4; 26:2^{2}, 43; 27:2, 16, 19, 20, 21; 30:2, 4, 11, 14^{2}; 31:9^{2}, 10^{2}, 11^{2}, 13, 15, 18, 20, 27, 30, 35, 51, 52; 32:13, 15, 26; 33:3, 4, 52^{4}; 35:3, 7, 29, Deu 1:1, 3, 7, 18, 19, 22, 31; 2:7, 16, 32, 33, 34, 36, 37; 3:1, 2, 3, 4, 5, 7, 10^{3}, 13^{2}, 14, 18, 21^{2}; 4:3, 4, 6, 8, 9, 10, 19^{2}, 29^{2}, 30, 34, 49; 5:1, 3, 13, 22, 23, 26, 27^{2}, 28, 29, 31, 33; 6:2^{2}, 5^{3}, 19, 22, 24, 25; 7:6, 7, 14, 15^{2}, 16, 18, 19; 8:1, 2, 13; 9:10, 18; 10:12^{3}, 14, 15; 11:3, 6, 7, 8, 13^{2}, 22^{2}, 23, 25, 32; 12:1, 2, 5, 7, 8, 10, 11^{2}, 14, 18, 28; 13:3^{2}, 9, 11, 15, 16^{2}, 18; 14:2, 9, 11, 19, 20, 22, 28, 29; 15:5, 10^{2}, 18, 19; 16:3, 4, 15^{2}, 16, 18; 17:7, 10, 13, 14, 19^{2}; 18:1, 5, 6, 7, 18; 19:8, 9; 20:11, 13, 14, 15, 18; 21:6, 17, 21^{2}; 22:19, 29; 23:6, 20; 24:8, 19; 25:16^{2}, 18, 19; 26:2, 11, 12, 13, 14, 16^{2}, 18, 19; 27:1, 3, 8, 9, 14, 15, 16, 17, 18, 19, 20, 21, 22, 23, 24, 25, 26; 28:1^{2}, 2, 8, 10, 12, 15^{2}, 20, 25, 26, 32, 33, 37, 40, 42, 45, 52^{4}, 55, 58, 60, 64; 29:2^{4}, 9, 10^{2}, 21^{2}, 24, 27, 29; 30:1^{2}, 2^{3}, 3, 6^{2}, 7, 8, 9, 10^{2}; 31:1, 5, 7, 9, 11^{2}, 12, 18, 28, 30; 32:4, 27, 44, 45^{2}, 46^{2}; 33:3, 12; 34:1, 2^{2}, 11^{4}, 12, Jos 1:2, 4, 5, 7, 8, 14, 16; 2:3, 9, 13, 18, 22, 23, 24^{2}; 3:1, 11, 13, 15, 17^{2}; 4:1, 10, 11, 14^{2}, 18, 24; 5:1^{2}, 4^{2}, 5^{2}, 6, 8; 6:3, 5, 17^{2}, 19, 21, 22, 23^{2}, 24, 25, 27; 7:3, 9, 15, 23, 24^{2}, 25; 8:1, 3, 4, 5, 11, 14, 15, 16, 21, 24^{3}, 25^{2}, 26, 33, 34^{2}, 35^{2}; 9:1^{2}, 5, 9, 10, 11, 18, 19^{2}, 21, 24^{2}; 10:2, 5, 6, 7^{2}, 9, 15, 21, 24, 25, 29, 31, 34, 36, 38, 39, 40^{2}, 41, 42, 43; 11:4, 5, 6, 7, 10, 11, 12^{2}, 14, 15, 16^{3}, 17, 18, 19, 21^{2}, 23; 12:1, 5, 24; 13:2^{2}, 4, 5, 6^{2}, 9, 10, 11^{2}, 12, 16, 17, 21^{2}, 25, 30^{2}; 15:32, 46; 16:9; 17:16; 19:8; 20:9; 21:19, 26, 33, 39, 41, 42, 43, 44^{2}, 45^{2}; 22:2^{2}, 5^{3}, 20; 23:1, 2, 3^{2}, 4, 6, 14^{4}, 15^{2}; 24:1, 2, 3, 17^{2}, 18, 27^{2}, 31, Jdg 1:25; 2:4, 7^{3}, 10, 18; 3:1, 3, 19, 29; 4:13^{2}, 15^{2}, 16; 5:31; 6:9, 13^{2}, 31, 33, 35, 37, 39, 40; 7:1, 6, 7, 8, 12, 14, 16, 18^{2}, 21, 22, 23, 24^{2}; 8:10^{2}, 12, 27, 34, 35; 9:2^{2}, 3^{2}, 6^{2}, 14, 25, 34, 44, 45, 46, 47, 48, 49, 51^{2}, 57; 10:8, 18; 11:8, 11, 20, 21^{2}, 22, 24, 26; 12:4; 13:13, 14, 23; 14:3; 16:2^{2}, 17, 18^{2}, 27, 30, 31; 19:20, 25, 29, 30; 20:1, 2^{2}, 6, 7, 8, 10^{2}, 11, 12, 16, 17, 25, 26, 33, 34, 35, 37, 44, 46^{2}, 48^{2}; 21:5, Rut 2:11, 21; 3:5, 11^{2}, 16; 4:9^{3}, 11, 1Sm 1:4, 11, 21; 2:14^{2}, 22^{2}, 23, 28^{2}, 32, 33; 3:12, 17, 20; 4:1, 5, 13; 5:5, 8, 11; 6:4, 18; 7:2, 3^{2}, 5, 13, 15, 16; 8:4, 5, 7, 8, 10, 20, 21; 9:6, 19, 20^{2}, 21; 10:9, 11, 18, 19, 20, 24^{3}, 25; 11:1, 2^{2}, 3, 4, 7, 15^{2}; 12:1^{2}, 7, 18, 19^{2}, 20^{2}, 24; 13:3, 4, 7, 19; 14:7, 15, 20, 22, 25, 38, 39, 40, 47, 52; 15:3, 6, 8, 9^{2}, 11; 17:11, 19, 24, 46, 47; 18:5, 6, 14, 16, 22, 30; 19:1, 5, 7, 18, 24^{2}; 20:6; 22:1, 4, 6, 7, 8, 11^{2}, 14, 15^{2}, 16, 22; 23:8, 20, 23^{2}; 24:2; 25:1, 6, 7, 9, 12, 16, 17, 21^{2}, 22, 30; 26:12, 24; 27:11; 28:3, 4, 20^{2}; 29:1; 30:6, 16^{2}, 18, 19, 20, 22, 31; 31:6, 12, 2Sm 1:11; 2:9, 23, 28, 29, 30, 32; 3:12, 18, 19, 21^{2}, 23, 25, 29, 31, 32, 34, 35, 36^{2}, 37^{2}; 4:1, 7; 5:1, 3, 5, 17; 6:1, 2, 5^{2}, 11, 12, 14, 15, 19^{2}, 21; 7:1, 3, 7^{2}, 9, 11, 17^{2}, 21, 22; 8:4, 11, 14^{2}, 15^{2}; 9:7, 9^{2}, 11, 12; 10:7, 17, 19; 11:1, 9, 18, 19, 22; 12:12, 29, 31^{2}; 13:21, 23, 25, 27, 29, 30, 31, 32, 33, 36; 14:19^{2}, 25; 15:6, 10, 14, 16,

17, 18^{4}, 22^{2}, 23^{3}, 24^{2}, 30; 16:4, 6^{3}, 8, 11, 14, 15, 18, 21^{2}, 22, 23; 17:2, 3^{2}, 4, 10, 11, 12, 13, 14, 16, 22, 24; 18:4, 5^{2}, 8, 17, 31, 32; 19:2, 5, 6, 7, 8^{2}, 9^{2}, 11, 14^{2}, 20, 28, 30, 38, 39, 40, 41^{2}, 42; 20:2, 7, 12, 13, 14^{2}, 15, 22, 23; 21:5, 14; 22:1, 23, 31; 23:5, 6, 39; 24:2, 7, 8, 23, 1Kg 1:3, 9^{2}, 19, 20, 25, 39, 40, 41, 49; 2:2, 3, 4^{2}, 15, 26, 44; 3:13, 15, 28; 4:1, 7, 10, 11, 12, 21^{2}, 24^{2}, 25, 27, 30^{2}, 31^{2}, 34^{2}; 5:8, 10, 13; 6:12, 18, 22, 29, 38^{2}; 7:5, 9, 14, 25, 33, 37, 40, 45, 47, 48, 51; 8:1, 2, 3, 4, 5, 14^{2}, 16, 22, 23, 38, 39^{2}, 40, 43^{2}, 48^{2}, 50, 53, 54, 55, 56^{2}, 58, 60, 62, 63, 65, 66; 9:1, 3, 4, 7, 9, 19^{2}, 20; 10:2, 3, 4, 13, 15, 21^{2}, 23, 29; 11:8, 13, 16, 25, 28, 32, 34, 37, 38, 41, 42; 12:1, 3, 12, 16, 18, 20^{2}, 21, 23; 13:11, 32; 14:8, 9, 13, 18, 21, 22, 24, 26, 29; 15:3, 5, 6, 7, 12, 14, 16, 18, 20^{2}, 22, 23^{3}, 27, 29, 31, 32, 33; 16:7, 11, 12, 13, 14, 16, 17, 25, 26, 30, 33; 18:5^{2}, 19, 20, 21, 24, 30^{2}, 36, 39; 19:1^{2}, 18; 20:1, 4, 7, 8^{2}, 9, 10, 13, 15, 28; 22:10, 12, 17, 19, 22, 23, 28, 39^{2}, 43, 2Kg 3:6, 19, 21^{2}, 25; 4:3, 4, 13; 5:12, 15^{2}; 7:15; 8:4, 6^{2}, 9, 21, 23; 9:5, 7, 14; 10:5, 9^{2}, 11^{2}, 17, 18, 19^{3}, 21^{2}, 22, 30, 31, 33, 34^{2}; 11:1, 9, 14, 18, 19, 20; 12:2, 4, 9, 18^{2}, 19; 13:8, 11, 12, 22; 14:14^{2}, 21, 24, 28; 15:3, 35:8, 12, 15^{2}; 36:10, 24, 25^{2}, 29, 33, 34; 37:16, 22, 23, 24; 38:4^{3}, 5, 6^{2}, 7, 8, 9, 11, 13, 15, 20^{2}; 39:4, 11, 13, 17, 18, 20, 21, 23, 26; 40:4^{2}; 41:17; 43:11^{5}; 44:5^{4}, 6, 7, 9, 14^{2}, 24, 30^{4}; 45:16, 17, 22; 47:12; 48:19, Dan 1:15, 17^{2}, 19, 20^{2}; 9:6, 7^{2}, 11, 13, 14, 16^{2}; 11:2^{2}, 16, 37, 43; 12:7, Hos 2:11^{2}; 4:3; 5:2; 7:2, 4, 6, 7^{2}, 10; 9:1, 4, 8, 15; 10:14; 12:1, 8; 13:2, 10; 14:2, Jol 1:2, 5, 12, 14, 19; 2:1, 6, 12, 28, 32; 3:2, 4, 9, 11, 12, 18, Ams 2:3; 3:2^{2}; 4:6^{2}; 5:16^{2}, 17; 7:10; 8:8, 10^{2}; 9:1, 5^{2}, 9, 10, 12, 13, Obd 1:7, 15, 16, Jon 2:3, Mic 1:2, 5, 7^{3}; 2:12; 3:7, 9; 4:5; 5:9, 11; 6:16; 7:2, 16, 19, Nah 1:4, 5; 2:10^{2}; 3:1, 7, 10, 12, 19, Hab 1:9, 15; 2:5^{2}, 6, 8^{2}, 17, 19, 20, Zep 1:4, 8, 11^{2}, 18^{2}; 2:3, 11^{2}, 14; 3:7^{2}, 8^{2}, 9, 14, 19^{2}, 20, Hag 1:11, 12, 14; 2:4, 7^{2}, 17, Zec 1:11; 2:13; 4:2; 5:6; 6:5; 7:5, 14; 8:12, 17; 9:1; 10:11; 11:10; 12:2, 3^{3}, 6, 9, 14; 14:2, 5, 9, 12, 14, 16, 19, 21, Mal 2:9, 10; 3:12; 4:1^{2}, 4

all כֹּל (A)

Ezr 5:7; 6:17; 7:16, 21, 25, Dan 2:12, 30, 38, 39, 40, 44, 48; 3:2, 3, 7^{2}; 4:1^{2}, 6, 12^{2}, 18, 21, 28, 35, 37; 5:8, 19, 22, 23; 6:7, 24, 25^{2}, 26; 7:7, 14, 16, 19, 23, 27

all *ἅπας*

Mat 6:32; 24:39; 28:11, Mrk 1:27; 11:32; 16:15, Lke 3:21; 4:6, 40; 5:26; 8:37; 9:15; 19:48; 20:6, Act 2:7; 4:31; 5:12, 16; 11:10; 16:3, 28; 27:33, Eph 6:13, Jas 3:2, 1Es 8:66; 9:10, AEs 16:24, Sir 17:19; 24:34, 1Mc 10:30; 15:8, 2Mc 11:2; 13:6; 14:9, 3Mc 3:5, 18, 21; 5:2; 6:12, 23; 7:6, 4Mc 1:9; 6:20; 15:24

all *πᾶς*

Gen 31:1, 1Sm 18:28; 30:2, Hag 2:2, Mat 1:17; 2:3, 4, 16^{2}; 3:5^{2}, 15; 4:8, 9, 24; 5:11, 15, 18; 6:29, 32, 33; 8:16, 34; 9:35; 10:22, 30; 11:13, 28; 12:15, 23; 13:32, 34, 41^{2}, 44, 46, 51, 56^{2}; 14:20, 35; 15:37; 18:25, 31, 32, 34; 19:20; 21:10, 12, 26; 22:10, 27, 28; 23:5, 8, 27, 35, 36; 24:2, 8, 9, 14, 30, 33, 34, 47; 25:5, 7, 31, 32; 26:1, 27, 31, 33, 35, 52, 56, 70; 27:1, 22, 25, 45; 28:18, 19, 20, Mrk 1:5^{2}, 32; 2:12^{2}, 13; 3:28; 4:13, 31, 32; 5:26, 40; 6:30, 33, 39, 41, 42, 50; 7:3, 14, 19, 23; 9:15, 35^{2}; 10:20, 44; 11:17, 18; 12:22, 28, 33, 43, 44; 13:4, 10, 13, 30, 37; 14:23, 27, 29, 31, 50, 53, 64, Lke 1:6, 48, 63, 65^{2}, 66, 71, 75; 2:1, 3, 10, 18, 19, 20, 31, 38, 47, 51; 3:3, 6, 16, 19, 20; 4:5, 7, 15, 20, 22, 25, 28, 36; 5:9; 6:10, 17, 19^{2}, 26; 7:1, 16, 17, 18, 29, 35; 8:40, 45, 47, 52; 9:1, 7, 13, 17, 23, 43^{2}, 48; 11:50; 12:7, 15, 18, 27, 30, 41, 44; 13:2, 3, 4, 5, 17^{3}, 27, 28; 14:10, 18, 29, 33; 15:1, 13, 31; 16:14, 26; 17:10, 27, 29; 18:12, 21, 22, 43; 19:7, 37; 20:38, 45; 21:3, 4^{2}, 12, 17, 22, 24, 29, 32, 35, 36^{2}, 38; 23:48, 49; 24:9^{2}, 14, 19, 21, 25, 27^{2}, 47, Joh 1:7, 16; 2:15; 3:26; 4:29, 39, 45; 5:20, 22, 23, 28; 6:37, 39, 45; 7:21; 8:2; 10:4, 8, 29; 13:11, 18; 14:26; 15:15, 21; 16:13, 15; 17:2^{2}, 10, 21; 18:4, 20; 19:28, Act 1:1, 8, 14, 18, 19, 21; 2:1, 4, 12, 14, 17, 32, 36, 39, 44, 45; 3:9, 11, 16, 18, 21, 24, 25; 4:10^{2}, 16, 29, 33; 5:5, 11, 17, 20, 21, 34, 36, 37; 6:15; 7:10, 14, 22, 50; 8:1, 10, 27, 40; 9:14, 21, 26, 32, 35, 39, 40; 10:2, 12, 33^{2}, 36, 38, 39, 41, 43, 44; 11:14, 23; 12:11; 13:10^{2}, 22, 24, 29; 14:15, 16; 15:3, 12, 17; 16:26, 32, 33; 17:7, 11, 21, 26, 30; 18:2, 17, 23; 19:7, 10, 17^{2}, 19, 26, 34; 20:18, 19, 25, 26, 28, 32, 36, 37; 21:5, 18, 20, 21, 24, 27; 22:3, 10, 12, 15, 30; 23:1; 24:3, 5; 25:24; 26:2, 3, 4, 11, 14, 20, 29; 27:20, 24, 35, 36, 37, 44; 28:2, 30, Rom 1:5, 7, 8, 18, 29; 3:12, 22, 23; 4:11, 16^{2}; 5:12, 18^{2}; 7:8; 8:32, 37; 9:5, 6, 7, 17; 10:12^{2}, 16, 18; 11:26, 32; 12:4, 17, 18; 13:7; 14:5, 10; 15:11^{2}, 13, 14, 33; 16:4, 15, 16, 19, 26, 1Co 1:2, 5^{2}, 10; 3:22; 7:7, 17; 8:1, 7; 9:19, 23, 24; 10:1^{2}, 2, 3, 4, 17, 31; 12:6, 11, 12, 13^{2}, 19, 26^{2}, 29^{4}, 30^{3}; 13:2^{3}, 3; 14:5, 18, 23, 24^{3}, 31^{3}, 33; 15:7, 8, 19, 22^{2}, 25, 39, 51^{2}; 16:14, 20, 24, 2Co 1:1, 3, 4; 2:3^{2}, 5; 3:2, 18; 4:15; 5:10, 14^{2}, 15, 18; 7:4, 13, 15; 8:7, 18; 9:13; 11:28; 12:12, 19; 13:2, 13, 14, Gal 1:2; 2:14; 3:8, 26, 28; 4:1; 6:6, Eph 1:9, 15, 21, 23^{2}; 2:3; 3:8, 18, 19, 20, 21; 4:2, 6^{4}, 10, 13, 31^{2}; 5:3, 9; 6:16^{2}, 18^{4}, 24, Php 1:1, 3, 4, 7^{2}, 8, 9, 13, 25; 2:17, 21, 26, 29; 4:5, 7, 12, 22, Col 1:4, 9, 11^{2}, 15, 19, 28; 2:2, 3, 10, 13; 3:8, 11^{2}, 14, 16; 4:7, 12, 1Th 1:7; 2:15; 3:7, 9, 13; 4:6, 10; 5:5, 14, 15, 18, 26, 27, 2Th 1:4, 10; 2:9, 10, 12; 3:2, 16^{3}, 18, 1Ti 2:1^{2}, 2, 4, 6, 11; 4:10, 15; 5:2, 20; 6:1, 10, 2Ti 1:15; 3:9, 11, 12, 16; 4:8, 16, 17, 21, Tit 2:7, 11, 14, 15; 3:2, 15, Phm 1:5, 6, Heb 1:6, 11, 14; 2:11; 3:16; 4:4, 13; 5:9; 6:16; 8:11; 9:19^{2}, 21; 11:13, 39; 12:8, 11, 14, 23; 13:4, 24^{2}, 25, Jas 1:2, 7, 21; 2:10; 4:16; 5:12, 1Pe 1:15, 24^{2}; 2:1^{3}, 18; 3:8; 4:8; 5:5, 7, 10, 14, 2Pe 3:9, 11, 16, 1Jn 1:7, 9; 2:16, 19, 20; 5:17, 2Jn 1:1, 3Jn 1:2, Jde 1:15^{4}, 25, Rev 1:7; 2:23; 5:6, 13; 7:9, 11; 8:3, 7; 12:5; 13:8, 12, 16; 14:8; 15:4; 18:3, 12^{3}, 14, 17, 19, 23, 24; 19:5, 17, 21; 21:8, 1Es 1:13, 21, 25, 49^{2}, 53, 54, 56, 58; 2:8, 14; 3:1^{3}, 2, 14, 18, 20, 21; 4:2, 10, 19^{2}, 28, 36, 37^{3}, 39, 40, 41, 44, 47^{2}, 48, 49, 50, 53^{2}, 56, 57, 61; 5:3, 28, 35, 41, 46, 50, 52, 56, 58, 61, 62; 6:4, 10, 19; 7:8, 11^{2}, 12, 13; 8:4, 7^{2}, 13, 23, 24, 26, 49, 55, 65, 86, 93, 96; 9:3, 6, 12, 15, 16, 36, 40^{2}, 41, 45, 46, 47, 49, 50, 53, 54, Tob 1:3, 4^{3}, 5, 6, 7, 10, 20, 21; 2:6; 3:2^{2}, 4, 11; 4:3, 5^{2}, 7, 11, 12^{2}, 14, 16, 19^{2}; 8:5, 15^{2}; 11:14, 17; 12:5, 6, 19; 13:4, 5, 10, 12^{2}, 14^{2}, 18; 14:5, 6, 7, Jdt 1:6^{2}, 7^{3}, 9, 10, 11, 12^{2}, 13^{2}, 16; 2:2^{3}, 10, 14, 23, 24, 26, 27^{2}, 28; 3:3^{3}, 7, 8^{4}, 10; 4:1, 3, 5, 11, 14, 15; 5:1, 2^{2}, 4, 5, 14, 15^{2}, 16, 22; 6:1^{2}, 12, 16^{3}, 17; 7:1, 2, 6, 8^{2}, 12, 13, 16, 19, 20, 23^{2}, 26; 8:6, 9, 10, 14, 21, 28, 29; 9:4, 6, 12, 14; 10:1, 4, 5, 13, 20, 23; 11:1, 7, 9, 12, 16, 20; 12:15, 18; 13:1, 4, 13, 17, 18, 20; 14:4, 8, 10, 12, 13; 15:4^{2}, 5, 9, 10^{2}, 11^{3}, 12, 13^{3}; 16:1^{2}, 14, 16, 19, 22, 24, AEs 10:9, 10, 11; 13:2, 4, 5, 6, 8, 11, 18; 14:5^{2}, 12, 19; 15:2, 6, 16; 16:8, 11, 22, Wis 5:9; 6:7^{2}; 7:3, 6, 9, 11, 12, 16, 23; 8:3; 11:23; 12:7, 16^{2}; 13:1, 11; 14:25; 15:7, 13, 14, 15; 16:7, 25; 17:17; 18:12; 19:22, Sir 1:1, 9, 10; 3:13; 6:26, 37; 7:33, 36; 8:5, 7; 9:15; 10:2; 12:5; 13:16, 23; 14:17; 15:13; 16:30; 17:4, 14, 20, 32; 18:13; 19:20^{2}; 21:3; 22:6, 12; 23:12, 15, 17, 19; 24:7, 23; 25:24; 26:4, 5, 6; 29:12; 30:15; 31:22; 33:7, 10, 13, 15, 17, 22; 35:5; 36:1, 2, 11, 17; 37:15, 20, 21, 24; 38:10, 29, 31; 39:1, 14, 19, 26, 27, 29, 33, 35; 40:1, 8, 10, 12; 41:3; 42:7, 8, 17, 18, 22, 23^{2}; 43:25, 27, 28; 44:7, 18, 23; 45:1, 4, 16; 46:10, 18; 47:8^{2}; 48:15^{2}; 49:4; 50:9, 13, 17, 22, Bar 1:3, 4^{2}, 7, 21; 2:4^{2}, 7, 9, 12, 15, 27^{2}; 3:7, 8; 4:1, LJr 1:51, Aza 1:4^{3}, 5^{2}, 8^{2}, 9, 14, 20, 21, 35, 38, 39, 42, 43, 57, 58, 59, 68, Sus 1:4, 6, 30, 33, 47, 50, 60, 63, Bel 1:5, 12, Man 1:2, 15, 1Mc 1:9, 21, 22, 24, 28, 41, 43, 49, 51; 2:11, 18, 19, 23, 37, 40, 41, 43, 67, 70; 3:2^{2}, 6, 27, 34, 36; 4:11, 15, 22, 26, 33, 37, 51, 55, 59; 5:5, 13, 15, 23, 25, 26, 27, 28, 38, 42, 43, 44, 45, 53, 63^{2}; 6:10, 12, 14, 19, 25, 28, 41, 43, 58, 59; 7:5, 6, 7^{2}, 18, 22, 23, 24, 46^{2}; 8:1, 14, 16^{2}, 24; 9:11, 14, 20, 23^{2}, 28, 33, 34, 36, 40, 58^{2}, 60, 63; 10:5, 7, 29, 33, 34^{3}, 36, 41, 43, 47, 64, 89; 11:26, 29, 34^{2}, 35, 38^{2}, 39, 43, 47, 51, 53, 55, 60, 70; 12:32, 43, 44, 45, 48, 49, 52^{2}, 53; 13:4, 6, 9, 10, 22, 26, 29, 34, 48, 53; 14:4^{2}, 5, 9, 14, 35, 43^{2}, 46, 47; 15:1, 5, 7, 9, 10, 23, 27, 36, 2Mc 1:3, 22, 26; 2:14, 17^{2}, 25; 3:3, 11, 20, 24^{2}, 28, 34; 4:5, 42; 5:8, 15, 20, 26; 7:31, 34; 8:2, 14, 20, 24, 31; 9:8, 15, 16, 21; 10:17; 11:9, 11, 15; 12:21, 40, 41; 13:4, 12, 23; 14:36, 38; 15:7, 11, 12, 17, 20, 34, 36, 3Mc 1:1, 11^{2}, 16, 27, 29; 2:2, 28, 30; 3:1, 6, 20; 4:11, 16, 18; 5:7^{2}, 21, 29; 6:2, 6, 8, 12, 15, 16, 18, 26, 30, 32, 39; 7:1, 4, 22, 4Mc 1:11, 14, 19, 25, 35; 2:16, 22; 3:9, 18; 4:1, 12, 24; 5:23, 24; 8:29; 9:18, 26, 28; 12:1, 8, 11; 13:13, 17; 14:5; 15:12; 16:25; 17:19, 24

all omnis

2Es 1:8, 10, 11^{2}; 2:42; 3:11, 21, 26; 4:38; 5:7, 9, 23, 24^{2}, 25^{2}, 26^{2}, 27^{2}; 6:20, 23, 25, 33, 54^{2}, 55; 7:6, 29, 42, 48, 65, 68, 70, 87, 98, 104, 117; 8:15, 41^{3}; 9:45; 10:2^{2}, 3, 7, 8^{2}, 10^{2}, 23; 11:2^{2}, 8, 12, 19, 32, 40^{2}; 12:13, 24, 31, 37, 40^{2}, 42; 13:2, 4, 8, 11^{2}, 33, 36; 14:27; 15:9, 11, 20, 26, 29, 40, 41^{2}, 44^{2}, 48, 57, 62; 16:18, 20, 32, 54, 64^{2}, 67

all *(Translator supplied)

Gen 10:10; 32:11; 33:2; 42:17; 47:15, 18, 20; 48:15, Lev 11:20, 21, 27; 19:7; 26:44, Num 11:32; 17:13; 23:25, Deu 12:25; 18:17; 33:5, Jos 21:40, Jdg 16:3, 30, 2Sm 14:14; 18:28, 1Kg 4:24; 6:5; 12:31; 13:33, 2Kg 5:21, 22; 9:11; 15:36; 17:32, 1Ch 16:32, 2Ch 20:23; 30:21, Est 3:12^{2}; 4:11, Job 9:22; 11:20; 15:20; 31:37; 40:13, Ps 145:10, 19, Prv 11:24; 22:18; 27:24, Ecc 2:21, Sng 4:13; 5:10, Jer 3:5, 19, 24; 5:5; 32:20; 36:6; 47:2; 50:37, 39, Lam 5:19, Ezk 24:21; 31:14; 32:15, 29, 30; 35:7; 36:5; 41:16, Dan 2:35; 6:3; 10:3, Hos 1:6; 4:2, Jol 2:2; 3:20, Mic 1:10, Nah 3:4, Mrk 6:2, Lke 14:17; 20:31, Joh 11:49; 16:1, Act 24:9, Rom 8:39, 1Co 4:6, 9, 2Co 3:10, Gal 6:16, Eph 5:19, 1Ti 6:11, Heb 8:4, 2Pe 1:20; 3:3, 1Jn 3:24, 2Es 5:45^{2}; 7:78, 91; 16:26, Tob 4:12, Jdt 2:28; 4:10; 8:22; 11:2, 4; 13:8; 14:5; 15:2, Wis 5:17; 15:18; 16:17; 17:14, Sir 16:27; 24:33; 27:23; 29:15; 44:14, 16; 45:15; 48:12, Bar 4:20, Man 1:15, 1Mc 8:23, 2Mc 2:23; 6:11; 7:41; 9:17, 3Mc 2:21; 3:19, 4Mc 1:30; 2:9; 18:2

all *See also* alike, along, any, day, diligence, disheveled, eternity, even, expectations, generations, go, gone, if, king, manner, means, men, merciful, most, nations, night, no, nothing, nourishing, once, one, open, other, others, oversee, powerful, put, seeing, sides, strongest, time, together, wise.

above all 1. *μάλιστα*

2Ti 4:13 also the books, and above all the parchments. 1

all around 1. סָבִיב 2. *κυκλόθεν*

Ps 78:28 let them fall . . all around their habitations. 1
Lam 2: 3 he has burned like . . consuming all around. 1
Ezk 40: 5 a wall all around the outside of the temple area 1
41: 6 There were offsets all around the wall 1
Rev 4: 8 creatures . . full of eyes all around and within 2
1Mc 6:62 and gave orders to tear down the wall all around. 2

at all 1. גַּם 2. *μηδαμῶς* 3. *οὐδείς*

Jer 6:15 No, they were not at all ashamed; 1
8:12 they were not at all ashamed; they did not know how 1
23:32 so they do not profit this people at all †
2Co 12:11 I was not at all inferior 3
2Mc 7:25 Since the young man would not listen to him at all 2

all at once 1. פִּתְאֹם

Prv 7:22 All at once he follows her, as an ox goes 1

do all 1. כלה

Exd 5:14 Why have you not done all your task of making 1

all in vain 1. *μάταιος*

4Mc 16: 7 O seven childbirths all in vain 1

all kinds 1. כֹּל 2. *πᾶς*

Exd 1:14 bitter . . in all kinds of work in the field; 1
2Ch 32:27 treasuries . . for all kinds of costly vessels; 1
28 stalls for all kinds of cattle, and sheepfolds. 1
Ps 45:13 with all kinds of wealth. •
Ezk 17:23 cedar; and under it will dwell all kinds of beasts; 2

all over 1. *ὅλος*

Joh 13:10 but he is clean all over 1

all round 1. סָבִיב

Num34:12 shall be your land with its boundaries all round 1
35: 4 wall of the city outward a 1,000 cubits all round. 1

all sorts 1. כֹּל 2. *παμμιγής* 3. *παντοῖος*

Gen 24:10 departed, taking all sorts of choice gifts 1
40:17 basket there were all sorts of baked food 1
2Ch 2:14 and to do all sorts of engraving and execute 1
2Mc 5: 3 and armor of all sorts. 3
12:13 and inhabited by all sorts of Gentiles 2
3Mc 5:22 in devising all sorts of insults 3
7:16 crowned with all sorts of very fragrant flowers 3
4Mc 1:34 all sorts of foods that are forbidden to us 3

all that fills 1. מְלֹא

Ps 96:11 let the sea roar, and all that fills it; 1
98: 7 Let the sea roar, and all that fills it; 1
Isa 34: 1 Let the earth listen, and all that fills it; 1
42:10 Let the sea roar and all that fills it 1
Jer 8:16 and devour the land and all that fills it 1

all the better 1. *μᾶλλον*

1Ti 6: 2 rather they must serve all the better 1

all the more 1. אָכֵן 2. *ἐπὶ πολύ* 3. *μᾶλλον* 4. *περισσοτέρως* 5. *περισσῶς* 6. *πολὺ πλέον*

Zep 3: 7 But all the more they were eager 1
Mat 27:23 they shouted all the more 5
Mrk 15:14 they shouted all the more, "Crucify him. 5
Joh 5:18 why the Jews sought all the more to kill him 3
Act 9:22 Saul increased all the more in strength 3
2Co 7:15 his heart goes out all the more to you 4
12: 9 I will all the more gladly boast of my weaknesses 3
3Mc 1: 8 he was all the more eager to visit them 3
5:17 to make . . joyful by celebrating all the more. 2
4Mc 2: 6 I could prove to you all the more 6
13:24 they loved one another all the more. 3

all the people 1. *ὄχλος*

2Mc 11: 6 they and all the people . . besought the Lord 1

all the way 1. *ἄχρι* 2. *ἕως*

2Sm 3:16 went . . weeping after her all the way to Bahu'rim. •
2Co 10:14 we were the first to come all the way to you 1
1Mc 5:29 they went all the way to the stronghold of Dathema. 2

all things 1. כֹּל 2. כֹּל (A) 3. *ἅπας* 4. *πᾶς* 5. omnis

Gen 24: 1 the LORD had blessed Abraham in all things. 1
Deu 28:47 by reason of the abundance of all things 1
48 serve your enemies . . in want of all things; 1
57 she will eat them secretly, for want of all things 1
Jos 1:17 we obeyed Moses in all things, so we will obey you; 1
2Sm 14:20 to know all things that are on the earth 1
23: 5 an everlasting covenant, ordered in all things 1
2Kg 14: 3 he did in all things as Jo'ash his father had done. 1
1Ch 29:14 For all things come from thee 1
Job 42: 2 I know that thou canst do all things 1
Ps 8: 6 thou hast put all things under his feet 1
119:91 all things are thy servants. 1
Isa 44:24 I am the LORD, who made all things 1
Jer 17: 9 The heart is deceitful above all things 1
51:19 for he is the one who formed all things 1
Dan 2:40 iron breaks to pieces and shatters all things; 2
Mat 11:27 All things have been delivered to me by my Father; 4
17:11 and he is to restore all things; 4
19:26 but with God all things are possible. 4
Mrk 7:37 He had done all things well 4
9:12 Eli'jah does come first to restore all things 4
23 All things are possible to him who believes. 4
10:27 for all things are possible with God. 4
13:23 take heed; I have told you all things beforehand. 4
14:36 Abba, Father, all things are possible to thee 4
Lke 1: 3 having followed all things closely for some time past 4
10:22 All things have been delivered to me by my Father; 4
Joh 1: 3 all things were made through him 4
3:35 and has given all things into his hand. 4
4:25 when he comes, he will show us all things. 3
13: 3 the Father had given all things into his hands 4
14:26 he will teach you all things 4
16:30 Now we know that you know all things 4
Act 2:44 and had all things in common; 3
20:35 In all things I have shown you 4
Rom 8:32 will he not also give us all things with him? 4
11:36 and through him and to him are all things. 4
1Co 2:15 The spiritual man judges all things 4
3:21 For all things are yours 4
4:13 the offscouring of all things. 4
6:12 All things are lawful for me 4
12 not all things are helpful 4
12 All things are lawful for me 4
8: 6 from whom are all things and for whom we exist 4
6 through whom are all things 4
9:22 I have become all things to all men 4
25 exercises self-control in all things 4
10:23 All things are lawful 4
23 not all things are helpful 4
23 All things are lawful 4
23 not all things build up. 4
11:12 And all things are from God.) 4
13: 7 Love bears all things, believes all things 4
7 Love bears all things, believes all things 4
7 hopes all things, endures all things. 4
7 hopes all things, endures all things. 4
14:26 Let all things be done for edification. 4
40 all things should be done decently and in order. 4
15:27 For God has put all things in subjection 4
27 All things are put in subjection under him 4
27 he is excepted who put all things under him. 4
28 When all things are subjected to him 4
28 be subjected to him who put all things under him 4
2Co 11: 6 made this plain to you in all things. 4
Gal 3:10 who does not abide by all things written 4
22 the scripture consigned all things to sin 4
Eph 1:10 to unite all things in him 4
11 the purpose of him who accomplishes all things 4
22 he has put all things under his feet 4
22 the head over all things for the church. 4
3: 9 hidden for ages in God who created all things; 4

4:10 that he might fill all things.) 4
Php 2:14 Do all things without grumbling or questioning 4
3: 8 I have suffered the loss of all things 4
21 even to subject all things to himself. 4
4:13 I can do all things in him who strengthens me. 4
Col 1:16 for in him all things were created 4
16 all things were created through him 4
17 He is before all things 4
17 in him all things hold together. 4
20 through him to reconcile to himself all things 4
2:22 referring to things which all perish 4
1Ti 3:11 temperate, faithful in all things. 4
6:13 God who gives life to all things 4
Tit 1:15 To the pure all things are pure 4
Heb 1: 2 a Son, whom he appointed the heir of all things 4
2:10 for whom and by whom all things exist 4
3: 4 but the builder of all things is God.) 4
13:18 desiring to act honorably in all things. 4
1Pe 4: 7 The end of all things is at hand; 4
2Pe 1: 3 His divine power has granted to us all things 4
3: 4 all things have continued as they were 4
Rev 4:11 for thou didst create all things 4
21: 5 Behold, I make all things new. 4
1Es 3:12 truth is victor over all things. 4
4:35 truth is great, and stronger than all things. 4
8:21 Let all things prescribed . . be . . fulfilled 4
2Es 8:44 and for whose sake thou hast formed all things 5
11: 6 I saw how all things under heaven were subjected 5
16:62 Almighty God; who made all things and searches 5
AEs 13: 9 O Lord, Lord, King who rulest over all things 4
12 Thou knowest all things; thou knowest, O Lord 4
14:15 Thou hast knowledge of all things 4
16:18 God, who rules over all things 4
21 God, who rules over all things 4
Wis 1: 7 that which holds all things together 4
10 because a jealous ear hears all things 4
14 For he created all things that they might exist 4
7:22 wisdom, the fashioner of all things, taught me 4
24 she pervades and penetrates all things. 4
27 Though she is but one, she can do all things 4
27 she renews all things 4
8: 1 she orders all things well. 4
5 what is richer than wisdom who effects all things? 4
9: 1 who hast made all things by thy word 4
11 For she knows and understands all things 4
10: 2 and gave him strength to rule all things. 3
11:20 thou hast arranged all things by measure 4
23 thou canst do all things 4
24 For thou lovest all things that exist 4
26 Thou sparest all things, for they are thine 4
12: 1 For thy immortal spirit is in all things. 4
15 Thou . . rulest all things righteously 4
15: 1 patient, and ruling all things in mercy. 4
16:17 in the water, which quenches all things 4
18:14 For while gentle silence enveloped all things 4
16 and stood and filled all things with death 4
Sir 1: 4 Wisdom was created before all things 4
17:30 For all things cannot be in men 4
18:26 all things move swiftly before the Lord. 4
24: 8 the Creator of all things gave me a commandment 3
39:16 All things are the works of the Lord 4
17 in God's time all things will be sought after 4
34 all things will prove good in their season. 4
40:11 All things that are from the earth 4
42:24 All things are twofold, one opposite the other 4
43:22 A mist quickly heals all things 4
26 by his word all things hold together. 4
33 For the Lord has made all things 4
50:29 he will be strong for all things 4
Bar 3:32 he who knows all things knows her, he found her 4
Aza 1: 6 and have sinned in all things 4
54 Bless the Lord, all things that grow on the earth 4
Sus 1:42 who art aware of all things before they come to be 4
Man 1: 4 at whom all things shudder 4
2Mc 1:24 O Lord, Lord God, Creator of all things 4
7:23 and devised the origin of all things 4
12:22 who sees all things 4
15: 2 he who sees all things 4
3Mc 2: 3 the creator of all things and the governor of all 4
21 God, who oversees all things 4
5:28 This was the act of God who rules over all things 4
7:18 the king had generously provided all things to them 4
4Mc 11: 5 Is it because we revere the Creator of all things 4

all this 1. *τοσοῦτος*
Rev 18:17 In one hour all this wealth has been laid waste. 1

allege 1. *φάσκω*
3Mc 3: 7 alleging that these people were loyal 1

allegiance 1. יָד 2. מִשְׁמֶרֶת
1Ch 12:29 kept their allegiance to the house of Saul. 2
29:24 pledged their allegiance to King Solomon. 1
allegiance *See also* swear.

allegorically 1. *πνευματικῶς*
Rev 11: 8 city which is allegorically called Sodom 1

allegory 1. מָשָׁל 2. *ἀλληγορέω*
Ezk 17: 2 propound a riddle, and speak an allegory 1
20:49 saying of me, 'Is he not a maker of allegories? 1
24: 3 utter an allegory to the rebellious house 1
Gal 4:24 Now this is an allegory 2
allegory *See also* speak.

alliance 1. *συμμαχία*
1Mc 8:17 to Rome to establish friendship and alliance 1
20 sent us to you to establish alliance and peace 1
22 as a memorial of peace and alliance 1
12: 3 to renew the former friendship and alliance 1
8 a clear declaration of alliance and friendship. 1
16 our former friendship and alliance with them. 1
14:18 to renew with him the friendship and alliance 1
24 to confirm the alliance with the Romans. 1
15:17 to renew our ancient friendship and alliance. 1
2Mc 4:11 friendship and alliance with the Romans 1
3Mc 3:21 both because of their alliance with us 1
alliance *See also* make.

alliance in battle 1. *συμμαχία*
3Mc 3:14 by the gods' deliberate alliance with us in battle 1

allot 1. גּוֹרָל 2. היה 3. חֶבֶל 4. חלק 5. נחל 6. נפל 7. *κληροδοτέω* 8. *λαγχάνω* 9. *μερίζω* 10. *μερίς* 11. *προστάσσω* 12. *τάσσω*
Deu 4:19 LORD your God has allotted to all the peoples 4
29:26 worshiped them, gods . . not allotted to them; 4
32: 9 LORD'S portion . . Jacob his allotted heritage. 3
Jos 13: 6 only allot the land to Israel for an inheritance 6
29 it was allotted . . according to their families. 2
31 were allotted . . according to their families. •
14: 5 as the LORD commanded . . they allotted the land. 4
17: 1 To Machir . . were allotted Gilead and Bashan •
6 Gilead was allotted to the . . Manas'sites. •
18:11 the territory allotted to it fell between 1
21:20 cities allotted to them were out of . . E'phraim. •
40 As for the cities . . those allotted to them were •
23: 4 I have allotted . . those nations that remain 6
1Ch 6:62 Gershomites . . were allotted thirteen cities •
63 the Merar'ites . . were allotted twelve cities •
77 were allotted out of the tribe of Zeb'ulun •
26:15 and to his sons was allotted the storehouse. •
Neh 9:22 didst allot to them every corner; 4
Job 7: 3 I am allotted months of emptiness 5
Ezk 45: 1 When you allot the land as a possession 6
47:22 You shall allot it as an inheritance 6
22 with you they shall be allotted an inheritance 6
48:29 the land which you shall allot as an inheritance 6
Act 1:17 allotted his share in this ministry. 8
17:26 having determined allotted periods 11
Sir 11:18 this is the reward allotted to him 10
17:11 allotted to them the law of life. 7
45:20 he allotted to him the first of the first fruits 9
2Mc 8:27 allotted it to them as the beginning of mercy. 12

allotment 1. גּוֹרָל 2. מַחֲלֹקֶת
Jos 11:23 gave . . according to their tribal allotments. 2
12: 7 Joshua gave . . according to their allotments 2
16: 1 The allotment of . . Joseph went from the Jordan 1
17: 1 Then allotment was made to the tribe of Manas'seh 1
2 And allotments were made to the rest of the tribe •
Ezk 48:10 shall be the allotments of the holy portion •
10 the priests shall have an allotment measuring •
13 Levites shall have an allotment 25,000 cubits •
allotted *See* land, portion, territory, time.

allotted place 1. גּוֹרָל
Dan 12:13 stand in your allotted place at the end 1

allow 1. נוח 2. נתן 3. *ἀφίημι* 4. *δίδωμι* 5. *ἐάω* 6. *ἔξεστι* 7. *ἐξίημι* 8. *ἐπιτρέπω* 9. *συγχωρέω* 10. *συγχωρητέον* 11. *χορηγέω* 12. patior
Gen 30:27 Laban said to him, "If you will allow me to say so •
Exd 12:23 will not allow the destroyer to enter 2
Num21:23 Sihon would not allow Israel to pass through 2
Deu 18:14 LORD your God has not allowed you so to do. 2
Jdg 1:34 they did not allow them to come down to the plain; 2
3:28 Moabites, and allowed not a man to pass over. 2
15: 1 But her father would not allow him to go in. 2
2Sm 21:10 she did not allow the birds of the air to come upon 2
2Kg 10:24 man who allows any . . to escape shall forfeit •
1Ch 16:21 he allowed no one to oppress them; 1
Est 8:11 the king allowed the Jews . . to gather and defend 2
9:13 let the Jews . . be allowed tomorrow also to do 2
Ps 105:14 he allowed no one to oppress them; 1
Dan 1: 8 asked . . to allow him not to defile himself. •
Mat 19: 8 Moses allowed you to divorce your wives 8
20:15 Am I not allowed to do what I choose 6
23:13 nor allow those who would enter to go in. 3
Mrk 5:37 he allowed no one to follow him except Peter 3
10: 4 Moses allowed a man to write a certificate 8
11:16 he would not allow any one to carry anything 3
Lke 4:41 would not allow them to speak 5
Act 14:16 allowed all the nations to walk in their own ways; 5
16: 7 the Spirit of Jesus did not allow them; 5
28: 4 justice has not allowed him to live. 5
16 Paul was allowed to stay by himself 8
Rev 9: 5 were allowed to torture them for five months 4
13: 5 allowed to exercise authority for . . months; 4
7 Also it was allowed to make war on the saints 4
14 and by the signs which it is allowed to work 4
15 allowed to give breath to the image of the beast 4
16: 8 and it was allowed to scorch men with fire; 4
2Es 15:10 I will not allow them to live any longer 12
Sir 18:31 If you allow your soul to take pleasure 11
25:25 Allow no outlet to water 4
2Mc 2:31 the one . . should be allowed to strive for brevity 10
11:24 and ask that their own customs be allowed them. 9
3Mc 1:11 were allowed to enter 7
5:18 why the Jews had been allowed to remain alive 5

allow to escape 1. *ἀπολύω*
Sir 27:19 as you allow a bird to escape from your hand 1

allow to go 1. *προσεάω*
Act 27: 7 and as the wind did not allow us to go on 1

allow to take 1. *χορηγέω*
Sir 18:31 allow your soul to take pleasure in base desire 1

allowance 1. אֲרֻחָה 2. חֹק
Gen 47:22 priests . . lived on the allowance 2
1Kg 11:18 and assigned him an allowance of food •
2Kg 25:30 for his allowance, a regular allowance was given 1
30 a regular allowance was given him by the king 1
Jer 40: 5 So the captain of the guard gave him an allowance 1
52:34 for his allowance, a regular allowance was given 1
34 a regular allowance was given him by the king 1

fixed allowance 1. חֹק
Gen 47:22 the priests had a fixed allowance from Pharaoh 1

food allowance 1. לֶחֶם
Neh 5:14 neither . . ate the food allowance of the governor. 1
18 not demand the food allowance of the governor 1

alloy 1. בְּדִיל
Isa 1:25 smelt away your dross . . and remove all your alloy. 1

allure 1. סות 2. פתה
Job 36:16 He also allured you out of distress 1
Hos 2:14 Therefore, behold, I will allure her, and bring her 2

ally 1. אִישׁ בְּרִית 2. בַּעַל בְּרִית 3. חבר 4. *λαός ἐπὶ τὴν συμμαχίαν* 5. *συμμαχέω* 6. *συμμαχία* 7. *συμμάχομαι* 8. *σύμμαχος* 9. complector
Gen 14:13 of Eshcol and of Aner; these were allies of Abram. 2
Ps 94:20 Can wicked rulers be allied with thee 3
Hos 8:10 Though they hire allies among the nations •
Obd 1: 7 All your allies have deceived you 1
2Es 11:30 I saw how it allied the two heads with itself 9
Jdt 3: 6 took picked men from them as his allies. 6
7: 1 all the allies who had joined him 4
1Mc 8:20 we may be enrolled as your allies and friends. 8
24 any of their allies in all their dominion 8
28 to the enemy allies shall be given no grain, arms 8
31 made your yoke heavy upon our friends and allies 8
9:60 secretly sent letters to all his allies in Judea 8
10: 6 to become his ally 8
16 Come now, we will make him our friend and ally. 8
47 they remained his allies all his days. 5
11:60 all the army of Syria gathered to him as allies. 6
12:14 annoy you and our other allies and friends 8
14:40 friends and allies and brethren 8
15:17 as our friends and allies 8
2Mc 8:24 With the Almighty as their ally, they 7
11:10 having their heavenly ally 8
12:36 their ally and leader in the battle. 8

almighty 1. שַׁדַּי 2. *παγκρατής* 3. *παντοκράτωρ* 4. fortis 5. omnipotens
Gen 17: 1 I am God Almighty; walk before me, and be blameless. 1
28: 3 God Almighty bless you and make you fruitful 1
35:11 God said to him, "I am God Almighty 1
43:14 may God Almighty grant you mercy before the man 1
48: 3 Jacob said to Joseph, "God Almighty appeared 1
49:25 by God Almighty who will bless you 1
Exd 6: 3 I appeared . . as God Almighty, but by my name 1
Num24: 4 oracle of . . who sees the vision of the Almighty 1
16 who sees the vision of the Almighty 1
Rut 1:20 the Almighty has dealt very bitterly with me. 1
21 and the Almighty has brought calamity upon me? 1
Job 5:17 despise not the chastening of the Almighty. 1
6: 4 For the arrows of the Almighty are in me; 1
14 forsakes the fear of the Almighty. 1
8: 3 Or does the Almighty pervert the right? 1
5 seek God and make supplication to the Almighty 1
11: 7 Can you find out the limit of the Almighty? 1
13: 3 But I would speak to the Almighty 1
15:25 against God, and bids defiance to the Almighty 1
21:15 What is the Almighty, that we should serve him? 1
20 let them drink of the wrath of the Almighty. 1
22: 3 pleasure to the Almighty if you are righteous 1

17 and 'What can the Almighty do to us?' 1
23 you return to the Almighty and humble yourself 1
25 if the Almighty is your gold 1
26 then you will delight yourself in the Almighty 1
23:16 the Almighty has terrified me; 1
24: 1 are not times of judgment kept by the Almighty 1
27: 2 the Almighty, who has made my soul bitter; 1
10 Will he take delight in the Almighty? 1
11 what is with the Almighty I will not conceal. 1
13 which oppressors receive from the Almighty 1
29: 5 when the Almighty was yet with me 1
31: 2 my heritage from the Almighty on high? 1
35 Here is my signature! let the Almighty answer me! 1
32: 8 the spirit in a man, the breath of the Almighty 1
33: 4 the breath of the Almighty gives me life. 1
34:10 from the Almighty that he should do wrong. 1
12 the Almighty will not pervert justice. 1
35:13 an empty cry, nor does the Almighty regard it. 1
37:23 The Almighty-we cannot find him; he is great 1
40: 2 Shall a faultfinder contend with the Almighty? 1
Ps 68:14 When the Almighty scattered kings there 1
91: 1 who abides in the shadow of the Almighty 1
Isa 13: 6 as destruction from the Almighty it will come! 1
Ezk 1:24 many waters, like the thunder of the Almighty 1
10: 5 like the voice of God Almighty when he speaks. 1
Jol 1:15 and as destruction from the Almighty it comes. 1
2Co 6:18 be my sons and daughters, says the Lord Almighty. 3
Rev 1: 8 who is and who was and who is to come, the Almighty. 3
4: 8 sing, "Holy, holy, holy, is the Lord God Almighty 3
11:17 saying, "We give thanks to thee, Lord God Almighty 3
15: 3 wonderful are thy deeds, O Lord God the Almighty! 3
16: 7 I heard the altar cry, "Yea, Lord God the Almighty 3
14 for battle on the great day of God the Almighty. 3
19: 6 For the Lord our God the Almighty reigns. 3
15 of the fury of the wrath of God the Almighty. 3
21:22 for its temple is the Lord God the Almighty 3
1Es 9:46 God Most High, the God of hosts, the Almighty; 3
2Es 1:15 Thus says the Lord Almighty 5
22 Thus says the Lord Almighty 5
28 Thus says the Lord Almighty 5
33 Thus says the Lord Almighty 5
2: 9 So will I do to those . . says the Lord Almighty. 5
31 for I am merciful, says the Lord Almighty. 5
13:23 who have works and have faith in the Almighty. 4
16:62 the spirit of Almighty God 5
Jdt 4:13 before the sanctuary of the Lord Almighty. 3
8:13 You are putting the Lord Almighty to the test 3
15:10 May the Almighty Lord bless you for ever! 3
16: 6 the Lord Almighty has foiled them 3
17 The Lord Almighty will take vengeance on them 3
Wis 7:25 a pure emanation of the glory of the Almighty; 3
Sir 42:17 which the Lord the Almighty has established 3
50:14 the offering to the Most High, the Almighty 3
17 to worship their Lord, the Almighty, God Most High. 3
Bar 3: 1 'O Lord Almighty, God of Israel, the soul in anguish 3
4 O Lord Almighty, God of Israel, hear now the prayer 3
Man 1: 1 O Lord Almighty, God of our fathers, of Abraham 3
2Mc 1:25 who alone art just and almighty and eternal 3
3:22 While they were calling upon the Almighty Lord 2
30 now that the Almighty Lord had appeared. 3
5:20 what was forsaken in the wrath of the Almighty 3
6:26 I shall not escape the hands of the Almighty. 3
7:35 the judgment of the almighty, all-seeing God. 3
38 to bring to an end the wrath of the Almighty 3
8:11 not expecting the judgment from the Almighty 3
18 we trust in the Almighty God 3
24 With the Almighty as their ally, they 3
15: 8 the victory which the Almighty would give them. 3
32 the holy house of the Almighty; 3
3Mc 2: 2 holy among the holy ones, the only ruler, almighty 3
8 they praised you, the Almighty. 3
5: 7 they all called upon the Almighty Lord 3
6: 2 Almighty God Most High 3
18 the most glorious, almighty, and true God 3
28 the sons of the almighty and living God of heaven 3

almond 1. לוז 2. שָׁקֵד
Gen 30:37 took fresh rods of poplar and almond and plane 1
43:11 honey, gum, myrrh, pistachio nuts, and almonds. 2
Jer 1:11 And I said, "I see a rod of almond. 2
almond *See also* make.

ripe almond 1. שָׁקֵד
Num17: 8 rod of Aaron . . had sprouted . . bore ripe almonds. 1

almond tree 1. שָׁקֵד
Ecc 12: 5 the almond tree blossoms, the grasshopper drags 1

almost 1. כִּמְעַט 2. מְעַט 3. *μέλλω* 4. *σχεδόν* 5. paene
Exd 17: 4 this people? They are almost ready to stone me. 2
Ps 73: 2 But as for me, my feet had almost stumbled 1
119:87 They have almost made an end of me on earth; 1
Act 13:44 almost the whole city gathered together 4
19:26 almost throughout all Asia 4
21:27 When the seven days were almost completed 3
Heb 9:22 almost everything is purified with blood 4
2Es 7:48 but almost all who have been created! 5
10:10 and behold, almost all go to perdition 5
2Mc 5: 2 over all the city, for almost 40 days 4

alms 1. *ἐλεημοσύνη*
Mat 6: 2 Thus, when you give alms, sound no trumpet before 1
3 when you give alms, do not let your left hand know 1
4 that your alms may be in secret; and your Father 1
Lke 11:41 give for alms those things which are within; 1
12:33 Sell your possessions, and give alms 1
Act 3: 2 to ask alms of those who entered the temple. 1
3 he asked for alms. 1
10 the one who sat for alms at the Beautiful Gate 1
10: 2 gave alms liberally to the people 1
4 Your prayers and your alms have ascended 1
31 your alms have been remembered before God. 1
24:17 I came to bring to my nation alms and offerings. 1
Tob 4: 7 Give alms from your possessions 1
12: 8 It is better to give alms than to treasure up gold. 1
14: 2 He gave alms, and he continued to fear the Lord God 1
10 Ahikar gave alms and escaped the deathtrap 1
Sir 7:10 nor neglect to give alms. 1
12: 3 to him who does not give alms. 1
29: 8 do not make him wait for your alms. 1
35: 2 he who gives alms sacrifices a thank offering. 1

almsgiving 1. *ἐλεημοσύνη*
Tob 12: 8 fasting, almsgiving, and righteousness 1
9 For almsgiving delivers from death 1
14:11 consider what almsgiving accomplishes 1
Sir 3:30 so almsgiving atones for sin. 1
17:22 A man's almsgiving is like a signet with the Lord 1
29:12 Store up almsgiving in your treasury 1
40:17 almsgiving endures for ever. 1
24 almsgiving rescues better than both. 1

almug 1. אַלְמֻגִּים
1Kg 10:11 from Ophir a very great amount of almug wood 1
12 the king made of the almug wood supports 1
12 no such almug wood has come or been seen, to this day 1

aloe 1. אֲהָלוֹת 2. *ἄλοη*
Num24: 6 like aloes that the LORD has planted 1
Ps 45: 8 all fragrant with myrrh and aloes and cassia. 1
Prv 7:17 perfumed my bed with myrrh, aloes, and cinnamon. 1
Sng 4:14 with all trees of frankincense, myrrh and aloes 1
Joh 19:39 came bringing a mixture of myrrh and aloes 2

aloft 1. קוֹמָה 2. רום
Ezk 19:11 it towered aloft among the thick boughs; 1
Zec 14:10 But Jerusalem shall remain aloft upon its site 2
aloft *See also* soar.

alone 1. אֶחָד 2. אִישׁ אֶחָד 3. אַךְ 4. בְּגַף 5. בדד 6. בָּדָד 7. יַחַד 8. יַחְדָּו 9. לְבַד 10. לְבָדָד 11. רַק 12. רַק לְבַד 13. *εἰμί* 14. *εἷς* 15. *ἔρημος* 16. *κατὰ μόνας* 17. *μόνος* 18. *παρά* 19. solus
Gen 2:18 not good that the man should be alone; 9
32:24 Jacob was left alone; and a man wrestled with him 9
44:20 and he alone is left of his mother's children; 9
47:26 the land of the priests alone did not become 9
Exd 18:14 Why do you sit alone, and all the people stand 9
18 you are not able to perform it alone. 9
21: 4 be her master's and he shall go out alone. 4
24: 2 Moses alone shall come near to the LORD; 9
Lev 13:46 he shall dwell alone in a habitation outside 6
Num11:14 I am not able to carry all this people alone 9
17 that you may not bear it yourself alone. 9
23: 9 lo, a people dwelling alone 10
Deu 1: 9 I said to you, 'I am not able alone to bear you; 9
12 How can I bear alone the weight and burden of you 9
8: 3 man does not live by bread alone 9
32:12 LORD alone did lead him, and there was no foreign 6
33:28 Israel dwelt . . the fountain of Jacob alone 6
Jos 13:12 he alone was left of the remnant of the Reph'aim •
14 To the tribe of Levi alone Moses gave no 11
22:20 And he did not perish alone for his iniquity. 2
Jdg 3:20 as he was sitting alone in his cool roof chamber. 9
6:37 if there is dew on the fleece alone, and it is dry 9
1Sm 21: 1 Why are you alone, and no one with you? •
25:24 Upon me alone, my lord, be the guilt; •
2Sm 13:32 Amnon alone is dead, for by the command of Ab'salom 9
33 for Amnon alone is dead. 9
18:24 when he . . looked, he saw a man running alone. 9
25 If he is alone, there are tidings in his mouth. 9
26 watchman . . said, "See, another man running alone! 9
20:21 give up him alone, and I will withdraw 9
1Kg 3:18 we were alone; there was no one else with us 8
11:29 the two of them were alone in the open country. 9
2Kg 19:15 O LORD . . thou art the God, thou alone, of all 9
19 know that thou, O LORD, art God alone. 9
1Ch 29: 1 Solomon my son, whom alone God has chosen, is young 1
Ezr 4: 3 we alone will build to the LORD, the God of Israel 7
Neh 9: 6 Thou art the LORD, thou alone; thou hast made 9
Est 3: 6 But he disdained to lay hands on Mor'decai alone. 9
Job 1:15 I alone have escaped to tell you. 12
16 I alone have escaped to tell you. 12
17 I alone have escaped to tell you. 12
19 I alone have escaped to tell you. 12
9: 8 who alone stretched out the heavens 9
15:19 to whom alone the land was given 9
31:17 or have eaten my morsel alone 9
Ps 4: 8 for thou alone, O LORD, makest me dwell in safety. 10
62: 1 For God alone my soul waits in silence; 3
5 For God alone my soul waits in silence 3
71:16 I will praise thy righteousness, thine alone. 9
72:18 God of Israel, who alone does wondrous things. 9
83:18 them know that thou alone, whose name is the LORD 9
86:10 thou alone art God. 9
136: 4 to him who alone does great wonders 9
148:13 name of the LORD, for his name alone is exalted; 9
Prv 5:17 Let them be for yourself alone 9
9:12 if you scoff, you alone will bear it. 9
Ecc 4:10 but woe to him who is alone when he falls 1
11 they are warm; but how can one be warm alone? •
12 a man might prevail against one who is alone •
7:29 this alone I found, that God made man upright 9
Isa 2:11 the LORD alone will be exalted in that day. 9
17 the LORD alone will be exalted in that day. 9
5: 8 you are made to dwell alone in . . the land. 9
26:13 ruled over us, but thy name alone we acknowledge. 9
37:16 thou art the God, thou alone, of all the kingdoms 9
20 the earth may know that thou alone art the LORD. 9
44:24 the LORD . . who stretched out the heavens alone 9
49:21 I was left alone; whence then have these come?' 9
63: 3 I have trodden the wine press alone 9
Jer 15:17 I sat alone, because thy hand was upon me 6
49:31 that has no gates or bars, that dwells alone. 6
Lam 3:28 Let him sit alone in silence when he has laid it 6
Ezk 9: 8 And while they were smiting, and I was left alone •
14:16 they alone would be delivered 9
18 but they alone would be delivered. 9
40:46 sons of Zadok, who alone among the sons of Levi may •
Dan 10: 7 I, Daniel, alone saw the vision, 9
8 I was left alone and saw this great vision 9
Hos 8: 9 gone up to Assyria, a wild ass wandering alone; 5
Mic 7:14 dwell alone in a forest in the midst of a garden 10
Mat 4: 4 written, 'Man shall not live by bread alone 17
14:23 When evening came, he was there alone 17
18:15 tell him his fault, between you and him alone 17
Mrk 2: 7 Who can forgive sins but God alone? 14
4:10 when he was alone 16
6:47 he was alone on the land. 17
10:18 Why do you call me good? No one is good but God alone 14
Lke 4: 4 It is written, 'Man shall not live by bread alone.' 17
9:18 Now it happened that as he was praying alone 16
36 when the voice had spoken, Jesus was found alone. 17
10:40 my sister has left me to serve alone 17
18:19 No one is good but God alone. 14
Joh 6:22 his disciples had gone away alone. 17
8: 9 Jesus was left alone with the woman 17
16 it is not I alone that judge, but I and he who sent me. 17
29 who sent me is with me; he has not left me alone 17
12:24 it remains alone 17
16:32 will leave me alone 17
32 yet I am not alone, for the Father is with me. 17
Rom 4:23 the words . . were written not for his sake alone 17
11: 3 and I alone am left, and they seek my life. 17
Gal 6: 4 then his reason to boast will be in himself alone 17
1Th 3: 1 we were willing to be left behind at Athens alone 17
1Ti 6:16 who alone has immortality 17
2Ti 4:11 Luke alone is with me 17
Jas 2:24 justified by works and not by faith alone. 17
Rev 15: 4 O Lord? For thou alone art holy. 17
1Es 5:71 for we alone will build it for the Lord of Israel 17
8:25 Blessed be the Lord alone 17
2Es 7:44 and to you alone have I shown these things. 19
118 the fall was not yours alone, but ours also 19
8: 7 For thou alone dost exist 19
12:36 you alone were worthy to learn this secret 19
42 For of all the prophets you alone are left to us 19
13:53 And you alone have been enlightened about this 19
Tob 1: 6 I alone went often to Jerusalem for the feasts 17
8: 4 When the door was shut and the two were alone •
6 It is not good that the man should be alone 17
Jdt 5: 4 they alone, of all who live in the west 18
9:14 no other . . but thou alone! •
13: 2 Judith was left alone in the tent 17
AEs 13: 5 it alone, stands constantly in opposition 17
14: 3 help me, who am alone and have no helper but thee 17
14 save us by thy hand, and help me, who am alone 17
Wis 10: 1 when he alone had been created 17
17:21 over those men alone heavy night was spread 17
Sir 18: 2 the Lord alone will be declared righteous. 17
24: 5 Alone I have made the circuit 17
34 Observe that I have not labored for myself alone 17
33:17 I have not labored for myself alone 17
46: 8 these two alone were preserved 13
Sus 1:14 a time when they could find her alone. 17
36 As we were walking in the garden alone 17
Bel 1:14 in the presence of the king alone 17
1Mc 6:25 not against us alone 17
13: 4 I alone am left. 17
2Mc 1:24 who alone art King and art kind 17
25 who alone art bountiful 17
25 who alone art just and almighty and eternal 17
7:37 to make you confess that he alone is God 17
8:35 and made his way alone like a runaway slave 15

15:39 For just as it is harmful to drink wine alone 16
39 again, to drink water alone •
4Mc 7:18 these alone are able to control the passions 17
9:18 sons of the Hebrews alone are invincible 17
15:17 O woman, who alone gave birth 17
16:10 a widow and alone, with many sorrows. 17

alone *See also* leave, let.

along 1. אֶל 2. בְּ 3. בְּתוֹךְ 4. הלך 5. וְ 6. וְעַל 7. לְעֻמַּת 8. עבר 9. עַל 10. עַל יַד 11. עִם 12. *ἅμα* 13. *ἐν* 14. *ἐπί* 15. *καί* 16. *κατά* 17. *κατὰ πρόσωπον* 18. *μετά* 19. *παρά* 20. *σύν* 21. cum

Gen 21:14 putting it on her shoulder, along with the child 5
Exd 13:21 pillar of cloud to lead them along the way •
Lev 14:12 offer it . . along with the log of oil 5
31 a burnt offering, along with a cereal offering 9
51 the scarlet stuff, along with the living bird 5
Num 1:47 by their ancestral tribe along with them. •
13:29 Canaanites dwell by the sea, and along the Jordan. 10
34: 3 from the wilderness of Zin along the side of Edom 9
Jos 2:22 for the pursuers had made search all along the way 2
9: 1 the lowland all along the coast of the Great Sea 2
15: 3 goes up south of Ka'desh-bar'nea, along by Hezron 8
17: 4 give us an inheritance along with our brethren. 3
6 daughters . . received . . along with his sons. 3
7 then the boundary goes along southward •
21: 2 cities . . along with their pasture lands 5
11 They gave . . along with the pasture lands 5
23: 4 I have allotted . . along with all the nations 5
Jdg 7:12 Mid'ianites . . lay along the valley 2
9:25 they robbed all who passed by them along that way; 2
1Sm 1:24 she took him up . . along with a three-year-old bull 2
6:12 the cows went straight . . along one highway 2
18:27 David arose and went, along with his men 5
1Ch 4:33 along with all their villages 5
7: 4 along with them . . were units of the army 6
29 also along the borders of the Manas'sites 9
25: 7 The number of them along with their brethren 11
Ezr 3: 9 along with the sons of Hen'adad and the Levites •
Prv 7: 8 passing along the street near her corner 2
27:22 fool in a mortar . . along with crushed grain 3
Isa 3:16 mincing along as they go, tinkling with . . feet; 4
49: 9 They shall feed along the ways, on all bare 9
Ezk 1:20 they went, and the wheels rose along with them; 7
21 from the earth, the wheels rose along with them; 7
40:18 the pavement ran along the side of the gates 1
47: 6 Then he led me back along the bank of the river. •
18 along the Jordan between Gilead and the land •
19 thence along the Brook of Egypt to the Great Sea. †
48:28 thence along the Brook of Egypt to the Great Sea. •
Mat 13: 4 as he sowed, some seeds fell along the path 19
19 this is what was sown along the path. 19
29 you root up the wheat along with them. 12
15:29 and passed along the Sea of Galilee 19
22:16 disciples to him, along with the Hero'dians 18
Mrk 4: 4 as he sowed, some seed fell along the path 19
15 the ones along the path, where the word is sown; 19
Lke 8: 5 as he sowed, some fell along the path 19
12 The ones along the path are those who have heard; 19
9:57 As they were going along the road, a man said to him 13
Act 8:36 as they went along the road 16
21:24 purify yourself along with them •
23:15 You therefore, along with the council •
1Co 11:32 may not be condemned along with the world. 20
2Ti 2:22 along with those who call upon the Lord 18
2Es 3:22 the law . . along with the evil root 21
Jdt 1: 6 all those who lived along the Euphrates •
7 all who lived along the seacoast 17
2:23 the Ishmaelites who lived along the desert 17
24 all the hilltop cities along the brook Abron 14
28 the people who lived along the seacoast •
6: 8 will not die until you perish along with them. 18
9: 3 thou didst strike down slaves along with princes 14
Wis 7:11 All good things came to me along with her 18
10:17 she guided them along a marvelous way 13
Sir 2:12 Woe . . to the sinner who walks along two ways! 14
1Mc 6:33 and took his army by a forced march along the road 16
11: 4 they had piled them in heaps along his route. 13
12:50 been seized and had perished along with his men 15
15:41 go out and make raids along the highways of Judea •
3Mc 5:47 he . . rushed out in full force along with the beasts 20
4Mc 4:25 women . . along with their infants 18
8: 3 seven brothers . . along with their aged mother 18

along *See also* carry, coast, drag, enter, go, lead, move, pass, ride, sail, sit, take, walk.

all along 1. עַד הֵנָּה 2. *πάλαι*

1Sm 1:16 for all along I have been speaking out of . . anxiety 1
2Co 12:19 Have you been thinking all along 2

along the border 1. *παράκειμαι*

2Mc 9:25 the princes along the borders 1

along the coast 1. *κατά*

Act 27: 2 about to sail to the ports along the coast of Asia 1

along toward 1. *πρός*

Jdt 12: 5 Along toward the morning watch she arose 1

along with 1. בְּתוֹךְ 2. עַל

Jer 40: 1 bound in chains along with all the captives 1
Ezk 25:10 I will give it along with the Ammonites 2

alongside 1. אֶל פָּנִים 2. לְעֻמַּת 3. *παρά*

Ezk 45: 6 Alongside the portion set apart as the holy 2
7 alongside the holy district and the property 1
48:13 alongside the territory of the priests 2
18 of the length alongside the holy portion 2
18 it shall be alongside the holy portion. 2
1Mc 13:52 the temple hill alongside the citadel 3

aloof 1. מִנֶּגֶד 2. *ἐξ ἀναντίας*

2Sm 18:13 then you yourself would have stood aloof. 1
Ps 38:11 companions stand aloof from my plague 1
Obd 1:11 On the day that you stood aloof 1
Sir 37: 9 then stand aloof to see what will happen to you. 2

aloof *See also* keep.

aloud 1. בְּגָרוֹן 2. בְּקוֹל 3. בְּקוֹל גָּדוֹל 4. דמם 5. נשא קוֹל 6. נתן קוֹל 7. פֶּה 8. קוֹל 9. קוֹל גָּדוֹל 10. בְּחַיִל (A) 11. *λέγω* 12. *φωνή* 13. cum sono

Gen 29:11 Then Jacob kissed Rachel, and wept aloud. 5
45: 2 he wept aloud, so that the Egyptians heard it 6
Jdg 9: 7 he . . and cried aloud and said to them, "Listen to me 5
1Sm 11: 4 they reported . . and all the people wept aloud. 5
2Sm 15:23 all the country wept aloud as . . people passed by 9
1Kg 18:27 Cry aloud, for he is a god; either he is musing 3
28 they cried aloud, and cut themselves 3
Ps 3: 4 I cry aloud to the LORD, and he answers me 8
26: 7 singing aloud a song of thanksgiving 2
27: 7 Hear, O LORD, when I cry aloud, be gracious to me 8
66:17 I cried aloud to him, and he was extolled 7
77: 1 I cry aloud to God, aloud to God, that he may hear me. 8
1 I cry aloud to God, aloud to God, that he may hear me. 8
Isa 58: 1 Cry aloud, spare not, lift up your voice 1
Lam 2:18 Cry aloud to the Lord! O daughter of Zion! •
Ezk 24:17 Sigh, but not aloud; make no mourning for the dead. 4
27:30 and wail aloud over you, and cry bitterly. 8
Dan 3: 4 herald proclaimed aloud, "You are commanded 10
4:14 cried aloud and said thus, 'Hew down the tree 10
5: 7 king cried aloud to bring in the enchanters 10
Mat 9:27 two blind men followed him, crying aloud 11
Rev 18:15 fear of her torment, weeping and mourning aloud 11
1Es 9:41 he read aloud in the open square before the gate •
2Es 6:23 the trumpet shall sound aloud 13
1Mc 3:50 they cried aloud to Heaven, saying 12

aloud *See also* call, cry, groan, read, shout, sing.

already 1. גַּם 2. יֵשׁ 3. כְּבָר 4. עַתָּה 5. *ἔτι* 6. *ἤδη* 7. *πάλαι* 8. iam

Exd 1: 5 Joseph was already in Egypt. •
Num16:47 plague had already begun among the people; •
Deu 31:21 I know the purposes . . they are already forming •
Jos 23: 4 with all the nations that I have already cut off •
Jdg 8: 6 Are Zebah and Zalmun'na already in your hand 4
15 Are Zebah and Zalmun'na already in your hand 4
1Sm 17:12 the man was already old and advanced in years. •
2Kg 7:13 multitude of Israel that have already perished; •
2Ch 28:13 For our guilt is already great •
Neh 5: 5 some of our daughters . . already been enslaved; 2
Ecc 1:10 It has been already, in the ages before us. 3
2:12 after the king? Only what he has already done. 3
3:15 That which is, already has been; 3
15 that which is to be, already has been; 3
4: 2 the dead who are already dead more fortunate 3
6:10 Whatever has come to be has already been named 3
9: 6 their hate and their envy have already perished 3
7 God has already approved what you do. 3
Isa 56: 8 others to him besides those already gathered. •
Hos 8: 8 already they are among the nations 4
Mal 2: 2 indeed I have already cursed them 1
Mat 5:28 a woman lustfully has already committed 6
17:12 I tell you that Eli'jah has already come 6
Mrk 4:37 so that the boat was already filling. 6
11:11 as it was already late 6
15:44 Pilate wondered if he were already dead; 6
44 he asked him whether he was already dead. 7
Lke 12:49 would that it were already kindled! 6
21:30 know that the summer is already near. 6
Joh 3:18 he who does not believe is condemned already 6
4:35 see how the fields are already white for harvest 6
9:22 the Jews had already agreed 6
27 He answered them, "I have told you already 6
11:17 Laz'arus had already been in the tomb four days. 6
13: 2 when the devil had already put it into the heart 6
15: 3 You are already made clean by the word 6
19:33 came to Jesus and saw that he was already dead 6
Act 4: 3 it was already evening 6
27: 9 the voyage was already dangerous 6
9 the voyage was already dangerous 6
Rom 15:20 not where Christ has already been named •
1Co 4: 8 Already you are filled! 6
8 Already you have become rich! 6
5: 3 I have already pronounced judgment 6
7:18 time of his call already circumcised •
Php 3:12 Not that I have already obtained this 6
12 or am already perfect 6
2Th 2: 7 the mystery of lawlessness is already at work; 6
1Ti 5:15 For some have already strayed after Satan. 6
2Ti 2:18 holding that the resurrection is past already. 6
4: 6 For I am already on the point of being sacrificed; 6
1Jn 2: 8 and the true light is already shining. 6
4: 3 coming, and now it is in the world already. 6
2Es 2:13 The kingdom is already prepared for you; watch! 8
4:11 one who is already worn out by the corrupt world 8
5:55 as born of a creation which already is aging 8
14:11 and nine of its parts have already passed 8
18 the eagle . . is already hastening to come. 8
Tob 3: 8 You already have had seven 6
15 Already seven husbands of mine are dead 6
Wis 18: 9 already they were singing the praises 6
23 when the dead had already fallen on one another 6
19:16 those who had already shared the same rights. 6
1Mc 12: 7 Already in time past a letter was sent to Onias 5
2Mc 4:39 many of the gold vessels had already been stolen. 6
45 already as good as beaten 6
15:20 the enemy was already close at hand 6
3Mc 3:10 already some . . were pledging to protect them 6
4:20 the paper and the pens . . had already given out. 6
5:15 the hour of the banquet was already slipping by 6
6: 5 had already gained control of the whole world 6
4Mc 9:21 the ligaments . . were already severed 6
12: 2 when he saw that he was already in fetters 6

already *See also* charge, say, suffered.

also 1. *καί*

Sir 0: 1 but also that those who love learning 1
1 was himself also led to write something 1
1 that, by becoming conversant with this also, 1

also *See also* give, more.

altar 1. מִזְבֵּחַ 2. מַדְבַּח (A) 3. *βωμός* 4. *θυσιαστήριον* 5. altare

Gen 8:20 Then Noah built an altar to the LORD 1
20 Noah . . offered burnt offerings on the altar. 1
12: 7 he built there an altar to the LORD 1
8 and there he built an altar to the LORD 1
13: 4 to the place where he had made an altar 1
18 Hebron; and there he built an altar to the LORD. 1
22: 9 Abraham built an altar there 1
9 Isaac his son, and laid him on the altar 1
26:25 he built an altar there 1
33:20 There he erected an altar and called it 1
35: 1 dwell there; and make there an altar to the God who 1
3 to Bethel, that I may make there an altar to the God 1
7 there he built an altar, and called the place 1
Exd 17:15 Moses built an altar and called the name of it 1
20:24 An altar of earth you shall make for me 1
25 if you make me an altar of stone, you shall not 1
26 you shall not go up by steps to my altar 1
21:14 you shall take him from my altar, that he may die. 1
24: 4 he rose early in the morning, and built an altar 1
6 and half of the blood he threw against the altar. 1
27: 1 You shall make the altar of acacia wood 1
1 the altar shall be square, and its height 1
5 you shall set it under the ledge of the altar 1
5 the net shall extend halfway down the altar. 1
6 you shall make poles for the altar 1
7 the poles shall be upon the two sides of the altar 1
28:43 when they come near the altar to minister 1
29:12 the blood . . put it upon the horns of the altar 1
12 you shall pour out at the base of the altar. 1
13 you shall . . burn them upon the altar. 1
16 throw it against the altar round about. 1
18 burn the whole ram upon the altar; 1
20 throw the rest of the blood against the altar 1
21 take part of the blood that is on the altar 1
25 burn them on the altar in addition to the burnt 1
36 shall offer a sin offering for the altar 1
37 shall make atonement for the altar 1
37 consecrate it, and the altar shall be most holy; 1
37 whatever touches the altar shall become holy. 1
38 Now this is what you shall offer upon the altar 1
44 consecrate . . the altar; 1
30: 1 You shall make an altar to burn incense upon; 1
18 put it between the tent of meeting and the altar 1
20 when they come near the altar to minister 1
27 its utensils, and the altar of incense 1
28 the altar of burnt offering with all 1
31: 8 pure lampstand . . and the altar of incense 1
9 altar of burnt offering with all its utensils 1
32: 5 When Aaron saw this, he built an altar before it; 1
34:13 You shall tear down their altars 1
35:15 the altar of incense, with its poles 1
16 the altar of burnt offering, with its grating 1
37:25 He made the altar of incense of acacia wood; 1
38: 1 He made the altar of burnt offering also 1
3 he made all the utensils of the altar, the pots 1
4 he made for the altar a grating, a network 1
7 poles through the rings on the sides of the altar 1
30 the bronze altar and the bronze grating 1
30 he made . . all the utensils of the altar 1
39:38 the golden altar, the anointing oil 1
39 the bronze altar, and its grating of bronze 1

40: 5 you shall put the golden altar for incense 1
6 You shall set the altar of burnt offering before 1
7 laver between the tent of meeting and the altar 1
10 shall also anoint the altar of burnt offering 1
10 consecrate the altar; and the altar shall be most 1
10 consecrate the altar; and the altar shall be most 1
26 he put the golden altar in the tent of meeting 1
29 he set the altar of burnt offering at the door 1
30 between the tent of meeting and the altar 1
32 when they approached the altar, they washed; 1
33 court round the tabernacle and the altar 1
Lev 1: 5 throw the blood round about against the altar 1
7 Aaron the priest shall put fire on the altar 1
8 the wood that is on the fire upon the altar 1
9 the priest shall burn the whole on the altar 1
11 he shall kill it on the north side of the altar 1
11 shall throw its blood against the altar round 1
12 the wood that is on the fire upon the altar 1
13 shall offer the whole, and burn it on the altar 1
15 the priest shall bring it to the altar 1
15 wring off its head, and burn it on the altar 1
15 shall be drained out on the side of the altar 1
16 he shall . . cast it beside the altar on the east 1
17 shall burn it on the altar, upon the wood 1
2: 2 as its memorial portion upon the altar 1
8 to the priest, he shall bring it to the altar 1
9 its memorial portion and burn this on the altar 1
12 they shall not be offered on the altar 1
3: 2 throw the blood against the altar round about 1
5 burn it on the altar upon the burnt offering 1
8 throw its blood against the altar round about 1
11 the priest shall burn it on the altar as food 1
13 throw its blood against the altar round about 1
16 the priest shall burn them on the altar as food 1
4: 7 on the horns of the altar of fragrant incense 1
7 at the base of the altar of burnt offering 1
10 the priest shall burn them upon the altar 1
18 the blood on the horns of the altar 1
18 at the base of the altar of burnt offering 1
19 shall take from it and burn upon the altar 1
25 put it on the horns of the altar of burnt offering 1
25 blood at the base of the altar of burnt offering 1
26 all its fat he shall burn on the altar 1
30 put it on the horns of the altar of burnt offering 1
30 rest of its blood at the base of the altar 1
31 the priest shall burn it upon the altar 1
34 put it on the horns of the altar of burnt offering 1
34 rest of its blood at the base of the altar 1
35 the priest shall burn it on the altar 1
5: 9 blood of the sin offering on the side of the altar 1
9 blood shall be drained out at the base of the altar 1
12 priest shall . . burn this upon the altar 1
6: 9 upon the altar all night until the morning 1
9 the fire of the altar shall be kept burning on it 1
10 consumed the burnt offering on the altar 1
10 the ashes . . and put them beside the altar 1
12 The fire on the altar shall be kept burning on it 1
13 be kept burning upon the altar continually 1
14 before the LORD, in front of the altar 1
15 burn this as its memorial portion on the altar 1
7: 2 its blood shall be thrown on the altar round about 1
5 the priest shall burn them on the altar 1
31 The priest shall burn the fat on the altar 1
8:11 he sprinkled some of it on the altar seven times 1
11 anointed the altar and all its utensils 1
15 put it on the horns of the altar round about 1
15 purified the altar, and poured out the blood 1
15 poured out the blood at the base of the altar 1
16 and Moses burned them on the altar 1
19 threw the blood upon the altar round about 1
21 Moses burned the whole ram on the altar 1
24 Moses threw the blood upon the altar round about 1
28 burned them on the altar with the burnt offering 1
30 the blood which was on the altar, and sprinkled it 1
9: 7 Then Moses said to Aaron, "Draw near to the altar 1
8 So Aaron drew near to the altar, and killed 1
9 in the blood and put it on the horns of the altar 1
9 poured out the blood at the base of the altar 1
10 from the sin offering he burned upon the altar 1
12 he threw it on the altar round about 1
13 and he burned them upon the altar 1
14 burned them with the burnt offering on the altar 1
17 cereal offering . . and burned it upon the altar 1
18 blood, which he threw upon the altar round about 1
20 the breasts, and he burned the fat upon the altar 1
24 the burnt offering and the fat upon the altar 1
10:12 unleavened beside the altar, for it is most holy 1
14:20 offer . . the cereal offering on the altar 1
16:12 coals of fire from the altar before the LORD 1
18 shall go out to the altar which is before the LORD 1
18 and put it on the horns of the altar round about 1
20 holy place and the tent of meeting and the altar 1
25 the sin offering he shall burn upon the altar 1
33 for the tent of meeting and for the altar 1
17: 6 the priest shall sprinkle the blood on the altar 1
11 I have given it for you upon the altar 1
21:23 not come near the veil or approach the altar 1
22:22 an offering by fire upon the altar to the LORD 1
Num 3:26 the court which is around . . the altar 1
31 their charge was . . the lampstand, the altars 1
4:11 over the golden altar they shall spread a cloth 1
13 they shall take away the ashes from the altar 1
14 they shall put on it all the utensils of the altar *
14 basins, all the utensils of the altar; 1
26 court which is around the . . altar 1
5:25 cereal offering . . and bring it to the altar; 1
26 burn it upon the altar 1
7: 1 Moses . . anointed and consecrated the altar 1
10 offerings for the dedication of the altar 1
10 offered their offering before the altar. 1
11 for the dedication of the altar. 1
84 This was the dedication offering for the altar 1
88 This was the dedication offering for the altar 1
16:38 into hammered plates as a covering for the altar 1
39 were hammered out as a covering for the altar 1
46 censer, and put fire therein from off the altar 1
18: 3 shall not come near to . . the altar 1
5 you shall attend to . . the duties of the altar 1
7 for all that concerns the altar 1
17 You shall sprinkle their blood upon the altar 1
23: 1 said to Balak, "Build for me here seven altars 1
2 offered on each altar a bull and a ram. 1
4 I have prepared the seven altars 1
4 I have offered upon each altar a bull and a ram. 1
14 built seven altars, and offered a bull and a ram 1
14 offered a bull and a ram on each altar. 1
29 Build for me here seven altars 1
30 Balak . . offered a bull and a ram on each altar. 1
Deu 7: 5 you shall break down their altars 1
12: 3 you shall tear down their altars 1
27 offer . . on the altar of the LORD your God; 1
27 blood . . be poured out on the altar of the LORD 1
16:21 not plant any tree as an Ashe'rah beside the altar 1
26: 4 set it down before the altar of the LORD your God. 1
27: 5 there . . build an altar to the LORD your God 1
5 build an altar . . an altar of stones; 1
6 build an altar to the LORD . . of unhewn stones; 1
33:10 put . . whole burnt offering upon thy altar. 1
Jos 8:30 Joshua built an altar in Mount Ebal to the LORD 1
31 an altar of unhewn stones, upon which no man has 1
9:27 for the congregation and . . the altar of the LORD 1
22:10 Manas'seh built there an altar by the Jordan 1
10 an altar by the Jordan, an altar of great size. 1
11 built an altar at the frontier of the land 1
16 by building yourselves an altar this day 1
19 do not rebel . . by building yourselves an altar 1
19 an altar other than the altar of the LORD our God. 1
23 spare us not . . for building an altar to turn away 1
26 Let us now build an altar, not for burnt offering 1
28 Behold the copy of the altar of the LORD 1
29 turn . . by building an altar for burnt offering 1
29 the altar of the LORD our God that stands 1
34 The Reubenites and . . called the altar Witness; 1
Jdg 2: 2 you shall break down their altars.' 1
6:24 Then Gideon built an altar there to the LORD 1
25 father's bull . . and pull down the altar of Ba'al 1
26 build an altar to the LORD your God on the top 1
28 the altar of Ba'al was broken down, and the Ashe'rah 1
28 bull . . offered upon the altar which had been built 1
30 he has pulled down the altar of Ba'al and cut down 1
31 himself, because his altar has been pulled down. 1
32 Jerubba'al . . because he pulled down his altar. 1
13:20 the flame went up toward heaven from the altar 1
20 the angel . . ascended in the flame of the altar 1
21: 4 the people rose early, and built there an altar 1
1Sm 2:28 to be my priest, to go up to my altar, to burn incense 1
33 The man . . whom I shall not cut off from my altar 1
7:17 And he built there an altar to the LORD. 1
14:35 And Saul built an altar to the LORD; 1
35 it was the first altar that he built to the LORD. 1
2Sm 24:18 rear an altar to the LORD on the threshing floor 1
21 To buy the . . in order to build an altar to the LORD 1
25 And David built there an altar to the LORD 1
1Kg 1:50 went, and caught hold of the horns of the altar. 1
51 he has laid hold of the horns of the altar, saying 1
53 they brought him down from the altar. 1
2:28 LORD and caught hold of the horns of the altar. 1
29 Jo'ab has fled . . and behold, he is beside the altar 1
3: 4 to offer 1,000 burnt offerings upon that altar. 1
6:20 He also made an altar of cedar. 1
22 altar that belonged to the inner sanctuary 1
7:48 the golden altar, the golden table for the bread 1
8:22 Then Solomon stood before the altar of the LORD 1
31 swears his oath before thine altar in this house 1
54 he arose from before the altar of the LORD 1
64 the bronze altar . . was too small to receive 1
9:25 peace offerings upon the altar which he built 1
12:32 and he offered sacrifices upon the altar; 1
33 He went up to the altar which he had made in Bethel 1
33 and went up to the altar to burn incense. 1
13: 1 Jerobo'am was standing by the altar 1
2 cried against the altar by the word of the LORD 1
2 O altar, altar, thus says the LORD: 'Behold, a son 1
2 O altar, altar, thus says the LORD: 'Behold, a son 1
3 Behold, the altar shall be torn down 1
4 which he cried against the altar at Bethel 1
4 Jerobo'am stretched out his hand from the altar 1
5 The altar also was torn down 1
5 and the ashes poured out from the altar 1
32 the saying . . against the altar in Bethel 1
16:32 He erected an altar for Ba'al in the house of Ba'al 1
18:26 they limped about the altar which they had made. 1
30 he repaired the altar of the LORD 1
32 he built an altar in the name of the LORD. 1
32 And he made a trench about the altar 1
35 the water ran round about the altar 1
19:10 forsaken thy covenant, thrown down thy altars 1
14 forsaken thy covenant, thrown down thy altars 1
2Kg 11:11 guards stood . . around the altar and the house. 1
18 his altars and his images they broke in pieces 1
18 and they slew Mattan . . before the altars. 1
12: 9 and set it beside the altar on the right side 1
16:10 Ahaz . . he saw the altar that was at Damascus. 1
10 Ahaz sent to Uri'ah the priest a model of the altar 1
11 And Uri'ah the priest built the altar; 1
12 when the king came . . the king viewed the altar. 1
12 the king drew near to the altar, and went up on it 1
13 threw the blood of . . offerings upon the altar. 1
14 the bronze altar . . before the LORD he removed 1
14 the place between his altar and the house of the LORD 1
14 he removed . . and put it on the north side of his altar. 1
15 Upon the great altar burn the morning burnt offering 1
15 the bronze altar shall be for me to inquire by. 1
18:22 high places and altars Hezeki'ah has removed 1
22 shall worship before this altar in Jerusalem"? 1
21: 3 he erected altars for Ba'al, and made an Ashe'rah 1
4 And he built altars in the house of the LORD 1
5 And he built altars for all the host of heaven 1
23: 9 priests . . did not come up to the altar of the LORD 1
12 the altars on the roof . . he pulled down and broke 1
12 altars which Manas'seh had made . . he pulled down 1
15 the altar at Bethel . . he pulled down and he broke 1
15 that altar with the high place he pulled down 1
16 took the bones . . and burned them upon the altar 1
17 which you have done against the altar at Bethel. 1
20 he slew all the priests . . upon the altars 1
1Ch 6:49 made offerings upon the altar of burnt offering 1
49 made offering . . and upon the altar of incense 1
16:40 to the LORD upon the altar of burnt offering 1
21:18 David should go up and rear an altar to the LORD 1
22 that I may build on it an altar to the LORD 1
26 David built there an altar to the LORD 1
26 with fire . . upon the altar of burnt offering. 1
29 tabernacle . . and the altar of burnt offering 1
22: 1 and here the altar of burnt offering for Israel. 1
28:18 for the altar of incense made of refined gold 1
2Ch 1: 5 bronze altar that Bez'alel . . had made 1
6 Solomon went up there to the bronze altar 1
4: 1 He made an altar of bronze, twenty cubits long 1
19 things . . in the house of God: the golden altar 1
5:12 stood east of the altar with . . priests who were 1
6:12 Then Solomon stood before the altar of the LORD 1
22 and comes and swears his oath before thy altar 1
7: 7 because the bronze altar . . could not hold 1
9 kept the dedication of the altar seven days 1
8:12 offerings to the LORD upon the altar of the LORD 1
14: 3 took away the foreign altars and the high places 1
15: 8 he repaired the altar of the LORD 1
23:10 around the altar and the house. 1
17 his altars and his images they broke in pieces 1
17 slew Mattan the priest of Ba'al before the altars. 1
26:16 to burn incense on the altar of incense. 1
19 house of the LORD, by the altar of incense. 1
28:24 Ahaz . . made himself altars in . . Jerusalem. 1
29:18 the altar of burnt offering and all its utensils 1
19 behold, they are before the altar of the LORD. 1
21 to offer them on the altar of the LORD. 1
22 blood and threw it against the altar; 1
22 their blood was thrown against the altar; 1
22 their blood was thrown against the altar. 1
24 made a sin offering with their blood on the altar 1
27 burnt offering be offered on the altar. 1
30:14 removed the altars that were in Jerusalem 1
31: 1 all Israel . . broke down . . the altars 1
32:12 this same Hezeki'ah taken away his . . altars 1
12 Before one altar you shall worship 1
33: 3 erected altars to the Ba'als, and made Ashe'rahs 1
4 he built altars in the house of the LORD 1
5 he built altars for all the host of heaven 1
15 all the altars that he had built on the mountain 1
16 He also restored the altar of the LORD 1
34: 4 broke down the altars of the Ba'als 1
5 burned the bones of the priests on their altars 1
7 he broke down the altars, and beat the Ashe'rim 1
35:16 to offer burnt offerings on the altar of the LORD 1
Ezr 3: 2 built the altar of the God of Israel 1
3 set the altar in its place, for fear was upon them 1
7:17 offer them upon the altar of the house of your God 2
Neh 10:34 to burn upon the altar of the LORD our God 1
Ps 26: 6 in innocence, and go about thy altar, O LORD 1
43: 4 Then I will go to the altar of God 1
51:19 then bulls will be offered on thy altar. 1
84: 3 where she may lay her young, at thy altars 1
118:27 up to the horns of the altar! 1
Isa 6: 6 burning coal . . taken with tongs from the altar. 1
17: 8 they will not have regard for the altars 1
19:19 an altar to the LORD in . . the land of Egypt 1

27: 9 when he makes all the stones of the altars 1
36: 7 high places and altars Hezeki'ah has removed 1
7 You shall worship before this altar"? 1
56: 7 their sacrifices will be accepted on my altar; 1
60: 7 they shall come up with acceptance on my altar 1
Jer 11:13 the altars you have set up to shame 1
13 set up to shame, altars to burn incense to Ba'al. 1
17: 1 of their heart, and on the horns of their altars 1
2 while their children remember their altars 1
Lam 2: 7 The Lord has scorned his altar . . his sanctuary; 1
Ezk 6: 4 Your altars shall become desolate 1
5 scatter your bones round about your altars. 1
6 so that your altars will be waste and ruined 1
13 among their idols round about their altars 1
8: 5 behold, north of the altar gate, in the entrance 1
16 of the temple . . between the porch and the altar 1
9: 2 they went in and stood beside the bronze altar. 1
40:46 is for the priests who have charge of the altar; 1
47 and the altar was in front of the temple. 1
41:22 an altar of wood, three cubits high 1
43:13 These are the dimensions of the altar by cubits 1
13 this shall be the height of the altar 1
17 The steps of the altar shall face east. •
18 These are the ordinances for the altar 1
20 its blood, and put it on the four horns of the altar •
20 you shall cleanse the altar and make atonement •
22 the altar shall be cleansed, as it was cleansed 1
26 they make atonement for the altar and purify it 1
27 shall offer upon the altar your burnt offerings 1
45:19 the four corners of the ledge of the altar 1
47: 1 the threshold of the temple, south of the altar. 1
Hos 4:19 they shall be ashamed because of their altars. 4
8:11 E'phraim has multiplied altars for sinning 1
11 they have become to him altars for sinning. 1
10: 1 the more altars he built; 1
2 The LORD will break down their altars 1
8 Thorn and thistle shall grow up on their altars; 1
12:11 their altars also shall be like stone heaps 1
Jol 1:13 lament, O priests, wail, O ministers of the altar. 1
2:17 Between the vestibule and the altar 1
Ams 2: 8 they lay themselves down beside every altar 1
3:14 I will punish the altars of Bethel 1
14 and the horns of the altar shall be cut off 1
9: 1 I saw the LORD standing beside the altar 1
Zec 9:15 drenched like the corners of the altar. 1
14:20 of the LORD shall be as the bowls before the altar; 1
Mal 1: 7 By offering polluted food upon my altar. 1
10 you might not kindle fire upon my altar in vain! 1
2:13 You cover the LORD'S altar with tears 1
Mat 5:23 So if you are offering your gift at the altar 4
24 leave your gift there before the altar and go; 4
23:18 If any one swears by the altar, it is nothing 4
18 if any one swears by the gift that is on the altar •
19 which is greater, the gift or the altar 4
20 So he who swears by the altar 4
35 murdered between the sanctuary and the altar. 4
Lke 1:11 on the right side of the altar of incense. 4
11:51 perished between the altar and the sanctuary. 4
Act 17:23 I found also an altar with this inscription 3
Rom 11: 3 Lord . . they have demolished thy altars 4
1Co 9:13 those who serve at the altar 4
10:18 partners in the altar? 4
Heb 7:13 from which no one has ever served at the altar. 4
13:10 We have an altar 4
Jas 2:21 when he offered his son Isaac upon the altar? 4
Rev 6: 9 I saw under the altar the souls of those 4
8: 3 another angel came and stood at the altar 4
3 prayers of all the saints upon the golden altar 4
5 censer and filled it with fire from the altar 4
9:13 a voice from the four horns of the golden altar 4
11: 1 Rise and measure the temple of God and the altar 4
14:18 Then another angel came out from the altar 4
16: 7 I heard the altar cry, "Yea, Lord God the Almighty 4
1Es 1:18 sacrifices were offered on the altar of the Lord 4
4:52 to be offered on the altar every day 4
5:48 prepared the altar of the God of Israel 4
50 they erected the altar in its place 4
8:15 to offer sacrifices upon the altar of their Lord 4
2Es 10:21 our altar thrown down, our temple destroyed; 5
Tob 1: 6 give these to the priests . . at the altar. 4
Jdt 4: 3 the sacred vessels and the altar and the temple 4
12 They even surrounded the altar with sackcloth 4
8:24 and the temple and the altar rest upon us. 4
9: 8 to cast down the horn of thy altar with the sword. 4
AEs 14: 9 to quench thy altar and the glory of thy house 4
Wis 9: 8 an altar in the city of thy habitation 4
Sir 35: 6 anoints the altar 4
47: 9 He placed singers before the altar 4
50:11 went up to the holy altar 4
12 as he stood by the hearth of the altar 3
14 Finishing the service at the altars 3
15 he poured it out at the foot of the altar 3
Bar 1:10 offer them upon the altar of the Lord our God; 4
1Mc 1:21 entered the sanctuary and took the golden altar 4
47 to build altars and sacred precincts and shrines 3
54 sacrilege upon the altar of burnt offering. 4
54 built altars in the surrounding cities of Judah 3
59 they offered sacrifice on the altar 3
59 which was upon the altar of burnt offering. 4
2:23 to offer sacrifice upon the altar in Modein 3
24 he ran and killed him upon the altar. 3
25 he tore down the altar. 3
45 Mattathias . . went about and tore down the altars; 3
4:38 the sanctuary desolate, the altar profaned 4
44 what to do about the altar of burnt offering 4
45 So they tore down the altar 4
47 and built a new altar like the former one. 4
49 the altar of incense, and the table 4
50 Then they burned incense on the altar 4
53 on the new altar of burnt offering 4
56 So they celebrated the dedication of the altar 4
59 the days of dedication of the altar 4
5: 1 heard that the altar had been built 4
68 he tore down their altars 3
6: 7 which he had erected upon the altar in Jerusalem; 4
7:36 stood before the altar and the temple 4
2Mc 1:18 Nehemiah, who built the temple and the altar 4
19 took some of the fire of the altar 4
32 when the light from the altar shone back 4
2: 5 the tent and the ark and the altar of incense 4
19 the dedication of the altar 3
3:15 prostrated themselves before the altar 4
4:14 no longer intent upon their service at the altar 4
6: 5 The altar was covered with abominable offerings 4
10: 2 altars which had been built in the public square 3
3 and made another altar of sacrifice 4
26 Falling upon the steps before the altar 4
13: 8 he had committed many sins against the altar 3
14: 3 to have access again to the holy altar 4
33 and tear down the altar 4
15:31 stationed the priests before the altar 4

altar *See also* hearth.

altar for burning incense 1. מְקַטְּרָה
2Ch 30:14 the altars for burning incense they took away 1

incense altar 1. חַמָּן
Lev 26:30 I will . . cut down your incense altars 1
2Ch 14: 5 took out of . . Judah . . the incense altars. 1
34: 4 hewed down the incense altars which stood 1
7 hewed down all the incense altars throughout 1
Isa 27: 9 no . . incense altars will remain standing. 1
Ezk 6: 4 and your incense altars shall be broken; 1
6 your incense altars cut down 1

altar of incense 1. חַמָּן 2. *θυμιατήριον*
Isa 17: 8 either the Ashe'rim or the altars of incense. 1
Heb 9: 4 having the golden altar of incense 2

altar of sacrifice 1. *θυσιαστήριον*
2Mc 10: 3 and made another altar of sacrifice 1

alter 1. עבר 2. שנה 3. שנא (A) 4. *ἀλλοιόω* 5. *ἕτερος* 6. *καταστρέφω*
Ezr 6:11 I make a decree that if any one alters this edict 3
12 that shall put forth a hand to alter this 3
Est 1:19 let it be written . . so that it may not be altered 1
Ps 89:34 alter the word that went forth from my lips. 2
Lke 9:29 the appearance of his countenance was altered 5
Jdt 10: 7 and noted how her face was altered 4
3Mc 3:23 we may soon alter our policy. 6

alter a form of government 1. *ἐκπολιτεύω*
4Mc 4:19 and altered its form of government 1

alternation 1. *ἀλλαγή*
Wis 7:18 the alternations of the solstices 1

although 1. אֶפֶס כִּי 2. בְּלֹא 3. גַּם 4. וְ 5. כְּ 6. כִּי 7. עַל 8. *δέ* 9. *εἰ* 10. *καί* 11. *καίπερ* 12. *καίτοι* 13. *καίτοιγε* 14. *μέν*
Gen 31:37 Although you have felt through all my goods 6
50 although no man is with us, remember •
39:10 although she spoke to Joseph day after day 5
Exd 13:17 land of the Philistines, although that was near; 6
34: 9 although it is a stiff-necked people; 6
Num 14:44 although neither the ark of the covenant 4
Jos 17:14 but one lot . . although I am a numerous people 4
1Sm 1: 5 although he loved Hannah, he would give . . only 1
2Sm 21: 2 although . . Israel had sworn to spare them, Saul 4
1Kg 1: 1 although they covered him with clothes, he could •
18 Adoni'jah is king, although you . . do not know it. 4
2:28 Adoni'jah although he had not supported Ab'salom- 4
3: 7 made thy servant king . . although I am 4
18:12 will kill me, although I . . have revered the LORD 4
1Ch 12:17 although there is no wrong in my hands 2
Neh 6: 1 (although up to that time I had not set up the doors 3
Job 2: 3 although you moved me against him 4
10: 7 although thou knowest that I am not guilty 7
16:17 although there is no violence in my hands 7
32: 3 although they had declared Job to be in the wrong. 4
Ecc 8: 6 although man's trouble lies heavy upon him. 6
Isa 53: 9 in his death, although he had done no violence 7
Jer 14:15 prophesy in my name although I did not send them 4
25: 4 although the LORD persistently sent to you 4
Ezk 13: 7 said, 'Says the LORD,' although I have not spoken? 4
22 although I have not disheartened him 4
35:10 although the LORD was there 4
Hos 7:15 Although I trained and strengthened their arms 4
Joh 4: 2 (although Jesus himself did not baptize 13
21:11 although there were so many, the net was not torn. •
Act 15:24 although we gave them no instructions •
Rom 1:21 for although they knew God they did not honor him •
3:21 although the law and the prophets bear witness •
8:10 although your bodies are dead because of sin 14
1Co 2: 6 although it is not a wisdom of this age 8
8: 5 although there may be so-called gods in heaven 9
2Co 7:12 So although I wrote to you 9
Heb 4: 3 although his works were finished 12
5: 8 Although he was a Son 11
1Es 6:20 although it has been in process of construction •
2Es 9:10 although they received my benefits •
Jdt 11:13 although it is not lawful •
1Mc 11:25 Although . . men . . kept making complaints 10
3Mc 4:18 although most of them were still in the country 11
4Mc 3:10 although springs were plentiful there 11
15 David, although he was burning with thirst 11
4:13 although . . he had scruples about doing 11
5: 7 Although you have had them for so long a time •
7: 4 Although his sacred life was consumed •
9:21 Although the ligaments . . were . . severed •
13:27 although nature . . had augmented 11
15:24 Although she witnessed the destruction 11

altogether 1. אַךְ 2. יַחַד 3. יַחְדָּו 4. כֹּל 5. כָּלָה
Gen 18:21 whether they have done altogether according 5
46:15 altogether his sons and his daughters numbered 4
Deu 16:15 bless . . so that you will be altogether joyful. 1
Job 27:12 why then have you become altogether vain? †
Ps 19: 9 are true, and righteous altogether. 3
35:26 put to shame and confusion altogether 3
37:38 transgressors shall be altogether destroyed; 3
40:14 be put to shame and confusion altogether 2
139: 4 lo, O LORD, thou knowest it altogether. 4
Sng 5:16 His speech is . . and he is altogether desirable. 4

altogether *See also* fearful.

always 1. בְּכָל עֵת 2. כֹּל יָמִים 3. לֹא כרת 4. לָנֶצַח 5. נֵצַח 6. עוֹלָם 7. תְּמוֹל שִׁלְשֹׁם 8. תָּמִיד 9. *ἀεί* 10. *διὰ παντός* 11. *ἐν πᾶσιν* 12. *πάντοτε* 13. *πᾶς* 14. *πάσαι ἡμέραι* 15. *πάσας τὰς ἡμέρας* 16. *φθάνω* 17. omni tempore 18. semper 19. sempiternus
Exd 25:30 set the bread . . on the table before me always. 8
28:38 it shall always be upon his forehead 8
Deu 5:29 Oh that they had such a mind as this always 2
6:24 LORD commanded us . . for our good always 2
11: 1 love the LORD . . and keep his charge . . always. 2
12 eyes of the LORD your God are always upon it 8
14:23 may learn to fear the LORD your God always. 2
Jos 9:23 some of you shall always be slaves 3
1Sm 21: 5 women have been kept from us as always when I go 7
27:12 therefore he shall be my servant always. 6
2Sm 9: 7 and you shall eat at my table always. 8
10 Mephib'osheth . . shall always eat at my table. 8
13 for he ate always at the king's table. 8
1Kg 5: 1 for Hiram always loved David. 2
11:36 David my servant may always have a lamp before me 2
2Kg 17:37 and the law . . you shall always be careful to do. 2
2Ch 18: 7 never prophecies good . . but always evil. 2
Ps 9:18 For the needy shall not always be forgotten 4
16: 8 I keep the LORD always before me; 8
73:12 always at ease, they increase in riches. 6
103: 9 He will not always chide 5
Prv 5:19 be infatuated always with her love. 8
6:21 Bind them upon your heart always; 8
8:30 daily his delight, rejoicing before him always 1
28:14 Blessed is the man who fears the LORD always; 8
Ecc 9: 8 Let your garments be always white; 1
Isa 57:16 not contend for ever, nor will I always be angry; 5
Mat 18:10 in heaven their angels always behold the face 10
26:11 For you always have the poor with you 12
11 you will not always have me. 12
28:20 I am with you always, to the close of the age. 14
Mrk 5: 5 on the mountains he was always crying out 13
14: 7 For you always have the poor with you 12
7 but you will not always have me. 12
Lke 15:31 he said to him, 'Son, you are always with me 12
18: 1 to the effect that they ought always to pray 12
Joh 6:34 They said to him, "Lord, give us this bread always. 12
7: 6 your time is always here. 12
8:29 I always do what is pleasing to him. 12
11:42 I knew that thou hearest me always 12
12: 8 The poor you always have with you 12
8 The poor you always have with you 12
18:20 always taught in synagogues and in the temple 12
Act 2:25 I saw the Lord always before me 10
7:51 you always resist the Holy Spirit 9
24:16 I always take pains to have a clear conscience 10
Rom 1: 9 I mention you always in my prayers 12
1Co 1: 4 I give thanks to God always for you 12
15:58 always abounding in the work of the Lord 12
2Co 1:19 was not Yes and No; but in him it is always Yes. •
2:14 who in Christ always leads us in triumph 12
4:10 always carrying in the body the death of Jesus 12
11 always being given up to death for Jesus' sake 9

5: 6 So we are always of good courage 12
6:10 as sorrowful, yet always rejoicing 9
9: 8 so that you may always have enough of everything 12
Gal 4:18 it is always good to be made much 12
Eph 5:20 always and for everything giving thanks 12
Php 1: 4 always in every prayer of mine for you all 12
20 with full courage now as always 12
2:12 Therefore, my beloved, as you have always obeyed 12
4: 4 Rejoice in the Lord always 12
Col 1: 3 We always thank God, the Father of our Lord Jesus 12
4: 6 Let your speech always be gracious 12
12 always remembering you earnestly 12
1Th 1: 2 We give thanks to God always for you all 12
2:16 so as always to fill up the measure of their sins. 16
3: 6 and reported that you always remember us kindly 12
4:17 so we shall always be with the Lord. 12
5:15 always seek to do good to one another and to all. 12
16 Rejoice always 12
2Th 1: 3 We are bound to give thanks to God always for you 12
11 To this end we always pray for you 12
2:13 we are bound to give thanks to God always for you 12
2Ti 4: 5 As for you, always be steady, endure suffering 11
Tit 1:12 Cretans are always liars, evil beasts 9
Phm 1: 4 I thank my God always 12
Heb 3:10 They always go astray in their hearts 9
7:25 since he always lives to make intercession 12
1Pe 3:15 Always be prepared to make a defense to any one 9
2Pe 1:12 I intend always to remind you of these things 9
1Es 1:32 it was ordained that this should always be done 9
2Es 8:30 who have always put their trust in thy glory. 18
15:47 who have always lusted after you. 18
53 If you had not always killed my chosen people 17
16:20 nor be always mindful of the scourges. 19
AEs 13: 2 always acting reasonably and with kindness 9
16: 4 God, who always sees everything. 9
9 always judging . . with . . consideration. 9
Wis 11:21 it is always in thy power to show great strength 12
14:31 always pursues the transgression 9
17:11 it has always exaggerated the difficulties. 9
Sir 17:15 Their ways are always before him 10
23:10 the man who always swears and utters the Name 10
27:11 The talk of the godly man is always wise 10
38:29 he is always deeply concerned over his work 10
1Mc 2:65 always listen to him; he shall be your father. 15
2Mc 14:15 always upholds his own heritage 9
24 he kept Judas always in his presence 10
3Mc 7: 6 always taking their part 10
9 we always shall have . . as an antagonist 10

am *See* I.

amass 1. ἰσχύω 2. πληθύνω
Sir 43:15 In his majesty he amasses the clouds 1
47:18 amassed silver like lead. 2

amaze 1. תמה 2. ἀποθαυμάζω 3. ἐκθαμβέω 4. ἐκθαυμάζω 5. ἐκπλήσσω 6. ἐξίστημι 7. θαμβέω 8. θάμβος 9. θαυμάζω 10. θαυμαστός 11. exsisto 12. miror
Ecc 5: 8 If you see . . do not be amazed at the matter; 1
Mat 12:23 all the people were amazed, and said 6
Mrk 1:27 And they were all amazed 7
2:12 so that they were all amazed and glorified God 6
10:24 the disciples were amazed at his words 7
32 they were amazed 7
12:17 they were amazed at him. 4
16: 5 a . . man . . in a white robe; and they were amazed 3
6 And he said to them, "Do not be amazed 3
Lke 2:47 who heard him were amazed at his understanding 6
4:36 they were all amazed and said to one another 8
8:56 her parents were amazed 6
24:22 Moreover, some women of our company amazed us. 6
Act 2: 7 they were amazed and wondered, saying 6
12 all were amazed and perplexed 6
8: 9 and amazed the nation of Sama'ria 6
11 for a long time he had amazed them with his magic. 6
13 he was amazed. 6
9:21 all who heard him were amazed, and said 6
10:45 the believers . . were amazed 6
12:16 when they opened, they saw him and were amazed. 6
2Es 9: 9 those who have now abused my ways shall be amazed 12
13:11 When I saw it, I was amazed. 11
Tob 11:16 Those who saw him as he went were amazed 9
Jdt 15: 1 they were amazed at what had happened. 6
Wis 5: 2 will be amazed at his unexpected salvation. 6
13: 4 if men were amazed at their power and working 5
Sir 11:13 raises up his head, so that many are amazed at him. 2
43:18 the mind is amazed at its falling. 6
1Mc 15:32 when he saw . . he was amazed 6
4Mc 2: 1 why is it amazing 10
6:11 in fact . . he amazed even his torturers 9
14:11 Do not consider it amazing 10
17:16 Who were not amazed? 5

greatly amaze 1. ἐκθαμβέω
Mrk 9:15 the crowd, when they saw him, were greatly amazed 1

amazement 1. ἔκστασις 2. ἔκστασις μεγάλη
Mrk 5:42 immediately overcome with amazement. 2
Lke 5:26 amazement seized them all 1
Act 3:10 they were filled with wonder and amazement 1
amazement *See also* look.

most amazing 1. θαυμάσιος
4Mc 7:13 Most amazing, indeed 1

ambassador 1. מַלְאָךְ 2. צִיר 3. πρεσβεύω 4. πρέσβυς 5. πρεσβύτης
Isa 18: 2 which sends ambassadors by the Nile 2
Ezk 17:15 he rebelled against him by sending ambassadors 1
2Co 5:20 So we are ambassadors for Christ 3
Eph 6:20 which I am an ambassador in chains 3
Phm 1: 9 I, Paul, an ambassador and now a prisoner also 5
1Mc 9:70 he sent ambassadors to him to make peace with him 4
10:51 Then Alexander sent ambassadors to Ptolemy 4

ambition 1. φιλοτιμία
Wis 14:18 Then the ambition of the craftsman impelled 1
ambition *See also* make.

selfish ambition 1. ἐριθεία
Jas 3:14 if you have . . selfish ambition in your hearts 1
16 For where jealousy and selfish ambition exist 1

ambush 1. אֹרֶב 2. ארב 3. מַאֲרָב 4. מִסְתָּר 5. צפן 6. ἐνεδρεύω 7. ἔνεδρον
Jos 8: 2 lay an ambush against the city, behind it. 2
7 rise up from the ambush, and seize the city; 2
12 and set them in ambush between Bethel and Ai 2
14 there was an ambush against him behind the city. 2
19 And the ambush rose quickly out of their place 2
21 all Israel saw that the ambush had taken the city 2
Jdg 9:35 Abim'elech and the men . . rose from the ambush. 3
2Ch 13:13 Jerobo'am had sent an ambush around 3
13 the ambush was behind them. 3
20:22 set an ambush against the men of Ammon, Moab 2
Ezr 8:31 delivered us . . from ambushes by the way. 2
Ps 10: 8 He sits in ambush in the villages; 3
17:12 eager to tear, as a young lion lurking in ambush. 4
64: 4 shooting from ambush at the blameless 4
Prv 1:11 let us wantonly ambush the innocent; 5
Jer 9: 8 but in his heart he plans an ambush for him. 1
51:12 set up watchmen; prepare the ambushes; 2
Act 23:16 Now the son of Paul's sister heard of their ambush; 7
25: 3 planning an ambush to kill him on the way. 7
Sir 8:11 lest he lie in ambush against your words. 7
1Mc 1:36 It became an ambush against the sanctuary 7
5: 4 ambushed them on the highways. 6
9:40 Then they rushed upon them from the ambush 7
10:80 there was an ambush behind him 7
11:68 set an ambush against him in the mountains 7
ambush *See also* enemy, lie, man, place, set.

amen 1. אָמֵן 2. ἀμήν
Num 5:22 And the woman shall say, 'Amen, Amen.' 1
22 And the woman shall say, 'Amen, Amen.' 1
Deu 27:15 all the people shall answer and say, 'Amen.' 1
16 all the people shall say, 'Amen.' 1
17 all the people shall say, 'Amen.' 1
18 all the people shall say, 'Amen.' 1
19 all the people shall say, 'Amen.' 1
20 all the people shall say, 'Amen.' 1
21 all the people shall say, 'Amen.' 1
22 all the people shall say, 'Amen.' 1
23 all the people shall say, 'Amen.' 1
24 all the people shall say, 'Amen.' 1
25 all the people shall say, 'Amen.' 1
26 all the people shall say, 'Amen.' 1
1Kg 1:36 Amen! May the LORD, the God of my lord . . say so. 1
1Ch 16:36 all the people said "Amen!" and praised the LORD. 1
Neh 5:13 all the assembly said "Amen" and praised the LORD. 1
8: 6 all the people answered, "Amen, Amen," lifting up 1
6 all the people answered, "Amen, Amen," lifting up 1
Ps 41:13 from everlasting to everlasting! Amen and Amen. 1
13 from everlasting to everlasting! Amen and Amen. 1
72:19 may his glory fill the whole earth! Amen and Amen! 1
19 may his glory fill the whole earth! Amen and Amen! 1
89:52 Blessed be the LORD for ever! Amen and Amen. 1
52 Blessed be the LORD for ever! Amen and Amen. 1
106:48 let all the people say, "Amen!" Praise the LORD! 1
Jer 28: 6 prophet Jeremiah said, "Amen! May the LORD do so; 1
Mrk 16:20 by the signs that attended it. Amen. •
Rom 1:25 the Creator, who is blessed for ever! Amen. 2
9: 5 God who is over all be blessed for ever. Amen. 2
11:36 To him be glory for ever. Amen. 2
15:33 The God of peace be with you all. Amen. 2
16:27 glory for evermore through Jesus Christ! Amen. 2
1Co 14:16 say the "Amen" to your thanksgiving 2
16:24 My love be with you all in Christ Jesus. Amen. 2
2Co 1:20 That is why we utter the Amen through him 2
Gal 1: 5 to whom be the glory for ever and ever. Amen. 2
6:18 Christ be with your spirit, brethren. Amen. 2
Eph 3:21 to all generations, for ever and ever. Amen. 2
Php 4:20 glory for ever and ever. Amen. 2
1Ti 1:17 be honor and glory for ever and ever. Amen. 2
6:16 To him be honor and eternal dominion. Amen. 2
2Ti 4:18 To him be the glory for ever and ever. Amen. 2
Heb 13:21 to whom be glory for ever and ever. Amen. 2
25 Grace be with all of you. Amen. 2
1Pe 4:11 glory and dominion for ever and ever. Amen. 2
5:11 To him be the dominion for ever and ever. Amen. 2
2Pe 3:18 glory both now and to the day of eternity. Amen. 2
Jde 1:25 before all time and now and for ever. Amen. 2
Rev 1: 6 glory and dominion for ever and ever. Amen. 2
7 Behold, he is coming . . Even so. Amen. 2
3:14 words of the Amen, the faithful and true witness 2
5:14 the four living creatures said, "Amen! 2
7:12 saying, "Amen! Blessing and glory and wisdom 2
12 might be to our God for ever and ever! Amen. 2
19: 4 worshiped God . . saying, "Amen. Hallelujah! 2
22:20 Surely I am coming soon." Amen. Come, Lord Jesus! 2
1Es 9:47 all the multitude answered, "Amen. 2
Tob 8: 8 she said with him, "Amen. 2
Man 1:15 thine is the glory for ever. Amen. 2
3Mc 7:23 through all times! Amen. 2
4Mc 18:24 to whom be glory for ever and ever. Amen. 2

amend 1. יטב 2. ἐπιδιορθόω
Jer 7: 3 Amend your ways and your doings 1
5 For if you truly amend your ways and your doings 1
18:11 and amend your ways and your doings. 1
26:13 Now therefore amend your ways and your doings 1
35:15 amend your doings, and do not go after other gods 1
Tit 1: 5 that you might amend what was defective 2
amends *See* make.

amethyst 1. אַחְלָמָה 2. ἀμέθυστος
Exd 28:19 the third row a jacinth, an agate, and an amethyst; 1
39:12 the third row, a jacinth, an agate, and an amethyst; 1
Rev 21:20 the eleventh jacinth, the twelfth amethyst. 2

amid 1. בְּ 2. בְּבֵין 3. בְּתוֹךְ 4. תַּחַת 5. בְּ (A) 6. cum
Job 4:13 Amid thoughts from visions of the night 1
30:14 they come; amid the crash they roll on. 4
Isa 44: 4 They shall spring up like grass amid waters 2
Ezk 32:20 shall fail amid those who are slain by the sword 3
Dan 4:15 amid the tender grass of the field. 5
Ams 2: 2 and Moab shall die amid uproar, amid shouting 1
2 amid shouting and the sound of the trumpet; 1
Zec 4: 7 the top stone amid shouts of 'Grace, grace to it! •
2Es 8:27 who have kept thy covenants amid afflictions. 6
amiss *See* judge, never.

act amiss 1. ἀγνοέω
Sir 5:15 In great and small matters do not act amiss 1

do amiss 1. חטא
Lev 5:16 also make restitution for what he has done amiss 1

amnesty 1. ἀμνησικακία
3Mc 3:21 our amnesty toward their compatriots here 1

among 1. אֶל 2. אֵת 3. בְּ 4. בֵּין 5. בְּקֶרֶב 6. בְּתוֹךְ 7. גֵּו 8. לְ 9. מֵאֵת 10. מִן 11. מִקֶּרֶב 12. מִתּוֹךְ 13. עַל 14. עִם 15. קָצָה 16. קָצֶה 17. קֶרֶב 18. תָּוֶךְ 19. תַּחַת 20. בֵּין (A) 21. מִן (A) 22. ἀνὰ μέσον 23. διά 24. εἰς 25. εἰς μέσον 26. εἰς ὁδόν 27. ἐκ 28. ἐν 29. ἐνώπιον 30. ἐπί 31. καθίστημι ἐν 32. κατά 33. κύκλος 34. μέσος 35. μετά 36. μεταξύ 37. παρά 38. πρός 39. σύν 40. cum 41. de 42. in 43. inter 44. super
Gen 3: 8 hid themselves . . among the trees of the garden. 3
13:12 while Lot dwelt among the cities of the valley 3
17:10 Every male among you shall be circumcised. •
12 is eight days old among you shall be circumcised; •
23 every male among the men of Abraham's house 3
23: 4 I am a stranger and a sojourner among you; 14
4 a sojourner among you; give me property among you 14
6 Hear us, my lord; you are a mighty prince among us. 3
10 Now Ephron was sitting among the Hittites; 3
16 the weights current among the merchants. 8
24: 3 daughters of the Canaanites, among whom I dwell 3
3 daughters of the Canaanites, among whom I dwell 5
30:32 the spotted and speckled among the goats; 3
33 not speckled and spotted among the goats 3
33 among the goats and black among the lambs 3
41 the flock, that they might breed among the rods 3
33: 1 he divided the children among Leah and Rachel 13
34:22 that every male among us be circumcised as they 8
35: 2 Put away the foreign gods that are among you 3
39:14 See, he has brought among us a Hebrew to insult us; 8
17 whom you have brought among us, came in to me 3
40:20 head of the chief baker among his servants. 3
42: 5 Israel came to buy among the others who came 3
47: 2 from among his brothers he took five men 16
6 and if you know any able men among them, 3
Exd 2: 3 placed it among the reeds at the river's brink. 3
5 she saw the basket among the reeds and sent 3
7: 5 bring out the people of Israel from among them. 18
9:20 word of the LORD among the servants of Pharaoh 10
10: 1 that I may show these signs of mine among them 3
2 Egyptians and what signs I have done among them; 3

11 No! Go, the men among you, and serve the LORD •
12:31 and said, "Rise up, go forth from among my people 18
49 for the stranger who sojourns among you. 3
13: 2 first to open the womb among the people of Israel 3
13 Every first-born of man among your sons you shall 3
15:11 Who is like thee, O LORD, among the gods? 3
17: 7 by saying, "Is the LORD among us or not? 3
19: 5 you shall be my own possession among all peoples; 10
28: 1 bring near . . Aaron . . from among the people 18
29:45 I will dwell among the people of Israel 3
46 out of . . Egypt that I might dwell among them; 3
30:12 no plague among them when you number them. 3
31:14 that soul shall be cut off from among his people. 17
32:25 break loose, to their shame among their enemies) 3
33: 3 but I will not go up among you, lest I consume you 3
5 I should go up among you, I would consume you. 3
34:10 and all the people among whom you are shall see 3
35: 5 Take from among you an offering to the LORD; 2
10 let every able man among you come and make all 3
36: 8 all the able men among the workmen made 3
Lev 6:18 Every male among the children of Aaron may eat 3
22 The priest from among Aaron's sons 10
29 Every male among the priests may eat of it 3
7: 6 Every male among the priests may eat of it 3
33 he among the sons of Aaron who offers the blood 10
10: 3 I will show myself holy among those who are near me 3
11: 2 which you may eat among all the beasts 10
3 chews the cud, among the animals, you may eat 3
4 Nevertheless among those that chew the cud 10
13 you shall have in abomination among the birds 10
21 Yet among the winged insects that go on all fours 10
27 all that go on their paws, among the animals 3
29 unclean to you among the swarming things 3
31 These are unclean to you among all that swarm 3
16:29 the native or the stranger who sojourns among you 3
17: 4 that man shall be cut off from among his people 17
8 or of the strangers that sojourn among them 3
10 or of the strangers that sojourn among them 3
10 and will cut him off from among his people 17
12 No person among you shall eat blood 10
12 any stranger who sojourns among you 3
13 or of the strangers that sojourn among them 3
18:26 the native or the stranger who sojourns among you 3
29 shall be cut off from among their people 17
19:16 not go . . as a slanderer among your people 3
34 shall be to you as the native among you 10
20: 3 and will cut him off from among his people 17
5 and will cut off from among their people 17
6 I . . will cut him off from among his people 17
14 that there may be no wickedness among you 3
18 both . . shall be cut off from among their people 17
21: 1 defile himself for the dead among his people 3
4 defile himself . . among his people 3
10 The priest who is chief among his brethren 10
15 not profane his children among his people 3
22:32 I will be hallowed among the people of Israel 3
23:30 that person I will destroy from among his people 17
24:10 went out among the people of Israel 6
25:33 their possession among the people of Israel 3
44 from among the nations that are round about you 2
45 You may also buy from among the strangers •
26:11 I will make my abode among you 3
12 I will walk among you, and will be your God 3
22 I will let loose the wild beasts among you 3
25 I will send pestilence among you, and you shall be 3
33 I will scatter you among the nations 3
38 you shall perish among the nations 3
27:29 who is to be utterly destroyed from among men 10
Num 1:49 take a census of them among the people of Israel; 3
2:33 the Levites were not numbered among the people 3
3: 9 given to him from among the people of Israel. 9
12 the Levites from among the people of Israel 18
12 that opens the womb among the people of Israel. 10
41 all the first-born among the people of Israel 3
41 firstlings among the cattle of . . Israel. 3
42 all the first-born among the people of Israel 3
45 all the first-born among the people of Israel 3
4: 2 sons of Kohath from among the sons of Levi 18
18 Ko'hathites be destroyed from among the Levites; 18
5:21 execration and an oath among your people 3
27 shall become an execration among her people. 3
8: 6 Take the Levites from among the people of Israel 18
14 separate the Levites from among the people 18
16 given to me from among the people of Israel; 18
17 first-born among the people of Israel are mine 3
18 all the first-born among the people of Israel. 3
19 as a gift . . from among the people of Israel 18
19 there may be no plague among the people of Israel 3
9: 7 among the people of Israel? 3
14 if a stranger sojourns among you 2
11: 1 fire of the LORD burned among them, and consumed 3
3 fire of the LORD burned among them. 3
4 rabble that was among them had a strong craving; 3
20 you have rejected the LORD who is among you 5
21 The people among whom I am number 600,000 on foot; 5
26 they were among those registered 3
12: 6 said, "Hear my words: If there is a prophet among you 3
13: 2 send a man, every one a leader among them. 3
14: 6 who were among those who had spied out the land 10

11 all the signs which I have wrought among them? 3
13 bring up this people in thy might from among them 5
42 your enemies, for the LORD is not among you. 5
15:14 if . . any one is among you throughout 3
26 be forgiven, and the stranger who sojourns among 6
29 for him who is native among the people of Israel 3
29 for the stranger who sojourns among them. 3
30 shall be cut off from among his people. 17
16: 3 LORD is among them; why then do you exalt 6
21 Separate . . from among this congregation 18
47 plague had already begun among the people; 3
17: 6 the rod of Aaron was among their rods. 3
18: 6 Levites from among the people of Israel; 18
20 neither shall you have any portion among them; 6
20 portion and your inheritance among . . Israel. 6
23 among the people of Israel they shall have no 6
24 have no inheritance among the people of Israel. 6
19:10 to the stranger who sojourns among them 6
20:13 LORD . . showed himself holy among them. 3
21: 6 LORD sent fiery serpents among the people 3
23: 9 not reckoning itself among the nations! 3
21 the shout of a king is among them. 3
25:11 he was jealous with my jealousy among them 6
26:62 not numbered among the people of Israel 6
62 no inheritance given to them among . . Israel. 6
64 among these there was not a man of those numbered 3
27: 3 not among the company of those who gathered 3
4 possession among our father's brethren. 6
7 an inheritance among their father's brethren 6
31: 3 Arm men from among you for the war, 9
16 plague came among the congregation of the LORD. 3
17 therefore, kill every male among the little ones 3
32:30 shall have possessions among you in . . Canaan. 6
33: 4 first-born, whom the LORD had struck down among 3
35:15 refuge . . stranger and for the sojourner among 6
Deu 2:16 men of war . . were dead from among the people 17
4: 3 LORD your God destroyed from among you all 17
27 LORD will scatter you among the peoples 3
27 you will be left few in number among the nations 3
7:14 shall not be male or female barren among you 3
14 not be male or female barren . . among your cattle. 3
20 LORD your God will send hornets among them 3
13: 1 If a prophet arises among you, or a dreamer 5
11 do any such wickedness as this among you 5
13 certain base fellows have gone out among you 11
14 such an abominable thing has been done among you 3
14: 6 animal that . . chews the cud, among the animals 3
15: 4 there will be no poor among you (for the LORD 3
7 If there is among you a poor man 3
16:11 fatherless, and the widow who are among you 5
17: 2 If there is found among you, within . . your towns 5
15 One from among your brethren you shall set 11
18: 2 no inheritance among their brethren; the LORD 5
10 not be found among you any one who burns his son 3
15 raise up for you a prophet like me from among you 11
18 prophet like you from among their brethren; 17
19:20 never again commit any such evil among you. 5
21:11 see among the captives a beautiful woman 3
23:10 If there is among you any man who is not clean 3
14 that he may not see anything indecent among you 3
26:11 you, and the Levite, and the sojourner who is among 3
28:37 among all the peoples where the LORD will lead 3
43 sojourner who is among you shall mount above you 3
54 most tender and delicately bred among you 3
56 most tender and delicately bred woman among you 3
64 LORD will scatter you among all peoples 3
65 among these nations you shall find no ease 3
29:17 detestable things . . which were among them. 14
18 Beware lest there be among you a man or woman 3
18 lest there be among you a root bearing poisonous 3
30: 1 call them to mind among all the nations 3
31:16 land, where they go to be among them 3
17 evils come upon us because our God is not among us?' 5
32:26 make the remembrance . . cease from among men •
33:16 head of him that is prince among his brothers. •
Jos 1:14 but all the men of valor among you shall pass over •
3: 5 for tomorrow the LORD will do wonders among you. 5
10 you shall know that the living God is among you 5
4: 6 that this may be a sign among you 5
7:11 stolen . . and put them among their own stuff. 3
12 destroy the devoted things from among you. 17
13 take away the devoted things from among you. 17
21 when I saw among the spoil a beautiful mantle 3
8: 9 but Joshua spent that night among the people. 6
35 and the sojourners who lived among them. 3
9: 7 men of Israel said . . "Perhaps you live among us; 3
16 they heard . . and that they dwelt among them. 5
22 Why did you deceive us . . when you dwell among us? 5
10: 1 had made peace with Israel and were among them 5
13:22 Balaam also . . among the rest of their slain. 1
14: 3 the Levites he gave no inheritance among them. 6
15 this Arba was the greatest man among the Anakim. 3
15:13 he gave . . a portion among the people of Judah 3
17: 4 he gave them an inheritance among the brethren 6
9 The cities here . . among the cities of Manas'seh 6
18: 2 There remained among the people of Israel seven 3
7 The Levites have no portion among you 5
19:49 Israel gave an inheritance among them to Joshua 6
20: 9 and for the stranger sojourning among them 6

22:14 the head of a family among the clans of Israel. 8
19 and take for yourselves a possession among us; 6
23: 7 be mixed with these nations left here among you 2
12 the remnant of these nations left here among you 2
24:17 in all the way . . and among all the peoples 3
23 put away the foreign gods which are among you 5
Jdg 1:29 but the Canaanites dwelt in Gezer among them. 3
30 Canaanites dwelt among them, and became subject 3
32 the Asherites dwelt among the Canaanites 3
33 not drive out . . but dwelt among the Canaanites 3
2:12 other gods, from among the gods of the peoples •
3: 5 Israel dwelt among the Canaanites, the Hittites 3
5: 8 shield or spear to be seen among 40,000 in Israel? 3
9 who offered themselves . . among the people. 3
15 Among the clans of Reuben there were great 3
16 Why did you tarry among the sheepfolds, to hear 4
16 Among the clans of Reuben there were great 8
10:16 So they put away the foreign gods from among them 17
14: 3 a woman among the daughters of your kinsmen 3
3 kinsmen, or among all our people, that you must go 3
18: 1 no inheritance among the tribes of Israel had 3
25 Do not let your voice be heard among us, lest angry 14
20:12 is this that has taken place among you? 3
16 Among all these were 700 picked men 10
21:12 found among the inhabitants of Ja'besh-gil'ead 10
Rut 2: 2 and glean among the ears of grain after him 3
7 Pray, let me glean and gather among the sheaves 3
15 Let her glean even among the sheaves 4
4:10 dead may not be cut off from among his brethren 14
1Sm 4: 3 come among us and save us from . . our enemies. 5
17 has also been a great slaughter among the people; 3
6:19 LORD had made a . . slaughter among the people. 3
7: 3 put away the . . Ash'taroth from among you 18
9: 2 a man among the people of Israel more handsome 10
10:10 and he prophesied among them. 6
11 Is Saul also among the prophets? 3
12 became a proverb, "Is Saul also among the prophets? 3
22 Behold, he has hidden himself among the baggage. 1
23 when he stood among the people, he was taller 6
24 There is none like him among all the people. 3
14:15 camp, in the field, and among all the people; 3
30 the slaughter among the Philistines has not 3
34 Disperse yourselves among the people, and say 3
39 was not a man among all the people that answered 10
15: 6 Go, depart, go down from among the Amal'ekites 18
6 Ken'ites departed from among the Amal'ekites. 18
33 so shall your mother be childless among women. 10
16: 1 I have provided for myself a king among his sons. 3
19: 8 and made a great slaughter among them 3
24 Hence it is said, "Is Saul also among the prophets? 3
22:14 And who among all your servants is so faithful 3
23: 5 fought . . and made a great slaughter among them. 3
19 Does not David hide among us in the strongholds 14
23 search him out among all the thousands of Judah. 3
30:22 fellows among the men who had gone with David 10
2Sm 6:19 and distributed among all . . to each a cake 8
11:17 some . . servants of David among the people fell. 10
15:31 Ahith'ophel is among the conspirators 3
17: 9 slaughter among the people who follow Ab'salom.' 3
19:28 but you set . . among those who eat at your table. 3
22:50 I will extol thee, O LORD, among the nations 3
23: 9 next . . among the three mighty men was Elea'zar 3
23 He was renowned among the 30 10
24:16 who was working destruction among the people 3
1Kg 2: 7 and let them be among those who eat at your table; 3
5: 6 there is no one among us who knows how to cut 3
6:13 I will dwell among the children of Israel 6
8:53 separate them from among all the peoples •
9: 7 become a proverb and a byword among all peoples. 3
11:20 Genu'bath was in . . among the sons of Pharaoh. 6
12:31 and appointed priests from among all the people 15
13:33 made priests . . again from among all the people; 15
14: 7 Because I exalted you from among the people 18
21: 9 and set Naboth on high among the people; •
12 and set Naboth on high among the people. •
2Kg 4:13 She answered, "I dwell among my own people. 6
18 he went out . . to his father among the reapers. 1
9: 2 and go in and bid him rise from among his fellows 18
10:23 there is no servant of the LORD here among you 14
11: 2 and stole him away from among the king's sons 18
17:25 the LORD sent lions among them, which killed some 3
26 therefore he has sent lions among them 3
32 appointed from among themselves . . priests 15
18: 5 was none like him among all the kings of Judah 3
5 none like him . . nor among those who were before •
24 captain among the least of my master's servants •
35 Who among all the gods . . have delivered their 3
23: 9 they ate unleavened bread among their brethren. 6
1Ch 5: 2 though Judah became strong among his brothers 3
11:12 next . . among the three mighty men was Elea'zar 3
25 He was renowned among the 30 10
12: 1 were among the mighty men who helped him in war. 3
4 Ishma'iah of Gibeon, a mighty man among the 30 3
16: 8 make known his deeds among the peoples! 3
24 Declare his glory among the nations 3
24 his marvelous works among all the peoples! 3
31 let them say among the nations, "The LORD reigns! 3
35 gather and save us from among the nations 10
23:14 sons of Moses . . named among the tribe of Levi. 13

24: 4 chief men were found among the sons of Elea'zar •
4 more . . than among the sons of Ith'amar •
5 officers . . among both the sons of Elea'zar 3
26:19 among the Ko'rahites and the sons of Merar'i. 8
31 men of great ability among them were found 3
28: 4 and among my father's sons he took pleasure in me 3
2Ch 7:13 When I . . or send pestilence among my people 3
20 make it a proverb and a byword among all peoples. 3
11:22 Abi'jah . . as chief prince among his brothers 3
17: 9 they went about . . and taught among the people. 3
19: 4 Jehosh'aphat . . went out again among the people 3
22:11 stole him away from among the king's sons 18
24:16 buried him in the city of David among the kings 3
19 he sent prophets among them to bring them back 3
23 princes of the people from among the people 10
26: 6 elsewhere among the Philistines. 3
28:15 clothed all that were naked among them; 3
15 carrying all the feeble among them on asses 3
31:19 portions to every male among the priests 3
19 portions . . to every one among the Levites 3
32:14 Who among all the gods . . was able to deliver 3
36:23 Whoever is among you of all his people 3
Ezr 1: 3 Whoever is among you of all his people, may his God 3
2:62 their registration among those enrolled •
Neh 1: 8 unfaithful, I will scatter you among the peoples; 3
6: 6 It is reported among the nations, and Geshem also 3
7: 3 guards from among the inhabitants of Jerusalem •
64 among those enrolled in the genealogies •
9:17 wonders which thou didst perform among them; 14
11:17 Bakbuki'ah, the second among his brethren; 10
13:26 Among the many nations there was no king like him 3
Est 1:19 let it be written among the laws of the Persians 3
2: 6 carried away from Jerusalem among the captives 14
3: 8 scattered . . and dispersed among the peoples 4
4: 3 there was great mourning among the Jews 8
8:17 there was gladness and joy among the Jews, a feast 8
9:28 Purim . . never fall into disuse among the Jews 12
28 nor should . . cease among their descendants. 10
10: 3 and he was great among the Jews and popular 8
Job 1: 6 before the LORD, and Satan also came among them. 3
2: 1 Satan also came among them to present himself 3
8 to scrape himself, and sat among the ashes. 6
3: 6 let it not rejoice among the days of the year 3
8:17 about the stoneheap; he lives among the rocks. 34
12: 9 Who among all these does not know that the hand 3
15:10 Both the gray-haired and the aged are among us 3
19 no stranger passed among them). 3
17:10 I shall not find a wise man among you. 3
18:19 has no offspring or descendant among his people 3
22:24 gold of Ophir among the stones of the torrent bed 3
24:11 among the olive rows of the wicked they make oil; 4
29:25 as chief, and I dwelt like a king among his troops 3
30: 5 They are driven out from among men; 7
7 Among the bushes they bray; 4
32:12 or that answered his words, among you. 10
34: 4 let us determine among ourselves what is good. 4
37 he claps his hands among us 4
41: 6 Will they divide him up among the merchants? 4
42:15 gave them inheritance among their brothers. 6
Ps 9:11 Tell among the peoples his deeds! 3
12: 1 have vanished from among the sons of men. 10
8 as vileness is exalted among the sons of men. 8
18:49 I will extol thee, O LORD, among the nations 3
21:10 their children from among the sons of men. 10
22:18 they divide my garments among them 8
30: 3 from among those gone down to the Pit. 10
44:11 hast scattered us among the nations. 3
14 Thou hast made us a byword among the nations 3
14 made us . . a laughingstock among the peoples. 3
45: 9 of kings are among your ladies of honor; 3
46:10 I am God. I am exalted among the nations 3
54: 0 went and told Saul, "David is in hiding among us. 14
57: 9 give thanks to thee, O Lord, among the peoples; 3
9 I will sing praises to thee among the nations. 3
66: 5 he is terrible in his deeds among men. 13
9 who has kept us among the living 3
67: 2 upon earth, thy saving power among all nations. 3
68:13 though they stay among the sheepfolds- 4
18 receiving gifts among men 3
18 gifts among men, even among the rebellious •
30 Rebuke the beasts that dwell among the reeds •
69:28 let them not be enrolled among the righteous. 14
74: 9 there is none among us who knows how long. 2
77:14 who hast manifested thy might among the peoples. 3
78:45 He sent among them swarms of flies 3
60 at Shiloh, the tent where he dwelt among men 3
79:10 be known among the nations before our eyes! 3
80: 6 our enemies laugh among themselves. 8
81: 9 There shall be no strange god among you; 3
86: 8 There is none like thee among the gods, O Lord 3
87: 4 Among those who know me I mention Rahab 8
88: 4 I am reckoned among those who go down to the Pit; 14
5 like one forsaken among the dead 3
89: 6 Who among the heavenly beings is like the LORD 3
96: 3 Declare his glory among the nations 3
3 his marvelous works among all the peoples! 3
10 Say among the nations, "The LORD reigns! 3
99: 6 Moses and Aaron were among his priests 3
6 Samuel . . among those who called on his name. 3
104:12 birds of the air . . sing among the branches. 4
105: 1 make known his deeds among the peoples! 3
27 They wrought his signs among them, and miracles 3
37 there was none among his tribes who stumbled. 3
106:15 but sent a wasting disease among them. 3
27 disperse their descendants among the nations 3
29 plague broke out among them. 3
47 O LORD . . and gather us from among the nations 10
108: 3 give thanks to thee, O LORD, among the peoples 3
3 I will sing praises to thee among the nations. •
110: 6 He will execute judgment among the nations 3
120: 5 Woe is me, that . . I dwell among the tents of Kedar! 14
6 long . . my dwelling among those who hate peace. 14
126: 2 then they said among the nations, "The LORD 3
136:11 brought Israel out from among them 18
Prv 1:14 throw in your lot among us 3
6:19 a man who sows discord among brothers. 4
7: 7 I have seen among the simple 3
7 I have perceived among the youths 3
15:31 He whose ear heeds . . will abide among the wise. 3
23:20 Be not among winebibbers, or among gluttonous 3
20 Be not . . among gluttonous eaters of meat; 3
28 increases the faithless among men. 3
30:14 to devour the . . needy from among men. 10
30 the lion, which is mightiest among beasts 3
31:23 when he sits among the elders of the land. 14
Ecc 1:11 things yet to happen among those who come after. 14
7:28 One man among 1,000 I found 10
28 but a woman among all these I have not found. 3
9:17 better than the shouting of a ruler among fools. 3
Sng 1: 8 If you do not know, O fairest among women 3
2: 2 As a lily among brambles, so is my love 4
2 As a lily among . . so is my love among maidens. 4
3 As an apple tree among the trees of the wood, so is 3
3 an apple tree . . so is my beloved among young men. 4
16 he pastures his flock among the lilies. 3
4: 2 bear twins, and not one among them is bereaved. 3
5 like two fawns . . that feed among the lilies. 3
5: 9 What is your beloved . . O fairest among women? 3
10 and ruddy, distinguished among 10,000. 10
6: 1 has your beloved gone, O fairest among women? 3
3 he pastures his flock among the lilies. 3
6 all . . bear twins, not one among them is bereaved. 3
Isa 5:17 fatlings and kids shall feed among the ruins. •
8:16 seal the teaching among my disciples. 3
10: 4 Nothing . . but to crouch among the prisoners 19
4 among the prisoners or fall among the slain. 3
16 send wasting sickness among his stout warriors 3
12: 4 make known his deeds among the nations 3
16: 4 let the outcasts of Moab sojourn among you; 3
24:13 in the midst of the earth among the nations 6
29:19 the poor among men shall exult in the Holy One 3
30:14 among its fragments not a sherd is found 3
33:14 Who among us can dwell with the devouring fire? 8
14 Who among us can dwell with . . burnings? 8
36: 9 a single captain among the least of my master's •
20 Who among all the gods of these countries 3
38:11 man no more among the inhabitants of the world. 14
41:28 among these there is no counselor who 10
42:23 Who among you will give ear to this 3
43: 9 Who among them can declare this 3
12 when there was no strange god among you; 3
44:14 lets it grow strong among the trees of the forest; 3
48:14 Who among them has declared these things? 3
50:10 Who among you fears the LORD and obeys the voice 3
51:18 none to guide her among all the sons she has borne 10
18 by the hand among all the sons she has brought up. 3
57: 5 you who burn with lust among the oaks 3
6 Among the smooth stones of the valley 3
59:10 among those in full vigor we are like dead men. 3
61: 9 descendants shall be known among the nations 3
66:19 I will set a sign among them. 3
19 they shall declare my glory among the nations. 3
Jer 3:13 and scattered your favors among strangers 8
19 I thought how I would set you among my sons 3
4: 3 and sow not among thorns. 1
29 they enter thickets; they climb among rocks; 3
5:26 For wicked men are found among my people; 3
6:15 Therefore they shall fall among those who fall; 3
27 made you an assayer and tester among my people 3
8:12 Therefore they shall fall among the fallen; 3
17 For behold, I am sending among you serpents 3
9:16 I will scatter them among the nations 3
10: 7 for among all the wise ones of the nations 3
11: 9 There is revolt among the men of Judah 3
12:14 will pluck up the house of Judah from among them. 18
14:22 Are there any among the false gods of the nations 3
18:13 thus says the LORD: Ask among the nations 3
22:23 O inhabitant of Lebanon, nested among the cedars 3
23:18 For who among them has stood in the council •
25:16 the sword which I am sending among them. 4
20 and all the foreign folk among them; •
27 because of the sword which I am sending among you. 4
29: 8 your diviners who are among you deceive you 5
18 a hissing, and a reproach among all the nations 3
32 shall not have any one living among this people 3
30:11 of all the nations among whom I scattered you •
31: 8 among them the blind and the lame 3
32:20 and to this day in Israel and among all mankind 3
37: 4 was still going in and out among the people 3
12 to receive his portion there among the people. 3
39:14 So he dwelt among the people. 3
40: 5 and dwell with him among the people; 3
6 at Mizpah, and dwelt with him among the people 3
11 in Moab and among the Ammonites and in Edom 3
41: 8 there were ten men among them who said to Ish'mael 3
44: 8 and a taunt among all the nations of the earth? 3
46:18 the LORD of hosts, like Tabor among the mountains 3
48:27 Was he found among thieves 3
49: 3 lament, and run to and fro among the hedges! 3
14 and a messenger has been sent among the nations 3
15 behold, I will make you small among the nations 3
15 you small among the nations, despised among men. 3
50: 2 Declare among the nations and proclaim 3
23 How Babylon has become a horror among the nations! 3
46 and her cry shall be heard among the nations. 3
51:27 on the earth, blow the trumpet among the nations; 3
41 How Babylon has become a horror among the nations! 3
Lam 1: 1 a widow . . she that was great among the nations! 3
1 She that was a princess among the cities 3
2 among all her lovers she has none to comfort her; 10
3 she dwells now among the nations 3
17 Jerusalem has become a filthy thing among them. 4
2: 9 her king and princes are among the nations; 3
3:45 made us offscouring and . . among the peoples. 3
4:15 men said among the nations, "They shall stay 3
20 Under his shadow we shall live among . . nations. 3
Ezk 1: 1 as I was among the exiles by the river Chebar 6
13 moving to and fro among the living creatures; 4
2: 5 know that there has been a prophet among them. 3
3:15 I sat there overwhelmed among them seven days. 3
25 so that you cannot go out among the people; 3
4:13 among the nations whither I will drive them. 3
5:14 of reproach among the nations round about you 3
6: 8 When you have among the nations some who escape 3
9 will remember me among the nations 3
13 when their slain lie among their idols 3
7:11 neither shall there be preeminence among them. 3
8:11 the son of Shaphan standing among them. 6
10: 2 Go in among the whirling wheels 4
11: 1 I saw among them Ja-azani'ah the son of Azzur 3
16 Though I removed them far off among the nations 3
16 and though I scattered them among the countries 3
12:12 prince who is among them shall lift his baggage 3
15 when I disperse them among the nations 3
16 abominations among the nations where they go 3
13: 4 Your prophets have been like foxes among ruins 3
19 You have profaned me among my people 1
15: 2 branch which is among the trees of the forest? 3
6 wood of the vine among the trees of the forest 3
16:14 your renown went forth among the nations 3
18:18 and did what is not good among his people 3
19: 2 say: What a lioness was your mother among lions! 4
6 He prowled among the lions; he became a young lion 3
11 it towered aloft among the thick boughs; 4
20: 9 in the sight of the nations among whom they dwelt 3
23 that I would scatter them among the nations 3
38 I will purge out the rebels from among you 3
41 I will manifest my holiness among you 3
22:15 I will scatter you among the nations 3
26 so that I am profaned among them. 3
30 I sought for a man among them who should build up 10
23:10 she became a byword among women 8
25: 4 they shall set their encampments among you 3
10 may be remembered no more among the nations 3
26:20 dwell in the nether world, among primeval ruins •
27:36 The merchants among the peoples hiss at you; 3
28:19 All who know you among the peoples are appalled 3
24 thorn to hurt them among all their neighbors 10
25 from the peoples among whom they are scattered 3
29:12 40 years among cities that are laid waste. 6
12 I will scatter the Egyptians among the nations 3
12 and disperse them among the countries. 3
13 from the peoples among whom they were scattered; •
21 I will open your lips among them. 3
30:23 I will scatter the Egyptians among the nations 3
26 I will scatter the Egyptians among the nations 3
31: 3 and of great height, its top among the clouds. 4
10 it towered high and set its top among the clouds 4
14 or set their tops among the clouds 4
14 to death, to the nether world among mortal men 3
17 who dwelt under its shadow among the nations 3
18 in glory and in greatness among the trees of Eden? 3
18 you shall lie among the uncircumcised 3
32: 2 You consider yourself a lion among the nations •
9 when I carry you captive among the nations 3
12 all of them most terrible among the nations. •
25 They have made her a bed among the slain 3
25 they are placed among the slain. 6
28 shall be broken and lie among the uncircumcised 6
32 he shall be laid among the uncircumcised 3
33: 2 the people of the land take a man from among them •
33 will know that a prophet has been among them. 6
34:24 my servant David shall be prince among them; 3
35:11 I will make myself known among you, when I judge 3
36:19 I scattered them among the nations 3
21 Israel caused to be profaned among the nations 3
22 name, which you have profaned among the nations 3

23 name, which has been profaned among the nations 3
23 and which you have profaned among them; 3
30 the disgrace of famine among the nations. 3
37: 2 he led me round among them; 13
21 from the nations among which they have gone 4
39:21 I will set my glory among the nations; 3
28 because I sent them into exile among the nations 3
28 none of them remaining among the nations •
40:46 sons of Zadok, who alone among the sons of Levi may 10
44: 9 foreigners who are among the people of Israel 6
47:13 inheritance among the twelve tribes of Israel. 8
21 you shall divide this land among you 8
22 for the aliens who reside among you 3
22 and have begotten children among you. 3
22 an inheritance among the tribes of Israel. 6
48:29 as an inheritance among the tribes of Israel 8
Dan 1: 6 Among these were Daniel, Hanani'ah, Mish'a-el 3
19 among them all none was found like Daniel 10
2:25 I have found among the exiles from Judah a man 21
4:25 that you shall be driven from among men •
32 you shall be driven from among men •
33 driven from among men, and ate grass like an ox •
35 heaven and among the inhabitants of the earth; •
5:21 driven from among men, and his mind was made •
7: 8 came up among them another horn, a little one 20
9:16 become a byword among all who are round about us. 8
11:14 men of violence among your own people •
24 scattering among them plunder, spoil, and goods. 8
33 among the people who are wise shall make many •
Hos 5: 9 among the tribes of Israel I declare what is sure. 3
8: 8 they are among the nations as a useless vessel. 3
10 Though they hire allies among the nations 3
9:17 they shall be wanderers among the nations. 3
10:14 the tumult of war shall arise among your people 3
Jol 2:17 heritage a reproach, a byword among the nations. 3
17 Why should they say among the peoples 3
19 no more make you a reproach among the nations. 3
25 my great army, which I sent among you. 3
32 among the survivors shall be those whom the LORD 3
3: 2 they have scattered them among the nations 3
9 Proclaim this among the nations: Prepare war 3
Ams 1: 1 of Amos, who was among the shepherds of Teko'a 3
2:16 who is stout of heart among the mighty shall flee 3
4:10 I sent among you a pestilence after the manner 3
9: 9 shake the house of Israel among all the nations 3
Obd 1: 1 and a messenger has been sent among the nations 3
2 Behold, I will make you small among the nations 3
4 though your nest is set among the stars 4
Mic 2: 4 Among our captors he divides our fields. 8
5: 2 who are little to be among the clans of Judah 3
8 the remnant of Jacob shall be among the nations 3
8 like a lion among the beasts of the forest 3
8 like a young lion among the flocks of sheep 3
10 I will cut off your horses from among you 17
13 cut off your images and . . pillars from among you 17
14 I will root out your Ashe'rim from among you 17
7: 2 and there is none upright among men; 3
Hab 1: 5 Look among the nations, and see; 3
Zep 3:20 and praised among all the peoples of the earth 3
Hag 2: 3 Who is left among you that saw this house 3
5 My Spirit abides among you; fear not. 3
Zec 1: 8 He was standing among the myrtle trees 4
10 the man who was standing among the myrtle trees 4
11 angel . . who was standing among the myrtle trees 4
3: 7 the right of access among those who are standing 4
7:14 among all the nations which they had not known. 13
8:13 been a byword of cursing among the nations 3
10: 9 Though I scattered them among the nations 3
12: 6 Judah . . like a flaming torch among sheaves; 3
8 so that the feeblest among them on that day shall 3
Mal 1:10 there were one among you who would shut the doors 3
11 my name is great among the nations, says the LORD 3
11 my name is great among the nations, says the LORD 3
14 my name is feared among the nations. 3
Mat 2: 6 are by no means least among the rulers of Judah; 28
4:23 disease and every infirmity among the people. 28
10: 5 Go nowhere among the Gentiles 26
11:11 Truly, I say to you, among those born of women 28
13:22 As for what was sown among thorns 24
25 his enemy came and sowed weeds among the wheat 22
16: 7 they discussed it among themselves, saying 28
8 why do you discuss among yourselves the fact 28
20:26 It shall not be so among you 28
26 whoever would be great among you 28
27 whoever would be first among you 28
22:25 Now there were seven brothers among us 37
23:11 He who is greatest among you •
26: 5 lest there be a tumult among the people. 28
27:35 they divided his garments among them by casting lots; •
56 among whom were Mary Mag'dalene 28
28:15 story has been spread among the Jews to this day. 37
Mrk 1:27 so that they questioned among themselves 38
4: 7 Other seed fell among thorns 24
18 others are the ones sown among thorns 24
5: 3 who lived among the tombs 28
5 Night and day among the tombs 28
6: 4 among his own kin, and in his own house. 28
6 he went about among the villages teaching. 33
41 he divided the two fish among them all. •

10:43 it shall not be so among you 28
43 whoever would be great among you 28
44 whoever would be first among you 28
15: 7 among the rebels in prison 35
24 and divided his garments among them •
40 among whom were Mary Mag'dalene . . and Salo'me 28
Lke 1: 1 which have been accomplished among us 28
25 to take away my reproach among men. 28
42 Blessed are you among women 28
2:14 on earth peace among men with whom he is pleased! 28
44 they sought him among their kinsfolk 28
7:16 A great prophet has arisen among us! 28
28 among those born of women none is greater 28
49 began to say among themselves 28
8: 7 some fell among thorns 28
14 as for what fell among the thorns 24
27 he lived not in a house but among the tombs. 28
9:46 an argument arose among them 28
48 who is least among you all is the one who is great. 28
10:36 the man who fell among the robbers? 24
11:11 What father among you, if his son asks for a fish 27
16:15 what is exalted among men 28
21:24 and be led captive among all nations 24
22:17 Take this, and divide it among yourselves; 24
24 A dispute also arose among them 28
26 the greatest among you become as the youngest 28
55 Peter sat among them. 34
24: 5 Why do you seek the living among the dead? 35
Joh 1:14 And the Word became flesh and dwelt among us 28
26 but among you stands one whom you do not know 34
6: 9 but what are they among so many? 24
43 Do not murmur among yourselves. 35
52 The Jews then disputed among themselves, saying 38
7:12 much muttering about him among the people 28
35 to go to the Dispersion among the Greeks •
43 there was a division among the people over him. 28
8: 7 Let him who is without sin among you be the first •
9:16 There was a division among them. 28
10:19 There was again a division among the Jews 28
11:54 no longer went about openly among the Jews 28
12:20 among those who went up to worship at the feast 27
15:24 If I had not done among them the works 28
19:24 They parted my garments among them •
20:19 Jesus came and stood among them and said to them 25
26 Jesus came and stood among them, and said 25
21:23 The saying spread abroad among the brethren 24
Act 1:17 he was numbered among us 28
21 the Lord Jesus went in and out among us 30
4:12 no other name under heaven given among men 28
17 it may spread no further among the people 24
34 There was not a needy person among them 28
5:12 wonders were done among the people 28
6: 3 pick out from among you seven men of good repute •
8 did great wonders and signs among the people. 28
9:28 So he went in and out among them at Jerusalem 35
32 Now as Peter went here and there among them all 23
10: 7 from among those that waited on him •
45 the believers from among the circumcised •
12:18 there was no small stir among the soldiers 28
13:26 those among you that fear God 28
14:14 and rushed out among the multitude, crying 24
15: 7 in the early days God made choice among you 28
12 God had done through them among the Gentiles. 28
22 to choose men from among them •
22 leading men among the brethren 28
17:33 Paul went out from among them. 34
34 believed, among them Dionys'ius the Are-op'agite 28
18:11 teaching the word of God among them. 28
19:30 Paul wished to go in among the crowd 24
20:18 You yourselves know how I lived among you 35
25 all you among whom I have gone preaching 28
29 fierce wolves will come in among you 24
30 from among your own selves will arise men •
32 among all those who are sanctified. 28
21:19 things that God had done among the Gentiles 28
20 how many thousands there are among the Jews 28
21 you teach all the Jews who are among the Gentiles 32
23:10 go down and take him by force from among them 34
24: 5 an agitator among all the Jews •
21 which I cried out while standing among them 28
25: 5 let the men of authority among you go down with me 28
6 When he had stayed among them 28
26: 4 spent from the beginning among my own nation 28
18 a place among those who are sanctified by faith 28
27:22 no loss of life among you, but only of the ship. 27
28:25 as they disagreed among themselves 38
Rom 1: 5 for the sake of his name among all the nations 28
13 in order that I may reap some harvest among you 28
13 as well as among the rest of the Gentiles 28
24 dishonoring of their bodies among themselves 28
2:24 The name of God is blasphemed among the Gentiles 28
8:29 he might be the first-born among many brethren. 28
12: 3 I bid every one among you not to think of himself 28
15: 9 Therefore I will praise thee among the Gentiles 28
26 for the poor among the saints at Jerusalem; •
16: 6 Greet Mary, who has worked hard among you. 24
7 they are men of note among the apostles 28
1Co 1: 6 testimony to Christ was confirmed among you- 28
10 that there be no dissensions among you 28

11 there is quarreling among you, my brethren. 28
2: 2 For I decided to know nothing among you 28
6 Yet among the mature we do impart wisdom 28
3: 3 For while there is jealousy and strife among you 28
18 If any one among you thinks that he is wise 28
5: 1 there is immorality among you 28
1 of a kind that is not found even among pagans 28
2 be removed from among you. 34
13 Drive out the wicked person from among you. •
6: 5 there is no man among you wise enough to decide 28
9:11 If we have sown spiritual good among you •
11:18 I hear that there are divisions among you 28
19 for there must be factions among you 28
19 in order that those who are genuine among you 28
14:25 declare that God is really among you. 28
16:10 see that you put him at ease among you 38
2Co 1:19 Jesus Christ, whom we preached among you 28
2:15 among those who are being saved 28
15 among those who are perishing 28
8: 6 also complete among you this gracious work. 24
18 the brother who is famous among all the churches 28
10:15 our field among you may be greatly enlarged 28
12:12 The signs of a true apostle were performed among you 28
Gal 1:14 many of my own age among my people 28
16 I might preach him among the Gentiles 28
2: 2 the gospel which I preach among the Gentiles 28
3: 5 works miracles among you 28
Eph 2: 3 Among these we all once lived 28
5: 3 covetousness must not even be named among you 28
3 as is fitting among saints. •
Php 2: 5 Have this mind among yourselves 28
15 among whom you shine as lights in the world 28
Col 1: 6 so among yourselves, from the day you heard 28
27 how great among the Gentiles 28
4:11 men of the circumcision among my fellow workers •
16 when this letter has been read among you 37
1Th 1: 5 what kind of men we proved to be among you 28
9 what a welcome we had among you 38
5:12 respect those who labor among you 28
13 Be at peace among yourselves. 28
2Th 3: 1 as it did among you 38
1Ti 1:20 among them Hymenae'us and Alexander •
3:16 preached among the nations 28
6: 5 wrangling among men who are depraved in mind •
2Ti 1:15 among them Phy'gelus and Hermog'enes. •
2:17 Among them are Hymenae'us and Phile'tus •
3: 6 among them are those who . . 27
Heb 5: 1 every high priest chosen from among men •
13: 4 Let marriage be held in honor among all 28
Jas 2: 4 made distinctions among yourselves 28
3: 6 an unrighteous world among our members 31
13 Who is wise and understanding among you? 28
4: 1 and what causes fightings among you? 28
5:13 Is any one among you suffering? Let him pray. 28
14 Is any among you sick? Let him call for the elders 28
19 if any one among you wanders from the truth 28
1Pe 2:12 Maintain good conduct among the Gentiles 28
5: 1 So I exhort the elders among you, as a fellow elder 28
2Pe 2: 1 false prophets also arose among the people 28
1 just as there will be false teachers among you 28
8 saw and heard as he lived among them 28
1Jn 4: 9 In this the love of God was made manifest among us 28
Rev 2:13 An'tipas . . who was killed among you 37
6:15 hid . . among the rocks of the mountains 24
1Es 8:91 there was great weeping among the multitude. 28
2Es 1:14 and did great wonders among you 42
21 I divided fertile lands among you •
2: 7 Let them be scattered among the nations 42
26 for I will require them from among your number. •
3:33 I have traveled widely among the nations 42
5:28 and scattered thine only one among the many? 42
7:46 who among the living is there 41
46 who among men that has not transgressed •
76 nor number yourself among those 40
8:35 there is no one among those who have been born 41
35 and among those who have existed there is no one 41
49 not deemed yourself to be among the righteous 43
9:26 and there I sat among the flowers 42
29 O Lord, thou didst show thyself among us 42
10:16 and will be praised among women. 42
12:38 shall teach them to the wise among your people 41
14: 9 you shall be taken up from among men •
13 comfort the lowly among them •
17 evils be multiplied among its inhabitants. 44
46 to give them to the wise among your people. 41
15: 9 all the innocent blood from among them. •
16 For there shall be unrest among men •
Tob 1: 4 chosen from among all the tribes of Israel •
3: 4 the nations among which we have been dispersed. 28
4:12 from among the descendants of your fathers •
12 all took wives from among their brethren •
13 to take a wife for yourself from among them. •
6:15 to take a wife from among your own people •
11:17 rejoicing among all his brethren in Nineveh. •
13: 3 he has scattered us among them. 28
5 the nations among whom you have been scattered. 28
Jdt 1: 8 those among the nations of Carmel and Gilead 28
6: 2 to prophesy among us as you have done today 28
6 you shall fall among their wounded 28

8:22 he will bring upon our heads among the Gentiles 28
9: 4 their booty to be divided among thy beloved sons •
10:19 who have women like this among them 28
AEs 10: 9 wonders, which have not occurred among the nations 28
11 before God and among all the nations. 28
13 for ever among his people Israel. 28
13: 3 Haman, who excels among us in sound judgment 37
4 among all the nations in the world 28
14: 5 take . . from among all their ancestors •
16: 4 not only take away thankfulness from among men •
22 among your commemorative festivals 28
Wis 4:10 while living among sinners he was taken up. 36
18 and an outrage among the dead for ever 28
5: 5 Why has he been numbered among the sons of God? 28
5 why is his lot among the saints? 28
8:10 I shall have glory among the multitudes 28
15 among the people I shall show myself capable 28
9: 4 do not reject me from among thy servants. •
6 for even if one is perfect among the sons of men 28
12:17 dost rebuke any insolence among those who know it. 28
13: 7 as they live among his works they keep searching 28
13 a castoff piece from among them 27
Sir 1:15 She made among men an eternal foundation 35
15 among their descendants she will be trusted. 35
7: 7 do not disgrace yourself among the people. 28
16 Do not count yourself among the crowd of sinners; 28
11: 3 The bee is small among flying creatures 28
16:17 Among so many people I shall not be known 28
23:14 when you sit among great men 22
24: 7 Among all these I sought a resting place 35
25:18 Her husband takes his meals among the neighbors 22
26: 3 granted among the blessings of the man who fears 28
27:12 Among stupid people watch for a chance to leave 25
12 among thoughtful people stay on. 25
28: 9 inject enmity among those who are at peace. 22
23 it will burn among them and will not be put out 28
29:18 they have wandered among foreign nations. 28
30: 2 will boast of him among acquaintances. 22
31: 9 he has done wonderful things among his people. 28
18 If you are seated among many persons 22
32: 1 be among them as one of them 28
33:18 Hear me, you who are great among the people •
37:26 He who is wise among his people 28
39: 4 serve among great men and appear before rulers; 22
4 he tests the good and the evil among men. 28
41: 1 one who lives at peace among his possessions 28
42:11 notorious among the people •
44:23 distributed them among twelve tribes. 28
45:22 he has no portion among the people 28
49:16 Shem and Seth were honored among men 28
Bar 2: 4 desolation among all the surrounding peoples 28
13 among the nations where thou hast scattered us. 28
29 turn into a small number among the nations 28
3:11 that you are counted among those in Hades? 35
37 she appeared upon earth and lived among men. 28
LJr 1:67 show signs in the heavens and among the nations 28
Sus 1:64 Daniel had a great reputation among the people. 29
1Mc 1: 6 and divided his kingdom among them 28
2:18 you . . will be numbered among the friends of the king •
3:38 mighty men among the friends of the king •
4:58 There was very great gladness among the people 28
5: 2 the descendants of Jacob who lived among them. 28
2 they began to kill and destroy among the people. 28
63 in all Israel and among all the Gentiles •
6:35 distributed the beasts among the phalanxes; 24
7:13 Hasideans were first among the sons of Israel 28
23 the evil . . done among the sons of Israel 28
8: 2 brave deeds which they were doing among the Gauls 28
16 there is no envy or jealousy among them. 28
9:27 prophets ceased to appear among them. •
10:65 and enrolled him among his chief friends •
11:60 beyond the river and among the cities 28
12: 7 Arius, who was king among you 28
53 and blot out the memory of them from among men. •
13:17 lest he arouse great hostility among the people 38
15:35 they were causing great damage among the people 28
2Mc 1:27 set free those who are slaves among the Gentiles 28
7:16 Because you have authority among men 28
8:28 and distributed the rest among themselves •
9:28 among the mountains in a strange land. 28
12: 3 the Jews who lived among them 39
14:35 a temple for thy habitation among us; 28
3Mc 2: 2 holy among the holy ones, the only ruler, almighty 28
4 among whom were even giants 28
21 the first Father of all, holy among the holy ones 28
3: 5 they were established in good repute among all men. •
6 which was common talk among all; 28
19 they become the only people among all nations •
21 Among other things 28
23 they abominate those few among them 28
4: 2 among the Jews there was incessant mourning •
6: 1 famous among the priests of the country •
7:21 greater prestige among their enemies 28
4Mc 2:22 he enthroned the mind among the senses 23
14:15 For example, among birds •
151 1: 1 I was small among my brothers 28

among *See also* fall, live, move, number, sit, spread, walk.

among whom 1. שָׁם
2Kg 17:33 the nation from among whom they had been carried 1

amount 1. πλῆθος
Lev 27:23 the man shall give the amount of the valuation •
2Sm 12:30 brought forth the spoil . . a very great amount. •
1Kg 9:28 gold, to the amount of 420 talents; •
10:11 brought from Ophir a very great amount of almug •
2Kg 22: 4 Go up . . that he may reckon the amount of the money •
1Ch 20: 2 the spoil of the city, a very great amount. •
2Mc 3: 6 the amount of the funds could not be reckoned 1
12:43 to the amount of 2,000 drachmas of silver •

great amount 1. πολύς
Jdt 15: 7 the Israelites . . got a great amount of booty 1
1Mc 9:35 to store with them the great amount of baggage 1

huge amount 1. πολὺ σφόδρα
Jdt 2:18 a huge amount of gold and silver 1

immense amount 1. πολὺ σφόδρα
1Mc 3:41 they took silver and gold in immense amounts 1

same amount 1. זֶה
2Ch 27: 5 Ammonites paid him the same amount 1

ample 1. רָחָב 2. ἱκανός 3. περισσεύω 4. πολύς
Lke 12:19 Soul, you have ample goods laid up for many years; 4
Php 1:26 ample cause to glory in Christ Jesus 3
Sir 31:19 How ample a little is for a well-disciplined man! 2
47:23 ample in folly and lacking in understanding 1

amulet 1. לַחַשׁ
Isa 3:20 the perfume boxes, and the amulets; 1

amuse 1. παίζω
Sir 32:12 Amuse yourself there, and do what you have in mind 1

ancestor 1. אָב 2. γονεύς 3. πατήρ 4. πάτριος
5. πρόγονος 6. prior
Jos 19:47 after the name of Dan their ancestor. 1
Jdg 18:29 after the name of Dan their ancestor, who was born 1
Heb 7:10 for he was still in the loins of his ancestor 3
2Es 3:12 to be more ungodly than were their ancestors. 6
Jdt 5: 8 For they had left the ways of their ancestors 2
AEs 14: 5 take . . from among all their ancestors 5
Sir 8: 4 lest your ancestors be disgraced. 5
2Mc 8:19 when help came to their ancestors 5
11:25 according to the customs of their ancestors. 5
3Mc 5:31 a full and firm loyalty to my ancestors. 5
6:28 from the time of our ancestors until now 5
7: 7 toward us and our ancestors 5
4Mc 3: 8 the whole army of our ancestors had encamped. 5
5:29 the sacred oaths of my ancestors 5
9:24 the just Providence of our ancestors 4

ancestor of nation 1. ἐθνοπάτωρ
4Mc 16:20 Isaac, the ancestor of our nation 1

ancestral 1. אָב 2. πάτριος 3. προγονικός
Num 1:16 the leaders of their ancestral tribes 1
47 numbered by their ancestral tribe along 1
2Mc 8:17 the overthrow of their ancestral way of life. 3
14: 7 Therefore I have laid aside my ancestral glory 3
3Mc 1: 3 apostatized from the ancestral traditions 2
4Mc 4:23 if any . . should be found observing the ancestral law 2
5:33 to break the ancestral law by my own act. 2
8: 7 the ancestral tradition of your national life. 2
9: 1 transgress our ancestral commandments; 2
18: 5 to abandon their ancestral customs 2

anchor 1. ἄγκυρα 2. ἄσσον
Act 27:13 they weighed anchor and sailed along Crete 2
29 they let out four anchors from the stern 1
30 under pretense of laying out anchors 1
40 they cast off the anchors and left them in the sea 1
Heb 6:19 as a sure and steadfast anchor of the soul 1

ancient 1. מֵעוֹלָם 2. עוֹלָם 3. עַתִּיק 4. קֶדֶם 5. קַדְמֹנִי
6. עַתִּיק (A) 7. ἀρχαῖος 8. ἐξ ἀρχῆς
Deu 33:15 with the finest produce of the ancient mountains 4
1Sm 24:13 As the proverb of the ancients says 5
1Ch 4:22 (now the records are ancient). 3
Ps 24: 7 be lifted up, O ancient doors! 2
9 be lifted up, O ancient doors! 2
68:33 him who rides in the heavens, the ancient heavens; 4
Prv 22:28 Remove not the ancient landmark 2
23:10 Do not remove an ancient landmark or enter 2
Isa 19:11 I am a son of the wise, a son of ancient kings"? 4
58:12 And your ancient ruins shall be rebuilt; 2
61: 4 They shall build up the ancient ruins 2
Jer 5:15 It is an enduring nation, it is an ancient nation 1
6:16 and look, and ask for the ancient paths 2
18:15 have stumbled in their ways, in the ancient roads 2
Ezk 36: 2 The ancient heights have become our possession, 2
Dan 7: 9 one that was ancient of days took his seat; 6
13 came to the Ancient of Days and was presented 6
22 until the Ancient of Days came, and judgment 6
Mic 5: 2 whose origin is from of old, from ancient days. 2
2Pe 2: 5 if he did not spare the ancient world 7
Rev 12: 9 ancient serpent, who is called the Devil 7
20: 2 And he seized the dragon, that ancient serpent 7
Wis 13:10 a useless stone, the work of an ancient hand. 7
Sir 2:10 Consider the ancient generations and see 7
16: 7 He was not propitiated for the ancient giants 7
39: 1 will seek out the wisdom of all the ancients 7
1Mc 15:17 to renew our ancient friendship and alliance. 8

ancient *See also* time.

more ancient 1. παλαιός
AEs 16: 7 be seen not so much from the more ancient records 1

anew 1. ἄνωθεν 2. πάλιν ἄνωθεν
Joh 3: 3 unless one is born anew, he cannot see the kingdom 1
7 that I said to you, 'You must be born anew.' 1
Wis 19: 6 whole creation in its nature was fashioned anew 2

anew *See also* bear, show.

angel 1. אַבִּיר 2. מַלְאָךְ 3. מַלְאַךְ (A) 4. ἄγγελος
5. ἅγιος 6. angelus
Gen 16: 7 The angel of the LORD found her by a spring 2
9 The angel of the LORD said to her 2
10 The angel of the LORD also said to her 2
11 the angel of the LORD said to her 2
19: 1 The two angels came to Sodom in the evening; 2
15 When morning dawned, the angels urged Lot 2
21:17 and the angel of God called to Hagar from heaven 2
22:11 the angel of the LORD called to him from heaven 2
15 the angel of the LORD called to Abraham 2
24: 7 he will send his angel before you 2
40 LORD . . will send his angel with you and prosper 2
28:12 and behold, the angels of God were ascending 2
31:11 the angel of God said to me in the dream, 'Jacob,' 2
32: 1 Jacob went on his way and the angels of God met him; 2
48:16 the angel who has redeemed me from all evil, 2
Exd 3: 2 the angel of the LORD appeared to him in a flame 2
14:19 Then the angel of God who went before the host 2
23:20 Behold, I send an angel before you, to guard you 2
23 When my angel goes before you, and brings you 2
32:34 behold, my angel shall go before you. 2
33: 2 I will send an angel before you, and I will drive 2
Num20:16 sent an angel and brought us forth out of Egypt; 2
22:22 the angel of the LORD took his stand in the way 2
23 ass saw the angel of the LORD standing in the road 2
24 Then the angel of the LORD stood in a narrow path 2
25 when the ass saw the angel of the LORD, she pushed 2
26 Then the angel of the LORD went ahead, and stood 2
27 When the ass saw the angel of the LORD, 2
31 he saw the angel of the LORD standing in the way 2
32 angel of the LORD said to him, "Why have you struck 2
34 Balaam said to the angel of the LORD, "I have sinned 2
35 angel of the LORD said to Balaam, "Go with the men; 2
Jdg 2: 1 the angel of the LORD went up from Gilgal 2
4 When the angel of the LORD spoke these words 2
5:23 Curse Meroz, says the angel of the LORD 2
6:11 the angel of the LORD came and sat under the oak 2
12 angel of the LORD appeared to him and said to him 2
20 the angel of God said to him, "Take the meat 2
21 the angel of the LORD reached out the tip 2
21 the angel of the LORD vanished from his sight. 2
22 Gideon perceived that he was the angel of the LORD 2
22 now I have seen the angel of the LORD face to face. 2
13: 3 the angel of the LORD appeared to the woman 2
6 was like the countenance of the angel of God 2
9 and the angel of God came again to the woman 2
13 the angel of the LORD said to Mano'ah, "Of all that I 2
15 Mano'ah said to the angel of the LORD, "Pray, let us 2
16 the angel of the LORD said to Mano'ah, "If you detain 2
16 did not know that he was the angel of the LORD. 2
17 Mano'ah said to the angel of the LORD, "What is 2
18 the angel of the LORD said to him, "Why do you ask 2
20 the angel of the LORD ascended in the flame 2
21 The angel of the LORD appeared no more to Mano'ah 2
21 Mano'ah knew that he was the angel of the LORD. 2
1Sm 29: 9 you are as blameless in my sight as an angel of God; 2
2Sm 14:17 the king is like the angel of God to discern good 2
20 the wisdom of the angel of God to know all things 2
19:27 But my lord the king is like the angel of God; 2
24:16 when the angel stretched forth his hand 2
16 said to the angel who was working destruction 2
16 the angel of the LORD was by the threshing floor 2
17 when he saw the angel who was smiting the people 2
1Kg 13:18 an angel spoke to me by the word of the LORD, saying 2
19: 5 an angel touched him, and said to him, "Arise 2
7 the angel of the LORD came again a second time 2
2Kg 1: 3 the angel of the LORD said to Eli'jah the Tishbite 2
15 the angel of the LORD said to Eli'jah, "Go down 2
19:35 the angel of the LORD went forth, and slew 2
1Ch 21:12 angel of the LORD destroying . . Israel. 2
15 God sent the angel to Jerusalem to destroy it; 2
15 he said to the destroying angel, "It is enough; 2
15 the angel of the LORD was standing 2
16 and saw the angel of the LORD standing between 2
18 angel of the LORD commanded Gad to say to David 2
20 Ornan . . he turned and saw the angel 2
27 Then the LORD commanded the angel; 2

30 afraid of the sword of the angel of the LORD. 2
2Ch 32:21 LORD sent an angel, who cut off all the mighty 2
Job 4:18 his angels he charges with error; 2
33:23 If there be for him an angel, a mediator 2
Ps 34: 7 The angel of the LORD encamps around those who 2
35: 5 with the angel of the LORD driving them on! 2
6 with the angel of the LORD pursuing them! 2
78:25 Man ate of the bread of the angels; 1
49 and distress, a company of destroying angels. 2
91:11 For he will give his angels charge of you 2
103:20 Bless the LORD, O you his angels, you mighty ones 2
148: 2 Praise him, all his angels, praise him, all his host! 2
Isa 37:36 the angel of the LORD went forth 2
63: 9 and the angel of his presence saved them; 2
Dan 3:28 sent his angel and delivered his servants 3
6:22 My God sent his angel and shut the lions' mouths 3
Hos 12: 4 He strove with the angel and prevailed 2
Zec 1: 9 The angel who talked with me said to me 2
11 they answered the angel of the LORD 2
12 Then the angel of the LORD said, 'O LORD of hosts 2
13 words to the angel who talked with me. 2
14 the angel who talked with me said to me, 'Cry out 2
19 I said to the angel who talked with me 2
2: 3 behold, the angel who talked with me came forward 2
3 and another angel came forward to meet him 2
3: 1 priest standing before the angel of the LORD 2
3 Now Joshua was standing before the angel 2
4 angel said to those who were standing before him •
5 the angel of the LORD was standing by. 2
6 the angel of the LORD enjoined Joshua 2
4: 1 the angel who talked with me came again 2
4 I said to the angel who talked with me 2
5 Then the angel who talked with me answered me 2
5: 5 Then the angel who talked with me came forward 2
10 Then I said to the angel who talked with me 2
6: 4 Then I said to the angel who talked with me 2
5 the angel answered me, "These are going forth 2
12: 8 like God, like the angel of the LORD, at their head. 2
Mat 1:20 as he considered this, behold, an angel of the Lord 4
24 he did as the angel of the Lord commanded him; he 4
2:13 an angel of the Lord appeared to Joseph in a dream 4
19 Herod died, behold, an angel of the Lord appeared 4
4: 6 for it is written, 'He will give his angels charge 4
11 left him, and behold, angels came and ministered 4
13:39 and the reapers are angels. 4
41 The Son of man will send his angels 4
49 The angels will come out and separate 4
16:27 For the Son of man is to come with his angels 4
18:10 in heaven their angels always behold the face 4
22:30 but are like angels in heaven. 4
24:31 will send out his angels with a loud trumpet call 4
36 not even the angels of heaven, nor the Son 4
25:31 all the angels with him 4
41 fire prepared for the devil and his angels; 4
26:53 send me more than twelve legions of angels? 4
28: 2 an angel of the Lord descended from heaven 4
5 the angel said to the women, "Do not be afraid 4
Mrk 1:13 the angels ministered to him. 4
8:38 glory of his Father with the holy angels. 4
12:25 are like angels in heaven. 4
13:27 then he will send out the angels 4
32 not even the angels in heaven, nor the Son 4
Lke 1:11 there appeared to him an angel of the Lord 4
13 the angel said to him, "Do not be afraid, Zechari'ah 4
18 Zechari'ah said to the angel, "How shall I know this? 4
19 the angel answered him, "I am Gabriel 4
26 the angel Gabriel was sent from God 4
30 the angel said to her, "Do not be afraid, Mary 4
34 Mary said to the angel, "How shall this be 4
35 the angel said to her, "The Holy Spirit will come 4
38 the angel departed from her. 4
2: 9 an angel of the Lord appeared to them 4
10 the angel said to them, "Be not afraid 4
13 suddenly there was with the angel a multitude 4
15 When the angels went away from them into heaven 4
21 he was called Jesus, the name given by the angel 4
4:10 He will give his angels charge of you, to guard you,' 4
9:26 the glory of the Father and of the holy angels. 4
12: 8 also will acknowledge before the angels of God; 4
9 will be denied before the angels of God. 4
15:10 there is joy before the angels of God 4
16:22 and was carried by the angels to Abraham's bosom 4
24:23 saying that they had even seen a vision of angels 4
Joh 1:51 the angels of God ascending and descending 4
12:29 Others said, "An angel has spoken to him. 4
20:12 she saw two angels in white 4
Act 5:19 an angel of the Lord opened the prison doors 4
6:15 his face was like the face of an angel. 4
7:30 an angel appeared to him in the wilderness 4
35 the angel that appeared to him in the bush. 4
38 the angel who spoke to him at Mount Sinai 4
53 you who received the law as delivered by angels 4
8:26 an angel of the Lord said to Philip, "Rise and go 4
10: 3 he saw clearly in a vision an angel of God 4
7 When the angel who spoke to him had departed 4
22 was directed by a holy angel to send for you 4
11:13 he told us how he had seen the angel standing 4
12: 7 behold, an angel of the Lord appeared 4
8 the angel said to him, "Dress yourself 4

9 not know that what was done by the angel was real 4
10 immediately the angel left him. 4
11 Now I am sure that the Lord has sent his angel 4
15 They said, "It is his angel! 4
23 Immediately an angel of the Lord smote him 4
23: 8 there is no resurrection, neither angel, nor spirit; 4
9 What if a spirit or an angel spoke to him? 4
27:23 this very night there stood by me an angel 4
Rom 8:38 neither death, nor life, nor angels 4
1Co 4: 9 a spectacle to the world, to angels and to men. 4
6: 3 Do you not know that we are to judge angels? 4
11:10 a veil on her head, because of the angels. 4
13: 1 If I speak in the tongues of men and of angels 4
2Co 11:14 Satan disguises himself as an angel of light. 4
Gal 1: 8 even if we, or an angel from heaven, should preach 4
3:19 it was ordained by angels through 4
4:14 as an angel of God, as Christ Jesus. 4
Col 2:18 self-abasement and worship of angels 4
2Th 1: 7 with his mighty angels in flaming fire 4
1Ti 3:16 vindicated in the Spirit, seen by angels 4
5:21 of God and of Christ Jesus and of the elect angels 4
Heb 1: 4 having become as much superior to angels as . . 4
5 For to what angel did God ever say, "Thou art my Son 4
6 he says, "Let all God's angels worship him. 4
7 Of the angels he says, "Who makes his angels winds 4
7 Of the angels he says, "Who makes his angels winds 4
13 to what angel has he ever said, "Sit at my right hand 4
2: 2 For if the message declared by angels was valid 4
5 it was not to angels that God subjected the world 4
7 make him for a little while lower than the angels 4
9 for a little while was made lower than the angels 4
16 surely it is not with angels that he is concerned 4
12:22 innumerable angels in festal gathering 4
13: 2 thereby some have entertained angels unawares. 4
1Pe 1:12 things into which angels long to look. 4
3:22 angels, authorities, and powers subject to him. 4
2Pe 2: 4 if God did not spare the angels when they sinned 4
11 angels, though greater in might and power 4
Jde 1: 6 the angels that did not keep their own position 4
Rev 1: 1 he made it known by sending his angel 4
20 seven stars are the angels of the seven churches 4
2: 1 To the angel of the church in Ephesus write 4
8 And to the angel of the church in Smyrna write 4
12 And to the angel of the church in Per'gamum write 4
18 And to the angel of the church in Thyati'ra write 4
3: 1 And to the angel of the church in Sardis write 4
5 I will confess his name . . before his angels. 4
7 to the angel of the church in Philadelphia write 4
14 And to the angel of the church in La-odice'a write 4
5: 2 a strong angel proclaiming with a loud voice 4
11 I heard . . the voice of many angels 4
7: 1 After this I saw four angels standing 4
2 I saw another angel ascend from the rising . . sun 4
2 he called with a loud voice to the four angels 4
11 all the angels stood round the throne 4
8: 2 Then I saw the seven angels who stand before God 4
3 another angel came and stood at the altar 4
4 rose . . from the hand of the angel before God. 4
5 Then the angel took the censer and filled it 4
6 Now the seven angels who had the seven trumpets 4
7 The first angel blew his trumpet •
8 The second angel blew his trumpet 4
10 The third angel blew his trumpet, and a great star 4
12 The fourth angel blew his trumpet 4
13 trumpets which the . . angels are about to blow! 4
9: 1 And the fifth angel blew his trumpet, and I saw 4
11 as king over them the angel of the bottomless pit; 4
13 Then the sixth angel blew his trumpet, and I heard 4
14 saying to the sixth angel who had the trumpet 4
14 Release the four angels who are bound 4
15 So the four angels were released 4
10: 1 another mighty angel coming down from heaven 4
5 the angel whom I saw standing on sea and land 4
7 trumpet call to be sounded by the seventh angel 4
8 the scroll which is open in the hand of the angel 4
9 So I went to the angel and told him to give me 4
10 took the little scroll from the hand of the angel 4
11:15 Then the seventh angel blew his trumpet 4
12: 7 Michael and his angels fighting . . the dragon; 4
7 and the dragon and his angels fought 4
9 and his angels were thrown down with him. 4
14: 6 Then I saw another angel flying in midheaven 4
8 Another angel, a second, followed, saying 4
9 And another angel, a third, followed them, saying 4
10 tormented . . in the presence of the holy angels 4
15 another angel came out of the temple, calling 4
17 another angel came out of the temple in heaven 4
18 Then another angel came out from the altar 4
18 the angel who has power over fire 4
19 So the angel swung his sickle on the earth 4
15: 1 I saw . . seven angels with seven plagues 4
6 out of the temple came the seven angels 4
7 the four living creatures gave the seven angels 4
8 seven plagues of the seven angels were ended. 4
16: 1 voice from the temple telling the seven angels 4
2 first angel went and poured his bowl on the earth •
3 The second angel poured his bowl into the sea •
4 The third angel poured his bowl into the rivers •
5 And I heard the angel of water say 4

8 The fourth angel poured his bowl on the sun •
10 The fifth angel poured his bowl on the throne •
12 The sixth angel poured his bowl on the river •
17 The seventh angel poured his bowl into the air •
17: 1 one of the seven angels who had the seven bowls 4
7 But the angel said to me, "Why marvel? I will tell you 4
18: 1 I saw another angel coming down from heaven 4
21 Then a mighty angel took up a stone 4
19: 9 And the angel said to me, "Write this •
17 Then I saw an angel standing in the sun 4
20: 1 Then I saw an angel coming down from heaven 4
21: 9 Then came one of the seven angels 4
12 and at the gates twelve angels 4
17 144 cubits by a man's measure, that is, an angel's. 4
22: 6 the Lord . . sent his angel to show his servants 4
8 I fell down to worship at the feet of the angel 4
16 I Jesus have sent my angel to you 4
2Es 1:19 you ate the bread of angels. 6
2:44 Then I asked an angel, "Who are these, my lord? 6
46 Then I said to the angel, "Who is that young man 6
48 Then the angel said to me, "Go, tell my people 6
4: 1 Then the angel that had been sent to me 6
5:15 the angel who had come and talked with me held me 6
20 as Uriel the angel had commanded me. 6
31 the angel who had come to me on a previous night 6
6: 3 before the innumerable hosts of angels 6
7: 1 the angel who had been sent to me 6
85 are guarded by angels in profound quiet. 6
95 and guarded by angels in profound quiet 6
8:21 before whom the hosts of angels stand trembling 6
10:28 Where is the angel Uriel, who came to me at first? 6
29 behold, the angel who had come to me at first came 6
12:51 seven days, as the angel had commanded me •
16:66 will you hide your sins before God and his angels? 6
Tob 5: 4 he found Raphael, who was an angel 4
6 The angel replied, "I will go with you 4
16 may his angel attend you 4
21 For a good angel will go with him 4
6: 3 the angel said to him, "Catch the fish. 4
4 Then the angel said to him, "Cut open the fish 4
5 the young man did as the angel told him 4
6 the young man said to the angel, "Brother Azarias 4
10 the angel said to the young man 4
13 the young man said to the angel, "Brother Azarias 4
15 the angel said to him 4
8: 3 the angel bound him. 4
15 let all thy angels . . bless thee for ever. 4
11:14 blessed are all thy holy angels. 4
12: 5 he called the angel and said to him 4
6 the angel called the two of them privately •
15 I am Raphael, one of the seven holy angels 4
22 the angel of the Lord had appeared to them. 4
AEs 15:13 I saw you, my lord, like an angel of God 4
Wis 10:10 gave him knowledge of angels 5
16:20 thou didst give thy people food of angels 4
Sir 48:21 his angel wiped them out. 4
LJr 1: 7 my angel is with you 4
Aza 1:26 the angel of the Lord came down into the furnace 4
37 Bless the Lord, you angels of the Lord 4
Sus 1:55 the angel of God has received the sentence 4
59 for the angel of God is waiting with his sword 4
Bel 1:34 the angel of the Lord said to Habakkuk 4
36 Then the angel of the Lord took him 4
39 the angel of God immediately returned Habakkuk 4
1Mc 7:41 thy angel went forth and struck down 185,000 4
2Mc 11: 6 to send a good angel to save Israel. 4
15:22 thou didst send thy angel in the time of Hezekiah 4
23 now, O Sovereign of the heavens, send a good angel 4
3Mc 6:18 two glorious angels of fearful aspect 4
4Mc 4:10 angels on horseback . . appeared from heaven 4
7:11 conquered the fiery angel 4

angel *See also* equal.

anger 1. אַף 2. חֵמָה 3. כעס 4. כַּעַס 5. קֶצֶף 6. קצף 7. רוּחַ 8. רגז (A) 9. *ἀγανακτέω* 10. *ἀπoργίζoμαι* 11. *θυμός* 12. *θυμόω* 13. *μῆνις* 14. *ὀργή* 15. *ὀργίζω* 16. *ὀργίλoς* 17. *παρoργίζω* 18. *παρoργισμός* 19. inrito 20. iracundia

Gen 27:45 until your brother's anger turns away 1
30: 2 Jacob's anger was kindled against Rachel 1
39:19 his master heard . . his anger was kindled. 1
44:18 let not your anger burn against your servant; 1
49: 6 for in their anger they slay men 1
7 Cursed be their anger, for it is fierce; 1
Exd 4:14 the anger of the LORD was kindled against Moses 1
11: 8 And he went out from Pharaoh in hot anger. 1
32:19 Moses' anger burned hot, and he threw the tables 1
22 Aaron said, "Let not the anger of my lord burn hot; 1
34: 6 a God merciful and gracious, slow to anger 1
Num11: 1 when the LORD heard it, his anger was kindled 1
10 anger of the LORD blazed hotly 1
33 anger of the LORD was kindled against the people 1
12: 9 anger of the LORD was kindled against them 1
14:18 LORD is slow to anger, and abounding in steadfast 1
22:22 God's anger was kindled because he went; 1
27 Balaam's anger was kindled, and he struck the ass 1
24:10 Balak's anger was kindled against Balaam 1
25: 3 anger of the LORD was kindled against Israel; 1

4 that the fierce anger of the LORD may turn away 1
32:10 LORD'S anger was kindled on that day, and he swore 1
13 the LORD'S anger was kindled against Israel 1
14 increase still more the fierce anger of the LORD 1
Deu 1:34 LORD heard your words, and was angered, 6
6:15 lest the anger of the LORD your God be kindled 1
7: 4 anger of the LORD would be kindled against you 1
9:19 For I was afraid of the anger and hot displeasure 1
11:17 anger of the LORD be kindled against you 1
13:17 LORD may turn from the fierceness of his anger 1
19: 6 lest the avenger of blood in hot anger pursue *
29:20 rather the anger of the LORD and his jealousy 1
23 which the LORD overthrew in his anger and wrath- 1
24 What means the heat of this great anger?' 1
27 therefore the anger of the LORD was kindled 1
28 uprooted . . in anger and fury and great wrath 1
31:17 my anger will be kindled against them in that day 1
32:22 For a fire is kindled by my anger, and it burns 1
Jos 7: 1 the anger of the LORD burned against the people 1
26 then the LORD turned from his burning anger. 1
23:16 the anger of the LORD will be kindled against you 1
Jdg 2:14 the anger of the LORD was kindled against Israel 1
20 the anger of the LORD was kindled against Israel; 1
3: 8 the anger of the LORD was kindled against Israel 1
6:39 Gideon said . . "Let not thy anger burn against me 1
8: 3 Then their anger against him was abated 7
9:30 When Zebul . . heard . . his anger was kindled. 1
10: 7 the anger of the LORD was kindled against Israel 1
14:19 In hot anger he went back to his father's house. 1
1Sm 11: 6 and his anger was greatly kindled. 1
17:28 and Eli'ab's anger was kindled against David 1
20:30 Then Saul's anger was kindled against Jonathan 1
34 And Jonathan rose from the table in fierce anger 1
2Sm 6: 7 the anger of the LORD was kindled against Uzzah; 1
11:20 then, if the king's anger rises, and if he says to you 2
12: 5 David's anger was . . kindled against the man; 1
24: 1 the anger of the LORD was kindled against Israel 1
1Kg 15:30 the anger to which he provoked the LORD 4
21:22 I will . . for the anger to which you have provoked 4
2Kg 13: 3 the anger of the LORD was kindled against Israel 1
23:26 by which his anger was kindled against Judah 1
24:20 because of the anger of the LORD . . he cast them 1
1Ch 13:10 the anger of the LORD was kindled against Uzzah; 1
2Ch 21:16 against Jeho'ram the anger of the Philistines 7
Ezr 5:12 our fathers had angered the God of heaven 8
Neh 9:17 thou art a God . . slow to anger and abounding 1
Est 1:12 the king . . and his anger burned within him. 2
2: 1 when the anger of King Ahasu-e'rus had abated 2
7:10 Then the anger of the king abated. 2
Job 4: 9 by the blast of his anger they are consumed. 1
9: 5 when he overturns them in his anger; 1
13 God will not turn back his anger; 1
18: 4 You who tear yourself in your anger 1
20:23 God will send his fierce anger into him 1
21:17 That God distributes pains in his anger? 1
35:15 now, because his anger does not punish 1
36:13 The godless in heart cherish anger; 1
33 who is jealous with anger against iniquity. 1
40:11 Pour forth the overflowings of your anger 1
Ps 6: 1 O LORD, rebuke me not in thy anger, nor chasten me 1
7: 6 Arise, O LORD, in thy anger, lift thyself up 1
27: 9 Turn not thy servant away in anger 1
30: 5 For his anger is but for a moment 1
37: 8 Refrain from anger, and forsake wrath! 1
38: 1 O LORD, rebuke me not in thy anger, nor chasten me 5
55: 3 in anger they cherish enmity against me. 1
69:24 let thy burning anger overtake them. 1
74: 1 thy anger smoke against the sheep of thy pasture? 1
76: 7 stand before thee when once thy anger is roused? 1
77: 9 Has he in anger shut up his compassion?" Selah 1
78:21 against Jacob, his anger mounted against Israel; 1
31 the anger of God rose against them and he slew 1
38 he restrained his anger often 1
49 He let loose on them his fierce anger, wrath 1
50 He made a path for his anger; he did not spare them 1
79: 6 Pour out thy anger on the nations that do not know 2
85: 3 thou didst turn from thy hot anger. 1
5 Wilt thou prolong thy anger to all generations? 1
86:15 slow to anger and abounding in steadfast love 1
90: 7 For we are consumed by thy anger; 1
11 Who considers the power of thy anger 1
95:11 swore in my anger that they . . not enter my rest. 1
102:10 because of thy indignation and anger; 5
103: 8 slow to anger and abounding in steadfast love. 1
106:32 They angered him at the waters of Mer'ibah 6
40 anger of the LORD was kindled against his people 1
124: 3 when their anger was kindled against us; 1
145: 8 slow to anger and abounding in steadfast love. 1
Prv 14:29 He who is slow to anger has great understanding 1
15: 1 but a harsh word stirs up anger. 1
18 but he who is slow to anger quiets contention. 1
16:32 He who is slow to anger is better than the mighty 1
19:11 Good sense makes a man slow to anger 1
21:14 A gift in secret averts anger; 1
22:24 Make no friendship with a man given to anger 1
24:18 LORD . . be displeased, and turn away his anger 1
27: 4 Wrath is cruel, anger is overwhelming; 1
29:11 A fool gives full vent to his anger 7
22 man given to anger causes much transgression. 2
30:33 pressing anger produces strife. 1
Ecc 7: 9 Be not quick to anger, for anger lodges 3
9 for anger lodges in the bosom of fools. 4
10: 4 If the anger of the ruler rises against you 7
Isa 5:25 Therefore the anger of the LORD was kindled 1
25 For all this his anger is not turned away 1
7: 4 at the fierce anger of Rezin and Syria 1
9:12 For all this his anger is not turned away 1
17 For all this his anger is not turned away 1
21 For all this his anger is not turned away 1
10: 4 For all this his anger is not turned away 1
5 Ah, Assyria, the rod of my anger, the staff of my fury! 1
25 my anger will be directed to their destruction. 1
12: 1 thy anger turned away, and thou didst comfort me. 1
13: 3 have summoned my mighty men to execute my anger 1
9 the LORD comes . . with wrath and fierce anger 1
13 the LORD of hosts in the day of his fierce anger. 1
14: 6 in anger with unrelenting persecution. 1
30:27 the LORD comes from far, burning with his anger 1
30 in furious anger and a flame of devouring fire 1
42:25 he poured upon him the heat of his anger 1
48: 9 For my name's sake I defer my anger 1
63: 3 I trod them in my anger and trampled them in my 1
6 I trod down the peoples in my anger 1
66:15 like the stormwind, to render his anger in fury 1
Jer 2:35 I am innocent; surely his anger has turned from me.' 1
4: 8 the fierce anger of the LORD has not turned back 1
26 before the LORD, before his fierce anger. 1
7:20 Behold, my anger and my wrath will be poured out 1
10:24 not in thy anger, lest thou bring me to nothing. 1
12:13 because of the fierce anger of the LORD. 1
15:14 in my anger a fire is kindled which shall burn 1
17: 4 in my anger a fire is kindled 1
18:23 deal with them in the time of thine anger. 1
21: 5 in anger, and in fury, and in great wrath. 1
23:20 The anger of the LORD will not turn back 1
25:37 because of the fierce anger of the LORD. 1
38 and because of his fierce anger. 1
30:24 The fierce anger of the LORD will not turn back 1
32:31 This city has aroused my anger and wrath 1
37 the countries to which I drove them in my anger 1
33: 5 men whom I shall smite in my anger and my wrath 1
36: 7 for great is the anger and wrath 1
42:18 As my anger and my wrath were poured out 1
44: 6 my wrath and my anger were poured forth 1
49:37 I will bring evil upon them, my fierce anger 1
51:45 save his life from the fierce anger of the LORD! 1
52: 3 Surely because of the anger of the LORD 1
Lam 1:12 LORD inflicted on the day of his fierce anger. 1
2: 1 the Lord in his anger has set . . Zion under a cloud! 1
1 he has not remembered . . in the day of his anger. 1
3 cut down in fierce anger all the might of Israel; 1
21 in the day of thy anger thou hast slain them 1
22 on the day of the anger of the LORD none escaped 1
3:43 hast wrapped thyself with anger and pursued us 1
66 Thou wilt pursue them in anger and destroy them 1
4:11 full vent to his wrath, he poured out his hot anger; 1
Ezk 5:13 Thus shall my anger spend itself 1
15 when I execute judgments on you in anger and fury 1
7: 3 I will let loose my anger upon you 1
8 my wrath upon you, and spend my anger against you 1
13:13 and there shall be a deluge of rain in my anger 1
20: 8 wrath upon them and spend my anger against them 1
21 and spend my anger against them 1
22:20 so I will gather you in my anger and in my wrath 1
25:14 they shall do in Edom according to my anger 1
35:11 I will deal with you according to the anger 1
43: 8 so I have consumed them in my anger. 1
Dan 9:16 anger and thy wrath turn away from thy city 1
11:20 shall be broken, neither in anger nor in battle. 1
Hos 7: 6 all night their anger smolders; 1
8: 5 My anger burns against them. 1
11: 9 I will not execute my fierce anger 1
13:11 I have given you kings in my anger 1
14: 4 for my anger has turned from them. 1
Jol 2:13 for he is gracious and merciful, slow to anger 1
Ams 1:11 his anger tore perpetually, and he kept his wrath 1
Jon 3: 9 God may yet repent and turn from his fierce anger 1
4: 2 a gracious God and merciful, slow to anger 1
Mic 5:15 And in anger and wrath I will execute vengeance 1
7:18 He does not retain his anger for ever 1
Nah 1: 3 The LORD is slow to anger and of great might 1
6 Who can endure the heat of his anger? 1
Hab 3: 8 Was thy anger against the rivers 1
12 thou didst trample the nations in anger. 1
Zep 2: 2 there comes upon you the fierce anger of the LORD 1
3: 8 upon them my indignation, all the heat of my anger; 1
Zec 10: 3 My anger is hot against the shepherds 1
Mat 18:34 in anger his lord delivered him to the jailers 15
Mrk 3: 5 he looked around at them with anger 14
Lke 14:21 the householder in anger said to his servant 15
2Co 12:20 perhaps there may be quarreling, jealousy, anger 11
Gal 5:20 idolatry, sorcery, enmity, strife, jealousy, anger 11
Eph 4:26 do not let the sun go down on your anger. 18
31 wrath and anger and clamor and slander 14
Col 3: 8 now put them all away: anger, wrath, malice, slander 14
1Ti 2: 8 lifting holy hands without anger or quarreling; 14
Heb 11:27 not being afraid of the anger of the king 11
Jas 1:19 Let every man be quick to hear . . slow to anger 14
20 anger of man does not work the righteousness of God. 14
Rev 14:10 poured unmixed into the cup of his anger 14
1Es 1:52 in his anger against his people 12
2Es 1: 7 But they have angered me 19
10: 5 and answered her in anger and said 20
Tob 1:18 in his anger he put many to death 11
Jdt 2: 7 I am coming against them in my anger 11
9: 8 and bring down their power in thy anger 11
AEs 15: 7 he looked at her in fierce anger 11
Wis 10: 3 departed from her in his anger 14
18:21 he withstood the anger 11
19: 1 were assailed to the end by pitiless anger 11
Sir 1:22 Unrighteous anger cannot be justified 11
22 a man's anger tips the scale to his ruin. 11
3:16 whoever angers his mother is cursed by the Lord. 17
4: 2 nor anger a man in want. 17
5: 6 his anger rests on sinners. 11
10:18 nor fierce anger for those born of women. 14
26: 8 There is great anger when a wife is drunken 14
28 because of a third anger comes over me 11
27:30 Anger and wrath, these also are abominations 13
28: 3 Does a man harbor anger against another 14
10 will be his anger 11
19 who has not been exposed to its anger 11
30:24 Jealousy and anger shorten life 11
31:30 Drunkenness increases the anger of a fool 11
36: 7 Rouse thy anger and pour out thy wrath 14
39:28 in their anger they scourge heavily 11
28 calm the anger of their Maker. 11
40: 5 there is anger and envy and trouble and unrest 11
45:18 in wrath and anger. 14
19 in the wrath of his anger they were destroyed 14
Bar 1:13 the anger of the Lord and his wrath have not 11
2:13 Let thy anger turn away from us, for we are left 11
20 For thou hast sent thy anger and thy wrath upon us 11
4: 6 you were handed over . . because you angered God 17
1Mc 2:24 He gave vent to righteous anger 11
44 and struck down sinners in their anger 14
49 it is a time of ruin and furious anger. 14
3:27 he was greatly angered 15
7:35 in anger he swore this oath 11
35 he went out in great anger. 11
15: 6 the king was greatly angered. 15
2Mc 4:38 inflamed with anger 11
40 were becoming aroused and filled with anger 14
5:17 the Lord was angered for a little while 10
10:35 fired with anger because of the blasphemies 11
13: 4 the King of kings aroused the anger of Antiochus 11
14:45 Still alive and aflame with anger, he rose 11
3Mc 6:22 Then the king's anger was turned to pity and tears 14
4Mc 1: 4 namely anger, fear, and pain. 11
24 Anger . . is an emotion 11
2:16 just as it repels anger 11
17 he did nothing against them in anger 11
17 controlled his anger by reason. 11
19 saying, "Cursed be their anger"? 11
20 For if reason could not control anger 11
3: 3 No one of us can eradicate anger from the mind 11
3 reason can help to deal with anger. 11
4:21 The divine justice was angered by these acts 9
8: 9 if by disobedience you rouse my anger 16

anger *See also* bear, given, keep, look, move, provoke, slow.

fierce anger 1. חֲרוֹן אַף 2. חֳרִי אַף

2Ch 25:10 returned home in fierce anger. 2
29:10 that his fierce anger may turn away from us. 1
30: 8 that his fierce anger may turn away from you. 1
Jer 4:26 before the LORD, before his fierce anger. 1

overpowering anger 1. *ὀργή*

3Mc 5: 1 king . . was filled with overpowering anger and wrath 1

angrily 1. *μετ' ὀργῆς*

3Mc 6:23 he wept and angrily threatened his friends 1

angry 1. אנף 2. זעם 3. זעף 4. חֵמָה 5. חרה 6. חרה אַף 7. חרה ל 8. חרר 9. כעס 10. מַר נֶפֶשׁ 11. עבר 12. עשן 13. קצף 14. רגז 15. רעע 16. בנס (A) 17. *δεινάζω* 18. *ἐπoργίζομαι* 19. *θυμομαχέω* 20. *θυμόω* 21. *μηνιάω* 22. *μηνίω* 23. *ὀργίζω* 24. *παροργίζω* 25. *χαλεπαίνω* 26. *χολάω* 27. adzelor 28. indignor

Gen 4: 5 Cain was very angry, and his countenance fell. 5
6 Why are you angry, and why has your countenance 5
18:30 let not the Lord be angry, and I will speak. 5
32 Then he said, "Oh let not the Lord be angry 5
31:35 Let not my lord be angry that I cannot rise 5
34: 7 the men were indignant and very angry, because he 5
40: 2 Pharaoh was angry with his two officers 13
41:10 When Pharaoh was angry with his servants 13
45: 5 do not be distressed, or angry with yourselves 5
Exd 16:20 and Moses was angry with them. 13
Lev 10:16 he was angry with Elea'zar and Ith'amar 13
Num16:15 Moses was very angry, and said to the LORD 5
22 wilt thou be angry with all the congregation? 13
31:14 Moses was angry with the officers of the army 13
Deu 1:37 The LORD was angry with me also on your account 1

3:26 LORD was angry with me on your account 11
4:21 LORD was angry with me on your account 1
9: 8 LORD was so angry with you that he was ready 1
20 LORD was so angry with Aaron that he was ready 1
Jos 22:18 he will be angry with the whole congregation 13
Jdg 18:25 heard among us, lest angry fellows fall upon you 10
1Sm 15:11 Samuel was angry; and he cried to the LORD 5
18: 8 Saul was very angry, and this saying displeased 5
20: 7 if he is angry, then know that evil is determined 5
29: 4 the commanders . . were angry with him; 13
2Sm 3: 8 Then Abner was very angry over the words 5
6: 8 David was angry because the LORD had broken 5
13:21 When King David heard . . he was very angry. 5
19:42 Why then are you angry over this matter? 7
22: 8 the earth reeled and . . because he was angry. 7
1Kg 8:46 If they sin . . and thou art angry with them 1
11: 9 the LORD was angry with Solomon 1
2Kg 5:11 Na'aman was angry, and went away, saying, "Behold 13
13:19 Then the man of God was angry with him, and said 13
17:18 Therefore the LORD was very angry with Israel 1
1Ch 13:11 David was angry because the LORD 5
2Ch 6:36 If they sin against thee . . and thou art angry 1
16:10 Then Asa was angry with the seer 9
25:10 And they became very angry with Judah 6
15 Therefore the LORD was angry with Amazi'ah 6
26:19 Then Uzzi'ah was angry. 3
19 became angry with the priests leprosy broke out 3
28: 9 because the LORD . . was angry with Judah 4
Ezr 9:14 Wouldst thou not be angry with us 1
Neh 4: 1 Sanbal'lat . . was angry and greatly enraged 5
7 heard . . they were very angry; 5
5: 6 I was very angry when I heard their outcry 5
13: 8 very angry, and I threw all the . . furniture 15
Job 32: 2 He was angry at Job because he justified himself 6
3 he was angry also at Job's three friends 6
Ps 2:12 kiss his feet, lest he be angry, and you perish 1
4: 4 Be angry, but sin not; commune with your own hearts 14
18: 7 trembled and quaked, because he was angry. 5
60: 1 thou hast been angry; oh, restore us. 1
79: 5 How long, O LORD? Wilt thou be angry for ever? 1
80: 4 how long . . be angry with thy people's prayers? 12
85: 5 Wilt thou be angry with us for ever? 1
112:10 wicked man sees it and is angry; 9
Prv 22:14 he with whom the LORD is angry will fall into it. 2
25:23 backbiting tongue, angry looks. 2
Ecc 5: 6 why should God be angry at your voice, and destroy 13
Sng 1: 6 My mother's sons were angry with me 8
Isa 12: 1 O LORD, for though thou wast angry with me 1
47: 6 was angry with my people, I profaned my heritage; 13
54: 9 I have sworn that I will not be angry with you 13
57:16 not contend for ever, nor will I always be angry; 13
17 Because of . . his covetousness I was angry 13
17 I smote him, I hid my face and was angry; 13
64: 5 Behold, thou wast angry, and we sinned; 13
9 Be not exceedingly angry, O LORD 13
Jer 3: 5 will he be angry for ever *
12 says the LORD; I will not be angry for ever. *
Lam 5:22 Art thou exceedingly angry with us? 13
Ezk 16:42 I will be calm, and will no more be angry. 9
Dan 2:12 king was angry and very furious, and commanded 16
Jon 4: 1 displeased Jonah exceedingly, and he was angry. 5
4 the LORD said, "Do you do well to be angry? 5
9 to Jonah, "Do you do well to be angry for the plant? 5
9 he said, "I do well to be angry, angry enough to die. 5
9 he said, "I do well to be angry, angry enough to die. *
Zec 1: 2 The LORD was very angry with your fathers. 13
15 I am very angry with the nations that are at ease; 13
15 while I was angry but a little 13
Mal 1: 4 the people with whom the LORD is angry for ever. 2
Mat 5:22 every one who is angry with his brother shall be 23
22: 7 The king was angry, and he sent his troops 23
Lke 15:28 he was angry and refused to go in 23
Joh 7:23 are you angry with me 26
Act 12:20 Herod was angry with the people of Tyre and Sidon; 19
Eph 4:26 Be angry but do not sin 23
Rev 12:17 Then the dragon was angry with the woman 23
1Es 8:88 Wast thou not angry enough with us 23
2Es 8:30 Be not angry with those who are deemed worse 28
34 what is man, that thou art angry with him 28
16:48 the more angry I will be with them for their sins 27
Tob 5:13 Do not be angry with me 23
Jdt 1:12 Then Nebuchadnezzar was very angry 20
Sir 4: 3 Do not add to the troubles of an angry mind 24
10: 6 Do not be angry with your neighbor for any injury 21
28: 7 do not be angry with your neighbor 22
Bel 1: 8 Then the king was angry, and he called his priests 20
Man 1:13 Do not be angry with me for ever or lay up evil for me 22
1Mc 11:22 When he heard this he was angry 23
2Mc 7:33 if our living Lord is angry for a little while 18
13:25 so angry that they wanted to annul its terms. 17
4Mc 2:17 When Moses was angry with Dathan and Abiram 20
9:10 the tyrant not only was angry 25

angry *See also* make, stay.

become angry 1. חרה 2. חרה אַף 3. קצף 4. *ὀργίζω*

Gen 31:36 Then Jacob became angry, and upbraided Laban; 1
Jdg 19: 2 his concubine became angry with him, and she went 4
Est 2:21 Bigthan and Teresh . . became angry and sought 3
Job 32: 2 Then Eli'hu . . became angry. 2
5 he became angry. 2
1Mc 5: 1 they became very angry 4
6:59 they became angry and did all these things. 4

anguish 1. חול 2. חִיל 3. חַלְחָלָה 4. יָגוֹן 5. מוּצָק 6. מֵעֶה 7. מָצוֹק 8. מְצוּקָה 9. עִיר 10. צוּקָה 11. צַר 12. צָרָה 13. קְפָדָה 14. שָׁבָץ 15. שֶׁבֶר 16. עצב (A) 17. *ἄγχω* 18. *ἀγωνία* 19. *ἀγωνιάω* 20. *ἀλγέω* 21. *βασανίζω* 22. *θλῖψις* 23. *ὀδυνάω* 24. *ὀδύνη* 25. *πόνος* 26. *στενός* 27. *στενοχωρία* 28. *συνοχή* 29. *ὠδίνω* 30. angustia

Deu 2:25 hear . . and shall tremble and be in anguish 1
2Sm 1: 9 Stand . . and slay me; for anguish has seized me 14
Job 7:11 I will speak in the anguish of my spirit; 11
15:24 distress and anguish terrify him; 8
Ps 48: 6 trembling . . anguish as of a woman in travail. 2
55: 4 My heart is in anguish within me 1
116: 3 I suffered distress and anguish. 4
119:143 Trouble and anguish have come upon me 7
Prv 1:27 when distress and anguish come upon you. 10
Isa 8:22 distress and darkness, the gloom of anguish; 10
9: 1 will be no gloom for her that was in anguish 5
13: 8 they will be in anguish like a woman in travail. 1
21: 3 Therefore my loins are filled with anguish; 3
23: 5 Egypt, they will be in anguish over . . Tyre. 1
30: 6 Through a land of trouble and anguish 10
65:14 cry out . . and shall wail for anguish of spirit. 15
Jer 4:19 My anguish, my anguish! I writhe in pain! 6
19 My anguish, my anguish! I writhe in pain! 6
31 anguish as of one bringing forth her first child 12
6:24 anguish has taken hold of us 12
15: 8 I have made anguish and terror fall upon them 9
49:24 anguish and sorrows have taken hold of her 12
50:43 anguish seized him, pain as of a woman in travail. 12
Ezk 7:25 When anguish comes, they will seek peace 13
30: 4 anguish shall be in Ethiopia 3
9 and anguish shall come upon them 3
Dan 6:20 cried out in a tone of anguish and said to Daniel 16
Jol 2: 6 Before them peoples are in anguish 3
Nah 2:10 anguish is on all loins, all faces grow pale! 3
Zep 1:15 day of distress and anguish, a day of ruin 8
Zec 9: 5 be afraid; Gaza too, and shall writhe in anguish; *
Lke 16:24 I am in anguish in this flame.' 23
25 now he is comforted here, and you are in anguish. 23
Joh 16:21 she no longer remembers the anguish 22
Rom 9: 2 great sorrow and unceasing anguish in my heart. 24
2Co 2: 4 much affliction and anguish of heart 28
Rev 12: 2 in her pangs of birth, in anguish for delivery. 21
16:10 men gnawed their tongues in anguish 25
2Es 2:27 when the day of tribulation and anguish comes 30
16:19 tribulation and anguish are sent as scourges 30
Tob 3: 1 in my grief I wept, and I prayed in anguish, saying 24
Wis 4:19 they will suffer anguish 24
5: 3 in anguish of spirit they will groan, and say 27
Sir 48:19 they were in anguish, like women in travail. 29
Bar 3: 1 soul in anguish and the wearied spirit cry out 26
2Mc 3:16 disclosed the anguish of his soul. 18
21 the high priest in his great anguish. 19
9: 9 while he was still living in anguish and pain 24
4Mc 11:11 gasping for breath and in anguish of body 17
14:17 in the anguish of love 20

anguish *See also* feel.

animal 1. בְּהֵמָה 2. חַיָּה 3. טֶבַח 4. מִקְנֶה 5. *κνώδαλον* 6. *κτῆνος* 7. *τετράπους*

Gen 3:14 cursed are you . . above all wild animals; 2
6:20 and of the animals according to their kinds 1
7: 2 Take with you seven pairs of all clean animals 1
2 and a pair of the animals that are not clean 1
8 Of clean animals and of animals 1
8 clean animals and of animals that are not clean 1
23 man and animals and creeping things and birds 1
8:17 birds and animals and every creeping thing 1
20 Noah . . took of every clean animal 1
29: 7 it is not time for the animals to be gathered 4
43:16 and slaughter an animal and make ready 3
Lev 3: 1 if he offers an animal from the herd *
6 his offering . . is an animal from the flock *
7:25 the fat of an animal of which an offering by fire 1
26 eat no blood . . whether of fowl or of animal 1
11: 3 chews the cud, among the animals, you may eat 1
26 Every animal which parts the hoof but is not 1
27 among the animals that go on all fours 2
39 if any animal of which you may eat dies 1
22:22 Animals blind or disabled or mutilated *
24 Any animal which has its testicles bruised *
25 neither shall you offer . . any such animals *
27: 9 If it is an animal such as men offer as an offering 1
11 if it is an unclean animal such as is not offered 1
11 man shall bring the animal before the priest 1
26 a firstling of animals . . belongs to the LORD 1
27 if it is an unclean animal, then he shall buy it 1
32 every tenth animal of all that pass under *
Deu 14: 4 animals you may eat: the ox, the sheep, the goat 1
6 Every animal that parts the hoof and has the hoof 1
6 animal that . . chews the cud, among the animals 1
1Kg 18: 5 save . . alive, and not lose some of the animals. 1
Jer 27: 5 with the men and animals that are on the earth 1
Mal 1: 8 When you offer blind animals in sacrifice *
Act 10:12 animals and reptiles and birds of the air. 7
11: 6 I observed animals and beasts of prey 7
Rom 1:23 mortal man or birds or animals or reptiles. 7
1Co 15:39 there is one kind for men, another for animals 6
Wis 11:15 irrational serpents and worthless animals 5
16: 1 tormented by a multitude of animals. 5
19:19 land animals were transformed *
1Mc 1:47 to sacrifice swine and unclean animals 6
4Mc 1:34 when we crave seafood and fowl and animals 7

animal that dies 1. נְבֵלָה

Lev 7:24 The fat of an animal that dies of itself 1

wild animal 1. *θηρίον*

2Mc 5:27 and kept himself . . alive . . as wild animals do 1
10: 6 wandering in the . . caves like wild animals. 1
3Mc 4: 9 They were brought on board like wild animals 1

ankle 1. *σφυδρόν*

Act 3: 7 his feet and ankles were made strong. 1

ankle-deep 1. אֶפֶס

Ezk 47: 3 led me through the water; and it was ankle-deep. 1

anklet 1. עֶכֶס 2. *χλιδῶν*

Isa 3:18 take away . . finery of the anklets, the headbands 1
Jdt 10: 4 put on her anklets and bracelets and rings 2

annex 1. *προστίθημι*

1Mc 10:38 let them be so annexed to Judea 1

annihilate 1. אבד 2. *ἐξαναλίσκω* 3. *ἐξουδενόω* 4. *καταφθορά*

Est 3:13 to destroy, to slay, and to annihilate all Jews 1
7: 4 be destroyed, to be slain, and to be annihilated. 1
8:11 defend . . to destroy, to slay, and to annihilate 1
AEs 13:15 the eyes of our foes are upon us to annihilate us 4
Sir 47: 7 annihilated his adversaries the Philistines 3
1Mc 5:15 to annihilate us. 2

annihilation 1. *ἀφανισμός*

AEs 16:15 who were consigned to annihilation 1

anniversary 1. *καιρός*

4Mc 1:10 On this anniversary it is fitting 1

announce 1. דבר 2. נגד 3. קרא 4. שׁמע 5. *ἀναγγέλλω* 6. *ἀπαγγέλλω* 7. *εὐαγγελίζω* 8. adnuntio

Jdg 13:23 shown us . . or now announced to us such things 4
Isa 21: 6 Go, set a watchman, let him announce what he sees. 2
10 LORD of hosts, the God of Israel, I announce to you 2
44: 7 Who has announced from of old the things to come? *
48: 5 before they came to pass I announced them to you 4
63: 1 It is I, announcing vindication, mighty to save. 1
Jer 4:16 announce to Jerusalem, "Besiegers come 4
Lam 1:21 Bring thou the day thou hast announced 3
1Pe 1:12 the things which have now been announced to you 5
Rev 10: 7 as he announced to his servants the prophets 7
2Es 7:99 This is the order . . as henceforth is announced ‡
11:16 I announce this to you before you disappear. 8
Jdt 11:19 it was announced to me, and I was sent to tell you. 6
Sir 16:22 Who will announce his acts of justice? 5

announce beforehand 1. *προκαταγγέλλω*

Act 7:52 they killed those who announced beforehand 1

annoy 1. *διαπονέομαι* 2. *δυσχέρεια* 3. *παρενοχλέω*

Act 4: 2 annoyed because they were teaching the people 1
16:18 Paul was annoyed 1
1Mc 10:35 annoy any of them about any matter. 3
63 let no one annoy him for any reason. 3
12:14 We were unwilling to annoy you 3
2Mc 9:21 I suffered an annoying illness 2

annoyance 1. *ἐνοχλέω*

1Es 2:29 go no further to the annoyance of kings. 1

annual 1. בְּשָׁנָה

2Ch 8:13 commandment . . for . . the three annual feasts- 1

annually 1. *κατ' ἐνιαυτόν*

2Kg 3: 4 Mesha . . had to deliver annually to the king *
4Mc 4:17 he would pay the king 3,660 talents annually. 1

annul 1. כפר 2. פרר 3. *ἀθετέω* 4. *ἀκυρόω*

Isa 14:27 LORD of hosts has purposed, and who will annul it? 2
28:18 Then your covenant with death will be annulled 1
Zec 11:10 annulling the covenant which I had made with all 2
11 it was annulled on that day 2
14 annulling the brotherhood between Judah 2
Gal 3:15 no one annuls even a man's will, or adds to it 3
17 annul a covenant previously ratified by God 4
2Mc 13:25 so angry that they wanted to annul its terms. 3
14:28 he had to annul their agreement 3

anoint 1. בֶּן יִצְהָר 2. דשן 3. מִמְשַׁח 4. משח 5. מִשְׁחָה 6. מָשִׁיחַ 7. סוך 8. סכך 9. ἀλείφω 10. ἐγχρίω 11. ἐπιχρίω 12. λιπαίνω 13. μυρίζω 14. χρίσις 15. χρῖσμα 16. χρῖσμα ἔχω 17. χριστός 18. χρίω

Gen 31:13 I am the God of Bethel, where you anointed a pillar 4
Exd 25: 6 oil for the lamps, spices for the anointing oil 5
28:41 shall anoint them and ordain them 4
29: 7 you shall take the anointing oil 5
7 and pour it on his head and anoint him. 4
21 take . . the anointing oil, and sprinkle it 5
29 to be anointed in them and ordained in them. 4
36 and shall anoint it, to consecrate it. 4
30:25 you shall make of these a sacred anointing oil 5
25 a holy anointing oil it shall be. 5
26 you shall anoint with it the tent of meeting 4
30 you shall anoint Aaron and his sons 4
31 This shall be my holy anointing oil throughout 5
31:11 anointing oil and the fragrant incense 5
35: 8 oil for the light, spices for the anointing oil 5
15 the anointing oil and the fragrant incense 5
28 oil for the light, and for the anointing oil 5
37:29 He made the holy anointing oil also, and the pure 5
39:38 the golden altar, the anointing oil 5
40: 9 Then you shall take the anointing oil, and anoint 5
9 anoint the tabernacle and all that is in it 4
10 You shall also anoint the altar of burnt 4
11 You shall also anoint the laver and its base 4
13 you shall anoint him and consecrate him 4
15 anoint them, as you anointed their father 4
15 anoint them, as you anointed their father 4
15 their anointing shall admit them to a perpetual 4
Lev 4: 3 if it is the anointed priest who sins 6
5 the anointed priest shall take some of the blood 6
16 Then the anointed priest shall bring some 6
6:20 offer to the LORD on the day when he is anointed 4
22 among Aaron's sons, who is anointed to succeed him 6
7:36 on the day that they were anointed 4
8: 2 Take . . the anointing oil, and the bull of the sin 5
10 The Moses took the anointing oil, and anointed 5
10 Moses . . anointed the tabernacle and all that 4
11 anointed the altar and all its utensils 4
12 poured some of the anointing oil on Aaron's head 5
12 and anointed him, and consecrated him 4
30 took some of the anointing oil and of the blood 5
10: 7 for the anointing oil of the LORD is upon you 5
16:32 the priest who is anointed and consecrated 4
21:10 upon whose head the anointing oil is poured 5
12 for the consecration of the anointing oil 5
Num 3: 3 anointed priests, whom he ordained to minister 4
4:16 charge of . . and the anointing oil 5
7: 1 Moses . . had anointed and consecrated it 4
1 Moses . . anointed and consecrated the altar 4
10 altar on the day it was anointed; 4
84 for the altar, on the day when it was anointed 4
88 offering for the altar, after it was anointed. 4
35:25 high priest who was anointed with the holy oil. 4
Deu 28:40 but you shall not anoint yourself with the oil; 7
Jdg 9: 8 trees once went forth to anoint a king over them; 4
15 If in good faith you are anointing me king over 4
Rut 3: 3 Wash therefore and anoint yourself 7
1Sm 2:10 LORD will . . and exalt the power of his anointed. 6
35 go in and out before my anointed for ever. 6
9:16 I will send . . a man . . and you shall anoint him 4
10: 1 Has not the LORD anointed you to be prince 18
1 the LORD has anointed you to be prince over his 4
12: 3 before the LORD and before his anointed. 6
5 The LORD . . and his anointed is witness this day 6
15: 1 The LORD sent me to anoint you king over . . Israel; 4
17 The LORD anointed you king over Israel. 4
16: 3 and you shall anoint for me him whom I name to you. 4
6 Surely the LORD's anointed is before him. 6
12 And the LORD said, "Arise, anoint him; for this is he. 4
13 and anointed him in the midst of his brothers; 4
24: 6 do this thing to my lord, the LORD's anointed 6
6 LORD forbid . . seeing he is the LORD's anointed. 6
10 'I will not . . for he is the LORD's anointed.' 6
26: 9 put forth his hand against the LORD's anointed 6
11 put forth my hand against the LORD's anointed; 6
16 kept watch over your lord, the LORD's anointed. 6
23 put forth my hand against the LORD's anointed. 6
2Sm 1:14 put . . your hand to destroy the LORD's anointed? 6
16 saying, 'I have slain the LORD's anointed.' 6
21 the shield of Saul, not anointed with oil. 6
2: 4 there they anointed David king over . . Judah. 4
7 house of Judah has anointed me king over them. 4
3:39 And I am this day weak, though anointed king; 4
5: 3 and they anointed David king over Israel. 4
17 that David had been anointed king over Israel 4
12: 7 I anointed you king over Israel, and I delivered 4
20 David arose . . and washed, and anointed himself 8
14: 2 do not anoint yourself with oil, but behave like 7
19:10 But Ab'salom, whom we anointed over us, is dead 4
21 to death . . because he cursed the LORD's anointed? 6
22:51 shows steadfast love to his anointed, to David 6
23: 1 David . . the anointed of the God of Jacob 6
1Kg 1:34 let Zadok . . and Nathan . . anoint him king over 4
39 took the horn of oil . . and anointed Solomon. 4
45 Zadok . . and Nathan . . have anointed him king 4
5: 1 they had anointed him king in place of his father; 4
19:15 you shall anoint Haz'ael to be king over Syria; 4
16 Jehu . . you shall anoint to be king over Israel; 4
16 Eli'sha . . you shall anoint to be prophet 4
2Kg 9: 3 'Thus says the LORD, I anoint you king over Israel.' 4
6 Thus says the LORD . . I anoint you king 4
12 Thus says the LORD, I anoint you king over Israel.' 4
11:12 and they proclaimed him king, and anointed him; 4
23:30 took Jeho'ahaz . . and anointed him, and made him 4
1Ch 11: 3 they anointed David king over Israel 4
14: 8 David had been anointed king over all Israel 4
29:22 and they anointed him as prince for the LORD 4
2Ch 22: 7 LORD had anointed to destroy the house of Ahab. 4
23:11 Jehoi'ada and his sons anointed him, 4
28:15 provided . . food and drink, and anointed them; 7
Ps 2: 2 against the LORD and his anointed, saying 6
18:50 and shows steadfast love to his anointed 6
20: 6 Now I know that the LORD will help his anointed; 6
23: 5 thou anointest my head with oil, my cup overflows. 2
28: 8 he is the saving refuge of his anointed. 6
45: 7 Therefore God, your God, has anointed you 4
84: 9 look upon the face of thine anointed! 6
89:20 with my holy oil I have anointed him; 4
38 thou art full of wrath against thy anointed. 6
51 which they mock the footsteps of thy anointed. 6
132:17 I have prepared a lamp for my anointed. 6
141: 5 but let the oil of the wicked never anoint my head; 12
Isa 45: 1 Thus says the LORD to his anointed, to Cyrus 6
61: 1 the LORD has anointed me to bring good tidings 4
Lam 4:20 The breath of our nostrils, the LORD'S anointed 6
Ezk 16: 9 and anointed you with oil. 7
28:14 With an anointed guardian cherub I placed you; 3
Dan 9:24 to anoint a most holy place. 4
10: 3 nor did I anoint myself at all, 7
Hos 8:10 cease for a little while from anointing king 18
Ams 6: 6 and anoint themselves with the finest oils 4
Mic 6:15 tread olives, but not anoint yourselves with oil; 7
Hab 3:13 forth . . for the salvation of thy anointed. 6
Zec 4:14 These are the two anointed who stand by the Lord 1
Mat 6:17 when you fast, anoint your head and wash your face 9
Mrk 6:13 anointed with oil many that were sick 9
14: 8 anointed my body beforehand for burying. 13
16: 1 so that they might go and anoint him. 9
Lke 4:18 he has anointed me to preach good news to the poor 18
7:38 anointed them with the ointment. 9
46 You did not anoint my head with oil 9
46 she has anointed my feet with ointment. 9
Joh 9: 6 and anointed the man's eyes with the clay 11
11 made clay and anointed my eyes and said to me 11
11: 2 It was Mary who anointed the Lord with ointment 9
12: 3 anointed the feet of Jesus 9
Act 4:26 against the Lord and against his Anointed'– 17
27 thy holy servant Jesus, whom thou didst anoint 18
10:38 how God anointed Jesus of Nazareth 18
Heb 1: 9 has anointed thee with the oil of gladness 18
Jas 5:14 let them pray over him, anointing him with oil 9
1Jn 2:20 you have been anointed by the Holy One 16
27 the anointing which you received from him 15
27 as his anointing teaches you about everything 15
Rev 3:18 salve to anoint your eyes, that you may see. 10
Tob 6: 8 anoint . . a man who has white films in his eyes 10
11: 8 You therefore must anoint his eyes with the gall; 10
Jdt 10: 3 anointed herself with precious ointment 18
16: 8 She anointed her face with ointment 9
Sir 35: 6 anoints the altar 12
45:15 ordained him, and anointed him with holy oil 18
46:13 established the kingdom and anointed rulers 18
19 before the Lord and his anointed 17
48: 8 who anointed kings to inflict retribution 18
2Mc 1:10 who is of the family of the anointed priests 17
151 1: 4 and anointed me with his anointing oil. 18
4 and anointed me with his anointing oil. 14

anointed one 1. מָשִׁיחַ

1Ch 16:22 Touch not my anointed ones, do my prophets no harm! 1
2Ch 6:42 do not turn away the face of thy anointed one! 1
Ps 105:15 Touch not my anointed ones, do my prophets no harm! 1
132:10 do not turn away the face of thy anointed one. 1
Dan 9:25 to the coming of an anointed one, a prince 1
26 62 weeks, an anointed one shall be cut off 1

anointing *See* oil.

another 1. אַח 2. אֶחָד 3. אָחוֹת 4. אַחֵר 5. אִישׁ 6. אֵלֶּה 7. בְּכֹה 8. גַּם 9. זֶה 10. זוּר 11. יסף 12. כָּכָה 13. נֶפֶשׁ 14. עוֹד 15. עָמִית 16. פְּנֵי רֵעַ 17. רֵעַ 18. רְעוּת 19. שֵׁנִי 20. אָחֳרָן (A) 21. דָּא (A) 22. ἄλλος 23. ἀλλότριος 24. ἄνθρωπος 25. αὐτός 26. βρῶμα 27. δόξα 28. εἷς 29. ἕκαστος 30. ἕτερος 31. ἔτι ἅπαξ 32. ἡμέρα 33. θυγάτηρ 34. λίθος 35. ὁ δέ 36. ὃς δέ 37. οὗτος 38. πάλιν 39. προστίθημι 40. τίς 41. aliquis 42. alius 43. unus

Gen 4:25 God has appointed for me another child 4
8:10 He waited another seven days 14
12 Then he waited another seven days 14
11: 3 they said to one another, "Come, let us make bricks 17
7 they may not understand one another's speech. 17
25: 1 Abraham took another wife, whose name was 11
26:21 Then they dug another well, and they quarreled 4
22 he moved from there and dug another well 4
31 rose early and took oath with one another; 1
29:27 in return for serving me another seven years. 4
30 and served Laban for another seven years. 4
30:24 saying, "May the LORD add to me another son! 4
35:17 Fear not; for now you will have another son. 8
37: 9 Then he dreamed another dream, and told it to his 14
9 Behold, I have dreamed another dream; 14
19 They said to one another, "Here comes this 1
42:21 Then they said to one another, "In truth we are 1
28 turned trembling to one another, saying 1
43: 6 to tell the man that you had another brother? 14
7 father still alive? Have you another brother?' •
33 and the men looked at one another in amazement. 17
Exd 10:23 they did not see one another, nor did any rise 1
16:15 Israel saw it, they said to one another, "What is it? 1
21:10 If he takes another wife to himself, he shall not 4
14 if a man willfully attacks another to kill him 17
35 When one man's ox hurts another's, so that it dies 17
25:20 with their wings, their faces one to another; 1
26: 3 Five curtains shall be coupled to one another; 3
3 five curtains shall be coupled to one another. 3
5 the loops shall be opposite one another. 3
19 two bases under another frame for its two tenons; 2
21 and two bases under another frame; 2
25 and two bases under another frame. 2
36:10 he coupled five curtains to one another 2
10 other five curtains he coupled to one another. 2
12 the loops were opposite one another. 2
24 bases under another frame for its two tenons. 2
26 and two bases under another frame. 2
37: 9 their wings, with their faces one to another; 1
Lev 7:10 all the sons of Aaron, one as well as another 1
19:11 You shall not . . lie to one another 15
20 a woman who is a slave, betrothed to another man •
25:14 you shall not wrong one another 1
17 You shall not wrong one another, 15
46 not rule, one over another, with harshness 1
26:37 They shall stumble over one another 1
27:20 sold the field to another man, it shall not be 4
Num 8: 8 take another young bull for a sin offering. 19
14: 4 they said to one another, "Let us choose a captain 1
23:13 Balak said to him, "Come with me to another place 4
27 Come now, I will take you to another place; 4
36: 7 not be transferred from one tribe to another; •
9 no . . transferred from one tribe to another; 4
Deu 4:34 take a nation . . from the midst of another nation •
17: 8 between one kind of homicide and another •
8 between . . one kind of legal right and another •
8 between . . one kind of assault and another •
20: 5 die in the battle and another man dedicate it. 4
6 lest he die . . and another man enjoy its fruit. 4
7 die in the battle and another man take her.' 4
22:22 man is found lying with the wife of another man •
24: 2 if she goes and becomes another man's wife 4
28:30 betroth a wife, and another man shall lie with her; 4
32 sons . . shall be given to another people 4
29:28 cast them into another land, as at this day.' 4
Jdg 2:10 there arose another generation after them 4
10:18 people, the leaders of Gilead, said one to another 17
11: 2 for you are the son of another woman. 4
Rut 2: 8 do not go to glean in another field or leave this 4
22 lest in another field you be molested. 4
3:14 but arose before one could recognize another; 17
1Sm 10: 3 one carrying . . another carrying three loaves 2
3 and another carrying a skin of wine. 2
6 prophesy . . and be turned into another man. 4
9 When he turned . . God gave him another heart; 4
13:18 another company turned toward Beth-hor'on 2
18 and another company turned toward the border 2
17:30 And he turned away from him toward another 4
2Sm 3:11 Ish-bo'sheth could not answer Abner another word •
11:25 for the sword devours now one and now another; 9
18:20 you may carry tidings another day 4
26 And the watchman saw another man running; 4
26 watchman . . said, "See, another man running alone! •
1Kg 13:10 he went another way, and did not return by the way 4
18: 6 Obadi'ah went in another direction by himself. 2
20:29 they encamped opposite one another seven days. 6
37 The he found another man, and said, "Strike me 4
21: 6 or else . . I will give you another vineyard for it'; •
22: 7 Is there not here another prophet of the LORD 14
20 And one said one thing, and another said another. 9
20 And one said one thing, and another said another. 7
2Kg 1:11 the king sent to him another captain of 50 men 4
4: 6 she said to her son, "Bring me another vessel. 14
6 And he said to her, "There is not another. 14
7: 8 then they came back, and entered another tent 4
11: 6 another third being at the gate Sur and a third •
21:16 he had filled Jerusalem from one end to another †
1Ch 2:26 Jerah'meel also had another wife, whose name was 4
16:20 from one kingdom to another people 4
2Ch 18: 6 Is there not here another prophet of the LORD 14
19 And one said one thing and another said another. 9
19 And one said one thing and another said another. 12
20:23 they all helped to destroy one another. 17
25:12 The men of Judah captured another 10,000 alive •
30:23 to keep the feast for another seven days; 4

23 kept it for another seven days with gladness. •
32: 5 outside it he built another wall; 4
Neh 3:11 repaired another section 19
19 Ezer . . repaired another section opposite 19
20 repaired another section from the Angle 19
21 Mer'emoth . . repaired another section 19
24 of Hen'adad repaired another section 19
27 Teko'ites repaired another section opposite 19
30 Hanani'ah . . Hanun . . repaired another section. 19
4:19 we are separated on the wall, far from one another. 1
9: 3 for another fourth of it they made confession •
Est 1:19 let the king give her royal position to another 18
4:14 deliverance will rise . . from another quarter 4
Job 1:16 While he was yet speaking, there came another 9
17 there came another, and said, "The Chalde'ans 9
18 While he was yet speaking, there came another 9
19:27 my eyes shall behold, and not another. 10
21:25 Another dies in bitterness of soul 9
31: 8 then let me sow, and another eat; 4
10 then let my wife grind for another 4
41:16 near to another that no air can come between 2
17 They are joined one to another; 1
Ps 16: 4 who choose another god multiply their sorrows; 4
75: 7 putting down one and lifting up another. 9
105:13 from one kingdom to another people 4
109: 8 May his days be few; may another seize his goods! 4
145: 4 One generation shall laud thy works to another •
Prv 11:24 another withholds what he should give •
13: 7 another pretends to be poor, yet has great wealth. •
23:35 When shall I awake? I will seek another drink. 14
25: 9 do not disclose another's secret; 4
27: 2 Let another praise you, and not your own mouth; 10
17 sharpens iron, and one man sharpens another. 16
28:17 If a man is burdened with the blood of another 13
Ecc 4:10 who is alone . . and has not another to lift him up. 19
7:27 adding one thing to another to find the sum 2
Sng 5: 9 What is your beloved more than another beloved •
9 What is your beloved more than another beloved •
Isa 3: 5 the people will oppress one another, every man 5
6: 3 one called to another and said: "Holy, holy, holy 9
13: 8 They will look aghast at one another; 17
44: 5 another will call himself by the name of Jacob 9
5 and another will write on his hand, 'The LORD'S,' 9
48:11 My glory I will not give to another. 4
65:22 They shall not build and another inhabit; 4
22 they shall not plant and another eat; 4
Jer 3: 1 she goes from him and becomes another man's wife 4
7: 5 if you truly execute justice one with another 17
13:14 And I will dash them one against another 1
18: 4 and he reworked it into another vessel 4
22:26 into another country, where you were not born 4
23:27 by their dreams which they tell one another 17
30 prophets . . who steal my words from one another. 17
25:26 kings of the north, far and near, one after another 1
26:20 There was another man who prophesied 8
36:16 they turned one to another in fear; 17
28 Take another scroll and write on it 4
32 Then Jeremiah took another scroll 4
46:16 they said one to another, 'Arise, and let us go back 17
51:31 One runner runs to meet another •
31 one messenger to meet another, to tell the king †
46 one year and afterward a report in another year •
Ezk 1: 9 their wings touched one another; 3
11 wings, each of which touched the wing of another 5
23 were stretched out straight, one toward another; 3
3:13 sound of the wings . . as they touched one another 3
4:17 and look at one another in dismay, and waste away 1
12: 3 from your place to another place in their sight. 4
17: 7 there was another great eagle with great wings 2
19: 5 she took another of her whelps 2
22:11 another lewdly defiles his daughter-in-law; 5
11 another in you defiles his sister 5
24:23 in your iniquities and groan to one another. 1
33:30 say to one another, each to his brother 2
37:16 then take another stick and write upon it 2
41: 6 stories, one over another, 30 in each story. †
11 and another door toward the south; 2
45: 5 Another section, 25,000 cubits •
Dan 2:39 After you shall arise another kingdom inferior 20
44 nor . . its sovereignty be left to another people. 20
5:17 yourself, and give your rewards to another; 20
7: 3 great beasts . . different from one another. 21
5 behold, another beast, a second one, like a bear. 20
6 another, like a leopard, with four wings of a bird 20
8 came up among them another horn, a little one 20
24 arise, and another shall arise after them; 20
8:13 another holy one said to the one that spoke 2
Hos 3: 3 not play the harlot, or belong to another man; •
Jol 1: 3 and their children another generation. 4
2: 8 They do not jostle one another 1
Ams 4: 7 upon one city, and send no rain upon another city; 2
Jon 1: 7 they said to one another, "Come, let us cast lots 17
Zec 2: 3 and another angel came forward to meet him 4
8:16 that you shall do: Speak the truth to one another 17
17 devise evil in your hearts against one another 17
21 the inhabitants of one city shall go to another 2
11: 9 that are left devour the flesh of one another. 18
Mal 2:10 Why then are we faithless to one another 1
3:16 those who feared the LORD spoke with one another; 17
Mat 2:12 departed to their own country by another way. 22
8: 9 I say to one, 'Go,' and he goes, and to another, 'Come,' 22
21 Another of the disciples said to him 30
11: 3 or shall we look for another? 30
13:23 in one case a hundredfold, in another 60 36
23 in one case a hundredfold, in another 60 36
24 Another parable he put before them, saying 22
31 Another parable he put before them, saying 22
33 He told them another parable 22
19: 9 and marries another, commits adultery. 22
21:33 Hear another parable 22
35 beat one, killed another, and stoned another. 36
35 beat one, killed another, and stoned another. 36
22: 5 went off, one to his farm, another to his business 36
24: 2 one stone upon another 34
25:15 to one he gave five talents, to another two 36
15 to another two, to another one 36
26:22 and began to say to him one after another 29
71 when he went out to the porch, another maid saw him 22
Mrk 10:11 Whoever divorces his wife and marries another 22
12 if she divorces her husband and marries another 22
12: 4 Again he sent to them another servant 22
5 he sent another, and him they killed 22
13: 2 There will not be left here one stone upon another 34
14:19 to say to him one after another, "Is it I? 28
58 I will build another, not made with hands.' 22
16:12 After this he appeared in another form to two 30
Lke 6: 6 On another sabbath 30
7: 8 to another, 'Come,' and he comes 22
19 Are you he . . or shall we look for another? 22
20 'Are you he . . or shall we look for another?' 22
9:56 And they went on to another village. 30
59 To another he said, "Follow me. 30
61 Another said, "I will follow you, Lord 30
14:19 another said, 'I have bought five yoke of oxen 30
20 another said, 'I have married a wife 30
31 what king, going to encounter another king in war 30
16: 7 Then he said to another, 'And how much do you owe?' 30
12 you have not been faithful in that which is another's 23
18 divorces his wife and marries another 30
19:20 Then another came, saying 30
44 they will not leave one stone upon another in you; 34
20:11 he sent another servant 39
21: 6 there shall not be left here one stone upon another 34
22:59 still another insisted, saying, "Certainly 22
Joh 4:37 'One sows and another reaps.' 22
5: 7 while I am going another steps down before me. 22
32 there is another who bears witness to me 22
43 if another comes in his own name 22
14:16 he will give you another Counselor, to be with you 22
18:15 so did another disciple 22
19:37 again another scripture says 30
21:18 another will gird you 22
Act 1:20 'His office let another take.' 30
2:12 all were amazed . . saying to one another 22
7:18 till there arose over Egypt another king 30
12:17 Then he departed and went to another place. 30
13:35 Therefore he says also in another psalm 30
17: 7 saying that there is another king, Jesus. 30
19:32 Now some cried one thing, some another †
21:34 Some in the crowd shouted one thing, some another; †
Rom 2: 1 you have no excuse . . when you judge another; 30
7: 3 an adulteress if she lives with another man 30
3 and if she marries another man 30
4 so that you may belong to another 30
23 another law at war with the law of my mind 30
9:21 one vessel for beauty and another for menial use? 36
14: 4 to pass judgment on the servant of another? 23
5 One man esteems one day as better than another •
15:20 lest I build on another man's foundation 23
1Co 3: 4 and another, "I belong to Apol'los 30
4: 6 puffed up in favor of one against another. 30
7: 7 one of one kind and one of another. 37
11:21 one is hungry and another is drunk. 36
12: 8 to another the utterance of knowledge 22
9 to another faith by the same Spirit 30
9 to another gifts of healing by the one Spirit 22
10 to another the working of miracles 22
10 to another prophecy 22
10 to another the ability to distinguish . . spirits 22
10 to another various kinds of tongues 30
10 to another the interpretation of tongues. 22
14:30 If a revelation is made to another sitting 22
15:39 there is one kind for men, another for animals 22
39 another for birds, and another for fish. 22
39 another for birds, and another for fish. 22
40 the glory of the terrestrial is another. 30
41 one glory of the sun, and another glory of the moon 22
41 another glory of the stars 22
2Co 2: 1 not to make you another painful visit. 38
3:18 from one degree of glory to another 27
10:16 work already done in another's field. 23
11: 4 For if some one comes and preaches another Jesus 22
Gal 1: 7 not that there is another gospel 22
Col 3:13 if one has a complaint against another 40
1Th 5:11 encourage one another and build one another up 28
Heb 4: 8 God would not speak later of another day. 22
5: 6 as he says also in another place 30
7:11 need . . for another priest to arise 30
13 belonged to another tribe 30
15 when another priest arises 30
Jas 2:25 when she . . sent them out another way? 30
Rev 6: 4 And out came another horse, bright red; 22
7: 2 I saw another angel ascend from the rising . . sun 22
8: 3 another angel came and stood at the altar 22
10: 1 Then I saw another mighty angel coming down 22
12: 3 another portent appeared in heaven; 22
13:11 I saw another beast which rose out of the earth; 22
14: 6 Then I saw another angel flying in midheaven 22
8 Another angel, a second, followed, saying 22
9 And another angel, a third, followed them, saying 22
15 another angel came out of the temple, calling 22
17 another angel came out of the temple in heaven 22
18 Then another angel came out from the altar 22
15: 1 Then I saw another portent in heaven 22
18: 1 I saw another angel coming down from heaven 22
4 Then I heard another voice from heaven saying 22
20:12 another book was opened, which is the book of life 22
2Es 3:32 Or has another nation known thee besides Israel? 42
6: 6 through me and not through another. 42
6 through me and not through another. 42
7: 6 Another example: There is a city 42
105no one shall ever pray for another on that day 41
105neither shall any one lay a burden on another ‡
12:14 12 kings shall reign in it, one after another. 43
13:12 another multitude which was peaceable. 42
39 another multitude that was peaceable 42
40 and they were taken into another land. 42
15:38 from the north, and another part from the west. 42
16:27 one man will long to see another •
Tob 6:12 cannot give her to another man 30
Wis 16:14 A man in his wickedness kills another •
19: 3 they reached another foolish decision 30
Sir 0: 2 when translated into another language 30
11:12 There is another who is slow and needs help •
14:15 leave the fruit of your labors to another 30
18 one dies and another is born. 30
20: 5 while another is detested •
6 while another keeps silent •
23:23 brought forth children by another man. 23
28: 3 Does a man harbor anger against another 24
29: 5 A man will kiss another's hands 25
22 sumptuous food in another man's house. 23
32: 9 when another is speaking, do not babble. 30
33: 7 Why is any day better than another 32
19 do not give your property to another 30
34:23 When one builds and another tears down 28
24 When one prays and another curses 28
36:18 yet one food is better than another. 26
21 one daughter is better than another. 33
40:29 When a man looks to the table of another 23
29 He pollutes himself with another man's food 23
Bar 2: 3 we should eat . . another the flesh of his daughter. 24
4: 3 Do not give your glory to another 30
1Mc 5:37 Timothy gathered another army 22
10:16 So he said, "Shall we find another such man? 28
13:28 erected seven pyramids, opposite one another 28
2Mc 3:37 to send on another mission to Jerusalem 31
4: 8 from another source of revenue, 80 talents. 22
19 to expend it for another purpose. 30
26 Jason . . was supplanted by another man 30
10: 3 and made another altar of sacrifice 30
4Mc 13:11 another said, "Bear up nobly 35
12 another reminded them, "Remember whence 35

another *See also* agree, belong, dispute, face, fight, look, nation, one, pretend, sing, time, way.

another man 1. אַחֵר 2. *ἄλλος* 3. *ἀλλότριος* 4. *ἕτερος* 5. *ὃς δέ* 6. *ὕπανδρος*

Exd 22: 5 beast loose and it feeds in another man's field 1
Rom 14: 5 while another man esteems all days alike. 5
1Co 3:10 another man is building upon it 2
10:29 liberty . . be determined by another man's scruples? 2
1Ti 5:22 nor participate in another man's sins 3
Sir 9: 9 Never dine with another man's wife 6
41:21 gazing at another man's wife; 6
2Mc 4:26 Jason . . was supplanted by another man 4

another there 1. *ἀλλαχῆ*

Wis 18:18 one here and another there, hurled down half dead 1

answer 1. אֵמֶר 2. אמר 3. דָּבָר 4. חֵלֶק 5. מַעֲנֶה 6. נגד 7. עַל פִּי 8. ענה 9. ענה וְאמר 10. שׁוּב 11. שׁוּב דָּבָר 12. שׁוּב מִלָּה 13. ענה (A) 14. פִּתְגָם (A) 15. תוּב פִּתְגָם (A) 16. *ἀποκρίνομαι* 17. *ἀπόκρισις* 18. *ἀπολογέομαι* 19. *εἶπον* 20. *ἐκ* 21. *ἐπακούω* 22. *ἐπιφωνέω* 23. *ὅς* 24. *πρός* 25. *ὑπακούω* 26. *φημί* 27. *φθέγγομαι ἀπόκρισιν* 28. dico 29. respondeo

Gen 18:27 Abraham answered, "Behold, I have taken 8
29 He answered, "For the sake of 40 I will not do it. 2
30 He answered, "I will not do it, if I find 30 there. 2
31 He answered, "For the sake of twenty I will not 2
32 answered, "For the sake of ten I will not destroy 2
23: 5 The Hittites answered Abraham 8
10 Ephron the Hittite answered Abraham 8
14 Ephron answered Abraham 8

24:50 Laban and Bethu'el answered, "The thing comes 8
27: 1 said to him, "My son"; and he answered, "Here I am. 2
20 He answered, "Because the LORD your God 2
24 really my son Esau?" He answered, "I am. 2
32 Who are you?" He answered, I am your son 2
37 Isaac answered Esau, "Behold, I have made him 8
39 Then Isaac his father answered him 8
30:33 my honesty will answer for me later, when you 8
31:14 Then Rachel and Leah answered him 8
31 Jacob answered Laban, "Because I was afraid 8
43 Then Laban answered and said to Jacob 8
33: 8 Jacob answered, "To find favor in the sight of my 2
34:13 The sons of Jacob answered Shechem 8
35: 3 the God who answered me in the day of my distress 8
38:17 He answered, "I will send you a kid from the flock. 2
40:18 Joseph answered, "This is its interpretation 8
41:16 Joseph answered Pharaoh, "It is not in me; 8
42:22 Reuben answered them, "Did I not tell you 8
43: 7 What we told him was in answer to these questions; 7
45: 3 But his brothers could not answer him 8
47:16 Joseph answered, "Give your cattle, 2
30 He answered, "I will do as you have said. 2
50: 6 Pharaoh answered, "Go up, and bury your father 2
Exd 2:14 He answered, "Who made you a prince and a judge 2
4: 1 Moses answered, "But behold, they will not believe 8
19: 8 all the people answered together and said 8
19 Moses spoke, and God answered him in thunder. 8
24: 3 all the people answered with one voice, and said 8
Num22:18 Balaam answered and said to the servants 8
23:12 answered, "Must I not take heed to speak 8
26 Balaam answered Balak, "Did I not tell you 8
32:31 sons of Gad and the sons of Reuben answered, "As 8
Deu 1:14 you answered me, 'The thing that you have spoken 8
41 Then you answered me, 'We have sinned 8
20:11 if its answer to you is peace and it opens to you 8
25: 9 she shall answer and say, 'So shall it be done 8
27:15 all the people shall answer and say, 'Amen.' 8
Jos 1:16 And they answered Joshua, "All that .. we will do 8
7:20 Achan answered Joshua, "Of a truth I have sinned 8
9:24 They answered Joshua, "Because it was told 8
22:21 said in answer to the heads of the families 8
24:16 Then the people answered, "Far be it from us 8
Jdg 5:29 nay, she gives answer to herself 1
7:14 his comrade answered, "This is no other 8
8: 8 men of Penu'el answered him as the men of Succoth 8
8 answered him as the men of Succoth had answered. 8
18 They answered "As you are, so were they, every one 2
25 And they answered, "We will willingly give them. 2
11:13 king of the Ammonites answered the messengers 2
19:28 Get up, let us be going." But there was no answer. 8
20: 4 the Levite .. answered and said, "I came to Gib'e-ah 8
Rut 2: 4 And they answered, "The LORD bless you. 2
6 And the servant .. answered, "It is the Moabite 8
11 Bo'az answered her, "All that you have done 8
3: 9 said, "Who are you?" And she answered, "I am Ruth 2
1Sm 1:15 But Hannah answered, "No, my lord 9
17 Then Eli answered, "Go in peace 8
4:17 He who brought the tidings answered and said 8
20 Fear not .. " But she did not answer or give heed. 8
5: 8 They answered, "Let the ark .. be brought around 2
6: 4 They answered, "Five golden tumors and .. mice 2
7: 9 Samuel cried .. and the LORD answered him. 8
8:18 the LORD will not answer you in that day. 8
9: 8 The servant answered Saul again, "Here, I have 8
12 They answered, "He is; behold, he is just ahead 8
19 Samuel answered Saul, "I am the seer; go up before me 8
21 Saul answered, "Am I not a Benjaminite 8
10:12 man of the place answered, "And who is their father? 8
14:37 But he did not answer him that day. 8
39 not a man among all the people that answered him. 8
41 O LORD .. why hast thou not answered thy servant 29
16:18 One of the young men answered, "Behold, I have seen 8
17:27 And the people answered him in the same way 2
30 and the people answered him again as before. 10
58 David answered, "I am the son of your servant Jesse 2
19:17 And Michal answered Saul, "He said to me, 'Let me go; 2
20:10 tell me if your father answers you roughly? 8
28 Jonathan answered Saul, "David earnestly asked 8
32 Jonathan answered Saul his father, "Why should he 8
21: 4 the priest answered David, "I have no common bread 8
5 And David answered the priest, "Of a truth 8
22: 9 Then answered Do'eg the E'domite .. "I saw the son 8
12 Hear now .. " And he answered, "Here I am, my lord. 2
14 Then Ahim'elech answered the king 8
23: 4 the LORD answered him, "Arise, go down to Kei'lah; 8
25:10 Nabal answered David's servants, "Who is David? 8
26:14 Will you not answer, Abner?" Then Abner answered 8
14 Abner answered, "Who are you that calls to the king? 8
28: 6 the LORD did not answer him, either by dreams 8
15 Saul answered, "I am in great distress; 2
15 God has turned away .. and answers me no more 8
30: 8 He answered him, "Pursue; for you shall surely 2
2Sm 1: 4 Tell me." And he answered, "The people have fled 2
7 saw me, and called to me. And I answered, 'Here I am.' 2
8 'Who are you?' I answered him, 'I am an Amal'ekite.' 2
13 And he answered, "I am the son of a sojourner 2
2:20 Is it you, As'ahel?" And he answered, "It is I. 2
3:11 Ish-bo'sheth could not answer Abner another word 10
4: 9 David answered Rechab and Ba'anah his brother 8
9: 6 And he answered, "Behold, your servant. 2
13:12 She answered him, "No, my brother, do not force me; 2
14: 5 She answered, "Alas, I am a widow; 2
18 the king answered the woman, "Do not hide from me 8
19 The woman answered and said, "As surely as you live 8
32 Ab'salom answered Jo'ab, "Behold, I sent word to you 2
15:21 But It'tai answered the king, "As the LORD lives 8
16: 2 Ziba answered, "The asses are for the king's 2
18:29 Ahi'ma-az answered, "When Jo'ab sent your servant 2
32 the Cushite answered, "May the enemies of my lord 2
19:21 Abi'shai the son of Zeru'iah answered 8
26 He answered, "My lord, O king, my servant deceived 2
38 the king answered, "Chimham shall go over with me 2
42 All the men of Judah answered the men of Israel 8
43 And the men of Israel answered the men of Judah 8
20:17 the woman said, "Are you Jo'ab?" He answered, "I am. 2
17 Listen to .. " And he answered, "I am listening. 2
20 Jo'ab answered, "Far be it from me .. that I should 8
22:42 they cried to the LORD, but he did not answer them. 8
24:13 consider, and decide what answer I shall return 3
1Kg 1:28 Then King David answered, "Call Bathshe'ba to me. 8
36 Benai'ah .. answered the king, "Amen! May the LORD 8
43 Jonathan answered Adoni'jah, "No, for our lord King 8
2:22 King Solomon answered his mother, "And why do you 8
30 saying, "Thus said Jo'ab, and thus he answered me. 8
3:27 the king answered and said, "Give the living child 8
10: 3 Solomon answered all her questions; 6
12: 6 How do you advise me to answer this people? 10
7 and speak good words to them when you answer them 8
9 What do you advise that we answer this people 10
13 the king answered the people harshly 8
16 the people answered the king, "What portion 10
18: 8 he answered him, "It is I. 2
18 he answered, "I have not troubled Israel; 2
21 And the people did not answer him a word. 8
24 the God who answers by fire, he is God. 8
24 And all the people answered, "It is well spoken. 8
26 called on the name of Ba'al .. "O Ba'al, answer us! 8
26 there was no voice, and no one answered. 8
29 there was no voice; no one answered, no one heeded. 8
37 Answer me, O LORD .. that this people may know 8
37 O LORD, answer me, that this people may know 8
20: 4 the king of Israel answered, "As you say, my lord 8
11 the king of Israel answered, "Tell him 8
14 Who shall begin the battle?" He answered, "You. 2
21: 6 and he answered, 'I will not give you my vineyard.' 2
20 He answered, "I have found you 2
22:15 he answered him, "Go up and triumph; 2
2Kg 1: 8 They answered him, "He wore a garment of haircloth 2
10 Eli'jah answered the captain of 50 8
12 Eli'jah answered them, "If I am a man of God 8
2: 5 he answered, "Yes, I know it; hold your peace. 2
3: 8 Jeho'ram answered, "By the way of the wilderness 2
11 one of the king of Israel's servants answered 2
4:13 She answered, "I dwell among my own people. 2
14 Geha'zi answered, "Well, she has no son 2
26 And she answered, "It is well. 2
6: 2 Let us go to the Jordan .. " And he answered, "Go. 2
3 go with your servants." And he answered, "I will go. 2
22 He answered, "You shall not slay them. 2
28 What is your trouble?" She answered, "This woman 2
7:19 the captain had answered the man of God 8
8:12 He answered, "Because I know the evil 2
13 Eli'sha answered, "The LORD has shown me 2
14 he answered, "He told me that you would .. recover. 2
9:19 Jehu answered, "What have you to do with peace? 2
22 He answered, "What peace can there be 2
10:13 And they answered, "We are the kinsmen 2
15 Jehon'adab answered, "It is." Jehu said, "If it is 2
18:36 people were silent and answered him not a word 8
36 the king's command was, "Do not answer him. 8
20:10 Hezeki'ah answered, "It is an easy thing 2
15 Hezeki'ah answered, "They have seen all that is 2
1Ch 21:12 decide what answer I shall return to him who sent 3
26 and he answered him with fire from heaven upon 8
28 the LORD had answered him at the threshing floor 8
2Ch 1:11 God answered Solomon, "Because this was 2
2:11 Then Huram the king of Tyre answered in a letter 2
9: 2 Solomon answered all her questions; 6
10: 6 How do you advise me to answer this people? 11
9 What do you advise that we answer this people 11
13 the king answered them harshly 8
16 the people answered the king 10
18: 3 He answered him, "I am as you are, my people 2
14 And he answered, "Go up and triumph; 2
25: 9 man of God answered, "The LORD is able to give you 2
31:10 Azari'ah the chief priest .. answered him 2
32:24 answered him and gave him a sign. 2
Ezr 4:17 king sent an answer: "To Rehum the commander 14
5: 5 then answer be returned by letter concerning it. •
10:12 Then all the assembly answered with a loud voice 8
Neh 6: 4 I answered them in the same manner. 10
8: 6 all the people answered, "Amen, Amen," lifting up 8
Est 4:13 Mor'decai told them to return answer to Esther •
7: 3 Then Queen Esther answered, "If I have found favor 9
Job 1: 7 Satan answered the LORD, "From going to and fro 8
9 Then Satan answered the LORD, "Does Job fear God 8
2: 2 Satan answered the LORD, "From going to and fro 8
4 Then Satan answered the LORD, "Skin for skin! 8
4: 1 Then Eli'phaz the Te'manite answered 8
5: 1 Call now; is there any one who will answer you? 8
6: 1 Then Job answered 8
8: 1 Then Bildad the Shuhite answered 8
9: 1 Then Job answered 8
3 one could not answer him once in 1,000 8
14 can I answer him, choosing my words with him? 8
15 Though I am innocent, I cannot answer him; 8
16 If I summoned him and he answered me 8
32 For he is not a man, as I am, that I might answer him 8
11: 1 Then Zophar the Na'amathite answered 8
12: 1 Then Job answered 8
4 I, who called upon God and he answered me 8
13:22 Then call, and I will answer; 8
14:15 Thou wouldest call, and I would answer thee; 8
15: 1 Then Eli'phaz the Te'manite answered 8
2 Should a wise man answer with windy knowledge 8
16: 1 Then Job answered 8
3 what provokes you that you answer? 8
18: 1 Then Bildad the Shuhite answered 8
19: 1 Then Job answered 8
7 Behold, I cry out, 'Violence!' but I am not answered; 8
20: 1 Then Zophar the Na'amathite answered 8
2 Therefore my thoughts answer me 10
3 out of my understanding a spirit answers me. 8
21: 1 Then Job answered 8
34 nothing left of your answers but falsehood. 10
22: 1 Then Eli'phaz the Te'manite answered 8
23: 1 Then Job answered 8
5 I would learn what he would answer me 8
25: 1 Then Bildad the Shuhite answered 8
26: 1 Then Job answered 8
30:20 I cry to thee and thou dost not answer me; 8
31:14 When he makes inquiry, what shall I answer him? 10
35 Here is my signature! let the Almighty answer me! 8
32: 1 these three men ceased to answer Job 8
3 he was angry .. because they had found no answer 5
5 was no answer in the mouth of these three men 5
6 Eli'hu the son of Bar'achel the Buzite answered 8
12 that confuted Job, or that answered his words 8
14 I will not answer him with your speeches. 10
15 They are discomfited, they answer no more; 8
16 because they stand there, and answer no more? 8
• 17 I also will give my answer; 4
20 I must open my lips and answer. 8
33: 5 Answer me, if you can; set your words in order 10
12 in this you are not right. I will answer you. 8
13 He will answer none of my words'? 8
32 If you have anything to say, answer me; 10
34:36 because he answers like wicked men. 10
35: 4 I will answer you and your friends with you. 12
12 There they cry out, but he does not answer 8
38: 1 Then the LORD answered Job out of the whirlwind 8
40: 2 He who argues with God, let him answer it. 8
3 Then Job answered the LORD 8
4 I am of small account; what shall I answer thee? 10
5 I have spoken once, and I will not answer; 8
6 Then the LORD answered Job out of the whirlwind 8
42: 1 Then Job answered the LORD 8
Ps 3: 4 to the LORD, and he answers me from his holy hill. 8
4: 1 Answer me when I call, O God of my right! 8
13: 3 Consider and answer me, O LORD my God; 8
17: 6 I call upon thee, for thou wilt answer me, O God; 8
18:41 they cried to the LORD, but he did not answer them. 8
20: 1 The LORD answer you in the day of trouble! 8
6 he will answer him from his holy heaven 8
9 O LORD; answer us when we call. 21
22: 2 O my God, I cry by day, but thou dost not answer; 8
27: 7 when I cry aloud, be gracious to me and answer me! 8
34: 4 I sought the LORD, and he answered me 8
38:15 it is thou, O LORD my God, who wilt answer. 8
55: 2 Attend to me, and answer me; 8
60: 5 give victory by thy right hand and answer us! 8
65: 5 By dread deeds thou dost answer us 8
69:13 in the abundance of thy steadfast love answer me. 8
16 Answer me, O LORD, for thy steadfast love is good; 8
17 for I am in distress, make haste to answer me. 8
81: 7 I answered you in the secret place of thunder; 8
86: 1 Incline thy ear, O LORD, and answer me 8
7 I call on thee, for thou dost answer me. 8
91:15 When he calls to me, I will answer him; 8
99: 6 They cried to the LORD, and he answered them. 8
8 O LORD our God, thou didst answer them; 8
102: 2 answer me speedily in the day when I call! 8
108: 6 give help by thy right hand, and answer me! 8
118: 5 LORD answered me and set me free. 8
21 I thank thee that thou hast answered me 8
119:26 When I told of my ways, thou didst answer me; 8
42 then shall I have an answer for those who taunt me 8
145 With my whole heart I cry; answer me, O LORD! 8
120: 1 In my distress I cry to the LORD, that he may answer 8
138: 3 On the day I called, thou didst answer me 8
143: 1 faithfulness answer me, in thy righteousness! 8
7 Make haste to answer me, O LORD! My spirit fails! 8
Prv 1:28 Then they will call upon me, but I will not answer; 8
15: 1 A soft answer turns away wrath 5
28 The mind of the righteous ponders how to answer 8
16: 1 but the answer of the tongue is from the LORD. 5
18:13 If one gives answer before he hears 3

23 poor use entreaties . . rich answer roughly. 8
22:21 that you may give a true answer to those who sent 1
24:26 He who gives a right answer kisses the lips. 3
26: 4 Answer not a fool according to his folly 8
5 Answer a fool according to his folly 8
16 than seven men who can answer discreetly. 10
27:11 Be wise . . that I may answer him who reproaches 11
19 As in water face answers to face, so the mind of man *
Ecc 10:19 wine gladdens . . and money answers everything. 8
Isa 10:30 Hearken, O La'ishah! Answer her, O An'athoth! 8
14:32 What will one answer the messengers 8
21: 9 And he answered, "Fallen, fallen is Babylon; 8
30:19 of your cry; when he hears it, he will answer you. 8
36:21 they were silent and answered him not a word 8
21 for the king's command was, "Do not answer him. 8
39: 4 Hezeki'ah answered, "They have seen all 2
41:17 I the LORD will answer them 8
28 no counselor who, when I ask, gives an answer. 3
46: 7 it does not answer or save him from his trouble. 8
49: 8 the LORD: "In a time of favor I have answered you 8
50: 2 Why . . When I called, was there no one to answer? 8
58: 9 Then you shall call, and the LORD will answer; 8
65:12 because, when I called, you did not answer 8
24 Before they call I will answer 8
66: 4 because, when I called, no one answered 8
Jer 7:13 and when I called you, you did not answer 8
27 You shall call to them, but they will not answer 8
11: 5 Then I answered, "So be it, LORD. 8
22: 9 And they will answer, "Because they forsook 2
23:35 What has the LORD answered? 8
37 to the prophet, 'What has the LORD answered you? 8
33: 3 Call to me and I will answer you, and will tell you 8
35: 6 But they answered, "We will drink no wine 2
17 I have called to them and they have not answered. 8
36:18 Baruch answered them, "He dictated 2
38:27 he answered them as the king had instructed him. 6
42: 4 and whatever the LORD answers you I will tell you; 8
44:15 in the land of Egypt, answered Jeremiah 8
20 all the people who had given him this answer 3
Ezk 14: 4 I the LORD will answer him myself 8
7 I the LORD will answer him myself; 8
37: 3 And I answered, "O Lord GOD, thou knowest. 2
Dan 2: 5 king answered the Chalde'ans, "The word from me 13
7 answered a second time, "Let the king tell 13
8 The king answered, "I know with certainty 13
10 Chalde'ans answered the king, "There is not a man 13
27 Daniel answered the king, "No wise men, enchanters 13
3:16 Shadrach . . and Abed'nego answered the king 13
16 have no need to answer you in this matter. 15
24 counselors . . answered the king, "True, O king. 13
25 He answered, "But I see four men loose, walking 13
4:19 Belteshaz'zar answered, "My lord, may the dream 13
5:17 Daniel answered before the king, "Let your gifts 13
6:12 king answered, "The thing stands fast, 13
13 Then they answered before the king, 13
Hos 2:15 there she shall answer as in the days of her youth 8
21 that day, says the LORD, I will answer the heavens 8
21 the heavens and they shall answer the earth; 8
22 and the earth shall answer the grain, the wine 8
22 the oil, and they shall answer Jezreel; 8
14: 8 It is I who answer and look after you. 8
Jol 2:19 The LORD answered and said to his people 8
Ams 7:14 Then Amos answered Amazi'ah, "I am no prophet 8
Jon 2: 2 to the LORD, out of my distress, and he answered me; 8
Mic 3: 4 they will cry to the LORD, but he will not answer 8
7 cover their lips, for there is no answer from God. 5
6: 3 In what have I wearied you? Answer me! 8
5 and what Balaam the son of Be'or answered him 8
Hab 2: 1 and what I will answer concerning my complaint. 10
2 And the LORD answered me: "Write the vision; 8
Hag 2:12 does it become holy?" The priests answered, "No 8
13 The priests answered, "It does become unclean. 8
Zec 1:10 answered, 'These are they whom the LORD has sent 8
11 they answered the angel of the LORD 8
13 the LORD answered gracious and comforting 8
19 What are these?" And he answered me, "These are 2
21 He answered, "These are the horns which scattered 2
4: 5 Then the angel who talked with me answered me 8
5: 2 What do you see?" I answered, "I see a flying scroll; 2
6: 5 the angel answered me, "These are going forth 8
10: 6 for I am the LORD their God and I will answer them. 8
13: 9 They will call on my name, and I will answer them. 8
Mal 2:12 any to witness or answer, or to bring an offering 8
Mat 3:15 But Jesus answered him, "Let it be so now; 16
4: 4 But he answered, "It is written, 'Man shall not live 16
8: 8 the centurion answered him, "Lord, I am not worthy 16
11: 4 Jesus answered them, "Go and tell John 16
12:39 he answered them 16
13:11 he answered them, "To you it has been given to know 16
37 He answered, "He who sows the good seed 16
14:28 Peter answered him 16
15: 3 He answered them 16
13 He answered 16
23 he did not answer her a word 16
24 He answered 16
26 he answered 16
28 Then Jesus answered her 16
16: 2 He answered them 16
17 Jesus answered him 16
17:17 Jesus answered 16
19: 4 He answered, "Have you not read 16
20:22 Jesus answered, "You do not know 16
21:21 Jesus answered them, "Truly, I say to you 16
24 Jesus answered them, "I also will ask you 16
24 and if you tell me the answer 23
27 So they answered Jesus, "We do not know. 16
29 he answered, 'I will not'; but afterward he repented 16
30 he answered, 'I go, sir,' but did not go. 16
22:29 Jesus answered them, "You are wrong 16
46 no one was able to answer him a word 16
24: 2 he answered them, "You see all these, do you not? 16
4 Jesus answered them, "Take heed that no one leads 16
25:26 his master answered him 16
37 Then the righteous will answer him 16
40 the King will answer them, 'Truly, I say to you 16
44 Then they also will answer 16
45 Then he will answer them, 'Truly, I say to you 16
26:23 He answered, "He who has dipped his hand in the dish 16
66 They answered, "He deserves death. 16
27:14 he gave him no answer, not even to a single charge; 16
25 all the people answered, "His blood be on us 16
Mrk 6:37 he answered them, "You give them something to eat. 16
7:28 she answered him, "Yes, Lord; yet even the dogs 16
8: 4 his disciples answered him, "How can one feed 16
29 Peter answered him, "You are the Christ. 16
9:17 one of the crowd answered him, "Teacher 16
19 he answered them, "O faithless generation 16
10: 3 He answered them, "What did Moses command you? 16
11:22 Jesus answered them, "Have faith in God. 16
29 answer me, and I will tell you by what authority 16
30 from heaven or from men? Answer me. 16
33 So they answered Jesus, "We do not know. 16
12:28 seeing that he answered them well, asked him 16
29 Jesus answered, "The first is, 'Hear, O Israel 16
34 when Jesus saw that he answered wisely 16
14:40 they did not know what to answer him. 16
60 Have you no answer to make? 16
61 he was silent and made no answer 16
15: 2 he answered him, "You have said so. 16
4 Pilate again asked him, "Have you no answer to make? 16
5 Jesus made no further answer 16
9 he answered them, "Do you want me to release for you 16
Lke 1:19 the angel answered him, "I am Gabriel 16
2:47 amazed at his understanding and his answers. 17
3:11 he answered them, "He who has two coats 16
16 John answered them all, "I baptize you with water; 16
4: 4 Jesus answered him, "It is written 16
8 Jesus answered him, "It is written 16
12 Jesus answered him, "It is said, 'You shall not tempt 16
5: 5 Simon answered, "Master, we toiled all night 16
22 he answered them, "Why do you question 16
31 Jesus answered them, "Those who are well 16
6: 3 Jesus answered, "Have you not read what David did 16
7:22 he answered them, "Go and tell John 16
40 Jesus answering said to him, "Simon 16
40 he answered, "What is it, Teacher? 26
43 Simon answered, "The one, I suppose 16
8:50 Jesus on hearing this answered him, "Do not fear; 16
9:19 they answered, "John the Baptist 16
20 Peter answered, "The Christ of God. 16
41 Jesus answered, "O faithless and perverse 16
49 John answered, "Master, we saw a man 16
10:27 he answered, "You shall love the Lord your God 16
28 You have answered right; do this, and you will live. 16
41 the Lord answered her, "Martha, Martha 16
11: 7 he will answer from within, 'Do not bother me 16
45 One of the lawyers answered him, "Teacher 16
12:11 what you are to answer or what you are to say; 18
13: 2 he answered them, "Do you think 16
8 he answered him, 'Let it alone, sir, this year also 16
15 Then the Lord answered him, "You hypocrites! 16
25 He will answer you, 'I do not know 16
15:29 he answered his father, 'Lo, these many years 16
17:20 he answered them, "The kingdom of God is not coming 16
19:40 He answered, "I tell you, if these were silent 16
20: 3 He answered them, "I also will ask you a question; 16
7 So they answered that they did not know 16
26 marveling at his answer they were silent. 17
39 some of the scribes answered, "Teacher 16
21:14 not to meditate beforehand how to answer 18
22:68 if I ask you, you will not answer. 16
23: 3 he answered him, "You have said so. 16
24:18 Then one of them, named Cle'opas, answered him 16
Joh 1:21 Are you the prophet?" And he answered, "No. 16
22 Let us have an answer for those who sent us. 17
26 John answered them, "I baptize with water; 16
48 Jesus answered him, "Before Philip called you 16
49 Nathan'a-el answered him, "Rabbi 16
50 Jesus answered him, "Because I said to you 16
2:19 Jesus answered them, "Destroy this temple 16
3: 3 Jesus answered him, "Truly, truly, I say to you 16
5 Jesus answered, "Truly, truly, I say to you 16
10 Jesus answered him, "Are you a teacher of Israel 16
27 John answered, "No one can receive anything 16
4:10 Jesus answered her, "If you knew the gift of God 16
17 The woman answered him, "I have no husband. 16
5: 7 The sick man answered him, "Sir, I have no man 16
11 he answered them, "The man who healed me said 16
17 Jesus answered them, "My Father is working still 16
6: 7 Philip answered him 16
26 Jesus answered them, "Truly, truly, I say to you 16
29 Jesus answered them, "This is the work of God 16
43 Jesus answered them, "Do not murmur 16
68 Simon Peter answered him, "Lord, to whom 16
70 Jesus answered them, "Did I not choose you 16
7:16 Jesus answered them, "My teaching is not mine 16
20 The people answered, "You have a demon! 16
21 Jesus answered them, "I did one deed 16
46 The officers answered 16
47 The Pharisees answered them, "Are you led astray 16
8:14 Jesus answered, "Even if I do bear witness 16
19 Jesus answered, "You know neither me nor my Father 16
33 They answered him, "We are descendants of Abraham 16
34 Jesus answered them, "Truly, truly, I say to you 16
39 They answered him, "Abraham is our father. 16
48 The Jews answered him, "Are we not right in saying 16
49 Jesus answered, "I have not a demon 16
54 Jesus answered, "If I glorify myself 16
9: 3 Jesus answered, "It was not that this man sinned 16
11 He answered, "The man called Jesus made clay 16
20 His parents answered, "We know that this is our son 16
25 He answered, "Whether he is a sinner, I do not know; 16
27 He answered them, "I have told you already 16
30 The man answered, "Why, this is a marvel! 16
34 They answered him, "You were born in utter sin 16
36 He answered, "And who is he, sir 16
10:25 Jesus answered them, "I told you 16
32 Jesus answered them, "I have shown you 16
33 The Jews answered him, "It is not for a good work 16
34 Jesus answered them, "Is it not written in your law 16
11: 9 Jesus answered, "Are there not twelve hours 16
12:23 Jesus answered them, "The hour has come 16
30 Jesus answered, "This voice has come for your sake 16
34 The crowd answered him, "We have heard 16
13: 7 Jesus answered him, "What I am doing 16
8 Jesus answered him, "If I do not wash you 16
26 Jesus answered, "It is he 16
36 Jesus answered, "Where I am going 16
38 Jesus answered, "Will you lay down your life for me? 16
14:23 Jesus answered him, "If a man loves me 16
16:31 Jesus answered them, "Do you now believe? 16
18: 5 They answered him, "Jesus of Nazareth. 16
8 Jesus answered, "I told you that I am he 16
20 Jesus answered him, "I have spoken openly 16
22 Is that how you answer the high priest? 16
23 Jesus answered him, "If I have spoken wrongly 16
30 They answered him 16
34 Jesus answered, "Do you say this of your own accord 16
35 Pilate answered, "Am I a Jew? 16
36 Jesus answered, "My kingship is not of this world; 16
37 Jesus answered, "You say that I am a king 16
19: 7 The Jews answered him. "We have a law 16
9 But Jesus gave no answer. 17
11 Jesus answered him, "You would have no power 16
15 The chief priests answered, "We have no king 16
22 Pilate answered, "What I have written 16
20:28 Thomas answered him, "My Lord and my God! 16
21: 5 They answered him, "No. 16
Act 4:19 Peter and John answered them, "Whether it is right 16
5:29 Peter and the apostles answered, "We must obey God 16
8:24 Simon answered, "Pray for me to the Lord 16
9:13 Anani'as answered, "Lord 16
11: 9 the voice answered a second time from heaven 16
12:13 a maid named Rhoda came to answer. 25
19:15 the evil spirit answered them, "Jesus I know 16
21:13 Then Paul answered, "What are you doing 16
22: 8 I answered, 'Who are you, Lord?' 16
28 The tribune answered, "I bought this citizenship 16
25:12 Then Festus . . answered 16
16 I answered them that it was not the custom 16
2Co 1:11 granted us in answer to many prayers. 20
5:12 so that you may be able to answer 24
Col 4: 6 you may know how you ought to answer every one. 16
1Es 6:13 They answered us, 'We are the servants of the Lord 16
9:47 all the multitude answered, "Amen. 22
2Es 2:45 He answered and said to me 29
47 He answered and said to me, "He is the Son of God 29
4: 1 the angel . . whose name was Uriel, answered 29
6 I answered and said, "Who of those 29
13 He answered me and said, "I went into a forest 29
19 I answered and said, "Each has made a foolish plan 29
20 He answered me and said, "You have judged rightly 29
22 Then I answered and said, "I beseech you, my lord 29
26 He answered me and said, "If you are alive 29
33 Then I answered and said, "How long 29
34 He answered me and said, "You do not hasten faster 29
36 Jeremiel the archangel answered them and said 29
38 Then I answered and said, "O sovereign Lord 29
40 He answered me and said, "Go and ask a woman 29
44 I answered and said, "If I have found favor 29
52 He answered me and said, "Concerning the signs 29
5:43 Then I answered and said, "Couldst thou not 29
53 she herself will answer you 28
6: 7 I answered and said, "What will be the dividing 29
11 I answered and said, "O sovereign Lord 29
13 He answered and said to me, "Rise to your feet 29
7:17 Then I answered and said, "O sovereign Lord, behold 29

45 I answered and said, "O sovereign Lord, I said 29
49 He answered me and said, "Listen to me, Ezra 29
59 He answered me and said, "Weigh within yourself 29
70 He answered me and said, "When the Most High made 29
73 how will they answer in the last times? 29
75 I answered and said, "If I have found favor 29
76 He answered me and said, "I will show you that also 29
100 I answered and said, "Will time therefore 29
102 I answered and said, "If I have found favor 29
104 He answered me and said, "Since you have found 29
106 I answered and said, "How then do we find 29
112 He answered me and said, "This present world 29
116 I answered and said, "This is my first and last word 29
127 He answered and said, "This is the meaning 29
132 I answered and said, "I know, O Lord 29
8: 1 He answered me and said, "The Most High made 29
4 I answered and said, "Then drink your fill 29
25 as long as I have understanding I will answer. 29
37 He answered me and said, "Some things 29
42 I answered and said, "If I have found favor 29
46 He answered me and said, "Things that are present 29
62 Then I answered and said 29
9: 1 He answered me and said, "Measure carefully 29
14 I answered and said 29
17 He answered me and said, "As is the field 29
10: 5 and answered her in anger and said 29
38 He answered me and said, "Listen to me 29
12:45 Then I answered them and said 29
13:20 He answered me and said 29
14:19 Then I answered and said, "Let me speak 29
23 He answered me and said, "Go and gather the people 29
Tob 5: 1 Then Tobias answered him 16
11 he answered, "Are you looking for a tribe 19
7: 3 They answered him 19
10: 7 she answered him, "Be still and stop deceiving me; 19
Jdt 6:17 He answered and told them what had taken place 16
14:15 when no one answered 21
Sir 4: 8 answer him peaceably and gently. 16
5:11 Be quick to hear, and be deliberate in answering. 27
12 If you have understanding, answer your neighbor; 16
8: 9 learn how to give an answer in time of need. 17
11: 8 Do not answer before you have heard 16
20: 6 is one who keeps silent because he has no answer 17
46: 6 the great Lord answered him 21
Sus 1:54 He answered, "Under a mastic tree. 19
58 He answered, "Under an evergreen oak. 19
Bel 1: 5 He answered, " . . I do not revere man-made idols 19
17 He answered, "They are unbroken, O king. 19
1Mc 2:19 Mattathias answered and said in a loud voice 16
36 they did not answer them or hurl a stone at them 16
13: 8 they answered in a loud voice, "You are our leader 16
15:35 Athenobius did not answer him a word 16
2Mc 14: 5 He answered 26

answer *See also* give, make.

answer back 1. *ἀνταποκρίνομαι*
Rom 9:20 But who are you, a man, to answer back to God? 1

answer no 1. nego
2Es 5:11 And it will answer, 'No.' 1

ant 1. נְמָלָה
Prv 6: 6 Go to the ant, O sluggard; 1
30:25 ants are a people not strong, yet they provide 1

antagonist 1. *ἀνταγωνίζομαι* 2. *ἀνταγωνιστής* 3. *ἀντίκειμαι*
3Mc 7: 9 in everything and inescapably as an antagonist 3
4Mc 3: 5 reason . . is their antagonist. 2
17:14 The tyrant was the antagonist 1

antelope 1. תְּאוֹ
Deu 14: 5 the ibex, the antelope, and the mountain-sheep 1
Isa 51:20 the head of every street like an antelope in a net; 1

antichrist 1. *ἀντίχριστος*
1Jn 2:18 and as you have heard that antichrist is coming 1
18 so now many antichrists have come; 1
22 This is the antichrist, he who denies 1
4: 3 This is the spirit of the antichrist 1
2Jn 1: 7 such a one is the deceiver and the antichrist. 1

antimony 1. אֶבֶן פּוּךְ 2. פּוּךְ
1Ch 29: 2 quantities of . . antimony, colored stones 1
Isa 54:11 behold, I will set your stones in antimony 2

anvil 1. פַּעַם 2. *ἄκμονος*
Isa 41: 7 him who strikes the anvil 1
Sir 38:28 So too is the smith sitting by the anvil 2

anxiety 1. דְּאָגָה 2. שִׂיחַ 3. *βαρέω* 4. *μέριμνα* 5. *μεριμνάω* 6. *προσδοκία* 7. *σύννους* 8. *φροντίς*
1Sm 1:16 speaking out of my great anxiety and vexation. 2
Prv 12:25 Anxiety in a man's heart weighs him down 1
2Co 5: 4 we sigh with anxiety 3
11:28 my anxiety for all the churches. 4
Php 4: 6 Have no anxiety about anything 5
1Pe 5: 7 Cast all your anxieties on him 4
1Es 8:71 sat down in anxiety and grief. 7
Sir 30:24 anxiety brings on old age too soon. 4
31: 1 anxiety about it removes sleep. 4
2 Wakeful anxiety prevents slumber 4
2Mc 3:21 the anxiety of the high priest 6
4Mc 16: 8 the more grievous anxieties of your upbringing. 8

anxiety *See also* free.

deathly anxiety 1. *ἀγών*
AEs 14: 1 Esther the queen, seized with deathly anxiety 1

anxious 1. דאג 2. כרה (A) 3. *μεριμνάω* 4. *προσδοκία* 5. *ταράσσω* 6. satago 7. timoratus
1Sm 10: 2 your father . . is anxious about you, saying 1
Jer 17: 8 and is not anxious in the year of drought 1
Dan 7:15 As for me, Daniel, my spirit within me was anxious 2
Mat 6:25 I tell you, do not be anxious about your life 3
27 which of you by being anxious can add one cubit 3
28 And why are you anxious about clothing? Consider 3
31 do not be anxious, saying, 'What shall we eat?' 3
34 Therefore do not be anxious about tomorrow 3
34 for tomorrow will be anxious for itself. 3
10:19 do not be anxious how you are to speak 3
Lke 10:41 you are anxious and troubled about many things; 3
12:11 do not be anxious how or what you are to answer 3
22 do not be anxious about your life 3
25 which of you by being anxious can add a cubit 3
26 why are you anxious about the rest? 3
1Co 7:32 The unmarried man is anxious about the affairs 3
Php 2:20 who will be genuinely anxious for your welfare. 3
2Es 2:27 Do not be anxious 6
3: 3 I began to speak anxious words to the Most High 7
Sir 40: 2 their anxious thought is the day of death 4
Bar 3:18 those who scheme to get silver, and are anxious 3
2Mc 15:19 being anxious over the encounter 5

anxious *See also* mind, toil.

anxious about 1. *μεριμνάω*
1Co 7:33 the married man is anxious about worldly affairs 1
34 is anxious about the affairs of the Lord 1
34 the married woman is anxious about worldly affairs 1

become anxious 1. דאג
1Sm 9: 5 cease to care . . and become anxious about us. 1

anxious beforehand 1. *προμεριμνάω*
Mrk 13:11 do not be anxious beforehand 1

less anxious 1. *ἄλυπος*
Php 2:28 I may be less anxious. 1

anxiously 1. *ὀδυνάω*
Lke 2:48 your father and I have been looking for you anxiously. 1

anxiously *See also* wait.

any 1. אֶחָד 2. אַחֵר 3. אַיִן 4. אִישׁ 5. יסף 6. כֹּה 7. כֹּל 8. מִן 9. כֹּל (A) 10. *ἀπό* 11. *εἷς* 12. *ἕν τι* 13. *μηδείς* 14. *ὅς* 15. *ὃς ἄν* 16. *ὅσος* 17. *οὐδείς* 18. *οὐθείς* 19. *οὔτε* 20. *πᾶς* 21. *τις* 22. *τίς* 23. aliqui 24. alius 25. non 26. numquid 27. omnis
Gen 3: 1 more subtle than any other wild creature 7
1 Did God say, 'You shall not eat of any tree 7
4:15 lest any who came upon him should kill him. 7
17:12 bought with your money from any foreigner 7
14 Any uncircumcised male who is not circumcised *
31:14 Is there any portion or inheritance left to us *
36:31 before any king reigned over the Israelites. *
37: 3 loved Joseph more than any other of his children 7
43:34 portion was five times as much as any of theirs. 7
47: 6 and if you know any able men among them, *
Exd 10:23 nor did any rise from his place for three days; 4
11: 7 against any of the people of Israel 7
12: 9 Do not eat any of it raw or boiled with water *
39 they prepared for themselves any provisions. *
46 you shall not carry forth any of the flesh 8
16:19 Let no man leave any of it till the morning. 8
18:22 any small matter they shall decide themselves; 7
26 any small matter they decided themselves. 7
20: 4 any likeness of anything that is in heaven 7
10 in it you shall not do any work, you, or your son 7
21:23 If any harm follows, then you shall give life *
22: 9 for any kind of lost thing, of which one says 7
10 an ass or an ox or a sheep or any beast to keep 7
20 Whoever sacrifices to any god, save to the LORD *
22 You shall not afflict any widow or orphan. 7
25 If you lend money to any of my people with you who *
31 you shall not eat any flesh that is torn by beasts *
28:38 Aaron shall take upon himself any guilt *
29:34 if any of the flesh for the ordination 8
30:33 Whoever compounds any like it or whoever puts *
33 whoever puts any of it on an outsider shall be cut 8
38 Whoever makes any like it to use as perfume *
31:14 whoever does any work on it *
15 whoever does any work on the sabbath day shall be *
32:24 I said to them, 'Let any who have gold take it off'; *
34:10 in all the earth or in any nation 7
35: 2 whoever does any work on it shall be put to death; *
24 found acacia wood of any use in the work 7
35 by any sort of workman or skilled designer. 7
36: 1 to know how to do any work in the construction 7
Lev 1: 2 When any man of you brings an offering to the LORD *
2:11 you shall burn no leaven nor any honey 7
4: 2 If any one sins unwittingly in any of the things 7
2 If anyone sins . . and does any one of them 8
5: 4 any sort of rash oath that men swear 7
4 he shall in any of these be guilty 1
5 When a man is guilty in any of these, he shall 1
15 sins . . in any of the holy thing of the LORD 8
17 sins, doing any of the things which the LORD has 1
6: 3 in any of all the things which men do and sin 1
7 he shall be forgiven for any of the things 1
27 when any of its blood is sprinkled on a garment 8
30 any blood is brought into the tent of meeting 8
7:15 he shall not leave any of it until the morning 8
18 If any of the flesh of the sacrifice of his peace 8
19 Flesh that touches any unclean thing shall not 7
21 or an unclean beast or any unclean abomination 7
24 The fat . . may be put to any other use 7
26 eat no blood . . in any of your dwellings 7
27 Whoever eats of any blood, that person shall be 7
10:14 you shall eat in any clean place, you and your sons *
11:32 anything upon which any of them falls 7
32 any vessel that is used for any purpose 7
32 any vessel that is used for any purpose 7
33 if any of them falls into any earthen vessel 7
33 if any of them falls into any earthen vessel 7
34 Any food in it which may be eaten . . be unclean 7
39 if any animal of which you may eat dies 8
43 abominable with any swarming thing that swarms 7
44 not defile yourselves with any swarming thing 7
12: 4 she shall not touch any hallowed thing 7
14:54 This is the law for any leprous disease 7
15: 2 When any man has a discharge from his body 4
9 any saddle on which he who has the discharge 7
24 if any man lies with her, and her impurity is on him *
17: 3 If any man of the house of Israel kills an ox 4
8 Any man of the house of Israel *
10 If any man of the house of Israel *
10 If any man . . eats any blood, I will set my face 7
12 any stranger who sojourns among you *
13 Any man also of the people of Israel *
13 who takes in hunting any beast or bird *
14 You shall not eat the blood of any creature 7
18:21 shall not give any of your children . . to Molech 8
23 shall not lie with any beast and defile yourself 7
23 neither shall any woman give herself to a beast *
24 Do not defile yourselves by any of these things 7
29 For whoever shall do any of these abominations 7
30 to practice any of these abominable customs 8
19:18 You shall not take vengeance or bear any grudge *
26 You shall not eat any flesh with the blood in it *
28 You shall not make any cuttings in your flesh *
28 or tattoo any marks upon you: I am the LORD *
20: 2 Any man of the people of Israel, or of the strangers *
2 who gives any of his children to Molech 8
16 If a woman approaches any beast and lies with it 7
21: 5 nor make any cuttings in their flesh *
9 the daughter of any priest, if she profanes 4
11 he shall not go in to any dead body, nor defile 7
22: 3 If any one of all your descendants throughout 7
6 the person who touches any such shall be unclean *
24 Any animal which has its testicles bruised *
25 neither shall you offer . . any such animals 7
23:30 whoever does any work on this same day 7
27: 9 all of such that any man gives to the LORD is holy *
10 if he makes any exchange of beast for beast *
31 If a man wishes to redeem any of his tithe 8
Num 3:38 any one else who came near was to be put to death. *
5: 6 When a man or woman commits any of the sins 7
10 whatever any man gives to the priest shall be his. *
12 If any man's wife goes astray and acts *
6: 3 shall not drink any juice of grapes or eat grapes 7
9 if any man dies very suddenly beside him *
9:10 If any man of you or of your descendants *
18: 7 any one else who comes near shall be put to death. *
20 neither shall you have any portion among them; *
31 may eat it in any place, you and your households; 7
19:11 He who touches the dead body of any person 7
13 Whoever touches . . body of any man who has died *
21: 9 if a serpent bit any man, he would look *
30: 6 under . . any thoughtless utterance of her lips *
9 any vow of a widow or of a divorced woman *
13 Any vow and any binding oath to afflict herself 7
13 Any vow and any binding oath to afflict herself 7
31:19 whoever of you has killed any person *
19 whoever has touched any slain *
35:11 manslayer who kills any person without intent *
15 that any one who kills any person without intent *
26 manslayer shall at any time go beyond the bounds *
36: 3 married to any of the sons of the other tribes 1
8 inheritance in any tribe of the people of Israel *
Deu 2: 5 for I will not give you any of their land 8
9 not give you any of their land for a possession 8
19 not give you any of the land of the sons of Ammon 8
4:16 a graven image . . in the form of any figure 7
17 likeness of any beast that is on the earth 7

17 likeness of any winged bird that flies in the air 7
18 likeness of any fish that is in the water 7
33 Did any people ever hear the voice of a god •
34 has any god ever attempted to go and take a nation •
5: 8 'You shall not make . . any likeness of anything 7
14 not do any work, you, or your son, or your daughter 7
14 your ox, or your ass, or any of your cattle 7
25 if we hear the voice of the LORD our God any more 5
7: 7 not . . more in number than any other people 7
12:15 slaughter and eat flesh within any of your towns 7
17 You may not eat . . any of your votive offerings 7
21 then you may kill any of your herd or your flock 8
13:11 never again do any such wickedness as this among •
14: 1 not . . make any baldness on your foreheads •
3 You shall not eat any abominable thing. 7
15: 7 in any of your towns within your land 1
21 if it has any blemish, if it is lame or blind •
21 blind, or has any serious blemish whatever 7
16: 4 nor shall any of the flesh . . remain all night 8
5 not offer . . within any of your towns 1
21 not plant any tree as an Ashe'rah beside the altar 7
17: 1 ox . . in which is a blemish, any defect whatever; 7
2 found among you, within any of your towns 1
3 worshipped . . moon or any of the host of heaven 7
8 If any case arises requiring decision •
8 any case . . which is too difficult for you •
18: 6 Levite comes from any of your towns out of all Israel 1
10 not be found among you any one who burns his son •
10 any one who practices divination, a soothsayer •
19: 3 so that any manslayer can flee to them. 7
4 If any one kills his neighbor unintentionally •
11 if any man hates his neighbor, and lies in wait •
15 not prevail against a man for any crime or for any 7
15 for any wrong in connection with any offense 7
15 for any wrong in connection with any offense 7
16 If a malicious witness rises against any man •
20 never again commit any such evil among you. •
21: 1 any one is found slain, lying in the open country •
22: 3 so . . do with any lost thing of your brother's •
6 come upon a bird's nest, in any tree or on the ground 7
8 may not bring the guilt . . if any one fall from it. •
23:10 among you any man who is not clean by reason •
18 not bring . . in payment for any vow 7
24 you shall not put any in your vessel. •
24: 5 he shall not . . be charged with any business; 7
26:13 I have not transgressed any of thy commandments 8
14 have not . . removed any of it while I was unclean 8
14 I have not . . offered any of it to the dead; 8
27:21 'Cursed be he who lies with any kind of beast.' 7
28:14 if you do not turn aside from any of the words 7
55 not give to any of them any of the flesh 1
55 not give . . any of the flesh of his children whom 8
Jos 5: 1 and there was no longer any spirit in them •
6:10 neither shall any word go out of your mouth •
18 lest . . you take any of the devoted things •
10:21 moved his tongue against any of the people 4
11:14 and they did not leave any that breathed. 7
Jdg 2:19 they did not drop any of their practices •
21 drive out before them any of the nations that 4
3: 1 Israel who had no experience of any war in Canaan; 7
4:20 and if any man comes and asks you, 'Is any one here?' •
7: 4 and any of whom I say to you, 'This man shall not go 7
11:25 are you any better than Balak the son of Zippor •
12: 5 when any of the fugitives of E'phraim said, "Let me •
13:14 let her drink wine . . or eat any unclean thing; 7
16:13 I shall become weak, and be like any other man. •
20: 8 We will not any of us go to his tent, and none of us 4
21: 7 will not give them any of our daughters for wives? •
1Sm 2:13 The custom . . when any man offered sacrifice 7
9: 2 he was taller than any of the people. 7
10:23 he was taller than any of the people 7
13:22 nor spear found in the hand of any of the people 7
14:52 when Saul saw any strong man, or any valiant man 7
52 when Saul saw any strong man, or any valiant man 7
26:12 No man saw it, or knew it, nor did any awake; 3
30:22 we will not give them any of the spoil . . we have •
2Sm 2: 1 Shall I go up into any of the cities of Judah? 1
7: 7 did I speak a word with any of the judges of Israel 1
10:19 Syrians feared to help the Ammonites any more. •
15: 2 when any man had a suit to come before the king 7
19:29 Why speak any more of your affairs? I have decided •
42 Or has he given us any gift? •
1Kg 6: 7 hammer nor axe nor any tool of iron was heard 7
7:14 full of wisdom . . for making any work in bronze. 7
8:37 their enemy besieges them in any of their cities; 11
38 supplication is made by any man or by all 7
10:20 The like of it was never made in any kingdom. 7
13:33 any who would, he consecrated to be priests •
14:11 Any one belonging to Jerobo'am who dies •
2Kg 5:17 will not . . sacrifice to any god but the LORD. 2
10:24 allows any of those whom I give into your hands •
12: 5 wherever any need of repairs is discovered. •
12 and for any outlay upon the repairs of the house. 7
13 trumpets, or any vessels of gold, or of silver 7
18:33 Has any of the gods . . ever delivered his land 4
23:25 Before . . nor did any like him arise after him. •
1Ch 1:43 the land of Edom before any king reigned over •
17: 6 did I speak a word with any of the judges of Israel 1
23:26 tabernacle or any of the things for its service 7

28 and any work for the service of the house of God; •
28:21 willing man who has skill for any kind of service; 7
29:25 such royal majesty as had not been on any king 7
2Ch 2:14 and to do . . engraving and execute any design 7
6:28 enemies besiege them in any of their cities; •
29 whatever prayer . . is made by any man or by all 7
8:15 king had commanded . . concerning any matter 7
9:19 The like of it was never made in any kingdom. 7
23:19 no one should enter who was in any way unclean. 7
32:15 for no god of any nation or kingdom has been able 7
Ezr 6:11 I make a decree that if any one alters this edict 9
12 overthrow any king or people that shall put 9
7:13 any one of the people of Israel or their priests 9
24 upon any one of the priests, the Levites 9
9:14 that there should be no remnant, nor any to escape? •
Neh 10:31 if the peoples . . bring in wares or any grain 7
Est 4:11 if any man or woman goes . . there is but one law; 7
13 that . . you will escape any more than all •
8:11 annihilate any armed force . . that might attack 7
11 any armed force of any people or province •
Job 4:20 they perish for ever without any regarding it. •
5: 1 Call now; is there any one who will answer you? •
6: 6 or is there any taste in the slime of the purslane? •
13 no help in me, and any resource is driven from me. •
30 Is there any wrong on my tongue? •
10:18 Would that I had died before any eye had seen me •
21:22 Will any teach God knowledge •
22: 3 Is it any pleasure to the Almighty if you are •
25: 3 Is there any number to his armies? •
27: 6 my heart does not reproach me for any of my days. •
31: 7 if any spot has cleaved to my hands; •
19 if I have seen any one perish for lack of clothing •
32:21 I will not show partiality to any person •
21 or use flattery toward any man. •
34:23 For he has not appointed a time for any man to go •
27 had no regard for any of his ways 7
31 any one said to God, 'I have borne chastisement; •
31 borne chastisement; I will not offend any more; •
36: 5 Behold, God is mighty, and does not despise any; •
29 any one understand the spreading of the clouds •
37:24 men fear him; he does not regard any who are wise 7
Ps 12: 1 Help, LORD; for there is no longer any that is godly; •
14: 2 to see if there are any that act wisely •
53: 2 to see if there are any that are wise •
74: 9 there is no longer any prophet •
82: 7 die like men, and fall like any prince. 1
86: 8 nor are there any works like thine. •
109:12 nor any to pity his fatherless children! •
115:17 nor do any that go down into silence. 7
135:17 nor is there any breath in their mouths. •
139:24 see if there be any wicked way in me •
141: 4 Incline not my heart to any evil •
147:20 He has not dealt thus with any other nation; 7
Prv 1:17 For in vain is a net spread in the sight of any bird; 7
3:31 do not choose any of his ways; 7
6: 7 Without having any chief, officer or ruler •
14:34 but sin is a reproach to any people. •
30:30 lion, which . . does not turn back before any; 7
Ecc 1:11 nor will there be any remembrance of later •
2: 7 and flocks, more than any who had been before me 7
9: 6 no more for ever any share in all that is done •
Sng 4:10 and the fragrance of your oils than any spice! 7
Isa 33:20 nor will any of its cords be broken. 7
35: 9 nor shall any ravenous beast come up on it; •
36: 6 will pierce the hand of any man who leans on it. •
18 Has any of the gods of the nations delivered •
43:10 no god was formed, nor shall there be any after me. •
44: 8 a God besides me? There is no Rock; I know not any. •
54:15 If any one stirs up strife, it is not from me; •
56: 2 and keeps his hand from doing any evil. 7
Jer 9: 4 and put no trust in any brother; 7
12:17 But if any nation will not listen •
14:22 Are there any among the false gods of the nations •
16: 7 nor shall any one give him the cup of consolation •
17: 6 in the desert, and shall not see any good come. •
22 out of your houses on the sabbath or do any work 7
18: 7 If at any time I declare concerning a nation •
9 And if at any time I declare concerning a nation •
18 let us not heed any of his words. 7
23: 4 neither shall any be missing, says the LORD. •
27: 8 But if any nation or kingdom will not serve •
11 any nation which will bring its neck under •
13 as the LORD has spoken concerning any nation •
36:24 nor any of his servants who heard all these words 7
37:17 and said, "Is there any word from the LORD? •
41: 4 after the murder of Gedali'ah, before any one knew •
44:26 no more be invoked by the mouth of any man of Judah 7
Lam 1:12 Look and see if there is any sorrow like my sorrow •
3: 2 and brought me into darkness without any light; •
4:12 kings . . or any of the inhabitants of the world 7
Ezk 1:17 they went in any of their four directions •
5:10 and any of you who survive I will scatter 7
7:16 if any survivors escape •
10:11 they went in any of their four directions •
12:24 For there shall be no more any false vision 7
28 None of my words will be delayed any longer •
14: 4 Any man of the house of Israel who takes his idols 4
11 nor defile themselves any more •
22 Yet, if there should be left in it any survivors •

15: 2 how does the wood of the vine surpass any wood 7
3 Do men take a peg from it to hang any vessel on? 7
16: 5 No eye pitied you, to do any of these things to you 1
15 and lavished your harlotries on any passer-by. 7
25 offering yourself to any passer-by 7
18: 7 does not oppress any one •
8 does not lend at interest or take any increase •
16 does not wrong any one, exacts no pledge •
23 Have I any pleasure in the death of the wicked †
32 For I have no pleasure in the death of any one •
20:28 wherever they saw any high hill or any leafy tree 7
28 wherever they saw any high hill or any leafy tree 7
24: 6 piece after piece, without making any choice. †
32:13 no foot of man shall trouble them any more •
33: 4 then if any one who hears the sound of the trumpet •
37:23 or with any of their transgressions; 7
39:10 out of the field or cut down any out of the forests •
15 pass through the land and any one sees a man's bone •
44:13 nor come near any of my sacred things 7
46:16 If the prince makes a gift to any of his sons 6
18 The prince shall not take any of the inheritance 8
48:14 They shall not sell or exchange any of it; •
Dan 2:10 such a thing of any magician or enchanter 9
30 as for me, not because of any wisdom that I have •
3:27 fire had not had any power over the bodies •
28 serve and worship any god except their own God. 9
29 Any people, nation, or language that speaks 9
6: 4 could find no ground for complaint or any fault 9
5 not find any ground for complaint against 9
7 makes petition to any god or man for 30 days 9
12 that any man who makes petition to any god or man 9
12 petition to any god or man within 30 days 9
11:37 he shall not give heed to any other god 7
Ams 8: 7 Surely I will never forget any of their deeds. 7
Hag 2:12 or pottage, or wine, or oil, or any kind of food 7
13 contact with a dead body touches any of these 7
Zec 8:10 there was no wage for man or any wage for beast •
10 neither was there any safety from the foe 3
13: 3 if any one again appears as a prophet •
14:17 if any of the families of the earth do not go up •
Mal 1: 9 will he show favor to any of you? says the LORD •
2:12 any to witness or answer, or to bring an offering •
Mat 16: 5 they had forgotten to bring any bread. •
19: 3 Is it lawful to divorce one's wife for any cause? 20
27:15 to release for the crowd any one prisoner •
Mrk 2:26 which it is not lawful for any but the priests •
5:35 Why trouble the Teacher any further? •
6:11 if any place will not receive you 15
16:18 if they drink any deadly thing, it will not hurt 22
Lke 4:40 all those who had any that were sick •
6: 4 it is not lawful for any but the priests to eat •
20:40 For they no longer dared to ask him any question. 17
23:14 guilty of any of your charges against him; 17
Joh 7:48 Have any of the authorities . . believed in him? 22
16:29 Ah, now you are speaking plainly, not in any figure! 17
20:23 If you forgive the sins of any, they are forgiven; 22
23 if you retain the sins of any, they are retained. 22
21: 5 Jesus said to them, "Children have you any fish? 22
Act 2:45 distributed them to all, as any had need. 22
4:32 any of the things which he possessed 22
35 distribution was made to each as any had need. 22
8:16 for it had not yet fallen on any of them 17
9: 2 if he found any belonging to the Way, men or women 22
10:28 I should not call any man common or unclean. 13
13:15 Brethren, if you have any word of exhortation 22
20:24 I do not account my life of any value 17
24:18 without any crowd or tumult. •
25:16 not the custom of the Romans to give up any one 22
26: 8 Why is it thought incredible by any of you •
27:34 since not a hair is to perish from the head of any 17
42 lest any should swim away and escape; 22
28:21 reported or spoken any evil about you. 22
Rom 8:33 Who shall bring any charge against God's elect? •
13: 9 You shall not covet," and any other commandment 22
15:23 I no longer have any room for work in these regions •
1Co 1: 7 you are not lacking in any spiritual gift 13
4: 3 I should be judged by you or by any human court •
7:12 if any brother has a wife who is an unbeliever 22
13 If any woman has a husband who is an unbeliever 22
35 not to lay any restraint upon you •
9: 7 without eating any of its fruit •
15 I have made no use of any of these rights 17
15 to secure any such provision •
10:25 without raising any question 13
27 eat . . without raising any question 13
11: 4 Any man who prays or prophesies with his head 20
5 any woman who prays or prophesies with her head 20
12:16 that would not make it any less a part of the body. †
14:27 If any speak in a tongue 22
15:10 On the contrary, I worked harder than any of them 20
2Co 1: 4 able to comfort those who are in any affliction 20
11: 9 and will refrain from burdening you in any way. 20
12:17 through any of those whom I sent to you? 22
13: 1 Any charge must be sustained 20
Gal 5: 6 nor uncircumcision is of any avail 22
6: 1 Brethren, if a man is overtaken in any trespass 22
Eph 5: 5 has any inheritance in the kingdom of Christ •
Php 2: 1 So if there is any encouragement in Christ 22
1 any incentive of love 22

1 any participation in the Spirit 22
1 any affection and sympathy 22
4: 8 whatever is gracious, if there is any excellence 22
12 in any and all circumstances 20
1Th 2: 9 worked night and day, that we might not burden any 22
2Th 2: 3 Let no one deceive you in any way 13
3: 6 any brother who is living in idleness 20
8 that we might not burden any of you. 22
11 mere busybodies, not doing any work. 13
1Ti 1: 3 not to teach any different doctrine *
5:16 If any believing woman has . . widows 22
19 Never admit any charge against an elder *
2Ti 2:21 ready for any good work. 20
Tit 1:16 detestable, disobedient, unfit for any good deed. 20
3: 1 to be obedient, to be ready for any honest work 20
Heb 3:12 lest there be in any of you an evil . . heart 22
4: 1 lest any of you be judged to have failed 22
12 sharper than any two-edged sword 20
10: 2 would no longer have any consciousness of sin. 13
18 there is no longer any offering for sin. *
Jas 1: 5 If any of you lacks wisdom, let him ask God 22
5:12 do not swear . . with any other oath 22
13 Is any cheerful? Let him sing praise. 22
14 Is any among you sick? Let him call for the elders 22
2Pe 3: 9 not wishing that any should perish 22
2Jn 1:10 do not receive him . . or give him any greeting; *
3Jn 1: 5 when you render any service to the brethren *
Rev 7: 1 blow on earth or sea or against any tree. 20
16 sun shall not strike them, nor any scorching heat 20
9: 4 not to harm . . any green growth or any tree 20
4 not to harm . . any green growth or any tree 20
18:22 a craftsman of any craft shall be found 20
1Es 1:24 beyond any other people or kingdom 20
4:18 gold and silver or any other beautiful thing 20
19 gold or silver or any other beautiful thing. 20
5:53 all who had made any vow to God *
6:32 if any should transgress . . 16
32 nullify any of the things herein written 21
8:22 no tribute or any other tax *
22 to be laid on any of the priests or Levites 20
22 no one has authority to impose any tax upon them. 21
9: 4 if any did not meet there within two or three days 16
2Es 2:23 When you find any who are dead *
43 of great stature, taller than any of the others 27
3:28 Are the deeds of those . . any better? 26
7:66 nor do they know of any torment or salvation *
9:34 the sea a ship, or any dish food or drink 24
10:45 before any offering was offered in it. 25
53 where there was no foundation of any building *
12:15 for a longer time than any other of the 12. *
13: 9 hand nor held a spear or any weapon of war; 23
Tob 1:18 put to death any who came fleeing from Judea 21
3: 8 have had no benefit from any of them. 11
14 I am innocent of any sin with man 20
4: 7 Do not turn your face away from any poor man 20
14 the wages of any man who works for you 20
18 do not despise any useful counsel. 20
Jdt 2:13 to transgress any of your sovereign's commands 12
4: 7 it was easy to stop any who tried to enter *
5:20 if there is any unwitting error in this people *
8:15 power to protect us within any time he pleases 14
18 any tribe or family or people or city of ours 19
20 he will not disdain us or any of our nation. 10
11:13 it is not lawful for any of the people 17
12:10 did not invite any of his officers. 17
20 in any one day since he was born. *
AEs 13:12 not in insolence or pride or for any love of glory *
14:15 I . . abhor the bed . . of any alien. 20
Wis 7: 9 Neither did I liken to her any priceless gem *
24 For wisdom is more mobile than any motion; 20
12:13 For neither is there any god besides thee *
14 nor can any king or monarch confront thee *
17 dost rebuke any insolence among those who know it. *
Sir 7:13 Refuse to utter any lie 20
8: 7 Do not rejoice over any one's death *
10: 6 Do not be angry with your neighbor for any injury 20
12:13 Who will pity . . any who go near wild beasts? 20
22:18 will not stand firm against any fear. 20
22 in these cases any friend will flee. 20
25:13 Any wound, but not a wound of the heart! 20
13 Any wickedness, but not the wickedness of a wife! 20
14 Any attack, but not an attack from those who hate! 20
14 any vengeance, but not the vengeance of enemies! 20
19 Any iniquity is insignificant 20
26:12 drinks from any water near him 20
33: 7 Why is any day better than another *
20 do not let any one take your place. 20
36:18 The stomach will take any food 20
21 A woman will accept any man 20
37:11 with an idler about any work 20
11 in any matter of counsel. 20
29 have an insatiable appetite for any luxury 20
40:16 The reeds by any water or river bank 20
16 will be plucked up before any grass. 20
27 covers a man better than any glory. 20
42:12 Do not look upon any one for beauty 20
46:19 I have not taken any one's property 20
47:22 nor cause any of his works to perish 10
48:12 all his days he did not tremble before any ruler *
Bar 2:19 any righteous deeds of our fathers or our kings *
LJr 1:25 They are bought at any cost 20
56 they can offer no resistance to a king or any enemies. *
Aza 1:14 For we, O Lord, have become fewer than any nation 20
1Mc 3:28 ordered them to be ready for any need. 20
8:24 any of their allies in all their dominion 20
26 without receiving any return. 18
30 any addition or deletion that they may make 15
10:35 annoy any of them about any matter. 21
35 annoy any of them about any matter. 20
43 in any of its precincts 20
43 because he owes money to the king or has any debt 20
63 bring charges against him about any matter 13
63 let no one annoy him for any reason. 20
13: 5 to spare my life in any time of distress 20
39 We pardon any errors and offenses committed *
40 if any of you are qualified to be enrolled 21
14:44 permitted to nullify any of these decisions 21
45 Whoever . . nullifies any of them 21
15:21 Therefore if any pestilent men have fled to you 21
2Mc 3:29 deprived of any hope of recovery 20
38 If you have any enemy 21
4:27 he did not pay regularly any of the money 17
9:24 if . . any unwelcome news came 21
11:31 none of them shall be molested in any way 17
3Mc 2:30 if any of them prefer 21
3:19 and are unwilling to regard any action as sincere. 17
27 whoever shelters any of the Jews 21
29 useless for all time to any mortal creature. 20
4:13 not omitting any detail of their punishment. 13
5: 6 the Jews were left without any aid 20
7: 5 without any inquiry or examination 20
8 with no one in any place doing them harm at all 20
9 if we devise any evil against them 21
9 or cause them any grief at all *
14 any whom they met of their fellow-countrymen *
22 those who held any restored it 21
4Mc 4:23 if any of them should be found 21
24 When . . he had not been able in any way 13
5: 3 If any were not willing to eat defiling food 21
13 it will excuse you from any transgression 20
17 we should not transgress it in any respect. 17
23 we endure any suffering willingly; 20
7:22 to endure any suffering for the sake of virtue 20
8: 2 any who ate defiling food should be freed *
2 if any were to refuse *
27 the youths . . neither said any of these things 17
9:29 How sweet is any kind of death 20
10: 7 they were not able in any way to break his spirit 13
16:11 shall I have any of my sons to bury me. 21
12 did not wail with such a lament for any of them 17
12 nor did she dissuade any of them from dying 21
19 therefore you ought to endure any suffering 20

any *See also* case, less, longer, means, more, other, time, way.

any after 1. οὐκέτι
Mrk 12:34 after that no one dared . . any question. 1

any at all
Num22:38 Have I now any power at all to speak anything? †

any kind 1. כֹּל
Ps 107:18 they loathed any kind of food 1

any man 1. אִישׁ 2. אֲשֶׁר 3. οὐδείς 4. τίς
Exd 34:24 neither shall any man desire your land 1
Lev 7: 8 the priest who offers any man's burnt offering 1
Num33:54 wherever the lot falls to any man, that shall be his 2
Jos 2:11 and there was no courage left in any man 1
1Sm 12: 4 You have not . . taken anything from any man's hand. 1
2Sm 21: 4 is it for us to put any man to death in Israel. 1
2Kg 18:21 will pierce the hand of any man who leans on it. 1
Mat 16:24 If any man would come after me 4
Mrk 4:23 If any man has ears to hear, let him hear. 4
8:34 said to them, "If any man would come after me 4
Lke 9:23 he said to all, "If any man would come after me 4
Joh 7:17 if any man's will is to do his will 4
18:31 It is not lawful for us to put any man to death. 3
1Co 3:14 If the work which any man has built 4
15 If any man's work is burned up, he will suffer loss 4
Eph 2: 9 not because of works, lest any man should boast. 4
Php 3: 4 If any other man thinks he has reason 4
Tit 1: 6 if any man is blameless, the husband of one wife 4
2Mc 13: 6 any man guilty of sacrilege *

any more 1. עוֹד 2. μηκέτι
Jer 20: 9 not mention him, or speak any more in his name 1
31:40 It shall not be uprooted or overthrown any more 1
Ezk 23:27 to the Egyptians or remember them any more. 1
24:13 you shall not be cleansed any more 1
36:15 let you hear any more the reproach of the nations 1
37:23 They shall not defile themselves any more 1
39: 7 I will not let my holy name be profaned any more; 1
28 of them remaining among the nations any more; 1
29 I will not hide my face any more from them 1
Lke 8:49 do not trouble the Teacher any more. 2

any one 1. אָדָם 2. אֶחָד 3. אִישׁ 4. אִישׁ אִישׁ 5. אֲשֶׁר 6. כֹּל 7. כֹּל אֲשֶׁר 8. מִי 9. נֶפֶשׁ 10. ἄνθρωπος 11. ἐάν 12. ἕκαστος 13. ἐκεῖνος 14. μηδείς 15. ὅς 16. ὃς ἄν 17. ὅστις 18. οὐδείς 19. πᾶς 20. τις 21. τίς 22. nemo 23. quis
Gen 4:15 If any one slays Cain, vengeance shall be taken 6
19:12 the men said to Lot, "Have you any one else here? 8
12 sons, daughters, or any one you have in the city 6
31:32 Any one with whom you find your gods *
Exd 12:15 for if any one eats what is leavened 6
19 for if any one eats what is leavened 6
22:10 is driven away, without any one seeing it *
Lev 2: 1 When any one brings a cereal offering 9
4: 2 If any one sins unwittingly in any of the things 9
13 If . . they do any one of the things which the LORD 2
22 sins, doing unwittingly any one of all the things 2
27 If any one of the common people sins unwittingly 9
27 sins unwittingly in doing any one of the things 2
5: 1 any one sins in that he hears a public adjuration 9
2 Or if any one touches an unclean thing 9
4 Or if any one utters with his lips a rash oath 9
13 sin which he has committed in any one of these 2
15 If any one commits a breach of faith and sins 9
17 If any one sins, doing any of the things 9
6: 2 If any one sins and commits a breach of faith 9
7:21 if any one touches an unclean thing 9
15: 5 any one who touches his bed shall wash 3
11 Any one whom he that has the discharge touches 6
33 for any one, male or female, who has a discharge *
18: 6 None of you shall approach any one near of kin 6
22:18 When any one of the house of Israel . . presents 4
21 when any one offers a sacrifice of peace 3
Num15:14 is sojourning with you, or any one is among you 5
19:22 any one who touches it shall be unclean 9
35:15 that any one who kills any person without intent 6
30 If any one kills a person, the murderer shall 6
Jos 2:19 If any one goes out of the doors of your house 6
19 but if a hand is laid upon any one who is with you 6
20: 9 any one who killed . . without intent could flee 6
Jdg 4:20 man comes and asks you, 'Is any one here?' say, No. 3
18: 7 they were far . . and had no dealings with any one. 1
28 from Sidon, and they had no dealings with any one. 1
2Sm 9: 1 Is there still any one left of the house of Saul 5
14:10 If any one says anything to you, bring him to me *
19:22 Shall any one be put to death in Israel this day? 3
20:12 And any one who came by, seeing him, stopped; 6
1Kg 14:11 any one who dies in the open country the birds *
16: 4 Any one belonging to Ba'asha who dies in the city *
4 and any one of his who dies in the field *
21:24 Any one belonging to Ahab who dies in the city *
24 any one of his who dies in the open country *
2Kg 4:29 If you meet any one, do not salute him; 3
29 and if any one salutes you, do not reply; 3
10: 5 We will not make any one king; do whatever is good 3
11:15 and slay with the sword any one who follows her. *
2Ch 23:14 any one who follows her is to be slain *
Ezr 10: 8 that if any one did not come within three days 7
Isa 27: 3 Lest any one harm it, I guard it night and day; *
Jer 29:32 shall not have any one living among this people 3
Ezk 14: 7 For any one of the house of Israel 4
33: 6 and the sword comes, and takes any one of them; 9
45:20 for any one who has sinned through error 3
Mat 5:39 But if any one strikes you on the right cheek, turn 17
40 and if any one would sue you and take your coat *
41 if any one forces you to go one mile, go with him two 17
8: 4 See that you say nothing to any one; but go 14
10:14 if any one will not receive you or listen 16
11:27 any one to whom the Son chooses to reveal him. 11
12:19 nor will any one hear his voice in the streets; 21
13:19 When any one hears the word of the kingdom 19
15: 5 you say, 'If any one tells his father or his mother 16
21: 3 If any one says anything to you, you shall say, 'The 21
22:46 did any one dare to ask him any more questions. 21
23:16 If any one swears by the temple, it is nothing 16
16 if any one swears by the gold of the temple 16
18 If any one swears by the altar, it is nothing 16
18 if any one swears by the gift that is on the altar 15
24:23 Then if any one says to you, 'Lo, here is the Christ!' 21
Mrk 1:44 said to him, "See that you say nothing to any one 14
7:24 he entered a house, and would not have any one know 18
9: 8 they no longer saw any one with them but Jesus 18
30 he would not have any one know it; 21
35 If any one would be first, he must be last of all 21
11: 3 If any one says to you, 'Why are you doing this?' 21
16 he would not allow any one to carry anything 21
25 forgive, if you have anything against any one 21
13:21 then if any one says to you, 'Look, here is the Christ!' 21
16: 8 they said nothing to any one, for they were afraid. 18
Lke 8:43 and could not be healed by any one 18
14: 8 When . . invited by any one to a marriage feast 21
26 If any one comes to me 21
17: 7 Will any one of you . . say to him 21
19: 8 if I have defrauded any one of anything 21
31 If any one asks you, 'Why are you untying it?' 21
20:18 when it falls on any one it will crush him. 16
Joh 4:33 Has any one brought him food? 21
6:46 Not that any one has seen the Father 21
51 if any one eats of this bread, he will live for ever; 21

7:37 If any one thirst, let him come to me and drink. 21
8:33 and have never been in bondage to any one 18
51 if any one keeps my word, he will never see death. 21
52 and you say, 'If any one keeps my word 21
9:22 if any one should confess him to be Christ 21
31 if any one is a worshiper of God and does his will 21
32 that any one opened the eyes of a man born blind. 21
10: 9 if any one enters by me, he will be saved 21
11: 9 If any one walks in the day, he does not stumble 21
10 if any one walks in the night, he stumbles 21
57 if any one knew where he was 21
12:26 If any one serves me, he must follow me 21
26 if any one serves me, the Father will honor him. 21
47 If any one hears my sayings and does not keep them 21
13:20 he who receives any one whom I send receives me; 21
Act 4:17 to speak no more to any one in this name. 14
8:19 any one . . may receive the Holy Spirit *
10:28 to visit any one of another nation *
35 any one who fears him . . is acceptable to him. *
47 Can any one forbid water for baptizing 21
19:38 the craftsmen . . have a complaint against any one 21
24:12 they did not find me disputing with any one 21
Rom 6:16 if you yield . . to any one as obedient slaves *
8: 9 Any one who does not have the Spirit of Christ 21
14:14 it is unclean for any one who thinks it unclean. 13
20 but it is wrong for any one to make others fall 10
1Co 1:15 lest any one should say that you were baptized 21
16 I do not know whether I baptized any one else.) 21
3:12 Now if any one builds on the foundation with gold 21
17 If any one destroys God's temple 21
18 If any one among you thinks that he is wise 21
5:11 not to associate with any one 21
7:18 Was any one at the time of his call uncircumcised? 21
18 Was any one at the time of his call uncircumcised? 21
36 If any one thinks that he is not behaving 21
8: 2 If any one imagines that he knows something 21
10 For if any one sees you, a man of knowledge, at table 21
9:15 I would rather die than have any one deprive me 18
10:12 Therefore let any one who thinks that he stands *
11:16 If any one is disposed to be contentious 21
29 For any one who eats and drinks *
34 if any one is hungry, let him eat at home 21
14: 7 how will any one know what is played? *
9 how will any one know what is said *
16 how can any one in the position of an outsider say *
37 If any one thinks that he is a prophet, or spiritual 21
38 If any one does not recognize this 21
16:22 If any one has no love for the Lord 21
2Co 2: 5 if any one has caused pain, he has caused it not 21
10 Any one whom you forgive, I also forgive 21
5:17 if any one is in Christ, he is a new creation 21
6: 3 We put no obstacle in any one's way 14
10: 7 If any one is confident that he is Christ's 21
11: 9 I did not burden any one 18
21 whatever any one dares to boast 21
Gal 1: 9 If any one is preaching to you a gospel 21
6: 3 if any one thinks he is something 21
Eph 6: 8 knowing that whatever good any one does 12
1Th 4: 9 you have no need to have any one write to you *
2Th 3: 8 we did not eat any one's bread without paying 21
10 If any one will not work, let him not eat. 21
14 If any one refuses to obey what we say 21
1Ti 1: 8 if any one uses it lawfully 21
3: 1 If any one aspires to the office of bishop 21
5: 8 If any one does not provide for his relatives 21
6: 3 If any one teaches otherwise 21
2Ti 2:21 If any one purifies himself from what is ignoble 21
Jas 1:23 For if any one is a hearer of the word and not a doer 21
26 If any one thinks he is religious 21
3: 2 if any one makes no mistakes in what he says 21
5:13 Is any one among you suffering? Let him pray. 21
19 if any one among you wanders from the truth 21
1Pe 3:15 Always be prepared to make a defense to any one 19
1Jn 2: 1 if any one does sin, we have an advocate 21
15 If any one loves the world 21
27 and you have no need that any one should teach you; 21
3:15 Any one who hates his brother is a murderer 19
17 if any one has the world's goods 15
4:20 If any one says, "I love God," and hates his brother 21
5:16 If any one sees his brother committing . . sin 21
18 We know that any one born of God does not sin 19
2Jn 1: 9 Any one who goes ahead and does not abide 19
10 If any one comes to you and does not bring 21
Rev 3:20 if any one hears my voice and opens the door 21
11: 5 if any one would harm them, fire pours out 21
5 if any one would harm them, thus he is doomed 21
13: 9 If any one has an ear, let him hear 21
10 If any one is to be taken captive 21
10 if any one slays with the sword 21
14: 9 If any one worships the beast and its image 21
20:15 if any one's name was not found written in the book 21
21:27 nor any one who practices abomination *
22:18 if any one adds to them, God will add to him 21
19 if any one takes away from the words of the book 21
1Es 2: 5 If any one of you, therefore, is of his people 20
2Es 3:31 hast not shown to any one 20
5:11 or any one who does right *
7: 5 If any one, then, wishes to reach the sea 23
105 neither shall any one lay a burden on another ‡
Tob 1:17 if I saw any one of my people dead 20
4:15 what you hate, do not do to any one 14
6: 7 if a demon or evil spirit gives trouble to any one 20
8:12 let us bury him without any one knowing about it. 14
Jdt 11: 1 I have never hurt any one 10
AEs 13:14 I will not bow down to any one but to thee 18
Wis 6: 7 For the Lord of all will not stand in awe of any one *
8: 7 if any one loves righteousness 20
8 if any one longs for wide experience 20
12:11 it was not through fear of any one 20
Sir 15:20 He has not commanded any one to be ungodly 18
20 he has not given any one permission to sin. 18
22: 2 any one that picks it up will shake it off his hand. 19
LJr 1:14 though unable to destroy any one who offends it. *
27 If any one sets one of them upright 20
27 If any one sets one of them upright 20
40 Why then must any one think that they are gods *
44 Why then must any one think that they are gods *
56 must any one admit or think that they are gods? *
1Mc 1:57 the book . . was found in the possession of any one 20
57 if any one adhered to the law 20
2Mc 1:19 the place was unknown to any one. 19
3Mc 3:28 Any one willing to give information *
7:21 to confiscation of their belongings by any one. 14

any one else 1. זוּר

Num 1:51 if any one else comes near, he shall be 1
3:10 if any one else comes near, he shall be put to death. 1

any part 1. מִן 2. *πᾶς*

Lev 11:25 whoever carries any part of their carcass 1
35 upon which any part of their carcass falls 1
37 if any part of their carcass falls upon the seed 1
38 if . . any part of their carcass falls on it 1
1Mc 10:33 into any part of my kingdom 2

any person 1. נֶפֶשׁ

Jos 20: 3 manslayer who kills any person without intent 1

any place

Mrk 6:55 to any place where they heard he was. *

any place whatever 1. אָנֶה וָאָנָה

1Kg 2:36 do not go forth from there to any place whatever. 1
42 the day you go forth and go to any place whatever 1

any sort 1. מְאוּמָה

Deu 24:10 When you make your neighbor a loan of any sort 1
2Mc 5:10 he had no funeral of any sort *

any such

1Mc 15: 8 any such future debts shall be canceled for you *

any thing 1. *τίς*

Eph 5:27 without spot or wrinkle or any such thing 1

anybody 1. *πάντοτε* 2. *πᾶσα σάρξ*

2Ti 3: 7 who will listen to anybody 1
Sir 33:29 Do not act immoderately toward anybody 2

anything 1. אַיִן 2. דָּבָר 3. יתר 4. כֹּל 5. כֹּל אֲשֶׁר 6. כֹּל דָּבָר 7. כְּלִי 8. כֹּל כְּלִי 9. כֹּל מְאוּמָה 10. מְאוּמָה 11. מָה 12. מְלָאכָה 13. מִלָּה 14. שְׁאֵלָה (A) 15. *ἅπας* 16. *εἷς* 17. *μηδείς* 18. *ὅσος* 19. *οὐδείς* 20. *οὐδέν* 21. *πᾶν ῥῆμα* 22. *πᾶς* 23. *σκεῦος* 24. *τις* 25. *τίς* 26. nihil

Gen 14:23 or anything that is yours, lest you should say 4
18:14 Is anything too hard for the LORD? 2
22:12 Do not . . do anything to him; 10
30:31 You shall not give me anything; 10
39: 6 he had no concern for anything but the food 10
8 my master has no concern about anything 11
9 he kept back anything from me except yourself 10
23 paid no heed to anything that was in Joseph's 9
Exd 12:10 anything that remains until the morning *
20: 4 likeness of anything that is in heaven above 4
17 covet . . anything that is your neighbor's. 4
22:14 If a man borrows anything of his neighbor, and it *
35:29 heart moved them to bring anything for the work 4
36: 6 man nor woman do anything more for the offering *
Lev 6: 5 or anything about which he has sworn falsely 4
11:10 anything in the seas or the rivers 4
32 anything upon which any of them falls 4
13:48 in a skin or in anything made of skin 4
49 in anything made of skin, it is a leprous disease 4
52 woolen or linen, or anything of skin 4
53 garment in warp or woof or in anything of skin 4
57 appears . . in anything of skin, it is spreading 4
58 the garment, warp or woof, or anything of skin 4
59 disease . . in anything of skin, to decide 4
15: 6 whoever sits on anything 7
10 whoever touches anything that was under him 4
22 whoever touches anything upon which she sits 8
23 the bed or anything upon which she sits 7
19: 6 anything left over until the third day *
20:25 abominable by beast or by bird or by anything 4
22: 4 Whoever touches anything that is unclean 4
20 You shall not offer anything that has a blemish 4
27:10 He shall not substitute anything for it *
28 no devoted thing . . of anything that he has 4
Num 15:29 one law for him who does anything unwittingly *
30 person who does anything with a high hand *
22:38 Have I now any power at all to speak anything? 10
30: 9 anything by which she has bound herself 4
35:22 if he . . hurled anything on him without lying in wait 8
Deu 4:18 likeness of anything that creeps on the ground 4
23 form of anything which the LORD . . has forbidden 4
25 by making a graven image in the form of anything 4
5: 8 'You shall not make . . any likeness of anything *
21 not desire . . anything that is your neighbor's.' 4
14:21 You shall not eat anything that dies of itself; 4
22: 5 woman . . not wear anything that pertains to a man *
23:14 that he may not see anything indecent among you 2
19 interest on anything that is lent for interest. 6
Jdg 13:14 may not eat of anything that comes from the vine 4
18:10 there is no lack of anything that is in the earth. 6
19:19 with your servants; there is no lack of anything. 6
1Sm 3:17 if you hide anything from me of all that he told 2
10:16 of the kingdom . . he did not tell him anything. 10
12: 4 oppressed us or taken anything from any . . hand. 10
5 you have not found anything in my hand. 10
19: 3 and if I learn anything I will tell you. 11
20:26 Saul did not say anything that day; for he thought 10
21: 2 Let no one know anything of the matter 10
22:15 Let not the king impute anything to his servant 2
25:15 whether . . spoil or anything that had been taken; 5
30:19 whether . . spoil or anything that had been taken; 5
2Sm 3:35 if I taste bread or anything else till the sun 10
13: 2 it seemed impossible . . to do anything to her. 10
14:10 If any one says anything to you, bring him to me *
18 Do not hide from me anything I ask you. 2
19 from anything that my lord the king has said. 4
1Kg 10:21 silver, it was not considered as anything 10
15: 5 turn aside from anything that he commanded him 4
2Ch 9:20 silver was not considered as anything *
Job 20:20 he will not save anything in which he delights. *
31:16 I have withheld anything that the poor desired *
33:32 If you have anything to say, answer me; 13
Ps 101: 3 not set before my eyes anything that is base. 2
Ecc 3:14 nothing . . added to it, nor anything taken from it; 1
6: 5 it has not seen the sun or known anything; *
7:14 may not find out anything that will be after him. 10
12:12 My son, beware of anything beyond these. 3
Jer 32:27 is anything too hard for me? 6
42:21 obeyed the voice of the LORD your God in anything 5
Ezk 15: 3 Is wood taken from it to make anything? 12
4 it is charred, is it useful for anything? 12
5 it is charred, can it ever be used for anything! 12
29:18 army got anything from Tyre to pay for the labor *
44:18 not gird . . with anything that causes sweat. *
31 The priests shall not eat of anything 4
Dan 3:29 speaks anything against the God of Shadrach 14
Jon 3: 7 man nor beast, herd nor flock, taste anything; 10
Mat 5:37 anything more than this comes from evil. *
9:33 Never was anything like this seen in Israel. *
18:19 agree on earth about anything they ask 22
21: 3 If any one says anything to you, you shall say, 'The 25
Mrk 2:12 saying, "We never saw anything like this! *
4:22 nor is anything secret, except to come to light. *
7:12 then you no longer permit him to do anything 19
8:23 he asked him, "Do you see anything? 25
9:22 if you can do anything, have pity on us and help us. 25
29 cannot be driven out by anything but prayer. 19
11:13 he went to see if he could find anything on it. 25
16 to carry anything through the temple. 23
25 forgive, if you have anything against any one 25
13:15 nor enter his house, to take anything away; 25
Lke 8:17 nor anything secret that shall not be known *
9:36 told no one . . anything of what they had seen. 19
11: 7 I cannot get up and give you anything'? *
8 though he will not get up and give him anything *
15:16 no one gave him anything. *
19: 8 if I have defrauded any one of anything 25
48 they did not find anything they could do 25
22:35 did you lack anything?" They said, "Nothing. 25
24:41 he said to them, "Have you anything here to eat? 25
Joh 1: 3 without him was not anything made that was made. 16
46 Can anything good come out of Nazareth? 25
3:27 No one can receive anything except what is given 20
14:14 if you ask anything in my name, I will do it. 25
16:23 if you ask anything of the Father, he will give it 25
Act 10:14 never eaten anything that is common or unclean. 22
17:25 as though he needed anything 25
19:39 if you seek anything further 25
20:20 declaring to you anything that was profitable 19
24:19 if they have anything against me. 25
25: 5 if there is anything wrong about the man 25
11 committed anything for which I deserve to die 25
Rom 8:39 nor depth, nor anything else in all creation 25
13: 8 Owe no one anything, except to love one another; 17
14: 2 One believes he may eat anything 22
21 or do anything that makes your brother stumble. *
15:18 For I will not venture to speak of anything 25
1Co 3: 7 nor he who waters is anything 25
4: 4 I am not aware of anything against myself 19
6:12 I will not be enslaved by anything. 25
7:19 For neither circumcision counts for anything 19

9:12 we endure anything rather than put an obstacle 22
10:19 That food offered to idols is anything 25
19 that an idol is anything? 25
14:35 If there is anything they desire to know 25
2Co 2:10 What I have forgiven, if I have forgiven anything 25
3: 5 competent of ourselves to claim anything 25
13: 8 For we cannot do anything against the truth 25
Gal 6:15 For neither circumcision counts for anything 25
Eph 5:13 when anything is exposed by the light 22
13 for anything that becomes visible is light. 22
Php 1:28 not frightened in anything by your opponents. 17
3:15 if in anything you are otherwise minded 25
4: 8 if there is anything worthy of praise 25
1Th 1: 8 so that we need not say anything. 25
5: 1 you have no need to have anything written to you. *
1Ti 6: 7 we cannot take anything out of the world; 25
Phm 1:18 If he . . owes you anything *
Jas 1: 7 will receive anything from the Lord. 25
1Jn 5:14 if we ask anything according to his will he hears 25
Rev 22: 3 There shall no more be anything accursed 22
1Es 4:39 instead of anything that is unrighteous 22
2Es 2:28 they shall not be able to do anything against you 26
Tob 2: 4 before I tasted anything *
12:11 I will not conceal anything from you 21
Jdt 8:13 but you will never know anything! 19
Wis 10:12 godliness is more powerful than anything. 22
11:24 thou wouldst not have made anything 24
25 How would anything have endured 24
25 anything not called forth by thee *
Sir 8:12 if you do lend anything, be as one who has lost it. *
10: 6 do not attempt anything by acts of insolence. 17
19:13 if he did anything, so that he may do it no more. 24
25: 3 how then can you find anything in your old age? *
29:26 if you have anything at hand, let me have it to eat. 24
Bel 1: 7 it never ate or drank anything. *
1Mc 8:30 both . . shall determine to add or delete anything *
10:35 authority to exact anything from them *
2Mc 9:24 if anything unexpected happened 24
3Mc 2: 3 those who have done anything in insolence 24
9 though you have no need of anything 15
4Mc 2: 5 or anything that is your neighbor's 18

anything *See also* accomplishing, no.

without anything 1. μηδείς
4Mc 9:12 without accomplishing anything 1

anywhere 1. בְּכֹל
Gen 19:17 do not look back or stop anywhere in the valley; 1

apace 1. הלך 2. מְאֹד
2Sm 18:25 And he came apace, and drew near. 1
Jer 48:16 and his affliction hastens apace. 2

apart 1. חוּץ 2. לְבַד 3. מִלְּבַד 4. ἄνευ 5. κατ' ἰδίαν 6. μόνος 7. χωρίς
Gen 21:28 Abraham set seven ewe lambs of the flock apart. 2
29 these seven ewe lambs which you have set apart? 2
30:40 he put his own droves apart 2
Num 6:21 apart from what else he can afford; 3
Jdg 20:17 the men of Israel, apart from Benjamin, mustered 2
Ps 16: 2 Thou art my Lord; I have no good apart from thee. 4
Ecc 2:25 apart from him who can eat or . . have enjoyment? 1
Mat 14:13 to a lonely place apart 5
17: 1 and led them up a high mountain apart. 5
Mrk 9: 2 led them up a high mountain apart by themselves; 6
Lke 9:10 withdrew apart to a city called Beth-sa'ida. 5
Joh 15: 5 for apart from me you can do nothing. 7
Rom 3:21 righteousness . . manifested apart from law 7
28 man is justified by faith apart from works of law. 7
4: 6 God reckons righteousness apart from works 7
7: 8 Apart from the law sin lies dead. 7
9 I was once alive apart from the law 7
2Co 11:28 And, apart from other things 7
Heb 11:40 apart from us they should not be made perfect. 7
Jas 2:18 Show me your faith apart from your works 7
20 that faith apart from works is barren? 7
26 For as the body apart from the spirit is dead 7
26 so faith apart from works is dead. 7
Wis 11:20 Even apart from these 7

apart *See also* dwell, portion, set, wrench.

ape 1. קוֹף
1Kg 10:22 bringing gold, silver, ivory, apes, and peacocks. 1
2Ch 9:21 (ships) bringing . . ivory, apes, and peacocks. 1

apiece 1. אֶחָד 2. גֻּלְגֹּלֶת 3. לַגֻּלְגֹּלֶת
Exd 16:16 you shall take an omer apiece, according 2
22 gathered twice as much bread, two omers apiece; 1
Num 3:47 you shall take five shekels apiece; 3
7:86 golden dishes . . weighing ten shekels apiece *
Ezk 41:24 The doors had two leaves apiece *

apologize 1. παρακαλέω
Act 16:39 so they came and apologized to them 1

apology *See* add.

apostasy 1. מְשׁוּבָה 2. ἀποστασία
Jer 2:19 and your apostasy will reprove you. 1
5: 6 their apostasies are great. 1
1Mc 2:15 king's officers who were enforcing the apostasy 2

apostasy *See also* commit, join.

apostatize 1. ἀπαλλοτριόω
3Mc 1: 3 apostatized from the ancestral traditions 1

apostle 1. ἀπόστολος
Mat 10: 2 The names of the twelve apostles are these 1
Mrk 6:30 The apostles returned to Jesus, and told him all 1
Lke 6:13 chose from them twelve, whom he named apostles; 1
9:10 the apostles told him what they had done 1
11:49 I will send them prophets and apostles 1
17: 5 The apostles said to the Lord, "Increase our faith! 1
22:14 he sat at table, and the apostles with him. 1
24:10 who told this to the apostles; 1
Act 1: 2 the apostles whom he had chosen. 1
26 he was enrolled with the eleven apostles. 1
2:37 said to Peter and the rest of the apostles 1
42 devoted themselves to the apostles' teaching 1
43 signs were done through the apostles. 1
4:33 the apostles gave their testimony 1
35 laid it at the apostles' feet 1
36 who was surnamed by the apostles Barnabas 1
37 laid it at the apostles' feet. 1
5: 2 laid it at the apostles' feet. 1
12 done . . by the hands of the apostles 1
18 they arrested the apostles 1
29 Peter and the apostles answered, "We must obey God 1
40 when they had called in the apostles 1
6: 6 These they set before the apostles 1
8: 1 except the apostles. 1
14 Now when the apostles at Jerusalem heard 1
18 through the laying on of the apostles' hands 1
9:27 took him, and brought him to the apostles 1
11: 1 the apostles and the brethren who were in Judea 1
14: 4 some with the apostles. 1
14 when the apostles Barnabas and Paul heard of it 1
15: 2 to Jerusalem to the apostles and the elders 1
4 were welcomed by the church and the apostles 1
6 The apostles and the elders were gathered together 1
22 it seemed good to the apostles and the elders 1
23 The brethren, both the apostles and the elders 1
16: 4 decisions . . reached by the apostles 1
Rom 1: 1 Paul . . called to be an apostle 1
11:13 Inasmuch then as I am an apostle to the Gentiles 1
16: 7 they are men of note among the apostles 1
1Co 1: 1 by the will of God to be an apostle of Christ Jesus 1
4: 9 God has exhibited us apostles as last of all 1
9: 1 Am I not free? Am I not an apostle? 1
2 If to others I am not an apostle, at least I am to you; 1
5 as the other apostles 1
12:28 God has appointed in the church first apostles 1
29 Are all apostles? Are all prophets? 1
15: 7 he appeared to James, then to all the apostles. 1
9 the least of the apostles, unfit to be called 1
9 unfit to be called an apostle 1
2Co 1: 1 Paul, an apostle of Christ Jesus by the will of God 1
11: 5 inferior to these superlative apostles. 1
13 disguising themselves as apostles of Christ. 1
12:11 inferior to these superlative apostles 1
12 The signs of a true apostle were performed among you 1
Gal 1: 1 Paul an apostle–not from men nor through man 1
17 to those who were apostles before me 1
19 I saw none of the other apostles 1
Eph 1: 1 Paul, an apostle of Christ Jesus by the will of God 1
2:20 the foundation of the apostles and prophets 1
3: 5 been revealed to his holy apostles and prophets 1
4:11 his gifts were that some should be apostles 1
Col 1: 1 Paul, an apostle of Christ Jesus by the will of God 1
1Th 2: 6 might have made demands as apostles of Christ. 1
1Ti 1: 1 Paul, an apostle of Christ Jesus by command of God 1
2: 7 For this I was appointed a preacher and apostle 1
2Ti 1: 1 Paul, an apostle of Christ Jesus by the will of God 1
11 appointed a preacher and apostle and teacher 1
Tit 1: 1 a servant of God and an apostle of Jesus Christ 1
Heb 3: 1 the apostle and high priest of our confession. 1
1Pe 1: 1 Peter, an apostle of Jesus Christ 1
2Pe 1: 1 Peter, a servant and apostle of Jesus Christ 1
3: 2 commandment of the Lord . . through your apostles. 1
Jde 1:17 predictions of the apostles of our Lord Jesus 1
Rev 2: 2 tested those who call themselves apostles 1
18:20 O heaven, O saints and apostles and prophets 1
21:14 twelve names of the twelve apostles of the Lamb. 1

false apostle 1. ψευδαπόστολος
2Co 11:13 such men are false apostles, deceitful workmen 1

apostleship 1. ἀποστολή
Act 1:25 this ministry and apostleship 1
Rom 1: 5 we have received grace and apostleship 1
1Co 9: 2 you are the seal of my apostleship in the Lord. 1

appall 1. בעת 2. שַׁמָּה 3. שׁמם 4. ἐκταράσσω
Ezr 9: 3 pulled hair from my head . . and sat appalled. 3
4 sat appalled until the evening sacrifice. 3
Job 17: 8 Upright men are appalled at this 3
18:20 They of the west are appalled at his day 3
21: 5 Look at me, and be appalled 3
Ps 40:15 Let them be appalled because of their shame 3
70: 3 Let them be appalled because of their shame 3
143: 4 my heart within me is appalled. 3
Isa 21: 4 My mind reels, horror has appalled me; 1
63: 5 I was appalled, but there was no one to uphold; 3
Jer 2:12 Be appalled, O heavens, at this, be shocked 3
4: 9 the priests shall be appalled 3
5:30 An appalling and horrible thing has happened 2
49:20 their fold shall be appalled at their fate. 3
50:13 one who passes by Babylon shall be appalled 3
45 their fold shall be appalled at their fate. 3
Ezk 19: 7 the land was appalled and all who were in it 3
26:16 and tremble every moment, and be appalled at you. 3
27:35 the inhabitants of the coastlands are appalled 3
28:19 All who know you among the peoples are appalled 3
Dan 8:27 appalled by the vision and did not understand it. 3
Wis 17: 3 terribly alarmed, and appalled by specters. 4

make appalled 1. שׁמם
Ezk 32:10 I will make many peoples appalled at you 1

apparel 1. בֶּגֶד 2. לְבוּשׁ 3. ἐσθής 4. ἱμάτιον 5. ἱματισμός 6. καταστολή
Jdg 17:10 I will give you . . and a suit of apparel 1
2Sm 1:24 who put ornaments of gold upon your apparel. 2
Isa 63: 1 he that is glorious in his apparel 2
2 Why is thy apparel red, and thy garments 2
Lke 23:11 then, arraying him in gorgeous apparel 3
24: 4 behold, two men stood by them in dazzling apparel; 3
Act 10:30 behold, a man stood before me in bright apparel 3
20:33 I coveted no one's silver or gold or apparel. 5
1Ti 2: 9 modestly and sensibly in seemly apparel 6
Jdt 10: 3 arrayed herself in her gayest apparel 4
AEs 14: 2 she took off her splendid apparel 4

apparel *See also* rich.

apparition 1. ἐπιφάνεια 2. φαντασία
Wis 18:17 apparitions in dreadful dreams 2
2Mc 5: 4 the apparition might prove to have been . . good 1

appeal 1. צעק 2. ἐντυγχάνω 3. ἐπερώτημα 4. ἐπικαλέω 5. παρακαλέω 6. παράκλησις 7. ποιέω παράκλησιν 8. πρόσωπον 9. ὑπομιμνήσκω 10. concupiscentia
2Kg 8: 3 she went forth to appeal to the king for her house 1
5 the woman . . appealed to the king for her house 1
Mat 26:53 Do you think that I cannot appeal to my Father 5
Act 25:11 I appeal to Caesar. 4
12 You have appealed to Caesar 4
21 when Paul had appealed to be kept in custody 4
25 as he himself appealed to the emperor 4
26:32 if he had not appealed to Caesar. 4
28:19 I was compelled to appeal to Caesar 4
Rom 12: 1 I appeal to you therefore, brethren 5
15:30 I appeal to you, brethren, by our Lord Jesus Christ 5
16:17 I appeal to you, brethren, to take note 5
1Co 1:10 I appeal to you, brethren, by the name of our Lord 5
2Co 8:17 For he not only accepted our appeal 6
1Th 2: 3 our appeal does not spring from error 6
Phm 1: 9 yet for love's sake I prefer to appeal to you–I, Paul 5
10 I appeal to you for my child, Ones'imus 5
Heb 13:22 I appeal to you, brethren 5
1Pe 3:21 but as an appeal to God for a clear conscience 3
Jde 1: 3 appealing to you to contend for the faith 5
2Es 6:44 and of varied appeal to the taste 10
Wis 8:21 so I appealed to the Lord and besought him 2
13:18 For health he appeals to a thing that is weak 4
18:22 appealing to the oaths and covenants 9
Sir 41:21 rejecting the appeal of a kinsman 8
47: 5 For he appealed to the Lord, the Most High 4
51:10 I appealed to the Lord, the Father of my lord 4
1Mc 8:32 If now they appeal again for help against you 2
2Mc 4:36 the Jews in the city appealed to him 2
7:24 Antiochus not only appealed to him in words 7
37 appealing to God to show mercy soon to our nation 4

appeal *See also* heed, make.

appeal for mercy 1. חנן
Job 9:15 I must appeal for mercy to my accuser. 1

appear 1. גלה 2. מַרְאֶה 3. עמד 4. פנה 5. פָּנִים 6. ראה 7. נפק (A) 8. ἀνατέλλω 9. ἀναφαίνω 10. ἀνίστημι 11. ἀπαντάω 12. γίνομαι 13. δοκέω 14. ἐμφανίζω 15. ἐπιφαίνω 16. ἐπιφάνεια 17. ἔρχομαι 18. ἐφίστημι 19. ὀπτάνομαι 20. ὀπτασία 21. ὅρασις 22. ὁράω 23. παραγίνομαι 24. προσποιέω 25. προφαίνομαι 26. φαίνω 27. φανερόω 28. φαντάζομαι 29. ὡς 30. advento 31. appareo 32. apparesco 33. conpareo 34. facies 35. orior 36. video 37. viso
Gen 1: 9 and let the dry land appear. 6
12: 7 Then the LORD appeared to Abram, and said 6
7 altar to the LORD, who had appeared to him. 6
17: 1 the LORD appeared to Abram, and said to him 6
18: 1 the LORD appeared to him by the oaks of Mamre 6

26: 2 the LORD appeared to him and said, Do not go down 6
24 the LORD appeared to him the same night and said 6
35: 1 make there an altar to the God who appeared to you 6
9 God appeared to Jacob again, when he came 6
46:28 sent Judah . . to appear before him in Goshen; ‡
48: 3 Jacob said to Joseph, "God Almighty appeared 6
Exd 3: 2 the angel of the LORD appeared to him in a flame 6
16 LORD . . has appeared to me, saying, "I have 6
4: 1 for they will say, 'The LORD did not appear to you.' 6
5 and the God of Jacob, has appeared to you. 6
6: 3 I appeared to Abraham, to Isaac, and to Jacob, as God 6
14:27 sea returned . . when the morning appeared; 4
16:10 the glory of the LORD appeared in the cloud. 6
23:15 None shall appear before me empty-handed. 6
17 shall all your males appear before the LORD God. 6
34:20 And none shall appear before me empty. 6
23 all your males appear before the LORD God 6
24 when you go up to appear before the LORD your God 6
Lev 9: 4 for today the LORD will appear to you.' 6
6 the glory of the LORD will appear to you 6
23 the glory of the LORD appeared to all the people 6
13: 3 the disease appears to be deeper than the skin 2
4 if the spot . . appears no deeper than the skin 2
7 he shall appear again before the priest 6
14 when raw flesh appears . . he shall be unclean 6
20 if it appears deeper than the skin and its hair 2
25 if . . it appears deeper than the skin 2
30 if it appears deeper than the skin, and the hair 2
31 if . . it appears no deeper than the skin 2
32 the itch appears to be no deeper than the skin 2
34 if . . it appears to be no deeper than the skin 2
57 then if it appears again in the garment, in warp 6
14:37 if it appears to be deeper than the surface 6
16: 2 I will appear in the cloud upon the mercy seat 6
Num14:10 glory . . appeared at the tent of meeting to all 6
16:19 glory of the LORD appeared to all 6
42 covered it, and the glory of the LORD appeared. 6
20: 6 And the glory of the LORD appeared to them 6
Deu 16:16 all your males shall appear before the LORD 6
16 shall not appear before the LORD empty-handed; 6
19:17 both parties . . shall appear before the LORD 3
31:11 when all Israel comes to appear before the LORD 6
15 LORD appeared in the tent in a pillar of cloud; 6
Jdg 6:12 angel of the LORD appeared to him and said to him 6
13: 3 angel of the LORD appeared to the woman and said 6
10 the man who came to me . . has appeared to me. 6
21 The angel of the LORD appeared no more to Mano'ah 6
19:26 as morning appeared, the woman came and fell down 4
1Sm 1:22 bring him, that he may appear in the presence 6
3:21 And the LORD appeared again at Shiloh 6
1Kg 3: 5 the LORD appeared to Solomon in a dream by night; 6
9: 2 the LORD appeared to Solomon a second time 6
2 a second time, as he had appeared to him at Gibeon. 6
11: 9 the LORD . . who had appeared to him twice 6
2Ch 1: 7 In that night God appeared to Solomon 6
3: 1 where the LORD had appeared to David his father 6
7:12 Then the LORD appeared to Solomon in the night 6
Ps 21: 9 make them as a blazing oven when you appear. 5
102:16 For the LORD . . will appear in his glory; 6
Prv 27:25 When the grass is gone, and the new growth appears 6
Sng 2:12 The flowers appear on the earth 6
Isa 49: 9 to those who are in darkness, 'Appear.' 1
Jer 31: 3 the LORD appeared to him from afar. 6
Ezk 8: 2 below what appeared to be his loins it was fire 2
10: 1 appeared above them something like a sapphire 6
8 The cherubim appeared to have the form of a human 6
21:24 so that in all your doings your sins appear 6
Dan 5: 5 fingers of a man's hand appeared and wrote 7
8: 1 third year . . vision appeared to me, Daniel 6
1 after that which appeared to me at the first. 6
11:31 Forces from him shall appear 3
Zec 9:14 Then the LORD will appear over them 6
Mal 3: 2 who can stand when he appears? 6
Mat 1:20 an angel of the Lord appeared to him in a dream 26
2: 7 from them what time the star appeared; 26
13 an angel of the Lord appeared to Joseph in a dream 26
19 an angel of the Lord appeared in a dream to Joseph 26
13:26 then the weeds appeared also. 26
17: 3 behold, there appeared to them Moses and Eli'jah 22
23:27 which outwardly appear beautiful 26
28 So you also outwardly appear righteous to men 26
24:30 then will appear the sign of the Son of man 26
27:53 went into the holy city and appeared to many. 14
Mrk 1: 4 John the baptizer appeared in the wilderness 12
9: 4 there appeared to them Eli'jah with Moses; 22
16: 9 he appeared first to Mary Magdalene 26
12 After this he appeared in another form to two 27
14 Afterward he appeared to the eleven themselves 27
Lke 1:11 there appeared to him an angel of the Lord 22
2: 9 an angel of the Lord appeared to them 18
9: 8 by some that Eli'jah had appeared 26
31 who appeared in glory and spoke of his departure 22
19:11 the kingdom of God was to appear immediately. 9
24:28 He appeared to be going further 24
34 has appeared to Simon! 22
Joh 7:27 when the Christ appears 17
31 When the Christ appears 17
Act 1: 3 appearing to them during 40 days 19
2: 3 there appeared to them tongues as of fire 22
7: 2 The God of glory appeared to our father Abraham 22
26 he appeared to them as they were quarreling 22
30 an angel appeared to him in the wilderness 22
35 the angel that appeared to him in the bush. 22
9:17 the Lord Jesus who appeared to you on the road 22
12: 7 behold, an angel of the Lord appeared 18
13:31 he appeared to those who came up with him 22
16: 9 a vision appeared to Paul in the night 22
26:16 I have appeared to you for this purpose 22
16 those in which I will appear to you 22
27:20 when neither sun nor stars appeared for many a day 15
1Co 15: 5 that he appeared to Cephas, then to the twelve. 22
6 Then he appeared to more than 500 brethren 22
7 he appeared to James, then to all the apostles. 22
8 he appeared also to me. 22
2Co 5:10 For we must all appear before the judgment seat 27
13: 7 not that we may appear to have met the test 26
Col 3: 4 When Christ who is our life appears 27
4 you also will appear with him in glory. 27
2Th 2: 8 destroy him by his appearing and his coming. 16
1Ti 6:14 until the appearing of our Lord Jesus Christ; 16
2Ti 1:10 manifested through the appearing of our Savior 16
4: 1 by his appearing and his kingdom 16
8 also to all who have loved his appearing. 16
Tit 2:11 has appeared for the salvation of all men 15
13 the appearing of the glory of our great God 16
3: 4 loving kindness of God our Savior appeared 15
Heb 9:11 when Christ appeared as a high priest 23
24 now to appear in the presence of God on our behalf. 14
26 he has appeared once for all at the end of the age 27
28 will appear a second time, not to deal with sin 22
11: 3 was made out of things which do not appear. 26
Jas 4:14 For you are a mist that appears for a little time 26
1Pe 4:18 where will the impious and sinner appear? 26
1Jn 2:28 so that when he appears we may have confidence 27
3: 2 it does not yet appear what we shall be 27
2 we know that when he appears we shall be like him 27
5 You know that he appeared to take away sins 27
8 The reason the Son of God appeared 27
Rev 4: 3 he . . appeared like jasper and carnelian 21
12: 1 a great portent appeared in heaven, a woman 22
3 another portent appeared in heaven; 22
15: 2 I saw what appeared to be a sea of glass 29
1Es 5:40 until a high priest should appear 10
2Es 3: 6 right hand had planted before the earth appeared. 30
33 Yet their reward has not appeared 33
6:22 Sown places shall suddenly appear unsown 31
40 so that thy works might then appear. 31
7:26 that the city which now is not seen shall appear 32
36 Then the pit of torment shall appear 31
114and truth has appeared. 35
9: 3 there shall appear in the world earthquakes 36
10:41 The woman who appeared to you a little while ago 31
42 but an established city has appeared to you- 31
12:11 the fourth kingdom which appeared in a vision 37
15:28 a terrifying sight, appearing from the east! 34
Tob 12:19 I merely appeared to you and did not eat or drink 19
22 the angel of the Lord had appeared to them. 22
Wis 6:16 she graciously appears to them in their paths 28
17: 4 dismal phantoms with gloomy faces appeared. 14
Sir 35: 4 Do not appear before the Lord empty-handed 22
37:18 four turns of fortune appear 8
39: 4 serve among great men and appear before rulers; 22
43: 2 The sun, when it appears, making proclamation 20
16 At his appearing the mountains are shaken 20
22 when the dew appears, it refreshes from the heat. 11
Bar 3:37 she appeared upon earth and lived among men. 22
1Mc 4: 6 At daybreak Judas appeared in the plain 22
19 a detachment appeared, coming out of the hills. 22
9:23 all the doers of injustice appeared. 8
27 since the time that prophets ceased to appear 22
2Mc 1:33 the liquid had appeared 26
2: 8 the glory of the Lord and the cloud will appear 22
3:25 there appeared to them a . . horse 22
26 Two young men also appeared to him 25
30 now that the Almighty Lord had appeared. 15
33 the same young men appeared again to Heliodorus 26
5: 2 there appeared golden-clad horsemen 26
10:29 there appeared to the enemy from heaven 26
11: 8 there . . a horseman appeared at their head 26
12:16 the . . lake . . appeared to be running over with blood. 26
22 when Judas' first division appeared 15
14:20 it had appeared that they were of one mind 26
15:13 Then likewise a man appeared 15
3Mc 2:30 he might not appear to be an enemy to all 26
3: 4 For this reason they appeared hateful to some; 26
5: 6 to the Gentiles it appeared that . . 13
4Mc 4:10 angels on horseback . . appeared from heaven 25
7:20 when some persons appear to be dominated 26

appear as prophet 1. נבא
Zec 13: 3 if any one again appears as a prophet 1

appear before 1. ראה פָּנִים
Isa 1:12 When you come to appear before me 1

appear in a body 1. ἐπισυνάγω
1Mc 7:12 a group of scribes appeared in a body before Alcimus 1

appear in glory 1. כבד
Hag 1: 8 that I may appear in my glory, says the LORD. 1

appear in public 1. ὀπτασία
AEs 14:16 upon my head on the days when I appear in public 1

appear later 1. ἐπακολουθέω
1Ti 5:24 the sins of others appear later. 1

make appear righteous 1. צדק
Ezk 16:51 and have made your sisters appear righteous 1
52 you have made your sisters appear righteous. 1

appearance 1. מַרְאֶה 2. עַיִן 3. תֹּאַר 4. רֵו (A) 5. εἰδέα 6. εἶδος 7. ἐπιφάνεια 8. εὐπρέπεια 9. ἰδέα 10. λόγος 11. ὁμοίωμα 12. ὅρασις 13. ὄψις 14. πρόσωπον 15. facies
Exd 24:17 the appearance of the glory of the LORD was like 1
Lev 13:43 swelling . . like the appearance of leprosy 1
Num 9:15 over the tabernacle like the appearance of fire 1
16 continually . . appearance of fire by night. 1
11: 7 manna . . its appearance like that of bdellium. 2
1Sm 16: 7 Do not look on his appearance or on the height 1
17:42 was but a youth, ruddy and comely in appearance. 1
28:14 What is his appearance?" And she said, "An old man 3
Job 4:16 I could not discern its appearance. 1
Sng 5:15 His appearance is like Lebanon 1
Isa 52:14 astonished at him-his appearance was so marred 1
Ezk 1: 5 And this was their appearance: they had the form 1
16 As for the appearance of the wheels 1
16 their appearance was like the gleaming •
26 of a throne, in appearance like sapphire; 1
27 upward from what had the appearance of his loins 1
27 gleaming bronze, like the appearance of fire 1
27 from what had the appearance of his loins I saw 1
27 I saw as it were the appearance of fire 1
28 Like the appearance of the bow 1
28 the appearance of the brightness round about. 1
28 Such was the appearance of the likeness 1
8: 2 lo, a form that had the appearance of a man; 1
2 it was like the appearance of brightness 1
10: 9 the appearance of the wheels was like sparkling 1
10 as for their appearance, the four had the same 1
22 faces whose appearance I had seen by the river 1
40: 3 there was a man, whose appearance was like bronze 1
43:10 its appearance and plan, that they may be ashamed 12
Dan 1:13 our appearance and the appearance of the youths 1
13 our appearance and the appearance of the youths 1
15 seen that they were better in appearance 1
2:31 its appearance was frightening. 4
3:25 appearance of the fourth is like a son of the gods. 4
8:15 before me one having the appearance of a man. 1
10: 6 his face like the appearance of lightning 1
18 one having the appearance of a man touched me 1
Jol 2: 4 appearance is like the appearance of horses 1
4 appearance is like the appearance of horses 1
Mat 16: 3 how to interpret the appearance of the sky 14
28: 3 His appearance was like lightning 5
Lke 9:29 the appearance of his countenance was altered 6
12:56 to interpret the appearance of the earth and sky; 14
Joh 7:24 Do not judge by appearances 13
Col 2:23 These have indeed an appearance of wisdom 10
Rev 9: 7 In appearance the locusts were like horses 11
1Es 4:18 then see a woman lovely in appearance and beauty 6
2Es 15:34 and their appearance is very threatening 15
Jdt 8: 7 She was beautiful in appearance 6
11:23 You are not only beautiful in appearance 6
Wis 14:17 they imagined their appearance far away 13
15: 5 whose appearance arouses yearning in fools 13
19 they are not so beautiful in appearance 13
17: 6 worse than that unseen appearance. 13
Sir 11: 2 nor loathe a man because of his appearance. 12
19:29 A man is known by his appearance 12
25:17 The wickedness of a wife changes her appearance 12
43: 1 the appearance of heaven in a spectacle of glory. 6
LJr 1:63 be compared with them in appearance or power. 9
Sus 1:31 Now Susanna was . . beautiful in appearance. 6
2Mc 2:21 the appearances which came from heaven 7
3:16 To see the appearance of the high priest 9
4Mc 8: 4 struck by their appearance and nobility 8

good appearance 1. μορφή
Tob 1:13 and good appearance in the sight of Shalmaneser 1

handsome appearance 1. εὐμορφία
4Mc 8:10 your youth and handsome appearance. 1

outward appearance 1. עַיִן
1Sm 16: 7 man looks on the outward appearance, but the LORD 1

radiant appearance 1. הוֹד
Dan 10: 8 my radiant appearance was fearfully changed 1

appease 1. אבה 2. כפר 3. נחם 4. καταπραΰνω
Gen 32:20 For he thought, "I may appease him with the present 2
Prv 6:35 nor be appeased though you multiply gifts. 1
16:14 wise man will appease it. 2

Isa 57: 6 Shall I be appeased for these things? 3
2Mc 13:26 convinced them, appeased them 4

append

1Mc 12: 7 you are our brethren, as the appended copy shows. •

appendage 1. יֹתֶרֶת

Exd 29:13 take . . the appendage of the liver 1
22 take . . the appendage of the liver 1
Lev 3: 4 the appendage of the liver which he shall take 1
10 the appendage of the liver which he shall take 1
15 the appendage of the liver which he shall take 1
4: 9 the appendage of the liver which he shall take 1
7: 4 the appendage of the liver which he shall take 1
8:16 he took . . the appendage of the liver 1
25 he took . . the appendage of the liver 1
9:10 the kidneys and the appendage of the liver 1
19 the kidneys, and the appendage of the liver 1

appetite 1. חַיָּה 2. נֶפֶשׁ 3. κοιλία 4. ὄρεξις

Deu 14:26 you desire . . whatever your appetite craves; 2
Job 6: 7 My appetite refuses to touch them; 2
33:20 loathes bread, and his appetite dainty food. 2
38:39 or satisfy the appetite of the young lions 1
Prv 6:30 if he steals to satisfy his appetite 2
13:25 righteous has enough to satisfy his appetite 2
16:26 A worker's appetite works for him; 2
23: 2 put a knife . . if you are a man given to appetite. 2
Ecc 6: 7 the toil . . yet his appetite is not satisfied. 2
Isa 5:14 Therefore Sheol has enlarged its appetite 2
56:11 The dogs have a mighty appetite; 2
Rom 16:18 such persons . . serve . . their own appetites 3
Wis 16: 2 a delicacy to satisfy the desire of appetite; 4
3 might lose the least remnant of appetite 4
Sir 18:30 restrain your appetites. 4
4Mc 1:33 because reason is able to rule over appetites 4
35 the emotions of the appetites are restrained 4

insatiable appetite 1. ἀπληστεύομαι

Sir 37:29 have an insatiable appetite for any luxury 1

applaud 1. κατευφημέω

3Mc 7:13 When they had applauded him in fitting manner 1

apple 1. אִישׁוֹן 2. בָּבָה 3. תַּפּוּחַ

Deu 32:10 cared for him, he kept him as the apple of his eye. 1
Ps 17: 8 Keep me as the apple of the eye; 1
Prv 7: 2 keep my teachings as the apple of your eye; 1
25:11 fitly spoken is like apples of gold in a setting 3
Sng 2: 5 Sustain me with raisins, refresh me with apples; 3
7: 8 and the scent of your breath like apples 3
Jol 1:12 Pomegranate, palm, and apple, all the trees 3
Zec 2: 8 he who touches you touches the apple of his eye. 2

apple of one's eye 1. κόρη

Sir 17:22 like the apple of his eye. 1

apple tree 1. תַּפּוּחַ

Sng 2: 3 As an apple tree among the trees of the wood, so is 1
8: 5 Under the apple tree I awakened you. 1

evenly applied 1. ישר

1Kg 6:35 with gold evenly applied upon the carved work. 1

apply 1. בוא 2. מרח 3. נתן 4. שׁית 5. ἐπιδίδωμι 6. μετασχηματίζω 7. πίπτω 8. προΐστημι 9. προσφέρω 10. vaco

Prv 22:17 apply your mind to my knowledge; 4
23:12 Apply your mind to instruction and your ear 1
Ecc 1:13 I applied my mind to seek and to search out 3
17 I applied my mind to know wisdom and . . madness 3
8: 9 while applying my mind to all that is done 3
16 When I applied my mind to know wisdom 3
Isa 38:21 take a cake of figs, and apply it to the boil 2
1Co 4: 6 I have applied all this to myself and Apol'los 6
Tit 3: 8 may be careful to apply themselves to good deeds 8
14 learn to apply themselves to good deeds 8
2Es 13:54 and have applied yourself to mine 10
Sir 6:32 if you apply yourself you will become clever. 5
2Mc 4:20 it was applied to the construction of triremes. 7
4Mc 11:19 To his back they applied sharp spits 9

apply only to the people 1. κοινός

AEs 15:10 our law applies only to the people. Come near 1

appoint 1. זמן 2. חֹק 3. חֻקָּה 4. יכח 5. יסד 6. יעד 7. כון 8. לקח 9. מוֹעֵד 10. מנה 11. מִשְׁמֶרֶת 12. נתן 13. עמד 14. עשׂה 15. פקד 16. צוה 17. צוה לְ 18. קרא 19. שׂום 20. שׁית 21. שׁתת 22. מנה (A) 23. נתן (A) 24. ἀναδείκνυμι 25. ἀποδείκνυμι 26. ἀπόκειμαι 27. ἀποτάσσω 28. διαταγή 29. διατάσσω 30. διατίθημι 31. ἐπιτρέπω 32. ἡμέρα 33. ἵστημι 34. καθίστημι 35. κληρόω 36. λαμβάνω 37. ὁρίζω 38. ποιέω 39. προσημαίνω 40. προχειρίζω 41. τακτός 42. τάσσω 43. τίθημι 44. χειροτονέω 45. instituo 46. sum

Gen 4:25 God has appointed for me another child 20
24:14 let her be the one whom thou hast appointed 4
44 whom the LORD has appointed for my master's son.' 4
41:34 Let Pharaoh proceed to appoint overseers over 15
Exd 21:13 then I will appoint for you a place to which he may 19
30:16 shall appoint it for the service of the tent 12
31: 6 behold, I have appointed with him Oho'liab 12
Lev 26:16 I will appoint over you sudden terror, 15
Num 1:50 appoint the Levites over the tabernacle 15
3:10 you shall appoint Aaron and his sons 15
36 the appointed charge of the sons of Merar'i 11
4:19 appoint them each to his task and to his burden 19
49 commandment of the LORD . . they were appointed 15
27:16 LORD . . appoint a man over the congregation 15
Deu 1:13 men . . and I will appoint them as your heads.' 19
16:18 appoint judges and officers in all your towns 12
20: 9 commanders . . appointed at the head of the people. 15
Jos 4: 4 called the twelve men . . whom he had appointed 7
20: 2 Appoint the cities of refuge, of which I spoke 12
8 they appointed Bezer in the wilderness 12
1Sm 8: 5 appoint for us a king to govern us like all 19
11 take your sons and appoint them to his chariots 19
12 and he will appoint for himself commanders 19
12: 6 The LORD . . who appointed Moses and Aaron 14
13:11 you did not come within the days appointed 9
14 LORD has appointed him . . prince over his people 16
25:30 and has appointed you prince over Israel 17
2Sm 6:21 who chose . . to appoint me as prince over Israel 16
7:10 And I will appoint a place for my people Israel 19
11 from the time that I appointed judges 16
20: 5 he delayed beyond the set time . . appointed him. 6
1Kg 1:35 I have appointed him to be ruler over Israel 16
12:31 and appointed priests from among all the people 14
32 Jerobo'am appointed a feast on the fifteenth day 14
2Kg 7:17 Now the king had appointed the captain 15
8: 6 So the king appointed an official for her, saying 12
17:32 and appointed . . all sorts of people as priests 14
25:22 he appointed Gedali'ah the son of . . governor. 15
23 the king of Babylon had appointed Gedali'ah 15
1Ch 6:48 the Levites were appointed for all the service 12
9:29 Others . . were appointed over the furniture 10
15:16 chiefs of the Levites to appoint their brethren 13
17 the Levites appointed Heman the son of Jo'el; 13
16: 4 appointed certain of the Levites as ministers 12
7 David first appointed that thanksgiving be sung 12
42 The sons of Jedu'thun were appointed to the gate. •
17: 9 I will appoint a place for my people Israel 19
10 that I appointed judges over my people Israel 16
26:29 Chenani'ah and his sons were appointed •
32 King David appointed him and his brethren 15
2Ch 3: 1 at the place that David had appointed 7
8:14 he appointed the divisions of the priests 13
11:15 he appointed his own priests for the high places 13
22 Rehobo'am appointed Abi'jah . . as chief prince 13
19: 5 He appointed judges in the land 13
8 Jehosh'aphat appointed certain Levites 13
20:21 he appointed those who were to sing to the LORD 13
31: 2 Hezeki'ah appointed the divisions 13
33: 8 land which I appointed for your fathers 13
35: 2 He appointed the priests to their offices 13
Ezr 3: 8 appointed the Levites, from twenty years old 13
7:25 appoint magistrates and judges who may judge 22
10:14 taken foreign wives come at appointed times 1
Neh 5:14 appointed . . governor in the land of Judah 16
7: 1 gatekeepers . . Levites had been appointed 15
3 Appoint guards from among the inhabitants 13
9:17 appointed a leader to return to their bondage 12
10:34 at times appointed, year by year, to burn 1
12:31 appointed two great companies which gave 13
44 that day men were appointed over the chambers 15
13: 4 appointed over the chambers of the house 12
31 wood offering, at appointed times 1
Est 2: 3 And let the king appoint officers . . to gather 15
4: 5 Hathach . . who had been appointed to attend her 13
Job 14: 5 thou hast appointed his bounds that he cannot 14
13 that thou wouldest appoint me a set time 20
23:14 For he will complete what he appoints for me; 2
30:23 death, and to the house appointed for all living. 9
34:23 For he has not appointed a time for any man to go 19
Ps 7: 6 awake, O my God; thou hast appointed a judgment. 16
49:14 Like sheep they are appointed for Sheol; 21
75: 2 At the set time which I appoint I will judge 8
78: 5 testimony in Jacob, and appointed a law in Israel 19
104: 8 to the place which thou didst appoint for them. 5
109: 6 Appoint a wicked man against him; 15
119:138 Thou hast appointed thy testimonies 16
Ecc 3:17 God will judge . . for he has appointed a time •
Jer 1: 5 I appointed you a prophet to the nations. 12
5:24 keeps . . the weeks appointed for the harvest.' 3
15: 3 will appoint over them four kinds of destroyers 15
33:20 and night will not come at their appointed time •
40: 5 whom the king of Babylon appointed governor 15
7 men heard that the king of Babylon had appointed 15
11 and had appointed Gedali'ah the son of Ahi'kam 15
41: 2 whom the king of Babylon had appointed governor 15
47: 7 against the seashore he has appointed it. 6
49:19 and I will appoint over her whomever I choose. 15
50:44 I will appoint over her whomever I choose. 15
51:27 appoint a marshal against her, bring up horses 15
Ezk 36:38 at Jerusalem during her appointed feasts 9
44:14 I will appoint them to keep charge of the temple 12
24 laws and my statutes in all my appointed feasts 9
46:11 At the feasts and the appointed seasons 9
Dan 1:10 king, who appointed your food and your drink 10
11 steward . . appointed over Daniel, Hanani'ah 10
2:16 Daniel . . besought the king to appoint him a time 23
24 king had appointed to destroy the wise men 22
49 appointed Shadrach, Meshach, and Abed'nego 22
3:12 Jews . . appointed over the affairs 22
Hos 1:11 and they shall appoint for themselves one head; 19
6:11 For you also, O Judah, a harvest is appointed. 20
11: 7 so they are appointed to the yoke 18
Jon 1:17 LORD appointed a great fish to swallow up Jonah; 10
4: 6 the LORD God appointed a plant, and made it come up 10
7 God appointed a worm which attacked the plant 10
8 the sun rose, God appointed a sultry east wind 10
Mrk 3:14 he appointed twelve, to be with him 38
Lke 3:13 Collect no more than is appointed you. 29
10: 1 After this the Lord appointed 70 others 24
Joh 15:16 I chose you and appointed you 43
Act 3:20 he may send the Christ appointed for you, Jesus 40
6: 3 whom we may appoint to this duty. 34
12:21 On an appointed day Herod put on his royal robes 41
14:23 had appointed elders for them in every church 44
15: 2 appointed to go up to Jerusalem to the apostles 42
17:31 judge the world . . by a man whom he has appointed 37
22:10 will be told all that is appointed for you to do.' 42
14 God of our fathers appointed you to know his will 40
26:16 to appoint you to serve and bear witness 40
28:23 When they had appointed a day for him 42
Rom 13: 2 resists what God has appointed 28
1Co 12:28 God has appointed in the church first apostles 43
2Co 8:19 appointed by the churches to travel with us 44
Eph 1:12 have been destined and appointed to live 35
1Ti 1:12 by appointing me to his service 43
2: 7 For this I was appointed a preacher and apostle 43
2Ti 1:11 For this gospel I was appointed a preacher 43
Tit 1: 5 appoint elders in every town as I directed you 34
Heb 1: 2 a Son, whom he appointed the heir of all things 43
3: 2 He was faithful to him who appointed him 38
5: 1 every high priest . . is appointed to act on behalf 34
5 but was appointed by him who said to him •
7:28 Indeed, the law appoints men in their weakness 34
28 the oath . . appoints a Son who has been made perfect •
8: 3 every high priest is appointed to offer gifts 34
9:27 just as it is appointed for men to die once 26
1Es 5:58 they appointed the Levites 33
6:27 those who were appointed as local rulers in Syria 27
8:23 appoint judges and justices to judge 24
9:12 come at the time appointed 36
2Es 3: 7 immediately thou didst appoint death for him 45
4:27 to bring . . in their appointed times 46
8:52 a city is built, rest is appointed ‡
Tob 1:21 appointed Ahikar, the son of my brother Anael 42
22 had appointed him second to himself 34
Jdt 5:18 departed from the way which he had appointed 30
Sir 17:17 He appointed a ruler for every nation 34
33: 8 he appointed the different seasons and feasts; •
11 appointed their different ways; •
Bar 1:14 on the days of the feasts and at appointed seasons. 32
Sus 1: 5 two elders . . were appointed as judges. 25
Man 1: 7 thou hast appointed repentance for sinners 37
8 not appointed repentance for the righteous 43
8 appointed repentance for me, who am a sinner. 43
1Mc 1:51 he appointed inspectors over all the people 38
3:55 After this Judas appointed leaders of the people 34
6:55 had appointed to bring up Antiochus his son 34
10:20 we have appointed you today to be the high priest 34
34 sabbaths and new moons and appointed days 25
69 Demetrius appointed Apollonius 34
14:42 and appoint men over its tasks and over the country 34
16:11 appointed governor over the plain of Jericho 34
2Mc 5:22 more barbarous than the man who appointed him; 34
8: 9 Ptolemy promptly appointed Nicanor 40
22 He appointed his brothers also 42
23 Besides, he appointed Eleazar to read aloud •
9:23 my father . . appointed his successor 24
25 I have appointed my son Antiochus to be king 24
10:11 appointed one Lysias 24
14:12 he . . appointed him governor of Judea, 24
26 he had appointed . . Judas, to be his successor 24
3Mc 5:13 since they had escaped the appointed hour 39
4Mc 4:16 and appointed Onias's brother Jason as high priest. 34
18 the king appointed him high priest 31

appoint as treasurer 1. אצר

Neh 13:13 I appointed as treasurers over the storehouses 1

appointed *See* duty, feast, festival, hour, season, signal, time.

appointed place 1. מִפְקָד

Ezk 43:21 it shall be burnt in the appointed place 1

appointment 1. יעד 2. מוֹעֵד 3. מִפְקָד 4. מִשְׁפָּט

1Sm 20:35 Jonathan went . . to the appointment with David 2

2Ch 31:13 by the appointment of Hezeki'ah . . and Azari'ah 3
Ps 119:91 By thy appointment they stand this day; 4
Ams 3: 3 together, unless they have made an appointment? 1

appointment *See also* make.

apportion 1. חלק 2. מנה 3. נחל 4. נפל בְּחֶבֶל 5. נתן 6. διαιρέω 7. ἐξαριθμέω 8. καταμερίζω 9. μερίζω

Jos 18: 2 whose inheritance had not yet been apportioned. 1
10 there Joshua apportioned the land to the people 1
2Ch 31:14 to apportion the contribution reserved 5
Job 7: 3 nights of misery are apportioned to me. 2
Ps 78:55 he apportioned them for a possession 4
Isa 49: 8 to apportion the desolate heritages; 3
1Co 12:11 who apportions to each one individually 6
2Co 10:13 keep to the limits God has apportioned us 9
Heb 7: 2 to him Abraham apportioned a tenth part 9
Sir 1: 9 he saw her and apportioned her 7
19 He saw her and apportioned her 7
44: 2 The Lord apportioned to them great glory 1
3Mc 6:31 they apportioned to celebrants the place 8

appreciate 1. εὑρίσκω

Sir 31:22 in the end you will appreciate my words 1

approach 1. בוא 2. מִפְּנֵי 3. נגשׁ 4. קָרֵב 5. קָרֵב 6. קרב 7. קרב אֶל 8. קרב (A) 9. ἀνάβασις 10. ἐγγίζω 11. εἰσέρχομαι πρός 12. ἐπέρχομαι 13. ἐφίστημι 14. ἔφοδος 15. προσάγω 16. πρόσβασιν ποιέω 17. πρόσβασις 18. προσεγγίζω 19. προσέρχομαι 20. προσίημι 21. προσπορεύομαι 22. πρόσωπον 23. συνεγγίζω 24. τόπος 25. appropinquo 26. venio

Gen 20: 4 Now Abim'elech had not approached her, so he said 6
27:41 days of mourning for my father are approaching; 6
Exd 40:32 when they approached the altar, they washed; 6
Lev 18: 6 None of you shall approach any one near of kin 6
14 you shall not approach his wife; she is your aunt 6
19 You shall not approach a woman to uncover her 6
20:16 If a woman approaches any beast and lies with it 6
21:17 None . . may approach to offer the bread 6
23 not come near the veil or approach the altar 3
22: 3 If any one . . approaches the holy things 6
Deu 2:19 when you approach the frontier of the sons of Ammon 6
31:14 Behold, the days approach when you must die; 6
Jos 8: 5 I, and all . . with me, will approach the city. 7
1Sm 9:18 Then Saul approached Samuel in the gate, and said 3
2Kg 11: 8 and whoever approaches the ranks is to be slain. 1
Ezr 4: 2 approached Zerub'babel and the heads of fathers' 3
9: 1 officials approached me and said, "The people 3
Est 5: 2 Then Esther approached and touched the top 6
Job 31:37 like a prince I would approach him. 6
Isa 41: 1 let them approach, then let them speak; 3
Jer 30:21 I will make him draw near, and he shall approach me 3
21 for who would dare of himself to approach me? 3
37:11 withdrawn . . at the approach of Pharaoh's army 2
Ezk 18: 6 or approach a woman in her time of impurity 6
42:13 the priests who approach the LORD shall eat 5
44:16 they shall approach my table, to minister to me 6
45: 4 and approach the LORD to minister to him; 4
Dan 7:16 approached one of those who stood there 8
Lke 12:33 where no thief approaches and no moth destroys. 10
Act 9: 3 Now as he journeyed he approached Damascus 10
1Es 5:68 So they approached Zerubbabel and Jeshua 19
2Es 5:50 Or is she now approaching old age? 25
10:25 so that I was too frightened to approach her ‡
12:21 the time when its end approaches 25
13: 9 he saw the onrush of the approaching multitude 26
Tob 6: 9 When they approached Ecbatana 18
14 he harms no one except those who approach her. 15
17 when you approach her, rise up, both of you 21
Jdt 4: 2 very greatly terrified at his approach 22
7 the approach was narrow 17
7: 7 examined the approaches to the city 9
12:13 Bagoas . . approached her and said 11
Wis 1: 5 ashamed at the approach of unrighteousness. 12
Sir 1:28 do not approach him with a divided mind. 19
9:13 if you approach him, make no misstep 19
21: 2 for if you approach sin, it will bite you 19
41:22 do not approach her bed 13
1Mc 3:16 When he approached the ascent of Beth-horon 10
5:42 When Judas approached the stream of water 10
11: 4 When he approached Azotus 10
13:23 When he approached Baskama, he killed Jonathan 10
2Mc 11: 5 Invading Judea, he approached Beth-zur 23
12:21 When Timothy learned of the approach of Judas 14
21 because of the narrowness of all the approaches. 24
3Mc 1:26 and began now to approach 16
5:14 approached the king and nudged him. 19
4Mc 14:19 sting those who approach their hive 20

approach *See also* sign.

appropriate 1. ἀνήκω 2. ἄξιος 3. ἀφορίζω 4. καθήκω 5. πρέπω

1Mc 10:40 from appropriate places. 1
12:11 both in our feasts and on other appropriate days 4
2Mc 11:36 that we may make proposals appropriate for you. 4
3Mc 7:19 landed in peace with appropriate thanksgiving 5
4Mc 3:20 had both appropriated money to them 3
5:11 adopt a mind appropriate to your years 2

most appropriate 1. validus

2Es 10: 8 It is most appropriate to mourn now 1

approval 1. ἔπαινος 2. εὐδοκία 3. χάρις

Jer 44:19 was it without our husbands' approval •
Rom 13: 3 do what is good, and you will receive his approval 1
1Pe 2:20 you have God's approval. 3
Sir 2:16 Those who fear the Lord will seek his approval 2
32:10 approval precedes a modest man. 3

approval *See also* give, receive.

approve 1. ברר 2. טוֹב בְּעֵינַיִם 3. עוד 4. ראה 5. רצה 6. δοκιμάζω 7. δόκιμος 8. ἐπιγινώσκω 9. εὐδοκέω 10. εὐδοκία 11. κρίνω 12. παραινέω 13. συνευδοκέω 14. χάρις 15. probo

1Sm 29: 6 Nevertheless the lords do not approve of you. 2
1Ch 7:40 men of Asher, heads of fathers' houses, approved 1
Job 29:11 when the eye saw, it approved; 3
Ecc 9: 7 God has already approved what you do. 5
Lam 3:36 to subvert a man . . the Lord does not approve. 4
Act 22:20 I also was standing by and approving 13
Rom 1:32 but approve those who practice them. 13
2:18 know his will and approve what is excellent 6
14:18 is acceptable to God and approved by men. 7
22 no reason to judge himself for what he approves. 6
16:10 Greet Apel'les, who is approved in Christ. 7
Php 1:10 so that you may approve what is excellent 6
1Th 2: 4 just as we have been approved by God 6
2Ti 2:15 to present yourself to God as one approved 7
1Pe 2:19 one is approved if, mindful of God, he endures pain 14
1Es 4:39 All men approve her deeds 9
6:22 if it is approved by our lord the king 11
2Es 5:27 thou hast given the law which is approved by all. 15
Sir 11:17 what he approves will have lasting success. 10
42: 8 will be approved before all men. 6
2Mc 4: 3 one of Simon's approved agents 6
3Mc 7:12 approving the truth of what they said 12
4Mc 15:27 She did not approve the deliverance 8

apron 1. חֲגוֹרָה 2. σιμικίνθιον

Gen 3: 7 leaves together and made themselves aprons. 1
Act 19:12 aprons were carried away from his body to the sick 2

apt 1. ἀκριβής

Prv 15:23 To make an apt answer is a joy to a man •
Sir 18:29 pour forth apt proverbs. 1

apt *See also* teacher.

arbitrarily 1. ἑκούσιος

4Mc 8:25 Not even the law itself would arbitrarily slay 1

arc 1. κυκλόω

Sir 43:12 It encircles the heaven with its glorious arc; 1

arch 1. camera

2Es 16:59 who has spread out the heaven like an arch 1

archangel 1. ἀρχάγγελος 2. archangelus

1Th 4:16 will descend from heaven . . with the archangel's call 1
Jde 1: 9 archangel Michael, contending with the devil 1
2Es 4:36 Jeremiel the archangel answered them and said 2

archer 1. בַּעַל חִצִּים 2. דרך 3. ירה 4. ירה אִישׁ בַּקֶּשֶׁת 5. קֶשֶׁת 6. רַב 7. רֹמֵה קֶשֶׁת 8. τοξότης 9. sagittarius

Gen 49:23 The archers fiercely attacked him 1
1Sm 31: 3 hard upon Saul, and the archers found him; 4
3 and he was badly wounded by the archers. 3
2Sm 11:24 the archers shot at your servants from the wall; 3
1Ch 10: 3 Saul, and the archers found him; 3
3 Saul . . was wounded by the archers. 3
2Ch 35:23 the archers shot King Josi'ah; and the king said 3
Job 16:13 his archers surround me. 6
Prv 26:10 Like an archer who wounds everybody is he who 6
Isa 21:17 the remainder of the archers . . will be few; 5
Jer 4:29 At the noise of horseman and archer 7
50:29 Summon archers against Babylon 6
51: 3 Let not the archer bend his bow 2
2Es 16: 7 Can one turn back an arrow shot by a strong archer? 9
16 an arrow shot by a mighty archer does not return 9
Jdt 2:15 together with 12,000 archers on horseback 8
1Mc 9:11 the slingers and the archers went ahead 8

archive 1. בֵּית גְּנַז (A) 2. סְפַר (A) 3. ἀποδείκνυμι 4. βιβλιοφυλάκιον

Ezr 5:17 let search be made in the royal archives there 1
6: 1 house of the archives where the documents 2
1Es 6:21 in the royal archives of our lord the king 4
23 royal archives that were deposited in Babylon. 4
1Mc 14:23 put a copy of their words in the public archives 3

arduous 1. ἰσχυρός

Wis 10:12 in his arduous contest she gave him the victory 1

area 1. גְּבוּל 2. περίβολος

Gen 23:17 field, throughout its whole area, was made over 1
Deu 19: 3 divide into three parts the area of the land 1
Ezk 40: 5 a wall all around the outside of the temple area •
42:15 measuring the interior of the temple area •
15 and measured the temple area round about. •
45: 6 of the city an area 5,000 cubits broad •
4Mc 4:11 half dead in the temple area that was open to all 2

sacred area 1. מִקְדָּשׁ

Ezk 43:21 it shall be burnt . . outside the sacred area. 1

arena 1. γυμνασία

4Mc 11:20 summoned to an arena of sufferings for religion 1

wrestling arena 1. παλαίστρα

2Mc 4:14 the unlawful proceedings in the wrestling arena 1

argue 1. יכח 2. ריב 3. שׁפט 4. διαλέγομαι 5. διαλογίζομαι 6. διαμάχομαι 7. ἐρίζω 8. συζητέω

Job 13: 3 I desire to argue my case with God. 1
15: 3 Should he argue in unprofitable talk 1
40: 2 He who argues with God, let him answer it. 1
Prv 25: 9 Argue your case with your neighbor himself 2
Isa 43:26 Put me in remembrance, let us argue together; 3
Mat 21:25 And they argued with one another 5
Mrk 8:11 The Pharisees came and began to argue with him 8
9:14 scribes arguing with them. 8
11:31 they argued with one another 5
Act 17: 2 for three weeks he argued with them 4
17 he argued in the synagogue with the Jews 4
18: 4 he argued in the synagogue every sabbath 4
19 went into the synagogue and argued with the Jews. 4
19: 8 arguing and pleading about the kingdom of God; 4
9 and argued daily in the hall of Tyran'nus. 4
24:25 as he argued about justice and self-control 4
Sir 8: 3 Do not argue with a chatterer 6
11: 9 argue about a matter which does not concern you 7

argument 1. שׁפט 2. תּוֹכַחַת 3. διαλογισμός 4. λέγω 5. λογισμός 6. λόγος

Job 23: 4 and fill my mouth with arguments. 2
Prv 29: 9 If a wise man has an argument with a fool, the fool 1
Lke 9:46 an argument arose among them 3
2Co 10: 5 We destroy arguments and every proud obstacle 5
4Mc 1: 5 Their attempt at argument is ridiculous! 4
8:16 what arguments might have been used 6

argument *See also* make.

ariel 1. אֲרִיאֵל

2Sm 23:20 a doer of great deeds; he smote two ariels of Moab. 1
1Ch 11:22 doer of great deeds; he smote two ariels of Moab. 1

aright 1. ישׁר 2. כֵּן 3. לַמִּשְׁפָּט

Prv 15:21 but a man of understanding walks aright. 1
Isa 28:26 For he is instructed aright; his God teaches him. 3
Jer 8: 6 and listened, but they have not spoken aright; 2

aright *See also* direct, lead, order.

set aright 1. כון

Job 11:13 If you set your heart aright 1

arise 1. היה 2. זרח 3. נשׂא 4. עור 5. עמד 6. קום 7. קוּם (A) 8. ἀνίστημι 9. ἀντανίστημι 10. ἄρχω 11. γίνομαι 12. ἐγείρω 13. εἰσέρχομαι 14. ἐνίστημι 15. ἐξανίστημι 16. ἵστημι 17. καθίστημι 18. exsurgo 19. nascor 20. proficiscor 21. surgo

Gen 13:17 Arise, walk through the length and the breadth 6
19:15 angels urged Lot, saying, "Arise, take your wife 6
33 know when she lay down or when she arose. 6
35 and the younger arose, and lay with him; 6
35 not know when she lay down or when she arose. 6
21:18 Arise, lift up the lad, and hold him fast 6
22: 3 Abraham . . arose and went to the place 6
19 they arose and went together to Beer-sheba; 6
24:10 and he arose, and went to Mesopota'mia 6
54 When they arose in the morning, he said, "Send me 6
61 Then Rebekah and her maids arose 6
27:31 Let my father arise, and eat of his son's game 6
43 arise, flee to Laban my brother in Haran 6
28: 2 Arise, go to Paddan-aram to the house of Bethu'el 6
31:13 Now arise, go forth from this land, and return 6
17 Jacob arose, and set his sons and his wives 6
21 He fled with all that he had, and arose and crossed 6
32:22 The same night he arose and took his two wives 6
35: 1 God said to Jacob, "Arise, go up to Bethel 6
3 then let us arise and go up to Bethel 6
37: 7 and lo, my sheaf arose and stood upright; 6
38:19 she arose and went away, and taking off her veil 6
41:30 after them there will arise seven years 6
43: 8 Send the lad with me, and we will arise and go 6
13 also your brother, and arise, go again to the man; 6
15 and they arose and went down to Egypt 6
Exd 1: 8 Now there arose a new king over Egypt 6
Num 10:35 Arise, O LORD, and let thy enemies be scattered; 6

Deu 9:12 LORD said to me, 'Arise, go down quickly from here; 6
10:11 Arise, go on your journey at the head of the people 6
13: 1 If a prophet arises among you, or a dreamer 6
17: 8 If any case arises requiring decision *
8 then you shall arise and go up to the place 6
34:10 not arisen a prophet since in Israel like Moses 6
Jos 1: 2 arise, go over this Jordan you and all this people 6
7:10 Arise, why have you thus fallen upon your face? 6
8: 1 take all the fighting men . . and arise, go up to Ai; 6
3 Joshua arose, and all the fighting men, to go up 6
24: 9 Then Balak . . arose and fought against Israel; 6
Jdg 2:10 there arose another generation after them 6
3:20 from God for you." And he arose from his seat. 6
4: 9 Deb'orah arose, and went with Barak to Kedesh. 6
5: 7 ceased until you arose, Deb'orah, arose as a mother 6
7 you arose, Deb'orah, arose as a mother in Israel. 6
12 Arise, Barak, lead away your captives, O son 6
7: 9 LORD said to him, "Arise, go down against the camp; 6
15 and said, "Arise; for the LORD has given the host 6
8:21 And Gideon arose and slew Zebah and Zalmun'na; 6
10: 1 arose to deliver Israel Tola the son of Pu'ah 6
3 After him arose Ja'ir the Gileadite, who judged 6
13:11 Mano'ah arose and went after his wife, and came 6
16: 3 at midnight he arose and took hold of the doors 6
18: 9 Arise, and let us go up against them; for we have 6
19: 3 her husband arose and went after her, to speak 6
20: 8 all the people arose as one man, saying, "We will not 6
18 The people of Israel arose and went up to Bethel 6
Rut 3:14 but arose before one could recognize another; 6
1Sm 3: 6 Samuel arose and went to Eli, and said, "Here I am 6
8 And he arose and went to Eli, and said, "Here I am 6
9: 3 Take . . and arise, go and look for the asses. 6
26 Saul arose, and both he and Samuel went out 6
13:15 Samuel arose, and went up from Gilgal to Gib'e-ah 6
14:38 and know and see how this sin has arisen today. 1
16:12 And the LORD said, "Arise, anoint him; for this is he. 6
17:35 if he arose against me, I caught him by his beard 6
48 When the Philistine arose and came and drew near 6
18:27 David arose and went . . and killed 200 6
23: 4 Arise, go down to Kei'lah; for I will give 6
13 David and his . . arose and departed from Kei'lah 6
24 And they arose, and went to Ziph ahead of Saul. 6
24: 4 David arose and . . cut off the skirt of Saul's robe 6
8 David also arose, and went out of the cave 6
26: 2 Saul arose and went down to the wilderness 6
27: 2 David arose and went over, he and the 600 men 6
28:23 he arose from the earth, and sat upon the bed. 6
31:12 valiant men arose, and went all night 6
2Sm 2:14 Let the young men arise and play before us. 6
14 And Jo'ab said, "Let them arise. 6
15 Then they arose and passed over by number 6
3:21 I will arise and go, and will gather all Israel 6
6: 2 David arose and went . . from Ba'ale-judah 6
11: 2 when David arose from his couch and was walking 6
12:20 Then David arose from the earth, and washed 6
21 but when the child died, you arose and ate food. 6
13:15 And Amnon said to her, "Arise, be gone. 6
29 Then all the king's sons arose, and each . . fled. 6
31 Then the king arose, and rent his garments 6
14:23 So Jo'ab arose and went to Geshur 6
31 Then Jo'ab arose and went to Ab'salom at his house 6
15: 9 Go in peace." So he arose, and went to Hebron. 6
14 Arise, and let us flee; or . . there will be no escape 6
17:21 Arise, and go quickly over the water; 6
22 David arose, and all the people who were with him 6
19: 7 Now therefore arise, go out and speak kindly 6
8 Then the king arose, and took his seat in the gate. 6
24:11 when David arose in the morning, the word . . came 6
1Kg 1:50 he arose, and went, and caught hold of the horns 6
2:40 Shim'e-i arose and saddled an ass, and went to Gath 6
3:12 and none like you shall arise after you. 6
20 she arose at midnight, and took my son from beside 6
8:54 he arose from before the altar of the LORD 6
11:40 Jerobo'am arose, and fled into Egypt, to Shishak 6
14: 2 Arise, and disguise yourself, that it be not known 6
4 she arose, and went to Shiloh, and came to the house 6
12 Arise therefore, go to your house. 6
17 Jerobo'am's wife arose, and departed 6
17: 9 Arise, go to Zar'ephath . . and dwell there. 6
10 So he arose and went to Zar'ephath; 6
19: 3 he was afraid, and he arose and went for his life 6
5 an angel . . said to him, "Arise and eat. 6
7 Arise and eat, else the journey will be too great 6
8 he arose, and ate and drank 6
21 he arose and went after Eli'jah, and ministered 6
21: 7 Arise, and eat bread, and let your heart be 6
15 Arise, take possession of the vineyard of Naboth 6
16 Ahab arose to go down to the vineyard of Naboth 6
18 Arise, go down to meet Ahab . . who is in Sama'ria; 6
2Kg 1: 3 Arise, go up to meet the messengers . . and say 6
15 So he arose and went down with him to the king 6
4:30 So he arose and followed her. 6
7: 5 So they arose at twilight to go to the . . Syrians; 6
8: 1 Arise, and depart with your household 6
2 So the woman arose, and did according to the word 6
9: 6 So he arose, and went into the house; 6
11: 1 she arose and destroyed all the royal family. 6
12:20 His servants arose and made a conspiracy 6
23:25 Before . . nor did any like him arise after him. 6
25:26 all the people . . arose, and went to Egypt; 6
1Ch 10:12 all the valiant men arose 6
20: 4 there arose war with the Philistines at Gezer; 5
22:16 gold, silver, bronze, and iron. Arise and be doing! 6
19 Arise and build the sanctuary of the LORD God 6
2Ch 6:41 now arise, O LORD God, and go to thy resting place 6
22:10 she arose and destroyed all the royal family 6
29:12 Then the Levites arose, Mahath the son of Ama'sai 6
30:27 the priests and the Levites arose and blessed 6
Ezr 3: 2 Then arose Jeshua . . with his fellow priests 6
5: 2 arose and began to rebuild the house of God 7
10: 4 Arise, for it is your task, and we are with you; 6
5 Then Ezra arose and made the leading priests 6
Neh 2:12 Then I arose in the night, I and a few men with me; 6
20 we his servants will arise and build; 6
4:14 I looked, and arose, and said to the nobles 6
5: 1 Now there arose a great outcry of the people 1
7:65 priest with Urim and Thummim should arise. 5
Job 1:20 Then Job arose, and rent his robe 6
7: 4 When I lie down I say, 'When shall I arise?' 6
25: 3 Upon whom does his light not arise? 6
Ps 3: 7 Arise, O LORD! Deliver me, O my God! 6
7: 6 Arise, O LORD, in thy anger, lift thyself up 6
9:19 Arise, O LORD! Let not man prevail; 6
10:12 Arise, O LORD; O God, lift up thy hand; 6
12: 5 because the needy groan, I will now arise 6
17:13 Arise, O LORD! confront them, overthrow them! 6
27: 3 heart shall not fear; though war arise against me 6
68: 1 Let God arise, let his enemies be scattered; 6
74:22 Arise, O God, plead thy cause; 6
76: 9 when God arose to establish judgment to save all 6
78: 6 arise and tell them to their children 6
82: 8 Arise, O God, judge the earth; 6
102:13 Thou wilt arise and have pity on Zion; 6
132: 8 Arise, O LORD, and go to thy resting place 6
Prv 6: 9 When will you arise from your sleep? 6
Sng 2:10 Arise, my love, my fair one, and come away; 6
13 Arise, my love, my fair one, and come away. 6
5: 5 I arose to open to my beloved, and my hands dripped 6
Isa 21: 5 eat, they drink. Arise, O princes, oil the shield! 6
23:12 daughter of Sidon; arise, pass over to Cyprus 6
26:14 they are shades, they will not arise; 6
31: 2 will arise against the house of the evildoers 6
33:10 Now I will arise," says the LORD 6
49: 7 Kings shall see and arise; princes 6
52: 2 from the dust, arise, O captive Jerusalem; 6
60: 1 Arise, shine; for your light has come 6
2 but the LORD will arise upon you 2
Jer 1:17 arise, and say to them everything that I command 6
2:27 time of their trouble they say, 'Arise and save us!' 6
28 Let them arise, if they can save you 6
13: 4 and arise, go to the Euphra'tes, and hide it there 6
6 the LORD said to me, "Arise, go to the Euphra'tes 6
18: 2 Arise, and go down to the potter's house 6
26:17 certain of the elders of the land arose and spoke 6
31: 6 Arise, and let us go up to Zion, to the LORD our God. 6
46:16 Arise, and let us go back to our own people 6
Lam 2:19 Arise, cry out in the night, at the . . watches! 6
Ezk 3:12 and as the glory of the LORD arose from its place *
22 and he said to me, "Arise, go forth into the plain 6
23 So I arose and went forth into the plain; 6
Dan 2:39 After you shall arise another kingdom inferior 7
6:19 king arose and went in haste to the den of lions. 7
7: 5 it was told, 'Arise, devour much flesh.' 7
17 four kings who shall arise out of the earth. 7
24 horns, out of this kingdom ten kings shall arise 7
24 arise, and another shall arise after them; 7
8:22 in place of which four others arose *
22 four kingdoms shall arise from his nation 5
23 king of bold countenance . . shall arise. 5
11: 2 Behold, three more kings shall arise in Persia; 5
3 Then a mighty king shall arise, who shall rule 5
4 when he has arisen, his kingdom shall be broken 5
7 branch from her roots shall arise in his place; 5
20 arise in his place one who shall send an exactor 5
21 In his place shall arise a contemptible person 5
12: 1 time shall arise Michael, the great prince 5
Hos 10:14 the tumult of war shall arise among your people 6
Jon 1: 2 Arise, go to Nin'eveh, that great city 6
6 Arise, call upon your god! 6
3: 2 Arise, go to Nin'eveh, that great city, and proclaim 6
3 Jonah arose and went to Nin'eveh 6
6 he arose from his throne, removed his robe 6
Mic 2:10 Arise and go, for this is no place to rest; 6
4:13 Arise and thresh, O daughter of Zion 6
6: 1 Arise, plead your case before the mountains 6
Hab 1: 3 strife and contention arise. 3
2: 7 Will not your debtors suddenly arise 6
19 to a wooden thing, Awake; to a dumb stone, Arise! 4
Zep 3: 8 for the day when I arise as a witness. 6
Mat 8:24 behold, there arose a great storm on the sea 11
9:25 took her by the hand, and the girl arose. 12
12:41 The men of Nin'eveh will arise at the judgment 8
42 The queen of the South will arise at the judgment 12
13:21 and when tribulation or persecution arises 11
24:11 many false prophets will arise 12
24 For false Christs and false prophets will arise 12
Mrk 4:17 then, when tribulation or persecution arises 11
37 a great storm of wind arose 11
5:41 which means, "Little girl, I say to you, arise. 12
7:24 And from there he arose 8
9:27 lifted him up, and he arose. 8
13:22 False Christs and false prophets will arise 12
Lke 1:39 In those days Mary arose 8
4:38 he arose and left the synagogue 8
6:48 when a flood arose 11
7:14 he said, "Young man, I say to you, arise. 12
16 A great prophet has arisen among us! 12
8:54 he called, saying, "Child, arise. 12
9:46 an argument arose among them 13
11:31 The queen of the South will arise at the judgment 12
32 The men of Nin'eveh will arise at the judgment 8
15:14 a great famine arose in that country 11
18 I will arise and go to my father 8
20 he arose and came to his father 8
22:24 A dispute also arose among them 11
23: 1 Then the whole company of them arose 8
Joh 3:25 Now a discussion arose between John's disciples 11
Act 5:36 before these days Theu'das arose 8
37 Judas the Galilean arose 8
6: 9 some of those . . arose and disputed with Stephen. 8
7:18 till there arose over Egypt another king 8
8: 1 a great persecution arose against the church 11
9: 8 Saul arose from the ground 12
11:19 the persecution that arose over Stephen 11
15:39 And there arose a sharp contention 11
19:23 About that time there arose no little stir 11
20:30 will arise men speaking perverse things 8
23: 7 a dissension arose 11
9 Then a great clamor arose 11
Eph 5:14 it is said, "Awake, O sleeper, and arise from the dead 8
Heb 7:11 need . . for another priest to arise 8
15 when another priest arises 8
2Pe 2: 1 false prophets also arose among the people 11
Rev 12: 7 Now war arose in heaven, Michael and his angels 11
1Es 2: 8 Then arose the heads of families 17
5:58 Jeshua arose, and his sons and brethren 16
6: 2 arose and began to build the house of the Lord 16
8:95 Arise and take action, for it is your task 8
96 Then Ezra arose 8
2Es 11:12 behold, on the right side one wing arose 21
13 Then the next wing arose and reigned 18
12: 2 the two wings . . arose and set themselves up ‡
13 when a kingdom shall arise on earth 18
18 great struggles shall arise 19
20 Eight kings shall arise in it 18
32 who will arise from the posterity of David ‡
13: 2 behold, a wind arose from the sea 18
57 Then I arose and walked in the field 20
Tob 8: 9 Raguel arose and went and dug a grave 8
10:10 Raguel arose and gave him his wife Sarah 8
Jdt 7:29 Then great and general lamentation arose 11
12: 5 Along toward the morning watch she arose 8
14:19 shouts arose in the midst of the camp. 11
Sir 17:23 Afterward he will arise and requite them 15
47:21 a disobedient kingdom arose out of Ephraim. 10
48: 1 Then the prophet Elijah arose like a fire 8
Bar 3:19 to Hades, and others have arisen in their place. 9
5: 5 Arise, O Jerusalem, stand upon the height and look 8
Bel 1:39 Daniel arose and ate 8
1Mc 13:44 a great tumult arose in the city. 11
14:41 until a trustworthy prophet should arise 8
16: 5 Early in the morning they arose 8
2Mc 5: 5 When a false rumor arose that Antiochus was dead 11
3Mc 3:24 a sudden disorder should later arise against us 14
5:32 an affection arising from our nurture in common *
4Mc 5:13 any transgression that arises out of compulsion. 11

arise *See also* contradiction.

arise early 1. שכם

Gen 31:55 Early in the morning Laban arose 1
Jos 8:10 And Joshua arose early in the morning 1
Jdg 19: 5 they arose early in the morning, and he prepared 1
8 he arose early in the morning to depart; 1
9 tomorrow you shall arise early in the morning 1
2Kg 19:35 when men arose early in the morning, behold 1
Isa 37:36 and when men arose early in the morning 1

ark 1. אָרוֹן 2. תֵּבָה 3. κιβωτός 4. arca

Gen 6:14 Make yourself an ark of gopher wood; 2
14 make rooms in the ark, and cover it inside and out 2
15 the length of the ark 300 cubits 2
16 Make a roof for the ark, and finish it to a cubit 2
16 for the ark, and finish it to a cubit above; 2
18 and you shall come into the ark, you, your sons 2
19 you shall bring two of every sort into the ark 2
7: 1 Go into the ark, you and all your household 2
7 him went into the ark, to escape the waters 2
9 two and two, male and female, went into the ark 2
13 three wives of his sons with them entered the ark 2
15 They went into the ark with Noah 2
17 and the waters increased, and bore up the ark 2
18 the earth; and the ark floated on the face 2
23 those that were with him in the ark. 2
8: 1 that were with him in the ark. 2
4 the ark came to rest upon the mountains 2
6 Noah opened the window of the ark 2

9 she returned to him to the ark 2
9 took her and brought her into the ark with him. 2
10 again he sent forth the dove out of the ark; 2
13 Noah removed the covering of the ark, and looked 2
16 Go forth from the ark, you and your wife 2
19 the earth, went forth by families out of the ark. 2
9:10 the earth with you, as many as came out of the ark. 2
18 The sons of Noah who went forth from the ark 2
Exd 25:10 They shall make an ark of acacia wood; 1
14 on the sides of the ark, to carry the ark by them. 1
14 on the sides of the ark, to carry the ark by them. 1
15 The poles shall remain in the rings of the ark; 1
16 you shall put into the ark the testimony 1
21 you shall put the mercy seat on the top of the ark; 1
21 in the ark you shall put the testimony 1
22 cherubim that are upon the ark of the testimony 1
26:33 bring the ark of the testimony in thither within 1
34 mercy seat upon the ark of the testimony 1
30: 6 the veil that is by the ark of the testimony 1
26 you shall anoint . . the ark of the testimony 1
31: 7 tent of meeting, and the ark of the testimony 1
35:12 the ark with its poles, the mercy seat, and the veil 1
37: 1 Bez'alel made the ark of acacia wood; 1
5 poles into the rings on the sides of the ark 1
5 on the sides of the ark, to carry the ark. 1
39:35 the ark of the testimony with its poles 1
40: 3 you shall put in it the ark of the testimony 1
3 and you shall screen the ark with the veil. 1
5 golden altar . . before the ark of the testimony 1
20 he took the testimony and put it into the ark 1
20 and put the poles on the ark, and set the mercy seat 1
20 and set the mercy seat above on the ark; 1
21 he brought the ark into the tabernacle 1
21 and screened the ark of the testimony; 1
Lev 16: 2 before the mercy seat which is upon the ark 1
Num 3:31 their charge was to be the ark, the table 1
4: 5 cover the ark of the testimony with it; 1
7:89 mercy seat that was upon the ark of the testimony 1
10:33 ark of the covenant of the LORD went before them 1
35 whenever the ark set out, Moses said, "Arise, O LORD 1
14:44 neither the ark of the covenant of the LORD 1
Deu 10: 1 come up to me . . and make an ark of wood. 1
2 you shall put them in the ark.' 1
3 I made an ark of acacia wood, and hewed two tables 1
5 put the tables in the ark which I had made; 1
8 Levi to carry the ark of the covenant of the LORD 1
31: 9 sons of Levi, who carried the ark of the covenant 1
25 who carried the ark of the covenant of the LORD 1
26 put it by the side of the ark of the covenant 1
Jos 3: 3 see the ark of the covenant of the LORD your God 1
6 Take up the ark of the covenant, and pass on before 1
6 And they took up the ark of the covenant, and went 1
8 the priests who bear the ark of the covenant 1
11 the ark of the covenant of the Lord . . is to pass 1
13 feet of the priests who bear the ark of the LORD 1
14 the priests bearing the ark of the covenant 1
15 when those who bore the ark had come to the Jordan 1
15 feet of the priests bearing the ark were dipped 1
17 who bore the ark of the covenant of the LORD 1
4: 5 Pass on before the ark of the LORD your God 1
7 cut off before the ark of the covenant of the LORD; 1
9 of the priests bearing the ark of the covenant 1
10 the priests who bore the ark stood in the midst 1
11 the ark of the LORD and the priests passed over 1
16 the priests who bear the ark of the testimony 1
18 when the priests bearing the ark of the covenant 1
6: 4 bear seven trumpets of rams' horns before the ark; 1
6 Take up the ark of the covenant 1
6 seven . . rams' horns before the ark of the LORD. 1
7 the armed men pass on before the ark of the LORD. 1
8 the ark of the covenant of the LORD following 1
9 and the rear guard came after the ark 1
11 he caused the ark of the LORD to compass the city 1
12 and the priests took up the ark of the LORD. 1
13 bearing the . . horns before the ark of the LORD 1
13 and the rear guard came after the ark of the LORD 1
7: 6 fell . . upon his face before the ark of the LORD 1
8:33 all Israel . . stood on opposite sides of the ark 1
33 priests who carried the ark of the covenant 1
Jdg 20:27 for the ark of the covenant of God was there 1
1Sm 3: 3 the temple of the LORD, where the ark of God was. 1
4: 3 bring the ark of the covenant of the LORD here 1
4 sent to Shiloh, and brought from there the ark 1
4 were there with the ark of the covenant of God. 1
5 the ark of the covenant of the LORD came 1
6 the ark of the LORD had come to the camp 1
11 And the ark of God was captured; 1
13 for his heart trembled for the ark of God. 1
17 and the ark of God has been captured. 1
18 When he mentioned the ark of God, Eli fell over 1
19 the tidings that the ark of God was captured 1
21 because the ark of God had been captured 1
22 glory has . . for the ark of God has been captured. 1
5: 1 When the Philistines captured the ark of God 1
2 Philistines took the ark of God . . and set it up 1
3 face downward . . before the ark of the LORD. 1
4 face downward . . before the ark of the LORD 1
7 The ark of the God of Israel must not remain 1
8 What shall we do with the ark of the God of Israel? 1

8 Let the ark of the God of Israel be brought around 1
8 they brought the ark of the God of Israel there. 1
10 So they sent the ark of God to Ekron. 1
10 when the ark of God came to Ekron 1
10 brought . . the ark of the God of Israel to slay us 1
11 Send away the ark of the God of Israel 1
6: 1 The ark of the LORD was in the country 1
2 What shall we do with the ark of the LORD? 1
3 If you send away the ark of the God of Israel 1
8 take the ark of the LORD and place it on the cart 1
11 And they put the ark of the LORD on the cart 1
13 when they lifted up their eyes and saw the ark 1
15 Levites took down the ark of the LORD and the box 1
18 stone, beside which they set . . the ark of the LORD 1
19 because they looked into the ark of the LORD; 1
21 Philistines have returned the ark of the LORD. 1
7: 1 the men . . came and took up the ark of the LORD 1
1 Elea'zar, to have charge of the ark of the LORD. 1
2 the day that the ark was lodged at Kir'iath-je'arim 1
14:18 Saul said to Ahi'jah, "Bring hither the ark of God. 1
18 the ark of God went at that time with the people 1
2Sm 6: 2 went . . to bring up from there the ark of God 1
3 And they carried the ark of God upon a new cart 1
4 were driving the new cart with the ark of God; 1
4 with the ark of God; and Ahi'o went before the ark. 1
6 Uzzah put out his hand to the ark of God 1
7 because he put forth his hand to the ark; •
7 and he died there beside the ark of God. 1
9 he said, "How can the ark of the LORD come to me? 1
10 David was not willing to take the ark of the LORD 1
11 the ark of the LORD remained . . three months; 1
12 The LORD has blessed . . because of the ark of God. 1
12 David went and brought up the ark of God 1
13 who bore the ark of the LORD had gone six paces 1
15 David and . . Israel brought up the ark of the LORD 1
16 As the ark of the LORD came into the city of David 1
17 And they brought in the ark of the LORD, and set it 1
7: 2 I dwell . . but the ark of God dwells in a tent. 1
11:11 The ark and Israel and Judah dwell in booths; 1
15:24 Levites, bearing the ark of the covenant of God; 1
24 and they set down the ark of God 1
25 Carry the ark of God back into the city. 1
29 So Zadok and Abi'athar carried the ark of God back 1
1Kg 2:26 you bore the ark of the Lord GOD before David my 1
3:15 stood before the ark of the covenant of the LORD 1
6:19 to set there the ark of the covenant of the LORD. 1
8: 1 assembled . . to bring up the ark of the covenant 1
3 elders . . came, and the priests took up the ark. 1
4 they brought up the ark of the LORD, the tent 1
5 congregation . . were with him before the ark 1
6 brought the ark of the covenant of the LORD 1
7 spread out their wings over the place of the ark 1
7 made a covering above the ark and its poles. 1
9 There was nothing in the ark except the two 1
21 a place for the ark, in which is the covenant 1
1Ch 6:31 the house of the LORD, after the ark rested there. 1
13: 3 Then let us bring again the ark of our God to us; 1
5 to bring the ark of God from Kir'iath-je'arim. 1
6 to bring up from there the ark of God 1
7 they carried the ark of God upon a new cart 1
9 Uzzah put out his hand to hold the ark 1
10 smote him because he put forth his hand to the ark; 1
12 he said, "How can I bring the ark of God home to me? 1
13 David did not take the ark home into the city 1
14 the ark of God remained with the household 1
15: 1 he prepared a place for the ark of God 1
2 No one but the Levites may carry the ark of God 1
2 LORD chose them to carry the ark of the LORD 1
3 to bring up the ark of the LORD to its place 1
12 so that you may bring up the ark of the LORD 1
14 to bring up the ark of the LORD, the God of Israel. 1
15 carried the ark of God upon their shoulders 1
23 and Elka'nah were to be gatekeepers for the ark. 1
24 should blow the trumpets before the ark of God. 1
24 Jehi'ah also were to be gatekeepers for the ark. 1
25 to bring up the ark of the covenant of the LORD 1
26 carrying the ark of the covenant of the LORD 1
27 all the Levites who were carrying the ark 1
28 brought up the ark of the covenant of the LORD 1
29 ark of the covenant of the LORD came to the city 1
16: 1 brought the ark of God, and set it inside the tent 1
4 Levites as ministers before the ark of the LORD 1
6 before the ark of the covenant of God. 1
37 there before the ark of the covenant of the LORD 1
37 to minister continually before the ark 1
17: 1 ark of the covenant of the LORD is under a tent. 1
22:19 so that the ark of the covenant of the LORD 1
28: 2 house . . for the ark of the covenant of the LORD 1
18 and covered the ark of the covenant of the LORD. 1
2Ch 1: 4 David had brought up the ark of God 1
5: 2 to bring up the ark of the covenant of the LORD 1
4 and the Levites took up the ark. 1
5 they brought up the ark, the tent of meeting 1
6 and all the congregation . . were before the ark 1
7 brought the ark of the covenant of the LORD 1
8 spread out their wings over the place of the ark 1
8 cherubim made a covering above the ark and its 1
10 was nothing in the ark except the two tables 1
6:11 there I have set the ark, in which is the covenant 1

41 go to thy resting place, thou and the ark of thy 1
8:11 the places to which the ark of the LORD has come 1
35: 3 Put the holy ark in the house which Solomon 1
Ps 132: 8 resting place, thou and the ark of thy might. 1
Jer 3:16 no more say, "The ark of the covenant of the LORD. 1
Mat 24:38 until the day when Noah entered the ark 3
Lke 17:27 until the day when Noah entered the ark 3
Heb 9: 4 the ark of the covenant 3
11: 7 Noah . . took heed and constructed an ark 3
1Pe 3:20 during the building of the ark 3
Rev 11:19 ark of his covenant was seen within his temple; 3
1Es 1: 3 put the holy ark of the Lord in the house 3
2Es 10:22 the ark of our covenant has been plundered 4
2Mc 2: 4 the tent and the ark should follow with him 3
5 the tent and the ark and the altar of incense 3
4Mc 15:31 Just as Noah's ark . . endured the waves 3

arm 1. זְרוֹעַ 2. זְרוֹעַ יָד 3. יָד 4. צַד 5. דְּרָע (A)
6. ἀγκάλη 7. βραχίων 8. τράχηλος 9. χείρ 10. ὦμος
11. brachium

Gen 24:22 two bracelets for her arms weighing ten gold 3
30 he saw . . the bracelets on his sister's arms 3
47 I put . . the bracelets on her arms. 3
49:24 bow remained unmoved, his arms were made agile 2
Exd 6: 6 I will redeem you with an outstretched arm 1
15:16 because of the greatness of thy arm, they are 1
Deu 4:34 by a mighty hand and an outstretched arm 1
5:15 with a mighty hand and an outstretched arm; 1
7:19 saw, the . . mighty hand, and the outstretched arm 1
9:29 bring out . . by thy outstretched arm.' 1
11: 2 consider . . mighty hand and his outstretched arm 1
26: 8 with a mighty hand and an outstretched arm 1
33:20 Gad . . tears the arm, and the crown of the head. 1
27 underneath are the everlasting arms. 1
Jdg 15:14 the ropes which were on his arms became as flax 1
16:12 he snapped the ropes off his arms like a thread. 1
2Sm 1:10 I took . . and the armlet which was on his arm 1
22:35 He trains my hands . . so that my arms can bend a bow 1
1Kg 8:42 and thy mighty hand, and of thy outstretched arm) 1
2Kg 5:18 my master goes . . leaning on my arm, and I bow 3
17:36 with great power and with an outstretched arm; 1
2Ch 6:32 for the sake of . . hand, and thy outstretched arm 1
32: 8 With him is an arm of flesh; but with us is the LORD 1
Job 22: 9 the arms of the fatherless were crushed. 1
26: 2 How you have saved the arm that has no strength! 1
31:22 let my arm be broken from its socket. 1
35: 9 call for help because of the arm of the mighty. 1
38:15 their uplifted arm is broken. 1
40: 9 Have you an arm like God, and can you thunder 1
Ps 10:15 Break thou the arm of the wicked and evildoer; 1
18:34 for war, so that my arms can bend a bow of bronze. 1
37:17 For the arms of the wicked shall be broken; 1
44: 3 nor did their own arm give them victory; 1
3 hand, and thy arm, and the light of thy countenance; 1
77:15 Thou didst with thy arm redeem thy people 1
89:10 didst scatter thy enemies with thy mighty arm. 1
13 Thou hast a mighty arm; strong is thy hand 1
21 my arm also shall strengthen him. 1
98: 1 right hand and his holy arm have gotten him 1
136:12 with a strong hand and an outstretched arm 1
Prv 31:17 She . . makes her arms strong. 1
Sng 5:14 His arms are rounded gold, set with jewels. 3
8: 6 Set me . . upon your heart, as a seal upon your arm; 1
Isa 17: 5 gathers . . grain and his arm harvests the ears 1
30:30 and the descending blow of his arm to be seen 1
33: 2 Be our arm every morning, our salvation 1
40:10 GOD comes with might, and his arm rules for him; 1
11 he will gather the lambs in his arms 1
44:12 with hammers, and forges it with his strong arm; 1
48:14 and his arm shall be against the Chalde'ans. 1
51: 5 has gone forth, and my arms will rule the peoples; 1
5 coastlands wait for me, and for my arm they hope. 1
9 Awake, awake, put on strength, O arm of the LORD; 1
52:10 The LORD has bared his holy arm before the eyes 1
53: 1 to whom has the arm of the LORD been revealed? 1
59:16 then his own arm brought him victory 1
60: 4 and your daughters shall be carried in the arms. 4
62: 8 has sworn by his right hand and by his mighty arm 1
63: 5 no one to uphold; so my own arm brought me victory 1
12 who caused his glorious arm to go at the right 1
Jer 17: 5 man who trusts in man and makes flesh his arm 1
21: 5 with outstretched hand and strong arm, in anger 1
27: 5 I who by my great power and my outstretched arm 1
32:17 great power and by thy outstretched arm! 1
21 with a strong hand and outstretched arm 1
48:25 The horn of Moab is cut off, and his arm is broken 1
Ezk 4: 7 the siege of Jerusalem, with your arm bared; 1
13:20 I will tear them from your arms; 1
16:11 with ornaments, and put bracelets on your arms 3
17: 9 not take a strong arm or many people to pull it 1
20:33 with a mighty hand and an outstretched arm 1
34 with a mighty hand and an outstretched arm 1
30:21 I have broken the arm of Pharaoh king of Egypt; 1
22 and will break his arms, both the strong arm 1
22 both the strong arm and the one that was broken; •
24 I will strengthen the arms of the king of Babylon 1
24 but I will break the arms of Pharaoh 1
25 but the arms of Pharaoh shall fall; 1

25 but the arms of Pharaoh shall fall; 1
Dan 2:32 head of . . gold, its breast and arms of silver 5
10: 6 arms and legs like the gleam of burnished bronze 1
11: 6 but she shall not retain the strength of her arm 1
Hos 7:15 Although I trained and strengthened their arms 1
11: 3 taught E'phraim to walk, I took them up in my arms; 1
Zec 11:17 May the sword smite his arm and his right eye! 1
17 Let his arm be wholly withered 1
Lke 1:51 He has shown strength with his arm 7
2:28 he took him up in his arms and blessed God and said 6
Joh 12:38 to whom has the arm of the Lord been revealed? 7
Act 13:17 with uplifted arm he led them out of it. 7
2Es 15:11 with a mighty hand and with an uplifted arm 11
AEs 15: 8 took her in his arms until she came to herself 6
Wis 5:16 with his arm he will shield them. 7
11:21 who can withstand the might of thy arm? 7
16:16 were scourged by the strength of thy arm 7
Sir 21:21 like a bracelet on the right arm. 7
36: 6 make thy hand and thy right arm glorious. 7
38:30 He moulds the clay with his arm 7
Bar 2:11 with great power and outstretched arm 7
2Mc 12:35 one . . bore down upon him and cut off his arm 10
15:24 By the might of thy arm 7
30 ordered them to cut off Nicanor's head and arm 9
32 He showed them . . that profane man's arm 9
3Mc 5:49 falling into one another's arms 8
4Mc 9:11 bound his hands and arms with thongs on each side. 7
10: 6 breaking his fingers and arms and legs 7

arm (2) 1. חגר 2. חלץ 3. חֲמֻשִׁים 4. לבשׁ 5. מָגֵן 6. מלא 7. נשׂא 8. נשׁק 9. *δύναμις* 10. *ἔνοπλος* 11. *θωρακίζω* 12. *καθοπλίζω* 13. *ὁπλίζω* 14. *ὁπλοδοτέω* 15. *ὅπλον* 16. *ὁπλοποιέω* 17. *πανοπλία*

Num31: 3 Arm men from among you for the war, 2
5 there were provided . . 12,000 armed for war. 2
32:27 every man . . armed for war, before the LORD to battle 2
29 every man who is armed to battle before the LORD 2
30 if they will not pass over with you armed 2
32 We will pass over armed before the LORD 2
Deu 3:18 pass over armed before your brethren the people 2
Jos 1:14 all the men of valor . . shall pass over armed 3
4:12 passed over armed before the people of Israel 3
Jdg 10:17 Ammonites were called to arms, and they encamped *
12: 1 The men of E'phraim were called to arms *
18:11 600 men . . armed with weapons of war, set forth 1
16 men . . armed with their weapons of war, stood 1
17 with the 600 men armed with weapons of war 1
1Sm 17: 5 and he was armed with a coat of mail 4
2Sm 23: 7 the man . . arms himself with iron and the shaft 6
1Ch 12:24 bearing shield and spear were 6,800 armed troops 2
34 were 37,000 men armed with shield and spear. *
37 120,000 men armed with all the weapons of war. *
2Ch 14: 8 an army . . armed with bucklers and spears 7
17:17 with 200,000 men armed with bow and shield 8
18 Jeho'zabad with a 180,000 armed for war. 2
Ps 78: 9 The E'phraimites, armed with the bow, turned back 8
Prv 6:11 want like an armed man. 5
24:34 want like an armed man. 5
Isa 30:32 with brandished arm he will fight with them. *
1Pe 4: 1 arm yourselves with the same thought 13
Jdt 14: 3 they will seize their arms and go into the camp 17
Wis 5:17 and will arm all creation to repel his enemies; 16
18:22 not by strength of body, and not by force of arms 15
1Mc 1:35 they stored up arms and food 15
5:43 they threw away their arms 15
6: 6 that the Jews had grown strong from the arms 15
35 1,000 men armed with coats of mail 11
37 upon each were four armed men 9
41 the clanking of their arms 15
7:44 they threw down their arms and fled. 15
8:26 not give or supply grain, arms, money, or ships 15
28 shall be given no grain, arms, money, or ships 15
10: 6 to recruit troops, to equip them with arms 15
21 and equipped them with arms in abundance. 15
11:51 they threw down their arms and made peace 15
12:27 to keep their arms at hand 15
14:32 he armed the men of his nation's forces 14
33 where . . the arms of the enemy had been stored 15
2Mc 4:40 Lysimachus armed about 3,000 men 12
8:18 For they trust to arms and acts of daring," he said 15
9: 2 the people rushed to the rescue with arms 15
10:23 Having success at arms in everything 15
27 they took up their arms 15
11: 7 Maccabeus himself was the first to take up arms 15
15: 5 I command you to take up arms 15
11 He armed each of them 12
21 the varied supply of arms 15
21 he knew that it is not by arms 15
3Mc 1: 2 Theodotus . . took . . the best of the Ptolemaic arms 15
23 They shouted to their fellows to take arms 15
5:48 the following armed forces 10
6:21 turned back upon the armed forces following 10
4Mc 3:12 armed themselves fully 12
4:10 going up with his armed forces to seize the money 12
5: 1 with his armed soldiers standing about him 10
7:11 our father Aaron, armed with the censer 12

fully arm 1. *ἐξοπλίζω* 2. *καθωπλίζω*

Lke 11:21 a strong man, fully armed, guards his own palace 2
2Mc 5: 2 in companies fully armed with lances 1

arm rest 1. יָד

1Kg 10:19 on each side of the seat were arm rests 1
19 and two lions standing beside the arm rests 1
2Ch 9:18 on each side of the seat were arm rests 1
18 two lions standing beside the arm rests 1

strong arm 1. זְרוֹעַ

Ps 83: 8 are the strong arm of the children of Lot. Selah 1

arm with a scythe 1. *δρεπανηφόρος*

2Mc 13: 2 300 chariots armed with scythes. 1

armament 1. *πανοπλία*

Sir 46: 6 so that the nations might know his armament 1

armed *See* force, troop.

armed man 1. חלץ 2. חֲמֻשִׁים 3. *ἔνοπλος* 4. *ὅπλον*

Num32:21 every armed man of you will pass over the Jordan 1
Jos 6: 7 let the armed men pass on before the ark 1
9 And the armed men went before the priests 1
13 and the armed men went before them 1
Jdg 7:11 he went down . . to the outposts of the armed men 2
2Ch 28:14 the armed men left the captives and the spoil 1
Isa 15: 4 therefore the armed men of Moab cry aloud; 1
2Mc 5:26 then rushed into the city with his armed men 4
14:22 Judas posted armed men in readiness 3

ready armed 1. חלץ

Jos 4:13 about 40,000 ready armed for war passed over 1

armlet 1. אֶצְעָדָה 2. כּוּמָז 3. צְעָדָה

Exd 35:22 earrings and signet rings and armlets, all sorts 2
Num31:50 LORD'S offering . . armlets and bracelets 1
2Sm 1:10 I took . . and the armlet which was on his arm 1
Isa 3:20 the headdresses, the armlets, the sashes 3

armor 1. חֲגוֹרָה 2. כְּלִי 3. מַד 4. *θωρακισμός* 5. *θώραξ* 6. *κάλυμμα* 7. *ὅπλον* 8. *πανοπλία* 9. *σκευή* 10. *σκεῦος*

Jdg 9:54 called hastily to the young man his armor-bearer 2
1Sm 14: 1 said to the young man who bore his armor, "Come 2
6 Jonathan said to the young man who bore his armor 2
7 And his armor-bearer said to him, "Do all that 2
12 the men . . hailed Jonathan and his armor-bearer 2
12 Jonathan said to his armor-bearer, "Come up 2
13 Then Jonathan . . and his armor-bearer after him. 2
13 and his armor-bearer killed them after him; 2
14 which Jonathan and his armor-bearer made 2
17 Jonathan and his armor-bearer were not there. 2
16:21 Saul loved him . . and he became his armor-bearer. 2
17:38 Then Saul clothed David with his armor; 3
39 And David girded his sword over his armor 3
54 but he put his armor in his tent. 2
18: 4 of the robe . . and gave it to David, and his armor 3
31: 4 Saul said to his armor-bearer, "Draw your sword 2
4 But his armor-bearer would not; for he feared 2
5 when his armor-bearer saw that Saul was dead 2
6 Saul died, and his three sons, and his armor-bearer 2
9 they cut off his head, and stripped off his armor 2
10 They put his armor in the temple of Ash'taroth; 2
2Sm 18:15 And ten young men, Jo'ab's armor-bearers 2
23:37 Na'harai of Be-er'oth, the armor-bearer of Jo'ab 2
1Kg 20:11 Let not him that girds on his armor boast himself *
2Kg 3:21 all who were able to put on armor . . were called 1
1Ch 10: 4 Then Saul said to his armor-bearer 2
4 But his armor-bearer would not; 2
5 when his armor-bearer saw that Saul was dead 2
9 they stripped him and took his head and his armor 2
10 they put his armor in the temple of their gods 2
11:39 Na'harai of Be-er'oth, the armor-bearer of Jo'ab 2
Ezk 23:12 warriors clothed in full armor, horsemen riding *
38: 4 and horsemen, all of them clothed in full armor *
Lke 11:22 he takes away his armor in which he trusted 8
Rom 13:12 Let us . . put on the armor of light; 7
1Mc 3: 3 he girded on his armor of war and waged battles 9
4: 6 armor and swords such as they desired. 6
30 the man who carried his armor. 10
6:43 one of the beasts was equipped with royal armor. 5
2Mc 5: 3 and armor of all sorts. 4

armor *See also* put, suit.

armor and weapons 1. *πανοπλία*

2Mc 3:25 was seen to have armor and weapons of gold. 1
10:30 protecting him with their own armor and weapons 1

full armor 1. *πανοπλία*

2Mc 15:28 Nicanor, lying dead, in full armor. 1

scale armor 1. דֶּבֶק

1Kg 22:34 between the scale armor and the breastplate; 1
2Ch 18:33 between the scale armor and the breastplate; 1

whole armor 1. *πανοπλία*

Eph 6:11 Put on the whole armor of God 1
13 Therefore take the whole armor of God 1
Wis 5:17 The Lord will take his zeal as his whole armor 1

armory 1. אוֹצָר 2. בֵּית כֵּלִים 3. נֶשֶׁק

2Kg 20:13 spices, the precious oil, his armory, all that was 2
Neh 3:19 opposite the ascent to the armory at the Angle. 3
Isa 39: 2 his whole armory, all that was found 2
Jer 50:25 The LORD has opened his armory 1

armpit 1. אַצִּיל יָד

Jer 38:12 Put the rags and clothes between your armpits 1

arms *See* bear, collect, parade, take, tie.

army 1. גְּדוּד 2. זְרוֹעַ 3. חַיִל 4. חלץ 5. מַחֲנֶה 6. מַעֲרָכָה 7. עַם 8. צָבָא 9. חַיִל (A) 10. *δύναμις* 11. *δυνατός* 12. *λαός* 13. *ὁ παρά* 14. *ὁ περί* 15. *παράταξις* 16. *παρεμβολή* 17. *πλῆθος* 18. *στράτευμα* 19. *στρατιά* 20. *στρατόπεδον* 21. *στρατός* 22. exercitus

Gen 21:22 Abim'elech and Phicol the commander of his army 8
32 Phicol the commander of his army rose up 8
26:26 adviser and Phicol the commander of his army. 8
32: 2 when Jacob saw them he said, "This is God's army! 5
Exd 14: 6 his chariot and took his army with him 7
9 chariots and his horsemen and his army 3
Num31:14 Moses was angry with the officers of the army 3
48 officers who were over the thousands of the army 8
Deu 11: 4 what he did to the army of Egypt, to their horses 3
20: 1 see . . an army larger than your own 7
24: 5 newly married, he shall not go out with the army 8
Jos 5:14 as commander of the army of the LORD I . . now come. 8
15 the commander of the LORD's army said to Joshua 8
10: 5 and went up with all their armies and encamped 5
Jdg 4: 2 Jabin . . the commander of his army was Sis'era 8
7 Sis'era, the general of Jabin's army, to meet you 8
15 Sis'era and all his chariots and all his army 5
16 Barak pursued the chariots and the army 5
16 all the army of Sis'era fell by the edge 5
7:21 and all the army ran; they cried out and fled. 5
22 against his fellow and against all the army; 5
22 and the army fled as far as Beth-shit'tah 5
8: 6 your hand, that we should give bread to your army? 8
10 and Zalmun'na were in Karkor with their army 5
10 were left of all the army of the people of the East; 5
11 Gideon went up . . and attacked the army; 5
11 attacked the army; for the army was off its guard. 5
12 and he threw all the army into a panic. 5
9:29 to Abim'elech, 'Increase your army, and come out.' 8
20:26 all the people of Israel, the whole army, went up 7
1Sm 12: 9 Sis'era, commander of the army of . . Hazor 8
14:50 the name of the commander of his army was Abner 8
17: 1 Philistines gathered their armies for battle; 5
21 the Philistines drew up . . army against army. 6
21 the Philistines drew up . . army against army. 6
26 who . . should defy the armies of the living God? 6
36 he has defied the armies of the living God. 6
45 the LORD of hosts, the God of the armies of Israel 6
55 he said to Abner, the commander of the army 8
23: 3 we go . . against the armies of the Philistines? 6
26: 5 Abner the son of Ner, the commander of his army; 8
5 Saul . . while the army was encamped around him. 7
7 David and Abi'shai went to the army by night; 7
7 lay Saul . . and Abner and the army lay around him. 7
14 David called to the army, and to Abner . . saying 7
28: 1 you and your men are to go out with me in the army. 5
5 When Saul saw the army of the Philistines 5
19 LORD will give the army of Israel . . into the hand 5
2Sm 2: 8 Now Abner the son of Ner, commander of Saul's army 8
3:23 When Jo'ab and all the army that was with him came 8
5:24 gone out . . to smite the army of the Philistines. 5
8: 9 David had defeated the whole army of Hadade'zer 3
16 Jo'ab the son of Zeru'iah was over the army; 8
10:16 Shobach the commander of the army of Hadade'zer 8
18 and wounded Shobach the commander of their army 8
17:25 had set Ama'sa over the army instead of Jo'ab. 8
18: 2 And David sent forth the army 7
4 army marched out by hundreds and by thousands. 7
6 the army went out into the field against Israel; 7
19:13 God do so . . if you are not commander of my army 8
20:23 Now Jo'ab was in command of all the army of Israel; 8
24: 2 king said to Jo'ab and the commanders of the army 3
4 against Jo'ab and the commanders of the army. 3
4 Jo'ab and the commanders of the army went out 3
1Kg 1:19 Abi'athar . . and Jo'ab the commander of the army; 8
25 the king's sons, Jo'ab the commander of the army 8
2: 5 the two commanders of the armies of Israel, Abner 8
32 Abner . . commander of the army of Israel 8
32 and Ama'sa . . commander of the army of Judah. 8
35 king put Benai'ah . . over the army in place of Jo'ab 8
4: 4 Benai'ah . . was in command of the army; Zadok 8
11:15 Jo'ab the commander of the army went up 8
21 Jo'ab the commander of the army was dead 8
15:20 Ben-ha'dad . . sent the commanders of his armies 3
16:16 Israel made Omri, the commander of the army, king 8
20: 1 Ben-ha'dad . . gathered all his army together; 3

19 the servants . . and the army which followed 3
25 muster an army like the army that you have lost 3
25 muster an army like the army that you have lost 3
22:36 about sunset a cry went through the army 5
2Kg 3: 9 there was no water for the army or for the beasts 5
4:13 to the king or to the commander of the army? 8
5: 1 Na'aman, commander of the army of the king of Syria 8
6:14 he sent . . horses and chariots and a great army; 3
15 an army with horses and chariots was round about 3
24 Ben-ha'dad king of Syria mustered his entire army 5
7: 6 the Lord had made the army of the Syrians hear 5
6 chariots, and of horses, the sound of a great army 3
14 the king sent them after the army of the Syrians 5
8:21 smote the E'domites . . but his army fled home. 7
9: 5 the commanders of the army were in council; 3
11:15 commanded the captains . . set over the army 3
13: 7 was not . . an army of more than 50 horsemen 7
18:17 and the Rab'shakeh with a great army from Lachish 3
25: 1 Nebuchadnez'zar . . came with all his army 3
5 But the army of the Chalde'ans pursued the king 3
5 and all his army was scattered from him. 3
10 the army of the Chalde'ans . . broke down the walls 3
19 and the secretary of the commander of the army 8
1Ch 7: 4 were units of the army for war, 36,000 8
10: 7 saw that the army had fled •
11:15 when the army of Philistines was encamped 5
26 The mighty men of the armies were As'ahel 3
12:14 These Gadites were officers of the army 8
21 men of valor, and were commanders in the army. 8
22 until there was a great army, like an army of God. 5
22 until there was a great army, like an army of God. 5
14:15 before you to smite the army of the Philistines. 5
16 smote the Philistine army from Gibeon to Gezer. 5
18: 9 David had defeated the whole army of Hadade'zer 3
15 Jo'ab the son of Zeru'iah was over the army; 8
19: 7 chariots and the king of Ma'acah with his army 7
8 he sent Jo'ab and all the army of the mighty men. 8
16 with Shophach the commander of the army 8
18 also Shophach the commander of their army. 8
20: 1 Jo'ab led out the army, and ravaged the country 8
21: 2 David said to Jo'ab and the commanders of the army 7
26:26 officers . . and the commanders of the army 8
27: 3 chief of all the commanders of the army 8
34 Jo'ab was commander of the king's army. 8
2Ch 13: 3 having an army of valiant men of war 3
14: 8 Asa had an army of 300,000 from Judah 3
9 with an army of 1,000,000 men and 300 chariots 3
13 they were broken before the LORD and his army. 5
16: 4 sent the commanders of his armies against 3
7 the army of the king of Syria has escaped you. 3
8 the Ethiopians and the Libyans a huge army 3
20:21 as they went before the army, and say 4
23:14 the captains who were set over the army 3
24:23 the army of the Syrians came up against Jo'ash. 3
24 the army of the Syrians had come with few men 3
24 LORD delivered into their hand a very great army 3
25: 7 O king, do not let the army of Israel go with you 8
9 talents which I have given to the army of Israel? 1
10 Amazi'ah discharged the army that had come to him 1
13 the men of the army whom Amazi'ah sent back 1
26:11 Uzzi'ah had an army of soldiers, fit for war 8
13 Under their command was an army of 307,500 8
14 Uzzi'ah prepared for all the army shields, spears 8
28: 9 he went out to meet the army that came to Sama'ria 8
33:11 brought upon them the commanders of the army 8
14 put commanders of the army in all the fortified 3
Neh 2: 9 sent with me officers of the army and horsemen. 3
4: 2 said in the presence . . of the army of Sama'ria 3
Est 1: 3 all his princes and servants, the army chiefs 3
Job 25: 3 Is there any number to his armies? 1
Ps 33:16 A king is not saved by his great army; 3
44: 9 abased us, and hast not gone out with our armies. 8
60:10 Thou dost not go forth, O God, with our armies. 8
68:12 The kings of the armies, they flee, they flee! 8
108:11 Thou dost not go forth, O God, with our armies. 8
Sng 6: 4 terrible as an army with banners. •
10 Who is this . . terrible as an army with banners? •
13 look upon the . . as upon a dance before two armies? 5
Isa 36: 2 to King Hezeki'ah at Jerusalem, with a great army. 3
43:17 brings forth chariot and horse, army and warrior 3
Jer 32: 2 the army of the king of Babylon was besieging 3
34: 1 all his army and all the kingdoms of the earth 3
7 when the army of the king of Babylon was fighting 3
21 into the hand of the army of the king of Babylon 3
35:11 for fear of the army of the Chalde'ans 3
11 for fear of . . the army of the Syrians. 3
37: 5 The army of Pharaoh had come out of Egypt; 3
7 Behold, Pharoah's army which came to help you 3
10 For even if you should defeat the whole army 3
11 Now when the Chalde'an army had withdrawn 3
11 withdrawn . . at the approach of Pharaoh's army 3
38: 3 into the hand of the army of the king of Babylon 3
39: 1 Nebuchadrez'zar king of Babylon and all his army 3
5 But the army of the Chalde'ans pursued them 3
46: 2 Concerning the army of Pharaoh Neco 3
52: 4 king of Babylon came with all his army 3
8 But the army of the Chalde'ans pursued the king 3
8 and all his army was scattered from him. 3
14 And all the army of the Chalde'ans 3
25 the secretary of the commander of the army 8
Ezk 17:15 that they might give him horses and a large army. 7
17 Pharaoh with his mighty army and great company 3
27:10 Lud and Put were in your army as your men of war; 3
29:18 king of Babylon made his army labor hard 3
18 neither he nor his army got anything from Tyre 3
19 it shall be the wages for his army. 3
32:31 Pharaoh and all his army, slain by the sword 3
38: 4 all your army, horses and horsemen, all of them 3
15 riding on horses, a great host, a mighty army; 3
Dan 3:20 ordered certain mighty men of his army to bind 9
11: 7 come against the army and enter the fortress 3
13 come on with a great army and abundant supplies. 3
22 Armies shall be utterly swept away before him 2
25 against the king of the south with a great army; 3
25 war with an exceedingly great and mighty army; 3
26 army . . swept away, and many shall fall down slain 3
Jol 2: 5 like a powerful army drawn up for battle. 7
11 The LORD utters his voice before his army 3
25 my great army, which I sent among you. 3
Lke 21:20 when you see Jerusalem surrounded by armies 20
Heb 11:34 put foreign armies to flight. 16
Rev 19:14 And the armies of heaven . . followed him 18
19 kings . . with their armies gathered to make war 18
19 to make war against him . . and against his army. 18
1Es 4:10 All his people and his armies obey him 10
2Es 1:10 Pharaoh with his servants, and all his army. 22
15:33 fear and trembling shall come upon their army 22
Jdt 1: 4 so that his armies could march out in force 11
13 overthrew the whole army of Arphaxad 10
2: 4 Holofernes, the chief general of his army 10
7 cover . . the earth with the feet of my armies 10
14 generals, and officers of the Assyrian army 10
19 he set out with his whole army 10
22 From there Holofernes took his whole army 10
3: 6 Then he went down to the seacoast with his army 10
10 assemble all the supplies for his army. 10
5: 1 Holofernes, the general of the Assyrian army 10
3 How large is their army 10
3 Who rules over them as king, leading their army? 19
24 they will be devoured by your vast army. 19
6: 1 Holofernes, the commander of the Assyrian army 10
6 the sword of my army and the spear of my servants 19
7: 1 The next day Holofernes ordered his whole army 19
7 and then returned to his army. 12
9 lest his army be defeated. 10
11 not a man of your army will fall. 12
17 the army of the Ammonites moved forward 16
18 rest of the Assyrian army encamped in the plain 19
20 The whole Assyrian army, their infantry 16
26 to the army of Holofernes and to all his forces 12
10:13 Holofernes the commander of your army 10
11:18 then you shall go out with your whole army 10
13:15 Holofernes, the commander of the Assyrian army 10
14: 3 rouse the officers of the Assyrian army 10
19 When the leaders of the Assyrian army heard this 10
16:12 they perished before the army of my Lord. 15
Wis 12: 8 didst send wasps as forerunners of thy army 20
1Mc 1: 4 He gathered a very strong army 10
2:44 They organized an army, and struck down sinners 10
66 he shall command the army for you 19
3:13 Seron, the commander of the Syrian army, heard 10
15 again a strong army of ungodly men went up 16
17 when they saw the army coming to meet them 16
19 not on the size of the army 10
23 he rushed suddenly against Seron and his army 16
27 a very strong army. 16
57 Then the army marched out 16
4:10 crush this army before us today. 16
20 They saw that their army had been put to flight •
21 when they also saw the army of Judas 16
30 When he saw that the army was strong, he prayed 16
31 So do thou hem in this army 16
34 there fell of the army of Lysias 5,000 men 16
37 So all the army assembled 16
5:28 Then Judas and his army quickly turned back 16
34 when the army of Timothy realized 16
37 Timothy gathered another army 16
40 Now as Judas and his army drew near 16
43 the whole army followed him 12
49 Judas ordered proclamation to be made to the army 16
6: 5 the armies which had gone into the land of Judah 16
6 spoils which they had taken from the armies 16
33 and took his army by a forced march along the road 16
38 on the two flanks of the army 16
40 the king's army was spread out on the high hills 16
41 the army was very large and strong. 16
42 Judas and his army advanced to the battle 16
42 600 men of the king's army fell. 16
48 The soldiers of the king's army went up to Jerusalem 16
7: 2 the army seized Antiochus and Lysias 10
4 So the army killed them 10
14 A priest of the line of Aaron has come with the army 10
32 About 500 men of the army of Nicanor fell 13
35 Unless Judas and his army are delivered 16
38 Take vengeance on this man and on his army 16
39 the Syrian army joined him. 10
42 So also crush this army before us today 16
43 So the armies met in battle 16
43 The army of Nicanor was crushed 16
44 When his army saw that Nicanor had fallen 16
8: 6 with cavalry and chariots and a very large army. 10
9: 1 Nicanor and his army had fallen in battle 10
1 and with them the right wing of the army. •
7 When Judas saw that his army had slipped away 16
11 the army of Bacchides marched out from the camp 10
11 the archers went ahead of the army 10
13 The earth was shaken by the noise of the armies 16
14 the strength of his army were on the right 16
34 he with all his army crossed the Jordan. 18
10: 2 he assembled a very large army 10
49 the army of Demetrius fled 16
53 he and his army were crushed by us 16
73 my cavalry and such an army in the plain 10
77 3,000 cavalry and a large army 10
78 the armies engaged in battle. 16
80 they surrounded his army 16
11:60 all the army of Syria gathered to him as allies. 10
63 had come to Kadesh in Galilee with a large army 10
67 Jonathan and his army encamped by the waters 16
68 the army of the foreigners met him in the plain; 16
70 commanders of the forces of the army. 10
12:42 When Trypho saw that he had come with a large army 10
13: 1 Trypho had assembled a large army 10
11 with him a considerable army 10
12 with a large army to invade the land of Judah 10
20 Simon and his army 16
14: 3 he went and defeated the army of Demetrius 16
16: 6 Then he and his army lined up against them 12
7 Then he divided the army 12
8 Cendebeus and his army were put to flight 16
2Mc 5:24 with an army of 22,000 18
8: 5 As soon as Maccabeus got his army organized •
12 the arrival of the army 20
21 then he divided his army into four parts. 18
24 wounded and disabled most of Nicanor's army 19
35 the destruction of his own army! 21
9: 9 the whole army felt revulsion at his decay. 20
10:28 the two armies joined battle •
35 twenty young men in the army of Maccabeus 14
12:20 Maccabeus arranged his army in divisions 19
38 Then Judas assembled his army 18
13:13 before the king's army could enter Judea 18
14: 1 a strong army and a fleet 17
21 A chariot came forward from each army •
15:20 their army drawn up for battle 19
3Mc 5: 3 those of his friends and of the army 19
6: 4 Pharaoh . . destroyed together with his arrogant army 19
17 and brought an uncontrollable terror upon the army. 20
4Mc 3: 8 around which the whole army . . had encamped. 21
4:11 and propitiate the wrath of the heavenly army. 21

army *See also* serve.

even larger army 1. *πλεοναστός*

1Mc 4:35 to invade . . with an even larger army 1

great army 1. *πλῆθος*

Jdt 2:16 as a great army is marshaled for a campaign. 1
2Mc 13: 1 Antiochus Eupator was coming with a great army 1

aroma 1. *εὐωδία* 2. *ὀσμή*

2Co 2:15 For we are the aroma of Christ to God 1
Sir 24:15 I gave forth the aroma of spices 2

aromatic 1. בֹּשֶׂם

Exd 30:23 Take . . of aromatic cane 250 1

around 1. אַחֲרֵי 2. סָבִיב 3. עַל סָבִיב 4. *κυκλόθεν* 5. *κύκλος* 6. *κυκλόω* 7. *περί* 8. *πέριξ* 9. *πρός*

Gen 41:48 in every city the food from the fields around it. 2
Exd 25:24 and make a molding of gold around it. 2
25 shall make around it a frame a handbreadth wide 2
25 make . . a molding of gold around the frame. 2
27:17 the pillars around the court shall be filleted 2
28:32 with a woven binding around the opening 2
33 make pomegranates . . around its skirts 2
37: 2 and made a molding of gold around it. 2
11 and made a molding of gold around it. 2
12 he made around it a frame a handbreadth wide 2
12 made a molding of gold around the frame. 2
39:23 a garment, with a binding around the opening 2
Lev 25:31 the villages which have no wall around them 2
Num 1:50 and shall encamp around the tabernacle. 2
53 the Levites shall encamp around the tabernacle 2
3:26 the court which is around the tabernacle 3
4:26 court which is around the tabernacle 2
11:32 they spread them out . . all around the camp. 2
Deu 21: 2 cities which are around him that is slain; 2
1Sm 26: 5 Saul . . while the army was encamped around him. 2
7 lay Saul . . and Abner and the army lay around him. 2
2Sm 22:12 He made darkness around him his canopy 2
1Kg 3: 1 house of the LORD and the wall around Jerusalem. 2
6: 5 and he made side chambers all around. 2
6 around the outside of the house he made offsets 2
2Kg 2:24 he turned around, and when he saw them, he cursed 1
11:11 guards stood . . around the altar and the house. 2
25: 4 though the Chalde'ans were around the city. 2

10 all . . broke down the walls around Jerusalem. 2
2Ch 23:10 around the altar and the house. 2
Neh 12:29 built . . villages around Jerusalem. 2
Ps 18:11 He made darkness his covering around him 2
34: 7 of the LORD encamps around those who fear him 2
76:11 let all around him bring gifts to him 2
128: 3 children . . olive shoots around your table. 2
Jer 6: 3 they shall pitch their tents around her 2
Ezk 42:20 It had a wall around it, 500 cubits long 2
43:13 broad, with a rim of one span around its edge. 2
17 with a rim around it half a cubit broad 2
45: 2 with 50 cubits for an open space around it. 2
46:23 around each of the four courts was a row 2
Nah 3: 8 Thebes that sat by the Nile, with water around her 2
Mat 3: 4 leather girdle around his waist; and his food was 7
8:18 Now when Jesus saw great crowds around him 7
Mrk 1: 6 a leather girdle around his waist 7
Act 5:16 gathered from the towns around Jerusalem 8
Rev 5:11 Then I looked, and I heard around the throne 5
Jdt 5:22 all the men standing around the tent 6
15: 3 had camped in the hills around Bethulia 5
Sir 50:12 with a garland of brethren around him 4
Bar 2: 4 into subjection to all the kingdoms around us 5
1Mc 5:10 The Gentiles around us have gathered together 5
38 All the Gentiles around us have gathered to him 5
57 let us go and make war on the Gentiles around us. 5
6:18 kept hemming Israel in around the sanctuary. 5
11:55 All the troops . . gathered around him 9
12:27 he stationed outposts around the camp. 5
3Mc 1:27 When those who were around him observed this 7
3: 8 saw an unexpected tumult around these people 7
6: 1 Eleazar . . directed the elders around him to cease 7
4Mc 3: 8 around which the whole army . . had encamped. 7
9:13 the noble youth was stretched out around this 7
11:10 twisted his back around the wedge on the wheel 7
14: 7 move in choral dance around religion 7

around *See also* all, bring, circle, come, earth, flow, fly, gather, go, look, march, press, prowl, ring, run, send, set, shine, stand, tear, turn, wall, wheel, wrap.

arouse 1. עור 2. *αἴρω* 3. *διεγείρω* 4. *εἰς ἔρχομαι* 5. *ἐξαγείρω* 6. *κινέω* 7. *παρίστημι* 8. *παρορμάω* 9. excito 10. inflammo 11. suscito

Isa 45:13 I have aroused him in righteousness 1
Jer 32:31 This city has aroused my anger and wrath •
Act 21:30 Then all the city was aroused 6
Rom 7: 5 our sinful passions, aroused by the law •
2Pe 1:13 to arouse you by way of reminder 3
3: 1 in both of them I have aroused your sincere mind 3
2Es 4:37 he will not move or arouse them 9
6:37 For my spirit was greatly aroused 10
11:37 a creature . . was aroused out of the forest 11
Wis 15: 5 whose appearance arouses yearning in fools 4
Sus 1:45 God aroused the holy spirit of a young lad 5
1Mc 6:34 to arouse them for battle. 7
10:74 his spirit was aroused 6
13:17 lest he arouse great hostility among the people 2
2Mc 13: 4 the King of kings aroused the anger of Antiochus 5
15:10 when he had aroused their courage 3
17 so noble and so effective in arousing valor 8

become aroused 1. *ἐπεγείρω*

2Mc 4:40 since the crowds were becoming aroused 1

arrange 1. *διατάσσω* 2. *κοσμέω* 3. *μηχανάομαι* 4. *οἰκονομέω* 5. *συνίστημι* 6. *συντάσσω* 7. *τίθημι*

Act 20:13 so he had arranged 1
1Co 12:18 as it is, God arranged the organs in the body 7
Wis 11:20 thou hast arranged all things by measure 1
Sir 47:10 arranged their times throughout the year 2
50:14 arranging the offering to the Most High 2
Sus 1:14 they arranged for a time when they could find her 6
2Mc 12:20 Maccabeus arranged his army in divisions 1
3Mc 3: 2 While these matters were being arranged 4
4: 1 a feast at public expense was arranged 5
5: 5 and arranged for their continued custody 3
6:31 arranged for a banquet of deliverance 5
35 when they had arranged the . . choral group 5

arrange in advance 1. *προκαταρτίζω*

2Co 9: 5 and arrange in advance for this gift 1

arrange in an order 1. *κοσμέω*

Sir 16:27 He arranged his works in an eternal order 1

arrange to sleep 1. *κατακλίνω*

3Mc 1: 3 and arranged that a . . man should sleep in the tent 1

arrange with care 1. תקן

Ecc 12: 9 and arranging proverbs with great care. 1

arrangement 1. מִשְׁפָּט 2. עֵרֶךְ 3. תְּכוּנָה 4. dispositio

Exd 40: 4 in the table, and set its arrangements in order; 2
Ezk 42:11 with the same exits and arrangements and doors. 1
43:11 portray the temple, its arrangement, its exits 3
Heb 9: 9 According to this arrangement •
2Es 6:45 the arrangement of the stars to come into being; 4

arrangement *See also* make.

array 1. הֲדָרָה 2. לבשׁ 3. עמד 4. ערך 5. *ἐνδύω* 6. *ἑτοιμάζω* 7. *κοσμέω* 8. *κόσμος* 9. *παράταξις* 10. *περιβάλλω* 11. *στέλλω* 12. *στολή*

Gen 41:42 and arrayed him in garments of fine linen 2
Jdg 6:31 Jo'ash said to all who were arrayed against him 3
2Sm 10: 9 he chose . . and arrayed them against the Syrians; 4
10 and he arrayed them against the Ammonites. 4
17 the Syrians arrayed themselves against David 4
1Kg 22:10 sitting on their thrones, arrayed in their robes 2
1Ch 12:38 All these, men of war, arrayed in battle order 4
16:29 Worship the LORD in holy array; 1
19:10 and arrayed them against the Syrians; 4
11 and they were arrayed against the Ammonites. 4
2Ch 5:12 arrayed in fine linen, with cymbals, harps 2
18: 9 sitting on their thrones, arrayed in their robes; 2
20:21 to sing to the LORD and praise him in holy array 1
Est 6: 9 array the man whom the king delights to honor 2
11 Haman took the robes . . and he arrayed Mor'decai 2
Job 6: 4 the terrors of God are arrayed against me. 4
Ps 29: 2 worship the LORD in holy array. 1
55:18 many are arrayed against me. •
96: 9 Worship the LORD in holy array; 1
Jer 50: 9 and they shall array themselves against her; 4
42 arrayed as a man for battle against you 4
Zep 1: 8 and all who array themselves in foreign attire. 2
Mat 6:29 his glory was not arrayed like one of these. 10
Lke 12:27 even Solomon in all his glory was not arrayed 10
23:11 then, arraying him in gorgeous apparel 10
Joh 19: 2 put it on his head, and arrayed him in a purple robe; 10
Rev 9: 7 the locusts were like horses arrayed for battle; 6
17: 4 The woman was arrayed in purple and scarlet 10
19:14 arrayed in fine linen, white and pure 5
Jdt 7:11 do not fight against them in battle array 9
10: 3 arrayed herself in her gayest apparel 5
12:15 arrayed herself in all her woman's finery 7
AEs 15: 6 clothed in the full array of his majesty 12
Sir 43: 9 a gleaming array in the heights of the Lord. 8
3Mc 1:19 who had recently been arrayed for marriage 11

array *See also* draw, muster, set.

battle array 1. מִלְחָמָה 2. *παράταξις*

1Ch 19: 9 Ammonites came out and drew up in battle array 1
1Es 2:30 with horsemen and a multitude in battle array 2

array in attire 1. *περιβάλλω*

AEs 15: 1 arrayed herself in splendid attire. 1

array in one's garments 1. *στολίζω*

1Es 1: 2 arrayed in their garments 1
5:59 the priests stood arrayed in their garments 1
7: 9 priests . . arrayed in their garments 1

properly array 1. *εὐπρεπῶς*

1Es 1:10 the Levites, properly arrayed 1

arrest 1. *ἐπιβάλλω τάς χεῖρας* 2. *ἐπιλαμβάνω* 3. *κρατέω* 4. *παραδίδωμι* 5. *πιάζω* 6. *συλλαμβάνω*

Mat 4:12 Now when he heard that John had been arrested 4
21:46 But when they tried to arrest him, they feared 3
26: 4 took counsel together in order to arrest Jesus 3
Mrk 1:14 Now after John was arrested 4
12:12 they tried to arrest him 3
14: 1 how to arrest him by stealth, and kill him; 3
Joh 7:30 they sought to arrest him 5
32 Pharisees sent officers to arrest him. 5
44 Some of them wanted to arrest him 5
8:20 but no one arrested him 5
10:39 Again they tried to arrest him 5
11:57 let them know, so that they might arrest him. 5
Act 1:16 Judas who was guide to those who arrested Jesus. 6
4: 3 they arrested them 1
5:18 they arrested the apostles 1
12: 3 he proceeded to arrest Peter also 6
21:33 Then the tribune came up and arrested him 2
2Mc 7: 1 were arrested and were being compelled 6
14:39 Nicanor . . sent more than 500 soldiers to arrest him; 6
40 by arresting him he would do them an injury. 6
4Mc 16:15 when you and your sons were arrested together 6

arrival 1. בוא 2. *ἔφοδος* 3. *παρουσία*

Num10:21 tabernacle was set up before their arrival. 1
Jdt 10:18 her arrival was reported from tent to tent 3
1Mc 11:44 the king rejoiced at their arrival. 2
2Mc 8:12 the arrival of the army 3

arrive 1. בוא 2. נגע 3. עלה 4. *ἄρχω* 5. *γίνομαι* 6. *διακομίζω* 7. *εἰσέρχομαι* 8. *ἐνίστημι* 9. *ἐπιπορεύομαι* 10. *ἔρχομαι* 11. *ἐφίστημι* 12. *καταντάω* 13. *καταπλέω* 14. *κατέρχομαι* 15. *παραγίνομαι* 16. *παράγω* 17. *πάρειμι* 18. *παρίστημι* 19. *προσπίπτω*

Gen 19:22 I can do nothing till you arrive there. 1
Exd 10:26 must serve the LORD until we arrive there. 1
Jdg 3:27 When he arrived, he sounded the trumpet 1
11:18 and arrived on the east side of the land of Moab 1
19:10 rose up and departed, and arrived opposite Jebus 1
1Sm 4:13 When he arrived, Eli was sitting upon his seat 1
2Sm 3:22 the servants of David arrived . . from a raid 1
16:14 And the king, and all the people . . arrived weary 1
1Kg 19:15 when you arrive, you shall anoint Haz'ael 1
2Kg 6:32 before the messenger arrived Eli'sha said 1
9: 2 when you arrive, look there for Jehu 1
16:11 before King Ahaz arrived from Damascus. 1
18:17 When they arrived, they came and stood 3
Est 6:14 the king's eunuchs arrived and brought Haman 2
Jer 41: 5 80 men arrived from Shechem and Shiloh 1
43: 7 And they arrived at Tah'panhes. 1
Ezk 16: 7 and became tall and arrived at full maidenhood; 1
Zec 6:10 and Jedai'ah, who have arrived from Babylon; and go 1
Lke 8:26 they arrived at the country of the Ger'asenes 13
11: 6 a friend of mine has arrived on a journey 15
Act 11:11 three men arrived at the house in which we were 11
13: 5 When they arrived at Sal'amis 5
14:27 when they arrived 15
17:10 when they arrived 15
18: 5 When Silas and Timothy arrived from Macedo'nia 14
27 When he arrived 15
21: 7 we arrived at Ptolema'is 12
23:35 I will hear you when your accusers arrive. 15
25:13 Agrippa . . arrived at Caesare'a to welcome Festus. 12
27: 7 arrived with difficulty off Cni'dus 5
28:13 we made a circuit and arrived at Rhe'gium 12
1Co 16: 3 when I arrive, I will send those whom you accredit 15
2Ti 1:17 when he arrived in Rome he searched for me 5
3: 7 can never arrive at a knowledge of the truth. 10
3Jn 1: 3 the brethren arrived and testified to the truth 10
1Es 8: 6 arrived in Jerusalem on the new moon 15
61 we arrived in Jerusalem 7
Tob 2: 1 When I arrived home 14
7: 1 arrived at the house of Raguel 15
10: 1 they did not arrive 4
Jdt 16:18 When they arrived at Jerusalem 10
1Mc 3:40 when they arrived they encamped near Emmaus 10
15:15 Numenius and his companions arrived from Rome 10
2Mc 2:28 arriving at the outlines of the condensation. 9
3: 9 When he had arrived at Jerusalem 15
24 he arrived at the treasury with his bodyguard 17
4:21 upon arriving at Joppa 15
5:25 When this man arrived in Jerusalem 15
15:31 when he arrived there 15
3Mc 1: 9 After he had arrived in Jerusalem 6
2:25 When he arrived in Egypt 6
3:20 when we arrived in Egypt victorious 6
25 as soon as this letter shall arrive 19
4: 1 In every place, then, where this decree arrived 19
5:26 Hermon arrived and invited him to come out 18
6:16 the king arrived at the hippodrome 16
7:17 When they had arrived at Ptolemais 15
4Mc 2: 8 to cancel the debt when the seventh year arrives. 8

arrogance 1. גַּאֲוָה 2. גָּאוֹן 3. גֹּדֶל 4. עָתָק 5. שַׁאֲנָן 6. *ἀλαζονεία* 7. *ἀνάστεμα* 8. *θρασύνω* 9. *μεγαλαυχία* 10. *ὑπερηφανία* 11. *ὑπερηφάνως* 12. *ὑψαυχενέω* 13. *φρόνημα* 14. *φρύαγμα*

1Sm 2: 3 let not arrogance come from your mouth; 4
2Kg 19:28 and your arrogance has come into my ears 5
Ps 10: 2 In arrogance the wicked hotly pursue the poor; 1
36:11 Let not the foot of arrogance come upon me 1
Prv 8:13 Pride and arrogance and the way of evil 2
Isa 9: 9 who say in pride and in arrogance of heart 3
16: 6 of his arrogance, his pride, and his insolence– 1
37:29 your arrogance has come to my ears 5
Jer 48:29 of his loftiness, his pride, and his arrogance 1
Jas 4:16 As it is, you boast in your arrogance. 6
Jdt 6:19 O Lord God of heaven, behold their arrogance 10
9:10 crush their arrogance by the hand of a woman. 7
AEs 16:12 unable to restrain his arrogance 10
Wis 5: 8 What has our arrogance profited us? 10
Sir 10: 7 Arrogance is hateful before the Lord 10
22:22 reviling, arrogance, disclosure of secrets 10
48:18 made great boasts in his arrogance. 10
1Mc 1:24 spoke with great arrogance. 10
2:49 Arrogance and reproach have now become strong 10
2Mc 5:21 thinking in his arrogance that . . 10
7:36 receive just punishment for your arrogance. 10
9: 4 in his arrogance he said 11
7 but was even more filled with arrogance 10
8 in his superhuman arrogance 6
11 he began to lose much of his arrogance 10
13: 9 The king with barbarous arrogance was coming 13
15: 6 in his utter boastfulness and arrogance 12
3Mc 1:26 he, in his arrogance, took heed of nothing 8
2:17 exult in the arrogance of their tongue, saying 10
6:16 all the arrogance of his forces. 14
4Mc 2:15 lust for power, vainglory, boasting, arrogance 9
8:19 this arrogance that threatens to destroy us? 6

arrogant 1. גְּבַהּ לֵב 2. גֹּדֶל 3. הלל 4. זֵד 5. יָהִיר 6. עֶבְרָה 7. עָתָק 8. רְחַב 9. *ἀγέρωχος* 10. *αὐθάδης* 11. *ὑπερηφανία* 12. *ὑπερήφανος* 13. *φυσιόω*

Ps 73: 3 For I was envious of the arrogant 3
94: 4 They pour out their arrogant words, they boast 7
101: 5 man of haughty looks and arrogant heart 8

Prv 16: 5 Every one who is arrogant is an abomination 1
21:24 proud, haughty man who acts with arrogant pride. 6
Isa 10:12 he will punish the arrogant boasting of the king 2
13:11 I will put an end to the pride of the arrogant 4
Hab 2: 5 the arrogant man shall not abide. 5
Mal 3:15 Henceforth we deem the arrogant blessed; 4
4: 1 the arrogant and all evildoers will be stubble; 4
1Co 4:18 Some are arrogant, as though I were not coming 13
5: 2 you are arrogant! Ought you not rather to mourn? 13
13: 5 it is not arrogant or rude 13
2Ti 3: 2 lovers of self, lovers of money, proud, arrogant 12
Tit 1: 7 he must not be arrogant or quick-tempered 10
Wis 14: 6 when arrogant giants were perishing 12
Sir 23: 8 the reviler and the arrogant are tripped by them. 12
1Mc 2:47 They hunted down the arrogant men 11
3Mc 1:25 to change his arrogant mind 9
5:13 to show . . to the arrogant Gentiles. 12
4Mc 4:15 an arrogant and terrible man 12
9:30 the arrogant design of your tyranny 12

arrogant man 1. גֵּאֶה
Ps 140: 5 Arrogant men have hidden a trap for me 1

arrogant people 1. φυσιόω
1Co 4:19 find out not the talk of these arrogant people 1

arrogantly 1. בְּגֵאוּת 2. ὑπερηφανία 3. ὑπερηφάνως
Ps 17:10 with their mouths they speak arrogantly. 1
1Mc 7:34 defiled them and spoke arrogantly 3
47 the right hand which he so arrogantly stretched out 3
3Mc 2: 5 who acted arrogantly 2
arrogantly *See also* behave, deal.

arrow 1. בֵּן 2. בֶּן־קֶשֶׁת 3. חֵץ 4. חֵצִי 5. נֶשֶׁק 6. βέλος 7. σχίζα 8. τόξευμα 9. sagitta
Num24: 8 pierce them through with his arrows. 3
Deu 32:23 evils upon them; I will spend my arrows upon them; 3
42 I will make my arrows drunk with blood 3
1Sm 20:20 And I will shoot three arrows to the side of it 3
21 I will send the lad, saying, 'Go, find the arrows.' 3
21 'Look, the arrows are on this side of you, take them,' 3
22 if I say . . 'Look, the arrows are beyond you,' then go; 3
36 he said . . "Run and find the arrows which I shoot. 3
36 As the lad ran, he shot an arrow beyond him. 4
37 And when the lad came to the place of the arrow 4
37 Jonathan called . . "Is not the arrow beyond you? 4
38 Jonathan's lad gathered up the arrows 3
2Sm 22:15 And he sent out arrows, and scattered them; 3
2Kg 9:24 shot Joram . . so that the arrow pierced his heart 4
13:15 Eli'sha said to him, "Take a bow and arrows"; 3
15 Take a bow and arrows"; so he took a bow and arrows. 3
17 The LORD's arrow of victory, the arrow of victory 3
17 LORD's arrow . . the arrow of victory over Syria! 3
18 And he said, "Take the arrows"; and he took them. 3
19:32 not come into this city or shoot an arrow there 3
1Ch 12: 2 bowmen, and could shoot arrows and sling stones 3
2Ch 26:15 engines . . to shoot arrows and great stones. 3
Job 6: 4 For the arrows of the Almighty are in me; 3
20:24 a bronze arrow will strike him through. 5
41:28 The arrow cannot make him flee; 2
Ps 7:13 deadly weapons, making his arrows fiery shafts. 3
11: 2 they have fitted their arrow to the string 3
18:14 he sent out his arrows, and scattered them; 3
38: 2 thy arrows have sunk into me, and thy hand has come 3
45: 5 Your arrows are sharp in the heart of the king's 3
57: 4 their teeth are spears and arrows 3
64: 3 who aim bitter words like arrows 3
7 God will shoot his arrow at them; 3
76: 3 There he broke the flashing arrows, the shield •
77:17 thy arrows flashed on every side. 3
91: 5 of the night, nor the arrow that flies by day 3
120: 4 A warrior's sharp arrows, with glowing coals 3
127: 4 Like arrows in the hand of a warrior are the sons 3
144: 6 send out thy arrows and rout them! 3
Prv 7:23 till an arrow pierces its entrails; 3
25:18 like a war club, or a sword, or sharp arrow. 3
26:18 madman who throws firebrands, arrows, and death 3
Isa 5:28 their arrows are sharp, all their bows bent 3
7:24 With bow and arrows men will come there 3
37:33 come into this city, or shoot an arrow there 3
49: 2 he made me a polished arrow 3
Jer 9: 8 Their tongue is a deadly arrow; 3
50: 9 Their arrows are like a skilled warrior 3
14 you that bend the bow; shoot at her, spare no arrows 3
51:11 Sharpen the arrows! Take up the shields! 3
Lam 3:12 he bent his bow and set me as a mark for his arrow. 3
13 He drove into my heart the arrows of his quiver; 1
Ezk 5:16 I loose against you my deadly arrows of famine 3
16 deadly arrows of famine, arrows for destruction •
21:21 he shakes the arrows, he consults the teraphim 3
39: 3 make your arrows drop out of your right hand. 3
9 shields and bucklers, bows and arrows, handpikes 3
Hab 3: 9 from thy bow, and put the arrows to the string. •
11 at the light of thine arrows as they sped 3
Zec 9:13 Judah as my bow; I have made E'phraim its arrow. •
14 and his arrow go forth like lightning; 3
2Es 16: 7 Can one turn back an arrow shot by a strong archer? 9
13 and his arrows that he shoots are sharp 9
16 Just as an arrow shot by a mighty archer 9
Wis 5:12 when an arrow is shot at a target 6
Sir 19:12 Like an arrow stuck in the flesh of the thigh 6
26:12 open her quiver to the arrow. 6
1Mc 6:51 machines to shoot arrows, and catapults. 6
10:80 shot arrows at his men 7
2Mc 10:30 showered arrows and thunderbolts 8
arrows *See* machine.

arsenal 1. תַּלְפִּיּוֹת
Sng 4: 4 neck is like the tower . . built for an arsenal 1

art 1. מַעֲשֶׂה 2. ἔργον 3. τέχνη
2Ch 16:14 kinds of spices prepared by the perfumer's art; 1
Act 17:29 a representation by the art . . of man. 3
Wis 17: 7 The delusions of their magic art lay humbled 3
Sir 49: 1 prepared by the art of the perfumer 2

evil art 1. κακότεχνος
Wis 15: 4 the evil intent of human art misled us 1

magic art 1. περίεργος 2. φαρμακεία
Act 19:19 a number of those who practiced magic arts 1
Wis 18:13 because of their magic arts 2

secret art 1. לַט
Exd 7:11 they also . . did the same by their secret arts. 1
22 magicians . . did the same by their secret arts; 1
8: 7 the magicians did the same by their secret arts 1
18 magicians tried by their secret arts to bring 1

article 1. כְּלִי 2. σκεῦος
Lev 11:32 whether it is an article of wood or a garment 1
Num31:20 purify every garment, every article of skin 1
20 purify . . every article of wood. 1
50 LORD'S offering . . articles of gold 1
51 received . . the gold, all wrought articles. 1
2Sm 8:10 Joram brought . . articles of silver, of gold 1
1Kg 10:25 his present, articles of silver and gold 1
1Ch 18:10 articles of gold, of silver, and of bronze; 1
2Ch 9:24 his present, articles of silver and of gold 1
Rev 18:12 all kinds of scented wood, all articles of ivory 2
12 articles of costly wood, bronze, iron and marble 2

artificial 1. עשׂה
Neh 3:16 repaired to . . the artificial pool 1

artisan 1. אָמוֹן
Jer 52:15 together with the rest of the artisans. 1

artist 1. τις
4Mc 17: 7 to paint the history of your piety as an artist 1

artistic
Exd 31: 4 to devise artistic designs, to work in gold •
artistic *See also* design.

ascend 1. סלק 2. עלה 3. קום 4. ἀναβαίνω 5. ascendo
Gen 28:12 and behold, the angels of God were ascending 2
Deu 32:49 Ascend this mountain of the Ab'arim, Mount Nebo 2
50 die on the mountain which you ascend 2
Jdg 13:20 the angel . . ascended in the flame of the altar 2
2Ch 21: 4 Jeho'ram had ascended the throne of his father 3
Ps 24: 3 Who shall ascend the hill of the LORD? 2
68:18 Thou didst ascend the high mount 2
139: 8 If I ascend to heaven, thou art there! 1
Prv 30: 4 Who has ascended to heaven and come down? 2
Isa 14:13 You said in your heart, 'I will ascend to heaven; 2
14 I will ascend above the heights of the clouds 2
Joh 1:51 the angels of God ascending and descending 4
3:13 No one has ascended into heaven but he who 4
6:62 the Son of man ascending where he was before? 4
20:17 for I have not yet ascended to the Father 4
17 I am ascending to my Father and your Father 4
Act 2:34 David did not ascend into the heavens 4
10: 4 have ascended as a memorial before God. 4
Rom10: 6 say in your heart, "Who will ascend into heaven? 4
Eph 4: 8 When he ascended on high he led a host of captives 4
9 In saying, "He ascended," what does it mean 4
10 He who descended is he who also ascended 4
Rev 7: 2 I saw another angel ascend from the rising . . sun 4
11: 7 the beast that ascends from the bottomless pit 4
17: 8 The beast . . is to ascend from the bottomless pit 4
2Es 4: 8 neither did I ever ascend into heaven.' 5
Tob 12:20 I am ascending to him who sent me 4
3Mc 5: 9 their entreaty ascended fervently to heaven. 4

ascent 1. מוֹרָד 2. מַעֲלֶה 3. מַעֲלָה 4. עלה 5. ἀνάβασις
Num34: 4 boundary shall turn south of the ascent of Akrab'bim 3
Jos 10:10 chased them by the way of the ascent of Beth-hor'on 3
11 they were going down the ascent of Beth-hor'on 1
15: 3 it goes out southward of the ascent of Akrab'bim 3
7 Gilgal, which is opposite the ascent of Adum'mim 3
18:17 Geli'loth, which is opposite the ascent of Adum'mim; 3
Jdg 1:36 the border . . ran from the ascent of Akrab'bim 3
8:13 returned from the battle by the ascent of Heres. 3
2Sm 15:30 David went up the ascent of the Mount of Olives 3
2Kg 9:27 they shot him in the chariot at the ascent of Gur 3
2Ch 20:16 behold, they will come up by the ascent of Ziz; 3
32:33 buried him in the ascent of the tombs 3
Neh 3:19 opposite the ascent to the armory at the Angle. 4
12:37 stairs of the city . . at the ascent of the wall 3
Ps 120: 0 A Song of Ascents. 2
121: 0 A Song of Ascents. 2
122: 0 A Song of Ascents. Of David. 2
123: 0 A Song of Ascents. 2
124: 0 A Song of Ascents. Of David. 2
125: 0 A Song of Ascents. 2
126: 0 A Song of Ascents. 2
127: 0 A Song of Ascents. Of Solomon. 2
128: 0 A song of Ascents. 2
129: 0 A Song of Ascents. 2
130: 0 A Song of Ascents. 2
131: 0 A Song of Ascents. Of David. 2
132: 0 A Song of Ascents. 2
133: 0 A Song of Ascents. 2
134: 0 A Song of Ascents. 2
Isa 15: 5 For at the ascent of Luhith they go up weeping; 3
Jer 48: 5 For at the ascent of Luhith they go up weeping; 3
Sir 25:20 A sandy ascent for the feet of the aged 5
1Mc 3:16 When he approached the ascent of Beth-horon 5

ascertain 1. חקר 2. ἀκριβόω 3. ἐπιγινώσκω
2Ch 4:18 weight of the bronze was not ascertained. 1
Mat 2: 7 ascertained from them what time the star 2
16 time which he had ascertained from the wise men. 2
Act 24:11 As you may ascertain 3

ascribe 1. יהב 2. נתן 3. δίδωμι
Deu 32: 3 Ascribe greatness to our God! 1
1Sm 18: 8 They have ascribed to David ten thousands 2
8 and to me they have ascribed thousands; 2
1Ch 16:28 ascribe to the LORD, O families of the peoples 1
28 ascribe to the LORD glory and strength! 1
29 Ascribe to the LORD the glory due his name; 1
Job 36: 3 ascribe righteousness to my Maker. 2
Ps 29: 1 Ascribe to the LORD, O heavenly beings 1
1 ascribe to the LORD glory and strength. 1
2 Ascribe to the LORD the glory of his name; 1
68:34 Ascribe power to God, whose majesty 2
96: 7 Ascribe to the LORD, O families of the peoples 1
7 ascribe to the LORD glory and strength! 1
8 Ascribe to the LORD the glory due his name; 1
Sir 10:28 ascribe to yourself honor 3
39:15 ascribe majesty to his name 3
Bar 2:17 the dead . . will not ascribe glory or justice 3
18 will ascribe to thee glory and righteousness 3

ascription 1. ῥῆμα
Sir 47: 8 with ascriptions of glory 1

ash 1. אֵפֶר 2. דֶּשֶׁן 3. עָפָר 4. פִּיחַ 5. κόνις 6. σποδός 7. τέφρα 8. cinis
Gen 18:27 to the Lord, I who am but dust and ashes. 1
Exd 9: 8 Take handfuls of ashes from the kiln 4
10 So they took ashes from the kiln, and stood before 4
Lev 1:16 on the east side, in the place for ashes 2
4:12 a clean place, where the ashes are poured out 2
12 where the ashes are poured out it shall be burned 2
6:10 he shall take up the ashes 2
11 carry forth the ashes outside the camp 2
Num19: 9 clean shall gather up the ashes of the heifer 1
10 he who gathers the ashes of the heifer shall wash 1
17 shall take some ashes of the burnt sin offering 3
2Sm 13:19 Tamar put ashes on her head, and rent the long robe 1
1Kg 13: 3 the ashes that are upon it shall be poured out.' 2
5 altar also was torn down, and the ashes poured out 2
2Kg 23: 4 he burned them . . and carried their ashes to Bethel. 3
Est 4: 1 rent his clothes and put on sackcloth and ashes 1
3 and most of them lay in sackcloth and ashes. 1
Job 2: 8 to scrape himself, and sat among the ashes. 1
13:12 Your maxims are proverbs of ashes 1
30:19 I have become like dust and ashes. 1
42: 6 I despise myself, and repent in dust and ashes. 1
Ps 102: 9 For I eat ashes like bread 1
147:16 he scatters hoarfrost like ashes. 1
Isa 44:20 He feeds on ashes; a deluded mind has led him 1
58: 5 and to spread sackcloth and ashes under him? 1
61: 3 in Zion–to give them a garland instead of ashes 1
Jer 6:26 gird on sackcloth, and roll in ashes; 1
25:34 Wail, you shepherds, and cry, and roll in ashes •
31:40 The whole valley of the dead bodies and the ashes 2
Lam 3:16 made my teeth grind . . and made me cower in ashes; 1
Ezk 27:30 They cast dust on their heads and wallow in ashes; 1
28:18 I turned you to ashes upon the earth 1
Dan 9: 3 with fasting and sackcloth and ashes. 1
Jon 3: 6 covered himself with sackcloth, and sat in ashes. 1
Mal 4: 3 they will be ashes under the soles of your feet 1
Mat 11:21 repented long ago in sackcloth and ashes. 6
Lke 10:13 sitting in sackcloth and ashes. 6
Heb 9:13 the ashes of a heifer 6
2Es 2: 9 lies in lumps of pitch and heaps of ashes 8
9:38 and there were ashes on her head. 8

13:11 but only the dust of ashes and the smell of smoke. 8
Jdt 4:15 With ashes upon their turbans 6
9: 1 and put ashes on her head 6
AEs 14: 2 she covered her head with ashes and dung 6
Wis 2: 3 the body will turn to ashes 7
15:10 His heart is ashes, his hope is cheaper than dirt 6
Sir 10: 9 How can he who is dust and ashes be proud? 6
17:32 all men are dust and ashes. 6
40: 3 the one who is humbled in dust and ashes 6
Bel 1:14 Then Daniel ordered his servants to bring ashes 7
1Mc 3:47 and sprinkled ashes on their heads 6
4:39 sprinkled themselves with ashes. 6
2Mc 4:41 took handfuls of the ashes that were lying about 6
13: 5 a tower . . 50 cubits high, full of ashes 6
5 which . . inclines precipitously into the ashes. 6
8 against the altar whose fire and ashes were holy 6
8 he met his death in ashes. 6
3Mc 4: 6 their myrrh-perfumed hair sprinkled with ashes 5

ash *See also* receive, put, take, turn.

ash heap 1. אַשְׁפֹּת

1Sm 2: 8 he lifts the needy from the ash heap, to make them 1
Ps 113: 7 lifts the needy from the ash heap 1
Lam 4: 5 who were brought up in purple lie on ash heaps. 1

ashamed 1. בוש 2. חפר 3. כלם 4. αἰδέομαι 5. αἰσχύνω 6. ἐλέγχω 7. ἐντρέπω 8. ἐπαισχύνομαι 9. καταισχύνω

Gen 2:25 wife were both naked, and were not ashamed. 1
2Sm 10: 5 meet them, for the men were greatly ashamed. 3
19: 3 as people steal in who are ashamed when they flee 3
2Kg 2:17 when they urged him till he was ashamed, he said 1
8:11 and stared at him, until he was ashamed. 1
1Ch 19: 5 for the men were greatly ashamed. 3
Ezr 8:22 ashamed to ask the king for a band of soldiers 1
9: 6 O my God, I am ashamed and blush to lift my face 1
Job 19: 3 are you not ashamed to wrong me? 1
Ps 6:10 my enemies shall be ashamed and sorely troubled; 1
25: 3 let them be ashamed who are wantonly 1
34: 5 be radiant; so your faces shall never be ashamed. 2
Isa 1:29 For you shall be ashamed of the oaks in which you 1
23: 4 Be ashamed, O Sidon, for the sea has spoken 1
24:23 moon will be confounded, and the sun ashamed; 1
26:11 them see thy zeal for thy people, and be ashamed. 1
29:22 Jacob shall no more be ashamed 1
45:24 be ashamed, all who were incensed against him. 1
54: 4 Fear not, for you will not be ashamed; 1
Jer 3: 3 you have a harlot's brow, you refuse to be ashamed. 3
6:15 ashamed when they committed abomination? 1
15 No, they were not at all ashamed; 1
8:12 ashamed when they committed abomination? 1
12 they were not at all ashamed; they did not know how 1
12:13 They shall be ashamed of their harvests 1
14: 3 they are ashamed and confounded 1
4 the farmers are ashamed, they cover their heads. 1
22:22 then you will be ashamed and confounded 1
31:19 I was ashamed, and I was confounded 1
48:13 Then Moab shall be ashamed of Chemosh 1
13 as the house of Israel was ashamed of Bethel 1
Ezk 16:27 who were ashamed of your lewd behavior. 3
52 So be ashamed, you also, and bear your disgrace 1
54 and be ashamed of all that you have done 3
61 and be ashamed when I take your sisters 3
36:32 Be ashamed and confounded for your ways 1
43:10 that they may be ashamed of their iniquities. 3
11 if they are ashamed of all that they have done 3
Hos 4:19 they shall be ashamed because of their altars. 1
10: 6 and Israel shall be ashamed of his idol. 1
Mic 7:16 nations shall . . be ashamed of all their might; 1
Zec 13: 4 every prophet will be ashamed of his vision 1
Mrk 8:38 whoever is ashamed of me and of my words 8
38 of him will the Son of man also be ashamed 8
Lke 9:26 For whoever is ashamed of me and of my words 8
26 of him will the Son of man be ashamed 8
16: 3 I am ashamed to beg. 5
Rom 1:16 For I am not ashamed of the gospel 8
6:21 get from the things of which you are now ashamed? 8
Php 1:20 my . . hope that I shall not be at all ashamed 5
2Th 3:14 that he may be ashamed. 7
2Ti 1: 8 Do not be ashamed then of testifying to our Lord 8
12 I am not ashamed, for I know whom I have believed 8
16 he was not ashamed of my chains 8
Heb 2:11 why he is not ashamed to call them brethren 8
11:16 God is not ashamed to be called their God 8
1Pe 4:16 as a Christian, let him not be ashamed 5
1Es 8:51 I was ashamed to ask the king for foot soldiers 7
74 I am ashamed and confounded before thy face. 5
Jdt 9: 3 was ashamed of the deceit they had practiced 4
Wis 1: 5 ashamed at the approach of unrighteousness. 6
13:17 he is not ashamed to address a lifeless thing. 5
Sir 4:26 Do not be ashamed to confess your sins 5
22:25 I will not be ashamed to protect a friend 5
41:17 Be ashamed of immorality 5
19 Be ashamed before the truth of God •
19 Be ashamed of selfish behavior at meals •
42: 1 Of the following things do not be ashamed 5
8 Do not be ashamed to instruct the stupid •
LJr 1:27 those who serve them are ashamed 5
Sus 1:11 ashamed to disclose their lustful desire 5
27 the servants were greatly ashamed 9
1Mc 4:31 let them be ashamed of their troops 5

ashamed *See also* make, need.

ashore 1. εἰς τὴν γῆν 2. ἐπὶ τὸν αἰγιαλόν

Mat 13:48 when it was full, men drew it ashore and sat down 2
Joh 21:11 hauled the net ashore, full of large fish, 153 1

ashore *See also* bring, cast, go.

aside 1. עִם 2. ἐκ μέσου 3. ἴδιος 4. κατ' ἰδίαν 5. παρά 6. ab

1Sm 9:23 the portion . . of which I said to you, 'Put it aside.' 1
Mat 20:17 he took the twelve disciples aside 4
1Co 16: 2 each of you is to put something aside 5
Col 2:14 this he set aside, nailing it to the cross. 2
2Es 10:24 and lay aside your many sorrows 6
2Mc 4:34 Menelaus, taking Andronicus aside 3

aside *See also* crowd, go, lay, put, set, stand, take, thrust, turn.

ask 1. אמר 2. בקש 3. בַּקָּשָׁה 4. דָּבָר 5. דרש 6. שאל 7. שְׁאֵלָה 8. אמר (A) 9. בעא (A) 10. שאל (A) 11. αἰτέω 12. ἀξιόω 13. δέω 14. εἶπον 15. ἐκζητέω 16. ἐξετάζω 17. ἐπερωτάω 18. ἐρωτάω 19. ζητέω 20. λέγω 21. μανθάνω 22. μετακαλέω 23. ὅπως 24. παραιτέομαι 25. παρακαλέω 26. πυνθάνομαι 27. interrogo 28. perrogo 29. peto 30. rogo

Gen 24:47 Then I asked her, 'Whose daughter are you?' 6
57 They said, "We will call the maiden, and ask her. 6
26: 7 When the men of the place asked him about his wife 6
32:17 When Esau . . asks you, 'To whom do you belong? 6
29 Then Jacob asked him, "Tell me, I pray, your name. 6
29 But he said, "Why is it that you ask my name? 6
37:15 and the man asked him, "What are you seeking? 6
38:21 he asked the men of the place, "Where is the harlot 6
40: 7 he asked Pharaoh's officers who were with him 6
44:19 My lord asked his servants, saying 6
Exd 3:13 God of your fathers . . ' and they ask me, 'What is his 1
22 each woman shall ask of her neighbor . . jewelry 6
5:14 foremen . . were beaten, and were asked, "Why have 1
8:31 the LORD did as Moses asked, and removed 4
11: 2 Speak now . . that they ask, every man of his 6
12:35 they had asked of the Egyptians jewelry 6
36 they let them have what they asked. 6
13:14 when . . your son asks you, 'What does this mean?' 6
18: 7 and they asked each other of their welfare 6
Deu 4:32 For ask now of the days that are past 6
32 ask from one end of heaven to the other •
6:20 When your son asks you in time to come, 'What is 6
13:14 inquire and make search and ask diligently; 6
32: 7 ask your father, and he will show you; your elders 6
Jos 4: 6 a sign . . when your children ask in time to come 6
21 When your children ask their fathers in time 6
9:14 and did not ask direction from the LORD. 6
15:18 she urged him to ask her father for a field; 6
19:50 gave him the city which he asked, Tim'nath-se'rah 6
Jdg 1:14 to him, she urged him to ask her father for a field; 6
4:20 and if any man comes and asks you, 'Is any one here?' 6
5:25 He asked water and she gave him milk 6
13: 6 I did not ask him whence he was, and he did not tell 6
18 Why do you ask my name, seeing it is wonderful? 6
18:15 young Levite . . and asked him of his welfare. 6
24 have I left? How then do you ask me, 'What ails you?' 1
Rut 3:11 do not fear, I will do for you all that you ask 1
1Sm 1:20 Samuel, for she said, "I have asked him of the LORD. 6
8:10 to the people who were asking a king from him. 6
12:13 whom you have chosen, for whom you have asked; 6
17 wickedness . . in asking for a king. 6
19 added . . this evil, to ask for ourselves a king. 6
19:22 and he asked, "Where are Samuel and David? 6
20: 6 David earnestly asked . . to run to Bethlehem 6
28 David . . asked leave of me to go to Bethlehem; 6
25: 8 Ask your young men, and they will tell you. 6
27:10 A'chish asked, "Against whom have you made a raid 1
28:16 Why then do you ask me, since the LORD has turned 6
2Sm 11: 7 David asked how Jo'ab was doing, and how the people 6
12:20 when he asked, they set food before him, and he ate. 6
14:18 Do not hide from me anything I ask you. 6
32 I may send you to the king, to ask, "Why have I come 1
20:18 to say in old time, 'Let them but ask counsel at Abel'; 6
1Kg 1: 6 father had never . . displeased him by asking, "Why 1
2:17 ask King Solomon . . to give me Ab'ishag 1
22 And why do you ask Ab'ishag . . for Adoni'jah? Ask 6
22 Ask for him the kingdom also; for he is my elder 6
3: 5 by night; and God said, "Ask what I shall give you. 6
10 It pleased the Lord that Solomon had asked this. 6
11 Because you have asked this, and have not asked 6
11 and have not asked for yourself long life 6
11 have asked for yourself understanding 6
13 give . . what you have not asked, both riches 6
10:13 whatever she asked besides what was given her 6
19: 4 and he asked that he might die, saying, "It is enough; 6
2Kg 2: 9 Ask what I shall do for you, before I am taken 6
10 he said, "You have asked a hard thing; 6
4:28 Then she said, "Did I ask my lord for a son? 6
6:28 And the king asked her, "What is your trouble? 1
8: 6 And when the king asked the woman, she told him. 6
1Ch 4:10 And God granted what he asked. 6
2Ch 1: 7 God . . said to him, "Ask what I shall give you. 6
11 you have not asked possessions, wealth, honor 6
11 and have not even asked long life, 6
11 have asked wisdom and knowledge for yourself 6
9:12 gave . . all that she desired, whatever she asked 6
Ezr 5: 4 They also asked them this, "What are the names 8
9 Then we asked those elders and spoke to them thus 10
10 asked them their names, for your information 10
7: 6 king granted him all that he asked 3
8:22 ashamed to ask the king for a band of soldiers 6
Neh 1: 2 I asked them concerning the Jews that survived 6
2: 8 king granted me what I asked, for the good hand •
13: 6 after some time I asked leave of the king 6
Est 2:15 she asked for nothing except what Hegai 2
Job 12: 7 But ask the beasts, and they will teach you; 6
21:29 Have you not asked those who travel the roads 6
31:30 I have not let my mouth sin by asking for his life 6
35: 3 That you ask, 'What advantage have I? 1
Ps 2: 8 Ask of me, and I will make the nations 6
21: 4 He asked life of thee; thou gavest it to him 6
27: 4 One thing have I asked of the LORD, that will I seek 6
35:11 they ask me of things that I know not. 6
105:40 They asked, and he brought quails 6
106:15 he gave them what they asked 7
119:82 I ask, "When wilt thou comfort me? 1
Prv 30: 7 Two things I ask of thee; deny them not to me 6
Ecc 4: 8 no end to all his toil . . so that he never asks •
7:10 For it is not from wisdom that you ask this. 6
Isa 7:11 Ask a sign of the LORD your God; 6
12 Ahaz said, "I will not ask 6
30: 2 to go down to Egypt, without asking for my counsel 6
41:28 no counselor who, when I ask, gives an answer. 6
58: 2 they ask of me righteous judgments 6
65: 1 I was ready to be sought by those who did not ask 6
Jer 6:16 and look, and ask for the ancient paths 6
15: 2 when they ask you, 'Where shall we go?' 1
5 Who will turn aside to ask about your welfare? 6
18:13 thus says the LORD: Ask among the nations 6
23:33 or a prophet, or a priest asks you 6
30: 6 Ask now, and see, can a man bear a child? 6
36:17 Then they asked Baruch, "Tell us, how did you write 6
38:14 king said to Jeremiah, "I will ask you a question; 6
27 all the princes came to Jeremiah and asked him 6
48:19 Ask him who flees and her who escapes; 6
50: 5 They shall ask the way to Zion 6
Ezk 36:37 I will let the house of Israel ask me to do for them 5
Dan 1: 8 therefore he asked the chief of the eunuchs 2
2:10 no . . king has asked such a thing of any magician 10
11 thing that the king asks is difficult 10
23 hast now made known to me what we asked of thee 9
27 can show . . the mystery which the king has asked 10
7:16 asked him the truth concerning all this. 9
Jon 4: 8 he asked that he might die, and said 6
Mic 7: 3 the prince and the judge ask for a bribe 6
Hag 2:11 Ask the priests to decide this question 6
Zec 7: 3 to ask the priests of the house of the LORD 1
10: 1 Ask rain from the LORD in the season of the spring 6
13: 6 one asks him, 'What are these wounds on your back?' 1
Mal 2:14 You ask, "Why does he not? 1
17 Or by asking, "Where is the God of justice? •
Mat 6: 8 Father knows what you need before you ask him. 11
7: 7 Ask, and it will be given you; seek, and you will find; 11
8 For every one who asks receives 11
9 Or what man of you, if his son asks him for bread 11
10 Or if he asks for a fish, will give him a serpent? 11
11 give good things to those who ask him! 11
12:10 they asked him, "Is it lawful to heal on the sabbath? 17
46 asking to speak to him. 19
14: 7 to give her whatever she might ask. 11
16: 1 to test him they asked him to show them a sign 17
13 he asked his disciples 18
17:10 the disciples asked him 17
18:19 agree on earth about anything they ask 11
19: 3 Pharisees came up to him and tested him by asking 20
17 he said . . "Why do you ask me about what is good? 18
20:20 kneeling before him she asked him 11
22 You do not know what you are asking 11
21:22 whatever you ask in prayer, you will receive 11
24 I also will ask you a question 18
22:23 they asked him a question 17
27:11 the governor asked him 17
20 elders persuaded the people to ask for Barab'bas 11
58 He went to Pilate and asked for the body of Jesus. 11
Mrk 3:32 your brothers are outside, asking for you. 19
4:10 asked him concerning the parables. 18
5: 9 Jesus asked him, "What is your name? 17
6:22 Ask me for whatever you wish, and I will grant it. 11
23 he vowed to her, "Whatever you ask me, I will give you 11
24 said to her mother, "What shall I ask? 11
25 asked, saying, "I want you to give me at once the head 11
7: 5 the Pharisees and the scribes asked him 17
17 his disciples asked him about the parable. 17
8: 5 he asked them, "How many loaves have you? 18
23 he asked him, "Do you see anything? 17
27 on the way he asked his disciples 17
29 he asked them, "But who do you say that I am? 17
9:11 they asked him, "Why do the scribes say 17
16 he asked them, "What are you discussing with them? 17

18 I asked your disciples to cast it out 14
21 Jesus asked his father, "How long has he had this? 17
28 his disciples asked him privately 17
32 they were afraid to ask him. 17
33 when he was in the house he asked them 17
10: 2 Pharisees came up and in order to test him asked 17
10 in the house the disciples asked him again 17
17 a man ran up and knelt before him, and asked him 17
35 we want you to do for us whatever we ask of you. 11
38 You do not know what you are asking 11
11:29 Jesus said to them, "I will ask you a question; 17
12:18 they asked him a question, saying 17
28 seeing that he answered them well, asked him 17
34 after that no one dared to ask him any question. 17
13: 3 James and John and Andrew asked him privately 17
14:60 stood up in the midst, and asked Jesus 17
61 the high priest asked him, "Are you the Christ 17
15: 2 Pilate asked him, "Are you the King of the Jews? 17
4 Pilate again asked him, "Have you no answer to make? 17
6 one prisoner for whom they asked. 24
8 the crowd came up and began to ask Pilate 11
43 went to Pilate, and asked for the body of Jesus. 11
44 he asked him whether he was already dead. 17
Lke 1:63 he asked for a writing tablet, and wrote, 11
3:10 the multitudes asked him, "What then shall we do? 17
14 Soldiers also asked him 17
5: 3 he asked him to put out a little from the land. 18
6: 9 Jesus said to them, "I ask you 17
7: 3 asking him to come and heal his slave. 18
36 One of the Pharisees asked him to eat with him 18
8: 9 his disciples asked him what this parable meant 17
30 Jesus then asked him, "What is your name? 17
37 all the people . . asked him to depart from them; 18
9:18 he asked them, "Who do the people say that I am? 17
45 they were afraid to ask him about this saying. 18
11: 9 I tell you, Ask, and it will be given you 11
10 every one who asks receives 11
11 What father among you, if his son asks for a fish 11
12 or if he asks for an egg, will give him a scorpion? 11
13 give the Holy Spirit to those who ask him! 11
37 a Pharisee asked him to dine with him 18
14:32 he sends an embassy and asks terms of peace. 18
15:26 asked what this meant. 26
17:20 Being asked by the Pharisees 17
18:18 a ruler asked him, "Good Teacher, what shall I do 17
40 when he came near, he asked him 17
19:31 If any one asks you, 'Why are you untying it?' 18
20: 3 I also will ask you a question; now tell me 18
21 They asked him, "Teacher 17
21: 7 they asked him, "Teacher, when will this be 17
22:64 they also blindfolded him and asked him 17
68 if I ask you, you will not answer. 18
23: 3 Pilate asked him, "Are you the King of the Jews? 18
6 he asked whether the man was a Galilean. 17
25 for insurrection and murder . . they asked for 11
52 went to Pilate and asked for the body of Jesus. 11
Joh 1:19 priests and Levites from Jerusalem to ask him 18
21 And they asked him, "What then? Are you Elijah? 18
25 They asked him, "Then why are you baptizing 18
4: 9 you, a Jew, ask a drink of me, a woman of Samar'ia? 11
10 you would have asked him, and he would have given 11
40 they asked him to stay with them; 18
52 So he asked them the hour when he began to mend 26
5:12 They asked him, "Who is the man who said to you 18
8: 7 as they continued to ask him 18
9: 2 his disciples asked him, "Rabbi, who sinned 18
15 The Pharisees again asked him 18
19 asked them, "Is this your son 18
21 Ask him; he is of age, he will speak for himself. 18
23 Therefore his parents said, "He is of age, ask him. 17
11:22 whatever you ask from God, God will give you. 11
14:13 Whatever you ask in my name, I will do it 11
14 if you ask anything in my name, I will do it. 11
15: 7 ask whatever you will, and it shall be done for you. 11
16 whatever you ask the Father in my name 11
16: 5 yet none of you asks me, 'Where are you going?' 18
19 Jesus knew that they wanted to ask him 18
19 he said to them, "Is this what you are asking 19
23 In that day you will ask nothing of me 18
23 if you ask anything of the Father, he will give it 11
24 Hitherto you have asked nothing in my name 11
24 ask, and you will receive, that your joy may be full. 11
26 In that day you will ask in my name 11
18: 7 Again he asked them, "Whom do you seek? 17
21 Why do you ask me? Ask those who have heard me 18
21 Why do you ask me? Ask those who have heard me 18
26 One of the servants . . asked 20
19:31 the Jews asked Pilate 18
38 asked Pilate that he might take away the body 18
21:12 none of the disciples dared ask him, "Who are you? 16
Act 1: 6 So when they had come together, they asked him 18
3: 2 to ask alms of those who entered the temple. 11
3 he asked for alms. 18
14 asked for a murderer to be granted to you 11
8:30 asked, "Do you understand what you are reading? 14
9: 2 asked him for letters to the synagogues 11
10:18 and called out to ask 26
29 I ask then why you sent for me. 26
32 ask for Simon who is called Peter 22
48 Then they asked him to remain for some days. 18
12:20 they asked for peace 11
13:21 Then they asked for a king; and God gave them Saul 11
28 yet they asked Pilate to have him killed. 11
16:39 took them out and asked them to leave the city. 18
18:20 When they asked him to stay for a longer period 18
23:18 Paul . . asked me to bring this young man to you 18
19 going aside asked him privately, "What is it 26
20 The Jews have agreed to ask you to bring Paul down 18
34 he asked to what province he belonged 17
25: 3 asking as a favor 11
15 asking for sentence against him. 11
20 I asked whether he wished to go to Jerusalem 20
28:20 therefore I have asked to see you 25
Rom 1:10 asking that somehow by God's will 13
10:18 But I ask, have they not heard? Indeed they have; 20
19 Again I ask, did Israel not understand? 20
20 shown myself to those who did not ask for me. 17
11: 1 I ask, then, has God rejected his people? By no means! 20
11 I ask, have they stumbled so as to fall? By no means! 20
1Co 14:35 let them ask their husbands at home 17
15:35 some one will ask, "How are the dead raised? 14
Gal 3: 2 Let me ask you only this 21
Eph 3:13 I ask you not to lose heart 11
20 far more abundantly than all that we ask or think 11
Php 4: 3 I ask you also, true yokefellow, help these women 18
Col 1: 9 asking that you may be filled with the knowledge 11
Jas 1: 5 If any of you lacks wisdom, let him ask God 11
6 let him ask in faith, with no doubting 11
4: 2 You do not have, because you do not ask. 11
3 You ask and do not receive 11
3 You . . do not receive, because you ask wrongly 11
1Jn 3:22 we receive from him whatever we ask 11
5:14 if we ask anything according to his will he hears 11
15 if we know that he hears us in whatever we ask 11
16 he will ask, and God will give him life 11
1Es 4:42 the king said to him, "Ask what you wish 11
46 now, O lord the king, this is what I ask and request 12
6:11 we asked these elders 26
12 we questioned them and asked them 11
8:51 I was ashamed to ask the king for foot soldiers 11
2Es 2: 4 Go, my children, and ask for mercy from the Lord.' 29
13 Ask and you will receive 29
44 Then I asked an angel, "Who are these, my lord? 27
4: 6 that you ask me concerning these things? 27
7 he said . . "If I had asked you, 'How many dwellings 27
9 now I have asked you only about fire and wind 27
25 It is about these things that I have asked. 27
28 For the evil about which you ask me has been sown 27
35 in their chambers ask about these matters 27
40 Go and ask a woman who is with child 27
52 Concerning the signs about which you ask me 28
5:11 one country shall ask its neighbor 27
37 the travail that you ask to understand. 30
39 the things which thou hast asked me? 27
46 He said to me, "Ask a woman's womb, and say to it 27
51 He replied to me, "Ask a woman who bears children 27
7:54 but ask the earth and she will tell you 27
8: 2 Just as, when you ask the earth, it will tell you 27
10: 9 Now ask the earth, and she will tell you 27
Tob 4: 2 I have asked for death 11
19 ask him that your ways may be made straight 11
7: 3 Raguel asked them, "Where are you from, brethren? 18
4 he asked them, "Is he in good health? 14
Jdt 6:16 Uzziah asked him what had happened. 17
10:12 and took her into custody, and asked her 17
AEs 13: 3 When I asked my counselors 26
16:13 asked for the destruction of Mordecai 11
Wis 13:19 he asks strength 11
19:11 when desire led them to ask for luxurious food; 11
Sir 32: 7 no more than twice, and only if asked. 17
33:19 lest you change your mind and must ask for it. 13
21 better that your children should ask from you 13
51:14 Before the temple I asked for her 12
Sus 1:40 and asked her who the young man was 17
1Mc 3:44 to pray and ask for mercy and compassion. 11
7:12 to ask for just terms. 15
10:72 Ask and learn who I am 18
11:28 Then Jonathan asked the king to free Judea 12
66 Then they asked him to grant them terms of peace 12
12: 4 asking them to provide . . safe conduct 23
13:45 asking Simon to make peace with them; 12
16:18 asking him to send troops to aid him •
19 asking them to come to him •
2Mc 2: 8 as Solomon asked that . . 12
3:31 Quickly some of Heliodorus' friends asked Onias 12
37 When the king asked Heliodorus . . he replied 17
7: 2 What do you intend to ask and learn from us? 18
7 and asked him, "Will you eat . . 17
11:17 and have asked about the matters indicated therein. 12
24 and ask that their own customs be allowed them. 12
14: 5 was asked about the disposition . . of the Jews. 17
15: 3 the thrice-accursed wretch asked 17
3Mc 6:37 asking for dismissal to their homes. 11
4Mc 1: 5 Some might perhaps ask 20
5:14 Eleazar asked to have a word. 11

ask a question 1. ἐπερωτάω 2. inquiro
Mat 22:35 one of them, a lawyer, asked him a question 1
41 Jesus asked them a question 1
46 did any one dare to ask him any more questions. 1
Lke 2:46 listening to them and asking them questions; 1
20:28 they asked him a question, saying, "Teacher 1
40 For they no longer dared to ask him any question. 1
2Es 8:55 Therefore do not ask any more questions 2

ask again 1. ἀπαιτέω
Lke 6:30 do not ask them again. 1

ask an accounting 1. חשב
2Kg 12:15 they did not ask an accounting from the men 1
22: 7 But no accounting shall be asked from them 1

ask back 1. ἀπαιτέω
Sir 20:15 today he lends and tomorrow he asks it back 1

ask in prayer 1. προσεύχομαι
Mrk 11:24 Therefore I tell you, whatever you ask in prayer 1

ask leave 1. αἰτέω
Act 7:46 and asked leave to find a habitation 1

ask much 1. רבה
Gen 34:12 Ask of me ever so much as marriage present 1

asleep 1. יָשֵׁן 2. נום 3. καθεύδω 4. κοιμάω 5. νυστάζω 6. dormio
1Sm 26:12 nor did any awake; for they were all asleep 1
1Kg 18:27 or perhaps he is asleep and must be awakened. 1
Nah 3:18 Your shepherds are asleep, O king of Assyria; 2
Mat 8:24 swamped by the waves; but he was asleep 3
28:13 stole him away while we were asleep.' 4
Mrk 4:38 he was in the stern, asleep on the cushion 3
13:36 lest he come suddenly and find you asleep. 3
14:37 Simon, are you asleep? Could you not watch one hour? 3
1Th 4:13 concerning those who are asleep 4
2Pe 2: 3 and their destruction has not been asleep. 5
2Es 7:32 the earth shall give up those who are asleep in it 6
Tob 8:13 went in, and found them both asleep. 3

asleep *See also* fall, fast, lie.

asp 1. פֶּתֶן 2. ἀσπίς
Deu 32:33 their wine is . . the cruel venom of asps. 1
Job 20:14 in his stomach; it is the gall of asps within him. 1
16 He will suck the poison of asps; 1
Isa 11: 8 sucking child . . play over the hole of the asp 1
Rom 3:13 The venom of asps is under their lips. 2

fearful aspect 1. φοβεροειδής
3Mc 6:18 two glorious angels of fearful aspect 1

aspire 1. ὀρέγω 2. φιλοτιμέομαι
1Th 4:11 to aspire to live quietly 2
1Ti 3: 1 If any one aspires to the office of bishop 1

ass 1. אָתוֹן 2. חֲמוֹר 3. עַיִר 4. ὄνος 5. ὑποζύγιον
Gen 22: 3 saddled his ass, and took two of his young men 2
5 Then Abraham said . . "Stay here with the ass; 2
24:35 maidservants, camels and asses. 2
30:43 menservants, and camels and asses. 2
32: 5 I have oxen, asses, flocks, menservants 2
34:28 took . . their asses, and whatever was in the city 2
36:24 as he pastured the asses of Zib'eon his father. 2
42:26 Then they loaded their asses with their grain 2
27 opened his sack to give his ass provender 2
43:18 to make slaves of us and seize our asses. 2
24 when he had given their asses provender 2
44: 3 the men were sent away with their asses. 2
13 rent their clothes, and every man loaded his ass 2
45:23 he sent as follows: ten asses loaded with the good 2
47:17 the horses, the flocks, the herds, and the asses 2
49:11 Binding . . his ass's colt to the choice vine 1
14 Is'sachar is a strong ass, crouching between 2
Exd 4:20 Moses . . set them on an ass, and went back 2
9: 3 plague upon . . the horses, the asses, the camels 2
13:13 Every firstling of an ass you shall redeem 2
20:17 covet . . his ox, or his ass, or anything 2
21:33 a pit . . and an ox or an ass falls into it 2
22: 4 whether it is an ox or an ass or a sheep 2
9 whether it is for ox, for ass, for sheep 2
10 If a man delivers to his neighbor an ass or an ox 2
23: 4 If you meet your enemy's ox or his ass going astray 2
5 If you see the ass of one who hates you lying under 2
12 that your ox and your ass may have rest 2
34:20 The firstling of an ass you shall redeem 2
Num16:15 I have not taken one ass from them, and I have not 2
22:21 Balaam rose in the morning, and saddled his ass 1
22 Now he was riding on the ass, and his two servants 1
23 ass saw the angel of the LORD standing in the road 1
23 the ass turned aside out of the road 1
23 Balaam struck the ass, to turn her into the road. 1
25 when the ass saw the angel of the LORD, she pushed 1
27 When the ass saw the angel of the LORD, 1
27 he struck the ass with his staff. 1
28 LORD opened the mouth of the ass, and she said 1
29 Balaam said to the ass, "Because you have 1
30 ass said to Balaam, "Am I not your ass 1

30 Am I not your ass, upon which you have ridden 1
32 Why have you struck your ass these three times? 1
33 ass saw me, and turned aside before me these three 1
31:28 tribute . . of the asses and of the flocks; 2
30 one drawn out of every 50 . . of the oxen, of the asses 2
34 61,000 asses 2
39 asses were 30,500, of which the LORD'S tribute 2
45 30,500 asses 2
Deu 5:14 your ox, or your ass, or any of your cattle 2
21 not desire . . his ox, or his ass, or anything 2
22: 3 so you shall do with his ass . . with his garment; 2
4 You shall not see your brother's ass or his ox 2
10 You shall not plow with an ox and an ass together. 2
28:31 your ass shall be violently taken away 2
Jos 6:21 men and women . . oxen, sheep, and asses 2
7:24 and daughters, and his oxen and asses and sheep 2
9: 4 and took worn-out sacks upon their asses 2
15:18 she alighted from her ass, and Caleb said to her 2
Jdg 1:14 she alighted from her ass, and Caleb said to her 2
5:10 Tell of it, you who ride on tawny asses, you who sit 1
6: 4 leave no sustenance . . and no sheep or ox or ass. 2
10: 4 he had 30 sons who rode on 30 asses; 3
12:14 40 sons and 30 grandsons, who rode on 70 asses; 3
15:15 he found a fresh jawbone of an ass, and put out his 2
16 With the jawbone of an ass, heaps upon heaps 2
16 with the jawbone of an ass have I slain 1,000 men 2
19: 3 He had with him his servant and a couple of asses. 2
10 He had with him a couple of saddled asses 2
19 We have straw and provender for our asses 2
21 into his house, and gave the asses provender; 2
28 he put her upon the ass; and the man rose up 2
1Sm 8:16 take . . and the best of your cattle and your asses 2
9: 3 Now the asses of Kish, Saul's father, were lost. 1
3 Take . . and arise, go and look for the asses. 1
5 lest my father cease to care about the asses 1
20 As for your asses that were lost three days ago 1
10: 2 The asses which you went to seek are found 1
2 your father has ceased to care about the asses 1
14 Where did you go?" And he said, "To seek the asses; 1
16 He told us plainly that the asses had been found. 1
12: 3 Whose ox have I taken? Or whose ass have I taken? 2
15: 3 infant and suckling, ox and sheep, camel and ass. 2
16:20 Jesse took an ass laden with bread 2
22:19 children and sucklings, oxen, asses and sheep 2
25:18 and 200 cakes of figs, and laid them on asses. 2
20 And as she rode on the ass . . David and his men came 2
23 Ab'igail . . made haste, and alighted from the ass 2
42 Ab'igail made haste and rose and mounted on an ass 2
27: 9 took . . the sheep, the oxen, the asses, the camels 2
2Sm 16: 1 Ziba . . met him, with a couple of asses saddled 2
2 The asses are for the king's household to ride on 2
17:23 he saddled his ass, and went off . . to his own city. 2
19:26 Saddle an ass for me, that I may ride upon it and go 2
1Kg 2:40 Shim'e-i arose and saddled an ass, and went to Gath 2
13:13 he said to his sons, "Saddle the ass for me. 2
13 they saddled the ass for him and he mounted it. 2
23 he saddled the ass for the prophet 2
24 body was . . in the road, and the ass stood beside it; 2
27 Saddle the ass for me." And they saddled it. 2
28 found his body . . and the ass and the lion 2
28 The lion had not eaten the body or torn the ass. 2
29 took up the body . . and laid it upon the ass 2
2Kg 4:22 Send me one of the servants and one of the asses 1
24 she saddled the ass, and she said to her servant 1
6:25 an ass's head was sold for 80 shekels of silver 2
7: 7 forsook . . tents, their horses, and their asses 2
10 nothing but the horses tied, and the asses tied 2
1Ch 5:21 50,000 camels, 250,000 sheep, 2,000 asses 2
12:40 bringing food on asses and on camels and on mules 2
2Ch 28:15 carrying all the feeble among them on asses 2
Ezr 2:67 their camels were 435, and their asses were 6,720. 2
Neh 7:69 their camels 435, and their asses 6,720. 2
13:15 heaps of grain and loading them on asses; 2
Job 1:14 were plowing and the asses feeding beside them; 1
24: 3 They drive away the ass of the fatherless; 2
Prv 26: 3 A whip for the horse, a bridle for the ass, and a rod 2
Isa 1: 3 ox knows its owner, and the ass its master's crib; 2
21: 7 horsemen in pairs, riders on asses 2
30: 6 carry their riches on the backs of asses 3
24 the oxen and the asses that till the ground 3
32:20 who let the feet of the ox and the ass range free. 2
Jer 22:19 With the burial of an ass he shall be buried 2
Ezk 23:20 whose members were like those of asses 2
Zec 9: 9 victorious is he, humble and riding on an ass 2
9 riding on an ass, on a colt the foal of an ass. 1
14:15 on the horses, the mules, the camels, the asses 2
Mat 21: 2 immediately you will find an ass tied 4
5 humble, and mounted on an ass 4
5 on an ass, and on a colt, the foal of an ass. 5
7 they brought the ass and the colt 4
Lke 13:15 untie his ox or his ass from the manger 4
Joh 12:15 behold, your king is coming, sitting on an ass's colt! 4
2Pe 2:16 a dumb ass spoke with human voice 5
1Es 5:43 245 mules, and 5,525 asses. 5
Jdt 2:17 He collected a vast number of camels and asses 4
Sir 33:24 Fodder and a stick and burdens for an ass 4

ass *See also* wild.

swift ass 1. עָרוֹד

Job 39: 5 Who has loosed the bonds of the swift ass 1

young ass 1. ὀνάριον

Joh 12:14 Jesus found a young ass and sat upon it 1

assail 1. בעת 2. קְרֹב עָל 3. שׁוּב יָד עַל 4. ἐπέρχομαι 5. ἐφίστημι 6. τιτρώσκω 7. ὑπέρ

2Sm 22: 5 the torrents of perdition assailed me; 1
Ps 18: 4 the torrents of perdition assailed me; 1
27: 2 When evildoers assail me, uttering slanders 2
Ezk 38:12 and carry off plunder; to assail the waste places 3
Lke 11:22 one stronger than he assails him and overcomes 4
Wis 18:17 unexpected fears assailed them; 5
19: 1 the ungodly were assailed to the end 5
2Mc 11: 9 ready to assail not only men 6
4Mc 15:32 the wintry storms that assail religion. 7

assailant 1. קוּם 2. ἐπανιστάνω

2Sm 22:40 thou didst make my assailants sink under me. 1
Ps 18:39 thou didst make my assailants sink under me. 1
44: 5 through thy name we tread down our assailants. 1
92:11 ears have heard the doom of my evil assailants. 1
109:28 Let my assailants be put to shame; 2
Lam 3:62 my assailants are against me all the day long. 1

assassin 1. σικάριος

Act 21:38 and led the 4,000 men of the Assassins out 1

assault 1. כבשׁ 2. לחם 3. נֶגַע 4. ἐπίθεσις 5. impetus

Deu 17: 8 between . . one kind of assault and another 3
21: 5 by their word . . every assault shall be settled. 3
Jos 10:31 and laid siege to it, and assaulted it 2
34 and they laid siege to it, and assaulted it; 2
36 went up . . to Hebron; and they assaulted it 2
38 Joshua . . turned back to Debir and assaulted it 2
Est 7: 8 Will he even assault the queen in my presence 1
2Es 15:19 but shall make an assault upon their houses 5
2Mc 5: 5 suddenly made an assault upon the city 4

dread assault 1. בְּעוּתִים

Ps 88:16 thy dread assaults destroy me. 1

assay 1. בחן

Jer 6:27 that you may know and assay their ways. 1

assayer 1. בחן

Jer 6:27 made you an assayer and tester among my people 1

assemble 1. אסף 2. יעד 3. קבץ 4. קָהָל 5. קהל 6. כנשׁ (A) 7. ἀθροίζω 8. ἀθρόος 9. ἀναλαμβάνω 10. ἐξεκκλησιάζω 11. ἐπισυνάγω 12. ἐπισυναγωγή 13. συλλέγω 14. συμπαραγίνομαι 15. συνάγω 16. συναθροίζω 17. συνέρχομαι 18. συντρέχω 19. advenio 20. conventio

Gen 49: 2 Assemble and hear, O sons of Jacob 3
Exd 35: 1 Moses assembled all the congregation 5
Lev 8: 3 assemble all the congregation at the door 5
4 the congregation was assembled at the door 5
Num 8: 9 assemble the whole congregation of . . Israel. 5
16: 3 and they assembled themselves together 5
19 Then Korah assembled all the congregation 5
42 congregation had assembled against Moses 5
20: 2 assembled themselves together against Moses 5
8 Take the rod, and assemble the congregation 5
Deu 31:12 Assemble the people, men, women, and little ones 5
28 Assemble to me all the elders of your tribes 5
Jos 18: 1 Then . . the people of Israel assembled at Shiloh 5
Jdg 20: 1 congregation assembled as one man to the LORD 5
1Sm 25: 1 all Israel assembled and mourned for him 3
28: 4 The Philistines assembled, and came 3
2Sm 20:14 and all the Bichrites assembled, and followed 5
1Kg 8: 1 Solomon assembled the elders of Israel 5
2 all the men of Israel assembled to King Solomon 5
5 congregation . . who had assembled before him 2
12:21 Rehobo'am . . assembled all the house of Judah 5
2Kg 10:18 Jehu assembled all the people, and said to them 3
1Ch 13: 5 David assembled all Israel 5
15: 3 David assembled all Israel at Jerusalem 5
23: 2 David assembled all the leaders of Israel 1
28: 1 David assembled at Jerusalem all the officials 5
2Ch 5: 2 Then Solomon assembled the elders of Israel 5
3 all the men of Israel assembled before the king 5
6 congregation . . who had assembled before him 2
11: 1 he assembled the house of Judah, and Benjamin 5
20: 4 Judah assembled to seek help from the LORD; 3
26 they assembled in the Valley of Bera'cah 5
25: 5 Then Amazi'ah assembled the men of Judah 3
29: 4 assembled them in the square on the east 1
30: 3 nor had the people assembled in Jerusalem 1
Ezr 10: 7 returned exiles . . should assemble at Jerusalem 3
9 assembled at Jerusalem within the three days; 3
Neh 7: 5 assemble the nobles and the officials 3
9: 1 people of Israel were assembled with fasting 1
Ps 48: 4 lo, the kings assembled, they came on together. 2
Prv 5:14 point of utter ruin in the assembled congregation. 4
Isa 11:12 and will assemble the outcasts of Israel 1
43: 9 and let the peoples assemble. 1
44:11 let them all assemble, let them stand forth 3
45:20 Assemble yourselves and come 3
48:14 Assemble, all of you, and hear! 3
Jer 4: 5 Assemble, and let us go into the fortified cities!' 1
12: 9 Go, assemble all the wild beasts; 1
26:17 and spoke to all the assembled people, saying 4
Ezk 11:17 and assemble you out of the countries 1
38: 7 all the hosts that are assembled about you 5
13 you assembled your hosts to carry off plunder 5
39:17 Assemble and come, gather from all sides 3
Dan 3: 2 Nebuchadnez'zar sent to assemble the satraps 6
3 assembled for the dedication of the image 6
11:10 war and assemble a multitude of great forces 1
Jol 2:16 Sanctify the congregation; assemble the elders; 3
Ams 3: 9 Assemble . . upon the mountains of Sama'ria 1
Mic 4: 6 In that day, says the LORD, I will assemble the lame 1
11 Now many nations are assembled against you 1
Zep 3: 8 to gather nations, to assemble kingdoms 3
Mat 2: 4 assembling all the chief priests and scribes 15
28:12 when they had assembled with the elders 15
Mrk 14:53 the elders and the scribes were assembled. 17
Lke 23:48 the multitudes who assembled to see the sight 14
1Co 5: 4 When you are assembled, and my spirit is present 15
11:18 in the first place, when you assemble as a church 17
14:23 If, therefore, the whole church assembles 17
2Th 2: 1 our assembling to meet him 12
Rev 16:14 to assemble them for battle on the great day 15
16 And they assembled them at . . Armaged'don. 15
1Es 8:41 I assembled them at the river called Theras 15
9: 3 they should assemble at Jerusalem 15
5 the men of . . Benjamin assembled at Jerusalem 11
2Es 6: 1 and before the assembled winds blew 20
13:37 he, my Son, will reprove the assembled nations 19
Jdt 3:10 in order to assemble all the supplies 13
1Mc 2:16 Mattathias and his sons were assembled. 15
3:44 the congregation assembled 7
46 So they assembled and went to Mizpah 15
52 Gentiles are assembled against us to destroy us; 15
58 who have assembled against us to destroy us 11
4:37 So all the army assembled 15
6:19 assembled all the people to besiege them. 10
28 He assembled all his friends 15
9: 7 he had no time to assemble them. 15
28 Then all the friends of Judas assembled and said 7
63 he assembled all his forces 15
10: 2 he assembled a very large army 15
48 Now Alexander the king assembled large forces 15
69 he assembled a large force 15
11:20 In those days Jonathan assembled the men of Judea 15
45 the men of the city assembled within the city 11
13: 1 Trypho had assembled a large army 15
10 So he assembled all the warriors 15
14: 1 Demetrius the king assembled his forces 15
2Mc 6:11 Others who had assembled in the caves near by 18
12:38 Then Judas assembled his army 9
3Mc 5:14 seeing that the guests were assembled 8
24 assembled for this most pitiful spectacle 16
34 and dismissed the assembled people 16

rebelliously assemble 1. ἐπισυνάγω

Sir 16:10 who rebelliously assembled 1

assemble together 1. קהל

Num 1:18 they assembled the . . congregation together 1

assembly 1. מוֹעֵד 2. מוֹשָׁב 3. מִקְרָא 4. עֵדָה 5. קָהָל 6. קְהִלָּה 7. ἐκκλησία 8. πλῆθος 9. συναγωγή 10. συστροφή

Exd 12: 6 when the whole assembly of the congregation 5
16 On the first day you shall hold a holy assembly 3
16 and on the seventh day a holy assembly; 3
16: 3 to kill this whole assembly with hunger. 5
Lev 4:13 the thing is hidden from the eyes of the assembly 5
14 the assembly shall offer a young bull 5
21 it is the sin offering for the assembly 5
16:17 for his house and for all the assembly of Israel 5
33 the priests and for all the people of the assembly 5
Num10: 7 when the assembly is to be gathered together 5
14: 5 before all the assembly of the congregation 5
15:15 For the assembly, there shall be one statute 5
16: 2 250 leaders . . chosen from the assembly 1
3 exalt yourselves above the assembly of the LORD? 5
33 they perished from the midst of the assembly. 5
47 ran into the midst of the assembly and behold 5
19:20 shall be cut off from the midst of the assembly 5
20: 4 Why have you brought the assembly of the LORD 5
6 Moses . . went from the presence of the assembly 5
10 Moses and Aaron gathered the assembly together 5
12 you shall not bring this assembly into the land 5
Deu 5:22 LORD spoke to all your assembly at the mountain 5
9:10 spoken with you . . on the day of the assembly. 5
10: 4 LORD had spoken to you . . on the day of the assembly; 5
18:16 desired of the LORD . . on the day of the assembly 5
23: 1 shall not enter the assembly of the LORD. 5
2 No bastard shall enter the assembly of the LORD; 5
2 none . . shall enter the assembly of the LORD. 5
3 No Ammonite . . shall enter the assembly of the LORD; 5

3 none . . shall enter the assembly of the LORD 5
8 born to them may enter the assembly of the LORD. 5
31:30 in the ears of all the assembly of Israel 5
33: 4 law, as a possession for the assembly of Jacob. 6
Jos 8:35 Joshua . . read before all the assembly of Israel 5
22:12 whole assembly of the people of Israel gathered 4
Jdg 20: 2 chiefs . . presented themselves in the assembly 5
21: 5 Which . . did not come up in the assembly 5
8 no one had come to the camp . . to the assembly. 5
1Sm 17:47 and that all this assembly may know that the LORD 5
1Kg 8:14 king . . blessed all the assembly of Israel 5
14 while all the assembly of Israel stood. 5
22 in the presence of all the assembly of Israel 5
55 he stood, and blessed all the assembly of Israel 5
65 and all Israel with him, a great assembly 5
12: 3 Jerobo'am and all the assembly of Israel came 5
20 they sent and called him to the assembly 4
1Ch 13: 2 David said to all the assembly of Israel 5
4 All the assembly agreed to do 5
28: 8 in the sight of . . the assembly of the LORD 5
29: 1 David the king said to all the assembly 5
10 blessed . . in the presence of all the assembly; 5
20 David said to all the assembly, "Bless the LORD 5
20 And all the assembly blessed the LORD, the God 5
2Ch 1: 3 Solomon, and all the assembly with him, went 5
5 And Solomon and the assembly sought the LORD. 5
6: 3 king . . and blessed all the assembly of Israel 5
3 while all the assembly of Israel stood. 5
12 in the presence of all the assembly of Israel 5
13 in the presence of all the assembly of Israel 5
20: 5 Jehosh'aphat stood in the assembly of Judah 5
14 in the midst of the assembly. 5
23: 3 all the assembly made a covenant with the king 5
28:14 before the princes and all the assembly. 5
29:23 he-goats . . brought to the king and the assembly 5
28 whole assembly worshiped, and the singers sang 5
31 assembly brought sacrifices and thank 5
32 burnt offerings which the assembly brought 5
30: 2 For the king and his princes and all the assembly 5
4 plan seemed right to . . all the assembly. 5
13 many people came . . a very great assembly. 5
17 many in the assembly who had not sanctified 5
23 the whole assembly agreed together to keep 5
24 Hezeki'ah . . gave the assembly 1,000 bulls 5
24 princes gave the assembly 1,000 bulls and 10,000 5
25 whole assembly of Judah, and the priests 5
25 whole assembly that came out of Israel 5
Ezr 2:64 whole assembly together was 42,360 5
10: 1 very great assembly of men, women, and children 5
12 Then all the assembly answered with a loud voice 5
14 Let our officials stand for the whole assembly; 5
Neh 5: 7 And I held a great assembly against them 6
13 all the assembly said "Amen" and praised the LORD. 5
7:66 The whole assembly together was 42,360 5
8: 2 Ezra . . brought the law before the assembly 5
17 all the assembly of those who had returned 5
13: 1 no Ammonite . . ever enter the assembly of God; 5
Job 30:28 I stand up in the assembly, and cry for help. 5
Ps 7: 7 Let the assembly of the peoples be gathered 4
89: 5 thy faithfulness in the assembly of the holy ones! 5
107:32 praise him in the assembly of the elders. 2
149: 1 song, his praise in the assembly of the faithful! 5
Prv 21:16 wanders . . will rest in the assembly of the dead. 5
26:26 his wickedness will be exposed in the assembly. 5
Isa 1:13 and sabbath and the calling of assemblies 3
4: 5 create . . over her assemblies a cloud by day 3
14:13 sit on the mount of assembly in the far north; 1
Jer 44:15 and all the women who stood by, a great assembly 5
Lam 1:15 he summoned an assembly against me to crush my 1
Mic 2: 5 cast the line by lot in the assembly of the LORD. 5
6: 9 Hear, O tribe and assembly of the city! •
Act 15:12 all the assembly kept silence 8
19:32 for the assembly was in confusion 7
39 it shall be settled in the regular assembly. 7
41 when he had said this, he dismissed the assembly. 7
23: 7 the assembly was divided. 8
Heb 12:23 to the assembly of the first-born 7
Jas 2: 2 a man . . comes into your assembly 9
Jdt 6:16 their young men and their women ran to the assembly 7
21 took him from the assembly to his own house 7
7:29 lamentation arose throughout the assembly 7
AEs 10:13 with an assembly and joy and gladness before God 9
Sir 6:34 Stand in the assembly of the elders. Who is wise? 8
7:14 Do not prattle in the assembly of the elders 8
15: 5 will open his mouth in the midst of the assembly. 7
16: 6 In an assembly of sinners a fire will be kindled 9
21: 9 An assembly of the wicked 9
17 will be sought in the assembly 7
23:24 She herself will be brought before the assembly 7
24: 2 In the assembly of the Most High 7
31:11 the assembly will relate his acts of charity. 7
Sus 1:41 The assembly believed them 9
60 Then all the assembly shouted loudly 9
1Mc 2:56 Caleb, because he testified in the assembly 7
4:59 all the assembly of Israel determined 7
5:16 a great assembly was called 7
14:19 read before the assembly in Jerusalem. 7
28 in Asaramel, in the great assembly of the priests 9
44 to convene an assembly in the country 10

assembly *See also* hold.

assembly of the elders 1. πρεσβυτέριον
Lke 22:66 the assembly of the elders of the people 1

solemn assembly 1. עֲצָרָה
Lev 23:36 it is a solemn assembly 1
Num29:35 eighth day you shall have a solemn assembly 1
Deu 16: 8 seventh day there shall be a solemn assembly 1
2Kg 10:20 Sanctify a solemn assembly for Ba'al. 1
2Ch 7: 9 on the eighth day they held a solemn assembly; 1
Neh 8:18 eighth day there was a solemn assembly 1
Isa 1:13 I cannot endure iniquity and solemn assembly. 1
Jol 1:14 Sanctify a fast, call a solemn assembly. 1
2:15 sanctify a fast; call a solemn assembly; 1
Ams 5:21 and I take no delight in your solemn assemblies. 1

assent 1. ἐπινεύω
2Mc 4:10 When the king assented and Jason came to office 1

assert 1. φάσκω
Act 25:19 who was dead, but whom Paul asserted to be alive. 1

assert righteousness 1. δίκαιος
Sir 7: 5 not assert your righteousness before the Lord 1

assertion *See* make.

assess 1. עבר
2Kg 12: 4 the money for which each man is assessed 1

assessment 1. עֵרֶךְ
2Kg 12: 4 –the money from the assessment of persons– 1
23:35 from every one according to his assessment 1

assign 1. אמר 2. מנה 3. נתן 4. ספר 5. עשה 6. פקד 7. שום 8. διατάσσω 9. διατίθημι 10. δίδωμι 11. μερίζω 12. προστάσσω 13. do
Num 4:27 assign to their charge all that they are to carry. 6
32 shall assign by name the objects which they 6
8:26 do to the Levites in assigning their duties. •
1Sm 29: 4 return to the place to which you . . assigned him; 6
2Sm 11:16 Jo'ab . . assigned Uri'ah to the place 3
1Kg 11:18 gave him a house, and assigned him an allowance 1
2Ch 2: 2 Solomon assigned 70,000 men 4
14 execute any design that may be assigned him 3
18 70,000 . . he assigned to bear burdens 5
Prv 8:29 when he assigned to the sea its limit 7
Ezk 4: 5 For I assign to you a number of days, 390 days 3
6 40 days I assign you, a day for each year. 3
45: 6 you shall assign for the possession of the city 3
47:23 there you shall assign him his inheritance 3
Dan 1: 5 king assigned them a daily portion of the rich 2
Lke 22:29 I assign to you, as my Father assigned to me 9
29 I assign to you, as my Father assigned to me 9
Rom12: 3 the measure of faith which God has assigned him. 11
1Co 3: 5 as the Lord assigned to each. 10
7:17 which the Lord has assigned to him 11
2Es 4:19 for the land is assigned to the forest 13
19 to the sea is assigned a place to carry its waves. •
21 For as the land is assigned to the forest 13
Sir 3:22 Reflect upon what has been assigned to you 12
1Mc 5:20 Then 3,000 men were assigned to Simon 11
6:35 picked horsemen were assigned to each beast. 8

assign a place 1. καταπαύω
Sir 24: 8 assigned a place for my tent 1

assign as an inheritance 1. נחל
Deu 21:16 assigns his possessions as an inheritance 1

assist 1. מִיַּד 2. נשא 3. עַל יַד 4. ἀντιλαμβάνω 5. ἐπαρκέω 6. συνεργέω 7. ὑπηρέτης
1Ch 23:28 their duty shall be to assist the sons of Aaron •
29 to assist also with the showbread •
2Ch 31:13 overseers assisting Conani'ah and Shim'e-i 1
15 faithfully assisting him in the cities 3
Ezr 1: 4 survivor . . be assisted by the men of his place 2
Act 13: 5 they had John to assist them. 7
1Ti 5:16 let her assist them 5
16 it may assist those who are real widows. 5
1Es 7: 2 assisting the elders of the Jews 6
Sir 29:20 Assist your neighbor according to your ability 4

assistance 1. ἀντίλημψις
Sir 51: 7 I looked for the assistance of men 1
3Mc 3:10 to exert more earnest efforts for their assistance. 1

assistant 1. עַל יָד
Neh 13:13 as their assistant Hanan the son of Zaccur, 1

associate 1. חָבֵר 2. ערב 3. כְּנָת (A) 4. αἱρετίς 5. ἐνδελεχίζω 6. κοινωνέω 7. κοινωνός 8. κολλάω 9. ὁ περί 10. προσπορεύομαι 11. συμμέτοχος 12. συνάγω 13. συναναμείγνυμι 14. συναπάγω 15. συνέταιρος 16. συνίστημι 17. συντάσσω 18. commisceo
Ezr 4: 7 rest of their associates wrote to Ar-ta-xerx'es 3
9 rest of their associates, the judges 3
17 rest of their associates who live in Sama'ria 3
23 Shim'shai the scribe and their associates 3
5: 3 She'thar-boz'enai and their associates came 3
6 She'thar-boz'enai and his associates 3
6: 6 She'thar-boz'enai, and your associates 3
13 She'thar-boz'enai, and their associates 3
Prv 20:19 do not associate with one who speaks foolishly. 2
Ezk 37:16 and the children of Israel associated with him 1
16 all the house of Israel associated with him 1
19 and the tribes of Israel associated with him; 1
Act 10:28 to associate with . . any one of another nation 8
Rom12:16 do not be haughty, but associate with the lowly; 14
1Co 5: 9 not to associate with immoral men; 13
11 not to associate with any one 13
Eph 5: 7 Therefore do not associate with them 11
1Es 2:16 the rest of their associates 17
25 the others associated with them 17
30 Shimshai the scribe and their associates 17
6: 3 Sathrabuzanes and their associates came to them 15
7 Sathrabuzanes, and their associates 15
27 and Sathrabuzanes, and their associates 15
7: 1 Sathrabuzanes, and their associates 15
2Es 7:76 be associated with those who have shown scorn 18
Wis 6:23 for envy does not associate with wisdom. 6
8: 4 an associate in his works. 4
Sir 9: 4 Do not associate with a woman singer 5
12:14 will pity a man who associates with a sinner 10
13: 1 whoever associates with a proud man 7
2 nor associate with a man 6
2 can the clay pot associate with the iron kettle? 6
16 all living beings associate by species 12
2Mc 1:33 Nehemiah and his associates 9
36 Nehemiah and his associates 9
8: 9 He associated with him Gorgias 16

associate *See also* business.

association 1. συναναστροφή
3Mc 2:31 their future association with the king. 1

assuage 1. חשך 2. כָּהָה 3. ἀνάπαυσις
Job 16: 5 the solace of my lips would assuage your pain. 1
6 If I speak, my pain is not assuaged 1
Nah 3:19 There is no assuaging your hurt 2
Sir 18:16 Does not the dew assuage the scorching heat? 3

assume 1. εἴ γε 2. ἐμποιέω 3. ὑπολαμβάνω
Eph 3: 2 assuming that you have heard of the stewardship 1
4:21 assuming that you have heard about him 1
1Es 5:38 the following had assumed the priesthood 2
Wis 13: 3 If . . men assumed them to be gods 3
3Mc 3:11 assuming that he would persevere constantly 3

assume authority 1. ἐξουσιάζω
1Mc 10:70 Why do you assume authority against us 1

assurance 1. אמן 2. βεβαίωσις 3. πίστις 4. ὑπόστασις
Deu 28:66 be in dread, and have no assurance of your life. 1
Act 17:31 of this he has given assurance to all men 3
Heb 11: 1 Now faith is the assurance of things hoped for 4
Wis 6:18 assurance of immortality 2

assurance *See also* give.

full assurance 1. πληροφορία
Heb 6:11 the full assurance of hope until the end 1
10:22 in full assurance of faith 1

assure 1. אֱמֶת 2. יָד לְיָד 3. ἵστημι 4. πληροφορία 5. dirigo 6. persuadeo
Prv 11:21 Be assured, an evil man will not go unpunished 2
16: 5 be assured, he will not go unpunished. 2
Jer 14:13 but I will give you assured peace in this place. 1
Col 2: 2 to have all the riches of assured understanding 4
2Es 7:131 joy over those to whom salvation is assured. 6
16:21 men will imagine that peace is assured for them 5
Sir 44:21 Therefore the Lord assured him by an oath 3

assure fully 1. πληροφορέω
Col 4:12 fully assured in all the will of God. 1

assured *See* rest.

assuredly 1. ἀσφαλῶς
Jos 23:13 know assuredly that the LORD . . will not †
Act 2:36 know assuredly that God has made him . . Lord 1

astonish 1. שמם 2. תוה (A) 3. ἐκπλήσσω 4. ἐξίστημι 5. θάμβος 6. θαυμάζω
Lev 26:32 who settle in it shall be astonished at it 1
1Kg 9: 8 every one . . will be astonished, and will hiss; 1
2Ch 7:21 every one passing by will be astonished, and say 1
Isa 52:14 As many were astonished at him–his appearance 1
Dan 3:24 King Nebuchadnez'zar was astonished and rose up 2
Mat 7:28 the crowds were astonished at his teaching 3

13:54 so that they were astonished, and said 3
19:25 they were greatly astonished, saying 3
22:33 they were astonished at his teaching. 3
Mrk 1:22 they were astonished at his teaching 3
6: 2 many who heard him were astonished, saying 3
7:37 they were astonished beyond measure, saying 3
10:26 they were exceedingly astonished, and said 3
11:18 the multitude was astonished at his teaching. 3
Lke 2:48 when they saw him they were astonished 3
4:32 they were astonished at his teaching 3
5: 9 For he was astonished, and all that were with him 5
9:43 all were astonished at the majesty of God 3
11:38 The Pharisee was astonished to see 6
Act 13:12 he was astonished at the teaching of the Lord. 3
Gal 1: 6 I am astonished 6
Jdt 11:16 things that will astonish the whole world 4
13:17 All the people were greatly astonished 4
2Mc 7:12 those . . were astonished at the young man's spirit 3

astonishing thing 1. פלא
Dan 11:36 speak astonishing things against the God 1

astonishment 1. ἔκστασις
Mrk 16: 8 trembling and astonishment had come upon them 1
astonishment *See also* object.

astound 1. תמה 2. תמה 3. ἔκθαμβος 4. ἐξίστημι 5. θαμβέομαι 6. καταπλήσσω
Job 26:11 tremble, and are astounded at his rebuke. 2
Ps 48: 5 As soon as they saw it, they were astounded 1
Jer 4: 9 and the prophets astounded. 2
Hab 1: 5 wonder and be astounded. For I am doing a work 1
Mrk 6:51 they were utterly astounded 4
Act 3:11 all the people ran together . . astounded. 3
1Mc 6: 8 he was astounded and badly shaken 5
2Mc 3:24 were astounded by the power of God 6

astounding thing 1. ἄξιος θαυμασμοῦ
2Mc 7:18 Therefore astounding things have happened. 1
astray *See* go, lead.

astrologer 1. גזר (A)
Dan 2:27 No wise men . . magicians, or astrologers 1
4: 7 magicians . . and the astrologers came in; 1
5: 7 enchanters, the Chalde'ans, and the astrologers. 1
11 chief of the . . Chalde'ans, and astrologers 1
asunder *See* break, burst, cut, divide, put, rend, split, tear.

athlete 1. ἀγωνίζομαι 2. ἀθλέω 3. ἀθλητής
1Co 9:25 Every athlete exercises self-control 1
2Ti 2: 5 An athlete is not crowned 2
4Mc 6:10 like a noble athlete the old man 3
17:15 and gave the crown to its own athletes. 3
16 admire the athletes of the divine legislation? 3

atone 1. כפר 2. ἐξιλάσκομαι
Lev 16:20 made an end of atoning for the holy place 1
Prv 16: 6 By loyalty and faithfulness iniquity is atoned 1
Isa 47:11 come upon you, for which you cannot atone; 1
Dan 9:24 atone for iniquity, to bring in everlasting 1
Sir 3: 3 Whoever honors his father atones for sins 2
30 so almsgiving atones for sin. 2
20:28 will atone for injustice. 2

atonement 1. כִּפֻּרִים 2. ἐξιλασμός
Exd 29:36 a bull as a sin offering for atonement. 1
30:10 with the blood of the sin offering of atonement 1
16 you shall take the atonement money 1
Lev 23:27 On the tenth day . . is the day of atonement 1
28 for it is a day of atonement, to make atonement 1
25: 9 on the day of atonement you shall send abroad 1
Num 5: 8 in addition to the ram of atonement 1
29:11 besides the sin offering of atonement 1
Sir 5: 5 Do not be so confident of atonement 2
35: 3 to forsake unrighteousness is atonement. 2
2Mc 12:45 Therefore he made atonement for the dead 2
atonement *See also* make, offering.

make atonement 1. כפר
Ezk 43:20 cleanse the altar and make atonement for it. 1
26 they make atonement for the altar and purify it 1
45:15 to make atonement for them, says the Lord GOD. 1
17 to make atonement for the house of Israel. 1
20 you shall make atonement for the temple. 1

attach 1. אחז 2. אסף 3. חבר 4. נתן 5. צמד 6. ἐπιτίθημι 7. περάπτω 8. προσκλίνω
Exd 28: 7 two shoulder-pieces attached to its two edges 3
14 shall attach the corded chains to the settings. 4
25 two cords you shall attach to the two settings 4
25 and so attach it in front to the shoulder-pieces 4
27 you shall make two rings of gold, and attach them 4
39:18 Two ends of the two cords they had attached 4
18 thus they attached it in front 4
20 rings of gold, and attached them in front 4
1Sm 14:52 any valiant man, he attached him to himself. 2
2Ch 9:18 which were attached to the throne 1
Ps 106:28 attached themselves to the Ba'al of Pe'or 5
Sir 11:31 to worthy actions he will attach blame. 6
2Mc 14:24 he was warmly attached to the man. 8
3Mc 3: 7 they attached no ordinary reproach to them. 7

attack 1. איב 2. לחם 3. מִלְחָמָה 4. נגח 5. נגע 6. נֶגַע 7. נכה 8. עלה 9. עָלוֹ עַל 10. פגע 11. צור 12. קום 13. קוּם אֶל 14. קוּם עַל 15. קרה 16. εἰς πόλεμον 17. ἐκπολεμέω 18. ἐμφέρω 19. ἐπαγωγή 20. ἐπί 21. ἐπιβάλλω 22. ἐπιβολή 23. ἐπίθεσις 24. ἐπιτίθημι 25. ἐφίστημι 26. ἔφοδος 27. κατά 28. ὅρμημα 29. παραγίνομαι 30. παρεμβάλλω 31. πατάσσω 32. πολεμέω 33. πόλεμος 34. προσβάλλω 35. προσβολή 36. ῥήγνυμι 37. συμβάλλω 38. συνάντησις 39. τύπτω 40. χείρ
Gen 34:30 they gather themselves against me and attack me 7
Deu 19:11 lies in wait for him, and attacks him, and wounds 14
22:26 man attacking and murdering his neighbor; 12
24: 8 Take heed, in an attack of leprosy, to be very 6
25:18 how he attacked you on the way, when you were faint 15
Jos 7: 3 about 2,000 or 3,000 men go up and attack Ai; 7
Jdg 1:12 He who attacks Kir'iath-se'pher and takes it, I will 7
6: 3 people of the East would come up and attack them; 9
8:11 Gideon went up . . and attacked the army; 7
1Sm 7:10 the Philistines drew near to attack Israel; 3
23: 2 Shall I go and attack these Philistines? 7
2 Go and attack the Philistines and save Kei'lah. 7
24: 7 David . . did not permit them to attack Saul. 13
2Sm 5: 8 up the water shaft to attack the lame and . . blind 5
11:25 strengthen your attack upon the city 3
17: 9 when some of the people fall at the first attack •
21:17 came to his aid, and attacked the Philistine 7
1Kg 2:32 he attacked and slew with the sword two men more 10
2Kg 3:24 the Israelites rose and attacked the Moabites 7
16: 7 rescue me from . . who are attacking me. 14
25:25 came . . and attacked and killed Gedali'ah 7
Est 8:11 annihilate any armed force . . that might attack 11
Ps 69: 4 would destroy me, those who attack me with lies. 1
109: 3 They beset me . . and attack me without cause. 2
Jer 6: 4 war against her; up, and let us attack at noon! 8
5 let us attack by night, and destroy her palaces! 8
Dan 11: 8 refrain from attacking the king of the north. •
40 time of the end the king of the south shall attack 4
Jon 4: 7 God appointed a worm which attacked the plant 7
Mat 7: 6 and turn to attack you. 36
Act 16:22 The crowd joined in attacking them 27
17: 5 attacked the house of Jason 25
18:10 no man shall attack you to harm you 24
1Es 4: 8 if he tells them to attack, they attack 31
8 if he tells them to attack, they attack 39
Jdt 2: 6 Go and attack the whole west country 38
AEs 16:20 who attack them at the time of their affliction. 24
Sir 25:14 Any attack, but not an attack from those who hate! 19
14 Any attack, but not an attack from those who hate! 19
1Mc 2:35 Then the enemy hastened to attack them. 33
41 fight against every man who comes to attack us 16
4: 2 attack them suddenly 31
3 to attack the king's force in Emmaus 31
30 who didst crush the attack of the mighty warrior 28
34 Then both sides attacked 37
5: 6 Then he crossed over to attack the Ammonites 20
16 who . . were being attacked by enemies. 32
27 are getting ready to attack the strongholds 30
30 and attacking the Jews within. 32
8:10 sent a general . . and attacked them 32
9:48 did not cross the Jordan to attack them. 20
67 Then he began to attack 39
11:20 to attack the citadel in Jerusalem 17
2Mc 4:40 launched an unjust attack 40
41 when the Jews became aware of Lysimachus' attack 23
5: 3 attacks and counterattacks made on this side 35
8: 7 the nights most advantageous for such attacks. 22
10:17 Attacking them vigorously 34
12: 6 attacked the murderers of his brethren 29
9 he attacked the people of Jamnia by night 21
10 5,000 Arabs with 500 horsemen attacked them. 34
13 He also attacked a certain city 21
13:15 he attacked the king's pavilion at night 21
22 attacked Judas and his men, was defeated; 34
26 how the king's attack and withdrawal turned out. 26
15: 1 he made plans to attack them 21
8 not to fear the attack of the Gentiles 26
17 they determined . . to attack bravely 18
4Mc 3: 7 David had been attacking the Philistines 34

attack again 1. προσκρούω
2Mc 13:19 was turned back, attacked again, and was defeated. 1

fierce attack 1. ὅρμημα
1Mc 6:47 when the Jews saw . . the fierce attack of the forces 1

fiercely attack 1. מרר
Gen 49:23 The archers fiercely attacked him 1

willfully attack 1. זיד
Exd 21:14 if a man willfully attacks another to kill him 1
attacking *See* try.

attain 1. בוא 2. יכל 3. נשׂג 4. ἀποφέρω 5. καταλαμβάνω 6. καταντάω 7. λαγχάνω 8. τυγχάνω 9. φθάνω 10. occurro
Gen 47: 9 they have not attained to the days of the years 3
2Sm 23:19 but he did not attain to the three. 1
23 but he did not attain to the three. 1
1Ch 11:21 he did not attain to the three. 1
25 but he did not attain to the three. 1
Ps 139: 6 too wonderful for me; it is high, I cannot attain 2
Lke 20:35 who are accounted worthy to attain to that age 8
Act 26: 7 to which our twelve tribes hope to attain 6
Rom 9:30 did not pursue righteousness have attained it 5
Eph 4:13 until we all attain to the unity of the faith 6
Php 3:11 I may attain the resurrection from the dead. 6
16 Only let us hold true to what we have attained. 9
2Es 13:18 but cannot attain it. 10
AEs 13: 3 has attained the second place in the kingdom 4
5 so that our kingdom may not attain stability. 8
Sir 27: 8 If you pursue justice, you will attain it 5
2Mc 14: 6 will not let the kingdom attain tranquillity. 8
3Mc 6: 1 who had attained a ripe old age 7

attain eminence 1. ὑπεραλόω
Sir 38:33 attain eminence in the public assembly 1

attain rest 1. ἀναπαύω
Sir 22:11 for he has attained rest 1

attainable
Heb 7:11 Now if perfection had been attainable •

attempt 1. נסה 2. αἴτιος 3. ἐπιχειρέω 4. ζητέω 5. ὁρμή 6. πειράζω 7. πεῖραν λαμβάνω 8. πειράω 9. πράσσω 10. surgo
Deu 4:34 has any god ever attempted to go and take a nation 1
Act 9:26 he attempted to join the disciples 6
14: 5 an attempt was made by both Gentiles and Jews 5
16: 7 they attempted to go into Bithyn'ia 6
Heb 11:29 the Egyptians, when they attempted to do the same 7
2Es 10: 2 and all my neighbors attempted to console me 10
Sir 10: 6 do not attempt anything by acts of insolence. 9
Bel 1:42 the men who had attempted his destruction 2
1Mc 12:39 Then Trypho attempted to become king in Asia 4
2Mc 2:23 we shall attempt to condense into a single book. 8
9: 2 and attempted to rob the temples 3
10:12 attempted to maintain peaceful relations 8
3Mc 2:32 they confidently attempted to save themselves 8
6:24 you are now attempting to deprive of dominion 3
4Mc 1: 5 Their attempt at argument is ridiculous! 3
3:21 just at that time certain men attempted a revolution •
8: 2 conspicuously defeated in his first attempt 8

attend 1. הלך לְרֶגֶל 2. לִפְנֵי 3. מִשְׁמֶרֶת 4. עֲבֹדָה 5. עִם 6. עמד 7. עמד לִפְנֵי 8. פקד 9. קשׁב 10. שׁמר 11. שׁמר מִשְׁמֶרֶת 12. שׁרת 13. ἐν 14. ἐπακολουθέω 15. ὁμιλέω 16. ποιέω 17. προνοέω 18. προσέχω 19. προσκαρτερέω 20. συμπορεύομαι 21. φροντίζω 22. intendo
Gen 39: 4 Joseph found favor in his sight and attended him 12
Num 1: 5 names of the men who shall attend you. 6
3: 8 shall . . attend to the duties for the people •
10 they shall attend to their priesthood; 10
28 8,600, attending to the duties of the sanctuary. 10
18: 3 attend you and attend to all duties of the tent; 11
3 attend you and attend to all duties of the tent; 11
4 shall join you, and attend to the tent of meeting 11
5 you shall attend to the duties of the sanctuary 10
7 sons with you shall attend to your priesthood 10
1Sm 25:42 Ab'igail . . and her five maidens attended her; 1
1Ch 23:32 shall attend the sons of Aaron, their brethren 3
27:32 and Jehi'el . . attended the king's sons. 5
2Ch 22: 8 Ahazi'ah's brothers, who attended Ahazi'ah 12
Ezr 8:20 David . . had set apart to attend the Levites. 4
Est 2: 2 Then the king's servants who attended him said 12
4: 5 Hathach . . who had been appointed to attend her 2
6: 3 The king's servants who attended him said 12
Ps 17: 1 Hear a just cause, O LORD; attend to my cry! 9
55: 2 Attend to me, and answer me; 9
Isa 42:23 Who . . will attend and listen for the time to come? 9
Jer 23: 2 and you have not attended to them. 8
2 Behold, I will attend to you for your evil doings 8
Ezk 44:11 they shall attend on the people, to serve them. 6
15 they shall attend on me to offer me the fat 7
Mrk 16:20 by the signs that attended it. Amen. 14
Act 2:46 And day by day, attending the temple together 19
Rom 13: 6 ministers of God, attending to this very thing. 19
2Co 3: 8 will not . . the Spirit be attended with greater splendor? 13
1Ti 4:13 attend to the public reading of scripture 18
1Es 4:11 no one may go away to attend to his own affairs 16
2Es 8:24 the petition of thy creature; attend to my words. 22
Tob 5:16 may his angel attend you 20
Sir 11:20 Stand by your covenant and attend to it 15
1Mc 16:14 and attending to their needs 21
4Mc 7:18 as many as attend to religion with a whole heart 17

cause to attend 1. עמד
Num 8:13 you shall cause the Levites to attend Aaron 1

attend to needs 1. ὑπηρετέω
Act 24:23 none . . be prevented from attending to his needs. 1

attendance 1. לִפְנֵי 2. מַעֲמָד
1Kg 10: 5 the attendance of his servants, their clothing 2
2Ch 9: 4 attendance of his servants, and their clothing 2
Est 7: 9 one of the eunuchs in attendance on the king 1

attendance upon 1. לִפְנֵי
Num 8:22 in attendance upon Aaron and his sons; 1

attendant 1. בוא 2. עמד 3. διάκονος 4. παρίστημι 5. ὑπηρέτης
Jdg 3:19 all his attendants went out from his presence. 2
Dan 11: 6 shall be given up, and her attendants, her child 1
Mat 22:13 the king said to the attendants, 'Bind him 3
Lke 4:20 he closed the book, and gave it back to the attendant 5
Jdt 13: 1 shut out the attendants from his master's presence 4

woman attending 1. נצב
1Sm 4:20 the women attending her said to her, "Fear not 1

attention 1. לֵב 2. νοῦς 3. πρόνοια 4. προσοχή 5. τόπος 6. φιληκοΐα
Prv 27:23 give attention to your herds; 1
1Es 9:41 all the multitude gave attention to the law. 2
Sir 0: 2 to read with good will and attention, 4
13:22 he speaks sensibly, and receives no attention. 5
2Mc 4: 6 without the king's attention 3
4Mc 15:21 attract the attention of their hearers 6
attention *See also* give, pay.

attentive 1. קשב 2. קַשָּׁב 3. קַשֻּׁב 4. ἀκροατής
2Ch 6:40 Now, O my God, let . . thy ears attentive to a prayer 3
7:15 eyes . . open and my ears attentive to the prayer 3
Neh 1: 6 let thy ear be attentive, and thy eyes open 2
11 ear be attentive to the prayer of thy servant 2
8: 3 ears of all . . were attentive to the book of the law. •
Ps 130: 2 Lord, hear my voice! Let thy ears be attentive 3
Prv 4: 1 be attentive, that you may gain insight; 1
20 My son, be attentive to my words; 1
5: 1 My son, be attentive to my wisdom 1
7:24 O sons . . be attentive to the words of my mouth. 1
Sir 3:29 an attentive ear is the wise man's desire. 4
attentive *See also* listener, make.

attentively 1. שמע
Exd 23:22 if you hearken attentively to his voice and do 1

attest 1. תְּעוּדָה 2. ἀποδείκνυμι 3. βεβαιόω 4. μαρτυρέω
Rut 4: 7 this was the manner of attesting in Israel. 1
Act 2:22 Jesus of Nazareth, a man attested to you by God 2
1Ti 5:10 she must be well attested for her good deeds 4
Heb 2: 3 it was attested to us by those who heard him 3
11: 5 he was attested as having pleased God. 4
39 all these, though well attested by their faith 4
attest *See also* get.

attire 1. מַלְבּוּשׁ 2. קִשֻּׁרִים 3. ἱματισμός 4. στολισμός
Jer 2:32 forget her ornaments, or a bride her attire? 2
Zep 1: 8 and all who array themselves in foreign attire. 1
1Ti 2: 9 gold or pearls or costly attire 3
Sir 19:30 A man's attire and open-mouthed laughter 4
attire *See also* array.
attitude *See* change.

attract 1. ἐφέλκω 2. κινέω
Wis 14:20 the multitude, attracted by the charm of his work 1
4Mc 1:33 when we are attracted to forbidden foods 2
15:21 attract the attention of their hearers 1

attractive 1. ἀξιόω 2. ὡραῖος
Sir 25: 5 How attractive is wisdom in the aged 2
LJr 1:43 because she was not as attractive as herself 1

attractive thing 1. ὡραῖος
Sir 25: 4 What an attractive thing 1

attribute 1. προσνέμω
4Mc 6:33 we properly attribute to it the power to govern. 1

audacious 1. θρασύς
3Mc 2: 6 varied punishments on the audacious Pharaoh 1
14 this audacious and profane man 1

audacity 1. θράσος 2. θρασύς
3Mc 2: 2 puffed up in his audacity and power. 2
21 had exalted himself in insolence and audacity. 2
26 he also continued with such audacity 1
audience *See* hall.

augment 1. רבה 2. συναύξω
Prv 28: 8 augments his wealth by interest and increase 1
4Mc 13:27 habits had augmented the affection of brotherhood 2

augur 1. נחש
Deu 18:10 divination, a soothsayer, or an augur, or a sorcerer 1
augury *See* practice.

august 1. σεμνός
4Mc 17: 5 does not stand so august as you 1

aunt 1. דּוֹדָה
Lev 18:14 you shall not approach his wife; she is your aunt 1

austerity 1. αὐστηρία
2Mc 14:30 this austerity did not spring from the best motives 1

authentic 1. ἀνυπόκριτος
Wis 18:16 the sharp sword of thy authentic command 1

author 1. ἀρχηγός 2. γενεσιάρχης
Act 3:15 killed the Author of life 1
Wis 13: 3 the author of beauty created them. 2

authority 1. הוד 2. יָד 3. מֶמְשָׁלָה 4. רבה 5. שִׁלְטוֹן 6. תֹּקֶף 7. ἀπό 8. ἀρχή 9. ἄρχων 10. δύναμις 11. ἐκ 12. ἐντολή 13. ἐξουσία 14. ἐπιταγή 15. ἐπὶ τῶν ἡνιῶν 16. ἡγεμών 17. ἰσχύς 18. κατά 19. κυριότης 20. τάσσω 21. ὑπεροχή
Gen 41:35 lay up grain under the authority of Pharaoh 2
Num 5:19 while you were under your husband's authority •
20 though you are under your husband's authority •
29 when a wife, though under her husband's authority •
27:20 You shall invest him with some of your authority 1
Est 9:29 Mor'decai the Jew gave full written authority 6
Prv 29: 2 righteous are in authority, the people rejoice; 4
16 When the wicked are in authority, transgression 4
Ecc 8: 8 power . . or authority over the day of death; 5
Isa 22:21 and will commit your authority to his hand; 3
Mat 7:29 for he taught them as one who had authority 13
8: 9 I am a man under authority, with soldiers under me; 13
9: 6 the Son of man has authority on earth to forgive 13
8 they glorified God, who had given such authority 13
10: 1 and gave them authority over unclean spirits 13
21:23 By what authority are you doing these things 13
23 who gave you this authority? 13
24 by what authority I do these things. 13
27 by what authority I do these things. 13
28:18 All authority in heaven and on earth 13
Mrk 1:22 he taught them as one who had authority 13
27 With authority he commands 13
2:10 Son of man has authority on earth to forgive sins"- 13
3:15 and have authority to cast out demons 13
6: 7 and gave them authority over the unclean spirits. 13
11:28 By what authority are you doing these things 13
28 who gave you this authority to do them? 13
29 tell you by what authority I do these things. 13
33 by what authority I do these things. 13
Lke 4: 6 I will give all this authority and their glory; 13
32 his word was with authority. 13
36 with authority and power he commands 13
5:24 Son of man has authority on earth to forgive 13
7: 8 I am a man set under authority 13
9: 1 gave them power and authority over all demons 13
10:19 have given you authority to tread upon serpents 13
12:11 the rulers and the authorities 13
19:17 you shall have authority over ten cities.' 13
20: 2 Tell us by what authority you do these things 13
2 who it is that gave you this authority. 13
8 by what authority I do these things. 13
20 authority and jurisdiction of the governor. 8
Joh 5:27 has given him authority to execute judgment 13
30 I can do nothing on my own authority 7
7:17 whether I am speaking on my own authority. 7
18 He who speaks on his own authority 7
26 Can it be that the authorities really know 9
48 Have any of the authorities . . believed in him? 9
8:28 I do nothing on my own authority 7
12:42 many even of the authorities believed in him 9
49 For I have not spoken on my own authority 11
14:10 I do not speak on my own authority 7
16:13 for he will not speak on his own authority 7
Act 1: 7 which the Father has fixed by his own authority. 13
9:14 here he has authority from the chief priests 13
26:10 by authority from the chief priests 13
12 the authority and commission of the chief priests. 13
Rom 13: 1 be subject to the governing authorities. 13
1 For there is no authority except from God 13
2 Therefore he who resists the authorities 13
3 Would you have no fear of him who is in authority? 13
6 for the authorities are ministers of God •
1Co 9: 8 Do I say this on human authority? •
15:24 every rule and every authority and power. 13
2Co 10: 8 even if I boast a little too much of our authority 13
11:17 I say not with the Lord's authority but as a fool 18
13:10 not have to be severe in my use of the authority 13
Eph 1:21 far above all rule and authority and power 13
Col 1:16 dominions or principalities or authorities 13
2:10 the head of all rule and authority. 13
Tit 2:15 exhort and reprove with all authority 14
3: 1 to be submissive to rulers and authorities 13
1Pe 3:22 angels, authorities, and powers subject to him. 13
2Pe 2:10 those who indulge . . and despise authority. 19
3Jn 1: 9 Diot'rephes . . does not acknowledge my authority. •
Jde 1: 8 these men . . reject authority, and revile 19
25 be glory, majesty, dominion, and authority 13
Rev 12:10 and the authority of his Christ have come 13
13: 2 dragon gave his power . . and great authority. 13
4 for he had given his authority to the beast 13
5 allowed to exercise authority for . . months; 13
7 authority was given it over every tribe 13
12 exercises all the authority of the first beast 13
17:12 they are to receive authority as kings 13
13 give over their power and authority to the beast; 13
18: 1 I saw another angel . . having great authority; 13
1Es 8:22 no one has authority to impose any tax upon them. 13
AEs 13: 2 not elated with presumption of authority 13
16: 5 many of those who are set in places of authority 13
Wis 10:14 and authority over his masters 13
Sir 17: 2 authority over the things upon the earth. 13
30:11 Give him no authority in his youth 13
45: 8 strengthened him with the symbols of authority 17
17 In his commandments he gave him authority 13
1Mc 6:28 He assembled . . those in authority. 15
10: 6 Demetrius gave him authority to recruit troops 13
8 had given him authority to recruit troops. 13
35 No one shall have authority to exact anything 13
38 obey no other authority but the high priest. 13
2Mc 3:24 the Sovereign of spirits and of all authority 13
4: 9 to establish by his authority a gymnasium 13
24 extolled him with an air of authority 13
7:16 Because you have authority among men 13
15:13 marvelous majesty and authority. 21
3Mc 3: 7 loyal neither to the king nor to his authorities 10
7: 1 all in authority in his government 20
12 without royal authority or supervision 13
4Mc 4: 5 On receiving authority to deal with this matter 13
6 He said that he had come with the king's authority 12
8: 7 have positions of authority in my government 16
authority *See also* assume, exercise, man, next.

city authority 1. πολιτάρχης
Act 17: 6 before the city authorities, crying 1
8 the people and the city authorities 1

authority over 1. αὐθεντέω 2. ἐξουσιάζω
Lke 22:25 those in authority over them 2
1Ti 2:12 to have authority over men 1

royal authority 1. τυραννίς
Wis 14:21 in bondage to misfortune or to royal authority 1

authorize 1. δίδωμι ἐξουσίαν
1Mc 1:13 He authorized them to observe the ordinances 1

autumn 1. חֹרֶף
Job 29: 4 as I was in my autumn days, when the friendship 1
Prv 20: 4 The sluggard does not plow in the autumn; 1
autumn *See also* rain.

avail 1. יעל 2. עמד 3. ערך 4. צלח 5. קום 6. ἰσχύω 7. ὑπομένω 8. ὠφελέω
Est 3: 4 to see whether Mor'decai's words would avail; 2
Job 36:19 Will your cry avail to keep you from distress 3
41:26 Though the sword reaches him, it does not avail; 5
Prv 21:30 No . . counsel, can avail against the LORD. •
Jer 7: 8 Behold, you trust in deceptive words to no avail. 1
Dan 11:27 shall speak lies at the same table, but to no avail; 4
Joh 6:63 the flesh is of no avail 8
Gal 5: 6 nor uncircumcision is of any avail 6
Wis 17: 5 avail to illumine that hateful night. 7

avail of the opportunity 1. χράομαι
1Co 7:21 avail yourself of the opportunity 1

avenge 1. דרש 2. דרש מִיַּד 3. ישע 4. נקם 5. נְקָמָה 6. נתן נְקָמוֹת 7. עשה נְקָמוֹת 8. ריב 9. שׁוב 10. ἐκδικέω 11. ἐκδίκησις 12. ἐπεξέρχομαι 13. ποιέω ἐκδίκησιν
Gen 4:24 If Cain is avenged sevenfold 4
Num 31: 2 Avenge the people of Israel on the Mid'ianites; 4
Deu 32:43 for he avenges the blood of his servants 4
Jdg 11:36 now that the LORD has avenged you on your enemies 7
15: 7 is what you do, I swear I will be avenged upon you 4
16:28 that I may be avenged upon the Philistines 4
1Sm 14:24 until . . evening and I am avenged on my enemies. 4
18:25 that he may be avenged of the king's enemies. 4
24:12 May the LORD judge . . may the LORD avenge me 4
25:33 kept me this day . . from avenging myself 3
39 Blessed be the LORD who has avenged the insult 8
2Sm 4: 8 the LORD has avenged my lord the king . . on Saul 6
16: 8 LORD has avenged . . the blood of the house of Saul 9
1Kg 2: 5 he murdered, avenging in time of peace blood 10
2Kg 9: 7 I may avenge on Jez'ebel the blood of my servants 4
2Ch 24:22 he was dying, he said, "May the LORD see and avenge! 2
Est 8:13 Jews were to be ready . . to avenge themselves 4
Ps 9:12 For he who avenges blood is mindful of them; 1

79:10 avenging of the outpoured blood of thy servants 5
Isa 1:24 vent my wrath . . and avenge myself on my foes. 4
Jer 5: 9 shall I not avenge myself on a nation such as this? 4
29 shall I not avenge myself on a nation such as this? 4
9: 9 shall I not avenge myself on a nation such as this? 4
46:10 a day of vengeance, to avenge himself on his foes. 4
Jol 3:21 I will avenge their blood 10
Nah 1: 2 The LORD is a jealous God and avenging 4
2 the LORD is avenging and wrathful; 4
Act 7:24 he defended the oppressed man and avenged him 13
Rom 12:19 Beloved, never avenge yourselves 10
Rev 6:10 how long before thou wilt judge and avenge 10
19: 2 he has avenged on her the blood of his servants. 10
Jdt 13:20 have avenged our ruin 12
1Mc 2:67 avenge the wrong done to your people. 10
6:22 to avenge our brethren? 11
9:42 when they had . . avenged the blood of their brother 10
13: 6 I will avenge my nation and the sanctuary 10
3Mc 7: 9 as an antagonist to avenge such acts. Farewell. 11

surely avenge 1. vindico

2Es 15: 9 I will surely avenge them," says the Lord 1

avenger 1. גאל 2. נקם 3. ἀλάστωρ 4. ἔκδικος

Num35:12 cities shall be for you a refuge from the avenger 1
19 avenger of blood shall himself put the murderer 1
21 avenger of blood shall put the murderer to death 1
24 between the manslayer and the avenger of blood 1
25 manslayer from the hand of the avenger of blood 1
27 avenger of blood finds him outside the bounds 1
27 avenger of blood slays the manslayer 1
Deu 19: 6 lest the avenger of blood in hot anger pursue 1
12 hand him over to the avenger of blood 1
Jos 20: 3 shall be . . a refuge from the avenger of blood. 1
5 And if the avenger of blood pursues him 1
9 not die by the hand of the avenger of blood 1
2Sm 14:11 that the avenger of blood slay no more 1
Ps 8: 2 a bulwark . . to still the enemy and the avenger. 2
44:16 at the sight of the enemy and the avenger. 2
99: 8 but an avenger of their wrongdoings. 2
1Th 4: 6 because the Lord is an avenger 4
Sir 30: 6 left behind him an avenger against his enemies 4
4Mc 11:23 I myself will bring a great avenger upon you 3

avert 1. כפה 2. עבר 3. עצר 4. שׁוב 5. ἀποστρέφω 6. ἀποτρέπω 7. μετατίθημι

2Sm 24:21 the plague may be averted from the people. 3
25 the LORD heeded . . and the plague was averted 3
1Ch 21:22 that the plague may be averted from the people. 3
Ezr 10:14 fierce wrath of our God . . be averted from us. 4
Est 8: 3 besought him . . to avert the evil design of Haman 2
Prv 21:14 A gift in secret averts anger; 1
Jer 11:15 Can vows and sacrificial flesh avert your doom? 2
Sir 4: 5 Do not avert your eye from the needy 5
14: 8 he averts his face and disregards people. 5
20:29 like a muzzle on the mouth they avert reproofs. 6
27: 1 whoever seeks to get rich will avert his eyes. 5
3Mc 1:16 to avert the violence of this evil design 7

avert with vengeance 1. μεταστρέφω

3Mc 5: 8 that he avert with vengeance the evil plot 1

avoid 1. סור 2. סור מֵעַל 3. פרע 4. שׁמר 5. ἀπέχω 6. ἀποτρέπω 7. διά 8. ἐκκλίνω 9. ἐκτρέπω 10. ἐξαιρέω 11. μή 12. περιίστημι 13. φευκτός 14. χάρις 15. non

2Ch 20:10 whom they avoided and did not destroy- 2
Ps 17: 4 I have avoided the ways of the violent. 4
Prv 4:15 Avoid it; do not go on it; 3
13:14 that one may avoid the snares of death. 1
14:27 that one may avoid the snares of death. 1
15:24 that he may avoid Sheol beneath. 1
16: 6 by the fear of the LORD a man avoids evil. 1
Rom 13: 5 one must be subject, not only to avoid God's wrath 7
16:17 those who create dissensions . . avoid them. 8
1Ti 6:20 Avoid the godless chatter and contradictions 9
2Ti 2:14 charge them . . to avoid disputing about words 11
16 Avoid such godless chatter 12
3: 5 Avoid such people. 6
Tit 3: 9 avoid stupid controversies, genealogies 12
2Es 7:21 what they should observe to avoid punishment. 15
Wis 2:16 he avoids our ways as unclean 5
17:10 though it nowhere could be avoided. 13
Sir 22:13 avoid him and you will find rest 8
37:31 he who is careful to avoid it prolongs his life. •
38:17 for one day, or two, to avoid criticism 14
2Mc 6:26 I should avoid the punishment of men 10

avoid quarreling 1. ἄμαχος

Tit 3: 2 to speak evil of no one, to avoid quarreling 1

await 1. ἀπεκδέχομαι 2. μένω 3. προσδέχομαι 4. ὑπομένω 5. expecto 6. maneo

Jer 3: 2 By the waysides you have sat awaiting lovers •
Hab 2: 3 For still the vision awaits its time; •
Act 20:23 imprisonment and afflictions await me. 2
Php 3:20 from it we await a Savior, the Lord Jesus Christ 1
Tit 2:13 awaiting our blessed hope 3
2Es 2:34 Await your shepherd 5
7:93 and the punishment that awaits them. 6
95 and the glory which awaits them in the last days. 6
8:59 the things which I have predicted await you ‡
59 and torment which are prepared await them •
Sir 16:22 who will await them? For the covenant is far off. 4

awake 1. יקץ 2. עור 3. קיץ 4. γίνομαι γρηγορέω 5. γρηγορέω 6. διεγείρω 7. ἐγείρω 8. ἐξεγείρω 9. ἔξυπνος γίνομαι 10. evigilo 11. expergefacio 12. vigilo

Gen 9:24 When Noah awoke from his wine 1
28:16 Then Jacob awoke from his sleep and said 1
41: 4 And Pharaoh awoke. 1
7 And Pharaoh awoke, and behold, it was a dream. 1
21 as gaunt as at the beginning. Then I awoke. 1
Jdg 5:12 Awake, awake, Deb'orah! Awake, awake, utter a song 2
12 Awake, awake, Deb'orah! Awake, awake, utter a song 2
12 Awake, awake, Deb'orah! Awake, awake, utter a song 2
12 Awake, awake, Deb'orah! Awake, awake, utter a song 2
16:14 he awoke from his sleep, and pulled away the pin 1
20 he awoke from his sleep, and said, "I will go out 1
1Sm 26:12 No man saw it, or knew it, nor did any awake; 3
1Kg 3:15 Solomon awoke, and behold, it was a dream. Then he 1
2Kg 4:31 and told him, "The child has not awaked. 3
Job 14:12 till the heavens are no more he will not awake 3
Ps 7: 6 awake, O my God; thou hast appointed a judgment. 2
17:15 when I awake, I shall be satisfied 3
35:23 Bestir thyself, and awake for my right 3
44:23 Awake! Do not cast us off for ever! 3
57: 8 Awake, my soul! Awake, O harp and lyre! 2
8 Awake, my soul! Awake, O harp and lyre! 2
8 harp and lyre! I will awake the dawn! 2
59: 5 Awake to punish all the nations; 3
73:20 They are like a dream when one awakes 3
20 on awaking you despise their phantoms. 2
78:65 Then the Lord awoke as from sleep 1
108: 1 I will sing and make melody! Awake, my soul! •
2 Awake, O harp and lyre! I will awake the dawn! 2
2 harp and lyre! I will awake the dawn! 2
139:18 When I awake, I am still with thee. 3
Prv 6:22 when you awake, they will talk with you. 3
23:35 When shall I awake? I will seek another drink. 3
Sng 4:16 Awake, O north wind, and come, O south wind! 2
5: 2 I slept, but my heart was awake. 2
Isa 26:19 O dwellers in the dust, awake and sing for joy! 3
29: 8 awakes with his hunger not satisfied 3
8 dreams he is drinking and awakes faint 3
51: 9 Awake, awake, put on strength, O arm of the LORD; 2
9 Awake, awake, put on strength, O arm of the LORD; 2
9 awake, as in days of old 2
52: 1 Awake, awake, put on your strength, O Zion; 2
1 Awake, awake, put on your strength, O Zion; 2
Jer 31:26 I awoke and looked, and my sleep was pleasant to me 3
Dan 12: 2 sleep in the dust of the earth shall awake 3
Jol 1: 5 Awake, you drunkards, and weep; 3
Hab 2: 7 and those awake who will make you tremble? 1
19 Woe to him who says to a wooden thing, Awake; 3
Zec 13: 7 Awake, O sword, against my shepherd 2
Mrk 4:39 he awoke and rebuked the wind, and said to the sea 6
Lke 8:24 awoke and rebuked the wind and the raging waves 6
12:37 whom the master finds awake when he comes 5
Eph 5:14 it is said, "Awake, O sleeper, and arise from the dead 7
Rev 3: 2 Awake, and strengthen what remains 4
3 If you will not awake, I will come like a thief 5
16:15 I am coming like a thief! Blessed is he who is awake 5
1Es 3: 3 went to sleep, and then awoke. 9
13 When the king awoke 8
2Es 5:14 Then I awoke, and my body shuddered violently 10
7:31 after seven days the world, which is not yet awake 12
35 righteous deeds shall awake 12
11:29 (the one which was in the middle) awoke 10
12: 3 Then I awoke in great perplexity of mind 12
13:13 Then in great fear I awoke 11
AEs 11:12 after he awoke he had it on his mind 6

awake *See also* keep, lie.

awake before 1. קדם

Ps 119:148 My eyes are awake before the watches of the night 1

awake manliness 1. ἐπανδρόω

2Mc 15:17 and awaking manliness in the souls of the young 1

awake out of sleep 1. ἐξυπνίζω

Joh 11:11 I go to awake him out of sleep. 1

stay awake 1. שׁקד

Ps 127: 1 watchman stays awake in vain. 1

awaken 1. יקץ 2. עור 3. קיץ 4. ἐξυπνόω

1Kg 18:27 or perhaps he is asleep and must be awakened. 1
Sng 2: 7 you stir not up nor awaken love until it please. 2
3: 5 stir not up nor awaken love until it please. 2
8: 4 I adjure . . that you stir not up nor awaken love 2
5 Under the apple tree I awakened you. 2
Ezk 7: 6 the end has come; it has awakened against you. 3
4Mc 5:11 not awaken from your foolish philosophy 4

award 1. στεφανόω

3Mc 3:28 will be awarded his freedom. 1

award *See also* give.

aware 1. ידע 2. γινώσκω 3. οἶδα 4. σύνοιδα

Sng 6:12 Before I was aware, my fancy set me in a chariot 1
Mat 12:15 Jesus, aware of this, withdrew from there 2
16: 8 Jesus, aware of this, said 2
22:18 Jesus, aware of their malice, said 2
26:10 Jesus, aware of this, said to them 2
Mrk 8:17 being aware of it, Jesus said to them 2
1Co 4: 4 I am not aware of anything against myself 4
2Ti 1:15 You are aware that all who are in Asia turned away 3
Tob 11: 2 Are you not aware, brother 2
Sir 21: 7 the sensible man, when he slips, is aware of it. 3
Sus 1:42 who art aware of all things before they come to be 3

become aware 1. ἐπιγινώσκω 2. συγγινώσκω 3. συνοράω

2Mc 4:41 when the Jews became aware of Lysimachus' attack 3
14:31 When the latter became aware that . . 2
4:33 When Onias became fully aware of these acts 1

away 1. אָחוֹר 2. בְּדֶרֶךְ 3. מֵאַחֲרֵי 4. מֵאֵצֶל 5. מִן 6. מִנֶּגֶד 7. מֵעַל 8. מִפְּנֵי 9. סור 10. αἴρω 11. ἄπειμι 12. ἀπό 13. ἐκ 14. ἐκδημέω 15. ἐκεῖθεν 16. ἐντεῦθεν 17. ἔξω 18. ἔχω 19. χωρίζω

Gen 27:39 Behold, away from the fatness of the earth 5
39 and away from the dew of heaven on high. 5
36: 6 he went into a land away from his brother Jacob. 8
Deu 2: 8 we went on, away from our brethren the sons of Esau •
8 away from the Arabah road from Elath •
Jdg 11:38 And he said, "Go." And he sent her away •
18:24 take my gods . . and go away, and what have I left? •
19: 2 she went away from him to her father's house •
1Sm 6: 7 but take their calves home, away from them. 3
20 And to whom shall he go up away from us? 7
17:30 And he turned away from him toward another 4
23:26 and David was making haste to get away from Saul 8
24:19 if a man finds his enemy, will he let him go away 2
26:20 my blood fall to the earth away from . . the LORD 6
1Kg 13:24 as he went away a lion met him on the road •
14: 8 tore the kingdom away from the house of David •
2Kg 11: 2 and stole him away from among the king's sons 5
Job 7:19 How long wilt thou not look away from me 5
14: 6 look away from him, and desist, that he may enjoy 5
28: 4 open shafts in a valley away from where men live; 5
Isa 14:19 you are cast out, away from your sepulchre 5
22: 4 Therefore I said: "Look away from me, let me weep 5
Jer 1:13 I see a boiling pot, facing away from the north. 8
32:40 that I will not turn away from doing good to them; 3
38:22 sunk in the mire, they turn away from you. 1
49:19 I will suddenly make them run away from her; 7
50:44 I will suddenly make them run away from her; 7
Lam 1: 8 yea, she herself groans, and turns her face away. 1
4:15 Away! Unclean!" men cried at them; 9
15 men cried at them; "Away! Away! Touch not! 9
15 men cried at them; "Away! Away! Touch not! 9
Ams 7:11 and Israel must go into exile away from his land 7
17 shall surely go into exile away from its land.' 7
Jon 1: 3 to Tarshish, away from the presence of the LORD. 5
Mat 5:29 out and throw it away; it is better that you lose 12
30 off and throw it away; it is better that you lose 12
13:48 but threw away the bad. 17
18: 8 or your foot . . cut it off and throw it away 12
9 pluck it out and throw it away 12
19:15 he laid his hands on them and went away. 15
Mrk 13:15 nor enter his house, to take anything away; 13
Lke 4:30 passing through the midst of them he went away. •
13:33 that a prophet should perish away from Jerusalem.' 17
14:35 men throw it away 17
23:18 they all cried out together, "Away with this man 10
Joh 2:16 the pigeons, "Take these things away; 16
19:15 They cried out, "Away with him, away with him 10
15 Away with him, away with him, crucify him! 10
Act 1:12 is near Jerusalem, a sabbath day's journey away; 18
21:36 the people followed, crying, "Away with him! 10
22:22 Away with such a fellow from the earth! 10
24:25 Go away for the present •
2Co 5: 6 we are away from the Lord 14
8 we would rather be away from the body and at home 14
9 So whether we are at home or away 14
10: 1 bold to you when I am away!- 11
13:10 I write this while I am away from you 11
Sir 8:19 lest you drive away your good luck. 7
Bar 5: 6 they went forth . . led away by their enemies •
2Mc 3:28 carried him away •
5:21 hurried away to Antioch 19

away *See also* bear, blow, break, bring, carry, cast, chase, cleanse, clear, come, crumble, cut, do, doom, drag, draw, drift, drive, even, fade, fall, far, flee, flow, fly, frighten, get, give, glide, go, hew, hide, hurl, keep, lay, lead, look, make, march, melt, pass, pine, pull, purge, put, remove, roll, rot, run, sail, scale, scare, send, slip, smelt, snatch, speed, stay, steal, strip, sweep, swim, swoon, take, tear, throw, thrust, turn, vanish, wander, wash, waste, wear, winnow, wipe, wither.

awe 1. δέος 2. φοβέω 3. φόβος

Lke 5:26 they glorified God and were filled with awe 3
Rom 11:20 So do not become proud, but stand in awe. 2
Heb 12:28 acceptable worship, with reverence and awe; 1
3Mc 7:21 being held in honor and awe 3

awe *See also* fill, hold, stand.

awe-inspiring 1. φοβερός

2Mc 1:24 awe-inspiring and strong and just and merciful 1

awesome 1. ירא

Gen 28:17 was afraid, and said, "How awesome is this place! 1

awful 1. ירא

Deu 28:58 that you may fear this glorious and awful name 1

awl 1. מַרְצֵעַ

Exd 21: 6 his master shall bore his ear through with an awl; 1
Deu 15:17 take an awl, and thrust it through his ear 1

awning 1. מְכַסֶּה

Ezk 27: 7 from the coasts of Eli'shah was your awning. 1

axe 1. בַּרְזֶל 2. גַּרְזֶן 3. חֶרֶב 4. מַגְזֵרָה 5. מַעֲצָד 6. קַרְדֹּם 7. ἀξίνη 8. πέλεκυς

Deu 19: 5 his hand swings the axe to cut down a tree 2
20:19 not destroy its trees by wielding an axe 2
Jdg 9:48 Abim'elech took an axe in his hand, and cut down 6
1Sm 13:20 to sharpen his plowshare, his mattock, his axe 6
21 and a third of a shekel for sharpening the axes 6
2Sm 12:31 to labor with saws and iron picks and iron axes 4
1Kg 6: 7 hammer nor axe nor any tool of iron was heard 2
1Ch 20: 3 to labor with saws and iron picks and axes; *
Ps 74: 5 they hacked the wooden trellis with axes. 6
Isa 10:15 Shall the axe vaunt itself over him who hews 2
34 cut down the thickets of the forest with an axe 1
Jer 10: 3 and worked with an axe by the hands of a craftsman. 5
46:22 march in force, and come against her with axes 6
Ezk 26: 9 with his axes he will break down your towers 3
Mat 3:10 Even now the axe is laid to the root of the trees; 7
Lke 3: 9 Even now the axe is laid to the root of the trees; 7
LJr 1:15 It has a dagger in its right hand, and has an axe 8

axe *See also* head.

axle 1. יָד 2. סֶרֶן 3. ἄξων

1Kg 7:30 stand had four bronze wheels and axles of bronze; 2
32 the axles of the wheels were of one piece 1
33 their axles, their rims, their . . were all cast. 1
Sir 33: 5 and his thoughts like a turning axle. 3
4Mc 9:20 were falling off the axles of the machine. 3

B

babble 1. בַּד 2. פֶּה 3. ἀδολεσχέω

Job 11: 3 Should your babble silence men, and when you mock 1
Prv 10:14 but the babbling of a fool brings ruin near. 2
Sir 32: 9 when another is speaking, do not babble. 3

babbler 1. ἀνὴρ γλωσσώδης 2. σπερμολόγος

Act 17:18 some said, "What would this babbler say? 2
Sir 9:18 A babbler is feared in his city 1

babe 1. ינק 2. נַעַר 3. עוֹלֵל 4. תַּעֲלוּלִים 5. βρέφος 6. νηπιάζω 7. νήπιος

Exd 2: 6 saw the child; and lo, the babe was crying. 2
Ps 8: 2 by the mouth of babes and infants 3
17:14 may they leave something over to their babes. 3
Isa 3: 4 make boys their princes, and babes shall rule 4
Lam 2:11 infants and babes faint in the streets 1
Mat 11:25 and revealed them to babes; 7
21:16 Out of the mouth of babes and sucklings 7
Lke 1:41 the babe leaped in her womb 5
44 the babe in my womb leaped for joy. 5
2:12 you will find a babe wrapped in swaddling cloths 5
16 the babe lying in a manger. 5
10:21 revealed them to babes 7
1Co 3: 1 as men of the flesh, as babes in Christ. 7
14:20 be babes in evil, but in thinking be mature. 6
1Pe 2: 2 Like newborn babes, long for . . spiritual milk 5
Jdt 7:27 witness the death of our babes before our eyes 7
Wis 10:21 and made the tongues of babes speak clearly. 7
12:24 they were deceived like foolish babes. 7
18: 5 had resolved to kill the babes of thy holy ones 7
1Mc 2: 9 Her babes have been killed in her streets 7

baby 1. βρέφος 2. νεογνὸν βρέφος 3. νήπιος

2Mc 6:10 with their babies hung at their breasts 1
8: 4 the lawless destruction of the innocent babies 3
3Mc 5:49 others with babies at their breasts 2
50 removing the babies from their breasts 3

back 1. אָחוֹר 2. אַחֲרֵי 3. אֲחֹרַנִּית 4. בוא 5. בֵּין יָדַיִם 6. גַּב 7. גֵּו 8. גַּו 9. הָלְאָה 10. כָּתֵף 11. מִבַּיִת 12. עֹרֶף 13. קָרַחַת 14. רְפִידָה 15. שׁוּב 16. שְׁכֶם 17. גַּב (A) 18. ἀπέχω 19. εἰσπορεύω 20. εἰς τὰ ὀπίσω 21. νῶτος 22. ὄπισθεν 23. ὀπίσω 24. ὀσφῦς 25. πάλιν

Gen 14:16 also brought back his kinsman Lot with his goods *
19: 9 they said, "Stand back! 9
17 do not look back or stop anywhere in the valley; 2
26 Lot's wife behind him looked back *
45:17 load your beasts and go back to the land of Canaan; 4
Exd 23:27 make all your enemies turn their backs to you. 12
26:12 shall hang over the back of the tabernacle. 1
33:23 you shall see my back; but my face shall not be 1
Lev 13:55 the leprous spot is on the back or on the front 13
Num24:25 Then Balaam rose, and went back to his place; 15
Deu 20: 5 Let him go back to his house, lest he die 15
6 Let him go back to his house, lest he die 15
7 Let him go back to his house, lest he die 15
8 Let him go back to his house, lest the heart 15
Jos 7: 8 what can I say, when Israel has turned their backs 12
12 they turn their backs before their enemies 12
8:20 when the men of Ai looked back, behold, the smoke 2
Jdg 20:42 they turned their backs before the men of Israel *
1Sm 10: 9 When he turned his back to leave Samuel 16
2Sm 1:22 the bow of Jonathan turned not back, and the sword 1
2:23 smote him . . so that the spear came out at his back; 2
22:41 Thou didst make my enemies turn their backs to me 12
1Kg 7: 8 own house . . in the other court back of the hall 11
9 costly stones . . sawed with saws, back and front 11
10:13 she turned and went back to her own land *
19 at the back of the throne was a calf's head 2
14: 9 and have cast me behind your back; 8
18:37 and that thou hast turned their hearts back. 3
2Kg 1: 6 Go back to the king who sent you, and say to him 15
20:10 rather let the shadow go back ten steps. 3
11 the LORD, and he brought the shadow back ten steps 3
2Ch 29: 6 turned their backs. 12
Neh 9:26 rebelled . . and cast thy law behind their back 8
Job 41:15 His back is made of rows of shields *
Ps 9: 3 When my enemies turned back, they stumbled 1
18:40 Thou didst make my enemies turn their backs to me 12
35: 4 Let them be turned back and confounded 1
40:14 let them be turned back and brought to dishonor 1
44:10 Thou hast made us turn back from the foe; 1
18 Our heart has not turned back 1
56: 9 Then my enemies will be turned back in the day 1
70: 2 Let them be turned back and brought to dishonor 1
114: 3 The sea looked and fled, Jordan turned back. 1
5 What ails you . . O Jordan, that you turn back? 1
129: 3 The plowers plowed upon my back; 6
Prv 10:13 but a rod is for the back of him who lacks sense. 7
14: 3 The talk of a fool is a rod for his back *
19:29 flogging for the backs of fools. 7
26: 3 bridle for the ass, and a rod for the back of fools. 7
29:11 but a wise man quietly holds it back. 1
Sng 3:10 He made its posts of silver, its back of gold 14
Isa 30: 6 carry their riches on the backs of asses 10
38: 8 make the shadow . . turn back ten steps. 3
17 for thou hast cast all my sins behind thy back. 7
44:25 who turns wise men back 1
50: 6 I gave my back to the smiters, and my cheeks 7
51:23 and you have made your back like the ground 7
59:14 Justice is turned back, 1
Jer 2:27 For they have turned their back to me 12
18:17 I will show them my back, not my face 12
31: 9 and with consolations I will lead them back *
32:33 have turned to me their back and not their face; 12
48:39 they wail! How Moab has turned his back in shame! 12
Lam 1:13 he spread a net for my feet; he turned me back; 1
Ezk 1:10 and the four had the face of an eagle at the back. *
2:10 and it had writing on the front and on the back 1
8:16 men, with their backs to the temple of the LORD 1
23:35 have forgotten me and cast me behind your back 8
40:13 Then he measured the gate from the back of the one *
13 back of the one side room to the back of the other *
47: 6 Then he led me back along the bank of the river. 15
Dan 7: 6 leopard, with four wings of a bird on its back; 17
Hos 2: 9 Therefore I will take back my grain in its time 15
Zec 13: 6 one asks him, 'What are these wounds on your back?' 5
Mat 24:18 let him who is in the field not turn back 23
Mrk 11: 3 will send it back here immediately.' 25
13:16 not turn back to take his mantle. 20
Lke 9:62 puts his hand to the plow and looks back is fit 20
17:31 likewise let him who is in the field not turn back. 20
24:23 they came back saying that they had even seen *
Joh 6:66 After this many of his disciples drew back 20
7:45 The officers then went back to the chief priests *
18: 6 they drew back and fell to the ground. 20
20:10 the disciples went back to their homes. 25
Rom 11:10 and bend their backs for ever. 21
24 be grafted back into their own olive tree. *
2Co 1:16 to come back to you from Macedo'nia 25
Phm 1:15 you might have him back for ever 18
Rev 5: 1 I saw . . a scroll written within and on the back 22
1Es 8:65 those who had come back from captivity *
Tob 2: 3 he came back and said *
12: 3 he has led me back to you safely, he cured my wife *
Sir 21:15 he dislikes it and casts it behind his back. 21
1Mc 4:16 Judas . . turned back from pursuing them 22
13:27 with polished stone at the front and back. 22
49 prevented from going out to the country and back 19
3Mc 3:24 these impious people behind our backs 21
4Mc 11:10 twisted his back around the wedge on the wheel 24
19 To his back they applied sharp spits 21
18:20 to the catapult and back again to more tortures *

back *See also* answer, ask, break, bring, buy, call, carry, come, curl, draw, drive, echo, fall, force, get, give, go, hold, keep, look, pay, press, push, put, receive, roll, send, set, shine, shrink, take, throw, thrust, turn, way.

back again 1. ἀνάγω

Wis 16:13 lead men down to the gates of Hades and back again. 1

backbiting 1. סָתַר

Prv 25:23 backbiting tongue, angry looks. 1

backbone 1. עָצֶה

Lev 3: 9 fat tail . . taking it away close by the backbone 1

backslide 1. מְשׁוּבָה 2. שׁוּב 3. שׁוֹבָב

Isa 57:17 went on backsliding in the way of his own heart. 3
Jer 8: 5 people turned away in perpetual backsliding? 1
14: 7 for our backslidings are many, we have sinned 1
Ezk 37:23 I will save them from all the backslidings 2

backward 1. אָחוֹר 2. אֲחֹרַנִּית

Gen 9:23 both their shoulders, and walked backward 2
49:17 that his rider falls backward. 1
1Sm 4:18 Eli fell over backward from his seat by the side 2
Job 23: 8 backward, but I cannot perceive him; 1
Ps 129: 5 who hate Zion be put to shame and turned backward! 1
Isa 28:13 that they may go, and fall backward, and be broken 1
50: 5 I was not rebellious, I turned not backward. 1
Jer 7:24 and went backward and not forward. 1
15: 6 says the LORD, you keep going backward; 1
46: 5 They are dismayed and have turned backward. 1

backward *See also* go, look.

bad 1. רֹעַ 2. רַע 3. רָעָה 4. רָעָה מִן 5. רעע 6. רְשַׁע 7. ἥσσων 8. κακός 9. μοχθηρός 10. πονηρός 11. σαπρός 12. φαῦλος 13. χειρίστως 14. χείρων 15. deterior 16. malus

Gen 24:50 from the LORD; we cannot speak to you bad or good. 2
31:24 say not a word to Jacob, either good or bad. 2
29 you speak to Jacob neither good nor bad.' 2
Lev 27:10 shall not . . exchange it, a good for a bad 2
10 a good for a bad, or a bad for a good 2
12 the priest shall value it as either good or bad 2
14 the priest shall value it as either good or bad 2
33 A man shall not inquire whether it is good or bad 2
Num13:19 whether the land that they dwell in is good or bad 2
24:13 to do either good or bad of my own will; 3
2Sm 13:22 But Ab'salom spoke to Amnon neither good nor bad; 2
19: 7 and this will be worse for you than all the evil 4
2Kg 2:19 but the water is bad, and the land is unfruitful. 2
Ps 41: 7 they imagine the worst for me. 3
Prv 13:17 A bad messenger plunges men into trouble 6
20:14 It is bad, it is bad," says the buyer; 2
14 It is bad, it is bad," says the buyer; 2
25:19 like a bad tooth or a foot that slips. 2
Ecc 5:14 and those riches were lost in a bad venture; 2
Jer 16:12 because you have done worse than your fathers 5
24: 2 but the other basket had very bad figs 2
2 very bad figs, so bad that they could not be eaten. 1
3 the good figs very good, and the bad figs very bad 2
3 the good figs very good, and the bad figs very bad 2
3 figs very bad, so bad that they cannot be eaten. 1
8 the bad figs which are so bad they cannot be eaten 2
8 the bad figs which are so bad they cannot be eaten 1
29:17 vile figs which are so bad they cannot be eaten. 1
Ezk 7:24 I will bring the worst of the nations to take 2
23:11 in her doting and in her harlotry, which was worse *
Mat 7:17 but the bad tree bears evil fruit. 11
18 nor can a bad tree bear good fruit. 11
9:16 and a worse tear is made. 14
12:33 or make the tree bad, and its fruit bad 11
33 or make the tree bad, and its fruit bad 11
45 worse than the first 14
13:48 but threw away the bad. 11
22:10 gathered all whom they found, both bad and good; 10
27:64 the last fraud will be worse than the first. 14
Mrk 2:21 the new from the old, and a worse tear is made. 14
5:26 no better but rather grew worse. 14
Lke 6:43 For no good tree bears bad fruit 11

43 nor again does a bad tree bear good fruit; 11
11:26 the last state . . becomes worse than the first. 14
13: 2 worse sinners than all the other Galileans •
4 do you think that they were worse offenders •
Joh 5:14 Sin no more, that nothing worse befall you. 14
Rom 9:11 and had done nothing either good or bad 12
13: 3 not a terror to good conduct, but to bad. 8
1Co 11:17 it is not for the better but for the worse. 7
15:33 Bad company ruins good morals. 8
1Ti 5: 8 and is worse than an unbeliever. 14
2Ti 3:13 go on from bad to worse, deceivers and deceived. •
13 go on from bad to worse, deceivers and deceived. 14
Heb 10:29 How much worse punishment . . will be deserved 14
2Pe 2:20 last state has become worse for them than the first. 14
2Es 7:87 The seventh way, which is worse than all the ways •
8:30 those who are deemed worse than beasts 16
14:16 evils worse than those which you have now seen 15
Wis 15:18 which are worse than all others 14
17: 6 worse than that unseen appearance. 14
Sir 6: 1 a bad name incurs shame and reproach 10
11:14 Good things and bad, life and death 8
22:11 the life of the fool is worse than death. 10
26: 5 all these are worse than death. 9
37:27 see what is bad for it and do not give it that. 10
39:34 no one can say, "This is worse than that 10
2Mc 5:23 worse than the others did 8
7:39 handled him worse than the others 13
3Mc 5:20 a savagery worse than that of Phalaris 8
6:26 accepted willingly the worst of human dangers 8

bad *See also* weather.

do bad 1. רעע
Jer 7:26 They did worse than their fathers. 1

bad off 1. ὑστερέω
1Co 8: 8 We are no worse off if we do not eat 1

bad thing 1. κακός
Sir 31:13 Remember that a greedy eye is a bad thing 1

badger 1. שָׁפָן
Ps 104:18 rocks are a refuge for the badgers. 1
Prv 30:26 badgers are a people not mighty, yet they make 1

badger *See also* rock.

badly 1. מְאֹד 2. σφόδρα
1Sm 31: 3 and he was badly wounded by the archers. 1
2Ch 35:23 king said . . Take me away, for I am badly wounded. 1
1Mc 6: 8 he was astounded and badly shaken 2

badly *See also* behave, deal.

baffle 1. צהב
Ezk 19: 5 When she saw that she was baffled •
Sir 10:10 A long illness baffles the physician 1

bag 1. חָרִיט 2. כִּיס 3. כְּלִי 4. צְרוֹר 5. πήρα
Gen 42:25 Joseph gave orders to fill their bags with grain 3
43:11 choice fruits of the land in your bags, and carry 3
Deu 25:13 not have in your bag two kinds of weights 2
1Sm 17:40 and put them in his shepherd's bag or wallet; 3
49 David put his hand in his bag and took out a stone 3
2Kg 5:23 and tied up two talents of silver in two bags 1
12:10 and they counted and tied up in bags the money •
Job 14:17 my transgression would be sealed up in a bag 4
Prv 7:20 he took a bag of money with him; 4
16:11 all the weights in the bag are his work. 2
Sng 1:13 My beloved is to me a bag of myrrh 4
Mic 6:11 acquit the man . . with a bag of deceitful weights? 2
Hag 1: 6 earns wages to put them into a bag with holes. 4
Mat 10:10 no bag for your journey, nor two tunics 5
Mrk 6: 8 a staff; no bread, no bag, no money in their belts; 5
Lke 9: 3 no staff, nor bag, nor bread, nor money 5
10: 4 Carry no purse, no bag, no sandals 5
22:35 When I sent you out with no purse or bag or sandals 5
36 let him who has a purse take it, and likewise a bag. 5
Jdt 10: 5 and filled a bag with parched grain 5
13:10 who placed it in her food bag 5
15 Then she took the head out of the bag and showed it 5

money bag 1. θυλάκιον
Tob 9: 5 Gabael brought out the money bags 1

baggage 1. כְּלִי 2. ἀποσκευή
1Sm 10:22 Behold, he has hidden himself among the baggage. 1
17:22 left the . . in charge of the keeper of the baggage 1
25:13 while 200 remained with the baggage. 1
30:24 so shall his share be who stays by the baggage; 1
Isa 10:28 at Michmash he stores his baggage; 1
Jer 46:19 Prepare yourselves baggage for exile 1
Ezk 12: 3 prepare for yourself an exile's baggage 1
4 You shall bring out your baggage by day 1
4 bring out your baggage . . as baggage for exile; 1
6 you shall lift the baggage upon your shoulder •
7 I brought out my baggage by day 1
7 brought out my baggage . . as baggage for exile 1
12 prince who is among them shall lift his baggage •
Jdt 7: 2 together with the baggage 2
1Mc 9:35 the great amount of baggage which they had. 2
39 and saw a tumultuous procession with much baggage; 2
2Mc 12:21 he sent off . . also the baggage 2

bagpipe 1. סוּמְפֹּנְיָה (A)
Dan 3: 5 hear the sound of the . . harp, bagpipe 1
7 heard the sound of . . harp, bagpipe •
10 hears the sound of . . harp, bagpipe 1
15 hear the sound of . . harp, bagpipe, and every kind 1

bake 1. אפה 2. בשל 3. מַאֲפֶה 4. מָעוֹג 5. עוג
6. תֻּפִינִים
Gen 19: 3 feast, and baked unleavened bread, and they ate. 1
40:17 basket there were all sorts of baked food 1
Exd 12:39 they baked unleavened cakes of the dough 1
16:23 bake what you will bake and boil what you will 1
23 bake what you will bake and boil what you will 1
Lev 2: 4 bring a cereal offering baked in the oven 3
5 if your offering is a cereal offering baked •
6:17 It shall not be baked with leaven 1
21 in baked pieces like a cereal offering 6
7: 9 every cereal offering baked in the oven 1
23:17 they shall be of fine flour, they shall be baked 1
24: 5 you shall take fine flour, and bake twelve cakes 1
26:26 ten women shall bake your bread in one oven 1
Num11: 8 like the taste of cakes baked with oil. •
1Sm 28:24 and kneaded it and baked unleavened bread of it 1
2Sm 13: 8 made cakes in his sight, and baked the cakes. 2
1Kg 17:12 I have nothing baked, only a handful of meal 4
19: 6 there was at his head a cake baked on hot stones •
Isa 44:15 warms himself, he kindles a fire and bakes bread; 1
19 in the fire, I also baked bread on its coals 1
Ezk 4:12 cake, baking it in their sight on human dung. 5
46:20 where they shall bake the cereal offering 1

baked *See* offering.

baker 1. אפה
Gen 40: 1 and his baker offended their lord the king 1
2 officers, the chief butler and the chief baker 1
5 they both dreamed—the butler and the baker 1
16 When the chief baker saw that 1
20 head of the chief baker among his servants. 1
22 but he hanged the chief baker 1
41:10 and put me and the chief baker in custody 1
13 to my office, and the baker was hanged. •
1Sm 8:13 daughters to be perfumers and cooks and bakers. 1
Jer 37:21 bread was given him daily from the bakers' street 1
Hos 7: 4 a heated oven, whose baker ceases to stir the fire 1

balance 1. מֹאזְנַיִם 2. מִפְלָשׂ 3. פֶּלֶס 4. מֹאזְנֵא (A)
5. ζυγός 6. πλάστιγξ 7. σταθμός 8. statera
Lev 19:36 You shall have just balances, just weights 1
Job 6: 2 all my calamity laid in the balances! 1
31: 6 Let me be weighed in a just balance 1
37:16 Do you know the balancings of the clouds 2
Ps 62: 9 men . . are a delusion; in the balances they go up; 1
Prv 11: 1 A false balance is an abomination to the LORD 1
16:11 A just balance and scales are the LORD'S; 3
Isa 40:12 mountains in scales and the hills in a balance? 1
Ezk 5: 1 take balances for weighing, and divide the hair. 1
45:10 You shall have just balances, a just ephah 1
Dan 5:27 TEKEL, you have been weighed in the balances 4
Hos 12: 7 A trader, in whose hands are false balances 1
Ams 8: 5 and deal deceitfully with false balances 1
Rev 6: 5 and its rider had a balance in his hand; 5
2Es 3:34 Now therefore weigh in a balance our iniquities 8
4:36 for he has weighed the age in the balance 8
Sir 21:25 will be weighed in the balance. 5
26:15 no balance can weigh the value of a chaste soul. 7
28:25 make balances and scales for your words 5
2Mc 9: 8 he could weigh the high mountains in a balance 6

bald 1. קֵרֵחַ 2. קָרְחָה
Lev 13:40 hair has fallen . . is bald but he is clean 1
Mic 1:16 make yourselves as bald as the eagle 2

bald *See also* forehead, head, locust, make.

make bald 1. קרח
Jer 16: 6 or cut himself or make himself bald for them. 1
Ezk 27:31 they make themselves bald for you 1
29:18 every head was made bald and every shoulder was 1

baldhead 1. קֵרֵחַ
2Kg 2:23 boys . . jeered at him, saying, "Go up, you baldhead! 1
23 saying, "Go up, you baldhead! Go up, you baldhead! 1

baldness 1. קָרְחָה
Deu 14: 1 not . . make any baldness on your foreheads 1
Isa 3:24 instead of well-set hair, baldness; 1
15: 2 On every head is baldness, every beard is shorn; 1
22:12 to baldness and girding with sackcloth; 1
Jer 47: 5 Baldness has come upon Gaza 1
Ezk 7:18 shame . . and baldness on all their heads. 1
Ams 8:10 I will bring . . baldness on every head; 1

baldness of the forehead 1. גַּבַּחַת
Lev 13:41 he has baldness of the forehead but he is clean 1

ball 1. דּוּר
Isa 22:18 and throw you like a ball into a wide land; 1

ballad *See* singer.

ballot 1. ψῆφος
4Mc 15:26 this mother held two ballots 1

balm 1. צֳרִי
Gen 37:25 with their camels bearing gum, balm, and myrrh 1
43:11 a present, a little balm and a little honey 1
Jer 8:22 Is there no balm in Gilead? Is there no physician 1
46:11 and take balm, O virgin daughter of Egypt! 1
51: 8 wail for her! Take balm for her pain; 1
Ezk 27:17 wheat, olives and early figs, honey, oil, and balm. 1

balsam tree 1. בָּכָא
2Sm 5:23 and come upon them opposite the balsam trees. 1
24 when you hear . . in the tops of the balsam trees 1
1Ch 14:14 and come upon them opposite the balsam trees. 1
15 sound of marching in the tops of the balsam trees 1

ban 1. בדל
Ezr 10: 8 banned from the congregation of the exiles. 1

band 1. אֲגֻדָּה 2. גְּדוּד 3. גור 4. חֶבֶל 5. חַיָּה 6. מְלֹא
7. עֵדָה 8. χείρ
1Sm 10: 5 you will meet a band of prophets coming down 4
10 When they came . . a band of prophets met him; 4
30: 8 Shall I pursue after this band? Shall I overtake 2
15 David said . . "Will you take me down to this band? 2
15 Swear . . and I will take you down to this band. 2
23 into our hand the band that came against us. 2
2Sm 2:25 Benjaminites gathered . . and became one band 1
23:13 a band of Philistines was encamped in the valley 5
2Kg 13:20 Now bands of Moabites used to invade the land 2
24: 2 the LORD sent against him bands of the Chalde'ans 2
2 bands of the Chalde'ans, and bands of the Syrians 2
2 bands of the Syrians, and bands of the Moabites 2
2 bands of the Moabites, and bands of the Ammonites 2
Ps 59: 3 fierce men band themselves against me. 3
86:14 band of ruthless men seek my life 7
Isa 31: 4 a band of shepherds is called forth against him 6
37:32 and out of Mount Zion a band of survivors. •
Hos 4:18 A band of drunkards, they give themselves •
1Mc 5: 6 where he found a strong band and many people 8

band (2) 1. סָבִיב 2. עֲבֹת 3. אֱסוּר (A)
1Kg 7:35 on the top . . was a round band half a cubit high; 1
Dan 4:15 bound with a band of iron and bronze 3
23 bound with a band of iron and bronze 3
Hos 11: 4 with cords of compassion, with the bands of love 2

band *See* skilfully, swathe.

magic band 1. כֶּסֶת
Ezk 13:18 Woe to the women who sew magic bands 1
20 Behold, I am against your magic bands 1

marauding band 1. גְּדוּד
1Kg 11:24 and became leader of a marauding band 1
2Kg 13:21 a marauding band was seen and the man was cast 1

band of men 1. גְּדוּד
2Ch 22: 1 band of men that came with the Arabs . . had slain 1

band of raiders 1. גְּדוּד
1Ch 12:21 They helped David against the band of raiders; 1

band of soldiers 1. חַיִל 2. σπεῖρα
Ezr 8:22 ask the king for a band of soldiers and horsemen 1
Joh 18: 3 Judas, procuring a band of soldiers 2
12 the band of soldiers . . seized Jesus 2

band of survivors 1. פְּלֵיטָה
2Kg 19:31 and out of Mount Zion a band of survivors. 1

raiding band 1. גְּדוּד
2Sm 4: 2 had two men who were captains of raiding bands; 1

swaddling band 1. חֲתֻלָּה
Job 38: 9 thick darkness its swaddling band 1

band together 1. גדד 2. גור
Ps 56: 6 They band themselves together, they lurk 2
94:21 band together against the life of the righteous 1
Hos 6: 9 so the priests are banded together ‡

bandage 1. אֲפֵר 2. חִתּוּל 3. καταδέω 4. κειρία
1Kg 20:38 and waited . . disguising himself with a bandage 1
41 made haste to take the bandage away from his eyes; 1
Ezk 30:21 bound up, to heal it by binding it with a bandage 2
Joh 11:44 his hands and feet bound with bandages 4
Sir 27:21 a wound may be bandaged 3

bandit 1. גְּדוּד
Hos 7: 1 thief breaks in, and the bandits raid without. 1

banish 1. אבד 2. גלה 3. נדח 4. שבת 5. αἴρω
6. ἀποστρέφω 7. ἐξάγω 8. φυγαδεύω 9. extinguo

2Sm 14:13 the king does not bring his banished one home 3
14 means not to keep his banished one an outcast. 3
Isa 24:11 all joy . . the gladness of the earth is banished. 2
Jer 25:10 I will banish from them the voice of mirth 1
Ezk 34:25 and banish wild beasts from the land 4
Rom 11:26 he will banish ungodliness from Jacob"; 6
2Es 8:53 illness is banished from you, and death is hidden; 9
1Mc 3:35 banish the memory of them from the place 5
2Mc 10:15 those who were banished from Jerusalem 8
4Mc 8:23 Why do we banish ourselves 7

banishment 1. שְׁרֹשִׁי (A)
Ezr 7:26 whether for death or for banishment 1

bank 1. גָּדָה 2. יָד 3. פָּנִים 4. שָׂפָה 5. *κρηπίς*
6. *τράπεζα* 7. *χάραξ* 8. *χεῖλος*
Gen 41: 3 stood by the other cows on the bank of the Nile. 4
17 dream I was standing on the banks of the Nile; 4
Deu 2:37 banks of the river Jabbok and the cities 2
Jos 3:15 the Jordan overflows all its banks 1
4:18 Jordan returned . . and overflowed all its banks 1
Jdg 11:26 all the cities that are on the banks of the Arnon 2
2Kg 2:13 and went back and stood on the bank 4
1Ch 12:15 when it was overflowing all its banks 1
Isa 8: 7 over all its channels and go over all its banks; 1
Ezk 47: 6 Then he led me back along the bank of the river. 4
7 I saw upon the bank of the river very many trees 4
12 And on the banks, on both sides of the river 4
Dan 8: 3 behold, a ram standing on the bank of the river. 3
6 ram . . seen standing on the bank of the river 3
16 I heard a man's voice between the banks of the U'lai *
10: 4 as I was standing on the bank of the great river 2
12: 5 one on this bank of the stream and one on that bank 4
5 one on this bank . . one on that bank of the stream. 4
Lke 19:23 Why then did you not put my money into the bank 6
43 when your enemies will cast up a bank about you 7
Sir 40:16 The reeds by any water or river bank 8
1Mc 9:43 he came . . to the banks of the Jordan. 5

steep bank 1. *κρημνός*
Mat 8:32 behold, the whole herd rushed down the steep bank 1
Mrk 5:13 rushed down the steep bank into the sea 1
Lke 8:33 the herd rushed down the steep bank into the lake 1

banker 1. *τραπεζίτης*
Mat 25:27 to have invested my money with the bankers 1

banner 1. דגל 2. דֶּגֶל 3. נֵס
Exd 17:15 the name of it, The LORD is my banner 3
16 saying, "A hand upon the banner of the LORD! *
Ps 60: 4 Thou hast set up a banner for those who fear thee 3
Sng 2: 4 He brought me . . and his banner over me was love. 2
6: 4 terrible as an army with banners. 1
10 Who is this . . terrible as an army with banners? 1
Jer 50: 2 set up a banner and proclaim, conceal it not 3
banner *See also* set.

banquet 1. יַיִן 2. מִשְׁתֶּה 3. מִשְׁתֵּי (A) 4. *δεῖπνον*
5. *δοχή* 6. *κώθωνα* 7. *πότος* 8. *συμποσία*
9. *συμπόσιον*
Est 1: 3 gave a banquet for all his princes and servants 2
5 the king gave . . a banquet lasting for seven days 2
9 Queen Vashti also gave a banquet for the women 2
2:18 the king gave a great banquet to all his princes 2
18 gave a great banquet . . it was Esther's banquet. 2
5:12 let no one come with the king to the banquet 2
6:14 to the banquet that Esther had prepared. 2
Sng 2: 4 He brought me to the banqueting house 1
Dan 5:10 queen . . came into the banqueting hall; 3
Mrk 6:21 when Herod on his birthday gave a banquet 4
Lke 14:12 When you give a dinner or a banquet 4
16 A man once gave a great banquet, and invited many; 4
17 at the time for the banquet he sent his servant 4
24 who were invited shall taste my banquet.' 4
1Es 3: 1 Now King Darius gave a great banquet 5
Jdt 6:21 gave a banquet for the elders 7
12:10 Holofernes held a banquet for his slave only 7
13: 1 because the banquet had lasted long. 7
Sir 31:31 Do not reprove your neighbor at a banquet of wine 9
32: 5 a concert of music at a banquet of wine. 9
49: 1 like music at a banquet of wine. 9
1Mc 16:15 he gave them a great banquet, and hid men there 7
2Mc 2:27 one who prepares a banquet 9
3Mc 5:15 the hour of the banquet was already slipping by 8
16 those present for the banquet 8
17 make the present portion of the banquet joyful 8
6:31 arranged for a banquet of deliverance 6
33 after convening a great banquet 9
banquet *See also* hall.

baptism 1. *βάπτισμα* 2. *βαπτισμός*
Mat 3: 7 the Pharisees and Sad'ducees coming for baptism 1
21:25 The baptism of John, whence was it? 1
Mrk 1: 4 preaching a baptism of repentance 1
10:38 to be baptized with the baptism 1
39 with the baptism with which I am baptized 1
11:30 Was the baptism of John from heaven or from men? 1
Lke 3: 3 preaching a baptism of repentance 1
7:29 baptized with the baptism of John; 1
12:50 a baptism to be baptized 1
20: 4 Was the baptism of John from heaven or from men? 1
Act 1:22 beginning from the baptism of John 1
10:37 after the baptism which John preached 1
13:24 a baptism of repentance 1
18:25 though he knew only the baptism of John. 1
19: 3 They said, "Into John's baptism. 1
4 John baptized with the baptism of repentance 1
Rom 6: 4 buried therefore with him by baptism into death 1
Eph 4: 5 one Lord, one faith, one baptism 1
Col 2:12 you were buried with him in baptism 2
1Pe 3:21 Baptism, which corresponds to this, now saves you 1

baptize 1. *βαπτίζω*
Mat 3: 6 they were baptized by him in the river Jordan 1
11 I baptize you with water for repentance, but he 1
11 to carry; he will baptize you with the Holy Spirit 1
13 to the Jordan to John, to be baptized by him. 1
14 I need to be baptized by you, and do you come to me? 1
16 when Jesus was baptized, he went up immediately 1
28:19 baptizing them in the name of the Father 1
Mrk 1: 5 and they were baptized by him in the river Jordan 1
8 I have baptized you with water 1
8 he will baptize you with the Holy Spirit 1
9 baptized by John in the Jordan. 1
10:38 to be baptized with the baptism 1
38 the baptism with which I am baptized? 1
39 with the baptism with which I am baptized 1
39 you will be baptized; 1
16:16 He who believes and is baptized will be saved 1
Lke 3: 7 the multitudes that came out to be baptized by him 1
12 Tax collectors also came to be baptized, and said 1
16 John answered them all, "I baptize you with water; 1
16 baptize you with the Holy Spirit and with fire. 1
21 Now when all the people were baptized 1
21 when Jesus also had been baptized 1
7:29 baptized with the baptism of John; 1
30 not having been baptized by him.) 1
12:50 a baptism to be baptized 1
Joh 1:25 They asked him, "Then why are you baptizing 1
26 John answered them, "I baptize with water; 1
28 beyond the Jordan, where John was baptizing. 1
31 but for this I came baptizing with water 1
33 but he who sent me to baptize with water said to me 1
33 this is he who baptizes with the Holy Spirit.' 1
3:22 there he remained with them and baptized. 1
23 John also was baptizing at Ae'non near Salim 1
23 and people came and were baptized. 1
26 to whom you bore witness, here he is, baptizing 1
4: 1 Jesus was making and baptizing more disciples 1
2 (although Jesus himself did not baptize 1
10:40 to the place where John at first baptized 1
Act 1: 5 for John baptized with water 1
5 you shall be baptized with the Holy Spirit. 1
2:38 Repent, and be baptized every one of you 1
41 So those who received his word were baptized 1
8:12 they were baptized, both men and women. 1
13 after being baptized he continued with Philip. 1
16 they had only been baptized 1
36 What is to prevent my being baptized? 1
38 he baptized him. 1
9:18 Then he rose and was baptized 1
10:47 Can any one forbid water for baptizing 1
48 baptized in the name of Jesus Christ 1
11:16 John baptized with water 1
16 you shall be baptized with the Holy Spirit.' 1
16:15 when she was baptized, with her household 1
33 he was baptized at once, with all his family. 1
18: 8 many . . believed and were baptized. 1
19: 3 he said, "Into what then were you baptized? 1
4 John baptized with the baptism of repentance 1
5 baptized in the name of the Lord Jesus. 1
22:16 now why do you wait? Rise and be baptized 1
Rom 6: 3 all of us who have been baptized into Christ 1
3 into Christ Jesus were baptized into his death? 1
1Co 1:13 were you baptized in the name of Paul? 1
14 I am thankful that I baptized none of you 1
15 say that you were baptized in my name. 1
16 I did baptize also the household of Steph'anas. 1
16 I do not know whether I baptized any one else.) 1
17 not send me to baptize but to preach the gospel 1
10: 2 all were baptized into Moses in the cloud 1
12:13 we were all baptized into one body 1
15:29 by being baptized on behalf of the dead 1
29 why are people baptized on their behalf? 1
Gal 3:27 For as many of you as were baptized into Christ 1

baptizer 1. *βαπτίζω*
Mrk 1: 4 John the baptizer appeared in the wilderness 1
6:14 John the baptizer has been raised from the dead; 1
24 she said, "The head of John the baptizer. 1

bar 1. אחז 2. בַּד 3. בְּרִיחַ 4. לָשׁוֹן 5. מוֹטָה 6. מְטִיל
7. מִנְעָל 8. *μοχλός*
Exd 26:26 you shall make bars of acacia wood 3
27 five bars for the frames of the other side 3
27 five bars for the frames of the side 3
28 The middle bar, halfway up the frames, shall pass 3
29 rings of gold for holders for the bars; 3
29 and you shall overlay the bars with gold. 3
35:11 its hooks and its frames, its bars, its pillars 3
36:31 he made bars of acacia wood, five for the frames 3
32 five bars for the frames of the other side 3
32 and five bars for the frames of the tabernacle 3
33 he made the middle bar to pass through 3
34 made their rings of gold for holders for the bars 3
34 and overlaid the bars with gold. 3
39:33 all its utensils, its hooks, its frames, its bars 3
Lev 26:13 I have broken the bars of your yoke 5
Num 3:36 appointed charge . . the bars, the pillars 3
4:31 frames . . with its bars, pillars, and bases 3
Deu 3: 5 cities fortified with high walls, gates, and bars 3
33:25 Your bars shall be iron and bronze; 7
Jos 7:21 I saw . . and a bar of gold weighing 50 shekels 4
24 and the silver and the mantle and the bar of gold 4
Jdg 16: 3 and pulled them up, bar and all, and put them on his 3
1Sm 23: 7 by entering a town that has gates and bars. 3
1Kg 4:13 60 great cities with walls and bronze bars); 3
2Ch 8: 5 fortified cities with walls, gates, and bars 3
14: 7 surround them with . . gates and bars; 3
Neh 3: 3 set its doors, its bolts, and its bars. 3
6 set its doors, its bolts, and its bars. 3
13 rebuilt . . set its doors, its bolts, and its bars 3
14 rebuilt . . set its doors, its bolts, and its bars. 3
15 covered . . set its doors, its bolts, and its bars; 3
7: 3 standing guard let them shut and bar the doors. 1
Job 17:16 Will it go down to the bars of Sheol? 2
38:10 prescribed bounds for it, and set bars and doors 3
40:18 his limbs like bars of iron. 6
Ps 107:16 cuts in two the bars of iron. 3
147:13 For he strengthens the bars of your gates; 3
Prv 18:19 but quarreling is like the bars of a castle. 3
Isa 43:14 I will send to Babylon and break down all the bars 3
45: 2 doors of bronze and cut asunder the bars of iron 3
Jer 28:13 Thus says the LORD: You have broken wooden bars 5
13 but I will make in their place bars of iron. 5
49:31 that has no gates or bars, that dwells alone. 3
51:30 her dwellings are on fire, her bars are broken. 3
Lam 2: 9 he has ruined and broken her bars; 3
Ezk 34:27 when I break the bars of their yoke, and deliver 5
38:11 without walls, and having no bars or gates 3
Hos 11: 6 consume the bars of their gates, and devour them 2
Ams 1: 5 I will break the bar of Damascus, and cut off 3
Jon 2: 6 I went down to the land whose bars closed upon me 3
Nah 3:13 fire has devoured your bars. 3
Sir 49:13 set up the gates and bars 8
LJr 1:18 make . . secure with doors and locks and bars 8
1Mc 9:50 with high walls and gates and bars. 8

barbarian 1. *βάρβαρος*
Rom 1:14 obligation both to Greeks and to barbarians 1
Col 3:11 barbarian, Scyth'ian, slave, free man 1
2Mc 2:21 pursued the barbarian hordes 1

barbarous 1. *βάρβαρος* 2. *βαρβαρόω* 3. *ξενίζω*
2Mc 10: 4 blasphemous and barbarous nations. 1
13: 9 The king with barbarous arrogance was coming 2
3Mc 3:24 traitors and barbarous enemies. 1
7: 3 to punish them with barbarous penalties 3

more barbarous 1. *βάρβαρος*
2Mc 5:22 more barbarous than the man who appointed him; 1

barbarously 1. *βαρβάρως*
2Mc 15: 2 Do not destroy so savagely and barbarously 1

barber 1. גַּלָּב
Ezk 5: 1 take a sharp sword; use it as a barber's razor 1

bare 1. גֶּרֶם 2. חשף 3. עֶרְיָה 4. צְחִיחַ 5. שפה
6. *γυμνός*
2Kg 9:13 his garment, and put it under him on the bare steps 1
Isa 13: 2 On a bare hill raise a signal, cry aloud to them; 5
52:10 The LORD has bared his holy arm before the eyes 2
Ezk 4: 7 the siege of Jerusalem, with your arm bared; 2
16: 7 your hair had grown; yet you were naked and bare. 3
22 your youth, when you were naked and bare 3
39 shall strip you . . and leave you naked and bare. 3
23:29 and leave you naked and bare 3
24: 7 she put it on the bare rock 4
8 I have set on the bare rock the blood she has shed 4
26: 4 scrape her soil from her, and make her a bare rock. 4
14 I will make you a bare rock; 4
1Co 15:37 a bare kernel 6
bare *See also* height, lay, make, rub, strip.

bare place 1. עָרָה
Isa 19: 7 There will be bare places by the Nile 1

barefoot 1. יָחֵף
2Sm 15:30 weeping . . barefoot and with his head covered; 1
Isa 20: 2 and he had done so, walking naked and barefoot- 1
3 my servant Isaiah has walked naked and barefoot 1
4 both the young and the old, naked and barefoot 1

barely 1. μόγις 2. μόλις 3. ὀλίγως
2Pe 2:18 they entice .. men who have barely escaped 3
3Mc 1:23 being barely restrained by the old men and the elders 2
7: 6 we barely spared their lives 1

bargain 1. בְּרִית 2. כרה
Job 6:27 and bargain over your friend. 2
41: 6 Will traders bargain over him? 2
Isa 57: 8 you have made a bargain for yourself with them •
Hos 12: 1 they make a bargain with Assyria 1

bark 1. נבח 2. φλοιός
Isa 56:10 they are all dumb dogs, they cannot bark; 1
Wis 13:11 and skilfully strip off all its bark 2

bark *See also* strip.

barley 1. שְׂעֹרָה 2. κριθή 3. κρίθινος
Exd 9:31 The flax and the barley were ruined 1
31 the barley was in the ear and the flax was in bud. 1
Lev 27:16 a sowing of a homer of barley shall be valued 1
Num 5:15 offering .. a tenth of an ephah of barley meal; 1
Deu 8: 8 a land of wheat and barley, of vines and fig trees 1
Jdg 7:13 lo, a cake of barley bread tumbled into the camp 1
Rut 1:22 they came .. at the beginning of barley harvest. 1
2:17 and it was about an ephah of barley. 1
23 until the end of the barley and wheat harvests; 1
3: 2 See, he is winnowing barley tonight 1
15 and he measured out six measures of barley 1
17 saying, "These six measures of barley he gave to me 1
2Sm 14:30 See, Jo'ab's field is next to mine, and he has barley 1
17:28 brought .. wheat, barley, meal, parched grain 1
21: 9 at the beginning of barley harvest. 1
1Kg 4:28 Barley also and straw .. they brought 1
2Kg 4:42 bringing .. twenty loaves of barley 1
7: 1 and two measures of barley for a shekel 1
16 and two measures of barley for a shekel 1
18 Two measures of barley shall be sold for a shekel 1
1Ch 11:13 There was a plot of ground full of barley 1
2Ch 2:10 crushed wheat, 20,000 cors of barley 1
15 Now therefore the wheat and barley, oil and wine 1
27: 5 gave him that year .. and 10,000 of barley. 1
Job 31:40 thorns .. and foul weeds instead of barley. 1
Isa 28:25 wheat in rows and barley in its proper place 1
Jer 41: 8 we have stores of wheat, barley, oil, and honey 1
Ezk 4: 9 you, take wheat and barley, beans and lentils 1
12 you shall eat it as a barley cake 1
13:19 for handfuls of barley and for pieces of bread 1
45:13 one sixth of an ephah from each homer of barley 1
Hos 3: 2 bought her for .. a homer and a lethech of barley. 1
Jol 1:11 wail, O vinedressers, for the wheat and the barley; 1
Joh 6: 9 a lad here who has five barley loaves and two fish; 3
13 fragments from the five barley loaves 3
Rev 6: 6 and three quarts of barley for a denarius 2
Jdt 8: 2 died during the barley harvest. 2

barn 1. אָסָם 2. מְגוּרָה 3. ἀποθήκη
Deu 28: 8 command the blessing upon you in your barns 1
Prv 3:10 then your barns will be filled with plenty 1
Hag 2:19 Is the seed yet in the barn? 2
Mat 6:26 they neither sow nor reap nor gather into barns 3
13:30 but gather the wheat into my barn. 3
Lke 12:18 I will pull down my barns, and build larger ones; 3
24 they have neither storehouse nor barn 3

barrack 1. παρεμβολή
Act 21:34 he ordered him to be brought into the barracks. 1
37 As Paul was about to be brought into the barracks 1
22:24 commanded him to be brought into the barracks 1
23:10 bring him into the barracks. 1
16 he went and entered the barracks and told Paul. 1
32 on the morrow they returned to the barracks 1

barren 1. גַּלְמוּד 2. עָצַר 3. עָקָר 4. ἀργός 5. στεῖρα 6. στειρόω 7. sterilis
Gen 11:30 Now Sar'ai was barren; she had no child. 3
25:21 Isaac prayed .. because she was barren; 3
29:31 he opened her womb; but Rachel was barren. 3
Exd 23:26 None shall .. be barren in your land; 3
Jdg 13: 2 his wife was barren and had no children. 3
3 Behold, you are barren and have no children; 3
1Sm 2: 5 The barren has borne seven, but she who has many 3
Job 3: 7 Yea, let that night be barren; 1
15:34 For the company of the godless is barren 1
Prv 30:16 Sheol, the barren womb, the earth ever thirsty 2
Isa 49:21 I was bereaved and barren, exiled and put away 1
54: 1 Sing, O barren one, who did not bear; 3
Lke 1: 7 they had no child, because Elizabeth was barren 5
36 the sixth month with her who was called barren. 5
23:29 Blessed are the barren 5
Jas 2:20 that faith apart from works is barren? 4
2Es 5: 1 and the land shall be barren of faith. 7
9:43 Your servant was barren and had no child 7
10:45 that she was barren for 30 years 7
Sir 42:10 though married, lest she be barren. 6

barren *See also* leave.

barren female 1. עָקָר
Deu 7:14 shall not be male or female barren among you 1

barren male 1. עָקָר
Deu 7:14 shall not be male or female barren among you 1

barren one 1. στεῖρα
Gal 4:27 Rejoice, O barren one who does not bear 1

barren woman 1. עָקָר 2. στεῖρα 3. sterilis
Job 24:21 They feed on the barren childless woman 1
Ps 113: 9 He gives the barren woman a home 1
2Es 10:46 then it was that the barren woman bore a son. 3
Wis 3:13 blessed is the barren woman who is undefiled 2

barrenness 1. νέκρωσις
Rom 4:19 he considered the barrenness of Sarah's womb. 1

barricade 1. σκάνδαλον
Jdt 5: 1 and set up barricades in the plains 1

barrier 1. גְּבוּל 2. חֹק 3. ὕψος
Jer 5:22 a perpetual barrier which it cannot pass; 2
Ezk 40:12 There was a barrier before the side rooms 1
1Mc 12:36 erect a high barrier 3

barter 1. ערב 2. μεταβολία
Ezk 27: 9 mariners were in you, to barter for your wares. 1
19 wrought iron, cassia, and calamus were bartered •
Sir 37:11 with a merchant about barter 2

base 1. אֶדֶן 2. חֵיק 3. יְסוֹד 4. יָרֵךְ 5. כֵּן 6. מְכוֹנָה 7. βάσις 8. ἐκ
Exd 25:31 The base and the shaft of the lampstand shall be 4
26:19 40 bases of silver you shall make 1
19 two bases under one frame for its two tenons 1
19 two bases under another frame for its two tenons; 1
21 their 40 bases of silver, two bases under one 1
21 forty bases of silver, two bases under one frame 1
21 and two bases under another frame; 1
25 shall be eight frames, with their bases of silver 1
25 with their bases of silver, sixteen bases; 1
25 two bases under one frame, and two bases 1
25 and two bases under another frame. 1
32 with hooks of gold, upon four bases of silver. 1
37 you shall cast five bases of bronze for them. 1
27:10 pillars shall be twenty and their bases twenty 1
11 pillars twenty and their bases twenty, of bronze 1
12 hangings .. with ten pillars and ten bases. 1
14 with three pillars and three bases. 1
15 with three pillars and three bases. 1
16 have four pillars and with them four bases. 1
17 be of silver, and their bases of bronze. 1
18 of fine twined linen and bases of bronze. 1
29:12 you shall pour out at the base of the altar. 3
30:18 a laver of bronze, with its base of bronze 5
28 all its utensils and the laver and its base; 5
31: 9 laver and its base 5
35:11 its bars, its pillars, and its bases; 1
16 all its utensils, the laver and its base; 5
17 its pillars and its bases, and the screen 1
36:24 he made 40 bases of silver under the twenty frames 1
24 two bases under one frame for its two tenons 1
24 two bases under another frame for its two 1
26 their 40 bases of silver, two bases under one 1
26 bases of silver, two bases under one frame 1
26 and two bases under another frame. 1
30 eight frames with their bases of silver 1
30 sixteen bases, under every frame two bases. 1
30 sixteen bases, under every frame two bases. 1
36 and he cast for them four bases of silver. 1
38 of gold, but their five bases were of bronze. 1
37:17 The base and the shaft of the lampstand were made 4
38: 8 he made the laver of bronze and its base of bronze 5
10 pillars were twenty and their bases twenty 1
11 their pillars twenty, their bases twenty 1
14 hangings .. three pillars and three bases. 1
15 hangings .. three pillars and three bases. 1
17 the bases for the pillars were of bronze 1
19 four bases were of bronze, their hooks of silver 1
27 were for casting the bases of the sanctuary 1
27 bases of the sanctuary, and the bases of the veil; 1
27 100 bases for the 100 talents, a talent for a base. 1
27 100 bases for the 100 talents, a talent for a base. 1
30 with it he made the bases for the door of the tent 1
31 the bases round about the court, and the bases 1
31 the court, and the bases of the gate of the court 1
39:33 frames, its bars, its pillars, and its bases; 1
39 all its utensils; the laver and its base; 5
40 hangings of the court, its pillars, and its bases 1
40:11 the laver and its base, and consecrate it. 5
18 Moses erected the tabernacle; he laid its bases 1
Lev 4: 7 at the base of the altar of burnt offering 3
18 he shall pour out at the base of the altar 3
25 blood at the base of the altar of burnt offering 3
30 rest of its blood at the base of the altar 3
34 rest of its blood at the base of the altar 3
5: 9 blood shall be drained out at the base of the altar 3
8:11 the laver and its base, to consecrate them 5
15 poured out the blood at the base of the altar 3
9: 9 poured out the blood at the base of the altar 3
Num 3:36 appointed charge .. the pillars, the bases 1
37 pillars .. with their bases and pegs and cords. 1
4:31 frames .. with its bars, pillars, and bases 1
32 pillars .. with their bases, pegs, and cords 1
8: 4 from its base to its flowers, it was hammered work; 4
Job 38: 6 On what were its bases sunk 1
Sng 5:15 His legs are alabaster .. set upon bases of gold. 1
Ezk 41:22 its corners, its base, and its walls were of wood. 7
43:13 its base shall be one cubit high 2
14 from the base on the ground to the lower ledge 2
17 and its base one cubit round about. 2
Zec 5:11 they will set the ephah down there on its base. 6
Rom 9:31 who pursued the righteousness which is based on law •
32 but as if it were based on works. 8
10: 5 the righteousness which is based on the law 8
6 But the righteousness based on faith says 8
Php 3: 9 not having a righteousness of my own, based on law 8
Sir 26:18 Like pillars of gold on a base of silver 7

base (2) 1. בְּלִיַּעַל 2. ἀδόκιμος 3. αἰσχρός 4. πονηρός
Deu 15: 9 be a base thought in your heart, and you say 1
Jdg 19:22 the men of the city, base fellows, beset the house 1
20:13 give up the men, the base fellows in Gib'e-ah 1
1Sm 30:22 all the wicked and base fellows among the men who 1
Ps 101: 3 not set before my eyes anything that is base. 1
Rom 1:28 God gave them up to a base mind 2
1Ti 6: 4 dissension, slander, base suspicions 4
Tit 1:11 teaching for base gain 3

base *See* desire, means.

base fellow 1. אִישׁ בְּלִיַּעַל 2. אִישׁ בֶּן בְּלִיַּעַל 3. קלה 4. בֶּן בְּלִיַּעַל
Deu 13:13 certain base fellows have gone out among you 3
1Kg 21:10 set two base fellows opposite him 2
13 the two base fellows came in and sat opposite him; 2
13 and the base fellows brought a charge 1
Isa 3: 5 insolent .. the base fellow to the honorable. 4

something base 1. κίβδηλος
Wis 2:16 We are considered by him as something base 1

base woman 1. בַּת בְּלִיַּעַל
1Sm 1:16 Do not regard your maidservant as a base woman 1

basely 1. κακός
4Mc 6:17 May we .. never think so basely 1

baseness 1. κακία
Sir 14: 6 this is the retribution for his baseness; 1
7 betrays his baseness in the end. 1

basic 1. ἀρχή
Sir 39:26 Basic to all the needs of man's life 1

basin 1. אַגָּן 2. אֲגַרְטָל 3. מִזְרָק 4. סַף 5. νιπτήρ
Exd 12:22 dip it in the blood which is in the basin 4
22 with the blood which is in the basin; 4
24: 6 Moses took half of the blood and put it in basins 1
27: 3 make .. shovels and basins and forks 3
38: 3 the pots, the shovels, the basins, the forks 3
Num 4:14 basins, all the utensils of the altar; 3
7:13 one silver basin of 70 shekels 3
19 one silver basin of 70 shekels 3
25 one silver basin of 70 shekels 3
31 one silver basin of 70 shekels 3
37 one silver basin of 70 shekels 3
43 one silver basin of 70 shekels 3
49 one silver basin of 70 shekels 3
55 one silver basin of 70 shekels 3
61 one silver basin of 70 shekels 3
67 one silver basin of 70 shekels 3
73 one silver basin of 70 shekels 3
79 one silver basin of 70 shekels 3
84 dedication offering .. twelve silver basins 3
85 weighing 130 shekels and each basin 70 3
2Sm 17:28 brought beds, basins, and earthen vessels, wheat 4
1Kg 7:40 Hiram also made .. the shovels, and the basins. 3
45 the pots, the shovels, and the basins, all these 3
50 The cups, snuffers, basins, dishes for incense 3
2Kg 12:13 not made .. basins of silver, snuffers, bowls 4
1Ch 28:17 pure gold for the forks, the basins, and the cups; 3
2Ch 4: 8 And he made 100 basins of gold. 3
11 Huram also made .. the shovels, and the basins. 3
22 basins, dishes for incense .. of pure gold; 3
Ezr 1: 9 number .. 1,000 basins of gold 2
9 number .. 1,000 basins of silver, 29 censers 2
Neh 7:70 governor gave to the treasury .. 50 basins 3
Jer 52:18 the shovels, and the snuffers, and the basins 3
19 the firepans, and the basins, and the pots 3
Joh 13: 5 Then he poured water into a basin 5

inner basin 1. ὅρμος
4Mc 13: 6 those who sail into the inner basin 1

basis 1. ἐκ
Rom 11: 6 it is no longer on the basis of works; 1

basket 1. דוד 2. טֶנֶא 3. כְּלוּב 4. סַל 5. תֵּבָה
6. *κλάσμα* 7. *κόφινος* 8. *σαργάνη* 9. *σπυρίς*
Gen 40:16 there were three cake baskets on my head 4
17 in the uppermost basket there were all sorts 4
17 eating it out of the basket on my head. 4
18 the three baskets are three days; 4
Exd 2: 3 she took for him a basket made of bulrushes 5
5 she saw the basket among the reeds and sent 5
29: 3 you shall put them in one basket and bring them 4
3 bring them in the basket, and bring the bull 4
23 out of the basket of unleavened bread 4
32 shall eat . . the bread that is in the basket 4
Lev 8: 2 two rams, and the basket of unleavened bread 4
26 out of the basket of unleavened bread 4
31 there eat it and the bread that is in the basket 4
Num 6:15 a basket of unleavened bread, cakes of fine flour 4
17 with the basket of unleavened bread; 4
19 take . . one unleavened cake out of the basket 4
Deu 26: 2 put it in a basket, and you shall go to the place 2
4 priest shall take the basket from your hand 2
28: 5 Blessed . . basket and your kneading-trough. 2
17 Cursed . . basket and your kneading-trough. 2
Jdg 6:19 the meat he put in a basket, and the broth he put 4
2Kg 10: 7 slew them . . and put their heads in baskets 1
Ps 81: 6 your hands were freed from the basket. 1
Jer 5:27 Like a basket full of birds, their houses are full 3
24: 1 showed me this vision: Behold, two baskets of figs 1
2 One basket had very good figs, like first-ripe 1
2 but the other basket had very bad figs 1
Ams 8: 1 GOD showed me: behold, a basket of summer fruit. 3
2 And I said, "A basket of summer fruit. 3
Mat 14:20 they took up twelve baskets 7
15:37 and they took up seven baskets 9
16: 9 and how many baskets you gathered? 7
10 and how many baskets you gathered? 9
Mrk 6:43 they took up twelve baskets 6
8: 8 the broken pieces left over, seven baskets full. 9
19 how many baskets full of broken pieces 7
20 how many baskets full of broken pieces 9
Lke 9:17 twelve baskets of broken pieces. 7
Joh 6:13 filled twelve baskets with fragments 7
Act 9:25 lowering him in a basket. 9
2Co 11:33 let down in a basket through a window in the wall 8

bastard 1. מַמְזֵר
Deu 23: 2 No bastard shall enter the assembly of the LORD; 1

bat 1. עֲטַלֵּף 2. *νυκτερίς*
Lev 11:19 the stork . . the hoopoe and the bat 1
Deu 14:18 stork, the heron . . the hoopoe and the bat. 1
Isa 2:20 cast forth their idols . . to the bats 1
LJr 1:22 Bats, swallows, and birds light on their bodies 2

bath 1. בַּת 2. בַּת (A) 3. *μετρητής*
1Kg 7:26 it held 2,000 baths. 1
38 he made ten lavers . . each laver held 40 baths 1
2Ch 2:10 cors of barley, 20,000 baths of wine 1
10 baths of wine, and 20,000 baths of oil. 1
4: 5 it held over 3,000 baths. 1
Ezr 7:22 up to . . 100 baths of wine 2
22 up to . . 100 baths of oil, and salt 2
Isa 5:10 ten acres of vineyard shall yield but one bath 1
Ezk 45:10 just balances, a just ephah, and a just bath. 1
11 ephah and the bath shall be of the same measure 1
11 the bath containing one tenth of a homer 1
14 as the fixed portion of oil, one tenth of a bath 1
14 the cor, like the homer, contains ten baths 1
1Es 8:20 100 baths of wine, and salt in abundance. 3

bathe 1. רחץ 2. *βαπτίζω* 3. *βάπτω* 4. *λούω*
5. *περικλύω*
Exd 2: 5 came down to bathe at the river, and her maidens 1
Lev 14: 8 shave off all his hair, and bathe himself in water 1
9 Then he shall wash his clothes, and bathe his body 1
15: 5 wash his clothes, and bathe himself in water 1
6 shall . . bathe himself in water, and be unclean 1
7 shall wash his clothes, and bathe himself 1
8 then he shall wash his clothes, and bathe himself 1
10 wash his clothes, and bathe himself in water 1
11 shall wash his clothes, and bathe himself in water 1
13 he shall bathe his body in running water 1
16 he shall bathe his whole body in water 1
18 both of them shall bathe themselves in water 1
21 shall wash his clothes, and bathe himself in water 1
22 shall wash his clothes, and bathe himself in water 1
27 shall wash his clothes, and bathe himself in water 1
16: 4 He shall bathe his body in water 1
24 he shall bathe his body in water in a holy place 1
26 shall wash his clothes and bathe his body in water 1
28 wash his clothes and bathe his body in water 1
17:15 shall wash his clothes, and bathe himself in water 1
16 if he does not wash them or bathe his flesh 1
22: 6 shall not eat . . unless he has bathed his body 1
Num19: 7 priest shall wash his clothes and bathe his body 1
8 wash his clothes . . and bathe his body in water 1
19 wash his clothes and bathe himself in water 1
Deu 23:11 evening comes on, he shall bathe himself in water 1
2Sm 11: 2 he saw from the roof a woman bathing; 1
Ps 58:10 he will bathe his feet in the blood of the wicked. 1
68:23 that you may bathe your feet in blood 3
Sng 5: 3 I had bathed my feet, how could I soil them? 1
12 His eyes are like doves . . bathed in milk 1
Ezk 16: 9 Then I bathed you with water 1
23:40 For them you bathed yourself, painted your eyes 1
Joh 13:10 He who has bathed does not need to wash 4
Jdt 10: 3 bathed her body with water 5
12: 7 bathed at the spring in the camp. 2
Sus 1:15 she went in . . and wished to bathe in the garden 4
17 and shut the garden doors so that I may bathe. 4

bathe in sweat 1. *ἱδρῶν*
4Mc 6:11 with his face bathed in sweat 1

battalion 1. *σπεῖρα*
Mat 27:27 they gathered the whole battalion before him. 1
Mrk 15:16 they called together the whole battalion 1

batter 1. כתת 2. שחת 3. *πατάσσω*
2Sm 20:15 and they were battering the wall, to throw it down. 2
Isa 24:12 in the city, the gates are battered into ruins. 1
1Mc 13:43 battered and captured one tower. 3

batter down 1. קרר
Isa 22: 5 day of . . a battering down of walls 1

battering *See* ram.

battle 1. כִּידוֹר 2. לחם 3. מַחֲנֶה 4. מִלְחָמָה 5. מַעֲרָכָה
6. נֶשֶׁק 7. צָבָא 8. קְרָב 9. תְּרוּעָה 10. *ἀγών* 11. *μάχη*
12. *παράταξις* 13. *πολεμέω* 14. *πόλεμος* 15. *στρατεία*
16. pugna
Gen 14: 8 they joined battle in the Valley of Siddim 4
Num21:33 came out against them . . to battle at Ed're-i. 4
31:21 said to the men of war who had gone to battle 4
27 between the warriors who went out to battle 4
28 tribute from the men of war who went out to battle 7
32:27 pass over . . before the LORD to battle 4
29 every man who is armed to battle before the LORD 4
Deu 2: 9 'Do not harass Moab or contend with them in battle 4
24 take possession, and contend with him in battle. 4
32 Sihon came out against us . . to battle at Jahaz. 4
3: 1 Og . . came out against us, . . to battle at Ed're-i. 4
20: 2 when you draw near to the battle, the priest shall 4
3 draw near . . to battle against your enemies 4
5 go back to his house, lest he die in the battle 4
6 go back to his house, lest he die in the battle 4
7 go back to his house, lest he die in the battle 4
29: 7 Sihon . . and Og . . came out against us to battle 4
Jos 4:13 passed over before the LORD for battle 4
8:14 made haste and went . . to meet Israel in battle; 4
11:19 was not a city that . . they took all in battle. 4
20 that they should come against Israel in battle 4
Jdg 8:13 Gideon the son of Jo'ash returned from the battle 4
20:14 to go out to battle against the people of Israel 4
18 go up first to battle against the Benjaminites? 4
20 Israel went out to battle against Benjamin; 4
23 Shall we again draw near to battle against our 4
28 yet again go out to battle against our brethren 4
34 came against Gib'e-ah . . and the battle was hard; 4
39 the men of Israel should turn in battle. 4
39 smitten down before us, as in the first battle 4
42 the battle overtook them, and those who came out 4
21:22 we did not take for each man . . his wife in battle 4
1Sm 4: 1 went out to battle against the Philistines; 4
2 and when the battle spread, Israel was defeated 4
2 slew about 4,000 men on the field of battle. 5
16 I am he who has come from the battle; 5
16 I fled from the battle today. 5
8:20 and go out before us and fight our battles. 4
13:22 on the day of the battle . . neither sword nor 4
14:20 Saul and all . . rallied and went into the battle; 4
22 they too followed hard after them in the battle. 4
23 and the battle passed beyond Beth-a'ven. 4
17: 1 Philistines gathered their armies for battle; 4
2 drew up in . . battle against the Philistines. 4
8 Why have you come out to draw up for battle? 4
13 sons of Jesse had followed Saul to the battle; 4
13 the names of his three sons who went to the battle 4
21 Israel and the Philistines drew up for battle •
28 for you have come down to see the battle. 4
47 the battle is the LORD's and he will give you 4
18:17 be valiant . . and fight the LORD's battles. 4
30 Then . . the Philistines came out to battle •
25:28 my lord is fighting the battles of the LORD; 4
26:10 or he shall go down into battle and perish. 4
29: 4 he shall not go down with us to battle 4
4 lest in the battle he become an adversary to us. 4
9 He shall not go up with us to the battle. 4
30:24 For as his share is who goes down into the battle 4
31: 3 The battle pressed hard upon Saul 4
2Sm 1: 4 The people have fled from the battle 4
25 the mighty fallen in the midst of the battle! 4
2:17 And the battle was very fierce that day; 4
3:30 he had killed . . As'ahel in the battle at Gibeon. 4
10: 8 Ammonites came out and drew up in battle array 4
9 When Jo'ab saw that the battle was set against him 4
13 Jo'ab . . drew near to battle against the Syrians; 4
11: 1 In . . the time when kings go forth to battle •
17:11 my counsel . . and that you go to battle in person. 8
18: 6 the battle was fought in the forest of E'phraim. 4
8 The battle spread over . . all the country; 4
19: 3 who are ashamed when they flee in battle. 4
10 Ab'salom, whom we anointed . . is dead in battle. 4
21:17 You shall no more go out with us to battle 4
22:40 thou didst gird me with strength for the battle; 4
23: 9 Philistines who were gathered there for battle 4
1Kg 8:44 thy people go out to battle against their enemy 4
20:14 Then he said, "Who shall begin the battle? 4
29 on the seventh day the battle was joined; 4
39 servant went out into the midst of the battle; 4
22: 4 Will you go with me to battle at Ramoth-gilead? 4
6 Shall I go to battle against Ramoth-gilead 4
15 Micai'ah, shall we go to Ramoth-gilead to battle 4
30 I will disguise myself and go into battle, but you 4
30 king . . disguised himself and went into battle. 4
34 Turn about, and carry me out of the battle 3
35 the battle grew hot . . and the king was propped up 4
2Kg 3: 7 will you go with me to battle against Moab? 4
26 Moab saw that the battle was going against him 4
14:11 he and Amazi'ah . . faced one another in battle •
1Ch 5:20 for they cried to God in the battle 4
10: 3 The battle pressed hard upon Saul 4
11:13 Philistines were gathered there for battle. 4
12:19 the Philistines for the battle against Saul. 4
33 equipped for battle with all the weapons of war 4
35 Of the Danites 28,600 men equipped for battle. 4
36 Of Asher 40,000 seasoned troops ready for battle. 4
14:15 go out to battle; for God has gone out before you 4
19: 7 Ammonites were mustered . . and came to battle. 4
10 the battle was set against him both in front 4
14 drew near before the Syrians for battle; 4
17 when David set the battle in array against 4
20: 1 spring . . the time when kings go forth to battle •
26:27 From spoil won in battles they dedicated gifts 4
2Ch 6:34 If thy people go out to battle against their 4
13: 3 Abi'jah went out to battle having an army 4
3 Jerobo'am drew up his line of battle against him 4
12 his priests with their battle trumpets 9
14 behold, the battle was before and behind them; 4
14:10 they drew up their lines of battle in the valley 4
18: 5 Shall we go to battle against Ramoth-gilead 4
14 Micai'ah, shall we go to Ramoth-gilead to battle 4
29 I will disguise myself and go into battle 4
29 and they went into battle. 4
33 Turn about, and carry me out of the battle 14
34 the battle grew hot that day 4
20: 1 came against Jehosh'aphat for battle. 4
15 Fear not . . for the battle is not yours but God's. 4
17 You will not need to fight in this battle; •
25:13 sent back, not letting them go with him to battle 4
21 faced one another in battle at Beth-she'mesh •
32: 8 the LORD . . to help us and to fight our battles. 4
35:22 but joined battle in the plain of Megid'do. 2
Job 15:24 against him, like a king prepared for battle. 1
38:23 the time of trouble, for the day of battle and war? 4
39:25 he says 'Aha!' He smells the battle from afar 4
41: 8 think of the battle; you will not do it again! 4
Ps 18:39 thou didst gird me with strength for the battle; 4
24: 8 LORD, strong and mighty, the LORD, mighty in battle! 4
55:18 He will deliver my soul in safety from the battle 8
78: 9 E'phraimites . . turned back on the day of battle. 8
89:43 thou hast not made him stand in battle. 4
140: 7 thou hast covered my head in the day of battle. 6
144: 1 LORD, my rock, who trains . . my fingers for battle; 4
Prv 21:31 The horse is made ready for the day of battle 4
Ecc 9:11 nor the battle to the strong, nor bread to the wise 4
Isa 3:25 fall by the sword and your mighty men in battle. 4
13: 4 The LORD of hosts is mustering a host for battle. 4
16: 9 upon your fruit . . the battle shout has fallen. •
21:15 from the bent bow, and from the press of battle. 4
22: 2 not slain with the sword or dead in battle. 4
27: 4 Would that I had thorns and briers to battle! 4
28: 6 those who turn back the battle at the gate. 4
30:32 battling with brandished arm he will fight 4
42:25 the heat of his anger and the might of battle; 4
Jer 6:23 upon horses, set in array as a man for battle 4
8: 6 like a horse plunging headlong into battle. 4
18:21 their youths be slain by the sword in battle. 4
46: 3 Prepare . . shield, and advance for battle! 4
49: 2 when I will cause the battle cry to be heard 4
14 and come against her, and rise up for battle! 4
50:22 The noise of battle is in the land 4
42 arrayed as a man for battle against you 4
Ezk 7:14 but none goes to battle, for my wrath is upon all 4
13: 5 it might stand in battle in the day of the LORD. 4
Dan 11:20 shall be broken, neither in anger nor in battle. 4
Hos 10:14 destroyed Beth-ar'bel on the day of battle; 4
Jol 2: 5 like a powerful army drawn up for battle. 4
Ams 1:14 strongholds, with shouting in the day of battle 4
Obd 1: 1 Rise up! let us rise against her for battle! 4
Zec 9:10 the battle bow shall be cut off 4
10: 3 will make them like his proud steed in battle. 4
4 out of them the tent peg, out of them the battle bow 4
5 Together they shall be like mighty men in battle 4
14: 2 all the nations against Jerusalem to battle 4
3 as when he fights on a day of battle. 8

1Co 14: 8 who will get ready for battle? 14
Rev 9: 7 the locusts were like horses arrayed for battle; 14
9 noise of many chariots . . rushing into battle. 14
16:14 to assemble them for battle on the great day 14
20: 8 Gog and Magog, to gather them for battle; 14
1Es 1:29 He joined battle with him in the plain of Megiddo 14
30 Take me away from the battle, for I am very weak. 11
2Es 15:30 and engage them in battle 16
16:40 Hear my words, O my people; prepare for battle 16
Jdt 1:13 defeated him in battle 14
5:18 they were utterly defeated in many battles 14
7:11 do not fight against them in battle array 13
14:13 to come down against us to give battle 14
Wis 12: 9 the righteous in battle 12
Sir 37: 5 in the face of battle take up the shield. 14
40: 6 like one who has escaped from the battle-front; 14
1Mc 1: 2 He fought many battles, conquered strongholds 14
18 He engaged Ptolemy king of Egypt in battle 14
2:32 prepared for battle against them 14
66 and fight the battle against the peoples. 14
3: 3 he girded on his armor of war and waged battles 14
13 who stayed with him and went out to battle 14
19 victory in battle depends 14
26 the Gentiles talked of the battles of Judas. 12
44 congregation assembled to be ready for battle 14
59 It is better for us to die in battle 14
4:13 they went forth from their camp to battle 14
17 there is a battle before us; 14
21 the army of Judas drawn up in the plain for battle 12
5: 7 He engaged in many battles with them 14
19 do not engage in battle with the Gentiles 14
21 fought many battles against the Gentiles 14
31 So Judas saw that the battle had begun 14
42 but make them all enter the battle. 14
59 came out of the city to meet them in battle. 14
67 On that day some priests . . fell in battle 14
67 they went out to battle unwisely. 14
6: 4 they withstood him in battle 14
33 his troops made ready for battle 14
34 to arouse them for battle. 14
42 Judas and his army advanced to the battle 12
7:31 to meet Judas in battle near Caphar-salama. 14
43 So the armies met in battle 14
43 he himself was the first to fall in the battle. 14
8: 5 they crushed in battle and conquered. 14
9: 1 Nicanor and his army had fallen in battle 14
7 the battle was imminent 14
13 the battle raged from morning till evening. 14
17 The battle became desperate 14
30 to fight our battle. 14
45 For look! the battle is in front of us and behind us; 14
47 So the battle began 14
10: 2 and marched out to meet him in battle. 14
15 men told him of the battles 14
49 The two kings met in battle, and the army 14
50 He pressed the battle strongly until the sun set 14
53 I met him in battle 11
78 the armies engaged in battle. 14
11:15 came against him in battle 14
69 emerged from their places and joined battle. 14
72 he turned back to the battle against the enemy 14
12:27 so as to be ready all night for battle 14
28 Jonathan and his men were prepared for battle 14
50 marching in close formation, ready for battle. 14
13: 9 Fight our battles 14
14 he was about to join battle with him 14
2Mc 8:20 the time of the battle with the Galatians 12
10:29 When the battle became fierce 11
12:36 their ally and leader in the battle. 14
14:18 their courage in battle for their country 10
3Mc 1: 4 two minas of gold if they won the battle. •
4Mc 9:24 Fight the sacred and noble battle for religion. 15

battle *See also* alliance, array, call, cry, drawn, engage, equip, go, join, line, meet, order, song, sound, tumult.

infantry battle 1. πεζομαχία
4Mc 17:24 courageous for infantry battle and siege 1

battlement 1. טִירָה 2. פִּנָּה 3. ἐπάλξις 4. προμαχών
Sng 8: 9 we will build upon her a battlement of silver; 1
Zep 1:16 and against the lofty battlements. 2
3: 6 their battlements are in ruins; 2
Tob 13:16 her towers and battlements with pure gold. 4
Sir 9:13 you are going about on the city battlements. 3

bay 1. לָשׁוֹן 2. κόλπος
Jos 15: 2 of the Salt Sea, from the bay that faces southward; 1
5 from the bay of the sea at the mouth of the Jordan; 1
18:19 boundary ends at the northern bay of the Salt Sea 1
Act 27:39 they noticed a bay with a beach 2

bazaar 1. חוּץ
1Kg 20:34 establish bazaars for yourself in Damascus 1

bdellium 1. בְּדֹלַח
Gen 2:12 land is good; bdellium and onyx stone are there. 1
Num11: 7 manna . . its appearance like that of bdellium. 1

beach 1. αἰγιαλός
Mat 13: 2 and the whole crowd stood on the beach. 1
Joh 21: 4 Just as day was breaking, Jesus stood on the beach; 1
Act 21: 5 and kneeling down on the beach we prayed 1
27:39 they noticed a bay with a beach 1
40 they made for the beach. 1

bead 1. כּוּמָז
Num31:50 LORD'S offering . . earrings, and beads 1

beam 1. גֵּב 2. כָּפִים 3. כרת 4. מָנוֹר 5. קוֹרָה
6. אָע (A) 7. δοκός 8. ἱμάντωσις 9. ξύλον
1Sm 17: 7 And the shaft of his spear was like a weaver's beam 4
2Sm 21:19 the shaft of whose spear was like a weaver's beam. 4
1Kg 6: 6 the supporting beams should not be inserted •
9 made the ceiling . . of beams and planks of cedar. 1
36 of hewn stone and one course of cedar beams. 3
7: 2 was built . . with cedar beams upon the pillars. 3
12 three courses of . . and a course of cedar beams; 3
1Ch 11:23 a spear like a weaver's beam; 4
20: 5 the shaft of whose spear was like a weaver's beam. 4
2Ch 3: 7 he lined the house with gold—its beams 5
34:11 to buy . . timber for binders and beams 5
Ezr 6:11 beam shall be pulled out of his house 6
Sng 1:17 the beams of our house are cedar, our rafters are 5
Hab 2:11 and the beam from the woodwork respond. 2
1Es 6:32 a beam should be taken out of his house 9
Sir 22:16 A wooden beam firmly bonded into a building 8
LJr 1:20 They are just like a beam of the temple 7
55 the gods will be burnt in two like beams. 7

beam (2) 1. ἀκτίς
Sir 43: 4 with bright beams it blinds the eyes. 1

beam *See* lay, make.

bean 1. פּוֹל
2Sm 17:28 brought . . meal, parched grain, beans and lentils 1
Ezk 4: 9 you, take wheat and barley, beans and lentils 1

bear 1. בֶּטֶן 2. גמל 3. הלך 4. חול 5. יבל 6. ילד
7. יִלּוֹד 8. יָלִיד 9. יצא 10. יצא מֵחֲלָצַיִם 11. יצא מֵרֶחֶם
12. כול 13. כתר 14. מֵמֵּעִים 15. מַשָּׂא 16. משך
17. נשא 18. נתן 19. סבל 20. עַל 21. עמס 22. ענה
23. עשה 24. פרה 25. שום 26. שית 27. ἀναφέρω
28. ἀνέχω 29. ἀποτίκτω 30. ἄστεκτος 31. βαστάζω
32. γένεσις 33. γενετή 34. γεννάω 35. γέννημα
36. γέννησις 37. γεννητός 38. γίνομαι 39. διά
40. δίδωμι 41. εἰς 42. ἐκ 43. ἐκφέρω 44. ἕλκω 45. ἔχω
46. κοιλία μητρός 47. μαρτυρέω 48. ποιέω 49. στέγω
50. τίκτω 51. τροποφορέω 52. ὑπέρ 53. ὑπομένω
54. ὑποφέρω 55. ὑφίστημι 56. φέρω 57. φορέω
58. fero 59. genero 60. gigno 61. nascor 62. pario
63. porto
Gen 1:11 earth put forth . . fruit trees bearing fruit 23
12 and trees bearing fruit in which is their seed 23
4: 1 and she conceived and bore Cain, saying 6
2 again, she bore his brother Abel. 6
13 My punishment is greater than I can bear. 17
17 she conceived and bore Enoch; and he built a city 6
18 To Enoch was born Irad; and Irad was the father 6
20 Adah bore Jabal; he was the father 6
22 Zillah bore Tubal-cain; he was the forger of all 6
25 Adam knew his wife again, and she bore a son 6
26 To Seth also a son was born 6
6: 1 of the ground, and daughters were born to them 6
10: 1 Japheth; sons were born to them after the flood. 6
21 the elder brother of Japheth, children were born 6
25 To Eber were born two sons 6
14:14 his trained men, born in his house, 318 of them 8
15: 3 and a slave born in my house will be my heir. •
16:11 and shall bear a son; you shall call his name 6
15 Hagar bore Abram a son; and Abram called the name 6
15 the name of his son, whom Hagar bore, Ish'mael. 6
16 when Hagar bore Ish'mael to Abram. 6
17:12 your generations, whether born in your house 8
13 both he that is born in your house 8
17 Shall a child be born to a man who is 100 years old? 6
19 Sarah your wife shall bear you a son 6
21 Isaac, whom Sarah shall bear to you at this season 6
23 all the slaves born in his house 8
27 all the men of his house, those born in the house 8
19:37 first-born bore a son, and called his name Moab; 6
38 The younger also bore a son, and called his name 6
21: 2 Sarah conceived, and bore Abraham a son 6
3 name of his son who was born to him 6
3 was born to him, whom Sarah bore him, Isaac. 6
5 years old when his son Isaac was born to him. 6
7 Yet I have borne him a son in his old age. 6
9 the Egyptian, whom she had borne to Abraham 6
22:20 Behold, Milcah also has borne children 6
23 These eight Milcah bore to Nahor 6
24 name was Reumah, bore Tebah, Gaham, Tahash 6
24:15 behold, Rebekah, who was born to Bethu'el 6
24 the son of Milcah, whom she bore to Nahor. 6
36 Sarah my master's wife bore a son to my master 6
47 Nahor's son, whom Milcah bore to him.' 6
25: 2 She bore him Zimran, Jokshan, Medan, Mid'ian 6
12 the Egyptian, Sarah's maid, bore to Abraham. 6
23 and two peoples, born of you, shall be divided; 14
26 Isaac was 60 years old when she bore them. 6
29:32 Leah conceived and bore a son 6
33 She conceived again and bore a son 6
34 Again she conceived and bore a son, and said 6
34 because I have borne him three sons"; 6
35 she conceived again and bore a son, and said 6
35 called his name Judah; then she ceased bearing. 6
30: 3 that she may bear upon my knees 6
5 Bilhah conceived and bore Jacob a son. 6
7 conceived again and bore Jacob a second son. 6
10 Then Leah's maid Zilpah bore Jacob a son. 6
12 Leah's maid Zilpah bore Jacob a second son. 6
17 she conceived and bore Jacob a fifth son. 6
19 conceived again, and she bore Jacob a sixth son. 6
20 will honor me, because I have borne him six sons 6
21 Afterwards she bore a daughter 6
23 She conceived and bore a son, and said 6
25 When Rachel had borne Joseph, Jacob said to Laban 6
31: 8 be your wages,' then all the flock bore spotted; 6
8 your wages,' then all the flock bore striped. 6
43 do . . to their children whom they have borne? 6
34: 1 the daughter of Leah, whom she had borne to Jacob 6
35:26 sons of Jacob who were born to him in Paddan-aram. 6
36: 4 Adah bore to Esau, El'iphaz; 6
4 Bas'emath bore Reu'el; 6
5 Oholiba'mah bore Je'ush, Jalam, and Korah. 6
5 sons of Esau who were born to him in the land 6
12 (Timna . . bore Am'alek to El'iphaz.) 6
14 she bore to Esau Je'ush, Jalam, and Korah. 6
18 these are the chiefs born of Oholiba'mah •
37:25 a caravan . . with their camels bearing gum, balm 17
38: 3 she conceived and bore a son 6
4 Again she conceived and bore a son 6
5 Yet again she bore a son 6
5 name Shelah. She was in Chezib when she bore him. 6
41:50 sons, whom As'enath . . bore to him. 6
44:27 said to us, 'You know that my wife bore me two sons; 6
46:15 these are the sons of Leah, whom she bore to Jacob 6
18 and these she bore to Jacob—sixteen persons. 6
20 to Joseph in the land of Egypt were born Manas'seh 6
20 whom As'enath . . bore to him. 6
22 these are the sons of Rachel, who were born 6
25 and these she bore to Jacob—seven persons in all 6
27 the sons of Joseph, who were born to him in Egypt 6
48: 5 now your two sons, who were born to you in the land 6
6 the offspring born to you after them shall be 6
49:15 he bowed his shoulder to bear 19
21 a hind let loose, that bears comely fawns. 18
50:23 children . . were born upon Joseph's knees. 6
Exd 1:22 Every son that is born to the Hebrews 6
2: 2 The woman conceived and bore a son; 6
22 She bore a son, and he called his name Gershom; 6
6:20 and she bore him Aaron and Moses 6
23 and she bore him Nadab, Abi'hu, Elea'zar 6
25 daughters of Pu'ti-el; and she bore him Phin'ehas. 6
19: 4 You have seen . . how I bore you on eagles' wings 17
20:16 You shall not bear false witness against 22
21: 4 a wife and she bears him sons or daughters 6
28:12 Aaron shall bear their names before the LORD 17
29 Aaron shall bear all the names of the sons of Israel 17
30 thus Aaron shall bear the judgment of the people 17
Lev 5: 1 yet does not speak, he shall bear his iniquity 17
17 he is guilty and shall bear his iniquity 17
7:18 he who eats of it shall bear his iniquity 17
10:17 you may bear the iniquity of the congregation 17
16:22 The goat shall bear all their iniquities 17
17:16 he shall bear his iniquity 17
18: 9 the daughter of your mother, whether born at home 6
9 whether . . at home or born abroad 6
19: 8 every one who eats it shall bear his iniquity 17
17 reason with your neighbor, lest you bear sin 17
20:17 he shall bear his iniquity 17
19 they shall bear their iniquity 17
20 they shall bear their sin, they shall die 17
22: 9 keep my charge, lest they bear sin for it and die 17
11 and those that are born in his house may eat 8
27 When a bull or sheep or goat is born 6
24:15 Whoever curses his God shall bear his sin 17
25:45 who have been born in your land 6
Num 5:31 but the woman shall bear her iniquity. 17
9:13 shall be cut off . . that man shall bear his sin. 17
11:17 they shall bear the burden of the people with you 17
17 that you may not bear it yourself alone. 17
14:34 you shall bear your iniquity, 40 years 17
17: 8 rod of Aaron . . had sprouted . . bore ripe almonds. 2
18: 1 bear iniquity in connection with the sanctuary; 17
1 shall bear iniquity in connection 17
22 lest they bear sin and die. 17
23 Levites . . shall bear their iniquity; 17
32 you shall bear no sin by reason of it 17
26:59 Joch'ebed . . who was born to Levi in Egypt; 6
59 she bore to Amram Aaron and Moses and Miriam 6
60 Aaron was born Nadab, Abi'hu, Elea'zar 6
30:15 then he shall bear her iniquity. 17
Deu 1: 9 I said to you, 'I am not able alone to bear you; 17
12 How can I bear alone the weight and burden of you 17

31 you have seen how the LORD your God bore you 17
31 how the LORD . . bore you, as a man bears his son 17
5:20 'Neither shall you bear false witness 22
15:19 firstling males that are born of your herd 6
21:15 two wives . . and they have borne him children 6
23: 8 third generation that are born to them may enter 6
25: 6 first son whom she bears shall succeed 6
28:57 afterbirth . . and her children whom she bears 6
29:18 root bearing poisonous and bitter fruit 24
32:11 out its wings, catching them, bearing them 17
Jos 3: 8 you shall command the priests who bear the ark 17
13 feet of the priests who bear the ark of the LORD 17
14 to pass over . . with the priests bearing the ark 17
15 when those who bore the ark had come to the Jordan 17
15 feet of the priests bearing the ark were dipped 17
17 priests who bore the ark of the covenant 17
4: 9 of the priests bearing the ark of the covenant 17
10 the priests who bore the ark stood in the midst 17
16 the priests who bear the ark of the testimony 17
18 when the priests bearing the ark of the covenant 17
5: 5 all the people that were born on the way . . had not 7
6: 4 And seven priests shall bear seven trumpets 17
6 and let seven priests bear seven trumpets 17
8 priests bearing the seven trumpets of rams' 17
13 the seven priests bearing the seven trumpets 17
Jdg 4:24 Israel bore harder and harder on Jabin the king 3
5:14 from Zeb'ulun those who bear the marshal's staff; 16
8:31 his concubine . . also bore him a son 6
11: 2 Gilead's wife also bore him sons; 6
13: 3 children; but you shall conceive and bear a son. 6
5 for lo, you shall conceive and bear a son. No razor 6
7 you shall conceive and bear a son; so then drink no 6
8 what we are to do with the boy that will be born. 6
24 the woman bore a son, and called his name Samson; 6
18:29 name of Dan their ancestor, who was born to Israel; 6
Rut 1:12 if I should have a husband . . and should bear sons 6
4:12 Perez, whom Tamar bore to Judah 6
13 the LORD gave her conception, and she bore a son. 6
15 for your daughter-in-law . . has borne him. 6
17 a name, saying, "A son has been born to Na'omi. 6
1Sm 1:20 in due time Hannah conceived and bore a son 6
2: 5 The barren has borne seven, but she who has many 6
21 and bore three sons and two daughters. 6
4:20 said to her, "Fear not, for you have borne a son. 6
14: 1 said to the young man who bore his armor, "Come 17
6 Jonathan said to the young man who bore his armor 17
7 And his armor-bearer said to him, "Do all that 17
12 the men . . hailed Jonathan and his armor-bearer 17
12 Jonathan said to his armor-bearer, "Come up 17
13 Then Jonathan . . and his armor-bearer after him. 17
13 and his armor-bearer killed them after him; 17
14 which Jonathan and his armor-bearer made 17
17 Jonathan and his armor-bearer were not there. 17
16:21 Saul loved him . . and he became his armor-bearer. 17
17:41 with his shield-bearer in front of him. 17
31: 4 Saul said to his armor-bearer, "Draw your sword 17
4 But his armor-bearer would not; for he feared 17
6 Saul died, and his three sons, and his armor-bearer 17
2Sm 3: 2 And sons were born to David at Hebron 6
5 These were born to David in Hebron. 6
5:13 and more sons and daughters were born to David. 6
14 names of those who were born to him in Jerusalem 7
6:13 when those who bore the ark . . had gone six paces 17
11:27 and she became his wife, and bore him a son. 6
12:14 the child that is born to you shall die. 6
15 the LORD struck the child that Uri'ah's wife bore 6
24 and she bore a son, and he called his name Solomon. 6
14:27 There were born to Ab'salom three sons 6
15:24 Levites, bearing the ark of the covenant of God; 17
16: 1 a couple of asses . . bearing 200 loaves of bread 20
19:19 let not the king bear it in mind. 25
21: 8 the two sons of Rizpah . . whom she bore to Saul 6
8 the five sons of Merab . . whom she bore to A'driel 6
1Kg 1: 6 handsome man; and he was born next after Ab'salom. 6
2:26 you bore the ark of the Lord GOD before David my 17
3:21 behold, it was not the child that I had borne. 6
8:19 your son who shall be born to you shall build 10
10: 2 a very great retinue, with camels bearing spices 17
11:20 the sister of Tah'penes bore him Genu'bath his son 6
13: 2 a son shall be born to the house of David, Josi'ah 6
14:28 the guard bore them and brought them back 17
2Kg 4:17 conceived, and she bore a son about that time 6
18:14 whatever you impose on me I will bear. 17
19:30 again take root downward, and bear fruit upward; 23
20:18 sons, who are born to you, shall be taken away; 6
1Ch 1:19 To Eber were born two sons: the name of the one was 6
32 she bore Zimran, Jokshan, Medan, Mid'ian, Ishbak 6
2: 3 Bath-shu'a the Canaanitess bore to him. 6
4 Tamar also bore him Perez and Zerah. 6
9 The sons of Hezron, that were born to him 6
17 Ab'igail bore Ama'sa, and the father of Ama'sa was 6
19 Caleb married Ephrath, who bore him Hur. 6
21 the daughter of Machir . . and she bore him Segub; 6
24 Eph'rathah . . she bore him Ashhur, the father 6
29 Ab'ihail, and she bore him Ahban and Molid. 6
35 gave his daughter . . and she bore him Attai. 6
46 Ephah . . bore Haran, Moza, and Gazez; 6
48 Ma'acah . . bore Sheber and Tir'hanah. 6
49 She also bore Sha'aph the father of Madman'nah 6
3: 1 the sons of David that were born to him in Hebron 6
4 six were born to him in Hebron 6
5 were born to him in Jerusalem: Shim'e-a, Shobab 6
4: 6 Na'arah bore him Ahuz'zam, Hepher, Te'meni 6
9 his name Jabez, saying, "Because I bore him in pain. 6
17 Bith'i-ah . . conceived and bore Miriam, Sham'mai 34
18 his Jewish wife bore Jered the father of Gedor 6
7:14 As'ri-el, whom his Aramean concubine bore; 6
14 she bore Machir the father of Gilead. 6
16 Ma'acah the wife of Machir bore a son 6
18 sister Hammo'lecheth bore Ishhod, Abi-e'zer 6
21 the men of Gath who were born in the land slew 6
23 his wife, and she conceived and bore a son; 6
12:24 The men of Judah bearing shield and spear were 17
22: 9 son shall be born to you; he shall be a man of peace. 6
26: 6 Shemai'ah were sons born who were rulers 6
2Ch 6: 9 your son who shall be born to you shall build 10
9: 1 camels bearing spices and very much gold 17
11:19 she bore him sons, Je'ush, Shemari'ah, and Zaham. 6
20 Ma'acah . . bore him Abi'jah, Attai, Ziza 6
12:11 guard came and bore them, and brought them back 17
Neh 9:30 Many years thou didst bear with them 16
Job 1: 2 were born to him seven sons and three daughters. 6
3: 3 Let the day perish wherein I was born 6
5: 7 man is born to trouble as the sparks fly upward. 6
11:12 when a wild ass's colt is born a man. 6
14: 1 Man that is born of a woman is of few days 6
15: 7 Are you the first man that was born? 6
14 he that is born of a woman, that he can be righteous? 6
21: 3 Bear with me, and I will speak 17
32 When he is borne to the grave 5
25: 4 How can he who is born of woman be clean? 6
34:31 any one said to God, 'I have borne chastisement; 17
36: 2 Bear with me a little, and I will show you 13
38:21 You know, for you were born 6
Ps 13: 2 How long must I bear pain in my soul 26
22:10 since my mother bore me thou hast been my God. 1
55:12 not an enemy who taunts me—then I could bear it; 17
68:29 temple at Jerusalem kings bear gifts to thee. 5
69: 7 For it is for thy sake that I have borne reproach 17
72: 3 the mountains bear prosperity for the people 17
87: 4 Ethiopia-"This one was born there," they say. 6
5 This one and that one were born in her"; 6
6 records . . "This one was born there." Selah 6
89:50 how I bear in my bosom the insults of the peoples 17
126: 6 goes forth weeping, bearing the seed for sowing 17
144:14 suffering no mischance or failure in bearing; 9
Prv 9:12 if you scoff, you alone will bear it. 17
17:17 brother is born for adversity. 6
25 foolish son is . . bitterness to her who bore him. 6
18:14 but a broken spirit who can bear? 17
23:25 let her who bore you rejoice. 6
25:18 man who bears false witness against 22
Ecc 2: 7 and had slaves who were born in my house; •
3: 2 a time to be born, and a time to die; 6
4:14 though . . in his own kingdom had been born poor. 6
Sng 6: 9 the darling . . flawless to her that bore her. 6
8: 5 there she who bore you was in travail. 6
Isa 1:14 become a burden to me, I am weary of bearing them. 17
7:14 a young woman shall conceive and bear a son 6
8: 3 the prophetess, and she conceived and bore a son. 6
9: 6 For to us a child is born, to us a son is given; 6
22: 6 Elam bore the quiver with chariots and horsemen 17
37:31 take root downward, and bear fruit upward; 23
39: 7 own sons, who are born to you, shall be taken away; 6
46: 3 Israel, who have been borne by me from your birth 21
4 I have made, and I will bear; 17
49:20 The children born in the time •
21 will say in your heart: 'Who has borne me these? 6
51: 2 to Abraham your father and to Sarah who bore you; 4
18 none to guide her among all the sons she has borne 6
52:11 purify . . you who bear the vessels of the LORD. 17
53: 4 he has borne our griefs and carried our sorrows; 17
11 and he shall bear their iniquities. 19
12 yet he bore the sin of many, and made intercession 17
54: 1 Sing, O barren one, who did not bear; 6
66: 8 Shall a land be born in one day? 4
Jer 1: 5 and before you were born I consecrated you; 11
10:19 this is an affliction and I must bear it. 17
15: 9 She who bore seven has languished; 6
10 Woe is me, my mother, that you bore me, 6
15 know that for thy sake I bear reproach. 17
16: 3 concerning the sons and daughters who are born 7
3 and concerning the mothers who bore them 6
17: 8 for it does not cease to bear fruit. 23
21 and do not bear a burden on the sabbath day 17
27 and not to bear a burden and enter by the gates 17
20:14 Cursed be the day on which I was born! 6
14 The day when my mother bore me 6
15 brought the news to my father, "A son is born to you 6
22:26 I will hurl you and the mother who bore you 6
26 into another country, where you were not born 6
29: 6 and daughters, that they may bear sons and daughters; 6
31:19 because I bore the disgrace of my youth. 17
44:22 The LORD could no longer bear your evil doings 17
50:12 and she who bore you shall be disgraced. 6
Lam 3:27 good . . that he bear the yoke in his youth. 17
5: 7 fathers sinned . . and we bear their iniquities. 19
Ezk 4: 4 you shall bear their punishment. 17
5 so long shall you bear the punishment 17
6 and bear the punishment of the house of Judah; 17
14:10 And they shall bear their punishment 17
16: 4 as for your birth, on the day you were born 6
5 you were abhorred, on the day that you were born. 6
20 sons and your daughters, whom you had borne to me 6
52 Bear your disgrace 17
52 So be ashamed, you also, and bear your disgrace 17
54 that you may bear your disgrace and be ashamed 17
58 You bear the penalty of your lewdness 17
17: 8 and bear fruit, and become a noble vine. 17
23 that it may bring forth boughs and bear fruit 23
23: 4 they bore sons and daughters. 6
35 bear the consequences of your lewdness 17
37 the sons whom they had borne to me. 6
49 you shall bear the penalty for your sinful 17
32:24 they bear their shame with those who go down 17
25 bear their shame with those who go down to the Pit; 17
30 who are slain by the sword, and bear their shame 17
36:15 you shall no longer bear the disgrace 17
44:10 went astray, shall bear their punishment. 17
12 that they shall bear their punishment. 17
13 they shall bear their shame 17
Hos 1: 3 Gomer . . and she conceived and bore him a son. 6
6 She conceived again and bore a daughter. 6
8 Not pitied, she conceived and bore a son. 6
2: 3 and make her as in the day she was born 6
5: 7 for they have borne alien children. 6
9:16 their root is dried up, they shall bear no fruit. 23
Jol 2:22 the tree bears its fruit 17
Ams 7:10 the land is not able to bear all his words. 12
Mic 6:16 so you shall bear the scorn of the peoples. 17
7: 9 I will bear the indignation of the LORD 17
Zep 3:18 that you will not bear reproach for it. 15
Zec 6:13 and shall bear royal honor, and shall sit and rule 17
13: 3 his father and mother who bore him will say to him 6
3 mother who bore him shall pierce him through 6
Mat 1:16 Joseph the husband of Mary, of whom Jesus was born 34
21 she will bear a son, and you shall call his name 50
23 virgin shall conceive and bear a son, and his name 50
25 knew her not until she had borne a son; 50
2: 1 Now when Jesus was born in Bethlehem of Judea 34
2 Where is he who has been born king of the Jews? 50
4 of them where the Christ was to be born. 34
3: 8 Bear fruit that befits repentance 48
10 tree therefore that does not bear good fruit 48
7:17 So, every sound tree bears good fruit 48
17 but the bad tree bears evil fruit. 48
18 A sound tree cannot bear evil fruit 48
18 nor can a bad tree bear good fruit. 48
19 Every tree that does not bear good fruit is cut 48
8:17 He took our infirmities and bore our diseases. 31
11:11 Truly, I say to you, among those born of women 37
13:26 when the plants came up and bore grain 48
17:17 How long am I to bear with you? 28
20:12 who have borne the burden of the day 31
26:24 better for that man if he had not been born. 34
Mrk 9:19 How long am I to bear with you? Bring him to me. 28
41 because you bear the name of Christ •
13: 9 to bear testimony before them. 41
14:21 better for that man if he had not been born. 34
Lke 1:13 your wife Elizabeth will bear you a son 36
31 you will conceive in your womb and bear a son 50
35 the child to be born will be called holy, the Son of God 34
2:11 born this day in the city of David a Savior 50
3: 8 Bear fruits that befit repentance 48
9 every tree . . that does not bear good fruit 48
6:43 For no good tree bears bad fruit 48
43 nor again does a bad tree bear good fruit; 48
7:28 among those born of women none is greater 37
9:41 how long am I to be with you and bear with you? 28
11:27 Blessed is the womb that bore you 31
13: 9 if it bears fruit next year, well and good 48
14:27 Whoever does not bear his own cross 31
21:13 This will be a time for you to bear testimony. 41
23:29 the wombs that never bore 34
Joh 1:13 who were born, not of blood 34
3: 3 unless one is born anew, he cannot see the kingdom 34
4 How can a man be born when he is old? 34
4 a second time into his mother's womb and be born? 34
5 unless one is born of water and the Spirit 34
6 That which is born of the flesh is flesh 34
6 and that which is born of the Spirit is spirit. 34
7 that I said to you, 'You must be born anew.' 34
8 so it is with every one who is born of the Spirit. 34
8:41 They said to him, "We were not born of fornication 34
43 It is because you cannot bear to hear my word. •
9: 2 who sinned . . that he was born blind? 34
19 Is this your son, who you say was born blind? 34
20 this is our son, and that he was born blind; 34
32 that any one opened the eyes of a man born blind. 34
34 They answered him, "You were born in utter sin 34
12:24 if it dies, it bears much fruit. 56
15: 2 Every branch of mine that bears no fruit 56
2 every branch that does bear fruit he prunes 56
2 he prunes, that it may bear more fruit. 56
4 As the branch cannot bear fruit by itself 56
5 he it is that bears much fruit 56
8 that you bear much fruit 56

16 that you should go and bear fruit 56
16:12 you cannot bear them now. 31
21 for joy that a child is born into the world. 34
18:37 For this I was born 34
19:17 and he went out, bearing his own cross 31
Act 7:20 At this time Moses was born 34
13:18 he bore with them in the wilderness. 51
15:10 neither our fathers nor we have been able to bear? 31
18:14 I should have reason to bear with you, O Jews; 28
22: 3 I am a Jew, born at Tarsus in Cili'cia 34
28 Paul said, "But I was born a citizen. 34
Rom 9:11 though they were not yet born 34
13: 4 be afraid, for he does not bear the sword in vain; 57
15: 1 ought to bear with the failings of the weak 31
1Co 11:12 so man is now born of woman 39
13: 7 Love bears all things, believes all things 49
15:49 Just as we have borne the image of the man of dust 57
49 we shall also bear the image of the man of heaven. 57
2Co 11: 1 bear with me in a little foolishness 28
1 Do bear with me! 28
19 For you gladly bear with fools, being wise 28
20 For you bear it if a man makes slaves of you 28
Gal 1:15 when he who had set me apart before I was born 46
4: 4 born of woman, born under the law 38
4 born of woman, born under the law 38
23 the son of the slave was born according to the flesh 34
27 Rejoice, O barren one who does not bear 50
29 who was born according to the flesh persecuted 34
29 who was born according to the Spirit •
5:10 he who is troubling you will bear his judgment 31
6: 2 Bear one another's burdens 31
5 For each man will have to bear his own load. 31
17 I bear on my body the marks of Jesus. 31
Php 2: 7 being born in the likeness of men. 38
3: 5 a Hebrew born of Hebrews; as to the law a Pharisee 42
1Th 3: 1 Therefore when we could bear it no longer 49
5 For this reason, when I could bear it no longer 49
1Ti 2: 6 testimony to which was borne at the proper time. •
2Ti 2:19 God's firm foundation stands, bearing this seal 45
Heb 1: 3 and bears the very stamp of his nature •
6: 8 if it bears thorns and thistles 43
9:28 Christ . . offered once to bear the sins of many 27
11:12 from one man . . were born descendants 34
23 Moses, when he was born, was hid for three months 34
13:13 and bear the abuse he endured. 56
22 bear with my word of exhortation 28
1Pe 2:24 He himself bore our sins in his body on the tree 27
2Pe 1:17 the voice was borne to him by the Majestic Glory 56
18 we heard this voice borne from heaven 56
2:12 creatures . . born to be caught and killed 34
1Jn 2:29 every one who does right is born of him. 34
3: 9 No one born of God commits sin; 34
9 and he cannot sin because he is born of God. 34
4: 7 and he who loves is born of God and knows God. 34
5: 4 For whatever is born of God overcomes the world; 34
10 the testimony that God has borne to his Son. 47
18 We know that any one born of God does not sin 34
18 but He who was born of God keeps him 34
Rev 2: 2 how you cannot bear evil men but have tested 31
6: 9 slain . . for the witness they had borne; 45
12:13 he pursued the woman who had borne the male child. 50
17 and bear testimony to Jesus 45
16: 2 the men who bore the mark of the beast 45
2Es 2: 2 The mother who bore them says to them, 'Go 59
4: 6 Who of those that have been born can do this 61
5:35 Why then was I born? 61
46 If you bear ten children, why one after another?' 62
51 He replied to me, "Ask a woman who bears children 62
52 Why are those whom you have borne recently 62
52 not like those whom you bore before •
53 Those born in the strength of youth 61
53 those born during the time of old age 61
55 as born of a creation which already is aging •
6: 8 because from him were born Jacob and Esau 61
7:63 better if the dust itself had not been born 61
65 all who have been born lament 61
68 who have been born are involved in iniquities 61
105 every one shall bear his own righteousness 63
127 every man who is born on earth shall wage 61
8: 6 every mortal who bears the likeness of a human 63
35 there is no one among those who have been born 60
9:22 the multitude . . which has been born in vain 61
10:10 from the beginning all have been born of her 61
12 which I brought forth in pain and bore in sorrow; 60
15 and bear bravely the troubles 58
46 then it was that the barren woman bore a son. 62
14:20 who will warn those who will be born hereafter? 61
Tob 13:11 bearing gifts in their hands 45
Jdt 7: 4 the hills will bear their weight. 55
12:18 in all the days since I was born. 32
20 in any one day since he was born. 34
AEs 14: 5 Ever since I was born 33
Wis 2: 2 Because we were born by mere chance 38
4: 6 children born of unlawful unions 34
5:13 we also, as soon as we were born, ceased to be 34
7: 3 when I was born, I began to breathe the common air 38
Sir 7:28 Remember . . through your parents you were born; 34
10:18 nor fierce anger for those born of women. 35
14:18 one dies and another is born. 34
22:15 of iron are easier to bear than a stupid man. 54
23:14 then you will wish that you had never been born 34
25 her branches will not bear fruit. 56
28:19 who has not borne its yoke 44
36:15 Bear witness to those 40
41: 9 When you are born, you are born to a curse 34
9 When you are born, you are born to a curse 34
44: 9 they have become as though they had not been born 38
49:15 no man like Joseph has been born, and his bones are 34
Bar 3:26 The giants were born there, who were famous of old 34
Man 1: 5 for thy glorious splendor cannot be borne 30
1Mc 2: 7 said, "Alas! Why was I born to see this 34
2Mc 7:20 she bore it with good courage 56
10: 7 bearing ivy-wreathed wands 45
4Mc 6: 9 he bore the pains and scorned the punishment 53
10: 2 the same mother bore me 34
11:15 Since to this end we were born and bred 34
13:21 they were born after an equal time of gestation 29
16: 6 After bearing seven children 50
16 you are called to bear witness for the nation. 52

bear (2) 1. דֹּב 2. דֹּב (A) 3. ἄρκος
1Sm 17:34 when there came a lion, or a bear, and took a lamb 1
36 Your servant has killed both lions and bears; 1
37 me from . . the lion and from the paw of the bear 1
2Sm 17: 8 they are enraged, like a bear robbed of her cubs 1
Prv 28:15 roaring lion or a charging bear is a wicked ruler 1
Isa 11: 7 The cow and the bear shall feed; 1
59:11 We all growl like bears, 1
Lam 3:10 He is to me like a bear lying in wait 1
Dan 7: 5 behold, another beast, a second one, like a bear. 2
Hos 13: 8 will fall upon them like a bear robbed of her cubs 1
Ams 5:19 as if a man fled from a lion, and a bear met him; 1
Rev 13: 2 the beast that I saw . . its feet were like a bear's 3
Wis 11:17 to send upon them a multitude of bears 3
Sir 25:17 darkens her face like that of a bear. 3
47: 3 with bears as with lambs of the flock. 3

bear *See* fail, hard.

bear a burden 1. מַשָּׂא 2. נשׂא 3. סָבַל
Exd 18:22 and they will bear the burden with you. 2
Num 4:24 service . . in serving and bearing burdens 1
47 could enter to do . . the work of bearing burdens 1
2Ch 2: 2 assigned 70,000 men to bear burdens 3
18 70,000 . . assigned to bear burdens 3

bear a child 1. ילד 2. γεννάω 3. τεκνογονέω 4. τεκνογονία 5. τίκτω
Gen 6: 4 and they bore children to them. 1
16: 1 Now Sar'ai, Abram's wife, bore him no children. 1
2 LORD has prevented me from bearing children; 1
17:17 Shall Sarah, who is 90 years old, bear a child? 1
18:13 'Shall I indeed bear a child, now that I am old?' 1
20:17 female slaves so that they bore children. 1
30: 1 When Rachel saw that she bore Jacob no children 1
9 Leah saw that she had ceased bearing children 1
Lev 12: 2 a woman conceives, and bears a male child 1
5 if she bears a female child, then she shall be 1
7 This is the law for her who bears a child 1
Isa 65:23 not labor in vain, or bear children for calamity; 1
Jer 30: 6 Ask now, and see, can a man bear a child? 1
Gal 4:24 bearing children for slavery; she is Hagar. 2
1Ti 2:15 woman will be saved through bearing children 4
5:14 I would have younger widows marry, bear children 3
Rev 12: 4 the woman who was about to bear a child 5

bear a grudge against 1. נטר
Lev 19:18 not . . bear any grudge against the sons 1

also bear witness 1. συμμαρτυρέω 2. συνεπιμαρτυρέω
Rom 2:15 while their conscience also bears witness 1
Heb 2: 4 while God also bore witness by signs and wonders 2

bear an image 1. עצב
Jer 44:19 we made cakes for her bearing her image 1

bear anew 1. ἀναγεννάω
1Pe 1: 3 we have been born anew to a living hope 1
23 You have been born anew, not of perishable seed 1

bear anger 1. קצף
Deu 9:19 the anger and hot displeasure which the LORD bore 1

bear arms 1. ἐνοπλίζω
Jdt 15:13 bearing their arms and wearing garlands 1

bear away 1. נשׂא
Jer 49:29 their camels shall be borne away from them 1

bear blame 1. חטא
Gen 43: 9 then let me bear the blame for ever; 1
44:32 I shall bear the blame in the sight of my father 1

cause to bear 1. נשׂא
Lev 22:16 so cause them to bear iniquity and guilt 1

bear death 1. θανατηφόρος
4Mc 15:26 one bearing death and the other deliverance 1

bear down upon 1. ἐπιφέρω
2Mc 12:35 one of the Thracian horsemen bore down upon him 1

bear false witness 1. ψευδομαρτυρέω
Mat 19:18 You shall not bear false witness 1
Mrk 10:19 Do not steal, Do not bear false witness 1
14:56 For many bore false witness against him 1
57 some stood up and bore false witness against him 1
Lke 18:20 Do not bear false witness 1
Sus 1:61 Daniel had convicted them of bearing false witness 1

bear fresh fruit 1. בכר
Ezk 47:12 they will bear fresh fruit every month 1

bear fruit 1. καρποφορέω 2. fructifero 3. fructifico
Mat 13:23 he indeed bears fruit, and yields 1
Mrk 4:20 hear the word and accept it and bear fruit 1
Rom 7: 4 in order that we may bear fruit for God. 1
5 at work in our members to bear fruit for death. 1
Col 1: 6 it is bearing fruit and growing 1
10 bearing fruit in every good work 1
2Es 3:33 and their labor has borne no fruit 3
16:25 The trees shall bear fruit, and who will gather it? 2
Wis 10: 7 plants bearing fruit that does not ripen 1

bear guilt 1. אשׁם
Hos 10: 2 now they must bear their guilt. 1
13:16 Sama'ria shall bear her guilt 1

bear loss 1. חטא
Gen 31:39 I bore the loss of it myself; 1

make bear guilt 1. אשׁם
Ps 5:10 Make them bear their guilt, O God; 1

bear patiently 1. ἐγκαρτερέω
4Mc 14: 9 but also bore the sufferings patiently 1

bear testimony 1. ἐκμαρτυρέω 2. μαρτυρέω 3. μαρτύριον
Mat 10:18 to bear testimony before them and the Gentiles. 3
Joh 5:32 the testimony which he bears to me is true. 2
2Mc 3:36 he bore testimony to all men 1

bear the name 1. ὀνομάζω
1Co 5:11 who bears the name of brother 1

bear tidings 1. בשׂר
Ps 68:11 great is the host of those who bore the tidings 1

bear twins 1. תאם
Sng 4: 2 a flock of shorn ewes . . all of which bear twins 1
6: 6 are like a flock of ewes . . all of them bear twins 1

bear untimely 1. ἔκτρωμα
1Co 15: 8 Last of all, as to one untimely born 1

bear up 1. נשׂא 2. עמס 3. αἴρω 4. βαστάζω 5. καρτερέω
Gen 7:17 and the waters increased, and bore up the ark 1
Ps 68:19 Blessed be the Lord, who daily bears us up; 2
91:12 On their hands they will bear you up 1
Prv 30:21 three things . . under four it cannot bear up 1
Mat 4: 6 On their hands they will bear you up 3
Lke 4:11 'On their hands they will bear you up 3
Rev 2: 3 and bearing up for my name's sake 4
4Mc 13:11 another said, "Bear up nobly 5

bear up under 1. ὑποφέρω
4Mc 14:12 the mother . . bore up under the rackings of each one 1

bear witness 1. ענה 2. ἀπομαρτυρέω 3. μαρτυρέω 4. μάρτυς 5. συμμαρτυρέω 6. testificor
Exd 23: 2 nor shall you bear witness in a suit 1
Joh 1: 7 He came . . to bear witness to the light 3
8 but came to bear witness to the light. 3
15 (John bore witness to him and cried 3
32 And John bore witness, "I saw the Spirit descend 3
34 And I have seen and have borne witness 3
2:25 and needed no one to bear witness of man; 3
3:11 and bear witness to what we have seen; 3
26 to whom you bore witness, here he is, baptizing 3
28 You yourselves bear me witness, that I said 3
32 He bears witness to what he has seen and heard 3
5:31 If I bear witness to myself 3
32 there is another who bears witness to me 3
33 and he has borne witness to the truth. 3
36 these very works . . bear me witness 3
37 the Father . . has himself borne witness to me 3
39 it is they that bear witness to me; 3
8:13 You are bearing witness to yourself 3
14 Even if I do bear witness to myself 3
18 I bear witness to myself 3
18 the Father who sent me bears witness to me. 3
10:25 they bear witness to me; 3

12:17 The crowd . . bore witness. 3
15:26 he will bear witness to me; 3
18:23 bear witness to the wrong 3
37 I was born . . to bear witness to the truth 3
19:35 He who saw it has borne witness 3
21:24 the disciple who is bearing witness to these 3
Act 10:43 To him all the prophets bear witness 3
14: 3 who bore witness to the word of his grace 3
15: 8 God who knows the heart bore witness to them 3
22: 5 as . . the whole council of elders bear me witness. 3
23:11 so you must bear witness also at Rome. 3
26:16 to appoint you to serve and bear witness 4
Rom 3:21 the law and the prophets bear witness to it 3
8:16 Spirit himself bearing witness with our spirit 5
9: 1 my conscience bears me witness in the Holy Spirit 5
10: 2 I bear them witness that they have a zeal for God 3
Gal 4:15 I bear you witness that, if possible 3
Col 4:13 I bear him witness that he has worked hard for you 3
Heb 10:15 the Holy Spirit also bears witness to us 3
11: 4 God bearing witness by accepting his gifts 3
1Jn 5: 9 he has borne witness to his Son. 3
Rev 1: 2 who bore witness to the word of God 3
2Es 7:94 witness which he who formed them bears 6
2Mc 12:30 the Jews . . bore witness to the good will 2

bear witness against 1. ἀντιμαρτυρέω 2. καταμαρτυρέω
Sus 1:43 these men have borne false witness against me. 2
49 these men have borne false witness against her. 2
2Mc 7: 6 which bore witness against the people to their faces 1

beard 1. זָקָן 2. שָׂפָם 3. πώγων
Lev 13:29 woman has a disease on the head or the beard 1
30 it is an itch, a leprosy of the head or the beard 1
14: 9 shall shave off his beard and his eyebrows 1
19:27 You shall not . . mar the edges of your beard 1
21: 5 nor shave off the edges of their beards 1
1Sm 17:35 I caught him by his beard, and smote him and killed 1
21:13 and let his spittle run down his beard. 1
2Sm 10: 4 and shaved off half the beard of each, and cut off 1
5 Remain at Jericho until your beards have grown 1
19:24 neither dressed his feet, nor trimmed his beard 2
20: 9 Jo'ab took Ama'sa by the beard with his right hand 1
1Ch 19: 5 Remain at Jericho until your beards have grown 1
Ezr 9: 3 pulled hair from my head and beard 1
Ps 133: 2 precious oil . . running down upon the beard 1
2 down upon the beard, upon the beard of Aaron 1
Isa 7:20 razor . . it will sweep away the beard also. 1
15: 2 On every head is baldness, every beard is shorn; 1
50: 6 and my cheeks to those who pulled out the beard; •
Jer 41: 5 with their beards shaved and their clothes torn 1
48:37 For every head is shaved and every beard cut off; 1
Ezk 5: 1 razor and pass it over your head and your beard; 1
1Es 8:71 pulled out hair from my head and beard 3
LJr 1:31 their heads and beards shaved 3

bearer 1. נשׂא 2. βαστάζω
Jdg 9:54 called hastily to the young man his armor-bearer 1
1Sm 17: 7 and his shield-bearer went before him. 1
31: 5 when his armor-bearer saw that Saul was dead 1
2Sm 18:15 And ten young men, Jo'ab's armor-bearers 1
23:37 Na'harai of Be-er'oth, the armor-bearer of Jo'ab 1
1Kg 5:15 Solomon also had 70,000 burden-bearers 1
1Ch 10: 4 Then Saul said to his armor-bearer 1
4 But his armor-bearer would not; 1
5 when his armor-bearer saw that Saul was dead 1
11:39 Na'harai of Be-er'oth, the armor-bearer of Jo'ab 1
Lke 7:14 the bearers stood still 2

burden bearer 1. סַבָּל
2Ch 34:13 were over the burden bearers and directed 1
Neh 4:10 The strength of the burden-bearers is failing 1

bearing 1. ἀπάντησις
2Mc 15:12 of modest bearing and gentle manner 1

beast 1. בְּהֵמָה 2. בֵּן 3. בְּעִיר 4. חַיָּה 5. טֶבַח 6. חֵיוָא (A) 7. θήρ 8. θηρίον 9. κνώδαλον 10. κτῆνος 11. animal 12. bestia
Gen 1:24 creeping things and beasts of the earth 4
25 God made the beasts of the earth 4
30 to every beast of the earth 4
2:19 out of the ground the LORD God formed every beast 4
20 names . . to every beast of the field; 4
6: 7 man and beast and creeping things 1
7:14 they and every beast according to its kind 4
21 moved upon the earth, birds, cattle, beasts 4
8: 1 God remembered Noah and all the beasts 4
19 every beast, every creeping thing, and every bird 4
9: 2 shall be upon every beast of the earth 4
5 of every beast I will require it and of man; 4
10 the birds, the cattle, and every beast of the earth 4
34:23 their property and all their beasts be ours? 1
36: 6 Esau took . . his cattle, all his beasts 1
37:20 we shall say that a wild beast has devoured him 4
33 a wild beast has devoured him; Joseph is without 4
45:17 Do this: load your beasts and go back to the land 3
Exd 8:17 and there came gnats on man and beast; 1
18 So there were gnats on man and beast. 1
9: 9 breaking out in sores on man and beast 1
10 boils breaking out in sores on man and beast. 1
19 upon every man and beast that is in the field 1
22 hail . . upon man and beast and every plant 1
25 struck . . both man and beast; and the hail struck 1
11: 7 of the people of Israel, either man or beast 1
12:12 smite all . . both man and beast; 1
13: 2 first to open the womb . . both of man and of beast 1
19:13 whether beast or man, he shall not live.' 1
22: 5 When a man . . lets his beast loose and it feeds 3
10 an ass or an ox or a sheep or any beast to keep 1
19 Whoever lies with a beast shall be put to death. 1
23:11 what they leave the wild beasts may eat. 4
29 lest . . the wild beasts multiply against you. 4
Lev 5: 2 whether the carcass of an unclean beast 4
7:21 or an unclean beast or any unclean abomination 1
24 and the fat of one that is torn by beast •
11: 2 which you may eat among all the beasts 1
46 This is the law pertaining to beast and bird 1
17:13 any beast or bird that may be eaten 4
18:23 shall not lie with any beast and defile yourself 1
23 woman give herself to a beast to lie with it 1
20:15 If a man lies with a beast, he shall be put to death 1
15 and you shall kill the beast 1
16 If a woman approaches any beast and lies with it 1
16 you shall kill the woman and the beast 1
25 between the clean beast and the unclean 1
25 not make yourselves abominable by beast 1
24:18 He who kills a beast shall make it good 1
21 He who kills a beast shall make it good 1
25: 7 for your cattle also and for the beasts 4
26: 6 I will remove evil beasts from the land 4
22 I will let loose the wild beasts among you 4
27:10 if he makes any exchange of beast for beast 1
10 if he makes any exchange of beast for beast 1
28 no devoted thing . . whether of man or beast 1
Num 3:13 first-born in Israel, both of man and of beast; 1
8:17 first-born . . are mine, both of man and of beast; 1
18:15 opens the womb of all flesh, whether man or beast 1
15 firstling of unclean beasts you shall redeem. 1
31:11 spoil and all the booty, both of man and of beast. 1
26 count of the booty . . both of man and of beast 1
47 one of every 50, both of persons and of beasts 1
35: 3 pasture lands shall be . . for all their beasts. 4
Deu 4:17 likeness of any beast that is on the earth 1
7:22 lest the wild beasts grow too numerous for you 4
27:21 'Cursed be he who lies with any kind of beast.' 1
28: 4 Blessed shall be . . the fruit of your beasts 1
26 body shall be food . . for the beasts of the earth; 1
32:24 I will send the teeth of beasts against them 1
Jdg 20:48 smote . . men and beasts and all that they found. 1
1Sm 17:44 birds of the air and to the beasts of the field. 1
2Sm 21:10 or the beasts of the field by night. 4
1Kg 4:33 he spoke . . of beasts, and of birds, and of reptiles 1
2Kg 3: 9 there was no water for the army or for the beasts 1
17 you shall drink, you, your cattle, and your beasts.' 1
4:24 Urge the beast on; do not slacken the pace for me •
14: 9 a wild beast of Lebanon passed by and trampled 4
2Ch 25:18 wild beast of Lebanon passed by and trampled 4
Ezr 1: 4 be assisted . . with goods and with beasts 1
6 aided them with . . goods, with beasts 1
Neh 2:12 no beast with me but the beast on which I rode. 1
12 no beast with me but the beast on which I rode. 1
14 no place for the beast that was under me to pass. 1
Job 5:22 shall not fear the beasts of the earth. 4
23 the beasts of the field shall be at peace with you. 4
12: 7 But ask the beasts, and they will teach you; 1
28: 8 The proud beasts have not trodden it; 2
35:11 who teaches us more than the beasts of the earth 1
37: 8 Then the beasts go into their lairs, 4
Ps 8: 7 sheep and oxen, and also the beasts of the field 1
36: 6 man and beast thou savest, O LORD. 1
49:12 he is like the beasts that perish. 1
20 in his pomp, he is like the beasts that perish. 1
50:10 For every beast of the forest is mine 4
68:30 Rebuke the beasts that dwell among the reeds 4
73:22 I was like a beast toward thee. 1
79: 2 flesh of thy saints to the beasts of the earth. 4
104:11 they give drink to every beast of the field; 4
20 when all the beasts of the forest creep forth. 4
135: 8 smote the first-born . . both of man and of beast; 1
147: 9 He gives to the beasts their food 1
148:10 Beasts and all cattle 4
Prv 9: 2 She has slaughtered her beasts 5
12:10 righteous . . regard for the life of his beast 1
30:30 the lion, which is mightiest among beasts 1
Ecc 3:18 to show them that they are but beasts. 1
19 fate of . . men and the fate of beasts is the same; 1
19 and man has no advantage over the beasts; 1
21 and the spirit of the beast goes down to the earth? 1
Isa 18: 6 be left . . to the beasts of the earth. 1
6 the beasts of the earth will winter upon them. 1
30: 6 An oracle on the beasts of the Negeb. 1
35: 9 nor shall any ravenous beast come up on it; 4
40:16 nor are its beasts enough for a burnt offering. 4
46: 1 Nebo stoops, their idols are on beasts and cattle; 4
1 are loaded as burdens on weary beasts. •
56: 9 All you beasts of the field, come to devour— 4
9 come to devour-all you beasts in the forest. 4
Jer 7:20 on this place, upon man and beast 1
33 birds of the air, and for the beasts of the earth; 1
9:10 both the birds of the air and the beasts have fled 1
12: 4 the beasts and the birds are swept away 1
15: 3 the birds of the air and the beasts of the earth 1
16: 4 birds of the air and for the beasts of the earth. 1
19: 7 birds of the air and to the beasts of the earth. 1
21: 6 the inhabitants of this city, both man and beast; 1
27: 6 I have given him also the beasts of the field 4
28:14 I have given to him even the beasts of the field 4
31:27 with the seed of man and the seed of beast. 1
32:43 It is a desolation, without man or beast; 1
33:10 which you say, 'It is a waste without man or beast 1
10 desolate, without man or inhabitant or beast 1
12 In this place which is waste, without man or beast 1
34:20 the birds of the air and the beasts of the earth. 1
36:29 and will cut off from it man and beast? 1
50: 3 both man and beast shall flee away. 1
51:62 nothing shall dwell in it, neither man nor beast 1
Ezk 4:14 eaten what died of itself or was torn by beasts •
5:17 I will send famine and wild beasts against you 4
8:10 kinds of creeping things, and loathsome beasts 1
14:13 famine upon it, and cut off from it man and beast 1
15 If I cause wild beasts to pass through the land 4
15 no man may pass through because of the beasts; 4
17 and I cut off from it man and beast; 1
19 with blood, to cut off from it man and beast; 1
21 sword, famine, evil beasts, and pestilence 4
21 and pestilence, to cut off from it man and beast! 1
17:23 cedar; and under it will dwell all kinds of beasts; 8
25:13 against Edom, and cut off from it man and beast; 1
29: 5 To the beasts of the earth and to the birds 4
8 and will cut off from you man and beast; 1
11 no foot of beast shall pass through it; 1
31: 6 beasts of the field brought forth their young; 4
13 will be all the beasts of the field. 4
32: 4 I will gorge the beasts of the whole earth 4
13 I will destroy all its beasts 1
13 nor shall the hoofs of beasts trouble them. 1
33:27 I will give to the beasts to be devoured; 4
34: 5 they became food for all the wild beasts. 4
8 my sheep have become food for all the wild beasts 4
25 and banish wild beasts from the land 4
28 nor shall the beasts of the land devour them; 4
36:11 I will multiply upon you man and beast; 1
38:20 the beasts of the field, and all creeping things 4
39: 4 and to the wild beasts to be devoured. 4
17 to all beasts of the field, 'Assemble and come 4
44:31 shall not eat of anything, whether bird or beast 1
Dan 2:38 given . . the beasts of the field, and the birds 6
4:12 beasts of the field found shade under it 6
14 let the beasts flee from under it 6
15 lot be with the beasts in the grass of the earth; 6
16 let a beast's mind be given to him; 6
21 under which beasts of the field found shade 6
23 let his lot be with the beasts of the field 6
25 dwelling shall be with the beasts of the field; 6
32 dwelling shall be with the beasts of the field; 6
5:21 mind was made like that of a beast 6
7: 3 four great beasts came up out of the sea 6
5 behold, another beast, a second one, like a bear. 6
6 beast had four heads; and dominion was given to it. 6
7 behold, a fourth beast, terrible and dreadful 6
7 different from all the beasts that were before 6
11 looked, the beast was slain, and its body 6
12 As for the rest of the beasts, 6
17 four great beasts are four kings who shall arise 6
19 know the truth concerning the fourth beast 6
23 Thus he said: 'As for the fourth beast, there 6
8: 4 no beast could stand before him, 4
Hos 2:12 and the beasts of the field shall devour them. 4
18 covenant on that day with the beasts of the field 4
4: 3 in it languish, and also the beasts of the field 4
Jol 1:18 How the beasts groan! 1
2:22 Fear not, you beasts of the field 1
Jon 3: 7 Let neither man nor beast, herd nor flock 1
8 but let man and beast be covered with sackcloth 1
Mic 5: 8 like a lion among the beasts of the forest 1
Hab 2:17 the destruction of the beasts will terrify you 1
Zep 1: 3 I will sweep away man and beast; 1
2:14 in the midst of her, all the beasts of the field; 4
Zec 8:10 there was no wage for man or any wage for beast 1
14:15 asses, and whatever beasts may be in those camps. 1
Lke 10:34 then he set him on his own beast 10
Tit 1:12 are always liars, evil beasts, lazy gluttons. 8
Heb 12:20 If even a beast touches the mountain 8
Jas 3: 7 For every kind of beast and bird, of reptile 8
Rev 11: 7 the beast that ascends from the bottomless pit 8
13: 1 I saw a beast rising out of the sea 8
2 And the beast that I saw was like a leopard 8
3 the whole earth followed the beast with wonder. 8
4 for he had given his authority to the beast 8
4 and they worshiped the beast, saying 8
4 Who is like the beast, and who can fight against it? 8
5 And the beast was given a mouth •
11 I saw another beast which rose out of the earth; 8
12 exercises all the authority of the first beast 8
12 makes . . inhabitants worship the first beast 8

14 it is allowed to work in the presence of the beast 8
14 bidding them to make an image for the beast 8
15 allowed to give breath to the image of the beast 8
15 so that the image of the beast should even speak 8
15 those who would not worship the image of the beast 8
17 the name of the beast or the number of its name. 8
18 let him . . reckon the number of the beast 8
14: 9 If any one worships the beast and its image 8
11 these worshipers of the beast and its image 8
15: 2 those who had conquered the beast and its image 8
16: 2 the men who bore the mark of the beast 8
10 angel poured his bowl on the throne of the beast 8
13 I saw, issuing . . from the mouth of the beast 8
17: 3 and I saw a woman sitting on a scarlet beast 8
7 and of the beast with seven heads and ten horns 8
8 The beast that you saw was, and is not 8
8 the dwellers . . will marvel to behold the beast 8
11 As for the beast that was and is not, it is an eighth 8
12 receive authority . . together with the beast. 8
13 give over their power and authority to the beast; 8
16 they and the beast will hate the harlot; 8
17 and giving over their royal power to the beast 8
19:19 And I saw the beast and the kings of the earth 8
20 And the beast was captured 8
20 those who had received the mark of the beast 8
20: 4 and who had not worshiped the beast or its image 8
10 where the beast and the false prophet were 8
2Es 5: 8 the wild beasts shall roam beyond their haunts 12
6:53 to bring forth before thee cattle, beasts 12
7:65 but let the beasts of the field be glad 12
8:30 those who are deemed worse than beasts 12
11:39 not the one that remains of the four beasts 11
40 all the beasts that have gone before 11
Jdt 11: 7 the beasts of the field and the cattle 8
AEs 16:24 most hateful for all time to beasts and birds. 8
Wis 11:18 or newly created unknown beasts full of rage 7
17: 9 yet, scared by the passing of beasts 9
19 the sound of the most savage roaring beasts 8
Sir 17: 4 granted them dominion over beasts and birds. 8
40: 8 With all flesh, both man and beast 10
Bar 3:16 and those who rule over the beasts on earth; 8
Aza 1:59 Bless the Lord, all beasts and cattle 8
1Mc 6:35 distributed the beasts among the phalanxes; 8
35 picked horsemen were assigned to each beast. 8
36 took their position . . wherever the beast was 8
37 were fastened upon each beast by special harness 8
43 one of the beasts was equipped with royal armor. 8
2Mc 9:15 throw out with their children to the beasts 8
11: 9 the wildest beasts or walls of iron. 7
3Mc 5:23 having equipped the beasts 8
29 the beasts and the armed forces were ready 8
31 a rich feast for the savage beasts 7
42 mangled by the knees and feet of the beasts 8
45 the beasts had been brought . . to . . madness 8
47 he . . rushed out in full force along with the beasts 8
6:16 arrived . . with the beasts 8
21 The beasts turned back upon the armed forces 8
4Mc 9:28 These leopard-like beasts tore out his sinews 7

beast *See also* fight, torn.

dead beast 1. מות
Exd 21:34 and the dead beast shall be his. 1
35 and the dead beast also they shall divide. 1
36 ox for ox, and the dead beast shall be his. 1

fatted beast 1. מְרִיא
Ams 5:22 and the peace offerings of your fatted beasts 1

fed beast 1. מְרִיא
Isa 1:11 burnt offerings of rams and the fat of fed beasts; 1

most savage beast 1. *θηριώδης*
4Mc 12:13 a man, were you not ashamed, you most savage beast 1

beast of prey 1. *θηρίον*
Act 11: 6 I observed animals and beasts of prey 1

slain beast 1. *σφάγιον*
Act 7:42 Did you offer to me slain beasts and sacrifices 1

stolen beast 1. גְּנֵבָה
Exd 22: 4 If the stolen beast is found alive in his 1

wild beast 1. בְּהֱמַת שָׂדֶה 2. חַיָּה 3. חַיַּת הַשָּׂדֶה 4. צִי 5. *θήρ* 6. *θηρίον*
1Sm 17:46 give the dead . . to the wild beasts of the earth; 2
Job 39:15 that the wild beast may trample them. 3
40:20 food for him where all the wild beasts play. 3
Ps 74:19 deliver the soul of thy dove to the wild beasts; 2
Isa 13:21 But wild beasts will lie down there 4
23:13 Chalde'ans . . destined Tyre for wild beasts. 4
34:14 wild beasts shall meet with hyenas 4
43:20 The wild beasts will honor me 3
Jer 12: 9 Go, assemble all the wild beasts; 3
50:39 wild beasts shall dwell with hyenas in Babylon 4
Hos 13: 8 as a wild beast would rend them. 3
Jol 1:20 Even the wild beasts cry to thee 1
Zep 2:15 desolation she has become, a lair for wild beasts 2
Mrk 1:13 and he was with the wild beasts; 6
Rev 6: 8 kill . . with pestilence and by wild beasts 6
Wis 7:20 and the tempers of wild beasts 6
12: 9 to destroy them at one blow by dread wild beasts 6
16: 5 the terrible rage of wild beasts 6
Sir 10:11 he will inherit creeping things, and wild beasts 6
12:13 Who will pity . . any who go near wild beasts? 6
39:30 the teeth of wild beasts, and scorpions 6
LJr 1:68 The wild beasts are better than they are 6
2Mc 4:25 the rage of a savage wild beast. 5
3Mc 6: 7 cast down . . to lions as food for wild beasts 5

beat 1. דוך 2. דפק 3. דקק 4. הלם 5. חבט 6. כָּתִית 7. כתת 8. נגע 9. נגף 10. נכה 11. נקף 12. סחף 13. ספד 14. רקע 15. שחט 16. שחק 17. תפף 18. *βασανίζω* 19. *δέρω* 20. *ἐπιβάλλω* 21. *θλάω* 22. *κίνησις* 23. *κολαφίζω* 24. *λείπω* 25. *μαστιγόω* 26. *πληγάς ἐπιτίθημι* 27. *πληγή* 28. *ποιέω* 29. *τύπτω* 30. plago
Exd 2:11 and he saw an Egyptian beating a Hebrew 10
5:14 foremen . . were beaten, and were asked, "Why have 10
16 And behold, your servants are beaten; 10
27:20 that they bring to you pure beaten olive oil 6
29:40 a fourth of a hin of beaten oil, and a fourth of a hin 6
30:36 you shall beat some of it very small, and put part 16
Lev 24: 2 to bring you pure oil from beaten olives 6
Num11: 8 ground it in mills or beat it in mortars 1
28: 5 mixed with a fourth of a hin of beaten oil. 6
Deu 24:20 When you beat your olive trees, you shall not 5
25: 2 then if the guilty man deserves to be beaten 10
2 judge shall cause him to lie down and be beaten 10
3 go on to beat him with more stripes than these 10
11 husband from the hand of him who is beating him 10
Jos 8:15 made a pretense of being beaten before them 8
Jdg 19:22 beset the house round about, beating on the door; 2
2Sm 2:17 Abner and the men of Israel were beaten before 9
1Kg 5:11 Solomon gave . . and 20,000 cors of beaten oil. 6
10:16 Solomon made . . large shields of beaten gold; 15
17 he made 300 shields of beaten gold; 15
2Kg 23: 6 burned it . . and beat it to dust and cast the dust 3
2Ch 9:15 Solomon made 200 large shields of beaten gold; 15
15 600 shekels of beaten gold went into each 15
16 he made 300 shields of beaten gold; 15
34: 7 beat the Ashe'rim and the images into powder 7
Neh 13:25 cursed them and beat some of them and pulled out 10
Prv 23:13 if you beat him with a rod, he will not die. 10
14 If you beat him with the rod you will save 10
35 they beat me, but I did not feel it. 4
28: 3 beating rain that leaves no food. 12
Sng 5: 7 they beat me, they wounded me, they took away my 10
Isa 2: 4 they shall beat their swords into plowshares 7
17: 6 Gleanings . . as when an olive tree is beaten– 11
24:13 as when an olive tree is beaten 11
32:12 Beat upon your breasts for the pleasant fields 13
Jer 10: 9 Beaten silver is brought from Tarshish 14
20: 2 Then Pashhur beat Jeremiah the prophet 10
37:15 at Jeremiah, and they beat him and imprisoned him 10
Jol 3:10 Beat your plowshares into swords 7
Jon 4: 8 the sun beat upon the head of Jonah 10
Mic 4: 3 they shall beat their swords into plowshares 7
Nah 2: 7 moaning like doves, and beating their breasts. 17
Mat 14:24 distant from the land, beaten by the waves 18
21:35 the tenants took his servants and beat one 19
24:49 begins to beat his fellow servants 29
Mrk 4:37 the waves beat into the boat 20
12: 3 they took him and beat him, and sent him away 19
5 some they beat and some they killed. 19
13: 9 you will be beaten in synagogues 19
Lke 10:30 robbers, who stripped him and beat him 26
12:45 to beat the menservants and the maidservants 29
48 who did not know, and did what deserved a beating 27
18:13 beat his breast, saying, 'God, be merciful to me 29
20:10 the tenants beat him 19
11 him also they beat and treated shamefully 19
22:63 who were holding Jesus mocked him and beat him; 19
23:48 all . . returned home beating their breasts. 29
Act 5:40 they beat them and charged them not to speak 19
16:37 beaten us publicly, uncondemned 19
18:17 and beat him in front of the tribunal 29
21:32 they stopped beating Paul. 29
22:19 I imprisoned and beat those who believed in thee. 19
1Co 9:26 I do not box as one beating the air; 19
2Co 6: 5 beatings, imprisonments, tumults, labors 27
11:23 with countless beatings, and often near death. 27
1Pe 2:20 if when you do wrong and are beaten for it 23
2Es 15:51 a wretched woman who is beaten and wounded 30
Tob 3: 9 Why do you beat us? If they are dead, go with them! 25
Wis 2: 2 a spark kindled by the beating of our hearts. 22
5:11 lashed by the beat of its pinions 27
Sir 30:12 beat his sides while he is young 21
2Mc 4:45 already as good as beaten 24
6:30 I am enduring terrible sufferings . . under this beating 25
9: 2 beat a shameful retreat. 28
4Mc 6:10 the old man, while being beaten, was victorious 29
9:12 beating him with scourges 29

beat against 1. *προσκόπτω*
Mat 7:27 the wind blew and beat against that house 1

beat down 1. כתת 2. מִרְמָס
Deu 1:44 Amorites . . beat you down in Se'ir as far as Hormah. 1
Isa 28:18 you will be beaten down by it. 2
Jer 46: 5 Their warriors are beaten down, and have fled 1

beat fine 1. שחק
2Sm 22:43 I beat them fine as the dust of the earth 1
Ps 18:42 I beat them fine as dust before the wind; 1

beat in pieces 1. דקק
Mic 4:13 you shall beat in pieces many peoples 1

beat loud 1. הלם
Jdg 5:22 loud beat the horses' hoofs with the galloping 1

beat off 1. *ἀμύνω*
2Mc 10:17 and beat off all who fought upon the wall 1

beat out 1. חבט
Jdg 6:11 Gideon was beating out wheat in the wine press 1
Rut 2:17 then she beat out what she had gleaned 1
Isa 28:27 but dill is beaten out with a stick 1

beat to pieces 1. כתת
Mic 1: 7 All her images shall be beaten to pieces 1

beat upon 1. *προσπίπτω*
Mat 7:25 the winds blew and beat upon that house 1

beat wildly 1. המה
Jer 4:19 the walls of my heart! My heart is beating wildly; 1

beat with a rod 1. *ῥαβδίζω*
Act 16:22 and gave orders to beat them with rods. 1
2Co 11:25 Three times I have been beaten with rods 1

beaten small 1. דַּק
Lev 16:12 and two handfuls of sweet incense beaten small 1

beating *See* receive.

beauteous 1. צְבִי
Jer 3:19 a heritage most beauteous of all nations. 1

beautiful 1. חֶמְדָּה 2. טוֹב 3. טוֹב מַרְאֶה 4. יפה 5. יָפֶה 6. יְפֵה פִי 7. יְפַת מַרְאֶה 8. יְפַת תֹּאַר 9. לִצְבִי 10. נאה 11. צְבִי 12. תִּפְאָרָה 13. *ἀστεῖος* 14. *εὐπρεπής* 15. *καλλίπαις* 16. *κάλλος* 17. *καλός* 18. *ὡραῖος* 19. decoris
Gen 12:11 I know that you are a woman beautiful to behold; 5
14 saw that the woman was very beautiful. 5
29:17 but Rachel was beautiful and lovely. 8
Deu 21:11 see among the captives a beautiful woman 8
Jos 7:21 among the spoil a beautiful mantle from Shinar 2
1Sm 16:12 Now he was ruddy, and had beautiful eyes, and was 5
25: 3 woman was of good understanding and beautiful 8
2Sm 11: 2 he saw . . and the woman was very beautiful. 3
13: 1 Now Ab'salom, David's son, had a beautiful sister 5
14:27 whose name was Tamar; she was a beautiful woman. 7
1Kg 1: 3 they sought for a beautiful maiden throughout 5
4 The maiden was very beautiful; and she became 5
Est 2: 2 Let beautiful young virgins be sought out 3
3 to gather all the beautiful young virgins 3
7 the maiden was beautiful and lovely 8
Ps 48: 2 beautiful in elevation, is the joy of all 5
Prv 4: 9 she will bestow on you a beautiful crown. 12
11:22 snout is a beautiful woman without discretion. 5
Ecc 3:11 He has made everything beautiful in its time; 5
Sng 1:15 Behold, you are beautiful, my love; 5
15 behold, you are beautiful; your eyes are doves. 5
16 you are beautiful, my beloved, truly lovely. 5
4: 1 Behold, you are beautiful, my love 5
1 Behold . . my love, behold, you are beautiful! 5
6: 4 You are beautiful as Tirzah, my love 5
Isa 2:16 against all the beautiful craft. 1
4: 2 the branch . . shall be beautiful and glorious 9
5: 9 houses shall be desolate, large and beautiful 2
52: 1 put on your beautiful garments, O Jerusalem 12
7 How beautiful upon the mountains are the feet 10
64:11 Our holy and beautiful house, 12
Jer 13:18 beautiful crown has come down from your head. 12
20 flock that was given you, your beautiful flock? 12
46:20 A beautiful heifer is Egypt 6
Ezk 7:20 beautiful ornament they used for vainglory 11
16:12 and a beautiful crown upon your head. 12
23:42 and beautiful crowns upon their heads. 12
31: 7 It was beautiful in its greatness 4
9 I made it beautiful in the mass of its branches 5
33:32 one who sings love songs with a beautiful voice 5
Mat 23:27 which outwardly appear beautiful 18
26:10 she has done a beautiful thing to me. 17
Mrk 14: 6 She has done a beautiful thing to me. 17
Act 3: 2 gate of the temple which is called Beautiful 18
10 at the Beautiful Gate of the temple 18
7:20 Moses . . was beautiful before God 13
Rom 10:15 How beautiful are the feet of those who preach 18
Heb 11:23 because they saw that the child was beautiful 13
1Es 4:18 gold and silver or any other beautiful thing 18
19 gold or silver or any other beautiful thing. 18

2Es 6: 3 before the beautiful flowers were seen 19
Tob 6:12 The girl is also beautiful and sensible 17
Jdt 8: 7 She was beautiful in appearance 17
10:14 she was in their eyes marvelously beautiful 16
11:23 You are not only beautiful in appearance 13
12:13 This beautiful maidservant will please come 17
Wis 5:16 a beautiful diadem from the hand of the Lord 16
13: 7 because the things that are seen are beautiful. 17
15:19 they are not so beautiful in appearance 17
Sir 24:14 like a beautiful olive tree in the field 14
25: 1 are beautiful in the sight of the Lord and of men; 18
26:17 so is a beautiful face on a stately figure. 16
18 so are beautiful feet with a steadfast heart. 18
43:11 exceedingly beautiful in its brightness. 18
Sus 1: 2 Susanna . . a very beautiful woman 17
31 Now Susanna was . . beautiful in appearance. 17
2Mc 3:26 gloriously beautiful and splendidly dressed 17
10: 7 ivy-wreathed wands and beautiful branches 18
4Mc 16:10 I who had so many and beautiful children 15

beautiful *See also* grow, make.

more beautiful 1. εὐπρεπής 2. καλός

Wis 7:29 For she is more beautiful than the sun 1
14:19 forced the likeness to take more beautiful form 2

most beautiful 1. καλός

3Mc 3:17 with magnificent and most beautiful offerings 1

beautiful thing 1. ὡραῖος

Sir 45:13 there never were such beautiful things 1

beautiful woman 1. καλός

Sus 1: 2 Susanna . . a very beautiful woman 1

beautify 1. יפה 2. מָרוּק 3. פאר

Ezr 7:27 to beautify the house of the LORD . . in Jerusalem 3
Est 2:12 was the regular period of their beautifying 2
Isa 60:13 the pine, to beautify the place of my sanctuary; 3
Jer 4:30 In vain you beautify yourself. 1

beauty 1. הָדָר 2. הוֹד 3. חֶסֶד 4. יָפֶה 5. יְפִי 6. מַרְאֶה 7. נֹעַם 8. צְבִי 9. תִּפְאָרָה 10. εὐμορφία 11. εὐπρέπεια 12. καλλονή 13. κάλλος 14. καλός 15. κόσμος 16. τιμή 17. decoris 18. species

Exd 28: 2 make holy garments . . for glory and for beauty. 9
40 you shall make them for glory and beauty. 9
2Sm 14:25 no one . . to be praised for his beauty as Ab'salom; 4
Est 1:11 to show the peoples and the princes her beauty; 5
Ps 27: 4 to behold the beauty of the LORD 7
45:11 the king will desire your beauty. 5
50: 2 the perfection of beauty, God shines forth. 5
96: 6 strength and beauty are in his sanctuary. 9
Prv 6:25 Do not desire her beauty in your heart 5
20:29 beauty of old men is their gray hair. 1
31:30 Charm is deceitful, and beauty is vain 5
Isa 3:24 instead of beauty, shame. 5
28: 1 to the fading flower of its glorious beauty 8
1 to the fading flower of its glorious beauty 9
4 the fading flower of its glorious beauty 8
4 the fading flower of its glorious beauty 9
5 be a crown of glory, and a diadem of beauty 9
33:17 Your eyes will see the king in his beauty; 5
40: 6 all its beauty is like the flower of the field. 3
44:13 the figure of a man, with the beauty of a man 9
53: 2 and no beauty that we should desire him. 6
62: 3 shall be a crown of beauty in the hand of the LORD 9
Lam 2:15 city which was called the perfection of beauty 5
Ezk 16:14 your renown . . because of your beauty 5
15 you trusted in your beauty, and played the harlot 5
25 your lofty place and prostituted your beauty 5
27: 3 O Tyre, you have said, 'I am perfect in beauty 5
4 your builders made perfect your beauty. 5
11 they made perfect your beauty. 5
28: 7 they shall draw their swords against the beauty 5
12 full of wisdom and perfect in beauty. 5
17 Your heart was proud because of your beauty; 5
31: 8 no tree in the garden of God was like it in beauty. 5
Hos 14: 6 his beauty shall be like the olive 2
Rom 9:21 to make out of the same lump one vessel for beauty 16
Jas 1:11 its flower falls, and its beauty perishes 11
1Es 4:18 then see a woman lovely in appearance and beauty 13
2Es 10:50 and the loveliness of her beauty. 17
15:54 Trick out the beauty of your face! 18
Jdt 1:14 turned its beauty into shame. 15
10: 7 they greatly admired her beauty, and said to her 13
19 they marveled at her beauty 13
23 they all marveled at the beauty of her face 13
11:21 either for beauty of face or wisdom of speech! 14
16: 7 undid him with the beauty of her countenance. 13
9 her beauty captivated his mind 13
AEs 15: 5 She was radiant with perfect beauty 13
Wis 7:10 I loved her more than health and beauty 10
8: 2 I became enamored of her beauty. 13
13: 3 through delight in the beauty of these things 12
3 the author of beauty created them. 13
5 from the greatness and beauty of created things 12
Sir 9: 8 look intently at beauty belonging to another; 13
8 many have been misled by a woman's beauty 13
25:21 Do not be ensnared by a woman's beauty 13
26:16 beauty of a good wife in her well-ordered home. 13
36:22 A woman's beauty gladdens the countenance 13
40:22 The eye desires grace and beauty 13
42:12 Do not look upon any one for beauty 13
43: 9 The glory of the stars is the beauty of heaven 13
18 The eye marvels at the beauty of its whiteness 13
47:10 He gave beauty to the feasts 11
Bar 5: 1 put on for ever the beauty of the glory from God. 11
LJr 1:24 As for the gold which they wear for beauty 13
Sus 1:32 that they might feed upon her beauty. 13
56 beauty has deceived you and lust has perverted 13
1Mc 1:26 the beauty of women faded. 13
2:12 behold, our holy place, our beauty, and our glory 12
3Mc 1: 9 impressed by its excellence and its beauty 11
4Mc 2: 1 for the enjoyment of beauty 13
8: 5 and greatly respect the beauty . . of such brothers 13

beauty *See also* surpass.

beauty of form 1. גִּזְרָה

Lam 4: 7 the beauty of their form was like sapphire. 1

because 1. אֶל 2. אֲשֶׁר 3. בְּ 4. בַּאֲשֶׁר 5. בִּגְלַל 6. בְּיַעַן 7. בַּעֲבוּר 8. בְּשֶׁל 9. וְ 10. יַעַן 11. יַעַן אֲשֶׁר 12. יַעַן כִּי 13. כְּ 14. כַּאֲשֶׁר 15. כִּי עַל כֵּן 16. לְ 17. לְמַעַן 18. מֵאֲשֶׁר 19. מִבִּלְתִּי 20. מִלִּפְנֵי 21. מִן 22. מִפְּנֵי 23. עַל 24. עַל אוֹדוֹת 25. עַל אֲשֶׁר 26. עַל דְּבַר 27. עַל דִּבְרַת 28. עַל כִּי 29. עַל כֵּן 30. עַל עֵקֶב 31. עִם 32. עֵקֶב 33. עֵקֶב אֲשֶׁר 34. עֵקֶב כִּי 35. תַּחַת 36. תַּחַת אֲשֶׁר 37. בְּ (A) 38. דִּי (A) 39. כָּל קֳבֵל (A) 40. כָּל קֳבֵל דִּי (A) 41. כָּל קֳבֵל דְּנָה (A) 42. לָקֳבֵל (A) 43. מִן (A) 44. מִן דִּי (A) 45. ἀνθ' ὧν 46. ἀντί 47. ἀπό 48. ἅτε 49. γάρ 50. διά 51. διότι 52. εἰς 53. ἐκ 54. ἐν 55. ἕνεκα 56. ἕνεκεν 57. ἐπεί 58. ἐπειδή 59. ἐπί 60. καθό 61. καθότι 62. κατά 63. ὅς 64. ὅτι 65. οὗ εἵνεκεν 66. παρά 67. ὑπέρ 68. ὑπό 69. χάρις 70. ὡς 71. ab 72. cum 73. de 74. enim 75. propter 76. propterea 77. quia 78. quod 79. quoniam

Gen 3:17 cursed is the ground because of you; 7
12:13 go well with me because of you 7
17 his house with great plagues because of Sar'ai 26
20: 3 Behold, you are a dead man, because of the woman 23
11 and they will kill me because of my wife. 26
18 of Abim'elech because of Sarah, Abraham's wife. 26
21:12 Be not displeased . . because of your slave woman; 23
12 Be not displeased because of the lad 23
22:18 bless themselves, because you have obeyed 33
26: 5 because Abraham obeyed my voice 32
9 I thought, 'Lest I die because of her.' 23
27:41 Now Esau hated Jacob because of the blessing 23
46 weary of my life because of the Hittite women. 22
29:20 a few days because of the love he had for her. 3
30:18 my hire because I gave my maid to my husband"; 2
27 that the LORD has blessed me because of you; 5
32:31 he passed Penu'el, limping because of his thigh. 23
34:13 answered . . Hamor deceitfully, because he had 2
27 plundered the city, because their sister had 2
36: 7 could not support them because of their cattle. 22
39:23 in Joseph's care, because the LORD was with him; 4
43:18 and they said, "It is because of the money 26
Exd 3: 7 their cry because of their taskmasters; 22
4:26 of blood," because of the circumcision. 16
5:21 because you have made us offensive in the sight 2
6: 9 not listen . . because of their broken spirit 21
13: 8 It is because of what the LORD did for me 7
15:16 because of the greatness of thy arm, they are 3
16: 7 the LORD, because he has heard your murmurings 3
8 because the LORD has heard your murmurings 3
17: 7 Massah and Mer'ibah, because of the faultfinding 23
7 and because they put the LORD to the proof 23
19:18 was wrapped in smoke, because the LORD descended 22
32:35 a plague . . because they made the calf 25
Lev 16:16 because of the uncleannesses of the people 21
16 because of their transgressions, all their sins 21
34 once in the year because of all their sins 21
19:17 your neighbor, lest you bear sin because of him 23
21: 3 (who is near to him because she has had no husband 2
26:39 pine away . . because of their iniquity 3
39 also because of the iniquities of their fathers 3
43 amends . . because they spurned my ordinances 6
Num 6:11 because he sinned by reason of the dead body. 18
11:20 because you have rejected the LORD who is among 12
12: 1 because of the Cushite woman whom he had married 24
11 do not punish us because we have done foolishly 2
13:24 because of the cluster which the men of Israel 24
14:16 'Because the LORD was not able to bring 19
24 Caleb, because he has a different spirit 32
20:12 Because you did not believe in me, to sanctify me 10
24 because you rebelled against my command 25
25:13 because he was jealous for his God 36
27:14 because you rebelled against my word 14
32:17 in the fortified cities because of the inhabitants 22
Deu 1:27 'Because the LORD hated us he has brought us forth 3
36 because he has wholly followed the LORD!' 11
2:25 tremble and be in anguish because of you.' 22
7: 7 It was not because you were more in number 21
12 because you hearken to these ordinances 32
8:20 because you would not obey the voice of the LORD 32
9: 4 Do not say . . 'It is because of my righteousness 3
4 it is because of the wickedness of these nations 3
5 Not because of your righteousness 3
6 land to possess because of your righteousness 3
18 because of all the sin which you had committed 23
28 Because the LORD was not able to bring them 21
28 because he hated them, he has brought them out 21
22:24 young woman because she did not cry for help 23
24 man because he violated his neighbor's wife; 23
29 shall be his wife, because he has violated her; 36
23: 4 because they did not meet you with bread 26
4 because they hired against you Balaam 2
28:20 evil of your doings, because you have forsaken 2
47 Because you did not serve the LORD your God 36
55 because he has nothing left him, in the siege 21
56 because she is so delicate and tender 21
67 because of the dread which your heart shall fear 21
29:25 because they forsook the covenant of the LORD 25
31:17 evils come upon us because our God is not among us?' 28
32: 5 no longer his children because of their blemish; •
19 because of the provocation of his sons 21
51 because you broke faith with me in the midst 25
51 because you did not revere me as holy in the midst 25
Jos 2:11 there was no courage . . in any man, because of you; 22
24 inhabitants . . are fainthearted because of us. 22
5: 1 heart melted . . because of the people of Israel. 22
6 Israel walked . . because they did not hearken 2
6: 1 Jericho was shut up . . because of the people 22
9: 9 come, because of the name of the LORD your God; 16
20 lest wrath be upon us, because of the oath 23
24 we feared greatly for our lives because of you 22
10:11 were more who died because of the hailstones 3
14:14 Hebron became . . because he wholly followed 11
Jdg 2:20 and he said, "Because this people have transgressed 11
6: 2 because of Mid'ian the people of Israel made 22
6 Israel was brought very low because of Mid'ian; 22
27 but because he was too afraid of his family 14
Rut 1:19 the whole town was stirred because of them; 23
4:12 and may your house be . . because of the children 21
1Sm 4:21 saying . . because the ark of God had been 1
21 and because of her father-in-law and her husband. 1
8:18 in that day you will cry out because of your king 20
15:23 Because you have rejected . . the LORD, he has also 10
17:32 Let no man's heart fail because of him; 23
18: 3 made a covenant with David, because he loved him 3
24: 5 David's heart smote him, because he had cut off 25
28:18 Because you did not obey . . the LORD has done this 14
20 filled with fear because of the words of Samuel; 21
30:16 because of all the great spoil they had taken 3
22 Because they did not go with us, we will not give 11
2Sm 2: 5 be blessed . . because you showed this loyalty 2
6 I will do good to you because you have done this 2
3:11 could not answer Abner . . because he feared him. 21
30 Jo'ab and . . slew Abner, because he had killed 25
6: 7 God smote him there because he put forth his hand 23
8 David was angry because the LORD had broken 25
12 The LORD has blessed . . because of the ark of God. 7
7:21 Because of thy promise, and according to thy own 7
8:10 to congratulate him because he had fought 25
12: 6 restore the lamb fourfold, because he did this 33
6 because he did this . . and because he had no pity. 25
25 he called his name Jedidi'ah, because of the LORD. 7
13: 2 he made himself ill because of his sister Tamar; 7
18:20 carry no tidings, because the king's son is dead. 15
19: 6 covered with shame . . because you love those who 16
21: 1 because he put the Gib'eonites to death. 25
7 because of the oath of the LORD 23
1Kg 2:32 because . . he attacked and slew with the sword 2
3: 6 because he walked before thee in faithfulness 14
11 God said to him, "Because you have asked this 11
19 this woman's son died . . because she lay on it. 2
5: 3 could not build . . because of the warfare 22
7:47 left . . unweighed, because there were so many 21
8:33 defeated . . because they have sinned 2
9: 9 Because they forsook the LORD their God 25
10: 9 Because the LORD loved Israel for ever 3
11:33 because he has forsaken me 11
14: 7 Because I exalted you from among the people 11
13 shall come to the grave, because in him there is 10
15 scatter them . . because they have made 11
16 give Israel up because of the sins of Jerobo'am 5
15: 5 because David did what was right 2
13 removed Ma'acah . . because she had an abominable 2
30 and because of the anger to which he provoked 3
16: 7 because of all the evil that he did 23
7 both . . and also because he destroyed it. 25
19 because of his sins which he committed 23
20:28 Because the Syrians have said, "The LORD is a god 11
36 Because you have not obeyed the voice of the LORD 11
42 Because you have let go . . therefore your life 10
21: 4 sullen because of what Naboth . . had said to him; 23
20 I have found you, because you have sold yourself 10
22 I will . . and because you have made Israel to sin. •
2Kg 1: 3 Is it because there is no God in Israel that you 21
6 Is it because there is no God in Israel that you 21
16 Because you have sent messengers to inquire 11
16 is it because there is no God in Israel 21

6:11 was greatly troubled because of this thing; 23
10:30 the LORD said to Jehu, "Because you have done well 11
12: 2 because Jehoi'ada the priest instructed him. 2
13:23 he turned toward them, because of his covenant 17
16:18 he removed . . because of the king of Assyria. 22
17:26 they are killing them, because they do not know 14
18:12 because they did not obey the voice 25
19: 6 be afraid because of the words . . you have heard 22
28 Because you have raged against me . . I will put my 10
21:11 Because Manas'seh . . has committed these 11
15 because they have done what is evil 11
22:13 great is the wrath . . because our fathers have 23
17 Because they have forsaken me and have burned 36
19 because your heart was . . I also have heard you 10
23:26 kindled . . because of all the provocations 23
25:24 not be afraid because of the Chalde'an officials; 21
1Ch 9: 1 exile . . because of their unfaithfulness. 3
12: 1 he could not move about freely because of Saul 22
13:10 smote him because he put forth his hand to the ark; 25
15:26 because God helped the Levites 3
18:10 because he had fought against Hadade'zer 25
29: 3 because of my devotion to the house of my God 3
9 rejoiced because these had given willingly 23
2Ch 1:11 Because this was in your heart 11
2:11 Because the LORD loves his people he has made you 3
7:22 'Because they forsook the LORD the God of their 25
9: 8 Because your God loved Israel 3
12: 5 had gathered at Jerusalem because of Shishak 22
13: 8 because you are a great multitude 9
15:16 because she had made an abominable image 2
16: 7 Because you relied on the king of Syria 3
8 Yet because you relied on the LORD 3
19: 2 Because of this, wrath has gone out against you 3
20:37 Because you have joined with Ahazi'ah 13
21: 7 because of the covenant which he had made 17
12 'Because you have not walked in the ways 36
15 your bowels come out because of the disease, 21
19 his bowels came out because of the disease 31
24:25 because of the blood of the son of Jehoi'ada 3
28: 6 because they had forsaken the LORD 3
9 Behold, because the LORD . . was angry with Judah 3
19 the LORD brought Judah low because of Ahaz 7
29:36 people rejoiced because of what God had done 23
32:20 prayed because of this and cried to heaven. 23
34:21 because our fathers have not kept the word 25
25 Because they have forsaken me and have burned 36
27 because your heart was penitent and you humbled 10
Ezr 3:11 because the foundation of the house of the LORD 23
4:14 Now because we eat the salt of the palace 40
5:12 because our fathers had angered the God 44
9: 4 because of the faithlessness of the . . exiles 23
15 none can stand before thee because of this. 23
10: 9 trembling because of this matter 23
9 trembling . . because of the heavy rain. 21
Neh 5: 3 mortgaging . . to get grain because of the famine. 3
15 I did not do so, because of the fear of God. 22
9:37 yield goes to the kings . . because of our sins; 3
38 Because of all this we make a firm covenant 3
13:29 because they have defiled the priesthood 23
Est 1:15 is to be done . . because she has not performed 25
8: 7 hanged . . because he would lay hands on the Jews. 25
9:26 because of all that was written in this letter 23
Job 20: 2 answer me, because of my haste within me. 7
32: 2 He was angry at Job because he justified himself 23
3 he was angry . . because they had found no answer 25
34:27 because they turned aside from following him 29
36 because he answers like wicked men. 23
35: 9 Because of the multitude of oppressions 21
9 call for help because of the arm of the mighty. 21
12 does not answer, because of the pride of evil men. 22
37:17 when the earth is still because of the south wind? 21
19 we cannot draw up our case because of darkness. 22
Ps 5: 8 LORD, in thy righteousness because of my enemies; 17
10 because of their many transgressions cast them out 3
6: 7 My eye wastes away because of grief, it grows weak 21
7 My eye . . it grows weak because of all my foes. 3
8: 2 thou hast founded a bulwark because of thy foes 17
12: 5 Because the poor are despoiled 21
5 because the needy groan, I will now arise 21
27:11 lead me on a level path because of my enemies. 17
31: 7 because thou hast seen my affliction 2
10 my strength fails because of my misery 3
37: 1 Fret not yourself because of the wicked 3
38: 3 in my flesh because of thy indignation; 22
3 there is no health in my bones because of my sin. 22
5 grow foul and fester because of my foolishness 22
8 I groan because of the tumult of my heart. 21
20 are my adversaries because I follow after good. 35
40:15 Let them be appalled because of their shame 30
41:12 But thou hast upheld me because of my integrity 3
42: 9 mourning because of the oppression of the enemy? 3
43: 2 mourning because of the oppression of the enemy? 3
48:11 of Judah rejoice because of thy judgments! 17
55: 3 because of the oppression of the wicked 22
19 because they keep no law, and do not fear God. 2
64: 8 Because of their tongue he will bring them 23
66:20 because he has not rejected my prayer 2
68:29 Because of thy temple at Jerusalem 21
69:18 set me free because of my enemies! 17

70: 3 Let them be appalled because of their shame 30
78:65 like a strong man shouting because of wine. 21
97: 8 rejoice, because of thy judgments, O God. 17
102: 5 Because of my loud groaning my bones cleave 21
10 because of thy indignation and anger; 22
107:17 because of their iniquities suffered 21
34 because of the wickedness of its inhabitants. 21
119:53 Hot indignation seizes me because of the wicked 21
62 praise . . because of thy righteous ordinances. 23
136streams of tears, because men do not keep thy law. 23
158because they do not keep thy commands. 2
Prv 1:24 Because I have called and you refused to listen 10
5:23 because of his great folly he is lost. 3
24:19 Fret not yourself because of evildoers 3
Ecc 4: 9 better than one, because they have a good reward 2
8: 2 and because of your sacred oath be not dismayed; 27
11 Because sentence . . is not executed speedily 2
12 it will be well . . because they fear before him; 2
13 will not be well with . . because he does not fear 2
Sng 1: 6 Do not gaze at me because I am swarthy 21
6 Do not gaze . . because the sun has scorched me. 21
Isa 3:16 Because the daughters of Zion are haughty 12
7: 4 faint because of these two smoldering stumps 21
5 Because Syria, with E'phraim . . has devised 12
22 because of the abundance of milk which they give 21
14:21 because of the guilt of their fathers 3
17: 9 deserted because of the children of Israel 22
19:17 fear because of the purpose which the LORD . . has 22
20: 5 confounded because of Ethiopia their hope 21
26:17 were we because of thee, O LORD; 22
29:13 Because this people draw near with their mouth 12
30:12 Because you despise this word 10
37: 6 Do not be afraid because of the words 22
21 Because you have prayed to me concerning 2
29 Because you have raged against me 10
38:15 has fled because of the bitterness of my soul. 23
40:26 because he is strong in power not one is missing. •
43: 4 Because you are precious in my eyes, and honored 18
48: 4 Because I know that you are obstinate 21
49: 7 shall prostrate themselves; because of the LORD 17
51:13 fear . . because of the fury of the oppressor 22
53:12 because he poured out his soul to death 36
54:15 strife with you shall fall because of you. 23
55: 5 shall run to you, because of the LORD your God 17
57:17 Because of the iniquity of his covetousness 3
61: 1 because the LORD has anointed me to bring good 10
65: 7 because they burned incense upon the mountains 2
12 because, when I called, you did not answer 10
66: 4 because, when I called, no one answered 10
Jer 3: 9 Because harlotry was so light to her 9
4: 4 because of the evil of your doings. 22
5:14 Because they have spoken this word 10
7:13 And now, because you have done all these things 10
32 bury in Topheth, because there is no room 21
9: 7 what else can I do, because of my people? 22
13 the LORD says: "Because they have forsaken my law 23
10:19 Woe is me because of my hurt! My wound is grievous. 23
11:17 because of the evil which the house of Israel 5
12:13 because of the fierce anger of the LORD. 21
13:25 says the LORD, because you have forgotten me 2
14: 4 Because of the ground . . the farmers are ashamed 7
15: 4 because of what Manas'seh . . did in Jerusalem. 5
16:11 Because your fathers have forsaken me 25
12 because you have done worse than your fathers •
18 because they have polluted my land 23
19: 4 Because the people have forsaken me 11
4 because they have filled this place •
8 and will hiss because of all its disasters. 23
11 because there will be no place else to bury. 21
20:17 because he did not kill me in the womb; 2
21:12 because of your evil doings. 22
22: 9 Because they forsook the covenant of the LORD 25
22 ashamed . . because of all your wickedness. 21
23: 9 because of the LORD and because of his holy words. 22
9 because of the LORD and because of his holy words. 22
10 because of the curse the land mourns 22
38 says the LORD, 'Because you have said these words 10
25: 8 Because you have not obeyed my words 11
16 crazed because of the sword which I am sending 22
27 because of the sword which I am sending among you. 22
37 because of the fierce anger of the LORD. 22
38 a waste because of the sword of the oppressor 22
38 and because of his fierce anger. 22
26: 3 to do to them because of their evil doings. 22
29:19 because they did not heed my words, says the LORD 36
22 Because of them this curse shall be used by all 21
23 because they have committed folly in Israel 11
31 Because Shemai'ah has prophesied to you 11
30:14 because your guilt is great, because your sins 23
14 guilt is great, because your sins are flagrant. •
15 pain is incurable. Because your guilt is great 23
15 guilt is great, because your sins are flagrant •
32:24 because of sword and famine and pestilence 22
32 because of all the evil of the sons of Israel 23
33: 5 from this city because of all their wickedness. 23
9 shall fear and tremble because of all the good 23
35:17 because I have spoken to them 10
18 Because you have obeyed the command of Jon'adab 11
41:18 to go to Egypt because of the Chaldeans 22

44: 3 because of the wickedness which they committed 22
23 It is because you burned incense 22
23 and because you sinned against the LORD 2
46:16 because of the sword of the oppressor. 22
47: 4 because of the day that is coming to destroy all 23
48: 7 because you trusted in your strongholds 10
49:17 and will hiss because of all its disasters. 23
50:13 Because of the wrath of the LORD she shall not be 21
13 be appalled, and hiss because of all her wounds. 23
16 because of the sword of the oppressor 22
51:64 because of the evil that I am bringing upon her. 22
52: 3 Surely because of the anger of the LORD 23
Lam 1: 3 Judah has gone into exile because of affliction 21
22 dealt with me because of all my transgressions; 23
2:11 heart is . . in grief because of the destruction 23
11 in grief . . because infants and babes faint 3
3:48 my eyes flow . . because of the destruction 23
5: 9 at the peril of our lives, because of the sword 22
Ezk 5: 7 Because you are more turbulent than the nations 10
9 because of all your abominations I will do 10
11 surely, because you have defiled my sanctuary 10
6:11 say, Alas! because of all the evil abominations 1
7:13 and because of his iniquity, none can maintain 3
12:19 because their land will be stripped of all 17
13: 8 Because you have uttered delusions 10
10 Because, yea, because they have misled my people 10
10 Because, yea, because they have misled my people 6
10 and because, when the people build a wall •
22 Because you have disheartened the righteous 10
14: 4 because of the multitude of his idols 3
15 no man may pass through because of the beasts; 22
15: 8 desolate, because they have acted faithlessly 10
16:14 among the nations because of your beauty 3
15 and played the harlot because of your renown 23
28 with the Assyrians, because you were insatiable; 21
31 were not like a harlot, because you scorned hire. 16
36 Because your shame was laid bare 10
36 with your lovers, and because of all your idols 23
36 and because of the blood of your children 13
43 Because you have not remembered the days 11
52 because of your sins in which you acted 3
63 never open your mouth again because of . . shame 22
17:18 Because he despised the oath 9
18 because he gave his hand and yet did all these •
18:28 Because he considered and turned away 9
20:16 because they rejected my ordinances 10
24 because they had not executed my ordinances 10
21: 4 Because I will cut off from you both righteous 11
7 you shall say, 'Because of the tidings. 1
24 Because you have made your guilt 10
24 because you have come to remembrance 10
22:19 Because you have all become dross, therefore 10
23:30 because you played the harlot with the nations 3
35 says the Lord GOD: Because you have forgotten me 10
24:13 Because I would have cleansed you 10
25: 3 Because you said, 'Aha!' over my sanctuary 10
6 Because you have clapped your hands 10
8 Thus says the Lord GOD: Because Moab said, Behold 10
12 Because Edom acted revengefully 10
15 Because the Philistines acted revengefully 10
26: 2 because Tyre said concerning Jerusalem 11
27:12 because of your great wealth of every kind; 21
16 trafficked . . because of your abundant goods; 21
18 goods, because of your great wealth of every kind; 21
28: 2 says the Lord GOD: "Because your heart is proud 10
6 Because you consider yourself as wise as a god 10
17 Your heart was proud because of your beauty; 3
29: 6 Because you have been a staff of reed 10
9 Because you said, 'The Nile is mine 10
20 because they worked for me, says the Lord GOD. 2
31:10 thus says the Lord GOD: Because it towered high 11
15 the trees of the field shall faint because of it. 23
32:10 their kings shall shudder because of you 23
33:10 sins are upon us, and we waste away because of them; 3
29 a waste because of all their abominations 23
34: 5 were scattered, because there was no shepherd; 21
8 because my sheep have become a prey 10
8 because my shepherds have not searched •
21 Because you push with side and shoulder 10
35: 5 Because you cherished perpetual enmity 10
6 because you are guilty of blood †
10 Because you said, 'These two nations 10
11 showed because of your hatred against them; 21
15 the house of Israel, because it was desolate 25
36: 2 says the Lord GOD: Because the enemy said of you 10
3 Because, yea, because they made you desolate, 10
3 Because, yea, because they made you desolate, 10
6 because you have suffered the reproach 10
13 Because men say to you, 'You devour men 10
39:23 because they dealt so treacherously with me 25
28 because I sent them into exile among the nations 3
44:12 Because they ministered to them before 11
13 bear their shame because of the abominations •
Dan 2: 8 because you see that the word from me is sure 40
12 Because of this the king was angry 41
30 as for me, not because of any wisdom that I have 37
40 because iron breaks to pieces and shatters 40
3:22 Because the king's order was strict 41
4: 9 because I know that the spirit of the holy gods 38

18 because all the wise men of my kingdom 40
5:10 because of the words of the king and his lords 42
12 because an excellent spirit, knowledge 40
19 because of the greatness that he gave him 43
6: 3 because an excellent spirit was in him; 39
4 because he was faithful, and no error or fault 40
22 because I was found blameless before him; 40
23 because he had trusted in his God. 38
7:11 looked . . because of the sound of the great words 43
9: 7 because of the treachery which they have 3
8 because we have sinned against thee. 2
10:12 I have come because of your words. 3
Hos 4:19 they shall be ashamed because of their altars. 21
7:16 because of the insolence of their tongue. 21
8: 1 because they have broken my covenant 10
9: 7 because of your great iniquity 23
15 Because of the wickedness of their deeds 23
10:15 done to you . . because of your great wickedness. 22
14: 1 you have stumbled because of your iniquity. 3
Jol 1: 5 wail . . because of the sweet wine 23
3: 2 because they have scattered them 2
19 because they have shed innocent blood 2
Ams 1: 3 punishment; because they have threshed Gilead 23
6 because they carried into exile a whole people 23
9 because they delivered up a whole people to Edom 23
11 because he pursued his brother with the sword 23
13 because they have ripped up women with child 23
2: 1 because he burned to lime the bones of the king 23
4 because they have rejected the law of the LORD 23
6 because they sell the righteous for silver 23
4:12 because I will do this to you, prepare to me 34
5:11 Therefore because you trample upon the poor 10
Jon 1:12 I know it is because of me that 8
4: 6 was exceedingly glad because of the plant. 23
Mic 3: 4 because they have made their deeds evil. 14
12 because of you Zion shall be plowed as a field; 5
6:13 making you desolate because of your sins. 23
7:13 will be desolate because of its inhabitants 23
17 and they shall fear because of thee. 21
Zep 3:11 because of the deeds by which you have rebelled 21
Hag 1: 9 Because of my house that lies in ruins 10
Zec 2: 4 because of the multitude of men and cattle in it. 21
9:11 for you also, because of the blood of my covenant 3
Mal 2:13 groaning because he no longer regards 21
14 Because the LORD was witness to the covenant 28
Mat 2:18 refused to be consoled, because they were no 64
7:25 it did not fall, because it had been founded 49
9:36 because they were harassed and helpless 64
10:41 He who receives a prophet because he is a prophet 52
41 because he is a righteous man 52
42 a cup of cold water because he is a disciple 52
11:20 because they did not repent. 64
13:13 because seeing they do not see 64
58 because of their unbelief. 50
14: 4 because John said to him 49
5 because they held him to be a prophet. 64
9 because of his oaths and his guests 50
15:32 because they have been with me now three days 64
17:20 He said to them, "Because of your little faith. 50
18:32 because you besought me; 57
20: 7 They said to him, 'Because no one has hired us.' 64
21:46 because they held him to be a prophet. 57
22:29 because you know neither the scriptures •
23:13 because you shut the kingdom of heaven 64
24:12 because wickedness is multiplied 50
26:31 You will all fall away because of me this night 54
33 Though they all fall away because of you 54
Mrk 1:34 because they knew him. 64
2: 4 because of the crowd 50
3: 9 because of the crowd, lest they should crush him; 50
4:29 because the harvest has come. 64
6: 6 he marveled because of their unbelief 50
17 because he had married her. 64
26 because of his oaths and his guests 50
34 because they were like sheep without a shepherd; 64
8: 2 because they have been with me now three days 64
9:38 we forbade him, because he was not following us. 64
41 because you bear the name of Christ 64
11:18 because all the multitude was astonished 49
16:14 because they had not believed those who saw him 64
Lke 1: 7 they had no child, because Elizabeth was barren 61
20 because you did not believe my words 45
2: 4 because he was of the house and lineage of David 50
7 because there was no place for them in the inn. 51
4:18 because he has anointed me to preach good news 65
41 because they knew that he was the Christ. 64
5:19 no way to bring him in, because of the crowd 50
6:48 because it had been well built. 50
8: 6 it withered away, because it had no moisture. 50
9: 7 he was perplexed, because it was said by some 50
49 we forbade him, because he does not follow with us. 64
53 because his face was set toward Jerusalem. 64
11: 8 because he is his friend 50
8 yet because of his importunity he will rise 50
13: 2 because they suffered thus? 64
14 indignant because Jesus had healed 64
14:14 you will be blessed, because they cannot repay 64
15:27 because he has received him safe and sound.' 64
17: 9 because he did what was commanded? 64
18: 5 yet because this widow bothers me 50
19: 3 because he was small of stature. 64
11 because he was near to Jerusalem 50
11 because they supposed •
17 Because you have been faithful in a very little 64
21 I was afraid of you, because you are a severe man; 64
44 because you did not know the time 45
20:36 because they are equal to angels 49
21:28 because your redemption is drawing near. 51
23: 8 desired to see him, because he had heard about him 50
Joh 1:50 Because I said to you, I saw you under the fig tree 64
2:25 because he knew all men 50
3:18 because he has not believed in the name 64
19 loved darkness . . because their deeds were e 49
23 Ae'non near Salim, because there was much water 64
4:39 believed in him because of the woman's testimony 50
41 And many more believed because of his word. 50
42 no longer because of your words that we believe 50
5:16 because he did this on the sabbath. 64
18 because he not only broke the sabbath 64
27 because he is the Son of man. 64
30 because I seek not my own will 64
39 because you think that . . you have eternal life; 64
6: 2 because they saw the signs which he did 64
18 The sea rose because a strong wind was blowing. •
26 you seek me, not because you saw signs 64
26 because you ate your fill of the loaves. 64
41 because he said, "I am the bread 64
57 I live because of the Father 50
57 he who eats me will live because of me. 50
7: 1 because the Jews sought to kill him. 64
7 because I testify of it that its works are evil. 64
23 because . . I made a man's whole body well? 64
30 because his hour had not yet come. 64
39 because Jesus was not yet glorified. 64
8:20 because his hour had not yet come. 64
37 because my word finds no place in you. 64
43 It is because you cannot bear to hear my word. 64
44 because there is no truth in him 64
45 because I tell the truth, you do not believe me. 64
9:22 because they feared the Jews 64
10:13 He flees because he is a hireling 64
17 the Father loves me, because I lay down my life 64
19 a division . . because of these words. 50
26 because you do not belong to my sheep. 64
33 because you, being a man, make yourself God. 64
36 because I said, 'I am the Son of God'? 64
11: 9 because he sees the light of this world. 64
10 he stumbles, because the light is not in him. 64
12: 6 because he was a thief 64
11 because . . many of the Jews were going away 64
41 Isaiah said this because he saw his glory 64
13:29 because Judas had the money box 57
14:12 because I go to the Father. 64
17 because it neither sees him nor knows him 64
19 because I live, you will live also. 64
28 because I go to the Father 64
15:19 because you are not of the world 64
21 because they do not know him who sent me. 64
27 because you have been with me from the beginning. 64
16: 3 because they have not known the Father, nor me. 64
4 because I was with you. 64
6 because I have said these things to you 64
9 concerning sin, because they do not believe in me; 64
10 because I go to the Father 64
11 because the ruler of this world is judged. 64
17 'because I go to the Father'? 64
21 because her hour has come 64
27 because you have loved me 64
17:14 because they are not of the world 64
18:18 made a charcoal fire, because it was cold 64
19: 7 because he has made himself the Son of God. 64
42 because of the Jewish day of Preparation 50
20:13 Because they have taken away my Lord 64
29 Have you believed because you have seen me? 64
21:17 because he said to him the third time 64
Act 2: 6 because each one heard them speaking 64
24 because it was not possible for him to be held 61
4: 2 annoyed because they were teaching the people 50
21 no way to punish them, because of the people 50
6: 1 because their widows were neglected 64
8:11 gave heed to him, because . . he had amazed them 50
20 because you thought you could obtain the gift 64
10:45 because the gift . . had been poured out 64
11:19 who were scattered because of the persecution 47
12:20 because their country depended . . for food. 50
23 because he did not give God the glory 45
13:27 because they did not recognize him •
14:12 because he was the chief speaker 58
16: 3 circumcised him because of the Jews 50
17:18 because he preached Jesus and the resurrection. 64
31 because he has fixed a day 61
18: 2 because Claudius had commanded 50
3 because he was of the same trade 50
20:38 sorrowing . . because of the word he had spoken 59
21:34 because of the uproar 50
35 because of the violence of the crowd; 50
22:11 I could not see because of the brightness of that light 47
18 because they will not accept your testimony 51
26: 3 because you are especially familiar •
27: 4 because the winds were against us. 50
9 because the fast had already gone by 50
12 because the harbor was not suitable to winter in •
28: 2 because it had begun to rain and was cold. 50
3 when a viper came out because of the heat 47
18 because there was no reason 50
20 since it is because of the hope of Israel 55
Rom 1: 8 because your faith is proclaimed 64
19 plain to them, because God has shown it to them. 49
25 because they exchanged the truth about God •
2: 1 because you, the judge, are doing the very same 49
18 because you are instructed in the law •
24 blasphemed among the Gentiles because of you. 50
3:25 because . . he had passed over former sins; 50
4:19 because he was about a 100 years old •
5: 5 because God's love has been poured 64
17 If, because of one man's trespass, death reigned •
6:15 Are we to sin because we are not under law 64
19 because of your natural limitations. 50
8:10 although your bodies are dead because of sin 50
10 spirits are alive because of righteousness 50
21 because the creation itself will be set free 64
27 because the Spirit intercedes for the saints 64
9: 7 of Abraham because they are his descendants; 64
11 not because of works but because of his call 53
11 not because of works but because of his call 53
32 Why? Because they did not pursue it through faith 64
10: 9 because, if you confess with your lips that Jesus 64
11:20 They were broken off because of their unbelief •
30 received mercy because of their disobedience •
14:23 because he does not act from faith; 64
15:15 because of the grace given me by God 50
1Co 1: 4 because of the grace of God which was given you 59
2:14 because they are spiritually discerned. 64
3:13 because it will be revealed with fire 64
4: 9 because we have become a spectacle 64
7: 2 because of the temptation to immorality 50
9:10 because the plowman should plow in hope 64
10:17 Because there is one bread, we who are many are one 64
30 because of that for which I give thanks? 67
11: 2 I commend you because you remember me 64
10 a veil on her head, because of the angels. 50
17 because when you come together 64
12:15 Because I am not a hand, I do not belong to the body 64
16 Because I am not an eye, I do not belong to the body 64
15: 9 because I persecuted the church of God. 51
15 because we testified of God 64
16:17 because they have made up for your absence; 64
2Co 1:15 Because I was sure of this, I wanted to come to you •
2:13 because I did not find my brother Titus there •
3: 7 because of its brightness, fading as this was 50
10 because of the splendor that surpasses it. 55
14 because only through Christ is it taken away. 64
4:18 because we look not to the things that are seen •
5:14 because we are convinced •
7: 9 As it is, I rejoice, not because you were grieved 64
9 because you were grieved into repenting 64
13 because his mind has been set at rest by you all. 64
16 because I have perfect confidence in you. 64
8:22 because of his great confidence in you. •
9:14 because of the surpassing grace of God in you. 50
11: 7 because I preached God's gospel without cost 64
11 why? Because I do not love you? God knows I do! 64
Gal 1:24 they glorified God because of me. 54
2: 4 because of false brethren secretly brought in 50
11 because he stood condemned. 64
16 because by works of the law 64
3:19 It was added because of transgressions 69
4: 6 because you are sons, God has sent the Spirit 64
13 you know it was because of a bodily ailment 50
Eph 1:15 because I have heard of your faith in the Lord •
2: 9 not because of works, lest any man should boast. 53
4:18 because of the ignorance that is in them 50
5: 6 for it is because of these things that 50
16 because the days are evil. 64
30 because we are members of his body. 64
Php 1: 7 because I hold you in my heart 50
14 in the Lord because of my imprisonment •
26 because of my coming to you again. 50
2:26 distressed because you heard that he was ill. 51
3: 8 because of the surpassing worth of knowing 50
Col 1: 4 because we have heard of your faith in Christ •
5 because of the hope laid up for you in heaven 50
1Th 2: 8 because you had become very dear to us. 51
18 because we wanted to come to you 51
4: 6 because the Lord is an avenger 51
5:13 because of their work 50
2Th 1: 3 because your faith is growing abundantly 64
10 because our testimony to you was believed. 64
2:10 because they refused to love the truth 45
13 because God chose you from the beginning 64
3: 9 It was not because we have not that right 64
1Ti 1:12 because he judged me faithful 64
13 I received mercy because I had acted ignorantly 64
4:10 because we have our hope set on the living God 64
Tit 3: 5 he saved us, not because of deeds done by us 53
Phm 1: 5 because I hear of your love •
7 because . . the saints have been refreshed 64

Heb 2: 9 because of the suffering of death 50
3:19 they were unable to enter because of unbelief. 50
4: 2 because it did not meet with faith in the hearers. •
6 failed to enter because of disobedience 50
5: 3 Because of this he is bound to offer sacrifice 50
7:18 because of its weakness and uselessness 50
23 because they were prevented by death 50
24 because he continues for ever. 50
11: 5 he was not found, because God had taken him 51
23 because they saw that the child was beautiful 51
31 because she had given friendly welcome •
Jas 1:10 because like the flower . . he will pass away. 64
4: 2 You do not have, because you do not ask. 50
3 You . . do not receive, because you ask wrongly 51
1Pe 2: 8 they stumble because they disobey the word •
21 because Christ also suffered for you 64
4:14 because the spirit of glory . . rests upon you. 64
2Pe 1: 4 the corruption . . in the world because of passion 54
21 because no prophecy ever came by . . man 49
2: 2 because of them the way of truth will be reviled. 50
3:12 because of which the heavens will be kindled 50
1Jn 2: 8 because the darkness is passing away 64
11 because the darkness has blinded his eyes. 64
12 because your sins are forgiven for his sake. 64
13 because you know him who is from the beginning 64
13 because you have overcome the evil one 64
13 because you know the Father. 64
14 because you know him who is from the beginning 64
14 I write to you, young men, because you are strong 64
21 not because you do not know the truth 64
21 I write to you . . because you know it 64
3: 9 and he cannot sin because he is born of God. 64
12 Because his own deeds were evil 64
14 because we love the brethren. 64
22 we receive . . because we keep his commandments 64
4:13 because he has given us of his own Spirit. 64
17 because as he is so are we in this world. 64
19 We love, because he first loved us. 64
5: 7 because the Spirit is the truth. 64
10 because he has not believed in the testimony 64
2Jn 1: 2 because of the truth which abides in us 50
Rev 3:10 Because you have kept my word 64
16 So, because you are lukewarm 64
8:11 men died of the water, because it was made bitter. 64
11:10 because these two prophets had been a torment 64
12:12 because he knows that his time is short! •
17: 8 the beast, because it was and is not and is to come. 64
1Es 1:14 because the priests were offering the fat 49
50 because he would have spared them 60
52 his anger . . because of their ungodly acts 50
3: 7 because of his wisdom he shall sit next to Darius 50
4:26 Many men have lost their minds because of women 50
26 Many men . . have become slaves because of them. 50
27 stumbled, or sinned, because of women. 50
62 because he had given them release and permission 64
5:61 because his goodness and his glory are for ever 64
65 because of the weeping of the people 50
7:15 Because he had changed the will of the king 64
8:77 because of our sins and the sins of our fathers 50
86 has come about because of our evil deeds 50
90 because of these things. 59
9: 6 shivering because of the bad weather 50
55 because they were inspired by the words 64
2Es 1:20 Because of the heat I covered you 75
25 Because you have forsaken me 79
34 because . . they have neglected my commandment 79
2: 2 'Go, my children, because I am a widow and forsaken. 77
3 because you have sinned before the Lord God 79
5 because they would not keep my covenant 77
7 because they have despised my covenant. 79
14 because I live, says the Lord. 77
15 establish their feet, because I have chosen you 79
16 because I recognize my name in them. 79
24 be quiet, my people, because your rest will come. 77
30 because I will deliver you, says the Lord. 77
31 because I will bring them out 79
32 because my springs run over 79
34 because he who will come at the end of the age 79
35 because the eternal light will shine upon you 77
3: 2 because I saw the desolation of Zion 79
4:26 because the age is hastening swiftly to its end. 79
27 because this age is full of sadness 79
5:34 but because of my grief I have spoken •
6: 8 because from him were born Jacob and Esau 79
15 because the word concerns the end 79
32 because your voice has surely been heard 79
55 because thou hast said that it was for us 79
7:60 because it is they who have made my glory 76
64 because we perish and know it. 79
72 because though they had understanding 79
74 not for their sake, but because of the times 75
81 The first way, because they have scorned the law 77
82 The second way, because they cannot now make 79
87 because they shall utterly waste away 79
92 because they have striven with great effort 79
93 because they see the perplexity 79
98 because they shall rejoice with boldness 79
124 because we have lived in unseemly places? 74
132 because he has mercy on those 78
133 gracious, because he is gracious to those 78
134 patient, because he shows patience toward those 79
135 bountiful, because he would rather give 79
136 because he makes his compassions abound 79
138 he is called giver, because if he did not give 79
139 judge, because if he did not pardon those •
8: 8 because thou dost give life to the body 79
31 thou, because of us sinners, are called merciful. 75
43 because it has not received thy rain 74
44 called thy own image because he is made like thee 79
49 because you have humbled yourself 79
50 because they have walked in great pride. 77
52 because it is for you that paradise is opened 74
9:20 because of the devices of those who had come 75
22 because with much labor I have perfected them. 77
32 for it could not, because it was thine. 79
33 because they did not keep what had been sown 78
10: 8 because we are all mourning, and to be sorrowful 79
8 and to be sorrowful, because we are all sorrowing; 79
20 be persuaded because of the troubles of Zion 75
20 be consoled because of the sorrow of Jerusalem. 75
32 I said, "Because you have forsaken me! 79
45 it is because there were 3,000 years in the world 75
12: 4 because you search out the ways of the Most High. 78
5 because of the great fear 71
13:18 because they understand what is reserved •
54 because you have forsaken your own ways 74
57 because of his wonders, which he did 73
58 because he governs the times 79
14:24 these five, because they are trained to write 77
32 because he is a righteous judge 72
15:13 because their seed shall fail 79
18 because of their pride the cities 75
19 plunder their goods, because of hunger for bread 75
19 and because of great tribulation. •
27 because you have sinned against him. 75
16:32 because no sheep will go along them. 78
33 shall mourn because they have no bridegrooms; •
33 because they have no husbands •
33 because they have no helpers. •
45 Because those who labor, labor in vain; 78
64 Because the Lord will strictly examine 78
Tob 1:12 because I remembered God with all my heart. 61
2: 9 because I was defiled •
3: 5 because we did not keep thy commandments 64
6 because I have heard false reproaches 64
8 because she had been given to seven husbands 64
17 because Tobias was entitled to possess her. 51
4:13 because shiftlessness is the mother of famine. 49
21 Do not be afraid . . because we have become poor 64
5:13 because I tried to learn your tribe and family. 64
6:11 because you are entitled to her 64
12 because you . . are entitled to the inheritance. 64
8: 7 I am not taking this sister of mine because of lust 50
16 Blessed art thou, because thou hast made me glad. 64
17 Blessed art thou, because thou hast had compassion 64
11: 1 because he had made his journey a success 64
16 Those who saw . . amazed because he could see. 64
13: 4 because he is our Lord and God 61
14: 8 because what . . Jonah said will . . happen. 64
Jdt 2: 6 because they disobeyed my orders. 64
5: 7 because they would not follow the gods 64
19 because it was uninhabited. 64
6: 2 because their God will defend them 64
7:15 because they rebelled 45
19 because all their enemies had surrounded them 64
21 because it was measured out to them to drink. 64
8: 9 because they were faint for lack of water 64
11: 7 not only do men serve him because of you 50
14 because . . the people . . have been doing this 64
12:18 because my life means more to me today 64
13: 1 because the banquet had lasted long. 50
20 because you did not spare your own life 45
AEs 12: 6 because of the two eunuchs of the king. 67
14: 7 because we glorified their gods 45
16:18 because the man . . has been hanged 50
Wis 1: 2 because he is found 64
4 because wisdom will not enter a deceitful soul 64
6 because God is witness of his inmost feelings 64
7 Because the Spirit . . has filled the world 64
10 because a jealous ear hears all things 64
11 because no secret word is without result 64
13 because God did not make death 64
16 because they are fit to belong to his party. 64
2: 2 Because we were born by mere chance 64
2 because the breath in our nostrils is smoke 64
5 because it is sealed up and no one turns back. 64
9 because this is our portion, and this our lot. 64
12 because he is inconvenient to us 64
15 because his . . life is unlike that of others 64
3: 5 because God tested them 64
9 because grace and mercy are upon his elect 64
4: 1 because it is known both by God and by men. 64
19 because he will dash them . . to the ground 64
5:14 Because the hope of the ungodly man is like chaff 64
16 because with his right hand he will cover them 64
6: 4 Because . . you did not rule rightly 64
5 because severe judgment falls 64
7 because he himself made both small and great 64
16 because she goes about seeking those worthy 64
7: 9 because all gold is but a little sand in her sight 64
10 because her radiance never ceases. 64
12 I rejoiced in them all, because wisdom leads them; 64
24 because of her pureness she pervades . . all things 50
8:10 Because of her I shall have glory 50
13 Because of her I shall have immortality 50
10: 3 he perished because in rage he slew his brother. •
4 When the earth was flooded because of him 50
8 For because they passed wisdom by •
21 because wisdom opened the mouth of the dumb 64
11:22 Because the whole world before thee 64
12:19 because thou givest repentance for sins. 64
13: 7 because the things that are seen are beautiful. 64
16 because he knows that it cannot help itself •
14: 3 because thou hast given it a path in the sea 64
8 because he did the work 64
11 because . . they became an abomination 64
21 because men . . bestowed on . . wood the name 64
29 for because they trust in lifeless idols •
30 because they thought wickedly of God 64
30 because in deceit they swore unrighteously •
15: 2 because we know that we are accounted thine. •
11 because he failed to know the one who formed him 64
16: 3 because of the odious creatures sent to them 50
9 because they deserved to be punished 64
18:13 because of their magic arts 50
19:13 they justly suffered because of their wicked acts; •
Sir 1:30 because you did not come in the fear of the Lord 64
7:35 because for such deeds you will be loved. 49
8: 8 because from them you will gain instruction 64
9 because from them you will gain understanding 64
14 because of his standing. 62
16 because blood is as nothing in his sight 64
11: 2 nor loathe a man because of his appearance. 54
14:16 because in Hades one cannot look for luxury. 64
15:11 Do not say, "Because of the Lord I left the right way"; 50
20: 6 is one who keeps silent because he has no answer 49
6 keeps silent because he knows when to speak. •
11 There are losses because of glory 56
22 lose it because of his foolish look. 47
22:26 if some harm should happen to me because of him 50
23: 1 let me not fall because of them! 54
25:24 because of her we all die. 50
26:28 because of a third anger comes over me 59
28:18 not so many as have fallen because of the tongue. 50
29: 7 Because of such wickedness, therefore 69
9 because of his need do not send him away empty. 62
31: 6 Many have come to ruin because of gold 69
33:30 because you have bought him with blood. 64
34:12 have escaped because of these experiences. 69
35: 5 to be done because of the commandment. 69
41: 7 they suffer reproach because of him. 50
44:26 Because of him his messenger finds the way 50
47:12 rose up a wise son who fared amply because of him; 50
Bar 1:17 because we have sinned before the Lord 63
2: 5 because we sinned against the Lord our God 64
19 it is not because of any righteous deeds of our 59
26 because of the wickedness of the house of Israel 50
3:28 so they perished because they had no wisdom 66
4: 6 you were handed over . . because you angered God 50
12 left desolate because of the sins of my children 50
12 because they turned away from the law of God. 51
22 because of the mercy which soon will come to you 59
LJr 1: 2 Because of the sins which you have committed 50
13 because of the dust from the temple 50
27 because . . these gods are made to stand 50
43 because she was not as attractive as herself 64
Aza 1: 5 all this . . because of our sins. 50
14 and are brought low . . because of our sins. 50
Sus 1: 4 because he was the most honored of them all. 50
18 did not see the elders, because they were hidden. 64
41 because they were elders of the people 70
63 because nothing shameful was found in her. 64
Bel 1: 5 Because I do not revere man-made idols 64
9 because he blasphemed against Bel 64
Man 1: 9 because of the multitude of my iniquities. 47
10 so that I am rejected because of my sins 67
1Mc 1:38 Because of them the residents of Jerusalem fled; 50
2:30 because evils pressed heavily upon them. 64
54 Phinehas . . because he was deeply zealous 54
55 because he fulfilled the command 54
56 Caleb, because he testified in the assembly 54
57 David, because he was merciful 54
58 Elijah because of great zeal for the law 54
60 Daniel because of his innocence 54
63 because he has returned to the dust 64
3:29 because of the dissension and disaster 69
46 because Israel formerly had a place of prayer 64
4: 5 because he said, "These men are fleeing from us. 64
5: 3 because they kept lying in wait for Israel 64
54 because not one of them had fallen 64
61 because . . they did not listen to Judas 64
6: 3 he could not, because his plan became known 64
8 because things had not turned out for him 64
9 because deep grief continually gripped him 64
13 I know that it is because of this 69
49 because they had no provisions there 64
53 because it was the seventh year 50

54 because famine had prevailed over the rest 64
9:60 unable to do it, because their plan became known. 64
10:42 because it belongs to the priests 50
43 because he owes money to the king or has any debt *
46 because they remembered the great wrongs 64
47 because he had been the first 64
70 I have become a laughingstock . . because of you 50
11:11 because he coveted his kingdom. 69
14 because the people of that region were in revolt. 64
33 because of the good will they show toward us. 69
13:18 Because Simon did not send him the money 64
22 he did not go because of the snow 50
51 because a great enemy had been crushed 64
14:35 because he had done all these things 50
35 because of the justice . . which he had maintained *
2Mc 2:11 because the sin offering had not been eaten. 50
24 because of the mass of material 50
3: 1 because of the piety of the high priest Onias 50
13 because of the king's commands which he had 50
18 because the holy place was about to . . 50
29 speechless because of the divine intervention 50
4:13 because of the surpassing wickedness of Jason 50
19 because that was inappropriate 50
30 because their cities had been given as a present 50
37 wept because of the moderation and good conduct 50
39 because many . . had already been stolen. *
50 because of the cupidity of those in power 50
5: 9 because of their kinship. 50
17 because of the sins of those who dwelt in the city 50
21 because his mind was elated. 50
6:11 because their piety kept them from defending 50
21 because of their long acquaintance with him 50
25 they should be led astray because of me 50
29 because the words . . were . . sheer madness. 50
30 because I fear him. 50
7: 9 because we have died for his laws. *
11 because of his laws I disdain them 50
16 Because you have authority among men *
18 because of our sins against our own God. *
20 because of her hope in the Lord. 50
32 For we are suffering because of our own sins. 50
8:15 because he had called them 55
25 obliged to return because the hour was late. 68
36 because they followed the laws ordained by him. 50
9: 9 because of his stench 68
10 Because of his intolerable stench 50
10:12 because of the wrong that had been done to them 50
13 because he had abandoned Cyprus 50
35 fired with anger because of the blasphemies 50
11:13 because the mighty God fought on their side *
12: 4 because they wished to live peaceably 70
7 because the city's gates were closed, he withdrew *
21 because of the narrowness of all the approaches. 50
24 because he held the parents of most of them 50
42 because of the sin of those who had fallen. 50
13: 3 because he thought that he would be established *
8 because he had committed many sins 57
17 because the Lord's help protected him. 50
14: 8 first because I am genuinely concerned *
8 second because I have regard also for . . *
17 because of the sudden consternation 50
15:17 because the city and . . temple were in danger. 50
3Mc 1:11 because not even members . . were allowed 50
21 because of what the king was profanely plotting. 59
29 because indeed all at that time preferred death 48
2:10 because you love the house of Israel *
12 because oftentimes . . you helped them 57
13 because of our many and great sins 50
16 because you graciously bestowed your glory 57
3: 4 because they worshiped God *
17 because when we proposed *
18 because of the benevolence which we have toward all 50
21 both because of their alliance with us 50
4: 2 groaned because of the unexpected destruction *
17 because of their innumerable multitude 50
5: 7 because . . they were forcibly confined 50
30 because . . his whole mind had been deranged 50
41 in a tumult because of its expectation 50
6:22 because of the things that he had devised 67
36 because of the deliverance that had come to them 69
7: 4 because of the ill-will 50
17 because of a characteristic of the place 50
4Mc 1:33 because reason is able to rule over appetites 64
34 we abstain because of domination by reason. 50
2: 2 because . . he overcame sexual desire. 64
3:12 because of the king's craving 59
20 because of their observance of the law 50
4: 3 because I am loyal to the king's government *
25 because they had circumcised their sons 64
5: 4 known to many . . because of his philosophy. 50
6: 7 because his body could not endure the agonies 47
7:16 If, therefore, because of piety 50
17 because not every one has prudent reason. 64
20 because of the weakness of their reason. 50
9: 6 because of their religion lived piously 50
7 if you take our lives because of our religion 50
9 because of your bloodthirstiness toward us 50
15 not because I am a murderer *
15 because I protect the divine law. *
10:10 because of our godly training and virtue 50
11 because of your impiety and bloodthirstiness 50
11: 5 Is it because we revere the Creator of all things 64
12 because . . you give us an opportunity *
12: 3 because of their disobedience. 50
12 Because of this 46
15 Then because he too was about to die, he said *
13:26 because . . their brotherly love more fervent 49
15: 4 because of their birthpangs 50
7 because of the many pains she suffered with each 50
8 yet because of the fear of God 50
9 because of the nobility of her sons 50
14 because of religion 50
24 disregarded all these because of faith in God. 50
17: 9 because of the violence of the tyrant 50
18 because of which they now stand 50
20 because of them our enemies did not rule 50
18: 4 Because of them the nation gained peace 50

because כִּי

Gen 2:3, 23; 3:10, 14, 17, 20; 8:21; 11:9; 16:11; 18:20; 19:13; 20:11; 21:13, 31; 22:16; 25:21, 28; 26:7, 9, 20; 27:20, 23; 28:11; 29:15, 32, 33, 34; 30:20; 31:30, 31; 32:32; 33:11²; 34:7, 19; 35:7; 37:3; 39:9; 41:57; 43:18, 32; 45:5; 47:20; 49:4; 50:17, Exd 1:19, 21; 2:10; 9:11; 12:39; 15:23; 18:11, 15; 29:33, 34; 31:14; 34:29; 40:35, Lev 10:13; 11:4, 5, 6, 7; 19:8, 20; 20:3; 21:23; 22:7, 25, Num 6:7, 12; 7:9; 9:13; 11:3, 34; 14:43; 15:25, 26, 31, 34; 19:13, 20; 22:3, 22, 29, 32; 26:62; 27:4; 30:5, 14; 32:11, 19, Deu 2:5, 9, 19; 4:37; 5:5; 7:8; 9:5, 25; 12:20; 13:5, 10; 14:7, 8, 24, 29; 15:2, 10, 16; 16:15; 18:12; 19:6; 22:19, 21, 27; 23:5, 7, 14; 24:1; 27:20; 28:45, 57, 62; 31:18, 29, Jos 5:7; 6:17, 25; 7:12, 15²; 9:18, 24; 10:2², 42; 14:9; 17:1, 6; 19:9; 20:5; 22:31, Jdg 1:19; 2:18; 3:12; 5:23; 6:31, 32; 8:20, 24; 9:18; 10:10; 11:13; 12:4; 14:17; 15:6; 17:13; 18:28; 20:36; 21:15, 22, 1Sm 1:5, 6; 2:1; 3:13; 6:19²; 9:12, 16, 24; 12:10, 22; 13:14; 14:29; 15:24; 16:7; 18:12; 19:4²; 20:18, 34; 21:8; 22:17; 23:15; 25:28; 26:12, 16, 21; 30:6, 13, 2Sm 1:10, 12; 10:3; 12:10, 14; 13:22; 14:15; 16:10; 19:21, 42; 22:8, 20, 1Kg 2:26²; 3:2, 26, 28; 8:11, 35, 64; 11:9; 13:21; 14:4; 17:7; 18:18; 21:2, 6, 29, 2Kg 1:17; 5:1; 8:12, 29; 15:16; 17:7; 24:20, 1Ch 4:9, 14, 41; 5:1, 9, 20, 22; 7:21, 23; 13:11; 15:13²; 19:3; 22:8, 2Ch 5:14; 6:24, 26; 7:2, 7; 11:14; 12:2; 13:18; 14:7; 16:10; 17:3; 21:3, 10; 22:6, 11; 24:16, 20, 24; 25:16, 20; 26:20; 27:6; 28:23; 30:3; 35:14; 36:15, Ezr 3:3, Neh 5:18; 6:12, 18; 8:12, Job 3:10; 6:20; 11:18; 15:25, 27; 20:20; 29:12; 30:11; 31:21, 25², 34; 32:1, 4, 16²; 34:33; 35:15; 39:11, 17, Ps 13:4, 6; 6:8; 8:7, 19; 8:5; 3:21; 7:40; 2:9; 3:3; 8:22; 6:17; 1:9, 14²; 07:30; 09:21; 16:1, 2; 19:74, 78, 131, 139, Prv 1:29; 21:7; 22:22, Ecc 2:17, 21; 5:20; 9:9; 12:3, 5, Isa 2:6; 3:8; 8:6; 14:20; 15:1²; 19:20; 26:3; 28:15; 31:1²; 52:15; 60:5, 9; 65:16, Jer 3:21; 4:17; 5:6; 6:19; 8:10, 14; 9:10, 19²; 10:2; 12:4; 13:17; 14:5, 6; 15:17; 19:15; 22:15; 26:11; 28:16; 29:15; 30:17; 31:15, 19; 39:18; 40:3; 41:18; 46:15, 23; 48:26, 42; 50:24; 51:11, Lam 1:5, 20, Ezk 3:7, 20, 21; 7:23; 18:18; 23:45; 47:12, Dan 9:9, 11, 16, 19, Hos 2:4; 4:6, 10, 13; 5:11; 8:11; 9:17; 10:13; 11:5; 13:16, Jol 1:10, 11, 13, 17, 18, 20, Jon 1:10, Mic 1:12; 2:1, 10; 7:9, 18, Hab 2:8, Zep 1:17; 2:10, Zec 9:5; 10:5, 6, Mal 2:2

because no 1. מִבְּלִי

Exd 14:11 Is it because there are no graves in Egypt 1

beckon 1. *κατανεύω* 2. *νεύω*

Lke 5: 7 they beckoned to their partners 1
Joh 13:24 Simon Peter beckoned to him and said, "Tell us 2

become 1. הוה 2. היה 3. היה לְ 4. הלך 5. לְ 6. הוא (A) 7. היה לְ (A) 8. *γίνομαι* 9. *εἰμί* 10. *εἰς* 11. *ἐμπίπτω* 12. *ἔχω* 13. *καθίστημι* 14. *παραλαμβάνω* 15. *ποῦ* 16. *τρέπω* 17. *φαίνω* 18. *ὡς* 19. facio 20. fio

Gen 2: 7 breath of life; and man became a living being. 2
10 there it divided and became four rivers. 2
24 cleaves to his wife, and they become one flesh. 2
3:22 Behold, the man has become like one of us 2
9:15 the waters shall never again become a flood 3
18:18 seeing that Abraham shall become a great 2
19:26 looked back, and she became a pillar of salt. 2
20:12 of my mother; and she became my wife. 2
21:20 the lad . . became an expert with the bow. 2
24:67 Rebekah, and she became his wife; and he loved her. 2
28: 3 multiply you, that you may become a company 2
32:10 and now I have become two companies. 2
34:15 you will become as we are and every male of you 2
16 we will dwell with you and become one people. 2
22 agree to dwell with us, to become one people 2
37:20 and we shall see what will become of his dreams. 2
39: 2 with Joseph, and he became a successful man; 2
47:20 The land became Pharaoh's; 2
26 the land . . alone did not become Pharaoh's. 2
48:19 my son, I know; he also shall become a people 2
19 and his descendants shall become a multitude 2
49:13 he shall become a haven for ships *
15 and became a slave at forced labor. 2
Exd 2:10 child grew . . and he became her son; 2
4: 3 So he cast it on the ground, and it became a serpent; 2
4 caught it, and it became a rod in his hand– 2
9 water . . will become blood upon the dry ground. 2
7: 9 cast it down . . that it may become a serpent.' 2
10 cast down his rod . . and it became a serpent. 2
12 cast down his rod, and they became serpents. 2
19 waters of Egypt . . that they may become blood; 2
8:16 the dust . . that it may become gnats throughout 2
17 dust of the earth became gnats throughout all 2
9: 9 it shall become fine dust over all the land 2
9 it shall become . . become boils breaking out 2
10 and it became boils breaking out in sores on man 2
24 never been in . . Egypt since it became a nation. 2
15: 2 and he has become my salvation; this is my God 2
22:24 your wives shall become widows 2
23:29 lest the land become desolate and the wild 2
32: 1 we do not know what has become of him. 2
23 we do not know what has become of him.' 2
34:12 lest it become a snare in the midst of you. 3
40: 9 all its furniture; and it shall become holy. 2
Lev 13:24 when . . the raw flesh of the burn becomes a spot 2
Num 5:27 woman shall become an execration among 3
11:20 month, until it . . becomes loathsome to you 3
14: 3 Our wives and our little ones will become a prey; 3
31 your little ones, who you said would become a prey 3
16:40 lest he become as Korah and as his company– 2
19:12 if he does not . . he will not become clean. *
26:10 together with Korah . . they became a warning. 3
Deu 1:39 your little ones, who you said would become a prey 3
7:26 bring an abominable thing . . become accursed like it 2
24: 2 if she goes and becomes another man's wife 3
26: 5 few in number; and there he became a nation, great 3
27: 9 this day you have become the people of the LORD 3
28:37 you shall become a horror, a proverb, and a byword 3
33: 5 Thus the LORD became king in Jesh'urun 2
Jos 7: 5 hearts of the people melted, and became as water. 3
12 they have become a thing for destruction. 3
9:21 they became hewers of wood and drawers of water 2
14:14 Hebron became the inheritance of Caleb 3
16:10 but have become slaves to do forced labor. 3
24:32 it became an inheritance of the descendants 3
Jdg 1:30 among them, and became subject to forced labor. 2
33 and of Beth-anath became subject to forced labor 2
35 them, and they became subject to forced labor. 2
2: 3 they shall become adversaries to you 2
8:27 and it became a snare to Gideon and to his family. 2
11:35 and you have become the cause of great trouble 2
39 it became a custom in Israel . . to lament 2
15:14 the ropes . . became as flax that has caught fire 2
16:13 If you weave . . then I shall become weak, and be 9
17: 5 installed one of his sons, who became his priest. 2
11 the young man became to him like one of his sons. 2
12 the young man became his priest, and was 2
18: 4 he has hired me, and I have become his priest. 2
Rut 1:11 yet sons . . that they may become your husbands? 3
4:13 Bo'az took Ruth and she became his wife; 3
16 Na'omi took the child . . and became his nurse. 3
1Sm 10:12 Therefore it became a proverb, "Is Saul also among 3
14:15 earth quaked; and it became a very great panic. 3
16:21 Saul loved him . . and he became his armor-bearer. 2
22: 2 gathered to him; and he became captain over them. 3
25:37 his heart died within . . and he became as a stone. 2
42 she went after . . David, and became his wife. 3
43 and both of them became his wives. 3
28:16 LORD has turned from you and become your enemy? 2
29: 4 lest in the battle he become an adversary to us. 3
2Sm 2:25 Benjaminites gathered . . and became one band 3
3: 1 the house of Saul became weaker and weaker. 4
5:10 And David became greater and greater 4
7:24 and thou, O LORD, didst become their God. 3
8: 2 And the Moabites became servants to David 3
6 the Syrians became servants to David 3
14 and all the E'domites became David's servants. 3
9:12 all who . . became Mephib'osheth's servants. *
11:27 David sent and brought . . and she became his wife 3
23:19 most . . of the 30, and became their commander; 2
1Kg 1: 4 she became the king's nurse and ministered to him; 2
2:15 kingdom has turned about and become my brother's 2
9: 7 Israel will become a proverb and a byword 2
8 this house will become a heap of ruins; 2
11:24 and became leader of a marauding band 2
12:30 this thing became a sin, for the people went 3
13: 6 hand was restored . . and became as it was before. 2
34 this thing became sin to the house of Jerobo'am 3
2Kg 17: 3 Hoshe'a became his vassal, and paid him tribute. 2
19:26 and have become like plants of the field 2
21:14 they shall become a prey . . to all their enemies 3
22:19 they should become a desolation and a curse 3
24: 1 and Jehoi'akim became his servant three years; 2
1Ch 11: 6 Jo'ab . . went up first, so he became chief. 3
21 renowned of the 30, and became their commander 3
17:22 and thou, O LORD, didst become their God. 3
18: 2 the Mo'abites became servants to David 2
6 the Syrians became servants to David 2
13 and all the E'domites became David's servants. 2
23:11 they became a father's house in one reckoning 3
2Ch 13: 9 becomes a priest of what are no gods. 3
16:12 his disease became severe; *
21: 5 Jeho'ram was 32 . . when he became king *
25:10 And they became very angry with Judah *
26:19 became angry with the priests leprosy broke out *
28:22 distress he became yet more faithless *
32:24 In those days Hezeki'ah became sick *
36:20 became servants to him and to his sons 3
Neh 6: 6 wish to become their king 1
Job 6:21 Such you have now become to me; 2
7:20 Why have I become a burden to thee? 2
15:28 which were destined to become heaps of ruins; *
19:15 I have become an alien in their eyes. 2
30: 9 now I have become their song, I am a byword to them. 2

Ps 31:12 I have become like a broken vessel. 2
37:26 his children become a blessing. •
69: 8 I have become a stranger to my brethren, an alien 2
10 my soul with fasting, it became my reproach. 2
11 I became a byword to them. 2
22 Let their own table before them become a snare; 3
79: 4 We have become a taunt to our neighbors 3
83:10 who became dung for the ground. 2
89:41 he has become the scorn of his neighbors. 2
94:22 the LORD has become my stronghold 3
106:36 served their idols, which became a snare to them. 3
114: 2 Judah became his sanctuary 3
118:14 LORD . . has become my salvation. 3
21 hast answered me and hast become my salvation. 3
22 rejected has become the head of the corner. 3
119:83 For I have become like a wineskin in the smoke 2
Prv 22:26 Be not one of those who . . become surety for debts. •
Isa 1:14 new moons . . they have become a burden to me 3
18 red like crimson, they shall become like wool. 2
21 How the faithful city has become a harlot 3
22 Your silver has become dross 3
31 the strong shall become tow, and his work a spark 3
7:23 every place . . will become briers and thorns. 2
25 will become a place where cattle are let loose 2
8:14 he will become a sanctuary, and a stone of offense 2
10:17 The light of Israel will become a fire 3
12: 2 the LORD GOD . . and he has become my salvation. 3
17: 1 cease to be a city, and will become a heap of ruins. 2
18: 5 and the flower becomes a ripening grape 2
19:17 Judah will become a terror to the Egyptians; 3
22:23 he will become a throne of honor to his father's 3
29:11 this has become to you like the words of a book 3
32:14 hill and the watchtower . . become dens for ever 2
15 and the wilderness becomes a fruitful field 3
34: 9 her land shall become burning pitch. 3
35: 7 the burning sand shall become a pool 3
7 the haunt of jackals shall become a swamp •
7 the grass shall become reeds and rushes. •
37:27 and have become like plants of the field 2
40: 4 the uneven ground shall become level 3
42:22 they have become a prey with none to rescue 3
44:12 he becomes hungry and his strength fails •
15 Then it becomes fuel for a man; 3
49: 5 the LORD, and my God has become my strength– 2
60:22 The least one shall become a clan 2
63: 8 not deal falsely; and he became their Savior. 3
19 We have become like those over whom thou hast 2
64: 6 We have all become like one who is unclean 2
10 Thy holy cities have become a wilderness 2
10 Zion has become a wilderness, 2
11 and all our pleasant places have become ruins 3
65:10 Sharon shall become a pasture for flocks 3
Jer 2:14 Why then has he become a prey? 2
21 have . . turned degenerate and become a wild vine? •
3: 1 she goes from him and becomes another man's wife 2
5:13 The prophets will become wind; 3
7:11 this house . . become a den of robbers in your eyes? 2
34 for the land shall become a waste. 3
11:13 For your gods have become as many as your cities 2
12: 8 My heritage has become to me like a lion 3
15:16 thy words became to me a joy 3
18:21 let their wives become childless and widowed. 2
20: 7 I have become a laughingstock all the day; 2
8 the word of the LORD has become for me a reproach 2
22: 5 that this house shall become a desolation. 2
23:14 all of them have become like Sodom to me 2
25:11 This whole land shall become a ruin and a waste 2
38 for their land has become a waste 2
26:18 Jerusalem shall become a heap of ruins 2
27:17 Why should this city become a desolation? 2
30:16 those who despoil you shall become a spoil 2
42:18 You shall become an execration, a horror, a curse 3
44: 6 they became a waste and a desolation 3
8 that you may be cut off and become a curse 3
12 they shall become an execration, a horror, a curse 3
22 therefore your land has become a desolation 3
46:19 For Memphis shall become a waste, a ruin 2
47: 2 and shall become an overflowing torrent; 2
48: 9 her cities shall become a desolation 2
34 the waters of Nimrim also have become desolate. 2
39 Moab has become a derision and a horror to all 2
49: 2 Rabbah . . it shall become a desolate mound 2
13 says the LORD, that Bozrah shall become a horror 2
17 Edom shall become a horror; 2
32 Their camels shall become booty 2
33 Hazor shall become a haunt of jackals 2
50:23 How Babylon has become a horror among the nations! 2
37 troops in her midst, that they may become women! 2
51:30 strength has failed, they have become women; 2
37 Babylon shall become a heap of ruins 2
41 How Babylon has become a horror among the nations! 2
43 Her cities have become a horror, a land of drought 2
Lam 1: 1 How like a widow has she become, she that was great 2
1 She that was a princess . . has become a vassal. 3
2 her friends . . they have become her enemies. 3
5 Her foes have become the head 3
6 Her princes have become like harts 2
8 sinned . . therefore she became filthy; 3
17 Jerusalem has become a filthy thing among them. 3
2: 5 The Lord has become like an enemy 2
3:14 I have become the laughingstock of all peoples 2
4: 3 but the daughter of my people has become cruel 5
8 their skin has . . become as dry as wood. 2
10 their own children; they became their food 3
5: 3 We have become orphans, fatherless; 2
17 For this our heart has become sick 2
Ezk 12:20 and the land shall become a desolation; 2
16: 8 says the Lord GOD, and you became mine. 2
57 you have become like her an object of reproach •
17: 6 it sprouted and became a low spreading vine 2
6 So it became a vine, and brought forth branches 2
8 and bear fruit, and become a noble vine. 2
23 and bear fruit, and become a noble cedar; 2
19: 3 he became a young lion, and he learned to catch 2
6 He prowled among the lions; he became a young lion 2
11 Its strongest stem became a ruler's scepter; 2
14 a lamentation, and has become a lamentation. 3
22:18 the house of Israel has become dross to me; 3
18 and lead in the furnace, have become dross. 3
19 Because you have all become dross, therefore 3
23: 4 They became mine, and they bore sons 3
10 she became a byword among women 2
24:11 that it may become hot, and its copper may burn •
26: 5 she shall become a spoil to the nations; 3
28: 5 your heart has become proud in your wealth •
34: 5 they became food for all the wild beasts. 3
8 because my sheep have become a prey 3
8 my sheep have become food for all the wild beasts 3
35: 4 cities waste, and you shall become a desolation; 2
36: 2 The ancient heights have become our possession, 3
3 became the possession of the rest of the nations 2
3 you became the talk and evil gossip of the people; •
4 cities, which have become a prey and derision 3
35 desolate has become like the garden of Eden 2
37:17 that they may become one in your hand. 3
44:12 and became a stumbling block of iniquity 2
Dan 2:35 became like the chaff of the summer threshing 6
35 stone . . became a great mountain and filled 7
6: 3 Daniel became distinguished above all 6
9:16 become a byword among all who are round about us. •
Hos 5: 9 E'phraim shall become a desolation 3
10 have become like those who remove the landmark; 2
8:11 they have become to him altars for sinning. 2
9:10 became detestable like the thing they loved. 2
11: 4 and I became to them as one, who eases the yoke 3
Jol 3:19 Egypt shall become a desolation 3
Jon 4: 5 till he should see what would become of the city. 2
Mic 3:12 Jerusalem shall become a heap of ruins 2
7: 1 For I have become as . . the summer fruit 2
Zep 2: 4 and Ash'kelon shall become a desolation; •
7 The seacoast shall become the possession 3
9 Moab shall become like Sodom 2
15 What a desolation she has become 3
Zec 2: 9 they shall become plunder for those who served 2
4: 7 Before Zerub'babel you shall become a plain; •
10: 7 Then E'phraim shall become like a mighty warrior 2
14: 9 the LORD will become king over all the earth; 3
Mat 4: 3 command these stones to become loaves of bread. 8
12:45 the last state of that man becomes worse 8
13:32 and becomes a tree 8
17: 2 and his garments became white as light. 8
18: 3 unless you turn and become like children 8
19: 5 and the two shall become one flesh'? 9
21:42 has become the head of the corner 8
23:15 when he becomes a proselyte 8
24:32 as soon as its branch becomes tender 8
28: 4 the guards trembled and became like dead men. 8
Mrk 1:17 Follow me and I will make you become fishers of men. 8
4:32 becomes the greatest of all shrubs 8
6:14 Jesus' name had become known 8
9: 3 garments became glistening, intensely white 8
10: 8 the two shall become one flesh 9
12:10 has become the head of the corner; 8
13:28 as soon as its branch becomes tender 8
Lke 4: 3 of God, command this stone to become bread. 8
6:16 Judas Iscariot, who became a traitor. 8
9:29 his raiment became dazzling white. 8
11:26 the last state . . becomes worse than the first. 8
30 For as Jonah became a sign to the men of Nin'eveh 8
13:19 it grew and became a tree 8
18:23 when he heard this he became sad 8
20:17 has become the head of the corner'? 8
22:26 the greatest among you become as the youngest 8
23:12 Herod and Pilate became friends with each other 8
Joh 1:12 he gave power to become children of God; 8
14 And the Word became flesh and dwelt among us 8
2: 9 the steward . . tasted the water now become wine 8
4:14 will become in him a spring of water welling up 8
9:27 Do you too want to become his disciples? 8
39 that those who see may become blind. 8
12:36 that you may become sons of light 8
17:23 that they may become perfectly one 9
Act 1:19 it became known to all the inhabitants 8
20 Let his habitation become desolate 8
22 one of these men must become with us a witness 8
4:11 which has become the head of the corner. 8
7:13 Joseph's family became known to Pharaoh. 8
29 and became an exile in the land of Mid'ian 8
40 we do not know what has become of him.' 8
9:42 it became known throughout all Joppa 8
10:10 he became hungry and desired something to eat; 8
12:18 no small stir . . over what had become of Peter. 8
19:17 this became known to all residents of Ephesus 8
23:10 when the dissension became violent 8
26:29 might become such as I am–except for these chains. 8
Rom 2:25 your circumcision becomes uncircumcision. 8
3:27 what becomes of our boasting? It is excluded. 15
4:18 that he should become the father of many nations; 8
7:13 through the commandment might become sinful 8
11: 9 Let their table become a snare and a trap, a pitfall 8
15: 8 Christ became a servant to the circumcised 8
1Co 3:13 each man's work will become manifest 8
18 let him become a fool that he may become wise. 8
18 let him become a fool that he may become wise. 8
4: 8 Already you have become rich! •
9 because we have become a spectacle 8
13 we have become, and are now, as the refuse 8
6:16 becomes one body with her 9
16 as it is written, "The two shall become one flesh. 10
17 united to the Lord becomes one spirit with him. 9
7:23 do not become slaves of men. 8
8: 9 somehow become a stumbling block to the weak. 8
9:20 To the Jews I became as a Jew, in order to win Jews 8
20 to those under the law I became as one under the law •
21 To those outside the law I became as one •
22 To the weak I became weak 8
22 I have become all things to all men 8
13:11 when I became a man, I gave up childish ways. 8
15:45 The first man Adam became a living being 8
45 the last Adam became a life-giving spirit. •
2Co 5:21 in him we might become the righteousness of God. 8
Gal 3:13 having become a curse for us–for it is written 8
4:12 Brethren, I beseech you, become as I am 8
12 I also have become as you are •
15 What has become of the satisfaction you felt? •
16 Have I then become your enemy 8
Eph 4:19 they have become callous •
5:31 the two shall become one flesh. 9
Php 1:13 so that it has become known 8
2: 8 became obedient unto death, even death on a cross 8
Col 1:23 of which I, Paul, became a minister. 8
25 of which I became a minister 8
1Th 1: 6 you became imitators of us and of the Lord 8
7 you became an example to all the believers 8
2: 8 because you had become very dear to us. 8
14 you, brethren, became imitators of the churches 8
1Ti 2:14 was deceived and became a transgressor. 8
Tit 3: 7 become heirs in hope of eternal life. 8
Heb 1: 4 having become as much superior to angels as . . 8
2:17 become a merciful and faithful high priest 8
5: 9 he became the source of eternal salvation 8
11 since you have become dull of hearing. 8
6: 4 have become partakers of the Holy Spirit 8
20 having become a high priest for ever 8
7:15 This becomes even more evident 9
16 who has become a priest 8
21 Those who formerly became priests 8
11: 7 became an heir of the righteousness 8
34 became mighty in war 8
Jas 2: 4 and become judges with evil thoughts? 8
10 whoever . . fails in one point has become guilty 8
11 you have become a transgressor of the law. 8
3: 1 Let not many of you become teachers, my brethren 8
1Pe 2: 7 stone . . has become the head of the corner 8
2Pe 1: 4 and become partakers of the divine nature. 8
2:20 last state has become worse for them than the first 8
Rev 6:12 and the sun became black as sackcloth 8
12 the full moon became like blood 8
8: 9 and a third of the sea became blood 8
11 A third of the waters became wormwood 8
11:15 The kingdom of the world has become the kingdom 8
16: 3 the sea, and it became like the blood of a dead man 8
4 the rivers . . and they became blood. 8
18: 2 It has become a dwelling place of demons 8
1Es 4:26 Many men . . have become slaves because of them. 8
43 in the day when you became king 14
2Es 3:16 and Jacob became a great multitude. 19
22 Thus the disease became permanent 19
5:35 Or why did not my mother's womb become my grave 20
10:28 my end has become corruption 19
11: 3 wings; but they became little, puny wings. 20
14:17 For the weaker the world becomes through old age 20
Tob 1: 9 When I became a man I married Anna 8
3: 6 that I may depart and become dust 8
6:15 she will become your wife 9
Jdt 5:10 there they became a great multitude 8
12:13 become today like one of the . . Assyrians 8
16:23 She became more and more famous 9
AEs 10: 6 The tiny spring which became a river 8
Wis 2:14 He became to us a reproof of our thoughts; 8
4:18 After this they will become dishonored corpses 9
8: 2 I became enamored of her beauty. 8
10:17 became a shelter to them by day 8
14:11 because . . they became an abomination 8
11 and became traps for the souls of men •
21 this became a hidden trap for mankind 8
16:11 become unresponsive to thy kindness. 8

Sir 0: 1 that, by becoming conversant with this also, 8
6: 1 do not become an enemy instead of a friend 8
29 will become for you a strong protection 9
32 if you apply yourself you will become clever. 9
33 if you incline your ear you will become wise. 9
7: 6 Do not seek to become a judge 8
18:33 become a beggar by feasting with borrowed money 8
24:17 blossoms became glorious and abundant fruit. •
31 my canal became a river, and my river became a sea. 8
31 my canal became a river, and my river became a sea. 8
31: 4 when he rests he becomes needy. 8
42:10 become pregnant in her father's house 8
43:19 when it freezes, it becomes pointed thorns. 8
44: 9 they have become as though they had not been born 8
46: 1 He became . . a great savior of God's elect 8
4 did not one day become as long as two? 8
Bel 1:28 The king has become a Jew; he has destroyed Bel 8
1Mc 1: 1 (He had previously become king of Greece.) •
4 they became tributary to him. 8
33 it became their citadel. 8
35 became a great snare. 8
36 It became an ambush against the sanctuary 8
38 she became a dwelling of strangers 8
38 she became strange to her offspring 8
2: 8 Her temple has become like a man without honor; 8
11 no longer free, she has become a slave. 8
53 kept the commandment, and became lord of Egypt. 8
55 Joshua . . became a judge in Israel. 8
6: 8 He took to his bed and became sick from grief 11
10: 6 to become his ally 9
70 I have become a laughingstock and reproach 8
14:17 Simon his brother had become high priest 8
30 and became their high priest 8
15: 9 so that your glory will become manifest 8
16:24 from the time that he became high priest 8
2Mc 1:33 When this matter became known 8
2:22 with great kindness became gracious to them- 8
3:24 became faint with terror. 16
4:16 became their enemies and punished them. 12
21 had become hostile to his government 8
50 having become the chief plotter 13
5:15 guided by Menelaus, who had become a traitor 8
9:17 he also would become a Jew 9
10:14 When Gorgias became governor of the region 8
29 When the battle became fierce 8
12:39 by that time it had become necessary 8
40 it became clear to all 8
14:27 The king became excited 8
3Mc 3:19 they become the only people among all nations 18
29 shall become useless for all time 17
6:34 would be destroyed and become food for birds 9
4Mc 1:11 they became the cause of the downfall of tyranny 13
6:19 become a pattern of impiety to the young 8
19 becoming an example 8
9:24 may become merciful to our nation 8
17:21 they having become, as it were, a ransom 8

become *See also* afraid, angry, anxious, aroused, aware, bright, broad, consolation, corrupt, defiled, desolate, desperate, disciplined, discouraged, drunk, dry, entangled, estrange, estranged, faint, false, fat, father, feeble, few, fool, foul, fresh, fugitive, full, futile, gaunt, great, guilty, hard, holy, hostile, hot, ill, impatient, impoverished, incensed, indignant, infuriated, involved, jealous, king, known, lame, like, manifest, many, mighty, obedient, obsolete, odious, old, pagan, poor, prosperous, proud, quiet, reconciled, rich, rigid, ruler, sick, skilled, sleek, son-in-law, strong, stubborn, subject, surety, sweet, tall, unclean, vain, visible, void, wailings, wanderer, warm, weak, wealthy, weary, wise, worthless.

becoming 1. נָאוֶה 2. decet

Prv 17: 7 Fine speech is not becoming to a fool; 1
2Es 8:49 you have humbled yourself, as is becoming for you 2

becomingly 1. *εὐσχημόνως*

Rom 13:13 conduct ourselves becomingly as in the day 1

bed 1. יָצוּעַ 2. יצע 3. מִטָּה 4. מַצָּע 5. מִשְׁכָּב 6. עֲרוּגָה 7. עֶרֶשׂ 8. מִשְׁכָּב (A) 9. *κλινάριον* 10. *κλίνη* 11. *κλινίδιον* 12. *κοίτη* 13. *στρωμνή* 14. cubile 15. lectus

Gen 47:31 Israel bowed himself upon the head of his bed. 3
48: 2 Israel summoned his strength, and sat up in bed. 3
49: 4 because you went up to your father's bed; 5
33 Jacob . . drew up his feet into the bed 3
Exd 8: 3 frogs . . shall come up . . on your bed 3
21:18 his fist and the man does not die but keeps his bed 5
Lev 15: 4 Every bed on which he who has the discharge lies 5
5 one who touches his bed shall wash his clothes 5
21 whoever touches her bed shall wash his clothes 5
23 the bed or anything upon which she sits 5
24 every bed on which he lies shall be unclean 5
26 Every bed on which she lies 5
26 shall be to her as the bed of her impurity 5
1Sm 19:13 Michal took an image and laid it on the bed 3
15 Bring him up to me in the bed, that I may kill him. 3
16 the image was in the bed, with the pillow 3
28:23 he arose from the earth, and sat upon the bed. 3
2Sm 4: 7 they came . . as he lay on his bed in his bedchamber 3
11 slain a righteous man in his . . house upon his bed 5
13: 5 Lie down on your bed, and pretend to be ill; 5
17:28 brought beds, basins, and earthen vessels, wheat 5
1Kg 1:47 And the king bowed himself upon the bed. 5
17:19 carried him up . . and laid him upon his own bed. 3
21: 4 he lay down on his bed, and turned away his face 3
2Kg 1: 4 not come down from the bed to which you have gone 3
6 not come down from the bed to which you have gone 3
16 not come down from the bed to which you have gone 3
4:10 put there for him a bed, a table, a chair, and a lamp 3
21 she went up and laid him on the bed of the man of God 3
32 Eli'sha . . saw the child lying dead on his bed. 3
2Ch 24:25 conspired against him . . slew him on his bed. 3
Job 7:13 When I say, 'My bed will comfort me 7
33:15 falls upon men, while they slumber on their beds 5
19 Man is also chastened with pain upon his bed 5
Ps 4: 4 commune with your own hearts on your beds 5
6: 6 every night I flood my bed with tears; 3
36: 4 He plots mischief while on his bed; 5
63: 6 I think of thee upon my bed, and meditate on thee 1
132: 3 I will not enter my house or get into my bed; 1
Prv 7:17 perfumed my bed with myrrh, aloes, and cinnamon. 5
22:27 why should your bed be taken from under you? 5
26:14 door turns . . so does a sluggard on his bed. 3
Sng 3: 1 Upon my bed by night I sought him 5
5:13 His cheeks are like beds of spices 6
6: 2 has gone down to his garden, to the beds of spices 6
Isa 14:11 maggots are the bed beneath you 2
28:20 For the bed is too short to stretch oneself on it 4
57: 2 rest in their beds who walk in their uprightness. 5
7 Upon a . . lofty mountain you have set your bed 5
8 for, deserting me, you have uncovered your bed 5
8 you have loved their bed, you have looked 5
Ezk 17: 7 From the bed where it was planted 6
10 wither away on the bed where it grew? 6
23:17 the Babylonians came to her into the bed of love 5
32:25 They have made her a bed among the slain 5
Dan 2:28 Your dream . . as you lay in bed are these 8
29 O king, as you lay in bed came thoughts 8
4: 5 as I lay in bed the fancies and the visions 8
10 visions of my head as I lay in bed were these 8
13 I saw in the visions of my head as I lay in bed 8
7: 1 dream and visions of his head as he lay in his bed. 8
Hos 7:14 but they wail upon their beds; 5
Ams 3:12 the corner of a couch and part of a bed. 7
6: 4 Woe to those who lie upon beds of ivory 3
Mic 2: 1 devise wickedness and work evil upon their beds! 5
Mat 9: 2 a paralytic, lying on his bed 10
6 Rise, take up your bed and go home. 10
Mrk 4:21 under a bushel, or under a bed, and not on a stand? 10
7:30 she went home, and found the child lying in bed 10
Lke 5:18 men were bringing on a bed a man who was paralyzed 10
19 and let him down with his bed through the tiles 11
24 I say to you, rise, take up your bed and go home. 11
8:16 puts it under a bed 10
11: 7 door is now shut, and my children are with me in bed; 12
17:34 in that night there will be two in one bed 10
Act 5:15 laid them on beds and pallets 9
1Es 3: 6 sleep on a gold bed •
2Es 3: 1 I was troubled as I lay on my bed 14
12:26 one of the kings shall die in his bed 15
Tob 8: 4 Tobias got up from the bed and said, "Sister, get up 10
14:11 As he said this he died in his bed 10
Jdt 8: 3 took to his bed and died in Bethulia his city 10
9: 3 thou gavest up . . their bed 13
10:21 Holofernes was resting on his bed 10
13: 1 they went to bed, for they all were weary 12
2 with Holofernes stretched out on his bed 10
4 Then Judith, standing beside his bed, said 10
6 She went up to the post at the end of the bed 10
7 She came close to his bed . . and said 10
9 Then she tumbled his body off the bed 13
15:11 all his silver dishes and his beds and his bowls 10
AEs 14:15 abhor the bed of the uncircumcised 12
Sir 31:19 He does not breathe heavily upon his bed. 12
40: 5 when one rests upon his bed 12
41:22 do not approach her bed 12
48: 6 famous men from their beds; 10
1Mc 6: 8 He took to his bed and became sick from grief 12

bed *See also* go, make, spread, stream.

cucumber bed 1. *σικυήρατον*

LJr 1:70 Like a scarecrow in a cucumber bed 1

marriage bed 1. *κοίτη*

Heb 13: 4 let the marriage bed be undefiled 1

torrent bed 1. נַחַל

Job 6:15 My brethren are treacherous as a torrent-bed 1
22:24 gold of Ophir among the stones of the torrent bed 1

bedchamber 1. חֲדַר מִטּוֹת 2. חֲדַר מִשְׁכָּב 3. *κοιτών*

Exd 8: 3 frogs which shall come up . . into your bedchamber 2
2Sm 4: 7 they came . . as he lay on his bed in his bedchamber 2
2Kg 6:12 the words that you speak in your bedchamber. 2
11: 2 and she put him and his nurse in a bedchamber. 1
2Ch 22:11 she put him and his nurse in a bedchamber. 1
Ecc 10:20 nor in your bedchamber curse the rich; 2
Jdt 13: 3 told her maid to stand outside the bedchamber 3
4 no one . . was left in the bedchamber 3
14:15 he opened it and went into the bedchamber 3
16:19 took for herself from his bedchamber 3

bedeck 1. *χρυσόω*

Rev 17: 4 and bedecked with gold and jewels and pearls 1
18:16 bedecked with gold, with jewels, and with pearls! 1

bedridden 1. *κατάκειμαι ἐπὶ κραβάττου*

Act 9:33 Aene'as, who had been bedridden for eight years 1

bedroom 1. *κοιτών*

1Es 3: 3 Darius the king went to his bedroom 1

bedstead 1. עֶרֶשׂ

Deu 3:11 behold, his bedstead was a bedstead of iron; 1
11 behold, his bedstead was a bedstead of iron; 1

bee 1. דְּבוֹרָה 2. *μέλισσα*

Deu 1:44 Amorites . . chased you as bees do and beat you 1
Jdg 14: 8 there was a swarm of bees in the body of the lion 1
Ps 118:12 surrounded me like bees, they blazed like a fire 1
Isa 7:18 for the bee which is in the land of Assyria. 1
Sir 11: 3 The bee is small among flying creatures 2
4Mc 14:19 since even bees . . defend themselves 2

befall 1. אנה 2. בוא 3. בוא אֶל 4. בוא עַל 5. היה 6. היה לְ 7. מצא 8. מִקְרֶה 9. נגע אֶל 10. קרא 11. קרה 12. *ἀπαντάω* 13. *γίνομαι* 14. *ἐπιπίπτω* 15. *ἔρχομαι* 16. *καταλαμβάνω* 17. *συμβαίνω* 18. *συναντάω* 19. *ὑπαντάω* 20. contingo 21. facio

Gen 41:36 famine which are to befall the land of Egypt 5
42: 4 for he feared that harm might befall him. 10
29 they told him all that had befallen them, saying 11
38 If harm should befall him on the journey 10
44:29 If . . harm befalls him, you will bring down my 11
49: 1 tell you what shall befall you in days to come. 10
Exd 1:10 if war befall us, they join our enemies and fight 10
Lev 10:19 yet such things as these have befallen me 10
Num 20:14 You know all the adversity that has befallen us 7
Deu 31:29 in the days to come evil will befall you 10
Jos 2:23 and they told him all that had befallen them. 7
Jdg 6:13 LORD is with us, why then has all this befallen us? 7
1Sm 2:34 this which shall befall your two sons, Hophni 3
20:26 Something has befallen him; he is not clean 8
1Ch 7:23 Beri'ah, because evil had befallen his house. 5
Est 6:13 Haman told . . everything that had befallen him. 11
9:26 because of . . and of what had befallen them 9
Job 3:25 fear comes upon me, and what I dread befalls me. 2
31: 3 Does not calamity befall the unrighteous •
Ps 91:10 no evil shall befall you 1
Prv 12:21 No ill befalls the righteous 1
15: 6 but trouble befalls the income of the wicked. •
Ecc 2:15 What befalls the fool will befall me also; 11
Isa 47:13 who at the new moons predict what shall befall 4
51:19 These two things have befallen you- 10
Jer 44:23 that this evil has befallen you, as at this day. 10
Lam 5: 1 Remember, O LORD, what has befallen us; 6
Dan 10:14 understand what is to befall your people 11
Ams 3: 6 Does evil befall a city, unless the LORD has done it? 5
Joh 5:14 Sin no more, that nothing worse befall you. 13
18: 4 Jesus, knowing all that was to befall him 15
Act 20:19 which befell me through the plots of the Jews; 17
22 not knowing what shall befall me there; 18
2Ti 3:11 what befell me at Antioch, at Ico'nium 13
2Es 3:10 the same fate befell them: as death came upon Adam 21
10:48 the destruction which befell Jerusalem. 21
12:43 the evils which have befallen us 20
Sir 7: 1 Do no evil, and evil will never befall you. 16
12:17 If calamity befalls you, you will find him there 19
25:19 may a sinner's lot befall her! 14
33: 1 No evil will befall the man who fears the Lord 12
Aza 1:10 shame and disgrace have befallen thy servants 13
2Mc 5:20 the misfortunes that befell the nation 13
11:13 he pondered over the defeat which had befallen him 13

make befall 1. מצא

Job 34:11 according to his ways he will make it befall him. 1

befit 1. נָאוֶה 2. *ἄξιος* 3. *ἀξίως* 4. *παρά* 5. *πρέπω*

Ps 33: 1 O you righteous! Praise befits the upright. 1
93: 5 holiness befits thy house, O LORD, for evermore. 1
Mat 3: 8 Bear fruit that befits repentance 2
Lke 3: 8 Bear fruits that befit repentance 2
Rom 16: 2 receive her in the Lord as befits the saints 3
1Ti 2:10 as befits women who profess religion. 5
Tit 2: 1 as for you, teach what befits sound doctrine. 5
3Jn 1: 6 to send them on . . as befits God's service. 3
1Es 4:46 this befits your greatness 4
Wis 13:15 then he makes for it a niche that befits it 2
3Mc 3:25 sure and shameful death that befits enemies. 5
4:10 they should undergo treatment befitting traitors •

befit holiness 1. *ἱεροπρεπής*

4Mc 11:20 O contest befitting holiness 1

before 1. אַיִן 2. אֶל 3. אֶל מוּל 4. אֶל פָּנִים 5. אֵת 6. אֶתְמוֹל שִׁלְשׁוֹם 7. אֵת פָּנִים 8. בְּ 9. בְּאַף 10. בְּטֶרֶם

11. בְּלֹא 12. בְּעֵינַיִם 13. בִּפְנֵי 14. בָּרִאשֹׁנָה 15. וְ 16. טֶרֶם 17. כְּ
18. לְ 19. לֹא 20. לְאַפַּיִם 21. לְכֹל 22. לְנֶגֶד 23. מֵאֶתְמוֹל שִׁלְשֹׁם
24. מוּל 25. מִטֶּרֶם 26. מִלְּ 27. מִלִּפְנֵי 28. מִן 29. מִנֶּגֶד 30. מֵעִם
31. מִפְּנֵי 32. מִתְּמוֹל שִׁלְשֹׁם 33. נֶגֶד 34. נֹכַח 35. עַד
36. עַד אֲשֶׁר לֹא 37. עַד לֹא 38. עוֹד 39. עַל 40. עַל פְּנֵי 41. עִם
42. פָּנִים 43. קֶדֶם 44. קַדְמָה 45. רִאשָׁה 46. רִאשׁוֹן
47. תְּמוֹל שִׁלְשֹׁם 48. לָקֳבֵל (A) 49. מִן קֳדָם (A) 50. קֳדָם (A)
51. ἅπαξ καὶ δίς 52. ἀπέναντι 53. ἀπό 54. ἀπὸ προσώπου
55. ἄχρι 56. διά 57. εἰς 58. εἰς πρόσωπον 59. ἐκ 60. ἔμπροσθεν
61. ἐν 62. ἔναντι 63. ἐναντίον 64. ἐνώπιον 65. ἐξ ἐναντίας
66. ἐπί 67. ἐχθὲς καὶ τρίτης ἡμέρας 68. ἕως 69. ἕως ἄν
70. ἕως οὗ 71. κατά 72. κατὰ πρόσωπον 73. κατέναντι
74. κατενώπιον 75. μετά 76. μετ᾽ οὐ 77. μέχρις οὗ 78. οὐ
79. πάλαι 80. παρά 81. παρὰ πόδας κεῖμαι 82. πάρειμι
83. παρουσία 84. πλησίον 85. πρίν 86. πρὶν ἄν 87. πρὶν ἤ
88. πρό 89. πρὸ προσώπου 90. πρός 91. πρόσωπον
92. πρότερος 93. προϋπάρχω 94. πρὸ χρόνου 95. πρῶτος
96. ὑπό 97. ab 98. ad 99. ante 100. ante facies 101. antequam
102. apud 103. contra 104. coram 105. facies 106. in 107. olim
108. prius 109. priusquam 110. quando adhuc 111. similiter

Gen 11:28 Haran died before his father Terah in the land 40
19: 4 before they lay down, the men of the city 16
13 the outcry . . has become great before the LORD 42
27 to the place where he had stood before the LORD; 42
20:16 and before every one you are righted. 18
23: 3 Abraham rose up from before his dead 42
18 presence of the Hittites, before all who went 8
24:15 Before he had done speaking, behold, Rebekah 16
45 Before I had done speaking in my heart 16
52 bowed himself to the earth before the LORD. 17
27: 4 that I may bless you before I die. 16
33 I ate it all before you came, and I have blessed 16
30:41 rods in the runnels before the eyes of the flock 18
31: 2 did not regard him with favor as before. 47
5 does not regard me with favor as he did before. 47
35 I cannot rise before you, for the way of women 31
37 Set it here before my kinsmen and your kinsmen 33
32:21 the present passed on before him; 40
33:12 Let us journey on our way, and I will go before you. 33
18 and he camped before the city. 42
37:10 to bow ourselves to the ground before you? 18
18 They saw him afar off, and before he came near 16
41:14 changed his clothes, he came in before Pharaoh. 2
50 Before the year of famine came 10
42: 6 brothers came, and bowed themselves before him 18
24 from them and bound him before their eyes. 18
45: 1 Joseph could not control himself before all 21
28 I will go and see him before I die. 10
47:15 Give us food; why should we die before your eyes? 33
19 Why should we die before your eyes 18
48: 5 in the land of Egypt before I came to you in Egypt 35
49: 8 your father's sons shall bow down before you. 18
Exd 1:19 they . . are delivered before the midwife comes 10
8:26 abominable to the Egyptians before their eyes 18
10: 3 will you refuse to humble yourself before me? 31
12:34 people took their dough before it was leavened 16
14:19 and the pillar of cloud moved from before them 42
25 Egyptians said, "Let us flee from before Israel; 42
18:19 You shall represent the people before God 24
19: 2 there Israel encamped before the mountain. 33
20: 3 You shall have no other gods before me. 40
20 that the fear of him may be before your eyes 39
22: 9 the case of both parties shall come before God; 35
26 restore it to him before the sun goes down; 35
23:15 None shall appear before me empty-handed. 42
17 shall all your males appear before the LORD God. 4
29 I will not drive them out from before you in one 42
30 I will drive them out from before you 42
31 and you shall drive them out before you. 42
27:21 the veil which is before the testimony 39
33:19 I will make all my goodness pass before you 40
34: 3 let no flocks or herds feed before that mountain. 3
6 The LORD passed before him, and proclaimed 40
10 Before all your people I will do marvels 33
11 Behold, I will drive out before you the Amorites 31
20 And none shall appear before me empty. 42
23 appear before the LORD God, the God of Israel. 42
24 For I will cast out nations before you 31
24 when you go up to appear before the LORD your God 42
Lev 3:12 then he shall offer it before the LORD 18
4:15 upon the head of the bull before the LORD 18
5:19 guilt offering he is guilty before the LORD 18
9: 5 brought what Moses commanded before the tent 4
10: 3 before all the people I will be glorified.' 40
4 carry your brethren from before the sanctuary 42
13: 7 he shall appear again before the priest 2
14:36 before the priest goes to examine the disease 16
16: 2 before the mercy seat which is upon the ark 4
18:24 the nations I am casting out before you defiled 31
19:32 You shall rise up before the hoary head 31
20:23 the nation which I am casting out before you 31
Num 10:21 tabernacle was set up before their arrival. 35
35 let them that hate thee flee before thee. 31
11:13 For they weep before me and say, 'Give us meat 39
33 While the meat was yet . . before it was consumed 16
13:30 Caleb quieted the people before Moses, and said 2
20: 8 tell the rock before their eyes to yield 18
10 gathered the assembly together before the rock 4
22:32 because your way is perverse before me; 22
25: 4 hang them in the sun before the LORD 18
27:14 to sanctify me at the waters before their eyes. 18
32:21 he has driven out his enemies from before him 42
33: 8 they set out from before Hahi'roth 42
52 all the inhabitants of the land from before you 42
55 do not drive out the inhabitants . . from before you 42
35:32 may return . . before the death of the high priest. 35
Deu 1:30 just as he did for you in Egypt before your eyes 18
2:12 sons of Esau . . destroyed them from before them 31
21 but the LORD destroyed them before them; 31
22 when he destroyed the Horites before them 31
4:34 LORD . . did for you in Egypt before your eyes? 18
38 driving out before you nations greater 31
5: 7 You shall have no other gods before me. 40
6:19 by thrusting out all your enemies from before you 42
22 LORD showed signs . . before our eyes; 18
7: 1 the LORD . . clears away many nations before you 42
22 LORD . . will clear away these nations before you 31
8:20 nations that the LORD makes to perish before you 42
9: 4 that the LORD is driving them out before you. 42
5 LORD your God is driving them out from before you 42
17 cast them . . and broke them before your eyes. 18
18 Then I lay prostrate before the LORD as before 46
12:29 When the LORD . . cuts off before you the nations 31
30 after they have been destroyed before you 31
16:16 appear before the LORD your God at the place 42
16 shall not appear before the LORD empty-handed; 42
17:12 stands to minister . . before the LORD your God 5
18:12 LORD your God is driving them out before you. 31
13 You shall be blameless before the LORD your God. 41
24:15 hire . . day he earns it, before the sun goes down 19
28:31 Your ox shall be slain before your eyes 18
31 ass . . violently taken away before your face 26
66 your life shall hang in doubt before you; 29
29: 2 LORD did before your eyes in the land of Egypt 18
31: 3 LORD . . will destroy these nations before you 27
11 Israel comes to appear before the LORD your God 7
11 read this law before all Israel in their hearing. 33
21 already forming, before I have brought them 10
32:52 For you shall see the land before you; 29
33:10 they shall put incense before thee 9
27 And he thrust out the enemy before you, and said 31
Jos 2: 8 Before they lay down, she came up to them 16
9 the inhabitants of the land melt away before you. 31
10 LORD dried up the water of the Red Sea before you 31
3: 1 and lodged there before they passed over. 16
4 for you have not passed this way before. 32
10 will . . drive out from before you the Canaanites 31
4: 7 waters of the Jordan were cut off before the ark 31
18 Jordan . . overflowed all its banks, as before. 47
5:13 a man stood before him with his drawn sword 22
8: 5 And when they come out against us, as before 14
6 they will say, 'They are fleeing from us, as before.' 14
11 all . . went up, and drew near before the city 33
33 stood . . before the Levitical priests 33
35 Joshua . . read before all the assembly of Israel 33
9:24 destroy all the inhabitants . . from before you; 42
10: 8 there shall not a man of them stand before you. 13
11 And as they fled before Israel 31
13: 6 drive them out from before the people of Israel; 42
23: 5 The LORD your God will push them back before you 31
9 LORD has driven out before you great . . nations; 31
13 continue to drive out these nations before you; 27
24: 8 and I destroyed them before you. 31
12 the hornet . . which drove them out before you 31
18 and the LORD drove out before us all the peoples 31
Jdg 2: 3 I will not drive them out before you; but they 31
21 I will not henceforth drive out before them any 31
5: 5 The mountains quaked before the LORD, yon Sinai 31
5 mountains quaked . . yon Sinai before the LORD 31
6: 9 I delivered you . . and drove them out before you 31
9:40 Abim'elech chased him, and he fled before him; 31
11:23 the Amorites from before his people Israel; 42
24 that the LORD our God has dispossessed before us 31
33 the Ammonites were subdued before the people 31
14:16 Samson's wife wept before him, and said, "You only 39
17 She wept before him the seven days 39
18 to him on the seventh day before the sun went down 10
16: 3 to the top of the hill that is before Hebron. 40
Rut 2:11 and came to a people that you did not know before. 47
3:14 but arose before one could recognize another; 10
1Sm 2:15 before the fat was burned, the priest's servant 10
18 Samuel was ministering before the LORD 7
4: 7 nothing like this has happened before. 6
9:13 find him, before he goes up to the high place to eat; 10
10:11 all who knew him before saw how he prophesied 23
12: 3 Here I am; testify against me before the LORD 33
3 before the LORD and before his anointed. 33
16 which the LORD will do before your eyes. 18
15:30 yet honor me now before the elders of my people 33
30 yet honor me now before . . and before Israel 33
16: 6 Surely the LORD's anointed is before him. 33
17:23 came up . . and spoke the same words as before. •
30 and the people answered him again as before. 46
18:26 Before the time had expired 19
19: 7 and he was in his presence as before. 6
8 great slaughter . . so that they fled before him. 31
21:13 he changed his behavior before them, and feigned 12
25:23 and fell before David on her face, and bowed 20
31: 1 the men of Israel fled before the Philistines 31
2Sm 2:24 came to the hill of Ammah, which lies before Gi'ah 40
26 How long will it be before you bid your people •
3:28 I and my kingdom are . . guiltless before the LORD 30
6:20 uncovering himself today before the eyes 18
7: 9 and have cut off all your enemies from before you; 42
23 by driving out before his people a nation 31
10:13 battle . . the Syrians; and they fled before him. 31
14 they likewise fled before Abi'shai 31
18 And the Syrians fled before Israel; 31
12:11 and I will take your wives before your eyes 18
12 but I will do this thing before all Israel 33
12 do this . . before all Israel, and before the sun. 33
20 when he asked, they set food before him, and he ate. 18
15: 2 had a suit to come before the king for judgment 2
18 all the 600 . . passed on before the king. 40
18:21 The Cushite bowed before Jo'ab, and ran. 18
28 bowed before the king with his face to the earth 18
19:28 but men doomed to death before my lord the king; 18
21: 6 that we may hang them up before the LORD at Gibeon 18
22:13 Out of the brightness before him . . fire flamed 33
23 For all his ordinances were before me 22
24 I was blameless before him 18
1Kg 1:23 he bowed before the king, with his face 18
7: 6 a porch in front . . and a canopy before them. 40
8: 1 assembled the elders . . before King Solomon 2
5 congregation . . who had assembled before him 39
8 from the holy place before the inner sanctuary; 40
25 a man before me to sit upon the throne of Israel 27
12: 6 the old men, who had stood before Solomon 42
13: 6 hand was restored . . and became as it was before. 14
14:24 the LORD drove out before the people of Israel. 31
20:27 the people of Israel encamped before them 33
21:26 the LORD cast out before the people of Israel.) 31
29 how Ahab has humbled himself before me? 27
29 Because he has humbled himself before me, I will 31
2Kg 1:13 and came and fell on his knees before Eli'jah 33
2: 9 Ask what I shall do for you, before I am taken 10
15 they came . . and bowed to the ground before him. 18
3:24 rose and attacked . . till they fled before them; 31
5:25 He went in, and stood before his master 2
6:32 before the messenger arrived Eli'sha said 10
13:14 Jo'ash . . went down to him, and wept before him 40
16: 3 the LORD drove out before the people of Israel. 31
11 Uri'ah . . made it, before King Ahaz arrived 35
17: 8 the LORD drove out before the people of Israel 31
11 nations . . the LORD carried away before them. 31
20: 4 before Isaiah had . . the word of the LORD came 19
21: 2 nations whom the LORD drove out before . . Israel. 31
9 whom the LORD destroyed before the people 31
22:19 and you humbled yourself before the LORD 31
25: 7 They slew the sons of Zedeki'ah before his eyes 18
1Ch 5:25 peoples . . whom God had destroyed before them. 31
10: 1 men of Israel fled before the Philistines 31
11:19 Far be it from me before my God that I should do 28
16:30 tremble before him, all the earth; 27
33 the trees of the wood sing for joy before the LORD 27
17: 8 have cut off all your enemies from before you; 42
21 in driving out nations before thy people 31
27 that it may continue for ever before thee; 18
19:14 and they fled before him. 31
15 the Ammonites . . likewise fled before Abi'shai 31
2Ch 5: 3 all the men of Israel assembled before the king 2
6 congregation . . who had assembled before him 39
9 from the holy place before the inner sanctuary; 40
6:16 'There shall never fail you a man before me to sit 27
8:14 offices of . . ministry before the priests 33
13:14 behold, the battle was before and behind them; 42
16 The men of Israel fled before Judah 31
19:10 that they may not incure guilt before the LORD 18
20: 7 drive out . . before thy people Israel 27
28: 3 the LORD drove out before the people of Israel. 31
32: 7 Do not be . . dismayed before the king of Assyria 31
33: 2 LORD drove out before the people of Israel. 31
9 LORD destroyed before the people of Israel. 31
12 humbled . . before the God of his fathers. 27
23 he did not humble himself before the LORD 27
34:27 because . . you humbled yourself before God 27
36:12 not humble himself before Jeremiah the prophet 27
Ezr 4:18 letter . . has been plainly read before me. 50
23 letter was read before Rehum and Shim'shai 50
7:19 you shall deliver before the God of Jerusalem. 50
28 before all the king's mighty officers. 18
10: 9 sat in the open square before the house of God •
Neh 4: 5 provoked thee to anger before the builders. 22
13:21 Why do you lodge before the wall? If you do so again 33
Est 5: 9 he neither rose nor trembled before him 28
Job 1: 6 came to present themselves before the LORD 39
2: 1 came to present themselves before the LORD 39
1 among them to present himself before the LORD. 39
4:16 A form was before my eyes; 18
17 Can mortal man be righteous before God? •
17 Can a man be pure before his Maker? 28
9: 2 it is so: but how can a man be just before God? 41
10:18 Would that I had died before any eye had seen me •
21 before I go whence I shall not return 10
15:32 It will be paid in full before his time 11
21: 8 and their offspring before their eyes. 18

22:16 They were snatched away before their time; 19
25: 4 How then can man be righteous before God? 41
26: 6 Sheol is naked before God 33
33:27 he sings before men, and says: 'I sinned 39
34:23 a time for any man to go before God in judgment. 2
35: 2 Do you say, 'It is my right before God,' 28
42:10 the LORD gave Job twice as much as he had before. •
Ps 5: 5 The boastful may not stand before thy eyes; 22
9: 3 they stumbled and perished before thee. 31
19 let the nations be judged before thee! 40
16: 8 I keep the LORD always before me; 22
18:12 Out of the brightness before him there broke 33
22 For all his ordinances were before me 22
23 I was blameless before him, and I kept myself 41
42 I beat them fine as dust before the wind; 40
22:25 my vows I will pay before those who fear him. 33
26: 3 For thy steadfast love is before my eyes 22
36: 1 there is no fear of God before his eyes. 22
37: 7 Be still before the LORD, and wait patiently 18
39:13 I may know gladness, before I depart and be no more! 10
44:15 All day long my disgrace is before me 33
50: 8 your burnt offerings are continually before me. 22
21 rebuke you, and lay the charge before you. 18
51: 3 my transgressions, and my sin is ever before me. 33
54: 3 they do not set God before them. Selah 22
66: 3 thy enemies cringe before thee. 18
68: 1 let those who hate him flee before him! 31
2 as wax melts before fire, let the wicked perish 31
2 as wax melts .. let the wicked perish before God! 31
72:11 May all kings fall down before him 18
78:30 before they had sated their craving †
55 He drove out nations before them; 31
79:10 be known among the nations before our eyes! 18
86:14 they do not set thee before them. 22
88: 1 I cry out in the night before thee. 33
89:23 I will crush his foes before him 31
36 his throne as long as the sun before me. 33
90: 2 Before the mountains were brought forth 10
8 Thou hast set our iniquities before thee 22
96: 9 tremble before him, all the earth! 31
97: 5 The mountains melt like wax before the LORD 27
5 before the LORD, before the Lord of all the earth. 27
7 all gods bow down before him. 18
101: 3 not set before my eyes anything that is base. 22
109:14 iniquity of his .. remembered before the LORD 2
15 Let them be before the LORD continually; 33
119:30 I set thy ordinances before me. •
46 will also speak of thy testimonies before kings 33
67 Before I was afflicted I went astray; 16
147I rise before dawn and cry for help; 8
168for all my ways are before thee. 33
129: 6 like the grass .. which withers before it grows up 44
138: 1 before the gods I sing thy praise; 33
139: 4 Even before a word is on my tongue, lo, O LORD 1
5 Thou dost beset me behind and before 43
Prv 4:25 your gaze be straight before you. 33
5:21 For a man's ways are before the eyes of the LORD 34
8:23 at the first, before the beginning of the earth. 28
25 Before the mountains had been shaped 10
26 before he had made the earth with its fields 37
15:11 Sheol and Abaddon lie open before the LORD 33
18:13 If one gives answer before he hears 10
30: 7 Two things .. deny them not to me before I die 10
30 lion, which .. does not turn back before any; 31
31 he-goat, and a king striding before his people. •
Ecc 1:10 It has been already, in the ages before us. 27
3:14 God .. in order that men should fear before him. 27
6: 8 knows how to conduct himself before the living? 33
7:17 why should you die before your time? 11
8:12 it will be well .. because they fear before him; 27
13 because he does not fear before God. 27
10:11 If the serpent bites before it is charmed 11
12: 1 in the days of .. before the evil days come 36
2 before the sun and the light .. are darkened 36
6 before the silver cord is snapped 36
Sng 6:12 Before I was aware, my fancy set me in a chariot 19
13 look upon the .. as upon a dance before two armies? •
Isa 1:16 remove the evil of your doings from before my eyes 33
2:10 in the dust from before the terror of the LORD 42
19 from before the terror of the LORD 42
21 from before the terror of the LORD 42
7: 2 as the trees of the forest shake before the wind. 31
16 For before the child knows how to refuse the evil 10
16 the land before whose two kings you are in dread 31
8: 4 for before the child knows how to cry 'My father' 10
6 melt in fear before Rezin and the son of Remali'ah; •
13:16 infants .. be dashed in pieces before their eyes; 18
17:14 Before morning, they are no more! 10
19:16 tremble with fear before the hand which the LORD 31
24:23 before his elders he will manifest his glory. 33
28: 4 will be like a first-ripe fig before the summer 10
30: 8 now, go, write it before them on a tablet 5
40:17 All the nations are as nothing before him 33
42: 9 before they spring forth I tell you of them. 10
44: 7 let him declare and set it forth before me. 18
15 makes it a graven image and falls down before it. 18
19 Shall I fall down before a block of wood? 18
47:14 No coal for warming .. no fire to sit before! 33
48: 5 before they came to pass I announced them to you 10
49:16 Behold .. your walls are continually before me. 33
52:10 his holy arm before the eyes of all the nations; 18
59:12 our transgressions are multiplied before thee 33
61:11 praise to spring forth before all the nations. 33
63:12 who divided the waters before them 31
65:24 Before they call I will answer 16
66: 7 Before she was in labor she gave birth; 10
7 before her pain came upon her she was delivered 10
Jer 1: 5 Before I formed you in the womb I knew you 10
5 and before you were born I consecrated you; 10
4:26 all its cities were laid in ruins before the LORD 31
26 before the LORD, before his fierce anger. 31
31 Woe is me! I am fainting before murderers. 18
5:22 says the LORD; Do you not tremble before me? 31
6: 7 sickness and wounds are ever before me. 40
21 I will lay before this people stumbling blocks 2
8: 2 they shall be spread before the sun and the moon 18
12: 1 yet I would plead my case before thee. 5
13:16 Give glory to .. God before he brings darkness 10
16 before your feet stumble on the .. mountains 10
27 How long will it be before you are made clean? 38
16: 9 make to cease from this place, before your eyes 18
17:16 that which came out of my lips was before thy face. 34
29:21 and he shall slay them before your eyes. 18
33: 4 against the siege mounds and before the sword 2
9 and a glory before all the nations of the earth 18
34: 5 fathers, the former kings who were before you 18
38:10 the prophet out of the cistern before he dies. 10
39: 6 the sons of Zedeki'ah at Riblah before his eyes; 18
41: 4 after the murder of Gedali'ah, before any one knew •
47: 1 the Philistines, before Pharaoh smote Gaza. 10
48:43 pit, and snare are before you, O inhabitant of Moab! 39
51:24 I will requite .. Chalde'a before your very eyes 18
52:10 slew the sons of Zedeki'ah before his eyes 18
Lam 2:19 Pour out your heart .. before the presence 34
Ezk 10: 2 And he went in before my eyes. 18
14: 3 and set .. their iniquity before their faces; 34
4 stumbling block of his iniquity before his face 34
7 stumbling block of his iniquity before his face 34
16:57 before your wickedness was uncovered? 10
21: 6 sigh with .. bitter grief before their eyes. 18
32:10 when I brandish my sword before them; 40
36:11 and will do more good to you than ever before. 45
23 I vindicate my holiness before their eyes. 18
37:20 are in your hand before their eyes 18
38:16 I vindicate my holiness before their eyes. 18
42:14 before they go near to that which is 15
Dan 2: 9 lying .. words before me till the times change. 50
24 bring me in before the king 50
25 brought in Daniel before the king in haste 50
31 image .. stood before you, and its appearance 48
3: 3 stood before the image that Nebuchadnez'zar 48
13 Then they brought these men before the king. 50
4: 6 all the wise men .. should be brought before me 50
8 At last Daniel came in before me–he who was named 50
5:13 Then Daniel was brought in before the king. 50
15 brought in before me to read this writing 50
17 Daniel answered before the king, "Let your gifts 50
19 all .. trembled and feared before him; 49
23 vessels of his house have been brought in before 50
6:10 prayed and gave thanks before his God 50
11 petition and supplication before his God. 50
12 said before the king, concerning the interdict 50
13 Then they answered before the king, 50
22 because I was found blameless before him; 50
22 also before you, O king, I have done no wrong. 50
24 before they reached the bottom of the den •
26 men tremble and fear before the God of Daniel 49
7: 7 different from all the beasts that were before 50
8 before which three of the first horns 50
10 stream of fire issued and came forth from before 50
10 10,000 times 10,000 stood before 50
13 Ancient of Days and was presented before him. 50
20 other horn .. before which three of them fell 50
8:15 behold, there stood before me one having 22
9: 2 must pass before the end of the desolations 18
10:16 said to him who stood before me, "O my lord, 22
11:22 Armies shall be utterly swept away before him 27
29 it shall not be this time as it was before. 46
Hos 7: 2 Now their deeds .. they are before my face. 33
Jol 1:16 Is not the food cut off before our eyes 33
2: 6 Before them peoples are in anguish 31
23 the early and the latter rain, as before. 46
Ams 2: 9 Yet I destroyed the Amorite before them 31
4: 3 the breaches, every one straight before her; 33
Mic 1: 4 valleys will be cleft, like wax before the fire 31
6: 1 Arise, plead your case before the mountains 5
6 and bow myself before God on high? 18
Nah 1: 5 The mountains quake before him, the hills melt; 28
5 the earth is laid waste before him 31
Hab 1: 3 Destruction and violence are before me; 22
9 terror of them goes before them. 42
2:20 let all the earth keep silence before him. 31
Zep 1: 7 Be silent before the Lord GOD! 31
2: 2 before you are driven away like the drifting 10
2 before there comes upon you the fierce anger 10
2 before there comes upon you the day of the wrath 10
3:20 when I restore your fortunes before your eyes 18
Hag 1:12 the people feared before the LORD. 31
2:15 Before a stone was placed upon a stone 25
Zec 2:13 Be silent, all flesh, before the LORD; 31
6: 5 after presenting themselves before the LORD 39
14: 4 the Mount of Olives which lies before Jerusalem 40
Mal 2: 9 you despised and abased before all the people 18
3:14 walking as in mourning before the LORD of hosts? 31
Mat 1:18 betrothed to Joseph, before they came together 85
5:12 the prophets who were before you. 88
16 your light so shine before men, that they may see 60
24 leave your gift there before the altar and go; 60
6: 1 Beware of practicing your piety before men 60
2 when you give alms, sound no trumpet before you 60
8 Father knows what you need before you ask him. 88
7: 6 and do not throw your pearls before swine 60
8: 2 behold, a leper came to him and knelt before him •
29 Have you come here to torment us before the time? 88
9:18 behold, a ruler came in and knelt before him •
10:18 you will be dragged before governors and kings 66
18 to bear testimony before them and the Gentiles. •
23 before the Son of man comes. 68
32 So every one who acknowledges me before men 60
32 I also will acknowledge before my Father 60
33 whoever denies me before men, I also will deny 60
33 before my Father who is in heaven. 60
11:10 'Behold, I send my messenger before thy face 88
10 who shall prepare thy way before thee.' 60
14: 6 daughter of Hero'di-as danced before the company 61
15:25 she came and knelt before him, saying •
16:28 before they see the Son of man coming 69
17: 2 he was transfigured before them 60
14 a man came up to him and kneeling before him said •
20:20 kneeling before him she asked him •
24:38 For as in those days before the flood 88
25:32 Before him will be gathered all the nations 60
26:34 this very night, before the cock crows 85
70 he denied it before them all, saying 60
75 Before the cock crows, you will deny me 85
27:11 Now Jesus stood before the governor 60
24 washed his hands before the crowd, saying 52
27 they gathered the whole battalion before him. 66
29 kneeling before him they mocked him, saying 60
62 the Pharisees gathered before Pilate 90
Mrk 1: 2 Behold, I send my messenger before thy face 88
2:12 took up the pallet and went out before them all 60
9: 1 before they see that the kingdom of God has come 69
2 he was transfigured before them 60
10:17 a man ran up and knelt before him, and asked him •
13: 9 stand before governors and kings for my sake 66
9 to bear testimony before them. •
30 before all these things take place. 77
14: 1 It was now two days before the Passover 75
30 this very night, before the cock crows twice 87
72 Before the cock crows twice 85
Lke 1: 6 they were both righteous before God 63
8 Now while he was serving as priest before God 62
15 for he will be great before the Lord 64
17 he will go before him in the spirit 64
75 in holiness and righteousness before him 64
76 you will go before the Lord to prepare his ways 64
2:21 before he was conceived in the womb. 88
26 before he had seen the Lord's Christ. 86
5:18 they sought to bring him in and lay him before Jesus; 64
19 through the tiles into the midst before Jesus. 60
25 immediately he rose before them 64
7:27 Behold, I send my messenger before thy face 88
27 who shall prepare thy way before thee.' 60
9:27 before they see the kingdom of God. 69
11:38 he did not first wash before dinner. 88
12: 6 not one of them is forgotten before God. 64
8 every one who acknowledges me before men 60
8 also will acknowledge before the angels of God; 60
9 he who denies me before men 64
9 will be denied before the angels of God. 64
11 when they bring you before the synagogues 66
58 you go with your accuser before the magistrate 66
14: 2 behold, there was a man before him who had dropsy. 60
15:10 there is joy before the angels of God 64
18 I have sinned against heaven and before you; 64
21 I have sinned against heaven and before you 64
16:15 You are those who justify yourselves before men 64
19:27 bring them here and slay them before me.' 60
21:12 before all this they will lay their hands on you 88
12 you will be brought before kings and governors 66
36 to stand before the Son of man. 60
22:15 to eat this passover with you before I suffer; 88
61 Before the cock crows today, you will deny me 85
23: 1 brought him before Pilate. 66
12 before this they had been at enmity 93
14 after examining him before you 64
24:19 a prophet mighty in deed and word before God 63
43 he took it and ate before them. 64
Joh 1:15 'He who comes after me ranks before me 60
15 ranks before me, for he was before me.'") 95
30 'After me comes a man who ranks before me 60
30 a man who ranks before me, for he was before me.' 95
48 Jesus answered him, "Before Philip called you 88
3:28 I am not the Christ, but I have been sent before him. 60
4:49 Sir, come down before my child dies. 85
5: 7 while I am going another steps down before me. 88

6:62 the Son of man ascending where he was before? 92
7:50 Nicode'mus, who had gone to him before 92
8:58 before Abraham was, I am. 85
9: 8 those who had seen him before as a beggar, said 92
10: 4 he goes before them, and the sheep follow him 60
8 All who came before me are thieves and robbers; 88
11:55 many went up . . before the Passover 88
12: 1 Six days before the Passover 88
37 Though he had done so many signs before them 60
13: 1 Now before the feast of the Passover 88
19 I tell you this now, before it takes place 88
14:29 now I have told you before it takes place 85
15:18 know that it has hated me before it hated you. 95
17: 5 glory which I had . . before the world was made. 88
24 given me . . before the foundation of the world. 88
Act 1: 5 before many days you shall be baptized 75
2:20 before the day of the Lord comes 85
25 I saw the Lord always before me 64
4:10 by him this man is standing before you well. 64
5:27 they set them before the council 61
36 before these days Theu'das arose 88
6: 6 These they set before the apostles 64
12 seized him and brought him before the council 57
7: 2 in Mesopota'mia, before he lived in Haran 87
10 favor and wisdom before Pharaoh, king of Egypt 63
20 Moses . . was beautiful before God •
45 which God thrust out before our fathers 54
8:21 your heart is not right before God. 62
32 As . . a lamb before its shearer is dumb 63
9:15 to carry my name before the Gentiles and kings 64
21 to bring them bound before the chief priests. 66
10: 4 have ascended as a memorial before God. 60
17 stood before the gate 66
30 behold, a man stood before me in bright apparel 64
31 your alms have been remembered before God. 64
12: 6 sentries before the door 88
13:24 Before his coming John had preached 89
16:19 dragged them . . before the rulers; 66
17: 6 before the city authorities, crying 66
18:12 brought him before the tribunal 66
19: 9 speaking evil of the Way before the congregation 64
22: 1 hear the defense which I now make before you. 90
30 he brought Paul down and set him before them. 57
23: 1 I have lived before God in all good conscience •
15 we are ready to kill him before he comes near. 88
30 to state before you what they have against him. 66
33 they presented Paul also before him. •
24: 1 They laid before the governor their case •
19 they ought to be here before you 66
20 when I stood before the council 66
21 I am on trial before you this day.' 66
25: 9 and there be tried on these charges before me? 66
10 Paul said, "I am standing before Caesar's tribunal 66
16 before the accused met the accusers face to face 87
26 Therefore I have brought him before you 66
26 especially before you, King Agrippa 66
26: 2 I think myself fortunate that it is before you 66
Rom 2:13 hearers of the law who are righteous before God 80
3:18 There is no fear of God before their eyes. 52
4: 2 something to boast about, but not before God. 90
5:13 sin indeed was in the world before the law 55
14: 4 It is before his own master that he stands •
16: 7 and they were in Christ before me. 88
1Co 2: 7 which God decreed before the ages 88
4: 5 do not pronounce judgment before the time 88
5 before the time, before the Lord comes 69
6: 1 does he dare go to law before the unrighteous 66
4 why do you lay them before those •
6 that before unbelievers? 66
2Co 5:10 For we must all appear before the judgment seat 60
7:14 so our boasting before Titus has proved true. 66
8:24 So give proof, before the churches, of your love 58
9: 5 to go on to you before me •
10: 7 Look at what is before your eyes 71
12:19 we have been defending ourselves before you 73
21 my God may humble me before you 90
Gal 1:15 when he who had set me apart before I was born 59
17 to those who were apostles before me 88
20 In what I am writing to you, before God, I do not lie!) 64
2: 2 privately before those who were of repute •
12 For before certain men came from James 88
14 I said to Cephas before them all 60
3: 1 before whose eyes 71
11 no man is justified before God by the law 80
23 Now before faith came 88
5:21 I warn you, as I warned you before •
Eph 1: 4 chose us in him before the foundation of the world 88
4 that we should be holy and blameless before him. 74
3:14 For this reason I bow my knees before the Father 90
Col 1:17 He is before all things 88
22 blameless and irreproachable before him 74
1Th 1: 3 remembering before our God and Father your work 60
2:19 crown of boasting before our Lord Jesus 60
3: 9 which we feel for your sake before our God 60
13 unblamable in holiness before our God and Father 60
1Ti 6:13 in his testimony before Pontius Pilate 66
2Ti 2: 2 have heard from me before many witnesses 56
14 charge them before the Lord 64
4:21 Do your best to come before winter 88
Heb 4:13 before him no creature is hidden 64
11: 5 Now before he was taken 88
Jas 1:27 pure and undefiled before God and the Father 80
4:10 Humble yourselves before the Lord 64
1Pe 1:20 destined before the foundation of the world 88
2Pe 2:11 a reviling judgment upon them before the Lord 80
1Jn 3:19 and reassure our hearts before him 60
21 we have confidence before God; 90
3Jn 1: 6 testified to your love before the church. 64
Jde 1:25 before all time and now and for ever. Amen. 88
Rev 1: 4 from the seven spirits who are before his throne 64
2:14 put a stumbling block before the sons of Israel 64
3: 5 I will confess his name before my Father 64
5 I will confess his name . . before his angels. 64
8 Behold, I have set before you an open door 64
9 make them come and bow down before your feet 64
4: 5 before the throne burn seven torches of fire 64
6 before the throne there is as it were a sea 64
10 the 24 elders fall down before him 64
10 they cast their crowns before the throne, singing 64
5: 8 the 24 elders fell down before the Lamb 64
6:10 how long before thou wilt judge and avenge 78
17 wrath has come, and who can stand before it? •
7: 9 standing before the throne and before the Lamb 64
9 standing before the throne and before the Lamb 64
11 they fell on their faces before the throne 64
15 Therefore are they before the throne of God 64
8: 2 Then I saw the seven angels who stand before God 64
3 upon the golden altar before the throne; 64
4 rose . . from the hand of the angel before God. 64
9:13 the four horns of the golden altar before God 64
11: 4 two lampstands which stand before the Lord 64
16 the 24 elders who sit on their thrones before God 64
12: 4 And the dragon stood before the woman 64
10 who accuses them day and night before our God. 64
13: 8 written before the foundation of the world 53
14: 3 and they sing a new song before the throne 64
3 and before the four living creatures 64
3 before the throne . . and before the elders. •
20:12 dead, great and small, standing before the throne 64
1Es 1: 5 minister before your brethren 60
11 before the people 60
3:22 before long they draw their swords. 76
5: 6 who spoke wise words before Darius 66
47 in the square before the first gate •
7:14 rejoicing before the Lord 62
8: 4 he found favor before the king 63
50 I proclaimed a fast . . before our Lord 62
74 I am ashamed and confounded before thy face. 71
90 Behold, we are now before thee in our iniquities; 64
91 lying upon the ground before the temple 60
9: 6 sat in the open square before the temple •
38 the open square before the east gate of the temple; •
41 in the open square before the gate of the temple 88
2Es 1:11 I have destroyed all nations before them 105
21 the Perizzites, and the Philistines before you. 105
2: 3 because you have sinned before the Lord God 104
3: 6 right hand had planted before the earth appeared. 101
8 did ungodly things before thee and scorned thee 104
13 when they were committing iniquity before thee 104
4: 3 and to put before you three problems. 104
14 that it may recede before us 104
48 and behold, a flaming furnace passed by before me 104
49 after this a cloud full of water passed before me 104
5:41 what will those do who were before us 99
50 let me speak before thee 104
52 not like those whom you bore before 99
54 are smaller . . than those who were before you 99
6: 1 before the portals of the world were in place 101
1 and before the assembled winds blew 101
2 before the rumblings of thunder sounded 101
2 and before the flashes of lightning shone 101
2 and before the foundations of paradise were laid 101
3 before the beautiful flowers were seen 101
3 before the powers of movement were established 101
3 before the innumerable hosts of angels 101
4 before the heights of the air were lifted up 101
4 before the measures of the firmaments 101
4 before the footstool of Zion was established 101
5 before the present years were reckoned 101
5 before the imaginations of those who now sin 101
5 before those who stored up treasures of faith 101
20 the books shall be opened before the firmament 100
32 has surely been heard before the Most High 102
35 I wept again and fasted seven days as before 111
42 and cultivated and be of service before thee. 104
53 to bring forth before thee cattle, beasts 104
55 All this I have spoken before thee, O Lord 104
7:87 before whom they sinned while they were alive 104
87 and before whom they are to be judged 104
8: 6 grant to thy servant that we may pray before thee 104
17 Therefore I will pray before thee for myself 104
19 and I will speak before thee. 104
19 before he was taken up. He said 109
42 If I have found favor before thee, let me speak. 104
48 you will be praiseworthy before the Most High 104
9:15 I said before, and I say now, and will say it again 107
18 before the world was made for them to dwell 101
27 my heart was troubled again as it was before. 99
28 I began to speak before the Most High, and said 104
10:34 do not forsake me, lest I die before my time. ‡
45 before any offering was offered in it. 110
57 you have been called before the Most High 102
11:16 I announce this to you before you disappear. 101
36 Then I heard a voice saying to me, "Look before you 103
43 your insolence has come up before the Most High 98
12: 7 if I have been accounted righteous before thee 102
7 if my prayer has indeed come up before thy face 99
13 all the kingdoms that have been before it. 99
24 all who were before them 99
32 and will cast up before them 104
33 he will set them living before his judgment seat 106
13:32 and the signs occur which I showed you before 99
14:22 If then I have found favor before thee 104
15:11 will smite Egypt with plagues, as before 108
16:12 and before the glory of his power. 97
53 I have not sinned before God and his glory. 104
65 when your sins come out before men 104
66 will you hide your sins before God and his angels? 104
Tob 1:21 before two of Sennacherib's sons killed him 70
2: 4 before I tasted anything 85
3: 3 those which my fathers committed before thee. 64
5 we did not walk in truth before thee. 64
8 before he had been with her as his wife 87
4: 2 explain to him about the money before I die? 85
5:17 as he goes in and out before us? 64
6: 7 make a smoke from these before the man or woman 64
14 if I go in I will die as those before me did 90
8:20 before the days of the feast were over 87
10:11 will prosper you, my children, before I die. 88
12 that I may rejoice before the Lord 64
11:17 Tobit gave thanks before them 64
12:12 I brought a reminder . . before the Holy One 64
13: 3 Acknowledge him before the nations 64
6 to do what is true before him 64
6 Turn back, you sinners, and do right before him 64
14:15 before he died 87
15 Before his death he rejoiced over Nineveh. 88
Jdt 3: 2 Behold, we . . lie prostrate before you 64
3 our sheepfolds with their tents, lie before you 89
4:11 prostrated themselves before the temple 72
11 and spread out their sackcloth before the Lord. 72
13 in Jerusalem before the sanctuary of the Lord 72
14 all the priests who stood before the Lord 64
5:13 Then God dried up the Red Sea before them 60
16 they drove out before them the Canaanites 91
21 we shall be put to shame before the whole world. 63
6:14 placed him before the magistrates of their city 66
7:14 before the sword reaches them 85
23 said before all the elders 63
25 to strew us on the ground before them with thirst 63
27 witness the death of our babes before our eyes 61
8:19 suffered a great catastrophe before our 64
35 may the Lord God go before you 60
10:16 when you stand before him 63
11:22 God has done well to send you before the people 60
12: 4 before the Lord carries out . . what he has determined 69
15 spread . . before Holofernes the soft fleeces 73
19 drank before him what her maid had prepared. 73
13:20 walking in the straight path before our God 64
14: 3 they will flee before you 54
5 before you do all this 88
16: 1 began this thanksgiving before all Israel 61
12 they perished before the army of my Lord. 59
20 before the sanctuary for three months 72
24 Before she died she distributed her property 88
AEs 10:11 before God and among all the nations. 64
13 with an assembly and joy and gladness before God 64
13:18 their death was before their eyes. 61
14: 6 now we have sinned before thee 64
13 Put eloquent speech in my mouth before the lion 64
15: 6 she stood before the king 64
16: 9 judging what comes before our eyes 96
Wis 2: 8 before they wither. 87
5:14 it is dispersed like smoke before the wind 96
7: 9 silver will be accounted as clay before her. 63
10: 5 and preserved him blameless before God •
11:22 Because the whole world before thee 63
12:12 who will come before thee to plead as an advocate •
27 him whom they had before refused to know. 79
14:20 the one whom shortly before they had honored 88
15: 8 this man who was made of earth a short time before 88
Sir 1: 4 Wisdom was created before all things 95
2:17 will humble themselves before him. 64
7: 5 not assert your righteousness before the Lord 62
5 nor display your wisdom before the king. 80
10: 7 Arrogance is hateful before the Lord 62
7 hateful before the Lord and before men •
11: 7 Do not find fault before you investigate 85
8 Do not answer before you have heard 85
28 Call no one happy before his death 88
14:13 Do good to a friend before you die 85
15:17 Before a man are life and death 62
17:15 Their ways are always before him 63
19 All their works are as the sun before him 63
20 all their sins are before the Lord. 62
18:19 Before you speak, learn 87
19 before you fall ill, take care of your health. 88

20 Before judgment, examine yourself 88
21 Before falling ill, humble yourself 85
23 Before making a vow, prepare yourself 85
26 all things move swiftly before the Lord. 62
19:17 Question your neighbor before you threaten him; 87
21:22 stands respectfully before it. 54
23: 3 then I will not fall before my adversaries 62
20 Before the universe was created 87
24 She herself will be brought before the assembly 57
24:10 In the holy tabernacle I ministered before him 64
27: 7 Do not praise a man before you hear him reason 88
29 pain will consume them before their death. 88
28:26 lest you fall before him who lies in wait. 73
31:18 do not reach out your hand before they do. 95
32:10 Lightning speeds before the thunder 88
34:20 Like one who kills a son before his father's eyes 62
35: 6 its pleasing odor rises before the Most High. 62
36: 4 us thou hast been sanctified before them 64
4 so in them be thou magnified before us; 64
38:15 He who sins before his Maker 62
39: 4 serve among great men and appear before rulers; 62
5 will make supplication before the Most High 62
19 The works of all flesh are before him 64
40:16 will be plucked up before any grass. 90
41:17 before your father or mother 53
17 Be ashamed . . of a lie, before a prince or a ruler; 53
18 of a transgression, before a judge or magistrate; 53
18 of iniquity, before a congregation or the people; 53
18 of unjust dealing, before your partner or friend; 53
19 Be ashamed before the truth of God 53
20 of silence, before those who greet you 53
22 abusive words, before friends 53
42: 8 will be approved before all men. 62
11 put you to shame before the great multitude. 61
45:13 Before his time 88
46: 3 Who before him ever stood so firm? 95
19 Before the time of his eternal sleep 88
19 Samuel called men to witness before the Lord 62
47: 9 He placed singers before the altar 73
48:10 calm the wrath of God before it breaks out in fury 88
12 all his days he did not tremble before any ruler 96
25 the hidden things before they came to pass. 87
50:13 before the whole congregation of Israel. 62
16 heard for remembrance before the Most High. 62
19 in prayer before him who is merciful 73
51: 2 Before those who stood by thou wast my helper 62
13 before I went on my travels 87
14 Before the temple I asked for her 62
30 Do your work before the appointed time 88
Bar 1: 5 they wept, and fasted, and prayed before the Lord; 63
17 because we have sinned before the Lord 62
18 statutes of the Lord which he set before us. 91
2:10 statutes of the Lord which he set before us. 72
19 we bring before thee our prayer for mercy 91
33 their fathers, who sinned before the Lord. 62
3: 2 have mercy, for we have sinned before thee. 63
4 sons of those who sinned before thee, who did not 63
7 iniquity of our fathers who sinned before thee. 63
LJr 1: 2 the sins which you have committed before God 63
5 you see the multitude before and behind them 60
27 placed before them just as before the dead. *
32 They howl and shout before their gods as some do 63
Aza 1:15 to make an offering before thee or to find mercy. 63
Sus 1:15 she went in as before with only two maids 67
29 They said before the people, "Send for Susanna 60
42 who art aware of all things before they come to be 85
Man 1: 4 all things shudder, and tremble before thy power 54
1Mc 1: 3 When the earth became quiet before him 64
18 Ptolemy turned and fled before him 54
3:22 He himself will crush them before us 89
23 they were crushed before him. 64
30 such funds as he had before for his expenses 51
4:10 crush this army before us today. 72
17 there is a battle before us; 65
60 and trampling them down as they had done before. 92
5: 1 the sanctuary dedicated as it was before 92
7 they were crushed before him 89
21 the Gentiles were crushed before him. 54
34 they fled before him 54
43 All the Gentiles were defeated before him 89
44 they could stand before Judas no longer. 72
52 into the large plain before Beth-shan. 72
54 before they returned in safety. 68
55 Simon . . was in Galilee before Ptolemais 72
6: 6 but had turned and fled before the Jews 54
7 surrounded . . with high walls as before 92
45 they parted before him on both sides. 53
51 he encamped before the sanctuary for many days. 66
59 let them live by their laws as they did before 92
7:12 a group of scribes appeared in a body before Alcimus 90
36 the priests went in and stood before the altar 72
42 So also crush this army before us today 64
9:44 today things are not as they were before. 67
10: 4 before he makes peace with Alexander against us 87
34 the three days before a feast 88
72 Men will tell you that you cannot stand before us 72
75 He encamped before Joppa 66
11:38 the land was quiet before him 64
52 the land was quiet before him. 64

65 Simon encamped before Beth-zur 66
12:24 with a larger force than before 92
14:19 read before the assembly in Jerusalem. 64
15: 5 the kings before me have granted you 88
2Mc 3:15 prostrated themselves before the altar 88
30 which a little while before was full of fear 92
4:44 three men . . presented the case before him. 66
47 if they had pleaded even before Scythians. 66
5: 8 Accused before Aretas the ruler of the Arabs 90
6:29 a little before had acted . . with good will 92
8:14 before he ever met them 85
17 keeping before their eyes the lawless outrage 88
26 For it was the day before the sabbath 88
10: 6 not long before, during the feast of booths 94
13 As a result he was accused before Eupator 90
24 Timothy, who had been defeated by the Jews before 92
26 Falling upon the steps before the altar 52
12:27 young men took their stand before the walls 88
13:13 before the king's army could enter Judea 85
14:14 the Gentiles . . who had fled before Judas *
15:21 perceiving the hosts that were before him 83
23 to carry terror and trembling before us. 60
31 stationed the priests before the altar 88
36 Syrian language–the day before Mordecai's day. 88
3Mc 1:24 the crowd, as before, was engaged in prayer 60
4: 4 the common object of pity before their eyes 88
8 seeing death immediately before them. 81
14 the hard labor . . briefly mentioned before 60
5:50 help which they had received before from heaven 60
4Mc 4:12 he would praise . . before all people. *
5: 4 one man . . was brought before the king 84
6 Before I begin to torture you, old man 85
8: 3 were brought before him 82
9:27 Before torturing him, they inquired 85
12: 4 be miserably tortured and die before your time 88
13: 3 by reason, which is praised before God 80
15 the danger of eternal torment lying before those *

before לִפְנֵי

Gen 7:1; 10:9^{2}; 13:9, 10; 17:1; 18:8, 22; 20:15; 23:12; 24:7, 33, 40, 51; 27:7^{2}, 10; 29:26; 30:30; 32:3, 16, 17, 20; 33:3, 14^{2}; 36:31; 40:9; 41:43; 43:9, 14, 15, 33; 44:14; 45:5, 7; 46:28^{2}; 47:6, 7; 48:15, 20; 50:16, 18, Exd 4:21; 7:9, 10; 9:10, 11, 13; 10:14; 11:10; 13:21, 22; 14:19; 16:9, 33, 34; 17:5, 6; 18:12; 19:7; 21:1; 23:20, 23, 27, 28^{2}; 25:30; 27:21; 28:12, 29, 30^{2}, 35, 38; 29:10, 11, 23, 24, 25, 26, 42; 30:6^{2}, 8, 16, 36; 32:1, 5, 23, 34; 33:2, 19; 34:34; 40:5, 6, 23, 25, 26, Lev 1:3, 5, 11; 3:1, 7, 8, 13; 4:4^{2}, 6, 7, 14, 15, 17, 18, 24; 6:7, 14, 25; 7:30; 8:26, 27, 29; 9:2, 4, 5, 21, 24; 10:1, 2, 15, 17, 19; 12:7; 14:11, 12, 16, 18, 23, 24, 27, 29, 31; 15:14, 15, 30; 16:1, 7, 10, 12, 13, 14, 15, 18, 30; 17:4; 18:27, 28, 30; 19:14, 22; 23:11, 20, 28, 40; 24:3, 4, 8; 26:7, 8, 17, 37; 27:8, 11, Num 3:4^{2}, 6, 7, 38^{2}; 5:16, 18, 25, 30; 6:16, 20; 7:3^{2}, 10; 8:9, 10, 11, 21; 9:6; 10:9, 10, 33; 11:20; 13:22; 14:5, 14, 37, 42, 43; 15:15, 25, 28; 16:2, 7, 9, 16, 17, 38, 40; 17:4, 7, 9, 10; 18:2, 19; 19:3; 20:3, 9; 22:33; 26:61; 27:2^{3}, 5, 17^{2}, 19, 21^{2}, 22; 31:50, 54; 32:4, 17, 20, 21, 22^{2}, 27, 29^{2}, 32; 33:7, 47; 35:12; 36:1, Deu 1:8, 21, 22, 30, 33, 38, 42, 45; 3:18; 4:8, 10, 32, 44; 6:25; 9:2, 3^{2}, 4, 18, 25; 10:8; 11:23, 26, 32; 12:7, 12, 18^{2}; 14:23, 26; 15:20; 16:11; 18:7; 19:17^{2}; 22:17; 23:14; 24:4, 13; 26:4, 5, 10^{2}, 13; 27:7; 28:7^{2}, 25^{2}; 29:10, 15; 30:1, 15, 19; 31:3, 8; 33:1, Jos 1:5, 14; 3:6^{2}, 11, 14; 4:5, 11, 12, 13; 6:4, 6, 7, 8, 9, 13^{2}, 26; 7:4, 5, 6, 8, 12^{2}, 13, 23; 8:5, 10, 15; 10:10, 14; 17:4; 18:1, 6, 8, 10; 19:51; 20:6, 9; 22:29; 24:1, 12, Jdg 3:2; 4:14, 15, 23; 6:18; 8:28; 11:11; 16:25; 20:23, 26^{2}, 28, 32, 35, 39, 42; 21:2, 1Sm 1:12, 15, 19; 2:28, 30, 35; 4:3, 17; 5:3, 4; 6:20; 7:6, 10; 8:11, 20; 9:15, 19, 24^{2}, 27; 10:5, 8, 19, 25; 11:15^{2}; 12:2^{2}, 7; 14:13; 15:33; 16:8, 10, 16; 17:7, 31, 57; 18:13, 16; 19:24; 20:1^{2}; 21:6, 7; 23:18; 25:19; 26:19; 28:22, 25; 30:20, 2Sm 2:14, 17; 3:31, 34; 5:3, 20, 24; 6:4, 5, 14, 16, 17, 21^{2}; 7:15, 16, 18, 26, 29; 13:9; 14:33; 15:1; 19:8, 17, 18; 21:9; 24:13, 1Kg 1:5, 23, 25, 28, 32; 2:4, 26, 45; 3:6, 12, 15, 16, 22, 24; 7:49; 8:5, 22, 23, 25^{2}, 28, 31, 33, 54, 59, 62, 64^{2}, 65; 9:3, 4, 6, 25; 10:8; 11:36; 12:8; 14:9; 15:3; 16:25, 30, 33; 17:1; 18:15, 46; 19:11^{2}, 19; 22:10, 21, 2Kg 4:12, 38, 43, 44; 5:15, 23; 6:22; 8:9; 10:4; 11:18; 16:14; 17:2; 18:5, 22; 19:14, 15, 26; 20:3; 21:11; 22:10, 19; 23:3, 25, 1Ch 1:43; 6:32; 11:3; 13:8, 10; 14:15; 15:24; 16:1, 4, 6, 27, 29, 37^{2}, 39; 17:13, 16, 24, 25; 19:7, 14, 18; 21:30; 22:5, 8, 18; 23:13, 31; 24:2; 29:15, 22, 25, 2Ch 1:5, 6, 10, 12, 13; 2:4, 6; 4:20; 5:6; 6:12, 14, 16, 19, 22, 24; 7:4, 7, 17, 19; 8:12; 9:7, 11; 10:6, 8; 13:15; 14:12^{2}, 13; 18:9, 20; 20:5, 9^{2}, 13, 18, 21; 23:17; 24:14; 25:8; 27:6; 28:14; 29:19; 31:20; 32:12; 33:19; 34:18, 24, 27^{2}, 31, Ezr 7:28; 8:21, 29; 9:9, 15^{2}; 10:1, 6, Neh 1:4, 6; 2:1; 5:15; 8:1, 2, 3; 9:8, 11, 24, 28, 35; 12:36; 13:4, 19, Est 1:3, 11, 17, 19; 3:7; 6:1, 9, 13^{2}; 7:6; 8:1, 5^{2}; 9:25, Job 4:19; 8:12, 16; 13:16; 15:4, 7; 17:6; 21:18, 33; 23:4; 33:5; 35:14; 41:10, 22; 42:11, Ps 5:8; 2:27, 29; 3:5; 4:0; 5:5; 0:3; 6:13; 1:7; 2:8; 8:3, 4, 7; 9:22; 2:9; 6:7; 9:11; 0:2; 3:13; 5:13; 6:9; 8:2; 5:6; 6:6, 13; 7:3; 8:6, 9; 02:0, 28; 06:23; 16:9; 19:169, 170; 41:2; 42:2^{2}; 43:2; 47:17, Prv 8:25, 30; 14:19; 15:33; 16:18^{2}; 17:14; 18:12^{2}, 16; 22:29^{2}; 23:1; 25:26; 27:4, Ecc 1:16; 2:7, 9; 5:2, 6; 9:1, Isa 8:4; 9:3; 17:13^{2}; 18:5; 23:18; 36:7; 37:14, 27; 38:3; 40:10; 41:2; 42:16; 43:10; 45:1^{2}, 2; 48:7, 19; 52:12; 53:2, 7; 55:12; 58:8; 62:11; 65:6; 66:22, 23, Jer 1:17; 2:22; 7:10; 9:13; 15:1, 9, 19; 18:17, 20, 23; 19:7; 21:8; 24:1; 26:4; 30:20; 31:36^{2}; 34:15, 18; 35:5, 19; 36:7, 9, 22; 37:20; 39:16; 40:4, 10; 42:2, 9; 44:10^{2}; 49:19, 37^{2}; 50:8, 44, Lam 1:5, 6, 22, Ezk 2:10; 3:20; 4:1; 6:4, 5; 8:1, 11; 9:6; 14:1; 16:18, 19, 50; 20:1; 22:30; 23:41; 28:17; 30:24; 33:22, 31; 36:17; 40:12; 41:22; 42:4; 43:24; 44:3, 12; 46:3, 9, Dan 1:5, 18, 19; 2:2; 8:4, 7; 9:10, 18, 20; 10:12; 11:16, Hos 6:2, Jol 2:3^{2}, 10, 11, 31, Ams 1:1; 9:4, Jon 1:2, Mic 2:13^{2}; 6:4, Nah 1:6, Hab 3:5, Hag 2:14, Zec 3:1, 3, 4, 8, 9; 4:7; 8:10; 14:20, Mal 3:1, 16; 4:5

before *See also* appear, awake, bring, carry, come, do, fall, go, hear, lay, mention, place, put, rise, say, set, sin, stand, straight, while.

long before 1. *πάλαι*

Wis 11:14 who long before had been cast out 1

beforehand 1. *ἔμπροσθεν* 2. *πρὸ καιροῦ* 3. *προλαμβάνω* 4. ante

Mrk 14: 8 anointed my body beforehand for burying. 3
2Es 8:52 and wisdom perfected beforehand. 4
16:38 about her womb for two or three hours beforehand 4
1Mc 6:36 These took their position beforehand 2
3Mc 6:22 the things that he had devised beforehand. 1

beforehand *See also* announce, anxious, know, make, meditate, preach, prepare, promise, speak, tell.

beforetime 1. לְפָנִים

Isa 41:26 and beforetime, that we might say, "He is right"? 1

beg 1. בקשׁ 2. נָא 3. שׁאל 4. *αἰτέω* 5. *ἀξιόω* 6. *δέομαι* 7. *ἐπαιτέω* 8. *ἐπαίτησις* 9. *ἐρωτάω* 10. *ἱκετεύω* 11. *παρακαλέω* 12. *προσαίτης* 13. peto

Gen 19: 7 said, "I beg you, my brothers 2
Est 7: 7 Haman stayed to beg his life from Queen Esther 1
Ps 37:25 forsaken or his children begging bread. 1
109:10 May his children wander about and beg; 3
Lam 4: 4 the children beg for food, but no one gives to them. 3
Mat 5:42 Give to him who begs from you, and do not refuse him 4
8:31 the demons begged him, "If you cast us out, send us 11
34 and when they saw him, they begged him to leave 11
15:23 And his disciples came and begged him, saying 9
Mrk 5:10 he begged him eagerly 11
12 they begged him, "Send us to the swine 11
17 they began to beg Jesus to depart 11
18 begged him that he might be with him. 11
7:26 begged him to cast the demon out of her daughter. 9
8:22 begged him to touch him. 11
Lke 6:30 Give to every one who begs from you 4
8:31 they begged him not to command them to depart 11
32 they begged him to let them enter these 11
38 The man from whom the demons had gone begged 6
9:38 I beg you to look upon my son, for he is my only child; 6
40 I begged your disciples to cast it out 6
16: 3 I am ashamed to beg. 7
27 he said, 'Then I beg you, father 9
18:35 a blind man was sitting by the roadside begging; 7
Joh 4:47 went and begged him to come down and heal his son 9
9: 8 Is not this the man who used to sit and beg? 12
Act 13:42 As they went out, the people begged 11
19:31 begged him not to venture into the theater. 11
21:12 we and the people there begged him not to go up 11
39 I beg you, let me speak to the people. 6
24: 4 I beg you in your kindness to hear us briefly. 11
26: 3 therefore I beg you to listen to me patiently. 6
2Co 2: 8 I beg you to reaffirm your love for him. 11
8: 4 begging us earnestly for the favor 6
10: 2 I beg of you that when I am present 6
Eph 4: 1 I therefore, a prisoner for the Lord, beg you 11
2Th 2: 1 we beg you, brethren 9
2Jn 1: 5 And now I beg you, lady, not as though I were writing 9
2Es 1:25 When you beg mercy of me, I will show you no mercy. 13
Wis 18: 2 they begged their pardon 6
19: 3 whom they had begged and compelled to depart. 10
Sir 40:28 it is better to die than to beg. 7
30 In the mouth of the shameless begging is sweet 8
1Mc 9:35 begged the Nabateans, who were his friends 11
3Mc 5:13 begged him . . to show . . his all-powerful hand 5

beg pardon 1. *παραιτέω*

3Mc 6:27 begging pardon for your former actions! 1

beget 1. ילד 2. *γεννάω* 3. *σπείρω* 4. genero

Lev 18:11 father's wife's daughter, begotten by your father 1
Deu 4:25 When you beget children and children's children 1
28:41 You shall beget sons and daughters 1
32:18 You were unmindful of the Rock that begot you 1
1Ch 14: 3 and David begot more sons and daughters. 1
Job 38:28 who has begotten the drops of dew? 1
Ps 2: 7 You are my son, today I have begotten you. 1
Prv 23:22 Hearken to your father who begot you 1
24 he who begets a wise son will be glad in him. 1
Ecc 6: 3 If a man begets 100 children . . but he does 1
Isa 45:10 who says to a father, 'What are you begetting?' 1
Jer 16: 3 and the fathers who begot them in this land 1
Ezk 18:10 If he begets a son who is a robber 1
14 if this man begets a son who sees all the sins 1
47:22 and have begotten children among you. 1
Act 13:33 'Thou art my Son, today I have begotten thee.' 2
Heb 1: 5 Thou art my Son, today I have begotten thee"? 2
5: 5 Thou art my Son, today I have begotten thee"; 2
2Es 16:46 they will beget their children. 4
4Mc 10: 2 the same father begot me and those who died 3

beggar 1. *ἐπαίτησις* 2. *προσαίτης* 3. *προσδέω* 4. *πτωχός*

Mrk 10:46 Bartimae'us, a blind beggar, the son of Timae'us 2
Joh 9: 8 those who had seen him before as a beggar, said 2
Sir 4: 3 nor delay your gift to a beggar. 3
18:33 become a beggar by feasting with borrowed money 4
25: 2 a beggar who is proud, a rich man who is a liar 4
40:28 My son, do not lead the life of a beggar 1

beggarly 1. *πτωχός*

Gal 4: 9 weak and beggarly elemental spirits 1

begin 1. אסר 2. היה 3. חלל 4. יסד 5. מִן 6. תְּחִלָּה 7. שׂרא (A) 8. ἀπό 9. ἄρξομαι 10. ἄρχω 11. βραχέως 12. γίνομαι 13. ἐκ 14. ἐνάρχομαι 15. ἐνάρχω 16. ἐξάρχω 17. εὔχομαι 18. ἐφίστημι 19. παρεμβάλλω 20. προενάρχομαι 21. πρῶτον 22. συνάπτω 23. adpropinquo 24. coepio 25. inchoo 26. incipio

Gen 4:26 time men began to call upon the name of the LORD. 3
6: 1 When men began to multiply on the face 3
11: 6 this is only the beginning of what they will do; 3
41:54 the seven years of famine began to come 3
44:12 he searched, beginning with the eldest 3
Num16:46 wrath has gone forth . . the plague has begun. 3
47 plague had already begun among the people; 3
25: 1 in Shittim the people began to play the harlot 3
Deu 2:24 begin to take possession, and contend with him 3
25 This day I will begin to put the dread and fear 3
31 'Behold, I have begun to give Sihon and his land 3
31 begin to take possession, that you may occupy 3
3:24 only begun to show thy servant thy greatness 3
16: 9 begin to count the seven weeks from the time 3
Jos 3: 7 I will begin to exalt you in the sight of Israel 3
18:12 their boundary began at the Jordan; 2
15 the southern side begins at the outskirts •
Jdg 10:18 Who is the man that will begin to fight 3
13: 5 and he shall begin to deliver Israel 3
25 And the Spirit of the LORD began to stir him 3
16:19 she began to torment him, and his strength left 3
22 the hair of his head began to grow again 3
19:25 And as the dawn began to break, they let her go. •
20:31 they began to smite and kill some of the people 3
39 Benjamin had begun to smite and kill about 3
40 when the signal began to rise out of the city 3
1Sm 3: 2 Eli, whose eyesight had begun to grow dim 3
13: 1 Saul was . . years old when he began to reign; •
2Sm 2:10 Ish-bo'shet . . was 40 years old when he began to reign •
5: 4 David was 30 years old when he began to reign •
24: 5 They crossed the Jordan, and began from Aro'er 19
1Kg 6: 1 he began to build the house of the LORD. •
14:21 Rehobo'am was 41 years old when he began to reign •
15: 1 Abi'jam began to reign over Judah. •
9 Asa began to reign over Judah •
25 Nadab . . began to reign over Israel •
33 Ba'asha . . began to reign over all Israel •
16: 8 Elah . . began to reign over Israel in Tirzah •
11 When he began to reign . . he killed all the house •
23 Omri began to reign over Israel •
29 Ahab the son of Omri began to reign over Israel •
20:14 Then he said, "Who shall begin the battle? 1
22:41 Jehosh'aphat . . began to reign over Judah •
42 Jehosh'aphat was 35 years old when he began •
51 Ahazi'ah . . began to reign over Israel in Sama'ria •
2Kg 8:16 Jeho'ram the son of . . began to reign. •
25 Ahazi'ah the son of Jeho'ram . . began to reign. •
26 Ahazi'ah was 22 years old when he began to reign •
9:29 In the eleventh year of . . Ahazi'ah began to reign •
10:32 the LORD began to cut off parts of Israel. 3
11:21 Jeho'ash was seven . . when he began to reign. •
12: 1 seventh year of Jehu Jeho'ash began to reign •
13: 1 Jeho'ahaz . . began to reign over Israel •
10 Jeho'ash . . began to reign over Israel in Sama'ria •
14: 1 Amazi'ah . . king of Judah, began to reign. •
2 He was 25 years old when he began to reign •
23 Jerobo'am . . began to reign in Sama'ria •
15: 1 Azari'ah the son of Amazi'ah . . began to reign. •
2 He was sixteen years old when he began to reign •
13 Shallum . . began to reign in the 39th year •
17 Men'ahem . . began to reign over Israel •
23 Pekahi'ah . . began to reign over Israel •
27 Pekah . . began to reign over Israel in Sama'ria •
32 Jotham the son of Uzzi'ah . . began to reign. •
33 He was 25 years old when he began to reign •
37 the LORD began to send Rezin . . and Pekah 3
16: 1 Ahaz the son of Jotham . . began to reign. •
2 Ahaz was twenty years old when he began to reign •
17: 1 Hoshe'a the son of Elah began to reign in Sama'ria •
18: 1 Hezeki'ah the son of Ahaz . . began to reign. •
2 He was 25 years old when he began to reign •
21: 1 Manas'seh was twelve . . when he began to reign •
19 Amon was 22 years old when he began to reign •
22: 1 Josi'ah was eight years old when he began to reign •
23:31 Jeho'ahaz was 23 years old when he began to reign •
36 Jehoi'akim was 25 years old when he began to reign •
25:27 in the year that he began to reign •
1Ch 1:10 he began to be a mighty one in the earth. 3
27:24 Jo'ab . . began to number, but did not finish; 3
2Ch 3: 1 Then Solomon began to build the house of the LORD 3
2 He began to build in the second month 3
12:13 Rehobo'am was 41 . . when he began to reign •
13: 1 Jerobo'am Abi'jah began to reign over Judah. •
20:22 when they began to sing and praise 3
31 Jehosh'aphat . . was 35 . . when he began to reign •
21:20 He was 32 years old when he began to reign •
22: 2 Ahazi'ah was 42 . . when he began to reign •
24: 1 Jo'ash was seven years old when he began to reign •
25: 1 25 years old when he began to reign •
26: 3 Uzzi'ah was sixteen . . when he began to reign •
27: 1 Jotham was 25 . . when he began to reign •
8 was 25 years old when he began to reign •
28: 1 Ahaz was twenty years old when he began to reign •
29: 1 Hezeki'ah began to reign when he was 25 •
17 began to sanctify on the first day of the first 3
27 burnt offering began, the song to the LORD began 3
27 burnt offering began, the song to the LORD began 3
31: 7 In the third month they began to pile up the heaps 3
10 Since they began to bring the contributions 3
33: 1 Manas'seh was twelve . . when he began to reign •
21 Amon was 22 . . when he began to reign •
34: 1 Josi'ah was eight years old when he began to reign •
3 he began to seek the God of David his father; 3
3 began to purge Judah and Jerusalem 3
36: 2 23 years old when he began to reign; •
5 Jehoi'akim was 25 . . when he began to reign •
9 Jehoi'achin was eight . . when he began to reign •
11 Zedeki'ah was 21 . . when he began to reign •
Ezr 3: 6 began to offer burnt offerings to the LORD. 3
5: 2 arose and began to rebuild the house of God 7
7: 9 first day of the first month he began to go up 4
Neh 4: 7 that the breaches were beginning to be closed 3
11:17 Mattani'ah . . leader to begin the thanksgiving 6
13:19 When it began to be dark at the gates of Jerusalem •
Est 6:13 If Mor'decai, before whom you have begun to fall, 3
9:23 the Jews undertook to do as they had begun 3
Job 38:12 you commanded the morning since your days began •
Jer 25:29 For behold, I begin to work evil at the city 3
Ezk 9: 6 And begin at my sanctuary. 3
6 they began with the elders 3
42:10 where the outside wall begins. •
48: 1 Beginning at the northern border, from the sea 5
Hos 9:15 in Gilgal; there I began to hate them. •
Jon 3: 4 Jonah began to go into the city 3
Mic 6:13 Therefore I have begun to smite you 9
Mat 4:17 From that time Jesus began to preach, saying 10
11: 7 they went away, Jesus began to speak to the crowds 10
20 Then he began to upbraid the cities 10
12: 1 they began to pluck heads of grain and to eat. 10
16:21 From that time Jesus began to show his disciples 10
22 Peter took him and began to rebuke him, saying 10
18:24 When he began the reckoning 10
24:49 begins to beat his fellow servants 10
26:22 and began to say to him one after another 10
37 he began to be sorrowful and troubled. 10
74 he began to invoke a curse on himself and to swear 10
Mrk 1:45 he went out and began to talk freely about it 10
2:23 his disciples began to pluck heads of grain. 10
4: 1 Again he began to teach beside the sea 10
5:17 they began to beg Jesus to depart 10
20 began to proclaim in the Decap'olis 10
6: 2 on the sabbath he began to teach in the synagogue; 10
7 began to send them out two by two 10
34 he began to teach them many things. 10
55 began to bring sick people on their pallets 10
8:11 The Pharisees came and began to argue with him 10
31 he began to teach them that the Son of man must 10
32 Peter took him, and began to rebuke him. 10
10:28 Peter began to say to him, "Lo, we have left 10
32 he began to tell them what was to happen to him 10
41 they began to be indignant at James and John. 10
47 he began to cry out and say, "Jesus, Son of David 10
11:15 And he . . began to drive out those who sold 10
12: 1 he began to speak to them in parables 10
13: 5 Jesus began to say to them, "Take heed 10
14:19 They began to be sorrowful 10
33 and began to be greatly distressed and troubled. 10
65 some began to spit on him, and to cover his face 10
69 began again to say to the bystanders 10
71 he began to invoke a curse on himself and to swear 10
15: 8 the crowd came up and began to ask Pilate 10
18 they began to salute him, "Hail, King of the Jews! 10
Lke 3: 8 do not begin to say to yourselves 10
23 Jesus, when he began his ministry 10
4:21 he began to say to them, "Today this scripture 10
5: 7 so that they began to sink. •
21 the scribes and the Pharisees began to question 10
7:15 the dead man sat up, and began to speak 10
24 he began to speak to the crowds concerning John 10
38 she began to wet his feet with her tears 10
49 began to say among themselves 10
9:12 Now the day began to wear away 10
11:29 When the crowds were increasing, he began to say 10
53 the scribes and the Pharisees began to press him 10
12: 1 he began to say to his disciples first 10
45 begins to beat the menservants 10
13:25 begin to stand outside and to knock at the door 10
26 Then you will begin to say, 'We ate and drank 10
14: 9 will begin with shame to take the lowest place. 10
18 they all alike began to make excuses 10
29 all who see it begin to mock him 10
30 saying, 'This man began to build 10
15:14 he began to be in want. 10
24 they began to make merry. 10
19:37 began to rejoice and praise God with a loud voice 10
45 began to drive out those who sold 10
20: 9 he began to tell the people this parable 10
21:28 Now when these things begin to take place, look up 10
22:23 they began to question one another 10
23: 2 they began to accuse him, saying, "We found this man 10
30 they will begin to say to the mountains, 'Fall on us'; 10
Joh 9:32 Never since the world began has it been heard 13
13: 5 began to wash the disciples' feet 10
Act 1: 1 dealt with all that Jesus began to do and teach 10
2: 4 began to speak in other tongues 10
11: 4 Peter began and explained to them in order 10
15 As I began to speak, the Holy Spirit fell on them 10
18:26 He began to speak boldly in the synagogue 10
24: 2 when he was called, Tertul'lus began to accuse him 10
27:18 they began next day to throw the cargo overboard; •
35 he broke it and began to eat. 10
28: 2 because it had begun to rain and was cold. 18
Rom 3: 2 To begin with, the Jews are entrusted 21
2Co 8:10 you began not only to do but to desire 20
Gal 3: 3 Having begun with the Spirit 14
Php 1: 6 I am sure that he who began a good work in you 14
1Pe 4:17 For the time has come for judgment to begin 10
17 if it begins with us, what will be the end of those 21
Rev 11:17 hast taken thy great power and begun to reign. •
1Es 1:39 when he began to reign in Judea and Jerusalem •
57 until the Persians began to reign •
2:30 began to hinder the builders 10
3:17 Then the first . . began and said 10
4: 1 Then the second . . began to speak 10
13 Then the third . . began to speak 10
33 he began to speak about truth 10
44 set apart when he began to destroy Babylon 17
5:53 began to offer sacrifices to God 10
6: 2 arose and began to build the house of the Lord 10
2Es 2:47 I began to praise those who had stood valiantly 24
3: 3 I began to speak anxious words to the Most High 24
12 When those who dwelt on earth began to multiply 24
12 and again they began to be more ungodly 24
5:22 and I began once more to speak words 24
6:29 where I was standing began to rock to and fro. ‡
36 I began to speak in the presence of the Most High. 24
9:28 I began to speak before the Most High, and said 25
10:41 whom you saw mourning and began to console- 25
49 you began to console her for what had happened. 25
14:10 and the times begin to grow old. 23
26 tomorrow at this hour you shall begin to write. 26
16: 6 when once it has begun to burn? 24
13 and will not miss when they begin to be shot 24
Tob 2:13 when she returned to me it began to bleat 10
5:17 Anna, his mother, began to weep, and said to Tobit •
7:15 Then they began to eat. 10
17 the girl began to weep •
8: 5 Tobias began to pray 10
10: 4 Then she began to mourn for him, and said 10
11:12 when his eyes began to smart he rubbed them •
Jdt 5:22 all the men . . began to complain •
16: 1 Then Judith began this thanksgiving 16
2 Begin a song to my God with tambourines 16
AEs 14:11 the man who began this against us. 10
Wis 7: 3 when I was born, I began to breathe the common air •
Sir 38:16 begin the lament 15
Sus 1: 8 and they began to desire her. 12
1Mc 3:25 Then Judas and his brothers began to be feared 10
4:59 beginning with the 25th day of the month 8
5: 2 they began to kill and destroy among the people. 10
31 So Judas saw that the battle had begun 10
7: 1 and there began to reign. •
9:40 and began killing them •
47 So the battle began 22
67 Then he began to attack 10
73 Jonathan began to judge the people 10
10: 1 They welcomed him, and there he began to reign. •
10 began to rebuild and restore the city. 10
11:46 began to fight. 10
54 the young boy Antiochus who began to reign •
13:42 the people began to write in their documents 10
15:40 came to Jamnia and began to provoke the people 10
2Mc 2:32 let us begin our narrative 10
9:11 he began to lose much of his arrogance 10
13:11 the people who had just begun to revive 11
3Mc 1:26 and began now to approach •
5:23 Hermon . . began to move them along •
6:20 Even the king began to shudder bodily •
21 and began trampling and destroying them. •
7:16 those . . began their departure from the city •
4Mc 1:12 I shall begin by stating my main principle 10
5: 6 Before I begin to torture you, old man 10
15 he began to address the people as follows 10
6: 8 rushed at him and began to kick him in the side •

begin one's session 1. συγκαθίζω

1Es 9:16 they began their sessions 1

only begin 1. ἐνάρχομαι

1Mc 9:55 he only began to tear it down 1

beginning 1. חלל 2. מִן 3. קֶדֶם 4. ראשׁ 5. רִאשׁוֹן 6. רֵאשִׁית 7. תְּחִלָּה 8. αἰών 9. αἰὼν χρόνου 10. ἀρχή 11. ἀρχῆθεν 12. ἄρχω 13. γένεσις 14. γίνομαι 15. ἐπιφώσκω 16. initio 17. initium 18. principium 19. saeculum

Gen 1: 1 In the beginning God created the heavens 6

10:10 The beginning of his kingdom was Ba'bel, Erech 6
13: 3 had been at the beginning, between Bethel and Ai 7
41:21 for they were still as gaunt as at the beginning. 7
Exd 12: 2 be for you the beginning of months; it shall be 4
Lev 23:32 on the ninth day of the month beginning at evening 2
Num10:10 feasts, and at the beginnings of your months 4
28:11 At the beginnings of your months you shall offer 4
Deu 3:12 I gave . . the territory beginning at Aro'er 2
11:12 from the beginning of the year to the end 6
Jdg 7:19 came . . at the beginning of the middle watch 4
Rut 1:22 they came . . at the beginning of barley harvest. 7
1Sm 3:12 all that I have spoken . . from beginning to end 1
2Sm 21: 9 at the beginning of barley harvest. 7
10 spread it . . from the beginning of harvest until 7
2Kg 17:25 at the beginning of their dwelling . . they did 7
Ezr 4: 6 reign of Ahasu-e'rus, in the beginning of his reign 7
Job 8: 7 though your beginning was small 6
42:12 the latter days of Job more than his beginning; 6
Ps 111:10 The fear of the LORD is the beginning of wisdom; 6
Prv 1: 7 fear of the LORD is the beginning of knowledge; 6
4: 7 The beginning of wisdom is this: Get wisdom 6
8:22 The LORD created me at the beginning of his work 6
23 at the first, before the beginning of the earth. 3
9:10 The fear of the LORD is the beginning of wisdom 7
17:14 beginning of strife is like letting out water; 6
20:21 An inheritance gotten hastily in the beginning 5
Ecc 3:11 find out what God has done from the beginning 4
7: 8 Better is the end of a thing than its beginning; 6
10:13 The beginning of the words . . is foolishness 7
Isa 1:26 and your counselors as at the beginning. 7
40:21 Has it not been told you from the beginning? 4
41: 4 calling the generations from the beginning? 4
26 Who declared it from the beginning 4
46:10 declaring the end from the beginning 6
48:16 from the beginning I have not spoken in secret 4
Jer 17:12 A glorious throne set on high from the beginning 5
26: 1 In the beginning of the reign of Jehoi'akim 6
27: 1 In the beginning of the reign of Zedeki'ah 6
28: 1 at the beginning of the reign of Zedeki'ah 6
49:34 in the beginning of the reign of Zedeki'ah 6
Lam 2:19 Arise, cry out . . at the beginning of the watches! 4
Ezk 40: 1 at the beginning of the year, on the tenth day 4
Dan 9:23 beginning of your supplications a word went 7
Ams 7: 1 locusts in the beginning of the shooting up 7
Mic 1:13 were the beginning of sin to the daughter of Zion 6
Mat 14:30 beginning to sink he cried out, "Lord, save me. 12
19: 4 he who made them from the beginning 10
8 but from the beginning it was not so. 10
20: 8 beginning with the last, up to the first.' 12
24: 8 all this is but the beginning of the birth-pangs. 10
21 from the beginning of the world until now 10
27:24 rather that a riot was beginning 14
Mrk 1: 1 The beginning of the Gospel of Jesus Christ 10
10: 6 from the beginning of creation 10
13: 8 this is but the beginning of the birth-pangs. 10
19 not been from the beginning of the creation 10
Lke 1: 2 who from the beginning were eyewitnesses 10
23:54 the sabbath was beginning. 15
24:27 beginning with Moses and all the prophets 12
47 beginning from Jerusalem. 12
Joh 1: 1 In the beginning was the Word 10
2 He was in the beginning with God; 10
8: 9 went away, one by one, beginning with the eldest 12
25 Even what I have told you from the beginning. 10
44 He was a murderer from the beginning 10
15:27 because you have been with me from the beginning. 10
16: 4 not say these things to you from the beginning 10
Act 1:22 beginning from the baptism of John 12
8:35 beginning with this scripture 12
10:37 beginning from Galilee 12
11:15 fell on them just as on us at the beginning. 10
26: 4 spent from the beginning among my own nation 10
2Co 3: 1 Are we beginning to commend ourselves again? 12
Php 4:15 in the beginning of the gospel 10
Col 1:18 he is the beginning, the first-born from the dead 10
2Th 2:13 God chose you from the beginning to be saved 10
Heb 1:10 Thou, Lord, didst found the earth in the beginning 10
7: 3 has neither beginning of days nor end of life 10
2Pe 3: 4 as they were from the beginning of creation. 10
1Jn 1: 1 That which was from the beginning 10
2: 7 commandment which you had from the beginning; 10
13 because you know him who is from the beginning 10
14 because you know him who is from the beginning 10
24 Let what you heard from the beginning abide 10
24 what you heard from the beginning abides in you 10
3: 8 for the devil has sinned from the beginning. 10
11 message which you have heard from the beginning 10
2Jn 1: 5 but the one we have had from the beginning 10
6 as you have heard from the beginning 10
Rev 3:14 the Amen . . the beginning of God's creation 10
21: 6 Alpha and the Omega, the beginning and the end. 10
22:13 Alpha and the Omega . . the beginning and the end 10
1Es 8:70 from the beginning of this matter 10
2Es 2:41 people, who have been called from the beginning 17
3: 4 didst thou not speak at the beginning 17
4:30 in Adam's heart from the beginning 17
42 that were committed to them from the beginning. 17
6: 1 At the beginning of the circle of the earth 17
7 and the beginning of the age that follows? 17

8 Jacob's hand held Esau's heel from the beginning. 17
9 Jacob is the beginning of the age that follows. 18
10 For the beginning of a man is his hand ‡
38 thou didst speak at the beginning of creation 17
7:30 as it was at the first beginnings 17
113 and the beginning of the immortal age to come ‡
8:19 The beginning of the words of Ezra's prayer 17
9: 4 from the days . . of old, from the beginning. 17
5 the beginning is evident, and the end manifest; 17
6 the beginnings are manifest in wonders 17
8 have sanctified for myself from the beginning. 19
10:10 from the beginning all have been born of her 17
14 so the earth also has from the beginning given 17
12:34 of which I spoke to you at the beginning. 16
13:14 From the beginning thou hast shown thy servant 16
14:22 in the world from the beginning 16
16:18 The beginning of sorrows 17
18 the beginning of famine, when many shall perish; 17
18 the beginning of wars 17
18 the beginning of calamities 17
Jdt 8:29 from the beginning of your life 10
AEs 13:15 that has been thine from the beginning. 10
Wis 6:17 The beginning of wisdom 10
22 from the beginning of creation 10
7: 5 no king has had a different beginning 10
18 the beginning and end and middle of times 10
9: 8 which thou didst prepare from the beginning. 10
12:11 they were an accursed race from the beginning 10
14: 6 even in the beginning 10
12 the beginning of fornication 10
13 neither have they existed from the beginning 10
27 the beginning and cause and end of every evil. 10
Sir 1:14 To fear the Lord is the beginning of wisdom 10
10:12 The beginning of man's pride 10
13 For the beginning of pride is sin 10
15:14 It was he who created man in the beginning 10
16:26 existed from the beginning by his creation 10
18: 7 When a man has finished, he is just beginning 12
24: 9 From eternity, in the beginning, he created me 10
25:24 From a woman sin had its beginning 10
36:11 as at the beginning. 10
15 those whom thou didst create in the beginning 10
37:16 Reason is the beginning of every work 10
39:25 From the beginning 10
32 from the beginning I have been convinced 10
44: 2 apportioned . . his majesty from the beginning. 8
2Mc 7:23 who shaped the beginning of man 13
8:27 allotted it to them as the beginning of mercy. 10
3Mc 3:21 affairs . . entrusted to them from the beginning; 11
5:11 from the beginning, night and day 9
6:26 from the beginning differed from all nations 10

beginning *See also* make.

begone 1. יצא 2. *ὑπάγω*
2Sm 16: 7 Begone, begone, you man of blood, you worthless 1
7 Begone, begone, you man of blood, you worthless 1
Isa 30:22 unclean things; you will say to them, "Begone! 1
Mat 4:10 Jesus said to him, "Begone, Satan! for it is written 2

only begotten 1. unigenitus
2Es 6:58 thy first-born, only begotten, zealous for thee 1

begrudge 1. *ὀφθαλμὸς πονηρός* 2. *φθονερός* 3. *φθονέω*
Mat 20:15 Or do you begrudge my generosity?' 1
Tob 4: 7 begrudge the gift when you make it 3
16 let your eye begrudge the gift when you made it. 3
Sir 14:10 A stingy man's eye begrudges bread 2

beguile 1. נכל 2. נשא 3. *ἀπατάω* 4. *παραλογίζομαι* 5. *πλανάω*
Gen 3:13 The woman said, "The serpent beguiled me, and I ate. 2
Num25:18 wiles, with which they beguiled you 1
Rev 2:20 Jez'ebel . . is teaching and beguiling 5
AEs 16: 6 beguile the . . good will of their sovereigns. 4
Sir 14:16 Give, and take, and beguile yourself 3

beguiling *See* speech.

behalf 1. אֵת 2. בַּעַד 3. לְ 4. מֵאֵת 5. עַל 6. עִם 7. *διά* 8. *περί* 9. *ὑπέρ* 10. pro
Lev 24: 8 on behalf of the people of Israel as a covenant 4
Jdg 9: 3 kinsmen spoke all these words on his behalf 5
1Kg 2:19 So Bathshe'ba went . . on behalf of Adoni'jah. 5
2Kg 4:13 Would you have a word spoken on your behalf 3
2Ch 16: 9 in behalf of those whose heart is blameless 6
20:17 see the victory of the LORD on your behalf, O Judah 6
Est 4:16 hold a fast on my behalf, and neither eat nor drink 5
Job 36: 2 for I have yet something to say on God's behalf. 3
Ps 109:21 my Lord, deal on my behalf for thy name's sake; 1
Isa 8:19 they consult the dead on behalf of the living? 2
Jer 11:14 or lift up a cry or prayer on their behalf 2
15:11 have not pleaded with thee on behalf of the enemy 1
29: 7 and pray to the LORD on its behalf 2
Act 24: 2 reforms are introduced on behalf of this nation •
Rom 15:30 with me in your prayers to God on my behalf 9
1Co 15:29 by being baptized on behalf of the dead 9
29 why are people baptized on their behalf? 9

2Co 1:11 so that many will give thanks on our behalf 9
5:20 We beseech you on behalf of Christ 9
12: 5 On behalf of this man I will boast 9
5 on my own behalf I will not boast 9
Eph 3: 1 prisoner for Christ Jesus on behalf of you Gentiles- 9
Col 1: 7 He is a faithful minister of Christ on our behalf 9
Phm 1:13 in order that he might serve me on your behalf 9
Heb 5: 1 high priest . . is appointed to act on behalf of men 9
6:20 Jesus has gone as a forerunner on our behalf 9
9:24 now to appear in the presence of God on our behalf. 9
2Es 4:34 but the Highest hastens on behalf of many. 10
Wis 16:24 relaxes on behalf of those who trust in thee. 9
Sir 29:13 will fight on your behalf against your enemy. 9
2Mc 1:26 on behalf of all thy people Israel 9
2:21 those who strove zealously on behalf of Judaism 9
11:15 every request in behalf of the Jews 8
4Mc 5:31 to be young in reason on behalf of piety. 7
14: 3 harmonious concord . . on behalf of religion! 8

behave 1. היה 2. מַעֲלָל 3. *ἀναστρέφω* 4. *περιπατέω*
1Sm 25: 3 but the man was churlish and ill-behaved; 2
2Sm 14: 2 behave like a woman who has been mourning 1
1Co 3: 3 of the flesh, and behaving like ordinary men? 4
2Co 1:12 we have behaved in the world 3
1Ti 3:15 how one ought to behave in the household of God 3

behave arrogantly 1. גבר
Job 36: 9 that they are behaving arrogantly. 1

behave badly 1. שחת
Jdg 2:19 turned back and behaved worse than their fathers 1

behave impiously 1. *ἀσεβέω*
2Mc 1:17 those who have behaved impiously. 1

behave properly 1. *ἀσχημονέω*
1Co 7:36 thinks that he is not behaving properly 1

behave toward 1. *χράομαι*
2Mc 12:14 those . . behaved most insolently toward Judas 1

behavior 1. דָּבָר 2. דֶּרֶךְ 3. טַעַם 4. *ἀναστροφή* 5. *γίνομαι* 6. *κατάστημα*
1Sm 21:13 he changed his behavior before them, and feigned 3
Est 1:18 ladies . . who have heard of the queen's behavior 1
Ezk 16:27 who were ashamed of your lewd behavior. 2
1Th 2:10 blameless was our behavior to you believers; 5
Tit 2: 3 older women likewise to be reverent in behavior 6
1Pe 3: 1 won without a word by the behavior of their wives 4
2 when they see your reverent and chaste behavior 4
16 those who revile your good behavior in Christ 4

pestilent behavior 1. *λοιμότης*
AEs 16: 7 accomplished through the pestilent behavior 1

selfish behavior 1. *πῆξις ἀγκῶνος*
Sir 41:19 Be ashamed of selfish behavior at meals 1

behead 1. סור ראשׁ 2. *ἀποκεφαλίζω* 3. *πελεκίζω*
2Sm 4: 7 they smote him, and slew him, and beheaded him. 1
Mat 14:10 he sent and had John beheaded in the prison 2
Mrk 6:16 John, whom I beheaded, has been raised. 2
27 He went and beheaded him in the prison 2
Lke 9: 9 Herod said, "John I beheaded 2
Rev 20: 4 beheaded for their testimony to Jesus 3
151 1: 7 I drew his own sword; I beheaded him 2

behind 1. אָחוֹר 2. אַחַר 3. אַחֲרֵי 4. בַּעַד 5. מֵאַחֲרֵי 6. מִבַּעַד לְ 7. *ἐξόπισθεν* 8. *κατά* 9. *κατόπισθεν* 10. *μετά* 11. *ὄπισθεν* 12. *ὀπίσω*
Gen 18:10 Sarah was listening at the tent door behind him 3
19:26 Lot's wife behind him looked back 3
22:13 looked, and behold, behind him was a ram 2
32:18 my lord Esau; and moreover he is behind us.' 3
20 Moreover your servant Jacob is behind us.' 3
Exd 11: 5 the maidservant who is behind the mill; 2
14:19 the angel . . moved and went behind them; 5
19 pillar of cloud . . stood behind them 3
Num 3:23 Gershonites . . encamp behind the tabernacle 3
Jos 8: 2 lay an ambush against the city, behind it. 5
4 lie in ambush against the city, behind it; 5
14 there was an ambush against him behind the city. 5
Jdg 20:40 the Benjaminites looked behind them; and behold 3
1Sm 11: 5 Saul was coming from the field behind the oxen; 3
21: 9 it is here wrapped in a cloth behind the ephod; 3
24: 8 And when Saul looked behind him, David bowed 3
2Sm 1: 7 when he looked behind him, he saw me, and called 3
2:20 Abner looked behind him and said, "Is it you, As'ahel? 3
25 And the Benjaminites gathered . . behind Abner 3
1Kg 14: 9 and have cast me behind your back; 3
2Kg 6:32 Is not the sound of his master's feet behind him? 3
9:18 Turn round and ride behind me. 2
19 Turn round and ride behind me. 2
25 you and I rode side by side behind Ahab his father 3
11: 6 and a third at the gate behind the guards) 2
19:21 she wags her head behind you-the daughter 3
2Ch 13:13 sent an ambush around to come on them from behind; 3
13 the ambush was behind them. 3

14 behold, the battle was before and behind them; 1
Neh 4:13 in the lowest parts of the space behind the wall 5
16 leaders stood behind all the house of Judah 3
9:26 rebelled . . and cast thy law behind their back 3
Job 41:32 Behind him he leaves a shining wake; 3
Ps 50:17 you cast my words behind you. 3
139: 5 Thou dost beset me behind and before 1
Sng 2: 9 Behold, there he stands behind our wall, gazing 2
4: 1 Your eyes are doves behind your veil. 6
3 halves of a pomegranate behind your veil. 6
6: 7 like halves of a pomegranate behind your veil. 6
Isa 26:20 shut your doors behind you; 4
30:21 your ears shall hear a word behind you 3
37:22 she wags her head behind you– 3
38:17 for thou hast cast all my sins behind thy back. 3
57: 8 Behind the door . . you have set up your symbol; 2
Ezk 3:12 I heard behind me the sound of a great earthquake; 2
23:35 have forgotten me and cast me behind your back 3
Jol 2: 3 and behind them a flame burns. 3
14 turn and repent, and leave a blessing behind him 3
Zec 1: 8 behind him were red, sorrel, and white horses. 3
Mat 9:20 came up behind him and touched the fringe 11
16:23 he turned and said to Peter, "Get behind me, Satan! 12
Mrk 5:27 came up behind him in the crowd 11
8:33 Get behind me, Satan! 12
Lke 7:38 standing behind him at his feet, weeping 12
8:44 came up behind him, and touched . . his garment 11
23:26 and laid on him the cross, to carry it behind Jesus. 11
Heb 6:19 enters into the inner shrine behind the curtain •
9: 3 Behind the second curtain stood a tent 10
Rev 1:10 and I heard behind me a loud voice like a trumpet 12
4: 6 creatures, full of eyes in front and behind 11
Tob 1:17 dead and thrown out behind the wall of Nineveh 12
11: 4 the dog went along behind them. 11
Wis 17: 3 behind a dark curtain of forgetfulness •
Sir 21:15 he dislikes it and casts it behind his back. 12
47:23 left behind him one of his sons, ample in folly 10
LJr 1: 5 you see the multitude before and behind them 11
1Mc 5:33 Then he came up behind them in three companies 7
9:45 For look! the battle is in front of us and behind us; 7
10:79 had secretly left 1,000 cavalry behind them. 9
80 there was an ambush behind him 9
3Mc 3:24 these impious people behind our backs 8

behind *See also* close, lag, leave, lie, stay.

remain behind 1. יצג 2. *ἀπολείπω*

Exd 10:24 let your flocks and your herds remain behind. 1
3Mc 1:17 those who remained behind in the city 2

behold 1. הֵא 2. הֵן 3. הִנֵּה 4. חזה 5. מַרְאֶה 6. נבט 7. ראה 8. ראה בְּ 9. שׁור 10. אֱלוּ (A) 11. אֲרוּ (A) 12. *βλέπω* 13. *εἶδον* 14. *ἐπιβλέπω* 15. *θεάομαι* 16. *θεωρέω* 17. *ἰδού* 18. *καθοράω* 19. *κατοπτρίζω* 20. *ὁράω* 21. *ὁρόω* 22. ecce 23. video

Gen 1:29 God said, "Behold, I have given you every plant 3
31 behold, it was very good. And there was evening 3
3:22 Behold, the man has become like one of us 2
4:14 Behold, thou hast driven me this day away 2
6:12 God saw the earth, and behold, it was corrupt; 3
13 behold, I will destroy them with the earth. 3
17 For behold, I will bring a flood of waters 3
8:13 behold, the face of the ground was dry. 3
9: 9 Behold, I establish my covenant with you 3
11: 6 the LORD said, "Behold, they are one people 2
12:11 I know that you are a woman beautiful to behold; 5
15: 3 Behold, thou hast given me no offspring; 2
4 behold, the word of the LORD came to him 3
17 behold, a smoking fire pot and a flaming torch 3
16: 2 Sar'ai said to Abram, "Behold now, the LORD has 3
6 Behold, your maid is in your power; 3
11 LORD said to her, "Behold, you are with child 3
17: 4 Behold, my covenant is with you 3
20 I have heard you; behold, I will bless him 3
18: 2 He lifted up his eyes and looked, and behold 3
27 Behold, I have taken upon myself to speak 3
31 He said, "Behold, I have taken upon myself to speak 3
19: 8 Behold, I have two daughters who have not known 3
19 behold, your servant has found favor 3
20 Behold, yonder city is near enough to flee to 3
21 He said to him, "Behold, I grant you this favor 3
28 and beheld, and lo, the smoke of the land went up 7
34 said to the younger, "Behold, I lay last night 2
20: 3 Behold, you are a dead man, because of the woman 3
15 Abim'elech said, "Behold, my land is before you; 3
16 Sarah he said, "Behold, I have given your brother 3
22: 7 He said, "Behold, the fire and the wood; 3
13 looked, and behold, behind him was a ram 3
20 Behold, Milcah also has borne children 3
24:13 Behold, I am standing by the spring of water 3
15 behold, Rebekah, who was born to Bethu'el 3
30 went to the man; and behold, he was standing 3
43 behold, I am standing by the spring of water; 3
45 behold, Rebekah came out with her water jar on her 3
51 Behold, Rebekah is before you, take her and go 3
63 looked, and behold, there were camels coming. 3
25:24 behold, there were twins in her womb. 3
26: 9 Behold, she is your wife; how then could you say 3
27: 2 Behold, I am old; I do not know the day of my death. 3
11 Behold, my brother Esau is a hairy man 2
36 behold, now he has taken away my blessing. 3
37 Isaac answered Esau, "Behold, I have made him 2
39 Behold, away from the fatness of the earth 3
42 Behold, your brother Esau comforts himself 3
28:12 and behold, the angels of God were ascending 3
13 behold, the LORD stood above it and said 3
15 Behold, I am with you and will keep you 3
29: 7 He said, "Behold, it is still high day 2
25 in the morning, behold, it was Leah; 3
33: 1 looked, and behold, Esau was coming 3
34:21 for behold, the land is large enough for them; 3
37: 7 behold, we were binding sheaves in the field 3
7 and behold, your sheaves gathered round it 3
9 Behold, I have dreamed another dream; 3
9 behold, the sun, the moon, and eleven stars were 3
38:29 drew back his hand, behold, his brother came out 3
41: 2 behold, there came up out of the Nile seven cows 3
3 behold, seven other cows, gaunt and thin, came up 3
5 and behold, seven ears of grain . . were growing 3
6 behold, after them sprouted seven ears 3
7 And Pharaoh awoke, and behold, it was a dream. 3
17 Then Pharaoh said to Joseph, "Behold, in my dream 3
41 Pharaoh said to Joseph, "Behold, I have set you 7
42: 2 he said, "Behold, I have heard that there is grain 3
13 and behold, the youngest is this day with our 3
35 emptied their sacks, behold, every man's bundle 3
44: 8 Behold, the money which we found in the mouth 2
16 behold, we are my lord's slaves 3
47:23 Joseph said to the people, "Behold, I have 2
48: 1 Joseph was told, "Behold, your father is ill"; 3
4 said to me, 'Behold, I will make you fruitful 3
21 Israel said to Joseph, "Behold, I am about to die 3
50:18 and said, "Behold, we are your servants. 3
Exd 1: 9 he said to his people, "Behold, the people of Israel 3
2:13 When he went out the next day, behold, two Hebrews 3
3: 9 now, behold, the cry of the people of Israel 3
4: 1 Moses answered, "But behold, they will not believe 2
6 he took it out, behold, his hand was leprous 3
7 behold, it was restored like the rest of his 3
14 and behold, he is coming out to meet you 3
23 behold, I will slay your first-born son.' 3
5: 5 Pharaoh said, "Behold, the people of the land 2
16 And behold, your servants are beaten; 3
6:12 said to the LORD, "Behold, the people of Israel have 2
30 Moses said . . "Behold, I am of uncircumcised lips; 2
7:16 and behold, you have not yet obeyed. 3
17 I am the LORD: behold, I will strike the water 3
8: 2 if you refuse to let them go, behold, I will plague 3
21 behold, I will send swarms of flies on you 3
29 Then Moses said, "Behold, I am going out from you 3
9: 3 behold, the hand of the LORD will fall with a very 3
7 Pharaoh sent, and behold, not one of the cattle 3
18 Behold, tomorrow about this time I will cause 3
10: 4 behold, tomorrow I will bring locusts 3
14:10 behold, the Egyptians were marching after them; 3
16: 4 Then the LORD said to Moses, "Behold, I will rain 3
10 they looked toward the wilderness, and behold 3
17: 6 Behold, I will stand before you there on the rock 3
23:20 Behold, I send an angel before you, to guard you 3
24: 8 Moses . . said, "Behold the blood of the covenant 3
11 they beheld God, and ate and drank. 4
14 and, behold, Aaron and Hur are with you; 3
31: 6 behold, I have appointed with him Oho'liab 3
32: 9 and behold, it is a stiff-necked people; 3
34 behold, my angel shall go before you. 3
33:21 the LORD said, "Behold, there is a place by me 3
34:10 he said, "Behold, I make a covenant. 3
11 Behold, I will drive out before you the Amorites 3
30 Moses, behold, the skin of his face shone 3
39:43 Moses saw all the work, and behold, they had done it; 3
Lev 10:16 the sin offering, and behold, it was burned 3
18 Behold, its blood was not brought into the inner 2
19 Aaron said to Moses, "Behold, today they have 2
Num 3:12 Behold, I have taken the Levites from among 3
12: 8 beholds the form of the LORD. 6
10 behold, Miriam was leprous, as white as snow. 3
10 towards Miriam, and behold, she was leprous. 3
16:42 tent of meeting; and behold, the cloud covered it 3
47 behold, the plague had already begun 3
17: 8 behold, the rod of Aaron . . had sprouted 3
12 Behold, we perish, we are undone, we are all undone. 2
18: 6 behold, I have taken your brethren the Levites 3
8 behold, I have given you whatever is kept 3
22: 5 Behold, a people has come out of Egypt; they cover 3
11 'Behold, a people has come out of Egypt 3
32 Behold, I have come forth to withstand you 3
23: 9 mountains I see him, from the hills I behold him; 9
11 behold, you have done nothing but bless them. 3
20 Behold, I received a command to bless 3
21 He has not beheld misfortune in Jacob; 6
24 Behold, a people! As a lioness it rises up 2
24:10 behold, you have blessed them these three times. 3
14 now, behold, I am going to my people; 3
17 I see him, but not now; I behold him, but not nigh 9
25: 6 behold, one of the people of Israel came 3
12 Behold, I give to him my covenant of peace; 3
31:16 Behold, these caused the people of Israel 2
32: 1 behold, the place was a place for cattle. 3
14 behold, you have risen in your fathers' stead 3
23 if you will not do so, behold, you have sinned 3
Deu 1: 8 Behold, I have set the land before you; go 7
10 behold, you are this day as the stars of heaven 3
21 Behold, the LORD your God has set the land before 7
2:24 behold, I have given into your hand Sihon 7
31 'Behold, I have begun to give Sihon and his land 7
3:11 behold, his bedstead was a bedstead of iron; 3
27 lift up your eyes . . and behold it with your eyes; 7
4: 5 Behold, I have taught you statutes 7
5:24 'Behold, the LORD our God has shown us his glory 2
9:13 seen . . and behold, it is a stubborn people; 3
16 I looked, and behold, you had sinned 3
10:14 Behold, to the LORD your God belong heaven 2
11:26 Behold, I set before you this day 7
13:14 behold, if it be true and certain that 3
26:10 behold, now I bring the first of the fruit 3
31:14 Behold, the days approach when you must die; 2
16 Behold, you are about to sleep with your fathers; 3
27 behold, while I am yet alive with you, today 2
Jos 2: 2 Behold, certain men of Israel have come here 3
18 Behold, when we come . . you shall bind this 3
3:11 Behold, the ark of the covenant . . is to pass over 3
5:13 he . . looked, and behold, a man stood before him 3
7:21 took them; and behold, they are hidden in the earth 3
22 Joshua sent . . and behold, it was hidden 3
8: 4 he commanded them, "Behold, you shall lie in ambush 7
20 behold, the smoke of the city went up to heaven; 3
9:12 was still . . but now, behold, it is dry and moldy 3
13 wineskins were new . . and behold, they are burst; 3
25 And now, behold, we are in your hand 3
14:10 now, behold, the LORD has kept me alive, as he said 3
22:11 Israel heard say, "Behold, the Reubenites 3
28 Behold the copy of the altar of the LORD 7
23: 4 Behold, I have allotted to you as an inheritance 7
24:27 Joshua said . . "Behold, this stone shall be 3
Jdg 1: 2 Judah shall go up; behold, I have given the land 3
4:22 behold, as Barak pursued Sis'era, Ja'el went out 3
6:15 Behold, my clan is the weakest in Manas'seh 3
28 behold, the altar of Ba'al was broken down 3
37 behold, I am laying a fleece of wool 3
7:13 Gideon came, behold, a man was telling a dream 3
13 telling a dream . . and he said, "Behold, I dreamed 3
8:15 he came . . and said, "Behold Zebah and Zalmun'na 3
9:31 Behold, Ga'al the son of Ebed and his kinsmen have 3
11:34 and behold, his daughter came out to meet him 3
13: 3 Behold, you are barren and have no children; 3
7 he said to me, 'Behold, you shall conceive and bear 3
10 Behold, the man who came to me the other day 3
14: 5 And behold, a young lion roared against him; 3
8 he turned aside to see . . and behold, there was 3
16 Behold, I have not told my father nor my mother 3
16:10 Behold, you have mocked me, and told me lies; 3
17: 2 behold, the silver is with me; I took it. 3
18: 9 have seen the land, and behold, it is very fertile. 3
12 called Ma'haneh-dan . . behold, it is west 3
19: 9 Behold, now the day has waned toward evening; pray 3
9 Behold, the day draws to its close; lodge here 3
16 behold, an old man was coming from his work 3
22 behold, the men . . beset the house round about 3
24 Behold, here are my virgin daughter and his 3
27 to go on his way, behold, there was his concubine 3
20: 7 Behold, you people of Israel, all of you, give 3
40 looked behind them; and behold, the whole 3
21: 8 behold, no one had come to the camp 3
9 For when the people were mustered, behold, not one 3
19 they said, "Behold, there is the yearly feast 3
Rut 2: 4 And behold, Bo'az came from Bethlehem; 3
3: 8 and turned over, and behold, a woman lay at his feet! 3
4: 1 and behold, the next of kin . . came by. So Bo'az said 3
1Sm 2:31 Behold, the days are coming, when I will cut off 3
3:11 the LORD said to Samuel, "Behold, I am about to do 3
5: 3 when the people . . behold, Dagon had fallen 3
4 when they rose . . behold, Dagon had fallen 3
8: 5 came . . and said to him, "Behold, you are old 3
9: 6 But he said to him, "Behold, there is a man of God 3
12 He is; behold, he is just ahead of you. 3
10: 8 go down before me . . and behold, I am coming to you 3
10 When they came . . behold, a band of prophets met 3
22 the LORD said, "Behold, he has hidden himself 3
12: 1 Samuel said . . "Behold, I have hearkened 3
2 And now, behold, the king walks before you; 3
2 I am old and gray, and behold, my sons are with you; 3
13 And now behold the king whom you have chosen 3
13 behold, the LORD has set a king over you. 3
13:10 As soon as he had finished . . behold, Samuel came; 3
14: 7 Do all that your mind . . behold, I am with you 3
8 Then said Jonathan, "Behold, we will cross over 3
16 the watchmen . . looked; and behold, the multitude 3
17 when they had numbered, behold, Jonathan and his 3
20 behold, every man's sword was against his fellow 3
26 when the people . . behold, the honey was dropping 3
33 they told Saul, "Behold, the people are sinning 3
15:12 Saul came . . and behold, he set up a monument 3
22 Behold, to obey is better than sacrifice 3
16:11 the youngest, but behold, he is keeping the sheep. 3
15 Behold now, an evil spirit from God is tormenting 3
18 Behold, I have seen a son of Jesse 3
17:23 behold, the champion, the Philistine . . came up 3

18:22 Behold, the king has delight in you 3
19:16 when the messengers came in, behold, the image was 3
19 Behold, David is at Nai'oth in Ramah. 3
22 And one said, "Behold, they are at Nai'oth in Ramah. 3
20: 2 You shall not die. Behold, my father does nothing 3
5 Behold, tomorrow is the new moon, and I should not 3
12 behold, if he is well disposed toward David 3
21 And behold, I will send the lad, saying 3
23 as for the matter .. behold, the LORD is between 3
21: 9 The sword of Goliath .. behold, it is here wrapped 3
23: 1 Now they told David, "Behold, the Philistines are 3
3 David's men said to him, "Behold, we are afraid here 3
24: 1 Behold, David is in the wilderness of En-ge'di. 3
4 LORD said to you, 'Behold, I will give your enemy 3
9 men who say, 'Behold, David seeks your hurt'? 3
20 now, behold, I know that you shall surely be king 3
25:14 Behold, David sent messengers out 3
19 Go on before me; behold, I come after you. 3
20 And as she rode .. behold, David and his men came 3
41 and said, "Behold, your handmaid is a servant 3
26:21 behold, I have played the fool, and have erred 3
24 Behold, as your life was precious .. so may my life 3
28: 7 his servants said to him, "Behold, there is a medium 3
21 Behold, your handmaid has hearkened to you; 3
30:16 behold, they were spread abroad over all the land 3
2Sm 1: 2 the third day, behold, a man came from Saul's camp 3
18 said it should be taught .. behold, it is written 3
3:12 Make your covenant with me, and behold, my hand 3
24 What have you done? Behold, Abner came to you; why 3
4: 6 behold, the doorkeeper .. had been cleaning 17
10 when one told me, 'Behold, Saul is dead,' 3
5: 1 the tribes .. came .. and said, "Behold, we are 3
9: 6 And he answered, "Behold, your servant. 3
12:11 Thus says the LORD, 'Behold, I will raise up evil 3
18 they said, "Behold, while the child was yet alive 3
13:24 Ab'salom came .. and said, "Behold, your servant has 3
34 and looked, and behold, many people were coming 3
35 Jon'adab said to the king, "Behold, the king's sons 3
36 finished speaking, behold, the king's sons came 3
14:21 Then the king said to Jo'ab, "Behold now, I grant this; 3
32 Ab'salom answered Jo'ab, "Behold, I sent word to you 3
15:15 said to the king, "Behold, your servants are ready 3
26 if he says .. behold, here I am, let him do to me 3
32 David .. behold, Hushai the Archite came 3
36 Behold, their two sons are with them there 3
16: 3 Ziba said .. "Behold, he remains in Jerusalem; 3
4 the king said to Ziba, "Behold, all that belonged 3
11 David said .. "Behold, my own son seeks my life; 3
17: 9 Behold, even now he has hidden .. in one of the pits 3
18:10 and told Jo'ab, "Behold, I saw Ab'salom hanging 3
31 And behold, the Cushite came; and the Cushite said 3
19: 1 It was told Jo'ab, "Behold, the king is weeping 3
8 people were all told, "Behold, the king is sitting 3
20 I have sinned; therefore, behold, I have come 3
20:21 the woman said .. "Behold, his head shall be thrown 3
1Kg 1:18 And now, behold, Adoni'jah is king, although you, my 3
25 behold, they are eating and drinking before him 3
42 he was still speaking, behold, Jonathan .. came; 3
51 it was told Solomon, "Behold, Adoni'jah fears King 3
2:29 Jo'ab has fled .. and behold, he is beside the altar 3
39 it was told Shim'e-i, "Behold, your slaves are in Gath 3
3:12 behold, I now do according to your word 3
12 I now do according to your word. Behold, I give you 3
15 Solomon awoke, and behold, it was a dream. Then he 3
21 When I rose .. to nurse my child, behold, it was dead; 3
21 when I looked .. behold, it was not the child that 3
8:27 Behold, heaven .. cannot contain thee; 3
10: 7 and behold, the half was not told me; 3
11:31 Behold, I am about to tear the kingdom 3
12:28 Behold your gods, O Israel, who brought you up 3
13: 1 behold, a man of God came out of Judah 3
2 Behold, a son shall be born to the house of David 3
3 Behold, the altar shall be torn down 3
25 behold, men passed by, and saw the body 3
14: 2 go to Shiloh; behold, Ahi'jah the prophet is there 3
5 Behold, the wife of Jerobo'am is coming to inquire 3
10 behold, I will bring evil upon the house 3
19 acts of Jerobo'am .. behold, they are written 3
15:19 Let there be a league .. behold, I am sending 3
16: 3 behold, I will .. sweep away Ba'asha and his house 3
17: 9 Behold, I have commanded a widow .. to feed you. 3
10 when he came .. behold, a widow was there 3
18: 7 as Obadi'ah was on the way, behold, Eli'jah met him; 3
8 Go, tell your lord, 'Behold, Eli'jah is here.' 3
11 'Go, tell your lord, "Behold, Eli'jah is here."' 3
14 'Go, tell your lord, "Behold, Eli'jah is here"'; 3
44 he said, "Behold, a little cloud like a man's hand 3
19: 5 he lay down .. and behold, an angel touched him 3
6 he looked, and behold, there was at his head a cake 3
9 and behold, the word of the LORD came to him 3
11 Go forth, and stand .. " And behold, the LORD passed 3
13 And behold, there came a voice to him, and said 3
20:13 behold, a prophet came near to Ahab king of Israel 3
13 Behold, I will give it into your hand this day; 3
31 Behold now, we have heard that the kings 3
36 behold, as soon as you .. a lion shall kill you. 3
39 servant went out .. and behold, a soldier turned 3
21:18 go down to meet .. behold, he is in the vineyard 3
21 Behold, I will bring evil upon you; 3

22:13 the messenger .. said to him, "Behold, the words 3
23 Now therefore behold, the LORD has put 3
25 Micai'ah said, "Behold, you shall see on that day 3
2Kg 2:11 as they still went on and talked, behold, a chariot 3
16 Behold now, there are .. 50 strong men; 3
19 Behold, the situation of this city is pleasant 3
3:20 The next morning .. behold, water came 3
4: 9 she said to her husband, "Behold now, I perceive 3
5:11 and went away, saying, "Behold, I thought that 3
15 Behold, I know that there is no God in all the earth 3
6:13 It was told him, "Behold, he is in Dothan. 3
15 When the servant .. went out, behold, an army 3
17 he saw; and behold, the mountain was full of horses 3
30 the people looked, and behold, he had sackcloth 3
7: 5 when they came .. behold, there was no one there. 3
6 said to one another, "Behold, the king of Israel 3
10 We came to the camp .. and behold, there was no one 3
8: 5 while he was telling .. behold, the woman 3
9: 5 when he came, behold, the commanders of the army 3
10: 4 and said, "Behold, the two kings could not stand 3
15:11 deeds of Zechari'ah, behold, they are written 3
15 the deeds of Shallum .. behold, they are written 3
26 deeds of .. behold, they are written in the Book 3
31 the acts of .. behold, they are written in the Book 3
17:26 he has sent lions .. and behold, they are killing 3
18:21 Behold, you are relying now on Egypt 3
19: 7 Behold, I will put a spirit in him, so that he shall 3
9 Behold, he has set out to fight against you 3
11 Behold, you have heard what the kings .. have done 3
35 when men arose .. behold, these were all dead 3
20: 5 I have seen your tears; behold, I will heal you; 3
17 Behold, the days are coming, when all .. shall be 3
21:12 Behold, I am bringing upon Jerusalem .. such evil 3
22:16 Thus says the LORD, Behold, I will bring evil 3
20 Therefore, behold, I will gather you 3
1Ch 11: 1 and said, "Behold, we are your bone and flesh. 3
17: 1 Behold, I dwell in a house of cedar 3
22: 9 Behold, a son shall be born to you; 3
28:21 behold the divisions of the priests 3
2Ch 2: 4 Behold, I am about to build a house for .. the LORD 3
6:18 Behold .. the highest heaven cannot contain 3
9: 6 behold, half the greatness of your wisdom 3
13:12 Behold, God is with us at our head 3
14 when Judah looked, behold, the battle was 3
16: 3 behold, I am sending to you silver and gold; 3
18:12 Behold, the words of the prophets with one accord 3
22 Now therefore behold, the LORD has put 3
24 Behold, you shall see on that day when you go 3
19:11 behold, Amari'ah the chief priest, is over you 3
20: 2 behold, they are in Haz'azon-ta'mar" 3
10 behold, the men of Ammon and Moab and Mount Se'ir 3
11 behold, they reward us by coming to drive us 3
16 behold, they will come up by the ascent of Ziz; 3
24 behold, they were dead bodies lying on the ground; 3
21:14 behold, the LORD will bring a great plague 3
23: 3 Behold, the king's son! Let him reign 3
26:20 behold, he was leprous in his forehead! 3
27: 7 behold, they are written in the Book of the Kings 3
28: 9 Behold, because the LORD .. was angry with Judah 3
26 behold, they are written in the Book of the Kings 3
29:19 behold, they are before the altar of the LORD. 3
32:32 behold, they are written in the vision of Isaiah 3
33:18 behold, they are in the Chronicles of the Kings 3
19 behold, they are written in the Chronicles 3
34:24 Thus says the LORD, Behold, I will bring evil 3
28 Behold, I will gather you to your fathers 3
35:25 behold, they are written in the Laments. 3
27 behold, they are written in the Book of the Kings 3
36: 8 behold, they are written in the Book of the Kings 3
Ezr 9:15 Behold, we are before thee in our guilt 3
Neh 9:36 Behold, we are slaves this day; 3
36 in the land .. behold, we are slaves. 3
Est 1:11 to show .. her beauty; for she was fair to behold 5
8: 7 Behold, I have given Esther the house of Haman 3
Job 1:12 Behold, all that he has is in your power; 3
19 behold, a great wind came across the wilderness 3
2: 6 the LORD said to Satan, "Behold, he is in your power; 3
4: 3 Behold, you have instructed many 3
5:17 Behold, happy is the man whom God reproves; 3
7: 8 The eye of him who sees me will behold me no more; 9
8:19 Behold, this is the joy of his way; 2
20 Behold, God will not reject a blameless man 2
9:12 Behold, he snatches away; who can hinder him? 2
19 If it is a contest of strength, behold him! 3
13:15 Behold, he will slay me; I have no hope; 2
18 Behold, I have prepared my case; 3
15:15 Behold, God puts no trust in his holy ones 2
16:19 Even now, behold, my witness is in heaven 3
19: 7 Behold, I cry out, 'Violence!' but I am not answered; 2
27 my eyes shall behold, and not another. 7
20: 9 nor will his place any more behold him. 9
21:16 Behold, is not their prosperity in their hand? 2
27 Behold, I know your thoughts 2
23: 8 Behold, I go forward, but he is not there; 2
9 on the left hand I seek him, but I cannot behold him; 4
24: 5 Behold, like wild asses in the desert they go 2
25: 5 Behold, even the moon is not bright 2
27:12 Behold, all of you have seen it yourselves; 2
28:28 Behold, the fear of the Lord, that is wisdom; 2

32:11 Behold, I waited for your words 2
12 behold, there was none that confuted Job 3
19 Behold, my heart is like wine that has no vent; 3
33: 2 Behold, I open my mouth; 3
6 Behold, I am toward God as you are; 2
7 Behold, no fear of me need terrify you; 3
10 Behold, he finds occasions against me 2
12 Behold, in this you are not right. 2
29 Behold, God does all these things, 2
34:29 When he hides his face, who can behold him 9
35: 5 behold the clouds, which are higher than you. 9
36: 5 Behold, God is mighty, and does not despise any; 2
22 Behold, God is exalted in his power; 2
25 men have looked on it; man beholds it from afar. 6
26 Behold, God is great, and we know him not; 2
30 Behold, he scatters his lightning about him 2
39:29 he spies out the prey; his eyes behold it afar off. 6
40: 4 Behold, I am of small account; what shall I answer 2
15 Behold, Be'hemoth, which I made as I made you; 3
16 Behold, his strength in his loins, and his power 3
23 Behold, if the river is turbulent 2
41: 9 Behold, the hope of a man is disappointed; 2
34 He beholds everything that is high; 7
Ps 7:14 Behold, the wicked man conceives evil 3
9:13 Behold what I suffer from those who hate me 7
11: 4 his eyes behold, his eyelids test 4
7 the upright shall behold his face. 4
17:15 for me, I shall behold thy face in righteousness; 4
15 I shall be satisfied with beholding thy form. 4
27: 4 to behold the beauty of the LORD 4
33:18 Behold, the eye of the LORD is on those who fear him 3
37:37 Mark the blameless man, and behold the upright 7
39: 5 Behold, thou hast made my days a few handbreadths 3
42: 2 When shall I come and behold the face of God? 7
46: 8 Come, behold the works of the LORD 4
51: 5 Behold, I was brought forth in iniquity, and in sin 2
6 Behold, thou desirest truth in the inward being; 2
54: 4 Behold, God is my helper; 3
63: 2 in the sanctuary, beholding thy power and glory. 7
73:12 Behold, these are the wicked; always at ease 3
84: 9 Behold our shield, O God; 7
87: 4 behold, Philistia and Tyre, with Ethiopia– 3
97: 6 all the peoples behold his glory. 7
119:18 that I may behold wondrous things out of thy law. 6
40 Behold, I long for thy precepts; 3
121: 4 Behold, he who keeps Israel will neither slumber 3
123: 2 Behold, as the eyes of servants look to the hand 3
133: 1 Behold, how good and pleasant it is when brothers 3
139:16 Thy eyes beheld my unformed substance; 7
Prv 1:23 behold, I will pour out my thoughts to you; 3
24:12 If you say, "Behold, we did not know this, 2
Ecc 1:14 behold, all is vanity and a striving after wind. 3
2: 1 But behold, this also was vanity. 3
11 I considered .. and behold, all was vanity 3
4: 1 behold, the tears .. and they had no one to comfort 3
5:18 Behold, what I have seen to be good .. is to eat 3
7:27 Behold, this is what I found, says the Preacher 7
29 Behold, this alone I found, that God made man 7
11: 7 and it is pleasant for the eyes to behold the sun. 7
Sng 1:15 Behold, you are beautiful, my love; 3
15 behold, you are beautiful; your eyes are doves. 3
16 Behold, you are beautiful, my beloved 3
2: 8 Behold, he comes, leaping upon the mountains 3
9 Behold, there he stands behind our wall, gazing 3
3: 7 Behold, it is the litter of Solomon! 3
11 Go .. O daughters of Zion, and behold King Solomon 8
4: 1 Behold, you are beautiful, my love 3
1 Behold .. my love, behold, you are beautiful! 3
Isa 3: 1 behold, the Lord, the LORD of hosts, is taking away 3
5: 7 he looked for justice, but behold, bloodshed; 3
7 bloodshed; for righteousness, but behold, a cry! 3
30 behold, darkness and distress; 3
6: 7 Behold, this has touched your lips; 3
7:14 Behold, a young woman shall conceive and bear 3
8: 7 behold, the Lord is bringing up against them 3
18 Behold, I and the children whom the LORD has given 3
22 they will look to the earth, but behold, distress 3
10:33 Behold .. the LORD of hosts will lop the boughs 3
12: 2 Behold, God is my salvation; 3
13: 9 Behold, the day of the LORD comes, cruel 3
17 Behold, I am stirring up the Medes against them 3
17: 1 Behold, Damascus will cease to be a city 3
14 At evening time, behold, terror! 3
19: 1 Behold, the LORD is riding on a swift cloud 3
20: 6 coastland will say in that day, 'Behold, this 3
21: 9 And, behold, here come riders, horsemen in pairs! 3
22:13 behold, joy and gladness, slaying oxen 3
17 Behold, the LORD will hurl you away violently 3
23:13 Behold the land of the Chalde'ans! 2
24: 1 Behold, the LORD will lay waste the earth 3
26:21 For behold, the LORD is coming forth 3
28: 2 Behold, the Lord has one who is mighty and strong; 3
16 thus says the Lord GOD, "Behold, I am laying in Zion 3
29:14 therefore, behold, I will again do marvelous 3
30:27 Behold, the name of the LORD comes from far 3
32: 1 Behold, a king will reign in righteousness 2
33: 7 Behold, the valiant ones cry without; 2
17 they will behold a land that stretches afar. 7
34: 5 behold, it descends for judgment upon Edom 3

35: 4 Behold, your God will come with vengeance 3
36: 6 Behold, you are relying on Egypt, that broken reed 3
37: 7 Behold, I will put a spirit in him 3
11 Behold, you have heard what the kings of Assyria 3
36 behold, these were all dead bodies. 3
38: 5 behold, I will add fifteen years to your life. 3
8 Behold, I will make the shadow cast 3
39: 6 Behold, the days are coming, when all that is 3
40: 9 say to the cities of Judah, "Behold your God! 3
10 Behold, the Lord GOD comes with might 3
10 behold, his reward is with him 3
15 Behold, the nations are like a drop from a bucket 2
15 behold, he takes up the isles like fine dust. 2
41:11 Behold, all who are incensed against you 2
15 Behold, I will make of you a threshing sledge 3
24 Behold, you are nothing, and your work is nought; 2
29 Behold, they are all a delusion; 2
42: 1 Behold my servant, whom I uphold 2
9 Behold, the former things have come to pass 3
43:19 Behold, I am doing a new thing; now it springs forth 3
44:11 Behold, all his fellows shall be put to shame 2
47:14 Behold, they are like stubble, the fire consumes 3
48: 7 lest you should say, 'Behold, I knew them.' 3
10 Behold, I have refined you, but not like silver; 3
49:16 Behold, I have graven you on the palms of my hands; 2
21 who has brought up these? Behold, I was left alone; 2
22 Behold, I will lift up my hand to the nations 3
50: 1 Behold, for your iniquities you were sold 2
2 Behold, by my rebuke I dry up the sea 2
9 Behold, the Lord GOD helps me; 2
9 Behold, all of them will wear out like a garment; 2
11 Behold, all you who kindle a fire 2
51:22 Behold I have taken from your hand the cup 3
52:13 Behold, my servant shall prosper 3
54:11 behold, I will set your stones in antimony 3
16 Behold, I have created the smith who blows 3
55: 4 Behold, I made him a witness to the peoples 2
5 Behold, you shall call nations that you know not 2
56: 3 let not the eunuch say, "Behold, I am a dry tree. 2
58: 3 Behold, in the day of your fast you seek your own 2
4 Behold, you fast only to quarrel and to fight 2
59: 1 Behold, the LORD'S hand is not shortened 2
9 we look for light, and behold darkness 3
60: 2 For behold, darkness shall cover the earth 3
62:11 Behold, the LORD has proclaimed to the end 3
11 Behold, your salvation comes; 3
11 behold, his reward is with him 3
64: 5 Behold, thou wast angry, and we sinned; 2
9 Behold, consider, we are all thy people. 2
65: 6 Behold, it is written before me: "I will not keep 3
13 says the Lord GOD: "Behold, my servants shall eat 3
13 behold, my servants shall drink, 3
13 behold, my servants shall rejoice, 3
14 behold, my servants shall sing for gladness 3
17 For behold, I create new heavens and a new earth; 3
18 for behold, I create Jerusalem a rejoicing 3
66:12 Behold, I will extend prosperity to her like 3
15 For behold, the LORD will come in fire 3
Jer 1: 6 Ah, Lord GOD! Behold, I do not know how to speak 3
9 Behold, I have put my words in your mouth. 3
18 And I, behold, I make you this day a fortified city 3
2:35 Behold, I will bring you to judgment for saying 3
3: 5 Behold, you have spoken 3
22 Behold, we come to thee; for thou art the LORD 3
4:13 Behold, he comes up like clouds 3
5:14 behold, I am making my words in your mouth a fire 3
15 Behold, I am bringing upon you a nation from afar 3
6:10 Behold, their ears are closed, they cannot listen; 3
10 behold, the word of the LORD is to them an object 3
19 behold, I am bringing evil upon this people 3
21 Therefore thus says the LORD: 'Behold 3
22 Thus says the LORD: "Behold, a people is coming 3
7: 8 Behold, you trust in deceptive words to no avail. 3
11 Behold, I myself have seen it, says the LORD. 3
20 Behold, my anger and my wrath will be poured out 3
32 behold, the days are coming, says the LORD 3
8: 8 behold, the false pen of the scribes has made it 3
15 for a time of healing, but behold, terror. 3
17 For behold, I am sending among you serpents 3
9: 7 Behold, I will refine them and test them 3
15 Behold, I will feed this people with wormwood 3
25 Behold, the days are coming, says the LORD 3
10:18 Behold, I am slinging out the inhabitants 3
22 Hark, a rumor! Behold, it comes!-a great commotion 3
11:11 Therefore, thus says the LORD, Behold 3
22 therefore thus says the LORD of hosts: "Behold 3
12:14 Behold, I will pluck them up from their land 3
13: 7 And behold, the waistcloth was spoiled; 3
13 Behold, I will fill with drunkenness 3
14:13 Ah, Lord GOD, behold, the prophets say to them 3
18 If I go out into the field, behold, those slain 3
18 if I enter the city, behold, the diseases of famine! 3
19 for a time of healing, but behold, terror. 3
16: 9 Behold, I will make to cease from this place 3
12 behold, every one of you follows his stubborn 3
14 behold, the days are coming, says the LORD 3
16 Behold, I am sending for many fishers 3
21 Therefore, behold, I will make them know 3
17:15 Behold, they say to me, "Where is the word 3
18: 6 Behold, like the clay in the potter's hand 3
11 Thus says the LORD, Behold, I am shaping evil 3
19: 3 Behold, I am bringing such evil upon this place 3
6 therefore, behold, days are coming, says the LORD 3
15 Behold, I am bringing upon this city 3
20: 4 Behold, I will make you a terror to yourself 3
21: 4 Behold, I will turn back the weapons of war 3
8 Behold, I set before you the way of life 3
13 Behold, I am against you 3
23: 2 Behold, I will attend to you for your evil doings 3
5 Behold, the days are coming, says the LORD 3
7 behold, the days are coming, says the LORD 3
15 Behold, I will feed them with wormwood 3
19 Behold, the storm of the LORD! Wrath has gone forth 3
30 behold, I am against the prophets, says the LORD 3
31 Behold, I am against the prophets, says the LORD 3
32 Behold, I am against those who prophesy lying 3
39 therefore, behold, I will surely lift you up 3
24: 1 showed me this vision: Behold, two baskets of figs 3
25: 9 behold, I will send for all the tribes of the north 3
29 For behold, I begin to work evil at the city 3
32 Behold, evil is going forth from nation to nation 3
26:14 But as for me, behold, I am in your hands. 3
27:16 saying, 'Behold, the vessels of the LORD'S house 3
28:16 thus says the LORD: 'Behold, I will remove you 3
29:17 Thus says the LORD of hosts, Behold 3
21 Behold, I will deliver them into the hand 3
32 thus says the LORD: Behold, I will punish Shemai'ah 3
30: 3 For behold, days are coming, says the LORD 3
18 Behold, I will restore the fortunes of the tents 3
23 Behold the storm of the LORD! Wrath has gone forth 3
31: 8 Behold, I will bring them from the north country 3
27 Behold, the days are coming, says the LORD 3
31 Behold, the days are coming, says the LORD 3
38 Behold, the days are coming, says the LORD 3
32: 3 Thus says the LORD: Behold, I am giving this city 3
7 Behold, Han'amel the son of Shallum your uncle 3
24 Behold, the siege mounds have come up to the city 3
24 has come to pass, and behold, thou seest it. 3
27 Behold, I am the LORD, the God of all flesh; 3
28 Behold, I am giving this city into the hands 3
37 Behold, I will gather them from all the countries 3
33: 6 Behold, I will bring to it health and healing 3
14 Behold, the days are coming, says the LORD 3
34: 2 Thus says the LORD: Behold, I am giving this city 3
17 behold, I proclaim to you liberty to the sword 3
22 Behold, I will command, says the LORD 3
35:17 Behold, I am bringing on Judah 3
37: 7 Behold, Pharoah's army which came to help you 3
38: 5 King Zedeki'ah said, "Behold, he is in your hands; 3
22 Behold, all the women left in the house of the king 3
39:16 Behold, I will fulfil my words against this city 3
40: 4 Now, behold, I release you today from the chains 3
42: 4 behold, I will pray to the LORD your God 3
43:10 Behold, I will send and take Nebuchadrez'zar 3
44: 2 Behold, this day they are a desolation 3
11 Behold, I will set my face against you for evil 3
26 Behold, I have sworn by my great name, 3
27 Behold, I am watching over them for evil 3
30 Behold, I will give Pharaoh Hophra king of Egypt 3
45: 4 Behold, what I have built I am breaking down 3
5 for, behold, I am bringing evil upon all flesh 3
46:25 Behold, I am bringing punishment upon Amon 3
47: 2 Thus says the LORD: Behold, waters are rising 3
48:12 behold, the days are coming, says the LORD 3
40 Behold, one shall fly swiftly like an eagle 3
49: 2 behold, the days are coming, says the LORD 3
5 Behold, I will bring terror upon you, says the Lord 3
15 behold, I will make you small among the nations 3
19 Behold, like a lion coming up from the jungle 3
22 Behold, one shall mount up and fly swiftly 3
35 Behold, I will break the bow of Elam 3
50: 9 For behold, I am stirring up 3
18 Behold, I am bringing punishment on the king 3
31 Behold, I am against you, O proud one, says the Lord 3
41 Behold, a people comes from the north; 3
44 Behold, like a lion coming up from the jungle 3
51: 1 Behold, I will stir up the spirit of a destroyer 3
25 Behold, I am against you, O destroying mountain 3
36 says the LORD: "Behold, I will plead your cause 3
47 Therefore, behold, the days are coming 3
52 behold, the days are coming, says the LORD 3
Lam 1: 9 O LORD, behold my affliction 7
11 Look, O LORD, and behold, for I am despised. 6
18 but hear, all you peoples, and behold my suffering; 7
20 Behold, O LORD, for I am in distress 7
3:63 Behold their sitting and their rising; 6
5: 1 Remember, O LORD . . behold, and see our disgrace! 6
Ezk 1: 4 behold, a stormy wind came out of the north 3
2: 9 I looked, behold, a hand was stretched out to me 3
3: 8 Behold, I have made your face hard 3
25 O son of man, behold, cords will be placed upon you 3
4: 8 And, behold, I will put cords upon you 3
14 Ah Lord GOD! behold, I have never defiled myself; 3
16 Son of man, behold, I will break the staff of bread 3
5: 8 therefore thus says the Lord GOD: Behold, I, even I 3
6: 3 Behold, I, even I, will bring a sword upon you 3
7: 5 Disaster after disaster! Behold, it comes. 3
6 it has awakened against you. Behold, it comes. 3
10 Behold, the day! Behold, it comes! 3
10 Behold, it comes! Your doom has come 3
8: 2 Then I beheld, and, lo, a form 7
4 behold, the glory of the God of Israel was there 3
5 So I lifted up my eyes toward the north, and behold 3
7 when I looked, behold, there was a hole in the wall. 3
14 and behold, there sat women weeping for Tammuz. 3
16 and behold, at the door of the temple of the LORD 3
10: 1 Then I looked, and behold, on the firmament 3
9 I looked, and behold, there were four wheels 3
11: 1 And behold, at the door of the gateway there were 3
12:27 Son of man, behold, they of the house of Israel say 3
13: 8 behold, I am against you, says the Lord GOD. 3
20 Behold, I am against your magic bands 3
15: 5 Behold, when it was whole, it was used for nothing; 3
16: 8 behold, you were at the age for love; 3
27 Behold, therefore, I stretched out my hand 3
37 therefore, behold, I will gather all your lovers 3
43 behold, I will requite your deeds upon your head 1
44 Behold, every one who uses proverbs will use this 3
49 Behold, this was the guilt of your sister Sodom 3
17: 7 behold, this vine bent its roots toward him 3
10 Behold, when it is transplanted, will it thrive? 3
12 Behold, the king of Babylon came to Jerusalem 3
18: 4 Behold, all souls are mine; 2
18 behold, he shall die for his iniquity. 3
20:47 Behold, I will kindle a fire in you 3
21: 3 Behold, I am against you 3
7 Behold, it comes and it will be fulfilled 3
22: 6 Behold, the princes of Israel in you, every one 3
13 Behold, therefore, I strike my hands together 3
19 behold, I will gather you into the midst 3
23:22 Behold, I will rouse against you your lovers 3
28 Behold, I will deliver you into the hands of those 3
24:16 Son of man, behold, I am about to take the delight 3
21 Behold, I will profane my sanctuary 3
25: 7 therefore, behold, I have stretched out my hand 3
8 Behold, the house of Judah is like all the other 3
16 Behold, I will stretch out my hand 3
26: 3 says the Lord GOD: Behold, I am against you, O Tyre 3
7 Behold, I will bring upon Tyre from the north 3
28: 7 behold, I will bring strangers upon you 3
22 says the Lord GOD: "Behold, I am against you, O Sidon 3
29: 3 Behold, I am against you, Pharaoh king of Egypt 3
8 Behold, I will bring a sword upon you, and will cut 3
10 therefore, behold, I am against you 3
19 Behold, I will give the land of Egypt 3
30:22 Behold, I am against Pharaoh king of Egypt 3
31: 3 Behold, I will liken you to a cedar in Lebanon 3
34:10 Behold, I am against the shepherds; 3
11 Behold, I, I myself will search for my sheep 3
17 Behold, I judge between sheep and sheep 3
20 Therefore, thus says the Lord GOD to them: Behold 3
35: 3 and say to it, Thus says the Lord GOD: Behold 3
36: 6 Behold, I speak in my jealous wrath 3
9 For, behold, I am for you, and I will turn to you 3
37: 2 behold, there were very many upon the valley; 3
5 Behold, I will cause breath to enter you 3
7 there was a noise, and behold, a rattling; 3
11 Behold, they say, 'Our bones are dried up 3
12 says the Lord GOD: Behold, I will open your graves 3
19 Behold, I am about to take the stick of Joseph 3
21 Behold, I will take the people of Israel 3
38: 3 says the Lord GOD: Behold, I am against you, O Gog 3
39: 1 says the Lord GOD: Behold, I am against you, O Gog 3
8 Behold, it is coming and it will be brought about 3
40: 3 When he brought me there, behold, there was a man 3
5 behold, there was a wall all around the outside 3
17 behold, there were chambers and a pavement 3
20 behold, there was a gate which faced toward •
24 behold, there was a gate on the south; 3
44 behold, there were two chambers in the inner •
43: 2 behold, the glory of the God of Israel 3
5 behold, the glory of the LORD filled the temple. 3
12 Behold, this is the law of the temple. 3
44: 4 I looked, and behold, the glory of the LORD filled 3
47: 1 behold, water was issuing from below 3
Dan 2:31 You saw, O king, and behold, a great image. 10
4:10 saw, and behold, a tree in the midst of the earth; 10
13 behold, a watcher, a holy one, came down 10
7: 2 behold, the four winds of heaven were stirring up 11
5 behold, another beast, a second one, like a bear. 11
7 behold, a fourth beast, terrible and dreadful 11
8 I considered the horns, and behold, there came up 10
8 behold, in this horn were eyes like the eyes 10
13 I saw in the night visions, and behold 11
8: 3 I raised my eyes and saw, and behold 3
5 As I was considering, behold, a he-goat came 3
15 behold, there stood before me one having 3
19 said, "Behold, I will make known to you what shall be 3
9:18 open thy eyes and behold our desolations 7
10: 5 I lifted up my eyes and looked, and behold, a man 3
10 behold, a hand touched me and set me trembling 3
16 behold, one in the likeness of the sons of men 3
11: 2 Behold, three more kings shall arise in Persia; 3
12: 5 Then I Daniel looked, and behold, two others stood 3
Hos 2:14 Therefore, behold, I will allure her, and bring her 3
9: 6 For behold, they are going to Assyria; 3
Jol 2:19 Behold, I am sending to you grain, wine, and oil 3

3: 1 For behold, in those days and at that time 3
Ams 2:13 Behold, I will press you down in your place 3
4: 2 that, behold, the days are coming upon you 3
6:11 For behold, the LORD commands 3
14 For behold, I will raise up against you a nation 3
7: 1 behold, he was forming locusts 3
4 behold, the Lord GOD was calling for a judgment 3
7 behold, the Lord was standing beside a wall 3
8: 1 GOD showed me: behold, a basket of summer fruit. 3
11 Behold, the days are coming," says the Lord GOD 3
9: 8 Behold, the eyes of the Lord GOD are upon 3
13 Behold, the days are coming," says the LORD 3
Obd 1: 2 Behold, I will make you small among the nations 3
Mic 1: 3 For behold, the LORD is coming forth 3
2: 3 Behold, against this family I am devising evil 3
7: 9 I shall behold his deliverance. 7
Nah 1:15 Behold, on the mountains the feet of him 3
2:13 Behold, I am against you, says the LORD of hosts 3
3: 5 Behold, I am against you, says the LORD of hosts 3
13 Behold, your troops are women in your midst. 3
Hab 1:13 Thou who art of purer eyes than to behold evil 7
2: 4 Behold, he whose soul is not upright in him 3
13 Behold, is it not from the LORD of hosts 3
19 Behold, it is overlaid with gold and silver 3
Zep 3:19 Behold, at that time I will deal 3
Zec 1: 8 behold, a man riding upon a red horse! 3
11 behold, all the earth remains at rest.' 3
18 I lifted my eyes and saw, and behold, four horns! 3
2: 1 behold, a man with a measuring line in his hand! 3
3 behold, the angel who talked with me came forward 3
9 Behold, I will shake my hand over them 3
3: 4 Behold, I have taken your iniquity away from you 7
8 behold, I will bring my servant the Branch. 3
9 behold, upon the stone which I have set before 3
4: 2 I said, "I see, and behold, a lampstand all of gold 3
5: 1 lifted my eyes and saw, and behold, a flying scroll! 3
7 behold, the leaden cover was lifted 3
9 and saw, and behold, two women coming forward! 3
6: 1 behold, four chariots came out 3
8 Behold, those who go toward the north country 7
12 Behold, the man whose name is the Branch 3
8: 7 Thus says the LORD of hosts: Behold, I will save 3
14: 1 Behold, a day of the LORD is coming 3
Mal 2: 3 Behold, I will rebuke your offspring 3
3: 1 Behold, I send my messenger to prepare the way 3
1 behold, he is coming, says the LORD of hosts. 3
4: 1 For behold, the day comes, burning like an oven 3
5 Behold, I will send you Eli'jah the prophet 3
Mat 1:20 as he considered this, behold, an angel of the Lord 17
23 Behold, a virgin shall conceive and bear a son 17
2: 1 days of Herod the king, behold, wise men 17
13 behold, an angel of the Lord appeared to Joseph 17
19 when Herod died, behold, an angel of the Lord 17
3:16 behold, the heavens were opened and he saw 17
4:11 Then the devil left him, and behold, angels came 17
8: 2 behold, a leper came to him and knelt before him 17
24 behold, there arose a great storm on the sea 17
29 behold, they cried out, "What have you to do with us 17
32 behold, the whole herd rushed down the steep bank 17
34 behold, all the city came out to meet Jesus 17
9: 2 behold, they brought to him a paralytic 17
3 behold, some of the scribes said to themselves 17
10 behold, many tax collectors and sinners came 17
18 behold, a ruler came in and knelt before him 17
20 behold, a woman who had suffered 17
32 As they were going away, behold, a dumb demoniac 17
10:16 Behold, I send you out as sheep 17
11: 7 What did you go out into the wilderness to behold? 15
8 Behold, those who wear soft raiment 17
10 'Behold, I send my messenger before thy face 17
19 and they say, 'Behold, a glutton and a drunkard 17
12:10 behold, there was a man with a withered hand 17
18 Behold, my servant whom I have chosen, my beloved 17
41 behold, something greater than Jonah is here. 17
42 behold, something greater than Solomon is here. 17
46 behold, his mother and his brothers stood 17
15:22 behold, a Canaanite woman from that region 17
17: 3 behold, there appeared to them Moses and Eli'jah 17
18:10 in heaven their angels always behold the face 12
19:16 behold, one came up to him, saying 17
20:18 Behold, we are going up to Jerusalem 17
30 behold, two blind men sitting by the roadside 17
21: 5 Behold, your king is coming to you 17
22: 4 Behold, I have made ready my dinner 17
23:38 Behold, your house is forsaken and desolate. 17
25: 6 'Behold, the bridegroom! Come out to meet him.' 17
26:45 Behold, the hour is at hand 17
51 behold, one of those who were with Jesus 17
27:51 behold, the curtain of the temple was torn in two 17
28: 2 behold, there was a great earthquake 17
7 behold, he is going before you to Galilee 17
9 behold, Jesus met them and said, "Hail! 17
11 behold, some of the guard went into the city 17
Mrk 1: 2 Behold, I send my messenger before thy face 17
3:11 whenever the unclean spirits beheld him 16
10:33 saying, "Behold, we are going up to Jerusalem; 17
15:35 some of the bystanders hearing it said, "Behold 20
Lke 1:20 behold, you will be silent and unable to speak 17
31 behold, you will conceive in your womb 17
36 behold, your kinswoman Elizabeth in her old age 17
38 Mary said, "Behold, I am the handmaid of the Lord 17
44 behold, when the voice of your greeting came 17
48 behold, henceforth all generations will call me 17
2:10 behold, I bring you good news of a great joy 17
34 Behold, this child is set for the fall and rising 17
48 Behold, your father and I have been looking 17
5:18 behold, men were bringing on a bed a man 17
6:23 for behold, your reward is great in heaven 17
7:12 behold, a man who had died was being carried out 17
24 What did you go out into the wilderness to behold? 15
25 Behold, those who are gorgeously appareled 17
27 Behold, I send my messenger before thy face 17
34 and you say, 'Behold, a glutton and a drunkard 17
37 behold, a woman of the city, who was a sinner 17
9:30 behold, two men talked with him, Moses and Eli'jah 17
38 behold, a man from the crowd cried, "Teacher 17
39 behold, a spirit seizes him 17
10: 3 Go your way; behold, I send you out as lambs 17
19 Behold, I have given you authority 17
25 behold, a lawyer stood up to put him to the test 17
11:31 behold, something greater than Solomon is here. 17
32 behold, something greater than Jonah is here. 17
41 behold, everything is clean for you. 17
13:30 behold, some are last who will be first 17
32 he said to them, "Go and tell that fox, 'Behold 17
35 Behold, your house is forsaken 17
14: 2 behold, there was a man before him who had dropsy. 17
17:21 behold, the kingdom of God is in the midst of you. 17
18:31 taking the twelve, he said to them, "Behold 17
19: 8 Zacchae'us stood and said to the Lord, "Behold 17
22:10 He said to them, "Behold 17
21 behold the hand of him who betrays me 17
31 Simon, Simon, behold, Satan demanded to have you 17
23:14 behold, I did not find this man guilty 17
15 Behold, nothing deserving death has been done 17
29 For behold, the days are coming when they will say 17
24: 4 behold, two men stood by them in dazzling apparel; 17
49 behold, I send the promise of my Father upon you; 17
Joh 1:14 we have beheld his glory, glory as of the only Son 15
29 Behold, the Lamb of God, who takes away the sin 20
36 and said, "Behold, the Lamb of God! 20
47 Behold, an Israelite indeed, in whom is no guile! 20
12:15 behold, your king is coming, sitting on an ass's colt! 17
17:24 to behold my glory which thou hast given me 16
19: 5 Pilate said to them, "Behold the man! 17
14 He said to the Jews, "Behold your King! 20
26 he said to his mother, "Woman, behold, your son! 20
27 Then he said to the disciple, "Behold, your mother! 20
Act 1:10 behold, two men stood by them in white robes 17
7:56 he said, "Behold, I see the heavens opened 17
8:27 behold, an Ethiopian, a eunuch 17
9:11 behold, he is praying 17
10:17 behold, the men that were sent by Cornelius 17
19 the Spirit said to him, "Behold 17
30 behold, a man stood before me in bright apparel 17
12: 7 behold, an angel of the Lord appeared 17
13:11 now, behold, the hand of the Lord is upon you 17
41 'Behold, you scoffers, and wonder, and perish 13
46 behold, we turn to the Gentiles. 17
20:22 now, behold, I am going to Jerusalem 17
25 now, behold, I know 17
Rom 9:33 Behold, I am laying in Zion a stone 17
2Co 3:18 beholding the glory of the Lord 19
5:17 the old has passed away, behold, the new has come. 17
6: 2 Behold, now is the acceptable time 17
2 behold, now is the day of salvation. 17
9 as dying, and behold we live 17
Jas 5: 4 Behold, the wages of the laborers 17
7 Behold, the farmer waits for the precious fruit 17
9 behold, the Judge is standing at the doors. 17
11 Behold, we call those happy who were steadfast. 17
1Pe 2: 6 Behold, I am laying in Zion a stone, a cornerstone 17
Jde 1:14 Behold, the Lord came with his holy myriads 17
Rev 1: 7 Behold, he is coming with the clouds 17
18 I died, and behold I am alive for evermore 17
2:10 Behold, the devil is about to throw some of you 17
22 Behold, I will throw her on a sickbed 17
3: 8 Behold, I have set before you an open door 17
9 Behcld, I will make those in the synagogue 17
9 behold, I will make them come and bow down before 17
20 Behold, I stand at the door and knock; 17
6: 2 I saw, and behold, a white horse, and its rider 17
5 And I saw, and behold, a black horse, and its rider 17
8 I saw, and behold, a pale horse, and its rider 17
12 When he opened the sixth seal, I looked, and behold •
7: 9 After this I looked, and behold, a great multitude 17
9:12 behold, two woes are still to come. 17
11:14 behold, the third woe is soon to come. 17
12: 3 appeared in heaven; behold, a great red dragon 17
17: 8 the dwellers . . will marvel to behold the beast 12
19:11 Then I saw heaven opened, and behold, a white horse! 17
21: 3 Behold, the dwelling of God is with men. 17
5 Behold, I make all things new. 17
22: 7 And behold, I am coming soon. 17
12 Behold, I am coming soon, bringing my recompense 17
1Es 8:90 Behold, we are now before thee in our iniquities; 17
2Es 4:48 I stood and looked, and behold, a flaming furnace 22
48 I looked, and behold, the smoke remained. 22
5: 1 behold, the days are coming 22
41 I said, "Yet behold, O Lord 22
6:17 and behold, a voice was speaking 22
18 it said, "Behold, the days are coming 22
29 While he spoke to me, behold, little by little 22
57 now, O Lord, behold, these nations 22
7:17 Then I answered and said, "O sovereign Lord, behold 22
26 For behold, the time will come, when the signs 22
98 for they hasten to behold the face of him 23
8:63 Behold, O Lord, thou hast now shown me 22
9:20 I considered my world, and behold, it was lost 22
20 and my earth, and behold, it was in peril 22
31 For behold, I sow my law in you 22
34 behold, it is the rule that . . 22
38 and behold, she was mourning and weeping 22
10:10 and behold, almost all go to perdition 22
25 behold, her face suddenly shone exceedingly 22
26 behold, she suddenly uttered a loud . . cry 22
27 I looked, and behold, the woman 22
29 behold, the angel who had come to me at first came 22
30 behold, I lay there like a corpse 22
32 and behold, I saw, and still see 22
44 whom you now behold as an established city ‡
49 behold, you saw her likeness, how she mourned 22
11: 1 and behold, there came up from the sea an eagle 22
2 I looked, and behold, he spread his wings 22
5 I looked, and behold, the eagle flew with his wings 22
7 I looked, and behold, the eagle rose 22
10 I looked, and behold, the voice did not come 22
11 and behold, there were 8 of them. 22
12 I looked, and behold, on the right side one wing 22
15 behold, a voice sounded, saying to it. 22
20 I looked, and behold, in due course the wings 22
22 after this I looked, and behold, the twelve wings 22
24 I looked, and behold, two little wings separated 22
25 I looked, and behold, these little wings planned 22
26 I looked, and behold, one was set up 22
28 I looked, and behold, the two that remained 22
29 while they were planning, behold, one of the heads 22
31 behold, the head turned with those 22
33 after this I looked, and behold, the middle head 22
35 I looked, and behold, the head on the right side 22
37 I looked, and behold, a creature like a lion 22
44 behold, they are ended, and his ages are completed! 22
12: 2 behold, the remaining head disappeared 22
3 I looked, and behold, they also disappeared 22
4 Behold, you have brought this upon me 22
5 Behold, I am still weary in mind 22
13 Behold, the days are coming when a kingdom 22
13: 2 behold, a wind arose from the sea 22
3 I looked, and behold, this wind made something 22
3 I looked, and behold, that man flew with the clouds ‡
5 After this I looked, and behold, an . . multitude 22
6 I looked, and behold, he carved out for himself 22
8 After this I looked, and behold, all 22
9 behold, when he saw the onrush 22
29 Behold, the days are coming 22
14: 1 behold, a voice came out of a bush opposite me 22
20 For behold, I will go, as thou hast commanded me 22
38 on the next day, behold, a voice called me, saying 22
39 Then I opened my mouth, and behold, a full cup 22
15: 1 Behold, speak in the ears of my people the words 22
5 Behold," says the Lord, "I bring evils upon the world 22
8 Behold, innocent and righteous blood cries out 22
10 Behold, my people is led like a flock 22
20 Behold," says God, "I call together all the kings 22
28 Behold, a terrifying sight 22
34 Behold, clouds from the east 22
16:14 Behold, calamities are sent forth 22
19 Behold, famine and plague 22
21 Behold, provision will be so cheap upon earth 22
36 Behold the word of the Lord, receive it 22
37 Behold, the calamities draw near 22
52 For behold, just a little while 22
54 Behold, the Lord knows all the works of men 22
67 Behold, God is the judge, fear him! 22
68 behold, the burning wrath of a great multitude 22
74 Behold, the days of tribulation are at hand 22
Tob 11: 6 Behold, your son is coming 20
14: 3 behold, I have grown old 20
Jdt 3: 2 Behold, we . . lie prostrate before you 17
3 Behold, our buildings, and all our land 17
6:19 O Lord God of heaven, behold their arrogance 18
9: 7 Behold now, the Assyrians 17
9 Behold their pride 12
AEs 11: 5 Behold, noise and confusion 20
6 behold, two great dragons came forward 20
8 behold, a day of darkness and gloom 20
Sir 16:18 Behold, heaven and the highest heaven 20
39:20 he beholds them 14
42:25 who can have enough of beholding his glory? 21
Bar 2:25 behold, they have been cast out to the heat of day 17
3: 8 Behold, we are today in our exile where thou hast 17
4:37 Behold, your sons are coming, whom you sent away; 17
Bel 1:11 the priests of Bel said, "Behold 17
1Mc 2:12 behold, our holy place, our beauty, and our glory 20
65 Now behold . . Simeon . . is wise in counsel; 17
3:52 behold, the Gentiles are assembled against us 17
4:36 Then said Judas and his brothers, "Behold 17

5:14 behold, other messengers . . came from Galilee 17
30 behold, a large company, that could not be counted 17
6:13 behold, I am perishing of deep grief 17
26 behold . . encamped against the citadel 17
11:68 behold, the army of the foreigners met him 17
16: 5 behold, a large force of infantry and horsemen 17
24 behold, they are written in the chronicles 17
4Mc 17: 7 those who first beheld it 16

being 1. נֶפֶשׁ 2. עוֹד 3. εἰμί 4. ψυχή
Gen 2: 7 breath of life; and man became a living being. 1
Ps 104:33 I will sing praise to my God while I have being. 2
146: 2 I will sing praises to my God while I have being. 2
Act 17:28 'In him we live and move and have our being' 3
Rom 2: 9 and distress for every human being who does evil 4
1Co 15:45 The first man Adam became a living being 4
Gal 4: 8 in bondage to beings that by nature are no gods; •
AEs 14:11 do not surrender thy scepter to what has no being; 3

heavenly being 1. בֶּן אֵלִים
Ps 29: 1 Ascribe to the LORD, O heavenly beings 1
89: 6 Who among the heavenly beings is like the LORD 1

human being 1. ἄνθρωπος 2. σάρξ 3. υἱὸς ἀνθρώπου 4. homo
Mat 24:22 no human being would be saved 2
Mrk 13:20 no human being would be saved 2
Rom 3:20 For no human being will be justified in his sight 2
1Co 1:29 so that no human being might boast 2
Jas 3: 8 no human being can tame the tongue 1
2Es 8: 6 mortal who bears the likeness of a human being 4
Jdt 8:16 nor like a human being, to be won over by pleading. 3
Wis 14:15 honored as a god what was once a dead human being 1
Sir 31:16 Eat like a human being what is set before you 1

inward being 1. טֻחוֹת
Ps 51: 6 Behold, thou desirest truth in the inward being; 1

living being 1. σάρξ
Sir 13:16 all living beings associate by species 1
14:17 All living beings become old like a garment 1
17: 4 He placed the fear of them in all living beings 1
18:13 compassion . . is for all living beings 1

beka 1. בֶּקַע
Exd 38:26 a beka a head (that is, half a shekel, 1

belch forth 1. λικμάω
Wis 11:18 or belch forth a thick pall of smoke 1

belief 1. πίστις
2Th 2:13 belief in the truth. 1
belief *See also* worthy.

believe 1. אמן 2. ἀπιστέω 3. ἐμπιστεύω 4. πιστεύω 5. πιστός 6. τίθημι 7. confido 8. credo
Gen 15: 6 he believed the LORD; and he reckoned it to him 1
45:26 his heart fainted, for he did not believe them. 1
Exd 4: 1 they will not believe me or listen to my voice 1
5 that they may believe that the LORD 1
8 If they will not believe you," God said, "or heed 1
8 the first sign, they may believe the latter sign. 1
9 If they will not believe even these two signs 1
31 the people believed; and when they heard 1
14:31 they believed in the LORD and in his servant 1
19: 9 may also believe you for ever. 1
Num14:11 how long will they not believe in me 1
20:12 Because you did not believe in me, to sanctify me 1
Deu 1:32 in spite of this word you did not believe the LORD 1
9:23 did not believe him or obey his voice. 1
1Kg 10: 7 I did not believe the reports until I came 1
2Kg 17:14 their fathers . . who did not believe in the LORD 1
2Ch 9: 6 I did not believe the reports until I came 1
20:20 Believe in the LORD your God 1
20 believe his prophets, and you will succeed. 1
32:15 do not believe him 1
Job 9:16 I would not believe that he was listening 1
15:22 He does not believe that he will return out 1
Ps 27:13 I believe that I shall see the goodness 1
78:32 despite his wonders they did not believe. 1
106:12 Then they believed his words; 1
119:66 Teach me . . for I believe in thy commandments. 1
Prv 14:15 The simple believes everything 1
26:25 when he speaks graciously, believe him not 1
Isa 7: 9 If you will not believe, surely you shall not be 1
28:16 'He who believes will not be in haste.' 1
43:10 that you may know and believe me and understand 1
53: 1 Who has believed what we have heard? 1
Jer 12: 6 believe them not, though they speak fair words 1
40:14 But Gedali'ah the son of Ahi'kam would not believe 1
Lam 4:12 The kings of the earth did not believe . . that foe 1
Jon 3: 5 the people of Nin'eveh believed God; 1
Hab 1: 5 a work . . that you would not believe if told. 1
Mat 8:13 Go; be it done for you as you have believed. 4
9:28 Do you believe that I am able to do this? 4
18: 6 one of these little ones who believe in me 4
21:25 'Why then did you not believe him?' 4
32 you did not believe him 4
32 the tax collectors and the harlots believed him; 4
32 you did not afterward repent and believe him. 4
24:23 do not believe it. 4
26 do not believe it. 4
27:42 we will believe in him. 4
Mrk 1:15 repent, and believe in the gospel. 4
5:36 Do not fear, only believe. 4
9:23 All things are possible to him who believes. 4
24 cried out and said, "I believe; help my unbelief! 4
42 one of these little ones who believe in me 4
11:23 believes that what he says will come to pass 4
24 believe that you have received it 4
31 he will say, 'Why then did you not believe him? 4
13:21 'Look, there he is!' do not believe it. 4
15:32 that we may see and believe 4
16:11 they would not believe it. 2
13 they did not believe them. 4
14 because they had not believed those who saw him 4
16 He who believes and is baptized will be saved 4
16 he who does not believe will be condemned. 2
17 these signs will accompany those who believe 4
Lke 1:20 because you did not believe my words 4
45 blessed is she who believed 4
8:12 that they may not believe and be saved. 4
13 they believe for a while 4
50 Do not fear; only believe, and she shall be well. 4
20: 5 he will say, 'Why did you not believe him?' 4
22:67 he said to them, "If I tell you, you will not believe; 4
24:11 they did not believe them. 2
25 slow of heart to believe 4
Joh 1: 7 that all might believe through him. 4
12 to all who received him, who believed in his name 4
50 I saw you under the fig tree, do you believe? 4
2:11 and his disciples believed in him. 4
22 and they believed the scripture and the word 4
23 many believed in his name when they saw the signs 4
3:12 told you earthly things and you do not believe 4
12 how can you believe if I tell you heavenly things? 4
15 whoever believes in him may have eternal life. 4
16 that whoever believes in him should not perish 4
18 He who believes in him is not condemned; 4
18 he who does not believe is condemned already 4
18 not believed in the name of the only Son of God. 4
36 He who believes in the Son has eternal life; 4
4:21 Woman, believe me, the hour is coming 4
39 Many Samaritans from that city believed in him 4
41 And many more believed because of his word. 4
42 no longer because of your words that we believe 4
48 Unless you see . . wonders you will not believe. 4
50 The man believed the word that Jesus spoke to him 4
53 and he himself believed, and all his household. 4
5:24 he who hears my word and believes him who sent me 4
38 for you do not believe him whom he has sent. 4
44 How can you believe 4
46 If you believed Moses, you would believe me 4
46 If you believed Moses, you would believe me 4
47 if you do not believe his writings 4
47 how will you believe my words? 4
6:29 that you believe in him whom he has sent. 4
30 that we may see, and believe you? 4
35 he who believes in me shall never thirst. 4
36 you have seen me and yet do not believe. 4
40 every one who sees the Son and believes in him 4
47 he who believes has eternal life. 4
64 there are some of you that do not believe 4
64 who those were that did not believe 4
69 we have believed 4
7: 5 For even his brothers did not believe in him. 4
31 Yet many of the people believed in him; they said 4
38 He who believes in me, as the scripture has said 4
39 which those who believed in him were to receive; 4
48 Have any . . of the Pharisees believed in him? 4
8:24 unless you believe that I am he. 4
30 As he spoke thus, many believed in him. 4
31 Jesus then said to the Jews who had believed 4
45 because I tell the truth, you do not believe me. 4
46 If I tell the truth, why do you not believe me? 4
9:18 The Jews did not believe that he had been blind 4
35 Do you believe in the Son of Man? 4
36 who is he, sir, that I may believe in him? 4
38 He said, "Lord, I believe"; and he worshiped him. 4
10:25 you do not believe 4
26 you do not believe 4
37 then do not believe me; 4
38 if I do them, even though you do not believe me 4
38 believe the works 4
42 many believed in him there. 4
11:15 that you may believe 4
25 who believes in me, though he die, yet shall he live 4
26 whoever lives and believes in me 4
26 Do you believe this? 4
27 I believe that you are the Christ, the Son of God 4
40 if you would believe you would see the glory of God? 4
42 they may believe that thou didst send me. 4
45 Many of the Jews therefore . . believed in him 4
48 every one will believe in him 4
12:11 Jews were going away and believing in Jesus. 4
36 While you have the light, believe in the light 4
37 yet they did not believe in him; 4
38 Lord, who has believed our report 4
39 Therefore they could not believe 4
42 many even of the authorities believed in him 4
44 He who believes in me, believes not in me 4
44 believes not in me but in him who sent me. 4
46 whoever believes in me 4
13:19 you may believe that I am he. 4
14: 1 believe in God, believe also in me. 4
1 believe in God, believe also in me. 4
10 Do you not believe that I am in the Father 4
11 Believe me that I am in the Father 4
11 or else believe me for the sake of the works 4
12 who believes in me will also do the works that I do; 4
29 so that when it does take place, you may believe. 4
16: 9 concerning sin, because they do not believe in me; 4
27 have believed that I came from the Father. 4
30 by this we believe that you came from God. 4
31 Jesus answered them, "Do you now believe? 4
17: 8 they have believed that thou didst send me. 4
20 those who believe in me through their word 4
21 the world may believe that thou hast sent me. 4
19:35 that you also may believe. 4
20: 8 also went in, and he saw and believed; 4
25 I will not believe. 4
27 do not be faithless, but believing. 5
29 Have you believed because you have seen me? 4
29 those who have not seen and yet believe. 4
31 these are written that you may believe 4
31 believing you may have life in his name. 4
Act 2:44 all who believed were together 4
4: 4 many of those who heard the word believed 4
32 company of those who believed were of one heart 4
8:12 when they believed Philip 4
13 Even Simon himself believed 4
9:26 for they did not believe that he was a disciple. 4
42 many believed in the Lord. 4
10:43 who believes in him receives forgiveness 4
11:17 when we believed in the Lord Jesus Christ 4
21 a great number that believed turned to the Lord. 4
13:12 Then the proconsul believed 4
39 by him every one that believes is freed 4
41 a deed you will never believe 4
48 as many as were ordained . . believed. 4
14: 1 so spoke that a great company believed 4
23 the Lord in whom they believed. 4
15: 7 hear the word of the gospel and believe. 4
11 we believe that we shall be saved 4
16:31 Believe in the Lord Jesus, and you will be saved 4
34 rejoiced . . that he had believed in God. 4
17:12 Many of them therefore believed 4
34 some men joined him and believed 4
18: 8 Crispus . . believed in the Lord 4
8 many of the Corinthians hearing Paul believed 4
27 helped those who through grace had believed 4
19: 2 receive the Holy Spirit when you believed? 4
4 to believe in the one who was to come after him 4
21:20 those who have believed 4
25 as for the Gentiles who have believed 4
22:19 I imprisoned and beat those who believed in thee. 4
24:14 believing everything laid down by the law 4
26:27 King Agrippa, do you believe the prophets? 4
27 I know that you believe. 4
Rom 3:22 faith in Jesus Christ for all who believe. 4
4: 3 Abraham believed God, and it was reckoned to him 4
11 all who believe without being circumcised 4
17 -in the presence of the God in whom he believed 4
18 In hope he believed against hope 4
24 It will be reckoned to us who believe in him 4
6: 8 we believe that we shall also live with him. 4
9:33 he who believes in him will not be put to shame. 4
10: 9 and believe in your heart that God raised him 4
10 man believes with his heart and so is justified 4
11 No one who believes in him will be put to shame 4
14 to call upon him in whom they have not believed? 4
14 to believe in him of whom they have never heard? 4
16 Lord, who has believed what he has heard from us? 4
13:11 nearer to us now than when we first believed; 4
14: 2 One believes he may eat anything 4
15:13 fill you with all joy and peace in believing 4
1Co 1:21 to save those who believe. 4
3: 5 Servants through whom you believed 4
11:18 I partly believe it 4
13: 7 Love bears all things, believes all things 4
15: 2 unless you believed in vain. 4
11 so we preach and so you believed. 4
2Co 4:13 as he had who wrote, "I believed, and so I spoke 4
13 we too believe, and so we speak 4
Gal 2:16 even we have believed in Christ Jesus 4
3: 6 Thus Abraham "believed God 4
22 might be given to those who believe. 4
Eph 1:13 you also, who . . have believed in him 4
19 greatness of his power in us who believe 4
Php 1:29 you should not only believe in him 4
1Th 4:14 since we believe that Jesus died and rose again 4
2Th 1:10 to be marveled at in all who have believed 4
10 because our testimony to you was believed. 4
2:11 to make them believe what is false 4
12 may be condemned who did not believe the truth 4
1Ti 1:16 an example to those who were to believe in him 4

3:16 believed on in the world, taken up in glory. 4
4: 3 those who believe and know the truth. 5
10 especially of those who believe. 5
6: 2 Those who have believing masters 5
2Ti 1:12 I am not ashamed, for I know whom I have believed 4
Tit 3: 8 those who have believed in God may be careful 4
Heb 4: 3 For we who have believed enter that rest 4
11: 6 must believe that he exists 4
Jas 2:19 You believe that God is one; you do well. 4
19 Even the demons believe–and shudder. 4
23 Abraham believed God 4
1Pe 1: 8 though you do not now see him you believe in him 4
2: 6 he who believes in him will not be put to shame. 4
7 To you therefore who believe, he is precious 4
7 but for those who do not believe 2
1Jn 3:23 we should believe in the name of his Son Jesus 4
4: 1 Beloved, do not believe every spirit 4
16 So we know and believe the love God has for us. 4
5: 1 Every one who believes that Jesus is the Christ 4
5 he who believes that Jesus is the Son of God? 4
10 He who believes in the Son of God 4
10 He who does not believe God has made him a liar 4
10 because he has not believed in the testimony 4
13 to you who believe in the name of the Son of God 4
Jde 1: 5 afterward destroyed those who did not believe. 4
1Es 4:28 now do you not believe me? 4
2Es 1:35 who without having heard me will believe 8
37 yet with the spirit they will believe the things 8
3:32 Or what tribes have so believed thy covenants 8
5:29 trodden down those who believed thy covenants. 8
6:33 and to say to you: 'Believe and do not be afraid! 7
7:130 did not believe him, or the prophets after him 8
9: 7 on account of the faith by which he has believed 8
Tob 2:14 I did not believe her 4
Jdt 14:10 he believed firmly in God, and was circumcised 4
Sir 19:15 do not believe everything you hear. 4
32:24 He who believes the law 4
Sus 1:41 The assembly believed them 4
1Mc 1:30 they believed him 3
2:59 Hannaniah, Azariah, and Mishael believed 4
10:46 they did not believe or accept them 4
3Mc 6:34 those who had previously believed 6
4Mc 5:25 we believe that the law was established by God 4
7:19 since they believe 4

believe firmly 1. πιστόω

2Ti 3:14 what you have learned and have firmly believed 1

fully believe 1. πείθω

Tob 14: 4 I fully believe what Jonah the prophet said 1

believer 1. ἔχω πιστά 2. πιστεύω 3. πιστός

Act 5:14 more than ever believers were added to the Lord 2
10:45 the believers from among the circumcised 3
15: 5 some believers . . rose up, and said 2
16: 1 the son of a Jewish woman who was a believer 3
19:18 Many also of those who were now believers came 2
1Co 14:22 a sign not for believers but for unbelievers 2
22 is not for unbelievers but for believers. 2
2Co 6:15 what has a believer in common with an unbeliever? 3
1Th 1: 7 example to all the believers in Macedo'nia 2
2:10 blameless was our behavior to you believers; 2
13 the word of God, which is at work in you believers. 2
1Ti 4:12 set the believers an example in speech 3
6: 2 are believers and beloved 3
Tit 1: 6 his children are believers 1

believing woman 1. πιστός

1Ti 5:16 If any believing woman has relatives who . . 1

belittle 1. בוז

Prv 11:12 He who belittles his neighbor lacks sense 1

bell 1. מְצִלָּה 2. פַּעֲמֹן 3. κώδων

Exd 28:33 pomegranates . . with bells of gold between 2
34 a golden bell and a pomegranate, a golden bell 2
34 a pomegranate, a golden bell and a pomegranate 2
39:25 They also made bells of pure gold 2
25 and put the bells between the pomegranates 2
26 a bell and a pomegranate, a bell and a pomegranate 2
26 a bell and a pomegranate, a bell and a pomegranate 2
Zec 14:20 shall be inscribed on the bells of the horses 1
Sir 45: 9 with very many golden bells round about 3

bellow 1. נבע

Ps 59: 7 There they are, bellowing with their mouths 1

bellows 1. מַפֻּחַ 2. ζώπυρον

Jer 6:29 The bellows blow fiercely, the lead is consumed 1
4Mc 8:13 iron claws and wedges and bellows 2

belly 1. בֶּטֶן 2. גָּחוֹן 3. חֹמֶשׁ 4. כָּרֵשׂ 5. מֵעֶה 6. מְעָא (A) 7. γαστήρ 8. κοιλία 9. venter

Gen 3:14 upon your belly you shall go 2
Lev 11:42 Whatever goes on its belly 2
Jdg 3:21 took the sword . . and thrust it into his belly; 1
22 for he did not draw the sword out of his belly; 1
2Sm 2:23 smote him in the belly with the butt of his spear 3
3:27 and there he smote him in the belly, so that he died 3
Job 20:15 God casts them out of his belly. 1
23 To fill his belly to the full God will send his 1
40:16 his power in the muscles of his belly. 1
Ps 17:14 May their belly be filled with what thou hast 1
Prv 13:25 but the belly of the wicked suffers want. 1
Sng 7: 2 belly is a heap of wheat, encircled with lilies. 1
Jer 51:34 he has filled his belly with my delicacies 4
Dan 2:32 arms of silver, its belly and thighs of bronze 6
Jon 1:17 Jonah was in the belly of the fish three days 5
2: 1 to the LORD his God from the belly of the fish 5
2 he answered me; out of the belly of Sheol I cried 1
Mat 12:40 three nights in the belly of the whale 8
Php 3:19 Their end is destruction, their god is the belly 8
2Es 15:35 be blood from the sword as high as a horse's belly 9
Sir 51: 5 from the depths of the belly of Hades 8
3Mc 6: 8 in the belly of a huge, sea-born monster 7
7:11 for the belly's sake 7

belong 1. היה 2. לְ 3. מִן 4. נחל 5. ἀνηκέω 6. ἀπό 7. αὐτός 8. γίνομαι 9. εἰμί 10. ἐκ 11. ἔχω 12. κατά 13. μετέχω 14. ὁ 15. οἰκεῖος 16. προσηκέω 17. ὑπάρχω

Gen 31:16 God has taken away from our father belongs to us 2
32:17 When Esau . . asks you, 'To whom do you belong? •
18 then you shall say, 'They belong to your servant •
38:25 By the man to whom these belong, I am with child. •
40: 8 Do not interpretations belong to God? 2
46:26 persons belonging to Jacob who came into Egypt 2
49:10 not depart . . until he comes to whom it belongs; ‡
Exd 9: 4 of all that belongs to the people of Israel. 2
Lev 6: 5 give it to him to whom it belongs 2
7: 9 all . . shall belong to the priest who offers it 2
14 it shall belong to the priest who throws 2
14:13 like the sin offering, belongs to the priest •
25:34 fields . . belonging to their cities may not be •
49 near kinsman belonging to his family 3
27:24 field shall return . . to whom the land belongs •
26 which as a firstling belongs to the LORD •
Num 1:50 and over all that belongs to it; •
16:30 swallows them up, with all that belongs to them •
32 men that belonged to Korah and all their goods. •
33 they and all that belonged to them went down •
25:14 fathers' house belonging to the Simeonites. 2
35: 5 this shall belong to them as pasture land 1
36: 3 inheritance of the tribe to which they belong; 1
4 inheritance of the tribe to which they belong; 1
Deu 10:14 Behold, to the LORD your God belong heaven •
23: 3 none belonging to them shall enter the assembly •
29:29 secret things belong to the LORD our God; 2
29 revealed belong to us and to our children for ever 2
Jos 2:13 my father and mother . . and all who belong to them 2
6:22 bring out . . the woman, and all who belong to her 2
23 brought out . . all who belonged to her; 2
25 Rahab the harlot . . and all who belonged to her 2
13: 4 and Mear'ah which belongs to the Sido'nians 2
15:21 The cities belonging to the tribe of . . Judah 2
17: 8 The land of Tap'puah belonged to Manas'seh 1
8 Tap'puah . . belonged to the sons of E'phraim. 2
9 The cities here . . belong to E'phraim. 2
18:14 Kir'iath-ba'al . . a city belonging to the tribe •
21:10 of the Ko'hathites who belonged to the Levites; 3
20 the rest . . belonging to the Ko'hathite families •
22:11 on the side that belongs to the people of Israel. •
Jdg 6:11 the oak at Ophrah, which belonged to Jo'ash 2
24 at Ophrah, which belongs to the Abiez'rites. •
18:27 Micah had made, and the priest who belonged to him 1
28 It was in the valley which belongs to Beth-rehob. •
19:12 of foreigners, who do not belong to the people 3
14 on them near Gib'e-ah, which belongs to Benjamin •
20: 4 I came to Gib'e-ah that belongs to Benjamin 2
Rut 2: 3 to come to the part of the field belonging to Bo'az 2
4: 3 land which belonged to our kinsman Elim'elech. 2
9 I have bought . . all that belonged to Elim'elech 2
9 and all that belonged to Chil'ion and to Mahlon. 2
1Sm 6:18 all the cities . . belonging to the five lords 2
17: 1 were gathered at Socoh, which belongs to Judah 2
25:21 nothing was missed of all that belonged to him; 2
22 I leave . . one male of all who belong to him. 2
27: 6 Ziklag has belonged to . . Judah to this day. 1
30:13 To whom do you belong? And where are you from? 2
14 made a raid . . upon that which belongs to Judah 2
2Sm 3:12 To whom does the land belong? Make your covenant •
6:12 of O'bed-e'dom and all that belongs to him •
9: 9 All that belonged to Saul . . I have given 1
16: 4 all that belonged to Mephib'osheth is now yours. 2
1Kg 4:10 Ben-hesed . . (to him belonged Socoh and all •
6:22 altar that belonged to the inner sanctuary 2
14:11 Any one belonging to Jerobo'am who dies 2
15:27 at Gib'bethon, which belonged to the Philistines; 2
16: 4 Any one belonging to Ba'asha who dies in the city 2
15 Gib'bethon, which belonged to the Philistines 2
17: 9 go to Zar'ephath, which belongs to Sidon, and dwell 2
19: 3 and came to Beer-sheba, which belongs to Judah 2
21:24 Any one belonging to Ahab who dies in the city 2
22: 3 Do you know that Ramoth-gilead belongs to us 2
2Kg 9:25 cast him on the . . ground belonging to Naboth •
12:16 The money from . . it belonged to the priests. 1
14:11 battle at Beth-she'mesh, which belongs to Judah. 2
28 Damascus and Hamath, which had belonged to Judah 2
24: 7 had taken all that belonged to the king of Egypt 1
1Ch 4:40 the former inhabitants there belonged to Ham. •
5: 2 yet the birthright belonged to Joseph •
7: 5 Their kinsmen belonging to . . Is'sachar 2
13: 6 Kir'iath-je'arim which belongs to Judah •
26:21 sons of the Gershonites belonging to Ladan 2
21 belonging to Ladan the Gershonite: Jehi'eli. 2
2Ch 21:17 possessions . . belonged to the king's house 2
25:21 Beth-she'mesh, which belongs to Judah. •
26:23 in the burial field which belonged to the kings •
31:19 fields of common land belonging to their cities •
34:33 territory that belonged to the people of Israel •
Ezr 2:59 not prove . . whether they belonged to Israel 3
Neh 7:61 their descent, whether they belonged to Israel 3
Est 1: 9 in the palace which belonged to King Ahasu-e'rus. 2
Ps 3: 8 Deliverance belongs to the LORD; 2
22:28 For dominion belongs to the LORD, and he rules 2
47: 9 For the shields of the earth belong to God; 2
62:11 I heard this: that power belongs to God; 2
12 that to thee, O Lord, belongs steadfast love. •
68:20 to God, the Lord, belongs escape from death. •
82: 8 for to thee belong all the nations! 4
89:18 For our shield belongs to the LORD 2
Prv 16: 1 The plans of the mind belong to man •
21:31 but the victory belongs to the LORD. •
Isa 8: 1 'Belonging to Ma'her-shal'al-hash-baz.' 2
Ezk 13:18 Will you hunt down souls belonging to my people 2
40:20 toward the north, belonging to the outer court. 2
42: 3 twenty cubits which belonged to the inner court 2
3 the pavement which belonged to the outer court 2
43:21 in the appointed place belonging to the temple •
44:30 all your offerings, shall belong to the priests; 1
45: 6 it shall belong to the whole house of Israel. 1
7 to the prince shall belong the land on both sides •
46:16 it shall belong to his sons, it is their property 1
48:12 it shall belong to them as a special portion 1
21 of the city shall belong to the prince. •
21 it shall belong to the prince. •
22 in the midst of that which belongs to the prince. 1
Dan 2:20 name of God . . to whom belong wisdom and might. •
9: 7 To thee, O Lord, belongs righteousness, but to us •
8 To us, O Lord, belongs confusion of face •
9 To the Lord our God belong mercy and forgiveness; •
Hos 3: 3 not play the harlot, or belong to another man; 1
Jon 2: 9 Deliverance belongs to the LORD! •
Zec 9: 1 For to the LORD belong the cities of Aram •
Mat 19:14 for to such belongs the kingdom of heaven. 9
20:14 Take what belongs to you, and go •
15 to do what I choose with what belongs to me •
Mrk 10:14 to such belongs the kingdom of God. •
Lke 14: 1 a ruler who belonged to the Pharisees •
18:16 to such belongs the kingdom of God. 9
23: 7 he belonged to Herod's jurisdiction 10
Joh 3:31 he who is of the earth belongs to the earth 9
10:26 because you do not belong to my sheep. 10
Act 2:10 Egypt and the parts of Libya belonging to Cyre'ne 12
4:37 sold a field which belonged to him 17
6: 9 Then some of those who belonged to the synagogue 10
9: 2 if he found any belonging to the Way, men or women •
12: 1 some who belonged to the church. 6
15: 5 who belonged to the party of the Pharisees 6
23:34 he asked to what province he belonged 9
27:23 the God to whom I belong and whom I worship 9
28: 7 lands belonging to the chief man of the island •
Rom 1: 6 who are called to belong to Jesus Christ •
7: 4 so that you may belong to another 8
8: 9 Any one who does not . . does not belong to him. •
9: 4 Israelites, and to them belong the sonship •
5 to them belong the patriarchs •
6 not all . . belong to Israel •
16:10 those who belong to the family of Aristobu'lus. 10
11 those . . who belong to the family of Narcis'sus. 10
1Co 1:12 I belong to Paul," or "I belong to Apol'los 9
12 I belong to Paul," or "I belong to Apol'los •
12 I belong to Cephas," or "I belong to Christ. •
12 I belong to Cephas," or "I belong to Christ. •
3: 4 For when one says, "I belong to Paul 9
4 and another, "I belong to Apol'los •
12:15 Because I am not a hand, I do not belong to the body 10
16 Because I am not an eye, I do not belong to the body 10
15:23 then at his coming those who belong to Christ. 14
2Co 4: 7 to show that the transcendent power belongs to God 9
Gal 5:24 those who belong to Christ Jesus •
Eph 4: 4 the one hope that belongs to your call •
22 which belongs to your former manner of life 12
Col 2:17 the substance belongs to Christ. •
1Th 5: 8 But, since we belong to the day, let us be sober •
Heb 6: 9 better things that belong to salvation. 11
7:13 belonged to another tribe 13
1Pe 4:11 To him belong glory and dominion 9
Rev 7:10 Salvation belongs to our God who sits upon •
17:11 it is an eighth but it belongs to the seven 10
19: 1 Salvation and glory and power belong to our God •
1Es 4:40 To her belongs the strength . . of all the ages •
5:37 could not prove . . that they belonged to Israel 10
2Es 9:13 those to whom the age belongs ‡
Tob 5: 8 I may learn to what tribe he belongs •

10 to what tribe and family do you belong? Tell me. 10
7: 3 We belong to the sons of Naphtali 10
Jdt 7:20 belonging to every inhabitant of Bethulia 7
8: 2 Her husband Manasseh, who belonged to her tribe *
10:12 To what people do you belong *
Wis 1:16 because they are fit to belong to his party. *
2:24 those who belong to his party experience it. *
Bar 1:15 Righteousness belongs to the Lord our God *
2: 6 Righteousness belongs to the Lord our God *
1Mc 5:62 they did not belong to the family of those men 10
10:42 because it belongs to the priests 5
12:23 your cattle and your property belong to us *
23 ours belong to you *
2Mc 3: 6 did not belong to the account of the sacrifices 16
10 some deposits belonging to widows and orphans *
15:12 trained . . in all that belongs to excellence 15
4Mc 4: 3 belong to King Seleucus. 16

belong still 1. ἐν
Col 2:20 you live as if you still belonged to the world 1

belong to another 1. ἀλλότριος
Sir 9: 8 look intently at beauty belonging to another; 1

belong to others 1. ἀλλότριος
Act 7: 6 aliens in a land belonging to others 1

belongings 1. ὑπάρχω
3Mc 7:21 confiscation of their belongings by any one. 1

prized belongings 1. יקר
Jer 20: 5 the city, all its gains, all its prized belongings 1

beloved 1. אהב 2. דוֹד 3. חֶמְדָּה 4. יְדִדוּת 5. יָדִיד
6. ἀγαπάω 7. ἀγάπη 8. ἀγαπητός 9. προσφιλής
10. φίλος
Deu 33:12 The beloved of the LORD, he dwells in safety by him; 5
2Sm 1:23 Saul and Jonathan, beloved and lovely! 1
Neh 13:26 beloved by his God, and God made him king 1
Ps 60: 5 That thy beloved may be delivered, give victory 5
108: 6 That thy beloved may be delivered 5
127: 2 for he gives to his beloved sleep. 5
Sng 1:13 My beloved is to me a bag of myrrh 2
14 My beloved is to me a cluster of henna blossoms 2
16 you are beautiful, my beloved, truly lovely. 2
2: 3 an apple tree . . so is my beloved among young men. 2
8 The voice of my beloved! Behold, he comes 2
9 My beloved is like a gazelle, or a young stag. 2
10 My beloved speaks and says to me: "Arise, my love 2
16 My beloved is mine and I am his 2
17 turn, my beloved, be like a gazelle 2
4:16 Let my beloved come to his garden 2
5: 2 Hark! my beloved is knocking. 2
4 My beloved put his hand to the latch 2
5 I arose to open to my beloved, and my hands dripped 2
6 I opened to my beloved, but my beloved had turned 2
6 I opened . . but my beloved had turned and gone. 2
8 I adjure you . . if you find my beloved 2
9 What is your beloved more than another beloved 2
9 What is your beloved more than another beloved 2
9 What is your beloved more than another beloved 2
9 What is your beloved more than another beloved 2
10 My beloved is all radiant and ruddy 2
16 This is my beloved and this is my friend 2
6: 1 Whither has your beloved gone, O fairest 2
1 Whither has your beloved turned 2
2 My beloved has gone down to his garden 2
3 I am my beloved's and my beloved is mine; 2
3 I am my beloved's and my beloved is mine; 2
7:10 I am my beloved's, and his desire is for me. 2
11 Come, my beloved, let us go forth into the fields 2
13 which I have laid up for you, O my beloved. 2
8: 5 Who is that coming up . . leaning upon her beloved 2
14 Make haste, my beloved, and be like a gazelle 2
Isa 5: 1 Let me sing for my beloved a love song concerning 2
1 My beloved had a vineyard on a very fertile hill. 2
Jer 11:15 What right has my beloved in my house 5
12: 7 I have given the beloved of my soul into the hands 4
Dan 11:37 give no heed . . to the one beloved by women; 3
Hos 3: 1 Go again, love a woman who is beloved of a paramour 1
Mat 3:17 my beloved Son, with whom I am well pleased. 8
12:18 my beloved with whom my soul is well pleased 8
17: 5 This is my beloved Son 8
Mrk 1:11 a voice came from heaven, "Thou art my beloved Son; 8
9: 7 This is my beloved Son; listen to him. 8
12: 6 He had still one other, a beloved son 8
Lke 3:22 my beloved Son; with thee I am well pleased. 8
20:13 I will send my beloved son 8
Act 15:25 with our beloved Barnabas and Paul 8
Rom 1: 7 To all God's beloved in Rome 8
9:25 her who was not beloved I will call 'my beloved.' 6
25 her who was not beloved I will call 'my beloved.' 6
11:28 but as regards election they are beloved 8
12:19 Beloved, never avenge yourselves 8
16: 5 Greet my beloved Epae'netus 8
8 Greet Amplia'tus, my beloved in the Lord. 8
9 Greet Urba'nus . . and my beloved Stachys. 8
12 Greet the beloved Persis, who has worked hard 8
1Co 4:14 to admonish you as my beloved children. 8
17 my beloved and faithful child in the Lord 8
10:14 Therefore, my beloved, shun the worship of idols. 8
15:58 Therefore, my beloved brethren, be steadfast 8
2Co 7: 1 Since we have these promises, beloved 8
12:19 all for your upbuilding, beloved. 8
Eph 1: 6 which he freely bestowed on us in the Beloved. 6
5: 1 be imitators of God, as beloved children. 8
6:21 Tych'icus the beloved brother 8
Php 2:12 Therefore, my beloved, as you have always obeyed 8
4: 1 stand firm thus in the Lord, my beloved. 8
Col 1: 7 Ep'aphras our beloved fellow servant 8
13 transferred us to the kingdom of his beloved Son 7
3:12 as God's chosen ones, holy and beloved 6
4: 7 he is a beloved brother and faithful minister 8
9 Ones'imus, the faithful and beloved brother 8
14 Luke the beloved physician and Demas greet you. 8
1Th 1: 4 For we know, brethren beloved by God 6
2Th 2:13 brethren beloved by the Lord 6
1Ti 6: 2 are believers and beloved 8
2Ti 1: 2 To Timothy, my beloved child 8
Phm 1: 1 To Phile'mon our beloved fellow worker 8
16 as a beloved brother, especially to me 8
Heb 6: 9 yet in your case, beloved 8
Jas 1:16 Do not be deceived, my beloved brethren. 8
19 Know this, my beloved brethren. 8
2: 5 Listen, my beloved brethren. 8
1Pe 2:11 Beloved, I beseech you as aliens and exiles 8
4:12 Beloved, do not be surprised at the fiery ordeal 8
2Pe 1:17 my beloved Son, with whom I am well pleased 8
3: 1 second letter that I have written to you, beloved 8
8 do not ignore this one fact, beloved 8
14 Therefore, beloved, since you wait for these 8
15 So also our beloved brother Paul wrote to you 8
17 beloved, knowing this beforehand, beware 8
1Jn 2: 7 Beloved, I am writing you no new commandment 8
3: 2 Beloved, we are God's children now; 8
21 Beloved, if our hearts do not condemn us 8
4: 1 Beloved, do not believe every spirit 8
7 Beloved, let us love one another; 8
11 Beloved, if God so loved us, we also ought to love 8
3Jn 1: 1 The elder to the beloved Ga'ius, whom I love 8
2 Beloved, I pray that all may go well with you 8
5 Beloved, it is a loyal thing you do 8
11 Beloved, do not imitate evil but imitate good. 8
Jde 1: 1 To those who are called, beloved in God the Father 6
3 Beloved, being very eager to write to you 8
17 you must remember, beloved, the predictions 8
20 But you, beloved, build yourselves up 8
Rev 20: 9 and surrounded . . the beloved city; 6
Jdt 9: 4 their booty to be divided among thy beloved sons 6
AEs 15: 5 she looked happy, as if beloved 9
Sir 4: 7 Make yourself beloved in the congregation 9
20:13 The wise man makes himself beloved 9
24:11 In the beloved city likewise 6
45: 1 was beloved by God and man 6
46:13 Samuel, beloved by his Lord, a prophet of the Lord 6
Bar 4:16 They led away the widow's beloved sons 8
Aza 1:12 for the sake of Abraham thy beloved 6
1Mc 6:11 I was kind and beloved in my power.' 6
3Mc 6:11 the destruction of your beloved people 6
4Mc 5:34 nor will I renounce you, beloved self-control. 10

beloved *See also* child.

greatly beloved 1. חמד 2. חֲמוּדָה
Dan 9:23 come to tell it to you, for you are greatly beloved; 1
10:11 said to me, "O Daniel, man greatly beloved, give heed 2
19 said, "O man greatly beloved, fear not, 2

below 1. לְמַטָּה 2. מַטָּה 3. מִתַּחַת 4. תַּחַת 5. κάτω
6. ὑποκάτω
Gen 35: 8 died, and she was buried under an oak below Bethel; 4
Jos 11:17 in the valley of Lebanon below Mount Hermon. 4
13: 5 from Ba'al-gad below Mount Hermon to the entrance 4
Jdg 7: 8 the camp of Mid'ian was below him in the valley. 4
1Sm 7:11 and smote them, as far as below Beth-car. 3
1Kg 4:12 which is beside Zarethan below Jezreel 3
7:29 both above and below the lions and oxen 3
1Ch 27:23 did not number those below twenty years of age 2
Job 26: 5 The shades below tremble 3
Jer 31:37 foundations of the earth below can be explored 2
Ezk 8: 2 below what appeared to be his loins it was fire 1
42: 9 Below these chambers was an entrance on the east 3
12 below the south chambers was an entrance *
47: 1 water was issuing from below the threshold 4
1 water was flowing down from below the south end 4
Mrk 14:66 as Peter was below in the courtyard 5
Joh 8:23 You are from below, I am from above; 5
Jdt 6:11 came to the springs below Bethulia. 6

below *See also* inscribe, world.

belt 1. אֵזוֹר 2. מֵזַח 3. מְזִיחַ 4. ζώνη
Job 12:21 and looses the belt of the strong. 3
Ps 109:19 like a belt with which he daily girds himself! 2
Ezk 23:15 girded with belts on their loins 1
Mat 10: 9 Take no gold, nor silver, nor copper in your belts 4
Mrk 6: 8 a staff; no bread, no bag, no money in their belts; 4

bemoan 1. נוד
Jer 15: 5 pity on you, O Jerusalem, or who will bemoan you? 1
16: 5 or go to lament, or bemoan them; 1
22:10 Weep not for him who is dead, nor bemoan him; 1
31:18 I have heard E'phraim bemoaning 1
48:17 Bemoan him, all you who are round about him 1
Nah 3: 7 Wasted is Nin'eveh; who will bemoan her? 1

bench 1. ζυγός
3Mc 4: 9 fastened by the neck to the benches of the boats 1

bend 1. דרך 2. כפן 3. נחת 4. עות 5. תאר 6. תלא
7. ἐπίκυφον 8. κάμπτω 9. κλίνω 10. κύπτω
11. συγκάμπτω 12. tendo
Jos 18:17 it bends in a northerly direction going 5
19:13 and going on to Rimmon it bends toward Ne'ah; *
2Sm 22:35 so that my arms can bend a bow of bronze. 3
Ps 7:12 will whet his sword; he has bent and strung his bow; 1
11: 2 for lo, the wicked bend the bow 1
18:34 for war, so that my arms can bend a bow of bronze. 3
37:14 The wicked draw the sword and bend their bows 1
Ecc 12: 3 keepers . . tremble, and the strong men are bent 4
Isa 5:28 their arrows are sharp, all their bows bent 1
21:15 swords, from the drawn sword, from the bent bow 1
Jer 9: 3 They bend their tongue like a bow; 1
50:14 you that bend the bow; shoot at her, spare no arrows 1
29 against Babylon, all those who bend the bow. 1
51: 3 Let not the archer bend his bow 1
Lam 2: 4 He has bent his bow like an enemy 1
3:12 he bent his bow and set me as a mark for his arrow. 1
Ezk 17: 7 behold, this vine bent its roots toward him 2
22: 6 have been bent on shedding blood. *
Dan 11:27 two kings, their minds shall be bent on mischief; *
Hos 11: 7 My people are bent on turning away from me; 6
Zec 9:13 For I have bent Judah as my bow; 1
Joh 8: 6 Jesus bent down 10
Rom 11:10 and bend their backs for ever. 11
2Es 16:13 For his right hand that bends the bow is strong 12
Bar 2:21 Bend your shoulders and serve the king 9
Man 1:11 now I bend the knee of my heart 9
3Mc 2: 1 bending his knees and extending his hands 8
4: 5 sluggish and bent with age 7

bend down 1. נטה 2. κατακύπτω 3. inclino
Hos 11: 4 and I bent down to them and fed them. 1
Joh 8: 8 once more he bent down and wrote with his finger 2
2Es 3:18 Thou didst bend down the heavens 3

bend low 1. שחח
Isa 60:14 who oppressed you shall come bending low to you; 1

bend over 1. ἐπιπίπτω 2. κύπτω 3. συγκρύπτω
Lke 13:11 she was bent over 3
Act 20:10 Paul went down and bent over him 1
Bar 2:18 person . . that goes about bent over and feeble 2

bend round 1. תאר
Jos 15: 9 then the boundary bends round to Ba'alah 1
11 then the boundary bends round to Shik'keron 1

beneath 1. בְּ 2. לְמַטָּה 3. מִבַּיִת 4. מַטָּה 5. מִלְמַטָּה
6. מִתַּחַת 7. תַּחַת 8. ἐν 9. κάτω 10. ὑπό 11. deorsum
Gen 49:25 blessings of the deep that couches beneath 7
Exd 20: 4 anything . . that is in the earth beneath 7
26:24 they shall be separate beneath, but joined 2
36:29 they were separate beneath, but joined at the top 5
Deu 4:39 know . . the LORD is God . . on the earth beneath; 7
5: 8 likeness of anything . . that is on the earth beneath 7
33:13 choicest gifts . . of the deep that couches beneath 7
Jos 2:11 is God in heaven above and on earth beneath. 6
1Kg 8:23 God like thee, in heaven above or on earth beneath 6
2Kg 6:30 he had sackcloth beneath upon his body– 3
Job 9:13 beneath him bowed the helpers of Rahab. 7
18:16 His roots dry up beneath, and his branches wither 6
Prv 15:24 that he may avoid Sheol beneath. 4
Ecc 2:22 and strain with which he toils beneath the sun? 7
Isa 14: 9 Sheol beneath is stirred up to meet you 7
11 maggots are the bed beneath you 7
51: 6 eyes to the heavens, and look at the earth beneath; 6
Hos 14: 7 They shall return and dwell beneath my shadow 1
Ams 2: 9 his fruit above, and his roots beneath. 6
Hab 3:16 my steps totter beneath me. 7
Act 2:19 signs on the earth beneath 9
2Es 6:41 and the other part remain beneath. 11
Jdt 13:15 here is the canopy beneath which he lay 8
Sir 51: 6 my life was very near to Hades beneath. 9
Bel 1:13 beneath the table 10

beneath *See also* stab.

benefactor 1. εὐεργετέω 2. εὐεργέτης
Lke 22:25 are called benefactors. 2
AEs 16: 2 the too great kindness of their benefactors 1
3 to scheme against their own benefactors. 2
13 Mordecai, our savior and perpetual benefactor 2
Wis 19:14 guests who were their benefactors. 2
2Mc 4: 2 the man who was the benefactor of the city 2
3Mc 3:19 in defiance of kings and their own benefactors 2

6:24 even me, your benefactor, you . . deprive 2
4Mc 8: 6 so I can be a benefactor to those who obey me. 1

beneficence 1. *κτίσμα καλόν*
3Mc 5:11 that beneficence . . bestowed by him 1

beneficent 1. *εὐεργετικός*
Wis 7:23 beneficent, humane, steadfast, sure 1

beneficial 1. *συμφέρω*
4Mc 5:11 the truth of what is beneficial 1

benefit 1. גְּמוּל 2. גמל 3. *ἀντιλαμβάνομαι* 4. *διά* 5. *εὐεργέτημα* 6. *λυσιτέλεια* 7. *ὀνίνημι* 8. *σύμφορος* 9. *χάριν ἔχω* 10. *ὠφελέω* 11. beneficium
2Ch 32:25 according to the benefit done to him 1
Ps 103: 2 Bless the LORD . . forget not all his benefits 1
Prv 11:17 A man who is kind benefits himself 2
1Co 4: 6 for your benefit, brethren 4
7:35 I say this for your own benefit 8
14: 6 how shall I benefit you 10
1Ti 6: 2 since those who benefit . . are believers 3
Phm 1:20 brother, I want some benefit from you in the Lord. 7
Heb 4: 2 the message which they heard did not benefit 10
13: 9 which have not benefited their adherents. 10
2Es 1: 9 on whom I have bestowed such great benefits? 11
17 Where are the benefits which I bestowed on you? 11
9:10 although they received my benefits 11
Tob 3: 8 have had no benefit from any of them. 7
Sir 5: 8 it will not benefit you in the day of calamity. 10
2Mc 2:27 seeks the benefit of others 6
5:20 afterward participated in its benefits 5
3Mc 5:20 the Jews were benefited by today's sleep 9
benefit *See also* receive.

material benefit 1. *σαρκικός*
1Co 9:11 is it too much if we reap your material benefits? 1

benevolence 1. *φιλανθρωπία* 2. *φιλανθρώπως*
3Mc 3:15 clemency and great benevolence 1
18 because of the benevolence which we have toward all 1
20 since we treat all nations with benevolence. 2

bequeath 1. נחל 2. *μερίζω*
Lev 25:46 You may bequeath them to your sons after you 1
4Mc 13:19 bequeathed through the fathers 2

bereave 1. שָׁכוּל 2. שַׁכּוּל 3. שכל 4. *ἐρημόω* 5. *καταλείπω* 6. *στερέω*
Gen 42:36 You have bereaved me of my children 3
43:14 If I am bereaved of my children, I am bereaved. 3
14 If I am bereaved of my children, I am bereaved. 3
Deu 32:25 In the open the sword shall bereave 3
Sng 4: 2 bear twins, and not one among them is bereaved. 2
6: 6 all . . bear twins, and not one among them is bereaved. 2
Isa 49:21 I was bereaved and barren, exiled and put away 1
Jer 15: 7 I have bereaved them, I have destroyed my people; 3
Lam 1:20 In the street the sword bereaves; 3
Hos 9:12 I will bereave them till none is left. 3
Bar 4:12 a widow and bereaved of many; I was left desolate 5
16 bereaved the lonely woman of her daughters. 4
4Mc 12: 6 who had been bereaved of so many sons 6

bereave of child 1. שכל
Ezk 36:12 you shall no longer bereave them of children. 1
13 you bereave your nation of children, 1
14 and no longer bereave your nation of children 1

bereavement 1. *ἀτεκνίας καιρός* 2. *πένθος*
Wis 14:15 consumed with grief at an untimely bereavement 2
4Mc 18: 9 did not have the grief of bereavement. 1
bereavement *See also* time.

bereft 1. זנח 2. שאר מִן 3. שכל 4. *ἀπορφανίζω* 5. *ἀποστερέω*
Gen 27:45 Why should I be bereft of you both in one day? 3
Rut 1: 5 the woman was bereft of her two sons 2
Lam 3:17 my soul is bereft of peace 1
1Th 2:17 since we were bereft of you, brethren 4
1Ti 6: 5 who are depraved in mind and bereft of the truth 5

berry 1. גַּרְגַּר
Isa 17: 6 three berries in the top of the highest bough 1

beryl 1. שֹׁהַם 2. תַּרְשִׁישׁ 3. *βήρυλλος*
Exd 28:20 the fourth row a beryl, an onyx, and a jasper; 2
39:13 the fourth row, a beryl, an onyx, and a jasper; 2
Ezk 28:13 topaz, and jasper, chrysolite, beryl, and onyx 1
Dan 10: 6 His body was like beryl, 2
Rev 21:20 the seventh chrysolite, the eighth beryl 3
Tob 13:17 beryl and ruby and stones of Ophir; 3

beseech 1. אָנָּא 2. אָנָּה 3. בקשׁ 4. חלה 5. חלה פָּנִים 6. חנן 7. נָא 8. בעה (A) 9. *αἰτέω* 10. *ἄξιος* 11. *ἀξιόω* 12. *δέομαι* 13. *δέω* 14. *ἐπικαλέω* 15. *ἐρωτάω* 16. *ἱκετεύω* 17. *καταξιόω* 18. *παρακαλέω* 19. deprecor 20. orabo 21. rogo
Gen 42:21 when he besought us and we would not listen; 6
Exd 32:11 Moses besought the LORD his God, and said, "O LORD 4
Num12:13 Moses cried . . "Heal her, O God, I beseech thee. 7
Deu 3:23 I besought the LORD at that time, saying 6
1Sm 23:11 O LORD . . I beseech thee, tell thy servant. 7
2Sm 12:16 David therefore besought God for the child; 3
2Kg 13: 4 Then Jeho'ahaz besought the LORD 5
19:19 save us, I beseech thee, from his hand 7
20: 3 Remember now, O LORD, I beseech thee, how I have 7
Ezr 8:23 fasted and besought our God for this 3
Est 8: 3 she fell at his feet and besought him with tears 6
Job 19:16 I must beseech him with my mouth. 6
Ps 116: 4 O LORD, I beseech thee, save my life! 2
118:25 Save us, we beseech thee, O LORD! 1
25 O LORD, we beseech thee, give us success! 1
Isa 38: 3 said, "Remember now, O LORD, I beseech thee 7
Dan 2:16 Daniel . . besought the king to appoint him a time 8
Ams 7: 2 I said, "O Lord GOD, forgive, I beseech thee! 7
5 Then I said, "O Lord GOD, cease, I beseech thee! 7
Jon 1:14 Therefore they cried to the LORD, "We beseech thee 1
4: 3 now, O LORD, take my life from me, I beseech thee 7
Mat 8: 5 came forward to him, beseeching him 18
14:36 besought him that they might only touch 18
18:29 So his fellow servant fell down and besought him 18
32 because you besought me; 18
Mrk 1:40 a leper came to him beseeching him, and kneeling 18
5:23 besought him, saying, "My little daughter 18
6:56 besought him that they might touch 18
7:32 they besought him to lay his hand upon him. 18
Lke 4:38 they besought him for her. 15
5:12 he fell on his face and besought him 12
7: 4 they besought him earnestly, saying, "He is worthy 18
8:28 I beseech you, do not torment me. 13
41 he besought him to come to his house 18
Joh 4:31 the disciples besought him, saying, "Rabbi, eat. 15
Act 16: 9 a man of Macedo'nia was standing beseeching him 18
15 she besought us, saying 18
2Co 5:20 We beseech you on behalf of Christ 13
12: 8 Three times I besought the Lord about this 18
Gal 4:12 Brethren, I beseech you, become as I am 13
1Th 4: 1 we beseech and exhort you in the Lord Jesus 15
5:12 we beseech you, brethren 15
1Pe 2:11 I beseech you as aliens and exiles to abstain 18
2Es 2:41 beseech the Lord's power 21
4:22 Then I answered and said, "I beseech you, my lord 19
5:56 I said, "O Lord, I beseech thee 21
9:44 I besought the Most High, night and day. 19
12: 6 Therefore I will now beseech the Most High 20
13:13 and I besought the Most High, and said 19
Wis 8:21 so I appealed to the Lord and besought him 13
Sir 50:19 the people besought the Lord Most High in prayer 13
Man 1:11 beseeching thee for thy kindness. 12
13 I earnestly beseech thee, forgive me, O Lord 9
2Mc 1: 8 We besought the Lord and we were heard 13
7:28 I beseech you, my child, to look at the heaven 11
8: 2 They besought the Lord to look upon the people 14
14 and at the same time besought the Lord 11
29 besought the merciful Lord 11
9:26 I therefore urge and beseech you 11
10: 4 they fell prostrate and besought the Lord 11
16 making solemn supplication and beseeching God 11
26 they besought him to be gracious to them 11
11: 6 with lamentations and tears, besought the Lord 16
12:11 The defeated nomads besought Judas 11
24 With great guile he besought them to let him go 10
42 turned to prayer, beseeching that . . 11
13:12 besought the merciful Lord with weeping 17
4Mc 4:11 with tears besought the Hebrews to pray for him 18

beset 1. סבב 2. צור 3. *ἐπέρχομαι* 4. *περίκειμαι* 5. obsideo
Ps 31:21 love to me when I was beset as in a besieged city. •
109: 3 They beset me with words of hate 1
139: 5 Thou dost beset me behind and before 2
Heb 5: 2 since he himself is beset with weakness. 4
2Es 15:33 an enemy in ambush shall beset them 5
Wis 17:14 beset them from the recesses of powerless Hades 3

beset round about 1. סבב
Jdg 19:22 the men . . beset the house round about, beating 1
20: 5 rose against me, and beset the house round about 1

beside 1. אֶל 2. אֵצֶל 3. אֵת 4. בְּ 5. בְּיַד 6. חטא 7. לְיַד 8. לְעֵבֶר 9. לְעֻמַּת 10. מְזוּזָה 11. מִן 12. מֵעַל 13. מִצַּד 14. עַל 15. עַל־יַד 16. עִם 17. *ἐξίστημι* 18. *ἐπί* 19. *παρά* 20. *πρός* 21. *σύν*
Gen 29: 2 lo, three flocks of sheep lying beside it; 14
Exd 2: 5 and her maidens walked beside the river; 15
Lev 1:16 he shall . . cast it beside the altar on the east 2
6:10 the ashes . . and put them beside the altar 2
10:12 eat it unleavened beside the altar 2
25:36 that your brother may live beside you 16
39 if your brother becomes poor beside you 16
47 If . . your brother beside him becomes poor 16
Num 6: 9 if any man dies very suddenly beside him 14
11:31 quails . . and let them fall beside the camp 14
23: 3 Stand beside your burnt offering, and I will go; 14
6 Moab were standing beside his burnt offering. 14
15 Stand here beside your burnt offering 14
17 lo, he was standing beside his burnt offering 14
24: 6 like gardens beside a river 14
6 like cedar trees beside the waters. 14
Deu 11:30 over against Gilgal, beside the oak of Moreh? 2
16:21 not plant any tree as an Ashe'rah beside the altar 2
32:39 I, even I, am he, and there is no god beside me; 16
Jos 3:16 far off, at Adam, the city that is beside Zar'ethan 13
12: 9 the king of Ai, which is beside Bethel, one; 13
22: 7 a possession beside their brethren in the land 16
Jdg 6:25 and cut down the Ashe'rah that is beside it; 14
28 and the Ashe'rah beside it was cut down 14
30 altar of Ba'al and cut down the Ashe'rah beside it. 14
7: 1 rose early and encamped beside the spring 14
11:34 child; beside her he had neither son nor daughter 11
Rut 2:14 she sat beside the reapers 13
1Sm 1: 9 on the seat beside the doorpost of the temple 14
5: 2 took the ark of God . . and set it up beside Dagon. 2
6:15 took down the ark . . and the box that was beside it 3
18 The great stone, beside which they set . . the ark 14
19: 3 stand beside my father in the field where you are 7
20:19 go to . . and remain beside yonder stone heap. 2
41 David rose from beside the stone heap 2
26: 3 Hachi'lah, which is beside the road on the east 14
2Sm 1: 9 And he said to me, 'Stand beside me and slay me; 14
10 I stood beside him, and slew him 14
4:12 killed them . . and hanged them beside the pool 14
6: 7 and he died there beside the ark of God. 16
12:17 And the elders of his house stood beside him 14
15: 2 rise early and stand beside the way of the gate; 15
23:18 and slew them, and won a name beside the three. 4
22 and won a name beside the three mighty men. 4
1Kg 1: 9 the Serpent's Stone, which is beside En-ro'gel 2
2:29 Jo'ab has fled . . and behold, he is beside the altar 2
3:20 arose at midnight, and took my son from beside me 2
4:12 all Beth-she'an which is beside Zarethan below 2
7:20 projection which was beside the network; 8
10:19 and two lions standing beside the arm rests 2
13:24 body was . . in the road, and the ass stood beside it; 2
24 the lion also stood beside the body. 2
28 the ass and the lion standing beside the body. 2
31 bury me . . lay my bones beside his bones. 2
21: 1 a vineyard in Jezreel, beside the palace of Ahab 2
22:19 host of heaven standing beside him on his right 14
2Kg 11:14 the captains and the trumpeters beside the king 1
12: 9 and set it beside the altar on the right side 2
1Ch 11:20 slew them, and won a name beside the three. 4
24 won a name beside the three mighty men. 4
2Ch 9:18 two lions standing beside the arm rests 2
23:13 captains and the trumpeters beside the king 14
Neh 2: 6 king said to me (the queen sitting beside him) 2
3:23 Azari'ah . . repaired beside his own house. 2
4:18 The man who sounded the trumpet was beside me. 2
8: 4 beside him stood Mattithi'ah, Shema, Anai'ah, Uri'ah 2
Job 1:14 were plowing and the asses feeding beside them; 15
41:25 at the crashing they are beside themselves. 6
Ps 23: 2 He leads me beside still waters; 14
Prv 3:29 neighbor who dwells trustingly beside you. 3
8: 2 On the heights beside the way 14
3 beside the gates in front of the town 7
30 then I was beside him, like a master workman; 2
34 watching daily . . waiting beside my doors. 10
Sng 1: 7 like one who wanders beside the flocks 14
8 pasture your kids beside the shepherd's tents. 14
5:12 His eyes are like doves beside springs of water 14
6:12 my fancy set me in a chariot beside my prince. •
Isa 32:20 Happy are you who sow beside all waters 14
Jer 17: 2 and their Ashe'rim, beside every green tree 14
36:21 all the princes who stood beside the king. 12
Ezk 1:15 upon the earth beside the living creatures 2
19 creatures went, the wheels went beside them; 2
3:13 and the sound of the wheels beside them 9
9: 2 they went in and stood beside the bronze altar. 2
10: 6 he went in and stood beside a wheel. 2
9 there were four wheels beside the cherubim 2
9 there were four wheels . . one beside each cherub; 2
16 the cherubim went, the wheels went beside them; 2
16 the wheels did not turn from beside them. 2
19 as they went forth, with the wheels beside them; 9
11:22 their wings, with the wheels beside them; 9
17: 5 he placed it beside abundant waters. 14
32:13 all its beasts from beside many waters; 14
40:49 were pillars beside the jambs on either side. 1
43: 6 While the man was standing beside me, I heard one 2
8 and their doorposts beside my doorposts 2
47:10 Fishermen will stand beside the sea; 14
Hos 13: 7 like a leopard I will lurk beside the way. 14
Ams 2: 8 they lay themselves down beside every altar 2
7: 7 behold, the Lord was standing beside a wall 14
9: 1 I saw the LORD standing beside the altar 14
Zec 4:12 trees, which are beside the two golden pipes 5
Mat 13: 1 went out of the house and sat beside the sea. 19
Mrk 2:13 He went out again beside the sea 19
3:21 for people were saying, "He is beside himself. 17
4: 1 Again he began to teach beside the sea 19
1 the whole crowd was beside the sea on the land. 20
5:21 he was beside the sea. 19
Joh 4: 6 Jesus . . sat down beside the well. 18

Act 4:14 seeing the man . . standing beside them 21
5:10 buried her beside her husband. 20
2Co 5:13 For if we are beside ourselves, it is for God 17
Rev 15: 2 standing beside the sea of glass 18
1Es 9:43 beside him stood Mattathiah, Shema, Anaiah 19
Tob 4: 4 bury her beside me in the same grave. 19
Jdt 6: 7 put you in one of the cities beside the passes *
7: 3 near Bethulia, beside the spring 18
18 which is near Chusi beside the brook Mochmur. 18
13: 4 Then Judith, standing beside his bed, said 19
1Mc 13:29 beside the suits of armor carved ships 19

beside *See also* lay, stand.

besides 1. אַחַר 2. אֶפֶס 3. בִּלְעֲדֵי 4. בֶּלֶת 5. בִּלְתִּי 6. גַּם 7. גַּם כִּי 8. וְ 9. זוּלָה 10. יוֹתֵר 11. לְ 12. לְבַד 13. לְבַד מִן 14. מִבַּלְעֲדֵי 15. מִלְּבַד 16. מִן 17. עוֹד 18. עַל 19. עִם 20. ἅμα 21. δέ 22. δὲ καί 23. εἶτα μέν 24. ἐκτός 25. ἐν 26. ἐπί 27. ἔτι 28. καί 29. ὁμοῦ 30. πλήν 31. πρός 32. πρὸς ἐπί 33. σύν 34. χωρίς 35. adhuc 36. post 37. praeter

Gen 20:12 Besides she is indeed my sister 6
26: 1 famine in the land, besides the former famine 15
28: 9 Esau . . took to wife, besides the wives he had 18
31:50 or if you take wives besides my daughters 18
Exd 12:37 besides women and children. 13
Lev 9:17 besides the burnt offering of the morning 15
23:38 besides the sabbaths of the LORD 12
38 besides your gifts, and besides all your votive 12
38 and besides all your votive offerings 12
38 and besides all your freewill offerings 12
Num13:28 besides, we saw the descendants of Anak there. 6
16:49 besides those who died in the affair of Korah. 15
28:10 besides the continual burnt offering 18
15 offered besides the continual burnt offering 18
23 offer these besides the burnt offering 15
24 offered besides the continual burnt offering 18
31 Besides the continual burnt offering 15
29: 6 besides the burnt offering of the new moon 15
11 besides the sin offering of atonement 15
16 besides the continual burnt offering 15
19 besides the continual burnt offering 15
22 besides the continual burnt offering 15
25 besides the continual burnt offering 15
28 besides the continual burnt offering 15
31 besides the continual burnt offering 15
34 besides the continual burnt offering 15
38 besides the continual burnt offering 15
Deu 3: 5 besides very many unwalled villages. 12
4:35 the LORD is God; there is no other besides him. 15
18: 8 besides what he receives from the sale 12
29: 1 besides the covenant which he had made with them 15
Jos 17: 5 ten portions, besides the land of Gilead 13
Jdg 8:26 gold; besides the crescents and the pendants 13
26 besides the collars that were about the necks 13
20:15 that drew the sword, besides the inhabitants 13
Rut 2:21 And Ruth the Moabitess said, "Besides, he said to me 7
4: 4 there is no one besides you to redeem it 9
1Sm 2: 2 There is none holy . . there is none besides thee; 4
2Sm 2:30 were missing . . nineteen men besides As'ahel. 8
7:22 is none like thee, and there is no God besides thee 9
17: 8 Besides, your father is expert in war; 8
1Kg 4:23 cattle, 100 sheep, besides harts, gazelles 13
5:16 besides Solomon's . . chief officers 13
10:13 whatever she asked besides what was given her 15
15 besides that which came from the traders 12
2Kg 21:16 Manas'seh . . besides the sin which he made Judah 13
1Ch 3: 9 besides the sons of the concubines; 15
9:13 besides their kinsmen 8
17:20 O LORD, and there is no God besides thee 9
29: 2 besides great quantities of onyx and stones *
2Ch 9:12 whatever she asked besides what she had brought 15
14 besides that which the traders and merchants 12
17:19 besides those whom the king had placed 15
29:35 Besides the great number of burnt offerings 6
Ezr 1: 4 besides freewill offerings for the house of God 19
6 besides all that was freely offered. 12
2:65 besides their menservants and maidservants 15
8:20 besides 220 of the temple servants, whom David 16
Neh 5:15 food and wine, besides 40 shekels of silver. 1
17 besides those who came to us from the nations 8
7:67 besides their menservants and maidservants 15
Ps 73:25 nothing upon earth that I desire besides thee. 19
Ecc 12: 9 Besides being wise, the Preacher also taught 10
Isa 26:13 other lords besides thee have ruled over us 9
43:11 I, I am the LORD, and besides me there is no savior. 14
44: 6 first and I am the last; besides me there is no god. 14
8 you are my witnesses! Is there a God besides me? 14
45: 5 there is no other, besides me there is no God; 9
6 from the west, that there is none besides me; 3
14 there is no other, no god besides him.' 2
21 there is no other god besides me 14
21 a . . God and a Savior; there is none besides me. 9
47: 8 in your heart, "I am, and there is no one besides me 17
10 in your heart, "I am, and there is no one besides me 17
56: 8 others to him besides those already gathered. 11
64: 4 no eye has seen a God besides thee 9
Dan 11: 4 plucked up and go to others besides these. 15
Hos 13: 4 and besides me there is no savior. 5
Mat 14:21 about 5,000 men, besides women and children. 34
15:38 4,000 men, besides women and children. 34
27:19 Besides, while he was sitting 21
Lke 16:26 besides all this, between us and you a great chasm 25
24:21 Yes, and besides all this, it is now the third day 33
Rom13:11 Besides this you know what hour it is 28
2Co 7:13 besides our own comfort 26
Eph 6:16 besides all these, taking the shield of faith 25
1Ti 5:13 Besides that, they learn to be idlers 20
Heb 12: 9 Besides, this, we have had earthly fathers 23
1Es 2: 7 besides the other things 33
5:41 besides menservants and maidservants 34
2Es 3:32 Or has another nation known thee besides Israel? 37
7:96 and besides they see the straits and toil 35
14:12 besides half of the tenth part. 36
Tob 5:15 besides, I will add to your wages 27
Wis 12:13 For neither is there any god besides thee 30
Sir 29:25 besides this you will hear bitter words 32
37:15 besides all this pray to the Most High 26
LJr 1:40 Besides, even the Chaldeans . . dishonor them; 27
56 Besides, they can offer no resistance to a king 22
Bel 1:10 besides their wives and children 24
41 there is no other besides thee. 30
2Mc 5:23 besides these Menelaus 31
6: 4 and besides brought in things for sacrifice 27
8:17 besides, the overthrow of their . . way of life. 27
23 Besides, he appointed Eleazar to read aloud 27
10:15 Besides this, the Idumeans . . were harassing 29
31 20,500 were slaughtered, besides 600 horsemen. 21
14: 4 besides these 31
3Mc 2:22 besides being paralyzed in his limbs 27
7:22 Besides they all recovered all 28

besiege 1. בַּמָּצוֹר 2. בנה עַל 3. חנה 4. מָצוֹר 5. נצר 6. סבב 7. עַל 8. צור 9. צור אֶל 10. צור עַל 11. צרר 12. שמר 13. παρεμβάλλω ἐπί 14. περικάθημαι 15. περικαθίζω 16. πολιορκέω 17. πολιορκία

Deu 20:12 makes war against you, then you shall besiege it; 8
19 When you besiege a city for a long time, making war 8
19 trees . . men that they should be besieged by you? 1
28:52 They shall besiege you in all your towns, until 11
52 besiege you in all your towns throughout 11
1Sm 11: 1 Nahash . . went up and besieged Ja'besh-gil'ead; 3
23: 8 go down to Kei'lah, to besiege David and his men. 9
2Sm 11: 1 ravaged the Ammonites, and besieged Rabbah. 8
16 as Jo'ab was besieging the city, he assigned Uri'ah 12
20:15 the men . . with Jo'ab came and besieged him in Abel 8
1Kg 8:37 if their enemy besieges them in . . their cities; 11
16:17 Omri went up . . and they besieged Tirzah. 8
20: 1 he went up and besieged Sama'ria, and fought 8
2Kg 6:24 Ben-ha'dad . . and went up, and besieged Sama'ria. 8
25 a great famine in Sama'ria, as they besieged it 10
16: 5 they besieged Ahaz but could not conquer him. 8
17: 5 to Sama'ria, and for three years he besieged it. 8
18: 9 Assyria came up against Sama'ria and besieged it 8
24:10 came up to Jerusalem, and the city was besieged. 1
11 came to . . while his servants were besieging it 10
25: 2 the city was besieged till the eleventh year 1
1Ch 20: 1 and came and besieged Rabbah. 11
2Ch 6:28 if . . enemies besiege them in . . their cities; 11
32: 9 Sennach'erib . . who was besieging Lachish 7
Ps 31:21 love to me when I was beset as in a besieged city. 4
Ecc 9:14 and a great king came against it and besieged it 6
Isa 1: 8 like a lodge in a . . field, like a besieged city. 5
29: 3 and I will besiege you with towers 8
Jer 21: 4 and against the Chalde'ans who are besieging you 8
9 to the Chalde'ans who are besieging you 8
32: 2 the king of Babylon was besieging Jerusalem 8
37: 5 the Chalde'ans who were besieging Jerusalem 8
39: 1 his army came against Jerusalem and besieged it; 8
52: 5 the city was besieged till the eleventh year 1
Lam 3: 5 he has besieged and enveloped me 2
1Mc 6:19 assembled all the people to besiege them. 15
20 They gathered together and besieged the citadel 15
24 the sons of our people besieged the citadel 14
11:21 Jonathan was besieging the citadel. 14
61 So he besieged it 15
15:25 Antiochus the king besieged Dor anew 13
2Mc 10:19 a force sufficient to besiege them 17
33 they besieged the fort for four days. 15
11: 6 Lysias was besieging the strongholds 16
4Mc 7: 4 besieged with many ingenious war machines 16

besiege *See also* hard.

besieger 1. נצר 2. πολιορκέω

Jer 4:16 Besiegers come from a distant land; 1
4Mc 7: 4 he conquered the besiegers 2

besmear 1. טפל

Ps 119:69 The godless besmear me with lies 1

best 1. magis

2Es 8:15 About all mankind thou knowest best 1

best *See also* do, good.

best man 1. רעה

Jdg 14:20 given to his companion, who had been his best man. 1

best possible 1. ἐνδεχομένως

2Mc 13:26 Lysias . . made the best possible defense 1

bestir 1. חרץ 2. עור 3. ἐγείρω

2Sm 5:24 when you hear the sound . . then bestir yourself; 1
Ps 35:23 Bestir thyself, and awake for my right 2
Isa 64: 7 that bestirs himself to take hold of thee; 2
Ezk 38:14 dwelling securely, you will bestir yourself 3
Jol 3:12 Let the nations bestir themselves, and come up 2

bestow 1. מגן 2. נתן 3. עשה 4. שום 5. שוה 6. ἀπονέμω 7. ἐπιβάλλω 8. περιτίθημι 9. προστίθημι 10. φέρω 11. χαρίζομαι 12. confero 13. praesto

Exd 32:29 may bestow a blessing upon you this day. 2
1Ch 29:25 and bestowed upon him such royal majesty 2
Est 6: 3 What . . has been bestowed on Mor'decai for this? 3
Ps 21: 5 splendor and majesty thou dost bestow upon him. 5
84:11 sun and shield; he bestows favor and honor. 2
Prv 4: 9 she will bestow on you a beautiful crown. 1
Ezk 16:14 the splendor which I had bestowed upon you 4
23: 7 She bestowed her harlotries upon them 2
Lke 7:21 on many that were blind he bestowed sight. 11
Php 2: 9 bestowed on him the name 11
1Pe 3: 7 bestowing honor on the woman as the weaker sex 6
2Es 1: 9 on whom I have bestowed such great benefits? 12
17 Where are the benefits which I bestowed on you? 13
Wis 14:21 men . . bestowed on objects of stone or wood the name 8
Sir 17:11 He bestowed knowledge upon them 9
47: 6 when the glorious diadem was bestowed upon him. 10
3Mc 5:11 is bestowed by him who grants it 7

bestow freely 1. χαριτόω

Eph 1: 6 which he freely bestowed on us in the Beloved. 1

bestow graciously 1. εὐδοκέω

3Mc 2:16 you graciously bestowed your glory upon your people 1

bestow honor 1. δοξάζω

1Mc 15: 9 we will bestow great honor upon you 1

bestow prosperity upon 1. יטב

1Sm 2:32 prosperity which shall be bestowed upon Israel; 1

bestow riches 1. πλουτέω

Rom10:12 and bestows his riches upon all who call upon him. 1

bestowed *See* gift.

bestower of crown 1. עטר

Isa 23: 8 Tyre, the bestower of crowns 1

bestride 1. צעד

Hab 3:12 Thou didst bestride the earth in fury 1

betake 1. διακομίζω

2Mc 4: 5 he betook himself to the king 1
9:29 betook himself to Ptolemy Philometor in Egypt. 1

betray 1. גלה 2. מכר 3. רמה 4. ἀποκαλύπτω 5. δῆλόν ποιέω 6. ἐκφαίνω 7. μηνύω 8. παραδίδωμι 9. προδίδωμι 10. προδότης 11. ψεύδω

1Ch 12:17 but if to betray me to my adversaries 3
Isa 16: 3 hide the outcasts, betray not the fugitive; 1
Nah 3: 4 who betrays nations with her harlotries 2
Mat 10: 4 and Judas Iscariot, who betrayed him. 8
24:10 then many will fall away, and betray one another 8
26:16 he sought an opportunity to betray him. 8
21 I say to you, one of you will betray me. 8
23 will betray me. 8
24 woe to that man by whom the Son of man is betrayed! 8
25 Judas, who betrayed him, said, "Is it I, Master? 8
45 Son of man is betrayed into the hands of sinners. 8
73 for your accent betrays you. 5
27: 4 I have sinned in betraying innocent blood. 8
Mrk 3:19 Judas Iscariot, who betrayed him. 8
14:10 went to the chief priests in order to betray him 8
11 he sought an opportunity to betray him. 8
18 Truly, I say to you, one of you will betray me 8
21 woe to that man by whom the Son of man is betrayed! 8
41 Son of man is betrayed into the hands of sinners. 8
Lke 22: 4 how he might betray him to them. 8
6 sought an opportunity to betray him to them 8
21 behold the hand of him who betrays me 8
22 woe to that man by whom he is betrayed! 8
48 would you betray the Son of man with a kiss? 8
Joh 6:64 who it was that would betray him. 8
71 he, one of the twelve, was to betray him. 8
12: 4 (he who was to betray him), said 8
13: 2 put it into the heart . . to betray him 8
11 For he knew who was to betray him 8
21 Truly, truly, I say to you, one of you will betray me. 8
18: 2 Now Judas, who betrayed him, also knew the place; 8
5 Judas, who betrayed him, was standing with them. 8
21:20 Lord, who is it that is going to betray you? 8

Act 7:52 whom you have now betrayed and murdered 10
1Co 11:23 the night when he was betrayed took bread 8
Sir 14: 7 betrays his baseness in the end. 6
27:16 Whoever betrays secrets destroys confidence 4
17 if you betray his secrets, do not run after him. 4
21 whoever has betrayed secrets is without hope. 4
2Mc 6:11 were betrayed to Philip 7
4Mc 4: 1 he fled . . with the purpose of betraying it. 9
13:18 or betray the brothers who have died before us. 11

betrayer 1. מִרְמָה 2. *παραδίδωμι*

Prv 14:25 but one who utters lies is a betrayer. 1
Mat 26:46 Rise, let us be going; see, my betrayer is at hand. 2
48 Now the betrayer had given them a sign, saying 2
27: 3 When Judas, his betrayer, saw 2
Mrk 14:42 Rise, let us be going; see, my betrayer is at hand. 2
44 Now the betrayer had given them a sign, saying 2

betroth 1. ארשׂ 2. חרף 3. *ἁρμόζω* 4. *μνηστεύομαι γυναῖκας* 5. *μνηστεύω* 6. *παρθένος*

Exd 22:16 If a man seduces a virgin who is not betrothed 1
Lev 19:20 a woman who is a slave, betrothed to another man 2
Deu 20: 7 what man is there that has betrothed a wife 1
22:23 If there is a betrothed virgin, and a man meets her 1
25 a man meets a young woman who is betrothed 1
27 though the betrothed young woman cried for help 1
28 If a man meets a virgin who is not betrothed 1
28:30 betroth a wife, and another man shall lie with her; 1
2Sm 3:14 my wife Michal, whom I betrothed at the price 1
Hos 2:19 And I will betroth you to me for ever; 1
19 I will betroth you to me in righteousness 1
20 I will betroth you to me in faithfulness; 1
Mat 1:18 his mother Mary had been betrothed to Joseph 5
Lke 1:27 a virgin betrothed to a man whose name was Joseph 5
2: 5 to be enrolled with Mary, his betrothed 5
1Co 7:36 is not behaving properly toward his betrothed 6
37 to keep her as his betrothed, he will do well. 6
38 So that he who marries his betrothed does well; 6
2Co 11: 2 I betrothed you to Christ 3
1Mc 3:56 were betrothed, or were planting vineyards 4

better 1. *καλός* 2. *κρείττων* 3. *λυσιτελέω* 4. *μᾶλλον* 5. *συμφέρω*

Ecc 5: 1 to listen is better than to offer the sacrifice *
Mat 5:29 out and throw it away; it is better that you lose 5
30 off and throw it away; it is better that you lose 5
18: 6 it would be better for him 5
8 it is better for you to enter life maimed or lame 1
9 it is better for you to enter life with one eye 1
26:24 It would have been better for that man 1
Mrk 9:42 it would be better for him 4
43 it is better for you to enter life maimed 1
45 it is better for you to enter life lame 1
46 it is better for you to enter the kingdom of God 1
14:21 better for that man if he had not been born. 1
Lke 17: 2 It would be better for him 3
Tob 3: 6 it is better for me to die than to live 3
12: 8 It is better to give alms than to treasure up gold. 1
Jdt 7:27 it would be better for us to be captured by them; 2
10:19 Surely not a man of them had better be left alive 1
Sir 16: 3 better than to have ungodly children. *
20: 2 How much better it is to reprove 1
LJr 1:59 better even the door of a house *
59 better also a wooden pillar in a palace *

better *See also* all, get, good.

any better off 1. *προέχω*

Rom 3: 9 What then? Are we Jews any better off? No, not at all; 1

how much better 1. אַף כִּי

1Sm 14:30 How much better if the people had eaten freely 1

better off than 1. *ὑπέρ*

Sir 40:18 he who finds treasure is better off than both. 1

better than 1. עַל 2. *παρά* 3. *ὑπέρ* 4. super

Dan 1:20 found them ten times better than all 1
Rom 14: 5 One man esteems one day as better than another 2
2Es 7:19 he said to me, "You are not a better judge than God 4
Sir 40:19 a blameless wife is accounted better than both. 3
20 the love of wisdom is better than both. 3
21 a pleasant voice is better than both. 3
23 a wife with her husband is better than both. 3
24 almsgiving rescues better than both. 3
26 the fear of the Lord is better than both 3
27 covers a man better than any glory. 3

between 1. אֶל מִבֵּית 2. בְּ 3. בֵּין 4. בְּתוֹךְ 5. לְ 6. עִם 7. עִם וְעִם 8. תַּחַת 9. בֵּין (A) 10. *ἀνὰ μέσον* 11. *διὰ μέσον* 12. *ἐκ* 13. *ἐνώπιον* 14. *μέσος* 15. *μετά* 16. *μεταξύ* 17. *πρός* 18. apud 19. inter

Gen 3:15 I will put enmity between you and the woman 3
15 enmity . . between your seed and her seed; 3
9:12 covenant which I make between me and you 3
13 a sign of the covenant between me and the earth. 3
15 my covenant which is between me and you 3
16 the everlasting covenant between God 3
17 I have established between me and all flesh 3
10:12 Resen between Nin'eveh and Calah; 3
13: 3 had been at the beginning, between Bethel and Ai 3
7 there was strife between the herdsmen of Abram's 3
8 Let there be no strife between you and me 3
8 Let there be no strife between you and me 3
15:17 a flaming torch passed between these pieces. 3
16: 5 May the LORD judge between you and me! 3
14 Beer-la'hai-roi; it lies between Kadesh and Bered. 3
17: 2 I will make my covenant between me and you 3
7 I will establish my covenant between me and you 3
10 covenant . . between me and you 3
11 a sign of the covenant between me and you. 3
20: 1 of the Negeb, and dwelt between Kadesh and Shur; 3
23:15 silver, what is that between you and me? 3
26:28 there be an oath between you and us 3
30:36 three days' journey between himself and Jacob; 3
31:37 kinsmen, that they may decide between us two. 3
44 and let it be a witness between you and me. 3
48 This heap is a witness between you and me today. 3
49 The LORD watch between you and me 3
50 remember, God is witness between you and me. 3
51 pillar, which I have set between you and me. 3
53 God of their father, judge between us. 3
32:16 put a space between drove and drove. 3
42:23 for there was an interpreter between them. 3
49:10 nor the ruler's staff from between his feet 3
14 a strong ass, crouching between the sheepfolds; 3
Exd 8:23 a division between my people and your people. 3
9: 4 will make a distinction between the cattle 3
11: 7 a distinction between the Egyptians and Israel. 3
13: 9 as a memorial between your eyes, that the law 3
16 shall be as . . frontlets between your eyes; 3
14: 2 encamp . . between Migdol and the sea 3
20 coming between the host of Egypt and the host 3
16: 1 Sin, which is between Elim and Sinai 3
18:16 I decide between a man and his neighbor 3
22:11 an oath by the LORD shall be between them both 3
25:22 from between the two cherubim that are upon 3
28:33 with bells of gold between them 4
30:18 you shall put it between the tent of meeting 3
31:13 for this is a sign between me and you 3
17 sign for ever between me and the people of Israel 3
39:25 and put the bells between the pomegranates 4
25 the robe round about, between the pomegranates; 4
40: 7 place the laver between the tent of meeting 3
30 he set the laver between the tent of meeting 3
Lev 10:10 You are to distinguish between the holy 3
10 between the unclean and the clean 3
11:47 to make a distinction between the unclean 3
47 between the living creature that may be eaten 3
20:25 distinction between the clean beast 3
25 between the clean beast and the unclean 3
26:46 which the LORD made between him and the people 3
Num 7:89 voice . . from between the two cherubim; 3
11:33 While the meat was yet between their teeth 3
13:23 they carried it on a pole between two of them; 2
16:48 he stood between the dead and the living; 3
21:13 boundary of Moab, between Moab and the Amorites. 3
22:24 stood in a narrow path between the vineyards *
26:56 divided . . between the larger and the smaller. 3
30:16 statutes . . as between a man and his wife 3
16 statutes . . between a father and his daughter 3
31:27 between the warriors who went out to battle 3
35:24 between the manslayer and the avenger of blood 3
Deu 1: 1 between Paran and Tophel, Laban, Haze'roth 3
16 'Hear the cases between your brethren, and judge 3
16 judge righteously between a man and his brother 3
5: 5 I stood between the LORD and you at that time 3
6: 8 they shall be as frontlets between your eyes. 3
11:18 they shall be as frontlets between your eyes. 3
17: 8 between one kind of homicide and another 3
25: 1 If there is a dispute between men, and they come 3
1 come into court, and the judges decide between *
28:57 afterbirth that comes out from between her feet 3
33:12 makes his dwelling between his shoulders. 3
Jos 3: 4 Yet there shall be a space between you and it 3
8: 9 went to the place . . and lay between Bethel and Ai 3
11 encamped on . . with a ravine between them and Ai. 3
12 and set them in ambush between Bethel and Ai 3
18:11 fell between the tribe of Judah and . . of Joseph. 3
22:25 the LORD has made . . a boundary between us and you 3
27 but to be a witness between us and you 3
27 between us and you, and between the generations 3
28 but to be a witness between us and you.' 3
34 it is a witness between us that the LORD is God. 3
24: 7 he put darkness between you and the Egyptians 3
Jdg 4: 5 the palm of Deb'orah between Ramah and Bethel 3
17 there was peace between Jabin the king of Hazor 3
9:23 God sent an evil spirit between Abim'elech 3
11:10 LORD will be witness between us; we will surely do 3
27 decide this day between the people of Israel 3
13:25 in Ma'haneh-dan, between Zorah and Esh'ta-ol. 3
15: 4 and put a torch between each pair of tails. 3
16:25 They made him stand between the pillars; 3
31 and buried him between Zorah and Esh'ta-ol 3
20:38 signal between the men of Israel and the men 5
1Sm 7:12 a stone and set it up between Mizpah and Jesha'nah 3
14 was peace also between Israel and the Amorites. 3
14:42 Cast the lot between me and my son Jonathan. 3
17: 1 and encamped between Socoh and Aze'kah 3
3 on the other side, with a valley between them. 3
6 a javelin of bronze . . between his shoulders. 3
20: 3 there is but a step between me and death. 3
23 as for . . the LORD is between you and me for ever. 3
42 'The LORD shall be between me and you . . for ever.' 3
42 between my descendants and your descendants 3
24:12 May the LORD judge between me and you 3
15 the LORD . . and give sentence between me and you 3
26:13 stood afar off . . with a great space between them; 3
2Sm 3: 1 a long war between the house of Saul and . . David; 3
6 was war between the house of Saul and . . of David 3
18: 9 and he was left hanging between heaven and earth 3
24 Now David was sitting between the two gates; 3
21: 4 not a matter of . . between us and Saul or his house; 7
7 the oath of the LORD which was between them 3
7 oath . . between them, between David and Jonathan 3
1Kg 3: 9 that I may discern between good and evil; for who 3
5:12 there was peace between Hiram and Solomon; 3
7:46 in the clay ground between Succoth and Zarethan. 3
14:30 there was war between Rehobo'am and Jerobo'am 3
15: 6 there was war between Rehobo'am and Jerobo'am 3
7 there was war between Abi'jam and Jerobo'am. 3
16 there was war between Asa and Ba'asha 3
19 Let there be a league between me and you 3
19 a league . . as between my father and your father 3
32 there was war between Asa and Ba'asha 3
18: 6 they divided the land between them 5
42 he bowed . . and put his face between his knees. 3
22:34 struck . . between the scale armor 3
2Kg 9:24 Jehu . . and shot Joram between the shoulders 3
11:15 Bring her out between the ranks; 1
17 made a covenant between the LORD and the king 3
17 and also between the king and the people. 3
16:14 place between his altar and the house of the LORD 3
25: 4 by the way of the gate between the two walls 3
1Ch 21:16 of the LORD standing between earth and heaven 3
2Ch 4:17 in the clay ground between Succoth and Zer'edah. 3
12:15 continual wars between Rehobo'am and Jerobo'am. *
13: 2 Now there was war between Abi'jah and Jerobo'am. 3
14:11 between the mighty and the weak. 3
16: 3 Let there be a league between me and you 3
3 a league . . as between my father and your father; 3
18:33 between the scale armor and the breastplate; 3
23:14 Bring her out between the ranks; 1
16 covenant between himself and all the people 3
Neh 3:32 between the upper chamber of the corner 3
Job 4:20 Between morning and evening they are destroyed; †
9:33 There is no umpire between us 3
26:10 at the boundary between light and darkness. 6
41:16 near to another that no air can come between 3
Ps 68:25 between them maidens playing timbrels 4
104:10 springs gush forth . . flow between the hills. 3
Prv 18:18 lot . . decides between powerful contenders. 3
Sng 1:13 to me a bag of myrrh, that lies between my breasts. 3
Isa 2: 4 He shall judge between the nations 3
5: 3 judge, I pray you, between me and my vineyard. 3
22:11 You made a reservoir between the two walls 3
59: 2 a separation between you and your God 3
Jer 34:18 they cut in two and passed between its parts 3
19 who passed between the parts of the calf; 3
38:12 Put the rags and clothes between your armpits 8
39: 4 garden through the gate between the two walls; 3
52: 7 a gate between the two walls, by the king's garden 3
Ezk 4: 3 place it as an iron wall between you and the city; 3
8: 3 the Spirit lifted me up between earth and heaven 3
16 of the temple . . between the porch and the altar 3
10: 2 with burning coals from between the cherubim 3
6 Take fire from between the whirling wheels 3
6 the whirling wheels, from between the cherubim 3
7 his hand from between the cherubim to the fire 3
7 to the fire that was between the cherubim 3
18: 8 executes true justice between man and man 3
20:12 my sabbaths, as a sign between me and them 3
20 that they may be a sign between me and you 3
22:26 no distinction between the holy and the common 3
26 difference between the unclean and the clean 3
34:17 I judge between sheep and sheep, rams and he-goats 3
20 will judge between the fat sheep and the lean 3
22 I will judge between sheep and sheep. 3
40: 7 and the space between the side rooms, five cubits; 3
41: 9 Between the platform of the temple *
18 a palm tree between cherub and cherub. 3
42:20 a separation between the holy and the common. 3
43: 8 with only a wall between me and them. 3
44:23 the difference between the holy and the common 3
23 distinguish between the unclean and the clean. 3
47:16 lies on the border between Damascus and Hamath) 3
18 from Hazar-e'non between Hauran and Damascus; 3
18 the Jordan between Gilead and the land of Israel; 3
48:22 The portion of the prince shall lie between 3
Dan 7: 5 had three ribs in its mouth between its teeth; 9
8: 5 goat had a conspicuous horn between his eyes. 3
16 I heard a man's voice between the banks of the U'lai 3
21 great horn between his eyes is the first king. 3
11:45 between the sea and the glorious holy mountain; 3
Hos 2: 2 put away . . adultery from between her breasts; 3
Jol 2:17 Between the vestibule and the altar 3
Mic 4: 3 He shall judge between many peoples 3

Zec 5: 9 lifted up the ephah between earth and heaven. 3
6: 1 chariots came out from between two mountains; 3
13 peaceful understanding shall be between them 3
9: 7 and its abominations from between its teeth; 3
11:14 the brotherhood between Judah and Israel. 3
Mal 2:14 covenant between you and the wife of your youth 3
3:18 you shall distinguish between the righteous 3
18 between one who serves God and one who does not 3
Mat 18:15 tell him his fault, between you and him alone 16
23:35 murdered between the sanctuary and the altar. 16
Lke 11:51 perished between the altar and the sanctuary. 16
15:12 he divided his living between them. *
16:26 between us and you a great chasm has been fixed 16
17:11 passing along between Sama'ria and Galilee. 11
Joh 3:25 a discussion . . between John's disciples and a Jew 15
19:18 one on either side, and Jesus between them. 14
Act 12: 6 Peter was sleeping between two soldiers 16
15: 9 he made no distinction between us and them 16
23: 7 between the Pharisees and the Sad'ducees *
Rom 10:12 there is no distinction between Jew and Greek; *
14:22 The faith . . keep between yourself and God; 13
1Co 6: 5 to decide between members of the brotherhood 10
12:10 the ability to distinguish between spirits *
Php 1:23 I am hard pressed between the two. 12
1Ti 2: 5 there is one mediator between God and men *
2Es 4:18 If now you were a judge between them *
6:10 between the heel and the hand 19
7: 8 there is only one path lying between them 19
8 that is, between the fire and the water *
11:28 the two . . were planning between themselves 18
Jdt 3:10 here he camped between Geba and Scythopolis 10
7:24 God be judge between you and us! 10
8: 3 the field between Dothan and Balamon. 10
11 pronounced this oath between God and you 10
Sir 13:18 What peace is there between a hyena and a dog? 17
18 what peace between a rich man and a poor man? 17
25: 1 agreement between brothers *
1 friendship between neighbors *
27: 2 driven firmly into a fissure between stones 10
2 sin is wedged in between selling and buying. 10
LJr 1:54 they are like crows between heaven and earth. 10
1Mc 3:18 no difference between saving by many or by few. *
7:28 Let there be no fighting between me and you 10
12:36 a high barrier between the citadel and the city 10
16: 5 a stream lay between them. 10

bevel 1.מוֹרָד

1Kg 7:29 Upon the frames . . were wreaths of beveled work. 1

bewail 1.בכה 2.κόπτω

Lev 10: 6 whole house of Israel, may bewail the burning 1
Deu 21:13 shall remain in your house and bewail . . a full month; 1
Jdg 11:37 I may go and wander . . and bewail my virginity 1
38 and she departed . . and bewailed her virginity 1
Lke 8:52 all were weeping and bewailing her 2
23:27 women who bewailed and lamented him. 2
1Mc 13:26 All Israel bewailed him with great lamentation 2

beware 1.זהר 2.שׁמר 3.חמה(A) 4.βλέπω 5.προσέχω 6.φυλάσσω

Deu 4:16 beware lest you act corruptly by making *
19 beware lest you lift up your eyes to heaven *
8:17 Beware lest you say in your heart, 'My power *
29:18 Beware lest there be among you a man or woman *
Jdg 13: 4 beware, and drink no wine or strong drink, and eat 2
13 Of all that I said to the woman let her beware. 2
2Kg 6: 9 Beware that you do not pass this place 2
Job 32:13 Beware lest you say, 'We have found wisdom; *
36:18 Beware lest wrath entice you into scoffing; 3
Ecc 12:12 My son, beware of anything beyond these. 1
Isa 36:18 Beware lest Hezeki'ah mislead you by saying *
Jer 9: 4 Let every one beware of his neighbor 2
Mat 6: 1 Beware of practicing your piety before men 5
7:15 Beware of false prophets 5
10:17 Beware of men; for they will deliver you up 5
16: 6 Take heed and beware of the leaven 5
11 Beware of the leaven of the Pharisees 5
12 he did not tell them to beware of the leaven 5
Mrk 8:15 Take heed, beware of the leaven of the Pharisees 4
12:38 in his teaching he said, "Beware of the scribes 4
Lke 12: 1 Beware of the leaven of the Pharisees 5
15 Take heed, and beware of all covetousness 6
20:46 Beware of the scribes 5
Act 13:40 Beware, therefore, lest there come upon you 4
2Ti 4:15 Beware of him yourself 6
2Pe 3:17 beware lest you be carried away with the error 6
Tob 4:12 Beware, my son, of all immorality 5
Wis 1:11 Beware then of useless murmuring 6
Sir 4:20 Observe the right time, and beware of evil 6
11:33 Beware of a scoundrel, for he devises evil 5
17:14 he said to them, "Beware of all unrighteousness. 5
22:26 whoever hears of it will beware of him. 6
28:26 Beware lest you err with your tongue 5

bewilder 1.συγχέω 2.excedo

Act 2: 6 they were bewildered 1
2Es 10:37 an explanation of this bewildering vision. 2

bewilderment 1.excessus 2.excessus mentis

2Es 10:28 into this overpowering bewilderment 2
13:30 bewilderment of mind shall come over those 1

bewitch 1.βασκαίνω

Gal 3: 1 O foolish Galatians! Who has bewitched you 1

beyond 1.אַיִן 2.אֶל פָּנִים 3.בְּעֵבֶר 4.הָלְאָה 5.הָלְאָה מִן 6.יוֹתֵר מִן 7.יֶתֶר 8.לֹא 9.לִבְלִי 10.מֵהָלְאָה 11.מִן 12.מֵעֵבֶר 13.מֵעַל 14.עבר 15.עֵבֶר 16.עַד אַיִן 17.עַל 18.עֲבַר(A) 19.ἐπάνω 20.ἐπέκεινα 21.ἕως οὗ παρῆλθον 22.λοιπός 23.οὐ 24.παρά 25.πέραν 26.περισσός 27.πολύς 28.ὑπέρ 29.χωρίς 30.prae 31.super

Gen 35:21 and pitched his tent beyond the tower of Eder. 11
49:26 blessings . . are mighty beyond the blessings 17
50:10 floor of Atad, which is beyond the Jordan 15
11 named A'bel-mizraim; it is beyond the Jordan. 15
Lev 15:25 has a discharge beyond the time of her impurity 17
Num22: 1 plains of Moab beyond the Jordan at Jericho. 12
32:19 on the other side of the Jordan and beyond; 4
32 inheritance shall remain with us beyond the Jordan. 12
34:15 received their inheritance beyond the Jordan 12
35:14 You shall give three cities beyond the Jordan 12
Deu 1: 1 Moses spoke to all Israel beyond the Jordan 3
5 Beyond the Jordan, in the land of Moab 3
3: 8 kings of the Amorites who were beyond the Jordan 3
20 land which the LORD . . gives them beyond the Jordan; 3
25 Let me . . see the good land beyond the Jordan 3
4:41 three cities in the east beyond the Jordan 3
46 beyond the Jordan in the valley 3
47 who lived to the east beyond the Jordan; 3
11:30 Are they not beyond the Jordan, west of the road 3
30:13 Neither is it beyond the sea, that you should say 12
Jos 1:14 the land which Moses gave you beyond the Jordan; 3
15 land which Moses . . gave you beyond the Jordan 3
2:10 to the two kings . . that were beyond the Jordan 3
5: 1 Amorites that were beyond the Jordan to the west 3
7: 7 we had been content to dwell beyond the Jordan! 3
9: 1 kings who were beyond the Jordan in the hill 3
10 kings of the Amorites who were beyond the Jordan 3
12: 1 took possession of their land beyond the Jordan 3
13: 8 which Moses gave . . beyond the Jordan eastward 3
27 the lower end of . . eastward beyond the Jordan. 15
32 of Moab, beyond the Jordan east of Jericho. 12
14: 3 to the two and one-half tribes beyond the Jordan; 12
16: 6 and passes along beyond it on the east to Jan-o'ah 14
18: 7 received their inheritance beyond the Jordan 12
20: 8 And beyond the Jordan . . they appointed Bezer 12
24: 2 Your fathers lived of old beyond the Euphra'tes 3
3 I took your father Abraham from beyond the River 15
14 gods which your fathers served beyond the River 3
15 the gods . . served in the region beyond the River 15
Jdg 5:17 Gilead stayed beyond the Jordan; 3
7:25 of Oreb and Zeeb to Gideon beyond the Jordan. 12
10: 8 the people of Israel that were beyond the Jordan 15
1Sm 20:22 if I say . . 'Look, the arrows are beyond you,' then go; 5
36 As the lad ran, he shot an arrow beyond him. 14
37 Jonathan called . . "Is not the arrow beyond you? 5
31: 7 men of Israel who . . and those beyond the Jordan 3
2Sm 10:16 the Syrians who were beyond the Euphra'tes; 12
16: 1 When David had passed a little beyond the summit 11
20: 5 he delayed beyond the set time . . appointed him. 11
1Kg 14:15 and scatter them beyond the Euphra'tes 12
2Kg 25:16 bronze of all these vessels was beyond weight. 8
1Ch 6:78 beyond the Jordan at Jericho 12
12:37 Of the Reubenites and . . from beyond the Jordan 15
19:16 the Syrians who were beyond the Euphra'tes 15
22: 3 as well as bronze in quantities beyond weighing 1
14 silver, and bronze and iron beyond weighing 1
2Ch 20: 2 coming against you from Edom, from beyond the sea; 15
Ezr 4:10 rest of the province Beyond the River, and now 18
11 servants . . of the province Beyond the River 18
16 no possession in the province Beyond the River. 18
17 rest of the province Beyond the River 18
20 ruled over the whole province Beyond the River 18
5: 3 governor of the province Beyond the River 18
6 governor of the province Beyond the River 18
6 governors . . in the province Beyond the River 18
6: 6 governor of the province Beyond the River 18
6 governors . . in the province Beyond the River 18
8 tribute of the province from Beyond the River. 18
13 governor of the province Beyond the River 18
7:21 treasurers in the province Beyond the River 18
25 judge . . people in the province Beyond the River 18
8:36 governors of the province Beyond the River; 15
Neh 2: 7 governors of the province Beyond the River 15
9 governors of the province Beyond the River 15
3: 7 governor of the province Beyond the River. 15
Job 9:10 who does great things beyond understanding 16
Ps 147: 5 his understanding is beyond measure. 1
Prv 6:15 in a moment he will be broken beyond healing. 1
29: 1 suddenly be broken beyond healing. 1
Ecc 12:12 My son, beware of anything beyond these. 6
Isa 5:14 Sheol has . . opened its mouth beyond measure 9
7:20 a razor which is hired beyond the River 3
18: 1 whirring wings . . beyond the rivers of Ethiopia; 15
52:14 appearance . . marred, beyond human semblance 11
14 and his form beyond that of the sons of men– 11
56:12 will be like this day, great beyond measure. 7
Jer 8:18 My grief is beyond healing, my heart is sick *
22:19 and cast forth beyond the gates of Jerusalem. 10
52:20 bronze of all these things was beyond weight. *
Ezk 41: 4 and its breadth, twenty cubits, beyond the nave. 2
Ams 5:27 I will take you into exile beyond Damascus 4
Zep 3:10 From beyond the rivers of Ethiopia 15
Mal 1: 5 Great is the LORD, beyond the border of Israel! 13
Mat 4:25 Judea and from beyond the Jordan. 25
19: 1 entered the region of Judea beyond the Jordan; 25
Mrk 3: 8 Jerusalem and Idume'a and from beyond the Jordan 25
10: 1 went to the region of Judea and beyond the Jordan 25
Joh 1:28 This took place in Bethany beyond the Jordan 25
3:26 Rabbi, he who was with you beyond the Jordan 25
Act 7:43 I will remove you beyond Babylon.' 20
1Co 1:16 Beyond that, I do not know 22
4: 6 learn by us not to go beyond what is written 28
10:13 not let you be tempted beyond your strength 28
2Co 4:17 weight of glory beyond all comparison †
8: 3 beyond their means, of their own free will 24
Gal 1:14 I advanced in Judaism beyond many of my own age 28
Heb 1: 9 the oil of gladness beyond thy comrades. 24
7: 7 It is beyond dispute 29
1Es 1:24 beyond any other people or kingdom 24
49 beyond all the unclean deeds of all the nations 28
4:42 Ask what you wish, even beyond what is written 27
2Es 5: 2 shall be increased beyond what you yourself see 31
2 and beyond what you heard of formerly. 31
28 and dishonored the one root beyond the others 31
12: 7 righteous before thee beyond many others 30
Jdt 1: 9 and beyond the Jordan as far as Jerusalem 25
10 even beyond Tanis and Memphis 19
15: 5 even beyond Damascus and its borders. 21
Sir 3:23 Do not meddle in what is beyond your tasks 26
8:13 Do not give surety beyond your means 28
13: 2 Do not lift a weight beyond your strength 28
Bar 3:18 are anxious, whose labors are beyond measure? 23
1Mc 7: 8 governor of the province Beyond the River 25
11:60 traveled beyond the river 25

beyond *See also* comprehension, go, land, limit, measure, pass, power, roam.

bid 1.אמר 2.אמר אֶל 3.אמר לְ 4.דִּבֶּר 5.דבר 6.דבר אֶל 7.מנה 8.צוה 9.εἶπον 10.κελεύω 11.λέγω 12.παραινέω

Gen 43:17 The man did as Joseph bade him, 1
Exd 16:24 So they laid it by till the morning, as Moses bade 8
Num15:38 bid them to make tassels on the corners 1
22:20 but only what I bid you, that shall you do. 5
35 only the word which I bid you, that shall you 5
Jos 4:12 passed over armed . . as Moses had bidden them; 6
5:14 What does my lord bid his servant? 5
6:10 shall not shout . . until the day I bid you shout; 1
8: 8 set the city on fire, doing as the LORD has bidden; 4
11: 9 And Joshua did to them as the LORD bade him; 1
1Sm 24:10 and some bade me kill you, but I spared you. 1
2Sm 2:26 before you bid your people turn from the pursuit 3
14:19 It was your servant Jo'ab who bade me; 8
16:11 and let him curse; for the LORD has bidden him. 1
2Kg 10: 5 your servants, and we will do all that you bid us. 2
Ps 61: 7 bid steadfast love and faithfulness watch over 7
Mat 14:28 Lord, if it is you, bid me come to you on the water. 10
Lke 9:54 do you want us to bid fire come down from heaven 9
12:13 bid my brother divide the inheritance with me. 9
Joh 12:50 I say as the Father has bidden me. 9
Act 27:22 I now bid you take heart 12
Rom 12: 3 by the grace given to me I bid every one among you 11
Tit 2: 2 Bid the older men be temperate, serious, sensible *
3 Bid the older women likewise to be reverent *
9 Bid slaves to be submissive to their masters *
Rev 13:14 bidding them to make an image for the beast 11

bid defiance 1.גבר

Job 15:25 against God, and bids defiance to the Almighty 1

bid farewell 1.ἀπασπάζομαι 2.ἀποδέχομαι

Act 21: 5 we prayed and bade one another farewell. 1
2Mc 3:35 having bidden Onias farewell 2

bid rise 1.קום

2Kg 9: 2 and go in and bid him rise from among his fellows 1

bier 1.מִטָּה 2.מִשְׁכָּב 3.σορός

2Sm 3:31 And King David followed the bier. 1
2Ch 16:14 They laid him on a bier which had been filled 2
Lke 7:14 he came and touched the bier 3

big 1.πολύς

Sir 37:11 with a lazy servant about a big task 1

bill 1.סֵפֶר 2.γράμμα

Deu 24: 1 writes her a bill of divorce and puts it 1
3 latter husband . . writes her a bill of divorce 1
Isa 50: 1 Where is your mother's bill of divorce 1

Lke 16: 6 he said to him, 'Take your bill 2
7 He said to him, 'Take your bill, and write 80.' 2

billow 1. גַּל 2. κλύδων
Ps 42: 7 thy waves and thy billows have gone over me. 1
Jon 2: 3 all thy waves and thy billows passed over me. 1
Wis 14: 5 and passing through the billows on a raft 2

billowy 1. κυμαίνω
Wis 5:10 like a ship that sails through the billowy water 1

bind 1. אלם 2. אִסָּר 3. אסר 4. אפד 5. חבש 6. חזק 7. ענד 8. עקד 9. צור 10. צרר 11. קשר 12. רכס 13. רתח 14. שקד 15. כפת (A) 16. δεσμεύω 17. δέω 18. διαδέω 19. δουλόω 20. ἐνεχυράζω 21. κατακλείω 22. κυριεύω 23. ὀφειλέτης 24. ὀφείλω 25. περίκειμαι 26. προσδέω 27. τελευτή 28. alligo
Gen 22: 9 Abraham . . bound Isaac his son 8
37: 7 behold, we were binding sheaves in the field 1
38:28 the midwife took and bound on his hand a scarlet 11
42:24 he took Simeon from them and bound him before 3
49:11 Binding his foal to the vine 3
Exd 28:28 they shall bind the breastpiece by its rings 12
29: 9 you shall gird them with girdles and bind caps 5
39:21 they bound the breastpiece by its rings 12
Lev 8: 7 skilfully woven band of the ephod, binding it 4
13 Moses . . bound caps on them, as the LORD 5
Num30: 2 swears an oath to bind himself by a pledge 3
3 Or when a woman . . binds herself by a pledge 3
4 her pledge by which she has bound herself 3
4 every pledge by which she has bound herself 3
5 no pledge by which she has bound herself 3
6 utterance . . by which she has bound herself 3
7 her pledges by which she has bound herself 3
8 utterance . . by which she bound herself; 3
9 anything by which she has bound herself 3
10 if she . . bound herself by a pledge with an oath 3
11 every pledge by which she bound herself 3
13 Any vow and any binding oath to afflict herself 2
Deu 6: 8 you shall bind them as a sign upon your hand 11
11: 8 you shall bind them as a sign upon your hand 11
Jos 2:18 you shall bind this scarlet cord in the window 11
21 and she bound the scarlet cord in the window. 11
Jdg 15:10 We have come up to bind Samson, 3
12 We have come down to bind you, that we may give you 3
13 No; we will only bind you and give you into their 3
13 they bound him with two new ropes, and brought him 3
16: 5 overpower him, that we may bind him to subdue him; 3
6 and how you might be bound, that one could subdue 3
7 If they bind me with seven fresh bowstrings 3
8 bowstrings . . and she bound him with them. 3
10 me lies; please tell me how you might be bound. 3
11 If they bind me with new ropes that have not been 3
12 Deli'lah took new ropes and bound him with them 3
13 and told me lies; tell me how you might be bound. 3
21 down to Gaza, and bound him with bronze fetters; 3
1Sm 25:29 my lord shall be bound in the bundle of the living 10
2Sm 3:34 Your hands were not bound 3
2Kg 17: 4 the king . . shut him up, and bound him in prison. 3
25: 7 and bound him in fetters, and took him to Babylon. 3
2Ch 33:11 bound him with fetters of bronze 3
36: 6 bound him in fetters to take him to Babylon. 3
Neh 6:18 For many in Judah were bound by oath to him •
Job 12:18 binds a waistcloth on their loins. 3
31:36 I would bind it on me as a crown; 7
36: 8 if they are bound in fetters and caught 3
13 they do not cry for help when he binds them. 3
38:31 Can you bind the chains of the Plei'ades 11
39:10 Can you bind him in the furrow with ropes 11
40:13 bind their faces in the world below. 5
Ps 118:27 Bind the festal procession with branches 3
149: 8 to bind their kings with chains 3
Prv 3: 3 bind them about your neck 11
6:21 Bind them upon your heart always; 11
7: 3 bind them on your fingers 11
26: 8 Like one who binds the stone in the sling 10
Isa 22:21 clothe him . . and will bind your girdle on him 6
49:18 you shall bind them on as a bride does. 11
61: 1 the opening of the prison to those who are bound; 3
Jer 39: 7 and bound him in fetters to take him to Babylon. 3
40: 1 when he took him bound in chains 3
51:63 you finish reading this book, bind a stone to it 11
52:11 of Zedeki'ah, and bound him in fetters 3
Lam 1:14 My transgressions were bound into a yoke; 14
Ezk 3:25 you shall be bound with them, so that you cannot go 3
5: 3 and bind them in the skirts of your robe. 9
24:17 Bind on your turban, and put . . shoes on your feet; 5
27:24 and in carpets of colored stuff, bound with cords 5
30:21 bound up, to heal it by binding it with a bandage 5
Dan 3:20 bind Shadrach, Meshach, and Abed'nego, and to cast 15
21 men were bound in their mantles, their tunics 15
23 fell bound into the burning fiery furnace. 15
24 Did we not cast three men bound into the fire? 15
4:15 bound with a band of iron and bronze •
23 bound with a band of iron and bronze •
Nah 3:10 and all her great men were bound in chains. 13
Mat 12:29 unless he first binds the strong man 17
13:30 Gather the weeds first and bind them in bundles 17
14: 3 For Herod had seized John and bound him 17
16:19 whatever you bind on earth shall be bound 17
19 shall be bound in heaven 17
18:18 Truly, I say to you, whatever you bind on earth 17
18 shall be bound in heaven 17
22:13 'Bind him hand and foot, and cast him into the outer 17
23: 4 They bind heavy burdens, hard to bear 16
27: 2 they bound him and led him away and delivered him 17
Mrk 3:27 unless he first binds the strong man 17
5: 3 no one could bind him any more 17
4 he had often been bound with fetters and chains 17
6:17 bound him in prison for the sake of Hero'di-as 17
15: 1 they bound Jesus and led him away 17
Lke 8:29 bound with chains and fetters 16
13:16 a daughter of Abraham whom Satan bound 17
Joh 11:44 his hands and feet bound with bandages 17
18:12 officers of the Jews seized Jesus and bound him. 17
24 Annas then sent him bound to Ca'iaphas 17
19:40 and bound it in linen cloths with the spices 17
Act 9: 2 he might bring them bound to Jerusalem. 17
14 to bind all who call upon thy name. 17
21 to bring them bound before the chief priests. 17
12: 6 bound with two chains 17
20:22 I am going to Jerusalem, bound in the Spirit 17
21:11 bound his own feet and hands, and said 17
11 So shall the Jews at Jerusalem bind the man 17
33 ordered him to be bound with two chains 17
22: 4 binding and delivering to prison 16
29 he had bound him. 17
28:20 I am bound with this chain. 25
Rom 7: 1 law is binding on a person only during his life? 22
2 a married woman is bound by law to her husband 17
1Co 7:15 in such a case the brother or sister is not bound. 19
27 Are you bound to a wife? Do not seek to be free. 17
39 A wife is bound to her husband as long as he lives. 17
Gal 5: 3 he is bound to keep the whole law. 23
2Th 1: 3 We are bound to give thanks to God always for you 24
2:13 we are bound to give thanks to God always for you 24
Heb 5: 3 Because of this he is bound to offer sacrifice 24
Rev 9:14 Release the four angels who are bound 17
20: 2 seized the dragon . . and bound him for a 1,000 years 17
1Es 1:40 bound him with a chain of brass 17
2Es 13:13 some of them were bound 28
Tob 3:17 to bind Asmodeus the evil demon 17
8: 3 the angel bound him. 17
Jdt 6:13 they bound Achior 17
8:16 Do not try to bind the purposes of the Lord our God; 20
Wis 17:17 with one chain of darkness they all were bound. 17
Sir 28:19 has not been bound with its fetters; 17
Bar 3:25 It is great and has no bounds; it is high 27
3Mc 3:25 bound securely with iron fetters 21
5: 5 and bound the hands of the wretched people 16
6:19 binding them with immovable shackles. 17
4Mc 9:11 bound his hands and arms with thongs on each side. 18
26 they bound him to the torture machine and catapult. 26
10: 3 the noble kinship that binds me to my brothers. •
11: 9 the guards bound him 17

bind about 1. אזר
Job 30:18 it binds me about like the collar of my tunic. 1

bind by oath 1. ἀναθεματίζω 2. ὀφείλω
Mat 23:16 he is bound by his oath.' 2
18 he is bound by his oath.' 2
Act 23:12 the Jews . . bound themselves by an oath 1
14 We have strictly bound ourselves by an oath 1
21 having bound themselves by an oath 1

bind firmly 1. חבר
Ps 122: 3 built as a city which is bound firmly together 1

bind together 1. σύνδεσμος 2. συνδέω
Col 3:14 which binds everything together in perfect harmony. 1
Sir 33: 4 bind together your instruction 2

bind up 1. חבש 2. צור 3. צרר 4. קשר 5. καταδεσμεύω 6. καταδέω
Gen 44:30 then, as his life is bound up in the lad's life 4
Exd 12:34 kneading bowls being bound up in their mantles 3
Deu 14:25 money, and bind up the money in your hand, and go 2
Job 5:18 For he wounds, but he binds up; 1
26: 8 He binds up the waters in his thick clouds 3
28:11 He binds up the streams so that they do not 1
Ps 147: 3 brokenhearted, and binds up their wounds. 1
Prv 22:15 Folly is bound up in the heart of a child 4
Isa 1: 6 they are not pressed out, or bound up, or softened 1
8:16 Bind up the testimony, seal the teaching 3
30:26 when the LORD binds up the hurt of his people 1
61: 1 he has sent me to bind up the brokenhearted 1
Ezk 30:21 and lo, it has not been bound up, to heal it 1
34: 4 the crippled you have not bound up 1
16 I will bind up the crippled 1
Hos 6: 1 he has stricken, and he will bind us up. 1
13:12 The iniquity of E'phraim is bound up 3
Lke 10:34 and went to him and bound up his wounds 6
Sir 30: 7 He who spoils his son will bind up his wounds 5

binder 1. חבר
2Ch 34:11 to buy . . timber for binders and beams 1

binder of sheaves 1. עמר
Ps 129: 7 the reaper . . or the binder of sheaves 1

binding 1. שָׂפָה
Exd 28:32 with a woven binding around the opening 1
39:23 a garment, with a binding around the opening 1
binding *See also* man.

bird 1. בַּעַל כָּנָף 2. עוֹף 3. פרח 4. צִפּוֹר 5. עוֹף (A) 6. צִפַּר (A) 7. ὄρνεον 8. ὄρνις 9. πετεινόν 10. πτηνόν 11. volatile
Gen 1:20 and let birds fly above the earth 2
21 every winged bird according to its kind 2
22 and let birds multiply on the earth 2
26 have dominion . . over the birds of the air 2
28 and have dominion over the birds of the air 2
30 beast of the earth, and to every bird of the air 2
2:19 every beast of the field and every bird of the air 2
20 names . . to the birds of the air 2
6: 7 creeping things and birds of the air 2
20 Of the birds according to their kinds 2
7: 3 seven pairs of the birds of the air also 2
8 animals that are not clean, and of birds 2
14 every bird according to its kind, 2
14 according to its kind, every bird of every sort. 4
21 moved upon the earth, birds, cattle, beasts 2
23 creeping things and birds of the air; 2
8:17 birds and animals and every creeping thing 2
19 every beast, every creeping thing, and every bird 2
20 clean animal and of every clean bird 2
9: 2 of the earth, and upon every bird of the air 2
10 the birds, the cattle, and every beast of the earth 2
15:10 other; but he did not cut the birds in two. 4
40:17 but the birds were eating it out of the basket 2
19 and the birds will eat the flesh from you. 2
Lev 1:14 offering to the LORD is a burnt offering of birds 2
11:13 you shall have in abomination among the birds 2
46 This is the law pertaining to beast and bird 2
14: 4 take . . two living birds and cedarwood 4
5 command them to kill one of the birds 4
6 He shall take the living bird with the cedarwood 4
6 dip them and the living bird in the blood 4
6 dip them . . in the blood of the bird 4
7 shall let the living bird go into the open field 4
50 shall kill one of the birds in an earthen vessel 4
51 the scarlet stuff, along with the living bird 4
51 dip them in the blood of the bird that was killed 4
52 cleanse the house with the blood of the bird 4
52 cleanse the house . . with the living bird 4
53 he shall let the living bird go out of the city 4
17:13 any beast or bird that may be eaten 2
20:25 and between the unclean bird and the clean 2
25 abominable by beast or by bird or by anything 2
Deu 4:17 likeness of any winged bird that flies in the air 4
14:11 You may eat all clean birds. 4
22: 6 come upon a bird's nest, in any tree or on the ground 4
28:26 dead body shall be food for all birds of the air 2
1Sm 17:44 I will give your flesh to the birds of the air 2
46 give the dead bodies . . to the birds of the air 2
2Sm 21:10 allow the birds of the air to come upon them by day 2
1Kg 4:33 he spoke . . of beasts, and of birds, and of reptiles 2
14:11 one who dies in . . the birds of the air shall eat; 2
16: 4 dies in the field the birds of the air shall eat. 2
21:24 who dies . . the birds of the air shall eat. 2
Job 12: 7 the birds of the air, and they will tell you; 2
28:21 concealed from the birds of the air. 2
35:11 makes us wiser than the birds of the air? 2
41: 5 Will you play with him as with a bird 4
Ps 8: 8 the birds of the air, and the fish of the sea 4
11: 1 can you say to me, "Flee like a bird to the mountains; 4
50:11 I know all the birds of the air 2
78:27 like dust, winged birds like the sand of the seas; 2
79: 2 thy servants to the birds of the air for food 2
102: 7 lie awake, I am like a lonely bird on the housetop. 4
104:12 birds of the air have their habitation; 2
17 In them the birds build their nests; 4
124: 7 escaped as a bird from the snare of the fowlers; 4
148:10 creeping things and flying birds! 4
Prv 1:17 For in vain is a net spread in the sight of any bird; 1
6: 5 like a bird from the hand of the fowler. 4
7:23 as a bird rushes into a snare; 4
27: 8 Like a bird that strays from its nest 4
Ecc 9:12 and like birds which are caught in a snare 4
10:20 a bird of the air will carry your voice 2
12: 4 and one rises up at the voice of a bird 4
Isa 16: 2 Like fluttering birds 2
31: 5 Like birds hovering, so the LORD . . will protect 4
Jer 4:25 and all the birds of the air had fled. 2
5:27 Like a basket full of birds, their houses are full 2
7:33 this people will be food for the birds of the air 2
9:10 both the birds of the air and the beasts have fled 2
12: 4 the beasts and the birds are swept away 2
15: 3 the birds of the air and the beasts of the earth 2
16: 4 their dead bodies shall be food for the birds 2
19: 7 will give their dead bodies for food to the birds 2

34:20 dead bodies shall be food for the birds of the air 2
Lam 3:52 I have been hunted like a bird by . . my enemies 4
Ezk 13:20 let the souls that you hunt go free like birds. 3
17:23 in the shade of its branches birds of every sort 4
29: 5 to the birds of the air I have given you as food. 2
31: 6 birds of the air made their nests in its boughs; 2
13 Upon its ruin will dwell all the birds of the air 2
32: 4 cause all the birds of the air to settle on you 2
38:20 the fish of the sea, and the birds of the air 2
39:17 Speak to the birds of every sort and to all beasts 4
44:31 shall not eat of anything, whether bird or beast 2
Dan 2:38 given . . the beasts . . and the birds of the air 5
4:12 birds of the air dwelt in its branches 6
14 beasts flee . . and the birds from its branches. 6
21 in whose branches the birds of the air dwelt– 6
33 till . . his nails were like birds' claws. 6
7: 6 leopard, with four wings of a bird on its back; 5
Hos 2:18 with the beasts of the field, the birds of the air 2
4: 3 languish . . and the birds of the air; 2
7:12 I will bring them down like birds of the air; 2
9:11 E'phraim's glory shall fly away like a bird– 2
11:11 they shall come trembling like birds from Egypt 4
Ams 3: 5 Does a bird fall in a snare on the earth 4
Zep 1: 3 I will sweep away the birds of the air 2
Mat 6:26 Look at the birds of the air: they neither sow 9
8:20 Foxes have holes, and birds of the air have nests; 9
13: 4 and the birds came and devoured them. 9
32 so that the birds of the air come and make nests 9
Mrk 4: 4 the birds came and devoured it. 9
32 the birds of the air can make nests in its shade. 9
Lke 8: 5 the birds of the air devoured it. 9
9:58 Foxes have holes, and birds of the air have nests; 9
12:24 Of how much more value are you than the birds! 9
13:19 the birds of the air made nests in its branches. 9
Act 10:12 animals and reptiles and birds of the air. 9
11: 6 beasts of prey and reptiles and birds of the air. 9
Rom 1:23 for images resembling mortal man or birds 9
1Co 15:39 another for birds, and another for fish. 10
Jas 3: 7 For every kind of beast and bird, of reptile 9
Rev 18: 2 a haunt of every foul and hateful bird; 7
19:17 he called to all the birds that fly in midheaven 7
21 and all the birds were gorged with their flesh. 7
2Es 5: 6 and the birds shall fly away together; 11
26 from all the birds that have been created 11
6:47 bring forth living creatures, birds, and fishes; 11
Jdt 11: 7 the cattle and the birds of the air 9
AEs 16:24 most hateful for all time to beasts and birds. 9
Wis 5:11 when a bird flies through the air 7
17:18 a melodious sound of birds 8
19:11 Afterward they saw also a new kind of birds 8
Sir 17: 4 granted them dominion over beasts and birds. 9
22:20 who throws a stone at birds scares them away 9
27: 9 Birds flock with their kind 9
19 as you allow a bird to escape from your hand 9
43:14 the clouds fly forth like birds. 9
17 He scatters the snow like birds flying down 9
Bar 3:17 those who have sport with the birds of the air 7
LJr 1:22 Bats, swallows, and birds light on their bodies 7
71 a thorn bush in a garden, on which every bird sits 7
Aza 1:58 Bless the Lord, all birds of the air 9
2Mc 15:33 said that he would give it piecemeal to the birds 7
4Mc 14:15 For example, among birds 9
bird *See also* food.

bird of prey 1. עַיִט
Gen 15:11 when birds of prey came down upon the carcasses 1
Job 28: 7 That path no bird of prey knows 1
Isa 18: 6 be left to the birds of prey of the mountains 1
6 the birds of prey will summer upon them 1
46:11 calling a bird of prey from the east 1
Jer 12: 9 Is my heritage to me like a speckled bird of prey? 1
9 Are the birds of prey against her round about? 1
Ezk 39: 4 I will give you to birds of prey of every sort 1

small bird 1. צִפּוֹר
Lev 14:49 he shall take two small birds 1

bird to pick 1. *οἰωνόβρωτος*
2Mc 9:15 to throw out . . for the birds to pick 1

birth 1. בֶּטֶן 2. זֶרַע 3. ילד 4. מוֹלֶדֶת 5. מַשְׁבֵּר 6. רֶחֶם 7. תּוֹלֵדוֹת 8. *γένεσις* 9. *γενετή* 10. *γένος* 11. *γίνομαι* 12. *κοιλία* 13. *κοιλία μητρός* 14. *μήτρα* 15. *τοκετός* 16. *φύσις* 17. nativitas 18. partus
Gen 5: 7 Seth lived after the birth of Enosh 807 years 3
10 Enosh lived after the birth of Kenan 815 years 3
13 Kenan lived after the birth of Ma-hal'alel 3
16 Ma-hal'alel lived after the birth of Jared 3
19 Jared lived after the birth of Enoch 800 years 3
22 walked with God after the birth of Methu'selah 3
26 Methu'selah lived after the birth of Lamech 3
30 Lamech lived after the birth of Noah 595 years 3
11:11 Shem lived after the birth of Arpach'shad 3
13 Arpach'shad lived after the birth of Shelah 3
15 Shelah lived after the birth of Eber 403 years 3
17 Eber lived after the birth of Peleg 430 years 3
19 Peleg lived after the birth of Re'u 209 years 3
21 Re'u lived after the birth of Serug 207 years 3
23 Serug lived after the birth of Nahor 200 years 3
25 Nahor lived after the birth of Terah 119 years 3
28 before his father Terah in the land of his birth 4
24: 7 house and from the land of my birth 4
25:13 sons . . named in the order of their birth 7
31:13 return to the land of your birth.' 4
Exd 28:10 their names . . in the order of their birth. 7
Jdg 13: 5 for the boy shall be a Nazirite to God from birth; 1
7 a Nazirite . . from birth to the day of his death.' 1
2Kg 19: 3 children have come to the birth, and there is no 5
Job 3: 1 opened his mouth and cursed the day of his birth. •
11 Why did I not die at birth 6
Ps 22:10 Upon thee was I cast from my birth 6
58: 3 they err from their birth, speaking lies. 1
71: 6 Upon thee I have leaned from my birth; 1
Ecc 7: 1 and the day of death, than the day of birth. 3
Isa 14:19 cast out . . like a loathed untimely birth •
37: 3 children have come to birth 5
46: 3 borne by me from your birth, carried from the womb; 1
48: 8 and that from birth you were called a rebel. 1
Jer 46:16 to our own people and to the land of our birth 4
Ezk 16: 3 and your birth are of the land of the Canaanites; 3
4 as for your birth, on the day you were born 3
Dan 9: 1 Darius . . by birth a Mede, who became king 2
Hos 9:11 no birth, no pregnancy, no conception! 3
Mat 1:18 the birth of Jesus Christ took place in this way. 8
19:12 For there are eunuchs who have been so from birth 12
Mrk 7:26 the woman was a Greek, a Syrophoeni'cian by birth. 10
Lke 1:14 many will rejoice at his birth; 8
Joh 9: 1 As he passed by, he saw a man blind from his birth. 9
Act 3: 2 a man lame from birth was being carried 12
14: 8 he was a cripple from birth, who had never walked. 13
Gal 2:15 who are Jews by birth and not Gentile sinners 16
2Es 4:42 makes haste to escape the pangs of birth 18
6:26 who from their birth have not tasted death 17
Sir 22: 3 the birth of a daughter is a loss. 11
23:14 you will curse the day of your birth. 15
50:22 who exalts our days from birth 14
2Mc 5:22 at Jerusalem, Philip, by birth a Phrygian 10
3Mc 1: 3 a Jew by birth who later changed his religion 10
birth *See also* bring, give, pang.

noble birth 1. *εὐγένεια* 2. *εὐγενής*
1Co 1:26 not many were of noble birth; 2
Wis 8: 3 She glorifies her noble birth by living with God 1
2Mc 14:42 and suffer outrages unworthy of his noble birth. 1

untimely birth 1. נֵפֶל
Job 3:16 Or why was I not as a hidden untimely birth 1
Ps 58: 8 like the untimely birth that never sees the sun. 1
Ecc 6: 3 I say that an untimely birth is better off than he 1

birth-pang 1. *ὠδίν* 2. *πάθος*
Mat 24: 8 all this is but the beginning of the birth-pangs. 1
Mrk 13: 8 this is but the beginning of the birth-pangs. 1
Sir 7:27 do not forget the birth pangs of your mother. 1
4Mc 15: 4 because of their birth-pangs 2
15 the birth-pangs you suffered for them! 1
15:16 the birth-pangs you suffered for them! 1
16: 8 In vain, my sons, I endured many birth-pangs for you 1

birthday 1. יוֹם ילד 2. *γενέθλιος ἡμέρα* 3. *γενέσια*
Gen 40:20 On the third day, which was Pharaoh's birthday 1
Mat 14: 6 when Herod's birthday came 3
Mrk 6:21 when Herod on his birthday gave a banquet 3
2Mc 6: 7 the monthly celebration of the king's birthday 2

birthright 1. בְּכֹרָה 2. *πρωτοτόκια*
Gen 25:31 Jacob said, "First sell me your birthright. 1
32 I am about to die; of what use is a birthright to me? 1
33 swore to him, and sold his birthright to Jacob. 1
34 Thus Esau despised his birthright. 1
27:36 He took away my birthright; 1
43:33 the first-born according to his birthright 1
1Ch 5: 1 his birthright was given to the sons of Joseph 1
1 in the genealogy according to the birthright; 1
2 yet the birthright belonged to Joseph 1
Heb 12:16 who sold his birthright for a single meal. 2

birthstool 1. אֹבֶן
Exd 1:16 When you . . see them upon the birthstool 1

bishop 1. *ἐπισκοπή* 2. *ἐπίσκοπος*
Php 1: 1 who are at Philip'pi, with the bishops and deacons 2
1Ti 3: 1 If any one aspires to the office of bishop 1
2 Now a bishop must be above reproach 2
Tit 1: 7 For a bishop, as God's steward, must be blameless 2

bit 1. מֶתֶג 2. *χαλινός*
2Kg 19:28 put my hook in your nose and my bit in your mouth 1
Ps 32: 9 mule . . which must be curbed with bit and bridle 1
Isa 37:29 put my hook in your nose and my bit in your mouth 1
Jas 3: 3 If we put bits into the mouths of horses 2

bit (2) 1. בָּקִיעַ
Ams 6:11 into fragments, and the little house into bits. 1

bite 1. נשך 2. *δάκνω* 3. *δῆγμα* 4. *ἐγκεντρίζω*
Gen 49:17 a viper . . that bites the horse's heels 1
Num21: 6 sent fiery serpents . . and they bit the people 1
8 every one who is bitten when he sees it, shall live. 1
9 if a serpent bit any man, he would look 1
Prv 23:32 At the last it bites like a serpent 1
Ecc 10: 8 serpent will bite him who breaks through a wall. 1
11 If the serpent bites before it is charmed 1
Jer 8:17 and they shall bite you," says the LORD. 1
Ams 5:19 hand against the wall, and a serpent bit him. 1
9: 3 command the serpent, and it shall bite them. 1
Gal 5:15 if you bite and devour one another take heed 2
Wis 16: 5 destroyed by the bites of writhing serpents 3
9 were killed by the bites of locusts and flies 3
11 To remind them of thy oracles they were bitten 4
Sir 21: 2 for if you approach sin, it will bite you 2

bitten by a serpent 1. *ὀφιόδηκτος*
Sir 12:13 Who will pity a snake charmer bitten by a serpent 1

bitter 1. מַר 2. מרה 3. מֹרָה 4. מרר 5. מְרֹרָה 6. תַּמְרוּר 7. *καρτερός* 8. *πικραίνω* 9. *πικρασμός* 10. *πικρός* 11. amarico 12. amaritudo 13. amarus
Gen 26:35 they made life bitter for Isaac and Rebekah. 3
27:34 with an exceedingly great and bitter cry 1
Exd 15:23 drink the water of Marah because it was bitter; 1
Deu 32:32 grapes of poison, their clusters are bitter; 5
Rut 1:13 it is exceedingly bitter to me for your sake 1
1Sm 30: 6 all the people were bitter in soul 4
2Sm 2:26 Do you not know that the end will be bitter? 1
2Kg 14:26 the affliction of Israel was very bitter 2
Est 4: 1 went out . . wailing with a loud and bitter cry; 1
Job 3:20 that is in misery, and life to the bitter in soul 1
23: 2 Today also my complaint is bitter 12
Ps 64: 3 who aim bitter words like arrows 1
Prv 5: 4 in the end she is bitter as wormwood 4
27: 7 one who is hungry everything bitter is sweet. 1
31: 6 Give . . wine to those in bitter distress; 1
Ecc 7:26 I found more bitter than death the woman whose 1
Isa 5:20 who put bitter for sweet and sweet for bitter! 1
20 who put bitter for sweet and sweet for bitter! 1
22: 4 Look away from me, let me weep bitter tears; 4
24: 9 strong drink is bitter to those who drink it. 4
Jer 2:19 Know and see that it is evil and bitter for you 1
4:18 This is your doom, and it is bitter; 1
6:26 make mourning . . most bitter lamentation; 6
31:15 heard in Ramah, lamentation and bitter weeping. 6
Ezk 27:31 in bitterness of soul, with bitter mourning. 1
Hos 12:14 E'phraim has given bitter provocation; 6
Ams 8:10 mourning . . and the end of it like a bitter day. 1
Hab 1: 6 the Chalde'ans, that bitter and hasty nation 1
Zep 1:14 the sound of the day of the LORD is bitter 1
Jas 3:14 if you have bitter jealousy . . in your hearts 10
Rev 10: 9 Take it and eat; it will be bitter to your stomach 8
2Es 1:22 in the wilderness, at the bitter stream 13
8:34 that thou art so bitter against it? 11
AEs 14: 8 we are in bitter slavery 9
Sir 29:25 besides this you will hear bitter words 10
38:17 Let your weeping be bitter 8
41: 1 O death, how bitter is the reminder of you 10
2Mc 6: 7 the Jews were taken, under bitter constraint 10
3Mc 1: 4 When a bitter fight resulted 7
2:24 but went away uttering bitter threats. 10
4:15 bitter haste and zealous intentness 10
6:31 instead of a bitter and lamentable death 10
4Mc 18:20 O bitter was that day–and yet not bitter– 10
20 O bitter was that day–and yet not bitter– 10
20 that bitter tyrant of the Greeks 10
bitter *See also* distress, fruit, grief, herb, lamentation, make, pain.

more bitter 1. *πικρός* 2. *χαλεπός*
Wis 19:13 practiced a more bitter hatred of strangers. 2
4Mc 15:16 O mother, tried now by more bitter pains 1

bitter thing 1. מְרֹרָה
Job 13:26 For thou writest bitter things against me 1

bitterly 1. גָּדוֹל 2. מַר 3. *κακός* 4. *πικρός* 5. *πικρῶς*
Jdg 5:23 Curse Meroz . . curse bitterly its inhabitants †
21: 2 they lifted up their voices and wept bitterly. 1
1Sm 1:10 She . . and prayed to the LORD, and wept bitterly. †
2Sm 13:36 king . . and all his servants wept very bitterly. 1
2Kg 20: 3 And Hezeki'ah wept bitterly. 1
Ezr 10: 1 for the people wept bitterly. †
Isa 33: 7 the envoys of peace weep bitterly. 2
38: 3 And Hezeki'ah wept bitterly. 1
Jer 13:17 my eyes will weep bitterly †
Lam 1: 2 She weeps bitterly in the night †
4 and she herself suffers bitterly. 2
Ezk 27:30 and wail aloud over you, and cry bitterly. 2
Mat 26:75 he went out and wept bitterly. 5
Lke 22:62 he went out and wept bitterly. 5
Sir 25:18 he cannot help sighing bitterly. 4
4Mc 12:14 you will wail bitterly 3
bitterly *See also* complain, deal, lament, weep.

less bitterly 1. ἡδύς
Sir 22:11 weep less bitterly for the dead 1

more bitterly 1. βαρύς 2. πικρός
3Mc 3: 1 but was still more bitterly hostile toward those 1
4Mc 6:16 as though more bitterly tormented by this counsel 2

bitterness 1. מֶמֶר 2. מַמְרוֹר 3. מַר 4. מָרָה 5. מְרוֹר 6. רֹאשׁ 7. πικρία
Num 5:18 priest shall have the water of bitterness 3
19 be free from this water of bitterness 3
23 wash them off into the water of bitterness; 3
24 make the woman drink the water of bitterness 3
1Sm 15:32 Surely the bitterness of death is past. 3
Job 7:11 I will complain in the bitterness of my soul. 3
9:18 get my breath, but fills me with bitterness. 2
10: 1 I will speak in the bitterness of my soul. 3
21:25 Another dies in bitterness of soul 4
Prv 14:10 The heart knows its own bitterness 4
17:25 foolish son is . . bitterness to her who bore him. 1
Isa 38:15 has fled because of the bitterness of my soul. 3
17 for my welfare that I had great bitterness; 3
Lam 1: 7 in the days of her affliction and bitterness •
3: 5 enveloped me with bitterness and tribulation; 6
15 He has filled me with bitterness 5
19 Remember my affliction and my bitterness •
Ezk 3:14 and I went in bitterness in the heat of my spirit 3
27:31 they weep over you in bitterness of soul 3
Act 8:23 For I see that you are in the gall of bitterness 7
Rom 3:14 Their mouth is full of curses and bitterness. 7
Eph 4:31 Let all bitterness and wrath . . be put away 7
Heb 12:15 no "root of bitterness" spring up 7
Wis 8:16 companionship with her has no bitterness 7
Sir 4: 6 in bitterness of soul 7
21:12 a cleverness which increases bitterness. 7
31:29 Wine drunk to excess is bitterness of soul 7

bitumen 1. חֵמָר
Gen 11: 3 had brick for stone, and bitumen for mortar. 1
14:10 Now the Valley of Siddim was full of bitumen pits; 1
Exd 2: 3 a basket . . and daubed it with bitumen and pitch; 1

black 1. חוּם 2. חשך 3. קדר 4. שָׁחֹר 5. μέλας 6. niger
Gen 30:32 spotted sheep and every black lamb 1
33 among the goats and black among the lambs 1
35 every lamb that was black, and put them in charge 1
40 striped and all the black in the flock of Laban; 1
Lev 13:31 if . . there is no black hair in it 4
37 if . . itch is checked, black hair has grown in it 4
Sng 5:11 his locks are wavy, black as a raven. 4
Jer 4:28 earth shall mourn, and the heavens above be black; 3
Lam 4: 8 Now their visage is blacker than soot 2
Mic 3: 6 the prophets, and the day shall be black over them; 3
Zec 6: 2 chariot had red horses, the second black horses 4
6 The chariot with the black horses goes toward 4
Mat 5:36 head, for you cannot make one hair white or black. 5
Rev 6: 5 And I saw, and behold, a black horse, and its rider 5
12 and the sun became black as sackcloth 5
2Es 7:125 but our faces shall be blacker than darkness? 6
black *See also* grow, turn.

blacken 1. קדר 2. μελανέω
Job 30:28 I go about blackened, but not by the sun; 1
LJr 1:21 when their faces have been blackened 2

blackness 1. כִּמְרִיר 2. קַדְרוּת 3. שַׁחַר
Job 3: 5 let the blackness of the day terrify it. 1
Isa 50: 3 I clothe the heavens with blackness 2
Jol 2: 2 blackness there is spread upon the mountains 3

blade 1. לַהַב 2. χόρτος
Jdg 3:22 the hilt also went in after the blade, and the fat 1
22 the fat closed over the blade, for he did not draw 1
Mrk 4:28 The earth produces of itself, first the blade 2
blade *See also* shoulder.

blame 1. αἴτιος 2. μέμφομαι 3. μέμψις 4. μωμάομαι 5. μῶμος
2Co 8:20 We intend that no one should blame us 4
Wis 13: 6 Yet these men are little to be blamed 3
Sir 11:31 to worthy actions he will attach blame. 5
41: 7 Children will blame an ungodly father 2
2Mc 13: 4 this man was to blame for all the trouble 1
blame *See also* bear, throw.

blameless 1. זכה 2. טוֹב 3. נקה 4. נָקִי 5. שָׁלֵם 6. תָּם 7. תָּמִים 8. תמם 9. זַכּוּ (A) 10. ἄκακος 11. ἀκηλίδωτος 12. ἄμεμπτος 13. ἀμέμπτως 14. ἄμωμος 15. ἀνέγκλητος 16. ἀπρόσκοπος
Gen 6: 9 was a righteous man, blameless in his generation; 7
17: 1 I am God Almighty; walk before me, and be blameless. 7
44:10 and the rest of you shall be blameless. 4
Deu 18:13 You shall be blameless before the LORD your God. 7
Jdg 15: 3 Samson said . . "This time I shall be blameless 3
1Sm 29: 9 you are as blameless in my sight as an angel of God; 2
2Sm 22:24 I was blameless before him 7
26 with the blameless man thou dost show thyself 7
2Ch 15:17 the heart of Asa was blameless all his days. 5
16: 9 in behalf of those whose heart is blameless 5
25: 2 yet not with a blameless heart. 5
Job 1: 1 was Job; and that man was blameless and upright 6
8 a blameless and upright man, who fears God 6
2: 3 a blameless and upright man, who fears God 6
9:20 though I am blameless, he would prove me perverse. 6
21 I am blameless; I regard not myself; 6
22 he destroys both the blameless and the wicked. 6
Ps 18:23 I was blameless before him, and I kept myself 7
25 with the blameless man thou dost show thyself 7
19:13 Then I shall be blameless, and innocent 8
37:18 The LORD knows the days of the blameless 7
51: 4 in thy sentence and blameless in thy judgment. 1
64: 4 shooting from ambush at the blameless 6
101: 2 I will give heed to the way that is blameless. 7
6 he who walks in the way that is blameless 7
119: 1 Blessed are those whose way is blameless 7
80 May my heart be blameless in thy statutes 7
Prv 11: 5 righteousness of the blameless keeps his way 7
20 but those of blameless ways are his delight. 7
28:10 blameless will have a goodly inheritance. 7
29:10 Bloodthirsty men hate one who is blameless 6
Ezk 28:15 You were blameless in your ways 7
Dan 6:22 because I was found blameless before him; 9
Lke 1: 6 righteous before God, walking . . blameless. 12
Eph 1: 4 that we should be holy and blameless before him. 14
Php 1:10 pure and blameless for the day of Christ 16
2:15 you may be blameless and innocent 12
3: 6 as to righteousness under the law blameless. 12
Col 1:22 blameless and irreproachable before him 14
1Th 2:10 blameless was our behavior to you believers; 13
5:23 kept sound and blameless 13
Tit 1: 6 if any man is blameless, the husband of one wife 15
7 For a bishop, as God's steward, must be blameless 15
Heb 7:26 such a high priest, holy, blameless, unstained 10
AEs 16:13 of Esther, the blameless partner of our kingdom 12
Wis 2:22 nor discern the prize for blameless souls; 14
4: 9 a blameless life is ripe old age. 11
10: 5 and preserved him blameless before God 12
15 A holy people and blameless race 12
18:21 a blameless man was quick to act as their champion; 12
Sir 31: 8 Blessed is the rich man who is found blameless 14
40:19 a blameless wife is accounted better than both. 14
1Mc 4:42 He chose blameless priests devoted to the law 14
blameless *See also* make, prove.

blameless man 1. תָּמִים
Job 8:20 Behold, God will not reject a blameless man 1
12: 4 me, a just and blameless man, am a laughingstock. 1
Ps 37:37 Mark the blameless man, and behold the upright 1

show blameless 1. תמם
2Sm 22:26 thou dost show thyself blameless; 1
Ps 18:25 thou dost show thyself blameless; 1

blamelessly 1. תָּמִים
Ps 15: 2 He who walks blamelessly, and does what is right 1

blaspheme 1. גדף 2. נקב 3. קבב 4. קלל 5. βλασφημέω 6. βλάσφημος 7. blasphemo
Lev 24:11 the Israelite woman's son blasphemed the Name 3
16 He who blasphemes the name of the LORD 2
16 when he blasphemes the Name, shall be put to death 2
1Sm 3:13 because his sons were blaspheming God 4
Ezk 20:27 In this again your fathers blasphemed me 1
Mat 9: 3 This man is blaspheming. 5
Mrk 3:29 whoever blasphemes against the Holy Spirit 5
Lke 12:10 he who blasphemes against the Holy Spirit 5
Joh 10:36 do you say . . 'You are blaspheming,' 5
Act 26:11 and tried to make them blaspheme 5
Rom 2:24 The name of God is blasphemed among the Gentiles 5
1Ti 1:13 though I formerly blasphemed and persecuted 6
20 that they may learn not to blaspheme. 5
Jas 2: 7 Is it not they who blaspheme that honorable name 5
Rev 13: 6 God, blaspheming his name and his dwelling 5
2Es 1:22 thirsty and blaspheming my name 7
Bel 1: 9 because he blasphemed against Bel 5
2Mc 10:34 The men within . . blasphemed terribly 5
12:14 railing at them and even blaspheming 5

blasphemer 1. βλασφημέω 2. βλάσφημος 3. μετὰ βλασφημίας
Act 19:37 blasphemers of our goddess. 1
Wis 1: 6 will not free a blasphemer from the guilt of his words; 2
Sir 3:16 Whoever forsakes his father is like a blasphemer 2
2Mc 9:28 the murderer and blasphemer 2
10:36 burned the blasphemers alive 2
15:24 blasphemers who come against thy holy people 3

blasphemous 1. βλασφημία 2. βλάσφημος 3. δύσφημος
Act 6:11 blasphemous words against Moses and God. 2
Rev 13: 1 and a blasphemous name upon its heads. 1
17: 3 beast which was full of blasphemous names 1
2Mc 10: 4 blasphemous and barbarous nations. 2
13:11 fall into the hands of the blasphemous Gentiles. 3
blasphemous *See also* word.

blasphemy 1. נֶאָצָה 2. βλασφημέω 3. βλασφημία 4. δυσφημία 5. blasphemia
Neh 9:18 when they . . had committed great blasphemies 1
26 disobedient . . committed great blasphemies. 1
Mat 12:31 every sin and blasphemy will be forgiven men 3
31 the blasphemy against the Spirit 3
26:65 You have now heard his blasphemy. 3
Mrk 2: 7 Why does this man speak thus? It is blasphemy! 2
3:28 whatever blasphemies they utter; 3
14:64 You have heard his blasphemy. 3
Lke 5:21 Who is this that speaks blasphemies? 3
Joh 10:33 It is not for a good work . . but for blasphemy 3
Rev 13: 6 it opened its mouth to utter blasphemies 3
2Es 1:23 I did not send fire upon you for your blasphemies 5
1Mc 2: 6 He saw the blasphemies being committed in Judah 3
7:38 remember their blasphemies 4
2Mc 8: 4 the blasphemies committed against his name 3
10:35 fired with anger because of the blasphemies 3
blasphemy *See also* speak.

blast 1. נְשָׁמָה 2. קוֹל 3. רוּחַ 4. שִׁדָּפוֹן 5. φωνή
Exd 15: 8 At the blast of thy nostrils the waters piled up 3
19:13 When the trumpet sounds a long blast •
16 a very loud trumpet blast, so that all 2
Deu 28:22 smite you . . with drought, and with blasting 4
2Sm 22:16 at the blast of the breath of his nostrils. 1
Job 4: 9 by the blast of his anger they are consumed. 3
Ps 18:15 O LORD, at the blast of the breath of thy nostrils. 1
Isa 25: 4 for the blast of the ruthless is like a storm 3
27: 8 he removed them with his fierce blast 3
Rev 8:13 woe . . at the blasts of the other trumpets 5
blast *See also* make.

blast of a trumpet 1. תְּרוּעָה
Lev 23:24 a memorial proclaimed with blast of trumpets 1

trumpet blast 1. שׁוֹפָר
Zep 1:16 a day of trumpet blast and battle cry 1

blaze 1. אֵשׁ 2. בער 3. חרה 4. לֶהָבָה 5. שְׂרֵפָה 6. ἐκκαίω 7. καίω 8. φλέγω 9. φλογίζω
Num11:10 anger of the LORD blazed hotly 3
16:37 to take up the censers out of the blaze; 5
Ps 21: 9 make them as a blazing oven when you appear. 1
118:12 they blazed like a fire of thorns; 6
Ezk 20:47 the blazing flame shall not be quenched 4
38:19 in my jealousy and in my blazing wrath I declare 1
Hos 7: 6 in the morning it blazes like a flaming fire. 2
Zec 12: 6 I will make the clans of Judah like a blazing pot 1
Heb 12:18 a blazing fire, and darkness, and gloom 7
Rev 8:10 great star fell from heaven, blazing like a torch 7
Wis 16:22 the fire that blazed in the hail 8
Sir 3:30 Water extinguishes a blazing fire 9

blaze up 1. ἀνάπτω
2Mc 1:22 a great fire blazed up, so that all marveled. 1
32 When this was done, a flame blazed up 1

bleach 1. λευκαίνω
Mrk 9: 3 as no fuller on earth could bleach them. 1

bleat 1. קוֹל 2. κράζω
1Sm 15:14 What then is this bleating of the sheep in my ears 1
Tob 2:13 when she returned to me it began to bleat 2

bleed 1. טָרִי
Isa 1: 6 but bruises and sores and bleeding wounds; 1

blemish 1. מוּם 2. שחת 3. κηλίς 4. μωμάομαι 5. μῶμος 6. σπιλάς
Lev 21:17 None . . who has a blemish may approach to offer 1
18 For no one who has a blemish shall draw near 1
21 No man . . who has a blemish shall come near 1
21 since he has a blemish, he shall not come near 1
23 because he has a blemish, that he may not profane 1
22:20 You shall not offer anything that has a blemish 1
21 must be perfect; there shall be no blemish in it 1
25 Since there is a blemish in them . . they will not 1
Num19: 2 red heifer . . in which there is no blemish 1
Deu 15:21 if it has any blemish, if it is lame or blind 1
21 blind, or has any serious blemish whatever 1
17: 1 ox or a sheep in which is a blemish 1
32: 5 no longer his children because of their blemish; 1
2Sm 14:25 to . . his head there was no blemish in him. 1
Job 11:15 then you will lift up your face without blemish; 1
Mal 1:14 and yet sacrifices to the LORD what is blemished; 2
2Pe 2:13 They are blots and blemishes 5
Jde 1:12 These are blemishes on your love feasts 6
Wis 13:14 and covering every blemish in it with paint; 3
Sir 11:33 lest he give you a lasting blemish. 5
34:18 the offering is blemished 4

without blemish 1. תָּמִים 2. ἀμώμητος 3. ἄμωμος
Exd 12: 5 Your lamb shall be without blemish, a male 1

29: 1 Take one young bull and two rams without blemish 1
Lev 1: 3 he shall offer a male without blemish 1
10 he shall offer a male without blemish 1
3: 1 shall offer it without blemish before the LORD 1
6 animal . . he shall offer it without blemish 1
4: 3 a young bull without blemish to the LORD 1
23 as his offering a goat, a male without blemish 1
28 his offering a goat, a female without blemish 1
32 he shall bring a female without blemish 1
5:15 bring . . a ram without blemish out of the flock 1
18 priest a ram without blemish out of the flock 1
6: 6 guilt offering to the LORD, a ram without blemish 1
9: 2 ram for a burnt offering, both without blemish 1
3 calf and a lamb, both a year old without blemish 1
14:10 take two male lambs without blemish, and one ewe 1
10 and one ewe lamb a year old without blemish 1
22:19 you shall offer a male without blemish 1
23:12 offer a male lamb a year old without blemish 1
18 seven lambs a year old without blemish 1
Num 6:14 one male lamb a year old without blemish 1
14 one ewe lamb a year old without blemish 1
14 one ram without blemish as a peace offering 1
28: 3 two male lambs a year old without blemish 1
9 two male lambs a year old without blemish 1
11 seven male lambs a year old without blemish; 1
19 see that they are without blemish; 1
31 See that they are without blemish. 1
29: 2 seven male lambs a year old without blemish; 1
8 they shall be to you without blemish; 1
13 they shall be without blemish; 1
17 fourteen male lambs a year old without blemish 1
20 fourteen male lambs a year old without blemish 1
23 fourteen male lambs a year old without blemish 1
26 fourteen male lambs a year old without blemish 1
29 fourteen male lambs a year old without blemish 1
32 fourteen male lambs a year old without blemish 1
36 seven male lambs a year old without blemish 1
Ezk 43:22 a he-goat without blemish for a sin offering; 1
23 you shall offer a bull without blemish 1
23 and a ram from the flock without blemish. 1
25 bull and a ram from the flock, without blemish 1
45:18 you shall take a young bull without blemish, 1
23 seven . . bulls and seven rams without blemish 1
46: 4 shall be six lambs without blemish and a ram 1
4 lambs without blemish and a ram without blemish; 1
6 offer a young bull without blemish, and six lambs 1
6 lambs and a ram, which shall be without blemish; 1
13 shall provide a lamb a year old without blemish 1
Eph 5:27 that she might be holy and without blemish. 3
Php 2:15 children of God without blemish 3
Heb 9:14 offered himself without blemish to God 3
1Pe 1:19 like that of a lamb without blemish or spot. 3
2Pe 3:14 to be found by him without spot or blemish 2
Jde 1:24 and to present you without blemish 3

blend 1. מַעֲשֶׂה 2. רֹקַח מַעֲשֵׂה 3. רֹקַח מִרְקַחַת

Exd 30:25 anointing oil blended as by the perfumer; 3
35 make an incense blended as by the perfumer 2
37:29 fragrant incense, blended as by the perfumer. 1

blending 1. *σύνθεσις*

Sir 49: 1 memory . . is like a blending of incense 1

bless 1. אֶשֶׁר 2. ברך 3. בְּרָכָה 4. ברך (A) 5. *εἰς εὐλογίαν* 6. *ἐνευλογέω* 7. *ἐν εὐλογίαις* 8. *εὐλογέω* 9. *εὐλογητός* 10. *κατευλογέω* 11. *μακαρίζω* 12. *μακάριος* 13. beatifico 14. beo

Gen 1:22 God blessed them, saying, "Be fruitful 2
28 God blessed them, and God said to them, "Be fruitful 2
2: 3 God blessed the seventh day and hallowed it 2
5: 2 created them, and he blessed them and named them 2
9: 1 God blessed Noah and his sons, and said to them 2
26 He also said, "Blessed by the LORD my God be Shem; 2
12: 2 I will bless you, and make your name great 2
3 I will bless those who bless you 2
3 I will bless those who bless you 2
3 by you all the families . . shall bless themselves. 2
14:19 he blessed him and said, "Blessed be Abram by God 2
19 he blessed him and said, "Blessed be Abram by God 2
20 blessed be God Most High 2
17:16 I will bless her, and moreover I will give you a son 2
16 I will bless her, and she shall be a mother 2
20 I have heard you; behold, I will bless him 2
18:18 the nations of the earth shall bless themselves 2
22:17 I will indeed bless you 2
18 all the nations of the earth bless themselves 2
24: 1 the LORD had blessed Abraham in all things. 2
27 Blessed be the LORD, the God of my master Abraham 2
31 He said, "Come in, O blessed of the LORD; 2
35 The LORD has greatly blessed my master 2
48 worshiped the LORD, and blessed the LORD 2
60 they blessed Rebekah, and said to her 2
25:11 After the death of Abraham God blessed Isaac 2
26: 3 I will be with you, and will bless you; 2
4 the nations of the earth shall bless themselves 2
12 The LORD blessed him 2
24 fear not, for I am with you and will bless you 2
29 You are now the blessed of the LORD. 2
27: 4 that I may bless you before I die. 2
7 and bless you before the LORD before I die. 2
10 so that he may bless you before he dies. 2
19 eat of my game, that you may bless me. 2
23 his brother Esau's hands; so he blessed him. 2
25 that I may eat of my son's game and bless you. 2
27 smell of his garments, and blessed him 2
27 the smell of a field which the LORD has blessed! 2
29 blessed be every one who blesses you! 2
29 blessed be every one who blesses you! 2
30 As soon as Isaac had finished blessing Jacob 2
31 eat of his son's game, that you may bless me. 2
33 and I have blessed him?–yes, and he shall 2
33 have blessed him?–yes, and he shall be blessed. 2
34 Bless me, even me also, O my father! 2
38 Bless me, even me also, O my father. 2
41 with which his father had blessed him 2
28: 1 Then Isaac called Jacob and blessed him 2
3 God Almighty bless you and make you fruitful 2
6 Esau saw that Isaac had blessed Jacob 2
6 he blessed him he charged him, "You shall not marry 2
14 all the families of the earth bless themselves. 2
30:27 that the LORD has blessed me because of you; 2
30 and the LORD has blessed you wherever I turned. 2
31:55 kissed . . his daughters and blessed them; 2
32:26 I will not let you go, unless you bless me. 2
29 you ask my name?" And there he blessed him. 2
35: 9 when he came from Paddan-aram, and blessed him. 2
39: 5 the LORD blessed the Egyptian's house 2
47: 7 and Jacob blessed Pharaoh. 2
10 Jacob blessed Pharaoh, and went out 2
48: 3 God Almighty appeared . . blessed me 2
9 Bring them to me . . that I may bless them. 2
15 he blessed Joseph, and said, "The God before 2
16 the angel . . bless the lads; and in them let my 2
20 he blessed them that day, saying, "By you Israel 2
49:25 God Almighty who will bless you with blessings 2
28 their father said to them as he blessed them 2
28 blessing each with the blessing suitable 2
Exd 12:32 be gone; and bless me also! 2
18:10 Jethro said, "Blessed be the LORD, who has 2
20:11 therefore the LORD blessed the sabbath day 2
24 I will come to you and bless you. 2
23:25 and I will bless your bread and your water; 2
39:43 had they done it. And Moses blessed them. 2
Lev 9:22 toward the people and blessed them 2
23 when they came out they blessed the people 2
Num 6:23 Thus you shall bless the people of Israel 2
24 The LORD bless you and keep you 2
27 upon the people of Israel, and I will bless them. 2
22: 6 for I know that he whom you bless is blessed 2
6 for I know that he whom you bless is blessed 2
12 shall not curse the people, for they are blessed. 2
23:11 behold, you have done nothing but bless them. 2
20 Behold, I received a command to bless 2
20 he has blessed, and I cannot revoke it. 2
25 Neither curse them at all, nor bless them at all. 2
24: 1 saw that it pleased the LORD to bless Israel 2
9 Blessed be every one who blesses you 2
9 Blessed be every one who blesses you 2
10 behold, you have blessed them these three times. 2
Deu 1:11 May the LORD . . bless you, as he has promised you! 2
2: 7 LORD . . blessed you in all the work of your hands; 2
7:13 he will love you, bless you, and multiply you; 2
13 also bless the fruit of your body and the fruit 2
14 You shall be blessed above all peoples; 2
8:10 shall bless the LORD your God for the good land 2
10: 8 stand before the LORD . . to bless in his name 2
12: 7 in which the LORD your God has blessed you. 2
14:24 when the LORD your God blesses you 2
29 LORD . . may bless you in all the work 2
15: 4 (for the LORD will bless you in the land 2
6 LORD your God will bless you, as he promised you 2
10 because for this the LORD your God will bless you 2
14 as the LORD . . has blessed you, you shall give 2
18 LORD your God will bless you in all that you do. 2
16:10 which you shall give as the LORD your God blesses 2
15 LORD . . will bless you in all your produce 2
21: 5 chosen them . . to bless in the name of the LORD 2
23:20 LORD . . may bless you in all that you undertake 2
24:13 that he may sleep in his cloak and bless you; 2
19 LORD . . bless you in all the work of your hands. 2
26:15 bless thy people Israel and the ground 2
27:12 stand upon Mount Ger'izim to bless the people 2
28: 3 Blessed shall you be in the city, and blessed 2
3 in the city, and blessed shall you be in the field. 2
4 Blessed shall be the fruit of your body 2
5 Blessed . . basket and your kneading-trough. 2
6 Blessed shall you be when you come in, and blessed 2
6 come in, and blessed shall you be when you go out. 2
8 bless you in the land which the LORD your God 2
12 to bless all the work of your hands; 2
29:19 one who . . blesses himself in his heart, saying 2
30:16 LORD your God will bless you in the land 2
33: 1 Moses . . blessed the children of Israel 2
11 Bless, O LORD, his substance, and accept the work 2
13 of Joseph he said, "Blessed by the LORD be his land 2
20 of Gad he said, "Blessed be he who enlarges Gad! 2
24 of Asher he said, "Blessed above sons be Asher; 2
Jos 8:33 that they should bless the people of Israel. 2
14:13 Joshua blessed him; and he gave Hebron to Caleb 2
17:14 I am . . since hitherto the LORD has blessed me? 2
22: 6 Joshua blessed them, and sent them away; 2
7 Joshua sent them away . . and blessed them 2
33 and the people of Israel blessed God 2
24:10 not listen to Balaam; therefore he blessed you; 2
Jdg 5: 2 people offered themselves . . bless the LORD! 2
9 among the people. Bless the LORD. 2
24 Most blessed of women be Ja'el, the wife of Heber 2
24 be Ja'el . . of tent-dwelling women most blessed. 2
13:24 Samson; and the boy grew, and the LORD blessed him. 2
17: 2 his mother said, "Blessed be my son by the LORD. 2
Rut 2: 4 And they answered, "The LORD bless you. 2
19 Blessed be the man who took notice of you. 2
20 And Na'omi said . . "Blessed be he by the LORD 2
3:10 May you be blessed by the LORD, my daughter; 2
4:14 Blessed be the LORD, who has not left you this day 2
1Sm 2:20 Then Eli would bless Elka'nah and his wife, and say 2
9:13 till he comes, since he must bless the sacrifice; 2
15:13 Blessed be you to the LORD; I have performed 2
23:21 And Saul said, "May you be blessed by the LORD; 2
25:32 Blessed be the LORD, the God of Israel, who sent you 2
33 Blessed be your discretion, and blessed be you 2
33 Blessed be your discretion, and blessed be you 2
39 Blessed be the LORD who has avenged the insult 2
26:25 Saul said to David, "Blessed be you, my son David! 2
2Sm 2: 5 May you be blessed by the LORD, because you showed 2
6:11 LORD blessed O'bed-e'dom and all his household. 2
12 The LORD has blessed the household of O'bed-e'dom 2
18 he blessed the people in the name of the LORD 2
20 David returned to bless his household. 2
7:29 may it please thee to bless the house of thy 2
29 the house of thy servant be blessed for ever. 2
14:22 Jo'ab . . and did obeisance, and blessed the king; 2
18:28 Blessed be the LORD your God, who has delivered up 2
19:39 and the king kissed Barzil'lai and blessed him 2
21: 3 that you may bless the heritage of the LORD? 2
22:47 and blessed be my rock, and exalted be my God 2
1Kg 1:48 Blessed be the LORD, the God of Israel, who has 2
2:45 King Solomon shall be blessed, and the throne 2
5: 7 Blessed be the LORD . . who has given to David 2
8:14 king . . blessed all the assembly of Israel 2
15 Blessed be the LORD, the God of Israel, who 2
55 he stood, and blessed all the assembly of Israel 2
56 Blessed be the LORD who has given rest 2
66 they blessed the king, and went to their homes 2
10: 9 Blessed be the LORD . . who has delighted in you 2
1Ch 4:10 Jabez . . saying, "Oh that thou wouldst bless me 2
13:14 the LORD blessed the household of O'bed-e'dom 2
16: 2 he blessed the people in the name of the LORD 2
36 Blessed be the LORD, the God of Israel 2
43 and David went home to bless his household. 2
17:27 please thee to bless the house of thy servant 2
27 what thou, O LORD, hast blessed is blessed for ever 2
27 what thou, O LORD, hast blessed is blessed for ever 2
26: 5 Pe-ul'lethai the eighth; for God blessed him. 2
29:10 David blessed the LORD in the presence of all 2
10 David said: "Blessed art thou, O LORD 2
20 said to all the assembly, "Bless the LORD your God. 2
20 And all the assembly blessed the LORD, the God 2
2Ch 2:12 Huram also said, "Blessed be the LORD God of Israel 2
6: 3 king . . and blessed all the assembly of Israel 2
4 he said, "Blessed be the LORD, the God of Israel, who 2
9: 8 Blessed be the LORD your God, who has delighted 2
20:26 Bera'cah, for there they blessed the LORD; 2
30:27 priests and the Levites . . blessed the people 2
31: 8 blessed the LORD and his people Israel. 2
10 for the LORD has blessed his people 2
Ezr 7:27 Blessed be the LORD, the God of our fathers 2
Neh 8: 6 Ezra blessed the Lord, the great God; 2
9: 5 Stand up and bless the LORD your God 2
5 Blessed be thy glorious name which is exalted 2
11: 2 people blessed all the men who willingly 2
Job 1:10 Thou hast blessed the work of his hands 2
21 blessed be the name of the LORD. 2
31:20 if his loins have not blessed me 2
42:12 the LORD blessed the latter days of Job 2
Ps 1: 1 Blessed is the man who walks not in the counsel 1
2:12 Blessed are all who take refuge in him. 1
5:12 For thou dost bless the righteous, O LORD; 2
16: 7 I bless the LORD who gives me counsel; 2
18:46 The LORD lives; and blessed be my rock 2
21: 6 Yea, thou dost make him most blessed for ever; 3
26:12 in the great congregation I will bless the LORD. 2
28: 6 Blessed be the LORD! for he has heard 2
9 O save thy people, and bless thy heritage; 2
29:11 May the LORD bless his people with peace! 2
31:21 Blessed be the LORD, for he has wondrously shown 2
32: 1 Blessed is he whose transgression is forgiven 1
2 Blessed is the man to whom the LORD imputes 1
33:12 Blessed is the nation whose God is the LORD 1
34: 1 I will bless the LORD at all times; 2
37:22 those blessed by the LORD shall possess the land 2
40: 4 Blessed is the man who makes the LORD his trust 1
41: 1 Blessed is he who considers the poor! 1
13 Blessed be the LORD, the God of Israel 2
45: 2 therefore God has blessed you for ever. 2
62: 4 They bless with their mouths 2

63: 4 I will bless thee as long as I live; 2
65: 4 Blessed is he whom thou dost choose 1
10 with showers, and blessing its growth. 2
66: 8 Bless our God, O peoples 2
20 Blessed be God, because he has not rejected my 2
67: 1 May God be gracious to us and bless us 2
6 God, our God, has blessed us. 2
7 God has blessed us; 2
68:19 Blessed be the Lord, who daily bears us up; 2
26 Bless God in the great congregation, the LORD 2
35 Blessed be God! 2
72:17 May men bless themselves by him 2
18 Blessed be the LORD, the God of Israel 2
19 Blessed be his glorious name for ever; 2
84: 4 Blessed are those who dwell in thy house 1
5 Blessed are the men whose strength is in thee 1
12 O LORD of hosts, blessed is the man who trusts 1
89:15 Blessed are the people who know the festal shout 1
52 Blessed be the LORD for ever! Amen and Amen. 2
94:12 Blessed is the man whom thou dost chasten, O LORD 1
96: 2 Sing to the LORD, bless his name; 2
100: 4 Give thanks to him, bless his name! 2
103: 1 Bless the LORD, O my soul; and all that is within me 2
1 all that is within me, bless his holy name! •
2 Bless the LORD, O my soul, and forget not 2
20 Bless the LORD, O you his angels, you mighty ones 2
21 Bless the LORD, all his hosts, his ministers 2
22 Bless the LORD, all his works, in all places 2
22 Bless the LORD, O my soul! 2
104: 1 Bless the LORD, O my soul! 2
35 Bless the LORD, O my soul! Praise the LORD! 2
106: 3 Blessed are they who observe justice 1
48 Blessed be the LORD, the God of Israel 2
107:38 By his blessing they multiply greatly; 2
109:28 Let them curse, but do thou bless! 2
112: 1 Blessed is the man who fears the LORD 1
2 generation of the upright will be blessed. 2
113: 2 Blessed be the name of the LORD from this time 2
115:12 The LORD has been mindful of us; he will bless us; 2
12 he will bless the house of Israel; 2
12 house of Israel; he will bless the house of Aaron; 2
13 he will bless those who fear the LORD 2
15 May you be blessed by the LORD 2
18 we will bless the LORD from this time forth 2
118:26 Blessed be he who enters in the name of the LORD! 2
26 We bless you from the house of the LORD 2
119: 1 Blessed are those whose way is blameless 1
2 Blessed are those who keep his testimonies 1
12 Blessed be thou, O LORD; teach me thy statutes! 2
124: 6 Blessed be the LORD, who has not given us as prey 2
128: 1 Blessed is every one who fears the LORD 1
4 thus shall the man be blessed who fears the LORD. 2
5 The LORD bless you from Zion! 2
129: 8 do not say . . We bless you in the name of the LORD! 2
132:15 I will abundantly bless her provisions; 2
134: 1 Come, bless the LORD, all you servants of the LORD 2
2 hands to the holy place, and bless the LORD! 2
3 May the LORD bless you from Zion 2
135:19 O house of Israel, bless the LORD! O house of Aaron 2
19 Israel . . O house of Aaron, bless the LORD! 2
20 O house of Levi, bless the LORD! 2
20 You that fear the LORD, bless the LORD! 2
21 Blessed be the LORD from Zion, he who dwells 2
144: 1 Blessed be the LORD, my rock, who trains my hands 2
145: 1 God and King, and bless thy name for ever and ever. 2
2 Every day I will bless thee, and praise thy name 2
10 O LORD, and all thy saints shall bless thee! 2
21 all flesh bless his holy name for ever and ever. 2
147:13 For he . . blesses your sons within you. 2
Prv 3:33 but he blesses the abode of the righteous. 2
5:18 Let your fountain be blessed 2
20: 7 blessed are his sons after him! 1
21 gotten hastily . . in the end not be blessed. 2
22: 9 He who has a bountiful eye will be blessed 2
27:14 He who blesses his neighbor with a loud voice 2
28:14 Blessed is the man who fears the LORD always; 1
29:18 but blessed is he who keeps the law. 1
30:11 those who . . do not bless their mothers. 2
Isa 19:25 whom the LORD of hosts has blessed, saying 2
25 Blessed be Egypt my people 2
30:18 blessed are all those who wait for him. 1
51: 2 when he was but one I called him, and I blessed him 2
56: 2 Blessed is the man who does this 1
61: 9 that they are a people whom the LORD has blessed. 2
65:16 he who blesses himself in the land shall bless 2
16 shall bless himself by the God of truth 2
23 shall be the offspring of the blessed of the LORD 2
66: 3 frankincense, like him who blesses an idol. 2
Jer 4: 2 then nations shall bless themselves in him 2
17: 7 Blessed is the man who trusts in the LORD 2
20:14 let it not be blessed! 2
31:23 The LORD bless you 2
Ezk 37:26 I will bless them and multiply them ‡
Dan 2:19 Then Daniel blessed the God of heaven. 4
20 Blessed be the name of God for ever and ever. 4
3:28 Blessed be the God of Shadrach, Meshach 4
4:34 blessed the Most High, and praised and honored 4
12:12 Blessed is he who waits and comes 1
Hag 2:19 From this day on I will bless you. 2
Zec 11: 5 those who sell them say, 'Blessed be the LORD 2
Mat 5: 3 Blessed are the poor in spirit, for theirs is 12
4 Blessed are those who mourn, for they shall be 12
5 Blessed are the meek, for they shall inherit 12
6 Blessed are those who hunger and thirst 12
7 Blessed are the merciful, for they shall obtain 12
8 Blessed are the pure in heart, for they shall see 12
9 Blessed are the peacemakers, for they shall be 12
10 Blessed are those who are persecuted 12
11 Blessed are you when men revile you 12
11: 6 blessed is he who takes no offense at me. 12
13:16 blessed are your eyes, for they see 12
14:19 he looked up to heaven, and blessed, and broke 8
16:17 Blessed are you, Simon Bar-Jona! 12
21: 9 Blessed is he who comes in the name of the Lord! 8
23:39 'Blessed is he who comes in the name of the Lord.' 8
24:46 Blessed is that servant 12
25:34 Come, O blessed of my Father 8
26:26 Jesus took bread, and blessed, and broke it 8
Mrk 6:41 blessed, and broke the loaves 8
8: 7 they had a few small fish; and having blessed them 8
10:16 he took them in his arms and blessed them 10
11: 9 Blessed is he who comes in the name of the Lord! 8
10 Blessed is the kingdom of our father David 8
14:22 he took bread, and blessed, and broke it, and gave it 8
61 Are you the Christ, the Son of the Blessed? 9
Lke 1:42 Blessed are you among women 8
42 blessed is the fruit of your womb! 8
45 blessed is she who believed 12
68 Blessed be the Lord God of Israel 9
2:28 he took him up in his arms and blessed God and said 8
34 Simeon blessed them and said to Mary his mother 8
6:20 and said: "Blessed are you poor 12
21 Blessed are you that hunger now 12
21 Blessed are you that weep now, for you shall laugh. 12
22 Blessed are you when men hate you 12
28 bless those who curse you 8
7:23 blessed is he who takes no offense at me. 12
9:16 he looked up to heaven, and blessed and broke them 8
10:23 Blessed are the eyes which see what you see! 12
11:27 Blessed is the womb that bore you 12
28 Blessed rather are those who hear the word of God 12
12:37 Blessed are those servants 12
38 and finds them so, blessed are those servants! 12
43 Blessed is that servant 12
13:35 'Blessed is he who comes in the name of the Lord!' 8
14:14 you will be blessed, because they cannot repay 12
15 Blessed is he who shall eat bread in the kingdom 12
19:38 saying, "Blessed is the King who comes 8
23:29 Blessed are the barren 12
24:30 blessed, and broke it, and gave it to them. 8
50 and lifting up his hands he blessed them. 8
51 While he blessed them, he parted from them 8
Joh 12:13 Blessed is he who comes in the name of the Lord 8
13:17 blessed are you if you do them. 12
20:29 Blessed are those who have not seen 12
Act 3:25 shall all the families of the earth be blessed.' 6
26 sent him to you first, to bless you 8
20:35 'It is more blessed to give than to receive.' 12
Rom 1:25 the Creator, who is blessed for ever! Amen. 9
4: 7 Blessed are those . . are forgiven 12
8 blessed is the man again 12
9: 5 God who is over all be blessed for ever. Amen. 9
12:14 Bless those who persecute you; 8
14 who persecute you; bless and do not curse them. 8
1Co 4:12 When reviled, we bless; when persecuted, we endure; 8
10:16 The cup of blessing which we bless 8
14:16 Otherwise, if you bless with the spirit 8
2Co 1: 3 Blessed be the God and Father of our Lord Jesus 9
11:31 he who is blessed for ever 9
Gal 3: 8 saying, "In you shall all the nations be blessed. 6
9 who are men of faith are blessed with Abraham 8
Eph 1: 3 Blessed be the God and Father of our Lord Jesus 9
3 who has blessed us in Christ 8
1Ti 1:11 glorious gospel of the blessed God 12
6:15 the blessed and only Sovereign 12
Tit 2:13 awaiting our blessed hope 12
Heb 6:14 saying, "Surely I will bless you and multiply you. 8
7: 1 met Abraham . . and blessed him; 8
6 blessed him who had the promises. 8
7 the inferior is blessed by the superior. 8
11:21 Jacob . . blessed each of the sons of Joseph 8
Jas 1:12 Blessed is the man who endures trial 12
25 he shall be blessed in his doing. 12
3: 9 With it we bless the Lord and Father 8
1Pe 1: 3 Blessed be the God and Father of our Lord Jesus 9
3: 9 but on the contrary bless 8
14 if you do suffer . . you will be blessed. 12
4:14 If you are reproached . . you are blessed 12
Rev 1: 3 Blessed is he who reads aloud the words 12
3 and blessed are those who hear, and who keep 12
14:13 Blessed are the dead who die in the Lord 12
13 Blessed indeed," says the Spirit •
16:15 I am coming like a thief! Blessed is he who is awake 12
19: 9 Blessed are those who are invited 12
20: 6 Blessed and holy is he who shares in the first 12
22: 7 Blessed is he who keeps the words of the prophecy 12
14 Blessed are those who wash their robes 12
1Es 4:36 heaven blesses her 8
40 Blessed be the God of truth! 9
60 Blessed art thou, who hast given me wisdom 9
8:25 Blessed be the Lord alone 9
9:46 Ezra blessed the Lord God Most High 8
2Es 7:45 Blessed are those who are alive 14
10:57 For you are more blessed than many 14
13:24 those who are left are more blessed than those 13
Tob 3:11 Blessed art thou, O Lord my God 9
11 blessed is thy holy and honored name for ever. 9
4:12 They were blessed in their children 8
19 Bless the Lord God on every occasion 8
7: 7 he blessed him and exclaimed 8
13 And he blessed them. 8
8: 5 Blessed art thou, O God of our fathers 9
5 and blessed by thy holy and glorious name for ever. 9
5 the heavens and all thy creatures bless thee. 8
15 Then Raguel blessed God and said 8
15 Blessed art thou, O God 9
15 Let thy saints and all thy creatures bless thee; 8
15 let . . thy chosen people bless thee for ever. 8
16 Blessed art thou, because thou hast made me glad. 9
17 Blessed art thou, because thou hast had compassion 9
9: 6 Gabael blessed Tobias and his wife. 8
10:11 when he had blessed them he sent them away, saying 8
11: 1 he blessed Raguel and his wife Edna 10
14 he wept and said, "Blessed art thou, O God 9
14 blessed is thy name for ever 9
14 blessed are all thy holy angels. 8
17 he blessed her, saying, "Welcome, daughter! 10
17 Blessed is God who has brought you to us 9
17 blessed are your father and your mother. •
13: 1 Blessed is God who lives for ever 9
1 blessed is his kingdom. •
12 blessed for ever will be all who love you. 8
14 How blessed are those who love you! 12
14 Blessed are those who grieved 12
18 and will give praise, saying, 'Blessed is God 9
Jdt 13:17 and said with one accord, "Blessed art thou, our God 9
18 you are blessed by the Most High God 9
18 blessed be the Lord God, who created the heavens 8
14: 7 Blessed are you in every tent of Judah! 8
15: 9 all blessed her with one accord and said to her 8
10 May the Almighty Lord bless you for ever! 8
12 gathered to see her, and blessed her 8
Wis 3:13 blessed is the barren woman who is undefiled 12
14 Blessed also is the eunuch •
14: 7 blessed is the wood 8
Sir 1:13 on the day of his death he will be blessed. 8
4:13 the Lord will bless the place she enters. 8
14: 1 Blessed is the man who does not blunder 12
2 Blessed is he whose heart does not condemn him 12
20 Blessed is the man who meditates on wisdom 12
31: 8 Blessed is the rich man who is found blameless 12
32:13 bless him who made you 8
33:12 some of them he blessed and exalted 8
34:15 Blessed is the soul of the man who fears the Lord! 12
39:14 bless the Lord for all his works; 8
35 bless the name of the Lord. 8
44:21 nations would be blessed through his posterity; 6
45: 1 Moses, whose memory is blessed. 7
7 He blessed him with splendid vestments 11
15 serve as priest and bless his people in his name. 8
46:11 may their memory be blessed! 7
48:11 Blessed are those who saw you 12
50:22 now bless the God of all 8
28 Blessed is he who concerns himself with these 12
51:12 I will bless the name of the Lord. 8
LJr 1:66 For they can neither curse nor bless kings; 8
Aza 1: 3 Blessed art thou, O Lord, God of our fathers 9
28 praised and glorified and blessed God 8
29 Blessed art thou, O Lord, God of our fathers 9
30 blessed is thy glorious, holy name 8
31 Blessed art thou in the temple of thy holy glory 8
32 Blessed art thou, who sittest upon cherubim 8
33 Blessed art thou upon the throne of thy kingdom 8
34 Blessed art thou in the firmament of heaven 8
35 Bless the Lord, all works of the Lord 8
36 Bless the Lord, you heavens 8
37 Bless the Lord, you angels of the Lord 8
38 Bless the Lord, all waters above the heaven 8
39 Bless the Lord, all powers 8
40 Bless the Lord, sun and moon 8
41 Bless the Lord, stars of heaven 8
42 Bless the Lord, all rain and dew 8
43 Bless the Lord, all winds 8
44 Bless the Lord, fire and heat 8
45 Bless the Lord, winter cold and summer heat 8
46 Bless the Lord, dews and snows 8
47 Bless the Lord, nights and days 8
48 Bless the Lord, light and darkness 8
49 Bless the Lord, ice and cold 8
50 Bless the Lord, frosts and snows 8
51 Bless the Lord, lightnings and clouds 8
52 Let the earth bless the Lord 8
53 Bless the Lord, mountains and hills 8
54 Bless the Lord, all things that grow on the earth 8
55 Bless the Lord, you springs 8
56 Bless the Lord, seas and rivers 8
57 Bless the Lord, you whales 8

58 Bless the Lord, all birds of the air 8
59 Bless the Lord, all beasts and cattle 8
60 Bless the Lord, you sons of men 8
61 Bless the Lord, O Israel 8
62 Bless the Lord, you priests of the Lord 8
63 Bless the Lord, you servants of the Lord 8
64 Bless the Lord, spirits . . of the righteous 8
65 Bless the Lord, you who are holy 8
66 Bless the Lord, Hananiah, Azariah, and Mishael 8
68 Bless him, all who worship the Lord, the God of gods 8
Sus 1:60 all the assembly shouted loudly and blessed God 8
1Mc 2:69 he blessed them, and was gathered to his fathers. 8
3: 7 his memory is blessed for ever. 5
4:30 Blessed art thou, O Savior of Israel 9
55 blessed Heaven, who had prospered them. 8
2Mc 1:17 Blessed in every way be our God 9
10:38 they blessed the Lord 8
12:41 they all blessed the ways of the Lord 8
15:29 they blessed the Sovereign Lord 8
34 they all, looking to heaven, blessed the Lord 8
34 blessed the Lord . . saying, "Blessed is he 9
3Mc 7:23 Blessed be the Deliverer of Israel 9
4Mc 7:15 O man of blessed age and of venerable gray hair 12
22 knows that it is blessed to endure any suffering 12
10:15 No, by the blessed death of my brothers 12
12: 1 he also . . had died a blessed death 12
17:18 and live through blessed eternity. 12
18:13 He praised Daniel . . and blessed him. 11

blessed *See* call, deem.

blessedness 1. μακαριότης
4Mc 4:12 would praise the blessedness of the holy place 1

blessing 1. בְּרָכָה 2. ἀγαθός 3. εὐλογέω 4. εὐλογία 5. εὔλογος 6. μακαρισμός 7. μερίς 8. χάρις 9. χάρισμα
Gen 12: 2 your name great, so that you will be a blessing. 1
27:12 bring a curse upon myself and not a blessing. 1
35 Your brother . . has taken away your blessing. 1
36 behold, now he has taken away my blessing. 1
36 he said, "Have you not reserved a blessing for me? 1
38 Have you but one blessing, my father? Bless me 1
41 Now Esau hated Jacob because of the blessing 1
28: 4 May he give the blessing of Abraham to you 1
39: 5 the blessing of the LORD was upon all that he had 1
49:25 will bless you with blessings of heaven above 1
25 blessings of the deep that couches beneath 1
25 blessings of the breasts and of the womb. 1
26 The blessings of your father are mighty 1
26 beyond the blessings of the eternal mountains 1
28 each with the blessing suitable to him. 1
Exd 32:29 may bestow a blessing upon you this day. 1
Lev 25:21 I will command my blessing upon you in the sixth 1
Deu 11:26 I set before you this day a blessing and a curse 1
27 blessing, if you obey the commandments 1
29 set the blessing on Mount Ger'izim and the curse 1
12:15 according to the blessing of the LORD your God 1
16:17 according to the blessing of the LORD your God 1
23: 5 LORD your God turned the curse into a blessing 1
28: 2 blessings shall come upon you and overtake you 1
8 command the blessing upon you in your barns 1
30: 1 come upon you, the blessing and the curse 1
19 set before you life and death, blessing and curse; 1
33: 1 This is the blessing with which Moses 1
23 O Naph'tali . . full of the blessing of the LORD 1
Jos 8:34 the words of the law, the blessing and the curse 1
2Sm 7:29 with thy blessing shall the house . . be blessed 1
Neh 9: 5 name . . exalted above all blessing and praise. 1
13: 2 yet our God turned the curse into a blessing. 1
Job 29:13 The blessing of him who was about to perish came 1
Ps 3: 8 thy blessing be upon thy people! Selah 1
21: 3 For thou dost meet him with goodly blessings; 1
24: 5 He will receive blessing from the LORD 1
37:26 his children become a blessing. 1
109:17 He did not like blessing; may it be far from him! 1
119:56 This blessing has fallen to me •
129: 8 do not say, "The blessing of the LORD be upon you! 1
133: 3 there the LORD has commanded the blessing 1
144:15 Happy the people to whom such blessings fall! •
Prv 10: 6 Blessings are on the head of the righteous 1
7 The memory of the righteous is a blessing 1
22 The blessing of the LORD makes rich 1
11:11 By the blessing of the upright a city is exalted 1
26 but a blessing is on the head of him who sells it. 1
24:25 delight, and a good blessing will be upon them. 1
28:20 A faithful man will abound with blessings 1
Isa 19:24 Israel . . a blessing in the midst of the earth 1
44: 3 I will pour . . my blessing on your offspring. 1
65: 8 Do not destroy it, for there is a blessing in it, 1
Ezk 34:26 and the places round about my hill a blessing; 1
26 they shall be showers of blessing. 1
44:30 that a blessing may rest on your house. 1
Jol 2:14 turn and repent, and leave a blessing behind him 1
Zec 8:13 so will I save you and you shall be a blessing. 1
Mal 2: 2 I will curse your blessings; 1
3:10 and pour down for you an overflowing blessing. 1
Lke 1:64 he spoke, blessing God. 5
24:53 were continually in the temple blessing God. 3
Act 13:34 give you the holy and sure blessings of David.' •
Rom 4: 6 So also David pronounces a blessing upon the man 6
9 Is this blessing pronounced only upon the circumcised 6
15:27 the Gentiles . . share in their spiritual blessings •
27 to be of service to them in material blessings. •
29 come in the fulness of the blessing of Christ. 4
1Co 9:23 that I may share in its blessings. •
10:16 The cup of blessing which we bless 4
2Co 1:11 the blessing granted us 9
9: 8 provide you with every blessing in abundance 8
Gal 3:14 that in Christ Jesus the blessing of Abraham 4
Eph 1: 3 blessed us . . with every spiritual blessing 4
Heb 6: 7 receives a blessing from God. 4
12:17 when he desired to inherit the blessing 4
Jas 3:10 From the same mouth come blessing and cursing. 4
1Pe 3: 9 that you may obtain a blessing. 4
Rev 5:12 to receive . . honor and glory and blessing! 4
13 to the Lamb be blessing and honor and glory 4
7:12 Blessing and glory and wisdom and thanksgiving 4
1Es 5:60 praising the Lord and blessing him 3
Tob 8:15 with every pure and holy blessing 4
Jdt 13:20 may he visit you with blessings 2
Wis 15:19 escaped both the praise of God and his blessing 4
18: 9 the same things, both blessings and dangers 2
Sir 3: 8 a blessing from him may come upon you. 4
9 a father's blessing strengthens the houses 4
7:32 so that your blessing may be complete. 4
11:22 blessing of the Lord is the reward of the godly 4
22 quickly God causes his blessing to flourish. 4
26: 3 A good wife is a great blessing 7
3 granted among the blessings of the man who fears 7
33:16 by the blessing of the Lord I excelled 4
34:17 he grants healing, life, and blessing. 4
36:17 according to the blessing of Aaron 4
39:22 His blessing covers the dry land like a river 4
40:17 Kindness is like a garden of blessings 4
27 The fear of the Lord is like a garden of blessing 4
44:23 The blessing of all men and the covenant 4
23 he acknowledged him with his blessings 4
47: 6 praised him for the blessings of the Lord 4
50:20 pronounce the blessing of the Lord with his lips 4
21 to receive the blessing from the Most High. 4
Aza 1: 1 singing hymns to God and blessing the Lord. 3

blessing *See also* give, invoke, pronounce.

blight 1. שׁדף 2. שְׁדֵפָה 3. שִׁדָּפוֹן 4. uredo
Gen 41: 6 seven ears, thin and blighted by the east wind. 1
23 ears, withered . . and blighted by the east wind 1
27 the seven empty ears blighted by the east wind 1
1Kg 8:37 famine . . pestilence or blight or mildew 3
2Kg 19:26 like tender grass . . blighted before it is grown? 2
2Ch 6:28 if there is pestilence or blight or mildew 3
Isa 37:27 like grass . . blighted before it is grown. •
Ams 4: 9 I smote you with blight and mildew; 3
Hag 2:17 I smote you . . with blight and mildew and hail; 3
2Es 15:13 and their trees shall be ruined by blight 4

blind 1. כהה 2. עור 3. עִוֵּר 4. עַוֶּרֶת 5. עלם 6. שעע 7. ἀμαυρός 8. ἀορασία 9. ἀποτυφλόω 10. τυφλός 11. τυφλόω
Exd 4:11 Who makes him dumb, or deaf, or seeing, or blind? 3
23: 8 no bribe, for a bribe blinds the officials 2
Lev 19:14 or put a stumbling block before the blind 3
21:18 a man blind or lame, or one who has a mutilated face 3
22:22 Animals blind or disabled or mutilated 4
Deu 15:21 if it has any blemish, if it is lame or blind 3
16:19 bribe blinds the eyes of the wise and subverts 2
28:29 grope at noonday, as the blind grope in darkness 3
1Sm 12: 3 have I taken a bribe to blind my eyes with it? 5
2Sm 5: 6 but the blind and the lame will ward you off 3
8 up the water shaft to attack the lame and . . blind 3
8 The blind and the lame shall not come 3
Job 29:15 I was eyes to the blind, and feet to the lame. 3
Ps 146: 8 the LORD opens the eyes of the blind. 3
Isa 29: 9 blind yourselves and be blind! 6
9 blind yourselves and be blind! 6
18 out of . . darkness the eyes of the blind shall see. 3
35: 5 Then the eyes of the blind shall be opened 3
42: 7 to open the eyes that are blind 3
16 I will lead the blind in a way that they know not 3
18 Hear, you deaf; and look, you blind, that you may see! 3
19 Who is blind but my servant 3
19 Who is blind as my dedicated one 3
19 or blind as the servant of the LORD? 3
43: 8 Bring forth the people who are blind 3
56:10 His watchmen are blind, they are all without 3
59:10 We grope for the wall like the blind 3
Jer 31: 8 the blind and the lame, the woman with child 3
Lam 4:14 They wandered, blind, through the streets 3
Ezk 6: 9 and blinded their eyes which turn wantonly •
Zep 1:17 that they shall walk like the blind 3
Zec 11:17 wholly withered, his right eye utterly blinded! 1
Mal 1: 8 When you offer blind animals in sacrifice 3
Mat 11: 5 the blind receive their sight and the lame walk 10
12:22 Then a blind and dumb demoniac was brought to him 10
15:14 Let them alone; they are blind guides 10
30 the lame, the maimed, the blind, the dumb 10
31 the lame walking, and the blind seeing 10
21:14 the blind and the lame came to him in the temple 10
23:16 Woe to you, blind guides, who say 10
17 You blind fools! 10
24 You blind guides, straining out a gnat 10
26 You blind Pharisee! 10
Mrk 10:46 Bartimae'us, a blind beggar, the son of Timae'us 10
Lke 4:18 to proclaim . . recovering of sight to the blind 10
7:21 on many that were blind he bestowed sight. 10
22 the blind receive their sight, the lame walk 10
14:13 invite the poor, the maimed, the lame, the blind 10
21 bring in the poor and maimed and blind and lame.' 10
Joh 5: 3 a multitude of invalids, blind, lame, paralyzed. 10
9: 1 As he passed by, he saw a man blind from his birth. 10
2 who sinned . . that he was born blind? 10
18 The Jews did not believe that he had been blind 10
19 Is this your son, who you say was born blind? 10
20 this is our son, and that he was born blind; 10
24 they called the man who had been blind 10
25 one thing I know, that though I was blind, now I see. 10
39 that those who see may become blind. 10
40 they said to him, "Are we also blind? 10
41 If you were blind, you would have no guilt 10
10:21 Can a demon open the eyes of the blind? 10
12:40 has blinded their eyes and hardened their heart 11
Act 13:11 you shall be blind and unable to see the sun for a time 10
Rom 2:19 if you are sure that you are a guide to the blind 10
2Co 4: 4 the god of this world has blinded the minds 11
2Pe 1: 9 For whoever lacks these things is blind 10
1Jn 2:11 because the darkness has blinded his eyes. 11
Rev 3:17 you are wretched, pitiable, poor, blind, and naked. 10
Wis 2:21 their wickedness blinded them 9
Sir 20:29 Presents and gifts blind the eyes of the wise; 9
43: 4 with bright beams it blinds the eyes. 7
LJr 1:37 They cannot restore sight to a blind man 10
2Mc 10:30 confused and blinded 8

blind man 1. עִוֵּר 2. τυφλός 3. caecus
Deu 27:18 'Cursed be he who misleads a blind man on the road.' 1
Mat 9:27 two blind men followed him, crying aloud 2
28 When he entered the house, the blind men came 2
15:14 if a blind man leads a blind man, both will fall 2
14 if a blind man leads a blind man, both will fall 2
20:30 behold, two blind men sitting by the roadside 2
23:19 You blind men! 2
Mrk 8:22 some people brought to him a blind man 2
23 he took the blind man by the hand 2
10:49 they called the blind man, saying to him 2
51 the blind man said to him, "Master 2
Lke 6:39 Can a blind man lead a blind man? 2
39 Can a blind man lead a blind man? 2
18:35 a blind man was sitting by the roadside begging; 2
Joh 9:13 the man who had formerly been blind. 2
17 they again said to the blind man 2
32 that any one opened the eyes of a man born blind. 2
11:37 he who opened the eyes of the blind man 2
2Es 2:21 let the blind man have a vision of my splendor. 3

blindfold 1. περικαλύπτω
Lke 22:64 they also blindfolded him and asked him 1

blindness 1. סַנְוֵרִים 2. עִוָּרוֹן
Gen 19:11 they struck with blindness the men 1
Deu 28:28 LORD will smite you with madness and blindness 2
2Kg 6:18 Strike this people, I pray thee, with blindness. 1
18 So he struck them with blindness 1
Zec 12: 4 every horse of the peoples with blindness. 2

block 1. בול 2. גדר 3. חסם 4. ξύλον 5. πάχος
Isa 44:19 Shall I fall down before a block of wood? 1
Lam 3: 9 he has blocked my ways with hewn stones 2
Ezk 39:11 it will block the travelers 3
Sir 31: 7 a stumbling block to those who are devoted to it 4
2Mc 4:41 some picked up stones, some blocks of wood 5

stumbling block 1. מִכְשׁוֹל 2. πρόσκομμα 3. σκάνδαλον
Lev 19:14 or put a stumbling block before the blind 1
Jer 6:21 I will lay before this people stumbling blocks 1
Ezk 3:20 I lay a stumbling block before him, he shall die; 1
7:19 it was the stumbling block of their iniquity. 1
14: 3 and set the stumbling block of their iniquity 1
4 and sets the stumbling block of his iniquity 1
7 and putting the stumbling block of his iniquity 1
44:12 and became a stumbling block of iniquity 1
Rom 14:13 put a stumbling block . . in the way of a brother. 2
1Co 1:23 a stumbling block to Jews and folly to Gentiles 3
8: 9 somehow become a stumbling block to the weak. 2
Gal 5:11 In that case the stumbling block of the cross 3
Rev 2:14 put a stumbling block before the sons of Israel 3

block up 1. ἐμφράσσω
Jdt 16: 4 their multitude blocked up the valleys 1
1Mc 2:36 or block up their hiding places 1
5:47 and blocked up the gates with stones. 1

blockade 1. πολιορκία
1Es 2:23 kept setting up blockades in it from of old 1

blood 1. דָּם 2. αἷμα 3. sanguis

Gen 4:10 The voice of your brother's blood is crying to me 1
11 to receive your brother's blood from your hand. 1
9: 4 eat flesh with its life, that is, its blood. 1
6 Whoever sheds the blood of man 1
6 by man shall his blood be shed; 1
37:22 Shed no blood; cast him into this pit here 1
26 if we slay our brother and conceal his blood? 1
31 killed a goat, and dipped the robe in the blood; 1
42:22 now there comes a reckoning for his blood. 1
49:11 he washes . . his vesture in the blood of grapes; 1
Exd 4: 9 water . . will become blood upon the dry ground. 1
25 Surely you are a bridegroom of blood to me! 1
26 she said, "You are a bridegroom of blood 1
7:17 the water . . and it shall be turned to blood 1
19 waters of Egypt . . that they may become blood; 1
19 and there shall be blood throughout all the land 1
20 all the water . . in the Nile turned to blood. 1
21 and there was blood throughout all the land 1
12: 7 Then they shall take some of the blood, and put it 1
13 The blood shall be a sign for you, upon the houses 1
13 and when I see the blood, I will pass over you 1
22 dip it in the blood which is in the basin 1
22 with the blood which is in the basin; 1
23 and when he sees the blood on the lintel 1
23:18 You shall not offer the blood of my sacrifice 1
24: 6 Moses took half of the blood and put it in basins 1
6 and half of the blood he threw against the altar. 1
8 Moses took the blood and threw it upon the people 1
8 Moses . . said, "Behold the blood of the covenant 1
29:12 shall take part of the blood of the bull and put it 1
12 the rest of the blood you shall pour out 1
16 take its blood and throw it against the altar 1
20 you shall kill the ram, and take part of its blood 1
20 throw the rest of the blood against the altar 1
21 take part of the blood that is on the altar 1
30:10 with the blood of the sin offering of atonement 1
34:25 You shall not offer the blood of my sacrifice 1
Lev 1: 5 Aaron's sons the priests shall present the blood 1
5 present the blood, and throw the blood round 1
11 Aaron's sons the priests shall throw its blood 1
15 its blood shall be drained out on the side 1
3: 2 throw the blood against the altar round about 1
8 shall throw its blood against the altar 1
13 throw its blood against the altar round about 1
17 a statute . . that you eat neither fat nor blood 1
4: 5 the anointed priest shall take some of the blood 1
6 the priest shall dip his finger in the blood 1
6 sprinkle part of the blood seven times 1
7 the priest shall put some of the blood 1
7 the rest of the blood of the bull he shall pour out 1
16 priest shall bring some of the blood of the bull 1
17 dip his finger in the blood and sprinkle it 1
18 he shall put some of the blood on the horns 1
18 the rest of the blood he shall pour out at the base 1
25 take some of the blood of the sin offering 1
25 pour out the rest of its blood at the base 1
30 the priest shall take some of its blood 1
30 pour out the rest of its blood at the base 1
34 take some of the blood of the sin offering 1
34 pour out the rest of its blood at the base 1
5: 9 sprinkle some of the blood of the sin offering 1
9 while the rest of the blood shall be drained out 1
6:27 when any of its blood is sprinkled on a garment 1
30 any blood is brought into the tent of meeting 1
7: 2 its blood shall be thrown on the altar round about 1
14 who throws the blood of the peace offerings 1
26 Moreover you shall eat no blood whatever 1
27 Whoever eats of any blood, that person shall be 1
33 offers the blood of the peace offerings 1
8:15 Moses killed it, and took the blood 1
15 purified the altar, and poured out the blood 1
19 threw the blood upon the altar round about 1
23 Moses killed it, and took some of its blood 1
24 Moses put some of the blood on the tips 1
24 Moses threw the blood upon the altar round about 1
30 took some of the anointing oil and of the blood 1
9: 9 the sons of Aaron presented the blood to him 1
9 he dipped his finger in the blood 1
9 poured out the blood at the base of the altar 1
12 Aaron's sons delivered to him the blood 1
18 Aaron's sons delivered to him the blood 1
10:18 Behold, its blood was not brought into the inner 1
12: 4 continue . . in the blood of her purifying 1
5 she shall continue in the blood of her purifying 1
7 she shall be clean from the flow of her blood 1
14: 6 dip them . . in the blood of the bird 1
14 The priest shall take some of the blood 1
17 upon the blood of the guilt offering 1
25 the priest shall take some of the blood 1
28 the place where the blood of the guilt offering 1
51 dip them in the blood of the bird that was killed 1
52 cleanse the house with the blood of the bird 1
15:19 When a woman has a discharge of blood 1
25 If a woman has a discharge of blood for many days 1
16:14 he shall take some of the blood of the bull 1
14 he shall sprinkle the blood with his finger 1
15 and bring its blood within the veil 1
15 the goat . . and do with its blood as he did 1
15 do . . as he did with the blood of the bull 1
18 and shall take some of the blood of the bull 1
18 the blood of the bull and of the blood of the goat 1
19 he shall sprinkle some of the blood upon it 1
27 whose blood was brought in to make atonement 1
17: 4 he has shed blood; and that man shall be cut off 1
6 the priest shall sprinkle the blood on the altar 1
10 If any man . . eats any blood, I will set my face 1
10 set my face against that person who eats blood 1
11 For the life of the flesh is in the blood 1
11 for it is the blood that makes atonement 1
12 No person among you shall eat blood 1
12 neither shall any stranger . . eat blood 1
13 shall pour out its blood and cover it with dust 1
14 For the life of every creature is the blood of it 1
14 You shall not eat the blood of any creature 1
14 for the life of every creature is its blood 1
19:26 You shall not eat any flesh with the blood in it 1
20: 9 cursed his father . . his blood is upon him 1
11 be put to death, their blood is upon them 1
12 have committed incest, their blood is upon them 1
13 they shall be put to death, their blood is upon them 1
16 they shall be put to death, their blood is upon them 1
18 and she has uncovered the fountain of her blood 1
27 their blood shall be upon them 1
Num18:17 You shall sprinkle their blood upon the altar 1
19: 4 shall take some of her blood with his finger 1
4 sprinkle some of her blood toward the front 1
5 flesh, and her blood, with her dung, shall be burned; 1
23:24 drinks the blood of the slain. 1
35:19 avenger of blood shall himself put the murderer 1
21 avenger of blood shall put the murderer to death 1
24 between the manslayer and the avenger of blood 1
25 manslayer from the hand of the avenger of blood 1
27 avenger of blood finds him outside the bounds 1
27 avenger of blood slays the manslayer 1
27 he shall not be guilty of blood. 1
33 for blood pollutes the land 1
33 no expiation . . for the blood that is shed in it 1
33 except by the blood of him who shed it. 1
Deu 12:16 Only you shall not eat the blood . . pour it out 1
23 Only be sure that you do not eat the blood; 1
23 do not eat the blood; for the blood is the life 1
27 offer . . burnt offerings, the flesh and the blood 1
27 the blood of your sacrifices shall be poured out 1
15:23 Only you shall not eat its blood; you shall pour 1
19: 6 lest the avenger of blood in hot anger pursue 1
10 lest innocent blood be shed in your land 1
12 hand him over to the avenger of blood 1
13 purge the guilt of innocent blood from Israel 1
21: 7 Our hands did not shed this blood, neither did our 1
8 set not the guilt of innocent blood in the midst 1
8 but let the guilt of blood be forgiven them.' 1
9 purge the guilt of innocent blood 1
32:14 of the blood of the grape you drank wine. 1
42 I will make my arrows drunk with blood 1
42 with the blood of the slain and the captives 1
43 for he avenges the blood of his servants 1
Jos 2:19 If any one goes . . his blood shall be upon his head 1
19 if a hand is laid . . his blood shall be on our head. 1
20: 3 shall be . . a refuge from the avenger of blood. 1
5 And if the avenger of blood pursues him 1
9 not die by the hand of the avenger of blood 1
Jdg 9:24 come and their blood be laid upon Abim'elech 1
1Sm 14:32 slew . . and the people ate them with the blood. 1
33 people are sinning . . by eating with the blood. 1
34 sin against the LORD by eating with the blood.' 1
19: 5 why then will you sin against innocent blood 1
25:31 for having shed blood without cause 1
26:20 Now therefore, let not my blood fall to the earth 1
2Sm 1:16 David said to him, "Your blood be upon your head; 1
22 From the blood of the slain . . fat of the mighty 1
3:27 he died, for the blood of As'ahel his brother. 1
28 guiltless before the LORD for the blood of Abner 1
4:11 shall I not now require his blood at your hand 1
14:11 that the avenger of blood slay no more 1
16: 7 Begone . . you man of blood, you worthless fellow! 1
8 has avenged . . all the blood of the house of Saul 1
8 See, your ruin is on you; for you are a man of blood. 1
20:12 Ama'sa lay wallowing in his blood in the highway. 1
23:17 Shall I drink the blood of the men who went 1
1Kg 2: 5 in time of peace blood which had been shed in war 1
5 putting innocent blood upon the girdle about my 1
9 bring his gray head down with blood to Sheol. 1
31 for the blood which Jo'ab shed without cause. 1
33 So shall their blood come back upon the head 1
37 shall die; your blood shall be upon your own head. 1
18:28 cut themselves . . until the blood gushed out 1
21:19 where dogs licked up the blood of Naboth 1
19 In the place . . shall dogs lick your own blood."' 1
22:35 the blood of the wound flowed into the bottom 1
38 the dogs licked up his blood 1
2Kg 3:22 the Moabites saw the water . . as red as blood. 1
23 This is blood; the kings have surely fought 1
9: 7 I may avenge on Jez'ebel the blood of my servants 1
7 and the blood of the all the servants of the LORD. 1
26 saw yesterday the blood of Naboth and . . his sons 1
26 I saw . . of Naboth and the blood of his sons 1
33 some of her blood spattered on the wall 1
16:13 and threw the blood of his peace offerings upon 1
15 throw upon it all the blood of the burnt offering 1
15 throw upon it . . all the blood of the sacrifice; 1
21:16 Manas'seh shed very much innocent blood 1
24: 4 and also for the innocent blood that he had shed; 1
4 for he filled Jerusalem with innocent blood 1
1Ch 22: 8 have shed much blood and have waged great wars; 1
8 because you have shed so much blood before me 1
28: 3 for you are a warrior and have shed blood. 1
2Ch 24:25 because of the blood of the son of Jehoi'ada 1
29:22 priests received the blood and threw it against 1
22 their blood was thrown against the altar; 1
22 their blood was thrown against the altar. 1
24 made a sin offering with their blood on the altar 1
30:16 the priests sprinkled the blood 1
35:11 priests sprinkled the blood 2
Job 16:18 O earth, cover not my blood 1
39:30 His young ones suck up blood; 1
Ps 9:12 For he who avenges blood is mindful of them; 1
16: 4 their libations of blood I will not pour out 1
50:13 eat the flesh of bulls, or drink the blood of goats? 1
55:23 men of blood and treachery shall not live 1
58:10 he will bathe his feet in the blood of the wicked. 1
68:23 that you may bathe your feet in blood 1
72:14 precious is their blood in his sight. 1
78:44 He turned their rivers to blood 1
79: 3 poured out their blood like water round about 1
10 avenging of the outpoured blood of thy servants 1
105:29 He turned their waters into blood 1
106:38 poured out innocent blood, the blood of their 1
38 poured out . . blood of their sons and daughters 1
38 land was polluted with blood. 1
139:19 O that . . men of blood would depart from me 1
Prv 1:11 Come with us, let us lie in wait for blood 1
16 they make haste to shed blood. 1
18 these men lie in wait for their own blood 1
6:17 hands that shed innocent blood 1
12: 6 The words of the wicked lie in wait for blood 1
28:17 If a man is burdened with the blood of another 1
30:33 pressing the nose produces blood 1
Isa 1:11 I do not delight in the blood of bulls, or of lambs 1
15 I will not listen; your hands are full of blood. 1
9: 5 every garment rolled in blood will be burned 1
15: 9 For the waters of Dibon are full of blood; 1
26:21 the earth will disclose the blood shed upon her 1
34: 3 the mountains shall flow with their blood. 1
6 The LORD has a sword; it is sated with blood 1
6 gorged with fat, with the blood of lambs and goats 1
7 Their land shall be soaked with blood 1
49:26 shall be drunk with their own blood as with wine. 1
59: 3 For your hands are defiled with blood 1
7 and they make haste to shed innocent blood; 1
66: 3 a cereal . . like him who offers swine's blood; 1
Jer 7: 6 or shed innocent blood in this place 1
19: 4 filled this place with the blood of innocents 1
22: 3 nor shed innocent blood in this place. 1
17 dishonest gain, for shedding innocent blood 1
26:15 you will bring innocent blood upon yourselves 1
46:10 and be sated, and drink its fill of their blood. 1
51:35 My blood be upon the inhabitants of Chalde'a 1
Lam 4:13 priests, who shed . . the blood of the righteous. 1
14 defiled with blood that none could touch 1
Ezk 3:18 but his blood I will require at your hand. 1
20 but his blood I will require at your hand. 1
5:17 pestilence and blood shall pass through you; 1
9: 9 the land is full of blood 1
14:19 and pour out my wrath upon it with blood 1
16: 6 passed by you, and saw you weltering in your blood 1
6 I said to you in your blood, 'Live 1
9 with water and washed off your blood from you 1
22 you were naked and bare, weltering in your blood. 1
36 and because of the blood of your children 1
38 as women who break wedlock and shed blood 1
38 and bring upon you the blood of wrath 1
18:10 a son who is a robber, a shedder of blood 1
13 surely die; his blood shall be upon himself. 1
21:32 your blood shall be in the midst of the land; 1
22: 3 A city that sheds blood in the midst of her 1
4 become guilty by the blood which you have shed 1
6 have been bent on shedding blood. 1
9 There are men in you who slander to shed blood 1
12 In you men take bribes to shed blood; 1
13 at the blood which has been in the midst of you. 1
27 like wolves tearing the prey, shedding blood 1
23:37 and blood is upon their hands; 1
45 and with the sentence of women that shed blood; 1
45 are adulteresses, and blood is upon their hands. 1
24: 7 the blood she has shed is still in the midst of her; 1
8 I have set on the bare rock the blood she has shed 1
28:23 pestilence into her, and blood into her streets; 1
32: 6 even to the mountains with your flowing blood; 1
33: 4 his blood shall be upon his own head. 1
5 his blood shall be upon himself. 1
6 his blood I will require at the watchman's hand. 1
8 but his blood I will require at your hand. 1
25 says the Lord GOD: You eat flesh with the blood 1
25 and lift up your eyes to your idols, and shed blood; 1
35: 6 I will prepare you for blood 1

6 prepare you for blood, and blood shall pursue you; 1
6 because you are guilty of blood 1
6 therefore blood shall pursue you. 1
36:18 for the blood which they had shed in the land 1
39:17 you shall eat flesh and drink blood. 1
18 and drink the blood of the princes of the earth 1
19 and drink blood till you are drunk 1
43:18 and for throwing blood against it 1
20 you shall take some of its blood 1
44: 7 when you offer to me my food, the fat and the blood. 1
15 attend on me to offer me the fat and the blood 1
45:19 shall take some of the blood of the sin offering 1
Hos 1: 4 punish the house of Jehu for the blood of Jezreel 1
6: 8 Gilead is a city . . tracked with blood. 1
Jol 2:30 portents . . blood and fire and columns of smoke. 1
31 The sun . . to darkness, and the moon to blood 1
3:19 they have shed innocent blood in their land. 1
21 I will avenge their blood 1
Jon 1:14 this man's life, and lay not on us innocent blood; 1
Mic 3:10 who build Zion with blood and Jerusalem 1
7: 2 they all lie in wait for blood 1
Hab 2: 8 for the blood of men and violence to the earth 1
12 Woe to him who builds a town with blood 1
17 for the blood of men and violence to the earth 1
Zep 1:17 their blood shall be poured out like dust 1
Zec 9: 7 I will take away its blood from its mouth 1
11 for you also, because of the blood of my covenant 1
15 they shall drink their blood like wine 2
Mat 16:17 For flesh and blood has not revealed this to you 2
23:30 in shedding the blood of the prophets.' 2
35 all the righteous blood shed on earth 2
35 from the blood of innocent Abel 2
35 to the blood of Zechari'ah the son of Barachi'ah 2
26:28 for this is my blood of the covenant 2
27: 4 I have sinned in betraying innocent blood. 2
6 since they are blood money. 2
8 has been called the Field of Blood to this day. 2
24 I am innocent of this man's blood 2
25 His blood be on us and on our children! 2
Mrk 5:25 woman who had had a flow of blood for twelve years 2
14:24 he said to them, "This is my blood of the covenant 2
Lke 8:43 woman who had had a flow of blood for twelve years 2
44 immediately her flow of blood ceased. 2
11:50 the blood of all the prophets 2
51 from the blood of Abel to the blood of Zechari'ah 2
51 from the blood of Abel to the blood of Zechari'ah 2
13: 1 the Galileans whose blood Pilate had mingled 2
22:20 the new covenant in my blood. 2
Joh 1:13 who were born, not of blood 2
6:53 eat the flesh of the Son of man and drink his blood 2
54 he who eats my flesh and drinks my blood 2
55 my blood is drink indeed. 2
56 who eats my flesh and drinks my blood abides in me 2
19:34 at once there came out blood and water. 2
Act 1:19 Akel'dama, that is, Field of Blood 2
2:19 blood, and fire, and vapor of smoke; 2
20 the moon into blood 2
5:28 you intend to bring this man's blood upon us. 2
15:20 from what is strangled and from blood. 2
29 from blood and from what is strangled 2
18: 6 Your blood be upon your heads! I am innocent 2
20:26 I am innocent of the blood of all of you 2
28 which he obtained with the blood of his own Son. 2
21:25 abstain . . from blood 2
22:20 when the blood of Stephen thy witness was shed 2
Rom 3:15 Their feet are swift to shed blood 2
25 whom God put forward as an expiation by his blood 2
5: 9 Since . . we are now justified by his blood 2
1Co 10:16 is it not a participation in the blood of Christ? 2
11:25 This cup is the new covenant in my blood 2
27 be guilty of profaning the body and blood of the Lord. 2
15:50 flesh and blood cannot inherit the kingdom 2
Gal 1:16 I did not confer with flesh and blood 2
Eph 1: 7 In him we have redemption through his blood 2
2:13 have been brought near in the blood of Christ. 2
6:12 we are not contending against flesh and blood 2
Col 1:20 making peace by the blood of his cross. 2
Heb 2:14 Since . . the children share in flesh and blood 2
9: 7 not without taking blood 2
12 taking not the blood of goats and calves 2
12 taking . . his own blood 2
13 the blood of goats and bulls 2
14 how much more shall the blood of Christ 2
18 was not ratified without blood. 2
19 he took the blood of calves and goats 2
20 saying, "This is the blood of the covenant 2
21 in the same way he sprinkled with the blood 2
22 almost everything is purified with blood 2
25 enters . . with blood not his own; 2
10: 4 the blood of bulls and goats 2
19 we have confidence . . by the blood of Jesus 2
29 profaned the blood of the covenant 2
11:28 kept the Passover and sprinkled the blood 2
12: 4 resisted to the point of shedding your blood. 2
24 the sprinkled blood 2
24 that speaks more graciously than the blood of Abel. •
13:11 whose blood is brought into the sanctuary 2
12 sanctify the people through his own blood. 2
20 by the blood of the eternal covenant 2
1Pe 1: 2 Jesus Christ and for sprinkling with his blood 2
19 with the precious blood of Christ 2
1Jn 1: 7 blood of Jesus his Son cleanses us from all sin. 2
5: 6 This is he who came by water and blood, Jesus 2
6 but with the water and the blood. 2
8 three witnesses, the Spirit, the water . . blood 2
Rev 1: 5 To him who . . freed us from our sins by his blood 2
5: 9 and by thy blood didst ransom men for God 2
6:10 thou wilt judge and avenge our blood on those 2
12 the full moon became like blood 2
7:14 made them white in the blood of the Lamb. 2
8: 7 there followed hail and fire, mixed with blood 2
9 and a third of the sea became blood 2
11: 6 power over the waters to turn them into blood 2
12:11 they have conquered him by the blood of the Lamb 2
14:20 and blood flowed from the wine press 2
16: 3 the sea, and it became like the blood of a dead man 2
4 the rivers . . and they became blood. 2
6 men have shed the blood of saints and prophets 2
6 and thou hast given them blood to drink. 2
17: 6 I saw the woman, drunk with the blood of the saints 2
6 drunk with . . the blood of the martyrs of Jesus. 2
18:24 And in her was found the blood of prophets 2
19: 2 he has avenged on her the blood of his servants. 2
13 He is clad in a robe dipped in blood 2
2Es 1:26 for you have defiled your hands with blood 3
32 their blood I will require of you, says the Lord. 3
5: 5 Blood shall drip from wood 3
15: 8 Behold, innocent and righteous blood cries out 3
9 all the innocent blood from among them. 3
22 those who shed innocent blood on earth. 3
35 there shall be blood from the sword 3
58 and drink their own blood in thirst for water. 3
Jdt 6: 4 their mountains will be drunk with their blood 2
9: 3 to be stained with blood 2
4 abhorred the pollution of their blood 2
AEs 16: 5 the shedding of innocent blood 2
10 really an alien to the Persian blood 2
Wis 7: 2 compacted with blood, from the seed of a man 2
11: 6 stirred up and defiled with blood 2
12: 5 sacrificial feasting on human flesh and blood. 2
14:25 all is a raging riot of blood and murder 2
Sir 8:16 because blood is as nothing in his sight 2
9: 9 in blood you be plunged into destruction. 1
11:32 a sinner lies in wait to shed blood. 2
12:16 his thirst for blood will be insatiable. 2
14:18 so are the generations of flesh and blood 2
17:31 So flesh and blood devise evil. 2
28:11 urgent strife sheds blood. 2
33:30 because you have bought him with blood. 2
34:21 whoever deprives them of it is a man of blood. 2
22 to deprive an employee . . is to shed blood. 2
39:26 milk and honey, the blood of the grape, and oil 2
50:15 poured a libation of the blood of the grape 2
Sus 1:46 I am innocent of the blood of this woman. 2
62 Thus innocent blood was saved that day. 2
1Mc 1:37 they shed innocent blood 2
7:17 The flesh of thy saints and their blood 2
9:38 they remembered the blood of John their brother 2
42 they had fully avenged the blood of their brother 2
2Mc 1: 8 burned the gate and shed innocent blood 2
8: 3 to hearken to the blood that cried out to him 2
12:16 the . . lake . . appeared to be running over with blood. 2
14:45 though his blood gushed forth 2
4Mc 3:15 what was regarded as equivalent to blood. 2
6: 6 his blood flowing 2
29 Make my blood their purification 2
7: 8 shielding it with their own blood 2
9:20 The wheel was completely smeared with blood 2
10: 8 drops of blood flowing from his entrails. 2
13:20 growing from the same blood 2
17:22 through the blood of those devout ones 2

blood *See also* defile, drain, guilt, shedding.

blood guiltiness 1. דָּם
Ps 51:14 Deliver me from blood guiltiness, O God 1

bloodguilt 1. דָּם
Exd 22: 2 there shall be no bloodguilt for him; 1
3 there shall be bloodguilt for him. 1
Lev 17: 4 bloodguilt shall be imputed to that man 1
1Sm 25:26 the LORD has restrained you from bloodguilt 1
33 kept me . . from bloodguilt and from avenging 1
2Sm 21: 1 There is bloodguilt on Saul and on his house 1
Hos 12:14 so his LORD will leave his bloodguilt upon him 1

bloodshed 1. דָּם 2. מִשְׂפָּח 3. αἷμα 4. ἔκχυσις αἵματος
2Ch 19:10 concerning bloodshed, law or commandment 1
Isa 5: 7 he looked for justice, but behold, bloodshed; 2
33:15 who stops his ears from hearing of bloodshed 1
Jer 48:10 is he who keeps back his sword from bloodshed. 1
Ezk 38:22 With . . bloodshed I will enter into judgment 1
Sir 22:24 so insults precede bloodshed. 3
27:15 The strife of the proud leads to bloodshed 4
40: 9 are death and bloodshed and strife and sword 3
2Mc 14:18 shrank from deciding the issue by bloodshed. 3

bloodshed *See also* guilt.

bloodstain 1. דָּם
Isa 4: 4 cleansed the bloodstains of Jerusalem 1

bloodthirstiness 1. μιαιφονία
4Mc 9: 9 because of your bloodthirstiness toward us 1
10:11 because of your impiety and bloodthirstiness 1

bloodthirsty 1. דָּם 2. αἱμοβόρος 3. μιαιφόνος
Ps 5: 6 LORD abhors bloodthirsty and deceitful men. 1
26: 9 with sinners, nor my life with bloodthirsty men 1
59: 2 save me from bloodthirsty men. 1
Prv 29:10 Bloodthirsty men hate one who is blameless 1
2Mc 4:38 he dispatched the bloodthirsty fellow 3
4Mc 10:17 the bloodthirsty, murderous . . Antiochus 2

bloody 1. דָּם
1Kg 2:32 LORD will bring back his bloody deeds upon his 1
Ezk 7:23 Because the land is full of bloody crimes 1
22: 2 will you judge, will you judge the bloody city? 1
24: 6 Woe to the bloody city 1
9 thus says the Lord GOD: Woe to the bloody city! 1
Nah 3: 1 Woe to the bloody city, all full of lies and booty 1

bloom 1. נצץ 2. פֶּרַח
Sng 6:11 see . . whether the pomegranates were in bloom. 1
7:12 whether . . and the pomegranates are in bloom. 1
Nah 1: 4 the bloom of Lebanon fades. 2

make bloom again 1. revirido
2Es 5:36 and make the withered flowers bloom again for me; 1

blossom 1. אֵב 2. נֵץ 3. נִצָּה 4. נצץ 5. סְמָדַר 6. פרח 7. פֶּרַח 8. צוץ 9. צִיץ 10. ἄνθος 11. βλαστός
Gen 40:10 as soon as it budded, its blossoms shot forth 2
Num17: 8 rod of Aaron . . produced blossoms, and it bore 9
Job 15:30 his blossom will be swept away by the wind. 11
33 and cast off his blossom, like the olive tree. 3
Ecc 12: 5 the almond tree blossoms, the grasshopper drags 4
Sng 2:13 The fig tree . . and the vines are in blossom; 5
15 for our vineyards are in blossom. 5
6:11 went down . . to look at the blossoms of the valley 1
7:12 see . . whether the grape blossoms have opened 5
Isa 5:24 as rottenness, and their blossom go up like dust; 7
18: 5 For before the harvest, when the blossom is over 7
27: 6 Israel shall blossom and put forth shoots 8
35: 1 the desert shall rejoice and blossom; 6
2 it shall blossom abundantly, and rejoice 6
Ezk 7:10 Your doom has come, injustice has blossomed 8
Hos 14: 5 he shall blossom as the lily 6
7 they shall blossom as the vine 6
Hab 3:17 Though the fig tree do not blossom 6
Sir 24:17 blossoms became glorious and abundant fruit. 10
39:14 put forth blossoms like a lily 10
51:15 From blossom to ripening grape 10

blossom *See also* henna, produce, put.

blossom forth 1. צוץ
Ps 72:16 may men blossom forth from the cities 1

make blossom 1. פרח
Isa 17:11 and make them blossom in the morning that you sow; 1

blot 1. μῶμος 2. σκάνδαλον 3. σπίλος
2Pe 2:13 They are blots and blemishes 3
Sir 7: 6 thus put a blot on your integrity. 2
20:24 A lie is an ugly blot on a man 1

blot out 1. כבה 2. כחד 3. מחה 4. ἐξαίρω 5. ἐξαλείφω 6. deleo
Gen 6: 7 the LORD said, "I will blot out man 3
7: 4 living thing that I have made I will blot out 3
23 He blotted out every living thing 3
23 they were blotted out from the earth. 3
Exd 17:14 I will . . blot out the remembrance of Am'alek 3
23:23 the Hivites, and the Jeb'usites, and I blot them out 2
32:32 forgive their sin–and if not, blot me, I pray thee, out 3
33 Whoever has sinned against me, him will I blot out 3
Deu 9:14 I may . . blot out their name from under heaven; 3
25: 6 that his name may not be blotted out of Israel. 3
19 blot out the remembrance of Am'alek from under 3
29:20 LORD would blot out his name from under heaven. 3
Jdg 21:17 that a tribe be not blotted out from Israel. 3
2Kg 14:27 that he would blot out the name of Israel 3
Neh 4: 5 let not their sin be blotted out from thy sight; 3
Ps 9: 5 thou hast blotted out their name for ever 3
51: 1 thy abundant mercy blot out my transgressions. 3
9 from my sins, and blot out all my iniquities. 3
69:28 Let them be blotted out of the book of the living; 3
109:13 his name be blotted out in the second generation! 3
14 let not the sin of his mother be blotted out! 3
Isa 43:25 blots out your transgressions for my own sake 3
Jer 18:23 nor blot out their sin from thy sight. 3
Ezk 32: 7 When I blot you out, I will cover the heavens 1
Act 3:19 that your sins may be blotted out 5
Rev 3: 5 I will not blot his name out of the book of life; 5
2Es 2: 7 let their names be blotted out from the earth 6
6:27 For evil shall be blotted out 6
7:139and blot out the multitude of their sins 6

Tob 4:19 do not let them be blotted out of your mind. 5
Sir 23:26 her disgrace will not be blotted out. 5
39: 9 it will never be blotted out 5
40:12 All bribery and injustice will be blotted out 5
41:11 the evil name of sinners will be blotted out. 5
44:13 their glory will not be blotted out. 5
18 all flesh should not be blotted out by a flood. 5
46:20 to blot out the wickedness of the people. 5
47:22 never blot out the descendants of his chosen one 5
1Mc 12:53 and blot out the memory of them from among men. 4
2Mc 12:42 that the sin . . might be wholly blotted out 5

blow 1. הלך 2. מצצר 3. נפח 4. נשב 5. נשף 6. פוח 7. תקע 8. πνεύω 9. πνέω 10. σαλπίζω 11. φυσάω 12. insuflo 13. spiro

Exd 15:10 Thou didst blow with thy wind, the sea covered 5
Num10: 3 when both are blown, all the congregation 7
4 if they blow only one, then the leaders 7
5 When you blow an alarm, the camps that are 7
6 when you blow an alarm the second time, the camps 7
6 alarm is to be blown whenever they are to set out. 7
7 you shall blow, but you shall not sound an alarm. 7
8 sons of Aaron . . shall blow the trumpets. 7
10 blow the trumpets over your burnt offerings 7
29: 1 It is a day for you to blow the trumpets •
Jos 6: 4 march . . the priests blowing the trumpets. 7
8 priests . . went forward, blowing the trumpets 7
9 went before the priests who blew the trumpets 7
9 while the trumpets blew continually. 7
13 priests . . passed on, blowing the trumpets 7
13 while the trumpets blew continually. 7
16 when the priests had blown the trumpets 7
20 the people shouted, and the trumpets were blown. 7
Jdg 7:18 When I blow the trumpet, I and all who are with me 7
18 When I blow . . then blow the trumpets also 7
19 and they blew the trumpets and smashed the jars 7
20 the three companies blew the trumpets and broke 7
20 and in their right hands the trumpets to blow; 7
22 When they blew the 300 trumpets 7
1Sm 13: 3 Saul blew the trumpet throughout all the land 7
2Sm 2:28 Jo'ab blew the trumpet; and all the men stopped 7
18:16 Jo'ab blew the trumpet, and the troops came back 7
20: 1 and he blew the trumpet, and said, "We have no 7
22 So he blew the trumpet, and they dispersed 7
1Kg 1:34 anoint him king . . then blow the trumpet, and say 7
39 anointed Solomon. Then they blew the trumpet; 7
2Kg 9:13 and they blew the trumpet, and proclaimed 7
11:14 the people . . rejoicing and blowing trumpets. 7
1Ch 15:24 priests, should blow the trumpets before the ark 2
16: 6 to blow trumpets continually, before the ark •
2Ch 13:14 the priests blew the trumpets. 2
23:13 all the people of the land . . blowing trumpets 7
Ps 81: 3 Blow the trumpet at the new moon, at the full moon 7
Ecc 1: 6 wind blows to the south, and . . round to the north; 1
Isa 18: 3 a signal . . look! When a trumpet is blown, hear! 7
27:13 in that day a great trumpet will be blown 7
40: 7 fades, when the breath of the LORD blows upon it; 4
24 when he blows upon them, and they wither 5
54:16 I . . created the smith who blows the fire of coals 3
Jer 4: 5 and say, "Blow the trumpet through the land; 7
6: 1 Blow the trumpet in Teko'a, and raise a signal 7
51:27 on the earth, blow the trumpet among the nations; 7
Ezk 7:14 They have blown the trumpet and made all ready; 7
21:31 I will blow upon you with the fire of my wrath; 6
22:20 to blow the fire upon it in order to melt it; 3
21 and blow upon you with the fire of my wrath 3
33: 3 and blows the trumpet and warns the people; 7
6 sees the sword . . and does not blow the trumpet 7
Hos 5: 8 Blow the horn in Gib'e-ah, the trumpet in Ramah. 7
Jol 2: 1 Blow the trumpet in Zion; 7
15 Blow the trumpet in Zion; sanctify a fast; 7
Ams 3: 6 Is a trumpet blown in a city, and the people are not 7
Mat 7:25 rain fell, and the floods came, and the winds blew 9
27 rain fell, and the floods came, and the wind blew 9
Lke 12:55 when you see the south wind blowing, you say 9
Joh 3: 8 The wind blows where it wills 9
6:18 The sea rose because a strong wind was blowing. 9
Rev 7: 1 that no wind might blow on earth or sea 9
8: 6 the seven angels . . made ready to blow them. 10
13 trumpets which the . . angels are about to blow! 10
2Es 6: 1 and before the assembled winds blew 13
11: 2 and all the winds of heaven blew upon him 12
Sir 28:12 If you blow on a spark, it will glow 11
43:16 at his will the south wind blows. 8
20 The cold north wind blows 8
LJr 1:61 the wind likewise blows in every land. 9

blow (2) 1. חַבּוּרָה 2. מַכָּה 3. נכה 4. תִּגְרָה 5. πληγή 6. ῥάπισμα

Num35:21 then he who struck the blow shall be put to death; •
2Sm 20:10 and shed his . . without striking a second blow; •
Ps 39:10 I am spent by the blows of thy hand. 4
Prv 17:10 than 100 blows into a fool. 3
20:30 Blows that wound cleanse away evil; 1
Isa 14: 6 that smote . . in wrath with unceasing blows 2
30:26 and heals the wounds inflicted by his blow. 2
30 and the descending blow of his arm to be seen •
Jer 14:17 with a great wound, with a very grievous blow. 2
30:14 for I have dealt you the blow of an enemy 2
Mrk 14:65 the guards received him with blows. 6
Act 16:23 when they had inflicted many blows upon them 5
Wis 12: 9 to destroy them at one blow by dread wild beasts •
Sir 22:22 disclosure of secrets, or a treacherous blow 5
27:25 a treacherous blow opens up wounds. 5
28:17 The blow of a whip raises a welt 5
17 a blow of the tongue crushes the bones. 5
1Mc 1:30 dealt it a severe blow, and destroyed many people 5
5: 3 He dealt them a heavy blow and humbled them 5
34 he dealt them a heavy blow 5
2Mc 3:26 inflicting many blows on him. 5
6:30 When he was about to die under the blows 5
9: 5 struck him an incurable and unseen blow 5

blow *See* deal, strike.

blow a trumpet 1. σαλπίζω

Rev 8: 7 The first angel blew his trumpet 1
8 The second angel blew his trumpet 1
10 The third angel blew his trumpet, and a great star 1
12 The fourth angel blew his trumpet 1
9: 1 And the fifth angel blew his trumpet, and I saw 1
13 Then the sixth angel blew his trumpet, and I heard 1
11:15 Then the seventh angel blew his trumpet 1
1Mc 4:13 Then the men with Judas blew their trumpets 1
9:12 the men with Judas also blew their trumpets. 1

blow away 1. נפח

Hag 1: 9 when you brought it home, I blew it away. 1

cause to blow 1. נסע

Ps 78:26 He caused the east wind to blow in the heavens 1

blow fiercely 1. נחר

Jer 6:29 The bellows blow fiercely, the lead is consumed 1

blow gently 1. ὑποπνέω

Act 27:13 when the south wind blew gently 1

make blow 1. נשב 2. עבר

Gen 8: 1 God made a wind blow over the earth, and the waters 2
Ps 147:18 he makes his wind blow, and the waters flow. 1

blow upon 1. נפח 2. פוח

Job 20:26 a fire not blown upon will devour him; 1
Sng 4:16 and come, O south wind! Blow upon my garden 2

blue 1. תְּכֵלֶת 2. ὑακίνθινος 3. ὑάκινθος

Exd 25: 4 blue and purple and scarlet stuff 1
26: 1 twined linen and blue and purple and scarlet 1
4 you shall make loops of blue on the edge 1
31 you shall make a veil of blue and purple 1
36 a screen . . of blue and purple and scarlet stuff 1
27:16 a screen . . of blue and purple and scarlet stuff 1
28: 5 They shall receive gold, blue and purple 1
6 ephod of gold, of blue and purple and scarlet 1
8 materials, of gold, blue and purple and scarlet 1
15 of gold, blue and purple and scarlet stuff 1
28 to the rings of the ephod with a lace of blue 1
31 you shall make the robe of the ephod all of blue. 1
33 shall make pomegranates of blue and purple 1
37 you shall fasten it on the turban by a lace of blue; 1
35: 6 blue and purple and scarlet stuff and fine 1
23 with whom was found blue or purple or scarlet 1
25 brought what they had spun in blue and purple 1
35 by an embroiderer in blue and purple and scarlet 1
36: 8 linen and blue and purple and scarlet stuff 1
11 he made loops of blue on the edge of the outmost 1
35 he made the veil of blue and purple and scarlet 1
37 screen . . of blue and purple and scarlet stuff 1
38:18 needlework in blue and purple and scarlet stuff 1
23 embroiderer in blue and purple and scarlet 1
39: 1 of the blue and purple and scarlet stuff 1
2 he made the ephod of gold, blue and purple 1
3 cut into threads to work into the blue and purple 1
5 of gold, blue and purple and scarlet stuff 1
8 of gold, blue and purple and scarlet stuff 1
21 rings of the ephod with a lace of blue 1
22 the robe of the ephod woven all of blue; 1
24 they made pomegranates of blue and purple 1
29 the girdle of fine twined linen and of blue 1
31 they tied to it a lace of blue, to fasten it 1
Num 4: 6 spread over that a cloth all of blue 1
7 they shall spread a cloth of blue 1
9 take a cloth of blue, and cover the lampstand 1
11 golden altar they shall spread a cloth of blue 1
12 put them in a cloth of blue, and cover them 1
15:38 to put upon the tassel of each corner a cord of blue; 1
Est 8:15 Mor'decai went . . in royal robes of blue and white 1
Ezk 27: 7 blue and purple from the coasts of Eli'shah was 1
24 in clothes of blue and embroidered work 1
Sir 6:30 her bonds are a cord of blue. 2
45:10 with a holy garment, of gold and blue and purple 3

blue *See also* cloth, fabric, hanging.

blunder 1. ὀλισθαίνω

Sir 14: 1 does not blunder with his lips 1

blunt 1. קהה

Ecc 10:10 If the iron is blunt, and one does not whet the edge 1

blush 1. חפר 2. כלם 3. ἐρυθριάω

Ezr 9: 6 O my God, I am ashamed and blush to lift my face 2
Isa 1:29 ashamed of . . and you shall blush for the gardens 1
Jer 6:15 they did not know how to blush. 2
8:12 they did not know how to blush. 2
Tob 2:14 I blushed for her 3

boar 1. חֲזִיר

Ps 80:13 The boar from the forest ravages it 1

boar *See also* wild.

board 1. לוּחַ 2. צֶלַע

Exd 27: 8 You shall make it hollow, with boards; 1
38: 7 he made it hollow, with boards. 1
1Kg 6:15 He lined the walls . . with boards of cedar; 2
15 he covered the floor . . with boards of cypress. 2
16 boards of cedar from the floor to the rafters 2
Sng 8: 9 we will enclose her with boards of cedar. 1

board (2)

Jon 1: 3 he paid the fare, and went on board, •

board *See* bring, go, put, take.

boast 1. אמר 2. בַּד 3. גדל 4. גדל פִּי 5. הלל 6. זכר 7. פְּרִי 8. תִּפְאָרָה 9. ἀλαζονεία 10. ἀλαζονεύομαι 11. αὐχέω 12. γαυρίαμα 13. γαυρόω 14. δοξάζω 15. ἐγκαυχάομαι 16. εἶπον 17. κατακαυχάομαι 18. καυχάομαι 19. καύχημα 20. καύχησις 21. κόμπος

1Kg 20:11 Let not him that girds on his armor boast himself 5
Ps 10: 3 For the wicked boasts of the desires of his heart 5
20: 7 Some boast of chariots, and some of horses; 6
7 we boast of the name of the LORD our God. 6
38:16 who boast against me when my foot slips! 3
44: 8 In God we have boasted continually 5
49: 6 boast of the abundance of their riches? 5
52: 1 Why do you boast, O mighty man, of mischief done 5
75: 4 I say to the boastful, "Do not boast 5
94: 4 arrogant words, they boast, all the evildoers. 1
Prv 20:14 but when he goes away, then he boasts. 5
25:14 man who boasts of a gift he does not give. 5
27: 1 Do not boast about tomorrow, for you do not know 5
Isa 10:12 he will punish the arrogant boasting of the king 7
16: 6 the pride of Moab . . his boasts are false. 2
20: 5 Ethiopia their hope and of Egypt their boast. 8
Jer 48:30 his boasts are false, his deeds are false. 2
49: 4 Why do you boast of your valleys 5
Obd 1:12 you should not have boasted 4
Zep 2:10 they scoffed and boasted against the people 3
Rom 2:17 and boast of your relation to God 18
23 You who boast in the law, do you dishonor God 18
3:27 what becomes of our boasting? It is excluded. 20
11:18 If you do boast, remember it is not you 17
1Co 1:29 so that no human being might boast 18
31 Let him who boasts, boast of the Lord. 18
31 Let him who boasts, boast of the Lord. 18
3:21 So let no one boast of men. 18
4: 7 why do you boast as if it were not a gift? 18
5: 6 Your boasting is not good. Do you not know 19
9:15 deprive me of my ground for boasting. 19
16 that gives me no ground for boasting 19
2Co 1:12 For our boast is this 20
7:14 so our boasting before Titus has proved true. 20
8:24 our boasting about you to these men. 20
9: 2 of which I boast about you 18
3 so that our boasting about you may not prove vain 19
10: 8 even if I boast a little too much of our authority 18
13 we will not boast beyond limit 18
15 We do not boast beyond limit, in other men's labors; 18
16 without boasting of work already done 18
17 Let him who boasts, boast of the Lord. 18
17 Let him who boasts, boast of the Lord. 18
11:10 this boast of mine shall not be silenced 20
12 in their boasted mission 18
16 so that I too may boast a little. 18
18 since many boast of worldly things 18
18 I too will boast.) 18
21 whatever any one dares to boast •
21 I also dare to boast of that. •
30 If I must boast 18
30 I will boast of the things that show my weakness. 18
12: 1 I must boast; there is nothing to be gained by it 18
5 On behalf of this man I will boast 18
5 on my own behalf I will not boast 18
6 Though if I wish to boast, I shall not be a fool 18
9 I will all the more gladly boast of my weaknesses 18
Eph 2: 9 not because of works, lest any man should boast. 18
1Th 2:19 For what is our hope or joy or crown of boasting 20
2Th 1: 4 Therefore we ourselves boast of you 15
Jas 1: 9 Let the lowly brother boast in his exaltation 18
3: 5 the tongue . . boasts of great things. 11
14 do not boast and be false to the truth. 17
4:16 As it is, you boast in your arrogance. 18
16 All such boasting is evil. 20
Jdt 16: 5 He boasted that he would burn up my territory 16

AEs 16: 4 carried away by the boasts of those who know 21
Wis 2:16 boasts that God is his father. 10
5: 8 what good has our boasted wealth brought us? 9
6: 2 you that . . boast of many nations. 13
17: 7 their boasted wisdom was scornfully rebuked. 9
Sir 10:27 one who goes about boasting, but lacks bread. 14
11: 4 Do not boast about wearing fine clothes 18
25: 6 their boast is the fear of the Lord. 19
30: 2 will boast of him among acquaintances. 18
31:10 Let it be for him a ground for boasting 20
47: 4 struck down the boasting of Goliath? 12
48: 4 who has the right to boast which you have? 18
3Mc 2:17 lest the transgressors boast in their wrath 18
4Mc 2:15 lust for power, vainglory, boasting, arrogance 9

boast *See also* make, reason.

loud boast 1. ὑπέρογκος
2Pe 2:18 For, uttering loud boasts of folly, they entice 1

boast over 1. κατακαυχάομαι
Rom 11:18 do not boast over the branches. 1

something to boast about 1. καύχημα
Rom 4: 2 he has something to boast about 1

boaster 1. ὑπέρογκος
Jde 1:16 loud-mouthed boasters, flattering people 1

boastful 1. הלל 2. ἀλαζών 3. γαυρόω 4. καύχησις 5. μεγαλορρημονέω 6. περπερεύομαι
Ps 5: 5 The boastful may not stand before thy eyes; 1
75: 4 I say to the boastful, "Do not boast 1
Rom 1:30 haughty, boastful, inventors of evil 2
1Co 13: 4 love is not jealous or boastful; 6
2Co 11:17 as a fool, in this boastful confidence; 4
3Mc 3:11 the king, boastful of his present good fortune 3
6: 4 lawless insolence and boastful tongue 5

boastfully 1. μεγαλαυχέω
2Mc 15:32 which had been boastfully stretched out 1

boastfully *See also* say.

boastfulness 1. כבד 2. ἀλαζονεία
2Ch 25:19 your heart has lifted you up in boastfulness. 1
2Mc 15: 6 in his utter boastfulness and arrogance 2
4Mc 1:26 In the soul it is boastfulness, covetousness 2

boat 1. πλοιάριον 2. πλοῖον 3. σκάφη 4. σκάφος
Mat 4:21 in the boat with Zeb'edee their father, mending 2
22 Immediately they left the boat and their father 2
8:23 he got into the boat, his disciples followed him. 2
24 so that the boat was being swamped by the waves; 2
9: 1 And getting into a boat he crossed over 2
13: 2 so that he got into a boat and sat there 2
14:13 he withdrew from there in a boat to a lonely place 2
22 Then he made the disciples get into the boat 2
24 the boat by this time was many furlongs distant 2
29 He said, "Come." So Peter got out of the boat 2
32 when they got into the boat, the wind ceased. 2
33 those in the boat worshiped him, saying 2
15:39 sending away the crowds, he got into the boat 2
Mrk 1:19 who were in their boat mending the nets. 2
20 they left their father Zeb'edee in the boat 2
3: 9 he told his disciples to have a boat ready for him 1
4: 1 so that he got into a boat and sat in it on the sea; 2
36 they took him with them in the boat, just as he was. 2
36 other boats were with him. 2
37 the waves beat into the boat 2
37 so that the boat was already filling. 2
5: 2 when he had come out of the boat 2
18 as he was getting into the boat 2
21 Jesus had crossed again in the boat to the other side •
6:32 they went away in the boat to a lonely place 2
45 he made his disciples get into the boat 2
47 when evening came, the boat was out on the sea 2
51 got into the boat with them and the wind ceased. 2
54 when they got out of the boat 2
8:10 he got into the boat with his disciples 2
13 he left them, and getting into the boat again •
14 they had only one loaf with them in the boat. 2
Lke 5: 2 he saw two boats by the lake 2
3 Getting into one of the boats, which was Simon's 2
3 he sat down and taught the people from the boat. 2
7 beckoned to their partners in the other boat 2
7 they came and filled both the boats 2
11 when they had brought their boats to land 2
8:22 One day he got into a boat with his disciples 2
37 so he got into the boat and returned. 2
Joh 6:17 got into a boat 2
19 walking on the sea and drawing near to the boat 2
21 they were glad to take him into the boat 2
21 immediately the boat was at the land 2
22 saw that there had been only one boat there 1
22 Jesus had not entered the boat with his disciples 2
23 However, boats from Tiber'i-as came near the place 1
24 they . . got into the boats and went to Caper'na-um 1
21: 3 They went out and got into the boat 2
6 Cast the net on the right side of the boat 2
8 the other disciples came in the boat 1
Act 27:16 we managed with difficulty to secure the boat; 3
30 had lowered the boat into the sea 3
32 Then the soldiers cut away the ropes of the boat 3
Sir 33: 2 like a boat in a storm. 2
2Mc 12: 3 to embark . . on boats which they had provided 4
6 burned the boats 4
3Mc 4: 9 fastened by the neck to the benches of the boats 2

bodily 1. σάρξ 2. σῶμα 3. σωματικός 4. σωματικῶς 5. carnalis
Lke 3:22 Holy Spirit descended upon him in bodily form 3
2Co 10:10 his bodily presence is weak 2
Gal 4:13 you know it was because of a bodily ailment 1
Eph 4:16 makes bodily growth and upbuilds itself in love. 2
Col 2: 9 in him the whole fulness of deity dwells bodily 4
1Ti 4: 8 for while bodily training is of some value 3
2Es 1:37 though they do not see me with bodily eyes 5
2Mc 3:17 terror and bodily trembling 2
3Mc 6:20 Even the king began to shudder bodily 2
4Mc 3:18 it can overthrow bodily agonies 2
10:20 we let our bodily members be mutilated. 2

bodily *See also* descent.

body 1. אול 2. בֶּטֶן 3. בָּשָׂר 4. גֵּוָה 5. גְּוִיָּה 6. גּוּפָה 7. חֹמֶשׁ 8. מֵעַ 9. מֵעֶה 10. נְבֵלָה 11. נֶפֶשׁ 12. עוֹר 13. עֲטִין 14. עֶצֶם 15. פֶּגֶר 16. קֵבָה 17. קֶרֶב 18. שְׁאֵר 19. גְּשֵׁם (A) 20. αὐτός 21. γυμνός 22. ἐκκλησία 23. κῶλον 24. ὁμοθυμαδόν 25. πλῆθος 26. πτῶμα 27. σάρξ 28. σκήνωμα 29. σπλάγχνον 30. σύστημα 31. σῶμα 32. σωματικός 33. χρώς 34. corpus 35. vas
Gen 25:25 came forth red, all his body like a hairy mantle; •
47:18 nothing left . . but our bodies and our lands. 5
Exd 22:27 covering, it is his mantle for his body; 12
30:32 It shall not be poured upon the bodies 3
Lev 6:10 and put his linen breeches upon his body 3
13: 2 When a man has on the skin of his body a swelling 3
2 a leprous disease on the skin of his body 3
3 examine the diseased spot on the skin of his body 3
3 than the skin of his body, it is a leprous disease 3
4 if the spot is white in the skin of his body 3
11 it is a chronic leprosy in the skin of his body 3
13 if the leprosy has covered all his body 3
18 when there is in the skin of one's body a boil 3
24 when the body has a burn on its skin 3
38 has spots on the skin of the body, white spots 3
39 spots on the skin of the body are of a dull white 3
43 the appearance of leprosy in the skin of the body 3
14: 9 and bathe his body in water, and he shall be clean 3
15: 2 When any man has a discharge from his body 3
3 whether his body runs with his discharge 3
3 or his body is stopped from discharge 3
7 touches the body of him who has the discharge 3
13 he shall bathe his body in running water 3
16 he shall bathe his whole body in water 3
19 which is her regular discharge from her body 3
16: 4 and shall have the linen breeches on his body 3
4 He shall bathe his body in water 3
24 he shall bathe his body in water in a holy place 3
26 shall wash his clothes and bathe his body in water 3
28 wash his clothes and bathe his body in water 3
21:11 he shall not go in to any dead body, nor defile 11
22: 6 unless he has bathed his body in water 3
Num 5:21 when the LORD makes . . your body swell; 2
22 make your body swell and your thigh fall away.' 2
27 body shall swell, and her thigh shall fall away 2
6: 6 he shall not go near a dead body. 11
8: 7 let them go with a razor over all their body 3
19: 7 priest shall wash his clothes and bathe his body 3
8 wash his clothes . . and bathe his body in water 3
13 Whoever touches . . body of any man who has died 11
25: 8 pierced both of them . . through her body. 16
Deu 7:13 also bless the fruit of your body and the fruit 2
21:23 his body shall not remain all night upon the tree 10
28: 4 Blessed shall be the fruit of your body 2
11 make you abound in . . the fruit of your body 2
18 Cursed shall be the offspring of your body 2
53 you shall eat the offspring of your own body 2
30: 9 prosperous in . . the fruit of your body 2
Jos 8:29 Joshua commanded, and they took his body down 10
Jdg 14: 8 a swarm of bees in the body of the lion, and honey. 5
1Sm 31:10 they fastened his body to the wall of Beth-shan. 5
12 took the body of Saul and the bodies of his sons 5
12 took the body of Saul and the bodies of his sons 5
2Sm 7:12 offspring . . who shall come forth from your body 9
20:10 so Jo'ab struck him with it in the body 7
1Kg 13:22 your body shall not come to the tomb 10
24 his body was thrown in the road 10
24 the lion also stood beside the body. 10
25 and saw the body thrown in the road, and the lion 10
25 the body . . and the lion standing by the body. 10
28 he went and found his body thrown in the road 10
28 the ass and the lion standing beside the body. 10
28 The lion had not eaten the body or torn the ass. 10
29 the prophet took up the body of the man of God 10
30 he laid the body in his own grave; 10
2Kg 6:30 he had sackcloth beneath upon his body– 3
19:35 when men arose . . these were all dead bodies. 15
1Ch 10:12 took away the body of Saul and . . of his sons 6
12 took away . . Saul and the bodies of his sons 6
Neh 9:37 power also over our bodies and over our cattle 5
Job 14:22 He feels only the pain of his own body 3
20:25 It is drawn forth and comes out of his body 4
21:24 his body full of fat 13
Ps 16: 9 my soul rejoices; my body also dwells secure. 3
31: 9 eye is wasted from grief, my soul and my body also. 2
32: 3 When I declared not my sin, my body wasted away 14
42:10 As with a deadly wound in my body 14
44:25 our body cleaves to the ground. 2
73: 4 have no pangs; their bodies are sound and sleek. 1
79: 2 given the bodies of thy servants to the birds 10
109:18 may it soak into his body like water 17
24 my body has become gaunt. 3
132:11 One of the sons of your body I will set 2
Prv 5:11 when your flesh and body are consumed 18
16:24 sweetness to the soul and health to the body. 14
18: 8 go down into the inner parts of the body. 2
26:22 go down into the inner parts of the body. 2
Ecc 2: 3 I searched . . how to cheer my body with wine 3
11:10 Remove . . and put away pain from your body; 3
Sng 5:14 His body is ivory work 8
Isa 10:18 the LORD will destroy, both soul and body 3
26:19 Thy dead shall live, their bodies shall rise. 10
37:36 behold, these were all dead bodies. 15
49: 1 from the body of my mother he named my name. 8
Jer 41: 5 their clothes torn, and their bodies gashed •
9 cistern into which Ish'mael cast all the bodies 15
Lam 4: 7 their bodies were more ruddy than coral 14
Ezk 1:11 wing of another, while two covered their bodies. 5
23 each creature had two wings covering its body. 5
Dan 3:27 not had any power over the bodies of those men; 19
28 yielded up their bodies rather than serve 19
4:33 body was wet with the dew of heaven 19
5:21 body was wet with the dew of heaven 19
7:11 body destroyed and given over to be burned 19
10: 6 His body was like beryl, 5
Mic 6: 7 give . . the fruit of my body for the sin of my soul? 2
Nah 3: 3 bodies without end–they stumble over the bodies 5
Hab 3:16 I hear, and my body trembles, my lips quiver 2
Hag 2:13 If one who is unclean by contact with a dead body •
Mat 5:29 than that your whole body be thrown into hell. 31
30 members than that your whole body go into hell. 31
6:22 The eye is the lamp of the body. So, if your eye 31
22 eye is sound, your whole body will be full of light; 31
23 your eye is not sound, your whole body will be full 31
25 drink, nor about your body, what you shall put on. 31
25 than food, and the body more than clothing? 31
10:28 do not fear those who kill the body 31
28 who can destroy both soul and body in hell. 31
14:12 his disciples came and took the body 26
24:28 Wherever the body is, there the eagles will be 26
26:12 In pouring this ointment on my body 31
26 Take, eat; this is my body. 31
27:52 many bodies of the saints who had fallen asleep 31
58 He went to Pilate and asked for the body of Jesus. 31
59 Joseph took the body 31
Mrk 5:29 she felt in her body that she was healed 31
6:29 they came and took his body, and laid it in a tomb. 26
14: 8 anointed my body beforehand for burying. 31
22 Take; this is my body. 31
51 with nothing but a linen cloth about his body 21
15:43 went to Pilate, and asked for the body of Jesus. 31
45 he granted the body to Joseph. 26
Lke 11:34 Your eye is the lamp of your body 31
34 your whole body is full of light 31
34 when it is not sound, your body is full of darkness. 31
36 whole body is full of light, having no part dark 31
12: 4 my friends, do not fear those who kill the body 31
22 nor about your body, what you shall put on. 31
23 the body more than clothing. 31
17:37 Where the body is, there the eagles will be 31
22:19 gave it to them, saying, "This is my body 31
23:52 went to Pilate and asked for the body of Jesus. 31
55 saw the tomb, and how his body was laid; 31
24: 3 when they went in they did not find the body. 31
23 did not find his body 31
Joh 2:21 But he spoke of the temple of his body. 31
7:23 on the sabbath I made a man's whole body well? •
19:31 to prevent the bodies from remaining on the cross 31
38 that he might take away the body of Jesus 31
38 So he came and took away his body. 31
40 They took the body of Jesus 31
20:12 sitting where the body of Jesus had lain 31
Act 6: 2 the twelve summoned the body of the disciples 25
9:40 then turning to the body he said, "Tabitha, rise. 31
12:20 they came to him in a body 24
19:12 aprons were carried away from his body to the sick 33
Rom 1:24 dishonoring of their bodies among themselves 31
4:19 weaken in faith when he considered his own body 31
6: 6 so that the sinful body might be destroyed 31
12 Let not sin . . reign in your mortal bodies 31
7: 4 have died to the law through the body of Christ 31
24 Who will deliver me from this body of death? 31
8:10 although your bodies are dead because of sin 31
11 will give life to your mortal bodies also 31
13 if . . put to death the deeds of the body 31

23 adoption as sons, the redemption of our bodies. 31
12: 1 to present your bodies as a living sacrifice 31
4 For as in one body we have many members 31
5 so we, though many, are one body in Christ 31
1Co 5: 3 For though absent in body I am present in spirit 31
6:13 The body is not meant for immorality 31
13 and the Lord for the body. 31
15 know that your bodies are members of Christ 31
16 becomes one body with her 31
18 is outside the body 31
18 the immoral man sins against his own body. 31
19 Do you not know that your body is a temple 31
20 So glorify God in your body. 31
7: 4 For the wife does not rule over her own body 31
4 the husband does not rule over his own body 31
34 how to be holy in body and spirit 31
9:27 I pommel my body and subdue it 31
10:16 is it not a participation in the body of Christ? 31
17 we who are many are one body 31
11:24 This is my body which is for you 31
27 be guilty of profaning the body and blood of the Lord. 31
29 who eats and drinks without discerning the body 31
12:12 For just as the body is one and has many members 31
12 all the members of the body, though many, are one 31
12 all the members of the body, though many, are one 31
13 we were all baptized into one body 31
14 body does not consist of one member but of many. 31
15 Because I am not a hand, I do not belong to the body 31
15 that would not make it any less a part of the body. 31
16 Because I am not an eye, I do not belong to the body 31
16 that would not make it any less a part of the body. 31
17 If the whole body were an eye 31
17 If the whole body were an ear •
18 as it is, God arranged the organs in the body 31
19 If all were a single organ, where would the body be? 31
20 As it is, there are many parts, yet one body. 31
22 the parts of the body which seem to be weaker 31
23 those parts of the body which we think less honorable 31
24 God has so composed the body 31
25 that there may be no discord in the body 31
27 you are the body of Christ 31
13: 3 if I deliver my body to be burned, but have not love 31
15:35 With what kind of body do they come? 31
37 what you sow is not the body which is to be 31
38 God gives it a body as he has chosen 31
38 to each kind of seed its own body. 31
40 There are celestial bodies 31
40 there are terrestrial bodies 31
44 It is sown a physical body 31
44 it is raised a spiritual body 31
44 If there is a physical body 31
44 there is also a spiritual body. •
2Co 4:10 always carrying in the body the death of Jesus 31
10 Jesus may also be manifested in our bodies. 31
5: 6 we know that while we are at home in the body 31
8 be away from the body and at home with the Lord. 31
10 according to what he has done in the body. 31
7: 1 every defilement of body and spirit 27
5 our bodies had no rest 27
12: 2 whether in the body or out of the body 31
2 whether in the body or out of the body 31
3 whether in the body or out of the body 31
3 whether in the body or out of the body 31
Gal 6:17 I bear on my body the marks of Jesus. 31
Eph 1:23 which is his body 31
2: 3 following the desires of body and mind 27
16 might reconcile us both to God in one body 31
4: 4 There is one body and one Spirit 31
12 for building up the body of Christ 31
16 the whole body, joined and knit together 31
5:23 Christ is the head of the church, his body 31
28 should love their wives as their own bodies 31
30 because we are members of his body. 31
Php 1:20 Christ will be honored in my body 31
3:21 who will change our lowly body 31
21 to be like his glorious body 31
Col 1:18 He is the head of the body, the church 31
22 now reconciled in his body of flesh by his death 31
24 for the sake of his body . . the church 31
2: 5 though I am absent in body 27
11 putting off the body of flesh 31
19 the whole body, nourished and knit together 31
23 self-abasement and severity to the body 31
3:15 to which indeed you were called in the one body. 31
1Th 5:23 may your spirit and soul and body be kept sound 31
Heb 3:17 who sinned, whose bodies fell in the wilderness 23
9:10 regulations for the body 27
10: 5 a body hast thou prepared for me; 31
10 the offering of the body of Jesus Christ 31
22 our bodies washed with pure water. 31
13: 3 since you also are in the body. 31
11 the bodies of those animals 31
Jas 2:16 the things needed for the body 31
26 For as the body apart from the spirit is dead 31
3: 2 a perfect man, able to bridle the whole body also. 31
3 we guide their whole bodies. 31
6 staining the whole body 31
1Pe 2:24 He himself bore our sins in his body on the tree 31
3:21 not as a removal of dirt from the body 27
2Pe 1:13 I think it right, as long as I am in this body 28
14 know that the putting off of my body will be soon 28
Jde 1: 9 Michael . . disputed about the body of Moses 31
2Es 1:32 slain them and torn their bodies in pieces 34
3: 5 it gave thee Adam, a lifeless body 34
5:14 Then I awoke, and my body shuddered violently 34
7:78 as the spirit leaves the body to return again 34
88 they shall be separated from their mortal body. 35
100 after they have been separated from the bodies 34
8: 8 because thou dost give life to the body 34
11:10 but from the midst of his body. 34
23 nothing remained on the eagle's body 34
45 and your whole worthless body 34
12: 3 and the whole body of the eagle was burned 34
17 but from the midst of his body 34
16:61 and put a heart in the midst of his body 34
Tob 1:18 When the bodies were sought by the king 31
2: 4 and removed the body to a place of shelter 20
7 I went and dug a grave and buried the body. 20
Jdt 1:16 a vast body of troops 25
10: 3 bathed her body with water 31
13: 8 and severed it from his body. •
9 Then she tumbled his body off the bed 31
AEs 14: 2 she utterly humbled her body 31
Wis 1: 4 nor dwell in a body enslaved to sin. 31
2: 3 the body will turn to ashes 31
8:20 rather, being good, I entered an undefiled body. 31
9:15 for a perishable body weighs down the soul 31
18:22 not by strength of body, and not by force of arms 31
Sir 30:14 a rich man who is severely afflicted in body. 31
15 and a robust body than countless riches 31
16 There is no wealth better than health of body 31
34:25 If a man washes after touching a dead body •
38:16 Lay out his body with the honor due him 31
41:11 The mourning of men is about their bodies 31
44:14 Their bodies were buried in peace 31
47:19 through your body 31
48:13 when he was dead his body prophesied. 31
51: 2 hast delivered my body from destruction 31
Bar 2:17 whose spirit has been taken from their bodies 29
LJr 1:22 birds light on their bodies and heads 31
71 like a dead body cast out in the darkness. •
Bel 1:32 they had been given two human bodies and two sheep 31
1Mc 3:13 a body of faithful men who stayed with him 22
11: 4 the charred bodies •
2Mc 6:30 I am enduring terrible sufferings in my body 31
7: 7 rather than have your body punished limb by limb? 31
37 I, like my brothers, give up body and life 31
9: 7 to torture every limb of his body. 31
9 so the ungodly man's body swarmed with worms 31
29 Philip, one of his courtiers, took his body home; 31
12:39 went to take up the bodies of the fallen 31
14:38 he had with all zeal risked body and life. 31
15:12 praying . . for the whole body of the Jews. 30
30 the man who was ever in body and soul the defender 31
3Mc 2:29 are also to be branded on their bodies by fire 31
7: 3 to gather together the Jews . . in a body 30
4Mc 1:20 by nature concerned with both body and soul. 31
27 in the body, indiscriminate eating, gluttony 31
28 two plants growing from the body and the soul 31
35 the impulses of the body are bridled by reason. 31
3: 1 reason rules . . over those of the body. 32
6: 7 because his body could not endure the agonies 31
7:13 his body no longer tense and firm 31
11:11 gasping for breath and in anguish of body 31
13:13 let us use our bodies as a bulwark for the law. 31
14:10 it consumed their bodies quickly. 31
17: 1 so that no one might touch her body. 31
18: 3 those who gave over their bodies in suffering 31

body *See also* appear, member.

dead body 1. גְוִיָּה 2. מות 3. נְבֵלָה 4. נֶפֶשׁ 5. פֶּגֶר 6. *πτῶμα*

Lev 26:30 cast your dead bodies upon the dead bodies 5
30 dead bodies upon the dead bodies of your idols 5
Num 6:11 because he sinned by reason of the dead body. 4
9: 6 unclean through touching the dead body of a man 4
7 unclean through touching the dead body of a man; 4
10 unclean through touching a dead body 4
14:29 your dead bodies shall fall in this wilderness; 5
32 your dead bodies shall fall in this wilderness. 5
33 last of your dead bodies lies in the wilderness. 5
19:11 He who touches the dead body of any person 2
16 Whoever . . touches . . a dead body, or a bone 2
Deu 28:26 dead body shall be food for all birds of the air 3
1Sm 17:46 I will give the dead bodies . . to the birds 5
2Ch 20:24 behold, they were dead bodies lying on the ground; 5
Isa 14:19 to . . the Pit, like a dead body trodden under foot 5
66:24 go forth and look on the dead bodies of the men 5
Jer 7:33 And the dead bodies of this people will be food 3
9:22 The dead bodies of men shall fall like dung 3
16: 4 their dead bodies shall be food for the birds 3
19: 7 will give their dead bodies for food to the birds 3
26:23 and cast his dead body into the burial place 3
31:40 The whole valley of the dead bodies and the ashes 5
33: 5 and to fill them with the dead bodies of men 5
34:20 Their dead bodies shall be food for the birds 3
36:30 his dead body shall be cast out to the heat by day 3
Ezk 6: 5 I will lay the dead bodies of the people of Israel 5
43: 7 and by the dead bodies of their kings 5
9 and the dead bodies of their kings far from me 5
Ams 8: 3 the dead bodies shall be many; 5
Nah 3: 3 heaps of corpses, dead bodies without end- 1
Hag 2:13 If one who is unclean by contact with a dead body 4
Rev 11: 8 their dead bodies will lie in the street 6
9 men . . gaze at their dead bodies and refuse 6

great body 1. *πολύς*

2Mc 6:31 but to the great body of his nation. 1

body of youth 1. *ἐφηβεῖον*

2Mc 4: 9 a gymnasium and a body of youth for it 1

bodyguard 1. טַבָּח 2. מִשְׁמַעַת 3. שׁמר לְראשׁ 4. *δορυφορία* 5. *δορυφόρος* 6. *ὁ περί* 7. *σωματοφύλαξ*

1Sm 22:14 king's son-in-law, and captain over your bodyguard 2
28: 2 Very well, I will make you my bodyguard for life. 3
2Sm 23:23 And David set him over his bodyguard. 2
2Kg 25: 8 Nebu'zarad'an, the captain of the bodyguard 1
1Ch 11:25 And David set him over his bodyguard. 2
Jer 52:12 Nebu'zarad'an the captain of the bodyguard 1
1Es 3: 4 the three young men of the bodyguard 7
1Mc 13:40 qualified to be enrolled in our bodyguard 6
2Mc 3:24 he arrived at the treasury with his bodyguard 5
28 with a great retinue and all his bodyguard 4
3Mc 2:23 friends and bodyguards . . quickly dragged him out 7

bog 1. טִיט

Ps 40: 2 out of the miry bog, and set my feet upon a rock 1

boil 1. בָּשֵׁל 2. בשל 3. זיד 4. נפח 5. רתח 6. תמם 7. *ἕψω*

Gen 25:29 Once when Jacob was boiling pottage, Esau came 3
Exd 12: 9 Do not eat any of it raw or boiled with water 2
16:23 and boil what you will boil, and all 2
23 and boil what you will boil, and all 2
23:19 You shall not boil a kid in its mother's milk. 2
29:31 ram of ordination, and boil its flesh 2
34:26 You shall not boil a kid in its mother's milk. 2
Lev 6:28 the earthen vessel in which it is boiled 2
28 if it is boiled in a bronze vessel 2
8:31 Moses said to Aaron and his sons, "Boil the flesh 2
Num 6:19 take the shoulder of the ram, when it is boiled 1
11: 8 people . . boiled it in pots, and made cakes of it; 2
Deu 14:21 You shall not boil a kid in its mother's milk. 2
16: 7 boil it and eat it at the place which the LORD 2
1Sm 2:13 servant would come, while the meat was boiling 2
15 he will not accept boiled meat from you, but raw. 2
1Kg 19:21 slew them, and boiled their flesh with the yokes 2
2Kg 4:38 and boil pottage for the sons of the prophets. 2
6:29 So we boiled my son, and ate him. 2
2Ch 35:13 boiled the holy offerings in pots, in caldrons 2
Job 41:20 smoke, as from a boiling pot and burning rushes. 4
Jer 1:13 What do you see?" And I said, "I see a boiling pot 4
Lam 4:10 women have boiled their own children; 2
Ezk 24: 5 boil its pieces, seethe also its bones in it. 5
10 kindle the fire, boil well the flesh 6
46:20 where the priests shall boil the guilt offering 2
24 shall boil the sacrifices of the people. 2
Zec 14:21 take of them and boil the flesh of the sacrifice 2
1Es 1:12 they boiled the sacrifices in brass pots 7
Bel 1:27 took pitch, fat, and hair, and boiled them together 7
33 He had boiled pottage 7

boil (2) 1. שְׁחִין

Exd 9: 9 it shall become . . become boils breaking out 1
10 and it became boils breaking out in sores on man 1
11 could not stand . . because of the boils 1
11 for the boils were upon the magicians and upon 1
Lev 13:18 when there is . . a boil that has healed 1
19 in the place of the boil . . comes a . . swelling 1
20 leprosy, it has broken out in the boil 1
23 it is the scar of the boil 1
Deu 28:27 LORD will smite you with the boils of Egypt 1
35 LORD will smite you . . with grievous boils 1
2Kg 20: 7 take and lay it on the boil, that he may recover 1
Isa 38:21 take a cake of figs, and apply it to the boil 1

cause to boil 1. בעה

Isa 64: 2 and the fire causes water to boil- 1

make boil 1. רתח

Job 41:31 He makes the deep boil like a pot; 1

bold 1. בטח 2. עַז 3. *ἀποτολμάω* 4. *θαρρέω* 5. *θρασύνω* 6. *θρασύς* 7. *κατατολμάω* 8. *παρρησία* 9. *παρρησιάζομαι* 10. *τολμάω* 11. *τολμηρός*

Prv 28: 1 but the righteous are bold as a lion. 1
Dan 8:23 king of bold countenance, one who understands 2
Rom 10:20 Then Isaiah is so bold as to say, "I have been found 3
2Co 3:12 Since we have such a hope, we are very bold 8
10: 1 bold to you when I am away!- 4
Php 1:14 bold to speak the word of God without fear. 10
Phm 1: 8 Accordingly, though I am bold enough in Christ 8
2Pe 2:10 Bold and wilful, they are not afraid to revile 11
Jdt 14:13 the slaves have been so bold as to come down 10

Wis 11:17 a multitude of bears, or bold lions 6
Sir 6:11 be bold with your servants; 9
2Mc 3:24 who had been so bold as to accompany him 7
3Mc 1:22 the bolder of the citizens would not tolerate 5

bold *See also* put.

boldly 1. *ἀφόβως* 2. *θαρραλέως* 3. *μετὰ παρρησίας* 4. *ταυρηδόν*
Prv 10:10 but he who boldly reproves makes peace. 3
Jde 1:12 love feasts, as they boldly carouse together 1
1Mc 4:18 afterward seize the plunder boldly. 3
4Mc 3:14 from it boldly brought the king a drink. 2
15:19 gazing boldly at the same agonies 4

boldly *See also* declare, preach, speak.

very boldly 1. *τολμηρός*
Rom 15:15 written to you very boldly by way of reminder 1

boldness 1. *θάρσος* 2. *θράσος* 3. *θρασύς* 4. *παρρησία* 5. *τόλμα* 6. fiducia
Act 4:13 Now when they saw the boldness of Peter and John 4
29 to speak thy word with all boldness 4
31 spoke the word of God with boldness. 4
Eph 3:12 in whom we have boldness 4
2Es 7:98 because they shall rejoice with boldness 6
Jdt 16:10 The Persians trembled at her boldness 5
Sir 25:25 Allow . . no boldness of speech in an evil wife. 4
1Mc 4:32 melt the boldness of their strength 2
35 the boldness which inspired those of Judas 1
3Mc 2: 4 who trusted in their strength and boldness 3
6:34 their fire-breathing boldness 5
4Mc 10: 5 Enraged by the man's boldness 4

boldness of speech 1. *παρρησία*
Sir 25:25 Allow . . no boldness of speech in an evil wife. 1

show boldness 1. *θαρρέω*
2Co 10: 2 not have to show boldness with such confidence 1

bolt 1. מַנְעוּל 2. נעל 3. *μοχλός*
2Sm 13:17 Put this woman out . . and bolt the door after her. 2
18 put her out, and bolted the door after her. 2
Neh 3: 3 set its doors, its bolts, and its bars. 1
6 set its doors, its bolts, and its bars. 1
13 rebuilt . . set its doors, its bolts, and its bars 1
14 rebuilt . . set its doors, its bolts, and its bars. 1
15 covered . . set its doors, its bolts, and its bars; 1
Sng 5: 5 my hands dripped . . upon the handles of the bolt. 1
Sir 28:25 make a door and a bolt for your mouth. 3
1Mc 12:38 he fortified it and installed gates with bolts. 3
13:33 high towers and great walls and gates and bolts 3

bond 1. אֵסוּר 2. אָסִיר 3. חַרְצֻבָּה 4. מוּסֵר 5. עצר 6. *δέσμιος* 7. *δεσμός* 8. *δέω* 9. *σύνδεσμος* 10. *χειρόγραφον*
Deu 32:36 sees . . there is none remaining, bond or free. 5
Jdg 15:14 caught fire, and his bonds melted off his hands. 1
1Kg 14:10 cut off . . every male, both bond and free in Israel 5
21:21 I . . will cut off from Ahab every male, bond or free 5
2Kg 9: 8 cut off . . every male, bond or free, in Israel. 5
14:26 for there was none left, bond or free 5
Job 12:18 He looses the bonds of kings 4
39: 5 Who has loosed the bonds of the swift ass 4
Ps 2: 3 Let us burst their bonds asunder 4
69:33 and does not despise his own that are in bonds. 2
107:14 broke their bonds asunder. 4
116:16 Thou hast loosed my bonds. 4
Isa 28:22 do not scoff, lest your bonds be made strong; 4
52: 2 loose the bonds from your neck, O captive 4
58: 6 that I choose: to loose the bonds of wickedness 3
Jer 2:20 you broke your yoke and burst your bonds; 4
5: 5 had broken the yoke, they had burst the bonds. 4
30: 8 and I will burst their bonds 4
Nah 1:13 and will burst your bonds asunder. 4
Lke 8:29 he broke the bonds 7
13:16 be loosed from this bond on the sabbath day? 8
Act 8:23 in the bond of iniquity. 9
22: 5 and bring them in bonds to Jerusalem to be punished. 8
Eph 4: 3 the unity of the Spirit in the bond of peace. 9
Col 2:14 having canceled the bond which stood against us 10
Sir 6:25 do not fret under her bonds. 7
30 her bonds are a cord of blue. 7
3Mc 4: 7 In bonds and in public view 6
5: 7 in their bonds they were forcibly confined 7
6:27 Loose and untie their unjust bonds! 7

bond *See also* put.

firmly bond 1. *ἐνδέω*
Sir 22:16 A wooden beam firmly bonded into a building 1

iron bond 1. *σιδηρόδεσμος*
3Mc 4: 9 driven under the constraint of iron bonds 1

bondage 1. עֶבֶד 2. עֲבֹדָה 3. עַבְדוּת 4. *δουλεία* 5. *δουλεύω* 6. servio 7. servitus
Exd 2:23 people of Israel groaned under their bondage 2
23 and their cry under bondage came up to God. 2
6: 6 I will deliver you from their bondage 2
9 broken spirit and their cruel bondage. 2
13: 3 came out from Egypt, out of the house of bondage 1
14 LORD brought us out . . from the house of bondage. 1
20: 2 brought you . . out of the house of bondage. 1
Deu 5: 6 LORD . . who brought you out of . . the house of bondage. 1
6:12 LORD, who brought you . . out of the house of bondage. 1
7: 8 LORD . . redeemed you from the house of bondage 1
8:14 LORD . . brought you . . , out of the house of bondage 1
13: 5 LORD . . redeemed you out of the house of bondage 1
10 LORD . . brought you . . out of the house of bondage. 1
26: 6 afflicted us, and laid upon us hard bondage. 2
Jos 24:17 up from . . Egypt, out of the house of bondage 1
Jdg 6: 8 I . . brought you out of the house of bondage; 1
Ezr 9: 8 grant us a little reviving in our bondage. 3
9 yet our God has not forsaken us in our bondage 3
Neh 9:17 leader to return to their bondage in Egypt. 3
Jer 34:13 out of the house of bondage, saying 1
Mic 6: 4 and redeemed you from the house of bondage; 1
Joh 8:33 and have never been in bondage to any one 5
Rom 8:21 creation . . set free from its bondage to decay 4
Gal 4: 8 in bondage to beings that by nature are no gods; 5
Heb 2:15 those who . . were subject to lifelong bondage. 4
1Es 8:80 Even in our bondage we were not forsaken 5
2Es 1: 7 out of the house of bondage? 7
2: 1 I brought this people out of bondage 7
14: 3 when my people were in bondage in Egypt; 6
Wis 14:21 in bondage to misfortune or to royal authority 5

bondage *See also* bring, hold.

bondmaid 1. אָמָה
Exd 23:12 the son of your bondmaid, and the alien, may be 1

bondman 1. עֶבֶד
Deu 15:17 he shall be your bondman for ever. 1
Ezr 9: 9 For we are bondmen; yet our God has not forsaken us 1

bondwoman 1. אָמָה
Deu 15:17 And to your bondwoman you shall do likewise. 1

bone 1. גֶּרֶם 2. עֶצֶם 3. גְּרֵם (A) 4. *ὀστέον*
Gen 2:23 the man said, "This at last is bone of my bones 2
23 the man said, "This at last is bone of my bones 2
29:14 Laban said . . "Surely you are my bone and flesh! 2
50:25 and you shall carry up my bones from here. 2
Exd 12:46 and you shall not break a bone of it. 2
13:19 Moses took the bones of Joseph with him; 2
19 you must carry my bones with you from here. 2
Num 9:12 none of it until the morning, nor break a bone of it; 2
19:16 Whoever . . touches . . a bone of a man, or a grave 2
18 sprinkle it . . upon him who touched the bone 2
24: 8 shall break their bones in pieces 2
Jos 24:32 The bones of Joseph . . were buried at Shechem 2
Jdg 9: 2 Remember also that I am your bone and your flesh. 2
1Sm 31:13 And they took their bones and buried them 2
2Sm 5: 1 and said, "Behold, we are your bone and flesh. 2
19:12 You are my kinsmen, you are my bone and my flesh; 2
13 say to Ama'sa, 'Are you not my bone and my flesh? 2
21:12 took the bones of Saul and the bones of his son 2
12 took . . the bones of his son Jonathan 2
13 and he brought up from there the bones of Saul 2
13 bones of Saul and the bones of his son Jonathan; 2
13 they gathered the bones of those who were hanged. 2
14 And they buried the bones of Saul and his son 2
1Kg 13: 2 and men's bones shall be burned upon you.' 2
31 bury me . . lay my bones beside his bones. 2
31 bury me . . lay my bones beside his bones. 2
2Kg 13:21 and as soon as the man touched the bones of Eli'sha 2
23:14 and filled their places with the bones of men. 2
16 and he sent and took the bones out of the tombs 2
18 And he said, "Let him be; let no man move his bones. 2
18 Let him be . . " So they let his bones alone 2
18 let his bones alone, with the bones of the prophet 2
20 the altars, and burned the bones of men upon them. 2
1Ch 10:12 they buried their bones under the oak in Jabesh 2
11: 1 and said, "Behold, we are your bone and flesh. 2
2Ch 34: 5 burned the bones of the priests on their altars 2
Job 2: 5 touch his bone and his flesh, and he will curse 2
4:14 trembling, which made all my bones shake. 2
7:15 strangling and death rather than my bones. 2
10:11 and knit me together with bones and sinews. 2
19:20 My bones cleave to my skin and to my flesh 2
20:11 His bones are full of youthful vigor 2
21:24 full of fat and the marrow of his bones moist. 2
30:17 The night racks my bones, and the pain 2
30 My skin turns black . . and my bones burn with heat. 2
33:19 with continual strife in his bones; 2
21 his bones which were not seen stick out. 2
40:18 His bones are tubes of bronze 2
Ps 6: 2 O LORD, heal me, for my bones are troubled. 2
22:14 all my bones are out of joint; my heart is like wax 2
17 I can count all my bones- 2
31:10 because of my misery, and my bones waste away. 2
34:20 He keeps all his bones; not one of them is broken. 2
35:10 All my bones shall say, "O LORD, who is like thee 2
38: 3 there is no health in my bones because of my sin. 2
51: 8 let the bones which thou hast broken rejoice. 2
53: 5 For God will scatter the bones of the ungodly; 2
102: 3 my bones burn like a furnace. 2
5 of my loud groaning my bones cleave to my flesh. 2
109:18 may it soak . . like oil into his bones! 2
141: 7 their bones be strewn at the mouth of Sheol. 2
Prv 3: 8 It will be . . refreshment to your bones. 2
12: 4 brings shame is like rottenness in his bones. 2
14:30 but passion makes the bones rot. 2
15:30 good news refreshes the bones. 2
17:22 but a downcast spirit dries up the bones. 1
25:15 soft tongue will break a bone. 1
Ecc 11: 5 you do not know how the spirit comes to the bones 2
Isa 38:13 like a lion he breaks all my bones; 2
58:11 with good things, and make your bones strong; 2
66:14 your bones shall flourish like the grass; 2
Jer 8: 1 says the LORD, the bones of the kings of Judah 2
1 the bones of its princes, the bones of the priests 2
1 the bones of its princes, the bones of the priests 2
1 bones of the priests, the bones of the prophets 2
1 and the bones of the inhabitants of Jerusalem 2
20: 9 as it were a burning fire shut up in my bones 2
23: 9 My heart is broken within me, all my bones shake; 2
Lam 1:13 he sent fire; into my bones he made it descend; 2
3: 4 made . . my skin waste away, and broken my bones; 2
4: 8 their skin has shriveled upon their bones 2
Ezk 6: 5 I will scatter your bones round about 2
24: 4 fill it with choice bones. 2
5 boil its pieces, seethe also its bones in it. 2
10 let the bones be burned up. 2
32:27 whose shields are upon their bones; 2
37: 1 in the midst of the valley; it was full of bones. 2
3 he said to me, "Son of man, can these bones live? 2
4 Again he said to me, "Prophesy to these bones, 2
4 say to them, O dry bones, hear the word of the LORD. 2
5 Thus says the Lord GOD to these bones 2
7 and the bones came together, bone to its bone. 2
7 and the bones came together, bone to its bone. 2
7 and the bones came together, bone to its bone. 2
11 these bones are the whole house of Israel. 2
11 Behold, they say, 'Our bones are dried up 2
39:15 pass through the land and any one sees a man's bone 2
Dan 6:24 lions . . broke all their bones in pieces. 3
Ams 2: 1 he burned to lime the bones of the king of Edom. 2
6:10 take him up to bring the bones out of the house 2
Mic 3: 2 who tear . . their flesh from off their bones; 2
3 and break their bones in pieces 2
Hab 3:16 rottenness enters into my bones, my steps totter 2
Mat 23:27 within they are full of dead men's bones 4
Lke 24:39 a spirit has not flesh and bones 4
Joh 19:36 Not a bone of him shall be broken. 4
Sir 26:13 her skill puts fat on his bones. 4
28:17 a blow of the tongue crushes the bones. 4
46:12 May their bones revive from where they lie 4
49:10 May the bones of the twelve prophets revive 4
15 his bones are cared for. 4
Bar 2:24 bones of our kings and the bones of our fathers 4
24 bones of our kings and the bones of our fathers 4
1Mc 13:25 Simon sent and took the bones of Jonathan 4
4Mc 6:26 When he was now burned to his very bones 4
9:21 the ligaments joining his bones 4
18:17 'Shall these dry bones live?' 4

bone *See also* gnaw.

book 1. כְּתָב 2. סֵפֶר 3. סִפְרָה 4. סְפַר (A) 5. סֵפֶר (A) 6. *βιβλίον* 7. *βίβλος* 8. *βύβλος* 9. *λόγος* 10. liber
Gen 5: 1 This is the book of the generations of Adam. 2
Exd 17:14 Write this as a memorial in a book and recite it 2
24: 7 Then he took the book of the covenant, and read it 2
32:32 blot me . . out of thy book which thou hast 2
33 against me, him will I blot out of my book. 2
Num 5:23 the priest shall write these curses in a book 2
Deu 17:18 write for himself in a book a copy of this law 2
28:58 do all the words . . which are written in this book 2
61 which is not recorded in the book of this law 2
29:20 curses written in this book would settle upon 2
21 curses . . written in this book of the law. 2
27 bringing . . all the curses written in this book; 2
30:10 keep . . which are written in this book of the law 2
31:24 finished writing the words of this law in a book 2
26 Take this book of the law, and put it by the side 2
Jos 1: 8 This book of the law shall not depart 2
8:31 as it is written in the book of the law of Moses 2
34 to all that is written in the book of the law. 2
10:13 Is this not written in the Book of Jashar? 2
18: 9 the land and set down in a book a description of it 2
23: 6 all that is written in the book of the law of Moses 2
24:26 Joshua wrote these . . in the book of the law of God; 2
1Sm 10:25 he wrote them in a book and laid it up 2
2Sm 1:18 it is written in the Book of Jashar. He said 2
1Kg 11:41 not written in the book of the acts of Solomon? 2
14:19 the Book of the Chronicles of the Kings 2
29 written in the Book of the Chronicles 2
15: 7 the Book of the Chronicles of the Kings of Judah? 2
23 the Book of the Chronicles of the Kings of Judah? 2
31 the Book of the Chronicles of the Kings of Israel? 2
16: 5 the Book of the Chronicles of the Kings of Israel? 2
14 the Book of the Chronicles of the Kings of Israel? 2
20 the Book of the Chronicles of the Kings of Israel? 2

27 the Book of the Chronicles of the Kings of Israel? 2
22:39 the Book of the Chronicles of the Kings of Israel? 2
45 the Book of the Chronicles of the Kings of Judah? 2
2Kg 1:18 the Book of the Chronicles of the Kings of Israel? 2
8:23 the Book of the Chronicles of the Kings of Judah? 2
10:34 the Book of the Chronicles of the Kings of Israel? 2
12:19 the Book of the Chronicles of the Kings of Judah? 2
13: 8 the Book of the Chronicles of the Kings of Israel? 2
12 the Book of the Chronicles of the Kings of Israel? 2
14: 6 what is written in the book of the law of Moses 2
15 the Book of the Chronicles of the Kings of Israel? 2
18 the Book of the Chronicles of the Kings of Judah? 2
28 the Book of the Chronicles of the Kings of Israel? 2
15: 6 the Book of the Chronicles of the Kings of Judah? 2
11 the Book of the Chronicles of the Kings 2
15 the Book of the Chronicles of the Kings 2
21 the Book of the Chronicles of the Kings of Israel? 2
26 the Book of the Chronicles of the Kings 2
31 the Book of the Chronicles of the Kings 2
36 the Book of the Chronicles of the Kings of Judah? 2
16:19 the Book of the Chronicles of the Kings of Israel? 2
20:20 the Book of the Chronicles of the Kings of Judah? 2
21:17 the Book of the Chronicles of the Kings of Judah? 2
25 the Book of the Chronicles of the Kings of Judah? 2
22: 8 I have found the book of the law in the house 2
8 Hilki'ah gave the book to Shaphan, and he read it. 2
10 Hilki'ah the priest has given me a book. 2
11 the king heard the words of the book of the law 2
13 Go, inquire . . concerning the words of this book 2
13 fathers have not obeyed the words of this book 2
16 I will bring evil . . all the words of the book 2
23: 2 all the words of the book of the covenant 2
3 words of this covenant . . written in this book; 2
21 as it is written in this book of the covenant. 2
24 written in the book that Hilki'ah . . found 2
28 the Book of the Chronicles of the Kings of Judah? 2
24: 5 the Book of the Chronicles of the Kings of Judah? 2
1Ch 9: 1 written in the Book of the Kings of Israel. 2
2Ch 16:11 the Book of the Kings of Judah and Israel. 2
17: 9 taught . . having the book of the law of the LORD 2
20:34 are recorded in the Book of the Kings of Israel. 2
24:27 in the Commentary on the Book of the Kings. 2
25: 4 what is written . . in the book of Moses 2
26 are they not written in the Book of the Kings 2
27: 7 in the Book of the Kings of Israel and Judah. 2
28:26 behold, they are written in the Book of the Kings 2
32:32 in the Book of the Kings of Judah and Israel. 2
34:14 Hilki'ah . . found the book of the law of the LORD 2
15 found the book of the law in the house of the LORD"; 2
15 Hilki'ah gave the book to Shaphan. 2
16 Shaphan brought the book to the king 2
18 Hilki'ah the priest has given me a book. 2
21 inquire . . concerning the words of the book 2
21 do according to all that is written in this book. 2
24 all the curses that are written in the book 2
30 read . . all the words of the book of the covenant 2
31 the covenant that were written in this book. 2
35:12 as it is written in the book of Moses. 2
27 behold, they are written in the Book of the Kings 2
36: 8 Book of the Kings of Israel and Judah; 2
Ezr 4:15 search . . book of the records of your fathers. 2
15 You will find in the book of the records and learn 2
6:18 as it is written in the book of Moses. 5
Neh 7: 5 found the book of the genealogy of those who came 2
8: 1 Ezra . . to bring the book of the law of Moses 2
3 ears of all . . were attentive to the book of the law. 2
5 Ezra opened the book in the sight of all 2
8 read from the book, from the law of God, clearly 2
18 by day . . he read from the book of the law of God. 2
9: 3 read from the book of the law of the LORD their God 2
12:23 Levi . . written in the Book of the Chronicles 2
13: 1 read from the book of Moses in the hearing 2
Est 2:23 And it was recorded in the Book of the Chronicles 2
6: 1 gave orders to bring the book of memorable deeds 2
10: 2 written in the Book of the Chronicles 2
Job 19:23 Oh that they were inscribed in a book! 2
Ps 40: 7 Lo, I come; in the roll of the book it is written of me; 2
56: 8 my tears in thy bottle! Are they not in thy book? 3
69:28 Let them be blotted out of the book of the living; 2
139:16 thy book were written, every one of them, the days 2
Ecc 12:12 Of making many books there is no end 2
Isa 29:11 this has become to you like the words of a book 2
12 when they give the book to one who cannot read 2
18 In that day the deaf shall hear the words of a book 2
30: 8 inscribe it in a book 2
34:16 Seek and read from the book of the LORD 2
Jer 25:13 against it, everything written in this book 2
30: 2 Write in a book all the words that I have spoken 2
45: 1 words in a book at the dictation of Jeremiah 2
51:60 Jeremiah wrote in a book all the evil 2
63 When you finish reading this book 2
Dan 7:10 court sat in judgment, and the books were opened. 4
9: 2 perceived in the books the number of years 2
10:21 tell you what is inscribed in the book of truth 1
12: 1 every one whose name . . found written in the book. 2
4 Daniel, shut up the words, and seal the book 2
Nah 1: 1 The book of the vision of Nahum of Elkosh. 2
Mal 3:16 a book of remembrance was written before him 2
Mat 1: 1 The book of the genealogy of Jesus Christ 7
Mrk 12:26 have you not read in the book of Moses 7
Lke 3: 4 As it is written in the book of the words of Isaiah 7
4:17 was given to him the book of the prophet Isaiah. 6
17 He opened the book 6
20 he closed the book, and gave it back to the attendant 6
20:42 For David himself says in the Book of Psalms 7
Joh 20:30 which are not written in this book; 6
21:25 the books that would be written. 6
Act 1: 1 In the first book, O The-oph'ilus 9
20 it is written in the book of Psalms 7
7:42 as it is written in the book of the prophets 7
19:19 a number of those . . brought their books together 7
Gal 3:10 abide by all things written in the book of the law 6
Php 4: 3 whose names are in the book of life. 7
2Ti 4:13 also the books, and above all the parchments. 6
Heb 9:19 sprinkled both the book itself and all the people 6
10: 7 as it is written of me in the roll of the book. 6
Rev 1:11 saying, "Write what you see in a book and send it 6
3: 5 I will not blot his name out of the book of life; 7
13: 8 name has not been written . . in the book of life 6
17: 8 names have not been written in the book of life 6
20:12 I saw the dead . . and books were opened. 6
12 another book was opened, which is the book of life 6
12 another book was opened, which is the book of life *
12 dead were judged by what was written in the books 6
15 name was not found written in the book of life 6
21:27 only those . . written in the Lamb's book of life 6
22: 7 keeps the words of the prophecy of this book. 6
9 with those who keep the words of this book. 6
10 the words of the prophecy of this book 6
18 hears the words of the prophecy of this book 6
18 add to him the plagues described in this book 6
19 if any one takes away from the words of the book 6
19 the holy city, which are described in this book. 6
1Es 1:11 as it is written in the book of Moses 6
33 written in the book of the histories of the kings 8
33 recorded in the book of the kings of Israel 6
5:49 the directions in the book of Moses the man of God. 7
7: 6 what was written in the book of Moses. 7
9 in accordance with the book of Moses 7
9:45 Then Ezra took up the book of the law 6
2Es 1: 1 The second book of the prophet Ezra 10
6:20 the books shall be opened before the firmament 10
12:37 write all . . that you have seen in a book 10
14:44 during the 40 days 94 books were written. 10
45 Make public the 24 books that you wrote first *
Tob 1: 1 The book of the acts of Tobit the son of Tobiel 7
12:20 Write in a book everything that has happened. 6
Sir 0: 1 the prophets and the other books of our fathers, 6
2 the prophecies, and the rest of the books 6
3 to the translation of the following book, 7
3 in order to complete and publish the book 6
24:23 is the book of the covenant of the Most High God 7
50:27 I have written in this book 6
Bar 1: 1 These are the words of the book which Baruch 6
3 Baruch read the words of this book in the hearing 6
3 of all the people who came to hear the book 7
14 you shall read this book which we are sending you 6
4: 1 She is the book of the commandments of God 7
1Mc 1:56 The books of the law which they found 6
57 Where the book of the covenant was found 6
3:48 they opened the book of the law 6
12: 9 since we have as encouragement the holy books 6
2Mc 2:13 collected the books about the kings 6
14 the books that had been lost on account of the war *
23 we shall attempt to condense into a single book. 6
6:12 Now I urge those who read this book 7
8:23 to read aloud from the holy book 7

boor 1. *ἀφρός*

Sir 21:23 A boor peers into the house from the door 1

boot 1. סאן

Isa 9: 5 For every boot of the tramping warrior in battle 1

booth 1. סֻכָּה 2. שׂךְ 3. *σκηνή* 4. *σκηνοπηγία*

Gen 33:17 built . . a house, and made booths for his cattle; 1
Lev 23:34 for seven days is the feast of booths to the LORD 1
42 You shall dwell in booths for seven days 1
42 all . . in Israel shall dwell in booths 1
43 I made the people of Israel dwell in booths 1
Deu 16:13 You shall keep the feast of booths seven days 1
16 appear . . at . . the feast of booths. 1
31:10 year of release, at the feast of booths 1
2Sm 11:11 The ark and Israel and Judah dwell in booths; 1
1Kg 20:12 as he was drinking with the kings in the booths 1
16 was drinking himself drunk in the booths 1
Ezr 3: 4 kept the feast of booths, as it is written 1
Neh 8:14 Israel . . dwell in booths during the feast 1
15 branches . . to make booths, as it is written. 1
16 people . . made booths for themselves 1
17 assembly . . made booths and dwelt in the booths; 1
17 assembly . . made booths and dwelt in the booths; 1
Job 27:18 like a booth which a watchman makes. 1
Isa 1: 8 Zion is left like a booth in a vineyard 1
Lam 2: 6 He has broken down his booth like that of a garden 2
Ams 9:11 I will raise up the booth of David that is fallen 1
Jon 4: 5 east of the city, and made a booth for himself 1
Zec 14:16 to worship . . and to keep the feast of booths. 1
18 that do not go up to keep the feast of booths. 1
19 that do not go up to keep the feast of booths. 1
Mat 17: 4 if you wish, I will make three booths here 3
Mrk 9: 5 let us make three booths 3
Lke 9:33 let us make three booths 3
1Es 5:51 They kept the feast of booths 4
2Mc 1: 9 now see that you keep the feast of booths 4
10: 6 not long before, during the feast of booths 3

booth *See also* feast.

booty 1. בַּז 2. מַלְקוֹחַ 3. מְשִׁסָּה 4. פֶּרֶק 5. שָׁלָל 6. *ἔχω* 7. *λάφυρον* 8. *προνομή* 9. *σκῦλον* 10. *ὠφέλεια*

Num31:11 took all the spoil and all the booty, both of man 2
12 brought the captives and the booty and the spoil 2
26 Take the count of the booty that was taken 2
27 divide the booty into two parts 2
32 Now the booty remaining of the spoil 2
Deu 2:35 cattle we took . . with the booty of the cities 5
2Ch 14:13 The men of Judah carried away very much booty. 5
Jer 49:32 Their camels shall become booty 1
Nah 3: 1 Woe to the bloody city, all full of lies and booty 4
Hab 2: 7 Then you will be booty for them. 3
Jdt 4:12 not to give up . . their wives as booty 8
9: 4 their booty to be divided among thy beloved sons 9
15: 7 the Israelites . . got a great amount of booty 7
LJr 1:58 and go off with this booty 6
1Mc 10:87 returned to Jerusalem with much booty. 9
2Mc 8:20 destroyed 120,000 and took much booty. 10

booty *See also* take.

border 1. גְּבוּל 2. גְּבוּלָה 3. יָד 4. יַרְכָה 5. לְבוֹא 6. פֵּאָה 7. קָצֶה 8. קָצוּ 9. שָׂפָה 10. תּוֹצָאָה 11. *ὅριον* 12. *συγκυρόω* 13. finis 14. terminus

Gen 14: 6 far as El-paran on the border of the wilderness; *
49:13 and his border shall be at Sidon. 4
Exd 16:35 they came to the border of the land of Canaan. 7
19:12 do not . . touch the border of it; 7
34:24 For I will . . enlarge your borders; 1
Lev 19: 9 you shall not reap your field to its very border 6
23:22 you shall not reap your field to its very border 6
Num20:23 Mount Hor, on the border of the land of Edom 1
21:15 extends to the seat of Ar, and leans to the border 1
Deu 3:14 as far as the border of the Gesh'urites 1
19: 8 if the LORD your God enlarges your border 1
Jos 4:19 in Gilgal on the east border of Jericho. 7
13:23 the border of the people of Reuben was the Jordan 1
17:18 clear it and possess it to its farthest borders; 10
18:16 boundary goes down to the border of the mountain 7
19 the boundary . . this is the southern border. 1
Jdg 1:36 the border of the Amorites ran from the ascent 1
7:22 as far as the border of A'bel-meho'lah, by Tabbath. 9
1Sm 6:12 after them as far as the border of Beth-she'mesh 1
13:18 and another company turned toward the border 1
27: 1 of seeking me . . within the borders of Israel 1
1Kg 4:21 the Euphra'tes to . . and to the border of Egypt; 1
2Kg 14:25 He restored the border of Israel 1
1Ch 4:10 saying, "Oh that thou wouldst . . enlarge my border 1
6:54 their settlements within their borders 1
7:29 also along the borders of the Manas'sites 3
2Ch 9:26 he ruled . . and to the border of Egypt. 1
26: 8 his fame spread even to the border of Egypt 5
Ps 147:14 He makes peace in your borders; he fills you 1
Isa 19:19 of Egypt, and a pillar to the LORD at its border. 1
26:15 thou hast enlarged all the borders of the land. 8
28:25 barley in its . . place, and spelt as the border? 2
60:18 or destruction within your borders; 1
Ezk 11:10 I will judge you at the border of Israel; 1
11 I will judge you at the border of Israel; 1
27: 4 Your borders are in the heart of the seas; 1
29:10 to Syene, as far as the border of Ethiopia. 1
47:16 which lies on the border between Damascus 1
16 Hazer-hatticon, which is on the border of Hauran. 1
17 which is on the northern border of Damascus 1
17 Damascus, with the border of Hamath to the north. 1
48: 1 Beginning at the northern border, from the sea 7
1 Hazar-e'non (which is on the northern border 1
21 cubits of the holy portion to the east border 1
21 from the 25,000 cubits to the west border 1
Jol 3: 6 removing them far from their own border. 1
Ams 1:13 in Gilead, that they might enlarge their border. 1
Obd 1: 7 deceived you, they have driven you to the border; 1
Mic 5: 6 into our land and treads within our border. 1
Zec 9: 2 Hamath also, which borders thereon 1
Mal 1: 5 Great is the LORD, beyond the border of Israel! 1
2Es 9: 8 in my land and within my borders 13
12:34 those who have been saved throughout my borders 13
13:48 who are found within my holy borders 14
Jdt 1: 5 the great plain which is on the borders of Ragae. 11
10 as far as the borders of Ethiopia. 11
2:25 came to the southern borders of Japheth 11
14: 4 you and all who live within the borders of Israel 11
15: 5 even beyond Damascus and its borders. 11
1Mc 2:46 that they found within the borders of Israel. 11
3:32 from the river Euphrates to the borders of Egypt. 11
5:60 were pursued to the borders of Judea 11
11:34 with all the region bordering them 12
59 from the Ladder of Tyre to the borders of Egypt. 11

14: 6 He extended the borders of his nation 11
33 Beth-zur on the borders of Judea 11
34 Gazara, which is on the borders of Azotus 11
15:30 outside the borders of Judea; 11

border *See also* along, land.

bore 1. נקב
2Kg 12: 9 took a chest, and bored a hole in the lid of it 1

bore through 1. רצע
Exd 21: 6 his master shall bore his ear through with an awl; 1

born in one's house 1. *οἰκογενής*
1Es 3: 1 all that were born in his house 1

borrow 1. לוה 2. נשה 3. עבט 4. שאל 5. *δανείζω*
Exd 22:14 If a man borrows anything of his neighbor, and it 4
Deu 15: 6 lend to many nations, but you shall not borrow; 3
28:12 lend to many nations, but you shall not borrow. 1
2Kg 4: 3 Go outside, borrow vessels of all your neighbors 4
6: 5 he cried out, "Alas, my master! It was borrowed. 4
Neh 5: 4 We have borrowed money for the king's tax 1
Ps 37:21 The wicked borrows, and cannot pay back 1
Jer 15:10 I have not lent, nor have I borrowed 2
Mat 5:42 do not refuse him who would borrow from you. 5
Wis 15:16 one whose spirit is borrowed formed them 5

borrow money 1. *δανεισμός*
Sir 18:33 become a beggar by feasting with borrowed money 1

borrower 1. לוה
Prv 22: 7 borrower is the slave of the lender. 1
Isa 24: 2 as with the lender, so with the borrower; 1
Sir 29: 6 the borrower has robbed him of his money *

bosom 1. דַּד 2. חֹב 3. חֵיק 4. חֹצֶן 5. חֵצֶן 6. *κόλπος* 7. sinus
Exd 4: 6 LORD said to him, "Put your hand into your bosom. 3
6 he put his hand into his bosom; and when he took it 3
7 Then God said, "Put your hand back into your bosom. 3
7 So he put his hand back into his bosom; 3
Num11:12 Carry them in your bosom, as a nurse carries 3
Deu 13: 6 If . . the wife of your bosom, . . , entices you 3
28:54 man . . grudge food to . . the wife of his bosom 3
56 woman . . will grudge to the husband of her bosom 3
Rut 4:16 Na'omi took the child and laid him in her bosom 3
2Sm 12: 3 and drink from his cup, and lie in his bosom 3
8 I gave . . and your master's wives into your bosom 3
1Kg 1: 2 let her lie in your bosom, that . . the king may be 3
3:20 took my son . . and laid it in her bosom, and laid 3
20 in her bosom, and laid her dead son in my bosom. 3
17:19 And he took him from her bosom, and carried him up 3
Job 23:12 treasured in my bosom the words of his mouth. 3
31:33 from men, by hiding my iniquity in my bosom 2
Ps 35:13 I prayed with head bowed on my bosom 3
74:11 why dost thou keep thy right hand in thy bosom? 3
79:12 sevenfold into the bosom of our neighbors 3
89:50 how I bear in my bosom the insults of the peoples 3
129: 7 binder of sheaves his bosom 5
Prv 5:20 Why . . embrace the bosom of an adventuress? 3
6:27 Can a man carry fire in his bosom 3
17:23 A wicked man accepts a bribe from the bosom 3
21:14 bribe in the bosom, strong wrath. 3
Ecc 7: 9 for anger lodges in the bosom of fools. 3
Isa 40:11 he will carry them in his bosom 3
49:22 and they shall bring your sons in their bosom 4
65: 6 I will repay, yea, I will repay into their bosom 3
7 I will measure into their bosom payment 3
Lam 2:12 their life is poured out on their mothers' bosom. 3
Ezk 23: 3 and their virgin bosoms handled. 1
8 had lain with her and handled her virgin bosom 1
21 when the Egyptians handled your bosom 1
Mic 7: 5 your mouth from her who lies in your bosom; 3
Lke 16:22 and was carried by the angels to Abraham's bosom 6
23 and saw Abraham far off and Laz'arus in his bosom. 6
Joh 1:18 the only Son, who is in the bosom of the Father 6
2Es 15:21 so I will do, and will repay into their bosom 7
55 The reward of a harlot is in your bosom 7
Sir 9: 1 Do not be jealous of the wife of your bosom 6

bosom *See also* friend.

both 1. בְּאֶחָד 2. גַּם 3. גַּם שְׁנַיִם 4. וְ 5. יַחְדָּו 6. כֵּן 7. מִן 8. עִם 9. שְׁנַיִם 10. *ἀμφότερος* 11. *ἄμφω* 12. *ἀπό* 13. *δύο* 14. *ἑκάτερος* 15. *καί* 16. *κοινῶς* 17. *τε* 18. et 19. uterque
Gen 2:25 the man and his wife were both naked 9
3: 7 the eyes of both were opened 9
9:23 garment, laid it upon both their shoulders 9
13: 6 that the land could not support both of them *
17:13 both he that is born in your house *
19: 4 the men of Sodom, both young and old †
11 the men . . both small and great †
36 Thus both the daughters of Lot were with child 9
21:31 because there both of them swore an oath. 9
22: 6 they went both of them together. 9
8 So they went both of them together. 9
24:25 We have both straw and provender enough 2
27:45 Why should I be bereft of you both in one day? 9
34:30 I shall be destroyed, both I and my household. *
40: 5 one night they both dreamed 9
43: 8 live and not die, both we and you and also our 2
44:16 we are . . slaves, both we and he also in whose hand 2
46:34 keepers of cattle . . both we and our fathers,' 2
47:19 Why should we die . . both we and our land? 2
48:13 Joseph took them both, E'phraim in his right hand 9
50: 9 went up with him both chariots and horsemen; 2
Exd 7:19 both in vessels of wood and in vessels of stone.' *
9:25 struck . . both man and beast; and the hail struck *
12:12 smite all . . both man and beast; †
31 go forth . . both you and the people of Israel; 2
38 and very many cattle, both flocks and herds. *
13: 2 first to open the womb . . both of man and of beast *
15 LORD slew . . both the first-born of man †
22: 9 the case of both parties shall come before God; 9
11 an oath by the LORD shall be between them both 9
26:24 thus shall it be with both of them; 9
32:15 tables that were written on both sides; 9
35:22 So they came, both men and women; *
34 he has inspired him to teach, both him and Oho'liab *
Lev 9: 2 ram for a burnt offering, both without blemish *
3 calf and a lamb, both a year old without blemish *
15:18 both of them shall bathe themselves in water *
16:21 Aaron shall lay both his hands upon the head 9
20:10 both the adulterer and the adulteress shall be *
11 both of them shall be put to death 9
12 both of them shall be put to death 9
13 both of them have committed an abomination 9
14 they shall be burned with fire, both he *
18 both of them shall be cut off 9
21:22 He may eat the bread . . both of the most holy *
22:28 you shall not kill both her and her young *
27:10 then both it and that for which it is exchanged *
33 then both it and that for which it is exchanged *
Num 3:13 first-born in Israel, both of man and of beast; *
5: 3 you shall put out both male and female *
7:13 both of them full of fine flour mixed with oil 9
19 both of them full of fine flour mixed with oil 9
25 both of them full of fine flour mixed with oil 9
31 both of them full of fine flour mixed with oil 9
37 both of them full of fine flour mixed with oil 9
43 both of them full of fine flour mixed with oil 9
49 both of them full of fine flour mixed with oil 9
55 both of them full of fine flour mixed with oil 9
61 both of them full of fine flour mixed with oil 9
67 both of them full of fine flour mixed with oil 9
73 both of them full of fine flour mixed with oil 9
79 both of them full of fine flour mixed with oil 9
8:17 first-born . . are mine, both of man and of beast; *
9:14 both for the sojourner and for the native. *
10: 3 when both are blown, all the congregation *
12: 5 Aaron and Miriam; and they both came forward. 9
20: 4 that we should die here, both we and our cattle? *
25: 8 pierced both of them . . through her body. 9
27:21 both he and all the people of Israel with him *
31:11 spoil and all the booty, both of man and of beast. *
26 count of the booty . . both of man and of beast *
47 one of every 50, both of persons and of beasts *
Deu 19:17 then both parties to the dispute shall appear 9
21:15 borne him children, both the loved and the disliked *
22:22 both of them shall die, the man . . and the woman; 2
24 shall bring them both out to the gate of that city 9
23:18 both . . are an abomination to the LORD your God. 9
29:11 both he who hews your wood and he who draws *
32:25 destroying both young man and virgin *
Jos 6:21 all in the city, both men and women, young and old †
8:25 both men and women, were 12,000 †
17:16 all the Canaanites . . both those in Beth-she'an *
Jdg 6: 5 both they and their camels could not be counted; 4
19: 8 until the day declines." So they ate, both of them. 9
Rut 1: 5 and both Mahlon and Chil'ion died 3
1Sm 2:26 continued to grow both in stature and in favor 4
34 the sign . . both of them shall die on the same day. 9
5: 4 head of Dagon and both his hands were . . cut off 9
6 and afflicted . . both Ashdod and its territory. *
9 afflicted the men of the city, both young and old *
6:18 all the cities . . both fortified cities 7
9:26 Saul arose, and both he and Samuel went out 9
12:14 if both you and the king . . will follow the LORD 2
25 you shall be swept away, both you and your king. 2
14:11 both of them showed themselves to the garrison 9
15: 3 do not spare them, but kill both man and woman 7
17:36 Your servant has killed both lions and bears; 2
20:11 they both went out into the field. 9
42 we have sworn both of us in the name of the LORD 9
22:19 both men and women, children and sucklings, oxen *
25:16 they were a wall to us both by night and by day 2
43 and both of them became his wives. 3
30: 2 taken . . all who were in it, both small and great; *
2Sm 6:19 the whole multitude of Israel, both men and women †
9:13 Now he was lame in both his feet. 9
10: 9 was set against him both in front and in the rear *
15:25 he will . . let me see both it and his habitation; *
16:23 so was . . esteemed, both by David and by Ab'salom. 2
17:18 so both of them went away quickly 9
19:14 Return, both you and all your servants. *
1Kg 3:13 what you have not asked, both riches and honor 2
6: 5 the house, both the nave and the inner sanctuary; *
25 both cherubim had the same measure and . . form. 9
7:29 both above and below the lions and oxen 6
14:10 cut off . . every male, both bond and free in Israel *
16: 7 word of the LORD came . . both because of all 4
2Kg 2: 7 they both were standing by the Jordan. 9
23: 2 all the people, both small and great; †
25:26 all the people, both small and great . . arose †
1Ch 7:24 who built both Lower and Upper Beth-hor'on *
12: 3 Ahi-e'zer, then Jo'ash, both sons of Shema'ah *
16: 3 distributed to all Israel, both men and women †
19:10 the battle was set against him both in front *
24: 5 officers . . among both the sons of Elea'zar *
29:12 Both riches and honor come from thee *
2Ch 24:14 both for the service and for the burnt offerings *
26:10 he had large herds, both in the Shephe'lah *
32:26 both he and the inhabitants of Jerusalem *
34:30 all the people both great and small; †
Neh 8: 2 assembly, both men and women and all who could *
12:40 both companies of those who gave thanks stood 9
Est 1: 5 all . . in Susa the capital, both great and small †
2:23 the men were both hanged on the gallows. 9
9:20 all the provinces of . . both near and far *
Job 9:22 he destroys both the blameless and the wicked. *
33 no umpire . . who might lay his hand upon us both. 9
15:10 Both the gray-haired and the aged are among us 2
Ps 4: 8 In peace I will both lie down and sleep; 5
49: 2 both low and high, rich and poor together! 2
76: 6 O God of Jacob, both rider and horse lay stunned. *
104:25 living things both small and great. 8
106: 6 Both we and our fathers have sinned; 8
115:13 bless . . who fear the LORD, both small and great. 8
135: 8 smote the first-born . . both of man and of beast; †
Prv 17:15 both alike an abomination to the LORD. 9
20:10 both alike an abomination to the LORD. 9
12 ear and the . . eye, the LORD has made them both. 9
24:22 who knows the ruin that will come from them both? 9
27: 3 but a fool's provocation is heavier than both. 9
29:13 LORD gives light to the eyes of both. 9
Ecc 2: 8 I got singers, both men and women *
4: 3 better than both is he who has not yet been 9
11: 6 do not know . . or whether both alike will be good. 9
Isa 1:31 both of them shall burn together 9
8:14 a rock of stumbling to both houses of Israel 9
10:18 the LORD will destroy, both soul and body †
20: 4 exiles, both the young and the old, naked *
Jer 4: 9 courage shall fail both king and princes; *
6:11 both husband and wife shall be taken 2
9:10 both the birds of the air and the beasts have fled *
10: 8 They are both stupid and foolish; 1
14:18 For both prophet and priest ply their trade 2
16: 6 Both great and small shall die in this land; *
21: 6 the inhabitants of this city, both man and beast; *
23:11 Both prophet and priest are ungodly; 2
32:14 both this sealed deed of purchase and this open *
44:17 as we did, both we and our fathers *
46:12 they have both fallen together. 9
50: 3 both man and beast shall flee away. †
51:12 the LORD has both planned and done what he spoke 2
Ezk 15: 4 when the fire has consumed both ends of it 9
16:53 both the fortunes of Sodom and her daughters *
61 your sisters, both your elder and your younger *
21: 3 will cut off from you both righteous and wicked. *
4 I will cut off from you both righteous and wicked *
19 both of them shall come forth from the same land. 9
23:13 that she was defiled; they both took the same way. 9
30:22 both the strong arm and the one that was broken; *
45: 7 to the prince shall belong the land on both sides †
47:12 And on the banks, on both sides of the river †
48:21 What remains on both sides of the holy portion †
Dan 8: 3 both horns were high, but one was higher †
9:24 seal both vision and prophet, *
Zec 5: 4 his house and consume it, both timber and stones. *
6:13 understanding shall be between them both. 9
Mat 9:17 and so both are preserved. 10
10:28 rather fear him who can destroy both soul and body 15
13:30 Let both grow together until the harvest 10
15:14 both will fall into a pit. 10
22:10 gathered all whom they found, both bad and good; 17
Lke 1: 6 they were both righteous before God 10
7 both were advanced in years. 10
5: 7 they came and filled both the boats 10
6:39 Will they not both fall into a pit? 10
7:42 When they could not pay, he forgave them both. 10
14: 9 he who invited you both will come and say to you *
22:66 both chief priests and scribes 17
Joh 11:48 and destroy both our holy place and our nation. 15
15:24 they have seen and hated both me and my Father. 15
20: 4 They both ran 13
Act 2:10 visitors from Rome, both Jews and proselytes 17
29 he both died and was buried 15
36 God has made him both Lord and Christ 15
4:27 both Herod and Pontius Pilate, with the Gentiles 17
5:14 multitudes both of men and women 17
7:35 God sent as both ruler and deliverer 15
8:12 they were baptized, both men and women. 17
38 both went down into the water 10
10:39 both in the country of the Jews and in Jerusalem. 17
14: 1 a great company . . both of Jews and of Greeks. 17
5 an attempt was made by both Gentiles and Jews 17

15: 3 they passed through both Phoeni'cia and Sama'ria 17
23 The brethren, both the apostles and the elders •
19:10 both Jews and Greeks. 17
17 all residents of Ephesus, both Jews and Greeks 17
20:21 testifying both to Jews and to Greeks 17
22: 4 delivering to prison both men and women 17
24:15 a resurrection of both the just and the unjust. 17
25:24 both at Jerusalem and here 17
26:22 I stand here testifying both to small and great 17
23 both to the people and to the Gentiles 17
28:23 both from the law of Moses and from the prophets. 17
Rom 1:12 by each other's faith, both yours and mine. 17
14 obligation both to Greeks and to barbarians 17
14 both to the wise and to the foolish 17
3: 9 all men, both Jews and Greeks, are under . . sin 17
14: 9 be Lord both of the dead and of the living. 15
1Co 1: 2 Lord Jesus Christ, both their Lord and ours •
24 to those who are called, both Jews and Greeks 17
6:13 God will destroy both one and the other 15
Eph 2:14 For he is our peace, who has made us both one 10
16 might reconcile us both to God in one body 10
18 for through him we both have access in one Spirit 10
6: 9 he who is both their Master and yours is in heaven 15
Php 1: 7 both in my imprisonment and in the defense 17
2:13 both to will and to work for his good pleasure. 15
1Th 2:15 who killed both the Lord Jesus and the prophets 15
1Ti 4:16 you will save both yourself and your hearers. 15
Phm 1:16 both in the flesh and in the Lord. 15
Heb 9:19 sprinkled both the book itself and all the people 17
21 both the tent and all the vessels used in worship. 15
2Pe 3: 1 in both of them I have aroused your sincere mind •
18 glory both now and to the day of eternity. Amen. 15
2Jn 1: 9 he who abides . . has both the Father and the Son. 15
Rev 11:18 those who fear thy name, both small and great •
13:16 all, both small and great, both rich and poor •
16 all, both small and great, both rich and poor 15
16 both rich and poor, both free and slave 15
19:18 and the flesh of all men, both free and slave 15
18 and the flesh of all men . . both small and great. 15
1Es 2:22 troubling both kings and other cities 15
6:26 the holy vessels . . both of gold and of silver 17
8:14 both gold and silver for bulls and rams and lambs 17
9:41 in the presence of both men and women 17
2Es 6:50 the seventh part . . could not hold them both. •
8: 9 which is kept shall both be kept by thy keeping. 19
9:19 which is supplied both with an unfailing table 18
Tob 3:16 The prayer of both was heard 11
5:15 if you both return safe and sound •
16 and good success to you both •
16 they both went out and departed 11
6: 5 they both continued on their way 11
17 when you approach her, rise up, both of you 11
7:12 The merciful God will guide you both for the best. •
8: 9 Then they both went to sleep for the night. 11
13 went in, and found them both asleep. 13
9: 6 In the morning they both got up early 16
11: 9 now I am ready to die." And they both wept. 11
12:16 They were both alarmed 13
Jdt 4: 2 alarmed both for Jerusalem and for the temple 15
13:13 They all ran together, both small and great 12
AEs 11: 6 great dragons came forward, both ready to fight 10
16:16 both for us and for our fathers 17
23 both now and hereafter it may mean salvation 15
Wis 4: 1 because it is known both by God and by men. 15
6: 7 because he himself made both small and great •
7:16 For both we and our words are in his hand 15
21 both what is secret and what is manifest 17
15: 7 both the vessels that serve clean uses 17
19 escaped both the praise of God and his blessing 15
18: 9 the same things, both blessings and dangers 15
Sir 0: 1 help the outsiders by both speaking and writing, 15
5: 6 both mercy and wrath are with him •
10: 7 injustice is outrageous to both. 11
18:17 Both are to be found in a gracious man. 11
20:25 the lot of both is ruin. 11
22: 5 will be despised by both. 11
28:12 both come out of your mouth. 11
40: 8 With all flesh, both man and beast 12
18 he who finds treasure is better off than both. 11
19 a blameless wife is accounted better than both. 11
20 the love of wisdom is better than both. 11
21 a pleasant voice is better than both. 11
22 the green shoots of grain more than both. 11
23 a wife with her husband is better than both. 11
24 almsgiving rescues better than both. 11
25 good counsel is esteemed more than both. 11
26 the fear of the Lord is better than both 11
Sus 1:10 Both were overwhelmed with passion for her 10
57 This is how you both have been dealing •
59 saw you in two, that he may destroy you both. •
1Mc 1:16 that he might reign over both kingdoms. 13
6:26 have fortified both the sanctuary and Beth-zur; 15
11:34 both the territory . . and the three districts 17
12:11 both in our feasts and on other appropriate days 17
2Mc 4: 5 the welfare, both public and private, of all the people •
5:15 a traitor both to the laws and to his country. 15
8:19 both the time of Sennacherib 15
14:46 he tore out his entrails, took them with both hands 14
3Mc 1: 1 all his forces, both infantry and cavalry 17
2:23 both friends and bodyguards . . dragged him out 17
3:21 both because of their alliance with us 17
21 both to deem them worthy of . . citizenship 15
23 both by speech and by silence 17
4:20 both the paper and the pens they used for writing 15
6:30 both wines and everything else 17
4Mc 1:20 by nature concerned with both body and soul. 15
21 The emotions of both pleasure and pain 15
32 reason obviously rules over both. 11
3:20 had both appropriated money to them 15
12:18 he will take vengeance both in this present life 15
13: 4 the brothers mastered both emotions and pains. 15
22 both general education and our discipline 15
15: 4 a wondrous likeness both of mind and of form. 17
18: 5 The tyrant Antiochus was both punished on earth 15

both *See also* parties, sides.

bother 1. *κόπον παρέχω*

Lke 11: 7 he will answer from within, 'Do not bother me 1
18: 5 yet because this widow bothers me 1

bottle 1. נֹאד 2. *ἀσκοπυτίνη* 3. *ἀσκός*

Ps 33: 7 He gathered the waters of the sea as in a bottle; 3
56: 8 put thou my tears in thy bottle! 1
Jdt 10: 5 gave her maid a bottle of wine and a flask of oil 2

bottom 1. חֵיק 2. קַרְקַע 3. תַּחַת 4. אַרְעִי (A) 5. *κάτω* 6. *ὅλος*

1Kg 22:35 blood . . flowed into the bottom of the chariot. 1
Ezk 46:23 with hearths made at the bottom of the rows 3
Dan 6:24 before they reached the bottom of the den 4
Ams 9: 3 they hide from my sight at the bottom of the sea 2
Mat 27:51 torn in two, from top to bottom 5
Mrk 15:38 torn in two, from top to bottom. 5
Joh 19:23 tunic was without seam, woven from top to bottom; 6

bottomless pit 1. *ἄβυσσος*

Rev 9: 1 given the key of the shaft of the bottomless pit; 1
2 he opened the shaft of the bottomless pit 1
11 as king over them the angel of the bottomless pit; 1
11: 7 the beast that ascends from the bottomless pit 1
17: 8 The beast . . is to ascend from the bottomless pit 1
20: 1 holding in his hand the key of the bottomless pit 1

bough 1. בֵּן 2. סְעַפָּה 3. סַרְעַפָּה 4. עָנָף 5. פֹּארָה 6. פֻּארָה 7. קָצִיר 8. שֵׁבֶט 9. *κλάδος*

Gen 49:22 Joseph is a fruitful bough 1
22 Joseph is . . a fruitful bough by a spring; 1
Lev 23:40 take . . boughs of leafy trees, and willows 4
Isa 10:33 will lop the boughs with terrifying power; 6
27:11 When its boughs are dry, they are broken; 7
Ezk 17:23 that it may bring forth boughs and bear fruit 4
19:11 it towered aloft among the thick boughs; 8
31: 5 its boughs grew large and its branches long 3
6 birds of the air made their nests in its boughs; 2
8 not rival it, nor the fir trees equal its boughs; 2
12 its boughs will lie broken 5
Wis 4: 4 For even if they put forth boughs for a while 9
Sir 14:26 will camp under her boughs; 9

bough *See also* go, lop.

high bough 1. אָמִיר

Isa 17: 6 three berries in the top of the highest bough 1

bound 1. גְּבוּל 2. גְּבוּלָה 3. חֵל 4. חֹק 5. קפץ 6. רקד 7. תַּכְלִית

Exd 23:31 I will set your bounds from the Red Sea to the sea 1
Num35:26 go beyond the bounds of his city of refuge 1
27 outside the bounds of his city of refuge 1
Deu 32: 8 he fixed the bounds of the peoples according 2
Jdg 2: 9 buried him within the bounds of his inheritance 1
1Kg 21:23 The dogs shall eat Jez'ebel within the bounds 3
Job 14: 5 hast appointed his bounds that he cannot pass 4
28: 3 search out to the farthest bound the ore in gloom 7
38:10 prescribed bounds for it, and set bars and doors 4
Ps 74:17 Thou hast fixed all the bounds of the earth; 1
104: 9 Thou didst set a bound which they should not pass 1
148: 6 he fixed their bounds which cannot be passed. 4
Sng 2: 8 he comes, leaping . . bounding over the hills. 5
Jer 5:22 I placed the sand as the bound for the sea 1
Hos 4: 2 they break all bounds and murder follows murder. •
Nah 3: 2 galloping horse and bounding chariot! 6

bound *See also* know, set.

far bound 1. קָצָת

Ps 65: 8 those who dwell at earth's farthest bounds 1

boundary 1. גְּבוּל 2. גְּבוּלָה 3. חֹק 4. תַּכְלִית 5. *ὁροθεσία*

Num21:13 extends from the boundary of the Amorites; 1
13 Arnon is the boundary of Moab 1
24 for Jazer was the boundary of the Ammonites. 1
22:36 city of Moab, on the boundary formed by the Arnon 1
36 at the city . . at the extremity of the boundary. 1
34: 3 your southern boundary shall be from the end 1
4 your boundary shall turn south of the ascent 1
5 boundary shall turn from Azmon to the Brook 1
6 western boundary, you shall have the Great Sea 1
6 Sea and its coast . . your western boundary. 1
7 your northern boundary: from the Great Sea 1
8 end of the boundary shall be at Zeded; 1
9 then the boundary shall extend to Ziphron 1
9 this shall be your northern boundary. 1
10 You shall mark out your eastern boundary 1
11 the boundary shall go down from Shepham to Riblah 1
11 boundary shall go down, and reach to the shoulder 1
12 boundary shall go down to the Jordan, and its end 1
12 your land with its boundaries all round. 2
Deu 2:18 day you are to pass over the boundary of Moab at Ar; 1
3:16 with the middle of the valley as a boundary 1
16 river Jabbok, the boundary of the Ammonites; 1
17 the Arabah also, with the Jordan as the boundary 1
Jos 12: 2 the river Jabbok, the boundary of the Ammonites 1
5 and all Bashan to the boundary of the Gesh'urites 1
5 Gilead to the boundary of Sihon king of Heshbon. 1
13: 3 from . . northward to the boundary of Ekron 1
4 to Aphek, to the boundary of the Amorites 1
10 cities . . as far as the boundary of the Ammonites; 1
23 the border . . was the Jordan as a boundary. 1
27 the kingdom of . . having the Jordan as a boundary 1
15: 1 lot . . reached southward to the boundary of Edom 1
2 south boundary ran from the end of the Salt Sea 1
4 This shall be your south boundary. 1
5 the east boundary is the Salt Sea 1
5 the boundary on the north side runs from the bay 1
6 the boundary goes up to Beth-hoglah, and passes 1
6 and the boundary goes up to the stone of Bohan 1
7 and the boundary goes up to Debir from the Valley 1
7 and the boundary passes along to . . En-she'mesh 1
8 then the boundary goes up by the valley of the son 1
8 and the boundary goes up to the top 1
9 boundary extends from the top of the mountain 1
9 then the boundary bends round to Ba'alah 1
10 the boundary circles west of Ba'alah to . . Se'ir 1
11 the boundary goes out to the shoulder of the hill 1
11 then the boundary bends round to Shik'keron 1
11 then the boundary comes to an end at the sea. 1
12 And the west boundary was the Great Sea with its 1
12 This is the boundary round about the people 1
21 in the extreme South, toward the boundary of Edom 1
16: 5 the boundary of their inheritance on the east was 1
6 and the boundary goes thence to the sea; 1
6 the boundary turns round toward Ta'anath-shi'loh 1
8 the boundary goes westward to the brook Kanah 1
17: 7 then the boundary goes along southward 1
8 Tap'puah on the boundary of Manas'seh belonged 1
9 Then the boundary went down to the brook Kanah. 1
9 the boundary of Manas'seh goes on the north side 1
10 Manas'seh's, with the sea forming its boundary; 1
18:12 their boundary began at the Jordan; 1
12 the boundary goes up the shoulder north 1
13 From there the boundary passes along southward 1
13 then the boundary goes down to At'aroth-ad'dar 1
14 Then the boundary goes in another direction 1
15 and the boundary goes from there to Ephron 1
16 then the boundary goes down to the border 1
19 the boundary passes on to the north 1
19 the boundary ends at the northern bay of the Salt 1
19:11 its boundary goes up westward, and on to Mar'eal 1
12 eastward . . to the boundary of Chis'loth-ta'bor; 1
14 the boundary turns about to Han'nathon 1
22 the boundary also touches Tabor, Shahazu'mah 1
22 and its boundary ends at the Jordan 1
29 then the boundary turns to Ramah, reaching 1
29 the boundary turns to Hosah, and it ends at the sea; 1
33 its boundary ran from Heleph, from the oak 1
34 the boundary turns westward to Az'noth-tabor 1
22:25 the LORD has made . . a boundary between us and you 1
Jdg 11:18 for the Arnon was the boundary of Moab 1
Job 26:10 at the boundary between light and darkness. 4
Prv 15:25 but maintains the widow's boundaries. 1
Isa 10:13 I have removed the boundaries of peoples 1
Ezk 45: 7 the western to the eastern boundary of the land. 1
47:13 boundaries by which you shall divide the land 1
15 This shall be the boundary of the land 1
17 the boundary shall run from the sea to Hazar-e'non 1
18 the boundary shall run from Hazar-e'non 1
20 the Great Sea shall be the boundary to a point 1
48:28 the boundary shall run from Tamar to the waters 1
Mic 7:11 In that day the boundary shall be far extended. 3
Act 17:26 the boundaries of their habitation 5

boundary *See also* boundary, form.

boundary by boundary 1. לִגְבוּלֹת

Jos 18:20 This is the inheritance . . boundary by boundary 1

boundless 1. *ἀμέτρητος* 2. *ἀπέραντος*

Sir 16:17 what is my soul in the boundless creation? 1
3Mc 2: 4 by bringing upon them a boundless flood. 1
9 created the boundless and immeasurable earth 2

bountiful 1. טוֹב 2. *χορηγός* 3. munificus

Prv 22: 9 He who has a bountiful eye will be blessed 1
2Es 7:135 bountiful, because he would rather give 3
2Mc 1:25 who alone art bountiful 2

bountifully 1. ἐπ' εὐλογίαις
2Co 9: 6 he who sows bountifully will also reap 1
6 sows bountifully will also reap bountifully. 1

bountifully *See also* deal.

bounty 1. טוֹבָה 2. יָד 3. תַּאֲוָה 4. תַּגְמוּל 5. δωρεά
Gen 49:26 beyond . . the bounties of the everlasting 3
1Kg 10:13 what was given her by the bounty of King Solomon. 2
Est 1: 7 wine was . . according to the bounty of the king. 2
Ps 65:11 Thou crownest the year with thy bounty; 1
116:12 What shall I render to the LORD for all his bounty 4
Wis 16:25 it served thy all-nourishing bounty 5

bow 1. יטה 2. ירד 3. כפף 4. כרע 5. מֵיתָר 6. נטה 7. קדד 8. שחה 9. שחח 10. κάμπτω 11. κλίνω
Gen 18: 2 he ran . . and bowed himself to the earth 8
19: 1 and bowed himself with his face to the earth 8
23: 7 Abraham rose and bowed to the Hittites 8
24:52 heard their words, he bowed himself to the earth 8
33: 3 He himself went on before them, bowing himself 8
37:10 brothers indeed come to bow ourselves 8
42: 6 brothers came, and bowed themselves before him 8
47:31 Israel bowed himself upon the head of his bed. 8
48:12 he bowed himself with his face to the earth. 8
49:15 he bowed his shoulder to bear 1
Num22:31 he bowed his head, and fell on his face. 7
Jdg 16:30 Then he bowed with all his might; and the house 1
Rut 2:10 she fell on her face, bowing to the ground, and said 8
1Sm 4:19 she bowed and gave birth; for her pains came 4
20:41 David rose from beside . . and bowed three times; 8
24: 8 David bowed with his face to the earth 7
25:23 and fell before David . . and bowed to the ground. 8
41 And she rose and bowed with her face to the ground 8
28:14 Saul . . bowed with his face to the ground 7
2Sm 14:33 and bowed himself on his face to the ground 8
18:21 The Cushite bowed before Jo'ab, and ran. 8
28 And he bowed . . with his face to the earth, and said 8
22:10 He bowed the heavens, and came down; 1
1Kg 1:16 Bathshe'ba bowed and did obeisance to the king 7
23 he bowed before the king, with his face 8
31 Bathshe'ba bowed with her face to the ground 7
47 And the king bowed himself upon the bed. 8
19:18 leave . . all the knees that have not bowed to Ba'al 4
2Kg 2:15 they came to meet him, and bowed to the ground 8
4:37 She came and fell at his feet, bowing to the ground; 8
5:18 when . . and I bow myself in the house of Rimmon 8
18 when I bow myself in the house of Rimmon 8
17:35 not fear other gods or bow yourselves to them 8
36 you shall fear . . you shall bow yourselves to him 8
2Ch 20:18 Then Jehosh'aphat bowed his head 7
29:29 all . . bowed themselves and worshiped. 4
Job 9:13 beneath him bowed the helpers of Rahab. 9
Ps 18: 9 He bowed the heavens, and came down; 1
21:12 you will aim at their faces with your bows. 5
22:29 before him shall bow all who go down to the dust 4
35:13 I prayed with head bowed on my bosom †
45:11 Since he is your lord, bow to him; 8
144: 5 Bow thy heavens, O LORD, and come down! 6
Isa 45:23 To me every knee shall bow 4
Lam 2:10 the maidens of Jerusalem have bowed their heads 2
Mic 6: 6 and bow myself before God on high? 3
Lke 24: 5 bowed their faces to the ground 11
Joh 19:30 he bowed his head and gave up his spirit. 11
Rom11: 4 7,000 men who have not bowed the knee to Ba'al". 10
14:11 As I live, says the Lord, every knee shall bow to me 10
Eph 3:14 For this reason I bow my knees before the Father 10
Php 2:10 at the name of Jesus every knee should bow 10
Sir 33:26 Yoke and thong will bow the neck 10

bow (2) 1. קֶשֶׁת 2. τόξον 3. arcus
Gen 9:13 I set my bow in the cloud, and it shall be a sign 1
14 the earth and the bow is seen in the clouds 1
16 When the bow is in the clouds, I will look upon it 1
21:20 the lad . . became an expert with the bow. 1
27: 3 take your weapons, your quiver and your bow 1
48:22 which I took . . with my sword and with my bow. 1
49:24 yet his bow remained unmoved 1
Jos 24:12 I sent . . it was not by your sword or by your bow. 1
1Sm 2: 4 The bows of the mighty are broken 1
18: 4 and even his sword and his bow and his girdle. 1
2Sm 1:22 the bow of Jonathan turned not back, and the sword 1
22:35 so that my arms can bend a bow of bronze. 1
1Kg 22:34 a certain man drew his bow at a venture 1
2Kg 6:22 taken captive with your sword and with your bow? 1
9:24 Jehu drew his bow . . and shot Joram 1
13:15 Eli'sha said to him, "Take a bow and arrows"; 1
15 Take a bow and arrows"; so he took a bow and arrows. 1
16 he said to the king . . "Draw the bow"; and he drew it. 1
1Ch 5:18 valiant men, who . . drew the bow, expert in war 1
2Ch 14: 8 280,000 men . . carried shields and drew bows; 1
17:17 with 200,000 men armed with bow and shield 1
18:33 a certain man drew his bow at a venture 1
26:14 prepared for all the army . . bows, and stones 1
Neh 4:13 with their swords, their spears, and their bows. 1
16 half held the spears, shields, bows 1
Job 29:20 glory fresh with me, and my bow ever new in my hand 1
Ps 7:12 will whet his sword; he has bent and strung his bow; 1
11: 2 for lo, the wicked bend the bow 1
18:34 for war, so that my arms can bend a bow of bronze. 1
37:14 The wicked draw the sword and bend their bows 1
15 their bows shall be broken. 1
44: 6 not in my bow do I trust, nor can my sword save me. 1
46: 9 he breaks the bow, and shatters the spear 1
60: 4 those who fear thee, to rally to it from the bow. 2
78: 9 The E'phraimites, armed with the bow, turned back 1
57 they twisted like a deceitful bow. 1
Isa 5:28 their arrows are sharp, all their bows bent 1
7:24 With bow and arrows men will come there 1
13:18 Their bows will slaughter the young men; 1
21:15 swords, from the drawn sword, from the bent bow 1
22: 3 rulers . . without the bow they were captured. 1
41: 2 like dust . . like driven stubble with his bow. 1
66:19 to Tarshish, Put, and Lud, who draw the bow 1
Jer 6:23 They lay hold on bow and spear, they are cruel 1
9: 3 They bend their tongue like a bow; 1
46: 9 men of Lud, skilled in handling the bow. 1
49:35 Behold, I will break the bow of Elam 1
50:14 you that bend the bow; shoot at her, spare no arrows 1
29 against Babylon, all those who bend the bow. 1
42 They lay hold of bow and spear; they are cruel 1
51: 3 Let not the archer bend his bow 1
56 her warriors are taken, their bows are broken 1
Lam 2: 4 He has bent his bow like an enemy 1
3:12 he bent his bow and set me as a mark for his arrow. 1
Ezk 1:28 Like the appearance of the bow 1
39: 3 then I will strike your bow from your left hand 1
9 shields and bucklers, bows and arrows, handpikes 1
Hos 1: 5 break the bow of Israel in the valley of Jezreel. 1
7 I will not deliver them by bow, nor by sword 1
2:18 and I will abolish the bow, the sword, and war 1
7:16 They turn to Ba'al; they are like a treacherous bow 1
Ams 2:15 he who handles the bow shall not stand 1
Hab 3: 9 Thou didst strip the sheath from thy bow 1
Zec 9:10 the battle bow shall be cut off 1
13 For I have bent Judah as my bow; 1
10: 4 out of them the tent peg, out of them the battle bow 1
Rev 6: 2 I saw . . a white horse, and its rider had a bow; 2
2Es 16:13 For his right hand that bends the bow is strong 3
Jdt 9: 7 they trust in shield and spear, in bow and sling 2
Wis 5:21 and will leap to the target as from a well-drawn bow 2

bow down 1. גהר 2. כנע 3. כפף 4. כרע 5. עוה 6. צעה 7. קדד 8. שוח 9. שחה 10. שחח 11. κύπτω 12. προσκυνέω 13. συγκύπτω
Gen 23:12 Then Abraham bowed down before the people 9
27:29 Let peoples serve you, and nations bow down to you. 9
29 may your mother's sons bow down to you. 9
33: 6 they and their children, and bowed down; 9
7 Leah . . and her children drew near and bowed down 9
7 Joseph and Rachel drew near, and they bowed down. 9
37: 7 gathered round it, and bowed down to my sheaf. 9
9 and eleven stars were bowing down to me. 9
43:26 and bowed down to him to the ground. 9
49: 8 your father's sons shall bow down before you. 9
Exd 11: 8 servants shall come down to me, and bow down to me 9
20: 5 you shall not bow down to them or serve them; 9
23:24 you shall not bow down to their gods, nor serve 9
Lev 26: 1 a figured stone in your land, to bow down to them 9
Num25: 2 people ate, and bowed down to their gods. 9
Deu 5: 9 you shall not bow down to them or serve them; 9
Jos 23: 7 or serve them, or bow down yourselves to them 9
16 and go and serve other gods and bow down to them. 9
Jdg 2:12 and bowed down to them; and they provoked 9
17 played . . after other gods and bowed down to them; 9
19 other gods, serving them and bowing down to them; 9
1Kg 2:19 the king rose to meet her, and bowed down to her; 9
18:42 he bowed himself down upon the earth 1
2Ch 7: 3 they bowed down with their faces to the earth 4
29:30 sang praises . . bowed down and worshiped. 7
Est 3: 2 And all . . bowed down and did obeisance to Haman; 4
2 But Mor'decai did not bow down or do obeisance. 4
5 Mor'decai did not bow down or do obeisance to him 4
Job 31:10 let others bow down upon her. 4
Ps 22:29 to him shall all the proud of the earth bow down; 9
35:14 laments his mother, bowed down and in mourning. 10
38: 6 I am utterly bowed down and prostrate; 5
44:25 For our soul is bowed down to the dust; 8
57: 6 They set a net for my steps; my soul was bowed down. 3
72: 9 May his foes bow down before him, and his enemies 4
81: 9 you shall not bow down to a foreign god. 9
86: 9 nations thou hast made shall come and bow down 9
95: 6 O come, let us worship and bow down, let us kneel 4
97: 7 all gods bow down before him. 9
107:12 Their hearts were bowed down with hard labor; 2
138: 2 I bow down toward thy holy temple and give thanks 9
145:14 LORD . . raises up all who are bowed down. 3
146: 8 The LORD lifts up those who are bowed down; 3
Prv 14:19 The evil bow down before the good 10
Isa 2: 8 they bow down to the work of their hands 9
5:15 Man is bowed down, and men are brought low 10
21: 3 I am bowed down so that I cannot hear 5
45:14 they shall come over in chains and bow down 9
46: 1 Bel bows down, Nebo stoops 4
2 They stoop, they bow down together 4
49:23 their faces to the ground they shall bow down 9
51:14 He who is bowed down shall speedily be released; 6
23 said to you, 'Bow down, that we may pass over'; 9
58: 5 Is it to bow down his head like a rush 3
60:14 all who despised you shall bow down at your feet; 9
65:12 and all of you shall bow down to the slaughter; 4
Jer 2:20 and under every green tree you bowed down 6
Lam 3:20 soul . . thinks of it and is bowed down within me. 8
Mic 5:13 shall bow down no more to the work of your hands; 9
Zep 1: 5 those who bow down on the roofs to the host 9
5 those who bow down and swear to the LORD 9
2:11 and to him shall bow down, each in its place 9
Rev 3: 9 make them come and bow down before your feet 12
Jdt 13:17 All the people . . bowed down and worshiped God 11
AEs 13:12 I . . refused to bow down to this proud Haman. 12
14 I will not bow down to any one but to thee 12
16:11 was continually bowed down to by all 12
Sir 19:26 There is a rascal bowed down in mourning 13
30:12 Bow down his neck in his youth •

bow down in worship 1. προσκυνέω
Sir 50:21 they bowed down in worship a second time 1

bow in worship 1. προσκυνέω
Heb 11:21 bowing in worship over the head of his staff. 1

bow low 1. ταπεινός
Sir 4: 7 bow your head low to a great man. 1

bow one's head 1. קדד
Gen 24:26 The man bowed his head and worshiped the LORD 1
48 Then I bowed my head and worshiped the LORD 1
43:28 And they bowed their heads and made obeisance. 1
Exd 4:31 when they heard . . they bowed their heads 1
12:27 the people bowed their heads and worshiped. 1
34: 8 And Moses made haste to bow his head 1
1Ch 29:20 bowed their heads, and worshipped the LORD 1
Neh 8: 6 bowed their heads and worshiped the LORD 1

bow the knee 1. אַבְרֵךְ
Gen 41:43 and they cried before him, "Bow the knee! 1

bowels 1. מֵעָה 2. גֵּו 3. σπλάγχνον
Num 5:22 that brings the curse pass into your bowels 2
2Sm 20:10 Jo'ab struck . . and shed his bowels to the ground 2
2Ch 21:15 severe sickness with a disease of your bowels 2
15 your bowels come out because of the disease, 2
18 after all this the LORD smote him in his bowels 2
19 his bowels came out because of the disease 2
Act 1:18 all his bowels gushed out. 3
Sir 10: 9 for even in life his bowels decay. 1
2Mc 9: 5 he was seized with a pain in his bowels 3
6 he had tortured the bowels of others 3

bowl 1. אַגָּן 2. גֻּלָּה 3. כְּפוֹר 4. מִזְרָק 5. מְנַקִּיָּה 6. סַף 7. סֵפֶל 8. צְלֹחִית 9. קֻבַּעַת כּוֹס 10. ὁλκεῖον 11. σκάφη 12. σκεῦος 13. φιάλη
Exd 25:29 make . . its flagons and bowls with which to pour 5
37:16 its plates and dishes for incense, and its bowls 5
Num 4: 7 put upon it . . the bowls, and the flagons 5
Jdg 5:25 she brought him curds in a lordly bowl. 7
6:38 dew from the fleece to fill a bowl with water. 7
1Kg 7:41 the two bowls of the capitals that were 2
41 networks to cover the two bowls of the capitals 2
42 cover the two bowls of the capitals that were 2
2Kg 2:20 He said, "Bring me a new bowl, and put salt in it. 8
12:13 not made . . basins of silver, snuffers, bowls 4
25:15 the firepans also, and the bowls. 4
1Ch 28:17 for the golden bowls and the weight of each; 3
17 for the silver bowls and the weight of each. 3
2Ch 4:12 the two pillars, the bowls, and the two capitals 2
12 networks to cover the two bowls of the capitals 2
13 to cover the two bowls of the capitals that were 2
Ezr 1:10 30 bowls of gold, 2,410 bowls of silver 3
10 30 bowls of gold, 2,410 bowls of silver 3
8:27 twenty bowls of gold worth 1,000 darics 3
Ecc 12: 6 or the golden bowl is broken 2
Sng 7: 2 Your navel is a rounded bowl that never lacks 1
Isa 51:17 have drunk to the dregs the bowl of staggering. 9
22 the bowl of my wrath you shall drink no more; 9
Jer 52:19 also the small bowls, and the firepans 6
Ams 6: 6 who drink wine in bowls, and anoint themselves 4
Zec 4: 2 lampstand all of gold, with a bowl on the top of it 2
3 olive trees by it, one on the right of the bowl 2
9:15 their blood like wine, and be full like a bowl 4
14:20 of the LORD shall be as the bowls before the altar; 4
Joh 19:29 A bowl full of vinegar stood there 12
Rev 5: 8 and with golden bowls full of incense 13
15: 7 seven golden bowls full of the wrath of God 13
16: 1 pour out . . the seven bowls of the wrath of God. 13
2 first angel went and poured his bowl on the earth 13
3 The second angel poured his bowl into the sea 13
4 The third angel poured his bowl into the rivers 13
8 The fourth angel poured his bowl on the sun 13
10 The fifth angel poured his bowl on the throne 13
12 angel poured his bowl on the river Euphra'tes 13
17 The seventh angel poured his bowl into the air 13
17: 1 one of the seven angels who had the seven bowls 13
21: 9 the seven bowls full of the seven last plagues 13
1Es 2:13 29 silver censers, 30 gold bowls, 2,410 silver bowls 13

13 2,410 silver bowls, and 1,000 other vessels. *
8:57 twenty golden bowls, and twelve bronze vessels *
Jdt 15:11 his beds and his bowls and all his furniture 10
Bel 1:33 had broken bread into a bowl 11
1Mc 1:22 the bowls, the golden censers, the curtain 13

bowl for libation 1. מְנַקִּיָּה
Jer 52:19 dishes for incense, and the bowls for libation. 1

kneading bowl 1. מִשְׁאֶרֶת
Exd 8: 3 into your ovens and your kneading bowls; 1
12:34 their kneading bowls being bound up 1

bowman 1. דרך קֶשֶׁת 2. נשק קֶשֶׁת
1Ch 8:40 warriors, bowmen, having many sons and grandsons 1
12: 2 bowmen, and could shoot arrows and sling stones 2

bowshot 1. קֶשֶׁת
Gen 21:16 a good way off, about the distance of a bowshot; 1

bowstring 1. יֶתֶר
Jdg 16: 7 fresh bowstrings which have not been dried 1
8 seven fresh bowstrings which had not been dried 1
9 But he snapped the bowstrings, as a string of tow 1

box 1. אַרְגָּז 2. בַּיִת
1Sm 6: 8 put in a box at its side the figures of gold 1
11 put the ark . . and the box with the golden mice 1
15 took down the ark . . and the box that was beside it 1
Isa 3:20 the perfume boxes, and the amulets; 2

box (2) 1. *πυκτεύω*
1Co 9:26 I do not box as one beating the air; 1

money box 1. *γλωσσόκομον*
Joh 12: 6 and as he had the money box 1
13:29 because Judas had the money box 1

boy 1. יֶלֶד 2. נַעַר 3. *ἀνηβάω* 4. *μειράκιον* 5. *νέος* 6. *παιδάριον* 7. *παῖς*
Gen 25:27 When the boys grew up, Esau was a skilful hunter 2
Jdg 13: 5 for the boy shall be a Nazirite to God from birth; 2
7 for the boy shall be a Nazirite to God from birth 2
8 what we are to do with the boy that will be born. 2
12 what is to be the boy's manner of life 2
24 Samson; and the boy grew, and the LORD blessed him. 2
1Sm 2:11 And the boy ministered to the LORD 2
18 Samuel was . . a boy girdled with a linen ephod. 2
21 the boy Samuel grew in the presence of the LORD. 2
26 the boy Samuel continued to grow both in stature 2
3: 1 Now the boy Samuel was ministering to the LORD 2
8 Eli perceived that the LORD was calling the boy. 2
2Kg 2:23 while he was going . . some small boys came out 2
24 two she-bears came . . and tore 42 of the boys 1
2Ch 34: 3 eighth year of his reign, while he was yet a boy 2
Isa 3: 4 make boys their princes, and babes shall rule 2
Lam 5:13 and boys stagger under loads of wood. 2
Jol 3: 3 and have given a boy for a harlot 1
Zec 8: 5 the city shall be full of boys and girls playing 1
Mat 17:18 and the boy was cured instantly. 7
Mrk 9:20 they brought the boy to him *
20 immediately it convulsed the boy *
26 it came out, and the boy was like a corpse *
Lke 2:43 the boy Jesus stayed behind in Jerusalem 7
9:42 healed the boy and gave him back to his father 7
1Mc 2:46 circumcised all the uncircumcised boys 6
6:17 Lysias had brought him up as a boy 5
11:54 the young boy Antiochus who began to reign 6
2Mc 5:13 destruction of boys, women, and children 3
24 to sell the women and boys as slaves. 5
4Mc 11:24 We six boys have paralyzed your tyranny! 4
12: 6 he sent for the boy's mother 7
9 Extremely pleased by the boy's declaration 7
15: 6 The mother of the seven boys 7

mere boy 1. *μειρακίσκος*
4Mc 11:13 the sixth, a mere boy, was led 1

bracelet 1. צָמִיד 2. שֵׁרָה 3. *χλιδῶν* 4. *ψέλιον*
Gen 24:22 took . . two bracelets for her arms 1
30 When he saw the ring, and the bracelets 1
47 I put . . the bracelets on her arms. 1
Num31:50 LORD'S offering . . armlets and bracelets 1
Isa 3:19 the pendants, the bracelets, and the scarfs; 2
Ezk 16:11 with ornaments, and put bracelets on your arms 1
23:42 they put bracelets upon the hands of the women 1
Jdt 10: 4 put on her anklets and bracelets and rings 4
Sir 21:21 like a bracelet on the right arm. 3

brackish 1. *πικρός*
Jas 3:11 from the same opening fresh water and brackish? 1

braggart 1. *λαπιστής*
Sir 20: 7 a braggart and fool goes beyond the right moment. 1

braid 1. *ἐμπλοκή*
1Pe 3: 3 outward adorning with braiding of hair 1

braided hair 1. *πλέγμα*
1Ti 2: 9 not with braided hair or gold or pearls 1

bramble 1. אָטָד 2. חוֹחַ
Jdg 9:14 all the trees said to the bramble, 'Come you 1
15 the bramble said to the trees, 'If in good faith you 1
15 if not, let fire come out of the bramble and devour 1
Sng 2: 2 As a lily among brambles, so is my love 2

bramble bush 1. *βάτος*
Lke 6:44 nor are grapes picked from a bramble bush. 1

bran 1. *πίτυρον*
LJr 1:43 burning bran for incense 1

branch 1. בַּד 2. בַּת 3. דָּלִיּוֹת 4. זְמוֹרָה 5. כַּף 6. כִּפָּה 7. נְטִישָׁה 8. נֵצֶר 9. סַלְסִלָּה 10. סַנְסִנִּים 11. סָעִיף 12. עֲבֹת 13. עָלֶה 14. עָנָף 15. עֳפָיִם 16. פֹּארָה 17. צֶמַח 18. קָנֶה 19. קָצִיר 20. שָׂרִיג 21. שָׂרֹק 22. שִׁבֹּלֶת 23. עֲנָף (A) 24. *βαΐον* 25. *θύρσος* 26. *κλάδος* 27. *κλῆμα* 28. *κλών*
Gen 40:10 and on the vine there were three branches; 20
12 the three branches are three days; 20
49:22 his branches run over the wall. 2
Exd 25:32 there shall be six branches going out 18
32 three branches of the lampstand out of one side 18
32 three branches of the lampstand out of the other 18
33 three cups . . on one branch 18
33 three cups . . on the other branch 18
33 -so for the six branches going out of the lampstand; 18
35 under each pair of the six branches going out 18
36 Their capitals and their branches shall be 18
37:18 there were six branches going out of its sides 18
18 three branches of the lampstand out of one side 18
18 three branches of the lampstand out of the other 18
19 cups . . with capital and flower on one branch 18
19 with capital and flower, on the other branch 18
19 for the six branches going out of the lampstand. 18
21 each pair of the six branches going out of it. 18
22 Their capitals and their branches were of one 18
Lev 23:40 take . . branches of palm trees, and boughs 5
Num13:23 and cut down from there a branch 4
Neh 8:15 Go out to the hills and bring branches of olive 13
Job 14: 9 bud and put forth branches like a young plant. 19
15:32 his branch will not be green. 6
18:16 roots dry up . . and his branches wither above. 19
29:19 with the dew all night on my branches 19
Ps 80:10 the mighty cedars with its branches; 14
11 it sent out its branches to the sea 19
104:12 birds of the air . . sing among the branches. 15
118:27 Bind the festal procession with branches 12
Sng 7: 8 climb the palm tree and lay hold of its branches. 10
Isa 4: 2 the branch of the LORD shall be beautiful 17
11: 1 of Jesse, and a branch shall grow out of his roots. 8
16: 8 lords of the nations . . struck down its branches 21
17: 6 four or five on the branches of a fruit tree 11
27:10 there he lies down, and strips its branches. 11
Jer 5:10 strip away her branches 7
6: 9 pass your hand again over its branches. 9
11:16 and its branches will be consumed. 3
23: 5 when I will raise up for David a righteous Branch 17
33:15 I will cause a righteous Branch to spring forth 17
48:32 vine of Sibmah! Your branches passed over the sea 7
Ezk 8:17 Lo, they put the branch to their nose. 4
17: 6 vine, and its branches turned toward him 3
6 So it became a vine, and brought forth branches 1
7 and shot forth its branches toward him 3
8 that it might bring forth branches, and bear 14
9 he not pull up its roots and cut off its branches *
23 in the shade of its branches birds of every sort 3
19:11 seen in its height with the mass of its branches. 3
14 And fire . . has consumed its branches and fruit 1
31: 3 a cedar . . with fair branches and forest shade 14
5 its boughs grew large and its branches long 16
6 under its branches all the beasts of the field 16
7 in its greatness, in the length of its branches; 3
8 were as nothing compared with its branches; 16
9 I made it beautiful in the mass of its branches 3
12 in all the valleys its branches will fall 3
13 upon its branches will be all the beasts 16
36: 8 shall shoot forth your branches 14
Dan 4:12 birds of the air dwelt in its branches 23
14 'Hew down the tree and cut off its branches 23
14 beasts flee . . and the birds from its branches. 23
21 in whose branches the birds of the air dwelt- 23
11: 7 branch from her roots shall arise in his place; 8
Jol 1: 7 their branches are made white. 20
Nah 2: 2 have stripped them and ruined their branches. 4
Zec 3: 8 behold, I will bring my servant the Branch. 17
4:12 What are these two branches of the olive trees 22
6:12 Behold, the man whose name is the Branch 17
Mal 4: 1 it will leave them neither root nor branch. 14
Mat 13:32 make nests in its branches. 26
21: 8 others cut branches from the trees 26
24:32 as soon as its branch becomes tender 26
Mrk 4:32 and puts forth large branches 26
13:28 as soon as its branch becomes tender 26
Lke 13:19 the birds of the air made nests in its branches. 26
Joh 12:13 they took branches of palm trees 24
15: 2 Every branch of mine that bears no fruit 27
2 every branch that does bear fruit he prunes *
4 As the branch cannot bear fruit by itself 27
5 I am the vine, you are the branches. 27
6 he is cast forth as a branch and withers 27
6 the branches are gathered, thrown into the fire *
Rom 11:16 and if the root is holy, so are the branches. 26
17 But if some of the branches were broken off 26
18 do not boast over the branches. 26
19 Branches were broken off so that I might be 26
21 For if God did not spare the natural branches 26
24 will . . natural branches be grafted back *
Jdt 15:12 she took branches in her hands 25
Wis 4: 5 The branches will be broken off 28
17:18 birds in wide-spreading branches 26
Sir 1:20 her branches are long life. 26
23:25 her branches will not bear fruit. 26
24:16 Like a terebinth I spread out my branches 26
16 my branches are glorious and graceful. 26
40:15 will not put forth many branches 26
2Mc 10: 7 ivy-wreathed wands and beautiful branches 26
branch *See also* full, palm, spread.

leafy branch 1. *στιβάς*
Mrk 11: 8 and others spread leafy branches 1

olive branch 1. *θαλλός*
2Mc 14: 4 the customary olive branches from the temple. 1

thick branch 1. שׂוֹבֶךְ
2Sm 18: 9 mule went under the thick branches of a great oak 1

vine branch 1. זְמוֹרָה
Ezk 15: 2 the vine branch which is among the trees 1

brand 1. אוּד 2. זֵק 3. *χαράσσω*
Isa 50:11 all you who kindle a fire, who set brands alight! 2
11 fire, and by the brands which you have kindled! 2
Ams 4:11 and you were as a brand plucked out of the burning; 1
Zec 3: 2 Is not this a brand plucked from the fire? 1
3Mc 2:29 are also to be branded on their bodies by fire 3

brandish 1. עוּף 2. עור 3. תְּנוּפָה 4. *κίνησις* 5. *κραδαίνω*
Isa 30:32 with brandished arm he will fight with them. 3
Ezk 32:10 when I brandish my sword before them; 1
Zec 9:13 I will brandish your sons, O Zion 2
2Mc 5: 3 brandishing of shields, massing of spears 4
11: 8 brandishing weapons of gold. 5

brass 1. נְחוּשָׁה 2. נְחֹשֶׁת 3. *χαλκεῖον* 4. *χάλκειος* 5. *χαλκός* 6. *χαλκοῦς* 7. aeramentum
Lev 26:19 I will make . . your earth like brass 1
Deu 28:23 heavens over your head shall be brass 2
Isa 48: 4 neck is an iron sinew and your forehead brass 1
1Es 1:12 they boiled the sacrifices in brass pots 3
40 bound him with a chain of brass 4
2Es 7:55 Say to her, 'You produce gold and silver and brass 7
56 and brass than silver, and iron than brass 7
56 and brass than silver, and iron than brass 7
Bel 1: 7 this is but clay inside and brass outside 5
1Mc 6:35 with brass helmets on their heads 6
39 the sun shone upon the shields of gold and brass 6

brave 1. בֶּן חַיִל 2. *ἀγαθός* 3. *ἀνδρεῖος* 4. *γενναῖος* 5. *θαρρέω*
Jdg 21:10 sent thither 12,000 of their bravest men 1
Tob 7:18 Be brave, my child 5
18 Be brave, my daughter. 5
Sir 19:10 Be brave! It will not make you burst! 5
2Mc 13:15 with a picked force of the bravest young men 2
15:11 the inspiration of brave words 2
4Mc 15:10 were righteous and self-controlled and brave 3
17:24 this made them brave and courageous 4
brave *See also* deed.

brave deed 1. *ἀνδραγαθία*
1Mc 5:56 Joseph . . heard of their brave deeds 1
8: 2 brave deeds which they were doing among the Gauls 1
9:22 his wars and the brave deeds that he did 1
10:15 the brave deeds that they had done 1
16:23 the brave deeds which he did 1

bravely 1. *ἀρρενωδῶς* 2. *γενναίως* 3. *θαρσαλέος* 4. fortiter
2Es 10:15 and bear bravely the troubles 4
2Mc 10:35 bravely stormed the wall 1
14:43 He bravely ran up on the wall 2
15:17 they determined . . to attack bravely 2
3Mc 1: 4 defend . . their children and wives bravely 3

noble bravery 1. *ἀνδραγαθία*
4Mc 1: 8 the noble bravery of those who died 1

brawler 1.המה
Prv 20: 1 Wine is a mocker, strong drink a brawler; 1

bray 1.נהק
Job 6: 5 Does the wild ass bray when he has grass 1
30: 7 Among the bushes they bray; 1

brazen 1.שַׁלִּיט
Ezk 16:30 did all these things, the deeds of a brazen harlot; 1

brazier 1.אָח 2.τήγανον
Jer 36:22 was a fire burning in the brazier before him. 1
23 and throw them into the fire in the brazier 1
23 consumed in the fire that was in the brazier. 1
4Mc 8:13 braziers and thumbscrews and iron claws 2
12:10 Running to the nearest of the braziers 2
19 he flung himself into the braziers 2

breach 1.בְּקִיעַ 2.בקע 3.פרץ 4.פֶּרֶץ 5.שֶׁבֶר
Gen 38:29 and she said, "What a breach you have made 4
Jdg 21:15 the LORD had made a breach in the tribes 4
1Kg 11:27 and closed up the breach of the city of David 4
Neh 4: 7 that the breaches were beginning to be closed 3
6: 1 reported . . that there was no breach left in it 4
Job 16:14 He breaks me with breach upon breach; 4
14 He breaks me with breach upon breach; 4
30:14 As through a wide breach they come; 4
Ps 60: 2 repair its breaches, for it totters. 5
89:40 Thou hast breached all his walls; 3
106:23 Moses, his chosen one, stood in the breach before 4
Isa 22: 9 you saw that the breaches of the city . . were many 1
58:12 you shall be called the repairer of the breach 4
Ezk 13: 5 You have not gone up into the breaches 4
22:30 and stand in the breach before me for the land 4
26:10 as one enters a city which has been breached. 2
30:16 Thebes shall be breached, and its walls broken 2
Ams 4: 3 And you shall go out through the breaches 4
9:11 booth . . that is fallen and repair its breaches 4
Mic 2:13 He who opens the breach will go up before them; •
breach *See also* make.

make a breach 1.בקע 2.פרץ
Gen 38:29 and she said, "What a breach you have made 2
Jer 39: 2 a breach was made in the city. 1
52: 7 Then a breach was made in the city; 1

breach of faith 1.מַעַל
Lev 5:15 If any one commits a breach of faith and sins 1
6: 2 If any one sins and commits a breach of faith 1
Jos 22:22 If it was in rebellion or in breach of faith 1

breach of trust 1.פֶּשַׁע
Exd 22: 9 For every breach of trust, whether it is for ox 1

bread 1.דָּגָן 2.לֶחֶם 3.ἄρτος 4.panis
Gen 3:19 In the sweat of your face you shall eat bread 2
14:18 king of Salem brought out bread and wine; 2
18: 5 while I fetch a morsel of bread 2
21:14 Abraham . . took bread and a skin of water 2
25:34 Jacob gave Esau bread and pottage of lentils 2
27:17 she gave the savory food and the bread 2
28:20 If God . . will give me bread to eat and clothing 2
31:54 mountain and called his kinsmen to eat bread; 2
54 they ate bread and tarried all night 2
41:54 but in all the land of Egypt there was bread. 2
55 the people cried to Pharaoh for bread; 2
43:25 for they heard that they should eat bread there. 2
32 Egyptians might not eat bread with the Hebrews 2
45:23 asses loaded with grain, bread, and provision 2
Exd 2:20 you left the man? Call him, that he may eat bread. 2
16: 3 when we . . ate bread to the full; 2
4 Behold, I will rain bread from heaven for you; 2
8 LORD gives . . in the morning bread to the full 2
12 in the morning you shall be filled with bread; 2
15 It is the bread which the LORD has given you 2
22 gathered twice as much bread, two omers apiece; 2
29 on the sixth day he gives you bread for two days; 2
32 that they may see the bread with which I fed you 2
18:12 came . . to eat bread with Moses' father-in-law 2
23:25 and I will bless your bread and your water; 2
25:30 you shall set the bread of the Presence 2
29: 2 unleavened bread, unleavened cakes mixed 2
23 one loaf of bread, and one cake of bread with oil 2
23 one cake of bread with oil, and one wafer 2
32 shall eat . . the bread that is in the basket 2
34 if any . . of the bread, remain until the morning 2
34:28 he neither ate bread nor drank water. 2
35:13 its utensils, and the bread of the Presence; 2
39:36 its utensils, and the bread of the Presence; 2
40:23 set the bread in order on it before the LORD; 2
Lev 7:13 his offering with cakes of leavened bread 2
8:26 took . . one cake of bread with oil, and one wafer 2
31 there eat it and the bread that is in the basket 2
32 the flesh and the bread you shall burn with fire 2
21: 6 for they offer . . the bread of their God 2
8 for he offers the bread of your God 2
17 may approach to offer the bread of his God 2
21 not come near to offer the bread of his God 2
22 He may eat the bread of his God 2
22:25 neither shall you offer as the bread of your God 2
23:14 you shall eat neither bread nor grain parched 2
17 bring . . two loaves of bread to be waved 2
18 you shall present with the bread seven lambs 2
20 the priest shall wave them with the bread 2
24: 7 it may go with the bread as a memorial portion 2
26: 5 you shall eat your bread to the full, and dwell 2
26 When I break your staff of bread 2
26 ten women shall bake your bread in one oven 2
26 and shall deliver your bread again by weight 2
Num 4: 7 over the table of the bread of the Presence •
7 continual bread also shall be on it; 2
14: 9 for they are bread for us; their protection 2
Deu 8: 3 man does not live by bread alone 2
9 in which you will eat bread without scarcity 2
9: 9 I neither ate bread nor drank water. 2
18 I neither ate bread nor drank water 2
16: 3 unleavened bread, the bread of affliction 2
23: 4 not meet you with bread and with water on the way 2
29: 6 not eaten bread, and you have not drunk wine 2
Jos 9:12 Here is our bread; it was still warm when we took it 2
Jdg 7:13 lo, a cake of barley bread tumbled into the camp 2
8: 5 give loaves of bread to the people who follow me; 2
6 your hand, that we should give bread to your army? 2
15 that we should give bread to your men who are 2
19: 5 Strengthen your heart with a morsel of bread 2
19 with bread and wine for me and your maidservant 2
Rut 2:14 Come here, and eat some bread, and dip your morsel 2
1Sm 2: 5 were full have hired themselves out for bread 2
36 implore . . for a piece of silver or a loaf of bread 2
36 Put me . . that I may eat a morsel of bread."' 2
9: 7 the bread in our sacks is gone, and there is no 2
10: 3 another carrying three loaves of bread 2
4 will greet you and give you two loaves of bread 2
16:20 Jesse took an ass laden with bread 2
21: 3 Give me five loaves of bread, or whatever is here. 2
4 I have no common bread at hand, but . . holy bread; 2
4 I have no common bread . . but there is holy bread; 2
6 the priest gave him the holy bread; 2
6 there was no bread there but . . of the Presence 2
6 was no bread there but the bread of the Presence 2
6 replaced by hot bread on the day it is taken away. 2
22:13 you have given him bread and a sword 2
25:11 Shall I take my bread and my water 2
28:22 let me set a morsel of bread before you; and eat 2
30:11 they gave him bread and he ate, they gave him water 2
12 he had not eaten bread or drunk . . for three days 2
2Sm 3:29 or who is slain by the sword, or who lacks bread! 2
35 the people came to persuade David to eat bread 2
35 if I taste bread or anything else till the sun 2
6:19 distributed . . to each a cake of bread, a portion 2
9:10 that your master's son may have bread to eat; 2
13: 5 Let my sister Tamar come and give me bread to eat 2
16: 1 a couple of asses . . bearing 200 loaves of bread 2
2 bread and summer fruit for the young men to eat 2
1Kg 7:48 the golden table for the bread of the Presence 2
13: 8 I will not eat bread or drink water in this place; 2
9 You shall neither eat bread, nor drink water 2
15 he said to him, "Come home with me and eat bread. 2
16 neither will I eat bread nor drink water with you 2
17 You shall neither eat bread nor drink water 2
18 Bring him back . . that he may eat bread and drink 2
19 he went back with him, and ate bread in his house 2
22 and have eaten bread and drunk water in the place 2
22 he said to you, "Eat no bread, and drink no water"; 2
23 after he had eaten bread and drunk, he saddled 2
17: 6 ravens brought him bread and meat in the morning 2
6 ravens brought . . bread and meat in the evening; 2
11 Bring me a morsel of bread in your hand. 2
18: 4 hid them . . and fed them with bread and water.) 2
13 and fed them with bread and water? 2
21: 7 Arise, and eat bread, and let your heart be 2
22:27 and feed him with scant fare of bread and water 2
2Kg 4:42 bringing . . bread of the first fruits 2
6:22 Set bread and water before them, that they may eat 2
18:32 of grain and wine, a land of bread and vineyards 2
1Ch 16: 3 loaf of bread, a portion of meat, and a cake 2
2Ch 4:19 altar, the tables for the bread of the Presence 2
18:26 feed him with scant fare of bread and water 2
Ezr 10: 6 neither eating bread nor drinking water; 2
Neh 9:15 give them bread from heaven for their hunger 2
13: 2 not meet . . Israel with bread and water 2
Job 3:24 For my sighing comes as my bread 2
15:23 He wanders abroad for bread, saying, 'Where is it?' 2
22: 7 you have withheld bread from the hungry. 2
28: 5 As for the earth, out of it comes bread; 2
33:20 that his life loathes bread 2
42:11 who had known him before, and ate bread with him 2
Ps 14: 4 evildoers who eat up my people as they eat bread 2
37:25 forsaken or his children begging bread 2
41: 9 bosom friend in whom I trusted, who ate of my bread 2
53: 4 who eat up my people as they eat bread 2
78:20 Can he also give bread, or provide meat 2
25 Man ate of the bread of the angels; 2
80: 5 Thou hast fed them with the bread of tears 2
102: 4 I forget to eat my bread. 2
9 For I eat ashes like bread 2
104:15 bread to strengthen man's heart. 2
105:16 When he . . broke every staff of bread 2
40 gave them bread from heaven in abundance. 2
127: 2 It is in vain . . eating the bread of anxious toil; 2
132:15 I will satisfy her poor with bread. 2
Prv 4:17 For they eat the bread of wickedness 2
6:26 for a harlot may be hired for a loaf of bread 2
9: 5 eat of my bread and drink of the wine I have mixed. 2
17 bread eaten in secret is pleasant. 2
12: 9 than one who plays the great man but lacks bread. 2
11 He who tills his land will have plenty of bread 2
20:13 open your eyes, and you will have plenty of bread. 2
17 Bread gained by deceit is sweet to a man 2
22: 9 blessed, for he shares his bread with the poor. 2
23: 6 Do not eat the bread of a man who is stingy; 2
25:21 If your enemy is hungry, give him bread to eat; 2
28:19 He who tills his land will have plenty of bread 2
21 but for a piece of bread a man will do wrong. 2
31:27 She . . does not eat the bread of idleness. 2
Ecc 9: 7 Go, eat your bread with enjoyment, and drink 2
11 nor the battle to the strong, nor bread to the wise 2
10:19 Bread is made for laughter, and wine gladdens 2
11: 1 Cast your bread upon the waters, 2
Isa 3: 1 whole stay of bread, and the whole stay of water; 2
7 n my house there is neither bread nor mantle 2
4: 1 We will eat our own bread and wear our own clothes 2
21:14 bring water, meet the fugitive with bread 2
30:20 though the Lord give you the bread of adversity 2
33:16 his bread will be given him, his water will be sure. 2
36:17 of grain and wine, a land of bread and vineyards. 2
44:15 warms himself, he kindles a fire and bakes bread; 2
19 in the fire, I also baked bread on its coals 2
51:14 go down to the Pit, neither shall his bread fail. 2
55: 2 your money for that which is not bread 2
10 giving seed to the sower and bread to the eater 2
58: 7 Is it not to share your bread with the hungry 2
Jer 16: 7 No one shall break bread for the mourner 3
37:21 and a loaf of bread was given him daily 2
21 until all the bread of the city was gone. 2
38: 9 hunger, for there is no bread left in the city. 2
41: 1 As they ate bread together there at Mizpah 2
42:14 or be hungry for bread, and we will dwell there, 2
Lam 1:11 All her people groan as they search for bread; 2
2:12 They cry to their mothers, "Where is bread and wine? 1
5: 6 We have given the hand . . to get bread enough. 2
9 We get our bread at the peril of our lives 2
Ezk 4: 9 and put them into a single vessel, and make bread 2
13 the people of Israel eat their bread unclean 2
15 dung, on which you may prepare your bread. 2
16 I will break the staff of bread in Jerusalem; 2
16 they shall eat bread by weight 2
17 I will do this that they may lack bread and water 2
5:16 famine upon you, and break your staff of bread. 2
12:18 Son of man, eat your bread with quaking 2
19 They shall eat their bread with fearfulness 2
13:19 for handfuls of barley and for pieces of bread 2
14:13 break its staff of bread and send famine upon it 2
16:19 Also my bread which I gave you 2
18: 7 commits no robbery, gives his bread to the hungry 2
16 but gives his bread to the hungry 2
24:17 nor eat the bread of mourners. 2
22 nor eat the bread of mourners. 2
44: 3 prince may sit in it to eat bread before the LORD; 2
Hos 2: 5 my lovers, who give me my bread and my water 2
9: 4 Their bread shall be like mourners' bread; 2
4 Their bread shall be like mourners' bread; 2
4 for their bread shall be for their hunger only; 2
Ams 4: 6 and lack of bread in all your places 2
7:12 flee away to the land of Judah, and eat bread there 2
8:11 not a famine of bread, nor a thirst for water 2
Hag 2:12 and touches with his skirt bread, or pottage 2
Mat 4: 4 written, 'Man shall not live by bread alone 3
6:11 Give us this day our daily bread; 3
7: 9 Or what man of you, if his son asks him for bread 3
12: 4 and ate the bread of the Presence 3
15:26 It is not fair to take the children's bread 3
33 Where are we to get bread enough in the desert 3
16: 5 they had forgotten to bring any bread. 3
7 We brought no bread. 3
8 the fact that you have no bread? 3
11 that I did not speak about bread 3
12 to beware of the leaven of bread 3
26:26 as they were eating, Jesus took bread, and blessed 3
Mrk 2:26 ate the bread of the Presence 3
6: 8 a staff; no bread, no bag, no money in their belts; 3
37 we go and buy 200 denarii worth of bread 3
7:27 for it is not right to take the children's bread 3
8: 4 feed these men with bread here in the desert? 3
14 Now they had forgotten to bring bread 3
16 We have no bread. 3
17 Why do you discuss the fact that you have no bread? 3
14:20 one who is dipping bread into the dish with me. •
22 he took bread, and blessed, and broke it, and gave it 3
Lke 4: 3 of God, command this stone to become bread. 3
4 It is written, 'Man shall not live by bread alone.' 3
6: 4 took and ate the bread of the Presence 3
7:33 has come eating no bread and drinking no wine 3
9: 3 no staff, nor bag, nor bread, nor money 3
11: 3 Give us each day our daily bread; 3
14:15 he who shall eat bread in the kingdom of God! 3

15:17 hired servants have bread enough and to spare 3
22:19 he took bread 3
24:30 When he was at table with them, he took the bread 3
35 he was known to them in the breaking of the bread. 3
Joh 6: 5 to buy bread, so that these people may eat? 3
7 200 denarii would not buy enough bread 3
23 the place where they ate the bread 3
31 'He gave them bread from heaven to eat.' 3
32 was not Moses who gave you the bread from heaven; 3
32 my Father gives you the true bread from heaven. 3
33 bread of God is that which comes down from heaven 3
34 They said to him, "Lord, give us this bread always. 3
35 Jesus said to them, "I am the bread of life 3
41 I am the bread which came down from heaven. 3
48 I am the bread of life. 3
50 This is the bread which comes down from heaven 3
51 I am the living bread which came down from heaven; 3
51 if any one eats of this bread, he will live for ever; 3
51 the bread which I shall give . . is my flesh. 3
58 This is the bread which came down from heaven 3
58 he who eats this bread will live for ever. 3
13:18 He who ate my bread 3
21: 9 a charcoal fire . . with fish lying on it, and bread. 3
13 Jesus came and took the bread and gave it to them 3
Act 2:42 the breaking of bread and the prayers. 3
46 breaking bread in their homes 3
20: 7 when we were gathered together to break bread 3
11 Paul had gone up and had broken bread and eaten 3
27:35 when he had said this, he took bread 3
1Co 10:16 The bread which we break 3
17 Because there is one bread, we who are many are one 3
17 we all partake of the one bread. 3
11:23 the night when he was betrayed took bread 3
26 For as often as you eat this bread 3
27 Whoever, therefore, eats the bread 3
28 eat of the bread and drink of the cup. 3
2Co 9:10 supplies seed to the sower and bread for food 3
2Th 3: 8 we did not eat any one's bread without paying 3
Heb 9: 2 the table and the bread of the Presence 3
1Es 9: 2 he did not eat bread or drink water 3
2Es 1:19 you ate the bread of angels. 4
5:18 Rise therefore and eat some bread 4
14:42 and ate their bread at night. 4
15:19 plunder their goods, because of hunger for bread 4
58 shall eat their own flesh in hunger for bread 4
Tob 1:17 I would give my bread to the hungry 3
4:16 Give of your bread to the hungry 3
17 Place your bread on the grave of the righteous 3
Jdt 10: 5 a cake of dried fruit and fine bread 3
Wis 16:20 supply them from heaven with bread ready to eat 3
21 the bread . . was changed •
Sir 10:27 one who goes about boasting, but lacks bread. 3
12: 5 hold back his bread, and do not give it to him 3
14:10 A stingy man's eye begrudges bread 3
15: 3 will feed him with the bread of understanding 3
20:16 those who eat my bread speak unkindly. 3
23:17 To a fornicator all bread tastes sweet 3
29:21 The essentials for life are water and bread 3
33:24 bread and discipline and work for a servant. 3
34:21 The bread of the needy is the life of the poor; 3
45:20 he prepared bread of first fruits in abundance; 3
Bel 1:33 had broken bread into a bowl 3
1Mc 4:51 They placed the bread on the table 3
2Mc 10: 3 and set out the bread of the Presence. 3

bread *See also* feast, loaf.

bread grain 1. לֶחֶם
Isa 28:28 Does one crush bread grain? 1

leavened bread 1. חָמֵץ
Exd 13: 3 no leavened bread shall be eaten. 1
7 no leavened bread shall be seen with you 1
23:18 the blood of my sacrifice with leavened bread 1
Deu 16: 3 You shall eat no leavened bread with it; 1

bread of the presence 1. πρόθεσις
1Mc 1:22 He took also the table for the bread of the Presence 1

unleavened bread 1. מַצָּה 2. ἄζυμος
Gen 19: 3 feast, and baked unleavened bread, and they ate. 1
Exd 12: 8 with unleavened bread and bitter herbs 1
15 Seven days you shall eat unleavened bread; 1
17 you shall observe the feast of unleavened bread 1
18 you shall eat unleavened bread, and so until 1
20 in all . . dwellings you shall eat unleavened bread. 1
13: 6 Seven days you shall eat unleavened bread 1
7 Unleavened bread shall be eaten for seven days; 1
23:15 You shall keep the feast of unleavened bread; 1
15 you shall eat unleavened bread for seven days 1
29:23 out of the basket of unleavened bread 1
34:18 The feast of unleavened bread you shall keep. 1
18 Seven days you shall eat unleavened bread 1
Lev 8: 2 two rams, and the basket of unleavened bread 1
26 out of the basket of unleavened bread 1
23: 6 the feast of unleavened bread to the LORD 1
6 seven days you shall eat unleavened bread 1
Num 6:15 a basket of unleavened bread, cakes of fine flour 1
17 with the basket of unleavened bread; 1
9:11 eat it with unleavened bread and bitter herbs. 1
28:17 seven days shall unleavened bread be eaten. 1
Deu 16: 3 seven days . . eat it with unleavened bread 1
8 For six days you shall eat unleavened bread; 1
16 appear . . at the feast of unleavened bread 1
1Sm 28:24 and kneaded it and baked unleavened bread of it 1
2Kg 23: 9 they ate unleavened bread among their brethren. 1
1Ch 23:29 cereal offering, the wafers of unleavened bread 1
2Ch 8:13 annual feasts–the feast of unleavened bread 1
30:13 came . . to keep the feast of unleavened bread 1
21 kept the feast of unleavened bread seven days 1
35:17 kept . . feast of unleavened bread seven days. 1
Ezr 6:22 kept the feast of unleavened bread seven days 1
Ezk 45:21 for seven days unleavened bread shall be eaten. 1
Mat 26:17 Now on the first day of Unleavened Bread 2
Mrk 14:12 on the first day of Unleavened Bread 2
Lke 22: 1 Now the feast of Unleavened Bread drew near 2
7 Then came the day of Unleavened Bread 2
Act 12: 3 This was during the days of Unleavened Bread. 2
20: 6 we sailed away . . after the days of Unleavened Bread 2
1Co 5: 8 with the unleavened bread of sincerity 2
1Es 1:10 having the unleavened bread 2
19 kept . . the feast of unleavened bread 2
7:14 kept the feast of unleavened bread seven days 2

breadth 1. אֹרֶךְ 2. מֶרְחָב 3. רֹחַב 4. פְּתָי (A) 5. εὖρος 6. πλάτος
Gen 6:15 its breadth 50 cubits, and its height 30 cubits. 3
13:17 Arise, walk through the length and the breadth 3
Exd 25:10 a cubit and a half its breadth 3
17 and a cubit and a half its breadth. 3
23 a cubit its breadth 3
26: 2 and the breadth of each curtain four cubits; 3
8 the breadth of each curtain four cubits; 3
16 a cubit and a half the breadth of each frame. 3
27:12 for the breadth of the court on the west side 3
13 The breadth of the court on the front to the east 3
18 the breadth 50, and the height five cubits 3
28:16 a span its length and a span its breadth. 3
30: 2 its length, and a cubit its breadth; 3
36: 9 and the breadth of each curtain four cubits; 3
15 the breadth of each curtain four cubits; 3
21 a cubit and a half the breadth of each frame. 3
37: 1 a cubit and a half its breadth, and a cubit 3
6 its length, and a cubit and a half its breadth. 3
10 two cubits was its length, a cubit its breadth 3
25 its length was a cubit, and its breadth was a cubit; 3
38: 1 and five cubits its breadth; it was square 3
18 twenty cubits long and 5 cubits high in its breadth 3
39: 9 a span its length and a span its breadth 3
Deu 3:11 its length, and four cubits its breadth 3
1Kg 7: 2 its breadth 50 cubits, and its height 30 cubits 3
6 length was 50 cubits, and its breadth 30 cubits; 3
2Ch 3: 3 60 cubits, and the breadth twenty cubits. 3
8 length, corresponding to the breadth 3
8 most holy place . . breadth was twenty cubits; 3
Ezr 6: 3 its height . . and its breadth 60 cubits 4
Isa 8: 8 wings will fill the breadth of your land 3
Ezk 40:11 Then he measured the breadth of the opening 3
11 and the breadth of the gateway, thirteen cubits. 1
13 a breadth of 25 cubits 3
20 He measured its length and its breadth. 3
21 and its breadth 25 cubits. 3
25 and its breadth 25 cubits. 3
29 and its breadth 25 cubits. 3
33 and its breadth 25 cubits. 3
36 and its breadth 25 cubits. 3
48 the breadth of the gate was fourteen cubits; 3
49 was twenty cubits, and the breadth twelve cubits; 3
41: 1 six cubits was the breadth of the jambs. 3
2 And the breadth of the entrance was ten cubits; 3
2 40 cubits, and its breadth, twenty cubits. 3
3 and the breadth of the entrance, six cubits; •
4 and its breadth, twenty cubits, beyond the nave. 3
5 and the breadth of the side chambers, four cubits 3
10 court was a breadth of twenty cubits round about 3
11 the breadth of the part that was left free 3
14 also the breadth of the east front of the temple 3
42: 2 100 cubits, and the breadth 50 cubits. 3
11 the same length and breadth, with the same exits 3
43:14 ledge, two cubits, with a breadth of one cubit; 3
14 four cubits, with a breadth of one cubit; 3
48: 8 25,000 cubits in breadth 3
9 in length, and 20,000 in breadth. 3
10 10,000 cubits in breadth on the western side 3
10 10,000 in breadth on the eastern side 3
13 cubits in length and 10,000 in breadth. 3
13 cubits and the breadth 20,000 3
15 5,000 cubits in breadth and 25,000 in length 3
Dan 3: 1 image of gold . . its breadth six cubits. 4
Jon 3: 3 great city, three days' journey in breadth. •
Hab 1: 6 who march through the breadth of the earth 2
Zec 2: 2 To measure Jerusalem, to see what is its breadth 3
5: 2 is twenty cubits, and its breadth ten cubits. 3
Eph 3:18 what is the breadth and length and height 6
Rev 21:16 its length the same as its breadth; 6
16 its length and breadth and height are equal. 6
1Es 6:25 and its breadth 60 cubits 6
Jdt 7: 3 they spread out in breadth over Dothan 5
Sir 1: 3 The height of heaven, the breadth of the earth 6

breadth *See also* length.

break 1. אבד 2. בוא 3. בקע 4. גדע 5. דכה 6. הרס 7. חבל 8. חלל 9. חַת 10. חתת 11. מַחְתֶּרֶת 12. מַסַּע 13. נָכֵא 14. נפץ 15. נתע 16. נתק 17. עבר 18. עלה 19. ענה 20. פרס 21. פֶּרֶץ 22. פרץ 23. פרק 24. פרר 25. פתח 26. קֹצֶר 27. רעע 28. רצץ 29. שֶׁבֶר 30. שבר 31. שִׁבָּרוֹן 32. רקק (A) 33. ἀθετέω 34. διαρήγνυμι 35. διαρρήσσω 36. διασκεδάννυμι 37. διαχέω 38. διορύσσω 39. ἐνθρύπτω 40. κατάγνυμι 41. κατακλάω 42. καταλύω 43. κλάσις 44. κλάω 45. λύω 46. παραβαίνω 47. παράβασις 48. παραβάτης 49. περικλάω 50. ῥάσσω 51. συνθρύπτω 52. συντρίβω 53. contero
Gen 17:14 his people; he has broken my covenant. 24
19: 9 man Lot, and drew near to break the door. 30
27:40 but when you break loose you shall break his yoke 23
32:24 wrestled with him until the breaking of the day. 18
26 Then he said, "Let me go, for the day is breaking. 18
Exd 6: 9 not listen . . because of their broken spirit 26
12:46 and you shall not break a bone of it. 30
22: 2 If a thief is found breaking in, and is struck 11
32:19 broke them at the foot of the mountain. 30
34: 1 were on the first tables, which you broke. 30
13 You shall . . break their pillars, and cut down 30
Lev 2: 6 you shall break it in pieces, and pour oil on it 25
6:28 the earthem vessel . . shall be broken 30
11:33 it shall be unclean, and you shall break it 30
15:12 vessel which he . . touches shall be broken 30
26:13 I have broken the bars of your yoke 30
15 if you . . break my covenant 24
19 I will break the pride of your power 30
26 When I break your staff of bread 29
44 so as to . . break my covenant with them 24
Num 9:12 none of it until the morning, nor break a bone of it; 30
10: 2 you shall use them . . for breaking camp. 12
15:31 Because he has . . broken his commandment 24
30: 2 he shall not break his word; he shall do 8
Deu 9:17 cast them . . and broke them before your eyes. 30
10: 2 words . . on the first tables which you broke 30
31:16 people . . will forsake me and break my covenant 24
20 turn . . and despise me and break my covenant. 24
Jdg 2: 1 I said, 'I will never break my covenant with you 24
7:20 companies blew the trumpets and broke the jars 30
19:25 And as the dawn began to break, they let her go. 18
1Sm 2: 4 The bows of the mighty are broken 9
4:18 Eli fell over backward . . and his neck was broken 30
9:26 Then at the break of dawn Samuel called to Saul 18
2Sm 23:16 Then the three mighty men broke through the camp 3
1Kg 15:19 go, break your league with Ba'asha king of Israel 24
2Kg 18: 4 He removed the high places, and broke the pillars 30
21 relying now on Egypt, that broken reed of a staff 28
1Ch 11:18 broke through the camp of the Philistines 3
2Ch 14:13 they were broken before the LORD and his army. 30
16: 3 go, break your league with Ba'asha king of Israel 24
Ezr 9:14 break thy commandments again and intermarry 24
Neh 4:21 held the spears from the break of dawn 18
Job 4:10 the teeth of the young lions, are broken. 15
16:14 He breaks me with breach upon breach; 22
17: 1 My spirit is broken, my days are extinct 7
24:20 wickedness is broken like a tree.' 30
29:17 I broke the fangs of the unrighteous 30
31:22 let my arm be broken from its socket. 30
38:15 their uplifted arm is broken. 30
Ps 2: 9 You shall break them with a rod of iron 27
3: 7 thou dost break the teeth of the wicked. 30
10:15 Break thou the arm of the wicked and evildoer; 30
29: 5 The voice of the LORD breaks the cedars 30
5 LORD breaks the cedars of Lebanon. 30
31:12 I have become like a broken vessel. 1
34:20 He keeps all his bones; not one of them is broken. 30
37:15 their bows shall be broken. 30
17 For the arms of the wicked shall be broken; 30
44:19 shouldst have broken us in the place of jackals 5
46: 9 he breaks the bow, and shatters the spear 30
51: 8 let the bones which thou hast broken rejoice. 5
17 sacrifice acceptable to God is a broken spirit; 30
17 a broken . . heart, O God, thou wilt not despise. 30
58: 6 O God, break the teeth in their mouths; 6
60: 1 O God, thou hast rejected us, broken our defenses; 22
69:20 Insults have broken my heart 30
74:13 thou didst break the heads of the dragons 30
76: 3 There he broke the flashing arrows, the shield 30
102:23 He has broken my strength in mid-course; 19
105:16 When he . . broke every staff of bread 30
119:126 for the LORD to act, for thy law has been broken. 24
124: 7 snare is broken, and we have escaped! 30
Prv 6:15 in a moment he will be broken beyond healing. 30
15: 4 but perverseness in it breaks the spirit. 29
13 but by sorrow of heart the spirit is broken. 13
18:14 but a broken spirit who can bear? 13
25:15 soft tongue will break a bone. 30
29: 1 suddenly be broken beyond healing. 30
Ecc 4:12 A threefold cord is not quickly broken. 16
12: 6 or the golden bowl is broken 28

6 or the pitcher is broken at the fountain 30
6 or the wheel broken at the cistern 28
Isa 5:27 is loose, not a sandal-thong broken; 16
8: 9 Be broken, you peoples, and be dismayed; give ear 27
15 stumble thereon; they shall fall and be broken; 30
9: 4 rod . . thou hast broken as on the day of Mid'ian. 10
14: 5 The LORD has broken the staff of the wicked 30
25 that I will break the Assyrian in my land 30
29 that the rod which smote you is broken 30
24: 5 violated . . broken the everlasting covenant. 24
19 The earth is utterly broken, the earth is rent 27
27:11 When its boughs are dry, they are broken; 30
28:13 that they may go, and fall backward, and be broken 30
30:13 iniquity . . like a break in a high wall 21
14 its breaking is like that of a potter's vessel 30
33: 8 Covenants are broken, witnesses are despised 24
20 nor will any of its cords be broken. 16
36: 6 relying on Egypt, that broken reed of a staff 28
38:13 like a lion he breaks all my bones; 30
42: 3 a bruised reed he will not break 30
58: 6 the oppressed go free, and to break every yoke? 16
Jer 2:13 broken cisterns, that can hold no water. 30
16 the men . . have broken the crown of your head. 27
20 For long ago you broke your yoke 30
34 you did not find them breaking in. 11
5: 5 But they all alike had broken the yoke 30
10:20 My tent is destroyed, and all my cords are broken; 16
11:10 and the house of Judah have broken my covenant 24
14:21 remember and do not break thy covenant with us. 24
15:12 Can one break iron, iron from the north, and bronze? 27
16: 7 No one shall break bread for the mourner 20
19:10 you shall break the flask in the sight of the men 30
11 will I break this people and this city 30
11 this city, as one breaks a potter's vessel 30
22:28 Is this man Coni'ah a despised, broken pot 14
23: 9 My heart is broken within me, all my bones shake; 30
28: 2 I have broken the yoke of the king of Babylon. 30
4 for I will break the yoke of the king of Babylon. 30
10 took the yoke-bars . . and broke them. 30
11 Even so will I break the yoke of Nebuchadnez'zar 30
12 the prophet Hanani'ah had broken the yoke-bars 30
13 Thus says the LORD: You have broken wooden bars 30
30: 8 that I will break the yoke from off their neck 30
31:32 my covenant which they broke 24
33:20 If you can break my covenant with the day 24
21 my covenant with David my servant may be broken 24
43:13 He shall break the obelisks of Heliop'olis 30
48:17 say, 'How the mighty scepter is broken 30
20 Moab is put to shame, for it is broken; wail and cry! 10
25 The horn of Moab is cut off, and his arm is broken 30
38 for I have broken Moab like a vessel 30
39 How it is broken! How they wail! 10
49:35 Behold, I will break the bow of Elam 30
50:23 hammer of the whole earth is cut down and broken! 30
51: 8 Suddenly Babylon has fallen and been broken; 30
30 her dwellings are on fire, her bars are broken. 30
Lam 2: 9 he has ruined and broken her bars; 30
3: 4 made . . my skin waste away, and broken my bones; 30
Ezk 4:16 Son of man, behold, I will break the staff of bread 30
5:16 famine upon you, and break your staff of bread. 30
6: 4 and your incense altars shall be broken; 30
6 your idols broken and destroyed 30
9 when I have broken their wanton heart 53
14:13 break its staff of bread and send famine upon it 30
16:59 despised the oath in breaking the covenant 24
17:15 Can he break the covenant and yet escape? 24
16 he despised, and whose covenant with him he broke 24
18 he despised the oath and broke the covenant 24
19 which he despised, and my covenant which he broke 24
21: 6 sigh with breaking heart and bitter grief 31
26: 2 Aha, the gate of the peoples is broken 30
29: 7 when they grasped you with the hand, you broke 28
7 when they leaned upon you, you broke 30
30: 8 set fire to Egypt, and all her helpers are broken. 30
18 when I break there the dominion of Egypt 29
21 I have broken the arm of Pharaoh king of Egypt; 30
22 and will break his arms, both the strong arm 30
22 both the strong arm and the one that was broken; 30
24 but I will break the arms of Pharaoh 30
32:28 you shall be broken 30
34:27 when I break the bars of their yoke, and deliver 29
44: 7 You have broken my covenant 24
Dan 2:40 like iron . . it shall break and crush all these. 32
8: 7 struck the ram and broke his two horns; 30
8 when he was strong, the great horn was broken 30
22 As for the horn that was broken, 30
25 but, by no human hand, he shall be broken. 30
11: 4 kingdom shall be broken and divided 30
20 within a few days he shall be broken 30
22 utterly swept away before him and broken 30
Hos 1: 5 I will break the bow of Israel in the valley 30
4: 2 they break all bounds and murder follows murder. 22
7: 1 they deal falsely, the thief breaks in 2
8: 1 because they have broken my covenant 17
6 The calf of Sama'ria shall be broken to pieces. *
Ams 1: 5 I will break the bar of Damascus, and cut off 30
Nah 1:13 And now I will break his yoke from off you 30
Zec 11:10 I took my staff Grace, and I broke it 4
14 Then I broke my second staff Union 4

Mat 6:19 consume and where thieves break in and steal 38
20 where thieves do not break in and steal. 38
12:20 he will not break a bruised reed 40
14:19 he looked up to heaven, and blessed, and broke 44
15:36 having given thanks he broke them and gave them 44
26:26 Jesus took bread, and blessed, and broke it 44
Mrk 6:26 he did not want to break his word to her. 33
41 blessed, and broke the loaves 41
8: 6 and having given thanks he broke them 44
19 I broke the five loaves for the 5,000 44
14: 3 she broke the flask and poured it over his head. 52
22 he took bread, and blessed, and broke it, and gave it 44
Lke 5: 6 as their nets were breaking 35
8:29 he broke the bonds 35
9:16 he looked up to heaven, and blessed and broke them 41
22:19 when he had given thanks he broke it and gave it 44
24:30 blessed, and broke it, and gave it to them. 44
35 he was known to them in the breaking of the bread. 43
Joh 5:18 because he not only broke the sabbath 45
7:23 so that the law of Moses may not be broken 45
10:35 (and scripture cannot be broken) 45
19:31 that their legs might be broken 40
32 the soldiers came and broke the legs of the first 40
33 they did not break his legs. 40
36 Not a bone of him shall be broken. 52
Act 2:42 the breaking of bread and the prayers. 43
46 breaking bread in their homes 44
20: 7 when we were gathered together to break bread 44
11 Paul had gone up and had broken bread and eaten 44
21:13 What are you doing, weeping and breaking my heart? 51
27:35 he broke it and began to eat. 44
Rom 2:23 do you dishonor God by breaking the law? 47
25 if you break the law, your circumcision becomes 48
27 you who have . . circumcision but break the law. 48
1Co 10:16 The bread which we break 44
11:24 when he had given thanks, he broke it, and said 44
Rev 5: 2 to open the scroll and break its seals? 45
Jdt 8:30 and made us take an oath which we cannot break. 46
9: 8 Break their strength by thy might 50
Sir 13: 2 will itself be broken. 52
21:14 The mind of a fool is like a broken jar 52
23:18 A man who breaks his marriage vows says 46
35:18 breaks the scepters of the unrighteous; 52
LJr 1:17 For just as one's dish is useless when it is broken 52
43 her cord was not broken. 34
Aza 1:11 do not break thy covenant 36
21 let their strength be broken. 52
Bel 1:33 had broken bread into a bowl 39
1Mc 6:62 he broke the oath he had sworn 33
15:27 he broke all the agreements he formerly had made 33
2Mc 10:28 Just as dawn was breaking 37
3Mc 2:20 those who are downcast and broken in spirit 52
4Mc 5:33 to break the ancestral law by my own act. 42
7: 5 broke the maddening waves of the emotion. 49
9:14 though broken in every member 44
10: 6 breaking his fingers and arms and legs 49

break *See also* day.

break a back 1. *ἐκσπονδυλίζομαι*
4Mc 11:18 his back was broken 1

break a neck 1. ערף
Isa 66: 3 sacrifices a lamb, like him who breaks a dog's neck 1

break a spirit 1. *ἄγω*
4Mc 10: 7 they were not able in any way to break his spirit 1

break a word 1. *διαψεύδω* 2. *ψεύδω*
1Mc 11:53 he broke his word about all that he had promised; 2
13:19 Trypho broke his word 1

break against 1. *προσρήσσω*
Lke 6:48 the stream broke against that house 1
49 a house . . against which the stream broke 1

break an oath 1. *ἐπιορκέω*
1Es 1:48 he broke his oath and rebelled 1

break asunder 1. נתץ 2. נתק 3. פרר
Job 16:12 I was at ease, and he broke me asunder; 3
Ps 107:14 broke their bonds asunder. 2
Nah 1: 6 and the rocks are broken asunder by him. 1

break away 1. פרץ
1Sm 25:10 servants . . breaking away from their masters. 1

break camp 1. *ἀναζεύγνυμι* 2. *ἀναζευγνύω*
Jdt 7: 1 to break camp and move against Bethulia 2
1Mc 12:32 Then he broke camp and went to Damascus 1

break down 1. הלם 2. הרס 3. חמס 4. חתת 5. ירד 6. נתץ 7. ערף 8. פרץ 9. קרר 10. שבר 11. *ἐπιβάλλω* 12. *λύω* 13. extero
Lev 14:45 he shall break down the house, its stones 6
Num24:17 it shall . . break down all the sons of Sheth. 9
Deu 7: 5 you shall break down their altars 6
Jdg 2: 2 you shall break down their altars.' 6
6:28 behold, the altar of Ba'al was broken down 6
8: 9 When I come again in peace, I will break down this 6
17 he broke down the tower of Penu'el, and slew the men 6
2Kg 14:13 broke down the wall of Jerusalem for 400 cubits 8
23: 7 he broke down the houses of the . . prostitutes 6
8 and he broke down the high places of the gates 6
25:10 all . . broke down the walls around Jerusalem. 6
2Ch 14: 3 broke down the pillars 10
25:23 broke down the wall of Jerusalem for 400 cubits 8
26: 6 broke down the wall of Gath and the wall of Jabneh 8
31: 1 all Israel . . broke down the high places 6
32: 5 built up all the wall that was broken down 8
33: 3 which his father Hezeki'ah had broken down 6
34: 4 broke down the altars of the Ba'als 6
7 he broke down the altars, and beat the Ashe'rim 6
36:19 broke down the wall of Jerusalem, and burned all 6
Neh 1: 3 wall of Jerusalem is broken down, and its gates 8
2:13 walls of Jerusalem which were broken down 8
4: 3 fox goes up . . he will break down their stone wall! 8
Job 19:10 He breaks me down on every side, and I am gone 6
Ps 28: 5 he will break them down and build them up no more. 2
52: 5 God will break you down for ever; 6
74: 6 then all its carved wood they broke down 1
80:12 Why then hast thou broken down its walls 8
Prv 24:31 its stone wall was broken down. 2
Ecc 3: 3 a time to break down, and a time to build up; 8
Isa 5: 5 break down its wall, and it shall be trampled 8
22:10 you broke down the houses to fortify the wall. 6
24:10 The city of chaos is broken down 10
43:14 I will send to Babylon and break down all the bars 5
Jer 1:10 to pluck up and to break down, to destroy 6
18: 7 that I will pluck up and break down and destroy it 6
31:28 watched over them to pluck up and break down 6
39: 8 and broke down the walls of Jerusalem. 6
45: 4 Behold, what I have built I am breaking down 2
48: 1 the fortress is put to shame and broken down; 4
52:14 broke down all the walls round about Jerusalem. 6
Lam 2: 2 in his wrath he has broken down the strongholds 2
6 He has broken down his booth like that of a garden 3
Ezk 13:14 I will break down the wall that you have daubed 2
16:39 and break down your lofty places; 6
26: 4 the walls of Tyre, and break down her towers; 2
9 with his axes he will break down your towers. 6
12 they will break down your walls 2
30:16 be breached, and its walls broken down. *
Hos 10: 2 The LORD will break down their altars 7
Mrk 14:72 he broke down and wept. 11
Eph 2:14 has broken down the dividing wall of hostility 12
1Es 1:55 broke down the walls of Jerusalem 12
2Es 15:61 you shall be broken down by them like stubble 13

break faith 1. מעל
Num 5: 6 men commit by breaking faith with the LORD 1
Deu 32:51 because you broke faith with me in the midst 1
Jos 7: 1 Israel broke faith in regard to the devoted 1
22:20 Did not Achan . . break faith in the matter 1
Ezr 10: 2 We have broken faith with our God 1

break forth 1. בקע 2. פצח 3. פרץ 4. פֶּרֶץ פרץ 5. פתח 6. *ῥήγνυμι*
2Sm 6: 8 because the LORD had broken forth upon Uzzah; 3
1Ch 13:11 because the LORD had broken forth upon Uzzah; 4
15:13 LORD our God broke forth upon us 3
Ps 98: 4 break forth into joyous song and sing praises! 2
Prv 3:20 by his knowledge the deeps broke forth 1
Isa 14: 7 quiet; they break forth into singing. 2
35: 6 For waters shall break forth in the wilderness 1
44:23 break forth into singing, O mountains 2
49:13 break forth, O mountains, into singing! 2
52: 9 Break forth together into singing 2
54: 1 break forth into singing and cry aloud 2
55:12 hills before you shall break forth into singing 2
58: 8 Then shall your light break forth like the dawn 1
Jer 1:14 Out of the north evil shall break forth 5
Gal 4:27 break forth and shout, you who are not in travail; 6

break in pieces 1. גרם 2. דכא 3. חתת 4. כתת 5. נפץ 6. נתץ 7. פצח 8. פצץ 9. שבר 10. דקק (A) 11. *διαθρύπτω* 12. *θραύω* 13. *συντρίβω*
Exd 23:24 and break their pillars in pieces. 9
Lev 11:35 it shall be broken in pieces 6
Num24: 8 shall break their bones in pieces 1
1Kg 19:11 rent the mountains, and broke in pieces the rocks 9
2Kg 11:18 his altars and his images they broke in pieces 9
18: 4 And he broke in pieces the bronze serpent 4
23:12 the altars . . he pulled down and broke in pieces *
14 And he broke in pieces the pillars 9
15 he pulled down and he broke in pieces its stones 13
25:13 the pillars . . the Chalde'ans broke in pieces 9
2Ch 15: 6 They were broken in pieces 4
23:17 his altars and his images they broke in pieces 9
31: 1 all Israel . . broke in pieces the pillars 9
34: 4 he broke in pieces the Ashe'rim and the graven 9
Job 19: 2 you torment me, and break me in pieces with words? 2
Isa 45: 2 I will break in pieces the doors of bronze 9
Jer 23:29 and like a hammer which breaks the rock in pieces? 8
48:12 empty his vessels, and break his jars in pieces. 5
51:20 weapon of war: with you I break nations in pieces; 5
21 with you I break in pieces the horse and his rider; 5

21 I break in pieces the chariot and the charioteer; 5
22 with you I break in pieces man and woman; 5
22 I break in pieces the old man and the youth; 5
22 I break in pieces the young man and the maiden; 5
23 I break in pieces the shepherd and his flock; 5
23 with you I break in pieces the farmer and his team; 5
23 I break in pieces governors and commanders. 5
56 are taken, their bows are broken in pieces; 3
52:17 the Chalde'ans broke in pieces, and carried all 9
Dan 2:34 smote the image . . and broke them in pieces; 10
35 iron . . gold, all together were broken in pieces 10
44 It shall break in pieces all these kingdoms 10
45 broke in pieces the iron, the bronze, the clay 10
6:24 lions . . broke all their bones in pieces. 10
7: 7 great iron teeth; it devoured and broke in pieces 10
19 which devoured and broke in pieces, 10
Mic 3: 3 and break their bones in pieces 7
Mrk 5: 4 the fetters he broke in pieces 13
Rev 2:27 as when earthen pots are broken in pieces 13
Sir 43:15 the hailstones are broken in pieces. 11
3Mc 6: 5 Sennacherib . . you, O Lord, broke in pieces 12

break in spirit 1. θραύω
2Mc 9:11 Then it was that, broken in spirit, he began . . 1

break in sunder 1. קוט
Job 8:14 His confidence breaks in sunder 1

break into 1. פרץ 2. διορύσσω
2Ch 24: 7 sons of Athali'ah . . had broken into the house 1
Prv 25:28 like a city broken into and left without walls. 1
Mat 24:43 would not have let his house be broken into. 2
Lke 12:39 he would not have left his house to be broken into. 2

break loose 1. פרע 2. רוד
Gen 27:40 but when you break loose you shall break his yoke 2
Exd 32:25 when Moses saw that the people had broken loose 1
25 (for Aaron had let them break loose, to their shame 1

make break out 1. בקע
Ezk 13:13 I will make a stormy wind break out in my wrath; 1

break of day 1. שְׁפַרְפָּר (A)
Dan 6:19 Then, at break of day, the king arose 1

break off 1. נתק 2. קטף 3. פרק (A) 4. διαλύω 5. ἐκκλάω 6. περικλάω 7. derelinquo
Job 17:11 My days are past, my plans are broken off 1
Ezk 17: 4 he broke off the topmost of its young twigs 2
22 I will break off from the topmost of its young 2
Dan 4:27 break off your sins by practicing 3
Rom 11:17 But if some of the branches were broken off 5
19 Branches were broken off so that I might be 5
20 They were broken off because of their unbelief 5
2Es 10: 5 Then I broke off the reflections 7
Wis 4: 5 The branches will be broken off 6
Sir 22:20 will break off the friendship. 4

break on the wheel 1. τροχίζω
4Mc 5: 3 were to be broken on the wheel and killed. 1

break open 1. διακόπτω
2Mc 10:36 Others broke open the gates 1

break out 1. בער 2. בקע 3. גלע 4. זרח 5. יצא 6. פרח 7. פרץ 8. צלח 9. שתר 10. ἐμπίπτω 11. emitto
Exd 9: 9 shall . . become boils breaking out in sores 6
10 and it became boils breaking out in sores on man 6
19:22 lest the LORD break out upon them. 7
24 the LORD, lest he break out against them. 7
22: 6 When fire breaks out and catches in thorns 5
Lev 13:12 if the leprosy breaks out in the skin 6
20 leprosy, it has broken out in the boil 6
25 leprosy; it has broken out in the burn 6
39 it is tetter that has broken out in the skin 6
42 it is leprosy breaking out on his bald head 6
14:43 If the disease breaks out again in the house 6
1Sm 5: 9 so that tumors broke out upon them. 9
2Ch 26:19 leprosy broke out on his forehead 4
Ps 106:18 Fire also broke out in their company; 1
29 plague broke out among them. 7
Prv 17:14 so quit before the quarrel breaks out. 3
18: 1 seeks . . to break out against all sound judgment. 3
Ezk 13:11 hailstones will fall, and a stormy wind break out; 2
Ams 5: 6 Seek the LORD and live, lest he break out like fire 8
2Es 5: 8 and fire shall often break out 11
Sir 48:10 calm the wrath of God before it breaks out in fury •
LJr 1:55 When fire breaks out in a temple of wooden gods 10

break out afresh 1. מאס
Job 7: 5 my skin hardens, then breaks out afresh. 1

break the law 1. ἀνομέω 2. παρανομία
1Es 9: 7 You have broken the law 1
4Mc 2:11 one rebukes her when she breaks the law. 2

break the neck 1. ערף
Exd 13:13 if . . not redeem it you shall break its neck. 1
34:20 if . . not redeem it you shall break its neck. 1
Deu 21: 4 break the heifer's neck there in the valley. 1
6 heifer whose neck was broken in the valley; 1

break the thread 1. ἀπορέω
4Mc 9:25 the saintly youth broke the thread of life. 1

break through 1. בקע 2. הרס 3. עבר 4. פרץ 5. διοδεύω
Exd 19:21 warn the people, lest they break through 2
24 the people break through to come up to the LORD 2
2Sm 5:20 The LORD has broken through my enemies before me 4
2Kg 3:26 he took with him . . swordsmen to break through 1
1Ch 14:11 God has broken through my enemies by my hand 4
Ps 18:12 there broke through his clouds hailstones 3
Ecc 10: 8 serpent will bite him who breaks through a wall. 4
Mic 2:13 they will break through and pass the gate 4
Aza 1:25 it broke through and burned those of the Chaldeans 5

break to pieces 1. חתת 2. דקק (A) 3. συνθλάω
1Sm 2:10 The adversaries . . shall be broken to pieces; 1
Isa 7: 8 E'phraim will be broken to pieces 1
Dan 2:40 iron breaks to pieces and shatters all things; 2
7:23 trample it down, and break it to pieces. 2
Lke 20:18 will be broken to pieces 3

break up 1. ניר 2. נפץ 3. נתס 4. שבר 5. λύω
1Kg 5: 9 and I will have them broken up there 2
Job 30:13 They break up my path, they promote my calamity; 3
Jer 4: 3 Break up your fallow ground 1
Hos 10:12 break up your fallow ground 1
Jon 1: 4 the ship threatened to break up. 4
Act 13:43 when the meeting of the synagogue broke up 5
27:41 the stern was broken up by the surf. 5

breakfast 1. ἀριστάω
Joh 21:12 Jesus said to them, "Come and have breakfast. 1
15 When they had finished breakfast 1

woman who breaks wedlock 1. נאף
Ezk 16:38 And I will judge you as women who break wedlock 1

breast 1. חָזֶה 2. לֵב 3. מֵעֶה 4. סְגוֹר לֵב 5. שֹׁד 6. שַׁד 7. חֲדִי (A) 8. κόλπος 9. μαστός 10. στῆθος 11. mamilla 12. pectus
Gen 49:25 blessings of the breasts and of the womb. 6
Exd 29:26 you shall take the breast of the ram 1
27 you shall consecrate the breast of the wave 1
Lev 7:30 he shall bring the fat with the breast 1
30 that the breast may be waved as a wave offering 1
31 but the breast shall be for Aaron and his sons 1
34 For the breast that is waved and the thigh 1
8:29 Moses took the breast, and waved it for a wave 1
9:20 they put the fat upon the breasts, and he burned 1
21 the breasts and the right thigh Aaron waved 1
10:14 the breast that is waved and the thigh 1
15 The thigh that is offered and the breast 1
Num 6:20 together with the breast that is waved 1
18:18 as the breast that is waved and as the right thigh 1
Job 3:12 Or why the breasts, that I should suck? 6
24: 9 who snatch the fatherless child from the breast 5
Ps 22: 9 thou didst keep me safe upon my mother's breasts. 6
14 heart is like wax, it is melted within my breast 3
131: 2 like a child quieted at its mother's breast; •
Sng 1:13 to me a bag of myrrh, that lies between my breasts. 6
4: 5 Your two breasts are like two fawns 6
7: 3 Your two breasts are like two fawns 6
7 and your breasts are like its clusters. 6
8 Oh, may your breasts be like clusters of the vine 6
8: 1 a brother to me, that nursed at my mother's breast! 6
8 We have a little sister, and she has no breasts. 6
10 I was a wall, and my breasts were like towers; 6
Isa 28: 9 weaned from the milk, those taken from the breast? 6
32:12 Beat upon your breasts for the pleasant fields 6
60:16 you shall suck the breast of kings; 5
66:11 and be satisfied with her consoling breasts; 5
Lam 4: 3 Even the jackals give the breast and suckle 6
Ezk 16: 7 your breasts were formed, and your hair had grown; 6
23: 3 there their breasts were pressed 6
21 your bosom and pressed your young breasts. 6
34 and pluck out your hair, and tear your breasts; 6
Dan 2:32 head of . . gold, its breast and arms of silver 7
Hos 2: 2 put away . . adultery from between her breasts; 6
9:14 Give them a miscarrying womb and dry breasts. 6
13: 8 I will tear open their breast 4
Nah 2: 7 moaning like doves, and beating their breasts. 2
Lke 11:27 the breasts that you sucked! 9
18:13 beat his breast, saying, 'God, be merciful to me 10
23:29 and the breasts that never gave suck!' 9
48 all . . returned home beating their breasts. 10
Joh 13:23 was lying close to the breast of Jesus; 8
25 lying thus, close to the breast of Jesus, he said 10
21:20 who had lain close to his breast at the supper 10
Rev 1:13 and with a golden girdle round his breast; 9
15: 6 and their breasts girded with golden girdles. 10
2Es 8:10 from the members . . (that is, from the breasts) 11
10 milk . . which is the fruit of the breasts 11
14:40 and wisdom increased in my breast 12
2Mc 3:19 girded with sackcloth under their breasts 9
6:10 with their babies hung at their breasts 9
3Mc 5:49 others with babies at their breasts 9
50 removing the babies from their breasts 9

breastpiece 1. חֹשֶׁן
Exd 25: 7 for the ephod and for the breastpiece. 1
28: 4 they shall make: a breastpiece, an ephod, a robe 1
15 you shall make a breastpiece of judgment 1
22 shall make for the breastpiece twisted chains 1
23 shall make for the breastpiece two rings of gold 1
23 two rings on the two edges of the breastpiece. 1
24 in the two rings at the edges of the breastpiece; 1
26 put them at the two ends of the breastpiece 1
28 they shall bind the breastpiece by its rings 1
28 that the breastpiece shall not come loose 1
29 names . . in the breastpiece of judgment upon 1
30 in the breastpiece of judgment you shall put 1
29: 5 put on Aaron . . the ephod, and the breastpiece 1
35: 9 for the ephod and for the breastpiece. 1
27 stones . . for the ephod and for the breastpiece 1
39: 8 He made the breastpiece, in skilled work 1
9 It was square; the breastpiece was made double 1
15 they made on the breastpiece twisted chains 1
16 two rings on the two edges of the breastpiece; 1
17 in the two rings at the edges of the breastpiece. 1
19 and put them at the two ends of the breastpiece 1
21 they bound the breastpiece by its rings 1
21 that the breastpiece should not come loose 1
Lev 8: 8 he placed the breastpiece on him 1
8 in the breastpiece he put the Urim and the Thummim 1

breastplate 1. שִׁרְיוֹן 2. ἐνδύω 3. θώραξ
1Kg 22:34 between the scale armor and the breastplate; 1
2Ch 18:33 between the scale armor and the breastplate; 1
Isa 59:17 He put on righteousness as a breastplate 1
Eph 6:14 put on the breastplate of righteousness 3
1Th 5: 8 put on the breastplate of faith and love 3
Rev 9: 9 they had scales like iron breastplates 3
17 the riders wore breastplates the color of fire 3
Wis 5:18 he will put on righteousness as a breastplate 3
Sir 43:20 the water puts it on like a breastplate. 2
1Mc 3: 3 Like a giant he put on his breastplate 3
6: 2 golden shields, breastplates, and weapons 3

breath 1. אַף 2. הֶבֶל 3. נֶפֶשׁ 4. נְשָׁמָה 5. רוּחַ 6. נִשְׁמָה (A) 7. ἀήρ 8. ἄσθμα 9. ἀτμίς 10. πνεῦμα 11. πνοή 12. ψυχή 13. spiramentum 14. spiritus
Gen 1:30 to . . everything that has the breath of life 3
2: 7 breathed into his nostrils the breath of life; 4
6:17 to destroy all flesh in which is the breath of life 5
7:15 flesh in which there was the breath of life. 5
22 dry land in whose nostrils was the breath of life 5
Jos 10:40 but utterly destroyed all that breathed 4
11:11 destroying . . there was none left that breathed 4
14 and they did not leave any that breathed. 4
2Sm 22:16 at the blast of the breath of his nostrils. 5
1Kg 15:29 he left to . . Jerobo'am not one that breathed 4
17:17 so severe that there was no breath left in him. 4
Job 4: 9 By the breath of God they perish, and by the blast 4
7: 7 Remember that my life is a breath; 5
16 Let me alone, for my days are a breath. 2
9:18 he will not let me get my breath 5
12:10 living thing and the breath of all mankind. 5
27: 3 as long as my breath is in me 4
32: 8 the spirit in a man, the breath of the Almighty 4
33: 4 the breath of the Almighty gives me life. 4
34:14 gather to himself his breath 4
37:10 By the breath of God ice is given 4
41:21 His breath kindles coals, and a flame comes forth 3
Ps 18:15 O LORD, at the blast of the breath of thy nostrils. 5
33: 6 all their host by the breath of his mouth. 5
39: 5 Surely every man stands as a mere breath! Selah 2
11 surely every man is a mere breath! Selah 2
62: 9 Men of low estate are but a breath 2
9 they are together lighter than a breath. 2
78:33 he made their days vanish like a breath 2
94:11 thoughts of man, that they are but a breath. 2
104:29 when thou takest away their breath, they die 5
135:17 nor is there any breath in their mouths. 5
144: 4 Man is like a breath, his days . . passing shadow. 2
146: 4 When his breath departs he returns to his earth; 5
Ecc 3:19 They all have the same breath 5
Sng 7: 8 and the scent of your breath like apples 1
Isa 2:22 Turn away from man in whose nostrils is breath 4
11: 4 with the breath of his lips . . slay the wicked. 5
30:28 his breath is like an overflowing stream 5
33 the breath of the LORD, like a stream of brimstone 4
33:11 your breath is a fire that will consume you. 5
40: 7 fades, when the breath of the LORD blows upon it; 5
42: 5 who gives breath to the people upon it 4
57:13 will carry them off, a breath will take them away. 2
Jer 10:14 images are false, and there is no breath in them. 5
51:17 images are false, and there is no breath in them. 5
Lam 4:20 The breath of our nostrils, the LORD'S anointed 5

Ezk 37: 5 Behold, I will cause breath to enter you 5
6 and put breath in you, and you shall live; 5
8 but there was no breath in them. 5
9 Then he said to me, "Prophesy to the breath 5
9 and say to the breath, Thus says the Lord GOD 5
9 Come from the four winds, O breath 5
10 the breath came into them, and they lived 5
Dan 5:23 but the God in whose hand is your breath 6
10:17 no strength remains . . no breath is left in me. 4
Hab 2:19 there is no breath at all in it. 5
Act 17:25 gives to all men life and breath and everything. 11
2Th 2: 8 slay him with the breath of his mouth 10
Rev 11:11 a breath of life from God entered them 10
13:15 allowed to give breath to the image of the beast 10
2Es 3: 5 thou didst breathe into him the breath of life 14
7:29 and all who draw human breath. 13
13:10 and from his lips a flaming breath 14
11 the stream of fire and the flaming breath 14
16:61 and gave him breath and life and understanding 14
Jdt 7:27 see our . . children draw their last breath. 12
Wis 2: 2 because the breath in our nostrils is smoke 11
7:25 For she is a breath of the power of God 9
11:18 such as breathe out fiery breath 8
20 men could fall at a single breath 10
20 scattered by the breath of thy power 10
15:15 nor nostrils with which to draw breath 7
Sir 33:20 While you are still alive and have breath in you 11
38:28 the breath of the fire melts his flesh 9
LJr 1:25 there is no breath in them. 10
2Mc 3:31 one who was lying quite at his last breath. 11
7: 9 when he was at his last breath, he said 11
22 It was not I who gave you life and breath 10
23 will in his mercy give life and breath back to you 10
4Mc 11:11 gasping for breath and in anguish of body 10
breath *See also* gasp.

breath of life 1. נְשָׁמָה
Isa 57:16 the spirit, and I have made the breath of life. 1

breathe 1. מַפָּח 2. נפח 3. נְשָׁמָה 4. *ἐμπνέω*
5. *ἔμπνους* 6. *ἐμφυσάω* 7. *πνέω* 8. *σπάω* 9. insuflo
Gen 2: 7 from the ground, and breathed into his nostrils 2
Deu 20:16 you shall save alive nothing that breathes 3
Job 11:20 their hope is to breathe their last. 1
Ps 150: 6 Let everything that breathes praise the LORD! 3
Sng 2:17 Until the day breathes and the shadows flee 2
4: 6 Until the day breathes and the shadows flee 2
Ezk 37: 9 breathe upon these slain, that they may live. 2
Joh 20:22 when he had said this, he breathed on them, and said 6
Act 9: 1 Saul, still breathing threats and murder 4
2Es 3: 5 thou didst breathe into him the breath of life 9
Wis 7: 3 when I was born, I began to breathe the common air 8
2Mc 7: 5 to take him to the fire, still breathing 5
9: 7 breathing fire in his rage against the Jews 7

breathe heavily 1. *ἀσθμαίνω*
Sir 31:19 He does not breathe heavily upon his bed. 1

breathe into 1. *ἐμφυσάω*
Wis 15:11 and breathed into him a living spirit. 1

breathe one's last 1. גוע 2. *ἀποπνέω* 3. *ἐκπνέω*
Gen 25: 8 Abraham breathed his last and died 1
17 he breathed his last and died 1
35:29 Isaac breathed his last; and he died 1
49:33 Jacob . . breathed his last, and was gathered 1
Job 14:10 man breathes his last, and where is he? 1
Mrk 15:37 Jesus uttered a loud cry, and breathed his last. 3
39 saw that he thus breathed his last 3
Lke 23:46 having said this he breathed his last. 3
4Mc 15:18 When the first-born breathed his last 2

breathe out 1. יָפֵחַ 2. פוח 3. *ἐκφυσάω* 4. *φυσάω*
Ps 27:12 risen against me, and they breathe out violence. 1
Prv 6:19 a false witness who breathes out lies 2
14: 5 but a false witness breathes out lies. 2
Wis 11:18 such as breathe out fiery breath 4
Sir 43: 4 it breathes out fiery vapors 3

delicately bred 1. ענג 2. עָנֹג
Deu 28:54 man who is the most tender and delicately bred 2
Jer 6: 2 The comely and delicately bred I will destroy 1

delicately bred woman 1. עָנֹג
Deu 28:56 most tender and delicately bred woman among you 1

breeches 1. מִכְנָס
Exd 28:42 you shall make for them linen breeches to cover 1
39:28 and the linen breeches of fine twined linen 1
Lev 6:10 and put his linen breeches upon his body 1
16: 4 and shall have the linen breeches on his body 1
Ezk 44:18 and linen breeches upon their loins; 1

linen breeches 1. *περισκελής*
Sir 45: 8 the linen breeches, the long robe, and the ephod. 1

breed 1. בֵּן 2. חמם 3. יחם 4. עבר 5. רבע 6. רמם
7. *ἀνατρέφω* 8. *γεννάω*
Gen 30:38 And since they bred when they came to drink 2
39 the flocks bred in front of the rods 2
41 Whenever the stronger of the flock were breeding 3
41 the flock, that they might breed among the rods 3
Exd 16:20 the morning, and it bred worms and became foul; 6
Lev 19:19 You shall not let your cattle breed 5
Est 8:10 on swift horses . . bred from the royal stud. 1
Job 21:10 Their bull breeds without fail; their cow calves 4
2Ti 2:23 you know that they breed quarrels. 8
4Mc 11:15 Since to this end we were born and bred 7

breed abundantly 1. שרץ
Gen 8:17 that they may breed abundantly on the earth 1

sheep breeder 1. נֹקֵד
2Kg 3: 4 Now Mesha king of Moab was a sheep breeder; 1

brevity 1. *σύντομος*
2Mc 2:31 be allowed to strive for brevity of expression 1

bribe 1. בֶּצַע 2. כֹּפֶר 3. מַתָּנָה 4. שחד 5. שֹׁחַד
6. שִׁלּוּם 7. *δωροκοπέω* 8. *χρῆμα*
Exd 18:21 who are trustworthy and who hate a bribe; 1
23: 8 you shall take no bribe, for a bribe blinds 5
8 no bribe, for a bribe blinds the officials 5
Deu 10:17 God, who is not partial and takes no bribe. 5
16:19 not take a bribe, for a bribe blinds the eyes 5
19 bribe blinds the eyes of the wise and subverts 5
27:25 'Cursed be he who takes a bribe to slay an innocent 5
1Sm 8: 3 they took bribes and perverted justice. 5
12: 3 have I taken a bribe to blind my eyes with it? 2
2Ch 19: 7 or partiality, or taking bribes. 5
Ps 15: 5 and does not take a bribe against the innocent. 5
26:10 whose right hands are full of bribes. 5
Prv 15:27 but he who hates bribes will live. 3
17: 8 A bribe is like a magic stone in the eyes of him 5
23 A wicked man accepts a bribe from the bosom 5
21:14 bribe in the bosom, strong wrath. 5
Ecc 7: 7 and a bribe corrupts the mind. 3
Isa 1:23 Every one loves a bribe and runs after gifts. 5
5:23 who acquit the guilty for a bribe 5
33:15 who shakes his hands, lest they hold a bribe 5
Ezk 16:33 bribing them to come to you from every side 4
22:12 In you men take bribes to shed blood; 5
Ams 5:12 you who afflict the righteous, who take a bribe 2
Mic 3:11 Its heads give judgment for a bribe 5
7: 3 the prince and the judge ask for a bribe 6
2Mc 4:45 promised a substantial bribe to Ptolemy 8
3Mc 4:19 had been bribed to contrive a means of escape 7
bribe *See also* offer.

bribery 1. שֹׁחַד 2. *δῶρον*
Job 15:34 fire consumes the tents of bribery. 1
Sir 40:12 All bribery and injustice will be blotted out 2

brick 1. לְבֵנָה 2. *πλίνθος*
Gen 11: 3 And they had brick for stone 1
Exd 1:14 hard service, in mortar and brick 1
5: 7 no longer give the people straw to make bricks 1
8 the number of bricks which they made heretofore 1
16 No straw . . yet they say to us, 'Make bricks!' 1
18 you shall deliver the same number of bricks. 1
19 by no means lessen your daily number of bricks. 1
Isa 9:10 The bricks have fallen, but we will build 1
65: 3 in gardens and burning incense upon bricks; 1
Ezk 4: 1 you, O son of man, take a brick and lay it before you 1
Jdt 5:11 and set them to making bricks 2
brick *See also* make.

make brick 1. לבן
Gen 11: 3 let us make bricks, and burn them thoroughly. 1

brick mold 1. מַלְבֵּן
Nah 3:14 tread the mortar, take hold of the brick mold! 1

brickkiln 1. מַלְבֵּן
2Sm 12:31 and made them toil at the brickkilns; 1
bridal *See* chamber.

bride 1. כַּלָּה 2. כְּלוּלָה 3. *γυνή* 4. *νύμφη*
5. *παρθένος*
2Sm 17: 3 back to you as a bride comes home to her husband. 4
Sng 4: 8 Come with me from Lebanon, my bride; come with me 1
9 You have ravished my heart, my sister, my bride 1
10 How sweet is your love, my sister, my bride! 1
11 Your lips distil nectar, my bride; 1
12 A garden locked is my sister, my bride 1
5: 1 I come to my garden, my sister, my bride 1
Isa 49:18 you shall bind them on as a bride does. 1
61:10 and as a bride adorns herself with her jewels. 1
62: 5 and as the bridegroom rejoices over the bride 1
Jer 2: 2 the devotion of your youth, your love as a bride 2
32 forget her ornaments, or a bride her attire? 1
7:34 voice of the bridegroom and . . voice of the bride; 1
16: 9 of the bridegroom and the voice of the bride. 1
25:10 of the bridegroom and the voice of the bride 1
33:11 voice of . . bridegroom and the voice of the bride 1
Hos 4:13 and your brides commit adultery. 1
14 nor your brides when they commit adultery; 1
Jol 2:16 leave his room, and the bride her chamber. 1
Joh 3:29 He who has the bride is the bridegroom; 4
2Co 11: 2 to present you as a pure bride to her one husband. 5
Rev 18:23 the voice of bridegroom and bride shall be heard 4
19: 7 and his Bride has made herself ready; 3
21: 2 prepared as a bride adorned for her husband; 4
9 Come, I will show you the Bride, the wife of the Lamb. 4
22:17 The Spirit and the Bride say, "Come. 4
Wis 8: 2 I desired to take her for my bride 4
Bar 2:23 of the bridegroom and the voice of the bride 4
1Mc 9:37 are conducting the bride 4

bridegroom 1. בַּעַל 2. חָתָן 3. *νυμφίος* 4. spondeo
Exd 4:25 Surely you are a bridegroom of blood to me! 2
26 she said, "You are a bridegroom of blood 2
Ps 19: 5 forth like a bridegroom leaving his chamber 2
Isa 61:10 as a bridegroom decks himself with a garland 2
62: 5 and as the bridegroom rejoices over the bride 2
Jer 7:34 voice of the bridegroom and . . voice of the bride; 2
16: 9 voice of gladness, the voice of the bridegroom 2
25:10 voice of gladness, the voice of the bridegroom 2
33:11 voice of . . bridegroom and the voice of the bride 2
Jol 1: 8 Lament . . for the bridegroom of her youth. 1
2:16 Let the bridegroom leave his room 2
Mat 9:15 as long as the bridegroom is with them? 3
15 The days will come, when the bridegroom is taken 3
25: 1 went to meet the bridegroom. 3
5 As the bridegroom was delayed 3
6 'Behold, the bridegroom! Come out to meet him.' 3
10 while they went to buy, the bridegroom came 3
Mrk 2:19 while the bridegroom is with them 3
19 As long as they have the bridegroom with them 3
20 when the bridegroom is taken away from them 3
Lke 5:34 while the bridegroom is with them? 3
35 when the bridegroom is taken away from them 3
Joh 2: 9 the steward of the feast called the bridegroom 3
3:29 He who has the bride is the bridegroom; 3
29 friend of the bridegroom . . rejoices greatly 3
29 the friend . . rejoices greatly at the bridegroom's voice; 3
Rev 18:23 the voice of bridegroom and bride shall be heard 3
2Es 16:33 shall mourn because they have no bridegrooms; 4
34 Their bridegrooms shall be killed in war 4
Bar 2:23 voice of the bridegroom and the voice 3
1Mc 1:27 Every bridegroom took up the lament 3
9:39 the bridegroom came out with his friends 3

bridle 1. מֶתֶג 2. רֶסֶן 3. *φιμόω* 4. *χαλιναγωγέω*
5. *χαλινός*
Ps 32: 9 mule . . which must be curbed with bit and bridle 2
39: 1 I will bridle my mouth †
Prv 26: 3 A whip for the horse, a bridle for the ass, and a rod 1
Isa 30:28 on the jaws . . a bridle that leads astray. 2
Jas 1:26 If any one . . does not bridle his tongue 4
3: 2 a perfect man, able to bridle the whole body also. 4
Rev 14:20 blood flowed . . as high as a horse's bridle 5
4Mc 1:35 the impulses of the body are bridled by reason. 3

gold bridle 1. *χρυσοχάλινος*
1Es 3: 6 have a chariot with gold bridles 1

golden bridle 1. *χρυσοχάλινος*
2Mc 10:29 on horses with golden bridles 1

brief 1. מְעַט 2. קָטֹן 3. *βραχύς* 4. *βραχυτελής*
5. *μικρός* 6. exilis
Ezr 9: 8 now for a brief moment favor has been shown 1
Isa 54: 7 For a brief moment I forsook you 2
2Es 12: 2 and their reign was brief and full of tumult. 6
30 the reign which was brief and full of tumult 6
Wis 15: 9 his life is brief 4
2Mc 6:25 for the sake of living a brief moment longer 5
7:36 after enduring a brief suffering 3

briefly 1. *βραχύς* 2. *διὰ βραχέων* 3. *δι' ὀλίγων*
4. *συντόμως*
Act 24: 4 I beg you in your kindness to hear us briefly. 4
Heb 13:22 I have written to you briefly. 2
1Pe 5:12 By Silva'nus . . I have written briefly to you 3
2Mc 6:17 we must go on briefly with the story. 3
3Mc 4:14 the hard labor . . briefly mentioned before 1

brier 1. בַּרְקָנִים 2. חֵדֶק 3. סַלּוֹן 4. סָרָב 5. סִרְפַּד
6. שַׁיִת 7. שָׁמִיר 8. vepres
Jdg 8: 7 flail . . with the thorns . . and with briers. 1
16 and he took thorns of the wilderness and briers 1
Isa 5: 6 not be . . hoed, and briers and thorns shall grow up; 7
7:23 every place . . will become briers and thorns. 7
24 for all the land will be briers and thorns; 7
25 not come there for fear of briers and thorns; 7
9:18 like a fire, it consumes briers and thorns; 7
10:17 burn and devour his thorns and briers in one day. 7
27: 4 Would that I had thorns and briers to battle! 6
32:13 soil of my people growing up in thorns and briers; 7
55:13 instead of the brier shall come up the myrtle; 5
Ezk 2: 6 though briers and thorns are with you 4
28:24 for . . Israel there shall be no more a brier 3

Mic 7: 4 The best of them is like a brier 2
2Es 16:32 and its fields shall be for briers 8

bright 1. אהל 2. אוֹר 3. אור 4. בָּהִיר 5. בַּר 6. נֹגַהּ
7. צהב 8. ἐκλάμπω 9. λαμπρός 10. λαμπρότης
11. φωτεινός

Ezr 8:27 two vessels of fine bright bronze as precious 7
Job 11:17 your life will be brighter than the noonday; •
25: 5 Behold, even the moon is not bright 1
37:21 look on the light when it is bright in the skies 4
Ps 139:12 not dark to thee, the night is bright as the day; 3
Prv 4:18 light . . which shines brighter and brighter †
Sng 6:10 fair as the moon, bright as the sun 5
Ezk 1:13 the fire was bright 6
32: 8 All the bright lights of heaven will I make dark 2
Mat 17: 5 when lo, a bright cloud overshadowed them 11
Lke 11:36 it will be wholly bright 11
Act 10:30 behold, a man stood before me in bright apparel 9
26:13 a light . . brighter than the sun 10
Rev 15: 6 seven angels . . robed in pure bright linen 9
19: 8 clothed with fine linen, bright and pure"- 9
22: 1 river of the water of life, bright as crystal 9
16 the offspring of David, the bright morning star. 9
Sir 17:31 What is brighter than the sun? 11
23:19 10,000 times brighter than the sun 11
43: 4 with bright beams it blinds the eyes. 8

bright *See also* make, red.

become bright 1. אור

1Sm 14:27 his hand to his mouth; and his eyes became bright. 1
29 my eyes have become bright, because I tasted 1

brighten 1. אור

Ezr 9: 8 that our God may brighten our eyes and grant us 1

brightness 1. זֹהַר 2. נֹגַהּ 3. נְגֹהָה 4. זִיו (A)
5. αὔγασμα 6. δόξα 7. claritas 8. splendor

2Sm 22:13 Out of the brightness . . coals of fire flamed 2
Ps 18:12 Out of the brightness before him there broke 2
Isa 59: 9 and for brightness, but we walk in gloom. 3
60: 3 and kings to the brightness of your rising. 2
19 nor for brightness shall the moon give light 2
62: 1 until her vindication goes forth as brightness 2
Ezk 1: 4 a great cloud, with brightness round about it 2
27 and there was brightness round about him. 2
28 the appearance of the brightness round about. 2
8: 2 it was like the appearance of brightness 1
10: 4 the court was full of the brightness of the glory 2
Dan 2:31 This image, mighty and of exceeding brightness 4
12: 3 shine like the brightness of the firmament; 1
Ams 5:20 and not light, and gloom with no brightness in it? 2
Hab 3: 4 His brightness was like the light 2
Act 22:11 I could not see because of the brightness of that light 6
2Co 3: 7 because of its brightness, fading as this was 6
2Es 6:45 thou didst command the brightness of the sun 8
7:42 night, or dawn or shining or brightness or light 7
Sir 43:11 exceedingly beautiful in its brightness. 5

brilliance 1. claritas

2Es 10:50 has shown you the brilliance of her glory 1

brilliant 1. ἔκλαμπρος 2. λαμπρός

Wis 17: 5 nor did the brilliant flames of the stars avail 1
20 was illumined with brilliant light 2

brim 1. שָׂפָה 2. ἄνω

1Kg 7:23 it was round, ten cubits from brim to brim 1
23 it was round, ten cubits from brim to brim 1
24 Under its brim were gourds, for 30 cubits 1
26 its brim was made like the brim of a cup 1
26 made like the brim of a cup, like the flower 1
2Ch 4: 2 molten sea . . round, ten cubits from brim to brim 1
2 molten sea . . round, ten cubits from brim to brim 1
5 its brim was made like the brim of a cup 1
5 its brim was made like the brim of a cup 1
Joh 2: 7 And they filled them up to the brim. 2

brimstone 1. גָּפְרִית

Gen 19:24 rained on Sodom and Gomor'rah brimstone and fire 1
Deu 29:23 whole land brimstone and salt, and a burnt-out 1
Job 18:15 brimstone is scattered upon his habitation. 1
Ps 11: 6 he will rain coals of fire and brimstone; 1
Isa 30:33 the breath of the LORD, like a stream of brimstone 1
34: 9 turned into pitch, and her soil into brimstone; 1
Ezk 38:22 rains and hailstones, fire and brimstone. 1

bring 1. אסף 2. אתה 3. בוא 4. גוז 5. גמל 6. היה
7. הלך 8. יבל 9. יהב 10. יסף 11. יצא 12. לקח
13. נגש 14. נהג 15. נחה 16. נסע 17. נשא 18. נתן
19. סבב 20. עלה 21. עלל 22. עמד 23. עשה 24. צעד
25. קרב 26. שום 27. שוב 28. שית 29. אתא (A)
30. אתה (A) 31. יבל (A) 32. סבל (A) 33. עלה (A)
34. עלל (A) 35. קרב (A) 36. ἄγω 37. ἀναβιβάζω
38. ἀνάγω 39. ἀπάγω 40. ἀποδίδωμι 41. βάλλω
42. γεννάω 43. γίνομαι 44. δίδωμι 45. εἰμί
46. εἰμὶ ποιέω 47. εἰς 48. εἰσάγω 49. εἰσφέρω
50. ἐκβάλλω 51. ἐκφέρω 52. ἐνίστημι 53. ἐξάγω
54. ἐπάγω 55. ἐπισπάω 56. ἐπιστρέφω
57. ἐπισυνάγω 58. ἐπιτίθημι 59. ἔρχομαι 60. ἔχω
61. καλέω 62. καταβάλλω 63. κατάγω 64. καταρτίζω
65. κατεργάζομαι 66. κατευθύνω 67. κομίζω
68. λαλέω 69. λαμβάνω 70. μετά 71. μετάγω
72. μεταπέμπω 73. μεταφέρω 74. παράγω
75. παραλαμβάνω 76. παρέχω 77. περιφέρω
78. ποιέω 79. προάγω 80. προπέμπω 81. προσάγω
82. προσφέρω 83. συμπαραλαμβάνω 84. τίθημι
85. φέρω 86. ad 87. adduco 88. adfero 89. deduco
90. do 91. educo 92. facio 93. facio venire 94. induco
95. porto 96. traicio

Gen 2:19 every bird of the air, and brought them to the man 3
22 made into a woman and brought her to the man. 3
4: 3 In the course of time Cain brought to the LORD 3
4 Abel brought of the firstlings of his flock 3
6:17 I will bring a flood of waters upon the earth 3
19 all flesh, you shall bring two of every sort 3
8: 9 took her and brought her into the ark with him. 3
14:16 also brought back his kinsman Lot with his goods •
15: 5 he brought him outside and said 11
7 I am the LORD who brought you from Ur 11
9 He said to him, "Bring me a heifer three years old 12
10 he brought him all these, cut them in two 12
18: 4 Let a little water be brought, and wash your feet 12
19 and justice; so that the LORD may bring to Abraham 3
19:10 their hands and brought Lot into the house 3
20: 9 that you have brought on me 3
24:67 Isaac brought her into the tent, and took Rebekah 3
26:10 and you would have brought guilt upon us. 3
27: 4 such as I love, and bring it to me that I may eat; 3
5 to the field to hunt for game and bring it 3
7 'Bring me game, and prepare for me savory food 3
10 you shall bring it to your father to eat 3
12 I shall seem to be mocking him, and bring a curse 3
14 took them and brought them to his mother; 3
25 Then he said, "Bring it to me, that I may eat 13
25 he brought it to him, and he ate; 13
25 and he brought him wine, and he drank. 3
31 savory food, and brought it to his father. 3
33 that hunted game and brought it to me, and I ate it 3
29:13 kissed him, and brought him to his house. 3
23 took his daughter Leah and brought her to Jacob; 3
30:14 in the field, and brought them to his mother Leah. 3
31:39 That which was torn by wild beasts I did not bring 3
33:11 Accept, I pray you, my gift that is brought to you 3
37: 2 and Joseph brought an ill report of them to their 3
32 robe with sleeves and brought it to their father 3
39:14 said to them, "See, he has brought among us a Hebrew 3
17 The Hebrew servant, whom you have brought 3
42:16 Send one of you, and let him bring your brother 12
20 bring your youngest brother to me; 3
34 Bring your youngest brother to me; 3
43: 2 the grain which they had brought from Egypt 3
16 to the steward of his house, "Bring the men 3
17 and brought the men to Joseph's house. 3
18 the men were afraid because they were brought 3
18 we are brought in, so that he may seek occasion 3
24 the man had brought the men into Joseph's house 3
26 Joseph came home, they brought into the house 3
45:19 take wagons . . and bring your father, and come. 17
46: 7 his offspring he brought with him into Egypt. 3
32 and they have brought their flocks, 3
47: 7 Then Joseph brought in Jacob his father, 3
14 Joseph brought the money into Pharaoh's house. 3
17 they brought their cattle to Joseph; 3
48: 9 And he said, "Bring them to me, I pray you, 12
Exd 2:10 and she brought him to Pharaoh's daughter 3
3:11 that I should . . bring the sons of Israel out 11
6: 8 I will bring you into the land which I swore 3
8: 7 magicians . . and brought frogs upon the land 20
9:19 in the field and is not brought home 1
10: 4 behold, tomorrow I will bring locusts 3
13 the LORD brought an east wind upon the land 14
13 the east wind had brought the locusts. 17
11: 1 Yet one plague more I will bring upon Pharaoh 3
13: 5 when the LORD brings you into the land 3
11 when the LORD brings you into the land 3
15:17 Thou wilt bring them in, and plant them on thy own 3
16: 5 sixth day, when they prepare what they bring 3
18:19 You shall . . bring their cases to God; 3
22 every great matter they shall bring to you 3
26 hard cases they brought to Moses 3
19: 4 on eagles' wings and brought you to myself. 3
24 Go down, and come up bringing Aaron with you; •
21: 6 then his master shall bring him to God 13
6 he shall bring him to the door or the doorpost; 13
22:13 it is torn by beasts, let him bring it as evidence; 3
23:19 first fruits . . you shall bring into the house 3
20 to bring you to the place which I have prepared. 3
23 When my angel goes before you, and brings you 3
26:33 bring the ark of the testimony in thither within 3
27:20 that they bring to you pure beaten olive oil 12
28:29 to bring them to continual remembrance before •
29: 3 you shall put them in one basket and bring them 25
3 bring them in the basket, and bring the bull •
4 You shall bring Aaron and his sons to the door 25
8 you shall bring his sons, and put coats on them 25
10 Then you shall bring the bull before the tent 25
30:16 it may bring the people of Israel to remembrance •
32: 2 rings of gold . . and bring them to me. 3
3 rings of gold . . and brought them to Aaron. 3
6 offerings and brought peace offerings; 13
21 that you have brought a great sin upon them? 3
34:26 you shall bring to the house of the LORD your God. 3
35: 5 let him bring the LORD'S offering: gold, silver 3
21 brought the LORD'S offering to be used 3
22 all . . brought brooches and earrings 3
23 rams' skins or goatskins, brought them. 3
24 brought it as the LORD'S offering; 3
24 wood of any use in the work, brought it. 3
25 women . . spun with their hands, and brought 3
27 the leaders brought onyx stones and stones 3
29 the people . . whose heart moved them to bring 3
29 people . . brought it as their freewill 3
36: 3 Israel had brought for doing the work 3
3 still kept bringing him freewill offerings 3
5 The people bring much more than enough for doing 3
6 So the people were restrained from bringing; 3
39:33 they brought the tabernacle to Moses 3
40: 4 you shall bring in the table, and set its 3
4 you shall bring in the lampstand, and set up 3
12 Then you shall bring Aaron and his sons 25
14 You shall bring his sons also and put coats 25
21 he brought the ark into the tabernacle 3
Lev 1: 2 When any man of you brings an offering to the LORD 25
2 you shall bring your offering of cattle 25
14 then he shall bring his offering of turtledoves 25
15 the priest shall bring it to the altar 25
2: 1 When any one brings a cereal offering 25
2 bring it to Aaron's sons the priests 3
4 When you bring a cereal offering baked 25
8 you shall bring the cereal offering that is made 3
8 to the priest, he shall bring it to the altar 13
11 No cereal offering which you bring to the LORD 25
12 first fruits you may bring them to the LORD 25
4: 4 He shall bring the bull to the door of the tent 3
5 the blood of the bull and bring it to the tent 3
14 and bring it before the tent of meeting 3
16 priest shall bring some of the blood of the bull 3
23 he shall bring as his offering a goat, a male 3
28 he shall bring for his offering a goat, a female 3
32 If he brings a lamb as his offering 3
32 he shall bring a female without blemish 3
5: 6 he shall bring his guilt offering to the LORD 3
7 he shall bring, as his guilt offering to the LORD 3
8 He shall bring them to the priest, who shall offer 3
11 then he shall bring, as his offering for the sin 3
12 he shall bring it to the priest, and the priest 3
15 he shall bring, as his guilt offering to the LORD 3
18 He shall bring to the priest a ram 3
6: 6 he shall bring to the priest his guilt offering 3
21 you shall bring it well mixed, in baked pieces 3
30 any blood is brought into the tent of meeting 3
7:13 he shall bring his offering with cakes 25
29 He shall bring his offering to the LORD 3
30 he shall bring with his own hands the offerings 3
30 he shall bring the fat with the breast 3
38 commanded . . bring their offerings to the LORD 25
8: 6 Moses brought Aaron and his sons, and washed them 25
13 Moses brought Aaron's sons, and clothed them 25
14 Then he brought the bull of the sin offering 13
24 Aaron's sons were brought, and Moses put some 25
9: 5 they brought what Moses commanded 12
7 bring the offering of the people 23
10:15 the breast that is waved they shall bring 3
18 Behold, its blood was not brought into the inner 3
12: 6 she shall bring to the priest at the door 3
13: 2 then he shall be brought to Aaron the priest 3
9 he shall be brought to the priest 3
14: 2 leper . . He shall be brought to the priest 3
23 eighth day he shall bring them for his cleansing 3
15:29 bring them to the priest, to the door of the tent 3
16:12 and he shall bring it within the veil 3
15 and bring its blood within the veil 3
27 whose blood was brought in to make atonement 3
17: 4 and does not bring it to the door of the tent 3
5 the people of Israel may bring their sacrifices 3
5 that they may bring them to the LORD, to the priest 3
9 and does not bring it to the door of the tent 3
18: 3 the land of Canaan, to which I am bringing you 3
19:21 he shall bring a guilt offering for himself 3
20:22 that the land where I am bringing you to dwell 3
23:10 When you . . reap its harvest, you shall bring 3
14 eat . . until you have brought the offering 3
15 the day that you brought the sheaf 3
17 You shall bring from your dwellings two loaves 3
24: 2 Command the people of Israel to bring you . . oil 12
11 And they brought him to Moses 3
26:25 I will bring a sword upon you, that shall execute 3
41 I . . brought them into the land of their enemies 3
27: 8 then he shall bring the person before the priest 22
11 then the man shall bring the animal 22
Num 5: 9 which they bring to the priest, shall be his; 25
15 then the man shall bring his wife to the priest 3
15 man shall . . bring the offering required of her 3

16 the priest shall bring her near 25
25 cereal offering . . and bring it to the altar; 25
6:10 On the eighth day he shall bring two turtledoves 3
12 bring a male lamb a year old for a guilt offering; 3
13 be brought to the door of the tent of meeting 3
7: 3 offered and brought their offerings before 3
11:16 bring them to the tent of meeting 12
31 brought quails from the sea, and let them fall 4
12:14 days, and after that she may be brought in again. 1
15 till Miriam was brought in again. 1
13:20 bring some of the fruit of the land. 12
23 they brought also some pomegranates and figs. •
32 brought to the people of Israel an evil report 11
14: 3 Why does the LORD bring us into this land, to fall 3
8 he will bring us into this land and give it to us 3
16 was not able to bring this people into the land 3
24 my servant Caleb . . I will bring into the land 3
31 But your little ones . . I will bring 3
15: 4 who brings his offering shall offer to the LORD 25
18 When you come into the land to which I bring you 3
25 because . . they have brought their offering 3
33 who found him . . brought him to Moses and Aaron 25
36 congregation brought him outside the camp 11
16:14 not brought us into a land flowing with milk 3
17 every one of you bring before the LORD his censer 25
18: 2 with you bring your brethren also 25
13 ripe fruits . . which they bring to the LORD 3
19: 2 Tell the people . . to bring you a red heifer 12
20: 4 Why have you brought the assembly of the LORD 3
5 to bring us to this evil place? It is no place 3
12 you shall not bring this assembly into the land 3
23: 7 From Aram Balak has brought me 15
25: 6 came and brought a Mid'ianite woman to his family 25
27: 5 Moses brought their case before the LORD. 25
17 who shall lead them out and bring them in; 3
31:12 Then they brought the captives and the . . spoil 3
50 we have brought the LORD'S offering 25
54 gold . . and brought it into the tent of meeting 3
32:17 until we have brought them to their place; 3
Deu 1:17 case that is too hard for you, you shall bring to me 25
4:38 to bring you in, to give you their land 3
5: 6 LORD . . who brought you out of the land of Egypt 11
6:10 when the LORD your God brings you into the land 3
12 LORD, who brought you out of the land of Egypt 11
21 LORD brought us out of Egypt with a mighty hand; 11
23 that he might bring us in and give us the land 3
7: 1 When the LORD your God brings you into the land 3
26 not bring an abominable thing into your house 3
8: 7 LORD your God is bringing you into a good land 3
14 forget the LORD . . who brought you out 11
15 who brought you water out of the flinty rock 11
9: 4 LORD has brought me in to possess this land'; 3
12 for your people whom you have brought from Egypt 11
26 brought out of Egypt with a mighty hand. 11
28 lest the land from which thou didst bring us say 11
28 LORD was not able to bring them into the land 3
11:29 when the LORD your God brings you into the land 3
12: 6 thither you shall bring your burnt offerings 3
11 thither you shall bring all that I command you 3
13: 5 LORD . . who brought you out of the land of Egypt 11
10 LORD . . who brought you out of the land of Egypt 11
14:24 so that you are not able to bring the tithe 17
16: 1 LORD your God brought you out of Egypt by night. 11
21:12 then you shall bring her home to your house 3
22: 2 bring it home to your house, and it shall be 1
8 may not bring the guilt of blood upon your house 26
14 brings an evil name upon her, saying, 'I took 11
19 brought an evil name upon a virgin of Israel; 11
23:18 not bring the hire of a harlot, or the wages of a dog 3
24:11 man . . shall bring the pledge out to you. 11
26: 8 LORD brought us out of Egypt with a mighty hand 11
9 brought us into this place and gave us this land 3
10 now I bring the first of the fruit of the ground 3
28:36 LORD will bring you, and your king . . to a nation 7
49 LORD will bring a nation against you from afar 17
61 LORD will bring upon you, until you are destroyed. 20
29:27 bringing upon it all the curses written 3
30: 5 LORD your God will bring you into the land 3
12 'Who will go up for us to heaven, and bring it to us 12
13 'Who will go over the sea for us, and bring it to us 12
31:20 For when I have brought them into the land 3
21 already forming, before I have brought them 3
23 shall bring the children of Israel into the land 3
33: 7 voice of Judah, and bring him in to his people. 3
Jos 6:23 and they brought all her kindred 11
7:23 And they took them . . and brought them to Joshua 3
8:23 But . . they took alive, and brought him to Joshua. 25
18: 6 describe the . . and bring the description here 3
23:15 the LORD will bring upon you all the evil things 3
24: 8 Then I brought you to the land of the Amorites 3
Jdg 1: 7 they brought him to Jerusalem, and he died there. 3
2: 1 you up from Egypt, and brought you into the land 3
5:25 she brought him curds in a lordly bowl. 25
6:19 brought them to him under the oak and presented 11
7:25 they brought the heads of Oreb and Zeeb to Gideon 3
11: 5 of Gilead went to bring Jephthah from the land 12
12: 9 and 30 daughters he brought in from outside 3
14:11 they brought 30 companions to be with him. 12
16: 8 the lords of the Philistines brought her seven 20

18 came up . . and brought the money in their hands. 20
18: 3 said to him, "Who brought you here? What are you 3
19:21 he brought him into his house, and gave the asses 3
20:10 to bring provisions for the people 12
21:12 they brought them to the camp at Shiloh 3
Rut 3:15 Bring the mantle you are wearing and hold it out. 9
1Sm 1:22 As soon as the child is weaned, I will bring him 3
24 she brought him to the house of the LORD at Shiloh; 3
25 slew the bull, and they brought the child to Eli. 3
4: 3 Let us bring the ark of the covenant of the LORD 12
4 sent to Shiloh, and brought from there the ark 17
5: 2 the ark . . and brought it into the house of Dagon 3
8 they brought the ark of the God of Israel there. 19
7: 1 took up the ark . . and brought it to the house 3
9: 7 But if we go, what can we bring the man? 3
7 and there is no present to bring to the man of God. 3
22 Samuel took . . and brought them into the hall 3
23 Bring the portion I gave you, of which I said to you 18
10:27 they despised him, and brought him no present. 3
11:12 Bring the men, that we may put them to death. 18
14:18 Saul said to Ahi'jah, "Bring hither the ark of God. 13
34 Let every man bring his ox or his sheep 13
34 So every one of the people brought his ox with him 13
15:15 They have brought them from the Amal'ekites 3
20 I have brought Agag the king of Am'alek 3
32 Bring here to me Agag the king of the Amal'ekites. 13
16:12 And he sent, and brought him in. Now he was ruddy 3
17 Provide for me a man . . and bring him to me. 3
17:18 See . . and bring some token from them. 12
54 took the head . . and brought it to Jerusalem; 3
57 Abner took him, and brought him before Saul 3
18:27 and David brought their foreskins 3
19: 7 And Jonathan brought David to Saul, and he was 3
20: 8 you have brought your servant into a . . covenant 3
8 why should you bring me to your father? 3
21: 8 I have brought neither my sword nor my weapons 12
14 man is mad; why then have you brought him to me? 3
15 you have brought this fellow to play the madman 3
25:27 this present which your servant has brought 3
35 Then David received . . what she had brought him; 3
27:11 neither man nor woman . . to bring tidings to Gath 3
30: 7 David said to Abi'athar . . "Bring me the ephod. 13
7 Abi'athar brought the ephod to David. 13
11 found an Egyptian . . and brought him to David; 12
2Sm 1:10 I took . . and I have brought them here to my lord. 3
3:13 not see my face, unless you first bring Michal 3
22 arrived . . from a raid, bringing much spoil 3
4: 8 and brought the head of Ish-bo'sheth to David 3
5: 2 it was you that led out and brought in Israel; 3
6: 3 and brought it out of the house of Abin'adab 17
17 And they brought in the ark of the LORD, and set it 3
7:18 Who am I . . that thou hast brought me thus far? 3
8: 2 the Moabites became . . and brought tribute. 17
6 the Syrians . . brought tribute. 17
7 David took . . and brought them to Jerusalem. 3
10 Joram brought with him articles of silver •
9: 5 Then King David sent and brought him 12
10 till the land . . and shall bring in the produce 3
11:27 David sent and brought her to his house 1
14:10 If any one says anything to you, bring him to me 3
23 Jo'ab arose . . and brought Ab'salom to Jerusalem. 3
16: 2 the king said to Ziba, "Why have you brought these? •
17:13 all Israel will bring ropes to that city 17
14 so that the LORD might bring evil upon Ab'salom. 3
28 brought beds, basins, and earthen vessels, wheat 13
23:16 drew water . . and took and brought it to David. 3
1Kg 1: 3 found Ab'ishag . . and brought her to the king. 3
38 on King David's mule, and brought him to Gihon. 7
2:19 and had a seat brought for the king's mother; 26
40 Shim'e-i went and brought his slaves from Gath. 3
3: 1 Pharaoh's daughter, and brought her into the city 3
24 king said, "Bring me a sword." So a sword was brought 12
24 So a sword was brought before the king. 3
4:21 they brought tribute and served Solomon all 13
28 and swift steeds they brought to the place where 3
7:13 King Solomon sent and brought Hiram from Tyre. 12
51 Solomon brought in the things . . dedicated 3
8: 6 Then the priests brought the ark of the covenant 3
32 by bringing his conduct upon his own head 18
9: 9 who brought their fathers out of . . Egypt 11
9 the LORD has brought all this evil upon them.' 3
28 they went to Ophir, and brought from there gold 12
28 and they brought it to King Solomon. 3
10:11 the fleet of Hiram, which brought gold from Ophir 17
11 fleet . . brought from Ophir a very great amount 3
22 the fleet . . used to come bringing gold, silver 17
25 Every one of them brought his present 3
14:10 I will bring evil upon the house of Jerobo'am 3
15:15 he brought into the house of the LORD the . . gifts 3
17: 6 ravens brought him bread and meat in the morning 3
10 Bring me a little water . . that I may drink. 12
11 as she was going to bring it, he called to her 12
11 Bring me a morsel of bread in your hand. 12
13 first make me a little cake of it and bring it to me 11
20:33 Then he said, "Go and bring him. 12
39 a soldier turned and brought a man to me, and said 3
21:21 Behold, I will bring evil upon you; 3
29 Because . . I will not bring the evil in his days; 3
29 but in his son's days I will bring the evil 3

22: 9 and said, "Bring quickly Micai'ah the son of Imlah. •
37 So the king died, and was brought to Sama'ria; 3
2Kg 2:20 He said, "Bring me a new bowl, and put salt in it. 12
20 Bring me a new bowl . . " So they brought it to him. 12
3:15 But now bring me a minstrel. 12
4: 5 as she poured they brought the vessels to her. 13
6 she said to her son, "Bring me another vessel. 13
20 he had lifted him, and brought him to his mother 3
41 Then bring meal." And he threw it into the pot 12
42 A man came . . bringing the man of God bread 3
5: 6 he brought the letter to the king of Israel 3
20 in not accepting from his hand what he brought. 3
6:19 I will bring you to the man whom you seek. 7
10: 8 They have brought the heads of the king's sons 3
11: 4 Jehoi'ada sent and brought the captains 12
9 each brought his men who were to go off duty 12
12: 4 the money which a man's heart prompts him to bring 3
14:20 they brought him upon horses; and he was buried 17
17:24 the king of Assyria brought people from Babylon 3
36 the LORD, who brought you out of the land of Egypt 20
20: 7 Bring a cake of figs. And let them take and lay it 12
20 how he made . . and brought water into the city 3
21:12 I am bringing upon Jerusalem and Judah such evil 3
22:16 I will bring evil upon this place and upon its 3
20 all the evil which I will bring upon this place.' 3
23: 8 he brought all the priests out of the cities 3
30 carried him . . and brought him to Jerusalem 3
24:16 the king of Babylon brought captive to Babylon 3
25:20 took them, and brought them to the king of Babylon 7
1Ch 5:26 brought them to Halah . . and the river Gozan 3
9:28 to count them when they were brought 3
10:12 the bodies . . and brought them to Jabesh. 3
11: 2 it was you that led out and brought in Israel; 3
18 drew water . . and took and brought it to David. 3
19 For at the risk of their lives, they brought it. 3
13: 5 to bring the ark of God from Kir'iath-je'arim. 3
14:17 LORD brought the fear of him upon all nations. 18
16: 1 brought the ark of God, and set it inside the tent 3
29 bring an offering, and come before him! 17
17:16 house, that thou hast brought me thus far? 3
18: 2 the Mo'abites . . brought tribute. 17
6 became servants to David, and brought tribute. 17
7 and brought them to Jerusalem. 3
21: 2 Go, number Israel . . and bring me a report 3
3 Why should he bring guilt upon Israel? 6
22: 4 and Tyrians brought great quantities of cedar 3
19 brought into a house built for the . . LORD. 3
2Ch 2:16 we will cut . . and bring it to you in rafts by sea 3
5: 1 Solomon brought in the things which David 3
7 the priests brought the ark . . to its place 3
6:23 requiting the guilty by bringing his conduct 18
7:22 therefore he has brought all this evil upon them' 3
8:18 talents of gold and brought it to King Solomon. 3
9:10 the servants . . who brought gold from Ophir 3
10 brought algum wood and precious stones. 3
12 whatever she asked besides what she had brought 3
14 that which the traders and merchants brought; 3
14 brought gold and silver to Solomon. 3
21 ships of Tarshish used to come bringing gold 17
24 Every one of them brought his present 3
15:11 from the spoil which they had brought 3
17: 5 all Judah brought tribute to Jehosh'aphat; 18
11 Philistines brought Jehosh'aphat presents 3
11 Arabs also brought him 7,700 rams 3
18: 8 Bring quickly Micai'ah the son of Imlah. •
22: 9 Ahazi'ah . . was brought to Jehu and put to death. 3
23: 8 They each brought his men, who were to go off duty 12
24: 6 to bring in from Judah and Jerusalem the tax 3
9 to bring in for the LORD the tax that Moses 3
10 princes and all the people . . brought their tax 3
11 chest was brought to the king's officers 3
14 brought the rest of the money before the king 3
25:14 he brought the gods of the men of Se'ir 3
23 Jo'ash . . brought him to Jerusalem 3
28 they brought him upon horses; and he was buried 17
26:18 it will bring you no honor from the LORD God. •
28: 5 brought them to Damascus. 3
8 and brought the spoil to Sama'ria. 3
13 said . . "You shall not bring the captives in here 3
15 brought them to their kinsfolk at Jericho 3
27 did not bring him into the tombs of the kings 3
29: 4 He brought in the priests and the Levites 3
21 they brought seven bulls, seven rams, seven lambs 3
23 he-goats . . brought to the king and the assembly 13
31 come near, bring sacrifices and thank offerings 3
31 assembly brought sacrifices and thank 3
31 of a willing heart brought burnt offerings. •
32 burnt offerings which the assembly brought 3
30:15 brought burnt offerings into the house 3
31: 5 brought in abundantly the tithe of everything. 3
6 also brought in the tithe of cattle and sheep 3
10 Since they began to bring the contributions 3
12 they faithfully brought in the contributions 3
32:23 many brought gifts to the LORD to Jerusalem 3
33:11 LORD brought upon them the commanders 3
11 bound . . and brought him to Babylon. 7
34: 9 delivered the money that had been brought 3
16 Shaphan brought the book to the king 3
24 I will bring evil upon this place 3

28 evil which I will bring upon this place 3
35:24 his servants . . brought him to Jerusalem. 7
36:10 Nebuchadnez'zar sent and brought him to Babylon 3
18 all these he brought to Babylon. 3
Ezr 3: 7 to bring cedar trees from Lebanon to the sea 3
4: 2 E'sar-had'don king of Assyria who brought us here. 20
5:14 taken . . and brought into the temple of Babylon 31
6: 3 place where . . burnt offerings are brought; 32
5 took . . and brought to Babylon 31
8:18 brought us a man of discretion, 3
30 to bring them to Jerusalem, to the house of our God. 3
Neh 1: 9 gather . . and bring them to the place 3
8: 1 Ezra . . to bring the book of the law of Moses 3
2 Ezra . . brought the law before the assembly 3
15 Go out to the hills and bring branches of olive 3
16 people went out and brought them and made booths 3
9:23 bring them into the land which thou hadst told 3
10:31 if the peoples . . bring in wares or any grain 3
34 offering, to bring it into the house of our God 3
35 obligate ourselves to bring the first fruits 3
36 also to bring to the house of our God 3
37 to bring the first of our coarse meal 3
37 bring to the Levites the tithes from our ground •
39 bring the contribution of grain, wine, and oil 3
11: 1 rest . . cast lots to bring one out of ten to live 3
12:27 bring them to Jerusalem to celebrate 3
13:12 Judah brought the tithe of the grain, wine, and oil 3
15 bringing in heaps of grain and loading them 3
15 brought into Jerusalem on the sabbath day; 3
16 brought in fish and all kinds of wares and sold 3
18 did not our God bring all this evil on us 3
19 no burden might be brought in on the sabbath day. 3
Est 1:11 to bring Queen Vashti before the king 3
17 commanded Queen Vashti to be brought before him 3
5: 5 Bring Haman quickly, that we may do as Esther •
6: 1 gave orders to bring the book of memorable deeds 3
8 let royal robes be brought . . and the horse 3
14 eunuchs arrived and brought Haman in haste 3
Job 5:13 the schemes of the wily are brought to a quick end. •
10:17 thou dost bring fresh hosts against me. •
12: 6 are secure, who bring their god in their hand. 3
22 and brings deep darkness to light. 11
14: 3 such a one and bring him into judgment with thee? 3
4 Who can bring a clean thing out of an unclean? 18
18:14 he trusted, and is brought to the king of terrors. 24
19:29 for wrath brings the punishment of the sword •
30:23 Yea, I know that thou wilt bring me to death 27
39:12 and bring your grain to your threshing floor? 1
42:11 all the evil that the LORD had brought upon him; 3
Ps 43: 3 let them lead me, let them bring me to thy holy hill 3
55: 3 they bring trouble upon me •
60: 9 Who will bring me to the fortified city? 8
66:11 Thou didst bring us into the net; 3
68:31 Let bronze be brought from Egypt; 2
72:10 may the kings of Sheba and Seba bring gifts! 25
76:11 let all around him bring gifts to him 8
78:54 he brought them to his holy land, to the mountain 3
71 he brought him to be the shepherd of Jacob 3
80: 8 Thou didst bring a vine out of Egypt; 16
96: 8 bring an offering, and come into his courts! 17
105:40 They asked, and he brought quails 3
107:30 brought them to their desired haven. 15
108:10 Who will bring me to the fortified city? 8
109: 6 let an accuser bring him to trial. †
126: 6 home with shouts of joy, bringing his sheaves 17
142: 7 Bring me out of prison, that I may give thanks 11
143:11 In thy righteousness bring me out of trouble! 11
Prv 10:14 but the babbling of a fool brings ruin near. •
16:15 favor . . the clouds that bring the spring rain. •
18: 6 A fool's lips bring strife 3
16 A man's gift . . brings him before great men. 15
19: 4 Wealth brings many new friends 10
21:27 how much more when he brings it with evil intent. 3
25: 8 do not hastily bring into court; 11
31:14 she brings her food from afar. 3
Ecc 3:22 who can bring him to see what will be after him? 3
11: 9 know that . . God will bring you into judgment. 3
12:14 For God will bring every deed into judgment 3
Sng 2: 4 He brought me to the banqueting house 3
3: 4 until I had brought him into my mother's house 3
8: 2 lead you and bring you into the house of my mother 3
10 I was in his eyes as one who brings peace. 11
11 each one was to bring for its fruit 1,000 3
Isa 1:13 Bring no more vain offerings; 3
3: 9 For they have brought evil upon themselves. 5
7:17 The LORD will bring upon you and upon your people 3
14: 2 will take them and bring them to their place 3
15: 9 yet I will bring upon Dibon even more 28
18: 7 gifts will be brought to the LORD of hosts 8
21:14 To the thirsty bring water, meet the fugitive 2
30: 5 that brings neither help nor profit •
31: 2 yet he is wise and brings disaster 3
40:23 who brings princes to nought 18
41:21 bring your proofs, says the King of Jacob. 13
22 Let them bring them, and tell us what is to happen. 13
42: 1 he will bring forth justice to the nations. 11
43: 5 I will bring your offspring from the east 3
6 bring my sons from afar and my daughters 3
9 Let them bring their witnesses to justify them 18
23 You have not brought me your sheep 3
48:15 have spoken and called him, I have brought him 3
49:22 and they shall bring your sons in their bosom 3
56: 7 these I will bring to my holy mountain 3
57: 6 to them . . you have brought a cereal offering. 20
58: 7 and bring the homeless poor into your house; 3
60: 6 They shall bring gold and frankincense 17
9 of Tarshish first, to bring your sons from far 3
11 men may bring to you the wealth of the nations 3
17 Instead of bronze I will bring gold 3
17 and instead of iron I will bring silver; 3
66: 4 and bring their fears upon them; 3
20 they shall bring all your brethren 3
20 as the Israelites bring their cereal offering 3
Jer 2: 7 I brought you into a plentiful land 3
17 Have you not brought this upon yourself 23
3:14 and I will bring you to Zion. 3
4: 6 stay not, for I bring evil from the north 3
18 ways and your doings have brought this upon you. 23
5:15 Behold, I am bringing upon you a nation from afar 3
6:19 behold, I am bringing evil upon this people 3
10: 9 Beaten silver is brought from Tarshish 3
11: 8 brought upon them all the words of this covenant 3
11 I am bringing evil upon them 3
23 For I will bring evil upon the men of An'athoth 3
12: 9 all the wild beasts; bring them to devour. 2
15: 8 I have brought against the mothers of young men 3
17:18 bring upon them the day of evil; 3
21 or bring it in by the gates of Jerusalem. 3
24 and bring in no burden by the gates of this city 3
26 bringing burnt offerings and sacrifices 3
26 and bringing thank offerings to . . the LORD. 3
18:22 thou bringest the marauder suddenly upon them! 3
19: 3 Behold, I am bringing such evil upon this place 3
15 Behold, I am bringing upon this city 3
23:12 for I will bring evil upon them 3
40 I will bring upon you everlasting reproach 18
24: 1 and had brought them to Babylon 3
25: 9 and I will bring them against this land 3
13 I will bring upon that land all the words 3
26:15 you will bring innocent blood upon yourselves 18
19 we are about to bring great evil upon ourselves. 23
23 they fetched Uri'ah from Egypt and brought him 3
27:11 nation which will bring its neck under the yoke 3
12 Bring your necks under the yoke of the king 3
31: 8 Behold, I will bring them from the north country 3
32:42 Just as I have brought all this great evil 3
42 I will bring upon them all the good that I promise 3
33: 6 Behold, I will bring to it health and healing 20
11 those who sing, as they bring thank offerings 3
35: 2 and bring them to the house of the LORD 3
4 I brought them to the house of the LORD 3
17 Behold, I am bringing on Judah 3
36:31 I will bring upon them, and upon the inhabitants 3
37:14 seized Jeremiah and brought him to the princes. 3
41: 5 bringing cereal offerings and incense •
42:17 from the evil which I will bring upon them. 3
44: 2 all the evil that I brought upon Jerusalem 3
45: 5 I am bringing evil upon all flesh, says the LORD; 3
48:44 I will bring these things upon Moab 3
49: 5 Behold, I will bring terror upon you, says the Lord 3
8 For I will bring the calamity of Esau upon him 3
32 I will bring their calamity from every side 3
36 I will bring upon Elam the four winds 3
37 I will bring evil upon them, my fierce anger 3
50: 9 I am stirring up and bringing against Babylon 20
51:64 because of the evil that I am bringing upon her. 3
52:26 and brought them to the king of Babylon at Riblah. 7
Lam 1:12 sorrow like my sorrow which was brought upon me 21
21 Bring thou the day thou hast announced 3
3: 2 he has driven and brought me into darkness 7
Ezk 5:16 when I bring more and more famine upon you 10
17 I will bring the sword upon you. 3
6: 3 Behold, I, even I, will bring a sword upon you 3
7:24 I will bring the worst of the nations to take 3
8: 3 and brought me in visions of God to Jerusalem 3
7 he brought me to the door of the court; 3
14 he brought me to the entrance of the north gate 3
16 he brought me into the inner court of the house 3
11: 1 The Spirit lifted me up, and brought me 3
8 I will bring the sword upon you, says the Lord GOD. 3
24 and brought me in the vision by the Spirit of God 3
12:13 I will bring him to Babylon 3
14:17 Or if I bring a sword upon that land, and say 3
22 for the evil that I have brought upon Jerusalem 3
22 for all that I have brought upon it. 3
16:38 and bring upon you the blood of wrath 18
17:12 her princes and brought them to him to Babylon. 3
20 in my snare, and I will bring him to Babylon 3
19: 4 they brought him with hooks to the land of Egypt. 3
9 in a cage, and brought him to the king of Babylon; 3
9 they brought him into custody 3
20:10 and brought them into the wilderness. 3
15 that I would not bring them into the land 3
28 For when I had brought them into the land 3
35 I will bring you into the wilderness 3
42 when I bring you into the land of Israel 3
23:22 I will bring them against you from every side 3
30 have brought this upon you 23
42 drunkards were brought from the wilderness; 3
26: 7 Behold, I will bring upon Tyre from the north 3
21 I will bring you to a dreadful end 18
27:15 they brought you in payment ivory tusks 27
28: 7 behold, I will bring strangers upon you 3
29: 8 I will bring a sword upon you, and will cut off 3
30:11 nations, shall be brought in to destroy the land; 3
33: 2 and say to them, If I bring the sword upon a land 3
34:13 and will bring them into their own land; 3
36:24 and bring you into your own land. 3
37:12 I will bring you home into the land of Israel. 3
21 from all sides, and bring them to their own land; 3
38:16 I will bring you against my land 3
17 that I would bring you against them? 3
40: 2 and brought me in the visions of God into the land 3
3 When he brought me there, behold, there was a man 3
4 you were brought here in order that I might show 3
17 Then he brought me into the outer court; 3
28 he brought me to the inner court by the south gate 3
32 he brought me to the inner court on the east side 3
35 Then he brought me to the north gate 3
44 he brought me from without into the inner court •
48 Then he brought me to the vestibule of the temple 3
41: 1 Then he brought me to the nave 3
42: 1 he brought me to the chambers which were 3
43: 1 Afterward he brought me to the gate 7
5 lifted me up, and brought me into the inner court; 3
44: 4 he brought me by way of the north gate to the front 3
46:19 Then he brought me through the entrance 3
Dan 1:18 king had commanded that they should be brought 3
18 chief . . brought them in before Nebuchadnez'zar. 3
2:24 bring me in before the king 33
25 Then Ar'ioch brought in Daniel before the king 34
3:13 Shadrach, Meshach, and Abed'nego be brought. 30
13 Then they brought these men before the king. 29
4: 6 all the wise men . . should be brought before me 33
5: 2 commanded that the vessels of gold . . be brought 30
3 brought in the golden and silver vessels 29
7 king cried aloud to bring in the enchanters 34
13 Then Daniel was brought in before the king. 34
13 exiles . . king my father brought from Judah. 29
15 brought in before me to read this writing 34
23 vessels of his house have been brought in before 29
6:16 Daniel was brought and cast into the den 29
17 stone was brought and laid upon the mouth 29
18 no diversions were brought to him, and sleep fled 35
24 men who had accused Daniel were brought and cast 29
9:12 by bringing upon us a great calamity; 3
14 ready the calamity and has brought it upon us; 3
24 bring in everlasting righteousness 3
11:17 shall bring terms of peace and perform them. •
Hos 2:14 allure her, and bring her into the wilderness 7
Ams 4: 1 who say to their husbands, 'Bring, that we may drink 3
4 bring your sacrifices every morning 3
5:25 Did you bring to me sacrifices and offerings 13
6:10 take him up to bring the bones out of the house 11
8:10 I will bring sackcloth upon all loins 20
Mic 1:15 I will again bring a conqueror upon you 3
Nah 2:11 where the lion brought his prey 3
Zep 3:10 my dispersed ones, shall bring my offering. 8
Hag 1: 8 to the hills and bring wood and build the house 3
9 when you brought it home, I blew it away. 3
Zec 3: 8 behold, I will bring my servant the Branch. 3
8: 8 bring them to dwell in the midst of Jerusalem; 3
10:10 I will bring them to the land of Gilead 3
Mal 1:13 You bring what has been taken by violence 3
13 lame or sick, and this you bring as your offering! 3
2:12 or to bring an offering to the LORD of hosts! 13
3:10 Bring the full tithes into the storehouse 3
Mat 4:24 all Syria, and they brought him all the sick 82
8:16 That evening they brought to him many 82
9: 2 behold, they brought to him a paralytic 82
32 behold, a dumb demoniac was brought to him. 82
10:34 Do not think that I have come to bring peace 41
34 I have not come to bring peace, but a sword. 41
12:20 till he brings justice to victory; 50
22 Then a blind and dumb demoniac was brought to him 82
45 he goes and brings with him seven other spirits 75
14:11 his head was brought on a platter 85
11 and she brought it to her mother. 85
18 he said, "Bring them here to me. 85
35 and brought to him all that were sick 82
15:30 crowds came to him, bringing with them the lame 60
16: 5 they had forgotten to bring any bread. 69
7 We brought no bread. 69
17:16 I brought him to your disciples 82
17 Bring him here to me. 85
18:24 one was brought to him who owed him 10,000 talents; 82
19:13 Then children were brought to him 82
21: 2 untie them and bring them to me. 36
7 they brought the ass and the colt 36
16 thou hast brought perfect praise'? 64
22:19 And they brought him a coin. 82
25:20 bringing five talents more, saying 82
Mrk 1:32 they brought to him all who were sick 85
2: 3 they came, bringing to him a paralytic 85
4:21 Is a lamp brought in to be put under a bushel 59
6:27 and gave orders to bring his head 85
28 brought his head on a platter 85

55 began to bring sick people on their pallets 77
7:32 they brought to him a man who was deaf 85
8:14 Now they had forgotten to bring bread 69
22 some people brought to him a blind man 85
9:17 I brought my son to you, for he has a dumb spirit; 85
19 How long am I to bear with you? Bring him to me. 85
20 they brought the boy to him 85
10:13 they were bringing children to him 82
11: 2 untie it and bring it. 85
7 they brought the colt to Jesus 85
12:15 Bring me a coin, and let me look at it. 85
16 they brought one 85
15:22 they brought him to the place called Gol'gotha 85
Lke 2:27 when the parents brought in the child Jesus 48
4:40 brought them to him 36
5:11 when they had brought their boats to land 63
18 men were bringing on a bed a man who was paralyzed 85
18 they sought to bring him in and lay him before Jesus; 49
19 no way to bring him in, because of the crowd 49
7:37 a woman . . brought an alabaster flask of ointment 67
9:41 Bring your son here. 81
10:34 and brought him to an inn, and took care of him. 36
11:26 Then he goes and brings seven other spirits 75
12:11 when they bring you before the synagogues 49
14:21 bring in the poor and maimed and blind and lame.' 48
15:22 Bring quickly the best robe, and put it on him; 51
23 bring the fatted calf and kill it 85
18:15 Now they were bringing even infants to him 82
40 Jesus stopped, and commanded him to be brought 36
19:27 bring them here and slay them before me.' 36
30 untie it and bring it here. 36
35 they brought it to Jesus 36
21:12 you will be brought before kings and governors 39
22:54 bringing him into the high priest's house 48
23: 1 brought him before Pilate. 36
14 said to them, "You brought me this man 82
Joh 1:42 He brought him to Jesus. Jesus looked at him 36
4:33 Has any one brought him food? 85
7:45 who said to them, "Why did you not bring him? 36
8: 3 The scribes and the Pharisees brought a woman 36
9:13 They brought to the Pharisees the man 36
10:16 I must bring them also 36
18:16 went out . . and brought Peter in. 48
29 What accusation do you bring against this man? 85
19: 4 See, I am bringing him out to you, that you may know 36
13 he brought Jesus out 36
39 came bringing a mixture of myrrh and aloes 85
21:10 Bring some of the fish that you have just caught. 85
Act 4:34 brought the proceeds of what was sold 85
37 brought the money 85
5: 2 brought only a part 85
16 bringing the sick 85
21 sent to the prison to have them brought. 36
26 captain with the officers went and brought them 36
27 when they had brought them 36
6:12 seized him and brought him before the council 36
7:45 Our fathers in turn brought it in with Joshua 48
9: 2 he might bring them bound to Jerusalem. 36
8 brought him into Damascus. 48
21 to bring them bound before the chief priests. 36
27 took him, and brought him to the apostles 36
10: 5 bring one Simon who is called Peter; 72
11:13 'Send to Joppa and bring Simon called Peter; 72
26 when he had found him, he brought him to Antioch. 36
12:25 bringing with them John 83
13:23 brought to Israel a Savior, Jesus, as he promised. 36
47 that you may bring salvation to . . the earth. 45
14:13 brought oxen and garlands to the gates 85
16:16 brought her owners much gain by soothsaying. 76
20 when they had brought them to the magistrates 81
30 brought them out and said 79
17:15 who conducted Paul brought him as far as Athens; 36
19 brought him to the Are-op'agus, saying 36
20 you bring some strange things to our ears 49
18:12 brought him before the tribunal 36
19:24 brought no little business to the craftsmen. 76
37 you have brought these men here 36
20:38 they brought him to the ship. 80
21:16 bringing us to the house of Mnason of Cyprus 36
28 moreover he also brought Greeks into the temple 48
34 he ordered him to be brought into the barracks. 36
22: 5 and bring them in bonds to Jerusalem to be punished. 36
23:10 bring him into the barracks. 36
18 took him and brought him to the tribune and said 36
18 Paul . . asked me to bring this young man to you 36
31 took Paul and brought him by night to Antip'atris. 36
24:17 I came to bring to my nation alms and offerings. 78
25: 6 ordered Paul to be brought. 36
17 and ordered the man to be brought in. 36
18 they brought no charge in his case 85
23 Then by command of Festus Paul was brought in. 36
Rom 4:15 For the law brings wrath 65
5:16 following one trespass brought condemnation 47
16 but the free gift . . brings justification. 47
7:13 Did that which is good, then, bring death to me? 43
1Co 14: 6 unless I bring you some revelation or knowledge 68
Eph 2:13 have been brought near in the blood of Christ. 43
1Th 4:14 God will bring with him those who have fallen 36
2Ti 4:11 Get Mark and bring him with you 36
13 bring the cloak that I left with Carpus at Tro'as 85
Heb 2:10 in bringing many sons to glory 36
1Pe 3:18 Christ also died . . that he might bring us to God 81
2Jn 1:10 comes to you and does not bring this doctrine 85
Rev 21:24 the kings of the earth shall bring their glory 85
26 bring into it the glory . . of the nations 85
22:12 Behold, I am coming soon, bringing my recompense 70
1Es 1:52 he gave command to bring against them the kings 37
4: 5 they bring everything to the king 67
17 Women make men's clothes; they bring men glory 78
22 bring everything and give it to women? 85
48 to bring cedar timber from Lebanon to Jerusalem 73
5:55 to bring cedar logs from Lebanon 74
69 Esarhaddon . . who brought us here. 71
8:47 brought us competent men of the sons of Mahli 36
80 brought us into favor with the kings 78
9:17 were brought to an end 36
18 were brought in and found to have foreign wives 57
39 they told Ezra . . to bring the law of Moses 67
40 Ezra the chief priest brought the law 67
2Es 1: 7 not I who brought them out of the land of Egypt 91
13 Surely it was I who brought you through the sea 96
2: 6 that you may bring confusion upon them 90
6 and bring their mother to ruin •
3: 9 again, in its time thou didst bring the flood 94
17 thou didst bring them to Mount Sinai. 87
4:27 it will not be able to bring the things 95
7:47 that the world to come will bring delight to few 92
48 and has brought us into corruption 89
10:28 he who brought me into this . . bewilderment 93
13:13 and some were bringing others as offerings. 87
23 He who brings the peril at that time 88
15: 5 Behold," says the Lord, "I bring evils upon the world 94
49 and bring you to destruction and death. 86
Tob 2: 2 bring whatever poor man . . you may find 36
6:14 and bring . . to the grave in sorrow on my account 63
9: 2 and bring him to the wedding feast. 36
11:17 Blessed is God who has brought you to us 36
14:10 how he brought him from light into darkness 36
Jdt 6:14 they untied him and brought him into Bethulia 39
8:22 all this he will bring upon our heads 56
23 For our slavery will not bring us into favor 66
10:17 they brought them to the tent of Holofernes. 36
11: 2 they have brought all this on themselves. 78
22 and to bring destruction upon those •
12: 5 the servants . . brought her into the tent 36
14: 5 bring Achior the Ammonite to me 61
18 brought disgrace upon . . King Nebuchadnezzar! 78
16: 3 brought me to his camp, in the midst of the people. •
AEs 11: 1 brought to Egypt the preceeding Letter of Purim 49
Wis 1:12 nor bring on destruction by the works of your hands; 55
6:19 immortality brings one near to God; 46
10:14 until she brought him the scepter of a kingdom 85
Sir 4:21 For there is a shame which brings sin 54
17:23 will bring their recompense on their heads. 40
20:26 The disposition of a liar brings disgrace •
22: 4 who acts shamefully brings grief to her father. 42
23:24 She herself will be brought before the assembly 53
30:24 anxiety brings on old age too soon. 36
33:22 bring no stain upon your honor. 44
37:30 for overeating brings sickness 45
48: 2 He brought a famine upon them 54
Bar 1: 9 and brought them to Babylon. 36
2: 5 They were brought low and not raised up 43
9 calamities . . the Lord has brought them upon us 54
19 we bring before thee our prayer for mercy 62
4:29 he . . will bring you everlasting joy 54
LJr 1:41 they bring him and pray Bel that the man may speak 82
Sus 1:17 She said to her maids, "Bring me oil and ointments 85
18 to bring what they had been commanded; 85
56 and commanded them to bring the other. 81
Bel 1:14 Then Daniel ordered his servants to bring ashes 85
1Mc 3:49 also brought the garments of the priesthood 85
4:45 lest it bring reproach upon them 43
7: 2 to bring them to him. 36
47 brought them and displayed them 85
9:26 brought them to Bacchides 36
13:32 he brought great calamity upon the land. 78
15:18 have brought a gold shield weighing 1,000 minas. 85
2Mc 1: 4 may he bring peace. 78
20 he ordered them to dip it out and bring it. 85
2: 5 he brought there the tent and the ark 49
3:18 the holy place was about to be brought into contempt. 59
4:43 Charges were brought against Menelaus 52
6: 4 and besides brought in things for sacrifice 49
10 two women were brought in for having circumcised 38
21 urged him to bring meat of his own providing 85
7: 7 they brought forward the second for their sport 36
18 After him they brought forward the sixth 36
8:34 who had brought the 1,000 merchants to buy the Jews 36
9: 8 Thus he . . was brought down to earth 43
14:41 they ordered that fire be brought 81
3Mc 1: 8 to bring him gifts of welcome 67
26 to bring the aforesaid plan to a conclusion. 58
3:14 it was brought to conclusion, according to plan 36
4:11 men had been brought to the place called Schedia 36
5:45 had been brought virtually to a state of madness 36
6:17 and brought an uncontrollable terror upon the army. 78
4Mc 1: 9 by despising sufferings that bring death •
3:14 from it boldly brought the king a drink. 67
6:24 the guards brought him to the fire. 38
8: 2 others of the Hebrew captives be brought 36
3 were brought before him 36
12 instruments of torture to be brought forward 84
9:26 the guards brought in the next eldest 36
10: 8 They immediately brought him to the wheel 36
18:20 in his burning rage brought those seven sons 36

bring *See also* hastily.

bring a captive 1. αἰχμαλωτεύω
AEs 11: 4 captives whom Nebuchadnezzar . . had brought 1

bring a charge 1. עוד 2. ריב 3. διαβάλλω 4. ἐντυγχάνω
1Kg 21:10 let them bring a charge against him, saying 1
13 base fellows brought a charge against Naboth 1
Neh 5: 7 I brought charges against the nobles 2
Lke 16: 1 and charges were brought to him 3
1Mc 10:63 no one is to bring charges against him 4

bring a charge against 1. ἐγκαλέω 2. καταγορεύω 3. κατηγορέω
Mrk 15: 4 See how many charges they bring against you. 3
Act 19:38 let them bring charges against one another. 1
Rom 8:33 Who shall bring any charge against God's elect? 1
1Mc 7:25 and brought wicked charges against them. 2

bring a cloud 1. ענן
Gen 9:14 When I bring clouds over the earth 1

bring a complaint 1. ריב
Job 31:13 when they brought a complaint against me; 1

bring a plague 1. נגף
2Ch 21:14 LORD will bring a great plague on your people 1

bring a sacrifice 1. זבח
Ps 50:23 He who brings thanksgiving as his sacrifice 1

bring about 1. בוא 2. היה 3. עשה 4. κατατίθημι
Gen 50:20 to bring it about that many people should be kept 3
2Sm 3:18 bring it about; for the LORD has promised David 3
1Kg 1:27 Has this thing been brought about by my lord 2
12:15 it was a turn of affairs brought about by the LORD 2
2Ch 10:15 for it was a turn of affairs brought about by God •
Jer 40: 3 the LORD has brought it about 1
Ezk 39: 8 Behold, it is coming and it will be brought about 2
Rom 1: 5 to bring about the obedience of faith •
16:26 to bring about the obedience of faith– •
AEs 13: 4 the unifying . . cannot be brought about 4

bring about death 1. מות
1Sm 28: 9 laying a snare for my life to bring about my death? 1

bring again 1. סבב 2. שוב 3. ἀνάγω 4. ἀποστρέφω
Gen 37:14 Go now . . and bring me word again. 2
43:21 money in full weight; so we have brought it again 2
48:21 but God . . will bring you again to the land 2
Deu 1:22 bring us word again of the way by which we must go 2
25 brought us word again, and said, 'It is a good land 2
28:60 bring upon you again all the diseases of Egypt 2
Jos 14: 7 and I brought him word again as it was in my heart. 2
Jdg 11: 9 If you bring me home again to fight 2
1Kg 2:30 Benai'ah brought the king word again, saying, "Thus 2
8:34 forgive . . and bring them again to the land 2
20: 9 messengers departed and brought him word again. 2
1Ch 13: 3 Then let us bring again the ark of our God to us; 1
2Ch 6:25 bring them again to the land which thou gavest 2
33:13 brought him again to Jerusalem into his kingdom. 2
Jer 12:15 and I will bring them again each to his heritage 2
Heb 13:20 who brought again from the dead our Lord Jesus 3
Bar 2:34 I will bring them again into the land 4

bring against 1. ἐπάγω 2. καταφέρω
Act 25: 7 bringing against him many serious charges 2
Bar 4:15 For he brought against them a nation from afar 1

bring aid 1. βοηθός
2Mc 3:39 and brings it aid 1

bring an accusation against 1. καταγορεύω
1Mc 7: 6 they brought . . this accusation against the people 1

bring around 1. סבב
1Sm 5: 8 Let the ark . . be brought around to Gath. 1
9 But after they had brought it around 1
10 They have brought around to us the ark of the God 1

bring ashore 1. ἐξωθέω
Act 27:39 planned if possible to bring the ship ashore. 1

bring away 1. נהג 2. ἐξάγω
1Sm 23: 5 fought with . . and brought away their cattle 1
LJr 1: 3 after that I will bring you away from there 2

bring back 1. בוא 2. ישב 3. עלה 4. שוב 5. הלך (A) 6. ἀνάγω 7. ἀνακομίζω 8. ἀναστρέφω

9. ἀποκαθίστημι 10. ἀποφέρω 11. εἰσάγω 12. ἐπιστρέφω
13. μετακομίζω 14. στρέφω 15. φέρω

Gen 14:16 Then he brought back all the goods 4
28:15 and will bring you back to this land; 4
42:37 Slay my two sons if I do not bring him back to you; 1
37 put him in my hands, and I will bring him back 4
43: 9 If I do not bring him back to you and set him before 1
44: 8 the money . . we brought back to you from the land 4
32 If I do not bring him back to you, then I shall bear 1
Exd 10: 8 So Moses and Aaron were brought back to Pharaoh; 4
15:19 the LORD brought back the waters of the sea upon 4
23: 4 you shall bring it back to him. 4
Num13:26 they brought back word to them and to all 4
22: 8 Lodge here this night, and I will bring back word 4
Deu 28:68 LORD will bring you back in ships to Egypt 4
Jos 22:32 returned . . and brought back word to them. 4
Jdg 19: 3 went . . to speak kindly to her and bring her back. 4
Rut 1:21 and the LORD has brought me back empty. 4
1Sm 30:19 Nothing was missing . . David brought back all. 4
2Sm 3:26 they brought him back from the cistern of Sirah; 4
12:23 why should I fast? Can I bring him back again? 4
14:21 I grant this; go, bring back the young man Ab'salom. 4
15: 8 the LORD will indeed bring me back to Jerusalem 4
25 he will bring me back and let me see both it and his 4
17: 3 and I will bring all the people back to you 4
19:10 why . . say nothing about bringing the king back? 4
11 be the last to bring the king back to his house 4
12 should you be the last to bring back the king?' 4
43 the first to speak of bringing back our king? 4
1Kg 2:32 The LORD will bring back his bloody deeds upon 4
44 LORD will bring back your evil upon your own head 4
13:18 Bring him back with you into your house 4
20 came to the prophet who had brought him back; 4
23 for the prophet whom he had brought back. 4
26 the prophet who had brought him back from the way 4
29 took up the body . . and brought it back to the city 4
14:28 the guard . . and brought them back to the guardroom. 4
2Kg 20:11 the LORD, and he brought the shadow back ten steps 4
22:20 And they brought back word to the king. 4
2Ch 12:11 and brought them back to the guardroom. 4
19: 4 Jehosh'aphat . . brought them back to the LORD 4
24:19 sent prophets . . to bring them back to the LORD; 4
34:28 they brought back word to the king. 4
Ezr 6: 5 be restored and brought back to the temple 5
Neh 13: 9 brought back thither the vessels of the house 4
Job 33:30 to bring back his soul from the Pit, 4
Ps 68:22 The Lord said, "I will bring them back from Bashan 4
22 I will bring them back from the depths of the sea 4
94:23 He will bring back on them their iniquity 4
Prv 19:24 will not even bring it back to his mouth. 4
26:15 wears him out to bring it back to his mouth. 4
Isa 49: 5 to be his servant, to bring Jacob back to him 4
Jer 16:15 For I will bring them back to their own land 4
23: 3 and I will bring them back to their fold 4
24: 6 and I will bring them back to this land. 4
27:16 vessels . . will . . be brought back from Babylon 2
22 Then I will bring them back and restore them 3
28: 3 Within two years I will bring back to this place 4
4 I will also bring back to this place Jeconi'ah 4
6 and bring back to this place from Babylon 4
29:10 I will fulfil to you my promise and bring you back 4
14 and I will bring you back to the place 4
30: 3 I will bring them back to the land which I gave 4
31:18 bring me back that I may be restored 4
32:37 I will bring them back to this place 4
34:22 and will bring them back to this city; 4
41:16 eunuchs, whom Joha'nan brought back from Gibeon. 4
Ezk 9:11 brought back word, saying, "I have done 4
29:14 and bring them back to the land of Pathros 4
34: 4 the strayed you have not brought back 4
16 I will bring back the strayed 4
39:27 when I have brought them back from the peoples 4
44: 1 Then he brought me back to the outer gate 4
47: 1 Then he brought me back to the door of the temple; 4
Jon 1:13 the men rowed hard to bring the ship back to land 4
Zec 10: 6 I will bring them back because I have compassion 4
Mat 27: 3 he repented and brought back the 30 pieces 14
Jas 5:19 and some one brings him back 12
20 brings back a sinner from the error of his way 12
1Es 1:31 after he was brought back to Jerusalem he died 9
4:24 he brings it back to the woman he loves. 10
Tob 12: 2 to give him half of what I have brought back. 15
5 Take half of all that you two have brought back. 15
14: 5 bring them back into their land 12
Jdt 11:14 to bring back to them permission from the senate. 13
Wis 16:14 he cannot bring back the departed spirit 8
Bar 5: 6 God will bring them back to you, carried in glory 11
1Mc 9:58 So now let us bring Bacchides back 6
2Mc 12:39 to bring them back to lie with their kinsmen 7

bring back safely 1. ἀποκαθίστημι

Tob 10:12 The Lord of heaven bring you back safely 1

bring before 1. παράγω 2. προάγω 3. προσάγω
4. προσφέρω

Act 25:26 Therefore I have brought him before you 2
Tob 12:12 I brought a reminder . . before the Holy One 3
2Mc 11:18 everything that needed to be brought before him 4
4Mc 5: 4 one man . . was brought before the king 1

bring calamity 1. רעע

Rut 1:21 and the Almighty has brought calamity upon me? 1
1Kg 17:20 hast thou brought calamity even upon the widow 1

cause to bring forth 1. ילד

Isa 66: 9 bring to the birth and not cause to bring forth? 1
9 shall I, who cause to bring forth, shut the womb? 1

bring darkness 1. חשך

Jer 13:16 Give glory to . . God before he brings darkness 1

bring death 1. מות 2. θανατηφόρος 3. mortalis

Job 9:23 When disaster brings sudden death, he mocks 1
33:22 his life to those who bring death. 1
2Es 7:119 but we have done deeds that bring death? 3
8:31 have passed our lives in ways that bring death ‡
4Mc 8:18 and venture upon a disobedience that brings death? 2

bring desolation upon 1. שמם

Ezk 30:12 I will bring desolation upon the land 1

bring destruction 1. חבל

Prv 13:13 despises the word brings destruction on himself 1

bring distress 1. צרר

Jer 10:18 I will bring distress on them 1
Zep 1:17 I will bring distress on men 1

bring double 1. διπλοῦς

Sir 20:10 there is a gift that brings a double return. 1

bring down 1. ירד 2. נגע 3. נדח 4. נחת 5. נפל
6. שחח 7. שפל 8. καταβαίνω 9. καταβιβάζω
10. κατάγω

Gen 39: 1 the Ish'maelites who had brought him down there. 1
42:38 you would bring down my gray hairs with sorrow 1
43: 7 that he would say, 'Bring your brother down'? 1
22 we have brought other money down in our hand 1
44:21 you said to your servants, 'Bring him down to me 1
29 you will bring down my gray hairs in sorrow 1
31 and your servants will bring down the gray hairs 1
45:13 Make haste and bring my father down here. 1
Deu 1:25 fruit of the land and brought it down to us 1
21: 4 elders of that city shall bring the heifer down 1
Jdg 7: 5 he brought the people down to the water; 1
16:21 seized him . . and brought him down to Gaza 1
1Sm 2: 6 The LORD . . he brings down to Sheol and raises up. 1
2Sm 15:14 lest he overtake us . . and bring down evil upon us 3
22:28 thy eyes are upon the haughty to bring them down. 7
48 God who . . brought down peoples under me 1
1Kg 1:33 to ride on my own mule, and bring him down to Gihon; 1
53 they brought him down from the altar. 1
2: 9 you shall bring his gray head down with blood 1
5: 9 My servants shall bring it down to the sea 1
17:23 and brought him down from the upper chamber 1
18:40 Eli'jah brought them down to the brook Kishon 1
2Kg 11:19 they brought the king down from the house 1
2Ch 23:20 brought the king down from the house of the LORD 1
Ps 18:27 but the haughty eyes thou dost bring down. 7
37:14 bend their bows, to bring down the poor and needy 5
59:11 make them totter by thy power, and bring them down 1
Prv 21:22 wise man . . brings down the stronghold 1
Isa 10:13 I have brought down those who sat on thrones. 1
14:11 Your pomp is brought down to Sheol 1
15 you are brought down to Sheol 1
25:12 fortifications of his walls he will bring down 6
Jer 49:16 I will bring you down from there, says the LORD. 1
51:40 I will bring them down like lambs 1
Lam 2: 2 he has brought down . . the kingdom and its rulers. 2
Ezk 13:14 and bring it down to the ground 2
31:18 You shall be brought down with the trees of Eden 1
Hos 7:12 I will bring them down like birds of the air; 1
Jol 3: 2 and bring them down to the valley of Jehosh'aphat 1
11 Bring down thy warriors, O LORD. 4
Ams 3:11 and bring down your defenses from you 1
9: 2 up to heaven, from there I will bring them down. 1
Obd 1: 3 Who will bring me down to the ground? 1
4 set among the stars, thence I will bring you down 1
Mat 11:23 You shall be brought down to Hades. 8
Lke 10:15 You shall be brought down to Hades. 8
Act 9:30 they brought him down to Caesare'a 10
22:30 he brought Paul down and set him before them. 10
23:15 give notice now to the tribune to bring him down 10
20 to bring Paul down to the council tomorrow 10
28 I brought him down to their council. 10
Rom10: 6 (that is, to bring Christ down) 10
Tob 3:10 I shall bring his old age down in sorrow to the grave. 10
Jdt 9: 8 and bring down their power in thy anger 10
Sir 48: 3 also three times brought down fire. 10
6 who brought kings down to destruction 10
Bar 3:29 taken her, and brought her down from the clouds? 9

bring evil 1. רעע

Jer 31:28 break down, to overthrow, destroy, and bring evil 1

bring extraordinary 1. פלא

Deu 28:59 LORD will bring . . extraordinary afflictions 1

bring forth 1. חול 2. ילד 3. יצא 4. מצא 5. נוב
6. נשא 7. עשה 8. פלח 9. צמח 10. שרץ 11. ἀποκυέω
12. βλαστάνω 13. δίδωμι 14. ἐκβάλλω 15. ἐξάγω
16. παρίστημι 17. τίκτω 18. creo 19. facio
20. germino 21. pario 22. procreo 23. produco
24. profero

Gen 1:12 The earth brought forth vegetation 3
20 waters bring forth swarms of living creatures 10
24 Let the earth bring forth living creatures 3
3:16 in pain you shall bring forth children 2
18 thorns and thistles it shall bring forth to you; 9
8:17 Bring forth with you every living thing that is 3
19:16 and they brought him forth and set him outside 3
17 when they had brought them forth, they said 3
24:53 the servant brought forth jewelry of silver 3
30:39 the flocks brought forth striped, speckled 2
41:47 years the earth brought forth abundantly 7
Exd 3:10 to Pharaoh that you may bring forth my people 3
12 when you have brought forth the people out 3
7: 4 then I will . . bring forth my hosts, my people 3
8:18 tried by their secret arts to bring forth gnats 3
29:46 I am the LORD their God, who brought them forth 3
32:11 thy people, whom thou has brought forth out 3
12 With evil intent did he bring them forth, to slay 3
Lev 25:21 that it will bring forth fruit for three years 7
38 God, who brought you forth out of the land of Egypt 3
42 whom I brought forth out of the land of Egypt 3
55 whom I brought forth out of the land of Egypt 3
26:13 God, who brought you forth out of the land of Egypt 3
45 whom I brought forth out of the land of Egypt 3
Num11:12 Did I bring them forth, that thou shouldst say to me 2
20:10 shall we bring forth water for you out of this rock? 3
16 sent an angel and brought us forth out of Egypt; 3
Deu 1:27 he has brought us forth out of the land of Egypt 3
4:20 LORD . . brought you forth out of the iron furnace 3
14:28 bring forth all the tithe of your produce 3
17: 5 then you shall bring forth to your gates 3
Jos 2: 3 Bring forth the men that have come to you 3
1Sm 12: 8 who brought forth your fathers out of Egypt 3
2Sm 12:30 And he brought forth the spoil of the city 3
31 And he brought forth the people who were in it 3
22:20 He brought me forth into a broad place; 3
2Kg 19: 3 and there is no strength to bring them forth. 2
1Ch 20: 2 he brought forth the spoil of the city 3
3 he brought forth the people who were in it 3
Neh 9: 7 choose Abram and bring him forth out of Ur 3
15 bring forth water for them from the rock 3
Job 10:18 Why didst thou bring me forth from the womb? 3
15: 7 Or were you brought forth before the hills? 1
35 They conceive mischief and bring forth evil 2
28:11 the thing that is hid he brings forth to light. 3
39: 1 Do you know when the mountain goats bring forth? 2
2 do you know the time when they bring forth 2
3 when they crouch, bring forth their offspring 8
Ps 7:14 pregnant with mischief, and brings forth lies. 2
18:19 He brought me forth into a broad place; 3
37: 6 will bring forth your vindication as the light 3
51: 5 Behold, I was brought forth in iniquity, and in sin 1
66:12 yet hou hast brought us forth to a spacious place. 3
90: 2 Before the mountains were brought forth 2
104:14 that he may bring forth food from the earth 3
135: 7 brings forth the wind from his storehouses. 4
Prv 8:24 When there were no depths I was brought forth 1
25 before the hills, I was brought forth; 1
10:31 The mouth of the righteous brings forth wisdom 5
25:23 The north wind brings forth rain; 1
27: 1 for you do not know what a day may bring forth. 2
Isa 26:18 we writhed, we have as it were brought forth wind. 2
33:11 You conceive chaff, you bring forth stubble; 2
37: 3 and there is no strength to bring them forth. 2
42: 3 he will faithfully bring forth justice. 3
43: 8 Bring forth the people who are blind 3
17 who brings forth chariot and horse 3
59: 4 conceive mischief and bring forth iniquity. 2
61:11 For as the earth brings forth its shoots 3
65: 9 I will bring forth descendants from Jacob 3
66: 8 Shall a nation be brought forth in one moment? 2
8 as Zion was in labor she brought forth her sons. 2
Jer 10:13 he brings forth the wind from his storehouses. 3
12: 2 they take root; they grow and bring forth fruit; 7
51:10 The LORD has brought forth our vindication; 3
16 he brings forth the wind from his storehouses. 3
Ezk 11: 7 you shall be brought forth out of the midst of it. 3
9 And I will bring you forth out of the midst of it 3
17: 6 So it became a vine, and brought forth branches 7
8 that it might bring forth branches, and bear 7
23 that it may bring forth boughs and bear fruit 6
28:18 I brought forth fire from the midst of you; 3
38: 4 hooks into your jaws, and I will bring you forth 3
46:21 Then he brought me forth to the outer court 3
Hos 9:16 Even though they bring forth, I will slay 2
Mic 5: 3 time when she who is in travail has brought forth; 2
7: 9 He will bring me forth to the light; 3
Hag 1:11 upon what the ground brings forth, upon men 3

Mat 12:35 out of his good treasure brings forth good 14
35 out of his evil treasure brings forth evil. 14
13: 8 and brought forth grain 13
Mrk 4: 8 seeds fell into good soil and brought forth grain 13
Heb 6: 7 For land which . . brings forth vegetation 17
Jas 1:15 sin when it is full-grown brings forth death. 11
18 Of his own will he brought us forth 11
5:18 and the earth brought forth its fruit. 12
Rev 12: 4 might devour her child when she brought it forth; 17
5 she brought forth a male child, one who is to rule 17
2Es 3:20 so that thy law might bring forth fruit in them. 19
5: 8 menstruous women shall bring forth monsters. 21
37 bring forth for me the winds shut up in them 23
49 For as an infant does not bring forth 21
49 a woman . . does not bring forth any longer •
6:40 that a ray of light be brought forth 24
47 to bring forth living creatures 22
53 thou didst command the earth to bring forth 18
7:62 O earth, what have you brought forth 21
9:31 it shall bring forth fruit in you 19
10:12 which I brought forth in pain and bore in sorrow; 21
14 then I say to you, 'As you brought forth in sorrow 21
16:32 and all its paths shall bring forth thorns 20
Wis 19:10 how . . the earth brought forth gnats 15
Sir 23:23 brought forth children by another man. 16
45: 1 the Lord brought forth a man of mercy 15

bring forth abundantly 1. שרץ
Gen 9: 7 bring forth abundantly on the earth and multiply 1

bring forth fruit 1. נוב 2. καρποφορέω 3. fructifico
Ps 92:14 They still bring forth fruit in old age 1
Lke 8:15 and bring forth fruit with patience. 2
2Es 11:42 those who brought forth fruit 3

bring forth one's first 1. בכר
Jer 4:31 anguish as of one bringing forth her first child 1

bring forth plentifully 1. εὐφορέω
Lke 12:16 The land of a rich man brought forth plentifully; 1

bring forth thousands 1. אלף
Ps 144:13 sheep bring forth thousands and ten thousands 1

bring forth young 1. ילד
Ezk 31: 6 beasts of the field brought forth their young; 1

bring forward 1. יצא 2. ἕλκω 3. κομίζω 4. παράγω 5. προσάγω
Zec 4: 7 he shall bring forward the top stone amid shouts 1
Wis 18:21 he brought forward the shield of his ministry 3
1Mc 10:82 Then Simon brought forward his force 2
2Mc 7:15 Next they brought forward the fifth 5
4Mc 9:11 Then . . the guards brought forward the eldest 4

bring glory 1. δοξάζω
1Mc 14:29 they brought great glory to their nation. 1

bring good 1. συμβάλλω
Wis 5: 8 what good has our boasted wealth brought us? 1

bring good news 1. בשר 2. εὐαγγελίζω
2Sm 4:10 told me . . and thought he was bringing good news 1
1Kg 1:42 for you are a worthy man and bring good news. 1
Lke 1:19 and to bring you this good news. 2
2:10 behold, I bring you good news of a great joy 2
8: 1 bringing the good news of the kingdom of God 2
Act 13:32 we bring you the good news 2
14:15 We also are men . . and bring you good news 2
1Th 3: 6 Timothy . . has brought us the good news 2

bring good tidings 1. בשר
Isa 52: 7 are the feet of him who brings good tidings 1
7 who publishes peace, who brings good tidings 1
61: 1 anointed me to bring good tidings to the afflicted; 1
Nah 1:15 the feet of him who brings good tidings 1

bring guilt 1. אָשְׁמָה
Lev 4: 3 who sins, thus bringing guilt on the people 1

bring guilt upon 1. חטא
Deu 24: 4 not bring guilt upon the land which the LORD 1

bring healing 1. מַרְפֵּא
Prv 12:18 but the tongue of the wise brings healing. 1
13:17 but a faithful envoy brings healing. 1

bring here 1. נגש 2. μεταβολή
1Sm 13: 9 Saul said, "Bring the burnt offering here to me 1
23: 9 he said to Abi'athar . . "Bring the ephod here. 1
AEs 14:18 since the day that I was brought here until now 2

bring home 1. בוא 2. שוב
2Sm 14:13 the king does not bring his banished one home 2
1Ch 13:12 he said, "How can I bring the ark of God home to me? 1
Zep 3:20 At that time I will bring you home 1
Zec 10:10 I will bring them home from the land of Egypt 2

bring into 1. בוא 2. εἰσάγω 3. εἰσφέρω
2Sm 13:10 Bring the food into the chamber, that I may eat 1
10 and brought them into the chamber to Amnon 1
2Kg 12: 4 All the money . . which is brought into the house 1
9 all the money that was brought into the house 1
13 money that was brought into the house of the LORD 1
16 the money from . . was not brought into the house 1
22: 4 the money . . brought into the house of the LORD 1
2Ch 15:18 he brought into the house of God the votive gifts 1
34:14 money . . brought into the house of the LORD 1
Sng 1: 4 The king has brought me into his chambers. 1
Act 21:29 Paul had brought him into the temple. 2
37 As Paul was about to be brought into the barracks 2
22:24 commanded him to be brought into the barracks 2
1Ti 6: 7 for we brought nothing into the world 3
Heb 1: 6 when he brings the first-born into the world 2
13:11 whose blood is brought into the sanctuary 3
Tob 7: 1 she brought them into the house. 2
Sir 11:29 Do not bring every man into your home 2
46: 8 to bring them into their inheritance 2
48:17 brought water into the midst of it 2
1Mc 4:49 and brought the lampstand . . into the temple. 3

bring into bondage 1. καταδουλόω
Gal 2: 4 that they might bring us into bondage– 1

bring into contempt 1. קלה 2. קלל 3. ἐξουδενέω
Isa 9: 1 he brought into contempt the land of Zeb'ulun 2
16:14 the glory of Moab will be brought into contempt 1
Jdt 13:17 who hast brought into contempt this day the enemies 3

bring into one's presence 1. παρίστημι
2Co 4:14 with Jesus and bring us with you into his presence. 1

bring into subjection 1. כבש 2. כנע 3. ἐνεξουσιάζω 4. καταδυναστεύω
Ps 106:42 brought into subjection under their power. 2
Jer 34:11 and brought them into subjection as slaves. 1
16 and you brought them into subjection 1
Sir 47:19 you were brought into subjection. 3
48:12 no one brought him into subjection. 4

bring judgment 1. דין
Gen 15:14 I will bring judgment on the nation 1

bring judgment upon 1. παραδίδωμι
2Mc 1:17 who has brought judgment upon those . . 1

bring low 1. דלל 2. כנע 3. כרע 4. מכך 5. צער 6. שחח 7. שפל 8. ταπεινός 9. ταπεινόω 10. ταπείνωσις
Jdg 6: 6 Israel was brought very low because of Mid'ian; 1
11:35 Alas, my daughter! you have brought me very low 3
1Sm 2: 7 poor and makes rich; he brings low, he also exalts. 7
2Ch 28:19 For the LORD brought Judah low because of Ahaz 2
Job 14:21 they are brought low, and he perceives it not. 5
40:12 Look on every one that is proud, and bring him low; 2
Ps 79: 8 for we are brought very low. 1
106:43 were brought low through their iniquity. 4
107:39 When they are diminished and brought low 6
116: 6 when I was brought low, he saved me. 1
142: 6 Give heed to my cry; for I am brought very low! 1
Prv 29:23 A man's pride will bring him low 7
Ecc 12: 4 and all the daughters of song are brought low; 6
Isa 2: 9 So man is humbled, and men are brought low– 7
11 The haughty looks of man shall be brought low 7
17 humbled, and the pride of men shall be brought low; 7
5:15 Man is bowed down, and men are brought low 7
10:33 be hewn down, and the lofty will be brought low. 7
17: 4 in that day the glory of Jacob will be brought low 1
26: 5 he has brought low the inhabitants of the height 6
Ezk 17:24 shall know that I the LORD bring low the high tree 7
Lke 3: 5 every mountain and hill shall be brought low 9
Jdt 13:20 when our nation was brought low 10
Sir 6:12 if you are brought low he will turn against you 9
33:12 some of them he cursed and brought low 9
Aza 1:14 and are brought low this day in all the world 8

make bring forth 1. ילד
Isa 55:10 water the earth, making it bring forth and sprout 1

bring more 1. יסף
Lev 26:21 I will bring more plagues upon you, sevenfold 1
Neh 13:18 Yet you bring more wrath upon Israel 1

bring near 1. נגש 2. קרב 3. ἐγγίζω 4. προσάγω
Gen 48:10 Joseph brought them near him; 1
13 Joseph took them . . and brought them near him. 1
Exd 28: 1 Then bring near to you Aaron your brother 2
Num 3: 6 Bring the tribe of Levi near, and set them before 2
16: 9 to bring you near to himself, to do service 2
10 he has brought you near him, and all your brethren 2
Jos 7:14 you shall be brought near by your tribes; 2
16 Joshua . . brought Israel near tribe by tribe 2
17 and he brought near the families of Judah 2
17 and he brought near the family of the Zer'ahites 2
18 and he brought near his household man by man 2
1Sm 10:20 Samuel brought all the tribes of Israel near 2
21 He brought the tribe of Benjamin near 2
21 he brought the . . Matrites near man by man 4
2Sm 13:11 But when she brought them near him to eat 1
Job 40:19 let him who made him bring near his sword! 1
Ps 65: 4 he whom thou dost choose and bring near, to dwell 2
Isa 46:13 I bring near my deliverance, it is not far off 2
Ezk 22: 4 you have brought your day near 2
Ams 6: 3 and bring near the seat of violence? 1
Sir 33:12 made holy and brought near to himself 3

bring news 1. בשר
Jer 20:15 Cursed be the man who brought the news 1

bring no regret 1. ἀμεταμέλητος
2Co 7:10 that leads to salvation and brings no regret 1

bring on board 1. κατάγω
3Mc 4: 9 They were brought on board like wild animals 1

bring on the way 1. עבר 2. προπέμπω
2Sm 19:40 all the people . . brought the king on his way. 1
Act 21: 5 they all . . brought us on our way 2

bring out 1. בוא 2. יצא 3. ἀνάγω 4. ἐκβάλλω 5. ἐκφέρω 6. ἐξάγω 7. προάγω 8. προφέρω 9. educo
Gen 14:18 king of Salem brought out bread and wine; 2
19: 5 Bring them out to us, that we may know them. 2
8 let me bring them out to you 2
8 let me bring them out to you 2
12 you have in the city, bring them out of the place; 2
38:24 Bring her out, and let her be burned. 2
25 As she was being brought out, she sent word 2
43:23 Then he brought Simeon out to them. 2
Exd 6: 6 I am the LORD, and I will bring you out 2
7 who has brought you out from under the burdens 2
13 a charge . . to bring the people of Israel out 2
26 Bring out the people of Israel . . by their hosts. 2
27 spoke . . about bringing out the people 2
7: 5 when I . . bring out the people of Israel 2
12:17 I brought your hosts out of the land of Egypt 2
39 of the dough which they had brought out of Egypt 2
42 by the LORD, to bring them out of the land of Egypt; 2
51 the LORD brought the people of Israel out 2
13: 3 the LORD brought you out from this place; 2
9 the LORD has brought you out of Egypt. 2
14 strength of hand the LORD brought us out of Egypt 2
16 strong hand the LORD brought us out of Egypt. 2
14:11 What have you done . . in bringing us out of Egypt? 2
16: 3 you have brought us out into this wilderness 2
6 it was the LORD who brought you out of the land 2
32 when I brought you out of the land of Egypt.' 2
18: 1 how the LORD had brought Israel out of Egypt. 2
19:17 Then Moses brought the people out of the camp 2
20: 2 God, who brought you out of the land of Egypt 2
Lev 19:36 your God, who brought you out of the land of Egypt 2
22:33 who brought you out of the land of Egypt 2
23:43 when I brought them out of the land of Egypt 2
24:14 Bring out of the camp him who cursed 2
23 they brought him who had cursed out of the camp 2
Num15:41 I am the LORD your God, who brought you out 2
17: 9 Then Moses brought out all the rods 2
20: 8 so you shall bring water out of the rock for them; 2
23:22 God brings them out of Egypt; 2
24: 8 God brings him out of Egypt; 2
Deu 4:37 brought you out of Egypt with his own presence 2
5:15 LORD . . brought you out thence with a mighty 2
6:23 he brought us out from there, that he might bring us 2
7: 8 the LORD has brought you out with a mighty hand 2
19 by which the LORD your God brought you out; 2
9:28 brought them out to slay them in the wilderness. 2
29 whom thou didst bring out by thy great power 2
21:19 take hold of him and bring him out to the elders 2
22:15 shall . . bring out the tokens of her virginity 2
21 bring out the young woman to the door 2
24 shall bring them both out to the gate of that city 2
29:25 when he brought them out of the land of Egypt 2
Jos 6:22 Go . . and bring out from it the woman 2
23 and brought out Rahab, and her father and mother 2
10:22 and bring those five kings out to me from the cave. 2
23 and brought those five kings out to him 2
24 when they brought those kings out to Joshua 2
24: 5 I sent Moses . . and afterwards I brought you out. 2
6 I brought your fathers out of Egypt, and you came 2
Jdg 2:12 who had brought them out of the land of Egypt; 2
6: 8 I . . brought you out of the house of bondage; 2
18 come to thee, and bring out my present, and set it 2
30 said to Jo'ash, "Bring out your son, that he may die 2
19:22 Bring out the man who came into your house, 2
24 here are my . . let me bring them out now. 2
Rut 2:18 she also brought out and gave her what food she had 2
2Sm 10:16 Hadade'zer sent, and brought out the Syrians 2
22:49 who brought me out from my enemies; 2
1Kg 8:16 the day that I brought . . Israel out of Egypt 2
21 when he brought them out of the land of Egypt. 2
51 heritage, which thou didst bring out of Egypt 2
53 thou didst bring our fathers out of Egypt, O Lord 2
2Kg 10:22 Bring out the vestments for all the worshipers 2
22 So he brought out the vestments for them. 2

26 they brought out the pillar . . and burned it. 2
11:12 Then he brought out the king's son 2
15 Bring her out between the ranks; 2
23: 4 to bring out of the temple . . all the vessels 2
6 he brought out the Ashe'rah from the house 2
1Ch 19:16 sent messengers and brought out the Syrians 2
2Ch 6: 5 'Since the day that I brought my people out 2
7:22 LORD . . who brought them out of the land of Egypt 2
23:11 Then he brought out the king's son 2
14 Jehoi'ada the priest brought out the captains 2
14 Bring her out between the ranks; 2
29:16 brought out all the uncleanness that they found 2
34:14 bringing out the money that had been brought 2
Ezr 1: 7 Cyrus . . brought out the vessels of the house 2
8 Cyrus king of Persia brought these out in charge 2
Ps 25:17 bring me out of my distresses. 2
107:14 he brought them out of darkness and gloom 2
136:11 who . . brought Israel out from among them 2
Isa 40:26 He who brings out their host by number 2
42: 7 to bring out the prisoners from the dungeon 2
Jer 7:22 day that I brought them out of the land of Egypt 2
8: 1 the bones . . shall be brought out of their tombs; 2
11: 4 when I brought them out of the land of Egypt 2
31:32 when I took them by the hand to bring them out 2
32:21 Thou didst bring thy people Israel out 2
34:13 when I brought them out of the land of Egypt 2
50:25 and brought out the weapons of his wrath 2
52:31 and brought him out of prison; 2
Ezk 12: 4 You shall bring out your baggage by day 2
7 I brought out my baggage by day 2
20: 6 that I would bring them out of the land of Egypt 2
9 in bringing them out of the land of Egypt. 2
14 nations, in whose sight I had brought them out. 2
22 nations, in whose sight I had brought them out. 2
34 I will bring you out from the peoples 2
38 I will bring them out of the land 2
41 when I bring you out from the peoples 2
27:26 rowers have brought you out into the high seas. 1
34:13 I will bring them out from the peoples 2
37: 1 he brought me out by the spirit of the LORD 2
38: 8 its people were brought out from the nations 2
46:20 in order not to bring them out into the outer 2
47: 2 Then he brought me out by way of the north gate 2
Dan 9:15 didst bring thy people out of the land of Egypt 2
Mat 13:52 like a householder who brings out of his treasure 4
Joh 10: 4 When he has brought out all his own 4
Act 5:19 an angel . . brought them out and said 6
12: 4 intending . . to bring him out to the people. 3
6 when Herod was about to bring him out 7
17 how the Lord had brought him out of the prison 6
17: 5 seeking to bring them out to the people. 7
1Es 2:10 Cyrus the king also brought out the holy vessels 5
11 When Cyrus king of the Persians brought these out 5
2Es 2: 1 I brought this people out of bondage 9
16 and will bring them out from their tombs 9
31 I will bring them out of the hiding places 9
15:11 I will bring them out with a mighty hand 9
Tob 9: 5 Gabael brought out the money bags 8
Bar 1:19 Lord brought our fathers out of the land of Egypt 6
20 he brought our fathers out of the land of Egypt 6
2:11 didst bring thy people out of the land of Egypt 6
24 bones . . would be brought out of their graves; 5

bring over 1. סבב 2. עבר 3. διαβιβάζω

Jos 7: 7 why hast thou brought this people over the Jordan 2
2Sm 2: 8 and brought him over to Mahana'im; 2
3:12 shall be with you to bring over all Israel to you. 1
19:15 Judah came . . to bring the king over the Jordan. 2
18 crossed . . to bring over the king's household 2
41 and brought the king and his . . over the Jordan 2
Wis 10:18 She brought them over the Red Sea 3

bring punishment 1. פקד

Jer 46:25 I am bringing punishment upon Amon of Thebes 1
50:18 I am bringing punishment on the king of Babylon 1

bring rain 1. גשם 2. מטר

Job 38:26 to bring rain on a land where no man is 2
Jer 14:22 the false gods of the nations that can bring rain? 1

bring relief 1. נחם

Gen 5:29 this one shall bring us relief from our work 1

bring reproach 1. חפר

Prv 19:26 son who causes shame and brings reproach. 1

bring ruin 1. אבד

Deu 28:63 LORD will take delight in bringing ruin upon you 1

bring safely 1. διασῴζω

Act 23:24 and bring him safely to Felix the governor. 1

bring secretly 1. παρεισάγω 2. παρείσακτος

Gal 2: 4 because of false brethren secretly brought in 2
2Pe 2: 1 secretly bring in destructive heresies 1

bring shame 1. בוש 2. αἰσχύνω 3. καταισχύνω

Prv 10: 5 but a son who sleeps in harvest brings shame. 1
12: 4 she who brings shame is like rottenness 1
29:15 left to himself brings shame to his mother. 1
Sir 4:20 do not bring shame on yourself. 2
42:14 it is a woman who brings shame and disgrace. 3

bring shame upon 1. חסד

Prv 25:10 lest he who hears you bring shame upon you 1

bring some 1. ἀναφέρω

1Es 4: 6 reap the harvest and bring some to the king 1

bring stealthily 1. גנב

Job 4:12 Now a word was brought to me stealthily 1

bring the curse 1. ארר

Num 5:18 water of bitterness that brings the curse. 1
19 water of bitterness that brings the curse. 1
22 may this water that brings the curse pass 1
24 the water of bitterness that brings the curse 1
24 water that brings the curse shall enter into her 1
27 water that brings the curse shall enter into her 1

bring tidings 1. בשר

1Sm 4:17 He who brought the tidings answered and said 1
2Sm 18:26 The king said, "He also brings tidings. 1

bring to an end 1. שבת 2. שכח 3. שלם 4. סוף (A) 5. שלם (A) 6. ἀποκτείνω 7. ἵστημι

Isa 21: 2 all the sighing she has caused I bring to an end. 1
38:12 from day to night thou dost bring me to an end; 3
13 from day to night thou dost bring me to an end. 3
Jer 48:35 I will bring to an end in Moab, says the LORD 1
Lam 2: 6 the LORD has brought to an end . . appointed feast 2
Dan 2:44 these kingdoms and bring them to an end 4
5:26 God has numbered . . and brought it to an end; 5
Ams 8: 4 and bring the poor of the land to an end 1
Eph 2:16 thereby bringing the hostility to an end. 6
2Mc 7:38 to bring to an end the wrath of the Almighty 7

bring to birth 1. שבר

Isa 66: 9 Shall I bring to the birth and not . . bring forth? 1

bring to completion 1. ἐπιτελέω

Php 1: 6 will bring it to completion at the day 1

bring to dishonor 1. כלם

Ps 40:14 let them be turned back and brought to dishonor 1
69: 6 those who seek thee be brought to dishonor 1
70: 2 Let them be turned back and brought to dishonor 1

bring to fulfilment 1. συντελέω

Tob 8:17 and bring their lives to fulfilment in health 1

bring to judgment 1. שפט

Jer 2:35 Behold, I will bring you to judgment for saying 1

bring to life 1. חיה 2. ζάω

1Sm 2: 6 The LORD kills and brings to life; 1
Rom 6:13 as men who have been brought from death to life 2

bring to light 1. φωτίζω

1Co 4: 5 who will bring to light the things now hidden 1
2Ti 1:10 brought life and immortality to light 1

bring to nothing 1. מעט 2. καταργέω

Jer 10:24 not in thy anger, lest thou bring me to nothing. 1
1Co 1:28 to bring to nothing things that are 2

bring to nought 1. פרר 2. שדד

Ps 33:10 LORD brings the counsel of the nations to nought; 1
Ezk 32:12 They shall bring to nought the pride of Egypt 2

bring to pass 1. בוא 2. היה 3. כלה 4. עשה

Gen 41:32 and God will shortly bring it to pass. 4
Jdg 20: 3 Tell us, how was this wickedness brought to pass? 2
2Kg 19:25 I planned from days of old what now I bring to pass 1
Prv 16:30 he who compresses his lips brings evil to pass. 3
Isa 37:26 I planned from days of old what now I bring to pass 1
46:11 I have spoken, and I will bring it to pass; 1

bring to remembrance 1. זכר

Num 5:15 bringing iniquity to remembrance. 1
1Kg 17:18 You have come to me to bring my sin to remembrance 1
Ezk 21:23 but he brings their guilt to remembrance 1

bring to ruin 1. כשל 2. סלף 3. עות

Ps 64: 8 of their tongue he will bring them to ruin; 1
146: 9 but the way of the wicked he brings to ruin. 3
Prv 19: 3 When a man's folly brings his way to ruin 2

bring to silence 1. דמם

Jer 48: 2 You also, O Madmen, shall be brought to silence; 1

bring to the light of day 1. τελεσφορέω

4Mc 13:20 they were brought to the light of day 1

bring to trial 1. שפט 2. ἄγω

Ps 37:33 let him be condemned when he is brought to trial. 1
Mrk 13:11 when they bring you to trial and deliver you up 2

bring together 1. אסף 2. συμφέρω

Jer 21: 4 I will bring them together into the midst 1
Act 19:19 a number of those . . brought their books together 2

bring trouble 1. עכר

Gen 34:30 You have brought trouble on me 1
Jos 6:18 lest when you . . and bring trouble upon it. 1
7:25 And Joshua said, "Why did you bring trouble on us? 1
25 The LORD brings trouble on you today. 1

bring up 1. אמן 2. אָמְנָה 3. גדל 4. חיה 5. יצא 6. עלה 7. רמם 8. ἄγω 9. ἀνάγω 10. ἀνατρέφω 11. ἐκτρέφω 12. προσάγω 13. συνεκτρόφος 14. συντρέφω 15. τρέφω 16. τροφεύω 17. educo 18. enutrio 19. nutrio

Gen 46: 4 Egypt, and I will also bring you up again; 6
50:24 visit you, and bring you up out of this land 6
Exd 3: 8 and to bring them up out of that land 6
17 I will bring you up out of the affliction of Egypt 6
17: 3 Why did you bring us up out of Egypt 6
32: 1 who brought us up out of the land of Egypt 6
4 who brought you up out of the land of Egypt! 6
7 whom you brought up out of the land of Egypt 6
8 who brought you up out of the land of Egypt!' 6
23 as for this Moses, the man who brought us up 6
33: 1 you and the people whom you have brought up 6
12 sayest to me, 'Bring up this people'; 6
Lev 11:45 I am the LORD who brought you up out of the land 6
Num14:13 for thou didst bring up this people in thy might 6
36 by bringing up an evil report against the land 5
37 the men who brought up an evil report of the land 5
16:13 brought us up out of a land flowing with milk 6
20:25 Aaron and Elea'zar . . bring them up to Mount Hor; 6
21: 5 Why have you brought us up out of Egypt to die 6
22:41 took Balaam and brought him up to Bamoth-ba'al; 6
Deu 20: 1 LORD . . brought you up out of the land of Egypt. 6
Jos 2: 6 she had brought them up to the roof, and hid them 6
7:24 and they brought them up to the Valley of Achor. 6
24:17 LORD . . brought us and our fathers up 6
32 The bones . . Israel brought up from Egypt 6
Jdg 2: 1 And he said, "I brought you up from Egypt 6
6:13 Did not the LORD bring us up from Egypt?' 6
15:13 they bound him . . and brought him up from the rock. 6
16:31 took him and brought him up and buried him 6
1Sm 2:14 all . . the fork brought up the priest would take 6
8: 8 from the day I brought them up out of Egypt even 6
10:18 I brought up Israel out of Egypt, and I delivered 6
12: 6 who . . brought your fathers up out of the land 6
19:15 Bring him up to me in the bed, that I may kill him. 6
28: 8 and bring up for me whomever I shall name to you. 6
11 the woman said, "Whom shall I bring up for you? 6
11 He said, "Bring up Samuel for me. 6
15 Why have you disturbed me by bringing me up? 6
2Sm 2: 3 And David brought up his men who were with him 6
6: 2 from Ba'ale-judah, to bring up from there the ark 6
12 David went and brought up the ark of God 6
15 David and . . Israel brought up the ark of the LORD 6
7: 6 since the day I brought up the people of Israel 6
12: 3 And he brought it up, and it grew up with him 4
21:13 and he brought up from there the bones of Saul 6
1Kg 8: 1 assembled . . to bring up the ark of the covenant 6
4 And they brought up the ark of the LORD 6
4 the priests and the Levites brought them up. 6
12:28 who brought you up out of the land of Egypt. 6
2Kg 10: 6 with the great men . . who were bringing them up. 3
17: 7 the LORD . . who had brought them up out of the land 6
25: 6 and brought him up to the king of Babylon 6
1Ch 13: 6 to bring up from there the ark of God 6
15: 3 to bring up the ark of the LORD to its place 6
12 so that you may bring up the ark of the LORD 6
14 to bring up the ark of the LORD, the God of Israel. 6
25 to bring up the ark of the covenant of the LORD 6
28 brought up the ark of the covenant of the LORD 6
2Ch 1: 4 David had brought up the ark of God 6
5: 2 to bring up the ark of the covenant of the LORD 6
5 they brought up the ark, the tent of meeting 6
5 the priests and the Levites brought them up. 6
8:11 Solomon brought Pharaoh's daughter up 6
36:17 Therefore he brought up against them the king 6
Ezr 1:11 5,469. All these did Shesh-baz'zar bring up 6
11 when the exiles were brought up from Babylonia 6
Neh 9:18 'This is your God who brought you up out of Egypt,' 6
10:38 Levites shall bring up the tithe of the tithes 6
12:31 I brought up the princes of Judah upon the wall 6
Est 2: 7 He had brought up Hadas'sah, that is Esther 1
20 obeyed . . just as when she was brought up by him. 2
Ps 30: 3 O LORD, thou hast brought up my soul from Sheol 6
71:20 from the depths of the earth thou wilt bring me up 6
81:10 who brought you up out of the land of Egypt. 6
Isa 1: 2 Sons have I reared and brought up 7
8: 7 the Lord is bringing up against them the waters 6
23: 4 reared young men nor brought up virgins. 7
49:21 who has brought up these? Behold, I was left alone; 3
51:18 by the hand among all the sons she has brought up. 3
63:11 who brought up out of the sea the shepherds of his 6
Jer 2: 6 the LORD who brought us up from the land of Egypt 6
11: 7 when I brought them up out of the land of Egypt 6
16:14 LORD lives who brought up the people of Israel 6

15 LORD lives who brought up the people of Israel 6
23: 7 LORD lives who brought up the people of Israel 6
8 'As the LORD lives who brought up and led 6
39: 5 they brought him up to Nebuchadrez'zar 6
51:27 bring up horses like bristling locusts. 6
52: 9 and brought him up to the king of Babylon 6
Lam 4: 5 who were brought up in purple lie on ash heaps. 1
Ezk 16:40 They shall bring up a host against you 6
19: 3 she brought up one of her whelps; 6
23:46 Bring up a host against them 6
26: 3 and will bring up many nations against you 6
3 against you, as the sea brings up its waves. 6
19 when I bring up the deep over you 6
39: 2 and drive you forward, and bring you up 6
Hos 9:12 if they bring up children, I will bereave them 3
12:13 the LORD brought Israel up from Egypt 6
Ams 2:10 Also I brought you up out of the land of Egypt 6
3: 1 family which I brought up out of the land of Egypt 6
9: 7 Did I not bring up Israel from the land of Egypt 6
Jon 2: 6 yet thou didst bring up my life from the Pit, O LORD 6
Mic 6: 4 For I brought you up from the land of Egypt 6
Hab 1:15 He brings all of them up with a hook 6
Lke 2:22 they brought him up to Jerusalem to present him 9
4:16 he came to Nazareth, where he had been brought up; 15
Act 7:20 he was brought up . . in his father's house; 10
21 and brought him up as her own son. 10
16:34 Then he brought them up into his house 9
22: 3 but brought up in this city at the feet of Gama'li-el 10
Rom 10: 7 (that is, to bring Christ up from the dead). 9
Eph 6: 4 bring them up in the discipline . . of the Lord. 11
1Es 1:38 brought him up out of Egypt. 9
4:16 women brought up . . men who plant the vineyards 11
20 A man leaves his own father, who brought him up 11
2Es 2: 3 I brought you up with gladness 17
15 embrace your sons; bring them up with gladness 17
8:12 Thou hast brought him up in thy righteousness 18
9:46 I brought him up with much care. 19
10:47 that she brought him up with much care 19
Tob 13: 2 he leads down to Hades, and brings up again 9
Bar 4: 8 forgot the everlasting God, who brought you up 16
1Mc 1: 6 who had been brought up with him from youth 13
6:15 and bring him up to be king. 11
17 Lysias had brought him up as a boy 11
55 had appointed to bring up Antiochus his son 11
11:39 Imalkue the Arab, who was bringing up Antiochus 15
13:43 made a siege engine, brought it up to the city 12
2Mc 7:27 and brought you up to this point in your life 8
3Mc 6: 7 Daniel . . you brought up to the light unharmed. 9
4Mc 10: 2 I was brought up on the same teachings? 10
13:24 and brought up in right living 14

bring up a child 1. *τεκνοτροφέω*
1Ti 5:10 as one who has brought up children 1

bring up against 1. *κατηγορέω*
Act 24:13 prove to you what they now bring up against me. 1

bring upon 1. נשׂא 2. *ἐπάγω* 3. *ποιέω* 4. *προσβάλλω* 5. induco 6. praesto
Exd 28:43 lest they bring guilt upon themselves and die. 1
Act 5:28 you intend to bring this man's blood upon us. 2
2Pe 2: 1 bringing upon themselves swift destruction. 2
5 he brought a flood upon the world of the ungodly; 2
2Es 12: 4 Behold, you have brought this upon me 6
15:12 punishment that the Lord will bring upon it. 5
Sir 1:30 thus bring dishonor upon yourself 2
2: 4 Accept whatever is brought upon you 2
4:17 she will bring fear and cowardice upon him 2
10:13 brought upon them extraordinary afflictions *
47:20 you brought wrath upon your children 2
Bar 4: 9 God has brought great sorrow upon me; 2
10 which the Everlasting brought upon them. 2
14 which the Everlasting brought upon them. 2
18 For he who brought these calamities upon you 2
27 be remembered by him who brought this upon you. 2
29 For he who brought these calamities upon you 2
Aza 1: 5 in all that thou hast brought upon us 2
5 thou hast brought all this upon us because of our sins. 2
8 all that thou hast brought upon us 2
1Mc 7: 7 see all the ruin which Judas has brought upon us 3
3Mc 2: 4 by bringing upon them a boundless flood. 2
4Mc 11:23 I myself will bring a great avenger upon you 4

bring victory 1. ישׁע
Isa 59:16 then his own arm brought him victory 1
63: 5 no one to uphold; so my own arm brought me victory 1

bring word 1. *ἀπαγγέλλω*
Mat 2: 8 and when you have found him bring me word 1

come bringing 1. בוא
1Ch 12:40 came bringing food on asses and on camels 1

brink 1. פֶּה 2. קָצָה 3. שָׂפָה
Exd 2: 3 placed it among the reeds at the river's brink. 3
7:15 Go to Pharaoh . . wait for him by the river's brink 3
Jos 3: 8 you come to the brink of the waters of the Jordan 2
15 the feet . . were dipped in the brink of the water 2
Isa 19: 7 bare places by the Nile, on the brink of the Nile 1

bristle 1. סָמַר
Jer 51:27 bring up horses like bristling locusts. 1

brittle 1. תבר (A)
Dan 2:42 kingdom shall be partly strong and partly brittle. 1

thing brought 1. *ἀκολουθέω*
Jdt 12: 2 provided from the things I have brought with me. 1

broad 1. רחב 2. רֹחַב 3. רָחָב 4. רְחַב יָדַיִם 5. *εὖρος* 6. *πλάτος* 7. spatiosus
Exd 3: 8 bring them up . . to a good and broad land 3
27: 1 altar . . five cubits long and five cubits broad; 2
Jdg 18:10 The land is broad; yea, God has given it 4
1Kg 6: 6 The lowest story was five cubits broad 2
6 the middle one was six cubits broad 2
6 and the third was seven cubits broad; 2
1Ch 4:40 the land was very broad, quiet, and peaceful; 1
Neh 3: 8 restored Jerusalem as far as the Broad Wall. 3
12:38 I followed them . . to the Broad Wall 3
Job 11: 9 longer than the earth, and broader than the sea. 3
37:10 the broad waters are frozen fast. 2
Ps 119:96 thy commandment is exceedingly broad. 3
Isa 33:21 a place of broad rivers and streams 4
Jer 51:58 The broad wall of Babylon shall be leveled 3
Ezk 40: 7 the side rooms, one reed long, and one reed broad; 2
30 25 cubits long and five cubits broad. 2
42 a cubit and a half long, and a cubit and a half broad 2
47 and 100cubits broad, foursquare; 2
41:12 yard on the west side was 70 cubits broad; 2
22 cubits high, two cubits long, and two cubits broad; 5
42:20 cubits long and 500 cubits broad 2
43:13 base shall be one cubit high, and one cubit broad 2
16 be square, twelve cubits long by twelve broad. 2
17 square, fourteen cubits long by fourteen broad 2
17 with a rim around it half a cubit broad *
45: 1 cubits long and 20,000 cubits broad; 2
3 cubits long and 10,000 broad 2
5 cubits long and 10,000 cubits broad 2
6 of the city an area 5,000 cubits broad 2
46:22 small courts, 40 cubits long and 30 broad; 2
Rev 20: 9 And they marched up over the broad earth 6
2Es 7: 3 so that it is broad and vast ‡
13 the entrances . . are broad and safe 7

broad *See also* make, pasture.

become broad 1. רחב
Ezk 41: 7 the side chambers became broader as they rose 1

broad part 1. latitudo
2Es 7: 5 how can he come to the broad part 1

broad place 1. מֶרְחָב 2. רַחַב
2Sm 22:20 He brought me forth into a broad place; 1
Job 36:16 into a broad place where there was no cramping 2
Ps 18:19 He brought me forth into a broad place; 1
31: 8 thou hast set my feet in a broad place. 1

broil 1. *ὀπτός*
Lke 24:42 They gave him a piece of broiled fish 1

broken *See* lie, piece.

brokenhearted 1. כאה לֵב 2. שבר לֵב
Ps 34:18 The LORD is near to the brokenhearted, and saves 2
109:16 pursued the poor . . and the brokenhearted 1
147: 3 heals the brokenhearted, and binds up 2
Isa 61: 1 he has sent me to bind up the brokenhearted 2

bronze 1. חַשְׁמַל 2. חַשְׁמַן 3. חשת 4. נָחוּשׁ 5. נְחוּשָׁה 6. נְחֹשֶׁת 7. נְחָשׁ (A) 8. *χάλκειος* 9. *χαλκοῦς*
Gen 4:22 the forger of all instruments of bronze 6
Exd 25: 3 this is the offering . . gold, silver, and bronze 6
26:11 you shall make 50 clasps of bronze 6
37 you shall cast five bases of bronze for them. 6
27: 2 and you shall overlay it with bronze. 6
3 all its utensils you shall make of bronze. 6
4 also make for it a grating, a network of bronze; 6
4 make four bronze rings at its four corners. 6
6 make poles . . and overlay them with bronze; 6
10 pillars . . bases . . of bronze 6
11 pillars twenty and their bases twenty, of bronze 6
17 be of silver, and their bases of bronze. 6
18 of fine twined linen and bases of bronze. 6
19 the pegs of the court, shall be of bronze. 6
30:18 You shall also make a laver of bronze 6
18 a laver of bronze, with its base of bronze 6
31: 4 to work in gold, silver, and bronze 6
35: 5 bring the LORD'S offering: gold, silver, and bronze 6
16 with its grating of bronze, its poles, and all its 6
24 who could make an offering of silver or bronze 6
32 to work in gold and silver and bronze 6
36:18 he made 50 clasps of bronze to couple the tent 6
38 of gold, but their five bases were of bronze. 6
38: 2 and he overlaid it with bronze. 6
3 all its utensils he made of bronze. 6
4 made . . a network of bronze, under its ledge 6
5 four corners of the bronze grating as holders 6
6 the poles . . and overlaid them with bronze. 6
8 he made the laver of bronze and its base of bronze 6
8 he made the laver of bronze and its base of bronze 6
10 were twenty and their bases twenty, of bronze 6
11 pillars twenty, their bases twenty, of bronze 6
17 the bases for the pillars were of bronze 6
19 four bases were of bronze, their hooks of silver 6
20 pegs . . for the court round about were of bronze. 6
29 the bronze that was contributed was 70 talents 6
30 the bronze altar and the bronze grating for it 6
30 the bronze altar and the bronze grating for it 6
39:39 the bronze altar, and its grating of bronze 6
39 the bronze altar, and its grating of bronze 6
Lev 6:28 if it is boiled in a bronze vessel 6
Num 16:39 Elea'zar the priest took the bronze censers 6
21: 9 Moses made a bronze serpent, and set it on a pole; 7
9 man, he would look at the bronze serpent and live. 6
31:22 only the gold, the silver, the bronze, the iron 6
Deu 33:25 Your bars shall be iron and bronze; 6
Jos 6:19 silver and gold, and vessels of bronze and iron 6
24 and gold, and the vessels of bronze and of iron 6
22: 8 many cattle, with silver, gold, bronze, and iron 6
1Sm 17: 5 He had a helmet of bronze on his head 6
5 weight of the coat was 5,000 shekels of bronze. 6
6 And he had greaves of bronze upon his legs 6
6 a javelin of bronze . . between his shoulders. 6
38 he put a helmet of bronze on his head 6
2Sm 8: 8 And from . . King David took very much bronze. 6
10 articles of silver, of gold, and of bronze; 6
21:16 whose spear weighed 300 shekels of bronze 6
22:35 so that my arms can bend a bow of bronze. 5
1Kg 4:13 60 great cities with walls and bronze bars); 6
7:14 his father was a man of Tyre, a worker in bronze; 6
14 full of wisdom . . for making any work in bronze. 6
15 He cast two pillars of bronze. 6
16 made two capitals of molten bronze, to set upon 6
27 He also made the ten stands of bronze; 6
30 stand had four bronze wheels and axles of bronze; 6
30 stand had four bronze wheels and axles of bronze; 6
38 he made ten lavers of bronze; each laver held 6
45 all these vessels . . were of burnished bronze. 6
47 the weight of the bronze was not found out. 6
8:64 the bronze altar . . was too small to receive 6
14:27 Rehobo'am made in their stead shields of bronze 6
2Kg 16:14 the bronze altar . . before the LORD he removed 6
15 the bronze altar shall be for me to inquire by. 6
17 and he took down the sea from off the bronze oxen 6
18: 4 broke . . the bronze serpent that Moses had made 6
25:13 the pillars of bronze . . the Chalde'ans broke 3
13 the pillars . . and the stands and the bronze sea 3
13 and carried the bronze to Babylon. 3
14 and all the vessels of bronze used in the temple 3
16 the bronze of all these vessels was beyond 3
17 one pillar . . and upon it was a capital of bronze; 3
17 a network and pomegranates, all of bronze 3
1Ch 15:19 The singers . . were to sound bronze cymbals; 6
18: 8 and from Cun . . David took very much bronze; 6
8 with it Solomon made the bronze sea 6
8 the pillars and the vessels of bronze. 6
10 articles of gold, of silver, and of bronze; 6
22: 3 as well as bronze in quantities beyond weighing 6
14 silver, and bronze and iron beyond weighing 6
16 gold, silver, bronze, and iron. Arise and be doing! 6
29: 2 and the bronze for the things of bronze 6
7 10,000 talents of silver, 18,000 talents of bronze 6
2Ch 1: 5 bronze altar that Bez'alel . . had made 6
6 Solomon went up there to the bronze altar 6
2: 7 a man skilled to work in gold, silver, bronze 6
14 He is trained to work in gold, silver, bronze, iron 6
4: 1 He made an altar of bronze, twenty cubits long 6
9 the court, and overlaid their doors with bronze; 6
16 for these Huram-abi made of burnished bronze 6
18 weight of the bronze was not ascertained. 6
6:13 Solomon had made a bronze platform . . and set it 6
7: 7 because the bronze altar . . could not hold 6
12:10 Rehobo'am made in their stead shields of bronze 6
24:12 workers in iron and bronze to repair 6
Ezr 8:27 two vessels of fine bright bronze as precious 6
Job 6:12 or is my flesh bronze? 4
20:24 a bronze arrow will strike him through. 5
40:18 His bones are tubes of bronze 5
41:27 counts iron as straw, and bronze as rotten wood. 5
Ps 18:34 for war, so that my arms can bend a bow of bronze. 5
68:31 Let bronze be brought from Egypt; 2
107:16 For he shatters the doors of bronze 6
Isa 45: 2 I will break in pieces the doors of bronze 5
60:17 Instead of bronze I will bring gold 6
17 instead of wood, bronze, instead of stones, iron. 6
Jer 1:18 a fortified city, an iron pillar, and bronze walls 6
6:28 they are bronze and iron 6
15:12 Can one break iron, iron from the north, and bronze? 6
20 I will make you . . a fortified wall of bronze; 6
52:17 And the pillars of bronze that were in the house 3
17 the bronze sea that were in the house of the LORD 3
17 in pieces, and carried all the bronze to Babylon. 6

18 dishes for incense, and all the vessels of bronze 3
20 the twelve bronze bulls which were under the sea 3
20 bronze of all these things was beyond weight. 3
22 Upon it was a capital of bronze; 3
22 a network and pomegranates, all of bronze 3
Ezk 1: 7 and they sparkled like burnished bronze. 6
27 I saw as it were gleaming bronze 1
8: 2 of brightness, like gleaming bronze. 1
9: 2 they went in and stood beside the bronze altar. 6
22:18 bronze and tin and iron and lead in the furnace 6
20 As men gather silver and bronze and iron and lead 6
27:13 and vessels of bronze for your merchandise. 6
40: 3 there was a man, whose appearance was like bronze 6
Dan 2:32 arms of silver, its belly and thighs of bronze 7
35 iron, the clay, the bronze, the silver, and the gold 7
39 arise . . yet a third kingdom of bronze 7
45 broke in pieces the iron, the bronze, the clay 7
4:15 bound with a band of iron and bronze 7
23 bound with a band of iron and bronze 7
5: 4 praised the gods of . . bronze, iron 7
23 gods of . . bronze, iron, wood, and stone 7
7:19 with its teeth of iron and claws of bronze; 7
10: 6 arms and legs like the gleam of burnished bronze 6
Mic 4:13 I will make your horn iron and your hoofs bronze; 5
Zec 6: 1 and the mountains were mountains of bronze. 6
Rev 9:20 demons and idols of gold and silver and bronze 9
18:12 articles of costly wood, bronze, iron and marble 9
1Es 8:57 twelve bronze vessels of fine bronze 9
57 twelve bronze vessels of fine bronze 9
Sir 28:20 its fetters are fetters of bronze; 8
1Mc 8:22 they wrote in reply, on bronze tablets 9
14:18 they wrote to him on bronze tablets 9
27 they made a record on bronze tablets 9
48 to inscribe this decree upon bronze tablets 9

bronze *See also* fetter, vessel.

burnished bronze 1. *χαλκολίβανον*

Rev 1:15 his feet were like burnished bronze 1
2:18 and whose feet are like burnished bronze. 1

gleaming bronze 1. חַשְׁמַל

Ezk 1: 4 the midst of the fire, as it were gleaming bronze. 1

thing of bronze 1. נְחֹשֶׁת

1Ch 29: 2 and the bronze for the things of bronze 1

brooch 1. חָח

Exd 35:22 all . . brought brooches and earrings 1

brood 1. בֵּן 2. תַּרְבּוּת 3. *γέννημα* 4. *νοσσιά* 5. *νοσσίον* 6. *πλῆθος* 7. filius

Num32:14 risen in your fathers' stead, a brood of sinful men 2
Job 30: 8 A senseless, a disreputable brood, 1
Jer 17:11 Like the partridge that gathers a brood *
Mat 3: 7 he said . . "You brood of vipers! Who warned you 3
12:34 You brood of vipers! how can you speak good 3
23:33 You serpents, you brood of vipers 3
37 as a hen gathers her brood under her wings 5
Lke 3: 7 You brood of vipers! 3
13:34 as a hen gathers her brood under her wings 4
2Es 1:30 as a hen gathers her brood under her wings 7
Wis 4: 3 the prolific brood of the ungodly 6

brook 1. אָפִיק 2. מַיִם 3. נַחַל 4. פֶּלֶג 5. *χειμάρρους*

Lev 23:40 take . . trees, and willows of the brook 3
Num34: 5 boundary . . turn from Azmon to the Brook of Egypt 3
Deu 2:13 'Now rise up, and go over the brook Zered.' 3
13 So we went over the brook Zered. 3
14 Ka'desh-bar'nea until we crossed the brook Zered 3
8: 7 good land, a land of brooks of water 3
9:21 threw the dust . . into the brook that descended 3
10: 7 Jot'bathah, a land with brooks of water. 3
Jos 15: 4 passes . . to Azmon, goes out by the Brook of Egypt 3
47 to the Brook of Egypt, and the Great Sea 3
16: 8 the boundary goes westward to the brook Kanah 3
17: 9 Then the boundary went down to the brook Kanah. 3
9 The cities here, to the south of the brook 3
9 boundary . . goes on the north side of the brook 3
19:11 then the brook which is east of Jok'ne-am; 3
1Sm 17:40 and chose five smooth stones from the brook 3
30: 9 and they came to the brook Besor 3
10 who were too exhausted to cross the brook Besor. 3
21 men . . who had been left at the brook Besor; 3
2Sm 15:23 and the king crossed the brook Kidron 3
17:20 They have gone over the brook of water. *
23:30 Benai'ah of . . Hid'dai of the brooks of Ga'ash 3
1Kg 2:37 on the day you go forth, and cross the brook Kidron 3
8:65 from the entrance of Hamath to the Brook of Egypt 3
15:13 down her image and burned it at the brook Kidron. 3
17: 3 Depart . . and hide yourself by the brook Cherith 3
4 You shall drink from the brook 3
5 he went and dwelt by the brook Cherith 3
6 and he drank from the brook. 3
7 the brook dried up, because there was no rain 3
18:40 Eli'jah brought them down to the brook Kishon 3
2Kg 23: 6 outside Jerusalem to the brook Kidron 3
6 he brought . . and burned it at the brook Kidron 3
12 and cast the dust of them into the brook Kidron. 3
24: 7 from the Brook of Egypt to the river Euphra'tes. 3
1Ch 11:32 Hurai of the brooks of Ga'ash 3
2Ch 7: 8 the entrance of Hamath to the Brook of Egypt. 3
15:16 crushed it, and burned it at the brook Kidron. 3
29:16 Levites . . carried it out to the brook Kidron. 3
32: 4 they stopped all the springs and the brook 3
Job 40:22 the willows of the brook surround him. 3
Ps 74:15 Thou didst cleave open springs and brooks; 3
110: 7 He will drink from the brook by the way; 3
Isa 15: 7 they carry away over the Brook of the Willows. 3
27:12 from the river Euphra'tes to the Brook of Egypt 3
30:25 there will be brooks running with water 4
Jer 15:18 Wilt thou be to me like a deceitful brook 2
31: 9 I will make them walk by brooks of water 3
40 and all the fields as far as the brook Kidron 3
Ezk 47:19 thence along the Brook of Egypt to the Great Sea. 3
48:28 thence along the Brook of Egypt to the Great Sea. 3
Jol 1:20 cry to thee because the water brooks are dried up 1
Ams 6:14 entrance of Hamath to the Brook of the Arabah. 3
Jdt 2: 8 every brook and river 5
24 all the hilltop cities along the brook Abron 5
7:18 which is near Chusi beside the brook Mochmur. 5

broom 1. מַטְאֲטֵא 2. רֹתֶם

Job 30: 4 to warm themselves the roots of the broom. 2
Isa 14:23 I will sweep it with the broom of destruction 1

broom tree 1. רֹתֶם

1Kg 19: 4 and came and sat down under a broom tree; 1
5 he lay down and slept under a broom tree; 1
Ps 120: 4 arrows, with glowing coals of the broom tree! 1

broth 1. מָרָק

Jdg 6:19 meat he put in a basket, and the broth he put in a pot 1
20 put them on this rock, and pour the broth over them. 1
Isa 65: 4 broth of abominable things is in their vessels; 1
Ezk 24:10 boil well the flesh, and empty out the broth *

brothel 1. *τέγος*

LJr 1:11 give some of it to the harlots in the brothel. 1

brother 1. אָח 2. אָח (A) 3. *ἀδελφή* 4. *ἀδελφός* 5. *ἀδελφότης* 6. *ἕτερος* 7. *ὁ* 8. frater

Gen 4: 2 again, she bore his brother Abel. 1
8 Cain said to Abel his brother, "Let us go out 1
8 Cain rose up against his brother Abel 1
9 the LORD said to Cain, "Where is Abel your brother? 1
9 I do not know; am I my brother's keeper? 1
10 The voice of your brother's blood is crying to me 1
11 opened its mouth to receive your brother's blood 1
21 His brother's name was Jubal; 1
9: 5 of man; of every man's brother I will require 1
22 of his father, and told his two brothers outside. 1
25 a slave of slaves shall he be to his brothers 1
10:21 the elder brother of Japheth, children were born 1
25 was divided, and his brother's name was Joktan. 1
12: 5 Sar'ai his wife, and Lot his brother's son 1
14:12 they also took Lot, the son of Abram's brother 1
13 the oaks of Mamre the Amorite, brother of Eshcol 1
19: 7 said, "I beg you, my brothers 1
20: 5 And she herself said, 'He is my brother.' 1
13 say of me, He is my brother.' 1
16 Sarah he said, "Behold, I have given your brother 1
22:20 has borne children to your brother Nahor 1
21 Uz the first-born, Buz his brother 1
23 Milcah bore to Nahor, Abraham's brother. 1
24:15 the wife of Nahor, Abraham's brother, came out 1
29 Rebekah had a brother whose name was Laban; 1
53 he also gave to her brother and to her mother 1
55 Her brother and her mother said, "Let the maiden 1
25:26 Afterward his brother came forth 1
27: 6 I heard your father speak to your brother Esau 1
11 Behold, my brother Esau is a hairy man 1
23 his hands were hairy like his brother Esau's 1
29 Be lord over your brothers 1
30 Esau his brother came in from his hunting. 1
35 he said, "Your brother came with guile 1
37 all his brothers I have given to him for servants 1
40 and you shall serve your brother; 1
41 then I will kill my brother Jacob. 1
42 Behold, your brother Esau comforts himself 1
43 arise, flee to Laban my brother in Haran 1
44 with him . . until your brother's fury turns away 1
45 until your brother's anger turns away 1
28: 2 daughters of Laban your mother's brother. 1
5 Bethu'el the Aramean, the brother of Rebekah 1
29: 4 Jacob said to them, "My brothers 1
10 the daughter of Laban his mother's brother 1
10 saw . . the sheep of Laban his mother's brother 1
10 watered the flock of Laban his mother's brother. 1
32: 3 before him to Esau his brother in the land of Se'ir 1
6 We came to your brother Esau 1
11 Deliver me . . from the hand of my brother 1
13 had with him a present for his brother Esau 1
17 When Esau my brother meets you, and asks you 1
33: 3 seven times, until he came near to his brother. 1
9 Esau said, "I have enough, my brother; 1
34:11 father and to her brothers, "Let me find favor 1
25 sons of Jacob, Simeon and Levi, Dinah's brothers 1
35: 1 to you when you fled from your brother Esau. 1
7 to him when he fled from his brother. 1
36: 6 he went into a land away from his brother Jacob. 1
37: 2 was shepherding the flock with his brothers; 1
4 when his brothers saw that their father loved 1
4 father loved him more than all his brothers 1
5 had a dream, and when he told it to his brothers 1
8 His brothers said to him, "Are you indeed to reign 1
9 another dream, and told it to his brothers 1
10 when he told it to his father and to his brothers 1
10 Shall I and your mother and your brothers indeed 1
11 his brothers were jealous of him 1
12 Now his brothers went to pasture their father's 1
13 Are not your brothers pasturing the flock 1
14 it is well with your brothers, and with the flock; 1
16 I am seeking my brothers," he said, "tell me 1
17 Joseph went after his brothers, and found them 1
23 Joseph came to his brothers, they stripped him 1
26 Then Judah said to his brothers, "What profit is it 1
26 if we slay our brother and conceal his blood? 1
27 not our hand be upon him, for he is our brother 1
27 our own flesh." And his brothers heeded him. 1
30 returned to his brothers, and said 1
38: 1 Judah went down from his brothers 1
8 Judah said to Onan, "Go in to your brother's wife 1
8 to her, and raise up offspring for your brother. 1
9 when he went in to his brother's wife he spilled 1
9 lest he should give offspring to his brother. 1
11 feared that he would die, like his brothers. 1
29 drew back his hand, behold, his brother came out 1
30 Afterward his brother came out with the scarlet 1
42: 3 ten of Joseph's brothers went down to buy grain 1
4 Jacob did not send Benjamin, Joseph's brother 1
4 Benjamin, Joseph's brother, with his brothers 1
6 Joseph's brothers came, and bowed themselves 1
7 Joseph saw his brothers, and knew them 1
8 Thus Joseph knew his brothers 1
13 said, "We, your servants, are twelve brothers 1
15 place unless your youngest brother comes here. 1
16 Send one of you, and let him bring your brother 1
19 let one of your brothers remain confined 1
20 bring your youngest brother to me; 1
21 In truth we are guilty concerning our brother 1
28 said to his brothers, "My money has been put back; 1
32 we are twelve brothers, sons of our father; 1
33 leave one of your brothers with me 1
34 Bring your youngest brother to me; 1
34 honest men, and I will deliver to you your brother 1
38 for his brother is dead, and he only is left. 1
43: 3 see my face, unless your brother is with you.' 1
4 If you will send our brother with us, we will go 1
5 see my face, unless your brother is with you.' 1
6 to tell the man that you had another brother? 1
7 father still alive? Have you another brother?' 1
7 that he would say, 'Bring your brother down'? 1
13 Take also your brother, and arise, go again 1
14 may send back your other brother and Benjamin. 1
29 and saw his brother Benjamin, his mother's son 1
29 Is this your youngest brother, of whom you spoke 1
30 made haste, for his heart yearned for his brother 1
44:14 When Judah and his brothers came to Joseph's 1
19 'Have you a father, or a brother?' 1
20 We have a father, an old man, and a young brother 1
20 the child of his old age; and his brother is dead 1
23 Unless your youngest brother comes down 1
26 If our youngest brother goes with us, then we will 1
26 unless our youngest brother is with us.' 1
33 let the lad go back with his brothers. 1
45: 1 when Joseph made himself known to his brothers. 1
3 Joseph said to his brothers, "I am Joseph; 1
3 But his brothers could not answer him 1
4 Joseph said to his brothers, "Come near to me 1
4 And he said, "I am your brother, Joseph 1
12 and the eyes of my brother Benjamin see 1
14 he fell upon his brother Benjamin's neck and wept 1
15 he kissed all his brothers and wept upon them; 1
15 and after that his brothers talked with him. 1
16 report was heard . . "Joseph's brothers have come 1
17 Say to your brothers, 'Do this: load your beasts 1
24 Then he sent his brothers away 1
46:31 Joseph said to his brothers and to his father's 1
31 say . . 'My brothers and my father's household 1
47: 1 My father and my brothers, with their flocks 1
2 from among his brothers he took five men 1
3 Pharaoh said to his brothers, "What is 1
5 Your father and your brothers have come to you. 1
6 settle your father and your brothers in the best 1
11 Then Joseph settled his father and his brothers 1
12 Joseph provided his father, his brothers, 1
48: 6 shall be called by the name of their brothers 1
19 nevertheless his younger brother shall be 1
22 I have given to you rather than to your brothers 1
49: 5 Simeon and Levi are brothers; 1
8 Judah, your brothers shall praise you; 1
26 brow of him who was separate from his brothers. 1
50: 8 as well as . . his brothers, and his father's 1
14 Joseph returned to Egypt with his brothers 1
15 Joseph's brothers saw that their father was dead 1

17 the transgression of your brothers and their sin 1
18 His brothers also came and fell down before him 1
24 Joseph said to his brothers, "I am about to die; 1
Exd 1: 6 Then Joseph died, and all his brothers 1
4:14 Is there not Aaron, your brother, the Levite? 1
7: 1 and Aaron your brother shall be your prophet. 1
2 and Aaron your brother shall tell Pharaoh to let 1
28: 1 Aaron your brother, and his sons with him 1
2 make holy garments for Aaron your brother 1
4 make holy garments for Aaron your brother 1
41 you shall put them upon Aaron your brother 1
32:27 go . . and slay every man his brother 1
29 each one at the cost of his son and of his brother 1
Lev 10: 4 carry your brethren from before the sanctuary 1
6 but your brethren, the whole house of Israel 1
16: 2 Tell Aaron your brother not to come at all times 1
18:14 uncover the nakedness of your father's brother 1
16 not uncover the nakedness of your brother's wife 1
16 brother's wife; she is your brother's nakedness 1
19:17 You shall not hate your brother in your heart 1
20:21 If a man takes his brother's wife, it is impurity 1
21 he has uncovered his brother's nakedness 1
21: 2 his father, his son, his daughter, his brother 1
10 The priest who is chief among his brethren 1
25:25 If your brother becomes poor, and sells part 1
25 come and redeem what his brother has sold 1
35 if your brother becomes poor 1
36 that your brother may live beside you 1
39 if your brother becomes poor beside you 1
46 over your brethren the people of Israel 1
47 If . . your brother beside him becomes poor 1
48 one of his brothers may redeem him 1
Num 6: 7 Neither for . . nor for brother or sister 1
8:26 minister to their brethren in the tent 1
16:10 all your brethren the sons of Levi with you? 1
18: 2 with you bring your brethren also 1
6 behold, I have taken your brethren the Levites 1
20: 3 died when our brethren died before the LORD! 1
8 you and Aaron your brother, and tell the rock 1
14 Thus says your brother Israel: You know 1
27: 4 possession among our father's brethren. 1
7 an inheritance among their father's brethren 1
9 then . . give his inheritance to his brothers. 1
10 if he has no brothers, then you shall give 1
10 give his inheritance to his father's brothers. 1
11 if his father has no brothers, then you shall give 1
13 as your brother Aaron was gathered 1
32: 6 your brethren go to the war while you sit here? 1
36: 2 give the inheritance of Zeloph'ehad our brother 1
Deu 1:16 'Hear the cases between your brethren, and judge 1
16 judge righteously between a man and his brother 1
28 Our brethren have made our hearts melt, saying 1
2: 4 territory of your brethren the sons of Esau 1
8 we went on, away from our brethren the sons of Esau 1
3:18 before your brethren the people of Israel. 1
20 until the LORD gives rest to your brethren 1
10: 9 no portion or inheritance with his brothers; 1
13: 6 If your brother . . entices you secretly, saying 1
15: 2 he shall not exact it of his neighbor, his brother 1
3 but whatever of yours is with your brother 1
7 there is among you a poor man, one of your brethren 1
7 not . . shut your hand against your poor brother 1
9 your eye be hostile to your poor brother 1
11 You shall open wide your hand to your brother 1
12 If your brother . . is sold to you, he shall serve 1
17:15 One from among your brethren you shall set 1
15 not put a foreigner . . who is not your brother. 1
20 his heart may not be lifted up above his brethren 1
18: 2 no inheritance among their brethren; the LORD 1
15 prophet . . from among you, from your brethren– 1
18 prophet like you from among their brethren; 1
19:18 if the witness . . accused his brother falsely 1
19 do to him as he had meant to do to his brother; 1
22: 1 not see your brother's ox or his sheep go astray 1
1 you shall take them back to your brother. 1
2 shall be with you until your brother seeks it; 1
3 so . . do with any lost thing of your brother's 1
4 You shall not see your brother's ass or his ox 1
23: 7 shall not abhor an E'domite, for he is your brother 1
19 not lend upon interest to your brother 1
20 to your brother you shall not lend upon interest; 1
24: 7 If a man is found stealing one of his brethren 1
14 not oppress . . whether he is one of your brethren 1
25: 3 lest . . your brother be degraded in your sight. 1
5 If brothers dwell together, and one of them dies 1
6 first son . . succeed to the name of his brother 1
7 refuses to perpetuate his brother's name 1
9 man who does not build up his brother's house.' 1
28:54 man . . grudge food to his brother, to the wife 1
32:50 as Aaron your brother died in Mount Hor 1
33: 9 he disowned his brothers, and ignored his children. 1
16 head of him that is prince among his brothers 1
24 be Asher; let him be the favorite of his brothers 1
Jos 1:14 pass over armed before your brethren and . . help 1
15 LORD gives rest to your brethren as well as to you 1
2:13 my father and mother, my brothers and sisters 1
18 gather . . your father and mother, your brothers 1
6:23 Rahab, and her father and mother and brothers 1
14: 8 my brethren . . made the heart of the people melt; 1
15:17 Oth'ni-el the son of Kenaz, the brother of Caleb 1
17: 4 give us an inheritance along with our brethren. 1
4 among the brethren of their father. 1
22: 3 you have not forsaken your brethren these many 1
4 the LORD your God has given rest to your brethren 1
7 a possession beside their brethren in the land 1
8 divide the spoil . . with your brethren. 1
Jdg 1: 3 Judah said to Simeon his brother, "Come up with me 1
13 Oth'ni-el the son of Kenaz, Caleb's younger brother 1
17 Judah went with Simeon his brother 1
3: 9 the son of Kenaz, Caleb's younger brother. 1
8:19 said, "They were my brothers, the sons of my mother; 1
9: 3 Abim'elech, for they said, "He is our brother. 1
5 and slew his brothers the sons of Jerubba'al 1
21 fled . . for fear of Abim'elech his brother. 1
24 blood be laid upon Abim'elech their brother 1
24 who strengthened his hands to slay his brothers. 1
56 against his father in killing his 70 brothers; 1
11: 3 Jephthah fled from his brothers, and dwelt 1
16:31 his brothers and all his family came down 1
18: 8 they came to their brethren at Zorah and Esh'ta-ol 1
8 their brethren said to them, "What do you report? 1
14 the five men . . said to their brethren, "Do you 1
19:23 No, my brethren, do not act so wickedly; 1
20:13 the voice of their brethren, the people of Israel 1
23 battle against our brethren the Benjaminites? 1
28 yet again go out to battle against our brethren 1
21: 6 had compassion for Benjamin their brother 1
22 when their fathers or their brothers come 1
Rut 4:10 dead may not be cut off from among his brethren 1
1Sm 14: 3 Ahi'jah the son of Ahi'tub, Ich'abod's brother 1
16:13 and anointed him in the midst of his brothers; 1
17:17 Take for your brothers an ephah of this . . grain 1
17 carry them quickly to the camp to your brothers; 1
18 See how your brothers fare, and bring some token 1
22 David left . . and went and greeted his brothers. 1
28 Now Eli'ab his eldest brother heard when he spoke 1
20:29 and my brother has commanded me to be there. 1
29 let me get away, and see my brothers. 1
22: 1 his brothers and all his father's house heard it 1
26: 6 David said . . to Jo'ab's brother Abi'shai 1
30:23 But David said, "You shall not do so, my brothers 1
2Sm 1:26 I am distressed for you, my brother Jonathan; 1
2:22 How . . could I lift up my face to your brother Jo'ab? 1
26 people turn from the pursuit of their brethren? 1
27 have given up the pursuit of their brethren 1
3: 8 of Saul . . to his brothers, and to his friends 1
27 he died, for the blood of As'ahel his brother. 1
30 Jo'ab and Abi'shai his brother slew Abner 1
30 he had killed their brother As'ahel in the battle 1
4: 6 so Rechab and Ba'anah his brother slipped in. 1
9 David answered Rechab and Ba'anah his brother 1
10:10 he put in the charge of Abi'shai his brother 1
13: 3 the son of Shim'e-ah, David's brother 1
4 I love Tamar, my brother Ab'salom's sister. 1
7 Go to your brother Amnon's house, and prepare food 1
8 Tamar went to her brother Amnon's house 1
10 and brought them . . to Amnon her brother. 1
12 She answered him, "No, my brother, do not force me; 1
16 But she said to him, "No, my brother; 4
20 And her brother Ab'salom said to her 1
20 Has Amnon your brother been with you? 1
20 Now hold your peace, my sister; he is your brother; 1
20 Tamar dwelt . . in her brother Ab'salom's house. 1
26 If not, pray let my brother Amnon go with us. 1
32 Jon'adab the son of Shim'e-ah, David's brother, said 1
14: 7 Give up the man who struck his brother 1
7 kill him for the life of his brother whom he slew'; 1
15:20 Go back, and take your brethren with you; 1
18: 2 of Abi'shai the son of Zeru'iah, Jo'ab's brother 1
19:41 Why have our brethren the men of Judah stolen you 1
20: 9 Jo'ab said to Ama'sa, "Is it well with you, my brother? 1
10 Then Jo'ab and Abi'shai his brother pursued Sheba 1
21:21 Jonathan, the son of Shim'e-i, David's brother 1
23:18 Abi'shai, the brother of Jo'ab, the son of Zeru'iah 1
24 As'ahel the brother of Jo'ab was one of the 30; 1
1Kg 1: 9 and he invited all his brothers, the king's sons 1
10 did not invite . . or Solomon his brother. 1
2: 7 met me when I fled from Ab'salom your brother. 1
15 kingdom has turned about and become my brother's 1
21 Let Ab'ishag . . be given to Adoni'jah your brother 1
22 he is my elder brother, and on his side are 1
9:13 What kind of cities are these . . my brother? 1
13:30 they mourned over him, saying, "Alas, my brother! 1
20:32 And he said, "Does he still live? He is my brother. 1
33 took it up . . and said, "Yes, your brother Ben-ha'dad. 1
2Kg 1:17 Jeho'ram, his brother, became king in his stead 4
23: 9 they ate unleavened bread among their brethren. 1
1Ch 1:19 two sons . . the name of his brother Joktan. 1
2:32 sons of Jada, Sham'mai's brother: Jether 1
42 The sons of Caleb the brother of Jerah'meel 1
4: 9 Jabez was more honorable than his brothers; 1
11 Chelub . . brother of Shuhah, . . father of Mehir 1
27 but his brothers had not many children 1
5: 2 though Judah became strong among his brothers 1
6:39 his brother Asaph, who stood on his right hand 1
44 On the left hand were their brethren the sons 1
48 their brethren the Levites were appointed 1
7:16 Peresh; and the name of his brother was Sheresh; 1
22 and his brothers came to comfort him. 1
34 The sons of Shemer his brother 1
35 The sons of Helem his brother 1
8:39 The sons of Eshek his brother: Ulam his first-born 1
11:20 Abi'shai, the brother of Jo'ab, was chief of the 30 1
26 mighty men . . were As'ahel the brother of Jo'ab 1
38 Jo'el the brother of Nathan 1
45 Jedi'a-el . . and Joha his brother, the Tizite 1
12:39 their brethren had made preparation for them. 1
13: 2 let us send abroad to our brethren 1
15: 5 Uri'el the chief, with 120 of his brethren; 1
6 Asai'ah the chief, with 220 of his brethren; 1
7 Jo'el the chief, with 130 of his brethren; 1
8 Shemai'ah the chief, with 200 of his brethren; 1
9 Eli'el the chief, with 80 of his brethren; 1
10 Ammin'adab the chief, with 112 of his brethren. 1
12 sanctify yourselves, you and your brethren 1
16 to appoint their brethren as the singers 1
17 of his brethren Asaph the son of Berechi'ah 1
17 of the sons of Merar'i, their brethren, Ethan 1
18 with them their brethren of the second order 1
16: 7 sung to the LORD by Asaph and his brethren. 1
37 David left Asaph and his brethren there 1
38 and also O'bed-e'dom and his 68 brethren 1
39 Zadok the priest and his brethren the priests 1
19:11 he put in the charge of Abi'shai his brother 1
15 likewise fled before Abi'shai, Jo'ab's brother 1
20: 5 Elha'nan . . slew Lahmi the brother of Goliath 1
7 Jonathan the son of Shim'e-a, David's brother 1
23:32 shall attend the sons of Aaron, their brethren 1
24:25 The brother of Micah, Isshi'ah; 1
31 head . . and his younger brother alike, cast lots 1
31 lots, just as their brethren the sons of Aaron 1
25: 7 The number of them along with their brethren 1
9 to Gedali'ah . . and his brethren and his sons 1
10 third to Zaccur, his sons and his brethren, twelve; 1
11 fourth to Izri, his sons and his brethren, twelve; 1
12 fifth to Nethani'ah, his sons and his brethren 1
13 sixth to Bukki'ah, his sons and his brethren 1
14 seventh to Jeshare'lah, his sons and his brethren 1
15 eighth to Jeshai'ah, his sons and his brethren 1
16 ninth to Mattani'ah, his sons and his brethren 1
17 tenth to Shim'e-i, his sons and his brethren, twelve; 1
18 eleventh to Az'arel, his sons and his brethren 1
19 twelfth to Hashabi'ah, his sons and his brethren 1
20 thirteenth, Shu'ba-el, his sons and his brethren 1
21 Mattithi'ah, his sons and his brethren, twelve; 1
22 fifteenth, to Jer'emoth, his sons and his brethren 1
23 sixteenth, to Hanani'ah, his sons and his brethren 1
24 to Joshbekash'ah, his sons and his brethren 1
25 eighteenth, to Hana'ni, his sons and his brethren 1
26 to Mallo'thi, his sons and his brethren, twelve; 1
27 twentieth, to Eli'athah, his sons and his brethren 1
28 to Hothir, his sons and his brethren, twelve; 1
29 to Giddal'ti, his sons and his brethren, twelve; 1
30 to Maha'zi-oth, his sons and his brethren, twelve; 1
31 Romam'ti-e'zer, his sons and his brethren, twelve. 1
26: 7 brethren were able men, Eli'hu and Semachi'ah. 1
8 sons of O'bed-e'dom with their sons and brethren 1
9 Meshelemi'ah had sons and brethren, able men 1
11 the sons and brethren of Hosah were thirteen. 1
12 had duties, just as their brethren did 1
22 sons of Jehi'eli, Zetham and Jo'el his brother 1
25 His brethren: from Elie'zer were his son Rehabi'ah 1
26 This Shelo'moth and his brethren were in charge 1
28 were in the care of Shelo'moth and his brethren. 1
30 Of the He'bronites, Hashabi'ah and his brethren 1
32 King David appointed him and his brethren 1
27: 7 As'ahel the brother of Jo'ab was fourth 1
18 for Judah, Eli'hu, one of David's brothers; 1
28: 2 and said: "Hear me, my brethren and my people. 1
2Ch 11: 4 shall not go up or fight against your brethren. 1
22 Abi'jah . . as chief prince among his brothers 1
19:10 whenever a case comes to you from your brethren 1
10 wrath may not come upon you and your brethren. 1
21: 2 He had brothers, the sons of Jehosh'aphat 1
4 slew all his brothers with the sword 1
13 killed your brothers, of your father's house 1
22: 8 Jehu . . met . . the sons of Ahazi'ah's brothers 1
29:15 They gathered their brethren 1
34 their brethren the Levites helped them 1
30: 7 Do not be like your fathers and your brethren 1
9 your brethren . . will find compassion 1
31:12 Conani'ah . . with Shim'e-i his brother as second; 1
13 assisting Conani'ah and Shim'e-i his brother 1
15 to distribute the portions to their brethren 1
35: 5 fathers' houses of your brethren the lay people 1
6 sanctify . . and prepare for your brethren 1
9 Shemai'ah and Nethan'el his brothers 1
15 their brethren the Levites prepared for them. 1
36: 4 the king of Egypt made Eli'akim his brother king 1
4 Neco took Jeho'ahaz his brother and carried him 1
10 made his brother Zedeki'ah king over Judah 1
Ezr 3: 8 together with the rest of their brethren 1
7:18 Whatever seems good to you and your brethren 2
8:17 telling them what to say to Iddo and his brethren 1
10:18 Jeshua the son of Jo'zadak and his brethren. 1
Neh 1: 2 Hana'ni, one of my brethren, came with certain men 1
3: 1 rose up with his brethren the priests 1

18 After him their brethren repaired: Bav'vai 1
4: 2 said in the presence of his brethren 1
14 fight for your brethren, your sons 1
23 neither I nor my brethren nor my servants 1
5: 1 great outcry . . against their Jewish brethren. 1
5 Now our flesh is as the flesh of our brethren 1
7 exacting interest, each from his brother. 1
8 We . . have bought back our Jewish brethren 1
8 but you even sell your brethren that they may be 1
10 Moreover I and my brethren and my servants 1
14 neither I nor my brethren ate the food allowance 1
7: 2 I gave my brother Hana'ni and Hanani'ah 1
10:10 their brethren, Shebani'ah, Hodi'ah, Keli'ta 1
29 join with their brethren, their nobles, and enter 1
11:12 their brethren who did the work of the house, 822; 1
13 his brethren, heads of fathers' houses, 245; 1
14 their brethren, mighty men of valor, 128; 1
17 Bakbuki'ah, the second among his brethren; 1
19 gatekeepers, Akkub, Talmon and their brethren 1
12: 7 chiefs of the priests and of their brethren 1
8 who with his brethren was in charge of the songs 1
9 Bakbuki'ah and Unno their brethren 1
24 Hashabi'ah . . with their brethren over against 1
13:13 their duty was to distribute to their brethren. 1
Est 10: 3 and popular with the multitude of his brethren 1
Job 1:13 drinking wine in their eldest brother's house; 1
18 drinking wine in their eldest brother's house; 1
6:15 My brethren are treacherous as a torrent-bed 1
19:13 He has put my brethren far from me 1
22: 6 For you have exacted pledges of your brothers 1
30:29 I am a brother of jackals, and a companion 1
42:11 Then came to him all his brothers and sisters 1
15 gave them inheritance among their brothers. 1
Ps 22:22 I will tell of thy name to my brethren; 1
35:14 as though I grieved for my friend or my brother; 1
50:20 You sit and speak against your brother; 1
69: 8 I have become a stranger to my brethren, an alien 1
122: 8 For my brethren and companions' sake I will say 1
133: 1 how good . . it is when brothers dwell in unity! 1
Prv 6:19 a man who sows discord among brothers. 1
17: 2 share the inheritance as one of the brothers. 1
17 brother is born for adversity. 1
18: 9 slack in his work is a brother to him who destroys. 1
19 A brother helped is like a strong city 1
24 friend who sticks closer than a brother. 1
19: 7 All a poor man's brothers hate him; 1
27:10 do not go to your brother's house in the day 1
10 neighbor . . near than a brother who is far away. 1
Ecc 4: 8 a person who has no one, either son or brother 1
Sng 8: 1 O that you were like a brother to me 1
Isa 3: 6 When a man takes hold of his brother in the house 1
9:19 like fuel for the fire; no man spares his brother. 1
19: 2 they will fight, every man against his brother 1
41: 6 and says to his brother, "Take courage! 1
66: 5 Your brethren who hate you and cast you out 1
20 bring all your brethren from all the nations 1
Jer 9: 4 and put no trust in any brother; 1
4 for every brother is a supplanter 1
12: 6 even your brothers and the house of your father 1
22:18 shall not lament for him, saying, 'Ah my brother!' 1
23:35 one to his neighbor and every one to his brother 1
31:34 each man teach his neighbor and each his brother 1
34: 9 so that no one should enslave a Jew, his brother. 1
17 by proclaiming liberty, every one to his brother 1
35: 3 Habazzini'ah, and his brothers, and all his sons 1
49:10 His children are destroyed, and his brothers 1
Ezk 11:15 Son of man, your brethren, even your brethren 1
15 even your brethren, your fellow exiles 1
18:18 he practiced extortion, robbed his brother 1
33:30 say to one another, each to his brother 1
38:21 every man's sword will be against his brother. 1
44:25 for brother or unmarried sister they may defile 1
Hos 2: 1 Say to your brother, "My people," and to your sister 1
12: 3 In the womb he took his brother by the heel 1
Ams 1:11 because he pursued his brother with the sword 1
Obd 1:10 For the violence done to your brother Jacob 1
12 not have gloated over the day of your brother 1
Mic 5: 3 his brethren shall return to the people 1
7: 2 and each hunts his brother with a net. 1
Zec 7: 9 show kindness and mercy each to his brother 1
10 none of you devise evil against his brother 1
Mal 1: 2 Is not Esau Jacob's brother?" says the LORD. 1
Mat 1: 2 Jacob the father of Judah and his brothers 4
11 Josi'ah the father of Jechoni'ah and his brothers 4
4:18 he saw two brothers, Simon who is called Peter 4
18 Simon who is called Peter and Andrew his brother 4
21 going on from there he saw two other brothers 4
21 son of Zeb'edee and John his brother, in the boat 4
5:22 one who is angry with his brother shall be liable 4
22 liable to judgment; whoever insults his brother 4
23 there remember that your brother has something 4
24 first be reconciled to your brother 4
47 And if you salute only your brethren, what more 4
7: 3 do you see the speck that is in your brother's eye 4
4 Or how can you say to your brother 4
5 to take the speck out of your brother's eye. 4
10: 2 and Andrew his brother 4
2 James the son of Zeb'edee, and John his brother; 4
21 Brother will deliver up brother to death 4
21 Brother will deliver up brother to death 4
12:46 behold, his mother and his brothers stood 4
48 Who is my mother, and who are my brothers? 4
49 he said, "Here are my mother and my brothers! 4
50 is my brother, and sister, and mother. 4
13:55 are not his brothers James and Joseph and Simon 4
14: 3 Hero'di-as, his brother Philip's wife; 4
17: 1 Peter and James and John his brother 4
18:15 If your brother sins against you, go and tell him 4
15 If he listens to you, you have gained your brother. 4
21 Lord, how often shall my brother sin against me 4
35 do not forgive your brother from your heart. 4
19:29 every one who has left houses or brothers 4
20:24 they were indignant at the two brothers. 4
22:24 his brother must marry the widow 4
24 raise up children for his brother.' 4
25 Now there were seven brothers among us 4
25 having no children left his wife to his brother. 4
23: 8 you have one teacher, and you are all brethren. 4
25:40 to one of the least of these my brethren 4
28:10 go and tell my brethren to go to Galilee 4
Mrk 1:16 he saw Simon and Andrew the brother of Simon 4
19 James the son of Zeb'edee and John his brother 4
3:17 John the brother of James 4
31 his mother and his brothers came 4
32 Your mother and your brothers are outside 4
33 he replied, "Who are my mother and my brothers? 4
34 he said, "Here are my mother and my brothers! 4
35 Whoever does the will of God is my brother 4
5:37 Peter and James and John the brother of James. 4
6: 3 brother of James and Joses and Judas and Simon 4
17 Hero'di-as, his brother Philip's wife 4
18 is not lawful for you to have your brother's wife. 4
10:29 there is no one who has left house or brothers 4
30 houses and brothers and sisters and mothers 4
12:19 if a man's brother dies and leaves a wife 4
19 and raise up children for his brother. 4
20 There were seven brothers; the first took a wife 4
13:12 brother will deliver up brother to death 4
12 brother will deliver up brother to death 4
Lke 3: 1 brother Philip tetrarch of the region 4
19 Hero'di-as, his brother's wife 4
6:14 whom he named Peter, and Andrew his brother 4
41 do you see the speck that is in your brother's eye 4
42 how can you say to your brother, 'Brother 4
42 how can you say to your brother, 'Brother 4
42 take out the speck that is in your brother's eye. 4
8:19 Then his mother and his brothers came to him 4
20 he was told, "Your mother and your brothers 4
21 My mother and my brothers are those who hear 4
12:13 bid my brother divide the inheritance with me. 4
14:12 do not invite your friends or your brothers 4
26 wife and children and brothers and sisters 4
15:27 he said to him, 'Your brother has come 4
32 your brother was dead, and is alive 4
16:28 for I have five brothers, so that he may warn them 4
17: 3 if your brother sins, rebuke him 4
18:29 house or wife or brothers or parents or children 4
20:28 Moses wrote for us that if a man's brother dies 4
28 raise up children for his brother. 4
29 Now there were seven brothers 4
21:16 even by parents and brothers and kinsmen 4
22:32 strengthen your brethren. 4
Joh 1:40 Andrew, Simon Peter's brother. 4
41 He first found his brother Simon, and said to him 4
2:12 with his mother and his brothers 4
6: 8 Andrew, Simon Peter's brother, said to him 4
7: 3 his brothers said to him, "Leave here 4
5 For even his brothers did not believe in him. 4
10 after his brothers had gone up to the feast 4
11: 2 It was Mary . . whose brother Laz'arus was ill. 4
19 to console them concerning their brother. 4
21 my brother would not have died. 4
23 Jesus said to her, "Your brother will rise again. 4
32 my brother would not have died. 4
20:17 go to my brethren and say to them 4
21:23 The saying spread abroad among the brethren 4
Act 1:14 Mary the mother of Jesus, and with his brothers. 4
15 In those days Peter stood up among the brethren 4
16 Brethren, the scripture had to be fulfilled 4
2:29 Brethren, I may say to you confidently 4
37 Brethren, what shall we do? 4
3:17 now, brethren, I know that you acted in ignorance 4
22 a prophet from your brethren as he raised me up. 4
6: 3 Therefore, brethren, pick out . . seven men 4
7: 2 Stephen said: "Brethren and fathers, hear me. 4
13 Joseph made himself known to his brothers 4
23 it came into his heart to visit his brethren 4
25 He supposed that his brethren understood 4
26 you are brethren, why do you wrong each other?' 4
37 a prophet from your brethren as he raised me up.' 4
9:17 laying his hands on him he said, "Brother Saul 4
30 when the brethren knew it 4
10:23 some of the brethren from Joppa accompanied him. 4
11: 1 the apostles and the brethren who were in Judea 7
12 These six brethren also accompanied me 4
29 send relief to the brethren who lived in Judea; 4
12: 2 killed James the brother of John with the sword; 4
17 he said, "Tell this to James and to the brethren. 4
13:15 Brethren, if you have any word of exhortation 4
26 Brethren, sons of the family of Abraham 4
38 Let it be known to you therefore, brethren 4
14: 2 poisoned their minds against the brethren. 4
15: 1 were teaching the brethren 4
3 they gave great joy to all the brethren. 4
7 Peter rose and said to them, "Brethren 4
13 Brethren, listen to me. 4
22 leading men among the brethren 4
23 The brethren, both the apostles and the elders 4
23 the brethren who are of the Gentiles in Antioch 4
32 exhorted the brethren with many words 4
33 they were sent off in peace by the brethren 4
36 let us return and visit the brethren 4
40 commended by the brethren 4
16: 2 He was well spoken of by the brethren 4
40 when they had seen the brethren 4
17: 6 they dragged Jason and some of the brethren 4
10 The brethren immediately sent Paul and Silas away 4
14 Then the brethren immediately sent Paul off 4
18:18 took leave of the brethren and sailed for Syria 4
27 the brethren encouraged him 4
21: 7 we greeted the brethren 4
17 the brethren received us gladly. 4
20 they said to him, "You see, brother 4
22: 1 Brethren and fathers, hear the defense 4
5 From them I received letters to the brethren 4
13 'Brother Saul, receive your sight.' 4
23: 1 Brethren, I have lived before God 4
5 I did not know, brethren, that he was the high priest; 4
6 Brethren, I am a Pharisee, a son of Pharisees 4
28:14 There we found brethren 4
15 the brethren there, when they heard of us, came 4
17 when they had gathered, he said to them, "Brethren 4
21 none of the brethren coming here has reported 4
Rom 1:13 I want you to know, brethren 4
7: 1 Do you not know, brethren 4
4 Likewise, my brethren, you have died to the law 4
8:12 So then, brethren, we are debtors, not to the flesh 4
29 he might be the first-born among many brethren. 4
9: 3 cut off from Christ for the sake of my brethren 4
10: 1 Brethren, my heart's desire and prayer to God 4
11:25 I want you to understand this mystery, brethren 4
12: 1 I appeal to you therefore, brethren 4
14:10 Why do you pass judgment on your brother? 4
10 Or you, why do you despise your brother? 4
13 never to put a . . hindrance in the way of a brother. 4
15 If your brother is being injured by what you eat 4
21 or do anything that makes your brother stumble. 4
15:14 I myself am satisfied about you, my brethren 4
30 I appeal to you, brethren, by our Lord Jesus Christ 4
16:14 Greet . . and the brethren who are with them. 4
17 I appeal to you, brethren, to take note 4
23 Eras'tus . . and our brother Quartus, greet you. 4
1Co 1: 1 Paul . . and our brother Sos'thenes 4
10 I appeal to you, brethren, by the name of our Lord 4
11 there is quarreling among you, my brethren. 4
26 For consider your call, brethren 4
2: 1 When I came to you, brethren 4
3: 1 I, brethren, could not address you as spiritual 4
4: 6 for your benefit, brethren 4
5:11 who bears the name of brother 4
6: 1 When one of you has a grievance against a brother 6
6 brother goes to law against brother 4
6 brother goes to law against brother 4
8 even your own brethren. 4
7:12 if any brother has a wife who is an unbeliever 4
15 in such a case the brother or sister is not bound. 3
24 So, brethren, in whatever state each was called 4
29 I mean, brethren, the appointed time has grown 4
8:11 the brother for whom Christ died. 4
12 Thus, sinning against your brethren 4
13 if food is a cause of my brother's falling 4
13 lest I cause my brother to fall. 4
9: 5 other apostles and the brothers of the Lord 4
10: 1 I want you to know, brethren 4
11:33 So then, my brethren, when you come together to eat 4
12: 1 Now concerning spiritual gifts, brethren 4
14: 6 Now, brethren, if I come to you speaking in tongues 4
20 Brethren, do not be children in your thinking 4
26 What then, brethren? 4
39 So, my brethren, earnestly desire to prophesy 4
15: 1 Now I would remind you, brethren 4
6 Then he appeared to more than 500 brethren 4
31 I protest, brethren, by my pride in you which I have 4
50 I tell you this, brethren 4
58 Therefore, my beloved brethren, be steadfast 4
16:11 I am expecting him with the brethren. 4
12 As for our brother Apol'los 4
12 to visit you with the other brethren 4
15 Now, brethren, you know that the household 4
20 All the brethren send greetings 4
2Co 1: 1 Timothy our brother 4
8 For we do not want you to be ignorant, brethren 4
2:13 because I did not find my brother Titus there 4
8: 1 We want you to know, brethren, about the grace 4
18 With him we are sending the brother who is famous 4
22 with them we are sending our brother 4
23 as for our brethren, they are messengers 4

9: 3 I am sending the brethren 4
5 necessary to urge the brethren to go on to you 4
11: 9 my needs were supplied by the brethren 4
12:18 I urged Titus to go, and sent the brother with him. 4
13:11 Finally, brethren, farewell 4
Gal 1: 2 all the brethren who are with me 4
11 I would have you know, brethren 4
19 except James the Lord's brother. 4
3:15 To give a human example, brethren 4
4:12 Brethren, I beseech you, become as I am 4
28 we, brethren, like Isaac, are children of promise. 4
31 So, brethren, we are not children of the slave 4
5:11 if I, brethren, still preach circumcision 4
13 For you were called to freedom, brethren 4
6: 1 Brethren, if a man is overtaken in any trespass 4
18 Christ be with your spirit, brethren. Amen. 4
Eph 6:21 Tych'icus the beloved brother 4
23 Peace be to the brethren, and love with faith 4
Php 1:12 I want you to know, brethren 4
14 most of the brethren have been made confident 4
2:25 to send to you Epaphrodi'tus my brother 4
3: 1 Finally, my brethren, rejoice in the Lord 4
13 Brethren, I do not consider 4
17 Brethren, join in imitating me 4
4: 1 Therefore, my brethren, whom I love and long 4
8 Finally, brethren, whatever is true 4
21 The brethren who are with me greet you. 4
Col 1: 1 Paul, an apostle . . and Timothy our brother 4
2 To the saints and faithful brethren in Christ 4
4: 7 he is a beloved brother and faithful minister 4
9 Ones'imus, the faithful and beloved brother 4
15 Give my greetings to the brethren at La-odice'a 4
1Th 1: 4 For we know, brethren beloved by God 4
2: 1 For you yourselves know, brethren 4
9 For you remember our labor and toil, brethren 4
14 you, brethren, became imitators of the churches 4
17 since we were bereft of you, brethren 4
3: 2 we sent Timothy, our brother and God's servant 4
7 for this reason, brethren, in all our distress 4
4: 1 Finally, brethren, we beseech and exhort you 4
6 wrong his brother in this matter 4
10 indeed you do love all the brethren 4
10 we exhort you, brethren, to do so more and more 4
13 we would not have you ignorant, brethren 4
5: 1 as to the times and the seasons, brethren 4
4 you are not in darkness, brethren 4
12 we beseech you, brethren 4
14 we exhort you, brethren, admonish the idlers 4
25 Brethren, pray for us. 4
26 Greet all the brethren with a holy kiss. 4
27 that this letter be read to all the brethren. 4
2Th 1: 3 to give thanks . . brethren, as is fitting 4
2: 1 we beg you, brethren 4
13 brethren beloved by the Lord 4
15 brethren, stand firm and hold to the traditions 4
3: 1 Finally, brethren, pray for us 4
6 Now we command you, brethren 4
6 any brother who is living in idleness 4
13 Brethren, do not be weary in well-doing. 4
15 warn him as a brother. 4
1Ti 4: 6 If you put these instructions before the brethren 4
5: 1 treat younger men like brothers 4
6: 2 on the ground that they are brethren 4
2Ti 4:21 Linus and Claudia and all the brethren. 4
Phm 1: 1 Paul . . and Timothy our brother 4
7 I have derived much joy . . my brother 4
16 as a beloved brother, especially to me 4
20 Yes, brother, I want some benefit from you 4
Heb 2:11 why he is not ashamed to call them brethren 4
12 saying, "I will proclaim thy name to my brethren 4
17 had to be made like his brethren in every respect 4
3: 1 Therefore, holy brethren . . consider Jesus 4
12 Take care, brethren, lest . . 4
7: 5 the people, that is, from their brethren 4
8:11 shall not teach . . every one his brother, saying 4
10:19 Therefore, brethren, since we have confidence 4
13:22 I appeal to you, brethren 4
23 our brother Timothy has been released 4
Jas 1: 2 Count it all joy, my brethren 4
9 Let the lowly brother boast in his exaltation 4
16 Do not be deceived, my beloved brethren. 4
19 Know this, my beloved brethren. 4
2: 1 My brethren, show no partiality 4
5 Listen, my beloved brethren. 4
14 What does it profit, my brethren 4
15 If a brother or sister is ill-clad 4
3: 1 Let not many of you become teachers, my brethren 4
10 My brethren, this ought not to be so. 4
12 Can a fig tree, my brethren, yield olives 4
4:11 Do not speak evil against one another, brethren. 4
11 He that speaks evil against a brother 4
11 speaks evil against . . or judges his brother 4
5: 7 Be patient, therefore, brethren 4
9 Do not grumble, brethren, against one another 4
10 As an example . . brethren, take the prophets 4
12 above all, my brethren, do not swear 4
19 My brethren, if any one among you wanders 4
1Pe 5:12 Silva'nus, a faithful brother as I regard him 4
2Pe 1:10 Therefore, brethren, be the more zealous 4

3:15 So also our beloved brother Paul wrote to you 4
1Jn 2: 9 and hates his brother is in the darkness still. 4
10 He who loves his brother abides in the light 4
11 he who hates his brother is in the darkness 4
3:10 nor he who does not love his brother. 4
12 not be like Cain who . . murdered his brother. 4
12 deeds were evil and his brother's righteous. 4
13 Do not wonder, brethren, that the world hates you. 4
14 because we love the brethren. 4
15 Any one who hates his brother is a murderer 4
16 we ought to lay down our lives for the brethren. 4
17 has the world's goods and sees his brother in need 4
4:20 If any one says, "I love God," and hates his brother 4
20 he who does not love his brother whom he has seen 4
21 he who loves God should love his brother also. 4
5:16 If any one sees his brother committing . . sin 4
3Jn 1: 3 the brethren arrived and testified to the truth 4
5 when you render any service to the brethren 4
10 he refuses himself to welcome the brethren 4
Jde 1: 1 Jude, a servant of Jesus . . and brother of James 4
Rev 1: 9 I John, your brother, who share with you in Jesus 4
6:11 their fellow servants and their brethren 4
12:10 the accuser of our brethren has been thrown down 4
19:10 I am a fellow servant with you and your brethren 4
22: 9 I am a fellow servant with you and your brethren 4
1Es 1: 5 minister before your brethren 4
6 prepare the sacrifices for your brethren 4
9 Jeconiah and Shemaiah and Nethanel his brother 4
13 their brethren the priests, the sons of Aaron 4
14 their brethren the priests, the sons of Aaron. 4
16 their brethren the Levites 4
37 made Jehoiakim his brother king of Judea 4
38 seized his brother Zarius 4
3:22 to be friendly with friends and brothers 4
4:61 told this to all his brethren. 4
5: 3 all their brethren were making merry 4
56 together with their brethren 4
58 Jeshua arose, and his sons and brethren 4
58 Kadmiel his brother 4
58 with their sons and brethren 4
7:12 for their brethren the priests 4
8:16 whatever you and your brethren are minded to do 4
46 ordered them to tell Iddo and his brethren 4
48 Hashabiah and Annunus and Jeshaiah his brother 4
77 our brethren and our kings and our priests 4
9:19 the son of Jozadak and his brethren 4
2Es 7:103 brothers for brothers 8
103 brothers for brothers 8
12:11 appeared in a vision to your brother Daniel. 8
14:33 your brethren are farther in the interior. 8
Tob 1: 3 I performed many acts of charity to my brethren 4
10 all my brethren . . ate the food of the Gentiles; 4
14 Gabael, the brother of Gabrias. 4
16 I performed many acts of charity to my brethren. 4
21 appointed Ahikar, the son of my brother Anael 4
2: 2 whatever poor man of our brethren you may find 4
4:12 all took wives from among their brethren 4
13 now, my son, love your brethren 4
13 in your heart do not disdain your brethren 4
5: 6 I have stayed with our brother Gabael. 4
10 Then Tobit said to him, "My brother 4
11 Tobit said to him, "I should like to know, my brother 4
13 Tobit said to him, "You are welcome, my brother 4
13 They did not go astray in the error of our brethren 4
13 My brother, you come of good stock. 4
6: 6 the young man said to the angel, "Brother Azarias 4
10 Brother, today we shall stay with Raguel 4
13 the young man said to the angel, "Brother Azarias 4
15 Now listen to me, brother 4
7: 3 Raguel asked them, "Where are you from, brethren? 4
4 he said to them, "Do you know our brother Tobit? 4
8 Then Tobias said to Raphael, "Brother Azarias 4
9: 2 Brother Azarias, take a servant and two camels 4
10:12 The Lord . . bring you back safely, dear brother 4
11: 2 Are you not aware, brother 4
17 rejoicing among all his brethren in Nineveh. 4
14: 4 Our brethren will be scattered over the earth 4
7 showing mercy to our brethren. 4
Jdt 7:30 Uzziah said to them, "Have courage, my brothers! 4
8:14 No, my brethren, do not provoke the Lord our God 4
22 the slaughter of our brethren 4
24 Now therefore, brethren, let us set an example 4
24 let us set an example to our brethren 4
26 the sheep of Laban, his mother's brother. 4
14: 1 Then Judith said to them, "Listen to me, my brethren 4
AEs 15: 9 What is it, Esther? I am your brother. Take courage; 4
Wis 10:10 fled from his brother's wrath 4
Sir 7:12 Do not devise a lie against your brother 4
18 a real brother for the gold of Ophir. 4
10:20 Among brothers their leader is worthy of honor 4
25: 1 agreement between brothers 4
29:10 for the sake of a brother or a friend 4
27 my brother has come to stay with me; 4
33:19 To son or wife, to brother or friend 4
31 If you have a servant, treat him as a brother 4
40:24 Brothers and help are for a time of trouble 4
45: 6 He exalted Aaron, the brother of Moses 4
50: 1 The leader of his brethren 1
12 with a garland of brethren around him 4

1Mc 2:17 supported by sons and brothers. 4
20 yet I and my sons and my brothers will live 4
40 If we all do as our brethren have done 4
41 let us not all die as our brethren died 4
65 Simeon your brother is wise in counsel 4
3: 2 All his brothers 4
25 Then Judas and his brothers began to be feared 4
42 Now Judas and his brothers saw 4
4:36 Then said Judas and his brothers, "Behold 4
59 Then Judas and his brothers and all the assembly 4
5:10 sent to Judas and his brothers a letter 4
13 all our brethren who were in the land of Tob 4
16 what they should do for their brethren 4
17 Then Judas said to Simon his brother 4
17 go and rescue your brethren in Galilee 4
17 I and Jonathan my brother will go to Gilead. 4
24 Judas Maccabeus and Jonathan his brother 4
25 happened to their brethren in Gilead 4
32 Fight today for your brethren! 4
55 Simon his brother was in Galilee 4
61 they did not listen to Judas and his brothers. 4
63 The man Judas and his brothers 4
65 Then Judas and his brothers went forth 4
6:22 to avenge our brethren? 4
7: 6 Judas and his brothers have destroyed 4
10 he sent messengers to Judas and his brothers 4
27 treacherously sent to Judas and his brothers 4
8:20 his brothers and the people of the Jews 4
9: 9 let us come back with our brethren and fight them; 4
10 let us die bravely for our brethren 4
19 Jonathan and Simon took Judas their brother 4
29 Since the death of your brother Judas 4
31 and took the place of Judas his brother. 4
33 Jonathan and Simon his brother 4
35 Jonathan sent his brother as leader 4
37 was reported to Jonathan and Simon his brother 4
38 they remembered the blood of John their brother 4
39 his friends and his brothers 4
42 they had fully avenged the blood of their brother 4
65 Jonathan left Simon his brother in the city 4
66 He struck down Odomera and his brothers 4
10: 5 to him and to his brothers and his nation. 4
15 the battles that . . his brothers had fought 4
18 King Alexander to his brother Jonathan, greeting 4
74 Simon his brother met him to help him. 4
11:30 King Demetrius to Jonathan his brother 4
59 Simon his brother he made governor 4
64 left his brother Simon in the country. 4
12: 6 to their brethren the Spartans, greeting. 4
7 stating that you are our brethren 4
11 as it is right and proper to remember brethren. 4
21 are brethren and are of the family of Abraham. 4
13: 3 what great things I and my brothers . . have done 4
4 By reason of this all my brothers have perished 4
5 for I am not better than my brothers. 4
8 in place of Judas and Jonathan your brother. 4
14 had risen up in place of Jonathan his brother 4
15 the money that Jonathan your brother owed 4
25 took the bones of Jonathan his brother 4
27 the tomb of his father and his brothers 4
28 for his father and mother and four brothers. 4
14:17 Simon his brother had become high priest 4
18 Judas and Jonathan his brothers. 4
20 rest of the Jewish people, our brethren 4
26 his brothers and the house of his father 4
29 Simon the son of Mattathias . . and his brothers 4
40 friends and allies and brethren 4
16: 2 I and my brothers and the house of my father 4
3 Take my place and my brother's 4
9 Judas the brother of John was wounded 4
21 his father and brothers had perished 4
2Mc 1: 1 The Jewish brethren in Jerusalem 4
1 To their Jewish brethren in Egypt 4
2:19 The story of Judas Maccabeus and his brothers 4
4: 7 Jason the brother of Onias 4
23 the brother of the previously mentioned Simon 4
26 after supplanting his own brother 4
29 his own brother Lysimachus 4
7: 1 seven brothers and their mother 4
4 the rest of the brothers and the mother 4
5 the brothers and their mother •
7 After the first brother had died in this way •
8 as the first brother had done. •
24 The youngest brother being still alive •
29 prove worthy of your brother 4
29 I may get you back again with your brothers. 4
36 our brothers . . have drunk of everflowing life 4
37 I, like my brothers, give up body and life 4
38 through me and my brothers 4
8:22 He appointed his brothers also 4
10:21 having sold their brethren for money 4
37 his brother Chaereas, and Apollophanes. 4
11: 7 to aid their brethren 4
22 King Antiochus to his brother Lysias, greeting. 4
12: 6 attacked the murderers of his brethren 4
24 because he held . . the brothers of some 4
25 for the sake of saving their brethren. 4
14:17 Simon, the brother of Judas 4
15:18 Their concern . . for brethren and relatives 4

3Mc 4:12 the ignoble misfortune of their brothers 4
4Mc 1: 8 Eleazar and the seven brothers and their mother. 4
4:16 and appointed Onias's brother Jason as high priest. 4
8: 3 seven brothers–handsome, modest, noble 4
5 the beauty and the number of such brothers 4
19 O men and brothers, should we not fear 4
9:23 Imitate me, brothers," he said. 4
10: 3 the noble kinship that binds me to my brothers. 5
13 give way to the same insanity as your brothers 4
15 No, by the blessed death of my brothers 4
16 a brother to those who have just been tortured. 4
11:14 I am younger in age than my brothers 4
20 so many of us brothers have been summoned 4
22 equipped with nobility, will die with my brothers 4
12: 2 had been fearfully reproached by the brothers 4
3 You see the result of your brothers' stupidity 4
16 not desert the excellent example of my brothers 4
13: 1 the seven brothers despised sufferings 4
4 the brothers mastered both emotions and pains. •
9 Brothers, let us die like brothers 4
11 While one said, "Courage, brother 4
18 each of the brothers who were being dragged away 4
18 Do not put us to shame, brother 4
18 or betray the brothers who have died before us. 4
20 There each of the brothers dwelt 4
23 the brothers were the more sympathetic 4
27 watching their brothers being maltreated 4
14: 3 harmonious concord of the seven brothers 4
7 O most holy seven, brothers in harmony! 4
17:13 the brothers contended. 4
151 1: 1 I was small among my brothers 4
5 My brothers were handsome and tall 4

brother *See also* love, manner, perform, slay, wife.

false brother 1. ψευδάδελφος

2Co 11:26 danger at sea, danger from false brethren; 1
Gal 2: 4 because of false brethren secretly brought in 1

father's brother 1. דּוֹד

Num36:11 were married to sons of their father's brothers. 1

husband's brother 1. יָבָם

Deu 25: 5 husband's brother shall go in to her, and take her 1
7 My husband's brother refuses to perpetuate 1

like a brother 1. ἀδελφικῶς

4Mc 13: 9 Brothers, let us die like brothers 1

brother-in-law *See* perform.

brotherhood 1. אָח אח 2. אַחֲוָה 3. ἀδελφός 4. ἀδελφότης

Ams 1: 9 did not remember the covenant of brotherhood. 1
Zec 11:14 the brotherhood between Judah and Israel. 2
1Co 6: 5 to decide between members of the brotherhood 3
1Pe 2:17 Honor all men. Love the brotherhood. Fear God. 4
5: 9 suffering is required of your brotherhood 4
1Mc 12:10 renew our brotherhood and friendship with you 4
17 concerning the renewal of our brotherhood. 4
4Mc 9:23 renounce our courageous brotherhood. 4
10:15 I will not renounce our noble brotherhood. 4
13:19 not ignorant of the affection of brotherhood 4
27 habits had augmented the affection of brotherhood 4

brotherly *See* affection, love.

brotherly-loving 1. φιλάδελφος

4Mc 13:21 brotherly-loving souls are nourished; 1

brow 1. מֵצַח מצח 2. קָדְקֹד קדקד 3. ὀφρῦς

Gen 49:26 may they be . . on the brow of him who was separate 2
Jer 3: 3 you have a harlot's brow, you refuse to be ashamed. 1
Lke 4:29 led him to the brow of the hill 3

bruise 1. דכא 2. מעך 3. פֶּצַע פצע 4. רצץ 5. שׁוּף 6. κατακόπτω 7. μώλωψ 8. συντρίβω

Gen 3:15 her seed; he shall bruise your head 5
15 head, and you shall bruise his heel. 5
Lev 22:24 which has its testicles bruised or crushed 2
Isa 1: 6 but bruises and sores and bleeding wounds; 3
42: 3 a bruised reed he will not break 4
53: 5 he was bruised for our iniquities; 1
10 Yet it was the will of the LORD to bruise him; 1
Mat 12:20 he will not break a bruised reed 8
Mrk 5: 5 bruising himself with stones. 6
Sir 23:10 will not lack bruises 7

brush 1. κληματίς

Aza 1:23 naphtha, pitch, tow, and brush. 1

brushwood 1. הֶמֶס 2. עֵץ

Jdg 9:48 took an axe . . and cut down a bundle of brushwood 2
Isa 64: 2 as when fire kindles brushwood 1

brutal 1. בער

Ezk 21:31 I will deliver you into the hands of brutal men 1

bucket 1. דְּלִי 2. vas

Num24: 7 Water shall flow from his buckets 1
Isa 40:15 Behold, the nations are like a drop from a bucket 1
2Es 6:56 their abundance to a drop from a bucket. 2

buckle 1. πόρπη

1Mc 10:89 he sent to him a golden buckle 1
11:58 dress in purple and wear a gold buckle. 1
14:44 to be clothed in purple or put on a gold buckle. 1

buckler 1. מָגֵן 2. סֹחֵרָה 3. צִנָּה

2Ch 14: 8 an army . . armed with bucklers and spears 3
Ps 35: 2 Take hold of shield and buckler 3
91: 4 his faithfulness is a shield and buckler. 2
Sng 4: 4 for an arsenal, whereon hang 1,000 bucklers 1
Jer 46: 3 Prepare buckler and shield, and advance 1
Ezk 23:24 on every side with buckler, shield, and helmet 3
38: 4 company, all of them with buckler and shield 3
39: 9 shields and bucklers, bows and arrows, handpikes 3

bud 1. גִּבְעֹל 2. פֶּרַח 3. פרח 4. βλαστάνω

Gen 40:10 as soon as it budded, its blossoms shot forth 3
Exd 9:31 the barley was in the ear and the flax was in bud. 1
Num17: 8 rod of Aaron . . had sprouted and put forth buds 2
Job 14: 9 yet at the scent of water it will bud 3
Sng 6:11 to . . see whether the vines had budded 3
7:12 let us go . . and see whether the vines have budded 3
Ezk 7:10 injustice has blossomed, pride has budded. 3
Heb 9: 4 Aaron's rod that budded 4
Sir 39:13 bud like a rose growing by a stream of water; 4

cause to bud 1. βλαστάνω

Sir 24:17 Like a vine I caused loveliness to bud 1

buffet 1. καταικίζω 2. κολαφίζω

1Co 4:11 we are ill-clad and buffeted and homeless 2
4Mc 7: 2 though buffeted by the stormings of the tyrant 1

bugle 1. σάλπιγξ

1Co 14: 8 if the bugle gives an indistinct sound 1

build 1. בנה 2. גדר 3. עשׂה 4. בנא (A) 5. בנה (A) 6. ἀνίστημι 7. δημιουργέω 8. ἐνδώμησις 9. ἔπαυλις 10. ἐποικοδομέω 11. ἵστημι 12. καθίστημι 13. κατασκευάζω 14. κτίζω 15. οἰκοδομέω 16. οἰκοδομή 17. οἰκοδόμος 18. ποιέω 19. συνοικοδομέω 20. aedifico

Gen 4:17 she conceived and bore Enoch; and he built a city 1
8:20 Then Noah built an altar to the LORD 1
10:11 went . . and built Nin'eveh, Reho'both-Ir 1
11: 4 Then they said, "Come, let us build ourselves a city 1
5 the tower, which the sons of men had built. 1
8 earth, and they left off building the city. 1
12: 7 he built there an altar to the LORD 1
8 and there he built an altar to the LORD 1
13:18 Hebron; and there he built an altar to the LORD. 1
22: 9 Abraham built an altar there 1
26:25 he built an altar there 1
33:17 journeyed to Succoth, and built himself a house 1
35: 7 there he built an altar, and called the place 1
Exd 1:11 and they built for Pharaoh store-cities 1
17:15 Moses built an altar and called the name of it 1
20:25 you shall not build it of hewn stones; 1
24: 4 he rose early in the morning, and built an altar 1
32: 5 When Aaron saw this, he built an altar before it; 1
Num13:22 (Hebron was built seven years before Zo'an 1
21:27 Come to Heshbon, let it be built, let the city 1
23: 1 said to Balak, "Build for me here seven altars 1
14 built seven altars, and offered a bull and a ram 1
29 Build for me here seven altars 1
32:16 We will build sheepfolds here for our flocks 1
24 Build cities for your little ones 1
34 the sons of Gad built Dibon, At'aroth, Aro'er 1
37 sons of Reuben built Heshbon, Elea'leh, Kiriatha'im 1
38 gave other names to the cities which they built. 1
Deu 6:10 great and goodly cities, which you did not build 1
8:12 when you . . have built goodly houses and live 1
13:16 heap of ruins for ever . . not be built again. 1
20: 5 What man is there that has built a new house 1
20 build siegeworks against the city that makes 1
22: 8 When you build a new house, you shall make 1
27: 5 there . . build an altar to the LORD your God 1
6 build an altar to the LORD . . of unhewn stones; 1
28:30 shall build a house, and you shall not dwell in it; 1
Jos 2:15 her house was built into the city wall •
8:30 Joshua built an altar in Mount Ebal to the LORD 1
22:10 the Gadites and . . Manas'seh built there an altar 1
11 the Gadites and . . Manas'seh have built an altar 1
16 by building yourselves an altar this day 1
19 do not rebel . . by building yourselves an altar 1
23 spare us not . . for building an altar to turn away 1
26 Let us now build an altar, not for burnt offering 1
29 turn . . by building an altar for burnt offering 1
24:13 I gave you . . and cities which you had not built 1
Jdg 1:26 went to the land of the Hittites and built a city 1
6:24 Then Gideon built an altar there to the LORD 1
26 build an altar to the LORD your God on the top 1
28 bull was offered upon the altar which had been built 1
21: 4 the people rose early, and built there an altar 1
1Sm 2:35 and I will build him a sure house, and he shall go 1
7:17 And he built there an altar to the LORD. 1
14:35 And Saul built an altar to the LORD; 1
35 it was the first altar that he built to the LORD. 1
2Sm 5: 9 David built the city round about from the Millo 1
11 carpenters and masons who built David a house. 1
7: 5 Would you build me a house to dwell in? 1
7 saying, "Why have you not built me a house of cedar? 1
13 He shall build a house for my name 1
27 made this revelation . . 'I will build you a house'; 1
24:21 To buy the . . in order to build an altar to the LORD 1
25 And David built there an altar to the LORD 1
1Kg 2:36 Build yourself a house . . and dwell there, and do 1
3: 1 until he had finished building his own house 1
2 because no house had yet been built for the name 1
5: 3 David . . could not build a house for the name 1
5 I purpose to build a house for the name of the LORD 1
5 'Your son . . shall build the house for my name.' 1
18 the timber and the stone to build the house. 1
6: 1 he began to build the house of the LORD. 1
2 The house which King Solomon built for the LORD 1
5 He also built a structure against the wall 1
7 When the house was built, it was with stone 1
7 was heard in the temple, while it was being built. 1
9 So he built the house, and finished it; 1
10 He built the structure against the whole house 1
12 Concerning this house which you are building 1
14 So Solomon built the house, and finished it. 1
16 He built twenty cubits of the rear of the house 1
16 he built this within as an inner sanctuary 1
36 He built the inner court with three courses 1
38 He was seven years in building it. 1
7: 1 Solomon was building his own house 1
2 He built the House of the Forest of Lebanon; 1
2 it was built upon three rows of cedar pillars •
8:13 I have built thee an exalted house 1
16 to build a house, that my name might be there; 1
17 to build a house for the name of the LORD 1
18 it was in your heart to build a house for my name 1
19 you shall not build the house, but your son 1
19 your son . . shall build the house for my name.' 1
20 I have built the house for the name of the LORD 1
27 how much less this house which I have built! 1
43 house which I have built is called by thy name. 1
44 and the house which I have built for thy name 1
48 and the house which I have built for thy name; 1
9: 1 finished building the house of the LORD 1
1 finished . . all that Solomon desired to build 3
3 consecrated this house which you have built 1
10 years, in which Solomon had built the two houses 1
15 forced labor . . to build the house of the LORD 1
19 whatever Solomon desired to build in Jerusalem 1
24 to her own house which Solomon had built for her; 1
24 then he built the Millo. 1
25 upon the altar which he built to the LORD 1
26 Solomon built a fleet of ships at E'zion-ge'ber 3
10: 4 the wisdom of Solomon, the house that he had built 1
11: 7 Solomon built a high place for Chemosh 1
27 Solomon built the Millo, and closed up the breach 1
38 I will be with you, and will build you a sure house 1
38 a sure house, as I built for David 1
12:25 Jerobo'am built Shechem in the hill country 1
25 and he went out from there and built Penu'el. 1
14:23 they also built for themselves high places 1
15:17 Ba'asha . . went up against Judah, and built Ramah 1
21 when Ba'asha heard . . he stopped building Ramah 1
22 its timber, with which Ba'asha had been building; 1
22 King Asa built Geba of Benjamin and Mizpah. 1
23 the acts of Asa . . and the cities which he built 1
16:24 and called . . the city which he built, Sama'ria 1
32 in the house of Ba'al, which he built in Sama'ria. 1
34 In his days Hi'el of Bethel built Jericho; 1
18:32 he built an altar in the name of the LORD. 1
22:39 acts of Ahab . . and the ivory house which he built 1
39 ivory house . . and all the cities that he built 1
2Kg 14:22 He built Elath and restored it to Judah 1
15:35 He built the upper gate of the house of the LORD. 1
16:11 And Uri'ah the priest built the altar; 1
18 covered way for the sabbath which had been built 1
17: 9 They built for themselves high places 1
21: 4 And he built altars in the house of the LORD 1
5 And he built altars for all the host of heaven 1
23:13 which Solomon . . had built for Ash'toreth 1
25: 1 they built siegeworks against it round about. 1
1Ch 6:10 in the house that Solomon built in Jerusalem 1
32 until Solomon had built the house of the LORD 1
7:24 who built both Lower and Upper Beth-hor'on 1
8:12 sons of Elpa'al . . Shemed, who built Ono and Lod 1
11: 8 he built the city round about from the Millo 1
14: 1 masons and carpenters to build a house for him. 1
15: 1 built houses for himself in the city of David; 3
17: 4 You shall not build me a house to dwell in. 1
6 saying, "Why have you not built me a house of cedar? 1
10 that the LORD will build you a house. 1
12 He shall build a house for me 1
25 revealed . . that thou wilt build a house for him; 1
21:22 that I may build on it an altar to the LORD 1

26 David built there an altar to the LORD 1
22: 2 dressed stones for building the house of God. 1
5 the house that is to be built for the LORD 1
6 charged him to build a house for the LORD 1
7 in my heart to build a house to the name of the LORD 1
8 you shall not build a house to my name 1
10 He shall build a house for my name. 1
11 may succeed in building the house of the LORD 1
19 Arise and build the sanctuary of the LORD God 1
19 into a house built for the name of the LORD. 1
28: 2 I had it in my heart to build a house of rest 1
2 and I made preparations for building. 1
3 God said . . 'You may not build a house for my name 1
6 Solomon your son who shall build my house 1
10 has chosen you to build a house for the sanctuary; 1
29:16 have provided for building thee a house 1
19 Grant to Solomon . . that he may build the palace 1
2Ch 2: 1 Solomon purposed to build a temple for . . LORD 1
3 sent him cedar to build himself a house to dwell 1
4 I am about to build a house for the name of the LORD 1
5 The house which I am to build will be great 1
6 But who is able to build him a house 1
6 Who am I to build a house for him 1
9 house I am to build will be great and wonderful. 1
12 a wise son . . who will build a temple for the LORD 1
3: 1 Then Solomon began to build the house of the LORD 1
2 He began to build in the second month 1
3 measurements for building the house of God 1
6: 2 I have built thee an exalted house 1
5 I chose no city . . in which to build a house 1
7 David . . to build a house for the name of the LORD 1
8 it was in your heart to build a house for my name 1
9 nevertheless you shall not build the house 1
9 your son . . shall build the house for my name.' 1
10 I have built the house for the name of the LORD 1
18 how much less this house which I have built! 1
33 house which I have built is called by thy name. 1
34 pray . . toward . . the house which I have built 1
38 pray toward . . and the house which I built 1
8: 1 in which Solomon had built the house of the LORD 1
4 He built Tadmor in the wilderness 1
4 all the store-cities which he built in Hamath. 1
5 He also built Upper . . and Lower Beth-hor'on 1
6 whatever Solomon desired to build in Jerusalem 1
11 from . . to the house which he had built for her 1
12 which he had built before the vestibule 1
9: 3 of Sheba had seen . . the house that he had built 1
11: 5 Rehobo'am . . built cities for defense in Judah. 1
6 He built Bethlehem, Etam, Teko'a 1
14: 6 He built fortified cities in Judah 1
7 he said to Judah, "Let us build these cities 1
7 So they built and prospered. 1
16: 1 Ba'asha . . went up against Judah, and built Ramah 1
5 when Ba'asha heard . . he stopped building Ramah 1
6 with which Ba'asha had been building 1
6 with them he built Geba and Mizpah. 1
17:12 He built in Judah fortresses and store-cities 1
20: 8 built thee in it a sanctuary for thy name, saying 1
36 He joined him in building ships to go to Tarshish 3
36 they built the ships in E'zion-ge'-ber. 3
26: 2 He built Eloth and restored it to Judah 1
6 built cities in the territory of Ashdod 1
9 Moreover Uzzi'ah built towers in Jerusalem 1
10 he built towers in the wilderness 1
27: 3 He built the upper gate of the house of the LORD 1
3 did much building on the wall of Ophel. 1
4 he built cities in the hill country of Judah 1
32: 5 outside it he built another wall; •
33: 4 he built altars in the house of the LORD 1
5 he built altars for all the host of heaven 1
14 built an outer wall for the city of David 1
15 all the altars that he had built on the mountain 1
19 sites on which he built high places and set up 1
35: 3 house which Solomon the son of David . . built; 1
36:23 charged me to build him a house at Jerusalem 1
Ezr 1: 2 LORD . . has charged me to build him a house 1
3: 2 built the altar of the God of Israel 1
4: 1 exiles were building a temple to the LORD 1
2 Let us build with you; for we worship your God 1
3 You have nothing to do with us in building a house 1
3 we alone will build to the LORD, the God of Israel 1
4 people of Judah, and made them afraid to build 1
5: 3 Who gave you a decree to build this house 4
4 names of the men who are building this building? 4
8 It is being built with huge stones 4
9 'Who gave you a decree to build this house 4
11 rebuilding the house . . built many years ago 5
11 which a great king of Israel built and finished. 5
16 from that time until now it has been in building 4
6:14 elders of the Jews built and prospered 4
14 finished their building by command of the God 4
Neh 2:17 Come, let us build the wall of Jerusalem 1
18 And they said, "Let us rise up and build. 1
20 we his servants will arise and build; 1
3: 1 rose up . . and they built the Sheep Gate. 1
2 next to him the men of Jericho built. 1
2 next to them Zaccur the son of Imri built. 1
3 sons of Hassena'ah built the Fish Gate; 1
15 built the wall of the Pool of Shelah of the king's 1
4: 1 Sanbal'lat heard that we were building the wall 1
3 Yes, what they are building–if a fox goes up on it 1
6 built the wall; and all the wall was joined 1
17 who were building on the wall. 1
18 sword girded at his side while he built. 1
6: 1 when it was reported . . that I had built the wall 1
6 that is why you are building the wall; 1
7: 1 wall had been built and I had set up the doors 1
4 people . . were few and no houses had been built. 1
12:29 singers had built for themselves villages 1
Job 20:19 he has seized a house which he did not build. 1
27:18 The house which he builds is like a spider's web 1
Ps 78:69 He built his sanctuary like the high heavens 1
89: 4 build your throne for all generations.'" Selah 1
122: 3 Jerusalem, built as a city which is bound firmly 1
127: 1 Unless the LORD builds the house, those who build 1
1 those who build it labor in vain. 1
Prv 9: 1 Wisdom has built her house 1
14: 1 Wisdom builds her house 1
24: 3 By wisdom a house is built 1
27 after that build your house. 1
Ecc 2: 4 I built houses and planted vineyards for myself; 1
9:14 and besieged it, building great siegeworks 1
Sng 4: 4 neck is like the tower . . built for an arsenal 1
8: 9 we will build upon her a battlement of silver; 1
Isa 5: 2 he built a watchtower in the midst of it 1
9:10 fallen, but we will build with dressed stones; 1
44:26 and of the cities of Judah, 'They shall be built 1
28 saying of Jerusalem, 'She shall be built,' 1
45:13 he shall build my city and set my exiles free 1
65:21 They shall build houses and inhabit them; 1
22 They shall not build and another inhabit; 1
66: 1 what is the house which you would build for me 1
Jer 1:10 and to overthrow, to build and to plant. 1
7:31 And they have built the high place of Topheth 1
18: 9 or a kingdom that I will build and plant it 1
19: 5 and have built the high places of Ba'al 1
22:13 to him who builds his house by unrighteousness 1
14 who says, 'I will build myself a great house 1
29: 5 Build houses and live in them; 1
28 exile will be long; build houses and live in them 1
31: 4 Again I will build you, and you shall be 1
4 Again I will build you, and you shall be built 1
28 so I will watch over them to build and to plant 1
32:31 from the day it was built to this day 1
35 They built the high places of Ba'al in the valley 1
35: 7 you shall not build a house; you shall not sow seed; 1
9 and not to build houses to dwell in. 1
45: 4 Behold, what I have built I am breaking down 1
52: 4 and built siegeworks against it round about. 1
Ezk 4: 2 and build a siege wall against it 1
11: 3 who say, 'The time is not near to build houses; 1
13:10 when the people build a wall, these prophets daub 1
16:24 you built yourself a vaulted chamber 1
25 you built your lofty place and prostituted 1
31 building your vaulted chamber at the head 1
17:17 cast up and siege walls built to cut off many lives 1
21:22 to cast up mounds, to build siege towers. 1
28:26 they shall build houses and plant vineyards. 1
Dan 4:30 Babylon, which I have built by my mighty power 4
9:25 forth of the word to restore and build Jerusalem 1
25 Then for 62 weeks it shall be built again 1
Hos 2: 6 and I will build a wall against her 2
8:14 has forgotten his Maker, and built palaces; 1
Ams 5:11 you have built houses of hewn stone 1
9: 6 who builds his upper chambers in the heavens 1
Mic 3:10 who build Zion with blood and Jerusalem 1
7:11 A day for the building of your walls! 1
Hab 2:12 Woe to him who builds a town with blood 1
Zep 1:13 Though they build houses, they shall not inhabit 1
Hag 1: 8 to the hills and bring wood and build the house 1
Zec 1:16 my house shall be built in it, says the LORD 1
5:11 To the land of Shinar, to build a house for it; 1
6:12 he shall build the temple of the LORD. 1
13 It is he who shall build the temple of the LORD 1
15 come and help to build the temple of the LORD; 1
8: 9 was laid, that the temple might be built. 1
9: 3 Tyre has built herself a rampart 1
Mal 1: 4 They may build, but I will tear down 1
Mat 7:24 like a wise man who built his house upon the rock; 15
26 a foolish man who built his house upon the sand; 15
16:18 on this rock I will build my church 15
21:33 dug a wine press in it, and built a tower 15
23:29 you build the tombs of the prophets 15
24: 1 point out to him the buildings of the temple. 16
26:61 to build it in three days.' 15
27:40 destroy the temple and build it in three days 15
Mrk 12: 1 built a tower, and let it out to tenants 15
13: 1 and what wonderful buildings! 16
2 Do you see these great buildings? 16
14:58 in three days I will build another 15
15:29 destroy the temple and build it in three days 15
Lke 4:29 brow of the hill on which their city was built 15
6:48 he is like a man building a house, who dug deep 15
48 because it had been well built. 15
49 like a man who built a house on the ground 15
7: 5 he loves our nation, and he built us our synagogue 15
11:47 Woe to you! for you build the tombs of the prophets 15
48 they killed them, and you build their tombs. 15
12:18 I will pull down my barns, and build larger ones; 15
14:28 desiring to build a tower 15
30 saying, 'This man began to build 15
17:28 they sold, they planted, they built 15
Joh 2:20 It has taken 46 years to build this temple 15
Act 7:47 it was Solomon who built a house for him. 15
49 What house will you build for me, says the Lord 15
Rom 15:20 lest I build on another man's foundation 15
1Co 3: 9 you are God's field, God's building. 16
12 Now if any one builds on the foundation with gold 10
14 which any man has built on the foundation 10
2Co 5: 1 we have a building from God 16
Heb 3: 4 For every house is built by some one 13
1Pe 2: 5 be yourselves built into a spiritual house 15
3:20 during the building of the ark 13
Rev 21:18 The wall was built of jasper 8
1Es 1: 3 the house which Solomon . . had built; 15
2: 4 commanded me to build him a house at Jerusalem 15
5 build the house of the Lord of Israel 15
8 go up to build the house in Jerusalem for the Lord; 15
18 are building that rebellious and wicked city 15
19 Now if this city is built and the walls finished 15
20 since the building of the temple is now going on •
24 if this city is built and its walls finished 15
28 to prevent these men from building the city 15
30 the building of the temple in Jerusalem ceased 16
4: 8 if he tells them to build, they build 15
8 if he tells them to build, they build 15
43 the vow which you made to build Jerusalem 15
45 You also vowed to build the temple 15
47 all who were going up with him to build Jerusalem. 15
48 to help him build the city. 15
51 be given for the building of the temple 16
53 all who came from Babylonia to build the city 14
55 until the day when . . Jerusalem built 15
63 to go up and build Jerusalem and the temple 15
5:53 though the temple of God was not yet built. 15
58 So the builders built the temple of the Lord. 15
63 came to the building of this one 16
67 were building the temple for the Lord God 15
68 We will build with you. 19
70 building the house for the Lord our God 15
71 for we alone will build it for the Lord of Israel 15
72 hindered their building; 15
73 they prevented the completion of the building 16
73 they were kept from building for two years 16
6: 2 arose and began to build the house of the Lord 15
4 By whose order are you building this house 15
6 they were not prevented from building 16
9 building . . a great new house for the Lord 15
11 At whose command are you building this house 15
14 the house was built many years ago 15
22 building of the house of the Lord in Jerusalem 16
24 the building of the house of the Lord in Jerusalem 15
27 to build this house of the Lord on its site. 15
28 I command that it be built completely 15
2Es 3:24 didst command him to build a city for thy name 20
5:25 from all the cities that have been built 20
7: 6 There is a city built and set on a plain 20
8:52 a city is built, rest is appointed 20
9:24 a field of flowers where no house has been built 20
10:46 after 3,000 years Solomon built the city 20
51 remain in the field where no house had been built 20
13:36 prepared and built, as you saw the mountain 20
Tob 13:16 Jerusalem will be built with sapphires 15
14: 5 will be rebuilt there with a glorious building 15
Jdt 1: 2 he is the king who built walls about Ecbatana 15
3 he built towers 100 cubits high 11
3: 3 Behold, our buildings, and all our land 9
Wis 9: 8 Thou hast given command to build a temple 15
14: 2 wisdom was the craftsman who built it; 13
Sir 21: 8 who builds his house with other people's money 17
22:16 A wooden beam firmly bonded into a building 16
34:23 When one builds and another tears down 17
40:19 Children and the building of a city 16
47:13 that he might build a house for his name 11
48:17 built pools for water. 15
49: 7 likewise to build and to plant. 15
12 in their days they built the house 15
1Mc 1:14 So they built a gymnasium in Jerusalem 15
47 to build altars and sacred precincts and shrines 15
54 built altars in the surrounding cities of Judah 15
3:56 he said to those who were building houses 15
4:47 and built a new altar like the former one. 15
53 altar of burnt offering which they had built. 18
5: 1 heard that the altar had been built 15
6:20 he built siege towers and other engines of war. 18
31 many days they fought and built engines of war; 18
8:15 they have built for themselves a senate chamber 18
9:50 built strong cities in Judea 15
10:11 to build the walls . . for better fortification 15
12 the strongholds that Bacchides had built 15
11:20 he built many engines of war to use against it. 18
12:35 planned with them to build strongholds in Judea 15
38 Simon built Adida in the Shephelah 15
13:27 Simon built a monument over the tomb of his father 15
30 This is the tomb which he built in Modein 18
38 the strongholds that you have built 15
48 built in it a house for himself. 15

14:36 who had built themselves a citadel 18
15: 7 the strongholds which you have built 15
16: 9 Cendebeus reached Kedron, which he had built. 15
15 little stronghold called Dok, which he had built; 15
23 the building of the walls which he built 16
23 the building of the walls which he built 15
2Mc 1:18 Nehemiah, who built the temple and the altar 15
10: 2 altars which had been built in the public square 7
14:33 I will build here a splendid temple to Dionysus. 6
3Mc 4:11 had been built with a monstrous perimeter wall 12
4Mc 14:16 building in precipitous chasms •

build a house 1. aedifico
2Es 16:42 and let him that builds a house be like one 1

build a nest 1. קנן
Ps 104:17 In them the birds build their nests; 1

build high 1. ὑψόω
1Mc 14:37 and built the walls of Jerusalem higher. 1

build into 1. συνοικοδομέω
Eph 2:22 you also are built into it 1

build more 1. רבה
Hos 10: 1 the more altars he built; 1

build on a housetop 1. κατὰ οἰκίαν ὀροφοιτόω
4Mc 14:15 by building on the housetops 1

build still higher 1. προσυψόω
1Mc 12:36 to build the walls of Jerusalem still higher 1

build up 1. בנה 2. גדר 3. סלל 4. ἐποικοδομέω 5. οἰκοδομέω 6. οἰκοδομή
Deu 25: 9 man who does not build up his brother's house.' 1
Rut 4:11 Rachel and Leah, who together built up . . Israel. 1
2Ch 32: 5 built up all the wall that was broken down 1
Ps 28: 5 he will break them down and build them up no more. 1
102:16 For the LORD will build up Zion 1
147: 2 LORD builds up Jerusalem; 1
Ecc 3: 3 a time to break down, and a time to build up; 1
Isa 57:14 shall be said, "Build up, build up, prepare the way 3
14 shall be said, "Build up, build up, prepare the way 3
60:10 Foreigners shall build up your walls 1
61: 4 They shall build up the ancient ruins 1
62:10 build up . . the highway, clear it of stones 3
10 build up, build up the highway, clear it of stones 3
Jer 12:16 they shall be built up in the midst of my people. 1
24: 6 I will build them up, and not tear them down; 1
42:10 then I will build you up and not pull you down; 1
Ezk 13: 5 or built up a wall for the house of Israel 2
22:30 for a man among them who should build up the wall 2
Act 9:31 the church . . had peace and was built up 5
20:32 which is able to build you up 5
1Co 8: 1 Knowledge" puffs up, but love builds up. 5
10:23 not all things build up. 5
14:12 strive to excel in building up the church. 6
2Co 10: 8 which the Lord gave for building you up 6
13:10 for building up and not for tearing down. 6
Gal 2:18 if I build up again those things which I tore down 5
Eph 4:12 for building up the body of Christ 6
Col 2: 7 rooted and built up in him 4
1Th 5:11 encourage one another and build one another up 5
Jde 1:20 build yourselves up on your most holy faith; 4
1Mc 12:37 So they gathered together to build up the city; 5
13:33 Simon built up the strongholds of Judea 5
15:39 and commanded him to build up Kedron 5
41 He built up Kedron and stationed there horsemen 5

build upon 1. ἐποικοδομέω
1Co 3:10 another man is building upon it 1
10 Let each man take care how he builds upon it. 1
Eph 2:20 built upon the foundation of the apostles 1

builder 1. בנה 2. κατασκευάζω 3. οἰκοδομέω 4. οἰκοδόμος 5. τεχνίτης
1Kg 5:18 Solomon's builders and Hiram's builders 1
18 and Hiram's builders and the men of Gebal did 1
2Kg 12:11 paid it . . to the carpenters and the builders 1
22: 6 carpenters, and to the builders, and to the masons 1
2Ch 34:11 They gave it to the carpenters and the builders 1
Ezr 3:10 builders laid the foundation of the temple 1
Neh 4: 5 provoked thee to anger before the builders. 1
18 each of the builders had his sword girded 1
Ps 118:22 The stone which the builders rejected 1
Isa 49:17 Your builders outstrip your destroyers 1
Ezk 27: 4 your builders made perfect your beauty. 1
Mat 21:42 The very stone which the builders rejected 3
Mrk 12:10 The very stone which the builders rejected 3
Lke 20:17 The very stone which the builders rejected 3
Act 4:11 is the stone which was rejected by you builders 4
Heb 3: 3 the builder of a house has more honor than the house. 2
4 but the builder of all things is God.) 2
11:10 the city . . whose builder and maker is God. 5
1Pe 2: 7 The very stone which the builders rejected 3
1Es 2:30 began to hinder the builders 3
5:58 So the builders built the temple of the Lord. 4
6: 4 the builders that are finishing these things? 4

master builder 1. ἀρχιτέκτων
1Co 3:10 like a skilled master builder 1
2Mc 2:29 the master builder of a new house 1

building 1. בַּיִת 2. בִּנְיָה 3. בִּנְיָן 4. בִּנְיָן (A) 5. aedificium
2Ch 34:11 timber for binders and beams for the buildings 1
Ezr 5: 4 names of the men who are building this building? 4
Ezk 41:12 The building that was facing the temple yard 3
12 the wall of the building was five cubits thick 3
13 the yard and the building with its walls 2
15 Then he measured the length of the building 3
42: 1 and opposite the building on the north. 3
2 The length of the building which was on the north •
5 the lower and middle chambers in the building. 3
10 opposite the yard and opposite the building 3
2Es 10:53 where there was no foundation of any building 5
54 no work of man's building could endure in a place 5
55 see the splendor and vastness of the building 5

bulge out 1. בעה
Isa 30:13 a high wall, bulging out, and about to collapse 1

bull 1. אַבִּיר 2. בֶּן בָּקָר 3. בָּקָר 4. פַּר 5. פַּר בֶּן בָּקָר 6. פַּר שׁוֹר 7. שׁוֹר 8. תּוֹר (A) 9. ταῦρος
Gen 32:15 40 cows and ten bulls, twenty she-asses 4
Exd 29: 1 Take one young bull and two rams without blemish 4
3 and bring the bull and the two rams. 4
10 Then you shall bring the bull before the tent 4
10 shall lay their hands upon the head of the bull 4
11 you shall kill the bull before the LORD 4
12 shall take part of the blood of the bull and put it 4
14 the flesh of the bull, and its skin, and its dung 4
36 every day you shall offer a bull as a sin offering 4
Lev 1: 5 Then he shall kill the bull before the LORD 2
4: 4 He shall bring the bull to the door of the tent 4
4 lay his hand on the head of the bull 4
4 he shall . . kill the bull before the LORD 4
5 the blood of the bull and bring it to the tent 4
7 the rest of the blood of the bull he shall pour out 4
8 all the fat of the bull of the sin offering 4
11 the skin of the bull and all its flesh 4
12 the whole bull he shall carry forth outside 4
15 shall lay their hands upon the head of the bull 4
15 the bull shall be killed before the LORD 4
16 the blood of the bull to the tent of meeting 4
20 Thus shall he do with the bull 4
20 as he did with the bull of the sin offering 4
21 he shall carry forth the bull outside the camp 4
21 burn it as he burned the first bull 4
8: 2 the bull of the sin offering, and the two rams 4
14 Then he brought the bull of the sin offering 4
14 their hands upon the head of the bull 4
17 the bull, and its skin, and its flesh, and its dung 4
9: 2 Take a bull calf for a sin offering, and a ram 2
16: 3 with a young bull for a sin offering and a ram 4
6 Aaron shall offer the bull as a sin offering 4
11 Aaron shall present the bull as a sin offering 4
11 he shall kill the bull as a sin offering 4
14 he shall take some of the blood of the bull 4
15 do . . as he did with the blood of the bull 4
18 and shall take some of the blood of the bull 4
27 the bull for the sin offering and the goat 4
22:19 a male . . of the bulls or the sheep or the goats 3
23 A bull or a lamb which has a part too long 7
27 When a bull or sheep or goat is born 7
23:18 present . . one young bull, and two rams 4
Num 7:87 cattle for the burnt offering twelve bulls 4
88 for the sacrifice of peace offerings 24 bulls 4
8:12 shall lay their hands upon the heads of the bulls; 4
15: 8 when you prepare a bull for a burnt offering 2
9 one shall offer with the bull a cereal offering 2
11 Thus it shall be done for each bull or ram 7
23: 1 provide for me here seven bulls and seven rams. 4
2 offered on each altar a bull and a ram. 4
4 I have offered upon each altar a bull and a ram. 4
14 offered a bull and a ram on each altar. 4
29 provide for me here seven bulls and seven rams. 4
30 Balak . . offered a bull and a ram on each altar. 4
28:11 burnt offering . . two young bulls, one ram 4
12 cereal offering . . for each bull; 4
14 offerings shall be half a hin of wine for a bull 4
19 burnt offering . . two young bulls, one ram 4
20 three tenths . . shall you offer for a bull 4
27 burnt offering . . two young bulls, one ram 4
28 three tenths of an ephah for each bull 4
29: 3 three tenths of an ephah for the bull 4
9 three tenths of an ephah for the bull 4
13 burnt offering . . thirteen young bulls 4
14 three tenths . . for each of the thirteen bulls 4
17 On the second day twelve young bulls, two rams 4
18 cereal . . offerings for the bulls, for the rams 4
20 On the third day eleven bulls, two rams, fourteen 4
21 cereal . . offerings for the bulls, for the rams 4
23 On the fourth day ten bulls, two rams, fourteen 4
24 cereal . . offerings for the bulls, for the rams 4
26 On the fifth day nine bulls, two rams, fourteen 4
27 cereal . . offerings for the bulls, for the rams 4
29 On the sixth day eight bulls, two rams, fourteen 4
30 cereal . . offerings for the bulls, for the rams 4
32 On the seventh day seven bulls, two rams, fourteen 4
33 cereal . . offerings for the bulls, for the rams 4
36 burnt offering . . one bull, one ram, seven 4
37 cereal . . offerings for the bull, for the ram 4
Deu 33:17 His firstling bull has majesty 7
Jdg 6:25 Take your father's bull . . and pull down 6
25 father's bull, the second bull seven years old 4
26 then take the second bull, and offer it as a burnt 4
28 and the second bull was offered upon the altar 4
1Sm 1:24 she took him up . . along with a three-year-old bull 4
25 they slew the bull, and they brought the child 4
1Kg 18:23 Let two bulls be given to us; 4
23 let them choose one bull for themselves 4
23 I will prepare the other bull 4
25 Choose for yourselves one bull and prepare it 4
26 they took the bull . . and they prepared it 4
33 and cut the bull in pieces and laid it on the wood. 4
1Ch 15:26 they sacrificed seven bulls and seven rams. 4
29:21 burnt offerings to the LORD, 1,000 bulls, 1,000 rams 4
2Ch 13: 9 comes to consecrate himself with a young bull 4
29:21 they brought seven bulls, seven rams, seven lambs 4
22 they killed the bulls, and the priests received 3
32 number of the burnt offerings . . 70 bulls 3
33 offerings were 600 bulls and 3,000 sheep 3
30:24 Hezeki'ah . . gave the assembly 1,000 bulls 4
24 princes gave the assembly 1,000 bulls and 10,000 4
35: 7 Josi'ah contributed . . 3,000 bulls; 3
8 for the passover offerings . . 300 bulls. 3
9 for the passover offerings . . 500 bulls. 3
12 And so they did with the bulls. 3
Ezr 6: 9 young bulls, rams, or sheep for burnt offerings 8
17 offered . . 100 bulls, 200 rams 8
7:17 with all diligence buy bulls, rams, and lambs 8
8:35 twelve bulls for all Israel, 96 rams 4
Job 21:10 Their bull breeds without fail; their cow calves 7
42: 8 Now therefore take seven bulls and seven rams 4
Ps 22:12 Many bulls encompass me, strong bulls of Bashan 4
12 strong bulls of Bashan surround me; •
50: 9 I will accept no bull from your house 4
13 Do I eat the flesh of bulls, or drink the blood 1
51:19 then bulls will be offered on thy altar. 4
66:15 I will make an offering of bulls and goats. Selah 3
68:30 herd of bulls with the calves of the peoples. 1
69:31 more than an ox or a bull with horns and hoofs. 4
Isa 1:11 in the blood of bulls, or of lambs, or of he-goats. 4
10:13 their treasures; like a bull I have brought down 1
Jer 46:15 Why has Apis fled? Why did not your bull stand? 1
50:27 Slay all her bulls, let them go down 4
52:20 the twelve bronze bulls which were under the sea 3
Ezk 39:18 of rams, of lambs, and of goats, of bulls, 4
43:19 says the Lord GOD, a bull for a sin offering. 5
21 You shall also take the bull of the sin offering 4
22 cleansed, as it was cleansed with the bull. 4
23 you shall offer a bull without blemish 5
25 a sin offering; also a bull and a ram from the flock 5
45:18 you shall take a young bull without blemish, 5
24 as a cereal offering an ephah for each bull 4
46: 7 an ephah with the bull and an ephah with the ram 4
Hos 12:11 if in Gilgal they sacrifice bulls 7
Heb 9:13 the blood of goats and bulls 9
10: 4 the blood of bulls and goats 9
1Es 6:29 for bulls and rams and lambs 9
7: 7 They offered . . 100 bulls, 200 rams, 400 lambs 9
8:14 both gold and silver for bulls and rams and lambs 9
65 12 bulls for all Israel, 96 rams 9
Sir 6: 2 lest your soul be torn in pieces like a bull. 9
38:25 whose talk is about bulls? 9
Aza 1:16 with burnt offerings of rams and bulls 9

mighty bull 1. אַבִּיר
Isa 34: 7 and young steers with the mighty bulls. 1

young bull 1. בֶּן בָּקָר 2. פַּר 3. פַּר בֶּן בָּקָר
Lev 4: 3 a young bull without blemish to the LORD 2
14 shall offer a young bull for a sin offering 2
Num 7:15 one young bull, one ram . . for a burnt offering; 2
21 one young bull, one ram . . for a burnt offering; 2
27 one young bull, one ram . . for a burnt offering; 2
33 one young bull, one ram . . for a burnt offering; 2
39 one young bull, one ram . . for a burnt offering; 2
45 one young bull, one ram . . for a burnt offering; 2
51 one young bull, one ram . . for a burnt offering; 2
57 one young bull, one ram . . for a burnt offering; 2
63 one young bull, one ram . . for a burnt offering; 2
69 one young bull, one ram . . for a burnt offering; 2
75 one young bull, one ram . . for a burnt offering; 2
81 one young bull, one ram . . for a burnt offering; 2
8: 8 them take a young bull and its cereal offering 2
8 take another young bull for a sin offering. 1
15:24 offer one young bull for a burnt offering 2
29: 2 burnt offering . . one young bull, one ram 2
8 burnt offering . . one young bull, one ram 2
Ezk 45:22 a young bull for a sin offering. 2
23 a burnt offering to the LORD seven young bulls 2

46: 6 day of the new moon he shall offer a young bull 3
11 cereal offering with a young bull shall be 2

bulrush 1. גֹּמֶא
Exd 2: 3 she took for him a basket made of bulrushes 1

bulwark 1. אֲגַם 2. אָשְׁיָה 3. חֵל 4. עֹז 5. ἑδραίωμα 6. φυλακή
Ps 8: 2 thou hast founded a bulwark because of thy foes 4
Isa 26: 1 he sets up salvation as walls and bulwarks. 3
Jer 50:15 she has surrendered; her bulwarks have fallen 2
51:32 the bulwarks are burned with fire 1
1Ti 3:15 the pillar and bulwark of the truth. 5
4Mc 13:13 let us use our bodies as a bulwark for the law. 6

bunch 1. אֲגֻדָּה
Exd 12:22 Take a bunch of hyssop and dip it in the blood 1

bunch of raisins 1. צִמּוּק
2Sm 16: 1 200 loaves of bread, 100 bunches of raisins 1

bundle 1. כְּנָפָה 2. צֶבֶת 3. צְרוֹר 4. שׂוֹךְ 5. שׂוֹכָה 6. δεσμή 7. πλῆθος
Gen 42:35 every man's bundle of money was in his sack; 3
35 and when they and their father saw their bundles 3
Jdg 9:48 took an axe . . and cut down a bundle of brushwood 5
49 every one of the people cut down his bundle 4
Rut 2:16 And also pull out some from the bundles for her 2
1Sm 25:29 my lord shall be bound in the bundle of the living 3
Jer 10:17 Gather up your bundle from the ground 1
Mat 13:30 Gather the weeds first and bind them in bundles 6
Act 28: 3 Paul had gathered a bundle of sticks 7

burden 1. טֹרַח 2. מַשָּׂא 3. סֹבֶל 4. סֵבֶל 5. סַבָּל 6. סִבְלָה 7. עבד 8. עשק 9. ἀβαρής 10. βαρέω 11. βάρος 12. βαρύνω 13. βαρύς 14. βρίθω 15. ἐπιβαρέω 16. θλῖψις 17. καταβαρέω 18. καταναρκάω 19. σωρεύω 20. φορτίον 21. baiulo 22. gravo 23. pondus
Exd 2:11 Moses . . looked on their burdens; 6
5: 4 Get to your burdens. 6
5 you make them rest from their burdens! 6
6: 6 out from under the burdens of the Egyptians 6
7 out from under the burdens of the Egyptians. 6
23: 5 see the ass . . lying under its burden 2
Num 4:19 appoint them each to his task and to his burden 2
11:11 dost lay the burden of all this people upon me? 2
14 the burden is too heavy for me. *
17 they shall bear the burden of the people with you 2
Deu 1:12 How can I bear alone the weight and burden of you 2
2Sm 15:33 If you go on with me, you will be a burden to me. 2
19:35 should your servant be an added burden to my lord 2
1Kg 5:15 Solomon also had 70,000 burden-bearers 5
2Kg 5:17 let there be given . . two mules' burden of earth; 2
Neh 4:17 Those who carried burdens were laden in such 4
13:15 also wine, grapes, figs, and all kinds of burdens 2
19 no burden might be brought in on the sabbath day. 2
Job 7:20 Why have I become a burden to thee? 2
Ps 38: 4 they weigh like a burden too heavy for me. 2
55:22 Cast your burden on the LORD, and he will sustain †
81: 6 I relieved your shoulder of the burden; 4
Prv 28:17 If a man is burdened with the blood of another 8
Isa 1:14 new moons . . they have become a burden to me 1
9: 4 the yoke of his burden, and the staff for his 3
10:27 his burden will depart from your shoulder 3
14:25 depart . . and his burden from their shoulder. 3
22:25 and the burden that was upon it will be cut off 2
43:23 I have not burdened you with offerings 7
24 But you have burdened me with your sins 7
46: 1 are loaded as burdens on weary beasts. 2
2 they cannot save the burden 2
Jer 17:21 and do not bear a burden on the sabbath day 2
22 And do not carry a burden out of your houses 2
24 and bring in no burden by the gates of this city 2
27 and not to bear a burden and enter by the gates 2
23:33 a priest asks you, 'What is the burden of the LORD? 2
33 You are the burden, and I will cast you off 2
34 one of the people who says, 'The burden of the LORD 2
36 'the burden of the LORD' you shall mention no more 2
36 for the burden is every man's own word 2
38 But if you say, 'The burden of the LORD,' 2
38 you have said these words, "The burden of the LORD 2
38 saying, "You shall not say, 'The burden of the LORD,' 2
Lam 3:14 the laughingstock . . the burden of their songs *
63 I am the burden of their songs. *
Mat 11:30 For my yoke is easy, and my burden is light. 20
20:12 who have borne the burden of the day 11
Lke 11:46 you load men with burdens hard to bear 20
46 you yourselves do not touch the burdens 20
Act 15:28 no greater burden than these necessary things 11
2Co 8:13 others should be eased and you burdened 16
11: 9 I did not burden any one 18
9 and will refrain from burdening you in any way. 9
12:13 except that I myself did not burden you 18
14 will not be a burden 18
16 granting that I myself did not burden you 17
Gal 6: 2 Bear one another's burdens 11
1Th 2: 9 worked night and day, that we might not burden any 15
2Th 3: 8 that we might not burden any of you. 15
1Ti 5:16 let the church not be burdened 10
2Ti 3: 6 capture weak women, burdened with sins 19
Rev 2:24 to you I say, I do not lay upon you any other burden; 11
2Es 3:21 For the first Adam, burdened with an evil heart 21
7:68 full of sins and burdened with transgressions. 22
105 neither shall any one lay a burden on another ‡
14:14 cast away from you the burdens of man 23
Wis 2:15 the very sight of him is a burden to us 13
9:15 this earthy tent burdens the thoughtful mind. 14
Sir 3:27 A stubborn mind will be burdened by troubles 12
21:16 A fool's narration is like a burden on a journey 20
33:24 Fodder and a stick and burdens for an ass 20

burden *See also* bear, bearer, lay, lift.

heavy burden 1. סִבְלָה 2. φορτίον
Exd 1:11 to afflict them with heavy burdens 1
Mat 23: 4 They bind heavy burdens, hard to bear 2

burdensome 1. כבד 2. βαρύνω 3. βαρύς
2Sm 13:25 let us not all go, lest we be burdensome to you. 1
1Jn 5: 3 And his commandments are not burdensome. 3
Sir 8:15 lest he be burdensome to you 2

burial 1. קְבוּרָה 2. קֶבֶר 3. ἐνταφιάζω 4. ἐνταφιασμός 5. ὀστέον 6. ταφή 7. τάφος 8. τυγχάνω
2Ch 26:23 buried him with his fathers in the burial field 1
Ecc 6: 3 but he does not enjoy . . and also has no burial 1
Isa 14:20 You will not be joined with them in burial 1
Jer 22:19 With the burial of an ass he shall be buried 1
Ezk 39:11 I will give to Gog a place for burial in Israel 2
Joh 12: 7 let her keep it for the day of my burial. 4
19:40 as is the burial custom of the Jews. 3
Heb 11:22 gave directions concerning his burial. 5
Sir 38:16 do not neglect his burial. 6
2Mc 13: 7 without even burial in the earth. 8
3Mc 6:31 prepared for their destruction and burial. 7

burial *See also* mound, place, prepare.

burial place 1. קֶבֶר
Jer 26:23 into the burial place of the common people. 1

buried *See* lie.

burier 1. קבר
Ezk 39:15 till the buriers have buried it 1

burlap 1. ὠμόλινον
Sir 40: 4 the one who is clothed in burlap; 1

burn 1. אֵשׁ 2. בָּאֵשׁ 3. בער 4. דלק 5. חרה 6. חָרוֹן 7. חרר 8. יצת 9. יצת בָּאֵשׁ 10. יקד 11. יְקוֹד 12. כוה 13. כְּוִיָּה 14. להט 15. מוֹקֵד 16. מִכְוָה 17. מִכְוַת אֵשׁ 18. מַקְטֵר 19. מִשְׂרֵפָה 20. עבר 21. עבר בָּאֵשׁ 22. עתם 23. קטר 24. קלה 25. שלק 26. שרף 27. שְׂרֵפָה 28. דלק (A) 29. יקד (A) 30. יְקֵדָה (A) 31. ἁγνίζω 32. ἀνακαίω 33. ἀναλίσκω 34. ἀποκαίω 35. διαπυρόω 36. ἐκκαίω 37. ἐμπίμπρημι 38. ἐμπυρίζω 39. ζέω 40. καίω 41. κατακαίω 42. κατακαύω 43. καταφλέγω 44. καῦσις 45. καυστικός 46. καύχομαι 47. πῦρ 48. πυρίζω 49. πυρόω 50: πύρωσις 51. τήκω 52. ὑφάπτω 53. φλέγω 54. φλογίζω 55. conburo 56. consumo 57. incendium 58. incendo
Gen 11: 3 let us make bricks, and burn them thoroughly. 26
38:24 Bring her out, and let her be burned. 26
44:18 let not your anger burn against your servant; 5
Exd 3: 2 the bush was burning, yet it was not consumed. 3
3 see this great sight, why the bush is not burnt. 3
12:10 anything that remains . . you shall burn. 26
21:25 burn for burn, wound for wound, stripe for stripe. 13
25 burn for burn, wound for wound, stripe for stripe. 13
22:24 my wrath will burn, and I will kill you 5
27:20 that a lamp may be set up to burn continually. *
29:13 you shall . . burn them upon the altar. 23
14 you shall burn with fire outside the camp; 26
18 burn the whole ram upon the altar; 23
25 burn them on the altar in addition to the burnt 23
34 then you shall burn the remainder with fire; 26
30: 1 You shall make an altar to burn incense upon; 18
7 Aaron shall burn fragrant incense on it; 23
7 when he dresses the lamps he shall burn it 23
8 he shall burn it, a perpetual incense 23
20 to burn an offering by fire to the LORD 23
32:20 he took the calf which they had made, and burnt it 26
40:27 burnt fragrant incense upon it; as the LORD had 23
Lev 1: 9 the priest shall burn the whole on the altar 23
13 the priest shall offer the whole, and burn it 23
15 wring off its head, and burn it on the altar 23
17 the priest shall burn it on the altar 23
2: 2 the priest shall burn this as its memorial 23
9 its memorial portion and burn this on the altar 23
11 you shall burn no leaven nor any honey 23
16 The priest shall burn as its memorial portion 23
3: 5 Then Aaron's sons shall burn it on the altar 23
11 the priest shall burn it on the altar as food 23
16 the priest shall burn them on the altar as food 23
4:10 the priest shall burn them upon the altar 23
12 and shall burn it on a fire of wood 26
12 where the ashes are poured out it shall be burned 26
19 shall take from it and burn upon the altar 23
21 burn it as he burned the first bull 26
21 burn it as he burned the first bull 26
26 all its fat he shall burn on the altar 23
31 the priest shall burn it upon the altar 23
35 the priest shall burn it on the altar 23
5:12 priest shall . . burn this upon the altar 23
6:12 the priest shall burn wood on it every morning 3
12 shall burn on it the fat of the peace offerings 23
15 burn this as its memorial portion on the altar 23
22 the whole of it shall be burned 23
23 offering of a priest shall be wholly burned *
30 sin offering . . it shall be burned with fire 26
7: 5 the priest shall burn them on the altar 23
17 on the third day shall be burned with fire 26
19 not be eaten; it shall be burned with fire 26
31 The priest shall burn the fat on the altar 23
8:16 and Moses burned them on the altar 23
17 the bull . . he burned with fire outside the camp 26
20 Moses burned the head and the pieces and the fat 23
21 Moses burned the whole ram on the altar 23
28 burned them on the altar with the burnt offering 23
32 the flesh and the bread you shall burn with fire 26
9:10 from the sin offering he burned upon the altar 23
11 The flesh and the skin he burned with fire 26
13 and he burned them upon the altar 23
14 burned them with the burnt offering on the altar 23
17 cereal offering . . and burned it upon the altar 23
20 the breasts, and he burned the fat upon the altar 23
10: 6 bewail the burning which the LORD has kindled 27
16 the sin offering, and behold, it was burned 26
13:24 when the body has a burn on its skin 17
24 when . . the raw flesh of the burn becomes a spot 16
25 leprosy; it has broken out in the burn 16
28 it is a swelling from the burn 16
28 for it is the scar of the burn 16
52 he shall burn the garment, whether diseased 26
52 leprosy; it shall be burned in the fire 26
55 shall burn it in the fire, whether the leprous 26
57 shall burn with fire that in which is the disease 26
16:25 the fat of the sin offering he shall burn 23
27 and their dung shall be burned with fire 26
28 he who burns them shall wash his clothes 26
17: 6 and burn the fat for a pleasing odor to the LORD 23
19: 6 anything left over . . shall be burned with fire 26
20:14 they shall be burned with fire, both he 26
21: 9 she shall be burned with fire 26
Num 5:26 burn it upon the altar 23
11: 1 fire of the LORD burned among them, and consumed 3
3 Tab'erah, because the fire of the LORD burned 3
16:39 censers, which those who were burned had offered; 26
40 should draw near to burn incense before the LORD 23
18:17 shall burn their fat as an offering by fire 23
19: 5 heifer shall be burned in his sight; 26
5 flesh, and her blood, with her dung, shall be burned; 26
6 into the midst of the burning of the heifer. 27
8 He who burns the heifer shall wash his clothes 26
17 shall take some ashes of the burnt sin offering 27
31:10 cities . . encampments, they burned with fire 26
Deu 4:11 mountain burned with fire to the heart of heaven 3
5:23 while the mountain was burning with fire 3
7: 5 you shall . . burn their graven images with fire. 26
25 graven images . . you shall burn with fire; 26
9:15 mountain was burning with fire; 3
21 calf . . and burned it with fire and crushed it 26
12: 3 and burn their Ashe'rim with fire; 26
31 even burn their sons and their daughters 26
13:16 burn the city and all its spoil with fire 26
18:10 any one who burns his son or his daughter 21
32:22 fire is kindled . . burns to the depths of Sheol 10
Jos 6:24 they burned the city with fire, and all within it; 26
7: 1 the anger of the LORD burned against the people 5
15 And he who is taken . . shall be burned with fire 26
25 they burned them with fire, and stoned them 26
26 then the LORD turned from his burning anger. 6
8:28 Joshua burned Ai, and made it . . a heap of ruins 26
11: 6 you shall . . burn their chariots with fire. 26
9 and burned their chariots with fire. 26
11 put to the sword . . and he burned Hazor with fire. 26
13 none of the cities . . on mounds did Israel burn 26
13 none . . except Hazor only; that Joshua burned. 26
Jdg 6:39 Gideon said . . "Let not thy anger burn against me 5
9:52 near to the door of the tower to burn it with fire. 26
12: 1 We will burn your house over you with fire. 26
14:15 lest we burn you and your father's house 26
15: 6 came up, and burned her and her father with fire. 26
18:27 smote them . . and burned the city with fire. 26
1Sm 2:15 before the fat was burned, the priest's servant 23
16 Let them burn the fat first, and then take 23
30: 1 They had overcome Ziklag, and burned it with fire 26
3 came to the city, they found it burned with fire 26
14 and we burned Ziklag with fire. 26
31:12 they came to Jabesh and burnt them there. 26
1Kg 9:16 gone up and captured Gezer and burnt it with fire 26
13: 2 and men's bones shall be burned upon you.' 26
15:13 Asa cut down her image and burned it at . . Kidron. 26

16:18 Zimri . . burned the king's house over him 26
2Kg 10:26 they brought out the pillar . . and burned it. 26
16: 3 He even burned his son as an offering 21
13 and burned his burnt offering 23
15 Upon the great altar burn the morning burnt offering 23
17:17 they burned their sons and . . as offerings 21
31 and the Sephar'vites burned their children 26
21: 6 And he burned his son as an offering 20
23: 4 he burned them outside Jerusalem in the fields 26
6 he brought . . and burned it at the brook Kidron 26
10 burn his son or his daughter as an offering 21
11 and he burned the chariots of the sun with fire. 26
15 crushing them . . also he burned the Ashe'rah. 26
16 took the bones . . and burned them upon the altar 26
20 the altars, and burned the bones of men upon them. 26
25: 9 he burned the house of the LORD, and the king's 26
1Ch 14:12 David gave command, and they were burned. 26
2Ch 2: 4 dedicate it to him for the burning of incense 23
4:20 lamps . . to burn before the inner sanctuary 3
13:11 that its lamps may burn every evening; 3
15:16 Asa cut down her image, crushed it, and burned it 26
28: 3 burned his sons as an offering 3
33: 6 he burned his sons as an offering in the valley 21
34: 5 burned the bones of the priests on their altars 26
36:19 burned the house of God, and broke down the wall 26
19 burned all its palaces with fire, and destroyed 26
Neh 2:17 Jerusalem lies in ruins with its gates burned. 9
10:34 to burn upon the altar of the LORD our God 3
Est 1:12 the king . . and his anger burned within him. 3
Job 30:30 My skin turns black . . and my bones burn with heat. 7
31:12 it would burn to the root all my increase. •
41:20 smoke, as from a boiling pot and burning rushes. •
Ps 38: 7 For my loins are filled with burning 24
39: 3 As I mused, the fire burned; 3
46: 9 he burns the chariots with fire! 26
69:24 let thy burning anger overtake them. 6
74: 8 they burned all the meeting places of God 26
79: 5 Will thy jealous wrath burn like fire? 3
80:16 have burned it with fire, they have cut it down; 26
89:46 How long will thy wrath burn like fire? 3
102: 3 my bones burn like a furnace. 7
140:10 Let burning coals fall upon them! 2
Prv 6:27 fire in his bosom and his clothes not be burned? 26
Isa 1: 7 your cities are burned with fire; 26
31 both . . shall burn together, with none to quench 3
4: 4 spirit of judgment and by a spirit of burning. 3
6:13 though a tenth remain in it, it will be burned 3
9: 5 every garment . . burned as fuel for the fire. 27
18 For wickedness burns like a fire, it consumes 3
19 wrath of the LORD of hosts the land is burned 22
10:16 and under his glory a burning will be kindled 11
16 will be kindled, like the burning of fire. 11
17 it will burn and devour his thorns and briers 3
30:27 the LORD comes from far, burning with his anger 3
33:12 the peoples will be as if burned to lime 19
12 like thorns cut down, that are burned in the fire. 8
14 Who . . can dwell with everlasting burnings? 15
34: 9 her land shall become burning pitch. 3
42: 3 and a dimly burning wick he will not quench; •
25 it burned him, but he did not take it to heart. 3
43: 2 through fire you shall not be burned. 12
44:16 Half of it he burns in the fire; 26
19 Half of it I burned in the fire 26
62: 1 and her salvation as a burning torch. 3
64:11 beautiful house . . has been burned by fire 27
65: 5 in my nostrils, a fire that burns all the day. 10
Jer 4: 4 go forth like fire, and burn with none to quench it 3
7:20 it will burn and not be quenched. 3
31 to burn their sons and their daughters 26
15:14 a fire is kindled which shall burn for ever. 10
17: 4 a fire is kindled which shall burn for ever. 10
19: 5 to burn their sons in the fire as burnt offerings 26
20: 9 there is in my heart as it were a burning fire 3
21:10 king of Babylon, and he shall burn it with fire. 26
12 go forth like fire, and burn with none to quench it 3
32:29 shall come and set this city on fire, and burn it 26
33:18 offer burnt offerings, to burn cereal offerings 23
34: 2 and he shall burn it with fire. 26
5 And as spices were burned for your fathers 19
5 so men shall burn spices for you and lament 26
22 they will fight against it, and take it, and burn it 26
36:22 there was a fire burning in the brazier 3
25 Gemari'ah urged the king not to burn the scroll 26
27 Now, after the king had burned the scroll 26
28 which Jehoi'akim the king of Judah has burned. 26
29 Thus says the LORD, You have burned this scroll 26
32 scroll which Jehoi'akim king of Judah had burned 26
37: 8 they shall take it and burn it with fire. 26
10 they would rise up and burn this city with fire. 26
38:17 and this city shall not be burned with fire 26
18 the Chalde'ans, and they shall burn it with fire 26
23 and this city shall be burned with fire. 26
39: 8 The Chalde'ans burned the king's house 26
43:12 he shall burn them and carry them away captive; 26
13 the gods of Egypt he shall burn with fire. 26
44:21 As for the incense that you burned in the cities 23
49: 2 and its villages shall be burned with fire; 8
51:25 and make you a burnt mountain. 27
32 the bulwarks are burned with fire 26
58 and her high gates shall be burned with fire. 8
52:13 he burned the house of the LORD 26
Lam 2: 3 he has burned like a flaming fire in Jacob 3
Ezk 1:13 that looked like burning coals of fire 3
5: 2 A third part you shall burn in the fire 3
4 cast them into the fire, and burn them in the fire; 26
10: 2 fill your hands with burning coals 1
16:41 they shall burn your houses 26
24:11 that it may become hot, and its copper may burn 7
39: 9 and make fires of the weapons and burn them 25
43:21 it shall be burnt in the appointed place 26
Dan 3: 6 cast into a burning fiery furnace. 29
11 cast into a burning fiery furnace. 29
15 cast into a burning fiery furnace; 29
17 able to deliver us from the burning fiery furnace; 29
20 cast them into the burning fiery furnace. 29
21 cast into the burning fiery furnace. 29
23 fell bound into the burning fiery furnace. 29
26 near to the door of the burning fiery furnace 29
7: 9 throne . . flames, its wheels were burning fire. 28
11 destroyed and given over to be burned with fire. 30
Hos 7: 6 For like an oven their hearts burn with intrigue; 32
8: 5 My anger burns against them. 5
Jol 1:19 and flame has burned all the trees of the field. 14
2: 3 and behind them a flame burns. 14
Ams 2: 1 he burned to lime the bones of the king of Edom. 26
4:11 and you were as a brand plucked out of the burning; 27
6:10 when a man's kinsman, he who burns him 26
Obd 1:18 they shall burn them and consume them 4
Mic 1: 7 all her hires shall be burned with fire 26
Nah 2:13 and I will burn your chariots in smoke 3
Mal 4: 1 For behold, the day comes, burning like an oven 3
Mat 3:12 the chaff he will burn with unquenchable fire. 41
13:30 in bundles to be burned 41
40 as the weeds are gathered and burned with fire 41
22: 7 destroyed . . murderers and burned their city 37
Lke 3:17 the chaff he will burn with unquenchable fire. 41
12:35 Let your loins be girded and your lamps burning 40
24:32 Did not our hearts burn within us 40
Joh 5:35 He was a burning and shining lamp 40
15: 6 gathered, thrown into the fire and burned. 40
Act 19:19 burned them in the sight of all 41
Rom 12:20 you will heap burning coals upon his head. 47
1Co 13: 3 if I deliver my body to be burned, but have not love 46
Heb 6: 8 its end is to be burned. 44
13:11 are burned outside the camp. 41
Rev 4: 5 before the throne burn seven torches of fire 40
8: 8 like a great mountain, burning with fire 40
18: 8 and she shall be burned with fire; 41
9 when they see the smoke of her burning; 50
18 and cried out as they saw the smoke of her burning 50
19:20 the lake of fire that burns with sulphur. 40
21: 8 in the lake that burns with fire and sulphur 40
1Es 1:55 they burned the house of the Lord 38
55 burned their towers with fire 38
4:45 which the Edomites burned 38
6:16 they pulled down the house, and burned it 38
2Es 12: 3 and the whole body of the eagle was burned 58
44 we also had been consumed in the burning of Zion! 57
14:21 For thy law has been burned 58
15:62 they shall burn with fire all your forests 56
16: 6 when once it has begun to burn? 58
53 for God will burn coals of fire on the head of him 55
Jdt 2:26 burned their tents 37
27 burned all their fields 37
Wis 13:12 and burn the castoff pieces of his work 33
16:19 at another time . . it burned more intensely than fire 53
Sir 8:10 lest you be burned in his flaming fire. 38
23:16 The soul heated like a burning fire 40
28:10 so will be the burning 36
10 so will be the burning 36
22 they will not be burned in its flame. 40
23 it will burn among them and will not be put out 36
43: 4 the sun burns the mountains three times as much 36
48: 1 his word burned like a torch. 40
Bar 1: 2 took Jerusalem and burned it with fire. 37
LJr 1:55 the gods will be burnt in two like beams. 41
Aza 1:25 it broke through and burned those of the Chaldeans 38
66 the midst of the burning fiery furnace 40
1Mc 1:31 He plundered the city, burned it with fire 37
54 sacrilege upon the altar of burnt offering. •
56 The books . . they tore to pieces and burned with fire. 38
59 which was upon the altar of burnt offering. •
3: 5 he burned those who troubled his people. 54
4:20 the Jews were burning the camp 38
38 the altar profaned, and the gates burned 42
5: 5 burned with fire their towers 38
28 he seized all its spoils and burned it with fire. 37
35 plundered it, and burned it with fire. 37
44 and burned the sacred precincts with fire 38
65 and burned its towers round about. 38
68 graven images of their gods he burned with fire; 42
6:31 the Jews sallied out and burned these with fire 38
10:84 Jonathan burned Azotus 38
84 he burned with fire. 38
85 with those burned alive 38
11: 4 those whom Jonathan had burned in the war 38
61 burned its suburbs with fire 38
12:29 they saw the fires burning. 40
16:10 John burned it with fire 38
2Mc 1: 8 burned the gate and shed innocent blood 48
33 Nehemiah . . had burned the materials of the sacrifice 31
8:33 burned those who had set fire to the sacred gates 52
10: 3 they burned incense and lighted lamps •
36 burned the blasphemers alive 41
12: 6 burned the boats 43
14:41 the doors burned 52
3Mc 4: 2 everywhere their hearts were burning 49
5:43 by burning to the ground the temple 47
4Mc 3:15 David, although he was burning with thirst 35
5:30 gouge out my eyes and burn my entrails. 51
6:25 There they burned him 43
26 When he was now burned to his very bones 41
27 I am dying in burning torments 45
9:17 Cut my limbs, burn my flesh, and twist my joints. 49
15:14 who saw them tortured and burned one by one 53
20 the flesh . . burned upon the flesh of other children 34
18:20 in his burning rage brought those seven sons 39

burn a sacrifice 1.קטר

2Ch 32:12 upon it you shall burn your sacrifices"? 1

burn down 1.שרף 2.ἐμπυρίζω 3.κατακαίω

2Kg 25: 9 every great house he burned down. 1
Jer 52:13 every great house he burned down. 1
Tob 14: 4 The house of God in it will be burned down 3
1Mc 11: 4 they showed him the temple of Dagon burned down 2

burn for incense 1.θυμιάω

LJr 1:43 burning bran for incense 1

burn hot 1.חרה

Exd 32:10 that my wrath may burn hot against them 1
11 why does thy wrath burn hot against thy people 1
19 Moses' anger burned hot, and he threw the tables 1
22 Aaron said, "Let not the anger of my lord burn hot; 1

burn hotly 1.ferveo

2Es 7:61 they are set on fire and burn hotly 1

burn incense 1.קטר 2.θυμιάω

1Sm 2:28 go up to my altar, to burn incense, to wear an ephod 1
1Kg 3: 3 he sacrificed and burnt incense at the high 1
9:25 offer up . . burning incense before the LORD. 1
11: 8 wives, who burned incense and sacrificed 1
12:33 and went up to the altar to burn incense. 1
13: 1 was standing by the altar to burn incense. 1
2 priests of the high places who burn incense 1
22:43 the people still sacrificed and burned incense 1
2Kg 12: 3 people continued to sacrifice and burn incense 1
14: 4 the people still sacrificed and burned incense 1
15: 4 the people still sacrificed and burned incense 1
35 the people still sacrificed and burned incense 1
16: 4 And he . . and burned incense on the high places 1
17:11 there they burned incense on all the high places 1
18: 4 the people of Israel had burned incense to it; 1
22:17 forsaken me and . . burned incense to other gods 1
23: 5 had ordained to burn incense in the high places 1
5 those also who burned incense to Ba'al, to the sun 1
8 places where the priests had burned incense 1
1Ch 23:13 for ever should burn incense before the LORD 1
2Ch 2: 6 except as a place to burn incense before him? 1
26:16 to burn incense on the altar of incense. 1
18 is not for you, Uzzi'ah, to burn incense to the LORD 1
18 who are consecrated to burn incense. 1
19 Now he had a censer in his hand to burn incense 1
28: 3 burned incense in the valley of the son of Hinnom 1
4 sacrificed and burned incense 1
25 he made high places to burn incense to other gods 1
29: 7 not burned incense or offered burnt offerings 1
11 to be his ministers and burn incense to him. 1
34:25 forsaken me and . . burned incense to other gods 1
Isa 65: 3 in gardens and burning incense upon bricks; 1
7 because they burned incense upon the mountains 1
Jer 1:16 they have burned incense to other gods 1
7: 9 burn incense to Ba'al, and go after other gods 1
11:12 and cry to the gods to whom they burn incense 1
13 set up to shame, altars to burn incense to Ba'al. 1
17 provoking me to anger by burning incense 1
18:15 they burn incense to false gods; 1
19: 4 and have profaned this place by burning incense 1
13 houses upon whose roofs incense has been burned 1
44: 3 they went to burn incense and serve other gods 1
5 to turn . . and burn no incense to other gods. 1
8 burning incense to other gods 1
17 we have vowed, burn incense to the queen of heaven 1
18 left off burning incense to the queen of heaven 1
19 When we burned incense to the queen of heaven 1
23 It is because you burned incense 1
25 to burn incense to the queen of heaven 1
48:35 offers sacrifice . . and burns incense to his god. 1
Hos 2:13 days of the Ba'als when she burned incense to them 1
11: 2 and burning incense to idols. 1
Hab 1:16 Therefore he . . burns incense to his seine; 1
Lke 1: 9 to enter the temple of the Lord and burn incense. 2
1Mc 1:55 and burned incense at the doors of the houses 2
4:50 Then they burned incense on the altar 2

burn through 1. διακαίω
4Mc 11:19 his entrails were burned through. 1

burn to death 1. succendo
2Es 10:22 our priests have been burned to death 1

burn together 1. συμφλογίζω
2Mc 6:11 Others . . were all burned together 1

burn up 1. בער 2. חרר 3. יצת 4. להט 5. להק 6. שׂרף בָּאֵשׁ 7. ἐκκαύω 8. ἐμπίπρημι 9. ἐμπυρίζω 10. εὑρίσκω 11. καταισχύνω 12. κατακαίω 13. succendo
Jdg 15: 5 and burned up the shocks and the standing grain 1
1Kg 14:10 as a man burns up dung until it is all gone. 1
Job 1:16 fell from heaven and burned up the sheep 1
Ps 97: 3 Fire . . burns up his adversaries round about. 5
106:18 flame burned up the wicked. 4
Isa 27: 4 against them, I would burn them up together. 3
Ezk 23:47 and burn up their houses. 6
24:10 let the bones be burned up. 2
Mal 4: 1 the day that comes shall burn them up 4
1Co 3:15 If any man's work is burned up, he will suffer loss 11
2Pe 3:10 and the works that are upon it will be burned up. 10
Rev 8: 7 and a third of the earth was burnt up 12
7 and a third of the trees were burnt up 12
7 and all green grass was burnt up. 12
17:16 and devour her flesh and burn her up with fire 12
2Es 13:11 and burned them all up 13
Jdt 6: 4 We will burn them up 12
16: 5 He boasted that he would burn up my territory 8
Sir 23:16 will never cease until the fire burns him up. 7
43:21 burns up the wilderness 7
1Mc 7:35 then if I return safely I will burn up this house. 9

burn wholly 1. ὁλοκαρπόομαι
Sir 45:14 His sacrifices shall be wholly burned 1

burn with fire 1. πυριφλεγής
3Mc 3:29 to be made unapproachable and burned with fire 1

burn with lust 1. חמם
Isa 57: 5 you who burn with lust among the oaks 1

burn with zeal 1. ζηλόω
1Mc 2:24 When Mattathias saw it, be burned with zeal 1
26 Thus he burned with zeal for the law 1

burned one 1. שׂרף
Neh 4: 2 heaps of rubbish, and burned ones at that? 1

burning *See* coal, heat, sand, wrath.

keep burning 1. יקד 2. עלה
Lev 6: 9 the fire of the altar shall be kept burning on it 1
12 The fire on the altar shall be kept burning on it 1
13 Fire shall be kept burning upon the altar 1
24: 2 that a light may be kept burning continually 2

burning place 1. תָּפְתֶּה
Isa 30:33 For a burning place has long been prepared; 1

burnish 1. מרט 2. מרק 3. קָלָל
1Kg 7:45 all these vessels . . were of burnished bronze. 1
2Ch 4:16 for these Huram-abi made of burnished bronze 2
Ezk 1: 7 and they sparkled like burnished bronze. 3
Dan 10: 6 arms and legs like the gleam of burnished bronze 3

burnished *See* bronze.

burnt *See* offering, sacrifice.

burnt-out *See* waste.

burst 1. בקע 2. חול 3. נפל 4. נתק 5. פרץ 6. פֶּרֶץ 7. ῥήγνυμι
Jos 9:13 wineskins were new . . and behold, they are burst; 1
2Sm 5:20 The LORD has broken . . like a bursting flood. 6
Job 32:19 like new wineskins, it is ready to burst. 1
Prv 3:10 your vats will be bursting with wine. 5
Jer 2:20 you broke your yoke and burst your bonds; 4
5: 5 had broken the yoke, they had burst the bonds. 4
23:19 it will burst upon the head of the wicked. 2
30: 8 and I will burst their bonds 4
23 it will burst upon the head of the wicked. 2
Jol 2: 8 they burst through the weapons 3
Mat 9:17 if it is, the skins burst, and the wine is spilled 7
Mrk 2:22 if he does, the wine will burst the skins 7
Lke 5:37 if he does, the new wine will burst the skins 7

burst asunder 1. נתק
Ps 2: 3 Let us burst their bonds asunder 1
Nah 1:13 and will burst your bonds asunder. 1

burst forth 1. בקע 2. גיח 3. ἀναδίδωμι
Gen 7:11 the fountains of the great deep burst forth 1
Job 38: 8 when it burst forth from the womb; 2
Ezk 32: 2 you burst forth in your rivers 2
Sir 1:23 then joy will burst forth for him. 3

make burst 1. ῥήγνυμι
Sir 19:10 Be brave! It will not make you burst! 1

burst open 1. διαρρήγνυμι 2. λάσκω
Act 1:18 falling headlong he burst open in the middle 2
Bel 1:27 The dragon ate them, and burst open 1

bursting *See* flood.

bury 1. טמן 2. קבר 3. ἐνταφιασμός 4. θάπτω 5. κατορύσσω 6. συγκομίζω 7. συνθάπτω 8. ταφή
Gen 15:15 you shall be buried in a good old age. 2
23: 4 that I may bury my dead out of my sight. 2
6 Bury your dead in the choicest of our sepulchres; 2
6 sepulchre, or hinder you from burying your dead. 2
8 If you are willing that I should bury my dead 2
11 of my people I give it to you; bury your dead. 2
13 accept it from me, that I may bury my dead there. 2
15 what is that between you and me? Bury your dead. 2
19 After this, Abraham buried Sarah his wife 2
25: 9 Isaac and Ish'mael his sons buried him in the cave 2
10 There Abraham was buried, with Sarah his wife. 2
35: 8 died, and she was buried under an oak below Bethel; 2
19 Rachel died, and she was buried on the way 2
29 and his sons Esau and Jacob buried him. 2
47:29 Do not bury me in Egypt 2
30 out of Egypt and bury me in their burying place. 2
48: 7 and I buried her there on the way to Ephrath 2
49:29 bury me with my fathers in the cave 2
31 There they buried Abraham and Sarah his wife; 2
31 there they buried Isaac and Rebekah his wife; 2
31 they buried Abraham . . and there I buried Leah- 2
50: 5 in the land of Canaan, there shall you bury me. 2
5 let me . . bury my father; then I will return. 2
6 Pharaoh answered, "Go up, and bury your father 2
7 Joseph went up to bury his father; 2
13 his sons . . buried him in the cave of the field 2
14 After he had buried his father, Joseph returned 2
14 all who had gone up with him to bury his father. 2
Num 11:34 there they buried the people who had the craving. 2
20: 1 Miriam died there, and was buried there. 2
33: 4 Egyptians were burying all their first-born 2
Deu 10: 6 Mose'rah. There Aaron died, and . . was buried; 2
21:23 bury him the same day, for a hanged man is accursed 2
34: 6 buried him in the valley in the land of Moab 2
Jos 24:30 And they buried him in his own inheritance 2
32 The bones of Joseph . . were buried at Shechem 2
33 Elea'zar . . died; and they buried him at Gib'e-ah 2
Jdg 2: 9 they buried him within the bounds 2
8:32 age, and was buried in the tomb of Jo'ash his father 2
10: 2 Then he died, and was buried at Shamir. 2
5 Ja'ir died, and was buried in Kamon. 2
12: 7 Jephthah . . died, and was buried in his city 2
10 Then Ibzan died, and was buried at Bethlehem. 2
12 Then Elon . . died, and was buried at Ai'jalon 2
15 Abdon . . died, and was buried at Pira'thon 2
16:31 brought him up and buried him between Zorah 2
Rut 1:17 where you die I will die, and there . . be buried. 2
1Sm 25: 1 they buried him in his house at Ramah. 2
28: 3 Israel had mourned . . him and buried him in Ramah 2
31:13 And they took their bones and buried them 2
2Sm 2: 4 It was the men of Ja'besh-gil'ead who buried Saul 2
5 you showed this loyalty to Saul . . and buried him! 2
32 As'ahel, and buried him in the tomb of his father 2
3:32 They buried Abner at Hebron; 2
4:12 took the head . . and buried it in the tomb of Abner 2
17:23 he died, and was buried in the tomb of his father. 2
21:14 And they buried the bones of Saul and his son 2
1Kg 2:10 his fathers, and was buried in the city of David. 2
31 Do as he has said, strike him down and bury him; 2
34 killed him; and he was buried in his own house 2
11:15 Jo'ab the commander . . went up to bury the slain 2
43 and was buried in the city of David his father; 2
13:29 and brought it back . . to mourn and to bury him. 2
31 after he had buried him, he said to his sons 2
31 bury me in the grave in which the man of God is 2
31 the grave in which the man of God is buried; 2
14:13 all Israel shall mourn for him, and bury him; 2
18 all Israel buried him and mourned for him 2
31 Rehobo'am . . was buried with his fathers 2
15: 8 and they buried him in the city of David. 2
24 was buried with his fathers in the city of David 2
16: 6 Ba'asha . . was buried at Tirzah; 2
28 Omri slept . . and was buried in Sama'ria 2
22:37 and they buried the king in Sama'ria. 2
50 Jehosh'aphat . . was buried with his fathers 2
2Kg 8:24 Joram slept . . and was buried with his fathers 2
9:10 eat Jez'ebel . . and none shall bury her. 2
28 and buried him in his tomb with his fathers 2
34 See now to this cursed woman, and bury her; 2
35 when they went to bury her, they found 2
10:35 Jehu slept . . and they buried him in Sama'ria. 2
12:21 And they buried him with his fathers in the city 2
13: 9 Jeho'ahaz slept . . and they buried him in Sama'ria; 2
13 Jo'ash was buried in Sama'ria with the kings 2
20 So Eli'sha died, and they buried him. 2
21 as a man was being buried, lo, a . . band was seen 2
14:16 Jeho'ash slept . . and was buried in Sama'ria 2
20 and he was buried in Jerusalem with his fathers 2
15: 7 and they buried him with his fathers in the city 2
38 Jotham slept . . and was buried with his fathers 2
16:20 Ahaz slept . . and was buried with his fathers 2
21:18 Manas'seh slept . . and was buried in the garden 2
26 And he was buried in his tomb in the garden of Uzza; 2
23:30 his servants . . and buried him in his own tomb. 2
1Ch 10:12 they buried their bones under the oak in Jabesh 2
2Ch 9:31 Solomon . . was buried in the city of David 2
12:16 Rehobo'am . . was buried in the city of David; 2
14: 1 they buried him in the city of David; 2
16:14 They buried him in the tomb which he had hewn out 2
21: 1 buried with his fathers in the city of David; 2
20 buried him in the city of David 2
22: 9 They buried him, for they said 2
24:16 buried him in the city of David among the kings 2
25 he died; and they buried him in the city of David 2
25 they did not bury him in the tombs of the kings. 2
25:28 buried with his fathers in the city of David. 2
26:23 buried him with his fathers in the burial field 2
27: 9 they buried him in the city of David; 2
28:27 buried him in the city, in Jerusalem 2
32:33 buried him in the ascent of the tombs 2
33:20 they buried him in his house; 2
35:24 died, and was buried in the tombs of his fathers. 2
Job 27:15 Those who survive him the pestilence buries 2
Ps 79: 3 there was none to bury them. 2
Prv 19:24 The sluggard buries his hand in the dish 1
26:15 The sluggard buries his hand in the dish; 1
Ecc 8:10 Then I saw the wicked buried; 2
Jer 7:32 for they will bury in Topheth 2
8: 2 and they shall not be gathered or buried; 2
14:16 victims of famine and sword, with none to bury 2
16: 4 shall not be lamented, nor shall they be buried; 2
6 they shall not be buried, and no one shall lament 2
19:11 Men shall bury in Topheth 2
11 because there will be no place else to bury. 2
20: 6 there you shall die, and there you shall be buried 2
22:19 With the burial of an ass he shall be buried 2
25:33 They shall not be lamented, or gathered, or buried; 2
Ezk 29: 5 you shall fall . . and not be gathered and buried. 2
39:11 there Gog and all his multitude will be buried; 2
12 the house of Israel will be burying them 2
13 All the people of the land will bury them; 2
14 bury those remaining upon the face of the land 2
15 till the buriers have buried it 2
Hos 9: 6 Memphis shall bury them. 2
Mat 8:21 Lord, let me first go and bury my father. 4
22 and leave the dead to bury their own dead. 4
14:12 took the body and buried it 4
27: 7 the potter's field, to bury strangers in. 8
Mrk 14: 8 anointed my body beforehand for burying. 3
Lke 9:59 he said, "Lord, let me first go and bury my father. 4
60 Leave the dead to bury their own dead 4
16:22 The rich man also died and was buried; 4
Act 2:29 he both died and was buried 4
5: 6 and carried him out and buried him. 4
9 the feet of those that have buried your husband 4
10 they carried her out and buried her 4
8: 2 Devout men buried Stephen 6
Rom 6: 4 We were buried therefore with him by baptism 7
1Co 15: 4 that he was buried 4
Col 2:12 you were buried with him in baptism 7
1Es 1:31 was buried in the tomb of his fathers. 4
Tob 1:17 I would bury him. 4
18 I buried them secretly 4
19 I was burying them 4
2: 7 I went and dug a grave and buried the body. 4
8 here he is burying the dead again! 4
9 On the same night I returned from burying him 4
4: 3 My son, when I die, bury me 4
4 bury her beside me in the same grave. 4
6:14 they have no other son to bury them. 4
8:12 let us bury him without any one knowing about it. 4
12:12 when you buried the dead 4
14: 6 will bury their idols. 5
10 Bury me properly, and your mother with me 4
12 when Anna died he buried her with his father. 4
Jdt 8: 3 they buried him with his fathers in the field 4
16:23 they buried her in the cave of her husband 4
Wis 18:12 the living were not sufficient even to bury them 4
Sir 44:14 Their bodies were buried in peace 4
1Mc 2:70 was buried in the tomb of his fathers at Modein. 4
7:17 there was none to bury them. 4
9:19 buried him in the tomb of their fathers at Modein 4
13:23 he killed Jonathan, and he was buried there. 4
25 buried him in Modein, the city of his fathers. 4
2Mc 9:15 whom he had not considered worth burying 8
4Mc 16:11 shall I have any of my sons to bury me. 4

burying place 1. קֶבֶר 2. קְבוּרָה
Gen 23: 4 property among you for a burying place 1
9 as a possession for a burying place. 1
20 possession for a burying place by the Hittites. 1
47:30 out of Egypt and bury me in their burying place. 2
49:30 bought . . to possess as a burying place. 1
50:13 bought . . to possess as a burying place. 1

bush 1. סְנֶה 2. שִׂיחַ 3. βάτος 4. φυτόν 5. rubus
Gen 21:15 she cast the child under one of the bushes. 2

Exd 3: 2 in a flame of fire out of the midst of a bush; 1
2 the bush was burning, yet it was not consumed. 1
3 see this great sight, why the bush is not burnt. 1
4 God called to him out of the bush, "Moses, Moses! 1
Deu 33:16 with the . . favor of him that dwelt in the bush. 1
Job 30: 4 They pick mallow and the leaves of bushes 2
7 Among the bushes they bray; 2
Mrk 12:26 in the passage about the bush 3
Lke 20:37 even Moses showed, in the passage about the bush 3
Act 7:30 in a flame of fire in a bush. 3
35 the angel that appeared to him in the bush. 3
2Es 14: 1 behold, a voice came out of a bush opposite me 5
3 Then he said to me, "I revealed myself in a bush 5
1Mc 4:38 they saw bushes sprung up as in a thicket 4
bush *See also* bramble.

thorn bush 1. נַעֲצוּץ 2. *ῥάμνος*
Isa 7:19 on all the thornbushes, and on all the pastures. 1
LJr 1:71 like a thorn bush in a garden 2

bushel 1. *ἀρτάβη* 2. *μόδιος*
Mat 5:15 lamp and put it under a bushel, but on a stand 2
Mrk 4:21 brought in to be put under a bushel, or under a bed 2
Lke 11:33 puts it in a cellar or under a bushel, but on a stand 2
Bel 1: 3 they spent on it twelve bushels of fine flour 1

business 1. דָּבָר 2. מְלָאכָה 3. מַעֲשֶׂה 4. עִנְיָן 5. *ἐμπορία* 6. *ἐργασία* 7. *κάθημαι* 8. *πρᾶγμα* 9. *πρᾶξις* 10. *χρεία*
Deu 24: 5 he shall not . . be charged with any business; 1
Jos 2:14 If you do not tell this business of ours 1
20 But if you tell this business of ours 1
Jdg 18: 3 doing in this place? What is your business here? *
1Sm 21: 8 because the king's business required haste. 1
25: 2 a man in Ma'on, whose business was in Carmel. 3
Est 3: 9 of those who have charge of the king's business 2
Ps 107:23 doing business on the great waters; 2
Ecc 1:13 it is an unhappy business that God has given 4
3:10 I have seen the business that God has given 4
4: 8 This also is vanity and an unhappy business. 4
5: 3 For a dream comes with much business 4
8:16 and to see the business that is done on earth 4
Dan 8:27 then I rose and went about the king's business; 2
Mat 22: 5 went off, one to his farm, another to his business 5
Joh 2:14 and the money-changers at their business. 7
Act 19:24 brought no little business to the craftsmen. 6
25 Men . . from this business we have our wealth. 6
Sir 38:24 he who has little business may become wise. 9
2Mc 4:23 to complete the records of essential business. 8
15: 5 to take up arms and finish the king's business. 10
business *See also* conduct.

business associate 1. *συμπραγματεύομαι*
3Mc 3:10 their neighbors and friends and business associates 1

do business 1. mercor
2Es 16:42 let him that does business be like one 1

busy 1. עלל 2. ענה 3. עשה 4. רוץ 5. *ἀναστρέφω* 6. *εἰμί* 7. *ἐν χερσὶν ἔχω*
1Kg 20:40 as your servant was busy . . he was gone. 3
2Ch 35:14 priests the sons of Aaron . . busied in offering *
Ps 141: 4 busy myself with wicked deeds in company 1
Ecc 1:13 God has given to the sons of men to be busy with. 2
3:10 God has given to . . men to be busy with. 2
Hag 1: 9 you busy yourselves each with his own house. 4
Wis 19: 3 while they were still busy at mourning 7
Sir 8: 8 busy yourself with their maxims 5
11:10 My son, do not busy yourself with many matters 6

busybody 1. *περιεργάζομαι* 2. *περίεργος*
2Th 3:11 mere busybodies, not doing any work. 1
1Ti 5:13 not only idlers but gossips and busybodies 2

butcher 1. *δήμιος*
2Mc 7:29 Do not fear this butcher 1

butler 1. מַשְׁקֶה
Gen 40: 1 after this, the butler of the king of Egypt 1
2 officers, the chief butler and the chief baker 1
5 they both dreamed–the butler and the baker 1
9 the chief butler told his dream to Joseph 1
13 his hand as formerly, when you were his butler. 1
20 and lifted up the head of the chief butler 1
21 He restored the chief butler to his butlership 1
23 Yet the chief butler did not remember Joseph 1
41: 9 Then the chief butler said to Pharaoh 1

butlership 1. מַשְׁקֶה
Gen 40:21 He restored the chief butler to his butlership 1

butt 1. אַחֲרֵי
2Sm 2:23 smote him in the belly with the butt of his spear 1

butter 1. חֶמְאָה
Ps 55:21 His speech was smoother than butter 1

buttock 1. שֵׁת
Isa 20: 4 naked and barefoot, with buttocks uncovered 1

buy 1. בִּמְחִיר בוא 2. כרה 3. לקח 4. מִקְנָה 5. קנה 6. שׁבר 7. קנא (A) 8. *ἀγοράζω* 9. *ἀγορασμός* 10. *κτάομαι* 11. *πρᾶσις* 12. *φέρω* 13. *ὠνέομαι* 14. emo
Gen 17:12 in your house, or bought with your money 4
13 he that is bought with your money 4
23 born in his house or bought with his money 4
27 those bought with money from a foreigner 4
33:19 he bought for 100 pieces of money the . . land 5
39: 1 Pot'i-phar . . bought him from the Ish'maelites 5
42: 3 brothers went down to buy grain in Egypt. 6
5 Thus the sons of Israel came to buy among 6
7 They said, "From the land of Canaan, to buy food. 6
10 No, my lord, but to buy food have your servants 6
43: 2 Go again, buy us a little food. 6
4 with us, we will go down and buy you food; 6
20 my lord, we came down the first time to buy food; 6
22 brought other money down in our hand to buy food. 6
44:25 when our father said, 'Go again, buy us a little food 6
47:14 money . . for the grain which they bought; 6
19 Buy us and our land for food, and we with our land 5
20 Joseph bought all the land of Egypt for Pharaoh; 5
22 Only the land of the priests he did not buy; 5
23 Behold, I have this day bought you and your land 5
49:30 cave . . which Abraham bought with the field 5
50:13 the cave . . which Abraham bought with the field 5
Exd 12:44 every slave that is bought for money may eat of it 4
21: 2 When you buy a Hebrew slave, he shall serve six 5
Lev 22:11 if a priest buys a slave as his property for money 5
25:14 If you . . buy from your neighbor 5
15 years after the jubilee, you shall buy 5
28 remain in the hand of him who bought it 5
30 be made sure in perpetuity to him who bought it 5
44 you may buy male and female slaves from among 5
45 You may also buy from among the strangers 5
50 He shall reckon with him who bought him 5
27:22 If he dedicates . . a field which he has bought 4
24 field shall return to him from whom it was bought 5
Deu 2: 6 buy water of them for money, that you may drink. 2
28:68 male and female slaves, but no man will buy you. 5
Jos 24:32 ground which Jacob bought from the sons of Hamor 5
Rut 4: 4 Buy it in the presence of those sitting here 5
5 The day you buy the field from the hand of Na'omi 5
5 you are also buying Ruth the Moabitess, the widow 5
8 the next of kin said to Bo'az, "Buy it for yourself 5
9 I have bought . . all that belonged to Elim'elech 5
10 Also Ruth . . I have bought to be my wife 5
2Sm 12: 3 but one little ewe lamb, which he had bought. 5
24:21 To buy the threshing floor of you, in order 5
24 king said . . "No, but I will buy it of you for a price; 5
24 David bought the threshing floor and the oxen 5
1Kg 16:24 He bought the hill of Sama'ria from Shemer 5
2Kg 12:12 as well as to buy timber and quarried stone 5
22: 6 as well as buying timber and quarried stone 5
1Ch 21:24 to Ornan, "No, but I will buy it for the full price; 5
2Ch 34:11 to buy quarried stone, and timber for binders 5
Ezr 7:17 with all diligence buy bulls, rams, and lambs 7
Neh 10:31 not buy from them on the sabbath or on a holy day; 3
Prv 17:16 fool have a price in his hand to buy wisdom 5
23:23 Buy truth, and do not sell it; 5
23 buy wisdom, instruction, and understanding. *
31:16 She considers a field and buys it; 3
Ecc 2: 7 I bought male and female slaves 5
Isa 43:24 You have not bought me sweet cane with money 5
55: 1 and he who has no money, come, buy and eat! 6
1 Come, buy wine and milk without money 6
Jer 13: 1 Go and buy a linen waistcloth 5
2 I bought a waistcloth according to the word 5
4 Take the waistcloth which you have bought 5
19: 1 Thus said the LORD, "Go, buy a potter's earthen flask 5
32: 7 to you and say, 'Buy my field which is at An'athoth 5
8 and said to me, 'Buy my field which is at An'athoth 5
8 and redemption is yours; buy it for yourself. 5
9 And I bought the field at An'athoth from Han'amel 5
15 vineyards shall again be bought in this land. 5
25 Buy the field for money and get witnesses 5
43 Fields shall be bought in this land 5
44 Fields shall be bought for money 5
Lam 5: 4 the wood we get must be bought. 1
Hos 3: 2 So I bought her for fifteen shekels of silver 2
Ams 8: 6 that we may buy the poor for silver 5
Zec 11: 5 Those who buy them slay them and go unpunished; 5
Mat 13:44 sells all that he has and buys that field. 8
46 went and sold all that he had and bought it. 8
14:15 into the villages and buy food for themselves. 8
21:12 drove out all who sold and bought in the temple 8
25: 9 go rather to the dealers and buy for yourselves.' 8
10 while they went to buy, the bridegroom came 8
27: 7 and bought with them the potter's field 8
Mrk 6:36 buy themselves something to eat. 8
37 we go and buy 200 denarii worth of bread 8
11:15 those who sold and those who bought in the temple 8
15:46 he bought a linen shroud 8
16: 1 the mother of James, and Salo'me, bought spices 8
Lke 9:13 go and buy food for all these people. 8
14:18 The first said to him, 'I have bought a field 8
19 another said, 'I have bought five yoke of oxen 8
17:28 they ate, they drank, they bought, they sold 8
22:36 who has no sword sell his mantle and buy one. 8
Joh 4: 8 had gone away into the city to buy food. 8
6: 5 How are we to buy bread, so that these people 8
7 200 denarii would not buy enough bread *
13:29 Buy what we need for the feast 8
Act 1:18 bought a field with the reward of his wickedness; 10
7:16 tomb that Abraham had bought for a sum of silver 13
22:28 I bought this citizenship for a large sum. 10
1Co 6:20 you were bought with a price 8
7:23 You were bought with a price 8
30 those who buy as though they had no goods 8
2Pe 2: 1 even denying the Master who bought them 8
Rev 3:18 I counsel you to buy from me gold refined by fire 8
13:17 that no one can buy or sell unless he has the mark 8
18:11 since no one buys their cargo any more 8
2Es 16:41 let him that buys be like one who will lose; 14
Sir 20:12 There is a man who buys much for a little 8
27: 2 sin is wedged in between selling and buying. 9
33:30 because you have bought him with blood. 10
Bar 1:10 buy with the money burnt offerings 8
3:30 Who . . found her, and will buy her for pure gold? 12
LJr 1:25 They are bought at any cost 8
1Mc 12:36 so that its garrison could neither buy nor sell. 8
13:49 to buy and sell 8
2Mc 8:11 inviting them to buy Jewish slaves 9
25 those who had come to buy them as slaves 9
34 who had brought the 1,000 merchants to buy the Jews 11

buy back 1. פדה 2. קנה
Lev 27:27 then he shall buy it back at your valuation 1
Neh 5: 8 We . . have bought back our Jewish brethren 2

buy grain 1. שׁבר
Gen 41:57 all the earth came . . to Joseph to buy grain 1
42: 2 grain in Egypt; go down and buy grain for us there 1

buyer 1. קנה 2. *ἀγοράζω*
Prv 20:14 It is bad, it is bad," says the buyer; 1
Isa 24: 2 as with the buyer, so with the seller; 1
Ezk 7:12 Let not the buyer rejoice, nor the seller mourn 1
Sir 37:11 with a buyer about selling 2

buyer of provisions 1. *ἀγοραστής*
Tob 1:13 I was his buyer of provisions. 1

buzzard 1. דָּאָה
Deu 14:13 buzzard, the kite, after their kinds; 1

bygone 1. רִאשׁוֹן
Job 8: 8 For inquire, I pray you, of bygone ages 1

bypath 1. נְתִיבָה
Jer 18:15 and have gone into bypaths, not the highway 1

bystander 1. *ἵστημι* 2. *ὁ ἐκεῖ* 3. *παρίστημι*
Mat 26:71 she said to the bystanders 2
73 After a little while the bystanders came up 1
27:47 some of the bystanders hearing it said 2
Mrk 14:69 began again to say to the bystanders 3
70 after a little while again the bystanders said 3
15:35 some of the bystanders hearing it said, "Behold 3

byway 1. אֹרַח עֲקַלְקַלָּה
Jdg 5: 6 ceased and travelers kept to the byways. 1

byword 1. חֶרְפָּה 2. מִלָּה 3. מָשָׁל 4. משל 5. שֵׁם 6. שְׁמוּעָה 7. שְׁנִינָה 8. *λαλιά* 9. *παραβολή*
Deu 28:37 you shall become a horror, a proverb, and a byword 7
1Kg 9: 7 Israel will become a proverb and a byword 7
2Ch 7:20 make it a proverb and a byword among all peoples. 7
Job 17: 6 He has made me a byword of the peoples 4
30: 9 now I have become their song, I am a byword to them. 2
Ps 44:14 Thou hast made us a byword among the nations 3
69:11 I became a byword to them. 3
Jer 24: 9 to be a reproach, a byword, a taunt, and a curse 3
Ezk 14: 8 I will make him a sign and a byword and cut him off 3
16:56 Was not your sister Sodom a byword in your mouth 6
23:10 she became a byword among women 5
Dan 9:16 become a byword among all who are round about us. 1
Jol 2:17 heritage a reproach, a byword among the nations. 4
Tob 3: 4 thou madest us a byword of reproach 9
Wis 5: 4 held in derision and made a byword of reproach 9
Sir 42:11 a byword in the city 8

byword of cursing 1. קְלָלָה
Zec 8:13 as you have been a byword of cursing 1

C

cage 1. סוּגַר 2. *κάρταλλος*
Ezk 19: 9 With hooks they put him in a cage, and brought him 1
Sir 11:30 Like a decoy partridge in a cage 2

cake 1. אֲשִׁישָׁה 2. דְּבֵלָה 3. חַלָּה 4. חֹרִי 5. כַּוָּן
6. לְבִבָה 7. לָשָׁד 8. נִקּוּד 9. עֻגָה 10. צְלִיל 11. *μάζας*
Gen 18: 6 measures of fine meal, knead it, and make cakes. 9
40:16 there were three cake baskets on my head 4
Exd 12:39 they baked unleavened cakes of the dough 9
29: 2 unleavened cakes mixed with oil, and unleavened 3
23 one loaf of bread, and one cake of bread with oil 3
Lev 2: 4 it shall be unleavened cakes of fine flour 3
7:12 offer with the thank offering unleavened cakes 3
12 cakes of fine flour well mixed with oil 3
13 his offering with cakes of leavened bread 3
14 of such he shall offer one cake from each offering •
8:26 he took one unleavened cake, and one cake of bread 3
26 took . . one cake of bread with oil, and one wafer 3
24: 5 you shall take fine flour, and bake twelve cakes 3
5 two tenths of an ephah shall be in each cake 3
Num 6:15 cakes of fine flour mixed with oil 3
19 take . . one unleavened cake out of the basket 3
11: 8 people . . boiled it in pots, and made cakes of it; 9
8 taste of it was like the taste of cakes baked 7
15:20 meal you shall present a cake as an offering; 3
Jdg 7:13 lo, a cake of barley bread tumbled into the camp 10
2Sm 6:19 distributed . . to each a cake of bread, a portion 3
13: 6 Tamar come and make a couple of cakes in my sight 6
8 made cakes in his sight, and baked the cakes. 6
10 And Tamar took the cakes she had made 6
1Kg 14: 3 Take with you ten loaves, some cakes, and a jar 8
17:13 first make me a little cake of it and bring it to me 9
19: 6 there was at his head a cake baked on hot stones 9
2Kg 20: 7 Bring a cake of figs. And let them take and lay it 2
Isa 38:21 Now Isaiah had said, "Let them take a cake of figs 2
Jer 7:18 knead dough, to make cakes for the queen of heaven; 5
44:19 we made cakes for her bearing her image 5
Ezk 4:12 you shall eat it as a barley cake 9
Hos 3: 1 they turn to other gods and love cakes of raisins. 1
7: 8 E'phraim is a cake not turned. 9
Bel 1:27 made cakes, which he fed to the dragon 11
cake *See also* make.

flat cake 1. חֲבִתִּים
1Ch 9:31 was in charge of making the flat cakes. 1

cake of dried fruit 1. *παλάθη*
Jdt 10: 5 a cake of dried fruit and fine bread 1

cake of figs 1. דְּבֵלָה
1Sm 25:18 clusters of raisins, and 200 cakes of figs 1
30:12 they gave him a piece of a cake of figs 1
1Ch 12:40 abundant provisions of meal, cakes of figs 1

cake of raisins 1. אֲשִׁישָׁה
2Sm 6:19 to each a cake of bread . . and a cake of raisins. 1
1Ch 16: 3 of bread, a portion of meat, and a cake of raisins. 1

unleavened cake 1. מַצָּה
Jos 5:11 they ate . . unleavened cakes and parched grain. 1
Jdg 6:19 a kid, and unleavened cakes from an ephah of flour; 1
20 God said . . "Take the meat and the unleavened cakes 1
21 and touched the meat and the unleavened cakes; 1
21 fire . . consumed . . the unleavened cakes; 1

calamity 1. אָוֶן 2. אֵיד 3. בֶּהָלָה 4. הַוָּה 5. חֲתַת
6. רַע 7. רָעָה 8. *ἐπαγωγή* 9. *κακός* 10. *πληγή*
11. *στενοχωρία* 12. *συμφορά* 13. malus
Deu 29:21 LORD would single him out . . for calamity 7
32:35 day of their calamity is at hand, and their doom 2
1Sm 10:19 your God, who saves you from all your calamities 6
2Sm 22:19 They came upon me in the day of my calamity; 2
Est 8: 6 to see the calamity that is coming to my people? 7
Job 6: 2 all my calamity laid in the balances! 4
21 you see my calamity, and are afraid. 5
30 Cannot my taste discern calamity? 4
9:23 he mocks at the calamity of the innocent. •
18:12 calamity is ready for his stumbling. 2
21:17 That their calamity comes upon them? 2
30 the wicked man is spared in the day of calamity 2
30:13 They break up my path, they promote my calamity; 4
31: 3 Does not calamity befall the unrighteous 2
23 For I was in terror of calamity from God 2
Ps 18:18 They came upon me in the day of my calamity; 2
35:26 altogether who rejoice at my calamity! 7
Prv 1:26 I also will laugh at your calamity; 2
27 when . . your calamity comes like a whirlwind 2
6:15 therefore calamity will come upon him suddenly; 2
17: 5 who is glad at calamity will not go unpunished. 2
20 one with a perverse tongue falls into calamity. 7
22: 8 He who sows injustice will reap calamity 1
24:16 but the wicked are overthrown by calamity. 7
27:10 brother's house in the day of your calamity. 2
28:14 hardens his heart will fall into calamity. 7
Isa 57: 1 For the righteous man is taken away from calamity 7
65:23 not labor in vain, or bear children for calamity; 3
Jer 18:17 my back, not my face, in the day of their calamity. 2
46:21 for the day of their calamity has come upon them 2
48:16 The calamity of Moab is near at hand 2
49: 8 For I will bring the calamity of Esau upon him 2
32 I will bring their calamity from every side 2
Ezk 35: 5 of the sword at the time of their calamity 2
Dan 9:12 by bringing upon us a great calamity; 7
13 all this calamity has come upon us, yet we have not 7
14 Therefore the LORD has kept ready the calamity 7
Obd 1:13 the gate of my people in the day of his calamity; 2
13 over his disaster in the day of his calamity; 2
13 have looted his goods in the day of his calamity. 2
2Co 6: 4 in afflictions, hardships, calamities 11
12:10 hardships, persecutions, and calamities 11
2Es 15:27 now calamities have come upon you the whole earth 13
16: 5 Calamities have been sent upon you 13
8 The Lord God sends calamities 13
14 Behold, calamities are sent forth 13
16 the calamities that are sent upon the earth 13
18 the beginning of calamities 13
18 when the calamities come? 13
21 then the calamities shall spring up on the earth 13
37 Behold, the calamities draw near 13
39 the calamities will not delay in coming forth 13
40 in the midst of the calamities be like strangers 13
AEs 16: 5 have been involved in irremediable calamities 12
Sir 2: 2 do not be hasty in time of calamity. 8
5: 8 it will not benefit you in the day of calamity. 8
12:17 If calamity befalls you, you will find him there 9
23:11 his house will be filled with calamities. 8
38:19 In calamity sorrow continues 8
40: 9 calamities, famine and affliction and plague. 8
Bar 1:20 there have clung to us the calamities 9
2: 7 calamities with which the Lord threatened us 9
9 And the Lord has kept the calamities ready 9
3: 4 so that calamities have clung to us. 9
4:18 For he who brought these calamities upon you 9
29 For he who brought these calamities upon you 9
LJr 1:48 For when war or calamity comes upon them 9
49 they cannot save themselves from war or calamity? 9
1Mc 13:32 he brought great calamity upon the land. 10
2Mc 6:12 not to be depressed by such calamities 12
16 Though he disciplines us with calamities 12
10:10 the principal calamities of the wars. 9
14:14 the misfortunes and calamities of the Jews 12
calamity *See also* bring.

calamity happen 1. *κακόω*
Sir 11:24 what calamity could happen to me in the future? 1

calamus 1. קָנֶה
Sng 4:14 nard and saffron, calamus and cinnamon 1
Ezk 27:19 wrought iron, cassia, and calamus were bartered 1

caldron 1. דּוּד 2. סִיר 3. קַלַּחַת 4. *λέβης*
1Sm 2:14 thrust it into the pan, or kettle, or caldron, or pot; 3
2Ch 35:13 boiled the holy offerings in pots, in caldrons 1
Ezk 11: 3 this city is the caldron, and we are the flesh. 2
7 they are the flesh, and this city is the caldron; 2
11 This city shall not be your caldron 2
Mic 3: 3 like meat in a kettle, like flesh in a caldron. 3
1Es 1:12 in brass pots and caldrons, with a pleasing odor 4
2Mc 7: 3 and gave orders that pans and caldrons be heated. 4
4Mc 8:13 rack and hooks and catapults and caldrons 4
12: 1 When he also, thrown into the caldron, had died 4
18:20 quenched fire with fire in his cruel caldrons 4

calf 1. בֵּן 2. בֶּן בָּקָר 3. עֵגֶל 4. עֶגְלָה 5. *δάμαλις*
6. *μόσχος*
Gen 18: 7 Abraham ran to the herd, and took a calf 2
8 took . . the calf which he had prepared 2
Exd 32: 4 fashioned it . . and made a molten calf; 3
8 they have made for themselves a molten calf 3
19 and saw the calf and the dancing, Moses' anger 3
20 he took the calf which they had made, and burnt it 3
24 into the fire, and there came out this calf. 3
35 because they made the calf which Aaron made. 3
Lev 9: 2 Take a bull calf for a sin offering, and a ram 3
3 Take . . a calf and a lamb, both a year old 3
8 Aaron . . killed the calf of the sin offering 3
Deu 9:16 you had made yourselves a molten calf; 3
21 sinful thing, the calf which you had made 3
1Sm 6: 7 yoke the cows . . but take their calves home 1
10 two milch cows . . and shut up their calves at home 1
14:32 and took sheep and oxen and calves, and slew them 2
28:24 Now the woman had a fatted calf in the house 3
1Kg 10:19 at the back of the throne was a calf's head 3
12:28 king took counsel, and made two calves of gold. 3
32 sacrificing to the calves that he had made. 3
2Kg 10:29 the golden calves that were in Bethel, and in Dan. 3
17:16 made for themselves molten images of two calves; 3
2Ch 11:15 appointed his own priests . . for the calves 3
13: 8 because you . . have with you the golden calves 3
Neh 9:18 Even when they had made . . a molten calf and said 3
Job 21:10 their cow calves, and does not cast her calf. •
Ps 29: 6 He makes Lebanon to skip like a calf 3
68:30 herd of bulls with the calves of the peoples. 3
106:19 made a calf in Horeb and worshiped 3
Isa 11: 6 the calf and the lion and the fatling together 3
27:10 there the calf grazes, there he lies down 3
Jer 14: 5 hind in the field forsakes her newborn calf •
31:18 I was chastened, like an untrained calf; 3
34:18 I will make like the calf which they cut in two 3
19 who passed between the parts of the calf; 3
46:21 soldiers in her midst are like fatted calves; 3
Ezk 1: 7 of their feet were like the sole of a calf's foot 3
Hos 8: 5 I have spurned your calf, O Sama'ria. 3
6 The calf of Sama'ria shall be broken to pieces. 3
10: 5 tremble for the calf of Beth-a'ven. 4
13: 2 Sacrifice to these, they say. Men kiss calves! 3
Ams 6: 4 eat . . and calves from the midst of the stall; 3
Mic 6: 6 with burnt offerings, with calves a year old? 3
Mal 4: 2 go forth leaping like calves from the stall. 3
Lke 15:23 bring the fatted calf and kill it 6
27 your father has killed the fatted calf 6
30 you killed for him the fatted calf!' 6
Heb 9:12 taking not the blood of goats and calves 6
19 he took the blood of calves and goats 6
1Es 1: 7 30,000 lambs and kids, and 3,000 calves 6
8 for the passover 2,600 sheep and 300 calves. 6
9 5,000 sheep and 700 calves. 6
Tob 1: 5 All the tribes . . used to sacrifice to the calf Baal 5
calf *See also* fat, make.

call 1. אמר 2. זעק 3. צעק 4. קרא 5. קרא לְ
6. קרא שֵׁם 7. שׂוּם 8. שׁוּב 9. שׁוע 10. שֵׁם 11. קרא (A)
12. *αἰτέω* 13. *ἀναγορεύω* 14. *εἶπον* 15. *εἰσκαλέομαι*
16. *ἐπικαλέω* 17. *ἐπίκλησις* 18. *ἐπιλέγω*

19. ἐπισυνάγω 20. ἐπονομάζω 21. καλέω 22. κλῆσις
23. κλητέος 24. κλητός 25. κράζω 26. λέγω
27. μετακαλέω 28. ὄνομα 29. ὄνομα ἔχω 30. ὀνομάζω
31. παρακαλέω 32. προσαγορεύω 33. προσκαλέω
34. πρόσκλησις 35. προσονομάζω 36. προσφωνέω
37. φωνέω 38. φωνή 39. χρηματίζω 40. ὧδε
41. advoco 42. invoco 43. nomino 44. testor 45. voco

Gen 1: 5 God called the light Day 4
5 the light Day, and the darkness he called Night 4
8 God called the firmament Heaven. 4
10 God called the dry land Earth 4
10 waters . . gathered together he called Seas 4
2:19 brought . . to the man to see what he would call them; 4
19 whatever the man called every living creature 4
23 flesh of my flesh; she shall be called Woman 4
3: 9 the LORD God called to the man 4
20 The man called his wife's name Eve 4
4:17 built a city, and called the name of the city 4
25 she bore a son and called his name Seth 4
26 was born, and he called his name Enosh. 4
26 time men began to call upon the name of the LORD. 4
5:29 called his name Noah, saying, "Out of the ground 4
11: 9 Therefore its name was called Ba'bel 4
12: 8 to the LORD and called on the name of the LORD. 4
18 Pharaoh called Abram, and said, "What is this 4
13: 4 there Abram called on the name of the LORD. 4
16:11 you shall call his name Ish'mael; 4
13 she called the name of the LORD who spoke to her 4
14 Therefore the well was called Beer-la'hai-roi; 4
15 Hagar bore Abram a son; and Abram called the name 4
17:15 you shall not call her name Sar'ai, but Sarah 4
19 and you shall call his name Isaac. 4
19: 5 they called to Lot, "Where are the men who came 4
22 Therefore the name of the city was called Zo'ar. 4
37 first-born bore a son, and called his name Moab; 4
38 bore a son, and called his name Ben-ammi; 4
20: 8 Abim'elech . . called all his servants 4
9 Then Abim'elech called Abraham, and said to him 4
21: 3 Abraham called the name of his son who was born 4
17 and the angel of God called to Hagar from heaven 4
31 Therefore that place was called Beer-sheba; 4
33 and called there on the name of the LORD 4
22:11 the angel of the LORD called to him from heaven 4
14 Abraham called the name of that place 4
15 the angel of the LORD called to Abraham 4
24:57 They said, "We will call the maiden, and ask her. 4
58 they called Rebekah, and said to her 4
25:25 like a hairy mantle; so they called his name Esau. 4
26 so his name was called Jacob. 4
30 Therefore his name was called Edom. 4
26: 9 Abim'elech called Isaac, and said 4
20 he called the name of the well Esek 4
21 he called its name Sitnah. 4
22 did not quarrel; so he called its name Reho'both 4
25 and called upon the name of the LORD 4
33 He called it Shibah; therefore the name 4
27: 1 called Esau his older son, and said to him 4
42 she sent and called Jacob her younger son 4
28: 1 Then Isaac called Jacob and blessed him 4
19 He called the name of that place Bethel; 4
29:32 she called his name Reuben; for she said 4
33 this son also"; and she called his name Simeon. 4
34 therefore his name was called Levi. 4
35 therefore she called his name Judah; 4
30: 6 given me a son"; therefore she called his name Dan 4
8 have prevailed"; so she called his name Naph'tali. 4
11 Good fortune!" so she called his name Gad. 4
13 will call me happy"; so she called his name Asher. 4
18 she called his name Is'sachar. 4
20 she called his name Zeb'ulun. 4
21 bore a daughter, and called her name Dinah. 4
24 she called his name Joseph 4
31: 4 Jacob sent and called Rachel and Leah 4
47 Laban called it Je'gar-sahadu'tha: but Jacob 4
47 Je'gar-sahadu'tha: but Jacob called it Galeed. 4
54 on the mountain and called his kinsmen to eat 4
32: 2 he called the name of that place Mahana'im. 4
28 he said, "Your name shall no more be called Jacob 1
30 Jacob called the name of the place Peni'el 4
33:17 the name of the place is called Succoth. 4
20 There he erected an altar and called it 4
35: 7 built an altar, and called the place El-bethel 4
8 so the name of it was called Al'lon-bacuth. 4
10 no longer shall your name be called Jacob 4
10 his name was called Israel. 4
15 Jacob called the name of the place where God 4
18 she called his name Ben-o'ni; 4
18 Ben-o'ni; but his father called his name Benjamin 4
38: 3 bore a son, and he called his name Er. 4
4 bore a son, and she called his name Onan. 4
5 bore a son, and she called his name Shelah. 4
29 Therefore his name was called Perez. 4
30 his hand; and his name was called Zerah. 4
39:14 she called to the men of her household and said 4
41: 8 and he sent and called for all the magicians 4
14 Then Pharaoh sent and called Joseph 4
45 Pharaoh called Joseph's name Zaph'enath-pane'ah 4
51 Joseph called the name of the first-born 4
52 The name of the second he called E'phraim 4
46:33 When Pharaoh calls you, and says, 4
47:29 Israel must die, he called his son Joseph 4
48: 6 they shall be called by the name of their 4
49: 1 Jacob called his sons, and said, "Gather 4
Exd 1:18 the king of Egypt called the midwives, and said 4
2: 7 Shall I go and call you a nurse from the Hebrew 4
8 So the girl went and called the child's mother. 4
20 you left the man? Call him, that he may eat bread. 4
22 She bore a son, and he called his name Gershom; 4
3: 4 God called to him out of the bush, "Moses, Moses! 4
8: 8 Then Pharaoh called Moses and Aaron, and said 4
25 Then Pharaoh called Moses and Aaron, and said, "Go 4
9:27 Then Pharaoh sent, and called Moses and Aaron 4
10:16 Then Pharaoh called Moses and Aaron in haste 4
24 Pharaoh called Moses, and said, "Go, serve the LORD; 4
12:21 Then Moses called all the elders of Israel 4
16:31 Now the house of Israel called its name manna; 4
17: 7 he called the name of the place Massah 4
15 Moses built an altar and called the name of it 4
19: 3 Moses went up to God, and the LORD called to him 4
7 So Moses came and called the elders of the people 4
20 the LORD called Moses to the top of the mountain 4
24:16 he called to Moses out of the midst of the cloud. 4
31: 2 See, I have called by name Bez'alel and son of Uri 4
33: 7 and he called it the tent of meeting. 4
34:31 Moses called to them; and Aaron and all 4
35:30 See, the LORD has called by name Bez'alel 4
36: 2 Moses called Bez'alel and Oho'liab and every able 4
Lev 1: 1 The LORD called Moses, and spoke to him 4
9: 1 On the eighth day Moses called Aaron and his sons 4
10: 4 Moses called Mish'a-el and Elza'phan 4
Num11: 3 name of that place was called Tab'erah 4
34 name of that place was called Kib'roth-hatta'avah 4
12: 5 LORD came down . . and called Aaron and Miriam; 4
13:16 Moses called Hoshe'a the son of Nun Joshua. 4
24 That place was called the Valley of Eshcol 4
16:12 Moses sent to call Dathan and Abi'ram 4
21: 3 so the name of the place was called Hormah. 4
22: 5 sent messengers to Balaam . . to call him, saying 4
20 If the men have come to call you, rise, go with them; 4
37 Did I not send to you to call you? 4
24:10 I called you to curse my enemies, and behold 4
32:41 their villages, and called them Hav'voth-ja'ir. 4
42 took Kenath . . and called it Nobah, 4
Deu 2:11 as Reph'idim, but the Moabites call them Emim. 4
20 but the Ammonites call them Zamzum'mim 4
3: 9 (the Sido'nians call Hermon Si'rion, while 4
9 Si'rion, while the Amorites call it Senir) 4
13 whole of that Bashan is called the land of Reph'aim. 4
14 Ja'ir . . called the villages after his own name 4
4: 7 as the LORD . . is to us, whenever we call upon him? 4
25: 8 elders of his city shall call him, and speak to him 4
10 the name of his house shall be called in Israel 4
28:10 see that you are called by the name of the LORD; 4
30: 1 call them to mind among all the nations 8
31:14 call Joshua, and present yourselves in the tent 4
33:19 They shall call peoples to their mountain; 4
Jos 4: 4 Joshua called the twelve men from the people 4
5: 9 name of this place is called Gilgal to this day. 4
6: 6 Joshua the son of Nun called the priests and said 4
7:26 name of that place is called the Valley of Achor. 4
19:47 and settled in it, calling Leshem, Dan 4
22:34 The Reubenites and . . called the altar Witness; 4
Jdg 1:17 So the name of the city was called Hormah. 4
26 Hittites and built a city, and called its name Luz; 4
2: 5 And they called the name of that place Bochim; 4
6:24 Gideon built . . and called it, The LORD is peace. 4
32 on that day he was called Jerubba'al, that is to say 4
8: 1 done to us, not to call us when you went to fight 4
31 bore him a son, and he called his name Abim'elech. 7
9:54 Then he called hastily to the young man 4
10: 4 30 cities, called Hav'voth-ja'ir to this day 4
17 Then the Ammonites were called to arms 3
12: 1 The men of E'phraim were called to arms 3
1 Why . . and did not call us to go with you? 4
2 and when I called you, you did not deliver me 2
13:24 the woman bore a son, and called his name Samson; 4
15:17 and that place was called Ra'math-le'hi. 4
18 very thirsty, and he called on the LORD and said 4
19 Therefore the name of it was called En-hakkor'e; 4
16:18 she sent and called the lords of the Philistines 4
19 she called a man, and had him shave off the seven 4
25 Call Samson, that he may make sport for us. 4
25 they called Samson out of the prison 4
28 Samson called to the LORD and said, "O Lord GOD 4
18:12 that place is called Ma'haneh-dan to this day; 4
22 the men . . were called out, and they overtook 2
Rut 1:20 Do not call me Na'omi, call me Mara 5
20 Do not call me Na'omi, call me Mara 5
21 Why call me Na'omi, when the LORD has afflicted me 5
1Sm 1:20 and bore a son, and she called his name Samuel 4
3: 4 Then the LORD called, "Samuel! Samuel! 4
5 ran to Eli, and said, "Here I am, for you called me. 4
5 But he said, "I did not call; lie down again. 4
6 the LORD called again, "Samuel!" And Samuel arose 4
6 went to Eli, and said, "Here I am, for you called me. 4
6 But he said, "I did not call, my son; lie down again. 4
8 And the LORD called Samuel again the third time. 4
8 went to Eli, and said, "Here I am, for you called me. 4
8 Eli perceived that the LORD was calling the boy. 5
9 Go, lie down; and if he calls you, you shall say 4
10 the LORD came . . calling as at other times 4
16 But Eli called Samuel and said, "Samuel, my son. 4
6: 2 the Philistines called for the priests 4
7:12 took a stone . . and called its name Ebene'zer; 4
9: 9 who is now . . prophet was formerly called a seer. •
9 who is now . . prophet was formerly called a seer. 4
26 Samuel called to Saul upon the roof 4
12:17 I will call upon the LORD, that he may send thunder 4
18 Samuel called upon the LORD, and the LORD sent 4
16: 8 Jesse called Abin'adab, and made him pass before 4
19: 7 Jonathan called David, and . . showed him all 4
20:37 Jonathan called after the lad and said 4
38 Jonathan called after the lad, "Hurry, make haste 4
23:28 therefore that place was called the Rock of Escape 4
24: 8 David also arose . . and called after Saul, "My lord 4
26:14 David called to the army, and to Abner . . saying 4
14 Abner answered, "Who are you that calls to the king? 4
29: 6 Then A'chish called David and said to him 4
2Sm 1: 7 when he looked . . he saw me, and called to me. 4
15 Then David called one of the young men and said, "Go 4
2:16 that place was called Hel'kath-hazzu'rim 4
26 Abner called to Jo'ab, "Shall the sword devour 4
5: 9 the stronghold, and called it the city of David. 4
20 the name of that place is called Ba'al-pera'zim. 4
6: 2 ark of God, which is called by the name of the LORD 4
8 and that place is called Pe'rez-uz'zah, to this day. 4
9: 2 whose name was Ziba, and they called him to David; 4
9 Then the king called Ziba, Saul's servant 4
12:24 and she bore a son, and he called his name Solomon. 4
25 he called his name Jedidi'ah, because of the LORD. 4
28 lest I take the city, and it be called by my name. 4
13:17 He called the young man who served him and said 4
15: 2 Ab'salom would call to him, and say, "From what city 4
17: 5 Call Hushai the Archite also, and let us hear 4
18:18 he called the pillar after his own name 4
18 and it is called Ab'salom's monument to this day. 4
26 and the watchman called to the gate and said 4
20:16 Then a wise woman called from the city, "Hear! Hear! 4
21 a man of . . E'phraim, called Sheba the son of Bichri 10
21: 2 the king called the Gib'eonites. 4
22: 7 I called upon the LORD; to my God I called. 4
1Kg 1:28 King David answered, "Call Bathshe'ba to me." So she 4
32 Call to me Zadok the priest, Nathan the prophet 4
7:21 pillar on the south and called its name Jachin; 4
21 the pillar on the north and called its name Bo'az. 4
8:43 all for which the foreigner calls to thee; 4
43 house which I have built is called by thy name. 4
52 giving ear to them whenever they call to thee. 4
9:13 So they are called the land of Cabul to this day. 4
12: 3 they sent and called him; and Jerobo'am . . came 4
20 they sent and called him to the assembly 4
16:24 and called the name of the city . . Sama'ria 4
17:10 he called to her and said, "Bring me a little water 4
11 as she was going . . he called to her and said 4
18: 3 Ahab called Obadi'ah, who was over the household. 4
24 you call on the name of your god 4
24 I will call on the name of the LORD; 4
25 call on the name of your god, but put no fire to it. 4
26 they prepared it, and called on the name of Ba'al 4
20: 7 the king of Israel called all the elders 4
2Kg 3:10 The LORD has called these three kings to give 4
13 No; it is the LORD who has called these three kings 4
4:12 he said to . . his servant, "Call this Shu'nammite. 4
12 When he had called her, she stood before him. 4
15 He said, "Call her." And . . she stood in the doorway. 4
15 when he had called her, she stood in the doorway. 4
22 she called to her husband, and said, "Send me one 4
36 summoned Geha'zi and said, "Call this Shu'nammite. 4
36 and said, "Call this Shu'nammite." So he called her. 4
5:11 come . . and stand, and call on the name of the LORD 4
6:11 he called his servants and said to them 4
7:10 So they came and called to the gatekeepers 4
8: 1 the LORD has called for a famine, and it will come 4
9: 1 Eli'sha . . called one of the sons of the prophets 4
10:19 Now therefore call to me all the prophets of Ba'al 4
14: 7 and took Sela by storm, and called it Jok'the-el 6
18: 4 the bronze serpent . . it was called Nehush'tan. 4
18 when they called for the king, there came out 4
1Ch 4: 9 and his mother called his name Jabez, saying 4
10 Jabez called on the God of Israel, saying 4
7:16 Ma'acah . . she called his name Peresh; 4
23 E'phraim . . called his name Beri'ah 4
11: 7 therefore it was called the city of David. 4
13: 6 which is called by the name of the LORD 4
11 and that place is called Pe'rez-uz'za to this day. 4
14:11 the name of that place is called Ba'al-pera'zim. 4
16: 8 O give thanks to the LORD, call on his name 4
21:26 called upon the LORD, and he answered him 4
22: 6 called for Solomon his son, and charged him 4
2Ch 3:17 pillars . . that on the south he called Jachin 4
6:33 all for which the foreigner calls to thee; 4
33 house which I have built is called by thy name. 4
7:14 if my people who are called by my name humble 4
10: 3 they sent and called him; 4
20:26 been called the Valley of Bera'cah to this day. 4

Ezr 2:61 Barzil'lai . . and was called by their name 4
Neh 5:12 I called the priests, and took an oath of them to do 4
7:63 Barzil'lai (who . . was called by their name). 4
Est 4: 5 Esther called for Hathach . . and ordered him 4
11 goes to the king . . without being called 4
11 I have not been called to come in to the king these 4
9:26 they called these days Purim, after the term Pur. 4
Job 5: 1 Call now; is there any one who will answer you? 4
12: 4 I, who called upon God and he answered me 4
13:22 Then call, and I will answer; 4
14:15 Thou wouldest call, and I would answer thee; 4
19:16 I call to my servant, but he gives me no answer; 4
31:24 gold my trust, or called fine gold my confidence; 1
42:14 he called the name of the first Jemi'mah; 4
Ps 4: 1 Answer me when I call, O God of my right! 4
3 the LORD hears when I call to him. 4
18: 6 In my distress I called upon the LORD; 4
20: 9 O LORD; answer us when we call. 4
28: 1 To thee, O LORD, I call; my rock, be not deaf to me 4
31:17 Let me not be put to shame, O LORD, for I call on thee; 4
42: 7 Deep calls to deep at the thunder of thy 4
50: 4 He calls to the heavens above and to the earth 4
55:16 I call upon God; and the LORD will save me. 4
56: 9 will be turned back in the day when I call. 4
61: 2 I call to thee, when my heart is faint. 4
63: 4 I will lift up my hands and call on thy name. •
72:12 For he delivers the needy when he calls 9
75: 1 call on thy name and recount thy wondrous deeds. ‡
79: 6 on the kingdoms that do not call on thy name! 4
80:18 give us life, and we will call on thy name! 4
81: 7 In distress you called, and I delivered you; 4
86: 5 abounding in steadfast love to all who call 4
7 In the day of my trouble I call on thee 4
91:15 When he calls to me, I will answer him; 4
99: 6 Samuel . . among those who called on his name. 4
102: 2 answer me speedily in the day when I call! 4
105: 1 O give thanks to the LORD, call on his name 4
116: 2 therefore I will call on him as long as I live. 4
4 Then I called on the name of the LORD: "O LORD 4
13 I will . . call on the name of the LORD 4
17 I will . . call on the name of the LORD. 4
118: 5 Out of my distress I called on the LORD; 4
138: 3 On the day I called, thou didst answer me 4
141: 1 Give ear to my voice, when I call to thee! 4
Prv 1:24 Because I have called and you refused to listen 4
7: 4 call insight your intimate friend; 4
8: 1 Does not wisdom call 4
4 To you, O men, I call, and my cry is to the sons of men. 4
9: 3 to call from the highest places in the town 4
15 calling to those who pass 4
16:21 The wise of heart is called a man of discernment 4
24: 8 plans to do evil will be called a mischief-maker. 4
Sng 3: 1 I called him, but he gave no answer. 21
5: 6 I sought him . . I called him, but he gave no answer 4
Isa 1:13 and sabbath and the calling of assemblies 4
26 you shall be called the city of righteousness 4
4: 1 only let us be called by your name; 4
3 he who is left . . will be called holy 4
5:20 Woe to those who call evil good and good evil 1
6: 3 one called to another and said: "Holy, holy, holy 4
4 thresholds shook at the voice of him who called 4
7:14 bear a son, and shall call his name Imman'u-el. 4
8: 3 Call his name Ma'her-shal'al-hash-baz; 4
12 Do not call conspiracy all that this people call 1
12 all that this people call conspiracy 1
9: 6 and his name will be called "Wonderful Counselor 4
12: 4 Give thanks to the LORD, call upon his name; 4
19:18 One of these will be called the City of the Sun. 1
21:11 One is calling to me from Se'ir 4
22:12 Lord GOD of hosts called to weeping and mourning 4
20 I will call my servant Eli'akim the son of Hilki'ah 4
30: 7 therefore I have called her "Rahab who sits still. 4
32: 5 The fool will no more be called noble 4
35: 8 a highway . . and it shall be called the Holy Way; 4
40:26 their host by number, calling them all by name; 4
41: 4 calling the generations from the beginning? 4
9 called from its farthest corners, saying to you 4
25 and he shall call on my name; 4
42: 6 I am the LORD, I have called you in righteousness 4
43: 1 I have redeemed you; I have called you by name 4
7 every one who is called by my name 4
22 Yet you did not call upon me, O Jacob; 4
44: 5 another will call himself by the name of Jacob 4
45: 3 I . . the God of Israel, who call you by your name. 4
4 I call you by your name, I surname you 4
46:11 calling a bird of prey from the east 4
47: 1 you shall no more be called tender and delicate. 4
5 no more be called the mistress of kingdoms. 4
48: 1 of Jacob, who are called by the name of Israel 4
2 For they call themselves after the holy city 4
8 and that from birth you were called a rebel. 4
12 Hearken to me, O Jacob, and Israel, whom I called! 4
13 when I call to them, they stand forth together. 4
15 have spoken and called him, I have brought him 4
49: 1 The LORD called me from the womb 4
50: 2 Why . . When I called, was there no one to answer? 4
51: 2 when he was but one I called him, and I blessed him 4
54: 5 Redeemer, the God of the whole earth he is called. 4
6 For the LORD has called you like a wife forsaken 4
55: 5 Behold, you shall call nations that you know not 4
56: 7 my house shall be called a house of prayer 4
58: 5 you call this a fast, and a day acceptable 4
9 Then you shall call, and the LORD will answer; 4
12 you shall be called the repairer of the breach 4
13 and call the sabbath a delight and the holy day 4
60:14 they shall call you the City of the LORD, 4
18 you shall call your walls Salvation 4
61: 3 that they may be called oaks of righteousness 4
6 but you shall be called the priests of the LORD 4
62: 2 and you shall be called by a new name 4
4 but you shall be called My delight is in her 4
12 And they shall be called The holy people 4
12 and you shall be called Sought out 4
63:19 like those who are not called by thy name. 4
64: 7 There is no one that calls upon thy name 4
65: 1 here am I," to a nation that did not call on my name. 4
12 because, when I called, you did not answer 4
15 his servants he will call by a different name. 4
24 Before they call I will answer 4
66: 4 because, when I called, no one answered 4
Jer 1:15 For, lo, I am calling all the tribes of the kingdoms 4
3: 4 Have you not just now called to me, 'My father 4
17 Jerusalem shall be called the throne of the LORD 4
19 And I thought you would call me, My Father 4
6:30 Refuse silver they are called 4
7:10 in this house, which is called by my name, and say 4
11 Has this house, which is called by my name 4
13 and when I called you, you did not answer 4
14 I will do to the house which is called by my name 4
27 You shall call to them, but they will not answer 4
30 in the house which is called by my name 4
32 when it will no more be called Topheth 1
9:17 Consider, and call for the mourning women to come; 4
10:25 and upon the peoples that call not on thy name; 4
11:14 for I will not listen when they call to me 4
16 The LORD once called you, 'A green olive tree 4
14: 9 and we are called by thy name; leave us not. 4
15:16 for I am called by thy name, O LORD, God of hosts. 4
19: 6 when this place shall no more be called Topheth 4
20: 3 The LORD does not call your name Pashhur 4
23: 6 And this is the name by which he will be called 4
25:29 work evil at the city which is called by my name 4
30:17 because they have called you an outcast 4
31: 6 For there shall be a day when watchmen will call 4
32:34 in the house which is called by my name 4
33: 3 Call to me and I will answer you, and will tell you 4
16 And this is the name by which it will be called 4
34:15 before me in the house which is called by my name; 4
35:17 I have called to them and they have not answered. 4
36: 4 Then Jeremiah called Baruch the son of Neri'ah 4
46:17 Call the name of Pharaoh, king of Egypt, 'Noisy one 4
Lam 1:19 I called to my lovers but they deceived me; 4
2:15 Is this the city which was called the perfection 1
3: 8 though I call and cry . . he shuts out my prayer; 2
21 But this I call to mind, and therefore I have hope 8
55 I called on thy name, O LORD, from the depths 4
57 Thou didst come near when I called on thee; 4
Ezk 9: 3 he called to the man clothed in linen 4
10:13 were called in my hearing the whirling wheels. 4
20:29 its name is called Bamah to this day 4
39:11 it will be called the Valley of Hamon-gog. 4
Dan 1: 7 Daniel he called Belteshaz'zar 7
7 Hanani'ah he called Shadrach •
7 Mish'a-el he called Meshach •
7 Azari'ah he called Abed'nego. •
5:12 Now let Daniel be called, 11
8:16 called, "Gabriel, make this man understand 4
9:18 behold . . the city which is called by thy name; 4
19 thy city and thy people are called by thy name. 4
Hos 1: 4 And the LORD said to him, "Call his name Jezreel; 4
6 the LORD said to him, "Call her name Not pitied 4
9 And the LORD said, "Call his name Not my people 4
2:16 says the LORD, you will call me, 'My husband,' 4
16 and no longer will you call me, 'My Ba'al.' 4
7: 7 and none of them calls upon me. 4
11 calling to Egypt, going to Assyria. 4
11: 1 and out of Egypt I called my son. 4
2 The more I called them, the more they went from me; 4
Jol 1:14 Sanctify a fast, call a solemn assembly. 4
2:15 sanctify a fast; call a solemn assembly; 4
32 that all who call upon the name of the LORD 4
32 the survivors shall be those whom the LORD calls. 4
Ams 5: 8 who calls for the waters of the sea, and pours them 4
16 They shall call the farmers to mourning 4
7: 4 the Lord GOD was calling for a judgment by fire 4
9: 6 who calls for the waters of the sea, and pours them 4
12 Edom and all the nations who are called by my name 4
Jon 1: 6 Arise, call upon your god! 4
2: 2 saying, "I called to the LORD, out of my distress 4
Zep 3: 9 that all of them may call on the name of the LORD 4
Hag 1:11 I have called for a drought upon the land 4
Zec 7:13 As I called, and they would not hear, so they called •
13 they called, and I would not hear," says the LORD 4
8: 3 Jerusalem shall be called the faithful city 4
13: 9 They will call on my name, and I will answer them. 4
Mal 1: 4 till they are called the wicked country 4
Mat 1:16 Jesus was born, who is called Christ. 26
21 son, and you shall call his name Jesus, for he will 21
23 his name shall be called Emman'u-el 21
25 she had borne a son; and he called his name Jesus. 21
2:15 the prophet, "Out of Egypt have I called my son. 21
23 he went and dwelt in a city called Nazareth 26
23 fulfilled, "He shall be called a Nazarene. 21
4:18 brothers, Simon who is called Peter and Andrew 26
21 mending their nets, and he called them. 21
5: 9 for they shall be called sons of God. 21
19 and teaches men so, shall be called least 21
19 and teaches them shall be called great 21
9: 9 he saw a man called Matthew 26
13 For I came not to call the righteous, but sinners. 21
10: 1 he called to him his twelve disciples 33
2 first, Simon, who is called Peter 26
25 If they have called the master of the house 16
11:16 and calling to their playmates 36
13:55 Is not his mother called Mary? 26
15:10 he called the people to him and said to them 33
32 Jesus called his disciples to him and said 33
18: 2 calling to him a child, he put him in the midst 33
20: 8 Call the laborers and pay them their wages 21
25 Jesus called them to him and said 33
32 Jesus stopped and called them, saying 37
21:13 'My house shall be called a house of prayer' 21
22: 3 sent his servants to call those who were invited 21
14 For many are called, but few are chosen. 24
43 inspired by the Spirit, calls him Lord, saying 21
45 If David thus calls him Lord, how is he his son? 21
23: 7 being called rabbi by men. 21
8 are not to be called rabbi 21
9 call no man your father on earth 21
10 Neither be called masters 21
25:14 called his servants 21
26: 3 the high priest, who was called Ca'iaphas 26
14 one of the twelve, who was called Judas Iscariot 26
36 to a place called Gethsem'ane 26
27: 8 that field has been called the Field of Blood 21
16 a notorious prisoner, called Barab'bas. 26
17 Barab'bas or Jesus who is called Christ? 26
22 what shall I do with Jesus who is called Christ? 26
33 when they came to a place called Gol'gotha 26
47 This man is calling Eli'jah. 37
Mrk 1:20 immediately he called them 21
2:17 I came not to call the righteous, but sinners. 21
3:13 called to him those whom he desired 33
23 he called them to him 33
31 standing outside they sent to him and called 21
6: 7 he called to him the twelve 33
7:14 he called the people to him again, and said 33
8: 1 he called his disciples to him, and said to them 33
34 he called to him the multitude 33
9:35 he sat down and called the twelve; 37
10:18 Why do you call me good? No one is good but God 26
42 Jesus called them to him and said to them 33
49 Jesus stopped and said, "Call him. 37
49 they called the blind man, saying to him 37
49 saying to him, "Take heart; rise, he is calling you. 37
11:17 My house shall be called a house of prayer 21
12:37 David himself calls him Lord; so how is he his son? 26
43 he called his disciples to him 33
14:32 they went to a place which was called Gethsem'ane; 28
15: 7 there was a man called Barab'bas. 26
12 do with the man whom you call the King of the Jews? 26
22 they brought him to the place called Gol'gotha •
35 Behold, he is calling Eli'jah. 37
Lke 1:13 you shall call his name John. 21
31 you shall call his name Jesus. 21
32 He . . will be called the Son of the Most High 21
35 the child to be born will be called holy, the Son of God 21
36 the sixth month with her who was called barren. 21
60 his mother said, "Not so, he shall be called John. 21
61 None of your kindred is called by this name. 21
62 inquiring what he would have him called. 21
76 you . . will be called the prophet of the Most High 21
2: 4 to the city of David, which is called Bethlehem 21
21 he was called Jesus, the name given by the angel 21
23 shall be called holy to the Lord") 21
5:32 I have not come to call the righteous, but sinners 21
6:13 when it was day, he called his disciples 36
15 Simon who was called the Zealot 21
46 Why do you call me 'Lord, Lord,' and not do what I tell 21
7:11 Soon afterward he went to a city called Na'in 21
19 John, calling to him two of his disciples 33
32 like children . . calling to one another 36
8: 2 Mary, called Mag'dalene 21
54 taking her by the hand he called, saying, "Child 37
9:10 withdrew apart to a city called Beth-sa'ida. 21
10:39 she had a sister called Mary 21
13:12 when Jesus saw her, he called her and said to her 36
15:19 I am no longer worthy to be called your son 21
21 I am no longer worthy to be called your son.' 21
26 he called one of the servants 33
16: 2 he called him and said to him, 'What is this 37
18:16 Jesus called them to him, saying 33
19 Why do you call me good? No one is good but God 26
19:13 Calling ten of his servants 21
15 to be called to him 37
29 at the mount that is called Olivet 21
20:37 where he calls the Lord the God of Abraham 26

44 David thus calls him Lord; so how is he his son? 21
21:37 went out and lodged on the mount called Olivet. 21
22: 1 which is called the Passover. 26
3 Then Satan entered into Judas called Iscariot 21
25 are called benefactors. 21
47 the man called Judas, one of the twelve, was leading 26
23:33 they came to the place which is called The Skull 21
Joh 1:42 You shall be called Cephas" (which means Peter). 21
48 Jesus answered him, "Before Philip called you 37
2: 9 the steward of the feast called the bridegroom 37
4: 5 So he came to a city of Samar'ia, called Sy'char 26
16 Go, call your husband, and come here. 37
25 Messiah is coming (he who is called Christ); 26
5: 2 a pool, in Hebrew called Beth-za'tha 18
18 also called God his Father 26
9:11 He answered, "The man called Jesus made clay 26
18 until they called the parents of the man 37
24 they called the man who had been blind 37
10: 3 he calls his own sheep by name and leads them out. 37
35 If he called them gods to whom the word of God came 14
11:16 Thomas, called the Twin 26
28 went and called her sister Mary, saying quietly 37
28 The Teacher is here and is calling for you. 37
54 but went . . to a town called E'phraim 26
12:17 when he called Laz'arus out of the tomb 37
13:13 You call me Teacher and Lord; and you are right 37
15:15 No longer do I call you servants 26
15 I have called you friends 14
18:33 Pilate . . called Jesus, and said to him 37
19:13 a place called The Pavement 26
17 to the place called the place of a skull 26
17 the place . . which is called in Hebrew Gol'gotha. 26
20:24 Now Thomas, one of the twelve, called the Twin 26
21: 2 Simon Peter, Thomas called the Twin 26
Act 1:12 from the mount called Olivet 21
19 the field was called in their language Akel'dama 21
23 they put forward two, Joseph called Barsab'bas 21
2:21 whoever calls on the name of the Lord 16
39 every one whom the Lord our God calls to him. 33
3: 2 gate of the temple which is called Beautiful 26
11 in the portico called Solomon's 21
4:18 So they called them and charged them not to speak 21
5:40 when they had called in the apostles 33
6: 9 synagogue of the Freedman (as it was called) 26
7:14 Joseph sent and called to him Jacob his father 27
8:10 that power of God which is called Great. 21
9:11 Rise and go to the street called Straight 21
21 those who called on this name 16
41 Then calling the saints and widows 37
10: 5 bring one Simon who is called Peter; 16
7 called two of his servants and a devout soldier 37
18 Simon who was called Peter was lodging there. 16
23 So he called them in to be his guests 15
28 I should not call any man common or unclean. 26
32 ask for Simon who is called Peter 16
11:13 'Send to Joppa and bring Simon called Peter; 16
26 were for the first time called Christians. 39
13: 1 Barnabas, Simeon who was called Niger 21
2 the work to which I have called them. 33
9 Saul, who is also called Paul •
14:12 Barnabas they called Zeus 21
12 Paul . . they called Hermes. •
15:17 all the Gentiles who are called by my name 16
22 They sent Judas called Barsab'bas, and Silas 21
37 wanted to take with them John called Mark. 21
16:10 concluding that God had called us 33
29 And he called for lights and rushed in 12
20:17 called to him the elders of the church. 27
22:16 and wash away your sins, calling on his name.' 16
23:17 Paul called one of the centurions and said 33
18 Paul the prisoner called me 33
23 Then he called two of the centurions and said 33
24: 2 when he was called, Tertul'lus began to accuse him 21
14 according to the Way, which they call a sect 26
27: 8 we came to a place called Fair Havens 21
14 soon a tempestuous wind, called the northeaster 21
16 a small island called Cauda 21
28: 1 then learned that the island was called Malta. 21
Rom 1: 1 Paul . . called to be an apostle 24
6 who are called to belong to Jesus Christ 24
7 God's beloved in Rome, who are called to be saints 24
2:17 if you call yourself a Jew and rely upon the law 20
4:17 calls into existence the things that do not exist 21
7: 3 Accordingly, she will be called an adulteress 39
8:28 who are called according to his purpose. 24
30 And those whom he predestined he also called; 21
30 and those whom he called he also justified; 21
9:11 not because of works but because of his call 21
24 even us whom he has called, not from the Jews only 21
25 Those who were not my people I will call 'my people,' 21
25 her who was not beloved I will call 'my beloved.' •
26 they will be called 'sons of the living God.' 21
11:29 For the gifts and the call of God are 22
1Co 1: 1 Paul, called by the will of God to be an apostle 24
2 called to be saints 24
2 call on the name of our Lord Jesus Christ 16
9 God is faithful, by whom you were called 21
24 to those who are called, both Jews and Greeks 24
26 For consider your call, brethren 22
7:15 God has called us to peace. 21
17 in which God has called him 21
18 Was any one at the time of his call uncircumcised? 21
20 remain in the state in which he was called. 21
21 Were you a slave when called? Never mind. 21
22 who was called in the Lord as a slave is a freedman 21
22 Likewise he who was free when called 21
24 So, brethren, in whatever state each was called 21
15: 9 unfit to be called an apostle 21
2Co 1:23 I call God to witness against me 16
Gal 1: 6 who called you in the grace of Christ 21
15 called me through his grace 21
5: 8 This persuasion is not from him who calls you. 21
13 For you were called to freedom, brethren 21
Eph 1:18 know what is the hope to which he has called you 22
2:11 called the uncircumcision 26
11 what is called the circumcision 26
4: 1 to lead a life worthy of the calling 22
1 the calling to which you have been called 21
4 just as you were called to the one hope 21
4 the one hope that belongs to your call 22
Php 3:14 prize of the upward call of God in Christ Jesus. 22
Col 3:15 to which indeed you were called in the one body. 21
4:11 Jesus who is called Justus 26
1Th 2:12 who calls you into his own kingdom and glory. 21
4: 7 God has not called us for uncleanness 21
16 will descend from heaven . . with the archangel's call 38
5:24 He who calls you is faithful, and he will do it. 21
2Th 1:11 that our God may make you worthy of his call 22
2:14 To this he called you through our gospel 21
1Ti 6:12 the eternal life to which you were called 21
2Ti 1: 9 who saved us and called us with a holy calling 21
9 who saved us and called us with a holy calling 22
Heb 2:11 why he is not ashamed to call them brethren 21
3: 1 holy brethren, who share in a heavenly call 22
13 as long as it is called "today 21
5: 4 he is called by God, just as Aaron was. 21
9: 2 it is called the Holy Place. 26
3 a tent called the Holy of Holies 26
15 those who are called 21
11: 8 when he was called to go out 21
16 God is not ashamed to be called their God 16
24 refused to be called the son of Pharaoh's daughter 26
Jas 2:23 and he was called the friend of God. 21
5:14 Let him call for the elders of the church 33
1Pe 1:15 as he who called you is holy, be holy yourselves 21
2: 9 called you out of darkness into . . light. 21
21 For to this you have been called 21
3: 6 as Sarah obeyed Abraham, calling him lord. 21
9 to this you have been called 21
15 make a defense to any one who calls you to account 12
5:10 who has called you to his eternal glory in Christ 21
2Pe 1: 3 through the knowledge of him who called us 21
10 more zealous to confirm your call and election 22
1Jn 3: 1 we should be called children of God; and so we are. 21
Jde 1: 1 To those who are called, beloved in God the Father 24
Rev 1: 9 I John . . was on the island called Patmos 21
2: 2 tested those who call themselves apostles 26
20 Jez'ebel, who calls herself a prophetess 26
24 learned what some call the deep things of Satan 26
6:16 calling to the mountains and the rocks, "Fall on us 26
7: 2 he called with a loud voice to the four angels 25
9:11 and in Greek he is called Apol'lyon. 29
11: 8 city which is allegorically called Sodom 21
12: 9 serpent, who is called the Devil and Satan 21
13:10 must he be slain. Here is a call for the endurance 40
18 This calls for wisdom 40
14:12 Here is a call for the endurance of the saints 40
15 another angel . . calling with a loud voice 25
18 another angel . . called with a loud voice 37
16:16 the place which is called in Hebrew Armaged'don. 21
17: 9 This calls for a mind with wisdom 40
14 those with him are called the chosen 24
19:11 He who sat upon it is called Faithful and True 21
13 the name by which he is called is The Word of God. 21
17 and with a loud voice he called to all the birds 25
1Es 3: 7 shall be called kinsman of Darius. 21
16 he said, "Call the young men 21
4:36 The whole earth calls upon truth 21
42 you shall sit next to me, and be called my kinsman. 21
63 the temple which is called by his name 30
5:38 was called by his name. 21
8:41 I assembled them at the river called Theras 26
2Es 1:40 who is also called the messenger of the Lord. 45
2:14 Call . . heaven and earth to witness 44
37 to him who has called you to heavenly kingdoms. 45
41 people, who have been called from the beginning 45
3: 1 I Salathiel, who am also called Ezra •
4:25 what will he do for his name, by which we are called? 42
6:49 the name of one thou didst call Behemoth 45
58 thy people, whom thou hast called thy first-born 45
7:132 that the Most High is now called merciful 45
138 he is called giver, because if he did not give •
8:31 thou, because of us sinners, are called merciful. 45
32 then thou wilt be called merciful. 45
44 and is called thy own image 43
9:26 I went . . into the field which is called Ardat 45
10:22 the name by which we are called has been profaned; 43
57 you have been called before the Most High 45
12:24 therefore they are called the heads of the eagle. 45
13:12 and call to him another multitude 41
45 and that country is called Arzareth. 45
55 and called understanding your mother. 45
14:38 on the next day, behold, a voice called me, saying 45
Tob 4: 2 Why do I not call my son Tobias 21
3 he called him and said 21
5: 8 He said, "Call him to me 37
7:13 Then he called his daughter Sarah 21
14 Next he called his wife Edna 21
16 Raguel called his wife Edna and said to her 21
9: 1 Then Tobias called Raphael and said to him 21
12: 1 Tobit then called his son Tobias and said to him 21
5 he called the angel and said to him 21
6 the angel called the two of them privately 21
14: 3 he called his son and grandsons 21
Jdt 2: 4 Nebuchadnezzar . . called Holofernes 21
14 and called together all the commanders, generals 21
5: 2 he called together all the princes of Moab 21
6:21 all that night they called on the God of Israel 16
7:26 Now call them in and surrender the whole city 16
9: 4 and called on thee for help 16
10: 2 called her maid and went down into the house 21
AEs 16:11 he was called our father 13
Wis 2:13 calls himself a child of the Lord. 30
14:22 they call such great evils peace. 32
18: 8 thou didst call us to thyself and glorify us. 33
Sir 5:14 Do not be called a slanderer 21
36:12 the people called by thy name 21
47:18 the Lord God, who is called the God of Israel 16
Bar 2:15 his descendants are called by thy name. 16
26 house which is called by thy name thou hast made 16
3:33 he . . called it, and it obeyed him in fear; 21
34 he called them, and they said, "Here we are! 21
5: 4 For your name will for ever be called by God 21
LJr 1:30 For why should they be called gods? 21
44 think that they are gods, or call them gods? 23
64 one must not think . . nor call them gods 23
Bel 1: 3 Now the Babylonians had an idol called Bel 28
8 he called his priests and said to them 21
1Mc 2: 3 Simon called Thassi 21
4 Judas called Maccabeus 21
5 Eleazar called Avaran 21
5 Jonathan called Apphus. 21
3: 1 Judas his son, who was called Maccabeus 21
5:16 a great assembly was called 19
6:10 So he called all his friends and said to them 21
14 Then he called for Philip, one of his friends 21
43 Eleazar, called Avaran, saw •
7:37 didst choose this house to be called by thy name 16
8:20 Judas, who is also called Maccabeus •
10:20 you are to be called the king's friend 21
11: 7 as far as the river called Eleutherus 21
47 So the king called the Jews to his aid 21
12:31 the Arabs who are called Zabadeans 21
37 he repaired the section called Chaphenatha. 21
16: 2 Simon called in his two older sons Judas and John 21
15 in the little stronghold called Dok 21
2Mc 1:36 his associates called this "nephthar 32
36 by most people it is called naphtha. 21
2:26 but calls for sweat and loss of sleep •
4: 7 Antiochus who was called Epiphanes 32
14 after the call to the discus 34
6: 2 and call it the temple of Olympian Zeus 35
2 to call the one in Gerizim the temple of Zeus •
7:25 the king called the mother to him 33
8: 1 Judas, who was also called Maccabeus •
15 because he had called them 17
9: 2 For he had entered the city called Persepolis 26
10: 9 Antiochus, who was called Epiphanes. 32
12 Ptolemy, who was called Macron 21
13 He heard himself called a traitor at every turn •
32 Timothy . . fled to a stronghold called Gazara 26
12:17 to Charax, to the Jews who are called Toubiani. 26
21 a place called Carnaim 26
32 After the feast called Pentecost 26
13:23 he was dismayed, called in the Jews, yielded 31
14: 6 Those of the Jews who are called Hasideans 26
16 at a village called Dessau. •
37 for his good will was called father of the Jews. 32
15:36 which is called Adar in the Syrian language 26
3Mc 4:11 had been brought to the place called Schedia 26
7:17 Ptolemais, called "rose-bearing 30
4Mc 12:17 I call on the God of our fathers 16
14:17 warning them with their own calls. 38
15:21 children in torture calling to their mother. 37
16: 9 have the happiness of being called grandmother. 21
16 noble is the contest to which you are called 21

call *See also* sound, trumpet.

call aloud 1. שׁוע

Job 19: 7 I call aloud, but there is no justice. 1

call back 1. סור 2. *μετακαλέω* 3. revoco

Isa 31: 2 he does not call back his words 1
1Es 1:50 sent by his messenger to call them back 2
2Es 4: 5 or call back for me the day that is past. 3

battle call 1. σημασία
1Mc 7:45 Jews . . kept sounding the battle call on the trumpets. 1

call blessed 1. אשׁר 2. μακαρίζω
Job 29:11 When the ear heard, it called me blessed 1
Ps 41: 2 he is called blessed in the land; 1
72:17 all nations call him blessed! 1
Prv 31:28 Her children rise up and call her blessed; 1
Mal 3:12 Then all nations will call you blessed 1
Lke 1:48 all generations will call me blessed; 2
Sir 31: 9 we will call him blessed 2
4Mc 1:10 I would also call them blessed for the honor 2

call common 1. κοινόω
Act 10:15 What God has cleansed, you must not call common. 1
11: 9 'What God has cleansed you must not call common.' 1

call down a curse upon 1. καταράομαι
Sir 4: 6 if . . he calls down a curse upon you 1

call falsely 1. ψευδώνυμος
1Ti 6:20 what is falsely called knowledge 1

call for help 1. שׁוע
Job 35: 9 call for help because of the arm of the mighty. 1
Ps 88: 1 O LORD, my God, I call for help by day; •

call forth 1. קרא 2. καλέω
Isa 31: 4 a band of shepherds is called forth against him 1
Wis 11:25 anything not called forth by thee 2

call happy 1. אשׁר 2. μακαρίζω
Gen 30:13 Happy am I! For the women will call me happy"; 1
Prv 3:18 those who hold her fast are called happy. 1
Sng 6: 9 The maidens saw her and called her happy; 1
Jas 5:11 Behold, we call those happy who were steadfast. 2
Wis 2:16 he calls the last end of the righteous happy 2
Sir 11:28 Call no one happy before his death 2
37:24 all who see him will call him happy. 2

must call 1. κλητέος
LJr 1:40 Why then must any one . . call them gods? 1

call out 1. זעק 2. צעק 3. קרא 4. εἶπον 5. κράζω 6. φωνέω
Jdg 4:13 Sis'era called out all his chariots, 900 chariots 1
6:34 the Abiez'rites were called out to follow him. 1
35 and they too were called out to follow him. 1
7:23 the men of Israel were called out from Naph'tali 2
24 So all the men of E'phraim were called out 2
18:22 the men . . were called out, and they overtook 1
1Sm 13: 4 the people were called out to join Saul 2
2Sm 18:25 And the watchman called out and told the king. 3
2Kg 3:21 all who were able . . were called out 2
7:11 Then the gatekeepers called out, and it was told 3
18:28 Rab'shakeh stood and called out in a loud voice 3
Isa 36:13 Then the Rab'shakeh stood and called out 3
Lke 8: 8 As he said this, he called out, "He who has ears 6
16:24 he called out, 'Father Abraham, have mercy 6
Act 10:18 and called out to ask 6
Rev 10: 3 called out with a loud voice, like a lion roaring; 5
3 when he called out, the seven thunders sounded. 5
18: 2 And he called out with a mighty voice 5
1Es 8:92 Then Shecaniah . . called out, and said to Ezra 6
Jdt 13:11 Judith called out from afar to the watchmen 4

call to account 1. דרשׁ 2. ἀνακρίνω 3. εὐθύνω
Ps 10:13 say in his heart, "Thou wilt not call to account"? 1
1Co 14:24 he is called to account by all. 2
3Mc 2:17 or call us to account for this profanation 3

call to judgment 1. קהל
Job 11:10 and calls to judgment, who can hinder him? 1

call to mind 1. זכר 2. μιμνήσκω
Ps 77:11 I will call to mind the deeds of the LORD; 1
Sir 42:15 I will now call to mind the works of the Lord 2

call to remembrance 1. μνημονεύω
AEs 13: 8 calling to remembrance all the works of the Lord 1

call to witness 1. עוד 2. ἐπιμαρτυρέω 3. μαρτύρομαι 4. testor
Deu 4:26 I call heaven and earth to witness against you 1
30:19 I call heaven and earth to witness against you 1
31:28 call heaven and earth to witness against them. 1
2Es 1:37 I call to witness the gratitude of the people 4
2:14 Call, O call heaven and earth to witness 4
36 I publicly call on my Savior to witness. 4
Jdt 7:28 We call to witness against you heaven and earth 3
Sir 46:19 Samuel called men to witness before the Lord 2

call together 1. זעק 2. צעק 3. συγκαλέω 4. convoco
Jos 8:16 people . . were called together to pursue them 1
1Sm 10:17 Samuel called the people together to the LORD 2
2Sm 20: 4 Call the men . . together to me within three days 1
Mrk 15:16 they called together the whole battalion 3
Lke 9: 1 And he called the twelve together 3
15: 6 when he comes home, he calls together his friends 3
9 she calls together her friends and neighbors 3
23:13 Pilate then called together the chief priests 3
Act 5:21 and called together the council 3
10:24 Cornelius . . had called together his kinsmen 3
28:17 he called together the local leaders of the Jews 3
2Es 15:20 I call together all the kings of the earth 4
Jdt 2: 2 He called together all his officers 3
6:16 They called together all the elders of the city 3
13:12 and called together the elders of the city 3
2Mc 15:31 and had called his countrymen together 3

trumpet call 1. σάλπιγξ
Mat 24:31 will send out his angels with a loud trumpet call 1

call upon 1. קרא 2. ἐπιβοάω 3. ἐπικαλέω 4. invoco
2Sm 22: 4 I call upon the LORD, who is worthy to be praised 1
7 In my distress I called upon the LORD; 1
Job 27:10 Will he call upon God at all times? 1
Ps 14: 4 as they eat bread, and do not call upon the LORD? 1
17: 6 I call upon thee, for thou wilt answer me, O God; 1
18: 3 I call upon the LORD, who is worthy to be praised 1
6 In my distress I called upon the LORD; 1
50:15 call upon me in the day of trouble; 1
53: 4 as they eat bread, and do not call upon God? 1
88: 9 Every day I call upon thee, O LORD; 1
141: 1 I call upon thee, O LORD; make haste to me! 1
145:18 The LORD is near to all who call upon him 1
18 LORD is near to . . all who call upon him in truth. 1
Prv 1:28 Then they will call upon me, but I will not answer; 1
Isa 55: 6 the LORD . . call upon him while he is near; 1
Jer 29:12 Then you will call upon me and come and pray to me 1
Act 9:14 to bind all who call upon thy name. 3
Rom 10:12 and bestows his riches upon all who call upon him. 3
13 For, "every one who calls upon the name of the Lord 3
14 to call upon him in whom they have not believed? 3
2Ti 2:22 those who call upon the Lord from a pure heart. 3
1Es 6:33 the Lord, whose name is there called upon 3
2Es 1:26 When you call upon me, I will not listen to you 4
2: 5 I call upon you, father, as a witness 4
Jdt 3: 8 and all their . . tribes should call upon him as god. 3
8:17 Therefore . . let us call upon him to help us 3
16: 2 exalt him, and call upon his name. 3
Wis 7: 7 I called upon God 3
11: 4 When they thirsted they called upon thee 3
14: 1 one . . calls upon a piece of wood 2
Sir 2:10 who ever called upon him and was overlooked? 3
46: 5 He called upon the Most High, the Mighty One 3
16 He called upon the Lord, the Mighty One 3
48:20 they called upon the Lord who is merciful 3
Bar 3: 7 in order that we should call upon thy name 3
2Mc 3:15 and called . . upon him who had given the law 3
22 While they were calling upon the Almighty Lord 3
31 asked Onias to call upon the Most High 3
12: 6 calling upon God the righteous Judge 3
15 calling upon the great Sovereign of the world 3
28 the Jews called upon the Sovereign 3
36 Judas called upon the Lord 3
13:10 to call upon the Lord day and night 3
14:34 and called upon the constant Defender of our nation 3
46 calling upon the Lord of life and spirit 3
15:21 and called upon the Lord who works wonders 3
22 he called upon him in these words 3
3Mc 1:27 they turned . . to call upon him who has all power 3
5: 7 they all called upon the Almighty Lord 3
6: 1 directed . . to cease calling upon the holy God 3

become callous 1. ἀπαλγέω
Eph 4:19 they have become callous 1

calm 1. שׁוה 2. שׁקט 3. γαλήνη 4. γαληνός 5. κοπάζω
Ps 131: 2 I have calmed and quieted my soul 1
Ezk 16:42 I will be calm, and will no more be angry. 2
Mat 8:26 and there was a great calm. 3
Mrk 4:39 the wind ceased, and there was a great calm. 3
Lke 8:24 they ceased, and there was a calm. 3
Sir 39:28 calm the anger of their Maker. 5
48:10 calm the wrath of God before it breaks out in fury 5
4Mc 13: 6 make it calm 4

calm dignity 1. εὐτάκτως
3Mc 2: 1 and extending his hands with calm dignity 1

calve 1. חול 2. פלט
Job 21:10 their cow calves, and does not cast her calf. 2
39: 1 Do you observe the calving of the hinds? 1

camel 1. גָּמָל 2. κάμηλος 3. camelus
Gen 12:16 maidservants, she-asses, and camels. 1
24:10 Then the servant took ten of his master's camels 1
11 he made the camels kneel down outside the city 1
14 'Drink, and I will water your camels' 1
19 she said, "I will draw for your camels also 1
20 to draw, and she drew for all his camels. 1
22 When the camels had done drinking 1
30 he was standing by the camels at the spring. 1
31 prepared the house and a place for the camels. 1
32 Laban ungirded the camels, and gave him straw 1
32 gave him straw and provender for the camels 1
35 gold, menservants and maidservants, camels 1
44 Drink, and I will draw for your camels also 1
46 Drink, and I will give your camels drink also.' 1
46 So I drank, and she gave the camels drink also. 1
61 Rebekah . . arose, and rode upon the camels 1
63 looked, and behold, there were camels coming. 1
64 when she saw Isaac, she alighted from the camel 1
30:43 menservants, and camels and asses. 1
31:17 arose, and set his sons and his wives on camels; 1
34 put them in the camel's saddle, and sat upon them. 1
32: 7 he divided . . the flocks and herds and camels 1
15 30 milch camels and their colts, 40 cows 1
37:25 a caravan . . with their camels bearing gum, balm 1
Exd 9: 3 plague upon . . the horses, the asses, the camels 1
Lev 11: 4 you shall not eat these: The camel, because it 1
Deu 14: 7 not eat . . the camel, the hare, and the rock badger 1
Jdg 6: 5 both they and their camels could not be counted; 1
7:12 and their camels were without number, as the sand 1
8:21 crescents . . on the necks of their camels. 1
26 collars that were about the necks of their camels. 1
1Sm 15: 3 infant and suckling, ox and sheep, camel and ass. 1
27: 9 took away the sheep, the oxen, the asses, the camels 1
30:17 400 young men, who mounted camels and fled. 1
1Kg 10: 2 a very great retinue, with camels bearing spices 1
2Kg 8: 9 all kinds of goods of Damascus, 40 camel loads. 1
1Ch 5:21 their livestock: 50,000 of their camels 1
12:40 bringing food on asses and on camels and on mules 1
27:30 Over the camels was Obil the Ish'maelite; 1
2Ch 9: 1 camels bearing spices and very much gold 1
14:15 and carried away sheep in abundance and camels. 1
Ezr 2:67 their camels were 435, and their asses were 6,720. 1
Neh 7:69 their camels 435, and their asses 6,720. 1
Job 1: 3 7,000 sheep, 3,000 camels 1
17 three companies, and made a raid upon the camels 1
42:12 had 14,000 sheep, 6,000 camels, 1,000 yoke of oxen 1
Isa 21: 7 riders on asses, riders on camels 1
30: 6 and their treasures on the humps of camels 1
60: 6 A multitude of camels shall cover you 1
Jer 49:29 their camels shall be borne away from them 1
32 Their camels shall become booty 1
Ezk 25: 5 I will make Rabbah a pasture for camels 1
Zec 14:15 on the horses, the mules, the camels, the asses 1
Mat 3: 4 a garment of camel's hair, and a leather girdle 2
19:24 Again I tell you, it is easier for a camel 2
23:24 straining out a gnat and swallowing a camel! 2
Mrk 1: 6 Now John was clothed in camel's hair 2
10:25 easier for a camel to go through the eye 2
Lke 18:25 For it is easier for a camel to go 2
1Es 5:43 435 camels, and 7,036 horses 2
2Es 15:36 a man's thigh and a camel's hock. 3
Tob 9: 2 Brother Azarias, take a servant and two camels 2
Jdt 2:17 He collected a vast number of camels and asses 2

camel's thorn 1. ἀσπάλαθος
Sir 24:15 Like cassia and camel's thorn 1

young camel 1. בִּכְרָה
Isa 60: 6 cover you, the young camels of Mid'ian and Ephah; 1
Jer 2:23 a restive young camel interlacing her tracks 1

camp 1. חנה 2. טִירָה 3. מַחֲנֶה 4. αὐλίζομαι 5. ἐπιστρατοπεδεύω 6. καταστρατοπεδεύω 7. παρεμβάλλω 8. παρεμβολή 9. στρατοπεδεία 10. στρατόπεδον 11. castrum
Gen 32:21 and he himself lodged that night in the camp. 3
33:18 and he camped before the city. 1
Exd 16:13 quails came up and covered the camp; 3
13 in the morning dew lay round about the camp. 3
17: 1 Israel . . camped at Reph'idim; 1
19:16 all the people who were in the camp trembled. 3
17 Then Moses brought the people out of the camp 3
29:14 you shall burn with fire outside the camp; 3
32:17 There is a noise of war in the camp. 3
19 as soon as he came near the camp and saw the calf 3
26 then Moses stood in the gate of the camp, and said 3
27 from gate to gate throughout the camp, and slay 3
33: 7 take the tent and pitch it outside the camp 3
7 outside the camp, far off from the camp; 3
7 the tent of meeting, which was outside the camp. 3
11 When Moses turned again into the camp 3
36: 6 word was proclaimed throughout the camp 3
Lev 4:12 whole bull he shall carry forth outside the camp 3
21 he shall carry forth the bull outside the camp 3
6:11 the ashes outside the camp to a clean place 3
8:17 the bull . . he burned with fire outside the camp 3
9:11 the skin he burned with fire outside the camp 3
10: 4 carry your brethren . . out of the camp 3
5 carried them in their coats out of the camp 3
13:46 dwell alone in a habitation outside the camp 3
14: 3 the priest shall go out of the camp, and the priest 3
8 after that he shall come into the camp 3
16:26 and afterward he may come into the camp 3
27 bull . . shall be carried forth outside the camp 3
28 and afterward he may come into the camp 3
17: 3 kills . . a goat in the camp, or kills it outside 3
3 If any man . . kills it outside the camp 3

24:10 son and a man of Israel quarreled in the camp 3
14 Bring out of the camp him who cursed 3
23 they brought him who had cursed out of the camp 3
Num 1:52 every man by his own camp and every man by his own 3
2: 3 shall be . . of the camp 3
9 The whole number of the camp of Judah 3
10 the standard of the camp of Reuben 3
16 The whole number of the camp of Reuben 3
17 with the camp of the Levites in the midst 3
17 Levites in the midst of the camps; 3
18 On the west side shall be the standard of the camp 3
24 The whole number of the camp of E'phraim 3
25 the camp of Dan by their companies 3
31 The whole number of the camp of Dan is 157,600 3
32 all in the camps who were numbered by their 3
4: 5 When the camp is to set out, Aaron and his sons 3
15 as the camp sets out, after that the sons of Kohath 3
5: 2 put out of the camp every leper 3
3 male and female, putting them outside the camp 3
3 that they may not defile their camp 3
4 Israel did so, and drove them outside the camp; 3
10: 2 you shall use them . . for breaking camp. 3
5 camps that are on the east side shall set out. 3
6 camps that are on the south side shall set out. 3
14 standard of the camp of the men of Judah set out 3
18 standard of the camp of Reuben set out by their 3
22 standard of the camp of the men of E'phraim set out 3
25 Then the standard of the camp of the men of Dan 3
25 Dan, acting as the rear guard of all the camps 3
34 whenever they set out from the camp. 3
11: 1 consumed some outlying parts of the camp. 3
9 When the dew fell upon the camp in the night 3
26 Now two men remained in the camp, one named Eldad 3
26 so they prophesied in the camp. 3
27 Eldad and Medad are prophesying in the camp. 3
30 Moses and the elders . . returned to the camp. 3
31 quails . . and let them fall beside the camp 3
31 let them fall . . round about the camp 3
32 they spread them out . . all around the camp. 3
12:14 Let her be shut up outside the camp seven days 3
15 Miriam was shut up outside the camp seven days; 3
13:19 dwell in are camps or strongholds 3
14:44 nor Moses, departed out of the camp. 3
15:35 stone him with stones outside the camp. 3
36 congregation brought him outside the camp 3
19: 3 she shall be taken outside the camp 3
7 afterwards he shall come into the camp; 3
9 deposit them outside the camp in a clean place; 3
31:12 at the camp on the plains of Moab by the Jordan 3
13 went forth to meet them outside the camp. 3
19 Encamp outside the camp seven days; 3
24 afterward you shall come into the camp. 3
Deu 2:14 men of war, had perished from the camp 3
15 against them, to destroy them from the camp 3
23: 9 go forth against your enemies and are in camp 3
10 not clean . . then he shall go outside the camp 3
10 outside the camp . . not come within the camp; 3
11 when the sun is down, he may come within the camp. 3
12 place outside the camp and you shall go out to it; 3
14 LORD your God walks in the midst of your camp 3
14 therefore your camp must be holy 3
29:11 your wives, and the sojourner who is in your camp 3
Jos 1:11 Pass through the camp, and command the people 3
3: 2 the officers went through the camp 3
5: 8 they remained in their places in the camp 3
6:11 and they came into the camp, and spent the night 3
11 they came into . . and spent the night in the camp. 3
14 marched around . . and returned into the camp. 3
18 make the camp of Israel a thing for destruction 3
23 and set them outside the camp of Israel. 3
9: 6 they went to Joshua in the camp at Gilgal, and said 3
10: 6 the men . . sent to Joshua at the camp in Gilgal 3
15 Then Joshua returned . . to the camp at Gilgal. 3
21 returned safe to Joshua in the camp at Makke'dah; 3
43 Then Joshua returned . . to the camp at Gilgal. 3
18: 9 then they came to Joshua in the camp at Shiloh 3
Jdg 7: 1 the camp of Mid'ian was north of them, by the hill 3
8 and the camp of Mid'ian was below him 3
9 Arise, go down against the camp; for I have given it 3
10 if you fear . . go down to the camp with Purah 3
11 be strengthened to go down against the camp. 3
11 outposts of the armed men that were in the camp. 3
13 of barley bread tumbled into the camp of Mid'ian 3
15 he returned to the camp of Israel, and said, "Arise; 3
17 when I come to the outskirts of the camp, do as I do. 3
18 the trumpets also on every side of all the camp 3
19 Gideon . . came to the outskirts of the camp 3
21 stood every man in his place round about the camp 3
11:18 and camped on the other side of the Arnon; 1
21: 8 no one had come to the camp from Ja'besh-gil'ead 3
12 they brought them to the camp at Shiloh 3
1Sm 4: 3 when the troops came to the camp 3
5 ark of the covenant of the LORD came into the camp 3
6 this great shouting in the camp of the Hebrews 3
6 the ark of the LORD had come to the camp 3
7 they said, "A god has come into the camp. 3
11:11 they came into the midst of the camp 3
13:17 raiders came out of the camp of the Philistines 3
14:15 there was a panic in the camp, in the field 3
19 the tumult in the camp . . increased more and more; 3
21 and who had gone up with them into the camp 3
17: 4 there came out from the camp of the Philistines 3
17 carry them quickly to the camp to your brothers; 3
53 and they plundered their camp. 3
26: 6 Who will go down with me into the camp to Saul? 3
2Sm 1: 2 a man came from Saul's camp, with his clothes rent 3
3 he said . . "I have escaped from the camp of Israel. 3
11:11 Jo'ab and the . . are camping in the open field; 1
23:16 broke through the camp of the Philistines 3
1Kg 16:16 made . . king over Israel that day in the camp. 3
2Kg 3:24 when they came to the camp . . the Israelites rose 3
6: 8 At such and such a place shall be my camp. 3
7: 4 come, let us go over to the camp of the Syrians; 3
5 they arose . . to go to the camp of the Syrians; 3
5 they came to the edge of the camp of the Syrians 3
7 and forsook . . leaving the camp as it was, and fled 3
8 when these lepers came to the edge of the camp 3
10 We came to the camp of the Syrians 3
12 they have gone out of the camp to hide themselves 3
16 went out, and plundered the camp of the Syrians. 3
19:35 slew 185,000 in the camp of the Assyrians; 3
1Ch 9:18 the gatekeepers of the camp of the Levites. 3
19 had been in charge of the camp of the LORD 3
11:18 broke through the camp of the Philistines 3
2Ch 22: 1 men that came with the Arabs to the camp had slain 3
31: 2 minister in the gates of the camp of the LORD 3
32:21 in the camp of the king of Assyria. 3
Ps 69:25 May their camp be a desolation 2
78:28 he let them fall in the midst of their camp 3
106:16 men in the camp were jealous of Moses and Aaron 3
Isa 37:36 slew . . in the camp of the Assyrians; 3
Ezk 4: 2 set camps also against it 3
Ams 4:10 the stench of your camp go up into your nostrils; 3
Zec 14:15 asses, and whatever beasts may be in those camps. 3
Heb 13:11 are burned outside the camp. 8
13 Therefore let us go forth to him outside the camp 8
Rev 20: 9 and surrounded the camp of the saints 8
2Es 1:15 I gave you camps for your protection 11
Tob 6: 1 came . . to the Tigris river and camped there. 4
Jdt 2:21 camped opposite Bectileth 5
3:10 here he camped between Geba and Scythopolis 6
6:11 the slaves took him and led him out of the camp 8
7:12 Remain in your camp 8
13 and camp there to keep watch 7
10:18 There was great excitement in the whole camp 8
12: 7 she remained in the camp for three days 8
7 bathed at the spring in the camp. 8
13:10 they passed through the camp 8
14: 3 they will seize their arms and go into the camp 8
19 shouts arose in the midst of the camp. 8
15: 3 had camped in the hills around Bethulia 7
5 what had happened in the camp of the enemy 8
6 The rest . . fell upon the Assyrian camp 8
11 the people plundered the camp for 30 days. 8
16: 3 and brought me to his camp, 8
Wis 19: 7 The cloud was seen overshadowing the camp 8
Sir 14:26 will camp under her boughs; 4
48:21 The Lord smote the camp of the Assyrians 8
1Mc 3:41 went to the camp to get the sons of Israel 8
4: 2 to fall upon the camp of the Jews 8
4 the division was still absent from the camp. 8
5 When Gorgias entered the camp of Judas by night 8
7 they saw the camp of the Gentiles 8
13 they went forth from their camp to battle 8
20 the Jews were burning the camp 8
23 Then Judas returned to plunder the camp 8
30 didst give the camp of the Philistines 8
5:38 Judas sent men to spy out the camp 8
41 camps on the other side of the river 7
6:32 Beth- zechariah, opposite the camp of the king. 8
9: 6 many slipped away from the camp 8
11 the army of Bacchides marched out from the camp 8
33 camped by the water of the pool of Asphar. 7
11:73 as far as Kadesh, to their camp 8
12:26 He sent spies to their camp 8
27 he stationed outposts around the camp. 8
28 they kindled fires in their camp and withdrew. 8
2Mc 13:14 he pitched his camp near Modein. 9
15 slew as many as 2,000 men in the camp 8
16 In the end they filled the camp with terror 8
15:22 slew . . 185,000 in the camp of Sennacherib. 8
4Mc 3:13 went searching throughout the enemy camp 10

camp *See also* break, move.

camp for the night 1. κοιμάω

1Mc 16: 4 and camped for the night in Modein. 1

campaign 1. מַחֲנֶה 2. πόλεμος

1Sm 29: 6 march out and in with me in the campaign; 1
Jdt 2:16 as a great army is marshaled for a campaign. 2

campaign *See also* carry.

can 1. יכל 2. δύναμαι 3. ἔχω 4. ἰσχύς 5. οἶδα 6. possum

Exd 8:18 magicians tried . . but they could not. 1
1Kg 5: 3 David . . could not build a house for the name 1
8:11 priests could not stand to minister 1
13: 4 dried up, so that he could not draw it back 1
14: 4 Ahi'jah could not see, for his eyes were dim 1
2Kg 3:26 to break through . . but they could not. 1
4:40 And they could not eat it. 1
16: 5 they besieged Ahaz but could not conquer him. 1
1Ch 21:30 David could not go before it to inquire of God 1
2Ch 5:14 priests could not stand to minister 1
7: 2 the priests could not enter the house of the LORD 1
29:34 could not flay all the burnt offerings 1
30: 3 could not keep it in its time because the priests 1
Ezr 2:59 could not prove their fathers' houses 1
Neh 7:61 but they could not prove their fathers' houses 1
Isa 7: 1 war against it, but they could not conquer it. 1
Jer 3: 5 but you have done all the evil that you could. 1
44:22 The LORD could no longer bear your evil doings 1
Ezk 47: 5 and it was a river that I could not pass through 1
Jon 1:13 to bring the ship back to land, but they could not 1
Mat 27:65 go, make it as secure as you can. 5
Mrk 6:19 wanted to kill him. But she could not 2
9:23 Jesus said to him, "If you can! 2
14: 8 She has done what she could 3
Lke 9:40 they could not. 2
19: 3 he sought to see who Jesus was, but could not 2
Joh 15: 4 neither can you, unless you abide in me. •
Act 8:31 he said, "How can I, unless some one guides me? 2
2Es 9:32 for it could not, because it was thine. 6
13: 7 I tried to see . . but I could not. 6
Wis 15:12 one must get money however one can, •
Sir 9:14 As much as you can, aim to know your neighbors 4
14:13 reach out and give to him as much as you can. 4
43:30 exalt him as much as you can 2
Bar 1: 6 they collected money, each giving what he could; 2
1Mc 6: 3 he could not, because his plan became known 2
4Mc 14:17 they do what they can to help their young 2

canal 1. יְאֹר 2. נָהָר 3. διῶρυξ

Exd 7:19 over their rivers, their canals, and their ponds 1
8: 5 the rivers, over the canals, and over the pools 1
Isa 19: 6 its canals will become foul 2
Sir 24:30 I went forth like a canal from a river 3
31 my canal became a river, and my river became a sea. 3

cancel 1. ἀθετέω 2. ἀφίημι 3. ἐξαλείφω 4. χρεοκοπέομαι

Col 2:14 having canceled the bond which stood against us 3
1Mc 10:33 cancel also the taxes on their cattle. 2
42 this too is canceled 2
11:36 not one of these grants shall be canceled 1
13:39 and cancel the crown tax which you owe 2
15: 8 any such future debts shall be canceled for you 2
4Mc 2: 8 to cancel the debt when the seventh year arrives. 4

cane 1. קָנֶה

Exd 30:23 Take . . of aromatic cane 250 1
Jer 6:20 or sweet cane from a distant land? 1

sweet cane 1. קָנֶה

Isa 43:24 You have not bought me sweet cane with money 1

cannot 1. לֹא יָכֹל 2. δύναμαι 3. οὐδὲ δύναμαι 4. non possum 5. sic

Gen 29: 8 they said, "We cannot until all the flocks are 1
Isa 29:11 he says, "I cannot, for it is sealed. 1
Jer 20: 9 and I am weary with holding it in, and I cannot. 1
Act 4:20 for we cannot but speak of what we have seen 2
Rom 8: 7 it does not submit to God's law, indeed it cannot; 3
2Es 4:41 I said, "No, lord, it cannot. 4
5:35 he said to me, "You cannot." And I said, 4
47 I said, "Of course it cannot 4
7:10 I said, "He cannot, lord." And he said to me 5

cannot *See also* bear.

canopy 1. חֻפָּה 2. סֻכָּה 3. עָב 4. κωνώπιον

2Sm 22:12 He made darkness around him his canopy 2
1Kg 7: 6 a porch in front . . and a canopy before them. 3
Ps 18:11 his canopy thick clouds dark with water. 2
Isa 4: 5 over all . . there will be a canopy and a pavilion. 1
Ezk 41:25 there was a canopy of wood in front 3
Jdt 10:21 under a canopy which was woven with purple 4
13: 9 and pulled down the canopy from the posts 4
15 here is the canopy beneath which he lay 4
16:19 the canopy which she took for herself 4

royal canopy 1. שַׁפְרִיר

Jer 43:10 he will spread his royal canopy over them. 1

cap 1. מִגְבָּעָה 2. פְּאֵר

Exd 28:40 shall make coats and girdles and caps; 1
29: 9 you shall . . bind caps on them; 1
39:28 fine linen, and the caps of fine linen 2
Lev 8:13 Moses . . bound caps on them, as the LORD 1

capable 1. ἀγαθός

Wis 8:15 among the people I shall show myself capable 1

capital 1. כַּפְתּוֹר 2. כֹּתֶרֶת 3. צֶפֶת 4. רֹאשׁ

Exd 25:31 its cups, its capitals, and its flowers shall be 1
33 made like almonds, each with capital and flower 1

33 three cups . . each with capital and flower 1
34 four cups . . with their capitals and flowers 1
35 a capital of one piece with it under each pair 1
36 Their capitals and their branches shall be 1
36:38 He overlaid their capitals, and their fillets 4
37:17 were made of hammered work; its cups, its capitals 1
19 cups . . with capital and flower on one branch 1
19 cups . . with capital and flower, on the other 1
20 cups . . with their capitals and flowers 1
21 a capital of one piece with it under each pair 1
22 Their capitals and their branches were of one 1
38:17 the overlaying of their capitals was also 4
19 the overlaying of their capitals and their 4
28 pillars, and overlaid their capitals 4
1Kg 7:16 made two capitals of molten bronze, to set upon 2
16 the height of the one capital was five cubits 2
16 the height of the other capital was five cubits. 2
17 made two nets . . for the capitals upon the tops 2
17 a net for the one capital, and a net for the other 2
17 the one capital, and a net for the other capital. 2
18 cover the capital that was upon the . . pillar; 2
18 he did the same with the other capital. 2
19 the capitals that were upon the tops 2
20 The capitals were upon the two pillars and also 2
20 there were . . and so with the other capital. 2
41 the two bowls of the capitals that were 2
41 two bowls of the capitals that were on the tops 2
42 bowls of the capitals that were upon the pillars; 2
2Kg 25:17 one pillar . . and upon it was a capital of bronze; 2
17 the height of the capital was three cubits; 2
17 a network . . upon the capital round about. 2
2Ch 3:15 with a capital of five cubits on the top of each. 3
4:12 the two pillars, the bowls, and the two capitals 2
12 the capitals that were on the top of the pillars; 2
13 the two bowls of the capitals that were upon 2
Jer 52:22 Upon it was a capital of bronze; 2
22 the height of the one capital was five cubits; 2
22 all of bronze, were upon the capital round about. 2
Ams 9: 1 Smite the capitals until the thresholds shake 1
Zep 2:14 the hedgehog shall lodge in her capitals; 1

capital (2) 1. בִּירָה 2. בִּירְתָא (A) 3. *πόλις βασιλείας*

Ezr 6: 2 Ecbat'ana, the capital which is in . . Media 2
Neh 1: 1 Now it happened . . as I was in Susa the capital 1
Est 1: 2 sat on his royal throne in Susa the capital 1
5 for all the people present in Susa the capital 1
2: 3 gather . . to the harem in Susa the capital 1
5 a Jew in Susa the capital whose name was Mor'decai 1
8 many maidens were gathered in Susa the capital 1
3:15 and the decree was issued in Susa the capital. 1
8:14 and the decree was issued in Susa the capital. 1
9: 6 In Susa the capital itself the Jews slew 1
11 the number of . . in Susa the capital was reported 1
12 In Susa the capital the Jews have slain five 1
Dan 8: 2 vision; and when I saw, I was in Susa the capital 1
1Mc 3:37 departed from Antioch his capital 3

captain 1. פֶּחָה 2. רֹאשׁ 3. רַב 4. רַב חֹבֵל 5. שַׂר 6. שַׂר מֵאוֹת 7. שָׁלִישׁ 8. רַב (A) 9. שַׁלִּיט (A) 10. *ἀρχηγός* 11. *ἄρχων* 12. *ἔπαρχος* 13. *ἡγεμών* 14. *κυβερνήτης* 15. *προστάτης* 16. *στρατηγός* 17. *χιλίαρχος*

Gen 37:36 officer of Pharaoh, the captain of the guard. 5
39: 1 the captain of the guard, an Egyptian 5
40: 3 in the house of the captain of the guard 5
4 The captain of the guard charged Joseph 5
41:10 put me . . in the house of the captain of the guard 5
12 with us, a servant of the captain of the guard; 5
Num14: 4 Let us choose a captain, and go back to Egypt. 2
31:48 the officers . . the captains of thousands 5
48 the officers . . the captains of hundreds 5
1Sm 22: 2 gathered to him; and he became captain over them. 5
14 king's son-in-law, and captain over your bodyguard 11
2Sm 4: 2 had two men who were captains of raiding bands; 5
1Kg 9:22 were his officials, his commanders, his captains 7
22:31 commanded the . . captains of his chariots 5
32 when the captains . . saw Jehosh'aphat, they said 5
33 when the captains . . saw that it was not the king 5
2Kg 1: 9 the king sent to him a captain of 50 men 5
10 Eli'jah answered the captain of 50 5
11 the king sent to him another captain of 50 men 5
13 Again the king sent the captain of a third 50 5
13 the third captain of 50 went up, and came 5
14 and consumed the two former captains of 50 5
7: 2 Then the captain . . said to the man of God 7
17 appointed the captain on whose hand he leaned 7
19 the captain had answered the man of God 7
11: 4 and brought the captains of the Carites 6
9 The captains did according to all that Jehoi'ada 6
10 the priest delivered to the captains the spears 6
14 the captains and the trumpeters beside the king 5
15 commanded the captains . . set over the army 5
19 he took the captains, the Carites, the guards 6
15:25 Pekah . . his captain, conspired against him 7
18:24 How then can you repulse a single captain 1
25: 8 Nebu'zarad'an, the captain of the bodyguard 3
10 the army . . who were with the captain of the guard 3
11 Nebu'zarad'an the captain of the guard carried 3
12 the captain of the guard left some of . . to be 3
15 gold the captain of the guard took away as gold 3
18 the captain of the guard took Serai'ah 3
20 Nebu'zarad'an the captain of the guard took them 3
23 the captains of the forces in the open country 5
26 all the people . . and the captains of the forces 5
2Ch 18:30 had commanded the captains of his chariots 5
31 when the captains . . saw Jehosh'aphat, they said 5
32 for when the captains of the chariots saw 5
23: 9 Jehoi'ada the priest delivered to the captains 5
13 captains and the trumpeters beside the king 5
14 Jehoi'ada the priest brought out the captains 5
20 he took the captains, the nobles, the governors 6
Job 39:25 the thunder of the captains, and the shouting. 5
Isa 3: 3 the captain of 50 and the man of rank 5
36: 9 a single captain among the least of my master's 1
Jer 39: 9 Then Nebu'zarad'an, the captain of the guard 3
10 Nebu'zarad'an, the captain of the guard, 3
11 Nebu'zarad'an, the captain of the guard, saying 3
13 Nebu'zarad'an the captain of the guard 3
40: 1 the captain of the guard had let him go from Ramah 3
2 The captain of the guard took Jeremiah and said 3
5 So the captain of the guard gave him an allowance 3
7 the captains of the forces in the open country 5
41:10 Nebu'zarad'an, the captain of the guard 3
43: 6 Nebu'zarad'an the captain of the guard had left 3
52:12 Nebu'zarad'an the captain of the bodyguard 3
14 Chalde'ans, who were with the captain of the guard 3
15 Nebu'zarad'an the captain of the guard 3
16 Nebu'zarad'an the captain of the guard left some 3
19 What was of gold the captain of the guard took 3
24 And the captain of the guard took Serai'ah 3
26 Nebu'zarad'an the captain of the guard took them 3
30 Nebu'zarad'an the captain of the guard 3
Dan 2:14 Ar'ioch, the captain of the king's guard 8
15 said to Ar'ioch, the king's captain 9
Jon 1: 6 the captain came and said to him, "What do you mean 4
Joh 18:12 the band of soldiers and their captain 17
Act 4: 1 the priests and the captain of the temple 16
5:24 the captain of the temple and the chief priests 16
26 captain with the officers went and brought them 16
27:11 to the captain and to the owner of the ship 14
Rev 19:18 to eat the flesh of kings, the flesh of captains 17
Jdt 14: 2 set a captain over them 10
12 they went to the generals and the captains 17
1Mc 16:19 he sent letters to the captains 17
2Mc 3: 4 who had been made captain of the temple 15
4:28 Sostratus the captain of the citadel 12
5:24 Apollonius, the captain of the Mysians †
12:19 who were captains under Maccabeus 13

captain over thousands 1. *χιλίαρχος*

1Es 1: 9 Ochiel and Joram, captains over thousands 1

captivate 1. *αἰχμαλωτίζω*

Jdt 16: 9 her beauty captivated his mind 1

captive 1. אָסִיר 2. אַסִּיר 3. בַּשֶּׁבִי 4. גּוֹלָה 5. גלה 6. גָּלוּת 7. שׁבה 8. שָׁבִי 9. שְׁבִי 10. שִׁבְיָה 11. שְׁבִית 12. *αἰχμαλωσία* 13. *αἰχμάλωτος* 14. *δέσμιος* 15. *δοριάλωτος* 16. *λεία* 17. *υἱὸς τῆς αἰχμαλωσίας* 18. captivus

Gen 31:26 my daughters like captives of the sword? 7
Exd 12:29 to the first-born of the captive who was 9
Num21: 1 against Israel, and took some of them captive. 9
29 has made his sons . . and his daughters captives 11
31:12 brought the captives and the booty and the spoil 9
19 purify yourselves and your captives 9
Deu 21:10 into your hands, and you take them captive 9
11 see among the captives a beautiful woman 10
13 shall put off her captive's garb, and shall remain 9
32:42 with the blood of the slain and the captives 9
Jdg 5:12 Arise, Barak, lead away your captives, O son 9
1Kg 8:46 carried away captive to the land of the enemy 7
47 the land to which they have been carried captive •
50 in the sight of those who carried them captive •
2Kg 24:14 He carried away . . 10,000 captives 5
16 the king of Babylon brought captive to Babylon 4
1Ch 3:17 sons of Jeconi'ah, the captive: Sheal'tiel his son 2
2Ch 6:36 so that they are carried away captive to a land 7
28:11 send back the captives from your kinsfolk 10
13 said . . "You shall not bring the captives in here 10
14 the armed men left the captives and the spoil 10
15 the men . . rose and took the captives 10
17 defeated Judah, and carried away captives. 9
Neh 4: 4 plundered in a land where they are captives. 10
Est 2: 6 among the captives carried away with Jeconi'ah 4
Ps 68:18 leading captives in thy train, and receiving 9
Isa 20: 4 Assyria lead away the Egyptians captives 9
49:24 or the captives of a tyrant be rescued? 9
25 Even the captives of the mighty shall be taken 9
52: 2 from the dust, arise, O captive Jerusalem; 9
2 bonds from your neck, O captive daughter of Zion. 8
61: 1 to proclaim liberty to the captives 7
Jer 40: 1 along with all the captives of Jerusalem 6
48:46 for your sons have been taken captive 3
Lam 1: 5 children have gone . . captives before the foe. 9
Ezk 32: 9 when I carry you captive among the nations 12
Hab 1: 9 They gather captives like sand. 9
Zec 9:11 set your captives free from the waterless pit. 1
Lke 4:18 has sent me to proclaim release to the captives 13
Eph 4: 8 When he ascended on high he led a host of captives 12
1Es 6: 5 the providence of the Lord was over the captives; 12
7:11 Not all of the returned captives were purified 17
12 for all the returned captives 17
2Es 1: 3 who was a captive in the country of the Medes 18
13:40 whom Shalmaneser . . led captive 18
Tob 7: 3 who are captives in Nineveh. 13
13:10 May he cheer those within you who are captives 13
Jdt 2: 9 I will lead them away captive 12
AEs 11: 4 He was one of the captives 12
Wis 17: 2 they themselves lay as captives of darkness 14
LJr 1: 1 those who were to be taken to Babylon as captives 13
2 you will be taken to Babylon as captives 13
1Mc 9:70 and obtain release of the captives. 12
72 He restored to him the captives 12
14: 7 He gathered a host of captives 12
2Mc 1:19 when our fathers were . . led captive to Persia *
3Mc 1: 5 many captives also were taken. 15
4Mc 8: 2 others of the Hebrew captives be brought 16

captive *See also* bring, carry, hold, lead, make, take.

captivity 1. גּוֹלָה 2. גלה 3. גָּלוּת 4. שְׁבִי 5. שִׁבְיָה 6. *αἰχμαλωσία* 7. *αἰχμάλωτος* 8. captivitas 9. captivus

Deu 28:41 not be yours; for they shall go into captivity. 4
Jdg 18:30 until the day of the captivity of the land. 2
2Kg 24:15 he took into captivity from Jerusalem 1
2Ch 6:37 supplication . . in the land of their captivity 4
38 if they repent . . in the land of their captivity 4
29: 9 our sons and our . . wives are in captivity 4
Ezr 2: 1 people . . who came up out of the captivity 4
3: 8 who had come to Jerusalem from the captivity. 4
8:35 At that time those who had come from captivity 4
9: 7 been given . . to the sword, to captivity 4
Neh 7: 6 came up out of the captivity of those exiles 4
8:17 all . . who had returned from the captivity 4
Ps 78:61 delivered his power to captivity 4
Isa 46: 2 but themselves go into captivity. 4
Jer 1: 3 the captivity of Jerusalem in the fifth month. 2
15: 2 those who are for captivity, to captivity. 4
2 those who are for captivity, to captivity. 4
20: 6 who dwell in your house, shall go into captivity; 4
22:22 and your lovers shall go into captivity; 4
30:10 offspring from the land of their captivity. 4
16 foes, every one of them, shall go into captivity; 4
43:11 to captivity those who are doomed to captivity 4
11 to captivity those who are doomed to captivity 4
46:27 your offspring from the land of . . captivity. 4
48:46 and your daughters into captivity. 5
52:31 in the 37th year of the captivity 3
Lam 1:18 my maidens and . . men have gone into captivity. 4
Ezk 12:11 they shall go into exile, into captivity. 4
30:17 and the women shall go into captivity. 4
18 her daughters shall go into captivity. 4
Dan 11:33 fall by sword and flame, by captivity and plunder 4
Ams 9: 4 they go into captivity before their enemies 4
Nah 3:10 Yet she was carried away, she went into captivity; 4
Rev 13:10 If . . to be taken captive, to captivity he goes; 6
1Es 5: 7 who came up out of their sojourn in captivity 6
56 all who had come to Jerusalem from the captivity; 6
67 those who had returned from captivity 6
6: 8 the Jews, who had been in captivity 6
28 who have returned from the captivity of Judea 6
7: 6 the rest of those from the captivity 6
10 The people of Israel who came from the captivity 6
13 the people of Israel who came from the captivity 6
8:65 those who had come back from captivity 6
77 to the sword and captivity and plundering 6
9: 3 to all who had returned from the captivity 6
4 those who had returned from the captivity. 6
15 those who had returned from the captivity 6
2Es 10:22 our Levites have gone into captivity 8
13:40 led away from their own land into captivity 9
16:46 in captivity and famine they will beget 8
Tob 3: 4 thou gavest us over to plunder, captivity, and death; 6
15 in the land of my captivity 6
13: 6 I give him thanks in the land of my captivity 6
Jdt 4: 3 they had only recently returned from the captivity 6
8:22 the captivity of the land 6
9: 4 thou gavest . . their daughters to captivity 6
Bar 4:10 I have seen the captivity of my sons 6
1Mc 2: 9 have been carried into captivity 7

captivity *See also* go, place, take.

captor 1. שׁבה

1Kg 8:47 supplication . . in the land of their captors 1
2Ch 30: 9 find compassion with their captors, and return 1
Ps 137: 3 For there our captors required of us songs 1
Isa 14: 2 will take captive those who were their captors 1
Mic 2: 4 Among our captors he divides our fields. 1

capture 1. אסר 2. לכד 3. לקח 4. שׁבה 5. תפשׂ 6. *αἰχμαλωσία* 7. *αἰχμαλωτίζω* 8. *ἀπολαμβάνω* 9. *γίνομαι εἰς διαρπαγήν* 10. *ζωγρέω*

11. *καταλαμβάνω* 12. *κρατέω* 13. *κυριεύω* 14. *λαμβάνω* 15. *πιάζω* 16. *προκαταλαμβάνω* 17. *συλλαμβάνω*

Gen 34:29 in the houses, they captured and made their prey. 4
Deu 2:34 we captured all his cities at that time 2
35 with the booty of the cities which we captured. 2
Jos 19:47 after capturing it and putting it to the sword 2
1Sm 4:11 And the ark of God was captured; 3
17 and the ark of God has been captured. 3
19 the tidings that the ark of God was captured 3
21 because the ark of God had been captured 3
22 glory has . . for the ark of God has been captured. 3
5: 1 When the Philistines captured the ark of God 3
23:26 closing in upon David and his men to capture them 5
30:20 David also captured all the flocks and herds; 3
1Kg 9:16 gone up and captured Gezer and burnt it with fire 2
20:21 went out, and captured the horses and chariots 14
2Kg 14:13 Jeho'ash king of Israel captured Amazi'ah 5
15:29 Tig'lath-pile'ser . . came and captured I'jon 3
17: 6 the king of Assyria captured Sama'ria 2
25: 6 Then they captured the king, and brought him up 5
2Ch 22: 9 Ahazi'ah . . captured while hiding in Sama'ria 2
25:12 The men of Judah captured another 10,000 alive 4
23 Jo'ash king of Israel captured Amazi'ah 3
Neh 9:25 captured fortified cities and a rich land 2
Prv 6:25 do not let her capture you with her eyelashes; 3
Isa 22: 3 rulers . . without the bow they were captured. 1
3 All of you who were found were captured 1
Jer 34: 3 but shall surely be captured and delivered 5
50:46 At the sound of the capture of Babylon 5
52: 9 Then they captured the king 5
Ezk 21:23 guilt to remembrance, that they may be captured. 5
Mat 26:55 with swords and clubs to capture me 17
Mrk 14:48 with swords and clubs to capture me? 17
2Ti 2:26 after being captured by him to do his will. 10
3: 6 capture weak women, burdened with sins 7
Rev 19:20 And the beast was captured 15
Tob 14:15 Nebuchadnezzar and Ahasuerus had captured. 7
Jdt 1:14 came to Ecbatana, captured its towers 12
15 He captured Arphaxad in the mountains of Ragae 14
5:18 their cities were captured by their enemies. 12
7:27 it would be better for us to be captured by them; 9
8:21 For if we are captured all Judea will be captured 14
21 For if we are captured all Judea will be captured 14
10:13 he can go and capture all the hill country 13
13 without losing one of his men, captured or slain. †
Bar 4:14 remember the capture of my sons and daughters 6
24 the neighbors of Zion have now seen your capture 6
1Mc 1:19 they captured the fortified cities 11
5:11 capture the stronghold to which we have fled 16
13 the enemy have captured their wives 7
30 engines of war to capture the stronghold 11
9:58 he will capture them all in one night. 17
11:56 Trypho captured the elephants 14
13:43 battered and captured one tower. 11
2Mc 8: 6 He captured strategic positions 8
10 by selling the captured Jews into slavery. 6
25 They captured the money 14
36 the capture of the people of Jerusalem 6
10:22 immediately captured the two towers. 11
14:41 When the troops were about to capture the tower 11

caravan 1. אֹרַח 2. אֹרְחָה 3. שכן בָּאֳהָלִים

Gen 37:25 looking up they saw a caravan of Ish'maelites 2
Jdg 5: 6 caravans ceased and travelers kept 1
8:11 went up by the caravan route east of Nobah 3
Job 6:18 The caravans turn aside from their course; 1
19 The caravans of Tema look, the travelers of Sheba 1
Isa 21:13 Arabia you will lodge, O caravans of De'danites. 1

carbuncle 1. אֶבֶן אֶקְדָּח 2. בָּרֶקֶת 3. נֹפֶךְ

Exd 28:17 sardius, topaz, and carbuncle shall be the first 2
39:10 of sardius, topaz, and carbuncle was the first row; 2
Isa 54:12 pinnacles of agate, your gates of carbuncles 1
Ezk 28:13 beryl, and onyx, sapphire, carbuncle, and emerald; 3

carcass 1. גְּוִיָּה 2. חָלָל 3. מַפֶּלֶת 4. נְבֵלָה 5. פֶּגֶר

Gen 15:11 when birds of prey came down upon the carcasses 5
Lev 5: 2 whether the carcass of an unclean beast 4
2 whether the carcass of an unclean beast 4
2 or a carcass of unclean swarming things 4
11: 8 not eat, and their carcasses you shall not touch 4
11 their carcasses you shall have in abomination 4
24 whoever touches their carcass shall be unclean 4
25 whoever carries . . their carcass shall wash 4
27 whoever touches their carcass shall be unclean 4
28 he who carries their carcass shall wash 4
35 upon which any part of their carcass falls 4
36 whatever touches their carcass shall be unclean 4
37 if any part of their carcass falls upon the seed 4
38 if . . any part of their carcass falls on it 4
39 he who touches its carcass shall be unclean 4
40 he who eats of its carcass shall wash his clothes 4
40 he also who carries the carcass shall wash 4
Deu 14: 8 flesh . . and their carcasses you shall not touch. 4
Jdg 14: 8 he turned aside to see the carcass of the lion 3
9 had taken the honey from the carcass of the lion. 1
Ps 89:10 Thou didst crush Rahab like a carcass 2
Jer 16:18 with the carcasses of their detestable idols 4
Ezk 32: 5 and fill the valleys with your carcass. ‡

care 1. דרשׁ 2. חפץ 3. חֵפֶץ 4. מְאֹד 5. עַל 6. שׂים לֵב 7. שַׂרְעַפִּים 8. *ἐπιμέλεια* 9. *μέλει* 10. *μέριμνα* 11. *μεριμνάω* 12. *πονέω* 13. *προσοχή* 14. *φροντίς* 15. labor

Gen 33:13 flocks and herds giving suck are a care to me; 5
1Sm 9: 5 lest my father cease to care about the asses *
2Sm 18: 3 For if we flee, they will not care about us. 6
3 If half of us die, they will not care about us. 6
Job 21:21 For what do they care for their houses after them 3
Ps 94:19 cares of my heart are many, thy consolations 7
142: 4 no refuge remains to me, no man cares for me. 1
Jer 2:10 or send to Kedar and examine with care; 4
22:28 a despised, broken pot, a vessel no one cares for? 2
30:14 All your lovers . . they care nothing for you; 1
17 an outcast: 'It is Zion, for whom no one cares!' 1
48:38 a vessel for which no one cares, says the LORD. 3
Mat 13:22 but the cares of the world . . choke the word 10
22:16 teach the way of God . . and care for no man; 9
Mrk 4:19 the cares of the world, and the delight in riches 10
38 Teacher, do you not care if we perish? 9
12:14 we know that you are true, and care for no man 9
Lke 8:14 they are choked by the cares and riches 11
10:40 Lord, do you not care that my sister has left me 9
21:34 drunkenness and cares of this life 10
Joh 10:13 is a hireling and cares nothing for the sheep. 9
12: 6 This he said, not that he cared for the poor 9
1Co 12:25 members may have the same care for one another. 11
1Pe 5: 7 Cast . . anxieties on him, for he cares about you 9
1Es 6:10 being completed with all splendor and care. 8
2Es 9:46 I brought him up with much care. 15
Wis 7: 4 I was nursed with care in swaddling cloths. 14
8: 9 counsel and encouragement in cares and grief. 14
12:13 whose care is for all men 9
20 if thou didst punish with such great care 13
13:13 he takes and carves with care in his leisure 8
Sir 13: 5 he will drain your resources and he will not care. 12

care (2) 1. אֵת 2. בין 3. דרשׁ 4. יָד 5. עֲבֹדָה 6. עַל 7. פקד 8. פְּקֻדָּה 9. רעה 10. שׁמר 11. *ἐπιμέλεια* 12. *ἐπιμελέομαι* 13. *ἐπισκέπτομαι* 14. *παρά* 15. *ποιμαίνω* 16. *χείρ* 17. curo

Gen 39:22 the prison committed to Joseph's care 4
23 anything that was in Joseph's care 4
Num 7: 9 charged with the care of the holy things 5
Deu 11:12 land which the LORD your God cares for; 3
32:10 encircled him, he cared for him, he kept him 2
Jdg 19:20 I will care for all your wants; only, do not spend *
1Sm 25:29 of the living in the care of the LORD your God; 1
2Sm 20: 3 concubines whom he had left to care for the house 10
1Ch 15:13 we did not care for it in the way that is ordained. 3
23:28 having the care of the courts and the chambers 6
26:28 were in the care of Shelo'moth and his brethren. 4
29: 8 in the care of Jehi'el the Gershonite. 4
2Ch 13:11 care for the golden lampstand *
Job 10:12 thy care has preserved my spirit. 8
Ps 8: 4 and the son of man that thou dost care for him? 7
Jer 23: 2 concerning the shepherds who care for my people 9
4 set shepherds over them who will care for them 9
Zec 10: 3 the LORD of hosts cares for his flock 7
11:16 a shepherd who does not care for the perishing 7
Act 20:28 to care for the church of God 15
27: 3 leave to go to his friends and be cared for. 11
1Ti 3: 5 how can he care for God's church? 12
Heb 2: 6 What is . . the son of man, that thou carest for him? 13
2Es 2:21 care for the injured and the weak 17
Jdt 12:11 the Hebrew woman who is in your care 14
Sir 38:15 may he fall into the care of a physician. 16
49:15 his bones are cared for. 13
2Mc 11:23 be undisturbed in caring for their own affairs. 11

care *See also* arrange, free, take.

earnest care 1. *σπουδή*

2Co 8:16 who puts the same earnest care for you 1

much care 1. labor

2Es 10:47 that she brought him up with much care 1

tender care 1. טִפֻּחִים

Lam 2:20 offspring, the children of their tender care? 1

very great care 1. *ἐπιμελῶς*

1Es 7: 2 supervised the holy work with very great care 1

carefree 1. שָׁלֵו

Ezk 23:42 The sound of a carefree multitude was with her; 1

careful 1. שׁמר 2. *ἀγρυπνία* 3. *προσέχω* 4. *σκοπέω* 5. *φροντίζω*

Deu 5: 1 you shall learn them and be careful to do them. 1
32 careful to do therefore as the LORD your God 1
6: 3 Hear therefore, O Israel, and be careful to do them; 1
25 if we are careful to do all this commandment 1
7:11 therefore be careful to do the commandment 1
8: 1 All the commandment . . you shall be careful to do 1
11:22 if you will be careful to do all this commandment 1
32 shall be careful to do all the statutes 1
12: 1 which you shall be careful to do in the land 1
28 Be careful to heed all these words 1
32 Everything . . you shall be careful to do; 1
15: 5 being careful to do all this commandment 1
16:12 you shall be careful to observe these statutes. 1
17:10 careful to do according to all that they direct 1
19: 9 provided you are careful to keep all this 1
23:23 be careful to perform what has passed your lips 1
24: 8 Take heed . . to be very careful to do according 1
8 as I commanded them, so you shall be careful to do. 1
26:16 therefore be careful to do them with all 1
28: 1 being careful to do all his commandments 1
13 obey the commandments . . being careful to do 1
15 not . . be careful to do all his commandments 1
58 If . . not careful to do all the words of this law 1
29: 9 be careful to do the words of this covenant 1
31:12 may . . be careful to do all the words of this law 1
32:46 may be careful to do all the words of this law. 1
Jos 1: 7 being careful to do according to all the law 1
8 be careful to do according to all that is written 1
2Kg 10:31 Jehu was not careful to walk in the law of the LORD 1
17:37 and the law . . you shall always be careful to do. 1
21: 8 be careful to do according to all that 1
1Ch 22:13 you will prosper if you are careful to observe 1
2Ch 33: 8 if only they will be careful to do all that 1
Ezk 18: 9 and is careful to observe my ordinances 1
19 and has been careful to observe all my statutes 1
20:19 and be careful to observe my ordinances 1
21 and were not careful to observe my ordinances 1
36:27 and be careful to observe my ordinances. 1
37:24 and be careful to observe my statutes. *
Lke 11:35 be careful lest the light in you be darkness. 4
Tit 3: 8 may be careful to apply themselves to good deeds 5
Sir 37:31 he who is careful to avoid it prolongs his life. 3
38:26 he is careful about fodder for the heifers. 2
27 he is careful to finish his work. 2
28 he is careful to complete its decoration. 2
30 he is careful to clean the furnace. 2

carefully 1. *ἀκριβῶς* 2. *ἐπιμελῶς* 3. diligenter

Gen 43: 7 They replied, "The man questioned us carefully †
Job 13:17 Listen carefully to my words †
21: 2 Listen carefully to my words †
Prv 23: 1 observe carefully what is before you; †
Eph 5:15 Look carefully then how you walk 1
2Es 16:30 who search carefully through the vineyard 3
2Mc 8:31 stored them all carefully in strategic places 2
4Mc 11:18 He was carefully stretched tight upon it 2

carefully *See also* measure.

careless 1. בטח 2. *ἀργός*

Prv 14:16 but a fool throws off restraint and is careless. 1
Mat 12:36 will render account for every careless word 2

cargo 1. *γόμος* 2. *φορτίον*

Act 21: 3 there the ship was to unload its cargo. 1
27:10 not only of the cargo and the ship 2
Rev 18:11 since no one buys their cargo any more 1
12 cargo of gold, silver, jewels and pearls 1

cargo *See also* throw.

carnal 1. *σάρκινος*

Rom 7:14 We know that the law is spiritual; but I am carnal 1

carnally 1. שִׁכְבַת זֶרַע

Lev 19:20 If a man lies carnally with a woman who is a slave 1
Num 5:13 if a man lies with her carnally, and it is hidden 1

carnally *See also* lie.

carnelian 1. אֹדֶם 2. *σάρδιον*

Ezk 28:13 carnelian, topaz, and jasper, chrysolite, beryl 1
Rev 4: 3 he . . appeared like jasper and carnelian 2
21:20 the fifth onyx, the sixth carnelian 2

carouse 1. *κῶμος* 2. *πότος* 3. *συνευωχέομαι*

Gal 5:21 envy, drunkenness, carousing, and the like 1
1Pe 4: 3 living in . . drunkenness, revels, carousing 2
2Pe 2:13 They are . . carousing with you. 3

carouse together 1. *συνευωχέομαι*

Jde 1:12 love feasts, as they boldly carouse together 1

carpenter 1. חָרָשׁ 2. חָרַשׁ עֵץ 3. *τέκτων*

2Sm 5:11 sent . . cedar trees, also carpenters and masons 2
2Kg 12:11 paid it . . to the carpenters and the builders 2
22: 6 to the carpenters, and to the builders 1
1Ch 14: 1 king of Tyre sent . . also masons and carpenters 2
22:15 stonecutters, masons, carpenters 2
2Ch 24:12 hired masons and carpenters to restore 1
34:11 They gave it to the carpenters and the builders 1
Ezr 3: 7 gave money to the masons and the carpenters 1
Isa 44:13 The carpenter stretches a line, he marks it out 2
Mat 13:55 Is not this the carpenter's son? 3
Mrk 6: 3 Is not this the carpenter, the son of Mary 3
1Es 5:54 they gave money to the masons and the carpenters 3
LJr 1:45 They are made by carpenters and goldsmiths 3

carpet 1. גְּנָזִים
Ezk 27:24 and in carpets of colored stuff, bound with cords 1

rich carpet 1. מַד
Jdg 5:10 Tell of it . . you who sit on rich carpets 1

carrier 1. *παρακομίζω*
2Mc 4:20 by the decision of its carriers 1

carrion *See* vulture.

carry 1. אמן 2. בוא 3. גלה 4. היה 5. הלך 6. חתה 7. יבל 8. יצא 9. מַשָּׂא 10. נהל 11. נשא 12. סבב 13. סבל 14. עלה 15. עשה 16. רכב 17. *αἴρω* 18. *ἀπάγω* 19. *ἀποφέρω* 20. *βαστάζω* 21. *διακονέω* 22. *εἰς* 23. *εἰσφέρω* 24. *κουφίζω* 25. *παρακομίζω* 26. *περιφέρω* 27. *φέρω* 28. porto
Gen 42:19 and let the rest go and carry grain for the famine 2
44: 1 sacks with food, as much as they can carry 11
45:27 wagons which Joseph had sent to carry him 11
46: 5 the sons of Israel carried Jacob their father 11
5 wagons which Pharaoh had sent to carry him. 11
47:30 let me lie with my fathers; carry me out of Egypt 11
50:13 for his sons carried him to the land of Canaan 11
Exd 13:19 God will visit you; then you must carry my bones 14
25:14 on the sides of the ark, to carry the ark by them. 11
27 as holders for the poles to carry the table. 11
28 and the table shall be carried with these. 11
27: 7 two sides of the altar, when it is carried. 11
30: 4 holders for poles with which to carry it. 11
37: 5 on the sides of the ark, to carry the ark. 11
14 as holders for the poles to carry the table. 11
15 the poles of acacia wood to carry the table 11
27 as holders for the poles with which to carry it. 11
38: 7 put the poles . . to carry it with them; 11
Lev 10: 4 said to them, "Draw near, carry your brethren 11
5 So they drew near, and carried them in their coats 11
11:25 whoever carries any part of their carcass 11
28 he who carries their carcass shall wash 11
40 he also who carries the carcass shall wash 11
15:10 he who carries such a thing shall wash 11
Num 1:50 they are to carry the tabernacle and all its 11
4:15 sons of Kohath shall come to carry these 11
15 things . . which the sons of Kohath are to carry. 9
25 they shall carry the curtains of the tabernacle 11
27 to carry, and in all that they have to do; 9
27 assign to their charge all that they are to carry. 9
31 this is what they are charged to carry 9
32 the objects which they are required to carry. 9
49 each to his task of serving or carrying; 9
7: 9 things which had to be carried on the shoulder. 11
10:17 sons . . who carried the tabernacle, set out. 11
21 Ko'hathites set out, carrying the holy things 11
11:12 Carry them in your bosom, as a nurse carries 11
12 Carry . . as a nurse carries the sucking child 11
14 I am not able to carry all this people alone 11
13:23 they carried it on a pole between two of them; 11
16:46 carry it quickly to the congregation 5
Deu 10: 8 Levi to carry the ark of the covenant of the LORD 11
28:38 carry much seed into the field, and shall gather 8
31: 9 sons of Levi, who carried the ark of the covenant 11
25 Levites who carried the ark of the covenant 11
Jos 3: 3 ark . . being carried by the Levitical priests 11
8:33 priests who carried the ark of the covenant 11
Jdg 3:18 sent away the people that carried the tribute. 11
16: 3 shoulders and carried them to the top of the hill 14
1Sm 5: 1 they carried it from Ebene'zer to Ashdod; 2
10: 3 three men . . one carrying three kids, another 11
3 another carrying three loaves of bread 11
3 and another carrying a skin of wine. 11
20:40 Go and carry them to the city. 2
2Sm 6: 3 And they carried the ark of God upon a new cart 16
8: 7 shields . . carried by the servants of Hadade'zer •
13:13 As for me, where could I carry my shame? 5
20:12 he carried Ama'sa out of the highway 12
1Kg 5:16 had charge of the people who carried on the work. 15
9:23 had charge of the people who carried on the work. 15
18:12 the Spirit . . will carry you whither I know not; 11
2Kg 4:19 The father said . . "Carry him to his mother. 11
5:23 and they carried them before Geha'zi. 11
20:17 all that is in . . shall be carried to Babylon; 11
23: 4 he burned them . . and carried their ashes to Bethel. 11
24:13 and carried off all the treasures 8
25:13 and carried the bronze to Babylon. 11
1Ch 5:18 valiant men, who carried shield and sword 11
13: 7 they carried the ark of God upon a new cart 16
15: 2 No one but the Levites may carry the ark of God 11
2 LORD chose them to carry the ark of the LORD 11
13 Because you did not carry it the first time •
15 carried the ark of God upon their shoulders 11
26 helped the Levites who were carrying the ark 11
27 all the Levites who were carrying the ark 11
18: 7 which were carried by the servants of Hadade'zer 4
23:26 Levites no longer need to carry the tabernacle 11
2Ch 14: 8 280,000 men . . carried shields and drew bows; 11
20:25 they took . . until they could carry no more. 9
28:15 carrying all the feeble among them on asses 10
35: 3 you need no longer carry it upon your shoulders. 9
24 servants . . carried him in his second chariot 16
36: 4 Neco took Jeho'ahaz . . and carried him to Egypt. 2
7 carried part of the vessels of the . . LORD 2
Neh 4:17 Those who carried burdens were laden in such 11
Job 10:19 carried from the womb to the grave. 7
24:10 hungry, they carry the sheaves; 11
31:36 Surely I would carry it on my shoulder; 11
Ps 28: 9 be thou their shepherd, and carry them for ever. 11
Prv 6:27 Can a man carry fire in his bosom 6
Ecc 10:20 a bird of the air will carry your voice 5
Isa 23: 7 city . . whose feet carried her to settle afar? 7
30: 6 carry their riches on the backs of asses 11
39: 6 be carried to Babylon; nothing shall be left 11
40:11 he will carry them in his bosom 11
46: 1 these things you carry are loaded as burdens 11
3 borne by me from your birth, carried from the womb; 11
4 I am He, and to gray hairs I will carry you. 13
4 I will bear; I will carry and will save. 13
7 They lift it upon their shoulders, they carry it 13
49:22 daughters shall be carried on their shoulders. 11
53: 4 he has borne our griefs and carried our sorrows; 13
60: 4 and your daughters shall be carried in the arms. 1
63: 9 lifted . . up and carried them all the days of old. 11
66:12 you shall suck, you shall be carried upon her hip 11
Jer 10: 5 they have to be carried, for they cannot walk. 11
17:22 And do not carry a burden out of your houses 8
20: 5 and seize them, and carry them to Babylon. 2
27:22 They shall be carried to Babylon 2
28: 3 away from this place and carried to Babylon. 2
52:17 in pieces, and carried all the bronze to Babylon. 11
Ezk 12: 7 in the dark, carrying my outfit upon my shoulder 11
17: 4 its young twigs and carried it to a land of trade 2
32: 9 when I carry you captive among the nations 2
Hos 10: 6 Yea, the thing itself shall be carried to Assyria 7
12: 1 and oil is carried to Egypt. 7
Jol 3: 5 carried my rich treasures into your temples. 2
Ams 1: 6 because they carried into exile a whole people 3
Hag 2:12 'If one carries holy flesh in the skirt of his 11
Mat 3:11 whose sandals I am not worthy to carry; he will 20
27:32 this man they compelled to carry his cross. 17
Mrk 2: 3 bringing to him a paralytic carried by four men. 17
14:13 a man carrying a jar of water will meet you 20
15:21 to carry his cross. 17
Lke 10: 4 Carry no purse, no bag, no sandals 20
16:22 and was carried by the angels to Abraham's bosom 19
22:10 a man carrying a jar of water will meet you 20
23:26 and laid on him the cross, to carry it behind Jesus. 27
Joh 5:10 it is not lawful for you to carry your pallet. 17
21:18 carry you where you do not wish to go. 27
Act 3: 2 a man lame from birth was being carried 20
9:15 he is a chosen instrument of mine to carry my name 20
21:35 he was actually carried by the soldiers 20
1Co 16: 3 to carry your gift to Jerusalem. 19
2Co 4:10 always carrying in the body the death of Jesus 26
8:19 in this gracious work which we are carrying on 21
Rev 17: 7 and of the beast . . that carries her. 20
1Es 1: 4 You need no longer carry it upon your shoulders 17
13 carried them to all the people 19
8:13 to carry to Jerusalem the gifts 19
60 carried them to the temple of the Lord. 23
2Es 4:19 to the sea is assigned a place to carry its waves. 28
AEs 15: 4 while the other followed carrying her train. 24
Wis 5:14 like chaff carried by the wind 27
14: 1 the ship which carries him. 27
18:16 carrying the sharp sword 27
Sir 6:25 Put your shoulder under her and carry her 20
Bar 5: 6 carried in glory, as on a royal throne. 17
LJr 1: 4 which are carried on men's shoulders 17
26 they are carried on men's shoulders 27
1Mc 2: 9 have been carried into captivity 18
4:30 the man who carried his armor. 17
5:30 carrying ladders and engines of war 17
2Mc 3:28 carried him away 27
4:19 to carry 300 silver drachmas for the sacrifice 25
19 who carried the money, however, thought best 25
23 to carry the money to the king 25
7:27 I carried you nine months in my womb 26
8:31 carried the rest of the spoils to Jerusalem. 27
9: 8 carried in a litter 25
10 no one was able to carry the man 25
15:23 to carry terror and trembling before us. 22
30 carry them to Jerusalem. 27

carry *See also* give.

carry about 1. נשׂא 2. *περιφέρω*
Isa 45:20 no knowledge who carry about their wooden idols 1
Eph 4:14 carried about with every wind of doctrine 2

carry along 1. *παραφέρω*
Jde 1:12 waterless clouds, carried along by the winds; 1

carry away 1. גּוֹלָה 2. גלה 3. גנב 4. הלך 5. יצא 6. לקח 7. נהג 8. נשׂא 9. שׁבה 10. גלה (A) 11. נשׂא (A) 12. *ἄγω* 13. *ἀποικίζω* 14. *ἀποφέρω* 15. *βαστάζω* 16. *ἐκφέρω* 17. *ἐπαίρω* 18. *μετάγω* 19. *μετοικίζω* 20. *συναπάγω* 21. *φέρω*
Gen 31:26 cheated me, and carried away my daughters 7
2Sm 5:21 and David and his men carried them away. 8
1Kg 8:46 they are carried away captive to the land 9
15:22 they carried away the stones of Ramah 8
2Kg 17: 6 and he carried the Israelites away to Assyria 2
11 as the nations did whom the LORD carried away 2
26 nations which you have carried away and placed 2
27 one of the priests whom you carried away thence; 2
28 priests whom they had carried away from Sama'ria 2
33 from among whom they had been carried away. 2
18:11 The king of Assyria carried the Israelites away 2
24:14 He carried away all Jerusalem, and . . the princes 2
15 And he carried away Jehoi'achin to Babylon; 2
1Ch 5:26 king of Assyria, and he carried them away 2
2Ch 6:36 so that they are carried away captive to a land 9
14:13 The men of Judah carried away very much booty. 8
15 and carried away sheep in abundance and camels. 9
16: 6 carried away the stones of Ramah and its timber 8
21:17 carried away all the possessions they found 9
28:17 defeated Judah, and carried away captives. 9
Ezr 1: 7 vessels . . Nebuchadnez'zar had carried away 5
5:12 carried away the people to Babylonia. 10
Est 2: 6 a Jew . . who had been carried away from Jerusalem 2
6 among the captives carried away with Jeconi'ah 2
6 whom Nebuchadnez'zar . . had carried away. 2
Job 15:12 Why does your heart carry you away 6
20:28 possessions of his house will be carried away 2
21:18 like chaff that the storm carries away? 3
24:18 swiftly carried away upon the face of the waters; •
Ps 49:17 For when he dies he will carry nothing away; 6
Ecc 5:15 nothing . . which he may carry away in his hand. 4
Isa 8: 4 the spoil of Sama'ria will be carried away 8
15: 7 they carry away over the Brook of the Willows. 8
41:16 winnow them and the wind shall carry them away 8
Ezk 30: 4 her wealth is carried away 6
38:13 to carry away silver and gold, to take away cattle 8
Dan 2:35 wind carried them away, so that not a trace of them 11
Nah 3:10 Yet she was carried away, she went into captivity; 1
Joh 20:15 she said to him, "Sir, if you have carried him away 15
Act 19:12 aprons were carried away from his body to the sick 14
Gal 2:13 carried away by their insincerity. 20
2Pe 3:17 carried away with the error of lawless men 20
Rev 17: 3 And he carried me away . . into a wilderness 14
21:10 And in the Spirit he carried me away 14
1Es 1:41 carried them away, and stored them in his temple 14
54 they took and carried away to Babylon. 14
2:10 which Nebuchadnezzar had carried away 18
5: 7 had carried away to Babylon 19
6:26 house in Jerusalem and carried away to Babylon 14
AEs 16: 4 carried away by the boasts of those who know 17
Bar 1: 8 which had been carried away from the temple 16
9 after Nebuchadnezzar . . had carried away 13
3Mc 3:18 they were carried away by their traditional conceit 21
4: 6 and were carried away unveiled 12

carry away captive 1. גלה 2. שׁבה 3. *αἰχμαλωτεύω* 4. *αἰχμαλωτίζω* 5. *προνομεύω* 6. captivo
Jer 41:14 Ish'mael had carried away captive from Mizpah 2
16 Ish'mael . . had carried away captive from Mizpah •
43:12 he shall burn them and carry them away captive; 2
52:15 captain of the guard carried away captive some 1
28 whom Nebuchadrez'zar carried away captive 1
29 he carried away captive from Jerusalem •
30 the captain of the guard carried away captive 1
1Es 6:16 carried the people away captive to Babylon 3
2Es 15:63 They shall carry your children away captive 6
Tob 1:10 Now when I was carried away captive to Nineveh 4
Sir 48:15 till they were carried away captive 5

carry away into exile 1. גלה
1Ch 5: 6 king of Assyria carried away into exile; 1

carry away the prize 1. *ἀθλοφόρος*
4Mc 15:29 who carried away the prize of the contest 1

carry back 1. שׁוב 2. *ἀναφέρω* 3. *μετατίθημι*
Gen 43:12 carry back with you the money that was returned 1
2Sm 15:25 Carry the ark of God back into the city. 1
29 So Zadok and Abi'athar carried the ark of God back 1
Act 7:16 they were carried back to Shechem 3
1Es 2:15 they were carried back by Sheshbazzar 2

carry before 1. *προάγω*
Jdt 10:22 with silver lamps carried before him. 1

carry captive 1. גלה 2. שׁבה
1Kg 8:47 the land to which they have been carried captive 2
48 land of their enemies, who carried them captive 2
50 in the sight of those who carried them captive 2
2Kg 15:29 and he carried the people captive to Assyria. 1
16: 9 and took it, carrying its people captive to Kir 1
2Ch 6:37 land to which they have been carried captive 2
38 land . . to which they were carried captive 2
Ezr 2: 1 Nebuchadnez'zar . . had carried captive 1
Jer 20: 4 he shall carry them captive to Babylon 1
22:12 in the place where they have carried him captive 1
52:27 So Judah was carried captive out of its land. 1
Ezk 6: 9 the nations where they are carried captive 2

carry down 1. ירד
Gen 37:25 on their way to carry it down to Egypt. 1
43:11 and carry down to the man a present, a little balm 1

carry forth 1. יצא
Exd 12:46 you shall not carry forth any of the flesh 1
Lev 4:12 the whole bull he shall carry forth outside 1
21 he shall carry forth the bull outside the camp 1
6:11 put on other garments, and carry forth the ashes 1
14:45 he shall carry them forth out of the city 1
16:27 bull . . shall be carried forth outside the camp 1

carry further 1. יסף
Ezk 23:14 she carried her harlotry further; 1

carry good news 1. בשר
1Sm 31: 9 and sent messengers . . to carry the good news 1
1Ch 10: 9 carry the good news to their idols 1

carry in a chariot 1. רכב
2Kg 9:28 servants carried him in a chariot to Jerusalem 1
23:30 And his servants carried him dead in a chariot 1

carry into exile 1. גלה 2. ἀποικίζω
2Kg 25:11 the rest . . Nebu'zarad'an . . carried into exile. 1
1Ch 8: 6 they were carried into exile to Mana'hath); 1
Neh 7: 6 whom Nebuchadnez'zar . . had carried into exile; 1
Jer 39: 9 carried into exile . . the rest of the people 1
Bar 2:14 the sight of those who have carried us into exile; 2

carry off 1. בוא 2. בזז 3. גזל 4. גנב 5. נהג 6. נשׂא 7. עלה 8. פלט 9. שׁבה 10. ἀποφέρω 11. ἁρπάζω 12. ἐκνήφω 13. rapio
Jdg 21:23 number, from the dancers whom they carried off; 3
1Sm 30: 2 they killed no one, but carried them off 5
2Kg 5: 2 the Syrians . . had carried off a little maid 9
7: 8 they carried off silver and gold and clothing 6
8 entered another tent, and carried off things 6
1Ch 5:21 They carried off their livestock 9
18:11 which he had carried off from all the nations 6
Job 27:20 in the night a whirlwind carries him off. 4
Isa 5:29 they growl and seize their prey, they carry it off 8
40:24 and the tempest carries them off like stubble. 6
57:13 idols deliver you! The wind will carry them off 6
Ezk 29:19 he shall carry off its wealth and despoil it 6
38:12 to seize spoil and carry off plunder; to assail 2
13 you assembled your hosts to carry off plunder 2
Dan 11: 8 He shall also carry off to Egypt their gods 1
Hos 5:14 I, even I, will rend and go away, I will carry off 6
Obd 1:11 on the day that strangers carried off his wealth 9
Nah 2: 7 its mistress is stripped, she is carried off 7
2Es 10:22 our righteous men have been carried off 13
16:68 they shall carry off some of you 13
Sir 31: 2 a severe illness carries off sleep. 12
Bar 4:26 taken away like a flock carried off by the enemy. 11
2Mc 5:21 Antiochus carried off 1,800 talents 10

carry on a campaign 1. στρατεύω
2Mc 15:17 they determined not to carry on a campaign 1

carry on openly 1. גלה
Ezk 23:18 When she carried on her harlotry so openly 1

carry on war 1. στρατεύω
2Co 10: 3 we are not carrying on a worldly war 1

carry out 1. בצע 2. יצא 3. עשׂה 4. ἄγω 5. ἐκκομίζω 6. ἐκπληρόω 7. ἐκφέρω 8. ἐπιτελέω 9. ποιέω 10. συντελέω
1Sm 28:18 carry out his fierce wrath against Am'alek 3
1Kg 22:34 Turn about, and carry me out of the battle 2
2Kg 10:30 you have done well in carrying out what is right 3
2Ch 18:33 Turn about, and carry me out of the battle 2
29: 5 carry out the filth from the holy place. 2
16 Levites . . carried it out to the brook Kidron. 2
Ps 37: 7 over the man who carries out evil devices! 3
Isa 30: 1 who carry out a plan, but not mine; 3
Lam 2:17 The LORD . . has carried out his threat; 1
Ezk 12: 6 lift the baggage . . and carry it out in the dark; 2
Lke 7:12 behold, a man who had died was being carried out 5
Act 5: 6 and carried him out and buried him. 7
9 they will carry you out. 7
10 they carried her out and buried her 7
15 they even carried out the sick into the streets 7
27:43 kept them from carrying out their purpose •
Rev 17:17 to carry out his purpose by being of one mind 9
Jdt 12: 4 before the Lord carries out . . what he has determined 9
13: 5 to carry out my undertaking 9
LJr 1:62 they carry out his command. 10
2Mc 3: 8 in fact to carry out the king's purpose. 8
15: 5 in carrying out his abominable design. 8
3Mc 1: 2 determined to carry out the plot he had devised 6
5: 4 Hermon . . proceeded faithfully to carry out the orders. 10
19 he had carried out completely the order given him 4

carry out registration 1. ἀπογράφω
3Mc 6:38 their registration was carried out 1

carry out revenge 1. ἐκδικέω
Jdt 2: 1 there was talk . . about carrying out his revenge 1

carry over 1. עבר
Jos 4: 3 Take twelve stones . . and carry them over with you 1
8 and they carried them over with them to the place 1

carry quickly 1. רוץ
1Sm 17:17 carry them quickly to the camp to your brothers; 1
2Ch 35:13 carried them quickly to all the lay people. 1

carry round 1. סבב
2Ch 33:14 carried it round Ophel, and raised it 1

carry the war 1. גרה
Dan 11:10 again shall carry the war as far as his fortress. 1

carry the world 1. κοσμοφορέω
4Mc 15:31 carrying the world in the universal flood 1

carry through 1. διακομίζω 2. διαφέρω
Mrk 11:16 to carry anything through the temple. 2
3Mc 2: 7 but carried through safely those who . . 1

carry tidings 1. בשׂר
2Sm 18:19 Let me run, and carry tidings to the king 1
20 Jo'ab said . . "You are not to carry tidings today; 1
20 you may carry tidings another day 1
20 but today you shall carry no tidings 1

carry up 1. עלה 2. ἀναφέρω
Gen 50:25 and you shall carry up my bones from here. 1
Exd 33:15 do not carry us up from here. 1
1Kg 17:19 and carried him up into the upper chamber 1
Lke 24:51 and was carried up into heaven. 2

carrying *See* frame.

cart 1. עֲגָלָה 2. ἅμαξα 3. χάρα
1Sm 6: 7 take and prepare a new cart and two milch cows 1
7 yoke the cows to the cart, but take their calves 1
8 take the ark of the LORD and place it on the cart 1
10 and took two milch cows and yoked them to the cart 1
11 And they put the ark of the LORD on the cart 1
14 The cart came into the field of Joshua 1
14 split up the wood of the cart and offered the cows 1
2Sm 6: 3 And they carried the ark of God upon a new cart 1
3 and Uzzah and Ahi'o . . were driving the new cart 1
1Ch 13: 7 they carried the ark of God upon a new cart 1
7 and Uzzah and Ahi'o were driving the cart. 1
Isa 5:18 Woe to those . . who draw sin as with cart ropes 1
28:27 nor is a cart wheel rolled over cummin; 1
28 he drives his cart wheel over it with his horses 1
Ams 2:13 as a cart full of sheaves presses down. 1
1Es 5:55 carts to the Sidonians and the Tyrians 3
Jdt 15:11 and loaded her mule and hitched up her carts 2
Sir 33: 5 The heart of a fool is like a cart wheel 2

carve 1. חקק 2. חֲרֹשֶׁת 3. מִקְלַעַת 4. עשׂה 5. פתח 6. קלע 7. γλύφω 8. ἐγγλύφω 9. ἐντυπόω 10. sculpo
Exd 31: 5 in carving wood, for work in every craft. 2
35:33 cutting stones for setting, and in carving wood 2
1Kg 6:18 The cedar . . was carved in the form of gourds 3
29 He carved all the walls of the house round about 6
29 with carved figures of cherubim and palm trees 3
35 he carved cherubim and palm trees and open 6
7:36 and on its panels, he carved cherubim, lions 5
2Ch 3: 7 and he carved cherubim on the walls. 5
Isa 22:16 carve a habitation for yourself in the rock? 1
Ezk 41:17 the nave were carved likenesses •
19 They were carved on the whole temple round about; 4
20 cherubim and palm trees were carved on the wall. 4
25 And on the doors of the nave were carved cherubim 4
25 palm trees, such as were carved on the walls; 4
2Co 3: 7 carved in letters on stone 9
2Es 13: 7 or place from which the mountain was carved 10
Wis 13:13 he takes and carves with care in his leisure 7
1Mc 13:29 beside the suits of armor carved ships 8

carve out 1. sculpo
2Es 13: 6 he carved out for himself a great mountain 1
36 the mountain carved out without hands. 1

carved *See* wood, work.

carving 1. מִקְלַעַת
1Kg 6:32 carvings of cherubim, palm trees, and open 1
7:31 At its opening there were carvings; 1

case 1. דָּבָר 2. דִּבְרֵי רִיבוֹת 3. דִּין 4. מִשְׁפָּט 5. רִיב 6. αἰτία 7. ἀρά 8. δικαιολογία 9. ἐπί 10. καθάπερ 11. κρίσις 12. κριτήριον 13. μέρος 14. ὅς 15. περί 16. τὰ κατά 17. pro
Exd 18:19 people before God, and bring their cases to God; 1
26 hard cases they brought to Moses 1
22: 9 the case of both parties shall come before God; 1
Num 5:29 This is the law in cases of jealousy, when a wife •
8:19 in case the people of Israel should come near •
27: 5 Moses brought their case before the LORD. 4
Deu 1:16 'Hear the cases between your brethren, and judge •
17 case that is too hard for you, you shall bring to me 1
17: 8 If any case arises requiring decision 1
8 any case . . which is too difficult for you 2
22:26 case is like that of a man attacking 1
Jos 20: 4 stand . . and explain his case to the elders 1
2Ch 19:10 whenever a case comes to you from your brethren 5
Job 13: 3 I desire to argue my case with God. •
18 Behold, I have prepared my case; 4
23: 4 I would lay my case before him 4
35:14 that the case is before him, and you are waiting 3
Prv 25: 9 Argue your case with your neighbor himself 5
Isa 41:21 Set forth your case, says the LORD; 5
43:26 set forth your case, that you may be proved right. •
45:21 Declare and present your case; •
Jer 12: 1 yet I would plead my case before thee. 4
Mat 19:10 If such is the case of a man with his wife 6
Act 23:15 you were going to determine his case more exactly 15
24:22 I will decide your case. 16
25:14 Festus laid Paul's case before the king, saying 16
18 they brought no charge in his case 15
28:18 no reason for the death penalty in my case. •
1Co 6: 2 are you incompetent to try trivial cases? 12
4 If then you have such cases 12
7:15 in such a case the brother or sister is not bound. •
2Co 3:10 Indeed, in this case, what once had splendor 13
4: 4 In their case the god of this world has blinded •
9: 3 may not prove vain in this case 13
Gal 5:11 In that case the stumbling block of the cross 7
Tit 3:14 so as to help cases of urgent need •
Heb 6: 9 yet in your case, beloved 15
1Pe 2:12 in case they speak against you as wrongdoers 14
1Es 9:17 the cases of the men who had foreign wives •
2Es 4:20 but why have you not judged so in your own case? •
8:51 think of your own case 17
Sir 0: 2 and to be indulgent in cases where, •
4: 9 do not be fainthearted in judging a case. •
11: 9 nor sit with sinners when they judge a case. •
22:22 in these cases any friend will flee. •
35:13 will not show partiality in the case of a poor man; 9
19 till he judges the case of his people 11
LJr 1:64 they are not able either to decide a case 11
2Mc 2: 8 as they were shown in the case of Moses 9
29 such in my judgment is the case with us. 9
4:44 three men . . presented the case before him. 8
6:14 in the case of the other nations 10
4Mc 5:21 for in either case the law is equally despised. •
15:11 in the case of none of them 9

case *See also* draw, lay, plead, state.

any case 1. πάντως
2Mc 3:13 this money must in any case be confiscated 1

disputed case 1. רִיב
2Ch 19: 8 to decide disputed cases. 1

one case 1. ὃς μέν
Mat 13:23 in one case a hundredfold, in another 60 1

present case 1. νῦν
Act 5:38 So in the present case I tell you 1

writing case 1. קֶסֶת 2. קֶסֶת סֹפֵר
Ezk 9: 2 clothed in linen, with a writing case at his side. 2
3 the man . . who had the writing case at his side. 2
11 the man . . with the writing case at his side 1

cassia 1. קִדָּה 2. קְצִיעָה 3. κιννάμωμον
Exd 30:24 of cassia 500, according to the shekel 1
Ps 45: 8 all fragrant with myrrh and aloes and cassia. 2
Ezk 27:19 wrought iron, cassia, and calamus were bartered 1
Sir 24:15 Like cassia and camel's thorn 3

cast 1. טול 2. ידד 3. ידה 4. ירה 5. ירט 6. ירשׁ 7. לוט 8. מגר 9. נגע 10. נטה 11. נטשׁ 12. נפל 13. נשׂא 14. נתן 15. עלה 16. שׂום 17. שׁכל 18. שׁלח 19. שׁלך 20. שׁפל 21. רמא (A) 22. ἀποστρέφω 23. βάλλω 24. δίδωμι 25. ἐκβάλλω 26. ἐπιρίπτω 27. ῥίπτω
Gen 21:15 she cast the child under one of the bushes. 19
37:22 Shed no blood; cast him into this pit here 19
24 they took him and cast him into a pit. 19
39: 7 his master's wife cast her eyes upon Joseph 13
Exd 1:22 Every son . . you shall cast into the Nile 19
4: 3 he said, "Cast it to the ground." So he cast it 19
3 So he cast it on the ground, and it became a serpent; 19
15: 4 chariots and his host he cast into the sea; 4
22:31 you shall cast it to the dogs. 19
Lev 1:16 he shall . . cast it beside the altar on the east 19
16: 8 Aaron shall cast lots upon the two goats 14
26:30 cast your dead bodies upon the dead bodies 14
Num19: 6 cast them into the midst of the burning 19
35:23 stone . . and without seeing him cast it upon him 12
Deu 9:17 two tables, and cast them out of my two hands 19
29:28 cast them into another land, as at this day.' 19
Jos 8:29 and cast it at the entrance of the gate of the city 19
18: 6 and I will cast lots for you here before the LORD 4
8 and I will cast lots for you here before the LORD 19

10 Joshua cast lots . . in Shiloh before the LORD; 19
Jdg 8:25 every man cast in it the earrings of his spoil. 19
1Sm 18:11 and Saul cast the spear, for he thought, "I will pin 1
20:33 But Saul cast his spear at him to smite him; 1
2Sm 11:21 Did not a woman cast an upper millstone upon him 19
1Kg 14: 9 and have cast me behind your back; 19
19:19 Eli'jah passed . . and cast his mantle upon him. 19
2Kg 2:16 caught him up and cast him upon some mountain 19
9:25 Take him up, and cast him on the plot of ground 19
26 take him up and cast him on the plot of ground 19
13:21 and the man was cast into the grave of Eli'sha; 19
23 nor has he cast them from his presence until now. 19
17:20 until he had cast them out of his sight. 19
19:18 and have cast their gods into the fire; 14
23: 6 beat it . . and cast the dust of it upon the graves 19
12 and cast the dust of them into the brook Kidron. 19
1Ch 24:31 head . . and his younger brother alike, cast lots 12
25: 8 they cast lots for their duties, small and great 12
26:13 cast lots by fathers' houses, small and great 12
14 They cast lots also for his son Zechari'ah 12
Neh 9:11 thou didst cast their pursuers into the depths 19
26 rebelled . . and cast thy law behind their back 19
10:34 likewise cast lots, the priests, the Levites 12
11: 1 rest . . cast lots to bring one out of ten to live 12
Est 3: 7 they cast Pur, that is the lot, before Haman 12
7 cast it month after month till the twelfth month *
9:24 and had cast Pur, that is the lot, 12
Job 16:11 casts me into the hands of the wicked. 5
18: 8 For he is cast into a net by his own feet 18
20:15 God casts them out of his belly. 6
21:10 their cow calves, and does not cast her calf. 17
30:19 God has cast me into the mire 4
Ps 2: 3 bonds asunder, and cast their cords from us. 19
17:11 they set their eyes to cast me to the ground. 10
22:10 Upon thee was I cast from my birth 19
18 for my raiment they cast lots. 12
50:17 you cast my words behind you. 19
55:22 Cast your burden on the LORD, and he will sustain 19
60: 8 Moab is my washbasin; upon Edom I cast my shoe; 19
89:44 Thou hast . . cast his throne to the ground. 8
108: 9 Moab is my washbasin; upon Edom I cast my shoe; 19
140:10 Let them be cast into pits, no more to rise! 12
147: 6 LORD . . casts the wicked to the ground. 20
Prv 16:33 The lot is cast into the lap 1
19:15 Slothfulness casts into a deep sleep 12
Ecc 11: 1 Cast your bread upon the waters, 18
Isa 19: 8 mourn and lament, all who cast hook in the Nile; 19
25: 7 the covering that is cast over all peoples 7
12 will bring down, lay low, and cast to the ground 9
26: 5 lays it low to the ground, casts it to the dust. 9
34:17 He has cast the lot for them 12
37:19 have cast their gods into the fire; 14
38: 8 I will make the shadow cast by the declining sun *
17 for thou hast cast all my sins behind thy back. 19
Jer 22: 7 choicest cedars, and cast them into the fire. 12
28 and cast into a land which they do not know? 19
26:23 and cast his dead body into the burial place 19
38: 6 they took Jeremiah and cast him into the cistern 19
9 to Jeremiah . . by casting him into the cistern; 19
41: 7 slew them, and cast them into a cistern. ‡
9 cistern into which Ish'mael cast all the bodies 19
51:63 and cast it into the midst of the Euphra'tes 19
Lam 2:10 they have cast dust on their heads 15
3:53 flung me . . into the pit and cast stones on me; 3
Ezk 5: 4 you shall take some, and cast them into the fire 19
7:19 They cast their silver into the streets 19
23:35 have forgotten me and cast me behind your back 19
26:12 soil they will cast into the midst of the waters. 16
27:30 They cast dust on their heads and wallow in ashes; 15
28:16 I cast you as a profane thing from the mountain *
17 I cast you to the ground; 19
32: 4 I will cast you on the ground 11
Dan 3: 6 shall . . be cast into a burning fiery furnace. 21
11 shall be cast into a burning fiery furnace. 21
15 immediately be cast into a . . fiery furnace; 21
20 cast them into the burning fiery furnace. 21
21 cast into the burning fiery furnace. 21
24 Did we not cast three men bound into the fire? 21
6: 7 shall be cast into the den of lions. 21
12 shall be cast into the den of lions? 21
16 Daniel was brought and cast into the den 21
24 men who had accused Daniel were brought and cast 21
Jol 3: 3 and have cast lots for my people 2
Obd 1:11 and foreigners . . cast lots for Jerusalem 2
Jon 1: 7 they said to one another, "Come, let us cast lots 12
7 So they cast lots, and the lot fell upon Jonah. 12
2: 3 For thou didst cast me into the deep 19
Mic 2: 5 you will have none to cast the line by lot 19
7:19 wilt cast all our sins into the depths of the sea. 19
Nah 3:10 for her honored men lots were cast 2
Zec 11:13 Then the LORD said to me, "Cast it into the treasury 19
13 and cast them into the treasury in the house 19
Mat 4:18 Andrew his brother, casting a net into the sea; 23
17:27 go to the sea and cast a hook 23
21:21 'Be taken up and cast into the sea,' 23
39 they took him and cast him out of the vineyard 25
22:13 and cast him into the outer darkness; 25
25:30 cast the worthless servant 25
27:35 divided his garments among them by casting lots; 23
Mrk 9:22 often cast him into the fire and into the water 23
11:23 'Be taken up and cast into the sea,' 23
15:24 casting lots for them 23
Lke 12:49 I came to cast fire upon the earth 23
17: 2 if . . he were cast into the sea 27
23:34 they cast lots to divide his garments. 23
Joh 15: 6 he is cast forth as a branch and withers 23
19:24 for my clothing they cast lots. 23
21: 6 Cast the net on the right side of the boat 23
6 they cast it 23
Act 1:26 they cast lots for them 24
1Pe 5: 7 Cast all your anxieties on him 26
1Jn 4:18 but perfect love casts out fear. 23
Rev 4:10 they cast their crowns before the throne, singing 23
12: 4 the stars of heaven, and cast them to the earth. 23
Jdt 6:12 kept them from coming up by casting stones 23
Sir 21:15 he dislikes it and casts it behind his back. 22
37: 8 lest he cast the lot against you 23

cast (2) 1. יצק 2. מוּצָק 3. מוּצֶקֶת 4. נסך 5. צור 6. צרף 7. χωνεύω

Exd 25:12 you shall cast four rings of gold for it 1
26:37 you shall cast five bases of bronze for them. 1
36:36 and he cast for them four bases of silver. 1
37: 3 he cast for it four rings of gold 1
13 He cast for it four rings of gold, and fastened 1
38: 5 He cast four rings on the four corners 1
27 The 100 talents of silver were for casting 1
1Kg 7:15 He cast two pillars of bronze. 5
24 the gourds were . . cast with it when it was cast. 1
24 the gourds were . . cast with it when it was cast. 1
30 The supports were cast, with wreaths at the side 1
33 rims, their spokes, and their hubs, were all cast. 1
37 all of them were cast alike, of the same measure 2
46 In the plain of the Jordan the king cast them 1
2Ch 4: 3 were in two rows, cast with it when it was cast. 1
3 were in two rows, cast with it when it was cast. 3
17 In the plain of the Jordan the king cast them 1
Isa 40:19 The idol! a workman casts it 4
19 with gold, and casts for it silver chains. 6
44:10 Who fashions a god or casts an image 4
LJr 1:24 when they were being cast, they had no feeling. 7

cast a net 1. ἀμφιβάλλω

Mrk 1:16 Simon and Andrew . . casting a net in the sea 1

cast against 1. καταφέρω

Act 26:10 I cast my vote against them. 1

cast ashore 1. ἐκβράζω

2Mc 5: 8 he was cast ashore in Egypt; 1

cast away 1. מאס 2. נטשׁ 3. שׁלך 4. proicio

1Sm 12:22 the LORD will not cast away his people 2
Ps 51:11 Cast me not away from thy presence 3
Ecc 3: 5 a time to cast away stones, and a time to gather 3
6 a time to keep, and a time to cast away; 3
Isa 31: 7 every one shall cast away his idols of silver 1
Jer 7:29 Cut off your hair and cast it away; 3
23:39 lift you up and cast you away from my presence 2
Ezk 18:31 Cast away from you all the transgressions 3
20: 7 I said to them, Cast away the detestable things 3
8 not every man cast away the detestable things 3
2Es 14:14 cast away from you the burdens of man 4

cast contempt 1. חרף

2Ch 32:17 he wrote letters to cast contempt on the LORD 1

cast down 1. הרס 2. ידה 3. ירד 4. כשׁל 5. נוח 6. נפל 7. סלף 8. שׁחח 9. שׁלך 10. καθαιρέω 11. καταβάλλω 12. ῥίπτω

Exd 7: 9 Take your rod and cast it down before Pharaoh 9
10 Aaron cast down his rod before Pharaoh 9
12 For every man cast down his rod, and they became 9
2Ch 25: 8 God will cast you down before the enemy; 4
8 for God has power to help or to cast down. 4
Ezr 10: 1 weeping and casting himself down before 6
Job 29:24 light of my countenance they did not cast down. 6
Ps 42: 5 Why are you cast down, O my soul 8
6 My soul is cast down within me 8
11 Why are you cast down, O my soul 8
43: 5 Why are you cast down, O my soul 8
55:23 thou, O God, wilt cast them down into the lowest pit; 3
56: 7 in wrath cast down the peoples, O God! 3
Prv 21:12 wicked are cast down to ruin. 7
Isa 22:19 you will be cast down from your station. 1
28: 2 he will cast down to the earth with violence. 5
Jer 9:19 because they have cast down our dwellings. 9
Lam 2: 1 He has cast down . . to earth the splendor 9
Ezk 6: 4 I will cast down your slain before your idols. 6
19:12 was plucked up in fury, cast down to the ground; 9
31:16 when I cast it down to Sheol with those who go down 3
Dan 8: 7 cast him down to the ground and trampled upon him; 9
10 host of the stars it cast down to the ground 6
12 truth was cast down to the ground 9
11:12 shall cast down tens of thousands 6
Ams 5: 7 and cast down righteousness to the earth! 5
Zec 1:21 to cast down the horns of the nations who lifted 2
Jdt 9: 8 to cast down the horn of thy altar with the sword. 11
Sir 1:30 cast you down in the midst of the congregation 11
10:14 The Lord has cast down the thrones of rulers 10
3Mc 6: 7 Daniel . . was cast down into the ground to lions 12

firmly cast 1. יצק

Job 41:23 his flesh cleave together, firmly cast upon him 1

cast forth 1. נטשׁ 2. שׁלך

Ps 147:17 He casts forth his ice like morsels; 2
Isa 2:20 men will cast forth their idols of silver 2
Jer 22:19 and cast forth beyond the gates of Jerusalem. 2
Ezk 29: 5 I will cast you forth into the wilderness 1
Ams 4: 3 and you shall be cast forth into Harmon 2

cast headlong 1. טול

Ps 37:24 though he fall, he shall not be cast headlong 1

cast into 1. ἐμβάλλω

Lke 12: 5 who . . has power to cast into hell 1

cast into hell 1. ταρταρόω

2Pe 2: 4 God . . cast them into hell 1

cast lots 1. נפל 2. λαγχάνω

1Sm 14:42 Cast the lot between me and my son Jonathan. 1
Job 6:27 You would even cast lots over the fatherless 1
Joh 19:24 but cast lots for it to see whose it shall be 2

cast off 1. הלא 2. זנח 3. מאס 4. נטשׁ 5. שׁחת 6. שׁלח 7. שׁלך 8. ἀπορίπτω 9. ἀποσκορακίζω 10. ἀποτίθημι 11. περιαιρέω

Jdg 6:13 us up from Egypt?' But now the LORD has cast us off 4
2Kg 21:14 I will cast off the remnant of my heritage 4
23:27 I will cast off this city which I have chosen 3
1Ch 28: 9 if you forsake him, he will cast you off for ever. 2
Job 15:33 and cast off his blossom, like the olive tree. 7
30:11 they have cast off restraint in my presence. 6
Ps 27: 9 Cast me not off, forsake me not, O God 4
43: 2 why hast thou cast me off? Why go I mourning 2
44: 9 Yet thou hast cast us off and abased us 2
23 Awake! Do not cast us off for ever! 2
71: 9 Do not cast me off in the time of old age; 7
74: 1 O God, why dost thou cast us off for ever? 2
88:14 O LORD, why dost thou cast me off? 2
89:38 now thou hast cast off and rejected 2
Isa 41: 9 I have chosen you and not cast you off"; 3
54: 6 like a wife of youth when she is cast off 3
Jer 23:33 You are the burden, and I will cast you off 4
31:37 I will cast off all the descendants of Israel 3
Lam 3:31 For the Lord will not cast off for ever 2
Hos 9:17 My God will cast them off 3
Ams 1:11 and cast off all pity, and his anger tore 5
Mic 4: 7 and those who were cast off, a strong nation; 1
Act 27:40 they cast off the anchors and left them in the sea 11
Rom 13:12 Let us then cast off the works of darkness 10
Sir 6:21 he will not be slow to cast her off. 8
1Mc 11:55 All the troops that Demetrius had cast off 9

cast off restraint 1. פרע

Prv 29:18 no prophecy the people cast off restraint 1

cast one's young 1. שׁכל

Exd 23:26 None shall cast her young or be barren 1

cast out 1. גרשׁ 2. זנח 3. ירשׁ 4. נדה 5. נדח 6. פנה 7. ריק 8. שׁלח 9. שׁלך 10. ἐκβάλλω 11. ἐκρίπτω 12. ῥίπτω 13. prodo 14. proicio

Gen 21:10 she said to Abraham, "Cast out this slave woman 1
Exd 34:24 For I will cast out nations before you 3
Lev 18:24 the nations I am casting out before you defiled 8
20:23 the nation which I am casting out before you 8
1Kg 9: 7 the house . . I will cast out of my sight; 8
21:26 the LORD cast out before the people of Israel.) 3
2Kg 10:25 the guard and the officers cast them out 9
24:20 he cast them out from his presence. 9
2Ch 7:20 and this house . . I will cast out of my sight 9
11:14 cast them out from serving as priests of the LORD 2
Ps 5:10 because of their many transgressions cast them out 5
18:42 I cast them out like the mire of the streets. 7
Isa 14:19 you are cast out, away from your sepulchre 9
34: 3 Their slain shall be cast out 9
66: 5 who hate you and cast you out for my name's sake 4
Jer 7:15 And I will cast you out of my sight 9
15 as I cast out all your kinsmen, all the offspring 9
14:16 shall be cast out in the streets of Jerusalem 9
36:30 his dead body shall be cast out to the heat by day 9
52: 3 that he cast them out from his presence. 9
Ezk 16: 5 but you were cast out on the open field 9
31:11 as its wickedness deserves. I have cast it out. 1
Ams 8: 3 in every place they shall be cast out in silence. 9
Jon 2: 4 Then I said, 'I am cast out from thy presence; 1
Zep 3:15 he hast cast out your enemies. 6
Mat 7:22 and cast out demons in your name 10
8:16 and he cast out the spirits with a word 10
31 the demons begged him, "If you cast us out, send us 10
9:33 when the demon had been cast out 10
34 He casts out demons by the prince of demons. 10

10: 1 authority over unclean spirits, to cast them out 10
8 cleanse lepers, cast out demons 10
12:24 that this man casts out demons. 10
26 if Satan casts out Satan, he is divided 10
27 if I cast out demons by Be-el'zebul 10
27 by whom do your sons cast them out? 10
28 if it is by the Spirit of God that I cast out demons 10
17:19 Why could we not cast it out? 10
Mrk 1:34 and cast out many demons 10
39 preaching . . and casting out demons. 10
3:15 and have authority to cast out demons 10
22 by the prince of demons he casts out the demons. 10
23 How can Satan cast out Satan? 10
6:13 they cast out many demons, and anointed with oil 10
7:26 begged him to cast the demon out of her daughter. 10
9:18 I asked your disciples to cast it out 10
28 Why could we not cast it out? 10
38 we saw a man casting out demons in your name 10
12: 8 and cast him out of the vineyard. 10
16: 9 from whom he had cast out seven demons. 10
17 in my name they will cast out demons 10
Lke 6:22 and cast out your name as evil 10
9:40 I begged your disciples to cast it out 10
49 we saw a man casting out demons in your name 10
11:14 Now he was casting out a demon that was dumb 10
15 He casts out demons by Be-el'zebul 10
18 you say that I cast out demons by Be-el'zebul. 10
19 if I cast out demons by Be-el'zebul 10
19 by whom do your sons cast them out? 10
20 if it is by the finger of God that I cast out demons 10
13:32 I cast out demons and perform cures today 10
20:12 this one they wounded and cast out. 10
15 they cast him out of the vineyard and killed him. 10
Joh 6:37 him who comes to me I will not cast out. 10
9:34 And they cast him out. 10
35 Jesus heard that they had cast him out 10
12:31 now shall the ruler of this world be cast out; 10
Act 7:58 Then they cast him out of the city and stoned him; 10
16:37 do they now cast us out secretly 10
27:19 they cast out with their own hands the tackle 12
Gal 4:30 Cast out the slave and her son 10
2Es 1:30 I will cast you out from my presence. 14
10:22 our little ones have been cast out 13
16:23 the dead shall be cast out like dung 14
Wis 11:14 who long before had been cast out 12
Sir 7:26 you have a wife who pleases you, do not cast her out; 10
Bar 2:25 behold, they have been cast out to the heat of day 11
LJr 1:71 like a dead body cast out in the darkness. 12
1Mc 13:48 He cast out of it all uncleanness 10
2Mc 5:10 He who had cast out many to lie unburied 11

cast reproach upon 1. כלם
Job 19: 3 These ten times you have cast reproach upon me; 1

cast up 1. סלל 2. שׁפך 3. ἀναβράσσω 4. παρεμβάλλω 5. infulcio 6. reicio
2Sm 20:15 they cast up a mound against the city, and it stood 2
2Kg 19:32 or cast up a siege mound against it. 2
Job 19:12 they have cast up siegeworks against me 1
30:12 they cast up against me their ways 1
Isa 37:33 or cast up a siege mound against it. 2
Jer 6: 6 cast up a siege mound against Jerusalem. 2
Ezk 4: 2 and cast up a mound against it; 2
17:17 will not help him in war, when mounds are cast up 2
21:22 to cast up mounds, to build siege towers. 2
Lke 19:43 when your enemies will cast up a bank about you 4
2Es 5: 7 the sea of Sodom shall cast up fish 6
12:32 and will cast up before them 5
Wis 10:19 and cast them up from the depth of the sea. 3

cast up foam 1. ἐπαφρίζω
Jde 1:13 casting up the foam of their own shame 1

castanet 1. מְנַעַנְעִ
2Sm 6: 5 lyres and harps and tambourines and castanets 1

castle 1. אַרְמוֹן 2. בִּירָה
Neh 7: 2 I gave . . Hanani'ah the governor of the castle 2
Prv 18:19 but quarreling is like the bars of a castle. 1

castoff piece 1. ἀπόβλημα
Wis 13:12 and burn the castoff pieces of his work 1
13 a castoff piece from among them 1

cat 1. αἴλουρος
LJr 1:22 so do cats. 1

catapult 1. καταπέλτης 2. πετροβόλος 3. σφενδόνη
Wis 5:22 will be hurled as from a catapult 2
1Mc 6:51 machines to shoot arrows, and catapults. 3
4Mc 8:13 rack and hooks and catapults and caldrons 1
9:26 they bound him to the torture machine and catapult. 1
11: 9 bound him and dragged him to the catapult; 1
26 and the catapults painless 1
18:20 brought . . to the catapult 1

cataract 1. צִנּוֹר
Ps 42: 7 calls to deep at the thunder of thy cataracts; 1

catastrophe 1. πτῶμα
Jdt 8:19 they suffered a great catastrophe 1

catch 1. אחז 2. דוג 3. חזק 4. טרף 5. לָכַד 6. לכד 7. לקח 8. מצא 9. ספה 10. תמך 11. תפשׂ 12. ἄγρα 13. ἁλίσκομαι 14. ἅλωσις 15. δράσσομαι 16. ἐπιλαμβάνομαι 17. ἐπιτυγχάνω 18. εὑρίσκω 19. ζωγρέω 20. θηρεύω 21. καταλαμβάνω 22. πιάζω 23. συναρπάζω
Gen 22:13 a ram, caught in a thicket by his horns; 1
39:12 caught him by his garment, saying, "Lie with me 11
Exd 4: 4 it by the tail"- so he put out his hand and caught it 3
22: 6 When fire breaks out and catches in thorns 8
Deu 32:11 out its wings, catching them, bearing them 7
Jdg 1: 6 they pursued him, and caught him, and cut off his 1
8:14 he caught a young man of Succoth, and questioned 6
15: 4 Samson went and caught 300 foxes 6
1Sm 17:35 if he arose against me, I caught him by his beard 3
2Sm 2:16 And each caught his opponent by the head 3
Job 36: 8 in fetters and caught in the cords of affliction 6
Ps 9:15 in the net . . has their own foot been caught. 6
10: 2 caught in the schemes which they have devised. 11
Prv 3:26 LORD . . will keep your foot from being caught. 5
5:22 he is caught in the coils of his sin. 10
6: 2 if you are . . caught in the words of your mouth; 6
31 if he is caught, he will pay sevenfold; 8
7:22 he follows her . . as a stag is caught fast *
12:27 A slothful man will not catch his prey 17
Ecc 9:12 and like birds which are caught in a snare 1
Sng 2:15 Catch us the foxes . . that spoil the vineyards 1
Isa 13:15 and whoever is caught will fall by the sword. 9
24:18 he who climbs . . shall be caught in the snare. 6
Jer 2:26 As a thief is shamed when caught 8
5:26 lying in wait. They set a trap; they catch men. 6
16:16 fishers, says the LORD, and they shall catch them; 2
48:44 he who climbs out . . shall be caught in the snare. 6
50:24 you did not know it; you were found and caught 11
Ezk 19: 3 a young lion, and he learned to catch prey; 4
6 he learned to catch prey; he devoured men. 4
Mat 14:31 reached out his hand and caught him, saying to him 16
Lke 5: 4 and let down your nets for a catch. 12
9 the catch of fish which they had taken; 12
10 henceforth you will be catching men. 19
11:54 to catch at something he might say. 20
20:26 to catch him by what he said 16
Joh 8: 3 a woman who had been caught in adultery 21
4 this woman has been caught in the act of adultery 21
21: 3 that night they caught nothing. 22
10 Bring some of the fish that you have just caught. 22
Act 27:15 the ship was caught and could not face the wind 23
1Co 3:19 it is written, "He catches the wise 15
2Pe 2:12 creatures . . born to be caught and killed 14
Tob 6: 3 the angel said to him, "Catch the fish. 16
Sir 9: 4 lest you be caught in her intrigues. 13
27:19 will not catch him again. 20
26 he who sets a snare will be caught in it. 13
29 will be caught in a snare 13
34: 2 As one who catches at a shadow 15
Aza 1:25 the Chaldeans whom it caught about the furnace. 18
Sus 1:58 did you catch them being intimate with each other? 21
1Mc 6:24 put to death as many of us as they have caught 18
2Mc 13:21 he was sought for, caught, and put in prison. 21

catch fast 1. חזק
2Sm 18: 9 Ab'salom was . . and his head caught fast in the oak 1

catch fire 1. בער
Jdg 15:14 the ropes . . became as flax that has caught fire 1

catch hold 1. חזק 2. ἔχω
1Kg 1:50 went, and caught hold of the horns of the altar. 1
2:28 Jo'ab fled . . and caught hold of the horns 1
2Kg 4:27 when she came . . she caught hold of his feet. 1
2Mc 12:35 Dositheus . . caught hold of Gorgias 2

catch sight of 1. προσνοέω
Tob 11: 6 she caught sight of him coming 1

catch up 1. אחז 2. נשׂא 3. ἀναλαμβάνω 4. ἁρπάζω
2Kg 2:16 the Spirit of the LORD has caught him up 2
Est 1: 6 hangings caught up with cords of fine linen 1
Act 8:39 the Spirit of the Lord caught up Philip 4
2Co 12: 2 a man in Christ . . caught up to the third heaven 4
3 this man was caught up into Paradise 4
1Th 4:17 we . . shall be caught up together with them 4
Rev 12: 5 her child was caught up to God and to his throne 4
Jdt 6:12 they caught up their weapons and ran out of the city 3
Wis 4:11 He was caught up 4

caterpillar 1. חָסִיל
1Kg 8:37 or blight or mildew or locust or caterpillar; 1
2Ch 6:28 if there is . . mildew or locust or caterpillar; 1
Ps 78:46 He gave their crops to the caterpillar 1
Isa 33: 4 spoil is gathered as the caterpillar gathers; 1

cattle 1. אַלּוּף 2. אֶלֶף 3. בְּהֵמָה 4. בְּעִיר 5. בָּקָר 6. מְלָאכָה 7. מִקְנֶה 8. שׁוֹר 9. βόσκημα 10. βουκόλιον 11. θρέμμα 12. κτῆνος 13. iumentum 14. pecus
Gen 1:24 their kinds: cattle and creeping things 3
25 the cattle according to their kinds 3
26 have dominion . . over the cattle 3
2:20 The man gave names to all cattle 3
3:14 done this, cursed are you above all cattle 3
4:20 those who dwell in tents and have cattle. 7
7:14 all the cattle according to their kinds 3
21 moved upon the earth, birds, cattle, beasts 3
8: 1 remembered . . all the cattle that were with him 3
9:10 the birds, the cattle, and every beast of the earth 3
13: 2 was very rich in cattle, in silver, and in gold. 7
7 strife between the herdsmen of Abram's cattle 7
7 Abram's cattle and the herdsmen of Lot's cattle. 7
30:29 and how your cattle have fared with me. 7
31: 9 Thus God has taken away the cattle of your father 7
18 he drove away all his cattle, all his livestock 7
18 he had gained, the cattle in his possession 7
33:14 slowly, according to the pace of the cattle 6
17 built . . a house, and made booths for his cattle; 7
34: 5 but his sons were with the cattle in the field 7
23 Will not their cattle, their property 7
36: 6 Esau took . . his cattle, all his beasts 7
7 could not support them because of their cattle. 7
46: 6 They also took their cattle and their goods 7
32 shepherds, for they have been keepers of cattle; 7
34 have been keepers of cattle from our youth 7
47: 6 put them in charge of my cattle. 7
16 Joseph answered, "Give your cattle, 7
16 I will give you food in exchange for your cattle 7
17 they brought their cattle to Joseph; 7
17 food in exchange for all their cattle that year. 7
18 and the herds of cattle are my lord's; 3
Exd 9: 3 very severe plague upon your cattle which are 7
4 a distinction between the cattle of Israel 7
4 The cattle of Israel and the cattle of Egypt 7
6 all the cattle of the Egyptians died 7
6 of the cattle of the people of Israel not one 7
7 not one of the cattle of the Israelites was dead. 7
19 get your cattle . . into safe shelter 7
20 made his slaves and his cattle flee into the houses 7
21 left his slaves and his cattle in the field. 7
10:26 Our cattle also must go with us; 7
11: 5 and all the first-born of the cattle. 3
12:29 smote . . and all the first-born of the cattle. 3
38 and very many cattle, both flocks and herds. 7
13:12 All the firstlings of your cattle that are males 3
15 first-born of man and the first-born of cattle. 3
17: 3 our children and our cattle with thirst? 7
20:10 or your maidservant, or your cattle 3
34:19 the womb is mine, all your male cattle 7
Lev 1: 2 you shall bring your offering of cattle 3
5: 2 or a carcass of unclean cattle or a carcass 3
19:19 not let your cattle breed with a different kind 3
25: 7 for your cattle also and for the beasts 3
26:22 I will . . destroy your cattle, and make you few 3
Num 3:41 cattle of the Levites instead of all 3
41 firstlings among the cattle of . . Israel. 3
45 Take . . the cattle of the Levites instead 3
45 cattle of the Levites instead of their cattle; 3
7:87 cattle for the burnt offering twelve bulls 5
88 cattle for the sacrifice of peace offerings 5
20: 4 that we should die here, both we and our cattle? 4
8 give drink to the congregation and their cattle. 4
11 congregation drank, and their cattle. 4
19 if we drink of your water, I and my cattle 7
31: 9 they took as booty all their cattle, their flocks 3
30 one drawn out of every 50 . . of all the cattle 3
33 72,000 cattle 5
38 The cattle were 36,000, of which the LORD'S tribute 5
44 36,000 cattle 5
32: 1 sons of Gad had a very great multitude of cattle; 7
1 behold, the place was a place for cattle 7
4 land which the LORD smote . . is a land for cattle; 7
4 land for cattle; and your servants have cattle. 7
26 Our . . wives, our flocks, and all our cattle 3
35: 3 their pasture lands shall be for their cattle 3
Deu 2:35 only the cattle we took as spoil for ourselves 3
3: 7 cattle and the spoil of the cities we took 3
19 your wives, your little ones, and your cattle 7
19 your cattle (I know that you have many cattle) 7
5:14 your ox, or your ass, or any of your cattle 3
7:13 bless . . the increase of your cattle 2
14 not be male or female barren . . among your cattle. 3
11:15 he will give grass in your fields for your cattle 3
13:15 destroying it utterly . . and its cattle 3
20:14 cattle, and everything else in the city 3
28: 4 Blessed shall be . . the increase of your cattle 2
11 make you abound in . . the fruit of your cattle 3
18 Cursed shall be . . the increase of your cattle 2
51 eat the offspring of your cattle and the fruit 3
51 not leave you . . the increase of your cattle 2
30: 9 prosperous in . . the fruit of your cattle 3
Jos 1:14 Your wives, your little ones, and your cattle 7
8: 2 its spoil and its cattle you shall take as booty 3
27 the cattle and the spoil of that city Israel took 3
11:14 And all the spoil of these cities and the cattle 3
14: 4 with their pasture lands for their cattle 7

21: 2 along with their pasture lands for our cattle. 3
22: 8 Go . . with much wealth, and with very many cattle 7
Jdg 6: 5 would come up with their cattle and their tents 7
18:21 little ones and the cattle and the goods in front 7
1Sm 8:16 take . . and the best of your cattle and your asses 10
23: 5 fought with . . and brought away their cattle 7
30:20 and the people drove those cattle before him 7
1Kg 4:23 fat oxen, and twenty pasture-fed cattle 5
2Kg 3:17 you shall drink, you, your cattle, and your beasts.' 7
1Ch 5: 9 cattle had multiplied in the land of Gilead. 7
7:21 because they came down to raid their cattle. 7
28: 1 the stewards of all the property and cattle 7
2Ch 14:15 they smote the tents of those who had cattle 7
20:25 found cattle in great numbers, goods, clothing 12
31: 6 also brought in the tithe of cattle and sheep 5
32:28 stalls for all kinds of cattle, and sheepfolds. 3
Neh 9:37 power also over our bodies and over our cattle 3
10:36 bring . . first-born of our sons and of our cattle 3
Job 18: 3 Why are we counted as cattle? 3
Ps 50:10 is mine, the cattle on 1,000 hills. 3
78:48 He gave over their cattle to the hail 4
104:14 Thou dost cause the grass to grow for the cattle 3
107:38 he does not let their cattle decrease. 3
144:14 may our cattle be heavy with young 1
148:10 Beasts and all cattle 3
Isa 7:25 will become a place where cattle are let loose 8
30:23 your cattle will graze in large pastures; 7
46: 1 Nebo stoops, their idols are on beasts and cattle; 3
63:14 Like cattle that go down into the valley 3
Jer 9:10 and the lowing of cattle is not heard; 7
49:32 become booty, their herds of cattle a spoil. 7
Ezk 38:12 the people . . who have gotten cattle and goods 7
13 take away cattle and goods, to seize great spoil 7
Jol 1:18 The herds of cattle are perplexed 5
Jon 4:11 more than 120,000 persons . . and also much cattle 3
Hag 1:11 upon men and cattle, and upon all their labors. 3
Zec 2: 4 because of the multitude of men and cattle in it. 3
Joh 4:12 drank from it himself, and his sons, and his cattle? 11
Rev 18:13 cattle and sheep, horses and chariots, and slaves 12
1Es 2: 7 with gifts and with horses and cattle 12
9 with silver and gold, with horses and cattle 12
5: 1 menservants and maidservants, and their cattle. 12
8:50 our children and the cattle that were with us. 12
9: 4 their cattle should be seized for sacrifice 12
2Es 6:53 to bring forth before thee cattle, beasts 13
8:29 who have had the ways of cattle 14
Tob 10:10 half of his property in slaves, cattle, and money. 12
Jdt 4:10 their wives and their children and their cattle 12
5: 9 much gold and silver and very many cattle. 12
8: 7 cattle, and fields 12
11: 7 the beasts of the field and the cattle 12
12 they have planned to kill their cattle 12
Sir 7:22 Do you have cattle? Look after them 12
Aza 1:59 Bless the Lord, all beasts and cattle 12
1Mc 1:32 seized the cattle. 12
2:30 they, their sons, their wives, and their cattle 12
38 with their wives and children and cattle 12
10:33 cancel also the taxes on their cattle. 12
12:23 your cattle and your property belong to us 12
2Mc 12:11 promising to give him cattle 9

caulk 1. חזק
Ezk 27: 9 her skilled men were in you, caulking your seams; 1

caulker 1. חזק בֶּדֶק
Ezk 27:27 your mariners and your pilots, your caulkers 1

cause 1. דָּבָר 2. דִּבְרָה 3. דִּין 4. היה 5. מִשְׁפָּט 6. נתן 7. עשה 8. רִיב 9. *αἰτία* 10. *αἴτιος* 11. *ἀφορμή* 12. *δημιουργός* 13. *διά* 14. *δίδωμι* 15. *εἰς* 16. *κατασκευάζω* 17. *καταφθείρω* 18. *κρίσις* 19. *παρέχω* 20. *πόθεν* 21. *ποιέω* 22. *χράω* 23. facio
Exd 23: 8 a bribe . . subverts the cause of those who are 1
24:14 whoever has a cause, let him go to them. 1
Lev 24:19 a man causes a disfigurement in his neighbor 6
Num31:16 these caused the people of Israel . . to act 4
Deu 16:19 bribe . . subverts the cause of the righteous. 1
28: 7 LORD will cause your enemies who rise against 6
25 LORD will cause you to be defeated before 6
Jdg 6:31 contend for Ba'al? Or will you defend his cause? •
1Sm 5: 9 LORD was against . . causing a very great panic •
24:15 give sentence . . and see to it, and plead my cause 8
2Sm 15: 4 every man with a suit or cause might come to me 5
20: 6 lest he get . . cities, and cause us trouble. ‡
1Kg 8:45 then hear . . and maintain their cause. 5
49 hear . . and maintain their cause 5
59 and may he maintain the cause of his servant 5
59 maintain . . and the cause of his people Israel 5
2Ch 6:35 then hear . . and maintain their cause. 5
39 hear thou . . and maintain their cause 5
Neh 4: 8 together to come . . and to cause confusion 7
Est 1:17 causing them to look with contempt upon their †
Job 5: 8 seek God, and to God would I commit my cause; 2
29:16 I searched out the cause of him whom I did not know. 8
31:13 If I have rejected the cause of my manservant 5
Ps 9: 4 For thou hast maintained my just cause; 3
22: 8 He committed his cause to the LORD; •
35:23 awake for my right, for my cause, my God 8
43: 1 defend my cause against an ungodly people; 8
45: 4 ride forth victoriously for the cause of truth 1
56: 5 All day long they seek to injure my cause; 1
74:22 Arise, O God, plead thy cause; 8
106:46 He caused them to be pitied by all those who held 6
111: 4 caused his wonderful works to be remembered; 7
119:154 Plead my cause and redeem me; give me life 8
140:12 LORD maintains the cause of the afflicted 3
Prv 10: 4 A slack hand causes poverty 7
10 He who winks the eye causes trouble 6
22:23 for the LORD will plead their cause and despoil 8
23:11 Redeemer . . will plead their cause against you. 8
29:22 man given to anger causes much transgression. •
Isa 1:23 the widow's cause does not come to them. 8
21: 2 all the sighing she has caused I bring to an end. •
34: 8 a year of recompense for the cause of Zion. 8
Jer 5:28 they judge not . . the cause of the fatherless 3
11:20 for to thee have I committed my cause. 8
20:12 for to thee have I committed my cause. 8
22:16 He judged the cause of the poor and needy; 3
30:13 There is none to uphold your cause 3
50:34 He will surely plead their cause 8
51:36 I will plead your cause and take vengeance 8
Lam 3:36 to subvert a man in his cause 8
58 Thou hast taken up my cause, O Lord 8
59 Thou hast seen . . O LORD; judge thou my cause. 5
Ezk 32:30 all the terror which they caused by their might; •
36:27 and cause you to walk in my statutes •
44:18 not gird . . with anything that causes sweat. •
Mic 7: 9 until he pleads my cause and executes judgment 8
Mat 19: 3 Is it lawful to divorce one's wife for any cause? 9
Act 19:40 no cause that we can give to justify this 10
2Co 2: 5 he has caused it not to me †
5:12 giving you cause to be proud of us 11
Jas 4: 1 What causes wars, and what causes fightings 20
1 and what causes fightings among you? 20
Rev 13:15 and to cause those who would not worship 21
16 Also it causes all . . to be marked 21
2Es 15: 2 cause them to be written on paper 23
39 the tempest that was to cause destruction 23
Jdt 9:14 cause thy whole nation and every tribe to know 21
Wis 12:16 sovereignty over all causes thee to spare all. 21
14:27 the beginning and cause and end of every evil. 9
17:13 prefers ignorance of what causes the torment. 9
Sir 18:15 nor cause grief by your words •
25:23 a wounded heart are caused by an evil wife. •
23 caused by the wife •
29: 4 cause trouble to those who help them. 19
36:20 A perverse mind will cause grief 14
LJr 1:54 They cannot judge their own cause 18
1Mc 3:29 the dissension and disaster which he had caused 16
42 to cause their final destruction. 15
15:31 for the destruction that you have caused 17
35 they were causing great damage among the people 21
2Mc 3:24 caused so great a manifestation 21
4: 1 had been the real cause of the misfortune. 12
47 Menelaus, the cause of all the evil, he acquitted 10
4Mc 1:11 they became the cause of the downfall of tyranny 10
16 knowledge of . . the causes of these. 9
3:21 and caused many and various disasters. 22
16:14 O mother, soldier of God in the cause of religion 13

cause for stumbling 1. *σκάνδαλον*
1Jn 2:10 and in it there is no cause for stumbling. 1

just cause 1. צֶדֶק
Ps 17: 1 Hear a just cause, O LORD; attend to my cry! 1

cause of falling 1. *σκανδαλίζω*
1Co 8:13 if food is a cause of my brother's falling 1

cause of great trouble 1. עכר
Jdg 11:35 you have become the cause of great trouble to me; 1

cause of grief 1. פּוּקָה
1Sm 25:31 my lord shall have no cause of grief, or pangs 1

cause of sin 1. *σκάνδαλον*
Mat 13:41 gather out of his kingdom all causes of sin 1

without cause 1. חִנָּם 2. רֵיקָם 3. *ἀναίτιος* 4. *δωρεάν*
1Sm 19: 5 will you sin . . by killing David without cause? 1
25:31 for having shed blood without cause 1
1Kg 2:31 for the blood which Jo'ab shed without cause. 1
Job 2: 3 against him, to destroy him without cause. 1
9:17 and multiplies my wounds without cause; 1
Ps 7: 4 with evil or plundered my enemy without cause 2
35: 7 For without cause they hid their net for me; 1
7 without cause they dug a pit for my life. 1
19 those wink the eye who hate me without cause. 1
38:19 Those who are my foes without cause are mighty •
69: 4 More . . are those who hate me without cause; 1
109: 3 attack me without cause. 1
119:161 Princes persecute me without cause 1
Prv 23:29 has wounds without cause? Who has redness of eyes? 1
24:28 not a witness against your neighbor without cause 1
Lam 3:52 by those who were my enemies without cause; 1
Ezk 14:23 I have not done without cause all that I have done 1
Joh 15:25 'They hated me without a cause.' 4
4Mc 12:14 for having slain without cause the contestants 3

causeless 1. חִנָּם
Prv 26: 2 curse that is causeless does not alight. 1

caution 1. *διαστέλλω*
Mrk 8:15 he cautioned them, saying, "Take heed 1

cautious 1. ירא 2. *εὐλαβέομαι*
Prv 14:16 A wise man is cautious and turns away from evil 1
Sir 18:27 A wise man is cautious in everything 2

cavalry 1. *ἱππεύς* 2. *ἱππικός* 3. *ἵπποι σὺν ἀναβάταις* 4. *ἵππος*
Rev 9:16 The number of the troops of cavalry was twice 2
Jdt 1:13 all his cavalry and all his chariots. 4
2: 5 120,000 foot soldiers and 12,000 cavalry. 3
22 his infantry, cavalry, and chariots 1
6: 3 They cannot resist the might of our cavalry. 4
7: 2 170,000 infantry and 12,000 cavalry 1
6 Holofernes led out all his cavalry 4
20 their infantry, chariots, and cavalry 1
16: 4 their cavalry covered the hills. 4
1Mc 1:17 with chariots and elephants and cavalry 1
3:39 and 7,000 cavalry 4
4: 1 and 1,000 picked cavalry 4
7 with cavalry round about it 4
28 and 5,000 cavalry to subdue them. 4
31 be ashamed of their troops and their cavalry. 4
8: 6 with cavalry and chariots and a very large army. 4
9: 4 20,000 foot soldiers and 2,000 cavalry. 4
11 The cavalry was divided into two companies 4
10:73 now you will not be able to withstand my cavalry 4
77 he mustered 3,000 cavalry 4
77 he had a large troop of cavalry 4
79 Apollonius had secretly left 1,000 cavalry behind 4
82 for the cavalry was exhausted 4
83 the cavalry was dispersed in the plain 4
12:49 Trypho sent troops and cavalry into Galilee 4
13:22 So Trypho got all his cavalry ready to go 4
15:13 with him were 120,000 warriors and 8,000 cavalry. 4
38 gave him troops of infantry and cavalry. 2
16: 7 the cavalry of the enemy were very numerous. 4
2Mc 10:24 collected the cavalry from Asia 4
11: 2 gathered about 80,000 men and all his cavalry 4
4 his thousands of cavalry, and his 80 elephants. 1
12:20 120,000 infantry and 2,500 cavalry. 1
33 he came out with 3,000 infantry and 400 cavalry. 1
13: 2 5,300 cavalry, 22 elephants 1
15:20 the cavalry deployed on the flanks 4
3Mc 1: 1 all his forces, both infantry and cavalry 2

cave 1. חֹר 2. מְעָרָה 3. *οἶκος ἀντρώδης* 4. *ὀπή* 5. *σπήλαιον*
Gen 19:30 he dwelt in a cave with his two daughters. 2
23: 9 that he may give me the cave of Mach-pe'lah 2
11 and I give you the cave that is in it; 2
17 the field with the cave which was in it 2
19 buried Sarah his wife in the cave of the field 2
20 The field and the cave that is in it 2
25: 9 his sons buried him in the cave of Mach-pe'lah 2
49:29 bury me . . in the cave that is in the field 2
30 in the cave that is in the field at Mach-pe'lah 2
32 the field and the cave that is in it were 2
50:13 his sons . . buried him in the cave of the field 2
Jos 10:16 fled, and hid themselves in the cave at Makke'dah. 2
17 have been found, hidden in the cave at Makke'dah. 2
18 Roll great stones against the mouth of the cave 2
22 Open the mouth of the cave, and bring . . out to me 2
22 and bring those five kings out to me from the cave. 2
23 brought those five kings out to him from the cave 2
27 threw them into the cave where they had hidden 2
27 set great stones against the mouth of the cave 2
Jdg 6: 2 Israel made . . the caves and the strongholds. 2
1Sm 13: 6 the people hid themselves in caves and in holes 2
22: 1 David . . and escaped to the cave of Adullam; 2
24: 3 came to the sheepfolds . . where there was a cave; 2
3 David and his men were sitting in the . . cave. 2
7 Saul rose up and left the cave, and went . . his way. 2
8 David also arose, and went out of the cave 2
10 the LORD gave you today into my hand in the cave; 2
2Sm 23:13 and came . . to David at the cave of Adullam 2
1Kg 18: 4 took . . prophets and hid them by fifties in a cave 2
13 how I hid 100 men . . by fifties in a cave 2
19: 9 there he came to a cave, and lodged 2
13 went out and stood at the entrance of the cave. 2
1Ch 11:15 to the rock to David at the cave of Adullam 2
Ps 57: 0 of David, when he fled from Saul, in the cave. 2
142: 0 A Maskil of David, when he was in the cave. 2
Isa 2:19 shall enter the caves of the rocks and the holes 2
Ezk 33:27 those who are . . in caves shall die 2
Nah 2:11 Where is the lions' den, the cave of the young lions •
12 he filled his cave with prey 1
Joh 11:38 it was a cave, and a stone lay upon it. 5
Heb 11:38 in dens and caves of the earth. 4
Rev 6:15 every one, slave and free, hid in the caves 5
Jdt 16:23 they buried her in the cave of her husband 5

2Mc 2: 5 Jeremiah came and found a cave 3
6:11 Others who had assembled in the caves near by 5
10: 6 wandering in the mountains and caves 5

cavern 1. נְקָרָה
Isa 2:21 to enter the caverns of the rocks and the clefts 1

cease 1. אפס 2. בטל 3. דמה 4. דמם 5. חדל 6. חרשׁ 7. כלה 8. מוּסָר 9. מושׁ 10. סוף 11. עמד 12. עמד מִן 13. רום 14. שׁבת 15. שׁתק 16. תמם 17. בטל (A) 18. *ἀδιαλείπτως* 19. *ἀνάπαυσιν ἔχω* 20. *ἀπολείπω* 21. *ἀπόλλυμι* 22. *ἀργέω* 23. *διαλείπω* 24. *ἐκλείπω* 25. *ἡσυχάζω* 26. *ἵστημι* 27. *καταλήγω* 28. *καταπαύω* 29. *κοπάζω* 30. *λήγω* 31. *μή* 32. *ξηραίνω* 33. *οὐ* 34. *παύω* 35. cesso 36. desino 37. intermissio
Gen 8:22 and winter, day and night, shall not cease. 14
18:11 it had ceased to be with Sarah after the manner 5
29:35 called his name Judah; then she ceased bearing. 16
30: 9 Leah saw that she had ceased bearing children 12
41:49 stored up grain . . until he ceased to measure it 5
Exd 9:29 the thunder will cease, and there will be no more 5
33 the thunder and the hail ceased, and the rain 5
34 the rain and the hail and the thunder had ceased 5
Deu 15:11 For the poor will never cease out of the land; 5
Jos 5:12 And the manna ceased on the morrow, when they ate 14
Jdg 5: 6 caravans ceased and travelers kept 5
7 The peasantry ceased in Israel, they ceased 5
7 The peasantry . . they ceased until you arose 5
20:28 Shall we yet again go out . . or shall we cease? 5
1Sm 2: 5 but those who were hungry have ceased to hunger. 5
7: 8 Do not cease to cry to the LORD . . that he may save 6
9: 5 lest my father cease to care about the asses 5
12:23 sin against the LORD by ceasing to pray for you; 5
2Ch 16: 5 stopped building Ramah, and let his work cease. 14
35:21 Cease opposing God, who is with me, lest he destroy 5
Ezr 4:24 it ceased until the second year . . of Darius 17
Est 9:28 should the commemoration of these days cease 10
Job 3:17 There the wicked cease from troubling 5
14: 7 sprout again, and that its shoots will not cease. 5
32: 1 these three men ceased to answer Job 14
Ps 35:15 whom I knew not slandered me without ceasing; 4
36: 3 he has ceased to act wisely and do good. 5
77: 8 Has his steadfast love for ever ceased? 1
Prv 19:27 Cease, my son, to hear instructions only to stray 5
22:10 quarreling and abuse will cease. 14
26:20 where there is no whisperer, quarreling ceases. 15
Ecc 12: 3 and the grinders cease because they are few 2
Isa 1:16 remove the evil of your doings . . cease to do evil 5
14: 4 How the oppressor has ceased 14
4 how the oppressor . . the insolent fury ceased! 14
16: 4 and destruction has ceased 7
17: 1 Behold, Damascus will cease to be a city 8
24: 8 the noise of the jubilant has ceased 5
29:20 ruthless . . come to nought and the scoffer cease 7
33: 1 When you have ceased to destroy, O 16
8 highways lie waste, the wayfaring man ceases. 14
Jer 14:17 with tears night and day, and let them not cease 3
17: 8 for it does not cease to bear fruit. 9
31:36 then shall the descendants of Israel cease 14
51:30 The warriors of Babylon have ceased fighting 5
Lam 3:22 The steadfast love of the LORD never ceases ‡
49 My eyes will flow without ceasing 3
5:15 The joy of our hearts has ceased; 14
Ezk 45: 9 cease your evictions of my people, says the Lord 13
Hos 7: 4 a heated oven, whose baker ceases to stir the fire 14
8:10 they shall cease for a little while 29
Ams 7: 5 Then I said, "O Lord GOD, cease, I beseech thee! 5
Jon 1:15 the sea ceased from its raging. 11
Mat 14:32 when they got into the boat, the wind ceased. 29
Mrk 4:39 said to the sea, "Peace! Be still!" And the wind ceased 29
5:29 immediately the hemorrhage ceased 32
6:51 got into the boat with them and the wind ceased. 29
Lke 5: 4 when he had ceased speaking, he said to Simon 34
7:45 she has not ceased to kiss my feet. 23
8:24 they ceased, and there was a calm. 34
44 immediately her flow of blood ceased. 26
11: 1 when he ceased, one of his disciples said to him 34
Act 5:42 they did not cease teaching 34
6:13 This man never ceases to speak words 34
20: 1 After the uproar ceased 34
31 I did not cease night or day to admonish every one 34
21:14 when he would not be persuaded, we ceased and said 25
1Co 13: 8 as for tongues, they will cease 34
Eph 1:16 I do not cease to give thanks for you 34
Col 1: 9 we have not ceased to pray for you 34
Heb 4:10 ceases from his labors as God did from his. 28
10: 2 would they not have ceased to be offered 34
1Pe 4: 1 whoever has suffered . . has ceased from sin 34
Rev 4: 8 and day and night they never cease to sing 19
1Es 2:30 the building of the temple in Jerusalem ceased 22
2Es 10: 4 but without ceasing mourn and fast until I die. 37
15:22 my sword will not cease from those 35
16:67 Cease from your sins, and forget your iniquities 36
Jdt 10: 1 Judith had ceased crying out to the God of Israel 34
Wis 5:13 we also, as soon as we were born, ceased to be 24
Sir 16:27 they do not cease from their labors. 24
17:28 thanksgiving has ceased 21
23:16 will never cease until the fire burns him up. 34
17 he will never cease until he dies. 29
28: 6 cease from enmity 34
38:23 let his remembrance cease 28
Bar 2:23 I will make to cease from the cities of Judah 24
Aza 1:23 king's servants . . did not cease feeding the . . fires 23
1Mc 9:27 since the time that prophets ceased to appear 33
73 Thus the sword ceased from Israel 28
2Mc 6: 1 and cease to live by the laws of God 31
9: 5 As soon as he ceased speaking 27
15: 7 Maccabeus did not cease to trust 18
3Mc 1:12 did not cease to maintain that he ought to enter 20
3:16 who never cease from their folly. 30
6:32 They ceased their chanting of dirges 27
4Mc 8:29 as soon as the tyrant had ceased counseling them 34

cease *See also* direct.

cause to cease 1. שׁבת 2. *καταπαύω*
Dan 9:27 shall cause sacrifice and offering to cease; 1
Sir 45: 3 By his words he caused signs to cease 2

make cease 1. שׁבת 2. שׁבת לְבִלְתִּי 3. שׁכך 4. בטל (A)
Num17: 5 thus I will make to cease from me the murmurings 3
Deu 32:26 make the remembrance . . cease from among men 1
Jos 22:25 might make our children cease to worship 2
Ezr 4:21 make a decree that these men be made to cease 4
23 and by force and power made them cease 4
Ps 46: 9 He makes wars cease to the end of the earth; 1
Jer 7:34 And I will make to cease from the cities of Judah 1
16: 9 Behold, I will make to cease from this place 1
48:33 I have made the wine cease from the wine presses; 1

never cease 1. *ἀκοίμητος*
Wis 7:10 because her radiance never ceases. 1

cease speaking 1. *σιωπάω*
1Es 4:41 He ceased speaking 1

cease to care about 1. נטשׁ דְּבָרִים
1Sm 10: 2 your father has ceased to care about the asses 1

cease to exist 1. *ἐκλείπω*
Sir 14:19 Every product decays and ceases to exist 1
24: 9 for eternity I shall not cease to exist. 1

cease to play 1. *ἐκλείπω*
1Mc 3:45 the flute and the harp ceased to play. 1

without ceasing 1. *ἀδιαλείπτως*
Rom 1: 9 without ceasing I mention you always 1
2Mc 13:12 lying prostrate for three days without ceasing 1

cedar 1. אֶרֶז 2. אֹרֶן 3. *κέδρινος* 4. *κέδρος*
Jdg 9:15 of the bramble and devour the cedars of Lebanon.' 1
2Sm 5:11 Hiram king of Tyre sent . . cedar trees 1
7: 2 I dwell in a house of cedar, but the ark 1
7 saying, "Why have you not built me a house of cedar? 1
1Kg 4:33 trees, from the cedar that is in Lebanon 1
5: 6 command that cedars of Lebanon be cut for me; 1
8 in the matter of cedar and cypress timber. 1
10 the timber of cedar and cypress that he desired 1
6: 9 made the ceiling . . of beams and planks of cedar. 1
10 it was joined to the house with timbers of cedar. 1
15 He lined the walls . . with boards of cedar; 1
16 boards of cedar from the floor to the rafters 1
18 The cedar within the house was carved in the form 1
18 all was cedar, no stone was seen. 1
20 He also made an altar of cedar. 1
36 of hewn stone and one course of cedar beams. 1
7: 2 it was built upon three rows of cedar pillars 1
2 was built . . with cedar beams upon the pillars. 1
3 it was covered with cedar above the chambers 1
7 was finished with cedar from floor to rafters. 1
11 And above were costly stones . . and cedar. 1
12 three courses of . . and a course of cedar beams; 1
9:11 supplied . . cedar and cypress timber and gold 1
10:27 he made cedar as plentiful as the sycamore 1
2Kg 14: 9 A thistle on Lebanon sent to a cedar on Lebanon 1
19:23 I felled its tallest cedars, its choicest 1
1Ch 14: 1 king of Tyre sent . . cedar trees, also masons 1
17: 1 Behold, I dwell in a house of cedar 1
6 saying, "Why have you not built me a house of cedar? 1
22: 4 cedar timbers without number; 1
4 and Tyrians brought great quantities of cedar 1
2Ch 1:15 king . . made cedar as plentiful as the sycamore 1
2: 3 dealt with David my father and sent him cedar 1
8 cedar, cypress, and algum timber from Lebanon 1
9:27 king made . . cedar as plentiful as the sycamore 1
25:18 A thistle on Lebanon sent to a cedar on Lebanon 1
Ezr 3: 7 to bring cedar trees from Lebanon to the sea 1
Job 40:17 He makes his tail stiff like a cedar; 1
Ps 29: 5 The voice of the LORD breaks the cedars 1
5 LORD breaks the cedars of Lebanon. 1
37:35 towering like a cedar of Lebanon. 4
80:10 the mighty cedars with its branches; 1
92:12 The righteous . . grow like a cedar in Lebanon. 1
104:16 cedars of Lebanon which he planted. 1
148: 9 fruit trees and all cedars! 1
Sng 1:17 the beams of our house are cedar, our rafters are 1
5:15 His appearance is like . . choice as the cedars. 1
8: 9 we will enclose her with boards of cedar. 1
Isa 2:13 all the cedars of Lebanon, lofty and lifted up; 1
9:10 cut down, but we will put cedars in their place. 1
14: 8 rejoice at you, the cedars of Lebanon, saying 1
37:24 I felled its tallest cedars 1
41:19 I will put in the wilderness the cedar 1
44:14 He cuts down cedars; or he chooses a holm tree 1
14 he plants a cedar and the rain nourishes it. 2
Jer 22: 7 and they shall cut down your choicest cedars 1
14 and cuts out windows for it, paneling it with cedar 1
15 think you are a king because you compete in cedar? 1
23 O inhabitant of Lebanon, nested among the cedars 1
Ezk 17: 3 came to Lebanon and took the top of the cedar; 1
22 will take a sprig from the lofty top of the cedar 1
23 and bear fruit, and become a noble cedar; 1
27: 5 they took a cedar from Lebanon to make a mast 1
31: 3 Behold, I will liken you to a cedar in Lebanon 1
8 The cedars in the garden of God could not rival it 1
Ams 2: 9 whose height was like the height of the cedars 1
Zec 11: 1 O Lebanon, that the fire may devour your cedars! 1
2 Wail, O cypress, for the cedar has fallen 1
1Es 4:48 to bring cedar timber from Lebanon to Jerusalem 3
5:55 to bring cedar logs from Lebanon 3
Sir 24:13 I grew tall like a cedar in Lebanon 4
50:12 like a young cedar on Lebanon 4

cedar *See also* work.

cedar tree 1. אֶרֶז
Num24: 6 like cedar trees beside the waters. 1

cedarwood 1. עֵץ אֶרֶז
Lev 14: 4 take . . cedarwood and scarlet stuff and hyssop 1
6 He shall take the living bird with the cedarwood 1
49 take two small birds, with cedarwood and scarlet 1
51 shall take the cedarwood and the hyssop 1
52 cleanse the house . . with the cedarwood 1
Num19: 6 priest shall take cedarwood and hyssop 1

ceiling 1. סִפֻּן 2. *φάτνωμα*
1Kg 6:15 from the floor . . to the rafters of the ceiling 1
2Mc 1:16 Opening the secret door in the ceiling 2

ceiling *See also* make.

celebrant 1. *κλισία*
3Mc 6:31 they apportioned to celebrants the place 1

celebrate 1. עשׂה 2. עבד (A) 3. *ἄγω* 4. *γεραίρω* 5. *εὐφροσύνη* 6. *ἔχω ἐπίσημον* 7. *περί* 8. *ποιέω* 9. *ποιέω πότον*
Ezr 6:16 celebrated the dedication of this house of God 2
Neh 12:27 bring them . . to celebrate the dedication 1
Ezk 45:21 you shall celebrate the feast of the passover •
Tob 6:12 we will celebrate the marriage. 8
11:19 Tobias' marriage was celebrated for seven days 3
Wis 14:23 or celebrate secret mysteries •
1Mc 4:56 So they celebrated the dedication of the altar 8
7:48 celebrated that day as a day of great gladness. 3
49 this day should be celebrated each year 3
9:37 sons of Jambri are celebrating a great wedding 8
10:58 celebrated her wedding at Ptolemais 8
13:52 that every year they should celebrate this day 3
2Mc 1:18 shall celebrate the purification of the temple 3
18 you also may celebrate the feast of booths 3
2:16 we are about to celebrate the purification 3
8:33 While they were celebrating the victory 3
10: 6 celebrated it for eight days with rejoicing 3
15:36 to celebrate the thirteenth day 6
3Mc 5:17 to make . . joyful by celebrating all the more 4
36 king . . urged the guests to return to their celebrating. 5
6:30 celebrate their rescue with all joyfulness 3
33 a great banquet to celebrate these events 7
7:18 There they celebrated their deliverance 9

cause to celebrate 1. זכר
Ps 45:17 I will cause your name to be celebrated 1

celebrate the festival 1. *ἑορτάζω*
1Co 5: 8 Let us, therefore, celebrate the festival 1

celebration 1. הלל
2Ch 23:13 singers . . leading in the celebration. 1
2Mc 6: 7 the monthly celebration of the king's birthday •

festal celebration 1. *ἑόρτασμα*
Wis 19:16 after receiving them with festal celebrations 1

celebration of a wondrous deed 1. *ἀρεταλογία*
Sir 36:14 celebration of thy wondrous deeds 1

celestial 1. *ἐπουράνιος*
1Co 15:40 There are celestial bodies 1
40 the glory of the celestial is one 1

cell 1. חָנוּת 2. *οἴκημα*
Jer 37:16 When Jeremiah had come to the dungeon cells 1
Act 12: 7 a light shone in the cell 2

cellar 1. אוֹצָר 2. *κρύπτη*

1Ch 27:27 produce of the vineyards for the wine cellars 1
Lke 11:33 puts it in a cellar or under a bushel, but on a stand 2

cemetery 1. *πολυάνδριον*

2Mc 9: 4 I will make Jerusalem a cemetery of Jews. 1
14 to level to the ground and to make a cemetery 1

censer 1. מַחֲלָף 2. מַחְתָּה 3. מִקְטֶרֶת 4. *θυΐσκη* 5. *θυμιατήριον* 6. *λιβανωτός* 7. *πυρεῖον*

Lev 10: 1 the sons of Aaron, each took his censer 2
16:12 he shall take a censer full of coals of fire 2
Num16: 6 Do this: take censers, Korah and all his company; 2
17 let every one of you take his censer 2
17 every one of you bring before the LORD his censer 2
17 bring . . before the LORD his censer, 250 censers; 2
17 you also, and Aaron, each his censer. 2
18 every man took his censer, and they put fire 2
37 to take up the censers out of the blaze; 2
38 the censers of these men who have sinned 2
39 Elea'zar the priest took the bronze censers 2
46 Take your censer, and put fire therein from off 2
2Ch 26:19 Now he had a censer in his hand to burn incense 3
Ezr 1: 9 number . . 1,000 basins of silver, 29 censers 1
Ezk 8:11 Each had his censer in his hand 3
Rev 8: 3 angel . . stood at the altar with a golden censer; 6
5 Then the angel took the censer and filled it 6
1Es 2:13 29 silver censers, 30 gold bowls, 4
Sir 50: 9 like fire and incense in the censer 7
1Mc 1:22 the bowls, the golden censers, the curtain 4
4Mc 7:11 our father Aaron, armed with the censer 5

censure 1. מוּסָר 2. *αἰτιάομαι* 3. *ἀκατάγνωστος*

Job 20: 3 I hear censure which insults me 1
Tit 2: 8 sound speech that cannot be censured 3
4Mc 2:19 censure the households of Simeon and Levi 2

census 1. סְפָר 2. פקד 3. *ἀπογραφή*

Exd 30:13 Each who is numbered in the census shall give 2
14 Every one who is numbered in the census 2
38:26 for every one who was numbered in the census 2
Num26: 4 Take a census of the people, from twenty years old *
2Ch 2:17 after the census . . which David . . had taken; 1
Act 5:37 in the days of the census 3
3Mc 4:17 no longer able to take the census of the Jews 3

census *See also* take.

center 1. טַבּוּר 2. תָּוֶךְ

Jdg 9:37 men are coming down from the center of the land 1
Ezk 5: 5 I have set her in the center of the nations 2
38:12 people . . who dwell at the center of the earth. 1

centurion 1. *ἑκατοντάρχης* 2. *κεντυρίων*

Mat 8: 5 he entered Caper'na-um, a centurion came forward 1
8 the centurion answered him, "Lord, I am not worthy 1
13 to the centurion Jesus said, "Go; be it done for you 1
27:54 When the centurion and those who were with him 1
Mrk 15:39 when the centurion, who stood facing him, saw 2
44 summoning the centurion 2
45 he learned from the centurion that he was dead 2
Lke 7: 2 Now a centurion had a slave who was dear to him 1
6 the centurion sent friends to him, saying to him 1
23:47 Now when the centurion saw what had taken place 1
Act 10: 1 Cornelius, a centurion 1
22 they said, "Cornelius, a centurion 1
21:32 He at once took soldiers and centurions 1
22:25 Paul said to the centurion who was standing by 1
26 When the centurion heard that 1
23:17 Paul called one of the centurions and said 1
23 Then he called two of the centurions and said 1
24:23 he gave orders to the centurion 1
27: 1 a centurion of the Augustan Cohort, named Julius. 1
6 There the centurion found a ship of Alexandria 1
11 centurion paid more attention to the captain 1
31 Paul said to the centurion and the soldiers 1
43 the centurion, wishing to save Paul 1

cereal *See* offering.

certain 1. אֶחָד 2. אִישׁ 3. מִן 4. גְּבַר (A) 5. יַצִּיב (A) 6. *τις* 7. quidam

Gen 28:11 he came to a certain place, and stayed there *
38: 1 Judah . . turned in to a certain Adullamite 2
2 Judah saw the daughter of a certain Canaanite 2
Num 9: 6 there were certain men who were unclean *
Deu 13:13 certain base fellows have gone out among you 2
Jos 2: 2 certain men of Israel have come here tonight *
Jdg 9:53 a certain woman threw an upper millstone 1
13: 2 there was a certain man of Zorah, of the tribe 1
19: 1 a certain Levite was sojourning in the remote 2
Rut 1: 1 a certain man of Bethlehem in Judah went *
1Sm 1: 1 There was a certain man of Ramatha'im-zo'phim 1
21: 7 a certain man of the servants of Saul was there 2
2Sm 12: 1 There were two men in a certain city 1
18:10 a certain man saw it, and told Jo'ab, "Behold, 1
1Kg 20:35 a certain man of the sons of the prophets said 1
22:34 a certain man drew his bow at a venture *
1Ch 16: 4 appointed certain of the Levites as ministers 3
25: 1 for the service certain of the sons of Asaph *
2Ch 13: 7 certain worthless scoundrels gathered about 2
18:33 a certain man drew his bow at a venture *
19: 8 appointed certain Levites and priests 3
28:12 Certain chiefs also of the men of E'phraim 2
Neh 1: 2 Hana'ni . . came with certain men out of Judah; *
11: 4 Jerusalem lived certain of the sons of Judah 3
36 certain divisions of the Levites in Judah 3
12:35 certain of the priests' sons with trumpets 3
Est 3: 8 There is a certain people scattered abroad 1
Jer 26:17 certain of the elders of the land arose and spoke 2
22 Then King Jehoi'akim sent to Egypt certain men *
Ezk 14: 1 Then came certain of the elders of Israel to me; 2
20: 1 certain of the elders of Israel came to inquire 2
Dan 2:45 dream is certain, and its interpretation sure. 5
3: 8 at that time certain Chalde'ans came forward 4
12 There are certain Jews whom you have appointed 4
20 ordered certain mighty men of his army to bind 4
Lke 7:41 A certain creditor had two debtors 6
11: 1 He was praying in a certain place 6
18: 2 He said, "In a certain city there was a judge 6
Act 13: 6 they came upon a certain magician 6
25:19 they had certain points of dispute with him 6
Heb 4: 7 again he sets a certain day, "Today 6
2Es 9: 1 when you see that a certain part . . are past 7
AEs 13: 4 there is scattered a certain hostile people 6
1Mc 11:21 certain lawless men who hated their nation 6
25 certain lawless men of his nation 6
15: 3 certain pestilent men have gained control 6
2Mc 4:40 under the leadership of a certain Auranus 6
12:13 He also attacked a certain city 6
35 a certain Dositheus, one of Bacenor's men 6
14: 3 a certain Alcimus . . formerly been high priest 6
37 A certain Razis, one of the elders of Jerusalem 6
3Mc 1: 2 a certain Theodotus . . crossed over by night 6
6: 1 Then a certain Eleazar . . prayed as follows 6
7: 3 Certain of our friends 6
4Mc 3:11 a certain irrational desire 6
4: 1 Now there was a certain Simon 6
5: 1 sitting in state . . on a certain high place 6

certain (2) 1. ידע 2. כון 3. persevero

Deu 13:14 behold, if it be true and certain that 2
17: 4 if it is true and certain that such an abominable 2
1Kg 2:37 on the day . . know for certain that you shall die; 1
42 Know for certain that on the day . . you shall die'? 1
Jer 26:15 Only know for certain that if you put me to death †
2Es 8:22 and whose utterances are certain 3

certain man 1. *τις*

Joh 11: 1 Now a certain man was ill, Laz'arus of Bethany 1
Gal 2:12 For before certain men came from James 1
3Mc 1: 3 a certain insignificant man 1
4Mc 3:21 just at that time certain men attempted a revolution 1

certain one 1. *δεῖνα*

Mat 26:18 Go into the city to a certain one, and say to him 1

certain person 1. *τις*

1Ti 1: 3 you may charge certain persons 1
6 Certain persons . . have wandered away 1
19 certain persons . . made shipwreck of . . faith 1

certainly 1. *ἀληθῶς* 2. *ἀλλά* 3. *ἀλλὰ καί* 4. *γέ* 5. *γίνομαι* 6. *γοῦν* 7. *ἐπ' ἀληθείας* 8. *ὄντως* 9. *οὐ μή* 10. *πάντως*

Lev 10:18 You certainly ought to have eaten it †
Num24:11 I said, 'I will certainly honor you,' †
1Sm 25:28 the LORD will certainly make my lord a sure house †
2Sm 5:19 I will certainly give the Philistines †
2Kg 8:10 Go, say to him, 'You shall certainly recover'; †
10 LORD has shown me that he shall certainly die. †
14 He told me that you would certainly recover. †
Jer 36:29 the king of Babylon will certainly come †
Mat 26:73 Certainly you are also one of them 1
Mrk 14:70 Certainly you are one of them 1
Lke 22:59 Certainly this man also was with him 7
23:47 Certainly this man was innocent! 8
Act 21:22 They will certainly hear that you have come. 10
Rom 6: 5 we shall certainly be united with him 3
Gal 2:17 is Christ then an agent of sin? Certainly not! 5
3:21 against the promises of God? Certainly not; 5
Sir 12: 2 if not by him, certainly by the Most High. 2
31:12 do not say, "There is certainly much upon it! 4
LJr 1:46 The men . . will certainly not live very long themselves 9
2Mc 3:38 certainly is about the place some power of God. 1
7:31 you . . will certainly not escape the hands of God. 9
4Mc 2: 2 It is for this reason, certainly 6

most certainly 1. *ὁμολογουμένως*

4Mc 7:16 most certainly devout reason is governor 1

certainty 1. כון 2. יַצִּיב מִן (A)

Jos 9:24 it was told to your servants for a certainty †
1Sm 26: 4 and learned of a certainty that Saul had come. 1
Jer 42:19 Know for a certainty that I have warned you †
22 know for a certainty that you shall die †
Dan 2: 8 I know with certainty that you are trying to gain 2

certificate 1. *βιβλίον*

Mat 19: 7 to give a certificate of divorce 1
Mrk 10: 4 allowed a man to write a certificate of divorce 1

certificate of divorce 1. *ἀποστάσιον*

Mat 5:31 let him give her a certificate of divorce.' 1

chafe 1. *σαλεύω*

Sir 26: 7 An evil wife is an ox yoke which chafes 1

chaff 1. חֲשַׁשׁ 2. מוֹץ 3. קַשׁ 4. עוּר (A) 5. *ἄχυρον* 6. *χνοῦς*

Job 13:25 thou frighten a driven leaf and pursue dry chaff? 3
21:18 like chaff that the storm carries away? 2
Ps 1: 4 but are like chaff which the wind drives away. 2
35: 5 Let them be like chaff before the wind 2
83:13 like whirling dust, like chaff before the wind. 3
Isa 17:13 like chaff on the mountains before the wind 2
29: 5 multitude of the ruthless like passing chaff. 2
33:11 You conceive chaff, you bring forth stubble; 1
41:15 and you shall make the hills like chaff; 2
Jer 13:24 I will scatter you like chaff driven by the wind 3
Dan 2:35 like the chaff of the summer threshing floors; 4
Hos 13: 3 the chaff that swirls from the threshing floor 2
Zep 2: 2 you are driven away like the drifting chaff 2
Mat 3:12 the granary, but the chaff he will burn 5
Lke 3:17 the chaff he will burn with unquenchable fire. 5
Wis 5:14 like chaff carried by the wind 6

chain 1. אֲזִק 2. זֵק 3. מַעֲדַנּוֹת 4. נְחֹשֶׁת 5. רָבִיד 6. רַתֹּקָה 7. שַׁרְשְׁרָה 8. הַמְנִכָא (A) 9. *ἅλυσις* 10. *δεσμός*

Gen 41:42 of fine linen, and put a gold chain about his neck; 5
Exd 28:14 two chains of pure gold, twisted like cords; 7
14 shall attach the corded chains to the settings. 7
22 shall make for the breastpiece twisted chains 7
39:15 on the breastpiece twisted chains like cords 7
1Kg 6:21 he drew chains of gold across, in front 6
7:17 nets of checker work with wreaths of chain work 7
2Ch 3: 5 nave he lined . . and made palms and chains on it. 7
16 He made chains like a necklace and put them 7
16 pomegranates, and put them on the chains. 7
Job 38:31 Can you bind the chains of the Plei'ades 3
Ps 149: 8 to bind their kings with chains 2
Isa 40:19 with gold, and casts for it silver chains. 6
45:14 they shall come over in chains and bow down 2
Jer 40: 1 when he took him bound in chains 1
4 Now, behold, I release you today from the chains 1
Lam 3: 7 he has put heavy chains on me; 4
Ezk 16:11 bracelets on your arms, and a chain on your neck. 5
Dan 5: 7 purple, and have a chain of gold about his neck 8
16 purple, and have a chain of gold about your neck 8
29 purple, a chain of gold was put about his neck 8
Nah 3:10 and all her great men were bound in chains. 2
Mrk 5: 3 even with a chain; 9
4 he had often been bound with fetters and chains 9
4 but the chains he wrenched apart 9
Lke 8:29 bound with chains and fetters 9
Act 12: 6 bound with two chains 9
7 the chains fell off his hands. 9
21:33 ordered him to be bound with two chains 9
26:29 might become such as I am-except for these chains. 10
28:20 I am bound with this chain. 9
Eph 6:20 which I am an ambassador in chains 9
2Ti 1:16 he was not ashamed of my chains 9
Heb 11:36 even chains and imprisonment. 10
Jde 1: 6 kept by him in eternal chains in the nether gloom 10
Rev 20: 1 the key of the bottomless pit and a giant chain. 9
1Es 1:40 bound him with a chain of brass 10
Wis 17:17 with one chain of darkness they all were bound. 9

chair 1. כִּסֵּא

2Kg 4:10 put there for him a bed, a table, a chair, and a lamp 1

chalkstone 1. אֶבֶן גִּר

Isa 27: 9 stones of the altars like chalkstones crushed 1

chamber 1. חֶדֶר 2. חֻפָּה 3. לִשְׁכָּה 4. נִשְׁכָּה 5. עֲלִיָּה 6. פְּנִימָה 7. צֵלָע 8. *θάλαμος* 9. *παστοφόριον* 10. *ταμιεῖον* 11. promptuarius

Gen 43:30 And he entered his chamber and wept there. 1
Deu 32:25 in the chambers shall be terror, destroying 1
Jdg 3:24 He is only relieving himself in the . . cool chamber. 1
15: 1 and he said, "I will go in to my wife in the chamber. 1
2Sm 13:10 Bring the food into the chamber, that I may eat 1
10 and brought them into the chamber to Amnon 1
18:33 and went up to the chamber over the gate, 5
1Kg 1:15 So Bathshe'ba went to the king into his chamber 1
7: 3 it was covered with cedar above the chambers 7
2Kg 4:11 he turned into the chamber and rested there. 5
23:11 by the chamber of Nathan-melech the chamberlain 3
1Ch 9:26 chambers and the treasures of the house of God. 3
33 dwelling in the chambers of the temple 3
23:28 having the care of the courts and the chambers 3
28:12 the plan of all . . all the surrounding chambers 3

2Ch 31:11 to prepare chambers in the house of the LORD; 3
Ezr 8:29 within the chambers of the house of the LORD. 3
10: 6 Ezra . . went to the chamber of Jehoha'nan 3
Neh 3:30 Meshul'lam . . repaired opposite his chamber. 4
10:37 priests, to the chambers of the house of our God; 3
38 bring up . . to the chambers, to the storehouse. 3
39 grain, wine, and oil to the chambers 3
12:44 men . . appointed over the chambers for the stores 4
13: 4 appointed over the chambers of the house 3
5 prepared for Tobi'ah a large chamber 3
7 preparing for him a chamber in the courts 4
8 furniture of Tobi'ah out of the chamber. 3
9 I gave orders and they cleansed the chambers; 3
Job 9: 9 Orion, the Plei'ades and the chambers of the south; 1
37: 9 From its chamber comes the whirlwind 1
Ps 19: 5 forth like a bridegroom leaving his chamber 2
45:13 The princess is decked in her chamber 6
104: 3 hast laid the beams of thy chambers on the waters 5
105:30 with frogs, even in the chambers of their kings. 1
Prv 7:27 going down to the chambers of death. 1
Sng 1: 4 The king has brought me into his chambers. 1
3: 4 and into the chamber of her that conceived me. 1
8: 2 and into the chamber of her that conceived me. 10
Isa 26:20 Come, my people, enter your chambers 1
Jer 35: 2 to the house of the LORD, into one of the chambers; 3
4 into the chamber of the sons of Hanan 3
4 which was near the chamber of the princes 3
4 above the chamber of Ma-asei'ah the son of Shallum 3
36:10 in the chamber of Gemari'ah the son of Shaphan 3
12 to the king's house, into the secretary's chamber; 3
20 having put the scroll in the chamber of Eli'shama 3
21 he took it from the chamber of Eli'shama 3
Ezk 40:17 behold, there were chambers and a pavement 3
17 30 chambers fronted on the pavement. 3
38 There was a chamber with its door 3
44 there were two chambers in the inner court 3
45 chamber which faces south is for the priests 3
46 the chamber which faces north is for the priests 3
41:10 chambers of the court was a breadth of twenty 3
42: 1 he brought me to the chambers which were 3
4 And before the chambers was a passage inward 3
5 Now the upper chambers were narrower 3
5 the lower and middle chambers in the building. *
6 the upper chambers were set back from the ground *
7 was a wall outside parallel to the chambers 3
7 toward the outer court, opposite the chambers 3
8 chambers on the outer court were 50 cubits 3
9 Below these chambers was an entrance on the east 3
10 opposite the building, there were chambers 3
11 they were similar to the chambers on the north 3
12 below the south chambers was an entrance 3
13 The north chambers and the south chambers 3
13 The north chambers and the south chambers 3
13 opposite the yard are the holy chambers 3
44:19 ministering, and lay them in the holy chambers; 3
46:19 north row of the holy chambers for the priests; 3
Jol 2:16 leave his room, and the bride her chamber. 2
1Es 8:59 in the chambers of the house of our Lord. 9
9: 1 the chamber of Jehohanan the son of Eliashib 9
2Es 4:35 the souls of the righteous in their chambers 11
41 the chambers of the souls are like the womb. 11
5: 9 and wisdom shall withdraw into its chamber 11
37 open for me the closed chambers 11
7:32 and the chambers shall give up the souls 11
95 being gathered into their chambers and guarded 11
8:20 and whose upper chambers are in the air *
3Mc 1:18 virgins who had been enclosed in their chambers 8

bridal chamber 1. *νυμφών* 2. *παστός*
Tob 6:13 each died in the bridal chamber. 1
16 When you enter the bridal chamber 1
1Mc 1:27 she who sat in the bridal chamber was mourning. 2
3Mc 1:19 Those women . . abandoned the bridal chambers 2
4: 6 who had just entered the bridal chamber 2

council chamber 1. *βουλευτήριον* 2. *χρηματιστήριον*
1Es 3:15 he took his seat in the council chamber 2
4Mc 15:25 as in the council chamber of her own soul 1

chamber for a priest 1. *παστοφόριον*
1Mc 4:57 they restored . . the chambers for the priests 1

inner chamber 1. חֶדֶר 2. חֶדֶר בְּחֶדֶר 3. *μυχός*
Jdg 16: 9 Now she had men lying in wait in an inner chamber. 1
12 the men lying in wait were in an inner chamber. 1
1Kg 20:30 Ben-ha'dad also fled, and entered an inner chamber 2
22:25 on that day when you go into an inner chamber 2
2Kg 9: 2 bid him rise . . and lead him to an inner chamber. 2
1Ch 28:11 its upper rooms, and its inner chambers 1
2Ch 18:24 you go into an inner chamber to hide yourself. 2
Wis 17: 4 not even the inner chamber . . protected them 3

chamber of a priest 1. *παστοφόριον*
1Mc 4:38 They saw also the chambers of the priests in ruins. 1

roof chamber 1. עֲלִיָּה
Jdg 3:20 as he was sitting alone in his cool roof chamber. 1
23 Ehud . . closed the doors of the roof chamber 1
24 saw that the doors of the roof chamber were locked 1
25 still did not open the doors of the roof chamber 1
2Kg 4:10 Let us make a small roof chamber with walls 1

senate chamber 1. *βουλευτήριον*
1Mc 8:15 they have built for themselves a senate chamber 1
19 they entered the senate chamber and spoke as follows 1
12: 3 they went to Rome and entered the senate chamber 1

side chamber 1. צֵלָע
1Kg 6: 5 and he made side chambers all around. 1
Ezk 41: 5 and the breadth of the side chambers, four cubits 1
6 the side chambers were in three stories 1
6 to serve as supports for the side chambers 1
7 the side chambers became broader as they rose 1
8 of the side chambers measured a full reed 1
9 outer wall of the side chambers was five cubits; 1
11 the doors of the side chambers opened on the part 1

upper chamber 1. מַעֲלָה 2. עֲלִיָּה 3. עֲלִי (A)
1Kg 17:19 and carried him up into the upper chamber 2
23 and brought him down from the upper chamber 2
2Kg 1: 2 fell through the lattice in his upper chamber 2
23:12 altars on the roof of the upper chamber of Ahaz 2
2Ch 3: 9 And he overlaid the upper chambers with gold. 2
Neh 3:31 upper chamber of the corner. 2
32 between the upper chamber of the corner 2
Dan 6:10 windows in his upper chamber open toward 3
Ams 9: 6 who builds his upper chambers in the heavens 1

vaulted chamber 1. גַּב
Ezk 16:24 you built yourself a vaulted chamber 1
31 your vaulted chamber at the head of every street 1
39 and they shall throw down your vaulted chamber 1

wedding chamber 1. thalamus
2Es 10: 1 when my son entered his wedding chamber 1
48 When my son entered his wedding chamber he died,' 1

chamberlain 1. סָרִיס 2. *ὁ ἐπὶ τοῖς κοιτῶνος*
2Kg 23:11 by the chamber of Nathan-melech the chamberlain 1
Est 1:10 the seven eunuchs who served . . as chamberlains *
Act 12:20 persuaded Blastus, the king's chamberlain 2

chameleon 1. תִּנְשֶׁמֶת
Lev 11:30 the lizard, the sand lizard, and the chameleon 1

champion 1. אִישׁ בֵּנַיִם 2. גִּבּוֹר 3. *ὑπερασπίστρια*
1Sm 17: 4 there came out . . a champion named Goliath 1
23 the champion, the Philistine of Gath . . came up 1
51 Philistines saw that their champion was dead 2
4Mc 15:29 vindicator of the law and champion of religion 3

chance 1. מִקְרֶה 2. פֶּגַע 3. קרא 4. קָרֶה 5. *εἰ* 6. *καιρός* 7. *παρατυγχάνω* 8. *συγκυρία* 9. *τόπος*
Deu 23:10 not clean by reason of what chances to him 4
1Sm 6: 9 not his hand . . it happened to us by chance. 1
2Sm 1: 6 By chance I happened to be on Mount Gilbo'a; 3
Ecc 9:11 but time and chance happen to them all. 2
Lke 10:31 Now by chance a priest was going down that road; 8
Act 17:17 he argued . . with those who chanced to be there. 7
27:12 on the chance that . . they could reach Phoenix 5
Heb 12:17 he was rejected for he found no chance to repent 9
Wis 12:10 thou gavest them a chance to repent 9
Sir 27:12 Among stupid people watch for a chance to leave 6

mere chance 1. *αὐτοσχεδίως*
Wis 2: 2 Because we were born by mere chance 1

chance to come upon 1. קרא
Deu 22: 6 If you chance to come upon a bird's nest, in any tree 1

chance to meet 1. קרא
2Sm 18: 9 Ab'salom chanced to meet the servants of David. 1

change 1. הפך 2. חלף 3. מור 4. סבב 5. שׂום 6. שׁנה 7. שׁנא (A) 8. *ἄλλαγμα* 9. *ἀλλάσσω* 10. *ἀλλοῖος* 11. *ἀλλοιόω* 12. *ἀλλοίωσις* 13. *ἐξίστημι* 14. *μεταβάλλω* 15. *μεταβολή* 16. *μετάθεσις* 17. *μετακιρνάομαι* 18. *μεταλλεύω* 19. *μεταμορφόω* 20. *μεταπίπτω* 21. *μεταστρέφω* 22. *μετασχηματίζω* 23. *μετατίθημι* 24. *παραλλάσσω* 25. *στρέφω* 26. *τροπή* 27. commuto 28. muto
Gen 31: 7 your father has cheated me and changed my wages 2
41 flock, and you have changed my wages ten times. 2
35: 2 and purify yourselves, and change your garments 2
41:14 and when he had shaved himself and changed his 2
Exd 14: 5 the mind of Pharaoh and his servants was changed 1
Lev 13:16 if the raw flesh . . is changed to white 1
55 if the diseased spot has not changed color 1
Num32:38 Nebo, and Ba'al-me'on (their names to be changed) 4
1Sm 21:13 he changed his behavior before them, and feigned 6
2Sm 12:20 and anointed himself, and changed his clothes; 2
14:20 In order to change the course of affairs 4
2Kg 23:34 and changed his name to Jehoi'akim. 4
24:17 and changed his name to Zedeki'ah. 4
2Ch 36: 4 changed his name to Jehoi'akim; 4
Est 9: 1 very day . . which had been changed to a day 1
Job 14:20 thou changest his countenance 6
38:14 It is changed like clay under the seal 1
Ps 15: 4 who swears to his own hurt and does not change; 3
46: 2 we will not fear though the earth should change 3
77:10 the right hand of the Most High has changed. 6
102:26 changest them like a raiment, and they pass away; 2
Ecc 8: 1 and the hardness of his countenance is changed. 6
Jer 2:11 Has a nation changed its gods 3
11 But my people have changed their glory 3
36 How lightly you gad about, changing your way! 6
13:23 Can the Ethiopian change his skin 1
48:11 and his scent is not changed. 3
Lam 4: 1 gold has grown dim, how the pure gold is changed! 6
Dan 2: 9 lying . . words before me till the times change. 7
21 He changes times and seasons; 7
3:19 expression of his face was changed against 7
4:16 let his mind be changed from a man's 7
5: 6 color changed, and his thoughts alarmed 7
9 greatly alarmed, and his color changed; 7
10 Let not your . . color change. 7
6: 8 sign the document, so that it cannot be changed 7
15 which the king establishes can be changed. 7
17 nothing might be changed concerning Daniel. 7
7:25 shall think to change the times and the law; 7
28 greatly alarmed me, and my color changed; 7
10: 8 my radiant appearance was fearfully changed 1
Hos 4: 7 I will change their glory into shame. 3
Mic 2: 4 ruined; he changes the portion of my people; 3
Zep 3: 9 I will change the speech of the peoples 1
19 and I will change their shame into praise 5
Mal 3: 6 For I the LORD do not change; 6
Act 6:14 change the customs which Moses delivered to us. 9
1Co 15:51 but we shall all be changed. 9
52 we shall be changed. 9
2Co 3:18 changed into his likeness 19
Gal 4:20 to be present with you now and to change my tone 9
Php 3:21 who will change our lowly body 22
Heb 1:12 they will be changed 9
7:12 when there is a change in the priesthood 23
12 necessarily a change in the law as well. 16
Jas 1:17 there is no variation or shadow due to change. 26
1Es 7:15 had changed the will of the king of the Assyrians 21
2Es 6:16 for they know that their end must be changed. 27
26 shall be changed and converted 28
8:22 they are changed to wind and fire ‡
Jdt 10: 7 noted how . . her clothing changed 14
AEs 15: 8 God changed the spirit of the king to gentleness 14
16: 9 by changing our methods 15
Wis 4:11 lest evil change his understanding 9
7:18 the changes of the seasons 15
12:10 their way of thinking would never change. 9
16:21 was changed to suit every one's liking. 17
25 changed into all forms 18
Sir 2: 4 in changes that humble you be patient. 8
6: 9 there is a friend who changes into an enemy 23
28 she will be changed into joy for you. 25
12:18 whisper much, and change his expression. 11
13:25 A man's heart changes his countenance 10
18:26 From morning to evening conditions change 14
25:17 The wickedness of a wife changes her appearance 11
27:11 the fool changes like the moon. 11
37:17 As a clue to changes of heart 12
1Mc 1:49 forget the law and change all the ordinances. 9
2Mc 3:16 his face and the change in his color 24
6:29 those . . now changed to ill will 14
11:24 our father's change to Greek customs 16
3Mc 1: 3 a Jew by birth who later changed his religion 14
25 to change his arrogant mind 13
3: 8 expected that matters would change; 20
5:42 changes of mind which had come about within him 15
4Mc 6:24 he had not been changed by their compassion 14
change *See also* make, persuade.

change attitude 1. *μεταβάλλω*
4Mc 15:14 This mother . . did not change her attitude. 1

change course 1. *μεταβάλλω*
4Mc 6:18 if we . . should now change our course 1

change one's manner of living 1. *μεταδιαιτέω*
4Mc 8: 8 by changing your manner of living. 1

change one's mind 1. נחם 2. *μεταβάλλω* 3. *μεταμέλομαι*
Ps 110: 4 The LORD has sworn and will not change his mind 1
Act 28: 6 they changed their minds 2
Heb 7:21 The Lord has sworn and will not change his mind 3
Wis 19: 2 they would change their minds and pursue them. 3
Sir 33:19 lest you change your mind and must ask for it. 3

change over 1. *μεταβαίνω*
2Mc 6: 9 who did not choose to change over to Greek customs 1

change places 1. μεθαρμόζω
Wis 19:18 the elements changed places with one another 1

change the way of life 1. ἐκδιαιτάω
4Mc 4:19 Jason changed the nation's way of life 1

channel 1. אָפִיק 2. יְאֹר 3. נַחַל 4. תְּעָלָה 5. vena
2Sm 22:16 Then the channels of the sea were seen 1
Job 28:10 He cuts out channels in the rocks 2
38:25 Who has cleft a channel for the torrents of rain 4
Ps 18:15 Then the channels of the sea were seen 1
Isa 8: 7 River . . it will rise over all its channels 1
11:15 smite it into seven channels that men may cross 3
2Es 13:44 and stopped the channels of the river 5
47 the Most High will stop the channels of the river 5

water channel 1. ὑδραγωγός
Sir 24:30 like a water channel into a garden. 1

chant 1. נתן 2. קנן
Ps 8: 1 Thou whose glory above the heavens is chanted 1
Ezk 32:16 This is a lamentation which shall be chanted; 2
16 the daughters of the nations shall chant it; 2
16 shall they chant it, says the Lord GOD. 2
3Mc 6:32 They ceased their chanting of dirges •

chaos 1. בֹּהוּ 2. לֹא סְדָרִים 3. תֹּהוּ 4. chaus
Job 10:22 the land of gloom and chaos 2
Isa 24:10 The city of chaos is broken down 3
34:11 and the plummet of chaos over its nobles. 1
45:18 he established it; he did not create it a chaos 3
19 I did not say to . . Jacob, 'Seek me in chaos.' 3
2Es 5: 8 There shall be chaos also in many places 4

char 1. חרר 2. ἐμπυρίζω
Ezk 15: 4 and the middle of it is charred, is it useful 1
5 when the fire has consumed it and it is charred 1
1Mc 11: 4 the charred bodies 2

character 1. δοκιμή 2. ἦθος 3. τρόπος 4. χαρακτήρ
Rom 5: 4 and endurance produces character 1
4 and character produces hope 1
Heb 6:17 the unchangeable character of his purpose •
Sir 0: 3 being prepared in character to live 2
2Mc 5:22 in character more barbarous than . . 3
4Mc 15: 4 We impress upon the character of a small child 4

character (2) 1. חֶרֶט 2. nota
Isa 8: 1 Take . . and write upon it in common characters 1
2Es 14:42 in characters which they did not know 2

characteristic 1. ἰδιότητα
3Mc 7:17 because of a characteristic of the place 1

charcoal 1. פֶּחָם
Prv 26:21 As charcoal to hot embers and wood to fire, so is 1
charcoal *See also* fire.

charge 1. יָד 2. משל 3. מִשְׁמֶרֶת 4. נצב עַל 5. נתן
6. עבר 7. עַל 8. עלה 9. עַל יַד 10. עשה
11. עשה מְלָאכָה 12. פָּנִים 13. פקד 14. פָּקִיד 15. רדה
16. שַׂר 17. שמר 18. שמר מִשְׁמֶרֶת 19. ἐν 20. ἐξουσία
21. ἐπί 22. ἐφίστημι 23. κλῆρος 24. κύριος 25. πρός
26. τάσσω 27. τάσσω ἐπί 28. praesum
Gen 24: 2 the oldest . . who had charge of all that he had 2
30:35 that was black, and put them in charge of his sons; 1
39: 4 house and put him in charge of all that he had. 1
6 he left all that he had in Joseph's charge; 1
40: 4 captain of the guard charged Joseph with them 13
47: 6 put them in charge of my cattle. 16
Num 3: 8 they shall have charge of all the furnishings 17
32 those who had charge of the sanctuary. 18
38 having charge of the rites within the sanctuary 17
7: 9 charged with the care of the holy things 7
31:30 Levites who have charge of the tabernacle 18
47 the Levites who had charge of the tabernacle 18
Deu 24: 5 he shall not . . be charged with any business; 6
Rut 2: 5 to his servant who was in charge of the reapers 4
6 the servant who was in charge of the reapers 4
1Sm 7: 1 Elea'zar, to have charge of the ark of the LORD. 17
17:22 left the . . in charge of the keeper of the baggage 9
2Sm 10:10 the rest of his men he put in the charge of Abi'shai 1
20:24 and Ador'am was in charge of the forced labor; 7
1Kg 4: 6 Ahi'shar was in charge of the palace; and Adoni'ram 7
6 Adoni'ram . . was in charge of the forced labor. 7
5:14 Adoni'ram was in charge of the levy. 7
16 were over the work, who had charge of the people 15
9:23 the chief officers . . had charge of the people 15
2Kg 6: 1 where we dwell under your charge is too small 12
7:17 king had appointed . . to have charge of the gate; •
10:22 He said to him who was in charge of the wardrobe 7
1Ch 9:19 were in charge of the work of the service 7
19 had been in charge of the camp of the LORD 7
23 in charge of the gates of the house of the LORD 7
26 in charge of the chambers and the treasures 7
27 and they had charge of opening it every morning. 7
28 Some . . had charge of the utensils of service 7
31 was in charge of making the flat cakes. 7
32 had charge of the showbread, to prepare it 7
19:11 the rest of his men he put in the charge of Abi'shai 1
23: 4 have charge of the work in the house of the LORD 7
26:20 had charge of the treasuries of the house of God 7
22 in charge of the treasuries of the house 7
24 chief officer in charge of the treasuries. 7
26 in charge of all the treasuries 7
27: 2 Jasho'beam . . in charge of the first division 7
4 Dodai . . in charge of the division of the second 7
6 Ammiz'abad his son was in charge of his division. 21
2Ch 23:18 whom David had organized to be in charge 7
24:12 had charge of the work of the house of the LORD 11
31:12 chief officer in charge of them was Conani'ah 7
Ezr 1: 8 brought these out in charge of Mith'redath 9
Neh 12: 8 who with his brethren was in charge of the songs 7
Est 2: 3 the king's eunuch who is in charge of the women; 17
8 in custody of Hegai who had charge of the women. 17
14 Sha-ash'gaz . . who was in charge of the concubines; 17
15 Hegai the . . eunuch, who had charge of the women 17
3: 9 of those who have charge of the king's business 10
Job 1:22 Job did not sin or charge God with wrong. 5
Jer 29:26 to have charge in the house of the LORD 14
Dan 12: 1 great prince who has charge of your people. 7
Nah 3: 3 Horsemen charging, flashing sword 8
Zec 3: 7 If you will walk in my ways and keep my charge 3
7 shall rule my house and have charge of my courts 17
Mrk 13:34 he leaves home and puts his servants in charge 20
Act 8:27 a minister . . in charge of all her treasure 21
1Pe 5: 2 Tend the flock of God that is your charge 19
3 not as domineering over those in your charge 23
1Es 5:58 to have charge of the work of the Lord 21
2Es 5:41 dost have charge of those who are alive at the end 28
Tob 1:22 and in charge of administration of the accounts •
Jdt 8:10 who was in charge of all she possessed 22
12:11 the eunuch who had charge of his personal affairs 22
14:13 the steward in charge of all his personal affairs 21
AEs 13: 6 the letters of Haman, who is in charge of affairs 27
1Mc 3:32 He left Lysias . . in charge of the king's affairs 21
9:25 and put them in charge of the country. 24
2Mc 3: 7 who was in charge of his affairs 21
6:21 who were in charge of that unlawful sacrifice 26
10:11 to have charge of the government 21
11: 1 who was in charge of the government 21
13: 2 who had charge of the government 21
23 who had been left in charge of the government 21
3Mc 5: 5 The servants in charge of the Jews went out 25
14 the person who was in charge of the invitations 26
6:30 summoned the official in charge of the revenues 21

charge (2) 1. לִפְנֵי 2. מִצְוָה 3. מִשְׁמֶרֶת 4. מִשְׁפָּט
5. עוד 6. פקד 7. פְּקֻדָּה 8. צוה 9. צוה עַל 10. שלח
11. διαμαρτύρομαι 12. διαστέλλω 13. ἐντολή
14. ἐπιτιμάω 15. λέγω 16. μαρτύρομαι
17. παραγγελία 18. παραγγέλλω
Gen 18:19 chosen him, that he may charge his children 8
26: 5 Abraham . . kept my charge, my commandments 3
28: 1 and charged him, "You shall not marry 8
6 he blessed him he charged him, "You shall not marry 8
49:29 Then he charged them, and said to them, 8
33 When Jacob finished charging his sons 8
Exd 4:28 the signs which he had charged him to do. 8
19:23 thou thyself didst charge us, saying 5
Lev 8:35 performing what the LORD has charged 3
18:30 keep my charge never to practice any of these 3
22: 9 They shall therefore keep my charge 3
Num 3:25 the charge of the sons of Gershon in the tent 3
31 their charge was to be the ark, the table 3
36 the appointed charge of the sons of Merar'i 7
4:16 Elea'zar . . shall have charge of the oil 7
27 assign to their charge all that they are to carry. 3
31 this is what they are charged to carry 3
8:26 in the tent of meeting, to keep the charge 3
9:19 people of Israel kept the charge of the LORD 3
23 they kept the charge of the LORD 3
Deu 1:16 I charged your judges at that time, 'Hear the cases 8
3:28 charge Joshua, and encourage and strengthen him; 8
11: 1 keep his charge, his statutes, his ordinances 3
17:18 which is in the charge of the Levitical priests; 1
27:11 Moses charged the people the same day, saying 8
Jos 18: 8 and Joshua charged those who went . . saying, "Go up 8
22: 3 careful to keep the charge of the LORD your God. 3
Rut 2: 9 Have I not charged the young men not to molest you? 8
1Sm 21: 2 The king has charged me with a matter, and said 8
2 of the matter . . with which I have charged you.' 8
1Kg 2: 1 drew near, he charged Solomon his son, saying 8
3 keep the charge of the LORD your God, walking 3
43 and the commandment with which I charged you? 8
4:28 they brought . . each according to his charge. 4
14: 6 I am charged with heavy tidings for you. 10
1Ch 22: 6 charged him to build a house for the LORD 8
23:32 they shall keep charge of the tent of meeting 3
2Ch 13:11 for we keep the charge of the LORD our God 3
19: 9 he charged them: "Thus you shall do 8
23: 6 all the people shall keep the charge of the LORD. 3
36:23 charged me to build him a house at Jerusalem 8
Ezr 1: 2 LORD . . has charged me to build him a house 6
Est 2:10 Mor'decai had charged her not to make it known. 9
20 Esther had not . . as Mor'decai had charged her; 9
4: 8 charge her to go to the king to make supplication 9
Jer 23:32 when I did not send them or charge them; 8
Ezk 40:46 is for the priests who have charge of the altar; 3
44: 8 And you have not kept charge of my holy things; 3
8 foreigners to keep my charge in my sanctuary. 3
14 I will appoint them to keep charge of the temple 3
15 sons of Zadok, who kept the charge of my sanctuary 3
16 to minister to me, and they shall keep my charge. 3
48:11 priests, the sons of Zadok, who kept my charge 3
Zec 3: 7 If you will walk in my ways and keep my charge 3
Mal 3:14 What is the good of our keeping his charge 3
Mat 9:30 And Jesus sternly charged them 15
10: 5 These twelve Jesus sent out, charging them 18
Mrk 5:43 he strictly charged them that no one should know 12
6: 8 charged them to take nothing for their journey 18
7:36 he charged them to tell no one 12
36 the more he charged them 12
8:30 he charged them to tell no one about him. 14
9: 9 he charged them to tell no one what they had seen 12
Lke 5:14 he charged him to tell no one 18
8:56 he charged them to tell no one what had happened. 18
9:21 he charged and commanded them 14
Joh 10:18 this charge I have received from my Father. 13
Act 1: 4 he charged them not to depart from Jerusalem 18
4:18 So they called them and charged them not to speak 18
5:28 We strictly charged you not to teach in this name 18
40 charged them not to speak in the name of Jesus 18
15: 5 to charge them to keep the law of Moses. 18
16:18 I charge you in the name of Jesus Christ 18
23 charging the jailer to keep them safely. 18
24 having received this charge 17
23:22 dismissed the young man, charging him, "Tell no one 18
1Th 2:11 and encouraged you and charged you 16
4:11 to work with your hands, as we charged you; 18
1Ti 1: 3 you may charge certain persons 18
5 whereas the aim of our charge is love 17
18 This charge I commit to you, Timothy, my son 17
5:21 I charge you to keep these rules without favor 11
6:14 I charge you to keep the commandment unstained 18
17 charge them not to be haughty 18
2Ti 2:14 charge them before the Lord 11
4: 1 I charge you in the presence of God 11

charge (3) 1. דָּבָר 2. פקד עַל 3. שׂום 4. αἰτία
5. αἰτίωμα 6. ἐγκαλέω 7. ἔγκλημα 8. κατηγορέω
9. κατηγορία 10. κρίσις 11. ῥῆμα 12. φημί
Exd 23: 7 Keep far from a false charge, and do not slay 1
Deu 19:15 two . . three witnesses, shall a charge be sustained. 1
22:14 charges her with shameful conduct, and brings 3
17 he has made shameful charges against her, saying 1
2Sm 3: 8 you charge me . . with a fault concerning a woman. 2
Job 4:18 his angels he charges with error; 3
Mat 27:14 he gave him no answer, not even to a single charge; 11
37 over his head they put the charge against him 4
Mrk 15:26 the inscription of the charge against him read 4
Lke 23:14 guilty of any of your charges against him; 8
Act 13:28 could charge him with nothing deserving death †
19:40 we are in danger of being charged with rioting today 6
23:28 the charge on which they accused him 4
29 charged with nothing deserving death 7
25: 7 bringing against him many serious charges 5
9 and there be tried on these charges before me? •
18 they brought no charge in his case 4
27 not to indicate the charges against him. 4
Rom 3: 8 as some . . slanderously charge us with saying. 12
2Co 13: 1 Any charge must be sustained 11
1Ti 5:19 Never admit any charge against an elder 9
Tit 1: 6 not open to the charge of being profligate 9
2Mc 4:43 Charges were brought against Menelaus 10
3Mc 4:19 charging that they had been bribed •
7: 7 acquitted . . of every charge of whatever kind. 4

charge (4) 1. נתן 2. פְּצִירָה
1Sm 13:21 the charge was a pim for the plowshares 2
Neh 10:32 obligation to charge ourselves yearly 1

charge (5) 1. נגח 2. עלה 3. רוץ 4. שקק 5. ὅρμημα
6. τρέχω
Prv 28:15 roaring lion or a charging bear is a wicked ruler 4
Dan 8: 4 I saw the ram charging westward and northward 1
Jol 2: 7 Like warriors they charge 3
Nah 3: 3 Horsemen charging, flashing sword 2
1Mc 4: 8 cavalry . . Do not . . be afraid when they charge. 5
2Mc 5: 2 golden-clad horsemen charging through the air 6
charge *See* bring, free, give, join, keep, lay, place, put, take.

charge against 1. κατηγορέω 2. λογίζομαι
Act 25:11 if there is nothing in their charges against me 1
2Ti 4:16 May it not be charged against them! 2
2Mc 4:47 Menelaus . . he acquitted of the charges against him 1

charge against (2) 1. ἐνσείω
2Mc 12:37 then he charged against Gorgias' men 1

charge already 1. προαιτιάομαι
Rom 3: 9 for I have already charged that all men 1

charge of fifties 1. *πεντηκοντάρχος*
1Mc 3:55 in charge of . . fifties and tens. 1

charge of thousands 1. *χιλίαρχος*
1Mc 3:55 in charge of thousands and hundreds 1

sternly charge 1. *ἐμβριμάομαι*
Mrk 1:43 And he sternly charged him 1

strictly charge 1. *διαστέλλω*
Mat 16:20 Then he strictly charged the disciples 1

charge to an account 1. *ἐλλογέω*
Phm 1:18 charge that to my account. 1

charge to bring against 1. *κατηγορέω*
Joh 8: 6 might have some charge to bring against him. 1
Act 28:19 though I had no charge to bring against my nation. 1

charge with an oath 1. שׁבע
1Sm 14:27 heard his father charge the people with the oath; 1
28 Your father . . charged the people with an oath 1

charger
Nah 2: 3 the chargers prance. •

chariot 1. מֶרְכָּב 2. מֶרְכָּבָה 3. עֲגָלָה 4. רֶכֶב 5. רְכוּב
6. *ἅρμα* 7. *δίφραξ* 8. *ῥέδη* 9. currus
Gen 41:43 he made him to ride in his second chariot; 2
46:29 Then Joseph made ready his chariot and went up 2
50: 9 went up with him both chariots and horsemen; 4
Exd 14: 6 So he made ready his chariot and took his army 4
7 and took 600 picked chariots 4
7 took . . all the other chariots of Egypt 4
9 all Pharaoh's horses and chariots and his 4
17 all his host, his chariots, and his horsemen. 4
18 Pharaoh, his chariots, and his horsemen. 4
23 Pharaoh's horses, his chariots, and his horsemen. 4
25 clogging their chariot wheels 2
26 come back . . upon their chariots, and upon 4
28 waters . . covered the chariots 4
15: 4 Pharaoh's chariots and his host he cast 2
19 Pharaoh with his chariots and his horsemen went 4
Deu 11: 4 did to . . their horses and to their chariots; 4
20: 1 see horses and chariots and an army larger 4
Jos 11: 4 they came . . with very many horses and chariots. 4
6 you shall . . burn their chariots with fire. 2
9 and burned their chariots with fire. 2
17:16 yet all the Canaanites . . have chariots of iron 4
18 drive out . . though they have chariots of iron 4
24: 6 pursued . . with chariots and horsemen 4
Jdg 1:19 of the plain, because they had chariots of iron. 4
4: 3 he had 900 chariots of iron 4
7 river Kishon with his chariots and his troops; 4
13 Sis'era called out all his chariots, 900 chariots 4
13 called out all his chariots, 900 chariots of iron 4
15 Sis'era and all his chariots and all his army 4
15 Sis'era alighted from his chariot and fled away 2
16 Barak pursued the chariots and the army 4
5:28 Why is his chariot so long in coming? Why tarry 4
28 Why tarry the hoofbeats of his chariots?' 2
1Sm 8:11 take your sons and appoint them to his chariots 2
11 to be his horsemen, and to run before his chariots; 2
12 to make . . and the equipment of his chariots. 4
13: 5 Philistines mustered . . 30,000 chariots 4
2Sm 1: 6 chariots and . . horsemen were close upon him. 4
8: 4 David . . left enough for 100 chariots. 4
10:18 David slew of the Syrians the men of 700 chariots 4
15: 1 Ab'salom got himself a chariot and horses 2
1Kg 1: 5 he prepared for himself chariots and horsemen 4
4:26 Solomon also had . . horses for his chariots 1
7:33 The wheels were made like a chariot wheel; 2
9:19 store-cities . . and the cities for his chariots 4
22 his captains, his chariot commanders 4
10:26 Solomon gathered . . chariots and horsemen; 4
26 he had 1,400 chariots and 12,000 horsemen 4
26 whom he stationed in the chariot cities 4
29 A chariot could be imported from Egypt 2
12:18 King Rehobo'am made haste to mount his chariot 2
16: 9 Zimri, commander of half his chariots, conspired 4
18:44 Go up, say to Ahab, 'Prepare your chariot and go down 6
20: 1 32 kings were with him, and horses and chariots; 4
21 went out, and captured the horses and chariots 4
25 horse for horse, and chariot for chariot; 4
25 horse for horse, and chariot for chariot; 4
33 and he caused him to come up into the chariot. 2
22:31 commanded the . . captains of his chariots 4
32 the captains of the chariots saw Jehosh'aphat 4
33 the captains of the chariots saw that it was not 4
35 the king was propped up in his chariot 2
35 blood . . flowed into the bottom of the chariot. 4
38 they washed the chariot by the pool of Sama'ria 4
2Kg 2:11 a chariot of fire and horses . . separated the two 4
12 father! the chariots of Israel and its horsemen! 4
5: 9 So Na'aman came with his horses and chariots 4
21 he alighted from the chariot to meet him, and said 2
26 when the man turned from his chariot to meet you? 2
6:14 he sent . . horses and chariots and a great army; 4
15 an army with horses and chariots was round about 4
17 mountain was full of horses and chariots of fire 4
7: 6 made the army . . hear the sound of chariots 4
8:21 Joram passed over to Za'ir with all his chariots 4
21 and his chariot commanders smote the E'domites 4
9:21 Make ready." And they made ready his chariot. 4
21 set out, each in his chariot, and went to meet Jehu 4
24 the arrow pierced . . and he sank in his chariot. 4
27 they shot him in the chariot at the ascent of Gur 2
10: 2 there are with you chariots and horses 4
15 And Jehu took him up with him into the chariot. 2
16 Come with me . . " So he had him ride in his chariot. 4
13: 7 an army of more than 50 horsemen and ten chariots 4
14 father! The chariots of Israel and its horsemen! 4
18:24 you rely on Egypt for chariots and for horsemen? 4
19:23 With my many chariots I have gone up the heights 4
23:11 and he burned the chariots of the sun with fire. 2
1Ch 18: 4 And David took from him a 1,000 chariots 4
4 but left enough for 100 chariots. 4
19: 6 of silver to hire chariots and horsemen 4
7 They hired 32,000 chariots and the king of Ma'acah 4
18 David slew of the Syrians the men of 7,000 chariots 4
28:18 his plan for the golden chariot of the cherubim 2
2Ch 1:14 gathered together chariots and horsemen; 4
14 he had 1,400 chariots 4
14 whom he stationed in the chariot cities 4
17 imported a chariot from Egypt for 600 2
8: 6 and all the cities for his chariots 4
9 commanders of his chariots, and his horsemen. 4
9:25 Solomon had 4,000 stalls for horses and chariots 2
25 whom he stationed in the chariot cities 4
10:18 King Rehobo'am made haste to mount his chariot 2
12: 3 with 1,200 chariots and 60,000 horsemen. 4
14: 9 with an army of 1,000,000 men and 300 chariots 2
16: 8 a huge army with exceedingly many chariots 4
18:30 had commanded the captains of his chariots 4
31 the captains of the chariots saw Jehosh'aphat 4
32 for when the captains of the chariots saw 4
34 king of Israel propped himself up in his chariot 2
21: 9 Jeho'ram passed over with . . all his chariots 4
9 surrounded him and his chariot commanders. 4
35:24 his servants took him out of the chariot 2
24 servants . . carried him in his second chariot 4
Ps 20: 7 Some boast of chariots, and some of horses; 4
46: 9 he burns the chariots with fire! 3
65:11 the tracks of thy chariot drip with fatness. •
104: 3 who makest the clouds thy chariot 5
Sng 1: 9 I compare you . . to a mare of Pharoah's chariots. 4
6:12 my fancy set me in a chariot beside my prince. 2
Isa 2: 7 and there is no end to their chariots. 2
22: 6 Elam bore the quiver with chariots and horsemen 4
7 Your choicest valleys were full of chariots 4
18 and there shall be your splendid chariots 2
31: 1 who trust in chariots because they are many 4
36: 9 you rely on Egypt for chariots and for horsemen? 4
37:24 With my many chariots I have gone up the heights 4
43:17 who brings forth chariot and horse 4
66:15 come in fire, and his chariots like the stormwind 2
20 offering to the LORD, upon horses, and in chariots 4
Jer 4:13 his chariots like the whirlwind; 2
17:25 kings . . riding in chariots and on horses 4
22: 4 riding in chariots and on horses 4
46: 9 Advance, O horses, and rage, O chariots! 4
47: 3 at the rushing of his chariots 4
50:37 A sword upon her horses and upon her chariots 4
51:21 I break in pieces the chariot and the charioteer; 4
Ezk 23:24 with chariots and wagons and a host of peoples; 4
26: 7 with horses and chariots, and with horsemen 4
10 noise of the horsemen and wagons and chariots 4
Dan 11:40 with chariots and horsemen, and with many ships; 4
Hos 10:13 Because you have trusted in your chariots 6
Jol 2: 5 As with the rumbling of chariots, 2
Mic 1:13 Harness the steeds to the chariots 2
5:10 I will cut off . . and will destroy your chariots; 2
Nah 2: 3 The chariots flash like flame when mustered 4
4 The chariots rage in the streets 4
13 and I will burn your chariots in smoke 4
3: 2 galloping horse and bounding chariot! 2
Hab 3: 8 ride upon thy horses, upon thy chariot of victory? 2
Hag 2:22 and overthrow the chariots and their riders; 2
Zec 6: 1 chariots came out from between two mountains; 2
2 The first chariot had red horses 2
3 the fourth chariot dappled gray horses. 2
6 The chariot with the black horses goes toward •
9:10 I will cut off the chariot from E'phraim 4
Act 8:28 seated in his chariot 6
29 Go up and join this chariot. 6
38 he commanded the chariot to stop 6
Rev 9: 9 like the noise of many chariots with horses 6
18:13 cattle and sheep, horses and chariots, and slaves 8
1Es 1:28 Josiah did not turn back to his chariot 6
31 he got into his second chariot 6
3: 6 have a chariot with gold bridles 6
2Es 15:29 nations . . shall come out with many chariots 9
Jdt 1:13 all his cavalry and all his chariots. 6
2:19 chariots and horsemen 6
22 his infantry, cavalry, and chariots 6
7:20 their infantry, chariots, and cavalry 6
Sir 48: 9 in a chariot with horses of fire; 6
49: 8 above the chariot of the cherubim. 6
1Mc 1:17 with chariots and elephants and cavalry 6
8: 6 with cavalry and chariots and a very large army. 6
2Mc 9: 7 so it came about that he fell out of his chariot 6
13: 2 300 chariots armed with scythes. 6
14:21 A chariot came forward from each army 7
3Mc 2: 7 pursued them with chariots and a mass of troops 6
6: 4 Pharaoh with his abundance of chariots 6
chariot *See also* carry, driver, horse, mount.

charioteer 1. רכב 2. *ἁρματηλάτης*
Jer 51:21 I break in pieces the chariot and the charioteer; 1
2Mc 9: 4 he ordered his charioteer to drive 2

chariotry 1. רֶכֶב
Ps 68:17 With mighty chariotry, twice 10,000 1

charity 1. *ἐλεημοσύνη*
Tob 2:14 your charities and your righteous deeds 1
4:10 For charity delivers from death 1
11 charity is an excellent offering 1
16 Give all your surplus to charity 1
charity *See also* act, deed.

charm 1. חֵן 2. כֶּשֶׁף 3. *εὔχαρις* 4. *χάρις*
Prv 31:30 Charm is deceitful, and beauty is vain 1
Nah 3: 4 betrays nations . . and peoples with her charms. 2
Wis 14:20 the multitude, attracted by the charm of his work 3
Sir 7:19 her charm is worth more than gold. 4
26:13 A wife's charm delights her husband 4
15 A modest wife adds charm to charm 4
15 A modest wife adds charm to charm 4

charm (2) 1. לַחַשׁ
Ecc 10:11 If the serpent bites before it is charmed 1
Isa 3: 3 the skilful magician and the expert in charms. 1
Jer 8:17 serpents, adders which cannot be charmed 1

deadly charm 1. כֶּשֶׁף
Nah 3: 4 the harlot, graceful and of deadly charms 1

charmer 1. בַּעַל לָשׁוֹן 2. חבר 3. לחשׁ 4. *ἐπαοιδός*
Deu 18:11 charmer, or a medium, or a wizard, or a necromancer. 2
Ps 58: 5 so that it does not hear the voice of charmers 3
Ecc 10:11 there is no advantage in a charmer. 1
Sir 12:13 Who will pity a snake charmer bitten by a serpent 4

chase 1. ברח 2. דלק 3. דלק אַחֲרֵי 4. פוּץ 5. רדף
6. *διώκω*
Lev 26: 7 you shall chase your enemies, and they shall fall 5
8 Five of you shall chase 100 5
8 100 of you shall chase 10,000 5
Deu 1:44 Amorites . . chased you as bees do and beat you 5
32:30 How should one chase 1,000, and two 5
Jos 7: 5 killed about . . and chased them before the gate 5
10:10 and chased them by the way of the ascent 5
11: 8 smote them and chased them as far as Great Sidon 5
Jdg 9:40 Abim'elech chased him, and he fled before him; 5
1Sm 17:53 came back from chasing the Philistines 3
Neh 13:28 therefore I chased him from me. 1
Job 18:11 frighten him . . and chase him at his heels. 4
Isa 17:13 will flee . . chased like chaff on the mountains 5
Lam 4:19 they chased us on the mountains, they lay in wait 2
Wis 2: 4 mist that is chased by the rays of the sun 6

chase away 1. ברח 2. נדד
Job 20: 8 he will be chased away like a vision of the night. 2
Prv 19:26 who does violence . . and chases away his mother 1

chasm 1. *φάραγχ* 2. *χάσμα*
Lke 16:26 between us and you a great chasm has been fixed 2
4Mc 14:16 building in precipitous chasms 1

chaste 1. *ἁγνός* 2. *ἐγκρατής* 3. *παρθένος*
Tit 2: 5 to be sensible, chaste, domestic, kind 1
1Pe 3: 2 when they see your reverent and chaste behavior 1
Rev 14: 4 not defiled themselves . . for they are chaste; 3
Sir 26:15 no balance can weigh the value of a chaste soul. 2

chasten 1. יכח 2. יסר 3. מוּסָר 4. תּוֹכַחַת 5. *παιδεύω*
2Sm 7:14 When he commits iniquity, I will chasten him 1
Job 5:17 despise not the chastening of the Almighty. 3
33:19 Man is also chastened with pain upon his bed 1
Ps 6: 1 not in thy anger, nor chasten me in thy wrath. 2
38: 1 not in thy anger, nor chasten me in thy wrath! 2
39:11 When thou dost chasten man with rebukes for sin 2
73:14 been stricken, and chastened every morning. 4
94:10 He who chastens the nations, does he not chastise? 2
12 Blessed is the man whom thou dost chasten, O LORD 2
118:18 The LORD has chastened me sorely 2
Isa 26:16 a prayer when thy chastening was upon them. 3
Jer 2:19 Your wickedness will chasten you 2
30:11 I will chasten you in just measure 2
31:18 Thou hast chastened me, and I was chastened 2
18 Thou hast chastened me, and I was chastened 2
46:28 I will chasten you in just measure 2
1Co 11:32 when we are judged by the Lord, we are chastened 5

Rev 3:19 Those whom I love, I reprove and chasten; 5
Wis 12:22 while chastening us thou scourgest our enemies 5

chastise 1.יכח 2.יסר 3.מוּסָר 4.κολάζω 5.μαστιγόω 6.μάστιξ 7.παιδεύω

Lev 26:18 then I will chastise you . . for your sins 2
28 I will . . chastise you myself sevenfold 2
Deu 21:18 though they chastise him, will not give heed 2
1Kg 12:11 My father chastised you with whips, but I will 2
11 but I will chastise you with scorpions.' 2
14 my father chastised you with whips, but I will 2
14 but I will chastise you with scorpions. 2
2Ch 10:11 My father chastised you with whips 2
11 but I will chastise you with scorpions.' •
14 my father chastised you with whips 2
14 but I will chastise you with scorpions. •
Ps 94:10 He who chastens the nations, does he not chastise? 1
Hos 5: 2 but I will chastise all of them. 3
7:12 I will chastise them for their wicked deeds. 2
10:10 against the wayward people to chastise them; 2
10 they are chastised for their double iniquity. 7
Lke 23:16 I will therefore chastise him and release him. 7
22 I will therefore chastise him and release him. 7
Heb 12: 6 chastises every son whom he receives. 5
Sir 22: 6 chastising and discipline are wisdom 6
4Mc 18: 5 and is being chastised after his death 4

chastisement 1.יכח 2.מוּסָר 3.עָוֹן 4.תּוֹכֵחָה 5.תּוֹכַחַת 6.verbero

Job 34:31 any one said to God, 'I have borne chastisement; •
Ps 149: 7 to wreak . . chastisement on the peoples 4
Prv 16:22 but folly is the chastisement of fools. 2
Isa 53: 5 upon him was the chastisement that made us whole 2
Lam 4: 6 the chastisement of the daughter of my people 3
Ezk 5:15 anger and fury, and with furious chastisements 5
25:17 upon them with wrathful chastisements. 5
Hab 1:12 O Rock, hast established them for chastisement. 1
2Es 15:12 for the plague of chastisement and punishment 6

chastity 1.σῶμα

Sir 7:24 Be concerned for their chastity 1

chatter 1.κενοφωνία

1Ti 6:20 Avoid the godless chatter and contradictions 1
2Ti 2:16 Avoid such godless chatter 1

chatterer 1.ἄνθρωπος γλωσσώδης

Sir 8: 3 Do not argue with a chatterer 1

cheap 1.εὐτελής 2.vilitas

2Es 16:21 Behold, provision will be so cheap upon earth 2
Wis 15:10 His heart is ashes, his hope is cheaper than dirt 1

cheat 1.גנב 2.גנב לֵבָב 3.נכל 4.תלל

Gen 31: 7 yet your father has cheated me 4
26 What have you done, that you have cheated me 2
27 Why did you flee secretly, and cheat me 1
Mal 1:14 Cursed be the cheat who has a male in his flock 3

check 1.עמד 2.ἀνακόπτω 3.πρός 4.πταίω

Lev 13: 5 if in his eyes the disease is checked 1
37 if in his eyes the itch is checked 1
Col 2:23 in checking the indulgence of the flesh. 3
2Mc 14:17 had been temporarily checked 4
4Mc 1:35 checked by the temperate mind 2

checker 1.שְׂבָכָה

1Kg 7:17 nets of checker work with wreaths of chain work 1

checker work 1.תַּשְׁבֵּץ

Exd 28: 4 an ephod, a robe, a coat of checker work, a turban 1

cheek 1.לְחִי 2.רַקָּה 3.σιαγών

Deu 18: 3 give to the priest . . the two cheeks 1
1Kg 22:24 came near and struck Micai'ah on the cheek 1
2Ch 18:23 Zedeki'ah . . struck Micai'ah on the cheek 1
Job 16:10 they have struck me insolently upon the cheek 1
Ps 3: 7 For thou dost smite all my enemies on the cheek 1
Sng 1:10 Your cheeks are comely with ornaments 1
4: 3 Your cheeks are like halves of a pomegranate 2
5:13 His cheeks are like beds of spices 1
6: 7 Your cheeks are like halves of a pomegranate 2
Isa 50: 6 and my cheeks to those who pulled out the beard; 1
Lam 1: 2 She weeps . . in the night, tears on her cheeks; 1
3:30 let him give his cheek to the smiter 1
Mic 5: 1 they strike upon the cheek the ruler of Israel. 1
Mat 5:39 any one strikes you on the right cheek, turn to him 3
Lke 6:29 To him who strikes you on the cheek 3
Sir 35:15 Do not the tears of the widow run down her cheek 3

cheer 1.יטב 2.משך 3.שׂמח 4.שׁעע 5.εὐφραίνω 6.εὐψυχέω

Jdg 9:13 Shall I leave my wine which cheers gods and men 3
Ps 94:19 thy consolations cheer my soul. 4
Ecc 2: 3 I searched . . how to cheer my body with wine 2
11: 9 let your heart cheer you in the days of your youth; 1
Php 2:19 so that I may be cheered by news of you. 6
Tob 13:10 May he cheer those within you who are captives 5
2Mc 15:11 he cheered them all by relating a dream 5

good cheer 1.בלג 2.εὔθυμος 3.εὐωχία 4.θαρρέω

Job 9:27 put off my sad countenance, and be of good cheer,' 1
Joh 16:33 be of good cheer, I have overcome the world. 4
Tob 11:11 saying, "Be of good cheer, father. 4
AEs 16:22 you shall observe this with all good cheer 3
2Mc 11:26 that they may know our policy and be of good cheer 2
3Mc 4: 8 instead of good cheer and youthful revelry 3

cheerful 1.טוֹב 2.יטב 3.שָׂמֵחַ 4.εὐθυμέω 5.ἱλαρός 6.λαμπρός 7.φαιδρός

1Kg 21: 7 Arise, and eat . . and let your heart be cheerful; 2
Prv 15:15 but a cheerful heart has a continual feast. 1
17:22 A cheerful heart is a good medicine 3
Zec 8:19 of joy and gladness, and cheerful feasts; 1
2Co 9: 7 God loves a cheerful giver. 5
Jas 5:13 Is any cheerful? Let him sing praise. 4
Sir 13:26 The mark of a happy heart is a cheerful face 5
26: 4 at all times his face is cheerful. 5
30:25 A man of cheerful and good heart 6
4Mc 13:13 looking at one another, cheerful and undaunted 7

cheerful *See also* make.

show cheerful 1.ἱλαρόω

Sir 35: 9 With every gift show a cheerful face 1

cheerfully 1.מַעֲדַנּוֹת 2.εὐθύμως

1Sm 15:32 And Agag came to him cheerfully. 1
Act 24:10 I cheerfully make my defense. 2

cheerfulness 1.ἱλαρότης

Rom 12: 8 he who does acts of mercy, with cheerfulness. 1

cheese 1.גְּבִינָה 2.חֲרִיץ חָלָב 3.שְׁפוֹת

1Sm 17:18 also take these ten cheeses to the commander 2
2Sm 17:29 brought . . sheep and cheese from the herd 3
Job 10:10 pour me out like milk and curdle me like cheese? 1

cherish 1.ראה 2.שׂום 3.שׁמר 4.θάλπω 5.προσδοκάω 6.τιθηνέω

Job 36:13 The godless in heart cherish anger; 2
Ps 66:18 If I had cherished iniquity in my heart 1
Ezk 35: 5 Because you cherished perpetual enmity •
Hos 4:10 they have forsaken the LORD to cherish harlotry. 3
Eph 5:29 nourishes and cherishes it 4
2Mc 7:14 cherish the hope that God gives 5
3Mc 3:15 cherish them with clemency 6

cherish enmity against 1.שׂטם

Ps 55: 3 in anger they cherish enmity against me. 1

cherub 1.כְּרוּב 2.χερούβ 3.χερουβείμ 4.χερουβίν

Gen 3:24 at the east . . of Eden he placed the cherubim 1
Exd 25:18 you shall make two cherubim of gold; 1
19 Make one cherub on the one end 1
19 Make . . one cherub on the other end; 1
19 shall you make the cherubim on its two ends. 1
20 The cherubim shall spread out their wings 1
20 mercy seat shall the faces of the cherubim be. 1
22 the two cherubim that are upon the ark 1
26: 1 with cherubim skilfully worked shall you make 1
31 in skilled work shall it be made, with cherubim. 1
36: 8 were made . . with cherubim skilfully worked. 1
35 with cherubim skilfully worked he made it. 1
37: 7 he made two cherubim of hammered gold; 1
8 one cherub on the one end, and one cherub 1
8 on the one end, and one cherub on the other end; 1
8 mercy seat he made the cherubim on its two ends. 1
9 The cherubim spread out their wings above 1
9 mercy seat were the faces of the cherubim. 1
Num 7:89 voice . . from between the two cherubim; 1
1Sm 4: 4 LORD of hosts, who is enthroned on the cherubim; 1
2Sm 6: 2 the LORD . . who sits enthroned on the cherubim. 1
22:11 He rode on a cherub, and flew . . upon the wings 1
1Kg 6:23 he made two cherubim of olivewood 1
24 Five cubits was . . one wing of the cherub 1
24 and five cubits . . the other wing of the cherub; 1
25 The other cherub also measured ten cubits; 1
25 both cherubim had the same measure and . . form. 1
26 The height of one cherub was ten cubits, and so was 1
26 ten cubits, and so was that of the other cherub. 1
27 He put the cherubim in the innermost part 1
27 the wings of the cherubim were spread out 1
27 a wing of the other cherub touched the other wall; 1
28 And he overlaid the cherubim with gold. 1
29 figures of cherubim and palm trees and open 1
32 of cherubim, palm trees, and open flowers; 1
32 spread gold upon the cherubim and . . palm trees. 1
35 carved cherubim and palm trees and open flowers; 1
7:29 on the panels . . were lions, oxen, and cherubim. 1
36 and on its panels, he carved cherubim, lions 1
8: 6 underneath the wings of the cherubim. 1
7 cherubim spread out their wings over the place 1
7 cherubim made a covering above the ark and its 1
2Kg 19:15 O LORD . . who art enthroned above the cherubim 1
1Ch 13: 6 the LORD who sits enthroned above the cherubim. 1
28:18 of the cherubim that spread their wings 1
2Ch 3: 7 and he carved cherubim on the walls. 1
10 most holy place he made two cherubim of wood 1
11 wings of the cherubim together extended twenty 1
11 wing . . touched the wing of the other cherub; 1
12 of this cherub, one wing . . touched the wall 1
12 was joined to the wing of the first cherub. 1
13 wings of these cherubim extended twenty cubits; 1
13 cherubim stood on their feet, facing the nave. •
14 he made the veil . . and worked cherubim on it. 1
5: 7 place, underneath the wings of the cherubim. 1
8 cherubim spread out their wings over the . . ark 1
8 cherubim made a covering above the ark and its 1
Ps 18:10 He rode on a cherub, and flew; he came swiftly 1
80: 1 who art enthroned upon the cherubim, shine forth 1
99: 1 sits enthroned upon the cherubim; 1
Isa 37:16 O LORD . . who art enthroned above the cherubim 1
Ezk 9: 3 gone up from the cherubim on which it rested 4
10: 1 firmament . . over the heads of the cherubim 1
2 the whirling wheels underneath the cherubim; 4
2 with burning coals from between the cherubim 1
3 Now the cherubim were standing on the south side 1
4 the glory of the LORD went up from the cherubim 4
5 the sound of the wings of the cherubim was heard 1
6 the whirling wheels, from between the cherubim 1
7 a cherub stretched forth his hand 1
7 his hand from between the cherubim to the fire 1
7 to the fire that was between the cherubim 1
8 The cherubim appeared to have the form of a human 1
9 there were four wheels beside the cherubim 1
9 there were four wheels . . one beside each cherub; 1
14 faces: the first face was the face of the cherub 1
15 And the cherubim mounted up. 1
16 when the cherubim went, the wheels went beside 1
16 the cherubim lifted up their wings to mount up 1
18 went forth . . and stood over the cherubim. 1
19 cherubim lifted up their wings and mounted up 1
20 and I knew that they were cherubim. 1
11:22 Then the cherubim lifted up their wings 1
28:14 With an anointed guardian cherub I placed you; 1
16 the guardian cherub drove you out from the midst 1
41:18 of cherubim and palm trees 1
18 a palm tree between cherub and cherub. 1
18 a palm tree between cherub and cherub. 1
18 Every cherub had two faces 1
20 cherubim and palm trees were carved on the wall. 1
25 And on the doors of the nave were carved cherubim 1
Heb 9: 5 above it were the cherubim of glory 2
Sir 49: 8 above the chariot of the cherubim. 3
Aza 1:32 Blessed art thou, who sittest upon cherubim 3

chest 1.אֲרוֹן

2Kg 12: 9 priest took a chest, and bored a hole in the lid 1
10 they saw that there was much money in the chest 1
2Ch 24: 8 the king commanded, and they made a chest 1
10 brought their tax and dropped it into the chest 1
11 chest was brought to the king's officers 1
11 would come and empty the chest and take it 1

chest *See also* treasure.

chew 1.גרר 2.עלה

Lev 11: 3 the hoof and is cloven-footed and chews the cud 2
4 Nevertheless among those that chew the cud 2
4 camel, because it chews the cud but does not part 2
5 it chews the cud but does not part the hoof 2
6 the hare, because it chews the cud but does not 2
7 swine . . does not chew the cud, is unclean to you 1
26 is not cloven-footed or does not chew the cud 2
Deu 14: 6 animal that . . chews the cud, among the animals 2
7 of those that chew the cud or have the hoof cloven 2
7 because they chew the cud but do not part the hoof 2
8 parts the hoof but does not chew the cud •

chew greedily 1.διαμασάομαι

Sir 31:16 do not chew greedily, lest you be hated. 1

chide 1.ריב

Ps 103: 9 He will not always chide 1

chief 1.אַבִּיר 2.אַיִל 3.אַלּוּף 4.גִּבּוֹר 5.גָּדוֹל 6.נצב 7.נָשִׂיא 8.פִּנָּה 9.קָצִין 10.ראשׁ 11.רִאשׁוֹן 12.שַׂר 13.רַב (A) 14.ἄρχων 15.ἡγέομαι 16.μέγας 17.πρώταρχος 18.πρῶτος 19.dux 20.princeps

Gen 36:15 These are the chiefs of the sons of Esau. 3
15 the chiefs Teman, Omar, Zepho, Kenaz 3
16 these are the chiefs of El'iphaz in the land 3
17 the chiefs Nahath, Zerah, Shammah, and Mizzah; 3
17 these are the chiefs of Reu'el in the land of Edom; 3
18 Esau's wife: the chiefs Je'ush, Jalam, and Korah 3
18 these are the chiefs born of Oholiba'mah 3
19 Esau (that is, Edom), and these are their chiefs. 3
21 these are the chiefs of the Horites 3
29 These are the chiefs of the Horites 3
29 Horites: the chiefs Lotan, Shobal, Zib'eon, Anah 3
30 Dishan; these are the chiefs of the Horites 3
40 These are the names of the chiefs of Esau 3
40 by their names: the chiefs Timna, Alvah, Jetheth 3
43 Mag'diel, and Iram; these are the chiefs of Edom 3

40: 2 officers, the chief butler and the chief baker 12
2 officers, the chief butler and the chief baker 12
9 the chief butler told his dream to Joseph 12
16 When the chief baker saw that 12
20 and lifted up the head of the chief butler 12
20 chief butler and the head of the chief baker 12
21 He restored the chief butler to his butlership 12
22 but he hanged the chief baker 12
23 Yet the chief butler did not remember Joseph 12
41: 9 Then the chief butler said to Pharaoh 12
10 and put me and the chief baker in custody 12
Exd 15:15 Now are the chiefs of Edom dismayed; 3
Lev 21:10 The priest who is chief among his brethren 5
Num 3:32 Elea'zar . . was to be chief over the leaders 7
25: 4 Take all the chiefs of the people, and hang them 10
Jos 10:24 Joshua . . and said to the chiefs of the men of war 9
22:14 and with him ten chiefs, one from each . . tribal 7
30 Phin'ehas . . and the chiefs of the congregation 7
32 Then Phin'ehas . . and the chiefs, returned 7
Jdg 20: 2 the chiefs of all the people, of all the tribes 8
1Sm 21: 7 Do'eg the E'domite, the chief of Saul's herdsmen. 1
2Sm 23: 8 Josheb-basshe'beth . . he was chief of the three; 10
18 Now Abi'shai . . was chief of the 30. 10
1Kg 5:16 Solomon's . . chief officers who were *
9:23 the chief officers who were over Solomon's work 6
2Kg 24:15 wives, his officials, and the chief men of the land 2
25:18 the captain . . took Serai'ah the chief priest 10
1Ch 1:51 The chiefs of Edom were: chiefs Timna, Al'iah 3
51 chiefs of Edom were: chiefs Timna, Al'iah, Jetheth 3
54 Mag'di-el, and Iram; these are the chiefs of Edom. 3
5: 7 his kinsmen . . the chief, Je-i'el, and Zechari'ah 10
12 Jo'el the chief, Shapham . . Ja'nai, and Shaphat 10
15 Ahi . . was chief in their fathers' houses; 10
7:40 men of Asher . . chief of the princes. 10
9:17 Shallum being the chief 10
26 for the four chief gatekeepers, who were Levites 4
11: 6 Jeb'usites first shall be chief and commander. 10
6 Jo'ab . . went up first, so he became chief. 10
10 Now these are the chiefs of David's mighty men 10
11 Jasho'be-am, a Hach'monite, was chief of the three; 10
20 Abi'shai, the brother of Jo'ab, was chief of the 30 10
12: 3 The chief was Ahi-e'zer, then Jo'ash, both sons 10
9 Ezer the chief, Obadi'ah second, Eli'ab third 10
18 Then the Spirit came upon Ama'sai, chief of the 30 10
20 chiefs of thousands in Manas'seh 10
32 200 chiefs, and all their kinsmen 10
15: 5 of the sons of Kohath, Uri'el the chief 12
6 of the sons of Merar'i, Asai'ah the chief 12
7 of the sons of Gershom, Jo'el the chief 12
8 of the sons of Eli-za'phan, Shemai'ah the chief 12
9 of the sons of Hebron, Eli'el the chief 12
10 of the sons of Uz'ziel, Ammin'adab the chief 12
16 David also commanded the chiefs of the Levites 12
16: 5 Asaph was the chief, and second to him were 10
23: 8 of Ladan: Jehi'el the chief, and Zetham, and Jo'el 10
11 Jahath was the chief, and Zizah the second; 10
16 The sons of Gershom: Sheb'uel the chief. 10
17 The sons of Elie'zer: Rehabi'ah the chief; 10
18 The sons of Izhar: Shelo'mith the chief. 10
19 sons of Hebron: Jeri'ah the chief, Amari'ah 10
20 The sons of Uz'ziel: Micah the chief 10
24: 4 chief men were found among the sons of Elea'zar 10
21 of the sons of Rehabi'ah, Isshi'ah the chief. 10
23 sons of Hebron: Jeri'ah the chief, Amari'ah *
25: 1 David and the chiefs of the service . . set apart 12
26:10 Hosah . . of Merar'i, had sons: Shimri the chief 10
10 not the first-born, his father made him chief 10
12 corresponding to their chief men, had duties 10
31 Jeri'jah was chief of the He'bronites 10
27: 3 chief of all the commanders of the army 10
5 Benai'ah, the son of Jehoi'ada the priest, as chief; 10
2Ch 8:10 these were the chief officers of King Solomon 12
11:22 Rehobo'am appointed Abi'jah . . as chief prince 10
19:11 Amari'ah the chief priest is over you 10
24: 6 king summoned Jehoi'ada the chief, and said to him 10
11 secretary and the officer of the chief priest 10
26:20 Azari'ah the chief priest, and all the priests 10
28:12 Certain chiefs also of the men of E'phraim 10
31:10 Azari'ah the chief priest . . answered him 10
35: 9 chiefs of the Levites, gave to the Levites 12
Ezr 7: 5 son of Elea'zar, son of Aaron the chief priest- 10
8:29 until you weigh them before the chief priests 12
Neh 10:14 chiefs of the people: Parosh, Pa'hath-mo'ab, Elam 10
11: 3 These are the chiefs of the province who lived 10
16 Shab'bethai . . of the chiefs of the Levites 10
12: 7 chiefs of the priests and of their brethren 10
24 chiefs of the Levites: Hashabi'ah, Sherebi'ah 10
46 days of David . . there was a chief of the singers 10
Est 1: 3 all his princes and servants, the army chiefs *
Job 12:24 from the chiefs of the people of the earth 10
29:25 I chose their way, and sat as chief 10
Ps 110: 6 he will shatter chiefs over the wide earth. 10
Prv 6: 7 Without having any chief, officer or ruler 9
Sng 4:14 myrrh and aloes, with all chief spices- 10
Jer 31: 7 and raise shouts for the chief of the nations; 10
52:24 the guard took Serai'ah the chief priest 10
Ezk 32:21 The mighty chiefs shall speak of them 2
38: 2 of Magog, the chief prince of Meshech and Tubal 10
3 O Gog, chief prince of Meshech and Tubal; 10
39: 1 O Gog, chief prince of Meshech and Tubal; 10
Dan 1: 7 chief of the eunuchs gave them names: Daniel 12
8 asked the chief of the eunuchs to allow him not 12
9 favor . . in the sight of the chief of the eunuchs; 12
10 chief of the eunuchs said to Daniel, "I fear lest my 12
11 said to the steward whom the chief of the eunuchs 12
18 chief of the eunuchs brought them in before 12
2:48 chief prefect over all the wise men of Babylon. 13
4: 9 O Belteshaz'zar, chief of the magicians 13
5:11 chief of the magicians, enchanters, Chalde'ans 13
10:13 but Michael, one of the chief princes, came to help 11
Act 14:12 because he was the chief speaker 15
1Es 8: 2 son of Eleazar, son of Aaron the chief priest. 18
2Es 5:16 Phaltiel, a chief of the people, came to me and said 19
15:16 for their king or the chief of their leaders. 20
1Mc 1:29 the king sent . . a chief collector of tribute 14
10:65 and enrolled him among his chief friends 18
11:27 to be regarded as one of his chief friends. 18
2Mc 4:50 the chief plotter against his fellow citizens. 16
8: 9 one of the king's chief friends 18
10:11 to be chief governor of Coelesyria and Phoenicia. 17

chief *See also* commander, general, officer, official, priest, shepherd, warrior.

chief man 1. אֵיל 2. אָצִיל 3. סָגָן 4. ראשׁ 5. *πρῶτος*

Exd 24:11 he did not lay his hand on the chief men 2
2Sm 23:13 And three of the 30 chief men went down 4
1Ch 7: 3 sons of Izrahi'ah . . five, all of them chief men; 4
8:28 according to their generations, chief men. 4
11:15 Three of the 30 chief men went down to the rock 4
Ezr 9: 2 hand of the officials and chief men 3
Ezk 17:13 The chief men of the land he had taken away 1
Act 28: 7 lands belonging to the chief man of the island 5

chiefly 1. *ὑπὲρ ἅπαν*

2Mc 8:35 having succeeded chiefly in . . 1

chieftain 1. נָשִׂיא 2. *ἄρχων*

1Ch 5: 6 Be-er'ah . . a chieftain of the Reubenites. 1
Jdt 7: 8 Then all the chieftains of the people of Esau 2

child 1. בֵּן 2. בנה 3. הרה 4. הָרָה 5. וָלָד 6. זֶרַע 7. טַף 8. ילד 9. יֶלֶד 10. ינק 11. נַעַר 12. עוֹלֵל 13. עלל 14. צֶאֱצָאִים 15. בֵּן (A) 16. *ἄνθρωπος* 17. *βρέφος* 18. *γαστήρ* 19. *γένεσις* 20. *γένημα* 21. *γεννάω* 22. *ἔγκυος* 23. *ἔκγονος* 24. *ἐν γαστρί* 25. *νέος* 26. *νήπιος* 27. *παιδίον* 28. *παιδοποιέω* 29. *παιδοποιία* 30. *παίδων γόνος* 31. *παῖς* 32. *σπέρμα* 33. *τέκνον* 34. *υἱός* 35. fetus 36. filius 37. infans 38. nascor 39. pario 40. parvulus 41. procreatio

Gen 3:16 in pain you shall bring forth children 1
4:25 appointed for me another child instead of Abel 6
10:21 To Shem also, the father of all the children 1
21 the elder brother of Japheth, children were born *
11:30 Now Sar'ai was barren; she had no child. 5
16:11 LORD said to her, "Behold, you are with child 4
17:17 Shall a child be born to a man who is 100 years old? 34
18:19 chosen him, that he may charge his children 1
19:36 Thus both the daughters of Lot were with child 3
21: 7 to Abraham that Sarah would suckle children? 1
8 the child grew, and was weaned; 9
14 putting it on her shoulder, along with the child 9
15 she cast the child under one of the bushes. 9
16 Let me not look upon the death of the child. 9
16 the child lifted up his voice and wept. 27
22:20 has borne children to your brother Nahor 1
25: 4 All these were the children of Ketu'rah. 1
22 The children struggled together within her; 1
30: 1 said to Jacob, "Give me children, or I shall die! 1
3 even I may have children through her. 2
26 Give me my wives and my children for whom I have 8
31:16 us and to our children; 1
43 The daughters are my daughters, the children are 1
43 do . . to their children whom they have borne? 1
32:11 slay us all, the mothers with the children. 1
22 took . . his two maids, and his eleven children 9
33: 1 he divided the children among Leah and Rachel 9
2 he put the maids with their children in front 9
2 in front, then Leah with her children, 9
5 raised his eyes and saw the women and children 9
5 Jacob said, "The children whom God has graciously 9
6 Then the maids drew near, they and their children 9
7 Leah likewise and her children drew near 9
13 to him, "My lord knows that the children are frail 9
14 lead on . . according to the pace of the children 9
36:25 These are the children of Anah 1
37: 3 loved Joseph more than any other of his children 1
38:24 moreover she is with child by harlotry. 4
25 By the man to whom these belong, I am with child. 4
42:36 You have bereaved me of my children *
43:14 If I am bereaved of my children, I am bereaved. *
44:20 We have . . a young brother, the child of his old 9
20 and he alone is left of his mother's children; *
45:10 you shall be near me, you and your children 1
10 your children and your children's children 1
10 your children and your children's children 1
48:11 and lo, God has let me see your children also. 6
50: 8 only their children, their flocks . . were left 7
23 saw E'phraim's children of the third generation 1
Exd 2: 3 a basket . . she put the child in it 9
6 When she opened it she saw the child; 9
6 This is one of the Hebrews' children. 9
7 call . . a nurse . . to nurse the child for you? 9
8 So the girl went and called the child's mother. 9
9 said to her, "Take this child away, and nurse him 9
9 So the woman took the child and nursed him. 9
10 the child grew, and she brought him 9
10:20 he did not let the children of Israel go. 1
24 serve the LORD; your children also may go with you; 7
12:26 when your children say to you, 'What do you mean 1
37 besides women and children. 7
17: 3 up out of Egypt, to kill us and our children 1
7 the faultfinding of the children of Israel 1
19: 6 you shall speak to the children of Israel. 1
20: 5 iniquity . . upon the children to the third 1
21: 4 the wife and her children shall be her master's 9
5 I love my master, my wife, and my children; 1
22 men strive together, and hurt a woman with child 4
22:24 become widows and your children fatherless. 1
34: 7 iniquity of the fathers upon the children 1
7 the children and the children's children 1
7 the children and the children's children 1
Lev 6:18 Every male among the children of Aaron may eat 1
18:21 shall not give any of your children . . to Molech 6
20: 2 who gives any of his children to Molech 6
3 he has given one of his children to Molech 6
4 when he gives one of his children to Molech 6
17 in the sight of the children of their people 1
21:15 that he may not profane his children 6
22:13 daughter . . has no child, and returns to her 6
25:41 then he shall go out from you, he and his children 1
54 released . . he and his children with him 1
Num 3: 4 they had no children. So Elea'zar and Ith'amar 1
5:28 she shall be free and shall conceive children. 6
14:18 visiting the iniquity of fathers upon children 1
33 your children shall be shepherds 1
Deu 1:36 Caleb . . shall see it, and to him and to his children 1
39 your children, who this day have no knowledge 1
2:34 destroyed every city, men, women, and children; 7
3: 6 destroying every city, men, women, and children. 7
4: 9 make them known to your children 1
9 make them known to your . . children's children- 1
9 make them known to your . . children's children- 1
10 that they may teach their children so.' 1
25 When you beget children and children's children 1
25 When you beget children and children's children 1
25 When you beget children and children's children 1
40 it may go well with you, and with your children 1
44 law . . Moses set before the children of Israel; 1
45 which Moses spoke to the children of Israel 1
46 whom Moses and the children of Israel defeated 1
5: 9 visiting the iniquity . . upon the children 1
29 go well with them . . their children for ever! 1
6: 7 you shall teach them diligently to your children 1
11: 2 (since I am not speaking to your children who 1
19 you shall teach them to your children 1
21 that your days and the days of your children 1
12:25 all may go well with you and with your children 1
28 go well with you and with your children after you 1
17:20 continue long in his kingdom, he and his children 1
21:15 two wives . . and they have borne him children 1
23: 8 children of the third generation that are born 1
24:16 fathers . . not be put to death for the children 1
16 nor . . children be put to death for the fathers; 1
28:54 grudge food . . to the last of the children 1
55 not give . . any of the flesh of his children whom 1
57 afterbirth . . and her children whom she bears 1
29:22 your children who rise up after you 1
29 revealed belong to us and to our children for ever 1
30: 2 return to the LORD your God, you and your children 1
31:13 their children, who have not known it, may hear 1
23 shall bring the children of Israel into the land 1
32: 5 dealt corruptly . . they are no longer his children 1
20 children in whom is no faithfulness. 1
46 that you may command them to your children 1
33: 1 Moses . . blessed the children of Israel 1
9 he disowned . . and ignored his children. 1
Jos 4: 6 a sign . . when your children ask in time to come 1
21 When your children ask . . in time to come 1
22 then you shall let your children know 1
5: 7 it was their children . . that Joshua 1
14: 9 inheritance for you and your children for ever 1
22:24 your children might say to our children 1
24 your children might say to our children 1
25 your children might make our children cease 1
25 might make our children cease to worship 1
27 lest your children say . . in time to come 1
27 your children say to our children in time to come 1
24: 4 but Jacob and his children went down to Egypt. 1
Jdg 10: 8 crushed and oppressed the children of Israel 1
11:34 she was his only child; beside her he had neither *
13: 2 his wife was barren and had no children. 8
3 Behold, you are barren and have no children; 8
Rut 4:12 because of the children that the LORD will give 6
16 Na'omi took the child and laid him in her bosom 9
1Sm 1: 2 Penin'nah had children, but Hannah had no 9

2 but Hannah had no children. 9
22 As soon as the child is weaned, I will bring him 11
24 she took him up . . and the child was young. 11
25 slew the bull, and they brought the child to Eli. 11
27 For this child I prayed; 11
2: 5 but she who has many children is forlorn. 1
20 The LORD give you children by this woman 6
4:19 Now his daughter-in-law . . was with child 4
21 And she named the child Ich'abod, saying 11
22:19 men and women, children and sucklings, oxen, asses 12
30:22 may lead away his wife and children, and depart. 1
2Sm 6:23 And Michal . . had no child to the day of her death. 9
11: 5 and she sent and told David, "I am with child. 4
12: 3 and it grew up with him and with his children; 1
14 the child that is born to you shall die. 1
15 the LORD struck the child that Uri'ah's wife bore 9
16 David therefore besought God for the child; 11
18 On the seventh day the child died. 9
18 feared to tell him that the child was dead; 9
18 while the child was yet alive, we spoke to him 9
18 how then can we say to him the child is dead? 9
19 David perceived that the child was dead; 9
19 and David said to his servants, "Is the child dead? 9
21 You fasted and wept for the child while it was 9
21 but when the child died, you arose and ate food. 9
22 While the child was still alive, I fasted and wept; 9
22 LORD . . be gracious to me, that the child may live?' 9
1Kg 3: 7 I am but a little child; I do not know how to go out 11
17 I gave birth to a child while she was in the house. •
21 When I rose . . to nurse my child, behold, it was dead; 1
21 behold, it was not the child that I had borne. 1
22 No, the living child is mine, and the dead child is 1
22 living child is mine, and the dead child is yours. 1
22 No, the dead child is yours, and the living child is 1
22 dead child is yours, and the living child is mine. 1
25 Divide the living child in two, and give half 9
26 give her the living child, and by no means slay it. 8
27 Give the living child to the first woman, and by no 8
6:13 I will dwell among the children of Israel 1
8:39 knowest the hearts of all the children of men); 1
9: 6 turn aside from following me, you or your children 1
11:17 Hadad fled . . Hadad being yet a little child. 11
14: 3 he will tell you what shall happen to the child. 11
12 your feet enter the city, the child shall die. 9
17 as she came to . . the house, the child died. 11
17:21 he stretched himself upon the child three times 9
21 LORD . . let this child's soul come into him again. 9
22 the soul of the child came into him again 9
23 Eli'jah took the child, and brought him down 9
20: 3 your fairest wives and children also are mine.' 1
5 Deliver to me . . your wives and your children"; 1
7 he sent to me for my wives and my children 1
2Kg 4: 1 the creditor has come to take my two children 9
18 When the child had grown, he went out one day 9
20 to his mother, the child sat on her lap till noon •
26 Is it well with you? . . Is it well with the child? 9
29 and lay my staff upon the face of the child. 11
30 the mother of the child said, "As the LORD lives 11
31 and laid the staff upon the face of the child 11
31 and told him, "The child has not awaked. 11
32 Eli'sha . . saw the child lying dead on his bed. 11
34 Then he went up and lay upon the child 9
34 the flesh of the child became warm. 9
35 the child sneezed seven times 11
35 child sneezed . . and the child opened his eyes. 11
5:14 was restored like the flesh of a little child 11
14: 6 not put to death the children of the murderers; 1
6 shall not be put to death for the children 1
6 or the children be put to death for the fathers; 1
17:31 Sephar'vites burned their children in the fire 1
34 which the LORD commanded the children of Jacob 1
41 So these nations . . their children likewise 1
41 their children . . and their children's children 1
41 their children . . and their children's children 1
19: 3 children have come to the birth, and there is no 1
1Ch 2:18 Caleb . . had children by his wife Azu'bah 8
4:27 but his brothers had not many children 1
6: 3 The children of Amram: Aaron, Moses, and Miriam. 1
14: 4 names of the children whom he had in Jerusalem 8
24: 2 Nadab and Abi'hu died . . and had no children 1
28: 8 inheritance to your children after you 1
2Ch 6:30 only, knowest the hearts of the children of men); 1
7: 3 all the children of Israel saw the fire come down 1
20:13 little ones, their wives, and their children. 1
21:14 will bring a great plague on . . your children 1
25: 4 he did not put their children to death 1
4 fathers . . not be put to death for the children 1
4 or the children be put to death for the fathers; 1
30: 9 your . . children will find compassion 1
Ezr 8:21 straight way for ourselves, our children 7
9:12 leave it for an inheritance to your children 1
10: 1 very great assembly of men, women, and children 9
3 to put away all these wives and their children 8
44 put them away with their children. 1
Neh 2:10 seek the welfare of the children of Israel. 1
5: 5 our children are as their children; 1
5 our children are as their children; 1
7:73 children of Israel were in their towns. 1
12:43 women and children also rejoiced. 9

13: 2 not meet the children of Israel with bread 1
24 half of their children spoke the language 1
Est 3:13 slay . . all Jews, young and old, women and children 7
8:11 annihilate any . . with their children and women 7
Job 8: 4 If your children have sinned against him 1
17: 5 the eyes of his children will fail. 1
20:10 His children will seek the favor of the poor 1
21: 8 Their children are established 6
11 like a flock, and their children dance. 9
24: 5 in the wilderness as food for their children. 11
27:14 If his children are multiplied 1
29: 5 when my children were about me; 11
38:32 or can you guide the Bear with its children? 1
Ps 11: 4 behold, his eyelids test, the children of men. 1
14: 2 looks down from heaven upon the children of men 1
17:14 may their children have more than enough; 1
21:10 their children from among the sons of men. 6
25:13 his children shall possess the land. 6
36: 7 The children of men take refuge in the shadow 1
37:25 forsaken or his children begging bread. 6
26 his children become a blessing. 6
28 but the children of the wicked shall be cut off. 6
69:36 the children of his servants shall inherit it 6
73:15 been untrue to the generation of thy children. 1
78: 4 We will not hide them from their children 1
5 our fathers to teach to their children; 1
6 might know them, the children yet unborn 1
6 arise and tell them to their children 1
83: 8 are the strong arm of the children of Lot. Selah 1
89:30 If his children forsake my law 1
90: 3 Thou . . sayest, "Turn back, O children of men! 1
16 thy glorious power to their children. 1
102:28 The children of thy servants shall dwell secure; 1
103:13 As a father pities his children 1
17 his righteousness to children's children 1
17 his righteousness to children's children 1
109: 9 his children be fatherless, and his wife a widow! 1
10 May his children wander about and beg; 1
113: 9 making her the joyous mother of children. 1
115:14 May the LORD give you increase . . your children! 1
128: 3 your children will be like olive shoots 1
6 May you see your children's children! 1
6 May you see your children's children! 1
131: 2 like a child quieted at its mother's breast; •
2 like a child that is quieted is my soul. •
148:12 together, old men and children! 11
Prv 13:22 leaves an inheritance to his children's children 1
22 leaves an inheritance to his children's children 1
14:26 his children will have a refuge. 1
20:11 Even a child makes himself known by his acts 11
22: 6 Train up a child in the way he should go 11
15 Folly is bound up in the heart of a child 11
23:13 Do not withhold discipline from a child; 11
29:15 child left to himself brings shame 11
31:28 Her children rise up and call her blessed; 1
Ecc 6: 3 If a man begets 100 children . . but he does •
10:16 Woe to you, O land, when your king is a child 11
Isa 3:12 My people-children are their oppressors 13
7:16 For before the child knows how to refuse the evil 11
8: 4 for before the child knows how to cry 'My father' 11
18 Behold, I and the children whom the LORD has given 9
9: 6 For to us a child is born, to us a son is given; 9
10:19 trees . . so few that a child can write them down. 11
11: 6 together, and a little child shall lead them. 11
13:18 no mercy . . their eyes will not pity children. 1
17: 3 Syria . . like the glory of the children of Israel 1
9 deserted because of the children of Israel 1
26:18 we were with child, we writhed 3
29:23 For when he sees his children, the work of my hands 9
30: 1 Woe to the rebellious children," says the LORD 1
37: 3 children have come to birth 1
38:19 makes known to the children thy faithfulness. 1
45:11 Will you question me about my children 1
49:20 The children . . of your bereavement will yet say 1
25 I will contend . . and I will save your children. 1
54: 1 For the children of the desolate one will be more 1
1 be more than the children of her that is married 1
57: 4 Are you not children of transgression 9
5 who slay your children in the valleys 9
59:21 of your mouth, or out of the mouth of your children 6
21 or out of the mouth of your children's children 6
21 or out of the mouth of your children's children 6
65:20 for the child shall die 100 years old 11
23 blessed . . and their children with them. 14
Jer 2: 9 with your children's children I will contend. 1
9 with your children's children I will contend. 1
30 In vain have I smitten your children 1
3:14 Return, O faithless children, says the LORD; 1
4:22 they know me not; they are stupid children 1
31 anguish as of one bringing forth her first child •
5: 7 Your children have forsaken me 1
6:11 Pour it out upon the children in the street 12
7:18 children gather wood, the fathers kindle fire 1
9:21 cutting off the children from the streets 12
10:20 my children have gone from me, and they are not; 1
17: 2 while their children remember their altars 1
18:21 Therefore deliver up their children to famine; 1
22:28 and his children hurled and cast into a land 6
30:20 Their children shall be as they were of old 1

31:15 Rachel is weeping for her children; 1
15 she refuses to be comforted for her children 1
17 your children shall come back to their own 1
20 Is E'phraim my dear son? Is he my darling child? 9
29 and the children's teeth are set on edge. 1
32:18 requite the guilt of fathers to their children 1
39 and the good of their children after them. 1
40: 7 and had committed to him men, women, and children 7
41:16 soldiers, women, children, and eunuchs 7
43: 6 the men, the women, the children, the princesses 7
44: 7 to cut off from you man and woman, infant and child 10
47: 3 the fathers look not back to the children 1
49:10 His children are destroyed, and his brothers 6
Lam 1: 5 her children have gone away, captives 12
16 a comforter is far . . my children are desolate 1
2:19 Lift your hands . . for the lives of your children 12
20 offspring, the children of their tender care? 12
4: 4 the children beg for food, but no one gives to them. 12
10 women have boiled their own children; 9
Ezk 16:21 that you slaughtered my children 1
36 the blood of your children that you gave to them 1
45 mother, who loathed her husband and her children; 1
45 who loathed their husbands and their children. 1
18: 2 and the children's teeth are set on edge 1
20:18 I said to their children in the wilderness 1
21 But the children rebelled against me; 1
23:39 For when they had slaughtered their children 1
37:16 and the children of Israel associated with him 1
25 their children and their children's children 1
25 their children and their children's children 1
25 their children and their children's children 1
47:22 and have begotten children among you. 1
Dan 6:24 den of lions-they, their children, and their wives; 15
11: 6 shall be given up, and her attendants, her child 9
Hos 1: 2 a wife of harlotry and have children of harlotry 9
2: 4 Upon her children also I will have no pity 1
4 no pity, because they are children of harlotry. 1
3: 4 For the children of Israel shall dwell many days 1
5 Afterward the children of Israel shall return 1
4: 6 I also will forget your children. 1
5: 7 for they have borne alien children. 1
9:12 if they bring up children, I will bereave them 1
10:14 were dashed in pieces with their children. 1
11: 1 When Israel was a child, I loved him 11
Jol 1: 3 Tell your children of it 1
3 and let your children tell their children 1
3 and let your children tell their children 1
3 and their children another generation. 1
2:16 gather the children, even nursing infants. 12
Mic 1:16 cut . . your hair, for the children of your delight; 1
Zec 10: 7 Their children shall see it and rejoice 1
9 with their children they shall live and return. 1
Mal 4: 6 turn the hearts of fathers to their children 1
6 turn . . the hearts of children to their fathers 1
Mat 1:18 found to be with child of the Holy Spirit; 18
2: 8 saying, "Go and search diligently for the child 27
9 to rest over the place where the child was. 27
11 going into the house they saw the child with Mary 27
13 Rise, take the child and his mother, and flee 27
13 Herod is about to search for the child, to destroy 27
14 he rose and took the child and his mother by night 27
18 Rachel weeping for her children; she refused 33
20 Rise, take the child and his mother, and go 27
20 those who sought the child's life are dead. 27
21 he rose and took the child and his mother, and went 27
3: 9 from these stones to raise up children to Abraham. 33
7:11 know how to give good gifts to your children 33
10:21 and the father his child 33
21 children will rise against parents 33
11:16 It is like children sitting in the market places 27
14:21 about 5,000 men, besides women and children. 27
15:26 It is not fair to take the children's bread 33
38 4,000 men, besides women and children. 27
18: 2 calling to him a child, he put him in the midst 27
3 unless you turn and become like children 27
4 Whoever humbles himself like this child 27
5 Whoever receives one such child in my name 27
25 with his wife and children and all that he had 33
19:13 Then children were brought to him 27
14 Jesus said, "Let the children come to me 27
29 sisters or father or mother or children or lands 33
21:15 the children crying out in the temple 31
22:24 If a man dies, having no children 33
24 raise up children for his brother.' 32
25 having no children left his wife to his brother. 32
23:15 twice as much a child of hell as yourselves. 34
37 I have gathered your children together 33
24:19 alas for those who are with child 24
27:25 His blood be on us and on our children! 33
Mrk 5:39 The child is not dead but sleeping. 27
40 and took the child's father and mother 27
40 and went in where the child was. 27
7:27 he said to her, "Let the children first be fed 33
27 for it is not right to take the children's bread 33
28 dogs under the table eat the children's crumbs. 27
30 she went home, and found the child lying in bed 27
9:24 Immediately the father of the child cried out 27
36 he took a child, and put him in the midst of them; 27
37 Whoever receives one such child in my name 27

10:13 they were bringing children to him 27
14 Let the children come to me, do not hinder them 27
15 receive the kingdom of God like a child 27
24 Children, how hard it is to enter 33
29 mother or father or children or lands 33
30 brothers and sisters and mothers and children 33
12:19 leaves a wife, but leaves no child 33
19 and raise up children for his brother. 32
20 when he died left no children; 32
21 the second took her, and died, leaving no children; 32
22 the seven left no children 32
13:12 the father his child 33
12 children will rise against parents 33
17 alas for those who are with child 24
Lke 1: 7 they had no child, because Elizabeth was barren 27
17 to turn the hearts of the fathers to the children 33
35 the child to be born will be called holy, the Son of God •
59 they came to circumcise the child 27
66 saying, "What then will this child be? 27
76 you, child, will be called the prophet 27
80 the child grew and became strong in spirit 27
2: 5 with Mary, his betrothed, who was with child. 22
17 which had been told them concerning this child; 27
27 when the parents brought in the child Jesus 27
34 this child is set for the fall and rising of many •
40 And the child grew and became strong 27
3: 8 is able from these stones to raise up children 33
7:32 They are like children sitting in the market place 27
35 Yet wisdom is justified by all her children. 33
8:51 the father and mother of the child. 31
54 he called, saying, "Child, arise. 31
9:47 he took a child and put him by his side 27
48 Whoever receives this child in my name 27
11: 7 door is now shut, and my children are with me in bed; 27
13 know how to give good gifts to your children 33
13:34 would I have gathered your children together 33
14:26 his own father and mother and wife and children 33
18:16 Let the children come to me, and do not hinder them; 27
17 receive the kingdom of God like a child 27
29 house or wife or brothers or parents or children 33
19:44 you and your children within you 33
20:28 the man must take the wife and raise up children 32
31 likewise all seven left no children and died. 33
21:23 Alas for those who are with child 24
23:28 weep for yourselves and for your children. 33
Joh 1:12 he gave power to become children of God; 33
4:49 Sir, come down before my child dies. 27
8:39 Jesus said to them, "If you were Abraham's children 33
11:52 to gather into one the children of God 33
16:21 when she is delivered of the child 27
21 for joy that a child is born into the world. 16
21: 5 Jesus said to them, "Children have you any fish? 27
Act 2:39 For the promise is to you and to your children 33
7: 5 though he had no child. 33
13:33 this he has fulfilled to us their children 33
21: 5 they all, with wives and children 33
21 telling them not to circumcise their children 33
Rom 2:20 a corrector of the foolish, a teacher of children 26
8:16 bearing witness . . that we are children of God 33
17 if children, then heirs, heirs of God 33
21 the glorious liberty of the children of God. 33
9: 7 and not all are children of Abraham 33
8 children of the flesh who are the children of God 33
8 children of the flesh who are the children of God 33
8 but the children of the promise are reckoned 33
10 when Rebecca had conceived children by one man •
29 If the Lord of hosts had not left us children 32
1Co 4:14 to admonish you as my beloved children. 33
17 my beloved and faithful child in the Lord 33
7:14 Otherwise, your children would be unclean 33
13:11 When I was a child, I spoke like a child 26
11 When I was a child, I spoke like a child 26
11 I thought like a child, I reasoned like a child; 26
11 I thought like a child, I reasoned like a child; 26
14:20 Brethren, do not be children in your thinking 27
2Co 6:13 In return–I speak as to children 33
12:14 children ought not to lay up for their parents 33
14 parents for their children. 33
Gal 4: 1 I mean that the heir, as long as he is a child 26
3 So with us; when we were children 26
25 for she is in slavery with her children. 33
27 the children of the desolate one are many more 33
27 more than the children of her that is married. •
28 we, brethren, like Isaac, are children of promise. 33
31 So, brethren, we are not children of the slave 33
Eph 2: 3 we were by nature children of wrath 33
4:14 so that we may no longer be children 26
5: 1 be imitators of God, as beloved children. 33
8 walk as children of light 33
6: 1 Children, obey your parents in the Lord 33
4 Fathers, do not provoke your children to anger 33
Php 2:15 be blameless and innocent, children of God 33
Col 3:20 Children, obey your parents in everything 33
21 Fathers, do not provoke your children 33
1Th 2: 7 like a nurse taking care of her children. 33
11 for you know how, like a father with his children 33
5: 3 as travail comes upon a woman with child 24
1Ti 1: 2 To Timothy, my true child in the faith 33
3: 4 keeping his children submissive 33
12 let them manage their children . . well 33
5: 4 If a widow has children or grandchildren 33
2Ti 1: 2 To Timothy, my beloved child 33
Tit 1: 4 To Titus, my true child in a common faith 33
6 his children are believers 33
Phm 1:10 I appeal to you for my child, Ones'imus 33
Heb 2:13 again, "Here am I, and the children God has given me. 27
14 therefore the children share in flesh and blood 27
5:13 he is a child. 26
11:23 because they saw that the child was beautiful 27
1Pe 1:14 As obedient children, do not be conformed 33
3: 6 you are now her children if you do right 33
2Pe 2:14 hearts trained in greed. Accursed children! 33
1Jn 2:13 I write to you, children 27
18 Children, it is the last hour; 27
3: 1 we should be called children of God; and so we are. 33
2 Beloved, we are God's children now; 33
10 By this it may be seen who are the children of God 33
10 and who are the children of the devil 33
5: 1 Every one who believes . . is a child of God 21
1 every one who loves the parent loves the child. 21
2 By this we know that we love the children of God 33
2Jn 1: 1 The elder to the elect lady and her children 33
4 to find some of your children following the truth 33
13 The children of your elect sister greet you. 33
3Jn 1: 4 to hear that my children follow the truth. 33
Rev 2:23 and I will strike her children dead. 33
12: 2 she was with child and she cried out in her pangs 24
4 might devour her child when she brought it forth; 33
5 she brought forth a male child, one who is to rule 34
5 her child was caught up to God and to his throne 33
13 he pursued the woman who had borne the male child. •
1Es 1:53 young man or virgin, old man or child 25
4:53 their children and all the priests who came. 33
6:31 libations . . for the king and his children 31
8:50 our children and the cattle that were with us. 33
85 for an inheritance to your children for ever. 34
93 all our foreign wives, with their children 33
9:36 they put them away with their children. 33
2Es 1: 5 declare . . to their children the iniquities 36
5 so that they may tell their children's children 36
5 so that they may tell their children's children 36
28 a mother her daughters or a nurse her children 40
34 your sons will have no children 41
37 whose children rejoice with gladness 40
2: 2 'Go, my children, because I am a widow and forsaken. 36
4 Go, my children, and ask for mercy from the Lord.' 36
5 in addition to the mother of the children 36
19 by these I will fill your children with joy. 36
32 Embrace your children until I come 38
41 The number of your children . . is full 36
3:12 they produced children and peoples 36
4:40 her womb can keep the child within her any longer. 35
5:46 If you bear ten children, why one after another?' •
51 He replied to me, "Ask a woman who bears children •
6:21 premature children at three and four months 37
9:43 Your servant was barren and had no child 39
15:25 Depart, you faithless children! 36
57 Your children shall die of hunger 38
63 They shall carry your children away captive 38
16: 2 and wail for your children, and lament for them 36
38 Just as a woman with child, in the ninth month 36
38 and when the child comes forth from the womb 37
44 like those who will have no children 36
46 and take their children captive 36
46 they will beget their children. 38
Tob 3:10 But she said, "I am the only child of my father •
15 he has no child to be his heir 27
4:12 They were blessed in their children 33
5:17 Why have you sent our child away? 27
18 consider it as rubbish as compared to our child. 27
6:17 I suppose that you will have children by her. 27
7:10 for it is your right to take my child 27
18 Be brave, my child 33
10: 5 Am I not distressed, my child, that I let you go 33
7 stop deceiving me; my child has perished 27
11 The God of heaven will prosper you, my children 33
12 to see your children by my daughter Sarah 27
11: 9 I have seen you, my child; now I am ready to die. 27
14:11 now, my children, consider 27
Jdt 4:10 their wives and their children and their cattle 26
11 the men and women of Israel, and their children 27
7:14 their wives and children will waste away with famine 33
22 Their children lost heart 26
23 the women, and the children 27
27 see our . . children draw their last breath. 33
32 The women and children he sent home 33
9:13 the house possessed by thy children. 34
16: 5 and seize my children as prey 26
12 were wounded like the children of fugitives 31
AEs 13: 6 all, with their wives and children 33
Wis 2:13 calls himself a child of the Lord. 31
3:12 Their wives are foolish, and their children evil; 33
16 children of adulterers will not come to maturity 33
4: 6 children born of unlawful unions 33
8:19 As a child I was by nature well endowed 31
10: 5 in the face of his compassion for his child. 33
12: 5 their merciless slaughter of children 33
25 as to thoughtless children 31
13:17 possessions and his marriage and children 33
14:15 a father . . made an image of his child 33
16:21 manifested thy sweetness toward thy children; 33
18: 5 one child had been exposed and rescued 33
5 thou didst . . take away a multitude of their children 33
9 the holy children of good men offered sacrifices 31
10 their piteous lament for their children 31
12 their most valued children had been destroyed. 19
19: 6 thy children might be kept unharmed. 31
Sir 3: 1 Listen to me your father, O children 33
2 the Lord honored the father above the children 33
5 will be gladdened by his own children 33
9 strengthens the houses of the children 33
11 it is a disgrace for children 33
7:23 Do you have children? Discipline them 33
11:28 a man will be known through his children. 33
14:26 he will place his children under her shelter 33
16: 1 Do not desire a multitude of useless children 33
3 better than to have ungodly children. 33
19:11 suffer pangs like a woman in labor with a child. 17
23: 7 Listen, my children 33
23 brought forth children by another man. 33
24 punishment will fall on her children. 33
25 Her children will not take root 33
25: 7 a man rejoicing in his children 33
30: 9 Pamper a child, and he will frighten you 33
33:21 better that your children should ask from you 33
40:15 The children of the ungodly 23
19 Children and the building of a city 33
41: 5 The children of sinners are abominable 33
5 children of sinners are abominable children 33
6 The inheritance of the children of sinners 33
7 Children will blame an ungodly father 33
14 My children, observe instruction and be at peace; 33
42: 5 of much discipline of children 33
44: 9 so have their children after them. 33
11 their inheritance to their children's children 1
11 their inheritance to their children's children 1
12 their children also, for their sake. 33
46: 9 his children obtained it for an inheritance; 32
47:20 you brought wrath upon your children 33
Bar 4:12 left desolate because of the sins of my children 33
15 nation . . who . . had no pity for a child. 27
19 Go, my children, go; for I have been left desolate. 33
21 Take courage, my children, cry to God 33
25 My children, endure with patience the wrath 33
27 Take courage, my children, and cry to God 33
32 the cities which your children served as slaves; 33
5: 5 see your children gathered from west and east 33
LJr 1:33 to clothe their wives and children. 27
Sus 1:30 And she came, with her parents, her children 33
Bel 1:10 besides their wives and children 33
15 the priests came with their wives and children 33
20 the footsteps of men and women and children. 27
21 seized the priests and their wives and children; 33
1Mc 1:32 they took captive the women and children 33
38 her children forsook her. 33
60 the women who had their children circumcised 33
2:38 with their wives and children and cattle 33
50 Now, my children, show zeal for the law 33
64 My children, be courageous 33
3:20 to destroy us and our wives and our children 33
45 not one of her children went in or out 20
5:13 captured their wives and children and goods 33
23 with their wives and children 33
45 with their wives and children and goods 33
8:10 the Romans took captive their wives and children; 33
13: 6 the sanctuary and your wives and children 33
45 The men in the city, with their wives and children 33
2Mc 5:13 destruction of boys, women, and children 33
6:10 having circumcised their children 33
7:28 I beseech you, my child, to look at the heaven 33
34 raise your hand against the children of heaven. 31
8:28 among themselves and their children. 27
9:15 throw out with their children to the beasts 26
20 If you and your children are well 33
12: 3 to embark, with their wives and children, on boats 33
21 he sent off the women and the children 33
14:25 he urged him to marry and have children; 28
15:18 Their concern for wives and children 33
3Mc 1: 4 defend . . their children and wives bravely 33
20 nurses abandoned even newborn children 33
3:25 together with their wives and children 33
27 old people or children or even infants 26
5:31 Were your parents or children present 30
49 parents and children, mothers and daughters 31
6: 3 look . . upon the children of the sainted Jacob 33
7: 2 We ourselves and our children are faring well 33
6 as a father does for his children 34
4Mc 2:12 It takes precedence over love for children 33
4: 9 the priests together with women and children 27
6:17 May we, the children of Abraham, never think 31
22 Therefore, O children of Abraham, die nobly 31
12: 2 he felt strong compassion for this child •
14:12 the rackings of each one of her children. 33
18 to demonstrate sympathy for children 33
20 sympathy for her children 33
15: 1 O reason of the children, tyrant over the emotions! 33
1 more desirable to the mother than her children! 33

4 We impress upon the character of a small child 31
8 disdained the temporary safety of her children. 33
12 each child singly and all together 31
15 the flesh of her children consumed by fire 33
20 When you saw the flesh of children 33
20 the flesh . . burned upon the flesh of other children 33
21 the voices of the children in torture 33
24 witnessed the destruction of seven children 33
25 the rackings of her children– 33
26 the other deliverance for her children. 33
16: 1 endured seeing her children tortured to death 33
6 After bearing seven children 31
9 Alas for my children 31
9 I shall not see your children 33
10 I who had so many and beautiful children •
17: 6 children were true descendants of father Abraham. 29
7 they saw the mother of the seven children 33
18: 1 O Israelite children 31
6 expressed also these principles to her children 33

child *See also* bear, bereave, bring, devoted, kill, loss, love, obtain, rob.

beloved child 1. מַחְמַד בֶּטֶן
Hos 9:16 I will slay their beloved children. 1

fatherless child 1. יָתוֹם
Job 24: 9 There are those who snatch the fatherless child 1
Ps 109:12 nor any to pity his fatherless children! 1
Jer 49:11 Leave your fatherless children, I will keep them 1

good child 1. *εὐτεκνία*
4Mc 18: 9 who lived out his life with good children 1

goodly child 1. טוֹב
Exd 2: 2 he was a goodly child, she hid him three months. 1

illegitimate child 1. *νόθος*
Heb 12: 8 then you are illegitimate children and not sons. 1

little child 1. טַף 2. *τεκνίον*
2Ch 31:18 all their little children, their wives 1
Ezk 9: 6 young men and maidens, little children and women 1
Joh 13:33 Little children, yet a little while I am with you. 2
Gal 4:19 Little children, with whom I am again in travail 2
1Jn 2: 1 My little children, I am writing this to you 2
12 I am writing to you, little children 2
28 now, little children, abide in him 2
3: 7 Little children, let no one deceive you. 2
18 Little children, let us not love in word or speech 2
4: 4 Little children, you are of God 2
5:21 Little children, keep yourselves from idols. 2

male child 1. יֶלֶד 2. *παῖς*
Exd 1:17 midwives . . let the male children live. 1
18 Why have you . . let the male children live? 1
Mat 2:16 killed all the male children in Bethlehem 2

no child 1. *ἄτεκνος*
Lke 20:28 if a man's brother dies, having a wife but no children 1

child of earth 1. *ἀπόγονος*
Wis 7: 1 a descendant of the first-formed child of earth; 1

only child 1. יָחִיד 2. *μονογενής*
Zec 12:10 mourn for him, as one mourns for an only child 1
Lke 9:38 I beg you to look upon my son, for he is my only child; 2
Tob 3:15 I am my father's only child 2
8:17 thou hast had compassion on two only children. 2

sucking child 1. ינק 2. עול
Num11:12 Carry . . as a nurse carries the sucking child 1
Deu 32:25 the sucking child with the man of gray hairs. 1
Isa 11: 8 sucking child . . play over the hole of the asp 1
49:15 Can a woman forget her sucking child 2

weaned child 1. גמל
Isa 11: 8 weaned child . . put his hand on the adder's den. 1

without child 1. *ἄτεκνος*
Lke 20:29 the first took a wife, and died without children; 1

woman with child 1. הָרָה 2. לאל 3. praegnans
2Kg 8:12 and rip up their women with child. 1
15:16 he ripped up all the women . . who were with child. 1
Ecc 11: 5 how the spirit . . in the womb of a woman with child 2
Isa 26:17 Like a woman with child, who writhes and cries out 1
Jer 31: 8 the woman with child and her who is in travail 1
Ams 1:13 they have ripped up women with child in Gilead 1
2Es 4:40 Go and ask a woman who is with child 3
6:21 women with child shall give birth 3
16:38 Just as a woman with child, in the ninth month 3

young child 1. עֲוִיל 2. עוֹלֵל
Job 19:18 Even young children despise me; 1
Mic 2: 9 from their young children you take away my glory 2

childbearing 1. הֵרָיוֹן
Gen 3:16 multiply your pain in childbearing; 1

childbirth 1. יוֹלֵדָה 2. *κυοφορία* 3. *λεχώ*
Hos 13:13 The pangs of childbirth come for him 1
LJr 1:29 women in menstruation or at childbirth 3
4Mc 16: 7 O seven childbirths all in vain 2

childhood 1. נֹעַר 2. *βρέφος* 3. *παιδιόθεν* 4. *παῖς*
Prv 29:21 He who pampers his servant from childhood 1
Mrk 9:21 he said, "From childhood. 3
2Ti 3:15 from childhood you have been acquainted 2
2Mc 6:23 and his excellent life even from childhood 4
15:12 had been trained from childhood 4

childish 1. *νήπιος*
1Co 13:11 when I became a man, I gave up childish ways. 1

childless 1. לֹא בֵּן 2. לֹא ילד 3. עֲרִירִי 4. שַׁכּוּל
5. שכל 6. *ἄτεκνος*
Gen 15: 2 give me, for I continue childless 3
Lev 20:20 bear their sin, they shall die childless 3
21 it is impurity . . they shall be childless 3
1Sm 15:33 so shall your mother be childless among women. 5
1Ch 2:30 and Seled died childless. 1
32 Jonathan; and Jether died childless. 1
Job 24:21 They feed on the barren childless woman 2
Jer 18:21 let their wives become childless and widowed. 4
22:30 says the LORD: "Write this man down as childless 3
Sir 16: 3 to die childless is better 6

childless *See also* make.

childlessness 1. *ἀτεκνία*
Wis 4: 1 Better than this is childlessness with virtue 1

chin 1. *γένειον*
4Mc 9:28 flayed all his flesh up to his chin 1
15:15 the flesh of the head to the chin exposed 1

chip 1. קֶצֶף
Hos 10: 7 perish, like a chip on the face of the waters. 1

chirp 1. צפף
Isa 8:19 the mediums and the wizards who chirp and mutter 1
10:14 that moved a wing, or opened the mouth, or chirped. 1

choice 1. בחר 2. ברר 3. חֶמְדָּה 4. מִבְחוֹר 5. מִבְחָר
6. מֶגֶד 7. רֵאשִׁית 8. *ἐκλέγω* 9. *ἐκλεκτός* 10. *εὐδοκία*
Gen 23: 6 Bury your dead in the choicest of our sepulchres; 5
Deu 33:14 with the choicest fruits of the sun 6
2Kg 3:19 conquer every . . and every choice city 4
19:23 its tallest cedars, its choicest cypresses; 4
Neh 5:18 one day was one ox and six choice sheep; 2
Prv 8:10 Take . . knowledge rather than choice gold; 1
19 my yield than choice silver. 1
10:20 The tongue of the righteous is choice silver; 1
Sng 4:13 an orchard . . with all choicest fruits 6
16 come to his garden, and eat its choicest fruits. 6
5:15 His appearance is like . . choice as the cedars. 1
Isa 22: 7 Your choicest valleys were full of chariots 5
37:24 its tallest cedars, its choicest cypresses; 5
Jer 22: 7 and they shall cut down your choicest cedars 5
25:34 and you shall fall like choice rams. 3
48:15 and the choicest of his young men have gone down 5
Ezk 20:40 contributions and the choicest of your gifts 7
23: 7 upon them, the choicest men of Assyria all of them; 5
24: 4 fill it with choice bones. 5
5 Take the choicest one of the flock 5
6 piece after piece, without making any choice. †
31:16 the trees of Eden, the choice and best of Lebanon 5
Sir 15:15 to act faithfully is a matter of your own choice. 10
24:15 like choice myrrh I spread a pleasant odor 9
1Mc 10:32 station in it men of his own choice to guard it. 8

choice *See also* fruit, garment, gift, make, portion, vine.

choice part 1. רֵאשִׁית
1Sm 2:29 upon the choicest parts of every offering 1

choirmaster 1. נצח
Ps 4: 0 To the choirmaster: with stringed instruments. 1
5: 0 To the choirmaster: for the flutes. 1
6: 0 To the choirmaster: with stringed instruments; 1
8: 0 To the choirmaster: according to The Gittith. 1
9: 0 To the choirmaster: according to Muth-labben. 1
11: 0 To the choirmaster. Of David. 1
12: 0 To the choirmaster: according to The Sheminith. 1
13: 0 To the choirmaster. A Psalm of David. 1
14: 0 To the choirmaster. Of David. 1
18: 0 To the choirmaster. A Psalm of David 1
19: 0 To the choirmaster. A Psalm of David. 1
20: 0 To the choirmaster. A Psalm of David. 1
21: 0 To the choirmaster. A Psalm of David. 1
22: 0 To the choirmaster . . A Psalm of David. 1
31: 0 To the choirmaster. A Psalm of David. 1
36: 0 To the choirmaster. A Psalm of David 1
39: 0 To the choirmaster: To Jeduthun. 1
40: 0 To the choirmaster. A Psalm of David. 1
41: 0 To the choirmaster. A Psalm of David. 1
42: 0 To the choirmaster. A Maskil 1
44: 0 To the choirmaster. A Maskil 1
45: 0 To the choirmaster: according to Lilies. 1
46: 0 To the choirmaster. A Psalm of the Sons of Korah. 1
47: 0 To the choirmaster. A Psalm of the Sons of Korah. 1
49: 0 To the choirmaster. A Psalm of the Sons of Korah. 1
51: 0 To the choirmaster. A Psalm of David 1
52: 0 To the choirmaster. A Maskil of David 1
53: 0 To the choirmaster: according to Mahalath. 1
54: 0 To the choirmaster: with stringed instruments. 1
55: 0 To the choirmaster: with stringed instruments. 1
56: 0 To the choirmaster: according to The Dove 1
57: 0 To the choirmaster: according to Do Not Destroy. 1
58: 0 To the choirmaster: according to Do Not Destroy. 1
59: 0 To the choirmaster: according to Do Not Destroy. 1
60: 0 To the choirmaster: according to Shushan Eduth. 1
61: 0 To the choirmaster: with stringed instruments. 1
62: 0 To the choirmaster: according to Jeduthun. 1
64: 0 To the choirmaster. A Psalm of David. 1
65: 0 To the choirmaster. A Psalm of David. A Song. 1
66: 0 To the choirmaster. A Song. A Psalm. 1
67: 0 To the choirmaster: with stringed instruments. 1
68: 0 To the choirmaster. A Psalm of David. A Song. 1
69: 0 To the choirmaster: according to Lilies. 1
70: 0 To the choirmaster. A Psalm of David 1
75: 0 To the choirmaster: according to Do Not Destroy. 1
76: 0 To the choirmaster: with stringed instruments. 1
77: 0 To the choirmaster: according to Jeduthun. 1
80: 0 To the choirmaster: according to Lilies. 1
81: 0 To the choirmaster: according to The Gittith. 1
84: 0 To the choirmaster: according to The Gittith. 1
85: 0 To the choirmaster. A Psalm of the Sons of Korah. 1
88: 0 choirmaster: according to Mahalath Leannoth. 1
109: 0 To the choirmaster. A Psalm of David. 1
139: 0 To the choirmaster. A Psalm of David. 1
140: 0 To the choirmaster. A Psalm of David. 1
Hab 3:19 To the choirmaster: with stringed instruments. 1

choke 1. *ἀποπνίγω* 2. *πνιγμός* 3. *πνίγω*
4. *συμπνίγω* 5. constringo
Mat 13: 7 and the thorns grew up and choked them. 3
22 and the delight in riches choke the word 4
Mrk 4: 7 the thorns grew up and choked it 4
19 enter in and choke the word 4
Lke 8: 7 and the thorns grew with it and choked it. 1
14 they are choked by the cares and riches 4
2Es 16:77 Woe to those who are choked by their sins 5
77 as a field is choked with underbrush 5
Sir 51: 4 from choking fire on every side 2

choose 1. אחז 2. בָּחִיר 3. בחר 4. ברר 5. חזה 6. ידע
7. יהב 8. לקח 9. מהר 10. נתן 11. קָרִיא 12. ראה
13. *αἱρετίζω* 14. *αἱρετός* 15. *αἱρέω* 16. *βούλομαι*
17. *ἐκλέγομαι* 18. *ἐκλεκτός* 19. *ἐκλογή*
20. *ἐπιδέχομαι* 21. *ἐπιλέγω* 22. *εὐδοκέω* 23. *θέλω*
24. *κατ' ἐκλογήν* 25. *λαμβάνω* 26. *ποιέω ἐκλεκτόν*
27. *προαιρέω* 28. *προχειρίζω* 29. *προχειροτονέω*
30. eligo
Gen 6: 2 took to wife such of them as they chose. 3
13:11 Lot chose for himself all the Jordan valley 3
18:19 No, for I have chosen him 6
Exd 17: 9 Moses said to Joshua, "Choose for us men, and go out 3
18:21 Moreover choose able men from all the people 5
25 Moses chose able men out of all Israel 3
Num14: 4 Let us choose a captain, and go back to Egypt. 10
16: 2 250 leaders . . chosen from the assembly 11
5 whom he will choose he will cause to come near 3
7 man whom the LORD chooses shall be the holy one. 3
17: 5 the rod of the man whom I choose shall sprout; 3
26: 9 Dathan and Abi'ram, chosen from the congregation 11
Deu 1:13 Choose wise, understanding, and experienced men 7
4:37 loved your fathers and chose their descendants 3
7: 6 chosen you to be a people for his own possession 3
7 that the LORD set his love upon you and chose you 3
10:15 LORD . . chose their descendants after them 3
12: 5 LORD your God will choose out of all your tribes 3
11 then to the place which the LORD . . will choose 3
14 at the place which the LORD will choose 3
18 place which the LORD your God will choose 3
21 If the place which the LORD your God will choose 3
26 shall go to the place which the LORD will choose 3
14: 2 LORD has chosen you to be a people 3
23 LORD . . will choose, to make his name dwell there 3
24 place . . which the LORD your God chooses, to set 3
25 go to the place which the LORD your God chooses 3
15:20 eat . . at the place which the LORD will choose. 3
16: 2 place . . LORD will choose, to make his name dwell 3
6 at the place which the LORD your God will choose 3
7 at the place which the LORD your God will choose; 3
11 at the place which the LORD your God will choose 3
15 feast . . at the place which the LORD will choose; 3
16 appear . . at the place which he will choose 3
17: 8 go up to the place . . LORD your God will choose 3
10 from that place which the LORD will choose; 3
15 set as king . . whom the LORD your God will choose. 3

18: 5 LORD .. has chosen him out of all your tribes 3
6 comes .. to the place which the LORD will choose 3
21: 5 LORD your God has chosen them to minister to him 3
23:16 place .. he shall choose within one of your towns 3
26: 2 go to the place .. LORD your God will choose 3
30:19 choose life, that you and your descendants 3
31:11 to appear .. at the place which he will choose 3
33:21 He chose the best of the land for himself 12
Jos 8: 3 and Joshua chose 30,000 mighty men of valor 3
9:27 to this day, in the place which he should choose. 3
24:15 choose this day whom you will serve 3
22 that you have chosen the LORD, to serve him. 3
Jdg 5: 8 When new gods were chosen, then war was 3
10:14 Go and cry to the gods whom you have chosen; 3
1Sm 2:28 I chose him out of all the tribes .. to be my priest 3
8:18 your king, whom you have chosen for yourselves; 3
10:24 Do you see him whom the LORD has chosen? 3
12:13 whom you have chosen, for whom you have asked; 3
13: 2 Saul chose 3,000 men of Israel; 3
16: 8 And he said, "Neither has the LORD chosen this one. 3
9 And he said, "Neither has the LORD chosen this one. 3
10 Samuel said .. "The LORD has not chosen these. 3
17: 8 Choose a man for yourselves, and let him come down 3
40 and chose five smooth stones from the brook 3
20:30 do I not know that you have chosen the son of Jesse 3
24: 2 Then Saul took 3,000 chosen men out of all Israel 3
26: 2 Saul arose and .. with 3,000 chosen men of Israel 3
2Sm 6:21 before the LORD, who chose me above your father 3
10: 9 Jo'ab .. chose some of the picked men of Israel 3
16:18 whom the LORD and .. have chosen, his I will be 3
17: 1 Let me choose 12,000 men 3
24:12 Three things I offer you; choose one of them 3
1Kg 3: 8 in the midst of thy people whom thou hast chosen 3
8:16 I chose no city .. in which to build a house 3
16 but I chose David to be over my people Israel.' 3
44 pray .. toward the city which thou hast chosen 3
48 their land .. the city which thou hast chosen 3
11:13 for the sake of Jerusalem which I have chosen. 3
32 the city which I have chosen out of all the tribes 3
34 for the sake of David my servant whom I chose 3
36 the city where I have chosen to put my name. 3
12:21 he assembled .. 180,000 chosen warriors 3
14:21 which the LORD had chosen out of all the tribes 3
18:23 let them choose one bull for themselves 3
25 Choose for yourselves one bull and prepare it 3
2Kg 21: 7 which I have chosen out of all the tribes 3
23:27 I will cast off this city which I have chosen 3
1Ch 9:22 chosen as gatekeepers at the thresholds, were 212 4
15: 2 LORD chose them to carry the ark of the LORD 3
16:41 the rest of those chosen and expressly named 4
19:10 he chose some of the picked men of Israel 3
21:10 Three things I offer you; choose one of them 3
24: 6 one father's house being chosen for Elea'zar 1
6 for Elea'zar and one chosen for Ith'amar. 1
28: 4 God of Israel chose me from all my father's house 3
4 chose Judah as leader, and in the house of Judah 3
5 of all my sons .. he has chosen Solomon my son 3
6 chosen him to be my son, and I will be his father. 3
10 LORD has chosen you to build a house 3
29: 1 Solomon my son, whom alone God has chosen, 3
2Ch 6: 5 I chose no city in all the tribes of Israel 3
5 I chose no man as prince over my people Israel; 3
6 I have chosen Jerusalem that my name may be there 3
6 I have chosen David to be over my people Israel.' 3
34 pray .. toward this city which thou hast chosen 3
38 pray toward .. the city which thou hast chosen 3
7:12 and have chosen this place for myself 3
16 For now I have chosen and consecrated this house 3
12:13 Jerusalem, the city which the LORD had chosen 3
29:11 not now be negligent, for the LORD has chosen you 3
33: 7 I have chosen out of all the tribes of Israel 3
Neh 1: 9 bring them to the place which I have chosen 3
9: 7 God who didst choose Abram and bring him forth 3
Est 2: 9 and with seven chosen maids from the king's 12
Job 7:15 that I would choose strangling and death 3
9:14 can I answer him, choosing my words with him? 3
15: 5 you choose the tongue of the crafty. 3
29:25 I chose their way, and sat as chief 3
34: 4 Let us choose what is right; 3
33 you must choose, and not I; 3
36:21 this you have chosen rather than affliction. 3
Ps 16: 4 Those who choose another god 9
25:12 instruct in the way that he should choose. 3
33:12 the people whom he has chosen as his heritage! 3
47: 4 He chose our heritage for us, the pride of Jacob 3
65: 4 Blessed is he whom thou dost choose 3
78:67 he did not choose the tribe of E'phraim; 3
68 he chose the tribe of Judah 3
70 He chose David his servant 3
105:26 sent Moses .. and Aaron whom he had chosen. 3
119:30 I have chosen the way of faithfulness 3
173help me, for I have chosen thy precepts. 3
132:13 For the LORD has chosen Zion; he has desired it 3
135: 4 For the LORD has chosen Jacob for himself 3
Prv 1:29 did not choose the fear of the LORD 3
3:31 do not choose any of his ways; 3
16:16 understanding is to be chosen rather than silver. 3
22: 1 good name .. be chosen rather than great riches 3
Isa 1:29 blush for the gardens which you have chosen. 3
7:15 knows how to refuse the evil and choose the good. 3
16 knows how to refuse the evil and choose the good 3
14: 1 The LORD .. will again choose Israel 3
40:20 He who is impoverished chooses for an offering 3
41: 8 you, Israel, my servant, Jacob, whom I have chosen 3
9 I have chosen you and not cast you off"; 3
24 an abomination is he who chooses you. 3
42: 1 my chosen, in whom my soul delights; 2
43:10 and my servant whom I have chosen 3
20 in the desert, to give drink to my chosen people 2
44: 1 O Jacob my servant, Israel whom I have chosen! 3
2 O Jacob my servant, Jeshu'run whom I have chosen. 3
14 he chooses a holm tree or an oak and lets it grow 8
45: 4 the sake of my servant Jacob, and Israel my chosen 2
49: 7 the Holy One of Israel, who has chosen you. 3
56: 4 who choose the things that please me 3
58: 5 the fast that I choose, a day for a man to humble ?
6 Is not this the fast that I choose 3
65: 9 my chosen shall inherit it, 2
12 in my eyes, and chose what I did not delight in. 3
15 You shall leave your name to my chosen for a curse 2
22 my chosen shall long enjoy the work of their 2
66: 3 These have chosen their own ways 3
4 I also will choose affliction for them 3
4 and chose that in which I did not delight. 3
Jer 33:24 has rejected the two families which he chose'? 3
26 will not choose one of his descendants to rule 8
49:19 and I will appoint over her whomever I choose. 3
50:44 I will appoint over her whomever I choose. 3
Ezk 20: 5 On the day when I chose Israel 3
Hag 2:23 for I have chosen you, says the LORD of hosts. 3
Zec 1:17 again comfort Zion and again choose Jerusalem. 3
2:12 and will again choose Jerusalem. 3
3: 2 The LORD who has chosen Jerusalem rebuke you! 3
Mat 11:27 any one to whom the Son chooses to reveal him. 16
12:18 Behold, my servant whom I have chosen, my beloved 13
20:14 I choose to give to this last as I give to you. 23
15 to do what I choose with what belongs to me 23
22:14 For many are called, but few are chosen. 18
Mrk 13:20 for the sake of the elect, whom he chose 17
Lke 6:13 called his disciples, and chose from them twelve 17
9:35 This is my Son, my Chosen; listen to him! 17
10:22 and any one to whom the Son chooses to reveal him. 16
42 Mary has chosen the good portion 17
14: 7 when he marked how they chose the places of honor 17
Joh 6:70 Did I not choose you, the twelve 17
13:18 I know whom I have chosen 17
15:16 You did not choose me, but I chose you 17
16 You did not choose me, but I chose you 17
19 I chose you out of the world 17
Act 1: 2 the apostles whom he had chosen. 17
24 show which one of these two thou hast chosen 17
6: 5 they chose Stephen 17
9:15 he is a chosen instrument of mine to carry my name 19
10:41 to us who were chosen by God as witnesses 29
13:17 The God of this people Israel chose our fathers 17
15:22 to choose men from among them 17
25 to choose men and send them to you 17
40 Paul chose Silas and departed 17
Rom 11: 5 there is a remnant, chosen by grace. 24
1Co 1:27 God chose what is foolish in the world 17
27 God chose what is weak in the world 17
28 God chose what is low and despised in the world 17
12:18 organs in the body, each one of them, as he chose. 23
15:38 God gives it a body as he has chosen 23
Eph 1: 4 even as he chose us in him 17
Php 1:22 Yet which I shall choose I cannot tell. 15
Col 1:27 To them God chose to make known 23
1Th 1: 4 he has chosen you; 19
2Th 2:13 God chose you from the beginning to be saved 15
Heb 5: 1 every high priest chosen from among men 25
11:25 choosing rather to share ill-treatment 15
Jas 2: 5 Has not God chosen those who are poor in the world 17
1Pe 1: 2 chosen and destined by God the Father 18
2: 4 in God's sight chosen and precious; 18
6 in Zion .. a cornerstone chosen and precious 18
9 you are a chosen race, a royal priesthood 18
Rev 17:14 those with him are called the chosen 18
1Es 5: 1 heads of fathers' houses were chosen to go up 17
8:10 who freely choose to do so, may go with you 13
9:16 Ezra .. chose for himself the leading men 21
2Es 2:15 because I have chosen you, says the Lord. 30
17 Do not fear, mother of sons, for I have chosen you 30
3:13 thou didst choose for thyself one of them 30
5:23 from all its trees thou hast chosen one vine 30
24 thou hast chosen for thyself one region 30
24 thou hast chosen for thyself one lily 30
6:54 the people whom thou hast chosen. 30
7:129Choose for yourself life, that you may live!' 30
15:53 If you had not always killed my chosen people 30
56 As you will do to my chosen people," says the Lord 30
Tob 1: 4 chosen from among all the tribes of Israel 17
8:15 let .. thy chosen people bless thee for ever. 18
Jdt 8:15 if he does not choose to help us 16
10:17 They chose from their number 100 men 21
11: 1 any one who chose to serve Nebuchadnezzar 13
AEs 16:21 God .. has made this day to be a joy to his chosen 18
Wis 7:10 I chose to have her rather than light 27
9: 7 Thou hast chosen me to be king of thy people 27
12:18 hast power to act whenever thou dost choose. 23
Sir 6:18 My son, from your youth up choose instruction 21
15:17 whichever he chooses will be given to him. 22
45: 4 he chose him out of all mankind. 17
16 He chose him out of all the living 17
49: 6 who set fire to the chosen city of the sanctuary 18
Bar 3:27 God did not choose them, nor give them the way 17
Sus 1:23 I choose not to do it and to fall into your hands 14
1Mc 1:63 They chose to die rather than to be defiled by food 20
2:19 and have chosen to do his commandments 13
3:38 Lysias chose Ptolemy the son of Dorymenes 21
4:42 He chose blameless priests devoted to the law 21
5:17 Choose your men and go and rescue your brethren 21
7: 8 So the king chose Bacchides 21
37 didst choose this house to be called by thy name 17
8:17 So Judas chose Eupolemus the son of John 21
9:25 Bacchides chose the ungodly 17
30 So now we have chosen you today to take his place 13
10:74 He chose 10,000 men 21
11:23 he chose some of the elders of Israel 21
12: 1 he chose men and sent them to Rome 21
16 We .. have chosen Numenius the son of Antiochus 21
45 choose for yourself a few men to stay with you 21
13:34 Simon also chose men and sent them to Demetrius 21
16: 4 So John chose .. 20,000 warriors 21
2Mc 1:25 didst choose the fathers and consecrate them 26
3: 7 The king chose Heliodorus 28
4:19 chosen as being Antiochian citizens •
5:19 the Lord did not choose the nation 17
6: 9 slay those who did not choose to change over 27
11:25 Accordingly, since we choose that .. 15
14:12 he immediately chose Nicanor 28
3Mc 2: 9 chose this city and sanctified this place 17
6:10 destroy us, Lord, by whatever fate you choose. 27

cannot but choose 1. *αἱρετός*

2Mc 7:14 One cannot but choose to die at the hands of men 1

choose likewise 1. *συνεκλεκτός*

1Pe 5:13 She who is at Babylon, who is likewise chosen 1

chop up 1. פרם

Mic 3: 3 and chop them up like meat in a kettle 1

choral group 1. *χορός*

3Mc 6:35 they had arranged the aforementioned choral group 1

chorus 1. *χορός*

3Mc 6:32 they formed choruses 1
4Mc 8: 4 grouped about their mother as if in a chorus 1
13: 8 For they constituted a holy chorus of religion 1
18:23 the chorus of the fathers 1

chorus *See also* form.

chosen *See* portion, warrior.

chosen man 1. בחר

Num11:28 Joshua .. minister of Moses, one of his chosen men 1
2Sm 6: 1 David .. gathered all the chosen men of Israel 1

chosen one 1. בָּחִיר 2. בחר 3. קרא 4. *ἐκλεκτός*

Num 1:16 These were the ones chosen 3
1Ch 16:13 sons of Jacob, his chosen ones! 1
Ps 89: 3 I have made a covenant with my chosen one 1
19 I have exalted one chosen from the people. 2
105: 6 sons of Jacob, his chosen ones! 1
43 led forth his .. chosen ones with singing. 1
106: 5 that I may see the prosperity of thy chosen ones 1
23 destroy them-had not Moses, his chosen one 1
Lke 23:35 if he is the Christ of God, his Chosen One! 4
Col 3:12 as God's chosen ones, holy and beloved 4
Sir 47:22 never blot out the descendants of his chosen one 4

chronic 1. ישן 2. *ἔμμονος*

Lev 13:11 it is a chronic leprosy in the skin of his body 1
Sir 30:17 and eternal rest than chronic sickness. 2

chronicle 1. דָּבָר 2. דִּבְרֵי יָמִים 3. יוֹם
4. *βιβλίον ἡμερῶν* 5. *βίβλος τῶν χρόνων*
6. *ὑπομνηματισμός*

1Kg 14:19 the Book of the Chronicles of the Kings 2
29 the Book of the Chronicles of the Kings of Judah? 2
15: 7 the Book of the Chronicles of the Kings of Judah? 2
23 the Book of the Chronicles of the Kings of Judah? 2
31 the Book of the Chronicles of the Kings of Israel? 2
16: 5 the Book of the Chronicles of the Kings of Israel? 2
14 the Book of the Chronicles of the Kings of Israel? 2
20 the Book of the Chronicles of the Kings of Israel? 2
27 the Book of the Chronicles of the Kings of Israel? 2
22:39 the Book of the Chronicles of the Kings of Israel? 2
45 the Book of the Chronicles of the Kings of Judah? 2
2Kg 1:18 the Book of the Chronicles of the Kings of Israel? 2
8:23 the Book of the Chronicles of the Kings of Judah? 2
10:34 the Book of the Chronicles of the Kings of Israel? 2
12:19 the Book of the Chronicles of the Kings of Judah? 2
13: 8 the Book of the Chronicles of the Kings of Israel? 2
12 the Book of the Chronicles of the Kings of Israel? 2
14:15 the Book of the Chronicles of the Kings of Israel? 2
18 the Book of the Chronicles of the Kings of Judah? 2

28 the Book of the Chronicles of the Kings of Israel? 2
15: 6 the Book of the Chronicles of the Kings of Judah? 2
11 Book of the Chronicles of the Kings of Israel. 2
15 Book of the Chronicles of the Kings of Israel. 2
21 the Book of the Chronicles of the Kings of Israel? 2
26 Book of the Chronicles of the Kings of Israel. 2
31 Book of the Chronicles of the Kings of Israel. 2
36 the Book of the Chronicles of the Kings of Judah? 2
16:19 the Book of the Chronicles of the Kings of Judah? 2
20:20 the Book of the Chronicles of the Kings of Judah? 2
21:17 the Book of the Chronicles of the Kings of Judah? 2
25 the Book of the Chronicles of the Kings of Judah? 2
23:28 the Book of the Chronicles of the Kings of Judah? 2
24: 5 the Book of the Chronicles of the Kings of Judah? 2
1Ch 27:24 was not entered in the chronicles of King David. 2
29:29 are written in the Chronicles of Samuel the seer 1
29 and in the Chronicles of Nathan the prophet 1
29 and in the Chronicles of Gad the seer 1
2Ch 12:15 written in the chronicles of Shemai'ah 1
20:34 written in the chronicles of Jehu 1
33:18 the Chronicles of the Kings of Israel. 1
19 written in the Chronicles of the Seers. 1
Neh 12:23 Levi . . written in the Book of the Chronicles 3
Est 2:23 And it was recorded in the Book of the Chronicles 2
6: 1 the book of memorable deeds, the chronicles 2
10: 2 in the Book of the Chronicles of the kings of Media 2
1Es 1:42 written in the chronicles of the kings. 5
2:22 find in the chronicles what has been written 6
1Mc 16:24 in the chronicles of his high priesthood 4

chrysolite 1. אֶבֶן תַּרְשִׁישׁ 2. תַּרְשִׁישׁ 3. χρυσόλιθος

Ezk 1:16 was like the gleaming of a chrysolite; 2
10: 9 of the wheels was like sparkling chrysolite. 1
28:13 carnelian, topaz, and jasper, chrysolite, beryl 2
Rev 21:20 the sixth carnelian, the seventh chrysolite 3

chrysoprase 1. χρυσόπρασος

Rev 21:20 the ninth topaz, the tenth chrysoprase 1

church 1. ἐκκλησία

Mat 16:18 on this rock I will build my church 1
18:17 tell it to the church 1
17 if he refuses to listen even to the church 1
Act 5:11 great fear came upon the whole church 1
8: 1 a great persecution arose against the church 1
3 Saul was ravaging the church 1
9:31 church throughout all Judea and Galilee 1
11:22 came to the ears of the church in Jerusalem 1
26 For a whole year they met with the church 1
12: 1 some who belonged to the church. 1
5 prayer for him was made to God by the church. 1
13: 1 Now in the church at Antioch there were prophets 1
14:23 had appointed elders for them in every church 1
27 they gathered the church together 1
15: 3 being sent on their way by the church 1
4 were welcomed by the church and the apostles 1
22 apostles and the elders, with the whole church 1
41 strengthening the churches. 1
16: 5 So the churches were strengthened in the faith 1
18:22 he went up and greeted the church 1
20:17 called to him the elders of the church. 1
28 to care for the church of God 1
Rom 16: 1 Phoebe, a deaconess of the church at Cen'chre-ae 1
4 all the churches of the Gentiles give thanks; 1
5 greet also the church in their house. 1
16 All the churches of Christ greet you. 1
23 Ga'ius, who is host to me and to the whole church 1
1Co 1: 2 To the church of God which is at Corinth 1
4:17 as I teach them everywhere in every church. 1
5:12 Is it not those inside the church 1
6: 4 who are least esteemed by the church? 1
7:17 This is my rule in all the churches. 1
10:32 to Jews or to Greeks or to the church of God 1
11:16 nor do the churches of God. 1
18 in the first place, when you assemble as a church 1
22 do you despise the church of God 1
12:28 God has appointed in the church first apostles 1
14: 4 he who prophesies edifies the church. 1
5 so that the church may be edified. 1
12 strive to excel in building up the church. 1
19 nevertheless, in church I would rather speak 1
23 If, therefore, the whole church assembles 1
28 let each of them keep silence in church 1
33 As in all the churches of the saints 1
34 the women should keep silence in the churches. 1
35 it is shameful for a woman to speak in church. 1
15: 9 because I persecuted the church of God. 1
16: 1 as I directed the churches of Galatia 1
19 The churches of Asia send greetings 1
19 together with the church in their house 1
2Co 1: 1 To the church of God which is at Corinth 1
8: 1 shown in the churches of Macedo'nia 1
18 the brother who is famous among all the churches 1
19 appointed by the churches to travel with us 1
23 messengers of the churches, the glory of Christ. 1
24 So give proof, before the churches, of your love 1
11: 8 I robbed other churches by accepting support 1
28 my anxiety for all the churches. 1
12:13 less favored than the rest of the churches 1
Gal 1: 2 To the churches of Galatia 1
13 how I persecuted the church of God violently 1
22 the churches of Christ in Judea; 1
Eph 1:22 the head over all things for the church. 1
3:10 through the church 1
21 to him be glory in the church and in Christ Jesus 1
5:23 as Christ is the head of the church 1
24 As the church is subject to Christ 1
25 Christ loved the church 1
27 might present the church to himself in splendor 1
29 cherishes it, as Christ does the church 1
32 am saying that it refers to Christ and the church; 1
Php 3: 6 as to zeal a persecutor of the church 1
4:15 no church entered into partnership with me 1
Col 1:18 He is the head of the body, the church 1
24 for the sake of his body . . the church 1
4:15 to Nympha and the church in her house. 1
16 have it read also in the church of the La-odice'ans; 1
1Th 1: 1 To the church of the Thessalo'nians 1
2:14 became imitators of the churches of God in Christ 1
2Th 1: 1 To the church of the Thessalo'nians 1
4 boast of you in the churches of God 1
1Ti 3: 5 how can he care for God's church? 1
15 which is the church of the living God 1
5:16 let the church not be burdened 1
Phm 1: 2 the church in your house 1
Jas 5:14 Let him call for the elders of the church 1
3Jn 1: 6 testified to your love before the church. 1
9 I have written something to the church; 1
10 stops those . . and puts them out of the church. 1
Rev 1: 4 John to the seven churches that are in Asia 1
11 in a book and send it to the seven churches 1
20 seven stars are the angels of the seven churches 1
20 the seven lampstands are the seven churches. 1
2: 1 To the angel of the church in Ephesus write 1
7 let him hear what the Spirit says to the churches 1
8 And to the angel of the church in Smyrna write 1
11 let him hear what the Spirit says to the churches 1
12 And to the angel of the church in Per'gamum write 1
17 let him hear what the Spirit says to the churches 1
18 And to the angel of the church in Thyati'ra write 1
23 And all the churches shall know that I am he 1
29 hear what the Spirit says to the churches.' 1
3: 1 And to the angel of the church in Sardis write 1
6 let him hear what the Spirit says to the churches 1
7 to the angel of the church in Philadelphia write 1
13 hear what the Spirit says to the churches.' 1
14 And to the angel of the church in La-odice'a write 1
22 hear what the Spirit says to the churches.' 1
22:16 to you with this testimony for the churches. 1

churlish 1. קָשֶׁה

1Sm 25: 3 but the man was churlish and ill-behaved; 1

churn up 1. fluctuo

2Es 16:12 the sea is churned up from the depths 1

cinnamon 1. קִנָּמוֹן 2. κιννάμωμον

Exd 30:23 of sweet-smelling cinnamon half as much 1
Prv 7:17 perfumed my bed with myrrh, aloes, and cinnamon. 1
Sng 4:14 nard and saffron, calamus and cinnamon 1
Rev 18:13 cinnamon, spice, incense, myrrh, frankincense 2

circle 1. חוּג 2. חֹק 3. סבב 4. κυκλόθεν 5. κύκλος 6. corona 7. orbis

Jos 15:10 the boundary circles west of Ba'alah to . . Se'ir 3
Job 26:10 described a circle upon the face of the waters 2
Prv 8:27 when he drew a circle on the face of the deep 1
Isa 40:22 It is he who sits above the circle of the earth 1
2Es 5:42 He said to me, "I shall liken my judgment to a circle; 6
6: 1 At the beginning of the circle of the earth 7
Wis 13: 2 the circle of the stars, or turbulent water 5
4Mc 14:17 by flying in circles around them 4

circle around 1. κυκλόω

Jdt 13:10 and circled around the valley 1
1Mc 13:20 he circled around by the way to Adora 1

circuit 1. כִּכָּר 2. סבב 3. סָבִיב 4. תְּקוּפָה 5. κύκλος

1Sm 7:16 went on a circuit . . to Bethel, Gilgal, and Mizpah; 2
1Ch 11: 8 round about from the Millo in complete circuit; 3
Neh 12:28 gathered . . from the circuit round Jerusalem 1
Ps 19: 6 of the heavens, and its circuit to the end of them; 4
Ecc 1: 6 and on its circuits the wind returns. 3
1Es 4:34 it makes the circuit of the heavens 5

circuit *See also* make.
circuitous *See* make.

circulate 1. ἐκχέω

3Mc 3: 2 a hostile rumor was circulated 1

circumcise 1. מול 2. περιτέμνω 3. περιτέμνω σάρκα ἀκροβυστίας 4. περιτομή

Gen 17:10 Every male among you shall be circumcised. 1
11 You shall be circumcised in the flesh 1
12 is eight days old among you shall be circumcised; 1
13 bought with your money, shall be circumcised. 1
14 Any uncircumcised male who is not circumcised 1
23 he circumcised the flesh of their foreskins 1
24 Abraham . . was circumcised in the flesh 1
25 was thirteen years old when he was circumcised 1
26 Abraham and his son Ish'mael were circumcised; 1
27 from a foreigner, were circumcised with him. 1
21: 4 Abraham circumcised his son Isaac 1
34:15 as we are and every male of you be circumcised. 1
17 if you will not listen to us and be circumcised 1
22 male among us be circumcised as they are 1
22 us be circumcised as they are circumcised. 1
24 and every male was circumcised 1
Exd 12:44 may eat of it after you have circumcised him. 1
48 let all his males be circumcised, then he may come 1
Lev 12: 3 the flesh of his foreskin shall be circumcised 1
Deu 10:16 Circumcise therefore the foreskin of your heart 1
30: 6 LORD your God will circumcise your heart 1
Jos 5: 2 and circumcise the people of Israel again 1
3 Joshua . . and circumcised the people of Israel 1
4 this is the reason why Joshua circumcised them 1
5 all the people who came out had been circumcised 1
5 yet all the people . . had not been circumcised 1
7 it was their children . . Joshua circumcised; 1
7 they had not been circumcised on the way. 1
8 When the circumcising of all the nation was done 1
Jer 4: 4 Circumcise yourselves to the LORD 1
9:25 when I will punish all those who are circumcised 1
Lke 1:59 they came to circumcise the child 2
2:21 at the end of eight days, when he was circumcised 2
Joh 7:22 you circumcise a man upon the sabbath. 2
Act 7: 8 circumcised him on the eighth day 2
10:45 the believers from among the circumcised 4
15: 1 you are circumcised according to the custom of Moses 2
5 It is necessary to circumcise them 2
16: 3 he took him and circumcised him 2
21:21 telling them not to circumcise their children 2
Rom 3:30 and he will justify the circumcised 4
4: 9 Is this blessing pronounced only upon the circumcised 4
12 likewise the father of the circumcised 4
12 circumcised who are not merely circumcised 4
15: 8 Christ became a servant to the circumcised 4
1Co 7:18 time of his call already circumcised 2
Gal 2: 3 not compelled to be circumcised 2
7 had been entrusted with the gospel to the circumcised 4
8 the mission to the circumcised 4
9 should go to the Gentiles and they to the circumcised; 4
6:12 compel you to be circumcised 2
13 they desire to have you circumcised 2
Php 3: 5 circumcised on the eighth day 4
Col 2:11 you were circumcised with a circumcision 2
3:11 circumcised and uncircumcised, barbarian 4
Jdt 14:10 he believed firmly in God, and was circumcised 3
1Mc 1:60 the women who had their children circumcised 2
61 their families and those who circumcised them; 2
2:46 they forcibly circumcised 2
2Mc 6:10 having circumcised their children 2
4Mc 4:25 because they had circumcised their sons 2

without being circumcised 1. δι' ἀκροβυστίας

Rom 4:11 all who believe without being circumcised 1

after one circumcises 1. περιτομή

Rom 4:10 Was it before or after he had been circumcised? 1
10 It was not after, but before he was circumcised. 1

before one circumcises 1. ἀκροβυστία

Rom 4:10 Was it before or after he had been circumcised? 1
10 It was not after, but before he was circumcised. 1

circumcision 1. מוּלָה 2. περιτέμνω 3. περιτομή 4. circumcisio

Exd 4:26 of blood," because of the circumcision. 1
Joh 7:22 Moses gave you circumcision 3
23 If on the sabbath a man receives circumcision 3
Act 7: 8 he gave him the covenant of circumcision 3
Rom 2:25 Circumcision . . is of value if you obey the law; 3
25 your circumcision becomes uncircumcision. 3
26 uncircumcision be regarded as circumcision? 3
27 you who have . . circumcision but break the law. 3
28 nor is true circumcision something external 3
29 and real circumcision is a matter of the heart 3
3: 1 Or what is the value of circumcision? 3
4:11 He received circumcision as a sign or seal 3
1Co 7:18 Let him not seek circumcision. 2
19 For neither circumcision counts for anything 3
Gal 5: 6 neither circumcision nor uncircumcision 3
11 if I, brethren, still preach circumcision 3
6:15 For neither circumcision counts for anything 3
Eph 2:11 what is called the circumcision 3
Php 3: 3 For we are the true circumcision 3
Col 2:11 a circumcision made without hands 3
11 in the circumcision of Christ; 3
4:11 men of the circumcision among my fellow workers 3
2Es 1:31 new moons, and circumcisions of the flesh. 4

circumcision *See also* party, receive, remove.

circumference 1. סבב 2. סָבִיב 3. περίμετρον

2Ch 4: 2 30 cubits measured its circumference. 2
Jer 52:21 its circumference was twelve cubits 1

Ezk 48:35 The circumference of the city shall be 18,000 2
Sir 50: 3 a reservoir like the sea in circumference. 3
circumference *See also* measure.

circumstance 1. עֵת
1Ch 29:30 accounts . . of the circumstances that came 1
Php 4:12 in any and all circumstances •
1Th 5:18 give thanks in all circumstances •
2Es 7:18 can endure difficult circumstances •
18 have suffered the difficult circumstances •
16:18 What shall they do in these circumstances •

humble circumstance 1. *ταπείνωσις*
Sir 20:11 raised their heads from humble circumstances. 1
circumstances *See* man.

cistern 1. בְּאֵר 2. בּוֹר 3. גֵּב 4. גֶּבֶא 5. *ἀποδοχεῖον* 6. *λάκκος* 7. *φρέαρ*
Lev 11:36 a spring or a cistern holding water shall be 2
Deu 6:11 cisterns hewn out, which you did not hew 2
1Sm 13: 6 hid themselves in . . and in tombs and in cisterns 2
2Sm 3:26 they brought him back from the cistern of Sirah; 2
2Kg 18:31 every . . will drink the water of his own cistern; 2
2Ch 26:10 he built towers . . and hewed out many cisterns 2
Neh 9:25 possession of . . cisterns hewn out, vineyards 2
Prv 5:15 Drink water from your own cistern 2
Ecc 12: 6 or the wheel broken at the cistern 2
Isa 30:14 or to dip up water out of the cistern. 4
36:16 one . . will drink the water of his own cistern; 2
Jer 2:13 and hewed out cisterns for themselves 1
13 broken cisterns, that can hold no water. 1
14: 3 they come to the cisterns, they find no water 3
38: 6 they took Jeremiah and cast him into the cistern 2
6 there was no water in the cistern, but only mire 2
7 that they had put Jeremiah into the cistern 2
9 to Jeremiah . . by casting him into the cistern; 2
10 and lift Jeremiah the prophet out of the cistern 2
11 he let down to Jeremiah in the cistern by ropes. 2
13 with ropes and lifted him out of the cistern. 2
41: 7 slew them, and cast them into a cistern. 2
9 cistern into which Ish'mael cast all the bodies 2
9 was the large cistern which King Asa had made 7
Jdt 7:21 their cisterns were going dry 6
8:31 the Lord will send us rain to fill our cisterns 6
Sir 50: 3 In his days a cistern for water was quarried out 5
2Mc 1:19 secretly hid it in the hollow of a dry cistern 7
10:37 They killed Timothy, who was hidden in a cistern 6

citadel 1. אַרְמוֹן 2. *ἄκρα* 3. *ἀκρόπολις* 4. *ἄκρος*
1Kg 16:18 he went into the citadel of the king's house 1
2Kg 15:25 slew him . . in the citadel of the king's house; 1
Ps 48: 3 Within her citadels God has shown himself a sure 1
13 go through her citadels; that you may tell 1
1Mc 1:33 it became their citadel. 4
3:45 the sons of aliens held the citadel 2
4: 2 Men from the citadel were his guides. 2
41 to fight against those in the citadel 2
6:18 Now the men in the citadel kept hemming Israel 2
20 They gathered together and besieged the citadel •
24 the sons of our people besieged the citadel •
26 have encamped against the citadel in Jerusalem 2
32 Then Judas marched away from the citadel 2
9:52 Gazara, and the citadel 2
53 put them under guard in the citadel at Jerusalem. 2
10: 6 the hostages in the citadel should be released 2
7 the men in the citadel. 2
9 the men in the citadel released the hostages 2
32 I release also my control of the citadel 2
11:20 to attack the citadel in Jerusalem 2
21 Jonathan was besieging the citadel. 2
41 remove the troops of the citadel from Jerusalem 2
12:36 a high barrier between the citadel and the city 2
13:21 Now the men in the citadel kept sending envoys 2
49 The men in the citadel at Jerusalem 2
50 cleansed the citadel from its pollutions. 2
52 the temple hill alongside the citadel 2
14: 7 he ruled over Gazara and Beth-zur and the citadel 2
36 who had built themselves a citadel 2
15:28 Gazara and the citadel in Jerusalem 2
2Mc 4:12 he founded a gymnasium right under the citadel 3
28 Sostratus the captain of the citadel 3
5: 5 Menelaus took refuge in the citadel. 3
15:31 he sent for those who were in the citadel. 4
35 he hung Nicanor's head from the citadel 4
4Mc 4:20 at the very citadel of our native land 4

citizen 1. בַּעַל 2. *πολίτης*
Jdg 9: 2 Say in the ears of all the citizens of Shechem 1
6 all the citizens of Shechem came together 1
18 Abim'elech . . king over the citizens of Shechem 1
20 let fire . . devour the citizens of Shechem 1
20 let fire come out from the citizens of Shechem 1
Lke 15:15 joined himself to one of the citizens 2
19:14 his citizens hated him 2
Act 21:39 from Tarsus in Cili'cia, a citizen of no mean city 2
22:28 Paul said, "But I was born a citizen. •
2Mc 4: 9 the men of Jerusalem as citizens of Antioch. †
5: 6 kept . . slaughtering his fellow citizens 2
23 In his malice toward the Jewish citizens 2
9:15 make, all of them, equal to citizens of Athens; †
19 To his worthy Jewish citizens 2
14: 8 I have regard also for my fellow citizens 2
3Mc 1:22 the bolder of the citizens would not tolerate 2
citizen *See also* love.

fellow citizen 1. *πολίτης* 2. *συμπολίτης*
Eph 2:19 you are fellow citizens with the saints 2
2Mc 4: 5 not accusing his fellow citizens 1
50 the chief plotter against his fellow citizens. 1
5: 8 as the executioner of . . his fellow citizens 1
23 who lorded it over his fellow citizens 1
15:30 the defender of his fellow citizens 1

citizenship 1. *πολιτεία*
Act 22:28 I bought this citizenship for a large sum. 1
3Mc 3:21 to deem them worthy of Alexandrian citizenship 1
23 they not only spurn the priceless citizenship 1

equal citizenship 1. *ἰσοπολίτης*
3Mc 2:30 shall have equal citizenship with the Alexandrians. 1

city 1. מְדִינָה 2. עִיר 3. עִיר וָעִיר 4. קִרְיָה 5. קֶרֶת 6. שַׁעַר 7. קִרְיָה (A) 8. *πόλις* 9. civitas
Gen 4:17 she conceived and bore Enoch; and he built a city 2
17 built a city, and called the name of the city 2
10:12 Nin'eveh and Calah; that is the great city. 2
11: 4 Then they said, "Come, let us build ourselves a city 2
5 the LORD came down to see the city and the tower 2
8 earth, and they left off building the city. 2
13:12 while Lot dwelt among the cities of the valley 2
18:24 Suppose there are 50 righteous within the city; 2
26 If I find at Sodom 50 righteous in the city 2
28 Wilt thou destroy the whole city for lack of five? 2
19: 4 before they lay down, the men of the city 2
12 sons, daughters, or any one you have in the city 2
14 for the LORD is about to destroy the city. 2
15 be consumed in the punishment of the city. 2
16 brought him forth and set him outside the city. 2
20 Behold, yonder city is near enough to flee to 2
21 I will not overthrow the city of which you have 2
22 Therefore the name of the city was called Zo'ar. 2
25 he overthrew those cities, and all the valley 2
25 overthrew . . all the inhabitants of the cities 2
29 when God destroyed the cities of the valley 2
29 when he overthrew the cities in which Lot dwelt. 2
23:10 of all who went in at the gate of his city 2
18 before all who went in at the gate of his city. 2
24:10 went to Mesopota'mia, to the city of Nahor. 2
11 kneel down outside the city by the well of water 2
13 the daughters of the men of the city are coming 2
26:33 therefore the name of the city is Beer-sheba 2
28:19 but the name of the city was Luz at the first. 2
33:18 Jacob came safely to the city of Shechem 2
18 and he camped before the city. 2
34:20 came to the gate of their city and spoke to the men 2
20 spoke to the men of their city, saying 2
24 all who went out of the gate of his city hearkened 2
24 all who went out of the gate of his city. 2
25 came upon the city unawares, and killed all 2
27 sons of Jacob . . plundered the city 2
28 took their flocks . . and whatever was in the city 2
35: 5 terror from God fell upon the cities that were 2
36:32 Edom, the name of his city being Din'habah. 2
35 in his stead, the name of his city being Avith. 2
39 the name of his city being Pau; 2
41:35 the authority of Pharaoh for food in the cities 2
48 and stored up food in the cities; 2
48 stored up in every city the food from the fields 2
44: 4 they had gone but a short distance from the city 2
13 and they returned to the city. 2
Exd 9:29 gone out of the city, I will stretch out my hands 2
33 So Moses went out of the city from Pharaoh 2
Lev 14:40 throw them into an unclean place outside the city 2
41 shall pour into an unclean place outside the city 2
45 he shall carry them forth out of the city 2
53 he shall let the living bird go out of the city 2
25:29 If a man sells a dwelling house in a walled city 2
30 then the house that is in the walled city 2
32 Nevertheless the cities of the Levites 2
32 the houses in the cities of their possession 2
33 house that was sold in a city of their possession 2
33 for the houses in the cities of the Levites are 2
34 fields . . belonging to their cities may not be 2
26:25 if you gather within your cities I will send 2
31 I will lay your cities waste 2
33 a desolation, and your cities shall be a waste 2
Num 13:19 whether the cities that they dwell in are camps 2
28 cities are fortified and very large; and besides 2
20:16 in Kadesh, a city on the edge of your territory. 2
21: 2 then I will utterly destroy their cities. 2
3 they utterly destroyed them and their cities; 2
25 Israel took all these cities, and Israel settled 2
25 Israel settled in all the cities of the Amorites 2
26 For Heshbon was the city of Sihon the king 2
27 be built, let the city of Sihon be established. 2
28 from Heshbon, flame from the city of Sihon. 4
22:36 Balak . . went out to meet him at the city of Moab 2
24:19 By Jacob . . survivors of cities be destroyed! 2
31:10 All their cities in the places where they dwelt 2
32:16 We will build . . cities for our little ones 2
17 little ones shall live in the fortified cities 2
24 Build cities for your little ones 2
26 shall remain there in the cities of Gilead; 2
33 the land and its cities with their territories 2
33 the cities of the land throughout the country. 2
36 Beth-nim'rah and Beth-har'an, fortified cities 2
38 gave other names to the cities which they built. 2
35: 2 give to the Levites . . cities to dwell in; 2
2 give . . pasture lands round about the cities. 2
3 The cities shall be theirs to dwell 2
4 pasture lands of the cities, which you shall give 2
4 shall reach from the wall of the city outward 2
5 you shall measure, outside the city 2
5 the city being in the middle; 2
5 belong to them as pasture land for their cities. 2
6 cities which you give to the Levites shall be 2
6 you give . . shall be the six cities of refuge 2
6 in addition to them you shall give 42 cities 2
7 All the cities which you give to the Levites 2
8 as for the cities which you shall give 2
8 each . . shall give of its cities to the Levites. 2
11 you shall select cities to be cities of refuge 2
11 you shall select cities to be cities of refuge 2
12 cities shall be for you a refuge from the avenger 2
13 cities . . you give shall by your six cities of refuge. 2
13 cities . . shall by your six cities of refuge. 2
14 You shall give three cities beyond the Jordan 2
14 shall give . . three cities in the land of Canaan 2
14 shall give . . cities . . , to be cities of refuge. 2
15 These six cities shall be for refuge 2
25 congregation . . restore him to his city of refuge 2
26 go beyond the bounds of his city of refuge 2
27 outside the bounds of his city of refuge 2
28 For the man must remain in his city of refuge 2
32 for him who has fled to his city of refuge 2
Deu 1:22 word again of . . the cities into which we shall come.' 2
28 the cities are great and fortified up to heaven; 2
2:34 we captured all his cities at that time 2
34 and utterly destroyed every city, men, women 2
35 cattle we took . . with the booty of the cities 2
36 from the city . . in the valley, as far as Gilead 2
36 there was not a city too high for us; the LORD 4
37 river Jabbok and the cities of the hill country 2
3: 4 we took all his cities at that time . . 60 cities 2
4 there was not a city which we did not take 4
4 we took all his cities at that time . . 60 cities 2
5 cities fortified with high walls, gates, and bars 2
6 destroying every city, men, women, and children. 2
7 cattle and the spoil of the cities we took 2
10 all the cities of the tableland and all Gilead 2
10 Sal'ecah and Ed're-i, cities of the kingdom of Og 2
12 half the hill country of Gilead with its cities; 2
19 shall remain in the cities which I have given you 2
4:41 Moses set apart three cities in the east 2
42 fleeing to one of these cities he might save his life 2
6:10 great and goodly cities, which you did not build 2
9: 1 cities great and fortified up to heaven 2
13:12 If you hear in one of your cities, which the LORD 2
13 have drawn away the inhabitants of the city 2
15 surely put the inhabitants of that city 2
16 burn the city and all its spoil with fire 2
19: 1 dwell in their cities and in their houses 2
2 set apart three cities for you in the land 2
5 may flee to one of these cities and save his life; 2
7 command you, You shall set apart three cities. 2
9 you shall add three other cities to these three 2
11 man flees into one of these cities 2
12 then the elders of his city shall send and fetch 2
20:10 When you draw near to a city to fight against it 2
14 cattle, and everything else in the city 2
15 do to all the cities which are very far from you 2
15 which are not cities of the nations here. 2
16 cities of these peoples that the LORD your God 2
19 When you besiege a city for a long time, making war 2
20 siegeworks against the city that makes war 2
21: 2 they shall measure the distance to the cities 2
3 elders of the city . . nearest to the slain man 2
4 elders of that city shall bring the heifer down 2
6 elders of that city nearest to the slain man 2
19 city at the gate of the place where he lives 2
20 shall say to the elders of his city, 'This our son 2
21 all the men of the city shall stone him to death 2
22:15 tokens of her virginity to the elders of the city 2
17 spread the garment before the elders of the city. 2
18 elders of that city shall take the man and whip 2
21 men of her city shall stone her to death 2
23 man meets her in the city and lies with her 2
24 shall bring them both out to the gate of that city 2
24 she did not cry for help though she was in the city 2
25: 8 elders of his city shall call him, and speak to him 2
28: 3 Blessed shall you be in the city, and blessed 2
16 Cursed shall you be in the city, and cursed 2
34: 3 Jericho the city of palm trees, as far as Zo'ar. 2
Jos 3:16 far off, at Adam, the city that is beside Zar'ethan 2
6: 3 You shall march around the city, all the men of war 2

3 all the men of war going around the city once. 2
4 you shall march around the city seven times 2
5 and the wall of the city will fall down flat 2
7 Go forward; march around the city 2
11 he caused the ark of the LORD to compass the city 2
14 they marched around the city once, and returned 2
15 and marched around the city in the same manner 2
15 they marched around the city seven times. 2
16 Shout; for the LORD has given you the city. 2
17 the city and all . . within it shall be devoted 2
20 the people went up into the city, every man 2
20 the people went up into . . and they took the city. 2
21 Then they utterly destroyed all in the city 2
24 they burned the city with fire, and all within it; 2
26 that rises up and rebuilds this city, Jericho. 2
8: 1 the king of Ai, and his people, his city, and his land; 2
2 lay an ambush against the city, behind it. 2
4 lie in ambush against the city, behind it; 2
4 do not go very far from the city 2
5 I, and all . . with me, will approach the city. 2
6 till we have drawn them away from the city; 2
7 rise up from the ambush, and seize the city; 2
8 And when you have taken the city 2
8 you shall set the city on fire, doing as the LORD 2
11 all . . went up, and drew near before the city 2
12 in ambush between . . to the west of the city. 2
13 the main encampment which was north of the city 2
13 and its rear guard west of the city. 2
14 his people, the men of the city, made haste 2
14 there was an ambush against him behind the city. 2
16 the people . . in the city were called together 2
16 they were drawn away from the city. 2
17 they left the city open, and pursued Israel. 2
18 stretched out the javelin . . toward the city. 2
19 they ran and entered the city and took it; 2
19 and they made haste to set the city on fire. 2
20 behold, the smoke of the city went up to heaven; 2
21 all Israel saw that the ambush had taken the city 2
21 saw . . and that the smoke of the city went up 2
22 the others came forth from the city against them; 2
27 the cattle and the spoil of that city Israel took 2
29 and cast it at the entrance of the gate of the city 2
9:17 and reached their cities on the third day. 2
17 Now their cities were Gibeon, Chephi'rah 2
10: 2 Gibeon was a great city, like . . the royal cities 2
2 Gibeon was a . . city, like one of the royal cities 2
19 pursue . . do not let them enter their cities; 2
20 remnant . . entered into the fortified cities 2
11:12 all the cities of those kings . . Joshua took 2
13 none of the cities . . on mounds did Israel burn 2
14 And all the spoil of these cities and the cattle 2
19 There was not a city that made peace 2
21 Joshua . . destroyed them with their cities. 2
13: 9 and the city that is in the middle of the valley 2
10 all the cities of Sihon king of the Amorites 2
16 and the city that is in the middle of the valley 2
17 Heshbon, and all its cities . . in the tableland; 2
21 that is, all the cities of the tableland 2
23 their families with their cities and villages. 2
25 territory was Jazer, and all the cities of Gilead 2
28 according to their families, with their cities 2
30 and all the towns of Ja'ir . . 60 cities 2
31 the cities of the kingdom of Og in Bashan; 2
14: 4 no portion was . . but only cities to dwell 2
12 Anakim were there, with great fortified cities 2
15: 9 and from there to the cities of Mount Ephron; 2
21 The cities belonging to the tribe . . were 2
32 in all, 29 cities, with their villages. 2
36 fourteen cities with their villages. 2
41 sixteen cities with their villages. 2
44 nine cities with their villages. 2
51 eleven cities with their villages. 2
54 nine cities with their villages. 2
57 ten cities with their villages. 2
59 six cities with their villages. 2
60 two cities with their villages. 2
62 Nibshan, the City of Salt, and En-ge'di 2
62 six cities with their villages. 2
17: 9 The cities here . . belong to E'phraim. 2
9 The cities here . . among the cities of Manas'seh 2
12 could not take possession of those cities; 2
18:14 Kir'iath-ba'al . . a city belonging to the tribe 2
21 Now the cities of the tribe of Benjamin 2
24 twelve cities with their villages 2
28 fourteen cities with their villages. 2
19: 6 thirteen cities with their villages; 2
7 four cities with their villages; 2
8 the villages round about these cities as far 2
15 twelve cities with their villages. 2
16 these cities with their villages. 2
22 sixteen cities with their villages. 2
23 the cities with their villages. 2
29 turns . . reaching to the fortified city of Tyre; 2
30 22 cities with their villages. 2
31 these cities with their villages. 2
35 The fortified cities are Ziddim, Zer, Hammath 2
38 nineteen cities with their villages. 2
39 the cities with their villages. 2
48 these cities with their villages. 2
50 gave him the city which he asked, Tim'nath-se'rah 2
50 and he rebuilt the city, and settled in it. 2
20: 2 Appoint the cities of refuge, of which I spoke 2
4 He shall flee to one of these cities 2
4 stand at the entrance of the gate of the city 2
4 and explain his case to the elders of that city; 2
4 shall take him into the city, and give him a place 2
6 he shall remain in that city until he has stood 2
9 These were the cities designated . . that any one 2
21: 2 commanded . . that we be given cities to dwell 2
3 gave . . the following cities and pasture lands 2
4 received by lot from . . thirteen cities. 2
5 Ko'hathites received by lot from . . ten cities. 2
6 Gersonites received by lot . . thirteen cities. 2
7 received from . . Zeb'ulun, twelve cities. 2
8 cities and their pasture lands . . Israel gave 2
9 gave the following cities mentioned by name 2
12 the fields of the city and its villages had been 2
13 gave Hebron, the city of refuge for the slayer 2
16 nine cities out of these two tribes; 2
18 and Almon with its pasture lands–four cities. 2
19 The cities . . were in all thirteen cities 2
19 The cities . . were in all thirteen cities 2
20 cities allotted to them were out of . . E'phraim. 2
21 given Shechem, the city of refuge for the slayer 2
22 Kib'za-im . . Beth-hor'on . . four cities; 2
24 Ai'jalon . . Gath-rim'mon . . four cities; 2
25 Ta'anach . . and Gath-rim'mon . . two cities. 2
26 The cities of the families of . . were ten in all 2
27 Golan . . the city of refuge for the slayer 2
27 Golan . . and Beesh'terah . . two cities; 2
29 Jarmuth . . En-gan'nim . . four cities; 2
31 Helkath . . and Rehob . . four cities; 2
32 Kedesh . . the city of refuge for the slayer 2
32 Ham'moth-dor . . and Kartan . . three cities. 2
33 The cities of the . . Gershonites were in all 2
33 in all thirteen cities with their pasture lands. 2
35 Dimnah . . Na'halal . . four cities; 2
37 Ked'emoth . . and Meph'a-ath . . four cities; 2
38 Ramoth . . the city of refuge for the slayer 2
39 Heshbon . . Jazer . . four cities in all. 2
40 the cities of the several Merar'ite families 2
40 those allotted . . were in all twelve cities. 2
41 cities of the Levites . . were in all 48 2
41 people . . were in all 48 cities 2
42 These cities had each its pasture lands 2
42 These cities had . . so it was with all these 2
24:13 I gave you . . and cities which you had not built 2
Jdg 1: 8 took it, and smote it . . and set the city on fire. 2
16 went up . . from the city of palms 2
17 So the name of the city was called Hormah. 2
23 (Now the name of the city was formerly Luz.) 2
24 the spies saw a man coming out of the city 2
24 Pray, show us the way into the city, and we will deal 2
25 he showed them the way into the city; 2
25 and they smote the city with the edge of the sword 2
26 went to the land of the Hittites and built a city 2
3:13 and they took possession of the city of palms. 2
8:16 he took the elders of the city and he took thorns 2
17 the tower of Penu'el, and slew the men of the city. 2
27 made an ephod of it and put it in his city, in Ophrah; 2
9:30 When Zebul the ruler of the city heard the words 2
31 and they are stirring up the city against you. 2
33 as the sun is up, rise early and rush upon the city; 2
35 and stood in the entrance of the gate of the city; 2
43 he looked and saw the men coming out of the city 2
44 and stood at the entrance of the gate of the city 2
45 Abim'elech fought against the city all that day; 2
45 he took the city, and killed the people . . in it; 2
45 and he razed the city and sowed it with salt. 2
51 there was a strong tower within the city 2
51 tower . . and all the people of the city fled to it 2
10: 4 and they had 30 cities, called Hav'voth-ja'ir 2
11:26 in all the cities that are on the banks 2
33 the neighborhood of Minnith, twenty cities 2
12: 7 died, and was buried in his city in Gilead. 8
14:18 the men of the city said to him on the seventh day 2
16: 2 then in wait for him all night at the gate of the city. 2
3 and took hold of the doors of the gate of the city 2
18:27 smote them . . and burned the city with fire. 2
28 And they rebuilt the city, and dwelt in it. 2
29 they named the city Dan, after the name of Dan 2
29 but the name of the city was La'ish at the first. 2
19:11 let us turn aside to this city of the Jeb'usites 2
12 will not turn aside into the city of foreigners 2
15 went in and sat down in the open square of the city; 2
17 saw the wayfarer in the open square of the city; 2
22 the men of the city, base fellows, beset the house 2
20:11 all the men of Israel gathered against the city 2
14 the Benjaminites came together out of the cities 2
15 mustered out of their cities on that day 2
31 Benjaminites . . were drawn away from the city 2
32 and draw them away from the city to the highways. 2
37 and smote all the city with the edge of the sword. 2
38 made a great cloud of smoke rise up out of the city 2
40 signal began to rise out of the city in a column 2
40 the whole of the city went up in smoke to heaven. 2
42 those who came out of the cities destroyed them 2
Rut 2:18 And she took it up and went into the city; 2
3:15 then she went into the city. 2
4: 2 he took ten men of the elders of the city, and said 2
1Sm 1: 3 go up . . from his city to worship and to sacrifice 2
4:13 when the man came into the city and told the news 2
13 when the man came . . all the city cried out. 2
5: 9 the hand of the LORD was against the city 2
9 and he afflicted the men of the city 2
11 was a deathly panic throughout the whole city. 2
12 and the cry of the city went up to heaven. 2
6:18 the cities of the Philistines belonging 2
18 both fortified cities and unwalled villages. 2
7:14 The cities . . were restored to Israel, from Ekron 2
8:22 Samuel then said . . "Go every man to his city. 2
9: 6 there is a man of God in this city 2
10 they went to the city where the man of God was. 2
11 As they went up the hill to the city, they met young 2
12 Make haste; he has come just now to the city 2
13 As soon as you enter the city, you will find him 2
14 they went up to the city. As they were entering 2
14 As they were entering the city, they saw Samuel 2
25 they came down from the high place into the city 2
27 they were going down to the outskirts of the city 2
10: 5 as you come to the city, you will meet . . prophets 2
15: 5 Saul came to the city of Am'alek, and lay in wait 2
16: 4 The elders of the city came to meet him trembling 2
18: 6 the women came out of all the cities of Israel 2
20: 6 asked leave of me to run to Bethlehem his city; 2
29 our family holds a sacrifice in the city 2
40 Go and carry them to the city. 2
42 And he rose . . and Jonathan went into the city. 2
22:19 Nob, the city of the priests, he put to the sword; 2
23:10 Saul seeks . . to destroy the city on my account. 2
27: 5 why should . . dwell in the royal city with you? 2
28: 3 mourned . . and buried him in Ramah, his own city. 2
30: 3 when David and his men came to the city, they found 2
29 in Racal, in the cities of the Jerah'meelites 2
29 for those . . in the cities of the Ken'ites 2
31: 7 they forsook their cities and fled; 2
2Sm 2: 1 Shall I go up into any of the cities of Judah? 2
5: 7 the stronghold of Zion, that is, the city of David. 2
9 the stronghold, and called it the city of David. 2
9 David built the city round about from the Millo 8
6:10 to take the ark of the LORD into the city of David; 2
12 and brought up the ark . . to the city of David 2
16 As the ark of the LORD came into the city of David 2
8: 8 from Betah and . . Bero'thai, cities of Hadade'zer 2
10: 3 sent his servants . . to search the city, and to spy 2
12 for our people, and for the cities of our God; 2
14 they likewise fled . . and entered the city. 2
11:16 as Jo'ab was besieging the city, he assigned Uri'ah 2
17 the men of the city came out and fought with Jo'ab; 2
20 he says . . 'Why did you go so near the city to fight? 2
25 strengthen your attack upon the city 2
12: 1 There were two men in a certain city 2
26 Jo'ab fought against . . and took the royal city. 2
27 moreover, I have taken the city of waters. 2
28 gather the rest . . and encamp against the city 2
28 lest I take the city, and it be called by my name. 2
30 And he brought forth the spoil of the city 2
31 thus he did to all the cities of the Ammonites. 2
15: 2 Ab'salom would call . . "From what city are you? 2
12 he sent for Ahith'opel . . from his city Giloh. 2
14 and smite the city with the edge of the sword. 2
24 until the people had all passed out of the city. 2
25 Carry the ark of God back into the city. 2
27 Look, go back to the city in peace, you and Abi'athar 2
34 But if you return to the city, and say to Ab'salom 2
37 So Hushai, David's friend, came into the city 2
17:13 If he withdraws into a city . . we shall drag it 2
13 all Israel will bring ropes to that city 2
17 for they must not be seen entering the city. 2
23 saddled his ass, and went off home to his own city. 2
18: 3 it is better that you send us help from the city. 2
19: 3 And the people stole into the city that day 2
37 Pray let . . return, that I may die in my own city 2
20: 6 pursue him, lest he get himself fortified cities 2
15 they cast up a mound against the city, and it stood 2
16 Then a wise woman called from the city, "Hear! Hear! 2
19 to destroy a city which is a mother in Israel; 2
21 give up him . . and I will withdraw from the city. 2
22 dispersed from the city, every man to his home. 2
24: 5 from the city that is in the middle of the valley 2
7 to all the cities of the Hivites and Canaanites; 2
1Kg 1:41 he said, "What does this uproar in the city mean? 4
45 there rejoicing, so that the city is in an uproar. 4
2:10 his fathers, and was buried in the city of David. 2
3: 1 daughter, and brought her into the city of David 2
4:13 60 great cities with walls and bronze bars); 2
8: 1 the ark . . out of the city of David, which is Zion. 2
16 I chose no city in all the tribes of Israel 2
37 their enemy besieges them in any of their cities; 6
44 pray . . toward the city which thou hast chosen 2
48 their land . . the city which thou hast chosen 2
9:11 Solomon gave to Hiram twenty cities in the land 2
12 to see the cities which Solomon had given him 2
13 Therefore he said, "What kind of cities are these 2
16 had slain the Canaanites who dwelt in the city 2
19 store-cities . . and the cities for his chariots 2
19 for his chariots, and the cities for his horsemen 2

24 went up from the city of David to her own house 2
10:26 whom he stationed in the chariot cities 2
11:27 and closed up the breach of the city of David 2
32 Jerusalem, the city which I have chosen 2
36 Jerusalem, the city where I have chosen 2
43 and was buried in the city of David his father; 2
12:17 people of Israel who dwelt in the cities of Judah. 2
13:25 told it in the city where the old prophet dwelt. 2
29 took up the body . . and brought it back to the city 2
32 high places which are in the cities of Sama'ria 2
14:11 Any one . . who dies in the city the dogs shall eat; 2
12 When your feet enter the city, the child 2
21 in Jerusalem, the city which the LORD had chosen 2
31 was buried with his fathers in the city of David. 2
15: 8 and they buried him in the city of David. 2
20 sent . . his armies against the cities of Israel 2
23 the acts of Asa . . and the cities which he built 2
24 was buried with his fathers in the city of David 2
16: 4 Any one . . who dies in the city the dogs shall eat; 2
18 when Zimri saw that the city was taken, he went 2
24 and called the name of the city . . Sama'ria 2
17:10 when he came to the gate of the city, behold, a widow 2
20: 2 he sent messengers into the city to Ahab 2
12 And they took their positions against the city. 2
19 these went out of the city, the servants 2
30 the rest fled into the city of Aphek; 2
30 entered an inner chamber in the city. 2
34 The cities which my father took . . I will restore; 2
21: 8 nobles who dwelt with Naboth in his city. 2
11 the men of his city . . did as Jez'ebel had sent word 2
11 the elders and the nobles who dwelt in his city 2
13 So they took him outside the city, and stoned him 2
24 who dies in the city the dogs shall eat; 2
22:26 take him back to Amon the governor of the city 2
36 Every man to his city, and every man to his country! 2
39 ivory house . . and all the cities that he built 2
50 was buried with his fathers in the city of David 2
2Kg 2:19 Now the men of the city said to Eli'sha, "Behold 2
19 Behold, the situation of this city is pleasant 2
23 some small boys came out of the city and jeered 2
3:19 you shall conquer every fortified city 2
19 conquer every . . and every choice city 2
25 And they overthrew the cities 2
6:14 and they came by night, and surrounded the city. 2
15 an army . . was round about the city. 2
19 This is not the way, and this is not the city; 2
7: 4 If we say, 'Let us enter the city,' . . we shall die 2
4 the famine is in the city, and we shall die there; 2
10 came and called to the gatekeepers of the city 2
12 When they come out of the city, we shall take them 2
12 we shall take them alive and get into the city.' 2
8:24 was buried with his fathers in the city of David; 2
9:15 let no one slip out of the city to go and tell 2
28 buried . . with his fathers in the city of David. 2
10: 1 sent them to Sama'ria, to the rulers of the city 9
2 chariots and horses, fortified cities also 2
5 over the palace, and he who was over the city 2
6 king's sons . . were with the great men of the city 2
11:20 the city was quiet after Athali'ah had been slain 2
12:21 buried him with his fathers in the city of David 2
13:25 took again from Ben-ha'dad . . the cities which he 2
25 and recovered the cities of Israel. 2
14:20 was buried in Jerusalem . . in the city of David. 2
15: 7 buried him with his fathers in the city of David 2
38 was buried with his fathers in the city of David 2
16:20 was buried with his fathers in the city of David; 2
17: 6 in Halah . . and in the cities of the Medes. 2
9 their towns, from watchtower to fortified city; 2
24 and placed them in the cities of Sama'ria 2
24 possession of Sama'ria, and dwelt in its cities. 2
26 carried away and placed in the cities of Sama'ria 2
29 every nation in the cities in which they dwelt; 2
18: 8 He smote . . from watchtower to fortified city. 2
11 put them in Halah . . and in the cities of the Medes 2
13 against all the fortified cities of Judah 2
30 this city will not be given into the hand 2
19:13 king of Arpad, the king of the city of Sepharva'im 2
25 you . . turn fortified cities into heaps of ruins 2
32 He shall not come into this city or shoot an arrow 2
33 he shall not come into this city, says the LORD. 2
34 I will defend this city to save it, for my own sake 2
20: 6 I will deliver you and this city out of the hand 2
6 I will defend this city for my own sake and for my 2
20 how he made . . and brought water into the city 2
23: 5 in the high places at the cities of Judah 2
8 brought . . the priests out of the cities of Judah 2
8 of the gate of Joshua the governor of the city 2
8 which were on one's left at the gate of the city. 2
17 And the men of the city told him, "It is the tomb 2
19 the shrines . . that were in the cities of Sama'ria 2
27 I will cast off this city which I have chosen 2
24:10 came up to Jerusalem, and the city was besieged. 2
11 Nebuchadnez'zar king of Babylon came to the city 2
25: 2 the city was besieged till the eleventh year 2
3 the famine was so severe in the city that 2
4 Then a breach was made in the city; 2
4 though the Chalde'ans were around the city. 2
11 the rest of the people who were left in the city 2
19 from the city he took an officer . . and five men 2
19 men of the . . council who were found in the city; 2
19 and 60 men . . who were found in the city. 2
1Ch 1:43 Bela . . the name of whose city was Din'habah. 2
46 and the name of his city was Avith. 2
50 Hadad . . and the name of his city was Pa'i 2
2:22 Ja'ir, who had 23 cities in the land of Gilead 2
4:31 These were their cities until David reigned. 2
32 Etam, A'in, Rimmon, Tochen , and Ashan, five cities 2
33 were round about these cities as far as Ba'al. 2
6:56 fields of the city and its villages 2
57 they gave the cities of refuge 2
60 All their cities . . were thirteen. 2
61 the Ko'hathites were given by lot . . ten cities. 2
62 Gershomites . . were allotted thirteen cities 2
63 twelve cities out of the tribes of Reuben, Gad 2
64 gave . . the cities with their pasture lands. 2
65 these cities which are mentioned by name. 2
66 cities of their territory out of the tribe 2
67 cities of refuge: Shechem . . Gezer 2
9: 2 dwell again in their possessions in their cities 2
10: 7 they forsook their cities and fled; 2
11: 5 stronghold of Zion, that is, the city of David. 2
7 therefore it was called the city of David. 2
8 he built the city round about from the Millo 2
8 and Jo'ab repaired the rest of the city. 2
13: 2 in the cities that have pasture lands 2
13 did not take the ark home into the city of David 2
15: 1 built houses for himself in the city of David; 2
29 ark . . of the LORD came to the city of David 2
18: 8 And from Tibhath and from Cun, cities of Hadade'zer 2
19: 7 Ammonites were mustered from their cities 2
9 in battle array at the entrance of the city 2
13 play the man . . for the cities of our God; 2
15 the Ammonites . . fled . . and entered the city. 2
20: 2 he brought forth the spoil of the city 2
3 David did to all the cities of the Ammonites. 2
27:25 over the treasuries in the country, in the cities 2
2Ch 1:14 whom he stationed in the chariot cities 2
5: 2 to bring up the ark . . out of the city of David 2
6: 5 I chose no city in all the tribes of Israel 2
28 enemies besiege them in any of their cities; 6
34 and they pray to thee toward this city which thou 2
38 pray toward . . the city which thou hast chosen 2
8: 2 Solomon rebuilt the cities which Huram had 2
4 all the store-cities which he built in Hamath. 2
5 fortified cities with walls, gates, and bars 2
6 Ba'alath, and all the store-cities . . Solomon had 2
6 and all the cities for his chariots 2
6 for his chariots, and the cities for his horsemen 2
11 up Pharoah's daughter from the city of David 2
9:25 whom he stationed in the chariot cities 2
31 Solomon . . was buried in the city of David 2
10:17 the people . . who dwelt in the cities of Judah. 2
11: 5 Rehobo'am . . built cities for defense in Judah. 2
10 fortified cities which are in Judah 2
12 he put shields and spears in all the cities 2
23 Judah and Benjamin, in all the fortified cities; 2
12: 4 he took the fortified cities of Judah 2
13 Jerusalem, the city which the LORD had chosen 2
16 Rehobo'am . . was buried in the city of David; 2
13:19 pursued Jerobo'am, and took cities from him 2
14: 1 they buried him in the city of David; 2
5 out of all the cities of Judah the high places 2
6 He built fortified cities in Judah 2
7 he said to Judah, "Let us build these cities 2
14 they smote all the cities round about Gerar 2
14 They plundered all the cities 2
15: 6 nation against nation and city against city 2
6 nation against nation and city against city 2
8 from the cities which he had taken 2
16: 4 his armies against the cities of Israel 2
4 conquered . . all the store-cities of Naph'tali. 2
14 hewn out for himself in the city of David. 2
17: 2 He placed forces in all the fortified cities 2
2 set garrisons . . in the cities of E'phraim 2
7 to teach in the cities of Judah; 2
9 they went about through all the cities of Judah 2
13 he had great stores in the cities of Judah. 2
19 king had placed in the fortified cities 2
18:25 take him back to Amon the governor of the city 2
19: 5 in the land in all the fortified cities of Judah 2
5 in all the fortified cities of Judah, city by city 2
5 in all the fortified cities of Judah, city by city 2
10 from your brethren who live in their cities 2
20: 4 from all the cities of Judah they came to seek 2
21: 1 buried with his fathers in the city of David; 2
3 great gifts . . together with fortified cities 2
20 buried him in the city of David 2
23: 2 Levites from all the cities of Judah 2
21 city was quiet, after Athali'ah had been slain 2
24: 5 Go out to the cities of Judah, and gather 2
16 buried him in the city of David among the kings 2
25 he died; and they buried him in the city of David 2
25:13 fell upon the cities of Judah 2
28 buried with his fathers in the city of David. 2
26: 6 built cities in the territory of Ashdod 2
27: 4 he built cities in the hill country of Judah 2
9 they buried him in the city of David; 2
28:15 at Jericho, the city of palm trees. 2
18 made raids on the cities in the Shephe'lah 2
25 In every city of Judah he made high places 2
27 buried him in the city, in Jerusalem 2
29:20 Hezeki'ah . . gathered the officials of the city 2
30:10 couriers went from city to city 2
10 couriers went from city to city 2
31: 1 all Israel . . went out to the cities of Judah 2
1 people of Israel returned to their cities 2
6 people . . who lived in the cities of Judah 2
15 assisting him in the cities of the priests 2
19 fields of common land belonging to their cities 2
19 men in the several cities who were designated 2
32: 1 encamped against the fortified cities 2
3 water of the springs that were outside the city; 2
5 he strengthened the Millo in the city of David. 2
6 in the square at the gate of the city 2
18 in order that they might take the city. 2
29 likewise provided cities for himself 2
30 down to the west side of the city of David. 2
33:14 built an outer wall for the city of David 2
14 in all the fortified cities in Judah. 2
15 he threw them outside of the city. 2
34: 6 in the cities of Manas'seh, E'phraim, and Simeon 2
8 he sent . . Ma-asei'ah the governor of the city 2
Ezr 4:10 deported and settled in the cities of Sama'ria 7
12 rebuilding that rebellious and wicked city; 7
13 if this city is rebuilt and the walls finished 7
15 learn that this city is a rebellious city 7
15 learn that this city is a rebellious city 7
15 That was why this city was laid waste. 7
16 if this city is rebuilt and its walls finished 7
19 found that this city from of old has risen 7
21 make a decree . . that this city be not rebuilt 7
10:14 all in our cities who have taken foreign wives 2
14 with them the elders and judges of every city 2
Neh 2: 3 when the city, the place of my fathers' sepulchres 2
5 Judah, to the city of my fathers' sepulchres 2
8 to make beams for . . the wall of the city 2
3:15 stairs that go down from the City of David. 2
7: 4 city was wide and large, but the people within it 2
9:25 captured fortified cities and a rich land 2
11: 1 one out of ten to live in Jerusalem the holy city 2
9 Judah . . of Hassen'u-ah was second over the city. 2
18 All the Levites in the holy city were 284. 2
12:37 went up . . by the stairs of the city of David 2
13:16 Men of Tyre also, who lived in the city, •
18 God bring all this evil on us and on this city? 2
Est 3:15 but the city of Susa was perplexed. 2
4: 1 and went out into the midst of the city 2
6 in the open square of the city in front 2
6: 9 conduct . . through the open square of the city 2
11 made him ride through the open square of the city 2
8:11 allowed the Jews who were in every city to gather 2
15 while the city of Susa shouted and rejoiced. 2
17 and in every city . . there was gladness and joy 3
9: 2 the Jews gathered in their cities . . to lay hands 2
28 generation, in every family, province, and city 2
Job 15:28 and has lived in desolate cities 2
24:12 From out of the city the dying groan 2
29: 7 When I went out to the gate of the city 5
39: 7 He scorns the tumult of the city; 4
Ps 9: 6 their cities thou hast rooted out; 2
31:21 love to me when I was beset as in a besieged city. 2
46: 4 a river whose streams make glad the city of God 2
48: 1 and greatly to be praised in the city of our God! 2
2 Zion, in the far north, the city of the great King. 4
8 so have we seen in the city of the LORD of hosts 2
8 city of the LORD of hosts, in the city of our God 2
55: 9 for I see violence and strife in the city. 2
59: 6 howling like dogs and prowling about the city. 2
14 howling like dogs and prowling about the city. 2
60: 9 Who will bring me to the fortified city? 2
69:35 will save Zion and rebuild the cities of Judah; 2
72:16 may men blossom forth from the cities 2
87: 1 On the holy mount stands the city he founded; †
3 Glorious things are spoken of you, O city of God. 2
101: 8 off all the evildoers from the city of the LORD. 2
107: 4 finding no way to a city to dwell in; 2
7 straight way, till they reached a city to dwell 2
36 hungry dwell, and they establish a city to live in; 2
108:10 Who will bring me to the fortified city? 2
122: 3 Jerusalem, built as a city which is bound firmly 2
127: 1 Unless the LORD watches over the city 2
Prv 1:21 at the entrance of the city gates she speaks 2
10:15 A rich man's wealth is his strong city; 4
11:10 goes well with the righteous, the city rejoices; 4
11 By the blessing of the upright a city is exalted 5
16:32 he who rules his spirit than he who takes a city. 2
18:11 A rich man's wealth is his strong city 4
19 A brother helped is like a strong city 8
21:22 A wise man scales the city of the mighty 2
25:28 like a city broken into and left without walls. 2
29: 8 Scoffers set a city aflame 4
Ecc 7:19 more than ten rulers that are in a city. 2
8:10 were praised in the city where they had done such 2
9:14 There was a little city with few men in it; 2
15 wise man, and he by his wisdom delivered the city. 2
10:15 that he does not know the way to the city. 2
Sng 3: 2 I will rise now and go about the city 2

3 watchmen found me, as they went about in the city. 2
5: 7 The watchmen found me, as they went about the city; 2
Isa 1: 7 country lies desolate, your cities are burned 2
8 like a lodge in a . . field, like a besieged city. 2
21 How the faithful city has become a harlot 4
26 you shall be called the city of righteousness 2
26 the city of righteousness, the faithful city. 4
6:11 How long, O Lord?" And he said: "Until cities lie waste 2
14:17 made . . like a desert and overthrew its cities 2
21 and fill the face of the world with cities. 2
31 Wail, O gate; cry, O city; melt in fear 2
17: 1 Behold, Damascus will cease to be a city 2
2 Her cities will be deserted for ever; 2
9 cities will be like the deserted places 2
19: 2 city against city, kingdom against kingdom; 2
2 city against city, kingdom against kingdom; 2
18 In that day there will be five cities in . . Egypt 2
18 One of these will be called the City of the Sun. 2
22: 2 you who are full of shoutings, tumultuous city 2
9 the breaches of the city of David were many 2
23: 7 exultant city whose origin is from days of old •
16 Take a harp, go about the city, O forgotten harlot! 2
24:10 The city of chaos is broken down 4
12 Desolation is left in the city 2
25: 2 For thou hast made the city a heap 2
2 made the city a heap, the fortified city a ruin; 4
2 the palace of aliens is a city no more 2
3 cities of ruthless nations will fear thee. 4
26: 1 We have a strong city; he sets up salvation 2
5 the inhabitants of the height, the lofty city. 4
27:10 For the fortified city is solitary 2
29: 1 Ho Ariel, Ariel, the city where David encamped! 4
32:13 yea, for all the joyous houses in the joyful city. 4
14 will be forsaken, the populous city deserted; 2
19 and the city will be utterly laid low. 2
33:20 Look upon Zion, the city of our appointed feasts! 4
36: 1 came up against all the fortified cities 2
15 this city will not be given into the hand 2
37:13 king of Arpad, the king of the city of Sepharva'im 2
26 make fortified cities crash into heaps of ruins 2
33 He shall not come into this city 2
34 he shall not come into this city, says the LORD. 2
35 For I will defend this city to save it 2
38: 6 this city out of the hand of the king of Assyria 2
6 I will deliver you . . and defend this city. 2
40: 9 say to the cities of Judah, "Behold your God! 2
42:11 Let the desert and its cities lift up their voice 2
44:26 and of the cities of Judah, 'They shall be built 2
45:13 he shall build my city and set my exiles free 2
48: 2 For they call themselves after the holy city 2
52: 1 beautiful garments, O Jerusalem, the holy city; 2
54: 3 possess . . and will people the desolate cities. 2
60:14 they shall call you the City of the LORD, 2
61: 4 they shall repair the ruined cities 2
62:12 be called Sought out, a city not forsaken. 2
64:10 Thy holy cities have become a wilderness 2
66: 6 an uproar from the city! A voice from the temple! 2
Jer 1:15 and against all the cities of Judah. 2
18 And I, behold, I make you this day a fortified city 2
2:15 his cities are in ruins, without inhabitant. 2
28 for as many as your cities are your gods, O Judah. 2
3:14 for I am your master; I will take you, one from a city 2
4: 5 Assemble, and let us go into the fortified cities!' 2
7 your cities will be ruins without inhabitant. 2
16 they shout against the cities of Judah. 2
26 all its cities were laid in ruins before the LORD 2
29 every city takes to flight; they enter thickets; 2
29 cities are forsaken, and no man dwells in them. 2
5: 6 A leopard is watching against their cities 2
17 your fortified cities in which you trust 2
6: 6 This is the city which must be punished; 2
7:17 see what they are doing in the cities of Judah 2
34 And I will make to cease from the cities of Judah 2
8:14 let us go into the fortified cities and perish 2
16 the city and those who dwell in it. 2
9:11 and I will make the cities of Judah a desolation 2
10:22 to make the cities of Judah a desolation 2
11: 6 Proclaim all these words in the cities of Judah 2
12 Then the cities of Judah . . will go 2
13 For your gods have become as many as your cities 2
13:19 The cities of Negeb are shut up, with none to open 2
14:18 if I enter the city, behold, the diseases of famine! 2
17:24 and bring in no burden by the gates of this city 2
25 then there shall enter by the gates of this city 2
25 and this city shall be inhabited for ever. 2
26 And people shall come from the cities of Judah 2
19: 8 And I will make this city a horror 2
11 will I break this people and this city 2
12 making this city like Topheth. 2
15 Behold, I am bringing upon this city 2
20: 5 Moreover, I will give all the wealth of the city 2
16 like the cities which the LORD overthrew 2
21: 4 bring them together into the midst of this city. 2
6 I will smite the inhabitants of this city 2
7 and the people in this city who survive 2
9 He who stays in this city shall die by the sword 2
10 For I have set my face against this city for evil 2
22: 6 make you a desert, an uninhabited city. •
8 And many nations will pass by this city 2

8 Why has the LORD dealt thus with this great city? 2
23:39 and the city which I gave to you and your fathers. 2
25:18 Jerusalem and the cities of Judah 2
29 For behold, I begin to work evil at the city 2
26: 2 and speak to all the cities of Judah which come 2
6 I will make this city a curse for all the nations 2
9 this city shall be desolate, without inhabitant'? 2
11 because he has prophesied against this city 2
12 against this house and this city all the words 2
15 blood . . upon this city and its inhabitants 2
20 He prophesied against this city 2
27:17 Why should this city become a desolation? 2
19 rest of the vessels which are left in this city. 2
29: 7 seek the welfare of the city where I have sent you 2
16 concerning all the people who dwell in this city 2
30:18 the city shall be rebuilt upon its mound 2
31:21 O virgin Israel, return to these your cities. 2
23 and in its cities, when I restore their fortunes 2
24 Judah and all its cities shall dwell there 2
38 when the city shall be rebuilt for the LORD 2
32: 3 I am giving this city into the hand of the king 2
24 siege mounds have come up to the city to take it 2
24 the city is given into the hands of the Chalde'ans 2
25 the city is given into the hands of the Chalde'ans 2
28 giving this city into the hands of the Chalde'ans 2
29 Chalde'ans who are fighting against this city 2
29 shall come and set this city on fire, and burn it 2
31 This city has aroused my anger and wrath 2
36 concerning this city of which you say, 'It is given 2
44 about Jerusalem, and in the cities of Judah 2
44 in the cities of the hill country 2
44 in the cities of the Shephe'lah 2
44 of the Shephe'lah, and in the cities of the Negeb; 2
33: 4 concerning the houses of this city 2
5 for I have hidden my face from this city 2
9 And this city shall be to me a name of joy, a praise •
10 in the cities of Judah and the streets 2
12 without man or beast, and in all of its cities 2
13 In the cities of the hill country 2
13 the hill country, in the cities of the Shephe'lah 2
13 of the Shephe'lah, and in the cities of the Negeb 2
13 about Jerusalem, and in the cities of Judah 2
34: 1 against Jerusalem and all of its cities 2
2 I am giving this city into the hand of the king 2
7 against all the cities of Judah that were left 2
7 these were the only fortified cities of Judah 2
22 and will bring them back to this city; 2
22 I will make the cities of Judah a desolation 2
36: 6 all the men of Judah who come out of their cities. 2
9 the people who came from the cities of Judah 2
37: 8 shall come back and fight against this city; 2
10 they would rise up and burn this city with fire. 2
21 until all the bread of the city was gone. 2
38: 2 He who stays in this city shall die by the sword 2
3 This city shall surely be given into the hand 2
4 hands of the soldiers who are left in this city 2
9 hunger, for there is no bread left in the city. 2
17 and this city shall not be burned with fire 2
18 then this city shall be given into the hand 2
23 and this city shall be burned with fire. 2
39: 2 a breach was made in the city. 2
4 they fled, going out of the city at night 2
9 the rest of the people who were left in the city 2
16 Behold, I will fulfil my words against this city 2
40: 5 appointed governor of the cities of Judah 2
10 and dwell in your cities that you have taken. 2
41: 7 When they came into the city, Ish'mael . . slew them 2
44: 2 upon Jerusalem and upon all the cities of Judah. 2
6 poured forth and kindled in the cities of Judah 2
17 our kings and our princes, in the cities of Judah 2
21 As for the incense that you burned in the cities 2
46: 8 I will destroy cities and their inhabitants. 2
47: 2 that fills it, the city and those who dwell in it. 2
48: 8 The destroyer shall come upon every city 2
8 come upon every city, and no city shall escape; 2
9 her cities shall become a desolation 2
15 The destroyer of Moab and his cities has come up 2
24 all the cities of the land of Moab, far and near. 2
28 Leave the cities, and dwell in the rock 2
41 the cities shall be taken 4
49: 1 and his people settled in its cities? 2
13 and all her cities shall be perpetual wastes. 2
18 Sodom and Gomor'rah and their neighbor cities •
25 How the famous city is forsaken, the joyful city! 2
25 How the famous city is forsaken, the joyful city! 4
50:32 I will kindle a fire in his cities 2
40 Sodom and Gomor'rah and their neighbor cities •
51:31 to tell the king of Babylon that his city is taken 2
43 Her cities have become a horror, a land of drought 2
52: 5 the city was besieged till the eleventh year 2
6 the famine was so severe in the city 2
7 Then a breach was made in the city; 2
7 the men of war fled and went out from the city 2
7 while the Chalde'ans were round about the city. 2
15 the rest of the people who were left in the city 2
25 from the city he took an officer 2
25 of the king's council, who were found in the city; 2
25 men . . who were found in the midst of the city. 2
Lam 1: 1 How lonely sits the city that was full of people! 2

1 She that was a princess among the cities 1
19 my priests and elders perished in the city 2
2:11 and babes faint in the streets of the city. 4
12 faint like wounded men in the streets of the city 2
15 Is this the city which was called the perfection 2
3:51 grief at the fate of all the maidens of my city. 2
Ezk 4: 1 and portray upon it a city, even Jerusalem; 2
3 place it as an iron wall between you and the city; 2
7 and you shall prophesy against the city. •
5: 2 shall burn in the fire in the midst of the city 2
2 and strike with the sword round about the city; •
6: 6 Wherever you dwell your cities shall be waste 2
7:15 in the city famine and pestilence devour. 2
23 the city is full of violence 2
9: 1 Draw near, you executioners of the city 2
4 And the LORD said to him, "Go through the city 2
5 Pass through the city after him, and smite; 2
7 they went forth, and smote in the city. 2
9 is full of blood, and the city full of injustice; 2
10: 2 and scatter them over the city. 2
11: 2 who give wicked counsel in this city; 2
3 this city is the caldron, and we are the flesh. •
6 You have multiplied your slain in this city 2
7 they are the flesh, and this city is the caldron; •
11 This city shall not be your caldron •
23 the LORD went up from the midst of the city 2
23 mountain which is on the east side of the city. 2
12:20 And the inhabited cities shall be laid waste 2
17: 4 and set it in a city of merchants. 2
19: 7 their strongholds, and laid waste their cities; 2
21:19 a signpost, make it at the head of the way to a city; 2
22: 2 will you judge, will you judge the bloody city? 2
3 A city that sheds blood in the midst of her 2
24: 6 Woe to the bloody city 2
9 thus says the Lord GOD: Woe to the bloody city! 2
25: 5 the cities of the Ammonites a fold for flocks. •
9 the flank of Moab from the cities on its frontier 2
26:10 as one enters a city which has been breached. 2
17 O city renowned, that was mighty on the sea 2
19 When I make you a city laid waste, like the cities 2
19 waste, like the cities that are not inhabited 2
29:12 her cities shall be a desolation 40 years 2
12 40 years among cities that are laid waste. 2
30: 7 her cities shall be in the midst of cities 2
7 in the midst of cities that are laid waste. 2
33:21 came to me and said, "The city has fallen. 2
35: 4 I will lay your cities waste 2
9 and your cities shall not be inhabited. 2
36: 4 the desolate wastes and the deserted cities 2
10 the cities shall be inhabited 2
33 I will cause the cities to be inhabited 2
35 ruined cities are now inhabited and fortified. 2
38 the waste cities be filled with flocks of men. 2
39: 9 those who dwell in the cities of Israel will go 2
16 A city Hamo'nah is there also. 2
40: 1 fourteenth year after the city was conquered 2
2 mountain, on which was a structure like a city 2
43: 3 which I had seen when he came to destroy the city 2
45: 5 as their possession for cities to live in. 8
6 you shall assign for the possession of the city 2
7 the holy district and the property of the city 2
48:15 in length, shall be for ordinary use for the city 2
15 In the midst of it shall be the city; 2
17 the city shall have open land 2
18 shall be food for the workers of the city. 2
19 workers of the city, from all the tribes of Israel 2
20 together with the property of the city. 2
21 holy portion and of the property of the city 2
22 of the Levites and the property of the city 2
30 These shall be the exits of the city 2
31 gates of the city being named after the tribes 2
35 The circumference of the city shall be 18,000 •
35 the name of the city henceforth shall be 2
Dan 9:16 anger . . wrath turn away from thy city Jerusalem 2
18 behold . . the city which is called by thy name; 2
19 thy city and thy people are called by thy name. 2
24 concerning your people and your holy city 2
26 prince . . destroy the city and the sanctuary. 2
11:15 siegeworks, and take a well-fortified city. 2
Hos 6: 8 Gilead is a city of evildoers 4
8:14 and Judah has multiplied fortified cities; 2
14 but I will send a fire upon his cities 2
11: 6 The sword shall rage against their cities 2
Jol 2: 9 They leap upon the city, they run upon the walls; 2
Ams 3: 6 Is a trumpet blown in a city, and the people are not 2
6 Does evil befall a city, unless the LORD has done it? 2
4: 6 I gave you cleanness of teeth in all your cities 2
7 I would send rain upon one city, and send no rain 2
7 upon one city, and send no rain upon another city; 2
8 three cities wandered to one city to drink water 2
8 three cities wandered to one city to drink water 2
5: 3 The city that went forth 1,000 shall have 2
6: 8 I will deliver up the city and all that is in it. 2
7:17 Your wife shall be a harlot in the city 2
9:14 and they shall rebuild the ruined cities 2
Obd 1:20 exiles . . shall possess the cities of the Negeb. 2
Jon 1: 2 Arise, go to Nin'eveh, that great city 2
3: 2 Arise, go to Nin'eveh, that great city, and proclaim 2
3 Now Nin'eveh was an exceedingly great city 2

4 Jonah began to go into the city 2
4: 5 Then Jonah went out of the city and sat to the east 2
5 went out of the city and sat to the east of the city 2
5 till he should see what would become of the city. 2
11 And should not I pity Nin'eveh, that great city 2
Mic 4:10 for now you shall go forth from the city 4
5:11 I will cut off the cities of your land 2
14 out your Ashe'rim . . and destroy your cities. 2
6: 9 The voice of the LORD cries to the city 2
9 Hear, O tribe and assembly of the city! •
Nah 3: 1 Woe to the bloody city, all full of lies and booty 2
Hab 2: 8 to the earth, to cities and all who dwell therein. 4
12 a town with blood, and founds a city on iniquity! 2
17 to the earth, to cities and all who dwell therein. 4
Zep 1:16 and battle cry against the fortified cities 2
2:15 This is the exultant city that dwelt secure 2
3: 1 rebellious and defiled, the oppressing city! 2
6 their cities have been made desolate 2
Zec 1:12 mercy on Jerusalem and the cities of Judah 2
17 My cities shall again overflow with prosperity 2
7: 7 in prosperity, with her cities round about her 2
8: 3 Jerusalem shall be called the faithful city 2
5 And the streets of the city shall be full of boys 2
20 yet come, even the inhabitants of many cities; 2
21 the inhabitants of one city shall go to another •
9: 1 For to the LORD belong the cities of Aram •
14: 2 the city shall be taken and the houses plundered 2
2 half of the city shall go into exile 2
2 the people shall not be cut off from the city. 2
Mat 2:23 he went and dwelt in a city called Nazareth 8
4: 5 Then the devil took him to the holy city, and set 8
5:14 A city set on a hill cannot be hid. 8
35 for it is the city of the great King. 8
8:33 The herdsmen fled, and going into the city 8
34 behold, all the city came out to meet Jesus 8
9: 1 he crossed over and came to his own city. 8
35 Jesus went about all the cities and villages 8
11: 1 to teach and preach in their cities. 8
20 Then he began to upbraid the cities 8
12:25 no city or house divided against itself 8
21:10 all the city was stirred, saying 8
17 went out of the city to Bethany and lodged there. 8
18 In the morning, as he was returning to the city 8
22: 7 destroyed . . murderers and burned their city 8
26:18 Go into the city to a certain one, and say to him 8
27:53 went into the holy city and appeared to many. 8
28:11 behold, some of the guard went into the city 8
Mrk 1:33 the whole city was gathered together 8
5:14 told it in the city and in the country 8
6:56 wherever he came, in villages, cities, or country 8
11:19 when evening came they went out of the city. 8
14:13 Go into the city 8
16 the disciples set out and went to the city 8
Lke 1:26 to a city of Galilee named Nazareth 8
39 into the hill country, to a city of Judah 8
2: 3 all went to be enrolled, each to his own city. 8
4 from Galilee, from the city of Nazareth, to Judea 8
4 to the city of David, which is called Bethlehem 8
11 born this day in the city of David a Savior 8
39 into Galilee, to their own city, Nazareth. 8
4:29 they rose up and put him out of the city 8
29 brow of the hill on which their city was built 8
31 he went down to Caper'na-um, a city of Galilee. 8
43 preach the good news . . to the other cities also 8
5:12 While he was in one of the cities 8
7:11 Soon afterward he went to a city called Na'in 8
12 As he drew near to the gate of the city 8
12 a large crowd from the city was with her. 8
37 behold, a woman of the city, who was a sinner 8
8: 1 he went on through cities and villages 8
27 there met him a man from the city who had demons 8
34 told it in the city and in the country. 8
39 proclaiming throughout the whole city 8
9:10 withdrew apart to a city called Beth-sa'ida. 8
14:21 Go out quickly to the streets and lanes of the city 8
18: 2 He said, "In a certain city there was a judge 8
3 a widow in that city who kept coming to him 8
19:17 you shall have authority over ten cities.' 8
19 he said . . 'And you are to be over five cities.' 8
41 when he drew near and saw the city he wept over it 8
21:21 let those who are inside the city depart •
22:10 when you have entered the city 8
23:19 an insurrection started in the city 8
24:49 stay in the city, until you are clothed with power 8
Joh 1:44 from Beth-sa'ida, the city of Andrew and Peter. 8
4: 5 So he came to a city of Samar'ia, called Sy'char 8
8 For his disciples had gone away into the city 8
28 left her water jar, and went away into the city 8
30 They went out of the city and were coming to him. 8
39 Many Samaritans from that city believed in him 8
19:20 the place . . was near the city 8
Act 4:27 truly in this city there were gathered together 8
7:58 Then they cast him out of the city and stoned him; 8
8: 5 Philip went down to a city of Sama'ria 8
8 there was much joy in that city. 8
9 who had previously practiced magic in the city 8
9: 6 rise and enter the city 8
10: 9 on their journey and coming near the city 8
11: 5 I was in the city of Joppa praying 8
12:10 they came to the iron gate leading into the city. 8
13:44 almost the whole city gathered together 8
50 the Jews incited . . the leading men of the city 8
14: 4 the people of the city were divided 8
6 fled to Lystra and Derbe, cities of Lycao'nia 8
13 whose temple was in front of the city 8
19 they stoned Paul and dragged him out of the city 8
20 he rose up and entered the city 8
21 When they had preached the gospel to that city 8
15:21 Moses has had in every city those who preach him 8
36 in every city where we proclaimed the word 8
16: 4 As they went on their way through the cities 8
12 the leading city of the district of Macedo'nia 8
12 We remained in this city some days; 8
14 Lydia, from the city of Thyati'ra 8
20 they are disturbing our city. 8
39 took them out and asked them to leave the city. 8
17: 5 they gathered a crowd, set the city in an uproar 8
16 as he saw that the city was full of idols. 8
18:10 I have many people in this city. 8
19:29 So the city was filled with the confusion; 8
35 the city of the Ephesians is temple keeper 8
20:23 the Holy Spirit testifies to me in every city 8
21: 5 till we were outside the city 8
29 Troph'imus the Ephesian with him in the city 8
30 Then all the city was aroused 8
39 from Tarsus in Cili'cia, a citizen of no mean city 8
22: 3 but brought up in this city at the feet of Gama'li-el 8
24:12 in the temple or in the synagogues, or in the city. 8
25:23 the prominent men of the city 8
26:11 I persecuted them even to foreign cities. 8
27: 8 Fair Havens, near which was the city of Lase'a. 8
Rom 16:23 Eras'tus, the city treasurer, and . . greet you. 8
2Co 11:26 danger from Gentiles, danger in the city 8
32 the governor under King Ar'etas guarded the city 8
Heb 11:10 the city which has foundations 8
16 he has prepared for them a city. 8
12:22 the city of the living God 8
13:14 For here we have no lasting city 8
14 we seek the city which is to come. •
2Pe 2: 6 the cities of Sodom and Gomor'rah to ashes 8
Jde 1: 7 Sodom and Gomor'rah and the surrounding cities 8
Rev 3:12 and the name of the city of my God 8
11: 2 they will trample over the holy city for 42 months. 8
8 city which is allegorically called Sodom 8
13 great earthquake, and a tenth of the city fell; 8
14:20 the wine press was trodden outside the city 8
16:19 The great city was split into three parts 8
19 and the cities of the nations fell 8
17:18 And the woman that you saw is the great city 8
18:10 alas! thou great city, thou mighty city, Babylon! 8
10 alas! thou great city, thou mighty city, Babylon! 8
16 Alas, alas, for the great city 8
18 What city was like the great city? •
18 What city was like the great city? 8
19 Alas, alas, for the great city 8
21 So shall Babylon the great city be thrown down 8
20: 9 and surrounded . . the beloved city; 8
21: 2 I saw the holy city, new Jerusalem, coming down 8
10 and showed me the holy city Jerusalem 8
14 And the wall of the city had twelve foundations 8
15 to measure the city and its gates and walls. 8
16 The city lies foursquare 8
16 and he measured the city with his rod 8
18 while the city was pure gold, clear as glass. 8
19 The foundations of the wall of the city 8
21 and the street of the city was pure gold 8
22 And I saw no temple in the city •
23 the city has no need of sun or moon to shine upon it 8
22: 2 through the middle of the street of the city; •
14 that they may enter the city by the gates. 8
19 God will take away his share . . in the holy city 8
1Es 2:18 are building that rebellious and wicked city 8
19 Now if this city is built and the walls finished 8
22 will learn that this city was rebellious 8
22 troubling both kings and other cities 8
23 That is why this city was laid waste. 8
24 if this city is built and its walls finished 8
26 this city from of old has fought against kings 8
28 to prevent these men from building the city 8
4:48 to help him build the city. 8
53 all who came from Babylonia to build the city 8
56 should be provided for all who guarded the city 8
6: 8 when we . . entered the city of Jerusalem 8
9 in the city of Jerusalem 8
2Es 3: 1 the 30th year after the destruction of our city 9
24 didst command him to build a city for thy name 9
25 the inhabitants of the city transgressed 9
27 deliver the city into the hands of thy enemies. 9
5:25 from all the cities that have been built 9
7: 6 There is a city built and set on a plain 9
9 If now that city is given to a man 9
26 that the city which now is not seen shall appear 9
8:52 a city is built, rest is appointed 9
10: 4 I intend not to return to the city, but to stay here 9
17 Therefore go into the city to your husband. 9
18 I will not go into the city, but I will die here. 9
27 there was an established city 9
42 but an established city has appeared to you- 9
44 whom you now behold as an established city 9
46 after 3,000 years Solomon built the city 9
54 the city of the Most High was to be revealed. 9
12:40 I had not returned to the city 9
50 the people went into the city, as I told them to do. 9
13:31 city against city, place against place 9
31 city against city, place against place 9
15:17 For a man will desire to go into a city 9
18 the cities shall be in confusion 9
42 they shall destroy cities and walls, mountains 9
57 and your cities shall be wiped out 9
60 as they pass they shall wreck the hateful city 9
62 they shall devour you and your cities 9
16:23 and its cities shall be demolished. 9
28 For out of a city, ten shall be left 9
47 the more they adorn their cities, their houses 9
70 For in many places and in neighboring cities 9
Tob 13: 9 O Jerusalem, the holy city, he will afflict you 8
Jdt 1: 1 the great city of Nineveh 8
14 Thus he took possession of his cities 8
2:24 destroyed all the hilltop cities 8
27 sacked their cities and ravaged their lands 8
3: 4 Our cities also and their inhabitants 8
6 and stationed garrisons in the hilltop cities 8
4:12 the cities they had inherited to be destroyed 8
5: 3 What cities do they inhabit? 8
18 their cities were captured by their enemies. 8
6: 7 put you in one of the cities beside the passes 8
12 When the men of the city saw them 8
12 they caught up their weapons and ran out of the city 8
14 Then the men of Israel came down from their city 8
14 placed him before the magistrates of their city 8
16 They called together all the elders of the city 8
7: 7 examined the approaches to the city 8
13 and they will give up their city 8
13 to keep watch that not a man gets out of the city. 8
22 and fell down in the streets of the city 8
23 gathered about Uzziah and the rulers of the city 8
26 Now call them in and surrender the whole city 8
32 the walls and towers of their city 8
32 they were greatly depressed in the city. 8
8: 3 took to his bed and died in Bethulia his city 8
9 to surrender the city to the Assyrians 8
10 Chabris and Charmis, the elders of her city 8
11 promising to surrender the city to our enemies 8
18 any tribe or family or people or city of ours 8
33 Stand at the city gate tonight •
33 promised to surrender the city to our enemies 8
10: 6 Then they went out to the city gate of Bethulia 8
6 the elders of the city, Chabris and Charmis. 8
9 Order the gate of the city to be opened for me 8
10 the men of the city watched her 8
13:12 When the men of her city heard her voice 8
12 they hurried down to the city gate 8
12 and called together the elders of the city 8
14: 2 take his weapons and go out of the city 8
9 made a joyful noise in their city. 8
AEs 11: 3 He was a Jew, dwelling in the city of Susa 8
16:24 Every city and country, without exception 8
Wis 9: 8 an altar in the city of thy habitation 8
Sir 9: 7 Do not look around in the streets of a city 8
13 you are going about on the city battlements. 8
18 A babbler is feared in his city 8
10: 2 like the ruler of the city 8
3 a city will grow 8
16: 4 a city will be filled with people 8
23:21 will be punished in the streets of the city 8
24:11 In the beloved city likewise 8
26: 5 The slander of a city, the gathering of a mob 8
28:14 destroyed strong cities 8
31:24 The city will complain 8
36:13 Have pity on the city of thy sanctuary, Jerusalem 8
26 a nimble robber that skips from city to city 8
26 a nimble robber that skips from city to city 8
38:32 Without them a city cannot be established 8
40:19 Children and the building of a city 8
42:11 a byword in the city 8
46: 2 stretched out his sword against the cities! 8
48:17 Hezekiah fortified his city 8
49: 6 who set fire to the chosen city of the sanctuary 8
50: 4 fortified the city to withstand a seige. 8
Bar 2:23 I will make to cease from the cities of Judah 8
4:32 the cities which your children served as slaves; 8
32 wretched will be the city •
Aza 1: 5 Jerusalem, the holy city of our fathers 8
1Mc 1:19 the fortified cities in the land of Egypt 8
29 the cities of Judah 8
30 he suddenly fell upon the city 8
31 He plundered the city, burned it with fire 8
33 Then they fortified the city of David 8
44 to Jerusalem and the cities of Judah 8
51 the cities of Judah to offer sacrifice 8
51 to offer sacrifice, city by city. 8
51 to offer sacrifice, city by city. 8
54 built altars in the surrounding cities of Judah 8
58 those found month after month in the cities. 8
2: 7 the ruin of my people, the ruin of the holy city 8
15 the king's officers . . came to the city of Modein 8
17 You are a leader, honored and great in this city 8

27 cried out in the city with a loud voice, saying 8
28 left all that they had in the city. 8
31 the troops in Jerusalem the city of David 8
3: 8 He went through the cities of Judah; 8
5:26 - all these cities were strong and large- 8
27 have been shut up in the other cities of Gilead; 8
28 he took the city 8
31 the cry of the city went up to Heaven 8
36 Bosor, and the other cities of Gilead. 8
44 he took the city 8
46 This was a large and very strong city on the road 8
47 the men of the city shut them out 8
50 he fought against the city 8
50 the city was delivered into his hands. 8
51 and razed and plundered the city •
51 Then he passed through the city over the slain. 8
59 came out of the city to meet them in battle. 8
68 he plundered the cities 8
6: 1 Elymais in Persia was a city famed for its wealth 8
3 he came and tried to take the city and plunder it 8
3 his plan became known to the men of the city 8
7 also Beth-zur, his city. 8
49 they evacuated the city 8
63 He found Philip in control of the city 8
63 took the city by force. 8
7: 1 sailed with a few men to a city by the sea 8
24 he prevented those in the city from going out •
32 the rest fled into the city of David. 8
9:50 built strong cities in Judea 8
52 He also fortified the city of Beth-zur, and Gazara 8
65 Jonathan left Simon his brother in the city 8
67 Simon and his men sallied out from the city 8
10:10 began to rebuild and restore the city. 8
63 Go forth with him into the middle of the city 8
71 for I have with me the power of the cities. 8
75 the men of the city closed its gates 8
76 the men of the city became afraid 8
86 the men of the city came out to meet him 8
11: 2 the people of the cities opened their gates to him 8
3 when Ptolemy entered the cities 8
3 he stationed forces as a garrison in each city. 8
8 King Ptolemy gained control of the coastal cities 8
45 the men of the city assembled within the city 8
45 the men of the city assembled within the city 8
46 Then the men of the city seized the main streets 8
46 the men . . seized the main streets of the city 8
47 and then spread out through the city 8
48 They set fire to the city 8
49 When the men of the city saw 8
49 the Jews had gained control of the city 8
50 stop fighting against us and our city. 8
60 beyond the river and among the cities 8
60 the people of the city met him and paid him honor. 8
66 took possession of the city 8
12:36 a high barrier between the citadel and the city 8
36 to separate it from the city 8
37 So they gathered together to build up the city; 8
13:25 buried him in Modein, the city of his fathers. 8
43 made a siege engine, brought it up to the city 8
44 The men in the siege engine leaped out into the city 8
44 a great tumult arose in the city. 8
45 The men in the city, with their wives and children 8
47 he expelled them from the city 8
14:10 He supplied the cities with food 8
17 he was ruling over the country and the cities in it 8
20 The rulers and the city of the Spartans 8
33 He fortified the cities of Judea, and Beth-zur 8
34 in those cities •
36 the men in the city of David in Jerusalem 8
37 the safety of the country and of the city 8
15: 4 those who have devastated many cities 8
14 He surrounded the city 8
14 he pressed the city hard from land and sea 8
19 against them and their cities and their country 8
28 they are cities of my kingdom. 8
30 hand over the cities which you have seized 8
31 the tribute money of the cities 8
16:14 Now Simon was visiting the cities of the country 8
18 to turn over to him the cities and the country. 8
2Mc 1:12 those who fought against the holy city. 8
2:22 freed the city 8
3: 1 While the holy city was inhabited 8
4 about the administration of the city market; 8
8 the cities of Coelesyria and Phoenicia 8
9 kindly welcomed by the high priest of the city 8
14 no little distress throughout the whole city. 8
4: 2 the man who was the benefactor of the city 8
22 welcomed magnificently by Jason and the city 8
30 because their cities had been given as a present •
32 he had sold to Tyre and the neighboring cities. 8
36 the Jews in the city appealed to him 8
38 led him about the whole city to that very place 8
39 acts of sacrilege . . in the city by Lysimachus 8
48 those who had spoken for the city 8
5: 2 over all the city, for almost 40 days 8
5 suddenly made an assault upon the city 8
5 at last the city was being taken 8
8 fleeing from city to city 8
8 fleeing from city to city 8

11 he left Egypt and took the city by storm. 8
17 because of the sins of those who dwelt in the city 8
26 then rushed into the city with his armed men 8
6: 8 was issued to the neighboring Greek cities 8
10 These . . they publicly paraded about the city 8
8: 3 to have mercy on the city 8
11 he immediately sent to the cities on the seacoast 8
17 the torture of the derided city 8
9: 2 For he had entered the city called Persepolis •
2 rob the temples and control the city 8
14 the holy city 8
10: 1 recovered the temple and the city; 8
27 a considerable distance from the city 8
36 they occupied the city. 8
11: 2 He intended to make the city a home for Greeks 8
12: 4 this was done by public vote of the city 8
13 He also attacked a certain city 8
16 They took the city by the will of God 8
27 Ephron, a fortified city where Lysias dwelt 8
28 they got the city into their hands 8
38 went to the city of Adullam 8
13:13 and get possession of the city. 8
14 the laws, temple, city, country, and commonwealth 8
15:14 prays much for the people and the holy city 8
17 the city and the sanctuary and the temple 8
19 those who had to remain in the city 8
37 the city has been in the possession of the Hebrews 8
3Mc 1: 6 decided to visit the neighboring cities 8
17 those who remained behind in the city 8
19 Those women . . flocked together in the city. 8
2: 9 chose this city and sanctified this place 8
31 maintaining the religion of their city 8
3: 8 The Greeks in the city, though wronged in no way 8
16 very great revenues to the temples in the cities 8
4: 3 What district or city 8
4 the generals in the several cities 8
11 the hippodrome . . in front of the city 8
11 to all coming back into the city 8
11 to those from the city going out into the country •
12 the Jews' compatriots from the city 8
5:24 The crowds of the city had been assembled 8
41 As a result the city is in a tumult 8
44 the places in the city most favorable 8
46 the city now being filled with countless masses 8
6: 5 Sennacherib . . was lifted up against your holy city 8
30 when he had returned to the city 8
41 wrote . . to the generals in the cities 8
7:16 those . . began their departure from the city 8
4Mc 7: 4 No city besieged 8

city *See also* authority, gate, inside, wall.

city of one's fathers 1. πατρίς
2Mc 8:33 in the city of their fathers 1

civilian 1. βίος
2Ti 2: 4 gets entangled in civilian pursuits 1

clad 1. כסה 2. לבש 3. περιβάλλω 4. στολὴ ἔχω
2Sm 13:18 thus were the virgin daughters . . clad of old. 2
1Kg 11:29 Now Ahi'jah had clad himself with a new garment; 1
Rev 3: 5 He who conquers shall be clad thus in white 3
4: 4 elders, clad in white garments, with golden 3
19:13 He is clad in a robe dipped in blood 3
2Mc 5: 2 there appeared golden-clad horsemen 4

claim 1. אמר 2. גאל 3. דָּבָר 4. ἀφορμή 5. καταξιόω 6. λογίζομαι 7. ποιέω 8. φάσκω
2Sm 15: 3 See, your claims are good and right; 3
Job 3: 5 Let gloom and deep darkness claim it. 2
Ecc 8:17 even though a wise man claims to know 1
Joh 8:53 And the prophets died! Who do you claim to be? 7
Rom 1:22 Claiming to be wise, they became fools 8
2Co 3: 5 competent of ourselves to claim anything 6
11:12 to do, in order to undermine the claim 4
12 who would like to claim 4
3Mc 4:11 claim to be inside the circuit of the city. 5

claim *See also* lay.

rightful claim 1. ἐξουσία
1Co 9:12 If others share this rightful claim upon you 1

clamor 1. צפף 2. קוֹל 3. שָׁאוֹן 4. κραυγή
Ps 74:23 Do not forget the clamor of thy foes 2
Isa 38:14 Like a swallow or a crane I clamor 1
Jer 25:31 The clamor will resound to the ends of the earth 3
Lam 2: 7 a clamor was raised in the house of the LORD 2
Act 23: 9 Then a great clamor arose 4
Eph 4:31 wrath and anger and clamor and slander 4

clamp 1. מְחַבְּרָה 2. ποδάγρα
1Ch 22: 3 iron for nails for the doors . . for clamps 1
4Mc 11:10 fitting iron clamps on them 2

clan 1. אַלּוּף 2. אֶלֶף 3. מִשְׁפָּחָה 4. פְּלַגָּה 5. cognatio
Gen 36:30 chiefs of the Horites, according to their clans 2
Num 1:16 These were . . the heads of the clans of Israel. 2
Jos 22:14 the head of a family among the clans of Israel. 2
Jdg 5:15 Among the clans of Reuben there were great 4
16 Among the clans of Reuben there were great 4
6:15 Behold, my clan is the weakest in Manas'seh 2
9: 1 them and to the whole clan of his mother's family 3
12: 9 30 daughters he gave in marriage outside his clan •
Isa 60:22 The least one shall become a clan 2
Mic 5: 2 who are little to be among the clans of Judah 2
Zec 9: 7 it shall be like a clan in Judah 1
12: 5 Then the clans of Judah shall say to themselves 1
6 I will make the clans of Judah like a blazing pot 1
2Es 3: 7 peoples and clans without number. 5

clang 1. ἀλαλάζω
1Co 13: 1 I am a noisy gong or a clanging cymbal. 1

clank 1. συγκρουσμός
1Mc 6:41 the clanking of their arms 1

clap 1. מחא 2. נכה 3. ספק 4. תקע 5. ἐπικροτέω 6. percussio
2Kg 11:12 and they clapped their hands, and said, "Long live 2
Job 27:23 It claps its hands at him, and hisses at him 3
34:37 he claps his hands among us 3
Ps 47: 1 Clap your hands, all peoples! Shout to God 4
98: 8 Let the floods clap their hands; 1
Isa 55:12 the trees of the field shall clap their hands. 1
Lam 2:15 All who pass along the way clap their hands at you; 3
Ezk 6:11 Clap your hands, and stamp your foot, and say, Alas! 2
21:14 clap your hands and let the sword come down twice 2
17 I also will clap my hands 2
25: 6 Because you have clapped your hands 1
Nah 3:19 hear the news of you clap their hands over you. 4
2Es 15:53 exulting and clapping your hands 6
Sir 12:18 he will shake his head, and clap his hands 5

clap of thunder 1. βροντή
Sir 40:13 crash like a loud clap of thunder in a rain. 1

loud clashing 1. תְּרוּעָה
Ps 150: 5 praise him with loud clashing cymbals! 1

clasp 1. קֶרֶס
Exd 26: 6 you shall make 50 clasps of gold 1
6 curtains one to the other with the clasps 1
11 you shall make 50 clasps of bronze 1
11 and put the clasps into the loops 1
33 you shall hang the veil from the clasps, and bring 1
36:13 he made 50 clasps of gold 1
13 coupled the curtains . . with clasps; 1
18 he made 50 clasps of bronze to couple the tent 1

clasp each other 1. לכד
Job 41:17 they clasp each other and cannot be separated. 1

class 1. ἐγκρίνω
2Co 10:12 venture to class or compare ourselves with some 1

claw 1. צִפֹּר (A) 2. χείρ
Dan 4:33 till . . his nails were like birds' claws. •
7:19 with its teeth of iron and claws of bronze; 1
4Mc 8:13 braziers and thumbscrews and iron claws 2

clay 1. חֹמֶר 2. טִיט 3. חֲסַף (A) 4. πηλός 5. fictilis 6. terra
2Ch 4:17 in the clay ground between Succoth and Zer'edah. •
Job 4:19 how much more those who dwell in houses of clay 1
10: 9 Remember that thou hast made me of clay; 1
13:12 your defenses are defenses of clay. 1
27:16 silver like dust, and pile up clothing like clay; 1
33: 6 I too was formed from a piece of clay. 1
38:14 It is changed like clay under the seal 1
Isa 29:16 Shall the potter be regarded as the clay; 1
41:25 as on mortar, as the potter treads clay. 2
45: 9 Does the clay say to him who fashions it 1
64: 8 we are the clay, and thou art our potter; 1
Jer 18: 4 And the vessel he was making of clay was spoiled 1
6 Behold, like the clay in the potter's hand 1
Dan 2:33 its feet partly of iron and partly of clay. 3
34 smote the image on its feet of iron and clay 3
35 the clay, the bronze, the silver, and the gold 3
41 toes partly of potter's clay and partly of iron 3
41 just as you saw iron mixed with the miry clay. 3
42 toes of the feet were partly iron and partly clay 3
43 As you saw the iron mixed with miry clay 3
43 not hold . . just as iron does not mix with clay. 3
45 broke in pieces the iron, the bronze, the clay 3
Nah 3:14 go into the clay, tread the mortar 2
Joh 9: 6 made clay of the spittle 4
6 and anointed the man's eyes with the clay 4
11 He answered, "The man called Jesus made clay 4
14 when Jesus made the clay and opened his eyes. 4
15 He put clay on my eyes, and I washed 4
Rom 9:21 Has the potter no right over the clay 4
2Es 7:52 will you add to them lead and clay? ‡
55 and also iron and lead and clay; 5
56 and lead than iron, and clay than lead.' 5
8: 2 it provides very much clay 6
Wis 7: 9 silver will be accounted as clay before her. 4

15: 7 he fashions out of the same clay 4
8 he forms a futile god from the same clay 4
10 his life is of less worth than clay 4
Sir 33:13 As clay in the hand of the potter 4
38:30 He moulds the clay with his arm 4
Bel 1: 7 this is but clay inside and brass outside 4

clay *See also* ground, pot, worker.

clean 1. בַּר 2. זַךְ 3. זכה 4. זכך 5. טָהוֹר 6. טהר 7. נָקִי 8. עטה 9. *καθαίρω* 10. *καθαρίζω* 11. *καθαρός*

Gen 7: 2 Take with you seven pairs of all clean animals 5
2 and a pair of the animals that are not clean 5
8 Of clean animals and of animals 5
8 clean animals and of animals that are not clean 5
8:20 Noah . . took of every clean animal 5
20 clean animal and of every clean bird 5
Lev 4:12 a clean place, where the ashes are poured out 5
6:11 the ashes outside the camp to a clean place 5
7:19 All who are clean may eat flesh 5
10:10 between the unclean and the clean 5
14 you shall eat in any clean place, you and your sons 5
11:32 until the evening; then it shall be clean 6
36 a cistern holding water shall be clean 5
37 seed for sowing that is to be sown, it is clean 5
47 distinction between the unclean and the clean 5
12: 7 she shall be clean from the flow of her blood 6
8 make atonement for her, and she shall be clean 6
13: 6 and he shall wash his clothes, and be clean 6
13 it has all turned white, and he is clean 5
17 priest shall pronounce . . he is clean 5
34 he shall wash his clothes, and be clean 6
37 the itch is healed, he is clean 5
39 tetter . . has broken out in the skin; he is clean 5
40 hair has fallen . . is bald but he is clean 5
41 he has baldness of the forehead but he is clean 5
58 shall then be washed a second time, and be clean 6
59 to decide whether it is clean or unclean 6
14: 4 him who is to be cleansed two living clean birds 5
8 he shall be clean; and after that he shall come 6
9 and bathe his body in water, and he shall be clean 6
20 make atonement for him, and he shall be clean 6
53 atonement for the house, and it shall be clean 6
57 to show when it is unclean and when it is clean 5
15: 8 who has the discharge spits on one who is clean 5
13 bathe . . in running water, and shall be clean 6
28 seven days, and after that she shall be clean 6
16:30 you shall be clean before the LORD 6
17:15 unclean until the evening; then he shall be clean 6
20:25 between the clean beast and the unclean 5
25 and between the unclean bird and the clean 5
22: 4 may eat of the holy things until he is clean 6
7 When the sun is down he shall be clean 6
Num 5:28 if the woman has not defiled herself and is clean 5
9:13 the man who is clean and is not on a journey, yet 5
18:11 every one who is clean in your house may eat of it. 5
13 every one who is clean in your house may eat of it. 5
19: 9 man who is clean shall gather up the ashes 5
9 deposit them outside the camp in a clean place; 5
12 shall cleanse himself . . and so be clean; 6
12 if he does not . . he will not become clean. 6
18 then a clean person shall take hyssop, and dip it 5
19 at evening he shall be clean. 6
31:23 pass through the fire, and it shall be clean. 6
24 on the seventh day, and you shall be clean; 6
Deu 12:15 unclean and the clean may eat of it 5
22 unclean and the clean alike may eat of it. 5
14:11 You may eat all clean birds. 5
20 All clean winged things you may eat. 5
15:22 unclean and the clean alike may eat it, as though 5
23:10 man who is not clean by reason of what chances 5
1Sm 20:26 he is not clean, surely he is not clean. 5
26 he is not clean, surely he is not clean. 5
2Sm 4: 6 the doorkeeper . . had been cleaning wheat 9
2Kg 5:10 flesh shall be restored, and you shall be clean. 6
12 Could I not wash in them, and be clean? 6
13 when he says to you, 'Wash, and be clean'? 6
14 his flesh was restored like . . and he was clean. 6
2Ch 30:17 the passover lamb for every one who was not clean 5
Ezr 6:20 purified themselves . . all of them were clean. 5
Job 11: 4 My doctrine is pure, and I am clean in God's eyes.' 1
15:14 What is man, that he can be clean? 3
15 the heavens are not clean in his sight; 4
17: 9 he that has clean hands grows stronger 5
25: 4 How can he who is born of woman be clean? 3
5 the stars are not clean in his sight; 4
33: 9 You say, 'I am clean, without transgression; 2
Ps 19: 9 the fear of the LORD is clean, enduring for ever; 5
24: 4 He who has clean hands and a pure heart 7
51: 7 Purge me with hyssop, and I shall be clean; 6
10 Create in me a clean heart, O God 5
Ecc 9: 2 the good and the evil, to the clean and the unclean 5
Isa 66:20 in a clean vessel to the house of the LORD. 5
Jer 43:12 he shall clean the land of Egypt, as a shepherd 8
12 as a shepherd cleans his cloak of vermin; 8
Ezk 22:26 difference between the unclean and the clean 5
36:25 I will sprinkle clean water upon you 5
25 you shall be clean from all your uncleannesses 6
37:11 our hope is lost; we are clean cut off •
44:23 distinguish between the unclean and the clean. 5
26 count . . seven days, and then he shall be clean. ‡
Zec 3: 5 I said, "Let them put a clean turban on his head. 5
5 they put a clean turban on his head 5
Mat 8: 3 saying, "I will; be clean. 10
23:26 that the outside also may be clean. 11
27:59 and wrapped it in a clean linen shroud 11
Mrk 1:41 I will; be clean. 10
Lke 5:13 I will; be clean. 10
11:41 behold, everything is clean for you. 11
Joh 13:10 he is clean all over; and you are clean 11
10 you are clean, but not every one of you. 11
11 that was why he said, "You are not all clean. 11
15: 3 You are already made clean by the word 11
Rom 14:20 Everything is indeed clean 11
Heb 10:22 with our hearts sprinkled clean •
Jdt 12: 9 she returned clean and stayed in the tent 11
Wis 15: 7 both the vessels that serve clean uses 11
Sir 38:30 he is careful to clean the furnace. 10

clean *See also* declare, keep, make, pronounce.

make clean 1. טהר

Jer 13:27 How long will it be before you are made clean? 1

clean person 1. טָהוֹר

Num19:19 clean person shall sprinkle upon the unclean 1

clean thing 1. טָהוֹר

Job 14: 4 Who can bring a clean thing out of an unclean? 1

cleanness 1. בַּר 2. נִקָּיוֹן

2Sm 22:21 according to the cleanness of my hands he 1
25 according to my cleanness in his sight. 1
Job 22:30 delivered through the cleanness of your hands. 1
Ps 18:20 according to the cleanness of my hands 1
24 the cleanness of my hands in his sight. 1
Ams 4: 6 I gave you cleanness of teeth in all your cities 2

cleanness *See also* rule.

cleanse 1. ברר 2. דוח 3. זכך 4. חטא 5. טהר 6. טָהֳרָה 7. מִשְׁעִי 8. רחץ 9. *καθαρίζω* 10. *καθαρισμός*

Lev 13: 7 he has shown himself . . for his cleansing 6
35 itch spreads in the skin after his cleansing 6
14: 2 law of the leper for the day of his cleansing 6
4 for him who is to be cleansed two living birds 5
7 upon him who is to be cleansed of leprosy 5
8 he who is to be cleansed shall wash his clothes 5
11 the priest who cleanses him shall set the man 5
11 priest . . shall set the man who is to be cleansed 5
14 the tip of the right ear of him who is be cleansed 5
17 right ear of him who is to be cleansed 5
18 put on the head of him who is to be cleansed 5
19 to make atonement for him who is to be cleansed 5
23 eighth day he shall bring them for his cleansing 6
25 the right ear of him who is to be cleansed 5
28 right ear of him who is to be cleansed 5
29 shall put on the head of him who is to be cleansed 5
31 atonement . . for him who is being cleansed 5
32 cannot afford the offerings for his cleansing 6
49 for the cleansing of the house he shall take two 4
52 Thus he shall cleanse the house with the blood 4
15:13 who has a discharge is cleansed of his discharge 5
13 count for himself seven days for his cleansing 6
28 But if she is cleansed of her discharge 5
16:19 cleanse it and hallow it from the uncleannesses 5
30 shall atonement be made for you, to cleanse you 5
Num 6: 9 shall shave his head on the day of his cleansing; 6
8: 6 Take the Levites . . and cleanse them. 5
7 thus you shall do to them, to cleanse them 5
7 wash their clothes and cleanse themselves. 5
15 when you have cleansed them and offered them 5
21 Aaron made atonement for them to cleanse them. 5
19:12 shall cleanse himself with the water 4
12 if he does not cleanse himself on the third day 4
13 touches . . and does not cleanse himself 4
19 thus on the seventh day he shall cleanse him 4
20 man who is unclean and does not cleanse himself 4
Jos 22:17 from which . . we have not cleansed ourselves 5
1Ch 23:28 the care of . . the cleansing of all that is holy 6
2Ch 29:15 went in . . to cleanse the house of the LORD. 5
16 priests went into the inner part . . to cleanse 5
18 We have cleansed all the house of the LORD 5
30:18 a multitude . . had not cleansed themselves 5
Neh 13: 9 I gave orders and they cleansed the chambers; 5
30 Thus I cleansed them from everything foreign 5
Job 9:30 If I wash myself . . and cleanse my hands with lye 3
Ps 51: 2 from my iniquity, and cleanse me from my sin! 5
Prv 30:12 own eyes but are not cleansed of their filth. 8
Isa 4: 4 washed away . . and cleansed the bloodstains 2
Jer 4:11 toward . . my people, not to winnow or cleanse 1
33: 8 I will cleanse them from all the guilt 5
Ezk 16: 4 nor were you washed with water to cleanse you 7
22:24 say to her, You are a land that is not cleansed 5
24:13 Because I would have cleansed you 5
13 you were not cleansed from your filthiness 5
13 you shall not be cleansed any more 5
36:25 from all your idols I will cleanse you. 5
33 On the day that I cleanse you 5
37:23 in which they have sinned, and will cleanse them; 5
39:12 burying them, in order to cleanse the land. 5
14 upon the face of the land, so as to cleanse it; 5
16 Thus shall they cleanse the land. 5
43:20 you shall cleanse the altar and make atonement 4
22 the altar shall be cleansed, as it was cleansed 4
22 cleansed, as it was cleansed with the bull. 4
23 When you have finished cleansing it 4
45:18 without blemish, and cleanse the sanctuary. 4
Dan 11:35 refine and to cleanse them and to make them white 1
Zec 13: 1 to cleanse them from sin and uncleanness. •
Mat 8: 3 And immediately his leprosy was cleansed. 9
10: 8 Heal the sick, raise the dead, cleanse lepers 9
11: 5 lame walk, lepers are cleansed and the deaf hear 9
23:25 you cleanse the outside of the cup 9
26 first cleanse the inside of the cup 9
Mrk 1:44 and offer for your cleansing what Moses commanded 10
Lke 4:27 none of them was cleansed 9
5:14 and make an offering for your cleansing 10
7:22 lepers are cleansed, and the deaf hear 9
11:39 Now you Pharisees cleanse the outside of the cup 9
17:14 as they went they were cleansed. 9
17 Were not ten cleansed? Where are the nine? 9
Act 10:15 What God has cleansed, you must not call common. 9
11: 9 'What God has cleansed you must not call common.' 9
15: 9 cleansed their hearts by faith. 9
2Co 7: 1 let us cleanse ourselves from every defilement 9
Eph 5:26 cleansed her by the washing of water with the word 9
Heb 10: 2 If the worshipers had once been cleansed 9
Jas 4: 8 Cleanse your hands, you sinners 9
2Pe 1: 9 forgotten that he was cleansed from his old sins 10
1Jn 1: 7 blood of Jesus his Son cleanses us from all sin. 9
9 and cleanse us from all unrighteousness. 9
Sir 23:10 will not be cleansed from sin. 9
38:10 cleanse your heart from all sin. 9
1Mc 4:36 let us go up to cleanse the sanctuary 9
41 until he had cleansed the sanctuary. 9
43 they cleansed the sanctuary 9
13:47 cleansed the houses in which the idols were 9
50 cleansed the citadel from its pollutions. 9

cleanse away 1. מרק

Prv 20:30 Blows that wound cleanse away evil; 1

cleanse out 1. *ἐκκαθαίρω*

1Co 5: 7 Cleanse out the old leaven 1

clear 1. ברא 2. טהר 3. מִשְׁקָע 4. נקה 5. נָקִי 6. סקל 7. פנה 8. צדק 9. צַח 10. *ἀγαθός* 11. *ἀναφαίνω* 12. *ἀπρόσκοπος* 13. *διακαθαρίζω* 14. *ἐμφανής* 15. *ἐπίδηλος* 16. *καθάριος* 17. *καθαρός* 18. *καλός* 19. *σαφής* 20. *τρανός* 21. *φαιδρός*

Gen 44:16 What shall we speak? Or how can we clear ourselves 8
Exd 21:19 he that struck him shall be clear; 4
28 but the owner of the ox shall be clear. 5
Num14:18 but he will by no means clear the guilty 4
Jos 17:18 though . . a forest, you shall clear it and possess 1
1Ch 28:19 All this he made clear by the writing •
Job 15: 9 What do you understand that is not clear to us? •
37:21 skies, when the wind has passed and cleared them. 2
Ps 19:12 Clear thou me from hidden faults. 4
80: 9 Thou didst clear the ground for it; 7
Isa 18: 4 from my dwelling like clear heat in sunshine 9
62:10 build up, build up the highway, clear it of stones 6
Ezk 34:18 to drink of clear water, that you must foul 3
Mat 3:12 and he will clear his threshing floor and gather 13
Lke 3:17 to clear his threshing floor 13
Act 24:16 I always take pains to have a clear conscience 12
1Ti 3: 9 must hold . . the faith with a clear conscience. 17
2Ti 1: 3 I thank God whom I serve with a clear conscience 17
Heb 13:18 we are sure that we have a clear conscience 18
1Pe 3:16 keep your conscience clear 10
21 but as an appeal to God for a clear conscience 10
Rev 21:18 while the city was pure gold, clear as glass. 17
Wis 6:22 make knowledge of her clear 14
7:22 holy, unique, manifold, subtle, mobile, clear 20
Sir 43: 1 the clear firmament 16
2Mc 6:30 It is clear to the Lord in his holy knowledge 21
12:40 it became clear to all 19
15:35 a clear and conspicuous sign to every one 15
4Mc 1: 4 it is also clear 11

clear *See also* declaration, eagerness, make, omen.

clear as crystal 1. *κρυσταλλίζω*

Rev 21:11 its radiance . . like a jasper, clear as crystal. 1

clear away 1. נשל

Deu 7: 1 the LORD . . clears away many nations before you 1
22 LORD . . will clear away these nations before you 1

clear ground 1. ברא

Jos 17:15 clear ground for yourselves in the land 1

make clear 1. שקע

Ezk 32:14 Then I will make their waters clear 1

clear of stone 1. סקל

Isa 5: 2 He digged it and cleared it of stones, and planted 1

clear out 1. יצא
Lev 26:10 clear out the old to make way for the new 1

clear the guilty 1. נקה
Exd 34: 7 who will by no means clear the guilty 1
Nah 1: 3 and the LORD will by no means clear the guilty. 1

clearly 1. בִּינָה 2. מַרְאֶה 3. פרש 4. ἀκριβῶς 5. δῆλος 6. νοέω 7. σαφής 8. τηλαυγῶς 9. φανερῶς
Num12: 8 With him I speak mouth to mouth, clearly 2
Neh 8: 8 read from the book, from the law of God, clearly 3
Jer 23:20 the latter days you will understand it clearly. 1
Mrk 8:25 was restored, and saw everything clearly. 8
Act 10: 3 he saw clearly in a vision an angel of God 9
Rom 1:20 clearly perceived in the things 6
Wis 19:18 This may be clearly inferred 4
2Mc 3:28 recognized clearly the sovereign power of God. 9
3Mc 4:19 he was clearly convinced about the matter 7
4Mc 2: 7 unless reason is clearly lord of the emotions? 5
clearly *See also* speak.

more clearly 1. σαφής
4Mc 3: 6 Now this can be explained more clearly 1

clearness 1. טֹהַר
Exd 24:10 like the very heaven for clearness. 1

cleave 1. בקע 2. פלח 3. excido
Ps 78:15 He cleft rocks in the wilderness 1
141: 7 rock which one cleaves and shatters on the land 2
Isa 48:21 he cleft the rock and the water gushed out. 1
Mic 1: 4 valleys will be cleft, like wax before the fire 1
Hab 3: 9 Thou didst cleave the earth with rivers. 1
2Es 1:20 did I not cleave the rock 3

cleave (2) 1. דבק 2. ספח 3. κολλάω 4. προσκολλάω
Gen 2:24 leaves . . his mother and cleaves to his wife 1
Num36: 7 every one . . shall cleave to the inheritance 1
9 tribe . . shall cleave to its own inheritance.' 1
Deu 10:20 LORD . . you shall serve him and cleave to him 1
11:22 commandment . . and cleaving to him 1
13: 4 you shall serve him and cleave to him. 1
17 None . . shall cleave to your hand; that the LORD 1
28:60 diseases of Egypt . . shall cleave to you. 1
30:20 loving . . obeying his voice, and cleaving to him; 1
Jos 22: 5 and to keep his commandments, and to cleave to him 1
23: 8 but cleave to the LORD your God as you have done 1
2Sm 23:10 hand was weary, and his hand cleaved to the sword; 1
2Kg 5:27 the leprosy of Na'aman shall cleave to you 1
Job 19:20 My bones cleave to my skin and to my flesh 1
29:10 their tongue cleaved to the roof of their mouth. 1
31: 7 if any spot has cleaved to my hands; 1
38:38 into a mass and the clods cleave fast together? 1
Ps 22:15 my tongue cleaves to my jaws; 1
44:25 our body cleaves to the ground. 1
101: 3 it shall not cleave to me. 1
102: 5 of my loud groaning my bones cleave to my flesh. 1
119:25 My soul cleaves to the dust; 1
31 I cleave to thy testimonies, O LORD; 1
137: 6 Let my tongue cleave to the roof of my mouth, if I do 1
Isa 14: 1 aliens . . will cleave to the house of Jacob. 2
Lam 4: 4 The tongue . . cleaves to the roof of its mouth 1
1Es 4:20 A man leaves . . and cleaves to his wife. 3
Sir 2: 3 Cleave to him and do not depart 3
6:34 Who is wise? Cleave to him. 4

cleave in love 1. חשק
Ps 91:14 Because he cleaves to me in love, I will deliver 1

make cleave 1. דבק
Deu 28:21 LORD will make the pestilence cleave to you 1
Ezk 3:26 I will make your tongue cleave to the roof 1

cleave open 1. בקע
Ps 74:15 Thou didst cleave open springs and brooks; 1

cleave together 1. דבק
Job 41:23 The folds of his flesh cleave together 1

cleft 1. חֲגָוִים 2. נָקִיק 3. נְקָרָה 4. סָעִיף 5. פלג 6. fissura
Exd 33:22 while my glory passes by I will put you in a cleft 3
Jdg 15: 8 down and stayed in the cleft of the rock of Etam. 4
11 Judah went down to the cleft of the rock of Etam 4
Job 38:25 Who has cleft a channel for the torrents of rain 5
Sng 2:14 O my dove, in the clefts of the rock, in the covert 1
Isa 2:21 to enter . . the clefts of the cliffs 4
7:19 the steep ravines, and in the clefts of the rocks 2
57: 5 valleys, and under the clefts of the rocks? 4
Jer 13: 4 and hide it there in a cleft of the rock. 3
16:16 and every hill, and out of the clefts of the rocks. 2
49:16 you who live in the clefts of the rock 1
Obd 1: 3 you who live in the clefts of the rock 1
2Es 16:28 in thick groves and clefts in the rocks. 6

clemency 1. ἐπιείκεια
3Mc 3:15 cherish them with clemency 1
7: 6 the clemency which we have toward all men 1

clerk *See* town.

clever 1. πανοῦργος 2. συνετός
1Co 1:19 the cleverness of the clever I will thwart. 2
Sir 6:32 if you apply yourself you will become clever. 1
21:12 He who is not clever cannot be taught 1
20 a clever man smiles quietly. 1
clever *See also* device.

cleverly 1. γενναίως
2Mc 14:31 he had been cleverly outwitted by the man 1
cleverly *See also* devise.

cleverness 1. πανουργία 2. σύνεσις
1Co 1:19 the cleverness of the clever I will thwart. 2
Sir 19:23 There is a cleverness which is abominable 1
25 is a cleverness which is scrupulous but unjust 1
21:12 a cleverness which increases bitterness. 1
34:10 he that has traveled acquires much cleverness. 1
cleverness *See also* display.

cliff 1. מַדְרֵגָה 2. סֶלַע
Sng 2:14 the clefts of the rock, in the covert of the cliff 1
Isa 2:21 to enter . . the clefts of the cliffs 2
Ezk 38:20 the cliffs shall fall 1

jutting cliff 1. πρόκρημνος
4Mc 7: 5 in setting his mind firm like a jutting cliff 1

climb 1. עלה 2. ἀναβαίνω
Sng 7: 8 I say I will climb the palm tree and lay hold of its 1
Isa 24:18 he who climbs out of the pit shall be caught 1
Jer 4:29 they enter thickets; they climb among rocks; 1
48:44 he who climbs out of the pit shall be caught 1
Joh 10: 1 but climbs in by another way 2

climb over 1. ὑπερβαίνω
4Mc 3:12 soldiers . . climbed over the enemy's ramparts. 1

climb up 1. עלה 2. ἀναβαίνω
1Sm 14:13 Then Jonathan climbed up on his hands and feet 1
Jol 2: 9 they climb up into the houses 1
Ams 9: 2 though they climb up to heaven 1
Lke 19: 4 and climbed up into a sycamore tree 2

cling 1. דבק 2. חבק 3. κολλάω 4. κρατέω 5. κράτος 6. προσκολλάω 7. cohero
Rut 1:14 and Orpah kissed her . . but Ruth clung to her. 1
1Kg 11: 2 Solomon clung to these in love. 1
2Kg 3: 3 he clung to the sin of Jerobo'am the son of Nebat 1
Job 24: 8 and cling to the rock for want of shelter. 2
Ps 63: 8 My soul clings to thee; thy right hand upholds me. 1
Jer 13:11 For as the waistcloth clings to the loins of a man 1
Lke 10:11 'Even the dust of your town that clings to our feet 3
Act 3:11 While he clung to Peter and John 4
2Es 12:19 eight little wings clinging to his wings 7
Sir 10:13 the man who clings to it pours out abominations. 5
13:16 a man clings to one like himself. 6
Bar 1:20 there have clung to us the calamities 3
3: 4 so that calamities have clung to us. 3

make cling 1. דבק
Jer 13:11 I made the whole house of Israel . . cling to me 1

cling so closely 1. εὐπερίστατος
Heb 12: 1 every weight, and sin which clings so closely 1

cloak 1. בֶּגֶד 2. כְּסוּת 3. מִטְפַּחַת 4. שַׂלְמָה 5. ἱμάτιον 6. πρόφασις 7. φαιλόνης 8. χλαμύς
Deu 22:12 tassels on the four corners of your cloak 2
24:13 restore . . pledge that he may sleep in his cloak 4
Isa 3:22 the mantles, the cloaks, and the handbags; 3
Jer 43:12 as a shepherd cleans his cloak of vermin; 1
Mat 5:40 your coat, let him have your cloak as well; 5
Mrk 15:17 they clothed him in a purple cloak •
20 they stripped him of the purple cloak •
1Th 2: 5 or a cloak for greed, as God is witness; 6
2Ti 4:13 bring the cloak that I left with Carpus at Tro'as 7
2Mc 12:35 grasping his cloak 8

clod 1. מֶגְרָפָה 2. רֶגֶב
Job 21:33 The clods of the valley are sweet to him; 2
38:38 into a mass and the clods cleave fast together? 2
Jol 1:17 The seed shrivels under the clods 1

clog 1. συνδέω
Exd 14:25 clogging their chariot wheels 1

close 1. אֵצֶל 2. לְעֻמַּת 3. נגע 4. קרב 5. ἀναγκαῖος 6. ἐν 7. ἐπί 8. καρδία 9. παρά 10. περισσοτέρως
Exd 25:27 Close to the frame the rings shall lie, as holders 2
37:14 Close to the frame were the rings, as holders 2
Lev 3: 9 fat tail . . taking it away close by the backbone 2
Jdg 20:34 did not know that disaster was close upon them. 3
41 for they saw that disaster was close upon them. 3
Isa 13:22 its time is close at hand and its days 4
Dan 8: 7 I saw him come close to the ram, and he was enraged 1
Joh 13:23 was lying close to the breast of Jesus; 6
25 lying thus, close to the breast of Jesus, he said 7
Act 10:24 called together his kinsmen and close friends. 5
Heb 2: 1 Therefore we must pay the closer attention 10
AEs 16: 7 investigation of matters close at hand. 9
Sir 16:24 pay close attention to my words. 8

close (2) 1. אטם 2. אטר 3. אפף 4. כסה 5. נקף 6. סגר 7. סכר 8. סתם 9. עטר 10. עלם 11. עצם 12. עצר 13. עָרֵל 14. צוּף 15. צפן 16. שית על 17. שעע 18. ἀποκλείω 19. καμμύω 20. κλείω 21. πτύσσω 22. συγκλείω 23. συντέλεια 24. claudo
Gen 8: 2 and the windows of the heavens were closed 7
20:18 For the LORD had closed all the wombs of the house 12
46: 4 and Joseph's hand shall close your eyes. 16
Num16:33 earth closed over them, and they perished 4
Jos 2: 5 when the gate was to be closed, at dark, the men went 6
Jdg 3:22 after the blade, and the fat closed over the blade 6
23 Ehud . . closed the doors of the roof chamber 6
1Sm 1: 5 only one . . because the LORD had closed her womb. 6
6 because the LORD had closed her womb. 6
23:26 Saul and his men were closing in 9
2Ch 32:30 Hezeki'ah closed the upper outlet of the waters 8
Neh 4: 7 that the breaches were beginning to be closed 8
6:10 meet . . and let us close the doors of the temple; 6
Job 17: 4 thou hast closed their minds to understanding 15
19: 6 put me in the wrong, and closed his net about me. 5
Ps 17:10 They close their hearts to pity; 6
69:15 or the pit close its mouth over me. 2
77: 4 Thou dost hold my eyelids from closing; •
88:17 they close in upon me together. 5
Prv 17:28 when he closes his lips, he is deemed intelligent. 1
21:13 He who closes his ear to the cry of the poor 1
Isa 29:10 and has closed your eyes, the prophets 11
32: 3 Then the eyes of those who see will not be closed 17
45: 1 to open doors . . that gates may not be closed 6
Jer 6:10 Behold, their ears are closed, they cannot listen; 13
Lam 3:54 water closed over my head; I said, 'I am lost.' 14
56 'Do not close thine ear to my cry for help!' 10
Jon 2: 5 The waters closed in over me 3
6 I went down to the land whose bars closed upon me •
Mat 13:15 and their eyes they have closed 19
39 the harvest is the close of the age 23
40 so will it be at the close of the age. 23
49 So it will be at the close of the age 23
24: 3 the close of the age? 23
28:20 I am with you always, to the close of the age. 23
Lke 4:20 he closed the book, and gave it back to the attendant 21
Act 28:27 their eyes they have closed 19
1Jn 3:17 sees . . in need, yet closes his heart against him 20
2Es 5:37 open for me the closed chambers 24
14:41 my mouth was opened, and was no longer closed. 24
Jdt 5: 1 had closed the passes in the hills 22
13: 1 Bagoas closed the tent from outside 22
Sir 11:27 at the close of a man's life 23
30:18 poured out upon a mouth that is closed 20
1Mc 10:75 the men of the city closed its gates 18
12:48 the men of Ptolemais closed the gates and seized him 18
2Mc 1:15 they closed the temple as soon as he entered it. 22
12: 7 because the city's gates were closed, he withdrew 22
close *See* come, draw, formation, friend, inshore, keep, lean, lie, stick.

close at hand 1. ἐγγύς 2. προσμείγνυμι 3. ὑπόγυος 4. in proximo
Joh 19:42 as the tomb was close at hand 1
2Es 2:34 he who will come . . is close at hand. 4
2Mc 12:31 the feast of weeks was close at hand. 3
15:20 the enemy was already close at hand 2

close behind 1. רֶגֶל 2. κατὰ πόδας
Hab 3: 5 pestilence, and plague followed close behind. 1
1Mc 9:16 they . . followed close behind Judas and his men. 2

close by 1. ἐγγύς 2. παρά
Sir 51:26 it is to be found close by. 1
2Mc 4:42 they killed close by the treasury. 2

close to death 1. גוע
Ps 88:15 Afflicted and close to death from my youth up 1

close up 1. סגר
Gen 2:21 took one . . and closed up its place with flesh; 1
1Kg 11:27 and closed up the breach of the city of David 1

close upon 1. דבק
2Sm 1: 6 chariots and the horsemen were close upon him. 1

closely 1. צַר 2. ἀκριβῶς 3. ἀτενίζω
Job 41:15 rows of shields, shut up closely as with a seal. 1
Lke 1: 3 having followed all things closely for some time past 2
Act 11: 6 Looking at it closely I observed animals 3
closely *See also* cling, look.

more closely 1. ἀκριβής
Act 23:20 to inquire somewhat more closely about him. 1

closet 1. חֶדֶר
Jdg 3:24 himself in the closet of the cool chamber. 1

cloth 1. בֶּגֶד 2. שִׂמְלָה 3. ῥάκος 4. σουδάριον
Lev 19:19 a garment of cloth made of two kinds of stuff •
Num 4: 6 spread over that a cloth all of blue 1
7 they shall spread a cloth of blue 1
8 they shall spread over them a cloth of scarlet 1
9 take a cloth of blue, and cover the lampstand 1
11 golden altar they shall spread a cloth of blue 1
12 put them in a cloth of blue, and cover them 1
13 the altar, and spread a purple cloth over it; 1
1Sm 21: 9 sword of Goliath . . is here wrapped in a cloth 2
Ezk 16:10 I clothed you also with embroidered cloth •
13 fine linen, and silk, and embroidered cloth; •
Mat 9:16 no one puts a piece of unshrunk cloth 3
Mrk 2:21 sews a piece of unshrunk cloth on an old garment; 3
Joh 11:44 his face wrapped with a cloth 4

cloth dyed blue 1. ὑάκινθος
1Mc 4:23 and cloth dyed blue and sea purple, and great riches. 1

linen cloth 1. ὀθόνιον 2. σινδών
Mrk 14:51 with nothing but a linen cloth about his body 2
52 he left the linen cloth and ran away naked. 2
Joh 19:40 and bound it in linen cloths with the spices 1
20: 5 he saw the linen cloths lying there 1
6 went into the tomb; he saw the linen cloths lying 1
7 and the napkin . . not lying with the linen cloths 1

swaddling cloth 1. σπάργανον
Wis 7: 4 I was nursed with care in swaddling cloths. 1

clothe 1. בִּלְבוּשׁ 2. כסה 3. כרבל 4. לבשׁ
5. לבשׁ (A) 6. ἀμφιέννυμι 7. ἐγκομβόομαι
8. ἐδιδύσκω 9. ἐνδιδύσκω 10. ἐνδύω 11. ἐν ἐσθῆτι
12. ἱματίζω 13. περιβάλλω 14. vestio
Gen 3:21 made . . garments of skins, and clothed them. 4
Lev 8: 7 clothed him with the robe, and put the ephod upon 4
13 Moses . . clothed them with coats, and girded 4
1Sm 17:38 Then Saul clothed David with his armor; 4
38 and clothed him with a coat of mail. 4
2Sm 1:24 over Saul, who clothed you daintily in scarlet 4
1Ch 15:27 David was clothed with a robe of fine linen 3
21:16 David and the elders, clothed in sackcloth 2
2Ch 6:41 Let thy priests . . be clothed with salvation 4
28:15 with the spoil they clothed all that were naked 4
15 they clothed them, gave them sandals 4
Est 4: 2 enter the king's gate clothed with sackcloth. 1
4 she sent garments to clothe Mor'decai 4
Job 7: 5 My flesh is clothed with worms and dirt; 4
8:22 Those who hate you will be clothed with shame 4
10:11 Thou didst clothe me with skin and flesh 4
29:14 I put on righteousness, and it clothed me; 4
37:22 God is clothed with terrible majesty. •
39:19 Do you clothe his neck with strength? 4
40:10 clothe yourself with glory and splendor. 4
Ps 35:26 Let them be clothed with shame and dishonor 4
65:13 the meadows clothe themselves with flocks 4
104: 1 Thou art clothed with honor and majesty 4
109:18 He clothed himself with cursing as his coat 4
29 May my accusers be clothed with dishonor; 4
132: 9 Let thy priests be clothed with righteousness 4
16 Her priests I will clothe with salvation 4
18 His enemies I will clothe with shame 4
Prv 23:21 drowsiness will clothe a man with rags. 4
31:21 for all her household are clothed in scarlet. 4
Isa 14:19 clothed with the slain 4
22:21 I will clothe him with your robe 4
37: 2 the senior priests, clothed with sackcloth 2
50: 3 I clothe the heavens with blackness 4
61:10 he has clothed me with the garments of salvation 4
Ezk 9: 2 with them was a man clothed in linen 4
3 #he called to the man clothed in linen 4
11 lo, the man clothed in linen, with the writing case 4
10: 2 And he said to the man clothed in linen 4
6 And when he commanded the man clothed in linen 4
7 put it into the hands of the man clothed in linen 4
16:10 I clothed you also with embroidered cloth 4
23: 6 warriors clothed in purple, governors 4
12 warriors clothed in full armor, horsemen riding 4
26:16 they will clothe themselves with trembling; 4
31:15 I will clothe Lebanon in gloom for it 4
34: 3 you clothe yourselves with the wool 4
38: 4 and horsemen, all of them clothed in full armor 4
Dan 5: 7 clothed with purple, and have a chain of gold 5
16 clothed with purple, and have a chain of gold 5
29 Daniel was clothed with purple, a chain of gold 5
10: 5 behold, a man clothed in linen, 4
12: 6 I said to the man clothed in linen, who was above 4
7 The man clothed in linen, who was above the waters 4
Hag 1: 6 you clothe yourselves, but no one is warm; 4
Zec 3: 3 Joshua was . . clothed with filthy garments. 4
4 I will clothe you with rich apparel. 4
5 turban on his head and clothed him with garments; 4
Mat 6:30 will he not . . clothe you, O men of little faith? •
11: 8 To see a man clothed in soft raiment? 6
25:36 I was naked and you clothed me 13
38 naked and clothe thee? 13
43 naked and you did not clothe me 13
Mrk 1: 6 Now John was clothed in camel's hair 10
5:15 sitting there, clothed and in his right mind 12
15:17 they clothed him in a purple cloak 9
Lke 7:25 A man clothed in soft clothing? 6
8:35 and found the man . . clothed and in his right mind 12
12:28 how much more will he clothe you •
16:19 who was clothed in purple and fine linen 8
24:49 stay in the city, until you are clothed with power 10
1Pe 5: 5 Clothe yourselves, all of you, with humility 7
Rev 1:13 clothed with a long robe and with a golden girdle 10
3:18 and white garments to clothe you 13
7: 9 clothed in white robes, with palm branches 13
13 Who are these, clothed in white robes 13
11: 3 power to prophesy . . clothed in sackcloth. 13
12: 1 a woman clothed with the sun 13
18:16 the great city that was clothed in fine linen 13
19: 8 it was granted her to be clothed with fine linen 13
1Es 3: 6 He shall be clothed in purple 13
2Es 2:20 defend the orphan, clothe the naked 14
AEs 15: 6 clothed in the full array of his majesty 10
Sir 40: 4 the one who is clothed in burlap; 13
45: 8 He clothed him with superb perfection 10
50:11 clothed himself with superb perfection 9
LJr 1:33 to clothe their wives and children. 10
1Mc 1:28 all the house of Jacob was clothed with shame. 10
10:62 and to clothe him in purple, and they did so. 10
64 and saw him clothed in purple 13
14:43 he should be clothed in purple and wear gold. 13
44 to be clothed in purple or put on a gold buckle. 13
2Mc 11: 8 clothed in white 11

clothe further 1. ἐπενδύομαι
2Co 5: 4 but that we would be further clothed 1

clothe in gloom 1. קדר
Ezk 31:15 I will clothe Lebanon in gloom for it 1

clothe in scarlet 1. תלע
Nah 2: 3 his soldiers are clothed in scarlet. 1

clothes 1. בֶּגֶד 2. גְּלוֹם 3. מַד 4. מֶלַח 5. שַׂלְמָה
6. שִׂמְלָה 7. ἀμφιέζω 8. ἀμφιέννυμι 9. ἐπενδύτης
10. ἱμάτιον 11. στολή 12. χιτών 13. vestimentum
Gen 37:29 Joseph was not in the pit, he rent his clothes 1
41:14 and changed his clothes, he came in before 6
44:13 Then they rent their clothes 6
Lev 10: 6 do not rend your clothes, lest you die 1
11:25 shall wash his clothes and be unclean 1
28 shall wash his clothes and be unclean 1
40 he who eats of its carcass shall wash his clothes 1
40 he . . shall wash his clothes and be unclean 1
13: 6 and he shall wash his clothes, and be clean 1
34 he shall wash his clothes, and be clean 1
45 The leper . . shall wear torn clothes 1
14: 8 he who is to be cleansed shall wash his clothes 1
9 Then he shall wash his clothes, and bathe his body 1
47 lies down in the house shall wash his clothes 1
47 he who eats in the house shall wash his clothes 1
15: 5 one who touches his bed shall wash his clothes 1
6 shall wash his clothes, and bathe himself 1
7 shall wash his clothes, and bathe himself 1
8 then he shall wash his clothes, and bathe himself 1
10 he . . shall wash his clothes, and bathe himself 1
11 shall wash his clothes, and bathe himself in water 1
13 and wash his clothes; and he shall bathe his body 1
21 whoever touches her bed shall wash his clothes 1
22 shall wash his clothes, and bathe himself in water 1
27 shall wash his clothes, and bathe himself in water 1
16:26 he . . shall wash his clothes and bathe his body 1
28 he who burns them shall wash his clothes 1
17:15 shall wash his clothes, and bathe himself in water 1
21:10 The priest . . shall not . . nor rend his clothes 1
Num 8: 7 wash their clothes and cleanse themselves. 1
21 purified themselves . . washed their clothes; 1
14: 6 Joshua . . and Caleb . . , rent their clothes 1
19: 7 priest shall wash his clothes and bathe his body 1
8 burns the heifer shall wash his clothes in water 1
10 he who gathers . . shall wash his clothes 1
19 he shall wash his clothes and bathe himself 1
21 water for impurity shall wash his clothes; 1
31:24 You must wash your clothes on the seventh day 1
Deu 29: 5 your clothes have not worn out upon you 5
Jos 7: 6 Joshua rent his clothes, and fell to the earth 6
9: 5 worn-out, patched sandals . . and worn-out clothes; 5
Jdg 3:16 girded it on his right thigh under his clothes. 3
11:35 when he saw her, he rent his clothes, and said, "Alas 1
1Sm 4:12 came to Shiloh . . with his clothes rent 3
19:13 put a pillow . . and covered it with the clothes. 1
24 And he too stripped off his clothes 1
2Sm 1: 2 with his clothes rent and earth upon his head. 1
11 Then David took hold of his clothes, and rent them; 1
3:31 Rend your clothes, and gird on sackcloth 1
12:20 and anointed himself, and changed his clothes; 6
19:24 nor trimmed his beard, nor washed his clothes 1
1Kg 1: 1 although they covered him with clothes, he could 1
21:27 when Ahab heard those words, he rent his clothes 1
2Kg 2:12 Then he took hold of his own clothes and rent them 1
5: 7 he rent his clothes and said, "Am I God 1
8 that the king of Israel had rent his clothes 1
8 Why have you rent your clothes? 1
6:30 When the king heard . . he rent his clothes 1
11:14 And Athali'ah rent her clothes, and cried, "Treason! 1
18:37 came to Hezeki'ah with their clothes rent 1
19: 1 he rent his clothes, and covered himself 1
22:11 when the king heard . . he rent his clothes. 1
19 and you have rent your clothes and wept before me 1
2Ch 23:13 Athali'ah rent her clothes, and cried, "Treason! 1
34:19 When the king heard . . he rent his clothes. 1
27 have rent your clothes and wept before me 1
Neh 4:23 none of us took off our clothes; 1
9:21 their clothes did not wear out and their feet 5
Est 4: 1 Mor'decai rent his clothes and put on sackcloth 1
Job 9:31 into a pit, and my own clothes will abhor me. 5
Prv 6:27 fire in his bosom and his clothes not be burned? 1
Isa 4: 1 We will eat our own bread and wear our own clothes 6
36:22 came to Hezeki'ah with their clothes rent 1
37: 1 When King Hezeki'ah heard it, he rent his clothes 1
Jer 38:12 Put the rags and clothes between your armpits 4
41: 5 with their beards shaved and their clothes torn 1
Ezk 16:39 they shall strip you of your clothes 1
23:26 They shall also strip you of your clothes 1
27:24 in clothes of blue and embroidered work 2
Mat 6:30 But if God so clothes the grass of the field 8
27:31 put his own clothes on him 10
Mrk 15:20 and put his own clothes on him 10
Lke 8:27 for a long time he had worn no clothes 10
12:28 if God so clothes the grass 7
Joh 21: 7 he put on his clothes, for he was stripped for work 9
1Es 4:17 Women make men's clothes; they bring men glory 11
2Es 9:38 her clothes were rent 13
LJr 1:31 the priests sit with their clothes rent 12
1Mc 2:14 Mattathias and his sons rent their clothes 10
3:47 rent their clothes. 10
4:39 Then they rent their clothes 10
13:45 went up on the wall with their clothes rent 10

fine clothes 1. ἱμάτιον
Sir 11: 4 Do not boast about wearing fine clothes 1

good clothes 1. שִׂמְלָה
Rut 3: 3 anoint yourself, and put on your best clothes 1

worn-out clothes 1. בְּלוֹאֵי מְלָחִים
Jer 38:11 and took from there old rags and worn-out clothes 1

clothing 1. בֶּגֶד 2. כְּסוּת 3. לְבוּשׁ 4. מְכַסֶּה 5. מַלְבּוּשׁ
6. שַׂלְמָה 7. שִׂמְלָה 8. תִּלְבֹּשֶׁת 9. ἔνδυμα 10. ἐσθής
11. ἔσθησις 12. ἱμάς 13. ἱμάτιον 14. ἱματισμός
15. σκέπασμα 16. στολή 17. tunica
Gen 28:20 give me bread to eat and clothing to wear 1
Exd 3:22 ask of her . . clothing, and you shall put them 7
12:35 jewelry of silver and of gold, and clothing; 7
21:10 not diminish her food, her clothing, or her 2
22: 9 for ass, for sheep, or clothing, or for any kind 6
Deu 8: 4 Your clothing did not wear out upon you 7
10:18 sojourner, giving him food and clothing. 7
Jos 22: 8 gold, bronze, and iron, and with much clothing; 6
1Kg 10: 5 the attendance of his servants, their clothing 5
2Kg 7: 8 they carried off silver and gold and clothing 1
2Ch 9: 4 attendance of his servants, and their clothing 5
4 his cupbearers, and their clothing 5
20:25 found cattle in great numbers, goods, clothing 1
Job 22: 6 and stripped the naked of their clothing. 1
24: 7 They lie all night naked, without clothing 3
10 They go about naked, without clothing; hungry 3
27:16 silver like dust, and pile up clothing like clay; 5
31:19 if I have seen any one perish for lack of clothing 3
Ps 69:11 When I made sackcloth my clothing 3
Prv 27:26 the lambs will provide your clothing 3
31:22 her clothing is fine linen and purple. 3
25 Strength and dignity are her clothing 3
Isa 23:18 supply abundant food and fine clothing 4
59: 6 Their webs will not serve as clothing; 1
17 he put on garments of vengeance for clothing 8
Jer 10: 9 their clothing is violet and purple; 3
Mat 6:25 than food, and the body more than clothing? 9
28 And why are you anxious about clothing? Consider 9
7:15 who come to you in sheep's clothing 9
Lke 7:25 A man clothed in soft clothing? 12
12:23 the body more than clothing. 9
Joh 19:24 for my clothing they cast lots. 14
1Ti 6: 8 if we have food and clothing 15
Jas 2: 2 For if a man with gold rings and in fine clothing 10
2 a poor man in shabby clothing also comes in 10
3 to the one who wears the fine clothing 10
1Pe 3: 3 adorning . . and wearing of fine clothing 13
2Es 2:45 they who have put off mortal clothing 17
Tob 1:17 I would give . . my clothing to the naked 13
4:16 Give . . of your clothing to the naked 13
Jdt 10: 7 noted how . . her clothing changed 16
Sir 29:21 clothing and a house to cover one's nakedness. 13
39:26 the blood of the grape, and oil and clothing. 13
LJr 1:33 take some of the clothing of their gods 14
1Mc 11:24 taking silver and gold and clothing 14

2Mc 3:33 dressed in the same clothing 11
cloths *See* wrap.

cloud 1. מַשְׂאֵת 2. נָשִׂיא 3. עָב 4. עָנָן 5. עֲנָנָה 6. עָרִיף 7. שַׁחַק 8. עֲנָן (A) 9. *νεφέλη* 10. *νέφος* 11. nubes
Gen 9:13 I set my bow in the cloud, and it shall be a sign 4
14 the earth and the bow is seen in the clouds 4
16 When the bow is in the clouds, I will look upon it 4
Exd 13:21 LORD went before them by day in a pillar of cloud 4
22 the pillar of cloud by day and the pillar of fire 4
14:19 and the pillar of cloud moved from before them 4
20 And there was the cloud and the darkness; 4
24 the LORD in the pillar of fire and of cloud looked 4
16:10 the glory of the LORD appeared in the cloud. 4
19: 9 Lo, I am coming to you in a thick cloud 4
16 a thick cloud upon the mountain 4
24:15 and the cloud covered the mountain. 4
16 Mount Sinai, and the cloud covered it six days; 4
16 he called to Moses out of the midst of the cloud. 4
18 Moses entered the cloud, and went up 4
33: 9 When Moses entered the tent, the pillar of cloud 4
10 saw the pillar of cloud standing at the door 4
34: 5 the LORD descended in the cloud and stood 4
40:34 Then the cloud covered the tent of meeting 4
35 not able to enter . . because the cloud abode upon it, 4
36 whenever the cloud was taken up 4
37 if the cloud was not taken up, then they did not go 4
38 the cloud of the LORD was upon the tabernacle 4
Lev 16: 2 I will appear in the cloud upon the mercy seat 4
13 the cloud of the incense may cover the mercy seat 4
Num 9:15 cloud covered the tabernacle, the tent 4
16 it was continually; the cloud covered it by day 4
17 whenever the cloud was taken up from over 4
17 in the place where the cloud settled down 4
18 as long as the cloud rested over the tabernacle 4
19 cloud continued over the tabernacle many days 4
20 cloud was a few days over the tabernacle 4
21 cloud remained from evening until morning; 4
21 cloud was taken up in the morning, they set out 4
21 when the cloud was taken up they set out. 4
22 that the cloud continued over the tabernacle 4
10:11 cloud was taken up from over the tabernacle 4
12 cloud settled down in the wilderness of Paran. 4
34 the cloud of the LORD was over them by day 4
11:25 LORD came down in the cloud and spoke to him 4
12: 5 LORD came down in a pillar of cloud, and stood 4
10 when the cloud removed from over the tent, behold 4
14:14 thy cloud stands over them and thou goest 4
14 thou goest before them, in a pillar of cloud by day 4
16:42 tent of meeting; and behold, the cloud covered it 4
Deu 1:33 who went before you . . in the cloud by day. 4
4:11 mountain . . wrapped in darkness, cloud, and gloom. 4
5:22 mountain out of the midst of the fire, the cloud 4
31:15 LORD appeared in the tent in a pillar of cloud; 4
15 pillar of cloud stood by the door of the tent. 4
Jdg 5: 4 heavens dropped, yea, the clouds dropped water. 3
20:38 when they made a great cloud of smoke rise up out 1
1Kg 8:10 a cloud filled the house of the LORD 4
11 could not stand to minister because of the cloud; 4
18:44 a little cloud like a man's hand is rising 3
45 the heavens grew black with clouds and wind 3
2Ch 5:13 the house of the LORD, was filled with a cloud. 4
14 could not stand to minister because of the cloud; 4
Neh 9:12 pillar of cloud thou didst lead them in the day 4
19 pillar of cloud . . not depart from them by day 4
Job 3: 5 deep darkness claim it. Let clouds dwell upon it; 5
7: 9 As the cloud fades and vanishes 4
20: 6 to the heavens, and his head reach to the clouds 3
26: 8 the cloud is not rent under them. 4
9 and spreads over it his cloud. 4
30:15 my prosperity has passed away like a cloud. 3
35: 5 behold the clouds, which are higher than you. 7
36:29 any one understand the spreading of the clouds 3
37:11 the clouds scatter his lightning. 4
15 causes the lightning of his cloud to shine? 4
16 Do you know the balancings of the clouds 3
38: 9 when I made clouds its garment 4
34 Can you lift up your voice to the clouds 3
36 Who has put wisdom in the clouds •
37 Who can number the clouds by wisdom? 7
Ps 18:11 his canopy thick clouds dark with water. 3
12 there broke through his clouds hailstones 3
36: 5 to the heavens, thy faithfulness to the clouds. 7
57:10 to the heavens, thy faithfulness to the clouds. 7
68: 4 lift up a song to him who rides upon the clouds; •
77:17 The clouds poured out water; the skies gave forth 3
78:14 In the daytime he led them with a cloud 4
97: 2 Clouds and thick darkness are round about him; 4
99: 7 He spoke to them in the pillar of cloud; 4
104: 3 who makest the clouds thy chariot 3
105:39 He spread a cloud for a covering 4
108: 4 thy faithfulness reaches to the clouds. 7
135: 7 who makes the clouds rise at the end of the earth 2
147: 8 He covers the heavens with clouds 3
Prv 3:20 by his knowledge . . clouds drop down the dew. 7
16:15 favor . . the clouds that bring the spring rain. 3
25:14 Like clouds and wind without rain is a man 2
Ecc 11: 3 If the clouds are full of rain 3
4 and he who regards the clouds will not reap. 3
12: 2 and the stars are darkened and the clouds return 3
Isa 4: 5 over her assemblies a cloud by day, and smoke 4
5: 6 command the clouds that they rain no rain upon it. 3
30 and the light is darkened by its clouds. 6
14:14 I will ascend above the heights of the clouds 3
18: 4 like a cloud of dew in the heat of harvest. 3
19: 1 Behold, the LORD is riding on a swift cloud 3
25: 5 as heat by the shade of a cloud 3
44:22 swept away your transgressions like a cloud 3
60: 8 Who are these that fly like a cloud, 3
Jer 4:13 Behold, he comes up like clouds 4
Lam 3:44 thou hast wrapped thyself with a cloud 4
Ezk 1: 4 wind came out of the north, and a great cloud 4
28 the bow that is in the cloud on the day of rain 4
8:11 and the smoke of the cloud of incense went up. 4
10: 3 and a cloud filled the inner court. 4
4 and the house was filled with the cloud 4
30: 3 day of the LORD is near; it will be a day of clouds 4
18 she shall be covered by a cloud 4
31: 3 and of great height, its top among the clouds. 9
10 it towered high and set its top among the clouds 9
14 or set their tops among the clouds 9
32: 7 I will cover the sun with a cloud 4
34:12 scattered on a day of clouds and thick darkness. 4
38: 9 you will be like a cloud covering the land 4
16 my people Israel, like a cloud covering the land. 4
Dan 7:13 clouds of heaven there came one like a son of man 8
Hos 6: 4 Your love is like a morning cloud, like the dew 4
Jol 2: 2 a day of clouds and thick darkness! 4
Nah 1: 3 and the clouds are the dust of his feet. 4
3:17 your scribes like clouds of locusts †
Zep 1:15 a day of clouds and thick darkness 4
Mat 17: 5 when lo, a bright cloud overshadowed them 9
5 and a voice from the cloud said 9
24:30 see the Son of man coming on the clouds of heaven 9
26:64 coming on the clouds of heaven. 9
Mrk 9: 7 a cloud overshadowed them 9
7 a voice came out of the cloud 9
13:26 then they will see the Son of man coming in clouds 9
14:62 coming with the clouds of heaven. 9
Lke 9:34 a cloud came and overshadowed them 9
34 they were afraid as they entered the cloud. 9
35 a voice came out of the cloud, saying, "This is my Son 9
12:54 When you see a cloud rising in the west 9
21:27 then they will see the Son of man coming in a cloud 9
Act 1: 9 a cloud took him out of their sight. 9
1Co 10: 1 our fathers were all under the cloud 9
2 all were baptized into Moses in the cloud 9
1Th 4:17 caught up together with them in the clouds 9
Heb 12: 1 surrounded by so great a cloud of witnesses 10
Jde 1:12 waterless clouds, carried along by the winds; 9
Rev 1: 7 Behold, he is coming with the clouds 9
10: 1 coming down from heaven, wrapped in a cloud 9
11:12 they went up to heaven in a cloud. 9
14:14 Then I looked, and lo, a white cloud 9
14 and seated on the cloud one like a son of man 9
15 calling . . to him that sat upon the cloud 9
16 he who sat upon the cloud swung his sickle 9
2Es 4:49 after this a cloud full of water passed before me 11
49 drops remained in the cloud. •
7:40 or cloud or thunder or lightning or wind or water 11
11: 2 and the clouds were gathered about him. 11
13: 3 behold, that man flew with the clouds of heaven; 11
20 to pass from the world like a cloud 11
15:34 Behold, clouds from the east 11
39 the winds . . shall prevail over the cloud 11
40 great and mighty clouds 11
Wis 2: 4 like the traces of a cloud 9
5:21 as from a well-drawn bow of clouds 10
19: 7 The cloud was seen overshadowing the camp 9
Sir 13:23 they extol to the clouds what he says 9
24: 4 my throne was in a pillar of cloud. 9
35:16 his prayer will reach to the clouds. 9
17 The prayer of the humble pierces the clouds 9
20 clouds of rain in the time of drought. 9
43:14 the clouds fly forth like birds. 9
15 In his majesty he amasses the clouds 9
50: 6 Like the morning star among the clouds 9
7 like the rainbow gleaming in glorious clouds; 9
10 like a cypress towering in the clouds. 9
Bar 3:29 taken her, and brought her down from the clouds? 9
LJr 1:62 commands the clouds to go over the whole world 9
Aza 1:51 Bless the Lord, lightnings and clouds 9
2Mc 2: 8 the glory of the Lord and the cloud will appear 9
cloud *See also* bring, set, storm.

cloud over 1. *ἐπινεφής*
2Mc 1:22 the sun, which had been clouded over, shone out 1

thick cloud 1. עָב 2. עָבֵי שְׁחָקִים
2Sm 22:12 He made . . thick clouds, a gathering of water. 2
Job 22:14 Thick clouds enwrap him, so that he does not see 1
26: 8 He binds up the waters in his thick clouds 1
37:11 He loads the thick cloud with moisture; 1

cloudburst 1. נֶפֶץ
Isa 30:30 with a cloudburst and tempest and hailstones. 1

cloudless 1. לֹא עָב
2Sm 23: 4 the sun shining forth upon a cloudless morning 1

cloven 1. פרס 2. שסע
Deu 14: 6 Every animal that . . has the hoof cloven in two 2
7 of those that chew the cud or have the hoof cloven 1

cloven-footed 1. שסע שֶׁסַע 2. שסע שֶׁסַע פַּרְסָה
Lev 11: 3 the hoof and is cloven-footed and chews the cud 2
7 because it parts the hoof and is cloven-footed 2
26 parts the hoof but is not cloven-footed 1

club 1. תּוֹתָח 2. *ξύλον* 3. *ῥάβδος*
Job 41:29 Clubs are counted as stubble; 1
Mat 26:47 with him a great crowd with swords and clubs 2
55 with swords and clubs to capture me 2
Mrk 14:43 with him a crowd with swords and clubs 2
48 with swords and clubs to capture me? 2
Lke 22:52 as against a robber, with swords and clubs? 2
Bel 1:26 I will slay the dragon without sword or club. 3

war club
Prv 25:18 like a war club, or a sword, or sharp arrow. •

clue 1. *ἴχνος*
Sir 37:17 As a clue to changes of heart 1

cluster 1. אֶשְׁכּוֹל 2. *βότρυς* 3. botrus 4. racemus
Gen 40:10 budded, its blossoms shot forth, and the clusters 1
Num13:23 branch with a single cluster of grapes 1
24 because of the cluster which the men of Israel 1
Deu 32:32 grapes of poison, their clusters are bitter; 1
Sng 1:14 My beloved is to me a cluster of henna blossoms 1
7: 7 and your breasts are like its clusters. 1
8 Oh, may your breasts be like clusters of the vine 1
Isa 65: 8 As the wine is found in the cluster 1
Mic 7: 1 there is no cluster to eat 1
Rev 14:18 and gather the clusters of the vine of the earth 2
2Es 9:21 and saved for myself one grape out of a cluster 3
16:30 some clusters may be left by those who search 4

cluster of grapes 1. botrus
2Es 12:42 like a cluster of grapes from the vintage 1

cluster of raisins 1. צִמּוּק
1Sm 25:18 parched grain, and 100 clusters of raisins 1
30:12 a piece of a cake . . and two clusters of raisins. 1
1Ch 12:40 clusters of raisins, and wine and oil, oxen 1

coal 1. גַּחֶלֶת 2. פֶּחָם 3. *ἄνθρακας* 4. *ἀνθρακιά* 5. *ἄνθραξ* 6. carbo
Lev 16:12 he shall take a censer full of coals of fire 1
2Sm 14: 7 Thus they would quench my coal which is left 1
22:13 Out of the brightness . . coals of fire flamed 1
Job 41:21 His breath kindles coals, and a flame comes forth 1
Ps 11: 6 On the wicked he will rain coals of fire 5
18:12 there broke through his clouds . . coals of fire. 1
13 uttered his voice, hailstones and coals of fire. 1
140:10 Let burning coals fall upon them! 1
Isa 44:12 fashions it and works it over the coals; 2
19 in the fire, I also baked bread on its coals 1
47:14 No coal for warming oneself is this 1
54:16 I . . created the smith who blows the fire of coals 2
Ezk 1:13 that looked like burning coals of fire 1
10: 2 fill your hands with burning coals 1
24:11 Then set it empty upon the coals 1
Rom 12:20 you will heap burning coals upon his head. 5
2Es 16:53 for God will burn coals of fire on the head of him 6
Sir 8:10 Do not kindle the coals of a sinner 3
4Mc 9:20 the heap of coals was being quenched 4

burning coal 1. רִצְפָּה 2. *ἀνθρακιά*
Isa 6: 6 in his hand a burning coal which he had taken 1
Sir 11:32 From a spark of fire come many burning coals 2

glowing coal 1. גַּחֶלֶת
2Sm 22: 9 glowing coals flamed forth from him. 1
Ps 18: 8 glowing coals flamed forth from him. 1
120: 4 arrows, with glowing coals of the broom tree! 1

hot coal 1. גַּחֶלֶת
Prv 6:28 walk upon hot coals and his feet not be scorched? 1

coal of fire 1. גַּחֶלֶת
Prv 25:22 for you will heap coals of fire on his head 1
coarse *See* meal.

coast 1. אִי 2. גְּבוּל 3. חוֹף 4. *ὅριον*
Num34: 6 western boundary . . the Great Sea and its coast; 2
Jos 9: 1 the lowland all along the coast of the Great Sea 3
Jdg 5:17 Asher sat still at the coast of the sea 3
Isa 23: 2 Be still, O inhabitants of the coast 1
6 to Tarshish, wail, O inhabitants of the coast! 1
Jer 2:10 For cross to the coasts of Cyprus and see 1
Ezk 27: 6 made your deck of pines from the coasts of Cyprus 1
7 blue and purple from the coasts of Eli'shah was 1
Jdt 1:12 as far as the coasts of the two seas. 4
coast *See also* along.

coast along 1. παραλέγομαι
Act 27: 8 Coasting along it with difficulty 1

coast-line 1. גְּבוּל
Jos 15:12 boundary was the Great Sea with its coast-line. 1
47 to . . and the Great Sea with its coast-line. 1

coastal 1. παραλία
1Mc 11: 8 King Ptolemy gained control of the coastal cities 1
coastal *See also* country.

coastland 1. אִי 2. παραλία
Gen 10: 5 From these the coastland peoples spread. 1
Est 10: 1 laid tribute . . and on the coastlands of the sea. 1
Ps 97: 1 LORD reigns; let . . the many coastlands be glad! 1
Isa 11:11 from Hamath, and from the coastlands of the sea. 1
20: 6 the inhabitants of this coastland will say 1
24:15 glory to the LORD; in the coastlands of the sea 1
41: 1 Listen to me in silence, O coastlands; 1
5 The coastlands have seen and are afraid 1
42: 4 and the coastlands wait for his law. 1
10 the coastlands and their inhabitants. 1
12 and declare his praise in the coastlands. 1
49: 1 Listen to me, O coastlands, and hearken 1
51: 5 the coastlands wait for me, and for my arm they 1
59:18 to the coastlands he will render requital. 1
60: 9 For the coastlands shall wait for me 1
66:19 to Tubal and Javan, to the coastlands afar off 1
Jer 25:22 and the kings of the coastland across the sea; 1
31:10 and declare it in the coastlands afar off; 1
47: 4 the remnant of the coastland of Caphtor. 1
Ezk 26:15 Will not the coastlands shake at the sound 1
27: 3 merchant of the peoples on many coastlands 1
15 many coastlands were your own special markets 1
35 the inhabitants of the coastlands are appalled 1
39: 6 on those who dwell securely in the coastlands; 1
Dan 11:18 shall turn his face to the coastlands 1
Jdt 5: 2 all the governors of the coastland 2
7: 8 the commanders of the coastland came to him 2

coat 1. כְּתֹנֶת 2. מַד 3. שִׁרְיוֹן 4. ἱμάτιον 5. χιτών
Exd 28: 4 an ephod, a robe, a coat of checker work, a turban 1
39 weave the coat in checker work of fine linen 1
40 for Aaron's sons you shall make coats and girdles 1
29: 5 put on Aaron the coat and the robe of the ephod 1
8 you shall bring his sons, and put coats on them 1
39:27 They also made the coats, woven of fine linen 1
40:14 bring his sons also and put coats on them 1
Lev 8: 7 he put on him the coat, and girded him 1
13 Moses . . clothed them with coats, and girded 1
10: 5 So they drew near, and carried them in their coats 1
16: 4 He shall put on the holy linen coat 1
1Sm 17: 5 and he was armed with a coat of mail 3
5 the weight of the coat was 5,000 shekels 3
2Sm 15:32 came . . with his coat rent and earth upon his 1
Ps 109:18 He clothed himself with cursing as his coat 2
Mat 5:40 if any one would sue you and take your coat, let him 5
Lke 3:11 He who has two coats, let him share 5
6:29 from him who takes away your coat 4
coat *See also* give.

coat of mail 1. סִרְיֹן 2. שִׁרְיוֹן 3. ἁλυσιδωτός 4. θώραξ
1Sm 17:38 and clothed him with a coat of mail. 2
2Ch 26:14 Uzzi'ah prepared . . helmets, coats of mail, bows 2
Neh 4:16 half held the . . bows, and coats of mail; 2
Job 41:13 Who can penetrate his double coat of mail? 4
Jer 46: 4 polish your spears, put on your coats of mail! 1
51: 3 let him not stand up in his coat of mail. 1
1Mc 6:35 1,000 men armed with coats of mail 3

cock 1. ἀλεκτρυών 2. ἀλέκτωρ
Prv 30:31 strutting cock, the he-goat, and a king striding 2
Mat 26:34 this very night, before the cock crows 2
74 immediately the cock crowed. 2
75 Before the cock crows, you will deny me 2
Mrk 14:30 this very night, before the cock crows twice 2
72 immediately the cock crowed a second time. 2
72 Before the cock crows twice 2
Lke 22:34 I tell you, Peter, the cock will not crow this day 2
60 while he was still speaking, the cock crowed. 2
61 Before the cock crows today, you will deny me 2
Joh 13:38 Truly, truly, I say to you, the cock will not crow 2
18:27 at once the cock crowed. 2
3Mc 5:23 as soon as the cock had crowed in the early morning 1

cockcrow 1. ἀλεκτοροφωνία
Mrk 13:35 at midnight, or at cockcrow, or in the morning– 1

written code 1. γράμμα
Rom 2:27 will condemn you who have the written code 1
7: 6 so that we serve not under the old written code 1
2Co 3: 6 not in a written code but in the Spirit 1
6 the written code kills, but the Spirit gives life. 1

coercive 1. ἀνάγκη
4Mc 9: 6 die despising your coercive tortures 1

coffer 1. γαζοφυλάκιον
1Mc 3:28 he opened his coffers 1

coffin 1. אָרוֹן
Gen 50:25 he was put in a coffin in Egypt. 1

cohort 1. σπεῖρα
Act 10: 1 what was known as the Italian Cohort 1
21:31 word came to the tribune of the cohort 1
27: 1 a centurion of the Augustan Cohort, named Julius. 1

coil 1. חֶבֶל
Prv 5:22 he is caught in the coils of his sin. 1

coin 1. δηνάριον 2. δραχμή 3. κέρμα
Mat 22:19 And they brought him a coin. 1
Mrk 12:15 Bring me a coin, and let me look at it. 1
Lke 15: 8 having ten silver coins, if she loses one coin 2
9 I have found the coin which I had lost.' 2
20:24 Show me a coin 1
Joh 2:15 and he poured out the coins of the money-changers 3

copper coin 1. λεπτός
Mrk 12:42 a poor widow came, and put in two copper coins 1
Lke 21: 2 he saw a poor widow put in two copper coins. 1

silver coin 1. δραχμή
Lke 15: 8 what woman, having 10 silver coins 1

coinage 1. κόμμα
1Mc 15: 6 I permit you to mint your own coinage 1

cold 1. צִנָּה 2. קַר 3. קֹר 4. קָרָה 5. קֶרַח 6. ψῦχος 7. ψυχρός 8. frigus
Gen 8:22 cold and heat, summer and winter, day and night 3
31:40 by day the heat consumed me, and the cold by night 5
Job 24: 7 and have no covering in the cold. 4
37: 9 cold from the scattering winds. 4
Ps 147:17 who can stand before his cold? 4
Prv 25:13 Like the cold of snow in the time of harvest 1
20 like one who takes off a garment on a cold day 4
25 Like cold water to a thirsty soul, so is good news 2
Jer 18:14 waters run dry, the cold flowing streams? 2
Nah 3:17 locusts settling on the fences in a day of cold– 4
Zec 14: 6 that day there shall be neither cold nor frost. •
Mat 10:42 even a cup of cold water 7
Joh 18:18 made a charcoal fire, because it was cold 6
Act 28: 2 because it had begun to rain and was cold. 6
2Co 11:27 often without food, in cold and exposure. 6
Rev 3:15 'I know your works: you are neither cold nor hot. 7
15 Would that you were cold or hot! 7
16 you are lukewarm, and neither cold nor hot 7
2Es 7:41 winter or frost or cold or hail or rain or dew 8
Sir 43:20 The cold north wind blows 7
Aza 1:49 Bless the Lord, ice and cold 6
4Mc 11:26 Your fire is cold to us 7
cold *See also* grow.

winter cold 1. ψῦχος
Aza 1:45 Bless the Lord, winter cold and summer heat 1

colic 1. στρόφος
Sir 31:20 distress of sleeplessness . . nausea and colic 1

collapse 1. כרע 2. נפל 3. κατεπικύπτω
Ps 20: 8 They will collapse and fall; but we shall rise 1
Isa 30:13 a high wall, bulging out, and about to collapse 2
AEs 15: 7 collapsed upon the head of the maid 3

collar 1. עֲנָק 2. פֶּה 3. צִינֹק 4. κλοιός
Jdg 8:26 besides the collars that were about the necks 1
Job 30:18 it binds me about like the collar of my tunic. 2
Ps 105:18 his neck was put in a collar of iron; •
133: 2 of Aaron, running down on the collar of his robes! 2
Jer 29:26 to put him in the stocks and collar. 3
Sir 6:24 Put . . your neck into her collar. 4
29 her collar a glorious robe. 4

collect 1. אמץ 2. אסף 3. אֲסֻפָּה 4. לקט 5. קבץ 6. ἐπισυνάγω 7. λαμβάνω 8. πράσσω 9. συνάγω 10. συναθροίζω 11. τελωνέομαι
Jdg 11: 3 worthless fellows collected round Jephthah 4
2Kg 22: 4 the keepers . . have collected from the people; 2
2Ch 24:11 and collected money in abundance. 2
34: 9 money . . which the Levites . . had collected 2
Ecc 12:11 like nails . . fixed are the collected sayings 3
Isa 22: 9 you collected the waters of the lower pool 5
Nah 2: 1 gird your loins; collect all your strength. 1
Hab 2: 5 and collects as his own all peoples. 5
Zec 14:14 shall be collected, gold, silver, and garments 2
Lke 3:13 Collect no more than is appointed you. 8
19:23 I should have collected it with interest?' 8
1Es 8:13 to collect for the Lord in Jerusalem all the gold 9
Jdt 2:17 He collected a vast number of camels and asses 7
Bar 1: 6 they collected money, each giving what he could; 9
1Mc 1:35 collecting the spoils of Jerusalem 9
3:31 collect the revenues from those regions 7
10:30 instead of collecting the third of the grain •
30 I will not collect them from the land of Judah 7
13:39 whatever other tax . . shall be collected no longer. 11
2Mc 2:13 collected the books about the kings 6
14 In the same way Judas also collected . . books 6
10:24 collected the cavalry from Asia 10

collect a tax 1. τελωνέομαι
1Mc 13:39 whatever other tax has been collected 1

collect arms 1. ὁπλολογέω
2Mc 8:27 when they had collected the arms of the enemy 1
31 Collecting the arms of the enemy 1

collect the tithe 1. עשׂר
Neh 10:37 for it is the Levites who collect the tithes 1

collection 1. קִבּוּץ 2. πρᾶξις
Isa 57:13 let your collection of idols deliver you! 1
2Mc 4:28 the collection of the revenue 2

collection man by man 1. κατ' ἀνδρολογίαν
2Mc 12:43 He also took up a collection, man by man 1

collector 1. λαμβάνω
Mat 17:24 the collectors of the half-shekel tax 1

chief tax collector 1. ἀρχιτελώνης
Lke 19: 2 he was a chief tax collector, and rich. 1

collector of tribute 1. φορολογία
1Mc 1:29 the king sent . . a chief collector of tribute 1

tax collector 1. τελώνης
Mat 5:46 Do not even the tax collectors do the same? 1
9:10 behold, many tax collectors and sinners came 1
11 Why . . eat with tax collectors and sinners? 1
10: 3 Thomas and Matthew the tax collector 1
11:19 a friend of tax collectors and sinners! 1
18:17 let him be to you as a Gentile and a tax collector. 1
21:31 the tax collectors and the harlots 1
32 the tax collectors and the harlots believed him; 1
Mrk 2:15 tax collectors and sinners were sitting with Jesus 1
16 he was eating with sinners and tax collectors 1
16 Why does he eat with tax collectors and sinners? 1
Lke 3:12 Tax collectors also came to be baptized, and said 1
5:27 he went out, and saw a tax collector, named Levi 1
29 was a large company of tax collectors and others 1
30 Why do you . . drink with tax collectors and sinners? 1
7:29 the people and the tax collectors justified God 1
34 a friend of tax collectors and sinners!' 1
15: 1 the tax collectors . . were all drawing near 1
18:10 one a Pharisee and the other a tax collector. 1
11 or even like this tax collector. 1
13 the tax collector . . beat his breast 1

colonnade 1. ξυστός 2. περίστυλον
Sir 22:17 the stucco decoration on the wall of a colonnade. 1
2Mc 4:46 taking the king aside into a colonnade 2

colony 1. ἀποικία 2. κολωνία
Act 16:12 Philip'pi . . a Roman colony 2
Wis 12: 7 receive a worthy colony of the servants of God. 1

color 1. עַיִן 2. זִיו (A) 3. χρόα 4. χρῶμα 5. color 6. tinctura
Lev 13:55 if the diseased spot has not changed color 1
Dan 5: 6 color changed, and his thoughts alarmed 2
9 greatly alarmed, and his color changed; 2
10 Let not your . . color change. 2
7:28 greatly alarmed me, and my color changed; 2
2Es 6:44 and flowers of inimitable color 5
9:17 as are the flowers, so are the colors 6
14:39 but its color was like fire. 5
Wis 15: 4 a figure stained with varied colors 4
2Mc 3:16 his face and the change in his color 3

color of fire 1. πύρινος
Rev 9:17 the riders wore breastplates the color of fire 1

color red 1. ἐρυθαίνω
Wis 13:14 and coloring its surface red 1
colored *See* spread, stone.

colored stuff 1. בְּרֹמִים
Ezk 27:24 and in carpets of colored stuff, bound with cords 1

many colors 1. רִקְמָה
Ezk 17: 3 A great eagle . . rich in plumage of many colors 1

colt 1. בֵּן 2. עַיִר 3. πῶλος
Gen 32:15 30 milch camels and their colts, 40 cows 1
49:11 Binding . . his ass's colt to the choice vine 1
Job 11:12 when a wild ass's colt is born a man. 2
Zec 9: 9 riding on an ass, on a colt the foal of an ass. 2
Mat 21: 2 an ass tied, and a colt with her 3
5 on an ass, and on a colt, the foal of an ass. 3
7 they brought the ass and the colt 3
Mrk 11: 2 you will find a colt tied 3

4 they went away, and found a colt tied at the door 3
5 What are you doing, untying the colt? 3
7 they brought the colt to Jesus 3
Lke 19:30 where on entering you will find a colt tied 3
33 as they were untying the colt, its owners said 3
33 Why are you untying the colt? 3
35 throwing their garments on the colt 3
Joh 12:15 behold, your king is coming, sitting on an ass's colt! 3

column 1. גֵּאוּת 2. דֶּלֶת 3. עַמּוּד 4. תִּימָרָה 5. *στῦλος*

Jdg 20:40 began to rise out of the city in a column of smoke 3
Sng 3: 6 What is that coming . . like a column of smoke 4
5:15 His legs are alabaster columns, set upon bases 3
Isa 9:18 and they roll upward in a column of smoke. 1
Jer 36:23 As Jehu'di read three or four columns 2
Jol 2:30 portents . . blood and fire and columns of smoke. 4
1Mc 13:29 erecting about them great columns 5
29 upon the columns he put suits of armor 5

comb 1. שָׂרִיק 2. *διαξαίνω*

Isa 19: 9 The workers in combed flax will be in despair 1
Jdt 10: 3 and combed her hair and put on a tiara 2

combat 1. מִלְחָמָה

2Ch 32: 6 he set combat commanders over the people 1

combine 1. conspiro

2Es 15:31 if they combine in great power and turn to pursue 1

combined *See* forces.

come 1. אַחֲרוֹן 2. אַחֲרִית 3. אתה 4. בוא 5. דֶּרֶךְ
6. היה 7. הלך 8. הִנֵּה 9. הפך 10. זעק 11. ידע 12. יהב
13. יצא 14. ירד 15. מָבוֹא 16. מוּבָא 17. מלא 18. מִנֶּגֶד
19. מצא 20. נָא 21. נגע 22. נגשׁ 23. נוח 24. נפל
25. נשׂא 26. עבר 27. עַד 28. עלה 29. פגע 30. פנה
31. צֶאֱצָאִים 32. צלח 33. קרא 34. קָרֵב 35. קרב
36. קרה 37. ראה 38. שׁוב 39. אתא (A) 40. מטא (A)
41. סלק (A) 42. עדה (A) 43. עלל (A) 44. *ἄγω*
45. *ἀκούω* 46. *ἀναβαίνω* 47. *ἀπέρχομαι* 48. *ἄρχω*
49. *αὔριον* 50. *ἀφικνέομαι* 51. *γένεσις* 52. *γίνομαι*
53. *δεῦρο* 54. *δεῦτε* 55. *διά* 56. *διανύω*
57. *διαφαύσκω* 58. *δίδωμι* 59. *διέρχομαι* 60. *ἐγγίζω*
61. *ἐγείρω* 62. *εἰμί* 63. *εἰς* 64. *εἰσέρχομαι* 65. *εἴσοδος*
66. *εἰσπορεύομαι* 67. *εἰσπορεύω* 68. *ἐκ*
69. *ἐκπορεύομαι* 70. *ἐκπορεύω* 71. *ἔλευσις*
72. *ἐνίστημι* 73. *ἐξέρχομαι* 74. *ἐπέρχομαι*
75. *ἐπιβάλλω* 76. *ἐπίβασις* 77. *ἐπιπορεύομαι*
78. *ἐπιστρέφω* 79. *ἔρχομαι* 80. *ἐφίστημι* 81. *ἔφοδος*
82. *ἔχω* 83. *ἥκω* 84. *θα* 85. *ἰδού* 86. *ἵημι*
87. *καθίστημι* 88. *καί* 89. *καταντάω* 90. *κατέρχομαι*
91. *κρατέω* 92. *μέλλω* 93. *παραγίνομαι* 94. *πάρειμι*
95. *παρεισέρχομαι* 96. *παρέρχομαι* 97. *παρίστημι*
98. *παρουσία* 99. *πίμπλημι* 100. *πορεύομαι*
101. *προάγω* 102. *προσάγω* 103. *προσβαίνω*
104. *προσέρχομαι* 105. *προσίημι* 106. *προσπίπτω*
107. *συμβαίνω* 108. *συμπληρόω* 109. *συνέρχομαι*
110. *φέρω* 111. *φθάνω* 112. accedo 113. advenio
114. convenio 115. educo 116. exeo 117. facio 118. fio
119. sum 120. venio

Gen 6: 4 the sons of God came in to the daughters of men 4
18 and you shall come into the ark, you, your sons 4
20 two of every sort shall come in to you 4
7: 6 when the flood of waters came upon the earth. 6
10 the waters of the flood came upon the earth. 6
10:14 Caslu'him (whence came the Philistines) 13
11: 3 they said to one another, "Come, let us make bricks 12
4 Then they said, "Come, let us build ourselves a city 12
7 Come, let us go down, and . . confuse their language 12
31 but when they came to Haran, they settled there. 4
12: 5 When they had come to the land of Canaan 4
13:18 Abram . . came and dwelt by the oaks of Mamre 4
14: 5 Ched-or-lao'mer and the kings . . came and subdued 4
7 then they turned back and came to Enmish'pat 4
13 Then one who had escaped came 4
15: 1 the word of the LORD came to Abram in a vision 6
4 behold, the word of the LORD came to him •
16: 8 you come from and where are you going? 4
17:16 of nations; kings of peoples shall come from her. 6
18: 5 pass on-since you have come to your servant. 26
21 according to the outcry which has come to me; 4
19: 1 The two angels came to Sodom in the evening; 4
5 Where are the men who came to you tonight? 4
8 for they have come under the shelter of my roof. 4
9 This fellow came to sojourn 4
23 sun had risen on the earth when Lot came to Zo'ar. 4
31 there is not a man on earth to come in to us 4
32 Come, let us make our father drink wine 7
20: 3 God came to Abim'elech in a dream by night 4
13 you must do me: at every place to which we come 4
22: 9 When they came to the place 4
24: 5 son back to the land from which you came? 13
31 He said, "Come in, O blessed of the LORD; 4
32 the man came into the house; and Laban ungirded 4
41 free from my oath, when you come to my kindred; 4
42 I came today to the spring, and said 4
50 The thing comes from the LORD; we cannot speak 13
62 Now Isaac had come from Beer-la'hai-roi 4
63 looked, and behold, there were camels coming. 4
25:29 Esau came in from the field, and he was famished. 4
26:27 Isaac said to them, "Why have you come to me 4
32 That same day Isaac's servants came and told him 4
27:30 Esau his brother came in from his hunting. 4
33 I ate it all before you came, and I have blessed 4
35 he said, "Your brother came with guile 4
28:11 he came to a certain place, and stayed there 29
29: 1 on his journey, and came to the land of the people 7
4 My brothers, where do you come from? •
6 Rachel his daughter is coming with the sheep! 4
9 Rachel came with her father's sheep; 4
30:16 When Jacob came from the field in the evening 4
16 You must come in to me; for I have hired you with my 4
30 For you had little before I came •
33 when you come to look into my wages with you. 4
38 troughs, where the flocks came to drink. 4
38 And since they bred when they came to drink 4
31:24 God came to Laban the Aramean in a dream by night 4
44 Come now, let us make a covenant, you and I; 7
32: 6 We came to your brother Esau 4
6 We came to . . Esau, and he is coming to meet you 7
8 thinking, "If Esau comes to the one company 4
11 for I fear him, lest he come and slay us all 4
33: 1 looked, and behold, Esau was coming 4
14 lead on slowly . . until I come to my lord in Se'ir. 4
18 Jacob came safely to the city of Shechem 4
34: 5 so Jacob held his peace until they came. 4
7 The sons of Jacob came in from the field 4
20 and his son Shechem came to the gate of their city 4
25 Dinah's brothers, took their swords and came upon 4
27 the sons of Jacob came upon the slain 4
35: 6 Jacob came to Luz (that is, Bethel) 4
9 when he came from Paddan-aram, and blessed him. 4
11 a company of nations shall come from you 6
27 Jacob came to his father Isaac at Mamre 4
37:10 Shall I and your mother . . indeed come to bow 4
13 Come, I will send you to them. 7
14 from the valley of Hebron, and he came to Shechem. 4
19 They said . . "Here comes this dreamer. 4
20 Come now, let us kill him and throw him into one 7
23 when Joseph came to his brothers 4
25 a caravan of Ish'maelites coming from Gilead 4
27 Come, let us sell him to the Ish'maelites 7
38:16 said, "Come, let me come in to you," for he did not 12
16 said, "Come, let me come in to you," for he did not 4
16 will you give me, that you may come in to me? 4
27 When the time of her delivery came 6
39:14 he came in to me to lie with me, and I cried out 4
16 his garment by her until his master came home 4
17 The Hebrew servant . . came in to me 4
40: 6 When Joseph came to them in the morning 4
41:14 changed his clothes, he came in before Pharaoh. 4
29 There will come seven years of great plenty 4
35 the food of these good years that are coming 4
50 Before the year of famine came 4
54 years of famine began to come, as Joseph had said. 4
57 Moreover, all the earth came to Egypt to Joseph 4
42: 5 Thus the sons of Israel came to buy among 4
5 Israel came to buy among the others who came 4
6 Joseph's brothers came, and bowed themselves 4
7 spoke roughly to them. "Where do you come from? 4
9 he said to them, "You are spies, you have come 4
10 lord, but to buy food have your servants come. 4
12 weakness of the land that you have come to see. 4
15 place unless your youngest brother comes here. 4
21 therefore is this distress come upon us. 4
29 When they came to Jacob their father in the land 4
36 take Benjamin; all this has come upon me. 6
43:21 when we came to the lodging place we opened 4
25 they made ready the present for Joseph's coming 4
26 When Joseph came home, they brought 4
44:14 Judah and his brothers came to Joseph's house 4
30 Now therefore, when I come to your servant 4
45:11 for there are yet five years of famine to come; •
16 report was heard . . "Joseph's brothers have come 4
18 come to me, and I will give you the best of the land 4
19 take wagons . . and bring your father, and come. 4
25 and came to the land of Canaan to their father 4
46: 1 Israel . . came to Beer-sheba, and offered 4
6 took . . goods . . and came into Egypt 4
8 the descendants of Israel, who came into Egypt 4
26 persons belonging to Jacob who came into Egypt 4
27 all the persons . . that came into Egypt, were 70. 4
28 and they came into the land of Goshen. 4
31 My brothers . . have come to me; 4
47: 1 my brothers . . have come from the land of Canaan; 4
4 They said to Pharaoh, "We have come to sojourn 4
5 Your father and your brothers have come to you. 4
15 all the Egyptians came to Joseph, and said, 4
18 when that year was ended, they came to him 4
48: 2 Your son Joseph has come to you"; 4
5 in the land of Egypt before I came to you in Egypt 4
7 For when I came from Paddan, Rachel to my sorrow 4
49: 1 tell you what shall befall you in days to come. 2
6 O my soul, come not into their council; 4
10 not depart . . until he comes to whom it belongs; 4
50:10 When they came to the threshing floor of Atad 4
18 His brothers also came and fell down before him 7
Exd 1: 1 the names of the sons of Israel who came to Egypt 4
10 Come, let us deal shrewdly with them 12
19 are delivered before the midwife comes to them. 4
2:16 seven daughters; and they came and drew water 4
17 The shepherds came and drove them away; 4
18 When they came to their father Reu'el 4
18 How is it that you have come so soon today? 4
3: 1 led his flock . . and came to Horeb, the mountain 4
9 the cry of the people of Israel has come to me 4
10 Come, I will send you to Pharaoh that you may bring 7
13 Moses said to God, "If I come to the people of Israel 4
5:15 the foremen . . came and cried to Pharaoh, "Why do 4
23 For since I came to Pharaoh to speak in thy name 4
8:17 and there came gnats on man and beast; 6
24 the LORD did so; there came great swarms of flies 4
9:32 for they are late in coming up.) •
10: 6 from the day they came on earth to this day.' 6
12 that they may come upon the land of Egypt 28
12:25 when you come to the land which the LORD will give 4
13:14 when in time to come your son asks you, 'What does •
14:20 coming between the host of Egypt and the host 4
15:23 When they came to Marah, they could not drink 4
27 Then they came to Elim, where there were twelve 4
16: 1 people of Israel came to the wilderness of Sin 4
22 leaders of the congregation came and told Moses 4
35 forty years, till they came to a habitable land; 4
35 they ate the manna, till they came to the border 4
17: 8 Then came Am'alek and fought with Israel 4
18: 5 Jethro . . came with his sons and his wife 4
6 Lo, your father-in-law Jethro is coming to you 4
12 and Aaron came with all the elders of Israel 4
15 Because the people come to me to inquire of God; 4
16 when they have a dispute, they come to me and I 4
19: 1 that day they came into the wilderness of Sinai. 4
2 set out . . and came into the wilderness 4
7 So Moses came and called the elders of the people 4
9 the LORD said to Moses, "Lo, I am coming to you 4
20:20 Do not fear; for God has come to prove you 4
24 in every place . . I will come to you and bless 4
21: 3 If he comes in single, he shall go out single; 4
3 if he comes in married, then his wife shall go out •
22: 9 the case of both parties shall come before God; 4
15 if it was hired, it came for its hire. 4
23:27 all the people against whom you shall come 4
24: 3 Moses came and told the people all the words 4
29:30 when he comes into the tent of meeting 4
32:26 Who is on the LORD'S side? Come to me. •
35:10 let every able man among you come and make all 4
21 they came, every one whose heart stirred him 4
22 So they came, both men and women; 4
36: 2 heart stirred him up to come to do the work; 35
4 every sort of task on the sanctuary came 4
Lev 11:34 Any food . . upon which water may come 4
12: 4 she shall not . . nor come into the sanctuary 4
13:16 then he shall come to the priest 4
19 there comes a white swelling or a reddish-white 6
14: 8 after that he shall come into the camp 4
34 When you come into the land of Canaan, which I give 4
35 then he who owns the house shall come and tell 4
48 if the priest comes and makes an examination 4
15:14 and come before the LORD to the door of the tent 4
17 garment and every skin on which the semen comes 6
16: 2 not to come at all times into the holy place 4
3 thus shall Aaron come into the holy place 4
23 Then Aaron shall come into the tent of meeting 4
26 and afterward he may come into the camp 4
28 and afterward he may come into the camp 4
19:23 When you come into the land and plant 4
23:10 When you come into the land which I give you 4
25: 2 When you come into the land which I give to you 4
22 until the ninth year, when its produce comes 4
25 his next of kin shall come and redeem 4
Num 4:15 sons of Kohath shall come to carry these 4
5:14 or if the spirit of jealousy comes upon him 26
14 or if the spirit of jealousy comes upon him 26
30 or when the spirit of jealousy comes upon a man 26
6: 5 no razor shall come upon his head; 26
9: 6 they came before Moses and Aaron on that day; 35
10:29 come with us, and we will do you good; for the LORD 7
13:22 They went up into the Negeb, and came to Hebron; 4
23 they came to the Valley of Eshcol, and cut down 4
26 they came to Moses and Aaron and to all 4
27 told him, "We came to the land to which you sent us; 4
33 (the sons of Anak, who come from the Nephilim); •
14:30 not one shall come into the land where I swore 4
15: 2 When you come into the land you are to inhabit 4
18 When you come into the land to which I bring you 4
16:43 Moses and Aaron came to the front of the tent 4
19: 2 red heifer . . upon which a yoke has never come. 28
7 afterwards he shall come into the camp; 4
14 every one who comes into the tent 4
20: 1 Israel . . came into the wilderness of Zin 4
22 people of Israel . . came to Mount Hor. 4
21: 1 that Israel was coming by the way of Atharim 4
7 people came to Moses, and said, "We have sinned 4
23 came to Jahaz, and fought against Israel. 4

27 Come to Heshbon, let it be built, let the city 4
22: 6 Come now, curse this people for me 7
7 elders . . came to Balaam, and gave him 4
9 God came to Balaam and said, "Who are these men 4
11 now come, curse them for me; 7
14 to Balak, and said, "Balaam refuses to come with us. 7
16 came to Balaam and said to him, "Thus says Balak 4
16 Let nothing hinder you from coming to me; 7
17 come, curse this people for me.' 7
20 God came to Balaam at night and said to him 4
20 If the men have come to call you, rise, go with them; 4
36 When Balak heard that Balaam had come, 4
37 Why did you not come to me? 7
38 Balaam said to Balak, "Lo, I have come to you! 4
39 Balaam . . Balak . . came to Kir'iath-hu'zoth. 4
23: 3 perhaps the LORD will come to meet me; 36
7 Come, curse Jacob for me, and come, denounce Israel!' 7
7 Come, curse Jacob for me, and come, denounce Israel!' 7
13 Balak said to him, "Come with me to another place 7
17 he came to him, and, lo, he was standing 4
27 Come now, I will take you to another place; 7
24: 2 And the Spirit of God came upon him 6
14 come, I will let you know what this people will do 7
20 but in the end he shall come to destruction. 27
24 ships shall come from Kittim and shall afflict 73
24 he also shall come to destruction. 27
25: 6 came and brought a Mid'ianite woman to his family 4
27:17 shall go out before them and come in before them 4
21 go out, and at his word they shall come 4
31:14 officers . . who had come from service in the war. 4
16 plague came among the congregation of the LORD. 6
24 afterward you shall come into the camp. 4
32: 2 sons of Gad and the sons of Reuben came and said 4
19 our inheritance has come to us on this side 4
33: 9 they set out from Marah, and came to Elim; 4
40 heard of the coming of the people of Israel. 4
36: 4 when the jubilee of the people of Israel comes 6
Deu 1:19 we set out . . and we came to Ka'desh-bar'nea. 4
20 'You have come to the hill country of the Amorites 4
22 word again of . . the cities into which we shall come.' 4
24 came to the Valley of Eshcol and spied it out. 4
31 way that you went until you came to this place.' 4
2:23 Caph'torim, who came from Caphtor, destroyed them 13
9: 7 from the day you came out of the land of Egypt 13
7 from . . until you came to this place 4
11: 5 did to you . . until you came to this place; 4
10 Egypt, from which you have come, where you sowed 13
12: 9 not as yet come to the rest and to the inheritance 4
14:29 shall come and eat and be filled; 4
16: 3 came out of the land of Egypt in hurried flight 13
3 remember the day . . came out of the land of Egypt. 13
6 passover . . at the time you came out of Egypt. 13
17: 9 coming to the Levitical priests, and to the judge 4
14 When you come to the land which the LORD . . gives 4
18: 6 Levite comes from any of your towns out of all Israel 4
6 Levite comes . . –and he may come when he desires– 4
9 When you come into the land which the LORD 4
23:10 outside the camp . . not come within the camp; 4
11 when evening comes on, he shall bathe himself 30
11 when the sun is down, he may come within the camp. 4
25: 1 dispute between men, and they come into court 22
17 Am'alek did to you . . as you came out of Egypt 13
26: 1 When you come into the land which the LORD 4
3 declare . . that I have come into the land 4
28: 2 blessings shall come upon you and overtake you 4
6 Blessed shall you be when you come in, and blessed 4
15 these curses shall come upon you and overtake 4
19 Cursed shall you be when you come in, and cursed 4
45 these curses shall come upon you and pursue you 4
29: 7 when you came to this place, Sihon . . and Og 4
16 how we came through the midst of the nations 26
22 generation to come, your children who rise up 1
22 foreigner who comes from a far land, would say 4
30: 1 when all these things come upon you, the blessing 4
31: 2 I am no longer able to go out and come in. 4
11 when all Israel comes to appear before the LORD 4
29 in the days to come evil will befall you 2
32:17 sacrificed to . . new gods that had come in of late 4
32 For their vine comes from the vine of Sodom *
44 Moses came and recited all the words of this song 4
33: 2 LORD came from Sinai, and dawned from Se'ir 4
2 he came from the ten thousands of holy ones 3
16 Let these come upon the head of Joseph 4
21 he came to the heads of the people, with Israel 3
Jos 2: 2 certain men of Israel have come here tonight 4
3 Bring forth the men that have come to you 4
3 they have come to search out all the land. 4
4 True, men came to me, but I did not know where 4
4 men came . . but I did not know where they came from; *
18 when we come into the land, you shall bind this 4
23 came down . . and passed over and came to Joshua 4
3: 1 and they came to the Jordan, and lodged there 4
8 you come to the brink of the waters of the Jordan 4
9 Come hither, and hear the words of the LORD 22
15 when those who bore the ark had come to the Jordan 4
5:14 as commander of the army of the LORD I . . now come. 4
6: 1 was shut up . . none went out, and none came in. 4
9 and the rear guard came after the ark 7
13 and the rear guard came after the ark of the LORD 7
9: 6 We have come from a far country . . make a covenant 4
8 Who are you? And where do you come from? 4
9 From a very far country your servants have come 4
11 We are your servants; come now, make a covenant *
12 we took it . . on the day we set forth to come to you 7
10: 9 Joshua came upon them suddenly 4
11: 5 and came and encamped . . at the waters of Merom 4
7 Joshua came . . upon them with all his people 4
21 Joshua came at that time, and wiped out the Anakim 4
14: 6 Then the people of Judah came to Joshua at Gilgal; 22
11 my strength . . for war, and for going and coming. 4
15: 4 goes out by . . and comes to its end at the sea. 6
11 then the boundary comes to an end at the sea. 6
18 When she came to him, she urged him to ask 4
17: 4 They came before Elea'zar the priest and Joshua 35
18: 4 that they may set out and . . and then come to me. 4
9 then they came to Joshua in the camp at Shiloh 4
21: 1 the heads . . came to Elea'zar the priest 22
22:10 And when they came to the region about the Jordan 4
15 And they came to the Reubenites, the Gadites 4
17 there came a plague upon the congregation 6
24: 6 I brought . . out of Egypt, and you came to the sea; 4
11 And you went over the Jordan and came to Jericho 4
Jdg 1:14 When she came to him, she urged him to ask her 4
3:10 The Spirit of the LORD came upon him, 6
20 Ehud came to him, as he was sitting alone 4
24 When he had gone, the servants came; 4
4:20 and if any man comes and asks you, 'Is any one here?' 4
22 Come, and I will show you the man whom 7
5:15 the princes of Is'sachar came with Deb'orah *
19 The kings came, they fought; then fought the kings 4
23 because they came not to the help of the LORD 4
28 Why is his chariot so long in coming? Why tarry 4
6: 5 would come up . . coming like locusts for number; 4
5 so that they wasted the land as they came in. 4
11 the angel . . came and sat under the oak at Ophrah 4
18 Do not depart from here . . until I come to thee 4
7:13 When Gideon came, . . a man was telling a dream 4
13 camp of Mid'ian, and came to the tent, and struck it 4
17 when I come to the outskirts of the camp, do as I do. 4
19 Gideon . . came to the outskirts of the camp 4
8: 4 Gideon came to the Jordan and passed over 4
15 he came to the men of Succoth, and said, "Behold 4
9:10 said to the fig tree, 'Come you, and reign over us.' 7
12 trees said to the vine, 'Come you, and reign over us.' 7
14 said to the bramble, 'Come you, and reign over us.' 7
15 over you, then come and take refuge in my shade; 4
24 violence done . . might come and their blood be 4
31 Ga'al . . and his kinsmen have come to Shechem 4
37 and one company is coming from the direction 4
52 Abim'elech came to the tower, and fought 4
57 and upon them came the curse of Jotham the son 4
11: 6 Come and be our leader, that we may fight 7
7 Why have you come to me now 4
12 that you have come to me to fight against my land? 4
13 Israel on coming from Egypt took away my land 28
16 the wilderness to the Red Sea and came to Kadesh. 4
29 the Spirit of the LORD came upon Jephthah 6
34 Then Jephthah came to his home at Mizpah; 4
13: 5 bear a son. No razor shall come upon his head 28
6 Then the woman came and told her husband 4
6 A man of God came to me, and his countenance was 4
8 let the man of God . . come again to us, and teach us 4
9 the angel of God came again to the woman as she sat 4
10 the man who came to me the other day has appeared 4
11 Mano'ah arose . . and came to the man and said 4
14 may not eat of anything that comes from the vine 13
14: 5 to Timnah, and he came to the vineyards of Timnah. 4
9 he came to his father and mother, and gave some 7
15:14 When he came to Lehi, the Philistines came 4
14 the Philistines came shouting to meet him; *
19 the hollow place . . and there came water from it; 13
16: 2 The Gazites were told, "Samson has come here 4
5 the lords of the Philistines came to her and said 28
17 A razor has never come upon my head; for I have been 28
17: 8 and as he journeyed, he came to the hill country 4
9 Micah said to him, "From where do you come? 4
18: 2 they came to the hill country of E'phraim 4
7 the five men departed, and came to La'ish 4
8 when they came . . their brethren said to them 4
10 you will come to an unsuspecting people. 4
13 they passed on . . and came to the house of Micah. 4
15 they turned aside thither, and came to the house 4
19 Keep quiet . . and come with us, and be to us 7
23 What ails you that you come with such a company? 10
27 the Danites came to La'ish, to a people quiet 4
19: 3 he came to her father's house; and when the girl's 100
3 girl's father saw him, he came with joy to meet him. *
11 Come now, let us turn aside . . and spend the night 7
13 Come and let us draw near to one of these places 7
16 an old man was coming from his work in the field 4
17 said, "Where are you going? and whence do you come? 4
18 of the hill country of E'phraim, from which I come. *
22 Bring out the man who came into your house, that we 4
23 seeing that this man has come into my house 4
26 the woman came and fell down at the door 4
20: 4 I came to Gib'e-ah that belongs to Benjamin 4
10 that when they come they may requite Gib'e-ah 4
26 the whole army, went up and came to Bethel 4
34 there came against Gib'e-ah 10,000 picked men 4
42 those who came out of the cities destroyed them *
21: 2 the people came to Bethel, and sat there till 4
8 no one had come . . from Ja'besh-gil'ead 4
22 fathers or their brothers come to complain to us 4
Rut 1:19 the two . . went on until they came to Bethlehem. 4
19 And when they came to Bethlehem, the whole town 4
22 And they came to Bethlehem at . . barley harvest. 4
2: 3 she happened to come to the part of the field 36
4 And behold, Bo'az came from Bethlehem; 4
7 she came, and she has continued 4
11 and came to a people that you did not know before. 7
12 under whose wings you have come to take refuge! 4
14 Come here, and eat some bread, and dip your morsel 22
3: 7 Then she came softly, and uncovered his feet 4
14 that the woman came to the threshing floor. 4
16 And when she came to her mother-in-law, she said 4
4: 4 is no one besides you . . and I come after you. *
11 the woman, who is coming into your house 4
1Sm 2: 3 let not arrogance come from your mouth; 13
13 the priest's servant would come, while the meat 4
14 to all the Israelites who came there. 4
15 the priest's servant would come and say to the man 4
27 And there came a man of God to Eli, and said to him 4
31 Behold, the days are coming, when I will cut off 4
36 every one who is left . . shall come to implore 4
3:10 And the LORD came and stood forth, calling 4
4: 1 And the word of Samuel came to all Israel. 6
3 when the troops came to the camp 4
3 come among us and save us from . . our enemies. 4
5 ark of the covenant of the LORD came into the camp 4
6 the ark of the LORD had come to the camp 4
7 they said, "A god has come into the camp. 4
12 and came to Shiloh the same day 4
13 when the man came into the city and told the news 4
14 Then the man hastened and came and told Eli. 4
16 I am he who has come from the battle; 4
19 bowed and gave birth; for her pains came upon her. 9
5:10 when the ark of God came to Ekron 4
6: 7 two . . cows upon which there has never come a yoke 28
14 The cart came into the field of Joshua 4
7: 1 the men of Kir'iath-je'arim came and took up the ark 4
8: 4 elders . . gathered together and came to Samuel 4
9: 5 When they came to the land of Zuph, Saul said to his 4
5 Come, let us go back, lest my father cease to care 7
9 he said, "Come, let us go to the seer"; 7
10 Well said; come, let us go." So they went to the city 7
12 Make haste; he has come just now to the city 4
13 the people will not eat till he comes 4
15 before Saul came, the LORD had revealed to Samuel 4
16 I have seen . . because their cry has come to me. 4
10: 3 go on . . further and come to the oak of Tabor; 4
5 After that you shall come to Gib'e-ath-elo'him 4
5 as you come to the city, you will meet . . prophets 4
8 I am coming to you to offer burnt offerings 14
8 Seven days you shall wait, until I come to you 4
10 When they came to Gib'e-ah . . prophets met him; 4
13 finished prophesying, he came to the high place. 4
22 they inquired again . . "Did the man come hither? 4
11: 4 When the messengers came to Gib'e-ah of Saul 4
5 Saul was coming from the field behind the oxen; 4
9 they said to the messengers who had come 4
9 the messengers came and told the men of Jabesh 4
11 they came into the midst of the camp 4
14 Samuel said to the people, "Come, let us go to Gilgal 7
12:12 when you saw that Nahash . . came against you 4
13: 8 He waited . . but Samuel did not come to Gilgal 4
10 As soon as he had finished . . behold, Samuel came; 4
11 you did not come within the days appointed 4
14: 1 Come, let us go over to the Philistine garrison 7
6 Come, let us go over to the garrison of these 7
9 If they say to us, 'Wait until we come to you,' 21
25 And all the people came into the forest; 4
38 Come hither, all you leaders of the people; 22
15: 5 Saul came to the city of Am'alek, and lay in wait 4
10 The word of the LORD came to Samuel 6
12 Saul came to Carmel, and . . he set up a monument 4
13 Samuel came to Saul, and Saul said to him 4
32 And Agag came to him cheerfully. 7
16: 2 and say, 'I have come to sacrifice to the LORD.' 4
4 Samuel did . . and came to Bethlehem. 4
4 The elders . . and said, "Do you come peaceably? 4
5 I have come to sacrifice to the LORD; 4
5 consecrate . . and come with me to the sacrifice. 4
6 When they came, he looked on Eli'ab and thought 4
11 for we will not sit down till he comes here. 4
21 And David came to Saul, and entered his service. 4
17:20 he came to the encampment as the host was going 4
34 when there came a lion, or a bear, and took a lamb 4
41 the Philistine came on and drew near to David 7
43 Am I a dog, that you come to me with sticks? 4
44 Come to me, and I will give your flesh to the birds 7
45 You come to me with a sword and with a spear 4
45 but I come to you in the name of the LORD of hosts 4
48 When the Philistine arose and came and drew near 7
18: 6 As they were coming home, when David returned 4
13 and he went out and came in before the people. 4
16 for he went out and came in before them. 4
19: 9 Then an evil spirit from the LORD came upon Saul 6

16 messengers came in . . the image was in the bed 4
18 David . . escaped, and he came to Samuel at Ramah 4
20 Spirit of God came upon the messengers of Saul 6
22 went to Ramah, and came to the great well . . in Secu; 4
23 and the Spirit of God came upon him also 6
23 he prophesied, until he came to Nai'oth in Ramah. 4
20: 1 David fled . . and came and said before Jonathan 4
9 determined . . that evil should come upon you 4
11 Come, let us go out into the field. 7
21 you are to come, for . . it is safe for you 4
24 when the new moon came, the king sat down to eat 6
27 Why has not the son of Jesse come to the meal 4
29 For this . . he has not come to the king's table. 4
37 And when the lad came to the place of the arrow 4
38 gathered up the arrows, and came to his master. 4
21: 1 Then came David to Nob to Ahim'elech the priest; 4
15 Shall this fellow come into my house? 4
22: 9 I saw the son of Jesse coming to Nob, to Ahim'elech 4
11 priests . . at Nob; and all of them came to the king. 4
23: 7 it was told Saul that David had come to Kei'lah. 4
10 Saul seeks to come to Kei'lah, to destroy the city 4
27 a messenger came to Saul, saying, "Make haste 4
27 messenger came . . saying, "Make haste and come; 7
24: 3 And he came to the sheepfolds by the way 4
25: 8 find favor in your eyes; for we come on a feast day. 4
9 When David's young men came, they said all this 4
11 give it to men who come from I do not know where? •
19 Go on before me; behold, I come after you. 4
34 unless you had made haste and come to meet me 4
36 And Ab'igail came to Nabal; 4
40 the servants of David came to Ab'igail at Carmel 4
26: 1 Then the Ziphites came to Saul at Gib'e-ah, saying 4
3 saw that Saul came after him into the wilderness 4
4 and learned of a certainty that Saul had come. 4
5 David rose and came to . . where Saul had encamped; 4
10 LORD will smite him; or his day shall come to die; 4
15 For one of the people came in to destroy the king 4
28: 4 Philistines . . came and encamped at Shunem; 4
8 and they came to the woman by night. 4
21 the woman came to Saul, and when she saw . . she said 4
29: 6 from the day of your coming to me to this day. 4
10 servants of your lord who came with you; 4
30: 1 David and his men came to Ziklag on the third day 4
3 when David and his men came to the city, they found 4
9 and they came to the brook Besor 4
21 Then David came to the 200 men 4
23 into our hand the band that came against us. 4
26 When David came to Ziklag, he sent . . the spoil 4
31: 4 lest these uncircumcised come and thrust me 4
7 and the Philistines came and dwelt in them. 4
8 when the Philistines came to strip the slain 4
12 they came to Jabesh and burnt them there. 4
2Sm 1: 2 a man came from Saul's camp, with his clothes rent 4
2 And when he came to David, he fell to the ground 4
3 David said to him, "Where do you come from? 4
13 And David said . . "Where do you come from? •
2: 4 the men of Judah came, and . . anointed David king 4
23 And all who came to the place . . stood still. 4
24 as the sun was . . they came to the hill of Ammah 4
29 they crossed the Jordan, and . . came to Mahana'im. 4
3:13 bring Michal . . when you come to see my face. 4
20 Abner came with twenty men to David at Hebron 4
23 When Jo'ab and all the army that was with him came 4
23 Abner . . came to the king, and he has let him go 4
24 Abner came to you; why is it that you have sent him 4
25 Abner the son of Ner came to deceive you 4
25 and to know your going out and your coming in 16
35 Then all the people came to persuade David to eat 4
4: 4 news about Saul and Jonathan came from Jezreel; 4
5 they came to the house of Ish-bo'sheth, as he was 4
5: 1 the tribes of Israel came to David at Hebron 4
3 the elders . . came to the king at Hebron; 4
6 who said to David, "You will not come in here 4
6 who said . . thinking, "David cannot come in here. 4
8 blind and the lame shall not come into the house. 4
13 David took more . . after he came from Hebron; 4
18 Now the Philistines had come and spread out 4
20 David came to Ba'al-pera'zim, and . . defeated them 4
23 and come upon them opposite the balsam trees. 4
6: 6 when they came to the threshing floor of Nacon 4
9 How can the ark of the LORD come to me? 4
16 As the ark of the LORD came into the city of David 4
7: 4 that . . night the word of the LORD came to Nathan 6
8: 5 Syrians . . came to help Hadade'zer king of Zobah 4
9: 6 Mephib'osheth . . came to David, and fell on his 4
10: 2 servants came into the land of the Ammonites. 4
11 if the Ammonites . . then I will come and help you. 7
14 Jo'ab returned . . and came to Jerusalem. 4
16 they came to Helam, with Shobach . . at their head. 4
17 and crossed the Jordan, and came to Helam. 4
11: 4 she came to him, and he lay with her. 4
7 When Uri'ah came to him, David asked how Jo'ab was 4
10 David said . . "Have you not come from a journey? 4
22 the messenger went, and came and told David all 4
12: 1 He came . . and said to him, "There were two men 4
4 Now there came a traveler to the rich man 4
4 to prepare for the wayfarer who had come to him 4
4 and prepared it for the man who had come to him. 4
13: 5 when your father comes to see you, say to him 4
5 Let my sister Tamar come and give me bread to eat 4
6 when the king came to see him, Amnon said 4
6 Pray let . . Tamar come and make a couple of cakes 4
11 and said to her, "Come, lie with me, my sister. 4
24 And Ab'salom came to the king, and said, "Behold 4
30 While they were on the way, tidings came to David 4
34 many people were coming from the Horona'im road 7
35 Jon'adab said . . "Behold, the king's sons have come; 4
36 the king's sons came, and lifted up their voice 4
14: 4 When the woman of Teko'a came to the king 4
15 Now I have come to say this to my lord the king 4
24 dwell apart . . he is not to come into my presence. 37
24 Ab'salom . . did not come into the king's presence. 37
28 without coming into the king's presence. 37
29 Ab'salom sent for Jo'ab . . but Jo'ab would not come 4
29 And he sent a second time, but Jo'ab would not come. 4
32 Come here, that I may send you to the king 4
32 Why have I come from Geshur? It would be better 4
33 he came to the king, and bowed himself on his face 4
15: 2 had a suit to come before the king for judgment 4
4 every man . . might come to me, and I would give him 4
6 to all of Israel who came to the king for judgment; 4
13 And a messenger came to David, saying 4
20 You came only yesterday, and shall I today 4
24 And Abi'athar came up, and lo, Zadok came also •
28 I will wait . . until word comes from you to inform 4
32 David came to the summit, where God was worshiped 4
32 Hushai . . came to meet him with his coat rent •
37 So Hushai, David's friend, came into the city 4
16: 5 When King David came to Bahu'rim, there came out 4
5 and as he came he cursed continually. 13
15 Ab'salom and all the people . . came to Jerusalem 4
16 And when Hushai . . came to Ab'salom, Hushai said 4
17: 2 I will come upon him while he is weary 4
6 And when Hushai came to Ab'salom, Ab'salom said 4
12 So we shall come upon him in some place 4
18 went . . and came to the house of a man at Bahu'rim 4
20 Ab'salom's servants came to the woman at the house 4
24 Then David came to Mahana'im. 4
27 When David came to Mahana'im, Shobi 4
18:22 Come what may, let me also run after the Cushite. 6
23 Come what may," he said, "I will run. 6
25 And he came apace, and drew near. 7
27 He is a good man, and comes with good tidings. 4
31 And behold, the Cushite came; and the Cushite said 4
19: 5 Then Jo'ab came into the house to the king, and said 4
7 worse . . than all the evil that has come upon you 4
8 and all the people came before the king. 4
11 when the word of all Israel has come to the king? 4
15 and Judah came to Gilgal to meet the king 4
20 I have come this day, the first . . to meet my lord 4
25 And when he came from Jerusalem to meet the king 4
30 since my lord the king has come safely home. 4
41 all the men of Israel came to the king, and said 4
20: 3 And David came to his house at Jerusalem; 4
8 When they were at . . Ama'sa came to meet them. 4
15 the men . . with Jo'ab came and besieged him in Abel 4
16 Hear! Tell Jo'ab, 'Come here, that I may speak to you.' 35
21:10 allow the birds of the air to come upon them by day 23
22: 7 he heard my voice, and my cry came to his ears. •
23:13 And three . . came about harvest time to David 4
24: 6 Then they came to Gilead, and to Kadesh 4
6 they came to Dan, and from Dan they went . . to Sidon 4
7 and came to the fortress of Tyre 4
8 they came to Jerusalem at the end of nine months 4
11 the word of the LORD came to the prophet Gad 6
13 Gad came to David and told him, and said to him 4
13 Shall three years of famine come . . in your land? 4
18 Gad came that day to David, and said to him, "Go up 4
20 the king and his servants coming on toward him; 26
21 Why has my lord the king come to his servant? 4
1Kg 1:12 come, let me give you counsel, that you may save 7
14 I also will come in after you and confirm 4
22 still speaking . . Nathan the prophet came in. 4
23 when he came in before the king, he bowed before 4
28 So she came into the king's presence, and stood 4
32 Call to me . . " So they came before the king. 4
35 he shall come and sit upon my throne; for he shall 4
42 Jonathan the son of Abi'athar the priest came; 4
42 Adoni'jah said, "Come in, for you are a worthy man 4
47 the king's servants came to congratulate our 4
53 And he came and did obeisance to King Solomon; 4
2:13 Adoni'jah . . came to Bathshe'ba the mother 4
13 she said, "Do you come peaceably? 4
28 When the news came to Jo'ab . . Jo'ab fled 4
30 Benai'ah came to the tent of the LORD, and said 4
3: 7 I do not know how to go out or come in. 4
15 Then he came to Jerusalem, and stood before 4
16 two harlots came to the king, and stood before 4
4:27 and for all who came to King Solomon's table, each 34
34 men came . . to hear the wisdom of Solomon 4
6:11 Now the word of the LORD came to Solomon 6
7:14 He came to King Solomon, and did all his work. 4
8: 3 all the elders of Israel came 4
31 If a man sins . . and comes and swears his oath 4
41 when a foreigner . . comes from a far country 4
42 when he comes and prays toward this house 4
9:12 when Hiram came from Tyre to see the cities 13
10: 1 she came to test him with hard questions. 4
2 She came to Jerusalem with a very great retinue 4
2 when she came to Solomon, she told him all 4
7 until I came and my own eyes had seen it; 4
10 never again came such an abundance of spices 4
12 no such almug wood has come or been seen 4
14 the weight of gold that came to Solomon 4
15 besides that which came from the traders •
22 the fleet . . used to come bringing gold, silver 4
11:18 They set out from Mid'ian and came to Paran 4
18 They . . came to Egypt, to Pharaoh king of Egypt 4
12: 1 all Israel had come to Shechem to make him king. 4
3 Jerobo'am and all the assembly of Israel came 4
12 Jerobo'am and all the people came to Rehobo'am 4
21 When Rehobo'am came to Jerusalem, he assembled 4
22 the word of God came to Shemai'ah the man of God 6
13: 1 man of God came out of Judah 4
7 Come home with me, and refresh yourself 4
9 drink water, nor return by the way that you came.' 7
10 did not return by the way that he came to Bethel. 4
11 his sons came and told him all that the man of God 4
12 the way which the man of God who came from Judah 4
14 Are you the man of God who came from Judah? 4
15 he said to him, "Come home with me and eat bread. 7
17 nor return by the way that you came.' 7
20 the word of the LORD came to the prophet 6
21 he cried to the man of God who came from Judah 4
22 your body shall not come to the tomb 4
25 they came and told it in the city 4
14: 4 went to Shiloh, and came to the house of Ahi'jah. 4
5 the wife of Jerobo'am is coming to inquire of you 4
5 When she came, she pretended to be another woman. 4
6 the sound of her feet, as she came in at the door 4
6 Come in, wife of Jerobo'am; why do you pretend 4
13 he only of Jerobo'am shall come to the grave 4
17 wife arose, and departed, and came to Tirzah. 4
17 as she came to the threshold of the house 4
15:17 no one to go out or come in to Asa king of Judah. 4
16: 1 word of the LORD came to Jehu . . against Ba'asha •
7 the word of the LORD came by the prophet Jehu 6
10 Zimri came in and struck him down and killed him 4
17: 2 And the word of the LORD came to him 6
8 Then the word of the LORD came to him 6
10 when he came to the gate of the city, behold, a widow 4
18 You have come to me to bring my sin to remembrance 4
18: 1 the word of the LORD came to Eli'jah . . saying, "Go 6
12 when I come and tell Ahab . . he will kill me 4
31 Jacob, to whom the word of the LORD came, saying 6
19: 3 and he arose and went . . and came to Beer-sheba 4
4 and came and sat down under a broom tree; 4
9 there he came to a cave, and lodged 4
9 the word of the LORD came to him, and he said to him •
13 And behold, there came a voice to him, and said •
20:22 Come, strengthen yourself, and consider well 7
43 king . . went to his house . . and came to Sama'ria. 4
21: 5 Jez'ebel his wife came to him, and said to him 4
13 the two base fellows came in and sat opposite him; 4
17 the word of the LORD came to Eli'jah the Tishbite 6
28 the word of the LORD came to Eli'jah the Tishbite 6
22:15 when he had come to the king, the king said to him 4
27 feed him with scant fare . . until I come in peace."' 4
2Kg 1: 6 There came a man to meet us, and said to us, 'Go back 28
7 who came to meet you and told you these things? 28
13 captain . . went up, and came and fell on his knees 4
2: 4 So they came to Jericho. 4
15 they came to meet him, and bowed to the ground 4
21 death nor miscarriage shall come from it. 6
3:15 the power of the LORD came upon him. 6
20 water came from the direction of Edom 4
24 when they came to the camp . . the Israelites rose 4
27 And there came great wrath upon Israel; 6
4: 1 the creditor has come to take my two children 4
7 She came and told the man of God, and he said, "Go 4
10 so that whenever he comes to us, he can go in there. 4
11 One day he came there, and he turned 4
25 So she set out, and came to the man of God 4
25 When the man of God saw her coming, he said 18
27 when she came to the mountain to the man of God 4
27 And Geha'zi came to thrust her away. 22
36 he called her. And when she came to him, he said 4
37 She came and fell at his feet, bowing to the ground; 4
39 and came and cut them up into the pot of pottage 4
42 A man came from Ba'al-shal'ishah, bringing 4
5: 8 Let him come now to me, that he may know 4
9 So Na'aman came with his horses and chariots 4
15 he returned . . and he came and stood before him; 4
22 There have just now come to me . . two young men 4
24 when he came to the hill, he took them 4
6: 4 when they came to the Jordan, they cut down trees. 4
14 and they came by night, and surrounded the city. 4
23 the Syrians came no more on raids into the land 4
32 Look, when the messenger comes, shut the door 4
7: 4 So now come, let us go over to the . . Syrians; 7
5 but when they came to the edge of the camp 4
6 Hittites and the kings of Egypt to come upon us. 4
8 when these lepers came to the edge of the camp 4
9 now therefore come, let us go and tell 7
10 So they came and called to the gatekeepers 4
10 We came to the camp of the Syrians 4
8: 1 called for a famine, and it will come upon the land 4

7 Eli'sha came to Damascus. Ben-ha'dad . . was sick; 4
7 when it was told him, "The man of God has come here 4
9 When he came and stood before him, he said 4
14 he departed from Eli'sha, and came to his master 4
9: 5 when he came, behold, the commanders of the army 4
11 Is all well? Why did this mad fellow come to you? 4
17 he spied the company of Jehu as he came, and said 4
19 a second horseman, who came to them, and said 4
30 When Jehu came to Jezreel, Jez'ebel heard of it; 4
10: 2 Now then, as soon as this letter comes to you 4
6 and come to me at Jezreel tomorrow at this time. 4
7 when the letter came . . they took the king's sons 4
8 the messenger came and told him, "They have 4
15 he met Jehon'adab . . coming to meet him; •
16 Come with me, and see my zeal for the LORD. 7
17 when he came to Sama'ria, he slew all that remained 4
21 Jehu sent . . all the worshipers of Ba'al came 4
21 there was not a man left who did not come. 4
11: 4 brought the captains . . and had them come to him 4
5 those who come off duty on the sabbath 4
7 two . . which come on duty in force on the sabbath 13
8 Be with the king . . goes out and when he comes in. 4
9 with those who were to come on duty on the sabbath 13
9 each brought his men . . and came to Jehoi'ada 4
14: 8 saying, "Come let us look one another in the face. 7
13 and came to Jerusalem, and broke down the wall 4
15:14 Men'ahem . . from Tirzah and came to Sama'ria 4
19 Pul the king of Assyria came against the land; 4
29 Tig'lath-pile'ser . . came and captured I'jon 4
16: 6 and the E'domites came to Elath, where they dwell 4
12 And when the king came from Damascus 4
17: 5 king of Assyria invaded . . and came to Sama'ria 28
28 one of the priests . . came and dwelt in Bethel 4
18:17 And they went up and came to Jerusalem. 4
17 they came and stood by the conduit of the upper 4
23 Come now, make a wager with my master the king 20
32 I come and take you away to a land like your own 4
37 Then Eli'akim . . and.., came to Hezeki'ah 4
19: 3 children have come to the birth, and there is no 4
5 When the servants of . . Hezeki'ah came to Isaiah 4
27 I know . . and your going out and coming in 4
28 and your arrogance has come into my ears 28
28 I will turn you back on the way by which you came. 4
32 He shall not come into this city or shoot an arrow 4
33 By the way that he came, by the same he shall return 4
33 he shall not come into this city, says the LORD. 4
20: 1 Isaiah the prophet . . came to him, and said to him 4
4 the word of the LORD came to him 6
14 Then Isaiah the prophet came to King Hezeki'ah 4
14 did these men say? And whence did they come to you? 4
14 They have come from a far country, from Babylon. 4
17 Behold, the days are coming, when all . . shall be 4
22: 9 Shaphan . . came to the king, and reported 4
23:17 the man of God who came from Judah and predicted 4
18 the bones of the prophet who came out of Sama'ria. 4
34 and he came to Egypt, and died there. 4
24: 3 this came upon Judah at the command of the LORD 6
11 Nebuchadnez'zar king of Babylon came to the city 4
20 it came to the point in Jerusalem and Judah that 6
25: 1 Nebuchadnez'zar . . came with all his army 4
8 Nebu'zarad'an . . came to Jerusalem. 4
23 when all the captains . . they came with their men 4
25 Ish'mael . . came with ten men, and attacked 4
1Ch 1:12 Caslu'him (whence came the Philis'tines) 13
2:53 from these came the Zo'rathites 13
55 These are the Ken'ites who came from Hammath 4
4:41 These . . came in the days of Hezeki'ah 4
7:22 and his brothers came to comfort him. 4
9:25 were obliged to come in every seven days 4
10: 4 these uncircumcised come and make sport of me. 4
7 the Philistines came and dwelt in them. 4
8 when the Philistines came to strip the slain 4
11: 3 the elders of Israel came to the king at Hebron; 4
5 said to David, "You will not come in here. 4
12: 1 Now these are the men who came to David at Ziklag 4
16 men of Benjamin and Judah came to the stronghold 4
17 If you have come to me in friendship to help me 4
19 David when he came with the Philistines 4
22 men kept coming to David to help him 4
23 armed troops, who came to David in Hebron 4
31 were expressly named to come and make David king. 4
38 All these . . came to Hebron with full intent 4
13: 9 when they came to the threshing floor of Chidon 4
14: 9 Now the Philistines had come and made a raid 4
14 and come upon them opposite the balsam trees. 4
15:29 ark of the covenant of the LORD came to the city 4
16:29 bring an offering, and come before him! 4
33 the LORD, for he comes to judge the earth. 4
17: 3 same night the word of the LORD came to Nathan 6
17 thy servant's house for a great while to come •
18: 5 Syrians of Damascus came to help Hadade'zer 4
19: 2 David's servants came to Hanun . . to console 4
3 Have not his servants come to you to search 4
7 who came and encamped before Med'eba. 4
7 Ammonites were mustered . . and came to battle. 4
9 the kings who had come were by themselves 4
15 Then Jo'ab came to Jerusalem. 4
17 crossed the Jordan, and came to them 4
20: 1 and came and besieged Rabbah. 4

21:11 Gad came to David and said . . "Thus says the LORD 4
21 As David came to Ornan, Ornan looked and saw David 4
22: 8 the word of the LORD came to me, saying 6
24:19 duty . . to come into the house of the LORD 4
27: 1 concerning the divisions that came and went 4
24 yet wrath came upon Israel for this 6
29:12 riches and honor come from thee, and thou rulest •
14 For all things come from thee •
16 all this abundance . . comes from thy hand •
30 circumstances that came upon him and upon 26
2Ch 1:10 wisdom and knowledge to go out and come 4
13 Solomon came from the high place at Gibeon 4
5: 4 all the elders of Israel came 4
6:22 made to take an oath, and comes and swears his oath 4
32 when a foreigner . . comes from a far country 4
32 when he comes and prays toward this house 4
8:11 places to which the ark . . has come are holy. 4
9: 1 she came to Jerusalem to test him 4
1 When she came to Solomon, she told him all that was 4
6 I did not believe the reports until I came 4
13 weight of gold that came to Solomon in one year 4
21 ships of Tarshish used to come bringing gold 4
10: 1 all Israel had come to Shechem to make him king. 4
3 Jerobo'am and all Israel came and said 4
5 He said to them, "Come to me again in three days. 38
12 Jerobo'am and all the people came to Rehobo'am 4
11: 1 When Rehobo'am came to Jerusalem 4
2 word of the LORD came to Shemai'ah the man of God 6
14 +evites left . . and came to Judah and Jerusalem 7
16 came after them from all the tribes of Israel 4
12: 3 people were without number who came with him 4
4 came as far as Jerusalem. 4
5 Then Shemai'ah the prophet came to Rehobo'am 4
7 word of the LORD came to Shemai'ah 6
11 guard came and bore them, and brought them back 4
13: 9 Whoever comes to consecrate himself 4
13 sent an ambush around to come on them from behind; 4
14: 9 came as far as Mare'shah. 4
11 in thy name we have come against this multitude. 4
15: 1 Spirit of God came upon Azari'ah the son of Oded 6
5 there was no peace . . to him who came 4
16: 1 that he might permit no one to go out or come 4
7 Hana'ni the seer came to Asa king of Judah 4
18:14 when he had come to the king, the king said to him 4
19:10 whenever a case comes to you from your brethren 4
10 wrath may not come upon you and your brethren. 6
20: 1 came against Jehosh'aphat for battle. 4
2 Some men came and told Jehosh'aphat 4
2 great multitude is coming against you from Edom 4
4 from all the cities of Judah they came to seek 4
9 If evil comes upon us, the sword, judgment 4
10 when they came from the land of Egypt 4
11 behold, they reward us by coming to drive us 4
12 this great multitude that is coming against us. 4
14 the Spirit of the LORD came upon Jaha'ziel 6
22 had come against Judah, so that they were routed. 4
24 Judah came to the watchtower of the wilderness 4
25 When Jehosh'aphat and his people came to take 4
28 They came to Jerusalem with harps and lyres 4
29 fear of God came on all the kingdoms 6
21:12 a letter came to him from Eli'jah . . saying 4
22: 1 band of men that came with the Arabs . . had slain 4
7 came there he went out with Jeho'ram to meet Jehu 4
23: 2 and they came to Jerusalem. 4
4 of you priests and Levites who come off duty 4
7 Be with the king when he comes 4
8 with those who were to come on duty on the sabbath; 13
24:11 would come and empty the chest and take it 4
17 the princes of Judah came and did obeisance 4
18 wrath came upon Judah and Jerusalem for this 6
23 They came to Judah and Jerusalem 4
24 the army of the Syrians had come with few men 4
25: 7 a man of God came to him and said 4
10 the army that had come to him from E'phraim 4
14 Amazi'ah came from the slaughter of the E'domites 4
17 Come, let us look one another in the face. 7
28: 9 he went out to meet the army that came to Sama'ria 4
12 stood up against those . . coming from the war 4
20 Til'gath-pilne'ser king of Assyria came against 4
29: 8 the wrath of the LORD came on Judah and Jerusalem 6
17 they came to the vestibule of the LORD; 4
30: 1 come to the house of the LORD at Jerusalem, to keep 4
5 the people should come and keep the passover 4
8 come to his sanctuary, which he has sanctified 4
11 humbled themselves and came to Jerusalem. 4
25 whole assembly that came out of Israel 4
25 sojourners who came out of the land of Israel 4
27 their prayer came to his holy habitation 4
31: 8 Hezeki'ah and the princes came and saw the heaps 4
32: 1 Sennach'erib king of Assyria came and invaded 4
2 Sennach'erib had come and intended to fight 4
4 Why should the kings of Assyria come and find 4
21 And when he came into the house of his god 4
25 wrath came upon him and Judah and Jerusalem. 6
26 wrath of the LORD did not come upon them 4
34: 9 came to Hilki'ah the high priest and delivered 4
35:21 I am not coming against you this day, but against 83
Ezr 2: 2 They came with Zerub'babel, Jeshua, Nehemi'ah 4
68 when they came to the house of the LORD 4

3: 1 When the seventh month came 21
8 second year of their coming to the house of God 4
8 who had come to Jerusalem from the captivity. 4
5: 3 Tat'tenai . . came to them and spoke to them thus 39
16 Shesh-baz'zar came and laid the foundations 39
7: 8 came to Jerusalem in the fifth month 4
9 first day of the fifth month he came to Jerusalem 4
8:13 Of the sons of Adoni'kam, those who came later •
32 We came to Jerusalem and there we remained 4
35 At that time those who had come from captivity 4
9:13 after all that has come upon us for our evil deeds 4
10: 8 that if any one did not come within three days 4
14 taken foreign wives come at appointed times 4
Neh 1: 2 Hana'ni . . came with certain men out of Judah; 4
2: 7 let me pass through until I come to Judah; 4
9 Then I came to the governors of the province 4
10 some one had come to seek the welfare 4
11 I came to Jerusalem and was there three days. 4
17 Come, let us build the wall of Jerusalem 7
4: 8 they all plotted together to come and fight 4
11 not know or see till we come into the midst of them 4
12 When the Jews who lived by them came they said 4
12 From all the places . . they will come up against •
5:17 besides those who came to us from the nations 4
6: 2 Come and let us meet together in one 7
7 now come, and let us take counsel together. 7
10 for they are coming to kill you, at night 4
10 at night they are coming to kill you. 4
17 Tobi'ah's letters came to them. 4
7: 7 came with Zerub'babel, Jeshua, Nehemi'ah, Azari'ah 4
73 seventh month had come, the children of Israel 21
9:32 all the hardship . . that has come upon us 19
33 thou hast been just in all that has come upon us 4
13: 7 came to Jerusalem, and I then discovered the evil 4
21 time on they did not come on the sabbath. 4
22 purify themselves and come and guard the gates 4
Est 1:12 Vashti refused to come at the king's command 4
17 Ahasu-e'rus commanded . . and she did not come 4
19 Vashti is to come no more before King Ahasu-e'rus 4
2:12 Now when the turn came for each maiden to go 21
15 the turn came for Esther . . to go in to the king 21
4: 3 wherever the king's command and his decree came 21
4 Esther's maids and her eunuchs came and told her 4
11 I have not been called to come in to the king these 4
14 have . . come to the kingdom for such a time as this? 21
5: 4 let the king and Haman come this day to a dinner 4
5 the king and Haman came to the dinner 4
8 the king and Haman come tomorrow to the dinner 4
8 the king and Haman come tomorrow to the dinner 49
12 Esther let no one come with the king 4
6: 5 And the king said, "Let him come in. 4
6 Haman came in, and the king said to him 4
8: 1 And Mor'decai came before the king 4
6 to see the calamity that is coming to my people? 19
17 wherever the king's command and his edict came 21
9:25 when Esther came before the king, he gave orders 4
25 his wicked plot . . should come upon his own head 38
Job 1: 6 when the sons of God came to present themselves 4
6 before the LORD, and Satan also came among them. 4
7 The LORD said to Satan, "Whence have you come? 4
14 there came a messenger to Job, and said 4
16 While he was yet speaking, there came another 4
17 there came another, and said, "The Chalde'ans 4
18 While he was yet speaking, there came another 4
19 behold, a great wind came across the wilderness 4
21 he said, "Naked I came from my mother's womb 13
2: 1 when the sons of God came to present themselves 4
1 Satan also came among them to present himself 4
2 the LORD said to Satan, "Whence have you come? 4
11 heard of all this evil that had come upon him 4
11 they came each from his own place 4
11 They made an appointment together to come 4
3: 6 let it not come into the number of the months. 4
21 who long for death, but it comes not •
24 For my sighing comes as my bread 4
26 I have no rest; but trouble comes. 4
4: 5 now it has come to you, and you are impatient; 4
5: 6 For affliction does not come from the dust 13
21 and shall not fear destruction when it comes. 4
26 You shall come to your grave in ripe old age 4
6:20 they come thither and are confounded. 4
9:32 that we should come to trial together. 4
13:13 I will speak, and let come on me what may. 26
16 a godless man shall not come before him. 4
14:14 I would wait, till my release should come. 4
16:22 For when a few years have come I shall go 3
17:10 come on again, all of you 4
19:12 His troops come on together; 4
20:25 It is drawn forth and comes out of his body 13
25 the glittering point comes out of his gall; 7
25 terrors come upon him. 7
21:17 That their calamity comes upon them? 4
22:21 be at peace; thereby good will come to you. 4
23: 3 that I might come even to his seat! 4
27: 9 Will God hear his cry, when trouble comes upon him? 4
28: 5 As for the earth, out of it comes bread; 13
20 Whence then comes wisdom? 4
29:13 blessing of him . . about to perish came upon me 4
30:14 As through a wide breach they come; 3

26 when I looked for good, evil came; 4
26 when I waited for light, darkness came. 4
33:26 he comes into his presence with joy. •
37: 2 the rumbling that comes from his mouth. 13
9 From its chamber comes the whirlwind 4
22 Out of the north comes golden splendor; 3
38:11 and said, 'Thus far shall you come, and no farther 4
41:16 near to another that no air can come between 4
42:11 Then came to him all his brothers and sisters 4
Ps 14: 7 deliverance for Israel would come out of Zion! •
17: 2 From thee let my vindication come! 13
22:25 From thee comes my praise in the . . congregation; •
30 shall tell of the Lord to the coming generation 4
24: 7 that the King of glory may come in. 4
9 that the King of glory may come in. 4
30: 5 for the night, but joy comes with the morning. •
33: 9 For he spoke, and it came to be; 6
34:11 Come, O sons, listen to me, I will teach you 7
37:13 at the wicked, for he sees that his day is coming. 4
40: 7 Lo, I come; in the roll of the book it is written of me; 4
41: 6 when one comes to see me, he utters empty words 4
42: 2 When shall I come and behold the face of God? 4
46: 8 Come, behold the works of the LORD 7
48: 4 lo, the kings assembled, they came on together. 26
50: 3 Our God comes, he does not keep silence 4
51: 0 when Nathan the prophet came to him 4
52: 0 when Doeg, the Edomite, came and told Saul 4
0 David has come to the house of Ahimelech. 4
53: 6 O that deliverance for Israel would come †
55: 5 Fear and trembling come upon me 4
15 Let death come upon them; let them go down to Sheol 25
59: 4 Rouse thyself, come to my help, and see! 33
62: 1 from him comes my salvation. •
65: 2 To thee shall all flesh come 4
66: 5 Come and see what God has done 7
16 Come and hear, all you who fear God 7
68:17 Lord came from Sinai into the holy place. •
69: 1 O God! For the waters have come up to my neck. 4
2 there is no foothold; I have come into deep waters 4
71:16 With the mighty deeds of the Lord GOD I will come 4
18 thy might to all the generations to come. 4
75: 6 not from the wilderness comes lifting up; •
78: 4 but tell to the coming generation 1
79: 1 O God, the heathen have come into thy inheritance; 4
11 Let the groans of the prisoners come before thee; 4
80: 2 Stir up thy might, and come to save us! 7
83: 4 They say, "Come, let us wipe them out as a nation; 7
86: 9 nations thou hast made shall come and bow down 4
88: 2 prayer come before thee, incline thy ear to my cry! 4
90: 9 our years come to an end like a sigh. ‡
95: 1 O come, let us sing to the LORD; 7
6 O come, let us worship and bow down, let us kneel 4
96: 8 bring an offering, and come into his courts! 4
13 before the LORD, for he comes, for he comes to judge 4
13 for he comes, for he comes to judge the earth. 4
98: 9 before the LORD, for he comes to judge the earth. 4
100: 2 Come into his presence with singing! 4
101: 2 Oh when wilt thou come to me? 4
102: 1 Hear my prayer, O LORD; let my cry come to thee! 4
13 time to favor her; the appointed time has come. 4
18 Let this be recorded for a generation to come 1
105:23 Then Israel came to Egypt; 4
31 He spoke, and there came swarms of flies 4
34 He spoke, and the locusts came, and young locusts 4
109:17 He loved to curse; let curses come on him! 4
110: 3 like dew your youth will come to you. •
119:41 Let thy steadfast love come to me, O LORD 4
77 Let thy mercy come to me, that I may live; 4
169 Let my cry come before thee, O LORD; 35
170 Let my supplication come before thee; 4
121: 1 From whence does my help come? 4
2 My help comes from the LORD, who made heaven •
8 keep your going out and your coming in 4
126: 6 come home with shouts of joy 4
134: 1 Come, bless the LORD, all you servants of the LORD 8
Prv 1:11 Come with us, let us lie in wait for blood 7
27 when . . your calamity comes like a whirlwind 3
27 when distress and anguish come upon you. 4
2: 6 from his mouth come knowledge and understanding; •
10 for wisdom will come into your heart 4
3:25 Do not be afraid . . when it comes; 4
6: 3 for you have come into your neighbor's power 4
15 therefore calamity will come upon him suddenly; 4
7:18 Come, let us take our fill of love till morning; 7
20 at full moon he will come home. 4
8: 6 from my lips will come what is right; •
9: 5 Come, eat of my bread and drink of the wine 7
11: 2 When pride comes, then comes disgrace; 4
2 When pride comes, then comes disgrace; 4
27 but evil comes to him who searches for it. 4
13: 3 he who opens wide his lips comes to ruin. •
18 Poverty . . come to him who ignores instruction •
14: 4 abundant crops come by the strength of the ox. •
18: 3 When wickedness comes, contempt comes also; 4
3 When wickedness comes, contempt comes also; 4
3 with dishonor comes disgrace. •
17 until the other comes and examines him. 4
21: 5 but every one who is hasty comes only to want. •
24:22 who knows the ruin that will come from them both? •

31:25 she laughs at the time to come. 1
Ecc 1: 4 A generation goes, and a generation comes 4
11 things yet to happen among those who come after. 6
2: 1 Come now, I will make a test of pleasure; 7
12 for what can the man do who comes after the king? 4
14 yet I perceived that one fate comes to all of them. 36
16 seeing that in the days to come all will have been 4
18 I must leave it to the man who will come after me; 6
4: 4 all toil and all skill in work come from . . envy •
5: 3 For a dream comes with much business 4
15 As he came from his mother's womb he shall go again 13
15 As he came . . he shall go again, naked as he came 4
16 This also is . . evil: just as he came, so shall he go; 4
6: 4 For it comes into vanity and goes into darkness 4
10 Whatever has come to be has already been named 6
9: 2 since one fate comes to all, to the righteous •
3 This is an evil in all . . that one fate comes to all; •
14 and a great king came against it and besieged it 4
11: 5 you do not know how the spirit comes to the bones 5
8 All that comes is vanity. 4
12: 1 in the days of . . youth, before the evil days come 4
Sng 2: 8 Behold, he comes, leaping upon the mountains 4
12 flowers appear . . the time of singing has come 21
4: 8 Come with me from Lebanon, my bride; come with me 53
8 from Lebanon, my bride; come with me from Lebanon. 4
16 Awake, O north wind, and come, O south wind! 4
16 Let my beloved come to his garden 4
5: 1 I come to my garden, my sister, my bride 4
7:11 Come, my beloved, let us go forth into the fields 7
Isa 1:12 When you come to appear before me 4
18 Come now, let us reason together, says the LORD 7
23 the widow's cause does not come to them. 4
2: 3 many peoples shall come, and say: "Come, let us go up 7
3 Come, let us go up to the mountain of the LORD 7
5 O house of Jacob, come, let us walk in the light 7
5:19 draw near, and let it come, that we may know it! 4
26 and lo, swiftly, speedily it comes! 4
7:17 bring . . such days as have not come 4
19 they will all come and settle in the . . ravines 4
24 With bow and arrows men will come there 4
25 you will not come there for fear of briers 4
10: 3 in the storm which will come from afar? 4
28 he has come to Ai'ath; he has passed through Migron 4
13: 5 come from a distant land . . the end of the heavens 4
6 as destruction from the Almighty it will come! 4
9 Behold, the day of the LORD comes, cruel 4
14: 9 Sheol . . is stirred up to meet you when you come 4
28 In the year that King Ahaz died came this oracle 6
31 For smoke comes out of the north 4
16:12 when he comes to his sanctuary to pray 4
19: 1 LORD is riding on a swift cloud and comes to Egypt; 4
23 the Assyrian will come into Egypt 4
20: 1 came to Ashdod and fought against it and took it,- 4
21: 1 it comes from the desert, from a terrible land. 4
9 And, behold, here come riders, horsemen in pairs! 4
12 Morning comes, and also the night. 3
12 If you will inquire, inquire; come back again. 3
22:15 Come, go to this steward, to Shebna 7
23: 5 When the report comes to Egypt •
26:20 Come, my people, enter your chambers 7
27: 6 In days to come Jacob shall take root 4
11 women come and make a fire of them. 4
13 will come and worship the LORD 4
28:15 scourge passes through it will not come to us; 4
29 This also comes from the LORD of hosts; 13
29: 4 from low in the dust your words shall come; •
4 your voice shall come from the ground 6
24 who err in spirit will come to understanding 11
30: 6 from where come the lioness and the lion •
8 for the time to come as a witness for ever. 1
13 whose crash comes suddenly, in an instant; 4
27 Behold, the name of the LORD comes from far 4
32:10 vintage . . fail, the fruit harvest will not come. 4
34: 1 the world, and all that comes from it. 31
35: 4 Behold, your God will come with vengeance 4
4 He will come and save you. 4
10 shall return, and come to Zion with singing; 4
36: 8 Come now, make a wager with my master the king •
17 until I come and take you away to a land 4
22 came to Hezeki'ah with their clothes rent 4
37: 3 children have come to birth 4
5 the servants of King Hezeki'ah came to Isaiah 4
24 I came to its remotest height, its densest forest 4
28 sitting down and your going out and coming in 4
29 your arrogance has come to my ears 28
29 I will turn you back on the way by which you came. 4
33 He shall not come into this city 4
34 By the way that he came, by the same he shall return 4
34 he shall not come into this city, says the LORD. 4
38: 1 Isaiah the prophet the son of Amoz came to him 4
4 Then the word of the LORD came to Isaiah 6
39: 3 Then Isaiah the prophet came to King Hezeki'ah 4
3 did these men say? And whence did they come to you? 4
3 have come to me from a far country, from Babylon. 4
6 the days are coming, when all that is in your house 4
40:10 Behold, the Lord GOD comes with might 4
41: 5 they have drawn near and come. 3
23 Tell us what is to come hereafter, that we may know 3
25 and he has come, from the rising of the sun 3

42: 5 who spread forth the earth and what comes from it 31
45:14 the Sabe'ans, men of stature, shall come over to you 26
20 Assemble yourselves and come 4
24 to him shall come and be ashamed 4
47: 9 These two things shall come to you in a moment 4
9 widowhood shall come upon you in full measure 4
11 evil shall come upon you 4
11 ruin shall come on you suddenly 4
48:16 from the time it came to be I have been there. 6
49:12 Lo, these shall come from afar 4
18 they all gather, they come to you. 4
21 I was left alone; whence then have these come?' •
50: 2 Why, when I came, was there no man? 4
51:11 shall return, and come to Zion with singing; 4
52: 1 shall no more come into you the uncircumcised 4
55: 1 Ho, every one who thirsts, come to the waters; 7
1 and he who has no money, come, buy and eat! 7
1 Come, buy wine and milk without money 7
3 Incline your ear, and come to me; 7
56: 1 righteousness, for soon my salvation will come 4
9 All you beasts of the field, come to devour- 3
12 Come," they say, "let us get wine 3
59:19 for he will come like a rushing stream 4
20 And he will come to Zion as Redeemer 4
60: 1 Arise, shine; for your light has come 4
3 And nations shall come to your light 7
4 they all gather together, they come to you; 4
4 your sons shall come from far, and your daughters 4
5 the wealth of the nations shall come to you. 4
6 all those from Sheba shall come. 4
13 The glory of Lebanon shall come to you 4
14 who oppressed you shall come bending low to you; 7
62:11 Behold, your salvation comes; 4
63: 1 this that comes from Edom, in crimsoned garments 4
4 and my year of redemption has come. 4
65:17 the former things shall not . . come into mind. 28
66: 7 before her pain came upon her she was delivered 4
15 For behold, the LORD will come in fire 4
18 and I am coming to gather all nations and tongues; 79
18 and they shall come and shall see my glory 4
23 all flesh shall come to worship before me 4
Jer 1: 2 to whom the word of the LORD came 6
3 It came also in the days of Jehoi'akim 6
4 Now the word of the LORD came to me saying 6
11 the word of the LORD came to me, saying, "Jeremiah 6
13 The word of the LORD came to me a second time 6
15 shall come and every one shall set his throne 4
2: 1 The word of the LORD came to me, saying 6
3 evil came upon them, says the LORD. 4
7 But when you came in you defiled my land 4
31 We are free, we will come no more to thee'? 4
3: 3 and the spring rain has not come; 6
16 It shall not come to mind, or be remembered 28
18 they shall come from the land of the north 4
22 we come to thee; for thou art the LORD our God. 3
4:12 a wind too full for this comes for me. 4
16 Warn the nations that he is coming; •
16 Besiegers come from a distant land; 4
5:12 He will do nothing; no evil will come upon us 4
31 but what will you do when the end comes? •
6: 3 Shepherds with . . flocks shall come against her; 4
20 To what purpose does frankincense come to me 4
22 Behold, a people is coming from the north country 4
26 for suddenly the destroyer will come upon us. 4
7: 1 The word that came to Jeremiah from the LORD 6
10 and then come and stand before me in this house 4
31 I did not command, nor did it come into my mind. 28
32 behold, the days are coming, says the LORD 4
8: 7 swallow, and crane keep the time of their coming; 4
15 We looked for peace, but no good came •
16 They come and devour the land 4
9:17 Consider, and call for the mourning women to come; 4
17 send for the skilful women to come; 4
25 Behold, the days are coming, says the LORD 4
10:22 Hark, a rumor! Behold, it comes!-a great commotion 4
11: 1 The word that came to Jeremiah from the LORD 6
12:12 in the desert destroyers have come; 4
13: 3 the word of the LORD came to me a second time 6
8 Then the word of the LORD came to me 6
20 and see those who come from the north. 4
14: 1 The word of the LORD which came to Jeremiah 6
3 they come to the cisterns, they find no water 4
15 Sword and famine shall not come on this land 6
19 We looked for peace, but no good came; •
16: 1 The word of the LORD came to me 6
14 behold, the days are coming, says the LORD 4
19 to thee shall the nations come 4
17: 6 in the desert, and shall not see any good come. 4
8 and does not fear when heat comes 4
15 Where is the word of the LORD? Let it come! 4
26 And people shall come from the cities of Judah 4
18: 1 The word that came to Jeremiah from the LORD 6
5 Then the word of the LORD came to me 6
18 Come, let us make plots against Jeremiah 7
18 Come, let us smite him with the tongue 7
19: 5 not command or decree, nor did it come into my mind; 28
6 therefore, behold, days are coming, says the LORD 4
14 Then Jeremiah came from Topheth 4
21: 1 the word which came to Jeremiah from the LORD 6

22:23 how you will groan when pangs come upon you 4
23: 5 Behold, the days are coming, says the LORD 4
7 behold, the days are coming, says the LORD 4
17 they say, 'No evil shall come upon you. 4
24: 4 Then the word of the LORD came to me 6
25: 1 The word that came to Jeremiah 6
3 to this day, the word of the LORD has come to me 6
34 your slaughter and dispersion have come 17
26: 1 this word came from the LORD 6
2 the cities of Judah which come to worship 4
27: 1 this word came to Jeremiah from the LORD. 6
3 the envoys who have come to Jerusalem 4
7 until the time of his own land comes; 4
28:12 the word of the LORD came to Jeremiah 6
29:12 Then you will call upon me and come and pray to me 7
30 Then the word of the LORD came to Jeremiah 6
30: 1 The word that came to Jeremiah from the LORD 6
3 For behold, days are coming, says the LORD 4
31: 9 With weeping they shall come 4
12 shall come and sing aloud on the height of Zion 4
27 Behold, the days are coming, says the LORD 4
31 Behold, the days are coming, says the LORD 4
38 Behold, the days are coming, says the LORD 4
32: 1 The word that came to Jeremiah from the LORD 6
6 Jeremiah said, "The word of the LORD came to me 6
7 son of Shallum your uncle will come to you and say 4
8 my cousin came to me in the court of the guard 4
26 The word of the LORD came to Jeremiah 6
29 shall come and set this city on fire, and burn it 4
33: 1 word of the LORD came to Jeremiah a second time 6
5 The Chalde'ans are coming in to fight 4
14 Behold, the days are coming, says the LORD 4
19 The word of the LORD came to Jeremiah 6
20 and night will not come at their appointed time 6
23 The word of the LORD came to Jeremiah 6
34: 1 The word which came to Jeremiah from the LORD 6
8 The word which came to Jeremiah from the LORD 6
12 word of the LORD came to Jeremiah from the LORD 6
35: 1 The word which came to Jeremiah from the LORD 6
11 we said, 'Come, and let us go to Jerusalem 4
12 Then the word of the LORD came to Jeremiah 6
36: 1 this word came to Jeremiah from the LORD 6
7 their supplication will come before the LORD 24
9 the people who came from the cities of Judah 4
14 Take in your hand the scroll . . and come. 7
14 took the scroll in his hand and came to them. 4
27 the word of the LORD came to Jeremiah 6
29 the king of Babylon will certainly come 4
37: 6 the word of the LORD came to Jeremiah the prophet 6
7 Behold, Pharoah's army which came to help you 13
16 When Jeremiah had come to the dungeon cells 4
19 The king of Babylon will not come against you 4
20 lord the king: let my humble plea come before you 24
38:25 have spoken with you and come to you and say to you 4
27 all the princes came to Jeremiah and asked him 4
39: 1 all his army came against Jerusalem 4
3 the princes of the king of Babylon came and sat 4
15 The word of the LORD came to Jeremiah 6
40: 1 The word that came to Jeremiah from the LORD 6
3 this thing has come upon you. 6
4 If it seems good to you to come with me to Babylon 4
4 to Babylon, come, and I will look after you well; 4
4 if it seems wrong to you to come with me to Babylon 4
4 but if it seems wrong to you to come . . do not come. *
10 before the Chalde'ans who will come to us; 4
12 they had been driven and came to the land of Judah 4
13 the leaders . . came to Gedali'ah at Mizpah 4
41: 1 the chief officers of the king, came with ten men 4
6 out from Mizpah to meet them, weeping as he came. 7
6 he said to them, "Come in to Gedali'ah 4
7 When they came into the city, Ish'mael . . slew them 4
42: 2 Let our supplication come before you 24
7 the word of the LORD came to Jeremiah. 6
43: 7 And they came into the land of Egypt 4
8 word of the LORD came to Jeremiah in Tah'panhes 6
11 He shall come and smite the land of Egypt 4
44: 1 The word that came to Jeremiah 6
8 in the land of Egypt where you have come to live 4
12 have set their faces to come to the land of Egypt 4
14 who have come to live in the land of Egypt 4
21 Did it not come into his mind? 28
28 the remnant of Judah, who came to the land of Egypt 4
46: 1 The word of the LORD which came to Jeremiah 6
13 the coming of Nebuchadrez'zar king of Babylon 4
18 and like Carmel by the sea, shall one come. 4
20 but a gadfly from the north has come upon her. 4
21 for the day of their calamity has come upon them 4
22 march in force, and come against her with axes 4
47: 1 The word of the LORD that came to Jeremiah 6
4 because of the day that is coming to destroy all 4
5 Baldness has come upon Gaza 4
48: 2 Come, let us cut her off from being a nation! 7
8 The destroyer shall come upon every city 4
12 behold, the days are coming, says the LORD 4
21 Judgment has come upon the tableland, upon Holon 4
49: 2 behold, the days are coming, says the LORD 4
4 saying, 'Who will come against me?' 4
9 If grape-gatherers came to you 4
9 If thieves came by night, would they not destroy *
14 and come against her, and rise up for battle! 4
34 The word of the LORD that came to Jeremiah 6
36 to which those driven out of Elam shall not come. 4
50: 4 and the people of Judah shall come together 4
4 Judah shall come together, weeping as they come; 7
5 saying, 'Come, let us join ourselves to the LORD 4
26 Come against her from every quarter; 4
27 Woe to them, for their day has come 4
31 your day has come, the time when I will punish you. 4
41 Behold, a people comes from the north; 4
51: 2 when they come against her from every side 6
10 come, let us declare in Zion the work of the LORD 4
13 your end has come, the thread of your life is cut. 4
33 and the time of her harvest will come. 4
46 when a report comes in one year 4
47 Therefore, behold, the days are coming 4
48 for the destroyers shall come against them 4
50 let Jerusalem come into your mind 28
51 aliens have come into the holy places 4
52 behold, the days are coming, says the LORD 4
53 yet destroyers would come from me upon her 4
56 for a destroyer has come upon her, upon Babylon; 4
60 all the evil that should come upon Babylon 4
61 said to Serai'ah: "When you come to Babylon 4
52: 4 king of Babylon came with all his army 4
Lam 1: 4 Zion mourn, for none come to the appointed feasts; 4
22 Let all their evil-doing come before thee; 4
3:38 the mouth of the Most High that good and evil come? 13
47 panic and pitfall have come upon us 6
4:18 our days were numbered; for our end had come. 4
Ezk 1: 3 the word of the LORD came to Ezekiel the priest 6
4 behold, a stormy wind came out of the north 4
5 And from the midst of it came the likeness *
25 there came a voice from above the firmament 6
3:15 I came to the exiles at Tel-abib 4
16 the word of the LORD came to me 6
4:14 nor has foul flesh come into my mouth. 4
6: 1 The word of the LORD came to me 6
7: 1 The word of the LORD came to me 6
2 end has come upon the four corners of the land. 4
5 Disaster after disaster! Behold, it comes. 4
6 An end has come, the end has come; 4
6 An end has come, the end has come; 4
6 it has awakened against you. Behold, it comes. 4
7 Your doom has come to you, O inhabitant of the land; 4
7 the time has come, the day is near, a day of tumult 4
10 Behold, it comes! Your doom has come 4
10 Behold, it comes! Your doom has come 13
12 The time has come, the day draws near. 4
25 When anguish comes, they will seek peace 4
26 Disaster comes upon disaster 4
9: 2 six men came from the direction of the upper gate 4
11: 5 I know the things that come into your mind. 28
14 the word of the LORD came to me 6
18 when they come there, they will remove from it all 4
12: 1 The word of the LORD came to me 6
8 In the morning the word of the LORD came to me 6
17 Moreover the word of the LORD came to me 6
21 the word of the LORD came to me 6
26 Again the word of the LORD came to me 6
13: 1 The word of the LORD came to me 6
14: 1 Then came certain of the elders of Israel to me; 4
2 the word of the LORD came to me 6
4 yet comes to the prophet, I the LORD will answer 4
7 yet comes to a prophet to inquire for himself 4
12 the word of the LORD came to me 6
15: 1 the word of the LORD came to me 6
16: 1 Again the word of the LORD came to me 6
13 You grew . . beautiful, and came to regal estate. 32
33 bribing them to come to you from every side 4
17: 1 The word of the LORD came to me 6
3 came to Lebanon and took the top of the cedar; 4
11 Then the word of the LORD came to me 6
12 Behold, the king of Babylon came to Jerusalem 4
18: 1 The word of the LORD came to me again 6
20: 1 certain of the elders of Israel came to inquire 4
2 the word of the LORD came to me 6
3 Is it to inquire of me that you come? 4
45 the word of the LORD came to me 6
21: 1 The word of the LORD came to me 6
7 When it comes, every heart will melt 4
7 Behold, it comes and it will be fulfilled 4
8 the word of the LORD came to me 6
14 clap your hands and let the sword come down twice *
18 The word of the LORD came to me again 6
19 ways for the sword of the king of Babylon to come; 4
20 mark a way for the sword to come to Rabbah 4
22 Into his right hand comes the lot for Jerusalem 6
25 wicked one, prince of Israel, whose day has come 4
27 until he comes whose right it is; 4
29 the unhallowed wicked, whose day has come 4
22: 1 Moreover the word of the LORD came to me, saying 6
3 blood in the midst of her, that her time may come 4
4 the appointed time of your years has come. 4
17 the word of the LORD came to me 6
23 the word of the LORD came to me 6
23: 1 The word of the LORD came to me 6
17 the Babylonians came to her into the bed of love 4
24 And they shall come against you from the north 4
39 they came into my sanctuary to profane it. 4
40 They even sent for men to come from far 4
40 far, to whom a messenger was sent, and lo, they came. 4
24: 1 the word of the LORD came to me 6
15 Also the word of the LORD came to me 6
20 I said to them, "The word of the LORD came to me 6
24 When this comes, then you will know 4
26 on that day a fugitive will come to you to report 4
25: 1 The word of the LORD came to me 6
26: 1 the word of the LORD came to me 6
27: 1 The word of the LORD came to me 6
33 When your wares came from the seas 13
36 you have come to a dreadful end 6
28: 1 The word of the LORD came to me 6
11 Moreover the word of the LORD came to me 6
19 you have come to a dreadful end 6
20 The word of the LORD came to me 6
29: 1 the word of the LORD came to me 6
17 the word of the LORD came to me 6
30: 1 The word of the LORD came to me 6
4 A sword shall come upon Egypt 4
9 and anguish shall come upon them 4
9 the day of Egypt's doom; for, lo, it comes! 4
20 the word of the LORD came to me 6
31: 1 the word of the LORD came to me 6
32: 1 the word of the LORD came to me 6
17 the word of the LORD came to me 6
33: 1 The word of the LORD came to me 6
3 if he sees the sword coming upon the land 4
4 and the sword comes and takes him away 4
6 if the watchman sees the sword coming 4
6 and the sword comes, and takes any one of them; 4
21 a man who had escaped from Jerusalem came to me 4
22 the evening before the fugitive came; 4
22 by the time the man came to me in the morning; 4
23 The word of the LORD came to me 6
30 Come, and hear what the word is that comes forth 4
31 they come to you as people come, and they sit 4
31 they come to you as people come, and they sit 15
33 When this comes–and come it will! 4
33 When this comes–and come it will! 4
34: 1 The word of the LORD came to me 6
35: 1 The word of the LORD came to me 6
7 I will cut off from it all who come and go. 26
36: 8 my people Israel; for they will soon come home. 4
16 The word of the LORD came to me 6
20 when they came to the nations 4
20 whereever they came, they profaned my holy name 4
21 profaned among the nations to which they came. 4
22 profaned among the nations to which you came. 4
37: 8 flesh had come upon them, and skin had covered 28
9 Come from the four winds, O breath 4
10 the breath came into them, and they lived 4
15 The word of the LORD came to me 6
38: 1 The word of the LORD came to me 6
9 You will advance, coming on like a storm 4
10 On that day thoughts will come into your mind 28
13 will say to you, 'Have you come to seize spoil? 4
15 come from your place out of the uttermost parts 4
18 on that day, when Gog shall come against the land 4
39: 8 Behold, it is coming and it will be brought about 4
17 Assemble and come, gather from all sides 4
43: 2 the glory of the God of Israel came from the east; 4
2 his coming was like the sound of many waters; *
3 which I had seen when he came to destroy the city 4
46: 9 When the people of the land come before the LORD 4
Dan 2: 2 So they came in and stood before the king. 4
29 in bed came thoughts of what would be hereafter 41
3: 2 come to the dedication of the image 39
26 servants of . . God, come forth, and come here! 39
27 no smell of fire had come upon them. 42
4: 7 magicians . . and the astrologers came in; 43
8 At last Daniel came in before me–he who was named 43
24 decree . . which has come upon my lord the king 40
28 All this came upon King Nebuchadnez'zar. 40
5: 8 Then all the king's wise men came in 43
7:13 clouds of heaven there came one like a son of man 39
13 came to the Ancient of Days and was presented 40
22 until the Ancient of Days came, and judgment 39
22 time came when the saints received the kingdom. 40
8: 5 he-goat came from the west across the . . earth 4
6 He came to the ram with the two horns 4
7 I saw him come close to the ram, and he was enraged 21
17 came near where I stood; and when he came 4
17 came, I was frightened and fell upon my face. 4
9:13 all this calamity has come upon us, yet we have not 4
21 Gabriel . . came to me in swift flight at the time 21
22 came and he said to me, "O Daniel, *
23 come to tell it to you, for you are greatly beloved; 4
25 to the coming of an anointed one, a prince *
26 people of the prince who is to come shall destroy 4
26 Its end shall come with a flood and to the end *
27 upon the wing . . come one who makes desolate *
10:12 I have come because of your words. 4
13 but Michael, one of the chief princes, came to help 4
14 came to make you understand what is to befall 4
14 For the vision is for days yet to come. *
16 by reason of the vision pains have come upon me 9
20 Then he said, "Do you know why I have come to you? 4

20 lo, the prince of Greece will come. 4
11: 6 shall come to the king of the north to make peace; 4
7 come against the army and enter the fortress 4
9 latter shall come into the realm of the king 4
10 which . . come on and overflow and pass through 4
13 come on with a great army and abundant supplies. 4
15 Then the king of the north shall come and throw up 4
16 But he who comes against him shall do according 4
17 come with the strength of his whole kingdom 4
21 come in without warning and obtain the kingdom 4
24 come into the richest parts of the province; 4
29 shall return and come into the south; 4
30 For ships of Kittim shall come against him 4
40 come into countries . . overflow and pass through. 4
41 He shall come into the glorious land. 4
45 yet he shall come to his end, with none to help him. 4
12:12 Blessed is he who waits and comes 21
Hos 1: 1 The word . . that came to Hose'a the son of Be-e'ri 6
3: 5 and they shall come in fear to the LORD *
6: 1 Come, let us return to the LORD; 7
3 he will come to us as the showers 4
9: 4 it shall not come to the house of the LORD. 4
7 The days of punishment have come 4
7 the days of recompense have come; 4
10 But they came to Ba'al-pe'or 4
10:10 I will come against the wayward people *
12 that he may come and rain salvation upon you. 4
11: 9 and I will not come to destroy. 4
12:11 they shall surely come to nought; 6
13:13 The pangs of childbirth come for him 4
15 the east wind, the wind of the LORD, shall come 4
14: 8 from me comes your fruit. 19
Jol 1: 1 The word of the LORD that came to Joel 6
15 and as destruction from the Almighty it comes. 4
2: 1 for the day of the LORD is coming, it is near 4
31 the great and terrible day of the LORD comes. 4
3:11 Hasten and come, all you nations round about 4
Ams 4: 2 that, behold, the days are coming upon you 4
4 Come to Bethel, and transgress; 4
5: 9 so that destruction comes upon the fortress. 4
6: 1 of the nations, to whom the house of Israel come! 4
8: 2 The end has come upon my people Israel; 4
11 Behold, the days are coming," says the Lord GOD 4
9:13 Behold, the days are coming," says the LORD 4
Obd 1: 5 If thieves came to you, if plunderers by night 4
5 If grape gatherers came to you 4
Jon 1: 1 Now the word of the LORD came to Jonah 6
6 the captain came and said to him, "What do you mean 35
7 they said to one another, "Come, let us cast lots 7
7 know on whose account this evil has come upon us. *
8 on whose account this evil has come upon us? *
8 What is your occupation? And whence do you come? 4
12 this great tempest has come upon you. *
2: 7 my prayer came to thee, into thy holy temple. 4
3: 1 Then the word of the LORD came to Jonah 6
Mic 1: 1 The word of the LORD that came to Micah 6
9 her wound is incurable; and it has come to Judah 4
15 the glory of Israel shall come to Adullam. 4
3:11 No evil shall come upon us. 4
4: 2 many nations shall come, and say: "Come, let us go up 7
2 Come, let us go up to the mountain of the LORD 7
8 Zion, to you shall it come 3
8 the former dominion shall come 4
5: 5 when the Assyrian comes into our land 4
6 the Assyrian when he comes into our land 4
7: 4 The day . . of their punishment, has come; 4
12 they will come to you, from Assyria to Egypt 4
Nah 1:15 never again shall the wicked come against you 26
3:19 For upon whom has not come your unceasing evil? 26
Hab 1: 8 Yea, their horsemen come from afar; 4
9 They all come for violence; 4
2: 3 it will surely come, it will not delay. 4
16 and shame will come upon your glory! *
3: 3 God came from Teman 4
Zep 1: 1 The word of the LORD which came to Zephani'ah 6
2: 2 there comes upon you the fierce anger of the LORD 4
2 before there comes upon you the day of the wrath 4
Hag 1: 1 the word of the LORD came by Haggai the prophet 6
2 the time has not yet come to rebuild the house 4
3 the word of the LORD came by Haggai the prophet 6
9 You have looked for much, and, lo, it came to little; *
14 they came and worked on the house of the LORD 4
2: 1 the word of the LORD came by Haggai the prophet 6
7 that the treasures of all nations shall come 4
10 the word of the LORD came by Haggai the prophet 6
16 When one came to a heap of twenty measures 4
16 when one came to the winevat to draw 50 measures 4
20 The word of the LORD came a second time to Haggai 6
Zec 1: 1 the word of the LORD came to Zechari'ah 6
7 the word of the LORD came to Zechari'ah 6
21 I said, "What are these coming to do?" He answered 4
21 these have come to terrify them, to cast down 4
2:10 lo, I come and I will dwell in the midst of you 4
4: 8 Moreover the word of the LORD came to me, saying 6
6: 9 the word of the LORD came to me 6
15 those who are far off shall come and help to build 4
7: 1 the word of the LORD came to Zechari'ah 6
4 Then the word of the LORD of hosts came to me; 6
8 the word of the LORD came to Zechari'ah, saying 6

12 great wrath came from the LORD of hosts. 6
8: 1 the word of the LORD of hosts came to me, saying 6
10 safety from the foe for him who went out or came in; 4
18 the word of the LORD of hosts came to me, saying 6
20 says the LORD of hosts: Peoples shall yet come 4
22 Many peoples and strong nations shall come 4
9: 9 O daughter of Jerusalem! Lo, your king comes to you; 4
10: 4 Out of them shall come the cornerstone 13
12: 9 all the nations that come against Jerusalem. 4
14: 1 Behold, a day of the LORD is coming 4
5 Then the LORD your God will come 4
16 the nations that have come against Jerusalem 4
18 then upon them shall come the plague 6
21 that all who sacrifice may come and take of them 4
Mal 3: 1 whom you seek will suddenly come to his temple; 4
1 behold, he is coming, says the LORD of hosts. 4
2 But who can endure the day of his coming 4
4: 1 For behold, the day comes, burning like an oven 4
1 the day that comes shall burn them up 4
5 the great and terrible day of the LORD comes. 4
6 lest I come and smite the land with a curse. 4
Mat 2: 1 wise men from the East came to Jerusalem, saying 93
2 in the East, and have come to worship him. 79
6 from you shall come a ruler who will govern my 73
8 bring me word, that I too may come and worship him. 79
9 in the East went before them, till it came to rest 79
3: 1 In those days came John the Baptist, preaching 93
7 the Pharisees and Sad'ducees coming for baptism 79
7 Who warned you to flee from the wrath to come? 92
11 he who is coming after me is mightier than I 79
13 Jesus came from Galilee to the Jordan to John 93
14 I need to be baptized by you, and do you come to me? 79
4: 3 the tempter came and said to him, "If you are the Son 104
11 left him, and behold, angels came and ministered 104
5: 1 when he sat down his disciples came to him. 104
17 Think not that I have come to abolish the law 79
17 the prophets; I have come not to abolish them 79
24 your brother, and then come and offer your gift. 79
37 anything more than this comes from evil. 62
6:10 Thy kingdom come. Thy will be done, On earth as it 79
7:15 false prophets, who come to you 79
25 rain fell, and the floods came, and the winds blew 79
27 rain fell, and the floods came, and the wind blew 79
8: 2 behold, a leper came to him and knelt before him 104
7 he said to him, "I will come and heal him. 79
8 I am not worthy to have you come under my roof; 64
9 I say to one, 'Go,' and he goes, and to another, 'Come,' 79
9 'Come,' and he comes, and to my slave, 'Do this,' 79
11 I tell you, many will come from east and west 83
28 when he came to the other side 79
29 Have you come here to torment us before the time? 79
9: 1 he crossed over and came to his own city. 79
10 behold, many tax collectors and sinners came 79
13 For I came not to call the righteous, but sinners. 79
14 Then the disciples of John came to him, saying 104
15 The days will come, when the bridegroom is taken 79
18 behold, a ruler came in and knelt before him 79
18 but come and lay your hand on her 79
23 when Jesus came to the ruler's house 79
28 the blind men came to him; and Jesus said to them 104
10:13 if the house is worthy, let your peace come upon it; 79
23 before the Son of man comes. 79
34 Do not think that I have come to bring peace 79
34 I have not come to bring peace, but a sword. 79
35 For I have come to set a man against his father 79
11: 3 said to him, "Are you he who is to come 79
14 he is Eli'jah who is to come. 79
18 For John came neither eating nor drinking 79
19 the Son of man came eating and drinking 79
28 Come to me, all who labor and are heavy laden 54
12:28 then the kingdom of God has come upon you. 111
32 either in this age or in the age to come. 92
42 she came from the ends of the earth 79
44 I will return to my house from which I came. 73
44 when he comes he finds it empty, swept 79
13: 4 and the birds came and devoured them. 79
10 the disciples came and said to him 104
19 the evil one comes and snatches away what is sown 79
25 his enemy came and sowed weeds among the wheat 79
27 the servants of the householder came and said 104
32 so that the birds of the air come and make nests 79
36 And his disciples came to him, saying 104
54 coming to his own country he taught them 79
14: 6 when Herod's birthday came 52
12 his disciples came and took the body 104
15 When it was evening, the disciples came to him 104
23 When evening came, he was there alone 52
25 in the fourth watch of the night he came to them 79
28 Lord, if it is you, bid me come to you on the water. 79
29 He said, "Come." So Peter got out of the boat 79
29 walked on the water and came to Jesus; 79
34 they came to land at Gennesaret. 79
15: 1 Then Pharisees and scribes came to Jesus 104
12 Then the disciples came and said to him 104
19 For out of the heart come evil thoughts, murder 73
23 And his disciples came and begged him, saying 104
25 she came and knelt before him, saying 79
30 great crowds came to him 104
16: 1 the Pharisees and Sad'ducees came 104

13 Now when Jesus came into the district 79
24 If any man would come after me 79
27 For the Son of man is to come with his angels 79
28 see the Son of man coming in his kingdom. 79
17: 7 Jesus came and touched them, saying 104
10 the scribes say that first Eli'jah must come? 79
11 He replied, "Eli'jah does come 79
12 I tell you that Eli'jah has already come 79
14 when they came to the crowd 79
19 Then the disciples came to Jesus privately 104
24 When they came to Caper'na-um 79
25 when he came home, Jesus spoke to him first, saying 79
18: 1 At that time the disciples came to Jesus, saying 104
7 For it is necessary that temptations come 79
7 woe to the man by whom the temptation comes! 79
19:14 Jesus said, "Let the children come to me 79
21 and come, follow me. 53
20: 8 when evening came, the owner of the vineyard said 52
9 when those hired about the eleventh hour came 79
10 Now when the first came 79
28 the Son of man came not to be served but to serve 79
21: 1 and came to Beth'phage, to the Mount of Olives 79
5 Behold, your king is coming to you 79
9 Blessed is he who comes in the name of the Lord! 79
14 the blind and the lame came to him in the temple 104
19 And he said to it, "May no fruit ever come from you 52
32 For John came to you in the way of righteousness 79
38 come, let us kill him 54
40 When therefore the owner of the vineyard comes 79
22: 3 but they would not come. 79
4 everything is ready; come to the marriage feast.' 54
11 But when the king came in to look at the guests 64
23 The same day Sad'ducees came to him 104
23:35 that upon you may come all the righteous blood 79
36 all this will come upon this generation. 83
39 'Blessed is he who comes in the name of the Lord.' 79
24: 1 when his disciples came to point out to him 104
3 the disciples came to him privately, saying 104
3 what will be the sign of your coming 98
5 For many will come in my name, saying 79
14 then the end will come. 83
27 For as the lightning comes from the east 73
27 so will be the coming of the Son of man. 98
30 see the Son of man coming on the clouds of heaven 79
37 so will be the coming of the Son of man. 98
39 they did not know until the flood came 79
39 so will be the coming of the Son of man. 98
42 you do not know on what day your Lord is coming. 79
43 in what part of the night the thief was coming 79
44 Son of man is coming at an hour you do not expect. 79
46 whom his master when he comes will find so doing. 79
50 the master of that servant will come on a day 83
25:10 while they went to buy, the bridegroom came 79
11 Afterward the other maidens came also, saying 79
19 the master of those servants came 79
27 at my coming I should have received 79
31 When the Son of man comes in his glory 79
34 Come, O blessed of my Father 54
36 I was in prison and you came to me.' 79
26: 2 after two days the Passover is coming 52
17 the disciples came to Jesus, saying 104
40 he came to the disciples and found them sleeping; 79
43 again he came and found them sleeping 79
45 Then he came to the disciples and said to them 79
47 Judas came, one of the twelve 79
64 coming on the clouds of heaven. 79
27: 1 When morning came 52
33 when they came to a place called Gol'gotha 79
49 let us see whether Eli'jah will come to save him. 79
53 coming out of the tombs after his resurrection 73
57 there came a rich man from Arimathe'a 79
28: 2 came and rolled back the stone, and sat upon it. 104
6 Come, see the place where he lay. 54
9 they came and took hold of his feet and worshiped 104
13 said, "Tell people, 'His disciples came by night 79
18 Jesus came and said to them 104
Mrk 1: 7 After me comes he who is mightier than I 79
9 In those days Jesus came from Nazareth of Galilee 79
11 a voice came from heaven, "Thou art my beloved Son; 52
14 after John was arrested Jesus came into Galilee 79
24 Have you come to destroy us? 79
31 he came and took her by the hand and lifted her up 104
40 a leper came to him beseeching him, and kneeling 79
45 people came to him from every quarter. 48
2: 3 they came, bringing to him a paralytic 79
17 I came not to call the righteous, but sinners. 79
18 people came and said to him 79
20 days will come, when the bridegroom is taken away 79
3: 3 Come here. 61
8 a great multitude, hearing all that he did, came 79
13 they came to him. 47
26 he cannot stand, but is coming to an end. 82
31 his mother and his brothers came 79
4: 4 the birds came and devoured it. 79
15 when they hear, Satan immediately comes 79
22 nor is anything secret, except to come to light. 79
29 because the harvest has come. 97
35 On that day, when evening had come, he said to them 52
5: 1 They came to the other side of the sea 79

14 people came to see what it was that had happened. 79
15 they came to Jesus, and saw the demoniac sitting 79
22 Then came one of the rulers of the synagogue 79
23 Come and lay your hands on her 79
33 came in fear and trembling 79
35 there came from the ruler's house 79
38 When they came to the house 79
6: 1 went away from there and came to his own country; 79
21 an opportunity came 52
22 For when Hero'di-as' daughter came in and danced 64
25 she came immediately with haste to the king 64
29 they came and took his body, and laid it in a tomb. 79
31 many were coming and going 79
35 it grew late, his disciples came to him and said 104
47 when evening came, the boat was out on the sea 52
48 about the fourth watch of the night he came 79
53 they came to land at Gennes'aret 79
56 wherever he came, in villages, cities, or country 67
7: 1 some of the scribes, who had come from Jerusalem 79
4 when they come from the market place •
15 the things which come out of a man are what defile 69
20 What comes out of a man is what defiles a man. 69
21 out of the heart of man, come evil thoughts 69
23 All these evil things come from within 69
25 heard of him, and came and fell down at his feet. 79
8: 3 some of them have come a long way. 83
11 The Pharisees came and began to argue with him 73
22 they came to Beth-sa'ida 79
34 said to them, "If any man wou'.l come after me 79
38 when he comes in the glory of his Father 79
9: 1 the kingdom of God has come with power. 79
7 a voice came out of the cloud 52
11 the scribes say that first Eli'jah must come 79
12 Eli'jah does come first to restore all things 79
13 I tell you that Eli'jah has come 79
14 when they came to the disciples 79
33 they came to Caper'na-um 79
10:14 Let the children come to me, do not hinder them 79
21 come, follow me. 53
30 in the age to come eternal life. 79
45 Son of man also came not to be served but to serve 79
46 they came to Jericho 79
50 he sprang up and came to Jesus. 79
11: 9 Blessed is he who comes in the name of the Lord! 79
10 kingdom of our father David that is coming 79
12 On the following day, when they came from Bethany 73
13 When he came to it, he found nothing but leaves 79
15 they came to Jerusalem 79
19 when evening came they went out of the city. 52
27 they came again to Jerusalem 79
27 the scribes and the elders came to him 79
12: 2 When the time came •
7 'This is the heir; come, let us kill him 54
9 He will come and destroy the tenants 79
14 they came and said to him, "Teacher 79
18 Sad'ducees came to him 79
42 a poor widow came, and put in two copper coins 79
13: 6 Many will come in my name, saying, 'I am he!' 79
26 then they will see the Son of man coming in clouds 79
33 for you do not know when the time will come. 62
35 when the master of the house will come 79
36 lest he come suddenly and find you asleep. 79
14: 3 a woman came with an alabaster flask of ointment 79
17 when it was evening he came with the twelve. 79
37 he came and found them sleeping 79
40 again he came and found them sleeping 79
41 he came the third time, and said to them 79
41 It is enough; the hour has come 79
43 while he was still speaking, Judas came 93
45 when he came, he went up to him at once, and said 79
62 coming with the clouds of heaven. 79
66 one of the maids of the high priest came; 79
15:21 who was coming in from the country 79
33 when the sixth hour had come 52
36 see whether Eli'jah will come to take him down. 79
42 when evening had come 52
Lke 1:28 he came to her and said, "Hail, O favored one 64
43 that the mother of my Lord should come to me? 79
44 when the voice of your greeting came to my ears 52
57 Now the time came for Elizabeth to be delivered 99
59 they came to circumcise the child 79
65 fear came on all their neighbors 52
2: 6 the time came for her to be delivered. 99
10 a great joy which will come to all the people; 62
22 when the time came for their purification 99
27 inspired by the Spirit he came into the temple; 79
51 he went down with them and came to Nazareth 79
3: 2 the word of God came to John the son of Zechari'ah 52
7 Who warned you to flee from the wrath to come? 92
12 Tax collectors also came to be baptized, and said 79
16 he who is mightier than I is coming 79
22 a voice came from heaven 52
4:16 he came to Nazareth, where he had been brought up; 79
25 when there came a great famine over all the land; 52
34 Have you come to destroy us? 79
42 the people sought him and came to him 79
5: 7 beckoned . . to come and help them 79
7 they came and filled both the boats 79
12 there came a man full of leprosy 85

17 who had come from every village of Galilee 79
32 I have not come to call the righteous, but sinners 79
35 days will come, when the bridegroom is taken away 79
6: 8 Come and stand here." And he rose and stood there. 61
17 who came to hear him 79
47 Every one who comes to me and hears my words 79
7: 3 asking him to come and heal his slave. 79
4 when they came to Jesus 93
6 for I am not worthy to have you come under my roof; 64
7 therefore I did not presume to come to you 79
8 to another, 'Come,' and he comes 79
8 to another, 'Come,' and he comes 79
14 he came and touched the bier 104
19 Are you he who is to come 79
20 when the men had come to him, they said 93
20 Are you he who is to come 79
33 For John the Baptist has come eating no bread 79
34 The Son of man has come eating and drinking; 79
45 from the time I came in she has not ceased to kiss 64
8: 4 people from town after town came to him 77
12 then the devil comes and takes away the word 79
17 that shall not be known and come to light. 79
19 Then his mother and his brothers came to him 93
35 they came to Jesus 79
41 there came a man named Ja'irus 79
41 he besought him to come to his house 64
47 she came trembling 79
49 a man from the ruler's house came and said 79
51 when he came to the house 79
9:12 the twelve came and said to him 104
23 he said to all, "If any man would come after me 79
26 when he comes in his glory 79
34 a cloud came and overshadowed them 52
35 a voice came out of the cloud, saying, "This is my Son 52
42 While he was coming, the demon tore him 104
10: 1 where he himself was about to come. 79
32 a Levite, when he came to the place and saw him 79
33 a Samaritan, as he journeyed, came to where he was; 79
11: 2 hallowed be thy name. Thy kingdom come. 79
20 then the kingdom of God has come upon you. 111
24 I will return to my house from which I came.' 73
25 when he comes he finds it swept and put in order. 79
31 she came from the ends of the earth 79
12:36 open to him at once when he comes and knocks. 79
37 whom the master finds awake when he comes 79
37 he will come and serve them. 96
38 If he comes in the second watch, or in the third 79
39 at what hour the thief was coming 79
40 the Son of man is coming at an unexpected hour. 79
43 his master when he comes will find so doing. 79
45 'My master is delayed in coming,' 79
46 the master of that servant will come 83
49 I came to cast fire upon the earth 79
51 you think that I have come to give peace on earth? 93
54 you say at once, 'A shower is coming' 79
13: 6 he came seeking fruit on it and found none. 79
7 Lo, these three years I have come seeking fruit 79
14 come on those days and be healed 79
25 'I do not know where you come from.' 62
27 I do not know where you come from; depart from me 62
29 men will come from east and west 83
31 At that very hour some Pharisees came, and said 104
35 'Blessed is he who comes in the name of the Lord!' 79
14: 9 he who invited you both will come and say to you 79
10 so that when your host comes he may say to you 79
17 'Come; for all is now ready.' 79
20 I have married a wife, and therefore I cannot come.' 79
21 So the servant came and reported this 93
23 compel people to come in 64
26 If any one comes to me 79
27 does not bear his own cross and come after me 79
31 who comes against him with 20,000? 79
15: 6 when he comes home, he calls together his friends 79
17 when he came to himself he said 79
20 he arose and came to his father 79
25 as he came and drew near to the house 79
27 he said to him, 'Your brother has come 83
30 when this son of yours came 79
16:21 moreover the dogs came and licked his sores. 79
28 lest they also come into this place of torment.' 79
17: 1 Temptations to sin are sure to come 79
1 woe to him by whom they come! 79
7 say to him when he has come in from the field 64
7 'Come at once and sit down at table'? 96
20 asked . . when the kingdom of God was coming 79
20 is not coming with signs to be observed; 79
22 The days are coming when you will desire to see 79
27 the flood came and destroyed them all. 79
18: 3 a widow in that city who kept coming to him 79
5 she will wear me out by her continual coming.' 79
8 Nevertheless, when the Son of man comes 79
16 Let the children come to me, and do not hinder them; 79
22 come, follow me. 53
30 in the age to come eternal life. 79
19: 5 when Jesus came to the place, he looked up and said 79
9 Today salvation has come to this house 52
10 the Son of man came to seek and to save the lost. 79
13 said to them, 'Trade with these till I come.' 79
18 the second came, saying, 'Lord 79

20 Then another came, saying 79
23 at my coming I should have collected it 79
38 the King who comes in the name of the Lord 79
43 the days shall come upon you 83
20:10 When the time came •
16 He will come and destroy those tenants 79
27 There came to him some Sadducees 104
21: 6 the days will come when there shall not be left 79
8 many will come in my name, saying, 'I am he!' 79
26 foreboding of what is coming on the world 74
27 then they will see the Son of man coming in a cloud 79
38 early in the morning all the people came to him •
22: 7 Then came the day of Unleavened Bread 79
14 when the hour came, he sat at table 52
18 until the kingdom of God comes. 79
40 when he came to the place he said to them, "Pray 52
45 when he rose from prayer, he came to the disciples 79
47 While he was still speaking, there came a crowd 85
66 When day came 52
23:26 who was coming in from the country 79
29 For behold, the days are coming when they will say 79
33 they came to the place which is called The Skull 79
42 remember me when you come into your kingdom. 79
55 The women who had come with him from Galilee 109
24:23 they came back saying that they had even seen 79
Joh 1: 7 He came for testimony, to bear witness 79
8 but came to bear witness to the light. •
9 The true light . . was coming into the world. 79
11 He came to his own home 79
15 'He who comes after me ranks before me 79
17 grace and truth came through Jesus Christ. 52
27 even he who comes after me 79
29 The next day he saw Jesus coming toward him 79
30 'After me comes a man who ranks before me 79
31 but for this I came baptizing with water 79
39 He said to them, "Come and see." They came and saw 79
39 They came and saw where he was staying; 79
46 Can anything good come out of Nazareth? 62
46 Philip said to him, "Come and see. 79
47 Jesus saw Nathan'a-el coming to him, and said of him 79
2: 4 Jesus said to her . . My hour has not yet come. 83
9 and did not know where it came 62
3: 2 This man came to Jesus by night and said to him 79
2 we know that you are a teacher come from God; 79
8 you do not know whence it comes or whither it goes; 79
19 that the light has come into the world 79
20 hates the light, and does not come to the light 79
21 But he who does what is true comes to the light 79
23 and people came and were baptized. 93
26 And they came to John, and said to him, "Rabbi 79
31 he who comes from heaven is above all. 79
31 He who comes from above is above all; 79
4: 5 So he came to a city of Samar'ia, called Sy'char 79
7 There came a woman of Samar'ia to draw water. 79
15 that I may not thirst, nor come here to draw. 59
16 Go, call your husband, and come here. 79
21 the hour is coming when neither on this mountain 79
23 But the hour is coming, and now is 79
25 I know that Messiah is coming 79
25 when he comes, he will show us all things. 79
27 Just then his disciples came. 79
29 Come, see a man who told me all that I ever did. 54
30 They went out of the city and were coming to him. 48
35 'There are yet four months, then comes the harvest'? 79
40 So when the Samaritans came to him, they asked him 79
45 he came to Galilee, the Galileans welcomed him 79
46 So he came again to Cana in Galilee 79
47 heard that Jesus had come from Judea to Galilee 83
54 when he had come from Judea to Galilee. 79
5:24 he does not come into judgment 79
25 Truly, truly, I say to you, the hour is coming 79
28 the hour is coming when all . . will hear 79
40 yet you refuse to come to me 79
43 I have come in my Father's name 79
43 if another comes in his own name 79
44 do not seek the glory that comes from the only God?. •
6: 5 seeing that a multitude was coming to him 79
14 the prophet who is to come into the world! 79
15 they were about to come and take him by force 79
16 When evening came 52
17 and Jesus had not yet come to them. 79
23 However, boats from Tiber'i-as came near the place 79
25 they said to him, "Rabbi, when did you come here? 52
35 he who comes to me shall not hunger 79
37 All that the Father gives me will come to me 83
37 him who comes to me I will not cast out. 79
44 No one can come to me 79
45 Every one . . comes to me. 79
65 This is why I told you that no one can come to me 79
69 . . come to know, that you are the Holy One of God •
7: 6 Jesus said to them, "My time has not yet come 94
27 Yet we know where this man comes from; 62
27 no one will know where he comes from. 79
28 You know me, and you know where I come from? 62
28 I have not come of my own accord 79
29 I know him, for I come from him, and he sent me. 62
30 because his hour had not yet come. 79
34 where I am you cannot come. 79
36 'Where I am you cannot come'? 79

37 If any one thirst, let him come to me and drink. 79
41 But some said, "Is the Christ to come from Galilee? 79
42 comes from Bethlehem, the village where David was? 79
8: 2 Early in the morning he came again to the temple 93
2 all the people came to him 79
14 I know whence I have come and whither I am going 79
14 do not know whence I come or whither I am going. 79
20 because his hour had not yet come. 79
21 where I am going, you cannot come. 79
22 since he says, 'Where I am going, you cannot come'? 79
42 I came not of my own accord, but he sent me. 79
9: 4 night comes, when no one can work. 79
29 we do not know where he comes from. 62
30 You do not know where he comes 62
39 Jesus said, "For judgment I came into this world 79
10: 8 All who came before me are thieves and robbers; 79
10 The thief comes only to steal and kill 79
10 I came that they may have life 79
12 sees the wolf coming and leaves the sheep 79
35 If he called them gods to whom the word of God came 52
41 many came to him; and they said, "John did no sign 79
11:17 Now when Jesus came 79
19 many of the Jews had come to Martha and Mary 79
20 When Martha heard that Jesus was coming 79
27 the Son of God, he who is coming into the world. 79
30 Now Jesus had not yet come to the village 79
32 Mary, when she came where Jesus was and saw him 79
33 and the Jews who came with her also weeping 109
34 They said to him, "Lord, come and see. 79
38 Then Jesus, deeply moved again, came to the tomb 79
43 Laz'arus, come out. 53
45 Many of the Jews therefore, who had come with Mary 79
48 the Romans will come 79
56 That he will not come to the feast? 79
12: 1 Jesus came to Bethany, where Laz'arus was 79
9 they came, not only on account of Jesus 79
12 a great crowd who had come to the feast heard 79
12 heard that Jesus was coming to Jerusalem. 79
13 Blessed is he who comes in the name of the Lord 79
15 behold, your king is coming, sitting on an ass's colt! 79
21 these came to Philip, who was from Beth-sa'ida 104
23 Jesus answered them, "The hour has come 79
27 No, for this purpose I have come to this hour. 79
28 Then a voice came from heaven 79
30 Jesus answered, "This voice has come for your sake 52
46 I have come as light into the world 79
47 for I did not come to judge the world 79
13: 1 when Jesus knew that his hour had come to depart 79
3 he had come from God and was going to God 73
6 He came to Simon Peter; and Peter said to him, "Lord 79
33 'Where I am going you cannot come.' 79
14: 3 I will come again and will take you to myself 79
6 no one comes to the Father, but by me. 79
18 I will not leave you desolate; I will come to you. 79
23 we will come to him and make our home with him. 79
28 'I go away, and I will come to you.' 79
30 the ruler of this world is coming 79
15:22 If I had not come and spoken to them 79
26 when the Counselor comes, whom I shall send to you 79
16: 2 indeed, the hour is coming 79
4 you, that when their hour comes you may remember 79
7 if I do not go away, the Counselor will not come 79
8 when he comes, he will convince the world 79
13 When the Spirit of truth comes 79
21 because her hour has come 79
25 the hour is coming 79
27 have believed that I came from the Father. 73
28 I came from the Father 73
28 have come into the world 79
30 by this we believe that you came from God. 73
32 The hour is coming, indeed it has come 79
32 The hour is coming, indeed it has come 79
17: 1 Father, the hour has come; glorify thy Son 79
8 and know in truth that I came from thee 73
11 they are in the world, and I am coming to thee 79
13 now I am coming to thee 79
18:37 for this I have come into the world 79
19:32 the soldiers came and broke the legs of the first 79
33 when they came to Jesus 79
38 So he came and took away his body. 79
39 who had at first come to him by night 79
39 came bringing a mixture of myrrh and aloes 79
20: 1 Mary Mag'dalene came to the tomb early 79
6 Simon Peter came, following him 79
19 Jesus came and stood among them and said to them 79
24 was not with them when Jesus came. 79
26 Jesus came and stood among them, and said 79
21: 8 the other disciples came in the boat 79
12 Jesus said to them, "Come and have breakfast. 54
13 Jesus came and took the bread and gave it to them 79
22 If it is my will that he remain until I come 79
23 If it is my will that he remain until I come 79
Act 1:11 Jesus . . will come in the same way as you saw him go 79
2: 1 When the day of Pentecost had come 108
2 suddenly a sound came from heaven 52
20 before the day of the Lord comes 79
43 fear came upon every soul 52
3:19 times of refreshing may come 79
4: 4 the number of the men came to about 5,000 52
5: 5 great fear came upon all who heard of it. 52
7 his wife came in, not knowing what had happened. 64
10 When the young men came in they found her dead 64
11 great fear came upon the whole church 52
15 as Peter came 79
21 the high priest came and those who were with him 93
22 when the officers came 93
24 wondering what this would come to. 52
25 And some one came and told them 93
36 were dispersed and came to nothing. 52
7:11 came a famine throughout all Egypt and Canaan 79
23 it came into his heart to visit his brethren 46
31 as he drew near to look, the voice of the Lord came 52
34 now come, I will send you to Egypt.' 53
52 the coming of the Righteous One 71
8:27 had come to Jerusalem to worship 79
36 they came to some water 79
40 till he came to Caesare'a. 79
9:12 Anani'as come in and lay his hands on him 64
17 on the road by which you came 79
21 he has come here for this purpose 79
26 when he had come to Jerusalem 93
38 Please come to us without delay. 59
39 when he had come, they took him to the upper room. 93
10: 3 angel of God coming in and saying to him 64
13 there came a voice to him, "Rise, Peter; kill and eat. 52
15 the voice came to him again a second time •
21 what is the reason for your coming? 94
22 to send for you to come to his house 63
29 So when I was sent for, I came without objection 79
33 you have been kind enough to come 93
45 from among the circumcised who came with Peter 109
11: 5 it came down to me. 79
20 who on coming to Antioch spoke to the Greeks also 79
22 came to the ears of the church in Jerusalem 45
23 When he came and saw the grace of God, he was glad; 93
12:10 they came to the iron gate leading into the city. 79
11 Peter came to himself, and said 52
13 a maid named Rhoda came to answer. 104
18 Now when day came, there was no small stir 52
20 they came to him in a body 94
13:13 and came to Perga in Pamphyl'ia 79
14 and came to Antioch of Pisid'ia 93
24 Before his coming John had preached 65
25 No, but after me one is coming 79
14:24 passed through Pisid'ia, and came to Pamphyl'ia. 79
15: 4 When they came to Jerusalem 93
25 it has seemed good to us, having come to one accord 52
36 after some days Paul said to Barnabas, "Come 78
16: 1 he came also to Derbe and to Lystra 89
7 when they had come opposite My'sia 79
15 come to my house and stay. 64
37 No! let them come themselves and take us out. 79
39 so they came and apologized to them 79
17: 1 they came to Thessaloni'ca 79
6 These men . . have come here also 94
13 they came there too 79
15 a command for Silas and Timothy to come to him 79
18: 2 lately come from Italy with his wife Priscilla 79
19 they came to Ephesus, and he left them there 89
24 a Jew named Apol'los . . came to Ephesus 89
19: 1 came to Ephesus 79
4 to believe in the one who was to come after him 79
6 the Holy Spirit came on them 79
18 Many also of those who were now believers came 48
19 and found it came to 50,000 pieces of silver. •
27 this trade of ours may come into disrepute 79
20: 2 he came to Greece. 79
6 in five days we came to them at Tro'as 79
14 we took him on board and came to Mityle'ne. 79
15 we came the following day opposite Chi'os 89
15 the day after that we came to Mile'tus. 79
18 when they came to him, he said to them 93
29 fierce wolves will come in among you 64
21: 1 we came by a straight course to Cos 79
8 On the morrow we departed and came to Caesare'a; 79
11 coming to us he took Paul's girdle 79
17 When we had come to Jerusalem 52
22 They will certainly hear that you have come. 79
31 word came to the tribune of the cohort 46
35 when he came to the steps 52
22:11 came into Damascus. 79
13 came to me, and standing by me said to me 79
27 So the tribune came and said to him 104
23:33 When they came to Caesare'a 64
24:17 I came to bring to my nation alms and offerings. 93
24 Felix came with his wife Drusil'la 93
25: 7 when he had come 93
23 Agrippa and Berni'ce came with great pomp 79
26:22 To this day I have had the help that comes from God •
27: 5 we came to Myra in Ly'cia. 90
8 we came to a place called Fair Havens 79
27 When the fourteenth night had come 52
29 prayed for day to come. 52
28: 6 saw no misfortune come to him 52
9 rest of the people . . also came and were cured. 104
13 on the second day we came to Pute'oli. 79
14 so we came to Rome. 79
15 came as far as the Forum of Ap'pius . . to meet us 79
23 they came to him at his lodging in great numbers. 79
30 welcomed all who came to him 66
Rom 1:10 I may now at last succeed in coming to you. 79
13 that I have often intended to come to you 79
3: 8 And why not do evil that good may come? 79
20 since through the law comes knowledge of sin. •
4:13 The promise . . did not come through the law •
5:14 Adam, who was a type of the one who was to come. 92
20 Law came in, to increase the trespass; 95
7: 9 when the commandment came, sin revived and I died; 79
10: 3 the righteousness that comes from God •
17 So faith comes from what is heard •
17 what is heard comes by the preaching of Christ. •
11:11 salvation has come to the Gentiles •
25 a hardening has come upon part of Israel 52
25 until the full number of the Gentiles come in 64
26 it is written, "The Deliverer will come from Zion 83
15:12 further Isaiah says, "The root of Jesse shall come 62
22 I have so often been hindered from coming to you. 79
23 since I have longed for many years to come to you 79
27 if the Gentiles have come to share in their •
29 I know that when I come to you 79
29 come in the fulness of the blessing of Christ. 79
32 that by God's will I may come to you with joy 79
1Co 2: 1 When I came to you, brethren 79
1 I did not come proclaiming to you 79
4: 5 before the time, before the Lord comes 79
18 as though I were not coming to you. 79
19 I will come to you soon, if the Lord wills 79
21 What do you wish? Shall I come to you with a rod 79
7: 5 then come together again, lest Satan tempt you 62
10:11 upon whom the end of the ages has come. 89
11:26 you proclaim the Lord's death until he comes. 79
34 I will give directions when I come. 79
13:10 when the perfect comes 79
14: 6 Now, brethren, if I come to you speaking in tongues 79
15:21 For as by a man came death •
21 by a man has come also the resurrection •
23 then at his coming those who belong to Christ. 98
24 Then comes the end, when he delivers the kingdom •
35 With what kind of body do they come? 79
16: 2 so that contributions need not be made when I come. 79
10 When Timothy comes, see that you put him at ease 79
12 it was not at all his will to come now 79
12 He will come when he has opportunity. 79
17 I rejoice at the coming of Steph'anas 98
22 Our Lord, come! 84
2Co 1:15 I wanted to come to you first 79
16 to come back to you from Macedo'nia 79
23 I refrained from coming to Corinth. 79
2: 3 so that when I came I might not suffer pain 79
12 When I came to Tro'as 79
3: 5 to claim anything as coming from us •
7 if . . death . . came with such splendor 52
10 has come to have no splendor at all •
11 For if what faded away came with splendor •
18 this comes from the Lord who is the Spirit. •
5:17 the old has passed away, behold, the new has come. 52
7: 5 For even when we came into Macedo'nia 79
6 comforted us by the coming of Titus 98
7 not only by his coming but also by the comfort 98
9: 4 lest if some Macedo'nians come with me and find 79
10:14 we were the first to come all the way to you 111
11: 4 For if some one comes and preaches another Jesus 79
9 the brethren who came from Macedo'nia 79
12:14 Here for the third time I am ready to come to you. 79
20 I fear that perhaps I may come and find you 79
21 I fear that when I come again my God may humble me 79
13: 1 This is the third time I am coming to you 79
2 if I come again I will not spare them- 79
10 in order that when I come 94
Gal 1:12 it came through a revelation of Jesus Christ. •
2:11 when Cephas came to Antioch 79
12 For before certain men came from James 79
12 when they came he drew back and separated 79
3:14 Abraham might come upon the Gentiles 52
17 the law, which came 430 years afterward 52
19 till the offspring should come 79
23 Now before faith came 79
24 the law was our custodian until Christ came •
25 now that faith has come 79
4: 4 when the time had fully come 79
9 now that you have come to know God •
Eph 1:21 but also in that which is to come; 92
2: 7 in the coming ages 74
17 he came and preached peace to you who were far off 79
5: 6 comes upon the sons of disobedience. 79
Php 1:11 which come through Jesus Christ •
26 because of my coming to you again. 98
27 so that whether I come and see you or am absent 79
2:24 shortly I myself shall come also. 79
Col 1: 6 which has come to you 94
2:17 These are only a shadow of what is to come 92
3: 6 On account of these the wrath of God is coming. 79
4:10 if he comes to you, receive him) 79
1Th 1: 5 for our gospel came to you not only in word 52
10 Jesus who delivers us from the wrath to come. 79
2:16 God's wrath has come upon them at last! 111
18 because we wanted to come to you 79

19 before our Lord Jesus at his coming? 98
3: 6 now that Timothy has come to us from you 79
13 at the coming of our Lord Jesus 98
4:15 who are left until the coming of the Lord 98
5: 2 the day of the Lord will come like a thief 79
3 as travail comes upon a woman with child •
23 blameless at the coming of our Lord Jesus 98
2Th 1:10 when he comes on that day to be glorified 79
2: 1 concerning the coming of our Lord Jesus Christ 98
2 to the effect that the day of the Lord has come. 72
3 that day will not come •
3 unless the rebellion comes first 79
8 destroy him by his appearing and his coming. 98
9 The coming of the lawless one 98
1Ti 1:15 Jesus came into the world to save sinners 79
2: 4 to come to the knowledge of the truth. 79
3:14 I hope to come to you soon 79
4: 8 the present life and also for the life to come. 92
13 Till I come, attend to the . . reading 79
2Ti 2:25 they will repent and come to know the truth 63
3: 1 in the last days there will come times of stress. 72
4: 3 For the time is coming 62
6 the time of my departure has come. 80
9 Do your best to come to me soon. 79
13 When you come 79
21 Do your best to come before winter 79
Tit 3:12 do your best to come to me at Nicop'olis 79
Heb 2: 5 God subjected the world to come 92
6: 5 the powers of the age to come 92
7:28 the word of the oath, which came later than the law •
8: 8 The days will come, says the Lord 79
9:11 a high priest of the good things that have come 52
27 after that comes judgment •
10: 1 a shadow of the good things to come 92
7 I said, 'Lo, I have come to do thy will, O God,' 83
9 he added, "Lo, I have come to do thy will. 83
37 the coming one shall come and shall not tarry; 83
11: 7 the righteousness which comes by faith. •
12:18 you have not come to what may be touched 104
22 you have come to Mount Zion 104
13:14 we seek the city which is to come. 92
23 with whom I shall see you if he comes soon. 79
24 Those who come from Italy send you greetings. •
Jas 2: 2 a poor man in shabby clothing also comes in 64
3:10 From the same mouth come blessing and cursing. 73
4:13 Come now, you who say, "Today or tomorrow 44
5: 1 Come now, you rich, weep and howl for the miseries 44
7 Be patient . . until the coming of the Lord. 98
8 for the coming of the Lord is at hand. 98
1Pe 1:13 the grace that is coming to you at the revelation 110
2: 4 Come to him, to the living stone, rejected by men 104
4:12 fiery ordeal which comes upon you to prove you 52
17 For the time has come for judgment to begin •
2Pe 1:16 made known to you the power and coming of our Lord 98
21 no prophecy ever came by the impulse of man 110
3: 3 scoffers will come in the last days 79
4 and saying, "Where is the promise of his coming? 98
10 But the day of the Lord will come like a thief 83
12 and hastening the coming of the day of God 98
1Jn 2:18 and as you have heard that antichrist is coming 79
18 so now many antichrists have come; 79
28 and not shrink from him in shame at his coming 98
4: 2 that Jesus Christ has come in the flesh is of God 79
3 antichrist, of which you heard that it was coming 79
5: 6 This is he who came by water and blood, Jesus 79
20 we know that the Son of God has come 83
2Jn 1: 7 the coming of Jesus Christ in the flesh; 79
10 If any one comes to you and does not bring 79
3Jn 1:10 So if I come, I will bring up what he is doing 79
Jde 1:14 Behold, the Lord came with his holy myriads 79
Rev 1: 4 from him who is and who was and who is to come 79
7 Behold, he is coming with the clouds 79
8 the Lord God, who is and who was and who is to come 79
2: 5 I will come to you and remove your lampstand 79
16 Repent then. If not, I will come to you soon and war 79
25 only hold fast what you have, until I come. 83
3: 3 If you will not awake, I will come like a thief 83
3 you will not know at what hour I will come upon you 83
9 make them come and bow down before your feet 83
10 hour of trial which is coming on the whole world 79
11 I am coming soon; hold fast what you have 79
20 opens the door, I will come to him and eat with him 64
4: 8 Lord God Almighty, who was and is and is to come! 79
6: 1 creatures say, as with a voice of thunder, "Come! 79
3 I heard the second living creature say, "Come! 79
5 I heard the third living creature say, "Come! 79
7 the voice of the fourth living creature say, "Come! 79
17 for the great day of their wrath has come 79
7:13 Who are these . . and whence have they come? 79
14 they who have come out of the great tribulation; 79
8: 3 another angel came and stood at the altar 79
9: 3 Then from the smoke came locusts on the earth 73
12 behold, two woes are still to come. 79
11:14 behold, the third woe is soon to come. 79
18 The nations raged, but thy wrath came 79
12:10 and the authority of his Christ have come 52
14: 7 Fear God . . for the hour of his judgment has come; 79
15 reap, for the hour to reap has come 79
15: 4 All nations shall come and worship thee 83
16: 2 and foul and evil sores came upon the men 52
15 ("Lo, I am coming like a thief! 79
17: 1 one of the seven angels . . came and said to me 79
1 Come, I will show you the judgment 53
8 the beast, because it was and is not and is to come. 94
10 seven kings . . one is, the other has not yet come 79
10 when he comes he must remain only a little while. 79
18: 8 so shall her plagues come in a single day 83
10 Babylon! In one hour has thy judgment come. 79
19: 5 And from the throne came a voice crying 73
7 for the marriage of the Lamb has come 79
17 Come, gather for the great supper of God 54
21: 9 Then came one of the seven angels 79
9 Come, I will show you the Bride, the wife of the Lamb. 53
22: 7 And behold, I am coming soon. 79
12 Behold, I am coming soon, bringing my recompense 79
17 The Spirit and the Bride say, "Come. 79
17 And let him who hears say, "Come. 79
17 And let him who is thirsty come 79
19 Surely I am coming soon." Amen. Come, Lord Jesus! 79
20 Surely I am coming soon." Amen. Come, Lord Jesus! 79
1Es 3:16 they were summoned, and came in. 64
4:16 From women they came 52
16 the vineyards from which comes wine. 52
53 all who came from Babylonia to build the city 103
53 their children and all the priests who came. 103
5: 8 They came with Zerubbabel and Jeshua 79
44 when they came to the temple of God 93
47 When the seventh month came 72
56 after their coming to the temple of God 93
56 all who had come to Jerusalem from the captivity; 93
57 after they came to Judea and Jerusalem. 79
63 came to the building of this one 79
64 while many came with trumpets and a joyful noise •
66 they came to find out what the sound . . meant. 79
6: 3 Sathrabuzanes . . came to them and said 94
20 after coming here 93
7:10 The people of Israel who came from the captivity •
13 the people of Israel who came from the captivity •
8: 1 Ezra came, the son of Seraiah, son of Azariah 103
21 wrath may not come upon the kingdom of the king 52
61 so we came to Jerusalem. 79
65 those who had come back from captivity 93
68 the principal men came to me and said 104
78 now in some measure mercy has come to us from thee 52
9:12 come at the time appointed 93
2Es 1: 4 The word of the Lord came to me, saying 117
35 I will give your houses to a people that will come 120
37 the gratitude of the people that is to come 120
38 and see the people coming from the east; 120
2:24 be quiet, my people, because your rest will come. 120
27 when the day of tribulation and anguish comes 120
32 Embrace your children until I come 120
33 When I came to them they rejected me 120
34 because he who will come at the end of the age 113
3:10 as death came upon Adam, so the flood upon them. •
29 when I came here 120
4:14 Come, let us go and make war against the sea 120
15 the waves of the sea also made a plan and said, 'Come!120
16 for the fire came and consumed it; 120
28 sown, but the harvest of it has not yet come. 120
29 where the good has been sown will not come. 120
30 will produce until the time of threshing comes! 120
35 And when will come the harvest of our reward? 120
45 whether more time is to come than has passed 120
46 but I do not know what is to come. 119
5: 1 behold, the days are coming 120
15 the angel who had come and talked with me held me120
16 Phaltiel, a chief of the people, came to me and said 120
19 and then you may come to me 120
31 the angel who had come to me on a previous night 120
36 Count up for me those who have not yet come 120
41 or we, or those who come after us? •
55 those who come after you will be smaller than you •
6: 6 just as the end shall come through me •
18 it said, "Behold, the days are coming 120
30 he said to me, "I have come to show you these things120
54 from him we have all come 115
7: 2 the words that I have come to speak to you. 120
5 how can he come to the broad part 120
16 considered in your mind what is to come 119
21 those who came into the world, when they came 120
21 those who came into the world, when they came 120
26 For behold, the time will come, when the signs 120
47 that the world to come will bring delight to few 119
69 if we were not to come into judgment after death 120
70 the world and Adam and all who have come from him120
75 we shall be kept in rest until those times come 120
96 and shall inherit what is to come 119
113and the beginning of the immortal age to come 119
132those who have not yet come into the world; 113
8: 1 but the world to come for the sake of few. 119
2 but only a little dust from which gold comes 118
5 not of your own will did you come into the world †
18 the swiftness of the judgment that is to come. 119
52 the age to come is prepared, plenty is provided 119
9:20 the devices of those who had come into it. 113
25 then I will come and talk with you. 120
29 when they came into the . . wilderness; 120
47 when he grew up and I came to take a wife for him 120
10: 3 and fled, and came to this field, as you see. 120
10 and others will come; and behold, almost all go 120
13 the multitude that is now in it goes as it came'; 120
28 Where is the angel Uriel, who came to me at first? 120
29 the angel who had come to me at first came to me 120
29 the angel who had come to me at first came to me 120
11:10 and behold, the voice did not come from his heads 116
13 while it was reigning it came to its end 120
14 while it was reigning its end came also 120
39 the end of my times might come through them? 120
40 You, the fourth that has come, have conquered 120
12:13 the days are coming when a kingdom shall arise 120
17 coming not from the eagle's heads 116
32 and will come and speak to them ‡
34 he will make them joyful until the end comes 120
40 and came to me and spoke to me, saying 120
48 but I have come to this place to pray 120
49 and after these days I will come to you. 120
13:13 many people came to him, some of whom were joyful12
20 Yet it is better to come into these things 120
28 the . . multitude which came to conquer him 120
29 Behold, the days are coming 120
30 bewilderment of mind shall come over those 120
34 as you saw, desiring to come and conquer him. 120
36 Zion will come and be made manifest to all people 120
46 and now, when they are about to come again 120
14:18 the eagle . . is already hastening to come. 120
25 you shall come here, and I will light in your heart 120
35 For after death the judgment will come 120
36 let no one come to me now 112
15:27 now calamities have come upon the whole earth 120
30 and with great power they shall come 113
33 fear and trembling shall come upon their army 119
44 They shall come to her and surround her 114
59 you shall come and suffer fresh afflictions 120
16:14 shall not return until they come over the earth. 120
18 when the calamities come? 120
50 when he comes who will defend him 120
Tob 1:18 put to death any who came fleeing from Judea 79
2: 3 he came back and said 79
5:13 My brother, you come of good stock. 62
6: 1 they came at evening to the Tigris river 79
7:11 when each came to her he died in the night 67
9: 6 got up early and came to the wedding feast 79
11: 6 she caught sight of him coming 79
6 Behold, your son is coming 79
18 Ahikar and his nephew Nadab came 93
12:18 For I did not come as a favor on my part 79
13:11 Many nations will come from afar 83
Jdt 1:14 came to Ecbatana, captured its towers 50
2: 7 I am coming against them in my anger 73
25 came to the southern borders of Japheth 79
3: 4 come and deal with them 79
5 The men came to Holofernes and told him all this. 93
9 Then he came to the edge of Esdraelon, near Dothan 79
5: 4 why have they . . refused to come out and meet me? 79
5 No falsehood shall come from your servant's mouth. 73
6: 5 take revenge on this race that came out of Egypt. •
11 came to the springs below Bethulia. 93
7: 8 commanders of the coastland came to him and said 104
31 if these days pass by, and no help comes for us 79
8:11 They came to her, and she said to them 79
9: 5 the things that are now, and those that are to come 74
10:12 where are you coming 79
18 they came and stood around her as she waited 79
23 Judith came into the presence of Holofernes 79
11: 3 tell me why you . . have come over to us 79
3 since you have come to safety. 83
18 I will come and tell you 79
19 till you come to Jerusalem 79
12:13 This beautiful maidservant will please come 79
16 Then Judith came in and lay down 64
13: 1 When evening came, his slaves quickly withdrew 52
10 came to its gates. 79
14: 2 as soon as morning comes and the sun rises 57
6 when he came and saw the head of Holofernes 79
13 they came to Holofernes' tent 93
15: 5 Those in . . all the hill country also came 93
8 came to witness the good things 79
16: 4 The Assyrian came down from the mountains 79
4 he came with myriads of his warriors 79
AEs 10: 4 Mordecai said, "These things have come from God. 52
11 came to the hour and moment and day of decision 79
11:10 there came a great river, with abundant water; 52
11 light came, and the sun rose •
15: 8 took her in his arms until she came to herself 87
16: 9 judging what comes before our eyes 79
Wis 1: 9 a report of his words will come to the Lord 83
2: 6 Come, therefore, let us enjoy the good things 54
4:20 come with dread when their sins are reckoned up 79
5:11 afterward no sign of its coming is found there; 76
6:22 will tell you what wisdom is and how she came to be 52
7: 7 the spirit of wisdom came to me. 79
11 All good things came to me along with her 79
14 the gifts that come from instruction. •
8:13 remembrance to those who come after me. •
9: 6 yet without the wisdom that comes from thee •
12:12 who will come before thee to plead as an advocate 79

14: 7 the wood by which righteousness comes. 52
17:12 surrender of the helps that come from reason; •
18 Whether there came a whistling wind •
18:20 a plague came upon the multitude in the desert 52
19:14 when they came to them 94
15 punishment of some sort will come upon the former •
Sir 0: 3 When I came to Egypt in the . . reign of Euergetes 93
1: 1 All wisdom comes from the Lord •
30 because you did not come in the fear of the Lord 104
3:11 For a man's glory comes from honoring his father •
5:13 Glory and dishonor come from speaking •
14 shame comes to the thief 62
6:19 Come to her like one who plows and sows 104
26 Come to her with all your soul 104
11:14 poverty and wealth, come from the Lord. 62
32 From a spark of fire come many burning coals •
12: 3 No good will come to the man who persists in evil 62
19: 9 when the time comes he will hate you. •
21: 5 his judgment comes speedily. 79
24:19 Come to me, you who desire me 104
27:27 he will not know where it came from. 83
31: 6 Many have come to ruin because of gold 58
38: 2 for healing comes from the Most High 62
39:31 when their times come •
40: 7 wonders that his fear came to nothing. 63
10 on their account the flood came. 52
42:13 for from garments comes the moth 70
13 from a woman comes woman's wickedness. •
43: 7 From the moon comes the sign for feast days •
44:17 a remnant was left . . when the flood came. 52
47:25 till vengeance came upon them. 79
Bar 1: 3 of all the people who came to hear the book 79
2: 7 calamities . . have come upon us. 79
30 land of their exile they will come to themselves 78
4:14 Let the neighbors of Zion come 79
22 joy has come to me from the Holy One 79
22 mercy . . will come to you from your . . Savior. 83
24 your salvation by God, which will come to you 74
36 see the joy that is coming to you from God! 79
37 Behold, your sons are coming, whom you sent away; 79
37 they are coming, gathered from east and west 79
5: 9 mercy and righteousness that come from him. •
LJr 1: 3 when you have come to Babylon 64
Sus 1: 4 and the Jews used to come to him 102
6 and all who had suits at law came to them. 48
28 the two elders came, full of their wicked plot 79
30 And she came, with her parents, her children 79
36 this woman came in with two maids 64
37 Then a young man . . came to her and lay with her. 79
42 who art aware of all things before they come to be 51
50 And the elders said to him, "Come, sit among us 53
52 your sins have now come home 83
Bel 1:15 In the night the priests came with their wives 79
16 Early in the morning the king rose and came •
40 the king came to mourn for Daniel 79
40 When he came to the den he looked in 79
1Mc 1: 1 who came from the land of Kittim 73
20 came to Jerusalem with a strong force. 46
29 he came to Jerusalem with a large force. 79
64 very great wrath came upon Israel. 52
2:15 the king's officers . . came to the city of Modein 79
16 Many from Israel came to them 104
18 be the first to come and do what the king commands 104
41 fight against every man who comes to attack us 79
3:17 when they saw the army coming to meet them 79
19 strength comes from Heaven. •
20 They come against us in great pride 79
4:12 saw them coming against them 79
29 They came into Idumea and encamped at Beth-zur 79
46 until there should come a prophet 93
60 coming and trampling them down 93
5:11 They are preparing to come 79
12 Now then come and rescue us from their hands 79
14 behold, other messengers . . came from Galilee 93
39 ready to come and fight against you 79
46 So they came to Ephron 79
53 till he came to the land of Judah. 79
6: 3 So he came and tried to take the city 79
5 Then some one came to him in Persia 79
11 I said to myself, 'To what distress I have come! 79
29 mercenary forces came to him 79
31 They came through Idumea 79
7: 5 Then there came to him all the lawless 79
10 came with a large force into the land of Judah 79
11 they saw that they had come with a large force. 79
14 A priest of the line of Aaron has come with the army 79
27 So Nicanor came to Jerusalem with a large force 79
28 I shall come with a few men to see you 83
29 So he came to Judas 79
30 Nicanor had come to him with treacherous intent 79
8: 1 they pledged friendship to those who came to them 104
9 The Greeks planned to come and destroy them 79
24 If war comes first to Rome 72
27 if war comes first to the nation of the Jews 107
9:10 If our time has come 60
43 he came with a large force on the sabbath day 79
60 He started to come with a large force 79
64 Then he came and encamped against Bethbasi 79
69 had counseled him to come into the country 79
72 came no more into their territory. 79
10: 7 Then Jonathan came to Jerusalem 79
16 Come now, we will make him our friend and ally. 88
57 came to Ptolemais 79
59 the king wrote to Jonathan to come to meet him. 79
67 Demetrius the son of Demetrius came from Crete 79
85 The number . . came to 8,000 men. 52
11: 9 He sent envoys to Demetrius the king, saying, "Come 53
15 came against him in battle 79
22 he set out and came to Ptolemais 79
44 when they came to the king 79
60 When he came to Askalon 79
63 the officers of Demetrius had come to Kadesh 94
12:15 have the help which comes from Heaven for our aid •
40 he marched forth and came to Beth-shan. 79
41 he came to Beth-shan. 79
42 Trypho saw that he had come with a large army 79
45 come with me to Ptolemais 53
13:20 Trypho came to invade the country and destroy it 79
21 urging him to come to them 79
14:21 we rejoiced at their coming. 81
22 envoys of the Jews, have come to us 79
15:11 he came in his flight to Dor, which is by the sea; 79
17 envoys of the Jews have come to us as our friends 79
31 Otherwise we will come and conquer you. 93
32 Athenobius . . came to Jerusalem 79
40 So Cendebeus came to Jamnia 93
16: 3 may the help which comes from Heaven be with you. 68
5 a large force . . was coming to meet them •
19 asking them to come to him 93
22 he seized the men who came to destroy him 79
2Mc 1:14 Antiochus came to the place 93
15 Antiochus had come with a few men 104
2: 5 Jeremiah came and found a cave 79
21 the appearances which came from heaven 52
3: 9 stated why he had come 94
39 and destroys those who come to do it injury. 93
4:10 When the king assented and Jason came to office 91
34 Andronicus came to Onias 93
44 When the king came to Tyre 89
6: 7 when the feast of Dionysus came 52
8: 6 Coming without warning 79
12 Word came to Judas 106
16 who were wickedly coming against them 93
18 to strike down those who are coming against us 79
19 when help came to their ancestors 52
20 by the help that came to them from heaven •
25 those who had come to buy them as slaves 93
9: 3 news came to him of what had happened to Nicanor 106
11 to come to his senses under the scourge of God 79
10:24 He came on, intending to take Judea by storm. 94
11: 2 came against the Jews 93
12: 7 intending to come again 83
17 they came to Charax 56
22 terror and fear came over the enemy 52
38 As the seventh day was coming on, they purified 75
13: 1 Antiochus Eupator was coming with a great army 93
9 was coming to show the Jews things far worse 79
14: 7 and have now come here 79
15 When the Jews heard of Nicanor's coming 81
15: 8 when help had come to them from heaven •
20 all were now looking forward to the coming decision 62
24 blasphemers who come against thy holy people 93
3Mc 2:10 when we come to this place and pray. 79
3:16 we came on to Jerusalem also 101
6:36 because of the deliverance that had come to them 52
7: 6 Since we have come to realize •
4Mc 1:23 Fear precedes pain and sorrow comes after. •
3: 8 when evening fell, he came 79
4: 2 he came to Apollonius, governor of Syria 83
3 I have come here because I am loyal 86
6 He said that he had come with the king's authority 83
6:13 some of the king's retinue came to him and said 105
9:31 the joys that come from virtue 55
32 the threats that come from impiety •
11: 3 I have come of my own accord 96
13:12 reminded them, "Remember whence you came 62

come *See also* message, news, perception, reckoning, summon, time, while, word, wrath.

come about 1. היה 2. γίνομαι 3. συμβαίνω
2Sm 13:35 as your servant said, so it has come about. 1
2Ch 22: 7 downfall of Ahazi'ah should come about 1
29:36 for the thing came about suddenly. 1
1Es 8:86 has come about because of our evil deeds 2
2Mc 3: 2 it came about that . . 3
9: 7 so it came about that he fell out of his chariot 3
13: 7 By such a fate it came about that . . 3
3Mc 1: 5 so it came about that the enemy was routed 3
5:42 changes of mind which had come about within him 2

come after 1. ἐπιγίνομαι
LJr 1:47 lies and reproach for those who come after. 1

come afterward 1. ἐπιγίνομαι
3Mc 2: 5 an example to those who should come afterward. 1

come afterwards 1. καθεξῆς
Act 3:24 from Samuel and those who came afterwards 1

come again 1. שׁוב
Gen 22: 5 go yonder and worship, and come again to you. 1
28:21 that I come again to my father's house in peace 1
Exd 24:14 Tarry here for us, until we come to you again; 1
Lev 14:39 the priest shall come again on the seventh day 1
Jos 2:23 Then the two men came down again from the hills 1
18: 8 Go up and down . . and come again to me; 1
Jdg 8: 9 I come again in peace, I will break down this tower. 1
1Kg 12: 5 Depart for three days, then come again to me. 1
12 as the king said, "Come to me again the third day. 1
17:21 LORD . . let this child's soul come into him again. 1
22 the soul of the child came into him again 1
19: 7 the angel of the LORD came again a second time 1
20: 5 The messengers came again, and said, "Thus says 1
2Kg 4:38 Eli'sha came again to Gilgal 1
2Ch 10:12 as the king said, "Come to me again the third day. 1
Ps 78:39 but flesh, a wind that passes and comes not again. 1
Prv 3:28 Go, and come again, tomorrow I will give it"– 1
Zec 4: 1 the angel who talked with me came again 1

come against 1. קרא 2. ἐπέρχομαι
Jos 11:20 that they should come against Israel in battle 1
1Mc 8: 4 They also subdued the kings who came against them 2

come around 1. סבב
Hab 2:16 the LORD'S right hand will come around to you 1

come away 1. הלך 2. יצא 3. δεῦτε
Sng 2:10 Arise, my love, my fair one, and come away; 1
13 Arise, my love, my fair one, and come away. 1
Jer 2:37 you will come away with your hands upon your head 2
Mrk 6:31 Come away by yourselves to a lonely place 3

come back 1. בוא 2. שׁוב 3. שׁוב ובוא 4. תְּשׁוּבָה 5. ἀναβαίνω 6. ἐπανέρχομαι 7. ἐπανήκω 8. ἐπάνοδος 9. ἐπιστρέφω 10. ἔρχομαι 11. καταπορεύομαι 12. ὑποστρέφω
Gen 8:11 the dove came back to him in the evening 1
15:16 shall come back here in the fourth generation; 2
Exd 14:26 the water may come back upon the Egyptians 2
Rut 2: 6 It is the Moabite maiden, who came back with Na'omi 2
4: 3 Na'omi, who has come back from the country of Moab 2
1Sm 7:17 he would come back to Ramah, for his home was there 4
17:53 And the Israelites came back from chasing 2
23:23 See . . and come back to me with sure information. 2
25:12 young men . . came back and told him all this. 3
27: 9 but took away . . and came back to A'chish. 3
2Sm 18:16 and the troops came back from pursuing Israel; 2
19:15 So the king came back to the Jordan; and Judah came 3
24 from . . until the day he came back in safety. 1
1Kg 2:33 So shall their blood come back upon the head 2
13:22 but have come back, and have eaten bread 2
2Kg 2:18 they came back to him, while he tarried at Jericho 2
4:22 quickly go to the man of God, and come back again. 2
7: 8 then they came back, and entered another tent 2
9:18 reached them, but he is not coming back. 2
20 He reached them, but he is not coming back. 2
36 When they came back and told him, he said 2
1Ch 21: 4 Jo'ab departed . . and came back to Jerusalem. 1
Est 2:14 in the morning she came back to the second harem 2
Ps 59: 6 Each evening they come back, howling like dogs 2
14 Each evening they come back, howling like dogs 2
Prv 2:19 none who go to her come back 2
12:14 and the work of a man's hand comes back to him. 2
26:27 stone will come back upon him who starts it 2
Jer 31:16 they shall come back from the land of the enemy. 2
17 children shall come back to their own country. 2
37: 8 And the Chalde'ans shall come back and fight 2
41:14 all the people . . turned about and came back 2
Lke 10:35 I will repay you when I come back.' 6
Joh 9: 7 So he went and washed and came back seeing. 10
Tob 5:21 he will come back safe and sound 12
Jdt 5:19 they . . have come back 5
Sir 4:18 Then she will come straight back to him 7
38:21 Do not forget, there is no coming back 8
1Mc 9: 9 let us come back with our brethren and fight them; 9
3Mc 4:11 to all coming back into the city 11

come back again 1. שׁוב אתה
Isa 21:12 If you will inquire, inquire; come back again. 1

come before 1. קדם 2. παραγίνομαι
2Kg 19:32 or come before it with a shield or cast up a siege 1
Ps 88:13 in the morning my prayer comes before thee. 1
Isa 37:33 or come before it with a shield 1
Mic 6: 6 With what shall I come before the LORD 1
6 Shall I come before him with burnt offerings 1
Lke 19:16 The first came before him, saying, 'Lord 2

come by 1. בוא 2. עבר
Rut 4: 1 the next of kin, of whom Bo'az had spoken, came by. 2
2Sm 20:12 And any one who came by, seeing him, stopped; 1

come by agreement 1. רגשׁ (A)
Dan 6: 6 came by agreement to the king and said to him, 1

11 men came by agreement and found Daniel making 1
15 men came by agreement to the king, and said 1

cause to come 1. בוא 2. עלה

Exd 8: 5 cause frogs to come upon the land of Egypt!' 2
Job 34:28 that they caused the cry of the poor to come to him 1
Ezk 37: 6 and will cause flesh to come upon you 2

cause to come near 1. קרב

Num16: 5 LORD . . will cause him to come near to him; 1
5 whom he will choose he will cause to come near 1

cause to come up 1. עלה

1Kg 20:33 and he caused him to come up into the chariot. 1

come close 1. ἐγγίζω

Jdt 13: 7 She came close to his bed . . and said 1

come down 1. ירד 2. נחת 3. נחת (A) 4. καταβαίνω 5. κατέρχομαι 6. συγκαταβαίνω 7. descendo

Gen 11: 5 the LORD came down to see the city and the tower 1
15:11 when birds of prey came down upon the carcasses 1
43:20 my lord, we came down the first time to buy food; 1
44:23 Unless your youngest brother comes down 1
45: 9 God has made me lord of all Egypt; come down to me 1
Exd 2: 5 Now the daughter of Pharaoh came down to bathe 1
3: 8 I have come down to deliver them out of the hand 1
9:19 for the hail shall come down upon every man 1
11: 8 all these your servants shall come down to me 1
19:11 the LORD will come down upon Mount Sinai 1
20 the LORD came down upon Mount Sinai, to the top 1
32: 1 the people saw that Moses delayed to come down 1
34:29 When Moses came down from Mount Sinai 1
29 in his hand as he came down from the mountain 1
Lev 9:22 he came down from offering the sin offering 1
Num11:17 I will come down and talk with you there; 1
25 LORD came down in the cloud and spoke to him 1
12: 5 LORD came down in a pillar of cloud, and stood 1
14:45 who dwelt in that hill country came down 1
20:28 Moses and Elea'zar came down from the mountain. 1
Deu 9:15 I turned and came down from the mountain 1
10: 5 Then I turned and came down from the mountain 1
28:24 from heaven it shall come down upon you until 1
43 you shall come down lower and lower. 1
52 walls . . come down throughout all your land; 1
Jos 2:23 Then the two men came down again from the hills 1
3:13 the waters coming down from above shall stand 1
16 waters coming down from above stood and rose up 1
Jdg 1:34 they did not allow them to come down to the plain; 1
7:24 Come down against the Mid'ianites and seize 1
9:36 Look, men are coming down from the mountain tops! 1
37 men are coming down from the center of the land 1
15:12 We have come down to bind you, that we may give you 1
16:31 his brothers and all his family came down 1
1Sm 6:21 the ark . . Come down and take it up to you. 1
9:25 they came down from the high place into the city 1
10: 5 band of prophets coming down from the high place 1
13:12 the Philistines will come down upon me at Gilgal 1
17: 8 Choose a man . . and let him come down to me. 1
28 Why have you come down? And with whom 1
28 for you have come down to see the battle. 1
23: 6 Abi'athar . . came down with an ephod in his hand. 1
11 Will Saul come down, as thy servant has heard? 1
11 And the LORD said, "He will come down. 1
20 Now come down, O king 1
20 according to all your heart's desire to come down 1
25:20 and came down under cover of the mountain 1
20 David and his men came down toward her; 1
2Sm 19:16 Shim'e-i . . made haste to come down with the men 1
20 the first . . to come down to meet my lord the king. 1
24 And Mephib'osheth . . came down to meet the king; 1
31 Now Barzil'lai . . had come down from Ro'gelim; 1
22:10 He bowed the heavens, and came down; 1
1Kg 2: 8 when he came down to meet me at the Jordan, I swore 1
22: 2 Jehosh'aphat . . came down to the king of Israel. 1
2Kg 1: 4 You shall not come down from the bed 1
6 you shall not come down from the bed 1
9 O man of God, the king says, 'Come down.' 1
10 let fire come down from heaven and consume you 1
10 Then fire came down from heaven, and consumed him 1
11 this is the king's order, 'Come down quickly!' 1
12 let fire come down from heaven and consume you 1
12 Then the fire of God came down from heaven 1
14 fire came down from heaven, and consumed the two 1
16 you shall not come down from the bed 1
6:18 when the Syrians came down . . Eli'sha prayed 1
33 the king came down to him and said, "This trouble is 1
7:17 man of God had said when the king came down 1
9:16 And Ahazi'ah . . had come down to visit Joram. 1
10:13 and we came down to visit the royal princes 1
1Ch 7:21 because they came down to raid their cattle. 1
2Ch 7: 1 ended his prayer, fire came down from heaven 1
3 all the children of Israel saw the fire come down 1
Neh 6: 3 I am doing a great work and I cannot come down. 1
3 work stop while I leave it and come down to you? 1
9:13 Thou didst come down upon Mount Sinai, and speak 1
Ps 18: 9 He bowed the heavens, and came down; 1
38: 2 thy hand has come down on me. 2
144: 5 Bow thy heavens, O LORD, and come down! 1
Prv 30: 4 Who has ascended to heaven and come down? 1
Isa 31: 4 LORD . . will come down to fight upon Mount Zion 1
47: 1 Come down and sit in the dust, O virgin daughter 1
55:10 For as the rain and the snow come down from heaven 1
64: 1 that thou wouldst rend the heavens and come down 1
3 thou camest down, the mountains quaked at thy 1
Jer 13:18 beautiful crown has come down from your head. 1
21:13 you who say, 'Who shall come down against us 2
48:18 Come down from your glory, and sit on the parched 1
Ezk 27:29 down from their ships come all that handle 1
30: 6 her proud might shall come down; 1
32:21 They have come down, they lie still 1
Dan 4:13 a watcher, a holy one, came down from heaven. 3
23 holy one, coming down from heaven and saying, 3
Mic 1: 3 and will come down and tread upon the high places 1
12 evil has come down from the LORD to the gate 1
Mat 8: 1 When he came down from the mountain 4
17: 9 as they were coming down the mountain 4
27:40 If you are the Son of God, come down from the cross. 4
42 let him come down now from the cross 4
Mrk 3:22 the scribes who came down from Jerusalem said 4
9: 9 as they were coming down the mountain 4
15:30 save yourself, and come down from the cross! 4
32 Let the Christ, the King of Israel, come down now 4
Lke 6:17 he came down with them and stood on a level place 4
8:23 a storm of wind came down on the lake 4
9:37 when they had come down from the mountain 5
54 do you want us to bid fire come down from heaven 4
17:31 let him . . not come down to take them away 4
19: 5 Zacchae'us, make haste and come down 4
6 he made haste and came down 4
Joh 4:47 he went and begged him to come down and heal 4
49 Sir, come down before my child dies. 4
6:33 the bread of God . . which comes down from heaven 4
38 I have come down from heaven, not to do my own will 4
41 I am the bread which came down from heaven. 4
42 does he now say, 'I have come down from heaven'? 4
50 This is the bread which comes down from heaven 4
51 I am the living bread which came down from heaven; 4
58 This is the bread which came down from heaven 4
Act 7:34 I have come down to deliver them 4
8:15 who came down and prayed for them 4
9:32 he came down also to the saints that lived at Lydda. 5
11:27 in these days prophets came down from Jerusalem 5
14:11 The gods have come down to us in the likeness of men! 4
15: 1 some men came down from Judea 4
21:10 a prophet named Ag'abus came down from Judea. 5
24: 1 the high priest Anani'as came down with some elders 4
22 When Lys'ias the tribune comes down 4
Jas 1:17 coming down from the Father of lights 4
3:15 This wisdom is not such as comes down from above 5
Rev 3:12 the new Jerusalem which comes down from my God 4
10: 1 another mighty angel coming down from heaven 4
12:12 for the devil has come down to you in great wrath 4
13:13 even making fire come down from heaven to earth 4
18: 1 I saw another angel coming down from heaven 4
20: 1 Then I saw an angel coming down from heaven 4
9 but fire came down from heaven and consumed them 4
21: 2 new Jerusalem, coming down out of heaven from God 4
10 Jerusalem coming down out of heaven from God 4
1Es 1:29 the commanders came down against King Josiah. 4
2Es 13:12 I saw the same man come down from the mountain 7
Tob 3:17 Sarah . . came down from her upper room. 4
Jdt 6:14 Then the men of Israel came down from their city 4
14:13 to come down against us to give battle 4
Sir 50:20 Simon came down 4
Aza 1:26 the angel of the Lord came down into the furnace 6
1Mc 10:71 come down to the plain to meet us 4
2Mc 2:10 fire came down from heaven 4
10 the fire came down 4

come forth 1. דרך 2. יצא 3. נפק (A) 4. ἐκπορεύομαι 5. ἐξέρχομαι 6. ἔξοδος 7. ἥκω 8. procedo 9. prodeo

Gen 17: 6 and kings shall come forth from you. 2
25:25 The first came forth red, all his body like a hairy 2
26 Afterward his brother came forth 2
Exd 5:20 met Moses . . as they came forth from Pharaoh; 2
Lev 9:24 fire came forth from before the LORD 2
10: 2 fire came forth from the presence of the LORD 2
16:24 and put on his garments, and come forth 2
Num11:20 Why did we come forth out of Egypt?"' 2
16:35 fire came forth . . and consumed the 250 men 2
20:11 water came forth abundantly 2
22:32 Behold, I have come forth to withstand you 2
24:17 star shall come forth out of Jacob, and a scepter 1
26: 4 who came forth out of the land of Egypt, were 2
Deu 14:22 which comes forth from the field year by year 2
21: 2 your elders and your judges shall come forth 2
23: 4 on the way, when you came forth out of Egypt 2
24: 9 Miriam on the way as you came forth out of Egypt. 2
Jos 5: 6 the men of war that came forth out of Egypt 2
8:22 the others came forth from the city against them; 2
Jdg 11:31 whoever comes forth from the doors of my house 2
1Sm 24:13 'Out of the wicked comes forth wickedness'; 2
2Sm 7:12 offspring . . who shall come forth from your body 2
1Kg 2:30 The king commands, 'Come forth.'" But he said, "No 2
20:33 Then Ben-ha'dad came forth to him; 2
Job 3:11 die at birth, come forth from the womb and expire? 2
14: 2 He comes forth like a flower, and withers; 2
23:10 when he has tried me, I shall come forth as gold. 2
26: 4 whose spirit has come forth from you? 2
38:29 From whose womb did the ice come forth 2
41:20 Out of his nostrils comes forth smoke 2
21 a flame comes forth from his mouth. 2
Ps 19: 5 which comes forth like a bridegroom 2
109: 7 When he is tried, let him come forth guilty; 2
Ecc 7:18 he who fears God shall come forth from them all. 2
Isa 11: 1 shall come forth a shoot from the stump of Jesse 2
14:29 from the serpent's root will come forth an adder 2
26:21 the LORD is coming forth out of his place 2
48: 1 and who came forth from the loins of Judah; 2
49: 9 saying to the prisoners, 'Come forth,' 2
Jer 20:18 Why did I come forth from the womb to see toil 2
30:21 their ruler shall come forth from their midst; 2
Ezk 5: 4 a fire will come forth into all . . of Israel. 2
14:22 sons and daughters, when they come forth to you 2
21:19 both of them shall come forth from the same land. 2
33:30 what the word is that comes forth from the LORD 2
Dan 3:26 servants of . . God, come forth, and come here! 3
7:10 stream of fire issued and came forth from before 3
8: 9 Out of one of them came forth a little horn 2
Jol 3:18 shall come forth from the house of the LORD 2
Mic 1: 3 behold, the LORD is coming forth out of his place 2
11 the inhabitants of Za'anan do not come forth; 2
5: 2 shall come forth for me one who is to be ruler 2
Lke 6:19 for power came forth from him and healed them all. 5
Joh 5:29 and come forth 4
8:42 I proceeded and came forth from God 7
2Es 6:44 For immediately fruit came forth 8
16:38 and when the child comes forth from the womb 9
39 will not delay in coming forth upon the earth 9
Sir 24: 3 I came forth from the mouth of the Most High 5
40: 1 the day they come forth from their mother's womb 6
Sus 1: 5 Iniquity came forth from Babylon 5
1Mc 1:10 From them came forth a sinful root 5
11 In those days lawless men came forth from Israel 5

come forward 1. יצא 2. נגש 3. עמד 4. קרב (A) 5. ἐξέρχομαι 6. ἵστημι 7. παραγίνομαι 8. προάγω 9. προέρχομαι 10. προσέρχομαι 11. προσπορεύομαι

Num12: 5 Aaron and Miriam; and they both came forward. 1
Deu 20: 2 priest shall come forward and speak to the people 2
21: 5 priests the sons of Levi shall come forward 2
1Sm 17:16 the Philistine came forward and took his stand 2
1Kg 22:21 a spirit came forward and stood before the LORD 1
2Ch 18:20 a spirit came forward and stood before the LORD 1
Ezr 3:10 priests . . came forward with trumpets 3
Dan 3: 8 at that time certain Chalde'ans came forward 4
Zec 2: 3 behold, the angel who talked with me came forward 1
3 and another angel came forward to meet him 1
5: 5 Then the angel who talked with me came forward 1
9 and saw, and behold, two women coming forward! 1
Mat 8: 5 he entered Caper'na-um, a centurion came forward 10
25:20 he who had received the five talents came forward 10
22 he also who had the two talents came forward 10
24 He also who had received the one talent came forward 10
26:60 though many false witnesses came forward 10
60 At last two came forward 10
Mrk 10:35 James and John, the sons of Zeb'edee, came forward 11
Joh 18: 4 Jesus . . came forward and said to them 5
Act 27:21 Paul then came forward among them and said, "Men 6
Jdt 10:22 he came forward to the front of the tent 5
AEs 11: 6 behold, two great dragons came forward 9
Sir 2: 1 My son, if you come forward to serve the Lord 10
1Mc 2:23 a Jew came forward in the sight of all 10
2Mc 5:18 as soon as he came forward 8
14:21 A chariot came forward from each army 9
4Mc 12: 1 the seventh and youngest of all came forward. 7

fully come 1. πληρόω

Joh 7: 8 my time has not yet fully come. 1

come here 1. παραγίνομαι 2. παρέρχομαι 3. advenio

Act 28:21 none of the brethren coming here has reported 1
2Es 4:12 to come here and live in ungodliness 3
Sir 29:26 Come here, stranger, prepare the table 2

come home 1. ἀναλύω 2. ἐπιστρέφω

2Sm 17: 3 back to you as a bride comes home to her husband. 2
Lke 12:36 to come home from the marriage feast 1

come in sight 1. ἀναφαίνω

Act 21: 3 When we had come in sight of Cyprus 1

come into 1. בוא 2. קדם 3. עלל (A) 4. εἰσέρχομαι 5. ἐπιβαίνω

Jos 2: 1 And they went, and came into the house of a harlot 1
6:11 and they came into the camp, and spent the night 1
2Sm 4: 7 When they came into the house, as he lay on his bed 1
2Kg 4:32 When Eli'sha came into the house, he saw the child 1
Ps 66:13 I will come into thy house with burnt offerings; 1
95: 2 Let us come into his presence with thanksgiving; 2
Dan 5:10 queen . . came into the banqueting hall; 3
Act 25: 1 Now when Festus had come into his province 5
28:16 when we came into Rome 4

Rom 5:12 as sin came into the world through one man 4
Heb 10: 5 when Christ came into the world, he said 4
Jas 2: 2 a man . . comes into your assembly 4

come into being 1. היה 2. γίνομαι 3. φαίνω 4. fio 5. germino
Jon 4:10 which came into being in a night, and perished 1
2Es 6:45 the arrangement of the stars to come into being; 4
10: 9 so many who have come into being upon her. 5
2Mc 7:22 I do not know how you came into being in my womb 3
28 Thus also mankind comes into being. 2

come later 1. אַחֲרוֹן
Ecc 4:16 Yet those who come later will not rejoice in him. 1

come like a whirlwind 1. סער
Hab 3:14 who came like a whirlwind to scatter me 1

come loose 1. זחח
Exd 28:28 that the breastpiece shall not come loose 1
39:21 that the breastpiece should not come loose 1

make come 1. בוא 2. יצא
Jos 24: 7 he . . made the sea come upon them and cover them; 1
Ps 78:16 He made streams come out of the rock 2

make come true 1. קום
Jer 28: 6 make the words . . you have prophesied come true 1

make come up 1. עלה
Num20: 5 why have you made us come up out of Egypt 1
Jon 4: 6 appointed a plant, and made it come up over Jonah 1

make come upon 1. קרא
Jer 32:23 thou hast made all this evil come upon them. 1

come mightily 1. צלח
Jdg 14: 6 the Spirit of the LORD came mightily upon him 1
19 the Spirit of the LORD came mightily upon him 1
15:14 and the Spirit of the LORD came mightily upon him 1
1Sm 10: 6 spirit of the LORD will come mightily upon you 1
10 and the spirit of God came mightily upon him 1
11: 6 And the spirit of God came mightily upon Saul 1
16:13 the Spirit of the LORD came mightily upon David 1

come near 1. בוא 2. נגשׁ 3. קָרֵב 4. קרב 5. קרב (A) 6. ἐγγίζω 7. προσέρχομαι 8. συνεγγίζω 9. accedo 10. adpropinquo
Gen 27:21 Isaac said to Jacob, "Come near, that I may feel 2
26 said to him, "Come near and kiss me, my son. 2
27 he came near and kissed him; and he smelled 2
33: 3 seven times, until he came near to his brother. 2
37:18 before he came near to them they conspired 4
45: 4 Joseph said to his brothers, "Come near to me 2
4 Come near to me, I pray you." And they came near. 2
Exd 3: 5 Then he said, "Do not come near; put off your shoes 4
12:48 be circumcised, then he may come near and keep it; 4
14:20 night passed without one coming near the other 4
16: 9 Say . . 'Come near before the LORD, for he has heard 4
19:22 the priests who come near to the LORD consecrate 2
22: 8 the owner of the house shall come near to God 4
24: 2 Moses alone shall come near to the LORD; 2
2 but the others shall not come near 2
28:43 when they come near the altar to minister 2
30:20 when they come near the altar to minister 2
32:19 as soon as he came near the camp and saw the calf 4
34:30 and they were afraid to come near him. 2
32 afterward all the people of Israel came near 2
Lev 21:21 shall come near to offer the LORD'S offerings 2
21 not come near to offer the bread of his God 2
23 he shall not come near the veil or approach 1
Num 1:51 any one else comes near, he shall be put to death. 3
3:10 if any one else comes near, he shall be put to death. 3
38 any one else who came near was to be put to death. 3
4:19 when they come near to the most holy things 2
8:19 people . . should come near the sanctuary. 2
17:13 Every one who comes near . . shall die. 3
13 Every one . . who comes near to the tabernacle 3
18: 3 not come near to the vessels of the sanctuary 4
4 no one else shall come near you. 4
7 any one else who comes near shall be put to death. 3
22 Israel shall not come near the tent of meeting 4
31:48 the officers . . of the army . . came near to Moses 4
32:16 Then they came near to him, and said, "We will build 2
36: 1 came near and spoke before Moses 4
Deu 1:22 Then all of you came near me, and said, 'Let us send 4
4:11 came near and stood at the foot of the mountain 4
5:23 you came near to me, all the heads of your tribes 4
22:14 I took this woman, and when I came near her 4
Jos 3: 4 Yet there shall be a space . . do not come near it. 4
7:14 and the tribe . . shall come near by families; 4
14 and the family . . shall come near by households; 4
14 the household . . shall come near man by man. 4
10:24 Come near, put your feet upon the necks of these 4
24 they came near, and put their feet on their necks. 4
Jdg 20:24 Israel came near against the Benjaminites 4
2Sm 15: 5 whenever a man came near to do obeisance to him 4
20:17 came near her; and the woman said, "Are you Jo'ab? 4
1Kg 18:21 Eli'jah came near to all the people, and said 2
30 Then Eli'jah said to all the people, "Come near to me"; 2
30 Come near . . "; and all the people came near to him. 2
36 Eli'jah the prophet came near and said, "O LORD 2
20:13 behold, a prophet came near to Ahab king of Israel 2
22 the prophet came near to the king of Israel 2
28 a man of God came near and said to the king 2
22:24 Zedeki'ah . . came near and struck Micai'ah 2
2Kg 5:13 his servants came near and said to him, "My father 2
2Ch 18:23 Then Zedeki'ah . . came near and struck Micai'ah 2
29:31 come near, bring sacrifices and thank offerings 2
Ps 91: 7 but it will not come near you. 2
10 no scourge come near your tent. 4
Isa 50: 8 Who is my adversary? Let him come near to me. 2
54:14 and from terror, for it shall not come near you. 4
65: 5 who say, "Keep to yourself, do not come near me 2
Jer 42: 1 people from the least to the greatest, came near 2
Lam 3:57 Thou didst come near when I called on thee; 4
Ezk 40:46 may come near to the LORD to minister to him. 3
44:13 They shall not come near to me, to serve me 2
13 nor come near any of my sacred things 2
15 shall come near to me to minister to me; 4
Dan 3:26 Then Nebuchadnez'zar came near to the door 5
6:12 Then they came near and said before the king 5
20 When he came near to the den where Daniel was 5
Lke 10: 9 'The kingdom of God has come near to you.' 6
11 the kingdom of God has come near.' 6
18:40 when he came near, he asked him 6
21:20 then know that its desolation has come near. 6
Act 10: 9 as they were . . coming near the city 6
23:15 we are ready to kill him before he comes near. 6
2Es 5:19 and do not come near me for seven days 9
14:18 and falsehood shall come near 10
Tob 6: 5 until they came near to Ecbatana. 6
11: 1 until they came near to Nineveh. 6
17 When Tobit came near to Sarah his daughter-in-law 6
AEs 15:10 our law applies only to the people. Come near 7
2Mc 10:27 when they came near to the enemy they halted. 8

come out 1. בוא 2. יצא 3. מוֹצָא 4. עלה 5. פכה 6. ἐκκύπτω 7. ἐκπορεύομαι 8. ἐξέρχομαι 9. ἔξοδος 10. παραγίνομαι 11. πρέρχομαι 12. exeo 13. procedo
Gen 9:10 with . . as many as came out of the ark. 2
15:14 they shall come out with great possessions. 2
24:13 daughters . . are coming out to draw water. 2
15 Rebekah . . came out with her water jar 2
43 let the young woman who comes out to draw 2
45 behold, Rebekah came out with her water jar on her 2
38:28 midwife . . saying, "This came out first. 2
29 drew back his hand, behold, his brother came out 2
30 Afterward his brother came out with the scarlet 2
43:31 Then he washed his face and came out; 2
Exd 4:14 and behold, he is coming out to meet you 2
13: 3 this day, in which you came out from Egypt 2
8 the LORD did for me when I came out of Egypt.' 2
17: 6 strike the rock, and water shall come out of it 2
23:15 in the month of Abib, for in it you came out of Egypt. 2
28:35 shall be heard . . when he comes out, lest he die. 2
32:24 I threw it . . and there came out this calf. 2
34:18 for in the month Abib you came out from Egypt. 2
34 he took the veil off, until he came out; 2
34 and when he came out, and told the people of Israel 2
Lev 9:23 when they came out they blessed the people 2
16:17 until he comes out and has made atonement 2
Num 1: 1 after they had come out of the land of Egypt 2
9: 1 after they had come out of the land of Egypt, saying 2
11:20 a whole month, until it comes out at your nostrils 2
12: 4 Come out, you three, to the tent of meeting. 2
4 And the three of them came out. 2
12 consumed when he comes out of his mother's womb. 2
16:27 Dathan and Abi'ram came out and stood at the door 2
20:18 not pass through, lest I come out with the sword 2
20 Edom came out against them with many men 2
21:33 Og the king of Bashan came out against them 2
22: 5 Behold, a people has come out of Egypt; they cover 2
11 'Behold, a people has come out of Egypt 2
33:38 people of Israel had come out of the land of Egypt 2
Deu 1:44 Amorites . . came out against you and chased you 2
2:32 Sihon came out against us . . to battle at Jahaz. 2
3: 1 Og the king of Bashan came out against us 2
4:45 spoke to . . Israel when they came out of Egypt 2
46 Israel defeated when they came out of Egypt. 2
28: 7 come out against you one way, and flee before you 2
57 afterbirth that comes out from between her feet 2
29: 7 Sihon . . and Og . . came out against us to battle 2
Jos 2:10 dried up the water . . when you came out of Egypt 2
5: 4 all the males of the people who came out of Egypt 2
4 on the way . . after they had come out of Egypt. 2
5 all the people who came out had been circumcised 2
5 born on the way . . after they had come out of Egypt 2
8: 5 And when they come out against us, as before 2
6 and they will come out after us 2
11: 4 they came out, with all their troops, a great host 2
19: 1 The second lot came out for Simeon 2
17 The fourth lot came out for Is'sachar 2
24 The fifth lot came out for the tribe of Asher 2
32 The sixth lot came out for the tribe of Naph'tali 2
40 The seventh lot came out for the tribe of Dan 2
21: 4 The lot came out for the . . Ko'hathites. 2
Jdg 1:24 the spies saw a man coming out of the city 2
3:22 he did not draw . . and the dirt came out. 2
4:18 And Ja'el came out to meet Sis'era 2
9:15 if not, let fire come out of the bramble and devour 2
20 but if not, let fire come out from Abim'elech 2
20 let fire come out from the citizens of Shechem 2
29 to Abim'elech, 'Increase your army, and come out.' 2
33 he and the men . . with him come out against you 2
43 he looked and saw the men coming out of the city 2
11:34 his daughter came out to meet him with timbrels 2
14:14 Out of the eater came something to eat. 2
14 Out of the strong came something sweet. 2
20: 1 people of Israel came out, from Dan to Beer-sheba 2
21 Benjaminites came out of Gib'e-ah, and felled 2
21:21 if the daughters of Shiloh come out to dance 2
21 come out of the vineyards and seize each man 2
1Sm 9:11 they met young maidens coming out to draw water 2
14 they saw Samuel coming out toward them on his way 2
11: 7 Whoever does not come out after Saul and Samuel 2
7 and they came out as one man. 2
13:17 raiders came out of the camp of the Philistines 2
14:11 Look, Hebrews are coming out of the holes 2
17: 4 there came out from the camp of . . a champion 2
8 Why have you come out to draw up for battle? 2
18: 6 the women came out of all the cities of Israel 2
30 Then . . the Philistines came out to battle 2
30 as often as they came out David had more success 2
23:15 Saul had come out to seek his life. 2
24:14 After whom has the king of Israel come out? 2
26:20 the king of Israel has come out to seek my life 2
2Sm 2:23 smote him . . so that the spear came out at his back; 2
3:26 When Jo'ab came out from David's presence 2
6:20 But Michal . . came out to meet David, and said 2
10: 8 Ammonites came out and drew up in battle array 2
11:17 the men of the city came out and fought with Jo'ab; 2
23 The men . . and came out against us in the field; 2
16: 5 there came out a man of the family of the house 2
1Kg 6: 1 after . . Israel came out of the land of Egypt 2
8: 9 of Israel, when they came out of the land of Egypt. 2
10 when the priests came out of the holy place 2
20:17 Men are coming out from Sama'ria. 2
18 If they have come out for peace, take them alive; 2
18 if they have come out for war, take them alive. 2
2Kg 2: 3 the sons of the prophets . . came out to Eli'sha 2
23 some small boys came out of the city and jeered 2
24 And two shebears came out of the woods 2
5:11 I thought that he would surely come out to me 2
7:12 When they come out of the city, we shall take them 2
9:11 When Jehu came out to the servants of his master 2
18:18 when they . . there came out to them Eli'akim 2
31 Make your peace with me and come out to me; 2
21:15 since the day their fathers came out of Egypt 2
24: 7 king of Egypt did not come again out of his land 2
1Ch 19: 9 Ammonites came out and drew up in battle array 2
26:14 Zechari'ah . . and his lot came out for the north. 2
15 O'bed-e'dom's came out for the south •
16 For Shuppim and Hosah it came out for the west •
2Ch 5:10 people of Israel, when they came out of Egypt. 2
11 Now when the priests came out of the holy place 2
14: 9 Zerah the Ethiopian came out against them 2
21:15 your bowels come out because of the disease, 2
19 his bowels came out because of the disease 2
Neh 4:21 from the break of dawn till the stars came out. 2
Prv 7:15 now I have come out to meet you, to seek you eagerly 2
Isa 36: 3 there came out to him Eli'akim the son of Hilki'ah 2
16 Make your peace with me and come out to me; 2
Jer 7:25 the day that your fathers came out of . . Egypt 2
17:16 that which came out of my lips was before thy face. 3
30:19 Out of them shall come songs of thanksgiving 2
36: 6 all the men of Judah who come out of their cities. 1
37: 5 The army of Pharaoh had come out of Egypt; 2
41: 6 And Ish'mael the son of Nethani'ah came out 2
Ezk 47: 2 the water was coming out on the south side. 5
Dan 3:26 Shadrach . . and Abed'nego came out from the fire. •
9:22 O Daniel, I have now come out to give you wisdom 2
11:11 come out and fight with the king of the north; 2
Hos 2:15 at the time when she came out of the land of Egypt. 4
Mic 7:15 in the days when you came out of the land of Egypt 2
Nah 1:11 Did one not come out from you 2
Hag 2: 5 the promise that I made you when you came out 2
Zec 6: 1 chariots came out from between two mountains; 2
7 When the steeds came out, they were impatient 2
Mat 8:28 two demoniacs met him, coming out of the tombs 8
32 Go." So they came out and went into the swine; 8
34 behold, all the city came out to meet Jesus 8
13:49 The angels will come out and separate 8
15:11 what comes out of the mouth, this defiles a man. 7
18 what comes out of the mouth 7
22 a Canaanite woman from that region came out 8
17:18 Jesus rebuked him, and the demon came out of him 8
25: 6 'Behold, the bridegroom! Come out to meet him.' 8
26:55 Have you come out as against a robber 8
Mrk 1:25 Be silent, and come out of him! 8
26 the unclean spirit . . came out of him. 8
38 for that is why I came out. 8
5: 2 when he had come out of the boat 8
8 Come out of the man, you unclean spirit! 8
13 unclean spirits came out, and entered the swine; 8

9:25 come out of him, and never enter him again. 8
26 it came out, and the boy was like a corpse 8
13: 1 as he came out of the temple 7
14:48 Have you come out as against a robber 8
Lke 1:22 when he came out, he could not speak to them 8
3: 7 the multitudes that came out to be baptized by him 7
4:35 Be silent, and come out of him! 8
35 he came out of him, having done him no harm. 8
36 he commands the unclean spirits, and they come out. 8
41 And demons also came out of many 8
8:29 commanded the unclean spirit to come out of the man 8
33 Then the demons came out of the man 8
15:28 His father came out and entreated him 8
22:39 And he came out, and went . . to the Mount of Olives 8
52 who had come out against him 10
52 Have you come out as against a robber, with swords 8
Joh 11:44 The dead man came out 8
19: 5 Jesus came out, wearing the crown of thorns 8
34 at once there came out blood and water. 8
20: 3 Peter then came out with the other disciple 8
Act 7: 7 they shall come out and worship me in this place.' 8
8: 7 unclean spirits came out of many 8
16:18 I charge you . . to come out of her 8
18 it came out that very hour. 8
36 now therefore come out and go in peace. 8
19:12 diseases left them and the evil spirits came out 7
28: 3 when a viper came out because of the heat 8
2Co 6:17 come out from them, and be separate from them 8
Eph 4:29 Let no evil talk come out of your mouths 7
Rev 6: 4 And out came another horse, bright red; 8
14:15 another angel came out of the temple, calling 8
17 another angel came out of the temple in heaven 8
18 Then another angel came out from the altar •
15: 6 out of the temple came the seven angels 8
16:17 and a loud voice came out of the temple 8
18: 4 Come out of her, my people 8
20: 8 and will come out to deceive the nations 8
2Es 9:29 when they came out from Egypt 12
13:27 fire and a storm coming out of his mouth 12
14: 1 behold, a voice came out of a bush opposite me 12
15:29 nations . . shall come out with many chariots 12
16:65 when your sins come out before men 13
Tob 8:14 she came out and told them that he was alive. 8
Jdt 10:20 all his servants came out and led her into the tent. 8
13: 3 to wait for her to come out 9
Sir 28:12 both come out of your mouth. 7
50: 5 as he came out of the inner sanctuary! 9
1Mc 2:27 Let every one . . come out with me! 8
33 Come out and do what the king commands 8
34 they said, "We will not come out 8
4:19 a detachment appeared, coming out of the hills. 6
5:59 Gorgias and his men came out of the city 8
7:33 Some of the priests came out of the sanctuary 8
46 men came out of all the villages of Judea round about 8
9:36 the sons of Jambri from Medeba came out 8
39 the bridegroom came out with his friends 8
10:86 the men of the city came out to meet him 8
2Mc 4:34 to come out from the place of sanctuary 11
5:26 put to the sword all those who came out to see them 8
12:33 he came out with 3,000 infantry and 400 cavalry. 8
3Mc 5:26 Hermon arrived and invited him to come out 9
27 being struck by the unusual invitation to come out 9

come out in leaf 1. *προβάλλω*
Lke 21:30 as soon as they come out in leaf 1

come over 1. הָיָה לְ 2. עבר 3. *διαβαίνω* 4. *ἐπέρχομαι* 5. *ἐπιπίπτω* 6. *περιχέω*
1Sm 10:11 What has come over the son of Kish? 1
26:22 Let one of the young men come over and fetch it. 2
2Sm 19:33 Come over with me, and I will provide for you 2
Isa 45:14 they shall come over in chains and bow down 2
Act 16: 9 Come over to Macedo'nia and help us. 3
Jdt 14: 3 Then fear will come over them, and they will flee 5
15: 2 Fear and trembling came over them 5
Sir 26:28 because of a third anger comes over me 4
2Mc 3:17 bodily trembling had come over the man 6
27 deep darkness came over him 6

come round 1. חַי
2Kg 4:16 At this season, when the time comes round 1

come safely to land 1. *διασῴζω*
Wis 14: 5 they come safely to land. 1

come short 1. resto
2Es 8:47 you come far short of being able to love 1

come swiftly 1. דאה 2. חוש
Deu 32:35 their doom comes swiftly. 2
Ps 18:10 he came swiftly upon the wings of the wind. 1

come there 1. *ἐπέρχομαι*
Act 14:19 Jews came there from Antioch and Ico'nium; 1

thing to come 1. אתה 2. בוא 3. *ἔρχομαι* 4. *μέλλω*
Isa 41:22 or declare to us the things to come. 2
44: 7 Who has announced from of old the things to come? 1
Joh 16:13 he will declare to you the things that are to come. 3
Rom 8:38 nor things present, nor things to come, nor powers 4
Wis 8: 8 and infers the things to come 4

come to a full end 1. תמם
Num14:35 in this wilderness they shall come to a full end 1

come to a halt 1. עמד
Neh 12:39 came to a halt at the Gate of the Guard. 1

come to aid 1. עזר
2Sm 21:17 But Abi'shai the son of Zeru'iah came to his aid 1

come to an end 1. גמר 2. כלה 3. סוף 4. שבת 5. *ἐκλείπω* 6. *καταστρέφω* 7. *τελευτή* 8. solvo
Ezr 10:17 come to the end of all the men who had married 2
Job 7: 6 and come to their end without hope. 2
Ps 7: 9 O let the evil of the wicked come to an end 1
Isa 10:25 in a . . while my indignation will come to an end 2
21:16 year . . all the glory of Kedar will come to an end; 2
66:17 shall come to an end together, says the LORD. 3
Lam 3:22 his mercies never come to an end; 2
Ezk 30:18 of Egypt, and her proud might shall come to an end; 4
33:28 her proud might shall come to an end; 4
Dan 12: 7 shattering of the power . . comes to an end 2
Ams 3:15 the great houses shall come to an end 3
2Es 7:114 sinful indulgence has come to an end 8
Wis 2: 1 there is no remedy when a man comes to his end 7
Sir 49: 4 the kings of Judah came to an end; 5
2Mc 9:28 the murderer . . came to the end of his life 6

come to ear 1. *ἀκούω*
Mat 28:14 if this comes to the governor's ears 1

come to fulness 1. *πληρόω*
Col 2:10 you have come to fulness of life in him 1

come to help 1. עזר 2. *ἀντιπαρέρχομαι* 3. *ἀρήγω* 4. *βοηθέω*
Ps 44:26 Rise up, come to our help! Deliver us 1
Rev 12:16 But the earth came to the help of the woman 4
Wis 16:10 thy mercy came to their help and healed them. 2
3Mc 4:16 that are not able . . to come to one's help 3

come to honor 1. כבד
Job 14:21 His sons come to honor, and he does not know it; 1

come to knowledge 1. ידע
Est 2:22 And this came to the knowledge of Mor'decai 1

come to life 1. *ζάω*
Rev 2: 8 the first and the last, who died and came to life. 1
20: 4 They came to life, and reigned with Christ 1
5 The rest of the dead did not come to life 1

come to maturity 1. *ἀτέλεστος*
Wis 3:16 children of adulterers will not come to maturity 1

come to mind 1. *ἐκνήφω*
1Co 15:34 Come to your right mind, and sin no more 1

come to nought 1. אבד 2. אפס 3. פרר
Ps 112:10 desire of the wicked man comes to nought. 1
Prv 10:28 expectation of the wicked comes to nought. 1
11: 7 expectation of the godless comes to nought. 1
Isa 8:10 Take counsel together, but it will come to nought; 3
29:20 For the ruthless shall come to nought 2
Ezk 12:22 days grow long, and every vision comes to nought 1

come to poverty 1. ירש
Gen 45:11 lest you . . and all that you have, come to poverty 1
Prv 20:13 Love not sleep, lest you come to poverty; 1
23:21 drunkard and the glutton will come to poverty 1

come to remembrance 1. זכר
Ezk 21:24 because you have come to remembrance 1

come to ruin 1. לבט
Prv 10: 8 but a prating fool will come to ruin. 1
12:12 The strong tower of the wicked comes to ruin •
Hos 4:14 people without understanding . . come to ruin. 1

come to shame 1. בוש
Isa 30: 5 every one comes to shame through a people 1

come to terms 1. *δέω δεξιάς*
1Mc 6:58 Now then let us come to terms with these men 1

come to want 1. מַחְסוֹר
Prv 22:16 who . . gives to the rich, will only come to want. 1

come together 1. אסף 2. קבץ 3. קרב 4. קשש 5. *ἀναλύω* 6. *ἐπισυνέχω* 7. *συνάγω* 8. *σύνειμι* 9. *συνέρχομαι*
Jdg 6:33 all . . and the people of the East came together 1
9: 6 all the citizens of Shechem came together 1
10:17 and the people of Israel came together 1
20:14 the Benjaminites came together out of the cities 1
1Ch 13: 2 that they may come together to us. 2
2Ch 30:13 many people came together in Jerusalem to keep 1
Neh 8:13 came together to Ezra the scribe in order 1
Ezk 37: 7 and the bones came together, bone to its bone. 3
Zep 2: 1 Come together and hold assembly 4
Zec 12: 3 the nations of the earth will come together 1
Mat 1:18 betrothed to Joseph, before they came together 9
22:34 they came together. 7
Mrk 3:20 and the crowd came together again 9
Lke 8: 4 And when a great crowd came together 8
Joh 18:20 where all Jews come together 9
Act 1: 6 So when they had come together, they asked him 9
2: 6 at this sound the multitude came together 9
16:13 and spoke to the women who had come together. 9
19:32 most . . did not know why they had come together. 9
25:17 When therefore they came together here 9
1Co 11:17 because when you come together 9
33 So then, my brethren, when you come together to eat 9
34 lest you come together to be condemned 9
14:26 When you come together, each one has a hymn 9
1Es 9:55 they came together. 6
Wis 5:12 the air, thus divided, comes together at once 5

come true 1. בוא 2. קרה
Num11:23 see whether my word will come true for you or not. 2
Deu 18:22 if the word does not come to pass or come true 1
Jdg 13:12 when your words come true, what is to be the boy's 1
17 when your words come true, we may honor you? 1
1Sm 9: 6 a man of God . . all that he says comes true. 1

come up 1. בוא 2. עלה 3. סלק (A) 4. *ἀναβαίνω* 5. *ἀνάβασις* 6. *ἄρχω* 7. *βλαστάνω* 8. *ἐγγίζω* 9. *ἐξέρχομαι* 10. *ἔρχομαι* 11. *ἐφίστημι* 12. *προσαναβαίνω* 13. *προσέρχομαι* 14. *συναναβαίνω* 15. ascendo
Gen 24:16 to the spring, and filled her jar, and came up. 2
41: 2 behold, there came up out of the Nile seven cows 2
3 cows . . came up out of the Nile after them 2
18 seven cows, fat and sleek, came up out of the Nile 2
19 seven other cows came up after them 2
27 seven lean and gaunt cows that came up after them 2
Exd 2:23 and their cry under bondage came up to God. 2
8: 3 frogs which shall come up into your house 2
4 the frogs shall come up on you and on your people 2
6 the frogs came up and covered the land of Egypt. 2
10:14 the locusts came up over all the land of Egypt 2
16:13 quails came up and covered the camp; 2
19:13 they shall come up to the mountain. 2
23 The people cannot come up to Mount Sinai; 2
24 Go down, and come up bringing Aaron with you; 2
24 the people break through to come up to the LORD 2
24: 1 said to Moses, "Come up to the LORD, you and Aaron 2
2 and the people shall not come up with him. 2
12 The LORD said to Moses, "Come up to me 2
34: 2 come up in the morning to Mount Sinai 2
3 shall come up with you, and let no man be seen 2
Num16:12 Dathan and Abi'ram . . said, "We will not come up. 2
14 We will not come up. 2
32:11 Surely none of the men who came up out of Egypt 2
Deu 10: 1 come up to me on the mountain, and make an ark 2
Jos 2: 8 she came up to them on the roof 2
4:16 the priests . . to come up out of the Jordan. 2
17 commanded the priests, "Come up out of the Jordan. 2
18 priests . . came up from the midst of the Jordan 2
19 The people came up out of the Jordan on the tenth 2
10: 4 Come up to me, and help me, and let us smite Gibeon; 2
6 come up to us quickly, and save us, and help us; 2
33 Then Horam king of Gezer came up to help Lachish; 2
18:11 The lot of the tribe of Benjamin . . came up 2
19:10 The third lot came up for the tribe of Zeb'ulun 2
Jdg 1: 3 Come up with me into the territory allotted 2
4: 5 the people of Israel came up to her for judgment. 2
6: 3 people of the East would come up and attack them; 2
5 they would come up with their cattle and their 2
11:16 when they came up from Egypt, Israel went through 2
12: 3 why then have you come up to me this day, to fight 2
14: 2 he came up, and told his father and mother, 2
15: 6 the Philistines came up, and burned her 2
9 the Philistines came up and encamped in Judah 2
10 Judah said, "Why have you come up against us? 2
10 have come up to bind Samson, to do to him as he did 2
16:18 Come up this once, for he has told me all his mind. 2
18 the lords of the Philistines came up to her 2
19:30 people of Israel came up out of the land of Egypt 2
21: 5 Which . . did not come up in the assembly 2
5 him who did not come up to the LORD to Mizpah 2
8 What one . . did not come up to the LORD to Mizpah? 2
1Sm 13: 5 they came up and encamped in Michmash 2
14:10 But if they say, 'Come up to us,' then we will go up; 2
12 Come up to us, and we will show you a thing. 2
12 Come up after me; for the LORD has given them 2
15: 2 opposing them . . when they came up out of Egypt. 2
6 to . . Israel when they came up out of Egypt. 2
17:23 Goliath . . came up out of the ranks 2
25 Have you seen this man who has come up? 2
25 Surely he has come up to defy Israel; 2
28:13 I see a god coming up out of the earth. 2
14 An old man is coming up; and he is wrapped in a robe. 2

2Sm 5:22 the Philistines came up yet again 2
15:24 And Abi'athar came up, and lo, Zadok came also 2
17:21 After they had gone, the men came up out of the well 2
1Kg 1:35 You shall then come up after him, and he shall come 2
14:25 Shishak king of Egypt came up against Jerusalem; 2
20:22 the king of Syria will come up against you. 2
2Kg 3:21 that the kings had come up to fight against them 2
12:10 the king's secretary and the high priest came up 2
15:14 Men'ahem . . came up from Tirzah 2
16: 5 Then Rezin . . and Pekah . . came up to wage war 2
7 Come up, and rescue me from the hand of the king 2
17: 3 Against him came up Shalmane'ser king of Assyria; 2
18: 9 Assyria . . came up against Sama'ria and besieged 2
13 Sennach'erib king of Assyria came up against all 2
25 I have come up against this place to destroy it? 2
23: 9 priests . . did not come up to the altar of the LORD 2
24: 1 Nebuchadnez'zar king of Babylon came up 2
10 the servants of . . came up to Jerusalem 2
2Ch 12: 2 Shishak king of Egypt came up against Jerusalem 2
9 Shishak king of Egypt came up against Jerusalem; 2
20:16 behold, they will come up by the ascent of Ziz; 2
21:17 they came up against Judah, and invaded it 2
24:23 the army of the Syrians came up against Jo'ash. 2
36: 6 Against him came up Nebuchadnez'zar 2
Ezr 2: 1 people . . who came up out of the captivity 2
59 following were those who came up from Tel-me'lah 2
4:12 Jews who came up from you to us have gone 3
Neh 4:12 From all the places . . they will come up against •
7: 5 genealogy of those who came up at the first 2
6 people . . who came up out of the captivity 2
61 following were those who came up from Tel-me'lah 2
12: 1 who came up with Zerub'babel the son of She-al'ti-el 2
Job 5:26 a shock of grain comes up to the threshing floor 2
7: 9 he who goes down to Sheol does not come up; 2
Prv 25: 7 for it is better to be told, "Come up here 2
Sng 3: 6 What is that coming up from the wilderness 2
4: 2 shorn ewes that have come up from the washing 2
6: 6 flock of ewes, that have come up from the washing 2
8: 5 Who is that coming up from the wilderness 2
Isa 7: 1 came up to Jerusalem to wage war against it 2
11:16 Israel when they came up from the land of Egypt. 2
14: 8 you were laid low, no hewer comes up against us.' 2
35: 9 nor shall any ravenous beast come up on it; 2
36: 1 Assyria came up against all the fortified 2
10 I have come up against this land to destroy it? 2
55:13 Instead of the thorn shall come up the cypress; 2
13 instead of the brier shall come up the myrtle; 2
60: 7 they shall come up with acceptance on my altar 2
Jer 4:13 Behold, he comes up like clouds 2
9:21 For death has come up into our windows 2
26:10 they came up from the king's house 2
32:24 siege mounds have come up to the city to take it 1
35:11 when Nebuchadrez'zar king of Babylon came up 2
48:15 The destroyer of Moab and his cities has come up 2
18 For the destroyer of Moab has come up against you; 2
49:19 Behold, like a lion coming up from the jungle 2
50: 3 out of the north a nation has come up against her 2
44 Behold, like a lion coming up from the jungle 2
51:42 The sea has come up on Babylon; 2
Ezk 38:16 you will come up against my people Israel 2
Dan 7: 3 four great beasts came up out of the sea 3
8 came up among them another horn, a little one 3
20 other horn which came up and before which three 3
8: 3 higher one came up last. 2
8 there came up four conspicuous horns 2
Jol 1: 6 For a nation has come up against my land 2
3: 9 Let all the men of war draw near, let them come up. 2
12 and come up to the valley of Jehosh'aphat; 2
Jon 1: 2 for their wickedness has come up before me. 2
4: 7 when dawn came up the next day 2
Nah 2: 1 The shatterer has come up against you. 2
Mat 8:19 a scribe came up and said to him 13
9:20 came up behind him and touched the fringe 13
13:26 when the plants came up and bore grain 7
17:14 a man came up to him and kneeling before him said 13
27 cast a hook, and take the first fish that comes up 4
18:21 Then Peter came up and said to him 13
19: 3 Pharisees came up to him and tested him by asking 13
16 behold, one came up to him, saying 13
20:20 the mother of the sons of Zeb'edee came up to him 13
21:23 came up to him as he was teaching, and said 13
26: 7 a woman came up to him 13
49 he came up to Jesus at once and said, "Hail, Master! 13
50 Then they came up and laid hands on Jesus 13
69 a maid came up to him, and said 13
73 After a little while the bystanders came up 13
Mrk 1:10 when he came up out of the water 4
5:27 came up behind him in the crowd 10
10: 2 Pharisees came up and in order to test him asked 13
12:28 one of the scribes came up and heard 13
15: 8 the crowd came up and began to ask Pilate 4
41 women who came up with him to Jerusalem. 14
Lke 2:38 And coming up at that very hour she gave thanks 11
8:44 came up behind him, and touched . . his garment 13
20: 1 the scribes with the elders came up 11
23:36 coming up and offering him vinegar 13
Joh 19: 3 they came up to him, saying, "Hail, King of the Jews! 6
Act 8:31 he invited Philip to come up and sit with him. 4
39 when they came up out of the water 4
13:31 he appeared to those who came up with him 14
21:33 Then the tribune came up and arrested him 8
Rev 4: 1 the first voice . . said, "Come up hither 4
11:12 voice from heaven saying to them, "Come up hither! 4
1Es 1:40 Nebuchadnezzar . . came up against him 4
2:18 the Jews who came up from you to us 4
5: 7 the men of Judea who came up out of . . captivity 4
36 The following are those who came up 4
8: 3 This Ezra came up from Babylon as a scribe 4
5 There came up with him to Jerusalem 14
2Es 8:41 all that have been sown will come up in due season ‡
43 For if the farmer's seed does not come up 15
11: 1 and behold, there came up from the sea an eagle 15
43 your insolence has come up before the Most High 15
12: 7 if my prayer has indeed come up before thy face 15
11 The eagle which you saw coming up from the sea 15
13: 3 a man come up out of the heart of the sea ‡
5 the man who came up out of the sea. 15
25 a man come up from the heart of the sea 15
32 whom you saw as a man coming up from the sea. 15
51 the man coming up from the heart of the sea? 15
Jdt 6:12 all the slingers kept them from coming up 5
12: 8 When she came up from the spring 4
Wis 19:12 to give them relief, quails came up from the sea. 4
Sir 48:18 In his days Sennacherib came up 4
1Mc 5:33 Then he came up behind them in three companies 9
2Mc 2: 6 Some . . came up to mark the way 13
10:36 Others who came up in the same way 12

come upon 1. אתה 2. בוא 3. לבשׁ 4. מצא 5. עלה 6. קדם 7. קרא 8. קרה 9. *γίνομαι* 10. *ἐνίστημι* 11. *ἐπεισέρχομαι* 12. *ἐπέρχομαι* 13. *εὑρίσκω* 14. *ἐφίστημι* 15. *ἔχω* 16. contingo

Gen 4:15 lest any who came upon him should kill him. 4
44:34 see the evil that would come upon my father. 4
Exd 18: 8 all the hardship that had come upon them 4
Lev 19:19 nor shall there come upon you a garment of cloth 5
Deu 4:30 all these things come upon you in the latter days 4
22:27 because he came upon her in the open country 4
31:17 many evils and troubles will come upon them 4
17 'Have not these evils come upon us because our God 4
21 when many evils and troubles have come upon them 4
Jdg 1: 5 They came upon Ado'ni-be'zek at Bezek, and fought 4
1Sm 28:10 no punishment shall come upon you for this 8
2Sm 22:19 They came upon me in the day of my calamity; 6
1Ch 12:18 Then the Spirit came upon Ama'sai, chief of the 30 3
Job 3:25 For the thing that I fear comes upon me 1
4:14 dread came upon me, and trembling 7
15:21 in prosperity the destroyer will come upon him. 2
20:22 all the force of misery will come upon him. 2
Ps 18:18 They came upon me in the day of my calamity; 6
35: 8 Let ruin come upon them unawares! 2
36:11 Let not the foot of arrogance come upon me 2
44:17 All this has come upon us 2
119:143 Trouble and anguish have come upon me 4
Prv 6:11 poverty will come upon you like a vagabond 2
10:24 What the wicked dreads will come upon him 2
24:34 poverty will come upon you like a robber 2
28:22 does not know that want will come upon him. 2
Jer 13:22 Why have these things come upon me? 7
41:12 They came upon him at the great pool 4
Ezk 32:11 sword of the king of Babylon shall come upon you. 2
Hab 3:16 day of trouble to come upon people who invade us. 5
Mat 18:28 came upon one of his fellow servants 13
27:32 As they went out, they came upon a man of Cyre'ne 13
Mrk 16: 8 trembling and astonishment had come upon them 15
Lke 1:35 The Holy Spirit will come upon you 12
21:34 and that day come upon you suddenly like a snare; 14
35 it will come upon all 11
Act 1: 8 when the Holy Spirit has come upon you 12
4: 1 the Sad'ducees came upon them 14
6:12 they came upon him and seized him 14
8:24 nothing of what you have said may come upon me. 12
13: 6 they came upon a certain magician 13
40 lest there come upon you what is said 12
23:27 when I came upon them with the soldiers 14
1Th 5: 3 then sudden destruction will come upon them 14
Jas 5: 1 howl for the miseries that are coming upon you. 12
2Es 10:15 the troubles that have come upon you. 16
Wis 6: 5 he will come upon you terribly and swiftly 14
12:27 the utmost condemnation came upon them. 12
16: 4 upon those oppressors . . want should come 12
5 the terrible rage . . came upon thy people 12
19:13 The punishments did not come upon the sinners 12
Sir 3: 8 a blessing from him may come upon you. 12
Bar 4: 9 For she saw the wrath that came upon you from God 12
25 the wrath that has come upon you from God 12
35 For fire will come upon her from the Everlasting 12
LJr 1:48 For when war or calamity comes upon them 12
1Mc 1:11 many evils have come upon us. 13
6:13 because of this . . these evils have come upon me; 13
2Mc 1: 7 the critical distress which came upon us 12
2:14 on account of the war which had come upon us 9
6: 9 the misery that had come upon them. 10
9:18 the judgment of God had justly come upon him 12

yet to come 1. sum

2Es 7:136 to those who are gone and to those yet to come 1

comeliness 1. הָדָר

Isa 53: 2 he had no form or comeliness that we should look 1

comely 1. יָפֶה 2. נאה 3. נָאוֶה 4. שֶׁפֶר

Gen 49:21 a hind let loose, that bears comely fawns. 4
1Sm 17:42 was but a youth, ruddy and comely in appearance. 1
Sng 1: 5 I am very dark, but comely, O daughters 3
10 Your cheeks are comely with ornaments 2
2:14 your voice is sweet, and your face is comely. 3
6: 4 beautiful as Tirzah, my love, comely as Jerusalem 3
Jer 6: 2 The comely and delicately bred I will destroy 3

before one comes to maturity 1. *ἀτέλεστος*

Wis 4: 5 before they come to maturity 1

comfort 1. בדר עַל לֵב 2. נִחוּם 3. נחם 4. נֶחָמָה 5. *ἀποδέχομαι* 6. *παρακαλέω* 7. *παράκλησις* 8. *παρηγορία* 9. consolo

Gen 24:67 Isaac was comforted after his mother's death. 3
27:42 Esau comforts himself by planning to kill you. 3
37:35 all his daughters rose up to comfort him; 3
35 but he refused to be comforted 3
38:12 when Judah was comforted, he went up to Timnah 3
50:21 Thus he reassured them and comforted them. 1
Rut 2:13 you have comforted me and spoken kindly 3
2Sm 12:24 Then David comforted his wife, Bathshe'ba 3
13:39 he was comforted about Amnon, seeing he was dead. 3
1Ch 7:22 and his brothers came to comfort him. 3
Job 2:11 to come to condole with him and comfort him. 3
7:13 When I say, 'My bed will comfort me 3
21:34 How then will you comfort me with empty nothings? 3
29:25 like one who comforts mourners. 3
42:11 they showed him sympathy and comforted him 3
Ps 23: 4 thy rod and thy staff, they comfort me. 3
71:21 Thou wilt increase my honor, and comfort me 3
77: 2 my soul refuses to be comforted. 3
86:17 LORD, hast helped me and comforted me. 3
119:50 This is my comfort in my affliction 4
76 Let thy steadfast love be ready to comfort me 3
82 I ask, "When wilt thou comfort me? 3
Ecc 4: 1 and they had no one to comfort them! 3
1 and there was no one to comfort them. 3
Isa 12: 1 thy anger turned away, and thou didst comfort me. 3
22: 4 do not labor to comfort me for the destruction 3
40: 1 Comfort, comfort my people, says your God. 3
1 Comfort, comfort my people, says your God. 3
49:13 For the LORD has comforted his people 3
51: 3 For the LORD will comfort Zion; 3
3 Zion; he will comfort all her waste places 3
12 I, I am he that comforts you; 3
19 famine and sword; who will comfort you? 3
52: 9 Jerusalem; for the LORD has comforted his people 3
54:11 O afflicted one, storm-tossed, and not comforted 3
57:18 I will lead him and requite him with comfort 2
61: 2 vengeance of our God; to comfort all who mourn; 3
66:13 As one whom his mother comforts, so I will comfort 3
13 whom his mother comforts, so I will comfort you; 3
13 you shall be comforted in Jerusalem. 3
Jer 16: 7 for the mourner, to comfort him for the dead; 3
31:13 I will comfort them, and give them gladness 3
15 she refuses to be comforted for her children 3
Lam 1: 2 among all her lovers she has none to comfort her; 3
17 Zion . . but there is none to comfort her 3
21 Hear how I groan; there is none to comfort me. 3
2:13 What can I liken to you, that I may comfort you 3
Ezk 31:16 will be comforted in the nether world. 3
32:31 he will comfort himself for all his multitude 3
Zec 1:13 gracious and comforting words to the angel 2
17 the LORD will again comfort Zion 3
Mat 5: 4 who mourn, for they shall be comforted. 6
Lke 16:25 now he is comforted here, and you are in anguish. 6
Act 9:31 in the comfort of the Holy Spirit 7
20:12 were not a little comforted. 6
2Co 1: 3 Father of mercies and God of all comfort 7
4 who comforts us in all our affliction 6
4 so that we may be able to comfort 6
4 with the comfort 7
4 with which we ourselves are comforted by God. 6
5 we share abundantly in comfort too. 7
6 it is for your comfort and salvation 7
6 if we are comforted, it is for your comfort 6
6 if we are comforted, it is for your comfort 7
7 you will also share in our comfort. 7
2: 7 so you should rather turn to forgive and comfort 6
7: 4 I have great pride in you; I am filled with comfort 7
6 God, who comforts the downcast 6
6 comforted us by the coming of Titus 6
7 also by the comfort with which he was comforted 7
7 by the comfort with which he was comforted in you 6
13 Therefore we are comforted 6
13 besides our own comfort 7
Col 4:11 they have been a comfort to me. 8
1Th 3: 7 comforted about you through your faith; 6
4:18 comfort one another with these words. 6
2Th 2:16 gave us eternal comfort and good hope 7
17 comfort your hearts and establish them 6
Phm 1: 7 I have derived much joy and comfort from your love 7
2Es 12: 8 that thou mayest fully comfort my soul. 9

14:13 comfort the lowly among them 9
Tob 7:17 the mother comforted her daughter in her tears 5
AEs 15: 8 he comforted her with soothing words, and said 6
16 all his servants sought to comfort her. 6
Sir 30:23 Delight your soul and comfort your heart 6
38:17 then be comforted for your sorrow. 6
23 be comforted for him when his spirit is departed. 6
48:24 comforted those who mourned in Zion. 6
49:10 they comforted the people of Jacob 6
Bar 4:30 for he who named you will comfort you. 6

comfort *See also* find, take.

comforter 1. נחם

2Sm 10: 3 because David has sent comforters to you 1
1Ch 19: 3 because David has sent comforters to you 1
Job 16: 2 miserable comforters are you all. 1
Ps 69:20 for comforters, but I found none. 1
Lam 1: 9 her fall is terrible, she has no comforter. 1
16 eyes . . with tears; for a comforter is far from me 1
Nah 3: 7 whence shall I seek comforters for her? 1

coming one 1. *ἔρχομαι*

Heb 10:37 yet a little while, and the coming one shall come 1

command

1. אֹמֶר 2. אמר 3. אִמְרָה 4. דָּבָר 5. דבר
6. יָד 7. מַאֲמָר 8. מִצְוָה 9. מִשְׁפָּט 10. עַל 11. פֶּה
12. פָּקִיד 13. צְדָקָה 14. צוה 15. קוֹל 16. אמר (A)
17. טְעֵם (A) 18. מִלָּה (A) 19. *ἄρχων* 20. *διατάσσω*
21. *δίδωμι ἐντολήν* 22. *εἶπον* 23. *εντέλλομαι*
24. *ἐντέλλω* 25. *ἐντολή* 26. *ἐντολὴν λαμβάνω*
27. *ἐπί* 28. *ἐπιταγή* 29. *ἐπιτάσσω* 30. *κατὰ τὸν λόγον*
31. *κελεύω* 32. *λόγιον* 33. *λόγος* 34. *παραγγέλλω*
35. *περιπατέω* 36. *προηγέομαι* 37. *πρόσταγμα*
38. *προστάσσω* 39. *ῥῆμα* 40. *σημαίνω* 41. *τάσσω*
42. *ὑποτάσσω* 43. dico 44. dispositio 45. impero
46. iubeo 47. iussum 48. mando 49. praecipio

Gen 2:16 the LORD God commanded the man, saying 14
3:11 tree of which I commanded you not to eat? 14
17 tree of which I commanded you, ‘You shall not eat 14
6:22 Noah did this; he did all that God commanded him. 14
7: 5 Noah did all that the LORD had commanded him. 14
9 into the ark with Noah, as God had commanded Noah. 14
16 of all flesh, went in as God had commanded him; 14
21: 4 he was eight days old, as God had commanded him. 14
27: 8 my son, obey my word as I command you. 14
41:40 people shall order themselves as you command; 11
44: 1 Then he commanded the steward of his house 14
45:19 Command them also, ‘Do this: take wagons •
21 gave . . according to the command of Pharaoh 11
47:11 gave them . . as Pharaoh had commanded. 14
50: 2 Joseph commanded his servants the physicians 14
12 Thus his sons did for him as he had commanded them; 14
Exd 1:17 did not do as the king of Egypt commanded them 5
22 Then Pharaoh commanded all his people 14
5: 6 The same day Pharaoh commanded the taskmasters 14
7: 2 You shall speak all that I command you; 14
6 Moses and Aaron . . did as the LORD commanded 14
10 Moses and Aaron . . did as the LORD commanded; 14
20 Moses and Aaron did as the LORD commanded; 14
8: 9 Be pleased to command me when I am to entreat •
27 sacrifice to the LORD . . as he will command us. 2
12:28 as the LORD had commanded Moses and Aaron 14
50 as the LORD commanded Moses and Aaron 14
16:16 This is what the LORD has commanded 14
23 This is what the LORD has commanded: ‘Tomorrow is 5
32 Moses said, “This is what the LORD has commanded 14
34 As the LORD commanded Moses, so Aaron placed it 14
18:23 If you do this, and God so commands you, then you 14
19: 7 these words which the LORD had commanded him. 14
23:15 as I commanded you, you shall eat unleavened 14
24:12 tables of stone, with the law and the commandment 8
27:20 you shall command the people of Israel 14
29:35 according to all that I have commanded you; 14
31: 6 that they may make all that I have commanded you 14
11 all that I have commanded you they shall do. 14
32: 8 quickly out of the way which I commanded them; 14
34: 4 went up on Mount Sinai, as the LORD had commanded 14
11 Observe what I command you this day. 14
18 eat unleavened bread, as I commanded you 14
34 told the people of Israel what he was commanded 14
35: 1 the things which the LORD has commanded you 14
4 This is the thing which the LORD has commanded. 14
10 come and make all that the LORD has commanded 14
29 work which the LORD had commanded by Moses 14
36: 1 with all that the LORD has commanded. 14
5 the work which the LORD has commanded us to do. 14
38:22 made all that the LORD commanded Moses; 14
39: 1 as the LORD had commanded Moses. 14
5 twined linen; as the LORD had commanded Moses. 14
7 sons of Israel; as the LORD had commanded Moses. 14
21 as the LORD had commanded Moses. 14
26 as the LORD had commanded Moses. 14
29 as the LORD had commanded Moses. 14
31 as the LORD had commanded Moses. 14
32 all that the LORD had commanded Moses; 14
42 all that the LORD had commanded Moses 14
43 as the LORD had commanded, so had they done it. 14
40:16 according to all that the LORD commanded him 14
19 the tent over it, as the LORD had commanded Moses. 14
21 as the LORD had commanded Moses. 14
23 the LORD; as the LORD had commanded Moses. 14
25 as the LORD had commanded Moses. 14
27 as the LORD had commanded Moses. 14
29 as the LORD had commanded Moses. 14
32 as the LORD commanded Moses. 14
Lev 6: 9 Command Aaron and his sons, saying, This is the law 14
7:36 the LORD commanded this to be given them 14
38 which the LORD commanded Moses on Mount Sinai 14
38 on the day that he commanded the people of Israel 14
8: 4 Moses did as the LORD commanded him 14
5 thing which the LORD has commanded to be done 14
9 the holy crown, as the LORD commanded Moses 14
13 bound caps on them, as the LORD commanded Moses 14
17 outside the camp, as the LORD commanded Moses 14
21 to the LORD, as the LORD commanded Moses 14
29 ram of ordination, as the LORD commanded Moses 14
31 eat it . . as I commanded, saying, ‘Aaron and his 14
34 LORD has commanded to be done to make atonement 14
35 lest you die; for so I am commanded 14
36 all the things which the LORD commanded by Moses 14
9: 5 they brought what Moses commanded 14
6 the thing which the LORD commanded you to do 14
7 make atonement . . as the LORD has commanded 14
10 upon the altar, as the LORD commanded Moses 14
21 wave offering . . as Moses commanded 14
10: 1 such as he had not commanded them 14
13 to the LORD; for so I am commanded 14
15 a due for ever; as the LORD has commanded 14
18 eaten it in the sanctuary, as I commanded 14
13:54 then the priest shall command that they wash 14
14: 4 the priest shall command them to take for him 14
5 the priest shall command them to kill one 14
36 Then the priest shall command that they empty 14
40 then the priest shall command that they take out 14
16:34 And Moses did as the LORD commanded him 14
17: 2 This is the thing which the LORD has commanded 14
24: 2 Command the people of Israel to bring you . . oil 14
23 Israel did as the LORD commanded Moses 14
25:21 I will command my blessing upon you in the sixth 14
27:34 commandments which the LORD commanded Moses 14
Num 1:19 the LORD commanded Moses. So he numbered them 14
54 according to all that the LORD commanded Moses. 14
2:33 not numbered . . as the LORD commanded Moses. 14
34 According to all that the LORD commanded Moses 14
3:16 Moses numbered them . . as he was commanded. 14
42 Moses numbered . . as the LORD commanded him. 14
51 word of the LORD, as the LORD commanded Moses. 14
4:27 service . . at the command of Aaron and his sons 11
49 numbered by him, as the LORD commanded Moses. 14
5: 2 Command the people of Israel that they put out 14
8: 3 set up its lamps . . as the LORD commanded Moses. 14
20 according to all that the LORD commanded Moses 14
22 as the LORD had commanded Moses concerning 14
9: 5 according to all that the LORD commanded Moses 14
8 hear what the LORD will command concerning you. 14
18 At the command of the LORD the people of Israel 11
18 at the command of the LORD they encamped; 11
20 then according to the command of the LORD 11
20 according to the command of the LORD they set out. 11
23 At the command of the LORD they encamped 11
23 at the command of the LORD they set out; 11
23 at the command of the LORD by Moses. 11
10:13 set out . . at the command of the LORD by Moses. 11
13: 3 sent . . according to the command of the LORD 11
14:41 Why . . you trangressing the command of the LORD 11
15:23 all that the LORD has commanded you by Moses 14
36 stoned him . . as the LORD commanded Moses. 14
17:11 Moses; as the LORD commanded him, so he did. 14
19: 2 statute of the law which the LORD has commanded 14
20: 9 Moses took the rod . . as he commanded him. 14
24 because you rebelled against my command 11
27 Moses did as the LORD commanded; 14
22:18 could not go beyond the command of the LORD 11
23:20 Behold, I received a command to bless •
26: 4 Take a census . . ” as the LORD commanded Moses. 14
27:11 as the LORD commanded Moses.’ 14
22 Moses did as the LORD commanded him; 14
23 commissioned him as the LORD directed 14
28: 2 Command the people of Israel, and say to them 14
29:40 just as the LORD had commanded Moses. 14
30: 1 This is what the LORD has commanded. 14
16 statutes which the LORD commanded Moses 14
31: 7 against Mid'ian, as the LORD commanded Moses 14
21 statute of the law which the LORD has commanded 14
31 Moses and Elea'zar . . did as the LORD commanded 14
41 gave the tribute . . as the LORD commanded Moses. 14
47 as the LORD commanded Moses. 14
49 counted the men of war who are under our command 6
32:25 Your servants will do as my lord commands. 14
33: 2 wrote down . . by command of the LORD; 11
38 went up Mount Hor at the command of the LORD 11
34: 2 Command the people of Israel, and say to them 14
13 Moses commanded the people of Israel, saying 14
13 land . . which the LORD has commanded to give 14
29 the LORD commanded to divide the inheritance 14
35: 2 Command the people of Israel, that they give 14
36: 2 LORD commanded my lord to give the land 14
2 my lord was commanded by the LORD to give 14
5 Moses commanded the people of Israel 14
6 LORD commands concerning the daughters 14
10 daughters . . did as the LORD commanded Moses; 14
13 which the LORD commanded by Moses to . . Israel 14
Deu 1:18 I commanded you at that time all the things 14
19 we set out . . as the LORD our God commanded us; 14
26 rebelled against the command of the LORD your God; 11
41 go up and fight, just as the LORD our God commanded 14
43 you rebelled against the command of the LORD 11
2: 4 command the people, You are about to pass through 14
3:18 I commanded you at that time, saying, ‘The LORD 14
21 I commanded Joshua at that time, ‘Your eyes 14
4: 2 You shall not add to the word which I command you 14
2 commandments of the LORD . . which I command 14
5 taught you . . as the LORD my God commanded me 14
13 his covenant, which he commanded you to perform 14
14 LORD commanded me at that time to teach you 14
40 you shall keep . . which I command you this day 14
5:12 keep it holy, as the LORD your God commanded you. 14
15 LORD your God commanded you to keep the sabbath 14
16 ‘Honor . . as the LORD your God commanded you; 14
32 do . . as the LORD your God has commanded you; 14
33 the way which the LORD your God has commanded 14
6: 1 the LORD your God commanded me to teach you 14
2 statutes and his commandments, which I command 14
6 these words which I command you this day 14
17 commandments . . which he has commanded you. 14
20 which the LORD our God has commanded you?’ 14
24 LORD commanded us to do all these statutes 14
25 do all this commandment . . as he has commanded 14
7:11 be careful to do . . which I command you this day. 14
8: 1 All the commandment which I command you this day 14
11 by not keeping . . which I command you this day 14
9:12 out of the way which I commanded them; 14
16 from the way which the LORD had commanded 14
10: 5 there they are, as the LORD commanded me. 14
13 which I command you this day for your good? 14
11: 8 commandment which I command you this day 14
13 obey my commandments which I command you 14
22 do all this commandment which I command you to do 14
27 obey the commandments . . which I command you 14
28 turn . . from the way which I command you this day 14
12:11 thither you shall bring all that I command you 14
14 there you shall do all that I am commanding you. 14
21 then you may kill . . as I have commanded you; 14
28 heed all these words which I command you 14
32 Everything that I command you you shall 14
13: 5 way in which the LORD . . commanded you to walk. 14
18 his commandments which I command you this day 14
15: 5 do all this commandment which I command you 14
11 poor will never cease . . therefore I command 14
15 therefore I command you this today. 14
18:18 he shall speak to them all that I command him. 14
20 speak . . which I have not commanded him to speak 14
19: 7 Therefore I command you, You shall set apart 14
9 this commandment, which I command you this day 14
20:17 destroy . . as the LORD your God has commanded; 14
24: 8 as I commanded them, so you shall be careful to do. 14
18 therefore I command you to do this. 14
22 therefore I command you to do this. 14
26:13 all thy commandments which thou hast commanded 14
14 done according to all that thou hast commanded 14
16 LORD . . commands you to do these statutes 14
27: 1 Moses and the elders . . commanded the people 14
1 Keep all the commandment which I command you 14
4 stones, concerning which I command you this day 14
10 commandments . . which I command you this day. 14
28: 1 his commandments which I command you this day 14
8 LORD will command the blessing upon you 14
13 commandments . . which I command you this day 14
14 from any of the words which I command you this day 14
15 commandments . . which I command you this day 14
45 his commandments . . which he commanded you. 14
29: 1 covenant which the LORD commanded Moses to make 14
30: 2 obey his voice in all that I command you this day 14
8 keep all his commandments which I command you 14
11 this commandment which I command you this day 14
16 commandments . . which I command you this day 14
31: 5 commandment which I have commanded you. 14
10 Moses commanded them, “At the end of every seven 14
25 Moses commanded the Levites who carried the ark 14
29 turn aside from the way which I have commanded 14
32:46 that you may command them to your children 14
33: 4 when Moses commanded us a law, as a possession 14
21 executed the commands and just decrees of the LORD 13
34: 9 Israel . . did as the LORD had commanded Moses. 14
Jos 1: 7 all the law which Moses my servant commanded you; 14
9 Have I not commanded you? Be strong 14
10 Joshua commanded the officers of the people 14
11 Pass through the camp, and command the people 14
13 Remember the word which Moses . . commanded you 14
16 All that you have commanded us we will do 14
18 disobeys your words, whatever you command him 14
3: 3 and commanded the people, “When you see the ark 14
8 you shall command the priests who bear the ark 14
4: 3 and command them, ‘Take twelve stones from here 14
8 And the men of Israel did as Joshua commanded 14

10 everything . . that the LORD commanded Joshua 14
10 to all that Moses had commanded Joshua. 14
16 Command the priests who bear the ark . . to come up 14
17 Joshua therefore commanded the priests, "Come up 14
6: 8 And as Joshua had commanded the people 2
10 Joshua commanded the people, "You shall not shout 14
7:11 my covenant which I commanded them; 14
8: 4 he commanded them, "Behold, you shall lie in ambush 14
8 when . . you shall..; see, I have commanded you. 14
27 the word of the LORD which he commanded Joshua. 14
29 and at the going down of the sun Joshua commanded 14
31 as Moses the servant of the LORD had commanded 14
33 as Moses . . had commanded at the first 14
35 There was not a word of all that Moses commanded 14
9:24 the LORD your God had commanded his servant 14
10:27 Joshua commanded, and they took them down 14
40 left none . . as the LORD God of Israel commanded. 14
11:12 as Moses the servant of the LORD had commanded. 14
15 As the LORD had commanded Moses his servant 14
15 As the LORD had . . so Moses commanded Joshua 14
15 of all that the LORD had commanded Moses. 14
20 be exterminated, as the LORD commanded Moses. 14
13: 6 allot the land . . as I have commanded you. 14
14: 2 as the LORD had commanded Moses for the nine 14
5 people of Israel did as the LORD commanded Moses; 14
17: 4 LORD commanded Moses to give us an inheritance 14
19:50 By command of the LORD they gave him the city 11
21: 2 The LORD commanded through Moses that we be 14
3 by command of the LORD the people . . gave 11
8 as the LORD had commanded through Moses. 14
22: 2 You have kept all that Moses . . commanded you 14
2 obeyed my voice in all that I have commanded you; 14
5 and the law which Moses . . commanded you 14
9 had possessed themselves by command of the LORD 11
23:16 covenant of the LORD . . which he commanded you 14
Jdg 2: 2 But you have not obeyed my command. What is this 15
20 my covenant which I commanded their fathers 14
3: 4 LORD, which he commanded their fathers by Moses. 14
19 O king." And he commanded, "Silence." And all his 2
4: 6 LORD, the God of Israel, commands you, 'Go, gather 14
13:14 thing; all that I commanded her let her observe. 14
21:10 sent . . their bravest men, and commanded them, 14
20 they commanded the Benjaminites, saying, "Go 14
1Sm 2:29 sacrifices and my offerings which I commanded 14
13:13 you have not kept the . . which he commanded you; 14
14 you have not kept what the LORD commanded you. 14
16: 4 Samuel did what the LORD commanded, and came 5
16 Let our lord now command your servants, who are 2
17:20 David rose . . and went, as Jesse had commanded him; 14
18:22 And Saul commanded his servants, "Speak to David 14
20:29 and my brother has commanded me to be there. 14
2Sm 4:12 David commanded his young men, and they killed 14
5:25 And David did as the LORD commanded him 14
7: 7 judges . . whom I commanded to shepherd my people 14
9:11 all that my lord the king commands his servant 14
13:28 Then Ab'salom commanded his servants 14
28 then kill him. Fear not; have I not commanded you? 14
29 did to Amnon as Ab'salom had commanded. 14
32 by the command of Ab'salom . . from the day 11
18: 2 the army, one third under the command of Jo'ab 6
2 one third under the command of Abi'shai the son 6
2 and one third under the command of It'tai 6
12 the king commanded you and Abi'shai and It'tai 14
20:23 Now Jo'ab was in command of all the army of Israel; 10
23 Benai'ah . . was in command of the Cher'ethites 10
21:14 and they did all that the king commanded. 14
24:19 David went up . . as the LORD commanded. 14
1Kg 2:30 The king commands, 'Come forth.'" But he said, "No 2
46 the king commanded Benai'ah . . and he went out 14
4: 4 Benai'ah . . was in command of the army; Zadok 10
5: 6 command that cedars of Lebanon be cut for me; 14
17 At the king's command, they quarried out 14
8:58 his ordinances, which he commanded our fathers. 14
9: 4 doing according to all that I have commanded you 14
11:10 had commanded him concerning this thing 14
10 he did not keep what the LORD commanded. 14
11 covenant and my statutes which I have commanded 14
38 if you will hearken to all that I command you 14
13: 9 so was it commanded me by the word of the LORD 14
21 which the LORD your God commanded you 14
15: 5 turn aside from anything that he commanded him 14
17: 4 I have commanded the ravens to feed you there. 14
9 I have commanded a widow there to feed you. 14
20:35 said to his fellow at the command of the LORD 4
22:31 the king of Syria had commanded the . . captains 14
2Kg 5:13 My father, if the prophet had commanded you to do 5
11: 5 he commanded them, "This is the thing 14
9 did according to all that Jehoi'ada . . commanded 14
15 Jehoi'ada . . commanded the captains who were set 14
14: 6 what is written . . where the LORD commanded 14
16:15 King Ahaz commanded Uri'ah the priest, saying 14
16 Uri'ah the priest did . . as King Ahaz commanded. 14
17:13 all the law which I commanded your fathers 14
15 concerning whom the LORD had commanded them 14
27 Then the king of Assyria commanded, "Send 14
34 which the LORD commanded the children of Jacob 14
35 The LORD made a covenant . . and commanded them 14
18: 6 commandments which the LORD commanded Moses. 14
12 his covenant, even all that Moses . . commanded; 14
36 for the king's command was, "Do not answer 8
21: 8 to do according to all that I have commanded them 14
8 the law that my servant Moses commanded them. 14
22:12 the king commanded Hilki'ah . . and Ahi'kam 14
23: 4 And the king commanded Hilki'ah the high priest 14
21 And the king commanded all the people 14
35 He . . according to the command of Pharaoh. 11
24: 3 this came upon Judah at the command of the LORD 11
25:19 officer who had been in command of the men of war 12
1Ch 6:49 all that Moses the servant of God had commanded. 14
10:13 he did not keep the command of the LORD 4
12:32 and all their kinsmen under their command. 11
14:16 David did as God commanded him 14
15:15 commanded according to the word of the LORD. 14
16 David also commanded the chiefs of the Levites 2
16:15 mindful . . of the word that he commanded 14
40 the law of the LORD which he commanded Israel. 14
17: 6 whom I commanded to shepherd my people 14
21: 6 for the king's command was abhorrent to Jo'ab. 4
18 angel of the LORD commanded Gad to say to David 2
27 Then the LORD commanded the angel; 2
22: 2 David commanded to gather together the aliens 2
13 which the LORD commanded Moses for Israel. 14
17 David also commanded all the leaders of Israel 14
24:19 as the LORD God of Israel had commanded him. 14
27: 6 Benai'ah who was . . in command of the 30; 10
28:21 all the people will be wholly at your command. 4
2Ch 7:13 When I . . command the locust to devour the land 14
17 doing according to all that I have commanded you 14
8:14 for so David the man of God had commanded. 8
15 not turn aside from what the king had commanded 8
14: 4 commanded Judah to seek the LORD 2
18:30 Now the king of Syria had commanded the captains 14
23: 8 all that Jehoi'ada the priest commanded. 14
24: 8 the king commanded, and they made a chest 2
21 by command of the king they stoned him 8
25: 4 in the book of Moses, where the LORD commanded 14
26:13 Under their command was an army of 307,500 6
29:15 and went in as the king had commanded 8
21 commanded the priests the sons of Aaron to offer 2
24 king commanded that the burnt offering 2
27 Hezeki'ah commanded that the burnt offering 2
30 king and the princes commanded the Levites 2
30: 6 as the king had commanded, saying 8
12 to do what the king and the princes commanded 8
31: 4 commanded the people . . to give the portion due 2
5 As soon as the command was spread abroad 4
11 Hezeki'ah commanded them to prepare chambers 2
32:12 Hezeki'ah . . commanded Judah and Jerusalem 2
33: 8 be careful to do all that I have commanded them 14
16 commanded Judah to serve the LORD the God 2
34:20 king commanded Hilki'ah, Ahi'kam the son 14
35:10 according to the king's command. 8
15 in their place according to the command of David 8
16 according to the command of King Josi'ah. 8
21 God has commanded me to make haste. 2
Ezr 4: 3 as King Cyrus the king of Persia has commanded us. 14
6:14 finished their building by command of the God 17
7:23 Whatever is commanded by the God of heaven 17
9:11 thou didst command by thy servants the prophets 14
Neh 1: 7 which thou didst command thy servant Moses. 14
8 word . . didst command thy servant Moses, saying 14
8:14 LORD had commanded by Moses that the people 14
9:14 command them commandments and statutes 14
11:23 there was a command from the king concerning 8
12:45 according to the command of David and . . Solomon. 8
13:19 I commanded that the doors should be shut 2
22 I commanded the Levites that they should purify 2
Est 1:10 he commanded Mehu'man, Biztha, Harbo'na, Bigtha 2
12 Vashti refused to come at the king's command 4
15 she has not performed the command of King 7
17 Ahasu-e'rus commanded Queen Vashti to be brought 2
3: 2 for the king had so commanded concerning him. 14
3 Why do you transgress the king's command? 8
12 an edict, according to all that Haman commanded 14
4: 3 wherever the king's command and his decree came 4
8: 9 that Mor'decai commanded concerning the Jews 14
14 rode out in haste, urged by the king's command; 4
17 wherever the king's command and his edict came 4
9: 1 command and edict were about to be executed 4
14 the king commanded this to be done; 2
32 The command of Queen Esther fixed . . Purim 7
Job 9: 7 who commands the sun, and it does not rise; 2
36:10 commands that they return from iniquity. 2
32 lightning, and commands it to strike the mark. 14
37:12 to accomplish all that he commands them 14
15 Do you know how God lays his command upon them *
38:12 Have you commanded the morning since your days 14
39:27 Is it at your command that the eagle mounts up 11
Ps 33: 9 he commanded, and it stood forth. 14
42: 8 By day the LORD commands his steadfast love; 14
68:11 Lord gives the command; 1
78: 5 a law . . which he commanded our fathers to teach 14
23 Yet he commanded the skies above 14
105: 8 He is mindful of . . the word that he commanded 14
106:34 not destroy the peoples, as the LORD commanded 2
107:25 For he commanded, and raised the stormy wind 2
111: 9 he has commanded his covenant for ever. 14
119: 4 Thou hast commanded thy precepts to be kept 14
158 because they do not keep thy commands. 32
133: 3 there the LORD has commanded the blessing 14
147:15 He sends forth his command to the earth; 3
148: 5 For he commanded and they were created. 14
8 stormy wind fulfilling his command! 4
Prv 8:29 waters might not transgress his command 11
Ecc 8: 2 Keep the king's command 11
5 He who obeys a command will meet no harm 8
Isa 5: 6 command the clouds that they rain no rain upon it. 14
10: 6 and against the people of my wrath I command him 14
13: 3 I myself have commanded my consecrated ones 14
34:16 For the mouth of the LORD has commanded 14
36:21 for the king's command was, "Do not answer him. 8
45:11 or command me concerning the work of my hands? 14
12 the heavens, and I commanded all their host. 14
48: 5 and my molten image commanded them.' 14
Jer 1: 7 and whatever I command you you shall speak. 14
17 and say to them everything that I command you. 14
7:22 I did not speak to your fathers or command them 14
23 But this command I gave them, 'Obey my voice 4
23 and walk in all the way that I command you 14
31 which I did not command 14
11: 4 which I commanded your fathers 14
4 Listen to my voice, and do all that I command you. 14
8 this covenant, which I commanded them to do 14
13: 5 hid it by the Euphra'tes, as the LORD commanded me. 14
6 waistcloth which I commanded you to hide there. 14
14:14 I did not send them, nor did I command them 14
17:22 keep the sabbath day holy, as I commanded 14
19: 5 burnt offerings to Ba'al, which I did not command 14
26: 2 all the words that I command you to speak to them; 14
8 all that the LORD had commanded him to speak 14
29:23 lying words which I did not command them. 14
32:23 did nothing of all thou didst command them to do. 14
35 to Molech, though I did not command them 14
34:22 Behold, I will command, says the LORD 14
35: 6 our father, commanded us, 'You shall not drink wine 14
8 that he commanded us, to drink no wine all our days 14
10 done all that Jon'adab our father commanded us. 14
14 The command which Jon'adab the son of Rechab gave 4
14 for they have obeyed their father's command. 8
16 have kept the command which their father gave 8
18 Because you have obeyed the command of Jon'adab 8
18 and done all that he commanded you 14
36:26 And the king commanded Jerah'meel the king's son 14
38:10 Then the king commanded E'bed-mel'ech 14
50:21 and do all that I have commanded you. 14
51:59 The word which Jeremiah the prophet commanded 14
52:25 he took an officer who had been in command 12
Lam 1:17 the LORD has commanded against Jacob that 14
3:37 Who has commanded and it came to pass 2
Ezk 9:11 word, saying, "I have done as thou didst command me. 14
10: 6 And when he commanded the man clothed in linen 14
12: 7 And I did as I was commanded. 14
24:18 on the next morning I did as I was commanded. 14
37: 7 I prophesied as I was commanded; 14
10 I prophesied as he commanded me 14
Dan 1:18 king had commanded that they should be brought 2
2: 2 Then the king commanded that the magicians 2
12 commanded that all the wise men of Babylon 16
46 King . . commanded that an offering and incense 16
3: 4 commanded, O peoples, nations, and languages 16
13 commanded that Shadrach, Meshach, and Abed'nego 16
28 set at nought the king's command, and yielded up 18
4:26 commanded to leave the stump of the roots 16
5: 2 Belshaz'zar . . commanded that the vessels of gold 16
29 Belshaz'zar commanded, and Daniel was clothed 16
6:16 king commanded, and Daniel was brought 16
23 commanded that Daniel be taken up out of the den. 16
24 king commanded, and those men who had accused 16
Ams 2:12 and commanded the prophets, saying, 'You shall not 14
6:11 For behold, the LORD commands 14
9: 3 I will command the serpent, and it shall bite 14
4 I will command the sword, and it shall slay them; 14
9 I will command, and shake the house of Israel 14
Zep 2: 3 all you humble of the land, who do his commands; 9
Zec 1: 6 my statutes, which I commanded my servants 14
9:10 he shall command peace to the nations; 5
Mal 2: 1 now, O priests, this command is for you. 8
4 So shall you know that I have sent this command 8
4: 4 the statutes and ordinances that I commanded 14
Mat 1:24 he did as the angel of the Lord commanded him; he 38
4: 3 If you are the Son of God, command these stones 22
8: 4 and offer the gift that Moses commanded 38
14: 9 he commanded it to be given; 31
15: 4 For God commanded 'Honor your father 22
35 commanding the crowd to sit down on the ground 34
17: 9 coming down the mountain, Jesus commanded them 23
19: 7 Why then did Moses command 23
20:21 Command that these two sons of mine may sit 22
28:20 all that I have commanded you 23
Mrk 1:27 he commands even the unclean spirits 29
44 and offer for your cleansing what Moses commanded 38
6:39 Then he commanded them all to sit down 29
8: 6 he commanded the crowd to sit down on the ground; 34
7 having blessed them, he commanded 22
9:25 You dumb and deaf spirit, I command you 29
10: 3 He answered them, "What did Moses command you? 23
13:34 commands the doorkeeper to be on watch. 23

Lke 4: 3 of God, command this stone to become bread. 22
36 he commands the unclean spirits, and they come out. 29
5:14 as Moses commanded, for a proof to the people. 38
8:25 commands even wind and water, and they obey him? 29
29 commanded the unclean spirit to come out of the man 34
31 they begged him not to command them to depart 29
9:21 he . . commanded them to tell this to no one 34
14:22 Sir, what you commanded has been done 29
15:29 I never disobeyed your command 25
17: 9 because he did what was commanded? 20
10 when you have done all that is commanded you 20
18:40 Jesus stopped, and commanded him to be brought 31
19:15 he commanded these servants 22
Joh 8: 5 Now in the law Moses commanded us to stone such. 23
14:31 I do as the Father has commanded me 23
15:14 You are my friends if you do what I command you. 23
17 This I command you, to love one another. 23
Act 4:15 when they had commanded them to go aside 31
8:38 he commanded the chariot to stop 31
10:33 hear all that you have been commanded by the Lord 38
42 he commanded us to preach to the people 34
48 he commanded them to be baptized 38
13:47 so the Lord has commanded us, saying 23
17:15 a command for Silas and Timothy to come to him 25
30 now he commands all men everywhere to repent 34
18: 2 Claudius had commanded all the Jews to leave 20
22:24 commanded him to be brought into the barracks 31
30 and commanded the chief priests . . to meet 31
23: 2 the high priest Anani'as commanded . . to strike him 29
10 the tribune . . commanded the soldiers to go down 31
35 he commanded him to be guarded 31
25:21 I commanded him to be held 31
23 Then by command of Festus Paul was brought in. 31
Rom 16:26 according to the command of the eternal God 28
1Co 7: 6 I say this by way of concession, not of command. 28
25 I have no command of the Lord 28
9:14 In the same way, the Lord commanded 20
14:37 is a command of the Lord. 25
2Co 8: 8 I say this not as a command 28
1Th 4:12 that you may command the respect of outsiders 35
2Th 3: 4 and will do the things which we command. 34
6 Now we command you, brethren 34
12 Now such persons we command and exhort 34
1Ti 1: 1 by command of God our Savior 28
4:11 Command and teach these things. 34
5: 7 Command this 34
Tit 1: 3 by command of God our Savior; 28
14 commands of men who reject the truth. 25
Phm 1: 8 to command you to do what is required 29
Heb 9:20 the covenant which God commanded you. 23
1Jn 3:23 love one another, just as he has commanded us. 21
2Jn 1: 4 just as we have been commanded by the Father. 26
1Es 1:18 according to the command of King Josiah. 28
2: 4 commanded me to build him a house at Jerusalem 40
4: 5 do not disobey the king's command 33
57 he also commanded to be done 29
5:51 as it is commanded in the law 29
71 as Cyrus the king of the Persians has commanded 38
6:11 At whose command are you building this house 38
19 with the command that . . 29
23 Darius commanded that search be made 38
27 Darius commanded Sisinnes the governor of Syria 38
28 I command that it be built completely 29
32 he commanded that . . 38
7: 4 they completed it by the command of the Lord God 37
8:19 I, Artaxerxes the king, have commanded 38
9:53 the Levites commanded all the people, saying 31
2Es 1:35 Those . . will do what I have commanded. 49
2:33 I, Ezra, received a command from the Lord 49
3: 4 and didst command the dust 45
24 didst command him to build a city for thy name 43
5:20 as Uriel the angel had commanded me. 48
6:40 Then thou didst command 43
41 didst command him to divide and separate 45
42 On the third day thou didst command the waters 45
45 thou didst command the brightness of the sun 45
46 thou didst command them to serve man 45
47 thou didst command the seventh part 43
48 as it was commanded 46
53 On the sixth day thou didst command the earth 45
8:10 thou hast commanded that from the members 45
14 with so great labor was fashioned by thy command 47
22 at whose command they are changed ‡
22 and whose command is terrible 44
10:59 the following one, as he had commanded me. 43
12:51 seven days, as the angel had commanded me 48
14: 5 Then I commanded him, saying 49
20 For behold, I will go, as thou hast commanded me 49
27 Then I went as he commanded me 49
31 the ways which the Most High commanded you. 49
37 I took the five men, as he commanded me 48
Tob 1: 8 as Deborah my father's mother had commanded me 24
3: 6 command my spirit to be taken up 29
6 Command that I now be released from my distress 29
13 Command that I be released from the earth 22
15 command that respect be shown to me 29
4:19 So, my son, remember my commands 25
5: 1 do everything that you have commanded me; 23
6:15 the words with which your father commanded you 24
Jdt 2: 3 every one who had not obeyed his command 33
13 to transgress any of your sovereign's commands 39
5: 9 Then their God commanded them to leave 22
12: 1 Then he commanded them to bring her 31
6 Let my lord now command 29
7 Holofernes commanded his guards not to hinder 38
Wis 14:16 at the command of monarchs 28
16: 6 to remind them of thy law's command. 25
18:16 the sharp sword of thy authentic command 28
19: 6 complying with thy commands 28
Sir 7:31 give him his portion, as is commanded you 23
15:20 He has not commanded any one to be ungodly 24
24:23 the law which Moses commanded us 24
39:16 whatever he commands will be done in his time. 37
18 At his command whatever pleases him is done 37
31 they will rejoice in his commands 25
43: 5 at his command it hastens on its course. 33
10 At the command of the Holy One 33
13 By his command he sends the driving snow 37
48:22 which Isaiah the prophet commanded 24
Bar 2: 9 in all his works which he has commanded us to do. 23
28 thou didst command him to write thy law 23
5: 8 tree have shaded Israel at God's command. 37
LJr 1: 1 to give them the message which God had commanded 29
62 commands the clouds to go over the whole world 29
62 they carry out his command. 41
Aza 1: 7 as thou hast commanded us 23
Sus 1:18 to bring what they had been commanded; 38
56 and commanded them to bring the other. 31
Man 1: 3 who hast shackled the sea by thy word of command 37
1Mc 1:43 the Gentiles accepted the command of the king. 33
50 whoever does not obey the command of the king 33
51 commanded the cities . . to offer sacrifice 24
2:18 be the first to come and do what the king commands 37
23 according to the king's command. 37
31 men who had rejected the king's command 25
33 do what the king commands, and you will live. 30
34 nor will we do what the king commands 33
55 because he fulfilled the command 33
66 he shall command the army for you 19
68 heed what the law commands. 37
3:14 who scorn the king's command. 33
39 destroy it, as the king had commanded. 33
42 also learned what the king had commanded to do 24
4:27 nor had they turned out as the king had commanded 24
6:23 to live by what he said and to follow his commands. 37
7: 9 he commanded him to take vengeance 24
26 he commanded him to destroy the people. 24
10: 6 he commanded that the hostages . . be released 22
37 just as the king has commanded in the land of Judah 38
81 his men stood fast, as Jonathan commanded 29
11: 2 Alexander the king had commanded them 25
12:17 We have commanded them to go also to you 24
23 We therefore command 24
27 Jonathan commanded his men to be alert 29
43 commanded his friends and his troops to obey him 29
15:39 He commanded him to encamp against Judea 24
39 and commanded him to build up Kedron 24
2Mc 3: 7 sent him with commands to effect the removal 25
13 because of the king's commands which he had 25
5:12 he commanded his soldiers 31
24 and commanded him to slay all the grown men 38
6:21 which had been commanded by the king 38
7: 4 he commanded that . . 38
30 I will not obey the king's command 37
30 I obey the command of the law 37
8: 9 in command of no fewer than 20,000 Gentiles 42
22 each to command a division 36
9: 8 he could command the waves of the sea 29
10:13 Unable to command the respect due his office •
12:20 Maccabeus . . set men in command of the divisions 27
14:16 At the command of the leader 38
27 commanding him to send Maccabeus to Antioch 31
31 and commanded them to hand the man over. 31
15: 3 who had commanded the keeping of the sabbath day. 38
5 I command you to take up arms 38
3Mc 4:11 he commanded that they should be enclosed 38
4Mc 6: 4 Obey the king's commands! 25
8: 2 then in violent rage he commanded 31
9:11 at his command the guards brought forward . . 31

command *See also* cry, give, take.

full command 1. *περικρατέω*
4Mc 7:17 Not every one has full command of his emotions 1
14:11 reason had full command over these men 1

command of elephants 1. *ἐλεφαντάρχης*
2Mc 14:12 who had been in command of the elephants 1

command strictly 1. mando
2Es 7:21 For God strictly commanded those 1

thing commanded 1. מִצְוָה
Lev 4: 2 in any of the things which the LORD has commanded 1
13 the things which the LORD has commanded 1
22 the things which the LORD his God has commanded 1
27 the things which the LORD has commanded not to be 1
5:17 the things which the LORD has commanded not to be 1

commander 1. חקק 2. נָגִיד 3. סָגָן 4. פֶּחָה 5. צוה
6. קָצִין 7. שַׂר 8. שַׂר צְבָאוֹת 9. בְּעֵל טְעֵם (A)
10. *ἀρχιστράτηγος* 11. *ἄρχων* 12. *δυνάστης* 13. *ἐπί*
14. *ἡγεμών* 15. *ἡγέομαι* 16. *στρατηγέω*
17. *στρατηγός* 18. *φυλάρχης*
Gen 21:22 Abim'elech and Phicol the commander of his army 7
32 Phicol the commander of his army rose up 7
26:26 adviser and Phicol the commander of his army. 7
Num31:14 officers of the army, the commanders of thousands 7
14 officers of the army . . commanders of hundreds 7
52 offering . . from the commanders of thousands 7
52 offering . . from . . the commanders of hundreds 7
54 received . . from the commanders of thousands 7
Deu 1:15 heads over you, commanders of thousands 7
15 heads over you . . commanders of hundreds 7
15 heads over you, commanders . . of fifties 7
15 heads over you, commanders . . of tens 7
20: 9 commanders . . appointed at the head of the people. 8
33:21 for there a commander's portion was reserved; 1
Jos 5:14 as commander of the army of the LORD I . . now come. 7
15 the commander of the LORD's army said to Joshua 7
Jdg 4: 2 Jabin . . the commander of his army was Sis'era 7
5: 9 My heart goes out to the commanders of Israel 1
14 from Machir marched down the commanders 1
1Sm 8:12 he will appoint . . commanders of thousands 7
12 commanders of . . and commanders of fifties 7
12: 9 Sis'era, commander of the army of . . Hazor 7
14:50 the name of the commander of his army was Abner 7
17:18 take these 10 cheeses to the commander 7
55 he said to Abner, the commander of the army 7
18:13 and made him a commander of 1,000; 7
22: 7 will he make you all commanders of thousands 7
7 will he make you . . and commanders of hundreds 7
26: 5 Abner the son of Ner, the commander of his army; 7
29: 3 the commanders of the Philistines said 7
3 said to the commanders of the Philistines 7
4 the commanders of the Philistines were angry 7
4 the commanders of the Philistines said to him 7
9 the commanders of the Philistines have said 7
2Sm 2: 8 Now Abner the son of Ner, commander of Saul's army 7
10:16 Shobach the commander of the army of Hadade'zer 7
18 and wounded Shobach the commander of their army 7
18: 1 and set over them commanders of thousands 7
1 set over them . . and commanders of hundreds. 7
5 when the king gave orders to all the commanders 7
19: 6 commanders and servants are nothing to you; 7
13 God do so . . if you are not commander of my army 7
23:19 most . . of the 30, and became their commander; 7
24: 2 king said to Jo'ab and the commanders of the army 11
4 against Jo'ab and the commanders of the army. 7
4 Jo'ab and the commanders of the army went out 7
1Kg 1:19 Abi'athar . . and Jo'ab the commander of the army; 7
25 the king's sons, Jo'ab the commander of the army 10
2: 5 the two commanders of the armies of Israel, Abner 7
32 Abner . . commander of the army of Israel 7
32 and Ama'sa . . commander of the army of Judah. 7
9:22 they were his officials, his commanders 7
22 his captains, his chariot commanders 7
11:15 Jo'ab the commander of the army went up 7
21 Jo'ab the commander of the army was dead 7
15:20 Ben-ha'dad . . sent the commanders of his armies 7
16: 9 Zimri, commander of half his chariots, conspired 7
16 Israel made Omri, the commander of the army, king 7
20:24 remove . . and put commanders in their places; 4
2Kg 4:13 to the king or to the commander of the army? 7
5: 1 Na'aman, commander of the army of the king of Syria 7
8:21 and his chariot commanders smote the E'domites 7
9: 5 the commanders of the army were in council; 7
5 and he said, "I have an errand to you, O commander. 7
5 And he said, "To you, O commander. 7
25:19 and the secretary of the commander of the army 7
1Ch 11: 6 Jeb'usites first shall be chief and commander. 7
21 renowned of the 30, and became their commander 7
12:21 men of valor, and were commanders in the army. 7
28 and 22 commanders from his own father's house. 7
34 1,000 commanders with whom were 37,000 men 7
13: 1 commanders of thousands and of hundreds 7
15:25 David and . . and the commanders of thousands 7
19:16 with Shophach the commander of the army 7
18 also Shophach the commander of their army. 7
21: 2 David said to Jo'ab and the commanders of the army 7
26:26 officers . . and the commanders of the army 7
27: 1 commanders of thousands and hundreds 7
3 chief of all the commanders of the army 7
5 The third commander . . was Benai'ah, 7
8 The fifth commander . . was Shamhuth 7
34 Jo'ab was commander of the king's army. 7
28: 1 the commanders of thousands, the commanders 7
1 of thousands, the commanders of hundreds 7
29: 6 the commanders of thousands and of hundreds 7
2Ch 1: 2 to the commanders of thousands and of hundreds 7
8: 9 commanders of his chariots, and his horsemen. 7
11:11 fortresses strong, and put commanders in them 2
16: 4 sent the commanders of his armies against 7
17:14 Of Judah, the commanders of thousands 7
14 Adnah the commander, with 300,000 mighty men 7
15 next to him Jehoha'nan the commander, with 280,000 7
21: 9 Then Jeho'ram passed over with his commanders 7

9 surrounded him and his chariot commanders. 7
23: 1 entered into a compact with the commanders 7
25: 5 under commanders of thousands and of hundreds 7
26:11 Hanani'ah, one of the king's commanders. 7
28: 7 slew . . Azri'kam the commander of the palace 2
32: 6 he set combat commanders over the people 7
21 cut off all the mighty warriors and commanders 2
33:11 brought upon them the commanders of the army 7
14 put commanders of the army in all the fortified 7
Ezr 4: 8 Rehum the commander and Shim'shai the scribe 9
9 then wrote Rehum the commander, Shim'shai 9
17 To Rehum the commander and Shim'shai the scribe 9
Isa 10: 8 for he says: "Are not my commanders all kings? 7
55: 4 a leader and commander for the peoples. 5
Jer 42: 1 Then all the commanders of the forces 7
8 the commanders of the forces who were with him 7
43: 4 Joha'nan the son of Kare'ah and all the commanders 7
5 commanders of the forces took all the remnant 7
51:23 I break in pieces governors and commanders. 3
57 her wise men, her governors, her commanders 3
52:25 the secretary of the commander of the army 7
Ezk 23: 6 governors and commanders, all of them desirable 3
12 Assyrians, governors and commanders, warriors 3
23 desirable young men, governors and commanders 3
Dan 11:18 commander shall put an end to his insolence; 6
1Es 1:29 the commanders came down against King Josiah. 11
Jdt 2:14 and called together all the commanders, generals 12
5: 2 the commanders of Ammon 17
6: 1 Holofernes, the commander of the Assyrian army 10
7: 8 the commanders of the coastland came to him 17
10:13 Holofernes the commander of your army 10
13:15 Holofernes, the commander of the Assyrian army 10
14:12 they sent word to their commanders 15
1Mc 3:13 Seron, the commander of the Syrian army, heard 11
5:56 Azariah, the commanders of the forces 11
6:28 all his friends, the commanders of his forces 11
57 said to the king, to the commanders of the forces 14
60 The speech pleased the king and the commanders 11
61 the king and the commanders gave them their oath 11
11:70 commanders of the forces of the army. 11
12:24 the commanders of Demetrius had returned 11
13:42 commander and leader of the Jews. 17
53 so he made him commander of all the forces 15
14: 2 he sent one of his commanders to take him alive. 11
47 be commander and ethnarch of the Jews and priests 17
2Mc 4:29 Crates, the commander of the Cyprian troops. 13
8:32 They killed the commander of Timothy's forces 18
10:32 where Chaereas was commander. 16

commander in chief 1. תַּרְתָּן
Isa 20: 1 the commander in chief, who was sent by Sargon 1

commander-in-chief 1. ἐπιστράτηγος
1Mc 15:38 Then the king made Cendebeus commander-in-chief 1

commandment 1. דָּבָר 2. מִצְוָה 3. עַל פִּי 4. פֶּה 5. פִּקּוּד 6. ἐντολή 7. πρόσταγμα 8. constituo 9. diligentia 10. mandatum
Gen 26: 5 Abraham . . kept my charge, my commandments 2
Exd 15:26 If you . . give heed to his commandments 2
16:28 refuse to keep my commandments and my laws? 2
17: 1 moved on . . according to the commandment 4
20: 6 those who love me and keep my commandments. 2
34:28 words of the covenant, the ten commandments. 1
38:21 as they were counted at the commandment of Moses 3
Lev 22:31 So you shall keep my commandments and do them 2
26: 3 walk in my statutes and observe my commandments 2
14 if you . . will not do all these commandments 2
15 so that you will not do all my commandments 2
27:34 These are the commandments which the LORD 2
Num 3:39 numbered at the commandment of the LORD 4
4:37 numbered according to the commandment 4
41 according to the commandment of the LORD. 4
45 according to the commandment of the LORD 4
49 According to the commandment of the LORD 4
15:22 err, and do not observe all these commandments 2
31 Because he has . . broken his commandment 2
39 remember all the commandments of the LORD, to do 2
40 you shall remember and do all my commandments 2
36:13 These are the commandments and the ordinances 2
Deu 4: 2 may keep the commandments of the LORD your God 2
13 to perform, that is, the ten commandments; 1
40 shall keep his statutes and his commandments 2
5:10 those who love me and keep my commandments. 2
29 to fear me and to keep all my commandments 2
31 tell you all the commandment and the statutes 2
6: 1 Now this is the commandment, the statutes 2
2 keeping all his statutes and his commandments 2
17 diligently keep the commandments of the LORD 2
25 do all this commandment before the LORD our God 2
7: 9 those who love him and keep his commandments 2
11 therefore be careful to do the commandment 2
8: 1 All the commandment which I command you this day 2
2 whether you would keep his commandments, or not. 2
6 shall keep the commandments of the LORD your God 2
11 by not keeping his commandments 2
9:23 against the commandment of the LORD your God 4
10: 4 he wrote on the tables . . the ten commandments 1
13 keep the commandments and statutes of the LORD 2
11: 1 keep his charge . . and his commandments 2
8 You shall therefore keep all the commandment 2
13 if you will obey my commandments which I command 2
22 if you will be careful to do all this commandment 2
27 if you obey the commandments of the LORD your God 2
28 not obey the commandments of the LORD your God 2
13: 4 fear him, and keep his commandments and obey 2
18 keeping all his commandments which I command 2
15: 5 being careful to do all this commandment 2
17:20 not turn aside from the commandment, either 2
19: 9 careful to keep all this commandment 2
26:13 according to all thy commandments which thou 2
13 I have not transgressed any of thy commandments 2
17 keep his statutes and his commandments 2
18 that you are to keep all his commandments 2
27: 1 Keep all the commandment which I command you 2
10 keeping his commandments and his statutes 2
28: 1 being careful to do all his commandments 2
9 if you keep the commandments of the LORD your God 2
13 if you obey the commandments of the LORD your God 2
15 not . . be careful to do all his commandments 2
45 to keep his commandments and his statutes 2
30: 8 keep all his commandments which I command you 2
10 keep his commandments and his statutes 2
11 this commandment which I command you this day 2
16 If you obey the commandments of the LORD your God 6
16 by keeping his commandments and his statutes 2
31: 5 do to them according to all the commandment 2
Jos 1:18 rebels against your commandment and disobeys 4
15:13 According to the commandment of the LORD 4
17: 4 according to the commandment of the LORD he gave 4
22: 5 observe the commandment and the law which Moses 2
5 walk in all his ways, and to keep his commandments 2
Jdg 2:17 who had obeyed the commandments of the LORD 2
3: 4 Israel would obey the commandments of the LORD 2
1Sm 12:14 not rebel against the commandment of the LORD 4
15 but rebel against the commandment of the LORD 4
13:13 not kept the commandment of the LORD your God 2
15:11 and has not performed my commandments. 1
13 I have performed the commandment of the LORD. 1
24 I have transgressed the commandment of the LORD 4
1Kg 2: 3 his statutes, his commandments, his ordinances 2
43 not kept your oath . . and the commandment 2
3:14 my ways, keeping my statutes and my commandments 2
6:12 and keep all my commandments and walk in them 2
8:58 keep his commandments, his statutes 2
61 walking in . . and keeping his commandments 2
9: 6 do not keep my commandments and my statutes 2
11:34 David . . kept my commandments and my statutes; 2
38 keeping my statutes and my commandments 2
13:21 and have not kept the commandment which the LORD 2
14: 8 like my servant David, who kept my commandments 2
18:18 you have forsaken the commandments of the LORD 2
2Kg 17:13 Turn . . and keep my commandments and my statutes 2
16 they forsook all the commandments of the LORD 2
19 keep the commandments of the LORD their God 2
34 the commandment which the LORD commanded 2
37 and the law and the commandment which he wrote 2
18: 6 the commandments which the LORD commanded 2
23: 3 to keep his commandments and his testimonies 2
1Ch 28: 7 in keeping my commandments and my ordinance 2
8 all the commandments of the LORD your God; 2
29:19 with a whole heart he may keep thy commandments 2
2Ch 7:19 and forsake my statutes and my commandments 2
8:13 offering according to the commandment of Moses 2
14: 4 to keep the law and the commandment. 2
17: 4 God of his father and walked in his commandments 2
19:10 concerning bloodshed, law or commandment 2
24:20 do you transgress the commandments of the LORD 2
29:25 according to the commandment of David and of Gad 2
25 commandment was from the LORD 2
31:21 in accordance with the law and the commandments 2
34:31 walk after the LORD and to keep his commandments 2
Ezr 7:11 Ezra . . learned in matters of the commandments 2
9:10 For we have forsaken thy commandments 2
14 break thy commandments again and intermarry 2
10: 3 those who tremble at the commandment of our God; 2
Neh 1: 5 those who love him and keep his commandments; 2
7 have not kept the commandments, the statutes 2
9 keep my commandments and do them 2
9:13 give them . . good statutes and commandments. 2
14 command them commandments and statutes 2
16 did not obey thy commandments; 2
29 did not obey thy commandments, but sinned 2
34 not kept thy law or heeded thy commandments 2
10:29 observe and do all the commandments of the LORD 2
12:24 according to the commandment of David 2
13: 5 given by commandment to the Levites, singers 2
Job 23:12 not departed from the commandment of his lips; 2
Ps 19: 8 the commandment of the LORD is pure 2
78: 7 the works of God, but keep his commandments; 2
89:31 if they . . do not keep my commandments 2
103:18 covenant and remember to do his commandments. 5
112: 1 who greatly delights in his commandments! 2
119: 6 having my eyes fixed on all thy commandments. 2
10 let me not wander from thy commandments! 2
19 hide not thy commandments from me! 2
21 accursed ones, who wander from thy commandments; 2
32 I will run in the way of thy commandments 2
35 Lead me in the path of thy commandments 2
47 for I find my delight in thy commandments 2
48 I revere thy commandments, which I love 2
60 I . . do not delay to keep thy commandments. 2
66 Teach me . . for I believe in thy commandments. 2
73 that I may learn thy commandments. 2
86 All thy commandments are sure; 2
96 thy commandment is exceedingly broad. 2
98 Thy commandment makes me wiser than my enemies 2
115 that I may keep the commandments of my God. 2
127 Therefore I love thy commandments above gold 2
131 I pant, because I long for thy commandments. 2
143 but thy commandments are my delight. 2
151 O LORD, and all thy commandments are true. 2
166 O LORD, and I do thy commandments. 2
172 of thy word, for all thy commandments are right. 2
176 for I do not forget thy commandments. 2
Prv 2: 1 My son, if you . . treasure up my commandment 2
3: 1 but let your heart keep my commandments; 2
4: 4 keep my commandments, and live; 2
6:20 My son, keep your father's commandment 2
23 commandment is a lamp and the teaching a light 2
7: 1 My son . . treasure up my commandments with you; 2
2 keep my commandments and live 2
10: 8 The wise of heart will heed commandments 2
13:13 who respects the commandment will be rewarded. 2
19:16 He who keeps the commandment keeps his life; 2
Ecc 12:13 Fear God, and keep his commandments; 2
Isa 29:13 fear of me is a commandment of men learned by rote; 2
48:18 O that you had hearkened to my commandments! 2
Dan 9: 4 those who love him and keep his commandments 2
5 aside from thy commandments and ordinances; 2
Mat 5:19 relaxes one of the least of these commandments 6
15: 3 And why do you transgress the commandment of God 6
19:17 If you would enter life, keep the commandments. 6
22:36 which is the great commandment in the law? 6
38 This is the great and first commandment. 6
40 On these two commandments depend all the law 6
Mrk 7: 8 You leave the commandment of God 6
9 a fine way of rejecting the commandment of God 6
10: 5 he wrote you this commandment. 6
19 You know the commandments 6
12:28 Which commandment is the first of all? 6
31 no other commandment greater than these. 6
Lke 1: 6 walking in all the commandments and ordinances 6
18:20 You know the commandments 6
23:56 they rested according to the commandment. 6
Joh 12:49 has himself given me commandment what to say 6
50 I know that his commandment is eternal life. 6
13:34 A new commandment I give to you 6
14:15 If you love me, you will keep my commandments. 6
21 He who has my commandments and keeps them 6
15:10 If you keep my commandments 6
10 just as I have kept my Father's commandments 6
12 This is my commandment, that you love one another 6
Rom 7: 8 But sin, finding opportunity in the commandment 6
9 when the commandment came, sin revived and I died; 6
10 the very commandment which promised life 6
11 For sin, finding opportunity in the commandment 6
12 and the commandment is holy and just and good. 6
13 through the commandment might become sinful 6
13: 9 The commandments, "You shall not commit adultery *
9 You shall not covet," and any other commandment 6
1Co 7:19 keeping the commandments of God. 6
Eph 2:15 the law of commandments and ordinances 6
6: 2 (this is the first commandment with a promise) 6
1Ti 6:14 I charge you to keep the commandment unstained 6
Heb 7: 5 have a commandment in the law 6
18 On the one hand, a former commandment is set aside 6
9:19 when every commandment . . had been declared 6
2Pe 2:21 the holy commandment delivered to them. 6
3: 2 commandment of the Lord . . through your apostles. 6
1Jn 2: 3 we know him, if we keep his commandments. 6
4 but disobeys his commandments is a liar 6
7 Beloved, I am writing you no new commandment 6
7 I am writing you . . an old commandment 6
7 old commandment is the word which you have heard 6
8 Yet I am writing you a new commandment 6
3:22 we receive . . because we keep his commandments 6
23 this is his commandment, that we should believe 6
24 All who keep his commandments abide in him 6
4:21 And this commandment we have from him 6
5: 2 when we love God and obey his commandments. 6
3 the love of God, that we keep his commandments. 6
3 And his commandments are not burdensome. 6
2Jn 1: 5 as though I were writing you a new commandment 6
6 this is love, that we follow his commandments; 6
6 this is the commandment, as you have heard 6
Rev 12:17 make war . . on those who keep the commandments 6
14:12 saints, those who keep the commandments of God 6
1Es 1: 6 according to the commandment of the Lord 7
4:52 in accordance with the commandment 6
8: 7 the law of the Lord or the commandments 6
82 we have transgressed thy commandments 7
2Es 1:34 because . . they have neglected my commandment 10
2: 1 I gave them commandments through my servants 10
33 and refused the Lord's commandment. 10
3: 7 thou didst lay upon him one commandment of thine; 9

19 thy commandment to the posterity of Israel. 9
33 though they are unmindful of thy commandments. 10
35 what nation has kept thy commandments so well? 10
36 individual men who have kept thy commandments 10
7:37 whose commandments you have despised! 9
45 who are alive and keep thy commandments! 8
72 and though they received the commandments 10
15:24 do not observe my commandments," says the Lord; 10
16:76 You who keep my commandments and precepts 10
Tob 3: 4 For they disobeyed thy commandments 6
5 because we did not keep thy commandments 6
4: 5 to sin or to transgress his commandments 6
14: 9 keep the law and the commandments 7
Wis 9: 9 what is right according to thy commandments. 6
Sir 1:26 If you desire wisdom, keep the commandments 6
6:37 meditate at all times on his commandments 6
10:19 Those who transgress the commandments. 6
15:15 If you will, you can keep the commandments 6
23:27 to heed the commandments of the Lord. 6
28: 6 be true to the commandments. 6
7 Remember the commandments 6
29: 1 keeps the commandments. 6
9 Help a poor man for the commandment's sake 6
11 according to the commandments of the Most High 6
32:23 for this is the keeping of the commandments. 6
24 gives heed to the commandments 6
35: 1 he who heeds the commandments 6
5 to be done because of the commandment. 6
37:12 whom you know to be a keeper of the commandments 6
45: 5 gave him the commandments face to face 6
17 In his commandments he gave him authority 6
Bar 3: 9 Hear the commandments of life, O Israel; give ear 6
4: 1 She is the book of the commandments of God 7
13 walk in the ways of God's commandments 6
Aza 1: 6 have not obeyed thy commandments; 6
1Mc 2:19 and have chosen to do his commandments 6
53 Joseph . . kept the commandment 6
10:14 who had forsaken the law and the commandments 7
2Mc 1: 4 open your heart to his law and his commandments 7
2: 2 not to forget the commandments of the Lord 7
3Mc 7:11 sake had transgressed the divine commandments 7
4Mc 9: 1 transgress our ancestral commandments; 6
13:15 who transgress the commandment of God. 6
16:24 die rather than violate God's commandment. 6

commandment *See also* give.

commemoration 1. זֵכֶר
Est 9:28 nor should the commemoration of these days 1

commemorative 1. ἐπώνυμος
AEs 16:22 among your commemorative festivals 1

commend 1. הלל 2. שבח 3. ἐπαινέω 4. παραδίδωμι 5. παρατίθημι 6. παρίστημι 7. συνίστημι
Prv 12: 8 A man is commended according to his good sense 1
Ecc 8:15 I commend enjoyment . . for this will go with him 2
Lke 16: 8 The master commended the dishonest steward 3
Act 14:26 where they had been commended to the grace of God 4
15:40 commended . . to the grace of the Lord. 4
20:32 now I commend you to God 5
Rom 16: 1 I commend to you our sister Phoebe 7
1Co 8: 8 Food will not commend us to God 6
11: 2 I commend you because you remember me 3
17 in the following instructions I do not commend 3
22 Shall I commend you in this? No, I will not. 3
2Co 3: 1 Are we beginning to commend ourselves again? 7
4: 2 commend ourselves to every man's conscience 7
5:12 We are not commending ourselves to you again 7
6: 4 we commend ourselves in every way 7
10:12 with some of those who commend themselves 7
18 not the man who commends himself that is accepted 7
18 the man whom the Lord commends. 7
12:11 I ought to have been commended by you 7
Wis 7:14 commended for the gifts 7
1Mc 12:43 commended him to all his friends 7
2Mc 9:25 often entrusted and commended to most of you 7

commendation 1. ἔπαινος
1Co 4: 5 Then every man will receive his commendation 1

commentary 1. מִדְרָשׁ
2Ch 24:27 in the Commentary on the Book of the Kings. 1

commission 1. דָּת 2. צוה 3. ἀποστέλλω 4. ἐκ 5. ἐπιτροπή 6. οἰκονομία 7. πρόσταγμα 8. χρίω
Num27:19 you shall commission him in their sight. 2
Deu 31:14 present yourselves . . that I may commission him. 2
23 LORD commissioned Joshua the son of Nun and said 2
Ezr 8:36 delivered the king's commissions to the king's 1
Act 26:12 the authority and commission of the chief priests. 5
1Co 9:17 I am entrusted with a commission. 6
2Co 1:21 has commissioned us; 8
2:17 as men of sincerity, as commissioned by God 4
1Es 8: 8 written commission from Artaxerxes the king 7
2Mc 1:20 having been commissioned by the king of Persia 3

commit 1. גזל 2. גלה 3. גלל 4. חטא 5. מעל 6. נתן 7. נתן בְּיַד 8. עזב 9. עשה 10. פקד 11. פשע 12. שום 13. ἁμαρτάνω 14. γίνομαι 15. δίδωμι 16. ἐργάζομαι 17. καταδεσμεύω 18. κατεργάζομαι 19. παραδίδωμι 20. παρατίθημι 21. πιστεύω 22. ποιέω 23. πράσσω 24. συντελέω 25. admitto 26. ago 27. commendo 28. committo 29. facio
Gen 39:22 the keeper of the prison committed to Joseph's 6
Lev 4: 3 let him offer for the sin which he has committed 4
14 when the sin which they have committed 4
23 if the sin which he has committed is made known 4
28 when the sin which he has committed is made known 4
28 a goat . . for his sin which he has committed 4
35 atonement for the sin which he has committed 4
5: 5 he shall confess the sin he has committed 4
6 to the LORD for the sin which he has committed 4
10 for him for the sin which he has committed 4
13 sin which he has committed in any one of these 4
6: 4 the deposit which was committed to him 10
19:22 atonement . . for his sin which he has committed 4
22 the sin which he has committed shall be forgiven 4
20:12 they have committed incest, their blood is upon 9
13 both of them have committed an abomination 9
26:40 treachery which they committed against me 5
Num 5: 6 When a man or woman commits any of the sins 9
6 any of the sins that men commit by breaking faith •
7 he shall confess his sin which he has committed; 9
Deu 9:18 because of all the sin which you had committed 4
19:15 any offense that he has committed; 4
20 rest . . shall never again commit any such evil 9
21:22 man has committed a crime punishable by death •
Jos 22:16 What is this treachery which you have committed 5
Jdg 9:56 crime . . which he committed against his father 9
20: 6 they have committed abomination 9
10 all the wanton crime which they have committed 9
1Kg 8:50 transgressions which they have committed 11
14:22 with their sins which they committed 4
27 and committed them to the hands of the officers 10
16:19 his sins which he committed, doing evil 4
19 his sin which he committed, making Israel to sin. 9
2Kg 21:11 Manas'seh . . has committed these abominations 9
17 and all that he did, and the sin that he committed 4
2Ch 12:10 committed them to the hands of the officers 10
34:16 committed to your servants they are doing. 7
Neh 9:18 when they . . had committed great blasphemies 9
26 disobedient . . committed great blasphemies. 9
Job 5: 8 would seek God, and to God would I commit my cause; 12
Ps 10:14 the hapless commits himself to thee; 8
22: 8 He committed his cause to the LORD; •
31: 5 Into thy hand I commit my spirit; 10
37: 5 Commit your way to the LORD; trust in him 3
Prv 16: 3 Commit your work to the LORD 3
Isa 22:21 and will commit your authority to his hand; 6
Jer 2:13 for my people have committed two evils 9
6:15 ashamed when they committed abomination? 9
8:12 ashamed when they committed abomination? 9
11:20 for to thee have I committed my cause. 2
16:10 What is the sin that we have committed 4
20:12 for to thee have I committed my cause. 2
29:23 because they have committed folly in Israel 9
37:21 gave orders, and they committed Jeremiah 10
40: 7 and had committed to him men, women, and children 10
41:10 had committed to Gedali'ah the son of Ahi'kam. 10
44: 3 because of the wickedness which they committed 9
7 Why do you commit this great evil 9
9 wickedness of your wives, which they committed 9
22 and the abominations which you committed; 9
Ezk 3:20 from his righteousness and commits iniquity 9
6: 9 for the evils which they have committed 9
8: 6 that the house of Israel are committing here 9
9 abominations that they are committing here. 9
13 still greater abominations which they commit. 9
17 to commit the abominations which they commit 9
17 to commit the abominations which they commit 9
9: 4 the abominations that are committed in it. 9
16:43 Have you not committed lewdness in addition 9
51 you have committed more abominations than they •
51 the abominations which you have committed. 9
18: 7 commits no robbery, gives his bread to the hungry 1
12 oppresses the poor and needy, commits robbery 1
12 his eyes to the idols, commits abomination 9
16 exacts no pledge, commits no robbery 1
21 away from all his sins which he has committed 9
22 the transgressions which he has committed 9
24 and commits iniquity and does the same 9
24 for . . the sin he has committed, he shall die. 4
26 When a righteous man . . commits iniquity 9
26 for the iniquity which he has committed 9
27 turns away from the wickedness he has committed 9
28 all the transgressions which he had committed 9
31 the transgressions which you have committed 11
20:43 for all the evils that you have committed. 9
22: 9 men commit lewdness in your midst. 9
11 commits abomination with his neighbor's wife; 9
29 practiced extortion and committed robbery; 1
23:24 I will commit the judgment to them 6
44 to Oho'lah and to Ohol'ibah to commit lewdness. 22
48 and not commit lewdness as you have done. 9
33:13 in his righteousness and commits iniquity 9
13 iniquity that he has committed he shall die. 9
15 in the statutes of life, committing no iniquity; 9
16 None of the sins that he has committed 4
18 and commits iniquity, he shall die for it. 9
26 You resort to the sword, you commit abominations 9
29 their abominations which they have committed. 9
43: 8 their abominations which they have committed 9
44:13 the abominations which they have committed. 9
Dan 9: 7 treachery which they have committed against 5
Hos 6: 9 on the way to Shechem, yea, they commit villainy. 9
Mal 2:11 abomination has been committed in Israel 9
Mrk 15: 7 who had committed murder in the insurrection 22
Lke 12:48 to whom men commit much 20
23:46 Father, into thy hands I commit my spirit! 20
Joh 8:34 every one who commits sin is a slave to sin. 22
Act 8: 3 committed them to prison. 19
14:23 they committed them to the Lord 20
25:11 committed anything for which I deserve to die 23
Rom 1:27 men committing shameless acts with men 18
6:17 standard . . to which you were committed 19
1Co 6:18 Every other sin which a man commits 22
2Co 11: 7 Did I commit a sin in abasing myself 22
1Ti 1:18 This charge I commit to you, Timothy, my son 20
Jas 2: 9 But if you show partiality, you commit sin 16
5:15 and if he has committed sins, he will be forgiven. 22
1Pe 2:22 He committed no sin; 22
2Pe 2: 4 God . . committed them to pits of nether gloom 19
1Jn 3: 4 Every one who commits sin is guilty 22
8 He who commits sin is of the devil; 22
9 No one born of God commits sin; 22
5:16 his brother committing what is not a mortal sin 13
Rev 20: 4 those to whom judgment was committed. 15
2Es 1: 5 iniquities which they have committed against me 25
26 and your feet are swift to commit murder. 28
2:23 commit them to the grave and mark it 27
3:13 when they were committing iniquity before thee 29
4:42 that were committed to them from the beginning. 27
7:32 the souls which have been committed to them. 27
72 because . . they committed iniquity 29
126 For while we lived and committed iniquity 29
138 those who have committed iniquities 29
14:31 you and your fathers committed iniquity 29
15: 8 ungodly deeds which they impiously commit 26
16:67 your iniquities, never to commit them again 26
Tob 3: 3 those which my fathers committed before thee. 13
Jdt 11:17 tell me when they have committed their sins. 22
13:16 yet he committed no act of sin with me 22
Sir 7: 8 Do not commit a sin twice 17
Sus 1:52 sins . . which you have committed in the past 22
1Mc 1:24 He committed deeds of murder 22
2: 6 He saw the blasphemies being committed in Judah 14
13:39 any errors and offenses committed to this day •
16:17 So he committed an act of great treachery 22
2Mc 4: 3 even murders were committed 24
39 When many acts of sacrilege had been committed 14
8: 4 the blasphemies committed against his name 14
17 which the Gentiles had committed 24
12:42 the sin which had been committed 14
13: 8 he had committed many sins against the altar 24
14 committing the decision to the Creator 15
3Mc 2: 4 those who in the past committed injustice 22
17 the defilement committed by these men •
4Mc 4: 7 committed deposits to the sacred treasury 21

commit adultery 1. נאף 2. μοιχάω 3. μοιχεύω
Exd 20:14 You shall not commit adultery. 1
Lev 20:10 commits adultery with the wife of his neighbor 1
Deu 5:18 'Neither shall you commit adultery. 1
Prv 6:32 He who commits adultery has no sense; 1
Jer 3: 9 she polluted the land, committing adultery 1
5: 7 When I fed them . . they committed adultery 1
7: 9 Will you steal, murder, commit adultery 1
23:14 have seen a horrible thing: they commit adultery 1
29:23 they have committed adultery 1
Ezk 23:37 For they have committed adultery 1
37 with their idols they have committed adultery; 1
43 Then I said, Do not men now commit adultery 3
Hos 4: 2 killing, stealing, and committing adultery; 1
13 and your brides commit adultery. 1
14 nor your brides when they commit adultery; 1
Mat 5:27 'You shall not commit adultery.' 3
28 who looks . . lustfully has already committed adultery 3
32 marries a divorced woman commits adultery. 2
19: 9 whoever . . marries another, commits adultery. 2
18 You shall not commit adultery 3
Mrk 10:11 and marries another, commits adultery against her; 2
12 she commits adultery. 2
19 Do not kill, Do not commit adultery 3
Lke 16:18 Every one who . . marries another commits adultery 3
18 he who marries a woman . . commits adultery. 3
18:20 Do not commit adultery, Do not kill, Do not steal 3
Rom 2:22 You who say that one must not commit adultery 3
22 You who say . . do you commit adultery? 3
13: 9 The commandments, "You shall not commit adultery 3
Jas 2:11 For he who said, "Do not commit adultery 3
11 If you do not commit adultery but do kill 3
Rev 2:22 those who commit adultery with her I will throw 3
Sir 23:23 she has committed adultery through harlotry 3

commit an act of sacrilege 1. ἀσεβέω
1Es 1:49 committed many acts of sacrilege 1

commit an error 1. שׁגג
Num15:28 for the person who commits an error, when he sins 1

commit an offense 1. ἀγνοέω 2. πλημμελέω
Sir 23:23 committed an offense against her husband 2
3Mc 3: 9 when it had committed no offense. 1

commit an outrage 1. ἀσεβέω
2Mc 4:38 he had committed the outrage against Onias 1

commit apostasy 1. παραπίπτω
Heb 6: 6 if they then commit apostasy 1

commit breach of faith 1. מעל
Lev 5:15 If any one commits a breach of faith and sins 1
6: 2 If any one sins and commits a breach of faith 1

commit fornication 1. πορνεύω 2. πόρνος
Rev 17: 2 kings of the earth have committed fornication 1
18: 3 kings of the earth have committed fornication 1
9 committed fornication and were wanton 1
Sir 23:16 man who commits fornication with his near of kin 2

commit harlotry 1. זנה
Hos 1: 2 for the land commits great harlotry 1

commit in an ungodly way 1. ἀσεβέω
Jde 1:15 deeds . . committed in such an ungodly way 1

commit iniquity 1. עוה
2Sm 7:14 When he commits iniquity, I will chasten him 1
Ps 106: 6 have committed iniquity, we have done wickedly. 1
Jer 9: 5 they commit iniquity and are too weary to repent. 1

make commit sin 1. חטא
2Kg 17:21 Jerobo'am . . and made them commit great sin. 1

commit perjury 1. ἐφορκέω
Wis 14:28 or live unrighteously, or readily commit perjury; 1

commit sin 1. חטא 2. ἁμαρτάνω
Lev 5: 7 offering . . for the sin which he has committed 1
11 his offering for the sin which he has committed 1
Ezk 16:51 Sama'ria has not committed half your sins; 1
Tob 12:10 those who commit sin are the enemies of their . . lives 2
Sir 27: 1 Many have committed sin for a trifle 2
LJr 1: 2 the sins which you have committed before God 2
Man 1: 9 the sins I have committed 2
4Mc 4:12 he had committed a sin deserving of death 2

commit sin unwittingly 1. שׁגה
Lev 4:13 If . . Israel commits a sin unwittingly 1

commit treachery 1. מעל
Jos 22:31 because you have not committed this treachery 1

commit treason 1. מעל 2. παραβασιλεύω
Ezk 17:20 for the treason he has committed against me. 1
3Mc 6:24 You are committing treason 2

commit unwittingly 1. שׁגג
Lev 5:18 the error which he committed unwittingly 1

common 1. אִישׁ 2. אֱנוֹשׁ 3. חֹל 4. רֹב 5. δημόσιος 6. ἴσος 7. κοινός 8. μερίς
Lev 10:10 distinguish between the holy and the common 3
Num16:29 If these men die the common death of all men •
Deu 3:11 according to the common cubit.) 1
1Sm 21: 4 I have no common bread at hand, but . . holy bread; 3
5 are holy, even when it is a common journey; 3
2Ch 1:15 king made silver and gold as common . . as stone •
9:27 king made silver as common in Jerusalem as stone •
Isa 8: 1 Take . . and write upon it in common characters 2
Jer 23:28 What has straw in common with wheat? •
Ezk 22:26 no distinction between the holy and the common 3
23:42 with men of the common sort drunkards were 4
42:20 a separation between the holy and the common. 3
44:23 the difference between the holy and the common 3
Act 2:44 and had all things in common; 7
4:32 they had everything in common. 7
5:18 put them in the common prison. 5
10:14 never eaten anything that is common or unclean. 7
28 I should not call any man common or unclean. 7
11: 8 nothing common . . has ever entered my mouth.' 7
2Co 6:15 what has a believer in common with an unbeliever? 8
Tit 1: 4 To Titus, my true child in a common faith 7
Jde 1: 3 eager to write to you of our common salvation 7
Wis 7: 3 when I was born, I began to breathe the common air 7
6 one entrance into life, and a common departure. 6
2Mc 8:29 they made common supplication 7
3Mc 2:33 depriving them of common fellowship 7
4: 4 perceiving the common object of pity 7
7:17 in accord with the common desire 7
common *See also* call, good, land, life, make, nurture, talk, zeal.

common man 1. δημότης 2. ἰδιώτης
Act 4:13 perceived that they were uneducated, common men 2
Wis 18:11 the common man suffered the same loss as the king; 1

common people 1. בְּנֵי הָעָם 2. עַם הָאָרֶץ
Lev 4:27 If any one of the common people sins unwittingly 2
2Kg 23: 6 cast . . upon the graves of the common people. 1
Jer 26:23 into the burial place of the common people. 1

common to man 1. ἀνθρώπινος
1Co 10:13 No temptation . . that is not common to man 1

commonwealth 1. πολιτεία 2. πολίτευμα
Eph 2:12 alienated from the commonwealth of Israel 1
Php 3:20 our commonwealth is in heaven 2
2Mc 13:14 the laws, temple, city, country, and commonwealth 1
4Mc 3:20 recognized their commonwealth- 1

commotion 1. רַעַשׁ 2. συστροφή 3. ταραχή
Jer 10:22 Hark, a rumor! Behold, it comes!-a great commotion 1
Act 19:40 to justify this commotion. 2
Sir 11:34 he will upset you with commotion 3

commune 1. אמר 2. ἀδολεσχέω
Ps 4: 4 commune with your own hearts on your beds 1
77: 6 I commune with my heart in the night; 2

communicate 1. κοινωνέω 2. λαλέω 3. μεταδίδωμι
Tob 7: 9 he communicated the proposal to Raguel 3
3Mc 4:11 communicate with the king's forces 1
16 are not able even to communicate 2

communicate holiness 1. קדשׁ
Ezk 44:19 lest they communicate holiness to the people 1
46:20 and so communicate holiness to the people. 1

communication 1. χρηματισμός
2Mc 11:17 have delivered your signed communication 1

community 1. ἔθνος 2. παροικία 3. πολίτευμα 4. σύστεμα 5. τόπος
1Mc 1:25 Israel mourned deeply in every community 5
2Mc 12: 7 and root out the whole community of Joppa. 3
3Mc 2:27 to inflict public disgrace upon the Jewish community 1
3: 9 such a great community 4
6:36 in their whole community 2

compact 1. בְּרִית 2. πήγνυμι
2Ch 23: 1 Jehoi'ada . . entered into a compact 1
Wis 7: 2 compacted with blood, from the seed of a man 2

companion 1. אָח 2. אַלּוּף 3. חָבֵר 4. חֲבֶרֶת 5. ידע 6. מֵרֵעַ 7. רֵעַ 8. רעה 9. רֵעָה 10. חָבֵר (A) 11. ἑταῖρος 12. κοινωνός 13. ὁ μετά 14. ὁ παρά 15. ὁ περί 16. ὁ σύν 17. παρακαθεύδω 18. συμβιωτής
Exd 32:27 slay . . every man his companion, and every man 7
Jdg 11:37 I may go and . . bewail . . I and my companions. 9
38 she departed, she and her companions 9
14:11 they brought 30 companions to be with him. 6
20 Samson's wife was given to his companion 6
15: 2 you . . hated her; so I gave her to your companion. 6
6 taken his wife and given her to his companion. 6
Job 30:29 of jackals, and a companion of ostriches. 7
Ps 38:11 companions stand aloof from my plague 7
45:14 she is led to the king, with her virgin companions 9
55:13 you, my equal, my companion, my familiar friend. 2
20 My companion stretched out his hand •
88: 8 Thou hast caused my companions to shun me; 5
18 my companions are in darkness. 5
119:63 I am a companion of all who fear thee 3
122: 8 For my brethren and companions' sake I will say 7
Prv 2:17 who forsakes the companion of her youth 2
13:20 but the companion of fools will suffer harm. 8
28: 7 but a companion of gluttons shames his father. 8
24 companion of a man who destroys. 3
Sng 1: 7 wanders beside the flocks of your companions? 3
8:13 my companions are listening for your voice; 3
Isa 1:23 princes are rebels and companions of thieves. 3
Jer 41: 8 and did not kill them with their companions. 1
Dan 2:13 sought Daniel and his companions, to slay them. 10
17 Hanani'ah, Mish'a-el, and Azari'ah, his companions 10
18 Daniel and his companions might not perish 10
Mal 2:14 though she is your companion and your wife 4
Jdt 10:20 Holofernes' companions and all his servants 17
Sir 6:10 there is a friend who is a table companion 12
37: 2 when a companion and friend turns to enmity? 11
4 Some companions rejoice 11
5 Some companions help a friend 11
40:23 A friend or a companion never meets one amiss 11
Aza 1:26 with Azariah and his companions 15
Bel 1: 2 Daniel was a companion of the king 18
1Mc 3:14 I will make war on Judas and his companions 16
12:52 they mourned for Jonathan and his companions 13
15:15 Numenius and his companions arrived from Rome 14
2Mc 5:27 and kept himself and his companions alive 13
8: 1 Judas . . and his companions 16
12 when he told his companions 16
3Mc 6: 6 The three companions in Babylon 11
companion *See also* traveling.

dinner companion 1. σύνδειπνος
Sir 9:16 Let righteous men be your dinner companions 1

drinking companion 1. συμπότης
3Mc 2:25 by the previously mentioned drinking companions 1

companion in travel 1. συνέκδημος
Act 19:29 who were Paul's companions in travel. 1

traveling companion 1. ὁδοιπορέω
Sir 42: 3 with traveling companions 1

companionship 1. συναναστροφή 2. συνήθεια
Wis 8:16 companionship with her has no bitterness 1
4Mc 13:22 this common nurture and daily companionship 2
27 nature and companionship and virtuous habits 2

company 1. אֵת 2. חֶבְרָה 3. לַהֲקָה 4. מַחֲנֶה 5. מִשְׁלַחַת 6. סוֹד 7. עֵדָה 8. עֲצָרָה 9. צָבָא 10. קָהָל 11. רֹאשׁ 12. שִׁפְעָה 13. ἀρχή 14. ἐκ 15. κλισία 16. λαός 17. μέρος 18. μέσος 19. ὁ μετά 20. ὁμιλία 21. ὁ περί 22. ὄχλος 23. παρεμβολή 24. πλῆθος 25. σπεῖρα 26. σπειρηδόν 27. συμπόσιον 28. συναγωγή 29. συνοδία
Gen 28: 3 that you may become a company of peoples. 10
32: 7 flocks and herds and camels, into two companies 4
8 If Esau comes to the one company and destroys it 4
8 destroys it, then the company which is left will 4
10 and now I have become two companies. 4
33: 8 What do you mean by all his company which I met? 4
35:11 a nation and a company of nations shall come 10
48: 4 and I will make of you a company of peoples 10
49: 6 O my spirit, be not joined to their company; 10
50: 9 horsemen; it was a very great company. 4
Num 1:52 shall pitch their tents by their companies 9
2: 3 standard of the camp of Judah by their companies 9
9 the camp of Judah, by their companies, is 186,400 9
10 the camp of Reuben by their companies 9
16 camp of Reuben, by their companies, is 151,450 9
18 the camp of E'phraim by their companies 9
24 camp of E'phraim, by their companies, is a 108,100 9
25 the camp of Dan by their companies 9
32 all . . who were numbered by their companies 9
10:14 men of Judah set out first by their companies; 9
18 camp of Reuben set out by their companies; 9
22 men of E'phraim set out by their companies; 9
25 men of Dan . . set out by their companies; 9
16: 5 said to Korah and all his company, "In the morning 7
6 Do this: take censers, Korah and all his company; 7
11 you and all your company have gathered together; 7
16 said to Korah, "Be present, you and all your company 7
40 lest he become as Korah and as his company- 7
26: 9 Dathan and Abi'ram . . in the company of Korah 7
10 together with Korah, when that company died 7
27: 3 not among the company of those who gathered 7
3 against the LORD in the company of Korah 7
Jdg 7:16 he divided the 300 men into three companies 11
20 the three companies blew the trumpets and broke 11
9:34 laid wait against Shechem in four companies. 11
37 and one company is coming from the direction 11
43 his men and divided them into three companies 11
44 Abim'elech and the company . . with him rushed 11
44 while the two companies rushed upon all who were 11
18:23 What ails you that you come with such a company? •
1Sm 11:11 Saul put the people in three companies; 11
13:17 And raiders came out . . in three companies; 11
17 one company turned toward Ophrah, to the land 11
18 another company turned toward Beth-hor'on 11
18 and another company turned toward the border 11
19:20 when they saw the company of the prophets 3
2Kg 5:15 he returned to the man . . he and all his company 4
9:17 he spied the company of Jehu as he came, and said 12
17 he spied the company . . and said, "I see a company. 12
Neh 12:31 appointed two great companies which gave •
38 other company of those who gave thanks went •
40 both companies of those who gave thanks stood •
Job 1:17 The Chalde'ans formed three companies 11
15:34 For the company of the godless is barren 7
16: 7 worn me out; he has made desolate all my company. 7
34: 8 who goes in company with evildoers 2
Ps 22:16 a company of evildoers encircle me; 7
26: 5 I hate the company of evildoers 10
50:18 you keep company with adulterers. †
78:49 and distress, a company of destroying angels. 5
106:17 earth opened . . covered the company of Abi'ram. 7
18 Fire also broke out in their company; 7
111: 1 company of the upright, in the congregation. 6
141: 4 wicked . . in company with men who work iniquity; 1
Jer 9: 2 all adulterers, a company of treacherous men. 8
15:17 I did not sit in the company of merrymakers 6
31: 8 a great company, they shall return here. 10
50: 9 against Babylon a company of great nations 10
Ezk 17:17 Pharaoh with his mighty army and great company 10
27:27 you, with all your company that is in your midst 10

32:22 Assyria is there, and all her company 10
23 the Pit, and her company is round about her grave; 10
38: 4 a great company, all of them with buckler 10
Mat 14: 6 daughter of Hero'di-as danced before the company 18
Mrk 6:39 sit down by companies upon the green grass. 27
Lke 2:44 supposing him to be in the company 29
5:29 was a large company of tax collectors and others 22
9:14 Make them sit down in companies, about 50 each. 15
23: 1 Then the whole company of them arose 24
24:22 Moreover, some women of our company amazed us. 14
Act 1:15 the company of persons was in all about 100 22
4:32 company of those who believed were of one heart 24
11:24 a large company was added to the Lord. 22
26 and taught a large company of people 22
13:13 Now Paul and his company set sail from Paphos 21
14: 1 so spoke that a great company believed 24
19:26 and turned away a considerable company of people 22
Rom 15:32 come . . and be refreshed in your company. •
1Co 15:33 Bad company ruins good morals. 20
Jdt 14:11 they went out in companies to the passes 25
Wis 8:18 in the experience of her company, understanding 20
Sir 45:18 their men and the company of Korah 28
1Mc 2:42 there united with them a company of Hasideans 28
5:30 behold, a large company, that could not be counted 16
33 Then he came up behind them in three companies 13
45 a very large company 23
9:11 The cavalry was divided into two companies 17
12 Flanked by the two companies 17
2Mc 1: 7 after Jason and his company revolted 19
5: 2 in companies fully armed with lances 26

company *See also* enjoy, keep, travel.

company by company 1. לְצִבְאוֹת
Num 1: 3 Aaron shall number them, company by company. 1

large company 1. ἄθροισμα
1Mc 3:13 Judas had gathered a large company 1

small company 1. ὀλιγοστός
1Mc 3:16 Judas went out to meet him with a small company. 1

comparable 1. ἀντιπαραβάλλω
Sir 23:12 is an utterance which is comparable to death 1

compare 1. דמה 2. היה כְּ 3. כְּ 4. משל 5. ערך 6. שוה 7. ἀφομοιόω 8. ἔφισος 9. λογίζομαι 10. ὁμοιόω 11. πρός 12. συγκρίνω 13. συμβάλλω 14. similo
1Kg 3:13 no . . king shall compare with you, all your days. 2
Est 7: 4 for our affliction is not to be compared 6
Job 28:19 The topaz of Ethiopia cannot compare with it 5
Ps 40: 5 none can compare with thee! 5
89: 6 For who in the skies can be compared to the LORD? 5
Prv 3:15 nothing you desire can compare with her. 6
8:11 all that you may desire cannot compare with her. 6
Sng 1: 9 I compare you, my love, to a mare of . . chariots. 1
Isa 40:18 you liken God, or what likeness compare with him? 5
25 To whom then will you compare me 1
46: 5 equal, and compare me, that we may be alike? 4
Lam 2:13 What can I say for you, to what compare you 1
Ezk 31: 8 were as nothing compared with its branches; 3
Mat 11:16 to what shall I compare this generation? 10
13:24 The kingdom of heaven may be compared to a man 10
18:23 Therefore the kingdom of heaven may be compared 10
22: 2 The kingdom of heaven may be compared to a king 10
25: 1 Then the kingdom of heaven shall be compared 10
Mrk 4:30 With what can we compare the kingdom of God 10
Lke 7:31 To what then shall I compare the men 10
13:18 to what shall I compare it? 10
20 To what shall I compare the kingdom of God? 10
Rom 8:18 the sufferings . . are not worth comparing •
2Co 10:12 venture to class or compare ourselves with some 12
12 and compare themselves with one another 12
2Es 6:56 thou hast compared their abundance to a drop 14
8:47 often compared yourself to the unrighteous ‡
Tob 5:18 consider it as rubbish as compared to our child. •
Wis 7:29 Compared with the light 12
Sir 9:10 a new one does not compare with him 8
22: 1 The indolent may be compared to a filthy stone 13
2 may be compared to the filth of dunghills 13
25:19 insignificant compared to a wife's iniquity 11
27:24 hated many things, but none to be compared to him; 10
Bar 3:35 This is our God; no other can be compared to him! 9
LJr 1:63 these idols are not to be compared with them 7

comparison 1. כְּ 2. σύγκρισις
Jdg 8: 2 What have I done now in comparison with you? 1
3 what have I been able to do in comparison with you? 1
2Co 4:17 weight of glory beyond all comparison †
Wis 7: 8 wealth as nothing in comparison with her. 2

compass 1. סבב
1Kg 7:24 were gourds . . compassing the sea round about; 1
2Ch 4: 3 gourds . . compassing the sea round about; 1

compass (2) 1. מְחוּגָה
Isa 44:13 with planes, and marks it with a compass; 1

cause to compass 1. סבב
Jos 6:11 he caused the ark of the LORD to compass the city 1

compassion 1. חמל 2. חֵן 3. נִחוּם 4. נֹחַם 5. נחם 6. רחם 7. רַחֲמִים 8. ἐλεέω 9. ἔλεος 10. κατοικτίρω 11. οἰκτιρέω 12. οἰκτιρμός 13. οἰκτίρμων 14. οἰκτίρω 15. παρακαλέω 16. σπλαγχνίζομαι 17. σπλάγχνον 18. σπλάγχνον οἰκτιρμοῦ 19. συμπαθέω 20. misericordia
Deu 13:17 show you mercy, and have compassion on you 6
32:36 LORD will . . have compassion on his servants 5
Jdg 21: 6 people of Israel had compassion for Benjamin 5
15 the people had compassion on Benjamin 5
1Sm 23:21 be blessed . . for you have had compassion on me. 1
1Kg 8:50 grant them compassion in the sight of those who 7
50 grant . . that they may have compassion on them 6
2Kg 13:23 LORD was gracious . . and had compassion on them 6
2Ch 30: 9 find compassion with their captors, and return 7
36:15 he had compassion on his people 1
17 had no compassion on young man or virgin 1
Ps 77: 9 Has he in anger shut up his compassion?" Selah 7
79: 8 let thy compassion come speedily to meet us 7
135:14 LORD will . . have compassion on his servants. 5
145: 9 his compassion is over all that he has made. 7
Isa 9:17 and has no compassion on their fatherless 6
14: 1 The LORD will have compassion on Jacob 6
27:11 he who made them will not have compassion on them 6
49:13 and will have compassion on his afflicted. 6
15 have no compassion on the son of her womb? 6
54: 7 but with great compassion I will gather you. 7
8 everlasting love I will have compassion on you 6
10 says the LORD, who has compassion on you. 6
63:15 heart and thy compassion are withheld from me. 7
Jer 12:15 I will again have compassion on them 6
13:14 I will not pity or spare or have compassion 6
21: 7 not pity them, or spare them, or have compassion. 6
30:18 and have compassion on his dwellings; 6
Lam 3:32 though he cause grief, he will have compassion 6
Ezk 16: 5 of these things to you out of compassion for you; 1
Dan 1: 9 gave Daniel favor and compassion in the sight 7
Hos 11: 4 I led them with cords of compassion •
8 my compassion grows warm and tender. 3
13:14 Compassion is hid from my eyes. 4
Zec 1:16 I have returned to Jerusalem with compassion; 7
10: 6 I will bring them back because I have compassion 6
12:10 I will pour out . . a spirit of compassion 2
Mat 9:36 When he saw the crowds, he had compassion for them 16
14:14 and he had compassion on them 16
15:32 I have compassion on the crowd 16
Mrk 6:34 he had compassion on them 16
8: 2 I have compassion on the crowd 16
Lke 7:13 he had compassion on her and said to her 16
10:33 when he saw him, he had compassion 16
15:20 his father saw him and had compassion 16
Rom 9:15 I will have compassion on whom I have compassion 14
15 I will have compassion on whom I have compassion 14
Col 3:12 compassion, kindness, lowliness, meekness 18
Heb 10:34 For you had compassion on the prisoners 19
2Es 7:33 and compassion shall pass away 20
136 abundant in compassion 20
136 because he makes his compassions abound 20
Tob 8:17 thou hast had compassion on two only children. 8
Wis 10: 5 in the face of his compassion for his child. 17
Sir 18:13 The compassion of man is for his neighbor 9
13 the compassion of the Lord is for . . beings 9
14 compassion on those who accept his discipline 8
Bar 2:27 all thy kindness and in all thy great compassion 12
1Mc 3:44 to pray and ask for mercy and compassion. 12
2Mc 7: 6 in truth has compassion on us 15
6 'And he will have compassion on his servants.' 15
4Mc 5:12 and have compassion on your old age 11
6:24 he had not been changed by their compassion 13
8:10 Even I, your enemy, have compassion for your youth 14
20 and have compassion on our mother's age 10

compassion *See also* feel.

great compassion 1. εὔσπλαγχνος
Man 1: 7 of great compassion, long-suffering 1

show compassion 1. ἐλεέω
4Mc 12: 6 to show compassion on her 1

compassion upon 1. רחם
Deu 30: 3 LORD your God will . . have compassion upon you 1
2Sm 23: 4 the sun shining forth upon a cloudless morning 1
2Kg 12:11 builders who worked upon the house of the LORD 1
22:16 evil upon this place and upon its inhabitants 1
Isa 8:11 spoke thus to me with his strong hand upon me 1
26:21 the earth will disclose the blood shed upon her 1
Ezk 7: 7 and not of joyful shouting upon the mountains. 1
16:38 and bring upon you the blood of wrath 1
Mic 7:19 He will again have compassion upon us 1
Hab 3: 8 ride upon thy horses, upon thy chariot of victory? 1
Zec 3: 9 upon the stone which I have set before Joshua 1
9: 1 The word of the LORD . . will rest upon Damascus. 1
14:10 But Jerusalem shall remain aloft upon its site 1

compassionate 1. חַנּוּן 2. רחום 3. רַחֲמָנִי 4. οἰκτίρμων 5. πολύσπλαγχνος
Exd 22:27 cries to me, I will hear, for I am compassionate. 1
Ps 78:38 Yet he, being compassionate, forgave 2
Lam 4:10 The hands of compassionate women have boiled 3
Jas 5:11 how the Lord is compassionate and merciful. 5
Sir 2:11 For the Lord is compassionate and merciful 4

compatriot 1. ὁμοεθνεῖς 2. ὁμόφυλος
3Mc 3:21 our amnesty toward their compatriots here 2
4:12 the Jews' compatriots from the city 1

compel 1. אנס 2. נדח 3. ἀγγαρεύω 4. ἀναγκάζω 5. κατὰ ἀνάγκην
Exd 3:19 not let you go unless compelled by a mighty hand. •
Est 1: 8 drinking . . no one was compelled; 1
Prv 7:21 with her smooth talk she compels him. 2
Lam 5:13 Young men are compelled to grind at the mill; •
Mat 27:32 this man they compelled to carry his cross. 3
Mrk 15:21 they compelled a passer-by, Simon of Cyre'ne 3
Lke 14:23 compel people to come in 4
Act 28:19 I was compelled to appeal to Caesar 4
Gal 2: 3 not compelled to be circumcised 4
14 how can you compel the Gentiles to live like Jews? 4
6:12 compel you to be circumcised 4
1Es 4: 6 they compel one another to pay taxes to the king. 4
Jdt 8:30 they compelled us to do for them 4
2Mc 6: 1 to compel the Jews to forsake the laws 4
7 they were compelled to walk in the procession 4
7: 1 were being compelled by the king 4
15: 2 the Jews who were compelled to follow him said 5
4Mc 4:26 tried to compel everyone in the nation 4
5: 2 to compel them to eat pork 4
27 It would be tyrannical for you to compel us 4
8: 2 being unable to compel an aged man 4
9 will compel me to destroy each and every one of you 4
18: 5 able to compel the Israelites to become pagans 4

compel to depart 1. ἐκβάλλω
Wis 19: 3 whom they had begged and compelled to depart. 1

compensation 1. כֹּפֶר
Prv 6:35 He will accept no compensation 1

compete 1. חרה 2. ἀθλέω 3. ἀντερείδω 4. τρέχω
Jer 12: 5 how will you compete with horses? 1
22:15 think you are a king because you compete in cedar? 1
1Co 9:24 in a race all the runners compete 4
2Ti 2: 5 unless he competes according to the rules. 2
Wis 15: 9 he competes with workers in gold and silver 3

competence 1. ἱκανός
2Co 3: 5 our competence is from God 1

competent 1. כֹּחַ 2. ἐπιστήμων 3. ἱκανός
Dan 1: 4 competent to serve in the king's palace 1
2Co 3: 5 Not that we are competent of ourselves to claim 3
1Es 8:47 brought us competent men of the sons of Mahli 2

competent *See also* make.

competition *See* enter.

compile 1. ἀνατάσσομαι
Lke 1: 1 many have undertaken to compile a narrative 1

compiler 1. συγγραφεύς
2Mc 2:28 leaving . . exact details to the compiler 1

complacence 1. שַׁלְוָה
Prv 1:32 complacence of fools destroys them; 1

complacent 1. בטח
Isa 32: 9 you complacent daughters, give ear to my speech. 1

complacent one 1. בטח
Isa 32:11 who are at ease, shudder, you complacent ones; 1

complacent woman 1. בטח
Isa 32:10 you will shudder, you complacent women; 1

complain 1. אנן 2. יכח 3. ריב 4. שִׂיחַ 5. שיח 6. γογγύζω 7. διαγογγύζω 8. λέγω 9. murmuro
Gen 21:25 Abraham complained to Abim'elech about a well 2
Num 11: 1 people complained in the hearing of the LORD 1
Jdg 21:22 fathers or their brothers come to complain to us 3
Job 7:11 I will complain in the bitterness of my soul. 5
Prv 23:29 Who has strife? Who has complaining? 4
Jer 2:29 Why do you complain against me? 3
12: 1 Righteous art thou, O LORD, when I complain to thee; 3
Lam 3:39 Why should a living man complain 1
Php 4:11 Not that I complain of want 8
2Es 1:15 and in them you complained. 9
16 but to this day you still complain. 9
Jdt 5:22 all the men . . began to complain 6
Sir 31:24 The city will complain 7

complain bitterly 1. σχετλιάζω
4Mc 3:12 When his guards complained bitterly 1

complaint 1. שִׂיחַ 2. תּוֹכַחַת 3. *λόγος* 4. *μομφή*

Job 7:13 will comfort me, my couch will ease my complaint,' 1
9:27 If I say, 'I will forget my complaint 1
10: 1 I will give free utterance to my complaint; 1
21: 4 As for me, is my complaint against man? 1
23: 2 Today also my complaint is bitter 1
Ps 64: 1 Hear my voice, O God, in my complaint; 1
102: 0 pours out his complaint before the LORD. 1
142: 2 I pour out my complaint before him 1
Hab 2: 1 and what I will answer concerning my complaint. 2
Act 19:38 If . . the craftsmen . . have a complaint against 3
Col 3:13 if one has a complaint against another 4

complaint *See also* bring, give, ground, make.

complete 1. בצע 2. כָּלָה 3. כלה 4. מלא 5. שלם 6. שָׁלֵם 7. *ἀνταναπληρόω* 8. *ἀπαρτισμός* 9. *ἄρτιος* 10. *ἐπὶ πέρας ἄγω* 11. *ἐπιτελέω* 12. *κατανύω* 13. *οἰκοδομέω* 14. *ὁλόκληρος* 15. *πᾶς* 16. *πληρόω* 17. *συντέλεια* 18. *συντελέω* 19. *τελειόω* 20. *τελέω* 21. compleo 22. finio 23. impleo 24. suppleo

Gen 15:16 iniquity of the Amorites is not yet complete. 6
29:21 may go in to her, for my time is completed. 4
27 Complete the week of this one 4
28 Jacob did so, and completed her week; 4
Exd 5:13 Complete your work, your daily task 3
Lev 8:33 until the days of your ordination are completed 4
12: 4 until the days of her purifying are completed 4
6 when the days of her purifying are completed 4
Num 6: 5 until the time is completed 4
13 time of his separation has been completed 4
1Ch 11: 8 round about from the Millo in complete circuit; *
2Ch 8:16 So the house of the LORD was completed. 6
12:12 so as not to make a complete destruction; 2
Est 1: 5 And when these days were completed, 4
Job 23:14 For he will complete what he appoints for me; 5
36:11 they complete their days in prosperity 3
Jer 25:12 Then after 70 years are completed 4
29:10 When 70 years are completed for Babylon 4
Ezk 4: 6 when you have completed these, you shall lie down 3
8 till you have completed the days of your siege. 3
5: 2 when the days of the siege are completed; 4
43:27 when they have completed these days 3
Zec 4: 9 his hands shall also complete it. 1
Lke 14:28 whether he has enough to complete it? 8
Act 21:27 When the seven days were almost completed 18
Rom 15:28 When therefore I have completed this 11
2Co 8: 6 also complete among you this gracious work. 11
10 it is best for you now to complete *
11 matched by your completing it 11
10: 6 when your obedience is complete. 16
Php 2: 2 complete my joy by being of the same mind 16
Col 1:24 in my flesh I complete what is lacking 7
2Ti 3:17 that the man of God may be complete 9
Jas 1: 4 that you may be perfect and complete 14
2:22 and faith was completed by works 19
1Jn 1: 4 we are writing this that our joy may be complete. 16
2Jn 1:12 so that our joy may be complete. 16
Rev 6:11 until the number . . should be complete 16
1Es 4:51 until it was completed 13
6:10 being completed with all splendor and care. 18
7: 4 they completed it by the command of the Lord God 18
2Es 3:23 the times passed and the years were completed 22
4:36 When the number . . is completed 23
40 when her nine months have been completed 23
6:19 and when the humiliation of Zion is complete 24
35 in order to complete the three weeks 24
11:44 behold, they are ended, and his ages are completed! 21
Tob 14: 5 until the times of the age are completed. 16
Wis 15: 3 For to know thee is complete righteousness 14
Sir 0: 3 in order to complete and publish the book 10
7:32 so that your blessing may be complete. 19
26: 2 he will complete his years in peace. 16
37:11 about completing his work 17
38:28 he is careful to complete its decoration. 17
50:19 so they completed his service. 19
1Mc 3:49 the Nazirites who had completed their days; 16
13:10 hastened to complete the walls of Jerusalem 20
2Mc 4:23 to complete the records of essential business. 20
9: 4 until he completed the journey 12
15: 1 to attack them with complete safety 15
3Mc 5:27 this had been so zealously completed for him. 20
4Mc 4:19 in complete violation of the law 15

such complete 1. *ὁλόκληρος*

4Mc 15:17 who alone gave birth to such complete devotion! 1

completely 1. כֹּל 2. *διὰ τέλους* 3. *δουλεία* 4. *εἰς τέλος* 5. *ἐπὶ τέλος* 6. *καθ' ἅπαν* 7. *κατὰ πᾶν* 8. *μέγας* 9. *ὅλος* 10. *ὁλοσχερῶς* 11. *παντελῶς* 12. *πάντοθεν*

Exd 11: 1 he will drive you away completely. †
Prv 28: 5 who seek the LORD understand it completely. 1
1Es 6:28 I command that it be built completely 10
Jdt 14:13 in order to be destroyed completely. 4
AEs 13: 7 leave our government completely secure 2
1Mc 8:18 was completely enslaving Israel. 3
2Mc 4:16 wished to imitate completely 6
14:46 with his blood now completely drained from him 11
3Mc 5: 1 the king, completely inflexible 7
12 completely frustrated in his inflexible plan. 8
19 he had carried out completely the order given him 5
27 completely overcome by incomprehension 7
4Mc 9:20 The wheel was completely smeared with blood 12
11:10 he was completely curled back like a scorpion 9

completeness 1. *τελειότης*

Wis 12:17 when men doubt the completeness of thy power 1

completion 1. *ἐπιτελέω* 2. *συμπλήρωσις* 3. *συντέλεια* 4. *τελείωσις* 5. *τέλεος*

1Es 1:58 until the completion of 70 years. 2
5:73 they prevented the completion of the building 1
6:20 it has not yet reached completion.' 3
2Mc 2: 9 the dedication and completion of the temple. 4
3Mc 1:22 would not tolerate the completion of his plans 5

completion *See also* bring.

complex 1. *πολύπλοκος*

4Mc 14:13 how complex is a mother's love for her children 1

most complex 1. *πολυτρόπος*

4Mc 1:25 which is the most complex of all the emotions. 1

complimentary 1. *ἔνδοξος*

Prv 25:27 so be sparing of complimentary words. 1

comply 1. *ὑπηρετέω*

Wis 19: 6 complying with thy commands 1

compose 1. *ἐκζητέω* 2. *συγκεράννυμι*

1Co 12:24 God has so composed the body 2
Sir 44: 5 those who composed musical tunes 1

composition 1. מַתְכֹּנֶת

Exd 30:32 you shall make no other like it in composition; 1
37 you shall make according to its composition 1

compound 1. רקח 2. *μεῖγμα*

Exd 30:33 Whoever compounds any like it or whoever puts 1
Sir 38: 8 the pharmacist makes of them a compound 2

comprehend 1. בין 2. ידע 3. שמע 4. *γινώσκω* 5. *καταλαμβάνω* 6. *κατανοέω* 7. *μεταλαμβάνω* 8. capio 9. conprehendo

Job 37: 5 great things which we cannot comprehend. 2
38:18 Have you comprehended the expanse of the earth? 1
Isa 33:19 obscure speech which you cannot comprehend 3
1Co 2:11 So also no one comprehends the thoughts of God 4
Eph 3:18 may have power to comprehend with all the saints 5
2Es 3:31 shown to any one how thy way may be comprehended. ‡
4: 2 do you think you can comprehend . . the Most High? 9
11 can your mind comprehend the way of the Most High? 8
12:38 are able to comprehend and keep these secrets. 8
Jdt 8:14 and find out his mind or comprehend his thought 6
3Mc 3: 1 When the impious king comprehended this situation 7

comprehension 1. *σύνεσις*

Sir 1:19 knowledge and discerning comprehension 1

beyond comprehension 1. inconprehensibilis

2Es 8:21 and whose glory is beyond comprehension 1

most comprehensive 1. *περιεκτικός*

4Mc 1:20 The two most comprehensive types 1

compress 1. קרץ

Prv 16:30 he who compresses his lips brings evil to pass. 1

compulsion 1. *ἀναγκάζω* 2. *ἀνάγκη*

2Co 9: 7 not reluctantly or under compulsion 2
Phm 1:14 your goodness might not be by compulsion 2
Bel 1:30 under compulsion he handed Daniel over to them. 1
4Mc 5:13 any transgression that arises out of compulsion. 2
16 there is no compulsion more powerful 2
8:14 when you transgress under compulsion. 2
22 for fearing the king when we are under compulsion. 2
24 Let us not struggle against compulsion 2

compute 1. חשב

Lev 27:18 then the priest shall compute the money-value 1
23 then the priest shall compute the valuation 1

comrade 1. רֵעַ 2. *ἑταῖρος* 3. *μέτοχος*

Jdg 7:13 man was telling a dream to his comrade; and he said 1
14 his comrade answered, "This is no other 1
Heb 1: 9 the oil of gladness beyond thy comrades. 3
3Mc 2:25 abetted by . . drinking companions and comrades 2

conceal 1. חבה 2. כחד 3. כסה 4. סתר 5. צפן 6. *ἐν ἀποκρύφοις* 7. *κρυπτός* 8. *κρύπτω* 9. *παρακαλύπτω* 10. abscondo

Gen 37:26 if we slay our brother and conceal his blood? 3
Deu 13: 8 nor shall you spare him, nor shall you conceal him; 3
Job 14:13 that thou wouldest conceal me 4
27:11 what is with the Almighty I will not conceal. 2
28:21 concealed from the birds of the air. 4
31:33 if I have concealed my transgressions from men 3
Ps 27: 5 he will conceal me under the cover of his tent 4
40:10 I have not concealed thy steadfast love 2
Prv 10: 6 but the mouth of the wicked conceals violence. 3
11 but the mouth of the wicked conceals violence. 3
18 He who conceals hatred has lying lips 3
12:23 A prudent man conceals his knowledge 3
25: 2 It is the glory of God to conceal things 4
28:13 conceals his transgressions will not prosper 3
Jer 16:17 nor is their iniquity concealed from my eyes. 5
49:10 he is not able to conceal himself. 1
50: 2 set up a banner and proclaim, conceal it not 2
Lke 9:45 it was concealed from them 9
2Es 2: 8 Woe to you, Assyria, who conceal the unrighteous 10
Tob 12:11 I will not conceal anything from you 8
Sir 11: 4 his works are concealed from men. 7
16:21 so most of his works are concealed. 6

concede 1. *συνομολογέω*

4Mc 13: 1 everyone must concede 1

conceit 1. לֵב 2. *ἑαυτοῦ* 3. *κενοδοξία* 4. *τῦφος* 5. *φυσίωσις*

Job 37:24 not regard any who are wise in their own conceit. 1
Rom 11:25 Lest you be wise in your own conceits 2
2Co 12:20 anger, selfishness, slander, gossip, conceit 5
Php 2: 3 Do nothing from selfishness or conceit 3
3Mc 3:18 they were carried away by their traditional conceit 4

conceit *See also* puff, swell.

conceited 1. *φρόνιμος παρ' ἑαυτόν*

Rom 12:16 associate with the lowly; never be conceited. 1

conceive 1. הָרָה 2. הרה 3. זרע 4. חבל 5. חשב 6. יחם 7. *ἀναβαίνω* 8. *γεννάω* 9. *ἐν γαστρί ἔχω* 10. *ἐνθυμέομαι* 11. *καταβολὴ σπέρματος* 12. *κοίτην ἔχω* 13. *συλλαμβάνω*

Gen 4: 1 and she conceived and bore Cain, saying 2
17 Cain knew his wife, and she conceived 2
16: 4 he went in to Hagar, and she conceived; 2
4 and when she saw that she had conceived 2
5 and when she saw that she had conceived 2
21: 2 Sarah conceived, and bore Abraham a son 2
25:21 his prayer, and Rebekah his wife conceived. 2
29:32 Leah conceived and bore a son 2
33 She conceived again and bore a son 2
34 Again she conceived and bore a son, and said 2
35 she conceived again and bore a son, and said 2
30: 5 Bilhah conceived and bore Jacob a son. 2
7 Rachel's maid Bilhah conceived again 2
17 God hearkened to Leah, and she conceived and bore 2
19 Leah conceived again, and she bore Jacob a sixth 2
23 She conceived and bore a son, and said 2
38: 3 she conceived and bore a son 2
4 Again she conceived and bore a son 2
18 went in to her, and she conceived by him. 2
Exd 2: 2 The woman conceived and bore a son; 2
Lev 12: 2 Say to the people of Israel, If a woman conceives 3
Num 5:28 she shall be free and shall conceive children. 3
11:12 Did I conceive all this people? Did I bring them 2
Jdg 13: 3 have no children; but you shall conceive and bear 2
5 for lo, you shall conceive and bear a son. No razor 1
7 Behold, you shall conceive and bear a son; 1
1Sm 1:20 in due time Hannah conceived and bore a son 2
2:21 she conceived and bore three sons and two 2
2Sm 11: 5 And the woman conceived; and she sent and told 2
2Kg 4:17 the woman conceived, and she bore a son 2
1Ch 4:17 Bith'i-ah . . conceived and bore Miriam, Sham'mai 2
7:23 his wife, and she conceived and bore a son; 2
Job 3: 3 the night which said, 'A man-child is conceived.' 2
15:35 They conceive mischief and bring forth evil 2
Ps 7:14 Behold, the wicked man conceives evil 4
35:20 in the land they conceive words of deceit. 5
51: 5 in iniquity, and in sin did my mother conceive me. 6
Sng 3: 4 and into the chamber of her that conceived me. 2
8: 2 and into the chamber of her that conceived me. 13
Isa 7:14 a young woman shall conceive and bear a son 1
8: 3 the prophetess, and she conceived and bore a son. 2
33:11 You conceive chaff, you bring forth stubble; 2
59: 4 they conceive mischief and bring forth 2
13 conceiving and uttering from the heart lying 2
Hos 1: 3 Gomer . . and she conceived and bore him a son. 2
6 She conceived again and bore a daughter. 2
8 When she had weaned Not pitied, she conceived 2
2: 5 she that conceived them has acted shamefully. 2
Mat 1:20 for that which is conceived in her is of the Holy 8
23 Behold, a virgin shall conceive and bear a son 9
Lke 1:24 After these days his wife Elizabeth conceived 13
31 you will conceive in your womb and bear a son 13
36 Elizabeth in her old age has also conceived a son; 13
2:21 before he was conceived in the womb. 13
Rom 9:10 when Rebecca had conceived children by one man 12
1Co 2: 9 nor the heart of man conceived 7
Heb 11:11 By faith Sarah . . received power to conceive 11
Jas 1:15 desire when it has conceived gives birth to sin; 13
3Mc 1:10 and conceived a desire to enter the holy of holies. 10
25 the plan that he had conceived. 10

conceive an idea 1. οἴομαι
2Mc 9: 4 he conceived the idea of turning upon the Jews 1

cunningly conceive 1. חפשׂ
Ps 64: 6 We have thought out a cunningly conceived plot. 1

conception 1. הֵרָיוֹן
Rut 4:13 he went in to her, and the LORD gave her conception 1
Hos 9:11 no birth, no pregnancy, no conception! 1

concern 1. דָּבָר 2. חמל 3. ידע 4. ἀναστρέφω 5. ἀσχολέω 6. ἐκτενία 7. ἐνθυμόω 8. ἐπιλαμβάνω 9. μέλει 10. περί 11. προσέχω 12. φρονέω 13. φροντίζω 14. φροντίς 15. φροντιστέον 16. χρεία 17. cogito 18. de
Gen 39: 6 and having him he had no concern for anything 3
8 my master has no concern about anything 3
Num18: 7 for all that concerns the altar 1
Ezk 12:10 This oracle concerns the prince in Jerusalem 10
36:21 I had concern for my holy name 2
1Co 9: 9 Is it for oxen that God is concerned? 9
Php 4:10 now at length you have revived your concern 12
10 you were indeed concerned for me 12
Heb 2:16 surely it is not with angels that he is concerned 8
2Es 6:15 because the word concerns the end 18
16 that the speech concerns them 18
8:38 For indeed I will not concern myself 17
Wis 6:17 concern for instruction is love of her 14
15: 9 he is not concerned that he is destined to die 14
Sir 7:24 Be concerned for their chastity 11
8:13 be concerned as one who must pay. 13
11: 9 argue about a matter which does not concern you 16
39: 1 will be concerned with prophecies; 5
50:28 Blessed is he who concerns himself with these 4
Bar 3:31 No one . . is concerned about the path to her. 7
2Mc 2:29 must be concerned with the whole construction 15
14: 8 concerned for the interests of the king 12
15:18 Their concern for wives and children 10
3Mc 6:41 magnanimously expressing his concern 6

concerned by nature 1. φύω
4Mc 1:20 is by nature concerned with both body and soul. 1

where is concerned 1. ὑπέρ
4Mc 9:18 where virtue is concerned. 1

concerning 1. אֶל 2. בְּ 3. בֵּין לְ 4. לְ 5. עַל 6. עַל אֹדוֹת 7. עַל דְּבַר 8. בְּ (A) 9. עַל (A) 10. εἰς 11. ἐπί 12. περί 13. ὑπέρ 14. ab 15. de 16. in
Gen 12:20 Pharaoh gave men orders concerning him; 5
24: 9 swore to him concerning this matter. 5
42:21 In truth we are guilty concerning our brother 5
47:26 made it a statute concerning the land of Egypt 5
Exd 8:12 and Moses cried to the LORD concerning the frogs 7
25: 9 concerning the pattern of the tabernacle •
Num 8:20 LORD commanded Moses concerning the Levites 4
22 commanded Moses concerning the Levites 5
9: 8 hear what the LORD will command concerning you. 4
30:12 proceeds out of her lips concerning her vows 4
12 her vows, or concerning her pledge of herself 4
32:28 Moses gave command concerning them to Elea'zar 4
36: 6 commands concerning the daughters of Zeloph'ehad 4
Deu 26:17 declared this day concerning the LORD •
18 LORD has declared this day concerning you •
27: 4 stones, concerning which I command you this day •
Jos 14: 6 the LORD said to Moses . . concerning you and me. 6
23:14 which the LORD your God promised concerning you; 5
15 which the LORD . . has promised concerning you 1
Jdg 21: 5 a great oath concerning him who did not come up 4
Rut 4: 7 custom . . concerning redeeming and exchanging 5
1Sm 3:12 all that I have spoken concerning his house 1
12: 7 plead with you . . concerning all the saving •
25:30 all the good that he has spoken concerning you 5
2Sm 3: 8 you charge me . . with a fault concerning a woman. •
7:25 the word . . spoken concerning thy servant 5
25 thou hast spoken . . and concerning his house 5
10: 2 sent . . to console him concerning his father. 1
14: 8 Go . . and I will give orders concerning you. 5
1Kg 2: 4 establish his word which he spoke concerning me 5
27 word of the LORD . . concerning the house of Eli 5
6:12 Concerning this house . . if you will walk •
10: 1 fame of Solomon concerning the name of the LORD 4
11: 2 the nations concerning which the LORD had said •
10 had commanded him concerning this thing 5
14: 5 is coming to inquire of you concerning her son; 1
22: 8 he never prophesies good concerning me 5
18 that he would not prophesy good concerning me 5
23 the LORD has spoken evil concerning you. 5
2Kg 10:10 the LORD spoke concerning the house of Ahab; 5
19: 9 when the king heard concerning Tirha'kah king 1
21 the word that the LORD has spoken concerning him 5
32 says the LORD concerning the king of Assyria 1
22:13 Go, inquire . . concerning the words of this book 5
13 according to all that is written concerning us. 5
1Ch 11:10 the word of the LORD concerning Israel. 5
17:23 which thou hast spoken concerning thy servant 5
23 thou hast spoken . . and concerning his house 5
19: 2 to console him concerning his father. 5
5 When David was told concerning the men 5
22:11 as he has spoken concerning you. 5
27: 1 concerning the divisions that came and went •
28:19 writing from the hand of the LORD concerning it •
2Ch 8:15 king had commanded . . concerning any matter 4
15 had commanded concerning . . the treasuries. 4
9:29 concerning Jerobo'am the son of Nebat? 5
18: 7 never prophesies good concerning me, but always 5
17 would not prophesy good concerning me, but evil? 5
22 the LORD has spoken evil concerning you. 5
19:10 concerning bloodshed, law or commandment 3
23: 3 as the LORD spoke concerning the sons of David. 5
34:21 inquire . . concerning the words of the book 5
Ezr 5: 5 then answer be returned by letter concerning it. 9
6: 3 Concerning the house of God at Jerusalem •
Neh 1: 2 I asked them concerning the Jews that survived 5
2 I asked them . . concerning Jerusalem. 5
6: 7 set up prophets to proclaim concerning you 5
11:23 there was a command from the king concerning 5
24 all matters concerning the people. 4
13:14 Remember me, O my God, concerning this 5
Est 3: 2 for the king had so commanded concerning him. 4
8: 9 that Mor'decai commanded concerning the Jews 1
Job 27:11 I will teach you concerning the hand of God; 2
35: 8 Your wickedness concerns a man like yourself 4
36:33 Its crashing declares concerning him 5
41:12 I will not keep silence concerning his limbs •
Ps 7: 0 sang to the LORD concerning Cush a Benjaminite. 7
71:10 For my enemies speak concerning me 4
Isa 1: 1 which he saw concerning Judah and Jerusalem 5
2: 1 Isaiah . . saw concerning Judah and Jerusalem. 5
5: 1 my beloved a love song concerning his vineyard 4
13: 1 The oracle concerning Babylon which Isaiah •
14:26 purpose . . purposed concerning the whole earth; 5
15: 1 An oracle concerning Moab. •
16:13 the LORD spoke concerning Moab in the past. 1
17: 1 An oracle concerning Damascus. •
19: 1 An oracle concerning Egypt. •
21: 1 oracle concerning the wilderness of the sea. •
11 The oracle concerning Dumah. •
13 The oracle concerning Arabia. 2
22: 1 The oracle concerning the valley of vision. •
23: 1 The oracle concerning Tyre. •
11 the LORD has given command concerning Canaan 1
29:22 says the LORD . . concerning the house of Jacob 1
32: 6 to utter error concerning the LORD 1
37: 9 heard concerning Tirha'kah king of Ethiopia 5
21 you have prayed to me concerning Sennach'erib 1
22 the word that the LORD has spoken concerning him 5
33 says the LORD concerning the king of Assyria 1
45:11 or command me concerning the work of my hands? 5
Jer 7:22 command them concerning burnt offerings 7
11:21 says the LORD concerning the men of An'athoth 5
12:14 says the LORD concerning all my evil neighbors 5
14: 1 which came to Jeremiah concerning the drought 5
10 Thus says the LORD concerning this people 4
15 concerning the prophets who prophesy in my name 5
16: 3 For thus says the LORD concerning the sons 5
3 and concerning the mothers who bore them 5
18: 7 If at any time I declare concerning a nation 5
8 if that nation, concerning which I have spoken 5
9 And if at any time I declare concerning a nation 5
22: 6 For thus says the LORD concerning the house 5
11 For thus says the LORD concerning Shallum 1
18 thus says the LORD concerning Jehoi'akim 1
23: 2 concerning the shepherds who care for my people 5
9 Concerning the prophets: My heart is broken 4
15 the LORD of hosts concerning the prophets 5
25: 1 to Jeremiah concerning all the people of Judah 5
27:13 as the LORD has spoken concerning any nation 1
19 concerning the pillars, the sea, the stands 1
21 concerning the vessels which are left 5
29:16 Thus says the LORD concerning the king 1
16 concerning all the people who dwell in this city 1
21 concerning Ahab the son of Kola'iah and Zedeki'ah 1
31 says the LORD concerning Shemai'ah of Nehel'am 1
30: 4 the LORD spoke concerning Israel and Judah 1
32:36 concerning this city of which you say, 'It is given 1
33: 4 concerning the houses of this city 5
34: 4 O Zedeki'ah . . ! Thus says the LORD concerning you 5
36:29 And concerning Jehoi'akim king of Judah 5
30 the LORD concerning Jehoi'akim king of Judah 5
39:11 Babylon gave command concerning Jeremiah 5
44: 1 that came to Jeremiah concerning all the Jews 1
46: 1 Jeremiah the prophet concerning the nations. 5
2 Concerning the army of Pharaoh Neco 5
47: 1 to . . the prophet concerning the Philistines 1
48: 1 Concerning Moab. Thus says the LORD of hosts 4
49: 1 Concerning the Ammonites. Thus says the LORD 4
7 Concerning Edom. Thus says the LORD of hosts 4
23 Concerning Damascus. 4
28 Concerning Kedar and the kingdoms of Hazor 4
34 came to Jeremiah the prophet concerning Elam 1
50: 1 word which the LORD spoke concerning Babylon 1
1 concerning the land of the Chalde'ans 1
51:11 his purpose concerning Babylon is to destroy it 5
12 done what he spoke concerning the inhabitants 1
60 words that are written concerning Babylon. 1
62 say, 'O LORD, thou hast said concerning this place 1
Ezk 12:19 says the Lord GOD concerning the inhabitants 4
13:16 who prophesied concerning Jerusalem and saw 1
18: 2 this proverb concerning the land of Israel 5
21:28 Thus says the Lord GOD concerning the Ammonites 1
28 the Ammonites, and concerning their reproach; 1
26: 2 because Tyre said concerning Jerusalem 5
36: 6 prophesy concerning the land of Israel, 5
44: 5 I shall tell you concerning all the ordinances 4
12 I have sworn concerning them, says the Lord GOD 5
Dan 1:20 matter . . concerning which the king inquired •
2:18 mercy of the God . . concerning this mystery 9
5:29 proclamation was made concerning him, 9
6:12 said before the king, concerning the interdict 9
17 nothing might be changed concerning Daniel. 8
7:16 asked him the truth concerning all this. 9
19 know the truth concerning the fourth beast 9
20 concerning the ten horns that were on its head 9
8:13 concerning the continual burnt offering •
9:24 concerning your people and your holy city 5
Ams 1: 1 words of Amos . . which he saw concerning Israel 5
7: 3 The LORD repented concerning this; 5
6 The LORD repented concerning this; 5
Obd 1: 1 Thus says the Lord GOD concerning Edom 4
Mic 1: 1 to Micah . . which he saw concerning Sama'ria 5
3: 5 concerning the prophets who lead my people 5
Nah 1: 1 An oracle concerning Nin'eveh. •
Hab 2: 1 and what I will answer concerning my complaint. 5
Zec 12: 1 An Oracle The word of the LORD concerning Israel 5
Mat 11: 7 began to speak to the crowds concerning John 12
Mrk 4:10 asked him concerning the parables. 12
Lke 1: 4 the truth concerning the things 12
2:17 which had been told them concerning this child; 12
3:15 all men questioned in their hearts concerning John 12
4:14 and a report concerning him went out 12
5:15 the report went abroad concerning him 12
7:17 this report concerning him spread 12
24 he began to speak to the crowds concerning John 12
24:19 they said to him, "Concerning Jesus of Nazareth 12
27 the things concerning himself. 12
Joh 11:19 to console them concerning their brother. 12
16: 8 concerning sin and righteousness and judgment 12
9 concerning sin, because they do not believe in me; 12
10 concerning righteousness 12
11 concerning judgment 12
Act 1:16 concerning Judas who was guide 12
2:25 David says concerning him, 'I saw the Lord 10
4: 9 concerning a good deed done to a cripple 11
18:25 and taught accurately the things concerning Jesus 12
19:23 there arose no little stir concerning the Way. 12
25:16 concerning the charge laid against him. 12
Rom 1: 3 the gospel concerning his Son 12
4:20 made him waver concerning the promise of God 10
7: 2 is discharged from the law concerning the husband •
9:27 And Isaiah cries out concerning Israel 13
1Co 7: 1 concerning the matters about which you wrote. 12
25 Now concerning the unmarried, I have no command 12
8: 1 Now concerning food offered to idols 12
12: 1 Now concerning spiritual gifts, brethren 12
16: 1 Now concerning the contribution for the saints 12
Col 4:10 concerning whom you have . . instructions 12
1Th 1: 9 report concerning us what a welcome we had 12
4: 9 But concerning love of the brethren 12
13 concerning those who are asleep 12
2Th 2: 1 concerning the coming of our Lord Jesus Christ 13
Heb 7:16 a legal requirement concerning bodily descent •
11: 7 being warned by God concerning events as yet unseen 12
22 gave directions concerning his burial. 12
1Jn 1: 1 concerning the word of life- 12
1Es 1:24 concerning those who sinned and acted wickedly 12
4:54 He wrote also concerning their support •
6: 6 word could be sent to Darius concerning them 12
22 send us directions concerning these things. 12
7:15 the will of the king . . concerning them 11
2Es 4: 6 that you ask me concerning these things? 15
52 Concerning the signs about which you ask me 15
52 I was not sent to tell you concerning your life 15
5: 1 Now concerning the signs 15
39 and how can I speak concerning the things 15
6:34 vain thoughts concerning the former times 16
34 lest you be hasty concerning the last times.' 14
7:78 Now, concerning death, the teaching is 15
90 Therefore this is the teaching concerning them 15
94 the witness which he . . bears concerning them •
8:51 inquire concerning the glory of those 15
15: 8 be silent . . concerning their ungodly deeds 15
AEs 10: 5 the dream that I had concerning these matters 12
12: 2 he informed the king concerning them. 12
Sir 17:14 gave commandment . . concerning his neighbor. 12
23: 7 Listen . . to instruction concerning speech •
Sus 1: 5 Concerning them the Lord had said 12
1Mc 8:15 constantly deliberate concerning the people 12
31 concerning the wrongs 12
9:55 or give commands concerning his house. 12
11:31 the letter which we wrote concerning you 12
12:17 concerning the renewal of our brotherhood. 12
21 found in writing concerning the Spartans 12
22 please write us concerning your welfare; 12
2Mc 8:12 Word came . . concerning Nicanor's invasion 12

11:20 concerning these matters and their details 13
4Mc 5:10 by holding a vain opinion concerning the truth 12
29 concerning the keeping of the law 12

concerning whom 1. אֲשֶׁר
2Kg 17:15 nations . . concerning whom the LORD 1

concert 1. σύγκριμα
Sir 32: 5 a concert of music at a banquet of wine. 1

concerted 1. συνάγω
3Mc 1:28 The continuous, vehement, and concerted cry 1

concession 1. συγγνώμη 2. φιλάνθρωπος
1Co 7: 6 I say this by way of concession, not of command. 1
2Mc 4:11 the existing royal concessions to the Jews 2

conciliate 1. παρακαλέω
1Co 4:13 when slandered, we try to conciliate 1

concisely 1. κεφαλαιόω
Sir 32: 8 Speak concisely, say much in few words 1

conclude 1. λογίζομαι 2. νοέω 3. περανθέντος, 4. συμβιβάζω 5. concludo
Act 16:10 concluding that God had called us 4
2Es 2:40 conclude the list of your people 5
1Mc 6: 9 he concluded that he was dying. 1
2Mc 14:30 Maccabeus . . concluded that . . 2
3Mc 4:11 the voyage was concluded as the king had decreed 3

conclusion 1. τέλος
3Mc 1:26 to bring the aforesaid plan to a conclusion. 1
3:14 it was brought to conclusion, according to plan 1

concord 1. συμφωνία
4Mc 14: 3 O sacred and harmonious concord 1

concubine 1. אִשָּׁה פִּלֶגֶשׁ 2. פִּלֶגֶשׁ 3. לְחֵנָה (A) 4. παλλακή
Gen 22:24 Moreover, his concubine, whose name was Reumah 2
25: 6 to the sons of his concubines Abraham gave gifts 2
35:22 Bilhah his father's concubine; and Israel heard 2
36:12 (Timna was a concubine of El'iphaz, Esau's son; 2
Jdg 8:31 his concubine who was in Shechem also bore him 2
19: 1 who took to himself a concubine from Bethlehem 1
2 his concubine became angry with him, and she went 2
9 the man and his concubine and his servant rose up 2
10 saddled asses, and his concubine was with him. 2
24 here are my virgin daughter and his concubine; 2
25 man seized his concubine, and put her out to them; 2
27 there was his concubine lying at the door 2
29 and laying hold of his concubine he divided her 2
20: 4 I came . . I and my concubine, to spend the night. 2
5 meant to kill me, and they ravished my concubine 2
6 I took my concubine and cut her in pieces, and sent 2
2Sm 3: 7 Now Saul had a concubine, whose name was Rizpah 2
7 Why have you gone in to my father's concubine? 2
5:13 David took more concubines and wives 2
15:16 the king left ten concubines to keep the house. 1
16:21 Go in to your father's concubines, whom he has left 2
22 and Ab'salom went in to his father's concubines 2
19: 5 and the lives of your wives and your concubines 2
20: 3 the king took the ten concubines whom he had left 1
21:11 Rizpah . . daughter of Ai'ah, the concubine of Saul 2
1Kg 11: 3 He had 700 wives . . and 300 concubines; 2
1Ch 1:32 The sons of Ketu'rah, Abraham's concubine 2
2:46 Ephah also, Caleb's concubine, bore Haran, Moza 2
48 Ma'acah, Caleb's concubine, bore Sheber 2
3: 9 besides the sons of the concubines; 2
7:14 As'ri-el, whom his Aramean concubine bore; 2
2Ch 11:21 above all his wives and concubines 2
21 (he took eighteen wives and 60 concubines 2
Est 2:14 Sha-ash'gaz . . who was in charge of the concubines; 2
Ecc 2: 8 I got . . and many concubines, man's delight. •
Sng 6: 8 There are 60 queens and 80 concubines 2
9 the queens and concubines also, and they praised 2
Dan 5: 2 king and his lords, his wives, and his concubines 3
3 king and his lords, his wives, and his concubines 3
23 lords, your wives, and your concubines have drunk 3
1Es 4:29 Apame, the king's concubine 4
2Mc 4:30 Antiochis, the king's concubine. 4

condemn 1. אשׁם 2. רשׁע 3. שׁפט 4. καταγινώσκω 5. καταδικάζω 6. κατακρίνω 7. κατάκρισις 8. κρίμα 9. κρίνω 10. condemno 11. vinco
Exd 22: 9 he whom God shall condemn shall pay double 2
Deu 25: 1 innocent and condemning the guilty 2
1Kg 8:32 judge thy servants, condemning the guilty 2
Job 9:20 I am innocent, my own mouth would condemn me; 2
29 I shall be condemned; why then do I labor in vain? 2
10: 2 I will say to God, Do not condemn me; 2
15: 6 Your own mouth condemns you, and not I; 2
34:17 Will you condemn him who is righteous and mighty 2
29 When he is quiet, who can condemn? 2
40: 8 Will you condemn me that you may be justified? 2
Ps 34:21 those who hate the righteous will be condemned. 1
22 none . . who take refuge in him will be condemned. 1
37:33 let him be condemned when he is brought to trial. 2
94:21 condemn the innocent to death. 2
109:31 to save him from those who condemn him to death. †
141: 6 given over to those who shall condemn them 3
Prv 12: 2 but a man of evil devices he condemns. 2
17:15 justifies . . and he who condemns the righteous 2
Mat 12: 7 you would not have condemned the guiltless. 5
37 and by your words you will be condemned. 5
41 and condemn it 6
42 and condemn it 6
20:18 and they will condemn him to death 6
27: 3 Judas, his betrayer, saw that he was condemned 6
Mrk 10:33 they will condemn him to death 6
14:64 they all condemned him as deserving death. 6
16:16 he who does not believe will be condemned. 6
Lke 6:37 condemn not, and you will not be condemned 5
37 condemn not, and you will not be condemned 5
11:31 arise . . and condemn them 6
32 arise . . and condemn it 6
19:22 I will condemn you out of your own mouth 9
24:20 condemned to death, and crucified him. 8
Joh 3:17 God sent the Son . . not to condemn the world 9
18 He who believes in him is not condemned; 9
18 he who does not believe is condemned already 9
8:10 Woman, where are they? Has no one condemned you? 6
11 Jesus said, "Neither do I condemn you 6
Act 13:27 fulfilled these by condemning him. 9
Rom 2: 1 in passing judgment . . you condemn yourself 6
27 will condemn you who have the written code 9
3: 7 why am I still being condemned as a sinner? 9
8: 3 he condemned sin in the flesh 6
34 who is to condemn? Is it Christ Jesus, who died, yes 6
14:23 But he who has doubts is condemned, if he eats 6
1Co 11:32 we are chastened so that we may not be condemned 6
34 lest you come together to be condemned 8
2Co 7: 3 I do not say this to condemn you 7
Gal 2:11 because he stood condemned. 4
2Th 2:12 may be condemned who did not believe the truth 9
Heb 11: 7 by this he condemned the world 6
Jas 5: 6 You have condemned . . the righteous man 5
2Pe 2: 6 he condemned them to extinction 6
1Jn 3:20 whenever our hearts condemn us; 4
21 Beloved, if our hearts do not condemn us 4
2Es 4:18 and which to condemn? 10
7:115 him who has been condemned in the judgment 11
Wis 2:20 Let us condemn him to a shameful death 5
4:16 will condemn the ungodly who are living 6
16 youth . . will condemn the prolonged old age •
12:15 condemn him who does not deserve to be punished. 5
17:11 condemned by its own testimony 5
Sir 14: 2 Blessed is he whose heart does not condemn him 4
19: 5 who rejoices in wickedness will be condemned 4
Sus 1:41 and they condemned her to death. 6
48 Have you condemned a daughter of Israel 6
53 condemning the innocent 6
Man 1:13 do not condemn me to the depths of the earth 5

condemn to death 1. θανατόω
1Mc 1:57 the decree of the king condemned him to death. 1

condemnation 1. שְׁפָט 2. κατάγνωσις 3. καταδικάζω 4. καταδίκη 5. κατάκριμα 6. κατάκρισις 7. κρίμα 8. κρίσις
Prv 19:29 Condemnation is ready for scoffers 1
Mrk 12:40 They will receive the greater condemnation. 7
Lke 20:47 They will receive the greater condemnation. 7
Rom 3: 8 Their condemnation is just. 7
5:16 following one trespass brought condemnation 5
18 one man's trespass led to condemnation for all 5
8: 1 no condemnation for those who are in Christ 5
2Co 3: 9 splendor in the dispensation of condemnation 6
1Ti 3: 6 fall into the condemnation of the devil; 7
5:12 so they incur condemnation 7
Jas 5:12 that you may not fall under condemnation. 8
2Pe 2: 3 from of old their condemnation has not been idle 7
Jde 1: 4 were designated for this condemnation 7
Wis 11:10 as a stern king does in condemnation. 3
12:27 the utmost condemnation came upon them. 4
Sir 5:14 severe condemnation to the double-tongued. 2
condemnation *See also* sentence.

condensation 1. ἐπιτομή
2Mc 2:28 arriving at the outlines of the condensation. 1

condense 1. ἐπιτέμνω
2Mc 2:23 we shall attempt to condense into a single book. 1

condition 1. דָּבָר 2. חֹק 3. פָּנִים 4. ἐπί 5. καιρός 6. κατά 7. σάρξ 8. τρόπος
Gen 34:15 Only on this condition will we consent to you •
22 Only on this condition will the men agree •
Exd 2:25 people of Israel, and God knew their condition. •
1Sm 11: 2 On this condition I will make a treaty with you •
2Ch 12:12 moreover, conditions were good in Judah. 1
Prv 27:23 Know well the condition of your flocks 3
Jer 32:11 containing the terms and conditions 2
Dan 1:10 poorer condition than the youths . . of your own age. 3
Gal 4:14 though my condition was a trial to you 7
Sir 18:26 From morning to evening conditions change 5
1Mc 6:61 On these conditions the Jews evacuated 4
2Mc 9:22 I do not despair of my condition 6
4Mc 11:11 In this condition, gasping for breath 8

proper condition 1. מַתְכֹּנֶת
2Ch 24:13 house of God to its proper condition 1

condole 1. נוּד
Job 2:11 to come to condole with him and comfort him. 1
Isa 51:19 befallen you-who will condole with you? 1

conduct 1. דָּבָר 2. דֶּרֶךְ 3. הלך 4. כּוּל 5. פֹּעַל 6. רכב 7. ἄγω 8. ἀγωγή 9. ἀναστρέφω 10. ἀναστροφή 11. ἀντίληψις 12. γίνομαι 13. ἑαυτοῦ 14. ἔργον 15. καθίστημι 16. ὁδός 17. περιπατέω 18. ποιέω 19. ποίησις νόμου 20. πολιτεύω 21. via
Deu 22:14 charges her with shameful conduct, and brings 1
1Kg 8:32 by bringing his conduct upon his own head 2
2Ch 6:23 requiting the guilty by bringing his conduct 2
Est 6: 9 and let him conduct the man on horseback 6
Ps 112: 5 who conducts his affairs with justice. 4
Prv 21: 8 but the conduct of the pure is right. 5
Ecc 6: 8 knows how to conduct himself before the living? 3
Ezk 36:17 their conduct before me was like the uncleanness 2
19 with their conduct and their deeds I judged them. 2
Act 17:15 who conducted Paul brought him as far as Athens; 15
Rom 1:28 to a base mind and to improper conduct. 18
13: 3 For rulers are not a terror to good conduct 14
13 conduct ourselves becomingly as in the day 17
Col 4: 5 Conduct yourselves wisely toward outsiders 17
2Th 3: 9 to give you in our conduct an example to imitate. 13
1Ti 4:12 an example in speech and conduct, in love, in faith 10
2Ti 3:10 Now you have observed my teaching, my conduct 8
1Pe 1:15 be holy yourselves in all your conduct; 10
17 conduct yourselves with fear 9
2:12 Maintain good conduct among the Gentiles 10
2Es 10:39 For he has seen your righteous conduct 21
Tob 4:14 be disciplined in all your conduct. 10
Sir 11:26 to reward a man . . according to his conduct. 16
51:19 in my conduct I was strict 19
1Mc 9:37 are conducting the bride 7
2Mc 11:26 and go on happily in the conduct of their own affairs. 11
3Mc 3: 4 and conducted themselves by his law 20
4:15 The registration . . was therefore conducted 12

conduct business 1. negotior
2Es 16:47 Those who conduct business 1

good conduct 1. εὐταξία
2Mc 4:37 the moderation and good conduct of the deceased; 1

safe conduct 1. μετ' εἰρήνης
1Mc 12: 4 to provide for the envoys safe conduct 1

wise conduct 1. חָכְמָה
Prv 10:23 but wise conduct is pleasure to a man 1

conduit 1. תְּעָלָה
2Kg 18:17 came and stood by the conduit of the upper pool 1
20:20 how he made the pool and the conduit and brought 1
Isa 7: 3 at the end of the conduit of the upper pool 1
36: 2 And he stood by the conduit of the upper pool 1

confederate 1. אִישׁ שָׁלוֹם
Obd 1: 7 your confederates have prevailed against you; 1

confer 1. היה דָּבָר 2. διαλέγω 3. ἐπιτίθημι 4. κοινολογέομαι 5. προσανατίθημι 6. συλλαλέω 7. συμβάλλω
2Sm 3:17 Abner conferred with the elders of Israel 1
1Kg 1: 7 He conferred with Jo'ab . . and with Abi'athar 1
Lke 22: 4 and conferred with the chief priests and officers 6
Act 4:15 they conferred with one another 7
25:12 when he had conferred with his council 6
Gal 1:16 I did not confer with flesh and blood 5
Sir 10: 5 confers his honor upon the person of the scribe. 3
1Mc 15:28 He sent . . Athenobius . . to confer with him, saying 4
2Mc 11:20 I have ordered . . to confer with you. 2

confer upon 1. ἐπιτρέπω
4Mc 4:17 if the office were conferred upon him 1

conference 1. κοινολογία 2. συμμίσγω
1Mc 11:22 to meet him for a conference at Ptolemais 2
2Mc 14:22 they held the proper conference. 1

confess 1. זכר 2. ידה 3. נגד 4. ספר 5. ἐξομολογέω 6. ὁμολογέω 7. ὁμολογουμένως 8. confiteor
Lev 5: 5 he shall confess the sin he has committed 2
16:21 confess over him all the iniquities of the people 2
26:40 if they confess their iniquity 2
Num 5: 7 he shall confess his sin which he has committed; 2
Neh 1: 6 confessing the sins of the people of Israel 2
9: 2 stood and confessed their sins 2
Ps 32: 5 I will confess my transgressions to the LORD"; 2
38:18 I confess my iniquity, I am sorry for my sin. 3

Prv 28:13 confesses and forsakes them will obtain mercy. 2
Isa 48: 1 and confess the God of Israel, but not in truth 1
Ezk 12:16 that they may confess all their abominations 4
Dan 9:20 confessing my sin and the sin of my people Israel 2
Mat 3: 6 in the river Jordan, confessing their sins. 5
Mrk 1: 5 confessing their sins. 5
Joh 1:20 He confessed, he did not deny, but confessed 6
20 He confessed, he did not deny, but confessed 6
9:22 if any one should confess him to be Christ 6
12:42 for fear of the Pharisees they did not confess it 6
Act 19:18 confessing and divulging their practices. 5
Rom 10: 9 if you confess with your lips that Jesus is Lord 6
10 and he confesses with his lips and so is saved. 6
Php 2:11 every tongue confess that Jesus Christ is Lord 5
1Ti 3:16 Great indeed, we confess, is the mystery 7
Jas 5:16 Therefore confess your sins to one another 5
1Jn 1: 9 If we confess our sins, he is faithful and just 6
2:23 He who confesses the Son has the Father also. 6
4: 2 every spirit which confesses that Jesus Christ 6
3 every spirit which does not confess Jesus 6
15 Whoever confesses that Jesus is the Son of God 6
Rev 3: 5 I will confess his name before my Father 6
2Es 2:45 and they have confessed the name of God 8
47 whom they confessed in the world 8
Tob 12:22 confessed the great and wonderful works of God 5
AEs 12: 3 when they confessed they were led to execution. 6
Sir 4:26 Do not be ashamed to confess your sins 6
Sus 1:14 they confessed their lust. 6
2Mc 6: 6 nor so much as confess himself to be a Jew. 6
4Mc 13: 5 How then can one fail to confess 6

confess a fault 1. ἀνθομολογέω
Sir 20: 2 the one who confesses his fault 1

make confess 1. ἐξομολογέω
2Mc 7:37 to make you confess that he alone is God 1

confession 1. ὁμολογία
1Ti 6:12 you were called when you made the good confession 1
13 who . . before Pontius Pilate made the good confession 1
Heb 3: 1 the apostle and high priest of our confession. 1
4:14 let us hold fast our confession. 1
10:23 Let us hold fast the confession of our hope 1
1Es 9: 8 Now then make confession and give glory 1

confession *See also* make.

confidence 1. אמן 2. בטח 3. בִּטָּחוֹן 4. כֶּסֶל 5. כִּסְלָה 6. מִבְטָח 7. סוֹד 8. ἀσφάλεια 9. ἐλπίς 10. θαρρέω 11. παρρησία 12. πείθω 13. πεποίθησις 14. πίστις 15. πιστός 16. ὑπόστασις
2Kg 18:19 On what do you rest this confidence of yours? 3
Job 4: 6 Is not your fear of God your confidence 5
8:14 His confidence breaks in sunder 4
11:18 you will have confidence, because there is hope; 2
29:24 I smiled on them when they had no confidence; 1
31:24 gold my trust, or called fine gold my confidence; 6
Prv 3:26 for the LORD will be your confidence 4
32 but the upright are in his confidence. 7
14:26 In the fear of the LORD one has strong confidence 6
Isa 36: 4 On what do you rest this confidence of yours? 3
Jer 48:13 Israel was ashamed of Bethel, their confidence. 6
Mic 7: 5 have no confidence in a friend; 2
2Co 3: 4 Such is the confidence that we have 13
7: 4 I have great confidence in you 11
16 because I have perfect confidence in you. 10
8:22 because of his great confidence in you. 13
10: 2 not have to show boldness with such confidence 13
11:17 as a fool, in this boastful confidence; 16
Gal 5:10 I have confidence in the Lord 12
Eph 3:12 confidence of access through our faith in him. 13
2Th 3: 4 we have confidence in the Lord about you 12
1Ti 3:13 great confidence in the faith which is in Christ 11
Heb 3: 6 we are his house if we hold fast our confidence 11
14 if only we hold our first confidence firm 16
4:16 Let us then with confidence draw near 11
10:19 Therefore, brethren, since we have confidence 11
35 Therefore do not throw away your confidence 11
1Pe 1:21 Through him you have confidence in God 15
1Jn 2:28 so that when he appears we may have confidence 11
3:21 we have confidence before God; 11
4:17 we may have confidence for the day of judgment 11
5:14 this is the confidence which we have in him 11
Wis 5: 1 righteous man will stand with great confidence 11
Sir 27:16 Whoever betrays secrets destroys confidence 14
37:26 will inherit confidence 14
1Mc 9:58 his men are living in quiet and confidence 12
10:71 If you now have confidence in your forces 12
2Mc 15: 7 did not cease to trust with all confidence 9
11 confidence in shields and spears 8

confidence *See also* put, reason, take.

foolish confidence 1. כֶּסֶל
Ps 49:13 the fate of those who have foolish confidence 1

confident 1. בטח 2. ἄφοβος 3. πείθω 4. πίστις 5. ὑπόστασις 6. confido
Job 6:20 are disappointed because they were confident; 1
40:23 he is confident though Jordan rushes against 1
Ps 27: 3 war arise against me, yet I will be confident. 1
2Co 9: 4 for being so confident. 5
10: 7 If any one is confident that he is Christ's 3
Phm 1:21 Confident of your obedience, I write to you 3
2Es 7:98 and shall be confident without confusion 6
Jdt 2: 5 take with you men confident in their strength 3
Sir 5: 5 Do not be so confident of atonement 2
49:10 delivered them with confident hope. 4

confident *See also* make.

confidently 1. ἀδεής 2. ἐν πίστει 3. θαρρέω 4. μετὰ παρρησίας 5. μετὰ πίστεως
Act 2:29 I may say to you confidently of the patriarch 4
Heb 13: 6 Hence we can confidently say 3
Sir 41:16 not everything is confidently esteemed 2
3Mc 2:32 they confidently attempted to save themselves 1
5:44 they confidently posted the armed forces 5

confine 1. אסר 2. διακεῖμαι 3. κλείω 4. περιέχω 5. φρουρέω
Gen 39:20 place where the king's prisoners were confined 1
40: 3 in the prison where Joseph was confined. 1
5 who were confined in the prison–each his own 1
Gal 3:23 we were confined under the law 5
Sir 23:19 His fear is confined to the eyes of men •
Man 1: 3 who hast confined the deep 3
3Mc 4:10 they were confined under a solid deck 2
5: 7 they were forcibly confined on every side 4

remain confined 1. אסר
Gen 42:19 let one of your brothers remain confined 1

confirm 1. אמן 2. חזק 3. חצק 4. מלא 5. עמד 6. קום 7. βεβαίαν ποιέω 8. βεβαιόω 9. ἐπιστοποιέω 10. ἵστημι 11. πιστόω 12. στερεόω
Lev 26: 9 and will confirm my covenant with you 6
Deu 8:18 that he may confirm his covenant which he swore 6
9: 5 that he may confirm the word which the LORD swore 6
27:26 'Cursed be he who does not confirm the words 6
Rut 4: 7 to confirm a transaction, the one drew off his 6
2Sm 7:25 confirm for ever the word which thou hast spoken 6
1Kg 1:14 I also will come in after you and confirm 4
8:26 let thy word be confirmed, which thou hast spoken 1
2Kg 15:19 help him to confirm his hold of the royal power. 2
1Ch 16:17 which he confirmed as a statute to Jacob 5
17:14 confirm him in my house and in my kingdom for ever 5
2Ch 6:17 O LORD, God of Israel, let thy word be confirmed 1
Est 9:29 gave full . . confirming this second letter 6
Ps 105:10 which he confirmed to Jacob as a statute 5
119:38 Confirm to thy servant thy promise 6
106I have sworn an oath and confirmed it 6
Isa 44:26 who confirms the word of his servant 6
Jer 44:25 Then confirm your vows and perform your vows! 6
Dan 9:12 confirmed his words, which he spoke against us 6
11: 1 stood up to confirm and strengthen him. 3
Mat 18:16 that every word may be confirmed 10
Mrk 16:20 confirmed the message 8
Rom 15: 8 to confirm the promises given to the patriarchs 8
1Co 1: 6 testimony to Christ was confirmed among you- 8
2Pe 1:10 more zealous to confirm your call and election 7
Sir 3: 2 confirmed the right of the mother over her sons. 12
29: 3 Confirm your word and keep faith with him 12
42:25 One confirms the good things of the other 12
Bar 2: 1 'So the Lord confirmed his word, which he spoke 10
24 thou hast confirmed thy words, which thou didst 10
1Mc 11:27 He confirmed him in the high priesthood 10
34 We have confirmed as their possession 10
57 I confirm you in the high priesthood 10
12: 1 to confirm and renew the friendship with them. 10
14:24 to confirm the alliance with the Romans. 10
38 Demetrius confirmed him in the high priesthood 10
15: 5 now . . I confirm to you all the tax remissions 10
2Mc 12:25 when . . he had confirmed his solemn promise 11
4Mc 18:17 He confirmed the saying of Ezekiel 9

confirmation 1. βεβαίωσις
Php 1: 7 in the defense and confirmation of the gospel. 1
Heb 6:16 disputes an oath is final for confirmation. 1

confiscate 1. διαρπάζω
Tob 1:20 Then all my property was confiscated 1

must confiscate 1. ἀναλημπτέος
2Mc 3:13 this money must in any case be confiscated 1

confiscation 1. ענש (A) 2. διασεισθέντες
Ezr 7:26 whether . . for confiscation of his goods 1
3Mc 7:21 to confiscation of their belongings by any one. 2

conflict 1. צָבָא 2. ἀγών 3. μεταξύ ἀλλήλων
Dan 10: 1 word was true, and it was a great conflict. 1
Rom 2:15 their conflicting thoughts accuse . . them 3
Php 1:30 engaged in the same conflict which you saw 2

conform 1. σύμμορφος 2. συσχηματίζω
Ps 119:85 men who do not conform to thy law. •
Rom 8:29 to be conformed to the image of his Son 1
12: 2 Do not be conformed to this world 2
1Pe 1:14 do not be conformed to the passions 2

confound 1. בוש 2. בלע 3. חפר 4. כלם 5. ἐντρέπω 6. συγχέω 7. συνταράσσω
2Kg 19:26 inhabitants . . are dismayed and confounded 1
Job 6:20 they come thither and are confounded. 3
Ps 14: 6 You would confound the plans of the poor 1
35: 4 Let them be turned back and confounded 3
Isa 19: 3 emptied out, and I will confound their plans; 2
20: 5 Then they shall be dismayed and confounded 1
24:23 moon will be confounded, and the sun ashamed; 3
33: 9 Lebanon is confounded and withers away; 3
37:27 shorn of strength, are dismayed and confounded 1
41:11 against you shall be put to shame and confounded; 4
45:16 All of them are put to shame and confounded 4
17 put to shame or confounded to all eternity. 4
50: 7 helps me; therefore I have not been confounded; 4
54: 4 be not confounded, for you will not be put to shame; 4
Jer 14: 3 they are ashamed and confounded 4
22:22 then you will be ashamed and confounded 4
31:19 and I was confounded, because I bore the disgrace 4
49:23 Hamath and Arpad are confounded 1
Ezk 16:63 that you may remember and be confounded 1
36:32 Be ashamed and confounded for your ways 4
Jol 1:11 Be confounded, O tillers of the soil 1
Zec 9: 5 Ekron also, because its hopes are confounded. 1
10: 5 they shall confound the riders on horses. 1
Act 9:22 confounded the Jews who lived in Damascus 6
1Es 8:74 I am ashamed and confounded before thy face. 5
Wis 10: 5 when the nations . . had been confounded 6
1Mc 3: 6 all the evildoers were confounded 7

confront 1. ענה 2. קדם 3. קדם פָּנִים 4. ἀντοφθαλμέω 5. κατέναντι
Deu 31:21 this song shall confront them as a witness 1
2Sm 22: 6 the snares of death confronted me. 2
Ps 17:13 Arise, O LORD! confront them, overthrow them! 3
18: 5 the snares of death confronted me. 2
Wis 12:14 nor can any king or monarch confront thee 4
Sir 34: 3 the likeness of a face confronting a face. 5

confuse 1. בלל 2. בלע 3. דהם 4. פלג 5. ἀλλοῖος 6. συγχέω
Gen 11: 7 there confuse their language 1
9 because there the LORD confused the language 1
Ps 55: 9 O Lord, confuse their tongues; 4
Isa 3:12 mislead . . and confuse the course of your paths. 2
28: 7 they are confused with wine, they stagger 2
Jer 14: 9 Why shouldst thou be like a man confused 3
Sir 40: 5 his sleep at night confuses his mind. 5
2Mc 10:30 confused and blinded 6

confusion 1. בֹּשֶׁת 2. בֹּשֶׁת פָּנִים 3. כְּלִמָּה 4. מְבוּכָה 5. מְהוּמָה 6. עִוְעִים 7. תֹּהוּ 8. תּוֹעָה 9. תִּמָּהוֹן 10. αἰσχύνη 11. ἀκαταστασία 12. θόρυβος 13. συγχέω 14. σύγχυσις 15. ταραχή 16. confundo 17. confusio 18. turbatio 19. turbo
Deu 7:23 over to you, and throw them into great confusion 5
28:20 send upon you curses, confusion, and frustration 5
28 LORD will smite you with . . confusion of mind; 9
1Sm 14:20 and there was very great confusion. 5
Neh 4: 8 together to come . . and to cause confusion 8
Isa 19:14 LORD . . mingled within her a spirit of confusion; 6
22: 5 a day of tumult and trampling and confusion 4
34:11 He shall stretch the line of confusion over it 7
45:16 the makers of idols go in confusion together. 3
Jer 7:19 Is it not themselves, to their own confusion? 2
Dan 9: 7 but to us confusion of face, as at this day 1
8 To us, O Lord, belongs confusion of face 1
Mic 7: 4 now their confusion is at hand. 4
Act 19:29 So the city was filled with the confusion; 14
32 for the assembly was in confusion 13
21:31 all Jerusalem was in confusion. 13
1Co 14:33 For God is not a God of confusion but of peace 11
2Es 2: 6 that you may bring confusion upon them 17
7:87 utterly waste away in confusion 17
98 and shall be confident without confusion 16
9: 3 wavering of leaders, confusion of princes 18
15:18 the cities shall be in confusion 19
16:21 earth–the sword, famine, and great confusion. 17
Tob 4:13 For in pride there is ruin and great confusion; 11
AEs 11: 5 Behold, noise and confusion 12
Wis 14:26 confusion over what is good 12
Bar 1:15 confusion of face, as at this day, to us, to the men 10
2: 6 confusion of face to us and our fathers 10
2Mc 13:16 filled the camp with terror and confusion 15
3Mc 6:19 filled them with confusion and terror 15

confusion *See also* put, throw.

wild confusion 1. φύρδην
2Mc 4:41 and threw them in wild confusion at Lysimachus 1

confute 1. יכח 2. רשע 3. διακατελέγχομαι 4. ἐλέγχω
Job 32:12 behold, there was none that confuted Job 1
Isa 54:17 you shall confute every tongue that rises 2

Act 18:28 for he powerfully confuted the Jews in public 3
Tit 1: 9 to confute those who contradict it. 4

congeal 1. קָפָא
Exd 15: 8 the deeps congealed in the heart of the sea. 1

congenial 1. πρὸς τὴν ψυχὴν αὐτοῦ
Sir 27:16 he will never find a congenial friend. 1

congratulate 1. ברך 2. χαρίζομαι
2Sm 8:10 to . . David, to greet him, and to congratulate him 1
1Kg 1:47 king's servants came to congratulate our lord 1
1Ch 18:10 and to congratulate him because he had fought 1
3Mc 1: 8 to congratulate him on what had happened 2

congregation 1. מַקְהֵל 2. עֵדָה 3. קָהָל 4. ἐκκλησία 5. πλῆθος 6. συναγωγή
Exd 12: 3 Tell all the congregation of Israel that 2
6 when the whole assembly of the congregation 2
19 cut off from the congregation of Israel 2
47 All the congregation of Israel shall keep it. 2
16: 1 all the congregation of the people of Israel 2
2 the whole congregation of the people of Israel 2
9 the whole congregation of the people of Israel 2
10 spoke to the whole congregation of the people 2
22 the leaders of the congregation came and told 2
17: 1 All the congregation of the people of Israel 2
34:31 Aaron and all the leaders of the congregation 2
35: 1 Moses assembled all the congregation 2
4 Moses said to all the congregation of the people 2
20 all the congregation of the people of Israel 2
38:25 the silver from those of the congregation 2
Lev 4:13 If the whole congregation of Israel commits a sin 2
15 the elders of the congregation 2
8: 3 assemble all the congregation at the door 2
4 the congregation was assembled at the door 2
5 Moses said to the congregation, "This is the thing 2
9: 5 all the congregation drew near and stood 2
10: 6 lest wrath come upon all the congregation 2
17 you may bear the iniquity of the congregation 2
16: 5 from the congregation of the people of Israel 2
19: 2 to all the congregation of the people of Israel 2
24:14 and let all the congregation stone him 2
16 all the congregation shall stone him 2
Num 1: 2 Take a census of all the congregation 2
16 were the ones chosen from the congregation 2
18 assembled the whole congregation together 2
53 that there may be no wrath upon the congregation 2
3: 7 duties . . for the whole congregation 2
4:34 leaders of the congregation numbered the sons 2
8: 9 assemble the whole congregation of . . Israel. 2
20 all the congregation of the people of Israel 2
10: 2 shall use them for summoning the congregation 2
3 all the congregation shall gather themselves 2
13:26 came to . . all the congregation of the people 2
26 brought back word . . to all the congregation 2
14: 1 Then all the congregation raised a loud cry; 2
2 whole congregation said to them, "Would that we 2
5 assembly of the congregation of the people 2
7 said to all the congregation of the people 2
10 congregation said to stone them with stones. 2
27 How long shall this wicked congregation murmur 2
35 this will I do to all this wicked congregation 2
36 made all the congregation to murmur against him 2
15:24 without the knowledge of the congregation 2
24 all the congregation shall offer one young bull 2
25 make atonement for all the congregation 2
26 all the congregation of the people of Israel 2
33 to Moses and Aaron, and to all the congregation. 2
35 all the congregation shall stone him 2
36 congregation brought him outside the camp 2
16: 2 with . . 250 leaders of the congregation 2
3 For all the congregation are holy, every one 2
9 separated you from the congregation of Israel 2
9 to stand before the congregation to minister 2
19 assembled all the congregation against them 2
19 glory . . appeared to all the congregation. 2
21 Separate . . from among this congregation 2
22 wilt thou be angry with all the congregation? 2
24 Say to the congregation, Get away from about 2
26 said to the congregation, "Depart, I pray you 2
41 all the congregation . . murmured against 2
42 congregation had assembled against Moses 2
45 Get away from the midst of this congregation 2
46 carry it quickly to the congregation 2
19: 9 shall be kept for the congregation of . . Israel 2
20: 1 people of Israel, the whole congregation, came 2
2 Now there was no water for the congregation; 2
8 Take the rod, and assemble the congregation 2
8 give drink to the congregation and their cattle. 2
11 congregation drank, and their cattle. 2
22 Israel, the whole congregation, came to Mount 2
27 went up . . in the sight of all the congregation. 2
29 all the congregation saw that Aaron was dead 2
25: 6 sight of the whole congregation of the people 2
7 Phin'ehas . . rose and left the congregation 2
26: 2 census of all the congregation of the people 2
9 Dathan and Abi'ram, chosen from the congregation 2
27: 2 stood before . . all the congregation 2
14 during the strife of the congregation 2
16 LORD . . appoint a man over the congregation 2
17 congregation of the LORD may not be as sheep 2
19 stand before . . all the congregation 2
20 all the congregation . . of Israel may obey. 2
21 all . . Israel with him, the whole congregation. 2
22 before Elea'zar . . and the whole congregation 2
31:12 brought . . to the congregation of the people 2
13 all the leaders of the congregation 2
16 plague came among the congregation of the LORD. 2
26 heads of the fathers' houses of the congregation; 2
27 between the warriors . . all the congregation. 2
43 now the congregation's half was 337,500 sheep 2
32: 2 said to . . the leaders of the congregation 2
4 land . . LORD smote before the congregation of Israel 2
35:12 not die until he stands before the congregation 2
24 then the congregation shall judge 2
25 congregation shall rescue the manslayer 2
25 congregation shall restore him to his city 2
Jos 9:15 the leaders of the congregation swore to them. 2
18 the leaders of the congregation had sworn 2
18 the congregation murmured against the leaders. 2
19 But all the leaders said to all the congregation 2
21 and drawers of water for all the congregation 2
27 of water for the congregation and for the altar 2
18: 1 the whole congregation of . . Israel assembled 2
20: 6 has stood before the congregation for judgment 2
9 not . . till he stood before the congregation. 2
22:16 Thus says the whole congregation of the LORD 2
17 came a plague upon the congregation of the LORD 2
18 angry with the whole congregation of Israel 2
20 wrath fell upon all the congregation of Israel? 2
30 Phin'ehas . . and the chiefs of the congregation 2
Jdg 20: 1 the congregation assembled . . to the LORD 2
21:10 the congregation sent thither 12,000 2
13 the whole congregation sent word 2
16 the elders of the congregation said, "What shall 2
1Kg 8: 5 the congregation of Israel, who had assembled 2
2Ch 5: 6 King Solomon and all the congregation of Israel 2
7: 8 all Israel with him, a very great congregation 3
24: 6 tax levied . . on the congregation of Israel 3
Ezr 10: 8 banned from the congregation of the exiles. 3
Ps 1: 5 nor sinners in the congregation of the righteous; 2
22:22 in the midst of the congregation I will praise 3
25 From thee comes my praise in the . . congregation; 3
26:12 in the great congregation I will bless the LORD. 1
35:18 Then I will thank thee in the great congregation; 3
40: 9 news of deliverance in the great congregation; 3
10 thy faithfulness from the great congregation. 3
74: 2 Remember thy congregation 2
107:32 them extol him in the congregation of the people 3
111: 1 company of the upright, in the congregation. 2
Prv 5:14 point of utter ruin in the assembled congregation. 2
Jer 6:18 hear, O nations, and know, O congregation 2
30:20 their congregation shall be established 2
Lam 1:10 thou didst forbid to enter thy congregation. 3
Jol 2:16 gather the people. Sanctify the congregation; 3
Act 7:38 he who was in the congregation in the wilderness 4
15:30 having gathered the congregation together 5
19: 9 speaking evil of the Way before the congregation 5
Heb 2:12 in the midst of the congregation 4
Sir 1:30 cast you down in the midst of the congregation 6
4: 7 Make yourself beloved in the congregation 6
24:23 an inheritance for the congregations of Jacob. 6
33:18 you leaders of the congregation, hearken. 4
39:10 the congregation will proclaim his praise; 4
41:18 of iniquity, before a congregation or the people; 6
44:15 the congregation proclaims their praise. 4
46: 7 they withstood the congregation 4
14 By the law of the Lord he judged the congregation 6
50:13 before the whole congregation of Israel. 4
20 lifted up his hands over the whole congregation 4
1Mc 3:44 the congregation assembled 6

great congregation 1. מַקְהֵל
Ps 68:26 Bless God in the great congregation, the LORD 1

conjugal
1Co 7: 3 husband should give to his wife her conjugal rights •

connect 1. חֹבֶרֶת 2. קָרַב 3. ἐπιβάλλω
Exd 36:17 on the edge of the other connecting curtain. 1
Neh 13: 4 Eli'ashib . . who was connected with Tobi'ah 2
2Mc 3: 3 all the expenses connected with the service 3

connection 1. בְּ (A) 2. δι' ὅν 3. εἰς
Num18: 1 bear iniquity in connection with the sanctuary; •
1 iniquity in connection with your priesthood. •
Deu 19:15 for any wrong in connection with any offense •
Dan 6: 5 find it in connection with the law of his God. 1
Heb 7:14 in connection with that tribe Moses said 3
1Mc 13:15 in connection with the offices he held 2

connivance 1. γνώμη
2Mc 4:39 by Lysimachus with the connivance of Menelaus 1

conquer 1. בקע 2. לחם 3. מְבוּסָה 4. נכה 5. ἐκπολεμέω 6. καταγωνίζομαι 7. κατακρατέω 8. κατακυριεύω 9. κατεργάζομαι 10. κρατέω 11. νικάω 12. τροπόω 13. devinco 14. expugno
1Kg 15:20 conquered Ijon, Dan, A'bel-beth-ma'acah 4
2Kg 3:19 you shall conquer every fortified city 4
25 and the slingers surrounded and conquered it. 4
16: 5 they besieged Ahaz but could not conquer him. 2
2Ch 16: 4 conquered I'jon, Dan, A'bel-ma'im 4
Isa 7: 1 war against it, but they could not conquer it. 2
6 let us conquer it for ourselves 1
18: 2 a nation mighty and conquering 3
7 a nation mighty and conquering 3
Ezk 40: 1 fourteenth year after the city was conquered 4
Heb 11:33 who through faith conquered kingdoms 6
Rev 2: 7 To him who conquers I will grant to eat of the tree 11
11 He who conquers shall not be hurt 11
17 To him who conquers I will give some . . manna 11
26 He who conquers and who keeps my works 11
3: 5 He who conquers shall be clad thus in white 11
12 He who conquers, I will make him a pillar 11
21 He who conquers, I will grant him to sit with me 11
21 as I myself conquered and sat down with my Father 11
5: 5 the Lion . . the Root of David, has conquered 11
6: 2 and he went out conquering and to conquer. 11
2 and he went out conquering and to conquer. 11
11: 7 the beast . . will make war upon them and conquer 11
12:11 they have conquered him by the blood of the Lamb 11
13: 7 to make war on the saints and to conquer them. 11
15: 2 those who had conquered the beast and its image 11
17:14 and the Lamb will conquer them 11
21: 7 He who conquers shall have this heritage 11
1Es 4: 4 they go, and conquer mountains, walls, and towers. 9
2Es 5: 9 and all friends shall conquer one another 14
11:40 You . . have conquered all the beasts 13
13:28 the . . multitude which came to conquer him 14
34 as you saw, desiring to come and conquer him. 14
Wis 16:10 thy sons were not conquered 11
18:22 He conquered the wrath not by strength of body 11
1Mc 1: 2 He fought many battles, conquered strongholds 10
5:44 Thus Carnaim was conquered 12
8: 5 they crushed in battle and conquered. 7
10 they plundered them, conquered the land 7
15:30 the places which you have conquered 8
31 Otherwise we will come and conquer you. 5
4Mc 1:11 By their endurance they conquered the tyrant 11
3:17 can conquer the drives of the emotions 11
6:33 now that reason has conquered the emotions 11
7: 4 he conquered the besiegers 11
11 conquered the fiery angel 11
13: 2 they had been conquered by these emotions. 11
7 conquered the tempest of the emotions. 11
16:14 you have conquered even a tyrant 11
17:24 he ravaged and conquered all his enemies. 11

conqueror 1. ירשׁ
Jer 8:10 I will give . . their fields to conquerors 1
Mic 1:15 I will again bring a conqueror upon you 1
conqueror *See also* more.

conscience 1. לֵב 2. συνείδησις
1Sm 25:31 have no cause of grief, or pangs of conscience 1
Act 23: 1 I have lived before God in all good conscience 2
24:16 I always take pains to have a clear conscience 2
Rom 2:15 while their conscience also bears witness 2
9: 1 my conscience bears me witness in the Holy Spirit 2
13: 5 but also for the sake of conscience. 2
1Co 8: 7 their conscience, being weak, is defiled. 2
10 if his conscience is weak 2
12 wounding their conscience when it is weak 2
10:25 without . . question on the ground of conscience. 2
27 without . . question on the ground of conscience. 2
28 for conscience' sake– 2
29 I mean his conscience, not yours–do not eat it 2
2Co 1:12 the testimony of our conscience 2
4: 2 commend ourselves to every man's conscience 2
5:11 I hope it is known also to your conscience. 2
1Ti 1: 5 that issues from a pure heart and a good conscience 2
19 holding faith and a good conscience 2
19 By rejecting conscience •
3: 9 must hold . . the faith with a clear conscience. 2
4: 2 liars whose consciences are seared 2
2Ti 1: 3 I thank God whom I serve with a clear conscience 2
Tit 1:15 their very minds and consciences are corrupted. 2
Heb 9: 9 cannot perfect the conscience of the worshiper 2
14 purify your conscience from dead works 2
10:22 our hearts sprinkled clean from an evil conscience 2
13:18 we are sure that we have a clear conscience 2
1Pe 3:16 keep your conscience clear 2
21 but as an appeal to God for a clear conscience 2
Wis 17:11 distressed by conscience 2

consciousness 1. συνείδησις
Heb 10: 2 would no longer have any consciousness of sin. 1

consecrate 1. מִלֵּא יָד 2. נזר 3. נֵזֶר 4. קָדוֹשׁ 5. קֹדֶשׁ 6. קדשׁ 7. ἁγιάζω 8. ἀφιερόω 9. καθαγιάζω 10. sanctifico

Exd 13: 2 Consecrate to me all the first-born; 6
19:10 Go to the people and consecrate them today 6
14 So Moses . . consecrated the people; 6
22 let the priests . . consecrate themselves 6
23 bounds about the mountain, and consecrate it.' 6
22:31 You shall be men consecrated to me; therefore you 5
28: 3 to consecrate him for my priesthood. 6
41 anoint them and ordain them and consecrate 6
29: 1 this is what you shall do to them to consecrate 6
27 you shall consecrate the breast of the wave 6
33 to ordain and consecrate them 6
36 and shall anoint it, to consecrate it. 6
37 make atonement for the altar, and consecrate it 6
44 I will consecrate the tent of meeting 6
44 Aaron also and his sons I will consecrate 6
30:29 you shall consecrate them, that they may be most 6
30 consecrate them, that they may serve me 6
40: 9 and consecrate it and all its furniture; 6
10 consecrate the altar; and the altar shall be most 6
11 the laver and its base, and consecrate it. 6
13 you shall anoint him and consecrate him 6
Lev 7:35 consecrated to them on the day they were *
8:10 all that was in it, and consecrated them 6
11 the laver and its base, to consecrate them 6
12 and anointed him, and consecrated him 6
15 consecrated it, to make atonement for it 6
30 so he consecrated Aaron and his garments 6
11:44 For I am the LORD your God: consecrate yourselves 6
16:32 the priest who is anointed and consecrated 1
20: 7 Consecrate yourselves therefore, and be holy 6
21: 8 You shall consecrate him, for he offers the bread 6
10 who has been consecrated to wear his garments 1
Num 3:13 I consecrated for my own all the first-born 6
6: 9 he defiles his consecrated head 3
11 And he shall consecrate his head that same day. 6
18 Nazirite shall shave his consecrated head 3
18 shall take the hair from his consecrated head 3
7: 1 Moses . . had anointed and consecrated it 6
1 Moses . . anointed and consecrated the altar 6
8:17 on the day that I . . consecrated them for myself 6
11:18 Consecrate yourselves for tomorrow 6
Deu 15:19 you shall consecrate to the LORD your God; 6
33: 3 all those consecrated to him were in his hand; 4
Jdg 17: 3 I consecrate the silver to the LORD from my hand 6
1Sm 7: 1 they consecrated his son, Elea'zar, to have charge 6
16: 5 consecrate yourselves, and come with me 6
5 And he consecrated Jesse and his sons 6
1Kg 8:64 the king consecrated the middle of the court 6
9: 3 I have consecrated this house 6
7 the house which I have consecrated for my name 6
13:33 any who would, he consecrated to be priests 1
1Ch 23:13 was set apart to consecrate the most holy things 6
29: 5 consecrating himself today to the LORD? 1
2Ch 7: 7 Solomon consecrated the middle of the court 6
16 For now I have chosen and consecrated this house 6
20 this house, which I have consecrated for my name 6
13: 9 Whoever comes to consecrate himself 1
26:18 who are consecrated to burn incense. 6
29:31 You have now consecrated yourselves to the LORD; 1
31: 6 dedicated things which had been consecrated 6
Neh 3: 1 consecrated it and set its doors; 6
1 consecrated it as far as the Tower of the Hundred 6
Jer 1: 5 and before you were born I consecrated you; 6
Ezk 43:26 for the altar and purify it, and so consecrate it. 1
48:11 This shall be for the consecrated priests 6
Hos 9:10 and consecrated themselves to Ba'al 2
Zep 1: 7 the LORD has . . consecrated his guests. 6
Joh 10:36 the Father consecrated and sent into the world 7
17:19 for their sake I consecrate myself 7
19 that they also may be consecrated in truth. 7
1Co 7:14 For the unbelieving husband is consecrated 7
14 the unbelieving wife is consecrated 7
1Ti 4: 5 for then it is consecrated by the word of God 7
2Ti 2:21 consecrated and useful to the master of the house 7
1Es 5:52 at all the consecrated feasts. 7
2Es 2:18 I have consecrated and prepared for you 10
5:25 thou hast consecrated Zion for thyself 10
Tob 1: 4 was consecrated and established 7
Jdt 4: 3 the altar and the temple had been consecrated 7
6:19 the faces of those who are consecrated to thee. 7
9:13 they have planned . . against thy consecrated house 7
11:13 the wine and oil, which they had consecrated 7
Sir 49: 7 he had been consecrated in the womb as prophet 7
1Mc 4:48 consecrated the courts. 7
2Mc 1:25 didst choose the fathers and consecrate them 7
2: 8 the place should be specially consecrated. 9
15:18 first fear was for the consecrated sanctuary. 9
3Mc 6: 3 a people of your consecrated portion 7
4Mc 13:13 with all our hearts consecrate ourselves to God 8
17:19 All who are consecrated are under your hands. 7
20 who have been consecrated for the sake of God 7

consecrated *See* offering.

consecrated one 1. קֹדֶשׁ

Isa 13: 3 I myself have commanded my consecrated ones 1

consecrated thing 1. קֹדֶשׁ

Num18: 8 consecrated things of the people of Israel; 1

consecration 1. מִלּוּא 2. נֵזֶר 3. *ἁγιασμός*

Lev 7:37 of the guilt offering, of the consecration 1
21:12 for the consecration of the anointing oil 2
Num 6:19 after he has shaven the hair of his consecration 2
2Mc 2:17 the kingship and priesthood and consecration 3

consent 1. אבה 2. אות 3. *ἀφίημι* 4. *γνώμη* 5. *εὐδοκέω* 6. *συγκατατίθημι* 7. *συνευδοκέω* 8. consentio

Gen 34:15 Only on this condition will we consent to you 2
41:44 and without your consent no man shall lift up *
Jdg 11:17 also to the king of Moab, but he would not consent. 1
1Kg 20: 8 all the people said to him, "Do not heed or consent. 1
Prv 1:10 My son, if sinners entice you, do not consent. 1
Mat 3:15 all righteousness." Then he consented. 3
Lke 11:48 consent to the deeds of your fathers 7
23:51 who had not consented to their purpose and deed 6
Act 8: 1 Saul was consenting to his death 7
1Co 7:12 she consents to live with him 7
13 he consents to live with her 7
Phm 1:14 I preferred to do nothing without your consent 4
1Es 6:22 was done with the consent of King Cyrus 4
7: 4 with the consent of Cyrus and Darius 4
2Es 16:69 who consent to eat shall be held in derision 8
1Mc 11:29 The king consented, and wrote a letter to Jonathan 5
2Mc 11:24 the Jews do not consent 7

consent *See also* give.

consequence 1. *ἀκολουθία* 2. ex

Ezk 23:35 bear the consequences of your lewdness *
2Es 8:33 receive their reward in consequence of their 2
4Mc 1:21 pleasure and pain have many consequences. 1

consequently 1. *διό* 2. *ὅθεν*

Heb 7:25 Consequently he is able for all time to save 2
10: 5 Consequently . . he said 1

consider 1. אמר לְלֵב 2. אשׁשׁ 3. בין 4. דמה 5. זמם 6. חשׁב 7. ידע 8. כון 9. נבט 10. נתן 11. פנה בְּ 12. ראה 13. שׂום 14. שׂום לֵב 15. שׂיח 16. שׂכל 17. שׁוב אֶל לֵב 18. שׁית לֵב 19. שׂכל (A) 20. *ἀναθεωρέω* 21. *ἀναλογίζομαι* 22. *ἀξιόω* 23. *βλέπω* 24. *γίνομαι* 25. *διαγινώσκω* 26. *διαλογίζομαι* 27. *διανοέω* 28. *ἐμβλέπω* 29. *ἐνθυμέομαι* 30. *ἐννοέω* 31. *ἐξετάζω* 32. *ἐπιλογίζομαι* 33. *ἐπισκέπτομαι* 34. *ἐπίσκεψις* 35. *ἐφοράω* 36. *ἔχω* 37. *ἡγέομαι* 38. *καθοράω* 39. *καταμανθάνω* 40. *κατανοέω* 41. *κρίνον* 42. *λογίζομαι* 43. *νοέω* 44. *νομίζω* 45. *ὁράω* 46. *ὅσος* 47. *συνοράω* 48. *φροντίζω* 49. accipio 50. adtendo 51. aestimo 52. cogito 53. considero 54. existimo

Exd 33:13 Consider too that this nation is thy people. 12
Deu 11: 2 consider this day . . the discipline of the LORD 7
2 consider the discipline of the LORD your God *
32: 7 of old, consider the years of many generations; 3
Jdg 18:14 Now therefore consider what you will do. 7
19:30 this day; consider it, take counsel, and speak. 13
1Sm 12:24 consider what great things he has done for you. 12
25:17 know this and consider what you should do; 12
2Sm 24:13 Now consider, and decide what answer 7
1Kg 10:21 silver, it was not considered as anything 6
2Kg 5: 7 Am I God . . ? Only consider, and see how he is seeking 7
2Ch 9:20 silver was not considered as anything 6
19: 6 said to the judges, "Consider what you do 12
Job 1: 8 Have you considered my servant Job 14
2: 3 said to Satan, "Have you considered my servant Job 14
8: 8 consider what the fathers have found; 8
11:11 when he sees iniquity, will he not consider it? 3
18: 2 Consider, and then we will speak. 3
23:15 when I consider, I am in dread of him. 3
37:14 stop and consider the wondrous works of God. 3
Ps 13: 3 Consider and answer me, O LORD my God; 9
25:18 Consider my affliction and my trouble 12
19 Consider how many are my foes 12
41: 1 Blessed is he who considers the poor! 16
45:10 Hear, O daughter, consider, and incline your ear; 12
77: 5 I consider the days of old, I remember the years 6
90:11 Who considers the power of thy anger 7
106: 7 fathers . . not consider thy wonderful works; 16
107:43 let men consider the steadfast love of the LORD. 3
119:95 but I consider thy testimonies. 3
159 Consider how I love thy precepts! 12
Prv 6: 6 consider her ways, and be wise. 12
17:28 Even a fool who keeps silent is considered wise; 6
21:29 but an upright man considers his ways. 3
24:32 Then I saw and considered it; 18
31:16 She considers a field and buys it; 5
Ecc 2:11 Then I considered all that my hands had done 11
12 turned to consider wisdom and madness and folly; 12
7:13 Consider the work of God; 12
14 and in the day of adversity consider; 12
Isa 41:20 men . . may consider and understand together 13
22 that we may consider them, that we may know 14
43:18 Remember not . . nor consider the things of old. 3
44:19 No one considers, nor is there knowledge 17
46: 8 Remember this and consider, recall it to mind 2
53: 8 generation, who considered that he was cut off 15
64: 9 Behold, consider, we are all thy people. 9
Jer 9:17 Consider, and call for the mourning women to come; 3
Ezk 18:28 Because he considered and turned away 12
28: 2 though you consider yourself as wise as a god 10
6 Because you consider yourself as wise as a god 10
32: 2 You consider yourself a lion among the nations 4
Dan 7: 8 I considered the horns, and behold, there came up 19
8: 5 As I was considering, behold, a he-goat came 3
9:23 therefore consider the word and understand 3
Hos 7: 2 But they do not consider that I remember all 1
Hag 1: 5 Consider how you have fared. 14
7 Consider how you have fared. 14
2:15 Pray now, consider what will come to pass 14
18 Consider from this day onward 14
18 of the LORD'S temple was laid, consider 14
Mat 1:20 as he considered this, behold, an angel of the Lord 29
6:28 you anxious about clothing? Consider the lilies 39
Lke 12:24 Consider the ravens: they neither sow nor reap 40
27 Consider the lilies, how they grow 40
Act 15: 6 gathered together to consider this matter. 45
Rom 4:19 weaken in faith when he considered his own body 40
19 he considered the barrenness of Sarah's womb. *
6:11 you also must consider yourselves dead to sin 42
8:18 I consider that the sufferings of this present 42
1Co 1:26 For consider your call, brethren 23
10:18 Consider the people of Israel 23
Php 3:13 I do not consider that I have made it my own 42
Phm 1:17 if you consider me your partner 36
Heb 3: 1 Therefore, holy brethren . . consider Jesus 40
10:24 let us consider how to stir up one another to love 40
11:11 since she considered him faithful 37
19 He considered that God was able to raise men 42
26 He considered abuse suffered for the Christ 37
12: 3 Consider him who endured . . such hostility 21
13: 7 consider the outcome of their life 20
2Es 4:31 Consider now for yourself how much fruit 51
50 he said to me, "Consider it for yourself 52
5:54 Therefore you also should consider 53
7:16 why have you not considered in your mind 49
84 they shall consider the torment laid up 53
126 we did not consider what we should suffer 52
9:20 I considered my world, and behold, it was lost 53
45 and considered my distress, and gave me a son 50
11:36 Look before you and consider what you see. 53
13:16 For as I consider it in my mind, alas for those 54
Tob 5:18 consider it as rubbish as compared to our child. 24
14:11 consider what almsgiving accomplishes 45
Wis 1:16 summoned death; considering him a friend 37
2:16 We are considered by him as something base 42
8:17 When I considered these things inwardly 42
15:12 he considered our existence an idle game 42
Sir 2:10 Consider the ancient generations and see 28
7: 9 He will consider the multitude of my gifts 35
11: 7 first consider, and then reprove. 43
33:17 Consider that I have not labored for myself 40
42:18 considers their crafty devices 27
50: 4 He considered how to save his people from ruin 48
Bar 2:16 Lord, look down . . and consider us. 30
1Mc 10:38 they are considered to be under one ruler 42
2Mc 2:24 considering the flood of numbers involved 47
29 has to consider only what is suitable 31
9:15 whom he had not considered worth burying 25
11:36 as soon as you have considered them 33
14:20 When the terms had been fully considered 34
3Mc 2:33 considering them to be enemies of the . . nation 41
3:11 not considering the might of the supreme God 38
15 we considered that we should not rule 37
5:16 after considering this 42
50 considered the help which they had received 47
4Mc 2:14 Do not consider it paradoxical 44
3:15 David . . considered it an altogether fearful danger 42
4: 7 considering it outrageous 44
5:13 For consider this 29
17 we consider that we should not transgress it 22
8:11 Will you not consider this 26
16 Let us consider, on the other hand 42
19 consider the threats of torments 42
9: 4 we consider this pity . . more grievous 44
14:11 Do not consider it amazing 37
15: 5 Considering that mothers are the weaker sex 46
16: 5 Consider this also. 32

consider in mind 1. *διαλογίζομαι*

Lke 1:29 considered . . what sort of greeting this might be 1

consider seriously 1. *ἐνθυμέομαι*

4Mc 8:21 let us seriously consider 1
27 nor even seriously considered them. 1

consider well 1. ידע וראה 2. שׁית לֵב

1Kg 20:22 consider well what you have to do; 1
Ps 48:13 consider well her ramparts 2
Jer 31:21 consider well the highway 2

consider worthy 1. *ἀξιόω*

1Ti 5:17 be considered worthy of double honor 1

considerable 1. ἐπὶ πλεῖον 2. ἱκανός 3. πολύς
Act 19:26 and turned away a considerable company of people 2
Sir 0: 1 acquiring considerable proficiency in them, 2
1Mc 12:10 considerable time has passed 3
13:11 with him a considerable army 2
2Mc 10:27 and advanced a considerable distance 1
3Mc 1:23 created a considerable disturbance in the holy place 2

considerately 1. κατὰ γνῶσιν
1Pe 3: 7 Likewise you husbands, live considerately 1

consideration 1. ἀπάντησις
AEs 16: 9 with more equitable consideration. 1

no consideration 1. ἀλογέω
2Mc 12:24 and no consideration would be shown them. 1

out of consideration 1. διά
1Co 10:28 then out of consideration for the man 1

consign 1. פקד 2. παραδίδωμι 3. συγκλείω
Isa 38:10 I am consigned to the gates of Sheol 1
Rom 11:32 For God has consigned all men to disobedience 3
Gal 3:22 the scripture consigned all things to sin 3
AEs 16:15 who were consigned to annihilation 2

consist 1. εἰμί
Lke 12:15 a man's life does not consist in the abundance 1
1Co 4:20 For the kingdom of God does not consist in talk *
12:14 body does not consist of one member but of many. 1
Jdt 5: 3 in what does their power or strength consist? *

consistent 1. εἷς
Sir 5:10 let your speech be consistent. 1

consolation 1. נֶחָמָה 2. תַּנְחוּם 3. παράκλησις 4. παραμυθία 5. παραμύθιον
Job 6:10 This would be my consolation; I would even exult 1
15:11 Are the consolations of God too small for you 2
21: 2 let this be your consolation. 2
Ps 94:19 thy consolations cheer my soul. 2
Jer 16: 7 any one give him the cup of consolation to drink 2
31: 9 and with consolations I will lead them back 3
Lke 2:25 looking for the consolation of Israel 3
6:24 you have received your consolation. 3
1Co 14: 3 encouragement and consolation. 4
Wis 3:18 no consolation in the day of decision. 5
consolation *See also* become, give.

become a consolation 1. נחם
Ezk 16:54 becoming a consolation to them. 1

console 1. נחם 2. תַּנְחוּם 3. παρακαλέω 4. παραμυθέομαι 5. παρηγορέω 6. consolo 7. consolor
2Sm 10: 2 sent . . to console him concerning his father. 1
1Ch 19: 2 to console him concerning his father. 1
2 came to Hanun . . to console him. 1
Isa 66:11 and be satisfied with her consoling breasts; 2
Ezk 14:22 you will be consoled for the evil 1
23 They will console you, when you see their ways 1
Mat 2:18 refused to be consoled, because they were no 3
Joh 11:19 to console them concerning their brother. 4
31 were with her in the house, consoling her 4
2Es 10: 2 and all my neighbors attempted to console me 7
3 when they all had stopped consoling me 7
20 be consoled because of the sorrow of Jerusalem. 6
41 whom you saw mourning and began to console- 6
49 you began to console her for what had happened. 6
16:23 there shall be no one to console them 7
Jdt 6:20 they consoled Achior, and praised him greatly. 3
Sir 35:17 he will not be consoled until it reaches the Lord; 3
3Mc 3: 8 They did try to console them 3
4Mc 12: 2 tried to console him, saying 5

consort 1. בוא 2. κολλάω
Ps 26: 4 with false men, nor do I consort with dissemblers; 1
Sir 19: 2 the man who consorts with harlots 2

conspicuous 1. חָזוּת 2. ἐπίσημος 3. πρόδηλος 4. φαιδρός
Dan 8: 5 goat had a conspicuous horn between his eyes. 1
8 there came up four conspicuous horns 1
1Ti 5:24 The sins of some men are conspicuous 3
25 also good deeds are conspicuous 3
1Mc 11:37 and put up in a conspicuous place 2
14:48 to put them up in a conspicuous place 2
2Mc 15:35 a clear and conspicuous sign to every one 4

conspicuously 1. περιφανῶς
4Mc 8: 2 when the tyrant was conspicuously defeated 1

conspiracy 1. קֶשֶׁר 2. ἐπιβουλή 3. συνωμοσία
2Sm 15:12 And the conspiracy grew strong 1
1Kg 16:20 acts of Zimri, and the conspiracy which he made 1
2Kg 12:20 His servants arose and made a conspiracy 1
14:19 they made a conspiracy against him in Jerusalem 1
15:15 deeds of Shallum, and the conspiracy which he 1
30 Then Hoshe'a . . made a conspiracy against Pekah 1
2Ch 25:27 they made a conspiracy against him in Jerusalem 1
Isa 8:12 Do not call conspiracy all that this people call 1
12 all that this people call conspiracy 1
Act 23:13 There were more than 40 who made this conspiracy. 3
2Mc 5: 7 in the end got only disgrace from his conspiracy 2
conspiracy *See also* make.

conspirator 1. קֶשֶׁר
2Sm 15:31 Ahith'ophel is among the conspirators 1

conspirator against 1. ἐπίβουλος
2Mc 14:26 that conspirator against the kingdom, Judas 1

conspire 1. יעץ 2. קשר 3. רגש 4. συμφρονέω 5. συστρέφω
1Sm 22: 8 that all of you have conspired against me? 2
13 Saul said . . "Why have you conspired against me 2
1Kg 15:27 Ba'asha . . conspired against him; 2
16: 9 his servant Zimri . . conspired against him. 2
16 Zimri has conspired, and he has killed the king"; 2
2Kg 9:14 Thus Jehu . . conspired against Joram. 2
10: 9 It was I who conspired against my master 2
15:10 Shallum the son of Jabesh conspired against him 2
25 Pekah . . his captain, conspired against him 2
21:23 And the servants of Amon conspired against him 2
24 all those who had conspired against King Amon 2
2Ch 24:21 conspired against him, and by command of the king 2
25 his servants conspired against him 2
26 Those who conspired against him were Zabad 2
33:24 his servants conspired against him and killed 2
25 slew all . . who had conspired against King Amon; 2
Ps 2: 1 Why do the nations conspire, and the peoples plot 3
83: 5 Yea, they conspire with one accord; 1
Ams 7:10 saying, "Amos has conspired against you 2
Bel 1:28 conspired against the king, saying 5
3Mc 3: 2 by men who conspired to do them ill 4

conspire against 1. נכל 2. ἐπισυνίστημι
Gen 37:18 before he came . . they conspired against him 1
Sir 45:18 Outsiders conspired against him, and envied him 2

constant 1. διὰ παντός 2. πολλάκις 3. προσκαρτερέω
Rom 12:12 be constant in prayer. 3
2Mc 14:34 and called upon the constant Defender of our nation 1
3Mc 5:41 in constant danger of being plundered. 2

constantly 1. ἀδιάλειπτος 2. ἀδιαλείπτως 3. διὰ παντός 4. διηνεκής
Act 10: 2 prayed constantly to God. 3
1Th 1: 2 constantly mentioning you in our prayers 2
2:13 we also thank God constantly for this 2
5:17 pray constantly 2
2Ti 1: 3 when I remember you constantly in my prayers. 1
AEs 13: 5 stands constantly in opposition to all men 3
1Mc 8:15 constantly deliberate concerning the people 3
12:11 We therefore remember you constantly 2
3Mc 3:11 persevere constantly in his same purpose 4
22 Since they incline constantly to evil 4
constantly *See also* stay.

constellation 1. כְּסִיל 2. מַזָּלוֹת 3. θέσις
2Kg 23: 5 to the sun, and the moon, and the constellations 2
Isa 13:10 their constellations will not give their light; 1
Wis 7:19 the constellations of the stars 3
29 excels every constellation of the stars. 3

consternation 1. חפז 2. ἀφασία
Ps 116:11 I said in my consternation, "Men are all a vain 1
2Mc 14:17 because of the sudden consternation 2

constitute 1. ἵστημι
4Mc 13: 8 For they constituted a holy chorus of religion 1

constitution 1. ἕξις
Sir 30:14 well and strong in constitution 1

constrain 1. צוק 2. ἀναγκάζω 3. παραβιάζομαι 4. συνέχω
Job 32:18 the spirit within me constrains me. 1
Lke 12:50 how I am constrained until it is accomplished! 4
24:29 they constrained him, saying, "Stay with us 3
2Mc 11:14 constraining him to be their friend. 2

constraint 1. ἀναγκαστῶς 2. ἀνάγκη
1Pe 5: 2 Tend . . not by constraint but willingly 1
2Mc 6: 7 the Jews were taken, under bitter constraint 2
3Mc 4: 9 driven under the constraint of iron bonds 2

construct 1. κατασκευάζω
Heb 11: 7 Noah . . took heed and constructed an ark 1
4Mc 4:20 not only was a gymnasium constructed 1

construction 1. מְלָאכָה 2. מַעֲשֶׂה 3. עֲבֹדָה 4. καταβολή 5. κατασκευή 6. οἰκοδομέω
Exd 36: 1 any work in the construction of the sanctuary 3
38:24 in all the construction of the sanctuary 1
1Kg 7:28 This was the construction of the stands 2
Neh 4:16 half of my servants worked on construction 1
Ezk 1:16 of the wheels and their construction 2
16 their construction being as it were a wheel 2
1Es 6:20 although it has been in process of construction 6
2Mc 2:29 must be concerned with the whole construction 4
4:20 it was applied to the construction of triremes. 5

consul 1. ὕπατος
1Mc 15:16 Lucius, consul of the Romans, to King Ptolemy 1
22 The consul wrote the same thing to Demetrius *

consult 1. דרשׁ 2. יעץ 3. עֲמֹד לְ 4. שׁאל 5. βουλεύω 6. γίνομαι 7. ἐξερευνάω 8. συμβουλεύω
Deu 17: 9 consult them, and they shall declare to you 1
2Sm 16:23 was as if one consulted the oracle of God; 4
1Ch 10:13 Saul . . also consulted a medium 1
13: 1 David consulted with the commanders 2
Ezr 2:63 priest to consult Urim and Thummim. 3
Ps 71:10 those who watch for my life consult together 2
Isa 8:19 when they say to you, "Consult the mediums 1
19 should not a people consult their God? 1
19 Should they consult the dead 1
19: 3 they will consult the idols and the sorcerers 1
31: 1 do not look to . . or consult the LORD! 1
40:14 Whom did he consult for his enlightenment 2
Ezk 21:21 he shakes the arrows, he consults the teraphim 4
Sir 8:17 Do not consult with a fool 8
9:14 consult with the wise. 8
37:10 Do not consult 5
11 Do not consult with a woman about her rival *
LJr 1:48 the priests consult together 5
1Mc 3:48 were consulting the images of their idols. 7
9:59 they went and consulted with him. 8
2Mc 13:13 After consulting privately with the elders 6

consult together 1. יעץ
Ps 83: 3 consult together against thy protected ones. 1

consultation 1. συμβούλιον
Mrk 15: 1 the whole council held a consultation 1

consume 1. אכל 2. אסף 3. בלע 4. בער 5. גרם 6. חסל 7. כלה 8. כרת 9. מסה 10. ספה 11. צמת 12. רעה 13. רעע 14. שׂרף 15. תמם 16. שׁמד (A) 17. ἀναλίσκω 18. ἀναλόω 19. ἀφανίζω 20. βιβρώσκω 21. δαπανάω 22. διαλύω 23. ἐκκαίω 24. ἐξαναλίσκω 25. ἐσθίω 26. καταβιβρώσκω 27. καταδαπανάομαι 28. κατακαίω 29. καταναλίσκω 30. καταποθέω 31. καταφλέγω 32. κατεσθίω 33. μαραίνω 34. πυρπολέω 35. τήκω 36. τρύχω 37. ὑπερτήκω 38. consumo 39. devoratio 40. devoro 41. excomedo 42. succendo
Gen 19:15 two daughters who are here, lest you be consumed 10
17 flee to the hills, lest you be consumed. 10
31:40 Thus I was; by day the heat consumed me 1
41:30 land of Egypt; the famine will consume the land 7
Exd 3: 2 the bush was burning, yet it was not consumed. 1
15: 7 thy fury, it consumes them like stubble. 1
22: 6 standing grain or the field is consumed 1
32:10 burn hot against them and I may consume them; 7
12 to consume them from the face of the earth'? 7
33: 3 go up among you, lest I consume you in the way 7
5 I should go up among you, I would consume you. 7
Lev 6:10 which the fire has consumed the burnt offering 1
9:24 And fire . . consumed the burnt offering 1
Num 11: 1 consumed some outlying parts of the camp. 1
33 While the meat was yet . . before it was consumed 8
12:12 as one dead, of whom the flesh is half consumed 1
16:21 that I may consume them in a moment. 7
35 consumed the 250 men offering the incense. 1
45 Get away . . that I may consume them in a moment. 7
25:11 so that I did not consume the people of Israel 7
32:13 generation that had done evil . . was consumed. 15
Deu 5:25 For this great fire will consume us; 1
28:21 until he has consumed you off the land which you 7
38 gather little in; for the locust shall consume 6
Jos 24:20 then he will turn and do you harm, and consume you 7
Jdg 6:21 fire . . consumed the flesh and the unleavened 1
1Sm 15:18 and fight against them until they are consumed. 7
2Sm 21: 5 The man who consumed us and planned to destroy us 7
22:38 and did not turn back until they were consumed. 7
39 I consumed them; I thrust them through 7
23: 7 and they are utterly consumed with fire. 14
1Kg 18:38 fire . . fell, and consumed the burnt offering 1
2Kg 1:10 let fire come . . and consume you and your 50. 1
10 Then fire came . . and consumed him and his 50. 1
12 let fire come . . and consume you and your 50. 1
12 fire of God came . . and consumed him and his 50 1
14 fire came down from heaven, and consumed the two 1
2Ch 7: 1 fire . . consumed the burnt offering 1
Ezr 9:14 angry with us till thou wouldst consume us 7
Job 1:16 the sheep and the servants, and consumed them; 1
4: 9 by the blast of his anger they are consumed. 7
15:34 fire consumes the tents of bribery. 1
18:13 By disease his skin is consumed 1
13 the first-born of death consumes his limbs. 1

20:26 what is left in his tent will be consumed. 12
22:20 what they left the fire has consumed.' 1
31:12 that would be a fire which consumes unto Abaddon 1
Ps 18:37 and did not turn back till they were consumed. 7
21: 9 in his wrath; and fire will consume them. 1
39:11 thou dost consume like a moth what is dear to him; 9
59:13 consume them in wrath, consume them till they are 7
13 in wrath, consume them till they are no more 7
69: 9 For zeal for thy house has consumed me 1
71:13 May my accusers be put to shame and consumed; 7
83:14 As fire consumes the forest 4
90: 7 For we are consumed by thy anger; 7
104:35 Let sinners be consumed from the earth 15
119:20 My soul is consumed with longing 5
139My zeal consumes me, because my foes forget 11
Prv 5:11 when your flesh and body are consumed 7
Ecc 10:12 but the lips of a fool consume him. 3
Isa 1:28 those who forsake the LORD shall be consumed. 7
9:18 like a fire, it consumes briers and thorns; 1
26:11 Let the fire for thy adversaries consume them. 1
33:11 your breath is a fire that will consume you. 1
43: 2 and the flame shall not consume you. 4
47:14 they are like stubble, the fire consumes them; 14
Jer 5: 3 thou hast consumed them 7
6:29 the lead is consumed by the fire; 15
9:16 the sword after them, until I have consumed them. 7
10:25 they have devoured him and consumed him 7
11:16 and its branches will be consumed. 13
14:12 but I will consume them by the sword, by famine 7
15 By . . famine those prophets shall be consumed. 15
27: 8 until I have consumed it by his hand. 15
36:23 until the entire scroll was consumed in the fire 15
44:12 and they shall all be consumed; 15
12 by the sword and by famine they shall be consumed; 15
18 and have been consumed by the sword 15
27 shall be consumed by the sword and by famine 15
49:37 the sword after them, until I have consumed them; 7
Lam 2: 3 he has burned like . . consuming all around. 1
4:11 a fire in Zion, which consumed its foundations. 1
Ezk 5:12 and be consumed with famine in the midst of you; 7
15: 4 when the fire has consumed both ends of it 1
5 when the fire has consumed it and it is charred 1
7 from the fire, the fire shall yet consume them; 1
19:12 stem was withered; the fire consumed it. 1
14 And fire . . has consumed its branches and fruit 1
22:15 I will consume your filthiness out of you. 15
31 I have consumed them with the fire of my wrath; 7
24:11 filthiness . . melted in it, its rust consumed. 15
28:18 fire from the midst of you; it consumed you 1
34:29 shall no more be consumed with hunger in the land 2
43: 8 so I have consumed them in my anger. 7
Dan 7:26 consumed and destroyed to the end. 16
Hos 11: 6 consume the bars of their gates, and devour them 7
Obd 1:18 they shall burn them and consume them 1
Nah 1:10 Like entangled thorns they are consumed 1
Zep 1:18 all the earth shall be consumed; 1
3: 8 all the earth shall be consumed. 1
Zec 5: 4 it shall abide in his house and consume it 7
Mal 3: 6 therefore you, O sons of Jacob, are not consumed. 7
Mat 6:19 where moth and rust consume and where thieves 19
20 in heaven, where neither moth nor rust consumes 19
Lke 9:54 fire come down from heaven and consume them? 17
Joh 2:17 Zeal for thy house will consume me. 32
Rom 1:27 men . . consumed with passion for one another 23
Gal 5:15 you are not consumed by one another. 17
Heb 10:27 fire which will consume the adversaries. 25
12:29 for our God is a consuming fire. 29
Rev 11: 5 fire pours out . . and consumes their foes; 32
20: 9 but fire came down from heaven and consumed them 32
2Es 4:16 for the fire came and consumed it; 38
7:87 and be consumed with shame 38
12:44 we also had been consumed in the burning of Zion! 42
15:23 and will consume the foundations of the earth 40
16:15 until it consumes the foundations of the earth. 41
77 It is shut off and given up to be consumed by fire. 39
Jdt 11:13 decided to consume the first fruits of the grain 24
AEs 11:11 consumed those held in honor. 32
Wis 5:13 were consumed in our wickedness. 27
14:15 consumed with grief at an untimely bereavement 36
16:18 consume the creatures sent against the ungodly 31
19:21 Flames . . failed to consume the flesh 33
Sir 23:16 will not be quenched until it is consumed 30
27:29 pain will consume them before their death. 29
36: 9 be consumed in the fiery wrath 26
43:21 He consumes the mountains 32
45:19 to consume them in flaming fire. 29
LJr 1:63 sent from above to consume mountains and woods 24
72 they will finally themselves be consumed 20
Bel 1:13 to go in regularly and consume the provisions. 18
1Mc 6:53 had consumed the last of the stores. 32
2Mc 1:23 while the sacrifice was being consumed 21
31 the materials of the sacrifice were consumed 17
2:10 fire . . consumed the whole burnt offerings. 17
11 Moses said, "They were consumed because . . 17
4Mc 3:11 undid and consumed him. 31
7: 4 his sacred life was consumed by tortures 34
12 though being consumed by the fire 37
14:10 it consumed their bodies quickly. 22
15:15 the flesh of her children consumed by fire 35
18:14 the flame shall not consume you.' 28

utterly consume 1. בער 2. *καταναλίσκομαι*
1Kg 14:10 and will utterly consume the house of Jerobo'am 1
Wis 16:16 and utterly consumed by fire. 2

consume with fire 1. *καταφλέγω*
3Mc 2: 5 consumed with fire and sulphur the men of Sodom 1

consummation 1. *συντέλεια*
Sir 39:28 in the time of consummation 1

consumption 1. שַׁחֶפֶת
Lev 26:16 I will appoint over you . . consumption, and fever 1
Deu 28:22 LORD will smite you with consumption . . fever 1

contact
Lev 22: 4 unclean through contact with the dead *
Num 5: 2 unclean through contact with the dead; *
Hag 2:13 If one who is unclean by contact with a dead body *

contain 1. בַּיִת 2. כול 3. נשא 4. *ἐκεῖ* 5. *ἐν* 6. *χωρέω*
1Kg 8:27 and the highest heaven cannot contain thee; 2
18:32 trench . . as great as would contain two measures 1
2Ch 2: 6 heaven, even highest heaven, cannot contain him? 2
6:18 heaven and the highest heaven cannot contain 2
Jer 32:11 sealed deed of purchase, containing the terms *
Ezk 12:19 their land will be stripped of all it contains *
23:32 and held in derision, for it contains much; 2
45:11 the bath containing one tenth of a homer 3
14 the cor, like the homer, contains ten baths *
Joh 21:25 the world itself could not contain the books 6
Heb 9: 4 which contained a golden urn holding the manna 5
1Mc 6: 2 containing golden shields, breastplates 4
12: 8 the letter, which contained a clear declaration 5

contemporary
2Es 5:54 that you and your contemporaries are smaller *

contempt 1. בוז 2. בִּזָּיוֹן 3. דֵּרָאוֹן 4. קָלוֹן 5. קלל 6. שְׁאָט 7. *ἐξουδενέω* 8. *ἐξουδένωσις* 9. *καταφρονέω* 10. *καταφρόνησις* 11. contemptus 12. inproperium
Gen 16: 4 she looked with contempt on her mistress. 5
5 she looked on me with contempt. 5
Est 1:17 to look with contempt upon their husbands †
18 and there will be contempt and wrath in plenty. 2
Job 12: 5 there is contempt for misfortune; 1
21 He pours contempt on princes 1
31:34 the contempt of families terrified me 1
Ps 31:18 against the righteous in pride and contempt. 1
107:40 he pours contempt upon princes 1
119:22 take away from me their scorn and contempt 1
123: 3 for we have had more than enough of contempt. 1
4 who are at ease, the contempt of the proud. 1
Prv 18: 3 When wickedness comes, contempt comes also; 1
Ezk 36: 5 with wholehearted joy and utter contempt 6
Dan 12: 2 some to shame and everlasting contempt. 3
Hab 2:16 will be sated with contempt instead of glory. 4
2Es 9: 9 those who have rejected them with contempt 11
16:69 shall be held in derision and contempt 12
Wis 4:18 They will see, and will have contempt for him 7
14:30 through contempt for holiness. 9
1Mc 1:39 her honor into contempt. 8
2Mc 3:18 the holy place was about to be brought into contempt. 10

contempt *See also* bring, cast, hold, treat.

contemptible *See* make.

contemptible person 1. בזה
Dan 11:21 In his place shall arise a contemptible person 1

contemptuous 1. *περιφρονέω* 2. contemno
2Es 8:56 and were contemptuous of his law 2
4Mc 8:28 For they were contemptuous of the emotions 1

contemptuous *See also* dealing.

contemptuously *See* treat.

contend 1. גרה 2. חזק 3. יכח 4. יָרִיב 5. מַצּוּת 6. נצה 7. עשק 8. ריב 9. *ἀγωνίζομαι* 10. *διακρίνω* 11. *διαμάχομαι* 12. *ἐπαγωνίζομαι* 13. *πάλη*
Gen 26:20 Esek, because they contended with him. 7
Num20: 3 people contended with Moses, and said, "Would that 8
13 Mer'ibah, where the people of Israel contended 8
26: 9 who contended against Moses and Aaron 6
9 Korah, when they contended against the LORD 6
Deu 2: 5 do not contend with them; for I will not give you 1
9 'Do not harass Moab or contend with them in battle 1
19 sons of Ammon, do not harass them or contend 1
24 take possession, and contend with him in battle. 1
33: 7 With thy hands contend for him, and be a help 8
Jdg 6:31 Will you contend for Ba'al? Or will you defend 8
31 Whoever contends for him shall be put to death 8
31 If he is a god, let him contend for himself 8
32 that is to say, "Let Ba'al contend against him 8
Neh 13:25 I contended with them and cursed them and beat 8
Job 9: 3 If one wished to contend with him, one could not 8
10: 2 let me know why thou dost contend against me. 8
13:19 Who is there that will contend with me? 8
23: 6 he contend with me in the greatness of his power? 8
33:13 Why do you contend against him, saying 8
40: 2 Shall a faultfinder contend with the Almighty? 8
Ps 35: 1 Contend, O LORD, with those who contend with me; 8
1 Contend, O LORD, with those who contend with me; 4
Prv 3:30 Do not contend with a man for no reason 8
Isa 3:13 The LORD has taken his place to contend 8
27: 8 by exile thou didst contend with them; 8
41:12 You shall seek those who contend with you 5
49:25 I will contend with those who contend with you 8
25 I will contend with those who contend with you 8
50: 8 Who will contend with me? 8
57:16 For I will not contend for ever, nor will I always 8
Jer 2: 9 Therefore I still contend with you, says the LORD 8
9 with your children's children I will contend. 8
Dan 10:21 none who contends by my side 2
Hos 4: 4 Yet let no one contend, and let none accuse 8
Mic 6: 2 and he will contend with Israel. 3
Act 23: 9 some of the scribes . . stood up and contended 11
Eph 6:12 we are not contending against flesh and blood 13
Jde 1: 3 appealing to you to contend for the faith 12
9 archangel Michael, contending with the devil 10
Sir 8: 1 Do not contend with a powerful man 11
4Mc 17:13 the brothers contended. 9

powerful contender 1. עָצוּם
Prv 18:18 lot . . decides between powerful contenders. 1

content 1. יאל 2. יטב 3. *ἀρκέω* 4. *αὐτάρκης* 5. *διαρκέω* 6. *εὐδοκέω* 7. *εὐδοκία*
Exd 2:21 Moses was content to dwell with the man 1
Lev 10:20 when Moses heard that, he was content 2
Jos 7: 7 we had been content to dwell beyond the Jordan! 1
Jdg 17:11 And the Levite was content to dwell with the man; 1
2Kg 14:10 Be content with your glory, and stay at home; *
Ezk 16:47 Yet you were not content to walk in their ways *
Lke 3:14 be content with your wages. 3
2Co 12:10 I am content with weaknesses, insults, hardships 6
Php 4:11 I have learned, in whatever state I am, to be content. 4
1Ti 6: 8 with these we shall be content. 3
Heb 13: 5 be content with what you have 3
3Jn 1:10 And not content with that, he refuses 3
Sir 29:23 Be content with little or much. 7
2Mc 5:15 Not content with this 3
3Mc 2:26 He was not content 5

content (2) 1. *ἔχω* 2. *ὁ ἐν* 3. *περιέχω* 4. concipio
2Es 16:57 who has measured the sea and its contents; 4
LJr 1:59 the door of a house that protects its contents 2
1Mc 11:29 its contents were as follows 1
15: 2 its contents were as follows 3
2Mc 9:18 This was its content 3

contention 1. מָדוֹן 2. רִיב
Prv 15:18 but he who is slow to anger quiets contention. 2
Jer 15:10 a man of strife and contention to the whole land! 1
Hos 4: 4 for with you is my contention, O priest. *
Hab 1: 3 strife and contention arise. 1

sharp contention 1. *παροξυσμός*
Act 15:39 And there arose a sharp contention 1

contentious 1. מָדוֹן 2. מִדְיָן 3. *φιλόνικος*
Prv 21: 9 than in a house shared with a contentious woman. 2
19 than with a contentious and fretful woman. 1
25:24 than in a house shared with a contentious woman. 2
27:15 continual dripping . . contentious woman are alike; 2
1Co 11:16 If any one is disposed to be contentious 3

contentiousness 1. *φιλονεικία*
4Mc 8:26 Why does such contentiousness excite us 1

contentment 1. *αὐτάρκεια*
1Ti 6: 6 is great gain in godliness with contentment; 1

contest 1. כֹּחַ 2. *ἀγών* 3. certamen
Job 9:19 If it is a contest of strength, behold him! 1
2Es 7:127This is the meaning of the contest 3
Wis 4: 2 victor in the contest for prizes 2
10:12 in his arduous contest she gave him the victory 2
4Mc 11:20 O contest befitting holiness 2
15:29 who carried away the prize of the contest 2
16:16 noble is the contest to which you are called 2
17:11 Truly the contest . . was divine 2

contest *See also* wage.

contestant 1. *ἀγωνιστής*
4Mc 12:14 having slain . . the contestants for virtue. 1

first contestant 1. *προαγωνίζομαι*
4Mc 17:13 Eleazar was the first contestant 1

contingent 1. *δῆμος*
Jdt 6: 1 in the presence of all the foreign contingents 1

continual 1. אֵיתָן 2. טרד 3. כֹּל הַיָּמִים 4. תָּמִיד
5. εἰς τέλος 6. ἐνδελεχισμός

Exd 28:29 to bring them to continual remembrance before 4
29:42 It shall be a continual burnt offering 4
Num 4: 7 continual bread also shall be on it; 4
16 charge of . . the continual cereal offering 4
28: 3 two male lambs . . as a continual offering. 4
6 It is a continual burnt offering 4
10 the continual burnt offering and its drink 4
15 offered besides the continual burnt offering 4
23 which is for a continual burnt offering. 4
24 offered besides the continual burnt offering 4
31 Besides the continual burnt offering 4
29: 6 besides . . the continual burnt offering 4
11 besides . . the continual burnt offering 4
16 besides the continual burnt offering 4
19 besides the continual burnt offering 4
22 besides the continual burnt offering 4
25 besides the continual burnt offering 4
28 besides the continual burnt offering 4
31 besides the continual burnt offering 4
34 besides the continual burnt offering 4
38 besides the continual burnt offering 4
2Ch 2: 4 and for the continual offering of the showbread 4
12:15 continual wars between Rehobo'am and Jerobo'am. 3
Ezr 3: 5 after that the continual burnt offerings 4
Neh 10:33 showbread, the continual cereal offering 4
33 continual burnt offering, the sabbaths 4
Job 33:19 with continual strife in his bones; 1
Prv 15:15 but a cheerful heart has a continual feast. 4
19:13 quarreling is a continual dripping of rain. 2
27:15 A continual dripping on a rainy day 2
Ezk 38: 8 Israel, which had been a continual waste; 4
46:14 ordinance for the continual burnt offering. 4
15 by morning, for a continual burnt offering. 4
Lke 18: 5 she will wear me out by her continual coming.' 5
1Es 5:52 thereafter the continual offerings 6
Jdt 4:14 Joakim . . offered the continual burnt offerings 6

continually 1. בְּכָל עֵת 2. הלך 3. הלך וָשׁוב
4. כֹּל יוֹם 5. עוֹד 6. תָּמִיד 7. תְּדִירָא (A) 8. ἀνακαινίζω
9. διὰ παντός 10. διατελέω 11. διηνεκῶς
12. εἰς τὸ διηνεκές 13. ἐνδελεχής 14. ἐνδελεχίζω
15. ἐνδελεχῶς 16. καθίστημι 17. perseveranter
18. sine intermissione

Gen 6: 5 of his heart was only evil continually. 4
8: 3 the waters receded from the earth continually. 3
Exd 27:20 that a lamp may be set up to burn continually. 6
28:30 upon his heart before the LORD continually. 6
29:38 two lambs a year old day by day continually. 6
Lev 6:13 be kept burning upon the altar continually 6
24: 2 that a light may be kept burning continually 6
3 keep it in order . . before the LORD continually 6
4 keep the lamps in order . . continually 6
8 set it in order . . continually on behalf 6
Num 9:16 it was continually; the cloud covered it by day 6
Deu 28:29 only oppressed and robbed continually 4
33 be only oppressed and crushed continually; 4
Jos 6: 9 while the trumpets blew continually. 2
13 passed on, blowing the trumpets continually; 2
13 while the trumpets blew continually. 2
1Sm 18:29 Saul was David's enemy continually. 4
2Sm 16: 5 and as he came he cursed continually. †
1Kg 10: 8 who continually stand before you and hear 6
14:30 there was war between . . and . . continually. 4
2Kg 4: 9 man of God, who is continually passing our way. 6
13: 3 he gave them continually into the hand of Haz'ael 4
1Ch 16: 6 to blow trumpets continually, before the ark 6
11 and his strength, seek his presence continually! 6
37 to minister continually before the ark 6
40 continually morning and evening 6
23:31 required of them, continually before the LORD. 6
2Ch 9: 7 servants, who continually stand before you 6
24:14 continually all the days of Jehoi'ada. 6
Job 1: 5 Thus Job did continually. 4
Ps 34: 1 his praise shall continually be in my mouth. 6
40:16 those who love thy salvation say continually 6
42: 3 while men say to me continually, "Where is your God? 4
10 they say to me continually, "Where is your God? 4
44: 8 In God we have boasted continually 4
50: 8 your burnt offerings are continually before me. 6
69:23 make their loins tremble continually. 6
71: 6 My praise is continually of thee. 6
14 I will hope continually, and will praise thee yet 6
72:15 May prayer be made for him continually 6
73:23 Nevertheless I am continually with thee; 6
74:23 of thy adversaries which goes up continually! 6
105: 4 seek his presence continually! 6
109:15 Let them be before the LORD continually; 6
119:44 I will keep thy law continually, for ever and ever; 6
109 I hold my life in my hand continually 6
117 have regard for thy statutes continually! 6
140: 2 stir up wars continually. 4
141: 5 for my prayer is continually against their 5
Prv 6:14 continually sowing discord; 1
Isa 21: 8 Upon a watchtower I stand . . continually by day 6
28:24 Does he who plows for sowing plow continually? 4
24 does he continually open and harrow his ground? •
49:16 Behold . . your walls are continually before me. 6
51:13 and fear continually all the day 6
52: 5 and continually all the day my name is despised. 6
58:11 And the LORD will guide you continually 6
60:11 Your gates shall be open continually; 6
65: 3 a people who provoke me to my face continually 6
Jer 23:17 They say continually to those who despise †
Lam 3:20 My soul continually thinks of it and is bowed †
Ezk 39:14 men to pass through the land continually 6
Dan 6:16 God, whom you serve continually, deliver you 7
20 has your God, whom you serve continually 7
Hos 12: 6 and wait continually for your God. 6
Lke 24:53 were continually in the temple blessing God. 9
Heb 9: 6 the priests go continually into the outer tent 9
10: 1 same sacrifices which are continually offered 12
13:15 let us continually offer up a sacrifice 9
2Es 9:25 pray to the Most High continually 18
10:39 you have sorrowed continually for your people 18
15: 8 the souls of the righteous cry out continually. 17
AEs 13: 4 continually disregard the ordinances 11
16:11 was continually bowed down to by all 10
Wis 10: 7 a continually smoking wasteland 16
Sir 17:19 his eyes are continually upon their ways. 13
20:19 continually on the lips of the ignorant. 14
24 it is continually on the lips of the ignorant. 14
23:10 continually examined under torture 13
37:18 it is the tongue that continually rules them. 13
45:14 be wholly burned twice every day continually. 13
51:11 I will praise thy name continually 15
Man 1:15 I will praise thee continually 9
1Mc 1:36 an evil adversary of Israel continually. 9
6: 9 because deep grief continually gripped him 8
15:25 continually throwing his forces against it 9
3Mc 4:16 was greatly and continually filled with joy 11

continually *See also* flash.

continue 1. ארך 2. היה 3. היה הלך 4. הלך 5. יסף
6. יצא 7. ישב 8. כון 9. משך 10. עוֹד 11. עמד 12. קום
13. רבה 14. γίνομαι 15. διαμένω 16. διατελέω
17. εἰμί 18. ἐμμένω 19. ἐπιμένω 20. ἔτι 21. λοιπός
22. μακροτονέω 23. μένω 24. παραμένω
25. περικάθημαι 26. προέρχομαι 27. προσμένω
28. προστίθημι 29. adhuc 30. adicio 31. nolo 32. teneo

Gen 7:17 The flood continued 40 days upon the earth; 2
8: 5 the waters continued to abate 3
15: 2 give me, for I continue childless 4
40: 4 and they continued for some time in custody. 2
Lev 12: 4 Then she shall continue for 33 days in the blood 7
5 she shall continue in the blood of her purifying 7
15:25 she shall continue in uncleanness •
Num 9:19 cloud continued over the tabernacle many days 1
21 if it continued for a day and a night •
22 that the cloud continued over the tabernacle 1
21:16 from there they continued to Beer; •
Deu 31: 1 Moses continued to speak these words 4
Jos 9:27 Joshua made them . . to continue to this day •
18: 5 Judah continuing in his territory on the south 11
19:27 then it continues in the north to Cabul 6
23:13 the LORD your God will not continue to drive out 5
Rut 2: 7 she has continued from early morning until now 11
1Sm 1:12 As she continued praying before the LORD 13
2:26 the boy Samuel continued to grow both in stature 4
13:14 But now your kingdom shall not continue; 12
2Sm 7:29 that it may continue for ever before thee; 2
1Kg 22: 1 Syria and Israel continued without war. 7
2Kg 12: 3 the people continued to sacrifice and burn 10
1Ch 17:27 that it may continue for ever before thee; 2
28: 7 if he continues resolute in keeping •
2Ch 29:28 all this continued until the burnt offering •
Neh 1: 4 I continued fasting and praying before the God •
Job 14: 2 he flees like a shadow, and continues not. 11
36: 1 Eli'hu continued, and said 5
Ps 36:10 O continue thy steadfast love to those who know 9
49: 9 that he should continue to live on for ever 10
72:17 for ever, his fame continue as long as the sun! •
101: 7 no man . . lies shall continue in my presence. 8
Prv 23:17 but continue in the fear of the LORD all the day. •
Isa 1: 5 Why . . be smitten, that you continue to rebel? 5
Jer 31: 3 I have continued my faithfulness to you. 9
Dan 1:21 Daniel continued until the first year of King •
Hos 10: 9 there they have continued. 11
Zec 14: 8 it shall continue in summer as in winter. 2
Lke 22:28 those who have continued with me in my trials; 15
Joh 8: 7 as they continued to ask him 19
31 If you continue in my word 23
35 The slave does not continue in the house for ever; 23
35 the son continues for ever. 23
Act 12:16 Peter continued knocking 19
13:43 urged them to continue in the grace of God. 27
14:22 exhorting them to continue in the faith 18
19:10 This continued for two years 14
27:33 you have continued in suspense and without food 16
Rom 6: 1 Are we to continue in sin that grace may abound? 19
9:11 that God's purpose of election might continue 23
11:22 provided you continue in his kindness; 19
2Co 11:12 what I do I will continue to do •
Php 1:25 I shall remain and continue with you all 24
Col 1:23 provided that you continue in the faith 19
1Ti 2:15 if she continues in faith and love and holiness 23
5: 5 continues in supplications and prayers 27
2Ti 3:14 as for you, continue in what you have learned 23
Heb 7: 3 he continues a priest for ever. 23
23 were prevented by death from continuing in office; 24
24 because he continues for ever. 23
8: 9 for they did not continue in my covenant 18
13: 1 Let brotherly love continue. 23
2Pe 3: 4 all things have continued as they were 15
1Jn 2:19 they would have continued with us; 23
2Es 9:13 Therefore, do not continue to be curious as to how 31
41 that I may weep for myself and continue to mourn 30
11:13 and it continued to reign a long time. 32
16:71 destroying those who continue to fear the Lord. 29
Tob 14: 2 He gave alms, and he continued to fear the Lord God 28
Jdt 16:15 thou wilt continue to show mercy. •
20 the people continued feasting in Jerusalem 17
Wis 16: 5 thy wrath did not continue to the end; 23
18:20 the wrath did not long continue. 23
Sir 38:19 In calamity sorrow continues 24
44:13 Their posterity will continue for ever 23
1Mc 10:26 have continued your friendship with us 18
27 now continue still to keep faith with us 18
11:22 he wrote Jonathan not to continue the siege 25
23 he gave orders to continue the siege •
2Mc 5:27 they continued to live on what grew wild 16
8: 1 those who had continued in the Jewish faith 23
26 they did not continue their pursuit. 22
3Mc 2:26 he also continued with such audacity 26
3: 3 The Jews . . continued to maintain good will •
5: 5 arranged for their continued custody 21
4Mc 5:10 you continue to despise me to your own hurt. 20

continue all night 1. διανυκτερεύω

Lke 6:12 and all night he continued in prayer to God. 1

continue long 1. ארך 2. ארך יָמִים

Deu 17:20 continue long in his kingdom, he and his children 2
Prv 28: 2 with men . . its stability will long continue. 1

continue on one's way 1. ὁδεύω 2. πορεύω

Tob 6: 5 they both continued on their way 1
11: 1 he continued on his way 2

continue steadfastly 1. προσκαρτερέω

Col 4: 2 Continue steadfastly in prayer 1

continue with 1. προσκαρτερέω

Act 8:13 after being baptized he continued with Philip. 1

continuous 1. אֶחָד 2. πυκνός

Zec 14: 7 there shall be continuous day 1
3Mc 1:28 The continuous, vehement, and concerted cry 2

continuously 1. ἀδιαλείπτως

2Mc 3:26 scourged him continuously 1

contract 1. συγγραφή 2. συνάλλαγμα

Tob 7:14 and took a scroll and wrote out the contract 1
1Mc 13:42 to write in their documents and contracts 2
14:43 all contracts in the country 1

contradict 1. ἀναντίρρητος 2. ἀντεῖπον
3. ἀντιλέγω

Lke 21:15 will be able to withstand or contradict. 2
Act 13:45 contradicted what was spoken by Paul 3
19:36 these things cannot be contradicted 1
Tit 1: 9 to confute those who contradict it. 3

contradiction 1. ἀντίθεσις

1Ti 6:20 Avoid the godless chatter and contradictions 1

contradiction arise 1. ἐναντιόομαι

4Mc 7:20 No contradiction therefore arises 1

contrary 1. קְרִי 2. ἀλλά 3. ἀνάπαλιν 4. ἀντίθετος
5. ἀντίκειμαι 6. ἀντιλέγω 7. ἀπειθέω 8. ἐναντίον
9. ἐναντίος 10. ἐναντιόω 11. παρά 12. τοὐναντίον

Lev 26:21 Then if you walk contrary to me 1
23 And if . . you . . walk contrary to me 1
24 then I also will walk contrary to you 1
27 And if . . you . . walk contrary to me 1
28 then I will walk contrary to you in fury 1
40 iniquity . . also in walking contrary to me 1
41 so that I walked contrary to them 1
Act 18:13 worship God contrary to the law. 11
Rom 3:31 By no means! On the contrary, we uphold the law. 2
10:21 my hands to a disobedient and contrary people. 6
11:24 grafted, contrary to nature, into a cultivated 11
1Co 15:10 On the contrary, I worked harder than any of them 2
Gal 1: 8 a gospel contrary to that which we preached 11
9 a gospel contrary to that which you received 11
2: 7 but on the contrary, when they saw 8
1Ti 1:10 whatever else is contrary to sound doctrine 5
1Pe 3: 9 but on the contrary bless 8
AEs 13: 4 have laws contrary to those of every nation 4

Wis 15: 7 those for contrary uses 9
19:21 Flames, on the contrary, failed to consume the flesh 3
Sir 41: 2 one who is contrary, and has lost his patience! 7
1Mc 14:45 Whoever acts contrary to these decisions 11
3Mc 3:22 they took this in a contrary spirit 12
4Mc 2: 8 he is forced to act contrary to his natural ways •
5:26 to eat meats that would be contrary to this. 10

contrary to the law 1. παρανομέω 2. παράνομος
Act 23: 3 yet contrary to the law you order me to be struck? 1
2Mc 4:11 and introduced new customs contrary to the law. 2

contribute 1. רום 2. תְּנוּפָה 3. βάλλω 4. κοινωνέω 5. μεταδίδωμι
Exd 38:29 the bronze that was contributed was 70 talents 2
2Ch 35: 7 Then Josi'ah contributed to the lay people 1
8 princes contributed willingly to the people 1
Mrk 12:43 all those who are contributing to the treasury. 3
44 For they all contributed out of their abundance; 3
Lke 21: 4 for they all contributed out of their abundance 3
Rom 12: 8 he who contributes, in liberality; 5
13 Contribute to the needs of the saints 4

contribution 1. מִנְחָה 2. תְּרוּמָה 3. κοινωνία 4. λογεία
2Ch 31: 3 The contribution of the king 1
10 Since they began to bring the contributions 2
12 they faithfully brought in the contributions 2
14 apportion the contribution reserved 2
Neh 10:37 bring . . of our coarse meal, and our contributions 2
39 bring the contribution of grain, wine, and oil 2
12:44 stores, the contributions, the first fruits 2
13: 5 previously put . . contributions for the priests. 2
Ezk 20:40 there I will require your contributions 2
Rom 15:26 pleased to make some contribution for the poor 3
1Co 16: 1 Now concerning the contribution for the saints 4
2 so that contributions need not be made when I come. 4
2Co 9:13 the generosity of your contribution for them 3

contrite 1. דכא 2. דַּכָּא 3. דכה 4. נָכֶה 5. συντρίβω
Ps 51:17 a . . contrite heart, O God, thou wilt not despise. 3
Isa 57:15 with him who is of a contrite and humble spirit 2
15 and to revive the heart of the contrite. 1
66: 2 he that is humble and contrite in spirit 4
Aza 1:16 with a contrite heart and a humble spirit 5

contrive 1. εἰς 2. ἐπινοέω 3. εὑρετής 4. τίθημι
Act 5: 4 How is it that you have contrived this deed 4
2Mc 7:31 who have contrived all sorts of evil 3
3Mc 4:19 had been bribed to contrive a means of escape 1
4Mc 10:16 Contrive tortures, tyrant, so that you may learn 2

maliciously contrive 1. κακότεχνος
4Mc 6:25 maliciously contrived instruments 1

control 1. אפק 2. διαιρέω 3. ἐγκρατής 4. ἐξουσία 5. κατακρατέω 6. κρατέω 7. κυριεύω 8. περικρατέω 9. συνέχω 10. σωφρονέω 11. ὑποχείριος
Gen 43:31 and controlling himself he said 1
45: 1 Joseph could not control himself before all 1
1Co 7:37 having his desire under control 4
2Co 5:14 For the love of Christ controls us 9
Tit 2: 6 urge the younger men to control themselves. 10
Sir 21:11 Whoever keeps the law controls his thoughts 5
1Mc 6:63 He found Philip in control of the city 7
8:16 to control all their land 7
10:32 I release also my control of the citadel 4
2Mc 3: 6 to fall under the control of the king. 4
9: 2 rob the temples and control the city 9
10:15 who had control of important strongholds 3
3Mc 1: 1 the regions which he had controlled 6
6: 5 had already gained control of the whole world 11
4Mc 1: 9 reason controls the emotions. 8
2: 6 reason is able to control desires. 6
17 controlled his anger by reason. 2
20 For if reason could not control anger 6
24 does not control forgetfulness and ignorance 6
7:18 are able to control the passions of the flesh 6
control *See also* gain, get, hold, outside, seize.

controversy 1. רִיב 2. ζήτημα 3. ζήτησις
Ezk 44:24 In a controversy they shall act as judges 1
Hos 4: 1 the LORD has a controversy with the inhabitants 1
Mic 6: 2 Hear, you mountains, the controversy of the LORD 1
2 for the LORD has a controversy with his people 1
Act 26: 3 all customs and controversies of the Jews 2
1Ti 6: 4 he has a morbid craving for controversy 3
2Ti 2:23 stupid, senseless controversies 3
Tit 3: 9 avoid stupid controversies, genealogies 3

convene 1. ἐξεκκλησιάζω 2. ἐπιστρέφω 3. συνάγω
1Mc 12:35 he convened the elders of the people 1
14:44 to convene an assembly in the country 2
3Mc 6:33 after convening a great banquet 3

convenience 1. καιρός
Sir 6: 8 a friend who is such at his own convenience 1

convenient 1. ἐπιτήδειος
1Mc 4:46 stored the stones in a convenient place 1

converge upon 1. ἐπισυνάγω
1Mc 15:12 for he knew that troubles had converged upon him 1

conversant 1. ἔνοχος
Sir 0: 1 that, by becoming conversant with this also, 1

conversation 1. דָּבָר 2. διαλογισμός 3. λογισμός 4. λόγος
Jer 38:27 for the conversation had not been overheard. 1
Lke 24:17 he said to them, "What is this conversation 4
AEs 12: 2 He overheard their conversation 3
Sir 9:15 your conversation be with men of understanding 2
19: 7 Never repeat a conversation 4

converse 1. סוֹד 2. ὁμιλέω
Ps 55:14 We used to hold sweet converse together; 1
Act 20:11 he conversed with them a long while 2
24:26 So he sent for him often and conversed with him. 2

conversion 1. ἐπιστροφή
Act 15: 3 reporting the conversion of the Gentiles 1

convert 1. ἐπιστροφή 2. προσήλυτος 3. converto
Act 13:43 many Jews and devout converts to Judaism 2
2Es 6:26 and converted to a different spirit. 3
Sir 49: 2 He was led aright in converting the people 1

first convert 1. ἀπαρχή
Rom 16: 5 Epae'netus, who was the first convert in Asia 1
1Co 16:15 were the first converts in Acha'ia 1

recent convert 1. νεόφυτος
1Ti 3: 6 He must not be a recent convert 1

convey 1. בְּיַד 2. יבל (A) 3. διαφέρω
Ezr 7:15 also to convey the silver and gold which the king 2
Est 1:12 at the king's command conveyed by the eunuchs. 1
15 Ahasu-e'rus conveyed by the eunuchs? 1
1Es 5:55 convey them in rafts to the harbor of Joppa 3

convict 1. אָשֵׁם 2. ἔλεγχος 3. ἐλέγχω 4. συνίστημι
2Sm 14:13 giving this decision the king convicts himself 1
Joh 8:46 Which of you convicts me of sin? 3
1Co 14:24 he is convicted by all 3
Jas 2: 9 are convicted by the law as transgressors. 3
Jde 1:15 to convict all the ungodly of all their deeds 3
Wis 1: 3 when his power is tested, it convicts the foolish; 3
9 to convict him of his lawless deeds; 2
4:20 their lawless deeds will convict them 3
Sus 1:61 Daniel had convicted them of bearing false witness 4

conviction 1. ἔλεγχος 2. πληροφορία
1Th 1: 5 in the Holy Spirit and with full conviction 2
Heb 11: 1 faith is . . the conviction of things not seen. 1

convince 1. δοκέω 2. ἐλεάω 3. ἐλέγχω 4. κρίνω 5. πείθω 6. πιστωθῆναι 7. στηρίζω 8. συμπείθω
Lke 16:31 neither will they be convinced 5
20: 6 they are convinced that John was a prophet. 5
Joh 16: 8 when he comes, he will convince the world 3
Act 26: 9 I . . was convinced that I ought to do many things 1
28:23 trying to convince them about Jesus 5
24 some were convinced by what he said 5
2Co 5:14 because we are convinced 4
Php 1:25 Convinced of this, I know that I shall remain 5
2Ti 4: 2 be urgent in season and out of season, convince 3
Jde 1:22 And convince some, who doubt; 2
Wis 16: 8 this also thou didst convince our enemies 5
Sir 39:32 from the beginning I have been convinced 7
2Mc 13:26 convinced them, appeased them 8
3Mc 3:26 fully convinced by these indications 5
4:19 he was clearly convinced about the matter 6
5: 5 The servants . . convinced that . . 1
4Mc 9:18 Through all these tortures I will convince you 5

fully convince 1. πληροφορέω
Rom 4:21 fully convinced that God was able to do 1
14: 5 Let every one be fully convinced in his own mind. 1

more convincingly 1. περισσότερος
Heb 6:17 when God desired to show more convincingly 1

convocation 1. מִקְרָא
Lev 23: 2 you shall proclaim as holy convocations 1
3 a sabbath of solemn rest, a holy convocation 1
4 These are . . the holy convocations 1
7 the first day you shall have a holy convocation 1
8 on the seventh day is a holy convocation 1
21 you shall hold a holy convocation 1
24 you shall observe . . a holy convocation 1
27 it shall be for you a time of holy convocation 1
35 On the first day shall be a holy convocation 1
36 the eighth day you shall hold a holy convocation 1
37 you shall proclaim as times of holy convocation 1
Num 28:18 the first day there shall be a holy convocation 1
25 seventh day you shall have a holy convocation; 1
26 you shall have a holy convocation; 1
29: 1 first day . . you shall have a holy convocation; 1
7 tenth day . . you shall have a holy convocation 1
12 fifteenth . . you shall have a holy convocation; 1

convulse 1. רעם 2. σπαράσσω 3. συσπαράσσω
Ezk 27:35 are horribly afraid, their faces are convulsed. 1
Mrk 1:26 the unclean spirit, convulsing him and crying 2
9:20 immediately it convulsed the boy 3
26 after crying out and convulsing him terribly 2
Lke 9:39 it convulses him till he foams, and shatters him 2
42 the demon tore him and convulsed him 3

cook 1. טַבָּח 2. טַבָּחָה 3. ἕψω
Lev 2: 7 offering is a cereal offering cooked in a pan •
1Sm 8:13 daughters to be perfumers and cooks and bakers. 2
9:23 Samuel said to the cook, "Bring the portion 1
24 the cook took up the leg and the upper portion 1
4Mc 6:15 We will set before you some cooked meat 3

cool 1. מְקֵרָה 2. קַר 3. רוּחַ 4. καταψύχω
Gen 3: 8 walking in the garden in the cool of the day 3
Jdg 3:20 as he was sitting alone in his cool roof chamber. 1
24 He is only relieving himself in the . . cool chamber. 1
Prv 17:27 who has a cool spirit is a man of understanding. 2
Lke 16:24 cool my tongue 4

coping 1. טֶפַח
1Kg 7: 9 from the foundation to the coping 1

copper 1. נְחוּשָׁה 2. נְחֹשֶׁת 3. λεπτός 4. χαλκός
Deu 8: 9 a land . . out of whose hills you can dig copper. 2
Job 28: 2 copper is smelted from the ore. 1
Ezk 24:11 that it may become hot, and its copper may burn 2
Mat 10: 9 Take no gold, nor silver, nor copper in your belts 4
Lke 12:59 till you have paid the very last copper. 3
Sir 12:10 like the rusting of copper, so is his wickedness. 4
copper *See also* coin, worker.

coppersmith 1. χαλκεύς
2Ti 4:14 Alexander the coppersmith did me great harm 1

copy 1. מִשְׁנֶה 2. עתק 3. פַּתְשֶׁגֶן 4. תַּבְנִית 5. פַּרְשֶׁגֶן (A) 6. ἀντίγραφον 7. ἀντίτυπος 8. μίμημα 9. ὑπόδειγμα
Deu 17:18 write for himself in a book a copy of this law 1
Jos 8:32 he wrote upon the stones a copy of the law of Moses 1
22:28 Behold the copy of the altar of the LORD 4
Ezr 4:11 copy of the letter that they sent–"To Ar-ta-xerx'es 5
23 the copy of King Ar-ta-xerx'es' letter was read 5
5: 6 copy of the letter which Tat'tenai . . sent 5
7:11 This is a copy of the letter which King 5
Est 3:14 A copy of the document was to be issued as a decree 3
4: 8 Mor'decai . . gave him a copy of the written decree 3
8:13 A copy of what was written was to be issued 3
Prv 25: 1 proverbs . . men of Hezeki'ah king of Judah copied. 2
Jer 32:11 the terms and conditions, and the open copy; •
Heb 8: 5 They serve a copy and shadow 9
9:23 the copies of the heavenly things 9
24 a copy of the true one 7
1Es 6: 7 A copy of the letter which Sisinnes . . wrote 6
8: 8 The following is a copy 6
AEs 13: 1 This is a copy of the letter 6
16: 1 The following is a copy of this letter 6
19 Therefore post a copy of this letter publicly 6
Wis 9: 8 a copy of the holy tent which thou didst prepare 8
LJr 1: 1 A copy of a letter which Jeremiah sent 6
1Mc 8:22 a copy of the letter which they wrote in reply 6
11:31 This copy of the letter 6
37 Now therefore take care to make a copy of this 6
12: 5 This is a copy of the letter which Jonathan wrote 6
7 you are our brethren, as the appended copy shows. 6
19 a copy of the letter which they sent to Onias 6
14:20 a copy of the letter which the Spartans sent 6
23 put a copy of their words in the public archives 6
23 they have sent a copy of this to Simon the high priest.' 6
27 This is a copy of what they wrote 6
49 to deposit copies of them in the treasury 6
15:24 They also sent a copy of these things to Simon 6

cor 1. כֹּר 2. כּוֹר (A) 3. κόρος 4. corum
1Kg 4:22 provision . . was 30 cors of fine flour 1
22 provision for one day was . . and 60 cors of meal 1
5:11 Solomon gave Hiram 20,000 cors of wheat as food 1
11 Solomon gave . . and 20,000 cors of beaten oil. 1
2Ch 2:10 20,000 cors of crushed wheat 1
10 crushed wheat, 20,000 cors of barley 1
27: 5 gave him that year . . and 10,000 cors of wheat 1
Ezr 7:22 up to . . 100 cors of wheat 2
Ezk 45:14 portion of oil, one tenth of a bath from each cor 1
14 the cor, like the homer, contains ten baths 4
1Es 8:20 likewise up to 100 cors of wheat 3

coral 1. פְּנִינִים 2. רָאמוֹת
Job 28:18 No mention shall be made of coral or of crystal; 2
Lam 4: 7 their bodies were more ruddy than coral 1
Ezk 27:16 embroidered work, fine linen, coral, and agate. 2

cord 1. חֶבֶל 2. חוּט 3. יֶתֶר 4. מִגְבָּלֹת 5. מֵיתָר 6. מַשְׂכֹּת 7. עֲבֹת 8. פָּתִיל 9. תִּקְוָה 10. תִּקְוַת חוּט 11. κλῶσμα 12. νευρά 13. σχοινίον

Gen 38:18 Your signet and your cord, and your staff 8
25 Mark . . the signet and the cord and the staff. 8
Exd 28:14 two chains of pure gold, twisted like cords; 4
14 shall attach the corded chains to the settings. 7
22 make . . twisted chains like cords, of pure gold; 7
24 the two cords of gold in the two rings at the edges 7
25 the two ends of the two cords you shall attach 7
35:18 the pegs of the court, and their cords; 5
39:15 on the breastpiece twisted chains like cords 7
17 they put the two cords of gold in the two rings 7
18 Two ends of the two cords they had attached 7
40 gate of the court, its cords, and its pegs; 5
Num 3:26 the screen for the door . . and its cords; 5
37 pillars . . with their bases and pegs and cords. 5
4:26 cords, and all the equipment for their service; 5
32 pillars . . with their bases, pegs, and cords 5
15:38 to put upon the tassel of each corner a cord of blue; 8
Jos 2:18 you shall bind this scarlet cord in the window 10
21 and she bound the scarlet cord in the window. 9
2Sm 22: 6 the cords of Sheol entangled me 1
Est 1: 6 hangings caught up with cords of fine linen 1
Job 30:11 Because God has loosed my cord and humbled me 3
36: 8 in fetters and caught in the cords of affliction 1
38:31 the Plei'ades, or loose the cords of Orion? 6
41: 1 or press down his tongue with a cord? 1
Ps 2: 3 bonds asunder, and cast their cords from us. 7
18: 4 The cords of death encompassed me 1
5 the cords of Sheol entangled me 1
119:61 Though the cords of the wicked ensnare me 1
129: 4 righteous; he has cut the cords of the wicked. 7
140: 5 trap for me, and with cords they have spread a net 1
Ecc 4:12 A threefold cord is not quickly broken. 2
12: 6 before the silver cord is snapped 1
Isa 5:18 those who draw iniquity with cords of falsehood 1
33:20 nor will any of its cords be broken. 1
54: 2 lengthen your cords and strengthen your stakes. 5
Jer 10:20 My tent is destroyed, and all my cords are broken; 5
Ezk 3:25 O son of man, behold, cords will be placed upon you 7
4: 8 And, behold, I will put cords upon you 7
27:24 and in carpets of colored stuff, bound with cords 1
Hos 11: 4 I led them with cords of compassion 1
Joh 2:15 And making a whip of cords, he drove them all 13
Sir 6:30 her bonds are a cord of blue. 11
LJr 1:43 the women, with cords about them 13
43 her cord was not broken. 13
2Mc 7: 1 compelled . . under torture with whips and cords 12

coriander 1. גַּד

Exd 16:31 it was like coriander seed, white, and the taste 1
Num11: 7 Now the manna was like coriander seed 1

cormorant 1. שָׁלָךְ

Lev 11:17 the owl, the cormorant, the ibis 1
Deu 14:17 pelican, the carrion vulture and the cormorant 1

corner 1. זָוִית 2. כָּנָף 3. כָּתֵף 4. מִקְצֹעַ 5. מִקְצֹעָה 6. פֵּאָה 7. פנה 8. פִּנָּה 9. פַּעַם 10. קָצָה 11. ἀρχή 12. γωνία 13. κανθός

Exd 25:26 the rings to the four corners at its four legs. 6
26:23 make two frames for corners of the tabernacle 5
24 they shall form the two corners. 5
27: 2 you shall make horns for it on its four corners; 8
4 make four bronze rings at its four corners. 10
36:28 made two frames for corners of the tabernacle 5
29 he made two of them thus, for the two corners. 5
37: 3 four rings of gold for its four corners 9
13 the rings to the four corners at its four legs. 6
38: 2 He made horns for it on its four corners; 8
5 four rings on the four corners of the bronze 10
Num15:38 make tassels on the corners of their garments 2
38 to put upon the tassel of each corner a cord of blue; 2
Deu 22:12 tassels on the four corners of your cloak 2
1Kg 7:30 at the four corners were supports for a laver. 9
34 four supports at the four corners of each stand; 8
39 set the sea on the southeast corner of the house. 3
2Kg 14:13 from the E'phraim Gate to the Corner Gate. 8
2Ch 4:10 set the sea at the southeast corner of the house. 3
25:23 from the E'phraim Gate to the Corner Gate. 7
26: 9 built towers in Jerusalem at the Corner Gate 8
15 engines . . to be on the towers and the corners 8
28:24 made . . altars in every corner of Jerusalem. 8
Neh 3:25 to the corner. Palal the son of Uzai repaired 8
31 upper chamber of the corner. 8
32 between the upper chamber of the corner 8
9:22 didst allot to them every corner; 6
Job 1:19 and struck the four corners of the house 8
37: 3 his lightning to the corners of the earth. 2
Ps 118:22 rejected has become the head of the corner. 8
Prv 7: 8 passing along the street near her corner 8
12 at every corner she lies in wait. 8
21: 9 It is better to live in a corner of the housetop 8
25:24 better to live in a corner of the housetop 8
Isa 11:12 Judah from the four corners of the earth. 2
Jer 9:26 in the desert that cut the corners of their hair; 6
25:23 Buz, and all who cut the corners of their hair; 6
31:40 to the corner of the Horse Gate toward the east 8
49:32 those who cut the corners of their hair 6
51:26 No stone shall be taken from you for a corner 8
Ezk 7: 2 end has come upon the four corners of the land. 2
41:22 its corners, its base, and its walls were of wood. 5
43:20 on the four corners of the ledge, and upon the rim 8
45:19 the four corners of the ledge of the altar 8
46:21 and led me to the four corners of the court; 4
21 and in each corner of the court there was a court 4
22 the four corners of the court were small courts 5
Ams 3:12 be rescued, with the corner of a couch and part 6
Zec 9:15 drenched like the corners of the altar. 1
14:10 the place of the former gate, to the Corner Gate 8
Mat 6: 5 pray in the synagogues and at the street corners 12
21:42 has become the head of the corner 12
Mrk 12:10 has become the head of the corner; 12
Lke 20:17 has become the head of the corner'? 12
Act 4:11 which has become the head of the corner. 12
10:11 a great sheet, let down by four corners 11
11: 5 a great sheet, let down from heaven by four corners 11
26:26 this was not done in a corner. 12
1Pe 2: 7 stone . . has become the head of the corner 12
Rev 7: 1 angels standing at the four corners of the earth 12
20: 8 nations . . at the four corners of the earth 12
Tob 11:13 scaled off from the corners of his eyes. 13
Sus 1:38 We were in a corner of the garden 12

corner *See also* pillar.

far corner 1. אָצִיל

Isa 41: 9 called from its farthest corners, saying to you 1

cornerstone 1. אֶבֶן פִּנָּה 2. פִּנָּה 3. ἀκρογωνιαῖος

Job 38: 6 were its bases sunk, or who laid its cornerstone 1
Isa 19:13 cornerstones of her tribes . . led Egypt astray. 2
28:16 a tested stone, a precious cornerstone 2
Zec 10: 4 Out of them shall come the cornerstone 2
Eph 2:20 Christ Jesus himself being the cornerstone 3
1Pe 2: 6 in Zion . . a cornerstone chosen and precious 3

coronation 1. πρωτοκλίσιον

2Mc 4:21 for the coronation of Philometor as king 1

corpse 1. גְּוִיָּה 2. נְבֵלָה 3. פֶּגֶר 4. νεκρός 5. πτῶμα 6. σῶμα 7. mortuus

2Kg 9:37 and the corpse of Jez'ebel shall be as dung 2
Ps 110: 6 among the nations, filling them with corpses; 1
Isa 5:25 their corpses were as refuse in . . the streets. 2
34: 3 and the stench of their corpses shall rise; 3
Nah 3: 3 hosts of slain, heaps of corpses, dead bodies 3
Mrk 9:26 it came out, and the boy was like a corpse 4
2Es 10:30 behold, I lay there like a corpse 7
Wis 4:18 After this they will become dishonored corpses 5
18:12 they . . had corpses too many to count 4
Sir 48: 5 You who raised a corpse from death and from Hades 4
1Mc 11: 4 and the corpses lying about 6
4Mc 15:20 corpses fallen on other corpses 4
20 corpses fallen on other corpses 4

correct 1. אשר 2. יסר 3. ἐλέγχω 4. μετατίθημι 5. παιδεύω

Prv 9: 7 He who corrects a scoffer gets himself abuse 2
Isa 1:17 seek justice, correct oppression; 1
Jer 10:24 Correct me, O LORD, but in just measure; 2
2Ti 2:25 correcting his opponents with gentleness 5
Wis 12: 2 Therefore thou dost correct little by little 3
4Mc 2:18 to correct some, and to render others powerless. 4

correction 1. מוּסָר 2. שֵׁבֶט 3. ἐπανόρθωσις 4. disciplina

Job 37:13 for correction, or for his land, or for love 2
Jer 2:30 smitten your children, they took no correction; 1
5: 3 but they refused to take correction. 1
Zep 3: 2 listens to no voice, she accepts no correction. 1
7 she will fear me, she will accept correction; 1
2Ti 3:16 profitable . . for reproof, for correction 3
2Es 16:19 as scourges for the correction of men. 4

corrector 1. διορθωτής 2. παιδευτής

Rom 2:20 a corrector of the foolish, a teacher of children 2
Wis 7:15 the corrector of the wise. 1

correspond 1. לְ 2. לְעֻמַּת 3. עַל פְּנֵי 4. ἀναλόγως 5. ἀντίτυπος 6. κατά 7. συστοιχέω

Exd 38:18 corresponding to the hangings of the court. 2
1Ch 23: 6 divisions corresponding to the sons of Levi 1
26:12 corresponding to their chief men, had duties 1
16 Watch corresponded to watch. 2
2Ch 3: 8 length, corresponding to the breadth 3
Neh 12:24 watch corresponding to watch. 2
Ezk 40:18 corresponding to the length of the gates; 2
41: 7 corresponding to the enlargement of the offset 6
45: 7 corresponding in length to one of the tribal 2
Gal 4:25 she corresponds to the present Jerusalem 7
2Co 11:15 Their end will correspond to their deeds. 6
1Pe 3:21 Baptism, which corresponds to this, now saves you 5
Wis 13: 5 comes a corresponding perception 4

corroboration 1. προσμαρτυρέω

3Mc 5:19 with the corroboration of his friends 1

corrosion 1. βρῶμα

LJr 1:12 save themselves from rust and corrosion 1

corrupt 1. אבר 2. אלח 3. שחת 4. שחת (A) 5. καταφθείρω 6. μιαίνω 7. φθείρω 8. corruptus

Gen 6:11 Now the earth was corrupt in God's sight 3
12 God saw the earth, and behold, it was corrupt; 3
12 for all flesh had corrupted their way 3
Exd 32: 7 your people . . have corrupted themselves; 3
Job 15:16 how much less one who is abominable and corrupt 2
Ps 14: 1 They are corrupt, they do abominable deeds 3
3 have all gone astray, they are all alike corrupt; 2
53: 1 They are corrupt, doing abominable iniquity; 3
Ecc 7: 7 and a bribe corrupts the mind. 1
Ezk 16:47 you were more corrupt than they in all your ways. 3
20:44 nor according to your corrupt doings 3
23:11 yet she was more corrupt than she in her doting 3
28:17 you corrupted your wisdom 3
Dan 2: 9 agreed to speak lying and corrupt words 4
Hos 9: 9 They have deeply corrupted themselves 3
Mal 2: 8 you have corrupted the covenant of Levi 3
2Co 7: 2 we have wronged no one, we have corrupted no one 7
Eph 4:22 is corrupt through deceitful lusts 7
2Ti 3: 8 men of corrupt mind and counterfeit faith; 5
Tit 1:15 to the corrupt and unbelieving nothing is pure; 6
15 their very minds and consciences are corrupted. 6
Rev 19: 2 judged the great harlot who corrupted the earth 7
2Es 4:11 one who is already worn out by the corrupt world 8
4Mc 18: 8 No seducer corrupted me on a desert plain 7

corrupt *See also* make.

become corrupt 1. corrumpo

2Es 9:19 those . . have become corrupt in their ways. 1

desperately corrupt 1. אנש

Jer 17: 9 heart is deceitful . . and desperately corrupt; 1

corruptible 1. corruptibilis 2. corruptus

2Es 7:31 that which is corruptible shall perish. 2
96 that they have now escaped what is corruptible 1
8:34 what is a corruptible race 1
14:13 And now renounce the life that is corruptible 2

corruption 1. מַשְׁחִית 2. עָוֹן 3. διαφθορά 4. φθορά 5. corruptela 6. corruptibilis 7. corruptio

2Kg 23:13 to the south of the mount of corruption 1
Hos 7: 1 the corruption of E'phraim is revealed 2
Act 2:27 nor let thy Holy One see corruption. 3
31 nor did his flesh see corruption. 3
13:34 no more to return to corruption 3
35 Thou wilt not let thy Holy One see corruption. 3
36 was laid with his fathers, and saw corruption; 3
37 he whom God raised up saw no corruption. 3
Gal 6: 8 will from the flesh reap corruption 4
2Pe 1: 4 escape from the corruption that is in the world 4
2:19 they themselves are slaves of corruption; 4
2Es 6:28 and corruption shall be overcome 5
7:48 and has brought us into corruption 7
111 when corruption has increased 6
113 in which corruption has passed away 5
8:53 hell has fled and corruption has been forgotten; ‡
10:28 my end has become corruption 7
Wis 14:12 the invention of them was the corruption of life 4
25 theft and deceit, corruption, faithlessness 4

corruption *See also* obtain.

corruptly *See* deal.

act corruptly 1. חבל 2. שחת

Deu 4:16 lest you act corruptly by making a graven image 2
25 if you act corruptly by making a graven image 2
9:12 your people . . have acted corruptly; 2
31:29 after my death you will surely act corruptly 2
Neh 1: 7 We have acted very corruptly against thee 1
Jer 6:28 all of them act corruptly. 2

cost 1. בְּ 2. שָׂכָר 3. נִפְקָה (A) 4. δαπάνη 5. δαπάνημα 6. εἰς 7. τιμή

Exd 32:29 each one at the cost of his son and of his brother 1
Num16:38 men who have sinned at the cost of their lives; 1
Deu 15:18 at half the cost of a hired servant he has served 2
Jos 6:26 At the cost of his first-born 1
26 at the cost of his youngest son 1
1Kg 2:23 if this word does not cost Adoni'jah his life! •
16:34 he laid its foundation at the cost of Abi'ram •
34 and set up its gates at the cost of . . Segub •
Ezr 6: 4 let the cost be paid from the royal treasury. 3
8 cost is to be paid to these men in full 3
Prv 7:23 he does not know that it will cost him his life. 1
Jer 42:20 you have gone astray at the cost of your lives. •
Lke 14:28 which of you . . does not first . . count the cost 4
1Es 6:25 the cost to be paid from the treasury of Cyrus 5
LJr 1:25 They are bought at any cost 7
1Mc 10:44 Let the cost of rebuilding . . be paid 4
45 the cost of rebuilding the walls of Jerusalem 4

45 the cost of rebuilding the walls in Judea *
2Mc 5: 6 success at the cost of one's kindred 6

cost nothing 1. חִנָּם
2Sm 24:24 offer burnt offerings . . which cost me nothing. 1
1Ch 21:24 offer burnt offerings which cost me nothing. 1

without cost 1. δωρεάν
2Co 11: 7 I preached God's gospel without cost to you? 1

costly 1. חֶמְדָּה 2. יקר 3. יָקָר 4. ἐπιθυμητός 5. πολυτελής 6. πολύτιμος 7. τίμιος 8. ὑπερήφανος
1Kg 5:17 they quarried out great, costly stones 3
7: 9 made of costly stones, hewn according to measure 3
10 The foundation was of costly stones, huge stones 3
11 costly stones, hewn according to measurement 3
2Ch 32:27 treasuries . . for all kinds of costly vessels; 1
Ps 49: 8 for the ransom of his life is costly 2
Joh 12: 3 Mary took a pound of costly ointment of pure nard 6
1Ti 2: 9 gold or pearls or costly attire 5
Rev 18:12 articles of costly wood, bronze, iron and marble 7
1Es 6: 9 with costly timber laid in the walls. 5
AEs 14: 2 instead of costly perfumes 8
Wis 2: 7 Let us take our fill of costly wine and perfumes 5
1Mc 1:23 the silver and the gold, and the costly vessels 4
costly *See also* gift, ornament, stone, ware.

very costly 1. πολυτελής
Mrk 14: 3 ointment of pure nard, very costly 1

cotton 1. כַּרְפַּס
Est 1: 6 white cotton curtains and blue hangings 1

white cotton 1. חוֹרָי
Isa 19: 9 be in despair, and the weavers of white cotton. 1

couch 1. יָצוּעַ 2. כרע 3. מִטָּה 4. מֵסַב 5. מִשְׁכָּב 6. עֶרֶשׂ 7. רבץ 8. שכן
Gen 4: 7 sin is couching at the door; its desire is for you 7
49: 4 you defiled it–you went up to my couch! 1
9 He stooped down, he couched as a lion 7
25 blessings of the deep that couches beneath 7
Num24: 9 couched, he lay down like a lion, and like a lioness; 2
Deu 33:13 choicest gifts . . of the deep that couches beneath 7
20 Gad couches like a lion, he tears the arm 8
2Sm 11: 2 when David arose from his couch and was walking 5
13 in the evening he went out to lie on his couch 5
1Ch 5: 1 but because he polluted his father's couch 1
Est 1: 6 and also couches of gold and silver 3
7: 8 Haman was falling on the couch where Esther was; 3
Job 7:13 will comfort me, my couch will ease my complaint,' 5
17:13 Sheol as my house, if I spread my couch in darkness 1
Ps 6: 6 I drench my couch with my weeping. 6
149: 5 faithful . . sing for joy on their couches. 5
Prv 7:16 I have decked my couch with coverings 6
Sng 1:12 While the king was on his couch, my nard gave forth 4
16 Our couch is green; 6
Ezk 19: 2 She couched in the midst of young lions 7
23:41 you sat upon a stately couch 3
Ams 3:12 be rescued, with the corner of a couch and part 3
6: 4 and stretch themselves upon their couches 6
could *See* can.

council 1. ישב 2. סוֹד 3. עֵדָה 4. ראה פָּנִים 5. βουλή 6. γερουσία 7. συμβούλιον 8. συνεδρία 9. συνέδριον
Gen 49: 6 O my soul, come not into their council; 2
2Kg 9: 5 the commanders of the army were in council; 1
25:19 took . . five men of the king's council 4
Job 15: 8 Have you listened in the council of God? 2
Ps 82: 1 God has taken his place in the divine council; 3
89: 7 God feared in the council of the holy ones 2
Jer 23:18 For who . . has stood in the council of the LORD 2
22 But if they had stood in my council 2
52:25 the men of war, and seven men of the king's council 4
Ezk 13: 9 they shall not be in the council of my people 2
Mat 5:22 his brother shall be liable to the council 9
10:17 they will deliver you up to councils 9
26:59 the chief priests and the whole council sought 9
Mrk 13: 9 they will deliver you up to councils 9
14:55 Now the chief priests and the whole council 9
15: 1 the whole council held a consultation 9
Lke 22:66 they led him away to their council, and they said 9
Joh 11:47 the Pharisees gathered the council, and said 9
Act 4:15 commanded them to go aside out of the council 9
5:21 the council and all the senate of Israel 9
27 they set them before the council 9
34 a Pharisee in the council named Gama'li-el 9
41 Then they left the presence of the council 9
6:12 seized him and brought him before the council 9
15 gazing at him, all who sat in the council saw 9
22:30 the chief priests and all the council to meet 9
23: 1 Paul, looking intently at the council, said 9
6 he cried out in the council 9
15 You therefore, along with the council 9
20 to ask you to bring Paul down to the council 9
28 I brought him down to their council. 9
24:20 when I stood before the council 9
25:12 when he had conferred with his council 7
1Es 2:17 the other judges of their council in Coelesyria 5
Jdt 6: 1 the disturbance made by the men outside the council 8
17 the council of Holofernes 8
11: 9 Now as for the things Achior said in your council 8
Sir 38:33 are not sought out for the council of the people 5
3Mc 1: 8 sent some of their council . . to greet him 6
4Mc 17:17 The tyrant himself and all his council marveled 7
council *See also* meeting, member.

council of elders 1. πρεσβυτέριον
Act 22: 5 the high priest and the whole council of elders 1
1Ti 4:14 the council of elders laid their hands upon you 1

counsel 1. דָּבָר 2. יעץ 3. מוֹעֵצָה 4. סוֹד 5. עֵצָה 6. פִּי 7. תַּחְבֻּלָה 8. מְלֵךְ (A) 9. βουλή 10. διαβούλιον 11. λογισμός 12. συμβουλεύω 13. συμβουλία 14. συμβούλιον 15. σύμβουλος 16. consilium
Num31:16 caused . . Israel, by the counsel of Balaam 1
Deu 32:28 For they are a nation void of counsel 5
Jdg 20: 7 Israel, all of you, give your advice and counsel 5
2Sm 15:31 turn the counsel of Ahith'ophel into foolishness. 5
34 you will defeat for me the counsel of Ahith'ophel. 5
16:20 Give your counsel; what shall we do? 5
23 the counsel which Ahith'ophel gave was 5
23 so was all the counsel of Ahith'ophel esteemed 5
17: 7 the counsel . . Ahith'ophel has given is not good. 5
11 my counsel is that all Israel be gathered to you 5
14 The counsel of Hushai the Archite is better 5
14 is better than the counsel of Ahith'ophel. 5
14 to defeat the good counsel of Ahith'ophel 5
15 Thus and so did Ahith'ophel counsel Ab'salom 5
15 and thus and so have I counseled. 5
21 thus . . has Ahith'ophel counseled against you. 5
23 Ahith'ophel saw that the counsel was not followed 5
20:18 to say in old time, 'Let them but ask counsel at Abel'; *
1Kg 1:12 come, let me give you counsel 5
12: 8 he forsook the counsel which the old men gave him 5
13 forsaking the counsel which the old men 5
14 according to the counsel of the young men, saying 5
1Ch 12:19 for the rulers of the Philistines took counsel 5
2Ch 10: 8 he forsook the counsel which the old men gave him 5
13 forsaking the counsel of the old men 5
14 according to the counsel of the young men, saying 5
22: 5 He even followed their counsel 5
25:16 done this and have not listened to my counsel. 5
Ezr 10: 3 according to the counsel of my lord 5
Est 5:14 This counsel pleased Haman, 1
Job 12:13 he has counsel and understanding. 5
21:16 The counsel of the wicked is far from me. 5
22:18 but the counsel of the wicked is far from me. 5
26: 3 How you have counseled him who has no wisdom 5
29:21 waited, and kept silence for my counsel. 5
38: 2 Who is this that darkens counsel by words 5
42: 3 this that hides counsel without knowledge? 5
Ps 1: 1 the man who walks not in the counsel of the wicked 5
5:10 O God; let them fall by their own counsels; 3
32: 8 I will counsel you with my eye upon you. 2
33:10 LORD brings the counsel of the nations to nought; 5
11 The counsel of the LORD stands for ever 5
73:24 Thou dost guide me with thy counsel 5
81:12 to follow their own counsels. 3
106:13 they did not wait for his counsel. 5
107:11 spurned the counsel of the Most High. 5
Prv 1:25 you have ignored all my counsel 5
30 would have none of my counsel 5
8:14 I have counsel and sound wisdom 5
12: 5 the counsels of the wicked are treacherous. 7
15:22 Without counsel plans go wrong 4
20:18 Plans are established by counsel; 5
21:30 No wisdom, no understanding, no counsel, can avail 5
Isa 8:10 Take counsel together, but it will come to nought; 5
11: 2 understanding, the spirit of counsel and might 5
16: 3 Give counsel, grant justice; 5
19:11 counselors of Pharaoh give stupid counsel. 5
28:29 the LORD of hosts; he is wonderful in counsel 5
29:15 those who hide deep from the LORD their counsel 5
30: 2 go down to Egypt, without asking for my counsel 6
44:26 and performs the counsel of his messengers; 5
46:10 My counsel shall stand, and I will accomplish 5
11 the man of my counsel from a far country. 5
47:13 You are wearied with your many counsels; 5
Jer 7:24 but walked in their own counsels 3
18:18 perish from the priest, nor counsel from the wise 5
32:19 great in counsel and mighty in deed; 5
49: 7 in Teman? Has counsel perished from the prudent? 5
Ezk 7:26 law perishes . . and counsel from the elders. 5
11: 2 who devise iniquity and who give wicked counsel 5
Dan 4:27 Therefore, O king, let my counsel be acceptable 8
Mic 6:16 and you have walked in their counsels; 3
Nah 1:11 evil against the LORD, and counseled villainy? 2
Mat 12:14 and took counsel against him, how to destroy him. 14
22:15 Then the Pharisees went and took counsel 14
27: 1 elders of the people took counsel against Jesus 14
7 So they took counsel 14
28:12 assembled with the elders and taken counsel 14
Mrk 3: 6 immediately held counsel with the Hero'di-ans 14
Act 13:36 served the counsel of God in his own generation 9
20:27 declaring to you the whole counsel of God. 9
Eph 1:11 according to the counsel of his will 9
Rev 3:18 I counsel you to buy from me gold refined by fire 12
2Es 1: 7 have angered me and despised my counsels. 16
2: 1 and made my counsels void. 16
18 According to their counsel I have consecrated 16
Tob 4:18 do not despise any useful counsel. 13
Wis 1: 9 the counsels of an ungodly man 10
8: 9 would give me good counsel and encouragement 15
9:13 For what man can learn the counsel of God? 9
17 Who has learned thy counsel 9
Sir 6: 2 not exalt yourself through your soul's counsel 9
23 do not reject my counsel. 13
19:22 is there prudence where sinners take counsel. 9
21:13 and his counsel like a flowing spring. 9
22:16 so the mind firmly fixed on a reasonable counsel 9
23: 1 do not abandon me to their counsel 9
24:29 and her counsel deeper than the great abyss. 9
25: 5 understanding and counsel in honorable men! 9
37: 7 Every counselor praises counsel 9
10 hide your counsel 9
13 establish the counsel of your own heart 9
16 counsel precedes every undertaking. 9
39: 7 He will direct his counsel and knowledge aright 9
43:23 By his counsel he stilled the great deep 11
1Mc 9:69 the lawless men who had counseled him to come 12
4Mc 6:16 as though more bitterly tormented by this counsel 13
8:29 as soon as the tyrant had ceased counseling them 12
counsel *See also* give, matter, take, wise.

good counsel 1. βουλή
Sir 25: 4 for the aged to possess good counsel! 1
40:25 good counsel is esteemed more than both. 1

counselor 1. אִישׁ עֵצָה 2. יעץ 3. אֲדַרְגָּזַר (A) 4. הַדָּבַר (A) 5. יָעֵט (A) 6. παράκλητος 7. συμβουλευτής 8. συμβουλεύω 9. σύμβουλος 10. συνδράω
2Sm 15:12 for Ahith'opel the Gi'lonite, David's counselor 2
1Ch 26:14 cast lots also for . . Zechari'ah, a shrewd counselor 2
27:32 Jonathan, David's uncle, was a counselor 2
33 Ahith'ophel was the king's counselor 2
2Ch 22: 3 his mother was his counselor in doing wickedly. 2
4 they were his counselors, to his undoing. 2
25:16 Have we made you a royal counselor? 2
Ezr 4: 5 hired counselors against them to frustrate 2
7:14 sent by the king and his seven counselors 5
15 silver and gold . . the king and his counselors 5
28 before the king and his counselors 2
8:25 offering . . which the king and his counselors 2
Job 3:14 with kings and counselors of the earth 2
12:17 He leads counselors away stripped 2
Ps 119:24 They testimonies . . they are my counselors. 1
Prv 11:14 in an abundance of counselors there is safety. 2
24: 6 abundance of counselors there is victory. 2
Isa 1:26 and your counselors as at the beginning. 2
3: 3 the counselor and the skilful magician 2
9: 6 and his name will be called "Wonderful Counselor 2
19:11 the wise counselors of Pharaoh give stupid 2
40:13 or as his counselor has instructed him? 1
41:28 among these there is no counselor who 2
Dan 3: 2 assemble the . . governors, the counselors 3
3 counselors, the treasurers, the justices 3
24 said to his counselors, "Did we not cast three men 4
27 satraps . . and the king's counselors gathered 4
4:36 counselors and my lords sought me 4
6: 7 presidents . . the counselors and the governors 4
Mic 4: 9 Has your counselor perished 2
Joh 14:16 he will give you another Counselor, to be with you 6
26 the Counselor, the Holy Spirit 6
15:26 when the Counselor comes, whom I shall send to you 6
16: 7 if I do not go away, the Counselor will not come 6
Rom 11:34 or who has been his counselor? 9
1Es 8:11 I and the seven friends who are my counselors 7
26 the king and his counselors and all his friends 8
55 king himself and his counselors and the nobles 9
AEs 13: 3 When I asked my counselors 9
Sir 37: 7 Every counselor praises counsel 9
8 Be wary of a counselor 9
42:21 he needs no one to be his counselor. 9
4Mc 5: 1 sitting in state with his counselors 10
9: 2 to the law and to Moses our counselor. 9
3 Tyrant and counselor of lawlessness 9

count 1. היה 2. חשב 3. כון 4. כסס 5. מנה 6. מִסְפָּר 7. נשא ראשׁ 8. ספר 9. פקד 10. ראשׁ 11. ἀριθμέω 12. ἀριθμός 13. εἰμί 14. ἐλλογέω 15. ἐξαριθμέω 16. ἡγέομαι 17. λογίζομαι 18. προσλογίζομαι 19. συμψηφίζω 20. ψηφίζω 21. numero
Gen 13:16 that if one can count the dust of the earth 5
16 the earth, your descendants also can be counted. 5
Exd 12: 4 you shall make your count for the lamb. 4
38:21 as they were counted at the commandment of Moses 9
Lev 15:13 then he shall count for himself seven days 8
28 she shall count for herself seven days 8
23:15 you shall count from the morrow 8
16 counting 50 days to the morrow after the seventh 8
25: 8 you shall count seven weeks of years, seven times 8

Num23:10 Who can count the dust of Jacob, or number 5
31:26 Take the count of the booty that was taken 10
49 Your servants have counted the men of war 7
Deu 16: 9 count seven weeks; begin to count the seven weeks 8
9 begin to count the seven weeks from the time 8
Jdg 6: 5 both they and their camels could not be counted; 6
1Kg 1:21 I and my son Solomon will be counted offenders. 1
3: 8 cannot be numbered or counted for multitude. 8
8: 5 that they could not be counted or numbered. 8
2Kg 12:10 and they counted and tied up in bags the money 5
1Ch 9:28 to count them when they were brought •
2Ch 5: 6 that they could not be counted or numbered. 8
Ezr 8:34 whole was counted and weighed, and the weight 6
Neh 13:13 appointed . . for they were counted faithful; 2
Job 13:24 hide thy face, and count me as thy enemy? 2
18: 3 Why are we counted as cattle? 2
19:11 wrath against me, and counts me as his adversary. 2
15 my maidservants count me as a stranger; 2
33:10 occasions against me, he counts me as his enemy; 2
41:27 He counts iron as straw, and bronze as rotten 2
29 Clubs are counted as stubble; 2
Ps 22:17 I can count all my bones- 8
109: 7 tried, let . . his prayer be counted as sin! •
119:119 the wicked of the earth thou dost count as dross; •
139:18 If I would count them, they are more than the sand. 8
22 hate . . perfect hatred; I count them my enemies. †
141: 2 Let my prayer be counted as incense before thee 3
Prv 27:14 early in the morning, will be counted as cursing. 2
Isa 22:10 you counted the houses of Jerusalem 8
33:18 Where is he who counted the towers? 8
18 Where is he who counted the towers? 8
Jer 33:13 pass under the hands of the one who counts them 5
Ezk 44:26 is defiled, he shall count for himself seven days 8
Lke 14:28 which of you . . does not first . . count the cost 20
Act 19:19 they counted the value of them 19
27 the temple . . may count for nothing 17
Rom 5:13 but sin is not counted where there is no law. 14
1Co 7:19 For neither circumcision counts for anything 13
2Co 5:19 not counting their trespasses against them 17
10: 2 with such confidence as I count on showing 17
Gal 6:15 For neither circumcision counts for anything 13
Php 2: 3 in humility count others better 16
6 not count equality with God a thing to be grasped 16
3: 7 I counted as loss for the sake of Christ. 16
8 Indeed I count everything as loss 16
8 count them as refuse 16
Jas 1: 2 Count it all joy, my brethren 16
2Pe 2:13 They count it pleasure to revel in the daytime. 16
3: 9 The Lord is not slow . . as some count slowness 16
15 count the forbearance of our Lord as salvation. 16
1Es 8:64 The whole was counted and weighed 12
2Es 11:11 I counted his opposing wings, and behold 21
Tob 9: 4 my father is counting the days 11
10: 1 Now his father Tobit was counting each day 17
Jdt 2:20 a multitude that could not be counted. 12
5:10 so great that they could not be counted. 12
Wis 14:30 just penalties will overtake them on two counts •
15: 9 he counts it his glory 16
Sir 1: 2 the days of eternity-who can count them? 15
7:16 Do not count yourself among the crowd of sinners; 18
Bar 3:11 that you are counted among those in Hades? 18
1Mc 5:30 behold, a large company, that could not be counted 12

count *See also* keep, many.

count a liar 1. כזב
Job 34: 6 in spite of my right I am counted a liar; 1

count as forbidden 1. ערל
Lev 19:23 then you shall count their fruit as forbidden 1

count happy 1. ברך 2. μακαρίζω
Ps 49:18 Though, while he lives, he counts himself happy 1
Wis 18: 1 and counted them happy for not having suffered 2

count out 1. ספר
Ezr 1: 8 Mith'redath . . counted them out to Shesh-baz'zar 1

count stolen 1. גנב
Gen 30:33 if found with me, shall be counted stolen. 1

count up 1. numero
2Es 5:36 Count up for me those who have not yet come 1

count worthy 1. ἀξιόω 2. καταξιόω
Act 5:41 were counted worthy to suffer dishonor for the name. 2
Heb 3: 3 Yet Jesus has been counted worthy of . . glory 1

countenance 1. אַף 2. מַרְאָה 3. פָּנִים 4. πρόσωπον 5. facies 6. visus
Gen 4: 5 Cain was very angry, and his countenance fell. 3
6 angry, and why has your countenance fallen? 3
Num 6:26 The LORD lift up his countenance upon you 3
Deu 28:50 nation of stern countenance, who shall not 3
Jdg 13: 6 man of God came . . and his countenance was like 2
6 was like the countenance of the angel of God 2
1Sm 1:18 and ate, and her countenance was no longer sad. 3
Job 9:27 I will put off my sad countenance 3
14:20 thou changest his countenance 3
29:24 light of my countenance they did not cast down. 3
Ps 4: 6 Lift up the light of thy countenance upon us 3
10: 4 In the pride of his countenance the wicked does 1
44: 3 hand, and thy arm, and the light of thy countenance; 3
80:16 may they perish at the rebuke of thy countenance! 3
89:15 who walk, O LORD, in the light of thy countenance 3
90: 8 our secret sins in the light of thy countenance. 3
Prv 15:13 A glad heart makes a cheerful countenance 3
Ecc 7: 3 by sadness of countenance the heart is made glad. 3
8: 1 and the hardness of his countenance is changed. 3
Dan 8:23 king of bold countenance, one who understands 3
Lke 9:29 the appearance of his countenance was altered 4
2Es 10:25 and her countenance flashed like lightning 6
15:63 and abolish the glory of your countenance. 5
Jdt 16: 7 undid him with the beauty of her countenance. 4
AEs 15:14 your countenance is full of grace. 4
Sir 13:25 A man's heart changes his countenance 4
36:22 A woman's beauty gladdens the countenance 4

countenance fall 1. στυγνάζω
Mrk 10:22 At that saying his countenance fell 1

counterattack 1. καταδρομή
2Mc 5: 3 attacks and counterattacks made on this side 1

counterfeit 1. ἀδόκιμος
2Ti 3: 8 men of corrupt mind and counterfeit faith; 1

counterfeit god 1. κίβδηλος
Wis 15: 9 he molds counterfeit gods. 1

countless 1. רב 2. ἀμέτρητος 3. ἀναρίθμητος 4. μυρίος 5. ὑπερβαλλόντως
Nah 3: 4 all for the countless harlotries of the harlot 1
1Co 4:15 For though you have countless guides in Christ 4
2Co 11:23 with countless beatings, and often near death. 5
Sir 30:15 and a robust body than countless riches 2
3Mc 5:46 filled with countless masses of people 3
6: 5 Sennacherib exulting in his countless forces 3

country 1. אֲדָמָה 2. אֶרֶץ 3. גְּבוּל 4. מָקוֹם 5. שָׂדֶה 6. ἀγρός 7. γῆ 8. ἔρημος τόπος 9. μέρος 10. μεσόγειος 11. πατρίς 12. τόπος 13. χώρα 14. regio
Gen 12: 1 Go from your country and your kindred 2
14: 7 and subdued all the country of the Amal'ekites 5
24: 4 will go to my country and to my kindred 2
25: 6 sent them . . eastward to the east country. 2
29:26 Laban said, "It is not so done in our country 4
30:25 that I may go to my own home and country. 2
32: 3 in the land of Se'ir, the country of Edom 5
9 O LORD who didst say to me, 'Return to your country 2
36:35 who defeated Mid'ian in the country of Moab 5
Exd 8: 2 behold, I will plague all your country with frogs; 3
10: 4 tomorrow I will bring locusts into your country 3
14 settled on the whole country of Egypt 3
19 locust was left in all the country of Egypt. 3
18:27 and he went his way to his own country. 2
Lev 25:24 And in all the country you possess 2
31 shall be reckoned with the fields of the country 5
Num32:33 the cities of the land throughout the country. •
Jos 9: 6 We have come from a far country . . make a covenant 2
9 From a very far country your servants have come 2
11 elders and all the inhabitants of our country 2
10:41 and all the country of Goshen, as far as Gibeon. 2
Jdg 11:19 Let us pass . . through your land to our country.' 4
21 land of the Amorites, who inhabited that country 2
16:24 our enemy . . the ravager of our country 2
18:14 men who had gone to spy out the country of La'ish 2
20: 6 all the country of the inheritance of Israel; 5
Rut 1: 1 went to sojourn in the country of Moab 5
2 They went into the country of Moab and remained 5
6 she started . . to return from the country of Moab 5
6 she had heard in the country of Moab that the LORD 5
22 Ruth . . who returned from the country of Moab. 5
2: 6 came back with Na'omi from the country of Moab. 5
4: 3 Na'omi, who has come back from the country of Moab 5
1Sm 6: 1 The ark . . was in the country of the Philistines 5
27: 5 let a place be given me in one of the country towns 5
7 David dwelt in the country of the Philistines 5
11 he dwelt in the country of the Philistines. 5
2Sm 15:23 all the country wept aloud as . . people passed by 2
18: 8 battle spread over the face of all the country; 2
1Kg 4:19 land of Gilead, the country of Sihon . . and of Og 2
8:41 when a foreigner . . comes from a far country 2
11:21 Let me depart, that I may go to my own country. 2
22 you are now seeking to go to your own country 2
20:27 but the Syrians filled the country. 2
22:36 Every man to his city, and every man to his country! 2
2Kg 3:20 water came . . till the country was filled 2
18:35 Who among all the gods of the countries have 2
35 have delivered their countries out of my hand 2
20:14 They have come from a far country, from Babylon. 2
1Ch 1:46 who defeated Mid'ian in the country of Moab 5
8: 8 Shahara'im had sons in the country of Moab 5
20: 1 and ravaged the country of the Ammonites 2
27:25 over the treasuries in the country, in the cities 5
29:30 and upon all the kingdoms of the countries. 2
2Ch 6:32 when a foreigner . . comes from a far country 2
12: 8 service of the kingdoms of the countries. 2
20:29 came on all the kingdoms of other countries 2
30:10 through the country of E'phraim and Manas'seh 2
Est 8:17 many from the peoples of the country declared 2
Ps 105:31 flies, and gnats throughout their country. 3
33 shattered the trees of their country. 3
Prv 25:25 Like cold water . . good news from a far country. 2
Isa 1: 7 Your country lies desolate . . cities are burned 2
8: 9 give ear, all you far countries; gird yourselves 2
36:20 Who among all the gods of these countries 2
20 have delivered their countries out of my hand 2
39: 3 have come to me from a far country, from Babylon. 2
46:11 the man of my counsel from a far country. 2
Jer 6:22 Behold, a people is coming from the north country 2
10:22 a great commotion out of the north country 2
16:15 the people of Israel out of the north country 2
15 out of . . the countries where he had driven them. 2
22:26 into another country, where you were not born 2
23: 3 out of all the countries where I have driven them 2
8 the house of Israel out of the north country 2
8 out of . . the countries where he had driven them. 2
28: 8 and pestilence against many countries 2
31: 6 will call in the hill country of E'phraim: •
8 Behold, I will bring them from the north country 2
17 children shall come back to their own country. 3
32:37 Behold, I will gather them from all the countries 2
46:10 in the north country by the river Euphra'tes. 2
50: 9 company of great nations, from the north country; 2
51: 9 Forsake her, and let us go each to his own country; 2
Ezk 5: 5 the center . . with countries round about her. 2
6 and against my statutes more than the countries 2
6: 8 when you are scattered through the countries 2
11:16 and though I scattered them among the countries 2
16 in the countries where they have gone. 2
17 and assemble you out of the countries 2
12:15 when I . . scatter them through the countries. 2
20:23 and disperse them through the countries 2
32 like the tribes of the countries, and worship 2
34 you out of the countries where you are scattered 2
41 the countries where you have been scattered; 2
42 country which I swore to give to your fathers. 2
22: 4 and a mocking to all the countries. 2
15 and disperse you through the countries 2
25: 7 and will make you perish out of the countries; 2
9 on its frontier, the glory of the country 2
29:12 desolation in the midst of desolated countries; 2
12 and disperse them among the countries. 2
30: 7 desolated in the midst of desolated countries 2
26 and disperse them throughout the countries. 2
32: 9 into the countries which you have not known. 2
34:13 and gather them from the countries 2
13 in all the inhabited places of the country. 2
35:10 These two nations and these two countries shall 2
36:19 they were dispersed through the countries; 2
24 and gather you from all the countries 2
Dan 11:40 come into countries . . overflow and pass through. 2
42 stretch out his hand against the countries 2
Hos 10: 1 as his country improved 2
Jon 1: 8 What is your country? And of what people are you? 2
4: 2 is not this what I said when I was yet in my country? 1
Zec 6: 6 the black horses goes toward the north country 2
6 the white ones go toward the west country •
6 and the dappled ones go toward the south country. 2
8 Behold, those who go toward the north country 2
8 have set my Spirit at rest in the north country. 2
8: 7 from the east country and from the west country; 2
7 from the east country and from the west country; 2
10: 9 yet in far countries they shall remember me •
Mal 1: 3 I have laid waste his hill country •
4 till they are called the wicked country 3
Mat 2:12 departed to their own country by another way. 13
8:28 to the country of the Gadarenes 13
13:54 coming to his own country he taught them 11
57 is not without honor except in his own country 11
Mrk 1: 5 there went out to him all the country of Judea 13
45 but was out in the country 8
5: 1 to the country of the Ger'asenes. 13
10 not to send them out of the country. 13
14 told it in the city and in the country 6
6: 1 went away from there and came to his own country; 11
4 without honor, except in his own country 11
36 to go into the country and villages round about 6
56 wherever he came, in villages, cities, or country 6
15:21 who was coming in from the country 6
16:12 as they were walking into the country. 6
Lke 4:23 do here also in your own country.' 11
24 no prophet is acceptable in his own country. 11
8:26 they arrived at the country of the Ger'asenes 13
34 told it in the city and in the country. 6
9:12 to go into the villages and country round about 6
15:13 and took his journey into a far country 13
14 a great famine arose in that country 13
15 one of the citizens of that country 13
19:12 A nobleman went into a far country 13
21:21 let not those who are out in the country enter it; 13
23:26 who was coming in from the country 6
Joh 4:44 that a prophet has no honor in his own country. 11
11:54 from there to the country near the wilderness 13

55 many went up from the country to Jerusalem 13
Act 10:39 both in the country of the Jews and in Jerusalem. 13
12:20 because their country depended . . for food. 13
20 their country depended on the king's country for food. •
19: 1 Paul passed through the upper country 9
26:20 throughout all the country of Judea 13
Heb 11:16 as it is, they desire a better country •
1Es 4:20 A man leaves . . his own country 13
21 his father or his mother or his country. 13
50 all the country which they would occupy 13
6: 8 when we went to the country of Judea 13
17 Cyrus reigned over the country of Babylonia 13
23 the fortress which is in the country of Media 13
8:13 may be found in the country of Babylonia 13
9:37 settled in Jerusalem and in the country 13
2Es 1: 3 who was a captive in the country of the Medes 14
5:11 one country shall ask its neighbor 14
13:45 and that country is called Arzareth. 14
Tob 1: 4 Now when I was in my own country 13
Jdt 2: 6 Go and attack the whole west country 7
23 south of the country of the Chelleans. •
5:18 and were led away captive to a foreign country 7
16:21 throughout the whole country. 7
AEs 16:24 Every city and country, without exception 13
Sir 47:17 the countries marveled at you. 13
Bar 3:10 that you are growing old in a foreign country 7
LJr 1:53 they cannot set up a king over a country 13
1Mc 1: 4 and ruled over countries, nations, and princes 13
3:29 the revenues from the country were small 13
7:20 He placed Alcimus in charge of the country 13
24 going out into the country. 13
8: 8 the country of India and Media and Lydia 13
9:24 the country deserted with them to the enemy. 13
25 and put them in charge of the country. 13
61 about 50 of the men of the country 13
65 while he went out into the country 13
69 had counseled him to come into the country 13
10:38 added to Judea from the country of Samaria 13
52 and gained control of our country; 13
11:62 he passed through the country as far as Damascus. 13
64 left his brother Simon in the country. 13
12:25 no opportunity to invade his own country. 13
33 and marched through the country as far as Askalon •
13:20 Trypho came to invade the country and destroy it 13
34 a request to grant relief to the country 13
49 prevented from going out to the country and back 13
14: 6 and gained full control of the country. 13
17 he was ruling over the country and the cities in it 13
28 the elders of the country 13
29 Since wars often occurred in the country 13
31 their enemies decided to invade their country 13
36 so that the Gentiles were put out of the country 13
37 fortified it for the safety of the country 13
42 and appoint men over its tasks and over the country 13
43 all contracts in the country 13
44 to convene an assembly in the country 13
15: 4 and intend to make a landing in the country 13
4 those who have destroyed our country 13
6 mint your own coinage as money for your country 13
15 with letters to the kings and countries 13
19 have decided to write to the kings and countries 13
19 against them and their cities and their country 13
21 fled to you from their country 13
23 to all the countries, and to Sampsames 13
16: 4 John chose out of the country 20,000 warriors 13
13 he determined to get control of the country 13
14 Now Simon was visiting the cities of the country 13
18 to turn over to him the cities and the country. 13
2Mc 4: 1 who had informed . . against his own country 11
5: 7 and fled again into the country of the Ammonites. †
8 abhorred as the executioner of his country 11
9 who had driven many from their own country into exile 11
15 a traitor both to the laws and to his country. 11
8:21 to die for their laws and their country 11
35 made his way . . across the country 10
9:23 made expeditions into the upper country 12
13: 3 not for the sake of his country's welfare 11
10 the law and their country and the holy temple 11
14 the laws, temple, city, country, and commonwealth 11
14: 2 and had taken possession of the country 13
9 Since you . . deign to take thought for our country 13
18 their courage in battle for their country 11
3Mc 4:11 to those from the city going out into the country 13
18 although most of them were still in the country 13
6: 1 famous among the priests of the country 13
25 have held the fortresses of our country? 13
4Mc 4: 1 he fled the country 11
5 he proceeded quickly to our country 11

country *See also* go.

coastal country 1. παραλία

1Mc 15:38 commander-in-chief of the coastal country 1

hill country 1. הַר 2. ὀρεινή 3. ὀρεινός 4. ὄρος 5. ὕψος τῆς γῆς

Gen 10:30 of Sephar to the hill country of the east. 1
31:21 set his face toward the hill country of Gilead. 1
23 after him into the hill country of Gilead. 1
25 Jacob had pitched his tent in the hill country 1
25 kinsmen encamped in the hill country of Gilead. 1
36: 8 Esau dwelt in the hill country of Se'ir; 1
9 the E'domites in the hill country of Se'ir. 1
Num13:17 into the Negeb . . and go up into the hill country 1
29 Amorites dwell in the hill country; 1
14:40 went up to the heights of the hill country, saying 1
44 go up to the heights of the hill country 1
45 Canaanites who dwelt in that hill country 1
Deu 1: 7 go to the hill country of the Amorites, and to all 1
7 Arabah, in the hill country and in the lowland 1
19 on the way to the hill country of the Amorites 1
20 'You have come to the hill country of the Amorites 1
24 they turned and went up into the hill country 1
41 thought it easy to go up into the hill country. 1
43 presumptuous and went up into the hill country. 1
44 Amorites who lived in that hill country came out 1
2:37 river Jabbok and the cities of the hill country 1
3:12 half the hill country of Gilead with its cities; 1
25 land beyond the Jordan, that goodly hill country 1
Jos 9: 1 who were beyond the Jordan in the hill country 1
10: 6 of the Amorites that dwell in the hill country 1
40 the whole land, the hill country and the Negeb 1
11: 2 the kings who were in the northern hill country 1
3 and the Jeb'usites in the hill country 1
16 all that land, the hill country and all the Negeb 1
16 and the hill country of Israel and its lowland 1
21 and wiped out the Anakim from the hill country 1
21 from Anab, and from all the hill country of Judah 1
21 and from all the hill country of Israel; 1
12: 8 in the hill country, in the lowland, in the Arabah 1
13: 6 inhabitants of the hill country from Lebanon 1
14:12 give me this hill country of which the LORD spoke 1
15:48 And in the hill country, Shamir, Jattir, Socoh 1
16: 1 up from Jericho into the hill country to Bethel; 1
17:15 the hill country of E'phraim is too narrow for you. 1
16 The hill country is not enough for us; 1
18 the hill country shall be yours 1
18:12 then up through the hill country westward; 1
19:50 Tim'nath-se'rah in the hill country of E'phraim; 1
20: 7 they set apart Kedesh . . in the hill country 1
7 and Shechem in the hill country of E'phraim 1
7 Kir'iath-ar'ba . . in the hill country of Judah. 1
21:11 Kir'iath-ar'ba . . in the hill country of Judah 1
21 pasture lands in the hill country of E'phraim 1
24: 4 I gave Esau the hill country of Se'ir to possess 1
30 Tim'nath-se'rah . . in the hill country of E'phraim 1
33 been given him in the hill country of E'phraim. 1
Jdg 1: 9 dwelt in the hill country, in the Negeb 1
19 Judah, and he took possession of the hill country 1
34 pressed the Danites back into the hill country 1
2: 9 Tim'nath-he'res, in the hill country of Ephraim 1
3:27 trumpet in the hill country of E'phraim; 1
27 Israel went down with him from the hill country 1
4: 5 Ramah and Bethel in the hill country of E'phraim; 1
7:24 throughout all the hill country of E'phraim 1
10: 1 lived at Shamir in the hill country of E'phraim. 1
12:15 E'phraim, in the hill country of the Amal'ekites. 1
17: 1 There was a man of the hill country of E'phraim 1
8 he came to the hill country of E'phraim 1
18: 2 they came to the hill country of E'phraim 1
13 on from there to the hill country of E'phraim 1
19: 1 the remote parts of the hill country of E'phraim 1
16 the man was from the hill country of E'phraim 1
18 to the remote parts of the hill country of E'phraim 1
1Sm 1: 1 Ramatha'im-zo'phim of the hill country of E'phraim 1
9: 4 they passed through the hill country of E'phraim 1
13: 2 in Michmash and the hill country of Bethel 1
14:22 hid themselves in the hill country of E'phraim 1
23:14 in the hill country of the Wilderness of Ziph. 1
2Sm 20:21 a man of the hill country of E'phraim, called Sheba 1
1Kg 4: 8 names: Ben-hur, in the hill country of E'phraim; 1
5:15 80,000 hewers of stone in the hill country 1
12:25 built Shechem in the hill country of E'phraim 1
2Kg 5:22 come to me from the hill country of E'phraim 1
1Ch 6:67 Shechem . . in the hill country of E'phraim 1
2Ch 2: 2 80,000 to quarry in the hill country 1
18 80,000 to quarry in the hill country 1
13: 4 which is in the hill country of E'phraim 1
15: 8 cities . . taken in the hill country of E'phraim 1
19: 4 from Beer-sheba to the hill country of E'phraim 1
21:11 he made high places in the hill country of Judah 1
27: 4 he built cities in the hill country of Judah 1
Jer 17:26 from the hill country, and from the Negeb 1
32:44 in the cities of the hill country 1
33:13 In the cities of the hill country 1
Lke 1:39 and went with haste into the hill country 3
65 through all the hill country of Judea; 3
Jdt 1: 6 He was joined by all the people of the hill country 2
2:22 and went up into the hill country 2
5: 3 what people . . lives in the hill country 2
15 they took possession of all the hill country. 2
19 and have settled in the hill country 2
6: 7 to take you back into the hill country 2
11 from the plain they went up into the hill country 2
7: 1 to seize the passes up into the hill country 2
18 and encamped in the hill country opposite Dothan 2
10:13 he can go and capture all the hill country 2
11: 2 your people who live in the hill country 2
15: 2 across the plain and through the hill country. 2
5 Those in Jerusalem and all the hill country 2
7 the villages and towns in the hill country 2
Sir 46: 9 he went up to the hill country 5
1Mc 10:70 do you assume authority against us in the hill country? 4

mountain country 1. הַר

Deu 2: 3 going about this mountain country long enough; 1

open country 1. מִגְרָשׁ 2. שָׂדֶה 3. ὕπαιθρος 4. campus

Deu 21: 1 any one is found slain, lying in the open country 2
22:25 if in the open country a man meets a young woman 2
27 because he came upon her in the open country 2
Jdg 20:31 in the highways . . and in the open country 2
1Sm 30:11 They found an Egyptian in the open country 2
2Sm 10: 8 men . . were by themselves in the open country. 2
1Kg 11:29 the two of them were alone in the open country. 2
14:11 any one who dies in the open country the birds 2
21:24 any one of his who dies in the open country 2
2Kg 7:12 to hide themselves in the open country 2
25:23 the captains of the forces in the open country •
1Ch 19: 9 were by themselves in the open country. 2
Jer 17: 3 on the mountains in the open country. 2
40: 7 the captains of the forces in the open country 2
13 the leaders of the forces in the open country 2
Ezk 48:15 for the city, for dwellings and for open country. 1
Mic 1: 6 I will make Sama'ria a heap in the open country 2
4:10 forth from the city and dwell in the open country; 2
2Es 15:57 all your people who are in the open country 4
2Mc 15:19 the encounter in the open country. 3

country round about 1. περίχωρος

Jdt 3: 7 these people and all in the country round about 1

surrounding country 1. περίχωρος

Lke 4:14 went out through all the surrounding country. 1
7:17 through . . Judea and all the surrounding country. 1
8:37 Then all the people of the surrounding country 1
Act 14: 6 and to the surrounding country; 1

countryman 1. בֶּן עַם 2. ἔθνος 3. ὁμοεθνής 4. ὁμόφυλος 5. συμφυλέτης

Jdg 14:16 you have put a riddle to my countrymen 1
17 Then she told the riddle to her countrymen. 1
1Th 2:14 from your own countrymen 5
Tob 1: 3 my brethren and countrymen 2
2Mc 4:10 he at once shifted his countrymen over to . . 4
12: 5 Judas heard of the cruelty visited on his countrymen 3
15:30 his youthful good will toward his countrymen 3
31 and had called his countrymen together 3

fellow countryman 1. ὁμοεθνῆ 2. ὁμοεθνής 3. ὁμοέθνος

2Mc 4: 2 the protector of his fellow countrymen 3
5: 6 over enemies and not over fellow countrymen. 2
3Mc 7:14 any whom they met of their fellow-countrymen 1

countryside 1. מִגְרָשׁ 2. χώρα

Ezk 27:28 of the cry of your pilots the countryside shakes 1
3Mc 3: 1 but was . . hostile toward those in the countryside 2

couple 1. חבר 2. צֶמֶד 3. שְׁנַיִם

Exd 26: 3 Five curtains shall be coupled to one another; 1
3 five curtains shall be coupled to one another. 1
6 shall . . couple the curtains one to the other 1
9 you shall couple five curtains by themselves 1
36:10 he coupled five curtains to one another 1
10 other five curtains he coupled to one another. 1
13 he . . coupled the curtains one to the other 1
16 He coupled five curtains by themselves 1
Jdg 19: 3 He had with him his servant and a couple of asses. 2
10 He had with him a couple of saddled asses 2
2Sm 13: 6 Tamar come and make a couple of cakes in my sight 3
16: 1 Ziba . . met him, with a couple of asses saddled 2
1Kg 17:12 I am gathering a couple of sticks, that I may go 3

couple together 1. חבר

Exd 26:11 and couple the tent together that it may be one 1
36:18 50 clasps of bronze to couple the tent together 1

courage 1. יָד 2. לֵב 3. לֵבָב 4. נֶפֶשׁ 5. רוּחַ 6. ἀνδρεία 7. ἀνδρεῖος 8. ἀρετή 9. γενναιότης 10. διάνοια 11. εὐανδρία 12. εὐψυχία 13. θαρρέω 14. θάρσος 15. θυμός 16. παρρησία 17. παρρησιάζομαι 18. πνεῦμα 19. ὑπομένω

Jos 2:11 and there was no courage left in any man 5
2Sm 4: 1 his courage failed, and all Israel was dismayed. 1
7:27 therefore thy servant has found courage to pray 2
1Ch 17:25 servant has found courage to pray before thee. •
Ps 107:26 their courage melted away in their evil plight; 4
Jer 4: 9 courage shall fail both king and princes; 2
Lam 1:16 comforter is far from me, one to revive my courage; 4
Ezk 22:14 Can your courage endure 2
Dan 11:25 he shall stir up his power and his courage 3
Act 28:15 Paul thanked God and took courage. 14

Php 1:20 with full courage now as always 16
1Th 2: 2 courage in our God to declare to you the gospel 17
Jdt 7:19 their courage failed 18
30 Uzziah said to them, "Have courage, my brothers! 13
11: 4 Have courage; you will live 13
Wis 8: 7 self-control and prudence, justice and courage; 7
LJr 1:59 it is better to be a king who shows his courage 6
1Mc 11:49 their courage failed 10
2Mc 6:20 who have the courage to refuse things 19
31 example of nobility and a memorial of courage 8
7:21 fired her woman's reasoning with a man's courage 15
14:18 their courage in battle for their country 12
15:10 when he had aroused their courage 15
17 by fighting hand to hand with all courage 11
4Mc 1: 4 those that stand in the way of courage 6
6 opposed to justice, courage, and self-control 6
11 marveled at their courage and endurance 6
18 justice, courage, and self-control. 6
5:23 it also trains us in courage 6
13:11 While one said, "Courage, brother 13
17: 2 showed the courage of your faith! 9
23 when he saw the courage of their virtue 7

courage *See also* give, lose, take.

good courage 1. אמץ 2. חזק 3. εὐθαρσής 4. εὐψύχως 5. θαρρέω

Deu 31: 6 Be strong and of good courage, do not fear 1
7 Be strong and of good courage; for you shall go 1
23 Be strong and of good courage; for you shall bring 1
Jos 1: 6 Be strong and of good courage; 1
9 Be strong and of good courage; be not frightened 1
18 Only be strong and of good courage. 1
10:25 Do not be afraid . . be strong and of good courage; 1
2Sm 10:12 Be of good courage, and let us play the man 2
1Ch 19:13 Be of good courage, and let us play the man 2
22:13 Be strong, and of good courage. 1
28:20 Be strong and of good courage, and do it. 1
2Ch 32: 7 Be strong and of good courage. Do not be afraid 1
Dan 10:19 peace be with you; be strong and of good courage. 1
2Co 5: 6 So we are always of good courage 5
8 We are of good courage 5
2Mc 7:20 she bore it with good courage 4
8:21 he filled them with good courage 3

courageous 1. אמץ 2. גבה 3. חזק 4. ἀνδρεῖος 5. ἀνδρίζω 6. γενναῖος 7. εὐψυχία 8. μεγαλοφρονέω 9. μεγαλόφρων

Jos 1: 7 Only be strong and very courageous 1
2Sm 13:28 Be courageous and be valiant. 3
2Ch 17: 6 His heart was courageous in the ways of the LORD; 2
1Co 16:13 be courageous, be strong. 5
Wis 8:15 show myself capable, and courageous in war. 4
Sir 28:15 Slander has driven away courageous women 4
1Mc 2:64 be courageous and grow strong in the law 5
3Mc 2:32 acted firmly with a courageous spirit 6
4Mc 2:23 temperate, just, good, and courageous. 4
6: 5 the courageous and noble man, as a true Eleazar 9
24 When they saw that he was so courageous 8
7:23 only the wise and courageous man 4
9:21 the courageous youth, worthy of Abraham 9
23 renounce our courageous brotherhood. 7
17:24 this made them brave and courageous 4

courageous spirit 1. εὐψυχία 2. καρτεροψυχία

4Mc 6:11 he amazed . . by his courageous spirit. 1
9:26 all were marveling at his courageous spirit 2

courageously 1. חזק 2. εὐθαρσῶς 3. θαρραλέως 4. θρασύς

2Ch 19:11 Deal courageously, and may the LORD be 1
1Mc 6:45 courageously ran into the midst of the phalanx 4
2Mc 7:10 and courageously stretched forth his hands 2
3Mc 1:23 die courageously for the ancestral law 3

courier 1. רוץ

2Ch 30: 6 couriers went throughout all Israel and Judah 1
10 couriers went from city to city 1
Est 3:13 Letters were sent by couriers to . . provinces 1
15 The couriers went in haste by order of the king 1
8:10 and letters were sent by mounted couriers 1
14 the couriers . . rode out in haste 1

course 1. ארח 2. דֶּרֶךְ 3. טוּר 4. מְסִלָּה 5. מְרוּצָה 6. פָּנִים 7. קַו 8. מַחֲלֹקֶת (A) 9. נִדְבָּךְ (A) 10. δόμος 11. δρόμος 12. ἴδιος 13. ὁδός 14. πορεία 15. τόπος 16. actus

Gen 4: 3 In the course of time Cain brought to the LORD 7
38:12 In course of time the wife of Judah •
Exd 2:23 In the course of those many days •
Jdg 5:20 the stars, from their courses they fought 4
2Sm 14:20 In order to change the course of affairs 6
1Kg 6:36 three courses of hewn stone and one course 3
36 of hewn stone and one course of cedar beams. 3
7:12 The great court had three courses of hewn stone 3
12 three courses of . . and a course of cedar beams; 3
Ezr 6: 4 with three courses of great stones 9
4 courses of great stones and one course of timber; 9
18 set . . the Levites in their courses 8
Job 6:18 The caravans turn aside from their course; 2
Ps 19: 5 like a strong man runs its course with joy. 1
Isa 3:12 mislead . . and confuse the course of your paths. 2
Jer 2:33 How well you direct your course to seek lovers! 2
8: 6 Every one turns to his own course 5
23:10 Their course is evil, and their might is not right. 5
Lke 13:32 the third day I finish my course. •
Act 13:25 as John was finishing his course, he said 11
20:24 if only I may accomplish my course 11
1Es 4:34 the sun is swift in its course 11
6:25 with three courses of hewn stone 10
25 one course of new native timber 10
2Es 8: 2 so is the course of the present world. 16
Wis 14: 3 thy providence, O Father, that steers its course •
18:14 and night in its swift course was now half gone 12
Sir 19:17 let the law of the Most High take its course. 15
43: 5 at his command it hastens on its course. 14
4Mc 14: 5 running the course toward immortality 13
15: 2 Two courses were open to this mother •

course (2) 1. δή 2. utique

2Es 5:47 I said, "Of course it cannot 2
4Mc 1: 2 virtue–I mean, of course, rational judgment. 1

course *See* change, due, follow, run, trace.

course of time 1. יָמִים מִיָּמִים

2Ch 21:19 In course of time . . his bowels came out 1

straight course 1. εὐθυδρομέω

Act 21: 1 we came by a straight course to Cos 1

court 1. חָצֵר 2. עֲזָרָה 3. תְּרַע (A) 4. αὐλή 5. ὁ περί 6. περιβολή

Exd 27: 9 You shall make the court of the tabernacle. 1
9 the court shall have hangings of fine twined 1
12 for the breadth of the court on the west side 1
13 The breadth of the court on the front to the east 1
16 For the gate of the court there shall be a screen 1
17 the pillars around the court shall be filleted 1
18 The length of the court shall be 100 cubits 1
19 and all its pegs and all the pegs of the court 1
35:17 the hangings of the court its pillars 1
17 its bases, and the screen for the gate of the court; 1
18 the pegs of the court, and their cords; 1
38: 9 he made the court; for the south side the hangings 1
9 hangings of the court were of fine twined linen 1
15 on this hand and that hand by the gate of the court 1
16 All the hangings round about the court were 1
17 and all the pillars of the court were filleted 1
18 the screen for the gate of the court was 1
18 corresponding to the hangings of the court. 1
20 all the pegs for the tabernacle and for the court 1
31 the bases round about the court, and the bases 1
31 the court, and the bases of the gate of the court 1
31 and all the pegs round about the court. 1
39:40 the hangings of the court, its pillars 1
40 its bases, and the screen for the gate of the court 1
40: 8 you shall set up the court round about, and hang up 1
8 hang up the screen for the gate of the court. 1
33 he erected the court round the tabernacle 1
33 set up the screen of the gate of the court. 1
Lev 6:16 in the court of the tent of meeting they shall eat 1
26 in a holy place it shall be eaten, in the court 1
Num 3:26 the hangings of the court, the screen for the door 1
26 the screen for the door of the court 1
37 also the pillars of the court round about 1
4:26 hangings of the court 1
26 screen for the entrance of the gate of the court 1
32 pillars of the court round about with their 1
1Kg 6:36 built the inner court with three courses of hewn 1
7: 8 own house . . in the other court back of the hall 1
9 from the court of the house of the LORD •
9 court of the house of the LORD to the great court. 1
12 The great court had three courses of hewn stone 1
12 so had the inner court of the house of the LORD 1
8:64 the middle of the court that was before the house 1
2Kg 20: 4 before Isaiah had gone out of the middle court 1
21: 5 built altars . . in the two courts of the house 1
23:12 had made in the two courts of the house of the LORD 1
1Ch 23:28 having the care of the courts and the chambers 1
28: 6 Solomon . . shall build my house and my courts 1
12 the plan of all that he had in mind for the courts 1
2Ch 4: 9 made the court of the priests, and the great court 1
9 made the court of the priests, and the great court 2
9 made the court . . and doors for the court 2
6:13 bronze platform . . and had set it in the court; 2
7: 7 Solomon consecrated the middle of the court 1
20: 5 in the house of the LORD, before the new court 1
23: 5 all the people shall be in the courts 1
24:21 stoned him with stones in the court of the house 1
29:16 into the court of the house of the LORD; 1
33: 5 built altars . . in the two courts of the house 1
Neh 3:25 upper house of the king at the court of the guard. 1
8:16 made booths . . in their courts and in the courts 1
16 made booths . . in the courts of the house of God 1
13: 7 chamber in the courts of the house of God. 1
Est 1: 5 a banquet . . in the court of the garden 1
2:11 Mor'decai walked in front of the court 1
4:11 if any . . goes to the king inside the inner court 1
5: 1 and stood in the inner court of the king's palace 1
2 the king saw Queen Esther standing in the court 1
6: 4 And the king said, "Who is in the court? 1
4 just entered the outer court of the king's palace 1
5 Haman is there, standing in the court. 1
Ps 65: 4 choose and bring near, to dwell in thy courts! 1
84: 2 soul longs, yea, faints for the courts of the LORD; 1
10 day in thy courts is better than 1,000 1
92:13 they flourish in the courts of our God. 1
96: 8 bring an offering, and come into his courts! 1
100: 4 Enter . . his courts with praise! 1
116:19 in the courts of the house of the LORD 1
135: 2 that stand in . . courts of the house of our God! 1
Isa 1:12 who requires of you this trampling of my courts? 1
62: 9 shall drink it in the courts of my sanctuary. 1
Jer 19:14 and he stood in the court of the LORD'S house 1
26: 2 Stand in the court of the LORD'S house, and speak 1
32: 2 and Jeremiah the prophet was shut up in the court 1
8 my cousin came to me in the court of the guard 1
12 Jews who were sitting in the court of the guard. 1
33: 1 while he was still shut up in the court of the guard 1
36:10 which was in the upper court, at the entry 1
20 they went into the court to the king 1
37:21 committed Jeremiah to the court of the guard; 1
21 Jeremiah remained in the court of the guard. 1
38: 6 cistern . . which was in the court of the guard 1
13 And Jeremiah remained in the court of the guard. 1
28 Jeremiah remained in the court of the guard 1
39:14 and took Jeremiah from the court of the guard. 1
15 while he was shut up in the court of the guard 1
Ezk 8: 3 to the entrance of the gateway of the inner court •
7 he brought me to the door of the court; 1
16 me into the inner court of the house of the LORD; 1
9: 7 and fill the courts with the slain. Go forth. 1
10: 3 and a cloud filled the inner court. 1
4 the court was full of the brightness of the glory 1
5 the cherubim was heard as far as the outer court 1
40:14 the vestibule of the gateway was the court. 1
17 Then he brought me into the outer court; 1
17 and a pavement, round about the court; 1
19 outer front of the inner court, 100 cubits. 1
20 toward the north, belonging to the outer court. 1
23 as on the east, was a gate to the inner court; 1
27 there was a gate on the south of the inner court; 1
28 he brought me to the inner court by the south gate 1
31 Its vestibule faced the outer court 1
32 he brought me to the inner court on the east side 1
34 Its vestibule faced the outer court 1
37 Its vestibule faced the outer court 1
44 he brought me from without into the inner court •
44 there were two chambers in the inner court 1
47 he measured the court, 100 cubits long 1
41:10 chambers of the court was a breadth of twenty •
42: 1 Then he led me out into the inner court 1
3 twenty cubits which belonged to the inner court 1
3 the pavement which belonged to the outer court 1
6 pillars like the pillars of the outer court; 1
7 parallel to the chambers, toward the outer court 1
8 chambers on the outer court were 50 cubits 1
9 as one enters them from the outer court 1
14 they shall not go out of it into the outer court 1
43: 5 lifted me up, and brought me into the inner court; 1
44:17 they enter the gates of the inner court, 1
17 they minister at the gates of the inner court, 1
19 they go out into the outer court to the people 1
21 shall drink wine, when he enters the inner court. 1
27 into the holy place, into the inner court 1
45:19 and the posts of the gate of the inner court. 1
46: 1 The gate of the inner court that faces east 1
20 not to bring them out into the outer court 1
21 Then he brought me forth to the outer court 1
21 and led me to the four corners of the court; 1
21 and in each corner of the court there was a court 1
21 and in each corner of the court there was a court 1
22 the four corners of the court were small courts 1
22 the four corners of the court were small courts 1
23 around each of the four courts was a row •
Dan 2:49 but Daniel remained at the king's court. 3
Zec 3: 7 shall rule my house and have charge of my courts 1
Lke 7:25 those who . . live in luxury are in kings' courts. •
Joh 18:15 he entered the court of the high priest 4
Rev 11: 2 do not measure the court outside the temple; 4
1Es 9: 1 went from the court of the temple 4
AEs 11: 3 a great man, serving in the court of the king. 4
12: 5 the king ordered Mordecai to serve in the court 4
Sir 50:11 he made the court of the sanctuary glorious. 6
1Mc 4:38 In the courts they saw bushes sprung up 4
48 consecrated the courts. 4
9:54 the wall of the inner court of the sanctuary 4
4Mc 5: 4 and known to many in the tyrant's court 5

court (2) 1. מִשְׁפָּט 2. רִיב 3. דִּין (A) 4. ἀγοραῖος 5. ἡμέρα 6. κριτήριον

Deu 25: 1 dispute between men, and they come into court 1
Prv 25: 8 do not hastily bring into court; 2
Dan 7:10 court sat in judgment, and the books were opened. 3

26 court shall sit in judgment, and his dominion 3
Mat 5:25 accuser, while you are going with him to court •
Act 19:38 the courts are open 4
1Co 4: 3 I should be judged by you or by any human court 5
Jas 2: 6 is it not they who drag you into court? 6
court *See* member.

courtesy 1. εὐπροσήγορος 2. χάρις
Sir 6: 5 a gracious tongue multiplies courtesies. 1
20:13 the courtesies of fools are wasted. 2

perfect courtesy 1. πραΰτης
Tit 3: 2 to show perfect courtesy toward all men. 1

courtier 1. μεγιστάν 2. σύντροφος
Mrk 6:21 a banquet for his courtiers and officers 1
2Mc 9:29 Philip, one of his courtiers, took his body home; 2

courtyard 1. חָצֵר 2. αὐλαία 3. αὐλή
Exd 8:13 frogs died out of . . and courtyards 1
2Sm 17:18 a man at Bahu'rim, who had a well in his courtyard; 1
Mat 26:58 as far as the courtyard of the high priest 3
69 Now Peter was sitting outside in the courtyard. 3
Mrk 14:54 right into the courtyard of the high priest 3
66 as Peter was below in the courtyard 3
Lke 22:55 had kindled a fire in the middle of the courtyard 3
Tob 2: 9 I slept by the wall of the courtyard 3
AEs 12: 1 Now Mordecai took his rest in the courtyard 3
1 who kept watch in the courtyard. 3
2Mc 14:41 were forcing the door of the courtyard 2
3Mc 2:27 he set up a stone on the tower in the courtyard 3
5:10 Hermon . . presented himself at the courtyard 3
46 entered at about dawn into the courtyard 3

cousin 1. בֶּן דּוֹד 2. דּוֹד 3. ἀνεψιός
Lev 25:49 or his uncle, or his cousin may redeem him 1
Jer 32: 8 my cousin came to me in the court of the guard 1
9 I bought the field . . from Han'amel my cousin 1
12 in the presence of Han'amel my cousin 2
Col 4:10 Mark the cousin of Barnabas 3
Tob 7: 2 How much the young man resembles my cousin Tobit! 3

covenant 1. בְּרִית 2. כרת 3. διαθήκη 4. συνθήκη 5. τίθημι χεῖρας ἐπὶ χεῖρας 6. dispositio 7. sponsio 8. testamentum 9. testimonium
Gen 6:18 I will establish my covenant with you; 1
9: 9 Behold, I establish my covenant with you 1
11 I establish my covenant with you 1
12 God said, "This is the sign of the covenant 1
13 a sign of the covenant between me and the earth. 1
15 I will remember my covenant which is between me 1
16 it and remember the everlasting covenant 1
17 God said to Noah, "This is the sign of the covenant 1
15:18 On that day the LORD made a covenant with Abram 1
17: 2 I will make my covenant between me and you 1
4 Behold, my covenant is with you 1
7 I will establish my covenant between me and you 1
7 their generations for an everlasting covenant 1
9 to Abraham, "As for you, you shall keep my covenant 1
10 This is my covenant, which you shall keep 1
11 a sign of the covenant between me and you. 1
13 shall my covenant be in your flesh 1
13 be in your flesh an everlasting covenant. 1
14 his people; he has broken my covenant. 1
19 Isaac. I will establish my covenant with him 1
19 my covenant with him as an everlasting covenant 1
21 I will establish my covenant with Isaac 1
21:27 to Abim'elech, and the two men made a covenant. 1
32 they made a covenant at Beer-sheba. 1
26:28 and let us make a covenant with you 1
31:44 Come now, let us make a covenant, you and I; 1
Exd 2:24 and God remembered his covenant with Abraham 1
6: 4 I also established my covenant with them 1
5 I have heard . . I have remembered my covenant. 1
19: 5 if you will obey my voice and keep my covenant 1
23:32 You shall make no covenant with them 1
24: 7 Then he took the book of the covenant, and read it 1
8 Behold the blood of the covenant which the LORD 1
31:16 their generations, as a perpetual covenant. 1
34:10 he said, "Behold, I make a covenant. 1
12 lest you make a covenant with the inhabitants 1
15 lest you make a covenant with the inhabitants 1
27 I have made a covenant with you and with Israel. 1
28 wrote upon the tables the words of the covenant 1
Lev 2:13 salt of the covenant with your God be lacking 1
24: 8 set it in order . . as a covenant for ever 1
26: 9 and will confirm my covenant with you 1
15 if you . . break my covenant 1
25 that shall execute vengeance for the covenant 1
42 then I will remember my covenant with Jacob 1
42 I will remember my covenant with Isaac 1
42 I will remember . . my covenant with Abraham 1
44 so as to . . break my covenant with them 1
45 I will for their sake remember the covenant 1
Num 10:33 ark of the covenant of the LORD went before them 1
14:44 neither the ark of the covenant of the LORD 1
18:19 it is a covenant of salt for ever before the LORD 1
25:12 Behold, I give to him my covenant of peace; 1
13 covenant of a perpetual priesthood 1
Deu 4:13 declared to you his covenant, which he commanded 1
23 lest you forget the covenant of the LORD your God 1
31 LORD . . will not . . forget the covenant 1
5: 2 The LORD our God made a covenant with us in Horeb. 1
3 Not with . . did the LORD make this covenant 1
7: 2 utterly destroy them; you shall make no covenant 1
9 LORD . . the faithful God who keeps covenant 1
12 LORD your God will keep with you the covenant 1
8:18 that he may confirm his covenant which he swore 1
9: 9 to receive . . the tables of the covenant 1
11 two tables of stone, the tables of the covenant. 1
15 two tables of the covenant were in my two hands. 1
10: 8 Levi to carry the ark of the covenant of the LORD 1
17: 2 who does what is evil . . in transgressing his covenant 1
29: 1 These are the words of the covenant 1
1 besides the covenant which he had made with them 1
9 be careful to do the words of this covenant 1
12 enter . . the sworn covenant of the LORD your God 1
14 is it with you only that I make this sworn covenant 1
21 accordance with all the curses of the covenant 1
25 because they forsook the covenant of the LORD 1
31: 9 sons of Levi, who carried the ark of the covenant 1
16 people . . will forsake me and break my covenant 1
20 turn . . and despise me and break my covenant. 1
25 who carried the ark of the covenant of the LORD 1
26 put it by the side of the ark of the covenant 1
33: 9 they observed thy word, and kept thy covenant. 1
Jos 3: 3 see the ark of the covenant of the LORD your God 1
6 Take up the ark of the covenant, and pass on before 1
6 And they took up the ark of the covenant, and went 1
8 the priests who bear the ark of the covenant 1
11 ark of the covenant of the Lord of all the earth 1
14 the priests bearing the ark of the covenant 1
17 who bore the ark of the covenant of the LORD 1
4: 7 cut off before the ark of the covenant of the LORD; 1
9 of the priests bearing the ark of the covenant 1
18 bearing the ark of the covenant of the LORD 1
6: 6 Take up the ark of the covenant 1
8 the ark of the covenant of the LORD following 1
7:11 transgressed my covenant which I commanded 1
15 he has transgressed the covenant of the LORD 1
8:33 who carried the ark of the covenant of the LORD 1
9: 6 from a far country; so now make a covenant with us. 1
7 then how can we make a covenant with you? 1
11 We are your servants . . make a covenant with us. 1
15 and made a covenant with them, to let them live; 1
16 after they had made a covenant with them 1
23:16 if you transgress the covenant of the LORD 1
24:25 Joshua made a covenant with the people that day 1
Jdg 2: 1 I said, 'I will never break my covenant with you 1
2 you shall make no covenant with the inhabitants 1
20 transgressed my covenant which I commanded 1
20:27 for the ark of the covenant of God was there 1
1Sm 4: 3 bring the ark of the covenant of the LORD here 1
4 the ark of the covenant of the LORD of hosts 1
4 were there with the ark of the covenant of God. 1
5 the ark of the covenant of the LORD came 1
18: 3 Then Jonathan made a covenant with David 1
20: 8 brought your servant into a sacred covenant 1
23:18 the two of them made a covenant before the LORD; 1
2Sm 3:12 Make your covenant with me, and . . my hand shall be 1
13 And he said, "Good; I will make a covenant with you; 1
21 that they may make a covenant with you 1
5: 3 King David made a covenant with them at Hebron 1
15:24 Levites, bearing the ark of the covenant of God; 1
23: 5 For he has made with me an everlasting covenant 1
1Kg 3:15 stood before the ark of the covenant of the LORD 1
6:19 to set there the ark of the covenant of the LORD. 1
8: 1 bring up the ark of the covenant of the LORD 1
6 brought the ark of the covenant of the LORD 1
21 in which is the covenant of the LORD which he made 1
23 keeping covenant and showing steadfast love 1
11:11 you have not kept my covenant and my statutes 1
19:10 the people of Israel have forsaken thy covenant 1
14 the people of Israel have forsaken thy covenant 1
20:34 So he made a covenant with him and let him go. 1
2Kg 11: 4 he made a covenant with them . . and he showed them 1
17 Jehoi'ada made a covenant between the LORD 1
13:23 because of his covenant with Abraham, Isaac 1
17:15 They despised his statutes, and his covenant 1
35 LORD made a covenant with them, and commanded 1
38 shall not forget the covenant that I have made 1
18:12 did not obey . . but transgressed his covenant 1
23: 2 all the words of the book of the covenant 1
3 king stood . . and made a covenant before the LORD 1
3 to perform the words of this covenant 1
3 and all the people joined in the covenant. 1
21 as it is written in this book of the covenant. 1
1Ch 11: 3 David made a covenant with them at Hebron 1
15:25 to bring up the ark of the covenant of the LORD 1
26 carrying the ark of the covenant of the LORD 1
28 brought up the ark of the covenant of the LORD 1
29 ark of the covenant of the LORD came to the city 1
16: 6 before the ark of the covenant of God. 1
15 He is mindful of his covenant for ever 1
16 the covenant which he made with Abraham •
17 as an everlasting covenant to Israel 1
37 there before the ark of the covenant of the LORD 1
17: 1 ark of the covenant of the LORD is under a tent. 1
22:19 so that the ark of the covenant of the LORD 1
28: 2 house . . for the ark of the covenant of the LORD 1
18 and covered the ark of the covenant of the LORD. 1
2Ch 5: 2 to bring up the ark of the covenant of the LORD 1
7 brought the ark of the covenant of the LORD 1
10 LORD made a covenant with the people of Israel •
6:11 the ark, in which is the covenant of the LORD 1
14 keeping covenant and showing steadfast love 1
7:18 I will establish . . as I covenanted with David 2
13: 5 to David and his sons by a covenant of salt? 1
15:12 they entered into a covenant to seek the LORD 1
21: 7 because of the covenant which he had made 1
23: 3 all the assembly made a covenant with the king 1
16 Jehoi'ada made a covenant between himself 1
29:10 it is in my heart to make a covenant with the LORD 1
34:30 read . . all the words of the book of the covenant 1
31 king . . made a covenant before the LORD 1
31 to perform the words of the covenant 1
32 Jerusalem did according to the covenant of God 1
Ezr 10: 3 Therefore let us make a covenant with our God 1
Neh 1: 5 God who keeps covenant and steadfast love 1
9: 8 thou . . didst make with him the covenant to give 1
32 God, who keepest covenant and steadfast love 1
13:29 defiled . . the covenant of the priesthood 1
Job 31: 1 I have made a covenant with my eyes; 1
41: 4 Will he make a covenant with you to take him 1
Ps 25:10 faithfulness, for those who keep his covenant 1
14 he makes known to them his covenant. 1
44:17 forgotten thee, or been false to thy covenant. 1
50: 5 my faithful ones, who made a covenant with me 1
16 or take my covenant on your lips? 1
55:20 against his friends, he violated his covenant. 1
74:20 Have regard for thy covenant; 1
78:10 They did not keep God's covenant, but refused 1
37 they were not true to his covenant. 1
83: 5 against thee they make a covenant- 1
89: 3 I have made a covenant with my chosen one 1
28 my covenant will stand firm for him. 1
34 I will not violate my covenant 1
39 hast renounced the covenant with thy servant; 1
103:18 to those who keep his covenant and remember to do 1
105: 8 He is mindful of his covenant for ever 1
9 covenant which he made with Abraham •
10 to Israel as an everlasting covenant 1
106:45 He remembered for their sake his covenant 1
111: 5 he is ever mindful of his covenant. 1
9 he has commanded his covenant for ever. 1
132:12 If your sons keep my covenant and my testimonies 1
Prv 2:17 who . . forgets the covenant of her God; 1
Isa 24: 5 violated . . broken the everlasting covenant. 1
28:15 you have said, "We have made a covenant with death 1
18 Then your covenant with death will be annulled 1
33: 8 Covenants are broken, witnesses are despised 1
42: 6 I have given you as a covenant to the people 1
49: 8 kept you and given you as a covenant to the people 1
54:10 and my covenant of peace shall not be removed 1
55: 3 I will make with you an everlasting covenant 1
56: 4 that please me and hold fast my covenant 1
6 does not profane it, and holds fast my covenant- 1
59:21 this is my covenant with them, says the LORD 1
61: 8 I will make an everlasting covenant with them. 1
Jer 3:16 no more say, "The ark of the covenant of the LORD. 1
11: 2 Hear the words of this covenant 1
3 who does not heed the words of this covenant 1
6 Hear the words of this covenant and do them. 1
8 brought upon them all the words of this covenant 1
10 and the house of Judah have broken my covenant 1
14:21 remember and do not break thy covenant with us. 1
22: 9 Because they forsook the covenant of the LORD 1
31:31 says the LORD, when I will make a new covenant 1
32 the covenant which I made with their fathers 1
32 my covenant which they broke 1
33 But this is the covenant which I will make 1
32:40 I will make with them an everlasting covenant 1
33:20 If you can break my covenant with the day 1
20 If you can break . . my covenant with the night 1
21 my covenant with David my servant may be broken 1
21 and my covenant with the Levitical priests •
25 If I have not established my covenant with day 1
34: 8 after King Zedeki'ah had made a covenant 1
10 the people who had entered into the covenant 1
13 I made a covenant with your fathers 1
15 and you made a covenant before me 1
18 the men who transgressed my covenant 1
18 and did not keep the terms of the covenant 1
50: 5 join . . to the LORD in an everlasting covenant 1
Ezk 16: 8 and entered into a covenant with you 1
59 despised the oath in breaking the covenant 1
60 yet I will remember my covenant with you 1
60 establish with you an everlasting covenant. 1
61 but not on account of the covenant with you. 1
62 I will establish my covenant with you 1
17:13 and made a covenant with him 1
14 that by keeping his covenant it might stand. 1
15 Can he break the covenant and yet escape? 1
16 he despised, and whose covenant with him he broke 1
18 he despised the oath and broke the covenant 1
19 which he despised, and my covenant which he broke 1

34:25 I will make with them a covenant of peace 1
37:26 I will make a covenant of peace with them; 1
26 it shall be an everlasting covenant with them; 1
44: 7 You have broken my covenant 1
Dan 9: 4 God, who keepest covenant and steadfast love 1
27 make a strong covenant with many for one week; 1
11:22 broken, and the prince of the covenant also. 1
28 heart shall be set against the holy covenant. 1
30 take action against the holy covenant. 1
30 heed to those who forsake the holy covenant. 1
32 seduce . . those who violate the covenant; 1
Hos 2:18 And I will make for you a covenant on that day 1
6: 7 But at Adam they transgressed the covenant; 1
8: 1 because they have broken my covenant 1
10: 4 with empty oaths they make covenants; 1
Ams 1: 9 did not remember the covenant of brotherhood. 1
Zec 9:11 for you also, because of the blood of my covenant 1
11:10 annulling the covenant which I had made with all 1
Mal 2: 4 that my covenant with Levi may hold, says the LORD 1
5 My covenant with him was a covenant of life 1
5 My covenant with him was a covenant of life •
8 you have corrupted the covenant of Levi 1
10 profaning the covenant of our fathers? 1
14 Because the LORD was witness to the covenant •
14 she is your companion and your wife by covenant. 1
3: 1 messenger of the covenant in whom you delight 1
Mat 26:28 for this is my blood of the covenant 3
Mrk 14:24 he said to them, "This is my blood of the covenant 3
Lke 1:72 to remember his holy covenant 3
22:20 the new covenant in my blood. 3
Act 3:25 the sons of the prophets and of the covenant 3
7: 8 he gave him the covenant of circumcision 3
Rom 9: 4 the covenants, the giving of the law, the worship 3
11:27 my covenant with them when I take away their sins. 3
1Co 11:25 This cup is the new covenant in my blood 3
2Co 3: 6 competent to be ministers of a new covenant 3
14 for to this day, when they read the old covenant 3
Gal 3:17 annul a covenant previously ratified by God 3
4:24 these women are two covenants 3
Eph 2:12 strangers to the covenants of promise 3
Heb 7:22 makes Jesus the surety of a better covenant. 3
8: 6 the covenant he mediates is better 3
7 For if that first covenant had been faultless •
8 when I will establish a new covenant 3
9 like the covenant that I made with their fathers 3
9 for they did not continue in my covenant 3
10 This is the covenant that I will make 3
13 In speaking of a new covenant •
9: 1 the first covenant had regulations for worship •
4 the ark of the covenant 3
4 the tables of the covenant; 3
15 Therefore he is the mediator of a new covenant 3
15 the transgressions under the first covenant. 3
18 Hence even the first covenant was not ratified •
20 saying, "This is the blood of the covenant 3
10:16 This is the covenant that I will make with them 3
29 profaned the blood of the covenant 3
12:24 to Jesus, the mediator of a new covenant 3
13:20 by the blood of the eternal covenant 3
Rev 11:19 ark of his covenant was seen within his temple; 3
2Es 2: 5 because they would not keep my covenant 8
7 because they have despised my covenant. 8
3:15 didst make with him an everlasting covenant 8
32 Or what tribes have so believed thy covenants 8
4:23 and the written covenants no longer exist; 6
5:29 trodden down those who believed thy covenants. 8
7:24 They scorned his law, and denied his covenants; 7
46 that has not transgressed thy covenant? 7
83 who have trusted the covenants of the Most High. 8
8:27 who have kept thy covenants amid afflictions. 9
10:22 the ark of our covenant has been plundered 8
Jdt 9:13 they have planned cruel things against thy covenant 3
AEs 14: 8 have covenanted with their idols 5
Wis 1:16 they made a covenant with him 4
12:21 oaths and covenants full of good promises! 4
18:22 the oaths and covenants given to our fathers. 3
Sir 11:20 Stand by your covenant and attend to it 3
16:22 who will await them? For the covenant is far off. 3
17:12 He established with them an eternal covenant 3
24:23 is the book of the covenant of the Most High God 3
28: 7 remember the covenant of the Most High 3
39: 8 will glory in the law of the Lord's covenant. 3
41:19 before the truth of God and his covenant 3
42: 2 of the law of the Most High and his covenant 3
44:12 Their descendants stand by the covenants 3
18 Everlasting covenants were made with him 3
20 was taken into covenant with him 3
20 he established the covenant in his flesh 3
23 The blessing of all men and the covenant 3
45: 5 to teach Jacob the covenant 3
7 He made an everlasting covenant with him 3
15 it was an everlasting covenant for him 3
24 Therefore a covenant of peace was established 3
25 A covenant was also established with David 3
47:11 he gave him the covenant of kings 3
Bar 2:35 I will make an everlasting covenant with them 3
Aza 1:11 do not break thy covenant 3
1Mc 1:11 Let us go and make a covenant with the Gentiles 3
15 abandoned the holy covenant 3
57 Where the book of the covenant was found 3
63 to profane the holy covenant 3
2:20 will live by the covenant of our fathers. 3
27 every one who . . supports the covenant 3
50 give your lives for the covenant of our fathers. 3
54 the covenant of everlasting priesthood. 3
4:10 remember his covenant with our fathers 3
11: 9 Come, let us make a covenant with each other 3
2Mc 1: 2 may he remember his covenant with Abraham 3
7:36 drunk of everflowing life under God's covenant; 3
8:15 the covenants made with their fathers 3
14:20 they agreed to the covenant. 4
26 he took the covenant that had been made 4
27 he was displeased with the covenant 4

covenant *See also* make.

firm covenant 1. אֲמָנָה
Neh 9:38 we make a firm covenant and write it 1

sworn covenant 1. אָלָה
Deu 29:19 when he hears the words of this sworn covenant 1

cover 1. אחז 2. חפה 3. טלל 4. טפל 5. יעט 6. כְּבָר 7. כסה 8. כפר 9. לאט 10. מלא 11. סכך 12. ספן 13. סֵתֶר 14. עטה 15. עטף 16. עטר 17. צָב 18. צָמִיד 19. צפה 20. צִפּוּי 21. קלע עַל 22. קרם 23. שכך 24. שׂוּף 25. ἐπικαλύπτω 26. καλύπτω 27. κατὰ ἔχω 28. κατακαλύπτω 29. περικαλύπτω 30. πίμπλημι 31. πληρόω 32. σκεπάζω 33. σκέπης 34. tego
Gen 6:14 in the ark, and cover it inside and out with pitch. 8
7:19 mountains under the whole heaven were covered; 7
20 covering them fifteen cubits deep. 7
9:23 covered the nakedness of their father; 7
24:65 she took her veil and covered herself. 7
38:15 be a harlot, for she had covered her face. 7
Exd 8: 6 the frogs came up and covered the land of Egypt. 7
10: 5 they shall cover the face of the land 7
15 For they covered the face of the whole land 7
14:28 The waters returned and covered the chariots 7
15: 5 The floods cover them; they went down 7
10 Thou didst blow with thy wind, the sea covered 7
16:13 quails came up and covered the camp; 7
21:33 when a man digs a pit and does not cover it 7
24:15 and the cloud covered the mountain. 7
16 Mount Sinai, and the cloud covered it six days; 7
26:13 shall hang over the sides . . to cover it. 7
28:42 linen breeches to cover their naked flesh; 7
29:13 shall take all the fat that covers the entrails 7
22 take . . the fat that covers the entrails 7
33:22 I will cover you with my hand until I have passed 23
40:34 Then the cloud covered the tent of meeting 7
Lev 3: 3 he shall offer the fat covering the entrails 7
9 the fat that covers the entrails, and all the fat 7
14 shall offer . . the fat covering the entrails 7
4: 8 the fat that covers the entrails and all the fat 7
7: 3 the fat tail, the fat that covers the entrails 7
9:19 that which covers the entrails, and the kidneys 7
13:12 breaks out . . so that the leprosy covers all 7
13 if the leprosy has covered all his body 7
45 leper . . shall cover his upper lip and cry 14
16:13 the cloud of the incense may cover the mercy seat 7
17:13 shall pour out its blood and cover it with dust 7
Num 4: 5 cover the ark of the testimony with it; 7
8 and cover the same with a covering of goatskin 7
9 cover the lampstand for the light, with its lamps 7
11 cover it with a covering of goatskin 7
12 cover them with a covering of goatskin, and put 7
15 have finished covering the sanctuary 7
7: 3 offering . . six covered wagons and twelve oxen 17
9:15 cloud covered the tabernacle, the tent 7
16 it was continually; the cloud covered it by day 7
16:42 tent of meeting; and behold, the cloud covered it 7
19:15 open vessel, which has no cover fastened upon it 18
22: 5 cover the face of the earth, and they are dwelling 7
11 a people . . covers the face of the earth; now come 7
Deu 22:12 corners of your cloak with which you cover 7
Jdg 4:18 into the tent, and she covered him with a rug. 7
19 skin of milk and gave him a drink and covered him. 7
1Sm 19:13 put a pillow . . and covered it with the clothes. 7
25:20 and came down under cover of the mountain 13
2Sm 15:30 weeping . . barefoot and with his head covered; 2
30 the people who were with him covered their heads 2
19: 4 The king covered his face, and the king cried 9
1Kg 1: 1 although they covered him with clothes, he could 7
6:15 he covered them on the inside with wood; 19
15 he covered the floor . . with boards of cypress. 19
32 He covered the two doors . . with carvings 21
7: 3 it was covered with cedar above the chambers 12
18 made pomegranates . . to cover the capital 7
41 the two networks to cover the two bowls 7
42 pomegranates . . to cover the two bowls 7
2Kg 3:25 every man threw a stone, until it was covered; 10
19: 1 his clothes, and covered himself with sackcloth 7
2 and the senior priests, covered with sackcloth 7
1Ch 28:18 spread their wings and covered the ark 11
2Ch 3: 5 nave he lined . . and covered it with fine gold 2
4:12 networks to cover the two bowls of the capitals 7
13 to cover the two bowls of the capitals that were 7
Neh 3:15 rebuilt it and covered it and set its doors 3
4: 5 Do not cover their guilt, and let not their sin 7
Est 6:12 Haman . . mourning and with his head covered. 2
7: 8 As the words left . . they covered Haman's face. 2
Job 9:24 he covers the faces of its judges– 7
14:17 thou wouldest cover over my iniquity. 4
15:27 because he has covered his face with his fat 7
16:18 O earth, cover not my blood 7
21:26 alike in the dust, and the worms cover them. 7
22:11 you cannot see, and a flood of water covers you. 7
23:17 by darkness, and thick darkness covers my face. 7
26: 9 He covers the face of the moon 1
36:30 about him, and covers the roots of the sea. 7
32 He covers his hands with the lightning 7
38:34 to the clouds, that a flood of waters may cover you? 7
40:22 For his shade the lotus trees cover him; 11
Ps 5:12 thou dost cover him with favor as with a shield. 16
27: 5 he will conceal me under the cover of his tent 13
32: 1 Blessed is he . . whose sin is covered. 7
44:15 shame has covered my face 7
19 and covered us with deep darkness. 7
68:13 wings of a dove covered with silver, its pinions 2
69: 7 shame has covered my face. 7
71:13 with scorn and disgrace may they be covered 14
73: 6 violence covers them as a garment. 15
80:10 The mountains were covered with its shade 7
84: 6 early rain also covers it with pools. 14
89:45 thou hast covered him with shame. Selah 14
91: 4 he will cover you with his pinions 11
104: 2 coverest thyself with light as with a garment 14
6 didst cover it with the deep as with a garment; 7
9 so that they might not again cover the earth. 7
106:11 waters covered their adversaries; 7
17 earth opened . . covered the company of Abi'ram. 7
139:11 If I say, "Let only darkness cover me 24
140: 7 thou hast covered my head in the day of battle. 11
147: 8 He covers the heavens with clouds 7
Prv 10:12 but love covers all offenses. 7
24:31 ground was covered with nettles 7
26:23 Like the glaze covering an earthen vessel 19
26 though his hatred be covered with guile 7
Ecc 6: 4 and in darkness its name is covered; 7
Isa 6: 2 each had six wings: with two he covered his face 7
2 each had six wings . . with two he covered his feet 7
11: 9 of the knowledge . . as the waters cover the sea. 7
26:21 disclose . . and will no more cover her slain. 7
29:10 and covered your heads, the seers. 7
30:22 defile your silver-covered graven images 20
37: 1 and covered himself with sackcloth 7
58: 7 when you see the naked, to cover him 7
59: 6 will not cover themselves with what they make. 7
60: 2 For behold, darkness shall cover the earth 7
6 A multitude of camels shall cover you 7
61:10 he has covered me with the robe of righteousness 5
Jer 3:25 and let our dishonor cover us; 7
14: 3 ashamed and confounded and cover their heads. 2
4 the farmers are ashamed, they cover their heads. 2
46: 8 He said, I will rise, I will cover the earth 7
51:42 she is covered with its tumultuous waves. 7
51 dishonor has covered our face 7
Ezk 1:11 wing of another, while two covered their bodies. 7
23 each creature had two wings covering its body. 7
7:18 horror covers them; shame is upon all faces 7
12: 6 you shall cover your face, that you may not see 7
12 he shall cover his face, that he may not see 7
16: 8 my skirt over you, and covered your nakedness; 7
10 in fine linen and covered you with silk. 7
18 took your embroidered garments to cover them 7
18: 7 and covers the naked with a garment 7
16 and covers the naked with a garment 7
24: 7 not pour it upon the ground to cover it with dust. 7
8 the blood she has shed, that it may not be covered. 7
17 do not cover your lips 14
22 you shall not cover your lips 14
26:10 will be so many that their dust will cover you; 7
19 the deep over you, and the great waters cover you 7
30:18 she shall be covered by a cloud 7
32: 7 When I blot you out, I will cover the heavens 7
7 I will cover the sun with a cloud 7
37: 6 and cover you with skin, and put breath in you, 22
8 skin had covered them; but there was no breath 22
38: 9 you will be like a cloud covering the land 7
16 my people Israel, like a cloud covering the land. 7
41:16 (now the windows were covered) 7
Hos 2: 9 and my flax, which were to cover her nakedness. 7
10: 8 and they shall say to the mountains, Cover us 7
Obd 1:10 shame shall cover you, and you shall be cut off 7
Jon 3: 6 covered himself with sackcloth, and sat in ashes. 7
8 but let man and beast be covered with sackcloth 7
Mic 3: 7 they shall all cover their lips 14
7:10 and shame will cover her who said to me 7
Hab 2:14 will be filled . . as the waters cover the sea. 7
3: 3 His glory covered the heavens 7
Zec 5: 7 behold, the leaden cover was lifted 6
Mal 2:13 You cover the LORD'S altar with tears 7

16 covering one's garment with violence 7
Mat 10:26 nothing is covered that will not be revealed 26
Mrk 14:65 some began to spit on him, and to cover his face 29
Lke 8:16 No one after lighting a lamp covers it 26
23:30 to the hills, 'Cover us.' 26
Rom 4: 7 those . . whose sins are covered; 25
1Co 11: 4 who prays or prophesies with his head covered 27
7 For a man ought not to cover his head 28
Heb 9: 4 the ark . . covered on all sides with gold 29
Jas 5:20 and will cover a multitude of sins. 26
1Pe 4: 8 since love covers a multitude of sins. 26
2Es 1:20 I covered you with the leaves of trees. 34
2:29 My hands will cover you 34
Jdt 2: 7 will cover the whole face of the earth 26
19 cover the whole face of the earth to the west 26
7:18 covered the whole face of the land 26
16: 4 their cavalry covered the hills. 26
AEs 14: 2 she covered her head with ashes and dung 30
2 she covered with her tangled hair. 30
15: 6 all covered with gold and precious stones •
Wis 5:16 because with his right hand he will cover them 32
Sir 16:30 he covered its surface 26
24: 3 covered the earth like a mist. 28
29:21 clothing and a house to cover one's nakedness. 26
37: 3 why were you formed to cover the land with deceit? 26
39:22 His blessing covers the dry land like a river 25
40:27 covers a man better than any glory. 26
47:15 Your soul covered the earth 25
48:12 It was Elijah who was covered by the whirlwind 32
LJr 1:68 they can flee to cover and help themselves. 33
1Mc 6:37 wooden towers, strong and covered 32
9:38 and went up and hid under cover of the mountain. 33
2Mc 6: 5 The altar was covered with abominable offerings 31

make cover 1. כסה
Jos 24: 7 he . . made the sea come upon them and cover them; 1

cover up 1. כסה 2. κρύπτω 3. συγκαλύπτω
Deu 23:13 turn back and cover up your excrement. 1
Mat 13:44 which a man found and covered up 2
Lke 12: 2 Nothing is covered up that will not be revealed 3

cover with paint 1. καταχρίω
Wis 13:14 and covering every blemish in it with paint; 1

cover with shame 1. בוש
2Sm 19: 5 You have . . covered with shame the faces of all 1

covered *See* way.

covering 1. כסה 2. כְּסוּי 3. כְּסוּת 4. לוֹט 5. מִכְסֶה 6. מְכַסֶּה 7. מָסָךְ 8. מְסֻכָּה 9. מַסֵּכָה 10. מַרְבַד 11. סֵתֶר 12. צִפּוּי 13. περιβόλαιον
Gen 8:13 Noah removed the covering of the ark, and looked 6
Exd 22:27 for that is his only covering, it is his mantle 3
26:14 for the tent a covering of tanned rams' skins 6
35:11 its tent and its covering, its hooks 6
36:19 made for the tent a covering of tanned rams' skins 6
39:34 the covering of tanned rams' skins and goatskins 6
40:19 over the tabernacle, and put the covering 6
Num 3:25 the tabernacle, the tent with its covering 6
4: 6 then they shall put on it a covering of goatskin 2
8 and cover the same with a covering of goatskin 6
10 put it . . in a covering of goatskin 6
11 cover it with a covering of goatskin 6
12 cover them with a covering of goatskin, and put 6
14 they shall spread upon it a covering of goatskin 2
25 carry . . the tent of meeting with its covering 6
25 carry . . the covering of goatskin that is on top 6
16:38 into hammered plates as a covering for the altar 12
39 were hammered out as a covering for the altar 12
2Sm 17:19 took and spread a covering over the well's mouth 7
2Ch 5: 8 cherubim made a covering above the ark and its 1
Job 24: 7 naked, without clothing, and have no covering 3
26: 6 naked before God, and Abaddon has no covering. 3
31:19 lack of clothing, or a poor man without covering; 3
Ps 18:11 He made darkness his covering around him 11
105:39 He spread a cloud for a covering 7
Prv 7:16 I have decked my couch with coverings 10
31:22 She makes herself coverings; 10
Isa 14:11 beneath you, and worms are your covering. 5
22: 8 He has taken away the covering of Judah. 7
25: 7 he will destroy . . the covering that is cast over 4
28:20 the covering too narrow to wrap oneself in it. 9
50: 3 and make sackcloth their covering. 3
Ezk 28:13 every precious stone was your covering 8
1Co 11:15 her hair is given to her for a covering. 13

covering *See also* make.

coverlet 1. מַכְבֵּר
2Kg 8:15 he took the coverlet and dipped it in water 1

covert 1. סֹךְ 2. סֻכָּה 3. סֵתֶר
Job 38:40 in their dens, or lie in wait in their covert? 2
40:21 in the covert of the reeds and in the marsh. 3
Ps 10: 9 he lurks in secret like a lion in his covert; 1
31:20 In the covert of thy presence thou hidest them 3
Sng 2:14 the clefts of the rock, in the covert of the cliff 3
Isa 32: 2 place from the wind, a covert from the tempest 3
Jer 25:38 Like a lion he has left his covert 1

covet 1. אהב 2. אוה 3. חמד 4. ἐπιθυμέω 5. ἐπιθυμία 6. ζηλόω 7. πλεονεξία
Exd 20:17 You shall not covet your neighbor's house; 3
17 you shall not covet your neighbor's wife 3
Deu 5:21 'Neither shall you covet your neighbor's wife; 3
7:25 not covet the silver or the gold that is on them 3
Jos 7:21 when I saw . . then I coveted them, and took them; 3
Ps 34:12 who desires life, and covets many days 1
Prv 21:26 All day long the wicked covets 2
Mic 2: 2 They covet fields, and seize them; 3
Mrk 7:22 coveting, wickedness, deceit, licentiousness 7
Act 20:33 I coveted no one's silver or gold or apparel. 4
Rom 7: 7 I should not have known what it is to covet 5
7 if the law had not said, "You shall not covet. 4
13: 9 You shall not covet," and any other commandment 4
Jas 4: 2 you covet and cannot obtain; so you fight 6
1Mc 11:11 because he coveted his kingdom. 4
4Mc 2: 5 You shall not covet your neighbor's wife 4
6 In fact, since the law has told us not to covet 4

covetous 1. πλεονέκτης 2. πλεονεξία
Eph 5: 5 one who is covetous (that is, an idolater) 1
Wis 10:11 When his oppressors were covetous 2

covetousness 1. בֶּצַע 2. ἐπιθυμία 3. πλεονεξία 4. φιλαργυρία
Isa 57:17 Because of the iniquity of his covetousness 1
Lke 12:15 Take heed, and beware of all covetousness 3
Rom 1:29 all . . wickedness, evil, covetousness, malice. 3
7: 8 sin . . wrought in me all kinds of covetousness. 2
Eph 5: 3 fornication and all impurity or covetousness 3
Col 3: 5 covetousness, which is idolatry. 3
4Mc 1:26 In the soul it is boastfulness, covetousness 4

cow 1. בָּקָר 2. פָּרָה 3. שׁוֹר
Gen 32:15 40 cows and ten bulls, twenty she-asses 2
41: 2 came up out of the Nile seven cows sleek and fat 2
3 behold, seven other cows, gaunt and thin, came up 2
3 stood by the other cows on the bank of the Nile. 2
4 the gaunt and thin cows ate up the seven sleek 2
4 thin cows ate up the seven sleek and fat cows. 2
18 seven cows, fat and sleek, came up out of the Nile 2
19 seven other cows came up after them 2
20 the thin and gaunt cows ate up the first seven 2
20 gaunt cows ate up the first seven fat cows 2
26 The seven good cows are seven years 2
27 seven lean and gaunt cows that came up after them 2
Exd 34:19 All . . the firstlings of cow and sheep. 3
Lev 22:28 whether the mother is a cow or a ewe 3
Num18:17 firstling of a cow . . you shall not redeem; 3
1Sm 6: 7 take and prepare a new cart and two milch cows 2
7 yoke the cows to the cart, but take their calves 2
10 and took two milch cows and yoked them to the cart 2
12 the cows went straight . . lowing as they went; 2
14 offered the cows as a burnt offering to the LORD. 2
Job 21:10 their cow calves, and does not cast her calf. 2
Isa 11: 7 The cow and the bear shall feed; 2
Ezk 4:15 let you have cow's dung instead of human dung 1
Ams 4: 1 Hear this word, you cows of Bashan 2

young cow 1. עֶגְלַת בָּקָר
Isa 7:21 a man will keep alive a young cow and two sheep; 1

coward 1. δειλιάζω 2. δειλός
Sir 34:14 nor play the coward, for he is his hope. 1
37:11 with a coward about war 2

coward *See also* play, prove.

cowardice 1. δειλία 2. μαλακοψυχάζω
Sir 4:17 she will bring fear and cowardice upon him 1
1Mc 4:32 Fill them with cowardice 1
4Mc 6:17 out of cowardice we feign a role unbecoming to us! 2
20 be a laughing stock to all for our cowardice 1

cowardly 1. ἄνανδρος 2. δειλανδρέω 3. δειλός 4. δειλόψυχος
Rev 21: 8 as for the cowardly, the faithless, the polluted 3
2Mc 8:13 were cowardly and distrustful of God's justice 2
4Mc 5:31 I am not so old and cowardly 1
8:16 if some of them had been cowardly and unmanly 4
13:10 Let us not be cowardly 2

cowardly thing 1. δειλός
Wis 17:11 For wickedness is a cowardly thing 1

cower 1. καταπτήσσω 2. πτήσσω
Sir 32:18 an insolent and proud man will not cower in fear. 1
4Mc 16:20 he did not cower. 2

cower in fear 1. πτηξάτω
3Mc 6:13 let the Gentiles cower today in fear of your . . might 1

make cower 1. כפש
Lam 3:16 made my teeth grind . . and made me cower in ashes; 1

crack 1. קוֹל
Nah 3: 2 The crack of whip, and rumble of wheel 1

crackle 1. קוֹל
Ecc 7: 6 For as the crackling of thorns under a pot, 1
Jol 2: 5 like the crackling of a flame of fire devouring 1

craft 1. מְלָאכָה 2. שְׂכִיָּה 3. ἐργατεία 4. μέθοδος 5. τέχνη
Exd 31: 5 in carving wood, for work in every craft. 1
35:33 in carving wood, for work in every skilled craft. 1
Isa 2:16 against all the beautiful craft. 2
Rev 18:22 a craftsman of any craft shall be found 5
AEs 16:13 with intricate craft and deceit 4
Wis 7:16 as are all understanding and skill in crafts. 3

craftily *See* deal.

craftiness 1. עֹרֶם 2. πανουργία
Job 5:13 He takes the wise in their own craftiness; 1
Lke 20:23 he perceived their craftiness, and said to them 2
1Co 3:19 He catches the wise in their craftiness 2
Eph 4:14 by their craftiness in deceitful wiles. 2

craftsman 1. חָכָם 2. חָרָשׁ 3. παρέχω 4. τέκτων 5. τεχνίτης 6. τεχνῖτις
Exd 35:35 work done by a craftsman or by a designer 2
38:23 a craftsman and designer and embroiderer 2
Deu 27:15 image . . a thing made by the hands of a craftsman 2
2Kg 24:14 and all the craftsmen and the smiths; 2
16 and the craftsmen and the smiths, 1,000 2
1Ch 4:14 Ge-har'ashim . . because they were craftsmen. 2
22:15 and all kinds of craftsmen without number •
29: 5 for all the work to be done by craftsmen 2
2Ch 2:14 with your craftsmen, the craftsmen of my lord 1
14 with your craftsmen, the craftsmen of my lord 1
Neh 11:35 Lod, and Ono, the valley of craftsmen. 2
Isa 40:20 he seeks out a skilful craftsman 2
41: 7 The craftsman encourages the goldsmith 2
44:11 and the craftsmen are but men; 2
Jer 10: 3 and worked with an axe by the hands of a craftsman. 2
9 They are the work of the craftsman 2
24: 1 princes of Judah, the craftsmen, and the smiths 2
29: 2 the craftsmen, and the smiths had departed 2
Hos 13: 2 idols . . all of them the work of craftsmen. 2
Act 19:24 brought no little business to the craftsmen. 3
38 Deme'trius and the craftsmen with him 5
Rev 18:22 a craftsman . . shall be found in thee no more; 5
Wis 13: 1 nor did they recognize the craftsman 5
14: 2 wisdom was the craftsman who built it; 6
18 Then the ambition of the craftsman impelled 5
Sir 9:17 will be praised for the skill of the craftsmen 5
38:27 So too is every craftsman and master workman 4
45:11 with twisted scarlet, the work of a craftsman; 5
LJr 1: 8 Their tongues are smoothed by the craftsman 4
45 nothing but what the craftsmen wish them to be. 5

craftsmanship 1. מְלָאכָה
Exd 31: 3 with knowledge and all craftsmanship 1
35:31 filled . . with all craftsmanship 1

crafty 1. חָכָם 2. עָרוּם 3. δόλιος 4. πανοῦργος
2Sm 13: 3 and Jon'adab was a very crafty man. 1
Job 5:12 He frustrates the devices of the crafty 2
15: 5 you choose the tongue of the crafty. 2
2Co 12:16 I was crafty, you say 4
Sir 11:29 many are the wiles of the crafty. 3

crafty device 1. πανοπούργευμα
Sir 42:18 considers their crafty devices 1

crag 1. סֶלַע 2. צוּר 3. שֵׁן
1Sm 14: 4 there was a rocky crag on the one side 3
4 on the one side and a rocky crag on the other side; 3
5 one crag rose on the north in front of Michmash 3
Job 39:28 makes his home in the fastness of the rocky crag. 3
Jer 18:14 Does the snow of Lebanon leave the crags 2
51:25 hand against you, and roll you down from the crags 1

cramp 1. מוּצָק
Job 36:16 into a broad place where there was no cramping 1

crane 1. עָגוּר
Isa 38:14 Like a swallow or a crane I clamor 1
Jer 8: 7 swallow, and crane keep the time of their coming; 1

crash 1. קוֹל 2. רֵעַ 3. שֶׁבֶר 4. שׁוֹאָה 5. ἐξηχέω 6. κτύπος
Job 30:14 they come; amid the crash they roll on. 4
36:33 Its crashing declares concerning him 2
41:25 at the crashing they are beside themselves. 3
Ps 77:18 The crash of thy thunder was in the whirlwind; 1
Isa 30:13 whose crash comes suddenly, in an instant; 3
Zep 1:10 Second Quarter, a loud crash from the hills. 3
Wis 17:19 the harsh crash of rocks hurled down 6
Sir 40:13 crash like a loud clap of thunder in a rain. 5

make crash 1. שאה
Isa 37:26 make fortified cities crash into heaps of ruins 1

crave 1. אוה 2. נֶפֶשׁ 3. שׁאל 4. תַּאֲוָה 5. ἐπιθυμία 6. ἐπιθυμέω 7. ὀρέγω

Num11:34 there they buried the people who had the craving. 1
Deu 12:20 you say, 'I will eat flesh,' because you crave flesh 1
14:26 you desire . . whatever your appetite craves; 3
Ps 78:18 tested God . . by demanding the food they craved. 2
29 well filled, for he gave them what they craved. 4
30 before they had sated their craving 4
Prv 13: 4 The soul of the sluggard craves, and gets nothing 1
Isa 32: 6 to leave the craving of the hungry unsatisfied 2
1Ti 6:10 it is through this craving that . . 7
4Mc 1:34 when we crave seafood and fowl and animals 6
3:12 because of the king's craving 5

morbid craving 1. νοσέω

1Ti 6: 4 he has a morbid craving for controversy 1

strong craving 1. אוה

Num11: 4 rabble that was among them had a strong craving; 1

wanton craving 1. אוה

Ps 106:14 they had a wanton craving in the wilderness 1

crawl 1. רמשׂ

Lev 11:44 any swarming thing that crawls upon the earth 1

crawling thing 1. זחל 2. רֶמֶשׂ

Deu 32:24 with venom of crawling things of the dust. 1
Mic 7:17 lick . . like the crawling things of the earth; 1
Hab 1:14 like crawling things that have no ruler. 2

craze 1. הלל

Jer 25:16 They shall drink and stagger and be crazed 1

create 1. ברא 2. קנה 3. καταρτίζω 4. κτίζω 5. κτίσμα 6. ποιέω 7. ποίημα 8. συγκτίζω 9. creatio 10. creo 11. facio

Gen 1: 1 In the beginning God created the heavens 1
21 God created the great sea monsters 1
27 God created man in his own image 1
27 in the image of God he created him; male and female 1
27 male and female he created them. 1
2: 4 heavens and the earth when they were created. 1
5: 1 When God created man, he made him in the likeness 1
2 Male and female he created them, and he blessed 1
2 them and named them Man when they were created. 1
6: 7 I will blot out man whom I have created 1
Num16:30 if the LORD creates something new 1
Deu 4:32 since the day that God created man upon the earth 1
32: 6 Is not he your father, who created you, who made you 2
Ps 51:10 Create in me a clean heart, O God 1
89:12 The north and the south, thou hast created them; 1
47 for what vanity thou hast created all . . men! 1
104:30 thou sendest forth thy Spirit, they are created; 1
148: 5 For he commanded and they were created. 1
Prv 8:22 The LORD created me at the beginning of his work 2
Isa 4: 5 Then the LORD will create over . . Mount Zion 1
40:26 and see: who created these? 1
41:20 the Holy One of Israel has created it. 1
42: 5 Thus says God, the LORD, who created the heavens 1
43: 1 now thus says the LORD, he who created you 1
7 whom I created for my glory, whom I formed 1
45: 7 I form light and create darkness 1
7 I make weal and create woe 1
8 I the LORD have created it. 1
12 I made the earth, and created man upon it; 1
18 says the LORD, who created the heavens (he is God!) 1
18 he established it; he did not create it a chaos 1
48: 7 They are created now, not long ago; 1
54:16 I . . created the smith who blows the fire of coals 1
16 I have also created the ravager to destroy; 1
57:18 creating for his mourners the fruit of the lips. 1
65:17 For behold, I create new heavens and a new earth; 1
18 and rejoice for ever in that which I create; 1
18 for behold, I create Jerusalem a rejoicing 1
Jer 31:22 For the LORD has created a new thing on the earth 1
Ezk 21:30 In the place where you were created 1
28:13 day that you were created they were prepared. 1
15 were blameless . . from the day you were created 1
Ams 4:13 he who forms the mountains, and creates the wind 1
Mal 2:10 Has not one God created us? 1
Mrk 13:19 the creation which God created until now 4
Rom16:17 take note of those who create dissensions 6
1Co 11: 9 Neither was man created for woman 4
Eph 2:10 we are his workmanship, created in Christ Jesus 7
15 create in himself one new man in place of the two 4
3: 9 hidden for ages in God who created all things; 4
4:24 created after the likeness of God 4
Col 1:16 for in him all things were created 4
16 all things were created through him 4
1Ti 4: 3 and enjoin abstinence from foods which God created 4
4 For everything created by God is good 5
Heb 1: 2 through whom also he created the world. 6
11: 3 the world was created by the word of God 3
Rev 4:11 for thou didst create all things 4
11 and by thy will they existed and were created. 4
10: 6 who created heaven and what is in it 4
1Es 6:13 the servants of the Lord who created the heaven 4
2Es 2:14 for I left out evil and created good 10
5:26 from all the birds that have been created 10
43 Couldst thou not have created at one time those 11
44 those who have been created in it. 10
49 so have I organized the world which I created. 10
6:41 thou didst create the spirit of the firmament 11
55 for us that thou didst create this world. 10
59 If the world has indeed been created for us 10
7:48 but almost all who have been created! 10
139 those who were created by his word 10
8: 3 Many have been created, but few shall be saved. 10
8 what thou hast created is preserved 9
8 thy creation which has been created in it. 10
9 womb gives up again what has been created in it 10
60 they themselves who were created have defiled 10
9:19 now those who have been created in this world 10
Jdt 13:18 blessed be the Lord God, who created the heavens 4
Wis 1:14 For he created all things that they might exist 4
2:23 for God created man for incorruption 4
10: 1 when he alone had been created 4
11:17 which created the world out of formless matter 4
13: 3 the author of beauty created them. 4
14:11 though part of what God created 5
Sir 1: 4 Wisdom was created before all things 4
9 The Lord himself created wisdom; 4
14 she is created with the faithful in the womb. 8
7:15 which were created by the Most High. 4
10:18 Pride was not created for men 4
15:14 It was he who created man in the beginning 6
17: 1 The Lord created man out of earth 4
18: 1 He who lives for ever created the whole universe; 4
23:20 Before the universe was created 4
24: 8 the one who created me 4
9 From eternity, in the beginning, he created me 4
31:13 What has been created more greedy than the eye? 4
27 It has been created to make men glad. 4
33:10 Adam was created of the dust. 4
36:15 those whom thou didst create in the beginning 4
38: 1 the Lord created him; 4
4 The Lord created medicines from the earth 4
12 the Lord created him 4
39:21 everything has been created for its use. 4
25 good things were created for good people 4
28 winds that have been created for vengeance 4
29 all these have been created for vengeance; 4
40: 1 Much labor was created for every man 4
10 All these were created for the wicked 4
49:14 No one like Enoch has been created on earth 4
Bel 1: 5 the living God, who created heaven and earth 4
2Mc 14:17 the sudden consternation created by the enemy. •
3Mc 1:23 created a considerable disturbance in the holy place 6
2: 9 created the boundless and immeasurable earth 4

newly created 1. νεόκτιστος

Wis 11:18 or newly created unknown beasts full of rage 1

created thing 1. κτίσμα 2. creatura

2Es 7:62 out of the dust like the other created things! 2
Wis 13: 5 from the greatness and beauty of created things 1

creation 1. ברא 2. יֵצֶר 3. γένεσις 4. κοσμοποιΐα 5. κόσμος 6. κτίσις 7. creata creatura 8. creatura 9. figmentum

Gen 2: 3 from all his work which he had done in creation. 1
Hab 2:18 For the workman trusts in his own creation 2
Mrk 10: 6 from the beginning of creation 6
13:19 not been from the beginning of the creation 6
16:15 preach the gospel to the whole creation. 6
Rom 1:20 Ever since the creation of the world 6
8:19 For the creation waits with eager longing 6
20 for the creation was subjected to futility 6
21 because the creation itself will be set free 6
22 the whole creation has been groaning in travail 6
23 not only the creation, but we ourselves •
39 nor depth, nor anything else in all creation 6
2Co 5:17 if any one is in Christ, he is a new creation 6
Gal 6:15 nor uncircumcision, but a new creation. 6
Col 1:15 the first-born of all creation; 6
Heb 9:11 that is, not of this creation 6
2Pe 3: 4 as they were from the beginning of creation. 6
Rev 3:14 the Amen . . the beginning of God's creation 6
2Es 5:44 The creation cannot make more haste 8
45 certainly give life at one time to thy creation? 7
45 and the creation will sustain them 8
55 as born of a creation which already is aging 8
56 through whom thou dost visit thy creation. 8
6:38 thou didst speak at the beginning of creation 8
7:75 when thou wilt renew the creation 8
8: 8 the womb . . endures thy creation 8
13 for he is thy creation; and thou wilt make him live 8
39 will rejoice over the creation of the righteous 9
45 for thou hast mercy on thy own creation. 8
47 able to love my creation more than I love it 8
13:26 who will himself deliver his creation 8
Jdt 9:12 King of all thy creation, hear my prayer! 6
Wis 2: 6 and make use of the creation to the full as in youth. 6
5:17 and will arm all creation to repel his enemies; 6
20 creation will join with him to fight 5
6:22 from the beginning of creation 3
16:24 creation, serving thee who hast made it 6
19: 6 the whole creation in its nature 6
Sir 16:17 what is my soul in the boundless creation? 6
26 existed from the beginning by his creation 1
49:16 Adam above every living being in the creation. 6
3Mc 2: 2 sovereign of all creation 6
7 the Ruler over the whole creation. 6
6: 2 governing all creation with mercy 6
4Mc 14: 7 just as the seven days of creation 4

creator 1. ברא 2. γενεσιουργός 3. κτίζω 4. κτίστης 5. ποιέω 6. creator

Ecc 12: 1 Remember also your Creator in . . your youth 1
Isa 40:28 the Creator of the ends of the earth. 1
43:15 I am the LORD, your Holy One, the Creator 1
Rom 1:25 served the creature rather than the Creator 3
Col 3:10 after the image of its creator. 3
1Pe 4:19 and entrust their souls to a faithful Creator. 4
2Es 5:44 cannot make more haste than the Creator 6
Jdt 9:12 Lord of heaven and earth, Creator of the waters 4
Wis 13: 5 a corresponding perception of their Creator. 2
Sir 4: 6 his Creator will hear his prayer. 5
24: 8 the Creator of all things gave me a commandment 4
2Mc 1:24 O Lord, Lord God, Creator of all things 4
7:23 the Creator of the world 4
13:14 the Creator of the world 4
3Mc 2: 3 the creator of all things and the governor of all 3
4Mc 5:25 the Creator of the world . . has shown sympathy 4
11: 5 Is it because we revere the Creator of all things 4

creature 1. בָּשָׂר 2. נֶפֶשׁ 3. עשׂה 4. קִנְיָן 5. θηρίον 6. κτῆνος 7. κτίσις 8. κτίσμα 9. φύσις 10. creatura 11. figmentum

Gen 1:20 waters bring forth swarms of living creatures 2
21 God created . . every living creature that moves 2
24 Let the earth bring forth living creatures 2
2:19 whatever the man called every living creature 2
9:10 with every living creature that is with you 2
12 me and you and every living creature that is 2
15 you and every living creature of all flesh; 2
16 God and every living creature of all flesh 2
Lev 11:10 of the living creatures that are in the waters 2
46 law pertaining to . . every living creature 2
17:14 For the life of every creature is the blood of it 1
14 You shall not eat the blood of any creature 1
14 for the life of every creature is its blood 1
Job 41:33 there is not his like, a creature without fear. 3
Ps 104:24 the earth is full of thy creatures. 4
Ezk 1:11 each creature had two wings •
23 each creature had two wings covering its body. •
47: 9 every living creature which swarms will live 2
Act 28: 4 saw the creature hanging from his hand 5
5 He, however, shook off the creature into the fire 5
Rom 1:25 served the creature rather than the Creator 7
Col 1:23 been preached to every creature under heaven 7
Heb 4:13 before him no creature is hidden 7
Jas 1:18 be a kind of first fruits of his creatures. 8
2Pe 2:12 like irrational animals, creatures of instinct •
Rev 5:13 I heard every creature in heaven and on earth 8
8: 9 a third of the living creatures in the sea died 8
2Es 5:45 If therefore all creatures will live at one time •
8:24 and give ear to the petition of thy creature; 11
11: 6 not even one creature that was on the earth. 10
37 I looked, and behold, a creature like a lion •
Tob 8: 5 the heavens and all thy creatures bless thee. 7
15 Let thy saints and all thy creatures bless thee; 7
Jdt 16:14 Let all thy creatures serve thee 7
Wis 9: 2 have dominion over the creatures thou hast made 8
12:27 they became incensed at those creatures •
16: 1 deservedly punished through such creatures •
3 because of the odious creatures sent to them •
19:19 land animals . . into water creatures •
19 and creatures that swim moved over to the land. •
Sir 43:25 huge creatures of the sea. 7
Bar 3:32 earth . . filled it with four-footed creatures; 6
Aza 1:57 whales and all creatures that move in the waters •
3Mc 3:29 useless for all time to any mortal creature. 9

flying creature 1. πετεινόν

Sir 11: 3 The bee is small among flying creatures 1

howling creature 1. אֹחַ

Isa 13:21 and its houses will be full of howling creatures; 1

huge creature of the sea 1. κῆτος

Sir 43:25 huge creatures of the sea. 1

living creature 1. חַי 2. חַיָּה 3. נֶפֶשׁ 4. animal

Gen 8:21 destroy every living creature as I have done. 1
Lev 11:46 to . . every living creature that swarms 3
47 between the living creature that may be eaten 2
47 the living creature that may not be eaten 2
Ezk 1: 5 came the likeness of four living creatures. 2
13 In the midst of the living creatures 2
13 moving to and fro among the living creatures; 2
14 And the living creatures darted to and fro 2
15 Now as I looked at the living creatures 2

15 upon the earth beside the living creatures 2
19 when the living creatures went, the wheels went 2
19 when the living creatures rose from the earth 2
20 the spirit of the living creatures 2
21 the spirit of the living creatures 2
22 Over the heads of the living creatures there was 2
3:13 the sound of the wings of the living creatures 2
10:15 These were the living creatures that I saw 2
17 the spirit of the living creatures was in them. 2
20 These were the living creatures that I saw 2
2Es 6:47 to bring forth living creatures 4
48 lifeless water produced living creatures 4
49 didst keep in existence two living creatures; ‡

creature of the wilderness 1. צִי
Ps 74:14 as food for the creatures of the wilderness. 1

sea creature 1. ἐνάλιος
Jas 3: 7 every kind . . of reptile and sea creature 1

swarming creature 1. שֶׁרֶץ
Gen 7:21 swarming creatures that swarm upon the earth 1
Lev 11:10 the swarming creatures in the waters 1

unfaithful creature 1. μοιχαλίς
Jas 4: 4 Unfaithful creatures! Do you not know 1

wild creature 1. חַיָּה
Gen 3: 1 more subtle than any other wild creature 1

winged creature 1. בַּעַל כְּנָפַיִם
Ecc 10:20 or some winged creature tell the matter. 1

credible *See* make.

credit 1. חשׁב 2. κλέος 3. λόγος 4. προσανοικοδομέω 5. χάρις
Lev 7:18 neither shall it be credited to him 1
Lke 6:32 If you love those who love you, what credit is that 5
33 what credit is that to you 5
34 what credit is that to you 5
Php 4:17 I seek the fruit which increases to your credit. 3
1Pe 2:20 For what credit is it, if when you do wrong 2
Sir 3:14 against your sins it will be credited to you; 4

creditor 1. בַּעַל מַשֵּׁה יָד 2. נשׁה 3. δανειστής
Exd 22:25 you shall not be to him as a creditor 2
Deu 15: 2 every creditor shall release what he has lent 1
2Kg 4: 1 the creditor has come to take my two children 2
Ps 109:11 May the creditor seize all that he has; 2
Isa 24: 2 as with the creditor, so with the debtor. 2
50: 1 which of my creditors is it to whom I have sold you? 2
Lke 7:41 A certain creditor had two debtors 3

creep 1. רמשׂ 2. רֶמֶשׂ
Gen 1:25 and everything that creeps upon the ground 2
26 every creeping thing that creeps upon the earth 1
30 and to everything that creeps on the earth 1
7: 8 of everything that creeps on the ground 1
14 every creeping thing that creeps on the earth 1
8:17 animals and every creeping thing that creeps 1
9: 2 upon everything that creeps on the ground 1
Deu 4:18 likeness of anything that creeps on the ground 1
Ezk 38:20 and all creeping things that creep on the ground 1

creep forth 1. רמשׂ
Ps 104:20 when all the beasts of the forest creep forth. 1

creeping thing 1. רֶמֶשׂ 2. שֶׁרֶץ 3. ἑρπετόν 4. reptilis
Gen 1:24 cattle and creeping things and beasts 1
26 every creeping thing that creeps upon the earth 1
6: 7 man and beast and creeping things 1
20 kinds, of every creeping thing of the ground 1
7:14 every creeping thing that creeps on the earth 1
23 man and animals and creeping things and birds 1
8:17 animals and every creeping thing that creeps 1
19 every beast, every creeping thing, and every bird 1
Lev 22: 5 whoever touches a creeping thing 2
Ps 148:10 creeping things and flying birds! 1
Ezk 8:10 round about, were all kinds of creeping things 1
38:20 and all creeping things that creep on the ground 1
Hos 2:18 of the air, and the creeping things of the ground; 1
2Es 6:53 cattle, beasts, and creeping things; 4
Sir 10:11 he will inherit creeping things, and wild beasts 3

crescent 1. שַׂהֲרֹן
Jdg 8:21 he took the crescents that were on the necks 1
26 gold; besides the crescents and the pendants 1
Isa 3:18 finery of . . the headbands, and the crescents; 1

crew 1. קָהָל
Ezk 27:34 and all your crew have sunk with you. 1

crib 1. אֵבוּס
Job 39: 9 Will he spend the night at your crib? 1
Isa 1: 3 ox knows its owner, and the ass its master's crib; 1

cricket 1. חַרְגֹּל
Lev 11:22 may eat . . the cricket according to its kind 1

crime 1. אָוֶן 2. חֵטְא 3. מִשְׁפָּט 4. עַוְלָה 5. עָוֹן 6. רָעָה 7. ἀδίκημα 8. αἰτία 9. αἴτιος 10. κακός
Deu 19:15 not prevail against a man for any crime or for any 5
21:22 man has committed a crime punishable by death 2
Jdg 9:56 Thus God requited the crime of Abim'elech 6
Ps 56: 7 recompense them for their crime; 1
64: 6 Who can search out our crimes? 4
Ezk 7:23 Because the land is full of bloody crimes 3
Lke 23: 4 I find no crime in this man. 9
22 I have found in him no crime deserving death •
Joh 18:38 I find no crime in him. 8
19: 4 that you may know that I find no crime in him. 8
6 for I find no crime in him. 8
2Mc 13: 6 notorious for other crimes. 10
4Mc 11: 3 you will incur punishment . . for even more crimes. 7
18:22 For these crimes divine justice pursued •
crime *See also* hatred, share.

heinous crime 1. זִמָּה
Job 31:11 For that would be a heinous crime; 1

wanton crime 1. נְבָלָה
Jdg 20:10 all the wanton crime which they have committed 1

criminal 1. κακοῦργος
Lke 23:32 Two others also, who were criminals, were led away 1
33 there they crucified him, and the criminals 1
39 the criminals who were hanged railed at him 1
2Ti 2: 9 suffering and wearing fetters like a criminal. 1

crimson 1. חמץ 2. תּוֹלָע
Isa 1:18 though they are red like crimson 2
63: 1 that comes . . in crimsoned garments from Bozrah 1
crimson *See also* fabric.

cringe 1. כחשׁ 2. συγκύπτω
Ps 66: 3 So great is thy power that thy enemies cringe 1
81:15 Those who hate the LORD would cringe toward him 1
Sir 12:11 he humbles himself and goes about cringing 2

come cringing 1. כחשׁ
2Sm 22:45 Foreigners came cringing to me; 1
Ps 18:44 they obeyed me; foreigners came cringing to me. 1

cripple 1. נכה 2. נָכֶה 3. שׁבר 4. ἄνθρωπος ἀσθενής 5. χωλός
2Sm 4: 4 Jonathan . . had a son who was crippled 2
9: 3 There is still a son . . he is crippled in his feet. 2
Ps 35:15 cripples whom I knew not slandered me 1
Ezk 34: 4 the crippled you have not bound up 3
16 I will bind up the crippled 3
Act 4: 9 concerning a good deed done to a cripple 4
14: 8 he was a cripple from birth, who had never walked. 5

crisis 1. καιρός
Sir 22:16 will not be afraid in a crisis. 1
Bar 3: 5 in this crisis remember thy power and thy name. 1

critical 1. ἀκμή
2Mc 1: 7 the critical distress which came upon us 1

criticism 1. διαβολή
Sir 38:17 for one day, or two, to avoid criticism 1

criticize 1. διακρίνω
Act 11: 2 the circumcision party criticized him 1

croak
Zep 2:14 the raven croak on the threshold; •

land crocodile 1. כֹּחַ
Lev 11:30 the gecko, the land crocodile, the lizard 1

crocus 1. חֲבַצֶּלֶת
Isa 35: 1 shall rejoice and blossom; like the crocus 1

crooked 1. הֲפַכְפַּךְ 2. עות 3. עִקֵּשׁ 4. עִקְּשׁוּת 5. פְּתַלְתֹּל 6. σκολιός
Deu 32: 5 they are a perverse and crooked generation. 5
2Sm 22:27 with the crooked thou dost show thyself 3
Ps 18:26 with the crooked thou dost show thyself 3
Prv 2:15 men whose paths are crooked 3
4:24 Put away from you crooked speech 4
6:12 wicked man . . goes about with crooked speech 4
8: 8 there is nothing twisted or crooked in them. 3
17:20 A man of crooked mind does not prosper 3
21: 8 The way of the guilty is crooked 1
Ecc 1:15 What is crooked cannot be made straight 2
Lke 3: 5 the crooked shall be made straight 6
Act 2:40 Save yourselves from this crooked generation. 6
Php 2:15 a crooked and perverse generation 6
Wis 13:13 a stick crooked and full of knots 6
crooked *See also* make.

crooked way 1. עֲקַלְקַל
Ps 125: 5 those who turn aside upon their crooked ways 1

crookedness 1. סֶלֶף
Prv 11: 3 crookedness of the treacherous destroys them. 1

crop 1. זֶרַע 2. יְבוּל 3. מֻרְאָה 4. תְּבוּאָה 5. γένημα 6. καρπός
Lev 1:16 he shall take away its crop with the feathers 3
25:15 and according to the number of years for crops 4
16 the number of the crops that he is selling to you 4
20 we may not sow or gather in our crop?' 4
Deu 22: 9 crop which you have sown and the yield 1
Neh 10:31 forego the crops of the seventh year •
Ps 78:46 He gave their crops to the caterpillar 2
Prv 14: 4 abundant crops come by the strength of the ox. 4
Lke 12:17 I have nowhere to store my crops?' 6
1Co 9:10 the thresher thresh in hope of a share in the crop. •
2Ti 2: 6 ought to have the first share of the crops. 6
Wis 16:19 to destroy the crops of the unrighteous land. 5
22 the crops of their enemies were being destroyed 6
26 it is not the production of crops that feeds man 6
Sir 7: 3 you will not reap a sevenfold crop. •
1Mc 11:34 from the crops of the land 5

cross 1. דרך 2. עבר 3. שׂכל 4. διαβαίνω 5. διαπεράομαι 6. διαπεράω 7. διαπορεύω 8. διέρχομαι 9. ἔρχομαι πέραν
Gen 31:21 and arose and crossed the Euphra'tes 2
32:10 for with only my staff I crossed this Jordan; 2
22 took . . eleven children, and crossed the ford 2
48:14 his right hand . . crossing his hands 3
Num34: 4 boundary shall turn south . . and cross to Zin 2
35:10 When you cross the Jordan into the land of Canaan 2
Deu 2:14 Ka'desh-bar'nea until we crossed the brook Zered 2
4:21 LORD . . swore that I should not cross the Jordan 2
Jdg 6:33 and crossing the Jordan they encamped 2
10: 9 the Ammonites crossed the Jordan to fight also 2
12: 1 and they crossed to Zaphon and said to Jephthah 2
1Sm 13: 7 people hid . . or crossed the fords of the Jordan 2
30:10 who were too exhausted to cross the brook Besor. 2
2Sm 2:29 they crossed the Jordan, and . . came to Mahana'im. 2
10:17 he gathered all Israel . . and crossed the Jordan 2
15:23 and the king crossed the brook Kidron 2
17:22 Then David arose . . and they crossed the Jordan; 2
22 by daybreak not one was left who had not crossed 2
24 Ab'salom crossed the Jordan with all . . Israel. 2
19:18 and they crossed the ford to bring over the king's •
18 Shim'e-i . . as he was about to cross the Jordan 2
24: 5 They crossed the Jordan, and began from Aro'er 2
1Kg 2:37 on the day you go forth, and cross the brook Kidron 2
2Kg 2: 9 When they had crossed, Eli'jah said to Eli'sha, "Ask 2
1Ch 12:15 These are the men who crossed the Jordan 2
19:17 crossed the Jordan, and came to them 2
Isa 11:15 into seven channels that men may cross dryshod. 1
Jer 2:10 For cross to the coasts of Cyprus and see 2
Mrk 5:21 Jesus had crossed again in the boat to the other side 6
Lke 16:26 none may cross from there to us.' 6
Act 18:27 when he wished to cross to Acha'ia 8
21: 2 having found a ship crossing to Phoeni'cia 6
Heb 11:29 the people crossed the Red Sea as if on dry land 4
Sir 8:16 do not cross the wilderness with him 7
1Mc 3:37 He crossed the Euphrates river 5
5:24 crossed the Jordan and went three days' journey 4
40 If he crosses over to us first 4
52 they crossed the Jordan into the large plain 4
9:34 he with all his army crossed the Jordan. 9
48 did not cross the Jordan to attack them. 4
12:30 they had crossed the Eleutherus river. 4

cross (2) 1. σταυρός
Mat 10:38 he who does not take his cross and follow me 1
16:24 let him deny himself and take up his cross 1
27:32 this man they compelled to carry his cross. 1
40 If you are the Son of God, come down from the cross. 1
42 let him come down now from the cross 1
Mrk 8:34 let him deny himself and take up his cross 1
15:21 to carry his cross. 1
30 save yourself, and come down from the cross! 1
32 come down now from the cross 1
Lke 9:23 take up his cross daily and follow me. 1
14:27 does not bear his own cross and come after me 1
23:26 and laid on him the cross, to carry it behind Jesus. 1
Joh 19:17 and he went out, bearing his own cross 1
19 Pilate also wrote a title and put it on the cross; 1
25 standing by the cross of Jesus were his mother 1
31 to prevent the bodies from remaining on the cross 1
1Co 1:17 lest the cross of Christ be emptied of its power. 1
18 For the word of the cross is folly 1
Gal 5:11 stumbling block of the cross has been removed. 1
6:12 not be persecuted for the cross of Christ. 1
14 except in the cross of our Lord Jesus Christ 1
Eph 2:16 reconcile us both . . through the cross 1
Php 2: 8 obedient unto death, even death on a cross. 1
3:18 live as enemies of the cross of Christ. 1
Col 1:20 making peace by the blood of his cross. 1
2:14 this he set aside, nailing it to the cross. 1
Heb 12: 2 endured the cross, despising the shame 1

cross over 1. עבר 2. ערב 3. διαβαίνω 4. διακομίζω 5. διαπεράω

Jos 5: 1 dried up the waters . . until they had crossed over 1
Jdg 11:32 Jephthah crossed over to the Ammonites to fight 2
12: 1 Why did you cross over to fight against 2
3 I took . . and crossed over against the Ammonites 2
1Sm 14: 8 Behold, we will cross over to the men 1
Isa 10:29 they have crossed over the pass 1
Jer 41:10 and set out to cross over to the Ammonites. 1
Ams 5: 5 not enter into Gilgal or cross over to Beer-sheba; 1
Mat 9: 1 And getting into a boat he crossed over 5
14:34 when they had crossed over, they came to land 5
Mrk 6:53 And when they had crossed over 5
Jdt 5:15 crossing over the Jordan 3
1Mc 5: 6 Then he crossed over to attack the Ammonites 5
41 we will cross over to him and defeat him. 5
43 Then he crossed over against them first 5
16: 6 so he crossed over first 5
6 when his men saw him, they crossed over after him. 5
3Mc 1: 2 and crossed over by night to the tent of Ptolemy 4

crouch 1. כרע 2. רבץ 3. שחח

Gen 49:14 a strong ass, crouching between the sheepfolds; 2
Job 38:40 when they crouch in their dens, or lie in wait 3
39: 3 when they crouch, bring forth their offspring 1
Isa 10: 4 Nothing . . but to crouch among the prisoners 1

crow 1. *ἐκέκραγεν* 2. *κορώνη* 3. *φωνέω*

Mat 26:34 this very night, before the cock crows 3
74 immediately the cock crowed. 3
75 Before the cock crows, you will deny me 3
Mrk 14:30 this very night, before the cock crows twice 3
72 immediately the cock crowed a second time. 3
72 Before the cock crows twice 3
Lke 22:34 I tell you, Peter, the cock will not crow this day 3
60 while he was still speaking, the cock crowed. 3
61 Before the cock crows today, you will deny me 3
Joh 13:38 Truly, truly, I say to you, the cock will not crow 3
18:27 at once the cock crowed. 3
LJr 1:54 they are like crows between heaven and earth. 2
3Mc 5:23 as soon as the cock had crowed in the early morning 1

crowd 1. *ἀγεληδόν* 2. *δῆμος* 3. *ὄχλος* 4. *πλῆθος* 5. *πληθύνω* 6. *πολύς* 7. *συνδρομή* 8. *συνθλίβω*

Mat 4:25 And great crowds followed him from Galilee 3
5: 1 Seeing the crowds, he went up on the mountain 3
7:28 the crowds were astonished at his teaching 3
8: 1 great crowds followed him; 3
18 Now when Jesus saw great crowds around him 3
9: 8 When the crowds saw it, they were afraid 3
23 flute players, and the crowd making a tumult 3
25 But when the crowd had been put outside, he went 3
33 the dumb man spoke; and the crowds marveled 3
36 When he saw the crowds, he had compassion for them 3
11: 7 they went away, Jesus began to speak to the crowds 3
13: 2 great crowds gathered about him 3
2 and the whole crowd stood on the beach. 3
34 All this Jesus said to the crowds in parables; 3
36 Then he left the crowds and went into the house. 3
14:13 But when the crowds heard it 3
15 send the crowds away to go into the villages 3
19 he ordered the crowds to sit down on the grass 3
19 and the disciples gave them to the crowds. 3
22 while he dismissed the crowds. 3
23 after he had dismissed the crowds 3
15:30 great crowds came to him 3
32 I have compassion on the crowd 3
33 bread enough . . to feed so great a crowd? 3
35 commanding the crowd to sit down on the ground 3
36 and the disciples gave them to the crowds. 3
39 sending away the crowds, he got into the boat 3
17:14 when they came to the crowd 3
19: 2 large crowds followed him, and he healed them 3
20:29 a great crowd followed him. 3
31 The crowd rebuked them, telling them to be silent; 3
21: 8 Most of the crowd spread their garments 3
9 the crowds that went before him 3
11 the crowds said, "This is the prophet Jesus 3
22:33 when the crowd heard it 3
23: 1 to the crowds and to his disciples 3
26:47 with him a great crowd with swords and clubs 3
55 At that hour Jesus said to the crowds 3
27:15 to release for the crowd any one prisoner 3
24 washed his hands before the crowd, saying 3
Mrk 2: 4 because of the crowd 3
13 and all the crowd gathered about him 3
3: 9 because of the crowd, lest they should crush him; 3
20 and the crowd came together again 3
32 a crowd was sitting about him; and they said to him 3
4: 1 a very large crowd gathered about him 3
1 the whole crowd was beside the sea on the land. 3
36 leaving the crowd, they took him with them 3
5:21 a great crowd gathered about him 3
24 a great crowd followed him and thronged about 3
27 came up behind him in the crowd 3
30 immediately turned about in the crowd, and said 3
31 You see the crowd pressing around you 3
6:45 while he dismissed the crowd. 3
8: 1 when again a great crowd had gathered 3
2 I have compassion on the crowd 3
6 he commanded the crowd to sit down on the ground; 3
6 and they set them before the crowd. 3
9:14 they saw a great crowd about them 3
15 immediately all the crowd, when they saw him 3
17 one of the crowd answered him, "Teacher 3
25 Jesus saw that a crowd came running together 3
10: 1 crowds gathered to him again 3
14:43 with him a crowd with swords and clubs 3
15: 8 the crowd came up and began to ask Pilate 3
11 the chief priests stirred up the crowd 3
15 So Pilate, wishing to satisfy the crowd 3
Lke 5:19 no way to bring him in, because of the crowd 3
6:17 with a great crowd of his disciples 3
19 all the crowd sought to touch him 3
7:11 his disciples and a great crowd went with him. 3
12 a large crowd from the city was with her. 3
24 he began to speak to the crowds concerning John 3
8: 4 And when a great crowd came together 3
19 they could not reach him for the crowd. 3
40 Now when Jesus returned, the crowd welcomed him 3
9:11 When the crowds learned it, they followed him 3
12 Send the crowd away, to go into the villages 3
16 and gave them . . to set before the crowd. 3
37 a great crowd met him. 3
38 behold, a man from the crowd cried, "Teacher 3
11:27 a woman in the crowd raised her voice and said 3
29 When the crowds were increasing, he began to say 3
19: 3 but could not, on account of the crowd 3
22:47 While he was still speaking, there came a crowd 3
Joh 5:13 there was a crowd in the place. 3
7:32 The Pharisees heard the crowd thus muttering 3
49 this crowd, who do not know the law, are accursed. 3
12: 9 When the great crowd of the Jews learned 3
12 a great crowd who had come to the feast heard 3
17 The crowd that had been with him 3
18 The reason why the crowd went to meet him 3
29 The crowd standing by heard it and said 3
34 crowd answered him, "We have heard from the law 3
Act 14:11 when the crowds saw what Paul had done 3
16:22 The crowd joined in attacking them 3
17:13 stirring up and inciting the crowds. 3
19:30 Paul wished to go in among the crowd 2
33 Some of the crowd prompted Alexander 3
35 when the town clerk had quieted the crowd, he said 3
21:27 stirred up all the crowd, and laid hands on him 3
34 Some in the crowd shouted one thing, some another; 3
35 because of the violence of the crowd; 3
24:12 they did not find me . . stirring up a crowd 3
18 without any crowd or tumult. 3
Jdt 2:20 Along with them went a mixed crowd 6
Sir 7:16 Do not count yourself among the crowd of sinners; 4
31:14 do not crowd your neighbor at the dish. 8
2Mc 3:18 People . . hurried out of their houses in crowds 1
4:40 since the crowds were becoming aroused 3
14:43 the crowd was now rushing in through the doors 3
43 and manfully threw himself down into the crowd. 3
45 he ran through the crowd 3
46 and hurled them at the crowd 3
3Mc 1:24 the crowd, as before, was engaged in prayer 4
28 cry of the crowds resulted in an immense uproar; 3
3: 8 the crowds that suddenly were forming 7
5:24 The crowds of the city had been assembled 4
41 it is crowded with masses of people 5
48 as well as by the trampling of the crowd 4

crowd *See also* gather.

crowd aside 1. *ἐκθλίβω*

Sir 16:28 They do not crowd one another aside 1

crowd one's way into 1. *κατά*

3Mc 5:46 crowding their way into the hippodrome 1

crowd together 1. *ἀθροίζω*

3Mc 1:20 they crowded together at the most high temple. 1

crown 1. כתר 2. כֶּתֶר 3. כֹּתֶרֶת 4. נֵזֶר 5. עטר 6. עֲטָרָה 7. עטר לְ 8. עַל 9. קָדְקֹד 10. *βασίλειος* 11. *διάδημα* 12. *καθίημι* 13. *κορυφή* 14. *μετά* 15. *στεφανηφορέω* 16. *στέφανος* 17. *στεφανόω* 18. *στέφω* 19. corona 20. corono

Exd 29: 6 put the holy crown upon the turban. 4
39:30 they made the plate of the holy crown of pure gold 4
Lev 8: 9 the holy crown, as the LORD commanded Moses 4
2Sm 1:10 I took the crown which was on his head 4
12:30 And he took the crown of their king from his head; 6
14:25 from the sole of his foot to the crown of his head 9
1Kg 7:31 Its opening was within a crown which projected 3
2Kg 11:12 the king's son, and put the crown upon him 4
1Ch 20: 2 David took the crown of their king from his head; 6
2Ch 23:11 put the crown upon him, and gave him the testimony; 4
Est 1:11 to bring Queen Vashti . . with her royal crown 2
2:17 he set the royal crown on her . . and made her queen 2
6: 8 and on whose head a royal crown is set; 2
8:15 robes of blue and white, with a great golden crown 6
Job 19: 9 and taken the crown from my head. 6
31:36 I would bind it on me as a crown; 6
Ps 8: 5 and dost crown him with glory and honor. 5
21: 3 thou dost set a crown of fine gold upon his head. 6
65:11 Thou crownest the year with thy bounty; 5
68:21 hairy crown of him who walks in his guilty ways. 9
89:19 I have set the crown upon one who is mighty •
39 thou hast defiled his crown in the dust. 4
103: 4 who crowns you with steadfast love and mercy 5
132:18 but upon himself his crown will shed its luster. 4
Prv 4: 9 she will bestow on you a beautiful crown. 6
12: 4 A good wife is the crown of her husband 6
14:18 but the prudent are crowned with knowledge. 1
24 The crown of the wise is their wisdom 6
16:31 A hoary head is a crown of glory; 6
17: 6 Grandchildren are the crown of the aged 6
27:24 does a crown endure to all generations? 4
Sng 3:11 with the crown with which his mother crowned him 6
11 with the crown with which his mother crowned him 7
7: 5 Your head crowns you like Carmel 8
Isa 28: 1 the proud crown of the drunkards of E'phraim 6
3 The proud crown of the drunkards of E'phraim 6
5 the LORD of hosts will be a crown of glory 6
62: 3 shall be a crown of beauty in the hand of the LORD 6
Jer 13:18 beautiful crown has come down from your head. 6
48:45 forehead of Moab, the crown of the sons of tumult. 9
Lam 5:16 The crown has fallen from our head; 6
Ezk 16:12 and a beautiful crown upon your head. 6
21:26 Remove the turban, and take off the crown; 6
23:42 and beautiful crowns upon their heads. 6
Zec 6:11 Take from them silver and gold, and make a crown 16
14 the crown shall be in the temple of the LORD 16
9:16 like the jewels of a crown they shall shine 4
Mat 27:29 plaiting a crown of thorns they put it on his head 16
Mrk 15:17 plaiting a crown of thorns they put it on him. 16
Joh 19: 2 the soldiers plaited a crown of thorns 16
5 Jesus came out, wearing the crown of thorns 16
Php 4: 1 my joy and crown 16
1Th 2:19 For what is our hope or joy or crown of boasting 16
2Ti 2: 5 An athlete is not crowned 17
4: 8 is laid up for me the crown of righteousness 16
Heb 2: 7 thou hast crowned him with glory and honor 17
9 crowned with glory and honor 17
Jas 1:12 he will receive the crown of life 16
1Pe 5: 4 you will obtain the unfading crown of glory. 16
Rev 2:10 and I will give you the crown of life. 16
3:11 hold fast . . so that no one may seize your crown. 16
4: 4 elders . . with golden crowns upon their heads. 16
10 they cast their crowns before the throne, singing 16
6: 2 its rider had a bow; and a crown was given to him 16
9: 7 on their heads . . what looked like crowns of gold 16
12: 1 and on her head a crown of twelve stars; 16
14:14 like a son of man, with a golden crown on his head 16
1Es 4:30 take the crown from the king's head 11
2Es 2:43 and on the head of each of them he placed a crown 19
45 now they are being crowned, and receive palms. 20
46 Who is that young man who places crowns on them 19
Jdt 15:13 they crowned themselves with olive wreaths 17
Wis 2: 8 Let us crown ourselves with rosebuds 18
4: 2 it marches crowned in triumph 15
5:16 Therefore they will receive a glorious crown 10
Sir 1:11 gladness and a crown of rejoicing. 16
18 The fear of the Lord is the crown of wisdom 16
6:31 put her on like a crown of gladness. 16
11: 5 one who was never thought of has worn a crown. 11
15: 6 He will find gladness and a crown of rejoicing 16
25: 6 Rich experience is the crown of the aged 16
40: 4 the man who wears purple and a crown 16
45:12 with a gold crown upon his turban 16
LJr 1: 9 make crowns for the heads of their gods 16
Bel 1:36 angel of the Lord took him by the crown of his head 13
1Mc 1: 9 They all put on crowns after his death 11
22 the curtain, the crowns 16
4:57 golden crowns and small shields 16
6:15 He gave him the crown and his robe and the signet 11
8:14 Yet for all this not one of them has put on a crown 11
10:20 he sent him a purple robe and a golden crown 16
29 payment of tribute and salt tax and crown levies 16
11:13 entered Antioch and put on the crown of Asia. 11
13 Thus he put two crowns upon his head 11
13 the crown of Egypt and that of Asia. •
54 who began to reign and put on the crown. 11
12:39 to become king in Asia and put on the crown 11
13:32 putting on the crown of Asia 11
37 received the gold crown and the palm branch 16
14: 5 To crown all his honors he took Joppa for a harbor 14
2Mc 14: 4 presenting to him a crown of gold and a palm 16
3Mc 7:16 crowned with all sorts of very fragrant flowers 12

crown *See also* bestower, give, levy, tax.

crown of head 1. קָדְקֹד

Deu 28:35 sole of your foot to the crown of your head. 1
33:16 these come . . upon the crown of the head of him 1
20 Gad . . tears the arm, and the crown of the head. 1
Job 2: 7 from the sole of his foot to the crown of his head. 1
Jer 2:16 the men . . have broken the crown of your head. 1

crucial 1. *χρεία*

Sir 4:23 Do not refrain from speaking at the crucial time 1

crucible 1. מַצְרֵף

Prv 17: 3 crucible is for silver, and the furnace 1
27:21 crucible is for silver . . furnace is for gold 1

crucify 1. ἀνασταυρόω 2. προσπήγνυμι 3. σταυρός 4. σταυρόω 5. συσταυρόω

Mat 20:19 to be mocked and scourged and crucified 4
23:34 some of whom you will kill and crucify 4
26: 2 Son of man will be delivered up to be crucified. 4
27:22 They all said, "Let him be crucified. 4
23 Let him be crucified. 4
26 delivered him to be crucified. 4
31 and led him away to crucify him. 4
35 when they had crucified him 4
38 Then two robbers were crucified with him 4
44 the robbers who were crucified with him 5
28: 5 I know that you seek Jesus who was crucified. 4
Mrk 15:13 they cried out again, "Crucify him. 4
14 they shouted all the more, "Crucify him. 4
15 he delivered him to be crucified. 4
20 they led him out to crucify him. 4
24 they crucified him, and divided his garments 4
25 it was the third hour, when they crucified him. 4
27 with him they crucified two robbers 4
32 Those who were crucified with him also reviled 5
16: 6 you seek Jesus of Nazareth, who was crucified. 4
Lke 23:21 they shouted out, "Crucify, crucify him! 3
21 they shouted out, "Crucify, crucify him! 3
23 he should be crucified 4
33 there they crucified him, and the criminals 4
24: 7 crucified, and on the third day rise. 4
20 condemned to death, and crucified him. 4
Joh 19: 6 they cried out, "Crucify him, crucify him! 4
6 they cried out, "Crucify him, crucify him! 4
6 Take him yourselves and crucify him 4
10 I have . . power to crucify you? 4
15 Away with him, away with him, crucify him! 4
15 Pilate said to them, "Shall I crucify your King? 4
16 he handed him over to them to be crucified. 4
18 There they crucified him, and with him two others 4
20 the place where Jesus was crucified 4
23 When the soldiers had crucified Jesus 4
32 the other who had been crucified with him; 5
41 Now in the place where he was crucified 4
Act 2:23 this Jesus . . you crucified and killed 2
36 Lord and Christ, this Jesus whom you crucified. 4
4:10 Jesus Christ of Nazareth, whom you crucified 4
Rom 6: 6 We know that our old self was crucified with him 5
1Co 1:13 Is Christ divided? Was Paul crucified for you? 4
23 we preach Christ crucified 4
2: 2 except Jesus Christ and him crucified. 4
8 they would not have crucified the Lord of glory. 4
2Co 13: 4 For he was crucified in weakness 4
Gal 2:20 I have been crucified with Christ 5
3: 1 Christ was publicly portrayed as crucified? 4
5:24 crucified the flesh with its passions 4
6:14 by which the world has been crucified to me 4
Heb 6: 6 since they crucify the Son of God 1
Rev 11: 8 great city . . where their Lord was crucified. 4

cruel 1. אַכְזָר 2. אַכְזָרִי 3. אַכְזְרִיּוּת 4. קָשֶׁה 5. קשה 6. רַע 7. ἀνελεήμων 8. πικρός 9. σκληρός 10. ὠμός 11. malignus

Gen 49: 7 Cursed . . their wrath, for it is cruel! 5
Exd 6: 9 broken spirit and their cruel bondage. 4
Deu 32:33 their wine is . . the cruel venom of asps. 1
Job 30:21 Thou hast turned cruel to me; 1
Ps 144:11 Rescue me from the cruel sword 6
Prv 12:10 but the mercy of the wicked is cruel. 2
17:11 cruel messenger will be sent against him. 2
27: 4 Wrath is cruel, anger is overwhelming; 3
Sng 8: 6 love is strong . . jealousy is cruel as the grave. 4
Isa 13: 9 Behold, the day of the LORD comes, cruel 2
Jer 6:23 they are cruel and have no mercy 2
50:42 they are cruel, and have no mercy. 2
Lam 4: 3 but the daughter of my people has become cruel 1
1Es 2:27 mighty and cruel kings ruled in Jerusalem 9
2Es 5:18 his flock in the power of cruel wolves. 11
Sir 13:12 Cruel is he who does not keep words to himself 7
2Mc 4:25 having the hot temper of a cruel tyrant 10
7:27 deriding the cruel tyrant 10
4Mc 6: 8 One of the cruel guards rushed at him 8
18:20 quenched fire with fire in his cruel caldrons 10

cruel *See also* oppressor.

cruel man 1. אַכְזָרִי 2. חמץ

Ps 71: 4 from the grasp of the unjust and cruel man. 2
Prv 11:17 but a cruel man hurts himself. 1

most cruel 1. κακός

3Mc 3: 1 and put to death by the most cruel means. 1

cruel thing 1. σκληρός

Jdt 9:13 they have planned cruel things against thy covenant 1

cruelly 1. בְּחָזְקָה 2. βάσανος

Jdg 4: 3 he . . oppressed the people of Israel cruelly 1
2Es 7:67 we shall be preserved . . but cruelly tormented †
4Mc 11: 1 this one died also, after being cruelly tortured 2

cruelly *See also* deal.

more cruelly 1. πικρός

4Mc 8: 2 these should be tortured even more cruelly. 1

cruelty 1. ὠμότης

2Mc 12: 5 Judas heard of the cruelty visited on his countrymen 1
3Mc 6:24 surpassing tyrants in cruelty 1
7: 5 cruelty more savage than . . Scythian custom 1

cruelty *See also* inflict.

crumb 1. ψιχίον

Mat 15:27 She said, "Yes, Lord, yet even the dogs eat the crumbs 1
Mrk 7:28 dogs under the table eat the children's crumbs. 1

crumble away 1. נבל

Job 14:18 the mountain falls and crumbles away 1

cruse 1. צַפַּחַת

1Kg 17:12 handful of meal in a jar, and a little oil in a cruse; 1
14 not be spent, and the cruse of oil shall not fail 1
16 neither did the cruse of oil fail 1

crush 1. גֶּרֶשׂ 2. דַּכָּא 3. דכא 4. דכה 5. דַּכָּה 6. דכע 7. דקק 8. המם 9. זור 10. כתשׁ 11. כתת 12. מחץ 13. מחק 14. מַכָּה 15. מָרוֹחַ 16. רעץ 17. רצץ 18. שׁאף 19. שׁבר 20. שׁוף 21. רעע (A) 22. βαρέω 23. θλίβω 24. θραύω 25. λικμάω 26. πατάσσω 27. στενοχωρέω 28. συγκλάω 29. συντρίβω

Lev 2:14 offer . . crushed new grain from fresh ears 1
21:20 an itching disease or scabs or crushed testicles 15
22:24 which has its testicles bruised or crushed 11
Num24:17 it shall crush the forehead of Moab 12
Deu 9:21 calf . . and burned it with fire and crushed it 11
23: 1 He whose testicles are crushed 5
28:33 be only oppressed and crushed continually; 17
33:11 crush the loins of his adversaries 12
Jdg 5:26 she struck Sis'era a blow, she crushed his head 13
9:53 upon Abim'elech's head, and crushed his skull. 17
10: 8 they crushed and oppressed . . Israel that year 16
2Sm 22:30 Yea, by thee I can crush a troop 17
43 I crushed them and stamped them down 7
2Kg 23:15 broke in pieces its stones, crushing them to dust; 7
2Ch 2:10 20,000 cors of crushed wheat 14
15:16 Asa cut down her image, crushed it, and burned it 7
Est 9:24 had cast Pur . . the lot, to crush and destroy them; 8
Job 4:19 in the dust, who are crushed before the moth. 3
5: 4 far from safety, they are crushed in the gate 6
6: 9 that it would please God to crush me 3
9:17 For he crushes me with a tempest 20
20:19 For he has crushed and abandoned the poor 17
22: 9 the arms of the fatherless were crushed. 3
34:25 they are crushed. 6
39:15 forgetting that a foot may crush them 9
Ps 10:10 The hapless is crushed, sinks down, and falls 4
18:29 Yea, by thee I can crush a troop; 17
34:18 The LORD . . saves the crushed in spirit. 2
38: 8 I am utterly spent and crushed; 4
72: 4 give deliverance . . and crush the oppressor! 3
74:14 Thou didst crush the heads of Leviathan 17
89:10 Thou didst crush Rahab like a carcass 3
23 I will crush his foes before him 11
94: 5 They crush thy people, O LORD 3
143: 3 enemy . . has crushed my life to the ground; 3
Prv 22:22 Do not . . crush the afflicted at the gate; 3
27:22 Crush a fool in a mortar with a pestle along 10
Isa 3:15 What do you mean by crushing my people 3
19:10 the pillars of the land will be crushed 3
28:28 Does one crush bread grain? 7
28 with his horses, he does not crush it. 7
41:15 you shall thresh the mountains and crush them 7
59: 5 and from one which is crushed a viper is hatched. 9
Jer 51:34 king of Babylon has devoured me, he has crushed me; 8
Lam 1:15 he summoned an assembly . . to crush my young men; 19
3:34 To crush under foot all the prisoners 3
Ezk 36: 3 made you desolate, and crushed you from all sides 18
Dan 2:40 like iron which crushes, it shall break and crush 21
40 like iron . . it shall break and crush all these. 21
Hos 5:11 E'phraim is oppressed, crushed in judgment 17
Ams 4: 1 Sama'ria, who oppress the poor, who crush the needy 17
Hab 3:13 Thou didst crush the head of the wicked 12
Zec 11: 6 they shall crush the earth, and I will deliver 11
Mrk 3: 9 because of the crowd, lest they should crush him; 23
Lke 20:18 when it falls on any one it will crush him. 25
Rom16:20 God . . will soon crush Satan under your feet. 29
2Co 1: 8 we were so utterly, unbearably crushed 22
4: 8 afflicted in every way, but not crushed 27
Jdt 9: 7 the Lord who crushest wars 29
10 crush their arrogance by the hand of a woman. 24
16: 3 For God is the Lord who crushes wars 29
Sir 28:17 a blow of the tongue crushes the bones. 28
35:18 till he crushes the loins of the unmerciful 29
36:10 Crush the heads of the rulers of the enemy, who say 29
47: 7 he crushed their power even to this day. 29
1Mc 3:22 He himself will crush them before us 29
23 they were crushed before him. 29
4:10 crush this army before us today. 29
14 The Gentiles were crushed and fled into the plain 29
30 who didst crush the attack of the mighty warrior 29
36 Behold, our enemies are crushed 29
5: 7 they were crushed before him 29
21 the Gentiles were crushed before him. 29
7:42 So also crush this army before us today 29
43 The army of Nicanor was crushed 29
8: 4 until they crushed them 29
5 they crushed in battle and conquered. 29
6 He was crushed by them; 29
9: 7 he was crushed in spirit 29
15 they crushed the right wing 29
16 the right wing was crushed 29
68 he was crushed by them 29
10:52 I crushed Demetrius 29
53 he and his army were crushed by us 29
12:31 he crushed them and plundered them. 26
13:51 because a great enemy had been crushed 29
14:13 the kings were crushed in those days. 29

crush to pieces 1. נפץ

Isa 27: 9 like chalkstones crushed to pieces 1

crush with suffering 1. καταπονέω

3Mc 2:13 we are crushed with suffering 1

crushed *See* grain.

cry 1. אמר 2. בכה 3. זעק 4. זְעָקָה 5. ענה 6. ערג 7. צְוָחָה 8. צעק 9. צְעָקָה 10. קוֹל 11. קרא 12. רִנָּה 13. רֶצַח 14. שׁוַע 15. שׁוע 16. שַׁוְעָה 17. תְּרוּעָה 18. קרא (A) 19. ἀναβοάω 20. βοάω 21. βοή 22. εἶπον 23. κλαίω 24. κράζω 25. κραυγάζω 26. κραυγή 27. λέγω 28. φωνέω 29. φωνή 30. clamo 31. sonitus vocis 32. vox

Gen 4:10 The voice of your brother's blood is crying to me 8
27:34 with an exceedingly great and bitter cry 9
39:15 when he heard that I lifted up my voice and cried 11
18 as soon as I lifted up my voice and cried, he left 11
41:43 and they cried before him, "Bow the knee! 11
55 Egypt was famished, the people cried to Pharaoh 8
45: 1 and he cried, "Make every one go out from me. 11
Exd 2: 6 saw the child; and lo, the babe was crying. 2
23 and their cry under bondage came up to God. 16
3: 7 have heard their cry because of their 9
9 the cry of the people of Israel has come to me 9
5: 8 for they are idle; therefore they cry, "Let us go 8
15 the foremen . . came and cried to Pharaoh, "Why do 8
8:12 and Moses cried to the LORD concerning the frogs 8
11: 6 there shall be a great cry throughout all 9
12:30 and there was a great cry in Egypt 9
14:15 The LORD said to Moses, "Why do you cry to me? 8
15:25 cried to the LORD; and the LORD showed him a tree 8
17: 4 Moses cried to the LORD, "What shall I do with this 8
22:23 cry out to me, I will surely hear their cry; 9
27 And if he cries to me, I will hear, for I am 8
32:18 or the sound of the cry of defeat, 5
Lev 13:45 cover his upper lip and cry, 'Unclean, unclean.' 11
Num11: 2 Then the people cried to Moses; and Moses prayed 8
12:13 Moses cried to the LORD, "Heal her, O God, I beseech 8
14: 1 Then all the congregation raised a loud cry; 10
16:34 all Israel . . round about them fled at their cry; 10
20:16 when we cried to the LORD, he heard our voice 8
Deu 15: 9 cry to the LORD against you, and it be sin in you. 11
24:15 lest he cry against you to the LORD, and it be sin 11
26: 7 Then we cried to the LORD the God of our fathers 8
Jos 24: 7 And when they cried to the LORD, he put darkness 8
Jdg 3: 9 the people of Israel cried to the LORD, the LORD 3
15 when the people of Israel cried to the LORD 3
4: 3 the people of Israel cried to the LORD for help; 8
6: 7 When . . Israel cried to the LORD on account 3
7:20 they cried, "A sword for the LORD and for Gideon! 11
9: 7 he . . and cried aloud and said to them, "Listen to me 11
10:10 Israel cried to the LORD, saying, "We have sinned 3
12 oppressed you; and you cried to me, and I delivered 8
14 Go and cry to the gods whom you have chosen; 3
1Sm 5:12 and the cry of the city went up to heaven. 16
7: 8 Do not cease to cry to the LORD . . that he may save 3
9 and Samuel cried to the LORD for Israel 3
9:16 I have seen . . because their cry has come to me. 9
12: 8 your fathers cried to the LORD and the LORD sent 3
10 they cried to the LORD, and said, "We have sinned 3
15:11 was angry; and he cried to the LORD all night. 3
2Sm 19: 4 and the king cried with a loud voice, "O my son 3
28 What further right have I, then, to cry to the king? 3
22: 7 he heard my voice, and my cry came to his ears. 16
42 they cried to the LORD, but he did not answer them. •
1Kg 8:28 hearkening to the cry and to the prayer 12
13: 2 the man cried against the altar . . and said 11
4 the saying . . which he cried against the altar 11
21 he cried to the man of God who came from Judah 11
32 the saying which he cried by the word of the LORD 11
17:20 he cried to the LORD, "O LORD my God 11
21 and cried to the LORD, "O LORD my God 11
18:27 Cry aloud, for he is a god; either he is musing 11
28 they cried aloud, and cut themselves 11
20:39 as the king passed, he cried to the king and said 8
22:36 about sunset a cry went through the army 12
2Kg 2:12 Eli'sha saw it and he cried, "My father, my father! 8
4: 1 the wife of one . . cried to Eli'sha 8

11:14 And Athali'ah rent her clothes, and cried, "Treason! 11
13:14 went down . . and wept before him, crying, "My father 1
20:11 Isaiah . . cried to the LORD, and he brought 11
1Ch 5:20 for they cried to God in the battle 3
2Ch 6:19 hearkening to the cry and to the prayer 12
13:14 and they cried to the LORD 8
14:11 Asa cried to the LORD his God 11
20: 9 we will . . cry to thee in our affliction 3
23:13 Athali'ah . . cried, "Treason! Treason! 1
32:20 prayed because of this and cried to heaven. 3
Neh 9: 4 cried with a loud voice to the LORD their God. 3
9 thou didst . . hear their cry at the Red Sea 4
27 in the time of their suffering they cried to thee 8
28 turned and cried to thee thou didst hear 3
Est 4: 1 went out . . wailing with a loud and bitter cry; 4
Job 16:18 let my cry find no resting place. 4
27: 9 Will God hear his cry, when trouble comes upon him? 9
29:12 because I delivered the poor who cried 15
30:20 I cry to thee and thou dost not answer me; 15
34:28 that they caused the cry of the poor to come to him 9
28 he heard the cry of the afflicted- 9
36:19 Will your cry avail to keep you from distress 14
38:41 the raven its prey, when its young ones cry to God 15
Ps 3: 4 I cry aloud to the LORD, and he answers me 11
5: 2 Hearken to the sound of my cry, my King and my God 15
9:12 he does not forget the cry of the afflicted. 9
17: 1 Hear a just cause, O LORD; attend to my cry! 12
18: 6 heard my voice, and my cry to him reached his ears. 16
41 they cried to the LORD, but he did not answer them. *
22: 2 O my God, I cry by day, but thou dost not answer; 11
5 To thee they cried, and were saved; 3
24 but has heard, when he cried to him. 15
27: 7 Hear, O LORD, when I cry aloud, be gracious to me 11
29: 9 in his temple all cry, "Glory! 1
30: 8 To thee, O LORD, I cried; 11
34: 6 This poor man cried, and the LORD heard him 11
15 the righteous, and his ears toward their cry. 16
39:12 Hear my prayer, O LORD, and give ear to my cry; 16
40: 1 the LORD; he inclined to me and heard my cry. 16
57: 2 I cry to God Most High, to God who fulfils 11
61: 1 Hear my cry, O God, listen to my prayer; 12
66:17 I cried aloud to him, and he was extolled 11
69: 3 I am weary with my crying; my throat is parched. 11
77: 1 I cry aloud to God, aloud to God, that he may hear me. 8
86: 3 O Lord, for to thee do I cry all the day. 11
6 hearken to my cry of supplication. 10
88: 2 prayer come before thee, incline thy ear to my cry! 12
13 I, O LORD, cry to thee; 15
89:26 He shall cry to me, 'Thou art my Father, my God 11
99: 6 They cried to the LORD, and he answered them. 11
102: 1 Hear my prayer, O LORD; let my cry come to thee! 16
106:44 regarded their distress, when he heard their cry. 12
107: 6 Then they cried to the LORD in their trouble 8
13 Then they cried to the LORD in their trouble 3
19 Then they cried to the LORD in their trouble 3
28 Then they cried to the LORD in their trouble 8
119:145 With my whole heart I cry; answer me, O LORD! 11
146 I cry to thee; save me 11
169 Let my cry come before thee, O LORD; 12
120: 1 In my distress I cry to the LORD, that he may answer 11
130: 1 Out of the depths I cry to thee, O LORD! 11
142: 1 I cry with my voice to the LORD 3
5 I cry to thee, O LORD; I say, Thou art my refuge 3
6 Give heed to my cry; for I am brought very low! 12
145:19 all who fear him, he also hears their cry, and saves 16
147: 9 food, and to the young ravens which cry. 11
Prv 8: 4 To you, O men, I call, and my cry is to the sons of men. 10
21:13 He who closes his ear to the cry of the poor 4
30:15 The leech has two daughters; "Give, give," they cry. *
Isa 5: 7 he looked . . for righteousness, but behold, a cry! 9
8: 4 for before the child knows how to cry 'My father' 11
13:22 Hyenas will cry in its towers 5
14:31 Wail, O gate; cry, O city; melt in fear 3
15: 5 road to Horona'im they raise a cry of destruction; 4
8 For a cry has gone round the land of Moab; 4
19:20 when they cry to the LORD because of oppressors 8
21: 8 Then he who saw cried: "Upon a watchtower I stand 11
30:19 be gracious to you at the sound of your cry; 3
33: 7 Behold, the valiant ones cry without; 8
34:14 the satyr shall cry to his fellow; 11
40: 2 and cry to her that her warfare is ended 11
3 A voice cries: "In the wilderness prepare the way 11
6 A voice says, "Cry!" And I said, "What shall I cry? 11
6 A voice says, "Cry!" And I said, "What shall I cry? 11
42: 2 He will not cry or lift up his voice 8
46: 7 If one cries to it, it does not answer or save him 8
58: 1 Cry aloud, spare not, lift up your voice 11
9 you shall cry, and he will say, Here I am. 15
65:19 the sound of weeping and the cry of distress. 10
Jer 4:31 For I heard a cry as of a woman in travail 10
31 the cry of the daughter of Zion gasping 10
7:16 for this people, or lift up cry or prayer for them 12
8:19 Hark, the cry of the daughter of my people 16
11:11 though they cry to me, I will not listen to them. 3
12 and the inhabitants of Jerusalem will go and cry 3
14 or lift up a cry or prayer on their behalf 12
12: 6 they are in full cry after you; believe them not 11
14: 2 and the cry of Jerusalem goes up. 7
12 Though they fast, I will not hear their cry 12
18:22 May a cry be heard from their houses 4
20:16 let him hear a cry in the morning 4
22:20 cry from Ab'arim, for all your lovers 8
25:34 Wail, you shepherds, and cry, and roll in ashes 3
36 Hark, the cry of the shepherds 9
30: 5 Thus says the LORD: We have heard a cry of panic 10
46:12 and the earth is full of your cry; 7
48: 3 Hark! a cry from Horona'im, 'Desolation 9
4 Moab is destroyed; a cry is heard as far as Zo'ar. 4
5 they have heard the cry of destruction. 9
20 Moab is put to shame, for it is broken; wail and cry! 3
49: 2 when I will cause the battle cry to be heard 17
3 for Ai is laid waste! Cry, O daughters of Rabbah! 8
21 their cry shall be heard at the Red Sea. 9
29 men shall cry to them: 'Terror on every side!' 11
50:46 and her cry shall be heard among the nations. 4
51:54 Hark! a cry from Babylon! 4
Lam 2:12 They cry to their mothers, "Where is bread and wine? 1
16 they hiss, they gnash their teeth, they cry 1
18 Cry aloud to the Lord! O daughter of Zion! 8
4:15 Away! Unclean!" men cried at them; 11
Ezk 8:18 though they cry in my ears with a loud voice 11
9: 1 Then he cried in my ears with a loud voice, saying 11
8 I fell upon my face, and cried, "Ah Lord GOD! 3
11:13 fell down upon my face, and cried with a loud voice 3
21:12 Cry and wail, son of man, for it is against my people; 3
22 to open the mouth with a cry, to lift up the voice 13
27:28 At the sound of the cry of your pilots 4
30 and wail aloud over you, and cry bitterly. 3
Dan 4:14 cried aloud and said thus, 'Hew down the tree 18
5: 7 king cried aloud to bring in the enchanters 18
Hos 7:14 They do not cry to me from the heart 3
8: 2 To me they cry, My God, we Israel know thee. 3
Jol 1:14 and cry to the LORD. 3
19 Unto thee, O LORD, I cry. 11
20 Even the wild beasts cry to thee 6
Jon 1: 2 go to Nin'eveh, that great city, and cry against it; 11
5 mariners were afraid, and each cried to his god; 3
14 Therefore they cried to the LORD, "We beseech thee 11
2: 2 he answered me; out of the belly of Sheol I cried 15
3: 4 he cried, " . . and Nin'eveh shall be overthrown! 11
8 with sackcloth, and let them cry mightily to God; 11
Mic 3: 4 they will cry to the LORD, but he will not answer 3
5 who cry "Peace" when they have something to eat 11
6: 9 The voice of the LORD cries to the city 11
Nah 2: 8 Halt! Halt!" they cry; but none turns back. *
Hab 1: 2 Or cry to thee "Violence!" and thou wilt not save? 3
Zep 1:10 a cry will be heard from the Fish Gate 9
Zec 1:17 Cry again, Thus says the LORD of hosts 11
6: 8 Then he cried to me, "Behold 3
Mat 3: 3 The voice of one crying in the wilderness 20
9:27 two blind men followed him, crying aloud 24
15:22 came out and cried 24
23 Send her away, for she is crying after us. 24
25: 6 at midnight there was a cry 26
27:46 Jesus cried with a loud voice 19
50 Jesus cried again with a loud voice 24
Mrk 1: 3 the voice of one crying in the wilderness 20
26 convulsing him and crying with a loud voice 28
15:34 at the ninth hour Jesus cried with a loud voice 20
37 Jesus uttered a loud cry, and breathed his last. 29
Lke 1:42 she exclaimed with a loud cry, "Blessed are you 26
3: 4 The voice of one crying in the wilderness 20
4:41 demons also came out of many, crying 25
9:38 behold, a man from the crowd cried, "Teacher 20
18: 7 who cry to him day and night 20
38 he cried, "Jesus, Son of David, have mercy on me! 20
23:23 demanding with loud cries 29
46 Then Jesus, crying with a loud voice, said, "Father 28
Joh 1:15 (John bore witness to him and cried 24
23 I am the voice of one crying in the wilderness 20
11:43 When he had said this, he cried with a loud voice 25
12:13 went out to meet him, crying, "Hosanna! 25
Act 7:60 he knelt down and cried with a loud voice 24
8: 7 unclean spirits . . crying with a loud voice 20
14:14 and rushed out among the multitude, crying 24
16:17 She followed Paul and us, crying 24
28 Paul cried with a loud voice, "Do not harm yourself 28
17: 6 before the city authorities, crying 20
19:32 Now some cried one thing, some another 24
21:36 the mob of the people followed, crying 24
Rom 8:15 the spirit of sonship. When we cry, "Abba! Father! 24
Gal 4: 6 his Son into our hearts, crying, "Abba! Father! 24
Heb 5: 7 with loud cries and tears 26
Jas 5: 4 cries of the harvesters have reached the ears 21
Rev 8:13 I heard an eagle crying with a loud voice 27
16: 7 I heard the altar cry, "Yea, Lord God the Almighty 27
19: 1 a great multitude in heaven, crying, "Hallelujah! 27
3 Once more they cried, "Hallelujah! 22
5 And from the throne came a voice crying 27
6 like the sound of mighty thunderpeals, crying 27
21: 4 neither shall there be mourning nor crying 26
2Es 10:26 she suddenly uttered a loud and fearful cry 31
27 I was afraid, and cried with a loud voice and said 30
11: 7 and uttered a cry to his wings, saying 32
Tob 13:18 all her lanes will cry 'Hallelujah!' 22
AEs 11:10 Then they cried to God 20
10 from their cry . . there came a great river 21
Wis 7: 3 my first sound was a cry, like that of all. 23
18:10 the discordant cry of their enemies echoed back 21
Sir 30: 7 his feelings will be troubled at every cry. 21
Bar 4:20 I will cry to the Everlasting all my days. 24
21 cry to God, and he will deliver you 20
27 Take courage, my children, and cry to God 20
Sus 1:44 The Lord heard her cry. 29
46 he cried with a loud voice, "I am innocent 20
1Mc 3:50 they cried aloud to Heaven, saying 20
4:10 now let us cry to Heaven 20
5:31 the cry of the city went up to Heaven 26
13:50 Then they cried to Simon to make peace with them 20
3Mc 1:16 they filled the temple with cries and tears; 26
28 cry of the crowds resulted in an immense uproar; 26
4: 2 mourning, lamentation, and tearful cries 21

cry *See also* raise.

cry aloud 1. זעק 2. צהל 3. צהל קול 4. צרח
5. קרא מלא 6. רום קול 7. רוע 8. רוע רֵעַ 9. רנן
10. *βοάω* 11. *κραυγάζω*

2Sm 13:19 and went away, crying aloud as she went. 1
Prv 1:20 Wisdom cries aloud in the street; 9
8: 3 at the entrance of the portals she cries aloud 9
Isa 10:30 Cry aloud, O daughter of Gallim! 3
13: 2 On a bare hill raise a signal, cry aloud to them; 6
15: 4 therefore the armed men of Moab cry aloud; 7
54: 1 break forth into singing and cry aloud 2
Jer 4: 5 cry aloud and say, 'Assemble, and let us go 5
Mic 4: 9 Now why do you cry aloud? Is there no king in you? 8
Zep 1:14 the mighty man cries aloud there. 4
Mat 12:19 He will not wrangle or cry aloud 11
1Mc 5:33 and cried aloud in prayer. 10

battle cry 1. תְּרוּעָה 2. *κραυγή*

Zep 1:16 a day of trumpet blast and battle cry 1
2Mc 12:37 he raised the battle cry, with hymns 2

empty cry 1. שָׁוְא

Job 35:13 Surely God does not hear an empty cry 1

cry for help 1. זעק 2. צעק 3. שׁוּעַ 4. שׁוע 5. שַׁוְעָה

Deu 22:24 she did not cry for help though she was in the city 2
27 woman cried for help there was no one to rescue 2
Jdg 6: 6 the people of Israel cried for help to the LORD. 1
Job 24:12 the soul of the wounded cries for help; 4
30:24 and in his disaster cry for help? 3
28 I stand up in the assembly, and cry for help. 4
36:13 they do not cry for help when he binds them. 4
Ps 18: 6 I called upon the LORD; to my God I cried for help. 4
41 They cried for help, but there was none to save 4
28: 2 voice of my supplication, as I cry to thee for help 4
30: 2 O LORD my God, I cried to thee for help 4
31:22 my supplications, when I cried to thee for help. 4
34:17 When the righteous cry for help, the LORD hears 2
119:147 I rise before dawn and cry for help; 4
Isa 38:13 I cry for help until morning; *
Lam 3: 8 though I . . cry for help, he shuts out my prayer; 4
56 my plea, 'Do not close thine ear to my cry for help!' 5
Hab 1: 2 O LORD, how long shall I cry for help 4

joyful cry 1. רְנָנָה

Job 3: 7 let no joyful cry be heard in it. 1

loud cry 1. *κραυγή*

Jdt 14:19 their loud cries and shouts arose 1

cry of command 1. *κέλευσμα*

1Th 4:16 will descend from heaven with a cry of command 1

cry of distress 1. צְוָחָה

Ps 144:14 there be no cry of distress in our streets! 1

cry out 1. זעק 2. זְעָקָה 3. נתן קול 4. פעה 5. צעק
6. קרא 7. רוע 8. רנן 9. זעק (A) 10. *ἀναβοάω*
11. *ἀνακράζω* 12. *βοάω* 13. *ἐπιβοάω* 14. *καταβοάω*
15. *καταβόησις* 16. *κράζω* 17. *κραυγάζω* 18. clamo
19. proclamo

Gen 27:34 he cried out with an exceedingly great . . cry 5
39:14 with me, and I cried out with a loud voice; 6
Exd 14:10 the people of Israel cried out to the LORD; 5
22:23 If you do afflict them, and they cry out to me, I will 5
Jdg 7:21 and all the army ran; they cried out and fled. 7
1Sm 4:13 when the man came . . all the city cried out. 1
5:10 when the ark . . the people of Ekron cried out 1
8:18 in that day you will cry out because of your king 1
28:12 When the woman . . she cried out with a loud voice; 1
2Sm 18:28 Then Ahi'ma-az cried out to the king, "All is well. 6
1Kg 22:32 to fight against him; and Jehosh'aphat cried out. 1
2Kg 4:40 But while they were eating . . they cried out 5
6: 5 he cried out, "Alas, my master! It was borrowed. 5
26 woman cried out . . saying, "Help, my lord, O king! 5
2Ch 18:31 Jehosh'aphat cried out, and the LORD helped him. 1
Job 19: 7 Behold, I cry out, 'Violence!' but I am not answered; 5
31:38 If my land has cried out against me 1
35: 9 because of . . oppressions people cry out; 1
12 There they cry out, but he does not answer 5
Ps 88: 1 I cry out in the night before thee. 5
Prv 1:21 on the top of the walls she cries out; 6

2: 3 yes, if you cry out for insight 6
21:13 himself cry out and not be heard. 6
Isa 15: 4 Heshbon and Ele-a'leh cry out 1
5 My heart cries out for Moab; his fugitives flee 1
26:17 who writhes and cries out in her pangs 1
42:13 he cries out, he shouts aloud 7
14 now I will cry out like a woman in travail 4
57:13 When you cry out, let your collection of idols 1
65:14 but you shall cry out for pain of heart 5
Jer 20: 8 For whenever I speak, I cry out, I shout 1
22:20 Go up to Lebanon, and cry out, and lift up your voice 5
30:15 Why do you cry out over your hurt? 1
47: 2 Men shall cry out 1
48:31 Therefore I wail for Moab; I cry out for all Moab; 1
34 Heshbon and Ele-a'leh cry out; 2
Lam 2:19 Arise, cry out in the night, at the .. watches! 8
Dan 6:20 cried out in a tone of anguish and said to Daniel 9
Ams 3: 4 Does a young lion cry out from his den, 3
Hab 2:11 For the stone will cry out from the wall 1
Zec 1: 4 fathers, to whom the former prophets cried out 6
14 Cry out, Thus says the LORD of hosts 6
Mat 8:29 behold, they cried out, "What have you to do with us 16
14:26 And they cried out for fear. 16
30 beginning to sink he cried out, "Lord, save me. 16
20:30 two blind men .. cried out, "Have mercy on us 16
31 but they cried out the more 16
21:15 the children crying out in the temple 16
Mrk 1:24 he cried out, "What have you to do with us 11
3:11 they fell down before him and cried out 16
5: 5 on the mountains he was always crying out 16
7 crying out with a loud voice, he said 16
6:49 they thought it was a ghost, and cried out; 11
9:24 Immediately the father of the child cried out 16
26 after crying out and convulsing him terribly 16
10:47 he began to cry out and say, "Jesus, Son of David 16
48 he cried out all the more, "Son of David, have mercy 16
11: 9 and those who followed cried out 16
15:13 they cried out again, "Crucify him. 16
Lke 4:33 and he cried out with a loud voice 11
8:28 he cried out and fell down before him 11
9:39 a spirit seizes him, and he suddenly cries out 16
18:39 he cried out all the more 16
19:40 the very stones would cry out. 16
23:18 they all cried out together, "Away with this man 11
Joh 12:44 Jesus cried out and said, "He who believes in me 16
18:40 They cried out again, "Not this man, but Barab'bas! 17
19: 6 they cried out, "Crucify him, crucify him! 17
12 but the Jews cried out 17
15 They cried out, "Away with him, away with him 17
Act 7:57 they cried out with a loud voice 16
19:28 they were enraged, and cried out 16
34 they all with one voice cried out 16
21:28 crying out, "Men of Israel, help! 16
22:23 as they cried out and waved their garments 17
23: 6 he cried out in the council 16
24:21 except this one thing which I cried out 16
Rom 9:27 And Isaiah cries out concerning Israel 16
Jas 5: 4 the wages .. which you kept back by fraud, cry out; 16
Rev 6:10 they cried out with a loud voice, "O Sovereign Lord 16
7:10 crying out with a loud voice, "Salvation 16
12: 2 she cried out in her pangs of birth 16
18:18 and cried out as they saw the smoke of her burning 16
19 as they wept and mourned, crying out, "Alas, alas 16
2Es 1:17 did you not cry out to me 19
15: 8 righteous blood cries out to me 18
8 the souls of the righteous cry out continually. 18
Tob 6:17 and cry out to the merciful God, and he will save you 12
Jdt 4: 9 every man of Israel cried out to God 10
12 and cried out in unison 12
15 they cried out to the Lord with all their might 12
5:12 Then they cried out to their God 10
6:18 the people .. cried out to him 12
7:19 The people of Israel cried out to the Lord their God 10
23 and cried out with a loud voice 10
29 they cried out to the Lord God with a loud voice. 12
9: 1 Judith cried out to the Lord with a loud voice 12
10: 1 Judith had ceased crying out to the God of Israel 12
14:16 he cried out with a loud voice and wept 12
AEs 10: 9 Israel, who cried out to God and were saved 12
13:18 all Israel cried out mightily 16
Sir 35:15 cries out against him who has caused them to fall? 15
Bar 3: 1 the wearied spirit cry out to thee. 16
Sus 1:24 Then Susanna cried out with a loud voice 10
42 Then Susanna cried out with a loud voice, and said 10
1Mc 2:27 Then Mattathias cried out in the city 11
4:40 and cried out to Heaven. 12
9:46 Cry out now to Heaven that you may be delivered 16
11:49 they cried out to the king with this entreaty 16
13:45 they cried out with a loud voice 12
2Mc 8: 3 to hearken to the blood that cried out to him 14
3Mc 5:51 and cried out in a very loud voice 10
4Mc 6: 4 while a herald opposite him cried out 13
16 Eleazar .. cried out 10

cry out for help 1.זעק
Exd 2:23 the people of Israel .. cried out for help 1

war cry 1.מִלְחָמָה
1Sm 17:20 the host was going forth .. shouting the war cry. 1

crystal 1.גָּבִישׁ 2.קֶרַח 3.κρύσταλλος
Job 28:18 No mention shall be made of coral or of crystal; 1
Ezk 1:22 likeness of a firmament, shining like crystal 2
Rev 4: 6 there is as it were a sea of glass, like crystal. 3
22: 1 river of the water of life, bright as crystal 3
crystal *See also* clear.

crystalline 1.κρυσταλλοειδής
Wis 19:21 the crystalline .. kind of heavenly food. 1

cub 1.אִישׁ 2.גור
2Sm 17: 8 like a bear robbed of her cubs in the field. •
Prv 17:12 Let a man meet a she-bear robbed of her cubs 1
Hos 13: 8 will fall upon them like a bear robbed of her cubs •
Nah 2:11 where his cubs were, with none to disturb? 2
cub *See also* lion.

cubit 1.אַמָּה 2.גֹּמֶד 3.אַמָּה(A) 4.πῆχυς
Gen 6:15 the length of the ark 300 cubits 1
15 its breadth 50 cubits, and its height 30 cubits. 1
15 its breadth 50 cubits, and its height 30 cubits. 1
16 for the ark, and finish it to a cubit above; 1
7:20 covering them fifteen cubits deep. 1
Exd 25:10 two cubits and a half shall be its length 1
10 a cubit and a half its breadth 1
10 and a cubit and a half its height. 1
17 two cubits and a half shall be its length 1
17 and a cubit and a half its breadth. 1
23 two cubits shall be its length 1
23 a cubit its breadth 1
23 and a cubit and a half its height. 1
26: 2 The length of each curtain shall be 28 cubits 1
2 and the breadth of each curtain four cubits; 1
8 The length of each curtain shall be 30 cubits 1
8 the breadth of each curtain four cubits; 1
13 the cubit on the one side, and the cubit 1
13 the cubit on the one side, and the cubit 1
16 Ten cubits shall be the length of a frame 1
16 a cubit and a half the breadth of each frame. 1
27: 1 altar .. five cubits long and five cubits broad; 1
1 altar .. five cubits long and five cubits broad; 1
1 the altar .. its height shall be three cubits. 1
9 hangings .. 100 cubits long for one side; 1
11 there shall be hangings 100 cubits long •
12 there shall be hangings for 50 cubits 1
13 breadth of the court .. shall be 50 cubits. 1
14 the gate shall be fifteen cubits, with three 1
15 the hangings shall be fifteen cubits •
16 there shall be a screen twenty cubits long 1
18 The length of the court shall be 100 cubits 1
18 the breadth 50, and the height five cubits 1
30: 2 A cubit shall be its length 1
2 its length, and a cubit its breadth; 1
2 and two cubits shall be its height; 1
36: 9 The length of each curtain was 28 cubits 1
9 and the breadth of each curtain four cubits; 1
15 The length of each curtain was 30 cubits 1
15 the breadth of each curtain four cubits; 1
21 Ten cubits was the length of a frame 1
21 a cubit and a half the breadth of each frame. 1
37: 1 two cubits and a half was its length 1
1 a cubit and a half its breadth, and a cubit 1
1 its breadth, and a cubit and a half its height. 1
6 two cubits and a half was its length 1
6 its length, and a cubit and a half its breadth. 1
10 two cubits was its length, a cubit its breadth 1
10 two cubits was its length, a cubit its breadth 1
10 its breadth, and a cubit and a half its height; 1
25 its length was a cubit, and its breadth was a cubit; 1
25 its length was a cubit, and its breadth was a cubit; 1
25 it was square, and two cubits was its height; 1
38: 1 five cubits was its length, and five cubits its 1
1 and five cubits its breadth; it was square 1
1 it was square, and three cubits was its height. 1
9 hangings .. were of fine twined linen, 100 cubits; 1
11 for the north side 100 cubits, their pillars 20 1
12 for the west side were hangings of 50 cubits 1
13 for the front of the east, 50 cubits. 1
14 hangings .. were fifteen cubits, with three 1
15 by the gate .. were hangings of fifteen cubits 1
18 it was twenty cubits long and five cubits high 1
18 it was twenty cubits long and five cubits high 1
Num11:31 about two cubits above the face of the earth. 1
35: 4 wall of the city outward a 1,000 cubits all round. 1
5 shall measure .. for the east side 2,000 cubits 1
5 shall measure .. for the south side 2,000 cubits 1
5 shall measure .. for the west side 2,000 cubits 1
5 shall measure .. for the north side 2,000 cubits 1
Deu 3:11 Nine cubits was its length, and four cubits 1
11 its length, and four cubits its breadth 1
11 according to the common cubit.) 1
Jos 3: 4 shall be a space .. a distance of about 2,000 cubits; 1
Jdg 3:16 himself a sword with two edges, a cubit in length; 2
1Sm 17: 4 whose height was six cubits and a span. 1
1Kg 6: 2 The house .. for the LORD was 60 cubits long 1
2 The house .. was 60 cubits long, twenty cubits wide •
2 The house .. twenty cubits wide, and 30 cubits high. 1
3 The vestibule .. was twenty cubits long 1
3 twenty cubits long .. and ten cubits deep 1
6 The lowest story was five cubits broad 1
6 the middle one was six cubits broad 1
6 and the third was seven cubits broad; 1
10 He built .. each story five cubits high 1
16 He built twenty cubits of the rear of the house 1
17 The house .. the nave .., was 40 cubits long. 1
20 The inner sanctuary was twenty cubits long 1
20 was twenty cubits long, twenty cubits wide 1
20 long, twenty cubits wide, and twenty cubits high; 1
23 he made two cherubim .. each ten cubits high. 1
24 Five cubits was the length of one wing 1
24 and five cubits .. the other wing of the cherub; 1
24 ten cubits from the tip of one wing to the tip 1
25 The other cherub also measured ten cubits; 1
26 The height of one cherub was ten cubits, and so was 1
7: 2 its length was 100 cubits 1
2 its breadth 50 cubits, and its height 30 cubits 1
2 its breadth 50 cubits, and its height 30 cubits 1
6 he made the Hall of Pillars; its length was 50 cubits 1
6 length was 50 cubits, and its breadth 30 cubits; 1
10 huge stones, stones of eight and ten cubits. 1
15 Eighteen cubits was the height of one pillar 1
15 twelve cubits measured its circumference; 1
16 the height of the one capital was five cubits 1
16 the height of the other capital was five cubits. 1
19 the capitals .. were of lily-work, four cubits. 1
23 it was round, ten cubits from brim to brim 1
23 ten cubits from brim to brim, and five cubits high 1
23 a line of 30 cubits measured its circumference. 1
24 Under its brim were gourds, for 30 cubits 1
27 each stand was four cubits long, four cubits wide 1
27 each stand was four cubits long, four cubits wide 1
27 long, four cubits wide, and three cubits high. 1
31 within a crown which projected upward one cubit; 1
31 its opening was round .. a cubit and a half deep. 1
32 and the height of a wheel was a cubit and a half. 1
35 on the top .. was a round band half a cubit high; 1
38 each laver measured four cubits 1
2Kg 14:13 broke down the wall of Jerusalem for 400 cubits 1
25:17 The height of the one pillar was eighteen cubits 1
17 the height of the capital was three cubits; 1
1Ch 11:23 a man of great stature, five cubits tall. 1
2Ch 3: 3 length, in cubits of the old standard, was 60 1
3 the length .. was 60 cubits, and the breadth 1
3 60 cubits, and the breadth twenty cubits. 1
4 The vestibule .. was twenty cubits long 1
4 its height was 120 cubits. •
8 most holy place; its length .. was twenty cubits; 1
8 most holy place .. breadth was twenty cubits; 1
11 The wings .. together extended twenty cubits 1
11 one wing of the one, of five cubits, touched 1
11 its other wing, of five cubits, touched the wing 1
12 cherub, one wing, of five cubits, touched the wall 1
12 the other wing, also of five cubits, was joined 1
13 wings of these cherubim extended twenty cubits; 1
15 he made two pillars 35 cubits high 1
15 with a capital of five cubits on the top of each. 1
4: 1 He made an altar of bronze, twenty cubits long 1
1 an altar of bronze .. and twenty cubits wide 1
1 made an altar of bronze .. and ten cubits high. 1
2 molten sea .. round, ten cubits from brim to brim 1
2 molten sea .. brim to brim, and five cubits high 1
2 round .. and a line of 30 cubits measured 1
3 were figures of gourds, for 30 cubits 1
6:13 bronze platform five cubits long, five .. wide 1
13 bronze platform five .. long, five cubits wide 1
13 bronze platform .. wide, and three cubits high 1
25:23 broke down the wall of Jerusalem for 400 cubits 1
Ezr 6: 3 height shall be 60 cubits and its breadth 3
3 its height .. and its breadth 60 cubits 3
Neh 3:13 repaired 1,000 cubits of the wall 1
Est 5:14 Let a gallows 50 cubits high be made 1
7: 9 gallows .. in Haman's house, 50 cubits high. 1
Jer 52:21 the height of the one pillar was eighteen cubits 1
21 its circumference was twelve cubits 1
22 the height of the one capital was five cubits; 1
Ezk 40: 5 reed in the man's hand was six long cubits 1
5 long cubits, each being a cubit and a handbreadth 1
7 and the space between the side rooms, five cubits; 1
8 the vestibule of the gateway, eight cubits; •
9 and its jambs, two cubits; 1
11 breadth of the opening of the gateway, ten cubits; 1
11 and the breadth of the gateway, thirteen cubits. 1
12 before the side rooms, one cubit on either side; 1
12 the side rooms were six cubits on either side. 1
13 25 cubits, from door to door. 1
14 He measured also the vestibule, twenty cubits; 1
15 inner vestibule of the gate was 50 cubits. 1
19 outer front of the inner court, 100 cubits. 1
21 its length was 50 cubits 1
21 and its breadth 25 cubits. 1
23 he measured from gate to gate, 100 cubits. 1
25 its length was 50 cubits 1
25 and its breadth 25 cubits. 1
27 gate to gate toward the south, 100 cubits. 1

29 its length was 50 cubits 1
29 and its breadth 25 cubits. 1
30 vestibules round about, 25 cubits long 1
30 25 cubits long and five cubits broad. 1
33 its length was 50 cubits 1
33 and its breadth 25 cubits. 1
36 windows round about; its length was 50 cubits 1
36 and its breadth 25 cubits. 1
42 a cubit and a half long, and a cubit and a half broad 1
42 a cubit and a half long, and a cubit and a half broad 1
42 a cubit and a half broad, and one cubit high 1
47 he measured the court, 100 cubits long 1
47 and 100cubits broad, foursquare; 1
48 of the vestibule, five cubits on either side; 1
48 the breadth of the gate was fourteen cubits; 4
48 of the gate were three cubits on either side. 1
49 The length of the vestibule was twenty cubits 1
49 was twenty cubits, and the breadth twelve cubits; 1
41: 1 six cubits was the breadth of the jambs. 1
2 And the breadth of the entrance was ten cubits; 1
2 the sidewalls of the entrance were five cubits 1
2 he measured the length of the nave 40 cubits 1
2 40 cubits, and its breadth, twenty cubits. 1
3 measured the jambs of the entrance, two cubits; 1
3 and the breadth of the entrance, six cubits; 1
3 and the sidewalls of the entrance, seven cubits. 1
4 he measured the length of the room, twenty cubits 1
4 and its breadth, twenty cubits, beyond the nave. 1
5 measured the wall of the temple, six cubits thick; 1
5 and the breadth of the side chambers, four cubits 1
8 measured a full reed of six long cubits. 1
9 outer wall of the side chambers was five cubits; 1
9 platform which was left free was five cubits. ‡
10 court was a breadth of twenty cubits round about 1
11 that was left free was five cubits round about. 1
12 yard on the west side was 70 cubits broad; 1
12 the wall of the building was five cubits thick 1
12 and its length 90 cubits. 1
13 he measured the temple, 100 cubits long; 1
13 building with its walls, 100 cubits long; 1
14 the temple and the yard, 100 cubits. 1
15 and its walls on either side, 100 cubits. 1
22 an altar of wood, three cubits high 1
22 cubits high, two cubits long, and two cubits broad; 1
22 cubits high, two cubits long, and two cubits broad; 4
42: 2 which was on the north side was 100 cubits 1
2 100 cubits, and the breadth 50 cubits. 1
3 Adjoining the twenty cubits which belonged *
4 was a passage inward, ten cubits wide 1
4 ten cubits wide and 100 cubits long 4
7 opposite the chambers, 50 cubits long. 1
8 chambers on the outer court were 50 cubits 1
8 opposite the temple were 100 cubits long. 1
16 500 cubits by the measuring reed. *
17 500 cubits by the measuring reed. *
18 500 cubits by the measuring reed. *
19 500 cubits by the measuring reed. *
20 It had a wall around it, 500 cubits long *
20 cubits long and 500 cubits broad *
43:13 These are the dimensions of the altar by cubits 1
13 cubits (the cubit being a cubit and a handbreadth 1
13 cubits (the cubit being a cubit and a handbreadth 1
13 its base shall be one cubit high 1
13 base shall be one cubit high, and one cubit broad 1
14 base on the ground to the lower ledge, two cubits 1
14 ledge, two cubits, with a breadth of one cubit; 1
14 smaller ledge to the larger ledge, four cubits ‡
14 four cubits, with a breadth of one cubit; 1
15 the altar hearth, four cubits; 1
15 projecting upward, four horns, one cubit high. 4
16 be square, twelve cubits long by twelve broad. *
17 square, fourteen cubits long by fourteen broad *
17 with a rim around it half a cubit broad 1
17 and its base one cubit round about. 1
45: 1 holy district, 25,000 cubits long *
1 cubits long and 20,000 cubits broad; *
2 a square plot of 500 by 500 cubits *
2 with 50 cubits for an open space around it. 1
3 a section 25,000 cubits long *
5 section, 25,000 cubits long *
5 cubits long and 10,000 cubits broad *
6 of the city an area 5,000 cubits broad *
6 25,000 cubits long; *
46:22 small courts, 40 cubits long and 30 broad; *
47: 3 the man measured 1,000 cubits 1
48: 8 25,000 cubits in breadth *
9 be 25,000 cubits in length, *
10 shall have an allotment measuring 25,000 cubits *
10 10,000 cubits in breadth on the western side *
13 25,000 cubits in length and 10,000 in breadth. *
13 The whole length shall be 25,000 cubits *
15 5,000 cubits in breadth and 25,000 in length *
16 its dimensions: the north side 4,500 cubits *
17 open land: on the north 250 cubits, on the south 250 *
18 holy portion shall be 10,000 cubits to the east *
20 set apart shall be 25,000 cubits square *
21 from the 25,000 cubits of the holy portion *
21 from the 25,000 cubits to the west border *
30 north side, which is to be 4,500 cubits by measure *
32 east side, which is to be 4,500 cubits, three gates *
33 south side, which is to be 4,500 cubits by measure *
34 On the west side, which is to be 4,500 cubits *
35 circumference of . . city shall be 18,000 cubits. *
Dan 3: 1 image of gold, whose height was 60 cubits 3
1 image of gold . . its breadth six cubits. 3
Zec 5: 2 a flying scroll; its length is twenty cubits 1
2 is twenty cubits, and its breadth ten cubits. 1
Mat 6:27 anxious can add one cubit to his span of life? 4
Lke 12:25 which of you . . can add a cubit to his span of life? 4
Rev 21:17 its wall, 144 cubits by a man's measure 4
1Es 6:25 its height to be 60 cubits 4
25 and its breadth 60 cubits 4
Jdt 1: 2 hewn stones three cubits thick 4
2 three cubits thick and six cubits long 4
2 he made the walls 70 cubits high 4
2 70 cubits high and 50 cubits wide; 4
3 he built towers 100 cubits high 4
3 100 cubits high and 60 cubits wide 4
4 he made its gates, which were 70 cubits high 4
4 70 cubits high and 40 cubits wide 4
Aza 1:24 streamed out above the furnace 49 cubits 4
2Mc 13: 5 there is a tower in that place, 50 cubits high 4

cucumber 1. קִשֻּׁאָה
Num11: 5 We remember the . . cucumbers, the melons 1

cucumber *See also* bed, field.

cud 1. גֵּרָה
Lev 11: 3 the hoof and is cloven-footed and chews the cud 1
4 Nevertheless among those that chew the cud 1
4 camel, because it chews the cud but does not part 1
5 it chews the cud but does not part the hoof 1
6 the hare, because it chews the cud but does not 1
7 swine . . does not chew the cud, is unclean to you 1
26 is not cloven-footed or does not chew the cud 1
Deu 14: 6 animal that . . chews the cud, among the animals 1
7 of those that chew the cud or have the hoof cloven 1
7 because they chew the cud but do not part the hoof 1
8 parts the hoof but does not chew the cud 1

cult *See* prostitute.

heathen cult 1. *θίασος*
Wis 12: 5 initiates from the midst of a heathen cult 1

cultivate 1. עבד 2. עֲבֹדָה 3. *γεωργέω* 4. *ἐργάζομαι* 5. *παιδεύω* 6. colo
Ps 104:14 plants for man to cultivate 2
Ecc 5: 9 an advantage to a land with cultivated fields. 1
Heb 6: 7 useful to those for whose sake it is cultivated 3
2Es 6:42 and cultivated and be of service before thee. 6
16:24 shall be left to cultivate the earth or to sow it. 6
Sir 20:28 Whoever cultivates the soil 4
21:23 a cultivated man remains outside. 5

cultivation 1. *γεώργιος* 2. cultura
2Es 8: 6 and cultivation of our understanding 2
Sir 27: 6 The fruit discloses the cultivation of a tree 1
6 discloses the cultivation of a man's mind. *

master cultivator 1. *παγγέωργος*
4Mc 1:29 the master cultivator, reason, weeds and prunes 1

cumi 1. *κοῦμ*
Mrk 5:41 he said to her, "Tal'itha cu'mi"; 1

cummin 1. כַּמֹּן 2. *κύμινον*
Isa 28:25 does he not scatter dill, sow cummin 1
27 nor is a cart wheel rolled over cummin; 1
27 beaten out with a stick, and cummin with a rod. 1
Mat 23:23 you tithe the mint and dill and cummin 2

cunning 1. חכם 2. עָקְבָה 3. ערם 4. עָרְמָה 5. שֵׂכֶל 6. תַּרְמִית 7. *κυβεία* 8. *πανουργία*
Jos 9: 4 they on their part acted with cunning 4
1Sm 23:22 it is told me that he is very cunning. 3
2Kg 10:19 Jehu did it with cunning in order to destroy 2
Ps 58: 5 voice of charmers or of the cunning enchanter. 1
119:118yea, their cunning is in vain. 6
Dan 8:25 By his cunning he shall make deceit prosper 5
2Co 4: 2 we refuse to practice cunning 8
11: 3 as the serpent deceived Eve by his cunning 8
Eph 4:14 by the cunning of men 7

cunningly *See* conceive.

cup 1. גָּבִיעַ 2. כּוֹס 3. כְּלִי אַגָּן 4. סַף 5. קַשְׂוָה 6. *κόνδυ* 7. *ποτήριον* 8. *σπονδεῖον* 9. calix
Gen 40:11 Pharaoh's cup was in my hand; and I took the grapes 2
11 grapes and pressed them into Pharaoh's cup 2
11 and placed the cup in Pharaoh's hand. 2
13 and you shall place Pharaoh's cup in his hand 2
21 and he placed the cup in Pharaoh's hand; 2
44: 2 put my cup, the silver cup, in the mouth of the sack 1
2 put my cup, the silver cup, in the mouth of the sack 1
4 Why have you stolen my silver cup? 6
12 and the cup was found in Benjamin's sack. 1
16 he also in whose hand the cup has been found. 1
17 the man in whose hand the cup was found shall be my 1
Exd 25:31 shall be made of hammered work; its cups 1
33 three cups made like almonds, each with capital 1
33 and three cups made like almonds 1
34 on the lampstand . . four cups made like almonds 1
37:17 were made of hammered work; its cups, its capitals 1
19 three cups made like almonds, each with capital 1
20 four cups made like almonds, with their capitals 1
2Sm 12: 3 it used to eat of his morsel, and drink from his cup 2
1Kg 7:26 made like the brim of a cup, like the flower 2
50 The cups, snuffers, basins, dishes for incense 4
1Ch 28:17 pure gold for the forks, the basins, and the cups; 5
2Ch 4: 5 its brim was made like the brim of a cup 2
Ps 11: 6 wind shall be the portion of their cup. 2
16: 5 The LORD is my chosen portion and my cup; 2
23: 5 thou anointest my head with oil, my cup overflows. 2
75: 8 For in the hand of the LORD there is a cup 2
116:13 I will lift up the cup of salvation 2
Prv 23:31 sparkles in the cup and goes down smoothly. 2
Isa 22:24 every . . vessel, from the cups to all the flagons. 3
51:17 drunk at the hand of the LORD the cup of his wrath 2
22 I have taken from your hand the cup of staggering; 2
65:11 and fill cups of mixed wine for Destiny; *
Jer 16: 7 any one give him the cup of consolation to drink 2
25:15 Take from my hand this cup of the wine of wrath 2
17 I took the cup from the LORD'S hand 2
28 if they refuse to accept the cup from your hand 2
35: 5 wine, and cups; and I said to them, "Drink wine. 2
49:12 did not deserve to drink the cup must drink it 2
51: 7 Babylon was a golden cup in the LORD'S hand 2
Lam 4:21 Rejoice . . but to you also the cup shall pass; 2
Ezk 23:31 therefore I will give her cup into your hand. 2
32 You shall drink your sister's cup which is deep 2
33 A cup of horror and desolation 2
33 desolation, is the cup of your sister Sama'ria; 2
Hab 2:15 makes his neighbors drink of the cup of his wrath *
16 The cup in the LORD'S right hand will come around 2
Zec 12: 2 Lo, I am about to make Jerusalem a cup of reeling 4
Mat 10:42 even a cup of cold water 7
20:22 Are you able to drink the cup that I am to drink? 7
23 He said to them, "You will drink my cup 7
23:25 you cleanse the outside of the cup 7
26 cleanse the inside of the cup and of the plate 7
26:27 he took a cup 7
39 My father, if it be possible, let this cup pass 7
Mrk 7: 4 washing of cups and pots and vessels of bronze.) 7
9:41 whoever gives you a cup of water to drink 7
10:38 Are you able to drink the cup that I drink 7
39 The cup that I drink you will drink 7
14:23 he took a cup 7
36 remove this cup from me 7
Lke 11:39 Now you Pharisees cleanse the outside of the cup 7
22:17 he took a cup, and when he had given thanks he said 7
20 likewise the cup after supper, saying, "This cup 7
20 This cup which is poured out for you 7
42 if thou art willing, remove this cup from me; 7
Joh 18:11 not drink the cup which the Father has given me? 7
1Co 10:16 The cup of blessing which we bless 7
21 You cannot drink the cup of the Lord 7
21 the cup of the Lord and the cup of demons 7
11:25 In the same way also the cup, after supper, saying 7
25 This cup is the new covenant in my blood 7
26 eat this bread and drink the cup 7
27 drinks the cup of the Lord in an unworthy manner 7
28 eat of the bread and drink of the cup. 7
Rev 14:10 poured unmixed into the cup of his anger 7
16:19 to make her drain the cup of the fury of his wrath. 7
17: 4 holding . . a golden cup full of abominations 7
18: 6 mix a double draught for her in the cup she mixed. 7
1Es 2:13 1,000 gold cups . . 29 silver censers 8
13 1,000 gold cups, 1,000 silver cups 8
3: 6 clothed in purple, and drink from gold cups *
2Es 14:39 and behold, a full cup was offered to me 9
Sir 50:15 he reached out his hand to the cup 8

cup for drink offerings 1. *σπονδεῖον*
1Mc 1:22 the cups for drink offerings 1

gold cup 1. *χρύσωμα*
1Mc 11:58 and granted him the right to drink from gold cups 1

cupbearer 1. מַשְׁקֶה 2. *οἰνοχόος*
1Kg 10: 5 his cupbearers, and his burnt offerings 1
2Ch 9: 4 his cupbearers, and their clothing 1
Neh 1:11 Now I was cupbearer to the king. 1
Tob 1:22 Now Ahikar was cupbearer, keeper of the signet 2

cupidity 1. *πλεονεξία*
2Mc 4:50 because of the cupidity of those in power 1

curb 1. בלם
Ps 32: 9 mule . . which must be curbed with bit and bridle 1

curd 1. חֶמְאָה
Gen 18: 8 Then he took curds, and milk, and the calf 1
Deu 32:14 Curds from the herd, and milk from the flock 1
Jdg 5:25 she brought him curds in a lordly bowl. 1
2Sm 17:29 brought . . honey and curds and sheep and cheese 1
Job 20:17 the streams flowing with honey and curds. 1

Prv 30:33 For pressing milk produces curds 1
Isa 7:15 He shall eat curds and honey 1
22 milk which they give, he will eat curds; 1
22 one . . left in the land will eat curds and honey. 1

curdle 1. קפא

Job 10:10 pour me out like milk and curdle me like cheese? 1

cure 1. אסף 2. רפא 3. θεραπεύω 4. ἰάομαι 5. ἴασις

2Kg 5: 3 He would cure him of his leprosy. 1
6 my servant, that you may cure him of his leprosy. 1
7 this man sends . . to me to cure a man of his leprosy? 1
11 wave his hand over the place, and cure the leper. 1
Hos 5:13 But he is not able to cure you or heal your wound. 2
Mat 17:18 and the boy was cured instantly. 3
Lke 6:18 troubled with unclean spirits were cured. 3
7:21 he cured many of diseases and plagues 3
9: 1 gave them power . . to cure diseases 3
11 cured those who had need of healing. 4
13:32 I cast out demons and perform cures today 5
Joh 5:10 the Jews said to the man who was cured 3
Act 28: 9 rest of the people . . also came and were cured. 3
Tob 6: 8 he will be cured. 4
12: 3 he has led me back to you safely, he cured my wife 3
Wis 16:12 For neither herb nor poultice cured them 3

curious 1. curiosus

2Es 9:13 Therefore, do not continue to be curious as to how 1

curl back 1. ἀνακλάω

4Mc 11:10 he was completely curled back like a scorpion 1

current 1. עבר 2. ῥέω

Gen 23:16 according to the weights current 1
Sir 4:26 do not try to stop the current of a river. 2

curse 1. אָלָה 2. ארר 3. ברך 4. חֵרֶם 5. מְאֵרָה 6. קבב 7. קלל 8. קְלָלָה 9. שְׁבוּעָה 10. תַּאֲלָה 11. ἀνάθεμα 12. ἀρά 13. βλασφημέω 14. ἐπικαταράομαι 15. ἐπικατάρατος 16. κατάρα 17. καταράομαι 18. καταράω 19. κατεράω

Gen 3:14 done this, cursed are you above all cattle 2
17 cursed is the ground because of you; 2
4:11 now you are cursed from the ground 2
5:29 Out of the ground which the LORD has cursed 2
8:21 I will never again curse the ground 7
9:25 he said, "Cursed be Canaan; 2
12: 3 and him who curses you I will curse; 7
3 and him who curses you I will curse; 2
27:12 bring a curse upon myself and not a blessing. 8
13 mother said to him, "Upon me be your curse, my son; 8
29 Cursed be every one who curses you 2
29 be every one who curses you 2
49: 7 Cursed be their anger, for it is fierce; 2
Exd 21:17 Whoever curses his father or his mother shall be 7
22:28 You shall not revile God, nor curse a ruler 2
Lev 19:14 You shall not curse the deaf 7
20: 9 For every one who curses his father or his mother 7
9 shall be put to death; he has cursed his father 7
24:11 the . . son . . cursed 7
14 Bring out of the camp him who cursed 7
15 Whoever curses his God shall bear his sin 7
23 they brought him who had cursed out of the camp 7
Num 5:21 priest make the woman take the oath of the curse 9
23 the priest shall write these curses in a book 1
22: 6 Come now, curse this people for me 2
6 I know that he . . whom you curse is cursed. 2
6 I know that he . . whom you curse is cursed. 2
11 now come, curse them for me; 6
12 shall not curse the people, for they are blessed. 2
17 come, curse this people for me.' 6
23: 7 Come, curse Jacob for me, and come, denounce Israel!' 2
8 How can I curse whom God has not cursed? 6
8 How can I curse whom God has not cursed? 6
11 I took you to curse my enemies, and behold 6
13 then curse them for me from there. 6
25 Neither curse them at all, nor bless them at all. 6
27 that you may curse them for me from there. 6
24: 9 cursed be every one who curses you. 2
9 be every one who curses you. 2
10 I called you to curse my enemies, and behold 6
Deu 11:26 I set before you this day a blessing and a curse 8
28 curse, if you do not obey the commandments 8
29 set the blessing . . and the curse on Mount Ebal. 8
23: 4 hired against you Balaam . . to curse you. 7
5 LORD your God turned the curse into a blessing 8
27:13 stand upon Mount Ebal for the curse: Reuben, Gad 8
15 'Cursed be the man who makes a graven or molten 2
16 'Cursed . . who dishonors his father or his mother.' 2
17 'Cursed . . who removes his neighbor's landmark.' 2
18 'Cursed be he who misleads a blind man on the road.' 2
19 'Cursed be he who perverts the justice due 2
20 'Cursed be he who lies with his father's wife 2
21 'Cursed be he who lies with any kind of beast.' 2
22 'Cursed be he who lies with his sister, whether 2
23 'Cursed be he who lies with his mother-in-law.' 2
24 'Cursed be he who slays his neighbor in secret.' 2
25 'Cursed be he who takes a bribe to slay an innocent 2
26 'Cursed be he who does not confirm the words 2
28:15 these curses shall come upon you and overtake 8
16 Cursed shall you be in the city, and cursed 2
16 in the city, and cursed shall you be in the field. 2
17 Cursed . . basket and your kneading-trough. 2
18 Cursed shall be the fruit of your body 2
19 Cursed shall you be when you come in, and cursed 2
19 come in, and cursed shall you be when you go out. 2
20 send upon you curses, confusion, and frustration 5
45 these curses shall come upon you and pursue you 8
29:20 curses written in this book would settle upon 1
21 accordance with all the curses of the covenant 1
27 bringing . . all the curses written in this book; 8
30: 1 come upon you, the blessing and the curse 8
7 LORD . . will put all these curses upon your foes 1
19 set before you life and death, blessing and curse; 8
Jos 6:26 Cursed before the LORD be the man that rises up 2
8:34 the words of the law, the blessing and the curse 8
9:23 you are cursed, and some of you shall . . be slaves 2
24: 9 and invited Balaam the son of Be'or to curse you 7
Jdg 5:23 Curse Meroz, says the angel of the LORD 2
23 Curse Meroz . . curse bitterly its inhabitants 2
9:57 and upon them came the curse of Jotham the son 8
21:18 sworn, "Cursed be he who gives a wife to Benjamin. 2
1Sm 14:24 Cursed be the man who eats food until . . evening 2
28 'Cursed be the man who eats food this day.' 2
17:43 And the Philistine cursed David by his gods. 7
26:19 but if it is men, may they be cursed before the LORD 2
2Sm 16: 5 and as he came he cursed continually. 7
7 Shim'e-i said as he cursed, "Begone, begone, you man 7
9 Why should this dead dog curse my lord the king? 7
10 If he is cursing because the LORD has said to him 7
10 because the LORD has said to him, 'Curse David,' 7
11 Let him alone, and let him curse; 7
12 repay me with good for this cursing of me today. 8
13 Shim'e-i went along . . and cursed as he went 7
19:21 to death . . because he cursed the LORD's anointed? 7
1Kg 2: 8 Shim'e-i . . who cursed me with a grievous curse 7
8 Shim'e-i . . who cursed me with a grievous curse 8
21:10 saying, 'You have cursed God and the king.' 3
13 the people, saying, "Naboth cursed God 3
2Kg 2:24 he cursed them in the name of the LORD. 7
22:19 they should become a desolation and a curse 8
2Ch 34:24 all the curses that are written in the book 1
Neh 10:29 enter into a curse and an oath to walk in God's law 1
13: 2 hired Balaam against them to curse them 7
2 yet our God turned the curse into a blessing. 8
25 I contended with them and cursed them and beat 7
Job 1: 5 sons have sinned, and cursed God in their hearts. 3
11 he will curse thee to thy face. 3
2: 5 he will curse thee to thy face. 3
9 hold fast your integrity? Curse God, and die. 3
3: 1 opened his mouth and cursed the day of his birth. 7
8 Let those curse it who curse the day 6
8 Let those curse it who curse the day 2
5: 3 but suddenly I cursed his dwelling. 6
24:18 their portion is cursed in the land; 7
31:30 my mouth sin by asking for his life with a curse 1
Ps 10: 3 man greedy for gain curses and renounces the LORD. 3
7 His mouth is filled with cursing and deceit 1
37:22 those cursed by him shall be cut off. 7
59:12 For the cursing and lies which they utter 1
62: 4 They bless . . but inwardly they curse. Selah 7
109:17 He loved to curse; let curses come on him! 8
17 He loved to curse; let curses come on him! •
18 He clothed himself with cursing as his coat 8
28 Let them curse, but do thou bless! 7
Prv 3:33 LORD'S curse is on the house of the wicked 5
11:26 The people curse him who holds back grain 6
20:20 If one curses his father or his mother 7
24:24 wicked, "You are innocent," will be cursed 6
26: 2 curse that is causeless does not alight. 8
27:14 early in the morning, will be counted as cursing. 8
28:27 but he who hides his eyes will get many a curse. 5
29:24 hears the curse, but discloses nothing. 1
30:10 lest he curse you, and you be held guilty. 7
11 There are those who curse their fathers 7
Ecc 7:21 lest you hear your servant cursing you; 7
22 many times you have yourself cursed others. 7
10:20 Even in your thought, do not curse the king 7
20 nor in your bedchamber curse the rich; 7
Isa 8:21 enraged and will curse their king and their God 7
24: 6 Therefore a curse devours the earth 1
65:15 You shall leave your name to my chosen for a curse 9
Jer 11: 3 Cursed be the man who does not heed the words 2
15:10 nor have I borrowed, yet all of them curse me. 7
17: 5 says the LORD: "Cursed is the man who trusts in man 2
20:14 Cursed be the day on which I was born! 2
15 Cursed be the man who brought the news 2
23:10 because of the curse the land mourns 1
24: 9 to be a reproach, a byword, a taunt, and a curse 8
25:18 a desolation and a waste, a hissing and a curse 8
26: 6 I will make this city a curse for all the nations 8
29:18 to be a curse, a terror, a hissing, and a reproach 1
22 Because of them this curse shall be used by all 8
42:18 You shall become an execration, a horror, a curse 8
44: 8 that you may be cut off and become a curse 8
12 they shall become an execration, a horror, a curse 8
22 and a waste and a curse, without inhabitant 8
48:10 Cursed is he who does the work of the LORD 2
10 and cursed is he who keeps back his sword 2
49:13 shall become a horror, a taunt, a waste, and a curse; 8
Lam 3:65 thy curse will be on them. 10
Dan 9:11 curse and oath which are written in the law 1
Zec 5: 3 Then he said to me, "This is the curse that goes out 1
14:11 inhabited, for there shall be no more curse; 4
Mal 1:14 Cursed be the cheat who has a male in his flock 2
2: 2 then I will send the curse upon you 5
2 I will curse your blessings; 2
2 indeed I have already cursed them 2
3: 9 You are cursed with a curse, for you are robbing me; 2
9 You are cursed with a curse, for you are robbing me; 5
4: 6 lest I come and smite the land with a curse. 4
Mat 25:41 Depart from me, you cursed, into the eternal fire 17
Mrk 11:21 The fig tree which you cursed has withered. 17
Lke 6:28 bless those who curse you 17
Rom 3:14 Their mouth is full of curses and bitterness. 12
12:14 who persecute you; bless and do not curse them. 17
1Co 12: 3 Jesus be cursed! 11
Gal 3:10 all who rely on works of the law are under a curse; 16
10 it is written, "Cursed be every one 15
13 Christ redeemed us from the curse of the law 16
13 having become a curse for us–for it is written 16
13 Cursed be every one who hangs on a tree"– 15
Heb 6: 8 it is worthless and near to being cursed 16
Jas 3: 9 and with it we curse men 17
10 From the same mouth come blessing and cursing. 16
Rev 16: 9 and they cursed the name of God 13
11 cursed the God of heaven for their pain and sores 13
21 till men cursed God for the plague of the hail 13
Tob 13:12 Cursed are all who hate you 15
Sir 3: 9 a mother's curse uproots their foundations. 16
16 whoever angers his mother is cursed by the Lord. 19
4: 5 nor give a man occasion to curse you; 17
21:27 When an ungodly man curses his adversary 18
27 he curses his own soul. 18
23:14 you will curse the day of your birth. 18
26 She will leave her memory for a curse 16
28:13 Curse the whisperer and deceiver 17
29: 6 he will repay him with curses and reproaches 16
33:12 some of them he cursed and brought low 17
34:24 When one prays and another curses 18
41: 9 When you are born, you are born to a curse 16
9 when you die, a curse is your lot. 16
10 so the ungodly go from curse to destruction. 16
Bar 1:20 the curse which the Lord declared through Moses 12
3: 8 to be reproached and cursed and punished 12
LJr 1:66 For they can neither curse nor bless kings; 17
4Mc 2:19 saying, "Cursed be their anger"? 15
151 1: 6 the Philistine, and he cursed me by his idols. 14

curse *See also* bring, invoke, name.

cursed woman 1. ארר

2Kg 9:34 See now to this cursed woman, and bury her; 1

cursing *See* byword.

curtain 1. דֹּק 2. יְרִיעָה 3. καταπέτασμα 4. παρακάλυμμα

Exd 26: 1 with ten curtains of fine twined linen and blue 2
2 The length of each curtain shall be 28 cubits 2
2 and the breadth of each curtain four cubits; 2
2 all the curtains shall have one measure. 2
3 Five curtains shall be coupled to one another; 2
3 the other five curtains shall be coupled to one 2
4 loops of blue on the edge of the outmost curtain 2
4 make loops on the edge of the outmost curtain 2
5 50 loops you shall make on the one curtain 2
5 loops you shall make on the edge of the curtain 2
6 shall . . couple the curtains one to the other 2
7 You shall also make curtains of goats' hair 2
7 eleven curtains shall you make. 2
8 The length of each curtain shall be 30 cubits 2
8 the breadth of each curtain four cubits; 2
8 the eleven curtains shall have the same measure. 2
9 you shall couple five curtains by themselves 2
9 couple . . six curtains by themselves 2
9 the sixth curtain you shall double over 2
10 shall make 50 loops on the edge of the curtain 2
10 shall make 50 loops on the edge of the curtain 2
12 the part that remains of the curtains of the tent 2
12 the half curtain that remains, shall hang over 2
13 what remains in the length of the curtains 2
36: 8 workmen made the tabernacle with ten curtains; 2
9 The length of each curtain was 28 cubits 2
9 and the breadth of each curtain four cubits; 2
9 all the curtains had the same measure. 2
10 he coupled five curtains to one another 2
10 other five curtains he coupled to one another. 2
11 of blue on the edge of the outmost curtain 2
11 he made them on the edge of the outmost curtain 2
12 he made 50 loops on the one curtain 2
12 edge of the curtain that was in the second set; 2
13 he . . coupled the curtains one to the other 2
14 He also made curtains of goats' hair for a tent 2
14 over the tabernacle; he made eleven curtains. 2
15 The length of each curtain was 30 cubits 2
15 the breadth of each curtain four cubits; 2

15 the eleven curtains had the same measure. 2
16 He coupled five curtains by themselves 2
16 He coupled . . six curtains by themselves. 2
17 50 loops on the edge of the outmost curtain 2
17 on the edge of the other connecting curtain. 2
Num 4:25 they shall carry the curtains of the tabernacle 2
Sng 1: 5 I am very dark . . like the curtains of Solomon. 2
Isa 40:22 who stretches out the heavens like a curtain 1
54: 2 and let the curtains of your habitations be 2
Jer 4:20 my tents are destroyed, my curtains in a moment. 2
10:20 to spread my tent again, and to set up my curtains. 2
49:29 be taken, their curtains and all their goods; 2
Hab 3: 7 the curtains of the land of Mid'ian did tremble. 2
Mat 27:51 behold, the curtain of the temple was torn in two 3
Mrk 15:38 the curtain of the temple was torn in two 3
Lke 23:45 the curtain of the temple was torn in two. 3
Heb 6:19 enters into the inner shrine behind the curtain 3
9: 3 Behind the second curtain stood a tent 3
10:20 through the curtain, that is, through his flesh 3
Wis 17: 3 behind a dark curtain of forgetfulness 4
1Mc 1:22 the bowls, the golden censers, the curtain 3
4:51 and hung up the curtains 3

white curtain 1. חור
Est 1: 6 white cotton curtains and blue hangings 1

cushion 1. *προσκεφάλαιον*
Mrk 4:38 he was in the stern, asleep on the cushion 1

custodian 1. *παιδαγωγός*
Gal 3:24 the law was our custodian until Christ came 1
25 we are no longer under a custodian; 1

custody 1. יָד 2. מְצוּדָה 3. מִשְׁמָר 4. *ἀσφάλεια* 5. *τήρησις*
Gen 40: 3 he put them in custody in the house of the captain 3
4 and they continued for some time in custody. 3
7 officers who were with him in custody in his 3
41:10 and put me and the chief baker in custody 3
Lev 24:12 they put him in custody, till the will of the LORD 3
Num15:34 They put him in custody 3
Est 2: 3 harem . . under custody of Hegai the king's eunuch 1
8 maidens were gathered . . in custody of Hegai 1
8 Esther also was . . and put in custody of Hegai 1
14 to the second harem in custody of Sha-ash'gaz 1
Ezk 19: 9 they brought him into custody 2
Act 4: 3 put them in custody until the morrow 5
3Mc 5: 5 arranged for their continued custody 4

custody *See also* keep, take.

custom 1. חֹק 2. חֻקָּה 3. מִשְׁפָּט 4. בְּלוֹ (A) 5. *δικαίωμα* 6. *ἐθίζω* 7. *ἐθισμός* 8. *ἔθος* 9. *ἔθω ποιεῖν* 10. *εἴωθα* 11. *θεσμός* 12. *νόμιμος* 13. *νόμος* 14. *συνήθεια*
Lev 18:30 to practice any of these abominable customs 2
20:23 you shall not walk in the customs of the nation 2
Jdg 11:39 it became a custom in Israel . . to lament 1
Rut 4: 7 Now this was the custom in former times in Israel 5
1Sm 2:13 The custom of the priests with the people was 3
27:11 Such was his custom all the while he dwelt 3
1Kg 18:28 and cut themselves after their custom 3
2Kg 11:14 standing by the pillar, according to the custom 3
17: 8 and walked in the customs of the nations 2
8 walked . . in the customs which the kings *
19 Judah also . . walked in the customs which Israel 2
Ezr 4:13 not pay tribute, custom, or toll 4
20 to whom tribute, custom, and toll were paid. 4
7:24 not be lawful to impose tribute, custom, or toll 4
Jer 10: 3 for the customs of the peoples are false. 2
Mrk 10: 1 again, as his custom was, he taught them. 10
Lke 1: 9 according to the custom of the priesthood 8
2:27 to do for him according to the custom of the law 6
42 they went up according to custom; 8
4:16 he went to the synagogue, as his custom was 10
22:39 went, as was his custom, to the Mount of Olives; 8
Joh 18:39 you have a custom that I should release one man 14
19:40 as is the burial custom of the Jews. 8
Act 6:14 change the customs which Moses delivered to us. 8
15: 1 you are circumcised according to the custom of Moses 8
16:21 advocate customs which it is not lawful for us 8
17: 2 Paul went in, as was his custom 10
21:21 not to circumcise . . or observe the customs. 8
25:16 was not the custom of the Romans to give up any one 8
26: 3 you are especially familiar with all customs 8
28:17 against the people or the customs of our fathers 8
Wis 14:16 the ungodly custom, grown strong with time 8
23 hold frenzied revels with strange customs 11
1Mc 1:14 a gymnasium . . according to Gentile custom 12
42 that each should give up his customs. 12
44 to follow customs strange to the land 12
10:89 such as it is the custom to give 8
2Mc 4:11 and introduced new customs contrary to the law. 7
6: 9 who did not choose to change over to Greek customs *
11:24 our father's change to Greek customs *
24 and ask that their own customs be allowed them. 12
25 according to the customs of their ancestors. 8
12:38 they purified themselves according to the custom 7
13: 4 by the method which is the custom in that place. 8
14:30 meeting him more rudely than had been his custom 6
3Mc 3: 2 the observance of their customs. 12
7: 5 a cruelty more savage than that of Scythian custom 13
4Mc 1:12 as my custom is 9
18: 5 to abandon their ancestral customs 8

customary 1. *καθήκω* 2. *νομίζω*
2Mc 14: 4 the customary olive branches from the temple. 2
31 were offering the customary sacrifices 1

cut 1. בֶּצַע 2. בקע 3. גדד 4. גלח 5. חטב 6. חֲרֹשֶׁת 7. כרת 8. נתח 9. פסל 10. קצץ 11. גזר (A) 12. *γλύφω* 13. *ἐκκόπτω* 14. *κατανύσσομαι* 15. *κείρω* 16. *κόπτω* 17. *τέμνω*
Gen 22: 3 and he cut the wood for the burnt offering 2
Exd 29:17 Then you shall cut the ram into pieces, and wash 8
31: 5 in cutting stones for setting, 6
34: 1 The LORD said to Moses, "Cut two tables of stone 9
4 Moses cut two tables of stone like the first; 9
35:33 in cutting stones for setting, 6
39: 3 gold leaf was hammered and cut into threads 10
Lev 22:24 testicles . . torn or cut, you shall not offer 7
Deu 14: 1 shall not cut yourselves or make any baldness 3
19: 5 into the forest with his neighbor to cut wood 5
2Sm 14:26 for at the end of every year he used to cut it; 4
26 when it was heavy on him, he cut it 4
1Kg 5: 6 command that cedars of Lebanon be cut for me; 7
6 who knows how to cut timber like the Sido'nians. 7
18:28 and cut themselves after their custom 3
2Ch 2: 8 your servants know how to cut timber in Lebanon. 7
10 give for your servants, the hewers who cut timber 7
16 will cut whatever timber you need from Lebanon 7
Ps 129: 4 righteous; he has cut the cords of the wicked. 10
144:12 corner pillars cut for the structure of a palace; 5
Jer 9:26 in the desert that cut the corners of their hair; 10
16: 6 or cut himself or make himself bald for them. 3
25:23 Buz, and all who cut the corners of their hair; 10
34:18 I will make like the calf which they cut in two 7
49:32 those who cut the corners of their hair 10
51:13 your end has come, the thread of your life is cut. 1
Ezk 16: 4 day you were born your navel string was not cut 7
Dan 2:45 stone was cut from a mountain by no human hand 11
Mat 21: 8 others cut branches from the trees 16
Mrk 11: 8 others spread leafy branches which they had cut 16
Act 2:37 when they heard this they were cut to the heart 14
18:18 At Cen'chre-ae he cut his hair, for he had a vow. 15
Rom 11:24 cut from what is by nature a wild olive tree 13
Sir 38:27 those who cut the signets of seals 12
4Mc 9:17 Cut my limbs, burn my flesh, and twist my joints. 17

cut asunder 1. גדע
Isa 45: 2 doors of bronze and cut asunder the bars of iron 1

cut away 1. *ἀποκόπτω*
Act 27:32 Then the soldiers cut away the ropes of the boat 1

cut down 1. גדע 2. גזר 3. גרע 4. חטב 5. כסח 6. כרת 7. כתר 8. נכה 9. נקף 10. עלל 11. קטף 12. *δενδροτομέω* 13. *ἐκκόπτω* 14. *καταστρώννυμι* 15. *κόπτω*
Exd 34:13 You shall . . cut down their Ashe'rim 6
Lev 26:30 I will . . cut down your incense altars 6
Num13:23 and cut down from there a branch 6
24 which the men of Israel cut down from there. 6
Deu 19: 5 his hand swings the axe to cut down a tree 6
20:19 may eat of them, but you shall not cut them down. 6
20 not trees for food you may destroy and cut down 6
Jdg 6:25 pull down the altar . . and cut down the Ashe'rah 6
26 the wood of the Ashe'rah which you shall cut down. 6
28 and the Ashe'rah beside it was cut down 7
30 pulled down the altar . . and cut down the Ashe'rah 6
9:48 took an axe . . and cut down a bundle of brushwood 6
49 every one of the people cut down his bundle 6
20:43 Cutting down the Benjaminites, they pursued 15
45 5,000 men of them were cut down in the highways 10
1Sm 11:11 cut down the Ammonites until the heat of the day; 8
1Kg 15:13 Asa cut down her image and burned it at . . Kidron. 6
2Kg 6: 4 when they came to the Jordan, they cut down trees. 2
18: 4 and broke the pillars, and cut down the Ashe'rah. 6
23:14 broke . . the pillars, and cut down the Ashe'rim 6
2Ch 15:16 Asa cut down her image, crushed it, and burned it 6
Job 8:12 While yet in flower and not cut down, they wither 11
14: 7 For there is hope for a tree, if it be cut down 6
Ps 80:16 have burned it with fire, they have cut it down; 5
Isa 9:10 the sycamores have been cut down 1
10:34 He will cut down the thickets of the forest 9
14:12 How you are cut down to the ground 1
22:25 the peg . . will be cut down and fall 1
33:12 like thorns cut down, that are burned in the fire. 5
44:14 He cuts down cedars; or he chooses a holm tree 6
Jer 10: 3 A tree from the forest is cut down 6
22: 7 and they shall cut down your choicest cedars 6
46:23 They shall cut down her forest, says the LORD 6
50:23 hammer of the whole earth is cut down and broken! 1
Lam 2: 3 He has cut down in . . anger all the might of Israel; 1
Ezk 5:11 therefore I will cut you down; 3
6: 6 your incense altars cut down 1
31:12 Foreigners . . will cut it down and leave it. 6
39:10 out of the field or cut down any out of the forests 4
Mat 3:10 good fruit is cut down and thrown into the fire. 13
7:19 tree . . is cut down and thrown into the fire. 13
Lke 3: 9 every tree . . is cut down and thrown into the fire. 13
13: 7 Cut it down; why should it use up the ground?' 13
9 if not, you can cut it down.' 13
1Es 4: 9 if he tells them to cut down, they cut down 13
9 if he tells them to cut down, they cut down 13
Jdt 3: 8 and cut down their sacred groves 13
14: 4 shall pursue them and cut them down as they flee. 14
15: 5 and cut them down as far as Choba 15
1Mc 6: 6 the armies they had cut down; 13
2Mc 5:12 to cut down relentlessly every one they met 15
10:35 and with savage fury cut down every one they met. 15
4Mc 2:14 The fruit trees of the enemy are not cut down 12

cut hair 1. גלח
2Sm 14:26 And when he cut the hair of his head 1

cut in pieces 1. חצב 2. נתח 3. קצץ
Jdg 20: 6 I took my concubine and cut her in pieces, and sent 2
1Sm 11: 7 He took a yoke of oxen, and cut them in pieces 2
1Kg 18:23 choose one bull . . and cut it in pieces and lay it 2
33 and cut the bull in pieces and laid it on the wood. 2
2Kg 24:13 and cut in pieces all the vessels of gold 3
2Ch 28:24 cut in pieces the vessels of the house of God 3
Isa 51: 9 Was it not thou that didst cut Rahab in pieces 1

cut in two 1. בתר 2. גדע 3. *σχίζω*
Gen 15:10 he brought him all these, cut them in two 1
10 other; but he did not cut the birds in two. 1
Ps 107:16 cuts in two the bars of iron. 2
Sus 1:55 and will immediately cut you in two. 3

cut into pieces 1. נתח
Lev 1: 6 flay the burnt offering and cut it into pieces 1
12 he shall cut it into pieces, with its head 1
8:20 when the ram was cut into pieces, Moses burned 1

cut off 1. בצע 2. בצר 3. גדע 4. גזז 5. גזר 6. גרע 7. דמה 8. דמם 9. חצץ 10. כחד 11. כרת 12. מול 13. מלל 14. נקה 15. סור 16. עלה 17. צמת 18. צרת 19. קסם 20. קצב 21. קצה 22. קצץ 23. קרע 24. שבת 25. קצץ (A) 26. *ἀποκόπτω* 27. *ἀποτέμνω* 28. *ἀφαιρέω* 29. *διασχίζω* 30. *ἐκκόπτω* 31. *ἐξαίρω* 32. *καθαιρέω* 33. *τέμνω* 34. abscido
Gen 9:11 all flesh be cut off by the waters of a flood 11
17:14 who is not . . shall be cut off from his people; 11
Exd 4:25 took a flint and cut off her son's foreskin 11
9:15 you would have been cut off from the earth; 10
12:15 that person shall be cut off from Israel. 11
19 person shall be cut off from the congregation 11
30:33 . . shall be cut off from his people.' 11
38 use as perfume shall be cut off from his people. 11
31:14 that soul shall be cut off from among his people. 11
Lev 7:20 person shall be cut off from his people 11
21 that person shall be cut off from his people 11
25 person . . shall be cut off from his people 11
27 that person shall be cut off from his people 11
17: 4 that man shall be cut off from among his people 11
9 that man shall be cut off from his people 11
10 and will cut him off from among his people 11
14 whoever eats it shall be cut off 11
18:29 shall be cut off from among their people 11
19: 8 that person shall be cut off from his people 11
20: 3 and will cut him off from among his people 11
5 and will cut off from among their people 11
6 I . . will cut him off from among his people 11
17 they shall be cut off in the sight of the children 11
18 both . . shall be cut off from among their people 11
22: 3 that person shall be cut off from my presence 11
23:29 on this same day shall be cut off from his people 11
Num 9:13 that person shall be cut off from his people 11
15:30 that person shall be cut off from among 11
31 that person shall be utterly cut off; 11
19:13 that person shall be cut off from Israel; 11
20 that person shall be cut off from the midst 11
Deu 12:29 When the LORD your God cuts off before you 11
19: 1 LORD . . cuts off the nations whose land the LORD 11
23: 1 He . . whose male member is cut off 11
25:12 cut off her hand; your eye shall have no pity. 22
Jos 3:16 those flowing down . . were wholly cut off; 11
4: 7 waters of the Jordan were cut off before the ark 11
7 the waters of the Jordan were cut off. 11
7: 9 surround us, and cut off our name from the earth; 11
23: 4 with all the nations that I have already cut off 11
Jdg 1: 6 and cut off his thumbs and his great toes. 22
7 with their thumbs and their great toes cut off 22
21: 6 One tribe is cut off from Israel this day. 3
Rut 4:10 that the name of the dead may not be cut off 11
1Sm 2: 9 but the wicked shall be cut off in darkness; 8
31 days are coming, when I will cut off your strength 3
33 The man . . whom I shall not cut off from my altar 11
5: 4 his hands were lying cut off upon the threshold; 11
17:46 and I will strike you down, and cut off your head; 15
51 took his sword . . and cut off his head with it. 11
20:15 and do not cut off your loyalty from my house 11
15 When the LORD cuts off every one of the enemies 11

16 name of Jonathan be cut off from . . house of David. 31
24: 4 David arose and stealthily cut off the skirt 11
5 because he had cut off Saul's skirt. 11
11 I cut off the skirt of your robe, and did not kill 11
21 Swear . . that you will not cut off my descendants 11
28: 9 how he has cut off the mediums and the wizards 11
31: 9 they cut off his head, and stripped off his armor 11
2Sm 4:12 they killed them, and cut off their hands and feet 22
7: 9 I have been . . and have cut off all your enemies 18
10: 4 and cut off their garments in the middle 11
20:22 they cut off the head of Sheba the son of Bichri 11
1Kg 9: 7 I will cut off Israel from the land 11
11:16 until he had cut off every male in Edom); 11
13:34 became sin . . so as to cut it off and to destroy it 10
14:10 and will cut off from Jerobo'am every male 11
14 a king . . who shall cut off the house of Jerobo'am 11
18: 4 when Jez'ebel cut off the prophets of the LORD 11
21:21 I . . will cut off from Ahab every male, bond or free 11
2Kg 6: 6 he cut off a stick, and threw it in there 20
9: 8 I will cut off from Ahab every male . . in Israel. 11
10:32 the LORD began to cut off parts of Israel. 21
16:17 King Ahaz cut off the frames of the stands 22
1Ch 17: 8 have cut off all your enemies from before you; 11
19: 4 cut off their garments in the middle 11
2Ch 32:21 cut off all the mighty warriors and commanders 10
Job 4: 7 Or where were the upright cut off? 10
6: 9 that he would let loose his hand and cut me off! 1
21:21 when the number of their months is cut off? 9
22:20 saying, 'Surely our adversaries are cut off 10
24:24 they are cut off like the heads of grain. 13
27: 8 the hope of the godless when God cuts him off 1
33:17 man aside from his deed, and cut off pride from man; •
36:20 night, when peoples are cut off in their place. 16
Ps 12: 3 May the LORD cut off all flattering lips 11
34:16 to cut off the remembrance of them from the earth. 11
37: 9 For the wicked shall be cut off; 11
22 those cursed by him shall be cut off. 11
28 but the children of the wicked shall be cut off. 11
38 the posterity of the wicked shall be cut off. 11
75:10 All the horns of the wicked he will cut off 3
76:12 who cuts off the spirit of princes 2
88: 5 no more, for they are cut off from thy hand. 5
101: 8 cutting off all the evildoers from the city 11
109:13 May his posterity be cut off; 11
15 may his memory be cut off from the earth! 11
118:10 in the name of the LORD I cut them off! 12
11 in the name of the LORD I cut them off! 12
12 in the name of the LORD I cut them off! 12
143:12 in thy steadfast love cut off my enemies 17
Prv 2:22 but the wicked will be cut off from the land 11
10:31 but the perverse tongue will be cut off. 11
23:18 your hope will not be cut off. 11
24:14 if you find it . . your hope will not be cut off. 11
26: 6 cuts off his own feet and drinks violence. 21
Isa 9:14 So the LORD cut off from Israel head and tail 11
10: 7 to destroy, and to cut off nations not a few; 11
11:13 and those who harass Judah shall be cut off; 11
14:22 and will cut off from Babylon name and remnant 11
18: 5 he will cut off the shoots with pruning hooks 11
22:25 and the burden that was upon it will be cut off 11
29:20 all who watch to do evil shall be cut off 11
38:12 he cuts me off from the loom; 1
48: 9 restrain it for you, that I may not cut you off. 11
19 their name would never be cut off or destroyed 11
53: 8 that he was cut off out of the land of the living 5
55:13 an everlasting sign which shall not be cut off. 11
56: 5 an everlasting name which shall not be cut off. 11
Jer 7:28 truth has perished; it is cut off from their lips. 11
29 Cut off your hair and cast it away; 4
9:21 cutting off the children from the streets 11
11:19 let us cut him off from the land of the living 11
36:23 the king would cut them off with a penknife 23
29 and will cut off from it man and beast? 24
44: 7 to cut off from you man and woman, infant and child 11
8 that you may be cut off and become a curse 11
11 set my face against you . . to cut off all Judah. 11
47: 4 to cut off from Tyre and Sidon every helper 11
48: 2 Come, let us cut her off from being a nation! 11
25 The horn of Moab is cut off, and his arm is broken 3
37 For every head is shaved and every beard cut off; 6
50:16 Cut off from Babylon the sower 11
51: 6 Be not cut off in her punishment 8
62 concerning this place that thou wilt cut it off 11
Ezk 14: 8 and cut him off from the midst of my people; 11
13 famine upon it, and cut off from it man and beast 11
17 and I cut off from it man and beast; 11
19 with blood, to cut off from it man and beast; 11
21 and pestilence, to cut off from it man and beast! 11
17: 9 he not pull up its roots and cut off its branches 19
17 cast up and siege walls built to cut off many lives 11
21: 3 will cut off from you both righteous and wicked. 11
4 I will cut off from you both righteous and wicked 11
23:25 They shall cut off your nose and your ears 15
25: 7 I will cut you off from the peoples 11
13 against Edom, and cut off from it man and beast; 11
16 I will cut off the Cher'ethites 11
29: 8 and will cut off from you man and beast; 11
30:15 and cut off the multitude of Thebes. 11
35: 7 I will cut off from it all who come and go. 11
37:11 our hope is lost; we are clean cut off 5
Dan 4:14 'Hew down the tree and cut off its branches 25
9:26 62 weeks, an anointed one shall be cut off 11
Hos 10:15 the king of Israel shall be utterly cut off. 7
Jol 1: 5 for it is cut off from your mouth. 11
9 and the drink offering are cut off from the house 11
16 Is not the food cut off before our eyes 11
Ams 1: 5 cut off the inhabitants from the Valley of Aven 11
8 I will cut off the inhabitants from Ashdod 11
2: 3 I will cut off the ruler from its midst 11
3:14 and the horns of the altar shall be cut off 3
Obd 1: 9 man from Mount Esau will be cut off by slaughter. 11
10 and you shall be cut off for ever. 11
14 at the parting of . . ways to cut off his fugitives; 11
Mic 1:16 Make yourselves bald and cut off your hair 4
5: 9 and all your enemies shall be cut off. 11
10 I will cut off your horses from among you 11
11 I will cut off the cities of your land 11
12 I will cut off sorceries from your hand 11
13 I will cut off your images and your pillars 11
Nah 1:12 they will be cut off and pass away. 4
14 I will cut off the graven image and the molten 11
15 he is utterly cut off. 11
2:13 I will cut off your prey from the earth 11
3:15 the fire devour you, the sword will cut you off. 11
Hab 2:10 shame to your house by cutting off many peoples; 21
3:17 Though . . the flock be cut off from the fold 5
Zep 1: 3 I will cut off mankind from the face of the earth 11
4 I will cut off from this place the remnant of Ba'al 11
11 all who weigh out silver are cut off. 11
3: 6 I have cut off nations; 11
Zec 5: 3 every one who steals shall be cut off henceforth 14
3 every one who swears falsely shall be cut off 14
9:10 I will cut off the chariot from E'phraim 11
10 the battle bow shall be cut off 11
13: 2 I will cut off the names of the idols from the land 11
8 two thirds shall be cut off and perish 11
14: 2 the rest of the people shall not be cut off 11
Mal 2:12 May the LORD cut off from the tents of Jacob 11
Mat 5:30 And if your right hand causes you to sin, cut it off 30
18: 8 or your foot . . cut it off and throw it away 30
26:51 and cut off his ear. 28
Mrk 9:43 if your hand causes you to sin, cut it off 26
45 if your foot causes you to sin, cut it off 26
14:47 struck the slave . . and cut off his ear. 28
Lke 22:50 and cut off his right ear. 28
Joh 18:10 and cut off his right ear 26
26 a kinsman of the man whose ear Peter had cut off 26
Rom 9: 3 that I myself were accursed and cut off from Christ •
11:22 otherwise you too will be cut off. 30
2Es 7:114 unbelief has been cut off 34
Jdt 14:15 with his head cut off and missing. 28
Wis 18:23 and cut off its way to the living. 29
1Mc 7:47 they cut off Nicanor's head 28
11:17 Zabdiel the Arab cut off the head of Alexander 28
2Mc 1:16 and dismembered them and cut off their heads 28
12:35 one . . bore down upon him and cut off his arm 32
15:30 ordered them to cut off Nicanor's head and arm 27
4Mc 10:19 See, here is my tongue; cut it off 33

cut off at rear 1. זנב
Deu 25:18 cut off at your rear all who lagged behind you; 1

cut off hair 1. *κείρω*
1Co 11: 6 then she should cut off her hair 1

cut off hands and feet 1. *ἀκρωτηριάζω*
2Mc 7: 4 and cut off his hands and feet 1

cut off supply 1. *πολιορκέω*
1Es 5:72 cut off their supplies 1

cut open 1. *ἀνατέμνω*
Tob 6: 4 Cut open the fish and take the heart 1

cut out 1. בקע 2. קרע 3. גזר (A) 4. *ἐκτέμνω*
Job 28:10 He cuts out channels in the rocks 1
Jer 22:14 and cuts out windows for it, paneling it with cedar 2
Dan 2:34 As you looked, a stone was cut out by no human hand 3
2Mc 15:33 he cut out the tongue of the ungodly Nicanor 4
4Mc 10:17 Antiochus gave orders to cut out his tongue. 4
21 you are cutting out a tongue 4
18:21 and cut out their tongues 4

cut out the tongue 1. *γλωσσοτομέω*
2Mc 7: 4 that the tongue of their spokesman be cut out 1
4Mc 12:13 to cut out the tongues of men 1

cut sharply 1. אחד
Ezk 21:16 Cut sharply to right and left 1

cut short 1. קצר 2. *ἐπιτέμνω*
Ps 89:45 Thou hast cut short the days of his youth; 1
2Mc 2:32 while cutting short the history itself. 2

cut to pieces 1. בתק 2. *διακόπτω* 3. *κατακόπτω* 4. *κατατιτρώσκω*
Ezk 16:40 and cut you to pieces with their swords. 1
2Mc 1:13 they were cut to pieces in the temple of Nanea 3
10:30 they were thrown into disorder and cut to pieces. 2
4Mc 6: 6 his sides were being cut to pieces. 4

cut up 1. פלח
2Kg 4:39 and came and cut them up into the pot of pottage 1

cutter 1. גָּזָם
Jol 2:25 the destroyer, and the cutter, my great army 1

cutting 1. שֶׂרֶט 2. שָׂרֶטֶת
Lev 19:28 You shall not make any cuttings in your flesh 1
21: 5 nor make any cuttings in their flesh 2

cutting *See also* locust, make.

cycle 1. *κύκλος* 2. *τροχός*
Jas 3: 6 setting on fire the cycle of nature 2
Wis 7:19 the cycles of the year 1

cymbal 1. מְצִלְתַּיִם 2. צֶלְצְלִים 3. *κύμβαλον*
2Sm 6: 5 and tambourines and castanets and cymbals. 2
1Ch 13: 8 making merry . . with . . cymbals and trumpets. 1
15:16 on harps and lyres and cymbals, to raise sounds 1
19 The singers . . were to sound bronze cymbals; 1
28 the sound of the horn, trumpets, and cymbals 1
16: 5 Asaph was to sound the cymbals 1
42 had trumpets and cymbals for the music 1
25: 1 prophesy with . . with harps, and with cymbals. 1
6 with cymbals, harps, and lyres for the service 1
2Ch 5:12 arrayed in fine linen, with cymbals, harps 1
13 song was raised, with trumpets and cymbals 1
29:25 Levites . . with cymbals, harps, and lyres 1
Ezr 3:10 Levites, the sons of Asaph, with cymbals 1
Neh 12:27 celebrate . . with cymbals, harps, and lyres. 1
Ps 150: 5 Praise him with sounding cymbals; 2
5 praise him with loud clashing cymbals! 2
1Co 13: 1 I am a noisy gong or a clanging cymbal. 3
1Es 5:59 the Levites, the sons of Asaph, with cymbals 3
Jdt 16: 2 sing to my Lord with cymbals 3
1Mc 4:54 with songs and harps and lutes and cymbals. 3
13:51 with harps and cymbals 3

cypress 1. בְּרוֹשׁ 2. עֵץ בְּרוֹשִׁים 3. *κυπάρισσος*
1Kg 5: 8 in the matter of cedar and cypress timber. 1
10 the timber of cedar and cypress that he desired 1
6:15 he covered the floor . . with boards of cypress. 1
34 and two doors of cypress wood; 1
9:11 supplied . . cedar and cypress timber and gold 1
2Kg 19:23 its tallest cedars, its choicest cypresses; 1
2Ch 2: 8 cedar, cypress, and algum timber from Lebanon 1
3: 5 nave he lined with cypress, and covered it 2
Isa 14: 8 The cypresses rejoice at you . . saying 1
37:24 its tallest cedars, its choicest cypresses; 1
41:19 I will set in the desert the cypress 1
55:13 Instead of the thorn shall come up the cypress; 1
60:13 come to you, the cypress, the plane, and the pine 1
Hos 14: 8 I am like an evergreen cypress 1
Zec 11: 2 Wail, O cypress, for the cedar has fallen 1
Sir 24:13 like a cypress on the heights of Hermon. 3
50:10 like a cypress towering in the clouds. 3

D

dagger 1. ἐγχειρίδιον
LJr 1:15 It has a dagger in its right hand, and has an axe 1

daily 1. יוֹם 2. יוֹם בְּיוֹם 3. יוֹם יוֹם 4. לַיּוֹם 5. תָּמִיד
6. ἐπιούσιος 7. ἐφήμερος 8. καθ' ἡμέραν
9. καθημερινός 10. cotidie
Exd 5:13 Complete your work, your daily task 2
19 by no means lessen your daily number of bricks. 2
16: 5 it will be twice as much as they gather daily. 1
Num28:24 same way you shall offer daily, for seven days 4
Ezr 3: 4 offered the daily burnt offerings by number 2
Neh 12:47 gave the daily portions for the singers •
Ps 68:19 Blessed be the Lord, who daily bears us up; 3
109:19 like a belt with which he daily girds himself! 5
Prv 8:30 daily his delight, rejoicing before him always 3
34 who listens to me, watching daily at my gates 3
Isa 58: 2 Yet they seek me daily and delight to know my ways 3
Jer 37:21 and a loaf of bread was given him daily 4
52:34 given him by the king according to his daily need 1
Ezk 43:25 you shall provide daily a goat for a sin offering; 4
45:23 and a he-goat daily for a sin offering. 4
46:13 for a burnt offering to the LORD daily; 4
Dan 1: 5 assigned them a daily portion of the rich food •
Mat 6:11 Give us this day our daily bread; 6
Lke 9:23 take up his cross daily and follow me. 8
11: 3 Give us each day our daily bread; 6
19:47 he was teaching daily in the temple 8
Act 3: 2 whom they laid daily at that gate of the temple 8
6: 1 neglected in the daily distribution. 9
16: 5 they increased in numbers daily. 8
17:11 examining the scriptures daily 8
19: 9 and argued daily in the hall of Tyran'nus. 8
2Co 11:28 there is the daily pressure upon me 8
Heb 7:27 He has no need . . to offer sacrifices daily 8
10:11 every priest stands daily at his service 8
Jas 2:15 If a brother or sister is . . in lack of daily food 7
1Es 6:30 for daily use as the priests . . may indicate 8
2Es 4:23 about those things which we daily experience 10
Jdt 12:15 received . . for her daily use 9
1Mc 6:57 We daily grow weaker, our food supply is scant 8
4Mc 13:22 this common nurture and daily companionship 8

daintily 1. עִם עֵדֶן 2. ὡς τρυφερεύομαι
2Sm 1:24 over Saul, who clothed you daintily in scarlet 1
AEs 15: 3 leaning daintily on one 2

dainty 1. מַנְעַמִּים 2. מַעֲדָן 3. תַּאֲוָה 4. λιπαρός
5. τρύφημα
Gen 49:20 be rich, and he shall yield royal dainties. 2
Job 33:20 loathes bread, and his appetite dainty food. 3
Ps 141: 4 let me not eat of their dainties! 1
Lam 4: 5 who feasted on dainties perish in the street; 2
Rev 18:14 thy dainties and thy splendor are lost to thee 4
Sir 31: 3 when he rests he fills himself with his dainties. 5

dam 1. אֵם
Exd 22:30 seven days it shall be with its dam; 1

damage 1. חֲבָל (A) 2. βλάβη 3. κακοποιέω
4. πληγή
Ezr 4:22 why should damage grow to the hurt of the king? 1
1Es 6:33 to hinder or damage that house of the Lord 3
Wis 11:19 not only could their damage exterminate men 2
1Mc 7:22 did great damage in Israel. 4
14:36 do great damage to its purity. 4
15:29 you have done great damage in the land 4
35 they were causing great damage among the people 4

dance 1. דוץ 2. חגג 3. חול 4. כרר 5. מָחוֹל
6. מְחוֹלָה 7. רקד 8. ὀρχέομαι 9. παίζω 10. χορεία
11. χορός 12. scirtor
Exd 15:20 went out after her with timbrels and dancing. 6
32:19 and saw the calf and the dancing, Moses' anger 6
Jdg 11:34 out to meet him with timbrels and with dances; 6
21:21 the daughters . . come out to dance in the dances 3
21 the daughters . . come out to dance in the dances 6
1Sm 18: 6 the women came out . . singing and dancing, to meet 6
21:11 Did they not sing to one another of him in dances 6
29: 5 David, of whom they sing to one another in dances 6
30:16 they were . . eating and drinking and dancing 2
2Sm 6:14 David danced before the LORD with all his might; 4
16 saw . . David leaping and dancing before the LORD; 4
1Ch 15:29 saw King David dancing and making merry; 7
Job 21:11 like a flock, and their children dance. 7
41:22 terror dances before him. 1
Ps 30:11 Thou hast turned for me my mourning into dancing; 5
149: 3 Let them praise his name with dancing 5
150: 4 Praise him with timbrel and dance; 5
Ecc 3: 4 a time to mourn, and a time to dance; 7
Sng 6:13 look upon the . . as upon a dance before two armies? 6
Isa 13:21 ostriches . . dwell, and there satyrs will dance. 7
Jer 31: 4 shall go forth in the dance of the merrymakers. 5
13 Then shall the maidens rejoice in the dance 5
Lam 5:15 our dancing has been turned to mourning. 5
Mat 11:17 'We piped to you, and you did not dance 8
14: 6 the daughter of Hero'di-as danced 8
Mrk 6:22 For when Hero'di-as' daughter came in and danced 8
Lke 7:32 We piped to you, and you did not dance 8
15:25 he heard music and dancing. 11
1Co 10: 7 sat down to eat and drink and rose up to dance. 9
2Es 6:21 and these shall live and dance. 12
Jdt 3: 7 welcomed him with garlands and dances 11
15:12 some of them performed a dance for her 11
13 she went before all the people in the dance 10

dance *See also* move.

dancer 1. חול
Jdg 21:23 number, from the dancers whom they carried off; 1
Ps 87: 7 Singers and dancers alike say, "All my springs 1

dandle 1. טפח 2. שׁעע
Isa 66:12 carried upon her hip, and dandled upon her knees. 2
Lam 2:22 those . . I dandled and reared my enemy destroyed. 1

danger 1. דָּבָר 2. רָעָה 3. κινδυνεύω 4. κίνδυνος
5. periclitor 6. periculum
1Sm 20:21 it is safe for you and there is no danger. 1
Prv 22: 3 A prudent man sees danger and hides himself; 2
27:12 A prudent man sees danger and hides himself; 2
Lke 8:23 they were filling with water, and were in danger. 3
Act 19:27 danger not only . . disrepute 3
40 we are in danger of being charged with rioting today 3
2Co 11:26 on frequent journeys, in danger from rivers 4
26 in danger from rivers, danger from robbers 4
26 danger from robbers, danger from my own people 4
26 danger from Gentiles, danger in the city 4
26 danger from Gentiles, danger in the city 4
26 danger in the city, danger in the wilderness 4
26 danger at sea, danger from false brethren; 4
26 danger at sea, danger from false brethren; 4
2Es 7: 9 he passes through the danger set before him? 6
12 they are few and evil, full of dangers 6
89 and withstood danger every hour 6
9: 8 survive the dangers that have been predicted 6
12:18 it shall be in danger of falling 5
13:19 they shall see great dangers and much distress 6
Tob 4: 4 she faced many dangers for you 4
AEs 14: 4 for my danger is in my hand. 4
Wis 14: 4 showing that thou canst save from every danger •
18: 9 the same things, both blessings and dangers 4
Sir 3:26 whoever loves danger will perish by it. 4
34:12 I have often been in danger of death 4
43:24 Those who sail the sea tell of its dangers 4
1Mc 11:23 put himself in danger 4
14:29 exposed themselves to danger 4
2Mc 1:11 Having been saved by God out of grave dangers 4
15:17 the sanctuary and the temple were in danger. 3
3Mc 5:41 in constant danger of being plundered. 3
6:26 accepted willingly the worst of human dangers 4
4Mc 3:15 David . . considered it an altogether fearful danger 4
13:15 the danger of eternal torment lying before those 4

dangerous 1. ἐπικίνδυνον 2. ἐπισφαλής
Act 27: 9 the voyage was already dangerous 2
3Mc 5:33 suffered an unexpected and dangerous threat 1

dapple 1. בָּרֹד
Zec 6: 3 the fourth chariot dappled gray horses. 1
6 and the dappled ones go toward the south country. 1

dare 1. ערב 2. κατατολμάω 3. τολμάω 4. audeo
Gen 49: 9 as a lioness; who dares rouse him up? •
Job 41:10 No one is so fierce that he dares to stir him up. •
Jer 30:21 for who would dare of himself to approach me? 1
Mat 22:46 did any one dare to ask him any more questions. 3
Mrk 12:34 after that no one dared to ask him any question. 3
Lke 20:40 For they no longer dared to ask him any question. 3
Joh 21:12 none of the disciples dared ask him, "Who are you? 3
Act 5:13 None of the rest dared join them 3
7:32 Moses trembled and did not dare to look. 3
Rom 5: 7 perhaps for a good man one will dare even to die. 3
1Co 6: 1 does he dare go to law before the unrighteous 3
2Co 11:21 whatever any one dares to boast 3
21 I also dare to boast of that. 3
2Es 13: 8 all . . were much afraid, yet dared to fight. 4
2Mc 4: 2 He dared to designate as a plotter 3
5:15 Antiochus dared to enter the most holy temple 2

daric 1. דַּרְכְּמוֹן
1Ch 29: 7 5,000 talents and 10,000 darics of gold 1
Ezr 2:69 gave to . . the work 61,000 darics of gold 1
8:27 twenty bowls of gold worth 1,000 darics 1
Neh 7:70 governor gave to the treasury 1,000 darics of gold 1
71 gave into the treasury . . 20,000 darics of gold 1
72 rest of the people gave was 20,000 darics of gold 1

daring 1. εὐτολμία 2. θράσος
Jdt 16:10 the Medes were daunted at her daring. 2
2Mc 13:18 having had a taste of the daring of the Jews 1

daring *See also* act.

dark 1. אֹפֶל 2. חשך 3. חָשֵׁךְ 4. חֲשֵׁכָה 5. לֹא אוֹר
6. מַחְשָׁךְ 7. עֲלָטָה 8. צלל 9. קדר 10. שָׁחֹר
11. αὐχμηρός 12. ἀφεγγής 13. σκοτεινός 14. σκοτία
15. obscurus
Gen 15:17 When the sun had gone down and it was dark 7
Jos 2: 5 when the gate was to be closed, at dark, the men went 3
Neh 13:19 When it began to be dark at the gates of Jerusalem 8
Job 3: 9 Let the stars of its dawn be dark; 2
6:16 which are dark with ice, and where the snow hides 9
12:25 They grope in the dark without light; 3
18: 6 The light is dark in his tent 2
24:14 The murderer rises in the dark 5
16 In the dark they dig through houses; 3
Ps 11: 2 to shoot in the dark at the upright in heart; 1
18:11 his canopy thick clouds dark with water. 4
35: 6 Let their way be dark and slippery 3
139:12 even the darkness is not dark to thee 2
Sng 1: 5 I am very dark, but comely, O daughters 10
Isa 13:10 the sun will be dark at its rising 2
29:15 whose deeds are in the dark, and who say 6
Ezk 8:12 in the dark, every man in his room of pictures? 3
12: 6 upon your shoulder, and carry it out in the dark; 7
7 I went forth in the dark, carrying my outfit 7
12 lift his baggage upon his shoulder in the dark 7
30:18 At Tehaph'nehes the day shall be dark 2
Mat 10:27 What I tell you in the dark, utter in the light 14
Lke 11:36 whole body is full of light, having no part dark 13
12: 3 have said in the dark shall be heard in the light 14
Joh 6:17 It was now dark 14
20: 1 early, while it was still dark 14
2Pe 1:19 as to a lamp shining in a dark place 11

2Es 12:42 and like a lamp in a dark place 15
Wis 17: 3 behind a dark curtain of forgetfulness 12
dark *See also* make, region, saying, speech.

dark place 1. מַחְשָׁךְ
Ps 74:20 the dark places of the land are full 1

darken 1. חָשַׁךְ 2. חשך 3. קדר 4. σκοτίζω 5. σκοτόω
Exd 10:15 covered . . so that the land was darkened 2
Job 22:11 your light is darkened, so that you cannot see 1
38: 2 Who is this that darkens counsel by words 2
Ps 69:23 Let their eyes be darkened 2
Ecc 12: 2 before the sun and the light . . are darkened 2
Isa 5:30 and the light is darkened by its clouds. 2
Jol 2:10 The sun and the moon are darkened 3
3:15 The sun and the moon are darkened 3
Ams 5: 8 into the morning, and darkens the day into night 2
8: 9 and darken the earth in broad daylight. 2
Mat 24:29 the sun will be darkened 4
Mrk 13:24 after that tribulation, the sun will be darkened 4
Rom 1:21 and their senseless minds were darkened. 4
11:10 their eyes be darkened so that they cannot see 4
Eph 4:18 they are darkened in their understanding 5
Rev 8:12 so that a third of their light was darkened; 4
9: 2 the sun and the air were darkened with the smoke 5
Sir 25:17 darkens her face like that of a bear. 5

darkness 1. אֹפֶל 2. אֲפֵלָה 3. חֹשֶׁךְ 4. חֲשֵׁכָה 5. מַאְפֵּל 6. מַחְשָׁךְ 7. עֵיפָה 8. תְּעֻפָה 9. חָשׁוֹךְ (A) 10. γνόφος 11. σκοτεινός 12. σκοτία 13. σκοτίζω 14. σκότος 15. σκοτόω 16. tenebrae
Gen 1: 2 and darkness was upon the face of the deep 3
4 and God separated the light from the darkness 3
5 the light Day, and the darkness he called Night 3
18 to separate the light from the darkness. 3
15:12 and lo, a dread and great darkness fell upon him. 4
Exd 10:21 toward heaven that there may be darkness over 3
21 over the land of Egypt, a darkness to be felt. 3
22 there was thick darkness in all the land of Egypt 3
14:20 And there was the cloud and the darkness; 3
Deu 4:11 mountain . . wrapped in darkness, cloud, and gloom. 3
5:23 heard the voice out of the midst of the darkness 3
28:29 grope at noonday, as the blind grope in darkness 2
Jos 24: 7 he put darkness between you and the Egyptians 5
1Sm 2: 9 but the wicked shall be cut off in darkness; 3
2Sm 22:12 He made darkness around him his canopy 3
29 Yea, thou art . . and my God lightens my darkness. 3
Job 3: 4 Let that day be darkness! May God above not seek it 3
5:14 They meet with darkness in the daytime 3
10:22 gloom and chaos, where light is as darkness. 1
11:17 its darkness will be like the morning. 8
12:22 He uncovers the deeps out of darkness 3
15:22 not believe that he will return out of darkness 3
23 He knows that a day of darkness is ready at his hand; 3
30 he will not escape from darkness; 3
17:12 The light,' they say, 'is near to the darkness.' 3
13 Sheol as my house, if I spread my couch in darkness 3
18:18 He is thrust from light into darkness 3
19: 8 he has set darkness upon my paths. 3
20:26 Utter darkness is laid up for his treasures; 3
23:17 for I am hemmed in by darkness, and thick darkness 3
26:10 at the boundary between light and darkness. 3
28: 3 Men put an end to darkness 3
29: 3 by his light I walked through darkness; 3
30:26 when I waited for light, darkness came. 1
37:19 we cannot draw up our case because of darkness. 3
38:19 where is the place of darkness 3
Ps 18:11 He made darkness his covering around him 3
28 the LORD my God lightens my darkness. 3
82: 5 nor understanding, they walk about in darkness; 4
88:12 Are thy wonders known in the darkness 3
18 my companions are in darkness. 6
91: 6 nor the pestilence that stalks in darkness 1
104:20 Thou makest darkness, and it is night 3
105:28 He sent darkness, and made the land dark; 3
107:10 Some sat in darkness and in gloom, prisoners 3
14 he brought them out of darkness and gloom 3
112: 4 Light rises in the darkness for the upright; 3
139:11 If I say, "Let only darkness cover me 3
12 even the darkness is not dark to thee 3
12 for darkness is as light with thee. 4
143: 3 has made me sit in darkness like those long dead. 6
Prv 2:13 to walk in the ways of darkness 3
7: 9 at the time of night and darkness. 2
20:20 his lamp will be put out in utter darkness. 3
Ecc 2:13 wisdom excels folly as light excels darkness. 3
14 but the fool walks in darkness; 3
5:17 and spent all his days in darkness and grief 3
6: 4 For it comes into vanity and goes into darkness 3
4 and in darkness its name is covered; 3
11: 8 remember that the days of darkness will be many. 3
Isa 5:20 put darkness for light and light for darkness 3
20 put darkness for light and light for darkness 3
30 behold, darkness and distress; 3
8:22 distress and darkness, the gloom of anguish; 4
9: 2 who walked in darkness have seen a great light; 3
29:18 out of . . darkness the eyes of the blind shall see. 3
42: 7 from the prison those who sit in darkness. 3
16 I will turn the darkness before them into light 6
45: 3 I will give you the treasures of darkness 3
7 I form light and create darkness 3
19 I did not speak in secret, in a land of darkness; 3
47: 5 go into darkness, O daughter of the Chalde'ans 3
49: 9 to those who are in darkness, 'Appear.' 3
50:10 servant, who walks in darkness and has no light 3
58:10 then shall your light rise in the darkness 3
59: 9 we look for light, and behold darkness 3
60: 2 For behold, darkness shall cover the earth 3
Jer 23:12 be to them like slippery paths in the darkness 2
Lam 3: 2 and brought me into darkness without any light; 3
6 he has made me dwell in darkness like the dead 6
Ezk 32: 8 and put darkness upon your land, says the Lord 3
Dan 2:22 he knows what is in the darkness 9
Jol 2: 2 a day of darkness and gloom, a day of clouds 3
31 The sun shall be turned to darkness 3
Ams 4:13 who makes the morning darkness, and treads 7
5:18 day of the LORD? It is darkness, and not light; 3
20 Is not the day of the LORD darkness, and not light 3
Mic 3: 6 and darkness to you, without divination. 3
7: 8 I sit in darkness, the LORD will be a light to me. 3
Nah 1: 8 and will pursue his enemies into darkness. 3
Zep 1:15 a day of darkness and gloom, a day of clouds 3
Mat 4:16 the people who sat in darkness have seen a great 14
6:23 will be full of darkness. If then the light in you 11
23 darkness. If then the light in you is darkness 14
23 you is darkness, how great is the darkness! 14
8:12 kingdom will be thrown into the outer darkness; 14
22:13 and cast him into the outer darkness; 14
25:30 into the outer darkness 14
27:45 there was darkness over all the land 14
Mrk 15:33 there was darkness over the whole land 14
Lke 1:79 to give light to those who sit in darkness 14
11:35 be careful lest the light in you be darkness. 14
22:53 this is your hour, and the power of darkness. 14
23:44 darkness over the whole land until the ninth hour 14
Joh 1: 5 The light shines in the darkness 12
5 and the darkness has not overcome it. 12
3:19 and men loved darkness rather than light 14
8:12 he who follows me will not walk in darkness 12
12:35 lest the darkness overtake you 12
35 he who walks in the darkness 12
46 may not remain in darkness. 12
Act 2:20 the sun shall be turned into darkness 14
13:11 Immediately mist and darkness fell upon him 14
26:18 they may turn from darkness to light 14
Rom 2:19 a light to those who are in darkness 14
13:12 Let us then cast off the works of darkness 14
1Co 4: 5 the things now hidden in darkness 14
2Co 4: 6 the God who said, "Let light shine out of darkness 14
6:14 what fellowship has light with darkness? 14
Eph 5: 8 for once you were darkness, but now you are light 14
11 Take no part in the unfruitful works of darkness 14
6:12 against the world rulers of this present darkness 14
Col 1:13 has delivered us from the dominion of darkness 14
1Th 5: 4 you are not in darkness, brethren 14
5 we are not of the night or of darkness. 14
Heb 12:18 a blazing fire, and darkness, and gloom 10
1Pe 2: 9 called you out of darkness into . . light. 14
2Pe 2:17 the nether gloom of darkness has been reserved. 14
1Jn 1: 5 God is light and in him is no darkness at all. 12
6 while we walk in darkness 14
2: 8 because the darkness is passing away 12
9 and hates his brother is in the darkness still. 12
11 he who hates his brother is in the darkness 12
11 is in the darkness and walks in the darkness 12
11 because the darkness has blinded his eyes. 12
Jde 1:13 gloom of darkness has been reserved for ever. 14
Rev 16:10 the beast, and its kingdom was in darkness; 15
1Es 4:24 he faces lions, and he walks in darkness 14
2Es 6:39 and darkness and silence embraced everything; 16
7:40 water or air, or darkness or evening or morning 16
125 but our faces shall be blacker than darkness? 16
14:20 For the world lies in darkness 16
Tob 4:10 keeps you from entering the darkness; 14
14:10 how he brought him from light into darkness 14
10 as he himself went down into the darkness. 14
AEs 11: 8 behold, a day of darkness and gloom 14
Wis 17: 2 they themselves lay as captives of darkness 14
17 with one chain of darkness they all were bound. 14
21 an image of the darkness 14
21 still heavier than darkness 14
18: 4 deprived of light and imprisoned in darkness 14
19:17 surrounded by yawning darkness 14
Sir 23:18 Darkness surrounds me, and the walls hide me 14
LJr 1:71 like a dead body cast out in the darkness. 14
Aza 1:48 Bless the Lord, light and darkness 14
2Mc 3:27 deep darkness came over him 14
3Mc 4:10 with their eyes in total darkness 13
darkness *See also* bring, full.

deep darkness 1. אֲפֵלָה 2. עֲרָפֶל 3. צַלְמָוֶת
Job 3: 5 Let gloom and deep darkness claim it. 3
10:21 not return, to the land of gloom and deep darkness 3
12:22 and brings deep darkness to light. 3
16:16 on my eyelids is deep darkness; 3
22:13 Can he judge through the deep darkness? 2
24:17 For deep darkness is morning to all of them; 3
17 are friends with the terrors of deep darkness. 3
28: 3 the ore in gloom and deep darkness. 3
34:22 There is no gloom or deep darkness 3
38:17 or have you seen the gates of deep darkness? 3
Ps 44:19 and covered us with deep darkness. 3
Prv 4:19 The way of the wicked is like deep darkness; 1
Isa 9: 2 those who dwelt in a land of deep darkness 3
Jer 2: 6 in a land of drought and deep darkness 3
13:16 turns it into gloom and makes it deep darkness. 2
Ams 5: 8 and turns deep darkness into the morning 3

thick darkness 1. אֹפֶל 2. אֲפֵלָה 3. מַאְפֵּלְיָה 4. עֲרָפֶל 5. γνόφος
Exd 20:21 drew near to the thick darkness where God was. 4
Deu 5:22 midst of the fire, the cloud, and the thick darkness 4
2Sm 22:10 and came down; thick darkness was under his feet. 4
1Kg 8:12 said that he would dwell in thick darkness. 4
2Ch 6: 1 said that he would dwell in thick darkness. 4
Job 3: 6 That night-let thick darkness seize it! 1
23:17 by darkness, and thick darkness covers my face. 1
38: 9 thick darkness its swaddling band 4
Ps 18: 9 thick darkness was under his feet. 4
97: 2 Clouds and thick darkness are round about him; 4
Isa 8:22 they will be thrust into thick darkness. 2
60: 2 cover the earth, and thick darkness the peoples; 4
Jer 2:31 Have I been . . to Israel . . a land of thick darkness? 3
Ezk 34:12 scattered on a day of clouds and thick darkness. 4
Jol 2: 2 a day of clouds and thick darkness! 4
Zep 1:15 a day of clouds and thick darkness 4
Sir 45: 5 led him into the thick darkness 5

darling 1. אֶחָד 2. שַׁעֲשֻׁעִים
Sng 6: 9 My dove . . is only one, the darling of her mother 1
Jer 31:20 Is E'phraim my dear son? Is he my darling child? 2

dart 1. מַסָּע 2. שֶׁבֶט 3. βέλος 4. κέντρον
2Sm 18:14 he took three darts in his hand, and thrust them 2
Job 41:26 not avail; nor the spear, the dart, or the javelin. 1
Eph 6:16 can quench all the flaming darts of the evil one. 3
4Mc 14:19 as though with an iron dart sting 4

dart (2) 1. רוץ 2. רצא
Ezk 1:14 And the living creatures darted to and fro 2
Nah 2: 4 gleam like torches, they dart like lightning. 1

dash 1. נגף 2. נפץ 3. ῥήγνυμι 4. τίθημι
Ps 91:12 lest you dash your foot against a stone. 1
137: 9 little ones and dashes them against the rock! 2
Jer 13:14 And I will dash them one against another 2
Jdt 16: 5 dash my infants to the ground 4
Wis 4:19 he will dash them speechless to the ground 3

dash against 1. conlido
2Es 15:35 They shall dash against one another 1

dash down 1. ῥήσσω
Mrk 9:18 wherever it seizes him, it dashes him down 1

dash in pieces 1. נפץ 2. רטש 3. שבר
Deu 7: 5 you shall . . dash in pieces their pillars 3
12: 3 you shall . . dash in pieces their pillars 3
2Kg 8:12 and dash in pieces their little ones 2
Ps 2: 9 dash them in pieces like a potter's vessel. 1
Isa 13:16 Their infants will be dashed in pieces 2
Hos 10:14 mothers were dashed in pieces with . . children. 2
13:16 their little ones shall be dashed in pieces 2
Nah 3:10 her little ones were dashed in pieces 2

dash out 1. ἐκπηδάω
Sus 1:39 and he opened the doors and dashed out. 1

dash to pieces 1. בקע 2. פצץ
2Ch 25:12 they were all dashed to pieces. 1
Job 16:12 he seized me by the neck and dashed me to pieces; 2

dash to the ground 1. ἐδαφίζω
Lke 19:44 and dash you to the ground 1

date set 1. προθεσμία
Gal 4: 2 until the date set by the father. 1

daub 1. חמר 2. טוח
Exd 2: 3 a basket . . and daubed it with bitumen and pitch; 1
Ezk 13:10 a wall, these prophets daub it with whitewash; 2
11 say to those who daub it with whitewash 2
12 Where is the daubing with which you daubed it? 2
14 I will break down the wall that you have daubed 2
15 and upon those who have daubed it with whitewash; 2
15 The wall is no more, nor those who daubed it 2
22:28 prophets have daubed for them with whitewash 2

daubing 1. טִיחַ
Ezk 13:12 Where is the daubing with which you daubed it? 1

daughter 1. בַּת 2. θυγάτηρ 3. νεᾶνις 4. παιδίον 5. filia

Gen 5: 4 and he had other sons and daughters. 1
7 and had other sons and daughters. 1
10 and had other sons and daughters. 1
13 Kenan . . had other sons and daughters. 1
16 Ma-hal'alel . . had other sons and daughters. 1
19 and had other sons and daughters. 1
22 Enoch . . had other sons and daughters. 1
26 and had other sons and daughters. 1
30 Lamech . . had other sons and daughters. 1
6: 1 of the ground, and daughters were born to them 1
2 the sons of God saw that the daughters of men 1
4 the sons of God came in to the daughters of men 1
11:11 Shem lived . . and had other sons and daughters. 1
13 Arpach'shad . . had other sons and daughters. 1
15 Shelah . . had other sons and daughters. 1
17 Eber lived . . and had other sons and daughters. 1
19 Peleg . . had other sons and daughters. 1
21 Re'u lived . . and had other sons and daughters. 1
23 years, and had other sons and daughters. 1
25 and had other sons and daughters. 1
29 Milcah, the daughter of Haran 1
19: 8 Behold, I have two daughters who have not known 1
12 Sons-in-law, sons, daughters, or any one 1
14 his sons-in-law, who were to marry his daughters 1
15 take your wife and your two daughters 1
16 seized . . his wife and his two daughters 1
30 Lot . . dwelt in the hills with his two daughters 1
30 he dwelt in a cave with his two daughters. 1
36 Thus both the daughters of Lot were with child 1
20:12 the daughter of my father but not the daughter 1
12 my father but not the daughter of my mother; 1
24: 3 a wife . . from the daughters of the Canaanites 1
13 the daughters of the men of the city are coming 1
23 said, "Tell me whose daughter you are. 1
24 She said to him, "I am the daughter of Bethu'el 1
37 my son from the daughters of the Canaanites 1
47 Then I asked her, 'Whose daughter are you?' 1
47 She said, The daughter of Bethu'el, Nahor's son 1
48 the right way to take the daughter of my master's 1
25:20 Rebekah, the daughter of Bethu'el the Aramean 1
26:34 Judith the daughter of Be-e'ri the Hittite 1
34 Esau . . took . . Bas'emath the daughter of Elon 1
28: 2 take as wife from there one of the daughters 1
9 the daughter of Ish'mael Abraham's son 1
29: 6 Rachel his daughter is coming with the sheep! 1
10 Now when Jacob saw Rachel the daughter of Laban 1
16 Now Laban had two daughters; 1
18 seven years for your younger daughter Rachel. 1
23 in the evening he took his daughter Leah 1
24 Laban gave his maid Zilpah to his daughter Leah 1
28 then Laban gave him his daughter Rachel to wife. 1
29 Bilhah to his daughter Rachel to be her maid. 1
30:21 Afterwards she bore a daughter 1
31:26 cheated me, and carried away my daughters 1
28 to kiss my sons and my daughters farewell? 1
31 you would take your daughters . . by force 1
41 fourteen years for your two daughters 1
43 The daughters are my daughters, the children are 1
43 The daughters are my daughters, the children are 1
43 But what can I do this day to these my daughters 1
50 If you ill-treat my daughters 1
50 or if you take wives besides my daughters 1
55 kissed . . his daughters and blessed them; 1
34: 1 Dinah the daughter of Leah, whom she had borne 1
3 his soul was drawn to Dinah the daughter of Jacob; 1
5 heard that he had defiled his daughter Dinah; 1
7 folly in Israel by lying with Jacob's daughter 1
8 my son Shechem longs for your daughter; 1
9 Make marriages with us; give your daughters 1
9 and take our daughters for yourselves. 1
16 Then we will give our daughters to you 1
16 we will take your daughters to ourselves 1
17 we will take our daughter, and we will be gone. 1
19 because he had delight in Jacob's daughter. 1
21 let us take their daughters in marriage 1
21 marriage, and let us give them our daughters. 1
36: 2 the Canaanites: Adah the daughter of Elon 1
2 Oholiba'mah the daughter of Anah 1
3 Bas'emath, Ish'mael's daughter, the sister 1
6 took his wives, his sons, his daughters, and all 1
14 sons of Oholiba'mah the daughter of Anah 1
18 born of Oholiba'mah the daughter of Anah 1
25 Dishon and Oholiba'mah the daughter of Anah. 1
39 name was Mehet'abel, the daughter of Matred 1
39 the daughter of Matred, daughter of Me'zahab. 1
37:35 All his sons and all his daughters rose up 1
38: 2 Judah saw the daughter of a certain Canaanite 1
12 of time the wife of Judah, Shua's daughter, died; 1
41:45 in marriage As'enath, the daughter of Poti'phera 1
50 As'enath, the daughter of Poti'phera priest of On 1
46: 7 his daughters, and his sons' daughters; all his 1
7 his daughters, and his sons' daughters; all his 1
15 to Jacob . . together with his daughter Dinah; 1
15 his sons and his daughters numbered 33 1
18 Laban gave to Leah his daughter; 1
20 whom As'enath, the daughter of Poti'phera 1
25 Bilhah, whom Laban gave to Rachel his daughter 1
Exd 1:16 but if it is a daughter, she shall live. 1
22 but you shall let every daughter live. 1
2: 1 a man . . went and took to wife a daughter of Levi. 1
5 Now the daughter of Pharaoh came down to bathe 1
7 his sister said to Pharaoh's daughter, "Shall I go 1
8 Pharaoh's daughter said to her, "Go. 1
9 Pharaoh's daughter said to her, "Take this child 1
10 and she brought him to Pharaoh's daughter 1
16 Now the priest of Mid'ian had seven daughters; 1
20 He said to his daughters, "And where is he? 1
21 the man, and he gave Moses his daughter Zippo'rah. 1
3:22 put them on your sons and on your daughters; 1
6:23 took . . Eli'sheba, the daughter of Ammin'adab 1
25 took to wife one of the daughters of Pu'ti-el; 1
10: 9 with our sons and daughters and with our flocks 1
20:10 you, or your son, or your daughter, your manservant 1
21: 4 a wife and she bears him sons or daughters 1
7 When a man sells his daughter as a slave 1
9 his son, he shall deal with her as a daughter. 1
31 If it gores a man's son or daughter, he shall be 1
32: 2 of your wives, your sons, and your daughters 1
34:16 you take of their daughters for your sons 1
16 their daughters play the harlot after their 1
Lev 10:14 you and your sons and your daughters with you 1
12: 6 purifying . . whether for a son or for a daughter 1
18: 9 your sister, the daughter of your father 1
9 of your father or the daughter of your mother 1
10 not uncover the nakedness of your son's daughter 1
10 your son's daughter or of your daughter's daughter 1
10 nakedness . . of your daughter's daughter 1
11 the nakedness of your father's wife's daughter 1
17 the nakedness of a woman and of her daughter 1
17 you shall not take her son's daughter 1
17 take . . her daughter's daughter to uncover her 1
17 take . . her daughter's daughter to uncover her 1
19:29 Do not profane your daughter 1
20:17 If a man takes his sister, a daughter of his father 1
17 takes . . a daughter of his mother, and sees her 1
21: 2 his father, his son, his daughter, his brother 1
9 the daughter of any priest, if she profanes 1
22:12 If a priest's daughter is married to an outsider 1
13 if a priest's daughter is a widow or divorced 1
24:11 name was Shelo'mith, the daughter of Dibri, 1
26:29 you shall eat the flesh of your daughters 1
Num18:11 given . . to your sons and daughters with you 1
19 I give to you, and to your sons and daughters 1
21:29 has made his sons . . and his daughters captives 1
25: 1 play the harlot with the daughters of Moab. 1
15 Cozbi the daughter of Zur, who was the head 1
18 Cozbi, the daughter of the prince of Mid'ian 1
26:33 Zeloph'ehad . . had no sons, but daughters 1
33 names of the daughters of Zeloph'ehad were 1
46 the name of the daughter of Asher was Serah. 1
59 Amram's wife was Joch'ebed the daughter of Levi 1
27: 1 Then drew near the daughters of Zeloph'ehad 1
1 names of his daughters were: Mahlah, Noah, Hoglah 1
7 The daughters of Zeloph'ehad are right; 1
8 cause his inheritance to pass to his daughter. 1
9 if he has no daughter, then you shall give 1
30:16 statutes . . between a father and his daughter 1
36: 2 inheritance of Zeloph'ehad . . to his daughters. 1
6 commands concerning the daughters of Zeloph'ehad 1
8 every daughter who possesses an inheritance 1
10 daughters of Zeloph'ehad did as the LORD 1
11 daughters of Zeloph'ehad, were married to sons 1
Deu 5:14 not do any work, you, or your son, or your daughter 1
7: 3 not . . giving your daughters to their sons 1
3 not . . taking their daughters for your sons. 1
12:12 rejoice . . you and your sons and your daughters 1
18 eat . . you and your son and your daughter 1
31 burn their sons and their daughters in the fire 1
13: 6 If . . your son, or your daughter, . . , entices you 1
16:11 rejoice . . you and your son and your daughter 1
14 rejoice . . you and your son and your daughter 1
18:10 any one who burns his son or his daughter 1
22:16 I gave my daughter to this man to wife 1
17 I did not find in your daughter the tokens 1
17 these are the tokens of my daughter's virginity.' 1
23:17 no cult prostitute of the daughters of Israel 1
27:22 sister, whether the daughter of his father 1
22 sister, whether the . . daughter of his mother.' 1
28:32 Your sons and your daughters shall be given 1
41 You shall beget sons and daughters 1
53 eat the . . flesh of your sons and daughters 1
56 will grudge to . . her son and to her daughter 1
32:19 provocation of his sons and his daughters. 1
Jos 7:24 took Achan . . and his sons and daughters 1
15:16 to him will I give Achsah my daughter as wife. 1
17 and he gave him Achsah his daughter as wife. 1
17: 3 Now Zeloph'ehad . . had no sons, but only daughters; 1
3 these are the names of his daughters: Mahlah, Noah 1
6 daughters of Manas'seh received an inheritance 1
Jdg 1:12 I will give him Achsah my daughter as wife. 1
13 and he gave him Achsah his daughter as wife. 1
3: 6 they took their daughters to themselves for wives 1
6 for wives, and their own daughters they gave 1
11:34 his daughter came out to meet him with timbrels 1
34 beside her he had neither son nor daughter. 1
35 Alas, my daughter! you have brought me very low 1
40 the daughters of Israel went . . to lament 1
40 year by year to lament the daughter of Jephthah 1
12: 9 30 sons; and 30 daughters he gave in marriage 1
9 and 30 daughters he brought in from outside 1
14: 1 he saw one of the daughters of the Philistines. 1
2 I saw one of the daughters of the Philistines 1
3 a woman among the daughters of your kinsmen 1
19:24 here are my virgin daughter and his concubine; 1
21: 1 No one of us shall give his daughter in marriage 1
7 will not give them any of our daughters for wives? 1
18 Yet we cannot give them wives of our daughters. 1
21 if the daughters of Shiloh come out to dance 1
21 each man his wife from the daughters of Shiloh 1
Rut 1:11 Turn back, my daughters, why will you go with me? 1
12 Turn back, my daughters, go your way, 1
13 No, my daughters, for it is exceedingly bitter 1
2: 2 And she said to her, "Go, my daughter. 1
8 Now, listen, my daughter, do not go to glean 1
22 It is well, my daughter, that you go out with his 1
3: 1 My daughter, should I not seek a home for you 1
10 "May you be blessed by the LORD, my daughter; 1
11 And now, my daughter, do not fear 1
16 she said, "How did you fare, my daughter? 1
18 Wait, my daughter, until you learn how the matter 1
1Sm 1: 4 to Penin'nah . . and to all her sons and daughters; 1
2:21 and bore three sons and two daughters. 1
8:13 He will take your daughters to be perfumers 1
14:49 and the names of his two daughters were these 1
50 Saul's wife was Ahin'o-am the daughter of Ahim'aaz. 1
17:25 the king . . will give him his daughter 1
18:17 Here is my elder daughter Merab; I will give her 1
19 Merab, Saul's daughter, should have been given 1
20 Now Saul's daughter Michal loved David; 1
27 And Saul gave him his daughter Michal for a wife. 1
25:44 Saul had given Michal his daughter . . to Palti 1
30: 3 wives and sons and daughters taken captive. 1
6 were bitter . . each for his sons and daughters. 1
19 whether small or great, sons or daughters, spoil 1
2Sm 1:20 lest the daughters of the Philistines rejoice 1
20 lest the daughters of the uncircumcised exult. 1
24 Ye daughters of Israel, weep over Saul 1
3: 3 Ab'salom the son of Ma'acah the daughter of Talmai 1
7 whose name was Rizpah, the daughter of Ai'ah; 1
13 first bring Michal, Saul's daughter, when you come 1
5:13 and more sons and daughters were born to David. 1
6:16 Michal the daughter of Saul looked out 1
20 Michal the daughter of Saul came . . to meet David 1
23 And Michal the daughter of Saul had no child 1
11: 3 Is not this Bathshe'ba, the daughter of Eli'am 1
12: 3 lie in his bosom, and it was like a daughter to him. 1
13:18 thus were the virgin daughters of the king clad 1
14:27 three sons, and one daughter whose name was Tamar; 1
17:25 who had married Ab'igal the daughter of Nahash 1
19: 5 and the lives of your sons and your daughters 1
21: 8 took the two sons of Rizpah the daughter of Ai'ah 1
8 and the five sons of Merab the daughter of Saul 1
10 Then Rizpah the daughter of Ai'ah took sackcloth 1
11 what Rizpah the daughter of Ai'ah . . had done 1
1Kg 3: 1 he took Pharaoh's daughter, and brought her 1
4:11 (he had Taphath the daughter of Solomon as his 1
15 he had taken Bas'emath the daughter of Solomon 1
7: 8 for Pharaoh's daughter whom he had taken 1
9:16 Pharaoh . . had given it as dowry to his daughter 1
24 Pharaoh's daughter went up from the city of David 1
11: 1 Solomon loved . . the daughter of Pharaoh 1
15: 2 name was Ma'acah the daughter of Abish'alom. 1
10 name was Ma'acah the daughter of Abish'alom. 1
16:31 he took for wife Jez'ebel the daughter of Ethba'al 1
22:42 mother's name was Azu'bah the daughter of Shilhi. 1
2Kg 8:18 for the daughter of Ahab was his wife. 1
9:34 and bury her; for she is a king's daughter. 1
11: 2 Jehosh'eba, the daughter of King Joram, sister 1
14: 9 saying, 'Give your daughter to my son for a wife'; 1
15:33 mother's name was Jeru'sha the daughter of Zadok. 1
17:17 burned their sons and . . daughters as offerings 1
18: 2 mother's name was Abi the daughter of Zechari'ah. 1
19:21 she scorns you–the virgin daughter of Zion; 1
21 she wags her head . . –the daughter of Jerusalem. 1
21:19 name was Meshul'lemeth the daughter of Haruz 1
22: 1 mother's name was Jedi'dah the daughter of Adai'ah 1
23:10 burn his son or his daughter as an offering 1
~~31 was~~ Hamu'tal the daughter of Jeremiah of Libnah. 1
36 name was Zebi'dah the daughter of Pedai'ah 1
24: 8 name was Nehush'ta the daughter of Elna'than 1
18 was Hamu'tal the daughter of Jeremiah of Libnah. 1
1Ch 1:50 his wife's name Mehet'abel the daughter of Matred 1
50 daughter of Matred, the daughter of Me'zahab. 1
2:21 Hezron went in to the daughter of Machir 1
34 Now Sheshan had no sons, only daughters; 1
35 Sheshan gave his daughter in marriage to Jarha 1
49 and the daughter of Caleb was Achsah. 1
3: 2 Ma'acah, the daughter of Talmai, king of Geshur; 1
5 Bath-shu'a, the daughter of Am'mi-el; 1
4:17 Bith'i-ah, the daughter of Pharaoh 1
27 Shim'e-i had sixteen sons and six daughters; 1
7:15 and Zeloph'ehad had daughters. 1
24 His daughter was She'erah 1
14: 3 and David begot more sons and daughters. 1

15:29 Michal the daughter of Saul looked out 1
23:22 Elea'zar died having no sons, but only daughters; 1
25: 5 had given Heman . . sons and three daughters. 1
2Ch 2:14 the son of a woman of the daughters of Dan 1
8:11 Solomon brought Pharaoh's daughter up 1
11:18 took as wife Ma'halath the daughter of Jer'imoth 1
18 Ab'ihail the daughter of Eli'ab the son of Jesse; 1
20 After her he took Ma'acah the daughter of Ab'salom 1
21 Rehobo'am loved Ma'acah the daughter of Ab'salom 1
21 had 28 sons and 60 daughters); 1
13: 2 Micai'ah the daughter of U'riel of Gib'e-ah. 1
21 had 22 sons and sixteen daughters. 1
20:31 Azu'bah the daughter of Shili. 1
21: 6 for the daughter of Ahab was his wife. 1
22:11 Jeho-shab'e-ath, the daughter of the king 1
11 Jeho-shab'e-ath, the daughter of King Jeho'ram 1
24: 3 for him two wives, and he had sons and daughters. 1
25:18 Give your daughter to my son for a wife 1
27: 1 name was Jeru'shah the daughter of Zadok. 1
28: 8 200,000 of their kinsfolk . . and daughters; 1
29: 1 Abi'jah the daughter of Zechari'ah. 1
9 our sons and our daughters . . are in captivity 1
31:18 wives, their sons, and their daughters 1
Ezr 2:61 wife from the daughters of Barzil'lai 1
9: 2 taken some of their daughters to be wives 1
12 Therefore give not your daughters to their sons 1
12 neither take their daughters for your sons 1
Neh 3:12 Shallum . . repaired, he and his daughters. 1
4:14 fight for your . . daughters, your wives 1
5: 2 With our sons and our daughters, we are many; 1
5 forcing our sons and our daughters to be slaves 1
5 some of our daughters . . already been enslaved; 1
6:18 Jehoha'nan had taken the daughter of Meshul'lam 1
7:63 wife of the daughters of Barzil'lai 1
10:28 wives, their sons, their daughters, all who have 1
30 not give our daughters to the peoples of the land 1
30 not give . . or take their daughters for our sons; 1
13:25 You shall not give your daughters to their sons 1
25 not . . take their daughters for your sons 1
Est 2: 7 brought up . . Esther, the daughter of his uncle 1
7 Mor'decai adopted her as his own daughter. 1
15 Esther the daughter of Ab'ihail the uncle 1
15 Mor'decai, who had adopted her as his own daughter 1
9:29 Queen Esther, the daughter of Ab'ihail 1
Job 1: 2 were born to him seven sons and three daughters. 1
13 his sons and daughters were eating and drinking 1
18 Your sons and daughters were eating 1
42:13 He had also seven sons and three daughters. 1
15 there were no women so fair as Job's daughters; 1
Ps 9:14 in the gates of the daughter of Zion I may rejoice 1
45: 9 daughters of kings are among your ladies 1
10 Hear, O daughter, consider, and incline your ear; 1
48:11 Let the daughters of Judah rejoice 1
97: 8 daughters of Judah rejoice 1
106:37 They sacrificed their sons and their daughters 1
38 poured out . . blood of their sons and daughters 1
137: 8 O daughter of Babylon, you devastator! 1
144:12 our daughters like corner pillars cut 1
Prv 30:15 The leech has two daughters; "Give, give," they cry. 1
Ecc 12: 4 and all the daughters of song are brought low; 1
Sng 1: 5 dark, but comely, O daughters of Jerusalem 1
2: 7 I adjure you, O daughters of Jerusalem 1
3: 5 I adjure you, O daughters of Jerusalem . . stir not 1
10 wrought within by the daughters of Jerusalem. 1
11 Go forth, O daughters of Zion, and behold 1
5: 8 I adjure you, O daughters of Jerusalem 1
16 This is my beloved . . O daughters of Jerusalem. 1
8: 4 I adjure you, O daughters of Jerusalem 1
Isa 1: 8 And the daughter of Zion is left like a booth 1
3:16 Because the daughters of Zion are haughty 1
17 smite . . the heads of the daughters of Zion 1
4: 4 washed away the filth of the daughters of Zion 1
10:30 Cry aloud, O daughter of Gallim! 1
32 shake . . fist at the mount of the daughter of Zion 1
15: 2 daughter of Dibon has gone up to the high places •
16: 1 lambs . . to the mount of the daughter of Zion. 1
2 the daughters of Moab at the fords of the Arnon. 1
22: 4 the destruction of the daughter of my people. 1
23:10 Overflow your land . . O daughter of Tarshish; 1
12 O oppressed virgin daughter of Sidon; 1
32: 9 you complacent daughters, give ear to my speech. 1
37:22 she scorns you–the virgin daughter of Zion; 1
22 her head behind you–the daughter of Jerusalem. 1
43: 6 bring . . my daughters from the end of the earth 1
47: 1 and sit in the dust, O virgin daughter of Babylon; 1
1 without a throne, O daughter of the Chalde'ans! 1
5 go into darkness, O daughter of the Chalde'ans 1
49:22 daughters shall be carried on their shoulders. 1
52: 2 bonds from your neck, O captive daughter of Zion. 1
56: 5 a name better than sons and daughters; 1
60: 4 and your daughters shall be carried in the arms. 1
62:11 Say to the daughter of Zion, "Behold 1
Jer 3:24 and their herds, their sons and their daughters. 1
4:11 A hot wind . . toward the daughter of my people 1
31 cry of the daughter of Zion gasping for breath 1
5:17 they shall eat up your sons and your daughters; 1
6: 2 I will destroy, the daughter of Zion. 1
23 for battle, against you, O daughter of Zion! 1
26 O daughter of my people, gird on sackcloth 1
7:31 to burn their sons and their daughters 1
8:19 Hark, the cry of the daughter of my people 1
21 For the wound of the daughter of my people 1
22 the health of the daughter of my people 1
9: 1 weep . . for the slain of the daughter of my people! 1
20 teach to your daughters a lament 1
11:22 sons and their daughters shall die by famine; 1
14:16 their wives, their sons, and their daughters. 1
17 for the virgin daughter of my people is smitten 1
16: 2 nor shall you have sons or daughters 1
3 concerning the sons and daughters who are born 1
19: 9 eat the flesh of their sons and their daughters 1
29: 6 Take wives and have sons and daughters; 1
6 and give your daughters in marriage 1
6 marriage, that they may bear sons and daughters; 1
31:22 How long will you waver, O faithless daughter? 1
32:35 to offer up their sons and daughters to Molech 1
35: 8 ourselves, our wives, our sons, or our daughters 1
41:10 king's daughters and all the people who were left 1
46:11 and take balm, O virgin daughter of Egypt! 1
24 The daughter of Egypt shall be put to shame 1
48:46 and your daughters into captivity. 1
49: 3 for Ai is laid waste! Cry, O daughters of Rabbah! 1
4 you boast of your valleys, O faithless daughter 1
50:42 for battle against you, O daughter of Babylon! 1
51:33 daughter of Babylon is like a threshing floor 1
52: 1 Hamu'tal the daughter of Jeremiah of Libnah. 1
Lam 1: 6 From the daughter of Zion has departed all her 1
15 as in a . . press the virgin daughter of Judah. 1
2: 1 Lord . . has set the daughter of Zion under a cloud! 1
2 broken . . strongholds of the daughter of Judah; 1
4 he has slain . . in the tent of the daughter of Zion; 1
5 he has multiplied in the daughter of Judah 1
8 to lay in ruins the wall of the daughter of Zion; 1
10 elders of the daughter of Zion sit . . in silence; 1
11 the destruction of the daughter of my people 1
13 What can I say for you . . O daughter of Jerusalem? 1
13 that I may comfort you, O virgin daughter of Zion? 1
15 and wag their heads at the daughter of Jerusalem; 1
18 Cry aloud to the Lord! O daughter of Zion! 1
3:48 the destruction of the daughter of my people. 1
4: 3 but the daughter of my people has become cruel 1
6 the chastisement of the daughter of my people 1
10 the destruction of the daughter of my people. 1
21 Rejoice and be glad, O daughter of Edom 1
22 punishment of your iniquity, O daughter of Zion 1
22 your iniquity, O daughter of Edom, he will punish 1
Ezk 13:17 your face against the daughters of your people 1
14:16 they would deliver neither sons nor daughters; 1
18 they would deliver neither sons nor daughters 1
20 they would deliver neither son nor daughter; 1
22 any survivors to lead out sons and daughters 1
16:20 And you took your sons and your daughters 1
27 your enemies, the daughters of the Philistines 1
44 proverb about you, 'Like mother, like daughter. 1
45 You are the daughter of your mother 1
46 who lived with her daughters to the north of you; 1
46 south of you, is Sodom with her daughters. 1
48 Sodom and her daughters have not done as you 1
48 not done as you and your daughters have done. 1
49 she and her daughters had pride, surfeit of food 1
53 both the fortunes of Sodom and her daughters 1
53 and the fortunes of Sama'ria and her daughters 1
55 As for your sisters, Sodom and her daughters 1
55 daughters shall return to their former estate; 1
55 daughters shall return to your former estate. 1
57 an object of reproach for the daughters of Edom 1
57 and for the daughters of the Philistines 1
61 and give them to you as daughters 1
22:11 defiles his sister, his father's daughter. 1
23: 2 there were two women, the daughters of one mother; 1
4 they bore sons and daughters. 1
10 they seized her sons and her daughters; 1
25 They shall seize your sons and your daughters 1
47 they shall slay their sons and their daughters 1
24:21 your sons and your daughters whom you left 1
25 heart's desire, and also their sons and daughters 1
26: 6 her daughters on the mainland shall be slain 1
8 He will slay with the sword your daughters 1
30:18 her daughters shall go into captivity. 1
32:16 the daughters of the nations shall chant it; 1
18 her and the daughters of majestic nations 1
44:25 however, for father or mother, for son or daughter 1
Dan 11: 6 daughter of the king of the south shall come 1
17 give him the daughter of women to destroy 1
Hos 1: 3 he went and took Gomer the daughter of Dibla'im 1
6 She conceived again and bore a daughter. 1
4:13 Therefore your daughters play the harlot 1
14 I will not punish your daughters 1
Jol 2:28 your sons and your daughters shall prophesy 1
3: 8 I will sell your sons and your daughters 1
Ams 7:17 sons and your daughters shall fall by the sword 1
Mic 1:13 were the beginning of sin to the daughter of Zion 1
4: 8 O tower of the flock, hill of the daughter of Zion 1
8 come, the kingdom of the daughter of Jerusalem. 1
10 Writhe and groan, O daughter of Zion 1
13 Arise and thresh, O daughter of Zion 1
7: 6 the daughter rises up against her mother 1
Zep 3:10 my suppliants, the daughter of my dispersed ones 1
14 Sing aloud, O daughter of Zion; shout, O Israel! 1
14 with all your heart, O daughter of Jerusalem! 1
Zec 2: 7 you who dwell with the daughter of Babylon. 1
10 Sing and rejoice, O daughter of Zion; for lo, I come 1
9: 9 Rejoice greatly, O daughter of Zion! 1
9 Shout aloud, O daughter of Jerusalem! 1
Mal 2:11 and has married the daughter of a foreign god. 1
Mat 9:18 saying, "My daughter has just died 2
22 Take heart, daughter; your faith has made you 2
10:35 and a daughter against her mother 2
37 and he who loves son or daughter more than me 2
14: 6 the daughter of Hero'di-as danced 2
15:22 my daughter is severely possessed by a demon. 2
28 And her daughter was healed instantly. 2
21: 5 Tell the daughter of Zion 2
Mrk 5:34 Daughter, your faith has made you well 2
35 Your daughter is dead 2
6:22 For when Hero'di-as' daughter came in and danced 2
7:26 begged him to cast the demon out of her daughter. 2
29 the demon has left your daughter. 2
Lke 1: 5 he had a wife of the daughters of Aaron 2
2:36 a prophetess, Anna, the daughter of Phan'uel 2
8:42 he had an only daughter, about twelve years of age 2
48 Daughter, your faith has made you well 2
49 Your daughter is dead; do not trouble the Teacher 2
12:53 mother against daughter 2
53 daughter against her mother 2
13:16 a daughter of Abraham whom Satan bound 2
23:28 Daughters of Jerusalem, do not weep for me 2
Joh 12:15 Fear not, daughter of Zion 2
Act 2:17 your sons and your daughters shall prophesy 2
7:21 Pharaoh's daughter adopted him 2
21: 9 four unmarried daughters, who prophesied. 2
2Co 6:18 be my sons and daughters, says the Lord Almighty. 2
Heb 11:24 refused to be called the son of Pharaoh's daughter 2
1Es 4:29 the daughter of the illustrious Bartacus 2
5: 1 with their wives and sons and daughters 2
38 Agia, one of the daughters of Barzillai 2
8:70 sons have married the daughters of these people 2
84 do not give your daughters in marriage 2
84 do not take their daughters for your sons 2
2Es 1:28 a mother her daughters or a nurse her children 5
15:47 you have decked out your daughters in harlotry 5
16:33 their daughters shall mourn 5
Tob 3: 7 Sarah, the daughter of Raguel, was reproached 2
9 May we never see a son or daughter of yours! 2
17 to give Sarah the daughter of Raguel in marriage •
17 Sarah the daughter of Raguel came down •
4:13 the sons and daughters of your people 2
6:10 he has an only daughter named Sarah 2
7: 8 his wife Edna and his daughter Sarah wept 2
11 I have given my daughter to seven husbands 4
13 Then he called his daughter Sarah 2
17 the mother comforted her daughter in her tears 2
18 Be brave, my daughter. 2
10:12 He said also to his daughter 2
12 to see your children by my daughter Sarah 2
12 See, I am entrusting my daughter to you 2
11:17 he blessed her, saying, "Welcome, daughter! 2
Jdt 8: 1 the daughter of Merari the son of Ox, son of Joseph 2
9: 4 thou gavest . . their daughters to captivity 2
10:12 She replied, "I am a daughter of the Hebrews 2
12:13 one of the daughters of the Assyrians 2
13:18 Uzziah said to her, "O daughter . . 2
16: 7 Judith the daughter of Merari undid him 2
Wis 9: 7 to be judge over thy sons and daughters. 2
Sir 7:24 Do you have daughters? 2
25 Give a daughter in marriage 2
22: 3 the birth of a daughter is a loss. 2
4 A sensible daughter obtains her husband 2
5 An impudent daughter disgraces father •
26:10 Keep strict watch over a headstrong daughter 2
36:21 one daughter is better than another. 2
42: 9 A daughter keeps her father secretly wakeful 2
11 Keep strict watch over a headstrong daughter 2
Bar 2: 3 we should eat . . another the flesh of his daughter. 2
4:10 the captivity of my sons and daughters 2
14 remember the capture of my sons and daughters 2
16 bereaved the lonely woman of her daughters. 2
Sus 1: 2 a wife named Susanna, the daughter of Hilkiah 2
3 had taught their daughter according to the law 2
29 Send for Susanna, the daughter of Hilkiah 2
48 Have you condemned a daughter of Israel 2
57 have been dealing with the daughters of Israel 2
57 but a daughter of Judah would not endure 2
63 praised God for their daughter Susanna 2
1Mc 9:37 a daughter of one of the great nobles of Canaan 2
10:54 give me now your daughter as my wife 2
57 he and Cleopatra his daughter 2
58 gave him Cleopatra his daughter in marriage 2
11: 9 I will give you in marriage my daughter 2
10 For I now regret that I gave him my daughter 2
12 So he took his daughter away from him 2
3Mc 5:49 parents and children, mothers and daughters 3
4Mc 15:28 as the daughter of God-fearing Abraham 2
18:20 those seven sons of the daughter of Abraham †

little daughter 1. θυγάτριον

Mrk 5:23 My little daughter is at the point of death 1
7:25 a woman, whose little daughter was possessed 1

daughter-in-law 1. כַּלָּה 2. νύμφη

Gen 11:31 his grandson, and Sar'ai his daughter-in-law 1
38:11 Then Judah said to Tamar his daughter-in-law 1
16 he did not know that she was his daughter-in-law. 1
24 Tamar your daughter-in-law has played the harlot 1
Lev 18:15 uncover the nakedness of your daughter-in-law 1
20:12 If a man lies with his daughter-in-law, both of them 1
Rut 1: 6 she started with her daughters-in-law to return 1
7 she set out from . . with her two daughters-in-law 1
8 Na'omi said to her two daughters-in-law, "Go, return 1
22 Ruth the Moabitess her daughter-in-law with her 1
2:22 Na'omi said to Ruth, her daughter-in-law, "It is well 1
4:15 your daughter-in-law who loves you . . has borne 1
1Sm 4:19 Now his daughter-in-law . . was with child 1
1Ch 2: 4 His daughter-in-law Tamar also bore him Perez 1
Ezk 22:11 another lewdly defiles his daughter-in-law; 1
Mic 7: 6 the daughter-in-law against her mother-in-law; 1
Mat 10:35 a daughter-in-law against her mother-in-law; 2
Lke 12:53 mother-in-law against her daughter-in-law 2
53 daughter-in-law against her mother-in-law. 2
Tob 11:16 Then Tobit went out to meet his daughter-in-law 2
17 When Tobit came near to Sarah his daughter-in-law 2
12:12 when you and your daughter-in-law Sarah prayed 2
14 to heal you and your daughter-in-law Sarah. 2

daunt 1. ענה 2. ταράσσω

Isa 31: 4 by their shouting or daunted at their noise 1
Jdt 16:10 the Medes were daunted at her daring. 2

dawn 1. אוֹר 2. זרח 3. נֹגַהּ 4. נֶשֶׁף 5. עלה
6. עֲלוֹת הַשַּׁחַר 7. שַׁחַר 8. ἀνατέλλω 9. ἀνατολή
10. βαθέως 11. γίνομαι 12. διαυγάζω 13. ἐπιφώσκω
14. ἑωθινός 15. ἵημι 16. ὄρθρος 17. ὑποφαίνω
18. ante lucem

Gen 19:15 When morning dawned, the angels urged Lot 5
Deu 33: 2 came from Sinai, and dawned from Se'ir upon us; 2
Jos 6:15 the seventh day they rose early at the dawn of day 6
Jdg 19:25 And as the dawn began to break, they let her go. 7
1Sm 9:26 Then at the break of dawn Samuel called to Saul 7
2Sm 23: 4 he dawns on them like the morning light 2
Neh 4:21 held the spears from the break of dawn 7
Job 3: 9 Let the stars of its dawn be dark; 4
7: 4 I am full of tossing till the dawn. 4
38:12 caused the dawn to know its place 7
41:18 his eyes are like the eyelids of the dawn. 7
Ps 22: 0 The Hind of the Dawn. A Psalm of David. 7
57: 8 Awake, O harp and lyre! I will awake the dawn! 7
97:11 Light dawns for the righteous 8
108: 2 Awake, O harp and lyre! I will awake the dawn! 7
119:147 I rise before dawn and cry for help; 4
Prv 4:18 path of the righteous is like the light of dawn 3
Sng 6:10 Who is this that looks forth like the dawn 7
Isa 8:20 for this word which they speak there is no dawn. 7
14:12 O Day Star, son of Dawn! How you are cut down 7
58: 8 Then shall your light break forth like the dawn 7
Hos 6: 3 his going forth is sure as the dawn; 7
Jon 4: 7 when dawn came up the next day 7
Mic 2: 1 When the morning dawns, they perform it 1
Zep 3: 5 each dawn he does not fail; 1
Mat 4:16 region and shadow of death light has dawned. 8
28: 1 toward the dawn of the first day of the week 13
Lke 24: 1 on the first day of the week, at early dawn 10
Act 27:33 As day was about to dawn 11
2Pe 1:19 until the day dawns and the morning star rises 12
2Es 7:42 or noon or night, or dawn or shining or brightness 18
Jdt 14:11 As soon as it was dawn 16
Wis 16:28 and must pray to thee at the dawning of the light; 9
Sir 24:32 again make instruction shine forth like the dawn 16
1Mc 5:30 At dawn they looked up 14
2Mc 10:28 Just as dawn was breaking 9
35 at dawn of the fifth day 17
13:17 This happened, just as day was dawning 17
3Mc 5:46 entered at about dawn into the courtyard 15

dawn of life 1. שַׁחֲרוּת

Ecc 11:10 for youth and the dawn of life are vanity. 1

dawn upon 1. ἐπισκέπτομαι ἀνατολή

Lke 1:78 when the day shall dawn upon us from on high 1

day 1. יוֹם 2. יוֹמָם 3. שַׁחַר 4. יוֹם (A) 5. ἐπί 6. ἡμέρα
7. καιρός 8. σήμερον 9. τότε 10. χρόνος 11. ψυχή
12. ὥρα 13. die 14. hodie 15. nunc

Gen 1: 5 God called the light Day 1
5 there was evening and there was morning, one day 1
8 there was morning, a second day 1
13 evening and there was morning, a third day 1
14 in . . the heavens to separate the day 1
14 let them be . . for seasons and for days and years 1
16 the greater light to rule the day 1
18 to rule over the day and over the night 1
19 was evening and there was morning, a fourth day 1
23 evening and there was morning, a fifth day 1
31 evening and there was morning, a sixth day. 1
2: 2 on the seventh day God finished his work 1
2 God . . rested on the seventh day 1
3 God blessed the seventh day and hallowed it 1
4 In the day that the LORD God made the earth 1
17 for in the day that you eat of it you shall die. 1
3: 8 walking in the garden in the cool of the day 1
14 dust you shall eat all the days of your life. 1
17 shall eat of it all the days of your life; 1
4:14 thou hast driven me this day away from the ground; 1
5: 4 The days of Adam after he became the father 1
5 Thus all the days that Adam lived were 930 years 1
8 Thus all the days of Seth were 912 years; 1
11 Thus all the days of Enosh were 905 years; 1
14 Thus all the days of Kenan were 910 years; 1
17 Thus all the days of Ma-hal'alel were 895 years; 1
20 Thus all the days of Jared were 962 years; 1
23 Thus all the days of Enoch were 365 years. 1
27 Thus all the days of Methu'selah were 969 years; 1
31 Thus all the days of Lamech were 777 years; 1
6: 3 he is flesh, but his days shall be 120 years. 1
4 The Nephilim were on the earth in those days 1
7: 4 For in seven days I will send rain upon the earth 1
4 send rain upon the earth 40 days and 40 nights; 1
10 after seven days the waters of the flood came 1
11 on the seventeenth day of the month 1
11 on that day all the fountains of the great deep 1
12 rain fell upon the earth 40 days and 40 nights. 1
13 On the very same day Noah and his sons 1
17 The flood continued 40 days upon the earth; 1
24 the waters prevailed upon the earth 150 days. 1
8: 3 At the end of 150 days the waters had abated; 1
4 on the seventeenth day of the month 1
5 in the tenth month, on the first day of the month •
6 At the end of 40 days Noah opened the window 1
10 He waited another seven days 1
12 Then he waited another seven days 1
13 the first day of the month, the waters were dried •
14 In the second month, on the 27th day of the month 1
22 and winter, day and night, shall not cease. 1
9:29 All the days of Noah were 950 years; 1
10:25 Peleg, for in his days the earth was divided 1
11:32 The days of Terah were 205 years; 1
14: 1 In the days of Am'raphel king of Shinar 1
15:18 On that day the LORD made a covenant with Abram 1
17:12 He that is eight days old among you 1
23 of their foreskins that very day, as God had said 1
26 That very day Abraham and his son Ish'mael 1
18: 1 the door of his tent in the heat of the day. 1
19:37 Moab; he is the father of the Moabites to this day. 1
38 he is the father of the Ammonites to this day. 1
21: 4 circumcised his son Isaac when he was eight days 1
8 great feast on the day that Isaac was weaned. 1
34 Abraham sojourned many days in the land 1
22: 4 On the third day Abraham lifted up his eyes 1
14 The LORD will provide; as it is said to this day 1
24:55 remain with us a while, at least ten days; •
25: 7 These are the days of the years of Abraham's life 1
24 When her days to be delivered were fulfilled 1
26: 1 former famine that was in the days of Abraham. 1
15 had dug in the days of Abraham his father. 1
18 which had been dug in the days of Abraham 1
32 That same day Isaac's servants came and told him 1
33 name of the city is Beer-sheba to this day. 1
27: 2 Behold, I am old; I do not know the day of my death. 1
41 Esau said to himself, "The days of mourning 1
45 Why should I be bereft of you both in one day? 1
29: 7 He said, "Behold, it is still high day 1
20 and they seemed to him but a few days 1
30:14 In the days of wheat harvest Reuben went 1
35 that day Laban removed the he-goats 1
36 he set a distance of three days' journey 1
31:22 told Laban on the third day that Jacob had fled 1
23 pursued him for seven days and followed close 1
39 whether stolen by day or stolen by night. 1
40 Thus I was; by day the heat consumed me 1
43 But what can I do this day to these my daughters 1
32:24 wrestled with him until the breaking of the day. 3
26 Then he said, "Let me go, for the day is breaking. 3
32 Therefore to this day the Israelites do not eat 1
33:13 if they are overdriven for one day, all the flocks 1
16 Esau returned that day on his way to Se'ir. 1
34:25 On the third day, when they were sore 1
35: 3 the God who answered me in the day of my distress 1
20 Rachel's tomb, which is there to this day. 1
28 Now the days of Isaac were 180 years. 1
29 gathered to his people, old and full of days; 1
37:34 Jacob . . mourned for his son many days. 1
39:10 although she spoke to Joseph day after day 1
10 although she spoke to Joseph day after day 1
11 one day, when he went into the house to do his work 1
40:12 the three branches are three days; 1
13 within three days Pharaoh will lift up your head 1
18 the three baskets are three days; 1
19 within three days Pharaoh will lift up 1
20 On the third day, which was Pharaoh's birthday 1
42:13 the youngest is this day with our father 1
17 put them all together in prison for three days. 1
18 On the third day Joseph said to them 1
32 the youngest is this day with our father 1
47: 8 said to Jacob, "How many are the days of the years 1
9 Jacob said to Pharaoh, "The days of the years of my 1
9 evil have been the days of the years of my life 1
9 they have not attained to the days of the years 1
9 my fathers in the days of their sojourning. 1
23 Behold, I have this day bought you and your land 1
26 a statute . . and it stands to this day 1
28 the days of Jacob, the years of his life, 1
48:15 the God who has led me all my life long to this day 1
20 he blessed them that day, saying, "By you Israel 1
49: 1 tell you what shall befall you in days to come. 1
50: 3 40 days were required for it 1
3 And the Egyptians wept for him 70 days. 1
4 when the days of weeping for him were past 1
10 and he made a mourning for his father seven days. 1
Exd 2:11 One day, when Moses had grown up, he went out 1
13 When he went out the next day, behold, two Hebrews 1
23 In the course of those many days 1
3:18 go a three days' journey into the wilderness 1
5: 3 let us go . . a three days' journey 1
6 The same day Pharaoh commanded the taskmasters 1
6:28 On the day when the LORD spoke to Moses in the land 1
7:25 Seven days passed after the LORD had struck 1
8:22 on that day I will set apart the land of Goshen 1
27 go three days' journey into the wilderness 1
9:18 in Egypt from the day it was founded until now. 1
10: 6 from the day they came on earth to this day.' 1
6 from the day they came on earth to this day.' 1
13 upon the land all that day and all that night; 1
22 darkness in all the land of Egypt three days; 1
23 nor did any rise from his place for three days; 1
28 for in the day you see my face you shall die. 1
12: 3 on the tenth day of this month they shall take •
6 keep it until the fourteenth day of this month 1
14 This day shall be for you a memorial day 1
14 This day shall be for you a memorial day 1
15 Seven days you shall eat unleavened bread; 1
15 on the first day you shall put away leaven 1
15 from the first day until the seventh day 1
15 from the first day until the seventh day 1
16 On the first day you shall hold a holy assembly 1
16 and on the seventh day a holy assembly; 1
16 no work shall be done on those days; •
17 for on this very day I brought your hosts out 1
17 therefore you shall observe this day 1
18 on the fourteenth day of the month at evening 1
18 so until the twenty-first day of the month 1
19 For seven days no leaven shall be found 1
41 at the end . . on that very day 1
51 on that very day the LORD brought the people 1
13: 3 Remember this day, in which you came out 1
4 This day you are to go forth, in the month of Abib. 1
6 Seven days you shall eat unleavened bread 1
6 and on the seventh day there shall be a feast 1
7 Unleavened bread shall be eaten for seven days; 1
8 you shall tell your son on that day, 'It is 1
21 the LORD went before them by day in a pillar 2
21 that they might travel by day and by night; 2
22 the pillar of cloud by day and the pillar of fire 2
14:30 Thus the LORD saved Israel that day from the hand 1
15:22 they went three days in the wilderness 1
16: 1 on the fifteenth day of the second month 1
4 go out and gather a day's portion every day 1
4 go out and gather a day's portion every day 1
5 On the sixth day, when they prepare what they 1
22 On the sixth day they gathered twice as much 1
26 Six days you shall gather it; but on the seventh 1
26 but on the seventh day, which is a sabbath 1
27 On the seventh day some of the people went out 1
29 on the sixth day he gives you bread for two days; 1
29 on the sixth day he gives you bread for two days; 1
29 let no man go out of his place on the seventh day. 1
30 So the people rested on the seventh day. 1
19: 1 that day they came into the wilderness of Sinai. 1
11 be ready by the third day; 1
11 for on the third day the LORD will come down 1
15 he said to the people, "Be ready by the third day; 1
16 On the morning of the third day there were 1
20: 8 Remember the sabbath day, to keep it holy. 1
9 Six days you shall labor, and do all your work; 1
10 the seventh day is a sabbath to the LORD your God; 1
11 for in six days the LORD made heaven and earth 1
11 the LORD . . rested the seventh day; 1
11 LORD blessed the sabbath day and hallowed it. 1
12 that your days may be long in the land 1
21:21 if the slave survives a day or two, he is not to be 1
22:30 seven days it shall be with its dam; 1
30 on the eighth day you shall give it to me. 1
23:12 Six days you shall do your work, but on the seventh 1
12 do your work, but on the seventh day you shall rest; 1
15 you shall eat unleavened bread for seven days 1
26 I will fulfil the number of your days. 1
24:16 Mount Sinai, and the cloud covered it six days; 1
16 and on the seventh day he called to Moses 1
18 Moses was on the mountain 40 days and 40 nights. 1
29:30 The son . . shall wear them seven days 1
35 through seven days shall you ordain them 1

36 every day you shall offer a bull as a sin offering 1
37 Seven days you shall make atonement 1
38 two lambs a year old day by day continually. 1
38 two lambs a year old day by day continually. 1
31:15 Six days shall work be done, but the seventh day 1
15 seventh day is a sabbath of solemn rest, holy 1
15 whoever does any work on the sabbath day shall be 1
17 in six days the LORD made heaven and earth 1
17 on the seventh day he rested, and was refreshed.' 1
32:28 there fell of the people that day about 3,000 men. 1
29 may bestow a blessing upon you this day. 1
34 Nevertheless, in the day when I visit, I will visit 1
34:11 Observe what I command you this day. 1
18 Seven days you shall eat unleavened bread 1
21 Six days you shall work, but on the seventh day 1
21 but on the seventh day you shall rest; 1
28 he was there with the LORD 40 days and 40 nights; 1
35: 2 Six days shall work be done, but on the seventh day 1
2 on the seventh day you shall have a holy sabbath 1
3 in all your habitations on the sabbath day. 1
40: 2 On the first day of the first month you shall 1
17 second year, on the first day of the month •
37 go onward till the day that it was taken up. 1
38 was upon the tabernacle by day, and fire was in it 2
Lev 6: 5 give it . . on the day of his guilt offering 1
20 offer to the LORD on the day when he is anointed 1
7:15 shall be eaten on the day of his offering 1
16 it shall be eaten on the day that he offers his 1
17 the sacrifice on the third day shall be burned 1
18 peace offering is eaten on the third day 1
35 the day they were presented to them as priests 1
36 on the day that they were anointed 1
38 on the day that he commanded the people of Israel 1
8:33 the door of the tent of meeting for seven days 1
33 for seven days, until the days of your ordination 1
33 for it will take seven days to ordain you 1
35 you shall remain day and night for seven days 2
35 you shall remain day and night for seven days 1
9: 1 On the eighth day Moses called Aaron and his sons 1
12: 2 then she shall be unclean seven days 1
3 on the eighth day the flesh of his foreskin shall 1
4 Then she shall continue for 33 days in the blood 1
4 until the days of her purifying are completed 1
5 in the blood of her purifying for 66 days 1
6 when the days of her purifying are completed 1
13: 4 shut up the diseased person for seven days 1
5 the priest shall examine him on the seventh day 1
5 then the priest shall shut him up seven days more 1
6 shall examine him again on the seventh day 1
21 then the priest shall shut him up seven days 1
26 the priest shall shut him up seven days 1
27 the priest shall examine him the seventh day 1
31 shut up the person . . for seven days 1
32 on the seventh day the priest shall examine 1
33 shut up the person . . for seven days more 1
34 on the seventh day the priest shall examine 1
50 priest shall shut up that . . for seven days 1
51 he shall examine the disease on the seventh day 1
54 and he shall shut it up seven days more 1
14: 2 law of the leper for the day of his cleansing 1
8 but shall dwell outside his tent seven days 1
9 on the seventh day he shall shave all his hair off 1
10 on the eighth day he shall take two male lambs 1
23 on the eighth day he shall bring them 1
38 go out . . and shut up the house seven days 1
39 the priest shall come again on the seventh day 1
15:13 then he shall count for himself seven days 1
14 on the eighth day he shall take two turtledoves 1
19 she shall be in her impurity for seven days 1
24 impurity is on him, he shall be unclean seven days 1
25 If a woman has a discharge of blood for many days 1
25 all the days of the discharge she shall continue 1
25 as in the days of her impurity, she shall be 1
26 bed on which she lies, all the days of her discharge 1
28 she shall count for herself seven days 1
29 on the eighth day she shall take two turtledoves 1
16:29 in the seventh month, on the tenth day of the month •
30 for on this day shall atonement be made for you 1
19: 6 It shall be eaten the same day you offer it 1
6 anything left over until the third day 1
7 If it is eaten at all on the third day, it is 1
22:27 it shall remain seven days with its mother 1
27 from the eighth day on it shall be acceptable 1
28 shall not kill both her and her young in one day 1
30 be eaten on he same day, you shall leave none of it 1
23: 3 Six days shall work be done; but on the seventh day 1
3 on the seventh day is a sabbath of solemn rest 1
5 the first month, on the fourteenth day of the month •
6 on the fifteenth day of the same month 1
6 seven days you shall eat unleavened bread 1
7 the first day you shall have a holy convocation 1
8 present an offering . . to the LORD seven days 1
8 on the seventh day is a holy convocation 1
12 on the day when you wave the sheaf, you shall offer 1
14 you shall eat neither . . until this same day 1
15 after the sabbath, from the day that you brought 1
16 50 days to the morrow after the seventh sabbath 1
21 you shall make proclamation on the same day 1
24 In the seventh month, on the first day of the month •
27 On the tenth day of this seventh month is the day •
27 On the tenth day . . is the day of atonement 1
28 you shall do no work on this same day; for it is a day 1
28 for it is a day of atonement, to make atonement 1
29 For whoever is not afflicted on this same day 1
30 whoever does any work on this same day 1
32 on the ninth day of the month beginning at evening •
34 On the fifteenth day of this seventh month 1
34 for seven days is the feast of booths to the LORD 1
35 On the first day shall be a holy convocation 1
36 Seven days you shall present offerings by fire 1
36 the eighth day you shall hold a holy convocation 1
37 drink offerings, each on its proper day 1
39 On the fifteenth day of the seventh month 1
39 you shall keep the feast of the LORD seven days 1
39 on the first day shall be a solemn rest 1
39 on the eighth day shall be a solemn rest 1
40 you shall take on the first day the fruit 1
40 rejoice before the LORD your God seven days 1
41 You shall keep it as a feast to the LORD seven days 1
42 You shall dwell in booths for seven days 1
24: 8 Every sabbath day Aaron shall set it in order 1
25: 9 send abroad the loud trumpet on the tenth day 1
9 on the day of atonement you shall send abroad 1
27:23 shall give . . on that day as a holy thing 1
Num 1: 1 on the first day of the second month •
18 on the first day of the second month •
3:13 on the day that I slew all the first-born 1
6: 4 All the days of his separation he shall eat 1
5 All the days of his vow of separation no razor 1
6 days that he separates himself to the LORD 1
8 days of his separation he is holy to the LORD. 1
9 shall shave his head on the day of his cleansing; 1
9 on the seventh day he shall shave it. 1
10 On the eighth day he shall bring two turtledoves 1
11 And he shall consecrate his head that same day. 1
12 to the LORD for the days of his separation 1
7: 1 On the day when Moses had finished setting up 1
10 altar on the day it was anointed; 1
11 shall offer their offering, one leader each day 1
12 offered his offering the first day was Nahshon 1
18 On the second day Nethan'el . . made an offering; 1
24 On the third day Eli'ab . . of the men of Zeb'ulun 1
30 On the fourth day Eli'zur . . of the men of Reuben 1
36 On the fifth day Shelu'mi-el . . of Simeon 1
42 On the sixth day Eli'asaph . . of the men of Gad 1
48 On the seventh day Eli'shama . . of E'phraim 1
54 On the eighth day Gama'liel . . of Manas'seh 1
60 On the ninth day Abi'dan . . of the men of Benjamin 1
66 On the tenth day Ahie'zer . . of the men of Dan 1
72 On the eleventh day Pa'giel . . of the men of Asher 1
78 On the twelfth day Ahi'ra . . of Naph'tali 1
84 for the altar, on the day when it was anointed 1
8:17 day that I slew all the first-born in the land 1
9: 3 fourteenth day of this month, in the evening 1
5 first month, on the fourteenth day of the month 1
6 that they could not keep the passover on that day; 1
6 they came before Moses and Aaron on that day; 1
11 In the second month on the fourteenth day 1
15 On the day that the tabernacle was set up 1
16 it was continually; the cloud covered it by day 6
19 cloud continued over the tabernacle many days 1
20 cloud was a few days over the tabernacle 1
21 if it continued for a day and a night 2
22 Whether it was two days, or a month, or a longer time 1
10:10 On the day of your gladness also 1
11 second month, on the twentieth day of the month •
33 set out . . three days' journey; 1
33 ark . . went before them three days' journey 1
34 the cloud of the LORD was over them by day 2
11:19 You shall not eat one day, or two days, or five days 1
19 You shall not eat one day, or two days, or five days 1
19 You shall not eat one day, or two days, or five days 1
19 You shall not eat . . ten days, or twenty days 1
19 You shall not eat . . ten days, or twenty days 1
31 about a day's journey on this side 1
31 about . . a day's journey on the other side 1
32 the people rose all that day, and all night 1
32 people rose . . all night, and all the next day 1
12:14 should she not be shamed seven days? 1
14 Let her be shut up outside the camp seven days 1
15 Miriam was shut up outside the camp seven days; 1
13:25 At the end of 40 days they returned from spying 1
14:14 thou goest before them, in a pillar of cloud by day 2
34 According to the number of the days in which you 1
34 40 days, for every day a year, you shall bear 1
34 for every day a year, you shall bear your iniquity 1
15:23 from the day the the LORD gave commandment 1
32 found a man gathering sticks on the sabbath day. 1
19:11 He who touches . . shall be unclean seven days; 1
12 cleanse himself . . on the third day 1
12 cleanse himself . . day and on the seventh day 1
12 if he does not cleanse himself on the third day 1
12 does not cleanse himself . . on the seventh day 1
14 every one . . shall be unclean seven days. 1
16 shall be unclean seven days. 1
19 sprinkle . . on the third day and on the seventh 1
19 sprinkle . . day and on the seventh day; 1
19 thus on the seventh day he shall cleanse him 1
20:29 all the house of Israel wept for Aaron 30 days 1
22:30 you have ridden all your life long to this day? 1
24:14 people will do to your people in the latter days. 1
25:18 their sister, who was slain on the day of the plague 1
28: 9 On the sabbath day two male lambs a year old 1
16 fourteenth day of the first month is the LORD'S 1
17 on the fifteenth day of this month is a feast; 1
17 seven days shall unleavened bread be eaten. 1
18 the first day there shall be a holy convocation 1
24 same way you shall offer daily, for seven days 1
25 seventh day you shall have a holy convocation; 1
26 On the day of the first fruits, when you offer 1
29: 1 On the first day of the seventh month •
1 It is a day for you to blow the trumpets 1
7 On the tenth day of this seventh month •
12 On the fifteenth day of the seventh month 1
12 you shall keep a feast to the LORD seven days; 1
17 On the second day twelve young bulls, two rams 1
20 On the third day eleven bulls, two rams, fourteen 1
23 On the fourth day ten bulls, two rams, fourteen 1
26 On the fifth day nine bulls, two rams, fourteen 1
29 On the sixth day eight bulls, two rams, fourteen 1
32 On the seventh day seven bulls, two rams, fourteen 1
35 eighth day you shall have a solemn assembly 1
30: 5 disapproval to her on the day that he hears of it 1
7 says nothing to her on the day that he hears; 1
8 if, on the day that her husband comes to hear of it 1
12 makes them null and void on the day that he hears 1
14 if her husband says nothing to her from day to day 1
14 if her husband says nothing to her from day to day 1
14 he said nothing to her on the day that he heard 1
31:19 Encamp outside the camp seven days; 1
19 purify . . on the third day and on the seventh day. 1
19 purify . . on the third day and on the seventh day. 1
24 You must wash your clothes on the seventh day 1
32:10 LORD'S anger was kindled on that day, and he swore 1
33: 3 set out . . the fifteenth day of the first month; 1
8 went a three days' journey in the wilderness of Etham 1
38 died . . on the first day of the fifth month. •
Deu 1: 2 eleven days' journey from Horeb by the way 1
3 40th year, on the first day of the eleventh month •
10 behold, you are this day as the stars of heaven 1
33 who went before you . . in the cloud by day. 2
39 your children, who this day have no knowledge 1
46 you remained at Kadesh many days 1
46 many days, the days that you remained there. 1
2: 1 for many days we went about Mount Se'ir. 1
18 day you are to pass over the boundary of Moab at Ar; 1
22 settled in their stead even to this day. 1
25 This day I will begin to put the dread and fear 1
30 might give him into your hand, as at this day. 1
3:14 Hav'voth-ja'ir, as it is to this day.) 1
4: 4 held fast to the LORD . . are all alive this day. 1
8 as all this law which I set before you this day? 1
9 depart from your heart all the days of your life; 1
10 how on the day that you stood before the LORD 1
10 fear me all the days that they live upon the earth 1
15 no form on the day that the LORD spoke to you 1
20 be a people of his own possession, as at this day. 1
26 heaven and earth to witness against you this day 1
30 all these things come upon you in the latter days 1
32 For ask now of the days that are past 1
32 since the day that God created man upon the earth 1
38 their land for an inheritance, as at this day; 1
39 know therefore this day, and lay it to your heart 1
40 you shall keep . . which I command you this day 1
40 that you may prolong your days in the land 1
5: 1 which I speak in your hearing this day 1
3 but with us, who are all of us here alive this day. 1
12 'Observe the sabbath day, to keep it holy 1
13 Six days you shall labor, and do all your work; 1
14 seventh day is a sabbath to the LORD your God; 1
15 your God commanded you to keep the sabbath day. 1
16 your days may be prolonged, and that it may go well 1
24 day seen God speak with man and man still live. 1
6: 2 all his statutes . . all the days of your life; 1
2 that your days may be prolonged. 1
6 these words which I command you this day 1
24 that he might preserve us alive, as at this day. 1
7:11 be careful to do . . which I command you this day. 1
8: 1 All the commandment which I command you this day 1
11 by not keeping . . which I command you this day 1
18 confirm his covenant . . as at this day. 1
19 solemnly warn you this day that you shall 1
9: 1 O Israel; you are to pass over the Jordan this day 1
3 Know therefore this day that he who goes over 1
7 from the day you came out of the land of Egypt 1
9 I remained on the mountain 40 days and 40 nights 1
10 spoken with you . . on the day of the assembly. 1
11 at the end of 40 days and 40 nights the LORD gave me 1
18 I lay prostrate . . 40 days and 40 nights; 1
24 rebellious . . from the day that I knew you. 1
25 before the LORD for these 40 days and 40 nights 1
10: 4 LORD had spoken to you . . on the day of the assembly; 1
8 set apart the tribe of Levi . . to this day. 1
10 I stayed on the mountain . . 40 days and 40 nights 1
13 which I command you this day for your good? 1
15 chose . . you above all peoples, as at this day. 1
11: 2 consider this day . . the discipline of the LORD 1

4 how the LORD has destroyed them to this day; 1
8 commandment which I command you this day 1
13 my commandments which I command you this day 1
21 that your days and the days of your children 1
21 that your days and the days of your children 1
26 I set before you this day a blessing and a curse 1
27 commandments . . which I command you this day 1
28 turn . . from the way which I command you this day 1
32 which I set before you this day. 1
12: 1 all the days that you live upon the earth. 1
8 not do . . all that we are doing here this day 1
13:18 his commandments which I command you this day 1
15: 5 commandment which I command you this day. 1
16: 3 seven days . . eat it with unleavened bread 1
3 all the days of your life you may remember the day 1
3 remember the day when you came out of . . Egypt. 1
4 No leaven . . in all your territory for seven days; 1
4 sacrifice on the evening of the first day 1
8 For six days you shall eat unleavened bread; 1
8 seventh day there shall be a solemn assembly 1
13 You shall keep the feast of booths seven days 1
15 seven days you shall keep the feast to the LORD 1
17: 9 to the judge who is in office in those days 1
19 he shall read in it all the days of his life 1
18:16 desired of the LORD . . on the day of the assembly 1
19: 9 this commandment, which I command you this day 1
17 priests and the judges . . in office in those days; 1
20: 3 say to them, 'Hear, O Israel, you draw near this day 1
21:16 then on the day when he assigns his possessions 1
23 bury him the same day, for a hanged man is accursed 1
22:19 be his wife; he may not put her away all his days. 1
29 he may not put her away all his days. 1
23: 6 not seek their peace . . all your days for ever. 1
24:15 you shall give him his hire on the day he earns it 1
25:15 that your days may be prolonged in the land 1
26: 3 I declare this day to the LORD your God 1
16 This day the LORD your God commands you to do 1
17 declared this day concerning the LORD 1
18 LORD has declared this day concerning you 1
27: 1 Keep . . commandment which I command you this day. 1
2 day you pass over the Jordan to the land 1
4 stones, concerning which I command you this day 1
9 this day you have become the people of the LORD 1
10 commandments . . which I command you this day. 1
11 Moses charged the people the same day, saying 1
28: 1 his commandments which I command you this day 1
13 commandments . . which I command you this day 1
14 from any of the words which I command you this day 1
15 commandments . . which I command you this day 1
32 eyes . . fail with longing for them all the day; 1
66 night and day you shall be in dread 2
29: 4 to this day the LORD has not given you a mind 1
10 stand this day all of you before the LORD your God; 1
12 sworn covenant . . LORD . . makes with you this day; 1
13 that he may establish you this day as his people 1
15 here with us this day as well as with him 1
15 stands here . . this day before the LORD our God. 1
18 heart turns away this day from the LORD our God 1
28 cast them into another land, as at this day.' 1
30: 2 obey his voice in all that I command you this day 1
8 commandments which I command you this day. 1
11 this commandment which I command you this day 1
15 See, I have set before you this day life and good 1
16 commandments . . which I command you this day 1
18 I declare to you this day, that you shall perish; 1
19 heaven and earth to witness against you this day 1
20 for that means life to you and length of days 1
31: 2 said to them, "I am 120 years old this day; 1
14 Behold, the days approach when you must die; 1
17 my anger will be kindled against them in that day 1
17 so that they will say in that day, 'Have not 1
18 surely hide my face in that day on account of all 1
22 Moses wrote this song the same day, and taught it 1
29 in the days to come evil will befall you 1
32: 7 Remember the days of old, consider the years 1
35 day of their calamity is at hand, and their doom 1
46 all the words . . I enjoin upon you this day 1
48 LORD said to Moses that very day 1
33:12 encompasses him all the day long 1
25 as your days, so shall your strength be. 1
34: 6 no man knows the place of his burial to this day. 1
8 wept . . in the plains of Moab 30 days; 1
8 then the days of weeping and mourning for Moses 1
Jos 1: 5 able to stand before you all the days of your life; 1
8 but you shall meditate on it day and night 2
11 within three days you are to pass over this 1
2:16 Go . . and hide yourselves there three days 1
22 into the hills, and remained there three days 1
3: 2 At the end of three days the officers went 1
7 This day I will begin to exalt you in the sight 1
4: 9 Joshua set up . . and they are there to this day. 1
14 On that day the LORD exalted Joshua in . . Israel; 1
14 had stood in awe of Moses, all the days of his life. 1
19 people came . . on the tenth day of the first month •
5: 9 This day I have rolled away the reproach of Egypt 1
9 name of this place is called Gilgal to this day. 1
10 passover on the fourteenth day of the month 1
11 on the morrow after the passover, on that very day 1
6: 3 Thus shall you do for six days. 1
4 and on the seventh day you shall march around 1
10 shall not shout . . until the day I bid you shout; 1
14 the second day they marched around the city once 1
14 And the second day . . So they did for six days. 1
15 the seventh day they rose early at the dawn of day 1
15 the seventh day they rose early at the dawn of day •
15 it was only on that day . . seven times. 1
25 and she dwelt in Israel to this day 1
7:26 a great heap of stones that remains to this day; 1
26 Therefore to this day the name of that place is 1
8:25 And all who fell that day . . were 12,000 1
28 made it . . a heap of ruins, as it is to this day. 1
29 heap of stones, which stands there to this day. 1
9:12 we took it . . on the day we set forth to come to you 1
16 At the end of three days after they had made 1
17 and reached their cities on the third day. 1
27 But Joshua made them that day hewers of wood 1
27 Joshua made them . . to continue to this day 1
10:12 the day when the LORD gave the Amorites over 1
13 did not hasten to go down for about a whole day. 1
14 There has been no day like it before or since 1
27 great stones . . which remain to this very day. 1
28 And Joshua took Makke'dah on that day, and smote it 1
32 and he took it on the second day, and smote it 1
35 and they took it on that day, and smote it 1
35 every person in it he utterly destroyed that day 1
13:13 dwell in the midst of Israel to this day. 1
14: 9 And Moses swore on that day, saying 1
10 and now, lo, I am this day 85 years old. 1
11 I am still as strong to this day as . . the day that 1
11 as strong . . as I was in the day that Moses sent me; 1
12 hill country of which the LORD spoke on that day; 1
12 you heard on that day how the Anakim were there 1
14 became the inheritance of Caleb . . to this day 1
15:63 dwell with . . Judah at Jerusalem to this day. 1
16:10 Canaanites have dwelt in . . E'phraim to this day 1
22: 3 not forsaken your brethren these many days 1
3 not forsaken . . these many days, down to this day 1
16 in turning away this day from following the LORD 1
16 by building yourselves an altar this day 1
18 that you must turn away this day from . . the LORD? 1
29 and turn away this day from following the LORD 1
23: 8 cleave to the LORD . . as you have done to this day. 1
9 no man has been able to withstand you to this day. 1
24:15 choose this day whom you will serve 1
25 Joshua made a covenant with the people that day 1
31 And Israel served the LORD all the days of Joshua 1
31 the days of Joshua, and all the days of the elders 1
Jdg 1:21 people of Benjamin in Jerusalem to this day. 1
26 called its name Luz; that is its name to this day. 1
2: 7 the people served the LORD all the days of Joshua 1
7 all the days of the elders who outlived Joshua 1
18 hand of their enemies all the days of the judge; 1
3:30 Moab was subdued that day under the hand 1
4:14 Up! For this is the day in which the LORD has given 1
23 on that day God subdued Jabin the king of Canaan 1
5: 1 Then sang Deb'orah and Barak . . on that day 1
6 In the days of Shamgar . . in the days of Ja'el 1
6 In the days of Shamgar . . in the days of Ja'el 1
6:24 To this day it still stands at Ophrah 1
27 too afraid . . to do it by day, he did it by night. 2
32 on that day he was called Jerubba'al, that is to say 1
8:28 the land had rest 40 years in the days of Gideon 1
9:18 have risen up against my father's house this day 1
19 honor with Jerubba'al and with his house this day 1
45 Abim'elech fought against the city all that day; 1
10: 4 30 cities, called Hav'voth-ja'ir to this day 1
15 to thee; only deliver us, we pray thee, this day. 1
11:27 the LORD . . decide this day between the people 1
40 went . . to lament . . four days in the year. 1
12: 3 why then have you come up to me this day, to fight 1
13: 7 a Nazirite . . from birth to the day of his death.' 1
10 the man who came to me the other day has appeared 1
14:12 tell me . . within the seven days of the feast 1
14 they could not in three days tell what the riddle 1
15 On the fourth day they said to Samson's wife 1
17 wept . . the seven days that their feast lasted; 1
17 on the seventh day he told her, because she 1
18 to him on the seventh day before the sun went down 1
15:19 it was called En-hakkor'e; it is at Lehi to this day. 1
20 he judged Israel in the days of the Philistines 1
17: 6 In those days there was no king in Israel; 1
18: 1 In those days there was no king in Israel. 1
1 And in those days the tribe of the Danites was 1
12 that place is called Ma'haneh-dan to this day; 1
30 were priests . . until the day of the captivity 1
19: 1 In those days, when there was no king in Israel 1
4 made him stay, and he remained with him three days; 1
5 on the fourth day they arose early in the morning 1
8 on the fifth day he arose early in the morning 1
8 and tarry until the day declines." So they ate 1
9 now the day has waned toward evening; pray tarry 1
9 the day draws to its close; lodge here and let 1
11 When they were near Jebus, the day was far spent 1
30 from the day that . . Israel came up out 1
30 been seen from the day . . until this day; 1
20:15 mustered . . on that day 26,000 men that drew 1
21 felled to the ground on that day 22,000 men 1
22 place where they had formed it on the first day. 1
24 against the Benjaminites the second day. 1
25 Benjamin went against them . . the second day 1
26 the LORD, and fasted that day until evening 1
27 ark of the covenant of God was there in those days 1
28 Phin'ehas . . ministered before it in those days) 1
30 Israel went up . . on the third day, and set 1
35 Israel destroyed 25,100 men of Benjamin that day 1
46 all who fell that day of Benjamin were 25,000 men 1
21: 6 One tribe is cut off from Israel this day. 1
25 In those days there was no king in Israel; 1
Rut 1: 1 In the days when the judges ruled 1
4: 5 The day you buy the field from the hand of Na'omi 1
9 You are witnesses this day that I have bought 1
10 you are witnesses this day. 1
14 who has not left you this day without next of kin; 1
1Sm 1: 4 On the day when Elka'nah sacrificed, he would give 1
11 I will give him to the LORD all the days of his life 1
2:31 Behold, the days are coming, when I will cut off 1
34 the sign . . both of them shall die on the same day. 1
3: 1 And the word of the LORD was rare in those days; 1
12 On that day I will fulfil . . all that I have spoken 1
4:12 and came to Shiloh the same day 1
5: 5 do not tread on the threshold . . to this day. 1
6:15 burnt offerings and . . sacrifices on that day 1
16 they returned that day to Ekron. 1
18 The great stone . . is a witness to this day 1
7: 2 From the day that the ark . . a long time passed 1
6 they gathered . . and fasted on that day, and said 1
10 the LORD thundered with a mighty voice that day 1
13 against the Philistines all the days of Samuel. 1
15 Samuel judged Israel all the days of his life. 1
8: 8 from the day I brought them up out of Egypt even 1
8 from the day I brought them up . . even to this day 1
18 in that day you will cry out because of your king 1
18 the LORD will not answer you in that day. 1
9:15 the day before Saul came, the LORD had revealed 1
20 As for your asses that were lost three days ago 1
24 Saul ate with Samuel that day. 1
10: 8 Seven days you shall wait, until I come to you 1
9 and all these signs came to pass that day. 1
19 you have this day rejected your God, who saves you 1
11: 3 Give us seven days respite that we may send 1
11 cut down the Ammonites until the heat of the day; 1
13 Saul said, "Not a man shall be put to death this day 1
12: 2 walked before you from my youth until this day. 1
5 The LORD . . and his anointed is witness this day 1
18 and the LORD sent thunder and rain that day; 1
13: 8 He waited seven days, the time appointed 1
11 you did not come within the days appointed 1
22 on the day of the battle . . neither sword nor 1
14: 1 One day Jonathan the son of Saul said . . "Come 1
23 So the LORD delivered Israel that day; 1
24 And the men of Israel were distressed that day; 1
28 'Cursed be the man who eats food this day.' 1
31 They struck down the Philistines that day 1
37 But he did not answer him that day. 1
41 why hast thou not answered thy servant this day? 14
45 for he has wrought with God this day. 1
52 There was hard fighting . . all the days of Saul; 1
15:28 LORD has torn the kingdom . . from you this day 1
35 did not see Saul again until the day of his death 1
16:13 Spirit . . came mightily upon David from that day 1
17:10 I defy the ranks of Israel this day; give me a man 1
12 In the days of Saul the man was already old 1
16 For 40 days the Philistine came forward 1
46 This day the LORD will deliver you into my hand 1
46 give the dead bodies . . this day to the birds 1
18: 2 Saul took him that day, and would not let him 1
9 Saul eyed David from that day on. 1
10 David was playing the lyre, as he did day by day. 1
10 David was playing the lyre, as he did day by day. 1
19:24 and lay naked all that day and all that night. 1
20:12 When . . about this time tomorrow, or the third day •
19 And on the third day you will be greatly missed; •
26 Saul did not say anything that day; for he thought 1
27 on the second day, the morrow after the new moon •
34 and ate no food the second day of the month 1
21: 6 replaced by hot bread on the day it is taken away. 1
7 a . . man of the servants of Saul was there that day 1
10 And David rose and fled that day from Saul 1
22: 8 stirred up . . to lie in wait, as at this day. 1
13 has risen against me, to lie in wait, as at this day? 1
18 Do'eg . . killed on that day 85 persons 1
22 I knew on that day, when Do'eg . . was there 1
23:14 Saul sought him every day 1
24: 4 Here is the day of which the LORD said to you 1
10 Lo, this day your eyes have seen how the LORD gave 1
18 you have declared this day how you have dealt 1
19 for what you have done to me this day. 1
25: 8 find favor in your eyes; for we come on a feast day. 1
16 they were a wall to us both by night and by day 2
32 the LORD . . who sent you this day to meet me! 1
33 who have kept me this day from bloodguilt 1
38 And about ten days later the LORD smote Nabal; 1
26: 8 God has given your enemy into your hand this day; 1
10 LORD will smite him; or his day shall come to die; 1
19 driven me out this day that I should have no share 1
21 my life was precious in your eyes this day; 1
24 as your life was precious this day in my sight 1

27: 1 I shall now perish one day by the hand of Saul; 1
6 that day A'chish gave him Ziklag; 1
6 Ziklag has belonged to . . Judah to this day. 1
7 the number of the days . . was a year 1
28: 1 In those days the Philistines gathered 1
18 the LORD has done this thing to you this day. 1
20 he had eaten nothing all day and all night. 1
29: 3 who has been with me now for days and years 1
3 I have found no fault in him to this day. 1
6 from the day of your coming to me to this day. 1
6 from the day of your coming to me to this day. 1
8 from the day I entered your service until now 1
30: 1 David and his men came to Ziklag on the third day 1
12 or drunk water for three days and three nights. 1
13 left me . . because I fell sick three days ago. 1
25 And from that day forward he made it a statute 1
25 made it a statute and an ordinance . . to this day. 1
31: 6 Saul died . . and all his men, on the same day 1
13 and buried them . . and fasted seven days. 1
2Sm 1: 1 David remained two days in Ziklag; 1
2 on the third day . . a man came from Saul's camp 1
2:17 And the battle was very fierce that day; 1
3: 8 This day I keep showing loyalty to . . Saul 1
35 persuade David to eat bread while it was yet day; 1
37 the people and all Israel understood that day 1
38 a prince and a great man has fallen this day 1
39 And I am this day weak, though anointed king; 1
4: 3 have been sojourners there to this day 1
5 about the heat of the day they came to the house 1
8 LORD has avenged my lord the king this day on Saul 1
5: 8 David said on that day, "Whoever would smite 1
6: 8 and that place is called Pe'rez-uz'zah, to this day. 1
9 And David was afraid of the LORD that day; 1
23 And Michal . . had no child to the day of her death. 1
7: 6 since the day I brought up the people of Israel 1
6 since the day I brought up . . to this day 1
12 When your days are fulfilled and you lie down 1
11:12 Uri'ah remained in Jerusalem that day 1
12:18 On the seventh day the child died. 1
13:32 determined from the day he forced his sister 1
14: 2 who has been mourning many days for the dead; 1
16:23 Now in those days the counsel which Ahith'ophel 1
18: 7 and the slaughter there was great on that day 1
8 and the forest devoured more people that day 1
18 and it is called Ab'salom's monument to this day. 1
20 you may carry tidings another day 1
31 LORD has delivered you this day from the power 1
19: 2 So the victory that day was turned into mourning 1
2 the people heard that day, "The king is grieving 1
3 And the people stole into the city that day 1
5 your servants, who have this day saved your life 1
19 your servant did wrong on the day . . the king left 1
20 I have come this day, the first . . to meet my lord 1
22 that you should this day be as an adversary to me? 1
22 Shall any one be put to death in Israel this day? 1
22 do I not know that I am this day king over Israel? 1
24 from the day the king departed until . . he came 1
24 from . . until the day he came back in safety. 1
35 I am this day 80 years old; can I discern 1
20: 3 they were shut up until the day of their death 1
4 Call . . Judah together to me within three days 1
21: 1 a famine in the days of David for three years 1
9 were put to death in the first days of harvest 1
10 allow the birds of the air to come upon them by day 2
12 on the day the Philistines killed Saul on Gilbo'a; 1
22: 1 David spoke . . this song on the day when the LORD 1
19 They came upon me in the day of my calamity; 1
23:10 and the LORD wrought a great victory that day; 1
20 slew a lion in a pit on a day when snow had fallen. 1
24: 8 at the end of nine months and twenty days. 1
13 there be three days' pestilence in your land? 1
18 Gad came that day to David, and said to him, "Go up 1
1Kg 1:25 he has gone down this day, and has sacrificed oxen 1
30 as I swore to you . . even so will I do this day. 1
48 to sit on my throne this day, my own eyes seeing it.' 1
2: 8 cursed me . . on the day when I went to Mahana'im; 1
24 Adoni'jah shall be put to death this day. 1
37 on the day you go forth . . you shall die; 1
38 So Shim'e-i dwelt in Jerusalem many days. 1
42 on the day you go forth and go to any place 1
3: 6 hast given him a son to sit on his throne this day. 1
13 no . . king shall compare with you, all your days. 1
14 if you will . . then I will lengthen your days. 1
18 on the third day after I was delivered, this woman 1
4:21 and served Solomon all the days of his life. 1
22 Solomon's provision for one day was 30 cors 1
25 dwelt in safety . . all the days of Solomon. 1
5: 7 Blessed be the LORD this day, who has given 1
8: 8 and they are there to this day. 1
16 the day that I brought . . Israel out of Egypt 1
24 and with thy hand hast fulfilled it this day. 1
28 the prayer which thy servant prays . . this day; 1
29 eyes may be open night and day toward this house 1
40 fear thee all the days that they live in the land 1
59 words . . be near to the LORD our God day and night 2
59 may he maintain . . as each day requires; †
61 be wholly true to the LORD . . as at this day. 1
64 The same day the king consecrated the . . court 1
65 the feast . . before the LORD our God, seven days. 1
66 On the eighth day he sent the people away; 1
9:13 So they are called the land of Cabul to this day. 1
21 made a forced levy . . and so they are to this day. 1
10:12 almug wood has come or been seen, to this day 1
21 was not considered . . in the days of Solomon. 1
11:12 I will not do it in your days 1
25 an adversary of Israel all the days of Solomon 1
34 I will make him ruler all the days of his life 1
12: 5 Depart for three days, then come again to me. 1
12 Jerobo'am . . came to Rehobo'am the third day 1
12 as the king said, "Come to me again the third day. 1
19 rebellion against the house of David to this day. 1
32 a feast on the fifteenth day of the eighth month 1
33 on the fifteenth day in the eighth month 1
13: 3 he gave a sign the same day, saying, "This is the sign 1
11 all that the man of God had done that day in Bethel; 1
15: 5 that he commanded him all the days of his life 1
6 there was war . . all the days of his life. 1
14 Asa was wholly true to the LORD all his days. 1
16 war between Asa and Ba'asha . . all their days. 1
32 war between Asa and Ba'asha . . all their days. 1
16:15 Zimri reigned seven days in Tirzah. 1
16 made . . king over Israel that day in the camp. 1
34 In his days Hi'el of Bethel built Jericho; 1
17:14 until the day that the LORD sends rain 1
15 she, and he, and her household ate for many days. 1
18: 1 After many days the word of the LORD came 1
36 LORD . . let it be known this day that thou art God 1
19: 4 he . . went a day's journey into the wilderness 1
8 and went . . 40 days and 40 nights to Horeb 1
20:13 Behold, I will give it into your hand this day; 1
29 they encamped opposite one another seven days. 1
29 on the seventh day the battle was joined; 1
29 Israel smote . . 100,000 foot soldiers in one day. 1
21:29 Because . . I will not bring the evil in his days; 1
29 but in his son's days I will bring the evil 1
22:25 you shall see on that day when you go . . to hide 1
35 the battle grew hot that day, and the king 1
46 who remained in the days of his father Asa 1
2Kg 2:17 for three days they sought him but did not find 1
22 So the water has been wholesome to this day 1
3: 9 when they had made a . . march of seven days 1
4: 8 One day Eli'sha went on to Shunem 1
11 One day he came there, and he turned 1
18 he went out one day to his father 1
6:29 And on the next day I said to her, 'Give your son 1
7: 9 This day is a day of good news; if we are silent 1
9 This day is a day of good news; if we are silent 1
8: 6 from the day that she left the land until now. 1
20 In his days Edom revolted from the rule of Judah 1
22 Edom revolted from the rule of Judah to this day. 1
10:27 house of Ba'al, and made it a latrine to this day. 1
32 In those days the LORD began to cut off parts 1
12: 2 Jeho'ash did what was right . . all his days 1
13:22 oppressed Israel all the days of Jeho'ahaz. 1
14: 7 called it Jok'the-el, which is its name to this day. 1
15: 5 he was a leper to the day of his death 1
18 he did not depart all his days from all the sins 1
29 In the days of Pekah king of Israel 1
37 In those days the LORD began to send Rezin 1
16: 6 came to Elath, where they dwell to this day. 1
17:23 Israel was exiled . . to Assyria until this day. 1
34 To this day they do according to the former 1
41 as their fathers did, so they do to this day. 1
18: 4 until those days the people . . burned incense 1
19: 3 Thus says Hezeki'ah, This day is a day of distress 1
3 This day is a day of distress, of rebuke 1
25 I planned from days of old what now I bring to pass 1
20: 1 In those days Hezeki'ah became sick 1
5 I will heal you; on the third day you shall go up 1
8 I . . go up to the house of the LORD on the third day? 1
17 Behold, the days are coming, when all . . shall be 1
17 which your fathers have stored up till this day 1
19 if there will be peace and security in my days? 1
21:15 since the day their fathers came out of Egypt 1
15 since the day their fathers . . even to this day. 1
23:22 since the days of the judges who judged Israel 1
22 or during all the days of the kings of Israel 1
29 In his days Pharaoh Neco king of Egypt went up 1
24: 1 In his days Nebuchadnez'zar king of Babylon came 1
25: 1 in the tenth month, on the tenth day of the month •
3 On the ninth day of the fourth month the famine •
8 In the fifth month, on the seventh day of the month •
27 in the twelfth month, on the 27th day of the month •
29 every day of his life he dined regularly 1
1Ch 1:19 Peleg (for in his days the earth was divided) 1
4:41 These . . came in the days of Hezeki'ah 1
41 and exterminated them to this day 1
43 and they have dwelt there to this day. 1
5:10 in the days of Saul they made war on the Hagrites 1
17 enrolled by genealogies in the days of Jotham 1
17 enrolled . . in the days of Jerobo'am 1
26 brought them to . . the river Gozan, to this day. 1
7: 2 their number in the days of David being 22,600 1
22 E'phraim their father mourned many days 1
9:25 were obliged to come in every seven days 1
33 for they were on duty day and night. 2
10:12 they . . fasted seven days. 1
11:22 slew a lion in a pit on a day when snow had fallen. 1
12:22 from day to day men kept coming to David to help 1
22 from day to day men kept coming to David to help •
39 with David for three days, eating and drinking 1
13: 3 for we neglected it in the days of Saul. 1
11 and that place is called Pe'rez-uz'za to this day. 1
12 David was afraid of God that day; 1
16: 7 Then on that day David first appointed 1
23 Tell of his salvation from day to day. 1
23 Tell of his salvation from day to day. 1
37 minister . . before the ark as each day required 1
17: 5 not dwelt in a house since the day I led up Israel 1
5 since the day I led up Israel to this day 1
11 days are fulfilled to go to be with your fathers 1
21:12 or else three days of the sword of the LORD 1
22: 9 I will give peace and quiet to Israel in his days. 1
23: 1 When David was old and full of days 1
26:17 On the east there were six each day 6
17 on the north four each day, on the south four 1
17 north four each day, on the south four each day 1
29:15 our days on the earth are like a shadow 1
21 and on the next day offered burnt offerings 1
22 they ate and drank before the LORD on that day 1
28 he died in a good old age, full of days, riches 1
2Ch 5: 9 the poles . . they are there to this day. 1
6: 5 'Since the day that I brought my people out 1
15 and with thy hand hast fulfilled it this day. 1
20 eyes may be open day and night toward this house 2
31 walk in thy ways all the days that they live 1
7: 8 Solomon held the feast for seven days 1
9 on the eighth day they held a solemn assembly; 1
9 kept the dedication of the altar seven days 1
9 for they had kept . . and the feast seven days. 1
10 On the 23rd day of the seventh month he 1
8: 8 made a forced levy and so they are to this day. 1
13 as the duty of each day required 1
14 he appointed . . as the duty of each day required 1
16 from the day the foundation . . was laid 1
9:20 not considered . . in the days of Solomon. 1
10: 5 He said to them, "Come to me again in three days. 1
12 all the people came to Rehobo'am the third day 1
12 as the king said, "Come to me again the third day. 1
19 against the house of David to this day. 1
13:20 did not recover his power in the days of Abi'jah; 1
14: 1 In his days the land had rest for ten years. 1
15:11 They sacrificed to the LORD on that day 1
17 the heart of Asa was blameless all his days. 1
18:24 Behold, you shall see on that day when you go 1
34 the battle grew hot that day 1
20:25 three days in taking the spoil, it was so much. 1
26 On the fourth day they assembled in the Valley 1
26 been called the Valley of Bera'cah to this day. 1
21: 8 In his days Edom revolted from the rule of Judah 1
10 Edom revolted from the rule of Judah to this day. 1
15 come out because of the disease, day by day.' 1
15 come out because of the disease, day by day.' 1
24: 2 all the days of Jehoi'ada the priest. 1
11 Thus they did day after day, and collected money 1
14 continually all the days of Jehoi'ada. 1
15 Jehoi'ada grew old and full of days, and died; 1
26: 5 set himself to seek God in the days of Zechari'ah 1
21 King Uzzi'ah was a leper to the day of his death 1
28: 6 Pekah . . slew 120,000 in Judah in one day 1
29:17 to sanctify on the first day of the first month •
17 and on the eighth day of the month they came 1
17 then for eight days they sanctified the house 1
17 on the sixteenth day of the first month 1
30:15 killed the passover lamb on the fourteenth day •
21 kept the feast of unleavened bread seven days 1
21 the priests praised the LORD day by day 1
21 the priests praised the LORD day by day 1
22 ate the food of the festival for seven days 1
23 to keep the feast for another seven days; 1
23 kept it for another seven days with gladness. 1
31:16 entered . . as the duty of each day required 1
32:24 In those days Hezeki'ah became sick 1
26 did not come upon them in the days of Hezeki'ah. 1
34:33 All his days they did not turn away 1
35: 1 lamb on the fourteenth day of the first month. •
16 all the service of the LORD was prepared that day 1
17 kept . . feast of unleavened bread seven days. 1
18 since the days of Samuel the prophet; 1
21 I am not coming against you this day, but against 1
25 spoken of Josi'ah in their laments to this day. 1
36: 9 reigned three months and ten days in Jerusalem. 1
21 All the days that it lay desolate it kept sabbath 1
Ezr 3: 4 daily burnt offerings . . as each day required. 1
6 From the first day of the seventh month 1
4: 2 since the days of E'sar-had'don king of Assyria 1
5 days of Cyrus king of Persia, even until the reign 1
7 in the days of Ar-ta-xerx'es, Bishlam 1
6: 9 let that be given to them day by day without fail 4
9 let that be given to them day by day without fail 4
15 finished on the third day of the month of Adar 4
19 On the fourteenth day of the first month •
22 kept the feast . . seven days with joy; 1
7: 9 first day of the first month he began to go up •
9 first day of the fifth month he came to Jerusalem •
8:15 Aha'va, and there we encamped three days. 1
31 departed from the river Aha'va on the twelfth day •

32 came to Jerusalem . . remained three days. 1
33 On the fourth day, within the house of our God 1
9: 7 From the days of our fathers to this day 1
7 From the days of our fathers to this day 1
7 plundering, and to utter shame, as at this day. 1
15 left a remnant that has escaped, as at this day. 1
10: 8 that if any one did not come within three days 1
9 assembled at Jerusalem within the three days; 1
9 ninth month, on the twentieth day of the month. •
13 Nor is this a work for one day or for two; 1
16 On the first day of the tenth month they sat down 1
17 by the first day of the first month they had come 1
Neh 1: 4 I sat down and wept, and mourned for days; 1
6 prayer . . I now pray before thee day and night 1
2:11 I came to Jerusalem and was there three days. 1
4: 2 Will they finish up in a day? Will they revive 1
9 set a guard as a protection . . day and night. 2
16 From that day on, half of my servants worked 1
22 may be a guard for us by night and may labor by day. 1
5:11 Return to them this very day their fields 1
18 prepared for one day was one ox and six choice 1
18 every ten days skins of wine in abundance; 1
6:15 finished on the 25th day of . . Elul •
15 wall was finished . . in 52 days. 1
17 Moreover in those days the nobles of Judah sent 1
8: 2 on the first day of the seventh month. 1
9 This day is holy to the LORD your God; 1
10 for this day is holy to our Lord; 1
11 Be quiet, for this day is holy; do not be grieved. 1
13 On the second day the heads of fathers' houses 1
17 from the days of Jeshua the son of Nun to that day 1
17 from the days of Jeshua the son of Nun to that day 1
18 day by day, from the first day to the last day 1
18 day by day, from the first day to the last day 1
18 day by day, from the first day to the last day 1
18 day by day, from the first day to the last day 1
18 kept the feast seven days; and on the eighth day 1
18 eighth day there was a solemn assembly 1
9: 1 Now on the 24th day of this month 1
3 read from . . the law . . for a fourth of the day; 1
10 thou didst get thee a name, as it is to this day. 1
12 pillar of cloud thou didst lead them in the day 2
19 pillar of cloud . . not depart from them by day 2
32 time of the kings of Assyria until this day. 1
36 Behold, we are slaves this day; 1
10:31 wares or any grain on the sabbath day to sell 1
31 not buy from them on the sabbath or on a holy day; 1
11:23 settled provision . . as every day required. 1
12: 7 chiefs of the priests . . in the days of Jeshua. 1
12 days of Joi'akim were priests, heads of fathers' 1
22 Levites, in the days of Eli'ashib, Joi'ada, Joha'nan 1
23 Book of the Chronicles until the days of Joha'nan 1
26 days of Joi'akim the son of Jeshua son of Jo'zadak 1
26 days of Nehemi'ah the governor and of Ezra 1
43 offered great sacrifices that day and rejoiced 1
44 that day men were appointed over the chambers 1
46 For in the days of David and Asaph of old there was 1
47 all Israel in the days of Zerub'babel 1
47 all Israel . . in the days of Nehemi'ah 1
13: 1 On that day they read from the book of Moses 1
15 In those days I saw in Judah men treading 1
15 brought into Jerusalem on the sabbath day; 1
15 warned them on the day when they sold food. 1
17 evil thing . . profaning the sabbath day? 1
19 no burden might be brought in on the sabbath day. 1
22 guard the gates, to keep the sabbath day holy. 1
23 days also I saw the Jews who had married women 1
Est 1: 1 In the days of Ahasu-e'rus . . who reigned 1
2 in those days when King Ahasu-e'rus sat . . in Susa 1
4 he showed . . for many days, 180 days 1
4 he showed the riches . . for many days, 180 days. 1
5 And when these days were completed, 1
5 the king gave . . a banquet lasting for seven days 1
10 On the seventh day . . he commanded Mehu'man 1
18 This very day the ladies . . will be telling it 1
2:11 And every day Mor'decai walked 1
21 in those days . . as Mor'decai was sitting 1
3: 4 spoke to him day after day and he would not listen 1
4 spoke to him day after day and he would not listen 1
7 they cast Pur . . before Haman day after day; 1
7 they cast Pur . . before Haman day after day; 1
12 summoned on the thirteenth day of the first month 1
13 and to annihilate all Jews . . in one day 1
13 in one day, the thirteenth day of the twelfth month •
14 proclamation to all . . to be ready for that day. 1
4:11 I have not been called . . these 30 days. 1
16 a fast . . and neither eat nor drink for three days 1
16 neither eat nor drink . . three days, night or day. 1
5: 1 On the third day Esther put on her royal robes 1
4 let the king and Haman come this day to a dinner 1
9 Haman went out that day joyful and glad of heart. 1
7: 2 on the second day . . the king again said to Esther 1
8: 1 On that day King Ahasu-e'rus gave to Queen Esther 1
9 in the third month . . on the 23rd day; •
12 to destroy . . upon one day throughout all 1
12 on the thirteenth day of the twelfth month •
13 and the Jews were to be ready on that day to avenge 1
9: 1 month of Adar, on the thirteenth day of the same 1
1 on the very day when the enemies of the Jews hoped 1
1 very day . . which had been changed to a day •
11 That very day the number of those slain in Susa 1
13 allowed . . to do according to this day's edict. 1
15 The Jews . . gathered also on the fourteenth day 1
17 was on the thirteenth day of the month of Adar 1
17 and on the fourteenth day they rested •
17 they . . made that a day of feasting and gladness. 1
18 on the thirteenth day and on the fourteenth •
18 gathered . . and rested on the fifteenth day •
18 making that a day of feasting and gladness. 1
19 Jews of . . hold the fourteenth day of the month 1
19 hold . . as a day for gladness and feasting 1
19 a day on which they send choice . . to one another. •
21 keep the fourteenth day of the month Adar 1
21 keep . . and also the fifteenth day of the same 1
22 they should keep . . as the days on which the Jews 1
22 should make them days of feasting and gladness 1
22 days for sending choice portions to one another •
26 they called these days Purim, after the term Pur. 1
27 that without fail they would keep these two days 1
28 that these days should be remembered and kept 1
28 these days of Purim should never fall 1
28 nor should the commemoration of these days •
31 that these days of Purim should be observed 1
Job 1: 4 go and hold a feast in the house of each on his day; 1
5 when the days of the feast had run their course 1
6 a day when the sons of God came to present 1
13 a day when his sons and daughters were eating 1
2: 1 Again there was a day when the sons of God came 1
13 on the ground seven days and seven nights 1
3: 1 opened his mouth and cursed the day of his birth. 1
3 Let the day perish wherein I was born 1
4 Let that day be darkness! May God above not seek it 1
5 let the blackness of the day terrify it. 1
6 let it not rejoice among the days of the year 1
8 Let those curse it who curse the day 1
7: 1 are not his days like the days of a hireling? 1
1 are not his days like the days of a hireling? 1
6 My days are swifter than a weaver's shuttle 1
16 Let me alone, for my days are a breath. 1
8: 9 know nothing, for our days on earth are a shadow. 1
9:25 My days are swifter than a runner; they flee away 1
10: 5 Are thy days as the days of man, or thy years 1
5 Are thy days as the days of man, or thy years 1
20 Are not the days of my life few? 1
12:12 and understanding in length of days. 1
14: 1 Man that is born of a woman is of few days 1
5 Since his days are determined 1
6 that he may enjoy, like a hireling, his day. 1
14 All the days of my service I would wait 1
15:20 The wicked man writhes in pain all his days 1
23 He knows that a day of darkness is ready at his hand; 1
17: 1 My spirit is broken, my days are extinct 1
11 My days are past, my plans are broken off 1
12 They make night into day; 1
18:20 They of the west are appalled at his day 1
20:28 dragged off in the day of God's wrath. 1
21:13 They spend their days in prosperity 1
30 the wicked man is spared in the day of calamity 1
30 that he is rescued in the day of wrath? 1
24: 1 why do those who know him never see his days? 1
16 by day they shut themselves up; 2
27: 6 my heart does not reproach me for any of my days. 1
29: 2 as in the days when God watched over me; 1
4 I was in my autumn days, when the friendship of God 1
18 I shall multiply my days as the sand 1
30:16 days of affliction have taken hold of me. 1
25 Did not I weep for him whose day was hard? 1
27 days of affliction come to meet me. 1
32: 7 Let days speak, and many years teach wisdom. 1
33:25 let him return to the days of his youthful vigor 1
36:11 they complete their days in prosperity 1
38:12 you commanded the morning since your days began 1
21 the number of your days is great! 1
23 the time of trouble, for the day of battle and war? 1
42:17 Job died, an old man, and full of days. 1
Ps 1: 2 on his law he meditates day and night. 2
7:11 a God who has indignation every day. 1
18: 0 on the day when the LORD delivered him 1
18 They came upon me in the day of my calamity; 1
19: 2 Day to day pours forth speech 1
2 Day to day pours forth speech 1
20: 1 The LORD answer you in the day of trouble! 1
21: 4 gavest it to him, length of days for ever and ever. 1
22: 2 O my God, I cry by day, but thou dost not answer; 2
23: 6 and mercy shall follow me all the days of my life; 1
25: 5 for thee I wait all the day long. 1
27: 4 in the house of the LORD all the days of my life 1
5 will hide me in his shelter in the day of trouble; 1
32: 3 my body wasted away through my groaning all day 1
4 For day and night thy hand was heavy upon me; 2
34:12 who desires life, and covets many days 1
35:28 and of thy praise all the day long. 1
37:13 at the wicked, for he sees that his day is coming. 1
18 The LORD knows the days of the blameless 1
19 in the days of famine they have abundance. 1
38: 6 all the day I go about mourning. 1
12 meditate treachery all the day long. 1
39: 4 my end, and what is the measure of my days; 1
5 Behold, thou hast made my days a few handbreadths 1
41: 1 The LORD delivers him in the day of trouble; 1
42: 3 My tears have been my food day and night 2
8 By day the LORD commands his steadfast love; 2
44: 1 what deeds thou didst perform in their days 1
1 didst perform in their days, in the days of old 1
15 All day long my disgrace is before me 1
22 Nay, for thy sake we are slain all the day long 1
50:15 call upon me in the day of trouble; 1
52: 1 mischief done against the godly? All the day 1
55:10 Day and night they go around it on its walls; 2
23 treachery shall not live out half their days. 1
56: 1 all day long foemen oppress me; 1
2 my enemies trample upon me all day long 1
5 All day long they seek to injure my cause; 1
9 will be turned back in the day when I call. 1
59:16 a fortress and a refuge in the day of my distress. 1
61: 8 praises to thy name, as I pay my vows day after day. 1
8 praises to thy name, as I pay my vows day after day. 1
71: 8 with thy praise, and with thy glory all the day. 1
15 of thy deeds of salvation all the day 1
24 will talk of thy righteous help all the day long 1
72: 7 In his days may righteousness flourish 1
15 blessings invoked for him all the day! 1
73:14 For all the day long I have been stricken 1
74:16 Thine is the day, thine also the night; 1
22 remember how the impious scoff at thee all the day! 1
77: 2 In the day of my trouble I seek the Lord; 1
5 I consider the days of old, I remember the years 1
78: 9 E'phraimites . . turned back on the day of battle. 1
33 he made their days vanish like a breath 1
42 or the day when he redeemed them from the foe; 1
81: 3 new moon, at the full moon, on our feast day. 1
84:10 day in thy courts is better than 1,000 1
86: 3 O Lord, for to thee do I cry all the day. 1
7 In the day of my trouble I call on thee 1
88: 1 O LORD, my God, I call for help by day; 1
9 Every day I call upon thee, O LORD; 1
17 They surround me like a flood all day long; 1
89:16 who exult in thy name all the day 1
29 his throne as the days of the heavens. 1
45 Thou hast cut short the days of his youth; 1
90: 9 For all our days pass away under thy wrath 1
12 teach us to number our days that we may get 1
14 that we may rejoice and be glad all our days. 1
15 Make us glad as many days as thou hast afflicted 1
91: 5 of the night, nor the arrow that flies by day 2
94:13 to give him respite from days of trouble 1
95: 8 Mer'ibah, as on the day of Massah in the wilderness 1
96: 2 tell of his salvation from day to day. 1
2 tell of his salvation from day to day. 1
102: 2 not hide thy face from me in the day of my distress! 1
2 answer me speedily in the day when I call! 1
3 For my days pass away like smoke 1
8 All the day my enemies taunt me 1
11 My days are like an evening shadow; 1
23 he has shortened my days. 1
24 I say, "take me not hence in the midst of my days 1
103:15 As for man, his days are like grass; 1
109: 8 May his days be few; may another seize his goods! 1
110: 3 day you lead your host upon the holy mountains. 1
5 shatter kings on the day of his wrath. 1
118:24 This is the day which the LORD has made; 1
119:91 By thy appointment they stand this day; 1
97 how I love thy law! It is my meditation all the day. 1
164 Seven times a day I praise thee 1
121: 6 The sun shall not smite you by day 2
128: 5 prosperity of Jerusalem all the days of you life! 1
136: 8 the sun to rule over the day 1
137: 7 O LORD, against the E'domites the day of Jerusalem 1
138: 3 On the day I called, thou didst answer me 1
139:12 not dark to thee, the night is bright as the day; 1
16 book were written . . days that were formed 1
140: 7 thou hast covered my head in the day of battle. 1
143: 5 I remember the days of old, I meditate on all that 1
144: 4 like a breath, his days are like a passing shadow. 1
145: 2 Every day I will bless thee, and praise thy name 1
146: 4 on that very day his plans perish. 1
Prv 3: 2 length of days and years of life 1
4:18 shines brighter and brighter until full day. 1
9:11 For by me your days will be multiplied 1
11: 4 Riches do not profit in the day of wrath 1
15:15 All the days of the afflicted are evil 1
16: 4 even the wicked for the day of trouble. 1
21:26 All day long the wicked covets 1
31 The horse is made ready for the day of battle 1
23:17 but continue in the fear of the LORD all the day. 1
24:10 If you faint in the day of adversity 1
25:20 like one who takes off a garment on a cold day 1
27: 1 for you do not know what a day may bring forth. 1
10 brother's house in the day of your calamity. 1
15 A continual dripping on a rainy day 1
28:16 who hates unjust gain will prolong his days. 1
31:12 She does him good . . all the days of her life. 1
Ecc 2: 3 to do . . during the few days of their life. 1
16 seeing that in the days to come all will have been 1
23 For all his days are full of pain 1
5:17 and spent all his days in darkness and grief 1
18 the few days of his life which God has given him 1

20 For he will not much remember the days of his life 1
6: 3 many years, so that the days of his years are many 1
12 while he lives the few days of his vain life 1
7: 1 and the day of death, than the day of birth. 1
1 and the day of death, than the day of birth. 1
10 Why were the former days better than these? 1
14 In the day of prosperity be joyful 1
14 and in the day of adversity consider; 1
8: 8 power . . or authority over the day of death; 1
13 neither will he prolong his days like a shadow 1
15 this will go with him . . through the days of life 1
16 how neither day nor night one's eyes see sleep; 1
9: 9 all the days of your vain life which he has given 1
11: 1 for you will find it after many days. 1
8 remember that the days of darkness will be many. 1
9 let your heart cheer you in the days of your youth; 1
12: 1 Remember also . . in the days of your youth 1
1 in the days of . . youth, before the evil days come 1
3 the day when the keepers of the house tremble 1
Sng 2:17 Until the day breathes and the shadows flee 1
3:11 his mother crowned him on the day of his wedding 1
11 on the day of the gladness of his heart. 1
4: 6 Until the day breathes and the shadows flee 1
8: 8 What shall we . . on the day when she is spoken for? 1
Isa 1: 1 which he saw . . in the days of Uzzi'ah, Jotham, Ahaz 1
2: 2 It shall come to pass in the latter days 1
11 the LORD alone will be exalted in that day. 1
12 the LORD . . has a day against all that is proud 1
17 the LORD alone will be exalted in that day. 1
20 In that day men will cast forth their idols 1
3: 7 in that day he will speak out, saying 1
18 In that day the Lord will take away the finery 1
4: 1 seven women shall take hold of one man in that day 1
2 In that day the branch of the LORD 1
5 cloud by day, and smoke . . by night; 2
6 for a shade by day from the heat, and for a refuge 2
5:30 They will growl over it on that day 1
7: 1 In the days of Ahaz the son of Jotham, son of Uzzi'ah 1
17 bring . . such days as have not come 1
17 the day that E'phraim departed from Judah– 1
18 In that day the LORD will whistle for the fly 1
20 In that day the Lord will shave with a razor 1
21 In that day a man will keep alive a young cow 1
23 In that day every place where there used to be 1
9: 4 rod . . thou hast broken as on the day of Mid'ian. 1
14 head and tail, palm branch and reed in one day– 1
10: 3 What will you do on the day of punishment 1
17 burn and devour his thorns and briers in one day. 1
20 In that day the remnant of Israel 1
27 in that day his burden will depart 1
32 This very day he will halt at Nob 1
11:10 In that day the root of Jesse shall stand 1
11 In that day the Lord will extend his hand 1
12: 1 You will say in that day 1
4 you will say in that day: "Give thanks to the LORD 1
13: 6 Wail, for the day of the LORD is near; 1
9 Behold, the day of the LORD comes, cruel 1
13 the LORD of hosts in the day of his fierce anger. 1
22 at hand and its days will not be prolonged. 1
17: 4 in that day the glory of Jacob will be brought low 1
7 In that day men will regard their Maker 1
9 In that day their strong cities will be like 1
11 you make them grow on the day that you plant them 1
11 flee away in a day of grief and incurable pain. 1
19:16 In that day the Egyptians will be like women 1
18 In that day there will be five cities in . . Egypt 1
19 In that day there will be an altar to the LORD 1
21 the Egyptians will know the LORD in that day 1
23 In that day there will be a highway from Egypt 1
24 In that day Israel will be the third with Egypt 1
20: 6 coastland will say in that day, 'Behold, this 1
21: 8 Upon a watchtower I stand . . continually by day 2
22: 5 a day of tumult and trampling and confusion 1
8 In that day you looked to the weapons of the House 1
12 In that day the Lord GOD of hosts called 1
20 In that day I will call my servant Eli'akim 1
25 In that day . . the peg that was fastened 1
23: 7 exultant city whose origin is from days of old 1
15 In that day Tyre will be forgotten 1
15 for 70 years, like the days of one king. 1
24:21 On that day the LORD will punish the host 1
22 and after many days they will be punished. 1
25: 9 It will be said on that day, "Lo, this is our God; 1
26: 1 In that day this song will be sung in the land 1
27: 1 In that day the LORD with his hard 1
2 In that day: "A pleasant vineyard, sing of it! 1
3 Lest any one harm it, I guard it night and day; 1
6 In days to come Jacob shall take root •
8 with his fierce blast in the day of the east wind. 1
12 In that day from the river Euphra'tes to the Brook 1
13 in that day a great trumpet will be blown 1
28: 5 In that day the LORD of hosts will be a crown 1
19 it will pass through, by day and by night; 1
29:18 In that day the deaf shall hear the words of a book 1
30:23 In that day your cattle will graze in large 1
25 in the day of the great slaughter 1
26 sun will be sevenfold, as the light of seven days 1
26 in the day when the LORD binds up the hurt 1
31: 7 that day every one shall cast away his idols 1

34: 8 For the LORD has a day of vengeance 1
10 Night and day it shall not be quenched; 2
37: 3 Thus says Hezeki'ah, 'This day is a day of distress 1
3 Thus says Hezeki'ah, 'This day is a day of distress 1
26 I planned from days of old what now I bring to pass 1
38: 1 In those days Hezeki'ah became sick 1
10 I said, In the noontide of my days I must depart; 1
12 from day to night thou dost bring me to an end; 1
13 from day to night thou dost bring me to an end. 1
19 the living, he thanks thee, as I do this day; 1
20 to stringed instruments all the days of our life 1
39: 6 the days are coming, when all that is in your house 1
6 which your fathers have stored up till this day 1
8 There will be peace and security in my days. 1
47: 9 two things shall come to you . . in one day; 1
49: 8 in a day of salvation I have helped you; 1
51: 9 as in days of old, the generations of long ago. 1
13 and fear continually all the day 1
52: 5 and continually all the day my name is despised. 1
6 in that day they shall know that it is I who speak; 1
53:10 see his offspring, he shall prolong his days; 1
54: 9 this is like the days of Noah to me: as I swore that •
56:12 will be like this day, great beyond measure. 1
58: 3 in the day of your fast you seek your own pleasure 1
4 Fasting like yours this day will not make 1
5 the fast that I choose, a day for a man to humble 1
5 call this a fast, and a day acceptable to the LORD? 1
13 from doing your pleasure on my holy day 1
13 a delight and the holy day of the LORD honorable; 1
60:11 day and night they shall not be shut; 2
19 The sun shall be no more your light by day 2
20 and your days of mourning shall be ended. 1
61: 2 and the day of vengeance of our God; 1
62: 6 all the day and all the night they shall never be 1
63: 4 For the day of vengeance was in my heart 1
9 lifted . . up and carried them all the days of old. 1
11 Then he remembered the days of old, 1
65: 2 I spread out my hands all the day to a rebellious 1
5 in my nostrils, a fire that burns all the day. 1
20 there be in it an infant that lives but a few days 1
20 or an old man who does not fill out his days 1
22 the days of a tree shall the days of my people be 1
22 the days of a tree shall the days of my people be 1
66: 8 Shall a land be born in one day? 1
Jer 1: 2 in the days of Josi'ah the son of Amon, king of Judah 1
3 It came also in the days of Jehoi'akim 1
10 See, I have set you this day over nations 1
18 And I, behold, I make you this day a fortified city 1
2:32 people have forgotten me days without number. 1
3: 6 The LORD said to me in the days of King Josi'ah 1
16 in those days, says the LORD, they shall no more say 1
18 In those days the house of Judah shall join 1
25 we and our fathers, from our youth even to this day; 1
4: 9 In that day, says the LORD, courage shall fail 1
5:18 But even in those days, says the LORD 1
6: 4 attack at noon!" "Woe to us, for the day declines 1
7:22 the day that I brought them out of the land 1
25 the day that your fathers came out of the land 1
25 came out of the land of Egypt to this day 1
25 sent . . the prophets to them, day after day; 1
25 sent . . the prophets to them, day after day; 1
32 behold, the days are coming, says the LORD 1
9: 1 that I might weep day and night for the slain 2
25 Behold, the days are coming, says the LORD 1
11: 5 a land flowing with milk and honey, as at this day. 1
7 even to this day, saying, Obey my voice. 1
12: 3 and set them apart for the day of slaughter. 1
13: 6 And after many days the LORD said to me 1
14:17 Let my eyes run down with tears night and day 1
15: 9 her sun went down while it was yet day; 2
16: 9 from this place, before your eyes and in your days 1
13 there you shall serve other gods day and night 2
14 behold, the days are coming, says the LORD 1
19 my stronghold, my refuge in the day of trouble 1
17:11 in the midst of his days they will leave him 1
16 nor have I desired the day of disaster 1
17 thou art my refuge in the day of evil. 1
18 bring upon them the day of evil; 1
21 and do not bear a burden on the sabbath day 1
22 or do any work, but keep the sabbath day holy 1
24 by the gates of this city on the sabbath day 1
24 but keep the sabbath day holy and do no work on it 1
27 do not listen to me, to keep the sabbath day holy 1
27 by the gates of Jerusalem on the sabbath day 1
18:17 my back, not my face, in the day of their calamity. 1
19: 6 therefore, behold, days are coming, says the LORD 1
20: 7 I have become a laughingstock all the day; 1
8 has become for me a . . derision all day long. 1
14 Cursed be the day on which I was born! 1
14 The day when my mother bore me 1
18 to see toil and sorrow, and spend my days in shame? 1
22:30 childless, a man who shall not succeed in his days; 1
23: 5 Behold, the days are coming, says the LORD 1
6 In his days Judah will be saved 1
7 behold, the days are coming, says the LORD 1
20 In the latter days you will understand it 1
25: 3 to this day, the word of the LORD has come to me 1
18 a hissing and a curse, as at this day; 1
33 those slain by the LORD on that day 1

34 the days of your slaughter and dispersion 1
26:18 Micah . . prophesied in the days of Hezeki'ah 1
27:22 until the day when I give attention to them 1
30: 3 For behold, days are coming, says the LORD 1
7 Alas! that day is so great there is none like it; 1
8 come to pass in that day, says the LORD of hosts 1
24 In the latter days you will understand this. 1
31: 6 For there shall be a day when watchmen will call 1
27 Behold, the days are coming, says the LORD 1
29 In those days they shall no longer say 1
31 Behold, the days are coming, says the LORD 1
33 make with the house of Israel after those days 1
35 says the LORD, who gives the sun for light by day 2
38 Behold, the days are coming, says the LORD 1
32:20 and to this day in Israel and among all mankind 1
20 and hast made thee a name, as at this day. 1
31 from the day it was built to this day 1
31 from the day it was built to this day 1
33:14 Behold, the days are coming, says the LORD 1
15 In those days and at that time I will cause 1
16 In those days Judah will be saved 1
20 If you can break my covenant with the day 1
20 so that day and night will not come 2
25 If I have not established my covenant with day 2
35: 1 in the days of Jehoi'akim the son of Josi'ah 1
7 but you shall live in tents all your days 1
7 that you may live many days in the land 1
8 that he commanded us, to drink no wine all our days 1
14 and they drink none to this day 1
36: 2 from the day I spoke to you, from the days of Josi'ah 1
2 spoke to you, from the days of Josi'ah until today. 1
6 and on a fast day in the hearing of all the people 1
30 his dead body shall be cast out to the heat by day 1
37:16 and remained there many days 1
38:28 until the day that Jerusalem was taken. 1
39: 2 in the fourth month, on the ninth day of the month •
16 shall be accomplished before you on that day. 1
17 But I will deliver you on that day, says the LORD 1
41: 4 On the day after the murder of Gedali'ah 1
42: 7 At the end of ten days the word of the LORD came 1
19 that I have warned you this day 1
21 I have this day declared it to you 1
44: 2 Behold, this day they are a desolation 1
6 a waste and a desolation, as at this day. 1
10 have not humbled themselves even to this day 1
22 without inhabitant, as it is this day. 1
23 that this evil has befallen you, as at this day. 1
46:10 That day is the day of the Lord GOD of hosts 1
10 That day is the day of the Lord GOD of hosts •
10 a day of vengeance, to avenge himself on his foes. 1
21 for the day of their calamity has come upon them 1
26 Egypt shall be inhabited as in the days of old 1
47: 4 because of the day that is coming to destroy all 1
48:12 behold, the days are coming, says the LORD 1
41 shall be in that day like the heart of a woman 1
47 restore the fortunes of Moab in the latter days 1
49: 2 behold, the days are coming, says the LORD 1
22 heart of the warriors of Edom shall be in that day 1
26 all her soldiers shall be destroyed in that day 1
39 in the latter days I will restore the fortunes 1
50: 4 In those days and in that time, says the LORD 1
20 In those days and in that time, says the LORD 1
27 Woe to them, for their day has come 2
30 all her soldiers shall be destroyed on that day 1
31 your day has come, the time when I will punish you. 1
51: 2 from every side on the day of trouble. 1
47 Therefore, behold, the days are coming 1
52 behold, the days are coming, says the LORD 1
52: 4 tenth month, on the tenth day of the month •
6 On the ninth day of the fourth month the famine •
11 and put him in prison till the day of his death. 1
12 In the fifth month, on the tenth day •
31 on the 25th day of the month •
33 every day of his life he dined . . at the king's 1
34 his daily need, until the day of his death 1
Lam 1: 7 remembers in the days of her affliction 1
7 precious things that were hers from days of old. 1
12 LORD inflicted on the day of his fierce anger. 1
13 he has left me stunned, faint all the day long. 1
21 Bring thou the day thou hast announced 1
2: 1 he has not remembered . . in the day of his anger. 1
7 a clamor . . as on the day of an appointed feast. 1
16 Ah, this is the day we longed for; now we have it; 1
18 tears stream down like a torrent day and night! 2
21 in the day of thy anger thou hast slain them 1
22 didst invite as to the day of an appointed feast 1
22 on the day of the anger of the LORD none escaped 1
3: 3 surely against me he turns . . the whole day long. 1
14 the burden of their songs all day long. 1
62 my assailants are against me all the day long. 1
4:18 our days were numbered; for our end had come. 1
5:21 Restore us . . Renew our days as of old! 1
Ezk 1: 1 in the fourth month, on the fifth day of the month •
2 On the fifth day of the month (it was the fifth year •
28 the bow that is in the cloud on the day of rain 1
2: 3 have transgressed against me to this very day. 1
3:15 I sat there overwhelmed among them seven days. 1
16 at the end of seven days, the word of the LORD came 1
4: 4 for the number of the days that you lie upon it 1

5 For I assign to you a number of days, 390 days 1
5 For I assign to you a number of days, 390 days 1
6 40 days I assign you, a day for each year. 1
6 40 days I assign you, a day for each year. 1
8 till you have completed the days of your siege. 1
9 the number of days that you lie upon your side 1
9 days that you lie upon your side, 390 days 1
10 food . . shall be by weight, twenty shekels a day; 1
5: 2 when the days of the siege are completed; 1
7: 7 the time has come, the day is near, a day of tumult 1
7 the time has come, the day is near, a day of tumult •
10 Behold, the day! Behold, it comes! 1
12 The time has come, the day draws near. 1
19 to deliver them in the day of the wrath of the LORD; 1
8: 1 in the sixth month, on the fifth day of the month •
12: 3 and go into exile by day in their sight; 2
4 You shall bring out your baggage by day 2
7 I brought out my baggage by day 2
22 days grow long, and every vision comes to nought 1
23 But say to them, The days are at hand 1
25 in your days, O rebellious house, I will speak 1
27 The vision that he sees is for many days hence 1
13: 5 it might stand in battle in the day of the LORD. 1
16: 4 as for your birth, on the day you were born 1
5 you were abhorred, on the day that you were born. 1
22 you did not remember the days of your youth 1
43 you have not remembered the days of your youth 1
56 a byword in your mouth in the day of your pride 1
60 my covenant with you in the days of your youth 1
20: 1 the fifth month, on the tenth day of the month •
5 On the day when I chose Israel 1
6 On that day I swore to them that I would bring them 1
29 its name is called Bamah to this day 1
31 yourselves with all your idols to this day. 1
21:25 wicked one, prince of Israel, whose day has come 1
29 the unhallowed wicked, whose day has come 1
22: 4 you have brought your day near 1
14 in the days that I shall deal with you? 1
24 or rained upon in the day of indignation. 1
23: 8 which she had practiced since her days in Egypt; •
19 her harlotry, remembering the days of her youth 1
38 they have defiled my sanctuary on the same day 1
39 on the same day they came into my sanctuary 1
24: 1 in the tenth month, on the tenth day of the month •
2 write down the name of this day, this very day. 1
2 write down the name of this day, this very day. 1
2 has laid siege to Jerusalem this very day. 1
25 on the day when I take from them their stronghold 1
26 on that day a fugitive will come to you to report 1
27 On that day your mouth will be opened 1
26: 1 In the eleventh year, on the first day of the month •
18 Now the isles tremble on the day of your fall; 1
27:27 into the heart of the seas on the day of your ruin. 1
28:13 On the day that you were created 1
15 were blameless . . from the day you were created 1
29: 1 the tenth month, on the twelfth day of the month •
17 in the first month, on the first day of the month •
21 On that day I will cause a horn to spring forth 1
30: 2 Thus says the Lord GOD: "Wail, 'Alas for the day! 1
3 For the day is near, the day of the LORD is near; 1
3 For the day is near, the day of the LORD is near; 1
3 day of the LORD is near; it will be a day of clouds 1
9 that day swift messengers shall go forth from me 1
9 shall come upon them on the day of Egypt's doom; 1
18 At Tehaph'nehes the day shall be dark 1
20 the first month, on the seventh day of the month •
31: 1 in the third month, on the first day of the month •
32: 1 in the twelfth month, on the first day of the month •
10 for his own life, on the day of your downfall. 1
17 on the fifteenth day of the month •
33:21 in the tenth month, on the fifth day of the month •
34:12 scattered on a day of clouds and thick darkness. 1
36:33 On the day that I cleanse you 1
38: 8 After many days you will be mustered; 1
10 On that day thoughts will come into your mind 1
14 On that day when my people Israel are dwelling 1
16 In the latter days I will bring you 1
17 Are you he of whom I spoke in former days 1
17 who in those days prophesied for years 1
18 on that day, when Gog shall come against the land 1
19 On that day there shall be a great shaking 1
39: 8 That is the day of which I have spoken. 1
11 On that day I will give to Gog a place for burial 1
13 on the day that I show my glory, says the Lord GOD. 1
22 I am the LORD their God, from that day forward. 1
40: 1 on the tenth day of the month •
1 on that very day, the hand of the LORD was upon me 1
43:18 On the day when it is erected for offering 1
22 on the second day you shall offer a he-goat 1
25 For seven days you shall provide daily a goat 1
26 Seven days shall they make atonement 1
27 when they have completed these days 1
27 then from the eighth day onward the priests 1
44:26 is defiled, he shall count for himself seven days 1
27 on the day that he goes into the holy place 1
45:18 In the first month, on the first day of the month •
20 You shall do the same on the seventh day •
21 first month, on the fourteenth day of the month 1
21 for seven days unleavened bread shall be eaten. 1
22 On that day the prince shall provide for himself 1
23 the seven days of the festival he shall provide 1
23 rams without blemish, on each of the seven days; 1
25 seventh month, on the fifteenth day of the month 1
25 for the seven days of the feast, he shall make 1
46: 1 The gate . . shall be shut on the six working days; 1
1 but on the sabbath day it shall be opened 1
1 on the day of the new moon it shall be opened. 1
4 prince offers to the LORD on the sabbath day 1
6 On the day of the new moon he shall offer 1
12 as he does on the sabbath day. Then he shall go out 1
Dan 1:12 Test your servants for ten days; let us be given 1
14 hearkened . . and tested them for ten days. 1
15 end of ten days it was seen that they were better 1
2:28 made known . . what will be in the latter days. 4
44 days of those kings the God of heaven will set up 4
4:34 end of the days I, Nebuchadnez'zar, lifted my eyes 4
5:11 days of your father light and understanding 4
26 MENE, God has numbered the days of your kingdom •
6: 7 makes petition to any god or man for 30 days 4
10 got down upon his knees three times a day 4
12 god or man within 30 days except to you, O king 4
13 but makes his petition three times a day. 4
7: 9 one that was ancient of days took his seat; 4
13 came to the Ancient of Days and was presented 4
22 until the Ancient of Days came, and judgment 4
8:26 vision, for it pertains to many days hence. 1
27 I, Daniel, was overcome and lay sick for some days; 1
9: 7 but to us confusion of face, as at this day 1
15 hast made thee a name, as at this day 1
10: 2 days I, Daniel, was mourning for three weeks. 1
4 On the 24th day of the first month 1
12 first day that you set your mind to understand 1
13 prince . . Persia withstood me 21 days; 1
14 what is to befall your people in the latter days. 1
14 For the vision is for days yet to come. 1
11:20 within a few days he shall be broken 1
33 though they shall fall . . for some days. 1
12:11 there shall be 1,290 days. 1
12 he who waits and comes to the 1,335 days. 1
13 in your allotted place at the end of the days. 4
Hos 1: 1 in the days of Uzzi'ah, Jotham, Ahaz, and Hezeki'ah 1
1 and in the days of Jerobo'am the son of Jo'ash 1
5 And on that day, I will break the bow of Israel 1
11 for great shall be the day of Jezreel. 1
2: 3 and make her as in the day she was born 1
13 I will punish her for the feast days of the Ba'als 1
15 there she shall answer as in the days of her youth 1
16 that day, says the LORD, you will call me, 1
18 And I will make for you a covenant on that day 1
21 that day, says the LORD, I will answer the heavens 1
3: 3 I said to her, "You must dwell as mine for many days; 1
4 For the children of Israel shall dwell many days 1
5 come . . to his goodness in the latter days. 1
4: 5 You shall stumble by day 1
5: 9 become a desolation in the day of punishment; 1
6: 2 After two days he will revive us; 1
2 on the third day he will raise us up 1
7: 5 On the day of our king the princes became sick 1
9: 5 What will you do on the day of appointed festival 1
5 and on the day of the feast of the LORD? 1
7 The days of punishment have come 1
7 the days of recompense have come; 1
9 corrupted themselves as in the days of Gib'e-ah 1
10: 9 From the days of Gib'e-ah, you have sinned, O Israel; 1
14 destroyed Beth-ar'bel on the day of battle; 1
12: 1 and pursues the east wind all day long; 1
9 in tents, as in the days of the appointed feast. 1
Jol 1: 2 Has such a thing happened in your days 1
2 in your days, or in the days of your fathers? 1
15 Alas for the day! For the day of the LORD is near 1
15 Alas for the day! For the day of the LORD is near 1
2: 1 for the day of the LORD is coming, it is near 1
2 a day of darkness and gloom, a day of clouds 1
2 a day of clouds and thick darkness! 1
11 For the day of the LORD is great and very terrible; 1
29 in those days, I will pour out my spirit. 1
31 before the great and terrible day of the LORD 1
3: 1 For behold, in those days and at that time 1
14 day of the LORD is near in the valley of decision. 1
18 in that day the mountains shall drip sweet wine 1
Ams 1: 1 concerning Israel in the days of Uzzi'ah king 1
1 and in the days of Jerobo'am the son of Jo'ash, 1
14 strongholds, with shouting in the day of battle 1
14 with a tempest in the day of the whirlwind; 1
2:16 the mighty shall flee away naked in that day 1
3:14 the day I punish Israel for his transgressions 1
4: 2 that, behold, the days are coming upon you 1
4 every morning, your tithes every three days; 1
5: 8 into the morning, and darkens the day into night 1
18 Woe to you who desire the day of the LORD! 1
18 Why would you have the day of the LORD? 1
20 Is not the day of the LORD darkness, and not light 1
6: 3 O you who put far away the evil day, and bring near 1
8: 3 The songs . . shall become wailings in that day 1
9 And on that day," says the Lord GOD 1
10 mourning . . and the end of it like a bitter day. 1
11 Behold, the days are coming," says the Lord GOD 1
13 In that day the fair virgins . . shall faint 1
9:11 In that day I will raise up the booth of David 1
11 and rebuild it as in the days of old; 1
13 Behold, the days are coming," says the LORD 1
Obd 1: 8 Will I not on that day, says the LORD, destroy 1
11 On the day that you stood aloof 1
11 on the day that strangers carried off his wealth 1
12 not have gloated over the day of your brother 1
12 your brother in the day of his misfortune; 1
12 the people of Judah in the day of their ruin; 1
12 should not have boasted in the day of distress. 1
13 the gate of my people in the day of his calamity; 1
13 over his disaster in the day of his calamity; 1
13 have looted his goods in the day of his calamity. 1
14 delivered up . . in the day of distress. 1
15 the day of the LORD is near upon all the nations. 1
Jon 1:17 Jonah was in the belly of the fish three days 1
3: 3 great city, three days' journey in breadth. 1
4 began to go into the city, going a day's journey. 1
4 Yet 40 days, and Nin'eveh shall be overthrown! 1
Mic 1: 1 Micah of Mo'resheth in the days of Jotham, 1
2: 4 In that day they shall take up a taunt song 1
3: 6 the prophets, and the day shall be black over them; 1
4: 1 It shall come to pass in the latter days 1
6 In that day, says the LORD, I will assemble the lame 1
5: 2 whose origin is from of old, from ancient days. 1
10 And in that day, says the LORD 1
7: 4 The day of their watchmen, of their punishment 1
11 A day for the building of your walls! 1
11 In that day the boundary shall be far extended. 1
12 In that day they will come to you 1
14 in Bashan and Gilead as in the days of old. 1
15 in the days when you came out of the land of Egypt 1
20 hast sworn to our fathers from the days of old. 1
Nah 1: 7 LORD is good, a stronghold in the day of trouble; 1
3:17 locusts settling on the fences in a day of cold- 1
Hab 1: 5 For I am doing a work in your days 1
3:16 I will quietly wait for the day of trouble to come 1
Zep 1: 1 Hezeki'ah, in the days of Josi'ah the son of Amon 1
7 For the day of the LORD is at hand; 1
8 And on the day of the LORD'S sacrifice- 1
9 On that day I will punish every one 1
10 On that day," says the LORD, "a cry will be heard 1
14 The great day of the LORD is near 1
14 the sound of the day of the LORD is bitter 1
15 A day of wrath is that day, a day of distress 1
15 A day of wrath is that day, a day of distress 1
15 A day of wrath is that day, a day of distress 1
15 a day of ruin and devastation, a day of darkness 1
15 a day of darkness and gloom, a day of clouds 1
15 a day of clouds and thick darkness 1
16 a day of trumpet blast and battle cry 1
18 deliver them on the day of the wrath of the LORD. 1
2: 2 comes upon you the day of the wrath of the LORD. 1
3 may be hidden on the day of the wrath of the LORD. 1
3: 8 for the day when I arise as a witness. 1
11 On that day you shall not be put to shame 1
16 On that day it shall be said to Jerusalem 1
18 as on a day of festival. 6
Hag 1: 1 in the sixth month, on the first day of the month 1
15 on the 24th day of the month, in the sixth month 1
2: 1 in the seventh month, on the 21st day of the month •
10 On the 24th day of the ninth month •
15 what will come to pass from this day onward. 1
18 Consider from this day onward 1
18 from the 24th day of the ninth month. 1
18 the day that the foundation of the LORD'S temple 1
19 From this day on I will bless you. 1
20 on the 24th day of the month •
23 On that day, says the LORD of hosts, I will take you 1
Zec 1: 7 On the 24th day of the eleventh month 1
2:11 shall join themselves to the LORD in that day 1
3: 9 remove the guilt of this land in a single day. 1
10 In that day, says the LORD of hosts 1
4:10 For whoever has despised the day of small things 1
6:10 and go the same day to the house of Josi'ah 1
7: 1 fourth day of the ninth month, which is Chislev. •
8: 6 of the remnant of this people in these days 1
9 you who in these days have been hearing these 1
9 since the day that the foundation of the house 1
10 For before those days there was no wage for man 1
11 the remnant of this people as in the former days 1
15 so again have I purposed in these days to do good 1
23 In those days ten men from the nations 1
9:16 On that day the LORD their God will save them 1
11:11 it was annulled on that day 1
12: 3 On that day I will make Jerusalem a heavy stone 1
4 On that day, says the LORD, I will strike 1
6 On that day I will make the clans of Judah 1
8 On that day the LORD will put a shield about 1
8 so that the feeblest among them on that day shall 1
9 on that day I will seek to destroy all the nations 1
11 On that day the mourning in Jerusalem will be 1
13: 1 On that day there shall be a fountain 1
2 on that day, says the LORD of hosts, I will cut off 1
4 On that day every prophet will be ashamed 1
14: 1 Behold, a day of the LORD is coming 1
3 as when he fights on a day of battle. 1
4 On that day his feet shall stand on the Mount 1
5 earthquake in the days of Uzzi'ah king of Judah. 1

6 that day there shall be neither cold nor frost. 1
7 there shall be continuous day 1
7 day (it is known to the LORD), not day and not night 1
8 On that day living waters shall flow out 1
9 on that day the LORD will be one and his name one. 1
13 on that day a great panic from the LORD shall fall 1
20 on that day there shall be inscribed on the bells 1
21 in the house of the LORD of hosts on that day. 1
Mal 3: 2 But who can endure the day of his coming 1
4 as in the days of old and as in former years. 1
7 From the days of your fathers you have turned 1
17 my special possession on the day when I act 1
4: 1 For behold, the day comes, burning like an oven 1
1 the day that comes shall burn them up 1
3 on the day when I act, says the LORD of hosts. 1
5 before the great and terrible day of the LORD 1
Mat 2: 1 Bethlehem of Judea in the days of Herod the king 6
3: 1 In those days came John the Baptist, preaching 6
4: 2 And he fasted 40 days and 40 nights 6
6:11 Give us this day our daily bread; 8
34 Let the day's own trouble be sufficient 6
34 day's own trouble be sufficient for the day. 6
7:22 On that day many will say to me, 'Lord, Lord 6
9:15 The days will come, when the bridegroom is taken 6
10:15 it shall be more tolerable on the day of judgment 6
11:12 From the days of John the Baptist until now 6
22 it shall be more tolerable on the day of judgment 6
23 it would have remained until this day. 8
24 it shall be more tolerable on the day of judgment 6
12:36 on the day of judgment men will render account 6
40 For as Jonah was three days and three nights 6
40 For as Jonah was three days and three nights 6
13: 1 That same day Jesus went out of the house and sat 6
14:15 This is a lonely place, and the day is now over 12
15:32 because they have been with me now three days 6
16:21 and be killed, and on the third day be raised. 6
17: 1 after six days Jesus took with him Peter 6
23 he will be raised on the third day 6
20: 2 for a denarius a day 6
6 he said to them, 'Why do you stand here idle all day? 6
12 the burden of the day and the scorching heat.' 6
19 he will be raised on the third day. 6
22:23 The same day Sad'ducees came to him 6
46 nor from that day did any one dare to ask him 6
23:30 saying, 'If we had lived in the days of our fathers 6
24:19 those who give suck in those days! 6
22 if those days had not been shortened 6
22 those days will be shortened. 6
29 after the tribulation of those days 6
36 of that day and hour no one knows 6
37 As were the days of Noah 6
38 For as in those days before the flood 6
38 until the day when Noah entered the ark 6
42 you do not know on what day your Lord is coming. 6
50 the master of that servant will come on a day 6
25:13 you know neither the day nor the hour. 6
26: 2 after two days the Passover is coming 6
17 Now on the first day of Unleavened Bread •
29 until that day when I drink it new with you 6
55 Day after day I sat in the temple teaching 6
55 Day after day I sat in the temple teaching 6
61 to build it in three days.' 6
27: 8 has been called the Field of Blood to this day. 8
40 destroy the temple and build it in three days 6
62 Next day, that is, after the day of Preparation •
63 'After three days I will rise again.' 6
64 to be made secure until the third day 6
28: 1 toward the dawn of the first day of the week •
15 story has been spread among the Jews to this day. 6
Mrk 1: 9 In those days Jesus came from Nazareth of Galilee 6
13 he was in the wilderness 40 days, tempted by Satan 6
2: 1 when he returned to Caper'na-um after some days 6
20 The days will come, when the bridegroom is taken 6
20 then they will fast in that day. 6
4:27 sleep and rise night and day 6
35 On that day, when evening had come, he said to them 6
5: 5 Night and day among the tombs 6
8: 1 In those days 6
2 because they have been with me now three days 6
31 be killed, and after three days rise again. 6
9: 2 And after six days Jesus took with him Peter 6
31 when he is killed, after three days he will rise. 6
10:34 after three days he will rise. 6
13:17 those who give suck in those days! 6
19 For in those days there will be . . tribulation 6
20 if the Lord had not shortened the days 6
20 he shortened the days. 6
24 in those days, after that tribulation 6
32 of that day or that hour no one knows 6
14: 1 It was now two days before the Passover 6
12 on the first day of Unleavened Bread 6
25 until that day when I drink it new in the kingdom 6
58 in three days I will build another 6
15:29 destroy the temple and build it in three days 6
16: 2 very early on the first day of the week •
9 Now when he rose early on the first day of the week •
Lke 1: 5 In the days of Herod, king of Judea 6
20 unable to speak until the day 6
24 After these days his wife Elizabeth conceived 6
25 done to me in the days when he looked on me 6
39 In those days Mary arose 6
59 on the eighth day they came to circumcise 6
75 before him all the days of our life. 6
78 when the day shall dawn upon us from on high †
80 till the day of his manifestation to Israel. 6
2: 1 In those days a decree went out 6
11 born this day in the city of David a Savior 8
21 at the end of eight days, when he was circumcised 6
37 with fasting and prayer night and day. 6
44 they went a day's journey 6
46 After three days they found him in the temple 6
4: 2 for 40 days in the wilderness 6
2 he ate nothing in those days 6
16 as his custom was, on the sabbath day 6
25 were many widows in Israel in the days of Eli'jah 6
42 when it was day he departed 6
5:17 On one of those days, as he was teaching 6
35 The days will come, when the bridegroom is taken 6
35 then they will fast in those days. 6
6:12 In these days he went out to the mountain to pray; 6
13 when it was day, he called his disciples 6
23 Rejoice in that day, and leap for joy 6
8:22 One day he got into a boat with his disciples 6
9:12 Now the day began to wear away 6
22 be killed, and on the third day be raised. 6
28 Now about eight days after these sayings 6
36 they kept silence and told no one in those days 6
37 On the next day 6
51 When the days drew near for him to be received up 6
10:12 it shall be more tolerable on that day for Sodom 6
12:46 on a day when he does not expect him 6
13:14 come on those days and be healed •
14 There are six days on which work ought to be done; 6
14 not on the sabbath day. 6
16 be loosed from this bond on the sabbath day? 6
32 the third day I finish my course. •
33 today and tomorrow and the day following •
14: 5 will not immediately pull him out on a sabbath day? 6
15:13 Not many days later, the younger son gathered all 6
17: 4 if he sins against you seven times in the day 6
22 he said to the disciples, "The days are coming 6
22 will desire to see one of the days of the Son of man 6
24 so will the Son of man be in his day. 6
26 As it was in the days of Noah 6
26 As it was in the days of Noah 6
27 until the day when Noah entered the ark 6
28 Likewise as it was in the days of Lot 6
29 on the day when Lot went out from Sodom 6
30 on the day when the Son of man is revealed. 6
31 On that day, let him 6
18: 7 who cry to him day and night 6
33 on the third day he will rise. 6
19:43 the days shall come upon you 6
20: 1 One day, as he was teaching the people 6
21: 6 the days will come when there shall not be left 6
22 these are days of vengeance 6
23 Alas . . for those who give suck in those days! 6
34 and that day come upon you suddenly like a snare; 6
37 every day he was teaching in the temple 6
22: 7 day . . on which the passover lamb had to be sacrificed. 6
34 I tell you, Peter, the cock will not crow this day 8
66 When day came 6
23:12 became friends with each other that very day 6
29 For behold, the days are coming when they will say 6
54 was the day of Preparation 6
24: 1 on the first day of the week, at early dawn •
7 crucified, and on the third day rise. 6
13 That very day two of them were going to a village 6
18 things that have happened there in these days? 6
21 it is now the third day since this happened. 6
29 it is toward evening and the day is now far spent 6
46 on the third day rise from the dead 6
Joh 1:39 and they stayed with him that day 6
2: 1 On the third day there was a marriage at Cana 6
12 and there they stayed for a few days. 6
19 this temple, and in three days I will raise it up. 6
20 and will you raise it up in three days? 6
4:40 and he stayed there two days. 6
43 After the two days he departed to Galilee. 6
5: 9 Now that day was the sabbath. 6
6:39 but raise it up at the last day. 6
40 I will raise him up at the last day. 6
44 I will raise him up at the last day. 6
54 I will raise him up at the last day. 6
7:37 On the last day of the feast, the great day 6
37 On the last day of the feast, the great day •
8:56 Abraham rejoiced that he was to see my day 6
9: 4 work the works of him who sent me, while it is day; 6
14 Now it was a sabbath day when Jesus made the clay 6
11: 6 he stayed 2 days longer in the place where he was. 6
9 Are there not twelve hours in the day? 6
9 If any one walks in the day, he does not stumble 6
17 Laz'arus had already been in the tomb four days. 6
24 rise again in the resurrection at the last day. 6
53 from that day on they took counsel 6
12: 1 Six days before the Passover 6
7 let her keep it for the day of my burial. 6
48 will be his judge on the last day. 6
14:20 In that day you will know that I am in my Father 6
16:23 In that day you will ask nothing of me 6
26 In that day you will ask in my name 6
19:31 (for that sabbath was a high day) 6
20: 1 Now on the first day of the week •
19 On the evening of that day 6
19 the first day of the week •
26 Eight days later 6
Act 1: 2 until the day when he was taken up 6
3 appearing to them during 40 days 6
5 before many days you shall be baptized 6
12 is near Jerusalem, a sabbath day's journey away; •
15 In those days Peter stood up among the brethren 6
22 until the day when he was taken up from us 6
2: 1 When the day of Pentecost had come 6
15 since it is only the third hour of the day; 6
17 in the last days it shall be, God declares 6
18 in those days I will pour out my Spirit 6
20 before the day of the Lord comes 6
20 the great and manifest day. •
29 his tomb is with us to this day. 6
41 there were added that day about 3,000 souls. 6
3:24 also proclaimed these days. 6
5:36 before these days Theu'das arose 6
37 in the days of the census 6
42 every day in the temple and at home 6
6: 1 Now in these days 6
7: 8 circumcised him on the eighth day 6
26 on the following day he appeared to them 6
41 they made a calf in those days 6
45 So it was until the days of David 6
8: 1 And on that day a great persecution arose 6
9: 9 for three days he was without sight 6
19 For several days he was with the disciples 6
23 When many days had passed 6
24 were watching the gates day and night, to kill him; 6
37 In those days she fell sick and died 6
43 in Joppa for many days with one Simon, a tanner. 6
10: 3 About the ninth hour of the day 6
30 Cornelius said, "Four days ago, about this hour 6
40 God raised him on the third day 6
48 Then they asked him to remain for some days. 6
11:27 in these days prophets came down from Jerusalem 6
28 this took place in the days of Claudius. 5
12: 3 This was during the days of Unleavened Bread. 6
18 Now when day came, there was no small stir 6
21 On an appointed day Herod put on his royal robes 6
13:14 on the sabbath day they went into the synagogue 6
31 for many days he appeared 6
41 I do a deed in your days 6
15: 7 in the early days God made choice among you 6
36 after some days Paul said to Barnabas, "Come 6
16:12 We remained in this city some days; 6
13 on the sabbath day we went outside the gate 6
18 this she did for many days 6
35 when it was day, the magistrates sent the police 6
17:17 he argued . . in the market place every day 6
31 he has fixed a day on which he will judge the world 6
18:18 After this Paul stayed many days longer 6
20: 6 we sailed away . . after the days of Unleavened Bread 6
6 in five days we came to them at Tro'as 6
6 Tro'as, where we stayed for seven days. 6
7 On the first day of the week •
15 we came the following day opposite Chi'os •
15 the next day we touched at Samos •
15 the day after that we came to Mile'tus. •
16 at Jerusalem, if possible, on the day of Pentecost 6
18 from the first day that I set foot in Asia 6
26 Therefore I testify to you this day 8
31 I did not cease night or day to admonish every one 6
21: 1 the next day to Rhodes . . from there to Pat'ara •
4 we stayed there for seven days 6
5 when our days there were ended 6
7 stayed with them for one day. 6
10 While we were staying for some days 6
15 After these days we made ready 6
18 On the following day Paul went in with us to James; •
26 the next day he purified himself with them 6
26 the days of purification would be fulfilled 6
27 When the seven days were almost completed 6
22: 3 being zealous for God as you all are this day. 8
23: 1 I have lived . . in all good conscience up to this day. 6
12 When it was day, the Jews made a plot 6
24: 1 after five days the high priest . . came down 6
11 it is not more than twelve days since I went up 6
21 I am on trial before you this day.' 8
24 After some days Felix came with his wife 6
25: 1 after three days he went up to Jerusalem 6
6 stayed among them not more than eight or ten days 6
13 Now when some days had passed 6
14 as they stayed there many days 6
26: 7 as they earnestly worship night and day 6
22 To this day I have had the help that comes from God 6
29 not only you but also all who hear me this day 8
27: 7 We sailed slowly for a number of days 6
19 the third day they cast out . . the tackle •
20 when neither sun nor stars appeared for many a day 6
29 prayed for day to come. 6

33 As day was about to dawn 6
33 Today is the fourteenth day 6
39 when it was day, they did not recognize the land 6
28: 7 entertained us hospitably for three days. 6
12 we stayed there for three days. 6
13 after one day a south wind sprang up 6
13 on the second day we came to Pute'oli. •
14 were invited to stay with them for seven days 6
17 After three days he called together . . leaders 6
23 When they had appointed a day for him 6
Rom 2: 5 storing up wrath for yourself on the day of wrath 6
16 on that day when . . God judges the secrets of men 6
8:36 we are being killed all the day long; 6
10:21 All day long I have held out my hands 6
11: 8 ears that should not hear, down to this very day. 6
13:12 the night is far gone, the day is at hand. 6
13 conduct ourselves becomingly as in the day 6
14: 5 One man esteems one day as better than another 6
5 while another man esteems all days alike. 6
6 He who observes the day, observes it in honor 6
1Co 1: 8 guiltless in the day of our Lord Jesus Christ. 6
3:13 the Day will disclose it 6
5: 5 may be saved in the day of the Lord Jesus. 6
10: 8 and 23,000 fell in a single day. 6
15: 4 that he was raised on the third day 6
16: 2 On the first day of every week •
2Co 1:14 on the day of the Lord Jesus. 6
3:14 for to this day, when they read the old covenant 6
15 Yes, to this day whenever Moses is read 8
4:16 our inner nature is being renewed every day. 6
6: 2 helped you on the day of salvation. 6
2 behold, now is the day of salvation. 6
Gal 1:18 remained with him fifteen days. 6
4:10 You observe days, and months, and seasons 6
Eph 4:30 you were sealed for the day of redemption. 6
5:16 because the days are evil. 6
6:13 that you may be able to withstand in the evil day 6
Php 1: 5 from the first day until now. 6
6 at the day of Jesus Christ. 6
10 pure and blameless for the day of Christ 6
2:16 so that in the day of Christ I may be proud 6
Col 1: 6 from the day you heard and understood 6
9 from the day we heard of it 6
1Th 2: 9 we worked night and day 6
3:10 praying earnestly night and day that we may see 6
5: 2 you yourselves know well that the day of the Lord 6
4 for that day to surprise you like a thief. 6
5 of light and sons of the day; 6
8 But, since we belong to the day, let us be sober 6
2Th 1:10 when he comes on that day to be glorified 6
2: 2 to the effect that the day of the Lord has come. 6
3 that day will not come •
3: 8 with toil and labor we worked night and day 6
1Ti 5: 5 in supplications and prayers night and day; 6
2Ti 1: 4 I long night and day to see you 6
12 to guard until that Day what has been entrusted 6
18 to find mercy from the Lord on that Day 6
3: 1 in the last days there will come times of stress. 6
4: 8 the righteous judge, will award to me on that Day 6
Heb 1: 2 in these last days he has spoken to us by a Son 6
3: 8 on the day of testing in the wilderness 6
13 exhort one another every day 6
4: 4 For he has . . spoken of the seventh day in this way •
4 God rested on the seventh day from all his works. 6
7 again he sets a certain day, "Today 6
8 God would not speak later of another day. 6
5: 7 In the days of his flesh, Jesus offered up prayers 6
7: 3 has neither beginning of days nor end of life 6
8: 8 The days will come, says the Lord 6
9 on the day when I took them by the hand 6
10 with the house of Israel after those days 6
10:16 after those days, says the Lord 6
25 all the more as you see the Day drawing near. 6
32 recall the former days 6
11:30 after they had been encircled for seven days. 6
Jas 5: 3 You have laid up treasure for the last days. 6
5 have fattened your hearts in a day of slaughter. 6
1Pe 2:12 and glorify God on the day of visitation. 6
3:10 He that would love life and see good days 6
20 when God's patience waited in the days of Noah 6
2Pe 1:19 until the day dawns and the morning star rises 6
2: 8 he was vexed in his righteous soul day after day 6
8 he was vexed in his righteous soul day after day 6
9 under punishment until the day of judgment 6
3: 3 scoffers will come in the last days 6
7 kept until the day of judgment and destruction 6
8 with the Lord one day is as a 1,000 years 6
8 and a 1,000 years as one day. 6
10 But the day of the Lord will come like a thief 6
12 and hastening the coming of the day of God 6
18 glory both now and to the day of eternity. Amen. 6
1Jn 4:17 we may have confidence for the day of judgment 6
Jde 1: 6 kept . . until the judgment of the great day; 6
Rev 1:10 I was in the Spirit on the Lord's day, and I heard 6
2:10 and for ten days you will have tribulation. 6
13 you did not deny . . even in the days of An'tipas 6
4: 8 and day and night they never cease to sing 6
6:17 for the great day of their wrath has come 6
7:15 and serve him day and night within his temple; 6

8:12 a third of the day was kept from shining 6
9: 6 in those days men will seek death and will not find it; 6
15 ready for the hour, the day, the month, and the year 6
10: 7 in the days of the trumpet call to be sounded 6
11: 3 to prophesy for 1,260 days, clothed in sackcloth. 6
6 no rain . . during the days of their prophesying 6
9 For three days and a half men from the peoples 6
11 after the three and a half days a breath of life 6
12: 6 to be nourished for 1,260 days. 6
10 who accuses them day and night before our God. 6
14:11 and they have no rest, day or night 6
16:14 for battle on the great day of God the Almighty. 6
18: 8 so shall her plagues come in a single day 6
20:10 they will be tormented day and night for ever 6
21:25 and its gates shall never be shut by day- 6
1Es 1: 1 the fourteenth day of the first month 6
17 were accomplished that day 6
19 kept the passover . . seven days. 6
32 have made lamentation for him to this day 6
44 reigned three months and ten days in Jerusalem. 6
4:21 With his wife he ends his days 11
34 returns to its place in one day. 6
43 in the day when you became king 6
52 to be offered on the altar every day 6
55 until the day when the temple should be finished 6
63 they feasted . . for seven days. 6
5:51 offered the proper sacrifices every day 6
69 ever since the days of Esarhaddon 6
7: 5 the 23rd day of the month of Adar •
10 the fourteenth day of the first month •
14 kept the feast of unleavened bread seven days 6
8:41 we encamped there three days 6
61 on the twelfth day of the first month •
62 When we had been there three days 6
76 we are in great sin to this day. 6
77 in shame until this day. 6
89 we are left as a root to this day. 8
9: 4 if any did not meet there within two or three days 6
5 assembled at Jerusalem within three days 6
5 on the twentieth day of the month. •
11 This is not a work we can do in one day or two 6
50 This day is holy to the Lord 6
52 for the day is holy to the Lord 6
53 This day is holy; do not be sorrowful. 6
2Es 1:16 but to this day you still complain. 15
31 for I have rejected your feast days, and new moons 13
2:13 pray that your days may be few 13
27 when the day of tribulation and anguish comes 13
4: 5 or call back for me the day that is past. 13
9 asked you only about fire and wind and the day 13
51 Do you think that I shall live until those days? 13
51 Or who will be alive in those days? 13
5: 1 behold, the days are coming 13
13 and fast for seven days 13
19 and do not come near me for seven days 13
20 I fasted seven days, mourning and weeping 13
21 after seven days the thoughts of my heart 13
6:18 it said, "Behold, the days are coming 13
31 will pray again and fast again for seven days 13
35 I wept again and fasted seven days as before 13
38 and didst say on the first day 13
41 Again, on the second day, thou didst create 13
42 On the third day thou didst command the waters 13
44 These were made on the third day. 13
45 On the fourth day thou didst command 13
47 On the fifth day thou didst command 13
51 which had been dried up on the third day 13
53 On the sixth day thou didst command the earth 13
7:30 turned back to primeval silence for seven days 13
31 after seven days the world, which is not yet awake 13
38 Thus he will speak to them on the day of judgment- 13
39 a day that has no sun or moon or stars •
84 torment laid up for themselves in the last days. •
95 and the glory which awaits them in the last days. •
101 They shall have freedom for seven days 13
101 during these seven days they may see the things 13
102 whether on the day of judgment the righteous 13
104 The day of judgment is decisive 13
105 no one shall ever pray for another on that day ‡
107 Joshua after him for Israel in the days of Achan 13
108 Samuel in the days of Saul ‡
110 for the people in the days of Sennacherib 13
113 the day of judgment will be the end of this age 13
9: 4 from the days that were of old 13
23 if you will let seven days more pass 13
27 after seven days, as I lay on the grass 13
44 every hour and every day during those 30 years 13
44 I besought the Most High, night and day. 13
47 I set a day for the marriage feast. 13
10: 2 I remained quiet until evening of the second day 13
59 to those who dwell on earth in the last days 13
12:13 the days are coming when a kingdom shall arise 13
23 In its last days the Most High will raise up •
28 he also shall fall by the sword in the last days. •
32 whom the Most High has kept until the end of days •
34 the day of judgment, of which I spoke to you 13
39 wait here seven days more, so that you may be shown 13
40 people heard that the seven days were past 13
49 and after these days I will come to you. 13

51 I sat in the field seven days 13
51 and my food was of plants during those days. 13
13: 1 After seven days I dreamed a dream in the night; 13
16 alas for those who will be left in those days! 13
18 what is reserved for the last days 13
20 and not to see what shall happen in the last days. •
29 Behold, the days are coming 13
40 in the days of King Hoshea 13
52 except in the time of his day. 13
56 after three more days I will tell you 13
58 And I stayed there three days. 13
14: 1 On the third day, while I was sitting under an oak 13
4 Mount Sinai, where I kept him with me many days; 13
22 those who wish to live in the last days may live. •
23 and tell them not to seek you for 40 days. 13
36 and let no one seek me for 40 days. 13
42 They sat 40 days, and wrote during the daytime 13
44 during the 40 days 94 books were written. 13
45 when the 40 days were ended 13
15:21 Just as they have done to my elect until this day 14
29 and from the day that they set out 13
16:17 Who will deliver me in those days? 13
31 in those days three or four shall be left by those 13
65 shall stand as your accusers in that day. 13
74 Behold, the days of tribulation are at hand 13
Tob 1: 2 in the days of Shalmaneser, king of the Assyrians 6
3 all the days of my life 6
16 In the days of Shalmaneser 6
21 not 50 days passed before . . 6
3: 7 On the same day, at Ecbatana in Media 6
4: 1 On that day Tobit remembered the money 6
3 Honor her all the days of your life 6
5 Remember the Lord our God all your days, my son 6
5 Live uprightly all the days of your life 6
9 against the day of necessity. 6
5:14 tell me, what wages am I to pay you-a drachma a day 6
8:19 a wedding feast . . which lasted fourteen days. 6
20 before the days of the feast were over 6
20 until the 14 days of the wedding feast were ended 6
9: 4 my father is counting the days 6
10: 1 Now his father Tobit was counting each day 6
1 when the days for the journey had expired 6
7 she went out every day to the road 6
7 until the fourteen days . . had expired 6
11:19 Tobias' marriage was celebrated for seven days 6
12:19 All these days I merely appeared to you 6
Jdt 1: 1 in the days of Arphaxad 6
5 it was in those days 6
15 and he utterly destroyed him, to this day. 6
16 and feasted for 120 days. 6
2: 1 on the 22nd day of the first month •
10 hold them for me till the day of their punishment. 6
21 They marched for three days from Nineveh 6
4:13 the people fasted many days throughout Judea 6
6: 5 said these words on the day of your iniquity 6
5 you shall not see my face again from this day 6
15 who in those days were Uzziah the son of Micah 6
19 look this day upon the faces of those . . consecrated 6
7: 2 all their warriors moved their camp that day; 6
6 On the second day 6
20 whole Assyrian army . . surrounded them for 34 days 6
21 did not have enough . . for a single day 6
28 Let him not do this day 8
30 Let us hold out for five more days 6
31 if these days pass by, and no help comes for us •
8: 6 She fasted all the days of her widowhood 6
9 to surrender the city . . after five days 6
11 the Lord turns and helps us within so many days. •
12 that have put God to the test this day 6
15 choose to help us within these five days 6
18 nor in these present days 6
18 as was done in days gone by- 6
33 within the days after which you have promised 6
11:15 on that very day they will be handed over to you 6
17 serves the God of heaven day and night 6
12: 7 she remained in the camp for three days 6
10 On the fourth day Holofernes held a banquet 6
14 it will be a joy to me until the day of my death! 6
16 ever since the day he first saw her. 6
18 in all the days since I was born. 6
20 in any one day since he was born. 6
13: 3 as she did every day 6
7 Give me strength this day, O Lord God of Israel! 6
11 even as he has done this day! 8
17 who hast brought into contempt this day the enemies 6
14: 8 Now tell me what you have done during these days. 6
8 from the day she left 6
10 remaining so to this day. 6
15:11 the people plundered the camp for 30 days. 6
16:17 in the day of judgment 6
22 she remained a widow all the days of her life 6
24 the house of Israel mourned for her seven days. 6
25 in the days of Judith 6
AEs 10:11 came to the hour and moment and day of decision 6
13 observe these days in the month of Adar 6
11: 2 on the first day of Nisan •
8 behold, a day of darkness and gloom 6
13: 6 on the fourteenth day of the twelfth month •
7 may in one day go down in violence to Hades 6

14:16 upon my head on the days when I appear in public 6
16 I do not wear it on the days when I am at leisure. 6
18 since the day that I was brought here until now 6
15: 1 On the third day, when she ended her prayer 6
16:20 the thirteenth day of the twelfth month, Adar •
20 on that very day they may defend themselves 6
21 God . . has made this day to be a joy to his chosen •
21 instead of a day of destruction for them. •
22 you shall observe this . . as a notable day 6
Wis 3:18 no consolation in the day of decision. 6
10:17 became a shelter to them by day 6
Sir 1: 2 the drops of rain, and the days of eternity 6
13 on the day of his death he will be blessed. 6
3:15 in the day of your affliction 6
5: 7 Do not . . postpone it from day to day 6
7 Do not . . postpone it from day to day 6
8 it will not benefit you in the day of calamity. 6
6: 8 will not stand by you in your day of trouble. 6
10 will not stand by you in your day of trouble. 6
11: 4 exalt yourself in the day that you are honored 6
25 In the day of prosperity, adversity is forgotten 6
25 and in the day of adversity 6
26 to reward a man on the day of death 6
14:14 Do not deprive yourself of a happy day 6
17: 2 He gave to men few days, a limited time 6
18: 9 The number of a man's days is great 6
10 so are a few years in the day of eternity. 6
24 Think of his wrath on the day of death 6
25 in the days of wealth think of poverty and need. 6
27 in days of sin he guards against wrongdoing. 6
22:12 Mourning for the dead lasts seven days 6
23:14 you will curse the day of your birth. 6
15 will never become disciplined all his days. 6
26: 1 the number of his days will be doubled. 6
33: 7 Why is any day better than another 6
9 some of them he made ordinary days. 6
23 At the time when you end the days of your life 6
36: 8 Hasten the day, and remember the appointed time 7
37:25 The life of a man is numbered by days 6
25 the days of Israel are without number. 6
38:17 for one day, or two, to avoid criticism 6
27 labors by night as well as by day 6
40: 1 from the day they come forth 6
1 till the day they return to the mother of all. 6
2 their anxious thought is the day of death 6
41: 3 remember your former days and the end of life •
13 The days of a good life are numbered 6
45:14 be wholly burned twice every day continually. 6
15 for his descendants all the days of heaven 6
46: 4 did not one day become as long as two? 6
7 in the days of Moses he did a loyal deed 6
47: 1 Nathan rose up to prophesy in the days of David. 6
7 he crushed their power even to this day. 8
13 Solomon reigned in days of peace 6
48:12 all his days he did not tremble before any ruler 6
18 In his days Sennacherib came up 6
23 In his days the sun went backward 6
49: 3 in the days of wicked men 6
12 in their days they built the house 6
50: 3 In his days a cistern for water was quarried out 6
8 like roses in the days of the first fruits 6
8 like a green shoot on Lebanon on a summer day; 6
22 who exalts our days from birth 6
23 grant that peace may be in our days in Israel 6
23 in our days in Israel, as in the days of old. 6
24 let him deliver us in our days! 6
51:10 not to forsake me in the days of affliction 6
Bar 1: 2 in the fifth year, on the seventh day of the month •
8 At the same time, on the tenth day of Sivan, Baruch •
11 days on earth may be like the days of heaven. 6
11 days on earth may be like the days of heaven. 6
12 we shall serve them many days and find favor 6
13 to this day the anger of the Lord and his wrath 6
14 on the days of the feasts and at appointed seasons. 6
15 confusion of face, as at this day, to us, to the men 6
19 From the day when the Lord brought our fathers 6
20 So to this day there have clung to us 6
2: 6 to us and our fathers, as at this day. 6
11 and hast made thee a name, as at this day 6
25 cast out to the heat of day and the frost of night. 6
28 on the day when thou didst command him to write 6
3:20 Young men have seen the light of day, and have •
4:20 I will cry to the Everlasting all my days. 6
35 fire will come upon her . . for many days 6
Aza 1:14 and are brought low this day in all the world 8
17 such may our sacrifice be in thy sight this day 8
47 Bless the Lord, nights and days 6
Sus 1:15 while they were watching for an opportune day 6
52 You old relic of wicked days 6
62 Thus innocent blood was saved that day. 6
64 And from that day onward Daniel had a great 6
Bel 1: 3 every day they spent on it twelve bushels 6
4 revered it and went every day to worship it 6
6 see how much he eats and drinks every day? 6
31 he was there for six days. 6
32 every day they had been given two human bodies 6
40 On the seventh day the king came to mourn 6
Man 1:15 all the days of my life 6
1Mc 1:11 In those days lawless men came forth from Israel 6
54 Now on the fifteenth day of Chislev 6
59 And on the 25th day of the month •
2: 1 In those days Mattathias the son of John 6
32 on the sabbath day. 6
34 so profane the sabbath day. 6
41 So they made this decision that day 6
41 So they made this decision that day 6
49 Now the days drew near for Mattathias to die 6
3:29 laws that had existed from the earliest days. 6
47 They fasted that day 6
49 the Nazirites who had completed their days; 6
4:25 Thus Israel had a great deliverance that day. 6
52 on the 25th day of the ninth month •
54 At the very season and on the very day 6
56 they celebrated . . for eight days 6
59 the days of dedication of the altar 6
59 the 25th day of the month of Chislev. 6
59 the 25th day of the month of Chislev. •
5:24 crossed the Jordan and went three days' journey 6
27 take and destroy all these men in one day. 6
34 As many as 8,000 of them fell that day. 6
50 fought against the city all that day 6
60 as many as 2,000 . . fell that day. 6
67 On that day some priests . . fell in battle 6
6: 9 He lay there for many days 6
31 for many days they fought and built engines of war 6
51 he encamped before the sanctuary for many days. 6
52 made engines of war . . and fought for many days 6
7:16 he seized 60 of them and killed them in one day 6
43 on the thirteenth day of the month of Adar •
45 The Jews pursued them a day's journey 6
48 celebrated that day as a day of great gladness. 6
48 celebrated that day as a day of great gladness. 6
49 they decreed that this day should be celebrated 6
49 celebrated each year on the thirteenth day of Adar 6
50 the land of Judah had rest for a few days. 6
8:10 and enslaved them to this day 6
9:20 they mourned many days and said 6
24 In those days a very great famine occurred 6
34 Bacchides found this out on the sabbath day 6
43 he came with a large force on the sabbath day 6
49 about 1,000 of Bacchides' men fell that day. 6
64 he fought against it for many days 6
10:30 I release them from this day and henceforth 8
30 from this day and for all time. 8
34 sabbaths and new moons and appointed days 6
34 let them all be days of immunity and release 6
34 let them all be days of immunity and release 6
47 they remained his allies all his days. 6
50 Demetrius fell on that day. 6
55 Happy was the day on which you returned 6
11:18 But King Ptolemy died three days later 6
20 In those days Jonathan assembled the men of Judea 6
40 he stayed there many days. 6
47 killed on that day as many as 100,000 men 6
48 seized much spoil on that day 6
65 and fought against it for many days and hemmed it in. 6
74 3,000 of the foreigners fell that day. 6
12:11 both in our feasts and on other appropriate days 6
13:26 mourned for him many days. 6
30 it remains to this day. 6
39 any errors and offenses committed to this day 6
43 In those days Simon encamped against Gazara 6
51 On the 23rd day of the second month •
52 that every year they should celebrate this day 6
14: 4 The land had rest all the days of Simon 6
4 as was the honor shown him, all his days. 6
13 the kings were crushed in those days. 6
27 On the eighteenth day of Elul, in the 172nd year •
36 in his days things prospered in his hands 6
16: 2 the wars of Israel from our youth until this day 6
2Mc 1:18 on the 25th day of Chislev •
2:12 Likewise Solomon also kept the eight days. 6
16 Will you therefore please keep the days? 6
3:14 he set a day and went in to direct the inspection 6
5: 2 over all the city, for almost 40 days 6
14 Within the total of three days 6
25 waited until the holy sabbath day 6
6:11 to observe the seventh day secretly •
11 in view of their regard for that most holy day. 6
7:20 she saw her seven sons perish within a single day 6
8:26 For it was the day before the sabbath •
27 who had preserved them for that day 6
10: 5 on the same day 6
5 on the 25th day of the same month •
6 celebrated it for eight days with rejoicing 6
8 should observe these days every year. 6
33 they besieged the fort for four days. 6
35 at dawn of the fifth day 6
11:30 those who go home by the 30th day of Xanthicus •
12:15 overthrew Jericho in the days of Joshua 10
38 As the seventh day was coming on, they purified •
39 On the next day •
13:10 to call upon the Lord day and night 6
12 lying prostrate for three days without ceasing 6
17 This happened, just as day was dawning 6
14: 4 During that day he kept quiet. 6
21 the leaders set a day 6
15: 1 to attack them . . on the day of rest. 6
2 the day which he . . has honored and hallowed 6
2 honored and hallowed above other days •
3 who had commanded the keeping of the sabbath day. 6
4 who ordered us to observe the seventh day •
36 never to let this day go unobserved 6
36 the thirteenth day of the twelfth month •
36 Syrian language–the day before Mordecai's day. 6
36 Syrian language–the day before Mordecai's day. 6
3Mc 4: 8 the remaining days of their marriage festival 6
14 to be destroyed in the space of a single day. 6
15 though uncompleted it stopped after 40 days. 6
5: 2 on the following day to drug all the elephants 6
11 from the beginning, night and day 6
18 to remain alive through the present day. 6
6:30 needed for a festival of seven days 6
36 observance of the aforesaid days as a festival 6
38 for 40 days 6
38 the three days 6
40 until the fourteenth day •
7:15 In that day they put to death more than 300 men 6
15 they kept the day as a joyful festival •
17 the fleet waited for them . . for seven days. 6
19 they decided to observe these days 6
4Mc 3: 7 had been attacking the Philistines all day long 6
14: 7 just as the seven days of creation 6
17:12 on that day virtue gave the awards 9
18:19 this is your life and the length of your days.' 6
20 O bitter was that day–and yet not bitter– 6

day *See also* break, bring, day, during, eighth, hold, night, once, stay, while, write.

day after 1. מָחֳרָת

Num33: 3 on the day after the passover the people 1

day after day 1. כָּל הַיָּמִים 2. καθ' ἡμέραν

Jdg 16:16 she pressed him hard with her words day after day 1
2Sm 13:37 And David mourned for his son day after day. 1
Mrk 14:49 Day after day I was with you in the temple 2
Lke 22:53 I was with you day after day in the temple 2
Sus 1:12 they watched eagerly, day after day, to see her. 2

all day 1. ἕως τῆς νυκτός

AEs 11:12 sought all day to understand it in every detail. 1

all the day 1. יוֹמָם

Ps 13: 2 in my soul, and have sorrow in my heart all the day? 1

day before the new moon 1. προνουμηνία

Jdt 8: 6 the day before the new moon 1

day before the sabbath 1. προσάββατον

Mrk 15:42 that is, the day before the sabbath 1
Jdt 8: 6 except the day before the sabbath 1

day break 1. אוֹר 2. πρωΐα

2Sm 2:32 all night, and the day broke upon them at Hebron. 1
Joh 21: 4 Just as day was breaking, Jesus stood on the beach; 2

day by day 1. לַיּוֹם 2. καθ' ἡμέραν

Num28: 3 offer . . day by day, as a continual offering 1
Act 2:46 And day by day, attending the temple together 2
47 the Lord added to their number day by day 2

each day 1. καθ' ἡμέραν

Lke 11: 3 Give us each day our daily bread; 1

every day 1. יוֹם בְּיוֹם 2. καθ' ἡμέραν

2Kg 25:30 a regular allowance . . every day a portion 1
Lke 16:19 and who feasted sumptuously every day. 2
1Co 15:31 I die every day! 2
Sus 1: 8 The two elders used to see her every day 2
1Mc 8:15 every day 320 senators constantly deliberate 2

feast day 1. מוֹעֵד 2. ἑορτή

1Ch 23:31 to the LORD on sabbaths, new moons, and feast days 1
Jdt 10: 2 on sabbaths and on her feast days; 2
Sir 43: 7 From the moon comes the sign for feast days 2

following day 1. מָחֳרָת 2. ἐπαύριον 3. ἔπειμι

Jdg 9:42 On the following day the men went out 1
Mrk 11:12 On the following day, when they came from Bethany 2
Act 10:24 on the following day they entered Caesare'a. 2
16:11 and the following day to Ne-ap'olis 3

latter day 1. אַחֲרִית

Job 8: 7 your latter days will be very great. 1
42:12 the LORD blessed the latter days of Job 1

next day 1. מָחֳרָת 2. αὔριον 3. ἑξῆς 4. ἐπαύριον 5. ἕτερος 6. crastinum

Gen 19:34 on the next day, the first-born said to the younger 1
1Sm 5: 3 when the people of Ashdod rose early the next day 1
30:17 from twilight until the evening of the next day; 1
Jon 4: 7 when dawn came up the next day 1
Mat 27:62 Next day, that is, after the day of Preparation 4
Lke 10:35 the next day he took out two denarii 2
Joh 1:29 The next day he saw Jesus coming toward him 4
35 The next day again John was standing 4

43 The next day Jesus decided to go to Galilee. 4
6:22 On the next day the people . . saw 4
12:12 The next day a great crowd . . heard 4
Act 10: 9 The next day, as they were on their journey 4
23 The next day he rose and went off with them 4
14:20 on the next day he went on with Barnabas to Derbe. 4
25: 6 the next day he took his seat on the tribunal 4
17 but on the next day took my seat on the tribunal 3
27: 3 The next day we put in at Sidon 5
18 they began next day to throw the cargo overboard; 3
2Es 14:38 on the next day, behold, a voice called me, saying 6
Jdt 7: 1 The next day Holofernes ordered . . to break camp 4
Sus 1:28 The next day, when the people gathered 4

day of rejoicing 1. χαρμόσυνος
Jdt 8: 6 and days of rejoicing of the house of Israel. 1

day of solemn rest 1. שַׁבָּתוֹן
Exd 16:23 Tomorrow is a day of solemn rest, a holy sabbath 1
Lev 23:24 you shall observe a day of solemn rest 1

day of the new moon 1. νεομηνία
Jdt 8: 6 the day of the new moon 1

day star 1. הֵילֵל
Isa 14:12 How you are fallen from heaven, O Day Star 1

third day 1. שְׁלִישִׁי
1Sm 20: 5 hide myself in the field till the third day 1

daybreak 1. עוֹר הַבֹּקֶר 2. αὐγή 3. ὄρθρος 4. πρωΐα
2Sm 17:22 by daybreak not one was left who had not crossed 1
Act 5:21 they entered the temple at daybreak and taught 3
20:11 conversed with them a long while, until daybreak 2
3Mc 5:24 they were eagerly waiting for daybreak. 4

daylight 1. יוֹם אוֹר 2. φῶς ἡμέρας
Ams 8: 9 and darken the earth in broad daylight. 1
Sir 33: 7 when all the daylight in the year is from the sun? 2

days *See* four, length, pass.

latter days 1. אַחֲרִית
Job 8: 7 your latter days will be very great. 1
42:12 the LORD blessed the latter days of Job 1

daytime 1. יוֹמָם 2. ἡμέρα 3. die
Job 5:14 They meet with darkness in the daytime 1
Ps 78:14 In the daytime he led them with a cloud 1
2Pe 2:13 They count it pleasure to revel in the daytime. 2
2Es 14:42 They sat 40 days, and wrote during the daytime 3
43 As for me, I spoke in the daytime 3
Tob 10: 7 she ate nothing in the daytime 2

daze 1. עלם
Nah 3:11 You also will be drunken, you will be dazed; 1

dazzle 1. ἀστράπτω 2. ἐξαστράπτω
Lke 9:29 his raiment became dazzling white. 2
24: 4 behold, two men stood by them in dazzling apparel; 1

deacon 1. διάκονος
Php 1: 1 who are at Philip'pi, with the bishops and deacons 1
1Ti 3: 8 Deacons likewise must be serious 1
12 Let deacons be the husband of one wife 1

deacon *See also* serve.

deaconess 1. διάκονος
Rom 16: 1 Phoebe, a deaconess of the church at Cen'chre-ae 1

dead 1. גוע 2. מָוֶת 3. מות 4. מֵת 5. נֶפֶשׁ 6. רְפָאִים 7. שׁדד 8. ἀπόλλυμι 9. θάνατος 10. θνῄσκω 11. κοίμησις 12. μεταλλάσσω 13. νεκρός 14. νεκρόω 15. οὗτος 16. mortuus
Gen 23: 3 Abraham rose up from before his dead 4
4 that I may bury my dead out of my sight. 4
6 Bury your dead in the choicest of our sepulchres; 4
6 sepulchre, or hinder you from burying your dead. 4
8 If you are willing that I should bury my dead 4
11 of my people I give it to you; bury your dead. 4
13 accept it from me, that I may bury my dead there. 4
15 what is that between you and me? Bury your dead. 4
42:38 for his brother is dead, and he only is left. 4
44:20 the child of his old age; and his brother is dead 4
50:15 Joseph's brothers saw that their father was dead 4
Exd 4:19 all the men who were seeking your life are dead. 3
9: 7 not one of the cattle of the Israelites was dead. 4
12:30 for there was not a house where one was not dead. 4
14:30 Israel saw the Egyptians dead upon the seashore. 4
Lev 11:31 whoever touches them when they are dead shall be 3
32 anything . . when they are dead shall be unclean 3
19:28 cuttings in your flesh on account of the dead 5
21: 1 defile himself for the dead among his people 5
11 he shall not go in to any dead body, nor defile 4
22: 4 unclean through contact with the dead 5
Num 5: 2 unclean through contact with the dead; 5
6: 6 he shall not go near a dead body. 4
16:48 he stood between the dead and the living; 4
19:18 sprinkle it . . upon him who touched the . . dead 4
20:29 all the congregation saw that Aaron was dead 1
Deu 2:16 men of war . . were dead from among the people 3
14: 1 you shall not cut yourselves . . for the dead. 4
25: 5 wife of the dead shall not be married outside 4
6 succeed to the name of his brother who is dead 4
26:14 I have not . . offered any of it to the dead; 4
Jos 1: 2 Moses my servant is dead; now therefore arise 4
Jdg 3:25 and there lay their lord dead on the floor. 4
4:22 there lay Sis'era dead, with the tent peg in his 4
5:27 at her feet . . where he sank, there he fell dead. 7
9:55 the men of Israel saw that Abim'elech was dead 4
16:30 the dead whom he slew at his death were more 4
20: 5 and they ravished my concubine, and she is dead. 3
Rut 1: 8 as you have dealt with the dead and with me. 4
2:20 kindness has not forsaken the living or the dead! 4
4: 5 buying Ruth the Moabitess, the widow of the dead 4
5 restore the name of the dead to his inheritance. 4
10 to be my wife, to perpetuate the name of the dead 4
10 that the name of the dead may not be cut off 4
1Sm 4:17 your two sons also, Hophni and Phin'ehas, are dead 3
19 that her father-in-law and her husband were dead 4
17:51 Philistines saw that their champion was dead 4
24:14 whom do you pursue? After a dead dog! After a flea! 4
25:39 When David heard that Nabal was dead, he said 4
31: 5 when his armor-bearer saw that Saul was dead 4
7 saw that . . and that Saul and his sons were dead 3
2Sm 1: 4 many of the people also have fallen and are dead; 3
4 and Saul and his son Jonathan are also dead. 3
5 How do you know that Saul and . . Jonathan are dead? 4
2: 7 and be valiant; for Saul your lord is dead 4
4:10 when one told me, 'Behold, Saul is dead,' 4
9: 8 that you should look upon a dead dog such as I? 4
11:21 say, 'Your servant Uri'ah the Hittite is dead also.' 4
24 some of the king's servants are dead; 3
24 and your servant Uri'ah the Hittite is dead also. 4
26 the wife . . heard that Uri'ah her husband was dead 4
12:18 feared to tell him that the child was dead; 4
18 how then can we say to him the child is dead? 4
19 David perceived that the child was dead; 4
19 and David said to his servants, "Is the child dead? 4
19 Is the child dead?" They said, "He is dead. 4
23 But now he is dead; why should I fast? 4
13:32 Amnon alone is dead, for by the command 4
33 to suppose that all the king's sons are dead; 3
33 for Amnon alone is dead. 4
39 he was comforted about Amnon, seeing he was dead. 4
14: 2 who has been mourning many days for the dead; 4
5 "Alas, I am a widow; my husband is dead. 3
16: 9 Why should this dead dog curse my lord the king? 4
18:20 carry no tidings, because the king's son is dead. 4
19: 6 if Ab'salom were alive and all of us . . dead today 4
10 Ab'salom, whom we anointed . . is dead in battle. 4
1Kg 3:20 in her bosom, and laid her dead son in my bosom. 4
21 When I rose . . to nurse my child, behold, it was dead; 4
22 living child is mine, and the dead child is yours. 4
22 No, the dead child is yours, and the living child is 4
23 'This is my son that is alive, and your son is dead'; 4
23 your son is dead, and my son is the living one.' 4
11:21 Jo'ab the commander of the army was dead 4
21:14 saying, "Naboth has been stoned; he is dead. 4
15 that Naboth had been stoned and was dead 3
15 Arise, take . . for Naboth is not alive, but dead. 4
16 as soon as Ahab heard that Naboth was dead 4
2Kg 4: 1 Your servant my husband is dead; 4
32 Eli'sha . . saw the child lying dead on his bed. 4
8: 5 how Eli'sha had restored the dead to life 4
11: 1 Now when Athali'ah . . saw that her son was dead 4
19:35 when men arose . . these were all dead bodies. 4
23:30 And his servants carried him dead in a chariot 4
1Ch 10: 5 when his armor-bearer saw that Saul was dead 4
7 saw . . that Saul and his sons were dead 3
2Ch 22:10 Now when Athali'ah . . saw that her son was dead 4
Job 1:19 it fell upon the young people, and they are dead; 3
Ps 31:12 I have passed out of mind like one who is dead; 4
88: 5 like one forsaken among the dead 4
10 Dost thou work wonders for the dead? 4
106:28 ate sacrifices offered to the dead; 4
115:17 The dead do not praise the LORD 4
143: 3 has made me sit in darkness like those long dead. 4
Prv 9:18 he does not know that the dead are there 6
21:16 wanders . . will rest in the assembly of the dead. 6
Ecc 4: 2 I thought the dead who are . . dead more fortunate 4
2 the dead who are already dead more fortunate 3
9: 3 they live, and after that they go to the dead. 4
4 for a living dog is better than a dead lion. 4
5 For the living know . . but the dead know nothing 4
10: 1 Dead flies make . . ointment give off an evil odor; 2
Isa 8:19 Should they consult the dead 4
22: 2 not slain with the sword or dead in battle. 4
26:14 They are dead, they will not live; 4
19 Thy dead shall live, their bodies shall rise. 4
37:36 behold, these were all dead bodies. 4
Jer 16: 7 for the mourner, to comfort him for the dead; 4
22:10 Weep not for him who is dead, nor bemoan him; 4
Lam 3: 6 dwell in darkness like the dead of long ago. 4
Ezk 24:17 Sigh, but not aloud; make no mourning for the dead. 4
44:25 defile themselves by going near to a dead person; 4
Mat 2:20 those who sought the child's life are dead. 10
8:22 and leave the dead to bury their own dead. 13
22 and leave the dead to bury their own dead. 13
10: 8 Heal the sick, raise the dead, cleanse lepers 13
11: 5 the dead are raised up, and the poor have good news 13
14: 2 he has been raised from the dead 13
17: 9 until the Son of man is raised from the dead. 13
22:31 as for the resurrection of the dead 13
32 He is not God of the dead, but of the living. 13
27:64 'He has risen from the dead,' 13
28: 7 he has risen from the dead 13
Mrk 6:14 John the baptizer has been raised from the dead; 13
9: 9 the Son of man should have risen from the dead 13
10 questioning what the rising from the dead meant 13
12:25 For when they rise from the dead 13
26 as for the dead being raised 13
27 He is not God of the dead, but of the living; 13
15:45 he learned from the centurion that he was dead •
Lke 7:22 the deaf hear, the dead are raised up 13
9: 7 John had been raised from the dead 13
60 Leave the dead to bury their own dead 13
60 Leave the dead to bury their own dead 13
15:24 this my son was dead, and is alive again 13
32 your brother was dead, and is alive 13
16:30 if some one goes to them from the dead 13
31 if some one should rise from the dead.' 13
20:35 to the resurrection from the dead 13
37 that the dead are raised, even Moses showed 13
38 Now he is not God of the dead, but of the living 13
24: 5 Why do you seek the living among the dead? 13
46 on the third day rise from the dead 13
Joh 2:22 When therefore he was raised from the dead 13
5:21 as the Father raises the dead and gives them life 13
25 when the dead will hear the voice of the Son of God 13
11:39 for he has been dead four days •
12: 1 whom Jesus had raised from the dead. 13
9 to see Laz'arus, whom he had raised from the dead. 13
17 raised him from the dead 13
19:33 came to Jesus and saw that he was already dead 10
20: 9 the scripture, that he must rise from the dead. 13
21:14 after he was raised from the dead. 13
Act 3:15 the Author of life, whom God raised from the dead. 13
4: 2 in Jesus the resurrection from the dead. 13
10 whom you crucified, whom God raised from the dead 13
5:10 When the young men came in they found her dead 13
10:41 after he rose from the dead. 13
42 judge of the living and the dead. 13
13:30 God raised him from the dead; 13
34 as for the fact that he raised him from the dead 13
17: 3 to suffer and to rise from the dead 13
31 given assurance . . by raising him from the dead 13
32 when they heard of the resurrection of the dead 13
20: 9 he fell down . . and was taken up dead. 13
23: 6 the hope and the resurrection of the dead 13
24:21 With respect to the resurrection of the dead 13
25:19 who was dead, but whom Paul asserted to be alive. 10
26: 8 thought incredible . . that God raises the dead? 13
23 by being the first to rise from the dead 13
28: 6 to swell up or suddenly fall down dead 13
Rom 1: 4 by his resurrection from the dead, Jesus Christ 13
4:17 God . . who gives life to the dead 13
19 his own body, which was as good as dead 14
24 him that raised from the dead Jesus our Lord 13
6: 4 so that as Christ was raised from the dead 13
9 Christ being raised from the dead will never die 13
11 you also must consider yourselves dead to sin 13
7: 4 belong . . to him who has been raised from the dead 13
8 Apart from the law sin lies dead. 13
8:10 although your bodies are dead because of sin 13
11 the Spirit of him who raised Jesus from the dead 13
11 he who raised Christ Jesus from the dead 13
34 Jesus, who died, yes, who was raised from the dead •
10: 7 (that is, to bring Christ up from the dead). 13
9 and believe . . that God raised him from the dead 13
11:15 their acceptance mean but life from the dead? 13
14: 9 be Lord both of the dead and of the living. 13
1Co 15:12 Now if Christ is preached as raised from the dead 13
12 there is no resurrection of the dead? 13
13 if there is no resurrection of the dead 13
15 if it is true that the dead are not raised. 13
16 For if the dead are not raised 13
20 in fact Christ has been raised from the dead 13
21 has come also the resurrection of the dead. 13
29 by being baptized on behalf of the dead 13
29 If the dead are not raised at all 13
32 If the dead are not raised, "Let us eat and drink 13
35 some one will ask, "How are the dead raised? 13
42 So is it with the resurrection of the dead. 13
52 the dead will be raised imperishable 13
2Co 1: 9 not on ourselves but on God who raises the dead; 13
Gal 1: 1 God the Father, who raised him from the dead- 13
Eph 1:20 when he raised him from the dead 13
2: 1 when you were dead through the trespasses 13
5 even when we were dead through our trespasses 13
5:14 it is said, "Awake, O sleeper, and arise from the dead 13
Php 3:11 I may attain the resurrection from the dead. 13
Col 1:18 he is the beginning, the first-born from the dead 13
2:12 who raised him from the dead. 13
13 were dead in trespasses 13
1Th 1:10 his Son from heaven, whom he raised from the dead 13
4:16 the dead in Christ will rise first; 13

2Ti 2: 8 Remember Jesus Christ, risen from the dead 13
4: 1 who is to judge the living and the dead 13
Heb 6: 1 foundation of repentance from dead works 13
2 the resurrection of the dead 13
9:14 purify your conscience from dead works 13
11:12 Therefore from one man, and him as good as dead 14
19 God was able to raise men even from the dead 13
35 Women received their dead by resurrection. 13
13:20 who brought again from the dead our Lord Jesus 13
Jas 2:17 So faith by itself, if it has no works, is dead. 13
26 For as the body apart from the spirit is dead 13
26 so faith apart from works is dead. 13
1Pe 1: 3 the resurrection of Jesus Christ from the dead 13
21 who raised him from the dead and gave him glory 13
4: 5 who is ready to judge the living and the dead. 13
6 the gospel was preached even to the dead 13
Rev 1: 5 Jesus Christ . . the first-born of the dead 13
17 When I saw him, I fell at his feet as though dead. 13
2:23 and I will strike her children dead. 9
3: 1 you have the name of being alive, and you are dead. 13
11:18 and the time for the dead to be judged 13
14:13 Blessed are the dead who die in the Lord 13
20: 5 The rest of the dead did not come to life 13
12 dead, great and small, standing before the throne 13
12 dead were judged by what was written in the books 13
13 And the sea gave up the dead in it 13
13 Death and Hades gave up the dead in them 13
2Es 2:16 I will raise up the dead from their places 16
23 When you find any who are dead 16
7:109 for the one who was dead, that he might live 16
16:23 the dead shall be cast out like dung 16
Tob 2: 8 here he is burying the dead again! 13
3:15 Already seven husbands of mine are dead 8
12:12 when you buried the dead 13
13 in order to go and lay out the dead 13
Jdt 2: 8 every . . river shall be filled with their dead 13
6: 4 their fields will be full of their dead 13
14:15 and found him thrown down on the platform dead 13
Wis 4:18 and an outrage among the dead for ever 13
14:15 honored as a god what was once a dead human being 13
15: 5 they desire the lifeless form of a dead image. 13
17 what he makes with lawless hands is dead 13
18:23 when the dead had already fallen on one another 13
19: 3 were lamenting at the graves of their dead 13
Sir 7:33 withhold not kindness from the dead. 13
17:28 From the dead, as from one who does not exist 13
22:11 Weep for the dead, for he lacks the light 13
11 weep less bitterly for the dead 13
12 Mourning for the dead lasts seven days 13
34:25 If a man washes after touching a dead body 13
38:16 My son, let your tears fall for the dead 13
21 you do the dead no good, and you injure yourself. 15
23 When the dead is at rest 13
48:13 when he was dead his body prophesied. 11
Bar 2:17 for the dead who are in Hades, whose spirit 10
3: 4 hear now the prayer of the dead of Israel 10
10 country, that you are defiled with the dead 13
LJr 1:27 placed before them just as before the dead. 13
71 like a dead body cast out in the darkness. 13
2Mc 5: 5 When a false rumor arose that Antiochus was dead 12
12:44 superfluous and foolish to pray for the dead 13
4Mc 8:21 if we disobey we are dead! 10

dead *See also* beast, body, half, lie, raise.

dead man 1. מות 2. *θνήσκω* 3. *νεκρός* 4. *τελευτάω*

Gen 20: 3 Behold, you are a dead man, because of the woman 1
Exd 12:33 haste; for they said, "We are all dead men. 1
Isa 59:10 among those in full vigor we are like dead men. 1
Mat 23:27 within they are full of dead men's bones 3
28: 4 the guards trembled and became like dead men. 3
Lke 7:15 the dead man sat up, and began to speak 3
Joh 11:39 Martha, the sister of the dead man, said to him, "Lord 4
44 The dead man came out 2
Rev 16: 3 the sea, and it became like the blood of a dead man 3

one dead 1. מות

Num12:12 Let her not be as one dead, of whom the flesh 1

dead person 1. מות

Num19:13 Whoever touches a dead person, the body of any man 1

dead thing 1. *νεκρός*

Wis 13:10 miserable, with their hopes set on dead things 1
18 for life he prays to a thing that is dead 1

deadly 1. בְּלִיַּעַל 2. בְּנֶפֶשׁ 3. הַוָּה 4. מָוֶת 5. מְמוֹת 6. רַע 7. שחט 8. *θανατηφόρος* 9. *τηλικοῦτος*

Ps 7:13 he has prepared his deadly weapons 4
17: 9 despoil me, my deadly enemies who surround me. 2
41: 8 They say, "A deadly thing has fastened upon him; 1
91: 3 will deliver you . . from the deadly pestilence; 3
Jer 9: 8 Their tongue is a deadly arrow; 7
16: 4 They shall die of deadly diseases. 5
Ezk 5:16 I loose against you my deadly arrows of famine 6
2Co 1:10 he delivered us from so deadly a peril 9
Jas 3: 8 the tongue . . full of deadly poison. 8

deadly *See also* charm, wound.

deadly thing 1. *θανάσιμος*

Mrk 16:18 if they drink any deadly thing, it will not hurt 1

deaf 1. חרשׁ 2. חֵרֵשׁ 3. *κωφός*

Exd 4:11 Who makes him dumb, or deaf, or seeing 2
Lev 19:14 You shall not curse the deaf 2
Ps 28: 1 To thee, O LORD, I call; my rock, be not deaf to me 1
58: 4 a serpent, like the deaf adder that stops its ear 2
Isa 29:18 In that day the deaf shall hear the words of a book 2
35: 5 be opened, and the ears of the deaf unstopped; 2
42:18 Hear, you deaf; and look, you blind, that you may see! 2
19 or deaf as my messenger whom I send? 2
43: 8 blind, yet have eyes, who are deaf, yet have ears! 2
Mic 7:16 hands on their mouths; their ears shall be deaf; 1
Mat 11: 5 lame walk, lepers are cleansed and the deaf hear 3
Mrk 7:32 they brought to him a man who was deaf 3
37 he even makes the deaf hear and the dumb speak. 3
9:25 You dumb and deaf spirit, I command you 3
Lke 7:22 lepers are cleansed, and the deaf hear 3

deaf man 1. חֵרֵשׁ

Ps 38:13 I am like a deaf man, I do not hear 1

deal 1. דָּבָר 2. עלל 3. עשה 4. פעל 5. *ἀπαντάω* 6. *διεξάγω* 7. *εἰς* 8. *ἐπί* 9. *ἔχω* 10. *ἦθος* 11. *καταχράομαι* 12. *κρίνω* 13. *πατάσσω* 14. *περί* 15. *ποιέω* 16. *πορεύω* 17. *πρᾶσις* 18. *συγχράομαι* 19. *χράομαι* 20. *χωρίς*

Gen 21:23 but as I have dealt loyally with you 3
23 but as I have dealt loyally with you 3
24:49 if you will deal loyally and truly with my master 3
47:29 and promise to deal loyally and truly with me. 3
Exd 5:15 Why do you deal thus with your servants? 3
21: 9 his son, he shall deal with her as a daughter. 3
31 shall be dealt with according to this same rule. 3
Num 4:19 deal thus with them, that they may live and not die 3
11:15 If thou wilt deal thus with me, kill me at once 3
Deu 7: 5 thus shall you deal with them 3
Jos 2:12 swear . . that as I have dealt kindly with you 3
12 you also will deal kindly with my father's house 3
14 we will deal kindly and faithfully with you 3
Jdg 9:16 if you have dealt well with Jerubba'al and his 3
18: 4 thus has Micah dealt with me: he has hired me 3
7 the Sido'nians and had no dealings with any one. 1
28 from Sidon, and they had no dealings with any one. 1
Rut 1: 8 Go, return . . May the LORD deal kindly with you 3
8 as you have dealt with the dead and with me. 3
1Sm 2:23 I hear of your evil dealings from all the people. 1
20: 8 Therefore deal kindly with your servant 3
24:18 you have dealt well with me 3
2Sm 10: 2 I will deal loyally with Hanun the son of Nahash 3
2 I will . . as his father dealt loyally with me. 3
18:13 if I had dealt treacherously against his life 3
1Kg 2: 5 how he dealt with the two commanders 3
7 deal loyally with the sons of Barzil'lai 3
2Kg 12:15 they did not ask . . for they dealt honestly. 3
21: 6 and dealt with mediums and with wizards. 3
22: 7 no accounting shall . . for they deal honestly. 3
1Ch 19: 2 David said, "I will deal loyally with Hanun 3
2 for his father dealt loyally with me. 3
2Ch 2: 3 As you dealt with David . . so deal with me. 3
3 As you dealt with David . . so deal with me. •
19:11 Deal courageously, and may the LORD be 3
33: 6 dealt with mediums and with wizards. 3
Neh 9:33 dealt faithfully and we have acted wickedly; 3
Job 42: 8 not to deal with you according to your folly; 3
Ps 103:10 He does not deal with us according to our sins 3
109:21 my Lord, deal on my behalf for thy name's sake; 3
119:65 Thou hast dealt well with thy servant, O LORD 3
124 Deal with thy servant according to thy 3
147:20 He has not dealt thus with any other nation; 3
Jer 6:13 from prophet to priest, every one deals falsely. 3
8:10 from prophet to priest every one deals falsely. 3
18:23 deal with them in the time of thine anger. 3
21: 2 perhaps the LORD will deal with us 3
22: 8 Why has the LORD dealt thus with this great city? 3
39:12 do him no harm, but deal with him as he tells you. 3
Lam 1:22 and deal with them as thou hast dealt with me 2
22 and deal with them as thou hast dealt with me 2
2:20 see! With whom hast thou dealt thus? 2
Ezk 8:18 I will deal in wrath; my eye will not spare 3
16:59 I will deal with you as you have done 3
20:44 I am the LORD, when I deal with you 3
22:14 in the days that I shall deal with you? 3
23:25 against you, that they may deal with you in fury. 3
29 they shall deal with you in hatred 3
31:11 surely deal with it as its wickedness deserves. 3
35:11 I will deal with you according to the anger 3
15 I will deal with you; you shall be desolate 3
39:24 I dealt with them according to their uncleanness 3
Dan 1:13 according to what you see deal with your servants. 3
11: 7 shall deal with them and shall prevail. 3
39 He shall deal with the strongest fortresses 3
Hos 7: 1 for they deal falsely, the thief breaks 4
Jol 2:26 your God, who has dealt wondrously with you. 3
Zep 3:19 I will deal with all your oppressors. 3
Zec 1: 6 As the LORD of hosts purposed to deal with us 3
6 for our ways and deeds, so has he dealt with us. 3
8:11 I will not deal with the remnant of this people •
Lke 16: 8 more shrewd in dealing with their own generation 7
Joh 4: 9 For Jews have no dealings with Samaritans. 18
Act 1: 1 I have dealt with all that Jesus began to do 15
1Co 7:31 those who deal with the world 19
31 as though they had no dealings with it 11
2Co 13: 3 He is not weak in dealing with you 7
4 in dealing with you we shall live with him 7
Heb 9:10 deal only with food and drink 8
28 will appear a second time, not to deal with sin 20
1Es 6: 5 Yet the elders of the Jews were dealt with kindly 9
Tob 3: 6 now deal with me according to thy pleasure; 15
Jdt 3: 4 deal with them in any way that seems good to you. 5
Sir 42: 5 of profit from dealing with merchants 17
50:22 deals with us according to his mercy. 15
Bar 2:27 'Yet thou hast dealt with us, O Lord our God 15
Aza 1:19 deal with us in thy forbearance 15
Sus 1:57 have been dealing with the daughters of Israel 15
1Mc 5: 3 He dealt them a heavy blow and humbled them 13
9:29 to deal with those of our nation who hate us. •
13:31 Trypho dealt treacherously with the young king 16
2Mc 6:14 he does not deal in this way with us 12
14:30 Nicanor was more austere in his dealings 6
3Mc 4:13 these men be dealt with in precisely the same fashion 15
4Mc 3: 3 reason can help to deal with anger. •
4: 5 On receiving authority to deal with this matter 14
5:24 in all our dealings we act impartially 10

deal a blow 1. נכה 2. *πατάσσω*

Jer 30:14 for I have dealt you the blow of an enemy 1
1Mc 1:30 dealt it a severe blow, and destroyed many people 2
5:34 he dealt them a heavy blow 2

deal arrogantly 1. זיד

Exd 18:11 when they dealt arrogantly with them. 1

deal bitterly 1. מרר

Rut 1:20 the Almighty has dealt very bitterly with me. 1

deal bountifully 1. גמל

Ps 13: 6 LORD, because he has dealt bountifully with me. 1
116: 7 for the LORD has dealt bountifully with you. 1
119:17 Deal bountifully with thy servant 1
142: 7 for thou wilt deal bountifully with me. 1

deal corruptly 1. שחת

Deu 32: 5 They have dealt corruptly with him, they are no 1
Isa 1: 4 offspring of evildoers, sons who deal corruptly! 1

deal craftily 1. נכל 2. *κατασοφίζομαι*

Ps 105:25 to deal craftily with his servants. 1
Act 7:19 He dealt craftily with our race 2

deal cruelly 1. קשה

Job 39:16 She deals cruelly with her young 1

deal deceitfully 1. עות

Ams 8: 5 and deal deceitfully with false balances 1

deal faithlessly 1. בגד

Exd 21: 8 since he has dealt faithlessly with her. 1
Hos 5: 7 They have dealt faithlessly with the LORD; 1
6: 7 there they dealt faithlessly with me. 1

deal falsely 1. כחש 2. שקר 3. חלל

Gen 21:23 you will not deal falsely with me 2
Exd 8:29 only let not Pharaoh deal falsely again by not 3
Lev 19:11 You shall not steal, nor deal falsely 1
Jos 24:27 lest you deal falsely with your God. 1
Isa 63: 8 they are my people, sons who will not deal falsely; 2

deal generously 1. חנן

Ps 112: 5 well with the man who deals generously and lends 1

deal gently 1. לְאַט 2. *μετριοπαθέω*

2Sm 18: 5 Deal gently for my sake with the young man 1
Job 15:11 or the word that deals gently with you? 1
Heb 5: 2 He can deal gently with the ignorant and wayward 2

deal graciously 1. חנן

Gen 33:11 Accept . . because God has dealt graciously 1

deal harshly 1. ענה 2. רעע

Gen 16: 6 Then Sar'ai dealt harshly with her 1
Num20:15 Egyptians dealt harshly with us and our fathers; 2

deal ill 1. רעע

Num11:11 Why has thou dealt ill with thy servant? 1

deal insolently 1. גדל

Ps 55:12 is not an adversary who deals insolently with me- 1

deal kindly 1. עָשִׂי חֶסֶד

Jdg 1:24 show us the way . . and we will deal kindly with you. 1

deal out 1. פלס 2. *παραδίδωμι*

Ps 58: 2 your hands deal out violence on earth. 1
Sir 42: 7 Whatever you deal out 2

deal perversely 1. עול
Isa 26:10 in the land of uprightness he deals perversely 1

deal proudly 1. זוד (A)
Dan 5:20 spirit was hardened so that he dealt proudly 1

deal shrewdly 1. חכם
Exd 1:10 Come, let us deal shrewdly with them 1

deal treacherously 1. בגד 2. מעל
Jdg 9:23 Shechem dealt treacherously with Abim'elech; 1
1Sm 14:33 And he said, "You have dealt treacherously; 1
Isa 24:16 For the treacherous deal treacherously 1
16 the treacherous deal very treacherously. 1
33: 1 with whom none has dealt treacherously! 1
1 made an end of dealing treacherously 1
1 you will be dealt with treacherously. 1
48: 8 I knew that you would deal very treacherously 1
Jer 12: 6 even they have dealt treacherously with you; 1
Lam 1: 2 her friends have dealt treacherously with her 1
Ezk 20:27 blasphemed me, by dealing treacherously with me 2
39:23 because they dealt so treacherously with me 2

deal unfaithfully 1. fraudo
2Es 7:72 they dealt unfaithfully 1

deal violently 1. zelo
2Es 15:52 Would I have dealt with you so violently 1

deal wantonly 1. פרע
2Ch 28:19 for he had dealt wantonly in Judah 1

deal well 1. יטב
Gen 12:16 for her sake he dealt well with Abram; 1
Exd 1:20 So God dealt well with the midwives; 1
1Sm 25:31 And when the LORD has dealt well with my lord 1

deal wisely 1. בין 2. שכל
2Ch 11:23 he dealt wisely, and distributed some of his sons 1
Prv 14:35 A servant who deals wisely has the king's favor 2
17: 2 A slave who deals wisely will rule over a son 2
Jer 23: 5 and he shall reign as king and deal wisely 2

deal worse 1. רעע
Gen 19: 9 Now we will deal worse with you than with them. 1

dealer 1. סחר 2. ערב 3. πωλέω
Ezk 27:21 the princes of Kedar were your favored dealers 1
27 your caulkers, your dealers in merchandise 2
Mat 25: 9 go rather to the dealers and buy for yourselves.' 3

contemptuous dealing 1. spretio
2Es 12:32 before them their contemptuous dealings. 1

unjust dealing 1. ἀδικία
Sir 41:18 of unjust dealing, before your partner or friend; 1

wise dealing 1. שכל
Prv 1: 3 receive instruction in wise dealing 1

dear 1. חמד 2. יַקִּיר 3. ἀγαπητός 4. ἔντιμος 5. carus
Ps 39:11 thou dost consume like a moth what is dear to him; 1
Jer 31:20 Is E'phraim my dear son? Is he my darling child? 2
Lke 7: 2 Now a centurion had a slave who was dear to him 4
2Es 7:104or a friend his dearest friend, to be ill or sleep 5
Tob 10:12 The Lord . . bring you back safely, dear brother 3
dear *See also* hold.

most dear 1. carus
2Es 6:58 zealous for thee, and most dear 1
7:103or friends for those who are most dear. 1

very dear 1. ἀγαπητός
1Th 2: 8 because you had become very dear to us. 1

death 1. בּוֹר 2. דָּם 3. הרג 4. מָוֶת 5. מות 6. מְמוֹת
7. מות (A) 8. αἵδης 9. ἀναίρεσις 10. ἀπώλεια
11. θάνατος 12. μεταλλάσσω 13. μόρος 14. νεκρός
15. νέκρωσις 16. τελευτάω 17. τελευτή 18. φόνος
19. morior 20. mors
Gen 21:16 for she said, "Let me not look upon the death 5
24:67 Isaac was comforted after his mother's death. •
25:11 After the death of Abraham God blessed Isaac 5
26:18 stopped them after the death of Abraham; 5
27: 2 Behold, I am old; I do not know the day of my death. 5
Exd 10:17 entreat . . to remove this death from me. 4
19:12 touches the mountain shall be put to death; 5
21:28 When an ox gores a man or a woman to death 5
Lev 16: 1 after the death of the two sons of Aaron 5
Num15:36 stoned him to death with stones, as the LORD 5
16:29 If these men die the common death of all men 5
23:10 Let me die the death of the righteous 5
35:25 live in it until the death of the high priest 5
28 city of refuge until the death of the high priest; 5
28 but after the death of the high priest 5
31 for the life of a murderer, who is guilty of death; 5
32 may return . . before the death of the high priest. 5
Deu 13:10 You shall stone him to death with stones 5
17: 5 stone that man or woman to death with stones. 5
21:21 men . . shall stone him to death with stones; 5
22 man has committed a crime punishable by death 4
22:21 men . . shall stone her to death with stones 5
24 you shall stone them to death with stones 5
26 woman there is no offense punishable by death 4
30:15 set before you . . life and good, death and evil. 4
19 set before you life and death, blessing and curse; 4
31:27 how much more after my death! 5
29 after my death you will surely act corruptly 5
33: 1 Moses . . blessed . . Israel before his death. 5
Jos 1: 1 After the death of Moses the servant of the LORD 4
2:13 save alive . . and deliver our lives from death. 4
20: 6 remain . . until the death of him who is high priest 4
Jdg 1: 1 After the death of Joshua the people of Israel 4
5:18 Zeb'ulun . . jeoparded their lives to the death; 5
13: 7 a Nazirite . . from birth to the day of his death.' 5
16:16 and urged him, his soul was vexed to death. 5
30 the dead whom he slew at his death were more 5
Rut 1:17 May the LORD . . if even death parts me from you. 4
2:11 you have done . . since the death of your husband 5
1Sm 4:20 about the time of her death the women . . said 5
15:32 Surely the bitterness of death is past. 4
35 did not see Saul again until the day of his death 5
20: 3 there is but a step between me and death. 4
22:22 I have occasioned the death of all the persons •
2Sm 1: 1 After the death of Saul, when David had returned 4
23 In life and in death they were not divided; 5
6:23 And Michal . . had no child to the day of her death. 5
15:21 wherever my lord . . whether for death or for life 4
19:28 all my father's house were but men doomed to death 4
20: 3 they were shut up until the day of their death 5
22: 5 For the waves of death encompassed me 4
6 the snares of death confronted me. 4
1Kg 2:26 Go to . . your estate; for you deserve death. But I 4
11:40 and was in Egypt until the death of Solomon. 5
12:18 and all Israel stoned him to death with stones. 5
21:10 Then take him out, and stone him to death. 5
13 took him outside the city, and stoned him to death 5
2Kg 1: 1 After the death of Ahab, Moab rebelled 5
2:21 death nor miscarriage shall come from it. 4
4:40 cried out, "O man of God, there is death in the pot! 4
14:17 lived fifteen years after the death of Jeho'ash 5
15: 5 he was a leper to the day of his death 4
20: 1 became sick and was at the point of death. 5
1Ch 2:24 After the death of Hezron, Caleb went 5
22: 5 materials in great quantity before his death. 5
2Ch 10:18 people of Israel stoned him to death 5
22: 4 for after the death of his father 5
24:15 Jehoi'ada . . was 130 years old at his death. 5
17 Now after the death of Jehoi'ada 5
25:25 lived fifteen years after the death of Jo'ash 5
26:21 King Uzzi'ah was a leper to the day of his death 5
32:33 all Judah . . did him honor at his death. 5
Ezr 7:26 whether for death or for banishment 7
Job 3:21 who long for death, but it comes not 4
5:20 In famine he will redeem you from death 4
7:15 that I would choose strangling and death 4
18:13 the first-born of death consumes his limbs. 4
28:22 Abaddon and Death say, 'We have heard a rumor of it 4
30:23 Yea, I know that thou wilt bring me to death 4
38:17 Have the gates of death been revealed to you 4
Ps 6: 5 For in death there is no remembrance of thee; 4
9:13 O thou who liftest me up from the gates of death 4
13: 3 lighten my eyes, lest I sleep the sleep of death; 4
18: 4 The cords of death encompassed me 4
5 the snares of death confronted me. 4
22:15 thou dost lay me in the dust of death. 4
30: 9 What profit is there in my death 2
33:19 that he may deliver their soul from death 4
49:14 Death shall be their shepherd; 4
55: 4 the terrors of death have fallen upon me. 4
15 Let death come upon them; let them go down to Sheol 4
56:13 For thou hast delivered my soul from death 4
68:20 to God, the Lord, belongs escape from death. 4
78:50 he did not spare them from death 4
89:48 What man can live and never see death? 4
94:21 condemn the innocent to death. 2
107:18 drew near to the gates of death. 4
109:16 pursued the poor and needy . . to their death. 5
31 to save him from those who condemn him to death. †
116: 3 The snares of death encompassed me; 4
8 For thou hast delivered my soul from death 4
15 Precious . . of the LORD is the death of his saints. 5
118:18 LORD . . has not given me over to death. 4
Prv 2:18 for her house sinks down to death 4
5: 5 Her feet go down to death; 4
7:27 going down to the chambers of death. 4
8:36 all who hate me love death. 4
10: 2 but righteousness delivers from death. 4
11: 4 but righteousness delivers from death. 4
12:28 but the way of error leads to death. 4
13:14 that one may avoid the snares of death. 4
14:12 but its end is the way to death. 4
27 that one may avoid the snares of death. 4
16:14 A king's wrath is a messenger of death 4
25 but its end is the way to death. 4
18:21 Death and life are in the power of the tongue 4
21: 6 fleeting vapor and a snare of death. 4
24:11 Rescue those who are being taken away to death; 4
26:18 madman who throws firebrands, arrows, and death 4
28:17 let him be a fugitive until death; let no one help 1
Ecc 7: 1 and the day of death, than the day of birth. 4
26 I found more bitter than death the woman whose 4
8: 8 power . . or authority over the day of death; 4
Sng 8: 6 love is strong as death, jealousy is cruel 4
Isa 25: 8 He will swallow up death for ever 4
28:15 you have said, "We have made a covenant with death 4
18 Then your covenant with death will be annulled 4
38: 1 became sick and was at the point of death. 5
18 Sheol cannot thank . . death cannot praise thee; 4
53: 9 with the wicked and with a rich man in his death 4
12 because he poured out his soul to death 4
Jer 8: 3 Death shall be preferred to life 4
9:21 For death has come up into our windows 4
18:21 May their men meet death by pestilence 3
21: 8 before you the way of life and the way of death. 4
26:11 This man deserves the sentence of death 4
16 This man does not deserve the sentence of death 4
52:11 and put him in prison till the day of his death. 5
34 his daily need, until the day of his death 5
Lam 1:20 in the house it is like death. 4
Ezk 18:23 Have I any pleasure in the death of the wicked 5
32 For I have no pleasure in the death of any one 5
28: 8 you shall die the death of the slain 6
10 You shall die the death of the uncircumcised 5
31:14 for they are all given over to death 4
33:11 I have no pleasure in the death of the wicked 5
Hos 13:14 Shall I redeem them from Death? 4
14 O Death, where are your plagues? 4
Hab 2: 5 as wide as Sheol; like death he has never enough. 4
Mat 2:15 remained there until the death of Herod. 17
4:16 region and shadow of death light has dawned. 11
10:21 Brother will deliver up brother to death 11
16:28 some standing here who will not taste death 11
20:18 and they will condemn him to death 11
26:38 My soul is very sorrowful, even to death 11
66 They answered, "He deserves death. 11
Mrk 9: 1 some standing here who will not taste death 11
10:33 they will condemn him to death 11
13:12 brother will deliver up brother to death 11
14:34 My soul is very sorrowful, even to death 11
64 they all condemned him as deserving death. 11
Lke 1:79 who sit in darkness and in the shadow of death 11
2:26 he should not see death 11
7: 2 who was sick and at the point of death. 16
9:27 are some standing here who will not taste death 11
22:33 I am ready to go with you to prison and to death. 11
23:15 nothing deserving death has been done by him; 11
22 I have found in him no crime deserving death 11
24:20 condemned to death, and crucified him. 11
Joh 5:24 has passed from death to life. 11
8:51 if any one keeps my word, he will never see death. 11
52 he will never taste death.' 11
11: 4 This illness is not unto death 11
13 Now Jesus had spoken of his death 11
12:33 He said this to show by what death he was to die. 11
18:32 to show by what death he was to die. 11
21:19 to show by what death he was to glorify God 11
Act 2:24 having loosed the pangs of death 11
8: 1 Saul was consenting to his death 9
13:28 could charge him with nothing deserving death 11
22: 4 I persecuted this Way to the death 11
23:29 charged with nothing deserving death 11
25:25 I found that he had done nothing deserving death; 11
26:31 This man is doing nothing to deserve death 11
Rom 5:10 reconciled to God by the death of his Son 11
12 sin came into the world . . death through sin 11
12 death spread to all men because all men sinned– 11
14 Yet death reigned from Adam to Moses 11
17 If, because of one man's trespass, death reigned 11
21 so that, as sin reigned in death 11
6: 3 into Christ Jesus were baptized into his death? 11
4 buried therefore with him by baptism into death 11
5 if we have been united with him in a death like his 11
9 death no longer has dominion over him. 11
10 The death he died he died to sin, once for all •
13 as men who have been brought from death to life 14
16 slaves . . either of sin, which leads to death 11
21 The end of those things is death. 11
23 For the wages of sin is death 11
7: 5 at work in our members to bear fruit for death. 11
10 the very commandment . . proved to be death to me. 11
13 Did that which is good, then, bring death to me? 11
13 sin, working death in me through what is good 11
24 Who will deliver me from this body of death? 11
8: 2 has set me free from the law of sin and death. 11
6 To set the mind on the flesh is death 11
38 neither death, nor life, nor angels 11
1Co 3:22 the world or life or death or the present 11
11:26 you proclaim the Lord's death until he comes. 11
15:21 For as by a man came death 11
26 The last enemy to be destroyed is death. 11
54 Death is swallowed up in victory. 11
55 O death, where is thy victory? 11
55 O death, where is thy sting? 11
56 The sting of death is sin 11
2Co 1: 9 felt that we had received the sentence of death 11

2:16 to one a fragrance from death to death 11
16 to one a fragrance from death to death 11
3: 7 Now if the dispensation of death 11
4:10 always carrying in the body the death of Jesus 15
11 always being given up to death for Jesus' sake 11
12 death is at work in us, but life in you. 11
7:10 worldly grief produces death. 11
11:23 with countless beatings, and often near death. 11
Php 1:20 whether by life or by death. 11
2: 8 became obedient unto death, even death on a cross 11
8 obedient unto death, even death on a cross. 11
27 Indeed he was ill, near to death 11
3:10 becoming like him in his death 11
Col 1:22 now reconciled in his body of flesh by his death 11
2Ti 1:10 who abolished death 11
Heb 2: 9 because of the suffering of death 11
9 that by the grace of God he might taste death 11
14 that through death he might destroy him 11
14 him who has the power of death, that is, the devil. 11
15 through fear of death 11
5: 7 to him who was able to save him from death 11
7:23 because they were prevented by death 11
9:15 since a death has occurred which redeems them 11
16 a will is involved, the death of the one who made it 11
17 a will takes effect only at death 14
11: 5 he should not see death 11
Jas 1:15 sin when it is full-grown brings forth death. 11
5:20 will save his soul from death 11
1Jn 3:14 We know that we have passed out of death into life 11
14 He who does not love abides in death. 11
Rev 1:18 and I have the keys of Death and Hades. 11
2:10 Be faithful unto death 11
11 He . . shall not be hurt by the second death 11
6: 8 a pale horse, and its rider's name was Death 11
9: 6 in those days men will seek death and will not find it; 11
6 they will long to die, and death will fly from them. 11
12:11 they loved not their lives even unto death. 11
20: 6 Over such the second death has no power 11
13 Death and Hades gave up the dead in them 11
14 Death and Hades were thrown into the lake of fire 11
14 This is the second death, the lake of fire; 11
21: 4 and death shall be no more 11
8 the lake that burns . . which is the second death. 11
1Es 8:24 whether by death or some other punishment 11
2Es 3: 7 immediately thou didst appoint death for him 20
10 as death came upon Adam, so the flood upon them. 20
6:26 who from their birth have not tasted death 20
7:48 into corruption and the ways of death 20
66 salvation promised to them after death. 20
69 if we were not to come into judgment after death 20
75 whether after death . . we shall be kept in rest 20
78 Now, concerning death, the teaching is 20
92 might not lead them astray from life into death. 20
117 in sorrow now and expect punishment after death? 19
126 consider what we should suffer after death. 20
8:38 or about their death, their judgment 20
53 illness is banished from you, and death is hidden; ‡
9:12 must in torment acknowledge it after death. 20
14:34 and after death you shall obtain mercy. 20
35 For after death the judgment will come 20
15: 5 the sword and famine and death and destruction. 20
26 he will hand them over to death and slaughter. 20
49 and bring you to destruction and death. 20
53 and talking about their death when you were drunk? 20
Tob 3: 4 thou gavest us over to plunder, captivity, and death; 11
4: 2 I have asked for death 11
10 For charity delivers from death 11
6:12 without incurring the penalty of death 11
12: 9 For almsgiving delivers from death 11
Jdt 7:27 we shall not witness the death of our babes 11
11:11 death will fall upon them 11
12:14 it will be a joy to me until the day of my death! 11
14: 5 sent him to us as if to his death. 11
AEs 13:18 their death was before their eyes. 11
Wis 1:12 Do not invite death by the error of your life 11
13 because God did not make death 11
13 he does not delight in the death of the living. 10
16 men by their words and deeds summoned death •
2: 5 there is no return from our death 17
20 Let us condemn him to a shameful death 11
24 through the devil's envy death entered the world 11
12:20 those deserving of death 11
16:13 For thou hast power over life and death 11
18:12 by the one form of death 11
16 and stood and filled all things with death 11
20 experience of death touched also the righteous 11
19: 5 they themselves might meet a strange death. 11
Sir 1:13 on the day of his death he will be blessed. 17
4:28 Strive even to death for the truth 17
8: 7 Do not rejoice over any one's death 14
9:13 you will not be worried by the fear of death 11
11:14 Good things and bad, life and death 11
26 to reward a man on the day of death 17
28 Call no one happy before his death 17
14:12 Remember that death will not delay 11
15:17 Before a man are life and death 11
18:22 do not wait until death to be released from it. 11
24 Think of his wrath on the day of death 17
22:11 the life of the fool is worse than death. 11
23:12 is an utterance which is comparable to death 11
26: 5 all these are worse than death. 11
27:29 pain will consume them before their death. 11
28: 6 remember destruction and death 11
21 its death is an evil death 11
21 its death is an evil death 11
30:17 Death is better than a miserable life 11
33:14 life the opposite of death 11
23 in the hour of death 17
34:12 I have often been in danger of death 11
37: 2 Is it not a grief to the death 11
18 good and evil, life and death 11
38:18 For sorrow results in death 11
40: 2 their anxious thought is the day of death 17
5 fear of death, and fury and strife 11
9 are death and bloodshed and strife and sword 11
41: 1 O death, how bitter is the reminder of you 11
2 O death, how welcome is your sentence 11
3 Do not fear the sentence of death 11
46:20 he prophesied and revealed to the king his death 17
48: 5 You who raised a corpse from death and from Hades 11
14 so in death his deeds were marvelous. 17
51: 6 My soul drew near to death 11
9 prayed for deliverance from death. 11
LJr 1:18 as though he were sentenced to death 11
36 They cannot save a man from death 11
Aza 1:66 saved us from the hand of death 11
Sus 1:22 For if I do this thing, it is death for me; 11
1Mc 9:23 After the death of Judas, the lawless emerged 17
29 Since the death of your brother Judas 16
2Mc 4:47 while he sentenced to death those unfortunate men 11
6:19 welcoming death with honor 11
22 that by doing this he might be saved from death 11
30 though I might have been saved from death 11
31 leaving in his death an example of nobility 11
7:14 when he was near death, he said 16
29 Accept death 11
13: 8 he met his death in ashes. 11
14 exhorting his men to fight nobly to the death 11
14:46 This was the manner of his death. 12
3Mc 1:29 because indeed all at that time preferred death 11
3:25 sure and shameful death that befits enemies. 18
4: 8 seeing death immediately before them. 8
5:42 he would send them to death without delay 8
51 they stood now at the gates of death. 8
6:29 since they now had escaped death. 11
31 those disgracefully treated and near to death 8
31 instead of a bitter and lamentable death 13
7:16 those who had held fast to God even to death 11
4Mc 1: 9 by despising sufferings that bring death 11
5:37 one who does not fear your violence even to death. 11
6:21 and not protect our divine law even to death. 11
30 he resisted even to the very tortures of death 11
7: 8 in sufferings even to death. 11
15 whom the faithful seal of death has perfected! 11
16 an aged man despised tortures even to death 11
9: 4 to be more grievous than death itself. 11
5 threatening us with death by torture 11
29 How sweet is any kind of death 11
10: 1 When he too had endured a glorious death 11
15 No, by the blessed death of my brothers 11
12: 1 he also . . had died a blessed death •
13: 1 seven brothers despised sufferings even unto death 11
27 maltreated and tortured to death. 11
14: 4 proved coward or shrank from death 11
5 hastened to death by torture 11
6 those holy youths . . agreed to go to death for its sake. 11
19 and defend it even to the death? 11
15:10 they obeyed her even to death 11
12 to death for the sake of religion. 11
19 the signs of the approach of death. 11
16: 1 endured seeing her children tortured to death 11
13 she implored them and urged them on to death 11
17: 1 she also was about to be seized and put to death 11
7 enduring their varied tortures to death. 11
10 and enduring torture even to death. 11
22 through . . their death as an expiation 11

death *See also* bear, bring, burn, close, condemn, die, man, penalty, point, put, shadow, torture.

cause death 1. מות 2. פוח נֶפֶשׁ

1Kg 17:18 You have come . . and to cause the death of my son! 1
Job 31:39 if I . . caused the death of its owners; 2

deathly 1. מָוֶת

1Sm 5:11 was a deathly panic throughout the whole city. 1

deathly *See also* anxiety.

deathtrap 1. παγὶς θανάτου

Tob 14:10 escaped the deathtrap which Nadab had set 1

debar 1. עצר

Jer 36: 5 I am debarred from going to the house of the LORD; 1

debate 1. ζήτησις

Act 15: 2 had no small dissension and debate with them 1
7 after there had been much debate, Peter rose 1

debater 1. συζητητής

1Co 1:20 Where is the debater of this age? 1

debauchery 1. ἀσέλγεια 2. ἀσωτία 3. κοίτη

Rom 13:13 not in debauchery and licentiousness 3
Eph 5:18 do not get drunk with wine, for that is debauchery; 2
Wis 14:26 adultery, and debauchery. 1
2Mc 6: 4 temple was filled with debauchery and reveling 2

debt 1. מַשָּׁאָה 2. מַשָּׁא יָד 3. נשא ל 4. נְשִׁי 5. δάνειον 6. ὀφειλέτης 7. ὀφειλή 8. ὀφείλημα 9. ὀφείλω 10. πρᾶγμα

1Sm 22: 2 in distress, and every one who was in debt 3
2Kg 4: 7 Go, sell the oil and pay your debts 4
Neh 10:31 forego . . the exaction of every debt. 2
Prv 22:26 Be not one of those who . . become surety for debts. 1
Mat 6:12 And forgive us our debts, As we also have forgiven 8
18:27 released him and forgave him the debt. 5
30 put him in prison till he should pay the debt. 9
32 'You wicked servant! I forgave you all that debt 7
34 till he should pay all his debt. 9
Rom 15:27 and indeed they are in debt to them 6
1Es 3:20 forgets all sorrow and debt. 8
1Mc 10:43 because he owes money to the king or has any debt 10
15: 8 Every debt you owe to the royal treasury 8
8 any such future debts shall be canceled for you •
4Mc 2: 8 to cancel the debt when the seventh year arrives. 5

debtor 1. אֲשֶׁר נשא בְּ 2. נשך 3. ὀφειλέτης 4. χρεοφειλέτης

Isa 24: 2 as with the creditor, so with the debtor. 1
Ezk 18: 7 but restores to the debtor his pledge •
Hab 2: 7 Will not your debtors suddenly arise 2
Mat 6:12 debts, As we also have forgiven our debtors; 3
Lke 7:41 A certain creditor had two debtors 4
16: 5 summoning his master's debtors one by one 4
Rom 8:12 So then, brethren, we are debtors, not to the flesh 3

decay 1. רמם 2. σαπρία 3. σήπη 4. σήπω 5. φθορά

Rom 8:21 creation . . set free from its bondage to decay 5
Sir 10: 9 for even in life his bowels decay. 1
14:19 Every product decays and ceases to exist 4
19: 3 Decay and worms will inherit him 3
2Mc 9: 9 the whole army felt revulsion at his decay. 2

deceased 1. μεταλάσσω

2Mc 4:37 the moderation and good conduct of the deceased; 1

deceit 1. מִרְמָה 2. רְמִיָּה 3. שֶׁקֶר 4. תַּרְמִית 5. ἀδίκως 6. ἀπάτη 7. δολιότης 8. δόλος 9. παραλογισμός 10. dolus

Job 15:35 their heart prepares deceit. 1
27: 4 my tongue will not utter deceit. 2
31: 5 my foot has hastened to deceit; 1
Ps 10: 7 filled with cursing and deceit and oppression; 1
17: 1 Give ear to my prayer from lips free of deceit! 1
32: 2 in whose spirit there is no deceit. 2
34:13 from evil, and your lips from speaking deceit. 1
35:20 in the land they conceive words of deceit. 1
36: 3 The words of his mouth are mischief and deceit; 1
50:19 your tongue frames deceit. 1
101: 7 No man who practices deceit shall dwell in my 2
Prv 12:17 but a false witness utters deceit. 1
20 Deceit is in the heart of those who devise evil 1
20:17 Bread gained by deceit is sweet to a man 3
26:24 He who hates . . harbors deceit in his heart; 1
Isa 53: 9 no violence, and there was no deceit in his mouth. 1
57: 4 of transgression, the offspring of deceit 3
Jer 8: 5 They hold fast to deceit, they refuse to return. 4
9: 6 deceit upon deceit, they refuse to know me 1
6 deceit upon deceit, they refuse to know me 1
14:14 divination, and the deceit of their own minds. 4
23:26 and who prophesy the deceit of their own heart 4
Dan 8:25 cunning . . make deceit prosper under his hand 1
Hos 11:12 and the house of Israel with deceit; 1
Mrk 7:22 coveting, wickedness, deceit, licentiousness 8
Act 13:10 full of all deceit and villainy 8
Rom 1:29 Full of envy, murder, strife, deceit, malignity 8
Col 2: 8 makes a prey of you by philosophy and empty deceit 6
2Es 6:27 and deceit shall be quenched; 10
11:40 you have dwelt on the earth with deceit. 10
Jdt 9: 3 was ashamed of the deceit they had practiced 6
10 By the deceit of my lips strike down the slave 6
AEs 16:13 with intricate craft and deceit 9
Wis 1: 5 a . . disciplined spirit will flee from deceit 8
14:25 theft and deceit, corruption, faithlessness 8
30 because in deceit they swore unrighteously 5
Sir 1:30 your heart was full of deceit. 8
19:26 inwardly he is full of deceit. 8
37: 3 why were you formed to cover the land with deceit? 7
Bel 1:18 and with you there is no deceit, none at all. 8
1Mc 8:28 do so without deceit. 8

deceit *See also* utter.

deceitful 1. אַכְזָב 2. מִרְמָה 3. עָקֹב 4. רְמִיָּה 5. שֶׁקֶר 6. תַּרְמִית 7. ἀπάτη 8. δόλιος 9. κακότεχνος 10. πλάνη 11. πλάνος

Ps 5: 6 LORD abhors bloodthirsty and deceitful men. 2
43: 1 from deceitful and unjust men deliver me! 2
52: 4 love all words that devour, O deceitful tongue. 2
78:57 they twisted like a deceitful bow. 4
109: 2 wicked and deceitful mouths are opened against 2
120: 2 Deliver me, O LORD, from . . deceitful tongue. 4
3 what more . . be done to you, you deceitful tongue? 4
Prv 31:30 Charm is deceitful, and beauty is vain 5
Jer 15:18 Wilt thou be to me like a deceitful brook 1
17: 9 The heart is deceitful above all things 3
Mic 6:11 acquit the man . . with a bag of deceitful weights? 2
12 and their tongue is deceitful in their mouth. 4
Zep 3:13 be found in their mouth a deceitful tongue. 6
2Co 11:13 such men are false apostles, deceitful workmen 8
Eph 4:14 by their craftiness in deceitful wiles. 10
22 is corrupt through deceitful lusts 7
1Ti 4: 1 giving heed to deceitful spirits 11
Jdt 9:13 Make my deceitful words to be their wound 7
Wis 1: 4 because wisdom will not enter a deceitful soul 9
4Mc 18: 8 nor did the destroyer, the deceitful serpent 7

deceitful thing 1. אַכְזָב
Mic 1:14 the houses of Achzib shall be a deceitful thing 1

deceitfully 1. בְּמִרְמָה 2. לְמִרְמָה 3. מִרְמָה 4. רְמִיָּה 5. δόλος
Gen 34:13 answered . . Hamor deceitfully, because he had 1
Job 13: 7 falsely for God, and speak deceitfully for him? 4
Ps 24: 4 to what is false, and does not swear deceitfully. 2
Jer 9: 8 tongue is a deadly arrow; it speaks deceitfully; 3
Dan 11:23 alliance is made . . he shall act deceitfully; 3
1Mc 13:17 Simon knew that they were speaking deceitfully 5
deceitfully *See also* deal.

deceitfulness 1. ἀπάτη
Heb 3:13 hardened by the deceitfulness of sin. 1

deceive 1. כחש 2. מִרְמָה 3. נשא 4. סות 5. פתה 6. רמה 7. שגג 8. שׁלה 9. תלל 10. תעה 11. ἀπατάω 12. ἀπάτη 13. ἀποπλανάω 14. δολιόω 15. ἐξαπατάω 16. παραλογίζομαι 17. πλανάω 18. φρεναπατάω 19. ψεύδω 20. fallo
Gen 29:25 Why then have you deceived me? 6
Lev 6: 2 by deceiving his neighbor in a matter of deposit 1
Deu 11:16 lest your heart be deceived, and you turn aside 5
Jos 9:22 Why did you deceive us . . when you dwell among us? 6
1Sm 19:17 Why have you deceived me thus, and let my enemy go 6
28:12 Why have you deceived me? You are Saul. 6
2Sm 3:25 Abner the son of Ner came to deceive you 5
19:26 My lord, O king, my servant deceived me; 6
2Kg 4:28 Did I ask . . for a son? Did I not say, Do not deceive me? 8
18:29 Do not let Hezeki'ah deceive you, for he will not be 3
19:10 Do not let your God . . deceive you by promising 3
2Ch 32:15 do not let Hezeki'ah deceive you or mislead you 3
Job 12:16 the deceived and the deceiver are his. 7
13: 9 Or can you deceive him, as one deceives a man? 9
9 Or can you deceive him, as one deceives a man? 9
15:31 him not trust in emptiness, deceiving himself; 10
Prv 14: 8 but the folly of fools is deceiving. 2
24:28 do not deceive with your lips. 5
26:19 man who deceives his neighbor and says, "I am only 6
Isa 36:14 says the king: 'Do not let Hezeki'ah deceive you 3
37:10 Do not let your God on whom you rely deceive you 3
Jer 4:10 Ah, Lord GOD, surely thou hast utterly deceived 3
9: 5 Every one deceives his neighbor 9
20: 7 O LORD, thou hast deceived me, and I was deceived; 5
7 O LORD, thou hast deceived me, and I was deceived; 5
10 Perhaps he will be deceived, then we can overcome 5
29: 8 your diviners who are among you deceive you 3
37: 9 Thus says the LORD, Do not deceive yourselves 3
38:22 saying, 'Your trusted friends have deceived you 4
49:16 The horror you inspire has deceived you 3
Lam 1:19 I called to my lovers but they deceived me; 6
Ezk 14: 9 if the prophet be deceived and speak a word 5
9 I, the LORD, have deceived that prophet 5
Obd 1: 3 The pride of your heart has deceived you 3
7 All your allies have deceived you 3
Zec 13: 4 not put on a hairy mantle in order to deceive 1
Rom 3:13 they use their tongues to deceive. 14
7:11 sin . . deceived me and by it killed me. 15
16:18 and by fair and flattering words they deceive 15
1Co 3:18 Let no one deceive himself 15
6: 9 Do not be deceived; neither the immoral 17
15:33 Do not be deceived 17
2Co 11: 3 as the serpent deceived Eve by his cunning 15
Gal 6: 3 he deceives himself. 18
7 Do not be deceived; God is not mocked 17
Eph 5: 6 Let no one deceive you with empty words 11
2Th 2: 3 Let no one deceive you in any way 15
1Ti 2:14 Adam was not deceived, but the woman was deceived 11
14 Adam was not deceived, but the woman was deceived 15
2Ti 3:13 go on from bad to worse, deceivers and deceived. 17
Jas 1:16 Do not be deceived, my beloved brethren. 17
22 hearers only, deceiving yourselves. 16
26 If any one . . deceives his heart 11
1Jn 1: 8 If we say we have no sin, we deceive ourselves 17
2:26 to you about those who would deceive you; 17
3: 7 Little children, let no one deceive you. 17
Rev 13:14 it deceives those who dwell on earth 17
18:23 and all nations were deceived by thy sorcery. 17
19:20 he deceived those who had received the mark 17
20: 3 that he should deceive the nations no more 17
8 and will come out to deceive the nations 17
10 the devil who had deceived them was thrown 17
2Es 10:36 Or is my mind deceived, and my soul dreaming? 20
Tob 10: 7 she answered him, "Be still and stop deceiving me; 17
Jdt 12:16 he had been waiting for an opportunity to deceive her 11
16: 8 and put on a linen gown to deceive him. 12
Wis 4:11 lest . . guile deceive his soul. 11
12:24 they were deceived like foolish babes. 19
Sir 13: 6 When he needs you he will deceive you 13
34: 7 For dreams have deceived many 17
Sus 1:56 beauty has deceived you and lust has perverted 15
Bel 1: 7 Do not be deceived, O king 17
2Mc 7:18 Do not deceive yourself in vain 17

deceiver 1. שׁגה 2. δίγλωσσος 3. πλανάω 4. πλάνος 5. φρεναπάτης
Job 12:16 the deceived and the deceiver are his. 1
2Ti 3:13 go on from bad to worse, deceivers and deceived. 3
Tit 1:10 empty talkers and deceivers 5
2Jn 1: 7 For many deceivers have gone out into the world 4
7 such a one is the deceiver and the antichrist. 4
Rev 12: 9 deceiver of the whole world–he was thrown down 3
Sir 28:13 Curse the whisperer and deceiver 2

decently 1. εὐσχημόνως
1Co 14:40 all things should be done decently and in order. 1

deception 1. ἀπάτη 2. παραλογισμός 3. ψευδής
2Th 2:10 with all wicked deception 1
Sir 34: 8 Without such deceptions 3
2Mc 1:13 a deception employed by the priests of Nanea. 2

deceptive 1. כָּזָב 2. שֶׁקֶר 3. תָּפֵל
Prv 11:18 A wicked man earns deceptive wages 2
23: 3 delicacies, for they are deceptive food. 1
Jer 7: 4 Do not trust in these deceptive words 2
8 Behold, you trust in deceptive words to no avail. 2
Lam 2:14 have seen for you false and deceptive visions; 3

decide 1. אמר 2. בחר 3. גזר 4. היה עִם לֵב 5. חרץ 6. יכח 7. פרד 8. ראה 9. שׁפט 10. ἀρέσκω 11. βουλεύω 12. βούλομαι 13. γινώσκω 14. διαγινώσκω 15. διακρίνω 16. δοκέω 17. εὐδοκέω 18. θέλω 19. ἵστημι 20. κρίνω 21. κρίσις 22. κριτής 23. λογίζομαι 24. ποιέω
Gen 31:37 kinsmen, that they may decide between us two. 6
Exd 18:16 I decide between a man and his neighbor 9
22 any small matter they shall decide themselves; 9
26 any small matter they decided themselves. 9
Lev 13:59 to decide whether it is clean or unclean *
Deu 25: 1 come into court, and the judges decide between 9
Jdg 11:27 the LORD . . decide this day between the people 9
2Sm 15:15 ready to do whatever my lord the king decides. 2
19:29 I have decided: you and Ziba shall divide the land. 1
24:13 consider, and decide what answer I shall return 8
1Kg 20:40 So shall your judgment be; you . . have decided it. 5
1Ch 21:12 decide what answer I shall return to him who sent 8
2Ch 19: 8 to decide disputed cases. *
24: 4 Jo'ash decided to restore the house of the LORD. 4
Job 22:28 You will decide on a matter 3
Prv 18:18 lot . . decides between powerful contenders. 7
Isa 2: 4 shall judge . . and shall decide for many peoples; 6
11: 3 what his eyes see, or decide by what his ears hear; 6
4 and decide with equity for the meek of the earth; 6
Mic 4: 3 and shall decide for strong nations afar off; 6
Hag 2:11 Ask the priests to decide this question *
Mrk 15:24 to decide what each should take. *
Lke 16: 4 I have decided what to do 13
Joh 1:43 The next day Jesus decided to go to Galilee. 18
Act 3:13 when he had decided to release him. 20
20:16 Paul had decided to sail past Ephesus 20
24:22 I will decide your case. 14
25:25 I decided to send him. 20
27: 1 when it was decided that we should sail for Italy 20
Rom 14:13 but rather decide never to put a stumbling block 20
1Co 2: 2 For I decided to know nothing among you 20
6: 5 there is no man among you wise enough to decide 15
Tit 3:12 I have decided to spend the winter there. 20
1Es 8:11 as I and . . my counselors have decided 16
Jdt 2: 3 it was decided 20
11:13 decided to consume the first fruits of the grain 20
Wis 15: 7 the worker in clay decides. 22
Sir 33:13 to give them as he decides. 21
LJr 1:64 they are not able either to decide a case 20
1Mc 6:19 So Judas decided to destroy them 23
8:26 as Rome has decided 16
28 as Rome has decided 16
9:69 Then he decided to depart to his own land. 11
14:31 their enemies decided to invade their country 12
41 the Jews and their priests decided 17
15:19 We therefore have decided to write to the kings 10
2Mc 3:23 Heliodorus went on with what had been decided. 14
11:36 which he decided are to be referred to the king 20
13:13 march out and decide the matter by the help of God 20
14:18 shrank from deciding the issue by bloodshed. 24
15:17 to decide the matter 20
21 as the Lord decides 20
3Mc 1: 6 decided to visit the neighboring cities 20
3:21 deciding . . to deem them worthy 12
6:30 deciding that they should celebrate 20
7:19 they decided to observe these days 19
4Mc 1:14 We shall decide just what reason is 15

decision 1. דָּבָר 2. דְּבַר מִשְׁפָּט 3. חָרוּץ 4. מִשְׁפָּט 5. תּוֹרָה 6. שְׁאֵלָה (A) 7. γνώμη 8. γνῶσις 9. διάγνωσις 10. δόγμα 11. ἕνεκεν 12. ἐπιτροπή 13. κρίμα 14. κρίνω 15. κρίσις 16. λογισμός 17. λόγος 18. σύγκριμα 19. φαίνω
Exd 18:16 know the statutes of God and his decisions. 5
20 teach them the statutes and the decisions 5
Deu 17: 8 If any case arises requiring decision 4
9 they shall declare to you the decision. 2
11 according to the decision which they pronounce 4
2Sm 14:13 giving this decision the king convicts himself 1
Prv 16:33 but the decision is wholly from the LORD. 4
Dan 4:17 the decision by the word of the holy ones 6
Jol 3:14 multitudes, in the valley of decision! 3
14 day of the LORD is near in the valley of decision. 3
Zep 3: 8 For my decision is to gather nations 4
Mrk 14:64 What is your decision? 19
Act 16: 4 delivered to them for observance the decisions 10
25:21 kept in custody for the decision of the emperor 9
1Es 8:10 In accordance with my gracious decision 14
9: 4 the decision of the ruling elders 13
AEs 10:11 came to the hour and moment and day of decision 15
Wis 3:18 no consolation in the day of decision. 9
19: 3 they reached another foolish decision 16
Sir 8:14 the decision will favor him 14
32:17 will find a decision according to his liking. 18
33: 8 By the Lord's decision they were distinguished 8
1Mc 14:44 permitted to nullify any of these decisions *
45 Whoever acts contrary to these decisions *
46 the right to act in accord with these decisions. 17
2Mc 4:20 by the decision of its carriers 11
11:25 our decision is that their temple be restored 14
13:14 committing the decision to the Creator 12
15:20 all were now looking forward to the coming decision 15
4Mc 9:27 they heard this noble decision. 7
decision *See also* make.

inspired decision 1. קֶסֶם
Prv 16:10 Inspired decisions are on the lips of a king; 1

decisive 1. audax 2. terminus
2Es 7:78 When the decisive decree has gone forth 2
104 The day of judgment is decisive 1

deck 1. יפה 2. כהן 3. לְבוּשׁ 4. עדה 5. עטף 6. רבד
Job 40:10 Deck yourself with majesty and dignity; 4
Ps 45:13 The princess is decked in her chamber 3
65:13 the valleys deck themselves with grain 5
Prv 7:16 I have decked my couch with coverings 6
Isa 61:10 as a bridegroom decks himself with a garland 2
Jer 4:30 that you deck yourself with ornaments of gold 4
10: 4 Men deck it with silver and gold; 1
Ezk 16:11 I decked you with ornaments 4
13 Thus you were decked with gold and silver; 4
23:40 and decked yourself with ornaments; 4
Hos 2:13 and decked herself with her ring and jewelry 4

deck (2) 1. קֶרֶשׁ 2. σανίδωμα
Gen 6:16 make it with lower, second, and third decks. *
Ezk 27: 6 made your deck of pines from the coasts of Cyprus 1
3Mc 4:10 they were confined under a solid deck 2
deck *See* gaily.

deck out 1. κοσμέω 2. exorno 3. orno
2Es 15:47 you have decked out your daughters in harlotry 3
16:50 when she decks herself out 2
LJr 1:11 They deck their gods out with garments like men 1

declaration 1. אַחֲוָה 2. ἐπαγγελία
Job 13:17 let my declaration be in your ears. 1
4Mc 12: 9 Extremely pleased by the boy's declaration 2

clear declaration 1. διασαφέω
1Mc 12: 8 a clear declaration of alliance and friendship. 1

declare 1. אמר 2. דבר 3. חוה 4. חרשׁ 5. ידע 6. נְאֻם 7. נגד 8. ספר 9. פרשׁ 10. קדשׁ 11. שׁמע 12. אמר (A) 13. ἀναγγέλλω 14. ἀναδείκνυμι 15. ἀπαγγέλλω 16. ἀποκρίνω 17. ἀποφαίνω 18. διασαφέω 19. διηγέομαι 20. εἶπον 21. ἐκδιηγέομαι 22. ἐξαγγέλλω 23. ἐπιμαρτυρέω 24. λαλέω 25. λέγω 26. ὁμολογέω 27. προσφέρω 28. προφέρω 29. συντάσσω 30. ὑποδείκνυμι λόγους 31. φάσκω 32. adnuntio 33. enarro 34. loquor 35. narro 36. renuntio
Exd 9:16 so that my name may be declared throughout all 8
Lev 23:44 Thus Moses declared to the people of Israel 2

24:12 the will of the LORD should be declared to them 9
Deu 4:13 declared to you his covenant, which he commanded 7
5: 5 I stood . . to declare to you the word of the LORD; 7
17: 9 they shall declare to you the decision. 7
10 Then . . do according to what they declare to you 7
11 not turn . . from the verdict which they declare 7
26: 3 I declare this day to the LORD your God 7
17 declared this day concerning the LORD 1
18 LORD has declared this day concerning you 1
27:14 Levites shall declare to all the men of Israel 1
30:18 I declare to you this day, that you shall perish; 7
1Sm 2:30 Therefore the LORD the God of Israel declares 6
30 I promised . . '; but now the LORD declares: 'Far be it 6
24:18 you have declared . . how you have dealt well 7
2Sm 7:11 the LORD declares to you that the LORD will make 7
1Kg 8:24 hast kept with . . what thou didst declare to him; 2
53 as thou didst declare through Moses, thy servant 2
1Ch 16:24 Declare his glory among the nations 8
17:10 Moreover I declare to you that the LORD 7
2Ch 6:15 kept . . what thou didst declare to him; 2
Neh 8:12 understood the words that were declared to them. 5
Job 12: 8 the fish of the sea will declare to you. 8
15:17 what I have seen I will declare 8
21:31 Who declares his way to his face 7
26: 3 and plentifully declared sound knowledge! 5
28:27 then he saw it and declared it; 8
32: 6 I was timid and afraid to declare my opinion 3
10 say, 'Listen to me; let me also declare my opinion 3
17 I also will declare my opinion. 3
33: 3 My words declare the uprightness of my heart •
23 to declare to man what is right for him; 7
34:33 therefore declare what you know. 2
36: 9 then he declares to them their work 7
33 Its crashing declares concerning him 7
38: 3 I will question you, and you shall declare to me. 5
18 Declare, if you know all this. 7
40: 7 I will question you, and you declare to me. 5
42: 4 I will question you, and you declare to me. 5
Ps 19: 2 night to night declares knowledge. 3
32: 3 When I declared not my sin, my body wasted away 4
50: 6 The heavens declare his righteousness 7
88:11 Is thy steadfast love declared in the grave 8
92: 2 to declare thy steadfast love in the morning 7
96: 3 Declare his glory among the nations 8
102:21 that men may declare in Zion the name of the LORD 8
119:13 I declare all the ordinances of thy mouth. 8
145: 4 to another, and shall declare thy mighty acts. 7
6 I will declare thy greatness. 8
147:19 He declares his word to Jacob 7
Isa 41:22 or declare to us the things to come. 11
26 Who declared it from the beginning 7
26 There was none who declared it 7
27 I first have declared it to Zion •
42: 9 have come to pass, and new things I now declare; 7
12 and declare his praise in the coastlands. 7
43: 9 Who among them can declare this 7
12 I declared and saved and proclaimed 7
21 I formed . . that they might declare my praise. 8
44: 7 let him declare and set it forth before me. 7
8 have I not told you from of old and declared it? 7
45:19 I . . speak the truth, I declare what is right. 7
21 Declare and present your case; 7
21 Who told this long ago? Who declared it of old? 7
46:10 declaring the end from the beginning 7
48: 3 The former things I declared of old 7
5 I declared them to you from of old 7
6 now see all this; and will you not declare it? 7
14 Who among them has declared these things? 7
20 declare this with a shout of joy, proclaim it 7
58: 1 declare to my people their transgression 7
66:19 they shall declare my glory among the nations. 7
Jer 4: 5 Declare in Judah, and proclaim in Jerusalem 7
15 For a voice declares from Dan and proclaims evil 7
5:20 Declare this in the house of Jacob 7
9:12 mouth of the LORD spoken, that he may declare it? 7
18: 7 If at any time I declare concerning a nation 2
9 And if at any time I declare concerning a nation 2
31:10 Hear the word of the LORD, O nations, and declare it 7
42:20 whatever the LORD our God says declare to us 7
21 I have this day declared it to you 7
44:25 and your wives have declared with your mouths 2
46:14 Declare in Egypt, and proclaim in Migdol; 7
50: 2 Declare among the nations and proclaim 7
28 to declare in Zion the vengeance of the LORD 7
51:10 let us declare in Zion the work of the LORD our God. 8
Ezk 22: 2 Then declare to her all her abominable deeds. 5
23:36 Then declare to them their abominable deeds. 5
38:19 in my jealousy and in my blazing wrath I declare 2
40: 4 declare all that you see to the house of Israel. 7
Dan 4:18 you, O Belteshaz'zar, declare the interpretation 12
Hos 5: 9 among . . Israel I declare what is sure. 5
Ams 4:13 and declares to man what is his thought; 7
Mic 3: 5 declare war against him who puts nothing 10
8 to declare to Jacob his transgression 7
Zec 9:12 today I declare that I will restore to you double. 7
Mat 7:23 And then will I declare to them, 'I never knew you; 26
11:25 At that time Jesus declared, "I thank thee, Father 20
26:33 Peter declared to him, "Though they all fall away 16
Mrk 12:36 himself, inspired by the Holy Spirit, declared 20
Lke 8:39 and declare how much God has done for you 19
47 declared in the presence of all the people 15
Joh 8:26 I declare to the world what I have heard from him. 24
16:13 he will declare to you the things that are to come. 13
14 he will take what is mine and declare it to you. 13
15 will take what is mine and declare it to you. 13
Act 2:17 in the last days it shall be, God declares 25
9:27 declared to them how . . he had seen the Lord 19
10:46 Then Peter declared 16
11:14 he will declare to you a message 24
13:41 if one declares it to you.' 21
14:27 declared all that God had done with them 13
15: 4 they declared all that God had done with them. 13
20:20 did not shrink from declaring to you anything 13
27 declaring to you the whole counsel of God. 13
26:20 declared first to those at Damascus 15
1Co 14:25 declare that God is really among you. 15
Col 4: 3 to declare the mystery of Christ 24
1Th 2: 2 courage in our God to declare to you the gospel 24
4:15 For this we declare to you by the word of the Lord 25
Tit 2:15 Declare these things 24
Heb 2: 2 For if the message declared by angels was valid 24
3 It was declared at first by the Lord 24
9:19 every commandment of the law had been declared 24
1Pe 2: 9 you may declare the wonderful deeds of him 22
5:12 and declaring that this is the true grace of God; 23
2Es 1: 5 Go and declare to my people their evil deeds 32
6:31 I will again declare to you greater things 36
48 the nations might declare thy wondrous works. 33
7:54 defer to her, and she will declare it to you. 35
8: 7 we are a work of thy hands, as thou hast declared. 34
36 righteousness and goodness will be declared 32
14: 5 and declared to him the end of the times ‡
Tob 8:20 Raguel declared by oath to Tobias 20
12: 6 worthily declaring the works of God 30
Sir 16:25 declare knowledge accurately. 15
39:10 Nations will declare his wisdom 19
42:15 will declare what I have seen 21
19 He declares what has been and what is to be 15
44: 8 so that men declare their praise. 21
15 Peoples will declare their wisdom 19
Bar 1:20 the curse which the Lord declared through Moses 29
2:20 thou didst declare by thy servants the prophets 24
2Mc 2: 7 he rebuked them and declared 20
6:23 he declared himself quickly 17
7: 6 as Moses declared in his song 18
9:14 he was now declaring to be free; 14
10:26 as the law declares. 18
14:32 when they declared on oath that they did not know 31
15: 4 when they declared 17
3Mc 4:17 the scribes declared to the king 27
7: 4 they declared that . . 28
11 For they declared that . . 28
151 1: 3 who will declare it to my Lord? The Lord himself; 13

declare *See also* even.

declare a Jew 1. יהד

Est 8:17 and many . . declared themselves Jews 1

declare boldly 1. *παρρησιάζομαι*

Eph 6:20 I may declare it boldly, as I ought to speak. 1

declare clean 1. *καθαρίζω*

Mrk 7:19 Thus he declared all foods clean.) 1

declare guilty 1. רשע

Isa 50: 9 Lord GOD helps me; who will declare me guilty? 1

declare innocent 1. *δικαιόω*

Sir 26:29 a tradesman will not be declared innocent of sin. 1

declare righteous 1. *δικαιόω*

Sir 18: 2 the Lord alone will be declared righteous. 1

declare unclean 1. טמא

Lev 14:36 lest all that is in the house be declared unclean 1

declare wrong 1. רשע

Job 32: 3 although they had declared Job to be in the wrong. 1

decline 1. ירד 2. נטה 3. פנה 4. *ἐπινεύω*

Jdg 19: 8 and tarry until the day declines." So they ate 2
2Kg 20:11 by which the sun had declined on the dial of Ahaz. 1
Isa 38: 8 I will make the shadow cast by the declining sun 1
8 back . . the ten steps by which it had declined. 1
Jer 6: 4 attack at noon!" "Woe to us, for the day declines 3
Act 18:20 When they asked him to stay . . he declined. 4

decorate 1. *κατακοσμέω*

1Mc 4:57 They decorated the front of the temple 1

decoration 1. *ζωγραφέω* 2. *κοσμέω* 3. *κόσμος* 4. *περίθεσις*

1Pe 3: 3 outward adorning with . . decoration of gold 4
Sir 22:17 the stucco decoration on the wall of a colonnade. 3
38:28 he is careful to complete its decoration. 2
1Mc 1:22 the gold decoration on the front of the temple 3
2Mc 2:29 one who undertakes its painting and decoration 1

decoy 1. *θηρευτής*

Sir 11:30 Like a decoy partridge in a cage 1

decrease 1. מעט 2. *ἐλαττόω*

Ps 107:38 he does not let their cattle decrease. 1
Jer 29: 6 multiply there, and do not decrease. 1
Joh 3:30 He must increase, but I must decrease. 2

decree 1. אֹמֶר 2. גזר 3. דבר 4. דָּת 5. חֹק 6. חקק 7. חרץ 8. חתך 9. טַעַם 10. כתב 11. סֵפֶר 12. עֵדָה 13. עֵדוּת 14. עמד דָּבָר 15. פִּתְגָם 16. גְּזֵרָה (A) 17. דָּת (A) 18. טַעַם (A) 19. טְעֵם (A) 20. *βουλή* 21. *γραφή* 22. *διαθήκη* 23. *διάταγμα* 24. *δικαίωμα* 25. *δόγμα* 26. *δογματίζω* 27. *ἐπικρίνω* 28. *ἵστημι* 29. *κρίμα* 30. *προορίζω* 31. *πρόσταγμα* 32. *προστάσσω* 33. *σύγκριμα* 34. *ψήφισμα* 35. sententia 36. terminus

Lev 6:18 as decreed for ever throughout your generations 5
22 offer it to the LORD as decreed for ever 5
2Ch 30: 5 decreed to make a proclamation throughout all 14
Ezr 4:19 made a decree, and search has been made 19
21 make a decree that these men be made to cease 19
21 city be not rebuilt, until a decree is made by me. 18
5: 3 Who gave you a decree to build this house 19
9 'Who gave you a decree to build this house 19
13 Cyrus . . made a decree that this house of God 19
17 see whether a decree was issued by Cyrus the king 19
6: 1 Darius the king made a decree, and search was made 19
3 Cyrus . . issued a decree: Concerning the house 19
8 I make a decree regarding what you shall do 19
11 I make a decree that if any one alters this edict 19
12 I Darius make a decree; let it be done 19
14 by decree of Cyrus and Darius and Ar-ta-xerx'es 19
7:13 I make a decree that any one of the people 19
21 make a decree to all the treasurers 19
Est 1:20 when the decree made by the king is proclaimed 15
2: 1 what she had done and what had been decreed 2
3: 9 let it be decreed that they be destroyed 10
14 A copy of the document was to be issued as a decree 4
15 and the decree was issued in Susa the capital. 4
4: 3 wherever the king's command and his decree came 4
8 Mor'decai . . gave him a copy of the written decree 4
8:13 A copy . . was to be issued as a decree 4
14 and the decree was issued in Susa the capital. 4
9:14 a decree was issued in Susa, and . . were hanged. 4
Job 20:29 the heritage decreed for him by God. 1
28:26 when he made a decree for the rain 5
Ps 2: 7 I will tell of the decree of the LORD: He said to me 5
58: 1 Do you indeed decree what is right, you gods? 3
81: 5 He made it a decree in Joseph, when he went out 13
93: 5 Thy decrees are very sure; 12
122: 4 as was decreed for Israel, to give thanks 13
Prv 8:15 By me kings reign, and rulers decree what is just; 6
31: 5 lest they drink and forget what has been decreed 6
Isa 10: 1 Woe to those who decree iniquitous decrees 6
1 Woe to those who decree iniquitous decrees 5
22 Destruction is decreed, overflowing 7
23 the LORD of hosts, will make a full end, as decreed 7
28:22 heard a decree of destruction from the Lord GOD 7
Jer 3: 8 I had sent her away with a decree of divorce; 11
19: 5 not command or decree, nor did it come into my mind; 3
Dan 2:13 decree went forth . . wise men were to be slain 17
15 Why is the decree of the king so severe? 17
3:10 You, O king, have made a decree 19
29 make a decree: Any people, nation, or language 19
4: 6 I made a decree that all the wise men of Babylon 19
17 The sentence is by the decree of the watchers 16
24 decree of the Most High, which has come upon my 16
6:26 I make a decree, that in all my royal dominion 19
9:24 70 weeks of years are decreed concerning 8
26 end there shall be war; desolations are decreed. 7
27 until the decreed end is poured out 7
Jon 3: 7 By the decree of the king and his nobles 9
Lke 2: 1 a decree went out from Caesar Augustus 25
Act 17: 7 are all acting against the decrees of Caesar 25
Rom 1:32 Though they know God's decree 24
1Co 2: 7 which God decreed before the ages 30
1Es 5:55 the decree which they had in writing from Cyrus 31
6:34 I, King Darius, have decreed that it be done 26
2Es 7:78 When the decisive decree has gone forth 35
10:16 if you acknowledge the decree of God to be just 36
Tob 1: 6 it is ordained . . by an everlasting decree 31
AEs 13: 6 Therefore we have decreed 32
Wis 11: 7 in rebuke for the decree to slay the infants 23
Sir 14:12 the decree of Hades has not been shown to you. 22
17 the decree from of old is, "You must surely die! 22
41: 3 this is the decree from the Lord for all flesh 29
1Mc 1:57 the decree of the king condemned him to death. 33
60 According to the decree 31
7:49 they decreed that this day should be celebrated 28
8: 7 decreed that he . . should pay a heavy tribute 28
13:52 Simon decreed 28
14:22 we have recorded in our public decrees, as follows 20
48 to inscribe this decree upon bronze tablets 21
2Mc 6: 8 At the suggestion of Ptolemy a decree was issued 34
10: 8 They decreed by public ordinance and vote 26
15:36 they all decreed by public vote 26

3Mc 4: 1 In every place, then, where this decree arrived 31
2 that had suddenly been decreed for them. 27
11 the voyage was concluded as the king had decreed 26
5:40 again revoking your decree in the matter? 26
4Mc 4:23 after he had plundered them he issued a decree 25
24 by means of his decrees 25
26 his decrees were despised by the people 25

just decree 1. מִשְׁפָּט
Deu 33:21 executed the commands and just decrees 1

dedicate 1. חנך 2. נוף 3. נתן 4. קֹדֶשׁ 5. קדשׁ 6. ἁγιάζω 7. ἀναδείκνυμι 8. ἀνατίθημι 9. ἐγκαινίζω 10. καθιδρύω
Exd 35:22 dedicating an offering of gold to the LORD. 2
Lev 22: 2 the holy things . . which they dedicate to me 5
3 holy things, which the people of Israel dedicate 5
27:14 When a man dedicates his house to be holy 5
15 if he who dedicates it wishes to redeem his house 5
16 If a man dedicates to the LORD part of the land 5
17 If he dedicates his field from the year 5
18 if he dedicates his field after the jubilee 5
19 if he who dedicates the field wishes to redeem it 5
22 If he dedicates to the LORD a field 5
26 a firstling . . no man may dedicate; whether ox 5
Deu 20: 5 built a new house and has not dedicated it? 1
5 die in the battle and another man dedicate it. 1
2Sm 8:11 these also King David dedicated to the LORD 5
11 with the silver and gold which he dedicated 5
1Kg 8:63 the king and . . dedicated the house of the LORD. 1
2Kg 12:18 gifts that . . the kings of Judah, had dedicated 5
23:11 horses that the kings . . had dedicated to the sun 3
1Ch 18:11 these also King David dedicated to the LORD 5
26:26 of the dedicated gifts which . . had dedicated. 5
27 From spoil won in battles they dedicated gifts 5
28 Also all that Samuel . . had dedicated 5
2Ch 2: 4 dedicate it to him for the burning of incense 5
7: 5 king and . . people dedicated the house of God. 1
Isa 23:18 her hire will be dedicated to the LORD; 4
Jdt 16:19 Judith also dedicated to God all the vessels 8
Sir 35: 9 dedicate your tithe with gladness. 6
1Mc 4:36 go up to cleanse the sanctuary and dedicate it. 9
54 it was dedicated with songs and harps and lutes 9
5: 1 the sanctuary dedicated as it was before 9
3Mc 2:14 holy place . . dedicated to your glorious name. 7
7:20 dedicating a place of prayer 10

dedicated *See* gift.

dedicated one 1. שׁלם
Isa 42:19 Who is blind as my dedicated one 1

dedicated thing 1. קֹדֶשׁ
1Kg 7:51 the things which David his father had dedicated 1
2Ch 5: 1 the things which David his father had dedicated 1
24: 7 all the dedicated things of the house of the LORD 1
31: 6 dedicated things which had been consecrated 1
12 brought in . . tithes and the dedicated things. 1

dedication 1. חֲנֻכָּה 2. חֲנֻכָּה (A) 3. ἐγκαινισμός
Num 7:10 offerings for the dedication of the altar 1
11 for the dedication of the altar. 1
2Ch 7: 9 kept the dedication of the altar seven days 1
Ezr 6:16 celebrated the dedication of this house of God 2
17 offered at the dedication of this house of God 2
Neh 12:27 dedication of the wall of Jerusalem they sought 1
27 bring them . . to celebrate the dedication 1
Ps 30: 0 A Song at the dedication of the Temple. 1
Dan 3: 2 come to the dedication of the image 2
3 assembled for the dedication of the image 2
1Es 7: 7 at the dedication of the temple of the Lord 3
1Mc 4:56 So they celebrated the dedication of the altar 3
59 the days of dedication of the altar 3
2Mc 2: 9 the dedication and completion of the temple. 3
19 the dedication of the altar 3

dedication *See also* offering.

deduction *See* make.

deed 1. גְּמוּל 2. גְּמוּלָה 3. דָּבָר 4. דֶּרֶךְ 5. יָד 6. מַעַל 7. מַעֲלָל 8. מַעֲשֶׂה 9. עֲבָד 10. פַּעַל 11. עֲלִילָה 12. עֲלִילִיָּה 13. עשׂה 14. פֹּעַל 15. ἔργον 16. πρᾶγμα 17. πρᾶξις 18. πράσσω 19. χείρ 20. facio 21. factum 22. operatio 23. opus
Gen 44:15 What deed is this that you have done? 8
Deu 11: 3 signs and his deeds which he did in Egypt 8
Jdg 9:16 and have done to him as his deeds deserved 5
1Sm 8: 8 According to all the deeds which they have done 8
19: 4 and . . his deeds have been of good service to you; 8
2Sm 12:14 by this deed you have utterly scorned the LORD 3
23:20 was a valiant man . . a doer of great deeds; 14
1Kg 2:32 LORD will bring back his bloody deeds upon his •
2Kg 14:28 Now the rest of the deeds of Amazi'ah 3
15:11 Now the rest of the deeds of Zechari'ah 3
15 Now the rest of the deeds of Shallum 3
21 the rest of the deeds of Men'aham, 3
26 the rest of the deeds of Pekahi'ah, 3
20:20 rest of the deeds of Hezeki'ah, 3
24: 5 Now the rest of the deeds of Jehoi'akim 3
1Ch 11:22 a valiant man of Kabzeel, a doer of great deeds; 14
16: 8 make known his deeds among the peoples! 11
2Ch 25:26 rest of the deeds of Amazi'ah, from first to last 3
Ezr 9:13 after all that has come upon us for our evil deeds 8
Est 1:17 this deed of the queen will be made known 3
Job 33:17 that he may turn man aside from his deed 8
Ps 9:11 Tell among the peoples his deeds! 11
14: 1 They are corrupt, they do abominable deeds 11
28: 4 according to the evil of their deeds; 6
33:15 of them all, and observes all their deeds. 8
44: 1 what deeds thou didst perform in their days 14
66: 3 Say to God, "How terrible are thy deeds! 8
5 he is terrible in his deeds among men. 11
77:11 I will call to mind the deeds of the LORD; 6
12 I will meditate . . and muse on thy mighty deeds. 11
105: 1 make known his deeds among the peoples! 11
107:22 let them . . tell of his deeds in songs of joy! 8
24 saw the deeds of the LORD, his wondrous works 8
118:17 I shall live, and recount the deeds of the LORD. 8
141: 4 busy myself with wicked deeds in company 11
145:13 LORD is . . gracious in all his deeds. 8
Prv 14:14 good man with the fruit of his deeds. 10
19:17 he will repay him for his deed. 1
Ecc 4: 3 and has not seen the evil deeds that are done 8
8:11 sentence against an evil deed is not executed 8
14 it happens according to the deeds of the wicked 8
14 according to the deeds of the righteous. 8
9: 1 the wise and their deeds are in the hand of God; 9
12:14 For God will bring every deed into judgment 8
Isa 3: 8 speech and their deeds are against the LORD 6
10 for they shall eat the fruit of their deeds. 6
5:12 they do not regard the deeds of the LORD 14
12: 4 make known his deeds among the nations 11
28:21 to do his deed-strange is his deed! 8
21 to do his deed-strange is his deed! 8
29:15 whose deeds are in the dark, and who say 8
59: 6 and deeds of violence are in their hands. 14
18 According to their deeds, so will he repay 2
Jer 5:28 They know no bounds in deeds of wickedness; 3
11:18 then thou didst show me their evil deeds. 6
25:14 I will recompense them according to their deeds 14
32:19 great in counsel and mighty in deed; 12
48:30 his boasts are false, his deeds are false. 13
50:29 Requite her according to her deeds 14
Ezk 9:10 I will requite their deeds upon their heads. 4
11:21 I will requite their deeds upon their own heads 4
16:30 did all these things, the deeds of a brazen harlot; 8
43 I will requite your deeds upon your head 4
36:19 with their conduct and their deeds I judged them. 11
31 your evil ways, and your deeds that were not good; 6
Hos 4: 9 and requite them for their deeds. 7
5: 4 Their deeds do not permit them to return 6
7: 2 Now their deeds encompass them 6
12 I will chastise them for their wicked deeds. •
9:15 Because of the wickedness of their deeds 6
12: 2 and requite him according to his deeds. 7
Jol 3: 4 If you are paying me back, I will requite your deed 1
7 and I will requite your deed upon your own head. 1
Ams 8: 7 Surely I will never forget any of their deeds. 8
Obd 1:15 your deeds shall return on your own head. 1
Mic 3: 4 because they have made their deeds evil. 6
Zep 3: 7 they were eager to make all their deeds corrupt. 11
11 because of the deeds by which you have rebelled 11
Zec 1: 4 from your evil ways and from your evil deeds.' 7
6 for our ways and deeds, so has he dealt with us. 7
Mat 11: 2 about the deeds of the Christ 15
19 Yet wisdom is justified by her deeds. 15
23: 5 They do all their deeds to be seen by men 15
Lke 11:48 consent to the deeds of your fathers 15
23:41 we are receiving the due reward of our deeds 18
51 who had not consented to their purpose and deed 17
24:19 a prophet mighty in deed and word before God 15
Joh 3:19 loved darkness . . because their deeds were e 15
20 lest his deeds should be exposed. 15
21 seen that his deeds have been wrought in God. 15
7:21 Jesus answered them, "I did one deed 15
Act 5: 4 you have contrived this deed in your heart 16
7:22 he was mighty in his words and deeds. 15
13:41 I do a deed in your days 15
41 a deed you will never believe 15
26:20 and perform deeds worthy of their repentance 15
Rom 8:13 if . . put to death the deeds of the body 17
15:18 obedience from the Gentiles, by word and deed 15
2Co 11:15 Their end will correspond to their deeds. 15
Col 1:21 doing evil deeds 15
3:17 whatever you do, in word or deed 15
1Ti 2:10 by good deeds 15
5:10 she must be well attested for her good deeds 15
25 also good deeds are conspicuous 15
6:18 They are to do good, to be rich in good deeds 15
2Ti 4:14 the Lord will requite him for his deeds. 15
Tit 1:16 they deny him by their deeds 15
16 detestable, disobedient, unfit for any good deed. 15
2: 7 in all respects a model of good deeds 15
14 who are zealous for good deeds. 15
3: 5 he saved us, not because of deeds done by us 15
8 may be careful to apply themselves to good deeds 15
14 learn to apply themselves to good deeds 15
1Pe 1:17 judges each one . . according to his deeds 15
2:12 they may see your good deeds and glorify God 15
2Pe 2: 8 he was vexed . . with their lawless deeds) 15
1Jn 3:12 Because his own deeds were evil 15
18 let us not love in word . . but in deed and in truth 15
Jde 1:15 to convict all the ungodly of all their deeds 15
Rev 14:13 for their deeds follow them! 15
15: 3 Great and wonderful are thy deeds, O Lord God 15
16:11 and did not repent of their deeds. 15
18: 6 and repay her double for her deeds; 15
1Es 1:23 the deeds of Josiah were upright 15
4:39 All men approve her deeds 15
8:86 because of our evil deeds and our great sins 15
2Es 3:28 Are the deeds of those . . any better? 20
31 Are the deeds of Babylon better than those of Zion? 20
7:119 but we have done deeds that bring death? 23
8:33 reward in consequence of their own deeds 23
14:35 the deeds of the ungodly will be disclosed. 21
15: 6 their harmful deeds have reached their limit. 22
48 imitated . . in all her deeds and devices 23
Tob 3: 2 all thy deeds and all thy ways are mercy and truth 15
4: 6 your ways will prosper through your deeds. 15
13: 9 he will afflict you for the deeds of your sons 15
Wis 1:16 men by their words and deeds summoned death 19
Sir 3: 8 Honor your father by word and deed 15
4:29 sluggish and remiss in your deeds. 15
7:35 because for such deeds you will be loved. •
11:27 his deeds will be revealed. 15
15:19 he knows every deed of man. 15
16:12 he judges a man according to his deeds. 15
14 will receive in accordance with his deeds. 15
20:16 there is no gratitude for my good deeds •
27:22 Whoever winks his eye plans evil deeds •
32:16 like a light they will kindle righteous deeds. •
35:19 till he repays the man according to his deeds 17
36: 8 let people recount thy mighty deeds. •
48:14 so in death his deeds were marvelous. 15
Bar 2:33 from their stubbornness and their wicked deeds; 16
1Mc 2:51 Remember the deeds of the fathers 15
3: 4 He was like a lion in his deeds 15
7 he made Jacob glad by his deeds 15
2Mc 3:36 the deeds of the supreme God 15
3Mc 1:27 not to overlook this unlawful and haughty deed. 17
2:25 he increased in his deeds of malice •
3:17 accepted our presence . . insincerely by deed 16
7:22 God perfectly performed great deeds •
4Mc 5:38 dominate . . either by word or by deed. 15
7: 9 by your deeds you made your words . . credible 15
11: 6 these deeds deserve honors, not tortures. •
16:14 in word and deed you have proved more powerful 15

deed (2) 1. סֵפֶר
Jer 32:10 I signed the deed, sealed it, got witnesses 1
11 Then I took the sealed deed of purchase 1
12 and I gave the deed of purchase to Baruch 1
12 the witnesses who signed the deed of purchase 1
14 Take these deeds 1
14 this sealed deed of purchase and this open deed 1
14 this sealed deed of purchase and this open deed 1
16 After I had given the deed of purchase to Baruch 1
44 deeds shall be signed and sealed and witnessed 1

deed *See* abominable, brave, celebration, dread, evil, glorious, good, great, lawless, licentious, loyal, memorable, mighty, righteous, saving, terrible, unclean, ungodly, unrighteous, vile, wicked, wonderful, wondrous.

do a brave deed 1. ἀνδραγαθέω
1Mc 5:61 thinking to do a brave deed 1
67 some priests, who wished to do a brave deed, fell 1

do a good deed 1. εὐεργεσία
Act 4: 9 concerning a good deed done to a cripple 1

deed of charity 1. ἐλεημοσύνη
Tob 12: 9 perform deeds of charity and of righteousness 1

deed of murder 1. φονοκτονία
1Mc 1:24 He committed deeds of murder 1

deed of salvation 1. תְּשׁוּעָה
Ps 71:15 of thy deeds of salvation all the day 1

deem 1. חשׁב 2. ἡγέομαι 3. παρά 4. habeo 5. iudico
Prv 17:28 when he closes his lips, he is deemed intelligent. 1
Isa 32:15 and the fruitful field is deemed a forest. 1
2Th 1: 6 since indeed God deems it just 3
2Es 8:30 those who are deemed worse than beasts 5
49 not deemed yourself to be among the righteous 5
13:14 and hast deemed me worthy to have my prayer heard 4
Wis 12:15 deeming it alien to thy power 2
17: 6 they deemed the things which they saw to be worse 2
2Mc 9:21 I have deemed it necessary 2

deem a fool 1. μωραίνω
Sir 23:14 be deemed a fool on account of your habits 1

deem blessed 1. אשׁר
Mal 3:15 Henceforth we deem the arrogant blessed; 1

deem worthy 1. καταξιόω
3Mc 3:21 to deem them worthy of Alexandrian citizenship 1
4Mc 18: 3 were deemed worthy to share in a divine inheritance. 1

deep 1. בְּקֶרֶב 2. מִלְמַעְלָה 3. מַעֲמַקִּים 4. מְצוּלָה
5. עמק 6. עָמֹק 7. צוּלָה 8. רֹחַב 9. שפל 10. שָׁפָל
11. תְּהוֹם 12. עֲמִיק (A) 13. ἄβυσσος 14. βάθος
15. βαθύς 16. βαρύς 17. ἐβαθύνω 18. μέγας
19. πολύς 20. abyssus 21. altus
Gen 1: 2 and darkness was upon the face of the deep 11
7:11 the fountains of the great deep burst forth 11
20 covering them fifteen cubits deep. 2
8: 2 the fountains of the deep and the windows 11
49:25 blessings of the deep that couches beneath 11
Exd 15: 8 the deeps congealed in the heart of the sea. 11
Lev 13: 3 the disease appears to be deeper than the skin 6
4 if the spot . . appears no deeper than the skin 6
20 if it appears deeper than the skin and its hair 10
21 if . . it is not deeper than the skin, but is dim 10
25 if . . it appears deeper than the skin 6
26 if . . it is no deeper than the skin, but is dim 10
30 if it appears deeper than the skin, and the hair 6
31 if . . it appears no deeper than the skin 6
32 the itch appears to be no deeper than the skin 6
34 if . . it appears to be no deeper than the skin 6
14:37 if it appears to be deeper than the surface 10
Deu 33:13 choicest gifts . . of the deep that couches beneath 11
2Sm 1:21 be no dew or rain . . nor upsurging of the deep! •
1Kg 6: 3 twenty cubits long . . and ten cubits deep 8
7:31 its opening was round . . a cubit and a half deep. •
Job 11: 8 Deeper than Sheol–what can you know? 6
12:22 He uncovers the deeps out of darkness 6
28:14 The deep says, 'It is not in me,' 11
38:16 or walked in the recesses of the deep? 11
30 the face of the deep is frozen. 11
41:31 He makes the deep boil like a pot; 4
32 one would think the deep to be hoary. 11
Ps 33: 7 as in a bottle; he put the deeps in storehouses. 11
36: 1 speaks to the wicked deep in his heart; 1
6 thy judgments are like the great deep; 11
42: 7 Deep calls to deep at the thunder of thy 11
7 Deep calls to deep at the thunder of thy 11
64: 6 For the inward mind and heart of a man are deep! 6
69: 2 I sink in deep mire, where there is no foothold; 4
2 there is no foothold; I have come into deep waters 3
14 let me be delivered . . from the deep waters. 3
15 the flood sweep over me, or the deep swallow me up 4
77:16 they were afraid, yea, the deep trembled. 11
78:15 and gave them drink abundantly as from the deep. 11
80: 9 it took deep root and filled the land. •
92: 5 O LORD! Thy thoughts are very deep! 5
104: 6 didst cover it with the deep as with a garment; 11
106: 9 he led them through the deep as through a desert. 11
107:24 saw . . his wondrous works in the deep. 4
135: 6 in heaven and on earth, in the seas and all deeps. 11
148: 7 Praise the LORD . . sea monsters and all deeps 11
Prv 3:20 by his knowledge the deeps broke forth 11
8:27 when he drew a circle on the face of the deep 11
28 when he established the fountains of the deep 11
18: 4 The words of a man's mouth are deep waters; 6
20: 5 The purpose in a man's mind is like deep water 6
22:14 The mouth of a loose woman is a deep pit; 6
23:27 For a harlot is a deep pit; 6
Ecc 7:24 That which is, is far off, and deep, very deep; 6
24 That which is, is far off, and deep, very deep; 6
Isa 7:11 a sign . . let it be deep as Sheol or high as heaven. 5
29: 4 Then deep from the earth you shall speak 9
15 those who hide deep from the LORD their counsel 5
44:27 says to the deep, 'Be dry, I will dry up your rivers 7
51:10 didst dry up the sea, the waters of the great deep; 11
Ezk 23:32 your sister's cup which is deep and large; 6
26:19 when I bring up the deep over you 11
31: 4 waters nourished it, the deep made it grow tall 11
15 I will make the deep mourn for it 11
40: 6 the threshold of the gate, one reed deep; 8
47: 5 the water had risen; it was deep enough to swim •
Dan 2:22 he reveals deep and mysterious things; 12
Ams 7: 4 and it devoured the great deep 11
Jon 2: 3 For thou didst cast me into the deep 4
5 closed in over me, the deep was round about me; 11
Hab 3:10 the deep gave forth its voice, it lifted its hands 11
Lke 5: 4 he said to Simon, "Put out into the deep 14
6:48 he is like a man building a house, who dug deep 17
Joh 4:11 you have nothing to draw with, and the well is deep; 15
Act 20: 9 He sank into a deep sleep 15
2Es 4: 7 or how many streams are at the source of the deep 20
8 I never went down into the deep 20
7: 7 and deep water on the left; 21
16:57 It is he who searches the deep and its treasures 20
Wis 4: 3 will strike a deep root or take a firm hold. 14
10:18 and led them through deep waters; 19
16:11 lest they should fall into deep forgetfulness 15
Sir 22: 7 who rouses a sleeper from deep slumber. 15
24:29 and her counsel deeper than the great abyss. •
Aza 1:32 and lookest upon the deeps 13
Man 1: 3 who hast confined the deep 13
1Mc 6: 9 because deep grief continually gripped him 18
13 behold, I am perishing of deep grief 18
2Mc 3:27 deep darkness came over him 19
3Mc 5:12 he was overcome by so pleasant and deep a sleep 15
47 he had filled his impious mind with a deep rage 16
deep *See also* darkness, go, grief, make, region, sleep, sympathy.

great deep 1. ἄβυσσος
Sir 43:23 By his counsel he stilled the great deep 1

deep thing 1. חֵקֶר 2. βαθύς
Job 11: 7 Can you find out the deep things of God? 1
Rev 2:24 learned what some call the deep things of Satan 2

too deep for words 1. ἀλάλητος
Rom 8:26 intercedes for us with sighs too deep for words. 1

deeply 1. מְאֹד 2. נֶפֶשׁ 3. עמק 4. ἐν αἰσθήσει
5. μέγας 6. σφόδρα 7. valde
1Sm 1:10 She was deeply distressed and prayed to the LORD •
Est 4: 4 When . . told her, the queen was deeply distressed; 1
Isa 31: 6 Turn to him from whom you have deeply revolted 3
49: 7 Thus says the LORD . . to one deeply despised 2
Hos 9: 9 They have deeply corrupted themselves 3
1Es 1:24 how they grieved the Lord deeply 4
2Es 9:38 and was deeply grieved at heart 7
41 embittered in spirit and deeply afflicted. 7
Tob 3:10 she was deeply grieved 6
6:17 fell in love with her and yearned deeply for her. 6
1Mc 1:25 Israel mourned deeply in every community 5
2:39 they mourned for them deeply. 6
12:52 all Israel mourned deeply. †
14:16 they were deeply grieved. 6
deeply *See also* drink, move, moved, sigh, zealous.

defame 1. βλασφημέω
1Ti 6: 1 name of God and the teaching may not be defamed. 1

defeat 1. חֲלוּשָׁה 2. נגף 3. נכה 4. פרר
5. δύναμαι πρός 6. ἔκβολος 7. ἐκπολεμέω
8. ἐλαττονόω 9. ἐλάττωμα 10. ἐξολεθρεύω
11. ἡσσάομαι 12. ἥττημα 13. ἥττων γίνομαι
14. θραῦσμα 15. ἰσχύω 16. κατακρατέω 17. κραταιόω
18. νικάω 19. πατάσσω 20. συντρίβω 21. τρέπω
22. vinco
Gen 14:17 return from the defeat of Ched-or-lao'mer 3
36:35 Hadad the son of Bedad, who defeated Mid'ian 3
Exd 32:18 or the sound of the cry of defeat, 1
Num14:45 came down, and defeated them and pursued them 3
22: 6 I shall be able to defeat them and drive them 3
Deu 1: 4 after he had defeated Sihon . . and Og 3
42 lest you be defeated before your enemies.' 2
2:33 we defeated him and his sons and all his people. 3
4:46 whom Moses and the children of Israel defeated 3
7: 2 when the LORD . . gives them . . , and you defeat 3
28: 7 cause your enemies . . to be defeated before you; 2
25 cause you to be defeated before your enemies; 2
29: 7 came out . . to battle, but we defeated them; 3
Jos 10:40 Joshua defeated the whole land 3
41 Joshua defeated them from Ka'desh-bar'nea to Gaza 3
12: 1 the kings . . whom the people of Israel defeated 3
6 Moses . . and the people of Israel defeated them; 3
7 whom Joshua and the people of Israel defeated 3
13:12 these Moses had defeated and driven out. 3
21 whom Moses defeated with the leaders of Mid'ian 3
Jdg 1: 4 LORD gave . . into their hand; and they defeated 3
5 fought against him, and defeated the Canaanites 3
10 they defeated She'shai and Ahi'man and Talmai. 3
17 and they defeated the Canaanites who inhabited 3
3:13 and went and defeated Israel; and they took 3
11:21 into the hand of Israel, and they defeated them; 3
20:35 the LORD defeated Benjamin before Israel; 2
36 the Benjaminites saw that they were defeated. 2
1Sm 4: 2 Israel was defeated by the Philistines 3
10 the Philistines fought, and Israel was defeated 2
13: 3 Jonathan defeated the garrison . . at Geba; 3
4 Israel heard . . Saul had defeated the garrison 3
15: 7 Saul defeated the Amal'ekites 3
2Sm 5:20 to Ba'al-pera'zim, and David defeated them there; 3
8: 1 David defeated the Philistines and subdued 3
2 he defeated Moab, and measured them with a line 3
3 David also defeated Hadade'zer the son of Rehob 3
9 David had defeated the whole army of Hadade'zer 3
10 had fought against Hadade'zer and defeated him; 3
10:15 Syrians saw . . they had been defeated by Israel 2
19 saw that they had been defeated by Israel 2
15:34 you will defeat for me the counsel of Ahith'ophel. 4
17:14 the LORD had ordained to defeat the good counsel 4
18: 7 And the men of Israel were defeated there 2
1Kg 8:33 thy people . . are defeated before the enemy 2
2Kg 10:32 Haz'ael defeated them throughout . . Israel 3
13:25 Jo'ash defeated him and recovered the cities 3
14:12 Judah was defeated by Israel, and every man fled 2
1Ch 1:46 who defeated Mid'ian in the country of Moab 3
14:11 went up to Ba'al-pera'zim, and David defeated them 3
18: 1 David defeated the Philistines and subdued 3
2 defeated Moab, and the Mo'abites became servants 3
3 David also defeated Hadade'zer king of Zobah 3
9 David had defeated the whole army of Hadade'zer 3
10 fought against Hadade'zer and defeated him; 3
19:16 Syrians saw . . they had been defeated by Israel 2
19 saw that they had been defeated by Israel 2
2Ch 6:24 thy people Israel are defeated before the enemy 2
13:15 God defeated Jerobo'am and all Israel 2
14:12 the LORD defeated the Ethiopians before Asa 2
25:22 Judah was defeated by Israel 2
28: 5 king of Syria, who defeated him and took captive 3
5 Israel, who defeated him with great slaughter. 3
17 E'domites had again invaded and defeated Judah 3
23 the gods of Damascus which had defeated him 3
Jer 37:10 For even if you should defeat the whole army 3
46: 2 which Nebuchadrez'zar king of Babylon defeated 3
1Co 6: 7 is defeat for you 12
Rev 12: 8 but they were defeated 15
2Es 7:128 that if he is defeated he shall suffer 22
Jdt 1:13 defeated him in battle 17
5:18 they were utterly defeated in many battles 10
20 then we will go up and defeat them. 7
7: 9 lest his army be defeated. 14
11:11 now, in order that my lord may not be defeated 6
1Mc 1: 1 defeated Darius, king of the Persians 19
3:11 he defeated and killed him 19
5:40 he will surely defeat us. 5
41 we will cross over to him and defeat him. 5
43 All the Gentiles were defeated before him 20
8: 2 how they had defeated them 16
6 They also defeated Antiochus the Great, king of Asia •
10:49 Alexander pursued him and defeated them. 15
14: 3 he went and defeated the army of Demetrius 19
2Mc 9: 2 Antiochus and his men were defeated 21
10:24 Timothy, who had been defeated by the Jews before 11
11:13 he pondered over the defeat which had befallen him 9
12:11 The defeated nomads besought Judas 8
13:19 was turned back, attacked again, and was defeated. 8
22 attacked Judas and his men, was defeated; 13
4Mc 8: 2 conspicuously defeated in his first attempt 18
9:30 being defeated by our endurance 18
11:20 in which we have not been defeated! 18

defect 1. דָּבָר רָע 2. תְּבַלֻּל
Lev 21:20 a man with a defect in his sight or an itching 2
Deu 17: 1 ox . . in which is a blemish, any defect whatever; 1

without defect 1. תָּמִים
Num19: 2 to bring you a red heifer without defect 1

defective 1. λείπω
Tit 1: 5 that you might amend what was defective 1

defend 1. גנן 2. יכח 3. ישע 4. נצל 5. סכך 6. עמד עַל
7. ריב 8. שׁפט 9. ἀμύνομαι 10. ἀμύνω 11. ἀπαμύνω
12. ἀπολογέομαι 13. βοηθέω 14. ἐπαμύνω 15. ποιέω
16. ὑπερασπίζω 17. ὑπέρμαχος 18. defendo
19. protego 20. tueor
Jdg 6:31 contend for Ba'al? Or will you defend his cause? 3
2Sm 23:12 took his stand in . . the plot, and defended it 4
2Kg 19:34 I will defend this city to save it, for my own sake 1
20: 6 I will defend this city for my own sake and for my 1
1Ch 11:14 in the midst of the plot, and defended it 4
Est 8:11 the Jews . . to gather and defend their lives 6
9:16 Jews who . . also gathered to defend their lives 6
Job 13:15 yet I will defend my ways to his face. 2
Ps 5:11 let them ever sing for joy; and do thou defend them 5
43: 1 defend my cause against an ungodly people; 7
45: 4 for the cause of truth and to defend the right; •
Isa 1:17 defend the fatherless, plead for the widow. 8
23 They do not defend the fatherless 8
19:20 a savior, and will defend and deliver them. 7
37:35 For I will defend this city to save it 1
38: 6 I will deliver you . . and defend this city. 1
Jer 5:28 they do not defend the rights of the needy. 8
Hos 13:10 where are all your princes, to defend you– •
Act 7:24 he defended the oppressed man and avenged him 9
2Co 12:19 we have been defending ourselves before you 12
2Es 2:20 give to the needy, defend the orphan 20
7:122 that the glory of the Most High will defend those 19
13:49 he will defend the people who remain. 19
16:50 who will defend him who searches out every sin 18
Jdt 5:21 their Lord will defend them 16
6: 2 because their God will defend them 16
AEs 16:20 on that very day they may defend themselves 10
Wis 10:20 and praised with one accord thy defending hand 17
16:17 the universe defends the righteous. 17
1Mc 8:32 we will defend their rights 15
2Mc 6:11 their piety kept them from defending themselves 13
3Mc 1: 4 exhorted them to defend themselves 13
27 to defend them in the present trouble 14
7: 6 the God of heaven surely defends the Jews 16
4Mc 14:19 and defend it even to the death? 11

defend against 1. ἐπαμύνω
4Mc 14:19 even bees . . defend themselves against intruders 1

defend the cause 1. שׁפט
Ps 72: 4 May he defend the cause of the poor of the people 1

defender 1. ἔνδον 2. πρωταγωνιστής 3. ὑπέρμαχος
2Mc 8:36 proclaimed that the Jews had a Defender 3
10:36 Others . . wheeled around against the defenders 1
14:34 and called upon the constant Defender of our nation 3
15:30 the defender of his fellow citizens 2

defense 1. גַּב 2. מָצוֹר 3. עֹז 4. ἀπολογία 5. βοήθεια 6. ὀχύρωσις
2Ch 11: 5 Rehobo'am . . built cities for defense in Judah. 2
Job 13:12 your defenses are defenses of clay. 1
12 your defenses are defenses of clay. 1
Ps 60: 1 O God, thou hast rejected us, broken our defenses; *
Jer 41: 9 cistern which King Asa had made for defense *
Ams 3:11 and bring down your defenses from you 3
Act 22: 1 hear the defense which I now make before you. 4
1Co 9: 3 This is my defense to those who would examine me. 4
Php 1: 7 both in my imprisonment and in the defense 4
16 I am put here for the defense of the gospel; 4
2Ti 4:16 At my first defense no one took my part 4
1Pe 3:15 Always be prepared to make a defense to any one 4
Wis 6:10 who have been taught them will find a defense. 4
Sir 34:16 a defense against falling. 5
1Mc 14:10 furnished them with the means of defense 6
defense *See also* make, place, say.

make a defense
Jer 33: 4 torn down to make a defense against the siege *

sure defense 1. מִשְׂגָּב
Ps 48: 3 God has shown himself a sure defense. 1
defenseless *See* leave.

defer 1. ארך 2. הדר פָּנִים 3. משך 4. adulor
Lev 19:15 not be partial to the poor or defer to the great 2
Prv 13:12 Hope deferred makes the heart sick 3
Isa 48: 9 For my name's sake I defer my anger 1
2Es 7:54 defer to her, and she will declare it to you. 4

deference 1. מַרְפֵּא 2. ἐντρέπω
Ecc 10: 4 deference will make amends for great offenses. 1
Sir 4:22 deference, to your downfall. 2

show deference 1. ἐντρέπω
Wis 6: 7 nor show deference to greatness 1
defiance *See* bid, hold.

defiantly 1. בְּיָד רָמָה
Exd 14: 8 people of Israel as they went forth defiantly. 1

defile 1. גאל 2. גֹּאַל 3. געל 4. חָלָל 5. חלל 6. טָמֵא 7. טמא 8. ענה 9. βεβηλόω 10. κοινός 11. κοινόω 12. λυμαίνομαι 13. μιαίνω 14. μιαρός 15. μίασμα 16. μιασμός 17. μολύνω 18. μύσος 19. συμμιαίνω 20. coinquino 21. maculo
Gen 34: 5 heard that he had defiled his daughter Dinah; 7
13 because he had defiled their sister Dinah. 7
27 the city, because their sister had been defiled; 7
49: 4 your father's bed; then you defiled it 5
Lev 11:43 you shall not defile yourselves with them 7
44 not defile yourselves with any swarming thing 7
15:31 by defiling my tabernacle that is in their midst 7
18:20 your neighbor's wife, and defile yourself with her 7
23 not lie with any beast and defile yourself with it 7
24 Do not defile yourselves by any of these things 7
24 by all these the nations . . defiled themselves 7
28 lest the land vomit you out, when you defile it 7
30 and never to defile yourselves by them 7
19:31 do not seek them out, to be defiled by them 7
20: 3 defiling my sanctuary and profaning my holy name 7
21: 1 none of them shall defile himself for the dead 7
3 virgin sister . . for her he may defile himself) 7
4 He shall not defile himself as a husband 7
7 shall not marry . . a woman who has been defiled 4
11 nor defile himself, even for his father 7
14 a woman who has been defiled, or a harlot 4
22: 8 he shall not eat, defiling himself by it 7
Num 5: 3 that they may not defile their camp 7
13 is undetected though she has defiled herself 7
14 he is jealous of his wife who has defiled herself; 7
14 jealous . . though she has not defiled herself; 7
20 if you have defiled yourself 7
27 then, if she has defiled herself 7
28 if the woman has not defiled herself and is clean 7
29 when a wife . . goes astray and defiles herself 7
6: 9 he defiles his consecrated head 7
12 be void, because his separation was defiled. 7
19:13 defiles the tabernacle of the LORD 7
20 since he has defiled the sanctuary of the LORD; 7
35:34 You shall not defile the land in which you live 7
Deu 21:23 not defile your land which the LORD your God 7
24: 4 may not take her . . after she has been defiled; 7
2Sm 1:21 For there the shield of the mighty was defiled 3
2Kg 23: 8 and defiled the high places where the priests 7
10 he defiled To'pheth . . that no one might burn his 7
13 And the king defiled the high places 7
16 and burned them upon the altar, and defiled it 7
Neh 13:29 because they have defiled the priesthood 2
Ps 79: 1 heathen . . have defiled thy holy temple; 7
89:39 thou hast defiled his crown in the dust. 5
Isa 23: 9 has purposed it, to defile the pride of all glory 5
30:22 Then you will defile your silver-covered graven 7
59: 3 For your hands are defiled with blood 1
Jer 2: 7 But when you came in you defiled my land 7
23 How can you say, 'I am not defiled 7
7:30 which is called by my name, to defile it. 7
19:13 shall be defiled like the place of Topheth. 6
32:34 set up their abominations . . to defile it. 7
Lam 4:14 defiled with blood that none could touch 1
Ezk 4:14 Ah Lord GOD! behold, I have never defiled myself; 7
5:11 surely, because you have defiled my sanctuary 7
9: 7 Then he said to them, "Defile the house 7
14:11 nor defile themselves any more 7
18: 6 does not defile his neighbor's wife 7
11 upon the mountains, defiles his neighbor's wife 7
15 does not defile his neighbor's wife 7
20: 7 do not defile yourselves with the idols of Egypt; 7
18 nor defile yourselves with their idols. 7
26 I defiled them through their very gifts 7
30 Will you defile yourselves 7
31 you defile yourselves with all your idols 7
22: 3 and that makes idols to defile herself! 7
4 and defiled by the idols which you have made; 7
11 another lewdly defiles his daughter-in-law; 7
11 another in you defiles his sister 8
23: 7 and she defiled herself with all the idols 7
13 I saw that she was defiled; 7
17 they defiled her with their lust; 7
38 they have defiled my sanctuary on the same day 7
28: 7 and defile your splendor. 5
33:26 each of you defiles his neighbor's wife; 7
36:17 they defiled it by their ways and their doings; 7
18 for the idols with which they had defiled it. 7
37:23 They shall not defile themselves any more 7
43: 7 house of Israel shall no more defile my holy name 7
8 They have defiled my holy name 7
44:25 They shall not defile themselves by going near 7
25 for brother . . they may defile themselves. 7
26 After he is defiled, he shall count for himself ‡
Dan 1: 8 resolved that he would not defile himself 1
8 asked . . to allow him not to defile himself. 1
Hos 5: 3 you have played the harlot, Israel is defiled. 7
6:10 E'phraim's harlotry is there, Israel is defiled. 7
9: 4 all who eat of it shall be defiled; 7
Zep 3: 1 Woe to her that is rebellious and defiled 1
Mat 15:11 not what goes into the mouth defiles a man 11
11 what comes out of the mouth, this defiles a man. 11
18 and this defiles a man. 11
20 These are what defile a man 11
20 to eat with unwashed hands does not defile a man. 11
Mrk 7: 2 ate with hands defiled, that is, unwashed. 10
5 but eat with hands defiled? 10
15 which by going into him can defile him 11
15 the things which come out of a man are what defile 11
18 into a man from outside cannot defile him 11
20 What comes out of a man is what defiles a man. 11
23 they defile a man. 11
Joh 18:28 might not be defiled, but might eat the passover. 13
Act 21:28 he has defiled this holy place. 11
1Co 8: 7 their conscience, being weak, is defiled. 17
2Pe 2:10 indulge in the lust of defiling passion 16
Jde 1: 8 these men in their dreamings defile the flesh 13
Rev 14: 4 who have not defiled themselves with women 17
2Es 1:26 for you have defiled your hands with blood 21
8:60 who were created have defiled the name of him 20
10:22 our virgins have been defiled 20
Tob 2: 9 because I was defiled 13
Jdt 9: 2 had loosed the girdle of a virgin to defile her 15
8 they intend to defile thy sanctuary 9
13:16 to defile and shame me. 15
Wis 7:25 nothing defiled gains entrance into her. 13
Sir 13: 1 Whoever touches pitch will be defiled 17
21:28 A whisperer defiles his own soul 17
42:10 while a virgin, lest she be defiled 9
47:20 defiled your posterity 9
Bar 3:10 country, that you are defiled with the dead 19
1Mc 1:37 they even defiled the sanctuary. 17
46 to defile the sanctuary and the priests 13
63 They chose to die rather than to be defiled by food 13
4:43 removed the defiled stones to an unclean place. 16
45 the Gentiles had defiled it 13
7:34 he mocked them and derided them and defiled them 13
14:36 defile the environs of the sanctuary 13
2Mc 6:25 while I defile and disgrace my old age. 18
14: 3 had wilfully defiled himself 17
4Mc 4:26 to eat defiling foods and to renounce Judaism. 14
7: 6 you neither defiled your sacred teeth 13
18: 8 defile the purity of my virginity. 12

defile with blood 1. λυθρώδης
Wis 11: 6 stirred up and defiled with blood 1
defiled *See* person.

become defiled 1. טמא 2. μιαίνω
Lev 18:25 the land became defiled, so that I punished 1
27 so that the land became defiled) 1
Heb 12:15 by it the many become defiled; 2
3Mc 7:14 their fellow-countrymen who had become defiled. 2

most defiled 1. μιαρός
2Mc 7:34 you, unholy wretch, you most defiled of all men 1

defiled person 1. κοινόω
Heb 9:13 the sprinkling of defiled persons 1

defilement 1. ἀκαθαρσία 2. μίασμα 3. μολυσμός
2Co 7: 1 let us cleanse ourselves from every defilement 3
2Pe 2:20 they have escaped the defilements of the world 2
2Mc 5:27 that they might not share in the defilement. 3
3Mc 2:17 Do not punish us for the defilement 1

definite 1. ἀσφαλής 2. ὁρίζω
Act 2:23 delivered up according to the definite plan . . of God 2
25:26 nothing definite to write to my lord about him 1

defraud 1. עשק 2. ἀποστερέω 3. συκοφαντέω
1Sm 12: 3 Or whom have I defrauded? Whom have I oppressed? 1
4 You have not defrauded us or oppressed us 1
Mrk 10:19 Do not defraud, Honor your father and mother.' 2
Lke 19: 8 if I have defrauded any one of anything 3
1Co 6: 7 Why not rather be defrauded? 2
8 you yourselves wrong and defraud 2
Sir 29: 7 afraid of being defrauded needlessly. 2

defray 1. χορηγέω
2Mc 3: 3 defrayed from his own revenues all the expenses 1

defy 1. אמץ עַל 2. חרף 3. מרה
1Sm 17:10 I defy the ranks of Israel this day; give me a man 2
25 Surely he has come up to defy Israel; 2
26 who is this . . that he should defy the armies 2
36 he has defied the armies of the living God. 2
45 God of the armies of Israel, whom you have defied. 2
2Sm 23: 9 they defied the Philistines who were gathered 2
2Ch 13: 7 gathered about him and defied Rehobo'am 1
Ps 139:20 men who maliciously defy thee 3
Isa 3: 8 their deeds . . defying his glorious presence. 3
defy *See also* proudly.

degenerate 1. סור
Jer 2:21 How then have you turned degenerate 1

degrade 1. קלה 2. ἀτιμία
Deu 25: 3 lest . . your brother be degraded in your sight. 1
1Co 11:14 for a man to wear long hair is degrading to him 2

degree
2Co 3:18 from one degree of glory to another *
2Mc 4: 3 When his hatred progressed to such a degree *

extraordinary degree 1. ἐξόχως
3Mc 5:31 and have exhibited to an extraordinary degree . . loyalty 1

low degree 1. ταπεινός
Lke 1:52 and exalted those of low degree; 1

deign
2Mc 14: 9 Since you . . deign to take thought for our country *

deity 1. θεῖον 2. θειότης 3. θεότης
Act 17:29 we ought not to think that the Deity is like gold 1
Rom 1:20 namely, his eternal power and deity 2
Col 2: 9 in him the whole fulness of deity dwells bodily 3

dejected 1. ταπεινός
Sir 25:23 A dejected mind, a gloomy face, and a wounded heart 1

dejectedly 1. אַט
1Kg 21:27 and lay in sackcloth, and went about dejectedly. 1

dejection 1. κατήφεια
Jas 4: 9 be turned to mourning and your joy to dejection. 1

delay 1. אחר 2. בוש 3. מהה 4. משך 5. עמד 6. בטל (A) 7. ἀναβολή 8. ἀναμένω 9. βραδύνω 10. μακρύνω 11. μέλλω 12. ὀκνέω 13. παρέλκω 14. παρέλκω χρόνον 15. χρονίζω 16. χρόνος 17. inpedio 18. moror 19. tardo
Gen 24:56 he said to them, "Do not delay me, since the LORD has 1
34:19 the young man did not delay to do the thing 1
43:10 for if we had not delayed, we would now have 3
Exd 22:29 You shall not delay to offer from the fulness 1
32: 1 the people saw that Moses delayed to come down 2
Jdg 3:26 Ehud escaped while they delayed, and passed 3
2Sm 20: 5 he delayed beyond the set time . . appointed him. 1
Ezr 6: 8 cost is to be paid . . in full and without delay 6
Ps 119:60 I . . do not delay to keep thy commandments. 3
Ecc 5: 4 When you vow a vow to God, do not delay paying it; 1
8: 3 go . . do not delay when the matter is unpleasant 5
Ezk 12:25 It will no longer be delayed, but in your days 4
28 None of my words will be delayed any longer 4
Dan 9:19 delay not, for thy own sake, O my God 1
Hab 2: 3 it will surely come, it will not delay. 1

Mat 24:48 'My master is delayed,' 15
25: 5 As the bridegroom was delayed 15
Lke 1:21 they wondered at his delay in the temple. 15
12:45 'My master is delayed in coming,' 15
Act 9:38 Please come to us without delay. 12
25:17 I made no delay, but on the next day took my seat 7
1Ti 3:15 if I am delayed 9
Rev 10: 6 that there should be no more delay 16
2Es 4:39 time of threshing is delayed for the righteous- 17
16:37 the calamities draw near, and are not delayed. 19
38 there will not be a moment's delay 19
39 the calamities will not delay in coming forth 18
Tob 5: 8 he said to him, "Go, and do not delay. 15
9: 4 if I delay long he will be greatly distressed. 15
Jdt 2:13 do not delay about it. 10
Sir 4: 3 nor delay your gift to a beggar. 13
5: 7 Do not delay to turn to the Lord 8
7:16 remember that wrath does not delay. 15
14:12 Remember that death will not delay 15
29: 5 at the time for repayment he will delay 14
35:18 the Lord will not delay 9
4Mc 6:23 you, guards of the tyrant, why do you delay? 11
9: 1 Why do you delay, O tyrant? 11

delay long 1. μακροθυμέω
Lke 18: 7 Will he delay long over them? 1

long delay 1. χρονίζω
Tob 10: 4 The lad has perished; his long delay proves it. 1

without delay 1. ἀνυπερθέτως 2. ταχέως
2Mc 14:27 to send . . to Antioch as a prisoner without delay. 2
3Mc 5:20 tomorrow without delay prepare the elephants 1
42 he would send them to death without delay 1

delectable
Sng 7: 6 How fair . . you are . . delectable maiden! ‡

delete 1. ἀφαιρέω
1Mc 8:30 both . . shall determine to add or delete anything 1

deletion 1. ἀφαιρέω
1Mc 8:30 any addition or deletion that they may make 1

deliberate 1. ἀπρόπτωτος 2. βουλεύω
1Mc 4:44 They deliberated what to do 2
8:15 constantly deliberate concerning the people 2
3Mc 3:14 by the gods' deliberate alliance with us in battle 1

deliberately 1. ἑκουσίως 2. θέλω
Heb 10:26 For if we sin deliberately 1
2Pe 3: 5 They deliberately ignore this fact 2

deliberation 1. βουλή 2. διαβουλίος
Sir 32:19 Do nothing without deliberation 1
44: 4 leaders of the people in their deliberations 2

delicacy 1. לֶחֶם חמד 2. מַטְעָם 3. עֵדֶן 4. ξένη γεῦσις 5. ξένος γεῦσις τροφή
Prv 23: 3 Do not desire his delicacies 2
6 man who is stingy; do not desire his delicacies; 2
Jer 51:34 he has filled his belly with my delicacies 3
Dan 10: 3 ate no delicacies, no meat or wine entered 1
Wis 16: 2 a delicacy to satisfy the desire of appetite; 5
3 might partake of delicacies. 4

delicate 1. עָנֹג 2. ענג
Deu 28:56 because she is so delicate and tender 2
Isa 47: 1 you shall no more be called tender and delicate. 1

delicately *See* bred.

delicious 1. ἐπιτερπής
2Mc 15:39 wine mixed with water is sweet and delicious 1

delicious morsel 1. להם
Prv 18: 8 words of a whisperer are like delicious morsels; 1
26:22 words of a whisperer are like delicious morsels; 1

delicious thing 1. ἡδύς
4Mc 5: 9 It is senseless not to enjoy delicious things 1

delight 1. גיל 2. חמד 3. חָפֵץ 4. חֵפֶץ 5. חפץ 6. מַחְמַד 7. מַעֲדָן 8. נעם 9. עֵדֶן 10. עדן 11. עלס 12. עֹנֶג 13. ענג 14. ריח 15. רצה 16. רָצוֹן 17. שׂושׂ 18. שִׂמְחָה 19. שעע 20. שַׁעֲשֻׁעִים 21. תַּאֲוָה 22. תַּעֲנוּג 23. ἀπατάω 24. ἀπάτη 25. ἐπιθύμημα 26. εὐδοκέω 27. εὐδοκία 28. εὐφραίνω 29. ἥδομαι 30. συνήδομαι 31. τέρπω 32. τέρψις 33. χαρά 34. χάρις 35. iucunditas
Gen 3: 6 that it was a delight to the eyes 21
34:19 because he had delight in Jacob's daughter. 5
Num14: 8 If the LORD delights in us, he will bring us 5
Deu 21:14 Then, if you have no delight in her, you shall let 5
1Sm 15:22 Has the LORD as great delight in burnt offerings 4
18:22 the king has delight in you, and all his servants 5
19: 1 But Jonathan, Saul's son, delighted much in David. 5
2Sm 22:20 he delivered me, because he delighted in me. 5
24: 3 why does my lord the king delight in this thing? 5
1Kg 10: 9 LORD . . who has delighted in you and set you 5
2Ch 9: 8 LORD . . who has delighted in you and set you 5
Neh 1:11 thy servants who delight to fear thy name; 3
9:25 filled and became fat, and delighted themselves 10
Est 2:14 the king delighted in her and she was summoned 5
6: 6 be done to the man whom the king delights to honor? 5
6 Whom would the king delight to honor more than me? 5
7 For the man whom the king delights to honor 5
9 array the man whom the king delights to honor 5
9 done to the man whom the king delights to honor.' 5
11 done to the man whom the king delights to honor. 5
Job 20:20 he will not save anything in which he delights. 2
22:26 then you will delight yourself in the Almighty 13
Ps 1: 2 his delight is in the law of the LORD 4
5: 4 thou art not a God who delights in wickedness; 3
16: 3 they are the noble, in whom is all my delight. 4
18:19 he delivered me, because he delighted in me. 5
22: 8 let him rescue him, for he delights in him! 5
35:27 LORD, who delights in the welfare of his servant! 3
36: 8 drink from the river of thy delights. 9
37:11 delight themselves in abundant prosperity. 13
23 he establishes him in whose way he delights; 5
40: 8 I delight to do thy will, O my God; 5
44: 3 for thou didst delight in them. 15
51:16 For thou hast no delight in sacrifice; 5
19 then wilt thou delight in right sacrifices 5
68:30 scatter the peoples who delight in war. 5
112: 1 who greatly delights in his commandments! 5
119:14 In the way of thy testimonies I delight 17
16 I will delight in thy statutes; 19
24 They testimonies are my delight 20
35 the path of thy commandments, for I delight in it. 5
70 heart is gross like fat, but I delight in thy law. 19
77 that I may live; for thy law is my delight. 20
92 If thy law had not been my delight 20
143but thy commandments are my delight. 20
174O LORD, and thy law is my delight. 20
147:10 His delight is not in the strength of the horse 5
Prv 1:22 How long will scoffers delight in their scoffing 2
2:14 who . . delight in the perversions of evil; 1
3:12 as a father the son in whom he delights. 15
7:18 Come, let us . . delight ourselves with love. 11
8:30 daily his delight, rejoicing before him always 20
31 delighting in the sons of men. 20
11: 1 but a just weight is his delight. 16
20 but those of blameless ways are his delight. 16
12:22 but those who act faithfully are his delight. 16
15: 8 but the prayer of the upright is his delight. 16
16:13 Righteous lips are the delight of a king 16
24:25 those who rebuke the wicked have delight 8
29:17 give you rest; he will give delight to your heart. 7
Ecc 2: 8 I got . . and many concubines, man's delight. 22
Isa 1:11 I do not delight in the blood of bulls, or of lambs 5
29 be ashamed of the oaks in which you delighted; 2
11: 3 his delight shall be in the fear of the LORD. 14
13:17 no regard for silver and do not delight in gold. 5
42: 1 my chosen, in whom my soul delights; 15
44: 9 and the things they delight in do not profit; 2
55: 2 what is good, and delight yourselves in fatness. 13
58: 2 Yet they seek me daily and delight to know my ways 5
2 they delight to draw near to God. 5
13 and call the sabbath a delight and the holy day 12
62: 4 but you shall be called My delight is in her 4
4 your land Married; for the LORD delights in you 5
65:12 in my eyes, and chose what I did not delight in. 5
66: 3 and their soul delights in their abominations 5
4 and chose that in which I did not delight. 5
11 drink deeply with delight from the abundance 13
Jer 9:24 for in these things I delight, says the LORD. 5
15:16 became to me a joy and the delight of my heart; 18
Ezk 24:16 I am about to take the delight of your eyes away 6
21 the pride of your power, the delight of your eyes 6
25 delight of their eyes and their heart's desire 6
Hos 8:13 but the LORD has no delight in them. 15
Mic 1:16 cut . . your hair, for the children of your delight; 22
7:18 for ever because he delights in steadfast love. 5
Mal 2:17 in the sight of the LORD, and he delights in them. 5
3: 1 messenger of the covenant in whom you delight 3
12 for you will be a land of delight, says the LORD 4
Mat 13:22 and the delight in riches choke the word 24
Mrk 4:19 the cares of the world, and the delight in riches 24
Rom 7:22 For I delight in the law of God, in my inmost self. 30
2Es 7:36 and opposite it the paradise of delight. 35
38 here are delight and rest 35
47 that the world to come will bring delight to few 35
Wis 1:13 he does not delight in the death of the living. 31
6:21 if you delight in thrones and scepters 29
8:18 in friendship with her, pure delight 32
13: 3 through delight in the beauty of these things 32
Sir 1:12 The fear of the Lord delights the heart 32
27 he delights in fidelity and meekness. 27
9:12 Do not delight in what pleases the ungodly; 26
21:16 delight will be found 34
26:13 A wife's charm delights her husband 32
30:23 Delight your soul and comfort your heart 23
45:12 the delight of the eyes, richly adorned. 25
51:15 my heart delighted in her 28
2Mc 15:39 so also the style of the story delights the ears 31
4Mc 1:22 desire precedes pleasure and delight follows 33

delight *See also* fill, find, take.

great delight 1. חמד 2. θυμήρης
Sng 2: 3 With great delight I sat in his shadow 1
Wis 3:14 a place of great delight in the temple of the Lord. 2

delightful 1. γλυκύς
4Mc 8:23 deprive ourselves of this delightful world? 1

deliver 1. גאל 2. חלץ 3. ילד 4. יצא 5. יְשׁוּעָה 6. ישׁע 7. מגן 8. מלט 9. מצא 10. נצל 11. נתן 12. סגר 13. פדה 14. פרע 15. פלט 16. פרק 17. שׁוב 18. שׁלח 19. שׁפט 20. יהב (A) 21. נצל (A) 22. שׁיזב (A) 23. שׁלם (A) 24. ἀναδίδωμι 25. ἀπαλλάσσω 26. ἀποδίδωμι 27. ἀπολύω 28. γεννάω 29. διακονέω 30. διασῴζω 31. διαταγή 32. ἐξαιρέω 33. ἐξαίρω 34. ἐπιδίδωμι 35. ἐπισκέπτομαι 36. λυτρόω 37. παραδίδωμι 38. προσπίπτω 39. ῥύομαι 40. σφραγίζω 41. τίκτω 42. eripio 43. libero 44. trado
Gen 9: 2 into your hand they are delivered. 11
14:20 who has delivered your enemies into your hand! 7
25:24 When her days to be delivered were fulfilled 3
32:11 Deliver me, I pray thee, 10
16 These he delivered into the hand of his servants 11
37:21 when Reuben heard it, he delivered him out 10
42:34 honest men, and I will deliver to you your brother 11
Exd 1:19 they . . are delivered before the midwife comes 3
2:19 They said, "An Egyptian delivered us out 10
3: 8 I have come down to deliver them out of the hand 10
5:18 you shall deliver the same number of bricks. 11
23 and thou hast not delivered thy people at all. 10
6: 6 I will deliver you from their bondage 10
18: 4 God . . delivered me from the sword of Pharaoh"). 10
8 Moses told . . how the LORD had delivered them. 10
9 rejoiced . . in that he had delivered them out 10
10 Blessed be the LORD, who has delivered you 10
11 because he delivered the people from under 10
22: 7 If a man delivers to his neighbor money or goods 11
10 If a man delivers to his neighbor an ass or an ox 11
23:31 for I will deliver the inhabitants of the land 11
Lev 9:12 Aaron's sons delivered to him the blood 9
13 they delivered the burnt offering to him 9
18 Aaron's sons delivered to him the blood 9
26:25 you shall be delivered into the hand of the enemy 11
Deu 32:39 there is none that can deliver out of my hand. 10
Jos 2:13 save alive . . and deliver our lives from death. 10
9:26 and delivered them out of the hand of the people 10
24:10 he blessed you; so I delivered you out of his hand. 10
Jdg 3: 9 people of Israel, who delivered them, Oth'niel 6
31 with an oxgoad; and he too delivered Israel. 6
6: 9 I delivered you from the hand of the Egyptians 10
14 Go . . and deliver Israel from the hand of Mid'ian; 6
15 Lord, how can I deliver Israel? Behold, my clan is 6
36 said to God, "If thou wilt deliver Israel by my hand 6
37 know that thou wilt deliver Israel by my hand 6
7: 2 against me, saying, 'My own hand has delivered me.' 6
7 With the 300 men . . I will deliver you 6
8:22 you have delivered us out of the hand of Mid'ian. 6
10: 1 arose to deliver Israel Tola the son of Pu'ah 6
11 Did I not deliver you from the Egyptians •
12 cried to me, and I delivered you out of their hand. 6
13 other gods; therefore I will deliver you no more. 6
14 let them deliver you in the time of your distress 6
15 to thee; only deliver us, we pray thee, this day. 10
12: 2 you did not deliver me from their hand. 6
3 when I saw that you would not deliver me 6
13: 5 and he shall begin to deliver Israel 6
1Sm 4: 8 Who can deliver us from the power of these mighty 10
7: 3 and he will deliver you out of the hand 10
10:18 I delivered you from the hand of the Egyptians 10
12:10 deliver us out of the hand of our enemies 10
11 the LORD . . delivered you out of the hand 10
14:23 So the LORD delivered Israel that day; 6
48 and smote the Amal'ekites, and delivered Israel 10
17:35 I went . . and delivered it out of his mouth; 10
37 The LORD who delivered me from the paw of the lion 10
37 The LORD who . . will deliver me from the hand 10
46 This day the LORD will deliver you into my hand 12
23: 5 David delivered the inhabitants of Kei'lah. 6
24:15 and plead my cause, and deliver me from your hand. 19
26:24 and may he deliver me out of all tribulation. 10
30:15 kill me, or deliver me into the hands of my master 12
2Sm 12: 7 and I delivered you out of the hand of Saul; 10
14:16 For the king will hear, and deliver his servant 10
18:19 the LORD has delivered him from . . his enemies. 19
31 LORD has delivered you this day from the power 19
19: 9 The king delivered us from the hand of our 10
22: 1 David . . on the day when the LORD delivered him 10
18 He delivered me from my strong enemy 10
20 he delivered me, because he delighted in me. 2
28 Thou dost deliver a humble people 6
44 Thou didst deliver me from strife 15
49 thou didst deliver me from men of violence. 10
1Kg 3:18 third day after I was delivered, this woman also 3
17:23 took the child . . and delivered him to his mother; 11
20: 5 Deliver to me your silver and your gold 11

2Kg 3: 4 Mesha . . had to deliver annually to the king 17
11:10 the priest delivered to the captains the spears 11
12:15 the men into whose hand they delivered the money 11
17:39 you shall fear the LORD . . and he will deliver you 10
18:29 he will not be able to deliver you out of my hand. 10
30 The LORD will surely deliver us 10
32 misleads you by saying, The LORD will deliver us. 10
33 Has any of the gods . . ever delivered his land 10
34 Have they delivered Sama'ria out of my hand? 10
35 Who . . have delivered their countries out of my 10
35 the LORD should deliver Jerusalem out of my hand?' 10
19:11 you have heard . . And shall you be delivered? 10
12 Have the gods of the nations delivered them 10
20: 6 I will deliver you and this city out of the hand 10
22: 7 for the money which is delivered into their hand 11
9 have delivered it into the hand of the workmen 11
1Ch 16:35 Deliver us, O God of our salvation, and gather 6
22:18 he has delivered the inhabitants of the land 11
2Ch 23: 9 Jehoi'ada the priest delivered to the captains 11
24:24 LORD delivered into their hand a very great army 11
25:15 gods . . which did not deliver their own people 10
32:11 The LORD our God will deliver us from the hand 10
13 gods . . at all able to deliver their lands 10
14 Who among all the gods . . was able to deliver 10
14 God should be able to deliver you from my hand? 10
15 no god . . has been able to deliver his people 10
15 How . . will your God deliver you out of my hand!' 10
17 have not delivered their people from my hands 10
17 God of Hezeki'ah will not deliver his people 10
34: 9 delivered the money that had been brought 11
10 delivered it to the workmen 11
17 delivered it into the hand of the overseers 11
Ezr 5:14 delivered to one whose name was Shesh-baz'zar 20
7:19 you shall deliver before the God of Jerusalem. 23
8:31 delivered us from the hand of the enemy 10
36 delivered the king's commissions to the king's 11
Neh 9:28 deliver them according to thy mercies. 10
Job 5: 4 there is no one to deliver them. 10
19 He will deliver you from six troubles; 10
6:23 Or, 'Deliver me from the adversary's hand'? 8
8: 4 sinned against him, he has delivered them 18
10: 7 there is none to deliver out of thy hand? 10
22:30 He delivers the innocent man; 8
30 delivered through the cleanness of your hands. 8
29:12 because I delivered the poor who cried 8
33:24 Deliver him from going down into the Pit 14
36:15 He delivers the afflicted by their affliction 2
39: 3 offspring, and are delivered of their young? 18
Ps 3: 7 Arise, O LORD! Deliver me, O my God! 6
6: 4 deliver me for the sake of thy steadfast love. 6
7: 1 save me from all my pursuers, and deliver me 10
17:13 Deliver my life from the wicked by thy sword 15
18: 0 on the day when the LORD delivered him 10
17 He delivered me from my strong enemy 10
19 he delivered me, because he delighted in me. 2
27 For thou dost deliver a humble people; 6
43 Thou didst deliver me from strife 15
48 who delivered me from my enemies; yea, thou didst 15
48 thou didst deliver me from men of violence. 10
22: 4 they trusted, and thou didst deliver them. 15
8 let him deliver him, let him rescue him 15
20 Deliver my soul from the sword 10
25:20 Oh guard my life, and deliver me; 10
31: 1 be put to shame; in thy righteousness deliver me! 15
8 hast not delivered me into the hand of the enemy; 12
15 deliver me from the hand of my enemies 10
33:16 a warrior is not delivered by his great strength. 10
19 that he may deliver their soul from death 10
34: 4 answered me, and delivered me from all my fears. 10
7 around those who fear him, and delivers them. 2
17 and delivers them out of all their troubles. 10
19 but the LORD delivers him out of them all. 10
35:10 who is like thee, thou who deliverest the weak 10
37:40 The LORD helps them and delivers them; 15
40 he delivers them from the wicked, and saves them 15
39: 8 Deliver me from all my transgressions. 10
40:13 Be pleased, O LORD, to deliver me! 10
41: 1 The LORD delivers him in the day of trouble; 8
43: 1 from deceitful and unjust men deliver me! 15
44:26 Deliver us for the sake of thy steadfast love! 13
50:15 I will deliver you, and you shall glorify me. 2
22 lest I rend, and there be none to deliver! 10
51:14 Deliver me from blood guiltiness, O God 10
54: 7 For thou hast delivered me from every trouble 10
55:18 He will deliver my soul in safety from the battle 13
56:13 For thou hast delivered my soul from death 10
59: 1 Deliver me from my enemies, O my God 10
2 deliver me from those who work evil, and save me 10
60: 5 That thy beloved may be delivered, give victory 2
69:14 let me be delivered from my enemies 10
70: 1 Be pleased, O God, to deliver me! 10
71: 2 In thy righteousness deliver me and rescue me; 10
11 seize him, for there is none to deliver him. 10
72:12 For he delivers the needy when he calls 10
74:19 Do not deliver the soul of thy dove to the wild 11
78:61 delivered his power to captivity 11
79: 9 deliver us, and forgive our sins, for thy name's sake! 10
81: 7 In distress you called, and I delivered you; 2
82: 4 deliver them from the hand of the wicked. 10
86:13 hast delivered my soul from the depths of Sheol. 10
89:48 Who can deliver his soul from the power of Sheol? 8
91: 3 he will deliver you from the snare of the fowler 10
14 Because he cleaves to me in love, I will deliver 15
97:10 delivers them from the hand of the wicked. 10
106: 4 help me when thou deliverest them; 5
10 delivered them from the power of the enemy. 1
43 Many times he delivered them 10
107: 6 LORD . . delivered them from their distress; 10
13 LORD . . delivered them from their distress; 6
19 LORD . . delivered them from their distress; 6
20 healed . . delivered them from destruction. 8
28 LORD . . delivered them from their distress; 4
108: 6 That thy beloved may be delivered 2
109:21 because thy steadfast love is good, deliver me! 10
116: 8 For thou hast delivered my soul from death 2
119:153 Look on my affliction and deliver me 2
170 deliver me according to thy word. 10
120: 2 Deliver me, O LORD, from lying lips 10
138: 7 thy right hand delivers me. 6
140: 1 Deliver me, O LORD, from evil men; 2
142: 6 Deliver me from my persecutors; for they are too 10
143: 9 Deliver me, O LORD, from my enemies! 10
144: 7 rescue me and deliver me from the many waters 10
11 deliver me from the hand of aliens 10
Prv 2:12 delivering you from the way of evil 10
10: 2 but righteousness delivers from death. 10
11: 4 but righteousness delivers from death. 10
6 The righteousness of the upright delivers them 10
8 The righteous is delivered from trouble 2
9 but by knowledge the righteous are delivered. 2
21 but those who are righteous will be delivered. 8
12: 6 but the mouth of the upright delivers men. 10
19:19 for if you deliver him, you . . have to do it again. 10
28:18 He who walks in integrity will be delivered 6
26 but he who walks in wisdom will be delivered. 8
31:24 she delivers girdles to the merchant. 11
Ecc 8: 8 will wickedness deliver those . . given to it. 8
9:15 wise man, and he by his wisdom delivered the city. 8
Isa 19:20 a savior, and will defend and deliver them. 10
20: 6 to whom we fled for help to be delivered 10
31: 5 he will protect and deliver it, he will spare 10
36:14 for he will not be able to deliver you. 10
15 by saying, "The LORD will surely deliver us; 10
18 mislead you by saying, "The LORD will deliver us. 10
18 Has any of the gods of the nations delivered 10
19 Have they delivered Sama'ria out of my hand? 10
20 have delivered their countries out of my hand 10
20 the LORD should deliver Jerusalem out of my hand?' 10
37:11 destroying them . . And shall you be delivered? 10
12 Have the gods of the nations delivered them 10
38: 6 I will deliver you and this city out of the hand 10
43:13 there is none who can deliver from my hand; 10
28 I delivered Jacob to utter destruction 11
44:17 prays to it and says, "Deliver me, for thou art my god! 10
20 led him astray, and he cannot deliver himself 10
47:14 cannot deliver themselves from the . . flame. 10
50: 2 cannot redeem? Or have I no power to deliver? 10
57:13 let your collection of idols deliver you! 10
64: 7 and hast delivered us into the hand 37
66: 7 before her pain . . she was delivered of a son. 8
Jer 1: 8 for I am with you to deliver you, says the LORD. 10
19 for I am with you, says the LORD, to deliver you. 10
7:10 and say, 'We are delivered!' 10
15:20 I am with you to save you and deliver you 10
21 I will deliver you out of the hand of the wicked 10
20:13 For he has delivered the life of the needy 10
21:12 and deliver from the hand of the oppressor 10
22: 3 and deliver from the hand of the oppressor 10
29:21 deliver them into the hand of Nebuchadrez'zar 11
34: 3 surely be captured and delivered into his hand; 11
37:17 You shall be delivered into the hand of the king 11
38:16 or deliver you into the hand of these men 11
39:17 But I will deliver you on that day, says the LORD 10
42:11 to save you and to deliver you from his hand. 10
43: 3 to deliver us into the hand of the Chalde'ans 11
46:24 she shall be delivered into the hand of a people 11
26 I will deliver them into the hand of those 11
Lam 2: 7 he has delivered into the hand of the enemy 12
5: 8 there is none to deliver us from their hand. 16
Ezk 7:19 silver and gold are not able to deliver them 10
13:21 and deliver my people out of your hand 10
23 I will deliver my people out of your hand. 10
14:14 they would deliver but their own lives 10
16 they would deliver neither sons nor daughters; 10
16 they alone would be delivered 10
18 they would deliver neither sons nor daughters 10
18 but they alone would be delivered. 10
20 they would deliver neither son nor daughter; 10
20 they would deliver but their own lives 10
16:27 and delivered you to the greed of your enemies 11
21:31 I will deliver you into the hands of brutal men 11
23: 9 I delivered her into the hands of her lovers 11
28 Behold, I will deliver you into the hands of those 11
33:12 shall not deliver him when he transgresses; 10
34:27 and deliver them from the hand of those 10
36:29 I will deliver you from all your uncleannesses; 6
Dan 3:15 god that will deliver you out of my hands? 22
17 God . . is able to deliver us from the . . furnace 22
17 God . . will deliver us out of your hand, O king. 22
28 sent his angel and delivered his servants 22
29 no other god who is able to deliver in this way. 21
6:14 distressed, and set his mind to deliver Daniel; 22
16 God, whom you serve continually, deliver you! 22
20 has your God . . able to deliver you from the lions 22
27 He delivers and rescues, he works signs 22
11:41 these shall be delivered out of his hand: Edom 8
12: 1 but at that time your people shall be delivered 8
Hos 1: 7 and I will deliver them by the LORD their God; 6
7 I will not deliver them by bow, nor by sword 6
Jol 2:32 call upon the name of the LORD shall be delivered; 8
Mic 5: 6 and they shall deliver us from the Assyrian 10
8 and tears in pieces, and there is none to deliver. 10
Zep 1:18 nor their gold shall be able to deliver them 10
Zec 11: 6 I will deliver none from their hand. 10
Mat 6:13 not into temptation, But deliver us from evil. 39
11:27 All things have been delivered to me by my Father; 37
17:22 Son of man is to be delivered into the hands of men 37
18:34 in anger his lord delivered him to the jailers 37
20:18 the Son of man will be delivered 37
19 deliver him to the Gentiles to be mocked 37
25:20 Master, you delivered to me five talents 37
22 Master, you delivered to me two talents 37
26:15 said, "What will you give me if I deliver him to you? 37
27: 2 delivered him to Pilate the governor. 37
26 delivered him to be crucified. 37
43 He trusts in God; let God deliver him now 39
Mrk 9:31 The Son of man will be delivered 37
10:33 Son of man will be delivered to the chief priests 37
33 deliver him to the Gentiles; 37
15: 1 led him away and delivered him to Pilate. 37
15 he delivered him to be crucified. 37
Lke 1: 2 just as they were delivered to us by those 37
57 Now the time came for Elizabeth to be delivered 41
74 delivered from the hand of our enemies 39
2: 6 the time came for her to be delivered. 41
4: 6 for it has been delivered to me 37
9:44 the Son of man is to be delivered 37
10:22 All things have been delivered to me by my Father; 37
18:32 For he will be delivered to the Gentiles 37
24: 7 must be delivered into the hands of sinful men 37
Joh 16:21 when she is delivered of the child 28
19:11 who delivered me to you has the greater sin. 37
Act 6:14 change the customs which Moses delivered to us. 37
7:34 I have come down to deliver them 32
53 you who received the law as delivered by angels 31
12: 4 delivered him to four squads of soldiers 37
15:30 they delivered the letter. 34
16: 4 delivered to them for observance the decisions 37
21:11 deliver him into the hands of the Gentiles.' 37
22: 4 delivering to prison both men and women 37
23:33 delivered the letter to the governor 24
26:17 delivering you from the people 32
27: 1 they delivered Paul . . to a centurion 37
28:17 yet I was delivered prisoner from Jerusalem 37
Rom 7:24 Who will deliver me from this body of death? 39
15:28 and have delivered to them what has been raised 40
31 I may be delivered from the unbelievers in Judea 39
1Co 5: 5 you are to deliver this man to Satan 37
11: 2 even as I have delivered them to you. 37
23 what I also delivered to you 37
13: 3 if I deliver my body to be burned, but have not love 37
15: 3 For I delivered to you as of first importance 37
24 Then comes the end, when he delivers the kingdom 37
2Co 1:10 he delivered us from so deadly a peril 39
10 set our hope that he will deliver us again. 39
10 set our hope that he will deliver us again. 39
3: 3 that you are a letter from Christ delivered by us 29
Gal 1: 4 to deliver us from the present evil age 32
Col 1:13 has delivered us from the dominion of darkness 39
1Th 1:10 Jesus who delivers us from the wrath to come. 39
2Th 3: 2 that we may be delivered from wicked and evil men; 39
1Ti 1:20 whom I have delivered to Satan 37
Heb 2:15 deliver all . . subject to lifelong bondage. 25
2Pe 2:21 the holy commandment delivered to them. 37
Jde 1: 3 faith . . once for all delivered to the saints. 37
1Es 6:18 they were delivered to Zerubbabel 37
8: 8 which was delivered to Ezra the priest 38
17 deliver the holy vessels of the Lord •
59 Be watchful and on guard until you deliver them 37
61 he delivered us from every enemy on the way 39
62 delivered in the house of our Lord to Meremoth 37
67 they delivered the king's orders 26
2Es 2:30 because I will deliver you, says the Lord. 42
3:27 deliver the city into the hands of thy enemies. 44
7:27 every one who has been delivered from the evils 43
96 from which they have been delivered 43
12:34 he will deliver in mercy the remnant of my people 43
13:26 who will himself deliver his creation 43
29 when the Most High will deliver those 43
14:26 and some you shall deliver in secret to the wise 44
29 and they were delivered from there 43
15:27 for God will not deliver you 43
16:17 Who will deliver me in those days? 43
67 and deliver you from all tribulation. 43
74 and I will deliver you from them. 43
Tob 4:10 For charity delivers from death 39
12: 9 For almsgiving delivers from death 39

14:11 consider . . how righteousness delivers 39
Jdt 6: 3 their God will not deliver them 39
8:33 the Lord will deliver Israel by my hand. 35
16: 3 he has delivered me out of the hands of my pursuers 32
AEs 10: 9 the Lord has delivered us from all these evils 39
Wis 2:18 deliver him from the hand of his adversaries. 39
10: 1 she delivered him from his transgression 32
13 delivered him from sin 39
15 wisdom delivered from a nation of oppressors. 39
16: 8 it is thou who deliverest from every evil. 39
11 then were quickly delivered 30
19: 9 praising thee, O Lord, who didst deliver them. 39
Sir 4: 9 Deliver him who is wronged 32
33: 1 in trial he will deliver him again and again. 32
48:20 delivered them by the hand of Isaiah. 36
49:10 delivered them with confident hope. 36
50:24 let him deliver us in our days! 36
51: 2 hast delivered my body from destruction 36
3 didst deliver me 36
8 thou dost deliver those who wait for thee 33
Bar 2:14 for thy own sake deliver us, and grant us favor 32
4:18 deliver you from the hand of your enemies. 32
21 deliver you from the power . . of the enemy. 32
LJr 1:54 or deliver one who is wronged 39
Aza 1:20 Deliver us in accordance with thy marvelous works 32
66 delivered us from the midst of the . . furnace 39
66 from the midst of the fire he has delivered us. 39
1Mc 2:60 was delivered from the mouth of the lions. 39
5:50 the city was delivered into his hands. 37
7:35 delivered into my hands this time 37
12:15 we were delivered from our enemies 39
17 greet you and deliver to you this letter from us 26
16: 2 so that we have delivered Israel many times. 39
2Mc 11:15 which Maccabeus delivered to Lysias in writing. 34
17 have delivered your signed communication 34
12:45 they might be delivered from their sin. 27

deliver again 1.שׁוּב
Lev 26:26 and shall deliver your bread again by weight 1

deliver over 1.מגר
Ezk 21:12 they are delivered over to the sword 1

deliver up 1.נתן 2.סגר 3.ἔκδοτος 4.παραδίδωμι
2Sm 18:28 the LORD . . who has delivered up the men 2
Jer 18:21 Therefore deliver up their children to famine; 1
Ezk 16:21 slaughtered my children and delivered them up 1
Ams 1: 6 exile a whole people to deliver them up to Edom. 2
9 because they delivered up a whole people to Edom 2
6: 8 I will deliver up the city and all that is in it. 2
Obd 1:14 you should not have delivered up his survivors 2
Mat 10:17 Beware of men; for they will deliver you up 4
19 When they deliver you up, do not be anxious 4
21 Brother will deliver up brother to death 4
24: 9 Then they will deliver you up to tribulation 4
26: 2 Son of man will be delivered up to be crucified. 4
27:18 it was out of envy that they had delivered him up. 4
Mrk 13: 9 they will deliver you up to councils 4
11 when they bring you to trial and deliver you up 4
12 brother will deliver up brother to death 4
15:10 the chief priests had delivered him up. 4
Lke 20:20 so as to deliver him up 4
21:12 delivering you up to the synagogues and prisons 4
16 You will be delivered up even by parents 4
23:25 Jesus he delivered up to their will. 4
24:20 our chief priests and rulers delivered him up 4
Act 2:23 delivered up according to the definite plan . . of God 3
3:13 Jesus, whom you delivered up 4

deliverance 1.הַצָּלָה 2.יְשׁוּעָה 3.יֶשַׁע 4.פַּלֵּט 5.פְּלֵיטָה 6.צֶדֶק 7.צְדָקָה 8.תְּשׁוּעָה 9.ῥῦσις 10.σωτηρία 11.σωτήριος
Jdg 15:18 Thou hast granted this great deliverance 8
1Sm 11: 9 'Tomorrow . . you shall have deliverance.' 8
13 the LORD has wrought deliverance in Israel. 8
2Ch 12: 7 but I will grant them some deliverance 5
Est 4:14 relief and deliverance will rise for the Jews 1
Ps 3: 8 Deliverance belongs to the LORD; 2
9:14 I may rejoice in thy deliverance. 2
14: 7 O that deliverance for Israel would come 2
22:31 proclaim his deliverance to a people yet unborn 7
32: 7 thou dost encompass me with deliverance. Selah 4
35: 3 Say to my soul, "I am your deliverance! 2
9 in the LORD, exulting in his deliverance. 2
40: 9 I have told the glad news of deliverance 6
51:14 my tongue will sing aloud of thy deliverance. 7
53: 6 O that deliverance for Israel would come 2
62: 7 On God rests my deliverance and my honor; 3
65: 5 thou dost answer us with deliverance, O God 6
Isa 26:18 We have wrought no deliverance in the earth 2
46:12 Hearken . . you who are far from deliverance 7
13 I bring near my deliverance, it is not far off 7
51: 1 Hearken to me, you who pursue deliverance 6
5 My deliverance draws near speedily 6
6 for ever, and my deliverance will never be ended. 7
8 but my deliverance will be for ever 7
56: 1 will come, and my deliverance be revealed. 7
Jon 2: 9 Deliverance belongs to the LORD! 2
Mic 7: 9 I shall behold his deliverance. 7
Act 7:25 God was giving them deliverance by his hand 10
Php 1:19 this will turn out for my deliverance 10
Jdt 8:17 while we wait for his deliverance 10
Wis 16: 6 received a token of deliverance 10
18: 7 The deliverance of the righteous 10
Sir 51: 9 prayed for deliverance from death. 9
1Mc 3: 6 deliverance prospered by his hand. 10
4:25 Thus Israel had a great deliverance that day. 10
56 offered a sacrifice of deliverance and praise. 11
5:62 those men through whom deliverance was given 10
3Mc 6:31 arranged for a banquet of deliverance 11
36 because of the deliverance that had come to them 10
7:16 had received the full enjoyment of deliverance 10
18 There they celebrated their deliverance 11
22 performed great deeds for their deliverance. 10
4Mc 15:26 one bearing death and the other deliverance 11
27 She did not approve the deliverance 10
deliverance *See also* give.

deliverer 1.יְשׁוּעָה 2.יֶשַׁע 3.נצל 4.פלט 5.λυτρωτής 6.ῥύομαι 7.ῥύστης
Jdg 3: 9 raised up a deliverer for the people of Israel 2
15 raised up for them a deliverer, Ehud, the son 2
18:28 there was no deliverer because it was far 3
2Sm 22: 2 The LORD is my rock . . my fortress . . my deliverer 4
Ps 18: 2 my fortress, and my deliverer, my God, my rock 4
40:17 Thou art my help and my deliverer; do not tarry 4
70: 5 Thou art my help and my deliverer 4
140: 7 O LORD, my Lord, my strong deliverer 1
144: 2 my fortress, my stronghold and my deliverer 4
Act 7:35 God sent as both ruler and deliverer 5
Rom 11:26 it is written, "The Deliverer will come from Zion 6
3Mc 7:23 Blessed be the Deliverer of Israel 7

delivery 1.ילד 2.τίκτω 3.partus
Gen 38:27 When the time of her delivery came 1
Rev 12: 2 in her pangs of birth, in anguish for delivery. 2
2Es 16:38 when the time of her delivery draws near 3

delude 1.נשׁא 2.תלל 3.παραλογίζομαι
Isa 19:13 and the princes of Memphis are deluded; 1
44:20 feeds on ashes; a deluded mind has led him astray 2
Col 2: 4 I say this in order that no one may delude you 3

deluge 1.שֶׁטֶף 2.κατακλύζω
Ezk 13:11 There will be a deluge of rain 1
13 and there shall be a deluge of rain in my anger 1
2Pe 3: 6 world . . was deluged with water and perished 2

delusion 1.אָוֶן 2.כָּזָב 3.שָׁוְא 4.שֶׁקֶר 5.תַּעְתֻּעִים 6.ἐμπαιγμα 7.πλάνη
Ps 62: 9 men of high estate are a delusion; 2
Isa 41:29 they are all a delusion; their works are nothing; 1
Jer 3:23 Truly the hills are a delusion 4
10:15 They are worthless, a work of delusion; 5
51:18 They are worthless, a work of delusion; 5
Ezk 13: 8 you have uttered delusions and seen lies 3
2Th 2:11 Therefore God sends upon them a strong delusion 7
Wis 17: 7 The delusions of their magic art lay humbled 6

delusive 1.שָׁוְא
Ezk 13: 7 Have you not seen a delusive vision 1
delusive *See also* vision.

delve 1.כרה
Num 21:18 well . . which the nobles of the people delved 1

demagoguery 1.δημαγωγία
1Es 5:73 by plots and demagoguery and uprisings 1

demand 1.בקשׁ 2.שׁאל 3.שׁלח 4.מִלָּה (A) 5.αἰτέω 6.αἴτημα 7.ἐν βάρει 8.ἐξαιτέω
1Kg 20: 9 All that you first demanded . . I will do; 3
Neh 5:18 not demand the food allowance of the governor 1
Ps 44:12 for a trifle, demanding no high price for them. †
78:18 tested God in their heart by demanding the food 2
Dan 2:10 not a man on earth who can meet the king's demand; 4
Lke 12:48 of him . . they will demand the more. 5
22:31 Simon, Simon, behold, Satan demanded to have you 8
23:23 demanding with loud cries 5
24 their demand should be granted. 6
1Co 1:22 For Jews demand signs and Greeks seek wisdom 5
1Th 2: 6 though we might have made demands 7
1Mc 15:35 As for Joppa and Gazara, which you demand 5
2Mc 7:10 When it was demanded 5
demand *See also* make.

legal demand 1.δόγμα
Col 2:14 the bond . . with its legal demands 1

demand to know 1.πυνθάνομαι
3Mc 5:18 the king . . with sharp threats demanded to know why 1

demolish 1.הרס 2.נתץ 3.שׁמד 4.κατασκάπτω 5.demolior
Num 33:52 demolish all their high places; 3
2Kg 10:27 they demolished the pillar of Ba'al 2
27 they . . demolished the house of Ba'al 2
Lam 2:17 as he ordained . . he has demolished without pity; 1
Rom 11: 3 Lord . . they have demolished thy altars 4
2Es 16:23 and its cities shall be demolished. 5
Jdt 3: 8 he demolished all their shrines 4

part demolished 1.καθαιρέω
1Mc 9:62 rebuilt the parts of it that had been demolished 1

demon 1.שֵׁד 2.δαιμονίζομαι 3.δαιμόνιον 4.δαίμων
Deu 32:17 They sacrificed to demons which were no gods 1
Ps 106:37 sons and their daughters to the demons; 1
Mat 7:22 and cast out demons in your name 3
8:31 the demons begged him, "If you cast us out, send us 4
9:33 when the demon had been cast out 3
34 He casts out demons by the prince of demons. 3
34 He casts out demons by the prince of demons. 3
10: 8 cleanse lepers, cast out demons 3
11:18 and they say, 'He has a demon'; 3
12:24 It is only by Be-el'zebul, the prince of demons 3
24 that this man casts out demons. 3
27 if I cast out demons by Be-el'zebul 3
28 if it is by the Spirit of God that I cast out demons 3
17:18 Jesus rebuked him, and the demon came out of him 3
Mrk 1:34 and cast out many demons 3
34 he would not permit the demons to speak 3
39 preaching . . and casting out demons. 3
3:15 and have authority to cast out demons 3
22 by the prince of demons he casts out the demons. 3
22 by the prince of demons he casts out the demons. 3
6:13 they cast out many demons, and anointed with oil 3
7:26 begged him to cast the demon out of her daughter. 3
29 the demon has left your daughter. 3
30 the child lying in bed, and the demon gone. 3
9:38 we saw a man casting out demons in your name 3
16: 9 from whom he had cast out seven demons. 3
17 in my name they will cast out demons 3
Lke 4:33 a man who had the spirit of an unclean demon 3
35 when the demon had thrown him down in the midst 3
41 demons also came out of many, crying 3
7:33 and you say, 'He has a demon.' 3
8: 2 Mary . . from whom seven demons had gone out 3
27 there met him a man from the city who had demons 3
29 was driven by the demon into the desert.) 3
30 he said, "Legion"; for many demons had entered him. 3
33 Then the demons came out of the man 3
35 found the man from whom the demons had gone 3
38 The man from whom the demons had gone begged 3
9: 1 gave them power and authority over all demons 3
42 the demon tore him and convulsed him 3
49 we saw a man casting out demons in your name 3
10:17 even the demons are subject to us in your name! 3
11:14 Now he was casting out a demon that was dumb 3
14 when the demon had gone out, the dumb man spoke 3
15 He casts out demons by Be-el'zebul 3
15 by Be-el'zebul, the prince of demons"; 3
18 you say that I cast out demons by Be-el'zebul. 3
19 if I cast out demons by Be-el'zebul 3
20 if it is by the finger of God that I cast out demons 3
13:32 I cast out demons and perform cures today 3
Joh 7:20 The people answered, "You have a demon! 3
8:48 you are a Samaritan and have a demon? 3
49 Jesus answered, "I have not a demon 3
52 Now we know that you have a demon 3
10:20 Many of them said, "He has a demon, and he is mad 3
21 These are not the sayings of one who has a demon. 2
21 Can a demon open the eyes of the blind? 3
1Co 10:20 they offer to demons and not to God 3
20 I do not want you to be partners with demons. 3
21 the cup of the Lord and the cup of demons 3
21 table of the Lord and the table of demons. 3
1Ti 4: 1 deceitful spirits and doctrines of demons 3
Jas 2:19 Even the demons believe–and shudder. 3
Rev 9:20 nor give up worshiping demons and idols of gold 3
18: 2 It has become a dwelling place of demons 3
Tob 3: 8 the evil demon Asmodeus had slain each of them 3
17 to bind Asmodeus the evil demon 3
6: 7 if a demon or evil spirit gives trouble to any one 3
14 a demon is in love with her 3
15 do not worry about the demon 3
17 Then the demon will smell it and flee away 3
8: 3 when the demon smelled the odor 3
Bar 4: 7 by sacrificing to demons and not to God. 3
35 for a long time she will be inhabited by demons. 3
demon *See also* possessed.

demoniac 1.δαιμονίζομαι
Mat 4:24 with various diseases and pains, demoniacs 1
8:28 country of the Gadarenes, two demoniacs met him 1
33 what had happened to the demoniacs. 1
9:32 behold, a dumb demoniac was brought to him. 1
12:22 Then a blind and dumb demoniac was brought to him 1
Mrk 5:15 came to Jesus, and saw the demoniac sitting there 1
16 to the demoniac and to the swine. 1

demonic 1.δαιμόνιος
Rev 16:14 for they are demonic spirits, performing signs 1

demonstrate 1. ἀποδείκνυμι 2. ἐπιδείκνυμι

4Mc 1: 8 I can demonstrate it best 1
9 All of these . . demonstrated that . . 2
14:18 to demonstrate sympathy for children 2
16: 2 Thus I have demonstrated 1

demonstration 1. ἀπόδειξις 2. ἐπιδείκνυμι

1Co 2: 4 in demonstration of the Spirit and of power 1
4Mc 3:19 a narrative demonstration of temperate reason. 1
13:10 be cowardly in the demonstration of our piety. 2

den 1. מְאוּרָה 2. מִנְהָרָה 3. מָעוֹן 4. מְעֹנָה 5. מְעָרָה 6. גֹּב (A) 7. λάκκος 8. σπήλαιον

Jdg 6: 2 made . . the dens which are in the mountains 2
Job 37: 8 go into their lairs, and remain in their dens. 4
38:40 when they crouch in their dens, or lie in wait 4
Ps 104:22 get them away and lie down in their dens. 4
Sng 4: 8 Depart . . from the dens of lions 4
Isa 11: 8 weaned child . . put his hand on the adder's den. 1
32:14 hill and the watchtower . . become dens for ever 5
Jer 7:11 this house . . become a den of robbers in your eyes? 5
Dan 6: 7 to you, O king, shall be cast into the den of lions. 6
12 shall be cast into the den of lions? 6
16 brought and cast into the den of lions. 6
17 stone was . . laid upon the mouth of the den 6
19 king arose and went in haste to the den of lions. 6
20 When he came near to the den where Daniel was 6
23 commanded that Daniel be taken up out of the den. 6
23 Daniel was taken up out of the den, 6
24 den of lions–they, their children, and their wives; 6
24 before they reached the bottom of the den 6
Ams 3: 4 Does a young lion cry out from his den, 3
Nah 2:11 Where is the lions' den, the cave of the young lions 3
12 his cave with prey and his dens with torn flesh. 4
Mat 21:13 but you make it a den of robbers. 8
Mrk 11:17 you have made it a den of robbers. 8
Lke 19:46 you have made it a den of robbers. 8
Heb 11:38 in dens and caves of the earth. 8
Bel 1:31 They threw Daniel into the lions' den 7
32 There were seven lions in the den 7
34 to Babylon, to Daniel, in the lions' den. 7
35 I know nothing about the den. 7
36 and set him down in Babylon, right over the den 7
40 When he came to the den he looked in 7
42 and threw into the den the men 7
4Mc 18:13 He praised Daniel in the den of the lions 7

denarius 1. δηνάριον

Mat 18:28 fellow servants who owed him a 100 denarii 1
20: 2 for a denarius a day 1
9 each of them received a denarius. 1
10 each of them also received a denarius. 1
13 did you not agree with me for a denarius? 1
Mrk 6:37 we go and buy 200 denarii worth of bread 1
14: 5 ointment . . sold for more than 300 denarii 1
Lke 7:41 one owed 500 denarii, and the other 50. 1
10:35 the next day he took out two denarii 1
Joh 6: 7 200 denarii would not buy enough bread 1
12: 5 Why was this ointment not sold for 300 denarii 1
Rev 6: 6 A quart of wheat for a denarius 1
6 and three quarts of barley for a denarius 1

denounce 1. זעם 2. נגד 3. βλασφημέω 4. κακηγορέω 5. μηνύω 6. arguo

Num23: 7 Come, curse Jacob for me, and come, denounce Israel!' 1
8 can I denounce whom the LORD has not denounced? 1
8 can I denounce whom the LORD has not denounced? 1
Jer 20:10 Denounce him! Let us denounce him! 2
10 Denounce him! Let us denounce him! 2
1Co 10:30 why am I denounced 3
2Es 12:32 he will denounce them for their ungodliness 6
2Mc 14:37 was denounced to Nicanor 5
4Mc 9:14 he denounced the tyrant, saying 4

dense 1. כָּבֵד 2. כַּרְמֶל

Exd 10:14 such a dense swarm of locusts as had never been 1
2Kg 19:23 its farthest retreat, its densest forest. 2
Isa 37:24 I came to its remotest height, its densest forest 2

deny 1. כחד 2. כחש 3. מנע 4. αἴρω 5. ἀνθίστημι 6. ἀπαρνέομαι 7. ἀρνέομαι 8. εἶπον 9. abnego 10. nego

Gen 18:15 Sarah denied, saying, "I did not laugh"; 2
Job 6:10 for I have not denied the words of the Holy One. 1
8:18 destroyed from his place, then it will deny him 2
Prv 30: 7 Two things . . deny them not to me before I die 3
9 and deny thee, and say, "Who is the LORD? 2
Isa 59:13 transgressing, and denying the LORD 2
Mat 10:33 whoever denies me before men, I also will deny 7
33 whoever denies me before men, I also will deny 7
16:24 let him deny himself and take up his cross 6
26:34 you will deny me three times. 6
35 Even if I must die with you, I will not deny you. 6
70 he denied it before them all, saying 7
72 again he denied it with an oath 7
75 you will deny me three times 6
Mrk 8:34 let him deny himself and take up his cross 6
14:30 you will deny me three times. 6
31 If I must die with you, I will not deny you. 6
68 he denied it, saying, "I neither know 7
70 again he denied it 7
72 you will deny me three times 6
Lke 8:45 When all denied it, Peter said, "Master 7
9:23 let him deny himself and take up his cross daily 7
12: 9 he who denies me before men 7
9 will be denied before the angels of God. 6
22:34 until you three times deny that you know me. 6
57 he denied it, saying, "Woman, I do not know him. 7
61 you will deny me three times. 6
Joh 1:20 He confessed, he did not deny, but confessed 7
13:38 till you have denied me three times. 7
18:25 He denied it and said, "I am not. 7
27 Peter again denied it 7
Act 3:13 denied in the presence of Pilate 7
14 you denied the Holy and Righteous One 7
4:16 we cannot deny it. 7
8:33 In his humiliation justice was denied him 4
2Ti 2:12 if we deny him, he also will deny us; 7
12 if we deny him, he also will deny us; 7
13 for he cannot deny himself. 7
3: 5 denying the power of it 7
Tit 1:16 they deny him by their deeds 7
2Pe 2: 1 even denying the Master who bought them 7
1Jn 2:22 he who denies that Jesus is the Christ 7
22 he who denies the Father and the Son. 7
23 No one who denies the Son has the Father. 7
Jde 1: 4 and deny our only Master and Lord, Jesus Christ. 7
Rev 2:13 you hold fast my name and you did not deny my faith 7
3: 8 you have kept my word and have not denied my name 7
2Es 7:24 They scorned his law, and denied his covenants; 9
37 Look now, and understand whom you have denied 10
Jdt 8:28 there is no one who can deny your words. 5
Bel 1:24 You cannot deny that this is a living god 8
4Mc 6:34 It would be ridiculous to deny it. *

depart 1. גלה 2. הלך 3. יצא 4. מוש 5. נטה 6. נסע 7. נסע וְהלךְ 8. סור 9. שוב 10. שור 11. שלח 12. עדה (A) 13. ἀναζεύγνυμι 14. ἀναλύω 15. ἀναχωρέω 16. ἀπαίρω 17. ἄπειμι 18. ἀπέρχομαι 19. ἀπολύω 20. ἀποτρέχω 21. ἀποχωρέω 22. ἀφίστημι 23. διΐστημι 24. ἐκλύω 25. ἐκχωρέω 26. ἔξειμι 27. ἐξέρχομαι 28. ἔξοδος 29. μεταβαίνω 30. παραβαίνω 31. πορεύομαι 32. συνεξορμάω 33. χωρίζω 34. discedo 35. proficiscor 36. transfero 37. vado

Gen 12: 4 Abram was 75 years old when he departed 3
14:12 in Sodom, and his goods, and departed. 2
21:14 And she departed, and wandered in the wilderness 2
24:10 took ten of his master's camels and departed 2
26:17 Isaac departed from there, and encamped 2
31 and Isaac set them on their way, and they departed 2
31:55 then he departed and returned home. 2
35:18 as her soul was departing (for she died) 3
42:26 Then they loaded . . and departed. 2
45:24 sent his brothers away, and as they departed 2
49:10 The scepter shall not depart from Judah 8
Exd 8:11 The frogs shall depart from you and your houses 8
29 the swarms of flies may depart from Pharaoh 8
13:22 the pillar of fire by night did not depart 4
16: 1 after they had departed from the land of Egypt. 3
18:27 Then Moses let his father-in-law depart 11
33: 1 The LORD said to Moses, "Depart, go up hence 2
11 Joshua . . did not depart from the tent. 4
35:20 Israel departed from the presence of Moses. 3
Lev 13:58 anything of skin from which the disease departs 8
Num10:30 I will depart to my own land and to my kindred. 2
12: 9 anger of the LORD was kindled . . and he departed; 2
14:44 nor Moses, departed out of the camp. 4
16:26 Depart . . from the tents of these wicked men 8
22: 7 departed with the fees for divination 2
Deu 4: 9 take heed . . lest they depart from your heart 8
24: 1 sends her out . . and she departs out of his house 3
Jos 1: 8 book of the law shall not depart out of your mouth 4
2:21 Then she sent them away, and they departed; 2
22 They departed, and went into the hills 2
Jdg 6:18 Do not depart from here . . until I come to thee 4
9:55 was dead, they departed every man to his home. 2
11:38 and she departed . . and bewailed her virginity 2
17: 8 the man departed from . . Bethlehem . . to live 2
18: 7 the five men departed, and came to La'ish 2
21 they turned and departed, putting the little 2
19: 8 he arose early in the morning to depart; 2
9 the man . . rose up to depart, his father-in-law 2
10 he rose up and departed, and arrived opposite 2
21:24 the people of Israel departed from there 2
1Sm 4:21 The glory has departed from Israel! 1
22 And she said, "The glory has departed from Israel 1
6: 6 did not they let the people go, and they departed? 2
10: 2 When you depart from me . . you will meet two men 2
15: 6 Go, depart, go down from among the Amal'ekites 8
6 the Ken'ites departed from . . the Amal'ekites. 8
16:14 Now the Spirit of the LORD departed from Saul 8
23 Saul . . and the evil spirit departed from him. 8
18:12 the LORD was with him but had departed from Saul. 8
20:42 And he rose and departed; and Jonathan went 2
22: 1 David departed from there and escaped 2
5 depart, and go into the land of Judah. 2
5 David departed, and went into the forest 2
23:13 David and his . . arose and departed from Kei'lah 3
29:10 and depart as soon as you have light. 2
30:22 may lead away his wife and children, and depart. 2
2Sm 6:19 Then all the people departed, each to his house. 2
11:12 Remain . . and tomorrow I will let you depart. 11
12:10 the sword shall never depart from your house 8
19:24 from the day the king departed until . . he came 2
22:22 and have not wickedly departed from my God. *
1Kg 11:21 Let me depart, that I may go to my own country. 11
12: 5 Depart for three days, then come again to me. 2
16 So Israel departed to their tents. 2
14:17 Jerobo'am's wife arose, and departed 2
17: 3 Depart from here and turn eastward 2
19:19 So he departed from there, and found Eli'sha 2
20: 9 the messengers departed and brought him word 2
36 as soon as he had departed . . a lion met him 2
38 the prophet departed, and waited for the king 2
2Kg 3: 3 sin of Jerobo'am . . he did not depart from it. 8
5:24 and he sent the men away, and they departed. 2
8: 1 Arise, and depart with your household 2
14 he departed from Eli'sha, and came to his master 2
10:15 when he departed from there, he met Jehon'adab 2
13: 2 followed the sins . . he did not depart from them. 8
6 they did not depart from the sins of . . Jerobo'am 8
11 he did not depart from all the sins of Jerobo'am 8
14:24 he did not depart from all the sins of Jerobo'am 8
15: 9 He did not depart from the sins of Jerobo'am 8
18 he did not depart all his days from all the sins 8
28 he did not depart from the sins of Jerobo'am 8
17:22 all the sins . . they did not depart from them 8
18: 6 he did not depart from following him, but kept 8
19:36 Sennach'erib . . departed, and went home 7
1Ch 16:43 Then all the people departed each to his house 2
19: 5 and they departed. When David was told 2
21: 4 Jo'ab departed and went throughout all Israel 3
2Ch 10:16 So all Israel departed to their tents. 2
21:20 he departed with no one's regret. 2
24:25 When they had departed from him 2
35:15 did not need to depart from their service 8
Ezr 8:31 Then we departed from the river Aha'va 6
Neh 9:19 pillar of cloud . . not depart from them by day 8
Job 21:14 They say to God, 'Depart from us! 8
22:17 They said to God, 'Depart from us,' 8
23:12 I have not departed from the commandment 4
28:28 and to depart from evil is understanding.' 8
Ps 6: 8 Depart from me, all you workers of evil; 8
9:17 The wicked shall depart to Sheol 9
18:21 and have not wickedly departed from my God. *
34:14 Depart from evil, and do good; seek peace 8
37:27 Depart from evil, and do good; so shall you abide 8
39:13 I may know gladness, before I depart and be no more! 2
44:18 nor have our steps departed from thy way 5
55:11 and fraud do not depart from its market place. 4
105:38 Egypt was glad when they departed 3
119:115 Depart from me, you evildoers 8
139:19 O that . . men of blood would depart from me 8
146: 4 When his breath departs he returns to his earth; 3
Prv 5: 7 do not depart from the words of my mouth. 8
17:13 evil will not depart from his house. 4
22: 6 when he is old he will not depart from it. 8
27:22 yet his folly will not depart from him. 8
Sng 4: 8 Depart from the peak of Ama'na, from . . Senir 10
Isa 7:17 the day that E'phraim departed from Judah– 8
10:27 his burden will depart from your shoulder 8
11:13 The jealousy of E'phraim shall depart 8
14:25 and his yoke shall depart from them 8
37:37 Then Sennach'erib king of Assyria departed 7
38:10 I said, In the noontide of my days I must depart; 2
52:11 Depart, depart, go out thence 8
11 depart, go out thence, touch no unclean thing; 8
54:10 For the mountains may depart and the hills be 4
10 but my steadfast love shall not depart from you 4
59:15 he who departs from evil makes himself a prey. 8
21 my words . . shall not depart out of your mouth 4
Jer 29: 2 and the smiths had departed from Jerusalem. 3
31:36 If this fixed order departs from before me 4
Lam 1: 6 From . . Zion has departed all her majesty. 3
Ezk 6: 9 their wanton heart which has departed from me 8
16:42 and my jealousy shall depart from you; 8
Dan 4:31 kingdom has departed from you 12
Hos 9:12 Woe to them when I depart from them! 8
10: 5 over its glory which has departed from it. 1
Zec 10:11 the scepter of Egypt shall depart. 8
Mat 2:12 they departed to their own country by another 15
13 Now when they had departed, behold, an angel 15
14 his mother by night, and departed to Egypt 15
7:23 'I never knew you; depart from me, you evildoers.' 21
9:24 he said, "Depart; for the girl is not dead 15
10:11 and stay with him until you depart. 27
16: 4 So he left them and departed. 18
25:41 Depart from me, you cursed, into the eternal fire 31
27: 5 he departed; and he went and hanged himself. 15
60 stone to the door of the tomb, and departed. 18
28: 8 they departed quickly from the tomb with fear 18
Mrk 5:17 to beg Jesus to depart from their neighborhood. 18
8:13 he departed to the other side. 18

Lke 1:38 the angel departed from her. 18
2:29 now lettest thou thy servant depart in peace 19
37 She did not depart from the temple 22
4:13 he departed from him until an opportune time. 22
42 when it was day he departed 27
5: 8 Depart from me, for I am a sinful man, O Lord. 27
8:31 not to command them to depart into the abyss. 18
37 all the people . . asked him to depart from them; 18
9: 4 stay there, and from there depart. 27
6 they departed and went through the villages 27
10:30 robbers . . departed, leaving him half dead. 18
13:27 depart from me, all you workers of iniquity!' 22
21:21 let those who are inside the city depart 25
Joh 4: 3 he left Judea and departed again to Galilee. 18
43 After the two days he departed to Galilee. 27
12:36 he departed and hid himself from them. 18
13: 1 to depart out of this world to the Father 29
Act 1: 4 he charged them not to depart from Jerusalem 33
7: 3 Depart from your land and from your kindred 27
4 Then he departed from the land of the Chalde'ans 27
9:17 So Anani'as departed and entered the house. 18
10: 7 When the angel who spoke to him had departed 18
12:17 Then he departed and went to another place. 27
15:40 Paul chose Silas and departed 27
16:40 they exhorted them and departed. 27
17:15 they departed. 26
18:23 After spending some time there he departed 27
20: 1 took leave of them and departed for Macedo'nia. 27
7 intending to depart on the morrow 27
11 he conversed with them . . and so departed. 27
21: 5 we departed and went on our journey 27
8 On the morrow we departed and came to Caesare'a; 27
22:21 he said to me, 'Depart 31
28:25 they departed, after Paul had made one statement 19
Php 1:23 My desire is to depart and be with Christ 14
1Ti 4: 1 in later times some will depart from the faith 22
2Ti 2:19 depart from iniquity. 22
1Es 1:16 no one needed to depart from his duties 30
3: 3 when they were satisfied they departed 14
8:11 Let as many as are so disposed . . depart with you 32
61 We departed from the river Theras 13
2Es 2:39 who have departed from the shadow of this age 36
3:22 but what was good departed 34
5:19 Then I said to him, "Depart from me 37
8: 5 and against your will you depart 35
15:25 Depart, you faithless children! 34
Tob 3: 6 that I may depart and become dust 19
5:16 they both went out and departed 18
14: 3 I have grown old and am about to depart this life. 20
Jdt 5:18 departed from the way which he had appointed 22
13:19 will never depart from the hearts of men 22
Wis 10: 3 when an unrighteous man departed from her 22
16:14 he cannot bring back the departed spirit 27
19: 2 though they . . permitted thy people to depart 17
Sir 2: 3 Cleave to him and do not depart 22
10:12 pride is to depart from the Lord 22
38:23 be comforted for him when his spirit is departed. 28
Aza 1: 6 have sinfully and lawlessly departed from thee 22
Sus 1: 7 When the people departed at noon 20
Bel 1:14 Then they went out . . and departed. 18
1Mc 1:24 Taking them all, he departed to his own land 18
2:19 departing . . from the religion of his fathers 22
3:37 departed from Antioch his capital 16
40 so they departed with their entire force 16
4:35 he departed to Antioch and enlisted mercenaries 16
5:29 He departed from there at night 16
6: 4 So he fled and in great grief departed from there 16
10 Sleep departs from my eyes 22
57 So he quickly gave orders to depart 18
63 Then he departed with haste 16
7:19 Then Bacchides departed from Jerusalem 16
9:36 departed with it. 18
69 Then he decided to depart to his own land. 18
72 then he turned and departed to his own land 18
10:13 each left his place and departed to his own land. 18
86 Then Jonathan departed from there 16
11:61 From there he departed to Gaza 18
13:12 Then Trypho departed from Ptolemais 16
24 Trypho turned back and departed to his own land. 18
2Mc 2: 3 the law should not depart from their hearts. 22
12:12 they departed to their tents. 33
18 departed from the region 24
3Mc 2:32 did not depart from their religion 23
5:21 each departed to his own home. 14
44 the friends and officers departed with great joy 14
7:13 shouted the Hallelujah and joyfully departed. 14
20 they departed unharmed, free, and overjoyed 14

depart *See also* compell, rise.

departure 1. *ἀναζεύγνυμι* 2. *ἀνάλυσις* 3. *ἄφιξις* 4. *ἄφοδος* 5. *ἔξοδος*

Lke 9:31 who appeared in glory and spoke of his departure 5
Act 20:29 after my departure fierce wolves will come 3
2Ti 4: 6 the time of my departure has come. 2
2Pe 1:15 after my departure you may be able . . to recall 5
Wis 3: 2 their departure was thought to be an affliction 5
7: 6 one entrance into life, and a common departure. 5
3Mc 7:10 immediately hurry to make their departure 4
16 those . . began their departure from the city 1

depend 1. בטח 2. *εἰμί* 3. *ἐκ* 4. *ἐν* 5. *ἐπέχω* 6. *ἐπί* 7. *κρεμάννυμι* 8. *κρεμάω*

Job 39:11 you depend on him because his strength is great 1
Mat 22:40 On these two commandments depend all the law 7
Rom 4:16 That is why it depends on faith 3
9:16 So it depends not upon man's will or exertion •
Php 3: 9 righteousness from God that depends on faith •
Jdt 8:24 their lives depend upon us 8
Sir 5: 8 Do not depend on dishonest wealth 5
31:20 Healthy sleep depends on moderate eating 6
38:24 depends on the opportunity of leisure 4
1Mc 3:19 victory in battle depends 2

depend for food 1. *τρέφω*

Act 12:20 their country depended on the king's country for food. 1

depend upon 1. *ἐκ* 2. *ἐν*

Rom 12:18 so far as it depends upon you, live peaceably 1
Jdt 9:11 For thy power depends not upon numbers 2

dependable 1. *πιστός*

Sir 33: 3 the law is as dependable as . . Urim. 1

dependent 1. טַף 2. *ὑποχείριος* 3. *χρείαν ἔχω*

Gen 47:12 according to the number of their dependents. 1
1Th 4:12 be dependent on nobody. 3
Wis 14:15 and handed on to his dependents secret rites 2

depict

Wis 18:24 upon his long robe the whole world was depicted •

deploy 1. *τάσσω*

2Mc 15:20 the cavalry deployed on the flanks 1

deport 1. גלה 2. *μεταγίνομαι*

Ezr 4:10 Osnap'par deported and settled in the cities 1
2Mc 2: 1 those who were being deported 2
2 instructed those who were being deported 2

deportation 1. *μετοικεσία*

Mat 1:11 at the time of the deportation to Babylon. 1
12 after the deportation to Babylon: Jechoni'ah was 1
17 and from David to the deportation to Babylon 1
17 from the deportation to Babylon to the Christ 1

depose 1. סור 2. שׁבת 3. נחת (A) 4. *ἀποκαθίστημι* 5. *ἀφαιρέω* 6. *καθαιρέω* 7. *μεθίστημι*

2Kg 23: 5 And he deposed the idolatrous priests 2
2Ch 36: 3 Then the king of Egypt deposed him in Jerusalem 1
Dan 5:20 deposed from his kingly throne, 3
Act 19:27 she may even be deposed from her magnificence 6
1Es 1:35 Then the king of Egypt deposed him from reigning 4
LJr 1:34 They cannot set up a king or depose one. 5
1Mc 8:13 those whom they wish they depose 7

deposit 1. נוח 2. פִּקָּדוֹן 3. *θησαυρίζω* 4. *κεῖμαι* 5. *παρακαταθήκη* 6. *παρακατατίθημι* 7. *τίθημι*

Lev 6: 2 in a matter of deposit or security 2
4 return . . the deposit which was committed 2
Num 17: 4 Then you shall deposit them in the tent 1
7 Moses deposited the rods before the LORD 1
19: 9 deposit them outside the camp in a clean place; 1
1Es 6:23 royal archives that were deposited in Babylon. 4
1Mc 14:49 to deposit copies of them in the treasury 7
2Mc 3:10 some deposits belonging to widows and orphans 6
15 who had given the law about deposits 5
15 keep them safe for those who had deposited them. 6
4Mc 4: 3 there are deposited tens of thousands in private funds 3
7 committed deposits to the sacred treasury 6

deprave 1. אלח 2. *διαφθείρω*

Ps 53: 3 they are all alike depraved; 1
1Ti 6: 5 wrangling among men who are depraved in mind 2

depraved man 1. *παμπόνηρος*

2Mc 14:27 the false accusations of that depraved man 1

depress 1. *ἐν ταπεινώσει* 2. *στέλλω*

Jdt 7:32 they were greatly depressed in the city. 1
2Mc 6:12 not to be depressed by such calamities 2

deprive 1. חסר 2. נטה 3. סור 4. *ἀπό* 5. *ἀποστερέω* 6. *ἀπὸ τῆς ψυχῆς* 7. *ἀστοχέω* 8. *ἀφυστερέω* 9. *ἐστέρημαι* 10. *κενόω* 11. *μεθίστημι* 12. *στερέω* 13. alieno

Job 12:20 He deprives of speech those who are trusted 3
Prv 18: 5 not good . . to deprive a righteous man of justice. 2
Ecc 4: 8 For whom am I . . depriving myself of pleasure? 1
Isa 5:23 for a bribe, and deprive the innocent of his right! 3
32: 6 and to deprive the thirsty of drink. 1
1Co 9:15 I would rather die than have any one deprive me 10
2Es 10:30 and I was deprived of my understanding 13
AEs 16:12 he undertook to deprive us of our kingdom 12
Wis 18: 4 their enemies deserved to be deprived of light 12
Sir 4: 1 My son, deprive not the poor of his living 5
7:19 Do not deprive yourself of a wise and good wife 7
14: 4 Whoever accumulates by depriving himself 6
14 Do not deprive yourself of a happy day 8
28:15 deprived them of the fruit of their toil. 12
34:21 whoever deprives them of it is a man of blood. 5
22 to deprive an employee of his wages 5
Aza 1:21 deprived of all power and dominion 4
2Mc 3:29 deprived of any hope of recovery 9
13:10 who were on the point of being deprived of the law 12
3Mc 1:12 Even if those men are deprived of this honor 12
2:33 depriving them of common fellowship and . . help. 12
5:32 have been deprived of life instead of these 12
6:12 deprived of life in the manner of traitors. 11
24 you are now attempting to deprive of dominion 11
4Mc 4: 7 should be deprived of them 12
8:23 deprive ourselves of this delightful world? 5

depth 1. יַרְכָה 2. מֶחְקָר 3. מַעֲמַקִּים 4. מְצוֹלָה 5. עמק 6. עֹמֶק 7. תְּהוֹם 8. תַּחְתִּי 9. *βάθος* 10. *βαθύς* 11. *κατώτατος* 12. *πέλαγος* 13. abyssus 14. profundus

Exd 15: 5 they went down into the depths like a stone. 4
Deu 32:22 fire is kindled . . burns to the depths of Sheol 8
Neh 9:11 thou didst cast their pursuers into the depths 4
Ps 63: 9 shall go down into the depths of the earth; 8
68:22 I will bring them back from the depths of the sea 4
71:20 from the depths of the earth thou wilt bring me up 7
86:13 hast delivered my soul from the depths of Sheol. 8
88: 6 Thou hast put me in the depths of the Pit 8
95: 4 In his hand are the depths of the earth; 2
107:26 mounted up to heaven, they went down to the depths; 7
130: 1 Out of the depths I cry to thee, O LORD! 3
139:15 intricately wrought in the depths of the earth. 8
Prv 8:24 When there were no depths I was brought forth 7
9:18 that her guests are in the depths of Sheol. 6
25: 3 As the heaven for height, and the earth for depth 6
Isa 14:15 brought down to Sheol, to the depths of the Pit. 1
44:23 shout, O depths of the earth; 8
51:10 that didst make the depths of the sea a way 3
63:13 who led them through the depths? 7
Jer 49: 8 Flee, turn back, dwell in the depths, O inhabitants 5
30 Flee, wander far away, dwell in the depths 5
Lam 3:55 I called on thy name . . from the depths of the pit; 8
Ezk 27:34 wrecked by the seas, in the depths of the waters; 3
Mic 7:19 wilt cast all our sins into the depths of the sea. 4
Zec 10:11 smitten, and all the depths of the Nile dried up. 4
Mat 13: 5 since they had no depth of soil 9
18: 6 and to be drowned in the depth of the sea. 12
Mrk 4: 5 since it had no depth of soil; 9
Rom 8:39 nor height, nor depth, nor anything else 9
11:33 O the depth of the riches and wisdom 9
1Co 2:10 even the depths of God. 9
Eph 3:18 the breadth and length and height and depth 9
2Es 3:18 move the world, and make the depths to tremble 13
5:25 from all the depths of the sea thou hast filled 13
8:23 whose look dries up the depths 13
13:52 explore or know what is in the depths of the sea 14
16:12 the sea is churned up from the depths 14
Jdt 8:14 You cannot plumb the depths of the human heart 9
Wis 10:19 and cast them up from the depth of the sea. 9
Sir 24: 5 have walked in the depths of the abyss. 10
51: 5 from the depths of the belly of Hades 9
Man 1:13 do not condemn me to the depths of the earth 11
3Mc 2: 7 you overwhelmed him in the depths of the sea 10

depute

2Sm 15: 3 there is no man deputed by the king to hear you. •

deputy 1. נצב 2. סְגָן 3. *διάδοχος*

1Kg 22:47 There was no king in Edom; a deputy was king. 1
Jer 51:28 the Medes, with their governors and deputies 2
2Mc 4:29 as deputy in the high priesthood 3

deputy *See also* act.

derange 1. *διασκεδάννυμι*

3Mc 5:30 because . . his whole mind had been deranged 1

deride 1. הלל 2. ליץ 3. לעג 4. קָלַס 5. רְחַב פֶּה 6. *βλασφημέω* 7. *ἐμπαίζω* 8. *ἐπεγγελάω* 9. *καταγελάω* 10. *καταμωκάομαι* 11. *ὀνειδίζω* 12. *χλευάζω*

1Sm 2: 1 My mouth derides my enemies, because I rejoice 5
Neh 2:19 derided us and despised us and said, "What is this 3
Ps 79: 4 mocked and derided by those round about us. 4
102: 8 those who deride me use my name for a curse. 1
119:51 Godless men utterly deride me, but I do not turn 2
Mat 27:39 those who passed by derided him, 6
Mrk 15:29 those who passed by derided him 6
Sir 13: 7 and finally he will deride you 10
LJr 1:43 she derides the woman next to her 11
1Mc 7:34 he mocked them and derided them and defiled them 9
2Mc 7:27 deriding the cruel tyrant 12
8:17 the torture of the derided city 7
4Mc 5:27 you may deride us for eating defiling foods 8

derision 1. חִידָה 2. לַעַג 3. לעג 4. קֶלֶס 5. שְׂחֹק 6. *γέλως* 7. derisus

Ps 2: 4 laughs; the LORD has them in derision. 3

44:13 the derision and scorn of those about us. 2
Jer 20: 8 has become for me a . . derision all day long. 4
48:26 in his vomit, and he too shall be held in derision. 5
27 Was not Israel a derision to you? 5
39 Moab has become a derision and a horror to all 5
Ezk 36: 4 cities, which have become a prey and derision 2
Hos 7:16 shall be their derision in the land of Egypt. 2
Hab 2: 6 taunt against him, in scoffing derision of him 1
2Es 16:69 shall be held in derision and contempt 7
Wis 5: 4 This is the man whom we once held in derision 6

derision *See also* hold.

derive 1. ἔχω

Phm 1: 7 I have derived much joy and comfort from your love 1

descend 1. ילד 2. ירד 3. נָחַת 4. נחת 5. ἀπόγονος
6. γίνομαι ἐκ σπέρματος 7. ἐκ
8. ἐξέρχομαι ἐκ τῆς ὀσφύος 9. καταβαίνω
10. καταβάσιος 11. καταφέρω 12. σπέρμα
13. συγκαταβαίνω 14. nascor

Gen 28:12 angels . . were ascending and descending on it! 2
Exd 19:18 was wrapped in smoke, because the LORD descended 2
33: 9 the pillar of cloud would descend and stand 2
34: 5 the LORD descended in the cloud and stood 2
Deu 9:21 brook that descended out of the mountain. 2
2Sm 21:20 and he also was descended from the giants. 1
22 These four were descended from the giants 1
1Ch 20: 6 and he also was descended from the giants. 1
8 These were descended from the giants in Gath; 1
Job 17:16 Shall we descend together into the dust? 4
Ps 7:16 on his own pate his violence descends. 2
49:14 straight to the grave they descend •
Isa 30:30 and the descending blow of his arm to be seen 3
34: 5 behold, it descends for judgment upon Edom 2
Ezk 26:20 I will thrust you down with those who descend 2
Mat 3:16 saw the Spirit of God descending like a dove 9
28: 2 an angel of the Lord descended from heaven 9
Mrk 1:10 the Spirit descending upon him like a dove; 9
Lke 3:22 Holy Spirit descended upon him in bodily form 9
Joh 1:32 I saw the Spirit descend as a dove from heaven 9
33 'He on whom you see the Spirit descend and remain 9
51 the angels of God ascending and descending 9
3:13 but he who descended from heaven, the Son of man. 9
7:42 the Christ is descended from David 12
Act 10:11 saw the heaven opened, and something descending 9
11: 5 in a trance I saw a vision, something descending 9
Rom 1: 3 descended from David according to the flesh 6
9: 6 For not all who are descended from Israel •
10: 7 or "Who will descend into the abyss? 9
Eph 4: 9 descended into the lower parts of the earth? 9
10 He who descended is he who also ascended 9
1Th 4:16 For the Lord himself will descend from heaven 9
2Ti 2: 8 descended from David, as preached in my gospel 12
Heb 7: 5 though these also are descended from Abraham. 8
14 evident that our Lord was descended from Judah 7
2Es 3:11 all the righteous who have descended from him. •
21 as were also all who were descended from him. 14
6:56 other nations which have descended from Adam 14
Jdt 5: 6 This people is descended from the Chaldeans. 5
Wis 10: 6 the fire that descended on the Five Cities. 10
13 She descended with him into the dungeon 13
3Mc 6:18 angels of fearful aspect descended 9
4Mc 16:20 wielding a sword and descending upon him 11

make descend 1. ירד

Lam 1:13 he sent fire; into my bones he made it descend; 1

descendant 1. בֵּן 2. דּוֹר 3. זֶרַע 4. יָלִיד 5. נֶכֶד
6. צֶאֱצָא מֵעָה 7. תּוֹלֵדוֹת 8. ἀπό 9. αὐτός 10. γενεά
11. γεννάω 12. γένος 13. γηγενής 14. ἔκγονος
15. καρπός τῆς ὀσφύος 16. σπέρμα 17. υἱός
18. υἱὸς τοῦ γένους 19. advenio 20. generatio 21. natus
22. semen

Gen 9: 9 with you and your descendants after you 3
11:10 These are the descendants of Shem. 7
27 Now these are the descendants of Terah. 7
12: 7 To your descendants I will give this land. 3
13:15 you see I will give to you and to your descendants 3
16 I will make your descendants as the dust 3
16 the earth, your descendants also can be counted. 3
15: 5 Then he said to him, "So shall your descendants be. 3
13 Know of a surety that your descendants will be 3
18 To your descendants I give this land 3
16:10 I will so greatly multiply your descendants 3
17: 7 between me and you and your descendants 3
7 to you and to your descendants after you. 3
8 and to your descendants after you 3
9 covenant, you and your descendants after you 3
10 me and you and your descendants after you 3
19 everlasting covenant for his descendants 3
21:12 through Isaac shall your descendants be named. 3
22:17 I will multiply your descendants as the stars 3
17 your descendants shall possess the gate 3
18 by your descendants shall all the nations 3
24: 7 To your descendants I will give this land,' 3
60 may your descendants possess the gate of those 3
25:12 These are the descendants of Ish'mael 7
19 the descendants of Isaac, Abraham's son 7
26: 3 to you and to your descendants I will give 3
4 I will multiply your descendants as the stars 3
4 will give to your descendants all these lands; 3
4 lands; and by your descendants all the nations 3
24 will bless you and multiply your descendants 3
28: 4 blessing . . to you and to your descendants 3
13 land . . I will give to you and to your descendants; 3
14 descendants shall be like the dust of the earth 3
14 by you and your descendants shall all 3
32:12 I will do you good, and make your descendants 3
35:12 the land to your descendants after you. 3
36: 1 These are the descendants of Esau (that is, Edom) 7
9 These are the descendants of Esau the father 7
46: 8 the names of the descendants of Israel, who came 7
48: 4 this land to your descendants after you 3
19 and his descendants shall become a multitude 3
Exd 1: 7 the descendants of Israel were fruitful 1
28:43 statute for him and for his descendants 3
30:21 to him and to his descendants throughout 3
32:13 I will multiply your descendants as the stars 3
13 this land . . I will give to your descendants 3
33: 1 saying, 'To your descendants I will give it.' 3
Lev 21:17 None of your descendants . . may approach 3
21 no man of the descendants of Aaron the priest 3
22: 3 your descendants throughout your generations 3
Num 9:10 If any man of you or of your descendants 2
13:22 Ahi'man . . and Talmai, the descendants of Anak 4
28 besides, we saw the descendants of Anak there. 4
14:24 his descendants shall possess it. 3
16:40 no one who . . is not of the descendants of Aaron 3
25:13 shall be to him, and to his descendants after him 3
Deu 1: 8 give to them and to their descendants after them.' 3
4:37 loved your fathers and chose their descendants 3
10:15 LORD . . chose their descendants after them 3
11: 9 to give to them and to their descendants, a land 3
23: 2 none of his descendants shall enter •
28:46 upon you . . and upon your descendants for ever. 3
30:19 life, that you and your descendants may live 3
31:21 unforgotten in the mouths of their descendants); 3
34: 4 swore . . 'I will give it to your descendants.' 3
Jos 15:14 Caleb drove out . . the descendants of Anak. 4
16: 1 The allotment of the descendants of Joseph went 1
17: 2 these were the male descendants of Manas'seh 1
21: 4 those Levites who were descendants of Aaron 1
10 cities . . which went to the descendants of Aaron 1
13 to the descendants of Aaron . . they gave Hebron 1
19 cities of the descendants of Aaron, the priests 1
22:28 If this should be said to us or to our descendants 2
24:32 an inheritance of the descendants of Joseph. 1
Jdg 1:16 the descendants of the Ken'ite, Moses' 1
4:11 the Ken'ites, the descendants of Hobab 1
Rut 4:18 Now these are the descendants of Perez 7
1Sm 20:42 between my descendants and your descendants 3
42 between my descendants and your descendants 3
24:21 Swear . . that you will not cut off my descendants 3
2Sm 21:16 Ish'bi-be'nob, one of the descendants of the giants 4
18 Saph . . was one of the descendants of the giants. 4
22:51 steadfast love . . to David, and his descendants 3
1Kg 2:33 head of Jo'ab and upon the head of his descendants 3
33 to David, and to his descendants, and to his house 3
9:21 their descendants who were left after them 1
11:39 I will for this afflict the descendants of David 3
2Kg 5:27 cleave to you, and to your descendants for ever. 3
17:20 the LORD rejected all the descendants of Israel 3
1Ch 1:33 All these were the descendants of Ketu'rah. 1
2:23 All these were the descendants of Machir, the father 1
33 These were the descendants of Jerah'meel. 1
50 These were the descendants of Caleb. 1
3:10 descendants of Solomon: Rehobo'am, Abi'jah his son 1
16 descendants of Jehoi'akim: Jeconi'ah his son 1
20: 4 who was one of the descendants of the giants; 4
27: 3 He was a descendant of Perez 1
2Ch 8: 8 from their descendants who were left after them 1
20: 7 give it for ever to the descendants of Abraham 3
Neh 9: 8 covenant to give to his descendants the land 3
23 multiply their descendants as the stars 1
24 descendants went in and possessed the land 1
11: 3 descendants of Solomon's servants. 1
Est 9:27 took it upon themselves and their descendants 3
28 nor should . . cease among their descendants. 3
31 had laid down for . . their descendants 3
Job 5:25 know also that your descendants shall be many 3
18:19 has no offspring or descendant among his people 5
Ps 18:50 to David and his descendants for ever. 3
89: 4 I will establish your descendants for ever 3
106:27 disperse their descendants among the nations 3
112: 2 His descendants will be mighty in the land; 3
Isa 14:20 May the descendants of evildoers nevermore be 3
44: 3 I will pour my Spirit upon your descendants 3
48:19 the sand, and your descendants like its grains; 6
54: 3 and your descendants will possess the nations 3
61: 9 Their descendants shall be known among 3
65: 9 I will bring forth descendants from Jacob 3
66:22 shall your descendants and your name remain. 3
Jer 23: 8 and led the descendants of the house of Israel 3
29:32 punish Shemai'ah of Nehel'am and his descendants; 3
31:36 then shall the descendants of Israel cease 3
37 I will cast off all the descendants of Israel 3
33:22 I will multiply the descendants of David 3
26 then I will reject the descendants of Jacob 3
26 will not choose one of his descendants to rule 3
Joh 8:33 "We are descendants of Abraham 16
37 I know that you are descendants of Abraham 16
Act 2:30 set one of his descendants upon his throne 15
Rom 4:13 The promise to Abraham and his descendants 16
16 and be guaranteed to all his descendants- 16
18 So shall your descendants be. 16
9: 7 of Abraham because they are his descendants; 16
7 Through Isaac shall your descendants be named. 16
8 of the promise are reckoned as descendants. 16
11: 1 I myself am an Israelite, a descendant of Abraham 16
2Co 11:22 Are they descendants of Abraham? So am I. 16
Heb 2:16 concerned . . with the descendants of Abraham. 16
7: 5 those descendants of Levi 17
11:12 from one man . . were born descendants •
18 Through Isaac shall your descendants be named. 16
2Es 3: 7 for him and for his descendants 21
15 thou wouldst never forsake his descendants 22
17 thou didst lead his descendants out of Egypt 22
19 to give the law to the descendants of Jacob 22
26 as Adam and all his descendants had done 20
7:118 but ours also who are your descendants. 19
9:30 and give heed to my words, O descendants of Jacob. 22
Tob 1: 1 of the descendants of Asiel 16
4:12 from among the descendants of your fathers 16
Jdt 8:32 through all generations of our descendants. 18
Wis 7: 1 a descendant of the first-formed child of earth; 13
Sir 1:15 among their descendants she will be trusted. 16
4:16 descendants will remain in possession of her. 10
44:11 prosperity will remain with their descendants 16
12 Their descendants stand by the covenants 16
45: 1 From his descendants the Lord brought forth 9
13 his sons and his descendants perpetually. 14
15 for his descendants all the days of heaven 16
21 which he gave to him and his descendants. 16
24 he and his descendants 16
25 so the heritage of Aaron is for his descendants. 16
47:22 never blot out the descendants of his chosen one 14
Bar 2:15 his descendants are called by thy name. 12
Aza 1:13 to make their descendants as many as the stars 16
1Mc 5: 2 to destroy the descendants of Jacob 12
2Mc 1:20 sent the descendants of the priests 14
7:17 will torture you and your descendants! 16
3Mc 6: 3 look upon the descendants of Abraham, O Father 16
36 for their descendants 10
4Mc 7:12 the descendant of Aaron, Eleazar †
13:19 bequeathed . . to their descendants 11
17: 6 children were true descendants of father Abraham. 8

descent 1. זֶרַע 2. מוֹרָד 3. κατάβασις

Jos 7: 5 and chased them . . and slew them at the descent. 2
8:14 went out early to the descent toward the Arabah •
Ezr 2:59 not prove their fathers' houses or their descent 1
Neh 7:61 but they could not prove . . nor their descent 1
Jer 48: 5 at the descent of Horona'im they have heard 2
Lke 19:37 at the descent of the Mount of Olives 3
Sir 43:17 its descent is like locusts alighting. 3
46: 6 at the descent of Beth-horon 3
1Mc 3:24 They pursued them down the descent of Beth-horon 3

bodily descent 1. σάρκινος

Heb 7:16 a legal requirement concerning bodily descent 1

foreign descent 1. עֵרֶב

Neh 13: 3 separated . . all those of foreign descent. 1

describe 1. חוג 2. כתב 3. נגד 4. ἀπαγγέλλω
5. γράφω 6. διηγέομαι 7. ἐκδιηγέομαι
8. κατὰ τὰ ῥήματα ταῦτα 9. dico

Jos 18: 6 you shall describe the land in seven divisions 2
Job 26:10 He has described a circle upon the face 1
Ezk 43:10 describe to the house of Israel the temple 3
Act 8:33 Who can describe his generation? 6
12:17 he described to them 6
Rev 22:18 add to him the plagues described in this book 5
19 the holy city, which are described in this book. 5
2Es 7:100 to see what you have described to me? 9
Jdt 7:28 the things which we have described! 8
14: 8 Then Judith described . . all that she had done 4
Sir 43:31 Who has seen him and can describe him? 7

describe *See also* hard.

description

Jos 18: 4 writing a description of it with a view to their •
6 describe . . and bring the description here to me; •
8 who went to write the description of the land •
8 Go up and down and write a description of the land •
9 the land and set down in a book a description of it •

desecrate 1. חלל 2. ὀνειδισμός

Ps 74: 7 they desecrated the dwelling place of thy name. 1
Jdt 4:12 the sanctuary to be profaned and desecrated 2

desecration *See* penalty.

desert 1. נפל 2. עזב 3. פרד 4. שלח
5. ἀπαυτομολέω 6. αὐτομολέω 7. ἀφίημι

8. ἀφίστημι 9. ἐγκαταλείπω 10. καταλείπω
11. μετατίθημι
1Sm 29: 3 and since he deserted to me I have found no fault 1
2Kg 25:11 and the deserters who had deserted to . . Babylon 1
1Ch 12:19 Some of the men of Manas'seh deserted to David 1
19 he will desert to his master Saul. 1
20 to Ziklag these men of Manas'seh deserted to him 1
2Ch 15: 9 great numbers had deserted to him from Israel 1
Prv 19: 4 but a poor man is deserted by his friend. 3
Isa 7:16 the land . . will be deserted. 2
17: 2 Her cities will be deserted for ever; 2
9 deserted places . . which they deserted 2
27:10 a habitation deserted and forsaken 4
32:14 will be forsaken, the populous city deserted; 2
Jer 37:13 saying, "You are deserting to the Chalde'ans. 1
14 And Jeremiah said, "It is false; I am not deserting 1
38:19 I am afraid of the Jews who have deserted 1
39: 9 those who had deserted to him 1
52:15 who had deserted to the king of Babylon 1
Ezk 36: 4 the desolate wastes and the deserted cities 2
Zep 2: 4 For Gaza shall be deserted 2
Zec 11:17 to my worthless shepherd, who deserts the flock! 2
Gal 1: 6 astonished that you are so quickly deserting 11
2Ti 4:10 has deserted me and gone to Thessaloni'ca; 9
16 all deserted me 9
Tob 1: 4 deserted the house of Jerusalem. 8
Wis 10:13 wisdom did not desert him 9
1Mc 2:21 to desert the law and the ordinances. 10
7:19 seized many of the men who had deserted to him 6
24 took vengeance on the men who had deserted 6
9:24 the country deserted with them to the enemy. 6
15:12 his troops had deserted him. 7
4Mc 12:16 not desert the excellent example of my brothers 5

desert (2) 1. חָרְבָּה 2. יְשִׁימוֹן 3. מִדְבָּר 4. עֲרָבָה
5. צִיָּה 6. ἐρημία 7. ἔρημος 8. desertum
Num21:20 top of Pisgah which looks down upon the desert. 2
23:28 to the top of Pe'or, that overlooks the desert. 2
Deu 32:10 He found him in a desert land, and in the howling 3
1Ch 5: 9 to the east as far as the entrance of the desert 3
Job 24: 5 asses in the desert they go forth to their toil 3
38:26 on the desert in which there is no man; 3
Ps 78:17 rebelling against the Most High in the desert. 5
40 in the wilderness and grieved him in the desert! 2
105:41 flowed through the desert like a river. 5
106: 9 he led them through the deep as through a desert. 3
14 put God to the test in the desert; 2
107:33 He turns rivers into a desert 3
35 He turns a desert into pools of water 3
Prv 21:19 It is better to live in a desert land 3
Isa 14:17 who made the world like a desert 3
16: 1 sent lambs . . from Sela, by way of the desert 3
8 its branches, which . . strayed to the desert; 3
21: 1 it comes from the desert, from a terrible land. 3
33: 9 Sharon is like a desert; 4
35: 1 the desert shall rejoice and blossom; 4
6 in the wilderness, and streams in the desert; 4
40: 3 make straight in the desert a highway for our God. 4
41:19 I will set in the desert the cypress 4
42:11 Let the desert and its cities lift up their voice 3
43:19 a way in the wilderness and rivers in the desert. 2
20 water in the wilderness, rivers in the desert 2
48:21 thirsted not when he led them through . . deserts; 1
50: 2 I dry up the sea, I make the rivers a desert; 3
51: 3 like Eden, her desert like the garden of the LORD; 4
63:13 Like a horse in the desert, they did not stumble. 3
Jer 2: 6 in the wilderness, in a land of deserts and pits 4
4:11 A hot wind from the bare heights in the desert 3
26 I looked, and lo, the fruitful land was a desert 3
5: 6 a wolf from the desert shall destroy them. 4
9: 2 O that I had in the desert a wayfarers' lodging 3
26 all who dwell in the desert that cut the corners 3
12:12 in the desert destroyers have come; 3
13:24 chaff driven by the wind from the desert. 3
17: 6 He is like a shrub in the desert 4
22: 6 yet surely I will make you a desert 3
25:24 the mixed tribes that dwell in the desert; 3
48: 6 Save yourselves! Be like a wild ass in the desert! 3
50:12 last of the nations, a wilderness dry and desert. 4
51:43 become a horror, a land of drought and a desert 4
Zep 2:13 a desolation, a dry waste like the desert. 3
Mal 1: 3 and left his heritage to jackals of the desert. 3
Mat 15:33 Where are we to get bread enough in the desert 6
Mrk 8: 4 feed these men with bread here in the desert? 6
Lke 8:29 was driven by the demon into the desert.) 7
Act 8:26 This is a desert road. 7
Heb 11:38 wandering over deserts and mountains 6
2Es 7:106 and Moses for our fathers who sinned in the desert 8
16:60 who has put springs of water in the desert 8
Jdt 2:23 the Ishmaelites who lived along the desert 7
Wis 5: 7 we journeyed through trackless deserts 7
18:20 a plague came upon the multitude in the desert 7
1Mc 1:39 Her sanctuary became desolate as a desert 7
4Mc 18: 8 No seducer corrupted me on a desert plain 6

desert (3) 1. גְּמוּל
Ps 94: 2 render to the proud their deserts! 1
desert *See* waste.

desert in panic 1. חתת
Isa 31: 9 and his officers desert the standard in panic 1
deserted *See* section.

deserted place 1. עֲזוּבָה
Isa 17: 9 cities will be like the deserted places 1

deserter 1. נפל
2Kg 25:11 and the deserters who had deserted to . . Babylon 1
Jer 52:15 the deserters who had deserted to the king 1

deserve 1. בֵּן 2. גְּמוּל 3. מִשְׁפָּט 4. αἰτία 5. αἴτιος
6. ἀξία 7. ἄξιος 8. ἄξιος εἰμί 9. ἀξιόω 10. δικαιόω
11. ἐν 12. ἔνοχος 13. κατά 14. κατάξιος 15. ὀφείλω
Deu 19: 6 mortally, though the man did not deserve to die 3
25: 2 then if the guilty man deserves to be beaten 1
Jdg 9:16 house, and have done to him as his deeds deserved- 2
1Kg 2:26 Go to . . your estate; for you deserve death. But I •
Ezr 9:13 punished us less than our iniquities deserved •
Job 11: 6 God exacts of you less than your guilt deserves. •
Jer 26:11 This man deserves the sentence of death •
16 This man does not deserve the sentence of death •
49:12 If those who did not deserve to drink the cup 3
Ezk 31:11 surely deal with it as its wickedness deserves. •
Mat 10:10 for the laborer deserves his food. 7
26:66 They answered, "He deserves death. 12
Mrk 14:64 they all condemned him as deserving death. 12
Lke 10: 7 the laborer deserves his wages 7
12:48 who did not know, and did what deserved a beating 7
23:15 nothing deserving death has been done by him; 7
22 I have found in him no crime deserving death 5
Act 13:28 could charge him with nothing deserving death 4
23:29 charged with nothing deserving death 7
25:11 committed anything for which I deserve to die 7
25 I found that he had done nothing deserving death; 7
26:31 This man is doing nothing to deserve death 7
Rom 1:32 that those who do such things deserve to die 8
1Ti 5:18 The laborer deserves his wages. 7
Heb 10:29 How much worse . . do you think will be deserved 9
Rev 2:23 I will give to each of you as your works deserve. 13
Tob 12: 4 The old man said, "He deserves it. 10
AEs 16:18 inflicted on him the punishment he deserved. 14
Wis 3:10 be punished as their reasoning deserves 13
12:15 condemn him who does not deserve to be punished. 15
20 those deserving of death 15
26 will experience the deserved judgment of God. 6
16: 9 they deserved to be punished by such things; 7
18: 4 their enemies deserved to be deprived of light 7
19: 4 the fate they deserved drew them on to this end 6
Sir 8: 5 remember that we all deserve punishment. 11
2Mc 4:38 repaid him with the punishment he deserved. 6
15:21 he gains the victory for those who deserve it. 7
3Mc 7:10 should receive the punishment they deserved. 15
4Mc 4:12 he had committed a sin deserving of death 7
11: 6 these deeds deserve honors, not tortures. 6

deserve to die 1. בֶּן מָוֶת
1Sm 26:16 deserve to die, because you have not kept watch 1
2Sm 12: 5 the man who has done this deserves to die; 1

deservedly 1. ἀξίως 2. αὐτάρκης
Wis 16: 1 deservedly punished through such creatures 1
4Mc 9: 9 will deservedly undergo . . eternal torment 2

design 1. מַחֲשָׁבָה 2. מַעֲשֶׂה 3. עֵצָה 4. βούλημα
5. διανοέω 6. ἐπιβάλλω 7. ἐπίνοια 8. λογισμός
9. νόημα 10. πρός
Exd 31: 4 to devise artistic designs, to work in gold 1
39: 3 into the fine twined linen, in skilled design. 2
2Ch 2:14 and to do . . engraving and execute any design 1
Job 10: 3 favor the designs of the wicked? 3
2Co 2:11 for we are not ignorant of his designs. 9
Jdt 9: 5 thou hast designed the things that are now 5
Wis 9:14 our designs are likely to fail 7
1Mc 11: 8 he kept devising evil designs against Alexander. 8
2Mc 6:12 these punishments were designed not to destroy 10
15: 5 in carrying out his abominable design. 4
3Mc 1:16 to avert the violence of this evil design 6
4Mc 9:30 the arrogant design of your tyranny 8
17: 2 frustrated his evil designs 7

artistic design 1. מַחֲשָׁבָה
Exd 35:32 to devise artistic designs, to work in gold 1

evil design 1. רָעָה
Est 8: 3 besought him . . to avert the evil design of Haman 1

designate 1. יעד 2. נקב 3. λέγω 4. ὁρίζω
5. προγράφω 6. προσαγορεύω
Exd 21: 8 her master, who has designated her for himself 1
9 If he designates her for his son, he shall deal 1
Jos 20: 9 cities designated for all the people of Israel 1
2Ch 31:19 men . . designated by name to distribute 2
Ezr 10:16 heads . . each of them designated by name. •
Rom 1: 4 designated Son of God in power 4
Heb 5:10 being designated by God a high priest 6
Jde 1: 4 were designated for this condemnation 5
2Mc 4: 2 He dared to designate as a plotter 3

designer 1. חשב
Exd 35:35 work done by a craftsman or by a designer 1
35 by any sort of workman or skilled designer. 1
38:23 a craftsman and designer and embroiderer 1

desirable 1. חֶמֶד 2. חֶמְדָּה 3. מַחְמַד 4. ἐπιθυμητός
5. desiderabilis
1Sm 9:20 And for whom is all that is desirable in Israel? 2
Sng 5:16 His speech is . . and he is altogether desirable. 3
Ezk 23: 6 desirable young men, horsemen riding on horses. 1
12 on horses, all of them desirable young men. 1
23 the Assyrians with them, desirable young men 1
2Es 7:57 which things are precious and desirable 5
Wis 8: 5 If riches are a desirable possession in life 4
desirable *See also* goods.

more desirable 1. ποθεινός
4Mc 15: 1 more desirable to the mother than her children! 1

desire 1. אֲבִיּוֹנָה 2. אוה 3. אמר 4. בחר 5. בקשׁ
6. דָּבָר 7. חמד 8. חָפֵץ 9. חֵפֶץ 10. חפץ 11. חֵשֶׁק
12. חשק 13. מַאֲוַי 14. מוֹרָשׁ 15. מַחְמָל 16. מַשָּׂא
17. מִשְׁאָלָה 18. נֶפֶשׁ 19. נשׂא נֶפֶשׁ 20. רָצוֹן 21. שׁאל
22. תַּאֲוָה 23. תִּקְוָה 24. תְּשׁוּקָה 25. ἀξιόω
26. βουλεύω 27. βουλή 28. βούλομαι 29. ἐθέλω
30. ἐπιθυμέω 31. ἐπιθυμητής 32. ἐπιθυμητός
33. ἐπιθυμία 34. ἐπιποθέω 35. εὐδοκία 36. ζητέω
37. θέλημα 38. θέλησις 39. θέλω 40. κατεπίθυμος
41. ὀρέγω 42. ὄρεξις 43. ποθέω 44. προαιρέω
45. πρόθυμος 46. concupisco 47. desidero 48. opto
49. volo
Gen 3: 6 the tree was to be desired to make one wise 7
16 yet your desire shall be for your husband 24
4: 7 sin is couching at the door; its desire is for you 24
Exd 10:11 serve the LORD, for that is what you desire. 5
15: 9 my desire shall have its fill of them. 18
34:24 neither shall any man desire your land, when you 7
Deu 5:21 not desire your neighbor's house, his field 2
12:15 slaughter and eat . . as much as you desire 2
20 you may eat as much flesh as you desire. 2
21 may eat within your towns as much as you desire. 2
14:26 spend the money for whatever you desire, oxen 2
18: 6 Levite comes . . -and he may come when he desires- 2
16 just as you desired of the LORD your God at Horeb 21
21:11 see . . a beautiful woman, and you desire for her 12
1Sm 18:25 The king desires no marriage present except 10
23:20 according to all your heart's desire to come down 2
2Sm 3:21 you may reign over all that your heart desires. 2
19:38 and all that you desire of me I will do for you. 4
23: 5 cause to prosper all my help and my desire? 9
1Kg 1:16 and the king said, "What do you desire? •
5: 8 I am ready to do all you desire in the matter 9
10 the timber of cedar and cypress that he desired 9
9: 1 finished . . all that Solomon desired to build 10
11 timber and gold, as much as he desired 9
19 to build . . whatever Solomon desired to build 11
10:13 gave to the queen of Sheba all that she desired 9
11:37 you shall reign over all that your soul desires 2
2Ch 8: 6 whatever Solomon desired to build in Jerusalem 11
9:12 gave to the queen of Sheba all that she desired 9
15:15 had sought him with their whole desire 20
Est 1: 8 had given orders . . to do as every man desired. 20
2:13 she was given whatever she desired to take 3
5: 5 Bring Haman . . that we may do as Esther desires. 6
Job 6: 8 and that God would grant my desire; 23
13: 3 I desire to argue my case with God. 10
17:11 my plans are broken off, the desires of my heart. 14
21:14 We do not desire the knowledge of thy ways. 10
23:13 who can turn him? What he desires, that he does. 2
31:16 I have withheld anything that the poor desired 9
33:32 answer me; speak, for I desire to justify you. 10
Ps 10: 3 For the wicked boasts of the desires of his heart 22
17 O LORD, thou wilt hear the desire of the meek; 22
19:10 More to be desired are they than gold 7
20: 4 May he grant you your heart's desire •
21: 2 Thou hast given him his heart's desire 22
34:12 What man is there who desires life 8
35:27 those who desire my vindication shout for joy 8
37: 4 he will give you the desires of your heart. 17
40: 6 Sacrifice and offering thou dost not desire; 10
14 let them be turned back . . who desire my hurt! 8
45:11 the king will desire your beauty. 2
51: 6 Behold, thou desirest truth in the inward being; 10
68:16 at the mount which God desired for his abode 7
70: 2 brought to dishonor who desire my hurt! 8
73:25 nothing upon earth that I desire besides thee. 10
107:30 brought them to their desired haven. 9
112: 8 until he sees his desire on his adversaries. •
10 desire of the wicked man comes to nought. 22
132:13 chosen Zion; he has desired it for his habitation 2
14 here I will dwell, for I have desired it. 2
140: 8 Grant not, O LORD, the desires of the wicked; 13
145:16 satisfiest the desire of every living thing. 20
19 He fulfils the desire of all who fear him 20

Prv 3:15 nothing you desire can compare with her. 9
6:25 Do not desire her beauty in your heart 7
8:11 all that you may desire cannot compare with her. 9
10:24 but the desire of the righteous will be granted. 22
11:23 desire of the righteous ends only in good; 22
13: 2 desire of the treacherous is for violence. 18
12 but a desire fulfilled is a tree of life. 22
19 A desire fulfilled is sweet to the soul; 22
19:22 What is desired in a man is loyalty 22
21:10 The soul of the wicked desires evil; 2
25 The desire of the sluggard kills him 22
23: 3 Do not desire his delicacies 2
6 man who is stingy; do not desire his delicacies; 2
24: 1 not envious of evil men, nor desire to be with them; 2
31: 4 it is not . . for rulers to desire strong drink; •
Ecc 2:10 whatever my eyes desired I did not keep from them; 21
6: 2 that he lacks nothing of all that he desires 2
9 Better is . . than the wandering of desire; 18
12: 5 grasshopper drags itself along and desire fails; 1
Sng 7:10 I am my beloved's, and his desire is for me. 24
Isa 26: 8 thy memorial name is the desire of our soul. 22
53: 2 and no beauty that we should desire him. 7
58:10 and satisfy the desire of the afflicted 18
11 and satisfy your desire with good things 18
Jer 17:16 nor have I desired the day of disaster 2
34:16 whom you had set free according to their desire 18
42:22 in the place where you desire to go to live. 10
44:14 Judah, to which they desire to return to dwell 19
50:19 and his desire shall be satisfied on the hills 18
Ezk 24:21 delight of your eyes, and the desire of your soul; 15
25 delight of their eyes and their heart's desire 16
Dan 7:19 desired to know the truth concerning the fourth •
Hos 6: 6 For I desire steadfast love and not sacrifice 10
Ams 5:18 Woe to you who desire the day of the LORD! 2
Mic 7: 1 no first-ripe fig which my soul desires. 2
Mal 2:15 what does he desire? Godly offspring. 5
Mat 9:13 Go and learn what this means, 'I desire mercy 39
12: 7 'I desire mercy, and not sacrifice,' 39
15:28 Be it done for you as you desire. 29
27:43 let God deliver him now, if he desires him 39
Mrk 3:13 called to him those whom he desired 39
4:19 and the desire for other things 33
Lke 5:39 no one after drinking old wine desires new 39
8:20 standing outside, desiring to see you. 39
10:24 many prophets and kings desired to see 29
29 he, desiring to justify himself, said to Jesus 29
14:28 desiring to build a tower 29
16:21 who desired to be fed 30
17:22 will desire to see one of the days of the Son of man 30
22:15 I have earnestly desired to eat this passover 30
23: 8 he had long desired to see him 29
20 desiring to release Jesus; 29
Joh 8:44 your will is to do your father's desires 33
17:24 Father, I desire that they also . . may be with me 39
Act 10:10 he became hungry and desired something to eat; 39
22:30 desiring to know . . why the Jews accused him 28
23:28 desiring to know the charge 28
24:27 desiring to do the Jews a favor 29
28:22 we desire to hear from you what your views are 25
Rom 9:22 What if God, desiring to show his wrath 29
10: 1 Brethren, my heart's desire and prayer to God 35
13:14 make no provision for the flesh, to gratify its desires. 33
1Co 7:15 if the unbelieving partner desires to separate •
37 having his desire under control 37
10: 6 not to desire evil as they did. 31
14:35 If there is anything they desire to know 39
2Co 8:10 you began not only to do but to desire 39
11 so that your readiness in desiring it 39
13: 3 since you desire proof that Christ is speaking 36
Gal 4:21 Tell me, you who desire to be under law 39
5:16 do not gratify the desires of the flesh. 33
17 the desires of the flesh are against the Spirit 30
17 the desires of the Spirit are against the flesh; •
24 the flesh with its passions and desires. 33
6:13 they desire to have you circumcised 39
Eph 2: 3 following the desires of body and mind 37
Php 1:23 My desire is to depart and be with Christ 33
Col 3: 5 fornication, impurity, passion, evil desire 33
1Th 2:17 we endeavored . . with great desire to see you 33
1Ti 1: 7 desiring to be teachers of the law 39
2: 4 who desires all men to be saved 39
8 I desire then that . . the men should pray 28
3: 1 he desires a noble task. 30
5:11 they desire to marry 39
6: 9 those who desire to be rich fall into temptation 28
9 into many senseless and hurtful desires 33
2Ti 3:12 all who desire to live a godly life in Christ 39
Tit 3: 8 I desire you to insist on these things 28
Heb 6:11 we desire each one of you to show . . 30
17 when God desired to show more convincingly 28
10: 5 Sacrifices and offerings thou hast not desired 39
8 Thou hast neither desired nor taken pleasure in 39
11:16 as it is, they desire a better country 41
12:17 when he desired to inherit the blessing 29
13:18 desiring to act honorably in all things. 39
Jas 1:14 when he is lured and enticed by his own desire. 33
15 desire when it has conceived gives birth to sin; 33
4: 2 You desire and do not have; so you kill. 30
Jde 1: 5 Now I desire to remind you 28

Rev 11: 6 with every plague, as often as they desire. 39
22:17 let him who desires take the water of life 29
2Es 2:41 your children, whom you desired 48
4: 4 I also will show you the way you desire to see 47
43 Then the things that you desire to see 46
8:32 For if thou hast desired to have pity on us 47
13:34 as you saw, desiring to come and conquer him. 49
15:17 For a man will desire to go into a city 46
Jdt 12:16 he was moved with great desire to possess her 40
16:22 Many desired to marry her 30
AEs 13: 2 to re-establish the peace which all men desire. 43
15 they desire to destroy the inheritance 30
Wis 4:12 roving desire perverts the innocent mind. 33
6:13 make herself known to those who desire her. 30
17 the most sincere desire for instruction 33
20 the desire for wisdom leads to a kingdom. 33
8: 2 I desired to take her for my bride 36
13: 6 while seeking God and desiring to find him. 39
14: 2 it was desire for gain that planned that vessel 42
15: 5 they desire the lifeless form of a dead image. 43
6 who either make or desire or worship them. 43
19 one would desire them 34
16: 2 a delicacy to satisfy the desire of appetite; 33
3 when they desired food 30
21 ministering to the desire of the one who took it 33
25 according to the desire of those who had need 38
19:11 when desire led them to ask for luxurious food; 33
Sir 1:26 If you desire wisdom, keep the commandments 30
3:29 an attentive ear is the wise man's desire. 33
5: 2 walking according to the desires of your heart. 33
6:37 your desire for wisdom will be granted. 33
14:14 let not your share of desired good pass by you. 33
16: 1 Do not desire a multitude of useless children 30
20: 4 Like a eunuch's desire to violate a maiden 33
24:19 Come to me, you who desire me 30
25:21 do not desire a woman for her possessions. 34
36:22 surpasses every human desire. 33
40:22 The eye desires grace and beauty 30
42:22 How greatly to be desired are all his works 32
Sus 1: 8 and they began to desire her. 33
11 their lustful desire to possess her. 33
1Mc 4: 6 armor and swords such as they desired. 28
2Mc 11:23 we desire that the subjects . . be undisturbed 28
28 If you are well, it is as we desire 28
15:38 that is what I myself desired 29
3Mc 1:10 and conceived a desire to enter the holy of holies. 26
5:26 indicating that what the king desired was ready 45
7: 2 God guiding our affairs according to our desire. 44
17 in accord with the common desire 27
4Mc 1:22 desire precedes pleasure and delight follows 33
31 Self-control . . is dominance over the desires. 33
32 Some desires are mental, others are physical 33
2: 1 the desires of the mind 33
4 to rule . . also over every desire. 33
6 reason is able to control desires. 33
3: 2 No one of us can eradicate that kind of desire 33
2 a way for us not to be enslaved by desire. 33
11 a certain irrational desire 33
12 respecting the king's desire 33
16 opposing reason to desire 33
5:23 we master all pleasures and desires 33

desire *See also* earnestly, set.

base desire 1. *ἐπιθυμία*
Sir 18:30 Do not follow your base desires 1
31 allow your soul to take pleasure in base desire 1

evil desire 1. הַוָּה 2. *ἐπιθυμία*
Mic 7: 3 the great man utters the evil desire of his soul; 1
Sir 23: 5 remove from me evil desire. 2

frenzied desire 1. *οἶστρος*
4Mc 3:17 and quench the flames of frenzied desires; 1

heart's desire 1. נֶפֶשׁ
Ps 35:25 to themselves, "Aha, we have our heart's desire! 1

sexual desire 1. *ἡδυπάθεια*
4Mc 2: 2 by mental effort he overcame sexual desire. 1
4 to rule over the frenzied urge of sexual desire 1

affectionately desirous 1. *ὁμείρομαι*
1Th 2: 8 So, being affectionately desirous of you 1

desist 1. חדל 2. *ἀφίστημι*
Job 14: 6 look away from him, and desist, that he may enjoy 1
Prv 23: 4 not . . acquire wealth; be wise enough to desist. 1
Sir 35:17 he will not desist until the Most High visits him 2

desolate 1. בּוּקָה 2. בֵּן חֲלוֹף 3. חרב 4. חָרְבָּה 5. יָחִיד 6. ישם 7. כחד 8. מְשַׁמָּה 9. שׁאה 10. שׁדד 11. שַׁמָּה 12. שָׁמֵם 13. שׁמם 14. שְׁמָמָה 15. *ἔρημος* 16. *ἐρημόω* 17. *ἐρήμωσις* 18. *ὀρφανός* 19. desertus
Gen 47:19 and that the land may not be desolate. 6
Exd 23:29 lest the land become desolate and the wild 14
Lev 26:34 enjoy its sabbaths as long as it lies desolate 13
Job 15:28 and has lived in desolate cities 7
Ps 40: 2 He drew me up from the desolate pit •
68: 6 God gives the desolate a home to dwell in; 5
Prv 31: 8 for the rights of all who are left desolate. 2
Isa 1: 7 Your country lies desolate . . cities are burned 14
7 it is desolate, as overthrown by aliens. 14
5: 9 many houses shall be desolate, large . . houses 11
6:11 without men, and the land is utterly desolate 9
49: 8 to apportion the desolate heritages; 13
54: 3 possess . . and will people the desolate cities. 13
62: 4 and your land shall no more be termed Desolate; 14
Jer 2:12 be shocked, be utterly desolate, says the LORD 3
4:30 And you, O desolate one, what do you mean 10
12:10 my pleasant portion a desolate wilderness. 14
11 made it a desolation; desolate, it mourns to me. 12
26: 9 this city shall be desolate, without inhabitant'? 3
33:10 and the streets of Jerusalem that are desolate 13
48:34 the waters of Nimrim also have become desolate. 8
49: 2 Rabbah . . it shall become a desolate mound 14
51:62 it shall be desolate for ever. 14
Lam 1: 4 all her gates are desolate, her priests groan; 13
16 a comforter is far . . my children are desolate 13
3:11 he led me off my way and . . he has made me desolate; 13
Ezk 6:14 and make the land desolate and waste 14
14:15 and they ravage it, and it be made desolate 14
16 but the land would be desolate. 14
15: 8 I will make the land desolate 14
25:13 I will make it desolate; from Teman even to Dedan 4
29:12 desolation in the midst of desolated countries; 13
30: 7 she shall be desolated in the midst of desolated 13
7 desolated in the midst of desolated countries 13
32:15 I make the land of Egypt desolate and when the land 14
33:28 the mountains of Israel shall be so desolate 13
35:14 of the whole earth I will make you desolate. 14
15 the house of Israel, because it was desolate 13
15 you shall be desolate, Mount Se'ir, and all Edom 14
36: 4 the desolate wastes and the deserted cities 13
34 the land that was desolate shall be tilled 13
35 that was desolate has become like the garden 13
35 the waste and desolate and ruined cities 13
36 and replanted that which was desolate; 13
Dan 9:17 shine upon thy sanctuary, which is desolate. 13
Jol 1:17 the storehouses are desolate; 13
2: 3 but after them a desolate wilderness 14
20 and drive him into a parched and desolate land 14
3:19 and Edom a desolate wilderness, 14
Mic 7:13 But the earth will be desolate 14
Nah 2:10 Desolate! Desolation and ruin! Hearts faint 1
Zec 7:14 Thus the land they left was desolate 13
14 the pleasant land was made desolate. 11
Mat 23:38 Behold, your house is forsaken and desolate. 15
24:15 So when you see the desolating sacrilege 17
Mrk 13:14 when you see the desolating sacrilege set up 17
Joh 14:18 I will not leave you desolate; I will come to you. 18
Act 1:20 Let his habitation become desolate 15
Rev 17:16 they will make her desolate and naked 16
2Es 1:33 Your house is desolate 19
5: 3 and men shall see it desolate. 19
16:23 for the earth shall be left desolate 19
32 for the earth shall be left desolate 19
Tob 14: 4 Jerusalem will be desolate 15
Bar 4:19 Go, my children, go; for I have been left desolate. 15
1Mc 1:54 they erected a desolating sacrilege 17
4:38 they saw the sanctuary desolate 16

desolate *See also* ground, land, lay, leave, lie, make.

become desolate 1. שׁמם 2. *ἐρημόω*
Lev 26:22 so that your ways shall become desolate 1
Ezk 6: 4 Your altars shall become desolate 1
1Mc 1:39 Her sanctuary became desolate as a desert 2

desolate one 1. שׁמם 2. *ἔρημος*
Isa 54: 1 For the children of the desolate one will be more 1
Gal 4:27 the children of the desolate one are many more 2

desolate place 1. שׁמם
Isa 49:19 Surely your waste and your desolate places 1

desolate woman 1. שׁמם
2Sm 13:20 Tamar dwelt, a desolate woman, in . . Ab'salom's 1

desolation 1. חָרְבָּה 2. מְבוּקָה 3. מְשַׁמָּה 4. שֹׁד 5. שַׁמָּה 6. שׁמם 7. שְׁמָמָה 8. *ἄβατος* 9. *ἐρημία* 10. *ἔρημος* 11. *ἐρήμωσις* 12. desertio 13. desolatio
Lev 26:33 your land shall be a desolation 7
2Kg 22:19 they should become a desolation and a curse 5
2Ch 30: 7 so that he made them a desolation, as you see. 5
Ps 46: 8 how he has wrought desolations in the earth. 5
69:25 May their camp be a desolation 6
Isa 13: 9 the LORD comes . . to make the earth a desolation 5
15: 6 the waters of Nimrim are a desolation; 3
17: 9 deserted . . and there will be desolation. 7
24:12 Desolation is left in the city 7
59: 7 desolation and destruction are in their 4
64:10 Zion . . a wilderness, Jerusalem a desolation. 7
Jer 4:27 The whole land shall be a desolation; 7
6: 8 lest I make you a desolation, an uninhabited land. 7
9:11 and I will make the cities of Judah a desolation 7
10:22 to make the cities of Judah a desolation 7
12:11 They have made it a desolation; 7

22: 5 that this house shall become a desolation. 1
25:18 its kings and princes, to make them a desolation 1
27:17 Why should this city become a desolation? 1
32:43 land of which you are saying, It is a desolation 7
34:22 I will make the cities of Judah a desolation 7
44: 2 Behold, this day they are a desolation 1
6 a waste and a desolation, as at this day. 7
22 therefore your land has become a desolation 1
48: 3 'Desolation and great destruction!' 4
9 her cities shall become a desolation 5
50: 3 which shall make her a land a desolation 5
13 but shall be an utter desolation; 7
51:29 to make the land of Babylon a desolation 5
Ezk 5:14 Moreover I will make you a desolation 1
7:23 and make a desolation. •
12:20 and the land shall become a desolation; 7
23:33 A cup of horror and desolation 7
29: 9 land of Egypt shall be a desolation and a waste. 7
10 the land of Egypt an utter waste and desolation 7
12 I will make the land of Egypt a desolation 7
12 her cities shall be a desolation 40 years 7
33:28 I will make the land a desolation and a waste; 7
29 when I have made the land a desolation and a waste 7
35: 3 I will make you a desolation and a waste. 7
4 cities waste, and you shall become a desolation; 7
7 I will make Mount Se'ir a waste and a desolation; 7
9 I will make you a perpetual desolation 7
36:34 shall be tilled, instead of being the desolation 7
Dan 9: 2 before the end of the desolations of Jerusalem 1
18 open thy eyes and behold our desolations 6
26 end there shall be war; desolations are decreed. 6
Hos 5: 9 E'phraim shall become a desolation 5
Jol 3:19 Egypt shall become a desolation 7
Mic 6:16 that I may make you a desolation 5
Nah 2:10 Desolate! Desolation and ruin! Hearts faint 2
Zep 2: 4 and Ash'kelon shall become a desolation; 7
13 and he will make Nin'eveh a desolation, a dry waste 7
15 What a desolation she has become 5
Lke 21:20 then know that its desolation has come near. 11
1Es 1:58 keep sabbath all the time of its desolation 11
8:81 raised Zion from desolation 10
2Es 3: 2 because I saw the desolation of Zion 12
12:48 to pray on account of the desolation of Zion 13
Jdt 8:22 the desolation of our inheritance 11
Bar 2: 4 to be a reproach and a desolation among all 8
23 land will be a desolation without inhabitants. 8
4:33 so she will be grieved at her own desolation. 9

desolation *See also* make.

desolator 1. שמם
Dan 9:27 decreed end is poured out on the desolator. 1

despair 1. אנשׁ 2. בושׁ 3. יאשׁ 4. לֹא אמן 5. שְׁמָמָה
6. ἀπελπίζω 7. ἀπογινώσκω 8. ἐξαπορέω
1Sm 27: 1 Saul will despair of seeking me any longer 3
Job 6:26 when the speech of a despairing man is wind? 3
24:22 they rise up when they despair of life. 4
Ps 69:20 have broken my heart, so that I am in despair. 1
Isa 19: 9 The workers in combed flax will be in despair 2
Ezk 7:27 The king mourns, the prince is wrapped in despair 5
2Co 1: 8 we despaired of life itself. 8
AEs 14:19 hear the voice of the despairing 6
Sir 22:21 do not despair 6
2Mc 9:22 I do not despair of my condition 7

despair *See also* drive, give.

become desperate 1. *βαρύνω*
1Mc 9:17 The battle became desperate 1

desperately *See* corrupt.

despise 1. בוז 2. בזה 3. זלל 4. מאס 5. נאץ 6. קלל
7. שׁוט 8. ἀτιμάζω 9. ἄτιμος 10. ἀτιμόω
11. βδελυκτός 12. ἐκπτύω 13. ἐκφαυλίζω
14. ἐξουδενέω 15. ἐξουδενόω 16. ἐξουθενέω
17. καταφρονέω 18. περιφρονέω 19. προσοχθίζω
20. ὑπερηφανέω 21. ὑπεροράω 22. ὑπερφρονέω
23. contemno 24. sperno
Gen 25:34 Thus Esau despised his birthright. 2
Num14:11 How long will this people despise me? 5
23 none of those who despised me shall see it. 5
31 shall know the land which you have despised. 4
15:31 Because he has despised the word of the LORD 2
16:30 know that these men have despised the LORD. 5
Deu 31:20 turn . . and despise me and break my covenant. 5
Jdg 9:38 Are not these the men whom you despised? 4
1Sm 2:30 those who despise me shall be lightly esteemed. 2
10:27 they despised him, and brought him no present. 2
15: 9 all that was despised and worthless 10
2Sm 6:16 and she despised him in her heart. 2
12: 9 Why have you despised the word of the LORD 2
10 never depart . . because you have despised me 2
19:43 Why then did you despise us? Were we not the first 6
2Kg 17:15 They despised his statutes, and his covenant 4
19:21 She despises you, she scorns you 2
1Ch 15:29 Michal . . despised him in her heart. 2
2Ch 36:16 despising his words, and scoffing at his 2
Neh 2:19 derided us and despised us and said, "What is this 2
4: 4 Hear, O our God, for we are despised; 1
Job 5:17 despise not the chastening of the Almighty. 4
10: 3 to oppress, to despise the work of thy hands 4
19:18 Even young children despise me; 4
36: 5 Behold, God is mighty, and does not despise any; 4
42: 6 therefore I despise myself, and repent 4
Ps 15: 4 in whose eyes a reprobate is despised 2
22: 6 scorned by men, and despised by the people. 2
24 he has not despised or abhorred the affliction 2
51:17 a . . contrite heart, O God, thou wilt not despise. 2
69:33 and does not despise his own that are in bonds. 2
73:20 on awaking you despise their phantoms. 2
102:17 will not despise their supplication. 2
106:24 Then they despised the pleasant land 4
119:141 I am small and despised 2
Prv 1: 7 fools despise wisdom and instruction. 2
30 despised all my reproof 5
3:11 My son, do not despise the LORD'S discipline 4
5:12 you say, "How . . my heart despised reproof! 5
6:30 Do not men despise a thief if he steals to satisfy 1
12: 8 but one of perverse mind is despised. 1
13:13 despises the word brings destruction on himself 1
14: 2 but he who is devious in his ways despises him. 1
21 He who despises his neighbor is a sinner 1
15: 5 A fool despises his father's instruction 5
20 but a foolish man despises his mother. 2
32 He who ignores instruction despises himself 4
19:16 he who despises the word will die. 2
23: 9 for he will despise the wisdom of your words. 1
22 do not despise your mother when she is old. 1
Ecc 9:16 though the poor man's wisdom is despised 2
Sng 8: 1 I would kiss you, and none would despise me. 1
Isa 1: 4 they have despised the Holy One of Israel 5
5:24 have despised the word of the Holy One of Israel. 5
30:12 Because you despise this word 4
33: 8 Covenants are broken, witnesses are despised 4
15 who despises the gain of oppressions 4
37:22 She despises you, she scorns you- 2
49: 7 Thus says the LORD . . to one deeply despised 2
52: 5 and continually all the day my name is despised. 5
53: 3 He was despised and rejected by men; 2
3 from whom men hide their faces he was despised 2
60:14 all who despised you shall bow down at your feet; 5
Jer 4:30 Your lovers despise you; they seek your life. 4
22:28 Is this man Coni'ah a despised, broken pot 2
23:17 to those who despise the word of the LORD 5
33:24 Thus they have despised my people 5
49:15 you small among the nations, despised among men. 2
Lam 1: 8 all who honored her despise her 3
11 Look, O LORD, and behold, for I am despised. 3
Ezk 16:57 Philistines, those round about who despise you. 7
59 who have despised the oath 2
17:16 who made him king, whose oath he despised 2
18 he despised the oath and broke the covenant 2
19 surely my oath which he despised, and my covenant 2
21:10 we make mirth? You have despised the rod, my son 4
13 what could it do if you despise the rod? 4
22: 8 You have despised my holy things 2
Ams 5:21 I hate, I despise your feasts, and I take no delight 4
Obd 1: 2 among . . nations, you shall be utterly despised. 2
Zec 4:10 For whoever has despised the day of small things 1
Mal 1: 6 to you, O priests, who despise my name. 2
6 You say, 'How have we despised thy name? 2
7 By thinking that the LORD'S table may be despised. 2
12 polluted, and the food for it may be despised. 2
2: 9 and so I make you despised and abased before all 2
Mat 6:24 devoted to one and despise the other. You cannot 17
18:10 that you do not despise one of these little ones; 17
Lke 16:13 will be devoted to the one and despise the other. 17
18: 9 to some who . . despised others 16
Rom 14: 3 Let not him who eats despise him who abstains 16
10 Or you, why do you despise your brother? 16
1Co 1:28 God chose what is low and despised in the world 16
11:22 do you despise the church of God 17
16:11 So let no one despise him 16
Gal 4:14 you did not scorn or despise me 12
1Th 5:20 do not despise prophesying 16
1Ti 4:12 Let no one despise your youth 17
Heb 12: 2 endured the cross, despising the shame 17
2Pe 2:10 those who indulge . . and despise authority. 17
2Es 1: 7 have angered me and despised my counsels. 24
2: 7 because they have despised my covenant. 24
7:37 whose commandments you have despised! 24
79 and who have despised his law 23
8:56 but they despised the Most High 24
9:11 and did not understand but despised it 24
Tob 4:18 do not despise any useful counsel. 17
Jdt 10:19 Who can despise these people 17
14: 5 the man who despised the house of Israel 13
Wis 3:11 whoever despises wisdom and instruction 14
12:24 animals which even their enemies despised 9
Sir 3:13 in all your strength do not despise him. 8
10:23 is not right to despise an intelligent poor man 8
19: 1 he who despises small things 16
22: 5 will be despised by both. 8
31:31 do not despise him in his merrymaking 15
38: 4 a sensible man will not despise them. 19
2Mc 1:27 look upon those who are rejected and despised 11
4:14 Despising the sanctuary 17
4Mc 1: 9 by despising sufferings that bring death 21
4:26 his decrees were despised by the people 17
5:10 you continue to despise me to your own hurt. 17
21 for in either case the law is equally despised. 20
6:21 if we should be despised by the tyrant as unmanly 17
7:16 because of piety an aged man despised tortures 18
9: 6 die despising your coercive tortures 21
13: 1 despised sufferings even unto death 22
9 who despised the same ordeal of the furnace. 17
14: 1 they not only despised their agonies 18
11 mind of woman despised even more diverse agonies 22
16: 2 a woman has despised the fiercest tortures. 22

despite 1. בְּ
Ps 78:32 despite his wonders they did not believe. 1
Sir 0: 2 despite our diligent labor in translating, •
4Mc 4: 1 despite all manner of slander •

despoil 1. בזז 2. גזל 3. נצל 4. קבע 5. שֹׁד 6. שׁדד
7. שׁלל 8. שׁלל שָׁלָל 9. שׁסה 10. שׁסס
11. λαμβάνω τὰ σκῦλα 12. σκυλεύω
Exd 3:22 thus you shall despoil the Egyptians. 3
12:36 Thus they despoiled the Egyptians. 3
1Sm 14:36 go down after the Philistines . . and despoil 1
Ps 12: 5 Because the poor are despoiled 5
17: 9 from the wicked who despoil me, my deadly enemies 6
35:10 the weak and needy from him who despoils him? 2
89:41 All that pass by despoil him; 10
Prv 22:23 LORD . . despoil of life those who despoil them. 4
23 LORD . . despoil of life those who despoil them. 4
Isa 17:14 This is the portion of those who despoil us 9
24: 3 The earth shall be . . utterly despoiled; 1
Jer 25:36 For the LORD is despoiling their pasture 6
30:16 those who despoil you shall become a spoil 10
Ezk 29:19 carry off its wealth and despoil it and plunder 8
39:10 they will despoil those who despoiled them, 7
10 they will despoil those who despoiled them, 7
Zec 11: 3 of the shepherds, for their glory is despoiled! 6
1Mc 3:20 to destroy us . . and to despoil us; 12
5: 3 humbled them and despoiled them. 11
22 he despoiled them. 11

destine 1. יסד 2. מנה 3. עתד 4. צפה 5. ἑτοιμάζω
6. κατὰ πρόγνωσιν 7. μέλλω 8. προγινώσκω
9. προορίζω 10. τίθημι 11. fio
Job 15:22 he is destined for the sword. 4
28 which were destined to become heaps of ruins; 3
Isa 23:13 Chalde'ans . . destined Tyre for wild beasts. 1
65:12 I will destine you to the sword 2
Hos 9:13 E'phraim's sons . . are destined for a prey; •
Eph 1: 5 He destined us in love to be his sons 9
12 have been destined and appointed to live 9
1Th 5: 9 For God has not destined us for wrath 10
1Pe 1: 2 chosen and destined by God the Father 6
20 destined before the foundation of the world 8
2: 8 they disobey . . as they were destined to do. 10
2Es 10:10 a multitude . . are destined for destruction. 11
Tob 6:17 she was destined for you from eternity 5
Wis 15: 9 he is not concerned that he is destined to die 7
17:21 the darkness that was destined to receive them; 7

destitute 1. עַרְעָר 2. רושׁ 3. καθυστερέω 4. ὑστερέω
Ps 82: 3 maintain the right of . . and the destitute. 2
102:17 he will regard the prayer of the destitute 1
Heb 11:37 destitute, afflicted, ill-treated- 4
Sir 37:20 he will be destitute of all food 3

destroy 1. אבד 2. אֲבַדֹּן 3. אכל 4. אסף 5. בלע
6. בער 7. דמה 8. דמם 9. היה לְשַׁמָּה 10. המם
11. הרג 12. הרם 13. חבל 14. חרם 15. חתת 16. יצת
17. ירשׁ 18. כחד 19. כָּלָה 20. כלה 21. כרת 22. כתת
23. מות 24. מחה 25. נכה 26. נקף 27. נתק 28. ספה
29. פרק 30. צמת 31. קֶטֶב 32. רַע 33. רעע 34. רשׁשׁ
35. שׁבר 36. שׁבת 37. שֹׁד 38. שׁדד 39. שׁוֹאָה
40. שׁחת 41. שׁמד 42. שׁמם 43. תמם 44. אבד (A)
45. ארב (A) 46. חבל (A) 47. סתר (A) 48. αἴρω
49. ἀναίρεσις 50. ἀναιρέω 51. ἀναίρω 52. ἀπόλλυμι
53. ἀπολλύω 54. ἀπόλλω 55. ἀπολύω 56. ἀπώλεια
57. ἀφανίζω 58. ἀφανισμός 59. ἀχρειόω
60. διαφθείρω 61. δίδωμι εἰς ἀφανισμόν
62. εἰς ὄλεθρον 63. ἐκκόπτω 64. ἐκτρίβω 65. ἐξαίρω
66. ἐξολεθρεύω 67. θραύω 68. καθαίρεσις
69. καθαιρέω 70. καταλύω 71. καταναλίσκω
72. καταργέω 73. κατασκάπτω 74. κατασπάω
75. καταστρέφω 76. καταφθείρω 77. λύω
78. ὀλεθρεύω 79. ὄλεθρος 80. πατάσσω 81. πορθέω
82. συναπολλύω 83. συντελέω 84. φθείρω
85. χειράω 86. consumo 87. corrumpo 88. demolio
89. destruo 90. devasto 91. disperdo 92. extermino
93. extero 94. obmutesco 95. perdo
Gen 6:13 behold, I will destroy them with the earth. 40
17 to destroy all flesh in which is the breath of life 40
8:21 neither will I ever again destroy every living 25
9:11 shall there be a flood to destroy the earth. 40
15 never again become a flood to destroy all flesh. 40

13:10 before the LORD destroyed Sodom and Gomor'rah. 40
18:23 Wilt thou indeed destroy the righteous 28
24 within the city; wilt thou then destroy the place 28
28 Wilt thou destroy the whole city for lack of five? 40
28 And he said, "I will not destroy it if I find 40
31 For the sake of twenty I will not destroy it. 40
32 For the sake of ten I will not destroy it. 40
19:13 for we are about to destroy this place 40
13 and the LORD has sent us to destroy it. 40
14 for the LORD is about to destroy the city. 40
29 when God destroyed the cities of the valley 40
32: 8 If Esau comes to the one company and destroys it 25
34:30 I shall be destroyed, both I and my household. 41
Exd 8: 9 entreat . . that the frogs be destroyed from you 21
12:13 no plague shall fall upon you to destroy you 40
15: 9 I will draw my sword, my hand shall destroy them.' 17
21:26 strikes the eye . . and destroys it 40
Lev 23:30 that person I will destroy from among his people 1
26:22 I will . . destroy your cattle, and make you few 21
30 I will destroy your high places 41
Num 4:18 Let not the . . Ko'hathites be destroyed 21
24:19 By Jacob . . survivors of cities be destroyed! 1
32:15 you will destroy all this people. 40
33:52 destroy all their figured stones 1
52 destroy all their molten images 1
Deu 1:27 give us into the hand of the Amorites, to destroy us. 41
2:12 sons of Esau . . destroyed them from before them 41
15 against them, to destroy them from the camp 10
21 but the LORD destroyed them before them; 41
22 when he destroyed the Horites before them 41
23 Caph'torim, who came from Caphtor, destroyed them 41
3: 6 destroying every city, men, women, and children. 14
4: 3 LORD your God destroyed from among you all 41
26 not live long . . but will be utterly destroyed. 41
31 LORD . . will not fail you or destroy you 40
6:15 destroy you from off the face of the earth. 41
7: 2 then you must utterly destroy them; 14
4 LORD . . would destroy you quickly. 41
10 requites . . those who hate him, by destroying 1
16 you shall destroy all the peoples that the LORD 3
20 left and hide themselves from you are destroyed. 1
23 into great confusion, until they are destroyed. 41
24 until you have destroyed them. 41
9: 3 LORD . . will destroy them and subdue them 41
8 LORD was so angry . . he was ready to destroy you. 41
14 let me alone, that I may destroy them 41
19 LORD . . was ready to destroy you. 41
20 so angry with Aaron that he was ready to destroy 41
25 because the LORD had said he would destroy you. 41
26 O Lord GOD, destroy not thy people and thy heritage 40
10:10 LORD was unwilling to destroy you. 40
11: 4 how the LORD has destroyed them to this day; 1
12: 2 You shall surely destroy all the places 1
3 destroy their name out of that place. 1
30 after they have been destroyed before you 41
20:17 utterly destroy . . Hittites and the Amorites 14
19 not destroy its trees by wielding an axe 40
20 not trees for food you may destroy and cut down 40
28:20 until you are destroyed and perish quickly 41
24 come down upon you until you are destroyed. 41
45 curses . . overtake you, till you are destroyed 41
48 yoke of iron . . until he has destroyed you. 41
51 shall eat . . until you are destroyed; 41
61 LORD will bring upon you, until you are destroyed. 41
63 LORD will take delight in . . destroying you; 41
31: 3 LORD . . will destroy these nations before you 41
4 as he did to Sihon and Og . . when he destroyed 41
32:25 destroying both young man and virgin •
33:27 And he thrust out the enemy . . and said, Destroy. 14
Jos 7: 7 to give us into . . of the Amorites, to destroy us? 1
12 no more, unless you destroy the devoted things 41
9:24 and to destroy all the inhabitants of the land 41
11:14 they smote . . until they had destroyed them 41
22:33 making war . . to destroy the land where 40
23:15 until he have destroyed you from off this good 41
24: 8 you took possession . . and I destroyed them 41
Jdg 4:24 until they destroyed Jabin king of Canaan. 21
6: 4 they would . . destroy the produce of the land 40
20:35 men of Israel destroyed 25,100 men of Benjamin 40
42 those who came out of the cities destroyed them 40
21:16 since the women are destroyed out of Benjamin? 41
1Sm 15: 6 go down from among . . lest I destroy you with them; 4
23:10 Saul seeks . . to destroy the city on my account. 40
24:21 not destroy my name out of my father's house. 41
26: 9 Do not destroy him; for who can . . and be guiltless? 40
15 For one of the people came in to destroy the king 40
2Sm 1:14 put . . your hand to destroy the LORD's anointed? 40
4:11 shall I not now . . destroy you from the earth? 6
14: 7 and so they would destroy the heir also. 41
11 that . . slay no more, and my son be not destroyed. 41
16 the man who would destroy me and my son together 41
20:19 you seek to destroy a city which is a mother 23
20 far be it, that I should swallow up or destroy! 40
21: 5 The man who consumed us and planned to destroy us 41
22:38 I pursued my enemies and destroyed them 41
41 those who hated me, and I destroyed them. 30
24:16 forth his hand toward Jerusalem to destroy it 40
1Kg 9:21 Israel were unable to destroy utterly 14
13:34 became sin . . so as to cut it off and to destroy it 41
15:29 killed all the house . . until he had destroyed it 41
16: 7 both . . and also because he destroyed it. 25
12 Thus Zimri destroyed all the house of Ba'asha 41
22:11 push the Syrians until they are destroyed.' 20
2Kg 8:19 Yet the LORD would not destroy Judah 40
10:19 Jehu did it . . in order to destroy the worshipers 1
11: 1 she arose and destroyed all the royal family. 1
13: 7 the king of Syria had destroyed them 1
23 turned toward them . . and would not destroy them; 40
18:25 I have come up against this place to destroy it? 40
25 Go up against this land, and destroy it.' 40
19:12 nations which my fathers destroyed, Gozan, Haran 40
18 were no gods . . therefore, they were destroyed. 1
21: 3 the high places which Hezeki'ah . . had destroyed; 1
9 the nations . . whom the LORD destroyed 41
24: 2 and sent them against Judah to destroy it 1
1Ch 4:41 These . . destroyed their tents and the Me-u'nim 25
43 they destroyed the remnant of the Amal'ekites 25
5:25 peoples . . whom God had destroyed before them. 41
21:12 destroying throughout all . . Israel. 40
15 God sent the angel to Jerusalem to destroy it; 40
15 when he was about to destroy it, the LORD saw 40
15 he said to the destroying angel, "It is enough; 40
2Ch 8: 8 whom the people of Israel had not destroyed- 20
12: 7 humbled themselves; I will not destroy them 40
18:10 push the Syrians until they are destroyed.' 20
19: 3 for you destroyed the Ashe'rahs out of the land 6
20:10 whom they avoided and did not destroy- 41
23 rose against . . destroying them utterly 41
23 they all helped to destroy one another. 40
37 LORD will destroy what you have made. 29
21: 7 Yet the LORD would not destroy the house of David 40
22: 7 LORD had anointed to destroy the house of Ahab. 21
10 she arose and destroyed all the royal family 1
24:23 destroyed all the princes of the people 40
25:16 I know that God has determined to destroy you 40
31: 1 until they had destroyed them all. 20
33: 9 evil than the nations whom the LORD destroyed 41
35:21 Cease opposing God, who is with me, lest he destroy 40
36:19 destroyed all its precious vessels. 40
Ezr 5:12 destroyed this house and carried away 47
6:12 put forth a hand . . to destroy this house of God 46
Neh 1: 3 Jerusalem . . its gates are destroyed by fire. 16
2: 3 its gates have been destroyed by fire? 3
13 its gates which had been destroyed by fire. 3
Est 3: 6 Haman sought to destroy all the Jews 41
9 let it be decreed that they be destroyed 1
13 to destroy, to slay, and to annihilate all Jews 41
7: 4 sold . . to be destroyed, to be slain 41
8: 5 letters . . which he wrote to destroy the Jews 1
11 defend . . to destroy, to slay, and to annihilate 41
9: 5 the Jews smote . . slaughtering, and destroying 2
6 the Jews slew and destroyed 500 men 1
24 had plotted against the Jews to destroy them 1
24 had cast Pur . . the lot, to crush and destroy them; 1
Job 2: 3 against him, to destroy him without cause. 5
4:20 Between morning and evening they are destroyed; 22
8:18 If he is destroyed from his place 5
9:22 he destroys both the blameless and the wicked. 20
10: 8 now thou dost turn about and destroy me. 5
12:23 He makes nations great, and he destroys them 1
14:19 so thou destroyest the hope of man. 1
19:26 after my skin has been thus destroyed 26
Ps 5: 6 Thou destroyest those who speak lies; 1
9: 5 thou hast destroyed the wicked; 1
11: 3 if the foundations are destroyed 12
18:40 those who hated me I destroyed. 30
21:10 You will destroy their offspring from the earth 1
37:38 transgressors shall be altogether destroyed; 41
55: 9 Destroy their plans, O Lord 5
57: 0 To the choirmaster: according to Do Not Destroy. 40
58: 0 To the choirmaster: according to Do Not Destroy. 40
59: 0 To the choirmaster: according to Do Not Destroy. 40
63: 9 those who seek to destroy my life shall go down 39
69: 4 mighty are those who would destroy me 30
73:19 How they are destroyed in a moment 9
74: 3 the enemy has destroyed everything 33
75: 0 To the choirmaster: according to Do Not Destroy. 40
78:38 forgave their iniquity, and did not destroy them; 40
45 devoured them, and frogs, which destroyed them. 40
47 He destroyed their vines with hail 11
49 and distress, a company of destroying angels. 32
83:10 who were destroyed at En-dor 41
88:16 thy dread assaults destroy me. 30
101: 5 Him who slanders . . secretly I will destroy. 30
8 morning I will destroy all the wicked in the land 30
106:23 Therefore he said he would destroy them- 41
23 to turn away his wrath from destroying them. 40
34 not destroy the peoples, as the LORD commanded 41
119:95 The wicked lie in wait to destroy me; 1
143:12 steadfast love . . destroy all my adversaries 1
145:20 but all the wicked he will destroy. 41
Prv 1:32 complacence of fools destroys them; 1
6:32 he who does it destroys himself. 40
11: 3 crookedness of the treacherous destroys them. 38
9 mouth the godless man would destroy his neighbor 40
14:11 The house of the wicked will be destroyed 41
18: 9 slack in his work is a brother to him who destroys. 40
28:24 companion of a man who destroys. 40
31: 3 Give not your . . ways to those who destroy kings. 24
Ecc 5: 6 why should God . . destroy the work of your hands? 13
7:16 why should you destroy yourself? 42
9:18 but one sinner destroys much good. 1
Isa 1:28 rebels and sinners shall be destroyed together •
10: 7 does not so think; but it is in his mind to destroy 41
18 his fruitful land the LORD will destroy 20
27 his yoke will be destroyed from your neck. 13
11: 9 shall not hurt or destroy in all my holy mountain; 40
15 utterly destroy the tongue of the sea of Egypt; 14
13: 5 his indignation, to destroy the whole earth. 13
9 earth a desolation and to destroy its sinners 41
14:20 because you have destroyed your land 40
21: 2 plunders, and the destroyer destroys. 38
23:11 concerning Canaan to destroy its strongholds. 41
25: 7 he will destroy on this mountain the covering 5
28: 2 like a storm of hail, a destroying tempest 31
33: 1 destroyer, who yourself have not been destroyed; 38
1 When you have ceased to destroy, O 38
1 have ceased to destroy, you will be destroyed; 38
36:10 I have come up against this land to destroy it? 40
10 said to me, Go up against this land, and destroy it.' 40
37:12 the nations which my fathers destroyed 40
19 were no gods . . therefore they were destroyed. 1
48:19 never be cut off or destroyed from before me. 41
51:13 the oppressor, when he sets himself to destroy? 40
54:16 I have also created the ravager to destroy; 13
65: 8 in the cluster, and they say, 'Do not destroy it 40
8 for my servants' sake, and not destroy them all. 40
25 shall not hurt or destroy in all my holy mountain 40
Jer 1:10 to break down, to destroy and to overthrow 1
4:20 Suddenly my tents are destroyed 38
5: 6 a wolf from the desert shall destroy them. 38
10 Go up through her vine-rows and destroy 40
17 cities . . they shall destroy with the sword. 34
6: 2 The comely and delicately bred I will destroy 7
5 let us attack by night, and destroy her palaces! 40
10:20 My tent is destroyed, and all my cords are broken; 38
11:19 Let us destroy the tree with its fruit 40
12:10 Many shepherds have destroyed my vineyard 40
17 then I will utterly pluck it up and destroy it 1
13:14 that I should not destroy them. 40
15: 3 the beasts of the earth to devour and destroy. 40
6 my hand against you and destroyed you; 40
7 I have bereaved them, I have destroyed my people; 1
17:18 destroy them with double destruction! 35
18: 7 that I will pluck up and break down and destroy it 1
22:20 cry . . for all your lovers are destroyed. 35
23: 1 Woe to the shepherds who destroy and scatter 1
24:10 until they shall be utterly destroyed 43
31:28 break down, to overthrow, destroy, and bring evil 1
36:29 will certainly come and destroy this land 40
46: 8 I will destroy cities and their inhabitants. 1
47: 4 that is coming to destroy all the Philistines 38
4 For the LORD is destroying the Philistines 38
48: 4 Moab is destroyed; a cry is heard as far as Zo'ar. 35
8 the plain shall be destroyed 41
18 he has destroyed your strongholds. 40
42 Moab shall be destroyed and be no longer a people 41
45 it has destroyed the forehead of Moab 3
49: 9 would they not destroy only enough 40
10 His children are destroyed, and his brothers 38
26 all her soldiers shall be destroyed in that day 8
28 against Kedar! Destroy the people of the east! 38
38 and destroy their king and princes, says the LORD. 1
50:30 all her soldiers shall be destroyed on that day 8
36 upon her warriors, that they may be destroyed! 15
51:11 his purpose concerning Babylon is to destroy it 40
20 with you I destroy kingdoms; 40
25 Behold, I am against you, O destroying mountain 40
25 mountain . . which destroys the whole earth; 40
Lam 2: 2 The Lord has destroyed . . all the habitations 5
5 Lord . . like an enemy, he has destroyed Israel; 5
5 he has destroyed all its palaces 5
8 he restrained not his hand from destroying; 5
16 We have destroyed her! Ah, this is the day we longed 5
22 those . . I dandled and reared my enemy destroyed. 20
3:66 and destroy them from under thy heavens, O LORD. 41
Ezk 5:16 destruction, which I will loose to destroy you 40
6: 3 and I will destroy your high places. 1
6 your idols broken and destroyed 36
9: 1 each with his destroying weapon in his hand. 40
8 wilt thou destroy all that remains of Israel 40
13:13 and great hailstones in wrath to destroy it. 19
14: 9 and will destroy him from the midst of my people 41
20:17 my eye spared them, and I did not destroy them 40
21:31 into the hands of brutal men, skilful to destroy. 40
22:27 destroying lives to get dishonest gain. 1
30 for the land, that I should not destroy it; 40
25: 7 perish out of the countries; I will destroy you. 41

15 to destroy in never-ending enmity; 40
16 and destroy the rest of the seacoast. 1
26: 4 They shall destroy the walls of Tyre 40
12 your walls and destroy your pleasant houses; 27
27:32 destroyed like Tyre in the midst of the sea? 94
30:11 nations, shall be brought in to destroy the land; 40
13 Thus says the Lord GOD: I will destroy the idols 1
32:13 I will destroy all its beasts 1
43: 3 which I had seen when he came to destroy the city 40
Dan 2:12 all the wise men of Babylon be destroyed. 44
24 king had appointed to destroy the wise men 44
24 Do not destroy the wise men of Babylon; 44
44 set up a kingdom which shall never be destroyed 46
4:23 'Hew down the tree and destroy it, 46
6:26 his kingdom shall never be destroyed 46
7:11 body destroyed and given over to be burned 45
14 his kingdom one that shall not be destroyed. 46
26 consumed and destroyed to the end. 44
8:24 destroy mighty men and the people of the saints. 40
25 Without warning he shall destroy many; 40
9:26 prince who is to come shall destroy the city 40
11:17 daughter of women to destroy the kingdom; 40
Hos 4: 5 and I will destroy your mother. 7
6 My people are destroyed for lack of knowledge; 7
10: 2 break down . . altars, and destroy their pillars. 38
8 the sin of Israel, shall be destroyed. 41
14 and all your fortresses shall be destroyed 38
14 as Shalman destroyed Beth-ar'bel 37
11: 9 I will not again destroy E'phraim; 40
9 and I will not come to destroy. •
13: 9 I will destroy you, O Israel; who can help you? 40
Jol 1:10 because the grain is destroyed, the wine fails 38
Ams 2: 9 Yet I destroyed the Amorite before them 41
9 I destroyed his fruit above, and his roots 41
9: 8 I will destroy it from the surface of the ground; 41
Obd 1: 5 plunderers by night-how you have been destroyed! 7
8 Will I not on that day . . destroy the wise men 1
Mic 2:10 uncleanness that destroys with a grievous 13
5:10 I will cut off . . and will destroy your chariots; 1
14 out your Ashe'rim . . and destroy your cities. 41
Zep 2: 5 and I will destroy you till no inhabitant is left. 1
13 his hand against the north, and destroy Assyria; 1
Hag 2:22 am about to destroy the strength of the kingdoms 41
Zec 11: 8 In one month I destroyed the three shepherds. 18
9 what is to be destroyed, let it be destroyed; 18
9 what is to be destroyed, let it be destroyed; 18
12: 9 on that day I will seek to destroy all the nations 41
Mal 3:11 that it will not destroy the fruits of your soil; 40
Mat 2:13 Herod . . to search for the child, to destroy him. 52
9:17 the wine is spilled, and the skins are destroyed; 52
10:28 rather fear him who can destroy both soul and body 52
12:14 and took counsel against him, how to destroy him. 55
22: 7 sent his troops and destroyed those murderers 52
26:61 I am able to destroy the temple of God 70
27:20 to ask for Barab'bas and destroy Jesus. 55
40 saying, "You who would destroy the temple 70
Mrk 1:24 Have you come to destroy us? 52
3: 6 how to destroy him. 55
9:22 into the water, to destroy him 55
11:18 scribes heard it and sought a way to destroy him; 55
12: 9 He will come and destroy the tenants 55
14:58 will destroy this temple that is made with hands 70
15:29 You who would destroy the temple 70
Lke 4:34 Have you come to destroy us? 52
5:37 the skins will be destroyed. 52
6: 9 to save life or to destroy it? 52
12:33 where no thief approaches and no moth destroys. 60
17:27 the flood came and destroyed them all. 52
29 destroyed them all- 52
19:47 principal men of the people sought to destroy 52
20:16 He will come and destroy those tenants 55
Joh 2:19 Destroy this temple, and in three days I 77
10:10 thief comes only to steal and kill and destroy 55
11:48 and destroy both our holy place and our nation. 48
Act 3:23 shall be destroyed from the people.' 66
6:14 Jesus of Nazareth will destroy this place 70
13:19 when he had destroyed seven nations in the land 69
Rom 6: 6 so that the sinful body might be destroyed 72
14:20 Do not, for the sake of food, destroy the work 70
1Co 1:19 I will destroy the wisdom of the wise 52
3:17 If any one destroys God's temple 84
17 God will destroy him 84
6:13 God will destroy both one and the other 72
8:11 so by your knowledge this weak man is destroyed 52
10: 9 destroyed by serpents; 52
10 destroyed by the Destroyer. 52
15:24 after destroying every rule 72
26 The last enemy to be destroyed is death. 72
2Co 4: 9 struck down, but not destroyed; 53
5: 1 if the earthly tent we live in is destroyed 70
10: 4 divine power to destroy strongholds 68
5 We destroy arguments and every proud obstacle 69
8 not for destroying you 68
Gal 1:13 and tried to destroy it; 81
23 now preaching the faith he once tried to destroy 81
2Th 2: 8 destroy him by his appearing and his coming. 72
Heb 2:14 destroy him who has the power of death 72
10:39 those who shrink back and are destroyed 56
Jas 4:12 he who is able to save and to destroy 52
2Pe 2:12 will be destroyed in the same destruction with them 84
1Jn 3: 8 to destroy the works of the devil. 77
Jde 1: 5 afterward destroyed those who did not believe. 52
10 they are destroyed. 84
Rev 8: 9 and a third of the ships were destroyed. 60
11:18 and for destroying the destroyers of the earth. 60
1Es 1:56 utterly destroyed all its glorious things. 59
4:44 set apart when he began to destroy Babylon 63
6:33 Therefore may the Lord . . destroy every king 57
8:88 to destroy us without leaving a root or seed 52
2Es 1:11 I have destroyed all nations before them 95
3: 9 thou didst bring the flood . . and destroy them. 95
30 and hast destroyed thy people 95
8:14 thou wilt suddenly and quickly destroy him 95
29 it not be thy will to destroy those 95
59 did not intend that men should be destroyed; 91
9:34 what was launched or what was put in is destroyed 92
35 they are destroyed 92
10:21 our altar thrown down, our temple destroyed; 89
11:42 you have destroyed the dwellings of those 89
12:33 then he will destroy them. 87
13:28 yet destroying the onrushing multitude 87
38 and will destroy them without effort by the law 95
49 when he destroys the multitude of the nations 95
15:11 as before, and will destroy all its land. 87
18 the houses shall be destroyed 93
33 shall beset them and destroy one of them 86
40 to destroy all the earth and its inhabitants 93
42 they shall destroy cities and walls, mountains 88
43 they shall go on . . and shall destroy her. 93
45 shall serve those who have destroyed her. 93
60 and shall destroy a part of your land 93
16:71 but plundering and destroying those 90
72 For they shall destroy and plunder their goods 90
Jdt 2: 3 every one . . should be destroyed. 78
24 destroyed all the hilltop cities 73
27 destroyed their flocks and herds 61
3: 8 given to him to destroy all the gods of the land 66
4: 1 plundered and destroyed all their temples; 61
12 the cities they had inherited to be destroyed 58
5:15 destroyed all the inhabitants of Heshbon 66
6: 3 He will send his forces and will destroy them 66
3 the king's servants will destroy them as one man. 80
7:13 thirst will destroy them 50
8:15 even to destroy us in the presence of our enemies. 78
11:15 they will be handed over to you to be destroyed. 79
13:14 has destroyed our enemies by my hand 67
14:13 in order to be destroyed completely. 66
15: 4 rush out upon their enemies to destroy them 49
AEs 10: 8 gathered to destroy the name of the Jews. 52
15 they desire to destroy the inheritance 52
17 not destroy the mouth of those who praise thee. 57
14: 9 to destroy thy inheritance 57
16:24 shall be destroyed in wrath with spear and fire. 71
Wis 1:11 a lying mouth destroys the soul. 51
12: 6 destroy by the hands of our fathers 52
8 to destroy them little by little 66
9 to destroy them at one blow by dread wild beasts 64
16: 5 destroyed by the bites of writhing serpents 60
19 to destroy the crops of the unrighteous land. 60
22 the crops of their enemies were being destroyed 76
27 For what was not destroyed by fire was melted 84
18: 5 thou didst destroy them . . by a mighty flood. 52
12 their most valued children had been destroyed. 60
13 yet, when their first-born were destroyed 79
Sir 6: 3 will devour your leaves and destroy your fruit 52
4 An evil soul will destroy him who has it 52
10:13 destroyed them utterly. 75
16 destroyed them to the foundations of the earth. 52
17 He has removed some of them and destroyed them 52
16: 9 those destroyed in their sins; 65
21: 2 destroy the souls of men. 50
22:27 so that my tongue may not destroy me! 52
27:16 Whoever betrays secrets destroys confidence 52
18 as a man destroys his enemy 52
18 destroyed the friendship of your neighbor. 52
28:13 he has destroyed many who were at peace. 52
14 destroyed strong cities 69
30:23 sorrow has destroyed many 52
31:25 wine has destroyed many. 52
36: 7 destroy the adversary and wipe out the enemy. 65
45:19 in the wrath of his anger they were destroyed 83
46: 6 he destroyed those who resisted 52
47:22 nor destroy the posterity of him who loved him 65
49: 7 to pluck up and afflict and destroy 52
LJr 1:14 though unable to destroy any one who offends it. 50
Sus 1:59 saw you in two, that he may destroy you both. 66
Bel 1:22 destroyed it and its temple. 75
28 he has destroyed Bel, and slain the dragon 74
Man 1:13 Do not destroy me with my transgressions! 82
1Mc 1:30 destroyed many people of Israel. 52
2:40 they will quickly destroy us from the earth. 78
3: 8 he destroyed the ungodly out of the land; 66
20 They come against us . . to destroy us 65
35 to wipe out and destroy the strength of Israel 65
39 to go into the land of Judah and destroy it 76
52 Gentiles are assembled against us to destroy us; 65
58 who have assembled against us to destroy us 65
5: 2 to destroy the descendants of Jacob 48
2 they began to kill and destroy among the people. 65
9 the Gentiles . . planned to destroy them 65
10 gathered together against us to destroy us. 65
13 and have destroyed about 1,000 men there. 53
27 take and destroy all these men in one day. 65
51 He destroyed every male by the edge of the sword 52
6:12 I sent to destroy the inhabitants of Judah 65
19 So Judas decided to destroy them 65
7: 6 his brothers have destroyed all your friends 52
26 he commanded him to destroy the people. 65
8: 9 The Greeks planned to come and destroy them 65
11 they destroyed and enslaved 76
9:73 he destroyed the ungodly out of Israel. 57
11: 4 Azotus and its suburbs destroyed 69
12:49 to destroy all Jonathan's soldiers. 52
53 nations round about them tried to destroy them 64
13: 1 invade the land of Judah and destroy it 64
6 gathered together out of hatred to destroy us. 64
20 Trypho came to invade the country and destroy it 64
15: 4 those who have destroyed our country 76
16:22 he seized the men who came to destroy him 53
22 had found out that they were seeking to destroy him. 53
2Mc 3:39 strikes and destroys those 53
4:11 he destroyed the lawful ways of living 70
5:14 80,000 were destroyed 76
6:12 these punishments were designed not to destroy 79
8: 3 the city which was being destroyed 76
20 destroyed 120,000 and took much booty. 52
10: 2 and also destroyed the sacred precincts. •
23 he destroyed more than 20,000 52
12:19 Sosipater . . marched out and destroyed those 52
23 and destroyed as many as 30,000 men. 60
15: 2 Do not destroy so savagely and barbarously 52
3Mc 2: 4 destroyed those who . . committed injustice 60
4 whom you destroyed by . . a boundless flood. •
4:14 at the end to be destroyed in . . a single day. 57
5:40 ordering . . that they be destroyed 57
6: 4 Pharaoh . . you destroyed together with his . . army 52
10 destroy us, Lord, by whatever fate you choose. 52
21 and began trampling and destroying them. 78
34 would be destroyed and become food for birds 62
7:12 they might destroy those everywhere 66
15 since they had destroyed the profaners. 85
4Mc 1: 6 is not for the purpose of destroying them 70
6:14 so irrationally destroying yourself 54
8: 9 you will compel me to destroy each and every one 52
11: 4 destroying us in this way? 81
17: 9 wished to destroy the way of life of the Hebrews. 70

destroy *See also* threaten.

utterly destroy 1.חרם 2.כלה 3.תמם
4.ἐξολεθρεύω 5.ὀλορρίζω

Exd 22:20 Whoever . . shall be utterly destroyed. 1
Lev 26:44 abhor them so as to destroy them utterly 2
27:29 No one devoted, who is to be utterly destroyed 1
Num21: 2 then I will utterly destroy their cities. 1
3 they utterly destroyed them and their cities; 1
Deu 2:34 and utterly destroyed every city, men, women 1
3: 6 And we utterly destroyed them, as we did to Sihon 1
c2 that city to the sword, destroying it utterly 1
Jos 2:10 what you did to . . whom you utterly destroyed. 1
6:21 Then they utterly destroyed all in the city 1
8:26 he had utterly destroyed all the inhabitants 1
10: 1 Joshua had taken Ai, and had utterly destroyed it 1
28 he utterly destroyed every person in it 1
35 every person in it he utterly destroyed that day 1
37 and utterly destroyed it with every person in it. 1
39 utterly destroyed every person in it; 1
40 but utterly destroyed all that breathed 1
11:11 put to the sword all . . utterly destroying them; 1
12 and smote them . . utterly destroying them 1
20 in order that they should be utterly destroyed 1
21 Joshua utterly destroyed them 1
Jdg 1:17 they defeated . . and utterly destroyed it. So the name 1
21:11 every male and . . you shall utterly destroy. 1
1Sm 15: 3 smite . . and utterly destroy all that they have; 1
8 and utterly destroyed all the people 1
9 that was good, and would not utterly destroy them; 1
9 all that was . . they utterly destroyed. 1
15 and the rest we have utterly destroyed. 1
18 Go, utterly destroy the sinners, the Amal'ekites 1
20 and I have utterly destroyed the Amal'ekites. 1
1Kg 9:21 Israel were unable to destroy utterly 1
2Kg 19:11 have done to all lands, destroying them utterly. 1
2Ch 32:14 nations which my fathers utterly destroyed 1
Isa 11:15 LORD will utterly destroy the tongue of the sea 1
37:11 have done to all lands, destroying them utterly. 1

Jer 24:10 until they shall be utterly destroyed 3
25: 9 I will utterly destroy them 1
50:21 and utterly destroy after them, says the LORD 1
50:26 and destroy her utterly; let nothing be left 1
51: 3 utterly destroy all her host. 1
Dan 11:44 to exterminate and utterly destroy many. 1
Jdt 1:15 and he utterly destroyed him, to this day. 4
AEs 13: 6 shall all . . be utterly destroyed by the sword 5

destroyer 1. הרס 2. חָסִיל 3. שדד 4. שחת 5. ἀπόλλυμι 6. διαφθείρω 7. λυμεών 8. ὀλεθρεύω 9. ὀλοθρευτής 10. ὀλοθρεύω

Exd 12:23 will not allow the destroyer to enter 4
Job 15:21 in prosperity the destroyer will come upon him. 3
Isa 16: 4 be a refuge to them from the destroyer. 3
21: 2 plunders, and the destroyer destroys. 3
33: 1 destroyer, who yourself have not been destroyed; 3
49:17 Your builders outstrip your destroyers 1
Jer 4: 7 a destroyer of nations has set out; 4
6:26 for suddenly the destroyer will come upon us. 3
12:12 in the desert destroyers have come; 3
15: 3 will appoint over them four kinds of destroyers •
8 against the mothers . . a destroyer at noonday; 3
22: 7 I will prepare destroyers against you 4
48: 8 The destroyer shall come upon every city 3
15 The destroyer of Moab and his cities has come up 3
18 For the destroyer of Moab has come up against you; 3
32 upon . . your vintage the destroyer has fallen. 3
51: 1 Behold, I will stir up the spirit of a destroyer 4
48 for the destroyers shall come against them 3
53 yet destroyers would come from me upon her 3
56 for a destroyer has come upon her, upon Babylon; 3
Jol 2:25 the destroyer, and the cutter, my great army 2
1Co 10:10 destroyed by the Destroyer. 9
Heb 11:28 the Destroyer of the first-born 10
Rev 11:18 and for destroying the destroyers of the earth. 6
Wis 18:25 To these the destroyer yielded, these he feared; 8
4Mc 2:14 preserves . . from the destroyers 5
18: 8 nor did the destroyer, the deceitful serpent 7

destroying *See* locust.

destruction 1. אבד 2. אֲבַדֹּן 3. אֵיד 4. בְּלִי 5. הַוָּה 6. חֶבֶל 7. כִּיד 8. כָּלָה 9. כִּלָּיוֹן 10. כרת 11. מות 12. מְחִתָּה 13. מַשְׁחִית 14. קֶטֶב 15. שֶׁבֶר 16. שִׁבָּרוֹן 17. שֹׁד 18. שָׁוְא 19. שְׁחִית 20. שחת 21. שמד 22. תַּבְלִית 23. ἀπόλλυμι 24. ἀπώλεια 25. ἀφανισμός 26. διαφθορά 27. ἔνδειξις 28. θραῦσμα 29. καθαίρεσις 30. καταστροφή 31. καταφθορά 32. ὀλέθριος 33. ὄλεθρος 34. πτῶσις 35. συντριβή 36. σύντριμμα 37. φθορά 38. contritio 39. exteritio 40. exterminium 41. interitus 42. perditio 43. ruina 44. violatio

Num24:20 but in the end he shall come to destruction. 1
24 he also shall come to destruction. 1
2Ch 26:16 he was strong he grew proud, to his destruction. 20
Est 4: 7 pay into the . . for the destruction of the Jews. 1
8 decree issued in Susa for their destruction 21
8: 6 can I endure to see the destruction of my kindred? 2
Job 5:21 and shall not fear destruction when it comes. 17
22 At destruction and famine you shall laugh 17
21:20 Let their own eyes see their destruction 7
30:12 cast up against me their ways of destruction. 3
Ps 5: 9 their heart is destruction 5
37:34 you will look on the destruction of the wicked. 10
52: 2 you are plotting destruction. 5
91: 6 nor the destruction that wastes at noonday. 14
107:20 healed . . delivered them from destruction. 19
Prv 10:29 LORD is . . destruction to evildoers. 12
16:18 Pride goes before destruction 15
17:19 he who makes his door high seeks destruction. 15
18:12 Before destruction a man's heart is haughty 15
19:18 do not set your heart on his destruction. 11
Isa 10:22 Destruction is decreed, overflowing 9
25 my anger will be directed to their destruction. 22
13: 6 as destruction from the Almighty it will come! 17
14:23 I will sweep it with the broom of destruction 21
15: 5 road to Horona'im they raise a cry of destruction; 15
16: 4 and destruction has ceased 17
22: 4 do not labor to comfort me for the destruction 17
26:14 thou hast visited them with destruction 21
28:22 heard a decree of destruction from the Lord GOD 8
30:28 to sift . . with the sieve of destruction 18
38:17 held back my life from the pit of destruction 4
51:19 devastation and destruction, famine and sword; 15
59: 7 and destruction are in their highways. 15
60:18 or destruction within your borders; 15
Jer 4: 6 evil from the north, and great destruction. 15
6: 1 for evil looms . . and great destruction. 15
7 violence and destruction are heard within her; 17
17:18 destroy them with double destruction! 16
20: 8 I cry out, I shout, "Violence and destruction! 17
48: 3 'Desolation and great destruction!' 15
5 they have heard the cry of destruction. 15
50:22 battle is in the land, and great destruction! 15
51:54 from Babylon! The noise of great destruction 15
Lam 2:11 the destruction of the daughter of my people 15
3:47 have come upon us, devastation and destruction; 15
48 the destruction of the daughter of my people. 15
4:10 they became their food in the destruction 15
Ezk 5:16 deadly arrows of famine, arrows for destruction 13
Hos 7:13 Destruction to them, for they have rebelled 17
8: 4 they made idols for their own destruction. 10
13:14 O Sheol, where is your destruction? 14
Jol 1:15 and as destruction from the Almighty it comes. 17
Ams 5: 9 who makes destruction flash forth against 17
9 so that destruction comes upon the fortress. 17
Mic 2:10 that destroys with a grievous destruction. 6
Hab 1: 3 Destruction and violence are before me; 17
2:17 the destruction of the beasts will terrify you 17
Mat 7:13 the way is easy, that leads to destruction 24
Rom 9:22 the vessels of wrath made for destruction 24
1Co 5: 5 for the destruction of the flesh 33
Php 1:28 This is a clear omen to them of their destruction 27
3:19 Their end is destruction, their god is the belly 24
1Th 5: 3 then sudden destruction will come upon them 33
2Th 1: 9 suffer the punishment of eternal destruction 33
1Ti 6: 9 plunge men into ruin and destruction. 24
2Pe 2: 1 bringing upon themselves swift destruction. 24
3 and their destruction has not been asleep. 24
12 these . . will be destroyed in the same destruction 37
3: 7 judgment and destruction of ungodly men. 24
16 the ignorant . . twist to their own destruction 24
2Es 1:16 at the destruction of your enemies 42
3: 1 the 30th year after the destruction of our city 43
7:131 there shall not be grief at their destruction 42
8:38 their judgment, or their destruction; 42
10:10 a multitude . . are destined for destruction. 40
48 the destruction which befell Jerusalem. 43
15: 5 the sword and famine and death and destruction. 41
39 the tempest that was to cause destruction 39
49 and bring you to destruction and death. 44
16: 2 for your destruction is at hand. 38
Tob 14:15 he heard of the destruction of Nineveh 24
Jdt 7:25 thirst and utter destruction. 24
11:22 and to bring destruction upon those 24
13: 5 the destruction of the enemies 28
16 was my face that tricked him to his destruction 24
AEs 16:13 asked for the destruction of Mordecai 24
21 instead of a day of destruction for them. 32
23 it may be a reminder of destruction. 24
Wis 1:12 nor bring on destruction by the works of your hands; 33
3: 3 their going from us to be their destruction 36
5: 7 paths of lawlessness and destruction 24
12:12 accuse thee for the destruction of nations 23
18: 7 the destruction of their enemies 24
Sir 9: 9 in blood you be plunged into destruction. 24
16: 9 a nation devoted to destruction 24
28: 6 remember destruction and death 31
31: 6 their destruction has met them face to face. 24
36: 9 may those who harm thy people meet destruction. 24
39:30 punishes the ungodly with destruction; 33
41:10 so the ungodly go from curse to destruction. 24
48: 6 who brought kings down to destruction 24
51: 2 hast delivered my body from destruction 24
12 for thou didst save me from destruction 24
Bar 4: 6 It was not for destruction that you were sold 24
25 but you will soon see their destruction 24
Bel 1:42 the men who had attempted his destruction 24
1Mc 3:42 to cause their final destruction. 24
43 Let us repair the destruction of our people 29
4:32 let them tremble in their destruction. 35
15:31 for the destruction that you have caused 31
2Mc 5:13 destruction of boys, women, and children 25
8: 4 the lawless destruction of the innocent babies 24
35 the destruction of his own army! 26
12:27 After the rout and destruction of these 24
13: 6 There they all push to destruction any man 33
3Mc 4: 2 groaned because of the unexpected destruction 32
5: 5 would experience its final destruction. 32
20 the destruction of the lawless Jews! 25
38 the destruction of the Jews tomorrow! 25
47 the grievous and pitiful destruction 30
6:11 the destruction of your beloved people 24
23 and saw them all fallen headlong to destruction 24
30 they had expected to meet their destruction. 33
31 prepared for their destruction and burial. 34
38 their destruction was set 24
4Mc 10:15 by the eternal destruction of the tyrant 33
15:24 witnessed the destruction of seven children 24

destruction *See also* bring, devote, devoted, doom, make, storm, vow, work.

cause destruction 1. שחת

Dan 8:24 cause fearful destruction, and shall succeed 1

thing for destruction 1. חֵרֶם

Jos 6:18 make the camp of Israel a thing for destruction 1
7:12 they have become a thing for destruction. 1

utter destruction 1. חֵרֶם

Isa 43:28 I delivered Jacob to utter destruction 1

destructive 1. ἀπώλεια 2. ὀλέθρος

2Pe 2: 1 secretly bring in destructive heresies 1
Wis 1:14 there is no destructive poison in them 2

detachment 1. μέρος

1Mc 4:19 a detachment appeared, coming out of the hills. 1

detail 1. מַעֲשֶׂה 2. ἕκαστος 3. ἐπιτάσσω 4. κατὰ μέρος 5. λόγος 6. μέρος 7. τρόπος

2Kg 16:10 and its pattern, exact in all its details. 1
Heb 9: 5 Of these things we cannot now speak in detail. 6
AEs 11:12 sought all day to understand it in every detail. 5
1Mc 4:41 Then Judas detailed men to fight 3
2Mc 2:30 to take trouble with details 4
11:20 concerning these matters and their details 4
14: 9 the details of this matter 2
3Mc 4:13 not omitting any detail of their punishment. 7
4Mc 4: 4 When Apollonius learned the details 2

exact detail 1. ἕκαστος

2Mc 2:28 leaving the responsibility for exact details 1

detain 1. עצר 2. ἐγκόπτω 3. συνέχω

Jdg 13:15 Pray, let us detain you, and prepare a kid for you. 1
16 If you detain me, I will not eat of your food; 1
1Sm 21: 7 was there that day, detained before the LORD; 1
Act 24: 4 to detain you no further 2
Tob 10: 2 he said, "Is it possible that he has been detained? •
1Mc 13:15 we are detaining him. 3

detect

Sir 36:19 so an intelligent mind detects false words. •

determine 1. אמץ 2. בוא לִפְנֵי 3. חרץ 4. חשב 5. יאל 6. ידע 7. יעץ 8. כלה 9. כלה מֵעִם 10. מנה 11. עשה 12. שום 13. βουλεύω 14. βούλομαι 15. γνώμη 16. διαγινώσκω 17. διανοέω 18. διαστέλλω 19. διΐστημι 20. δοκέω 21. ἵστημι 22. κρίνω 23. ὁρίζω 24. ὑπολαμβάνω 25. antepono

Gen 6:13 I have determined to make an end of all flesh; 2
Exd 21:22 and he shall pay as the judges determine. •
Rut 1:18 Na'omi saw that she was determined to go with her 1
1Sm 20: 7 if he is angry, then know that evil is determined 8
9 it was determined . . that evil should come upon 8
33 his father was determined to put David to death. 9
25:17 for evil is determined against our master 8
2Sm 13:32 this has been determined from the day he forced 12
2Kg 19:25 Have you not heard that I determined it long ago? 11
2Ch 25:16 I know that God has determined to destroy you 7
Est 7: 7 for he saw that evil was determined against him 8
Job 14: 5 Since his days are determined 3
34: 4 let us determine among ourselves what is good. 6
38: 5 Who determined its measurements 12
Ps 147: 4 He determines the number of the stars 10
Isa 37:26 Have you not heard that I determined it long ago? 11
Lam 2: 8 The LORD determined to lay in ruins the wall 4
Dan 11:36 for what is determined shall be done. 3
Hos 5:11 because he was determined to go after vanity. 5
Lke 22:22 For the Son of man goes as it has been determined; 23
Act 11:29 the disciples determined . . to send relief 23
17:26 having determined allotted periods 23
20: 3 he determined to return through Macedo'nia. 15
23:15 as though you were going to determine his case 16
1Co 7:37 determined this in his heart 22
10:29 why should my liberty be determined by another 22
2Es 7:42 by which all shall see what has been determined 25
Jdt 11:12 determined to use all that God . . has forbidden 16
12: 4 carries out . . what he has determined to do. 13
AEs 11:12 saw in this dream what God had determined to do 13
13: 2 I have determined 14
Wis 8: 9 I determined to take her to live with me 22
Sir 16:26 when he made them, he determined their divisions. 18
44:23 he determined his portions 18
1Mc 1:16 he determined to become king of the land of Egypt 24
3:31 determined to go to Persia 13
4:59 all the assembly of Israel determined 21
5: 2 they determined to destroy 13
16 to determine what they should do 13
8:30 If . . both parties shall determine to add 13
11:33 we have determined to do good 22
16:13 he determined to get control of the country 14
2Mc 8:10 Nicanor determined to make up . . the tribute 19
13:13 he determined to march out 13
15: 6 determined to erect a . . monument of victory 16
17 they determined not to carry on a campaign 16
3Mc 1: 2 determined to carry out the plot he had devised 17
26 determined to bring . . to a conclusion. 20

detest 1. בחל 2. שקץ 3. ἐχθραίνω 4. μισέω 5. μισητός

Deu 7:26 you shall utterly detest and abhor it; 2
Zec 11: 8 impatient with them, and they also detested me. 1
Sir 7:26 do not trust yourself to one whom you detest. 4
20: 5 detested for being too talkative. 5
1Mc 7:26 Nicanor . . who hated and detested Israel 3

detestable 1. שִׁקּוּץ 2. βδελυκτός 3. ἐχθρός
Hos 9:10 became detestable like the thing they loved. 1
Tit 1:16 detestable, disobedient, unfit for any good deed. 2
Wis 12: 4 thou didst hate for their detestable practices 3
detestable *See also* idol.

detestable thing 1. שִׁקּוּץ
Deu 29:17 have seen their detestable things, their idols 1
Ezk 5:11 my sanctuary with all your detestable things 1
7:20 they made . . their detestable things of it; 1
11:18 will remove from it all its detestable things 1
21 whose heart goes after their detestable things 1
20: 7 I said to them, Cast away the detestable things 1
8 the detestable things their eyes feasted 1
30 and go astray after their detestable things? 1
37:23 with their idols and their detestable things 1

devastate 1. דמם 2. הֲרִיסוּת 3. שׁמם 4. ἐρημόω 5. subverto 6. vasto
Lev 26:32 I will devastate the land 3
Isa 49:19 desolate places and your devastated land- 2
Jer 25:37 and the peaceful folds are devastated 1
2Es 15:30 and shall devastate a portion of the land 6
60 as they return from devastated Babylon. 5
1Mc 15: 4 those who have devastated many cities 4
29 You have devastated their territory 4

devastation 1. מְשׁוֹאָה 2. ספה 3. שְׁאֵת 4. שֹׁד 5. שׁמם
1Ch 21:12 or three months of devastation by your foes 2
Isa 51:19 devastation and destruction, famine and sword; 4
60:18 devastation or destruction within 4
61: 4 they shall raise up the former devastations; 5
4 the devastations of many generations. 5
Lam 3:47 have come upon us, devastation and destruction; 3
Zep 1:15 a day of ruin and devastation, a day of darkness 1

devastator 1. שׁדד
Ps 137: 8 O daughter of Babylon, you devastator! 1

device 1. חֶשְׁבּוֹן 2. מוֹעֵצָה 3. מַחֲשָׁבָה 4. ἐνθύμημα 5. κατασκευή 6. adinventio 7. cogitatio
Job 5:12 He frustrates the devices of the crafty 3
Prv 1:31 be sated with their own devices. 2
Ecc 7:29 but they have sought out many devices. 1
Isa 65: 2 way that is not good, following their own devices; 3
Jer 6:19 upon this people, the fruit of their devices 3
Lam 3:60 Thou hast seen . . all their devices against me. 3
61 Thou hast heard . . all their devices against me. 3
2Es 9:20 the devices of those who had come into it. 7
15:48 imitated . . in all her deeds and devices 6
Sir 35:19 repays . . according to their devices 4
3Mc 5:45 had been equipped with frightful devices 5
4Mc 8:15 and saw the dreadful devices •
device *See also* crafty.

clever device 1. πανούργευμα
Sir 1: 6 Her clever devices-who knows them? 1

evil device 1. זִמָּה 2. מְזִמָּה
Ps 26:10 men in whose hands are evil devices 1
37: 7 over the man who carries out evil devices! 2
Prv 12: 2 but a man of evil devices he condemns. 2

wicked device 1. זִמָּה
Isa 32: 7 he devises wicked devices to ruin the poor 1

devil 1. διάβολος
Mat 4: 1 the wilderness to be tempted by the devil. 1
5 Then the devil took him to the holy city, and set 1
8 Again, the devil took him to a very high mountain 1
11 Then the devil left him, and behold, angels came 1
13:39 the enemy who sowed them is the devil 1
25:41 into the eternal fire prepared for the devil 1
Lke 4: 2 tempted by the devil 1
3 The devil said to him, "If you are the Son of God 1
5 And the devil took him up •
13 when the devil had ended every temptation 1
8:12 then the devil comes and takes away the word 1
Joh 6:70 one of you is a devil? 1
8:44 You are of your father the devil 1
13: 2 when the devil had already put it into the heart 1
Act 10:38 healing all that were oppressed by the devil 1
13:10 said, "You son of the devil 1
Eph 4:27 give no opportunity to the devil. 1
6:11 able to stand against the wiles of the devil. 1
1Ti 3: 6 fall into the condemnation of the devil; 1
7 fall into reproach and the snare of the devil. 1
2Ti 2:26 they may escape from the snare of the devil 1
Heb 2:14 him who has the power of death, that is, the devil. 1
Jas 4: 7 Resist the devil and he will flee from you. 1
1Pe 5: 8 the devil prowls around like a roaring lion 1
1Jn 3: 8 He who commits sin is of the devil; 1
8 for the devil has sinned from the beginning. 1
8 to destroy the works of the devil. 1
10 and who are the children of the devil 1
Jde 1: 9 archangel Michael, contending with the devil 1
Rev 2:10 devil is about to throw some of you into prison 1
12: 9 serpent, who is called the Devil and Satan 1
12 for the devil has come down to you in great wrath 1
20: 2 that ancient serpent, who is the Devil and Satan 1
10 the devil who had deceived them was thrown 1
Wis 2:24 through the devil's envy death entered the world 1

devilish 1. δαιμονιώδης
Jas 3:15 wisdom . . is earthly, unspiritual, devilish. 1

devious 1. לוז 2. לָזוּת
Prv 2:15 men . . who are devious in their ways. 1
4:24 put devious talk far from you. 2
14: 2 but he who is devious in his ways despises him. 1

devise 1. ברא 2. הגה 3. זָמַם 4. חרשׁ 5. חשׁב 6. יעץ 7. מַחֲשָׁבָה 8. פעל 9. διαλογίζομαι 10. ἐνθυμέομαι 11. ἐξευρίσκω 12. εὕρεσις 13. κακοτεχνέω 14. μηχανάομαι 15. ποιέω 16. τεκταίνω 17. constituo
Exd 31: 4 to devise artistic designs, to work in gold 5
35:32 to devise artistic designs, to work in gold 5
2Sm 14:14 who devises means not to keep his banished one 5
1Kg 12:33 in the month which he had devised of his own heart; 1
Est 8: 3 the plot which he had devised against the Jews. 5
5 order . . to revoke the letters devised by Haman 7
9:25 plot which he had devised against the Jews 5
Ps 10: 2 caught in the schemes which they have devised. 5
21:11 if they devise mischief, they will not succeed. 5
35: 4 confounded who devise evil against me! 5
58: 2 Nay, in your hearts you devise wrongs; 8
Prv 6:14 with perverted heart devises evil 4
18 a heart that devises wicked plans 4
12:20 Deceit is in the heart of those who devise evil 4
14:22 Do they not err that devise evil? 4
22 who devise good meet loyalty and faithfulness. 4
24: 2 for their minds devise violence 2
9 The devising of folly is sin 3
Isa 7: 5 Remali'ah, has devised evil against you, saying 6
32: 7 he devises wicked devices to ruin the poor 6
8 he who is noble devises noble things 6
Jer 11:19 not know it was against me they devised schemes 5
18:11 and devising a plan against you. 5
Ezk 11: 2 these are the men who devise iniquity 5
38:10 you will devise an evil scheme 5
Dan 11:24 shall devise plans against strongholds 5
25 not stand, for plots shall be devised against 5
Hos 7:15 yet they devise evil against me. 5
Mic 2: 1 Woe to those who devise wickedness and work evil 5
3 Behold, against this family I am devising evil 5
6: 5 remember what Balak king of Moab devised 6
Hab 2:10 You have devised shame to your house 6
Zec 7:10 none of you devise evil against his brother 5
8:17 do not devise evil in your hearts 5
2Es 7:22 they devised for themselves vain thoughts 17
Wis 3:14 who has not devised wicked things against the Lord; 10
Sir 7:12 Do not devise a lie against your brother 4
11:33 Beware of a scoundrel, for he devises evil 16
13:26 to devise proverbs requires painful thinking. 12
17:31 So flesh and blood devise evil. 10
1Mc 11: 8 he kept devising evil designs against Alexander. 9
13:29 he devised an elaborate setting 15
2Mc 7:23 and devised the origin of all things 11
3Mc 1: 2 determined to carry out the plot he had devised •
5:22 in devising all sorts of insults 14
6:24 secretly devising acts of no advantage to the kingdom. 14
7: 9 if we devise any evil against them 13

devise a thing 1. μηχανάομαι
3Mc 5:28 the things he had previously devised. 1
6:22 the things that he had devised beforehand. 1

cleverly devise 1. σοφίζω
2Pe 1:16 For we did not follow cleverly devised myths 1

devise evil 1. זמם
Prv 30:32 if you have been devising evil, put your hand 1

devoid 1. διΐστημι 2. ἐλαττόω 3. μὴ ἔχω
Jde 1:19 worldly people, devoid of the Spirit. 3
AEs 16:10 quite devoid of our kindliness 1
Sir 16:23 This is what one devoid of understanding thinks; 2

devote 1. חרם 2. חֵרֶם 3. עבר 4. ἀντέχομαι 5. δίδωμι 6. εἰμί 7. ἐνθουσιάζω 8. ἐπακολουθέω 9. ἐπιδίδωμι 10. θελητής 11. προσέχω 12. προσκαρτερέω 13. προσφέρω 14. σχολάζω 15. τάσσω 16. dispono
Lev 18:21 of your children to devote them by fire to Molech 3
27:21 holy . . as a field that has been devoted 2
28 no devoted thing that a man devotes to the LORD 1
29 No one devoted, who is to be utterly destroyed 2
Jos 6:18 lest when you have devoted them you take any 1
Mic 4:13 and shall devote their gain to the LORD 1
Mat 6:24 or he will be devoted to one and despise 4
Lke 16:13 will be devoted to the one and despise the other. 4
Act 1:14 these with one accord devoted themselves to prayer 12
2:42 they devoted themselves 12
6: 4 we will devote ourselves to prayer 12
1Co 7: 5 that you may devote yourselves to prayer 14
16:15 devoted themselves to the service of the saints; 15
1Ti 4:15 Practice these duties, devote yourself to them 6
5:10 and devoted herself to doing good in every way. 8
2Es 13:55 for you have devoted your life to wisdom 16
Wis 14:30 devoting themselves to idols 11
Sir 0: 1 devoting himself . . to the reading of the law 5
3 I should myself devote some pains and labor 13
7:20 a hired laborer who devotes himself to you. 5
16: 9 a nation devoted to destruction •
31: 7 a stumbling block to those who are devoted to it 7
39: 1 he who devotes himself to the study of the law 9
1Mc 4:42 He chose blameless priests devoted to the law 10

devote effort 1. διαπονέω
2Mc 2:28 while devoting our effort to . . the outlines 1

devote for destruction 1. חֵרֶם
Jos 6:17 shall be devoted to the LORD for destruction; 1

devote to destruction 1. חָרַם
1Kg 20:42 the man whom I had devoted to destruction 1

more devoted to a child 1. φιλότεκνος
4Mc 15: 5 they are more devoted to their children. 1

devoted thing 1. חֵרֶם
Lev 27:28 no devoted thing that a man devotes to the LORD 1
28 every devoted thing is most holy to the LORD 1
Num18:14 Every devoted thing in Israel shall be yours. 1
Deu 13:17 None of the devoted things shall cleave 1
Jos 6:18 lest . . you take any of the devoted things 1
7: 1 broke faith in regard to the devoted things; 1
1 Achan . . of Judah, took some of the devoted things; 1
11 they have taken some of the devoted things; 1
12 destroy the devoted things from among you. 1
13 There are devoted things in the midst of you 1
13 until you take away the devoted things 1
15 he who is taken with the devoted things 1
22:20 break faith in the matter of the devoted things 1
1Ch 2: 7 transgressed in the matter of the devoted thing 1
Ezk 44:29 every devoted thing in Israel shall be theirs. 1

thing devoted to destruction 1. חֵרֶם
Jos 6:18 keep . . from the things devoted to destruction 1
1Sm 15:21 best of the things devoted to destruction 1

devotion 1. חֶסֶד 2. רצה 3. εὐσέβεια
1Ch 29: 3 because of my devotion to the house of my God 2
Jer 2: 2 I remember the devotion of your youth 1
2Co 11: 3 from a sincere and pure devotion to Christ. •
Jdt 8: 8 she feared God with great devotion. •
4Mc 14: 6 as though moved by an immortal spirit of devotion 3
15:17 who alone gave birth to such complete devotion! 3
devotion *See also* rigor.

undivided devotion 1. ἀπερισπάστως
1Co 7:35 secure your undivided devotion to the Lord. 1

devour 1. אכל 2. בלע 3. בער 4. לחם 5. אכל (A) 6. βρῶμα 7. δαπανάω 8. ἐσθίω 9. καταβιβρώσκω 10. κατάβρωμα 11. κατάβρωσις 12. καταπίνω 13. κατεσθίω 14. comedo 15. devoro
Gen 37:20 we shall say that a wild beast has devoured him 1
33 a wild beast has devoured him; Joseph is without 1
49:27 wolf, in the morning devouring the prey 1
Exd 24:17 glory of the LORD was like a devouring fire 1
Lev 10: 2 fire came forth . . and devoured them 1
Num13:32 land . . is a land that devours its inhabitants; 1
21:28 It devoured Ar of Moab, the lords of the heights 1
23:24 it does not lie down till it devours the prey 1
26:10 when the fire devoured 250 men; 1
Deu 4:24 LORD your God is a devouring fire, a jealous God. 1
9: 3 he who goes over before you as a devouring fire 1
31:17 hide my face from them, and they will be devoured; 1
32:22 burns . . devours the earth and its increase 1
24 devoured with burning heat and poisonous 4
42 my arrows . . and my sword shall devour flesh 1
Jdg 9:15 of the bramble and devour the cedars of Lebanon.' 1
20 let fire . . devour the citizens of Shechem 1
20 let fire come out . . and devour Abim'elech. 1
2Sm 2:26 Abner called . . "Shall the sword devour for ever? 1
11:25 for the sword devours now one and now another; 1
18: 8 forest devoured more people . . than the sword. 1
22: 9 Smoke went . . devouring fire from his mouth; 1
2Ch 7:13 When I . . command the locust to devour the land 1
Job 20:26 a fire not blown upon will devour him; 1
Ps 18: 8 devouring fire from his mouth; glowing coals 1
50: 3 before him is a devouring fire 1
52: 4 You love all words that devour 2
57: 4 I lie in the midst of lions that greedily devour •
78:45 among them swarms of flies, which devoured them 1
63 Fire devoured their young men, and their maidens 1
79: 7 devoured Jacob, and laid waste his habitation. 1
105:35 which devoured all the vegetation in their land 1
Prv 19:28 mouth of the wicked devours iniquity. 2
21:20 but a foolish man devours it. 2
30:14 to devour the poor from off the earth, the needy 1

Isa 1: 7 in your very presence aliens devour your land; 1
20 if you . . rebel, you shall be devoured by the sword; 1
3:14 It is you who have devoured the vineyard 3
5: 5 I will remove its hedge, and it shall be devoured; 3
24 as the tongue of fire devours the stubble 1
9:12 Philistines . . devour Israel with open mouth. 1
20 and they devour on the left, but are not satisfied; 1
20 not satisfied; each devours his neighbor's flesh 1
10:17 it will burn and devour his thorns and briers 1
24: 6 Therefore a curse devours the earth 1
29: 6 tempest, and the flame of a devouring fire. 1
30:27 and his tongue is like a devouring fire; 1
30 in furious anger and a flame of devouring fire 1
31: 8 and a sword, not of man, shall devour him; 1
33:14 Who among us can dwell with the devouring fire? 1
56: 9 All you beasts of the field, come to devour- 1
Jer 2:30 your own sword devoured your prophets 1
3:24 from our youth the shameful thing has devoured 1
5:14 this people wood, and the fire shall devour them. 1
8:16 They come and devour the land 1
10:25 for they have devoured Jacob; 1
25 they have devoured him and consumed him 1
12: 9 all the wild beasts; bring them to devour. 1
12 sword of the LORD devours from one end of the land 1
15: 3 the beasts of the earth to devour and destroy. 1
17:27 and it shall devour the palaces of Jerusalem 1
21:14 and it shall devour all that is round about her. 1
30:16 Therefore all who devour you shall be 1
16 Therefore all who devour you shall be devoured 1
46:10 The sword shall devour and be sated 1
14 for the sword shall devour round about you. 1
49:27 it shall devour the strongholds of Ben-ha'dad. 1
50: 7 All who found them have devoured them 1
17 First the king of Assyria devoured him 1
32 it will devour all that is round about him. 1
51:34 the king of Babylon has devoured me 1
Ezk 7:15 in the city famine and pestilence devour. 1
16:20 these you sacrificed to them to be devoured. 1
19: 3 he learned to catch prey; he devoured men. 1
6 he learned to catch prey; he devoured men. 1
20:47 it shall devour every green tree in you 1
22:25 they have devoured human lives; 1
23:25 your survivors shall be devoured by fire. 1
33:27 I will give to the beasts to be devoured; 1
34:28 nor shall the beasts of the land devour them; 1
35:12 are laid desolate, they are given us to devour. 1
36:13 You devour men, and you bereave your nation 1
14 therefore you shall no longer devour men 1
39: 4 and to the wild beasts to be devoured. 1
Dan 7: 5 it was told, 'Arise, devour much flesh.' 5
7 great iron teeth; it devoured and broke in pieces 5
19 which devoured and broke in pieces, 5
23 kingdom . . shall devour the whole earth 5
Hos 2:12 and the beasts of the field shall devour them. 1
5: 7 the new moon shall devour them with their fields. 1
7: 7 and they devour their rulers. 1
9 Aliens devour his strength, and he knows it not; 1
8: 7 if it were to yield, aliens would devour it. 2
14 and it shall devour his strongholds. 1
11: 6 and devour them in their fortresses. 1
13: 8 and there I will devour them like a lion 1
Jol 1:19 For fire has devoured the pastures 1
20 and fire has devoured the pastures 1
2: 3 Fire devours before them 1
5 a flame of fire devouring the stubble 1
Ams 1: 4 it shall devour the strongholds of Ben-ha'dad. 1
7 fire . . and it shall devour her strongholds. 1
10 Tyre, and it shall devour her strongholds. 1
12 it shall devour the strongholds of Bozrah. 1
14 Rabbah, and it shall devour her strongholds 1
2: 2 and it shall devour the strongholds of Ker'ioth 1
5 it shall devour the strongholds of Jerusalem. 1
4: 9 and your olive trees the locust devoured; 1
5: 6 and it devour, with none to quench it for Bethel 1
7: 4 and it devoured the great deep 1
Nah 2:13 and the sword shall devour your young lions; 1
3:13 fire has devoured your bars. 1
15 There will the fire devour you, the sword will cut 1
15 It will devour you like the locust. 1
Hab 1: 8 they fly like an eagle swift to devour. 1
3:14 rejoicing as if to devour the poor in secret. 1
Zec 9: 4 she shall be devoured by fire. 1
15 they shall devour and tread down the slingers; 1
11: 1 O Lebanon, that the fire may devour your cedars! 1
9 let those that are left devour the flesh of one 1
16 but devours the flesh of the fat ones, tearing off 1
12: 6 they shall devour to the right and to the left 1
Mat 13: 4 and the birds came and devoured them. 13
Mrk 4: 4 the birds came and devoured it. 13
12:40 who devour widows' houses 13
Lke 8: 5 the birds of the air devoured it. 13
15:30 who has devoured your living with harlots 13
20:47 who devour widows' houses 13
Gal 5:15 if you bite and devour one another take heed 13
1Pe 5: 8 the devil prowls . . seeking some one to devour. 12
Rev 12: 4 might devour her child when she brought it forth; 13
17:16 and devour her flesh and burn her up with fire 8
2Es 6:57 domineer over us and devour us. 15
11:31 it devoured the two little wings 14
35 the head . . devoured the one on the left. 15
12:27 the sword shall devour them. 14
28 the sword of one shall devour him who was with him; 14
15:62 they shall devour you and your cities 14
Jdt 5:24 they will be devoured by your vast army. 11
10:12 are about to be handed over to you to be devoured. 10
Sir 6: 3 will devour your leaves and destroy your fruit 13
51: 3 from the gnashings of teeth about to devour me 6
LJr 1:20 when worms from the earth devour them 13
Bel 1:21 devour what was on the table. 7
32 so that they might devour Daniel. 13
42 they were devoured immediately before his eyes. 9
2Mc 2:10 fire . . devoured the sacrifices 7

devourer 1. אכל
Mal 3:11 I will rebuke the devourer for you 1

devout 1. חָסִיד 2. εὐλαβής 3. εὐσέβεια 4. εὐσεβέω 5. εὐσεβής 6. σέβω
Isa 57: 1 devout men are taken away, 1
Lke 2:25 this man was righteous and devout 2
Act 2: 5 devout men from every nation under heaven. 2
8: 2 Devout men buried Stephen 2
10: 7 called two of his servants and a devout soldier 5
13:43 many Jews and devout converts to Judaism 6
50 the Jews incited the devout women of high standing 6
17: 4 as did a great many of the devout Greeks 6
22:12 one Anani'as, a devout man according to the law 2
Jdt 8:31 pray for us, since you are a devout woman 5
4Mc 1: 1 whether devout reason is sovereign 5
6:31 devout reason is sovereign over the emotions. 5
7: 4 the shield of his devout reason. 3
16 devout reason is governor of the emotions. 5
8: 1 in accordance with devout reason 3
11:23 enemy of those who are truly devout. 4
13: 1 devout reason is sovereign over the emotions. 5
15:23 devout reason, giving her heart a man's courage 5
16: 1 devout reason is sovereign over the emotions. 5
4 quenched so many . . by devout reason. 3
18: 2 devout reason is master of all emotions 5

devout man 1. εὐσεβής
Act 10: 2 a devout man who feared God 1

devout one 1. εὐσεβής
4Mc 17:22 through the blood of those devout ones 1

devout person 1. σέβω
Act 17:17 he argued . . with the Jews and the devout persons 1

dew 1. טַל 2. טַל (A) 3. δρόσος 4. ros
Gen 27:28 May God give you of the dew of heaven 1
39 and away from the dew of heaven on high. 1
Exd 16:13 in the morning dew lay round about the camp. 1
14 when the dew had gone up, there was on the face 1
Num11: 9 When the dew fell upon the camp in the night 1
Deu 32: 2 May my . . speech distil as the dew, as the gentle 1
33:28 yea, his heavens drop down dew. 1
Jdg 6:37 if there is dew on the fleece alone, and it is dry 1
38 he wrung enough dew from the fleece to fill a bowl 1
39 the fleece, and on all the ground let there be dew. 1
40 fleece only, and on all the ground there was dew. 1
2Sm 1:21 Gilbo'a, let there be no dew or rain upon you 1
17:12 light upon him as the dew falls on the ground; 1
1Kg 17: 1 there shall be neither dew nor rain these years 1
Job 29:19 with the dew all night on my branches 1
38:28 who has begotten the drops of dew? 1
Ps 110: 3 From the womb of the morning like dew your youth 1
133: 3 It is like the dew of Hermon 1
Prv 3:20 by his knowledge . . clouds drop down the dew. 1
19:12 but his favor is like dew upon the grass. 1
Sng 5: 2 my head is wet with dew, my locks with the drops 1
Isa 18: 4 like a cloud of dew in the heat of harvest. 1
26:19 For thy dew is a dew of light 1
19 For thy dew is a dew of light 1
Dan 4:15 Let him be wet with the dew of heaven; 2
23 let him be wet with the dew of heaven; 2
25 wet with the dew of heaven, 2
33 body was wet with the dew of heaven 2
5:21 body was wet with the dew of heaven 2
Hos 6: 4 Your love is . . like the dew that goes early away. 1
13: 3 they shall be . . like the dew that goes early away 1
14: 5 I will be as the dew to Israel; 1
Mic 5: 7 the midst of many peoples like dew from the LORD 1
Hag 1:10 the heavens above you have withheld the dew 1
Zec 8:12 the heavens shall give their dew; 1
2Es 7:41 winter or frost or cold or hail or rain or dew 4
Wis 11:22 like a drop of morning dew 3
Sir 18:16 Does not the dew assuage the scorching heat? 3
43:22 when the dew appears, it refreshes from the heat. 3
Aza 1:42 Bless the Lord, all rain and dew 3
46 Bless the Lord, dews and snows 3

dew *See also* moisten.

diadem 1. צָנִיף 2. צְפִירָה 3. διάδημα 4. μίτρα
Isa 28: 5 be a crown of glory, and a diadem of beauty 2
62: 3 and a royal diadem in the hand of your God. 1
Rev 12: 3 and ten horns, and seven diadems upon his heads. 3
13: 1 a beast . . with ten diadems upon its horns 3
19:12 and on his head are many diadems; 3
Wis 5:16 a beautiful diadem from the hand of the Lord 3
18:24 thy majesty on the diadem upon his head. 3
Sir 47: 6 when the glorious diadem was bestowed upon him. 3
Bar 5: 2 put on your head the diadem 4

diagnosis 1. פֵּשֶׁר
Sir 38:14 grant them success in diagnosis and in healing 1

dial 1. עלה
2Kg 20:11 by which the sun had declined on the dial of Ahaz. 1
Isa 38: 8 shadow cast by the declining sun on the dial of Ahaz 1
8 the sun turned back on the dial the ten steps 1

diamond 1. יַהֲלֹם 2. שָׁמִיר
Exd 28:18 second row an emerald, a sapphire, and a diamond; 1
39:11 an emerald, a sapphire, and a diamond; 1
Jer 17: 1 with a point of diamond it is engraved 2

dictate 1. קרא מִפֶּה 2. dico
Jer 36:18 He dictated all these words to me 1
2Es 14:42 and by turns they wrote what was dictated 2

dictation 1. פֶּה
Jer 36: 4 wrote upon a scroll at the dictation of Jeremiah 1
6 scroll which you have written at my dictation. 1
17 write all these words? Was it at his dictation? 1
27 which Baruch wrote at Jeremiah's dictation 1
32 who wrote on it at the dictation of Jeremiah 1
45: 1 words in a book at the dictation of Jeremiah 1

die 1. בֶּן מָוֶת 2. גוע 3. מָוֶת 4. מות 5. נְבֵלָה 6. ἀπογίνομαι 7. ἀποθνῄσκω 8. ἀπόλλυμι 9. γίνομαι νεκρός 10. ἐκλείπω ψυχή 11. ἐκψύχω 12. θάνατος 13. θανατόω 14. θνῄσκω 15. κάμνω 16. κοιμάω 17. μεταλλάσσω 18. μεταλλάσσω τὸν βίον 19. τελευτάω 20. τελευτή 21. dispergo 22. intereo 23. morior
Gen 2:17 for in the day that you eat of it you shall die. 4
3: 3 garden, neither shall you touch it, lest you die.' 4
4 the serpent said to the woman, "You will not die. 4
5: 5 days . . Adam lived were 930 years; and he died. 4
8 days of Seth were 912 years; and he died. 4
11 days of Enosh were 905 years; and he died. 4
14 days of Kenan were 910 years; and he died. 4
17 days of Ma-hal'alel were 895 years; and he died. 4
20 days of Jared were 962 years; and he died. 4
27 days of Methu'selah were 969 years; and he died. 4
31 the days of Lamech were 777 years; and he died. 4
6:17 everything that is on the earth shall die. 2
7:21 all flesh died that moved upon the earth 2
22 in whose nostrils was the breath of life died. 4
9:29 days of Noah were 950 years; and he died. 4
11:28 Haran died before his father Terah in the land 4
32 and Terah died in Haran. 4
19:19 lest the disaster overtake me, and I die. 4
20: 7 do not restore her, know that you shall surely die 4
23: 2 Sarah died at Kir'iath-ar'ba (that is, Hebron) 4
25: 8 Abraham breathed his last and died 4
17 he breathed his last and died 4
32 I am about to die; of what use is a birthright to me? 4
26: 9 I thought, 'Lest I die because of her.' 4
27: 4 that I may bless you before I die. 4
7 and bless you before the LORD before I die. 4
10 so that he may bless you before he dies. 4
30: 1 said to Jacob, "Give me children, or I shall die! 4
33:13 overdriven for one day, all the flocks will die. 4
35: 8 Deb'orah, Rebekah's nurse, died 4
18 as her soul was departing (for she died) 4
19 Rachel died, and she was buried on the way 4
29 Isaac breathed his last; and he died 4
36:33 Bela died, and Jobab the son of Zerah of Bozrah 4
34 Jobab died, and Husham of the land 4
35 Husham died, and Hadad the son of Bedad 4
36 Hadad died, and Samlah of Masre'kah reigned 4
37 Samlah died, and Shaul of Reho'both 4
38 Shaul died, and Ba'al-ha'nan the son of Achbor 4
39 Ba'al-ha'nan the son of Achbor died 4
38:11 feared that he would die, like his brothers. 4
12 of time the wife of Judah, Shua's daughter, died; 4
42: 2 buy grain . . that we may live, and not die. 4
20 verified, and you shall not die." And they did so. 4
43: 8 that we may live and not die, both we and you 4
44: 9 let him die, and we also will be my lord's slaves. 4
22 he should leave his father, his father would die. 4
31 when he sees that the lad is not with us, he will die 4
45:28 I will go and see him before I die. 4
46:12 but Er and Onan died in the land of Canaan 4
30 Now let me die, since I have seen your face 4
47:15 Give us food; why should we die before your eyes? 4
19 Why should we die before your eyes 4
19 give us seed, that we may live, and not die 4
29 when the time drew near that Israel must die 4
48: 7 Rachel to my sorrow died in the land of Canaan 4
21 Behold, I am about to die, but God will be with you 4
50: 5 I am about to die; in my tomb which I hewed out 4
16 Your father gave this command before he died 4

24 Joseph said to his brothers, "I am about to die; 4
25 Joseph died, being 110 years old; 4
Exd 1: 6 Then Joseph died, and all his brothers 4
2:23 the king of Egypt died. And the people of Israel 4
7:18 the fish in the Nile shall die, and the Nile shall 4
21 the fish in the Nile died; and the Nile became foul 4
8:13 the frogs died out of the houses and courtyards 4
9: 4 nothing shall die of all that belongs 4
6 all the cattle of the Egyptians died 4
6 of the cattle of . . Israel not one died. 4
19 upon every man and beast . . and they shall die. 4
10:28 for in the day you see my face you shall die. 4
11: 5 all the first-born in the land of Egypt shall die 4
14:11 you have taken us away to die in the wilderness? 4
12 the Egyptians than to die in the wilderness. 4
16: 3 said to them, "Would that we had died by the hand 4
20:19 but let not God speak to us, lest we die. 4
21:12 a man so that he dies shall be put to death. 4
14 you shall take him from my altar, that he may die. 4
18 his fist and the man does not die but keeps his bed 4
20 the slave dies under his hand, he shall be 4
35 When one man's ox hurts another's, so that it dies 4
22: 2 a thief . . is struck so that he dies 4
10 If . . it dies or is hurt or is driven away 4
14 If . . it is hurt or dies, the owner not being 4
28:35 shall be heard . . when he comes out, lest he die. 4
43 lest they bring guilt upon themselves and die. 4
30:20 they shall wash with water, lest they die. 4
21 wash their hands and their feet, lest they die 4
Lev 8:35 lest you die; for so I am commanded 4
10: 2 devoured them, and they died before the LORD 4
6 do not rend your clothes, lest you die 4
7 do not go out . . lest you die 4
9 Drink no wine . . lest you die 4
11:39 if any animal of which you may eat dies 4
15:31 lest they die in their uncleanness by defiling 4
16: 1 when they drew near before the LORD and died 4
2 the mercy seat which is upon the ark, lest he die 4
13 cover the mercy seat . . lest he die 4
17:15 every person that eats what dies of itself 5
20:20 bear their sin, they shall die childless 4
22: 8 That which dies of itself or is torn by beasts 5
9 keep my charge, lest they bear sin for it and die 4
Num 3: 4 Nadab and Abi'hu died before the LORD 4
4:15 must not touch the holy things, lest they die. 4
19 may live and not die when they come near 4
20 not go in to look . . lest they die. 4
6: 7 if they die, shall he make himself unclean; 4
9 if any man dies very suddenly beside him 4
14: 2 Would that we had died in the land of Egypt! 4
2 Or would that we had died in the wilderness! 4
35 in this wilderness . . they shall die. 4
37 died by plague before the LORD. 4
16:29 If these men die the common death of all men 4
49 Now those who died by the plague were 14,700 4
49 besides those who died in the affair of Korah. 4
17:10 an end of their murmurings . . lest they die. 4
13 near to the tabernacle of the LORD, shall die. 4
18: 3 lest they, and you, die. 4
22 lest they bear sin and die. 4
32 not profane the holy things . . lest you die.' 4
19:13 Whoever touches . . body of any man who has died 4
14 This is the law when a man dies in a tent 4
20: 1 people stayed in Kadesh; and Miriam died there 4
3 Would that we had died when our brethren died 2
3 died when our brethren died before the LORD! 2
4 that we should die here, both we and our cattle? 4
26 Aaron shall be gathered . . and shall die there. 4
28 Aaron died there on the top of the mountain. 4
21: 5 up out of Egypt to die in the wilderness? 4
6 so that many people of Israel died. 4
23:10 Let me die the death of the righteous 4
25: 9 those that died by the plague were 24,000. 4
26:10 together with Korah, when that company died 4
11 Notwithstanding, the sons of Korah did not die. 4
19 Er and Onan died in the land of Canaan. 4
61 Nadab and Abi'hu died when they offered unholy 4
65 They shall die in the wilderness. 4
27: 3 Our father died in the wilderness; 4
3 Our father died . . but died for his own sin; 4
8 If a man dies, and has no son 4
33:38 Aaron the priest went up Mount Hor . . died there 4
39 Aaron was 123 years old when he died on Mount Hor. 4
35:12 that the manslayer may not die until he stands 4
16 with an instrument of iron, so that he died 4
17 with a stone in the hand, by which a man may die 4
17 struck him down with a stone . . and he died 4
18 with a weapon of wood . . by which a man may die 4
18 with a weapon of wood . . and he died 4
20 hurled at him, lying in wait, so that he died 4
21 struck him down with his hand, so that he died 4
23 or used a stone, by which a man may die 4
23 without seeing him cast it . . so that he died 4
Deu 4:22 must die in this land, I must not go over the Jordan; 4
5:25 Now therefore why should we die? 4
25 if we hear the voice of the LORD . . we shall die. 4
10: 6 Mose'rah. There Aaron died, and . . was buried; 4
14:21 You shall not eat anything that dies of itself; 5
17: 6 witnesses he that is to die shall be put to death; 4
12 who acts presumptuously . . that man shall die; 4
18:16 me not . . see this great fire any more, lest I die.' 4
20 that same prophet shall die.' 4
19: 5 head . . strikes his neighbor so that he dies– 4
6 mortally, though the man did not deserve to die 3
11 attacks . . wounds him mortally so that he dies 4
12 over to the avenger of blood, so that he may die. 4
20: 5 go back to his house, lest he die in the battle 4
6 go back to his house, lest he die in the battle 4
7 go back to his house, lest he die in the battle 4
22:22 both of them shall die, the man . . and the woman; 4
25 then only the man who lay with her shall die. 4
24: 3 the latter husband dies, who took her to be his wife 4
7 then that thief shall die; 4
25: 5 If brothers dwell together, and one of them dies 4
31:14 Behold, the days approach when you must die; 4
32:50 die on the mountain which you ascend 4
50 as Aaron your brother died in Mount Hor 4
33: 6 Let Reuben live, and not die, nor let his men be few. 4
34: 5 Moses . . died there in the land of Moab 4
7 Moses was 120 years old when he died; 4
Jos 5: 4 all the males of the people . . had died on the way 4
10:11 the LORD threw down great stones . . and they died; 4
11 were more who died because of the hailstones 4
20: 9 so that he might not die by the hand of the avenger 4
24:29 Joshua the son of Nun, the servant of the LORD, died 4
33 Elea'zar the son of Aaron died; and they buried him 4
Jdg 1: 7 they brought him to Jerusalem, and he died there. 4
2: 8 Joshua the son of Nun, the servant of the LORD, died 4
19 whenever the judge died, they turned back 4
21 any of the nations that Joshua left when he died 4
3:11 40 years. Then Oth'ni-el the son of Kenaz died. 4
4: 1 in the sight of the LORD, after Ehud died. 4
21 lying fast asleep from weariness. So he died. 4
6:23 Peace be to you; do not fear, you shall not die. 4
30 Bring out your son, that he may die, for he has 4
8:32 Gideon the son of Jo'ash died in a good old age 4
33 As soon as Gideon died, the people of Israel 4
9:49 all the people of the Tower of Shechem also died 4
54 And his young man thrust him through, and he died. 4
10: 2 Then he died, and was buried at Shamir. 4
5 Ja'ir died, and was buried in Kamon. 4
12: 7 Jephthah the Gileadite died, and was buried 4
10 Then Ibzan died, and was buried at Bethlehem. 4
12 Then Elon the Zeb'ulunite died, and was buried 4
15 Abdon the son of Hillel . . died, and was buried 4
13:22 his wife, "We shall surely die, for we have seen God. 4
15:18 shall I now die of thirst, and fall into the hands 4
16:30 Samson said, "Let me die with the Philistines. 4
Rut 1: 3 But Elim'elech, the husband of Na'omi, died 4
5 and both Mahlon and Chil'ion died 4
17 where you die I will die, and there . . be buried. 4
17 where you die I will die, and there . . be buried. 4
1Sm 2:33 all the increase . . shall die by the sword of men. 4
34 the sign . . both of them shall die on the same day. 4
4:18 neck was broken and he died, for he was an old man 4
5:12 the men who did not die were stricken with tumors 4
12:19 Pray for your servants . . that we may not die 4
14:39 For as the LORD lives . . he shall surely die. 4
43 I tasted a little honey . . here I am, I will die. 4
44 God do so to me . . you shall surely die, Jonathan. 4
45 Shall Jonathan die, who has wrought . . victory 4
45 people ransomed Jonathan, that he did not die. 4
20: 2 he said to him, "Far from it! You shall not die. 4
14 show me the . . love of the LORD, that I may not die; 4
31 send and fetch him to me, for he shall surely die. 1
22:16 You shall surely die, Ahim'elech, you and all 4
25: 1 Now Samuel died; and all Israel . . mourned for him 4
37 his wife told him . . and his heart died within him 4
38 ten days later the LORD smote Nabal; and he died. 4
26:10 LORD will smite him; or his day shall come to die; 4
28: 3 Now Samuel had died, and all Israel had mourned 4
31: 5 he also fell upon his sword, and died with him. 4
6 Saul died, and his three sons, and his armor-bearer 4
2Sm 1:15 Go, fall upon him." And he smote him so that he died. 4
2:23 and he fell there, and died where he was. 4
23 to the place where As'ahel had fallen and died 4
3:27 and there he smote him in the belly, so that he died 4
33 Should Abner die as a fool dies? 4
33 Should Abner die as a fool dies? 4
4: 1 Saul's son . . heard that Abner had died at Hebron 4
6: 7 and he died there beside the ark of God. 4
10: 1 After this the king of the Ammonites died 4
18 and wounded Shobach . . so that he died there. 4
11:15 draw back . . that he may be struck down, and die. 4
21 millstone upon him . . so that he died at Thebez 4
12:13 LORD also has put away your sin; you shall not die. 4
14 the child that is born to you shall die. 4
18 On the seventh day the child died. 4
21 but when the child died, you arose and ate food. 4
14:14 We must all die, we are like water spilt 4
17:23 he died, and was buried in the tomb of his father. 4
18: 3 If half of us die, they will not care about us. 4
33 Would I had died instead of you, O Ab'salom, my son 4
19:23 And the king said to Shim'e-i, "You shall not die. 4
37 Pray let . . return, that I may die in my own city 4
20:10 Jo'ab struck him . . and he died. 4
24:15 and there died of the people . . 70,000 men. 4
1Kg 1:52 but if wickedness is found in him, he shall die. 4
2: 1 When David's time to die drew near, he charged 4
25 Benai'ah . . and he struck him down, and he died. 4
30 he said, "No, I will die here." Then Benai'ah brought 4
37 on the day . . know for certain that you shall die; 4
42 on the day you go forth . . you shall die'? 4
46 and he went out and struck him down, and he died 4
3:19 this woman's son died in the night, because she lay 4
13:31 he said to his sons, "When I die, bury me in the grave 4
14:11 Any one . . who dies in the city the dogs shall eat; 4
11 any one who dies in the open country the birds 4
12 your feet enter the city, the child shall die. 4
17 as she came to . . the house, the child died. 4
16: 4 Any one . . who dies in the city the dogs shall eat; 4
4 and any one of his who dies in the field 4
18 and burned the king's house over him . . and died 4
22 so Tibni died, and Omri became king. 4
17:12 prepare it . . that we may eat it, and die. 4
19: 4 and he asked that he might die, saying, "It is enough; 4
21:24 who dies in the city the dogs shall eat; 4
24 any one of his who dies in the open country 4
22:35 king was propped up . . until at evening he died; 4
37 So the king died, and was brought to Sama'ria; 4
2Kg 1: 4 'You shall not come . . but you shall surely die.' 4
6 you shall not come . . but shall surely die.' 4
16 you shall not come . . but you shall surely die.' 4
17 So he died according to the word of the LORD 4
3: 5 when Ahab died, the king of Moab rebelled 4
4:20 child sat on her lap till noon, and then he died. 4
7: 3 said to one another, "Why do we sit here till we die? 4
4 the famine is in the city, and we shall die there; 4
4 we shall die there; and if we sit here, we die also. 4
4 and if they kill us we shall but die. 4
17 people trod upon him in the gate, so that he died 4
20 the people trod upon him in the gate and he died. 4
8:10 LORD has shown me that he shall certainly die. 4
15 took . . and spread it over his face, till he died. 4
9:27 And he fled to Megid'do, and died there. 4
12:21 his servants, who struck him down, so that he died. 4
13:14 sick with the illness of which he was to die 4
20 So Eli'sha died, and they buried him. 4
24 When Haz'ael . . died, Ben-ha'dad his son became king 4
14: 6 but every man shall die for his own sin. 4
18:32 and take you away . . that you may live, and not die. 4
20: 1 Set your house in order; for you shall die 4
23:34 and he came to Egypt, and died there. 4
1Ch 1:44 When Bela died, Jobab the son of Zerah of Bozrah 4
45 When Jobab died, Husham of the land 4
46 When Husham died, Hadad the son of Bedad 4
47 When Hadad died, Samlah of Masre'kah reigned 4
48 When Samlah died, Sha'ul . . reigned 4
49 When Sha'ul died, Ba'al-ha'nan, the son of Achbor 4
50 When Ba'al-ha'nan died, Hadad reigned in his stead; 4
51 Hadad died. The chiefs of Edom were: chiefs Timna 4
2:19 When Azu'bah died, Caleb married Ephrath 4
30 and Seled died childless. 4
32 Jonathan; and Jether died childless. 4
10: 5 he also fell upon his sword, and died. 4
6 Saul died; he and his three sons and all his house 4
6 he . . and all his house died together. 4
13 Saul died for his unfaithfulness; 4
13:10 and he died there before God. 4
19: 1 after this Nahash the king of the Ammonites died 4
23:22 Elea'zar died having no sons, but only daughters; 4
24: 2 Nadab and Abi'hu died before their father 4
29:28 he died in a good old age, full of days, riches 4
2Ch 13:20 the LORD smote him, and he died. 4
16:13 dying in the 41st year of his reign. 4
18:34 then at sunset he died. 4
21:19 bowels came out . . and he died in great agony. 4
24:15 Jehoi'ada grew old and full of days, and died; 4
22 he was dying, he said, "May the LORD see and avenge! 4
25 he died; and they buried him in the city of David 4
25: 4 but every man shall die for his own sin. 4
32:11 may give you over to die by famine and by thirst 4
35:24 died, and was buried in the tombs of his fathers. 4
Est 2: 7 and when her father and her mother died 4
Job 2: 9 hold fast your integrity? Curse God, and die. 4
3:11 Why did I not die at birth 4
4:21 do they not die, and that without wisdom?' 4
10:18 Would that I had died before any eye had seen me 2
12: 2 you are the people, and wisdom will die with you. 4
13:19 For then I would be silent and die. 2
14: 8 and its stump die in the ground 4
10 But man dies, and is laid low; man breathes his last 4
14 If a man die, shall he live again? 4
21:23 One dies in full prosperity, being wholly at ease 4
25 Another dies in bitterness of soul 4
24:12 From out of the city the dying groan 4
27: 5 till I die I will not put away my integrity from me. 2
29:18 Then I thought, 'I shall die in my nest 2
34:20 In a moment they die; 4
36:12 perish by the sword, and die without knowledge. 2
14 They die in youth, and their life ends in shame. 4
42:17 Job died, an old man, and full of days. 4
Ps 41: 5 When will he die, and his name perish? 4
49:10 Yea, he shall see that even the wise die 4
17 For when he dies he will carry nothing away; 4
82: 7 nevertheless, you shall die like men 4
104:29 when thou takest away their breath, they die 2

118:17 I shall not die, but I shall live, and recount 4
Prv 5:23 He dies for lack of discipline 4
10:21 but fools die for lack of sense. 4
11: 7 When the wicked dies, his hope perishes 4
19 but he who pursues evil will die. 4
15:10 he who hates reproof will die. 4
19:16 he who despises the word will die. 4
23:13 if you beat him with a rod, he will not die. 4
30: 7 Two things . . deny them not to me before I die 4
Ecc 2:16 How the wise man dies just like the fool! 4
3: 2 a time to be born, and a time to die; 4
19 fate . . is the same; as one dies, so dies the other. 4
19 fate . . is the same; as one dies, so dies the other. 4
7:17 why should you die before your time? 4
9: 5 For the living know that they will die 4
Isa 5:13 their honored men are dying of hunger 4
6: 1 In the year that King Uzzi'ah died I saw the Lord 4
14:28 In the year that King Ahaz died came this oracle 4
22:13 Let us eat and drink, for tomorrow we die. 4
14 iniquity will not be forgiven you till you die. 4
18 into a wide land; there you shall die 4
38: 1 for you shall die, you shall not recover. 4
50: 2 fish stink for lack of water, and die of thirst. 4
51: 6 and they who dwell in it will die like gnats; 4
12 who are you that you are afraid of man who dies 4
14 he shall not die and go down to the Pit 4
59: 5 weave the spider's web; he who eats their eggs dies 4
65:20 for the child shall die 100 years old 4
66:24 for their worm shall not die, 4
Jer 11:21 Do not prophesy . . or you will die by our hand 4
22 the young men shall die by the sword; 4
22 sons and their daughters shall die by famine; 4
16: 4 They shall die of deadly diseases. 4
6 Both great and small shall die in this land; 4
20: 6 there you shall die, and there you shall be buried 4
21: 6 they shall die of a great pestilence. 4
9 He who stays in this city shall die by the sword 4
22:12 they have carried him captive, there shall he die 4
26 where you were not born, and there you shall die. 4
26: 8 the people laid hold of him, saying, "You shall die! 4
27:13 Why will you and your people die by the sword 4
28:16 This very year you shall die 4
17 in the seventh month, the prophet Hanani'ah died. 4
31:30 But every one shall die for his own sin; 4
34: 4 You shall not die by the sword. 4
5 You shall die in peace. 4
37:20 to the house of Jonathan . . lest I die there. 4
38: 2 He who stays in this city shall die by the sword 4
9 he will die there of hunger, for there is no bread 4
10 the prophet out of the cistern before he dies. 4
24 no one know of these words and you shall not die. 4
26 me back to the house of Jonathan to die there. 4
42:16 hard after you to Egypt; and there you shall die. 4
17 to go to Egypt to live there shall die by the sword 4
22 know . . that you shall die by the sword, by famine 4
44:12 they shall die by the sword and by famine; 4
Ezk 3:18 If I say to the wicked, 'You shall surely die,' 4
18 that wicked man shall die in his iniquity; 4
19 from his wicked way, he shall die in his iniquity; 4
20 I lay a stumbling block before him, he shall die; 4
20 he shall die for his sin 4
4:14 I have never eaten what died of itself or was torn 5
5:12 A third part of you shall die of pestilence 4
6:12 He that is far off shall die of pestilence; 4
12 he that is left . . shall die of famine. 4
7:15 he that is in the field dies by the sword; 4
11:13 Pelati'ah the son of Benai'ah died. 4
12:13 yet he shall not see it; and he shall die there. 4
13:19 putting to death persons who should not die 4
17:16 in Babylon he shall die. 4
18: 4 the soul that sins shall die. 4
13 he shall surely die; 4
17 he shall not die for his father's iniquity; 4
18 behold, he shall die for his iniquity. 4
20 The soul that sins shall die. 4
21 he shall surely live; he shall not die. 4
24 for . . the sin he has committed, he shall die. 4
26 and commits iniquity, he shall die for it; 4
26 iniquity which he has committed he shall die. 4
28 he shall surely live, he shall not die. 4
31 Why will you die, O house of Israel? 4
24:18 in the morning, and at evening my wife died. 4
28: 8 you shall die the death of the slain 4
10 You shall die the death of the uncircumcised 4
33: 8 to the wicked, O wicked man, you shall surely die 4
8 that wicked man shall die in his iniquity 4
9 he shall die in his iniquity 4
11 for why will you die, O house of Israel? 4
13 iniquity that he has committed he shall die. 4
14 though I say to the wicked, 'You shall surely die 4
15 he shall surely live, he shall not die. 4
18 and commits iniquity, he shall die for it. 4
27 and in caves shall die by pestilence. 4
44:31 bird or beast, that has died of itself or is torn. 5
Hos 13: 1 but he incurred guilt through Ba'al and died. 4
Ams 2: 2 and Moab shall die amid uproar, amid shouting 4
6: 9 if ten men remain in one house, they shall die. 4
7:11 Amos has said, 'Jerobo'am shall die by the sword 4
17 you yourself shall die in an unclean land 4
9:10 the sinners of my people shall die by the sword 4
Jon 4: 3 for it is better for me to die than to live. 4
8 he asked that he might die, and said 4
8 It is better for me to die than to live. 4
9 he said, "I do well to be angry, angry enough to die. 3
Hab 1:12 We shall not die. 4
Zec 11: 9 What is to die, let it die; 4
9 What is to die, let it die; 4
Mat 2:19 when Herod died, behold, an angel of the Lord 19
9:18 saying, "My daughter has just died 19
15: 4 let him surely die.' 19
22:25 the first married, and died 19
Mrk 7:10 let him surely die'; 19
9:47 where their worm does not die 19
Lke 7:12 behold, a man who had died was being carried out 14
Act 2:29 he both died and was buried 19
5: 5 he fell down and died 11
10 Immediately she fell down at his feet and died. 11
7:15 he died, himself and our fathers 19
12:23 he was eaten by worms and died. 11
25:11 committed anything for which I deserve to die 12
Rom 1:32 that those who do such things deserve to die 12
7: 4 you have died to the law through the body 13
1Co 7:39 If the husband dies 16
11:30 many of you are weak and ill, and some have died 16
Php 2:30 for he nearly died for the work of Christ 12
1Pe 2:24 we might die to sin and live to righteousness. 6
Rev 1:18 I died, and behold I am alive for evermore 9
2: 8 the first and the last, who died and came to life. 9
1Es 1:31 after he was brought back to Jerusalem he died 18
2Es 1:18 better . . than to die in this wilderness.' 23
7:29 after these years my son the Messiah shall die 23
78 that a man shall die 23
10: 1 when my son entered . . he fell down and died. 23
4 but without ceasing mourn and fast until I die. 23
18 I will not go into the city, but I will die here. 23
34 do not forsake me, lest I die before my time. 23
48 When my son entered his wedding chamber he died,' 23
12:26 one of the kings shall die in his bed 23
45 For we are no better than those who died there. 23
13:24 are more blessed than those who have died. 23
15: 4 For every unbeliever shall die in his unbelief. 23
57 Your children shall die of hunger 22
16:22 who survive the famine shall die by the sword. 21
Tob 6:13 each died in the bridal chamber. 8
14:11 As he said this he died in his bed 10
Jdt 6: 8 will not die until you perish along with them. 8
8: 3 took to his bed and died in Bethulia his city 19
Wis 3:18 If they die young, they will have no hope 19
4: 7 though he die early 19
16 The righteous man who had died 15
15: 9 he is not concerned that he is destined to die 15
Sir 8: 7 remember that we all must die. 19
10:10 the king of today will die tomorrow. 19
14:13 Do good to a friend before you die 19
18 one dies and another is born. 19
23:17 he will never cease until he dies. 19
30: 4 The father may die, and yet he is not dead 19
5 when he died he was not grieved; 20
37:31 Many have died of gluttony 19
Bar 4: 1 and those who forsake her will die. 7
Bel 1: 8 If you do not tell me . . .you shall die. 7
9 Daniel shall die 7
12 we will die; or else Daniel will 7
1Mc 2:37 for they said, "Let us all die in our innocence; 7
2Mc 4: 7 When Seleucus died 18
5: 9 he . . died in exile 8
6:30 When he was about to die under the blows 19
31 in this way he died 17
7: 5 brothers . . encouraged one another to die nobly, 19
7 After the first brother had died in this way 17
13 When he too had died 17
14 One cannot but choose to die at the hands of men 17
40 he died in his integrity 17
41 Last of all, the mother died, after her sons. 19
3Mc 1:23 die courageously for the ancestral law 19
4Mc 4:15 When King Seleucus died 19
6:22 die nobly for your religion! 19
10: 2 the same father begot me and those who died 7
11:13 After he too had died 19
22 equipped with nobility, will die with my brothers 14
12: 4 be miserably tortured and die before your time 14
18: 9 when these sons had grown up their father died 19

die *See also* deserve, doom.

die a good death 1. ἀπευθανατίζω
2Mc 6:28 a noble example of how to die a good death 1

cause to die 1. מות
Ps 105:29 waters into blood, and caused their fish to die. 1

die down 1. καταπαύω
Jdt 6: 1 When the disturbance . . died down 1

must die 1. morior
2Es 8:58 though knowing full well that they must die. 1

dies *See* animal, man.

differ 1. διαφέρω 2. διάφορος 3. ἔχω διαφοράν
Rom 12: 6 gifts that differ according to the grace given 2
1Co 15:41 star differs from star in glory. 1
Sir 0: 2 differ not a little as originally expressed. 3
3Mc 6:26 from the beginning differed from all nations 1

difference 1. διάστασις 2. διαφορά
Ezk 22:26 neither have they taught the difference *
44:23 They shall teach my people the difference *
1Mc 3:18 no difference between saving by many or by few. 2
3Mc 3: 7 they gossiped about the differences in worship 1

difference *See also* make.

different 1. אַחֵר 2. הֶפֶךְ 3. שׁנה 4. שׁנא (A) 5. שׁנה (A) 6. ἀλλοιόω 7. γένος 8. ἕτερος 9. alius
Num 14:24 Caleb, because he has a different spirit 1
Est 1: 7 in golden goblets, goblets of different kinds 3
3: 8 their laws are different from . . other people 3
Isa 65:15 his servants he will call by a different name. 1
Ezk 16:34 different from other women in your harlotries; 2
34 therefore you were different. 2
Dan 7: 3 great beasts . . different from one another. 4
7 different from all the beasts that were before 4
19 beast, which was different from all the rest 5
23 kingdom . . different from all the kingdoms 4
24 different from the former ones, 4
1Co 14:10 There are doubtless many different languages 7
2Co 11: 4 if you receive a different spirit 8
4 if you accept a different gospel 8
Gal 1: 6 turning to a different gospel– 8
2Es 5:53 Those . . are different from those 9
6:26 and converted to a different spirit. 9
Wis 7: 5 no king has had a different beginning 8
Sir 33: 8 he appointed the different seasons and feasts; 6
11 appointed their different ways; 6

different kind 1. כִּלְאַיִם
Lev 19:19 not let your cattle breed with a different kind 1

different opinion 1. סְעִפָּה
1Kg 18:21 will you go limping with two different opinions? 1

difficult 1. פלא 2. אנס (A) 3. יַקִּיר (A) 4. angustia 5. angustus
Deu 17: 8 any case . . which is too difficult for you 1
Dan 2:11 thing that the king asks is difficult 3
4: 9 know . . that no mystery is difficult for you 2
2Es 7:14 the difficult and vain experiences 5
18 can endure difficult circumstances 5
18 have suffered the difficult circumstances 4

difficult of access 1. δυσπρόσιτος
2Mc 12:21 that place was hard to besiege and difficult of access 1

too difficult 1. χαλεπός
Sir 3:21 Seek not what is too difficult for you 1

difficulty 1. δυσχέρεια 2. κοπιάω 3. μόλις 4. σκάνδαλον 5. στενοχωρία 6. χαλεπός 7. vix
Act 27: 7 arrived with difficulty off Cni'dus 3
8 Coasting along it with difficulty 3
16 we managed with difficulty to secure the boat; 3
Rom 16:17 those who create dissensions and difficulties 4
2Es 9:21 I saw and spared some with great difficulty 7
Wis 6:14 He . . will have no difficulty 2
17:11 it has always exaggerated the difficulties. 6
1Mc 13: 3 you know also the wars and the difficulties 5
2Mc 2:24 the difficulty there is 1
3Mc 5:15 when he had with difficulty roused him 3

dig 1. חפר 2. חצב 3. חתר 4. כרה 5. נקר 6. עזק 7. קור 8. ὀρύσσω 9. σκάπτω
Gen 21:30 you may be a witness for me that I dug this well. 1
26:15 the wells which his father's servants had dug 1
18 Isaac dug again the wells of water 1
18 the wells of water which had been dug 1
19 when Isaac's servants dug in the valley 1
21 Then they dug another well, and they quarreled 1
22 he moved from there and dug another well 1
25 And there Isaac's servants dug a well. 4
32 came and told him about the well which they had dug 1
Exd 7:24 Egyptians dug round about the Nile for water 1
21:33 when a man digs a pit and does not cover it 4
Num 21:18 well which the princes dug, which the nobles 1
Deu 8: 9 a land . . out of whose hills you can dig copper. 2
23:13 when you sit down outside, you shall dig a hole 1
2Kg 19:24 I dug wells and drank foreign waters 7
Job 3:21 and dig for it more than for hid treasures; 1
Ps 35: 7 without cause they dug a pit for my life. 1
57: 6 They dug a pit in my way, but they have fallen 4
94:13 until a pit is dug for the wicked. 4
119:85 Godless men have dug pitfalls for me 4
Prv 26:27 He who digs a pit will fall into it 4
Ecc 10: 8 He who digs a pit will fall into it; 1
Isa 5: 2 He digged it and cleared it of stones, and planted 6
37:25 I dug wells and drank waters 7
51: 1 and to the quarry from which you were digged. 5
Jer 13: 7 and dug, and I took the waistcloth from the place 1

18:20 Yet they have dug a pit for my life. 4
22 For they have dug a pit to take me, and laid snares 4
Ezk 8: 8 Then said he to me, "Son of man, dig in the wall"; 3
8 and when I dug in the wall, lo, there was a door. 3
12: 5 Dig through the wall in their sight, and go out 3
7 I dug through the wall with my own hands; 3
12 and shall go forth; he shall dig through the wall 3
Ams 9: 2 Though they dig into Sheol 3
Mat 21:33 dug a wine press in it, and built a tower 8
25:18 dug in the ground and hid his master's money. 8
Mrk 12: 1 and dug a pit for the wine press 8
Lke 6:48 he is like a man building a house, who dug deep 9
13: 8 till I dig about it and put on manure. 9
16: 3 I am not strong enough to dig 9
Tob 8: 9 Raguel arose and went and dug a grave 8
Sir 27:26 He who digs a pit will fall into it 8

dig a grave 1. ὀρύσσω
Tob 2: 7 I went and dug a grave and buried the body. 1

dig out 1. חפר
Ps 7:15 He makes a pit, digging it out, and falls 1

dig through 1. חתר
Job 24:16 In the dark they dig through houses; 1

dignify 1. κόσμιος
1Ti 3: 2 dignified, hospitable, an apt teacher 1

dignity 1. גֹּבַהּ 2. גְּדוּלָּה 3. הָדָר 4. שְׂאֵת 5. δόξα
6. μεγαλεῖος 7. ὑπεροχή
Est 6: 3 What honor or dignity has been bestowed 2
Job 40:10 Deck yourself with majesty and dignity; 1
Prv 31:25 Strength and dignity are her clothing 3
Hab 1: 7 their justice and dignity proceed 4
Sir 45:24 have the dignity of the priesthood for ever. 6
2Mc 6:23 worthy of his years and the dignity of his old age 7
15:13 distinguished by his gray hair and dignity 5
dignity *See also* calm.

diligence 1. προσοχή
Sir 11:18 is rich through his diligence and self-denial 1

all diligence 1. אָסְפַּרְנָא (A) 2. ἐπιμελῶς
Ezr 6:12 make a decree; let it be done with all diligence. 1
13 did with all diligence what Darius the king had 1
7:17 with all diligence buy bulls, rams, and lambs 1
21 requires of you, be it done with all diligence 1
1Es 6:34 done with all diligence as here prescribed. 2

diligent 1. חָרוּץ 2. שחר 3. ἐπιμονή
Prv 10: 4 but the hand of the diligent makes rich. 1
12:24 The hand of the diligent will rule 1
27 but the diligent man will get precious wealth. 1
13: 4 soul of the diligent is richly supplied. 1
24 but he who loves him is diligent to discipline 2
21: 5 plans of the diligent lead surely to abundance 1
Sir 38:27 each is diligent in making a great variety 3
diligent *See also* labor.

diligently 1. יטב 2. מְאֹד 3. קָשַׁב 4. אָסְפַּרְנָא (A)
5. ἀκριβῶς 6. ἐπιμελῶς
Exd 15:26 saying, "If you will diligently hearken †
Lev 10:16 Now Moses diligently inquired about the goat †
Deu 4: 9 Only take heed, and keep your soul diligently 2
6:17 You shall diligently keep the commandments †
13:14 inquire and make search and ask diligently; 1
17: 4 then you shall inquire diligently 1
19:18 judges shall inquire diligently 1
Ezr 5: 8 this work goes on diligently and prospers 4
Ps 119: 4 commanded thy precepts to be kept diligently. 2
Isa 21: 7 let him listen diligently, very diligently. 3
55: 2 Hearken diligently to me, and eat what is good †
Jer 12:16 if they will diligently learn the ways of my †
Zec 6:15 if you will diligently obey the voice of the LORD †
Mat 2: 8 saying, "Go and search diligently for the child 5
Lke 15: 8 seek diligently until she finds it? 6
diligently *See also* listen, seek, teach.

do diligently 1. יטב
Mic 7: 3 hands are upon what is evil, to do it diligently; 1

dill 1. קֶצַח 2. ἄνηθον
Isa 28:25 does he not scatter dill, sow cummin 1
27 Dill is not threshed with a threshing sledge 1
27 but dill is beaten out with a stick 1
Mat 23:23 you tithe mint and dill and cummin 2

dim 1. חשך 2. כבד 3. כֵּהָה 4. כהה 5. קום
Gen 27: 1 his eyes were dim so that he could not see 4
48:10 Now the eyes of Israel were dim with age 2
Lev 13: 6 if the diseased spot is dim and the disease has 3
21 if . . it is not deeper than the skin, but is dim 3
26 if . . it is no deeper than the skin, but is dim 3
28 if the spot . . is dim, it is a swelling 3
56 if the priest examines, and the disease is dim 3
Deu 34: 7 his eye was not dim, nor his natural force abated. 4
1Kg 14: 4 his eyes were dim because of his age. 5
Ecc 12: 3 those that look through the windows are dimmed 1
dim *See also* grow, make.

dimension 1. מִדָּה
Ezk 43:13 These are the dimensions of the altar by cubits 1
48:16 its dimensions: the north side 4,500 cubits 1

diminish 1. גרע 2. דלל 3. מעט 4. ἐλαττόω
5. ἐλάττωσις 6. σμικρύνω
Exd 21:10 he shall not diminish her food, her clothing 1
Lev 25:16 if the years are few you shall diminish the price 3
Ps 107:39 When they are diminished and brought low 3
Isa 19: 6 branches of Egypt's Nile will diminish and dry up 2
Ezk 16:27 and diminished your allotted portion 1
Sir 18: 6 It is not possible to diminish or increase them 4
31: 4 The poor man toils as his livelihood diminishes 5
Bar 2:34 and they will not be diminished. 6

dimly 1. כֵּהָה 2. ἐν αἰνίγματι
Isa 42: 3 and a dimly burning wick he will not quench; 1
1Co 13:12 now we see in a mirror dimly, but then face to face. 2

dine 1. אכל 2. אכל לֶחֶם 3. ἀριστάω 4. ἐσθίω
5. κάθημι
Gen 43:16 for the men are to dine with me at noon. 1
2Kg 25:29 he dined regularly at the king's table; 2
Jer 52:33 every day of his life he dined . . at the king's 1
Lke 11:37 a Pharisee asked him to dine with him 3
14: 1 when he went to dine at the house of a ruler 4
Sir 9: 9 Never dine with another man's wife 5

dinner 1. אֲרֻחָה 2. מִשְׁתֶּה 3. ἀγαθός 4. ἄριστον
Est 5: 4 let the king and Haman come this day to a dinner 2
5 the king and Haman came to the dinner 2
8 the king and Haman come tomorrow to the dinner 2
14 then go merrily with the king to the dinner. 2
Prv 15:17 Better is a dinner of herbs where love is 1
Mat 22: 4 Behold, I have made ready my dinner 4
Lke 11:38 he did not first wash before dinner. 4
14:12 When you give a dinner or a banquet 4
1Co 10:27 If one of the unbelievers invites you to dinner •
Tob 2: 1 a good dinner was prepared for me 3
12:13 did not hesitate to rise and leave your dinner 3
Bel 1:34 Take the dinner which you have to Babylon 3
37 Take the dinner which God has sent you. 4
dinner *See also* companion.

dip 1. בוא 2. טבל 3. βάπτω 4. ἐμβάπτω
Gen 37:31 killed a goat, and dipped the robe in the blood; 2
Exd 12:22 Take a bunch of hyssop and dip it in the blood 2
Lev 4: 6 the priest shall dip his finger in the blood 2
17 the priest shall dip his finger in the blood 2
9: 9 he dipped his finger in the blood 2
14: 6 dip them and the living bird in the blood 2
16 dip his right finger in the oil that is in his left 2
51 dip them in the blood of the bird that was killed 2
Num19:18 shall take hyssop, and dip it in the water 2
Deu 33:24 let him dip his foot in oil. 2
Jos 3:15 the feet . . were dipped in the brink of the water 2
Rut 2:14 eat some bread, and dip your morsel in the wine. 2
1Sm 14:27 tip of the staff . . and dipped it in the honeycomb 2
2Kg 5:14 he went down and dipped himself . . in the Jordan 2
8:15 the coverlet and dipped it in water and spread it 2
Jer 13: 1 put it on your loins, and do not dip it in water. 1
Mat 26:23 He who has dipped his hand in the dish with me 4
Mrk 14:20 one who is dipping bread into the dish with me. 4
Lke 16:24 send Laz'arus to dip the end of his finger in water 3
Joh 13:26 I shall give this morsel when I have dipped it 3
26 when he had dipped the morsel, he gave it to Judas 3
Rev 19:13 He is clad in a robe dipped in blood 3

dip out 1. ἀποβάπτω
2Mc 1:20 he ordered them to dip it out and bring it. 1

dip up 1. חשף
Isa 30:14 or to dip up water out of the cistern. 1

direct 1. אשר 2. דבר 3. יסר 4. יעד 5. ירה 6. ישר
7. כון 8. נצח 9. נתן 10. ערך 11. רום 12. שלח אֶל
13. βούλομα 14. διατάσσω 15. διδάσκω 16. εἶπον
17. εὐθύνω 18. κατά 19. κατευθύνω 20. κατόρθωσις
21. οἰκονομέω 22. συντάσσω 23. τάσσω 24. χείρ
25. χρηματίζω 26. dico 27. dispono 28. sermo
Num27:23 as the LORD directed through Moses. 2
Deu 17:10 careful to do according to all that they direct 5
24: 8 all that the Levitical priests shall direct you; 5
1Sm 7: 3 put away . . and direct your heart to the LORD 7
1Kg 5: 9 rafts to go by sea to the place you direct 12
1Ch 15:22 should direct the music, for he understood it. 3
29:18 thy people, and direct their hearts toward thee. 7
2Ch 32:30 directed them down to the west side of the city 6
34:13 were over the burden bearers and directed 8
Job 32:14 He has not directed his words against me 10
Ps 74: 3 Direct thy steps to the perpetual ruins; 11
Prv 16: 9 but the LORD directs his steps. 7
23:19 my son, and be wise, and direct your mind in the way. 1
Isa 10:25 my anger will be directed to their destruction. •
40:13 Who has directed the Spirit of the LORD 7
Jer 10:23 it is not in man who walks to direct his steps. 7
Ezk 21:16 right and left where your edge is directed. 4
23:25 I will direct my indignation against you 9
26: 9 He will direct the shock of his battering rams 9
Mat 21: 6 The disciples went and did as Jesus had directed 22
26:19 the disciples did as Jesus had directed them 22
27:10 as the Lord directed me. 22
28:15 they took the money and did as they were directed; 15
16 to the mountain to which Jesus had directed 23
Lke 8:55 he directed that something should be given her 14
Act 7:44 he who spoke to Moses directed him to make it 14
10:22 was directed by a holy angel to send for you 25
1Co 16: 1 as I directed the churches of Galatia 14
1Th 3:11 our Lord Jesus, direct our way to you; 19
2Th 3: 5 May the Lord direct your hearts to the love of God 19
Tit 1: 5 appoint elders in every town as I directed you 14
Jas 3: 4 wherever the will of the pilot directs. 13
2Es 9:26 I went, as he directed me, into the field 26
10:32 I did as you directed, and went out into the field 28
13:26 and he will direct those who are left. 27
Jdt 11: 7 who had sent you to direct every living soul 20
12: 8 prayed the Lord God of Israel to direct her way 19
AEs 16:16 who has directed the kingdom 19
Wis 6: 9 To you then, O monarchs, my words are directed •
Sir 25:26 If she does not go as you direct 24
37:15 he may direct your way in truth. 17
51:20 I directed my soul to her 19
1Mc 1:44 he directed them to follow customs strange •
4:47 Then they took unhewn stones, as the law directs 18
53 they rose and offered sacrifice, as the law directs 18
10:11 He directed those who were doing the work 16
2Mc 3:14 went in to direct the inspection of these funds. 21

direct (2) 1. παραχρῆμα
4Mc 14: 9 yes, not only heard the direct word of threat 1

direct aright 1. εὐθύνω 2. κατευθύνω
Sir 6:17 directs his friendship aright 1
38:10 Give up your faults and direct your hands aright 1
39: 7 He will direct his counsel and knowledge aright 2
49: 9 did good to those who directed their ways aright. 1

direct one's gaze 1. ἀτενίζω
Act 3: 4 Peter directed his gaze at him, with John, and said 1

direct one's step 1. ישר
Ps 119:128 Therefore I direct my steps by all thy precepts; 1

direct to cease 1. καταστέλλω
3Mc 6: 1 Eleazar . . directed the elders around him to cease 1

direct well 1. יטב
Jer 2:33 How well you direct your course to seek lovers! 1

direction 1. דַּבֶּרֶת 2. יָד 3. כְּתָב 4. מִכְתָּב 5. פֶּה
6. γραφή 7. διαγορεύω
Exd 38:21 the Levites under the direction of Ith'amar 2
Num 7: 8 under the direction of Ith'amar the son of Aaron 2
Deu 33: 3 receiving direction from thee 1
Jos 9:14 and did not ask direction from the LORD. 5
1Ch 25: 2 sons of Asaph, under the direction of Asaph 2
2 who prophesied under the direction of the king. 2
3 under the direction of their father Jedu'thun 2
6 all under the direction of their father 2
2Ch 23:18 under the direction of the Levitical priests 2
26:11 under the direction of Hanani'ah 2
35: 4 following the directions of David king 3
4 following . . directions of Solomon his son. 4
Ezr 3:10 praise the LORD, according to the directions 2
Jer 5:31 and the priests rule at their direction; 2
1Es 1: 5 in accordance with the directions of David 6
5:49 the directions in the book of Moses the man of God. 7
60 according to the directions of David •

direction (2) 1. בּוֹאֲכָה 2. דֶּרֶךְ 3. מָקוֹם 4. עֵבֶר
5. רֶבַע
Gen 10:19 from Sidon, in the direction of Gerar 1
19 and in the direction of Sodom, Gomor'rah, Admah 1
30 extended from Mesha in the direction of Sephar 1
13:10 like the land of Egypt, in the direction of Zo'ar; 1
25:18 is opposite Egypt in the direction of Assyria; 1
Deu 1:40 wilderness in the direction of the Red Sea.' 2
2: 1 the wilderness in the direction of the Red Sea 2
8 went in the direction of the wilderness of Moab. 2
Jos 8:15 and fled in the direction of the wilderness. 2
12: 3 and in the direction of Beth-jesh'imoth, to the sea 2
18:13 boundary passes along . . in the direction of Luz †
Jdg 9:37 coming from the direction of the Diviners' Oak. 2
20:42 turned . . in the direction of the wilderness; 2
1Sm 6:12 cows went . . in the direction of Beth-she'mesh 2
1Kg 18: 6 Ahab went in one direction by himself 2
6 Obadi'ah went in another direction by himself. 2
2Kg 3:20 water came from the direction of Edom 2
9:27 Ahazi'ah . . fled in the direction of Beth-haggan. 2
25: 4 And they went in the direction of the Arabah. 2
Isa 47:15 they wander about each in his own direction; 4
Jer 52: 7 And they went in the direction of the Arabah. 2

Ezk 1:17 they went in any of their four directions 5
8: 5 your eyes now in the direction of the north. 2
9: 2 six men came from the direction of the upper gate 2
10:11 they went in any of their four directions 5
11 but in whatever direction the front wheel faced 3

direction *See* go.

northerly direction 1. מִצָּפוֹן

Jos 18:17 it bends in a northerly direction going 1

directions *See* give, send.

directly forward 1. לְנֹכַח

Prv 4:25 Let your eyes look directly forward 1

dirge 1. קִינָה 2. θρῆνος 3. μέλι

Jer 9:20 a lament, and each to her neighbor a dirge. 1
3Mc 5:25 with most tearful supplication and mournful dirges 3
6:32 They ceased their chanting of dirges 2

funeral dirge 1. θρῆνος

1Mc 9:41 the voice of their musicians into a funeral dirge. 1

dirt 1. גּוּשׁ 2. טִיט 3. פַּרְשְׁדֹנָה 4. γῆ 5. ῥύπος

Jdg 3:22 out of his belly; and the dirt came out. 3
Job 7: 5 My flesh is clothed with worms and dirt; 1
Isa 57:20 cannot rest, and its waters toss up mire and dirt. 2
Zec 9: 3 like dust, and gold like the dirt of the streets. 2
1Pe 3:21 not as a removal of dirt from the body 5
Wis 15:10 His heart is ashes, his hope is cheaper than dirt 4

disable 1. שׁבר 2. μέλεσιν ἀναπείρους ποιέω

Lev 22:22 Animals blind or disabled or mutilated 1
2Mc 8:24 wounded and disabled most of Nicanor's army 2

disagree 1. ἀσύμφωνος

Act 28:25 as they disagreed among themselves 1

disagreement 1. διαφέρω

2Mc 3: 4 Simon . . had a disagreement with the high priest 1

disappear 1. צמת 2. שׁבת 3. ἀφίστημι 4. non appareo 5. non conpareo

Job 6:17 In time of heat they disappear; 1
Isa 17: 3 The fortress will disappear from E'phraim 2
2Es 11:13 it came to its end and disappeared 4
14 so that it disappeared like the first. 4
16 I announce this to you before you disappear. 4
18 and it also disappeared. 4
20 some . . that ruled, yet disappeared suddenly; 5
22 wings and the two little wings disappeared; 5
26 one was set up, but suddenly disappeared; 5
27 a second also, and this disappeared more quickly 5
33 the middle head also suddenly disappeared 5
12: 2 behold, the remaining head disappeared 5
3 I looked, and behold, they also disappeared 4
26 your seeing that the large head disappeared 4
Sir 39: 9 his memory will not disappear 3

surely disappear 1. non appareo

2Es 11:45 Therefore you will surely disappear, you eagle 1

disappoint 1. בושׁ 2. כזב 3. καταισχύνω

Job 6:20 are disappointed because they were confident; 1
41: 9 Behold, the hope of a man is disappointed; 2
Ps 22: 5 in thee they trusted, and were not disappointed. 1
Rom 5: 5 and hope does not disappoint us 3

disapproval *See* express.

disarm 1. ἀπεκδύομαι

Col 2:15 He disarmed the principalities and powers 1

disaster 1. אֵיד 2. אנשׁ 3. הַוָּה 4. מַכָּה 5. נֶכֶר 6. פִּיד 7. רַע 8. רָעָה 9. שֶׁבֶר 10. שׁוֹט 11. περίστασις 12. πληγή 13. συμφορά

Gen 19:19 flee to the hills, lest the disaster overtake me 8
Jdg 20:34 did not know that disaster was close upon them. 8
41 for they saw that disaster was close upon them. 8
Job 9:23 When disaster brings sudden death, he mocks 10
30:24 and in his disaster cry for help? 6
31: 3 and disaster the workers of iniquity? 5
Prv 24:22 for disaster from them will rise suddenly 1
Isa 31: 2 yet he is wise and brings disaster 7
47:11 disaster shall fall upon you 3
Jer 4:20 Disaster follows hard on disaster 9
20 Disaster follows hard on disaster 9
17:16 nor have I desired the day of disaster 2
19: 8 and will hiss because of all its disasters. 4
49:17 and will hiss because of all its disasters. 4
Ezk 7: 5 Thus says the Lord GOD: Disaster after disaster! 8
5 Thus says the Lord GOD: Disaster after disaster! 8
26 Disaster comes upon disaster 3
26 Disaster comes upon disaster 3
Obd 1:13 you should not have gloated over his disaster 8
Zep 3:18 I will remove disaster from you •
Zec 1:15 they furthered the disaster. 8
Wis 18:21 put an end to the disaster 13
1Mc 3:29 because of the dissension and disaster 12
8: 4 inflicted great disaster upon them 12
2Mc 4:16 For this reason heavy disaster overtook them 11
4Mc 3:21 and caused many and various disasters. 13

disbelieve 1. ἀπειθέω 2. ἀπιστέω 3. discredo

Lke 24:41 while they still disbelieved for joy 2
Act 19: 9 when some were stubborn and disbelieved 1
28:24 while others disbelieved. 2
2Es 16:36 do not disbelieve what the Lord says. 3
Wis 18:13 For though they had disbelieved everything 2

discard 1. זנח

2Ch 29:19 utensils which King Ahaz discarded in his reign 1

discern 1. בין 2. ידע בֵּין 3. נכר 4. שׁמע 5. ἀνακρίνω 6. γινώσκω 7. γνῶσις 8. γνωστός 9. διακρίνω 10. ἐνθυμέομαι 11. θεωρέω 12. κρίνω 13. κριτικός

Deu 32:29 wise . . they would discern their latter end! 1
2Sm 14:17 like the angel of God to discern good and evil. 4
19:35 can I discern what is pleasant and what is not? 2
1Kg 3: 9 that I may discern between good and evil; for who 1
11 asked . . understanding to discern what is right 4
12 I give you a wise and discerning mind, so that none 1
Job 4:16 I could not discern its appearance. 3
6:30 Cannot my taste discern calamity? 1
38:20 that you may discern the paths to its home? 1
Ps 19:12 But who can discern his errors? 1
139: 2 thou discernest my thoughts from afar. 1
Prv 14: 8 The wisdom of a prudent man is to discern his way 1
Isa 44:18 They know not, nor do they discern; 1
Hos 14: 9 whoever is discerning, let him know them; 1
1Co 2:14 because they are spiritually discerned. 5
11:29 who eats and drinks without discerning the body 9
Heb 4:12 discerning the thoughts . . of the heart. 13
Wis 2:22 nor discern the prize for blameless souls; 12
6:12 she is easily discerned by those who love her 11
9:13 who can discern what the Lord wills? 10
Sir 1:19 knowledge and discerning comprehension 7
Bar 3:14 you may at the same time discern where there is 6
Sus 1:42 O eternal God, who dost discern what is secret 8

discerning man 1. בין

Isa 29:14 discernment of . . discerning men shall be hid. 1

discernment 1. בִּינָה 2. טַעַם 3. תְּבוּנָה 4. αἴσθησις

Job 12:20 and takes away the discernment of the elders. 2
Isa 27:11 For this is a people without discernment; 1
29:14 discernment of . . discerning men shall be hid. 1
44:19 nor is there knowledge or discernment to say 3
Php 1: 9 with knowledge and all discernment 4

discernment *See also* man.

discharge 1. בדל 2. זוֹב 3. זוב 4. יָבַל 5. מִשְׁלַחַת 6. καταργέω

Lev 15: 2 When any man has a discharge from his body 3
2 from his body, his discharge is unclean 2
3 the law of his uncleanness for a discharge 2
3 whether his body runs with his discharge 2
3 or his body is stopped from discharge 2
4 Every bed on which he who has the discharge lies 3
6 on which he who has the discharge has sat 3
7 touches the body of him who has the discharge 3
8 who has the discharge spits on one who is clean 3
9 saddle on which he who has the discharge rides 3
11 Any one whom he that has the discharge touches 3
12 vessel which he who has the discharge touches 3
13 when he who has a discharge is cleansed 3
13 when he . . is cleansed of his discharge 2
15 make atonement for him . . for his discharge 2
19 When a woman has a discharge of blood 3
19 which is her regular discharge from her body 2
25 If a woman has a discharge of blood for many days 2
25 if she has a discharge beyond the time 3
25 all the days of the discharge she shall continue 2
26 bed on which she lies, all the days of her discharge 2
28 But if she is cleansed of her discharge 2
30 atonement for her . . for her unclean discharge 2
32 This is the law for him who has a discharge 3
33 for any one, male or female, who has a discharge 2
22: 4 who . . suffers a discharge may eat of the holy 3
22 Animals . . having a discharge or an itch 4
Num 5: 2 put out . . every one having a discharge 3
2Sm 3:29 never be without one who has a discharge 3
2Ch 25:10 Amazi'ah discharged the army that had come to him 1
Ecc 8: 8 there is no discharge from war 5
Rom 7: 2 she is discharged from the law 6
6 But now we are discharged from the law 6

disciple 1. לִמֻּד 2. μαθητεύω 3. μαθητής 4. μαθήτρια

Isa 8:16 seal the teaching among my disciples. 1
Mat 5: 1 when he sat down his disciples came to him. 3
8:21 Another of the disciples said to him 3
23 he got into the boat, his disciples followed him. 3
9:10 sat down with Jesus and his disciples. 3
11 Pharisees saw this, they said to his disciples 3
14 Then the disciples of John came to him, saying 3
14 Pharisees fast, but your disciples do not fast? 3
19 Jesus rose and followed him, with his disciples. 3
37 Then he said to his disciples 3
10: 1 he called to him his twelve disciples 3
24 A disciple is not above his teacher 3
25 it is enough for the disciple 3
42 a cup of cold water because he is a disciple 3
11: 1 instructing his twelve disciples 3
2 he sent word by his disciples 3
12: 1 his disciples were hungry 3
2 your disciples are doing what is not lawful to do 3
49 stretching out his hand toward his disciples 3
13:10 the disciples came and said to him 3
36 And his disciples came to him, saying 3
14:12 his disciples came and took the body 3
15 When it was evening, the disciples came to him 3
19 broke and gave the loaves to the disciples 3
19 and the disciples gave them to the crowds. 3
22 Then he made the disciples get into the boat 3
26 when the disciples saw him walking on the sea 3
15: 2 Why do your disciples transgress the tradition 3
12 Then the disciples came and said to him 3
23 And his disciples came and begged him, saying 3
32 Jesus called his disciples to him and said 3
33 the disciples said to him 3
36 he broke them and gave them to the disciples 3
36 and the disciples gave them to the crowds. 3
16: 5 When the disciples reached the other side 3
13 he asked his disciples 3
20 Then he strictly charged the disciples 3
21 From that time Jesus began to show his disciples 3
24 Then Jesus told his disciples 3
17: 6 When the disciples heard this 3
10 the disciples asked him 3
13 Then the disciples understood 3
16 I brought him to your disciples 3
19 Then the disciples came to Jesus privately 3
18: 1 At that time the disciples came to Jesus, saying 3
19:10 The disciples said to him, "If such is the case 3
13 The disciples rebuked the people; 3
23 Jesus said to his disciples, "Truly, I say to you 3
25 When the disciples heard this 3
20:17 he took the twelve disciples aside 3
21: 1 then Jesus sent two disciples 3
6 The disciples went and did as Jesus had directed 3
20 When the disciples saw it they marveled, saying 3
22:16 And they sent their disciples to him 3
23: 1 to the crowds and to his disciples 3
24: 1 when his disciples came to point out to him 3
3 the disciples came to him privately, saying 3
26: 1 he said to his disciples 3
8 when the disciples saw it, they were indignant 3
17 the disciples came to Jesus, saying 3
18 passover at your house with my disciples.' 3
19 the disciples did as Jesus had directed them 3
20 he sat at table with the twelve disciples; •
26 broke it, and gave it to the disciples and said 3
35 so said all the disciples. 3
36 he said to his disciples 3
40 he came to the disciples and found them sleeping; 3
45 Then he came to the disciples and said to them 3
56 Then all the disciples forsook him and fled. 3
27:57 who also was a disciple of Jesus. 2
64 lest his disciples go and steal him away 3
28: 7 Then go quickly and tell his disciples 3
8 ran to tell his disciples. 3
13 said, "Tell people, 'His disciples came by night 3
16 Now the eleven disciples went to Galilee 3
Mrk 2:15 sitting with Jesus and his disciples 3
16 said to his disciples 3
18 John's disciples and the Pharisees were fasting; 3
18 Why do John's disciples . . fast 3
18 the disciples of the Pharisees fast 3
18 your disciples do not fast? 3
23 his disciples began to pluck heads of grain. 3
3: 7 Jesus withdrew with his disciples to the sea 3
9 he told his disciples to have a boat ready for him 3
4:34 privately to his own disciples he explained 3
5:31 his disciples said to him, "You see the crowd 3
6: 1 his disciples followed him. 3
29 When his disciples heard of it 3
35 it grew late, his disciples came to him and said 3
41 broke the loaves, and gave them to the disciples 3
45 he made his disciples get into the boat 3
7: 2 they saw that some of his disciples ate 3
5 Why do your disciples not live 3
17 his disciples asked him about the parable. 3
8: 1 he called his disciples to him, and said to them 3
4 his disciples answered him, "How can one feed 3
6 he broke them and gave them to his disciples 3
10 he got into the boat with his disciples 3
27 Jesus went on with his disciples 3
27 on the way he asked his disciples 3
33 turning and seeing his disciples 3
34 the multitude with his disciples 3
9:14 when they came to the disciples 3
18 I asked your disciples to cast it out 3
28 his disciples asked him privately 3
31 for he was teaching his disciples, saying to them 3
10:10 in the house the disciples asked him again 3

13 the disciples rebuked them. 3
23 Jesus looked around and said to his disciples 3
24 the disciples were amazed at his words 3
46 as he was leaving Jericho with his disciples 3
11: 1 he sent two of his disciples 3
14 his disciples heard it. 3
12:43 he called his disciples to him 3
13: 1 one of his disciples said to him, "Look, Teacher 3
14:12 his disciples said to him, "Where will you have us 3
13 he sent two of his disciples, and said to them, "Go 3
14 where I am to eat the passover with my disciples?' 3
16 the disciples set out and went to the city 3
32 he said to his disciples, "Sit here, while I pray. 3
16: 7 But go, tell his disciples and Peter that he is going 3
Lke 5:30 their scribes murmured against his disciples 3
33 disciples of John fast often and offer prayers 3
33 so do the disciples of the Pharisees •
6: 1 his disciples plucked and ate some heads of grain 3
13 when it was day, he called his disciples 3
17 with a great crowd of his disciples 3
20 he lifted up his eyes on his disciples 3
40 A disciple is not above his teacher 3
7:11 his disciples and a great crowd went with him. 3
18 disciples of John told him of all these things. 3
19 John, calling to him two of his disciples 3
8: 9 his disciples asked him what this parable meant 3
22 One day he got into a boat with his disciples 3
9:14 he said to his disciples, "Make them sit down 3
16 gave them to the disciples 3
18 the disciples were with him 3
40 I begged your disciples to cast it out 3
43 he said to his disciples 3
54 when his disciples James and John saw it 3
10:23 Then turning to the disciples he said privately 3
11: 1 when he ceased, one of his disciples said to him 3
1 teach us to pray, as John taught his disciples. 3
12: 1 he began to say to his disciples first 3
22 he said to his disciples, "Therefore I tell you 3
14:26 he cannot be my disciple. 3
27 cannot be my disciple. 3
33 cannot be my disciple. 3
16: 1 He also said to the disciples, "There was a rich man 3
17: 1 he said to his disciples, "Temptations to sin 3
22 he said to the disciples, "The days are coming 3
18:15 when the disciples saw it, they rebuked them. 3
19:29 he sent two of the disciples 3
37 the whole multitude of the disciples 3
39 Teacher, rebuke your disciples. 3
20:45 he said to his disciples 3
22:11 where I am to eat the passover with my disciples?' 3
39 the disciples followed him. 3
45 when he rose from prayer, he came to the disciples 3
Joh 1:35 John was standing with two of his disciples; 3
37 The two disciples heard him say this 3
2: 2 invited to the marriage, with his disciples. 3
11 and his disciples believed in him. 3
12 with his mother . . and his disciples; 3
17 His disciples remembered that it was written 3
22 his disciples remembered that he had said this; 3
3:22 Jesus and his disciples went into the land 3
25 a discussion . . between John's disciples and a Jew 3
4: 1 making and baptizing more disciples than John 3
2 Jesus . . did not baptize, but only his disciples) 3
8 For his disciples had gone away into the city 3
27 Just then his disciples came. 3
31 the disciples besought him, saying, "Rabbi, eat. 3
33 So the disciples said to one another 3
6: 3 and there sat down with his disciples. 3
8 One of his disciples, Andrew 3
12 he told his disciples, "Gather up the fragments 3
16 his disciples went down to the sea 3
22 Jesus had not entered the boat with his disciples 3
22 his disciples had gone away alone. 3
24 Jesus was not there, nor his disciples 3
60 Many of his disciples, when they heard it, said 3
61 knowing in himself that his disciples murmured 3
66 After this many of his disciples drew back 3
7: 3 your disciples may see the works you are doing. 3
8:31 you are truly my disciples 3
9: 2 his disciples asked him, "Rabbi, who sinned 3
27 Do you too want to become his disciples? 3
28 they reviled him, saying, "You are his disciple 3
28 we are disciples of Moses. 3
11: 7 Then after this he said to the disciples 3
8 The disciples said to him, "Rabbi 3
12 The disciples said to him, "Lord 3
54 there he stayed with the disciples. 3
12: 4 Judas Iscariot, one of his disciples 3
16 His disciples did not understand this at first; 3
13: 5 began to wash the disciples' feet 3
22 The disciples looked at one another 3
23 One of his disciples, whom Jesus loved 3
35 all men will know that you are my disciples 3
15: 8 and so prove to be my disciples. 3
16:17 Some of his disciples said to one another 3
29 His disciples said, "Ah 3
18: 1 he went forth with his disciples 3
1 a garden, which he and his disciples entered. 3
2 Jesus often met there with his disciples. 3
15 so did another disciple 3
15 this disciple was known to the high priest 3
16 the other disciple, who was known to the high priest 3
17 Are not you also one of this man's disciples? 3
19 about his disciples and his teaching. 3
25 Are not you also one of his disciples? 3
19:26 and the disciple whom he loved standing near 3
27 Then he said to the disciple, "Behold, your mother! 3
27 the disciple took her to his own home. 3
38 Joseph of Arimathe'a, who was a disciple of Jesus 3
20: 2 went to Simon Peter and the other disciple 3
3 Peter then came out with the other disciple 3
4 the other disciple outran Peter 3
8 the other disciple, who reached the tomb first 3
10 the disciples went back to their homes. 3
18 Mary Mag'dalene went and said to the disciples 3
19 the doors being shut where the disciples were 3
20 the disciples were glad when they saw the Lord. 3
25 the other disciples told him 3
26 his disciples were again in the house 3
30 many other signs in the presence of the disciples 3
21: 1 revealed himself again to the disciples 3
2 two others of his disciples were together. 3
4 yet the disciples did not know that it was Jesus. 3
7 That disciple whom Jesus loved said to Peter 3
8 the other disciples came in the boat 3
12 none of the disciples dared ask him, "Who are you? 3
14 Jesus was revealed to the disciples 3
20 following them the disciple whom Jesus loved 3
23 The saying . . that this disciple was not to die; 3
24 the disciple who is bearing witness to these 3
Act 6: 1 when the disciples were increasing in number 3
2 the twelve summoned the body of the disciples 3
7 the number of the disciples multiplied greatly 3
9: 1 against the disciples of the Lord 3
10 there was a disciple at Damascus named Anani'as. 3
19 he was with the disciples at Damascus. 3
25 his disciples took him by night 3
26 he attempted to join the disciples 3
26 for they did not believe that he was a disciple. 3
36 Now there was at Joppa a disciple named Tabitha 4
38 the disciples . . sent two men to him entreating 3
11:26 the disciples were . . called Christians. 3
29 the disciples determined . . to send relief 3
13:52 the disciples were filled with joy 3
14:20 when the disciples gathered about him, he rose up 3
22 strengthening the souls of the disciples 3
28 remained no little time with the disciples. 3
15:10 by putting a yoke upon the neck of the disciples 3
16: 1 A disciple was there, named Timothy 3
18:23 strengthening all the disciples. 3
27 wrote to the disciples to receive him 3
19: 1 There he found some disciples. 3
9 he withdrew . . taking the disciples with him 3
30 the disciples would not let him; 3
20: 1 Paul sent for the disciples 3
30 to draw away the disciples after them. 3
21: 4 having sought out the disciples, we stayed there 3
16 some of the disciples from Caesare'a went with us 3
16 Mnason of Cyprus, an early disciple 3

disciple *See also* make.

fellow disciple 1. *συμμαθητής*

Joh 11:16 Thomas . . said to his fellow disciples 1

discipline 1. יסר 2. מוּסָר 3. *ἄσκησις* 4. *παιδεία* 5. *παιδευτής* 6. *παιδεύω* 7. erudio

Lev 26:23 if by this discipline you are not turned to me •
Deu 4:36 you hear his voice, that he might discipline you; 1
8: 5 as a man disciplines his son, the LORD your God 1
5 as a man . . the LORD your God disciplines you. 1
11: 2 consider the discipline of the LORD your God 2
Ps 50:17 For you hate discipline 2
Prv 3:11 My son, do not despise the LORD'S discipline 2
5:12 you say, "How I hated discipline 2
23 He dies for lack of discipline 2
6:23 reproofs of discipline are the way of life 2
12: 1 Whoever loves discipline loves knowledge 2
13:24 but he who loves him is diligent to discipline 2
15:10 severe discipline for him who forsakes the way; 2
19:18 Discipline your son while there is hope; 1
22:15 but the rod of discipline drives it far from him. 2
23:13 Do not withhold discipline from a child; 2
29:17 Discipline your son, and he will give you rest; 1
19 By mere words a servant is not disciplined 1
Jer 7:28 and did not accept discipline; 2
Eph 6: 4 bring them up in the discipline . . of the Lord. 4
Heb 12: 5 do not regard lightly the discipline of the Lord 4
6 For the Lord disciplines him whom he loves 6
7 It is for discipline that you have to endure 4
7 whom his father does not discipline? 6
8 If you are left without discipline 4
9 we have had earthly fathers to discipline us 5
10 they disciplined us for a short time 6
10 he disciplines us for our good •
11 For the moment all discipline seems painful 4
2Es 14:34 rule over your minds and discipline your hearts 7
Tob 4:14 be disciplined in all your conduct. 6
Wis 1: 5 a holy and disciplined spirit 4
3: 5 Having been disciplined a little 6
11: 9 though they were being disciplined in mercy 6
Sir 4:17 will torment him by her discipline 4
7:23 Do you have children? Discipline them 6
18:14 compassion on those who accept his discipline 4
22: 6 chastising and discipline are wisdom 4
23: 2 the discipline of wisdom over my mind! 4
26:14 nothing so precious as a disciplined soul. 6
30: 2 He who disciplines his son will profit by him 6
13 Discipline your son and take pains with him 6
32:14 He who fears the Lord will accept his discipline 4
33:24 bread and discipline and work for a servant. 4
38:33 they cannot expound discipline or judgment 4
42: 5 of much discipline of children 4
Bar 4:13 nor tread the paths of discipline 4
2Mc 6:12 not to destroy but to discipline our people. 4
16 Though he disciplines us with calamities 6
7:33 to rebuke and discipline us 4
10: 4 might be disciplined by him with forbearance 6
4Mc 13:22 our discipline in the law of God. 3

become disciplined 1. *παιδεύω*

Sir 23:15 will never become disciplined all his days. 1

well disciplined 1. *παιδεύω*

Sir 31:19 How ample a little is for a well-disciplined man! 1

disclose 1. גלה 2. גלה אֹזֶן 3. נגד 4. *ἀναγγέλλω* 5. *ἀναδείκνυμι* 6. *ἀποκαλύπτω* 7. *δηλόω* 8. *ἐκφαίνω* 9. *ἐμφαίνω* 10. *μηνύω* 11. *φαιδρός* 12. *φανερόω* 13. demonstro 14. ostendo

1Sm 20: 2 does nothing . . without disclosing it to me; 2
12 shall I not then send and disclose it to you? 2
13 if I do not disclose it to you, and send you away 2
22: 8 No one discloses to me when my son makes a league 2
8 none . . discloses to me that my son has stirred up 2
17 knew that he fled, and did not disclose it to me. 2
Prv 25: 9 do not disclose another's secret; 1
29:24 hears the curse, but discloses nothing. 3
Isa 26:21 the earth will disclose the blood shed upon her 1
Act 23:30 when it was disclosed to me 10
Rom 16:26 but is now disclosed 12
1Co 3:13 the Day will disclose it 7
4: 5 who . . will disclose the purposes of the heart. 12
14:25 the secrets of his heart are disclosed 11
2Es 4:43 the things . . will be disclosed to you. 13
7:26 the land which now is hidden shall be disclosed. 14
36 and the furnace of hell shall be disclosed 14
14:35 the deeds of the ungodly will be disclosed. 14
Sir 6: 9 will disclose a quarrel to your disgrace. 6
19: 8 unless it would be a sin for you, do not disclose it; 6
27: 6 The fruit discloses the cultivation of a tree 8
6 discloses the cultivation of a man's mind. •
Sus 1:11 ashamed to disclose their lustful desire 4
1Mc 7:31 learned that his plan had been disclosed 6
2Mc 2: 8 then the Lord will disclose these things 5
3:16 disclosed the anguish of his soul. 9

disclosure 1. *ἀποκάλυψις* 2. *ἐμφανισμός*

Sir 22:22 reviling, arrogance, disclosure of secrets 1
2Mc 3: 9 he told about the disclosure that had been made 2

discomfit 1. המם 2. חתת

Exd 14:24 discomfited the host of the Egyptians 1
Job 32:15 They are discomfited, they answer no more; 2

discomfort 1. רָעָה

Jon 4: 6 over his head, to save him from his discomfort. 1

discontented 1. מַר נֶפֶשׁ

1Sm 22: 2 was in debt, and every one who was discontented 1

discord 1. מָדוֹן 2. מִדְיָן 3. *σχίσμα*

Prv 6:14 continually sowing discord; 2
19 a man who sows discord among brothers. 1
1Co 12:25 that there may be no discord in the body 3

discordant 1. *ἀσύμφωνος*

Wis 18:10 the discordant cry of their enemies echoed back 1

discourage 1. נוא 2. רפה 3. רְפֵה יָדַיִם 4. רצץ 5. *ἀθυμέω*

Num32: 7 Why will you discourage the heart of . . Israel 1
9 discouraged the heart of the people of Israel 1
2Sm 17: 2 I will come . . while he is weary and discouraged 3
Ezr 4: 4 land discouraged the people of Judah 2
Isa 42: 4 be discouraged till he has established justice 4
1Mc 4:27 he was perplexed and discouraged 5

become discouraged 1. *ἀθυμέω*

Col 3:21 lest they become discouraged. 1

discourse 1. מָשָׁל 2. *διήγημα* 3. *διήγησις*

Num23: 7 Balaam took up his discourse, and said 1
18 Balaam took up his discourse, and said, "Rise, Balak 1
24: 3 took up his discourse, and said, "The oracle 1
15 he took up his discourse, and said, "The oracle 1

20 he looked on Am'alek, and took up his discourse 1
21 he looked on the Ken'ite, and took up his discourse 1
23 And he took up his discourse, and said 1
Job 27: 1 Job again took up his discourse, and said 1
29: 1 Job again took up his discourse, and said 1
Sir 8: 8 Do not slight the discourse of the sages 2
9 Do not disregard the discourse of the aged 2
39: 2 he will preserve the discourse of notable men 3

discover 1. בין 2. חקר 3. ידע 4. מצא 5. invenio
1Sm 22: 6 Now Saul heard that David was discovered 3
2Kg 12: 5 wherever any need of repairs is discovered. 4
Neh 13: 7 then discovered the evil that Eli'ashib had done 1
Ps 44:21 would not God discover this? 2
2Es 5:40 so you cannot discover my judgment 5

discredit 1. *βλασφημέω*
Tit 2: 5 the word of God may not be discredited. 1

discreet 1. בִּין
Gen 41:33 let Pharaoh select a man discreet and wise 1
39 there is none so discreet and wise as you are; 1

discreet man 1. *φρόνιμος*
Sir 21:24 a discreet man is grieved by the disgrace. 1

discreetly 1. טַעַם
Prv 26:16 than seven men who can answer discreetly. 1

discretion 1. טַעַם 2. מְזִמָּה 3. שֵׂכֶל 4. טְעֵם (A)
5. *αἵρεσις* 6. *κρίσις*
1Sm 25:33 Blessed be your discretion, and blessed be you 1
1Ch 22:12 LORD grant you discretion and understanding 3
2Ch 2:12 son, endued with discretion and understanding 3
Ezr 8:18 brought us a man of discretion, 3
Prv 1: 4 knowledge and discretion to the youth– 2
2:11 discretion will watch over you; 2
3:21 My son, keep sound wisdom and discretion; 2
5: 2 that you may keep discretion 2
8:12 I, wisdom . . find knowledge and discretion. 2
11:22 snout is a beautiful woman without discretion. 1
14:17 but a man of discretion is patient. 2
Dan 2:14 Daniel replied with prudence and discretion 4
Sir 33:29 do nothing without discretion. 6
1Mc 8:30 they shall do so at their discretion 5

discus 1. *δίσκος*
2Mc 4:14 after the call to the discus 1

discuss 1. *διαλαλέω* 2. *διαλέγομαι* 3. *διαλογίζομαι*
4. *ἐπιδείκνυμι* 5. *συζητέω* 6. *συλλογίζομαι*
Mat 16: 7 they discussed it among themselves, saying 3
8 why do you discuss among yourselves the fact 3
Mrk 8:16 they discussed it with one another, saying 3
17 Why do you discuss the fact that you have no bread? 3
9:16 he asked them, "What are you discussing with them? 5
33 What were you discussing on the way? 3
34 on the way they had discussed with one another 2
Lke 6:11 filled with fury and discussed with one another 1
20: 5 they discussed it with one another, saying 6
4Mc 1: 1 The subject that I am about to discuss 4

discuss from every side 1. *περίπατον ποιέω*
2Mc 2:30 to discuss matters from every side 1

discuss together 1. *συζητέω*
Lke 24:15 they were talking and discussing together, 1

discussion 1. *διήγησις* 2. *ζήτησις*
Joh 3:25 Now a discussion arose between John's disciples 2
Sir 9:15 your discussion be about the law of the Most High. 1

vain discussion 1. *ματαιολογία*
1Ti 1: 6 have wandered away into vain discussion 1

disdain 1. בזה 2. בזה בְּעֵינַיִם 3. מאס 4. *ἀπωθέω*
5. *ἀτιμάζω* 6. *ἐν οὐδενὶ τίθημι* 7. *ὑπερηφανεύομαι*
8. *ὑπεροράω*
1Sm 17:42 the Philistine . . saw David, he disdained him; 1
Est 3: 6 But he disdained to lay hands on Mor'decai alone. 2
Job 30: 1 I would have disdained to set with the dogs 3
Tob 4:13 in your heart do not disdain your brethren 7
Jdt 8:20 therefore we hope that he will not disdain us 8
Sir 8: 6 Do not disdain a man when he is old 5
2Mc 4:15 disdaining the honors prized by their fathers 6
7:11 because of his laws I disdain them 8
3Mc 3:22 disdained what is good 4
4Mc 15: 8 disdained the temporary safety of her children. 8

disease 1. חֳלִי 2. מַדְוֶה 3. מַחֲלֶה 4. מַחֲלָה 5. נֶגַע
6. תַּחֲלֻאִים 7. *ἀσθένεια* 8. *μάστιξ* 9. *νόσος*
10. infirmitas
Exd 15:26 I will put none of the diseases upon you which I 4
Lev 13: 2 a spot, and it turns into a leprous disease 5
3 the disease appears to be deeper than the skin 5
3 than the skin of his body, it is a leprous disease 5
5 if in his eyes the disease is checked 5
5 if . . the disease has not spread in the skin 5
6 if . . the disease has not spread in the skin 5
13 he shall pronounce him clean of the disease 5
17 if the disease has turned white, then the priest 5
20 it is the disease of leprosy, it has broken out 5
25 pronounce him unclean; it is a leprous disease 5
27 it is a leprous disease 5
29 When a man or woman has a disease on the head 5
30 the priest shall examine the disease 5
31 if the priest examines the itching disease 5
31 shut up the person with the itching disease 5
32 the priest shall examine the disease 5
44 he is unclean . . his disease is on his head 5
45 The leper who has the disease shall wear torn 5
46 remain unclean as long as he has the disease 5
47 When there is a leprous disease in a garment 5
49 if the disease shows greenish or reddish 5
49 it is a leprous disease and shall be shown 5
50 the priest shall examine the disease 5
50 and shut up that which has the disease 5
51 he shall examine the disease on the seventh day 5
51 If the disease has spread in the garment, in warp 5
51 the disease is a malignant leprosy; it is unclean 5
53 the disease has not spread in the garment in warp 5
54 that they wash the thing in which is the disease 5
55 though the disease has not spread, it is unclean 5
56 if the priest examines, and the disease is dim 5
57 shall burn with fire that in which is the disease 5
58 anything of skin from which the disease departs 5
59 This is the law for a leprous disease in a garment 5
14: 3 Then, if the leprous disease is healed in the leper 5
32 law for him in whom is a leprous disease 5
34 and I put a leprous disease in a house 5
35 seems to me to be some sort of disease in my house 5
36 before the priest goes to examine the disease 5
37 he shall examine the disease 5
37 if the disease is in the walls of the house 5
39 if the disease has spread in the walls 5
40 they take out the stones in which is the disease 5
43 If the disease breaks out again in the house 5
44 if the disease has spread in the house 5
48 and the disease has not spread in the house 5
48 the house clean, for the disease is healed 5
54 law for any leprous disease: for an itch 5
Deu 7:15 none of the evil diseases of Egypt . . will he inflict 2
28:60 bring upon you again all the diseases of Egypt 2
2Ch 16:12 his disease became severe; 1
12 yet even in his disease he did not seek the LORD 1
21:15 severe sickness with a disease of your bowels 3
15 your bowels come out because of the disease, 1
18 in his bowels with an incurable disease. 1
19 his bowels came out because of the disease 1
Job 18:13 By disease his skin is consumed •
Ps 103: 3 who forgives . . who heals all your diseases 6
Jer 14:18 if I enter the city, behold, the diseases of famine! 6
16: 4 They shall die of deadly diseases. 6
Mat 4:23 healing every disease and every infirmity 9
24 the sick, those afflicted with various diseases 9
8:17 He took our infirmities and bore our diseases. 9
9:35 and healing every disease and every infirmity. 9
10: 1 and to heal every disease and every infirmity. 9
Mrk 1:34 healed many who were sick with various diseases 9
3:10 so that all who had diseases pressed upon him 8
5:29 she was healed of her disease. 8
34 go in peace, and be healed of your disease. 8
Lke 4:40 any that were sick with various diseases 9
6:17 to be healed of their diseases 9
7:21 he cured many of diseases and plagues 9
9: 1 gave them power . . to cure diseases 9
Act 19:12 diseases left them and the evil spirits came out 9
28: 9 the rest of the people on the island who had diseases 7
2Es 3:22 Thus the disease became permanent 10

itching disease 1. גָּרָב 2. נֶתֶק
Lev 13:33 shut up the person with the itching disease 2
21:20 an itching disease or scabs or crushed testicles 1

wasting disease 1. רָזוֹן
Ps 106:15 but sent a wasting disease among them. 1

diseased 1. חלא 2. חלה 3. נֶגַע 4. *ἀσθενέω*
Lev 13:22 shall pronounce him unclean; it is diseased 3
43 if the diseased swelling is reddish-white 3
52 garment, whether diseased in warp or woof 3
1Kg 15:23 But in his old age he was diseased in his feet. 2
2Ch 16:12 Asa was diseased in his feet 1
Joh 6: 2 signs which he did on those who were diseased. 4
diseased *See also* spot.

diseased person 1. נֶגַע
Lev 13: 4 the priest shall shut up the diseased person 1
12 covers all the skin of the diseased person 1
17 shall pronounce the diseased person clean 1

diseased thing 1. נֶגַע
Lev 13:55 the priest shall examine the diseased thing 1

disfigure 1. נתן מום 2. *ἀφανίζω*
Lev 24:20 as he has disfigured a man, he shall be disfigured 1
20 as he has disfigured a man, he shall be disfigured 1
Mat 6:16 the hypocrites, for they disfigure their faces 2

disfigurement 1. מוּם
Lev 24:19 a man causes a disfigurement in his neighbor 1

disgrace 1. בושׁ 2. חפר 3. חֶרְפָּה 4. כלם 5. כְּלִמָּה
6. נְאָצָה 7. קָלוֹן 8. *αἰσχρός* 9. *αἰσχύνη* 10. *ἀτιμάζω*
11. *ἀτιμία* 12. *καταβάλλω* 13. *καταισχύνω* 14. *κηλίς*
15. *ὀνειδισμός* 16. *ὄνειδος* 17. *ψόγος*
Gen 34:14 for that would be a disgrace to us. 3
1Sm 11: 2 gouge out . . eyes, and thus put disgrace upon all 3
20:34 for David, because his father had disgraced him. 4
2Kg 19: 3 a day of distress, of rebuke, and of disgrace; 6
Job 10:15 I am filled with disgrace 7
Ps 44:15 All day long my disgrace is before me 5
71:13 with scorn and disgrace may they be covered 5
24 for they have been put to shame and disgraced 2
83:17 let them perish in disgrace. 2
Prv 3:35 wise will inherit honor, but fools get disgrace. 7
6:33 his disgrace will not be wiped away. 3
11: 2 When pride comes, then comes disgrace; 7
13:18 Poverty and disgrace come to him who ignores 7
18: 3 with dishonor comes disgrace. 3
Isa 30: 5 help nor profit, but shame and disgrace. 3
37: 3 day of distress, of rebuke, and of disgrace; 6
Jer 15: 9 she has been shamed and disgraced. 2
31:19 because I bore the disgrace of my youth. 3
50:12 and she who bore you shall be disgraced. 2
Lam 5: 1 Remember, O LORD . . behold, and see our disgrace! 3
Ezk 16:52 Bear your disgrace 5
52 So be ashamed, you also, and bear your disgrace 5
54 that you may bear your disgrace and be ashamed 5
36:15 you shall no longer bear the disgrace 3
30 may never again suffer the disgrace of famine 3
Mic 2: 6 disgrace will not overtake us. 5
3: 7 the seers shall be disgraced 1
Tob 3:10 if I do this, it will be a disgrace to him 16
Jdt 9: 2 polluted her womb to disgrace her 16
12:12 it will be a disgrace if we let such a woman go 8
14:18 brought disgrace upon . . King Nebuchadnezzar! 9
Sir 3:11 it is a disgrace for children 16
6: 9 will disclose a quarrel to your disgrace. 15
7: 7 do not disgrace yourself among the people. 12
8: 4 lest your ancestors be disgraced. 10
11: 6 Many rulers have been greatly disgraced 10
20:26 The disposition of a liar brings disgrace 11
21:24 a discreet man is grieved by the disgrace. 11
22: 1 every one hisses at his disgrace. 11
3 a disgrace to be the father 9
5 disgraces father and husband 13
23:26 her disgrace will not be blotted out. 16
25:22 There is wrath and impudence and great disgrace 9
42:14 it is a woman who brings shame and disgrace. 15
Aza 1:10 shame and disgrace have befallen thy servants 16
21 let them be disgraced 13
2Mc 5: 7 in the end got only disgrace from his conspiracy 9
6:25 while I defile and disgrace my old age. 14
3Mc 2:27 to inflict public disgrace upon the Jewish community 17
6:34 groaned as they . . were overcome by disgrace 9
disgrace *See also* suffer.

disgraceful 1. *αἰσχρός* 2. *αἰσχρῶς* 3. *αἰσχύνη*
1Co 11: 6 if it is disgraceful for a woman to be shorn 1
2Co 4: 2 renounced disgraceful, underhanded ways 3
2Mc 11:12 Lysias himself escaped by disgraceful flight. 2
disgracefully *See* treat.

act disgracefully 1. חפר
Prv 13: 5 wicked man acts shamefully and disgracefully. 1

disguise 1. חפשׂ 2. שׂוּם סֵתֶר 3. שׁנה
4. *μετασχηματίζω*
1Sm 28: 8 Saul disguised himself and put on . . garments 1
1Kg 14: 2 Arise, and disguise yourself, that it be not known 3
20:38 and waited . . disguising himself with a bandage 1
22:30 I will disguise myself and go into battle 1
30 the king of Israel disguised himself and went 1
2Ch 18:29 I will disguise myself and go into battle 1
29 king of Israel disguised himself; 1
35:22 disguised himself in order to fight with him. 1
Job 24:15 No eye will see me'; and he disguises his face. 2
2Co 11:13 disguising themselves as apostles of Christ. 4
14 Satan disguises himself as an angel of light. 4
15 if his servants also disguise themselves 4

disgust 1. קוּט
Ps 119:158I look at the faithless with disgust 1
disgust *See also* turn.

dish 1. כַּף 2. צַלַּחַת 3. *πίναξ* 4. *σκεῦος* 5. *τρύβλιον*
6. vas
Exd 25:29 you shall make its plates and dishes for incense 1
37:16 its plates and dishes for incense, and its bowls 1
Num 7:14 one golden dish of ten shekels, full of incense; 1
20 one golden dish of ten shekels, full of incense; 1
26 one golden dish of ten shekels, full of incense; 1

32 one golden dish of ten shekels, full of incense; 1
38 one golden dish of ten shekels, full of incense; 1
44 one golden dish of ten shekels, full of incense; 1
50 one golden dish of ten shekels, full of incense; 1
56 one golden dish of ten shekels, full of incense; 1
62 one golden dish of ten shekels, full of incense; 1
68 one golden dish of ten shekels, full of incense; 1
74 one golden dish of ten shekels, full of incense; 1
80 one golden dish of ten shekels, full of incense; 1
84 dedication offering . . twelve golden dishes 1
86 the twelve golden dishes, full of incense 1
86 all the gold of the dishes being 120 shekels; 1
1Kg 7:50 The cups, snuffers, basins, dishes for incense 1
2Kg 21:13 I will wipe Jerusalem as one wipes a dish 2
25:14 the snuffers, and the dishes for incense and all 1
2Ch 4:22 dishes for incense, and firepans, of pure gold; 1
24:14 utensils . . and dishes for incense, and vessels 1
Prv 19:24 The sluggard buries his hand in the dish 2
26:15 The sluggard buries his hand in the dish; 2
Jer 52:18 dishes for incense, and all the vessels of bronze 1
19 and the lampstands, and the dishes for incense 1
Mat 26:23 He who has dipped his hand in the dish with me 5
Mrk 14:20 one who is dipping bread into the dish with me. 5
Lke 11:39 the outside of the cup and of the dish 3
2Es 9:34 the sea a ship, or any dish food or drink 6
Sir 31:14 do not crowd your neighbor at the dish. 5
LJr 1:17 For just as one's dish is useless when it is broken 4

dish for incense 1. כַּף
Num 4: 7 put upon it the plates, the dishes for incense 1

silver dish 1. ἀργύρωμα
Jdt 12: 1 where his silver dishes were kept 1
15:11 all his silver dishes and his beds and his bowls 1

dishearten 1. כאב 2. כאה
Ezk 13:22 you have disheartened the righteous falsely 2
22 although I have not disheartened him 1

all disheveled 1. λύω
3Mc 1: 4 her locks all disheveled 1

dishonest 1. ἀδικία 2. ἄδικος
Lke 16: 8 The master commended the dishonest steward 1
10 he who is dishonest in a very little 2
10 is dishonest also in much. 2
Sir 5: 8 Do not depend on dishonest wealth 2
dishonest *See also* gain.

dishonestly 1. עָוֶל
Deu 25:16 all who do such things, all who act dishonestly 1

dishonor 1. חלל 2. כלם 3. כְּלִמָּה 4. נבל 5. קלה 6. קָלוֹן 7. קלל 8. עֶרְוָה (A) 9. ἄδοξος 10. ἀτιμάζω 11. ἀτιμία 12. ἄτιμος 13. καταισχύνω
Deu 27:16 'Cursed . . who dishonors his father or his mother.' 5
Ezr 4:14 not fitting for us to witness the king's dishonor 8
Ps 35: 4 Let them be put to shame and dishonor 2
26 Let them be clothed with shame and dishonor 3
69:19 my reproach, and my shame and my dishonor; 3
109:29 May my accusers be clothed with dishonor; 3
Prv 6:33 Wounds and dishonor will he get 6
18: 3 with dishonor comes disgrace. 6
Isa 23: 9 to dishonor all the honored of the earth. 7
61: 7 instead of dishonor you shall rejoice 3
Jer 3:25 and let our dishonor cover us; 3
14:21 do not dishonor thy glorious throne; 4
20:11 Their eternal dishonor will never be forgotten. 3
51:51 dishonor has covered our face 3
Lam 2: 2 brought . . to the ground in dishonor the kingdom 1
Joh 8:49 I honor my Father, and you dishonor me. 10
Rom 1:24 dishonoring of their bodies among themselves 10
2:23 do you dishonor God by breaking the law? 10
1Co 11: 4 with his head covered dishonors his head 13
5 with her head unveiled dishonors her head 13
15:43 It is sown in dishonor, it is raised in glory. 11
2Co 6: 8 in honor and dishonor 11
Jas 2: 6 But you have dishonored the poor man. 10
2Es 5:28 and dishonored the one root beyond the others ‡
Jdt 8:23 the Lord our God will turn it to dishonor. 11
Wis 4:18 After this they will become dishonored corpses 12
Sir 1:30 thus bring dishonor upon yourself 11
3:10 glorify yourself by dishonoring your father 11
10 your father's dishonor is no glory to you. 11
5:13 Glory and dishonor come from speaking 11
10:29 who will honor the man that dishonors his own life? 10
31 a man dishonored in wealth 9
29: 6 instead of glory will repay him with dishonor. 11
LJr 1:40 Besides, even the Chaldeans . . dishonor them; 10
1Mc 1:40 Her dishonor now grew as great as her glory 11
dishonor *See also* bring, suffer.

dishonorable 1. ἀτιμία
Rom 1:26 God gave them up to dishonorable passions. 1

disinherit 1. ירש
Num14:12 I will strike them . . and disinherit them 1

disjoint 1. ἐξαρθρόω
4Mc 10: 5 they disjointed his hands and feet 1

disjoint all members 1. ἐκμελίζω
4Mc 11:10 all his members were disjointed. 1

dislike 1. שׂנא 2. ἀπαρέσκω
Deu 21:15 two wives, the one loved and the other disliked 1
15 borne him children, both the loved and the disliked 1
15 if the first-born son is hers that is disliked 1
16 not . . in preference to the son of the disliked 1
17 first-born, the son of the disliked 1
24: 3 latter husband dislikes her and writes her 1
Prv 14:20 The poor is disliked even by his neighbor 1
Sir 21:15 when a reveler hears it, he dislikes it 2

dislocate 1. ἐκμελίζω 2. ἔξαρθρος
4Mc 9:13 his limbs were dislocated 2
10: 8 his vertebrae were being dislocated upon it 1

disloyal 1. ἀλλότρια φρονέω
2Mc 14:26 Nicanor was disloyal to the government 1

dismal 1. κατηφής 2. σκυθρωπός
Mat 6:16 you fast, do not look dismal, like the hypocrites 2
Wis 17: 4 dismal phantoms with gloomy faces appeared. 1

dismay 1. אשׁם 2. בהל 3. חַת 4. חתת 5. ירא 6. מוג 7. מְחִתָּה 8. שַׁמָּה 9. שִׁמָּמוֹן 10. שׁעה 11. שׁמם (A) 12. συγχέω 13. ταράσσω
Gen 42:35 their bundles of money, they were dismayed. 5
45: 3 for they were dismayed at his presence. 2
Exd 15:15 Now are the chiefs of Edom dismayed; 2
Deu 1:21 take possession . . do not fear or be dismayed.' 4
31: 8 not . . forsake you; do not fear or be dismayed. 4
Jos 1: 9 be not frightened, neither be dismayed; 4
8: 1 the LORD said to Joshua, "Do not fear or be dismayed; 4
10:25 Do not be afraid or dismayed; be strong 4
Jdg 20:41 the men of Benjamin were dismayed, for they saw 2
1Sm 17:11 they were dismayed and greatly afraid. 4
2Sm 4: 1 his courage failed, and all Israel was dismayed. 2
2Kg 19:26 inhabitants . . are dismayed and confounded 4
1Ch 22:13 and of good courage. Fear not, be not dismayed. 4
28:20 Fear not, be not dismayed; for the LORD God 4
2Ch 20:15 says the LORD . . 'Fear not, and be not dismayed 4
17 Fear not, and be not dismayed(O Judah); 4
32: 7 Do not be afraid or dismayed before the king 4
Job 4: 5 it touches you, and you are dismayed. 2
21: 6 When I think of it I am dismayed 2
39:22 He laughs at fear, and is not dismayed; 4
Ps 30: 7 thou didst hide thy face, I was dismayed. 2
83:17 Let them be put to shame and dismayed for ever; 2
104:29 When thou hidest thy face, they are dismayed; 2
Prv 21:15 justice is done, it is . . dismay to evildoers. 7
Ecc 8: 2 and because of your sacred oath be not dismayed; 2
Isa 8: 9 Be broken, you peoples, and be dismayed; give ear 4
9 far countries; gird yourselves and be dismayed; 4
9 gird yourselves and be dismayed. 4
13: 8 they will be dismayed. Pangs . . will seize them; 2
20: 5 Then they shall be dismayed and confounded 4
21: 3 I cannot hear, I am dismayed so that I cannot see. 2
37:27 shorn of strength, are dismayed and confounded 4
41:10 be not dismayed, for I am your God; 10
23 do harm, that we may be dismayed and terrified. 10
51: 7 of men, and be not dismayed at their revilings. 4
Jer 1:17 Do not be dismayed by them 4
17 dismayed by them, lest I dismay you before them. 4
8: 9 be put to shame, they shall be dismayed and taken; 4
21 I mourn, and dismay has taken hold on me. 8
10: 2 nor be dismayed at the signs of the heavens 4
2 because the nations are dismayed at them 4
14: 4 Because of the ground which is dismayed 4
17:18 let them be dismayed, but let me not be dismayed; 4
18 let them . . but let me not be dismayed; 4
23: 4 and they shall fear no more, nor be dismayed 4
30:10 says the LORD, nor be dismayed, O Israel; 4
46: 5 They are dismayed and have turned backward. 3
27 nor be dismayed, O Israel; 4
50: 2 Bel is put to shame, Mer'odach is dismayed. 4
2 images are put to shame, her idols are dismayed. 4
Ezk 2: 6 nor be dismayed at their looks 4
3: 9 fear them not, nor be dismayed at their looks 4
4:16 they shall drink water by measure and in dismay. 9
12:19 with fearfulness, and drink water in dismay 9
26:18 isles . . in the sea are dismayed at your passing. 2
Dan 4:19 Then Daniel . . was dismayed for a moment 11
Jol 1:18 even the flocks of sheep are dismayed. 1
Obd 1: 9 And your mighty men shall be dismayed, O Teman 4
Nah 2: 6 river gates are opened, the palace is in dismay; 6
Jdt 14:19 rent their tunics and were greatly dismayed 13
2Mc 13:23 he was dismayed, called in the Jews, yielded 12
dismay *See also* look.

dismember 1. ἐκμελίζω 2. μέλος ποιέω
2Mc 1:16 and dismembered them and cut off their heads 2
4Mc 10: 5 dismembering him by prying his limbs 1

dismiss 1. פטר 2. שׁלח 3. ἀπολύω 4. ἀποστέλλω 5. σκορπίζω 6. dimitto
Jdg 2: 6 When Joshua dismissed the people, the people 2
2Ch 23: 8 for Jehoi'ada . . did not dismiss the divisions. 1
Mat 14:22 while he dismissed the crowds. 3
23 after he had dismissed the crowds 3
Mrk 6:45 while he dismissed the crowd. 3
Act 19:41 when he had said this, he dismissed the assembly. 3
23:22 the tribune dismissed the young man 3
2Es 9:39 Then I dismissed the thoughts 6
Jdt 7:32 he dismissed the people to their various posts 5
Sus 1:36 shut the garden doors, and dismissed the maids. 3
1Mc 11:38 he dismissed all his troops 3
12:45 Dismiss them now to their homes 4
2Mc 7: 9 you dismiss us from this present life 3
14:23 dismissed the flocks of people 3
3Mc 5:34 and dismissed the assembled people 3

dismissal 1. ἀπόλυσις
3Mc 6:37 asking for dismissal to their homes. 1
40 they made the petition for their dismissal. 1

disobedience 1. ἀπείθεια 2. ἀπειθής 3. παρακοή
Rom 5:19 by one man's disobedience many were made sinners 3
11:30 received mercy because of their disobedience 2
32 For God has consigned all men to disobedience 1
2Co 10: 6 being ready to punish every disobedience 3
Eph 2: 2 is now at work in the sons of disobedience. 1
5: 6 comes upon the sons of disobedience. 1
Heb 2: 2 every transgression or disobedience 3
4: 6 failed to enter because of disobedience 1
11 no one fall by the same sort of disobedience. 1
4Mc 8: 9 if by disobedience you rouse my anger 1
18 and venture upon a disobedience that brings death? 1
12: 3 because of their disobedience. 1

disobedient 1. מרה 2. ἀνυπότακτος 3. ἀπειθέω 4. ἀπειθής
Neh 9:26 disobedient and rebelled against thee 1
Lke 1:17 the disobedient to the wisdom of the just 4
Act 26:19 I was not disobedient to the heavenly vision 4
Rom 1:30 inventors of evil, disobedient to parents 4
10:21 my hands to a disobedient and contrary people. 3
11:30 Just as you were once disobedient to God 3
31 so they have now been disobedient in order that 3
1Ti 1: 9 for the lawless and disobedient 2
2Ti 3: 2 disobedient to their parents, ungrateful, unholy 4
Tit 1:16 detestable, disobedient, unfit for any good deed. 4
3: 3 For we ourselves were once foolish, disobedient 4
Heb 3:18 those who were disobedient? 3
11:31 did not perish with those who were disobedient 3
Sir 16: 6 in a disobedient nation wrath was kindled. 3
47:21 a disobedient kingdom arose out of Ephraim. 4
Bar 1:19 we have been disobedient to the Lord our God 3
4Mc 9:10 those who are disobedient 3

disobey 1. בִּלְתִּי שמע 2. לֹא שמע 3. מרה 4. ἀπειθέω 5. μὴ τηρέω 6. παραβαίνω 7. παρακούω 8. παρέρχομαι 9. παρηκέω
Jos 1:18 rebels against . . and disobeys your words 2
1Kg 13:21 Because you have disobeyed the word of the LORD 3
26 the man of God, who disobeyed the word of the LORD; 3
Prv 24:21 LORD and the king, and do not disobey either 4
Jer 42:13 disobeying the voice of the LORD your God 1
Lke 15:29 I never disobeyed your command 8
1Pe 2: 8 they stumble because they disobey the word 4
1Jn 2: 4 but disobeys his commandments is a liar 5
1Es 4: 5 do not disobey the king's command 6
11 nor do they disobey him. 7
Tob 3: 4 For they disobeyed thy commandments 9
Jdt 2: 6 because they disobeyed my orders. 4
Sir 1:28 Do not disobey the fear of the Lord; 4
2:15 who fear the Lord will not disobey his words 4
16:28 they will never disobey his word. 4
23:23 first of all, she has disobeyed the law of the Most High 4
30:12 lest he become stubborn and disobey you 4
Bar 1:18 have disobeyed him, and have not heeded the voice 4
4Mc 8: 6 I am able to punish those who disobey my orders 4
11 if you disobey, nothing remains for you but to die 4
21 if we disobey we are dead! 4

disorder 1. ἀκαταστασία 2. ἀκόσμως 3. ἀταξία 4. ταραχή
2Co 12:20 slander, gossip, conceit, and disorder. 1
Jas 3:16 there will be disorder and every vile practice. 1
Wis 14:26 sex perversion, disorder in marriage, adultery 3
17: 8 the fears and disorders of a sick soul 4
2Mc 9: 1 Antiochus had retreated in disorder 2
10:30 they were thrown into disorder and cut to pieces. 4
3Mc 3:24 a sudden disorder should later arise against us 4

disorderly 1. ἄτακτος
3Mc 1:19 in a disorderly rush 1

disorganize 1. turbo
2Es 15:32 then these shall be disorganized and silenced 1

disown 1. לֹא נכר 2. נאר 3. ἀρνέομαι
Deu 33: 9 he disowned his brothers, and ignored his children. 1
Lam 2: 7 has scorned his altar, disowned his sanctuary; 2
1Ti 5: 8 he has disowned the faith 3

dispatch 1. ברא 2. שׁלח 3. ἀποκοσμέω 4. συντέμνω
2Kg 6:32 the king had dispatched a man from his presence; 2
Ezk 23:47 stone them and dispatch them with their swords; 1
Rom 9:28 Lord will execute . . with rigor and dispatch. 4
2Mc 4:38 he dispatched the bloodthirsty fellow 3

dispel 1. ἀποσκεδάννυμι 2. recludo
2Es 15:39 and shall dispel it 2
4Mc 5:11 dispel your futile reasonings 1

dispensation 1. διακονία
2Co 3: 7 Now if the dispensation of death 1
8 will not the dispensation of the Spirit 1
9 splendor in the dispensation of condemnation 1
9 the dispensation of righteousness 1

dispense
Prv 15: 2 The tongue of the wise dispenses knowledge •

disperse 1. זרה 2. נדח 3. נפץ 4. פוץ 5. פרד
6. διαλύω 7. διασκεδάννυμι 8. διαχέω 9. σκορπίζω
1Sm 14:34 Saul said, "Disperse yourselves among the people 4
2Sm 20:22 So he blew . . and they dispersed from the city 4
Neh 1: 9 though your dispersed be under the farthest 2
Est 3: 8 scattered . . and dispersed among the peoples 5
Ps 106:27 disperse their descendants among the nations •
Isa 11:12 the dispersed of Judah from the four corners 3
Ezk 12:15 when I disperse them among the nations 4
20:23 and disperse them through the countries 1
22:15 and disperse you through the countries 1
29:12 and disperse them among the countries. 1
30:23 and disperse them throughout the lands. 1
26 and disperse them throughout the countries. 1
36:19 they were dispersed through the countries; 1
Act 5:36 all who followed him were dispersed 6
Tob 3: 4 the nations among which we have been dispersed. 9
Wis 5:14 it is dispersed like smoke before the wind 8
1Mc 10:83 the cavalry was dispersed in the plain 9
3Mc 2:19 Wipe away our sins and disperse our errors 7

dispersed ones 1. פוץ
Zep 3:10 my suppliants, the daughter of my dispersed ones 1

dispersion 1. תְּפוֹצָה 2. διασπορά
Jer 25:34 your slaughter and dispersion have come 1
Joh 7:35 Does he intend to go to the Dispersion 2
Jas 1: 1 To the twelve tribes in the Dispersion 2
1Pe 1: 1 To the exiles of the Dispersion 2

display 1. ἐκτείνω 2. ἐνδείκνυμι 3. demonstro
1Ti 1:16 might display his perfect patience 2
2Es 7:104 and displays to all the seal of truth 3
1Mc 7:47 and displayed them just outside Jerusalem. 1

display cleverness 1. σοφίζω
Sir 32: 4 do not display your cleverness out of season. 1

display madness 1. μαίνομαι
4Mc 8: 5 not to display the same madness 1

display wisdom 1. σοφίζω
Sir 7: 5 nor display your wisdom before the king. 1

displease 1. עצב 2. עשׂה רַע בְּעֵינַיִם 3. רעע
4. רעע בְּעֵינַיִם 5. רעע בְּעֵינַיִם 6. βαρέως φέρω
7. δυσφορέω 8. μὴ ἀρέσκω
Gen 21:11 the thing was very displeasing to Abraham 5
12 Be not displeased because of the lad 4
38:10 what he did was displeasing in the sight 3
48:17 When Joseph saw . . it displeased him; 5
Num11:10 LORD blazed hotly, and Moses was displeased. 4
1Sm 8: 6 But the thing displeased Samuel when they said 4
18: 8 Saul was . . angry, and this saying displeased him; 4
29: 7 go . . that you may not displease the lords 2
2Sm 11:27 the thing . . David had done displeased the LORD. 4
1Kg 1: 6 His father had never . . displeased him by asking 1
1Ch 21: 7 God was displeased with this thing, and he smote 4
Neh 2:10 displeased them greatly that some one 3
Prv 24:18 lest the LORD see it, and be displeased 4
Isa 59:15 it displeased him that there was no justice. 4
Jon 4: 1 it displeased Jonah exceedingly 3
1Th 2:15 drove us out, and displease God and oppose all men 8
2Mc 4:35 grieved and displeased at the unjust murder 7
14:27 he was displeased with the covenant 6

displeasure 1. תְּנוּאָה
Num14:34 and you shall know my displeasure.' 1

hot displeasure 1. חֵמָה
Deu 9:19 the anger and hot displeasure which the LORD bore 1

disposal 1. ἐξουσία
Act 5: 4 after it was sold, was it not at your disposal? 1

dispose 1. διάκειμαι 2. δοκέω 3. ἐνθυμόω 4. θέλω
1Co 10:27 you are disposed to go 4
11:16 If any one is disposed to be contentious 2
1Es 8:11 Let as many as are so disposed, therefore, depart 3
3Mc 3:23 who are sincerely disposed toward us 1

dispose favorably 1. εὐνοέω
3Mc 7:11 never be favorably disposed toward . . government. 1

peaceably disposed 1. εἰρηνικός
2Mc 5:25 he pretended to be peaceably disposed 1

well disposed 1. טוֹב 2. εὐδοκέω 3. εὐμενής
1Sm 20:12 behold, if he is well disposed toward David 1
1Mc 8: 1 were well-disposed toward all who made an alliance 2
2Mc 12:31 exhorted them to be well disposed to their race 3

disposition 1. διάθεσις 2. ἦθος 3. πλάσμα
Jdt 8:29 your heart's disposition is right. 3
Sir 20:26 The disposition of a liar brings disgrace 2
2Mc 14: 5 was asked about the disposition . . of the Jews. 1

dispossess 1. ירשׁ 2. יְרֻשָּׁה 3. פוץ 4. κατάσχεσις
Num21:32 dispossessed the Amorites that were there. 1
24:18 Edom shall be dispossessed, Se'ir also 2
18 Se'ir also, his enemies, shall be dispossessed 2
32:39 dispossessed the Amorites who were in it. 1
Deu 2:12 sons of Esau dispossessed them, and destroyed 1
21 dispossessed them, and settled in their stead; 1
22 dispossessed them, and settled in their stead 1
7:17 nations are greater than I; how can I dispossess 1
9: 1 pass over . . to go in to dispossess nations 1
11:23 you will dispossess nations greater 1
12: 2 the nations whom you shall dispossess 1
29 cuts off . . nations whom you go in to dispossess 1
29 dispossess them and dwell in their land 1
18:14 these nations, which you are about to dispossess 1
19: 1 cuts off the nations . . and you dispossess them 1
31: 3 nations before you, so that you shall dispossess 1
Jdg 11:23 the LORD . . dispossessed the Amorites 1
24 that the LORD our God has dispossessed before us 1
Jer 49: 1 Why then has Milcom dispossessed Gad 1
2 then Israel shall dispossess those 1
2 shall dispossess those who dispossessed him 1
Ezk 46:18 so that none of my people shall be dispossessed 3
Act 7:45 when they dispossessed the nations 4

dispute 1. דָּבָר 2. דִּין 3. מָדוֹן 4. רִיב 5. ἀντιλογία
6. διάκρισις 7. διαλέγομαι 8. μάχομαι 9. συζητέω
10. φιλονεικία
Exd 18:16 when they have a dispute, they come to me and I 1
Deu 19:17 then both parties to the dispute shall appear 4
21: 5 by their word every dispute . . shall be settled. 4
25: 1 If there is a dispute between men, and they come 4
Prv 18:18 The lot puts an end to disputes 3
Ecc 6:10 he is not able to dispute with one stronger 2
Lke 22:24 A dispute also arose among them 10
Joh 6:52 The Jews then disputed among themselves, saying 8
Act 6: 9 some of those . . arose and disputed with Stephen. 9
9:29 he spoke and disputed against the Hellenists; 9
24:12 they did not find me disputing with any one 7
Rom 14: 1 welcome him, but not for disputes over opinions. 6
Heb 6:16 in all their disputes 5
7: 7 It is beyond dispute 5
Jde 1: 9 Michael . . disputed about the body of Moses 7
dispute *See also* point.

dispute about a word 1. λογομαχέω 2. λογομαχία
1Ti 6: 4 disputes about words, which produce envy 2
2Ti 2:14 charge them . . to avoid disputing about words 1

dispute with one another 1. συζητέω
Mrk 12:28 heard them disputing with one another 1
disputed *See* case.

disqualify 1. ἀδόκιμος 2. καταβραβεύω
1Co 9:27 I myself should be disqualified. 1
Col 2:18 Let no one disqualify you 2

disquiet 1. המה
Ps 42: 5 O my soul, and why are you disquieted within me? 1
11 O my soul, and why are you disquieted within me? 1
43: 5 O my soul, and why are you disquieted within me? 1

disregard 1. עבר 2. עלה עֵינַיִם 3. ἀθετέω 4. ἀμελέω
5. ἀστοχέω 6. ἐκλύω 7. ἐξουδενόω 8. καταλύω
9. παραπέμπω 10. παρέρχομαι 11. παρόρασις
12. παροράω 13. περιφρονέω 14. ὑπεροράω
15. φαυλίζω 16. neglego
Isa 40:27 and my right is disregarded by my God"? 1
Ezk 22:26 they have disregarded my sabbaths 2
1Th 4: 8 Therefore whoever disregards this 3
8 disregards not man but God 3
Tit 2:15 Let no one disregard you. 13
2Es 7:20 the law of God . . be disregarded! 16
Jdt 1:11 disregarded the orders of Nebuchadnezzar 15
11:10 my lord and master, do not disregard what he said 10
AEs 13: 4 continually disregard the ordinances 9
Wis 3:10 who disregarded the righteous man 4
Sir 8: 9 Do not disregard the discourse of the aged 5
14: 8 he averts his face and disregards people. 14
23:11 if he disregards it, he sins doubly 14
31:22 Listen to me, my son, and do not disregard me 7
2Mc 5:17 therefore he was disregarding the holy place. 11
4Mc 4:24 punishments were being disregarded 8
15:23 to disregard her temporal love for her children. 12
24 this noble mother disregarded all these 6

disreputable 1. בְּלִי שֵׁם
Job 30: 8 A senseless, a disreputable brood, 1

disrepute 1. ἀπελεγμός 2. ἄτιμος
Act 19:27 this trade of ours may come into disrepute 1
1Co 4:10 You are held in honor, but we in disrepute. 2

disrespectful 1. καταφρονέω
1Ti 6: 2 Those . . must not be disrespectful 1

dissemble 1. נכר
Prv 26:24 He who hates, dissembles with his lips 1

dissembler 1. עלם
Ps 26: 4 with false men, nor do I consort with dissemblers; 1

dissension 1. διχοστασία 2. ἔρις 3. στάσις
4. σχίσμα
Act 15: 2 had no small dissension and debate with them 3
23: 7 a dissension arose 3
10 when the dissension became violent 3
Rom 16:17 those who create dissensions and difficulties 1
1Co 1:10 that there be no dissensions among you 4
Gal 5:20 strife, jealousy, anger, selfishness, dissension 1
1Ti 6: 4 dissension, slander, base suspicions 2
Tit 3: 9 dissensions, and quarrels over the law 2
1Mc 3:29 because of the dissension and disaster 1

dissipation 1. ἀπάτη 2. κραιπάλη
Lke 21:34 weighed down with dissipation and drunkenness 2
2Pe 2:13 They are . . reveling in their dissipation 1

dissolve 1. הלך 2. διαχέω 3. καταλύω 4. λύω
Ps 58: 8 be like the snail which dissolves into slime 1
2Pe 3:10 and the elements will be dissolved with fire 4
11 Since all these things are thus to be dissolved 4
12 the heavens will be kindled and dissolved 4
Wis 2: 3 the spirit will dissolve like empty air. 2
4Mc 14: 8 encircled . . and dissolved it. 3

dissuade 1. ἀποστρέφω 2. ἀποτρέπω
1Mc 9: 9 they tried to dissuade him, saying 1
4Mc 16:12 nor did she dissuade any of them from dying 2

distaff 1. כִּישׁוֹר
Prv 31:19 She puts her hands to the distaff 1

distance 1. טחה 2. מִדָּה 3. רחב 4. רָחֹק 5. μακράν
6. μακρὰν ἀπέχω 7. μακρόθεν 8. πόρρωθεν
Gen 21:16 a good way off, about the distance of a bowshot; 1
30:36 he set a distance of three days' journey •
Exd 2: 4 his sister stood at a distance 4
Deu 21: 2 they shall measure the distance to the cities •
Jos 3: 4 shall be a space . . a distance of about 2,000 cubits; 2
2Kg 2: 7 also went, and stood at some distance from them 4
Ezk 40:19 he measured the distance from the inner front 3
Mat 8:30 was feeding at some distance from them. 5
26:58 Peter followed him at a distance 7
Mrk 11:13 seeing in the distance a fig tree in leaf 7
14:54 Peter had followed him at a distance 7
Lke 15:20 while he was yet at a distance 6
17:12 ten lepers, who stood at a distance 8
22:54 Peter followed at a distance; 7
23:49 the women . . stood at a distance 7
Wis 14:17 since they lived at a distance 5
Sir 13:10 do not remain at a distance 5
2Mc 8:25 After pursuing them for some distance •
10:27 and advanced a considerable distance •

remain at a distance 1. ἀφίστημι
Sir 13:10 do not remain at a distance 1

short distance 1. כִּבְרַת אֶרֶץ 2. לֹא רחק
Gen 44: 4 they had gone but a short distance from the city 2
2Kg 5:19 when Na'aman had gone from him a short distance 1

some distance 1. כִּבְרַת אֶרֶץ
Gen 35:16 when they were still some distance from Ephrath 1
48: 7 there was still some distance to go to Ephrath; 1

distant 1. מֶרְחָק 2. ἀπέχω
Isa 13: 5 come from a distant land . . the end of the heavens 1
Jer 4:16 Besiegers come from a distant land; 1
6:20 or sweet cane from a distant land? 1
Mat 14:24 the boat by this time was many furlongs distant 2
1Mc 8: 4 even though the place was far distant from them. 2
2Mc 12: 9 in Jerusalem, 30 miles distant. •

more distant 1. ulter

2Es 13:41 and go to a more distant region 1

distil 1. זקק 2. נזל 3. נטף

Deu 32: 2 May my . . speech distil as the dew, as the gentle 2
Job 36:27 the drops of water, he distils his mist in rain 1
Sng 4:11 Your lips distil nectar, my bride; 3
5:13 His lips are lilies, distilling liquid myrrh. 3

distinct 1. פלה 2. διαστολή 3. σαφής

Exd 33:16 in thy going with us, so that we are distinct 1
1Co 14: 7 do not give distinct notes 2
Wis 7:22 subtle, mobile, clear, unpolluted, distinct 3

distinction 1. διαστολή 2. ἐπιφανής 3. τιμή

Rom 3:22 all who believe. For there is no distinction; 1
10:12 there is no distinction between Jew and Greek; 1
Sir 45:12 a distinction to be prized, the work of an expert 3
2Mc 6:23 gray hairs . . he had reached with distinction 2

distinction *See also* make.

make a distinction 1. בדל

Ezk 22:26 they have made no distinction between the holy 1

distinctly 1. צַח

Isa 32: 4 stammerers will speak readily and distinctly. 1

distinguish 1. בדל 2. דגל 3. נכר 4. ראה 5. נצח (A) 6. ἀποδείκνυμι 7. διάκρισις 8. διαφέρω 9. διαχωρίζω 10. ἔνδοξος

Lev 10:10 You are to distinguish between the holy 1
Ezr 3:13 people could not distinguish the sound 3
Sng 5:10 and ruddy, distinguished among 10,000. 2
Ezk 44:23 and show them how to distinguish between *
Dan 6: 3 Daniel became distinguished above all 5
Mal 3:18 you shall distinguish between the righteous 4
Heb 5:14 to distinguish good from evil. 7
AEs 13: 3 is distinguished for his unchanging good will 6
Sir 33: 8 By the Lord's decision they were distinguished 9
11 the Lord distinguished them 9
1Mc 3:32 Lysias, a distinguished man of royal lineage 10
2Mc 15:13 distinguished by his gray hair and dignity 8

distinguish *See also* ability.

distort 1. διαστρέφω

Sir 19:25 people who distort kindness to gain a verdict. 1

distract 1. περισπάω

Lke 10:40 Martha was distracted with much serving 1
Sir 41: 2 very old and distracted over everything 1

without distraction 1. ἀπερίσπαστος

Sir 41: 1 a man without distractions 1

distraught 1. הום

Ps 55: 2 I am overcome by my trouble. I am distraught 1

distress 1. זְעָקָה 2. חול 3. כְּאֵב 4. מָצוֹק 5. מְצוּקָה 6. מֵצַר 7. מַר 8. נגשׂ 9. נֶפֶשׁ 10. עצב 11. צוק 12. צַר 13. צָרָה 14. צרר 15. כּאשׁ עַל (A) 16. ἀγωνία 17. ἀγωνιάω 18. ἀδημονέω 19. ἀνάγκη 20. βασανίζω 21. θλίβω 22. θλῖψις 23. λυπέω 24. μέλω 25. ὀδυνάω 26. ὀδύνη 27. πόνος 28. στενοχωρία 29. συνέχω 30. συνοχή 31. ταλαίπωρος 32. τρύχω 33. anxio 34. necessitas 35. patior 36. tribulatio

Gen 32: 7 Then Jacob was greatly afraid and distressed; 14
35: 3 the God who answered me in the day of my distress 13
42:21 we saw the distress of his soul, when he besought 13
21 therefore is this distress come upon us. 13
45: 5 now do not be distressed, or angry 10
Deu 28:53 siege and in the distress with which your enemies 4
53 distress with which your enemies shall distress 11
55 nothing left him, in the siege and in the distress 4
55 distress with which your enemy shall distress 11
57 want . . in the siege and in the distress 4
57 your enemy shall distress you in your towns. 11
Jdg 10: 9 so that Israel was sorely distressed. 14
14 let them deliver you in the time of your distress 13
1Sm 1:10 She was deeply distressed and prayed to the LORD 7
2:32 in distress you will look with envious eye on all 12
10:19 from all your calamities and your distresses; 13
14:24 And the men of Israel were distressed that day; 8
22: 2 every one who was in distress . . gathered to him; 4
28:15 Saul answered, "I am in great distress; 12
30: 6 And David was greatly distressed; 14
2Sm 1:26 I am distressed for you, my brother Jonathan; 12
22: 7 In my distress I called upon the LORD; 12
24:14 I am in great distress, let us fall into the hand 12
2Kg 19: 3 This day is a day of distress, of rebuke 13
1Ch 21:13 Then David said to Gad, "I am in great distress; 12
2Ch 15: 4 when in their distress they turned to the LORD 12
6 God troubled them with every sort of distress. 13
28:22 time of his distress he became yet more 14
33:12 when he was in distress he entreated the favor 14
Neh 9:37 we are in great distress. 13
Est 4: 4 When . . told her, the queen was deeply distressed; 2
Job 15:24 distress and anguish terrify him; 12
36:16 He also allured you out of distress 12
19 Will your cry avail to keep you from distress 12
Ps 4: 1 Thou hast given me room when I was in distress. 12
18: 6 In my distress I called upon the LORD; 12
25:17 bring me out of my distresses. 5
31: 9 Be gracious to me, O LORD, for I am in distress; 12
32: 6 at a time of distress, in the rush of great waters *
39: 2 I held my peace to no avail; my distress grew worse 3
59:16 a fortress and a refuge in the day of my distress. 12
69:17 for I am in distress, make haste to answer me. 12
78:49 anger, wrath, indignation, and distress 13
81: 7 In distress you called, and I delivered you; 13
102: 2 not hide thy face from me in the day of my distress! 12
106:44 regarded their distress, when he heard their cry. 12
107: 6 LORD . . delivered them from their distress; 5
13 LORD . . delivered them from their distress; 5
19 LORD . . delivered them from their distress; 5
28 LORD . . delivered them from their distress; 5
116: 3 I suffered distress and anguish. 13
118: 5 Out of my distress I called on the LORD; 6
120: 1 In my distress I cry to the LORD, that he may answer 13
Prv 1:27 when distress and anguish come upon you. 13
31: 6 Give . . wine to those in bitter distress; 9
Isa 5:30 behold, darkness and distress; 12
8:22 distress and darkness, the gloom of anguish; 13
25: 4 a stronghold to the needy in his distress 12
26:16 O LORD, in distress they sought thee 12
29: 2 Yet I will distress Ariel 11
7 against her and her stronghold and distress her 11
37: 3 Thus says Hezeki'ah, 'This day is a day of distress 13
65:19 the sound of weeping and the cry of distress. 1
Jer 15:11 in the time of trouble and in the time of distress! 13
19: 9 of his neighbor in the siege and in the distress 4
30: 7 it is a time of distress for Jacob; 13
Lam 1: 3 overtaken her in the midst of her distress. 6
20 Behold . . for I am in distress, my soul is in tumult 12
Dan 6:14 when he heard these words, was much distressed 15
Hos 5:15 and in their distress they seek me, saying 12
Obd 1:12 should not have boasted in the day of distress. 13
14 his survivors in the day of distress. 13
Jon 2: 2 saying, "I called to the LORD, out of my distress 13
Zep 1:15 A day of wrath is that day, a day of distress 13
Mat 8: 6 paralyzed at home, in terrible distress. 20
17:23 And they were greatly distressed. 23
18:31 they were greatly distressed 23
Lke 21:23 great distress shall be upon the earth 19
25 upon the earth distress of nations 30
Rom 2: 9 There will be tribulation and distress 28
8:35 Shall tribulation, or distress, or persecution 28
1Co 7:26 I think that in view of the present distress 19
Php 2:26 distressed because you heard that he was ill. 18
1Th 3: 7 in all our distress and affliction 19
2Es 6:37 and my soul was in distress. 33
9:45 and considered my distress, and gave me a son 36
10:50 sincerely grieved and profoundly distressed 35
13:19 they shall see great dangers and much distress 34
Tob 3: 6 Command that I now be released from my distress 19
9: 4 if I delay long he will be greatly distressed. 25
10: 3 he was greatly distressed. 23
5 Am I not distressed, my child, that I let you go 24
13:10 love those within you who are distressed 31
AEs 11: 8 tribulation and distress 28
14: 2 put on the garments of distress and mourning 28
Wis 11:11 they were equally distressed 32
17:11 distressed by conscience 29
Sir 31:20 distress of sleeplessness . . nausea and colic 27
Bar 2:18 the person that is greatly distressed, that goes 23
LJr 1:37 they cannot rescue a man who is in distress. 19
Sus 1:10 they did not tell each other of their distress 26
1Mc 2:53 Joseph in the time of his distress 28
5:16 their brethren who were in distress 22
6:11 I said to myself, 'To what distress I have come! 22
9:27 Thus there was great distress in Israel 22
68 They distressed him greatly 21
13: 5 to spare my life in any time of distress 22
2Mc 1: 7 the critical distress which came upon us 22
3:14 no little distress throughout the whole city. 17
15:19 were in no little distress 16

distress *See also* bring, cry.

bitter distress 1. נֶפֶשׁ מָרָה

2Kg 4:27 Let her alone, for she is in bitter distress; 1

greatly distress 1. קשה 2. ἐκθαμβέω 3. καταπονέω

Isa 8:21 pass through the land, greatly distressed 1
Mrk 14:33 and began to be greatly distressed and troubled. 2
2Pe 2: 7 greatly distressed by . . the wicked 3

distribute 1. חלק 2. נחל 3. נתן 4. פרק 5. διαδίδωμι 6. διαιρέω 7. διαμερίζω 8. κατακληροδοτέω 9. μερίζω 10. μερισμός

Jos 13:32 the inheritances which Moses distributed 2
14: 1 inheritances which . . distributed to them. 2
19:51 inheritances . . distributed by lot at Shiloh 2
2Sm 6:19 and distributed among all . . to each a cake 1
1Ch 16: 3 distributed to all Israel, both men and women 1
2Ch 11:23 he dealt wisely, and distributed some of his sons 4
31:15 to distribute the portions to their brethren 3
19 designated by name to distribute portions 3
35:12 distribute them according to the groupings 3
Neh 13:13 their duty was to distribute to their brethren. 1
Job 21:17 That God distributes pains in his anger? 1
38:24 way to the place where the light is distributed 1
Lke 18:22 Sell all that you have and distribute to the poor 5
Joh 6:11 he distributed them to those who were seated 5
Act 2: 3 distributed and resting on each one of them. 7
45 distributed them to all, as any had need. 7
Heb 2: 4 distributed according to his own will. 10
Jdt 16:24 Before she died she distributed her property 6
Sir 33:23 distribute your inheritance. 5
44:23 distributed them among twelve tribes. 9
1Mc 3:36 distribute their land. 8
6:35 distributed the beasts among the phalanxes; 6
2Mc 8:28 and distributed the rest among themselves 7

distribute freely 1. פזר

Ps 112: 9 has distributed freely, he has given to the poor; 1

distribute inheritance 1. נחל

Jos 19:49 had finished distributing the . . inheritances 1

distribution 1. διακονία

Act 6: 1 neglected in the daily distribution. 1

distribution *See also* make.

district 1. אֶרֶץ 2. מִדָּה 3. מְדִינָה 4. פֶּלֶךְ 5. תְּרוּמָה 6. γῆ 7. μερίς 8. μέρος 9. νομή 10. νόμος 11. ὅριον 12. τοπαρχία 13. τόπος

1Kg 20:14 the servants of the governors of the districts. 3
15 the servants of the governors of the districts 3
17 The servants of the governors of the districts 3
19 the servants of the governors of the districts 3
2Ch 11:23 through all the districts of Judah and Benjamin 1
Neh 3: 9 ruler of half the district of Jerusalem 4
12 ruler of half the district of Jerusalem 4
14 ruler of the district of Beth-hacche'rem 4
15 Shallum . . ruler of the district of Mizpah 4
16 ruler of half the district of Beth-zur 4
17 Hashabi'ah, ruler of half the district of Kei'lah 4
17 Hashabi'ah . . repaired for his district. 4
18 Bav'vai . . ruler of half the district of Kei'lah; 4
Ezk 45: 1 a portion of the land as a holy district *
3 in the holy district you shall measure 2
6 the portion set apart as the holy district *
7 the holy district and the property of the city 5
7 the holy district and the property of the city 5
Mat 2:22 he withdrew to the district of Galilee. 8
9:26 report of this went through all that district. 6
31 spread his fame through all that district. 6
15:21 and withdrew to the district of Tyre and Sidon. 8
16:13 into the district of Caesare'a Philip'pi 8
Mrk 8:10 went to the district of Dalmanu'tha. 8
Act 13:50 and drove them out of their district. 11
16:12 the leading city of the district of Macedo'nia 7
Jdt 4: 4 they sent to every district of Samaria 11
1Mc 10:30 the three districts added to it from Samaria 9
38 three districts that have been added to Judea 10
11:28 Judea and the three districts of Samaria 12
34 three districts of Aphairema and Lydda 10
57 set you over the four districts 10
3Mc 3:12 soldiers in Egypt and all its districts 13
4: 3 What district or city 10

mountain district 1. ὀρεινή

Jdt 5: 5 that dwells in the nearby mountain district 1

distrust 1. ἀπιστέω 2. ἀπιστία

Rom 4:20 No distrust made him waver 2
Wis 1: 2 those who do not distrust him. 1

distrustful 1. ἀπιστέω

2Mc 8:13 were cowardly and distrustful of God's justice 1

disturb 1. חרד 2. רגז 3. רהב 4. ἐκταράσσω 5. θορυβέω 6. ταράσσω 7. ταραχώδης 8. conturbo 9. excessus

1Sm 28:15 Why have you disturbed me by bringing me up? 2
2Sm 7:10 dwell in their own place, and be disturbed no more; 2
1Ch 17: 9 dwell in their own place, and be disturbed no more; 2
Sng 6: 5 Turn away your eyes from me, for they disturb me- 3
Nah 2:11 where his cubs were, with none to disturb? 1
Act 16:20 they are disturbing our city. 4
17: 8 were disturbed when they heard this. 6
2Es 5:33 Are you greatly disturbed in mind over Israel? 9
7:15 now why are you disturbed 8
Wis 17: 9 For even if nothing disturbing frightened them 7
18:19 dreams which disturbed them forewarned them 5
Sir 28: 9 a sinful man will disturb friends 6

disturbance 1. מְהוּמָה 2. θόρυβος 3. ταραχή 4. τραχύτης

2Ch 15: 5 great disturbances afflicted 1
Jdt 6: 1 When the disturbance . . died down 2
2Mc 3:30 was full of fear and disturbance 3
11:25 that this nation also be free from disturbance 3

3Mc 1:23 created a considerable disturbance in the holy place 4
disuse *See* fall.

diverse 1. *ποικίλος*
Prv 20:10 Diverse weights and diverse measures are both †
10 Diverse weights and diverse measures are both †
23 Diverse weights are an abomination to the LORD †
Heb 13: 9 led away by diverse and strange teachings 1

more diverse 1. *πολυτρόπος*
4Mc 14:11 mind of woman despised even more diverse agonies 1

diversion 1. דַּחֲוָה (A)
Dan 6:18 no diversions were brought to him, and sleep fled 1

divest 1. exuo
2Es 14:14 and divest yourself now of your weak nature 1

divide 1. בוא 2. בקע 3. גזר 4. הבר 5. חלק 6. חצה
7. נחל 8. נתח 9. פלג 10. פרד 11. פרר 12. פלג (A)
13. פרס (A) 14. *γίνομαι δίχα* 15. *διαδίδωμι*
16. *διαίρεσις* 17. *διαιρέω* 18. *διαμερίζω* 19. *δισσός*
20. *δόσις* 21. *μερίζω* 22. *μεσότοιχον* 23. *ποιέω*
24. *σχίζω* 25. *τέμνω* 26. divido 27. separatio
Gen 2:10 river . . divided and became four rivers. 10
10:25 Peleg, for in his days the earth was divided 9
14:15 he divided his forces against them by night 5
25:23 and two peoples, born of you, shall be divided; 10
32: 7 Jacob . . divided the people that were with him 6
33: 1 he divided the children among Leah and Rachel 6
49: 7 I will divide them in Jacob and scatter them 5
27 wolf . . at even dividing the spoil. 5
Exd 14:16 stretch out your hand over the sea and divide it 2
21 the sea dry land, and the waters were divided. 2
15: 9 I will overtake, I will divide the spoil 5
21:35 sell the live ox and divide the price of it; 6
35 and the dead beast also they shall divide. 6
Num26:53 To these the land shall be divided 5
55 the land shall be divided by lot; 5
56 Their inheritance shall be divided 5
Jos 13: 7 Now . . divide this land for an inheritance 5
18: 5 They shall divide it into seven portions 5
19:51 they finished dividing the land. 5
22: 8 divide the spoil . . with your brethren. 5
Jdg 5:30 Are they not finding and dividing the spoil? 5
7:16 he divided the 300 men into three companies 6
9:43 his men and divided them into three companies 6
19:29 hold of his concubine he divided her, limb by limb 8
2Sm 1:23 In life and in death they were not divided; 10
19:29 I have decided: you and Ziba shall divide the land. 5
1Kg 3:25 Divide the living child in two, and give half 3
26 It shall be neither mine nor yours; divide it. 3
16:21 the people of Israel were divided into two parts; 5
18: 6 they divided the land between them 5
1Ch 1:19 Peleg (for in his days the earth was divided) 9
Neh 9:11 thou didst divide the sea before them 2
Job 27:17 the innocent will divide the silver. 5
Ps 22:18 they divide my garments among them 5
68:12 women at home divide the spoil 5
74:13 Thou didst divide the sea by thy might; 11
78:13 He divided the sea and let them pass through it 2
136:13 to him who divided the Red Sea in sunder 3
Prv 16:19 better . . than to divide the spoil with the proud. 5
Isa 9: 3 as men rejoice when they divide the spoil. 5
18: 2 a nation . . whose land the rivers divide. 1
7 a nation . . whose land the rivers divide 1
33:23 Then prey and spoil in abundance will be divided; 5
47:13 let them . . save you, those who divide the heavens 4
53:12 I will divide him a portion with the great 5
12 and he shall divide the spoil with the strong; 5
63:12 who divided the waters before them 2
Ezk 5: 1 take balances for weighing, and divide the hair. 5
37:22 and no longer divided into two kingdoms. 6
42:12 and opposite them was a dividing wall. •
47:14 you shall divide it equally; 7
21 you shall divide this land among you 5
Dan 2:41 partly of iron, it shall be a divided kingdom; 12
5:28 PERES, your kingdom is divided and given 13
11: 4 kingdom shall be broken and divided 6
39 shall divide the land for a price. 5
Mic 2: 4 Among our captors he divides our fields. 5
Zec 14: 1 the spoil . . will be divided in the midst of you. 5
Mat 12:25 Every kingdom divided against itself 21
25 no city or house divided against itself 21
26 he is divided against himself 21
27:35 they divided his garments among them by casting lots 18
Mrk 3:24 If a kingdom is divided against itself 21
25 if a house is divided against itself 21
26 risen up against himself and is divided 21
6:41 he divided the two fish among them all. 21
15:24 they crucified him, and divided his garments 18
Lke 11:17 Every kingdom divided against itself is laid waste 18
17 a divided household falls. †
18 if Satan also is divided against himself 18
22 divides his spoil. 15
12:13 bid my brother divide the inheritance with me. 21
52 in one house there will be five divided 18
53 they will be divided 18
15:12 he divided his living between them. 17
22:17 Take this, and divide it among yourselves; 18
23:34 they cast lots to divide his garments. 18
Act 14: 4 the people of the city were divided 24
23: 7 the assembly was divided. 24
1Co 1:13 Is Christ divided? Was Paul crucified for you? 21
7:34 his interests are divided 21
Eph 2:14 has broken down the dividing wall of hostility 22
2Es 1:21 I divided fertile lands among you 26
6: 7 What will be the dividing of the times? 27
41 command him to divide and separate the waters 26
14:11 For the age is divided into twelve parts 26
Jdt 9: 4 their booty to be divided among thy beloved sons 16
Wis 5:12 the air, thus divided, comes together at once 25
Sir 1:28 do not approach him with a divided mind. 19
14:15 what you acquired by toil to be divided by lot? 16
42: 3 of dividing the inheritance of friends; 20
47:21 that the sovereignty was divided 14
1Mc 1: 6 and divided his kingdom among them 17
9:11 The cavalry was divided into two companies 17
16: 7 Then he divided the army 17
2Mc 8:21 then he divided his army into four parts. 23
30 they divided very much plunder 21

divide asunder 1. בדל
Lev 1:17 shall tear it . . but shall not divide it asunder 1

divide for inheritance 1. נחל
Num34:17 who shall divide the land to you for inheritance 1
18 of every tribe, to divide the land for inheritance 1
Ezk 47:13 you shall divide the land for inheritance 1

divide inheritance 1. נחל
Num34:29 the LORD commanded to divide the inheritance 1

divide into three parts 1. שלש
Deu 19: 3 divide into three parts the area of the land 1

divide into two parts 1. חצה
Num31:27 divide the booty into two parts 1

divide up 1. חלק 2. חצה
Job 41: 6 Will they divide him up among the merchants? 2
Ps 60: 6 With exultation I will divide up Shechem 1
108: 7 With exultation I will divide up Shechem 1
Jol 3: 2 scattered them . . and have divided up my land 1

divider 1. *μεριστής*
Lke 12:14 Man, who made me a judge or divider over you? 1

divination 1. מִקְסָם 2. קסם 3. קֶסֶם 4. *μαντεία*
5. *πύθων*
Num23:23 For there is . . no divination against Israel; 3
Deu 18:10 any one who practices divination, a soothsayer 3
1Sm 15:23 For rebellion is as the sin of divination 3
2Kg 17:17 and used divination and sorcery 3
Jer 14:14 are prophesying to you . . worthless divination 3
Ezk 12:24 any false vision or flattering divination 1
13: 7 and uttered a lying divination 1
23 see delusive visions nor practice divination; 3
21:21 at the head of the two ways, to use divination; 3
23 But to them it will seem like a false divination; 2
Mic 3: 6 and darkness to you, without divination. 2
Act 16:16 met by a slave girl who had a spirit of divination 5
Sir 34: 5 Divinations and omens and dreams are folly 4
divination *See also* fee, give, learn, practice, use.

divine 1. אֵל 2. אֱלֹהִים 3. *θεῖος* 4. *θειότης* 5. *θεός*
Ps 45: 6 Your divine throne endures for ever and ever. 2
82: 1 God has taken his place in the divine council; 1
Rom 3:25 in his divine forbearance he had passed over 5
2Co 10: 4 divine power to destroy strongholds 5
11: 2 I feel a divine jealousy for you 5
Col 1:25 the divine office which was given to me 5
1Ti 1: 4 rather than the divine training that is in faith; 5
2Pe 1: 3 His divine power has granted to us all things 3
4 and become partakers of the divine nature. 3
Wis 18: 9 and with one accord agreed to the divine law 4
2Mc 3:29 speechless because of the divine intervention 3
4:17 to show irreverence to the divine laws 3
3Mc 7:11 sake had transgressed the divine commandments 3
4Mc 1:16 the knowledge of divine and human matters 3
17 by which we learn divine matters reverently 3
4:13 by human treachery and not by divine justice. 3
21 The divine justice was angered by these acts 3
5:16 persuaded to govern our lives by the divine law 3
18 Even if . . our law were not truly divine 3
18 Even if . . we had wrongly held it to be divine 3
6:21 and not protect our divine law even to death. 3
7: 7 philosopher of divine life! 3
9 you made your words of divine philosophy credible. 3
8:22 Also, divine justice will excuse us 3
9: 9 undergo from the divine justice 3
15 because I protect the divine law. 3
32 the judgments of the divine wrath. 3
10:21 has been melodious with divine hymns. 3
11:27 those of the divine law that are set over us; 3
13:16 self-control, which is divine reason. 3
19 the divine and all-wise Providence 3
17:11 Truly the contest . . was divine 3
16 admire the athletes of the divine legislation? 3
18 they now stand before the divine throne 3
22 divine Providence preserved Israel 3
18: 3 were deemed worthy to share in a divine inheritance. 3
22 divine justice pursued . . the accursed tyrant. 3

divine (2) 1. נחש 2. קָסַם 3. קסם
Gen 44: 5 Is it not . . by this that he divines? 1
15 know that such a man as I can indeed divine? 1
1Sm 28: 8 And he said, "Divine for me by a spirit 3
Ezk 13: 6 They have spoken falsehood and divined a lie; 2
21:29 while they divine lies for you 3
22:28 seeing false visions and divining lies for them 3
Mic 3:11 its prophets divine for money; 3

diviner 1. בָּד 2. ענן 3. קסם
Deu 18:14 For these nations . . give heed . . to diviners; 3
Jdg 9:37 coming from the direction of the Diviners' Oak. 2
1Sm 6: 2 called for the priests and the diviners and said 3
Isa 2: 6 they are full of diviners . . and of soothsayers •
3: 2 the prophet, the diviner and the elder 3
44:25 the omens of liars, and makes fools of diviners; 3
Jer 27: 9 do not listen to your prophets, your diviners 3
29: 8 Do not let your prophets and your diviners 3
50:36 A sword upon the diviners, that they may become 1
Mic 3: 7 be disgraced, and the diviners put to shame; 3
Zec 10: 2 utter nonsense, and the diviners see lies; 3

divinity 1. *δαιμόνιος*
Act 17:18 He seems to be a preacher of foreign divinities 1

division 1. גְּדוּד 2. חלק 3. חֵלֶק 4. יָד 5. מַחֲלֹקֶת
6. פְּלֻגָּה (A) 7. *διαμερισμός* 8. *διαστολή* 9. *δύναμις*
10. *ἐφημερία* 11. *μερίς* 12. *μερισμός* 13. *παράταξις*
14. *παρεμβολή* 15. *σπεῖρα* 16. *σπειρηδόν*
17. *στολίζω* 18. *σχίσμα* 19. *τάξις*
Exd 8:23 Thus I will put a division between my people 8
Jos 18: 6 you shall describe the land in seven divisions 3
9 a description of it by towns in seven divisions; 3
2Kg 11: 7 the two divisions of you, which come on duty 4
1Ch 12:23 the numbers of the divisions of the armed troops 2
23: 6 David organized them in divisions 5
24: 1 The divisions of the sons of Aaron were these. 5
26: 1 As for the divisions of the gatekeepers 5
12 These divisions of the gatekeepers 5
19 These were the divisions of the gatekeepers 5
27: 1 concerning the divisions that came and went 5
1 each division numbering 24,000 5
2 Jasho'beam . . in charge of the first division 5
2 in his division were 24,000. 5
4 in charge of the division of the second month; 5
4 in his division were 24,000. 5
5 in his division were 24,000. 5
6 Ammiz'abad his son was in charge of his division. 5
7 in his division were 24,000. 5
8 in his division were 24,000. 5
9 in his division were 24,000. 5
10 in his division were 24,000. 5
11 in his division were 24,000. 5
12 in his division were 24,000. 5
13 in his division were 24,000. 5
14 in his division were 24,000. 5
15 in his division were 24,000. 5
28: 1 officers of the divisions that served the king 5
13 the divisions of the priests and of the Levites 5
21 divisions of the priests and the Levites 5
2Ch 5:11 without regard to their divisions; 5
8:14 he appointed the divisions of the priests 5
14 appointed . . gatekeepers in their divisions 5
23: 8 for Jehoi'ada . . did not dismiss the divisions. 5
26:11 army . . in divisions according to the numbers 1
31: 2 appointed the divisions of the priests 5
2 of the Levites, division by division 5
2 of the Levites, division by division 5
15 to their brethren . . by divisions. 5
16 according to their offices, by their divisions. 5
17 according to their offices, by their divisions. 5
35: 4 to your fathers' houses by your divisions 5
10 Levites in their divisions according 5
Ezr 6:18 set the priests in their divisions 6
Neh 11:36 certain divisions of the Levites in Judah 5
Lke 1: 5 Zechari'ah, of the division of Abi'jah 10
8 when his division was on duty 19
12:51 No, I tell you, but rather division; 7
Joh 7:43 there was a division among the people over him. 18
9:16 There was a division among them. 18
10:19 There was again a division among the Jews 18
1Co 11:18 I hear that there are divisions among you 18
Heb 4:12 piercing to the division of soul and spirit 12
1Es 1: 2 according to their divisions 17
Jdt 2:15 mustered the picked troops by divisions 13
Sir 16:26 when he made them, he determined their divisions. 11
1Mc 4: 1 this division moved out by night 14
4 the division was still absent from the camp. 9
2Mc 8:22 each to command a division 19
23 then, leading the first division himself 15

12:20 Maccabeus arranged his army in divisions 16
20 Maccabeus . . set men in command of the divisions 15
22 when Judas' first division appeared 15

divisions *See* set.

divorce 1. גרשׁ 2. כְּרִיתוּת 3. שׁלח 4. ἀπολύω 5. ἀποστάσιον 6. ἀφίημι

Lev 21: 7 marry a woman divorced from her husband 1
14 A widow, or one divorced, or a woman who has been 1
22:13 if a priest's daughter is a widow or divorced 1
Deu 24: 1 writes her a bill of divorce and puts it 2
3 latter husband . . writes her a bill of divorce 2
Isa 50: 1 Where is your mother's bill of divorce 2
Jer 3: 1 If a man divorces his wife and she goes from him 3
8 I had sent her away with a decree of divorce; 2
Mal 2:16 For I hate divorce, says the LORD the God of Israel 3
Mat 1:19 to shame, resolved to divorce her quietly. 4
5:31 It was also said, 'Whoever divorces his wife 4
32 I say to you that every one who divorces his wife 4
19: 3 Is it lawful to divorce one's wife for any cause? 4
7 to give a certificate of divorce 5
8 Moses allowed you to divorce your wives 4
9 I say to you: whoever divorces his wife 4
Mrk 10: 2 Is it lawful for a man to divorce his wife? 4
4 allowed a man to write a certificate of divorce 5
11 Whoever divorces his wife and marries another 4
12 if she divorces her husband and marries another 4
Lke 16:18 Every one who divorces his wife 4
18 he who marries a woman divorced from her husband 4
1Co 7:11 the husband should not divorce his wife. 6
12 he should not divorce her. 6
13 she should not divorce him. 6

divorce *See also* certificate.

divorced woman 1. גרשׁ 2. ἀπολύω

Num30: 9 any vow of a widow or of a divorced woman 1
Ezk 44:22 They shall not marry a widow, or a divorced woman 1
Mat 5:32 whoever marries a divorced woman commits adultery 2

divulge 1. ἀναγγέλλω 2. τίκτω

Act 19:18 confessing and divulging their practices. 1
Sir 8:18 for you do not know what he will divulge. 2

do 1. גְּמוּל 2. גמל 3. היה 4. יטב 5. כון 6. כלה 7. מַעַל 8. מַעֲלָל 9. מַעֲשֶׂה 10. מִפְעָל 11. מִשְׁמֶרֶת 12. עבד 13. עֲבֹדָה 14. עֲלִילָה 15. עשה 16. פעל 17. פֹּעַל 18. פְּעֻלָּה 19. שׂום 20. תמם 21. עבד (A) 22. ἀδύνατος 23. ἀνδραγαθέω 24. ἀνταποδίδωμι 25. γίνομαι 26. γινώσκω 27. διαπράσσω 28. δίδωμι 29. δράω 30. εἰμί 31. ἐκ 32. ἐν 33. ἐνδείκνυμι 34. ἐνεργάζομαι 35. ἐξεργάζομαι 36. ἐργάζομαι 37. ἔργον 38. ἐσθίω 39. εὐποιΐα 40. ἵστημι 41. κατατίθημι 42. κατεργάζομαι 43. λόγος 44. παρά 45. παρέχω 46. πάσχω 47. πείθω 48. περιπατέω 49. ποιέω 50. ποῖος 51. πρᾶγμα 52. πρᾶξις 53. πράσσω 54. συναναμείγνυμι 55. συντελέω 56. τελέω 57. τρόπος 58. χράω 59. ὠφελέω 60. ago 61. do 62. facio 63. fio 64. gero 65. opus

Gen 2: 2 God finished his work which he had done 15
2 rested . . from all his work which he had done. 15
3 from all his work which he had done in creation. 15
3:13 said to the woman, "What is this that you have done? 15
14 said to the serpent, "Because you have done this 15
4:10 What have you done? The voice of your brother's 15
8:21 destroy every living creature as I have done. 15
9:24 knew what his youngest son had done to him 15
11: 6 this is only the beginning of what they will do; 15
6 this is only the beginning of what they will do; 15
12:18 What is this you have done to me? 15
16: 5 May the wrong done to me be on you! I gave my maid •
6 is in your power; do to her as you please. 15
18: 5 your servant." So they said, "Do as you have said. 15
17 Shall I hide from Abraham what I am about to do 15
19 the LORD by doing righteousness and justice; 15
21 whether they have done altogether according 15
25 Far be it from thee to do such a thing 15
25 Shall not the Judge of all the earth do right? 15
29 He answered, "For the sake of 40 I will not do it. 15
30 He answered, "I will not do it, if I find 30 there. 15
19: 8 and do to them as you please; 15
8 only do nothing to these men 15
22 for I can do nothing till you arrive 15
20: 5 In the integrity of my heart . . I have done this. 15
6 Yes, I know that you have done this 15
9 What have you done to us? And how have I sinned 15
9 You have done to me things that ought not to be 15
9 to me things that ought not to be done. 15
13 I said to her, 'This is the kindness you must do me 15
21:12 whatever Sarah says to you, do as she tells you •
22 God is with you in all that you do; 15
26 Abim'elech said, "I do not know who has done this 15
22:12 Do not . . do anything to him; 15
16 because you have done this 15
24:15 Before he had done speaking, behold, Rebekah 6
19 camels also, until they have done drinking. 6
22 When the camels had done drinking 6
45 Before I had done speaking in my heart 6
66 told Isaac all the things that he had done. 15
26:10 Abim'elech said, "What is this you have done to us 15
29 that you will do us no harm, just as we have not 15
29 not touched you and have done to you nothing 15
27:19 I have done as you told me; now sit up and eat 15
37 What then can I do for you, my son? 15
45 until . . he forgets what you have done to him; 15
28:15 until I have done that of which I have spoken 15
29:25 Jacob said to Laban, "What is this you have done 15
26 Laban said, "It is not so done in our country 15
30:31 if you will do this for me, I will again feed 15
31:12 for I have seen all that Laban is doing to you. 15
16 now then, whatever God has said to you, do. 15
26 Laban said to Jacob, "What have you done 15
29 It is in my power to do you harm; 15
43 But what can I do this day to these my daughters 15
34: 7 for such a thing ought not to be done. 15
14 They said to them, "We cannot do this thing 15
39: 9 how then can I do this great wickedness, and sin 15
11 went into the house to do his work 15
22 and whatever was done there, he was the doer of it; 15
40:14 and do me the kindness, I pray you, to make mention 15
15 and here also I have done nothing that they 15
41:25 has revealed to Pharaoh what he is about to do. 15
28 God has shown to Pharaoh what he is about to do. 15
55 Egyptians, "Go to Joseph; what he says to you, do. 15
42:18 Joseph said to them, "Do this and you will live 15
25 for the journey. This was done for them. 15
28 What is this that God has done to us? 15
43:11 then do this: take some of the choice fruits 15
44: 5 You have done wrong in so doing.' 15
7 Far be it . . that they should do such a thing! 15
15 What deed is this that you have done? 15
17 he said, "Far be it from me that I should do so! 15
45:17 Say to your brothers, 'Do this: load your beasts 15
19 Command them also, 'Do this: take wagons 15
47:30 He answered, "I will do as you have said. 15
Exd 1:17 midwives . . did not do as the king . . commanded 15
18 Why have you done this, and let the male children 15
2: 4 stood . . to know what would be done to him. 15
3:16 I have observed you and what has been done to you 15
20 smite Egypt with all the wonders which I will do 15
4:15 and will teach you what you shall do. 15
17 this rod, with which you shall do the signs. 15
21 see that you do before Pharaoh all the miracles 15
28 the signs which he had charged him to do. •
6: 1 Now you shall see what I will do to Pharaoh; 15
8:26 Moses said, "It would not be right to do so; 15
9: 5 the LORD will do this thing in the land. 15
10: 2 tell . . what signs I have done among them; 19
12:16 no work shall be done on those days; 15
35 The people of Israel had also done as Moses told 15
14: 5 and they said, "What is this we have done 15
11 What have you done to us, in bringing us out 15
15:11 terrible in glorious deeds, doing wonders? 15
26 If you . . do that which is right in his eyes 15
17: 4 What shall I do with this people? 15
18: 1 Jethro . . heard of all that God had done 15
8 the LORD had done to Pharaoh and to the Egyptians 15
9 the good which the LORD had done to Israel 15
14 When Moses' father-in-law saw all that he was doing 15
14 What is this that you are doing for the people? 15
17 What you are doing is not good. 15
20 make them know . . what they must do. 15
23 If you do this, and God so commands you, then you 15
19: 8 All that the LORD has spoken we will do. 15
20: 9 Six days you shall labor, and do all your work; 15
10 in it you shall not do any work, you, or your son 15
21:11 if he does not do these three things for her 15
22:30 You shall do likewise with your oxen 15
23:11 You shall do likewise with your vineyard 15
12 Six days you shall do your work, but on the seventh 15
22 if you . . and do all that I say 15
24 nor serve them, nor do according to their works 15
24: 3 the words which the LORD has spoken we will do. 15
7 they said, "All that the LORD has spoken we will do 15
26:17 so shall you do for all the frames 15
29: 1 this is what you shall do to them to consecrate 15
31:11 all that I have commanded you they shall do. 15
15 Six days shall work be done, but the seventh day 15
32:14 the evil which he thought to do to his people. 15
21 Moses said to Aaron, "What did this people do to you 15
33: 5 that I may know what to do with you.' 15
17 This very thing that you have spoken I will do; 15
34:10 Before all your people I will do marvels 15
10 it is a terrible thing that I will do with you. 15
35: 1 which the LORD has commanded you to do. 15
2 Six days shall work be done, but on the seventh day 15
29 LORD had commanded by Moses to be done 15
35 work done by a craftsman or by a designer •
36: 1 to know how to do any work in the construction 15
2 heart stirred him up to come to do the work; 15
3 had brought for doing the work on the sanctuary. 15
4 so that all the able men who were doing every sort 15
4 came, each from the task that he was doing 15
5 much more than enough for doing the work 13
5 the work which the LORD has commanded us to do. 15
6 Let neither man nor woman do anything more 15
7 for the stuff they had was sufficient to do all 15
39:32 the people of Israel had done according to all 15
32 LORD had commanded Moses; so had they done. 15
42 so the people of Israel had done all the work. 15
43 Moses saw all the work, and behold, they had done it; 15
43 as the LORD had commanded, so had they done it. 15
Lev 4: 2 which the LORD has commanded not to be done 15
13 If . . they do any one of the things which the LORD 15
13 which the LORD has commanded not to be done 15
20 Thus shall he do with the bull 15
20 as he did . . so shall he do with this 15
22 sins, doing unwittingly any one of all the things 15
22 has commanded not to be done, and is guilty 15
27 sins unwittingly in doing any one of the things 15
27 has commanded not to be done, and is guilty 15
5:17 If any one sins, doing any of the things 15
17 which the LORD has commanded not to be done 15
6: 7 which one may do and thereby become guilty 15
8: 5 thing which the LORD has commanded to be done 15
34 As has been done today, the LORD has commanded 15
34 LORD has commanded to be done to make atonement 15
9: 6 the thing which the LORD commanded you to do 15
16:15 and do with its blood as he did with the blood 15
16 so he shall do for the tent of meeting 15
29 shall afflict yourselves, and shall do no work 15
18: 3 You shall not do as . . in the land of Egypt 15
3 not . . as they do in the land of Egypt 9
3 you shall not do as . . in the land of Canaan 15
3 not . . as they do in the land of Canaan 9
4 You shall do my ordinances and keep my statutes 15
5 my ordinances, by doing which a man shall live 15
26 and do none of these abominations 15
29 For whoever shall do any of these abominations 15
29 the persons that do them shall be cut off 15
19:15 You shall do no injustice in judgment 15
35 You shall do no wrong in judgment 15
37 all my statutes and all my ordinances, and do them 15
20: 8 Keep my statutes, and do them; I am the LORD 15
22 all my statutes and all my ordinances, and do them 15
22:31 So you shall keep my commandments and do them 15
23: 3 Six days shall work be done; but on the seventh day 15
3 you shall do no work; it is a sabbath to the LORD 15
7 convocation; you shall do no laborious work 15
8 convocation; you shall do no laborious work 15
21 you shall do no laborious work: it is a statute 15
25 You shall do no laborious work 15
28 you shall do no work on this same day; for it is a day 15
31 You shall do no work: it is a statute for ever 15
35 convocation; you shall do no laborious work 15
36 solemn assembly; you shall do no laborious work 15
24:19 as he has done it shall be done to him 15
19 as he has done it shall be done to him 15
25:18 Therefore you shall do my statutes 15
26: 3 observe my commandments and do them 15
14 if you . . will not do all these commandments 15
15 so that you will not do all my commandments 15
16 I will do this to you 15
Num 1:54 Thus did the people of Israel; they did according 15
54 they did according to all that the LORD 15
2:34 Thus did the people of Israel. 15
3:38 whatever had to be done for the people of Israel; 11
4: 3 to do the work in the tent of meeting. 15
23 for service, to do the work in the tent of meeting. 12
26 do all that needs to be done with regard to them. 12
26 do all that needs to be done with regard to them. 15
27 to carry, and in all that they have to do; 13
30 service, to do the work of the tent of meeting. 12
47 could enter to do the work of service 12
5: 4 Israel did so, and drove them outside the camp; 15
4 as the LORD said . . so the people of Israel did. 15
6:21 so shall he do according to the law 15
7: 5 used in doing the service of the tent of meeting 12
8: 3 And Aaron did so; he set up its lamps 15
7 thus you shall do to them, to cleanse them 15
11 may be theirs to do the service of the LORD. 12
19 to do the service for the people of Israel 12
20 Thus did Moses and Aaron . . to the Levites; 15
20 people of Israel did to them. 15
22 Levites went in to do their service in the tent 12
22 concerning the Levites, so they did to them. 15
26 minister . . and they shall do no service. 12
26 Thus shall you do to the Levites in assigning 15
9: 5 so the people of Israel did. 15
14 will keep the passover . . so shall he do; 15
14:28 'what you have said in my hearing I will do to you 15
35 this will I do to all this wicked congregation 15
15:11 Thus it shall be done for each bull or ram 15
12 so shall you do with every one according 15
13 who are native shall do these things in this way 15
14 pleasing odor to the LORD, he shall do as you do. 15
14 pleasing odor to the LORD, he shall do as you do. 15
24 then if it was done unwittingly 15
29 one law for him who does anything unwittingly 15
30 person who does anything with a high hand 15
34 not been made plain what should be done to him. 15
39 remember all the commandments of the LORD, to do 15
40 you shall remember and do all my commandments 15
16: 6 Do this: take censers, Korah and all his company; 15
9 to do service in the tabernacle of the LORD 12

28 LORD has sent me to do all these works 15
17:11 Thus did Moses; as the LORD commanded him 15
11 Moses; as the LORD commanded him, so he did. 15
18: 6 to do the service of the tent of meeting. 12
23 Levites shall do the service of the tent 12
20:27 Moses did as the LORD commanded; 15
21:34 do to him as you did to Sihon king of the Amorites 15
34 do to him as you did to Sihon king of the Amorites 15
22: 2 Balak . . saw all that Israel had done 15
17 whatever you say to me I will do; 15
18 not go beyond the command . . to do less or more. 15
20 but only what I bid you, that shall you do. 15
28 What have I done to you, that you have struck me 15
30 I ever accustomed to do so to you?" And he said, "No. 15
23: 2 Balak did as Balaam had said; and Balak and Balaam 15
11 Balak said to Balaam, "What have you done to me? 15
11 behold, you have done nothing but bless them. •
19 Has he said, and will he not do it? 15
26 All that the LORD says, that I must do'? 15
30 Balak did as Balaam had said, and offered 15
24:13 to do either good or bad of my own will; 15
14 people will do to your people in the latter days. 15
18 be dispossessed, while Israel does valiantly. 15
23 Alas, who shall live when God does this? 19
27:22 Moses did as the LORD commanded him; 15
28:25 you shall do no laborious work. 15
26 holy convocation; you shall do no laborious work 15
29: 1 convocation; you shall do no laborious work. 15
7 afflict yourselves; you shall do no work 15
12 holy convocation; you shall do no laborious work 15
35 solemn assembly: you shall do no laborious work. 15
30: 2 he shall do according to all that proceeds out 15
31:31 Moses and Elea'zar . . did as the LORD commanded 15
32: 8 Thus did your fathers when I sent them 15
13 generation that had done evil in the sight of the LORD 15
20 If you will do this, if you will take up arms 15
23 if you will not do so, behold, you have sinned 15
24 and do what you have promised 15
25 Your servants will do as my lord commands. 15
31 As the LORD has said to your servants, so we will do. 15
33:56 I will do to you as I thought to do to them. 15
56 I will do to you as I thought to do to them. 15
36:10 daughters . . did as the LORD commanded Moses; 15
Deu 1:14 'The thing that you have spoken is good for us to do.' 15
18 commanded you . . all the things that you should do. 15
44 Amorites . . chased you as bees do and beat you 15
3: 2 you shall do to him as you did to Sihon the king 15
21 that the LORD your God has done to these two kings; 15
21 so will the LORD do to all the kingdoms 15
24 what god . . can do such works and mighty acts 15
4: 1 which I teach you, and do them; that you may live 15
5 should do them in the land which you are entering 15
6 Keep them and do them; for that will be your wisdom 15
14 teach you . . that you might do them in the land 15
25 doing what is evil in the sight of the LORD 15
5: 1 you shall learn them and be careful to do them. 15
13 Six days you shall labor, and do all your work; 15
14 not do any work, you, or your son, or your daughter 15
27 speak to us . . we will hear and do it.' 15
31 do them in the land which I give them to possess.' 15
32 careful to do therefore as the LORD your God 15
6: 1 to teach you, that you may do them in the land 15
3 Hear therefore, O Israel, and be careful to do them; 15
18 do what is right and good in the sight of the LORD 15
24 LORD commanded us to do all these statutes 15
25 if we are careful to do all this commandment 15
7:11 therefore be careful to do the commandment 15
12 hearken to these ordinances, and keep and do them 15
19 so will the LORD your God do to all the peoples 15
8: 1 All the commandment . . you shall be careful to do 15
9:18 in doing what was evil in the sight of the LORD 15
10:21 your God, who has done for you these great 15
11:22 if you will be careful to do all this commandment •
22 do all this commandment which I command you to do 15
32 shall be careful to do all the statutes 15
12: 1 which you shall be careful to do in the land 15
4 You shall not do so to the LORD your God. 15
8 not do according to all that we are doing here 15
8 not do . . all that we are doing here this day 15
8 every man doing whatever is right in his own eyes; •
14 there you shall do all that I am commanding you. 15
25 when you do what is right in the sight of the LORD. 15
28 go well . . when you do what is good and right 15
30 serve their gods?-that I also may do likewise.' 15
31 You shall not do so to the LORD your God; 15
31 abominable thing . . they have done for their gods; 15
32 Everything . . you shall be careful to do; 15
13:11 shall . . never again do any such wickedness 15
14 such an abominable thing has been done among you 15
18 doing what is right in the sight of the LORD 15
14:29 bless . . all the work of your hands that you do. 15
15: 5 being careful to do all this commandment 15
17 And to your bondwoman you shall do likewise. 15
18 LORD your God will bless you in all that you do. 15
16: 8 seventh day . . you shall do no work on it. 15
17: 4 such an abominable thing has been done in Israel 15
5 bring . . man or woman who has done this evil thing 15
10 Then . . do according to what they declare to you 15
10 careful to do according to all that they direct 15
11 according to the instructions . . you shall do; 15
19 keeping . . this law and these statutes, and doing 15
18:14 LORD your God has not allowed you so to do. •
19:19 do to him as he had meant to do to his brother; 15
19 do to him as he had meant to do to his brother; 15
20:11 people who are found in it shall do forced labor •
15 do to all the cities which are very far from you 15
18 not teach you to do according to all their 15
18 abominable practices which they have done 15
21: 9 when you do what is right in the sight of the LORD. 15
22: 3 so you shall do with his ass . . with his garment; 15
3 so you shall do with his garment . . with any lost thing 15
3 so . . do with any lost thing of your brother's 15
26 But to the young woman you shall do nothing; 15
24: 8 very careful to do according to all that 15
8 as I commanded them, so you shall be careful to do. 15
18 therefore I command you to do this. 15
22 therefore I command you to do this. 15
25: 9 So shall it be done to the man who does not build up 15
16 all who do such things, all who act dishonestly 15
26:14 done according to all that thou hast commanded 15
16 LORD . . commands you to do these statutes 15
16 therefore be careful to do them with all 15
27:26 not confirm the words of this law by doing them.' 15
28: 1 being careful to do all his commandments 15
13 obey the commandments . . being careful to do 15
15 not . . be careful to do all his commandments 15
20 in all that you undertake to do 15
20 on account of the evil of your doings 8
58 If . . not careful to do all the words of this law 15
29: 9 be careful to do the words of this covenant 15
9 that you may prosper in all that you do. 15
24 'Why has the LORD done thus to this land? 15
29 that we may do all the words of this law. 15
30:12 bring it to us, that we may hear it and do it?' 15
13 bring it to us, that we may hear it and do it?' 15
14 your mouth and in your heart, so that you can do it. 15
31: 4 LORD will do to them as he did to Sihon and Og 15
5 do to them according to all the commandment 15
12 may . . be careful to do all the words of this law 15
18 on account of all the evil which they have done 15
29 will do what is evil in the sight of the LORD 15
32:46 may be careful to do all the words of this law. 15
34:11 signs . . which the LORD sent him to do in the land 15
Jos 1: 7 being careful to do according to all the law 15
8 be careful to do according to all that is written 15
16 All that you have commanded us we will do 15
3: 5 for tomorrow the LORD will do wonders among you. 15
5: 8 When the circumcising of all the nation was done 20
6: 3 Thus shall you do for six days. 15
7: 9 what wilt thou do for thy great name? 15
15 because he has done a shameful thing in Israel 15
19 give glory to . . and tell me now what you have done; 15
8: 2 and you shall do to Ai and its king as you did 15
8 set the city on fire, doing as the LORD has bidden; 15
9: 3 heard what Joshua had done to Jericho and to Ai 15
20 This we will do to them, and let them live 15
25 do as it seems good and right in your sight to do 15
25 do as it seems good and right . . to do to us. 15
10: 1 doing to Ai and its king as he had done to Jericho 15
1 doing to Ai and its king as he had done to Jericho 15
25 thus the LORD will do to all your enemies 15
28 he did to . . as he had done to the king of Jericho. 15
30 he did to . . as he had done to the king of Jericho. 15
32 and smote it . . as he had done to Libnah. 15
35 utterly destroyed . . as he had done to Lachish. 15
37 he left none remaining, as he had done to Eglon 15
39 as he had done to Hebron and . . so he did to Debir 15
11:20 For it was the LORD's doing to harden their hearts •
16:10 but have become slaves to do forced labor. •
22:24 What have you to do with the LORD, the God †
23: 3 all that the LORD . . has done to all these nations 15
6 be . . steadfast to keep and do all that is written 15
8 cleave to the LORD . . as you have done to this day. 15
Jdg 1: 7 as I have done, so God has requited me." And they 15
2: 2 my command. What is this you have done? 15
7 great work which the LORD had done for Israel. 15
10 the LORD or the work which he had done for Israel. 15
11 Israel did what was evil in the sight of the LORD 15
17 and they did not do so. 15
3: 7 Israel did what was evil in the sight of the LORD 15
12 again did what was evil in the sight of the LORD; 15
12 Israel, because they had done what was evil 15
4: 1 again did what was evil in the sight of the LORD 15
6: 1 Israel did what was evil in the sight of the LORD; 15
20 And he did so. 15
27 Gideon took . . and did as the LORD had told him; 15
27 too afraid . . to do it by day, he did it by night. 15
27 too afraid . . to do it by day, he did it by night. 15
29 they said to one another, "Who has done this thing? 15
29 Gideon the son of Jo'ash has done this thing. 15
40 God did so that night; for it was dry on the fleece 15
7:17 And he said to them, "Look at me, and do likewise; 15
17 when I come to the outskirts of the camp, do as I do. 15
17 when I come to the outskirts of the camp, do as I do. 15
8: 1 What is this that you have done to us, not to call us 15
2 What have I done now in comparison with you? 15
3 what have I been able to do in comparison with you? 15
35 for all the good that he had done to Israel. 15
9:16 house, and have done to him as his deeds deserved- 15
24 the violence done to the 70 sons of Jerubba'al •
33 you, you may do to them as occasion offers. 15
48 What you have seen me do, make haste to do 15
48 What you have seen me do, make haste to do 15
48 make haste to do, as I have done. •
10: 6 did what was evil in the sight of the LORD 15
15 We have sinned; do to us whatever seems good 15
11:10 witness between us; we will surely do as you say. 15
27 and you do me wrong by making war on me; 15
36 do to me according to what has gone forth 15
37 Let this thing be done for me; let me alone two 15
39 father, who did with her according to his vow 15
13: 1 again did what was evil in the sight of the LORD; 15
8 and teach us what we are to do with the boy 15
12 to be the boy's manner of life, and what is he to do? 9
14: 6 But he did not tell . . what he had done. 15
10 made a feast there; for so the young men used to do. 15
15: 3 to the Philistines, when I do them mischief. 15
6 the Philistines said, "Who has done this? 15
7 If this is what you do, I swear I will be avenged 15
10 come up to bind Samson, to do to him as he did to us. 15
10 come up to bind Samson, to do to him as he did to us. 15
11 What then is this that you have done to us? 15
11 he said . . "As they did to me, so have I done to them. 15
11 he said . . "As they did to me, so have I done to them. 15
17: 6 every man did what was right in his own eyes. 15
18: 3 What are you doing in this place? 15
14 Now therefore consider what you will do. 15
18 the priest said to them, "What are you doing? 15
19:23 seeing that . . do not do this vile thing. 15
24 Ravish them and do with them what seems good 15
24 but against this man do not do so vile a thing. 15
20: 9 what we will do to Gib'e-ah: we will go up against it 15
21: 7 What shall we do for wives for those who are left 15
11 This is what you shall do; every male and every 15
16 What shall we do for wives for those who are left 15
23 the Benjaminites did so, and took their wives 15
25 every man did what was right in his own eyes. 15
Rut 1:17 May the LORD do so to me and more also if even death 15
2:11 All that you have done . . has been fully told me 15
12 The LORD recompense you for what you have done 17
3: 4 go . . and lie down; and he will tell you what to do. 15
5 And she replied, "All that you say I will do. 15
6 went . . and did just as her mother-in-law had told 15
11 do not fear, I will do for you all that you ask 15
16 Then she told her all that the man had done for her 15
1Sm 1:23 Do what seems best to you, wait until you have 15
2:14 they did at Shiloh to all the Israelites 15
22 heard all that his sons were doing to all Israel 15
23 Why do you do such things? For I hear of your evil 15
35 who shall do according to what is in my heart 15
3:11 I am about to do a thing in Israel 15
17 May God do so to you and more also, if you hide 15
18 It is the LORD; let him do what seems good to him. 15
5: 8 What shall we do with the ark of the God of Israel? 15
6: 2 What shall we do with the ark of the LORD? 15
9 if . . then it is he who has done us this great harm; 15
10 The men did so, and took two milch cows 15
8: 8 all the deeds which they have done to me 15
8 According to all . . so they are also doing to you. 15
10: 2 What shall I do about my son? 15
7 do whatever your hand finds to do, for God is 15
7 do whatever your hand finds to do, for God is 15
8 until I come to you and show you what you shall do. 15
11: 7 Whoever does not . . so shall it be done to his oxen! 15
10 and you may do to us whatever seems good to you. 15
12:16 which the LORD will do before your eyes. 15
17 which you have done in the sight of the LORD 15
20 you have done all this evil, yet do not turn aside 15
13:11 Samuel said, "What have you done? 15
14: 7 Do all that your mind inclines to . . I am with you 15
36 And they said, "Do whatever seems good to you. 15
40 the people said to Saul, "Do what seems good to you. 15
43 Saul said to Jonathan, "Tell me what you have done. 15
44 God do so to me and more also; you shall surely die 15
48 And he did valiantly, and smote the Amal'ekites 15
15: 2 I will punish what Am'alek did to Israel 15
19 Why did you swoop on the spoil, and do what was evil 15
16: 3 and I will show you what you shall do; 15
4 Samuel did what the LORD commanded, and came 15
17:26 What shall be done for the man who kills this 15
27 So shall it be done to the man who kills him. 15
29 What have I done now? Was it not but a word? 15
19:18 and told him all that Saul had done to him. 15
20: 1 What have I done? What is my guilt? 15
2 my father does nothing . . without disclosing it 15
4 Whatever you say, I will do for you. 15
13 should it please my father to do you harm •
13 the LORD do so to Jonathan, and more also 15
32 Why should he be put to death? What has he done? 15
22: 3 let . . till I know what God will do for me. 15
24: 4 you shall do to him as it shall seem good to you. 15
6 LORD forbid that I should do this thing to my lord 15
19 LORD reward you with good for what you have done 15
25:17 know this and consider what you should do; 15
22 God do so to David and more also 15
26 enemies and those who seek to do evil to my lord •
30 when the LORD has done to my lord 15

26:16 This thing that you have done is not good. 15
18 For what have I done? What guilt is on my hands? 15
25 You will do many things and will succeed in them. 15
27:11 Lest they should . . and say, 'So David has done.' 15
28: 2 you shall know what your servant can do. 15
9 Surely you know what Saul has done 15
15 I have summoned you to tell me what I shall do. 15
17 The LORD has done to you as he spoke by me; 15
18 therefore the LORD has done this thing to you 15
29: 3 What are these Hebrews doing here? *
8 But what have I done? What have you found 15
30:23 You shall not do so . . with what the LORD has given 15
31:11 heard what the Philistines had done to Saul 15
2Sm 2: 6 I will do good to you because you have done this 15
6 do good to you because you have done this thing. 15
3: 9 God do so to Abner, and more also, if I do not 15
19 that Israel and . . Benjamin thought good to do. *
24 Jo'ab . . said, "What have you done? 15
25 to deceive . . and to know all that you are doing. 15
35 God do so to me and more also, if I taste bread 15
36 that the king did pleased all the people. 15
5:25 And David did as the LORD commanded him 15
7: 3 Go, do all that is in your heart; 15
23 and doing for them great and terrible things 15
25 confirm for ever . . and do as thou hast spoken; 15
9:11 According to all . . so will your servant do. 15
10: 3 Do you think, because David has sent comforters *
12 and may the LORD do what seems good to him. 15
11:11 as your soul lives, I will not do this thing. 15
27 the thing . . David had done displeased the LORD. 15
12: 5 the man who has done this deserves to die; 15
6 because he did this thing, and . . he had no pity. 15
9 you despised . . to do what is evil in his sight? 15
12 For you did it secretly; but I will do this thing 15
12 but I will do this thing before all Israel 15
18 how then can we . . ? He may do himself some harm. 15
21 What is this thing that you have done? 15
31 thus he did to all the cities of the Ammonites. 15
13: 2 it seemed impossible . . to do anything to her. 15
12 for such a thing is not done in Israel; 15
12 do not force me . . do not do this wanton folly. 15
16 is greater than the other which you did to me. 15
29 did to Amnon as Ab'salom had commanded. 15
14:20 to change . . affairs your servant Jo'ab did this. 15
15: 6 Thus Ab'salom did to all . . who came to the king 15
15 ready to do whatever my lord the king decides. *
26 here I am, let him do to me what seems good to him. 15
16:10 What have I to do with you, you sons of Zeru'iah? †
10 who then shall say, 'Why have you done so?' 15
20 Give your counsel; what shall we do? 15
17: 6 Thus has Ahith'ophel . . shall we do as he advises? 15
18: 4 king said . . "Whatever seems best to you I will do. 15
19:13 God do so to me, and more also, if you are not 15
18 to bring over the king's . . and to do his pleasure. 15
22 What have I to do with you, you sons of Zeru'iah †
27 do therefore what seems good to you. 15
37 and do for him whatever seems good to you. 15
38 and I will do for him whatever seems good to you; 15
38 and all that you desire of me I will do for you. 15
21: 3 What shall I do for you? And how . . make expiation 15
4 And he said, "What do you say that I shall do for you? 15
11 When David was told what Rizpah . . had done 15
14 and they did all that the king commanded. 15
23:17 Far be it from me, O LORD, that I should do this. 15
17 These things did the three mighty men. 15
22 These things did Benai'ah the son of Jehoi'ada 15
24:10 I have sinned greatly in what I have done. 15
12 choose one of them, that I may do it to you. 15
17 I have done . . but these sheep, what have they done? 15
1Kg 1: 6 by asking, "Why have you done thus and so? 15
30 as I swore to you . . even so will I do this day. 15
2: 3 prosper in all that you do and wherever you turn; 15
5 what Jo'ab . . did to me, how he dealt with the two 15
9 wise man; you will know what you ought to do to him 15
23 God do so to me and more also if this word does not 15
31 Do as he has said, strike him down and bury him; 15
38 as . . the king has said, so will your servant do. 15
44 all the evil that you did to David my father; 15
3:12 I now do according to your word. Behold, I give you 15
5: 8 I am ready to do all you desire in the matter 15
7:14 He came to King Solomon, and did all his work. 15
18 he did the same with the other capital. 15
40 Hiram finished . . that he did for King Solomon 15
51 work that . . Solomon did on the house of the LORD 15
8:43 hear . . and do according to all 15
9: 4 uprightness, doing . . all that I have commanded 15
8 Why has the LORD done thus to this land 15
11: 6 Solomon did what was evil in the sight of the LORD 15
8 so he did for all his foreign wives 15
12 for the sake of David your father I will not do it 15
25 an adversary . . doing mischief as Hadad did; *
25 an adversary . . doing mischief as Hadad did; *
33 walked in my ways, doing what is right in my sight 15
38 walk in my ways, and do what is right in my eyes 15
38 do what is right . . as David my servant did 15
41 acts of Solomon, and all that he did, and his wisdom 15
12:32 so he did in Bethel, sacrificing to the calves 15
13:11 all that the man of God had done that day in Bethel; 15
14: 4 Jerobo'am's wife did so; she arose, and went 15
8 followed me . . doing only that which was right 15
22 Judah did what was evil in the sight of the LORD 15
22 more than all that their fathers had done. 15
24 They did according to all the abominations 15
29 rest of the acts of Rehobo'am, and all that he did 15
15: 3 in all the sins which his father did before him; 15
5 David did what was right in the eyes of the LORD 15
7 The rest of the acts of Abi'jam, and all that he did 15
11 Asa did what was right in the eyes of the LORD 15
11 right in the eyes of the LORD, as David . . had done. *
23 the acts of Asa, all his might, and all that he did 15
26 He did what was evil in the sight of the LORD 15
31 the rest of the acts of Nadab, and all that he did 15
34 He did what was evil in the sight of the LORD 15
16: 5 the acts of Ba'asha, and what he did, and his might 15
7 all the evil that he did in the sight of the LORD 15
14 the rest of the acts of Elah, and all that he did 15
19 his sins . . doing evil in the sight of the LORD 15
25 Omri did what was evil in the sight of the LORD 15
25 and did more evil than all who were before him. 15
27 the rest of the acts of Omri which he did 15
30 Ahab . . did evil in the sight of the LORD 15
17: 5 he went and did according to the word of the LORD; 15
13 Fear not; go and do as you have said; 15
15 she went and did as Eli'jah said; 15
18:13 what I did when Jez'ebel killed the prophets 15
36 and that I have done all these things at thy word. 15
19: 1 Ahab told Jez'ebel all that Eli'jah had done 15
2 So may the gods do to me, and more also, if I do not 15
9 and he said to him, "What are you doing here, Eli'jah? *
13 and said, "What are you doing here, Eli'jah? *
20 Go back again; for what have I done to you? 15
20: 9 All that you first demanded . . I will do; 15
9 but this thing I cannot do.' 15
10 The gods do so to me, and more also, if the dust 15
22 consider well what you have to do; 15
24 do this: remove the kings, each from his post 15
25 And he hearkened to their voice, and did so. 15
21:11 the men of his city . . did as Jez'ebel had sent word 15
20 you have sold yourself to do what is evil 15
25 who sold himself to do what was evil 15
26 going after idols, as the Amorites had done 15
22:22 you shall succeed; go forth and do so.' 15
39 the rest of the acts of Ahab, and all that he did 15
43 doing what was right in the sight of the LORD; 15
52 He did what was evil in the sight of the LORD 15
53 in every way that his father had done. 15
2Kg 1:18 Now the rest of the acts of Ahazi'ah which he did 15
2: 9 Ask what I shall do for you, before I am taken 15
3: 2 He did what was evil in the sight of the LORD 15
13 What have I to do with you? Go to the prophets †
4: 2 What shall I do for you? Tell me; what have you 15
13 what is to be done for you? 15
14 he said, "What then is to be done for her? 15
5:13 prophet had commanded you to do some great thing *
13 if the prophet . . would you not have done it? 15
6:15 the servant said, "Alas, my master! What shall we do? 15
31 May God do so to me, and more also, if the head 15
7: 9 We are not doing right. This day is . . of good news; 15
8: 2 So the woman arose, and did according to the word 15
4 Tell me all the great things . . Eli'sha has done. 15
12 I know the evil that you will do to . . Israel; 15
13 What is . . that he should do this great thing? 15
18 he walked . . as the house of Ahab had done 15
18 And he did what was evil in the sight of the LORD. 15
23 the rest of the acts of Joram, and all that he did 15
27 and did what was evil in the sight of the LORD 15
27 did what was evil . . as the house of Ahab had done *
9:18 And Jehu said, "What have you to do with peace? †
19 Jehu answered, "What have you to do with peace? †
10: 5 your servants, and we will do all that you bid us. 15
5 do whatever is good in your eyes. 15
10 the LORD has done what he said by his servant 15
19 Jehu did it with cunning in order to destroy 15
30 and have done to the house of Ahab according 15
34 acts of Jehu, and all that he did, and all his might 15
11: 5 This is the thing that you shall do 15
9 captains did according to all that . . commanded 15
12: 2 Jeho'ash did what was right in the eyes of the LORD 15
19 the rest of the acts of Jo'ash, and all that he did 15
13: 2 He did what was evil in the sight of the LORD 15
8 acts of Jeho'ahaz and all that he did, and his might 15
11 He also did what was evil in the sight of the LORD; 15
12 the rest of the acts of Jo'ash, and all that he did 15
14: 3 And he did what was right in the eyes of the LORD 15
3 he did in all things as Jo'ash his father had done. 15
3 he did in all things as Jo'ash his father had done. 15
15 Now the rest of the acts of Jeho'ash which he did 15
24 And he did what was evil in the sight of the LORD; 15
28 rest of the acts of Jerobo'am and all that he did 15
15: 3 he did what was right in the eyes of the LORD 15
3 to all that his father Amazi'ah had done. 15
6 the rest of the acts of Azari'ah, and all that he did 15
9 And he did what was evil in the sight of the LORD 15
9 he did what was evil . . as his fathers had done. 15
18 And he did what was evil in the sight of the LORD; 15
21 rest of the deeds of Men'ahem, and all that he did 15
24 And he did what was evil in the sight of the LORD; 15
26 the rest of the deeds of Pekahi'ah, and all . . he did 15
28 And he did what was evil in the sight of the LORD; 15
31 the rest of the acts of Pekah, and all that he did 15
34 And he did what was right in the eyes of the LORD 15
34 to all that his father Uzzi'ah had done. 15
36 the rest of the acts of Jotham, and all that he did 15
16: 2 he did not do what was right in the eyes of the LORD 15
2 he did not do . . as his father David had done *
16 Uri'ah the priest did all this 15
19 Now the rest of the acts of Ahaz which he did 15
17: 2 And he did what was evil in the sight of the LORD 15
11 they did wicked things, provoking the LORD 15
12 the LORD had said to them, "You shall not do this. 15
15 commanded . . that they should not do like them. 15
17 and sold themselves to do evil in the sight 15
22 Israel walked in all the sins which Jerobo'am did; 15
34 they do according to the former manner. 15
37 and the law . . you shall always be careful to do. 15
40 but they did according to their former manner. 15
41 as their fathers did, so they do to this day. 15
41 as their fathers did, so they do to this day. 15
18: 3 And he did what was right in the eyes of the LORD 15
3 according to all that David his father had done. 15
19:11 what the kings of Assyria have done to all lands 15
31 The zeal of the LORD will do this. 15
20: 3 I have . . and have done what is good in thy sight. 15
9 the LORD will do the thing that he has promised 15
21: 2 And he did what was evil in the sight of the LORD 15
3 made an Ashe'rah, as Ahab king of Israel had done 15
6 He did much evil in the sight of the LORD 15
8 be careful to do according to all that 15
9 and Manas'seh seduced them to do more evil 15
9 to do more evil than the nations had done *
11 all that the Amorites did, who were before him 15
15 they have done what is evil in my sight 15
16 he made Judah to sin so that they did what was evil 15
17 and all that he did, and the sin that he committed 15
20 And he did what was evil in the sight of the LORD 15
20 evil . . as Manas'seh his father had done. 15
25 Now the rest of the acts of Amon which he did 15
22: 2 And he did what was right in the eyes of the LORD 15
13 have not obeyed . . to do according to all that is 15
23:17 things which you have done against the altar 15
19 he did to them according to all that he had done 15
19 according to all that he had done at Bethel. 9
28 the rest of the acts of Josi'ah, and all that he did 15
32 And he did what was evil in the sight of the LORD 15
32 did . . according to all that his fathers had done. 15
37 And he did what was evil in the sight of the LORD 15
37 he . . according to all that his fathers had done. 15
24: 3 sins of Manas'seh, according to all . . he had done 15
5 rest of the deeds of Jehoi'akim, and all that he did 15
9 And he did what was evil in the sight of the LORD 15
9 according to all that his father had done. 15
19 And he did what was evil in the sight of the LORD 15
19 according to all that Jehoi'akim had done. 15
1Ch 10:11 heard all that the Philistines had done to Saul 15
11:19 be it from me before my God that I should do this. 15
19 These things did the three mighty men. 15
24 These things did Benai'ah the son of Jehoi'ada 15
12:32 to know what Israel ought to do 15
13: 4 All the assembly agreed to do 15
14:16 David did as God commanded him 15
16:12 Remember the wonderful works that he has done 15
17: 2 Do all that is in your heart, for God is with you. 15
23 and do as thou hast spoken; 15
19:13 and may the LORD do what seems good to him. 15
20: 3 David did to all the cities of the Ammonites. 15
21: 8 sinned greatly in that I have done this thing. 15
10 choose one of them, that I may do it to you.' 15
17 But these sheep, what have they done? 15
23 let my lord the king do what seems good to him; 15
22:16 gold, silver, bronze, and iron. Arise and be doing! 15
23:24 who were to do the work for the service 15
25: 1 list of those who did the work and of their duties *
27:26 over those who did the work of the field 15
28:10 you to build a house . . be strong, and do it. 15
19 all the work to be done according to the plan. *
20 Be strong and of good courage, and do it. 15
29: 5 for all the work to be done by craftsmen *
2Ch 2:14 and to do all sorts of engraving and execute *
4:11 finished the work that he did for King Solomon 15
5: 1 work that Solomon did for the house of the LORD 15
6:33 hear . . and do according to all 15
7:11 all that Solomon had planned to do in the house 15
17 doing according to all that I have commanded you 15
21 'Why has the LORD done thus to this land and to this 15
12:14 he did evil, for he did not set his heart to seek 15
14: 2 Asa did what was good and right 15
18:21 you shall succeed; go forth and do so.' 15
19: 6 said to the judges, "Consider what you do 15
7 take heed what you do 15
9 Thus you shall do in the fear of the LORD 15
10 Thus you shall do, and you will not incur guilt. 15
20:12 do not know what to do, but our eyes are upon thee. 15
32 did what was right in the sight of the LORD. 15
35 Ahazi'ah king of Israel, who did wickedly. 15
21: 6 he walked . . as the house of Ahab had done; 15
6 And he did what was evil in the sight of the LORD. 15
22: 4 He did what was evil in the sight of the LORD 15

4 did what was evil . . as the house of Ahab had done; •
23: 4 This is the thing that you shall do 15
8 did according to all that Jehoi'ada the priest 15
24: 2 Jo'ash did what was right in the eyes of the LORD 15
11 Thus they did day after day, and collected money 15
16 because he had done good in Israel 15
25: 2 he did what was right in the eyes of the LORD 15
9 But what shall we do about the 100 talents 15
16 done this and have not listened to my counsel. 15
26: 4 he did what was right in the eyes of the LORD 15
4 all that his father Amazi'ah had done. 15
27: 2 he did what was right in the eyes of the LORD 15
2 all that his father Uzzi'ah had done 15
28: 1 he did not do what was right in the eyes of the LORD 15
29: 2 he did what was right in the eyes of the LORD 15
2 according to all that David his father had done. 15
6 done what was evil in the sight of the LORD our God; 15
36 people rejoiced because of what God had done 5
30:12 to give them one heart to do what the king 15
31:20 Thus Hezeki'ah did throughout all Judah; 15
20 he did what was good and right and faithful 15
21 every work . . he did with all his heart, and prospered. 15
32:13 have done to all the peoples of other lands? 15
25 according to the benefit done to him •
31 inquire about the sign that had been done 3
33 all Judah . . did him honor at his death. 15
33: 2 He did what was evil in the sight of the LORD 15
6 He did much evil in the sight of the LORD 15
8 be careful to do all that I have commanded them 15
9 did more evil than the nations whom the LORD 15
22 He did what was evil in the sight of the LORD 15
22 did . . evil . . , as Manas'seh his father had done. 15
34: 2 He did what was right in the eyes of the LORD 15
12 the men did the work faithfully. 15
13 directed all who did work in every kind 15
16 committed to your servants they are doing. 15
21 do according to all that is written in this book. 15
32 Jerusalem did according to the covenant of God 15
35: 6 to do according to the word of the LORD by Moses. 15
12 And so they did with the bulls. •
21 What have we to do with each other, king of Judah? †
36: 5 did what was evil in the sight of the LORD his God. 15
8 Jehoi'akim, and the abominations which he did 15
9 He did what was evil in the sight of the LORD. 15
12 did what was evil in the sight of the LORD his God. 15
Ezr 4: 3 You have nothing to do with us in building a house †
6: 8 regarding what you shall do for these elders 21
12 make a decree; let it be done with all diligence. 21
7:10 to study the law of the LORD, and to do it 15
18 Whatever seems good . . to do with the rest 21
18 do with the rest of the silver and gold 21
21 requires of you, be it done with all diligence 21
23 let it be done in full for the house of the God 21
9: 1 After these things had been done, the officials 6
10: 3 let it be done according to the law. 15
4 it is your task . . be strong and do it. 15
5 take oath that they would do as had been said. 15
11 make confession to the LORD . . and do his will; 15
12 It is so; we must do as you have said. 15
Neh 1: 9 and keep my commandments and do them 15
2:12 my God had put into my heart to do for Jerusalem. 15
16 officials did not know . . what I was doing; 15
16 officials, and the rest that were to do the work. 15
19 What is this thing that you are doing? 15
4: 2 What are these feeble Jews doing? 15
5: 9 I said, "The thing that you are doing is not good. 15
12 We will restore these . . We will do as you say. 15
12 took an oath of them to do as they had promised. 15
15 I did not do so, because of the fear of God. 15
19 all that I have done for this people. 15
6: 2 But they intended to do me harm. 15
3 I am doing a great work and I cannot come down. 15
8 No such things as you say have been done •
9 drop from the work, and it will not be done. 15
8:17 from . . Jeshua . . people of Israel had not done 15
9:24 that they might do with them as they would. 15
31 in thy great mercies thou didst not make an end 15
10:29 observe and do all the commandments of the LORD 15
13: 7 evil that Eli'ashib had done for Tobi'ah 15
14 good deeds that I have done for the house of my God 15
17 What is this evil thing which you are doing 15
27 then listen to you and do all this great evil 15
Est 1: 8 had given orders . . to do as every man desired. 15
15 what is to be done to Queen Vashti, 15
21 and the king did as Memu'can proposed; 15
2: 1 he remembered Vashti and what she had done 15
4 This pleased the king, and he did so. 15
3:11 is given . . to do with them as it seems good to you. 15
4: 1 When Mor'decai learned all that had been done 15
17 went . . and did everything as Esther had ordered 15
5: 5 Bring Haman . . that we may do as Esther desires. 15
8 and tomorrow I will do as the king has said. 15
6: 3 servants . . said, "Nothing has been done for him. 15
6 What shall be done to the man whom the king 15
9 Thus shall it be done to the man whom the king 15
10 do so to Mor'decai . . who sits at the king's gate. 15
11 Thus shall it be done to the man whom the king 15
7: 5 Who is he . . that would presume to do this? 15
9: 5 and did as they pleased to those who hated them. 15

12 What then have they done in the rest of the king's 15
13 allowed . . to do according to this day's edict. 15
14 the king commanded this to be done; 15
23 the Jews undertook to do as they had begun 15
Job 6:29 Turn, I pray, let no wrong be done. •
7:20 If I sin, what do I do to thee, thou watcher of men? 16
9:12 Who will say to him, 'What doest thou'? 15
11: 8 It is higher than heaven-what can you do? 16
12: 9 not know that the hand of the LORD has done this? 15
21:31 who requites him for what he has done? 15
22:17 and 'What can the Almighty do to us?' 16
31:14 what then shall I do when God rises up? 15
34:10 far be it from God that he should do wickedness •
32 if I have done iniquity, I will do it no more 16
35: 6 are multiplied, what do you do to him? 15
36:23 or who can say, 'Thou hast done wrong'? 16
42: 2 I know that thou canst do all things •
9 went and did what the LORD had told them; 15
Ps 1: 3 In all that he does, he prospers. 15
7: 3 if I have done this, if there is wrong in my hands 15
11: 3 are destroyed, what can the righteous do"? 16
14: 1 there is none that does good. 15
3 there is none that does good, no, not one. 15
15: 2 He who walks blamelessly, and does what is right 16
3 does no evil to his friend, nor takes up a reproach 15
5 He who does these things shall never be moved. 15
33: 4 all his work is done in faithfulness. •
34:14 Depart from evil, and do good; seek peace 15
37: 3 Trust in the LORD, and do good; 15
27 Depart from evil, and do good; so shall you abide 15
39: 9 not open my mouth; for it is thou who hast done it. 15
40: 8 I delight to do thy will, O my God; 15
50:21 These things you have done and I have been silent; 15
51: 4 sinned, and done that which is evil in thy sight 15
52: 9 thank thee for ever, because thou hast done it. 15
53: 1 there is none that does good. 15
3 there is none that does good, no, not one. 15
56: 4 I trust without a fear. What can flesh do to me? 15
11 in God I trust without fear. What can man do to me? 15
60:12 With God we shall do valiantly; 15
64: 9 what God has wrought, and ponder what he has done. 9
66: 5 Come and see what God has done 10
16 fear God, and I will tell what he has done for me. 15
69: 5 the wrongs I have done are not hidden from thee. •
71:19 Thou who hast done great things, O God 15
24 to shame and disgraced who sought to do me hurt. •
72:18 God of Israel, who alone does wondrous things. 15
78:11 They forgot what he had done 14
83: 9 Do to them as thou didst to Mid'ian 15
9 Do to them as thou didst to Mid'ian •
86:10 For thou art great and doest wondrous things 15
98: 1 O sing . . for he has done marvelous things! 15
103:18 covenant and remember to do his commandments. 15
20 O you his angels, you mighty ones who do his word 15
21 all his hosts, his ministers that do his will! 15
105: 5 Remember the wonderful works that he has done 15
106: 3 Blessed . . who do righteousness at all times! 15
21 Savior, who had done great things in Egypt 15
29 provoked the LORD to anger with their doings 7
35 with the nations and learned to do as they did. •
35 with the nations and learned to do as they did. 9
39 Thus they . . played the harlot in their doings. 7
107:23 doing business on the great waters; 15
108:13 With God we shall do valiantly; 15
109:27 thou, O LORD, hast done it! 15
115: 3 Our God . . does whatever he pleases. 15
118: 6 I do not fear. What can man do to me? 15
15 The right hand of the LORD does valiantly 15
16 the right hand of the LORD does valiantly! 15
23 This . . LORD's doing; it is marvelous in our eyes. •
119: 3 who also do no wrong, but walk in his ways! 16
121 I have done what is just and right; do not leave me 15
166 O LORD, and I do thy commandments. 15
126: 2 The LORD has done great things for them. 15
3 The LORD has done great things for us; we are glad. 15
135: 6 Whatever the LORD pleases he does 15
136: 4 to him who alone does great wonders 15
137: 8 Happy . . requites you with what you have done 2
143: 5 I meditate on all that thou hast done; 17
10 Teach me to do thy will, for thou art my God! 15
145:17 LORD is just . . and kind in all his doings. 9
Prv 2:14 who rejoice in doing evil 15
3:27 when it is in your power to do it. 15
30 Do not contend . . when he has done you no harm. 2
6: 3 then do this, my son, and save yourself 15
10:23 It is like sport to a fool to do wrong 15
16:12 It is an abomination to kings to do evil 15
21: 3 To do righteousness and justice is more 15
7 because they refuse to do what is just. 15
15 When justice is done, it is a joy to the righteous 15
24:29 Do not say, "I will do to him as he has done to me; 15
29 Do not say, "I will do to him as he has done to me; 15
29 not say, "I . . pay the man back for what he has done. 17
25: 8 for what will you do in the end, when your neighbor 15
30:20 adulteress . . says, "I have done no wrong. 16
31:29 Many women have done excellently 15
Ecc 1: 9 and what has been done is what will be done; 15
9 and what has been done is what will be done; 15
13 to seek . . by wisdom all that is done under heaven; 15

14 I have seen everything that is done under the sun; 15
2: 3 I might see what was good for the sons of men to do 15
11 Then I considered all that my hands had done 15
11 and the toil I had spent in doing it 15
12 for what can the man do who comes after the king? •
12 after the king? Only what he has already done. 15
17 what is done under the sun was grievous to me; 15
3:11 find out what God has done from the beginning 15
14 I know that whatever God does endures for ever; 15
4: 3 the evil deeds that are done under the sun. 15
5: 1 for they do not know that they are doing evil. 15
7:20 not a . . man on earth who does good and never sins. 15
8: 3 do not delay . . for he does whatever he pleases. 15
4 and who may say to him, "What are you doing? 15
9 applying my mind to all that is done under the sun 15
10 in the city where they had done such things. 15
11 the heart of the sons of men is fully set to do evil. 15
12 Though a sinner does evil 100 times 15
16 and to see the business that is done on earth 15
17 find out the work that is done under the sun. 15
9: 3 This is an evil in all that is done under the sun 15
6 have no . . share in all that is done under the sun. 15
7 God has already approved what you do. 9
10 Whatever your hand finds to do, do it 15
10 Whatever your hand finds . . do it with your might; 15
Sng 8: 8 What shall we do for our sister 15
Isa 1:16 remove the evil of your doings from before my eyes 7
3:11 what his hands have done shall be done to him. 1
11 what his hands have done shall be done to him. 15
5: 4 What more was there to do for my vineyard 15
4 What more . . for my vineyard, that I have not done 15
5 now I will tell you what I will do to my vineyard. 15
9: 7 The zeal of the LORD of hosts will do this. 15
10: 3 What will you do on the day of punishment 15
11 shall I not do to Jerusalem and her idols as I have 15
11 her idols as I have done to Sama'ria and her images? 15
13 he says: "By the strength of my hand I have done it 15
12: 5 praises to the LORD, for he has done gloriously; 15
16: 5 seeks justice and is swift to do righteousness. •
19:14 they have made Egypt stagger in all her doings 9
15 nothing . . palm branch or reed, may do. 15
20: 2 and he had done so, walking naked and barefoot- 15
22:16 What have you to do here and whom have you here •
24:13 as at the gleaning when the vintage is done. 6
25: 1 for thou hast done wonderful things 15
28:21 to do his deed-strange is his deed! 15
29:20 all who watch to do evil shall be cut off •
33:13 Hear, you who are far off, what I have done; 15
37:11 what the kings of Assyria have done to all lands 15
38: 3 and have done what is good in thy sight. 15
7 the LORD will do this thing that he has promised 15
15 he has spoken to me, and he himself has done it. 15
41: 4 Who has performed and done this 15
20 that the hand of the LORD has done this 15
42:16 These are the things I will do 15
43:19 Behold, I am doing a new thing; now it springs forth 15
44:23 Sing, O heavens, for the LORD has done it; 15
45: 7 I am the LORD, who do all these things. 15
46:10 from ancient times things not yet done, saying 15
11 bring it to pass; I have purposed, and I will do it. 15
48:11 For my own sake, for my own sake, I do it 15
53: 9 in his death, although he had done no violence 15
56: 1 says the LORD: "Keep justice, and do righteousness 15
2 and keeps his hand from doing any evil. 15
57:12 will tell of your righteousness and your doings 9
58:13 from doing your pleasure on my holy day 15
64: 3 When thou didst terrible things which we looked 15
65: 7 into . . bosom payment for their former doings. 18
8 I will do for my servants' sake, 15
Jer 2:23 know what you have done 15
3: 5 but you have done all the evil that you could. 15
7 After she has done all this she will return to me'; 15
4: 4 because of the evil of your doings. 7
18 ways and your doings have brought this upon you. 8
30 what do you mean that you dress in scarlet 15
5:12 and have said, 'He will do nothing; no evil will come •
13 Thus shall it be done to them!' 15
19 Why has . . our God done all these things to us?' 15
31 but what will you do when the end comes? 15
7: 3 Amend your ways and your doings 7
5 For if you truly amend your ways and your doings 7
10 only to go on doing all these abominations? 15
13 And now, because you have done all these things 15
14 I will do to the house which is called by my name 15
17 Do you not see what they are doing in the cities 15
30 For the sons of Judah have done evil in my sight 15
8: 6 no man repents . . saying, 'What have I done? 15
9: 7 for what else can I do, because of my people? 15
11: 4 Listen to my voice, and do all that I command you. 15
6 Hear the words of this covenant and do them. 15
8 this covenant, which I commanded them to do 15
15 when she has done vile deeds? 15
17 of Israel and the house of Judah have done 15
12: 5 how will you do in the jungle of the Jordan? 15
14:22 our hope on thee, for thou doest all these things. 15
16:12 because you have done worse than your fathers 15
17:10 according to the fruit of his doings. 8
22 out of your houses on the sabbath or do any work 15
24 but keep the sabbath day holy and do no work on it 15

18: 4 as it seemed good to the potter to do. 15
6 can I not do with you as this potter has done? 15
6 can I not do with you as this potter has done? •
8 repent of the evil that I intended to do to it. 15
10 the good which I had intended to do to it. 4
11 and amend your ways and your doings. 7
13 virgin Israel has done a very horrible thing. 15
19:12 Thus will I do to this place, says the LORD 15
21:12 because of your evil doings. 7
14 punish you according to the fruit of your doings 8
22: 3 Thus says the LORD: Do justice and righteousness 15
15 Did not your father eat and drink and do justice 15
23: 2 Behold, I will attend to you for your evil doings 7
22 their evil way, and from the evil of their doings. 8
25: 5 turn . . from his evil way and wrong doings 7
26: 3 that I may repent of the evil which I intend to do 15
3 to do to them because of their evil doings. 7
13 Now therefore amend your ways and your doings 7
14 Do with me as seems good and right to you. 15
28: 6 prophet Jeremiah said, "Amen! May the LORD do so; 15
29:32 to see the good that I will do to my people 15
30:15 I have done these things to you. 15
31:37 for all that they have done, says the LORD. 15
32:19 and according to the fruit of his doings; 8
23 did nothing of all thou didst command them to do. 15
30 and the sons of Judah have done nothing but evil 15
30 the sons of Israel have done nothing but provoke •
35 that they should do this abomination 15
33: 9 who shall hear of all the good that I do for them; 15
35:10 done all that Jon'adab our father commanded us. 15
15 amend your doings, and do not go after other gods 8
18 and done all that he commanded you 15
36: 3 will hear all the evil which I intend to do to them 15
38: 5 for the king can do nothing against you. •
39:12 Take him, look after him well and do him no harm 15
40: 3 has brought it about, and has done as he said. 15
16 You shall not do this thing 15
41:11 evil which Ish'mael the son of Nethani'ah had done 15
42: 3 way we should go, and the thing that we should do. 15
20 declare to us and we will do it. 15
44: 4 Oh, do not do this abominable thing that I hate! 15
17 But we will do everything that we have vowed 15
22 The LORD could no longer bear your evil doings 7
50:15 take vengeance on her, do to her as she has done. 15
15 take vengeance on her, do to her as she has done. 15
21 and do all that I have commanded you. 15
25 has a work to do in the land of the Chalde'ans. •
29 do to her according to all that she has done; 15
29 do to her according to all that she has done; 15
51:12 the LORD has both planned and done what he spoke 15
24 for all the evil that they have done in Zion 15
35 The violence done to me and to my kinsmen •
52: 2 according to all that Jehoi'akim had done. 15
Lam 1:21 enemies . . they are glad that thou hast done it. 15
2:17 The LORD has done what he purposed 15
3:59 Thou hast seen the wrong done to me, O LORD; •
Ezk 3:20 his righteous deeds which he has done shall not be 15
4:17 I will do this that they may lack bread and water •
5: 9 I will do with you what I have never yet done 15
9 I will do with you what I have never yet done 15
9 and the like of which I will never do again. 15
6:10 not said in vain that I would do this evil to them. 15
7:27 According to their way I will do to them 15
8: 6 Son of man, do you see what they are doing 15
12 what the elders of the house of Israel are doing 15
9:11 word, saying, "I have done as thou didst command me. 15
12: 4 in their sight, as men do who must go into exile. •
9 house, said to you, 'What are you doing?' 15
11 as I have done, so shall it be done to them; 15
11 as I have done, so shall it be done to them; 15
14:22 and you see their ways and their doings 14
23 when you see their ways and their doings; 14
23 I have not done without cause all that I have done 15
23 I have not done without cause all that I have done 15
16: 5 No eye pitied you, to do any of these things to you 15
47 or do according to their abominations; 15
48 Sodom and her daughters have not done as you 15
48 not done as you and your daughters have done. 15
54 and be ashamed of all that you have done 15
59 I will deal with you as you have done 15
63 all that you have done, says the Lord GOD. 15
17:24 I the LORD have spoken, and I will do it. 15
18:13 He has done all these abominable things; 15
14 who sees all the sins which his father has done 15
14 and fears, and does not do likewise 15
19 When the son has done what is lawful and right 15
22 for the righteousness which he has done 15
24 None of the righteous deeds which he has done 15
20:43 doings with which you have polluted yourselves; 14
44 nor according to your corrupt doings 14
21:13 what could it do if you despise the rod? •
24 so that in all your doings your sins appear 14
22:14 I the LORD have spoken, and I will do it. 15
23:38 Moreover this they have done to me 15
24:14 I will do it; I will not go back, I will not spare 15
14 according to . . your doings I will judge you 14
22 you shall do as I have done; 15
22 you shall do as I have done; 15
24 according to all that he has done you shall do. 15
24 according to all that he has done you shall do. 15
25:14 they shall do in Edom according to my anger 15
33:16 he has done what is lawful and right 15
31 they hear what you say but they will not do it; 15
32 for they hear what you say, but they will not do it. 15
36:17 they defiled it by their ways and their doings; 14
36 I, the LORD, have spoken, and I will do it. 15
37 I will let the house of Israel ask me to do for them 15
37:14 I, the LORD, have spoken, and I have done it 15
43:11 if they are ashamed of all that they have done 15
44:14 keep charge of the temple, to do all its service •
14 all its service and all that is to be done in it. 15
45:20 You shall do the same on the seventh day 15
Dan 4:35 stay his hand or say to him, "What doest thou? 21
6:10 before his God, as he had done previously. 21
22 also before you, O king, I have done no wrong. 21
9:12 under the whole heaven there has not been done 15
12 not been done the like of what has been done 15
14 righteous in all the works which he has done 15
11: 3 great dominion and do according to his will. 15
16 who comes . . shall do according to his own will 15
24 do what neither his fathers nor his fathers' 15
24 do what neither his fathers . . have done 15
36 king shall do according to his will; 15
36 for what is determined shall be done. 15
Hos 6: 4 What shall I do with you, O E'phraim? 15
4 What shall I do with you, O Judah? 15
9: 5 What will you do on the day of appointed festival 15
10: 3 and a king, what could he do for us? 15
15 Thus it shall be done to you, O house of Israel 15
14: 8 O E'phraim, what have I to do with idols? †
Jol 2:20 for he has done great things. 15
21 rejoice, for the LORD has done great things! 15
3:19 for the violence done to the people of Judah •
Ams 3: 6 Does evil befall a city, unless the LORD has done it? 15
10 They do not know how to do right," says the LORD 15
10 They do not know how to do right," says the LORD 15
4:12 Therefore thus I will do to you, O Israel; 15
12 because I will do this to you, prepare to me 15
Obd 1:10 For the violence done to your brother Jacob •
15 As you have done, it shall be done to you 15
15 As you have done, it shall be done to you 15
Jon 1:10 said to him, "What is this that you have done! 15
11 Then they said to him, "What shall we do to you 15
14 for thou, O LORD, hast done as it pleased thee. 15
3:10 the evil which he had said he would do to them; 15
10 he did not do it. 15
Mic 2: 7 the LORD impatient? Are these his doings? 8
6: 3 O my people, what have I done to you? 15
8 does the LORD require of you but to do justice 15
7:13 be desolate . . for the fruit of their doings. 7
Hab 1: 5 For I am doing a work in your days 16
2:17 The violence done to Lebanon will overwhelm you; •
Zep 2: 3 all you humble of the land, who do his commands; 16
3:13 they shall do no wrong and utter no lies 15
Zec 1:21 I said, "What are these coming to do?" He answered 15
7: 3 in the fifth month, as I have done for so many years? 15
8:16 These are the things that you shall do 15
Mal 2:13 And this again you do. You cover the LORD'S altar 15
Mat 1:24 he did as the angel of the Lord commanded him; he 49
5:19 who does them and teaches them shall be called 49
46 Do not even the tax collectors do the same? 49
47 what more are you doing than others? Do not even 49
47 than others? Do not even the Gentiles do the same? 49
6: 2 as the hypocrites do in the synagogues 49
3 your left hand know what your right hand is doing 49
10 Thy will be done, On earth as it is in heaven. 25
7:12 So whatever you wish that men would do to you, do 49
12 do so to them; for this is the law and the prophets. 49
21 he who does the will of my Father who is in heaven. 49
22 and do many mighty works in your name?' 49
24 who hears these words of mine and does them 49
26 and does not do them will be like a foolish man 49
8: 9 to my slave, 'Do this,' and he does it. 49
9 to my slave, 'Do this,' and he does it. 49
13 Go; be it done for you as you have believed. 25
29 What have you to do with us, O Son of God? †
9:28 Do you believe that I am able to do this? 49
29 According to your faith be it done to you. 25
11:20 where most of his mighty works had been done 25
21 for if the mighty works done in you had been done 25
21 for if the mighty works done in you had been done 25
23 For if the mighty works done in you had been done 25
23 For if the mighty works done in you had been done 25
12: 2 your disciples are doing what is not lawful to do 49
2 what is not lawful to do on the sabbath. 49
3 read what David did, when he was hungry 49
12 So it is lawful to do good on the sabbath. 49
50 For whoever does the will of my Father in heaven 49
13:28 He said to them, 'An enemy has done this.' 49
58 he did not do many mighty works there 49
15:28 Be it done for you as you desire. 25
16:27 then he will repay every man for what he has done. 52
17:12 but did to him whatever they pleased. 49
18:19 it will be done for them by my Father in heaven. 25
35 So also my heavenly Father will do 49
19:16 Teacher, what good deed must I do 49
20: 5 he did the same. 49
15 Am I not allowed to do what I choose 49
32 What do you want me to do for you? 49
21: 6 The disciples went and did as Jesus had directed 49
15 the wonderful things that he did 49
21 not only do what has been done to the fig tree 49
21 not only do what has been done to the fig tree •
21 it will be done. 25
23 By what authority are you doing these things 49
24 by what authority I do these things. 49
27 by what authority I do these things. 49
31 Which of the two did the will of his father? 49
36 they did the same to them. 49
40 what will he do to those tenants? 49
42 this was the Lord's doing 25
23: 3 but not what they do 37
5 They do all their deeds to be seen by men 49
23 these you ought to have done 49
24:46 whom his master when he comes will find so doing. 49
25:40 as you did it to one of the least of these 49
40 to . . the least of these my brethren, you did it to me.' 49
45 as you did it not to one of the least of these 49
45 as you did it not to one of the least of these 49
26:10 she has done a beautiful thing to me. 36
12 she has done it to prepare me for burial. 49
13 what she has done will be told in memory of her. 49
19 the disciples did as Jesus had directed them 49
42 if this cannot pass . . thy will be done. 25
27:19 Have nothing to do with that righteous man •
22 what shall I do with Jesus who is called Christ? 49
23 he said, "Why, what evil has he done? 49
28:15 they took the money and did as they were directed; 49
Mrk 1:24 What have you to do with us, Jesus of Nazareth? •
2:24 Look, why are they doing what is not lawful 49
25 he said to them, "Have you never read what David did 49
3: 4 Is it lawful on the sabbath to do good or to do harm 49
8 a great multitude, hearing all that he did, came 49
35 Whoever does the will of God is my brother 49
5: 7 What have you to do with me, Jesus •
19 tell them how much the Lord has done for you 49
20 how much Jesus had done for him 49
32 he looked around to see who had done it. 49
33 the woman, knowing what had been done to her, came 25
6: 5 he could do no mighty work there 49
30 told him all that they had done and taught. 49
7:12 then you no longer permit him to do anything 49
13 many such things you do. 49
37 He had done all things well 49
9:13 they did to him whatever they pleased 49
22 if you can do anything, have pity on us and help us. •
39 no one who does a mighty work in my name 49
10:17 what must I do to inherit eternal life? 49
35 we want you to do for us whatever we ask of you. 49
36 he said to them, "What do you want me to do for you? 49
51 Jesus said . . "What do you want me to do for you? 49
11: 3 If any one says to you, 'Why are you doing this?' 49
5 What are you doing, untying the colt? 49
23 it will be done for him. 30
28 By what authority are you doing these things 49
28 who gave you this authority to do them? 49
29 tell you by what authority I do these things. 49
33 by what authority I do these things. 49
12: 9 What will the owner of the vineyard do? 49
11 this was the Lord's doing 44
14: 6 She has done a beautiful thing to me. 36
7 whenever you will, you can do good to them; 49
8 She has done what she could 49
9 what she has done will be told in memory of her. 49
15: 8 to ask Pilate to do as he was wont to do for them. •
8 to ask Pilate to do as he was wont to do for them. 49
12 Then what shall I do with the man 49
14 Pilate said to them, "Why, what evil has he done? 49
Lke 1:25 Thus the Lord has done to me 49
49 for he who is mighty has done great things for me 49
2:27 to do for him according to the custom of the law 49
3:10 the multitudes asked him, "What then shall we do? 49
11 he who has food, let him do likewise. 49
12 Teacher, what shall we do? 49
14 And we, what shall we do? 49
19 for all the evil things that Herod had done 49
4:23 what we have heard you did at Caper'na-um, do here 25
23 do here also in your own country.' 49
34 Ah! What have you to do with us, Jesus of Nazareth? •
5: 6 when they had done this 49
6: 2 Why are you doing what is not lawful to do 49
2 doing what is not lawful to do on the sabbath? •
3 what David did when he was hungry 49
10 he did so, and his hand was restored. 49
11 what they might do to Jesus. 49
23 for so their fathers did to the prophets. 49
26 for their fathers did to the false prophets. 49
27 Love your enemies, do good to those who hate you 49
31 as you wish that men would do to you, do so to them. 49
31 as you wish that men would do to you, do so to them. 49
33 even sinners do the same. 49
46 Why do you call me 'Lord, Lord,' and not do what I tell 49
47 who comes to me and hears my words and does them 49
49 he who hears and does not do them 49
7: 4 He is worthy to have you do this for him 45
8 to my slave, 'Do this,' and he does it. 49
8 to my slave, 'Do this,' and he does it. 49

8:21 those who hear the word of God and do it. 49
28 What have you to do with me •
39 and declare how much God has done for you 49
39 proclaiming . . how much Jesus had done for him. 49
9: 7 Now Herod the tetrarch heard of all that was done 25
10 the apostles told him what they had done 49
15 And they did so, and made them all sit down. 49
43 they were all marveling at everything he did 49
10:13 if the mighty works done in you 25
13 if the mighty works . . had been done in Tyre 25
25 Teacher, what shall I do to inherit eternal life? 49
28 You have answered right; do this, and you will live. 49
37 Jesus said to him "Go and do likewise. 49
11:42 these you ought to have done 49
12: 4 after that have no more that they can do. 49
17 he thought to himself, 'What shall I do 49
18 he said, 'I will do this: I will pull down my barns 49
26 you are not able to do as small a thing as that •
43 his master when he comes will find so doing. 49
48 who did not know, and did what deserved a beating 49
13:17 the glorious things that were done by him. 25
14:22 Sir, what you commanded has been done 25
16: 3 the steward said to himself, 'What shall I do 49
4 I have decided what to do 49
17: 9 because he did what was commanded? 49
10 when you have done all that is commanded you 49
10 we have only done what was our duty.' 49
18:18 what shall I do to inherit eternal life? 49
41 What do you want me to do for you? 49
19:48 they did not find anything they could do 49
20: 2 Tell us by what authority you do these things 49
8 by what authority I do these things. 49
13 the owner of the vineyard said, 'What shall I do? 49
15 What then will the owner of the vineyard do to them? 49
22:19 Do this in remembrance of me. 49
23 which of them it was that would do this. 53
42 nevertheless not my will, but thine, be done. 25
23: 8 he was hoping to see some sign done by him. 25
15 nothing deserving death has been done by him; 53
22 Why, what evil has he done? 49
31 if they do this when the wood is green 49
34 forgive them; for they know not what they do 49
41 this man has done nothing wrong. 53
Joh 2: 4 O woman, what have you to do with me? •
5 said to the servants, "Do whatever he tells you. 49
11 first of his signs, Jesus did at Cana in Galilee 49
18 What sign have you to show us for doing this? 49
23 believed . . when they saw the signs which he did; 49
3: 2 for no one can do these signs that you do 49
2 for no one can do these signs that you do 49
20 For every one who does evil hates the light 53
21 But he who does what is true comes to the light 49
4:29 Come, see a man who told me all that I ever did. 49
34 My food is to do the will of him who sent me 49
39 woman's testimony, "He told me all that I ever did. 49
45 all that he had done in Jerusalem at the feast 49
54 This was now the second sign that Jesus did 49
5:16 because he did this on the sabbath. 49
19 the Son can do nothing of his own accord 49
19 only what he sees the Father doing 49
19 whatever he does, that the Son does likewise. 49
19 whatever he does, that the Son does likewise. 49
20 shows him all that he himself is doing 49
29 who have done good, to the resurrection of life 49
29 those who have done evil 53
30 I can do nothing on my own authority 49
36 these very works which I am doing 49
6: 2 signs which he did on those who were diseased. 49
6 he himself knew what he would do. 49
14 When the people saw the sign which he had done 49
28 What must we do, to be doing the works of God? 49
28 What must we do, to be doing the works of God? 49
30 what sign do you do, that we may see, and believe 49
38 I have come down from heaven, not to do my own will 49
7: 3 your disciples may see the works you are doing. 49
4 If you do these things, show yourself to the world. 49
17 if any man's will is to do his will 49
21 Jesus answered them, "I did one deed 49
31 will he do more signs than this man has done? 49
31 will he do more signs than this man has done? 49
51 giving him a hearing and learning what he does? 49
8:28 I do nothing on my own authority 49
29 I always do what is pleasing to him. 49
38 you do what you have heard from your father. 49
39 you would do what Abraham did 49
39 you would do what Abraham did 37
40 this is not what Abraham did. 49
41 You do what your father did. 49
41 You do what your father did. 37
44 your will is to do your father's desires 49
44 and has nothing to do with the truth 40
53 And the prophets died! Who do you claim to be? 49
9:16 How can a man who is a sinner do such signs? 49
26 They said to him, "What did he do to you? 49
31 if any one is a worshiper of God and does his will 49
33 If this man were not from God, he could do nothing. 49
10:25 The works that I do in my Father's name 49
32 for which of these do you stone me? 50
37 If I am not doing the works of my Father 49

38 if I do them, even though you do not believe me 49
41 many came to him; and they said, "John did no sign 49
11:45 who had come with Mary and had seen what he did 49
46 told them what Jesus had done. 49
47 What are we to do? For this man performs many signs 49
12:16 had been written of him and had been done to him. 49
18 they heard he had done this sign. 49
19 You see that you can do nothing 59
37 Though he had done so many signs before them 49
13: 7 Jesus answered . . "What I am doing you do not know 49
12 he said . . "Do you know what I have done to you? 49
12 he said . . "Do you know what I have done to you? 49
15 you also should do as I have done to you. 49
15 you also should do as I have done to you. 49
17 blessed are you if you do them. 49
27 What you are going to do, do quickly. 49
27 What you are going to do, do quickly. 49
14:10 the Father who dwells in me does his works. 49
12 who believes in me will also do the works that I do; 49
12 who believes in me will also do the works that I do; 49
12 greater works than these will he do 49
13 Whatever you ask in my name, I will do it 49
14 if you ask anything in my name, I will do it. 49
31 I do as the Father has commanded me 49
15: 5 for apart from me you can do nothing. 49
7 ask whatever you will, and it shall be done for you. 25
14 You are my friends if you do what I command you. 49
15 servant does not know what his master is doing; 49
21 all this they will do to you on my account 49
24 If I had not done among them the works 49
24 done among them the works which no one else did 49
16: 3 they will do this 49
17: 4 the work which thou gavest me to do; 49
18:35 what have you done? 49
19:25 So the soldiers did this. 49
20:30 Now Jesus did many other signs 49
21:25 there are also many other things which Jesus did; 49
Act 1: 1 dealt with all that Jesus began to do and teach 49
2:22 signs which God did through him in your midst 49
37 Brethren, what shall we do? 49
43 signs were done through the apostles. 25
4: 7 By what power or by what name did you do this? 49
16 saying, "What shall we do with these men? 49
28 to do whatever thy hand . . had predestined 49
5:12 Now many signs and wonders were done 25
35 take care what you do with these men. 53
6: 8 did great wonders and signs among the people. 49
7:51 As your fathers did, so do you. •
8: 6 when they heard him and saw the signs which he did. 49
9: 6 you will be told what you are to do. 49
13 how much evil he has done 49
10:35 any one who fears him and does what is right 36
39 we are witnesses to all that he did 49
11:30 they did so, sending it to the elders 49
12: 8 And he did so. And he said to him 49
9 not know that what was done by the angel was real 25
13:22 a man after my heart, who will do all my will.' 49
41 I do a deed in your days 36
14: 3 granting . . wonders to be done by their hands. 25
11 when the crowds saw what Paul had done 49
15 Men, why are you doing this? 49
27 declared all that God had done with them 49
15: 4 they declared all that God had done with them. 49
12 what signs and wonders God had done through them 49
29 you will do well. Farewell 53
16:18 this she did for many days 49
30 Men, what must I do to be saved? 49
19:11 did extraordinary miracles by the hands of Paul 49
14 Seven sons . . were doing this. 49
36 you ought to be quiet and do nothing rash. 53
21:13 What are you doing, weeping and breaking my heart? 49
14 The will of the Lord be done. 25
19 things that God had done among the Gentiles 49
22 What then is to be done? •
23 Do therefore what we tell you 49
33 He inquired who he was and what he had done. 49
22:10 I said, 'What shall I do, Lord?' 49
10 will be told all that is appointed for you to do.' 49
26 What are you about to do? 49
24:18 As I was doing this •
27 desiring to do the Jews a favor 41
25: 9 Festus, wishing to do the Jews a favor, said to Paul 41
25 I found that he had done nothing deserving death; 53
26: 9 I . . was convinced that I ought to do many things 53
10 I did so in Jerusalem 49
26 this was not done in a corner. 53
31 This man is doing nothing to deserve death 53
28:17 though I had done nothing against the people 53
Rom 1:32 that those who do such things deserve to die 53
32 they not only do them but approve 49
2: 1 you, the judge, are doing the very same things. 53
2 judgment . . falls upon those who do such things 53
3 and yet do them yourself 49
3 when you judge those who do such things 53
9 and distress for every human being who does evil 42
10 and honor and peace for every one who does good 36
14 Gentiles . . do by nature what the law requires 49
3: 8 And why not do evil that good may come? 49
12 no one does good, not even one. 49

4:21 that God was able to do what he had promised. 49
7:15 I do not do what I want 49
15 but I do the very thing I hate. 53
16 Now if I do what I do not want, I agree that the law is 49
17 So then it is no longer I that do it, but sin 42
18 I can will what is right, but I cannot do it. 42
19 For I do not do the good I want, but the evil I do not 49
19 but the evil I do not want is what I do. 53
20 Now if I do what I do not want, it is no longer I 49
20 it is no longer I that do it, but sin 42
21 when I want to do right, evil lies close at hand. 49
8: 3 For God has done what the law . . could not do •
3 what the law, weakened by the flesh, could not do 22
9:11 and had done nothing either good or bad 53
12:20 by so doing you will heap burning coals 49
13: 3 Then do what is good 49
4 But if you do wrong, be afraid 49
10 Love does no wrong to a neighbor; 36
14:21 or do anything that makes your brother stumble. •
15:27 they were pleased to do it •
1Co 3:13 test what sort of work each one has done. •
5: 2 Let him who has done this be removed 53
4 on the man who has done such a thing 42
12 For what have I to do with judging outsiders? •
7: 8 it is well for them to remain single as I do. •
36 let him do as he wishes: let them marry-it is no sin. 49
37 to keep her as his betrothed, he will do well. 49
38 So that he who marries his betrothed does well; 49
38 he who refrains from marriage will do better. 49
8: 8 We are . . no better off if we do. 38
9:17 For if I do this of my own will, I have a reward 53
23 I do it all for the sake of the gospel 49
10:31 So, whether you eat or drink, or whatever you do 49
31 do all to the glory of God. 49
33 just as I try to please all men in everything I do •
11:16 nor do the churches of God. •
24 Do this in remembrance of me. 49
25 Do this, as often as you drink it 49
14:15 What am I to do? I will pray with the spirit 30
26 Let all things be done for edification. 25
40 all things should be done decently and in order. 25
16: 1 so you also are to do. 49
10 he is doing the work of the Lord, as I am. 36
14 Let all that you do be done in love. •
14 Let all that you do be done in love. 25
2Co 1:17 Was I vacillating when I wanted to do this? •
5:10 according to what he has done in the body. 53
8:10 you began not only to do but to desire 49
9: 7 Each one must do as he has made up his mind •
10:11 we do when present. 37
11:11 why? Because I do not love you? God knows I do! •
12 what I do I will continue to do 49
12 what I do I will continue to do 49
12 they work on the same terms as we do. •
16 even if you do, accept me as a fool •
13: 7 we pray God that you may not do wrong 49
7 that you may do what is right 49
8 For we cannot do anything against the truth •
Gal 2:10 which very thing I was eager to do. 49
3: 5 do so by works of the law •
10 and do them. 49
12 He who does them shall live by them. 49
5:17 to prevent you from doing what you would. 49
21 those who do such things 53
6: 9 let us not grow weary in well-doing 49
10 as we have opportunity, let us do good to all men 36
Eph 2: 8 this is not your own doing, it is the gift of God- 31
3:20 is able to do far more abundantly 49
4:17 you must no longer live as the Gentiles do 48
5:12 to speak of the things that they do in secret 25
6: 6 as servants of Christ, doing the will of God 49
8 knowing that whatever good any one does 49
9 Masters, do the same to them 49
13 and having done all, to stand. 42
21 you also may know how I am and what I am doing 53
Php 1:16 The latter do it out of love •
2: 3 Do nothing from selfishness or conceit •
14 Do all things without grumbling or questioning 49
3:13 one thing I do, forgetting what lies behind •
4: 9 received and heard and seen in me, do 53
13 I can do all things in him who strengthens me. •
Col 1:21 doing evil deeds 32
3:17 whatever you do, in word or deed 49
17 do everything in the name of the Lord Jesus •
1Th 4: 1 just as you are doing, you do so more and more. 48
13 you may not grieve as others do who have no hope. •
5: 6 So then let us not sleep, as others do •
11 build one another up, just as you are doing. 49
15 always seek to do good to one another and to all. •
24 He who calls you is faithful, and he will do it. 49
2Th 2: 7 only he . . will do so until he is out of the way. •
3: 4 you are doing and will do 49
4 you are doing and will do 49
14 note that man, and have nothing to do with him 54
1Ti 4:16 by so doing you will save . . yourself 49
5:10 and devoted herself to doing good in every way. 37
21 doing nothing from partiality. 49
2Ti 1:12 therefore I suffer as I do •
2:26 after being captured by him to do his will. •

4: 5 do the work of an evangelist 49
14 Alexander the coppersmith did me great harm 33
Tit 3: 5 not because of deeds done by us in righteousness 49
Phm 1: 8 to command you to do what is required •
14 I preferred to do nothing without your consent 49
21 knowing that you will do even more than I say. 49
Heb 4:13 the eyes of him with whom we have to do. 43
6: 3 this we will do if God permits. 49
7:27 did this once for all when he offered up himself. 49
10: 7 I said, 'Lo, I have come to do thy will, O God,' 49
9 he added, "Lo, I have come to do thy will. 49
36 you may do the will of God 49
11:29 the Egyptians, when they attempted to do the same •
13: 6 I will not be afraid; what can man do to me? 49
16 Do not neglect to do good 39
17 Let them do this joyfully, and not sadly 49
19 I urge you the more earnestly to do this 49
21 you may do his will 49
Jas 1:25 he shall be blessed in his doing. 49
2: 8 If you really fulfill the . . law . . you do well. 49
19 You believe that God is one; you do well. 49
4:15 If the Lord wills . . we shall do this or that. 49
17 knows what is right to do and fails to do it 49
17 knows what is right to do and fails to do it 49
1Pe 2: 8 they disobey . . as they were destined to do. •
3:11 let him turn away from evil and do right; 49
12 the face of the Lord is against those that do evil 49
15 yet do it with gentleness and reverence; •
4: 3 for doing what the Gentiles like to do 42
3 for doing what the Gentiles like to do •
2Pe 1:10 for if you do this you will never fall; 49
19 You will do well to pay attention to this 49
1Jn 3:10 whoever does not do right is not of God 49
22 keep his commandments and do what pleases him. 49
4:18 For fear has to do with punishment •
3Jn 1: 5 Beloved, it is a loyal thing you do 49
6 You will do well to send them on their journey 49
10 So if I come, I will bring up what he is doing 49
Rev 2: 5 repent and do the works you did at first. 49
5 repent and do the works you did at first. •
22 unless they repent of her doings; 37
16:17 voice came . . from the throne, saying, "It is done! 25
19:10 but he said to me, "You must not do that! •
20:12 the dead were judged . . by what they had done. 37
13 and all were judged by what they had done. 37
21: 6 And he said to me, "It is done! 25
22:11 Let . . the righteous still do right 49
12 to repay every one for what he has done. 37
1Es 1:11 this they did in the morning. •
17 the things that had to do with the sacrifices •
26 What have we to do with each other, king of Judea? •
32 it was ordained that this should always be done 25
39 he did what was evil in the sight of the Lord. 49
44 He did what was evil in the sight of the Lord. 49
47 He also did what was evil in the sight of the Lord 49
2:28 to take care that nothing more be done 25
3:23 they do not remember what they have done. 53
24 since it forces men to do these things 49
4: 4 they do it 49
32 are not women strong, since they do such things? 53
35 Is he not great who does these things? 49
39 she does what is righteous 49
57 everything that Cyrus had ordered to be done 49
57 he also commanded to be done 49
5:69 For we obey your Lord just as you do •
70 You have nothing to do with us •
6:22 was done with the consent of King Cyrus 25
34 done with all diligence as here prescribed. 25
7: 6 the people . . did according to what was written 49
8:10 who freely choose to do so, may go with you •
16 whatever you and your brethren are minded to do 49
68 After these things had been done 56
96 take oath that they would do this 49
9: 9 do his will 49
10 We will do as you have said. 49
11 This is not a work we can do in one day or two •
2Es 1:21 What more can I do for you? says the Lord. 62
24 What shall I do to you, O Jacob? 62
30 But now, what shall I do to you? 62
34 and have done what is evil in my sight. 62
35 shown no signs will do what I have commanded. 62
2: 3 and have done what is evil in my sight. 62
4 now what can I do for you? 62
9 So will I do to those who have not listened to me 61
28 they shall not be able to do anything against you •
3:25 This was done for many years 62
26 in everything doing as Adam . . had done 62
26 as Adam and all his descendants had done 62
4: 6 Who of those that have been born can do this 62
25 what will he do for his name, by which we are called? 62
5:13 and if you pray again, and weep as you do now •
40 Just as you cannot do one of the things 62
41 what will those do who were before us 62
6:43 and at once the work was done. 63
47 and so it was done. 63
7:18 those who have done wickedly 64
21 what they should do to live 62
118 O Adam, what have you done? 62
119 but we have done deeds that bring death? 60

8:47 Never do so! •
63 the signs which thou wilt do in the last times 62
63 thou hast not shown me when thou wilt do them. •
10:18 She said to me, "I will not do so 62
59 what the Most High will do to those 62
11:33 just as the wings had done. •
12:41 and what harm have we done you 60
50 the people went into the city, as I told them to do. •
14:16 evils worse . . shall be done hereafter. 62
21 so no one knows the things which have been done 62
21 which have been done or will be done by thee. 65
48 And I did so. 62
15:21 Just as they have done to my elect until this day 62
21 so I will do, and will repay into their bosom 62
56 As you will do to my chosen people," says the Lord 62
56 so God will do to you 62
16:18 What shall they do in these circumstances 62
66 What will you do? Or how will you hide your sins 62
Tob 2: 8 be put to death for doing this 51
3:10 if I do this, it will be a disgrace to him 49
4: 3 do what is pleasing to her, and do not grieve her. 49
6 For if you do what is true 49
14 Watch yourself, my son, in everything you do 37
15 what you hate, do not do to any one 49
21 do what is pleasing in his sight. 49
5: 1 Father, I will do everything 49
7: 4 they said, "Yes, we do. 26
12: 6 for what he has done for you. 49
7 Do good, and evil will not overtake you. 49
13: 6 to do what is true before him 49
6 see what he will do with you 49
6 Turn back, you sinners, and do right before him 49
Jdt 2:15 as his lord had ordered him to do •
3: 2 Do with us whatever you will. 58
3 do with them whatever you please. 58
4: 1 had done to the nations 49
8 the Israelites did as Joakim . . had given order 49
6: 2 to prophesy among us as you have done today •
7:10 the Israelites, do not rely on their spears 47
16 he gave orders to do as they had said. 49
24 you have done us a great injury 49
28 Let him not do this day 49
31 I will do what you say. 49
8:18 as was done in days gone by– 25
26 Remember what he did with Abraham 49
30 they compelled us to do for them 49
32 I am about to do a thing 49
34 until I have finished what I am about to do. 49
34 until I have finished what I am about to do. 49
9: 2 thou hast said, 'It shall not be done' 30
2 'It shall not be done'-yet they did it. 49
5 thou hast done these things 49
9 give to me, a widow, the strength to do what I plan. •
10:10 When they had done this, Judith went out 49
11: 4 as they do the servants of my lord 25
11 when they do what is wrong. 49
14 the people living there have been doing this 49
15 and they proceed to do this 49
22 God has done well to send you before the people 49
23 if you do as you have said, your God shall be my God 49
12: 4 carries out . . what he has determined to do. •
14 Surely whatever pleases him I will do at once 49
13:11 even as he has done this day! 49
14: 5 before you do all this 49
8 Now tell me what you have done during these days. 49
8 Then Judith described . . all that she had done 49
10 Achior saw all that the God of Israel had done 49
15: 8 the good things which the Lord had done 49
10 You have done all this singlehanded 49
10 you have done great good to Israel 49
AEs 10: 9 God has done great signs and wonders 49
11:12 saw in this dream what God had determined to do 49
13: 5 doing all the harm they can 55
12 it was not . . for any love of glory that I did this 49
14 I did this, that I might not set the glory of man 49
14 I will not do these things in pride. 49
14: 5 didst do for them all that thou didst promise. 49
16:17 You will therefore do well 49
18 the man himself who did these things 35
Wis 3:14 the eunuch whose hands have done no lawless deed 36
7:27 Though she is but one, she can do all things •
11:13 they perceived it was the Lord's doing. •
23 thou canst do all things •
12:12 For who will say, "What hast thou done? 49
14:10 for what was done will be punished 53
10 will be punished together with him who did it. 29
Sir 2:14 What will you do when the Lord punishes you? 49
7: 1 Do no evil, and evil will never befall you. 49
12 nor do the like to a friend. 49
36 In all you do, remember the end of your life 43
8:18 do nothing that is to be kept secret 49
10:26 when you do your work 49
12: 1 If you do a kindness, know to whom you do it 49
1 If you do a kindness, know to whom you do it 49
2 Do good to a godly man, and you will be repaid 49
5 Do good to the humble 49
5 evil for all the good which you do to him. 49
14: 7 even if he does good, he does it unintentionally 49
7 even if he does good, he does it unintentionally 49

13 Do good to a friend before you die 49
15: 1 The man who fears the Lord will do this 49
11 for he will not do what he hates. 49
19:13 Question a friend, perhaps he did not do it 49
13 if he did anything, so that he may do it no more. 49
13 if he did anything, so that he may do it no more. 49
27:27 If a man does evil, it will roll back upon him 50
28: 2 Forgive your neighbor the wrong he has done •
31: 9 he has done wonderful things among his people. 49
10 had the power . . to do evil and did not do it? 49
10 had the power . . to do evil and did not do it? 49
18 do not reach out your hand before they do. •
32:12 Amuse yourself there, and do what you have in mind 49
19 Do nothing without deliberation 49
33:22 Excel in all that you do 37
29 do nothing without discretion. 49
34:26 goes again and does the same things 50
35: 5 to be done because of the commandment. •
39:16 whatever he commands will be done in his time. 30
18 At his command whatever pleases him is done •
42:15 By the words of the Lord his works are done. •
43:17 so do the tempest from the north •
46: 7 in the days of Moses he did a loyal deed 49
47: 8 In all that he did he gave thanks to the Holy One 37
48:14 As in his life he did wonders 49
16 Some of them did what was pleasing to God 49
22 For Hezekiah did what was pleasing to the Lord 49
50:22 who in every way does great things 49
29 For if he does them, he will be strong 49
51:30 Do your work before the appointed time 36
Bar 1:21 by serving other gods and doing what is evil 49
2: 2 Under the whole heaven there has not been done 49
2 done the like of what he has done in Jerusalem 49
9 in all his works which he has commanded us to do. •
LJr 1:32 as some do at a funeral feast for a man who has died. •
34 Whether one does evil to them or good 46
38 take pity on a widow or do good to an orphan. 49
44 Whatever is done for them is false 25
63 does what it is ordered 49
64 either to decide a case or to do good to men. 49
Aza 1: 4 For thou art just in all that thou hast done to us 49
7 we have not observed them or done them 49
8 all that thou hast done to us 49
8 thou hast done in true judgment. 49
20 Let all who do harm to thy servants be put to shame; 33
Sus 1:18 They did as she said, shut the garden doors 49
22 For if I do this thing, it is death for me; 53
22 and if I do not, I shall not escape your hands. 53
23 I choose not to do it and to fall into your hands 53
43 Yet I have done none of the things 49
62 they did to them as they had wickedly planned 49
62 had wickedly planned to do to their neighbor; •
Bel 1: 9 Let it be done as you have said. 25
15 as they were accustomed to do •
Man 1:10 have done what is evil in thy sight 49
1Mc 1:15 sold themselves to do evil. 49
52 they did evil in the land; 49
2:18 be the first to come and do what the king commands 49
18 as . . those . . left in Jerusalem have done. 49
19 and have chosen to do his commandments 32
33 do what the king commands, and you will live. 49
34 nor will we do what the king commands 49
40 If we all do as our brethren have done 49
40 If we all do as our brethren have done 49
51 deeds . . which they did in their generations 49
67 avenge the wrong done to your people. •
3:34 and gave him orders about all that he wanted done •
42 also learned what the king had commanded to do 49
50 What shall we do with these? 49
60 as his will in heaven may be, so he will do. 49
4:44 They deliberated what to do 49
46 a prophet to tell what to do with them. •
60 and trampling them down as they had done before. 49
5:16 to determine what they should do 49
6:12 now I remember the evils I did in Jerusalem 49
22 How long will you fail to do justice 49
27 they will do still greater things 49
7:22 did great damage in Israel. 49
23 the evil that Alcimus and those with him had done 49
23 it was more than the Gentiles had done. •
8: 2 brave deeds which they were doing among the Gauls 49
3 what they had done in the land of Spain 49
28 do so without deceit. •
30 they shall do so at their discretion 49
31 the wrongs which King Demetrius is doing 55
9:10 Far be it from us to do such a thing 49
22 the brave deeds that he did, and his greatness 49
60 they were unable to do it •
71 He agreed, and did as he said 49
10: 5 he will remember all the wrongs which we did to him 55
11 He directed those who were doing the work 49
11 build the walls . . and they did 49
15 the brave deeds that they had done 49
23 What is this that we have done? 49
27 repay you with good for what you do for us. 49
46 great wrongs which Demetrius had done in Israel 49
56 now I will do for you as you wrote 49
58 and celebrated . . with great pomp, as kings do. •
62 and to clothe him in purple, and they did so. 49

11: 5 They also told the king what Jonathan had done 49
33 we have determined to do good 49
40 He also reported to Imalkue what Demetrius had done 55
42 Not only will I do these things for you 49
43 you will do well to send me men who will help me 49
53 did not repay the favors which Jonathan had done 24
12:40 Jonathan might not permit him to do •
46 Jonathan trusted him and did as he said 49
13: 3 done for the laws and the sanctuary 49
9 all that you say to us we will do. 49
34 all that Trypho did was to plunder. 52
50 cried to Simon to make peace . . and he did so. 28
14:35 because he had done all these things 49
36 do great damage to its purity. 49
15:29 you have done great damage in the land 49
16: 1 reported . . what Cendebeus had done. 55
23 the brave deeds which he did 23
2Mc 1: 3 to do his will with a strong heart 49
22 When this was done and some time had passed 25
32 When this was done, a flame blazed up 25
5:27 and kept himself . . alive . . as wild animals do 57
6:22 that by doing this he might be saved from death 53
7: 8 as the first brother had done. •
16 you do what you please 49
8:29 When they had done this 27
9: 4 the injury done by those who had put him to flight; •
10: 4 when they had done this, they fell prostrate 49
12 because of the wrong that had been done to them 25
11:26 You will do well, therefore, to send word to them 49
12: 3 some men of Joppa did so ungodly a deed as this 55
4 this was done by public vote of the city •
43 In doing this he acted very well and honorably •
13: 9 those that had been done in his father's time. 25
14:23 and did nothing out of the way 53
40 by arresting him he would do them an injury. 34
15:38 that was the best I could do. •
3Mc 1: 7 By doing this 49
9 and did what was fitting for the holy place 49
2: 3 those who have done anything in insolence 53
5:17 When this was done 25
4Mc 2:17 he did nothing against them in anger 49
4: 7 did all that they could to prevent it. •
13 otherwise he had scruples about doing so •
5:10 you will do something even more senseless 49
14:17 they do what they can to help their young •
15: 4 have a deeper sympathy . . than do the fathers. •
16:25 as do Abraham and Isaac and Jacob •
18:16 'There is a tree of life for those who do his will.' 49

do *See also* abominable, abominably, again, all, amiss, bad, business, diligently, evil, foolishly, good, harm, hewing, homage, how, ill, injury, justice, much, nothing, obeisance, poorly, right, service, violence, well, wickedly, work, wrong.

do away 1. פרר 2. αἴρω 3. ἐξαίρω
Job 15: 4 But you are doing away with the fear of God 1
1Mc 14:14 and did away with every lawless and wicked man. 3
16:13 and made treacherous plans . . to do away with them. 2
19 He sent other men to Gazara to do away with John 2

do before 1. προπράσσω
1Es 1:33 the things that he had done before 1

must do 1. ὁράω
Rev 22: 9 he said to me, "You must not do that! 1

do one's best 1. σπουδάζω 2. σπουδαίως
2Ti 2:15 Do your best to present yourself to God as . . 1
4: 9 Do your best to come to me soon. 1
21 Do your best to come before winter 1
Tit 3:12 do your best to come to me at Nicop'olis 1
13 Do your best to speed Zenas . . on their way 2

doctrine 1. לֶקַח 2. διδασκαλία 3. διδαχή 4. λόγος
Job 11: 4 For you say, 'My doctrine is pure, and I am clean 1
Mat 15: 9 teaching as doctrines the precepts of men.' 2
Mrk 7: 7 teaching as doctrines the precepts of men.' 2
Rom 16:17 to the doctrine which you have been taught; 3
Eph 4:14 carried about with every wind of doctrine 2
Col 2:22 according to human precepts and doctrines 2
1Ti 1:10 whatever else is contrary to sound doctrine 2
4: 1 deceitful spirits and doctrines of demons 2
6 the good doctrine which you have followed. 2
Tit 1: 9 be able to give instruction in sound doctrine 2
2: 1 as for you, teach what befits sound doctrine. 2
10 they may adorn the doctrine of God our Savior. 2
Heb 6: 1 let us leave the elementary doctrine of Christ 4
2Jn 1: 9 and does not abide in the doctrine of Christ 3
9 he who abides in the doctrine has both the Father 3
10 comes to you and does not bring this doctrine 3

doctrine *See also* teach.

document 1. כְּתָב 2. גְּנַז (A) 3. כְּתָב (A) 4. συγγραφή
Ezr 6: 1 archives where the documents were stored. 2
Est 3:14 A copy of the document was to be issued as a decree 1
Dan 6: 8 establish the interdict and sign the document 3
9 King Darius signed the document and interdict. 3
10 Daniel knew that the document had been signed 3
1Mc 13:42 to write in their documents and contracts 4

doe 1. יַעֲלָה
Prv 5:19 lovely hind, a graceful doe. 1

doer 1. עשׂה 2. ἐργάζομαι 3. ποιέω 4. ποιητής
Gen 39:22 and whatever was done there, he was the doer of it; 1
2Sm 23:20 was a valiant man . . a doer of great deeds; •
1Ch 11:22 a valiant man of Kabzeel, a doer of great deeds; •
Rom 2:13 but the doers of the law who will be justified. 4
Jas 1:22 But be doers of the word, and not hearers only 4
23 For if any one is a hearer of the word and not a doer 4
25 being no hearer that forgets but a doer that acts 3
4:11 if you judge the law, you are not a doer of the law 4
1Mc 9:23 all the doers of injustice appeared. 2

doer of iniquity 1. noceo
2Es 6:19 when I require from the doers of iniquity 1

dog 1. כֶּלֶב 2. צוּר 3. κυνάριον 4. κύων
Exd 11: 7 against . . Israel . . not a dog shall growl; 1
22:31 you shall cast it to the dogs. 1
Deu 23:18 not bring the hire of a harlot, or the wages of a dog 1
Jdg 7: 5 that laps the water with his tongue, as a dog laps 1
1Sm 17:43 Am I a dog, that you come to me with sticks? 1
24:14 whom do you pursue? After a dead dog! After a flea! 1
2Sm 3: 8 Am I a dog's head of Judah? This day I keep showing 1
9: 8 that you should look upon a dead dog such as I? 1
16: 9 Why should this dead dog curse my lord the king? 1
1Kg 14:11 Any one . . who dies in the city the dogs shall eat; 1
16: 4 Any one . . who dies in the city the dogs shall eat; 1
21:19 where dogs licked up the blood of Naboth 1
19 In the place . . shall dogs lick your own blood."' 1
23 'The dogs shall eat Jez'ebel within . . Jezreel.' 1
24 who dies in the city the dogs shall eat; 1
22:38 the dogs licked up his blood 1
2Kg 8:13 Haz'ael said, "What is your servant, who is but a dog 1
9:10 And the dogs shall eat Jez'ebel in . . Jezreel 1
36 the dogs shall eat the flesh of Jez'ebel; 1
Job 30: 1 have disdained to set with the dogs of my flock. 1
Ps 22:16 Yea, dogs are round about me; 1
20 Deliver . . my life from the power of the dog! 1
59: 6 Each evening they come back, howling like dogs 1
14 Each evening they come back, howling like dogs 1
68:23 tongues of your dogs may have their portion 1
Prv 26:11 Like a dog that returns to his vomit is a fool 1
17 like one who takes a passing dog by the ears. 1
Ecc 9: 4 for a living dog is better than a dead lion. 1
Isa 56:10 they are all dumb dogs, they cannot bark; 1
11 The dogs have a mighty appetite; 1
66: 3 sacrifices a lamb, like him who breaks a dog's neck 1
Jer 15: 3 says the LORD: the sword to slay, the dogs to tear 1
Lam 4:18 Men dogged our steps so that we could not walk 2
Mat 7: 6 Do not give dogs what is holy; and do not throw 4
15:26 and throw it to the dogs. 3
27 She said, "Yes, Lord, yet even the dogs eat the crumbs 3
Mrk 7:27 throw it to the dogs. 3
28 Yes, Lord; yet even the dogs under the table eat 3
Lke 16:21 moreover the dogs came and licked his sores. 4
Php 3: 2 Look out for the dogs 4
2Pe 2:22 The dog turns back to his own vomit 4
Rev 22:15 Outside are the dogs and sorcerers 4
Tob 5:16 the young man's dog was with them. 4
11: 4 the dog went along behind them. 4
Jdt 11:19 not a dog will so much as open its mouth to growl 4
Sir 13:18 What peace is there between a hyena and a dog? 4

doing 1. ἔργον
Rom 2: 7 who by patience in well-doing seek for glory 1

mighty doing 1. גְּבוּרָה
Ps 106: 2 Who can utter the mighty doings of the LORD 1

domestic 1. οἰκουργός
Tit 2: 5 to be sensible, chaste, domestic, kind 1

dominance 1. κράτος
4Mc 6:34 to acknowledge the dominance of reason 1

dominance over 1. ἐπικράτεια
4Mc 1:31 Self-control . . is dominance over the desires. 1

dominant 1. αὐτοκράτωρ
4Mc 1: 7 that reason is dominant over the emotions 1

dominate 1. δεσπόζω 2. dominor
2Es 11:32 dominated its inhabitants 2
4Mc 5:38 you shall not dominate my religious principles 1

dominate by emotion 1. παθοκρατέω
4Mc 7:20 some . . appear to be dominated by their emotions 1

domination 1. ἐπικράτεια
4Mc 1:34 we abstain because of domination by reason. 1
3:18 spurn all domination by the emotions. 1
6:32 we would have testified to their domination. 1

domineer 1. dominor
2Es 6:57 domineer over us and devour us. 1

domineer over 1. κατακυριεύω
1Pe 5: 3 not as domineering over those in your charge 1

dominion 1. מַטֶּה 2. מְלוּכָה 3. מִמְשָׁל 4. מֶמְשָׁלָה 5. מֹשֵׁל 6. מֹשֵׁל 7. רדה 8. שָׁלְטָן (A) 9. ἀρχή 10. βασιλεία 11. βασίλειος 12. δυναστεία 13. ἐξουσία 14. κράτησις 15. κράτος 16. κυριεία 17. κυριότης
Gen 1:26 let them have dominion over the fish of the sea 7
28 and have dominion over the fish of the sea 7
37: 8 Or are you indeed to have dominion over us? 6
Jdg 14: 4 time the Philistines had dominion over Israel. 6
1Kg 4:24 he had dominion over all the region west 7
9:19 in Lebanon, and in all the land of his dominion. 4
2Ch 8: 6 to build . . in all the land of his dominion. 4
Neh 9:28 enemies, so that they had dominion over them; 7
Job 25: 2 Dominion and fear are with God; 6
Ps 19:13 sins; let them not have dominion over me! 6
22:28 For dominion belongs to the LORD, and he rules 2
72: 8 May he have dominion from sea to sea 7
103:22 all his works, in all places of his dominion. 4
114: 2 Judah . . his sanctuary, Israel his dominion. 4
145:13 dominion endures throughout all generations. 4
Jer 51:28 deputies, and every land under their dominion. 4
Ezk 30:18 when I break there the dominion of Egypt 1
Dan 4: 3 his dominion is from generation to generation. 8
22 your dominion to the ends of the earth. 8
34 for his dominion is an everlasting dominion 8
34 for his dominion is an everlasting dominion 8
6:26 all my royal dominion men tremble and fear 8
26 his dominion shall be to the end. 8
7: 6 beast had four heads; and dominion was given to it. 8
12 rest of the beasts, their dominion was taken away 8
14 to him was given dominion and glory and kingdom 8
14 his dominion is an everlasting dominion 8
14 his dominion is an everlasting dominion 8
26 dominion shall be taken away, to be consumed 8
27 kingdom and the dominion and the greatness 8
27 all dominions shall serve and obey them.' 8
11: 3 rule with great dominion and do according 3
4 nor according to the dominion with which he ruled 6
5 his dominion shall be a great dominion. 5
5 his dominion shall be a great dominion. 3
Mic 4: 8 the former dominion shall come 4
Zec 9:10 his dominion shall be from sea to sea 6
Eph 1:21 rule and authority and power and dominion 17
Col 1:13 has delivered us from the dominion of darkness 13
16 thrones or dominions or principalities 17
1Ti 6:16 To him be honor and eternal dominion. Amen. 15
1Pe 4:11 To him belong glory and dominion 15
5:11 To him be the dominion for ever and ever. Amen. 15
Jde 1:25 to the only God . . be glory, majesty, dominion 15
Rev 1: 6 to him be glory and dominion for ever and ever. 15
17:18 which has dominion over the kings of the earth. 10
AEs 14:12 King of the gods and Master of all dominion! 9
Wis 1:14 the dominion of Hades is not on earth. 11
6: 3 For your dominion was given you from the Lord 14
Sir 16:27 their dominion for all generations 9
24:11 in Jerusalem was my dominion. 13
Aza 1:21 deprived of all power and dominion 12
Bel 1: 5 and has dominion over all flesh. 16
1Mc 8:24 any of their allies in all their dominion 16
3Mc 6:24 attempting to deprive of dominion and life 9

dominion *See also* exercise, get, give.

dominion over 1. δεσπόζω 2. κατακυριεύω 3. κυριεύω
Rom 6: 9 death no longer has dominion over him. 3
14 For sin will have no dominion over you 3
Wis 9: 2 to have dominion over the creatures 1
Sir 17: 4 granted them dominion over beasts and birds. 2

under dominion 1. מֶמְשֶׁלֶת יָד
Jer 34: 1 all the kingdoms of the earth under his dominion 1

don 1. ἐνδύω
1Mc 14: 9 youths donned the glories and garments of war. 1

done *See* work.

well done 1. εὖ
Mat 25:21 Well done, good and faithful servant 1
23 Well done, good and faithful servant 1

doom 1. אַחֲרִית 2. דמם 3. חֵרֶם 4. חרם 5. עָתִיד 6. צְפִירָה 7. רָעָה 8. δέω 9. κρίμα 10. μόρος 11. ὀλέθριος 12. ταλαίπωρος
Deu 32:35 their doom comes swiftly. 5
2Sm 19:28 all my father's house were but men doomed to death •
2Kg 18:27 who are doomed with you to eat their own dung •
Ps 92:11 ears have heard the doom of my evil assailants. •
Isa 34: 2 he has doomed them, has given them over 4
5 upon Edom, upon the people I have doomed. 3
36:12 doomed with you to eat their own dung and drink •
Jer 4:18 This is your doom, and it is bitter; 7

8:14 for the LORD our God has doomed us to perish 2
11:15 Can vows and sacrificial flesh avert your doom? 7
43:11 those who are doomed to the pestilence •
11 to captivity those who are doomed to captivity •
11 to the sword those who are doomed to the sword. •
Lam 1: 9 she took no thought of her doom; 1
Ezk 7: 7 Your doom has come to you, O inhabitant of the land; 6
10 Behold, it comes! Your doom has come 6
30: 3 a day of clouds, a time of doom for the nations. •
9 the day of Egypt's doom; for, lo, it comes! •
Zec 11: 4 shepherd of the flock doomed to slaughter. •
7 the shepherd of the flock doomed to be slain •
Rev 11: 5 thus he is doomed to be killed. 8
Wis 18:15 into the midst of the land that was doomed 11
Sir 38:22 Remember my doom, for yours is like it 9
3Mc 5: 2 so that the Jews might meet their doom. 10
22 insults for those they thought to be doomed. 12

doom to destruction 1. שמד
Ps 92: 7 they are doomed to destruction for ever 1

doom to die 1. בֶּן תְּמוּתָה
Ps 79:11 thy great power preserve those doomed to die! 1
102:20 to set free those who were doomed to die; 1

doom to pass away 1. καταργέω
1Co 2: 6 rulers of this age, who are doomed to pass away. 1

door 1. דַּל 2. דֶּלֶת 3. פֶּתַח 4. תְּרַע (A) 5. αὐλαία 6. θύρα 7. θύρωμα
Gen 4: 7 sin is couching at the door; its desire is for you 3
6:16 and set the door of the ark in its side; 3
18: 1 as he sat at the door of his tent in the heat 3
2 When he saw them, he ran from the tent door 3
10 Sarah was listening at the tent door behind him 3
19: 6 Lot went out of the door to the men 3
6 the door to the men, shut the door after him 2
9 man Lot, and drew near to break the door. 2
10 into the house to them, and shut the door. 2
11 the men who were at the door of the house 3
11 wearied themselves groping for the door. 3
43:19 spoke with him at the door of the house 3
Exd 12:22 go out of the door of his house until the morning. 3
23 will pass over the door, and will not allow 3
21: 6 he shall bring him to the door or the doorpost; 2
26:36 you shall make a screen for the door of the tent 3
29: 4 You shall bring Aaron and his sons to the door 3
11 at the door of the tent of meeting 3
32 shall eat . . at the door of the tent of meeting. 3
42 offering . . at the door of the tent of meeting 3
33: 8 every man stood at his tent door, and looked 3
9 descend and stand at the door of the tent 3
10 cloud standing at the door of the tent 3
10 rise up and worship, every man at his tent door. 3
35:15 the screen for the door, at the door 3
15 screen for the door, at the door of the tabernacle; 3
36:37 He also made a screen for the door of the tent 3
38: 8 the . . women who ministered at the door 3
30 with it he made the bases for the door of the tent 3
39:38 the screen for the door of the tent; 3
40: 5 set up the screen for the door of the tabernacle. 3
6 altar . . before the door of the tabernacle 3
12 you shall bring Aaron and his sons to the door 3
28 he put in place the screen for the door 3
29 burnt offering at the door of the tabernacle 3
Lev 1: 3 he shall offer it at the door of the tent 3
5 the altar that is at the door of the tent 3
3: 2 kill it at the door of the tent of meeting 3
4: 4 He shall bring the bull to the door of the tent 3
7 which is at the door of the tent of meeting 3
18 which is at the door of the tent of meeting 3
8: 3 congregation at the door of the tent of meeting 3
4 the congregation was assembled at the door 3
31 Boil the flesh at the door of the tent of meeting 3
33 you shall not go out from the door of the tent 3
35 At the door of the tent of meeting 3
10: 7 do not go out from the door of the tent of meeting 3
12: 6 she shall bring to the priest at the door 3
14:11 the LORD, at the door of the tent of meeting 3
23 bring them . . to the door of the tent of meeting 3
38 go out of the house to the door of the house 3
15:14 before the LORD to the door of the tent of meeting 3
29 to the priest, to the door of the tent of meeting 3
16: 7 before the LORD at the door of the tent of meeting 3
17: 4 and does not bring it to the door of the tent 3
5 to the priest at the door of the tent of meeting 3
6 altar of the LORD at the door of the tent of meeting 3
9 does not bring it to the door of the tent of meeting 3
19:21 to the LORD, to the door of the tent of meeting 3
Num 3:25 the screen for the door of the tent of meeting 3
26 the hangings of the court, the screen for the door 3
4:25 screen for the door of the tent of meeting 3
6:10 to the priest to the door of the tent of meeting 3
13 be brought to the door of the tent of meeting 3
18 shave . . at the door of the tent of meeting 3
11:10 weeping . . every man at the door of his tent; 3
12: 5 LORD came . . and stood at the door of the tent 3
16:27 came out and stood at the door of their tents 3
20: 6 went . . to the door of the tent of meeting 3
25: 6 weeping at the door of the tent of meeting. 3
27: 2 stood . . at the door of the tent of meeting 3
Deu 15:17 awl, and thrust it through his ear into the door 2
22:21 bring . . to the door of her father's house 3
31:15 pillar of cloud stood by the door of the tent. 3
Jos 2:19 If any one goes out of the doors of your house 2
19:51 before . . LORD, at the door of the tent of meeting. 3
Jdg 3:23 Ehud . . closed the doors of the roof chamber 2
24 saw that the doors of the roof chamber were locked 2
25 still did not open the doors of the roof chamber 2
4:20 he said to her, "Stand at the door of the tent 3
9:52 and drew near to the door of the tower to burn it 3
11:31 comes forth from the doors of my house to meet me 2
16: 3 and took hold of the doors of the gate of the city 2
19:22 beset the house round about, beating on the door; 2
26 woman . . fell down at the door of the man's house 3
27 he opened the doors of the house and went out to go 2
27 lying at the door of the house, with her hands 3
1Sm 3:15 then he opened the doors of the house of the LORD. 2
21:13 and made marks on the doors of the gate 2
2Sm 11: 9 Uri'ah slept at the door of the king's house 3
13:17 Put this woman out . . and bolt the door after her. 2
18 put her out, and bolted the door after her. 2
1Kg 6:31 For the entrance . . he made doors of olivewood; 2
32 He covered the two doors of olivewood 2
34 and two doors of cypress wood; 2
34 the two leaves of the one door were folding 2
34 the two leaves of the other door were folding. 2
7:50 for the doors of the innermost part of the house 2
50 and for the doors of the nave of the temple. 2
14: 6 the sound of her feet, as she came in at the door 3
27 the guard, who kept the door of the king's house. 3
2Kg 4: 4 and shut the door upon yourself and your sons 2
5 and shut the door upon herself and her sons; 2
21 laid him on the bed . . and shut the door upon him •
33 he went in and shut the door upon the two of them 2
5: 9 Na'aman . . halted at the door of Eli'sha's house. 3
6:32 shut the door, and hold the door fast against him. 2
32 shut the door, and hold the door fast against him. 2
9: 3 Then open the door and flee; do not tarry. 2
10 Then he opened the door, and fled. 2
18:16 stripped the gold from the doors of the temple 2
1Ch 22: 3 iron for nails for the doors of the gates 2
2Ch 3: 7 lined the house with gold . . walls, and its doors; 2
4: 9 made the court . . and doors for the court 2
9 the court, and overlaid their doors with bronze; 2
22 for the inner doors to the most holy place 2
22 and for the doors of the nave of the temple 2
12:10 who kept the door of the king's house. 3
28:24 Ahaz . . shut up the doors of the house of the LORD; 2
29: 3 opened the doors of the house of the LORD 2
7 They also shut the doors of the vestibule 2
Neh 3: 1 consecrated it and set its doors; 2
3 set its doors, its bolts, and its bars. 2
6 set its doors, its bolts, and its bars. 2
13 rebuilt . . set its doors, its bolts, and its bars 2
14 rebuilt . . set its doors, its bolts, and its bars. 2
15 covered . . set its doors, its bolts, and its bars; 2
20 section from the Angle to the door of the house 3
21 section from the door of the house of Eli'ashib 3
6: 1 I had not set up the doors in the gates) 2
10 meet . . and let us close the doors of the temple; 2
7: 1 wall had been built and I had set up the doors 2
3 standing guard let them shut and bar the doors. 2
13:19 I commanded that the doors should be shut 2
Job 3:10 it did not shut the doors of my mother's womb 2
31: 9 I have lain in wait at my neighbor's door; 3
32 I have opened my doors to the wayfarer 2
34 so that I kept silence, and did not go out of doors– 3
38: 8 who shut in the sea with doors 2
10 prescribed bounds for it, and set bars and doors 2
41:14 Who can open the doors of his face? 2
Ps 24: 7 be lifted up, O ancient doors! 3
9 be lifted up, O ancient doors! 3
78:23 he commanded . . and opened the doors of heaven; 2
107:16 For he shatters the doors of bronze 2
141: 3 O LORD, keep watch over the door of my lips! 1
Prv 5: 8 do not go near the door of her house; 3
8:34 watching daily . . waiting beside my doors. 3
9:14 She sits at the door of her house 3
17:19 he who makes his door high seeks destruction. 3
26:14 As a door turns on its hinges, so does a sluggard 2
Ecc 12: 4 and the doors on the street are shut; 2
Sng 7:13 and over our doors are all choice fruits 3
8: 9 but if she is a door, we will enclose her 2
Isa 26:20 enter your chambers, and shut your doors 2
45: 1 to open doors before him that gates may not 2
2 I will break in pieces the doors of bronze 2
57: 8 Behind the door . . you have set up your symbol; 2
Ezk 8: 7 he brought me to the door of the court; 3
8 and when I dug in the wall, lo, there was a door. 3
16 and behold, at the door of the temple of the LORD 3
10:19 they stood at the door of the east gate 3
11: 1 at the door of the gateway there were 25 men; 3
33:30 by the walls and at the doors of the houses 3
40:13 25 cubits, from door to door. 3
13 25 cubits, from door to door. 3
38 was a chamber with its door in the vestibule 3
41:11 the doors of the side chambers opened on the part 3
11 one door toward the north, and another door 3
11 and another door toward the south; 3
17 to the space above the door, even to the inner room 3
20 from the floor to above the door 3
23 nave and the holy place had each a double door. 2
24 The doors had two leaves apiece 2
24 two swinging leaves for each door. 2
25 And on the doors of the nave were carved cherubim 2
42: 4 their doors were on the north. 3
11 with the same exits and arrangements and doors. 3
47: 1 Then he brought me back to the door of the temple; 3
Dan 3:26 near to the door of the burning fiery furnace 4
Hos 2:15 and make the Valley of Achor a door of hope. 3
Mic 7: 5 guard the doors of your mouth from her who lies 3
Zec 11: 1 Open your doors, O Lebanon 2
Mal 1:10 there were one among you who would shut the doors 2
Mat 6: 6 when you pray, go into your room and shut the door 6
25:10 the door was shut. 6
27:60 rolled a great stone to the door of the tomb 6
Mrk 1:33 gathered together about the door. 6
2: 2 not even about the door 6
11: 4 they went away, and found a colt tied at the door 6
15:46 he rolled a stone against the door of the tomb. 6
16: 3 the stone for us from the door of the tomb? 6
Lke 11: 7 door is now shut, and my children are with me in bed; 6
13:24 Strive to enter by the narrow door 6
25 the householder has risen up and shut the door 6
25 to knock at the door, saying, 'Lord, open to us.' 6
Joh 10: 1 he who does not enter the sheepfold by the door 6
2 he who enters by the door 6
7 I am the door of the sheep. 6
9 I am the door 6
18:16 while Peter stood outside at the door 6
20:19 the doors being shut where the disciples were 6
26 The doors were shut 6
Act 5: 9 Hark, the feet . . are at the door 6
19 an angel of the Lord opened the prison doors 6
23 the sentries standing at the doors 6
12: 6 sentries before the door 6
13 when he knocked at the door of the gateway 6
14:27 how he had opened a door of faith to the Gentiles. 6
16:26 immediately all the doors were opened 6
27 woke and saw that the prison doors were open 6
1Co 16: 9 for a wide door for effective work has opened 6
2Co 2:12 a door was opened for me in the Lord; 6
Col 4: 3 God may open to us a door for the word 6
Jas 5: 9 behold, the Judge is standing at the doors. 6
Rev 3: 8 Behold, I have set before you an open door 6
20 Behold, I stand at the door and knock; 6
20 if any one hears my voice and opens the door 6
4: 1 After this I looked, and lo, in heaven an open door! 6
1Es 4:49 should forcibly enter their doors; 6
Tob 8: 4 When the door was shut and the two were alone •
13 the maid opened the door and went 6
11:10 Tobit started toward the door, and stumbled 6
Jdt 14:14 Bagoas went in and knocked at the door of the tent 5
AEs 15: 6 When she had gone through all the doors 6
Wis 19:17 just as . . those at the door of the righteous man 6
17 each tried to find the way through his own door. 6
Sir 14:23 will also listen at her doors; 7
21:23 A boor peers into the house from the door 6
24 It is ill-mannered for a man to listen at a door 6
28:25 make a door and a bolt for your mouth. 6
LJr 1:18 make . . secure with doors and locks and bars 7
59 the door of a house that protects its contents 6
Sus 1:17 and shut the garden doors so that I may bathe. 6
18 They did as she said, shut the garden doors 6
18 and went out by the side doors 6
20 Look, the garden doors are shut, no one sees us 6
25 And one of them ran and opened the garden doors. 6
26 they rushed in at the side door 6
36 shut the garden doors, and dismissed the maids. 6
39 and he opened the doors and dashed out. 6
Bel 1:11 shut the door and seal it with your signet. 6
14 Then they went out, shut the door and sealed it 6
18 As soon as the doors were opened 6
21 they showed him the secret doors 6
1Mc 1:55 and burned incense at the doors of the houses 6
2Mc 1:16 Opening the secret door in the ceiling 6
14:41 were forcing the door of the courtyard 6
41 the doors burned 6
43 the crowd was now rushing in through the doors 7

door *See also* keep, maid.

next door 1. συνομορέω
Act 18: 7 his house was next door to the synagogue. 1

doorkeeper 1. סָפַף 2. תְּרַע (A) 3. θυρωρός
2Sm 4: 6 the doorkeeper of the house had been cleaning 3
Ezr 7:24 singers, the doorkeepers, the temple servants 2
Ps 84:10 rather be a doorkeeper in the house of my God than 1
Mrk 13:34 commands the doorkeeper to be on watch. 3

doorpost 1. אַמָּה 2. מְזוּזָה
Exd 12: 7 two doorposts and the lintel of the houses 2
22 touch . . the two doorposts with the blood 2
23 the blood on the lintel and on the two doorposts 2

21: 6 he shall bring him to the door or the doorpost; 2
Deu 6: 9 shall write them on the doorposts of your house 2
11:20 write them upon the doorposts of your house 2
1Sm 1: 9 on the seat beside the doorpost of the temple 2
1Kg 6:31 the lintel and the doorposts formed a pentagon. 2
33 made for the . . nave doorposts of olivewood 2
2Kg 18:16 the doorposts which Hezeki'ah . . had overlaid 1
Isa 57: 8 Behind . . doorpost you have set up your symbol; 2
Ezk 41:21 The doorposts of the nave were squared; 2
43: 8 and their doorposts beside my doorposts 2
8 and their doorposts beside my doorposts 2
45:19 and put it on the doorposts of the temple 2

doors *See* furnish.

doorstep 1. βαθμὸς θύρας
Sir 6:36 let your foot wear out his doorstep. 1

doorway 1. פֶּתַח
1Kg 7: 5 All the doorways and windows had square frames 1
2Kg 4:15 when he had called her, she stood in the doorway. 1

dot 1. κεραία
Mat 5:18 an iota, not a dot, will pass from the law until all 1
Lke 16:17 than for one dot of the law to become void. 1

dote 1. עגב 2. עֲגָבָה
Ezk 23: 5 and she doted on her lovers the Assyrians 1
7 all the idols of every one on whom she doted. 1
9 the hands of the Assyrians, upon whom she doted. 1
11 yet she was more corrupt than she in her doting 2
12 She doted upon the Assyrians 1
16 When she saw them she doted upon them 1
20 and doted upon her paramours there 1

double 1. כֶּפֶל 2. כפל 3. מִשְׁנֶה 4. שׁנה 5. שְׁנַיִם 6. δεύτερος 7. διπλάσιος 8. διπλοῦς
Gen 41:32 the doubling of Pharaoh's dream means that 4
43:12 Take double the money with you; 3
15 the present, and they took double the money 3
Exd 22: 4 he shall pay double. 5
7 if the thief is found, he shall pay double. 5
9 he . . shall pay double to his neighbor. 5
28:16 It shall be square and double, a span its length 2
39: 9 It was square; the breastpiece was made double 2
9 and a span its breadth when doubled. 2
2Kg 2: 9 let me inherit a double share of your spirit. 5
Job 41:13 Who can penetrate his double coat of mail? 1
Ps 12: 2 with . . a double heart they speak. †
Isa 40: 2 from the LORD'S hand double for all her sins. 1
Jer 17:18 destroy them with double destruction! 3
Ezk 41:23 nave and the holy place had each a double door. 5
Hos 10:10 they are chastised for their double iniquity. 5
Zec 9:12 today I declare that I will restore to you double. 3
2Co 1:15 so that you might have a double pleasure; 6
1Ti 5:17 be considered worthy of double honor 8
Rev 18: 6 and repay her double for her deeds; 8
6 mix a double draught for her in the cup she mixed. 8
Sir 26: 1 the number of his days will be doubled. 7
50: 2 laid the foundations for the high double walls 8

double *See also* bring, minded, portion, tongued.

double over 1. כפל
Exd 26: 9 the sixth curtain you shall double over 1

doubly 1. מִשְׁנֶה 2. δισσός
Jer 16:18 And I will doubly recompense their iniquity 1
Sir 23:11 if he disregards it, he sins doubly 2

doubt 1. ἀπιστέω 2. διακρίνω 3. διστάζω 4. haesito
Deu 28:66 your life shall hang in doubt before you; •
Mat 14:31 O man of little faith, why did you doubt? 3
21:21 if you have faith and never doubt 2
28:17 they worshiped him; but some doubted. 3
Mrk 11:23 does not doubt in his heart 2
Rom 14:23 But he who has doubts is condemned, if he eats 2
Jas 1: 6 let him ask in faith, with no doubting 2
6 he who doubts is like a wave of the sea 2
Jde 1:22 And convince some, who doubt; 2
2Es 16:75 Do not fear or doubt, for God is your guide. 4
Wis 12:17 when men doubt the completeness of thy power 1

no doubt 1. אָמְנָם 2. πάντως
Job 12: 2 No doubt you are the people 1
Act 28: 4 No doubt this man is a murderer 2

without doubt
Gen 37:33 Joseph is without doubt torn to pieces. †

doubtless 1. εἰ τυγχάνω 2. πάντως
Lke 4:23 Doubtless you will quote to me this proverb 2
1Co 14:10 There are doubtless many different languages 1

dough 1. בָּצֵק
Exd 12:34 people took their dough before it was leavened 1
39 of the dough which they had brought out of Egypt 1
2Sm 13: 8 And she took dough, and kneaded it, and made cakes 1
Jer 7:18 and the women knead dough, to make cakes 1
Hos 7: 4 the kneading of the dough until it is leavened. 1
Rom 11:16 If the dough offered as first fruits is holy •

dove 1. יוֹנָה 2. תֹּר 3. περιστερά 4. columba
Gen 8: 8 Then he sent forth a dove from him 1
9 the dove found no place to set her foot 1
10 again he sent forth the dove out of the ark; 1
11 the dove came back to him in the evening 1
12 sent forth the dove; and she did not return 1
2Kg 6:25 part of a kab of dove's dung for five shekels 1
Ps 55: 6 I say, "O that I had wings like a dove! I would fly away 1
56: 0 according to The Dove on Far-off Terebinths. 1
68:13 wings of a dove covered with silver, its pinions 1
74:19 Do not deliver the soul of thy dove to the wild 2
Sng 1:15 behold, you are beautiful; your eyes are doves. 1
2:14 O my dove, in the clefts of . . let me see your face 1
4: 1 Your eyes are doves behind your veil. 1
5: 2 my sister, my love, my dove, my perfect one; 1
12 His eyes are like doves beside springs of water 1
6: 9 My dove, my perfect one, is only one 1
Isa 38:14 Like . . a crane I clamor, I moan like a dove. 1
59:11 growl like bears, we moan and moan like doves; 1
60: 8 like a cloud, and like doves to their windows? 1
Jer 48:28 Be like the dove that nests 1
Ezk 7:16 like doves of the valleys, all of them moaning 1
Hos 7:11 E'phraim is like a dove, silly and without sense 1
11:11 trembling . . like doves from the land of Assyria; 1
Nah 2: 7 her maidens lamenting, moaning like doves 1
Mat 3:16 saw the Spirit of God descending like a dove 3
10:16 so be wise as serpents and innocent as doves. 3
Mrk 1:10 the Spirit descending upon him like a dove; 3
Lke 3:22 in bodily form, as a dove 3
Joh 1:32 I saw the Spirit descend as a dove from heaven 3
2Es 2:15 as does the dove 4
5:26 thou hast named for thyself one dove 4

down 1. בוא 2. לְמַטָּה 3. עַד 4. ἄχρι 5. εἰς 6. ἐν 7. ἕως 8. κατά 9. καταβαίνω 10. κάτω
Exd 9:23 thunder and hail, and fire ran down to the earth. •
27: 5 the net shall extend halfway down the altar. •
38: 4 a grating . . extending halfway down. 2
Lev 19:16 You shall not go up and down as a slanderer •
22: 7 When the sun is down he shall be clean 1
Deu 23:11 when the sun is down, he may come within the camp. 1
Jos 22: 3 not forsaken . . these many days, down to this day 3
2Ch 32:30 directed them down to the west side of the city 2
Ps 33:13 The LORD looks down from heaven, he sees all •
63: 9 shall go down into the depths of the earth; •
137: 7 Rase it, rase it! Down to its foundations! •
Ecc 3:21 and the spirit of the beast goes down to the earth? 2
Ezk 21:14 clap your hands and let the sword come down twice •
Mat 2:11 his mother, and they fell down and worshiped him. •
4: 6 If you are the Son of God, throw yourself down; 10
8:32 behold, the whole herd rushed down the steep bank 8
22:26 So too the second and third, down to the seventh. 7
Mrk 5:13 rushed down the steep bank into the sea 8
Lke 4: 9 throw yourself down from here; 10
8:33 the herd rushed down the steep bank into the lake 8
Joh 8: 6 Jesus bent down 10
Act 11: 5 it came down to me. 4
20: 9 he fell down from the third story 10
27:14 a tempestuous wind . . struck down from the land; 8
Rom 11: 8 ears that should not hear, down to this very day. 7
Rev 10: 4 and do not write it down. •
Tob 11: 5 Now Anna sat looking intently down the road 5
Jdt 10:15 hurrying down to the presence of our lord 9
13:12 they hurried down to the city gate 9
14: 6 he fell down on his face and his spirit failed him. •
16: 4 The Assyrian came down from the mountains •
Sir 42:16 The sun looks down on everything with its light 8
1Mc 3:24 They pursued them down the descent of Beth-horon 6
4:40 They fell face down on the ground •
2Mc 6:10 then hurled them down headlong from the wall. 8
9: 8 Thus he . . was brought down to earth 8

down *See also* batter, beat, bend, bow, break, bring, burn, carry, cast, come, cut, dash, die, drain, drop, even, fall, far, flow, fly, get, go, hew, hunt, hurl, kneel, lay, lead, let, lie, look, march, move, mow, pass, place, pour, press, pull, push, put, quiet, rain, roll, run, rush, saw, send, set, settle, sink, sit, smite, stamp, step, stoop, stream, strike, swallow, sweep, swoop, take, tear, throw, thrust, track, trample, tread, turn, upside, walk, weigh, weight, write.

down into 1. κατά
3Mc 6: 7 Daniel . . was cast down into the ground to lions 1

downcast 1. נָכֵא 2. רַע 3. καταπίπτω 4. ταπεινός
Gen 40: 7 Why are your faces downcast today? 2
Prv 17:22 but a downcast spirit dries up the bones. 1
2Co 7: 6 God, who comforts the downcast 4
3Mc 2:20 those who are downcast and broken in spirit 3

downcast *See also* look.

downfall 1. מַפֶּלֶת 2. מִשְׁבָּת 3. תְּבוּסָה 4. κατάλυσις 5. καταλύω 6. κατάπτωσις 7. πτῶσις
2Ch 22: 7 ordained by God that the downfall of Ahazi'ah 3
Ps 92:11 My eyes have seen the downfall of my enemies •
Prv 29:16 but the righteous will look upon their downfall. 1
Lam 1: 7 foe gloated over her, mocking at her downfall. 2
Ezk 32:10 for his own life, on the day of your downfall. 1
AEs 14:11 do not let them mock at our downfall 7
Sir 4:22 deference, to your downfall. 7
5:13 a man's tongue is his downfall. 7
13:13 you are walking about with your own downfall. 7
20:18 the downfall of the wicked will occur speedily. 7
25: 7 a man who lives to see the downfall of his foes; 7
3Mc 2:14 In our downfall 6
4Mc 1:11 they became the cause of the downfall of tyranny 5
11:25 is not this your downfall? 4

downtrodden 1. דַּךְ 2. עָנָו
Ps 74:21 Let not the downtrodden be put to shame; 1
147: 6 LORD lifts up the downtrodden 2

downward 1. ירד 2. לְמַטָּה
Deu 28:13 you shall tend upward only, and not downward; 2
Jos 18:16 it then goes . . and downward to En-rogel; 1
2Kg 19:30 remnant . . shall again take root downward 2
Isa 37:31 house of Judah shall again take root downward 2
Ezk 1:27 downward from what had the appearance of his 2

downward *See also* face.

dowry 1. זֶבֶד 2. שִׁלּוּחִים 3. φερνή
Gen 30:20 God has endowed me with a good dowry; 1
1Kg 9:16 Pharaoh . . had given it as dowry to his daughter 2
2Mc 1:14 to secure most of its treasures as a dowry. 3

drachma 1. δραχμή
Tob 5:14 tell me, what wages am I to pay you–a drachma a day 1
2Mc 4:19 to carry 300 silver drachmas for the sacrifice 1
10:20 on receiving 70,000 drachmas 1
12:43 to the amount of 2,000 drachmas of silver 1
3Mc 3:28 2,000 drachmas from the royal treasury 1

drag 1. סחב 2. ἄγω 3. ἕλκω 4. ἐπισπάω 5. κατασύρω 6. συναρπάζω 7. σύρω
2Sm 17:13 and we shall drag it into the valley 1
Jer 22:19 dragged and cast forth beyond the gates 1
Mat 10:18 you will be dragged before governors and kings 2
Lke 12:58 lest he drag you to the judge 5
Joh 21: 8 dragging the net full of fish 7
Act 14:19 they stoned Paul and dragged him out of the city 7
16:19 and dragged them into the market place 3
17: 6 they dragged Jason and some of the brethren 7
19:29 dragging with them Ga'ius and Aristar'chus 6
21:30 seized Paul and dragged him out of the temple 3
Jas 2: 6 is it not they who drag you into court? 3
4Mc 6: 1 dragged him violently 7
10:12 they dragged in the fourth, saying 4
11: 9 bound him and dragged him to the catapult; 3

drag along 1. סבל 2. ἕλκω
Ecc 12: 5 grasshopper drags itself along and desire fails; 1
3Mc 4: 7 they were violently dragged along 2

drag away 1. סחב 2. פרק 3. ἄγω 4. ἀποσπάω
Ps 7: 2 lest like a lion they rend me, dragging me away 2
Jer 49:20 little ones of the flock shall be dragged away; 1
50:45 little ones of their flock shall be dragged away; 1
Lam 1: 4 her maidens have been dragged away 3
4Mc 13:18 each of the brothers who were being dragged away 4

drag off 1. נגר 2. ἄγω 3. σύρω
Job 20:28 dragged off in the day of God's wrath. 1
Act 8: 3 he dragged off men and women 3
2Mc 12:35 and . . was dragging him off by main strength 2

drag out 1. גרר 2. ἐξέλκω
Hab 1:15 he drags them out with his net 1
3Mc 2:23 friends and bodyguards . . quickly dragged him out 2

dragnet 1. חֵרֶם
Ezk 32: 3 I will haul you up in my dragnet. 1

dragon 1. תַּנִּין 2. δράκων 3. draco
Ps 74:13 break the heads of the dragons on the waters. 1
Isa 27: 1 and he will slay the dragon that is in the sea. 1
51: 9 cut Rahab in pieces, that didst pierce the dragon 1
Ezk 29: 3 Pharaoh king of Egypt, the great dragon that lies 1
32: 2 but you are like a dragon in the seas; 1
Rev 12: 3 great red dragon, with seven heads and ten horns 2
4 And the dragon stood before the woman 2
7 Michael . . angels fighting against the dragon; 2
7 and the dragon and his angels fought 2
9 And the great dragon was thrown down 2
13 dragon saw that he had been thrown down to earth 2
16 river which the dragon had poured from his mouth 2
17 Then the dragon was angry with the woman 2
13: 2 to it the dragon gave his power and his throne 2
4 Men worshiped the dragon 2
11 and it spoke like a dragon. 2
16:13 I saw, issuing from the mouth of the dragon 2
20: 2 And he seized the dragon, that ancient serpent 2
2Es 15:29 The nations of the dragons of Arabia 3
31 then the dragons, remembering their origin 3
AEs 10: 7 The two dragons are Haman and myself. 2
11: 6 behold, two great dragons came forward 2

Sir 25:16 I would rather dwell with a lion and a dragon 2
Bel 1:23 a great dragon, which the Babylonians revered. 2
26 I will slay the dragon without sword or club. 2
27 made cakes, which he fed to the dragon 2
27 The dragon ate them, and burst open 2
28 he has destroyed Bel, and slain the dragon 2

drain 1. ἀποκενόω
Sir 13: 5 he will drain your resources and he will not care. 1
7 until he has drained you two or three times 1

drain blood 1. ἔξαιμος
2Mc 14:46 with his blood now completely drained from him 1

drain down 1. מצה
Ps 75: 8 all the wicked of the earth shall drain it down 1

make drain 1. δίδωμι
Rev 16:19 make her drain the cup of . . his wrath. 1

drain out 1. מצה
Lev 1:15 its blood shall be drained out on the side 1
5: 9 while the rest of the blood shall be drained out 1
Ezk 23:34 you shall drink it and drain it out 1

draught 1. πόμασιν
Ps 75: 8 he will pour a draught from it •
Rev 18: 6 mix a double draught for her in the cup she mixed. •
3Mc 5:45 the very fragrant draughts of wine 1

draw 1. אחז 2. דבק 3. דרך 4. מלא 5. משה 6. משך 7. נטש 8. עבר 9. פתח 10. ריק 11. רכב יָד 12. שלף 13. ἀναβιβάζω 14. ἀποσπάω 15. σπάω 16. habeo
Gen 34: 3 his soul was drawn to Dinah the daughter of Jacob; 2
Exd 2:10 she said, "Because I drew him out of the water. 5
15: 9 I will draw my sword, my hand shall destroy them.' 10
Num22:23 angel . . with a drawn sword in his hand; 12
31 saw the angel . . with his drawn sword in his hand; 12
31:30 take one drawn out of every 50, of the persons 1
Jos 5:13 stood before him with his drawn sword in his hand; 12
Jdg 8:10 there had fallen 120,000 men who drew the sword. 12
20 the youth did not draw his sword; for he was afraid 12
9:54 Draw your sword and kill me, lest men say of me 12
20: 2 of God, 400,000 men on foot that drew the sword. 12
15 mustered . . 26,000 men that drew the sword 12
17 Israel . . mustered 400,000 men that drew sword 12
25 of Israel; all these were men who drew the sword. 12
35 25,100 . . all these were men who drew the sword. 12
46 fell . . 25,000 men that drew the sword 12
1Sm 31: 4 Draw your sword, and thrust me through with it 12
2Sm 24: 9 there were . . valiant men who drew the sword 12
1Kg 6:21 he drew chains of gold across, in front 8
22:34 a certain man drew his bow at a venture 6
2Kg 9:24 Jehu drew his bow . . and shot Joram 4
13:16 he said to the king . . "Draw the bow"; 11
16 he said to the king . . "Draw the bow"; and he drew it. 11
1Ch 5:18 valiant men, who . . drew the bow, expert in war 3
10: 4 Draw your sword, and thrust me through with it 12
21: 5 Israel there were 1,100,000 men who drew the sword 12
5 and in Judah 470,000 who drew the sword. 12
16 and in his hand a drawn sword stretched out 12
2Ch 14: 8 280,000 men . . carried shields and drew bows; 3
18:33 a certain man drew his bow at a venture 6
Ps 10: 9 he seizes the poor when he draws him into his net. 6
35: 3 Draw the spear and javelin against my pursuers! 10
37:14 The wicked draw the sword and bend their bows 9
Sng 1: 4 Draw me after you, let us make haste. 6
Isa 5:18 those who draw iniquity with cords of falsehood 6
18 draw iniquity . . who draw sin as with cart ropes 6
21:15 swords, from the drawn sword, from the bent bow 7
66:19 to Tarshish, Put, and Lud, who draw the bow 6
Ezk 28: 7 they shall draw their swords against the beauty 10
30:11 and they shall draw their swords against Egypt 10
Mat 13:48 when it was full, men drew it ashore and sat down 13
26:51 Jesus stretched out his hand and drew his sword 14
Mrk 14:47 one of those who stood by drew his sword 15
Act 16:27 he drew his sword and was about to kill himself 15
1Es 3:22 before long they draw their swords. 15
2Es 7:29 and all who draw human breath. 16
151 1: 7 I drew his own sword; I beheaded him 15

draw (2) 1. חשׂף 2. שׁאב 3. ἀντλέω 4. ἄντλημα 5. ἕλκω 6. συνολκή
Gen 24:13 daughters . . are coming out to draw water. 2
19 she said, "I will draw for your camels also 2
20 she . . ran again to the well to draw 2
20 to draw, and she drew for all his camels. 2
43 let the young woman who comes out to draw 2
44 Drink, and I will draw for your camels also 2
45 and she went down to the spring, and drew. 2
Deu 29:11 both he who hews . . and he who draws your water 2
Rut 2: 9 go . . and drink what the young men have drawn. 2
1Sm 7: 6 and drew water and poured it out before the LORD 2
9:11 they met young maidens coming out to draw water 2
1Ch 11:18 drew water out of the well of Bethlehem 2
Isa 12: 3 you will draw water from the wells of salvation. 2
Nah 3:14 Draw water for the siege, strengthen your forts; 2
Hag 2:16 when one came to the winevat to draw 50 measures 1
Joh 4: 7 There came a woman of Samar'ia to draw water. 3
11 you have nothing to draw with, and the well is deep; 4
15 that I may not thirst, nor come here to draw. 3
6:44 unless the Father who sent me draws him 5
12:32 I . . will draw all men to myself. 5
18:10 Simon Peter, having a sword, drew it 5
Wis 15:15 nor nostrils with which to draw breath 6
19: 4 the fate they deserved drew them on to this end 5
3Mc 5:49 who were drawing their last milk. 5
4Mc 14:13 which draws everything toward an emotion 5

draw (3) 1. חקק
Prv 8:27 when he drew a circle on the face of the deep 1

draw (4) 1. γίνομαι
Joh 6:19 walking on the sea and drawing near to the boat 1

draw away 1. נדח 2. נתק 3. סות 4. ἀποσπάω 5. ἀφίστημι
Deu 4:19 you be drawn away and worship them and serve them 1
13:10 because he sought to draw you away from the LORD 1
13 have drawn away the inhabitants of the city 1
30:17 but are drawn away to worship other gods 1
Jos 8: 6 till we have drawn them away from the city; 2
16 they were drawn away from the city. 2
Jdg 20:31 Benjaminites . . were drawn away from the city 2
32 Let us flee, and draw them away from the city 2
2Ch 18:31 LORD helped him. God drew them away from him 3
Act 5:37 and drew away some of the people after him 5
20:30 to draw away the disciples after them. 4

draw back 1. שׁוב 2. ἀναποδίζω 3. ἀπέρχομαι 4. ὑποστέλλω
Gen 38:29 as he drew back his hand, behold, his brother came 1
Jos 8:26 Joshua did not draw back his hand . . until he had 1
2Sm 11:15 Set Uri'ah . . and then draw back from him 1
1Kg 13: 4 so that he could not draw it back to himself. 1
Joh 6:66 After this many of his disciples drew back 3
18: 6 they drew back and fell to the ground. 3
Gal 2:12 when they came he drew back and separated 4
2Mc 14:44 as they quickly drew back, a space opened 2

draw forth 1. יצא 2. שׁלף
Job 20:25 It is drawn forth and comes out of his body 2
Ezk 21: 3 and will draw forth my sword out of its sheath 1

make draw near 1. קרב
Jer 30:21 I will make him draw near, and he shall approach me 1

draw near 1. נגע 2. נגשׁ 3. נגשׁ וְבוא 4. קָרֹב 5. קָרֵב 6. קרב 7. קְרֵבָה 8. ἐγγίζω 9. προσέρχομαι 10. συμπληρόω 11. συνεγγίζω 12. adpropinquo
Gen 18:23 Then Abraham drew near, and said 2
19: 9 man Lot, and drew near to break the door. 2
33: 6 Then the maids drew near, they and their children 2
7 Leah likewise and her children drew near 2
7 Joseph and Rachel drew near, and they bowed down. 2
47:29 when the time drew near that Israel must die 6
Exd 14:10 When Pharaoh drew near, the people of Israel 6
20:21 while Moses drew near to the thick darkness 2
Lev 9: 5 all the congregation drew near and stood 6
7 Then Moses said to Aaron, "Draw near to the altar 6
8 So Aaron drew near to the altar, and killed 6
10: 4 said to them, "Draw near, carry your brethren 6
5 So they drew near, and carried them in their coats 6
16: 1 sons of Aaron, when they drew near before the LORD 6
21:18 For no one who has a blemish shall draw near 6
Num16:40 should draw near to burn incense before the LORD 6
27: 1 Then drew near the daughters of Zeloph'ehad 6
Deu 2:37 land of the sons of Ammon you did not draw near 6
20: 2 when you draw near to the battle, the priest shall 6
3 say to them, 'Hear, O Israel, you draw near this day 5
10 When you draw near to a city to fight against it 6
25:11 wife of the one draws near to rescue her husband 6
Jos 8:11 all . . went up, and drew near before the city 3
Jdg 9:52 and drew near to the door of the tower to burn it 2
19:13 Come and let us draw near to one of these places 6
20:23 Shall we again draw near to battle against our 2
1Sm 7:10 the Philistines drew near to attack Israel; 2
14:36 the priest said, "Let us draw near hither to God. 6
17:40 and he drew near to the Philistine. 2
41 the Philistine came on and drew near to David 5
48 Philistine . . came and drew near to meet David 6
30:21 when David drew near to the people he saluted 2
2Sm 10:13 Jo'ab and the people . . drew near to battle 2
18:25 And he came apace, and drew near. 5
1Kg 2: 1 When David's time to die drew near, he charged 6
2Kg 2: 5 The sons of the prophets . . drew near to Eli'sha 2
16:12 the king drew near to the altar, and went up on it 6
1Ch 19:14 drew near before the Syrians for battle; 2
Job 33:22 His soul draws near the Pit 6
Ps 69:18 Draw near to me, redeem me, set me free 6
88: 3 my life draws near to Sheol. 1
107:18 drew near to the gates of death. 1
119:150 They draw near who persecute me with evil 6
Ecc 5: 1 to draw near to listen is better than to offer 6
Isa 5:19 the purpose of the Holy One of Israel draw near 6
29:13 Because this people draw near with their mouth 2
34: 1 Draw near, O nations, to hear, and hearken, 6
41: 1 let us together draw near for judgment. 6
5 they have drawn near and come. 6
45:20 draw near together, you survivors of the nations! 2
48:16 Draw near to me, hear this: from the beginning 6
51: 5 My deliverance draws near speedily 6
57: 3 But you, draw near hither, sons of the sorceress 6
58: 2 they delight to draw near to God. 7
Lam 4:18 our end drew near; our days were numbered; 6
Ezk 7:12 The time has come, the day draws near. 1
9: 1 Draw near, you executioners of the city 6
43:19 of Zadok, who draw near to me to minister to me 4
Jol 3: 9 Let all the men of war draw near, let them come up. 2
Zep 3: 2 she does not draw near to her God. 6
Mal 3: 5 Then I will draw near to you for judgment; 6
Mat 21: 1 they drew near to Jerusalem 8
34 When the season of fruit drew near 8
Mrk 11: 1 when they drew near to Jerusalem, to Beth'phage 8
Lke 7:12 As he drew near to the gate of the city 8
9:51 When the days drew near for him to be received up 10
15: 1 sinners were all drawing near to hear him. 8
25 as he came and drew near to the house 8
18:35 As he drew near to Jericho 8
19:29 When he drew near to Beth'phage and Bethany 8
37 As he was now drawing near 8
41 when he drew near and saw the city he wept over it 8
21:28 because your redemption is drawing near. 8
22: 1 Now the feast of Unleavened Bread drew near 8
47 He drew near to Jesus to kiss him; 8
24:15 Jesus himself drew near and went with them. 8
28 they drew near to the village 8
Act 7:17 as the time of the promise drew near 8
31 as he drew near to look, the voice of the Lord came 9
22: 6 As I made my journey and drew near to Damascus 8
Heb 4:16 with confidence draw near to the throne of grace 9
7:19 through which we draw near to God. 8
25 to save those who draw near to God through him 9
10: 1 it can never . . make perfect those who draw near. 9
22 let us draw near with a true heart 9
25 all the more as you see the Day drawing near. 8
11: 6 whoever would draw near to God 9
Jas 4: 8 Draw near to God and he will draw near to you. 8
8 Draw near to God and he will draw near to you. 8
2Es 6:18 when I draw near to visit the inhabitants 12
8:61 Therefore my judgment is now drawing near; 12
12:21 when the middle of its time draws near 12
15:15 For the sword and misery draw near them 12
16:37 Behold, the calamities draw near 12
38 when the time of her delivery draws near 12
Jdt 8:27 the Lord scourges those who draw near to him 8
Sir 51: 6 My soul drew near to death 8
23 Draw near to me, you who are untaught 8
1Mc 2:49 Now the days drew near for Mattathias to die 8
5:40 his army drew near to the stream of water 8
2Mc 10:25 As he drew near 11

draw nigh 1. נגע
Ecc 12: 1 before the evil days come, and the years draw nigh 1

draw off 1. שׁלף
Rut 4: 7 the custom . . the one drew off his sandal and gave 1
8 the next of kin . . drew off his sandal. 1

draw one's last 1. ἐκλείπω
Jdt 7:27 or see our wives . . draw their last breath. 1

draw out 1. דלה 2. יצא 3. משה 4. משך 5. שׁאב 6. שׁלף 7. ἀντλέω
Jdg 3:22 for he did not draw the sword out of his belly; 6
4: 7 I will draw out Sis'era, the general of Jabin's army 4
1Sm 17:51 and took his sword and drew it out of its sheath 6
2Sm 22:17 he took me, he drew me out of many waters. 3
23:16 and drew water out of the well of Bethlehem 5
Job 41: 1 Can you draw out Levi'athan with a fishhook 4
Ps 18:16 he took me, he drew me out of many waters. 3
Prv 20: 5 but a man of understanding will draw it out. 1
Ezk 21: 5 shall know that I the LORD have drawn my sword out 2
Joh 2: 8 Now draw some out, and take it to the steward 7

draw to close 1. חנה
Jdg 19: 9 Behold, the day draws to its close; lodge here 1

draw up 1. אסף 2. גרע 3. משך 4. עלה 5. עמד 6. ערך
Gen 37:28 and they drew Joseph up and lifted him out 3
49:33 Jacob . . drew up his feet into the bed 1
Jdg 20:20 the men of Israel drew up the battle line against 6
1Sm 17: 8 Why have you come out to draw up for battle? 6
21 Israel and the Philistines drew up for battle 6
2Kg 3:21 were called out, and were drawn up at the frontier. 5
1Ch 19: 9 Ammonites came out and drew up in battle array 6
Job 36:27 For he draws up the drops of water 2
Ps 40: 2 He drew me up from the desolate pit 4
Jer 38:13 Then they drew Jeremiah up with ropes 3
Ezk 29: 4 I will draw you up out of the midst of your streams 4
Jol 2: 5 like a powerful army drawn up for battle. 6

draw up a case 1. ערך
Job 37:19 we cannot draw up our case because of darkness. 1

draw up a line 1. ערך
2Ch 13: 3 Jerobo'am drew up his line of battle against him 1
14:10 they drew up their lines of battle in the valley 1

draw up forces 1. ערך
1Ch 19:17 came to them, and drew up his forces against them. 1

draw up in array 1. ערך
2Sm 10: 8 Ammonites came out and drew up in battle array 1

draw up in line 1. ערך
1Sm 4: 2 The Philistines drew up in line against Israel 1
17: 2 and encamped . . and drew up in line of battle 1

draw water 1. דלה 2. שאב
Gen 24:11 evening, the time when women go out to draw water. 2
Exd 2:16 seven daughters; and they came and drew water 1
19 An Egyptian . . even drew water for us 1

drawer 1. שׁאב
Jos 9:21 they became hewers of wood and drawers of water 1
23 be slaves, hewers of wood and drawers of water 1
27 made them . . hewers of wood and drawers of water 1

drawn 1. פתח 2. ἀντλέω 3. σπασμός 4. σπάω
Ezk 21:28 say, A sword, a sword is drawn for the slaughter 1
Joh 2: 9 the servants who had drawn the water knew) 2
Sir 22:21 Even if you have drawn your sword 4
2Mc 5: 2 fully armed with lances and drawn swords- 3

drawn *See also* sword.

drawn up 1. דלה 2. ἀνασπάω 3. διατάσσω
4. ἕτοιμος
Ps 30: 1 I will extol thee, O LORD, for thou hast drawn me up 1
Act 11:10 all was drawn up again into heaven. 2
1Mc 4:21 the army of Judas drawn up in the plain for battle 4
2Mc 5: 3 troops of horsemen drawn up 3

drawn up for battle 1. ἐκτάσσω
2Mc 15:20 their army drawn up for battle 1

drawn up in formation 1. τάσσω
1Mc 12:26 the enemy were being drawn up in formation 1

well drawn 1. εὔκυκλος
Wis 5:21 and will leap to the target as from a well-drawn bow 1

dread 1. אֵים 2. אֵימָה 3. גור 4. דאג 5. חַת 6. יגר
7. מְגוֹרָה 8. מוֹרָא 9. עָרִיץ 10. ערץ 11. פחד 12. פַּחַד
13. קוץ 14. שׂער 15. δειλός 16. δεινός 17. τρόμος
18. φοβερός 19. φρικτός
Gen 9: 2 The fear of you and the dread of you 5
15:12 and lo, a dread and great darkness fell upon him. 2
Exd 1:12 Egyptians were in dread of the people of Israel. 13
15:16 Terror and dread fall upon them; 12
Num22: 3 Moab was in great dread of the people 3
Deu 1:29 I said to you, 'Do not be in dread or afraid of them. 10
2:25 put the dread and fear of you upon the peoples 12
7:21 You shall not be in dread of them; for the LORD 10
11:25 LORD . . will lay the fear . . and the dread of you 8
20: 3 do not fear, or tremble, or be in dread of them; 10
28:66 night and day you shall be in dread 11
67 because of the dread which your heart shall fear 12
31: 6 Be strong . . do not fear or be in dread of them 10
32:17 new gods . . your fathers had never dreaded. 14
1Sm 11: 7 Then the dread of the LORD fell upon the people 12
Job 3:25 fear comes upon me, and what I dread befalls me. 6
4:14 dread came upon me, and trembling 12
9:34 let not dread of him terrify me. 2
13:11 terrify you, and the dread of him fall upon you? 12
21 let not dread of thee terrify me. 2
23:15 when I consider, I am in dread of him. 11
Ps 31:11 an object of dread to my acquaintances; 12
64: 1 preserve my life from dread of the enemy 12
105:38 for dread of them had fallen upon it. 12
119:39 Turn away the reproach which I dread; 6
Prv 1:33 will be at ease, without dread of evil. 12
10:24 What the wicked dreads will come upon him 7
Isa 7:16 the land before whose two kings you are in dread 13
8:12 do not fear what they fear, nor be in dread. 10
13 let him be your fear, and let him be your dread. 10
57:11 Whom did you dread and fear, so that you lied 4
Jer 20:11 But the LORD is with me as a dread warrior; 9
Hab 1: 7 Dread and terrible are they; 1
Wis 4:20 come with dread when their sins are reckoned up 15
8:15 dread monarchs will be afraid of me 19
10:16 withstood dread kings with wonders and signs. 18
12: 9 to destroy them at one blow by dread wild beasts 16
1Mc 7:18 fear and dread of them fell upon all the people 17

dread *See also* assault, turn, wrath.

dread deed 1. ירא
Ps 45: 4 let your right hand teach you dread deeds! 1
65: 5 By dread deeds thou dost answer us 1

dreadful 1. אֵימְתָן (A) 2. δεινός 3. φόβου πλήρης
Dan 7: 7 terrible and dreadful and exceedingly strong; 1
Wis 5: 2 they will be shaken with dreadful fear 2
17: 6 a dreadful, self-kindled fire 3
18:17 apparitions in dreadful dreams 2
4Mc 8: 9 to destroy . . with dreadful punishments 2
15 and saw the dreadful devices 2

dreadful *See also* end.

dream 1. הזה 2. חֲלוֹם 3. חלם 4. חֵלֶם (A)
5. ἐνυπνιάζομαι 6. ἐνύπνιον 7. ὄναρ 8. ὄνειρος
9. somnio 10. somnium
Gen 20: 3 God came to Abim'elech in a dream by night 2
6 Then God said to him in the dream 2
28:12 he dreamed that there was a ladder set up 3
31:10 the flock I lifted up my eyes, and saw in a dream 2
11 the angel of God said to me in the dream, 'Jacob,' 2
24 God came to Laban the Aramean in a dream by night 2
37: 5 Now Joseph had a dream, and when he told 2
6 Hear this dream which I have dreamed 2
6 Hear this dream which I have dreamed 3
8 yet more for his dreams and for his words. 2
9 Then he dreamed another dream, and told it to his 3
9 Then he dreamed another dream, and told it to his 2
9 Behold, I have dreamed another dream; 3
9 Behold, I have dreamed another dream; 2
10 What is this dream that you have dreamed? 2
10 What is this dream that you have dreamed? 3
20 and we shall see what will become of his dreams. 2
40: 5 one night they both dreamed 3
5 -each his own dream, and each dream with its own 2
5 -each his own dream, and each dream with its own 2
8 They said to him, "We have had dreams 2
9 the chief butler told his dream to Joseph 2
9 said to him, "In my dream there was a vine before me 2
16 favorable, he said to Joseph, "I also had a dream 2
41: 1 Pharaoh dreamed that he was standing by the Nile 3
5 he fell asleep and dreamed a second time; 3
7 And Pharaoh awoke, and behold, it was a dream. 2
11 we dreamed on the same night, he and I 3
11 he and I, each having a dream with its own meaning. 3
11 he and I, each having a dream with its own meaning. 2
12 and when we told him, he interpreted our dreams 2
12 to each man according to his dream. 2
15 Pharaoh said to Joseph, "I have had a dream 2
15 when you hear a dream you can interpret it. 2
17 Behold, in my dream I was standing on the banks 2
22 also saw in my dream seven ears growing on one 2
25 said to Pharaoh, "The dream of Pharaoh is one; 2
26 good ears are seven years; the dream is one. 2
32 the doubling of Pharaoh's dream means that 2
42: 9 Joseph remembered the dreams which he had 2
9 remembered the dreams which he had dreamed 3
Num12: 6 I the LORD . . speak with him in a dream. 2
Deu 13: 1 If a prophet arises . . or a dreamer of dreams 2
3 shall not listen . . to that dreamer of dreams; 2
5 that dreamer of dreams shall be put to death 2
Jdg 7:13 man was telling a dream to his comrade; and he said 2
13 Behold, I dreamed a dream; and lo, a cake of barley 3
13 Behold, I dreamed a dream; and lo, a cake of barley 2
15 When Gideon heard the telling of the dream 2
1Sm 28: 6 either by dreams, or by Urim, or by prophets. 2
15 answers . . either by prophets or by dreams; 2
1Kg 3: 5 the LORD appeared to Solomon in a dream by night; 2
15 Solomon awoke, and behold, it was a dream. Then he 2
Job 7:14 then thou dost scare me with dreams 2
20: 8 He will fly away like a dream, and not be found; 2
33:15 In a dream, in a vision of the night, 2
Ps 73:20 They are like a dream when one awakes 2
126: 1 fortunes of Zion, we were like those who dream. 3
Ecc 5: 3 For a dream comes with much business 2
7 For when dreams increase, empty words grow many 2
Isa 29: 7 shall be like a dream, a vision of the night. 2
8 when a hungry man dreams he is eating and awakes 3
8 as when a thirsty man dreams he is drinking 3
56:10 dogs, they cannot bark; dreaming, lying down 1
Jer 23:25 prophesy lies in my name, saying, 'I have dreamed 3
25 saying, 'I have dreamed, I have dreamed!' 3
27 by their dreams which they tell one another 2
28 Let the prophet who has a dream tell the dream 2
28 Let the prophet who has a dream tell the dream 2
32 I am against those who prophesy lying dreams 2
29: 8 and do not listen to the dreams which they dream 2
8 and do not listen to the dreams which they dream *
Dan 1:17 understanding in all visions and dreams. 2
2: 1 second year . . Nebuchadnez'zar had dreams; 2
2 summoned, to tell the king his dreams. 2
3 I had a dream, and my spirit is troubled to know 2
3 spirit is troubled to know the dream. 2
4 Tell your servants the dream, and we will show 4
5 known to me the dream and its interpretation 4
6 if you show the dream and its interpretation 4
6 show me the dream and its interpretation. 4
7 Let the king tell his servants the dream 4
9 if you do not make the dream known to me 4
9 Therefore tell me the dream, and I shall know 4
26 make known to me the dream that I have seen 4
28 Your dream and the visions of your head as you lay 4
36 This was the dream; now we will tell the king 4
45 dream is certain, and its interpretation sure. 4
4: 5 I had a dream which made me afraid; 4
6 known to me the interpretation of the dream. 4
7 told them the dream, but they could not make known 4
8 Daniel came in . . and I told him the dream, saying 4
9 dream which I saw; tell me its interpretation. 4
18 This dream I, King Nebuchadnez'zar, saw. 4
19 not the dream or the interpretation alarm you. 4
19 My lord, may the dream be for those who hate you 4
5:12 interpret dreams, explain riddles, 4
7: 1 Daniel had a dream and visions of his head 4
1 Then he wrote down the dream, 4
Jol 2:28 your old men shall dream dreams 3
28 your old men shall dream dreams 2
Zec 10: 2 the dreamers tell false dreams 2
Mat 1:20 an angel of the Lord appeared to him in a dream 7
2:12 being warned in a dream not to return to Herod 7
13 an angel of the Lord appeared to Joseph in a dream 7
19 Lord appeared in a dream to Joseph in Egypt 7
22 go there, and being warned in a dream he withdrew 7
27:19 I have suffered much over him today in a dream. 7
Act 2:17 your old men shall dream dreams; 5
17 your old men shall dream dreams; 6
Jde 1: 8 these men in their dreamings defile the flesh 5
2Es 10:36 Or is my mind deceived, and my soul dreaming? 9
59 will show you in those dream visions 10
11: 1 On the second night I had a dream 10
12:35 This is the dream that you saw 10
13: 1 After seven days I dreamed a dream in the night; 9
1 After seven days I dreamed a dream in the night; 10
15 show me also the interpretation of this dream. 10
19 and much distress, as these dreams show. 10
53 the interpretation of the dream which you saw. 10
14: 8 the dreams that you have seen 10
AEs 10: 5 I remember the dream that I had 6
11: 2 Mordecai . . had a dream. 6
4 this was his dream 6
12 Mordecai saw in this dream 6
Wis 18:17 apparitions in dreadful dreams 8
19 dreams which disturbed them forewarned them 8
Sir 34: 1 dreams give wings to fools. 6
2 so is he who gives heed to dreams. 6
3 The vision of dreams is this against that 6
5 Divinations and omens and dreams are folly 6
7 For dreams have deceived many 6
2Mc 15:11 he cheered them all by relating a dream 8
4Mc 6: 5 as though being tortured in a dream; 8

like a dream 1. שֵׁנָה
Ps 90: 5 like a dream, like grass which is renewed 1

dreamer 1. בַּעַל חֲלֹמוֹת 2. חלם 3. somniator
Gen 37:19 They said . . "Here comes this dreamer. 1
Deu 13: 1 If a prophet arises . . or a dreamer of dreams 2
3 shall not listen . . to that dreamer of dreams; 2
5 that dreamer of dreams shall be put to death 2
Jer 27: 9 your diviners, your dreamers, your soothsayers 3
Zec 10: 2 the dreamers tell false dreams *

dreg 1. קֻבַּעַת 2. שֶׁמֶר
Ps 75: 8 the earth shall drain it down to the dregs. 2
Isa 51:17 have drunk to the dregs the bowl of staggering. 1

drench 1. מסה 2. רוה 3. שקה 4. μεθύω
Ps 6: 6 I drench my couch with my weeping. 1
Isa 16: 9 I drench you with my tears, O Heshbon and Ele-a'leh; 2
Ezk 32: 6 I will drench the land even to the mountains 3
Zec 9:15 drenched like the corners of the altar. *
Sir 24:31 I will water my orchard and drench my garden plot 4
39:22 drenches it like a flood. 4

dress 1. גָּזִית 2. יטב 3. עבד 4. עשׂה
Exd 30: 7 when he dresses the lamps he shall burn it 2
Deu 28:39 You shall plant vineyards and dress them 3
2Sm 19:24 he had neither dressed his feet, nor . . his beard 4
1Kg 5:17 to lay the foundation . . with dressed stones. 1
1Ch 22: 2 he set stonecutters to prepare dressed stones 1

dress (2) 1. לבשׁ 2. שִׁית 3. εἰμί 4. ζώννυμι
5. περιβάλλω 6. περιβολή 7. στολίζω
Prv 7:10 dressed as a harlot, wily of heart. 2
Jer 4:30 what do you mean that you dress in scarlet 1
Mrk 16: 5 they saw a young man . . dressed in a white robe; 5
Act 12: 8 Dress yourself and put on your sandals. 4
LJr 1:12 When they have been dressed in purple robes 5
1Mc 11:58 dress in purple and wear a gold buckle. 3
2Mc 3:26 gloriously beautiful and splendidly dressed 6
33 dressed in the same clothing 7

dressed *See* stone.

ready dressed 1. עשׂה
1Sm 25:18 two skins of wine, and five sheep ready dressed 1

dresser 1. בלס
Ams 7:14 I am a herdsman, and a dresser of sycamore trees 1

drift 1. עבר 2. διαφέρω

Zep 2: 2 you are driven away like the drifting chaff 1
Act 27:27 as we were drifting across the sea of A'dria 2

drift away 1. παραρρέω

Heb 2: 1 lest we drift away from it. 1

drink 1. מַשְׁקֶה 2. מִשְׁתֶּה 3. שקה 4. שִׁקּוּי 5. שתה 6. שְׁתִיָּה 7. שתה (A) 8. ἐκπίνω 9. οἶνος πολύς 10. πιέζω 11. πίνω 12. πίπτω 13. πόμα 14. πόσις 15. ποτόν 16. συμπίνω 17. bibo 18. potus

Gen 9:21 he drank of the wine, and became drunk 5
24:14 'Pray let down your jar that I may drink,' 5
14 maiden . . who shall say, 'Drink, and I will water 5
18 She said, "Drink, my lord"; 5
19 camels also, until they have done drinking. 5
22 When the camels had done drinking 5
43 Pray give me a little water from your jar to drink 3
44 Drink, and I will draw for your camels also 5
45 I said to her, 'Pray let me drink.' 3
46 She . . said, 'Drink, and I will give your camels 5
46 So I drank, and she gave the camels drink also. 5
54 he and the men who were with him ate and drank 5
25:34 and he ate and drank, and rose and went his way. 5
26:30 he made them a feast, and they ate and drank. 5
27:25 and he brought him wine, and he drank. 5
30:38 troughs, where the flocks came to drink. 5
38 And since they bred when they came to drink 5
43:34 they drank and were merry with him. 5
44: 5 Is it not from this that my lord drinks 5
Exd 7:18 will loathe to drink water from the Nile. 5
21 Egyptians could not drink water from the Nile; 5
24 the Egyptians dug . . for water to drink 5
24 for they could not drink the water of the Nile. 5
15:23 came to Marah, they could not drink the water 5
24 against Moses, saying, "What shall we drink? 5
17: 1 there was no water for the people to drink. 5
2 the people . . said, "Give us water to drink. 5
6 shall come out of it, that the people may drink. 5
24:11 they beheld God, and ate and drank. 5
32: 6 the people sat down to eat and drink, and rose up 5
34:28 he neither ate bread nor drank water. 5
Lev 10: 9 Drink no wine nor strong drink, you nor your sons 5
11:34 all drink which may be drunk 1
34 drink which may be drunk from every such vessel 5
Num 6: 3 he shall drink no vinegar made from wine 5
3 shall not drink any juice of grapes or eat grapes 5
20 after that the Nazirite may drink wine. 5
20: 5 evil place . . and there is no water to drink. 5
11 congregation drank, and their cattle. 5
17 neither will we drink water from a well; 5
19 if we drink of your water . . then I will pay for it; 5
21:22 we will not drink the water of a well; 5
23:24 drinks the blood of the slain. 5
33:14 where there was no water for the people to drink. 5
Deu 2: 6 buy water of them for money, that you may drink. 5
28 give me water for money, that I may drink; 5
9: 9 I neither ate bread nor drank water. 5
18 I neither ate bread nor drank water 5
11:11 land . . which drinks water by the rain 5
28:39 but you shall neither drink of the wine nor 5
29: 6 have not drunk wine or strong drink; 5
32:14 of the blood of the grape you drank wine. 5
38 who . . drank the wine of their drink offering? 5
Jdg 7: 5 likewise every one that kneels down to drink. 5
6 the rest of the people knelt down to drink water. 5
9:27 god, and ate and drank and reviled Abim'elech. 5
13: 4 beware, and drink no wine or strong drink, and eat 5
7 bear a son; so then drink no wine or strong drink 5
14 from the vine, neither let her drink wine 5
15:19 and when he drank, his spirit returned 5
19: 4 days; so they ate and drank, and lodged there. 5
6 the two men sat and ate and drank together; 5
21 and they washed their feet, and ate and drank. 5
Rut 2: 9 when you are thirsty, go to the vessels and drink 5
3: 3 until he has finished eating and drinking. 5
7 Bo'az had eaten and drunk, and his heart was merry 5
1Sm 1: 9 After they had eaten and drunk . . Hannah rose. 5
15 I have drunk neither wine nor strong drink 5
30:12 had not eaten bread or drunk water for three days 5
16 they were . . eating and drinking and dancing 5
2Sm 11:11 shall I then go to my house, to eat and to drink 5
13 he ate . . and drank, so that he made him drunk; 5
12: 3 it used to eat of his morsel, and drink from his cup 5
16: 2 and the wine for those who faint . . to drink. 5
19:35 Can your servant taste what he eats or . . drinks? 5
23:16 brought it to David. But he would not drink of it; 5
17 Shall I drink the blood of the men who went •
17 Therefore he would not drink it. 5
1Kg 1:25 behold, they are eating and drinking before him 5
4:20 Judah and Israel . . ate and drank and were happy. 5
10:21 All King Solomon's drinking vessels were of gold 1
13: 8 I will not eat bread or drink water in this place; 5
9 neither eat bread, nor drink water, nor return 5
16 neither will I eat bread nor drink water with you 5
17 You shall neither eat bread nor drink water 5
18 that he may eat bread and drink water.' 5
19 ate bread in his house, and drank water. 5
22 and have eaten bread and drunk water in the place 5
22 he said to you, "Eat no bread, and drink no water"; 5
23 after he had eaten bread and drunk, he saddled 5
16: 9 he was at Tirzah, drinking himself drunk 5
17: 4 You shall drink from the brook 5
6 and he drank from the brook. 5
10 Bring me a little water . . that I may drink. 5
18:41 Eli'jah said to Ahab, "Go up, eat and drink; 5
42 So Ahab went up to eat and to drink. 5
19: 6 And he ate and drank, and lay down again. 5
8 he arose, and ate and drank 5
20:12 Ben-ha'dad heard this message as he was drinking 5
16 Ben-ha'dad was drinking himself drunk 5
2Kg 3:17 be filled with water, so that you shall drink 5
6:22 Set bread and water . . that they may eat and drink 5
23 when they had eaten and drunk, he sent them away 5
7: 8 they went into a tent, and ate and drank 5
9:34 Then he went in and ate and drank; and he said 5
18:27 to eat their own dung and to drink their own urine? 5
31 every . . will drink the water of his own cistern; 5
19:24 I dug wells and drank foreign waters 5
1Ch 11:18 But David would not drink of it; 5
19 Shall I drink the lifeblood of these men? 5
19 Therefore he would not drink it. 5
12:39 with David for three days, eating and drinking 5
29:22 they ate and drank before the LORD on that day 5
2Ch 9:20 All King Solomon's drinking vessels were of gold 1
Ezr 3: 7 gave . . food, drink, and oil to the Sido'nians 2
10: 6 neither eating bread nor drinking water; 5
Neh 8:10 Go your way, eat the fat and drink sweet wine 5
12 all the people went their way to eat and drink 5
Est 1: 8 And drinking was according to the law 6
3:15 And the king and Haman sat down to drink; 5
4:16 a fast . . and neither eat nor drink for three days 5
5: 6 And as they were drinking wine, the king said 2
7: 2 And on the second day, as they were drinking wine 2
8 to the place where they were drinking wine 2
Job 1: 4 their three sisters to eat and drink with them. 5
13 his sons and daughters were eating and drinking 5
18 sons and daughters were eating and drinking 5
6: 4 are in me; my spirit drinks their poison; 5
15:16 corrupt, a man who drinks iniquity like water! 5
21:20 let them drink of the wrath of the Almighty. 5
Ps 50:13 eat the flesh of bulls, or drink the blood of goats? 5
78:44 so that they could not drink of their streams. 5
102: 9 mingle tears with my drink 4
110: 7 He will drink from the brook by the way; 5
Prv 4:17 drink the wine of violence. 5
5:15 Drink water from your own cistern 5
9: 5 eat of my bread and drink of the wine I have mixed. 5
23: 7 Eat and drink!" he says to you; but his heart is not 5
35 When shall I awake? I will seek another drink. •
26: 6 cuts off his own feet and drinks violence. 5
31: 4 not for kings to drink wine, or for rulers 5
5 lest they drink and forget what has been decreed 5
7 let them drink and forget their poverty 5
Ecc 2:24 that he should eat and drink, and find enjoyment 5
3:13 every one should eat and drink and take pleasure 5
5:18 is to eat and drink and find enjoyment in all 5
8:15 no good thing . . but to eat and drink, and enjoy 5
9: 7 Go, eat . . and drink your wine with a merry heart; 5
Sng 5: 1 I drink my wine with my milk. 5
1 Eat, O friends, and drink: drink deeply, O lovers! 5
Isa 5:22 Woe to those who are heroes at drinking wine 5
21: 5 they spread the rugs, they eat, they drink. 5
22:13 behold . . eating flesh and drinking wine. 5
13 Let us eat and drink, for tomorrow we die. 5
24: 9 No more do they drink wine with singing; 5
9 strong drink is bitter to those who drink it. 5
29: 8 thirsty man dreams he is drinking and awakes 5
32: 6 and to deprive the thirsty of drink. 1
36:12 to eat their own dung and drink their own urine? 5
16 one . . will drink the water of his own cistern; 5
37:25 I dug wells and drank waters 5
44:12 strength fails, he drinks no water and is faint. 5
51:17 you who have drunk at the hand of the LORD the cup 5
17 have drunk to the dregs the bowl of staggering. 5
22 the bowl of my wrath you shall drink no more; 5
62: 8 and foreigners shall not drink your wine 5
9 shall drink it in the courts of my sanctuary. 5
65:13 my servants shall drink, but you shall be thirsty; 5
Jer 2:18 by going to Egypt, to drink the waters of the Nile? 5
18 to Assyria, to drink the waters of the Euphra'tes? 5
16: 8 feasting to sit with them, to eat and drink. 5
22:15 Did not your father eat and drink and do justice 5
25:16 They shall drink and stagger and be crazed 5
26 And after them the king of Babylon shall drink. 5
27 Drink, be drunk and vomit, fall and rise no more 5
28 refuse to accept the cup from your hand to drink 5
28 Thus says the LORD of hosts: You must drink! 5
35: 5 wine, and cups; and I said to them, "Drink wine. 5
6 But they answered, "We will drink no wine 5
6 our father, commanded us, 'You shall not drink wine 5
8 that he commanded us, to drink no wine all our days 5
14 gave to his sons, to drink no wine, has been kept; 5
14 and they drink none to this day 5
49:12 If those who did not deserve to drink the cup 5
12 did not deserve to drink the cup must drink it 5
12 You shall not go unpunished, but you must drink. 5
51: 7 the nations drank of her wine 5
Lam 5: 4 We must pay for the water we drink 5
Ezk 4:11 And water you shall drink by measure 5
11 once a day you shall drink. 5
16 they shall drink water by measure and in dismay. 5
12:18 and drink water with trembling 5
19 with fearfulness, and drink water in dismay 5
23:32 You shall drink your sister's cup which is deep 5
34 you shall drink it and drain it out 5
25: 4 they shall drink your milk. 5
31:14 no trees that drink water may reach up to them 5
16 choice and best of Lebanon, all that drink water 5
34:18 to drink of clear water, that you must foul 5
19 and drink what you have fouled with your feet? 5
39:17 you shall eat flesh and drink blood. 5
18 and drink the blood of the princes of the earth 5
19 and drink blood till you are drunk 5
44:21 No priest shall drink wine, when he enters 5
Dan 1: 5 rich food . . and of the wine which he drank. 2
8 not defile . . with the wine which he drank; 2
10 king, who appointed your food and your drink 2
12 us be given vegetables to eat and water to drink. 5
16 their rich food and the wine they were to drink 2
5: 1 drank wine in front of the 1,000. 7
2 king and . . his concubines might drink from them. 7
3 king and . . his concubines drank from them. 7
4 They drank wine, and praised the gods of gold 7
23 you . . and your concubines have drunk wine 7
Hos 2: 5 give me . . my wool and my flax, my oil and my drink 4
Jol 3: 3 and have sold a girl for wine, and have drunk it. 5
Ams 2: 8 they drink the wine of those who have been fined. 5
4: 1 who say to their husbands, 'Bring, that we may drink 5
8 three cities wandered to one city to drink water 5
5:11 vineyards, but you shall not drink their wine. 5
6: 6 who drink wine in bowls, and anoint themselves 5
9:14 they shall plant vineyards and drink their wine 5
Obd 1:16 For as you have drunk upon my holy mountain 5
16 all the nations round about shall drink; 5
16 they shall drink, and stagger 5
Jon 3: 7 let them not feed, or drink water 5
Mic 6:15 you shall tread grapes, but not drink wine. 5
Hab 2:16 Drink, yourself, and stagger! 5
Zep 1:13 they shall not drink wine from them. 5
Hag 1: 6 you drink, but you never have your fill; 5
Zec 7: 6 when you eat and when you drink 5
6 eat for yourselves and drink for yourselves? 5
9:15 they shall drink their blood like wine 5
Mat 6:25 life, what you shall eat or what you shall drink 11
31 saying, 'What shall we eat?' or 'What shall we drink?' 11
11:18 For John came neither eating nor drinking 11
19 the Son of man came eating and drinking 11
20:22 Are you able to drink the cup that I am to drink? 11
22 Are you able to drink the cup that I am to drink? 11
23 He said to them, "You will drink my cup 11
24:38 before the flood they were eating and drinking 11
49 eats and drinks with the drunken 11
26:27 Drink of it, all of you; 11
29 I shall not drink again of this fruit of the vine 11
29 until that day when I drink it new with you 11
42 My Father, if this cannot pass unless I drink it 11
27:34 they offered him wine to drink, mingled with gall; 11
34 when he tasted it, he would not drink it. 11
Mrk 10:38 Are you able to drink the cup that I drink 11
38 Are you able to drink the cup that I drink 11
39 The cup that I drink you will drink 11
39 The cup that I drink you will drink 11
14:23 he gave it to them, and they all drank of it. 11
25 I shall not drink again of the fruit of the vine 11
25 when I drink it new in the kingdom of God. 11
16:18 if they drink any deadly thing, it will not hurt 11
Lke 1:15 he shall drink no wine nor strong drink 11
5:30 Why do you eat and drink with tax collectors 11
33 but yours eat and drink. 11
39 no one after drinking old wine desires new 11
7:33 has come eating no bread and drinking no wine 11
34 The Son of man has come eating and drinking; 11
10: 7 eating and drinking what they provide 11
12:19 take your ease, eat, drink, be merry.' 11
29 what you are to eat and what you are to drink 11
45 to eat and drink and get drunk 11
13:26 We ate and drank in your presence 11
17: 8 till I eat and drink 11
8 afterward you shall eat and drink'? 11
27 They ate, they drank, they married 11
28 they ate, they drank, they bought, they sold 11
22:18 I shall not drink of the fruit of the vine 11
30 you may eat and drink at my table in my kingdom 11
Joh 4: 7 Jesus said to her, "Give me a drink. 11
9 you, a Jew, ask a drink of me, a woman of Samar'ia? 11
10 who it is that is saying to you, 'Give me a drink,' 11
12 Jacob, who gave us the well, and drank from it 11
13 who drinks of this water will thirst again 11
14 whoever drinks of the water that I shall give him 11
6:53 eat the flesh of the Son of man and drink his blood 11
54 he who eats my flesh and drinks my blood 11
55 my blood is drink indeed. 14
56 who eats my flesh and drinks my blood abides in me 11
7:37 If any one thirst, let him come to me and drink. 11
18:11 not drink the cup which the Father has given me? 11

Act 9: 9 neither ate nor drank. 11
10:41 who ate and drank with him 16
23:12 an oath neither to eat nor drink 11
21 an oath neither to eat nor drink 11
Rom 14:17 For the kingdom of God is not food and drink 14
21 it is right not to eat meat or drink wine 11
1Co 9: 4 Do we not have the right to our food and drink? 11
10: 4 all drank the same supernatural drink 11
4 all drank the same supernatural drink 13
4 they drank from the supernatural Rock 11
7 sat down to eat and drink and rose up to dance. 11
21 You cannot drink the cup of the Lord 11
31 So, whether you eat or drink, or whatever you do 11
11:22 What! Do you not have houses to eat and drink in? 11
25 Do this, as often as you drink it 11
26 eat this bread and drink the cup 11
27 drinks the cup of the Lord in an unworthy manner 11
28 eat of the bread and drink of the cup. 11
29 any one who eats and drinks without discerning 11
29 eats and drinks judgment upon himself. 11
15:32 Let us eat and drink, for tomorrow we die. 11
Col 2:16 in questions of food and drink 14
Tit 2: 3 not to be slanderers or slaves to drink 9
Heb 6: 7 land which has drunk the rain that . . falls 11
9:10 food and drink and various ablutions 13
Rev 14:10 he also shall drink the wine of God's wrath 11
16: 6 and thou hast given them blood to drink. 11
18: 3 all nations have drunk the wine of her . . passion 11
1Es 3: 3 They ate and drank 11
6 clothed in purple, and drink from gold cups 11
18 It leads astray the minds of all who drink it. 11
22 When men drink 11
4:10 he reclines, he eats and drinks and sleeps 11
5:54 they gave money . . and food and drink 15
9: 2 he did not eat bread or drink water 11
51 go your way, eat the fat and drink the sweet 11
54 to eat and drink and enjoy themselves 11
2Es 8: 4 and drink wisdom, O my heart! ‡
9:24 and taste no meat and drink no wine 17
34 the sea a ship, or any dish food or drink 18
10: 4 and I will neither eat nor drink 17
14:38 Ezra, open your mouth and drink what I give you 17
40 I took it and drank; and when I had drunk it 17
40 I took it and drank; and when I had drunk it 17
15:58 and drink their own blood in thirst for water. 17
Tob 4:15 Do not drink wine to excess 11
7: 9 Raguel said to Tobias, "Eat, drink, and be merry; 11
12:19 I merely appeared to you and did not eat or drink 11
Jdt 7:21 did not have enough water to drink their fill 11
21 because it was measured out to them to drink. 11
12:11 to join us and eat and drink with us. 11
13 drink wine and be merry with us 11
17 Drink now, and be merry with us! 11
18 Judith said, "I will drink now, my lord 11
19 Then she took and ate and drank before him 11
20 drank a great quantity of wine 11
20 much more than he had ever drunk in any one day 11
AEs 14:17 I have not . . drunk the wine of the libations. 11
Sir 9:10 when it has aged you will drink it with pleasure. 10
24:21 those who drink me will thirst for more. 11
26:12 drinks from any water near him 11
31:27 if you drink it in moderation 11
28 Wine drunk in season and temperately 11
29 Wine drunk to excess is bitterness of soul 11
Bel 1: 6 see how much he eats and drinks every day? 11
7 it never ate or drank anything. 11
15 ate and drank everything. 8
1Mc 11:58 and granted him the right to drink from gold cups 11
2Mc 7:36 our brothers . . have drunk of everflowing life 12
15:39 For just as it is harmful to drink wine alone 11
39 again, to drink water alone •
3Mc 5:16 The king . . returned to his drinking 15
6:36 not for drinking and gluttony 15
4Mc 3:14 from it boldly brought the king a drink. 15
15 to drink what was regarded as . . blood. 15
16 he poured out the drink as an offering to God. 13

drink *See also* give, offer, offering, provide, serve.

drink deeply 1. מצץ 2. שכר
Sng 5: 1 Eat, O friends, and drink: drink deeply, O lovers! 2
Isa 66:11 that you may drink deeply with delight 1

drink freely 1. μεθύσκω
Joh 2:10 and when men have drunk freely, then the poor wine; 1

make drink 1. שקה 2. ποτίζω
Gen 19:32 Come, let us make our father drink wine 1
33 they made their father drink wine that night; 1
34 let us make him drink wine tonight also; 1
35 they made their father drink wine that night 1
Exd 32:20 and made the people of Israel drink it. 1
Num 5:24 make the woman drink the water of bitterness 1
26 afterward shall make the woman drink the water. 1
27 when he has made her drink the water, 1
Jer 25:15 make all the nations to whom I send you drink it. 1
17 and made all the nations . . drink it 1
Ams 2:12 But you made the Nazirites drink wine 1
Hab 2:15 Woe to him who makes his neighbors drink 1

1Co 12:13 all were made to drink of one Spirit. 2
Rev 14: 8 she who made all nations drink the wine 2

drink milk 1. γαλακτοποτέω
4Mc 13:21 they drank milk from the same fountains 1

drink one's fill 1. רוה 2. absorbo
Isa 34: 5 For my sword has drunk its fill in the heavens; 1
Jer 46:10 and be sated, and drink its fill of their blood. 1
2Es 8: 4 Then drink your fill of understanding, O my soul 2

drink only water 1. ὑδροποτέω
1Ti 5:23 No longer drink only water, but use a little wine 1

strong drink 1. שֵׁכָר 2. σίκερα
Lev 10: 9 Drink no wine nor strong drink, you nor your sons 1
Num 6: 3 separate himself from wine and strong drink; 1
3 no vinegar made from wine or strong drink 1
28: 7 pour out a drink offering of strong drink 1
Deu 14:26 whatever you desire . . wine or strong drink 1
29: 6 have not drunk wine or strong drink; 1
Jdg 13: 4 beware, and drink no wine or strong drink, and eat 1
7 bear a son; so then drink no wine or strong drink 1
14 neither let her drink wine or strong drink 1
1Sm 1:15 I have drunk neither wine nor strong drink 1
Prv 20: 1 Wine is a mocker, strong drink a brawler; 1
31: 4 it is not . . for rulers to desire strong drink; 1
6 Give strong drink to him who is perishing 1
Isa 5:11 rise . . that they may run after strong drink 1
22 valiant men in mixing strong drink 1
24: 9 strong drink is bitter to those who drink it. 1
28: 7 reel with wine and stagger with strong drink; 1
7 priest and the prophet reel with strong drink 1
7 with wine, they stagger with strong drink; 1
29: 9 stagger, but not with strong drink! 1
56:12 let us fill ourselves with strong drink; 1
Mic 2:11 I will preach to you of wine and strong drink 1
Lke 1:15 he shall drink no wine nor strong drink 2

drink up 1. שתה
Job 34: 7 man is like Job, who drinks up scoffing like water 1

drinker 1. שתה
Jol 1: 5 and wail, all you drinkers of wine 1

drinking *See* companion.

drip 1. דלף 2. נטף 3. רעף 4. σταλαγμός 5. stillo
Ps 65:11 the tracks of thy chariot drip with fatness. 3
12 The pastures of the wilderness drip 3
Prv 5: 3 For the lips of a loose woman drip honey 2
19:13 quarreling is a continual dripping of rain. 1
27:15 A continual dripping on a rainy day 1
Sng 5: 5 I arose to open . . and my hands dripped with myrrh 2
Jol 3:18 in that day the mountains shall drip sweet wine 2
Ams 9:13 the mountains shall drip sweet wine 2
2Es 5: 5 Blood shall drip from wood 5
4Mc 9:20 was being quenched by the drippings of gore 4

drippings of honeycomb 1. נֹפֶת
Ps 19:10 than honey and drippings of the honeycomb. 1
Prv 24:13 drippings of the honeycomb are sweet 1

drive 1. בוא 2. גרש 3. דחה 4. המם 5. מִנְהָג 6. נדח 7. נדף 8. נהג 9. נוס 10. נשב 11. נשל 12. עבר 13. שוב 14. שלח 15. ששא 16. תקע 17. טרד (A) 18. ἄγω 19. ἀνάγκη 20. ἀνατροπή 21. ἀπελαύνω 22. εἰσάγω 23. ἐλαύνω 24. συνελαύνω 25. τίθημι 26. φέρω 27. eicio
Exd 10:19 wind, which lifted the locusts and drove them 16
14:25 wheels so that they drove heavily; 8
Lev 26:36 sound of a driven leaf shall put them to flight 7
Num 5: 4 Israel did so, and drove them outside the camp; 14
22: 6 to defeat them and drive them from the land; 2
Deu 4:27 among the nations where the LORD will drive you. 8
30: 1 nations where the LORD your God has driven you 6
Jdg 4:21 softly to him and drove the peg into his temple 16
1Sm 30:20 and the people drove those cattle before him 8
2Sm 6: 3 and Uzzah and Ahi'o . . were driving the new cart 8
2Kg 9:20 And the driving is like the driving of Jehu 5
20 And the driving is like the driving of Jehu 5
20 the driving of Jehu . . for he drives furiously. 8
16: 6 the king . . and drove the men of Judah from Elath; 11
17:21 Jerobo'am drove Israel from following the LORD 6
1Ch 13: 7 and Uzzah and Ahi'o were driving the cart. 8
Job 6:13 no help in me, and any resource is driven from me. 6
13:25 Wilt thou frighten a driven leaf 7
Ps 35: 5 with the angel of the LORD driving them on! 3
Prv 20:26 A wise king . . drives the wheel over them. 13
Isa 28:28 he drives his cart wheel over it with his horses 4
41: 2 like dust . . like driven stubble with his bow. 7
59:19 stream, which the wind of the LORD drives. 9
Jer 8: 3 in all the places where I have driven them 6
13:24 I will scatter you like chaff driven by the wind 12
16:15 out of . . the countries where he had driven them. 6
23: 3 out of all the countries where I have driven them 6
8 out of . . the countries where he had driven them. 6
12 the darkness, into which they shall be driven 6
24: 9 in all the places where I shall drive them. 6
29:14 and all the places where I have driven you 6
18 among all the nations where I have driven them 6
32:37 the countries to which I drove them in my anger 6
40:12 from all the places to which they had been driven 6
43: 5 all the nations to which they had been driven 6
46:28 end of all the nations to which I have driven you 6
Lam 3: 2 he has driven and brought me into darkness 8
13 He drove into my heart the arrows of his quiver; 1
Ezk 4:13 among the nations whither I will drive them. 6
39: 2 I will turn you about and drive you forward 15
Dan 4:25 that you shall be driven from among men 17
32 you shall be driven from among men 17
33 driven from among men, and ate grass like an ox 17
5:21 driven from among men, and his mind was made 17
9: 7 all the lands to which thou hast driven them 6
Jol 2:20 and drive him into a parched and desolate land 6
Obd 1: 7 deceived you, they have driven you to the border; 14
Lke 8:29 was driven by the demon into the desert.) 23
Act 18:16 he drove them from the tribunal. 21
27:15 we gave way to it and were driven. 26
17 they lowered the gear, and so were driven. 26
Jas 3: 4 though they . . are driven by strong winds 23
2Pe 2:17 waterless springs and mists driven by a storm; 23
2Es 1:33 I will drive you out as the wind drives straw; •
16:72 and drive them out of their houses. 27
Wis 17:15 now were driven by monstrous specters 23
Sir 8:19 lest you drive away your good luck. 11
38:25 who drives oxen and is occupied with their work 23
1Mc 1:53 they drove Israel into hiding 25
2Mc 4:26 was driven as a fugitive into the land of Ammon. 24
9: 4 to drive without stopping 23
3Mc 4: 5 the violence with which they were driven 20
9 driven under the constraint of iron bonds 18
5: 2 and to drive them in 22
4Mc 3:17 can conquer the drives of the emotions 19

drive away 1. גרש 2. נדח 3. נדף 4. נהג 5. נוד 6. נשב 7. רדף 8. שבה 9. ἀφίστημι 10. διώκω 11. ἐκβάλλω 12. recutio
Gen 4:14 Behold, thou hast driven me this day away 1
15:11 upon the carcasses, Abram drove them away. 6
31:18 he drove away all his cattle, all his livestock 4
Exd 2:17 The shepherds came and drove them away; 1
11: 1 when he lets you go, he will drive you away 1
22:10 If . . it dies or is hurt or is driven away 8
Job 24: 3 They drive away the ass of the fatherless; 4
Ps 1: 4 but are like chaff which the wind drives away. 3
36:11 nor the hand of the wicked drive me away. 5
68: 2 As smoke is driven away, so drive them away; 3
2 As smoke is driven away, so drive them away; 3
Ecc 3:15 and God seeks what has been driven away. 7
Isa 19: 7 will dry up, be driven away, and be no more. 3
Jer 23: 2 scattered my flock, and have driven them away 2
50:17 Israel is a hunted sheep driven away by lions. 2
Mic 4: 6 and gather those who have been driven away 2
Zep 2: 2 you are driven away like the drifting chaff •
2Es 16: 5 and who is there to drive them away? 12
8 and who will drive them away? 12
Wis 5:14 like a light hoarfrost driven away by a storm 10
Sir 28:15 Slander has driven away courageous women 11
38:20 Do not give your heart to sorrow; drive it away 9

drive back 1. היה על 2. הלך 3. ἀποστρέφω
Exd 14:21 the LORD drove the sea back by a strong east wind 2
2Sm 11:23 but we drove them back to the entrance of the gate. 1
1Mc 7:46 and drove them back to their pursuers 3

drive far 1. גרש 2. רחק
Ps 31:22 said in my alarm, "I am driven far from thy sight. 1
Prv 22:15 but the rod of discipline drives it far from him. 2
Ezk 8: 6 to drive me far from my sanctuary? 2

drive firmly 1. πήγνυμι
Sir 27: 2 As a stake is driven firmly into a fissure 1

drive forth 1. שלח
Job 30:12 the rabble rise, they drive me forth, 1

drive hard 1. רדף
Lam 5: 5 With a yoke on our necks we are hard driven; 1

drive into exile 1. ἀποικίζω 2. ἀποξενόω
Sir 29:18 it has driven men of power into exile 1
2Mc 5: 9 he who had driven many . . into exile 2

drive mad 1. שגע
Deu 28:34 driven mad by the sight which your eyes shall see. 1

drive off 1. ἀπελαύνω 2. recutio
2Es 16: 6 Can one drive off a hungry lion in the forest 2
Wis 17: 8 promised to drive off the fears . . of a sick soul 1

drive out 1. אבד 2. גרש 3. ירש 4. נדד 5. נדח 6. ἐκβάλλω 7. ἐκβράζω 8. ἐκδιώκω 9. ἐκτινάσσω 10. ἐξαίρω 11. ἐξέρχομαι 12. σκορπίζω 13. proicio
Gen 3:24 He drove out the man; 2
Exd 6: 1 he will drive them out of his land. 2
10:11 they were driven out from Pharaoh's presence. 2

23:28 which shall drive out Hivite, Canaanite 2
29 I will not drive them out from before you in one 2
30 I will drive them out from before you 2
31 and you shall drive them out before you. 2
33: 2 I will drive out the Canaanites, the Amorites 2
34:11 Behold, I will drive out before you the Amorites 2
Num22:11 be able to fight against them and drive them out.' 2
32:21 until he has driven out his enemies from before 2
33:52 then you shall drive out all the inhabitants 3
55 if you do not drive out the inhabitants of the land 3
Deu 4:38 driving out before you nations greater 3
9: 3 so you shall drive them out, and make them perish 3
4 that the LORD is driving them out before you. 3
5 LORD your God is driving them out from before you 3
11:23 LORD will drive out all these nations before you 3
18:12 LORD your God is driving them out before you. 3
Jos 3:10 will . . drive out from before you the Canaanites 3
13: 6 I will myself drive them out 3
12 these Moses had defeated and driven out. 3
13 Yet . . Israel did not drive out the Gesh'urites 3
14:12 and I shall drive them out as the LORD said. 3
15:14 Caleb drove out from there the three sons of Anak 3
63 But the Jeb'usites . . Judah could not drive out; 3
16:10 However they did not drive out the Canaanites 3
17:13 they . . did not utterly drive them out. 3
18 you shall drive out the Canaanites 3
23: 5 push them back . . and drive them out of your sight; 3
9 LORD has driven out before you great . . nations; 3
13 continue to drive out these nations before you; 3
24:12 the hornet . . which drove them out before you 2
18 and the LORD drove out before us all the peoples 2
Jdg 1:19 but he could not drive out the inhabitants 3
20 and he drove out from it the three sons of Anak. 3
21 Benjamin did not drive out the Jeb'usites who 3
27 Manas'seh did not drive out the inhabitants 3
28 forced labor, but did not utterly drive them out. 3
29 E'phraim did not drive out the Canaanites who 3
30 Zeb'ulun did not drive out the inhabitants 3
31 Asher did not drive out the inhabitants of Acco 3
32 for they did not drive them out. 3
33 Naph'tali did not drive out the inhabitants 3
2: 3 So now I say, I will not drive them out before you; 2
21 I will not henceforth drive out before them any 3
23 left those nations, not driving them out at once 3
6: 9 I delivered you . . and drove them out before you 2
9:41 Zebul drove out Ga'al and his kinsmen 2
11: 7 Did you not . . and drive me out of my father's house? 2
1Sm 26:19 may they be cursed . . for they have driven me out 2
2Sm 7:23 by driving out before his people a nation 6
1Kg 14:24 which the LORD drove out before the people 3
2Kg 16: 3 whom the LORD drove out before . . Israel. 3
17: 8 nations whom the LORD drove out before . . Israel 3
21: 2 nations whom the LORD drove out before . . Israel. 3
1Ch 17:21 in driving out nations before thy people 2
2Ch 13: 9 Have you not driven out the priests of the LORD 5
20: 7 O our God, drived out the inhabitants of this land 3
11 by coming to drive us out of thy possession 2
28: 3 nations whom the LORD drove out 3
33: 2 LORD drove out before the people of Israel. 3
Job 18:18 into darkness, and driven out of the world. 4
30: 5 They are driven out from among men; 2
Ps 34: 0 so that he drove him out, and he went away. 2
44: 2 with thy own hand didst drive out the nations 3
78:55 He drove out nations before them; 2
80: 8 thou didst drive out the nations and plant it. 2
109:10 may they be driven out of the ruins they inhabit! 6
Prv 22:10 Drive out a scoffer, and strife will go out 2
Isa 27:13 those who were driven out to the land of Egypt 5
Jer 27:10 and I will drive you out, and you will perish. 5
15 with the result that I will drive you out 5
49: 5 and you shall be driven out 5
36 to which those driven out of Elam shall not come. 5
Ezk 28:16 the guardian cherub drove you out from the midst 1
Hos 9:15 I will drive them out of my house. 2
Mic 2: 9 The women of my people you drive out 2
Zep 2: 4 Ashdod's people shall be driven out at noon 2
Mat 21:12 drove out all who sold and bought in the temple 6
Mrk 1:12 The Spirit immediately drove him out 6
9:29 This kind cannot be driven out by anything 11
11:15 And he . . began to drive out those who sold 6
Lke 19:45 began to drive out those who sold 6
Joh 2:15 he drove them all . . out of the temple; 6
Act 13:50 and drove them out of their district. 6
1Co 5:13 Drive out the wicked person from among you. 10
1Th 2:15 drove us out, and displease God and oppose all men 8
2Es 1:21 I drove out the Canaanites, the Perizzites 13
33 I will drive you out as the wind drives straw; 13
Jdt 5: 8 they drove them out from the presence of their gods 6
12 the Egyptians drove them out of their sight. 6
14 and drove out all the people of the wilderness. 6
16 they drove out before them the Canaanites 6
Aza 1:26 and drove the fiery flame out of the furnace 9
1Mc 7: 6 and have driven us out of our land. 12
13:11 he drove out its occupants and remained there. 6
2Mc 1:12 he drove out those . . 7

drive to despair 1. ἐξαπορέω
2Co 4: 8 perplexed, but not driven to despair; 1

drive violently 1. violo
2Es 15:39 shall be driven violently toward the south 1

driven by the wind 1. ἀνεμίζω
Jas 1: 6 wave of the sea . . driven and tossed by the wind. 1

driver 1. נגשׂ
Job 39: 7 he hears not the shouts of the driver. 1
1Mc 6:37 also its Indian driver. •

driver of a chariot 1. רַכָּב
1Kg 22:34 he said to the driver of his chariot, "Turn about 1
2Ch 18:33 therefore he said to the driver of his chariot 1
driving *See* send.

dromedary 1. כִּרְכָּרָה
Isa 66:20 in litters, and upon mules, and upon dromedaries 1

droop 1. παρίημι
Heb 12:12 Therefore lift your drooping hands 1
Sir 25:23 Drooping hands and weak knees 1

drop 1. אֵגֶל 2. הֵלֶךְ 3. מַר 4. נָטָף 5. נטף 6. נפל 7. ערף 8. רְסִיס 9. רעף 10. רפה 11. שׁלך 12. καταβαίνω 13. ῥανίς 14. σταγών 15. gutta 16. stillicidium
Deu 32: 2 May my teaching drop as the rain, my speech distil 7
Jdg 2:19 they did not drop any of their practices 6
5: 4 the earth trembled, and the heavens dropped 5
4 heavens dropped, yea, the clouds dropped water. 5
1Sm 14:26 the honey was dropping, but no man put his hand 2
2Ch 24:10 brought their tax and dropped it into the chest 11
Neh 6: 9 Their hands will drop from the work 10
Job 29:22 not speak again, and my word dropped upon them. 5
36:27 For he draws up the drops of water 4
28 skies pour down, and drop upon man abundantly. 9
38:28 who has begotten the drops of dew? 2
Sng 5: 2 wet with dew, my locks with the drops of the night. 8
Isa 40:15 Behold, the nations are like a drop from a bucket 3
Rev 16:21 great hailstones . . dropped on men from heaven 12
2Es 4:49 drops remained in the cloud. 15
50 for as the rain is more than the drops 15
50 but drops and smoke remained. 15
6:56 their abundance to a drop from a bucket. 16
Wis 11:22 like a drop of morning dew 13
Sir 1: 2 The sand of the sea, the drops of rain 14
18:10 Like a drop of water from the sea 14
4Mc 10: 8 drops of blood flowing from his entrails. 14

drop down 1. ערף 2. רעף
Deu 33:28 yea, his heavens drop down dew. 1
Prv 3:20 by his knowledge . . clouds drop down the dew. 2

make drop 1. נפל 2. שׁלך
Job 29:17 and made him drop his prey from his teeth. 2
Ezk 39: 3 and will make your arrows drop out of your right 1

drop of water 1. gutta
2Es 9:16 as a wave is greater than a drop of water. 1

drop off 1. נשׁל
Deu 28:40 for your olives shall drop off. 1

droppings fall 1. ἀφοδεύω
Tob 2:10 their fresh droppings fell into my open eyes 1

dropsy 1. ὑδρωπικός
Lke 14: 2 behold, there was a man before him who had dropsy. 1

dross 1. סִיג
Ps 119:119 the wicked of the earth thou dost count as dross; 1
Prv 25: 4 Take away the dross from the silver 1
Isa 1:22 Your silver has become dross 1
25 I . . will smelt away your dross as with lye 1
Ezk 22:18 the house of Israel has become dross to me; 1
18 and lead in the furnace, have become dross. 1
19 Because you have all become dross, therefore 1

drought 1. בַּצָּרָה 2. בַּצֹּרֶת 3. חֹרֶב 4. צִיָּה 5. תַּלְאֻבָה 6. ἀβροχία
Deu 28:22 smite you . . with drought, and with blasting 3
Job 24:19 Drought and heat snatch away the snow waters; 4
Jer 2: 6 in a land of drought and deep darkness 4
14: 1 which came to Jeremiah concerning the drought 1
17: 8 and is not anxious in the year of drought 2
50:38 A drought upon her waters, that they may be dried 3
51:43 become a horror, a land of drought and a desert 4
Hos 13: 5 knew you in the wilderness, in the land of drought; 5
Hag 1:11 I have called for a drought upon the land 3
Sir 35:20 clouds of rain in the time of drought. 6

drove 1. עֵדֶר
Gen 30:40 he put his own droves apart 1
32:16 the hand of his servants, every drove by itself 1
16 put a space between drove and drove. 1
16 put a space between drove and drove. 1
19 instructed . . all who followed the droves 1

drown 1. שׁטף 2. ἀποπνίγω 3. βυθίζω 4. κατακλύζω 5. καταπίνω 6. καταποντίζω 7. πνίγω
Sng 8: 7 cannot quench love, neither can floods drown it. 1
Mat 18: 6 and to be drowned in the depth of the sea. 6
Mrk 5:13 drowned in the sea. 7
Lke 8:33 and the herd . . were drowned. 2
Heb 11:29 the Egyptians . . were drowned. 5
Wis 10:19 she drowned their enemies 4
2Mc 12: 4 the men . . took them out to sea and drowned them 3

drown in the sea 1. ποντόβροχος
3Mc 6: 4 by drowning them in the sea 1

drowsiness 1. נוּמָה
Prv 23:21 drowsiness will clothe a man with rags. 1
drowsy *See* grow.

drowsy man 1. νυστάζω
Sir 22: 8 who tells a story to a fool tells it to a drowsy man 1

drug 1. ποτίζω
3Mc 5: 2 on the following day to drug all the elephants 1
10 when he had drugged the pitiless elephants 1

drum 1. τύμπανον
1Es 5: 2 with the music of drums and flutes; 1

drunk 1. שׁכר 2. שִׁכֹּר 3. שִׁכָּרוֹן 4. μεθύσκω 5. μεθύω 6. inebrio
1Sm 25:36 Nabal's heart was merry . . for he was very drunk; 2
1Kg 16: 9 he was at Tirzah, drinking himself drunk 2
20:16 Ben-ha'dad was drinking himself drunk 2
Isa 29: 9 Be drunk, but not with wine; 1
49:26 shall be drunk with their own blood as with wine. 1
51:21 who are afflicted, who are drunk, but not with wine 1
Jer 25:27 Drink, be drunk and vomit, fall and rise no more 1
Ezk 39:19 and drink blood till you are drunk 3
Act 2:15 these men are not drunk, as you suppose 5
1Co 11:21 one is hungry and another is drunk. 5
1Th 5: 7 those who get drunk are drunk at night. 5
Rev 17: 6 I saw the woman, drunk with the blood of the saints 5
2Es 15:53 and talking about their death when you were drunk? 6
Jdt 6: 4 their mountains will be drunk with their blood 4
1Mc 16:16 When Simon and his sons were drunk, Ptolemy 4
drunk *See also* get, make.

become drunk 1. שׁכר 2. μεθύσκω
Gen 9:21 he drank of the wine, and became drunk 1
Lam 4:21 you shall become drunk and strip yourself bare. 1
Rev 17: 2 the dwellers on earth have become drunk. 2

drunkard 1. סָבָא 2. סבא 3. שִׁכֹּר 4. שתה שֵׁכָר 5. μέθυσος 6. οἰνοπότης 7. πάροινος
Deu 21:20 This our son . . is a glutton and a drunkard.' 2
Ps 69:12 the drunkards make songs about me. 4
Prv 23:21 drunkard and the glutton will come to poverty 2
26: 9 thorn that goes up into the hand of a drunkard 3
10 he who hires a passing fool or drunkard. •
Isa 28: 1 the proud crown of the drunkards of E'phraim 3
3 The proud crown of the drunkards of E'phraim 3
Ezk 23:42 drunkards were brought from the wilderness; 1
Hos 4:18 A band of drunkards, they give themselves •
Jol 1: 5 Awake, you drunkards, and weep; 3
Mat 11:19 and they say, 'Behold, a glutton and a drunkard 6
Lke 7:34 and you say, 'Behold, a glutton and a drunkard 6
1Co 5:11 if he . . is an idolater, reviler, drunkard 5
6:10 nor thieves, nor the greedy, nor drunkards 5
1Ti 3: 3 no drunkard, not violent but gentle 7
Tit 1: 7 a drunkard or violent or greedy for gain 7
Sir 19: 1 A workman who is a drunkard will not become rich; 5
4Mc 2: 7 a glutton, or even a drunkard 5

drunken 1. שִׁכֹּר 2. שׁכר 3. μέθυσος 4. μεθύω
1Sm 1:14 How long will you be drunken? Put away your wine 2
Jer 23: 9 I am like a drunken man, like a man overcome 1
Nah 3:11 You also will be drunken, you will be dazed; 2
Mat 24:49 eats and drinks with the drunken 4
Sir 26: 8 There is great anger when a wife is drunken 3
drunken *See also* make, stupor.

drunken man 1. שִׁכֹּר
Job 12:25 he makes them stagger like a drunken man. 1
Ps 107:27 they reeled and staggered like drunken men 1
Isa 19:14 Egypt . . as a drunken man staggers in his vomit. 1
24:20 The earth staggers like a drunken man, it sways 1

drunken woman 1. שִׁכֹּר
1Sm 1:13 therefore Eli took her to be a drunken woman. 1

drunkenness 1. שִׁכָּרוֹן 2. שְׁתִי 3. μέθη 4. οἰνοφλυγία
Ecc 10:17 feast . . for strength, and not for drunkenness! 2
Jer 13:13 will fill with drunkenness all the inhabitants 1
Ezk 23:33 you will be filled with drunkenness and sorrow. 1
Lke 21:34 weighed down with dissipation and drunkenness 3
Rom 13:13 not in reveling and drunkenness 3

Gal 5:21 envy, drunkenness, carousing, and the like 3
1Pe 4: 3 living in . . drunkenness, revels, carousing 4
Tob 4:15 let drunkenness go with you on your way. 3
Sir 31:30 Drunkenness increases the anger of a fool 3

dry 1. חָרֵב 2. חָרֵב חרב 3. חרב 4. יָבֵשׁ 5. יבשׁ 6. צִיָּה 7. צָמֵא 8. צמק 9. ἄνυδρον 10. ἐκκενόω 11. ξηρά 12. ξηρός

Gen 8:13 the waters were dried from off the earth; 3
13 behold, the face of the ground was dry. 3
14 the earth was dry. 5
Lev 7:10 every cereal offering, mixed with oil or dry 2
Num 6: 3 shall not drink . . or eat grapes, fresh or dried. 4
Deu 29:19 lead to the sweeping away of moist and dry alike. 7
Jos 9: 5 and all their provisions were dry and moldy. 4
12 it was still warm . . but now..it is dry and moldy; 4
Jdg 6:37 if there is dew . . and it is dry on all the ground 1
39 let it be dry only on the fleece, and on all 1
40 it was dry on the fleece only, and on all the ground 1
16: 7 fresh bowstrings which have not been dried 3
8 seven fresh bowstrings which had not been dried 3
Job 13:25 thou frighten a driven leaf and pursue dry chaff? 4
Ps 63: 1 my flesh faints for thee, as in a dry and weary land 6
Prv 17: 1 Better is a dry morsel with quiet 2
Isa 19: 5 dried up, and the river will be parched and dry; 3
27:11 When its boughs are dry, they are broken; 5
41:18 a pool of water, and the dry land springs of water. 6
44:27 the LORD . . who says to the deep, 'Be dry, 3
53: 2 a young plant, and like a root out of dry ground; 6
56: 3 let not the eunuch say, "Behold, I am a dry tree. 4
Jer 50:12 last of the nations, a wilderness dry and desert. 6
Lam 4: 8 their skin has . . become as dry as wood. 4
Ezk 17:24 and make the dry tree flourish. 4
19:13 in the wilderness, in a dry and thirsty land. 6
20:47 devour every green tree in you and every dry tree; 4
37: 2 and lo, they were very dry. 4
4 say to them, O dry bones, hear the word of the LORD. 4
Hos 9:14 Give them a miscarrying womb and dry breasts. 8
Nah 1:10 they are consumed, like dry stubble. 4
Lke 23:31 what will happen when it is dry? 12
Heb 11:29 the people crossed the Red Sea as if on dry land 11
Jdt 7:21 their cisterns were going dry 10
Wis 19: 7 and dry land emerging where water had stood before 12
2Mc 1:19 secretly hid it in the hollow of a dry cistern 9
4Mc 18:17 'Shall these dry bones live?' 12

dry *See also* grass, ground, land, make, run, stream-bed, waste.

become dry 1. חרב

Ps 106: 9 He rebuked the Red Sea, and it became dry; 1

make dry 1. יבשׁ

Jer 51:36 I will dry up her sea and make her fountain dry; 1

dry place 1. צָיוֹן

Isa 25: 5 like heat in a dry place. 1
32: 2 like streams of water in a dry place 1

dry rot 1. רָקָב

Hos 5:12 I am . . like dry rot to the house of Judah. 1

dry up 1. הפך 2. חרב 3. יָבֵשׁ 4. יבשׁ 5. נשׁת 6. נתן חָרְבָה 7. καταξηραίνω 8. ξηραίνω 9. arefacio 10. sicco

Gen 8: 7 the waters were dried up from the earth. 4
Num11: 6 now our strength is dried up 3
Jos 2:10 the LORD dried up the water of the Red Sea 4
4:23 LORD . . dried up the waters of the Jordan for you 4
23 Red Sea, which he dried up . . until we passed over 4
5: 1 the LORD had dried up the waters of the Jordan 4
1Kg 13: 4 And his hand, which he stretched out . . dried up 4
17: 7 the brook dried up, because there was no rain 4
2Kg 19:24 I dried up with the sole of my foot all the streams 2
Job 12:15 If he withholds the waters, they dry up; 4
14:11 a river wastes away and dries up 4
15:30 the flame will dry up his shoots 4
18:16 His roots dry up beneath, and his branches wither 4
Ps 22:15 my strength is dried up like a potsherd 4
32: 4 my strength was dried up as by the heat of summer. 1
74:15 thou didst dry up ever-flowing streams. 4
Prv 17:22 but a downcast spirit dries up the bones. 4
Isa 19: 5 the waters of the Nile will be dried up 5
6 branches of Egypt's Nile will diminish and dry up 2
7 all that is sown by the Nile will dry up 4
37:25 I dried up with the sole of my foot all the streams 2
42:15 mountains and hills, and dry up all their herbage; 4
15 the rivers into islands, and dry up the pools. 4
44:27 says to the deep, 'Be dry, I will dry up your rivers 4
50: 2 Behold, by my rebuke I dry up the sea 2
51:10 Was it not thou that didst dry up the sea 2
Jer 23:10 and the pastures of the wilderness are dried up. 4
50:38 drought upon her waters, that they may be dried up! 4
51:36 I will dry up her sea and make her fountain dry; 2
Ezk 17:24 dry up the green tree, and make the dry tree 4
19:12 cast down to the ground; the east wind dried it up; 4
30:12 I will dry up the Nile, and will sell the land 6
37:11 Behold, they say, 'Our bones are dried up 4
Hos 9:16 E'phraim is stricken, their root is dried up 4
13:15 and his fountain shall dry up 4
Jol 1:20 cry to thee because the water brooks are dried up 4
Nah 1: 4 he dries up all the rivers; 2
Zec 10:11 smitten, and all the depths of the Nile dried up. 4
Rev 16:12 the river Euphra'tes, and its water was dried up 8
2Es 6:42 six parts thou didst dry up 10
51 one of the parts which had been dried up 10
8:23 whose look dries up the depths 9
Jdt 5:13 Then God dried up the Red Sea before them 7
Sir 40:13 wealth of the unjust will dry up like a torrent 8

dryshod 1. בַּנְּעָלִים

Isa 11:15 into seven channels that men may cross dryshod. 1

due 1. בַּעַל 2. היה 3. חֹק 4. חֻקָּה 5. יאה 6. כְּ 7. ἀνήκω 8. ἄξιος 9. δεῖ 10. καθήκω 11. κατά 12. ὀφειλή 13. ὀφείλημα 14. πρέπει

Exd 23: 6 not pervert the justice due to your poor in his •
29:28 for Aaron and his sons as a perpetual due 3
Lev 7:34 as a perpetual due from the people of Israel 3
36 it is a perpetual due throughout their 4
10:13 because it is your due and your sons' due 3
13 because it is your due and your sons' due 3
14 for they are given as your due and your sons' due 3
14 for they are given as your due and your sons' due 3
15 it shall be yours, and your sons' with you, as a due 3
24: 9 offerings by fire to the LORD, a perpetual due 3
25:52 according to the years of service due from him •
Num18: 8 as a portion, and to your sons as a perpetual due. 3
11 I have given them . . as a perpetual due; 3
19 I give to you . . as a perpetual due; 3
29 you shall present every offering due to the LORD •
Deu 12:26 the holy things which are due from you 2
18: 3 this shall be the priests' due from the people •
24:17 not pervert the justice due to the sojourner •
27:19 who perverts the justice due to the sojourner •
1Ch 16:29 Ascribe to the LORD the glory due his name; •
2Ch 31: 4 to give the portion due to the priests •
Ps 7:17 to the LORD the thanks due to his righteousness 6
65: 1 Praise is due to thee, O God, in Zion; 14
96: 8 Acribe to the LORD the glory due his name; •
Prv 3:27 Do not withhold good from those to whom it is due 1
Jer 10: 7 For this is thy due; 5
Lke 23:41 we are receiving the due reward of our deeds 8
Rom 1:27 receiving in their own persons the due penalty 9
4: 4 his wages are not reckoned as a gift but as his due. 13
13: 7 Pay all of them their dues 12
7 Pay . . taxes to whom taxes are due •
7 revenue to whom revenue is due •
7 respect to whom respect is due •
7 honor to whom honor is due. •
Rev 16: 6 given them blood to drink. It is their due! 8
Sir 38: 1 Honor the physician with the honor due him •
16 Lay out his body with the honor due him 11
1Mc 10:36 that is due to all the forces of the king. 10
11:35 the other payments henceforth due to us 7
35 the tithes, and the taxes due to us 7
35 the salt pits and the crown taxes due to us 7
2Mc 8:10 to make up for the king the tribute due to the Romans •

due (2) 1. ἴδιος

Gal 6: 9 in due season we shall reap 1

due (3) 1. διά

Eph 4:18 due to their hardness of heart; 1
Jas 1:17 there is no variation or shadow due to change. •
Wis 14:22 they live in great strife due to ignorance •

due *See* reward.

due course 1. tempus

2Es 11:20 in due course the wings that followed also rose 1

due one's office 1. ἐξουσία

2Mc 10:13 Unable to command the respect due his office 1

due order 1. מַעֲרָכָה 2. עֲבוֹדָה

Jdg 6:26 build an altar . . with stones laid in due order; 1
1Ch 6:32 and they performed their service in due order. 2

rightful due 1. נַחֲלָה

Deu 18: 1 offerings . . to the LORD, and his rightful dues. 1

due season 1. מוֹעֵד 2. עֵת 3. tempus

Num28: 2 take heed to offer to me in its due season.' 1
Ps 104:27 to give them their food in due season. 2
145:15 thou gives them their food in due season. 2
2Es 8:41 all that have been sown will come up in due season 3
43 it has not received thy rain in due season 3

due time 1. תְּקוּפוֹת הַיָּמִים 2. καιρός 3. tempus

1Sm 1:20 in due time Hannah conceived and bore a son 1
1Pe 5: 6 that in due time he may exalt you. 2
2Es 10:16 you will receive your son back in due time 3
14:32 in due time he took from you what he had given. 3

dull 1. בער 2. בַּעַר 3. כבד 4. כֵּהֶה 5. νωθρός

Lev 13:39 spots on the skin of the body are of a dull white 4
Ps 92: 6 The dull man cannot know 2
94: 8 Understand, O dullest of the people! 1
Isa 59: 1 cannot save, or his ear dull, that it cannot hear; 3
Heb 5:11 since you have become dull of hearing. 5

dull *See also* grow.

dullness 1. מְגִנָּה

Lam 3:65 Thou wilt give them dullness of heart; 1

dumb 1. אלם 2. אִלֵּם 3. דּוּמָם 4. ἄλαλος 5. ἄφωνος 6. κωφός 7. mutus

Exd 4:11 Who makes him dumb, or deaf, or seeing 2
Ps 31:18 Let the lying lips be dumb 1
39: 2 I was dumb and silent, I held my peace to no avail; 1
9 I am dumb, I do not open my mouth; 1
Prv 31: 8 Open your mouth for the dumb 2
Isa 35: 6 and the tongue of the dumb sing for joy. 2
53: 7 and like a sheep that before its shearers is dumb 1
56:10 they are all dumb dogs, they cannot bark; 2
Ezk 3:26 so that you shall be dumb and unable to reprove 1
24:27 you shall speak and be no longer dumb. 1
33:22 my mouth was opened, and I was no longer dumb. 1
Dan 10:15 turned my face toward the ground and was dumb. 1
Hab 2:18 in his own creation when he makes dumb idols! 2
19 to a wooden thing, Awake; to a dumb stone, Arise! 3
Mat 9:32 behold, a dumb demoniac was brought to him. 6
12:22 Then a blind and dumb demoniac was brought to him 6
15:30 the lame, the maimed, the blind, the dumb 6
31 when they saw the dumb speaking 6
Mrk 7:37 he even makes the deaf hear and the dumb speak. 4
9:17 I brought my son to you, for he has a dumb spirit; 4
25 You dumb and deaf spirit, I command you 4
Lke 1:22 he made signs to them and remained dumb. 6
11:14 Now he was casting out a demon that was dumb 6
Act 8:32 As . . a lamb before its shearer is dumb 5
1Co 12: 2 you were led astray to dumb idols 5
2Pe 2:16 a dumb ass spoke with human voice 5
2Es 6:48 The dumb and lifeless water 7
Wis 10:21 because wisdom opened the mouth of the dumb 6

dumb man 1. אִלֵּם 2. ἐνεός 3. κωφός

Ps 38:13 like a dumb man who does not open his mouth. 1
Mat 9:33 the dumb man spoke; and the crowds marveled 3
12:22 he healed him, so that the dumb man spoke and saw. 3
Lke 11:14 when the demon had gone out, the dumb man spoke 3
LJr 1:41 when they see a dumb man, who cannot speak 2

dumbfounded *See* go.

dung 1. גֵּל 2. גָּלָל 3. דֹּמֶן 4. חֶרֶא 5. פֶּרֶשׁ 6. צְפִיעַ 7. κόπριον 8. stercus

Exd 29:14 the flesh of the bull, and its skin, and its dung 5
Lev 4:11 head, its legs, its entrails, and its dung 5
8:17 the bull, and its skin, and its flesh, and its dung 5
16:27 their skin and their flesh and their dung 5
Num19: 5 flesh, and her blood, with her dung, shall be burned; 5
1Kg 14:10 as a man burns up dung until it is all gone. 2
2Kg 6:25 part of a kab of dove's dung for five shekels 4
9:37 Jez'ebel shall be as dung upon the . . field 3
18:27 to eat their own dung and to drink their own urine? 4
Job 20: 7 he will perish for ever like his own dung; 1
Ps 83:10 who became dung for the ground. 3
Isa 36:12 to eat their own dung and drink their own urine? 4
Jer 8: 2 they shall be as dung on the . . ground. 3
9:22 men shall fall like dung upon the open field 3
16: 4 they shall be as dung 3
25:33 they shall be dung on the surface of the ground. 3
Ezk 4:12 cake, baking it in their sight on human dung. 2
15 let you have cow's dung instead of human dung 6
15 let you have cow's dung instead of human dung 1
Zep 1:17 poured out like dust, and their flesh like dung. 1
Mal 2: 3 will rebuke . . and spread dung upon your faces 5
3 dung upon your faces, the dung of your offerings 5
2Es 16:23 the dead shall be cast out like dung 8
AEs 14: 2 she covered her head with ashes and dung 7
1Mc 2:62 his splendor will turn into dung and worms. 7

dung-pit 1. מַדְמֵנָה

Isa 25:10 as straw is trodden down in a dung-pit. 1

dungeon 1. בּוֹר 2. בֵּית הַבּוֹר 3. מַסְגֵּר 4. λάκκος

Gen 40:15 that they should put me into the dungeon. 1
41:14 brought him hastily out of the dungeon; 1
Exd 12:29 to the first-born of the captive . . in the dungeon 2
Isa 42: 7 to bring out the prisoners from the dungeon 3
Jer 37:16 When Jeremiah had come to the dungeon cells 1
Wis 10:13 She descended with him into the dungeon 4

dunghill 1. נְוָלוּ (A) 2. κοπρία 3. κόπριον

Ezr 6:11 his house shall be made a dunghill. 1
Lke 14:35 is fit neither for the land nor for the dunghill; 2
Sir 22: 2 may be compared to the filth of dunghills 3

duration 1. χρόνος

3Mc 5:22 employ the duration of the night in sleep 1

during 1. בְּ 2. בְּ (A) 3. διά 4. ἐν 5. ἐν ἡμέραις 6. ἐπί 7. χρόνος 8. in 9. per 10. sub

Gen 41:34 the land of Egypt during the seven plenteous 1
47 During the seven plenteous years the earth 1
Lev 15:20 upon which she lies during her impurity 1

Num27:14 during the strife of the congregation 1
Jdg 16:30 more than those whom he had slain during his life. 1
2Kg 23:22 or during all the days of the kings of Israel •
Neh 8:14 Israel . . dwell in booths during the feast 1
Ecc 2: 3 to do . . during the few days of their life. •
Ezk 4: 9 During the number of days that you lie upon •
36:38 flock at Jerusalem during her appointed feasts 1
Dan 6:28 Daniel prospered during the reign of Darius 2
Mat 26: 5 Not during the feast, lest there be a tumult 4
Mrk 14: 2 Not during the feast, lest there be a tumult 4
Joh 13: 2 during supper •
Act 1: 3 appearing to them during 40 days 3
21 during all the time that the Lord Jesus went 4
12: 3 This was during the days of Unleavened Bread. •
13:17 during their stay in the land of Egypt 4
Rom 7: 1 law is binding on a person only during his life 7
Phm 1:13 during my imprisonment for the gospel; 4
1Pe 3:20 during the building of the ark •
Rev 11: 6 no rain . . during the days of their prophesying •
2Es 3:29 has seen many sinners during these 30 years ‡
5:53 those born during the time of old age 10
7:89 During the time that they lived in it 8
101 during these seven days they may see the things 8
9:23 do not fast during them, however; 8
44 every hour and every day during those 30 years 8
12:51 and my food was of plants during those days. 8
14:42 They sat 40 days, and wrote during the daytime 9
44 during the 40 days 94 books were written. 8
Jdt 2:27 he went down . . during the wheat harvest 5
8: 2 died during the barley harvest. 4
14: 8 Now tell me what you have done during these days. 4
2Mc 10: 6 not long before, during the feast of booths •
14: 4 During that day he kept quiet. •
3Mc 4:10 during the whole voyage •
7:19 they decided . . during the time of their stay. 6
4Mc 6:20 and during that time be a laughing stock to all •
13:20 and was shaped during the same period of time 4

during the day 1. interdie

2Es 5: 4 and the moon during the day. 1

dust 1. אָבָק 2. אֶרֶץ 3. דַּכָּא 4. עָפָר 5. שַׁחַק 6. *ἄμμος* 7. *γῆ* 8. *κονιορτός* 9. *κόνις* 10. *χοϊκός* 11. *χοῦς* 12. pulvis

Gen 2: 7 the LORD God formed man of dust from the ground 4
3:14 belly you shall go, and dust you shall eat 4
19 you are dust, and to dust you shall return. 4
19 you are dust, and to dust you shall return. 4
13:16 your descendants as the dust of the earth; 4
16 that if one can count the dust of the earth 4
18:27 to the Lord, I who am but dust and ashes. 4
28:14 descendants shall be like the dust of the earth 4
Exd 8:16 your rod and strike the dust of the earth 4
17 Aaron . . struck the dust of the earth 4
17 all the dust of the earth became gnats 4
Lev 17:13 shall pour out its blood and cover it with dust 4
Num 5:17 take some of the dust that is on the floor 4
23:10 Who can count the dust of Jacob, or number 4
Deu 9:21 grinding it . . until it was as fine as dust; 4
21 I threw the dust of it into the brook 4
28:24 will make the rain of your land powder and dust; 4
32:24 with venom of crawling things of the dust. 4
Jos 7: 6 and they put dust upon their heads. 4
1Sm 2: 8 He raises up the poor from the dust; 4
2Sm 16:13 cursed . . and threw stones at him and flung dust. 4
22:43 I beat them fine as the dust of the earth 4
1Kg 16: 2 I exalted you out of the dust and made you leader 4
18:38 and the wood, and the stones, and the dust 4
20:10 the dust of Sama′ria shall suffice for handfuls 4
2Kg 13: 7 and made them like the dust at threshing. 4
23: 6 burned it . . and beat it to dust and cast the dust 4
6 beat it . . and cast the dust of it upon the graves 4
12 and cast the dust of them into the brook Kidron. 4
15 broke in pieces its stones, crushing them to dust; 4
2Ch 1: 9 over a people as many as the dust of the earth. 4
Job 2:12 sprinkled dust upon their heads toward heaven. 4
4:19 houses of clay, whose foundation is in the dust 4
5: 6 For affliction does not come from the dust 4
10: 9 wilt thou turn me to dust again? 4
16:15 and have laid my strength in the dust. 4
17:16 Shall we descend together into the dust? 4
20:11 vigor, but it will lie down with him in the dust. 4
21:26 They lie down alike in the dust 4
22:24 if you lay gold in the dust 4
27:16 Though he heap up silver like dust 4
28: 6 place of sapphires, and it has dust of gold. 4
30:19 I have become like dust and ashes. 4
34:15 man would return to dust. 4
38:38 when the dust runs into a mass 4
40:13 Hide them all in the dust together; 4
42: 6 I despise myself, and repent in dust and ashes. 4
Ps 7: 5 my life to the ground, and lay my soul in the dust. 4
18:42 I beat them fine as dust before the wind; 4
22:15 thou dost lay me in the dust of death. 4
29 before him shall bow all who go down to the dust 4
30: 9 Will the dust praise thee? 4
44:25 For our soul is bowed down to the dust; 4
72: 9 his enemies lick the dust! 4
78:27 he rained flesh upon them like dust 4
89:39 thou hast defiled his crown in the dust. 2
90: 3 Thou turnest man back to the dust, and sayest 3
102:14 For thy servants . . have pity on her dust. 4
103:14 knows our frame; he remembers that we are dust. 4
104:29 they die and return to their dust. 4
113: 7 He raises the poor from the dust 4
119:25 My soul cleaves to the dust; 4
Prv 8:26 first of the dust of the world. 4
Ecc 3:20 all are from the dust, and all turn to dust again. 4
20 all are from the dust, and all turn to dust again. 4
12: 7 and the dust returns to the earth as it was 4
Isa 2:10 hide in the dust from . . the terror of the LORD 4
5:24 as rottenness, and their blossom go up like dust; 1
25:12 cast to the ground, even to the dust. 4
26: 5 lays it low to the ground, casts it to the dust. 4
19 O dwellers in the dust, awake and sing for joy! 4
29: 4 from low in the dust your words shall come; 4
4 and your speech shall whisper out of the dust. 4
5 your foes shall be like small dust 1
40:12 enclosed the dust of the earth in a measure 4
15 and are accounted as the dust on the scales; 5
41: 2 he makes them like dust with his sword 4
47: 1 and sit in the dust, O virgin daughter of Babylon; 4
49:23 bow down to you, and lick the dust of your feet. 4
52: 2 Shake yourself from the dust, arise, O captive 4
65:25 and dust shall be the serpent's food. 4
Lam 2:10 they have cast dust on their heads 4
21 In the dust of . . streets lie the young and the old; 2
3:29 let him put his mouth in the dust 4
Ezk 24: 7 not pour it upon the ground to cover it with dust. 4
26:10 will be so many that their dust will cover you; 1
27:30 They cast dust on their heads and wallow in ashes; 4
Dan 12: 2 many of those who sleep in the dust of the earth 4
Mic 1:10 in Beth-le-aph′rah roll yourselves in the dust. 4
7:17 they shall lick the dust like a serpent 4
Nah 1: 3 and the clouds are the dust of his feet. 1
Zep 1:17 their blood shall be poured out like dust 4
Zec 9: 3 heaped up silver like dust, and gold like the dirt 4
Mat 10:14 shake off the dust from your feet as you leave 8
Mrk 6:11 shake off the dust that is on your feet 11
Lke 9: 5 shake off the dust from your feet 8
10:11 'Even the dust of your town that clings to our feet 8
Act 13:51 they shook off the dust from their feet against them 8
22:23 waved their garments and threw dust into the air 8
1Co 15:47 The first man was from the earth, a man of dust 10
48 As was the man of dust 10
48 so are those who are of the dust 10
49 Just as we have borne the image of the man of dust 10
Rev 18:19 And they threw dust on their heads, as they wept 11
2Es 3: 4 and didst command the dust ‡
7:32 and the dust those who dwell silently in it 12
62 if the mind is made out of the dust 12
63 better if the dust itself had not been born 12
8: 2 but only a little dust from which gold comes 12
13:11 but only the dust of ashes and the smell of smoke. 12
15:44 then the dust and smoke shall go up to heaven 12
Tob 3: 6 that I may depart and become dust 7
Jdt 2:20 like the dust of the earth 6
Sir 10: 9 How can he who is dust and ashes be proud? 7
17:32 all men are dust and ashes. 7
33:10 Adam was created of the dust. 7
40: 3 the one who is humbled in dust and ashes 7
41:10 Whatever is from the dust returns to dust 7
10 Whatever is from the dust returns to dust 7
44:21 he would multiply him like the dust of the earth 11
LJr 1:13 because of the dust from the temple 8
17 the dust raised by the feet of those who enter. 8
1Mc 2:63 because he has returned to the dust 11
11:71 put dust on his head, and prayed. 7
2Mc 10:25 his men sprinkled dust upon their heads 7
14:15 they sprinkled dust upon their heads 7
3Mc 1:18 sprinkled their hair with dust 9
5:48 the Jews saw the dust raised by the elephants 8

dust *See also* fling, make.

fine dust 1. אָבָק 2. דַּק

Exd 9: 9 it shall become fine dust over all the land 1
Isa 40:15 behold, he takes up the isles like fine dust. 2

whirling dust 1. גַּלְגַּל

Ps 83:13 O my God, make them like whirling dust 1
Isa 17:13 the wind and whirling dust before the storm. 1

duty 1. דָּבָר 2. מְלָאכָה 3. מַעֲמָד 4. מִשְׁמָר 5. מִשְׁמֶרֶת 6. מִשְׁפָּט 7. עֲבֹדָה 8. *ἐφημερία* 9. *καθήκω* 10. *ὀφείλω* 11. *τάξις* 12. *χρεία*

Num 3: 7 They shall perform duties for him 5
8 shall . . attend to the duties for the people 5
28 8,600, attending to the duties of the sanctuary. 5
8:26 do to the Levites in assigning their duties. 5
18: 3 attend you and attend to all duties of the tent; •
5 you shall attend to the duties of the sanctuary 5
5 you shall attend to . . the duties of the altar 5
1Sm 10:25 told . . the rights and duties of the kingship; 6
2Kg 11: 7 two . . which come on duty in force on the sabbath •
9 with those who were to come on duty on the sabbath •
1Ch 9:33 for they were on duty day and night. 2
23:28 their duty shall be to assist the sons of Aaron 3
25: 1 list of those who did the work and of their duties 7
8 they cast lots for their duties, small and great 5
26:12 corresponding to their chief men, had duties 4
29 appointed to outside duties for Israel 2
2Ch 5:13 it was the duty of the trumpeters and singers •
8:13 as the duty of each day required 1
14 he appointed . . as the duty of each day required 1
23: 8 with those who were to come on duty on the sabbath; •
31:16 entered . . as the duty of each day required 1
Neh 13:13 their duty was to distribute to their brethren. •
30 established the duties of the priests 4
Ecc 12:13 Fear God . . for this is the whole duty of man. •
Ezk 18:11 who does none of these duties •
45:17 the prince's duty to furnish the burnt offerings •
Lke 1: 8 when his division was on duty 11
17:10 we have only done what was our duty.' 10
Act 6: 3 whom we may appoint to this duty. 12
1Ti 4:15 Practice these duties, devote yourself to them •
6: 2 Teach and urge these duties. •
1Es 1:16 no one needed to depart from his duties 8
Tob 1: 8 I would give to those to whom it was my duty 9
Sir 32: 2 when you have fulfilled your duties 12
2Mc 2:30 It is the duty of the original historian 9

duty *See also* off.

appointed duty 1. פְּקֻדָּה

1Ch 24: 3 to the appointed duties in their service. 1
19 had as their appointed duty in their service 1

duty of watching 1. מִשְׁמֶרֶת

1Ch 9:27 for upon them lay the duty of watching 1

religious duty 1. *εὐσεβέω*

1Ti 5: 4 learn their religious duty to their own family 1

ritual duty 1. *λατρεία*

Heb 9: 6 priests . . performing their ritual duties; 1

dwarf 1. דַּק

Lev 21:20 or a hunchback, or a dwarf, or a man with a defect 1

dwell 1. גור 2. דור 3. ישב 4. לון 5. מוֹשָׁב 6. מִשְׁכָּן 7. עמד 8. שכן 9. דור (A) 10. שכן (A) 11. שרא (A) 12. *εἰμί* 13. *ἐνοικέω* 14. *κάθημαι* 15. *καθίζω* 16. *καθίστημι* 17. *καταλύω* 18. *κατασκηνόω* 19. *κατασκήνωσις* 20. *κατοικέω* 21. *κατοίκησις* 22. *κατοίκος* 23. *μένω* 24. *οἰκέω* 25. *οἰκήτωρ* 26. *οἶκος* 27. *σκηνόω* 28. *συνοικέω* 29. commoror 30. habito 31. inhabito

Gen 4:16 Cain . . dwelt in the land of Nod, east of Eden. 3
20 father of those who dwell in tents 3
9:27 Japheth, and let him dwell in the tents of Shem; 8
13: 6 support both of them dwelling together; 3
6 great that they could not dwell together 3
7 the Per′izzites dwelt in the land. 3
12 Abram dwelt in the land of Canaan 3
12 while Lot dwelt among the cities of the valley 3
18 and came and dwelt by the oaks of Mamre 3
14: 7 also the Amorites who dwelt in Haz′azon-ta′mar. 3
12 son of Abram's brother, who dwelt in Sodom 3
16: 3 after Abram had dwelt ten years in the land 3
12 he shall dwell over against all his kinsmen. 8
19:29 when he overthrew the cities in which Lot dwelt. 3
30 Lot went up out of Zo′ar, and dwelt in the hills 3
30 for he was afraid to dwell in Zo′ar; 3
30 Lot . . dwelt in the hills with his two daughters 3
20: 1 of the Negeb, and dwelt between Kadesh and Shur; 3
15 land is before you; dwell where it pleases you. 3
22:19 and Abraham dwelt at Beer-sheba. 3
24: 3 daughters of the Canaanites, among whom I dwell 3
37 of the Canaanites, in whose land I dwell; 3
62 Isaac . . was dwelling in the Negeb. 3
25:11 And Isaac dwelt at Beer-la′hai-roi. 3
18 They dwelt from Hav′ilah to Shur 8
27 Jacob was a quiet man, dwelling in tents. 3
26: 2 Do not go down to Egypt; dwell in the land of which I 8
6 Isaac dwelt in Gerar. 3
17 in the valley of Gerar and dwelt there. 3
34:10 You shall dwell with us; and the land shall be open 3
10 the land shall be open to you; dwell and trade in it 3
16 we will dwell with you and become one people. 3
21 let them dwell in the land and trade in it 3
22 condition will the men agree to dwell with us 3
23 agree with them, and they will dwell with us. 3
35: 1 Arise, go up to Bethel, and dwell there; 3
22 While Israel dwelt in that land Reuben went 8
36: 7 were too great for them to dwell together; 3
8 Esau dwelt in the hill country of Se′ir; 3
37: 1 Jacob dwelt in the land of his father's 3
38:11 Tamar went and dwelt in her father's house. 3
45:10 you shall dwell in the land of Goshen 3
46:34 in order that you may dwell in the land of Goshen; 3
47: 4 let your servants dwell in the land of Goshen. 3
6 let them dwell in the land of Goshen; 3
27 Thus Israel dwelt in the land of Egypt 3
49:13 Zeb′ulun shall dwell at the shore of the sea; 8

50:22 Joseph dwelt in Egypt, he and his father's house; 3
Exd 2:21 Moses was content to dwell with the man 3
6: 4 the land in which they dwelt as sojourners. 1
8:22 the land of Goshen, where my people dwell 7
10:23 people of Israel had light where they dwelt. 5
12:40 The time that the people of Israel dwelt in Egypt 3
23:33 They shall not dwell in your land, lest they make 3
25: 8 sanctuary, that I may dwell in their midst. 8
29:45 I will dwell among the people of Israel 8
46 out of . . Egypt that I might dwell among them; 8
Lev 13:46 he shall dwell alone in a habitation outside 3
14: 8 but shall dwell outside his tent seven days 3
18: 3 in the land of Egypt, where you dwelt 3
20:22 that the land where I am bringing you to dwell 3
23:42 You shall dwell in booths for seven days 3
42 all . . in Israel shall dwell in booths 3
25:18 so you will dwell in the land securely 3
19 you will eat your fill, and dwell in it securely 3
29 If a man sells a dwelling house in a walled city 5
26: 5 you shall . . dwell in your land securely 3
35 in your sabbaths when you dwelt upon it 3
Num 5: 3 their camp, in the midst of which I dwell. 8
13:18 whether the people who dwell in it are strong 3
19 whether the land that they dwell in is good or bad 3
19 whether the cities that they dwell in are camps 3
28 Yet the people who dwell in the land are strong 3
29 Amal'ekites dwell in the land of the Negeb; 3
29 Amorites dwell in the hill country; 3
29 Canaanites dwell by the sea, and along the Jordan. 3
14:25 Canaanites dwell in the valleys 3
45 Canaanites who dwelt in that hill country 3
20:15 we dwelt in Egypt a long time; 3
21: 1 Canaanite, the king of Arad, who dwelt in the Negeb 3
31 Thus Israel dwelt in the land of the Amorites. 3
34 as you did to Sihon . . who dwelt at Heshbon. 3
22: 5 they are dwelling opposite me. 3
23: 9 lo, a people dwelling alone 8
25: 1 While Israel dwelt in Shittim the people 3
33:40 king of Arad, who dwelt in the Negeb in . . Canaan 3
55 shall trouble you in the land where you dwell. 3
35: 2 give to the Levites . . cities to dwell in; 3
3 The cities shall be theirs to dwell 3
32 no ransom . . that he may return to dwell in the land 3
34 land . . in the midst of which I dwell; 8
34 LORD dwell in the midst of the people of Israel. 8
Deu 3: 2 king of the Amorites, who dwelt at Heshbon.' 3
12:29 dispossess them and dwell in their land 3
13:12 cities, which the LORD . . gives you to dwell there 3
17:14 come to the land . . possess it and dwell in it 3
19: 1 dispossess them and dwell in their cities 3
23:16 he shall dwell with you, in your midst, in the place 3
25: 5 If brothers dwell together, and one of them dies 3
28:30 shall build a house, and you shall not dwell in it; 3
29:16 You know how we dwelt in the land of Egypt 3
30:20 you may dwell in the land which the LORD swore 3
33:12 The beloved of the LORD, he dwells in safety by him; 8
16 with the . . favor of him that dwelt in the bush. 8
28 Israel dwelt in safety, the fountain of Jacob 8
Jos 2:15 house was built . . so that she dwelt in the wall. 3
6:25 and she dwelt in Israel to this day 3
7: 7 we had been content to dwell beyond the Jordan! 3
9:10 and Og king of Bashan, who dwelt in Ash'taroth. •
16 they heard . . and that they dwelt among them. 3
22 Why did you deceive us . . when you dwell among us? 3
10: 6 of the Amorites that dwell in the hill country 3
12: 2 Sihon king of the Amorites who dwelt at Heshbon 3
4 and Og . . who dwelt at Ash'taroth and at Ed're-i 3
13:13 Geshur and Ma'acath dwell in the midst of Israel 3
21 the princes of Sihon, who dwelt in the land. 3
14: 4 no portion was . . but only cities to dwell 3
15:63 so the Jeb'usites dwell with the people of Judah 3
16:10 not drive out the Canaanites that dwelt in Gezer 3
10 the Canaanites have dwelt in the midst 3
17:12 Canaanites persisted in dwelling in that land. 3
16 all the Canaanites who dwell in the plain have 3
21: 2 LORD commanded . . we be given cities to dwell 3
24:13 cities . . you had not built, and you dwell therein; 3
15 the gods of the Amorites in whose land you dwell; 3
Jdg 1: 9 Canaanites who dwelt in the hill country 3
10 went against the Canaanites who dwelt in Hebron 3
21 drive out the Jeb'usites who dwelt in Jerusalem; 3
21 so the Jeb'usites have dwelt with the people 3
27 Canaanites persisted in dwelling in that land. 3
29 not drive out the Canaanites who dwelt in Gezer; 3
29 but the Canaanites dwelt in Gezer among them. 3
30 Canaanites dwelt among them, and became subject 3
32 the Asherites dwelt among the Canaanites 3
33 not drive out . . but dwelt among the Canaanites 3
35 the Amorites persisted in dwelling in Har-heres 3
3: 3 and the Hivites who dwelt on Mount Lebanon 3
5 Israel dwelt among the Canaanites, the Hittites 3
4: 2 army was Sis'era, who dwelt in Haro'sheth-ha-goiim. 3
5:24 be Ja'el . . of tent-dwelling women most blessed. •
6:10 the gods of the Amorites, in whose land you dwell 3
8:29 Jerubba'al . . went and dwelt in his own house. 3
9:21 Jotham . . fled, and went to Beer and dwelt there 3
41 Abim'elech dwelt at Aru'mah; and Zebul drove out 3
11: 3 Jephthah fled . . and dwelt in the land of Tob; 3
26 While Israel dwelt in Heshbon and its villages 3
17:11 And the Levite was content to dwell with the man; 3
18: 1 was seeking . . an inheritance to dwell in; 3
7 saw the people . . how they dwelt in security 3
28 And they rebuilt the city, and dwelt in it. 3
21:23 and rebuilt the towns, and dwelt in them. 3
1Sm 12:11 and delivered you . . and you dwelt in safety. 3
19:18 And he and Samuel went and dwelt at Nai'oth. 3
23:29 David . . dwelt in the strongholds of En-ge'di. 3
27: 3 David dwelt with A'chish at Gath, he and his men 3
5 let a place be given me . . that I may dwell there; 3
5 why should your servant dwell in the royal city 3
7 David dwelt in the country of the Philistines 3
11 he dwelt in the country of the Philistines. 3
31: 7 and the Philistines came and dwelt in them. 3
2Sm 2: 3 and they dwelt in the towns of Hebron. 3
5: 9 And David dwelt in the stronghold 3
7: 1 Now when the king dwelt in his house, and the LORD 3
2 I dwell in a house of cedar, but the ark 3
2 I dwell . . but the ark of God dwells in a tent. 3
5 Would you build me a house to dwell in? 3
6 I have not dwelt in a house since . . I brought up 3
10 that they may dwell in their own place 8
9:12 all who dwelt in Ziba's house became 5
13 Mephib'osheth dwelt in Jerusalem; 3
11:11 The ark and Israel and Judah dwell in booths; 3
13:20 Tamar dwelt, a desolate woman, in . . Ab'salom's 3
14:28 Ab'salom dwelt two full years in Jerusalem 3
15: 8 vowed a vow while I dwelt at Geshur in Aram, saying 3
1Kg 2:36 a house . . and dwell there, and do not go forth 3
38 So Shim'e-i dwelt in Jerusalem many days. 3
3:17 my lord, this woman and I dwell in the same house; 3
4:25 Judah and Israel dwelt in safety, from Dan even 3
6:13 I will dwell among the children of Israel 8
7: 8 His own house where he was to dwell . . was of like 3
8:12 said that he would dwell in thick darkness. 8
13 house, a place for thee to dwell in for ever. 3
27 But will God indeed dwell on the earth? 3
30 hear thou in heaven thy dwelling place; 3
39 hear . . in heaven thy dwelling place, and forgive 3
43 hear thou in heaven thy dwelling place 3
49 hear thou in heaven thy dwelling place 3
9:16 had slain the Canaanites who dwelt in the city 3
11:24 they went to Damascus and dwelt there 3
12:17 people of Israel who dwelt in the cities of Judah. 3
25 Jerobo'am built Shechem . . and dwelt there; 3
13:11 there dwelt an old prophet in Bethel. 3
25 told it in the city where the old prophet dwelt. 3
15:18 sent them to Ben-ha'dad . . who dwelt in Damascus 3
21 stopped building Ramah, and he dwelt in Tirzah. 3
17: 5 he went and dwelt by the brook Cherith 3
9 Arise, go to Zar'ephath . . and dwell there. 3
21: 8 the elders and the nobles who dwelt with Naboth 3
11 the elders and the nobles who dwelt in his city 3
2Kg 4:13 She answered, "I dwell among my own people. 3
6: 1 the place where we dwell . . is too small for us. 3
2 and let us make a place for us to dwell there. 3
13: 5 and the people of Israel dwelt in their homes 3
15: 5 he was a leper . . and he dwelt in a separate house. 3
16: 6 came to Elath, where they dwell to this day. 3
17:24 possession of Sama'ria, and dwelt in its cities. 3
25 at the beginning of their dwelling there 3
27 let him go and dwell there, and teach them the law 3
28 one of the priests . . came and dwelt in Bethel 3
29 every nation in the cities in which they dwelt; 3
19:36 Sennach'erib . . went home, and dwelt at Nin'eveh. 3
22:14 (now she dwelt in Jerusalem in the Second Quarter); 3
25:24 dwell in the land, and serve the king of Babylon 3
1Ch 2:55 families also of the scribes that dwelt at Jabez 3
4:23 they dwelt there with the king for his work. 3
28 They dwelt in Beer-sheba, Mola'dah, Ha'zar-shu'al 3
43 and they have dwelt there to this day. 3
5: 8 Bela . . son of Jo'el, who dwelt in Aro'er 3
9 He also dwelt to the east as far as the entrance 3
10 they dwelt in their tents throughout all 3
11 The sons of Gad dwelt . . in the land of Bashan 3
16 they dwelt in Gilead, in Bashan and in its towns 3
22 And they dwelt in their place until the exile. 3
23 the half-tribe of Manas'seh dwelt in the land 3
7:29 In these dwelt the sons of Joseph 3
8:28 These dwelt in Jerusalem. 3
29 Je-i'el the father of Gibeon dwelt in Gibeon 3
32 Now these also dwelt opposite their kinsmen. 3
9: 2 the first to dwell again in their possessions 3
3 some of the people . . dwelt in Jerusalem 3
16 who dwelt in the villages of the Netoph'athites. 3
33 dwelling in the chambers of the temple •
35 In Gibeon dwelt the father of Gibeon, Je-i'el 3
38 these also dwelt opposite their kinsmen 3
10: 7 the Philistines came and dwelt in them. 3
11: 7 David dwelt in the stronghold; 3
17: 1 Now when David dwelt in his house 3
1 Behold, I dwell in a house of cedar 3
4 You shall not build me a house to dwell in. 3
5 not dwelt in a house since the day I led up Israel 3
9 plant them, that they may dwell in their own place 8
23:25 and he dwells in Jerusalem for ever. 8
2Ch 2: 3 sent him cedar to build himself a house to dwell 3
6: 1 said that he would dwell in thick darkness. 8
2 exalted house, a place for thee to dwell 3
18 will God dwell indeed with man on the earth? 3
21 yea, hear thou from heaven thy dwelling place; 3
30 then hear thou from heaven thy dwelling place 3
33 hear thou from heaven thy dwelling place, and do 3
39 hear thou from heaven thy dwelling place 3
10:17 the people . . who dwelt in the cities of Judah. 3
11: 5 Rehobo'am dwelt in Jerusalem 3
16: 2 Ben-ha'dad king of Syria, who dwelt in Damascus 3
19: 4 Jehosh'aphat dwelt at Jerusalem; 3
20: 8 they have dwelt in it 3
26: 7 against the Arabs that dwelt in Gurba'al 3
21 being a leper dwelt in a separate house 3
30:25 sojourners who dwelt in Judah 3
34:22 now she dwelt in Jerusalem in the Second Quarter 3
Neh 8:14 people of Israel should dwell in booths during 3
17 assembly . . made booths and dwelt in the booths; 3
Job 3: 5 deep darkness claim it. Let clouds dwell upon it; 8
4:19 how much more those who dwell in houses of clay 8
11:14 let not wickedness dwell in your tents. 8
17: 2 my eye dwells on their provocation. 4
18:15 In his tent dwells that which is none of his; 8
21:28 Where is the tent in which the wicked dwelt?' 6
22: 8 the land, and the favored man dwelt in it. 3
29:25 as chief, and I dwelt like a king among his troops 8
30: 6 In the gullies of the torrents they must dwell 3
39:28 On the rock he dwells and makes his home 8
Ps 9:11 Sing praises to the LORD, who dwells in Zion! 3
15: 1 Who shall dwell on thy holy hill? 8
16: 9 my soul rejoices; my body also dwells secure. 8
23: 6 I shall dwell in the house of the LORD for ever. 3
24: 1 the world and those who dwell therein; 3
26: 8 thy house, and the place where thy glory dwells. 6
27: 4 that I may dwell in the house of the LORD 3
37: 3 you will dwell in the land, and enjoy security. 8
29 possess the land, and dwell upon it for ever. 8
61: 4 Let me dwell in thy tent for ever! 1
65: 4 choose and bring near, to dwell in thy courts! 8
8 those who dwell at earth's farthest bounds 3
68: 6 God gives the desolate a home to dwell in; 3
6 but the rebellious dwell in a parched land. 8
16 yea, where the LORD will dwell for ever! 8
18 that the LORD God may dwell there. 8
30 Rebuke the beasts that dwell among the reeds •
69:25 let no one dwell in their tents. 3
35 his servants shall dwell there and possess it; 3
36 those who love his name shall dwell in it. 8
74: 2 Remember Mount Zion, where thou hast dwelt. 8
78:60 at Shiloh, the tent where he dwelt among men 18
84: 4 Blessed are those who dwell in thy house 3
10 than dwell in the tents of wickedness. 2
85: 9 that glory may dwell in our land. 8
91: 1 He who dwells in the shelter of the Most High 3
94:17 soul . . soon have dwelt in the land of silence. 8
98: 7 world and those who dwell in it! 3
101: 6 faithful in the land, that they may dwell with me; 3
7 no . . practices deceit shall dwell in my house; 3
107: 4 finding no way to a city to dwell in; 5
7 straight way, till they reached a city to dwell 5
36 there he lets the hungry dwell 3
120: 5 Woe is me, that . . I dwell among the tents of Kedar! 8
132:14 here I will dwell, for I have desired it. 3
133: 1 how good . . it is when brothers dwell in unity! 3
135:21 Blessed . . from Zion, he who dwells in Jerusalem! 8
139: 9 dwell in the uttermost parts of the sea 8
140:13 upright shall dwell in thy presence. 3
Prv 1:33 he who listens to me will dwell secure 8
3:29 neighbor who dwells trustingly beside you. 3
8:12 I, wisdom, dwell in prudence 8
10:30 but the wicked will not dwell in the land. 8
Sng 8:13 O you who dwell in the gardens . . let me hear it. 3
Isa 6: 5 I dwell in the midst of a people of unclean lips; 3
8:18 the LORD of hosts, who dwells on Mount Zion. 8
9: 2 those who dwelt in a land of deep darkness 3
10:24 O my people, who dwell in Zion, be not afraid 3
11: 6 The wolf shall dwell with the lamb 1
13:20 It will never be inhabited or dwelt 8
21 its houses . . there ostriches will dwell 8
18: 3 inhabitants . . you who dwell on the earth 8
23:18 clothing for those who dwell before the LORD. 3
30:19 Yea, O people in Zion who dwell at Jerusalem; 3
32:16 Then justice will dwell in the wilderness 8
33: 5 The LORD is exalted, for he dwells on high; 8
14 Who among us can dwell with the devouring fire? 1
14 Who . . can dwell with everlasting burnings? 1
16 he will dwell on the heights; 8
24 the people who dwell there will be forgiven 3
34:11 the owl and the raven shall dwell in it. 8
17 to generation they shall dwell in it. 8
37:37 and went home and dwelt at Nin'eveh. 3
40:22 and spreads them like a tent to dwell in; 3
44:13 with the beauty of a man, to dwell in a house. 3
49:20 too narrow for me; make room for me to dwell in.' 3
51: 6 and they who dwell in it will die like gnats; 3
57:15 I dwell in the high and holy place 8
58:12 repairer . . the restorer of streets to dwell in. 3
65: 9 inherit it, and my servants shall dwell there. 8
Jer 2: 6 that none passes through, where no man dwells?' 3
4:29 cities are forsaken, and no man dwells in them. 3
7: 3 and I will let you dwell in this place. 8

7 then I will let you dwell in this place 8
8:16 the city and those who dwell in it. 3
9:26 all who dwell in the desert that cut the corners 3
10:17 O you who dwell under siege! 3
12: 4 For the wickedness of those who dwell in it 3
17: 6 He shall dwell in the parched places 8
20: 6 And you, Pashhur, and all who dwell in your house 3
23: 6 and Israel will dwell securely. 8
8 Then they shall dwell in their own land. 3
24: 8 and those who dwell in the land of Egypt. 3
25: 5 and dwell upon the land which the LORD has given 3
24 the mixed tribes that dwell in the desert; 8
27:11 to till it and dwell there, says the LORD. 3
29:16 concerning all the people who dwell in this city 3
31:24 Judah and all its cities shall dwell there 3
33:16 and Jerusalem will dwell securely. 8
35: 9 and not to build houses to dwell in. 3
15 you shall dwell in the land which I gave to you 3
39:14 So he dwelt among the people. 3
40: 5 and dwell with him among the people; 3
6 at Mizpah, and dwelt with him among the people 3
9 Dwell in the land, and serve the king of Babylon 3
10 As for me, I will dwell at Mizpah 3
10 and dwell in your cities that you have taken. 3
42:14 or be hungry for bread, and we will dwell there, 3
44: 1 all the Jews that dwelt in the land of Egypt 3
2 they are a desolation, and no one dwells in them 3
13 I will punish those who dwell in the land of Egypt 3
14 Judah, to which they desire to return to dwell 3
15 people who dwelt in Pathros in the land of Egypt 3
26 all you of Judah who dwell in the land of Egypt 3
47: 2 that fills it, the city and those who dwell in it. 3
48:28 Leave the cities, and dwell in the rock 8
49: 8 Flee, turn back, dwell in the depths, O inhabitants 3
18 no man shall dwell there, no man shall sojourn 3
30 Flee, wander far away, dwell in the depths 3
31 a nation at ease, that dwells securely 3
31 that has no gates or bars, that dwells alone. 8
33 no man shall dwell there, no man shall sojourn 3
50: 3 her land a desolation, and none shall dwell in it; 3
39 wild beasts shall dwell with hyenas in Babylon 3
39 in Babylon, and ostriches shall dwell in her; 3
40 says the LORD, so no man shall dwell there 3
51:13 O you who dwell by many waters, rich in treasures 8
43 drought and a desert, a land in which no one dwells 3
62 cut it off, so that nothing shall dwell in it 3
Lam 1: 3 she dwells now among the nations 3
Ezk 3:15 exiles at Tel-abib, who dwelt by the river Chebar. 3
6: 6 Wherever you dwell your cities shall be waste 5
12: 2 you dwell in the midst of a rebellious house 3
19 of the violence of all those who dwell in it. 3
17:16 the place where the king dwells who made him king •
23 cedar; and under it will dwell all kinds of beasts; 8
20: 9 in the sight of the nations among whom they dwelt •
27: 3 say to Tyre, who dwells at the entrance to the sea 3
28:25 then they shall dwell in their own land 3
26 they shall dwell securely in it 3
26 They shall dwell securely, when I execute 3
31: 6 under its shadow dwelt all great nations. 3
13 Upon its ruin will dwell all the birds of the air 8
17 yea, those who dwelt under its shadow 3
32:15 when I smite all who dwell in it 3
34:25 that they may dwell securely in the wilderness 3
28 they shall dwell securely 3
36:17 when the house of Israel dwelt in their own land 3
28 You shall dwell in the land which I gave 3
37:25 They shall dwell in the land where your fathers 3
25 shall dwell in the land where your fathers dwelt 3
25 children's children shall dwell there for ever; 3
38: 8 and now dwell securely, all of them. 3
11 fall upon the quiet people who dwell securely 3
11 all of them dwelling without walls 3
12 people . . who dwell at the center of the earth. 3
14 when my people Israel are dwelling securely 3
39: 6 on those who dwell securely in the coastlands; 3
9 those who dwell in the cities of Israel will go 3
26 when they dwell securely in their land 3
43: 7 I will dwell in the midst of the people of Israel 8
9 I will dwell in their midst for ever. 8
Dan 2:22 light dwells with him. 11
38 into whose hand he has given, wherever they dwell 9
4: 1 to all peoples . . that dwell in all the earth 9
12 birds of the air dwelt in its branches 9
21 in whose branches the birds of the air dwelt– 10
6:25 to all the peoples . . that dwell in all the earth 9
Hos 3: 3 I said to her, "You must dwell as mine for many days; 3
4 For the children of Israel shall dwell many days 3
4: 3 the land mourns, and all who dwell in it languish 3
14: 7 They shall return and dwell beneath my shadow 3
Jol 3:17 LORD your God, who dwell in Zion, my holy mountain. 8
21 for the LORD dwells in Zion. 8
Ams 3:12 people of Israel who dwell in Sama'ria be rescued 3
5:11 of hewn stone, but you shall not dwell in them; 3
8: 8 and every one mourn who dwells in it 3
9: 5 earth and it melts, and all who dwell in it mourn 3
Mic 4:10 forth from the city and dwell in the open country; 8
5: 4 And they shall dwell secure 3
7:14 dwell alone in a forest in the midst of a garden 8
Nah 1: 5 the world and all that dwell therein. 3
Hab 2: 8 to the earth, to cities and all who dwell therein. 3
17 to the earth, to cities and all who dwell therein. 3
Zep 2:15 This is the exultant city that dwelt secure 3
Hag 1: 4 for you yourselves to dwell in your paneled 3
Zec 2: 7 you who dwell with the daughter of Babylon. 3
10 I will dwell in the midst of you, says the LORD. 8
11 I will dwell in the midst of you, and you shall know 8
8: 3 to Zion, and will dwell in the midst of Jerusalem 8
8 bring them to dwell in the midst of Jerusalem; 8
9: 6 a mongrel people shall dwell in Ashdod; 3
14:11 Jerusalem shall dwell in security. 3
Mat 2:23 he went and dwelt in a city called Nazareth 20
4:13 leaving Nazareth he went and dwelt in Caper'na-um 20
12:45 and they enter and dwell there 20
23:21 swears by it and by him who dwells in it; 20
Lke 11:26 they enter and dwell there 20
13: 4 all the others who dwelt in Jerusalem? 20
21:35 all who dwell upon the face of the whole earth; 14
Joh 1:14 And the Word became flesh and dwelt among us 27
14:10 the Father who dwells in me does his works. 23
17 you know him, for he dwells with you 23
Act 2: 5 Now there were dwelling in Jerusalem Jews 20
14 Men of Judea and all who dwell in Jerusalem 20
26 moreover my flesh will dwell in hope. 18
7:48 Yet the Most High does not dwell in houses 20
Rom 7:17 no longer I . . but sin which dwells within me 24
18 For I know that nothing good dwells within me 24
20 no longer I . . but sin which dwells within me. 24
23 to the law of sin which dwells in my members. 12
8: 9 if in fact the Spirit of God dwells in you. 24
11 If the Spirit . . dwells in you 24
11 through his Spirit which dwells in you. 13
1Co 3:16 God's Spirit dwells in you? 24
Eph 3:17 Christ may dwell in your hearts through faith; 20
Col 1:19 in him all the fulness of God was pleased to dwell 20
2: 9 in him the whole fulness of deity dwells bodily 20
3:16 Let the word of Christ dwell in you richly 13
1Ti 6:16 dwells in unapproachable light 24
2Ti 1: 5 a faith that dwelt first in your grandmother 13
5 now, I am sure, dwells in you. •
2Pe 3:13 and a new earth in which righteousness dwells. 20
Rev 2:13 'I know where you dwell, where Satan's throne is; 20
13 who was killed among you, where Satan dwells. 20
3:10 to try those who dwell upon the earth. 20
6:10 avenge . . on those who dwell upon the earth? 20
8:13 Woe, woe, woe to those who dwell on the earth 20
11:10 those who dwell on the earth will rejoice 20
10 a torment to those who dwell on the earth. 20
12:12 Rejoice then, O heaven and you that dwell therein! 27
13: 6 his dwelling, that is, those who dwell in heaven. 27
8 and all who dwell on earth will worship it 20
14 it deceives those who dwell on earth 20
14: 6 gospel to proclaim to those who dwell on earth 14
21: 3 He will dwell with them 27
1Es 2: 5 he is the Lord who dwells in Jerusalem 18
2Es 3:12 When those who dwelt on earth began to multiply 30
4:21 also those who dwell upon earth 31
39 on account of the sins of those who dwell on earth. 31
5: 1 when those who dwell on earth shall be seized 31
6 whom those who dwell on earth do not expect 31
7:32 and the dust those who dwell silently in it 30
72 those who dwell on earth shall be tormented 29
8:17 I see the failings of us who dwell in the land 31
9: 9 those . . shall dwell in torments. 29
18 before the world was made for them to dwell 31
10:59 to those who dwell on earth in the last days 31
11: 5 over the earth and over those who dwell in it. 31
40 for so long you have dwelt on the earth 31
13:30 shall come over those who dwell on the earth. 31
46 Then they dwelt there until the last times 31
Tob 1: 4 the temple of the dwelling of the Most High 19
5:16 God who dwells in heaven will prosper your way 26
Jdt 5: 5 that dwells in the nearby mountain district 20
AEs 11: 3 He was a Jew, dwelling in the city of Susa 26
Wis 1: 4 nor dwell in a body enslaved to sin. 21
12: 3 Those who dwelt of old in thy holy land 25
Sir 1:10 She dwells with all flesh according to his gift •
4:15 whoever gives heed to her will dwell secure. 18
14:27 will dwell in the midst of her glory. 17
24: 4 I dwelt in high places 18
25:16 I would rather dwell with a lion and a dragon 28
16 rather . . than dwell with an evil wife. 28
50:26 the foolish people that dwell in Shechem. 22
Bar 1: 4 all who dwelt in Babylon by the river Sud. 20
3:13 God, you would be dwelling in peace for ever. 20
20 Young men . . have dwelt upon the earth; but they 20
1Mc 2: 7 to dwell there when it was given over to the enemy 15
29 many . . went down to the wilderness to dwell there 15
9:73 Jonathan dwelt in Michmash 24
10:10 Jonathan dwelt in Jerusalem 24
13:52 he and his men dwelt there. 24
53 he dwelt in Gazara. 24
14:34 Azotus, where the enemy formerly dwelt 24
2Mc 5:17 because of the sins of those who dwelt in the city 24
6: 2 as did the people who dwelt in that place. 24
12:27 Ephron, a fortified city where Lysias dwelt 20
30 when the Jews who dwelt there bore witness 16
4Mc 13:20 the brothers dwelt the same length of time 20

dwell apart 1. סבב

2Sm 14:24 the king said, "Let him dwell apart in his own house; 1
24 Ab'salom dwelt apart in his own house 1

dwell as an alien 1. peregrinor

2Es 14:29 At first our fathers dwelt as aliens in Egypt 1

cause to dwell 1. שׁכן (A)

Ezr 6:12 May the God who has caused his name to dwell there 1

make dwell 1. ישׁב 2. שׁכן 3. *κατοικίζω*

Lev 23:43 I made the people of Israel dwell in booths 1
Num14:30 land where I swore that I would make you dwell 2
Deu 12:11 LORD . . will choose, to make his name dwell there 2
14:23 place which he will choose, to make his name dwell 2
16: 2 place . . LORD will choose, to make his name dwell 2
6 LORD . . will choose, to make his name dwell in it 2
11 LORD . . choose, to make his name dwell there. 2
26: 2 LORD . . choose, to make his name dwell there. 2
1Sm 12: 8 who brought . . and made them dwell in this place. 1
Neh 1: 9 which I have chosen, to make my name dwell there 2
Ps 4: 8 for thou alone, O LORD, makest me dwell in safety. 1
Isa 5: 8 you are made to dwell alone in . . the land. 1
Jer 7:12 in Shiloh, where I made my name dwell at first 2
32:37 and I will make them dwell in safety. 1
Lam 3: 6 he has made me dwell in darkness like the dead 1
Hos 12: 9 I will again make you dwell in tents 1
Jas 4: 5 the spirit which he has made to dwell in us"? 3

dwell secure 1. שׁכן

Ps 102:28 The children of thy servants shall dwell secure; 1

dwell within 1. *ἐνοικέω*

2Ti 1:14 the Holy Spirit who dwells within us. 1

dweller 1. ישׁב 2. שׁכן 3. *κατοικέω*

Isa 26:19 O dwellers in the dust, awake and sing for joy! 2
Lam 4:21 O daughter of Edom, dweller in the land of Uz; 1
Rev 17: 2 the dwellers on earth have become drunk. 3
8 and the dwellers on earth . . will marvel 3

dwelling 1. דּוֹר 2. מוֹשָׁב 3. מָכוֹן 4. מְנוּחָה 5. מָעוֹן 6. מִשְׁכָּן 7. נָוֶה 8. שֶׁבֶת 9. שׁכן 10. מְדוֹר (A) 11. מְדָר (A) 12. מִשְׁכַּן (A) 13. *κατοικητήριον* 14. *κατοικία* 15. *οἰκητήριον* 16. *σκηνή* 17. habitatio

Gen 27:39 of the earth shall your dwelling be 2
Exd 12:20 in all your dwellings you shall eat unleavened 2
Lev 7:26 eat no blood . . in any of your dwellings 2
23: 3 a sabbath to the LORD in all your dwellings 2
14 a statute for ever . . in all your dwellings 2
17 You shall bring from your dwellings two loaves 2
21 it is a statute for ever in all your dwellings 2
31 a statute for ever . . in all your dwellings 2
Num16:24 Get away from about the dwelling of Korah, Dathan 6
27 got away from about the dwelling of Korah, Dathan 6
35:29 your generations in all your dwellings. 2
2Sm 7: 6 have been moving about in a tent for my dwelling. 6
1Ch 17: 5 from tent to tent and from dwelling to dwelling. 6
5 from tent to tent and from dwelling to dwelling. •
Ezr 7:15 God of Israel, whose dwelling is in Jerusalem 12
Job 5: 3 but suddenly I cursed his dwelling. 7
18:21 Surely such are the dwellings of the ungodly 6
38:19 Where is the way to the dwelling of light 9
Ps 43: 3 bring me to thy holy hill and to thy dwelling! 6
78:60 He forsook his dwelling at Shiloh, the tent 6
120: 6 Too long have I had my dwelling among those 9
Prv 21:20 treasure remains in a wise man's dwelling 7
24:15 wicked man against the dwelling of the righteous; 7
Isa 11:10 seek, and his dwellings shall be glorious. 4
18: 4 from my dwelling like clear heat in sunshine 3
32:18 in secure dwellings, and in quiet resting places. 6
38:12 My dwelling is plucked up and removed from me 1
Jer 9:19 because they have cast down our dwellings. 6
30:18 and have compassion on his dwellings; 6
51:30 her dwellings are on fire, her bars are broken. 6
Ezk 25: 4 among you and make their dwellings in your midst; 6
48:15 for the city, for dwellings and for open country. 2
Dan 2:11 gods, whose dwelling is not with flesh. 11
4:25 dwelling shall be with the beasts of the field; 10
32 dwelling shall be with the beasts of the field; 10
5:21 dwelling was with the wild asses; he was fed grass 10
Obd 1: 3 whose dwelling is high, who say in your heart 8
Zec 2:13 he has roused himself from his holy dwelling. 5
Act 15:16 rebuild the dwelling of David, which has fallen 16
2Co 5: 2 long to put on our heavenly dwelling 15
Jde 1: 6 the angels that . . left their proper dwelling 15
Rev 13: 6 God, blaspheming his name and his dwelling 16
21: 3 Behold, the dwelling of God is with men. 16
2Es 4: 7 How many dwellings are in the heart of the sea 17
5:38 except he whose dwelling is not with men? 17
11:42 you have destroyed the dwellings of those 17
1Mc 1:38 she became a dwelling of strangers 14
2Mc 3:39 he who has his dwelling in heaven 14
3Mc 2:15 your dwelling, the heaven of heavens 13

dwelling *See also* find, make.

dwelling place 1. מוֹשָׁב 2. מָעוֹן 3. מְעֹנָה 4. מָקוֹם 5. מִשְׁכָּן 6. *κατοικητήριον* 7. *σκήνωμα*

Gen 36:40 their families and their dwelling places 4
43 according to their dwelling places in the land 1
Lev 3:17 your generations, in all your dwelling places 1
Num24:21 Enduring is your dwelling place, and your nest 1
Deu 33:27 The eternal God is your dwelling place 2
1Ch 6:54 These are their dwelling places 1
2Ch 36:15 had compassion . . on his dwelling place; 2
Job 39: 6 and the salt land for his dwelling place? 5
Ps 49:11 their dwelling places to all generations 5
74: 7 they desecrated the dwelling place of thy name. 5
76: 2 in Salem, his dwelling place in Zion. 3
84: 1 How lovely is thy dwelling place, O LORD of hosts! 5
87: 2 more than all the dwelling places of Jacob. 5
90: 1 Lord . . our dwelling place in all generations. 2
132: 5 dwelling place for the Mighty One of Jacob. 5
7 Let us go to his dwelling place; let us worship 5
Ezk 37:27 My dwelling place shall be with them; 5
Eph 2:22 a dwelling place of God in the Spirit. 6
Rev 18: 2 It has become a dwelling place of demons 6
1Es 1:50 he would have spared them and his dwelling place. 7

dwells *See* place.

dwindle 1. מעט
Prv 13:11 Wealth hastily gotten will dwindle 1

dye
Job 38:14 it is dyed like a garment. •

dyed *See* work.

dyed stuff 1. צֶבַע
Jdg 5:30 spoil of dyed stuffs for Sis'era, spoil of dyed 1
30 for Sis'era, spoil of dyed stuffs embroidered 1

dynasty 1. *βασιλεύς*
3Mc 3: 3 unswerving loyalty toward the dynasty; 1

dysentery 1. *δυσεντερία*
Act 28: 8 lay sick with fever and dysentery 1

E

each 1. אֶחָד 2. אִישׁ 3. אִשָּׁה 4. גֶּבֶר 5. דָּבָר 6. כֹּל
7. ἀνά 8. ἀνήρ 9. εἷς 10. εἷς ἕκαστος 11. εἷς καθ' ἕν
12. ἕκαστος 13. ἑκάτερος 14. ἕτερος ἕκαστος 15. κατά
16. πάντοτε 17. πᾶς 18. τίς 19. singuli
20. unusquisque 21. uterque

Gen 1:11 each according to its kind, upon the earth *
12 their seed, each according to its kind *
10: 5 each with his own language 2
13:11 thus they separated from each other. 2
15:10 in two, and laid each half over against the other; 2
40: 5 –each his own dream, and each dream with its own 2
5 –each his own dream, and each dream with its own 2
41:11 he and I, each having a dream with its own meaning. 2
45:22 To each and all of them he gave festal garments; 2
49:28 blessing each with the blessing suitable 2
Exd 1: 1 sons of Israel . . each with his household 2
12: 4 according to what each can eat you shall make 2
16:16 the persons whom each of you has in his tent.' 2
18 each gathered according to what he could eat. 2
21 they gathered it, each as much as he could eat; 2
18: 7 and they asked each other of their welfare 2
25:33 three cups . . each with capital and flower *
33 three cups . . each with capital and flower *
35 a capital . . under each pair of the six branches *
26: 2 The length of each curtain shall be 28 cubits 1
2 and the breadth of each curtain four cubits; 1
8 The length of each curtain shall be 30 cubits 1
8 the breadth of each curtain four cubits; 1
16 a cubit and a half the breadth of each frame. 1
17 There shall be two tenons in each frame 1
28:21 like signets, each engraved with its name 2
30:12 each shall give a ransom for himself to the LORD 2
13 Each who is numbered in the census shall give 6
34 spices . . (of each shall there be an equal part) *
36: 4 able men . . came, each from the task that he was 2
9 The length of each curtain was 28 cubits 1
9 and the breadth of each curtain four cubits; 1
15 The length of each curtain was 30 cubits 1
15 the breadth of each curtain four cubits; 1
21 a cubit and a half the breadth of each frame. 1
22 Each frame had two tenons, for fitting together; 1
37:19 three cups made like almonds, each with capital 1
19 three cups made like almonds, each with capital *
21 a capital of one piece with it under each pair *
39:14 like signets, each engraved with its name 2
Lev 7:14 of such he shall offer one cake from each offering 6
10: 1 the sons of Aaron, each took his censer 2
23:37 drink offerings, each on its proper day 5
24: 5 two tenths of an ephah shall be in each cake 1
7 you shall put pure frankincense with each row *
25:10 when each of you shall return to his property 2
10 each of you shall return to his family 2
13 In this year of jubilee each of you shall return 2
Num 1: 4 there shall be with you a man from each tribe *
44 twelve men, each representing his fathers' house. 2
2: 2 Israel shall encamp each by his own standard 2
17 each in position, standard by standard. 2
4:19 appoint them each to his task and to his burden *
49 each to his task of serving or carrying; *
7: 3 wagon for every two . . for each one an ox; *
11 shall offer their offering, one leader each day *
85 each silver plate weighing 130 shekels 1
85 weighing 130 shekels and each basin 70 1
13: 2 each tribe of their fathers shall you send a man *
15: 5 offering, or for the sacrifice, for each lamb. 1
11 Thus it shall be done for each bull or ram 1
11 be done . . for each of the male lambs or the kids. *
38 to put upon the tassel of each corner a cord of blue; *
16:17 you also, and Aaron, each his censer. 2
17: 2 get from them rods, one for each fathers' house *
3 one rod for the head of each fathers' house. *
6 their leaders gave him rods, one for each leader *
9 they looked, and each man took his rod. *
23: 2 offered on each altar a bull and a ram. *
4 I have offered upon each altar a bull and a ram. *
14 offered a bull and a ram on each altar. *
30 Balak . . offered a bull and a ram on each altar. *
28: 7 offering shall be a fourth of a hin for each lamb; 1
12 cereal offering . . for each bull; 1
14 this is the burnt offering of each month †
21 tenth shall you offer for each of the seven lambs; 1
28 three tenths of an ephah for each bull 1
29 a tenth for each of the seven lambs; 1
29: 4 one tenth for each of the seven lambs; 1
10 a tenth for each of the seven lambs 1
14 three tenths . . for each of the thirteen bulls 1
14 two tenths for each of the two rams 1
15 a tenth for each of the fourteen lambs; 1
31: 4 send 1,000 from each of the tribes of Israel to the war *
5 1,000 from each tribe, 12,000 armed for war *
6 Moses sent them to the war, 1,000 from each tribe *
32:18 Israel have inherited each his inheritance. 2
35: 8 each, in proportion to the inheritance . . it inherits 2
36: 9 for each of the tribes of the people of Israel 2
Deu 1:23 I took twelve men of you, one man for each tribe; *
Jos 3:12 take twelve men . . from each tribe a man. *
4: 2 Take twelve men . . from each tribe a man *
4 whom he had appointed, a man from each tribe; *
5 and take up each of you a stone upon his shoulder 2
18: 4 Provide three men from each tribe, and I will send *
10 apportioned the land . . to each his portion. *
21:42 cities had each its pasture lands round about it; *
22:14 ten chiefs, one from each of the tribal families *
Jdg 2: 6 the people of Israel went each to his 2
15: 4 and put a torch between each pair of tails. *
16: 5 we will each give you 1,100 pieces of silver. 2
Rut 1: 8 Go, return each of you to her mother's house. 3
9 LORD grant that you may find a home, each of you 3
1Sm 30: 6 people were bitter . . each for his sons 2
2Sm 2:16 And each caught his opponent by the head 2
6:19 distributed . . to each a cake of bread, a portion 2
19 Then all the people departed, each to his house. 2
10: 4 and shaved off half the beard of each, and cut off *
13:29 all . . arose, and each mounted his mule and fled. 2
21:20 man of . . stature, who had six fingers on each hand *
20 who had six fingers . . and six toes on each foot *
1Kg 1:49 all the guests . . rose, and each went his own way. 2
4: 7 twelve officers . . each man had to make 1
27 officers supplied . . each one in his month; they 2
28 they brought . . each according to his charge. 2
6:10 He built . . each story five cubits high *
23 he made two cherubim . . each ten cubits high. *
27 wings touched each other in the middle †
7: 3 upon the 45 pillars, fifteen in each row. *
27 stands of bronze; each stand was four cubits long 1
30 each stand had four bronze wheels and axles 1
30 supports . . with wreaths at the side of each. 2
34 four supports at the four corners of each stand; 1
36 he carved . . according to the space of each 2
38 he made ten lavers . . each laver held 40 baths 1
38 each laver measured four cubits 1
38 and there was a laver for each of the ten stands. 1
42 two rows of pomegranates for each network 1
8:38 thy people Israel, each knowing the affliction 2
39 render to each whose heart thou knowest 2
59 may he maintain . . as each day requires; †
10:16 600 shekels of gold went into each shield. 1
17 three minas of gold went into each shield; 1
19 on each side of the seat were arm rests †
20 twelve lions stood there, one on each end of a step †
20:20 each killed his man; the Syrians fled 2
24 do this: remove the kings, each from his post 2
22:17 These have no master; let each return to his home 2
2Kg 6: 2 go to the Jordan and each of us get there a log 2
9:21 set out, each in his chariot, and went to meet Jehu 2
11: 8 surround . . each with his weapons in his hand; 2
9 each brought his men who were to go off duty 2
12: 5 let the priests take, each from his acquaintance; 2
1Ch 16: 3 to each a loaf of bread, a portion of meat 2
37 minister . . before the ark as each day required *
43 Then all the people departed each to his house 2
20: 6 who had six fingers on each hand, and six toes *
6 who had six fingers . . and six toes on each foot *
24:31 These also, the head of each father's house and his *
26:17 On the east there were six each day *
17 on the north four each day, on the south four *
17 north four each day, on the south four each day *
27: 1 each division numbering 24,000 1
28:14 for all golden vessels for each service *
14 weight of silver vessels for each service *
15 weight of gold for each lampstand and its lamps *
15 the use of each lampstand in the service *
16 weight of gold for each table for the showbread *
17 for the golden bowls and the weight of each; *
17 for the silver bowls and the weight of each. *
2Ch 3:15 with a capital of five cubits on the top of each. *
4:13 two rows of pomegranates for each network 1
6:29 each knowing his own affliction, and . . sorrow 2
30 hear thou . . and forgive, and render to each 2
8:13 as the duty of each day required *
14 he appointed . . as the duty of each day required *
9:15 600 shekels of . . gold went into each shield. 1
16 300 shekels of gold went into each shield; 1
18 on each side of the seat were arm rests *
19 one on each end of a step on the six steps. *
10:16 Each of you to your tents, O Israel! 2
18:16 let each return to his home in peace.' 2
23: 7 each with his weapons in his hand; 2
8 They each brought his men, who were to go off duty 2
31: 2 by division, each according to his service 2
16 entered . . as the duty of each day required *
35: 5 let there be for each a part of a father's house *
15 the gatekeepers were at each gate; *
21 What have we to do with each other, king of Judah? *
Ezr 1: 4 let each survivor, in whatever place he sojourns 6
2: 1 returned to . . Judah, each to his own town. 2
3: 4 daily burnt offerings . . as each day required. *
6: 5 brought back to the temple . . each to its place; 2
10:16 heads . . each of them designated by name. 6
Neh 4:15 we all returned to the wall, each to his work. 2
17 each with one hand labored on the work *
18 each of the builders had his sword girded 2
23 each kept his weapon in his hand. 2
5: 7 exacting interest, each from his brother. 2
7: 3 Appoint guards . . each to his station 2
3 Appoint guards . . each opposite his own house. 2
6 returned to Jerusalem and Judah, each to his town. 2
8:16 made booths for themselves, each on his roof 2
13:10 Levites . . had fled each to his field. 2
24 Judah, but the language of each people. *
30 established the duties . . each in his work; 2
Est 2:12 came for each maiden to go in to King Ahasu-e'rus *
Job 1: 4 go and hold a feast in the house of each on his day; 2
2:11 they came each from his own place 2
42:11 each of them gave him a piece of money and a ring 2
Ps 59: 6 Each evening they come back, howling like dogs *
14 Each evening they come back, howling like dogs *
Sng 3: 8 each with his sword at his thigh, against alarms 2
Isa 6: 2 Above him stood the seraphim; each had six wings 1
9:20 not satisfied; each devours his neighbor's flesh 2
14:18 kings . . lie in glory, each in his own tomb; 2
32: 2 Each will be like a hiding place from the wind 2
47:15 they wander about each in his own direction; 2
56:11 to their own way, each to his own gain, one and all. 2
Jer 5: 8 each neighing for his neighbor's wife. 2
6: 3 around her, they shall pasture, each in his place. 2
9: 8 each speaks peaceably to his neighbor *
20 a lament, and each to her neighbor a dirge. 3
12:15 and I will bring them again each to his heritage 2
15 each to his heritage and each to his land. 2
22: 7 destroyers against you, each with his weapons; 2
31:30 each man who eats sour grapes 6
34 each man teach his neighbor and each his brother 2

34:14 each of you must set free the fellow Hebrew 2
15 by proclaiming liberty, each to his neighbor 2
16 when each of you took back his male . . slaves 2
51: 9 Forsake her, and let us go each to his own country; 2
Ezk 1: 6 but each had four faces 1
6 had four faces, and each of them had four wings. 1
10 each had the face of a man in front; *
11 each creature had two wings 2
11 wings, each of which touched the wing of another 2
12 And each went straight forward; 2
15 a wheel . . one for each of the four of them. *
23 each creature had two wings covering its body. 2
4: 6 40 days I assign you, a day for each year. *
8:11 Each had his censer in his hand 2
9: 1 each with his destroying weapon in his hand. 2
10: 9 there were four wheels . . one beside each cherub; 1
21 Each had four faces, and each four wings 1
21 Each had four faces, and each four wings 1
33:20 I will judge each of you according to his ways. 2
26 each of you defiles his neighbor's wife; 2
30 say to one another, each to his brother 2
40: 5 long cubits, each being a cubit and a handbreadth *
41: 6 stories, one over another, 30 in each story. *
23 nave and the holy place had each a double door. *
24 two swinging leaves for each door. *
45:13 one sixth of an ephah from each homer of wheat *
13 one sixth of an ephah from each homer of barley *
14 portion of oil, one tenth of a bath from each cor *
23 rams without blemish, on each of the seven days; †
24 as a cereal offering an ephah for each bull *
24 an ephah for each ram, and a hin of oil to each ephah *
24 an ephah for each ram, and a hin of oil to each ephah *
46: 5 together with a hin of oil to each ephah. *
7 together with a hin of oil to each ephah. *
9 but each shall go out straight ahead. *
21 and in each corner of the court there was a court *
23 around each of the four courts was a row *
Jol 2: 7 They march each on his way, they do not swerve 2
8 not jostle one another, each marches in his path; 4
Jon 1: 5 mariners were afraid, and each cried to his god; 2
Mic 4: 5 all the peoples walk each in the name of its god 2
7: 2 and each hunts his brother with a net. 2
Zep 2:11 and to him shall bow down, each in its place 2
3: 5 each dawn he does not fail; *
Hag 1: 9 you busy yourselves each with his own house. 2
Zec 4: 2 with seven lips on each of the lamps *
7: 9 show kindness and mercy each to his brother 2
8: 4 each with staff in hand for very age. 2
11: 6 men to fall each into the hand of his shepherd 2
6 of his shepherd, and each into the hand of his king; *
12:12 The land shall mourn, each family by itself; *
14 each by itself, and their wives by themselves. *
14:13 each will lay hold on the hand of his fellow 2
Mat 20: 9 each of them received a denarius. 7
10 each of them also received a denarius. 7
25:15 to each according to his ability 12
Mrk 13:34 puts his servants in charge, each with his work 12
15:24 to decide what each should take. 18
Lke 2: 3 all went to be enrolled, each to his own city. 12
6:44 for each tree is known by its own fruit 12
9:14 Make them sit down in companies, about 50 each. 7
13:15 Does not each of you on the sabbath untie his ox 12
Joh 2: 6 jars . . each holding twenty or 30 gallons. 7
6: 7 buy enough bread for each of them to get a little 12
7:53 They went each to his own house. 12
19:23 made four parts, one for each soldier 12
Act 2: 3 distributed and resting on each one of them. 12
6 each one heard them speaking in his own language. 12
8 each of us in his own native language? 12
4:35 distribution was made to each as any had need. 12
17:27 Yet he is not far from each one of us 12
Rom 12: 3 each according to the measure of faith 12
14:12 each of us shall give account of himself to God. 12
15: 2 let each of us please his neighbor for his good 12
1Co 3: 5 as the Lord assigned to each. 12
8 each shall receive his wages 12
7: 7 each has his own special gift from God 12
24 So, brethren, in whatever state each was called 12
12: 7 To each is given the manifestation of the Spirit 12
11 who apportions to each one individually 12
18 organs in the body, each one of them, as he chose. 12
14:27 each in turn; and let one interpret. *
28 let each of them keep silence in church *
15:23 each in his own order: Christ the first fruits 12
38 to each kind of seed its own body. 12
16: 2 each of you is to put something aside 12
Eph 4: 7 grace was given to each of us 12
16 when each part is working properly 10
5:33 however, let each one of you love his wife 12
Php 2: 4 Let each of you look not only to his own interests 12
1Th 2:11 we exhorted each one of you 12
Heb 11:21 Jacob . . blessed each of the sons of Joseph 12
Jas 1:14 each person is tempted when he is lured 12
1Pe 1:17 if you invoke as Father him who judges each one 12
4:10 As each has received a gift, employ it 12
Rev 2:23 I will give to each of you as your works deserve. 12
4: 8 four living creatures, each . . with six wings 11
5: 8 fell down before the Lamb, each holding a harp 12
6:11 Then they were each given a white robe and told 12
21:21 each of the gates made of a single pearl 12
22: 2 tree of life . . yielding its fruit each month; 12
1Es 1:16 The gatekeepers were at each gate 12
3: 5 Let each of us state what one thing is strongest; 12
8 each wrote his own statement 12
5: 8 each to his own town 12
47 the sons of Israel were each in his own home 12
7: 9 the gatekeepers were at each gate. 12
9:13 with the elders and judges of each place 12
2Es 2:43 and on the head of each of them he placed a crown 19
4:19 I answered and said, "Each has made a foolish plan 21
5:47 it cannot, but only each in its own time. *
11: 8 let each sleep in his own place 20
Tob 1: 7 and spend the proceeds each year at Jerusalem; 12
3: 8 the evil demon Asmodeus had slain each of them *
6:13 each died in the bridal chamber. 17
7:11 when each came to her he died in the night *
10: 1 Now his father Tobit was counting each day 12
Jdt 12: 7 and went out each night to the valley of Bethulia 15
Wis 15: 7 and laboriously molds each vessel for our service 10
7 which shall be the use of each of these 14
19:17 each tried to find the way through his own door. 12
18 while each note remains the same 16
Sir 17:14 he gave commandment to each of them 12
38:27 each is diligent in making a great variety *
31 each is skilful in his own work. 12
Bar 1: 6 they collected money, each giving what he could; 12
21 each followed the intent of his own wicked heart 12
2: 8 by turning away, each of us, from the thoughts 12
Sus 1:14 and when each pressed the other for the reason *
1Mc 1: 8 his officers began to rule, each in his own place. 12
42 that each should give up his customs. 12
2:40 each said to his neighbor 8
3:56 each should return to his home 12
5:49 each should encamp where he was. 12
6:35 with each elephant they stationed 1,000 men 12
35 picked horsemen were assigned to each beast. 12
37 were fastened upon each beast by special harness 12
37 upon each were four armed men 12
54 they had been scattered, each to his own place. 12
10:13 each left his place and departed to his own land. 12
11: 3 he stationed forces as a garrison in each city. 12
2Mc 3:26 who stood on each side of him 13
7:21 She encouraged each of them 12
22 who set in order the elements within each of you. 12
8:22 each to command a division 13
22 to command a division, putting 1,500 men under each. 12
9:26 to maintain your present good will, each of you 12
13: 2 Each of them had a Greek force of 110,000 infantry 12
14:21 A chariot came forward from each army 12
15:11 He armed each of them 12
3Mc 1: 4 promising to give them each two minas of gold 12
5:21 each departed to his own home. 12
34 each to his own occupation. 12
7: 8 We also have ordered each and every one to return 12
18 to each as far as his own house. 12
20 brought safely . . each to his own place. 12
4Mc 1:20 each of these is by nature concerned with . . 13
29 each of which the master cultivator . . weeds 12
5: 2 to seize each and every Hebrew 9
8: 5 Young men, I admire each and every one of you 9
9 will compel me to destroy each and every one of you 9
13:13 Each of them and all of them together 10
18 each of the brothers who were being dragged away 10
20 There each of the brothers dwelt *
14:12 the rackings of each one of her children. 12
15: 7 because of the many pains she suffered with each 12
12 each child singly and all together *
19 you looked at the eyes of each one in his tortures 12
16:24 encouraged and persuaded each of her sons to die 10

each *See also* day, other, side, year.

each man 1. אִישׁ 2. ἕκαστος 3. ὅσος

Gen 41:12 giving an interpretation to each man 1
44: 1 and put each man's money in the mouth of his sack 1
Num 1: 4 each man being the head of the house 1
7: 5 give . . to each man according to his service. 1
17: 2 Write each man's name upon his rod 1
31:50 brought the LORD'S offering, what each man found 1
Jdg 21:21 come out . . and seize each man his wife 1
22 we did not take for each man . . his wife in battle 1
1Sm 30:22 each man may lead away his wife and children 1
2Kg 12: 4 the money for which each man is assessed 1
Jer 31:34 And no longer shall each man teach his neighbor 1
1Co 3:10 Let each man take care how he builds upon it. 2
13 each man's work will become manifest 2
7: 2 each man should have his own wife 2
Gal 6: 5 For each man will have to bear his own load. 2
1Es 2: 6 let each man, wherever he may live, be helped 3
Jdt 7: 5 Then each man took up his weapons 2
1Mc 11:38 each man to his own place 2
14:12 Each man sat under his vine and his fig tree 2
3Mc 6:25 Who . . has taken each man from his home 2

each one 1. אִישׁ 2. אִשָּׁה 3. ἕκαστος

Exd 32:29 each one at the cost of his son and of his brother 1
1Sm 10:25 sent all the people away, each one to his home. 1
Neh 3:28 repaired, each one opposite his own house. 1
Sng 8:11 each one was to bring for its fruit 1,000 1
Isa 34:15 the kites be gathered, each one with her mate. 2
1Co 1:12 each one of you says, "I belong to Paul 3
3:13 test what sort of work each one has done. 3
11:21 in eating, each one goes ahead with his own meal 3
14:26 When you come together, each one has a hymn 3
2Co 5:10 so that each one may receive good or evil 3
9: 7 Each one must do as he has made up his mind 3
Gal 6: 4 let each one test his own work 3
1Th 4: 4 each one of you know how to take a wife for himself 3
Heb 6:11 we desire each one of you to show . . 3
1Mc 2:19 departing each one from the religion of his fathers 3

each woman 1. אִשָּׁה 2. ἕκαστος

Exd 3:22 each woman shall ask of her neighbor . . jewelry 1
1Co 7: 2 and each woman her own husband. 2

eager 1. כסף 2. שכם 3. ἐκτενῆ 4. ζηλωτής 5. κατασπεύδω 6. προθυμέομαι 7. πρόθυμος 8. σπουδάζω 9. σπουδὴν ποιέω

Ps 17:12 They are like a lion eager to tear, as a young lion 1
Zep 3: 7 they were eager to make all their deeds corrupt. 2
Rom 1:15 I am eager to preach the gospel to you 7
1Co 14:12 you are eager for manifestations of the Spirit 4
Gal 2:10 which very thing I was eager to do. 8
Eph 4: 3 eager to maintain the unity of the Spirit 8
Jde 1: 3 Beloved, being very eager to write to you 9
Sir 18:14 who are eager for his judgments. 5
3Mc 1: 8 he was all the more eager to visit them 6
5:29 O king, according to your eager purpose. 3

eager *See also* expectation, longing.

more eager 1. πρόθυμος 2. σπουδαίως

Php 2:28 I am the more eager to send him, therefore 2
2Mc 15: 9 he made them the more eager. 1

eagerly 1. μετὰ σπουδῆς 2. πολύς 3. προθυμέομαι 4. προθύμως 5. σπουδαίως 6. φιλότιμος

Mrk 5:10 he begged him eagerly 2
2Ti 1:17 he searched for me eagerly and found me– 5
1Pe 5: 2 Tend . . not for shameful gain but eagerly 4
Sus 1:12 they watched eagerly, day after day, to see her. 6
1Mc 1:13 some of the people eagerly went to the king 3
2Mc 11: 7 Then they eagerly rushed off together. 4
3Mc 5:24 they were eagerly waiting for daybreak. 1

eagerly *See also* endeavor, seek, wait.

eagerness 1. προθυμία

Act 17:11 they received the word with all eagerness 1

eagerness to clear 1. ἀπολογία

2Co 7:11 what eagerness to clear yourselves 1

eagle 1. נֶשֶׁר 2. נְשַׁר (A) 3. ἀετός 4. aquila

Exd 19: 4 You have seen . . how I bore you on eagles' wings 1
Lev 11:13 an abomination: the eagle, the vulture, the osprey 1
Deu 14:12 shall not eat: the eagle, the vulture, the osprey 1
28:49 bring a nation . . as swift as the eagle flies 1
32:11 Like an eagle that stirs up its nest 1
2Sm 1:23 they were swifter than eagles 1
Job 9:26 They go by . . like an eagle swooping on the prey. 1
39:27 Is it at your command that the eagle mounts up 1
Ps 103: 5 so that your youth is renewed like the eagle's. 1
Prv 23: 5 flying like an eagle toward heaven. 1
30:19 the way of an eagle in the sky, the way of a serpent 1
Isa 40:31 they shall mount up with wings like eagles 1
Jer 4:13 his horses are swifter than eagles 1
48:40 Behold, one shall fly swiftly like an eagle 1
49:16 Though you make your nest as high as the eagle's 1
22 one shall mount up and fly swiftly like an eagle 1
Ezk 1:10 and the four had the face of an eagle at the back. 1
10:14 and the fourth the face of an eagle. 1
17: 3 A great eagle with great wings and long pinions 1
7 there was another great eagle with great wings 1
Dan 4:33 till his hair grew as long as eagles' feathers 2
7: 4 The first was like a lion and had eagles' wings. 2
Obd 1: 4 Though you soar aloft like the eagle 1
Mic 1:16 make yourselves as bald as the eagle 1
Hab 1: 8 they fly like an eagle swift to devour. 1
Mat 24:28 there the eagles will be gathered together. 3
Lke 17:37 there the eagles will be gathered together. 3
Rev 4: 7 the fourth living creature like a flying eagle. 3
8:13 I heard an eagle crying with a loud voice 3
12:14 woman was given the two wings of the great eagle 3
2Es 11: 1 and behold, there came up from the sea an eagle 4
5 I looked, and behold, the eagle flew with his wings 4
7 and behold, the eagle rose upon his talons 4
23 nothing remained on the eagle's body 4
37 he uttered a man's voice to the eagle, and spoke 4
45 Therefore you will surely disappear, you eagle 4
12: 1 saying these words to the eagle, I looked 4
3 and the whole body of the eagle was burned 4
11 The eagle which you saw coming up from the sea 4
17 coming not from the eagle's heads *
24 therefore they are called the heads of the eagle. 4
30 whom the Most High has kept for the eagle's end *
31 and roaring and speaking to the eagle 4
14:18 the eagle which you saw in the vision 4

ear 1. אֹזֶן 2. מְלִילָה 3. ἀκοή 4. οὖς 5. ὠτάριον
6. ὠτίον 7. auris

Gen 35: 4 gave . . the rings that were in their ears; 1
44:18 I pray you, speak a word in my lord's ears 1
50: 4 speak, I pray you, in the ears of Pharaoh, saying 1
Exd 17:14 recite it in the ears of Joshua, that I will 1
21: 6 his master shall bore his ear through with an awl; 1
29:20 tip of the right ear of Aaron and upon the tips 1
20 upon the tips of the right ears of his sons 1
32: 2 Take off the rings of gold which are in the ears 1
3 rings of gold which were in their ears 1
Lev 8:23 blood and put it on the tip of Aaron's right ear 1
24 the blood on the tips of their right ears 1
14:14 the priest shall put it on the tip of the right ear 1
17 priest shall put on the tip of the right ear 1
25 put it on the tip of the right ear of him who is to be 1
28 the tip of the right ear of him who is to be 1
Deu 15:17 awl, and thrust it through his ear into the door 1
23:25 grain, you may pluck the ears with your hand 2
29: 4 LORD has not given you . . ears to hear. 1
31:28 that I may speak these words in their ears 1
30 in the ears of all the assembly of Israel 1
Jdg 7: 3 proclaim in the ears of the people, saying 1
9: 2 Say in the ears of all the citizens of Shechem 1
3 all these words . . in the ears of all the men 1
17: 2 you uttered a curse, and also spoke it in my ears 1
1Sm 3:11 two ears of every one that hears it will tingle. 1
8:21 he repeated them in the ears of the LORD. 1
11: 4 reported the matter in the ears of the people; 1
15:14 What then is this bleating of the sheep in my ears 1
18:23 servants spoke those words in the ears of David. 1
25:24 pray let your handmaid speak in your ears 1
2Sm 7:22 according to all . . we have heard with our ears. 1
22: 7 he heard my voice, and my cry came to his ears. 1
2Kg 19:16 Incline thy ear, O LORD, and hear; open thy eyes 1
28 and your arrogance has come into my ears 1
21:12 the ears of every one who hears of it will tingle. 1
1Ch 17:20 all that we have heard with our ears. 1
2Ch 6:40 Now, O my God, let . . thy ears attentive to a prayer 1
7:15 eyes . . open and my ears attentive to the prayer 1
Neh 1: 6 let thy ear be attentive, and thy eyes open 1
11 O Lord, let thy ear be attentive to the prayer 1
8: 3 ears of all the people were attentive to the book 1
Job 4:12 stealthily, my ear received the whisper of it. 1
12:11 Does not the ear try words as the palate tastes 1
13: 1 my ear has heard and understood it. 1
17 let my declaration be in your ears. 1
15:21 Terrifying sounds are in his ears; 1
28:22 We have heard a rumor of it with our ears.' 1
29:11 When the ear heard, it called me blessed 1
33:16 then he opens the ears of men, and terrifies them 1
34: 3 the ear tests words as the palate tastes food. 1
36:10 He opens their ears to instruction, and commands 1
15 opens their ear by adversity. 1
42: 5 I had heard of thee by the hearing of the ear 1
Ps 10:17 thou wilt incline thy ear 1
17: 6 O God; incline thy ear to me, hear my words. 1
18: 6 heard my voice, and my cry to him reached his ears. 1
31: 2 Incline thy ear to me, rescue me speedily! 1
34:15 the righteous, and his ears toward their cry. 1
40: 6 but thou hast given me an open ear. †
44: 1 We have heard with our ears, O God 1
45:10 Hear, O daughter, consider, and incline your ear; 1
49: 4 I will incline my ear to a proverb; 1
58: 4 a serpent, like the deaf adder that stops its ear 1
71: 2 incline thy ear to me, and save me! 1
78: 1 incline your ears to the words of my mouth! 1
86: 1 Incline thy ear, O LORD, and answer me 1
88: 2 prayer come before thee, incline thy ear to my cry! 1
92:11 ears have heard the doom of my evil assailants. 1
94: 9 He who planted the ear, does he not hear? 1
102: 2 Incline thy ear to me; answer me speedily 1
115: 6 have ears, but do not hear; noses, but do not smell. 1
116: 2 Because he inclined his ear to me 1
130: 2 Lord, hear my voice! Let thy ears be attentive 1
135:17 they have ears, but they hear not 1
Prv 2: 2 making your ear attentive to wisdom 1
4:20 incline your ear to my sayings. 1
5: 1 incline your ear to my understanding; 1
13 I did not . . incline my ear to my instructors. 1
15:31 He whose ear heeds wholesome admonition 1
18:15 the ear of the wise seeks knowledge. 1
20:12 hearing ear and the seeing eye, the LORD has made 1
21:13 He who closes his ear to the cry of the poor 1
22:17 Incline your ear, and hear the words of the wise 1
23:12 Apply . . your ear to words of knowledge. 1
25:12 wise reprover to a listening ear. 1
26:17 like one who takes a passing dog by the ears. 1
28: 9 If one turns away his ear from hearing the law 1
Ecc 1: 8 the eye is not . . nor the ear filled with hearing. 1
Isa 6:10 the heart of this people fat, and their ears heavy 1
10 lest they see . . and hear with their ears 1
11: 3 what his eyes see, or decide by what his ears hear; 1
22:14 The LORD of hosts has revealed himself in my ears 1
30:21 your ears shall hear a word behind you 1
32: 3 and the ears of those who hear will hearken. 1
33:15 who stops his ears from hearing of bloodshed 1
35: 5 be opened, and the ears of the deaf unstopped; 1
37:17 Incline thy ear, O LORD, and hear; 1
29 your arrogance has come to my ears 1
42:20 his ears are open, but he does not hear. 1
43: 8 blind, yet have eyes, who are deaf, yet have ears! 1
48: 8 from of old your ear has not been opened. 1
49:20 The children . . will yet say in your ears 1
50: 4 he wakens my ear to hear as those who are taught. 1
5 The Lord GOD has opened my ear 1
55: 3 Incline your ear, and come to me; 1
59: 1 cannot save, or his ear dull, that it cannot hear; 1
Jer 5:21 have eyes, but see not, who have ears, but hear not. 1
6:10 Behold, their ears are closed, they cannot listen; 1
7:24 But they did not obey or incline their ear 1
26 yet they did not listen to me, or incline their ear 1
9:20 and let your ear receive the word of his mouth; 1
11: 8 Yet they did not obey or incline their ear 1
17:23 Yet they did not listen or incline their ear 1
19: 3 the ears of every one who hears of it will tingle. 1
25: 4 neither listened nor inclined your ears to hear 1
26:11 as you have heard with your own ears. 1
15 me to you to speak all these words in your ears. 1
34:14 did not listen to me or incline their ears to me. 1
35:15 But you did not incline your ear or listen to me. 1
44: 5 But they did not listen or incline their ear 1
Lam 3:56 my plea, 'Do not close thine ear to my cry for help!' 1
Ezk 3:10 receive in your heart, and hear with your ears. 1
8:18 though they cry in my ears with a loud voice 1
9: 1 Then he cried in my ears with a loud voice, saying 1
12: 2 who have ears to hear, but hear not; 1
16:12 I put a ring on your nose, and earrings in your ears 1
23:25 They shall cut off your nose and your ears 1
40: 4 look with your eyes, and hear with your ears, 1
44: 5 see with your eyes, and hear with your ears 1
Dan 9:18 O my God, incline thy ear and hear; open thy eyes 1
Ams 3:12 two legs, or a piece of an ear 1
Mic 7:16 hands on their mouths; their ears shall be deaf; 1
Zec 7:11 stopped their ears that they might not hear. 1
Mat 11:15 He who has ears to hear, let him hear. 4
13: 9 He who has ears, let him hear. 4
15 and their ears are heavy of hearing 4
15 and hear with their ears 4
16 and your ears, for they hear. 4
43 He who has ears, let him hear. 4
26:51 and cut off his ear. 6
Mrk 4: 9 he said, "He who has ears to hear, let him hear. 4
23 If any man has ears to hear, let him hear. 4
7:33 he put his fingers into his ears, and he spat 4
35 his ears were opened, his tongue was released 3
8:18 having ears do you not hear 4
14:47 struck the slave . . and cut off his ear. 5
Lke 1:44 when the voice of your greeting came to my ears 4
8: 8 He who has ears to hear, let him hear. 4
9:44 Let these words sink into your ears 4
14:35 He who has ears to hear, let him hear. 4
22:50 and cut off his right ear. 4
51 he touched his ear and healed him. 6
Joh 18:10 and cut off his right ear 5
26 a kinsman of the man whose ear Peter had cut off 6
Act 7:51 uncircumcised in heart and ears 4
57 stopped their ears and rushed together upon him. 4
11:22 came to the ears of the church in Jerusalem 4
17:20 you bring some strange things to our ears 3
28:27 their ears are heavy of hearing 4
27 hear with their ears 4
Rom 11: 8 eyes . . not see and ears that should not hear 4
1Co 2: 9 What no eye has seen, nor ear heard 4
12:16 if the ear should say, "Because I am not an eye 4
17 If the whole body were an ear 3
2Ti 4: 3 having itching ears 3
Jas 5: 4 reached the ears of the Lord of hosts. 4
1Pe 3:12 and his ears are open to their prayer. 4
Rev 2: 7 He who has an ear, let him hear what the Spirit says 4
11 He who has an ear, let him hear what the Spirit says 4
17 He who has an ear, let him hear what the Spirit says 4
29 He who has an ear, let him hear what the Spirit says 4
3: 6 He who has an ear, let him hear what the Spirit says 4
13 He who has an ear, let him hear what the Spirit says 4
22 He who has an ear, let him hear what the Spirit says 4
13: 9 If any one has an ear, let him hear 4
2Es 8:24 and give ear to the petition of thy creature; 7
10:56 you will hear as much as your ears can hear. 7
15: 1 Behold, speak in the ears of my people the words 7
Wis 1:10 because a jealous ear hears all things 4
15:15 nor ears with which to hear 4
Sir 3:29 an attentive ear is the wise man's desire. 4
4: 8 Incline your ear to the poor 4
6:33 if you incline your ear you will become wise. 4
16: 5 my ear has heard things more striking 4
17: 6 he gave them ears and a mind for thinking. 4
13 their ears heard the glory of his voice. 4
21: 5 goes from his lips to the ears of God 6
27:14 their quarrels make a man stop his ears. 6
38:28 he inclines his ear to the sound of the hammer 4
51:16 I inclined my ear a little and received her 4
Bar 2:16 Incline thy ear, O Lord, and hear; 4
31 give them a heart that obeys and ears that hear; 4
2Mc 15:39 so also the style of the story delights the ears 3

ear (2) 1. אָבִיב 2. שִׁבֹּלֶת 3. στάχυς

Gen 41: 6 behold, after them sprouted seven ears 2
7 the thin ears swallowed up the seven plump 2
7 swallowed up the seven plump and full ears. 2
22 saw in my dream seven ears growing on one stalk 2
23 seven ears, withered, thin, and blighted 2
24 the thin ears swallowed up the seven good ears. 2
24 the thin ears swallowed up the seven good ears. 2
26 and the seven good ears are seven years; 2
27 the seven empty ears blighted by the east wind 2
Exd 9:31 the barley was in the ear and the flax was in bud. 1
Isa 17: 5 gathers . . grain and his arm harvests the ears 2
Mrk 4:28 then the ear, then the full grain in the ear. 3
28 then the ear, then the full grain in the ear. 3

ear *See* come, give, perceive.

fresh ear 1. אָבִיב

Lev 2:14 offer . . crushed new grain from fresh ears 1

fresh ear of grain 1. כַּרְמֶל

2Kg 4:42 bringing . . and fresh ears of grain in his sack. 1

ear of grain 1. שִׁבֹּלֶת

Gen 41: 5 and behold, seven ears of grain, plump and good 1
Rut 2: 2 and glean among the ears of grain after him 1
Isa 17: 5 the ears of grain in the Valley of Reph'aim. 1

early 1. אָז 2. רִאשׁוֹן 3. שכם 4. ἀρχαῖος 5. ὀρθρίζω
6. ὄρθρος 7. πρόϊμος 8. πρωΐ 9. πρῶτος 10. φθάνω

Jos 8:14 made haste and went out early to the descent 3
Rut 2: 7 she has continued from early morning until now 1
1Sm 29:11 David set out with his men early in the morning 3
2Kg 6:15 servant . . rose early in the morning and went out 3
2Ch 17: 3 he walked in the earlier ways of his father; 2
Ps 127: 2 in vain that you rise up early and go late to rest 3
Hos 6: 4 Your love is . . like the dew that goes early away. 3
13: 3 they shall be . . like the dew that goes early away 3
Mat 20: 1 a householder who went out early in the morning 8
Mrk 16: 2 very early on the first day of the week 8
9 Now when he rose early on the first day of the week 8
Lke 24: 1 on the first day of the week, at early dawn 6
Joh 18:28 It was early 8
20: 1 Mary Mag'dalene came to the tomb early 8
Act 15: 7 in the early days God made choice among you 4
21 from early generations 4
21:16 Mnason of Cyprus, an early disciple 4
Jas 5: 7 until it receives the early and the late rain 7
Wis 4: 7 though he die early 10
Sir 4:12 those who seek her early will be filled with joy. 5
6:36 If you see an intelligent man, visit him early 5
31:20 he rises early, and feels fit 8
1Mc 3:29 laws that had existed from the earliest days. 9

early *See also* arise, fig, go, morning, rain, rise, start.

early in the morning 1. ὀρθρίζω 2. ὀρθρινός
3. ὄρθριος 4. ὄρθρος 5. πρωΐ

Lke 21:38 early in the morning all the people came to him 1
24:22 They were at the tomb early in the morning 2
Joh 8: 2 Early in the morning he came again to the temple 4
Bel 1:16 Early in the morning the king rose and came 5
1Mc 3:58 Be ready early in the morning to fight 5
4:52 Early in the morning on the 25th day 5
6:33 Early in the morning the king rose 5
11:67 Early in the morning they marched to the plain 5
16: 5 Early in the morning they arose 5
3Mc 5:10 Hermon . . presented himself . . early in the morning 3

right early 1. פנה בֹּקֶר

Ps 46: 5 God will help her right early. 1

earn 1. עשה 2. ἐσθίω

Deu 24:15 you shall give him his hire on the day he earns it •
Prv 11:18 A wicked man earns deceptive wages 1
2Th 3:12 to earn their own living. 2

earn a wage 1. שׂכר

Hag 1: 6 he who earns wages earns wages to put them 1
6 earns wages to put them into a bag with holes. 1

earn money 1. ἐριθεύομαι

Tob 2:11 Then my wife Anna earned money at women's work. 1

earnest 1. ἐκτενῶς 2. προθύμως 3. σπουδαῖος

Act 12: 5 earnest prayer for him was made to God 1
2Co 8:22 and found earnest in many matters 3
4Mc 1: 1 to pay earnest attention to philosophy. 2

earnest *See also* care.

more earnest 1. πᾶς 2. σπουδαῖος

2Co 8:22 who is now more earnest than ever 2
3Mc 3:10 to exert more earnest efforts for their assistance. 1

very earnest 1. σπουδαῖος

2Co 8:17 being himself very earnest 1

earnestly 1. ἐκτένεια 2. ἐκτενῶς 3. ἐπιθυμία
4. μετὰ πολλῆς 5. σπουδαίως 6. ὑπερεκπερισσοῦ

1Sm 20: 6 David earnestly asked . . to run to Bethlehem †
28 David earnestly asked . . to go to Bethlehem; †
Lke 7: 4 they besought him earnestly, saying, "He is worthy 5
22:15 I have earnestly desired to eat this passover 3
Act 26: 7 as they earnestly worship night and day 1
2Co 8: 4 begging us earnestly for the favor 4
1Th 3:10 praying earnestly night and day that we may see 6
1Pe 1:22 love one another earnestly from the heart. 2
Jdt 4:12 praying earnestly to the God of Israel 2
Man 1:13 I earnestly beseech thee, forgive me, O Lord †

earnestly *See also* remember, seek.

earnestly desire 1. ζηλόω

1Co 12:31 earnestly desire the higher gifts 1
14: 1 earnestly desire the spiritual gifts 1
39 So, my brethren, earnestly desire to prophesy 1

more earnestly 1. περισσοτέρως

Heb 13:19 I urge you the more earnestly to do this 1

earnestness 1. σπουδή

2Co 7:11 what earnestness this godly grief has produced 1
8: 7 in all earnestness, and in your love for us 1
8 to prove by the earnestness of others 1
Heb 6:11 to show the same earnestness 1

earring 1. נֶזֶם 2. עָגִיל 3. ἐνώτιον

Exd 35:22 all . . brought brooches and earrings 1
Num31:50 LORD'S offering . . signet rings, earrings 2
Jdg 8:24 give me every man of you the earrings of his spoil. 1
24 For they had golden earrings, because they were 1
25 every man cast in it the earrings of his spoil. 1
26 weight of the golden earrings that he requested 1
Ezk 16:12 I put a ring on your nose, and earrings in your ears 2
Jdt 10: 4 put on . . her earrings and all her ornaments 3

earth 1. אֲדָמָה 2. אֶרֶץ 3. עָפָר 4. אֲרַע (A) 5. אֲרַק (A) 6. יַבֶּשֶׁת (A) 7. γῆ 8. ἐπίγειος 9. orbis 10. orbis terrarum 11. terra 12. terrenus

Gen 1: 1 God created the heavens and the earth 2
2 The earth was without form and void 2
10 God called the dry land Earth 2
11 God said, "Let the earth put forth vegetation 2
11 each according to its kind, upon the earth 2
12 The earth brought forth vegetation 2
15 in . . the heavens to give light upon the earth 2
17 in . . the heavens to give light upon the earth 2
20 and let birds fly above the earth 2
22 and let birds multiply on the earth 2
24 God said, "Let the earth bring forth living 2
24 creeping things and beasts of the earth 2
25 God made the beasts of the earth 2
26 have dominion . . over all the earth 2
26 every creeping thing that creeps upon the earth 2
28 and fill the earth and subdue it; 2
28 every living thing that moves upon the earth. 2
29 plant . . which is upon the face of all the earth 2
30 to every beast of the earth 2
30 and to everything that creeps on the earth 2
2: 1 Thus the heavens and the earth were finished 2
4 the generations of the heavens and the earth 2
4 the LORD God made the earth and the heavens 2
5 when no plant of the field was yet in the earth 2
5 God had not caused it to rain upon the earth 2
6 a mist went up from the earth 2
4:12 be a fugitive and a wanderer on the earth. 2
14 I shall be a fugitive and a wanderer on the earth 2
6: 4 The Nephilim were on the earth in those days 2
5 the wickedness of man was great in the earth 2
6 that he had made man on the earth 2
11 Now the earth was corrupt in God's sight 2
11 the earth was filled with violence. 2
12 God saw the earth, and behold, it was corrupt; 2
12 flesh had corrupted their way upon the earth. 2
13 for the earth is filled with violence 2
13 behold, I will destroy them with the earth. 2
17 I will bring a flood of waters upon the earth 2
17 everything that is on the earth shall die. 2
7: 3 kind alive upon the face of all the earth. 2
4 For in seven days I will send rain upon the earth 2
6 when the flood of waters came upon the earth. 2
10 the waters of the flood came upon the earth. 2
12 rain fell upon the earth 40 days and 40 nights. 2
14 that creeps on the earth according to its kind 2
17 The flood continued 40 days upon the earth; 2
17 the ark, and it rose high above the earth. 2
18 waters . . increased greatly upon the earth; 2
19 the waters prevailed so mightily upon the earth 2
21 all flesh died that moved upon the earth 2
21 swarming creatures that swarm upon the earth 2
23 they were blotted out from the earth. 2
24 the waters prevailed upon the earth 150 days. 2
8: 1 wind blow over the earth, and the waters subsided; 2
3 the waters receded from the earth continually. 2
7 the waters were dried up from the earth. 2
9 were still on the face of the whole earth. 2
11 that the waters had subsided from the earth. 2
13 the waters were dried from off the earth; 2
14 the earth was dry. 2
17 every creeping thing that creeps on the earth– 2
17 that they may breed abundantly on the earth 2
17 and be fruitful and multiply upon the earth. 2
19 everything that moves upon the earth, went forth 2
22 While the earth remains, seedtime and harvest 2
9: 1 Be fruitful and multiply, and fill the earth. 2
2 shall be upon every beast of the earth 2
7 bring forth abundantly on the earth and multiply 2
10 the birds, the cattle, and every beast of the earth 2
11 shall there be a flood to destroy the earth. 2
13 a sign of the covenant between me and the earth. 2
14 When I bring clouds over the earth 2
16 of all flesh that is upon the earth. 2
17 me and all flesh that is upon the earth. 2
19 from these the whole earth was peopled. 2
10: 8 he was the first on earth to be a mighty man. 2
25 Peleg, for in his days the earth was divided 2
32 spread abroad on the earth after the flood. 2
11: 1 the whole earth had one language and few words. 2
4 abroad upon the face of the whole earth. 2
8 from there over the face of all the earth 2
9 confused the language of all the earth; 2
9 them abroad over the face of all the earth. 2
12: 3 by you all the families of the earth shall bless 1
13:16 your descendants as the dust of the earth; 2
16 that if one can count the dust of the earth 2
14:19 by God Most High, maker of heaven and earth; 2
22 LORD God Most High, maker of heaven and earth 2
18: 2 he ran . . and bowed himself to the earth 2
18 the nations of the earth shall bless themselves 2
25 Shall not the Judge of all the earth do right? 2
19: 1 and bowed himself with his face to the earth 2
23 sun had risen on the earth when Lot came to Zo'ar. 2
31 there is not a man on earth to come in to us 2
31 to come in to us after the manner of all the earth. 2
22:18 all the nations of the earth bless themselves 2
24: 3 God of heaven and of the earth, that you will not 2
52 heard their words, he bowed himself to the earth 2
26: 4 the nations of the earth shall bless themselves 2
15 Philistines had stopped and filled with earth 3
27:28 give you . . of the fatness of the earth 2
39 Behold, away from the fatness of the earth 2
28:12 there was a ladder set up on the earth 2
14 descendants shall be like the dust of the earth 2
14 all the families of the earth bless themselves. 1
41:47 seven plenteous years the earth brought forth 2
57 Moreover, all the earth came to Egypt to Joseph 2
57 the famine was severe over all the earth. 2
45: 7 to preserve for you a remnant on earth 2
48:12 he bowed himself with his face to the earth. 2
16 grow into a multitude in the midst of the earth. 2
Exd 8:16 your rod and strike the dust of the earth 2
17 Aaron . . struck the dust of the earth 2
17 all the dust of the earth became gnats 2
22 that I am the LORD in the midst of the earth. 2
9:14 that there is none like me in all the earth. 2
15 you would have been cut off from the earth; 2
16 name may be declared throughout all the earth. 2
23 thunder and hail, and fire ran down to the earth. 2
29 that you may know that the earth is the LORD'S. 2
33 the rain no longer poured upon the earth. 2
10: 6 from the day they came on earth to this day.' 1
15:12 thy right hand, the earth swallowed them. 2
19: 5 for all the earth is mine 2
20: 4 anything . . that is in the earth beneath 2
4 anything . . that is in the water under the earth; 2
11 for in six days the LORD made heaven and earth 2
24 An altar of earth you shall make for me 1
31:17 in six days the LORD made heaven and earth 2
32:12 to consume them from the face of the earth'? 1
33:16 other people that are upon the face of the earth? 1
34: 8 bow his head toward the earth, and worshiped. 2
10 such as have not been wrought in all the earth 2
Lev 11: 2 among all the beasts that are on the earth 2
21 legs . . with which to leap on the earth 2
29 the swarming things that swarm upon the earth 2
41 Every swarming thing that swarms upon the earth 2
42 the swarming things that swarm upon the earth 2
44 any swarming thing that crawls upon the earth 2
46 every living creature that swarms upon the earth 2
26:19 I will make . . your earth like brass 2
Num11:31 about two cubits above the face of the earth. 2
12: 3 than all men that were on the face of the earth. 1
14:21 as all the earth shall be filled with the glory 2
16:32 earth opened its mouth and swallowed them up 2
33 earth closed over them, and they perished 2
34 for they said, "Lest the earth swallow us up! 2
22: 5 cover the face of the earth, and they are dwelling 2
11 a people . . covers the face of the earth; now come 2
26:10 the earth opened its mouth and swallowed them up 2
Deu 3:24 what god is there in heaven or on earth who can do 2
4:10 fear me all the days that they live upon the earth 1
17 likeness of any beast that is on the earth 2
18 any fish that is in the water under the earth. 2
26 I call heaven and earth to witness against you 2
32 since the day that God created man upon the earth 2
36 on earth he let you see his great fire 2
39 know . . the LORD is God . . on the earth beneath; 2
5: 8 likeness of anything . . that is on the earth beneath 2
8 anything . . that is in the water under the earth; 2
6:15 destroy you from off the face of the earth. 1
7: 6 out of all the people . . on the face of the earth. 1
10:14 to the LORD . . belong . . , the earth with all that 2
11: 6 how the earth opened its mouth and swallowed 2
21 as long as the heavens are above the earth. 2
12: 1 all the days that you live upon the earth. 1
16 blood . . pour it out upon the earth like water. 2
24 you shall pour it out upon the earth like water. 2
13: 7 from the one end of the earth to the other 2
14: 2 out of all the peoples . . on the face of the earth. 1
28: 1 set you high above all the nations of the earth. 2
10 all the peoples of the earth shall see that 2
23 earth under you shall be iron. 2
25 be a horror to all the kingdoms of the earth. 2
26 body shall be food . . for the beasts of the earth; 2
49 bring . . from afar, from the end of the earth 2
64 scatter . . from one end of the earth to the other; 2
30:19 I call heaven and earth to witness against you 2
31:28 call heaven and earth to witness against them. 2
32: 1 let the earth hear the words of my mouth. 2
13 He made him ride on the high places of the earth 2
22 burns . . devours the earth and its increase 2
33:16 with the best gifts of the earth and its fulness 2
17 push the peoples . . to the ends of the earth; 2
Jos 2:11 is God in heaven above and on earth beneath. 2
3:11 ark of the covenant of the Lord of all the earth 2
13 bear the ark of the LORD, the Lord of all the earth 2
4:24 so that all the peoples of the earth may know that 2
5:14 And Joshua fell on his face to the earth 2
7: 6 and fell to the earth upon his face before the ark 2
9 surround us, and cut off our name from the earth; 2
21 they are hidden in the earth inside my tent 2
23:14 And now I am about to go the way of all the earth 2
Jdg 5: 4 the earth trembled, and the heavens dropped 2
18: 7 lacking nothing that is in the earth 2
10 there is no lack of anything that is in the earth. 2
1Sm 2: 8 For the pillars of the earth are the LORD'S 2
10 The LORD will judge the ends of the earth; 2
4: 5 gave a mighty shout, so that the earth resounded. 2
12 his clothes rent and with earth upon his head. 1
14:15 and even the raiders trembled; the earth quaked; 2
17:46 give the dead . . to the wild beasts of the earth; 2
46 that all the earth may know that there is a God 2
20:15 LORD cuts off every . . from the face of the earth 1
31 as long as the son of Jesse lives upon the earth 1
24: 8 David bowed with his face to the earth 2
26: 8 pin him to the earth with one stroke of the spear 2
20 Now therefore, let not my blood fall to the earth 2
28:13 I see a god coming up out of the earth. 2
23 he arose from the earth, and sat upon the bed. 2
2Sm 1: 2 with his clothes rent and earth upon his head. 1
4:11 shall I not now . . destroy you from the earth? 2
7: 9 like the name of the great ones of the earth. 2
23 What other nation on earth is like thy people 2
12:20 Then David arose from the earth, and washed 2
13:31 arose, and rent his garments, and lay on the earth; 2
14: 7 name nor remnant upon the face of the earth. 1
20 to know all things that are on the earth. 2
15:32 with his coat rent and earth upon his head. 1
18: 9 and he was left hanging between heaven and earth 2
28 bowed before the king with his face to the earth 2
22: 8 Then the earth reeled and rocked; 2
43 I beat them fine as the dust of the earth 2
23: 4 rain that makes grass to sprout from the earth. 2
1Kg 1:40 joy, so that the earth was split by their noise. 2
52 If . . not one of his hairs shall fall to the earth; 2
2: 2 I am about to go the way of all the earth. Be strong 2
4:34 men came . . from all the kings of the earth, who 2
8:23 God like thee, in heaven above or on earth beneath 2
27 But will God indeed dwell on the earth? 2
43 peoples of the earth may know thy name and fear 2
53 from among all the peoples of the earth, to be 2
60 that all the peoples of the earth may know 2
10:23 King Solomon excelled all the kings of the earth 2
24 the whole earth sought the presence of Solomon 2
13:34 and to destroy it from the face of the earth. 1
17:14 the day that the LORD sends rain upon the earth.' 1
18: 1 Go . . to Ahab; and I will send rain upon the earth. 1
42 he bowed himself down upon the earth 2
2Kg 5:15 there is no God in all the earth but in Israel; 2
17 let there be given . . two mules' burden of earth; 1
10:10 there shall fall to the earth nothing of the word 2
19:15 God, thou alone, of all the kingdoms of the earth; 2
15 O LORD . . thou hast made heaven and earth. 2
19 that all the kingdoms of the earth may know 2
1Ch 1:10 he began to be a mighty one in the earth. 2
19 Peleg (for in his days the earth was divided) 2
16:14 LORD our God; his judgments are in all the earth. 2
23 Sing to the Lord, all the earth! 2
30 tremble before him, all the earth; 2
31 Let the heavens be glad, and let the earth rejoice 2
33 the LORD, for he comes to judge the earth. 2
17: 8 like the name of the great ones of the earth. 2
21 What other nation on earth is like thy people 2
21:16 of the LORD standing between earth and heaven 2
22: 8 have shed so much blood before me upon the earth. 2
29:11 all . . in the heavens and in the earth is thine; 2

15 our days on the earth are like a shadow 2
2Ch 1: 9 over a people as many as the dust of the earth. 2
2:12 LORD . . who made heaven and earth 2
6:14 there is no God like thee, in heaven or on earth 2
18 will God dwell indeed with man on the earth? 2
33 that all the peoples of the earth may know thy 2
7: 3 they bowed down with their faces to the earth 2
9:22 King Solomon excelled all the kings of the earth 2
23 all the kings of the earth sought . . Solomon 2
16: 9 run to and fro throughout the whole earth 2
32:19 the gods of the peoples of the earth 2
36:23 given me all the kingdoms of the earth 2
Ezr 1: 2 given me all the kingdoms of the earth 2
5:11 'We are the servants of the God of heaven and earth 4
Neh 9: 1 assembled . . with earth upon their heads. 1
6 thou hast made . . the earth and all that is on it 2
Job 1: 7 From going to and fro on the earth 2
8 Job, that there is none like him on the earth 2
2: 2 From going to and fro on the earth 2
3 Job, that there is none like him on the earth 2
3:14 with kings and counselors of the earth 2
5:10 he gives rain upon the earth and sends waters 2
22 shall not fear the beasts of the earth. 2
25 your offspring as the grass of the earth. 2
7: 1 Has not man a hard service upon earth 2
21 For now I shall lie in the earth; thou wilt seek me 3
8: 9 know nothing, for our days on earth are a shadow. 2
19 out of the earth others will spring. 3
9: 6 who shakes the earth out of its place 2
24 The earth is given into the hand of the wicked; 2
11: 9 Its measure is longer than the earth 2
12: 8 the plants of the earth, and they will teach you; 2
24 from the chiefs of the people of the earth 2
14: 8 Though its root grow old in the earth 2
19 the torrents wash away the soil of the earth; 2
15:29 nor will he strike root in the earth; 2
16:18 O earth, cover not my blood 2
18: 4 in your anger, shall the earth be forsaken for you 2
17 His memory perishes from the earth 2
19:25 at last he will stand upon the earth; 3
20: 4 from of old, since man was placed upon earth 2
27 the earth will rise up against him. 2
24: 4 the poor of the earth all hide themselves. 2
26: 7 over the void, and hangs the earth upon nothing. 2
28: 2 Iron is taken out of the earth 3
5 As for the earth, out of it comes bread; 2
24 For he looks to the ends of the earth, 2
30: 6 must dwell, in holes of the earth and of the rocks. 3
34:13 Who gave him charge over the earth 2
35:11 who teaches us more than the beasts of the earth 2
37: 3 his lightning to the corners of the earth. 2
6 For to the snow he says, 'Fall on the earth'; 2
17 when the earth is still because of the south wind? 2
38: 4 when I laid the foundation of the earth? 2
13 that it might take hold of the skirts of the earth 2
18 Have you comprehended the expanse of the earth? 2
24 where the east wind is scattered upon the earth? 2
33 Can you establish their rule on the earth? 2
39:14 For she leaves her eggs to the earth 2
41:33 Upon earth there is not his like, a creature 3
Ps 2: 2 The kings of the earth set themselves 2
8 and the ends of the earth your possession. 2
10 O kings, be wise; be warned, O rulers of the earth. 2
8: 1 our Lord, how majestic is thy name in all the earth! 2
9 our Lord, how majestic is thy name in all the earth! 2
10:18 so that man who is of the earth may strike terror 2
18: 7 Then the earth reeled and rocked; 2
19: 4 yet their voice goes out through all the earth 2
21:10 You will destroy their offspring from the earth 2
22:27 All the ends of the earth shall remember and turn 2
29 to him shall all the proud of the earth bow down; 2
24: 1 The earth is the LORD'S and the fulness thereof 2
33: 5 earth is full of the steadfast love of the LORD. 2
8 Let all the earth fear the LORD 2
14 looks forth on all the inhabitants of the earth 2
34:16 to cut off the remembrance of them from the earth. 2
45:16 you will make them princes in all the earth. 2
46: 2 we will not fear though the earth should change 2
6 he utters his voice, the earth melts. 2
8 how he has wrought desolations in the earth. 2
9 He makes wars cease to the end of the earth; 2
10 among the nations, I am exalted in the earth! 2
47: 2 is terrible, a great king over all the earth. 2
7 For God is the king of all the earth; 2
9 For the shields of the earth belong to God; 2
48: 2 is the joy of all the earth, Mount Zion 2
10 so thy praise reaches to the ends of the earth. 2
50: 1 summons the earth from the rising of the sun 2
4 He calls to the heavens above and to the earth 2
57: 5 Let they glory be over all the earth! 2
11 Let thy glory be over all the earth! 2
58: 2 your hands deal out violence on earth. 2
11 surely there is a God who judges on earth. 2
59:13 God rules over Jacob to the ends of the earth. 2
61: 2 from the end of the earth I call to thee 2
63: 9 shall go down into the depths of the earth; 2
65: 5 God . . who art the hope of all the ends of the earth 2
8 those who dwell at earth's farthest bounds •
9 Thou visitest the earth and waterest it 2
66: 1 Make a joyful noise to God, all the earth; 2
4 earth worships thee; they sing praises to thee 2
67: 2 that thy way may be known upon earth 2
4 with equity and guide the nations upon earth. 2
6 The earth has yielded its increase; 2
7 let all the ends of the earth fear him! 2
68: 8 earth quaked, the heavens poured down rain 2
32 Sing to God, O kingdoms of the earth; sing praises 2
69:34 Let heaven and earth praise him 2
71:20 from the depths of the earth thou wilt bring me up 2
72: 6 like rain . . like showers that water the earth! 2
8 to sea, and from the River to the ends of the earth! 2
19 may his glory fill the whole earth! Amen and Amen! 2
73: 9 their tongue struts through the earth. 2
25 there is nothing upon earth that I desire 2
74:12 working salvation in the midst of the earth. 2
17 Thou hast fixed all the bounds of the earth; 2
75: 3 When the earth totters, and all its inhabitants 2
8 all the wicked of the earth shall drain it down 2
76: 8 the earth feared and was still 2
9 to save all the oppressed of the earth. Selah 2
12 who is terrible to the kings of the earth. 2
77:18 the earth trembled and shook. 2
78:69 like the earth, which he has founded for ever. 2
79: 2 flesh of thy saints to the beasts of the earth. 2
82: 5 all the foundations of the earth are shaken. 2
8 Arise, O God, judge the earth; 2
83:18 LORD, art the Most High over all the earth. 2
89:11 The heavens are thine, the earth also is thine; 2
27 make him . . highest of the kings of the earth. 2
90: 2 ever thou hadst formed the earth and the world 2
94: 2 Rise up, O judge of the earth; 2
95: 4 In his hand are the depths of the earth; 2
96: 1 sing to the LORD, all the earth! 2
9 tremble before him, all the earth! 2
11 Let the heavens be glad, and let the earth rejoice; 2
13 for he comes, for he comes to judge the earth. 2
97: 1 The LORD reigns; let the earth rejoice; 2
4 earth sees and trembles. 2
5 before the LORD, before the Lord of all the earth. 2
9 For thou, O LORD, art most high over all the earth; 2
98: 3 ends of the earth have seen the victory of our God. 2
4 Make a joyful noise to the LORD, all the earth; 2
9 before the LORD, for he comes to judge the earth. 2
99: 1 enthroned upon the cherubim; let the earth quake! 2
102:15 all the kings of the earth, thy glory. 2
19 from heaven the LORD looked at the earth 2
25 Of old thou didst lay the foundation of the earth 2
103:11 For as the heavens are high above the earth 2
104: 5 Thou didst set the earth on its foundations 2
9 so that they might not again cover the earth. 2
13 earth is satisfied with the fruit of thy work. 2
14 that he may bring forth food from the earth 2
24 the earth is full of thy creatures. 2
32 who looks on the earth and it trembles 2
35 Let sinners be consumed from the earth 2
105: 7 LORD our God; his judgments are in all the earth. 2
106:17 earth opened and swallowed up Dathan 2
108: 5 Let thy glory be over all the earth! 2
109:15 may his memory be cut off from the earth! 2
110: 6 he will shatter chiefs over the wide earth. 2
113: 6 who looks far down upon the heavens and the earth? 2
114: 7 Tremble, O earth, at the presence of the LORD 2
115:15 blessed by the LORD, who made heaven and earth! 2
16 but the earth he has given to the sons of men. 2
119:19 I am a sojourner on earth; 2
64 The earth, O LORD, is full of thy steadfast love; 2
87 They have almost made an end of me on earth; 2
90 thou hast established the earth, and it stands 2
119the wicked of the earth thou dost count as dross; 2
121: 2 help . . from the LORD, who made heaven and earth. 2
124: 8 LORD, who made heaven and earth. 2
134: 3 LORD bless . . he who made heaven and earth! 2
135: 6 in heaven and on earth, in the seas and all deeps. 2
7 who makes the clouds rise at the end of the earth 2
136: 6 to him who spread out the earth upon the waters 2
138: 4 kings of the earth shall praise thee, O LORD 2
139:15 intricately wrought in the depths of the earth. 2
146: 4 When his breath departs he returns to his earth; 1
6 who made heaven and earth, the sea, and all that 2
147: 8 he prepares rain for the earth 2
15 He sends forth his command to the earth; 2
148: 7 Praise the LORD from the earth, you sea monsters 2
11 Kings of the earth and all peoples 2
11 princes and all rulers of the earth! 2
13 his glory is above earth and heaven. 2
Prv 3:19 LORD by wisdom founded the earth; 2
8:16 by me princes rule, and nobles govern the earth. 7
23 at the first, before the beginning of the earth. 2
26 before he had made the earth with its fields 2
29 when he marked out the foundations of the earth 2
11:31 If the righteous is requited on earth 2
17:24 but the eyes of a fool are on the ends of the earth. 2
25: 3 As the heaven for height, and the earth for depth 2
30: 4 Who has established all the ends of the earth? 2
14 to devour the poor from off the earth, the needy 2
16 earth ever thirsty for water, and the fire 2
21 Under three things the earth trembles; 2
24 Four things on earth are small 2
Ecc 1: 4 A generation . . but the earth remains for ever. 2
3:21 and the spirit of the beast goes down to the earth? 2
5: 2 for God is in heaven, and you upon earth; 2
7:20 Surely there is not a righteous man on earth 2
8:14 There is a vanity which takes place on earth 2
16 and to see the business that is done on earth 2
11: 2 for you know not what evil may happen on earth. 2
3 clouds . . empty themselves on the earth; 2
12: 7 and the dust returns to the earth as it was 2
Sng 2:12 The flowers appear on the earth 2
Isa 1: 2 Hear, O heavens, and give ear, O earth; 2
2:19 when he rises to terrify the earth. 2
21 his majesty, when he rises to terrify the earth. 2
5:26 whistle for it from the ends of the earth; and lo 2
6: 3 the whole earth is full of his glory. 2
8:22 they will look to the earth, but behold, distress 2
10:14 eggs . . forsaken so I have gathered all the earth; 2
23 full end, as decreed, in the midst of all the earth. 2
11: 4 and decide with equity for the meek of the earth; 2
4 he shall smite the earth with the rod of his mouth 2
9 earth shall be full of the knowledge of the LORD 2
12 Judah from the four corners of the earth. 2
12: 5 let this be known in all the earth. 2
13: 5 his indignation, to destroy the whole earth. 2
9 the LORD comes . . to make the earth a desolation 2
13 and the earth will be shaken out of its place 2
14: 7 The whole earth is at rest and quiet; 2
9 the shades . . all who were leaders of the earth; 2
16 Is this the man who made the earth tremble 2
21 lest they rise and possess the earth 2
26 purpose . . purposed concerning the whole earth; 2
18: 3 inhabitants . . you who dwell on the earth 2
6 be left . . to the beasts of the earth. 2
6 the beasts of the earth will winter upon them. 2
19:24 Israel . . a blessing in the midst of the earth 2
23: 8 whose traders were the honored of the earth? 2
9 to dishonor all the honored of the earth. 2
17 kingdoms of the world upon the face of the earth. 2
24: 1 Behold, the LORD will lay waste the earth 2
3 The earth shall be utterly laid waste 2
4 The earth mourns and withers 2
4 the heavens languish together with the earth. 2
5 The earth lies polluted under its inhabitants; 2
6 Therefore a curse devours the earth 2
6 the inhabitants of the earth are scorched 2
11 all joy . . the gladness of the earth is banished. 2
13 thus it shall be in the midst of the earth among 2
16 From the ends of the earth we hear songs of praise 2
17 the snare are upon you, O inhabitant of the earth! 2
18 and the foundations of the earth tremble. 2
19 The earth is utterly broken, the earth is rent 2
19 the earth is rent asunder, the earth is violently 2
19 is rent asunder, the earth is violently shaken. 2
20 The earth staggers like a drunken man, it sways 2
21 in heaven, and the kings of the earth, on the earth. 1
21 in heaven, and the kings of the earth, on the earth. 1
25: 8 reproach . . he will take away from all the earth; 2
26: 9 For when thy judgments are in the earth 2
18 We have wrought no deliverance in the earth 2
21 to punish the inhabitants of the earth 2
21 the earth will disclose the blood shed upon her 2
28: 2 he will cast down to the earth with violence. 2
29: 4 Then deep from the earth you shall speak 2
34: 1 Let the earth listen, and all that fills it; 2
37:16 the God . . of all the kingdoms of the earth; 2
16 thou hast made heaven and earth. 2
20 that all the kingdoms of the earth may know that 2
40:12 enclosed the dust of the earth in a measure 2
21 understood from the foundations of the earth? 2
22 It is he who sits above the circle of the earth 2
23 and makes the rulers of the earth as nothing. 2
24 scarcely has their stem taken root in the earth 2
28 the Creator of the ends of the earth. 2
41: 5 the ends of the earth tremble; 2
9 you whom I took from the ends of the earth 2
42: 4 till he has established justice in the earth; 2
5 who spread forth the earth and what comes from it 2
10 a new song, his praise from the end of the earth! 2
43: 6 bring . . my daughters from the end of the earth 2
44:23 shout, O depths of the earth; 2
24 who spread out the earth-Who was with me?- 2
45: 8 the earth open, that salvation may sprout forth 2
12 I made the earth, and created man upon it; 2
18 (he is God!), who formed the earth and made it 2
22 Turn to me and be saved, all the ends of the earth! 2
48:13 My hand laid the foundation of the earth 2
20 proclaim it, send it forth to the end of the earth; 2
49: 6 my salvation may reach to the end of the earth. 2
13 Sing for joy, O heavens, and exult, O earth; 2
51: 6 eyes to the heavens, and look at the earth beneath; 2
6 like smoke, the earth will wear out like a garment 2
13 Maker, who . . laid the foundations of the earth 2
16 and laying the foundations of the earth 2
52:10 all the ends of the earth shall see the salvation 2
54: 5 Redeemer, the God of the whole earth he is called. 2
9 waters of Noah should no more go over the earth 2
55: 9 For as the heavens are higher than the earth 2
10 and return not thither but water the earth 2
58:14 I will make you ride upon the heights of the earth; 2

60: 2 For behold, darkness shall cover the earth 2
61:11 For as the earth brings forth its shoots 2
62: 7 Jerusalem and makes it a praise in the earth. 2
11 the LORD has proclaimed to the end of the earth 2
63: 6 and I poured out their lifeblood on the earth. 2
65:17 For behold, I create new heavens and a new earth; 2
66: 1 Heaven is my throne and the earth is my footstool; 2
22 new heavens and the new earth which I will make 2
Jer 4:23 I looked on the earth, and lo, it was waste and void; 2
28 For this the earth shall mourn 2
6:19 Hear, O earth; behold, I am bringing evil 2
22 stirring from the farthest parts of the earth. 2
7:33 birds of the air, and for the beasts of the earth; 2
9:24 justice, and righteousness in the earth; 2
10:10 At his wrath the earth quakes 2
11 gods who did not make the heavens and the earth 5
11 shall perish from the earth 4
12 It is he who made the earth by his power 2
13 he makes the mist rise from the ends of the earth. 2
15: 3 the birds of the air and the beasts of the earth 2
4 a horror to all the kingdoms of the earth 2
16: 4 birds of the air and for the beasts of the earth. 2
19 nations come from the ends of the earth and say 2
17:13 turn away from thee shall be written in the earth 2
19: 7 birds of the air and to the beasts of the earth. 2
23:24 Do I not fill heaven and earth? says the LORD. 2
24: 9 a horror to all the kingdoms of the earth 2
25:26 kingdoms . . which are on the face of the earth. 2
29 sword against all the inhabitants of the earth 2
30 against all the inhabitants of the earth. 2
31 The clamor will resound to the ends of the earth 2
32 stirring from the farthest parts of the earth! 2
33 extend from one end of the earth to the other. 2
26: 6 a curse for all the nations of the earth. 2
27: 5 and my outstretched arm have made the earth 2
5 with the men and animals that are on the earth 2
28:16 I will remove you from the face of the earth. 1
29:18 them a horror to all the kingdoms of the earth 2
31: 8 gather them from the farthest parts of the earth 2
22 For the LORD has created a new thing on the earth 2
37 foundations of the earth below can be explored 2
32:17 made the heavens and the earth by thy great power 2
33: 2 Thus says the LORD who made the earth 7
9 and a glory before all the nations of the earth 2
25 and night and the ordinances of heaven and earth 2
34: 1 all his army and all the kingdoms of the earth 2
17 a horror to all the kingdoms of the earth. 2
20 the birds of the air and the beasts of the earth. 2
44: 8 and a taunt among all the nations of the earth? 2
46: 8 He said, I will rise, I will cover the earth 2
12 and the earth is full of your cry; 2
49:21 At . . their fall the earth shall tremble; 2
50:23 hammer of the whole earth is cut down and broken! 2
34 that he may give rest to the earth 2
41 stirring from the farthest parts of the earth. 2
46 At . . capture of Babylon the earth shall tremble 2
51: 7 in the LORD'S hand, making all the earth drunken; 2
15 It is he who made the earth by his power 2
16 he makes the mist rise from the ends of the earth. 2
25 mountain . . which destroys the whole earth; 2
27 Set up a standard on the earth, blow the trumpet 2
41 Babylon . . the praise of the whole earth seized! 2
48 the heavens and the earth, and all that is in them 2
49 have fallen the slain of all the earth. 2
Lam 2: 1 has cast down from heaven to earth the splendor 2
15 the perfection of beauty, the joy of all the earth? 2
3:34 To crush . . all the prisoners of the earth 2
4:12 The kings of the earth did not believe . . that foe 2
Ezk 1:15 I saw a wheel upon the earth 2
19 when the living creatures rose from the earth 2
21 when those rose from the earth, the wheels rose 2
7:21 a prey, and to the wicked of the earth for a spoil; 2
8: 3 the Spirit lifted me up between earth and heaven 2
10:16 lifted up their wings to mount up from the earth 2
19 and mounted up from the earth in my sight 2
27:33 you enriched the kings of the earth. 2
28:18 I turned you to ashes upon the earth 2
29: 5 To the beasts of the earth and to the birds 2
31:12 the peoples of the earth will go from its shadow 2
32: 4 gorge the beasts of the whole earth with you. 2
34: 6 were scattered over all the face of the earth 2
27 and the earth shall yield its increase 2
35:14 For the rejoicing of the whole earth 2
38:12 people . . who dwell at the center of the earth. 2
20 all the men that are upon the face of the earth 1
39:18 and drink the blood of the princes of the earth 2
43: 2 the earth shone with his glory. 2
Dan 2:10 not a man on earth who can meet the king's demand; 6
35 great mountain and filled the whole earth. 4
39 kingdom of bronze . . rule over all the earth. 4
4: 1 to all peoples . . that dwell in all the earth 4
10 saw, and behold, a tree in the midst of the earth; 4
11 tree . . visible to the end of the whole earth. 4
15 leave the stump of its roots in the earth 4
15 lot be with the beasts in the grass of the earth; 4
20 visible to the end of the whole earth; 4
22 your dominion to the ends of the earth. 4
23 but leave the stump of its roots in the earth 4
35 inhabitants of the earth are accounted 4
35 heaven and among the inhabitants of the earth; 4
6:25 to all the peoples . . that dwell in all the earth 4
27 works signs and wonders in heaven and on earth 4
7:17 four kings who shall arise out of the earth. 4
23 beast, there shall be a fourth kingdom on earth 4
23 kingdom . . shall devour the whole earth 4
8: 5 he-goat came . . across the face of the whole earth 2
12: 2 many of those who sleep in the dust of the earth 1
Hos 2:21 the heavens and they shall answer the earth; 2
22 and the earth shall answer the grain, the wine 2
6: 3 as the spring rains that water the earth. 2
Jol 2:10 The earth quakes before them 2
30 give portents in the heavens and on the earth 2
3:16 and the heavens and the earth shake. 2
Ams 3: 2 have I known of all the families of the earth; 1
5 Does a bird fall in a snare on the earth 2
4:13 and treads on the heights of the earth- the LORD 2
5: 7 and cast down righteousness to the earth! 2
8 and pours them out upon the surface of the earth 2
8: 9 and darken the earth in broad daylight. 2
9: 5 The Lord, GOD of hosts, he who touches the earth 2
6 and founds his vault upon the earth; 2
6 and pours them out upon the surface of the earth- 2
9 a sieve, but no pebble shall fall upon the earth. 2
Mic 1: 2 hearken, O earth, and all that is in it; 2
3 and tread upon the high places of the earth. 2
4:13 their wealth to the Lord of the whole earth. 2
5: 4 for now he shall be great to the ends of the earth. 2
6: 2 Hear . . you enduring foundations of the earth; 2
7: 2 The godly man has perished from the earth 2
13 But the earth will be desolate 2
17 lick . . like the crawling things of the earth; 2
Nah 1: 5 the earth is laid waste before him 2
2:13 I will cut off your prey from the earth 2
Hab 1: 6 who march through the breadth of the earth 2
10 for they heap up earth and take it. 3
2: 8 for the blood of men and violence to the earth 2
14 For the earth will be filled with the knowledge 2
17 for the blood of men and violence to the earth 2
20 let all the earth keep silence before him. 2
3: 3 and the earth was full of his praise. Selah 2
6 He stood and measured the earth; 2
9 Thou didst cleave the earth with rivers. 2
12 Thou didst bestride the earth in fury 2
Zep 1: 2 sweep away everything from the face of the earth 1
3 I will cut off mankind from the face of the earth 1
18 all the earth shall be consumed; 2
18 sudden end . . of all the inhabitants of the earth. 2
2:11 yea, he will famish all the gods of the earth 2
3: 8 all the earth shall be consumed. 2
19 shame into praise and renown in all the earth. 2
20 and praised among all the peoples of the earth 2
Hag 1:10 the earth has withheld its produce. 2
2: 6 I will shake the heavens and the earth and the sea 2
21 I am about to shake the heavens and the earth 2
Zec 1:10 whom the LORD has sent to patrol the earth.' 2
11 We have patrolled the earth 2
11 behold, all the earth remains at rest.' 2
4:10 the eyes . . which range through the whole earth. 2
14 who stand by the Lord of the whole earth. 2
5: 9 lifted up the ephah between earth and heaven. 2
6: 5 before the LORD of all the earth. 2
7 were impatient to get off and patrol the earth. 2
7 he said, "Go, patrol the earth." So they patrolled 2
7 patrol the earth." So they patrolled the earth. 2
9:10 from the River to the ends of the earth. 2
11: 6 they shall crush the earth, and I will deliver 2
12: 1 stretched out the heavens and founded the earth 2
3 the nations of the earth will come together 2
14: 9 the LORD will become king over all the earth; 2
17 if any of the families of the earth do not go up 2
Mat 5: 5 the meek, for they shall inherit the earth. 7
13 You are the salt of the earth; but if salt has lost 7
18 For truly, I say to you, till heaven and earth pass 7
35 or by the earth, for it is his footstool 7
6:10 come. Thy will be done, On earth as it is in heaven. 7
19 Do not lay up for yourselves treasures on earth 7
9: 6 the Son of man has authority on earth to forgive 7
10:34 to bring peace on earth 7
11:25 I thank thee, Father, Lord of heaven and earth 7
12:40 three nights in the heart of the earth. 7
42 she came from the ends of the earth 7
16:19 whatever you bind on earth shall be bound 7
19 whatever you loose on earth 7
17:25 From whom do kings of the earth take toll 7
18:18 Truly, I say to you, whatever you bind on earth 7
18 whatever you loose on earth 7
19 Again I say to you, if two of you agree on earth 7
23: 9 call no man your father on earth 7
35 all the righteous blood shed on earth 7
24:30 then all the tribes of the earth will mourn 7
35 Heaven and earth will pass away 7
27:51 the earth shook, and the rocks were split; 7
28:18 All authority in heaven and on earth 7
Mrk 2:10 Son of man has authority on earth to forgive sins"- 7
4:28 The earth produces of itself, first the blade 7
31 the smallest of all the seeds on earth; 7
9: 3 as no fuller on earth could bleach them. 7
13:27 from the ends of the earth to the ends of heaven. 7
31 Heaven and earth will pass away 7
Lke 2:14 on earth peace among men with whom he is pleased! 7
5:24 authority on earth to forgive sins 7
10:21 I thank thee, Father, Lord of heaven and earth 7
11:31 she came from the ends of the earth 7
12:49 I came to cast fire upon the earth 7
51 you think that I have come to give peace on earth? 7
56 to interpret the appearance of the earth and sky; 7
16:17 it is easier for heaven and earth to pass away 7
18: 8 will he find faith on earth? 7
21:23 great distress shall be upon the earth 7
25 upon the earth distress of nations 7
33 Heaven and earth will pass away 7
35 all who dwell upon the face of the whole earth; 7
Joh 3:31 he who is of the earth belongs to the earth 7
31 he who is of the earth belongs to the earth 7
31 belongs to the earth, and of the earth he speaks; 7
12:24 a grain of wheat falls into the earth and dies 7
32 when I am lifted up from the earth 7
17: 4 I glorified thee on earth 7
Act 1: 8 all Judea and Sama'ria and to the end of the earth. 7
2:19 signs on the earth beneath 7
3:25 shall all the families of the earth be blessed.' 7
4:24 the heaven and the earth and the sea 7
26 The kings of the earth set themselves in array 7
7:49 'Heaven is my throne, and earth my footstool 7
8:33 his life is taken up from the earth. 7
10:11 great sheet, let down by four corners upon the earth. 7
13:47 to the uttermost parts of the earth.' 7
14:15 a living God who made the heaven and the earth 7
17:24 being Lord of heaven and earth 7
26 to live on all the face of the earth 7
22:22 Away with such a fellow from the earth! 7
Rom 9:17 so that my name may be proclaimed in all the earth 7
28 Lord will execute his sentence upon the earth 7
10:18 Their voice has gone out to all the earth 7
1Co 8: 5 may be so-called gods in heaven or on earth 7
10:26 For "the earth is the Lord's, and everything in it. 7
15:47 The first man was from the earth, a man of dust 7
Eph 1:10 things in heaven and things on earth. 7
3:15 every family in heaven and on earth is named 7
4: 9 descended into the lower parts of the earth? 7
6: 3 that you may live long on the earth. 7
Php 2:10 in heaven and on earth and under the earth 8
Col 1:16 in heaven and on earth, visible and invisible 7
20 all things, whether on earth or in heaven 7
3: 2 not on things that are on earth. 7
Heb 1:10 Thou, Lord, didst found the earth in the beginning 7
8: 4 Now if he were on earth, he would not be a priest 7
11:13 they were strangers and exiles on the earth. 7
38 in dens and caves of the earth. 7
12:25 they refused him who warned them on earth 7
26 His voice then shook the earth 7
26 shake not only the earth but also the heaven. 7
Jas 5: 5 You have lived on the earth in luxury 7
7 farmer waits for the precious fruit of the earth 7
12 do not swear, either by heaven or by earth 7
17 it did not rain on the earth. 7
18 and the earth brought forth its fruit. 7
2Pe 3: 5 an earth formed out of water and by means of water 7
7 the heavens and earth that now exist 7
10 and the earth . . will be burned up. 7
13 we wait for new heavens and a new earth 7
Rev 1: 5 Jesus Christ . . the ruler of kings on earth. 7
7 tribes of the earth will wail on account of him. 7
3:10 to try those who dwell upon the earth. 7
5: 3 no one in heaven or on earth or under the earth 7
3 no one in heaven or on earth or under the earth 7
6 seven spirits of God sent out into all the earth; 7
10 and they shall reign on the earth. 7
13 I heard every creature in heaven and on earth 7
13 every creature . . under the earth and in the sea 7
6: 4 rider was permitted to take peace from the earth 7
8 they were given power over a fourth of the earth 7
8 kill . . by wild beasts of the earth. 7
10 avenge . . on those who dwell upon the earth? 7
13 the stars of the sky fell to the earth 7
15 Then the kings of the earth and the great men 7
7: 1 angels standing at the four corners of the earth 7
1 holding back the four winds of the earth 7
1 that no wind might blow on earth or sea 7
2 angels who had been given power to harm earth 7
3 Do not harm the earth or the sea or the trees 7
8: 5 filled it with fire . . and threw it on the earth; 7
7 fire, mixed with blood, which fell on the earth; 7
7 and a third of the earth was burnt up 7
13 Woe, woe, woe to those who dwell on the earth 7
9: 1 and I saw a star fallen from heaven to earth 7
3 Then from the smoke came locusts on the earth 7
3 like the power of scorpions of the earth; 7
4 they were told not to harm the grass of the earth 7
10: 6 who created . . the earth and what is in it 7
11: 4 which stand before the Lord of the earth. 7
6 and to smite the earth with every plague 7
10 those who dwell on the earth will rejoice 7
10 a torment to those who dwell on the earth. 7
18 and for destroying the destroyers of the earth. 7
12: 4 the stars of heaven, and cast them to the earth. 7
9 the deceiver . . -he was thrown down to the earth 7

12 woe to you, O earth and sea, for the devil has come 7
13 dragon saw that he had been thrown down to earth 7
16 But the earth came to the help of the woman 7
16 earth opened its mouth and swallowed the river 7
13: 3 the whole earth followed the beast with wonder. 7
8 and all who dwell on earth will worship it 7
11 I saw another beast which rose out of the earth; 7
12 and makes the earth and its inhabitants worship 7
13 even making fire come down from heaven to earth 7
14 it deceives those who dwell on earth 7
14: 3 144,000 who had been redeemed from the earth. 7
6 gospel to proclaim to those who dwell on earth 7
7 and worship him who made heaven and earth 7
15 for the harvest of the earth is fully ripe. 7
16 he . . upon the cloud swung his sickle on the earth 7
16 swung his sickle . . and the earth was reaped. 7
18 and gather the clusters of the vine of the earth 7
19 So the angel swung his sickle on the earth 7
19 the angel . . gathered the vintage of the earth 7
16: 1 pour out on the earth the seven bowls of the wrath 7
2 first angel went and poured his bowl on the earth 7
18 such as had never been since men were on the earth 7
17: 2 kings of the earth have committed fornication 7
2 the dwellers on earth have become drunk. 7
5 mother . . of the earth's abominations. 7
8 and the dwellers on earth . . will marvel 7
18 which has dominion over the kings of the earth. 7
18: 1 and the earth was made bright with his splendor. 7
3 kings of the earth have committed fornication 7
3 the merchants of the earth have grown rich 7
9 the kings of the earth . . will weep and wail 7
11 the merchants of the earth weep and mourn for her 7
23 thy merchants were the great men of the earth 7
24 the blood . . of all who have been slain on earth. 7
19: 2 judged the great harlot who corrupted the earth 7
19 And I saw the beast and the kings of the earth 7
20: 8 nations . . at the four corners of the earth 7
9 And they marched up over the broad earth 7
11 from his presence earth and sky fled away 7
21: 1 Then I saw a new heaven and a new earth; 7
1 first heaven and the first earth had passed away 7
24 the kings of the earth shall bring their glory 7
1Es 4:34 The earth is vast, and heaven is high 7
36 The whole earth calls upon truth 7
6:13 the Lord who created the heaven and the earth. 7
8:77 were given over to the kings of the earth 7
2Es 2: 7 let their names be blotted out from the earth 11
14 Call, O call heaven and earth to witness 11
31 out of the hiding places of the earth 11
3: 4 when thou didst form the earth 11
6 right hand had planted before the earth appeared. 11
12 When those who dwelt on earth began to multiply 11
18 bend down the heavens and shake the earth 11
35 have the inhabitants of the earth not sinned 11
4:21 also those who dwell upon earth 11
21 can understand only what is on the earth 11
39 on account of the sins of those who dwell on earth. 11
5: 1 when those who dwell on earth shall be seized 11
6 whom those who dwell on earth do not expect 11
10 and unrestraint shall increase on earth. 11
23 O sovereign Lord, from every forest of the earth 11
48 Even so have I given the womb of the earth to those 11
6: 1 At the beginning of the circle of the earth 12
15 and the foundations of the earth will understand 11
18 I draw near to visit the inhabitants of the earth 11
24 the earth and those who inhabit it 11
26 the heart of the earth's inhabitants ‡
38 'Let heaven and earth be made,' 11
42 in the seventh part of the earth 11
53 thou didst command the earth to bring forth 11
7:32 the earth shall give up those who are asleep in it 11
54 but ask the earth and she will tell you 11
62 I replied and said, "O earth 11
72 those who dwell on earth shall be tormented 11
116 better if the earth had not produced Adam, or else 11
127 every man who is born on earth shall wage 11
8: 2 Just as, when you ask the earth, it will tell you 11
9:20 and my earth, and behold, it was in peril 9
10: 9 Now ask the earth, and she will tell you 11
12 My lamentation is not like the earth's 11
13 with the earth according to the way of the earth 11
13 with the earth according to the way of the earth 11
14 so the earth also has from the beginning given 11
26 so that the earth shook at the sound. 11
59 to those who dwell on earth in the last days 11
11: 2 and behold, he spread his wings over all the earth 11
5 to reign over the earth 11
6 not even one creature that was on the earth. 11
12 and it reigned over all the earth. 11
16 Hear me, you who have ruled the earth all this time; 11
32 this head gained control of the whole earth 11
34 also ruled over the earth and its inhabitants. 11
40 and over all the earth with grievous oppression; 9
40 for so long you have dwelt on the earth 10
41 you have judged the earth, but not with truth; 11
46 that the whole earth, freed from your violence 11
12: 3 and the earth was exceedingly terrified 11
13 when a kingdom shall arise on earth 11
23 and shall rule the earth 11
13:29 will deliver those who are on the earth. 11
30 shall come over those who dwell on the earth. 11
52 so no one on earth can see my Son 11
15:20 I call together all the kings of the earth 11
22 those who shed innocent blood on earth. 11
23 and will consume the foundations of the earth 11
27 now calamities have come upon the whole earth 11
29 their hissing shall spread over the earth 11
35 shall pour out a heavy tempest upon the earth 11
37 be fear and great trembling upon the earth 11
40 to destroy all the earth and its inhabitants 11
16:12 The earth and its foundations quake 11
14 shall not return until they come over the earth. 11
15 until it consumes the foundations of the earth. 11
16 the calamities that are sent upon the earth 11
21 Behold, provision will be so cheap upon earth 11
21 then the calamities shall spring up on the earth 11
22 who live on the earth shall perish by famine 11
23 for the earth shall be left desolate 11
24 shall be left to cultivate the earth or to sow it. 11
32 the earth shall be left desolate 11
39 will not delay in coming forth upon the earth 11
40 be like strangers on the earth. 11
50 who searches out every sin on earth. 11
52 and iniquity will be removed from the earth 11
55 He said, "Let the earth be made," and it was made 11
58 has suspended the earth over the water; 11
60 to send rivers from the heights to water the earth; 11
Tob 3:13 Command that I be released from the earth 7
7:18 the Lord of heaven and earth grant you joy 7
14: 4 Our brethren will be scattered over the earth 7
Jdt 2: 5 the Great King, the lord of the whole earth 7
7 Tell them to prepare earth and water 7
7 will cover the whole face of the earth 7
9 to the ends of the whole earth. 7
19 cover the whole face of the earth to the west 7
20 like the dust of the earth 7
6: 3 destroy them from the face of the earth 7
4 Nebuchadnezzar, the lord of the whole earth 7
7:28 heaven and earth and our God 7
9:12 Lord of heaven and earth, Creator of the waters 7
11: 1 Nebuchadnezzar, the king of all the earth. 7
7 Nebuchadnezzar the king of the whole earth 7
21 from one end of the earth to the other 7
13:18 blessed . . above all women on earth 7
18 who created the heavens and the earth 7
AEs 11: 5 thunders and earthquake, tumult upon the earth! 7
8 affliction and great tumult upon the earth! 7
13:10 For thou hast made heaven and earth 7
Wis 1: 1 Love righteousness, you rulers of the earth 7
14 the dominion of Hades is not on earth. 7
5:23 Lawlessness will lay waste the whole earth 7
6: 1 learn, O judges of the ends of the earth. 7
7: 3 fell upon the kindred earth 7
8: 1 from one end of the earth to the other •
9:16 We can hardly guess at what is on earth 7
18 thus the paths of those on earth were set right 7
10: 4 When the earth was flooded because of him 7
15: 7 when a potter kneads the soft earth 7
8 this man who was made of earth a short time before 7
8 this man . . goes to the earth from which he was taken •
18:16 and touched heaven while standing on the earth. 7
19:10 how . . the earth brought forth gnats 7
Sir 1: 3 The height of heaven, the breadth of the earth 7
10: 4 The government of the earth 7
16 destroyed them to the foundations of the earth. 7
17 extinguished the memory of them from the earth. 7
16:18 the abyss and the earth 7
19 mountains . . and the foundations of the earth 7
29 After this the Lord looked upon the earth 7
17: 1 The Lord created man out of earth 7
2 authority over the things upon the earth. •
24: 3 covered the earth like a mist. 7
6 In the waves of the sea, in the whole earth 7
36:17 all who are on the earth will know 7
38: 4 The Lord created medicines from the earth 7
8 from him health is upon the face of the earth. 7
39:31 be made ready on earth for their service 7
40:11 All things that are from the earth 7
11 turn back to the earth 7
43:17 The voice of his thunder rebukes the earth 7
19 He pours the hoarfrost upon the earth like salt 7
44:17 therefore a remnant was left to the earth 7
21 he would multiply him like the dust of the earth 7
21 from the River to the ends of the earth. 7
46:20 lifted up his voice out of the earth in prophecy 7
47:15 Your soul covered the earth 7
48:15 were scattered over all the earth 7
49:14 No one like Enoch has been created on earth 7
14 he was taken up from the earth. 7
51: 9 I sent up my supplication from the earth 7
Bar 1:11 days on earth may be like the days of heaven. 7
2:15 earth may know that thou art the Lord our God 7
3:16 and those who rule over the beasts on earth; 7
20 Young men . . have dwelt upon the earth; but they 7
23 sons . . who seek for understanding on the earth 7
32 He who prepared the earth for all time filled it 7
37 she appeared upon earth and lived among men. 7
LJr 1:20 when worms from the earth devour them 7
54 they are like crows between heaven and earth. 7
Aza 1:52 Let the earth bless the Lord 7
54 Bless the Lord, all things that grow on the earth 7
Bel 1: 5 the living God, who created heaven and earth 7
Man 1: 2 thou who hast made heaven and earth 7
13 do not condemn me to the depths of the earth 7
1Mc 1: 2 and put to death the kings of the earth. 7
3 He advanced to the ends of the earth 7
3 When the earth became quiet before him 7
9 they caused many evils on the earth. 7
2:37 heaven and earth testify for us 7
40 they will quickly destroy us from the earth. 7
3: 9 He was renowned to the ends of the earth 7
8: 4 who came against them from the ends of the earth 7
9:13 The earth was shaken by the noise of the armies 7
14:10 till his renown spread to the ends of the earth. 7
15: 9 glory will become manifest in all the earth. 7
2Mc 7:28 to look at the heaven and the earth 7
9: 8 Thus he . . was brought down to earth 7
13: 7 without even burial in the earth. 7
15: 5 he replied, "And I am a sovereign also, on earth 7
3Mc 2: 9 created the boundless and immeasurable earth 7
14 the holy place on earth 7
4Mc 18: 5 The tyrant Antiochus was both punished on earth 7

earth *See also* child.

earth around 1. ἔδαφος
3Mc 1:29 the walls and the whole earth around echoed 1

under the earth 1. καταχθόνιος
Php 2:10 in heaven and on earth and under the earth 1

earthen 1. חֶרֶשׂ 2. יצר 3. κεραμικός 4. ὀστράκινος
Lev 6:28 the earthen vessel in which it is boiled 1
11:33 if any of them falls into any earthen vessel 1
14: 5 kill one of the birds in an earthen vessel 1
50 shall kill one of the birds in an earthen vessel 1
15:12 the earthen vessel which he . . touches 1
Num 5:17 shall take holy water in an earthen vessel 1
2Sm 17:28 brought beds, basins, and earthen vessels, wheat 2
Jer 19: 1 Thus said the LORD, "Go, buy a potter's earthen flask 1
Lam 4: 2 they are reckoned as earthen pots 1
2Co 4: 7 we have this treasure in earthen vessels 4
Rev 2:27 as when earthen pots are broken in pieces 3

earthen *See also* vessel.

earthenware 1. חֶרֶשׂ 2. ὀστράκινος 3. fictilis
Jer 32:14 and put them in an earthenware vessel 1
2Ti 2:20 also of wood and earthenware 2
2Es 8: 2 very much clay from which earthenware is made 3

earthly 1. ἐπίγειος 2. ἐπὶ γῆς 3. κατὰ σάρκα 4. κοσμικός 5. σαρκικός 6. σάρξ
2Co 1:12 not by earthly wisdom but by the grace of God. 5
5: 1 For we know that if the earthly tent we live 1
Eph 6: 5 those who are your earthly masters 3
Col 3: 5 Put to death therefore what is earthly in you 2
22 those who are your earthly masters 3
Heb 9: 1 worship and an earthly sanctuary. 4
12: 9 we have had earthly fathers to discipline us 6
Jas 3:15 wisdom . . is earthly, unspiritual, devilish. 1

earthly thing 1. ἐπίγειος
Joh 3:12 If I have told you earthly things 1
Php 3:19 with minds set on earthly things. 1

earthquake 1. רַעַשׁ 2. σεισμός 3. συσσεισμός 4. motio locorum 5. terraemotus
1Kg 19:11 and after the wind an earthquake 1
11 but the LORD was not in the earthquake; 1
12 and after the earthquake a fire 1
Isa 29: 6 with thunder and with earthquake 1
Ezk 3:12 I heard behind me the sound of a great earthquake; 1
13 wheels . . that sounded like a great earthquake. 1
Ams 1: 1 he saw . . two years before the earthquake. 1
Zec 14: 5 you shall flee as you fled from the earthquake 1
Mat 24: 7 famines and earthquakes in various places 2
27:54 saw the earthquake and what took place 2
28: 2 behold, there was a great earthquake 2
Mrk 13: 8 there will be earthquakes in various places 2
Lke 21:11 there will be great earthquakes 2
Act 16:26 suddenly there was a great earthquake 2
Rev 6:12 I looked, and behold, there was a great earthquake; 2
8: 5 flashes of lightning, and an earthquake. 2
11:13 And at that hour there was a great earthquake 2
13 7,000 people were killed in the earthquake 2
19 peals of thunder, an earthquake, and heavy hail. 2
16:18 a great earthquake such as had never been 2
18 so great was that earthquake. 2
2Es 3:19 of fire and earthquake and wind and ice 5
9: 3 there shall appear in the world earthquakes 4
AEs 11: 5 thunders and earthquake, tumult upon the earth! 2
Sir 22:16 will not be torn loose by an earthquake 3
4Mc 17: 3 against the earthquake of the tortures. 2

earthwork 1. γέφυρα
2Mc 12:13 strongly fortified with earthworks and walls 1

earthy 1. γεώδης
Wis 9:15 this earthy tent burdens the thoughtful mind. 1
15:13 he makes from earthy matter fragile vessels 1

ease 1. נשא 2. רום 3. שאן 4. שַׁאֲנָן 5. שַׁלְאֲנָן 6. שלה 7. שָׁלֵו 8. שקט 9. שְׁלֵה (A) 10. ἄνεσις 11. ἀφόβως
Job 3:18 There the prisoners are at ease together; 3
26 I am not at ease, nor am I quiet; I have no rest; 6
7:13 will comfort me, my couch will ease my complaint,' 1
12: 5 In the thought of one who is at ease 4
16:12 I was at ease, and he broke me asunder; 7
21:23 full prosperity, being wholly at ease and secure 5
Ps 73:12 always at ease, they increase in riches. 7
123: 4 sated with the scorn of those who are at ease 4
Prv 1:33 he who listens to me . . will be at ease 3
Isa 32: 9 Rise up, you women who are at ease, hear my voice; 4
11 Tremble, you women who are at ease 4
Jer 30:10 Jacob shall return and have quiet and ease 3
46:27 Jacob shall return and have quiet and ease 3
48:11 Moab has been at ease from his youth 3
49:31 Rise up, advance against a nation at ease 7
Ezk 16:49 had pride, surfeit of food, and prosperous ease 8
Dan 4: 4 I, Nebuchadnez'zar, was at ease in my house 9
Hos 11: 4 as one, who eases the yoke on their jaws 2
Ams 6: 1 Woe to those who are at ease in Zion 4
Zec 1:15 I am very angry with the nations that are at ease; 4
1Co 16:10 see that you put him at ease among you 11
2Co 8:13 others should be eased and you burdened 10
ease *See also* find, take.

easily 1. בִּמְעַט 2. εὐχερῶς
Gen 26:10 One of the people might easily have lain 1
Wis 6:12 she is easily discerned by those who love her 2
easily *See also* melt, reconcile.

east 1. אָרִים 2. לִפְנֵי 3. מוֹצָא 4. מִזְרָח 5. מִזְרָחָה 6. מִזְרַח הַשֶּׁמֶשׁ 7. מִקֶּדֶם 8. עַל פְּנֵי 9. פָּנִים 10. קָדִים 11. קֶדֶם 12. קֵדְמָה 13. קִדְמָה 14. קַדְמֹנִי 15. ἀνατολή 16. ἀνατολὴ ἡλίου 17. ἀπηλιώτης 18. πρὸς ἀνατολάς 19. eurus 20. oriens 21. orientalis
Gen 2: 8 the LORD God planted a garden in Eden, in the east; 12
14 river is Tigris, which flows east of Assyria. 13
3:24 at the east of the garden of Eden 12
4:16 Cain . . dwelt in the land of Nod, east of Eden. 13
10:30 of Sephar to the hill country of the east. 12
11: 2 as men migrated from the east, they found a plain 12
12: 8 removed to the mountain on the east of Bethel 12
8 with Bethel on the west and Ai on the east; 12
13:11 and Lot journeyed east; 12
23:17 the field . . which was to the east of Mamre 2
19 the cave of the field of Mach-pe'lah east of Mamre 8
25: 6 sent them . . eastward to the east country. 12
9 the son of Zohar the Hittite, east of Mamre 8
28:14 to the west and to the east and to the north 11
29: 1 and came to the land of the people of the east. 12
49:30 at Mach-pe'lah, to the east of Mamre 8
50:13 at Mach-pe'lah, to the east of Mamre 8
Exd 10:13 the LORD brought an east wind upon the land 10
13 and when it was morning the east wind had brought *
14:21 the sea back by a strong east wind all night 10
27:13 The breadth of the court on the front to the east 4
38:13 for the front of the east, 50 cubits. 4
Num 3:38 to encamp before the tabernacle on the east 11
32:19 come to us on this side of the Jordan to the east. 4
33: 7 Pi-hahi'roth, which is east of Ba'al-ze'phon; 8
34: 3 from the end of the Salt Sea on the east; 11
11 shoulder of the sea of Chin'nereth on the east; 11
35: 5 shall measure . . for the east side 2,000 cubits 11
Deu 3:17 Salt Sea, under the slopes of Pisgah on the east. 4
4:41 Moses set apart three cities in the east 6
47 who lived to the east beyond the Jordan; 6
49 all the Arabah on the east side of the Jordan 5
Jos 4:19 in Gilgal on the east border of Jericho. 4
7: 2 to Ai, which is near Beth-a'ven, east of Bethel 7
11: 3 sent . . to the Canaanites in the east and the west 4
13: 3 from the Shihor, which is east of Egypt, northward 8
25 to Aro'er, which is east of Rabbah 8
32 the plains of Moab . . east of Jericho. 4
15: 5 the east boundary is the Salt Sea 11
16: 1 allotment . . went . . east of the waters of Jericho 4
5 the boundary . . on the east was At'aroth-ad'dar 4
6 on the east the boundary turns round 4
6 and passes along beyond it on the east to Jan-o'ah 4
17: 7 Asher to Mich-me'thath, which is east of Shechem; 8
10 on the north Asher . . and on the east Is'sachar 4
19:11 touches . . the brook which is east of Jok'ne-am; 8
13 it passes along on the east . . to Gath-hepher 12
34 touching . . Judah on the east at the Jordan. 6
20: 8 And beyond the Jordan east of Jericho 4
Jdg 6: 3 people of the East would come up and attack them; 12
33 and the Amal'ekites and the people of the East 12
7:12 the Amal'ekites and all the people of the East 12
8:10 were left of all the army of the people of the East; 12
11 by the caravan route east of Nobah and Jog'behah 12
20:43 from Nohah as far as opposite Gib'e-ah on the east. 6
21:19 is north of Bethel, on the east of the highway 6
1Sm 13: 5 encamped in Michmash, to the east of Beth-a'ven. 13
15: 7 Hav'ilah as far as Shur, which is east of Egypt. 8
26: 1 hill of Hachi'lah, which is on the east of Jeshi'mon? 9
3 Hachi'lah, which is . . on the east of Jeshi'mon. 9
1Kg 4:30 the wisdom of all the people of the east, and all 12
7:25 twelve oxen . . south, and three facing east; 4
11: 7 high place . . on the mountain east of Jerusalem. 8
17: 3 the brook Cherith, that is east of the Jordan. 8
5 the brook Cherith that is east of the Jordan. 8
2Kg 23:13 the high places that were east of Jerusalem 8
1Ch 5: 9 to the east as far as the entrance of the desert 4
10 tents throughout all the region east of Gilead. 4
9:24 on the four sides, east, west, north and south; 4
12:15 put to flight . . to the east and to the west. 4
26:14 The lot for the east fell to Shelemi'ah. 5
17 On the east there were six each day 4
2Ch 4: 4 stood upon twelve oxen . . and three facing east; 5
5:12 stood east of the altar with . . priests who were 4
20:16 the valley, east of the wilderness of Jeru'el. 9
29: 4 assembled them in the square on the east 4
31:14 Ko're . . keeper of the east gate 4
Neh 3:26 point opposite the Water Gate on the east 4
12:37 house of David, to the Water Gate on the east. 4
Job 1: 3 the greatest of all the people of the east. 12
18:20 horror seizes them of the east. 14
Ps 48: 7 By the east wind thou didst shatter the ships 10
75: 6 For not from the east or from the west 3
103:12 as far as the east is from the west 4
107: 3 gathered in from . . the east and from the west 4
Isa 2: 6 diviners from the east and of soothsayers 12
9:12 The Syrians on the east and the Philistines 12
11:14 they shall plunder the people of the east. 12
24:15 Therefore in the east give glory to the LORD; 1
41: 2 Who stirred up one from the east 4
43: 5 I will bring your offspring from the east 4
46:11 calling a bird of prey from the east 4
Jer 18:17 Like the east wind I will scatter them 10
49:28 against Kedar! Destroy the people of the east! 12
Ezk 8:16 their faces toward the east, worshiping the sun 11
16 men . . worshiping the sun toward the east. 11
10:19 the door of the east gate of the house of the LORD; 14
11: 1 to the east gate of the house of the LORD 14
1 gate of the house of the LORD, which faces east. 10
23 mountain which is on the east side of the city. 12
17:10 utterly wither when the east wind strikes it 10
19:12 cast down to the ground; the east wind dried it up 10
25: 4 I am handing you over to the people of the East 12
10 to the people of the East as a possession 12
27:26 The east wind has wrecked you 10
39:11 the Valley of the Travelers east of the sea; 13
40: 6 Then he went into the gateway facing east 10
10 three side rooms on either side of the east gate; 10
22 as those of the gate which faced toward the east; 10
23 opposite the gate on the north, as on the east 10
32 he brought me to the inner court on the east side 10
41:14 also the breadth of the east front of the temple 10
42: 9 Below these chambers was an entrance on the east 10
12 was an entrance on the east side, where one enters 10
15 he led me out by the gate which faced east 10
16 He measured the east side with the measuring 10
43: 1 he brought me to the gate, the gate facing east. 10
2 the glory of the God of Israel came from the east; 10
4 LORD entered the temple by the gate facing east 10
17 The steps of the altar shall face east. 10
44: 1 the sanctuary, which faces east; and it was shut. 10
45: 7 the city, on the west and on the east 11
46: 1 The gate of the inner court that faces east 10
12 the gate facing east shall be opened for him 10
47: 1 temple toward the east (for the temple faced east) 10
1 temple toward the east (for the temple faced east) 10
2 to the outer gate, that faces toward the east 10
18 On the east side, the boundary shall run 10
18 This shall be the east side. 10
48: 1 and extending from the east side to the west, 10
2 territory of Dan, from the east side to the west 10
3 territory of Asher, from the east side to the west 10
4 from the east side to the west, Manas'seh 10
5 of Manas'seh, from the east side to the west 10
6 from the east side to the west, Reuben, one portion 10
7 from the east side to the west, Judah, one portion. 10
8 territory of Judah, from the east side to the west 10
8 tribal portions, from the east side to the west 10
16 the east side 4,500, and the west side 4,500. 10
17 on the east 250, and on the west 250. 10
18 holy portion shall be 10,000 cubits to the east 10
21 cubits of the holy portion to the east border 10
23 tribes: from the east side to the west, Benjamin 10
24 from the east side to the west, Simeon, one portion 10
25 from the east side to the west, Is'sachar 10
26 the east side to the west, Zeb'ulun, one portion. 10
27 from the east side to the west, Gad, one portion. 10
32 On the east side, which is to be 4,500 cubits 10
Dan 8: 9 grew exceedingly great . . toward the east 4
11:44 tidings from the east and the north shall alarm 4
Ams 8:12 wander from sea to sea, and from north to east; 4
Jon 4: 5 went out of the city and sat to the east of the city 12
8 the sun rose, God appointed a sultry east wind 10
Zec 8: 7 from the east country and from the west country; 4
14: 4 which lies before Jerusalem on the east; 12
4 split in two from east to west 4
Mat 2: 1 wise men from the East came to Jerusalem, saying 15
2 For we have seen his star in the East, and have come 15
9 and lo, the star which they had seen in the East 15
8:11 I tell you, many will come from east and west 15
24:27 For as the lightning comes from the east 15
Lke 13:29 men will come from east and west 15
Rev 16:12 to prepare the way for the kings of the east. 16
21:13 on the east three gates, on the north three gates 15
1Es 5:47 before the first gate toward the east. 15
9:38 the open square before the east gate of the temple; 18
2Es 1:11 and scattered in the east the people 20
38 and see the people coming from the east; 20
15:20 from the east and from Lebanon 19
28 a terrifying sight, appearing from the east! 20
34 Behold, clouds from the east 20
39 the winds from the east shall prevail 20
39 by the east wind shall be driven violently 21
Jdt 7:18 toward the south and the east, toward Acraba 17
Bar 4:36 Look toward the east, O Jerusalem 15
37 they are coming, gathered from east and west 15
5: 5 stand upon the height and look toward the east 15
5 see your children gathered from west and east 15
1Mc 12:37 part of the wall on the valley to the east 17
east *See also* side, toward, wind.

east side 1. מִזְרָח 2. קֶדֶם 3. קֵדְמָה
Lev 1:16 beside the altar on the east side 3
Num 2: 3 Those to encamp on the east side 3
10: 5 camps that are on the east side shall set out. 3
34:11 from Shepham to Riblah on the east side of A'in; 2
1Ch 4:39 They journeyed . . to the east side of the valley 1
6:78 at Jericho, on the east side of the Jordan 1
9:18 in the king's gate on the east side 1

eastern 1. קָדִים 2. קֶדֶם 3. קֵדְמָה 4. קַדְמוֹן 5. קַדְמֹנִי
Num23: 7 king of Moab from the eastern mountains 3
34:10 You shall mark out your eastern boundary 2
Jos 18:20 Jordan forms its boundary on the eastern side. 2
Ezk 45: 7 extending from the western to the eastern 1
47: 8 This water flows toward the eastern region 4
18 to the eastern sea and as far as Tamar. 5
48:10 10,000 in breadth on the eastern side 1
Jol 2:20 drive . . his front into the eastern sea 5
Zec 14: 8 from Jerusalem, half of them to the eastern sea 5

eastward 1. לְמִזְרָח 2. מִזְרָחָה 3. מִזְרַח הַשֶּׁמֶשׁ 4. קָדִים 5. קֵדְמָה
Gen 13:14 southward and eastward and westward; 5
25: 6 sent them . . eastward to the east country. 5
Num34:15 beyond the Jordan at Jericho eastward 5
Deu 3:27 lift up your eyes . . southward and eastward 2
Jos 11: 8 and eastward as far as the valley of Mizpeh; 2
12: 1 their land . . with all the Arabah eastward 2
3 and the Arabah to the Sea of Chin'neroth eastward 2
13: 8 which Moses gave . . beyond the Jordan eastward 2
27 the lower end of . . eastward beyond the Jordan. 2
18: 7 their inheritance beyond the Jordan eastward 2
19:12 it goes in the other direction eastward 5
27 then it turns eastward, it goes to Beth-dagon 3
1Kg 17: 3 Depart from here and turn eastward 5
2Kg 10:33 from the Jordan eastward, all the land of Gilead 3
13:17 said, "Open the window eastward": and he opened it. 5
1Ch 7:28 Bethel and its towns, and eastward Na'aran 1
Ezk 47: 3 Going on eastward with a line in his hand 4

easy 1. קלל 2. εὔκοπος 3. εὐρύχωρος 4. εὐχερής 5. εὐχερῶς 6. κοῦφος 7. χρηστός 8. spatiosus
Exd 18:22 so it will be easier for you, 1
Prv 14: 6 but knowledge is easy for a man of understanding. 1
Mat 7:13 for the gate is wide and the way is easy 3
9: 5 For which is easier, to say, 'Your sins are forgiven,' 2
11:30 For my yoke is easy, and my burden is light. 7
19:24 Again I tell you, it is easier for a camel 2
Mrk 2: 9 Which is easier, to say to the paralytic 2
10:25 easier for a camel to go through the eye 2
Lke 5:23 Which is easier, to say, 'Your sins are forgiven you,' 2
16:17 it is easier for heaven and earth to pass away 2
18:25 For it is easier for a camel to go 2
2Es 7:18 while hoping for easier ones 8
18 and will not see the easier ones. 8
Jdt 4: 7 it was easy to stop any who tried to enter 5
7:10 not easy to reach the tops of their mountains. 4
Sir 11:21 easy in the sight of the Lord to enrich a poor man 6
26 it is easy in the sight of the Lord to reward a man 6
22:15 of iron are easier to bear than a stupid man. 2
1Mc 3:18 It is easy for many to be hemmed in by few 2
2Mc 2:27 just as it is not easy . . 4
easy *See also* make, think.

easy thing 1. קלל
2Kg 20:10 It is an easy thing for the shadow to lengthen ten 1

easy to handle 1. εὐκίνητος
Wis 13:11 may saw down a tree easy to handle 1

eat 1. אכל 2. בוא אל קֶרֶב 3. בְּפֶה 4. ברה 5. לחם 6. לְחֶם 7. לעט 8. רעה 9. אכל (A) 10. ἀπογεύω 11. βιβρώσκω 12. βρῶμα 13. βρώσιμος 14. βρῶσις

15. γεύομαι 16. δειπνέω 17. ἔδεσμα 18. ἔντερον
19. ἐσθίω 20. κατεσθίω 21. προσλαμβάνω
22. προσφέρω 23. συνεσθίω 24. τροφή 25. τρώγω
26. ψωμίζω 27. devoratio 28. gusto 29. manduco

Gen 2:16 You may freely eat of every tree of the garden; 1
17 of good and evil you shall not eat 1
17 for in the day that you eat of it you shall die. 1
3: 1 Did God say, 'You shall not eat of any tree 1
2 woman said to the serpent, "We may eat of the fruit 1
3 God said, 'You shall not eat of the fruit of the tree 1
5 For God knows that when you eat of it 1
6 make one wise, she took of its fruit and ate; 1
6 she also gave some to her husband, and he ate. 1
11 Have you eaten of the tree of which I commanded 1
11 tree of which I commanded you not to eat? 1
12 The woman . . gave me fruit of the tree, and I ate. 1
13 The woman said, "The serpent beguiled me, and I ate. 1
14 belly you shall go, and dust you shall eat 1
17 and have eaten of the tree of which I commanded 1
17 commanded you, 'You shall not eat of it,' 1
17 in toil you shall eat of it all the days 1
18 and you shall eat the plants of the field. 1
19 In the sweat of your face you shall eat bread 1
22 of the tree of life, and eat, and live for ever"- 1
6:21 take with you every sort of food that is eaten 1
9: 4 Only you shall not eat flesh with its life 1
14:24 take nothing but what the young men have eaten 1
18: 8 he stood by them under the tree while they ate. 1
19: 3 feast, and baked unleavened bread, and they ate. 1
24:33 Then food was set before him to eat; 1
33 but he said, "I will not eat until I have told 1
54 he and the men who were with him ate and drank 1
25:28 Isaac loved Esau, because he ate of his game; 3
30 Let me eat some of that red pottage 7
34 and he ate and drank, and rose and went his way. 1
26:30 he made them a feast, and they ate and drank. 1
27: 4 such as I love, and bring it to me that I may eat; 1
7 savory food, that I may eat it, and bless you 1
10 you shall bring it to your father to eat 1
19 now sit up and eat of my game 1
25 Then he said, "Bring it to me, that I may eat 1
25 he brought it to him, and he ate; 1
31 Let my father arise, and eat of his son's game 1
33 that hunted game and brought it to me, and I ate it 1
28:20 give me bread to eat and clothing to wear 1
31:38 I have not eaten the rams of your flocks. 1
46 made a heap; and they ate there by the heap. 1
54 mountain and called his kinsmen to eat bread; 1
54 they ate bread and tarried all night 1
32:32 the Israelites do not eat the sinew of the hip 1
37:25 Then they sat down to eat; and looking up they saw 1
39: 6 concern for anything but the food which he ate. 1
40:17 but the birds were eating it out of the basket 1
19 and the birds will eat the flesh from you. 1
41:21 when they had eaten them no one would have known 2
21 known that they had eaten them, 2
43: 2 when they had eaten the grain which they had 1
25 for they heard that they should eat bread there. 1
32 the Egyptians who ate with him by themselves 1
32 because the Egyptians might not eat bread 1
45:18 and you shall eat the fat of the land.' 1
Exd 2:20 you left the man? Call him, that he may eat bread. 1
10: 5 they shall eat what is left to you after the hail 1
5 they shall eat every tree of yours which grows 1
12 that they may . . eat every plant in the land 1
15 they ate all the plants in the land and all 1
12: 4 according to what each can eat you shall make 1
7 put it on . . the houses in which they eat them. 1
8 They shall eat the flesh that night, roasted; 1
8 with . . bitter herbs they shall eat it. 1
9 Do not eat any of it raw or boiled with water 1
11 In this manner you shall eat it: your loins girded 1
11 you shall eat it in haste. 1
15 Seven days you shall eat unleavened bread; 1
15 if any one eats what is leavened . . that person 1
16 what every one must eat, that only may be prepared 1
18 you shall eat unleavened bread, and so until 1
19 for if any one eats what is leavened 1
20 You shall eat nothing leavened; 1
20 your dwellings you shall eat unleavened bread. 1
43 passover: no foreigner shall eat of it; 1
44 may eat of it after you have circumcised him. 1
45 No sojourner or hired servant may eat of it. 1
46 In one house shall it be eaten; 1
48 But no uncircumcised person shall eat of it. 1
13: 3 no leavened bread shall be eaten. 1
6 Seven days you shall eat unleavened bread 1
7 Unleavened bread shall be eaten for seven days; 1
16: 3 when we sat by the fleshpots and ate bread 1
8 the LORD gives you in the evening flesh to eat 1
12 say to them, 'At twilight you shall eat flesh 1
15 the bread which the LORD has given you to eat. 1
16 Gather of it, every man of you, as much as he can eat; 1
18 each gathered according to what he could eat. 1
21 they gathered it, each as much as he could eat; 1
25 Moses said, "Eat it today, for today is a sabbath 1
35 the people of Israel ate the manna forty years 1
35 they ate the manna, till they came to the border 1
18:12 came . . to eat bread with Moses' father-in-law 1
21:28 its flesh shall not be eaten; 1
22:31 you shall not eat any flesh that is torn by beasts 1
23:11 lie fallow, that the poor of your people may eat; 1
11 what they leave the wild beasts may eat. 1
15 you shall eat unleavened bread for seven days 1
24:11 they beheld God, and ate and drank. 1
29:32 Aaron and his sons shall eat the flesh of the ram 1
33 They shall eat those things 1
33 but an outsider shall not eat of them 1
34 it shall not be eaten, because it is holy. 1
32: 6 the people sat down to eat and drink, and rose up 1
34:15 when . . one invites you, you eat of his sacrifice 1
18 Seven days you shall eat unleavened bread 1
28 he neither ate bread nor drank water. 1
Lev 3:17 a statute . . that you eat neither fat nor blood 1
6:16 the rest of it Aaron and his sons shall eat 1
16 it shall be eaten unleavened in a holy place 1
16 in the court of the tent of meeting they shall eat 1
18 Every male among the children of Aaron may eat 1
23 shall be wholly burned; it shall not be eaten 1
26 The priest who offers it for sin shall eat it 1
26 in a holy place it shall be eaten, in the court 1
29 Every male among the priests may eat of it 1
30 no sin offering shall be eaten from which any 1
7: 6 Every male among the priests may eat of it 1
6 it shall be eaten in a holy place; it is most holy 1
15 offerings for thanksgiving shall be eaten 1
16 it shall be eaten on the day that he offers his 1
16 on the morrow what remains of it shall be eaten 1
18 sacrifice of his peace offering is eaten 1
18 it shall be an abomination, and he who eats of it 1
19 touches any unclean thing shall not be eaten 1
19 All who are clean may eat flesh 1
20 the person who eats of the flesh of the sacrifice 1
21 touches . . and then eats of the flesh 1
23 You shall eat no fat, of ox, or sheep, or goat 1
24 any other use, but on no account shall you eat it 1
25 For every person who eats of the fat of an animal 1
26 Moreover you shall eat no blood whatever 1
27 Whoever eats of any blood, that person shall be 1
8:31 there eat it and the bread that is in the basket 1
31 saying, 'Aaron and his sons shall eat it' 1
10:12 eat it unleavened beside the altar 1
13 you shall eat it in a holy place 1
14 the thigh that is offered you shall eat 1
17 Why have you not eaten the sin offering 1
18 You certainly ought to have eaten it 1
19 If I had eaten the sin offering today 1
11: 2 These are the living things which you may eat 1
3 chews the cud, among the animals, you may eat 1
4 you shall not eat these: The camel, because it 1
8 Of their flesh you shall not eat 1
9 These you may eat, of all that are in the waters 1
9 in the seas or in the rivers, you may eat 1
11 flesh you shall not eat, and their carcasses 1
13 they shall not be eaten, they are an abomination 1
21 may eat those which have legs above their feet 1
22 you may eat: the locust according to its kind 1
34 Any food in it which may be eaten . . be unclean 1
39 if any animal of which you may eat dies 1
40 he who eats of its carcass shall wash his clothes 1
41 an abomination; it shall not be eaten 1
42 you shall not eat; for they are an abomination 1
47 between the living creature that may be eaten 1
47 the living creature that may not be eaten 1
14:47 he who eats in the house shall wash his clothes 1
17:10 If any man . . eats any blood, I will set my face 1
10 set my face against that person who eats blood 1
12 No person among you shall eat blood 1
12 neither shall any stranger . . eat blood 1
13 any beast or bird that may be eaten 1
14 You shall not eat the blood of any creature 1
14 whoever eats it shall be cut off 1
15 every person that eats what dies of itself 1
19: 6 It shall be eaten the same day you offer it 1
7 If it is eaten at all on the third day, it is 1
8 every one who eats it shall bear his iniquity 1
23 be forbidden to you, it must not be eaten 1
25 But in the fifth year you may eat of their fruit 1
26 You shall not eat any flesh with the blood in it 1
21:22 He may eat the bread of his God 1
22: 4 None . . may eat of the holy things until he is 1
6 the person . . shall not eat of the holy things 1
7 afterward he may eat of the holy things 1
8 That which . . is torn by beasts he shall not eat 1
10 An outsider shall not eat of a holy thing 1
10 a hired servant shall not eat of a holy thing 1
11 the slave may eat of it; and those that are born 1
11 that are born in his house may eat of his food 1
12 she shall not eat of the offering of the holy 1
13 she may eat of her father's food; yet no outsider 1
13 yet no outsider shall eat of it 1
14 if a man eats of a holy thing unwittingly 1
16 to bear iniquity . . by eating their holy thing 1
30 It shall be eaten on the same day 1
23: 6 seven days you shall eat unleavened bread 1
14 you shall eat neither bread nor grain parched 1
24: 9 they shall eat it in a holy place 1
25:12 you shall eat what it yields out of the field 1
19 The land will yield its fruit, and you will eat 1
20 if you say, 'What shall we eat in the seventh year 1
22 you will be eating old produce; until the ninth 1
22 until the ninth year . . you shall eat the old 1
26: 5 you shall eat your bread to the full, and dwell 1
10 you shall eat old store long kept 1
16 sow your seed in vain, for your enemies shall eat it 1
26 you shall eat, and not be satisfied 1
29 You shall eat the flesh of your sons 1
29 you shall eat the flesh of your daughters 1
Num 6: 3 shall not drink . . or eat grapes, fresh or dried. 1
4 eat nothing that is produced by the grapevine 1
9:11 eat it with unleavened bread and bitter herbs. 1
11: 4 Israel . . said, "O that we had meat to eat!. 1
5 We remember the fish we ate in Egypt for nothing 1
13 they weep . . and say, 'Give us meat, that we may eat.' 1
18 you shall eat meat; for you have wept 1
18 LORD will give you meat, and you shall eat. 1
19 You shall not eat one day, or two days, or five days 1
21 give them meat, that they may eat a whole month!' 1
15:19 when you eat of the food of the land 1
18:10 In a most holy place shall you eat of it; 1
10 every male may eat of it; it is holy to you. 1
11 every one who is clean in your house may eat of it. 1
13 every one who is clean in your house may eat of it. 1
31 may eat it in any place, you and your households; 1
25: 2 people ate, and bowed down to their gods. 1
28:17 seven days shall unleavened bread be eaten. 1
Deu 2: 6 food from them for money, that you may eat; 1
28 You shall sell me food for money, that I may eat 1
4:28 gods . . that neither see, nor hear, nor eat, nor smell. 1
6:11 when you eat and are full 1
8: 9 in which you will eat bread without scarcity 1
10 you shall eat and be full, and you shall bless 1
12 lest, when you have eaten and are full 1
9: 9 I neither ate bread nor drank water. 1
18 I neither ate bread nor drank water 1
11:15 for your cattle and you shall eat and be full. 1
12: 7 there you shall eat before the LORD your God 1
15 slaughter and eat flesh within any of your towns 1
15 unclean and the clean may eat of it 1
16 Only you shall not eat the blood . . pour it out 1
17 You may not eat within your towns the tithe 1
18 eat them before the LORD your God in the place 1
20 you say, 'I will eat flesh,' because you crave flesh 1
20 you may eat as much flesh as you desire. 1
21 may eat within your towns as much as you desire. 1
22 Just as the gazelle or the hart is eaten 1
22 the hart is eaten, so you may eat of it 1
22 unclean and the clean alike may eat of it. 1
23 Only be sure that you do not eat the blood; 1
23 you shall not eat the life with the flesh. 1
24 You shall not eat it; you shall pour it out 1
25 You shall not eat it; that all may go well with you 1
27 but the flesh you may eat. 1
14: 3 You shall not eat any abominable thing. 1
4 animals you may eat: the ox, the sheep, the goat 1
6 among the animals, you may eat. 1
7 Yet of those . . you shall not eat these 1
8 flesh you shall not eat, and their carcasses 1
9 Of all that are in the waters you may eat these 1
9 whatever has fins and scales you may eat. 1
10 does not have fins and scales you shall not eat; 1
11 You may eat all clean birds. 1
12 ones which you shall not eat: the eagle 1
19 winged insects . . shall not be eaten. 1
20 All clean winged things you may eat. 1
21 You shall not eat anything that dies of itself; 1
21 may give it to the alien . . that he may eat it 1
23 you shall eat the tithe of your grain, of your wine 1
26 eat there before the LORD your God and rejoice 1
29 shall come and eat and be filled; 1
15:20 eat it, you and your household, before the LORD 1
22 You shall eat it within your towns; 1
22 unclean and the clean alike may eat it, as though •
23 Only you shall not eat its blood; you shall pour 1
16: 3 You shall eat no leavened bread with it; 1
3 seven days . . eat it with unleavened bread 1
7 boil it and eat it at the place which the LORD 1
8 For six days you shall eat unleavened bread; 1
18: 1 eat the offerings by fire to the LORD 1
8 They shall have equal portions to eat 1
20:19 may eat of them, but you shall not cut them down. 1
23:24 neighbor's vineyard . . eat your fill of grapes 1
26:12 that they may eat within your towns and be filled 1
14 I have not eaten of the tithe while I was mourning 1
27: 7 sacrifice peace offerings, and shall eat there; 1
28:31 ox shall be slain . . and you shall not eat of it; 1
39 for the worm shall eat them. 1
51 eat the offspring of your cattle and the fruit 1
53 you shall eat the offspring of your own body 1
55 any of the flesh of his children whom he is eating 1
57 she will eat them secretly, for want of all things 1
29: 6 not eaten bread, and you have not drunk wine 1
31:20 when . . have eaten and are full and grown fat 1
32:13 he ate the produce of the field; 1
38 who ate the fat of their sacrifices, and drank 1
Jos 5:11 they ate of the produce of the land 1

12 when they ate of the produce of the land; 1
12 Israel . . ate of the fruit of the land of Canaan 1
24:13 you eat the fruit of vineyards and oliveyards 1
Jdg 9:27 god, and ate and drank and reviled Abim'elech. 1
13: 4 drink no wine . . and eat nothing unclean 1
7 drink no wine . . and eat nothing unclean 1
14 She may not eat of anything that comes 1
14 let her drink wine . . or eat any unclean thing; 1
16 If you detain me, I will not eat of your food; 1
14: 9 out into his hands, and went on, eating as he went; 1
9 and mother, and gave some to them, and they ate. 1
19: 4 days; so they ate and drank, and lodged there. 1
6 the two men sat and ate and drank together; 1
8 until the day declines." So they ate, both of them. 1
21 and they washed their feet, and ate and drank. 1
Rut 2:14 Come here, and eat some bread, and dip your morsel 1
14 and she ate until she was satisfied 1
3: 3 until he has finished eating and drinking. 1
7 Bo'az had eaten and drunk, and his heart was merry 1
1Sm 1: 7 Therefore Hannah wept and would not eat. 1
8 Hannah, why do you weep? And why do you not eat? 1
9 After they had eaten and drunk . . Hannah rose. 1
18 she said . . " Then the woman went her way and ate 1
2:36 Put me . . that I may eat a morsel of bread."' 1
9:13 find him, before he goes up to the high place to eat; 1
13 the people will not eat till he comes 1
13 afterward those eat who are invited. 1
19 today you shall eat with me, and in the morning 1
24 Eat; because it was kept for you until the hour 1
24 it was kept . . that you might eat with the guests. *
24 Saul ate with Samuel that day. 1
14:24 Cursed be the man who eats food until . . evening 1
28 'Cursed be the man who eats food this day.' 1
30 if the people had eaten freely today of the spoil 1
32 slew . . and the people ate them with the blood. 1
33 people are sinning . . by eating with the blood. 1
34 bring his ox or . . sheep, and slay them here, and eat; 1
34 sin against the LORD by eating with the blood.' 1
20:24 the new moon came, the king sat down to eat food. 1
34 Jonathan rose . . and ate no food the second day 1
28:20 he had eaten nothing all day and all night. 1
22 and eat, that you may have strength when you go 1
23 He refused, and said, "I will not eat. 1
25 put it before Saul and his servants; and they ate. 1
30:11 they gave him bread and he ate, they gave him water 1
12 when he had eaten, his spirit revived; 1
12 he had not eaten bread or drunk . . for three days 1
16 they were . . eating and drinking and dancing 1
2Sm 9: 7 and you shall eat at my table always. 1
10 that your master's son may have bread to eat; 1
10 Mephib'osheth . . shall always eat at my table. 1
11 Mephib'osheth ate at David's table 1
13 for he ate always at the king's table. 1
11:11 shall I then go to my house, to eat and to drink 1
13 he ate in his presence and drank 1
12: 3 it used to eat of his morsel, and drink from his cup 1
17 he would not, nor did he eat food with them. 4
20 when he asked, they set food before him, and he ate. 1
21 but when the child died, you arose and ate food. 1
13: 5 that I may see it, and eat it from her hand.' 1
6 let my sister . . that I may eat from her hand. 4
9 emptied it out before him, but he refused to eat. 1
10 Bring the food . . that I may eat from your hand. 4
11 But when she brought them near him to eat 1
16: 2 bread and summer fruit for the young men to eat 1
17:29 for David and the people with him to eat; 1
19:28 but you set . . among those who eat at your table. 1
35 Can your servant taste what he eats or . . drinks? 1
42 Have we eaten at all at the king's expense? 1
1Kg 1:25 behold, they are eating and drinking before him 1
2: 7 and let them be among those who eat at your table; 1
4:20 Judah and Israel . . ate and drank and were happy. 1
13: 8 I will not eat bread or drink water in this place; 1
9 You shall neither eat bread, nor drink water 1
15 he said to him, "Come home with me and eat bread. 1
16 neither will I eat bread nor drink water with you 1
17 You shall neither eat bread nor drink water 1
18 Bring him back . . that he may eat bread and drink 1
19 he went back with him, and ate bread in his house 1
22 and have eaten bread and drunk water in the place 1
22 he said to you, "Eat no bread, and drink no water"; 1
23 after he had eaten bread and drunk, he saddled 1
28 The lion had not eaten the body or torn the ass. 1
14:11 Any one . . who dies in the city the dogs shall eat; 1
11 one who dies in . . the birds of the air shall eat. 1
16: 4 Any one . . who dies in the city the dogs shall eat; 1
4 who dies in the field the birds . . shall eat. 1
17:12 prepare it . . that we may eat it, and die. 1
15 she, and he, and her household ate for many days. 1
18:19 prophets of Ashe'rah, who eat at Jez'ebel's table. 1
41 Eli'jah said to Ahab, "Go up, eat and drink; 1
42 So Ahab went up to eat and to drink. 1
19: 5 an angel . . said to him, "Arise and eat. 1
6 And he ate and drank, and lay down again. 1
7 Arise and eat, else the journey will be too great 1
8 he arose, and ate and drank 1
21 and gave it to the people, and they ate. 1
21: 4 turned away his face, and would eat no food. 1
5 Why is your spirit so vexed that you eat no food? 1
7 Arise, and eat bread, and let your heart be 1
23 'The dogs shall eat Jez'ebel within . . Jezreel.' 1
24 who dies in the city the dogs shall eat; 1
24 who dies . . the birds of the air shall eat. 1
2Kg 4: 8 a wealthy woman . . who urged him to eat some food. 1
8 whenever . . he would turn in there to eat food. 1
40 And they poured out for the men to eat. 1
40 But while they were eating . . they cried out 1
40 And they could not eat it. 1
41 and said, "Pour out for the men, that they may eat. 1
42 Eli'sha said, "Give to the men, that they may eat. 1
43 Give them to the men, that they may eat 1
43 says the LORD, 'They shall eat and have some left.' 1
44 they ate, and had some left, according to the word 1
6:22 Set bread and water . . that they may eat and drink 1
23 when they had eaten and drunk, he sent them away 1
28 Give your son, that we may eat him today 1
28 your son . . today, and we will eat my son tomorrow.' 1
29 So we boiled my son, and ate him. 1
29 I said to her, 'Give your son, that we may eat him'; 1
7: 2 You shall see it . . but you shall not eat of it. 1
8 they went into a tent, and ate and drank 1
19 You shall see it . . but you shall not eat of it. 1
9:10 And the dogs shall eat Jez'ebel in . . Jezreel 1
34 Then he went in and ate and drank; and he said 1
36 the dogs shall eat the flesh of Jez'ebel; 1
18:27 doomed . . to eat their own dung and to drink their 1
31 then every one of you will eat of his own vine 1
19:29 this year you shall eat what grows of itself 1
29 sow . . and plant vineyards, and eat their fruit. 1
23: 9 they ate unleavened bread among their brethren. 1
1Ch 12:39 with David for three days, eating and drinking 1
29:22 they ate and drank before the LORD on that day 1
2Ch 30:18 ate the passover otherwise than as prescribed. 1
22 people ate the food of the festival for seven 1
31:10 we have eaten and had enough and have plenty left; 1
Ezr 6:21 eaten by the people of Israel who had returned 1
9:12 that you may be strong, and eat the good of the land 1
10: 6 neither eating bread nor drinking water; 1
Neh 5: 2 let us get grain, that we may eat and keep alive. 1
14 neither I nor my brethren ate the food allowance 1
8:10 Go your way, eat the fat and drink sweet wine 1
12 all the people went their way to eat and drink 1
9:25 ate, and were filled and became fat, and delighted 1
Est 4:16 a fast . . and neither eat nor drink for three days 1
Job 1: 4 their three sisters to eat and drink with them. 1
13 his sons and daughters were eating and drinking 1
18 sons and daughters were eating and drinking 1
5: 5 His harvest the hungry eat 1
6: 6 that which is tasteless be eaten without salt 1
20:21 There was nothing left after he had eaten; 1
27:14 his offspring have not enough to eat. 6
31: 8 then let me sow, and another eat; 1
17 or have eaten my morsel alone 1
17 the fatherless has not eaten of it 1
39 if I have eaten its yield without payment 1
40:15 Behold, Be'hemoth . . he eats grass like an ox. 1
42:11 who had known him before, and ate bread with him 1
Ps 14: 4 evildoers who eat up my people as they eat bread 1
22:26 The afflicted shall eat and be satisfied; 1
41: 9 bosom friend in whom I trusted, who ate of my bread 1
50:13 Do I eat the flesh of bulls, or drink the blood 1
53: 4 who eat up my people as they eat bread 1
78:24 he rained down upon them manna to eat 1
25 Man ate of the bread of the angels; 1
29 they ate and were well filled 1
102: 4 I forget to eat my bread. 1
9 For I eat ashes like bread 1
106:20 God for the image of an ox that eats grass. 1
28 ate sacrifices offered to the dead; 1
127: 2 It is in vain . . eating the bread of anxious toil; 1
128: 2 You shall eat the fruit of the labor of your hands; 1
141: 4 let me not eat of their dainties! 5
Prv 1:31 therefore they shall eat the fruit of their way 1
4:17 For they eat the bread of wickedness 5
9: 5 eat of my bread and drink of the wine I have mixed. 5
17 bread eaten in secret is pleasant. *
13: 2 From the fruit of his mouth a good man eats good 1
18:21 those who love it will eat its fruits. 1
23: 1 When you sit down to eat with a ruler 5
6 Do not eat the bread of a man who is stingy; 5
7 Eat and drink!" he says to you; but his heart is not 1
8 will vomit up the morsels which you have eaten 1
24:13 My son, eat honey, for it is good 1
25:16 If you have found honey, eat only enough for you 1
27 It is not good to eat much honey 1
27:18 He who tends a fig tree will eat its fruit 1
30:17 ravens of the valley and eaten by the vultures. 1
20 adulteress: she eats, and wipes her mouth, and says 1
31:27 She . . does not eat the bread of idleness. 1
Ecc 2:24 that he should eat and drink, and find enjoyment 1
25 apart from him who can eat or . . have enjoyment? 1
3:13 every one should eat and drink and take pleasure 1
4: 5 The fool folds his hands, and eats his own flesh. 1
5:11 When goods increase, they increase who eat them; 1
12 sleep of a laborer, whether he eats little or much 1
18 is to eat and drink and find enjoyment in all 1
8:15 no good thing . . but to eat and drink, and enjoy 1
9: 7 Go, eat your bread with enjoyment, and drink 1
Sng 4:16 come to his garden, and eat its choicest fruits. 1
5: 1 I eat my honeycomb with my honey, I drink my wine 1
1 Eat, O friends, and drink: drink deeply, O lovers! 1
Isa 1:19 If . . obedient, you shall eat the good of the land; 1
3:10 for they shall eat the fruit of their deeds. 1
4: 1 We will eat our own bread and wear our own clothes 1
7:15 He shall eat curds and honey 1
22 milk which they give, he will eat curds; 1
22 one . . left in the land will eat curds and honey. 1
11: 7 and the lion shall eat straw like the ox. 1
21: 5 they spread the rugs, they eat, they drink. 1
22:13 behold . . eating flesh and drinking wine. 1
13 Let us eat and drink, for tomorrow we die. 1
29: 8 when a hungry man dreams he is eating and awakes 1
30:24 asses that till . . will eat salted provender 1
36:12 to eat their own dung and drink their own urine? 1
16 then every one of you will eat of his own vine 1
37:30 this year eat what grows of itself 1
30 and plant vineyards, and eat their fruit. 1
44:16 over the half he eats flesh, he roasts meat 1
19 on its coals, I roasted flesh and have eaten; 1
51: 8 and the worm will eat them like wool; 1
55: 1 and he who has no money, come, buy and eat! 1
2 Hearken diligently to me, and eat what is good 1
59: 5 weave the spider's web; he who eats their eggs dies 1
61: 6 you shall eat the wealth of the nations 1
62: 9 who garner it shall eat it and praise the LORD 1
65: 4 who eat swine's flesh, and broth of abominable 1
13 says the Lord GOD: "Behold, my servants shall eat 1
21 shall plant vineyards and eat their fruit. 1
22 they shall not plant and another eat; 1
25 the lion shall eat straw like the ox; 1
66:17 following one in the midst, eating swine's flesh 1
Jer 2: 3 All who ate of it became guilty; 1
7:21 to your sacrifices, and eat the flesh. 1
15:16 Thy words were found, and I ate them 1
16: 8 feasting to sit with them, to eat and drink. 1
19: 9 and every one shall eat the flesh of his neighbor 1
22:15 Did not your father eat and drink and do justice 1
24: 2 very bad figs, so bad that they could not be eaten. 1
3 figs very bad, so bad that they cannot be eaten. 1
8 the bad figs which are so bad they cannot be eaten 1
29: 5 plant gardens and eat their produce. 1
17 vile figs which are so bad they cannot be eaten. 1
28 and plant gardens and eat their produce. 1
31:29 no longer say: 'The fathers have eaten sour grapes 1
30 each man who eats sour grapes 1
41: 1 As they ate bread together there at Mizpah 1
Lam 2:20 Should women eat their offspring 1
Ezk 2: 8 open your mouth, and eat what I give you. 1
3: 1 he said to me, "Son of man, eat what is offered to you; 1
1 eat this scroll, and go, speak 1
3 Son of man, eat this scroll that I give you 1
3 I ate it; and it was in my mouth as sweet as honey. 1
4: 9 upon your side, 390 days, you shall eat it. 1
10 the food which you eat shall be by weight 1
10 once a day you shall eat it. 1
12 you shall eat it as a barley cake 1
13 Thus shall the people of Israel eat their bread 1
14 I have never eaten what died of itself or was torn 1
16 they shall eat bread by weight 1
5:10 fathers shall eat their sons in the midst of you 1
10 and sons shall eat their fathers; 1
12:18 Son of man, eat your bread with quaking 1
19 They shall eat their bread with fearfulness 1
16:13 you ate fine flour and honey and oil. 1
18: 2 The fathers have eaten sour grapes 1
6 if he does not eat upon the mountains 1
11 but eats upon the mountains 1
15 who does not eat upon the mountains 1
22: 9 and men in you who eat upon the mountains; 1
24:17 nor eat the bread of mourners. 1
22 nor eat the bread of mourners. 1
25: 4 they shall eat your fruit 1
33:25 says the Lord GOD: You eat flesh with the blood 1
34: 3 You eat the fat 1
19 And must my sheep eat what you have trodden 8
39:17 you shall eat flesh and drink blood. 1
18 You shall eat the flesh of the mighty 1
19 And you shall eat fat till you are filled, 1
42:13 the priests . . shall eat the most holy offerings; 1
44: 3 prince may sit in it to eat bread before the LORD; 1
29 They shall eat the cereal offering 1
31 The priests shall not eat of anything 1
45:21 for seven days unleavened bread shall be eaten. 1
Dan 1: 5 daily portion of the rich food which the king ate *
12 us be given vegetables to eat and water to drink. 1
13 youths who eat the king's rich food 1
15 than all the youths who ate the king's rich food. 1
4:33 driven from among men, and ate grass like an ox 9
10: 3 ate no delicacies, no meat or wine entered 1
11:26 who eat his rich food shall be his undoing; 1
Hos 4:10 They shall eat, but not be satisfied; 1
8:13 they sacrifice flesh and eat it; 1
9: 3 and they shall eat unclean food in Assyria. 1
4 all who eat of it shall be defiled; 1
10:13 you have eaten the fruit of lies. 1
Jol 1: 4 cutting locust left, the swarming locust has eaten 1
4 swarming locust left, the hopping locust has eaten 1

4 hopping locust left, the destroying locust has eaten. 1
2:25 the years which the swarming locust has eaten 1
26 You shall eat in plenty and be satisfied 1
Ams 6: 4 and eat lambs from the flock, and calves 1
7: 2 they had finished eating the grass of the land 1
12 flee away to the land of Judah, and eat bread there 1
9:14 and they shall make gardens and eat their fruit. 1
Mic 3: 3 who eat the flesh of my people, and flay their skin 1
6:14 You shall eat, but not be satisfied 1
7: 1 there is no cluster to eat 1
Hag 1: 6 you eat, but you never have enough; 1
Zec 7: 6 when you eat and when you drink 1
6 do you not eat for yourselves 1
Mat 6:25 life, what you shall eat or what you shall drink 19
31 saying, 'What shall we eat?' or 'What shall we drink?' 19
9:11 Why does your teacher eat with tax collectors 19
11:18 For John came neither eating nor drinking 19
19 the Son of man came eating and drinking 19
12: 1 they began to pluck heads of grain and to eat. 19
4 how he entered the house of God and ate the bread 19
4 which it was not lawful for him to eat 19
14:16 you give them something to eat. 19
20 they all ate and were satisfied 19
21 those who ate were about 5,000 men 19
15: 2 For they do not wash their hands when they eat. 19
20 to eat with unwashed hands does not defile a man. 19
27 She said, "Yes, Lord, yet even the dogs eat the crumbs 19
32 and have nothing to eat 19
37 they all ate and were satisfied 19
38 Those who ate were 4,000 men 19
24:38 eating and drinking, marrying 25
49 eats and drinks with the drunken 19
26:17 prepare for you to eat the passover? 19
21 as they were eating, he said, "Truly, I say to you 19
26 as they were eating, Jesus took bread, and blessed 19
26 Take, eat; this is my body. 19
Mrk 1: 6 ate locusts and wild honey. 19
2:16 when they saw that he was eating with sinners 19
16 Why does he eat with tax collectors and sinners? 19
26 ate the bread of the Presence 19
26 it is not lawful for any but the priests to eat 19
3:20 so that they could not even eat. 19
5:43 and told them to give her something to eat. 19
6:31 they had no leisure even to eat. 19
36 buy themselves something to eat. 19
37 he answered them, "You give them something to eat. 19
37 give it to them to eat? 19
42 they all ate and were satisfied. 19
44 those who ate the loaves were 5,000 men. 19
7: 2 they saw that some of his disciples ate 19
3 For the Pharisees, and all the Jews, do not eat 19
4 they do not eat unless they purify themselves 19
5 but eat with hands defiled? 19
28 dogs under the table eat the children's crumbs. 19
8: 1 they had nothing to eat 19
2 have nothing to eat; 19
8 they ate, and were satisfied 19
11:14 May no one ever eat fruit from you again. 19
14:12 prepare for you to eat the passover? 19
14 where I am to eat the passover with my disciples?' 19
18 as they were at table eating, Jesus said 19
18 one who is eating with me. 19
22 as they were eating, he took bread 19
Lke 4: 2 he ate nothing in those days 19
5:30 Why do you eat and drink with tax collectors 19
33 but yours eat and drink. 19
6: 1 his disciples plucked and ate some heads of grain 19
4 took and ate the bread of the Presence 19
4 it is not lawful for any but the priests to eat 19
7:33 For John the Baptist has come eating no bread 19
34 The Son of man has come eating and drinking; 19
36 One of the Pharisees asked him to eat with him 19
8:55 something should be given her to eat. 19
9:13 he said to them, "You give them something to eat. 19
17 all ate and were satisfied 19
10: 7 eating and drinking what they provide 19
8 eat what is set before you; 19
12:19 take your ease, eat, drink, be merry.' 19
22 anxious about your life, what you shall eat 19
29 what you are to eat and what you are to drink 19
45 to eat and drink and get drunk 19
13:26 We ate and drank in your presence 19
14:15 Blessed is he who shall eat bread in the kingdom 19
15: 2 This man receives sinners and eats with them. 23
16 the pods that the swine ate 19
23 let us eat and make merry; 19
17: 8 till I eat and drink 19
8 afterward you shall eat and drink'? 19
27 They ate, they drank, they married 19
28 they ate, they drank, they bought, they sold 19
22: 8 prepare the passover for us, that we may eat it. 19
11 where I am to eat the passover with my disciples?' 19
15 I have earnestly desired to eat this passover 19
16 I tell you I shall not eat it until it is fulfilled 19
30 you may eat and drink at my table in my kingdom 19
24:41 he said to them, "Have you anything here to eat? 13
43 he took it and ate before them. 19
Joh 4:31 the disciples besought him, saying, "Rabbi, eat. 19
32 I have food to eat of which you do not know. 19

6: 5 to buy bread, so that these people may eat? 19
13 fragments . . left by those who had eaten. 11
23 the place where they ate the bread 19
26 because you ate your fill of the loaves. 19
31 Our fathers ate the manna in the wilderness 19
31 'He gave them bread from heaven to eat.' 19
49 Your fathers ate the manna in the wilderness 19
50 a man may eat of it and not die. 19
51 if any one eats of this bread, he will live for ever; 19
52 How can this man give us his flesh to eat? 19
53 unless you eat the flesh of the Son of man 19
54 he who eats my flesh and drinks my blood 25
56 who eats my flesh and drinks my blood abides in me 25
57 he who eats me will live because of me. 25
58 not such as the fathers ate and died 19
58 he who eats this bread will live for ever. 25
13:18 He who ate my bread 25
18:28 might not be defiled, but might eat the passover. 19
Act 9: 9 neither ate nor drank. 19
10:10 he became hungry and desired something to eat; 15
13 there came a voice to him, "Rise, Peter; kill and eat. 19
14 never eaten anything that is common or unclean. 19
41 who ate and drank with him 23
11: 3 Why did you . . eat with them? 23
7 'Rise, Peter; kill and eat.' 19
20:11 Paul had gone up and had broken bread and eaten 15
23:12 an oath neither to eat nor drink 19
21 an oath neither to eat nor drink 19
27:35 he broke it and began to eat. 19
36 they all were encouraged and ate some food 21
38 when they had eaten enough 24
Rom 14: 2 One believes he may eat anything 19
2 while the weak man eats only vegetables. 19
3 Let not him who eats despise him who abstains 19
3 him who abstains pass judgment on him who eats; 19
6 He also who eats, eats in honor of the Lord 19
6 He also who eats, eats in honor of the Lord 19
15 If your brother is being injured by what you eat 12
15 Do not let what you eat cause the ruin of one 12
20 to make others fall by what he eats; 19
21 it is right not to eat meat or drink wine 19
23 But he who has doubts is condemned, if he eats 19
1Co 5:11 not even to eat with such a one. 23
8: 4 Hence, as to the eating of food offered to idols 14
7 some . . eat food as really offered to an idol 19
8 We are no worse off if we do not eat 19
10 not be encouraged . . to eat food offered to idols? 19
13 I will never eat meat 19
9: 7 without eating any of its fruit 19
10: 3 all ate the same supernatural food 19
7 The people sat down to eat and drink 19
18 who eat the sacrifices 19
25 Eat whatever is sold in the meat market 19
27 eat whatever is set before you 19
29 I mean his conscience, not yours-do not eat it 19
31 So, whether you eat or drink, or whatever you do 19
11:20 it is not the Lord's supper that you eat. 19
21 in eating, each one goes ahead with his own meal 19
22 What! Do you not have houses to eat and drink in? 19
26 For as often as you eat this bread 19
27 Whoever, therefore, eats the bread 19
28 Let a man examine himself, and so eat of the bread 19
29 For any one who eats and drinks 19
29 eats and drinks judgment upon himself. 19
33 So then, my brethren, when you come together to eat 19
34 if any one is hungry, let him eat at home 19
15:32 Let us eat and drink, for tomorrow we die. 19
Gal 2:12 he ate with the Gentiles 23
2Th 3: 8 we did not eat any one's bread without paying 19
10 If any one will not work, let him not eat. 19
Heb 13:10 those who serve the tent have no right to eat. 19
Jas 5: 3 their rust . . will eat your flesh like fire 19
Rev 2: 7 To him who conquers I will grant to eat of the tree 19
14 that they might eat food sacrificed to idols 19
20 and to eat food sacrificed to idols. 19
3:20 opens the door, I will come to him and eat with him 16
10: 9 Take it and eat; it will be bitter to your stomach 20
10 I took the little scroll . . and ate it; 20
10 when I had eaten it my stomach was made bitter. 19
19:18 to eat the flesh of kings, the flesh of captains 19
1Es 3: 3 They ate and drank 19
4:10 he reclines, he eats and drinks and sleeps 19
7:13 the people of Israel . . ate it 19
8:85 may be strong and eat the good things of the land 19
9: 2 he did not eat bread or drink water 15
51 go your way, eat the fat and drink the sweet 19
54 to eat and drink and enjoy themselves 19
2Es 1:19 you ate the bread of angels. 29
5:18 Rise therefore and eat some bread 28
6:52 thou hast kept them to be eaten by whom thou wilt 27
7:104 to be ill or sleep or eat or be healed in his stead 29
9:24 and eat only of the flowers of the field 29
24 and drink no wine, but eat only flowers *
26 and ate of the plants of the field 29
10: 4 and I will neither eat nor drink 29
12:51 and I ate only of the flowers of the field 29
14:42 and ate their bread at night. 29
15:58 shall eat their own flesh in hunger for bread 29
16:69 who consent to eat shall be held in derision *

Tob 1:10 my relatives ate the food of the Gentiles; 19
11 I kept myself from eating it 19
2: 1 I sat down to eat. 19
5 I washed myself and ate my food in sorrow. 19
13 for it is not right to eat what is stolen. 19
6: 5 they roasted and ate the fish. 19
7: 9 Raguel said to Tobias, "Eat, drink, and be merry; 19
11 Tobias said, "I will eat nothing here 15
15 Then they began to eat. 19
8: 1 When they had finished eating 16
10: 7 she ate nothing in the daytime 19
12:19 I merely appeared to you and did not eat or drink 19
Jdt 11:12 all that God by his laws has forbidden them to eat. 19
12: 2 Judith said, "I cannot eat it, lest it be an offense; 19
9 until she ate her food toward evening. 22
11 to join us and eat and drink with us. 19
15 that she might recline on them when she ate. 19
19 Then she took and ate and drank before him 19
AEs 14:17 thy servant has not eaten at Haman's table 19
Wis 4: 5 not ripe enough to eat, and good for nothing. 14
16: 2 thou didst prepare quails to eat *
20 thou didst supply them . . with bread ready to eat *
Sir 6:19 soon you will eat of her produce. 19
20:16 those who eat my bread speak unkindly. 19
24:21 Those who eat me will hunger for more 19
29:26 if you have anything at hand, let me have it to eat. 26
30:19 it can neither eat nor smell 19
25 will give heed to the food he eats. 17
31:16 Eat like a human being what is set before you 19
17 first to stop eating, for the sake of good manners *
20 Healthy sleep depends on moderate eating 18
45:21 for they eat the sacrifices to the Lord 19
Bar 2: 3 that we should eat, one the flesh of his son 19
Bel 1: 6 see how much he eats and drinks every day? 19
7 it never ate or drank anything. 11
8 tell me who is eating these provisions 20
9 if you prove that Bel is eating them 20
12 if you do not find that Bel has eaten it all 11
15 ate and drank everything. 20
27 The dragon ate them, and burst open 19
39 Daniel arose and ate 19
1Mc 1:62 and were resolved . . not to eat unclean food. 19
2Mc 2:11 because the sin offering had not been eaten. 11
6:18 forced to open his mouth to eat swine's flesh. 19
21 pretend that he was eating the flesh 19
7: 7 Will you eat rather than have your body punished 19
4Mc 4:26 to eat defiling foods and to renounce Judaism. 10
5: 2 to compel them to eat pork 10
6 I would advise you to save yourself by eating pork 10
26 to eat what will be most suitable for our lives 19
27 to eat in such a way that you may deride us 19
6:15 save yourself by pretending to eat pork. 10
8: 2 any who ate . . should be freed after eating 19
9:16 Agree to eat so that you may be released 19
27 they inquired if he were willing to eat 19
11:13 whether he was willing to eat and be released 19

eat *See also* give, persuade.

eat defiling food 1. *μιαροφαγέω* 2. *μιαροφαγία*

4Mc 5: 3 If any were not willing to eat defiling food 1
19 if we were to eat defiling food; 1
25 Therefore we do not eat defiling food 1
27 you may deride us for eating defiling foods 2
6:19 an example of the eating of defiling food. 2
7: 6 nor profaned . . by eating defiling foods. 2
8: 2 to compel an aged man to eat defiling foods 1
2 any who ate defiling food should be freed 1
12 out of fear to eat the defiling food. 1
29 counseling them to eat defiling food 1
11:16 to torture me for not eating defiling foods 1
25 to force us to eat defiling foods 2
13: 2 and had eaten defiling food 1

make eat 1. אכל 2. טעם (A)

Isa 49:26 I will make your oppressors eat their own flesh 1
Jer 19: 9 I will make them eat the flesh of their sons 1
Dan 4:25 made to eat grass like an ox, and you shall be wet 2
32 shall be made to eat grass like an ox; 2

eat meat 1. *σαρκοφαγέω* 2. *σαρκοφαγία*

4Mc 5: 8 should you abhor eating the very excellent meat 2
14 urged him . . to eat meat unlawfully 2
26 to eat meats that would be contrary to this. 1

eat nothing 1. *ἀσιτέω*

1Mc 3:17 we are faint, for we have eaten nothing today. 1

eat of a sacrifice 1. *σπλαγχνισμός*

2Mc 7:42 about the eating of sacrifices 1

eat one's fill 1. *ἐμπίμπλημι* 2. *χορτάζω*

Joh 6:12 when they had eaten their fill 1
26 because you ate your fill of the loaves. 2
Wis 13:12 and eat his fill. 1
Sir 24:19 eat your fill of my produce. 1

eat one's way 1. *νομὴν ἔχω*

2Ti 2:17 their talk will eat its way like gangrene 1

eat salt 1. מלח (A)
Ezr 4:14 Now because we eat the salt of the palace 1

something to eat 1. מַאֲכָל 2. נשך בְּשִׁנַּיִם
Jdg 14:14 Out of the eater came something to eat. 1
Mic 3: 5 who cry "Peace" when they have something to eat 2

eat up 1. אכל 2. בלע
Gen 41: 4 thin cows ate up the seven sleek and fat cows. 1
20 gaunt cows ate up the first seven fat cows 1
Lev 26:38 the land of your enemies shall eat you up 1
Num24: 8 he shall eat up the nations his adversaries 1
Deu 28:33 nation . . shall eat up the fruit of your ground 1
Ps 14: 4 all the evildoers who eat up my people 1
53: 4 who eat up my people as they eat bread 1
105:35 which . . ate up the fruit of their ground. 1
Isa 28: 4 he eats it up as soon as it is in his hand. 2
50: 9 like a garment; the moth will eat them up. 1
51: 8 For the moth will eat them up like a garment 1
Jer 5:17 They shall eat up your harvest and your food; 1
17 they shall eat up your sons and your daughters; 1
17 they shall eat up your flocks and your herds; 1
17 they shall eat up your vines and your fig trees; 1
Ams 7: 4 devoured the . . deep and was eating up the land. 1

eaten by worm 1. σκωληκόβρωτος
Act 12:23 he was eaten by worms and died. 1

eater 1. אכל
Jdg 14:14 Out of the eater came something to eat. 1
Isa 55:10 giving seed to the sower and bread to the eater 1
Nah 3:12 if shaken they fall into the mouth of the eater. 1

gluttonous eater 1. זלל
Prv 23:20 Be not . . among gluttonous eaters of meat; 1

indiscriminate eating 1. παντοφαγία
4Mc 1:27 in the body, indiscriminate eating, gluttony 1

ebony 1. הָבְנִי
Ezk 27:15 brought you in payment ivory tusks and ebony. 1

echo 1. ἠχέω 2. ἠχώ
Wis 17:19 an echo thrown back from a hollow of the mountains 2
3Mc 1:29 the walls and the whole earth around echoed 1

echo back 1. ἀντηχέω
Wis 18:10 the discordant cry of their enemies echoed back 1

edge 1. פֵּאָה 2. פֶּה 3. פָּנִים 4. צוּר 5. קָצָה 6. קָצֶה 7. שָׂפָה 8. κατὰ πρόσωπον 9. στόμα
Exd 13:20 encamped at Etham, on the edge of the wilderness. 6
17:13 Am'alek and his people with the edge of the sword. 2
26: 4 loops of blue on the edge of the outmost curtain 7
4 make loops on the edge of the outmost curtain 7
5 loops you shall make on the edge of the curtain 6
10 you shall make 50 loops on the edge 7
10 shall make 50 loops on the edge of the curtain 7
28: 7 two shoulder-pieces attached to its two edges 5
23 two rings on the two edges of the breastpiece. 5
24 in the two rings at the edges of the breastpiece; 5
26 put them . . on its inside edge next to the ephod. 7
36:11 of blue on the edge of the outmost curtain 7
11 he made them on the edge of the outmost curtain 7
12 he made 50 loops on the edge of the curtain 6
17 50 loops on the edge of the outmost curtain 7
17 on the edge of the other connecting curtain. 7
39: 4 shoulder-pieces, joined to it at its two edges. 5
16 two rings on the two edges of the breastpiece; 5
17 in the two rings at the edges of the breastpiece. 5
19 on its inside edge next to the ephod. 7
Lev 19:27 You shall not . . mar the edges of your beard 1
21: 5 nor shave off the edges of their beards 1
Num20:16 in Kadesh, a city on the edge of your territory. 6
21:24 Israel slew him with the edge of the sword 2
33: 6 Etham, which is on the edge of the wilderness. 6
37 at Mount Hor, on the edge of the land of Edom. 6
Deu 2:36 Aro'er . . on the edge of the valley of the Arnon 7
3:12 Aro'er, which is on the edge of the valley of the Arnon •
4:48 Aro'er . . on the edge of the valley of the Arnon 7
13:15 destroying it . . with the edge of the sword. 2
Jos 6:21 destroyed all . . with the edge of the sword. 2
8:24 all of them . . had fallen by the edge of the sword 2
24 and smote it with the edge of the sword. 2
10:28 smote it and its king with the edge of the sword; 2
30 and he smote it with the edge of the sword 2
32 and smote it with the edge of the sword 2
35 took it . . and smote it with the edge of the sword; 2
37 and took it, and smote it with the edge of the sword 2
39 and they smote them with the edge of the sword 2
11:12 took, and smote them with the edge of the sword 2
14 every man they smote with the edge of the sword 2
12: 2 Aro'er . . on the edge of the valley of the Arnon 7
13: 9 Aro'er . . on the edge of the valley of the Arnon 7
16 Aro'er . . on the edge of the valley of the Arnon 7
Jdg 1: 8 and took it, and smote it with the edge of the sword 2
25 and they smote the city with the edge of the sword 2
3:16 himself a sword with two edges, a cubit in length; 2
4:15 all his army before Barak at the edge of the sword; 2
16 the army of Sis'era fell by the edge of the sword; 2
18:27 came . . and smote them with the edge of the sword 2
20:37 and smote all the city with the edge of the sword. 2
48 and smote them with the edge of the sword 2
21:10 Go and smite . . with the edge of the sword; 2
1Sm 15: 8 destroyed . . people with the edge of the sword. 2
2Sm 15:14 and smite the city with the edge of the sword. 2
2Kg 7: 5 but when they came to the edge of the camp 6
8 when these lepers came to the edge of the camp 6
Job 1:15 and slew the servants with the edge of the sword; 2
17 and slew the servants with the edge of the sword; 2
Ps 89:43 Yea, thou hast turned back the edge of his sword 4
Ecc 10:10 If the iron is blunt, and one does not whet the edge 3
Jer 21: 7 He shall smite them with the edge of the sword; 2
Ezk 21:16 right and left where your edge is directed. 3
43:13 broad, with a rim of one span around its edge. 7
Lke 21:24 they will fall by the edge of the sword 9
Heb 11:34 escaped the edge of the sword 9
Jdt 2:27 put to death . . with the edge of the sword. 9
3: 9 Then he came to the edge of Esdraelon, near Dothan 8
Sir 28:18 Many have fallen by the edge of the sword 9
1Mc 5:28 killed every male by the edge of the sword 9
51 He destroyed every male by the edge of the sword 9

edict 1. דָּת 2. כְּתָב 3. פִּתְגָם (A) 4. διάταγμα
Ezr 6:11 I make a decree that if any one alters this edict 3
Est 2: 8 when the king's order and his edict were proclaimed 1
3:12 an edict, according to all that Haman commanded •
8: 8 an edict written in the name of the king 2
9 an edict was written . . concerning the Jews •
17 wherever the king's command and his edict came 1
9: 1 command and edict were about to be executed 1
13 allowed . . to do according to this day's edict. 1
Heb 11:23 they were not afraid of the king's edict. 4

edification 1. οἰκοδομή
1Co 14:26 Let all things be done for edification. 1

edify 1. οἰκοδομέω 2. οἰκοδομή 3. οἰκοδομὴν λαμβάνω
Rom15: 2 please his neighbor for his good, to edify him. 2
1Co 14: 4 He who speaks in a tongue edifies himself 1
4 he who prophesies edifies the church. 1
5 so that the church may be edified. 3
17 the other man is not edified. 1
Eph 4:29 only such as is good for edifying 2

educate 1. גדל 2. παιδεύω 3. πλανάω
Dan 1: 5 educated for three years, and at the end 1
Act 22: 3 educated according to . . the law of our fathers 2
Sir 10: 1 A wise magistrate will educate his people 2
34: 9 An educated man knows many things 3
4Mc 13:24 Since they had been educated by the same law 2

education 1. παιδεία
Sir 4:24 education through the words of the tongue. 1
21:19 To a senseless man education is fetters 1
21 education is like a golden ornament 1
4Mc 1:17 This, in turn, is education in the law 1
13:22 both general education and our discipline 1

effect 1. כָּזֶה 2. מַעֲשֶׂה 3. διά 4. ἐνεργέω 5. ἐργάζομαι 6. ἔργον 7. οὗτος 8. ποιέω 9. πρός 10. τρόπος 11. τύπος 12. ὡς
2Ch 34:22 went to Huldah . . spoke to her to that effect. 1
Isa 32:17 the effect of righteousness will be peace 2
Lke 18: 1 to the effect that they ought always to pray 9
Act 7: 6 God spoke to this effect 7
23:25 he wrote a letter to this effect 11
Rom 5:16 is not like the effect of that one man's sin. 3
2Th 2: 2 to the effect that the day of the Lord has come. 12
Jas 1: 4 let steadfastness have its full effect 6
5:16 prayer . . has great power in its effects. 4
Wis 8: 5 what is richer than wisdom who effects all things? 5
16:17 the fire had still greater effect 4
1Mc 8:30 If after these terms are in effect both parties •
2Mc 1:24 The prayer was to this effect 10
3: 7 to effect the removal of the aforesaid money. 8
11:16 The letter . . was to this effect 10
effect *See also* take.

no effect 1. interitus
2Es 4:23 the law of our fathers has been made of no effect 1

same effect 1. κατὰ τὰ αὐτά
1Mc 12: 2 He also sent letters to the same effect 1

without effect 1. ἀργός
Wis 14: 5 works of thy wisdom should not be without effect; 1

effective 1. δύναμαι 2. ἐργάζομαι
Wis 8: 6 if understanding is effective 2
2Mc 15:17 so noble and so effective in arousing valor 1

effective work 1. ἐνεργής
1Co 16: 9 for a wide door for effective work has opened 1

effort 1. ἐκτενής 2. ἐργασία 3. σπουδή 4. labor
Lke 12:58 make an effort to settle with him on the way 2
2Pe 1: 5 make every effort to supplement your faith 3
2Es 7:92 because they have striven with great effort 4
13:38 and will destroy them without effort by the law 4
3Mc 3:10 to exert more earnest efforts for their assistance. 1
effort *See also* devote, make.

mental effort 1. διάνοια
4Mc 2: 2 by mental effort he overcame sexual desire. 1

egg 1. בֵּיצָה
Deu 22: 6 nest . . with young ones or eggs and the mother 1
6 mother sitting upon the young or upon the eggs 1
Job 39:14 For she leaves her eggs to the earth 1
Isa 10:14 as men gather eggs that have been forsaken 1
59: 5 They watch adders' eggs, they weave 1
5 weave the spider's web; he who eats their eggs dies 1

eight 1. שְׁמֹנֶה 2. ὀκτώ 3. octo
Gen 17:12 He that is eight days old among you 1
21: 4 circumcised his son Isaac when he was eight days 1
22:23 These eight Milcah bore to Nahor 1
Exd 26:25 there shall be eight frames, with their bases 1
36:30 There were eight frames with their bases 1
Num 7: 8 four wagons and eight oxen he gave 1
29:29 On the sixth day eight bulls, two rams, fourteen 1
Jdg 3: 8 Israel served Cu'shan-rishatha'im eight years. 1
12:14 rode on 70 asses; and he judged Israel eight years. 1
1Sm 17:12 an Eph'rathite . . named Jesse, who had eight sons. 1
1Kg 7:10 huge stones, stones of eight and ten cubits. 1
2Kg 8:17 and he reigned eight years in Jerusalem. 1
22: 1 Josi'ah was eight years old when he began to reign 1
1Ch 24: 4 and eight of the sons of Ith'amar. 1
2Ch 21: 5 Jeho'ram . . reigned eight years in Jerusalem. 1
20 he reigned eight years in Jerusalem; 1
29:17 then for eight days they sanctified the house 1
34: 1 Josi'ah was eight years old when he began to reign 1
36: 9 Jehoi'achin was eight . . when he began to reign 1
Ecc 11: 2 Give a portion to seven, or even to eight 1
Jer 41:15 Ish'mael . . escaped from Joha'nan with eight men 1
Ezk 40: 8 the vestibule of the gateway, eight cubits; •
31 its stairway had eight steps. 1
34 and its stairway had eight steps. 1
37 its stairway had eight steps. 1
41 eight tables, on which the sacrifices were to be 1
Mic 5: 5 we will raise against him . . eight princes of men; 1
Lke 2:21 at the end of eight days, when he was circumcised 2
9:28 Now about eight days after these sayings 2
Joh 20:26 Eight days later 2
Act 9:33 Aene'as, who had been bedridden for eight years 2
25: 6 stayed among them not more than eight or ten days 2
1Pe 3:20 in which a few, that is, eight persons, were saved 2
2Es 11:11 and behold, there were eight of them. 3
12:19 eight little wings clinging to his wings 3
20 Eight kings shall arise in it 3
Tob 14: 2 after eight years he regained it 2
1Mc 4:56 they celebrated . . for eight days 2
59 observed with gladness and joy for eight days 2
2Mc 2:12 Likewise Solomon also kept the eight days. 2
10: 6 celebrated it for eight days with rejoicing 2

eighteen 1. שְׁמֹנֶה עֶשְׂרֵה 2. δέκα καὶ ὀκτώ 3. δέκα ὀκτώ 4. δεκαοκτώ
Jdg 3:14 served Eglon the king of Moab eighteen years. 1
10: 8 For eighteen years they oppressed . . Israel 1
1Kg 7:15 Eighteen cubits was the height of one pillar 1
2Kg 24: 8 Jehoi'achin was eighteen years old 1
25:17 The height of the one pillar was eighteen cubits 1
1Ch 26: 9 had sons and brethren, able men, eighteen. 1
2Ch 11:21 (he took eighteen wives and 60 concubines 1
Ezr 8:18 Sherebi'ah with his sons and kinsmen, eighteen. 1
Jer 52:21 the height of the one pillar was eighteen cubits 1
Lke 13: 4 eighteen upon whom the tower in Silo'am fell 4
11 had had a spirit of infirmity for eighteen years; 4
16 whom Satan bound for eighteen years 2
1Es 1:43 when he was made king he was eighteen years old 3
8:47 Sherebiah with his sons and kinsmen, eighteen; 3

eighteenth 1. שְׁמֹנֶה עֶשְׂרֵה 2. ὀκτωκαιδέκατος
1Kg 15: 1 Now in the eighteenth year of King Jerobo'am 1
2Kg 3: 1 In the eighteenth year of Jehosh'aphat 1
22: 3 In the eighteenth year of King Josi'ah 1
23:23 but in the eighteenth year of King Josi'ah 1
1Ch 24:15 to Hezir, the eighteenth to Hap'pizzez 1
25:25 eighteenth, to Hana'ni, his sons and his brethren 1
2Ch 13: 1 In the eighteenth year of King Jerobo'am 1
34: 8 Now in the eighteenth year of his reign 1
35:19 In the eighteenth year of the reign of Josi'ah 1
Jer 32: 1 was the eighteenth year of Nebuchadrez'zar. 1
52:29 in the eighteenth year of Nebuchadrez'zar 1
1Es 1:22 In the eighteenth year of the reign of Josiah 2
Jdt 2: 1 In the eighteenth year, on the 22nd day 2
1Mc 14:27 On the eighteenth day of Elul, in the 172nd year 2

eighth 1. שְׁמִינִי 2. שְׁמֹנֶה 3. ὄγδοος 4. octavus
Exd 22:30 on the eighth day you shall give it to me. 1
Lev 9: 1 On the eighth day Moses called Aaron and his sons 1

12: 3 on the eighth day the flesh of his foreskin shall 1
14:10 on the eighth day he shall take two male lambs 1
23 on the eighth day he shall bring them 1
15:14 on the eighth day he shall take two turtledoves 1
29 on the eighth day she shall take two turtledoves 1
22:27 from the eighth day on it shall be acceptable 1
23:36 the eighth day you shall hold a holy convocation 1
39 on the eighth day shall be a solemn rest 1
25:22 When you sow in the eighth year, you will be eating 1
Num 6:10 On the eighth day he shall bring two turtledoves 1
7:54 On the eighth day Gama'liel . . of Manas'seh 1
29:35 eighth day you shall have a solemn assembly 1
1Kg 6:38 in the month of Bul, which is the eighth month 1
8:66 On the eighth day he sent the people away; 1
12:32 a feast on the fifteenth day of the eighth month 1
33 on the fifteenth day in the eighth month 1
2Kg 24:12 took him prisoner in the eighth year of his reign 2
1Ch 12:12 Joha'nan eighth, Elza'bad ninth 1
24:10 the seventh to Hakkoz, the eighth to Abi'jah 1
25:15 eighth to Jeshai'ah, his sons and his brethren 1
26: 5 Is'sachar the seventh, Pe-ul'lethai the eighth; 1
27:11 Eighth . . was Sib'becai the Hu'shathite 1
11 for the eighth month, was Sib'becai 1
2Ch 7: 9 on the eighth day they held a solemn assembly; 1
29:17 and on the eighth day of the month they came 2
34: 3 eighth year of his reign, while he was yet a boy 2
Neh 8:18 eighth day there was a solemn assembly 1
Ezk 43:27 then from the eighth day onward the priests 1
Zec 1: 1 In the eighth month, in the second year of Darius 1
Lke 1:59 on the eighth day they came to circumcise 3
Act 7: 8 circumcised him on the eighth day 3
Rev 17:11 As for the beast that was and is not, it is an eighth 3
21:20 the seventh chrysolite, the eighth beryl 3
2Es 6:36 on the eighth night my heart was troubled 4

eighth day 1. ὀκταήμερος
Php 3: 5 circumcised on the eighth day 1

either 1. אוֹ 2. אִם 3. בֵּין 4. גַּם 5. וְ 6. כִּי 7. מִן
8. ἄμφω 9. ἀπό 10. γάρ 11. ἐάν τε 12. εἰ
13. ἑκάτερος 14. ἤ 15. ἤτοι 16. καί 17. μηδέ
18. μηθέτερος 19. μήτε 20. οὐ 21. οὔτε
Gen 31:24 say not a word to Jacob, either good or bad. 7
Exd 4:10 I am not eloquent, either heretofore or since 4
11: 7 of the people of Israel, either man or beast 7
Lev 12: 7 for her who bears a child, either male or female 1
13:59 disease . . either in warp or woof, or in anything 1
16:29 do no work, either the native or the stranger •
18:26 either the native or the stranger who sojourns •
27:12 the priest shall value it as either good or bad 3
14 the priest shall value it as either good or bad 3
Num 6: 2 When either a man or a woman makes a special vow 1
22:24 narrow path . . with a wall on either side. •
26 no way to turn either to the right or to the left. •
24:13 to do either good or bad of my own will; •
Deu 17:11 not turn . . either to the right hand or to the left. •
20 not turn . . either to the right hand or to the left; •
1Sm 20: 2 my father does nothing either great or small 1
27 not . . come to the meal, either yesterday or today? 4
28: 6 the LORD did not answer him, either by dreams 4
15 answers . . either by prophets or by dreams; 4
1Kg 18:27 he is a god; either he is musing, or he has gone aside 6
1Ch 12: 2 with either the right or the left hand; •
21:12 either three years of famine; 2
Prv 24:21 LORD and the king, and do not disobey either 18
Ecc 4: 8 a person who has no one, either son or brother 4
Isa 17: 8 their own fingers have made, either the Ashe'rim 5
Ezk 46:12 either a burnt offering or peace offerings •
Mat 5:34 I say to you, Do not swear at all, either by heaven 19
6:24 for either he will hate the one and love the other 10
12:32 either in this age or in the age to come. 21
33 Either make the tree good, and its fruit good 14
Lke 16:13 either he will hate the one and love the other 14
Act 24:12 either in the temple or in the synagogues 21
Rom 6:16 slaves . . either of sin, which leads to death 15
9:11 and had done nothing either good or bad 17
1Th 2: 5 never used either words of flattery, as you know 21
2Th 2: 2 either by spirit or by word, or by letter 19
15 taught . . either by word of mouth or by letter. 12
1Ti 1: 7 either what they are saying or . . 19
Jas 5:12 do not swear, either by heaven or by earth 19
1Jn 3: 6 no one who sins has either seen him or known him. 20
Rev 9:20 idols . . which cannot either see or hear or walk; 21
1Es 8:24 either fine or imprisonment. 14
Jdt 11:21 either for beauty of face or wisdom of speech! •
13: 4 no one, either small or great, was left 9
Wis 13: 2 either fire or wind or swift air 14
14:24 keep either their lives or their marriages pure 21
24 they either treacherously kill one another 14
28 For their worshipers either rave in exultation 14
15: 6 who either make or desire or worship them. 16
Sir 13:25 either for good or for evil. 11
20:30 what advantage is there in either of them? 8
41:14 what advantage is there in either of them? 8
LJr 1:35 they are not able to give either wealth or money; 21
64 they are not able either to decide a case 21
1Mc 4:35 how ready they were either to live or to die nobly 14
4Mc 5:20 in matters either small or great •
21 for in either case the law is equally despised. 13
38 dominate . . either by word or by deed. 21

either *See also* side.

elaborate setting 1. μηχάνημα
1Mc 13:29 he devised an elaborate setting 1

elapse 1. πληρόω
Act 24:27 when two years had elapsed 1

elate 1. ἐπαίρω 2. μετεωρισμός 3. μετωρίζω
4. φρενόομαι
AEs 13: 2 not elated with presumption of authority 1
2Mc 5:17 Antiochus was elated in spirit 3
21 because his mind was elated. 2
7:34 do not be elated in vain 3
11: 4 but was elated with his ten thousands of infantry 4

too elated 1. ὑπεραίρω
2Co 12: 7 to harass me, to keep me from being too elated. 1
7 to harass me, to keep me from being too elated. 1

elbow 1. ἀγκών
4Mc 10: 6 his fingers and arms and legs and elbows. 1

elder 1. גָּדוֹל 2. זָקֵן 3. רַב 4. סִיב (A) 5. שִׂיב (A)
6. μέγας 7. πρέσβυς 8. πρεσβύτερος 9. πρεσβύτης
10. πρεσβῦτις
Gen 25:23 the elder shall serve the younger. 3
50: 7 with him went up . . the elders of his household 2
7 went up . . all the elders of the land of Egypt 2
Exd 3:16 Go and gather the elders of Israel together 2
18 you and the elders of Israel shall go to the king 2
4:29 gathered together all the elders of the people 2
12:21 Moses called all the elders of Israel, and said 2
17: 5 taking with you some of the elders of Israel; 2
6 did so, in the sight of the elders of Israel. 2
18:12 and Aaron came with all the elders of Israel 2
19: 7 So Moses came and called the elders of the people 2
24: 1 Abi'hu, and 70 of the elders of Israel 2
9 Abi'hu, and 70 of the elders of Israel went up 2
14 he said to the elders, "Tarry here for us 2
Lev 4:15 the elders of the congregation 2
9: 1 Aaron and his sons and the elders of Israel 2
Num11:16 Gather for me 70 men of the elders of Israel 2
16 whom you know to be the elders of the people 2
24 he gathered 70 men of the elders of the people 2
25 the LORD came . . and put it upon the 70 elders; 2
30 Moses and the elders . . returned to the camp. 2
16:25 elders of Israel followed him. 2
22: 4 Moab said to the elders of Mid'ian, "This horde 2
7 elders of Moab and the elders of Mid'ian departed 2
7 elders of Moab and the elders of Mid'ian departed 2
Deu 5:23 all the heads of your tribes, and your elders; 2
19:12 then the elders of his city shall send and fetch 2
21: 2 your elders and your judges shall come forth 2
3 elders of the city . . nearest to the slain man 2
4 elders of that city shall bring the heifer down 2
6 elders of that city nearest to the slain man 2
19 take hold of him and bring him out to the elders 2
20 shall say to the elders of his city, 'This our son 2
22:15 tokens of her virginity to the elders of the city 2
16 father of the young woman shall say to the elders 2
17 spread the garment before the elders of the city. 2
18 elders of that city shall take the man and whip 2
25: 7 brother's wife . . go up to the gate to the elders 2
8 elders of his city shall call him, and speak to him 2
9 go up to him in the presence of the elders, and pull 2
27: 1 Now Moses and the elders of Israel commanded 2
29:10 heads . . your elders, and your officers, all 2
31: 9 gave it to . . and to all the elders of Israel. 2
28 Assemble to me all the elders of your tribes 2
32: 7 ask your . . elders, and they will tell you. 2
Jos 7: 6 Then Joshua rent . . he and the elders of Israel; 2
8:10 and went up, with the elders of Israel . . to Ai. 2
33 with their elders and officers and their judges 2
9:11 And our elders and all . . of our country said to us 2
20: 4 and explain his case to the elders of that city; 2
23: 2 summoned all Israel, their elders and heads 2
24: 1 and summoned the elders, the heads, the judges 2
31 all the days of the elders who outlived Joshua 2
Jdg 2: 7 all the days of the elders who outlived Joshua 2
8:14 wrote down . . the officials and elders 2
16 he took the elders of the city and he took thorns 2
11: 5 the elders of Gilead went to bring Jephthah 2
7 Jephthah said to the elders of Gilead, "Did you not 2
8 the elders of Gilead said to Jephthah, "That is why 2
9 Jephthah said to the elders of Gilead 2
10 the elders of Gilead said to Jephthah, "The LORD 2
11 Jephthah went with the elders of Gilead 2
21:16 the elders of the congregation said, "What shall 2
Rut 4: 2 he took ten men of the elders of the city, and said 2
4 and in the presence of the elders of my people. 2
9 Then Bo'az said to the elders and all the people 2
11 all the people who were at the gate, and the elders 2
1Sm 4: 3 the elders of Israel said, "Why has the LORD 2
8: 4 Then all the elders of Israel gathered together 2
11: 3 The elders of Jabesh said . . "Give us seven days 2
15:30 yet honor me now before the elders of my people 2
16: 4 The elders of the city came to meet him trembling 2
30:26 sent part . . to his friends, the elders of Judah 2
2Sm 3:17 Abner conferred with the elders of Israel 2
5: 3 elders of Israel came to the king 2
12:17 And the elders of his house stood beside him 2
17: 4 pleased Ab'salom and all the elders of Israel. 2
15 counsel Ab'salom and the elders of Israel; 2
19:11 Say to the elders of Judah, 'Why should you be 2
1Kg 8: 1 assembled the elders of Israel and all the heads 2
3 all the elders of Israel came 2
20: 7 the king . . called all the elders of the land 2
8 all the elders and all the people said to him 2
21: 8 she sent the letters to the elders and the nobles 2
11 the men of his city, the elders and the nobles 2
2Kg 6:32 Eli'sha . . and the elders were sitting with him. 2
32 Eli'sha said to the elders, "Do you see 2
10: 1 sent . . to the rulers of the city, to the elders 2
5 together with the elders and the guardians 2
23: 1 the elders of Judah and Jerusalem were gathered 2
1Ch 11: 3 the elders of Israel came to the king at Hebron; 2
15:25 David and the elders of Israel 2
21:16 David and the elders, clothed in sackcloth 2
2Ch 5: 2 Then Solomon assembled the elders of Israel 2
4 all the elders of Israel came 2
34:29 gathered . . the elders of Judah and Jerusalem. 2
Ezr 5: 5 eye of their God was upon the elders of the Jews 4
9 Then we asked those elders and spoke to them thus 5
6: 7 let the governor . . and the elders of the Jews 4
8 elders of the Jews for the rebuilding 4
14 elders of the Jews built and prospered 4
10: 8 by order of the officials and the elders 2
14 with them the elders and judges of every city 2
Job 12:20 and takes away the discernment of the elders. 2
Ps 105:22 to teach his elders wisdom. 2
107:32 praise him in the assembly of the elders. 2
Prv 31:23 when he sits among the elders of the land. 2
Isa 3: 2 the prophet, the diviner and the elder 2
5 the youth will be insolent to the elder 2
14 enters into judgment with the elders and princes 2
9:15 the elder and honored man is the head 2
24:23 before his elders he will manifest his glory. 2
Jer 19: 1 and take some of the elders of the people 2
26:17 certain of the elders of the land arose and spoke 2
29: 1 the prophet sent from Jerusalem to the elders 2
Lam 1:19 my priests and elders perished in the city 2
2:10 The elders of the daughter of Zion sit 2
4:16 no honor was shown . . no favor to the elders. 2
5:12 no respect is shown to the elders. 2
Ezk 7:26 law perishes . . and counsel from the elders. 2
8: 1 sat . . with the elders of Judah sitting before me 2
11 And before them stood 70 men of the elders 2
12 have you seen what the elders . . are doing 2
9: 6 began with the elders who were before the house. 2
14: 1 Then came certain of the elders of Israel to me; 2
16:61 your sisters, both your elder and your younger 1
20: 1 certain of the elders of Israel came to inquire 2
3 Son of man, speak to the elders of Israel 2
27: 9 elders of Gebal and her skilled men were in you 2
Jol 1:14 Gather the elders and all the inhabitants 2
2:16 Sanctify the congregation; assemble the elders; 2
Mat 15: 2 the tradition of the elders 8
16:21 from the elders and chief priests and scribes 8
21:23 the chief priests and the elders of the people 8
26: 3 Then the chief priests and the elders 8
47 from the chief priests and the elders of the people. 8
57 where the scribes and the elders had gathered. 8
27: 1 all the chief priests and the elders of the people 8
3 to the chief priests and the elders 8
12 accused by the chief priests and elders 8
20 Now the chief priests and the elders persuaded 8
41 with the scribes and elders, mocked him, saying 8
28:12 when they had assembled with the elders 8
Mrk 7: 3 observing the tradition of the elders; 8
5 according to the tradition of the elders 8
8:31 rejected by the elders and the chief priests 8
11:27 the scribes and the elders came to him 8
14:43 the chief priests and the scribes and the elders 8
53 the chief priests and the elders and the scribes 8
15: 1 the chief priests, with the elders and scribes 8
Lke 7: 3 he sent to him elders of the Jews 8
9:22 rejected by the elders and chief priests 8
15:25 Now his elder son was in the field 8
20: 1 the scribes with the elders came up 8
22:52 officers of the temple and elders 8
Act 4: 5 their rulers and elders and scribes 8
8 Rulers of the people and elders 8
23 what the chief priests and the elders had said 8
6:12 they stirred up the people and the elders 8
11:30 they did so, sending it to the elders 8
14:23 had appointed elders for them in every church 8
15: 2 to Jerusalem to the apostles and the elders 8
4 the apostles and the elders 8
6 The apostles and the elders were gathered together 8
22 it seemed good to the apostles and the elders 8
23 The brethren, both the apostles and the elders 8
16: 4 the apostles and elders who were at Jerusalem. 8
20:17 called to him the elders of the church. 8
21:18 all the elders were present. 8

23:14 they went to the chief priests and elders, and said 8
24: 1 the high priest Anani'as came down with some elders 8
25:15 the chief priests and the elders of the Jews 8
Rom 9:12 she was told, "The elder will serve the younger. 6
1Ti 5:17 the elders who rule well 8
19 Never admit any charge against an elder 8
Tit 1: 5 appoint elders in every town as I directed you 8
Jas 5:14 Let him call for the elders of the church 8
1Pe 5: 1 So I exhort the elders among you, as a fellow elder 8
5 you that are younger be subject to the elders. 8
2Jn 1: 1 The elder to the elect lady and her children 8
3Jn 1: 1 The elder to the beloved Ga'ius, whom I love 8
Rev 4: 4 and seated on the thrones were 24 elders 8
10 the 24 elders fall down before him 8
5: 5 Then one of the elders said to me, "Weep not; 8
6 and among the elders, I saw a Lamb standing 8
8 the 24 elders fell down before the Lamb 8
11 throne and the living creatures and the elders 8
14 and the elders fell down and worshiped. 8
7:11 round the elders and the four living creatures 8
13 Then one of the elders addressed me, saying 8
11:16 the 24 elders who sit on their thrones before God 8
14: 3 before the throne . . and before the elders. 8
19: 4 the 24 elders and the four living creatures 8
1Es 6: 5 Yet the elders of the Jews were dealt with kindly 8
8 we found the elders of the Jews 8
11 we asked these elders 8
27 the elders of the Jews 8
7: 2 assisting the elders of the Jews 8
9: 4 the decision of the ruling elders 8
13 with the elders and judges of each place 8
Jdt 6:16 They called together all the elders of the city 8
21 gave a banquet for the elders 8
7:23 said before all the elders 8
8:10 Chabris and Charmis, the elders of her city 8
10: 6 standing there with the elders of the city 8
13:12 and called together the elders of the city 8
Wis 8:10 and honor in the presence of the elders 8
Sir 6:34 Stand in the assembly of the elders. Who is wise? 7
7:14 Do not prattle in the assembly of the elders 7
Bar 1: 4 and in the hearing of the elders 8
Sus 1: 5 two elders . . were appointed as judges. 8
5 Iniquity came . . from elders who were judges 8
8 The two elders used to see her every day 8
16 And no one was there except the two elders 8
18 they did not see the elders 8
19 the two elders rose and ran to her, and said 9
24 and the two elders shouted against her. 9
27 And when the elders told their tale 9
28 the two elders came, full of their wicked plot 9
34 the two elders stood up in the midst of the people 9
36 The elders said, "As we were walking in the garden 9
41 they were elders of the people and judges; 8
50 And the elders said to him, "Come, sit among us 8
61 And they rose against the two elders 9
1Mc 1:26 rulers and elders groaned 7
7:33 some of the elders of the people 8
11:23 he chose some of the elders of Israel 8
12:35 he convened the elders of the people 8
13:36 to the elders and nation of the Jews, greeting. 8
14:20 to Simon the high priest and to the elders 8
28 the elders of the country 8
2Mc 13:13 After consulting privately with the elders 8
14:37 A certain Razis, one of the elders of Jerusalem 8
3Mc 1: 8 sent some of their . . elders to greet him 7
23 being barely restrained by the old men and the elders 8
25 the elders near the king 8
6: 1 Eleazar . . directed the elders around him to cease 7
4Mc 7:10 O elder, fiercer than fire 9
16:14 O mother . . elder and woman! 10

fellow elder 1. συμπρεσβύτερος
1Pe 5: 1 So I exhort the elders among you, as a fellow elder 1

elders *See* assembly, council.

next eldest 1. καθ' ἡλικίαν προτέρου δεύτερος
4Mc 9:26 the guards brought in the next eldest 1

elect 1. ἐκλεκτός 2. ἐκλογή 3. electus
Mat 24:22 for the sake of the elect 1
24 to lead astray, if possible, even the elect. 1
31 they will gather his elect from the four winds 1
Mrk 13:20 for the sake of the elect, whom he chose 1
22 to lead astray, if possible, the elect. 1
27 gather his elect from the four winds 1
Lke 18: 7 will not God vindicate his elect 1
Rom 8:33 Who shall bring any charge against God's elect? 1
11: 7 The elect obtained it, but the rest were hardened 2
1Ti 5:21 of God and of Christ Jesus and of the elect angels 1
2Ti 2:10 everything for the sake of the elect 1
Tit 1: 1 to further the faith of God's elect 1
2Jn 1: 1 The elder to the elect lady and her children 1
13 The children of your elect sister greet you. 1
2Es 15:21 Just as they have done to my elect until this day 3
16:73 the tested quality of my elect shall be manifest 3
74 Hear, my elect," says the Lord. 3
Wis 3: 9 because grace and mercy are upon his elect 1
4:15 God's grace and mercy are with his elect 1
Sir 46: 1 He became . . a great savior of God's elect 1

election 1. ἐκλογή
Rom 9:11 that God's purpose of election might continue 1
11:28 but as regards election they are beloved 1
2Pe 1:10 more zealous to confirm your call and election 1

element 1. στοιχεῖον 2. στοιχείωσις
2Pe 3:10 and the elements will be dissolved with fire 1
12 and the elements will melt with fire! 1
Wis 7:17 the activity of the elements; 1
19:18 the elements changed places with one another 1
2Mc 7:22 who set in order the elements within each of you. 2
4Mc 12:13 are made of the same elements as you 1

elemental spirit 1. στοιχεῖον
Gal 4: 3 slaves to the elemental spirits of the universe. 1
9 weak and beggarly elemental spirits 1
Col 2: 8 the elemental spirits of the universe 1
20 died to the elemental spirits of the universe 1

elementary 1. ἀρχή
Heb 6: 1 let us leave the elementary doctrine of Christ 1

elephant 1. ἐλέφας 2. θηρίον
1Mc 1:17 with chariots and elephants and cavalry 1
3:34 half of his troops and the elephants 1
6:30 32 elephants accustomed to war. 1
34 They showed the elephants the juice of grapes 1
35 with each elephant they stationed 1,000 men 1
37 upon the elephants were wooden towers *
46 He got under the elephant 1
8: 6 to fight against them with 120 elephants 1
11:56 Trypho captured the elephants 2
2Mc 11: 4 his thousands of cavalry, and his 80 elephants. 1
13: 2 5,300 cavalry, 22 elephants 1
15 He stabbed the leading elephant and its rider. 1
15:20 the elephants strategically stationed 2
21 the savagery of the elephants 2
3Mc 5: 1 he summoned Hermon, keeper of the elephants 1
2 on the following day to drug all the elephants 1
10 when he had drugged the pitiless elephants 1
20 tomorrow without delay prepare the elephants 1
38 Equip the elephants now once more 1
48 by the elephants going out at the gate 1

elephant *See also* keeper.

elephants *See* command, keeper.

elevation 1. נוֹף
Ps 48: 2 beautiful in elevation, is the joy of all 1

eleven 1. אַחַד עָשָׂר 2. עַשְׁתֵּי עָשָׂר 3. ἕνδεκα
Gen 32:22 took . . his two maids, and his eleven children 1
37: 9 behold, the sun, the moon, and eleven stars were 1
Exd 26: 7 eleven curtains shall you make. 2
8 the eleven curtains shall have the same measure. 2
36:14 over the tabernacle; he made eleven curtains. 2
15 the eleven curtains had the same measure. 2
Num29:20 On the third day eleven bulls, two rams, fourteen 2
Deu 1: 2 eleven days' journey from Horeb by the way 1
Jos 15:51 eleven cities with their villages. 1
2Kg 23:36 and he reigned eleven years in Jerusalem. 1
24:18 Zedeki'ah was . . and he reigned eleven years 1
2Ch 36: 5 he reigned eleven years in Jerusalem. 1
11 he reigned eleven years in Jerusalem. 1
Jer 52: 1 and he reigned eleven years in Jerusalem. 1
Mat 28:16 Now the eleven disciples went to Galilee 3
Mrk 16:14 Afterward he appeared to the eleven themselves 3
Lke 24: 9 told all this to the eleven and to all the rest. 3
33 they found the eleven gathered together 3
Act 1:26 he was enrolled with the eleven apostles. 3
2:14 Peter, standing with the eleven 3
1Es 1:46 he reigned eleven years. 3

eleventh 1. אַחַד עָשָׂר 2. עַשְׁתֵּי עָשָׂר 3. ἑνδέκατος
Num 7:72 On the eleventh day Pa'giel . . of the men of Asher 2
Deu 1: 3 year, on the first day of the eleventh month 2
1Kg 6:38 in the eleventh year . . the house was finished 1
2Kg 9:29 In the eleventh year of Joram . . Ahazi'ah began 1
25: 2 the city was besieged till the eleventh year 2
1Ch 12:13 Jeremiah tenth, Mach'bannai eleventh. 2
24:12 the eleventh to Eli'ashib, the twelfth to Jakim 2
25:18 eleventh to Az'arel, his sons and his brethren 2
27:14 Eleventh . . was Benai'ah of Pira'thon 2
14 Eleventh, for the eleventh month, was Benai'ah 2
Jer 1: 3 until the end of the eleventh year of Zedeki'ah 2
39: 2 in the eleventh year of Zedeki'ah 2
52: 5 till the eleventh year of King Zedeki'ah. 2
Ezk 26: 1 In the eleventh year, on the first day of the month 1
30:20 In the eleventh year, in the first month 1
31: 1 In the eleventh year, in the third month 1
Zec 1: 7 On the 24th day of the eleventh month 2
Mat 20: 6 about the eleventh hour he went out 3
9 when those hired about the eleventh hour came 3
Rev 21:20 the tenth chrysoprase, the eleventh jacinth 3
1Mc 16:14 in the eleventh month, which is the month of Shebat 3

eligible
Tob 6:11 for you are her only eligible kinsman. *

elixir 1. φαρμακός
Sir 6:16 A faithful friend is an elixir of life 1

eloquent 1. דָּבָר 2. εὔρυθμος 3. λόγιος 4. λόγος
Exd 4:10 Moses said . . "Oh, my Lord, I am not eloquent 1
Act 18:24 an eloquent man, well versed in the scriptures. 3
1Co 1:17 not with eloquent wisdom 4
AEs 14:13 Put eloquent speech in my mouth before the lion 2

else 1. אוֹ 2. אֵיךְ 3. אִם 4. אִם לֹא 5. זוּר 6. כְּ 7. כִּי 8. מְאוּמָה 9. עוֹד 10. ἄλλος 11. εἰ δὲ μή 12. εἰ μή 13. ἕτερος 14. λοιπός 15. τις 16. alius
Gen 19:12 the men said to Lot, "Have you any one else here? 9
42:16 or else, by the life of Pharaoh 4
Exd 8:21 Else, if you will not let my people go, behold, I will 7
22:27 in what else shall he sleep? *
Num 3:38 any one else who came near was to be put to death. 5
6:21 apart from what else he can afford; *
18: 4 no one else shall come near you. 5
7 any one else who comes near shall be put to death. 5
Deu 20:14 cattle, and everything else in the city *
Jdg 21:22 did you give . . else you would now be guilty. *
2Sm 3:35 if I taste bread or anything else till the sun 8
15:14 else there will be no escape for us from Ab'salom; 7
1Kg 3:18 there was no one else with us in the house, only we 5
19: 7 Arise and eat, else the journey will be too great 7
20:39 his life, or else you shall pay a talent of silver.' 1
21: 6 'Give me your vineyard . . or else, if it please you 1
1Ch 21:12 or else three days of the sword of the LORD 3
Neh 2: 2 This is nothing else but sadness of the heart. *
Job 32:22 else would my Maker soon put an end to me. 6
Ps 32: 9 bit and bridle, else it will not keep with you. *
Jer 9: 7 for what else can I do, because of my people? 2
19:11 because there will be no place else to bury. *
Jol 2:27 that I, the LORD, am your God and there is none else. 9
Zep 2:15 that said to herself, "I am and there is none else 9
Joh 14:11 or else believe me for the sake of the works 11
15:24 done among them the works which no one else did 10
Act 4:12 there is salvation in no one else 10
8:34 about himself or about some one else? 13
24:20 Or else let these men themselves say *
Rom 8:39 nor depth, nor anything else in all creation 13
1Co 1:16 I do not know whether I baptized any one else.) 10
7:11 or else be reconciled to her husband *
1Ti 1:10 whatever else is contrary to sound doctrine 13
1Es 4: 5 whatever spoil they take and everything else. 10
8:18 whatever else occurs to you as necessary 14
2Es 6:10 seek for nothing else, Ezra! 16
7:116or else, when it had produced him *
Bel 1:12 we will die; or else Daniel will *
29 or else we will kill you and your household. 12
1Mc 15:31 or else give me for them 500 talents of silver 12
4Mc 2:19 Why else did Jacob, our most wise father, censure 15

else *See also* any, everything, whatever.

some one else 1. ἕτερος
Lke 22:58 a little later some one else saw him and said 1

elsewhere
2Ch 26: 6 elsewhere among the Philistines. *
Ps 84:10 thy courts is better than 1,000 elsewhere. *
Jer 7:32 because there is no room elsewhere. *

elude 1. פטר מִפְּנֵי 2. ἐκκλίνω 3. λανθάνω
1Sm 19:10 he eluded Saul, so that he struck the spear 1
1Mc 9:47 he eluded him and went to the rear. 2
4Mc 3:13 Eluding the sentinels at the gates 3

emanation 1. ἀπόρροια
Wis 7:25 a pure emanation of the glory of the Almighty; 1

embalm 1. חנט 2. חֲנֻטִים
Gen 50: 2 commanded . . to embalm his father. 1
2 the physicians embalmed Israel; 1
3 for so many are required for embalming. 2
25 they embalmed him, and he was put in a coffin 1

embark 1. ἀνάγω 2. ἐμβαίνω 3. ἐπιβαίνω
Act 27: 2 embarking in a ship of Adramyt'tium 3
1Mc 15:37 Trypho embarked on a ship and escaped 2
2Mc 5: 9 having embarked to go to the Lacedaemonians 1
12: 3 to embark, with their wives and children, on boats 2

embarkation 1. εἰς πλοῖον ἐμβολή
3Mc 4: 7 as far as the place of embarkation. 1

embassy 1. πρεσβεία
Lke 14:32 he sends an embassy and asks terms of peace. 1
19:14 sent an embassy after him, saying, 'We do not want 1

hot ember 1. גַּחֶלֶת
Prv 26:21 As charcoal to hot embers and wood to fire, so is 1

embitter 1. חמץ 2. πικραίνω 3. amarus
Ps 73:21 When my soul was embittered 1

2Es 9:41 I am greatly embittered in spirit 3
1Mc 3: 7 He embittered many kings 2

embodiment 1. μόρφωσις
Rom 2:20 in the law the embodiment of knowledge and truth- 1

embrace 1. חבק 2. חֵיק 3. ἀσπάζομαι 4. ἐναγκάλισμα 5. ἐπιπίπτω ἐπὶ τράχηλον 6. ἐπισπάω 7. κοινός 8. περιλαμβάνω 9. περιπλέκω 10. συγγίνομαι 11. συμπεριλαμβάνω 12. amplector 13. circumfero 14. complector
Gen 16: 5 I gave my maid to your embrace 2
29:13 to meet him, and embraced him and kissed him 1
33: 4 Esau ran to meet him, and embraced him 1
48:10 and he kissed them and embraced them. 1
2Kg 4:16 he said, "At this season . . you shall embrace a son. 1
Prv 4: 8 she will honor you if you embrace her. 1
5:20 Why . . embrace the bosom of an adventuress? 1
Ecc 3: 5 a time to embrace, and a time to refrain 1
5 to embrace, and a time to refrain from embracing; 1
Sng 2: 6 O . . that his right hand embraced me! 1
8: 3 O that . . and that his right hand embraced me! 1
Lke 15:20 ran and embraced him and kissed him. 5
Act 20:10 embracing him said, "Do not be alarmed 11
37 they all wept and embraced Paul and kissed him. 5
2Es 2:15 Mother, embrace your sons 14
32 Embrace your children until I come 12
6:39 and darkness and silence embraced everything; 13
Tob 11: 9 Then Anna ran to meet them, and embraced her son 5
14 Then he saw his son and embraced him 5
Jdt 12:12 if we do not embrace her she will laugh at us. 6
AEs 15:12 he embraced her, and said, "Speak to me. 3
Sir 30:20 like a eunuch who embraces a maiden and groans. 8
Sus 1:39 We saw them embracing 10
3Mc 5:49 they kissed each other, embracing relatives 9
4Mc 1:24 an emotion embracing pleasure and pain. 7
13:21 For such embraces . . souls are nourished; 4

embroider 1. מַעֲשֶׂה 2. רקם 3. רִקְמָה
Exd 26:36 a screen . . embroidered with needlework. 2
27:16 fine twined linen, embroidered with needlework; 2
28:39 make a girdle embroidered with needlework. 2
36:37 fine twined linen, embroidered with needlework; 2
38:18 screen . . was embroidered with needlework 1
18 screen . . was embroidered with needlework 2
39:29 scarlet stuff, embroidered with needlework; 2
Jdg 5:30 for Sis'era, spoil of dyed stuffs embroidered 3
30 two pieces . . embroidered for my neck 3
Ezk 16:10 I clothed you also with embroidered cloth 3
13 fine linen, and silk, and embroidered cloth; 3
18 you took your embroidered garments to cover 3
26:16 and strip off their embroidered garments; 3
27: 7 fine embroidered linen from Egypt was your sail 3
embroider *See also* work.

embroiderer 1. רקם 2. ποικιλτός
Exd 35:35 by an embroiderer in blue and purple and scarlet 1
38:23 a craftsman and designer and embroiderer 1
Sir 45:10 the work of an embroiderer 2

emerald 1. בָּרֶקֶת 2. נֹפֶךְ 3. σμαράγδινος 4. σμάραγδος
Exd 28:18 second row an emerald, a sapphire, and a diamond; 2
39:11 the second row, an emerald, a sapphire 2
Ezk 27:16 they exchanged for your wares emeralds, purple 2
28:13 beryl, and onyx, sapphire, carbuncle, and emerald; 1
Rev 4: 3 a rainbow that looked like an emerald. 3
21:19 every jewel . . the fourth emerald 4
Tob 13:16 will be built with sapphires and emeralds 4
Jdt 10:21 gold and emeralds and precious stones. 4
Sir 32: 6 A seal of emerald in a rich setting of gold 4

emerge 1. ἀνάδυσις 2. ἐκκύπτω 3. ἐξανίστημι
Wis 19: 7 and dry land emerging where water had stood before 1
1Mc 9:23 the lawless emerged in all parts of Israel 2
11:69 Then the men in ambush emerged from their places 3

eminence 1. שְׂאֵת
Ps 62: 4 plan to thrust him down from his eminence. 1
eminence *See also* attain.

eminent 1. ἐκλεκτός 2. ἔνδοξος
Rom 16:13 Greet Rufus, eminent in the Lord 1
Sir 10:22 The rich, and the eminent, and the poor 2

more eminent man 1. ἔντιμος
Lke 14: 8 lest a more eminent man than you be invited by him; 1

eminently 1. πάνυ
2Mc 13: 8 this was eminently just 1

emission 1. יצא
Lev 15:16 if a man has an emission of semen, he shall bathe 1
18 lies with a woman and has an emission of semen •
32 and for him who has an emission of semen 1
22: 4 a man who has had an emission of semen 1

emotion 1. πάθος
4Mc 1: 1 devout reason is sovereign over the emotions 1
3 those emotions that hinder self-control 1
4 the emotions that hinder one from justice 1
5 If reason rules the emotions 1
6 For reason does not rule its own emotions 1
7 that reason is dominant over the emotions 1
9 reason controls the emotions. 1
13 whether reason is sovereign over the emotions. 1
14 what reason is and what emotion is 1
14 how many kinds of emotions there are 1
19 by means of it reason rules over the emotions. 1
20 two most comprehensive types of the emotions 1
21 The emotions of both pleasure and pain 1
24 an emotion embracing pleasure and pain. 1
25 which is the most complex of all the emotions. 1
29 so tames the jungle of habits and emotions. 1
30 over the emotions it is sovereign 1
30 rational judgment is sovereign over the emotions 1
35 the emotions of the appetites are restrained 1
2: 6 the emotions that hinder one from justice. 1
7 unless reason is clearly lord of the emotions? 1
9 can recognize that reason rules the emotions. 1
15 reason rules even the more violent emotions 1
16 repels all these malicious emotions 1
18 is able to get the better of the emotions 1
21 he planted in him emotions and inclinations 1
24 if reason is master of the emotions 1
3: 1 reason rules not over its own emotions 1
5 For reason does not uproot the emotions 1
17 can conquer the drives of the emotions 1
18 spurn all domination by the emotions. 1
6:31 devout reason is sovereign over the emotions. 1
32 if the emotions had prevailed over reason 1
33 now that reason has conquered the emotions 1
7: 1 steered . . over the sea of the emotions 1
5 broke the maddening waves of the emotion. 1
16 devout reason is governor of the emotions. 1
17 Not every one has full command of his emotions 1
22 would not be able to overcome the emotions 1
23 courageous man is lord of his emotions. 1
8:28 For they were contemptuous of the emotions 1
13: 1 devout reason is sovereign over the emotions. 1
2 if they had been slaves to their emotions 1
2 they had been conquered by these emotions. •
3 they prevailed over their emotions. 1
4 the brothers mastered both emotions and pains. 1
7 conquered the tempest of the emotions. 1
14: 1 mastered the emotions of brotherly love. 1
15: 1 O reason of the children, tyrant over the emotions! 1
4 the emotions of parents who love their children 1
23 in the very midst of her emotions 1
32 the flood of your emotions and the violent winds 1
16: 1 devout reason is sovereign over the emotions. 1
2 not only that men have ruled over the emotions 1
4 so many and such great emotions 1
18: 2 devout reason is master of all emotions 1
emotion *See also* dominate, feel, sovereignty.

emperor 1. βασιλεύς 2. σεβαστός
Act 25:21 kept in custody for the decision of the emperor 2
25 as he himself appealed to the emperor 2
1Pe 2:13 whether it be to the emperor as supreme 1
17 Fear God. Honor the emperor. 1

employ 1. διακονέω 2. ἐργάζομαι 3. καταχράω 4. χράω
1Co 9:13 who are employed in the temple service 2
1Pe 4:10 employ it for one another, as good stewards 1
2Mc 1:13 a deception employed by the priests of Nanea. 4
3Mc 5:22 employ the duration of the night in sleep 3

employed person 1. πραγματικός
1Es 8:22 persons employed in this temple 1

employee 1. μίσθιος
Sir 34:22 to deprive an employee of his wages 1

emptiness 1. שָׁוְא 2. תֹּהוּ
Job 7: 3 I am allotted months of emptiness 1
15:31 Let him not trust in emptiness 1
31 for emptiness will be his recompense. 1
Isa 40:17 by him as less than nothing and emptiness. 2

empty 1. בקק 2. הֶבֶל 3. ערה 4. פנה 5. פקד 6. ריק 7. רֵיק 8. רֵיקָם 9. שָׁוְא 10. תֹּהוּ 11. ἐκλείπω 12. ἔρημος 13. κενός 14. κενόω 15. σχολάζω 16. χαῦνος 17. vacuus
Gen 24:20 she quickly emptied her jar into the trough 3
37:24 The pit was empty, there was no water in it. 7
41:27 and the seven empty ears blighted by the east 7
42:35 As they emptied their sacks 6
Exd 3:21 and when you go, you shall not go empty 8
34:20 And none shall appear before me empty. 8
Lev 14:36 priest shall command that they empty the house 4
Jdg 7:16 into the hands of all of them and empty jars 7
Rut 1:21 and the LORD has brought me back empty. 8
1Sm 6: 3 If you send away the ark . . do not send it empty 8
20:18 will be missed, because your seat will be empty. 5
25 Abner sat by Saul . . but David's place was empty. 5
27 But on the second day . . David's place was empty. 5
2Sm 1:22 and the sword of Saul returned not empty. 8
2Kg 4: 3 borrow vessels . . empty vessels and not too few. 7
2Ch 24:11 would come and empty the chest and take it 3
Neh 5:13 may he be shaken out and emptied. 7
Job 22: 9 You have sent widows away empty 8
Ecc 5: 7 For when dreams increase, empty words grow many 2
11: 3 clouds . . empty themselves on the earth; 6
Isa 30: 7 For Egypt's help is worthless and empty 7
41:29 their molten images are empty wind. 10
55:11 from my mouth; it shall not return to me empty 8
59: 4 they rely on empty pleas, they speak lies 10
Jer 14: 3 no water, they return with their vessels empty; 8
48:11 he has not been emptied from vessel to vessel 6
12 tilters who will tilt him, and empty his vessels 6
51: 2 they shall empty her land 1
34 he has made me an empty vessel, he has swallowed 7
Ezk 24:10 boil well the flesh, and empty out the broth •
11 Then set it empty upon the coals 7
Hos 10: 4 with empty oaths they make covenants; 9
Hab 1:17 Is he then to keep on emptying his net 6
Zec 10: 2 tell false dreams, and give empty consolation. 2
Mat 12:44 when he comes he finds it empty, swept 15
Lke 1:53 the rich he has sent empty away. 13
1Co 1:17 lest the cross of Christ be emptied of its power. 14
Eph 5: 6 Let no one deceive you with empty words 13
Php 2: 7 emptied himself, taking the form of a servant 14
Col 2: 8 makes a prey of you by philosophy and empty deceit 13
2Es 6:22 storehouses shall suddenly be found to be empty; 17
7:25 Therefore, Ezra, empty things are for the empty 17
Jdt 7:20 until all the vessels of water . . were empty; 11
Wis 2: 3 the spirit will dissolve like empty air. 16
Sir 29: 9 because of his need do not send him away empty. 13
3Mc 5:43 empty of those who offered sacrifices there. 12
empty *See also* cry, nothing, plea, space, talk, talker, word.

empty out 1. בקק 2. יצק 3. נתך
2Sm 13: 9 she took the pan and emptied it out before him 2
2Kg 22: 9 Your servants have emptied out the money 3
2Ch 34:17 emptied out the money that was found in the house 3
Isa 19: 3 spirit of the Egyptians . . will be emptied out 1

empty thing 1. vacuus
2Es 7:25 Therefore, Ezra, empty things are for the empty 1

empty-handed 1. רֵיקָם 2. κενός
Gen 31:42 you would have sent me away empty-handed. 1
Exd 23:15 None shall appear before me empty-handed. 1
Deu 15:13 you shall not let him go empty-handed; 1
16:16 shall not appear before the LORD empty-handed; 1
Rut 3:17 not go back empty-handed to your mother-in-law. 1
Jer 50: 9 warrior who does not return empty-handed. 1
Mrk 12: 3 beat him, and sent him away empty-handed. 2
Lke 20:10 the tenants . . sent him away empty-handed. 2
11 and sent him away empty-handed. 2
Jdt 1:11 they sent back his messengers empty-handed 2
Sir 35: 4 Do not appear before the Lord empty-handed 2

enable 1. δύναμαι 2. ἐκποιέω
Php 3:21 by the power which enables him 1
Sir 42:17 The Lord has not enabled his holy ones to recount 2

enact 1. νομοθετέω
Heb 8: 6 since it is enacted on better promises. 1

enamor 1. ἐραστής
Wis 8: 2 I became enamored of her beauty. 1

encamp 1. חנה 2. שׁכן 3. תקע 4. καταλύω 5. παρεμβάλλω 6. στρατοπεδεύω
Gen 26:17 Isaac . . encamped in the valley of Gerar 1
31:25 Laban with his kinsmen encamped in the hill 3
Exd 13:20 they moved on from Succoth, and encamped at Etham 1
14: 2 Tell the people of Israel to turn back and encamp 1
2 you shall encamp over against it, by the sea. 1
9 his army, and overtook them encamped at the sea 1
15:27 and they encamped there by the water. 1
18: 5 he was encamped at the mountain of God. 1
19: 2 they encamped in the wilderness; 1
2 there Israel encamped before the mountain. 1
Num 1:50 they shall tend it, and shall encamp around 1
53 the Levites shall encamp around the tabernacle 1
2: 2 The people of Israel shall encamp each by his own 1
2 they shall encamp facing the tent of meeting 1
3 Those to encamp on the east side 1
5 Those to encamp next to him shall be the tribe 1
12 those to encamp next to him shall be the tribe 1
17 as they encamp, so shall they set out 1
27 those to encamp next to him shall be the tribe 1
34 so they encamped by their standards 1
3:23 The families of the Gershonites were to encamp 1
29 Kohath were to encamp on the south side 1
35 to encamp on the north side of the tabernacle. 1
38 to encamp before the tabernacle on the east 1
9:17 there the people of Israel encamped. 1

18 at the command of the LORD they encamped; 1
23 At the command of the LORD they encamped 1
10:31 you know how we are to encamp in the wilderness 1
12:16 people . . encamped in the wilderness of Paran. 1
21:10 people of Israel set out, and encamped in Oboth. 1
11 set out from Oboth, and encamped at I'ye-ab'arim 1
12 set out, and encamped in the Valley of Zered. 1
13 set out, and encamped on the other side 1
22: 1 Israel set out, and encamped in the plains of Moab 1
24: 2 Balaam . . saw Israel encamping tribe by tribe. 2
31:19 Encamp outside the camp seven days; 1
33: 5 people of Israel . . encamped at Succoth. 1
6 they set out from Succoth, and encamped at Etham 1
7 set out from Etham . . encamped before Migdol. 1
8 wilderness of Etham, and encamped at Marah. 1
9 came to Elim . . and they encamped there. 1
10 set out from Elim, and encamped by the Red Sea. 1
11 encamped in the wilderness of Sin. 1
12 wilderness of Sin, and encamped at Dophkah. 1
13 they set out from Dophkah, and encamped at Alush. 1
14 they set out from Alush, and encamped at Reph'idim 1
15 and encamped in the wilderness of Sinai 1
16 Sinai, and encamped at Kib'roth-hatta'avah. 1
17 Kib'roth-hatta'avah, and encamped at Haze'roth. 1
18 set out from Haze'roth, and encamped at Rithmah. 1
19 out from Rithmah, and encamped at Rim'mon-per'ez. 1
20 from Rim'mon-per'ez, and encamped at Libnah. 1
21 they set out from Libnah, and encamped at Rissah. 1
22 set out from Rissah, and encamped at Kehela'thah. 1
23 from Kehela'thah, and encamped at Mount Shepher. 1
24 out from Mount Shepher, and encamped at Hara'dah. 1
25 set out from Hara'dah, and encamped at Makhe'loth. 1
26 set out from Makhe'loth, and encamped at Tahath. 1
27 they set out from Tahath, and encamped at Terah. 1
28 they set out from Terah, and encamped at Mithkah. 1
29 set out from Mithkah, and encamped at Hashmo'nah. 1
30 out from Hashmo'nah, and encamped at Mose'roth. 1
31 from Mose'roth, and encamped at Bene-ja'akan. 1
32 from Bene-ja'akan, and encamped at Hor-haggid'gad. 1
33 from Hor-haggid'gad, and encamped at Jot'bathah. 1
34 set out from Jot'bathah, and encamped at Abro'nah. 1
35 from Abro'nah, and encamped at E'zion-ge'ber. 1
36 set out . . and encamped in the wilderness of Zin 1
37 set out from Kadesh, and encamped at Mount Hor 1
41 set out from Mount Hor, and encamped at Zalmo'nah. 1
42 set out from Zalmo'nah, and encamped at Punon. 1
43 they set out from Punon, and encamped at Oboth. 1
44 set out from Oboth, and encamped at I'ye-ab'arim 1
45 they set out from I'yim, and encamped at Dibon-gad. 1
46 Dibon-gad, and encamped at Al'mon-diblatha'im. 1
47 encamped in the mountains of Ab'arim, before Nebo. 1
48 encamped in the plains of Moab by the Jordan 1
49 encamped by the Jordan from Beth-jes'himoth 1
Jos 4:19 The people came up . . and they encamped in Gilgal 1
5:10 the people of Israel were encamped in Gilgal 1
8:11 drew near . . and encamped on the north side of Ai 1
10: 5 went up with all . . and encamped against Gibeon 1
11: 5 and encamped together at the waters of Merom 1
Jdg 6: 4 they would encamp against them and destroy 1
33 Jordan they encamped in the Valley of Jezreel. 1
7: 1 rose early and encamped beside the spring 1
9:50 Abim'elech went . . and encamped against Thebez 1
10:17 were called to arms, and they encamped in Gilead; 1
17 came together, and they encamped at Mizpah. 1
11:20 Sihon gathered . . and encamped at Jahaz 1
15: 9 the Philistines came up and encamped in Judah 1
18:12 600 men, armed . . went up and encamped 1
20:19 in the morning, and encamped against Gib'e-ah. 1
1Sm 4: 1 Israel went out . . they encamped at Ebene'zer 1
1 and the Philistines encamped at Aphek. 1
13: 5 they came up and encamped in Michmash 1
16 but the Philistines encamped at Michmash. 1
17: 1 and encamped between Socoh and Aze'kah 1
2 were gathered, and encamped in the valley of Elah 1
26: 3 Saul encamped on the hill of Hachi'lah 1
5 and came to the place where Saul had encamped; 1
5 Saul . . while the army was encamped around him. 1
28: 4 Philistines . . came and encamped at Shunem; 1
4 gathered . . Israel, and they encamped at Gilbo'a. 1
29: 1 the Israelites were encamped by the fountain 1
2Sm 12:28 gather the rest . . and encamp against the city 1
17:26 And Israel and Ab'salom encamped in the land 1
23:13 a band of Philistines was encamped in the valley 1
1Kg 16:15 Now the troops were encamped against Gib'bethon 1
16 the troops who were encamped heard it said 1
20:27 the people of Israel encamped before them 1
29 they encamped opposite one another seven days. 1
1Ch 11:15 when the army of Philistines was encamped 1
19: 7 who came and encamped before Med'eba. 1
2Ch 32: 1 encamped against the fortified cities 1
Ezr 8:15 Aha'va, and there we encamped three days. 1
Neh 11:30 encamped from Beer-sheba to . . Hinnom. 1
Job 19:12 against me, and encamp round about my tent. 1
Ps 27: 3 Though a host encamp against me 1
34: 7 of the LORD encamps around those who fear him 1
Isa 29: 1 Ho Ariel, Ariel, the city where David encamped! 1
3 I will encamp against you round about 1
Jer 50:29 Encamp round about her; let no one escape. 1
Zec 9: 8 Then I will encamp at my house as a guard 1
1Es 8:41 we encamped there three days 5
Jdt 7: 3 They encamped in the valley near Bethulia 5
17 they encamped in the valley 5
18 and encamped in the hill country opposite Dothan 5
18 rest of the Assyrian army encamped in the plain 5
Sir 14:24 he who encamps near her house 4
1Mc 2:32 they encamped opposite them 5
3:40 they encamped near Emmaus in the plain. 5
42 the forces were encamped in their territory. 5
57 encamped to the south of Emmaus. 5
4:29 They came into Idumea and encamped at Beth-zur 5
5: 5 he encamped against them 5
37 encamped opposite Raphon 5
39 they are encamped across the stream 5
42 Permit no man to encamp 5
49 each should encamp where he was. 5
50 So the men of the forces encamped 5
6:26 today they have encamped against the citadel 5
31 encamped against Beth-zur 5
32 encamped at Beth- zechariah 5
48 the king encamped in Judea and at Mount Zion. 5
51 he encamped before the sanctuary for many days. 5
7:19 Then Bacchides . . encamped in Beth-zaith 5
39 Nicanor . . encamped in Beth-horon 5
40 Judas encamped in Adasa with 3,000 men 5
9: 2 encamped against Mesaloth in Arbela 5
3 they encamped against Jerusalem; 5
5 Now Judas was encamped in Elasa 5
64 Then he came and encamped against Bethbasi 5
10:48 encamped opposite Demetrius. 5
69 encamped against Jamnia 5
75 He encamped before Joppa 5
86 encamped against Askalon 5
11:65 Simon encamped before Beth-zur 5
67 Jonathan and his army encamped by the waters 5
73 there they encamped. 5
13:13 Simon encamped in Adida, facing the plain. 5
43 In those days Simon encamped against Gazara 5
15:13 So Antiochus encamped against Dor 5
39 He commanded him to encamp against Judea 5
3Mc 1: 1 where Antiochus's supporters were encamped. 5
4Mc 3: 8 the whole army of our ancestors had encamped. 6

encampment 1. טִירָה 2. מַחֲנֶה 3. מַעְגָּל 4. מִשְׁכָּן
Gen 25:16 by their villages and by their encampments 1
Num24: 5 how fair are you . . encampments, O Israel! 4
31:10 All their cities . . and all their encampments 1
Jos 8:13 the main encampment which was north of the city 2
1Sm 17:20 he came to the encampment as the host was going 3
26: 5 Saul was lying within the encampment 3
7 there lay Saul sleeping within the encampment 3
Ezk 25: 4 they shall set their encampments among you 1

enchanter 1. אַשָּׁף 2. חבר 3. אָשַׁף (A)
Ps 58: 5 voice of charmers or of the cunning enchanter. 2
Dan 1:20 better than all the magicians and enchanters 1
2: 2 commanded that the magicians, the enchanters 1
10 such a thing of any magician or enchanter 3
27 No wise men, enchanters, magicians 3
4: 7 magicians, the enchanters, the Chalde'ans 3
5: 7 enchanters, the Chalde'ans, and the astrologers. 3
11 chief of the magicians, enchanters, Chalde'ans 3
15 wise men, the enchanters, have been brought 3

enchantment 1. חֶבֶר 2. נַחַשׁ
Num23:23 For there is no enchantment against Jacob 2
Isa 47: 9 and the great power of your enchantments. 1
12 Stand fast in your enchantments 1

encircle 1. נקף 2. סוג 3. *γυρόω* 4. *κυκλόθεν* 5. *κυκλόω* 6. *περιπλέκω*
Ps 22:16 a company of evildoers encircle me; 1
Sng 7: 2 belly is a heap of wheat, encircled with lilies. 2
Heb 11:30 after they had been encircled for seven days. 5
Sir 43:12 It encircles the heaven with its glorious arc; 3
45: 9 he encircled him with pomegranates 5
1Mc 10:11 encircle Mount Zion with squared stones 4
12:13 many wars have encircled us 5
3Mc 4: 8 their necks encircled with ropes instead of garlands 6
4Mc 14: 8 these youths . . encircled the sevenfold fear of tortures 5

enclose 1. בַּיִת 2. כול 3. סבב 4. צור עַל 5. *κατάκλειστος* 6. *παρεμβάλλω* 7. *περιφράσσω* 8. *συγκλείω* 9. concludo
Exd 28:11 you shall enclose them in settings of gold 3
39: 6 onyx stones were prepared, enclosed in settings 3
13 they were enclosed in settings of gold filigree. 3
Sng 8: 9 we will enclose her with boards of cedar. 4
Isa 40:12 enclosed the dust of the earth in a measure 2
Ezk 1:27 the appearance of fire enclosed round about; 1
Lke 5: 6 they enclosed a great shoal of fish 8
2Es 16:58 has enclosed the sea in the midst of the waters 9
2Mc 1:34 and enclosed the place and made it sacred. 7
3Mc 1:18 virgins who had been enclosed in their chambers 5
4:11 they should be enclosed in the hippodrome 6

enclosure 1. *περίβολος*
Sir 50: 2 high retaining walls for the temple enclosure. 1

sacred enclosure 1. *τέμενος*
3Mc 1: 7 by endowing their sacred enclosures with gifts 1

encompass 1. אפף 2. חדר 3. חפף 4. סבב 5. *περιβάλλω*
Deu 33:12 he encompasses him all the day long 3
2Sm 22: 5 For the waves of death encompassed me 1
Ps 18: 4 The cords of death encompassed me 1
22:12 Many bulls encompass me, strong bulls of Bashan 4
32: 7 thou dost encompass me with deliverance. Selah 4
40:12 For evils have encompassed me without number; 1
116: 3 The snares of death encompassed me; 1
Ezk 21:14 the great slaughter, which encompasses them 2
Hos 7: 2 Now their deeds encompass them 4
11:12 E'phraim has encompassed me with lies 4
3Mc 6:26 Who . . so lawlessly encompassed..those 5

encounter 1. *ἐμπίπτω* 2. *προσβολή* 3. *συμβάλλω* 4. *συναντάω* 5. *συνάντησις* 6. *συνερίζω*
Lke 14:31 what king, going to encounter another king in war 3
1Mc 5:25 They encountered the Nabateans 4
9:11 and took its stand for the encounter 5
2Mc 8:30 In encounters with the forces of Timothy 6
10:17 slew those whom they encountered 1
14:17 Simon . . had encountered Nicanor 3
15:19 the encounter in the open country. 2

encourage 1. חזק 2. חזק יָד 3. *ἐποτρύνω* 4. *εὐθαρσής* 5. *εὔθυμος* 6. *οἰκοδομέω* 7. *παραθάρσυνω* 8. *παρακαλέω* 9. *παραμυθέομαι* 10. *προτρέπω*
Deu 1:38 Joshua . . shall enter; encourage him 1
3:28 charge Joshua, and encourage and strengthen him; 1
2Sm 11:25 Thus shall you say to Jo'ab . . And encourage him. 1
2Ch 35: 2 encouraged them in the service of the house 1
Isa 41: 7 The craftsman encourages the goldsmith 1
Ezk 13:22 and you have encouraged the wicked 2
Act 18:27 the brethren encouraged him 10
27:36 all were encouraged and ate some food themselves. 5
1Co 8:10 might he not be encouraged 6
14:31 so that all may learn and all be encouraged; 8
Eph 6:22 that he may encourage your hearts. 8
Col 2: 2 that their hearts may be encouraged 8
4: 8 he may encourage your hearts 8
1Th 2:11 and encouraged you and charged you 9
5:11 Therefore encourage one another 8
14 encourage the fainthearted, help the weak 9
Heb 10:25 but encouraging one another 8
1Es 8:27 I was encouraged by the help of the Lord my God 4
Sir 17:24 encourages those whose endurance is failing. 8
1Mc 5:53 encouraging the people all the way 8
12:50 they encouraged one another 8
13: 3 he encouraged them, saying to them 8
2Mc 7: 5 the brothers . . encouraged one another to die nobly, 8
21 She encouraged each of them 8
11:32 I have also sent Menelaus to encourage you. 8
15: 9 Encouraging them from the law and the prophets 9
17 Encouraged by the words of Judas 8
3Mc 1: 6 to visit the . . cities and encourage them. 8
4Mc 13: 8 and encouraged one another, saying 7
14: 1 they encouraged them to face the torture 3
16:24 encouraged and persuaded each of her sons to die 8

mutually encourage 1. *συμπαρακαλέω*
Rom 1:12 that we may be mutually encouraged 1

encouragement 1. *λόγος* 2. *παραίνεσις* 3. *παράκλησις*
Act 4:36 Barnabas (which means, Son of encouragement) 3
20: 2 and had given them much encouragement 1
Rom 15: 4 by the encouragement of the scriptures 3
5 May the God of steadfastness and encouragement 3
1Co 14: 3 upbuilding and encouragement 3
Php 2: 1 So if there is any encouragement in Christ 3
Heb 6:18 might have strong encouragement 3
Wis 8: 9 would give me good counsel and encouragement 2
1Mc 10:24 I also will write them words of encouragement 3
12: 9 since we have as encouragement the holy books 3
encouragement *See also* give.

encouragingly 1. עַל לֵב 2. עַל לְבָב
2Ch 30:22 spoke encouragingly to all the Levites 1
32: 6 spoke encouragingly to them, saying 2

encrust 1. עלף
Sng 5:14 body is ivory work, encrusted with sapphires. 1

end 1. אַחֲרוֹן 2. אַחֲרֵי 3. אַחֲרִית 4. אֶפֶס 5. בלע 6. בַּעֲבוּר 7. גמר 8. היה תוֹצָאָה 9. חתת 10. יצא 11. כָּלָה 12. כלה 13. כָּנָף 14. כָּתֵף 15. לָכֵן 16. לְמַעַן 17. לָנֶצַח 18. מוש 19. מלא 20. נֵצַח 21. סוֹף 22. עֵקֶב 23. פֶּה 24. קֵץ 25. קֵצֶה 26. קָצָה 27. קָצֶה 28. קָצוּ 29. קְצָת 30. ראשׁ 31. רַב לָכֶם 32. שׁוב 33. שׁלם

34. תּוֹצָאָה 35. תַּכְלִית 36. תמם 37. תְּקוּפָה
38. דִּבְרָה (A) 39. סוֹף (A) 40. קְצָת (A) 41. ἄκρος
42. ἀποδίδωμι 43. ἀφίημι 44. διαλύω 45. ἐκλείπω
46. ἐξαρτίζω 47. ἐπιτελέω 48. ἔσχατος 49. καταπαύω
50. καταστροφή 51. λήγω 52. παύω 53. πέρας
54. πίμπλημι 55. πίπτω 56. πληρόω 57. συντέλεια
58. συντελέω 59. τελειόω 60. τελευτή 61. τελέω
62. τέλος 63. compleo 64. consummatio 65. dissolvo
66. finio 67. finis 68. pertranseo

Gen 6:13 I have determined to make an end of all flesh; 24
8: 3 At the end of 150 days the waters had abated; 27
6 At the end of 40 days Noah opened the window 24
23: 9 the cave . . is at the end of his field. 27
44:12 beginning with the eldest and ending 12
47:18 when that year was ended, they came to him 36
21 made slaves . . from one end of Egypt 27
Exd 12:41 at the end of 430 years, on that very day 24
23:16 the feast of ingathering at the end of the year 10
25:18 cherubim . . on the two ends of the mercy seat. 26
19 Make one cherub on the one end 26
19 Make . . one cherub on the other end; 26
19 shall you make the cherubim on its two ends. 26
26:28 bar . . shall pass through from end to end. 27
28 bar . . shall pass through from end to end. 27
28:25 the two ends of the two cords you shall attach 26
26 put them at the two ends of the breastpiece 26
34:22 the feast of ingathering at the year's end. 37
36:33 middle bar to pass through from end to end 27
33 from end to end halfway up the frames. 27
37: 7 on the two ends of the mercy seat he made them 26
8 on the one end, and one cherub on the other end; 26
8 on the one end, and one cherub on the other end; 26
8 mercy seat he made the cherubim on its two ends. 26
39:18 Two ends of the two cords they had attached 26
19 and put them at the two ends of the breastpiece 26
Lev 17: 5 This is to the end that the people of Israel 16
Num13:25 At the end of 40 days they returned from spying 24
23:10 let my end be like his! 3
24:20 but in the end he shall come to destruction. 3
34: 3 boundary shall be from the end of the Salt Sea 27
4 Zin, and its end shall be south of Ka'desh-bar'nea; 34
8 end of the boundary shall be at Zeded; 34
9 Ziphron, and its end shall be at Ha'zar-e'nan; 34
12 to the Jordan, and its end shall be at the Salt Sea. 34
Deu 4:32 ask from one end of heaven to the other 27
8:16 humble you and test you, to do you good in the end. 3
9:11 at the end of 40 days and 40 nights the LORD gave me 24
11:12 from the beginning . . to the end of the year. 3
13: 7 from the one end of the earth to the other 27
14:28 At the end of every three years you shall bring 27
15: 1 end of every seven years you shall grant a release. 24
28:49 bring . . from afar, from the end of the earth 27
64 scatter . . from one end of the earth to the other; 27
31:10 At the end of every seven years, at the set time 24
32:20 hide my face . . I will see what their end will be 3
33:17 push the peoples . . to the ends of the earth; 4
34: 8 days of . . mourning for Moses were ended. 36
Jos 3: 2 At the end of three days the officers went 27
9:16 At the end of three days after they had made 27
13:27 to the lower end of the Sea of Chin'nereth 27
15: 2 south boundary ran from the end of the Salt Sea 27
4 goes out by . . and comes to its end at the sea. 34
7 passes along to . . and ends at En-ro'gel; 8
8 at the northern end of the valley of Reph'aim; 27
11 then the boundary comes to an end at the sea. 34
16: 3 it goes . . then to Gezer, and it ends at the sea. 8
7 then it goes down from . . ending at the Jordan. 10
8 boundary goes westward to . . and ends at the sea. 8
17: 9 boundary of Manas'seh goes . . and ends at the sea; 8
18:12 and it ends at the wilderness of Beth-a'ven. 8
14 boundary goes . . and it ends at Kir'iath-ba'al 8
19 boundary ends at the northern bay of the Salt Sea 8
19 the northern bay . . at the south end of the Jordan 27
19:14 boundary . . and it ends at the valley of Iph'tahel; 8
22 and its boundary ends at the Jordan 8
29 the boundary turns to Hosah, and it ends at the sea; 8
33 ran . . as far as Lakkum; and it ended at the Jordan; 8
Jdg 11:39 at the end of two months, she returned to her 24
Rut 2:23 until the end of the barley and wheat harvests; 12
3: 7 he went to lie down at the end of the heap of grain. 27
1Sm 2:10 The LORD will judge the ends of the earth; 4
3:12 all that I have spoken . . from beginning to end. 12
2Sm 2:26 Do you not know that the end will be bitter? 1
14:26 for at the end of every year he used to cut it; 24
15: 7 at the end of four years Ab'salom said to the king 24
24: 8 they came to Jerusalem at the end of nine months 27
1Kg 2:39 it happened at the end of three years that two 24
8: 8 ends of the poles were seen from the holy place 30
9:10 At the end of twenty years . . Solomon had built 27
10:20 twelve lions stood there, one on each end of a step †
2Kg 8: 3 at the end of the seven years . . she went forth 27
10:21 the house . . was filled from one end to the other. 23
18:10 and at the end of three years he took it. 27
21:16 he had filled Jerusalem from one end to another 23
2Ch 5: 9 ends of the poles were seen from the holy place 30
7: 1 When Solomon had ended his prayer, fire came down 12
8: 1 At the end of twenty years, in which Solomon had 24
9:19 one on each end of a step on the six steps. *
20:16 you will find them at the end of the valley 21
21:19 at the end of two years, his bowels came out 24
24:23 At the end of the year the army of the Syrians 37
Ezr 9:11 filled it from end to end with their uncleanness. 23
11 filled it from end to end with their uncleanness. 23
Neh 3:21 from . . to the end of the house of Eli'ashib. 35
Job 5:13 the schemes of the wily are brought to a quick end. *
6:11 what is my end, that I should be patient? 24
16: 3 Shall windy words have an end? 24
22: 5 There is no end to your iniquities. 24
28: 3 Men put an end to darkness 24
24 For he looks to the ends of the earth, 26
31:40 The words of Job are ended. 36
34:36 Would that Job were tried to the end 20
36:14 They die in youth, and their life ends in shame. *
Ps 2: 8 and the ends of the earth your possession. 4
19: 4 and their words to the end of the world. 27
6 Its rising is from the end of the heavens 27
6 of the heavens, and its circuit to the end of them; 26
22:27 All the ends of the earth shall remember and turn 4
39: 4 LORD, let me know my end 24
46: 9 He makes wars cease to the end of the earth; 27
48:10 so thy praise reaches to the ends of the earth. 28
49:13 the end of those who are pleased 2
59:13 God rules over Jacob to the ends of the earth. 4
61: 2 from the end of the earth I call to thee 27
65: 5 God . . who art the hope of all the ends of the earth 28
67: 7 let all the ends of the earth fear him! 4
72: 8 to sea, and from the River to the ends of the earth! 4
20 The prayers of David, the son of Jesse, are ended. 12
73:17 then I perceived their end. 3
77: 8 Are his promises at an end for all time? 7
90: 9 our years come to an end like a sigh. ‡
98: 3 ends of the earth have seen the victory of our God. 4
102:27 thou art the same, and thy years have no end. 36
105:45 to the end that they should keep his statutes 6
107:27 reeled and staggered . . were at their wits' end. 5
119:33 way of thy statutes; and I will keep it to the end. 22
112to perform thy statutes for ever, to the end. 22
135: 7 who makes the clouds rise at the end of the earth 27
Prv 5: 4 in the end she is bitter as wormwood 3
11 at the end of your life you groan 3
10:28 The hope of the righteous ends in gladness *
11:23 desire of the righteous ends only in good; *
14:12 but its end is the way to death. 3
13 end of joy is grief. 3
16:25 but its end is the way to death. 3
17:24 but the eyes of a fool are on the ends of the earth. 27
20:21 gotten hastily . . in the end not be blessed. 3
25: 8 for what will you do in the end, when your neighbor 3
10 shame upon you, and your ill repute have no end. 32
29:21 pampers his servant . . end find him his heir. 3
30: 4 Who has established all the ends of the earth? 4
Ecc 3:11 done from the beginning to the end. 21
4: 8 no end to all his toil . . so that he never asks 24
16 there was no end of all the people; he was over all 24
7: 2 this is the end of all men 21
8 Better is the end of a thing than its beginning; 3
10:13 and the end of his talk is wicked madness. 3
12:12 Of making many books there is no end 24
13 The end of the matter; all has been heard. 21
Isa 2: 7 filled . . and there is no end to their treasures; 25
7 and there is no end to their chariots. 25
5:26 whistle for it from the ends of the earth; and lo 27
7: 3 at the end of the conduit of the upper pool 27
9: 7 his government and of peace there will be no end 24
13: 5 come from a distant land . . the end of the heavens 27
23:15 At the end of 70 years, it will happen to Tyre 24
17 At the end of 70 years, the LORD will visit 24
24:16 From the ends of the earth we hear songs of praise 13
26:14 to that end thou hast visited them 15
40: 2 and cry to her that her warfare is ended 19
28 the Creator of the ends of the earth. 26
41: 5 the ends of the earth tremble; 26
9 you whom I took from the ends of the earth 26
42:10 a new song, his praise from the end of the earth! 27
43: 6 bring . . my daughters from the end of the earth 27
45:22 Turn to me and be saved, all the ends of the earth! 4
46:10 declaring the end from the beginning 3
47: 7 lay these things to heart or remember their end. 3
48:20 proclaim it, send it forth to the end of the earth; 27
49: 6 my salvation may reach to the end of the earth. 27
51: 6 for ever, and my deliverance will never be ended. 9
52:10 all the ends of the earth shall see the salvation 4
60:20 and your days of mourning shall be ended. 33
62:11 the LORD has proclaimed to the end of the earth 27
Jer 1: 3 until the end of the eleventh year of Zedeki'ah 36
3: 5 will he be indignant to the end?' 17
5:31 but what will you do when the end comes? 3
8:20 The harvest is past, the summer is ended 12
10:13 he makes the mist rise from the ends of the earth. 27
12:12 sword of the LORD devours from one end of the land 27
16:19 nations come from the ends of the earth and say 4
17:11 and at his end he will be a fool. 3
25:31 The clamor will resound to the ends of the earth 27
33 shall extend from one end of the earth 27
34:14 At the end of six years each of you must set free 24
42: 7 At the end of ten days the word of the LORD came 24
44:27 sword and by famine, until there is an end of them. 12
51:13 your end has come, the thread of your life is cut. 24
16 he makes the mist rise from the ends of the earth. 27
Lam 4:18 our end drew near; our days were numbered; 24
18 our days were numbered; for our end had come. 24
Ezk 3:16 at the end of seven days, the word of the LORD came 27
7: 2 thus says the Lord GOD to the land of Israel: An end! 24
2 end has come upon the four corners of the land. 24
3 Now the end is upon you 24
6 An end has come, the end has come; 24
6 An end has come, the end has come; 24
11:13 wilt thou make a full end of the remnant of Israel? 12
15: 4 when the fire has consumed both ends of it 26
29:13 thus says the Lord GOD: At the end of 40 years 24
39:14 at the end of seven months they will make their 27
40: 9 the vestibule of the gate was at the inner end. *
15 to the end of the inner vestibule of the gate *
44: 6 let there be an end to all your abominations 31
47: 1 water was flowing down from below the south end 14
Dan 1: 5 three years, and at the end of that time 29
15 end of ten days it was seen that they were better 29
18 At the end of the time, when the king had commanded 29
4:11 tree . . visible to the end of the whole earth. 39
17 to the end that the living may know 38
20 visible to the end of the whole earth; *
22 your dominion to the ends of the earth. 39
29 end of twelve months he was walking on the roof 40
34 end of the days I, Nebuchadnez'zar, lifted my eyes 40
6:26 his dominion shall be to the end. 39
7:26 consumed and destroyed to the end. 39
28 Here is the end of the matter. 39
8:17 Understand . . vision is for the time of the end. 24
19 for it pertains to the appointed time of the end. 24
9: 2 before the end of the desolations of Jerusalem *
26 Its end shall come with a flood and to the end 24
26 flood and to the end there shall be war; 24
27 until the decreed end is poured out *
11:27 for the end is yet to be at the time appointed. 24
35 until the time of the end, for it is yet 24
40 time of the end the king of the south shall attack 24
45 yet he shall come to his end, with none to help him. 24
12: 4 seal the book, until the time of the end. 24
6 How long shall it be till the end of these wonders? 24
9 shut up and sealed until the time of the end. 24
13 go your way till the end; and you shall rest 24
13 in your allotted place at the end of the days. 24
Ams 8: 2 The end has come upon my people Israel; 24
10 mourning . . and the end of it like a bitter day. 3
Mic 5: 4 for now he shall be great to the ends of the earth. 4
Nah 2: 9 There is no end of treasure, or wealth 25
3: 1 full of lies and booty-no end to the plunder! 18
3 heaps of corpses, dead bodies without end- 25
Hab 2: 3 it hastens to the end-it will not lie. 24
Zep 1:18 for a full, yea, sudden end he will make 11
Zec 9:10 from the River to the ends of the earth. 4
Mat 10:22 But he who endures to the end will be saved. 62
12:42 she came from the ends of the earth 53
24: 6 this must take place, but the end is not yet. 62
13 he who endures to the end will be saved. 62
14 then the end will come. 62
31 from one end of heaven to the other. 41
26:58 he sat with the guards to see the end. 62
Mrk 3:26 he cannot stand, but is coming to an end. 62
13: 7 this must take place, but the end is not yet. 62
13 he who endures to the end will be saved. 62
27 from the ends of the earth to the ends of heaven. 41
27 from the ends of the earth to the ends of heaven. 41
Lke 1:23 when his time of service was ended 54
33 of his kingdom there will be no end. 62
2:21 at the end of eight days, when he was circumcised 54
43 when the feast was ended, as they were returning 59
4: 2 when they were ended, he was hungry. 58
13 when the devil had ended every temptation 58
7: 1 After he had ended all his sayings 56
11:31 she came from the ends of the earth 53
16:24 send Laz'arus to dip the end of his finger in water 41
21: 9 the end will not be at once. 62
Joh 13: 1 he loved them to the end. 62
Act 1: 8 all Judea and Sama'ria and to the end of the earth. 48
21: 5 when our days there were ended 46
Rom 6:21 The end of those things is death. 62
22 and its end, eternal life. 62
10: 4 For Christ is the end of the law 62
18 and their words to the ends of the world. 53
14: 9 For to this end Christ died and lived again *
1Co 1: 8 who will sustain you to the end 62
10:11 upon whom the end of the ages has come. 62
13: 8 Love never ends 55
15:24 Then comes the end, when he delivers the kingdom 62
2Co 3:13 see the end of the fading splendor. 62
11:15 Their end will correspond to their deeds. 62
Gal 3: 3 are you now ending with the flesh? 47
Eph 6:18 To that end keep alert with all perseverance *
Php 3:19 Their end is destruction, their god is the belly 62
2Th 1:11 To this end we always pray for you *
1Ti 4:10 For to this end we toil and strive *
Heb 1:12 thou art the same, and thy years will never end. 45
3:14 if only we hold . . firm to the end 62
6: 8 its end is to be burned. 62

11 the full assurance of hope until the end 62
7: 3 has neither beginning of days nor end of life 62
9:26 he has appeared once for all at the end of the age 57
1Pe 1:20 He . . was made manifest at the end of the times 48
4: 7 The end of all things is at hand; 62
17 what will be the end of those who do not obey 62
Rev 2:26 He . . who keeps my works until the end 62
15: 1 for with them the wrath of God is ended. 61
8 seven plagues of the seven angels were ended. 61
20: 3 no more, till the 1,000 years were ended. 61
5 until the 1,000 years were ended. 61
7 And when the 1,000 years are ended 61
21: 6 Alpha and the Omega, the beginning and the end. 62
22:13 Alpha and the Omega . . the beginning and the end 62
1Es 4:21 With his wife he ends his days 43
9:17 were brought to an end 53
2Es 2:34 because he who will come at the end of the age 67
3:14 to him only didst thou reveal the end of the times 67
4:26 because the age is hastening swiftly to its end. 68
5:41 dost have charge of those who are alive at the end 67
6: 6 just as the end shall come through me 67
7 when will be the end of the first age 67
9 For Esau is the end of this age 67
10 and the end of a man is his heel ‡
12 show thy servant the end of thy signs 67
15 because the word concerns the end 67
16 for they know that their end must be changed. 67
25 shall see my salvation and the end of my world. 67
7:112 This present world is not the end 67
113 the day of judgment will be the end of this age 67
8:54 in the end the treasure of immortality 67
9: 5 the beginning is evident, and the end manifest; 64
6 and the end in requital and in signs. 64
10:22 and our rejoicing has been ended 65
28 my end has become corruption 67
11:13 it came to its end and disappeared 67
14 while it was reigning its end came also 67
39 the end of my times might come through them? 67
44 behold, they are ended, and his ages are completed! 66
12: 6 that he may strengthen me to the end. 67
9 worthy to be shown the end of the times 67
21 the time when its end approaches 66
21 but two shall be kept until the end. 67
30 whom the Most High has kept for the eagle's end 67
32 whom the Most High has kept until the end of days 67
34 he will make them joyful until the end comes 67
14: 5 and declared to him the end of the times 67
9 until the times are ended. 66
45 when the 40 days were ended 63
16:13 they begin to be shot to the ends of the world. 67
Tob 8:20 until the fourteen days . . were ended 56
1 1 Here Tobit ended his words of praise. 52
Jdt 2: 9 to the ends of the whole earth. 41
10: 1 had ended all these words 58
11:21 from one end of the earth to the other 41
13: 6 She went up to the post at the end of the bed *
AEs 14:13 an end of him and those who agree with him. 57
15: 1 On the third day, when she ended her prayer 52
Wis 3:19 the end of an unrighteous generation 62
4:17 For they will see the end of the wise man 60
5: 4 his end was without honor. 60
6: 1 learn, O judges of the ends of the earth. *
7:18 the beginning and end and middle of times 62
8: 1 She reaches mightily from one end of the earth 53
11:14 at the end of the events they marveled at him 62
14:14 therefore their speedy end has been planned. 62
27 the beginning and cause and end of every evil. 53
16: 5 thy wrath did not continue to the end; 62
18:21 put an end to the disaster 53
19: 1 were assailed to the end by pitiless anger 62
4 the fate they deserved drew them on to this end 53
Sir 1:13 it will go well at the end 48
3:26 A stubborn mind will be afflicted at the end 48
7:36 In all you do, remember the end of your life 48
9:11 for you do not know what his end will be. 50
14: 7 betrays his baseness in the end. 48
18:12 sees and recognizes that their end will be evil; 50
21: 9 their end is a flame of fire. 57
10 at its end is the pit of Hades. 48
22: 8 at the end he will say, "What is it? 57
28: 6 Remember the end of your life 48
30:10 in the end you will gnash your teeth. 48
31:22 in the end you will appreciate my words 48
33:23 At the time when you end the days of your life 57
38:20 drive it away, remembering the end of life. 48
41: 3 remember your former days and the end of life 48
44:21 from the River to the ends of the earth. 41
50:19 till the order of worship of the Lord was ended 58
Bar 3:17 men trust, and there is no end to their getting; 62
1Mc 1: 3 He advanced to the ends of the earth 41
3: 9 He was renowned to the ends of the earth 48
8: 4 who came against them from the ends of the earth 41
14:10 till his renown spread to the ends of the earth. 41
2Mc 5: 7 and in the end . . got only disgrace from his conspiracy 62
8 Finally he met a miserable end 50
10: 9 Such then was the end of Antiochus 60
13 he took poison and ended his life. 45
13:16 In the end they filled the camp with terror 62
15:24 With these words he ended his prayer. 51
37 So I too will here end my story. 49
39 here will be the end. 60
3Mc 1: 2 to kill him and thereby end the war. 44
4:14 at the end to be destroyed in . . a single day. 62
5:49 the end of their most miserable suspense 62
6:16 Just as Eleazar was ending his prayer 51
4Mc 11:15 Since to this end we were born and bred *
12:19 so ended his life. 42

end *See also* bring, come, make, put, reach, stand.

come to end 1. כלה
Gen 41:53 The seven years of plenty . . came to an end; 1

dreadful end 1. בַּלָּהָה
Ezk 26:21 I will bring you to a dreadful end 1
27:36 you have come to a dreadful end 1
28:19 you have come to a dreadful end 1

extreme end 1. יַרְכָה
Ezk 46:19 I saw a place at the extreme western end of them. 1

full end 1. כָּלָה
Isa 10:23 For the Lord, the LORD of hosts, will make a full end 1
Jer 4:27 yet I will not make a full end. 1
5:10 and destroy, but make not a full end; 1
18 says the LORD, I will not make a full end of you. 1
30:11 I will make a full end of all the nations 1
11 but of you I will not make a full end. 1
46:28 I will make a full end of all the nations 1
28 but of you I will not make a full end. 1
Ezk 20:17 or make a full end of them in the wilderness. 1
Nah 1: 8 he will make a full end of his adversaries 1
9 He will make a full end; 1

inner end 1. בַּיִת
Ezk 40: 7 vestibule of the gate at the inner end, one reed. 1

last end 1. ἔσχατος
Wis 2:16 he calls the last end of the righteous happy 1

latter end 1. אַחֲרִית
Deu 32:29 wise . . they would discern their latter end! 1
Jer 12: 4 because men said, "He will not see our latter end. 1
Dan 8:19 what . . be at the latter end of the indignation; 1
23 at the latter end of their rule 1

north end 1. צָפוֹן
Jos 18:16 the mountain . . at the north end of the valley 1

end of life 1. אַחֲרִית 2. ἔκβασις 3. ἔσχατος 4. τελευτάω
4:
Prv 5:11 at the end of your life you groan 1
Heb 11:22 Joseph, at the end of his life 4
Wis 2:17 let us test what will happen at the end of his life; 2
Sir 2: 3 that you may be honored at the end of your life. 3

end of time 1. αἰών
Sir 48:25 He revealed what was to occur to the end of time 1

other end 1. קָצֶה
Deu 13: 7 from the one end of the earth to the other 1
Jer 12:12 devours from one end of the land to the other; 1
25:33 extend from one end of the earth to the other. 1

very end 1. תמם
Deu 31:24 finished writing . . law in a book, to the very end 1

endanger 1. חוב 2. סכן
Ecc 10: 9 and he who splits logs is endangered by them. 2
Dan 1:10 So you would endanger my head with the king. 1

endeavor 1. ἐπιχειρέω 2. ζητέω 3. πειράω 4. studium
Gal 2:17 if, in our endeavor to be justified in Christ 2
2Es 8:27 not the endeavors of those who act wickedly 4
27 but the endeavors of those who have kept *
2Mc 10:15 and endeavored to keep up the war. 1
11:19 I will endeavor . . to help promote your welfare 3

endeavor eagerly 1. σπουδάζω
1Th 2:17 we endeavored the more eagerly 1

endless 1. ἀπέραντος 2. πολυχρόνιος 3. inmensus
1Ti 1: 4 myths and endless genealogies 1
2Es 6:44 fruit came forth in endless abundance 3
4Mc 17:12 The prize was immortality in endless life. 2

endow 1. זבד 2. מלא 3. נחל 4. ἀπονέμω 5. ἐνδύω 6. do
Gen 30:20 God has endowed me with a good dowry; 1
Exd 28: 3 whom I have endowed with an able mind 2
Prv 8:21 endowing with wealth those who love me 3
2Es 4:22 why have I been endowed with . . understanding? 6
Sir 17: 3 He endowed them with strength like his own 5
3Mc 1: 7 by endowing their sacred enclosures with gifts 4

well endowed by nature 1. εὐφυής
Wis 8:19 As a child I was by nature well endowed 1

endowment 1. δόσις
Jas 1:17 Every good endowment . . is from above 1

endue 1. ידע
2Ch 2:12 son, endued with discretion and understanding 1
13 a skilled man, endued with understanding 1

endurance 1. καρτερία 2. ὑπομονή 3. ὑπομονόω
Lke 21:19 By your endurance you will gain your lives. 2
Rom 5: 3 knowing that suffering produces endurance 2
4 and endurance produces character 2
2Co 6: 4 through great endurance, in afflictions 2
Col 1:11 for all endurance and patience with joy 2
Heb 10:36 you have need of endurance 2
Rev 13:10 must he be slain. Here is a call for the endurance 2
14:12 Here is a call for the endurance of the saints 2
Sir 2:14 Woe to you who have lost your endurance! 2
17:24 encourages those whose endurance is failing. 2
4Mc 1:11 marveled at their courage and endurance 2
11 By their endurance they conquered the tyrant 2
6:13 partly out of admiration for his endurance 1
7: 9 through your glorious endurance 3
9: 8 through this severe suffering and endurance 2
30 being defeated by our endurance 2
11:12 to show our endurance for the law. 1
15:30 more manly than men in endurance! 2
17:12 tested them for their endurance 2
17 all his council marveled at their endurance 2
23 their endurance under the tortures 2
23 as an example for their own endurance 2

patient endurance 1. ὑπομονή
Rev 1: 9 share with you . . the patient endurance 1
2: 2 I know your works . . and your patient endurance 1
19 I know your works, your . . patient endurance 1
3:10 you have kept my word of patient endurance 1

endure 1. אֵיתָן 2. היה 3. חול 4. יכל 5. כול 6. כון 7. לְעוֹלָם 8. נֵצַח 9. עמד 10. עָתֵק 11. קום 12. קַיָּם (A) 13. ἀνέχω 14. ἀντέχω 15. διακαρτερέω 16. διαμένω 17. εἰμί 18. ἔχω 19. ζάω 20. καρτερέω 21. καρτερός 22. μένω 23. παραμένω 24. στέγω 25. συνέχω 26. ὑπάρχω 27. ὑπομένω 28. ὑπομονή 29. ὑποφέρω 30. φέρω 31. fero 32. patior 33. sustineo
Exd 18:23 then you will be able to endure, and all this 9
Num24:21 Enduring is your dwelling place, and your nest 1
1Ch 16:34 for his steadfast love endures for ever! *
41 for his steadfast love endures for ever. *
2Ch 5:13 is good, for his steadfast love endures for ever *
7: 3 is good, for his steadfast love endures for ever. *
6 -for his steadfast love endures for ever- *
20:21 for his steadfast love endures for ever. *
Ezr 3:11 steadfast love endures for ever toward Israel. *
Est 8: 6 how can I endure to see the calamity . . coming *
6 how can I endure to see the destruction of my *
Job 8:15 he lays hold of it, but it does not endure. 11
15:29 he will not be rich, and his wealth will not endure 11
20:21 therefore his prosperity will not endure. 3
Ps 19: 9 the fear of the LORD is clean, enduring for ever; 9
45: 6 Your divine throne endures for ever and ever. *
61: 6 the king; may his years endure to all generations! *
72: 5 May he live while the sun endures *
17 May his name endure for ever 2
89:36 His line shall endure for ever 2
37 shall stand firm while the skies endure." Selah *
100: 5 LORD is good; his steadfast love endures for ever *
101: 5 haughty . . and arrogant . . I will not endure. 4
102:12 thy name endures to all generations. *
24 whose years endure throughout all generations! *
26 They will perish, but thou dost endure; 9
104:31 May the glory of the LORD endure for ever 2
106: 1 for his steadfast love endures for ever! *
107: 1 for his steadfast love endures for ever! *
111: 3 his righteousness endures for ever. 9
10 His praise endures for ever! 9
112: 3 his righteousness endures for ever. 9
9 his righteousness endures for ever; 9
117: 2 faithfulness of the LORD endures for ever. *
118: 1 he is good; his steadfast love endures for ever! *
2 Israel say, "His steadfast love endures for ever. *
3 Aaron say, "His steadfast love endures for ever. *
4 His steadfast love endures for ever. *
29 for his steadfast love endures for ever! *
119:84 How long must thy servant endure? *
90 Thy faithfulness endures to all generations. *
160 of thy righteous ordinances endures for ever. *
135:13 Thy name, O LORD, endures for ever, thy renown, *
136: 1 for his steadfast love endures for ever. *
2 for his steadfast love endures for ever. *
3 for his steadfast love endures for ever; *
4 for his steadfast love endures for ever; *
5 for his steadfast love endures for ever; *
6 for his steadfast love endures for ever; *
7 for his steadfast love endures for ever; *
8 for his steadfast love endures for ever; *
9 for his steadfast love endures for ever; *
10 for his steadfast love endures for ever; *

11 for his steadfast love endures for ever; *
12 for his steadfast love endures for ever; *
13 for his steadfast love endures for ever; *
14 for his steadfast love endures for ever; *
15 for his steadfast love endures for ever; *
16 for his steadfast love endures for ever; *
17 for his steadfast love endures for ever; *
18 for his steadfast love endures for ever; *
19 for his steadfast love endures for ever; *
20 for his steadfast love endures for ever; *
21 for his steadfast love endures for ever; *
22 for his steadfast love endures for ever. *
23 for his steadfast love endures for ever; *
24 for his steadfast love endures for ever; *
25 for his steadfast love endures for ever. *
26 for his steadfast love endures for ever. *
138: 8 thy steadfast love, O LORD, endures for ever. *
145:13 dominion endures throughout all generations. *
Prv 8:18 with me, enduring wealth and prosperity. 10
12:19 Truthful lips endure for ever 6
18:14 A man's spirit will endure sickness; 5
21:28 but the word of a man who hears will endure. 8
27:24 does a crown endure to all generations? *
Ecc 2:16 of the fool there is no enduring remembrance 7
3:14 I know that whatever God does endures for ever; 2
Isa 1:13 I cannot endure iniquity and solemn assembly. 4
Jer 5:15 It is an enduring nation, it is an ancient nation 1
10:10 the nations cannot endure his indignation. 5
33:11 for his steadfast love endures for ever! *
Lam 5:19 thy throne endures to all generations. *
Ezk 22:14 Can your courage endure 9
Dan 4:34 kingdom endures from generation to generation; *
6:26 for he is the living God, enduring for ever; 12
11: 6 he and his offspring shall not endure; 9
Jol 2:11 is great and very terrible; who can endure it? 5
Mic 6: 2 Hear . . you enduring foundations of the earth; 1
Nah 1: 6 Who can endure the heat of his anger? 11
Mal 3: 2 But who can endure the day of his coming 5
Mat 10:22 But he who endures to the end will be saved. 27
13:21 but endures for a while 17
24:13 he who endures to the end will be saved. 27
Mrk 4:17 endure for a while 17
13:13 he who endures to the end will be saved. 27
Joh 6:27 the food which endures to eternal life 22
Rom 9:22 endured with much patience the vessels of wrath 30
1Co 4:12 When reviled, we bless; when persecuted, we endure; 13
9:12 we endure anything rather than put an obstacle 24
10:13 that you may be able to endure it. 29
13: 7 hopes all things, endures all things. 27
2Co 1: 6 when you patiently endure the same sufferings 28
9: 9 his righteousness endures for ever. 22
2Th 1: 4 in the afflictions which you are enduring. 13
2Ti 2:10 Therefore I endure everything 27
12 if we endure, we shall also reign with him 27
3:11 what persecutions I endured 29
4: 3 when people will not endure sound teaching 13
Heb 10:32 you endured a hard struggle with sufferings 27
11:27 he endured as seeing him who is invisible. 20
12: 2 endured the cross, despising the shame 27
3 Consider him who endured . . such hostility 27
7 It is for discipline that you have to endure 27
20 they could not endure the order that was given 30
13:13 and bear the abuse he endured. *
Jas 1:12 Blessed is the man who endures trial 27
1Pe 2:19 one is approved if, mindful of God, he endures pain 29
1Es 4:38 truth endures and is strong for ever 22
2Es 1: 9 How long shall I endure them 33
3:30 for I have seen how thou dost endure those who sin 33
7:18 can endure difficult circumstances 31
8: 8 the womb . . endures thy creation 32
10:54 no work of man's building could endure in a place 33
Jdt 11: 7 as his power endures 19
Wis 11:25 How would anything have endured 16
17:17 he was seized, and endured the inescapable fate; 22
Sir 1:23 A patient man will endure until the right moment 14
11:17 gift of the Lord endures for those who are godly 23
40:17 almsgiving endures for ever. 16
41:13 a good name endures for ever. 16
45:26 endure throughout their generations. *
51: 3 from the many afflictions that I endured 18
Bar 4: 1 She is . . the law that endures for ever 26
Aza 1:67 his mercy endures for ever. *
68 his mercy endures for ever. *
Sus 1:57 would not endure your wickedness. 27
1Mc 4:24 he is good, for his mercy endures for ever. *
10:15 the troubles that they had endured. 18
2Mc 2:27 we will gladly endure the uncomfortable toil 29
6:30 I am enduring terrible sufferings in my body 29
7:36 after enduring a brief suffering 29
9:12 when he could not endure his own stench 13
4Mc 5:23 we endure any suffering willingly; 27
6: 7 because his body could not endure the agonies 30
9 endured the tortures. 15
7:22 knows that it is blessed to endure any suffering 27
9: 6 the aged men . . lived piously while enduring torture 27
22 he nobly endured the rackings. 27
28 he steadfastly endured this agony and said 21
10: 1 When he too had endured a glorious death 20
13:27 endured for the sake of religion 13
15:31 stoutly endured the waves 27
32 endured nobly and withstood the wintry storms 25
16: 1 endured seeing her children tortured to death 27
8 In vain, my sons, I endured many birth-pangs for you 27
17 while an aged man endures such agonies 27
19 therefore you ought to endure any suffering 27
21 and endured it for the sake of God. 27
17: 4 maintaining firm an enduring hope in God. 28
7 enduring their varied tortures to death 27
10 and enduring torture even to death. 27

endure hardship 1. ענה

Ps 132: 1 David's favor, all the hardships he endured; 1

endure patiently 1. *μακροθυμέω* 2. *ὑπομονὴν ἔχω*

Heb 6:15 having patiently endured, obtained the promise. 1
Rev 2: 3 I know you are enduring patiently and bearing up 2

endure suffering 1. *κακοπαθέω* 2. *πάσχω*

2Ti 4: 5 As for you, always be steady, endure suffering 1
2Mc 9:28 having endured the more intense suffering 2

endure with patience 1. *μακροθυμέω*

Bar 4:25 My children, endure with patience the wrath 1

enemy 1. איב 2. איש אֹיֵב 3. עָר 4. צַר 5. צרר 6. קום 7. שׂנא 8. שׁוֹרֵר 9. עִיר (A) 10. *ἀντίκειμαι* 11. *ἀντίπαλος* 12. *ἀπεχθάνομαι* 13. *δυσμενής* 14. *ἐχθρεύω* 15. *ἐχθρός* 16. *νεκρός* 17. *πολέμιος* 18. *ὑπεναντίος* 19. adversarius 20. inimicus

Gen 14:11 the enemy took all the goods of Sodom *
20 who has delivered your enemies into your hand! 4
22:17 shall possess the gate of their enemies 1
49: 8 your hand shall be on the neck of your enemies; 1
Exd 1:10 if war befall us, they join our enemies and fight 7
15: 6 thy right hand, O LORD, shatters the enemy. 1
9 The enemy said, 'I will pursue, I will overtake 1
23: 4 If you meet your enemy's ox or his ass going astray 1
22 then I will be an enemy to your enemies 1
22 an enemy to your enemies and an adversary 1
27 I will make all your enemies turn their backs 1
32:25 break loose, to their shame among their enemies) 6
Lev 26: 7 you shall chase your enemies, and they shall fall 1
8 your enemies shall fall before you by the sword 1
16 sow your seed in vain, for your enemies shall eat it 1
17 you shall be smitten before your enemies 1
25 you shall be delivered into the hand of the enemy 1
32 your enemies who settle in it shall be astonished 1
34 while you are in your enemies' land 1
36 into their hearts in the lands of their enemies 1
37 have no power to stand before your enemies 1
38 the land of your enemies shall eat you up 1
39 are left shall pine away in your enemies' lands 1
41 I . . brought them into the land of their enemies 1
44 when they are in the land of their enemies 1
Num10: 9 you shall be saved from your enemies. 1
35 Arise, O LORD, and let thy enemies be scattered; 1
14:42 lest you be struck down before your enemies 1
23:11 I took you to curse my enemies, and behold 1
24:10 I called you to curse my enemies, and behold 1
18 Se'ir also, his enemies, shall be dispossessed 1
32:21 he has driven out his enemies from before him 1
35:23 he was not his enemy, and did not seek his harm; 1
Deu 1:42 lest you be defeated before your enemies.' 1
6:19 by thrusting out all your enemies from before you 1
12:10 gives you rest from all your enemies round about 1
20: 1 When you go forth to war against your enemies 1
3 draw near . . to battle against your enemies 1
4 LORD . . fight for you against your enemies 1
14 enjoy the spoil of your enemies, which the LORD 1
21:10 When you go forth to war against your enemies 1
23: 9 go forth against your enemies and are in camp 1
14 to save you and to give up your enemies before you 1
25:19 LORD . . given you rest from all your enemies 1
28: 7 LORD will cause your enemies who rise against 1
25 cause you to be defeated before your enemies; 1
31 your sheep shall be given to your enemies 1
48 therefore you shall serve your enemies whom 1
53 distress with which your enemies shall distress 1
55 distress with which your enemy shall distress 1
57 distress with which your enemy shall distress 1
68 offer yourselves for sale to your enemies 1
30: 7 put all these curses upon your foes and enemies 7
32:27 had I not feared provocation by the enemy, lest 1
31 even our enemies themselves being judges. 1
42 from the long-haired heads of the enemy.' 1
33:27 And he thrust out the enemy before you, and said 1
29 Your enemies shall come fawning to you; 1
Jos 7: 8 has turned their backs before their enemies! 1
12 Israel cannot stand before their enemies; 1
12 they turn their backs before their enemies 1
13 you cannot stand before your enemies 1
10:13 the nation took vengeance on their enemies. 1
19 pursue your enemies, fall upon their rear 1
25 thus the LORD will do to all your enemies 1
21:44 not one of all their enemies had withstood them 1
44 LORD had given all . . enemies into their hands. 1
22: 8 divide the spoil of your enemies 1
23: 1 given rest to Israel from all their enemies 1
Jdg 2:14 the power of their enemies round about 1
14 they could no longer withstand their enemies. 1
18 he saved them from the hand of their enemies 1
3:28 for the LORD has given your enemies the Moabites 1
5:31 So perish all thine enemies, O LORD! 1
8:34 rescued them from the hand of all their enemies 1
11:36 now that the LORD has avenged you on your enemies 1
16:23 Our god has given Samson our enemy into our hand. 1
24 god has given our enemy into our hand, the ravager 1
1Sm 2: 1 My mouth derides my enemies, because I rejoice 1
4: 3 come . . and save us from the power of our enemies. 1
10: 1 you will save them from the hand of their enemies 15
12:10 deliver us out of the hand of our enemies 1
11 and delivered you out of the hand of your enemies 1
14:24 until . . evening and I am avenged on my enemies. 1
30 had eaten . . of the spoil of their enemies 1
47 he fought against all his enemies on every side 1
18:25 that he may be avenged of the king's enemies. 1
29 Saul was David's enemy continually. 1
19:17 Why have you deceived me thus, and let my enemy go 1
20:15 LORD cuts off every one of the enemies of David 1
16 may the LORD take vengeance on David's enemies. 1
24: 4 I will give your enemy into your hand 1
19 if a man finds his enemy, will he let him go away 1
25:26 your enemies and those who seek . . be as Nabal. 1
29 and the lives of your enemies he shall sling out 1
26: 8 God has given your enemy into your hand this day; 1
28:16 LORD has turned from you and become your enemy? 3
29: 8 and fight against the enemies of my lord the king? 1
30:26 for you from the spoil of the enemies of the LORD"; 1
2Sm 3:18 save . . and from the hand of all their enemies. 1
4: 8 Ish-bo'sheth . . your enemy, who sought your life; 1
5:20 The LORD has broken through my enemies before me 1
7: 1 the LORD had given him rest from all his enemies 1
9 I have been . . and have cut off all your enemies 1
11 and I will give you rest from all your enemies. 1
18:19 has delivered him from the power of his enemies. 1
32 the enemies of my lord the king, and all who rise up 1
19: 9 king delivered us from the hand of our enemies 1
22: 1 delivered him from the hand of all his enemies 1
4 I call upon . . and I am saved from my enemies. 1
18 He delivered me from my strong enemy 1
38 I pursued my enemies and destroyed them 1
41 Thou didst make my enemies turn their backs to me 1
49 who brought me out from my enemies; 1
1Kg 3:11 long life or riches or the life of your enemies 1
5: 3 warfare with which his enemies surrounded him *
8:33 thy people . . are defeated before the enemy 1
37 if their enemy besieges them in . . their cities; 1
44 thy people go out to battle against their enemy 1
46 art angry with them, and dost give them to an enemy 1
46 carried away captive to the land of the enemy 1
48 land of their enemies, who carried them captive 1
21:20 Ahab . . to Eli'jah, "Have you found me, O my enemy? 1
2Kg 17:39 deliver you out of the hand of all your enemies. 1
21:14 and give them into the hand of their enemies 1
14 become a prey and a spoil to all their enemies 1
1Ch 14:11 God has broken through my enemies by my hand 1
17: 8 have cut off all your enemies from before you; 1
10 I will subdue all your enemies. 1
21:12 while the sword of your enemies overtakes you; 1
22: 9 I will give him peace from all his enemies 1
2Ch 6:24 thy people Israel are defeated before the enemy 1
28 if their enemies besiege them in . . cities; 1
34 If thy people . . battle against their enemies 1
36 art angry with them, and dost give them to an enemy 1
20:27 LORD had made them rejoice over their enemies. 1
29 LORD had fought against the enemies of Israel. 1
25: 8 God will cast you down before the enemy; 1
20 give them into the hand of their enemies *
26:13 an army . . to help the king against the enemy. 1
32:22 LORD saved . . from the hand of all his enemies; 1
Ezr 8:22 protect us against the enemy on our way; 1
31 delivered us from the hand of the enemy 1
Neh 4:11 our enemies said, "They will not know or see 4
15 When our enemies heard that it was known to us 1
5: 9 prevent the taunts of the nations our enemies? 1
6: 1 to Geshem the Arab and to the rest of our enemies 1
16 when all our enemies heard of it, all the nations 1
9:27 give them into the hand of their enemies 4
27 saved them from the hand of their enemies. 4
28 abandon them to the hand of their enemies 1
Est 3:10 to Haman the Ag'agite . . the enemy of the Jews. 5
7: 6 Esther said, "A foe and enemy! This wicked Haman! 2
8: 1 the house of Haman, the enemy of the Jews. 5
13 to avenge themselves upon their enemies. 1
9: 1 the enemies of the Jews hoped to get the mastery 1
5 the Jews smote all their enemies with the sword 1
10 the ten sons of Haman . . the enemy of the Jews; 5
16 and got relief from their enemies, 1
22 days . . the Jews got relief from their enemies 1
24 Haman . . the enemy of all the Jews, had plotted 5
Job 13:24 hide thy face, and count me as thy enemy? 1
27: 7 Let my enemy be as the wicked 1
33:10 occasions against me, he counts me as his enemy; 1
Ps 3: 7 For thou dost smite all my enemies on the cheek 1
5: 8 LORD, in thy righteousness because of my enemies; 8
6:10 my enemies shall be ashamed and sorely troubled; 1

7: 4 with evil or plundered my enemy without cause 5
5 let the enemy pursue me and overtake me 1
6 lift thyself up against the fury of my enemies; 5
8: 2 a bulwark . . to still the enemy and the avenger. 1
9: 3 When my enemies turned back, they stumbled 1
6 The enemy have vanished in everlasting ruins; 1
13: 2 How long shall my enemy be exalted over me? 1
4 lest my enemy say, "I have prevailed over him"; 1
17: 9 despoil me, my deadly enemies who surround me. 1
18: 0 delivered him from the hand of all his enemies 1
3 I am saved from my enemies. 1
17 He delivered me from my strong enemy 1
37 I pursued my enemies and overtook them; 1
40 Thou didst make my enemies turn their backs to me 1
48 who delivered me from my enemies; yea, thou didst 1
21: 8 Your hand will find out all your enemies; 1
23: 5 a table before me in the presence of my enemies; 5
25: 2 let not my enemies exult over me. 1
27: 6 now my head shall be lifted up above my enemies 1
11 lead me on a level path because of my enemies. 8
31: 8 hast not delivered me into the hand of the enemy; 1
15 deliver me from the hand of my enemies 1
37:20 enemies of the LORD are like the glory 1
41: 2 dost not give him up to the will of his enemies. 1
5 My enemies say of me in malice: "When will he die 1
11 in that my enemy has not triumphed over me. 1
42: 9 mourning because of the oppression of the enemy? 1
43: 2 mourning because of the oppression of the enemy? 1
44:10 our enemies have gotten spoil. 7
16 at the sight of the enemy and the avenger. 1
45: 5 are sharp in the heart of the king's enemies; 1
54: 5 He will requite my enemies with evil; 8
7 my eye has looked in triumph on my enemies. 1
55: 3 by the noise of the enemy 1
12 not an enemy who taunts me–then I could bear it; 1
56: 2 my enemies trample upon me all day long 8
9 Then my enemies will be turned back in the day 1
59: 1 Deliver me from my enemies, O my God 1
10 my God will let me look in triumph on my enemies. 8
61: 3 art my refuge, a strong tower against the enemy. 1
64: 1 preserve my life from dread of the enemy 1
66: 3 So great is thy power that thy enemies cringe 1
68: 1 Let God arise, let his enemies be scattered; 1
21 But God will shatter the heads of his enemies 1
69:14 let me be delivered from my enemies 7
18 set me free because of my enemies! 1
71:10 For my enemies speak concerning me 1
72: 9 his enemies lick the dust! 1
74: 3 the enemy has destroyed everything 1
10 Is the enemy to revile thy name for ever? 1
18 Remember this, O LORD, how the enemy scoffs 1
78:53 but the sea overwhelmed their enemies. 1
80: 6 our enemies laugh among themselves. 1
81:14 I would soon subdue their enemies 1
83: 2 For lo, thy enemies are in tumult; 1
89:10 didst scatter thy enemies with thy mighty arm. 1
22 The enemy shall not outwit him 1
42 thou hast made all his enemies rejoice. 1
51 with which thy enemies taunt, O LORD 1
92: 9 For, lo, thy enemies, O LORD, for, lo, thy enemies 1
9 O LORD, for, lo, thy enemies shall perish; 1
11 My eyes have seen the downfall of my enemies •
102: 8 All the day my enemies taunt me 1
106:10 delivered them from the power of the enemy. 1
42 Their enemies oppressed them 1
110: 1 till I make your enemies your footstool. 1
119:98 Thy commandment makes me wiser than my enemies 1
127: 5 when he speaks with his enemies in the gate. 1
132:18 His enemies I will clothe with shame 1
138: 7 out thy hand against the wrath of my enemies 1
139:22 hate . . perfect hatred; I count them my enemies. 1
143: 3 enemy has pursued me; he has crushed my life 1
9 Deliver me, O LORD, from my enemies! 1
12 in thy steadfast love cut off my enemies 1
Prv 16: 7 makes even his enemies to be at peace with him. 1
24:17 Do not rejoice when your enemy falls 1
25:21 If your enemy is hungry, give him bread to eat; 7
27: 6 profuse are the kisses of an enemy. 7
Isa 1:24 vent my wrath on my enemies, and . . on my foes. 4
9:11 against them, and stirs up their enemies. 1
59:18 wrath to his . . requital to his enemies; 1
62: 8 your grain to be food for your enemies 1
63:10 therefore he turned to be their enemy 1
66: 6 of the LORD, rendering recompense to his enemies! 1
14 and his indignation is against his enemies. 1
Jer 6:25 for the enemy has a sword, terror is on every side. 1
12: 7 beloved of my soul into the hands of her enemies. 1
15: 9 I will give to the sword before their enemies 1
11 have not pleaded with thee on behalf of the enemy 1
14 I will make you serve your enemies 1
17: 4 and I will make you serve your enemies 1
18:17 I will scatter them before the enemy. 1
19: 7 people to fall by the sword before their enemies 1
9 their enemies and those who seek their life 1
20: 4 They shall fall by the sword of their enemies 1
5 the kings of Judah into the hand of their enemies 1
21: 7 and into the hand of their enemies 1
30:14 for I have dealt you the blow of an enemy 1
31:16 they shall come back from the land of the enemy. 1
34:20 I will give them into the hand of their enemies 1
21 I will give into the hand of their enemies 1
44:30 Hophra king of Egypt into the hand of his enemies 1
30 Babylon, who was his enemy and sought his life. 1
46:22 for her enemies march in force •
49:37 I will terrify Elam before their enemies 1
50: 7 and their enemies have said, 'We are not guilty 4
Lam 1: 2 her friends . . they have become her enemies. 1
5 foes have become the head, her enemies prosper 1
9 O LORD, behold . . for the enemy has triumphed! 1
10 The enemy has stretched out his hands over all 4
16 are desolate, for the enemy has prevailed. 1
21 All my enemies have heard of my trouble; 1
2: 3 withdrawn . . right hand in the face of the enemy; 1
4 He has bent his bow like an enemy 1
5 The Lord has become like an enemy 1
7 he has delivered into the hand of the enemy 1
16 All your enemies rail against you; 1
17 he has made the enemy rejoice over you 1
22 those . . I dandled and reared my enemy destroyed. 1
3:46 All our enemies rail against us; 1
52 by those who were my enemies without cause; 1
4:12 did not believe . . that foe or enemy could enter 1
Ezk 16:27 and delivered you to the greed of your enemies 7
36: 2 Because the enemy said of you, 'Aha!' 1
39:27 and gathered them from their enemies' lands 1
Dan 4:19 may . . its interpretation for your enemies! 9
Hos 8: 3 the enemy shall pursue him. 1
Ams 9: 4 they go into captivity before their enemies 1
Mic 2: 8 But you rise against my people as an enemy; 1
4:10 will redeem you from the hand of your enemies. 1
5: 9 and all your enemies shall be cut off. 1
7: 6 a man's enemies are the men of his own house. 1
8 Rejoice not over me, O my enemy; 1
10 Then my enemy will see, and shame will cover her 1
Nah 1: 2 and keeps wrath for his enemies. 1
8 and will pursue his enemies into darkness. 1
3:11 you will seek a refuge from the enemy. 1
Zep 3:15 he hast cast out your enemies. 1
Mat 5:43 love your neighbor and hate your enemy.' 15
44 I say to you, Love your enemies and pray for those 15
13:25 his enemy came and sowed weeds among the wheat 15
28 He said to them, 'An enemy has done this.' 15
39 the enemy who sowed them is the devil 15
22:44 till I put thy enemies under thy feet'? 15
Mrk 12:36 till I put thy enemies under thy feet.' 15
Lke 1:71 that we should be saved from our enemies 15
74 delivered from the hand of our enemies 15
6:27 Love your enemies, do good to those who hate you 15
35 love your enemies, and do good, and lend 15
10:19 authority . . over all the power of the enemy 15
19:27 as for these enemies of mine 15
43 when your enemies will cast up a bank about you 15
20:43 till I make thy enemies a stool for thy feet.' 15
Act 2:35 till I make thy enemies a stool for thy feet.' 15
13:10 you enemy of all righteousness 15
Rom 5:10 while we were enemies we were reconciled to God 15
11:28 As regards the gospel they are enemies of God 15
12:20 No, "if your enemy is hungry, feed him; 15
1Co 15:25 until he has put all his enemies under his feet. 15
26 The last enemy to be destroyed is death. 15
Gal 4:16 Have I then become your enemy 15
Php 3:18 live as enemies of the cross of Christ. 15
2Th 3:15 Do not look on him as an enemy 15
1Ti 5:14 give the enemy no occasion to revile us. 10
Heb 1:13 till I make thy enemies a stool for thy feet"? 15
10:13 until his enemies should be made a stool 15
Jas 4: 4 makes himself an enemy of God. 15
1Es 4: 4 if he sends them out against the enemy, they go 17
5:66 the enemies of the tribe of Judah and Benjamin 15
8:61 he delivered us from every enemy on the way 15
2Es 1:11 I have slain all their enemies. 19
16 at the destruction of your enemies 20
3:27 deliver the city into the hands of thy enemies. 20
30 and hast preserved thy enemies 20
6:24 friends shall make war on friends like enemies 20
Tob 12:10 who commit sin are the enemies of their own lives. 17
Jdt 5:18 their cities were captured by their enemies. 18
7:19 because all their enemies had surrounded them 15
8:11 promising to surrender the city to our enemies 15
15 even to destroy us in the presence of our enemies. 15
19 before our enemies. 15
33 promised to surrender the city to our enemies 15
35 to take revenge upon our enemies. 15
13: 5 the enemies who have risen up against us. 15
11 to show . . his strength against our enemies 15
14 has destroyed our enemies by my hand 15
17 the enemies of thy people. 15
18 to strike the head of the leader of our enemies. 15
15: 4 rush out upon their enemies to destroy them. 17
5 with one accord they fell upon the enemy •
5 what had happened in the camp of the enemy 15
16:11 my weak people shouted and the enemy trembled; •
11 the enemy were turned back. •
AEs 13: 6 utterly destroyed by the sword of their enemies 15
14: 6 thou hast given us into the hands of our enemies 15
Wis 5:17 and will arm all creation to repel his enemies; 15
10:12 She protected him from his enemies 15
19 she drowned their enemies 15
11: 3 They withstood their enemies 17
5 very things by which their enemies were punished 15
8 how thou didst punish their enemies. 18
12:20 the enemies of thy servants 15
22 while chastening us thou scourgest our enemies 15
24 animals which even their enemies despised •
15:14 all the enemies who oppressed thy people. 15
18 The enemies of thy people •
16: 4 how their enemies were being tormented. 15
8 this also thou didst convince our enemies 15
22 the crops of their enemies were being destroyed 15
18: 1 Their enemies heard their voices •
4 their enemies deserved to be deprived of light •
7 the destruction of their enemies 15
8 thou didst punish our enemies 18
10 the discordant cry of their enemies echoed back 15
Sir 6: 1 do not become an enemy instead of a friend 15
4 make him the laughingstock of his enemies. 15
9 there is a friend who changes into an enemy 15
13 Keep yourself far from your enemies 15
12: 8 nor will an enemy be hidden in adversity. 15
9 A man's enemies are grieved when he prospers 15
10 Never trust your enemy 15
16 An enemy will speak sweetly with his lips 15
16 an enemy will weep with his eyes 15
18:31 make you the laughingstock of your enemies. 15
20:23 needlessly make him an enemy. 15
23: 3 my enemy will not rejoice over me. 15
25:14 any vengeance, but not the vengeance of enemies! 15
15 no wrath worse than an enemy's wrath. 15
27:18 as a man destroys his enemy 16
29: 6 he has needlessly made him his enemy 15
13 will fight on your behalf against your enemy. 15
30: 3 will make his enemies envious 15
6 left behind him an avenger against his enemies 15
36: 7 destroy the adversary and wipe out the enemy. 15
10 Crush the heads of the rulers of the enemy, who say 15
42:11 a laughingstock to your enemies 15
45: 2 made him great in the fears of his enemies. 15
46: 1 to take vengeance on the enemies 15
5 when enemies pressed him on every side 15
16 when his enemies pressed him on every side 15
47: 7 For he wiped out his enemies on every side 15
49: 9 For God remembered his enemies with storm 15
51: 8 dost save them from the hand of their enemies. 15
Bar 3:10 why is it that you are in the land of your enemies 15
4: 6 you were handed over to your enemies 18
18 deliver you from the hand of your enemies. 15
21 deliver you from the power and hand of the enemy. 15
25 Your enemy has overtaken you 15
26 taken away like a flock carried off by the enemy. 15
5: 6 they went forth . . led away by their enemies 15
LJr 1:56 they can offer no resistance to a king or any enemies. 17
Aza 1: 9 hast given us into the hands of lawless enemies 15
1Mc 2: 7 to dwell there when it was given over to the enemy 15
35 Then the enemy hastened to attack them. •
4:18 stand now against our enemies and fight them 15
36 Behold, our enemies are crushed 15
5:13 the enemy have captured their wives •
16 who . . were being attacked by enemies. •
27 the enemy are getting ready to attack •
6:38 to harass the enemy •
7:29 the enemy were ready to seize Judas. 17
46 they out flanked the enemy •
8:23 may sword and enemy be far from them. 15
26 to the enemy who makes war •
28 to the enemy allies shall be given no grain, arms •
9: 6 When they saw the huge number of the enemy forces •
8 Let us rise and go up against our enemies 18
24 the country deserted with them to the enemy. •
29 like him to go against our enemies and Bacchides 15
46 delivered from the hands of our enemies. 15
48 the enemy did not cross the Jordan •
10:26 and have not sided with our enemies 15
81 the enemy's horses grew tired. •
11:72 he turned back to the battle against the enemy •
12:15 we were delivered from our enemies 15
15 our enemies were humbled. 15
26 the enemy were being drawn up in formation •
28 When the enemy heard 18
13:51 because a great enemy had been crushed 15
14:26 they have fought and repulsed Israel's enemies 15
29 resisted the enemies of their nation 18
31 their enemies decided to invade their country 15
33 where . . the arms of the enemy had been stored 17
34 Azotus, where the enemy formerly dwelt 17
15:33 unjustly taken by our enemies. 15
16: 7 the cavalry of the enemy were very numerous. 18
2Mc 3:38 If you have any enemy 17
4:16 became their enemies and punished them. 17
5: 6 setting up trophies of victory over enemies 17
8: 6 and put to flight not a few of the enemy. 17
16 exhorted them not to be frightened by the enemy 17
24 they slew more than 9,000 of the enemy 17
27 when they had collected the arms of the enemy 17
31 Collecting the arms of the enemy •
10:21 by setting their enemies free 17
26 to be an enemy to their enemies 14
26 to be an enemy to their enemies 15

27 when they came near to the enemy they halted. 17
29 there appeared to the enemy from heaven 18
30 they showered . . thunderbolts upon the enemy 18
11:11 They hurled themselves like lions against the enemy 17
12:22 terror and fear came over the enemy 17
28 with power shatters the might of his enemies 17
13:21 Rhodocus . . gave secret information to the enemy 17
14:17 the sudden consternation created by the enemy. 11
22 to prevent sudden treachery on the part of the enemy 17
15:20 the enemy was already close at hand 17
26 Judas and his men met the enemy in battle 17
3Mc 1: 5 the enemy was routed in the action 11
2:13 subjected to our enemies 15
30 he might not appear to be an enemy to all 12
33 considering them to be enemies of the . . nation 17
3:24 traitors and barbarous enemies. 17
25 sure and shameful death that befits enemies. 13
4: 4 even some of their enemies 15
6: 6 turning the flame against all their enemies. 18
10 rescue us from the hand of the enemy 15
15 when they were in the land of their enemies 15
19 They opposed the forces of the enemy 18
7:21 greater prestige among their enemies 15
4Mc 2:14 The fruit trees of the enemy are not cut down 15
14 one preserves the property of enemies 15
3:11 the water in the enemy's territory 17
12 soldiers . . climbed over the enemy's ramparts. 17
13 went searching throughout the enemy camp 17
8:10 Even I, your enemy, have compassion for your youth 17
9:15 enemy of heavenly justice, savage of mind 15
11:23 enemy of those who are truly devout. 17
17:20 our enemies did not rule over our nation 17
24 he ravaged and conquered all his enemies. 17
18: 4 they ravaged the enemy. 17

enemy in ambush 1. subsessor
2Es 15:33 an enemy in ambush shall beset them 1

energy 1. ἐνέργεια
Col 1:29 the energy which he mightily inspires within me. 1

enforce 1. תקף (A) 2. ἐργάζομαι 3. καταναγκάζω
Dan 6: 7 ordinance and enforce an interdict 1
Heb 11:33 enforced justice, received promises 2
1Mc 2:15 king's officers who were enforcing the apostasy 3

engage 1. עשׂה 2. ἀναστρέφω 3. γίνομαι 4. ἔχω 5. συνάπτω 6. συνέχω 7. συνίστημι 8. συντίθημι 9. cogito 10. consto
2Ch 24:13 those who were engaged in the work labored 1
Lke 22: 5 they were glad, and engaged to give him money. 8
Php 1:30 engaged in the same conflict which you saw 4
2Es 9:39 the thoughts with which I had been engaged 9
10: 5 the reflections with which I was still engaged •
15:30 and engage them in battle 10
Wis 17:20 was engaged in unhindered work 6
1Mc 1:18 He engaged Ptolemy king of Egypt in battle 7
10:78 the armies engaged in battle. 5
3Mc 1:24 the crowd, as before, was engaged in prayer 2
4Mc 17:11 the contest in which they were engaged 3

engage in battle 1. συμμίσγω 2. συνάπτω
1Mc 4:14 and engaged in battle 2
5: 7 He engaged in many battles with them 2
19 do not engage in battle with the Gentiles 2
10:82 and engaged the phalanx in battle 2
2Mc 14:16 and engaged them in battle 1

engine 1. חִשָּׁבוֹן
2Ch 26:15 In Jerusalem he made engines 1

engine of war 1. μηχανή 2. μηχανὴ ὀργανικός
1Mc 5:30 carrying ladders and engines of war 1
6:20 he built siege towers and other engines of war. 1
31 many days they fought and built engines of war; 1
51 engines of war to throw fire and stones 1
52 The Jews also made engines of war to match theirs 1
11:20 he built many engines of war to use against it. 1
15:25 continually . . making engines of war 1
2Mc 12:15 without battering-rams or engines of war 2

siege engine 1. ἑλέπολις
1Mc 13:25 made a siege engine, brought it up to the city 1
44 The men in the siege engine leaped out into the city 1

war engine 1. ὄργανον
2Mc 12:27 great stores of war engines . . were there. 1

engrave 1. חרשׁ 2. פִּתּוּחַ 3. פתח 4. γλύμμα 5. γλυφή 6. κολάπτω
Exd 28: 9 two onyx stones, and engrave on them the names 3
11 As a jeweler engraves signets, so shall you 2
11 shall you engrave the two stones with the names 3
21 like signets, each engraved with its name 2
36 plate of pure gold, and engrave on it 3
36 engrave on it, like the engraving of a signet 2
39: 6 engraved like the engravings of a signet 3
6 engraved like the engravings of a signet 2
14 like signets, each engraved with its name 2
30 wrote upon it an inscription, like the engraving 2
2Ch 2: 7 trained also in engraving, to be 3
14 and to do all sorts of engraving and execute 2
Jer 17: 1 it is engraved on the tablet of their heart 1
Zec 3: 9 I will engrave its inscription, says the LORD 3
Wis 18:24 engraved on the four rows of stones 5
Sir 45:11 with precious stones engraved like signets 4
11 for a reminder, in engraved letters 6

engraving 1. נֶקֶב
Ezk 28:13 in gold were your settings and your engravings. 1

enhance 1. ἀποτελέω 2. αὔξησις 3. μεγάλης τινὸς κοινωνέω
2Mc 5:16 to enhance the glory and honor of the place. 2
15:39 enhances one's enjoyment 1
3Mc 2:31 they expected to enhance their reputation 3

enjoin 1. עוד 2. פקד 3. קום 4. קום עַל
Deu 32:46 all the words . . I enjoin upon you this day 1
Est 9:21 sent letters . . enjoining them that they should 4
31 as Mor'decai the Jew and Queen Esther enjoined 3
Zep 3: 7 lose sight of all that I have enjoined upon her 2
Zec 3: 6 the angel of the LORD enjoined Joshua 1
1Ti 4: 3 and enjoin abstinence from foods which God created •

enjoy 1. אכל 2. חלל 3. עשׂה טוֹב 4. ראה 5. ראה בְּטוֹב 6. רעה 7. רצה 8. שׂבע מִן 9. שׂמח 10. שׂמח בְּ 11. ἀπόλαυσις 12. ἀπολαύω 13. ἐντρυφάω 14. ἐπιδέχομαι 15. ἐσθίω 16. εὐδοκέω 17. εὐφραίνω 18. ἔχω 19. τυγχάνω 20. χράομαι 21. fruniscor
Lev 26:34 Then the land shall enjoy its sabbaths 7
34 then the land shall rest, and enjoy its sabbaths 7
43 land shall . . enjoy its sabbaths while it lies 7
Deu 20: 6 lest he die . . and another man enjoy its fruit. 2
14 enjoy the spoil of your enemies, which the LORD 1
2Ch 36:21 until the land had enjoyed its sabbaths. 7
Neh 9:36 fathers to enjoy its fruit and its good gifts 1
Job 14: 6 look away from him, and desist, that he may enjoy 7
Ps 34:12 covets many days, that he may enjoy good? 4
37: 3 you will dwell in the land, and enjoy security. 6
Prv 14: 9 scorns the wicked, but the upright enjoy his favor. •
Ecc 2: 1 I will make a test of pleasure; enjoy yourself. 5
21 leave all to be enjoyed by a man who did not toil •
3:12 be happy and enjoy themselves as long as they 3
22 a man should enjoy his work, for that is his lot; 10
5:19 wealth and possessions and power to enjoy them 1
6: 2 yet God does not give him power to enjoy them 1
2 power to enjoy them, but a stranger enjoys them; 1
3 but he does not enjoy life's good things 8
6 Even though he should live . . yet enjoy no good 4
8:15 to eat and drink, and enjoy himself 9
9: 9 Enjoy life with the wife whom you love 4
Jer 2: 7 into a plentiful land to enjoy its fruits 1
31: 5 planters shall plant, and shall enjoy the fruit. 2
Act 24: 2 Since through you we enjoy much peace 19
1Ti 6:17 richly furnishes us with everything to enjoy. 11
Heb 11:25 to enjoy the fleeting pleasures of sin. 18
1Es 1:58 Until the land has enjoyed its sabbaths 16
9:54 to eat and drink and enjoy themselves 17
2Es 7:96 they are to receive and enjoy in immortality. 21
AEs 16:11 far enjoyed the good will that we have 19
Wis 2: 6 let us enjoy the good things that exist 12
Sir 11:19 I have found rest, and now I shall enjoy my goods! 15
14: 5 He will not enjoy his own riches. 17
37:28 not every person enjoys everything. 16
41: 1 still has the vigor to enjoy his food! 14
2Mc 11:31 for the Jews to enjoy their own food and laws 20
4Mc 3:20 our fathers were enjoying profound peace 18
5: 9 It is senseless not to enjoy delicious things 12
8: 5 to yield to me and enjoy my friendship. 12
8 enjoy your youth 13
16:18 have had a share in the world and have enjoyed life 12

enjoy company 1. ἐμπίμπλημι 2. ὁμιλέω
Rom 15:24 once I have enjoyed your company for a little. 1
Jdt 12:12 let such a woman go without enjoying her company 2

enjoy fruit 1. חלל
Deu 20: 6 planted a vineyard and has not enjoyed its fruit? 1
6 lest he die . . and another man enjoy its fruit. 1

long enjoy 1. בלה
Isa 65:22 my chosen shall long enjoy the work of their 1

enjoy rest 1. requiesco
2Es 7:95 they understand the rest which they now enjoy 1

enjoyment 1. חושׁ 2. טוֹב 3. שִׂמְחָה 4. ἀπόλαυσις 5. εὐφροσύνη 6. μετουσία 7. χάρις
Ecc 2:24 eat and drink, and find enjoyment in his toil. 2
25 apart from him who . . or who can have enjoyment? 1
5:18 eat and drink and find enjoyment in all the toil 2
8:15 I commend enjoyment . . for this will go with him 3
9: 7 Go, eat your bread with enjoyment, and drink 3
Wis 2: 9 everywhere let us leave signs of enjoyment 5
2Mc 15:39 enhances one's enjoyment 7
3Mc 7:16 had received the full enjoyment of deliverance 4
4Mc 2: 1 for the enjoyment of beauty 6

enjoyment *See also* find, get.

enlarge 1. פתה 2. קרע 3. רבה 4. רחב 5. רחק 6. שׂמח 7. μεγαλύνω
Gen 9:27 God enlarge Japheth, and let him dwell 1
Exd 34:24 For I will . . enlarge your borders; 4
Deu 12:20 When the LORD your God enlarges your territory 4
19: 8 if the LORD your God enlarges your border 4
33:20 of Gad he said, "Blessed be he who enlarges Gad! 4
1Ch 4:10 saying, "Oh that thou wouldst . . enlarge my border 3
Job 12:23 he enlarges nations, and leads them away. 6
Ps 119:32 when thou enlargest my understanding! 4
Isa 5:14 Therefore Sheol has enlarged its appetite 4
26:15 thou hast enlarged all the borders of the land. 5
54: 2 Enlarge the place of your tent 4
Jer 4:30 that you enlarge your eyes with paint? 2
Ams 1:13 in Gilead, that they might enlarge their border. 4
2Co 10:15 our field among you may be greatly enlarged 7

enlargement 1. πρόσθεμα
Ezk 41: 7 corresponding to the enlargement of the offset 1

enlighten 1. אור 2. ἐπίγνωσις 3. φωτίζω 4. inlumino
Ps 19: 8 the LORD is pure, enlightening the eyes; 1
Joh 1: 9 The true light that enlightens every man 3
Rom 10: 2 a zeal for God, but it is not enlightened. 2
Eph 1:18 having the eyes of your hearts enlightened 3
Heb 6: 4 those who have once been enlightened 3
10:32 after you were enlightened 3
2Es 13:53 And you alone have been enlightened about this 4
Sir 45:17 to enlighten Israel with his law. 3

enlightenment 1. בין
Isa 40:14 Whom did he consult for his enlightenment 1

enlist 1. προσλαμβάνω 2. στρατολογέω
2Ti 2: 4 to satisfy the one who enlisted him. 2
2Mc 8: 1 enlisted those . . in the Jewish faith 1

enlist a mercenary 1. ξενολογέω
1Mc 4:35 he departed to Antioch and enlisted mercenaries 1

enmity 1. אֵיבָה 2. שׂנא 3. ἀπέχθεια 4. διαβολή 5. δυσμένεια 6. ἔχθρα 7. ἐχθραίνω 8. ἐχθρός
Gen 3:15 I will put enmity between you and the woman 1
Num 35:21 or in enmity struck him down with his hand 1
22 But if he stabbed him suddenly without enmity 1
Deu 4:42 without being at enmity with him in time past 2
19: 4 kills . . without having been at enmity with him 2
6 since he was not at enmity with his neighbor 2
Jos 20: 5 he killed . . unwittingly, having had no enmity 2
Ezk 25:15 to destroy in never-ending enmity; 1
35: 5 Because you cherished perpetual enmity 1
Lke 23:12 they had been at enmity with each other. 6
Gal 5:20 idolatry, sorcery, enmity, strife, jealousy, anger 6
Jas 4: 4 friendship with the world is enmity with God? 8
Sir 28: 6 cease from enmity 7
9 inject enmity among those who are at peace. 4
37: 2 when a companion and friend turns to enmity? 8
1Mc 11:12 their enmity became manifest. 8
2Mc 14:39 wishing to exhibit the enmity which he had 5
3Mc 4: 1 the inveterate enmity . . was now made evident 3
4Mc 2:14 reason . . can prevail even over enmity 8

enough 1. דַּי 2. הוֹן 3. כֹּל 4. מְעַט 5. מצא 6. עַד 7. רַב 8. שׂבע 9. שָׂבְעָה 10. ἀπέχω 11. ἀρκετός 12. ἀρκέω 13. αὐτάρκης 14. αὐτάρκεια 15. ἀφικνέομαι 16. ἐκποιέω 17. ἐπὶ τοσοῦτον 18. ἕως 19. ἕως τοῦ νῦν 20. ἱκανός 21. κορέννυμι 22. πίμπλημι 23. πολύς 24. τοσοῦτος
Gen 19:20 Behold, yonder city is near enough to flee to •
24:25 We have both straw and provender enough 7
33: 9 Esau said, "I have enough, my brother; 7
11 and because I have enough. 3
34:21 for behold, the land is large enough for them; •
45:28 Israel said, "It is enough; Joseph my son is still 7
Exd 9:28 there has been enough of this thunder and hail 7
36: 5 The people bring much more than enough for doing 1
Deu 1: 6 'You have stayed long enough at this mountain; •
2: 3 going about this mountain country long enough; •
Jos 17:16 The hill country is not enough for us; 5
22:17 Have we not had enough of the sin at Pe'or 4
Jdg 6:38 he wrung enough dew from the fleece to fill a bowl •
2Sm 8: 4 David . . left enough for 100 chariots. •
24:16 and said . . "It is enough; now stay your hand. 7
1Kg 12:28 You have gone up to Jerusalem long enough. 7
19: 4 It is enough; now, O LORD, take away my life; 7
1Ch 18: 4 but left enough for 100 chariots. •
21:15 he said to the destroying angel, "It is enough; 7
2Ch 31:10 we have eaten and had enough and have plenty left; 8
Job 27:14 his offspring have not enough to eat. 8
Ps 123: 3 for we have had more than enough of contempt. 8
Prv 13:25 righteous has enough to satisfy his appetite •

23: 4 not . . acquire wealth; be wise enough to desist. •
25:16 If you have found honey, eat only enough for you 1
27:27 there will be enough goats' milk for your food 1
30:15 never satisfied; four never say, "Enough 2
16 fire which never says, "Enough. 2
Isa 1:11 I have had enough of burnt offerings of rams 8
40:16 nor are its beasts enough for a burnt offering. 1
56:11 a mighty appetite; they never have enough. 9
Jer 49: 9 destroy only enough for themselves? 1
Ezk 34:18 Is it not enough for you to feed on the good 4
45: 9 Thus says the Lord GOD: Enough, O princes of Israel! 7
47: 5 the water had risen; it was deep enough to swim •
Obd 1: 5 would they not steal only enough for themselves? 1
Jon 4: 9 he said, "I do well to be angry, angry enough to die. 6
Nah 2:12 The lion tore enough for his whelps 1
Hab 2: 5 as wide as Sheol; like death he has never enough. 8
Hag 1: 6 you eat, but you never have enough; 9
Mat 10:25 it is enough for the disciple 11
15:33 Where are we to get bread enough in the desert 24
25: 9 Perhaps there will not be enough for us 12
Mrk 14:41 It is enough; the hour has come 10
Lke 14:28 whether he has enough to complete it? •
16: 3 I am not strong enough to dig •
22:38 he said to them, "It is enough. 20
Joh 6: 7 200 denarii would not buy enough bread 12
Act 27:38 when they had eaten enough 21
1Co 6: 5 there is no man among you wise enough to decide •
14:17 For you may give thanks well enough •
2Co 2: 6 this punishment by the majority is enough; 20
9: 8 so that you may always have enough of everything 13
Phm 1: 8 though I am bold enough in Christ to command you 23
1Es 8:88 Wast thou not angry enough with us 18
Tob 5:19 the life that is given to us by the Lord is enough 20
Jdt 7:21 did not have enough water to drink their fill •
Wis 14:22 Afterward it was not enough for them to err 12
18:25 merely to test the wrath was enough. 20
Sir 5: 1 nor say, "I have enough. 14
11:24 Do not say, "I have enough 14
39:11 if he goes to rest, it is enough for him. 16
42:25 who can have enough of beholding his glory? 22
43:30 you cannot praise him enough. 15
1Mc 2:33 they said to them, "Enough of this! 19
2Mc 7:42 Let this be enough 17

enough *See also* get, hot, kind, more, readily, ripe, strong, wide.

enough and to spare 1. περισσεύω

Lke 15:17 my father's hired servants have bread enough 1

enrage 1. זעם 2. כעס 3. מַר נֶפֶשׁ 4. מרר 5. קָצַף 6. קצף 7. קצף מְאֹד 8. רגז 9. διαπρίω 10. διοργίζω 11. ὀργίζω 12. πικρῶς φέρω 13. πλήρης θυμοῦ

2Sm 17: 8 his men are mighty men, and that they are enraged 3
Neh 4: 1 Sanbal'lat . . was angry and greatly enraged 2
Est 1:12 At this the king was enraged, and his anger burned 7
Isa 8:21 when they are hungry, they will be enraged 6
34: 2 For the LORD is enraged against all the nations 5
Jer 37:15 And the princes were enraged at Jeremiah 6
Ezk 16:43 but have enraged me with all these things; 8
Dan 8: 7 enraged against him and struck the ram 4
11:30 he shall . . be enraged and take action 1
Act 5:33 When they heard this they were enraged 9
19:28 When they heard this they were enraged 13
Bel 1:21 the king was enraged, and he seized the priests 11
1Mc 6:28 The king was enraged when he heard this 11
9:69 So he was greatly enraged at the lawless men 11
3Mc 3: 1 not only was he enraged against those Jews 10
4Mc 9:10 also was enraged, as at those who are ungrateful. 11
10: 5 Enraged by the man's boldness 12

enrich 1. דשן 2. עשר 3. πλουτέω 4. πλουτίζω

1Sm 17:25 the man who kills him, the king will enrich 2
Ps 65: 9 and waterest it, thou greatly enrichest it; 2
Prv 11:25 A liberal man will be enriched 1
28:25 but he who trusts in the LORD will be enriched. 1
Ezk 27:33 you enriched the kings of the earth. 2
1Co 1: 5 that in every way you were enriched in him 4
2Co 9:11 You will be enriched in every way for great generosity 4
Jdt 15: 6 plundered it, and were greatly enriched. 3
Sir 11:21 easy in the sight of the Lord to enrich a poor man 4

enrol 1. יחש 2. כתב 3. ἀναγράφω 4. ἀπὸ γραφῆς 5. ἀπογράφω 6. γράφω 7. ἐγγράφω 8. καταλέγω 9. προγράφω 10. συγκαταψηφίζομαι

2Ch 31:18 priests were enrolled with all their 1
19 to every one among the Levites who was enrolled. 1
Ps 69:28 let them not be enrolled among the righteous. 2
Ezk 13: 9 enrolled in the register of the house of Israel 2
Lke 2: 1 all the world should be enrolled. 5
3 all went to be enrolled, each to his own city. 5
5 to be enrolled with Mary, his betrothed 5
Act 1:26 he was enrolled with the eleven apostles. 10
1Ti 5: 9 Let a widow be enrolled 8
11 refuse to enrol younger widows •
Heb 12:23 who are enrolled in heaven 5
1Es 8:30 Zechariah, and with him 150 men enrolled. 4
1Mc 8:20 we may be enrolled as your allies and friends. 6
10:36 Let Jews be enrolled in the king's forces 9
65 and enrolled him among his chief friends 6
13:40 if any of you are qualified to be enrolled 6
40 let them be enrolled 7
2Mc 4: 9 to enrol the men of Jerusalem 3

enrol by genealogy 1. יחש

1Ch 5:17 All of these were enrolled by genealogies 1
7: 5 87,000 mighty warriors, enrolled by genealogy. 1
40 Their number enrolled by genealogies 1
9: 1 all Israel was enrolled by genealogies; 1
22 enrolled by genealogies in their villages. 1
2Ch 31:16 except those enrolled by genealogy 1
Neh 7: 5 assemble . . to be enrolled by genealogy. 1

enrol in the genealogy 1. יחש

1Ch 5: 1 so that he is not enrolled in the genealogy 1
Ezr 2:62 among those enrolled in the genealogies 1
Neh 7:64 among those enrolled in the genealogies 1

enrollment 1. יחש 2. ἀπογραφή

2Ch 31:17 The enrollment of the priests was according 1
Lke 2: 2 This was the first enrollment 2

enrollment by genealogy 1. יחש

1Ch 7: 7 their enrollment by genealogies was 22,034. 1
9 their enrollment by genealogies . . was 20,200 1

ensign 1. אוֹת 2. נֵס

Num 2: 2 with the ensigns of their fathers' houses; 1
Isa 11:10 the root of Jesse shall stand as an ensign 2
12 He will raise an ensign for the nations 2
62:10 lift up an ensign over the peoples. 2
Ezk 27: 7 from Egypt was your sail, serving as your ensign; 2

enslave 1. כבש 2. עבד 3. δουλεύω 4. δουλόω 5. ἐξουσιάζω 6. καταδουλόω 7. κατάχρεος 8. servio

Neh 5: 5 some of our daughters . . already been enslaved; 1
Jer 34: 9 so that no one should enslave a Jew, his brother. 2
10 so that they would not be enslaved again; 2
Ezk 34:27 from the hand of those who enslaved them. 2
Act 7: 6 who would enslave them and ill-treat them 4
Rom 6: 6 and we might no longer be enslaved to sin. 3
1Co 6:12 I will not be enslaved by anything. 5
2Pe 2:19 whatever overcomes a man, to that he is enslaved. 4
2Es 10:22 our young men have been enslaved 8
Wis 1: 4 nor dwell in a body enslaved to sin. 7
1Mc 8:10 enslaved them to this day. 6
11 they destroyed and enslaved 4
18 was completely enslaving Israel. 6
3Mc 2: 6 who had enslaved your holy people Israel. 6
4Mc 3: 2 a way for us not to be enslaved by desire. 4

ensnare 1. יקשׁ 2. לכד 3. מוֹקֵשׁ 4. נקשׁ 5. עוד 6. κατασοφίζω 7. προσπίπτω

Deu 7:25 not . . take it for yourselves, lest you be ensnared 1
12:30 take heed that you be not ensnared to follow them 4
Job 34:30 that he should not ensnare the people. 3
Ps 35: 8 let the net which they hid ensnare them; 2
119:61 Though the cords of the wicked ensnare me 5
Prv 5:22 The iniquities of the wicked ensnare him 2
12:13 man is ensnared by the transgression of his lips 3
29: 6 An evil man is ensnared in his transgression 3
Jdt 10:19 they will be able to ensnare the whole world! 6
Sir 25:21 Do not be ensnared by a woman's beauty 7

entangle 1. בוך 2. לקח 3. סבב 4. סבך 5. ἐμπλέκω 6. παγιδεύω

Exd 14: 3 They are entangled in the land; 1
2Sm 22: 6 the cords of Sheol entangled me 3
Ps 18: 5 the cords of Sheol entangled me 3
Prv 22:25 learn his ways and entangle yourself in a snare. 2
Nah 1:10 Like entangled thorns they are consumed 4
Mat 22:15 and took counsel how to entangle him in his talk. 6
2Pe 2:20 again entangled in them and overpowered 5

entangled *See* get.

become entangled 1. ἐνέχω

3Mc 6:10 our lives have become entangled in impieties 1

enter 1. בוא 2. בוא אֶל 3. בוא בְּ 4. בוא בְּתוֹךְ 5. בוא לְ 6. לקח 7. מָבוֹא 8. עבר 9. עלה 10. עמד 11. γινώσκω 12. εἰσβάλλω 13. εἰσέρχομαι 14. εἴσειμι 15. εἴσοδος 16. εἰσπορεύομαι 17. ἔρχομαι 18. ἔρχομαι εἰς 19. παραγίνομαι 20. παρεισπορεύομαι 21. συνεισέρχομαι 22. ὑπέρχομαι 23. ingredior 24. introeo 25. venio

Gen 7:13 three wives of his sons with them entered the ark 1
16 they that entered, male and female of all flesh 1
12:11 When he was about to enter Egypt, he said to Sar'ai 1
14 When Abram entered Egypt the Egyptians saw that 1
19: 3 they turned aside to him and entered his house; 1
31:33 went out of Leah's tent, and entered Rachel's. 1
41:46 Joseph . . entered the service of Pharaoh 10
43:30 And he entered his chamber and wept there. 1
Exd 12:23 destroyer to enter your houses to slay you. 1
24:18 Moses entered the cloud, and went up 1
33: 9 When Moses entered the tent, the pillar of cloud 1
40:35 Moses was not able to enter the tent of meeting 1
Lev 14:46 he who enters the house while it is shut up 1
16:17 he enters to make atonement in the holy place 1
Num 4: 3 all who can enter the service, to do the work 1
23 number them, all who can enter for service 1
30 number them, every one that can enter the service 1
35 every one that could enter the service, for work 1
39 every one that could enter the service for work 1
43 every one that could enter the service, for work 1
47 every one that could enter to do the work 1
5:24 water that brings the curse shall enter into her 1
27 water that brings the curse shall enter into her 1
20:24 Aaron . . shall not enter the land which I have 1
34: 2 When you enter the land of Canaan (this is the land 1
Deu 1:38 Joshua . . who stands before you, he shall enter; 1
4: 5 land . . you are entering to take possession of it. 1
21 swore . . that I should not enter the good land 1
7: 1 land which you are entering to take possession 1
11:10 land which you are entering to take possession 1
29 land which you are entering to take possession 1
23: 1 shall not enter the assembly of the LORD. 1
2 No bastard shall enter the assembly of the LORD; 1
2 none . . shall enter the assembly of the LORD. 1
3 No Ammonite . . shall enter the assembly of the LORD; 1
3 none . . shall enter the assembly of the LORD 1
8 born to them may enter the assembly of the LORD. 1
20 land which you are entering to take possession 1
27: 3 pass over to enter the land which the LORD 1
28:21 land which you are entering to take possession 1
63 land which you are entering to take possession 1
29:12 enter . . the sworn covenant of the LORD your God 8
30:16 land which you are entering to take possession 1
18 land . . going over the Jordan to enter and possess. 1
Jos 2: 3 men that have come to you, who entered your house; 5
8:19 they ran and entered the city and took it; 1
10:19 pursue . . do not let them enter their cities; 2
20 remnant . . entered into the fortified cities 1
Jdg 9:46 they entered the stronghold of the house 1
11:18 but they did not enter the territory of Moab 1
18: 9 be slow to go, and enter in and possess the land. 1
17 five men . . went up, and entered and took 1
19:29 when he entered his house, he took a knife 1
1Sm 5: 5 priests . . and all who enter the house of Dagon 1
7:13 and did not again enter the territory of Israel. 1
9:13 As soon as you enter the city, you will find him 1
14 As they were entering the city, they saw Samuel 4
14:26 And when the people entered the forest, behold 1
23: 7 shut himself in by entering a town that has gates 3
2Sm 10:14 they likewise fled . . and entered the city. 1
15:37 just as Ab'salom was entering Jerusalem. 1
17:17 for they must not be seen entering the city. 1
1Kg 11: 2 You shall not enter into marriage with them 1
14:12 When your feet enter the city, the child 1
20:30 Ben-ha'dad also fled, and entered an inner chamber 1
2Kg 6:20 As soon as they entered Sama'ria Eli'sha said 1
7: 4 If we say, 'Let us enter the city,' . . we shall die 1
8 then they came back, and entered another tent 1
9:31 as Jehu entered the gate, she said, "Is it peace 1
10:21 And they entered the house of Ba'al 1
12: 9 right side as one entered the house of the LORD; 1
19:23 I entered its farthest retreat, its densest 1
1Ch 19:15 the Ammonites . . fled . . and entered the city. 1
27:24 was not entered in the chronicles of King David. 9
2Ch 7: 2 the priests could not enter the house of the LORD 1
15:12 they entered into a covenant to seek the LORD 1
23: 1 Jehoi'ada . . entered into a compact 6
6 Let no one enter the house of the LORD 1
6 priests and ministering Levites; they may enter 1
7 whoever enters the house shall be slain. 1
19 no one should enter who was in any way unclean. 1
26:16 entered the temple of the LORD to burn incense 1
31:16 all who entered the house of the LORD as the duty 1
Ezr 9:11 land which you are entering, to take possession 1
Neh 2:15 I turned back and entered by the Valley Gate 1
9:23 told their fathers to enter and possess. 1
10:29 join . . enter into a curse and an oath to walk 1
13: 1 no Ammonite . . ever enter the assembly of God; 1
Est 4: 2 no one might enter the king's gate clothed 2
6: 4 Haman had just entered the outer court 5
Job 22: 4 reproves you, and enters into judgment with you? 1
38:16 Have you entered into the springs of the sea 1
22 Have you entered the storehouses of the snow 1
Ps 5: 7 I through . . steadfast love will enter thy house 1
37:15 their sword shall enter their own heart 1
45:15 led along as they enter the palace of the king. 1
95:11 swore in my anger that they . . not enter my rest. 1
100: 4 Enter his gates with thanksgiving, and his courts 1
118:19 enter through them and give thanks to the LORD. 1
20 righteous shall enter through it. 1
26 Blessed be he who enters in the name of the LORD! 1
132: 3 I will not enter my house or get into my bed; 1
143: 2 Enter not into judgment with thy servant; 1
Prv 4:14 Do not enter the path of the wicked 1
23:10 Do not . . enter the fields of the fatherless; 1
Isa 2:10 Enter into the rock, and hide in the dust 1
19 men shall enter the caves of the rocks 1
21 to enter the caverns of the rocks and the clefts 1
3:14 The LORD enters into judgment with the elders 1
13: 2 wave . . for them to enter the gates of the nobles. 1
24:10 every house is shut up so that none can enter. 1

26: 2 nation which keeps faith may enter in. 1
20 Come, my people, enter your chambers 1
59:14 for truth . . and uprightness cannot enter. 1
Jer 4:29 every city takes to flight; they enter thickets; 1
7: 2 all you men of Judah who enter these gates 1
9:21 into our windows, it has entered our palaces 1
14:18 if I enter the city, behold, the diseases of famine! 1
16: 5 says the LORD: Do not enter the house of mourning 1
17:19 Benjamin Gate, by which the kings of Judah enter 1
20 of Jerusalem, who enter by these gates. 1
25 then there shall enter by the gates of this city 1
27 and enter by the gates of Jerusalem 1
21:13 or who shall enter our habitations? 1
22: 2 and your people who enter these gates. 1
4 then there shall enter the gates of this house 1
32:23 they entered and took possession of it. 1
35 did not command them, nor did it enter into my mind 9
34:10 the people who had entered into the covenant 1
42:15 If you set your faces to enter Egypt 1
52:12 Nebu'zarad'an . . entered Jerusalem. 1
Lam 1:10 thou didst forbid to enter thy congregation. 1
4:12 foe or enemy could enter the gates of Jerusalem. 1
Ezk 2: 2 when he spoke to me, the Spirit entered into me 1
3:24 the Spirit entered into me, and set me upon my feet; 1
7:22 robbers shall enter and profane it 1
13: 9 nor shall they enter the land of Israel; 1
16: 8 and entered into a covenant with you 1
20:38 but they shall not enter the land of Israel. 1
26:10 when he enters your gates as one enters a city 1
10 as one enters a city which has been breached. 7
42: 9 as one enters them from the outer court 1
12 on the east side, where one enters the passage 1
14 When the priests enter the holy place 1
43: 4 glory of the LORD entered the temple by the gate 1
44: 2 it shall not be opened, and no one shall enter by it; 1
2 for the LORD, the God of Israel, has entered by it; 1
3 he shall enter by way of the vestibule of the gate 1
9 No foreigner . . shall enter my sanctuary. 1
16 they shall enter my sanctuary 1
17 they enter the gates of the inner court, 1
21 shall drink wine, when he enters the inner court. 1
46: 2 prince shall enter by the vestibule of the gate 1
8 When the prince enters, he shall go 1
9 he who enters by the north gate to worship 1
9 he who enters by the south gate 1
9 return by way of the gate by which he entered 1
47: 8 when it enters the stagnant waters of the sea 1
Dan 10: 3 no delicacies, no meat or wine entered my mouth 1
11: 7 enter the fortress of the king of the north 1
Jol 2: 9 they enter through the windows like a thief. 1
Ams 5: 5 do not seek Bethel, and do not enter into Gilgal 1
Obd 1:11 and foreigners entered his gates 1
13 You should not have entered the gate of my people 1
Hab 3:16 rottenness enters into my bones, my steps totter 1
Zec 5: 4 it shall enter the house of the thief 1
Mat 5:20 Pharisees, you will never enter the kingdom 13
7:13 Enter by the narrow gate; for the gate is wide 13
13 and those who enter by it are many. 13
21 Not every one who says to me, 'Lord, Lord,' shall enter 13
8: 5 As he entered Caper'na-um, a centurion came 13
14 when Jesus entered Peter's house 18
9:28 When he entered the house, the blind men came 18
10: 5 and enter no town of the Samaritans 13
11 whatever town or village you enter 13
12 As you enter the house, salute it. 13
12: 4 how he entered the house of God and ate the bread 13
9 and entered their synagogue. 18
29 Or how can one enter a strong man's house 13
45 and they enter and dwell there 13
18: 3 you will never enter the kingdom of heaven. 13
8 it is better for you to enter life maimed or lame 13
9 it is better for you to enter life with one eye 13
19: 1 entered the region of Judea beyond the Jordan; 18
17 If you would enter life, keep the commandments. 13
23 to enter the kingdom of heaven. 13
24 than for a rich man to enter the kingdom of God. 13
21:10 when he entered Jerusalem 13
12 Jesus entered the temple of God 13
23 when he entered the temple 18
23:13 you neither enter yourselves 13
13 nor allow those who would enter to go in. 13
24:38 until the day when Noah entered the ark 13
25:21 enter into the joy of your master.' 13
23 enter into the joy of your master.' 13
26:41 that you may not enter into temptation 13
Mrk 1:21 he entered the synagogue and taught. 13
29 entered the house of Simon and Andrew 18
45 so that Jesus could no longer openly enter a town 13
2:26 how he entered the house of God 13
3: 1 Again he entered the synagogue 13
27 no one can enter a strong man's house 13
4:19 enter in and choke the word 16
5:12 Send us to the swine, let us enter them. 13
13 unclean spirits came out, and entered the swine; 13
39 when he had entered, he said to them 13
6:10 he said to them, "Where you enter a house, stay there 13
7:17 when he had entered the house, and left the people 13
19 since it enters, not his heart but his stomach 16
24 he entered a house, and would not have any one know 13
8:26 Do not even enter the village. 13
9:25 come out of him, and never enter him again. 13
28 when he had entered the house 13
43 it is better for you to enter life maimed 13
45 it is better for you to enter life lame 13
46 to enter the kingdom of God with one eye 13
10:15 shall not enter it. 13
23 to enter the kingdom of God! 13
24 how hard it is to enter the kingdom of God! 13
25 than for a rich man to enter the kingdom of God. 13
11: 2 immediately as you enter it you will find a colt 16
11 he entered Jerusalem, and went into the temple; 13
15 he entered the temple 13
13:15 let him . . not go down, nor enter his house 13
14:14 wherever he enters, say to the householder 13
38 pray that you may not enter into temptation 17
16: 5 And entering the tomb, they saw a young man 13
Lke 1: 9 it fell to him by lot to enter the temple 13
40 she entered the house of Zechari'ah 13
4:38 left the synagogue, and entered Simon's house. 13
6: 4 how he entered the house of God 13
6 when he entered the synagogue and taught 13
7: 1 he entered Caper'na-um. 13
44 I entered your house 13
8:16 that those who enter may see the light. 16
30 he said, "Legion"; for many demons had entered him. 13
32 they begged him to let them enter these 13
33 the demons . . entered the swine 13
51 he permitted no one to enter with him 13
9: 4 whatever house you enter, stay there 13
34 they were afraid as they entered the cloud. 13
52 who went and entered a village of the Samaritans 13
10: 5 Whatever house you enter, first say, 'Peace 13
8 Whenever you enter a town and they receive you 13
10 whenever you enter a town 13
38 Now as they went on their way, he entered a village; 13
11:26 they enter and dwell there 13
33 those who enter may see the light. 16
52 you did not enter yourselves 13
52 you hindered those who were entering. 13
13:24 Strive to enter by the narrow door 13
24 many . . will seek to enter and will not be able. 13
17:12 as he entered a village, he was met by ten lepers 13
27 until the day when Noah entered the ark 13
18:17 shall not enter it. 13
24 How hard it is . . to enter the kingdom of God! 16
25 for a rich man to enter the kingdom of God. 13
19: 1 He entered Jericho and was passing through. 13
30 where on entering you will find a colt tied 16
45 he entered the temple 13
21:21 let not those who are out in the country enter it; 13
22: 3 Then Satan entered into Judas called Iscariot 13
10 when you have entered the city 13
10 follow him into the house which he enters 16
40 Pray that you may not enter into temptation. 13
46 pray that you may not enter into temptation. 13
24:26 suffer these things and enter into his glory? 13
Joh 3: 4 Can he enter a second time into his mother's womb 13
5 he cannot enter the kingdom of God. 13
6:22 Jesus had not entered the boat with his disciples 21
10: 1 he who does not enter the sheepfold by the door 13
2 he who enters by the door 13
9 if any one enters by me, he will be saved 13
13:27 after the morsel, Satan entered into him 13
18: 1 a garden, which he and his disciples entered. 13
28 They themselves did not enter the praetorium 13
33 Pilate entered the praetorium again 13
19: 9 he entered the praetorium again and said 13
Act 1:13 when they had entered 13
3: 2 to ask alms of those who entered the temple. 16
8 stood and walked and entered the temple 13
5:21 they entered the temple at daybreak and taught 13
8: 3 and entering house after house 16
9: 6 rise and enter the city 13
17 So Anani'as departed and entered the house. 13
10:24 on the following day they entered Caesare'a. 13
25 When Peter entered, Cornelius met him 13
11: 8 nothing . . unclean has ever entered my mouth.' 13
12 we entered the man's house. 13
14: 1 entered together into the Jewish synagogue 13
20 he rose up and entered the city 13
22 saying that . . we must enter the kingdom of God. 13
19: 8 he entered the synagogue 13
21: 8 we entered the house of Philip the evangelist 13
23:16 he went and entered the barracks and told Paul. 13
25:23 and they entered the audience hall 13
1Co 14:23 outsiders or unbelievers enter 13
24 an unbeliever or outsider enters 13
Heb 3:11 'They shall never enter my rest.' 13
18 swear that they should never enter his rest 13
19 they were unable to enter because of unbelief. 13
4: 1 while the promise of entering his rest remains 13
3 For we who have believed enter that rest 13
3 They shall never enter my rest 13
5 They shall never enter my rest. 13
6 Since therefore it remains for some to enter it 13
6 failed to enter because of disobedience 13
10 whoever enters God's rest 13
11 Let us therefore strive to enter that rest 13
6:19 a hope that enters into the inner shrine 13
9:12 he entered once for all into the Holy Place 13
24 For Christ has entered 13
25 as the high priest enters the Holy Place yearly 13
10:19 we have confidence to enter the sanctuary 15
Rev 11:11 a breath of life from God entered them 13
15: 8 and no one could enter the temple 13
21:27 But nothing unclean shall enter it 13
22:14 that they may enter the city by the gates. 13
1Es 6: 8 when we . . entered the city of Jerusalem 18
8:83 'The land which you are entering 13
2Es 7:80 such spirits shall not enter into habitations 23
123 paradise shall be revealed . . but we shall not enter 23
10: 1 when my son entered his wedding chamber 24
48 When my son entered his wedding chamber he died,' 25
Tob 3:17 Tobit returned and entered his house 13
4:10 keeps you from entering the darkness; 13
5: 9 he entered and they greeted each other. 13
6:16 When you enter the bridal chamber 13
12:15 enter into the presence of . . of the Holy One. 16
Wis 1: 4 because wisdom will not enter a deceitful soul 13
2:24 through the devil's envy death entered the world 13
3:13 who has not entered into a sinful union 11
8:16 When I enter my house, I shall find rest with her 13
20 rather, being good, I entered an undefiled body. 18
10:16 She entered the soul of a servant of the Lord 13
14:14 through the vanity of men they entered the world 13
Sir 4:13 the Lord will bless the place she enters. 16
Bar 3:15 her place? And who has entered her storehouses? 13
LJr 1:17 the dust raised by the feet of those who enter. 16
Bel 1:21 through which they were accustomed to enter 16
1Mc 1:21 He arrogantly entered the sanctuary 13
4: 5 When Gorgias entered the camp of Judas by night 18
5:42 but make them all enter the battle. 18
6:62 when the king entered Mount Zion 13
7: 2 he was entering the royal palace of his fathers 16
8:19 they entered the senate chamber and spoke as follows 13
10:83 They fled to Azotus and entered Beth-dagon 13
11: 3 when Ptolemy entered the cities 16
13 Then Ptolemy entered Antioch 13
12: 3 they went to Rome and entered the senate chamber 13
48 when Jonathan entered Ptolemais 13
48 all who had entered with him 21
13:47 then entered it with hymns and praise. 13
51 the Jews entered it with praise and palm branches 13
15:14 and permitted no one to leave or enter it. 16
2Mc 1:15 they closed the temple as soon as he entered it. 13
3:28 this man who had just entered the . . treasury 13
5:15 Antiochus dared to enter the most holy temple 13
8: 1 secretly entered the villages 20
9: 2 For he had entered the city called Persepolis 13
13:13 before the king's army could enter Judea 12
3Mc 1: 9 Then, upon entering the place 19
10 and conceived a desire to enter the holy of holies. 13
11 were allowed to enter 14
12 did not cease to maintain that he ought to enter 13
13 when he entered every other temple 13
15 why should not I at least enter 13
2:28 shall enter their sanctuaries 14
3:17 we proposed to enter their inner temple 13
18 excluded us from entering 15
4: 6 who had just entered the bridal chamber 22
5:46 entered at about dawn into the courtyard 13

enter *See also* try.

enter along 1. *συνεισέρχομαι*

Joh 18:15 he entered the court . . along with Jesus 1

cause to enter 1. בוא

Ezk 37: 5 Behold, I will cause breath to enter you 1

forcibly enter 1. *ἐπέρχομαι*

1Es 4:49 should forcibly enter their doors; 1

enter into 1. בוא 2. *εἰσέρχομαι*

Isa 57: 2 he enters into peace; they rest in their beds 1
Hos 4:15 Enter not into Gilgal, nor go up to Beth-a'ven 1
Joh 4:38 and you have entered into their labor. 2

enter into judgment 1. שפט

Jer 25:31 he is entering into judgment with all flesh 1
Ezk 17:20 to Babylon and enter into judgment with him 1
20:35 I will enter into judgment with you face to face. 1
36 As I entered into judgment with your fathers 1
36 I will enter into judgment with you, says the Lord 1
38:22 With . . bloodshed I will enter into judgment 1
Jol 3: 2 I will enter into judgment with them there 1

enter into partnership 1. *κοινωνέω*

Php 4:15 no church entered into partnership with me 1

enter service 1. הָיָה לִפְנֵי 2. עָמַד לִפְנֵי

1Sm 16:21 And David came to Saul, and entered his service. 2
29: 8 from the day I entered your service until now 1

enter suit 1. קרא

Isa 59: 4 No one enters suit justly, 1

enter the competition 1. ἐναθλέω
4Mc 17:13 the mother . . entered the competition 1

enter upon 1. εἰσκυκλέω 2. ἐπιβαίνω
Sir 51:15 my foot entered upon the straight path 2
2Mc 2:24 who wish to enter upon the narratives of history 1

enter violently 1. βιάζω
Lke 16:16 every one enters it violently 1

entertain 1. ξενίζω
Act 28: 7 who received us and entertained us hospitably 1
Heb 13: 2 thereby some have entertained angels unawares. 1

entertainment 1. ἀκρόαμα
Sir 32: 4 Where there is entertainment 1

enthrone 1. יָשַׁב 2. ἐνθρονίζομαι 3. κάθημαι
1Sm 4: 4 LORD of hosts, who is enthroned on the cherubim; 1
2Kg 19:15 O LORD . . who art enthroned above the cherubim 1
1Ch 13: 6 the LORD who sits enthroned above the cherubim. •
Ps 22: 3 art holy, enthroned on the praises of Israel. 1
55:19 humble them, he who is enthroned from of old; 1
61: 7 May he be enthroned for ever before God; 1
102:12 But thou, O LORD, art enthroned for ever; 1
123: 1 O thou who art enthroned in the heavens! 1
Isa 37:16 O LORD . . who art enthroned above the cherubim 1
Bar 3: 3 For thou art enthroned for ever, and we are 3
4Mc 2:22 he enthroned the mind among the senses 2

enthrone upon 1. יָשַׁב
Ps 80: 1 who art enthroned upon the cherubim, shine forth 1

enthroned *See* sit.

entice 1. סוּת 2. פָּתָה 3. ἀπάτησις 4. δελεάζω
Deu 13: 6 entices you secretly, saying, 'Let us go and serve 1
Jdg 14:15 Entice your husband to tell us what the riddle is 2
16: 5 Entice him, and see wherein his great strength 2
1Kg 22:20 'Who will entice Ahab, that he may go up and fall 2
21 spirit came forward . . saying, 'I will entice him.' 2
22 You are to entice him, and you shall succeed; 2
2Ch 18:19 LORD said, 'Who will entice Ahab the king of Israel 2
20 saying, 'I(a spirit) will entice him.' 2
21 said, 'You are to entice him, and you shall succeed; 2
Job 31: 9 If my heart has been enticed to a woman 2
27 my heart has been secretly enticed 2
36:18 Beware lest wrath entice you into scoffing; 1
Prv 1:10 My son, if sinners entice you, do not consent. 2
16:29 A man of violence entices his neighbor 2
Jas 1:14 when he is lured and enticed by his own desire. 4
2Pe 2:14 They entice unsteady souls. 4
18 entice with licentious passions of the flesh 4
Jdt 10: 4 to entice the eyes of all men who might see her. 3

entire 1. כָּל 2. תָּמִים 3. πᾶς
Lev 3: 9 he shall offer its fat, the fat tail entire 2
Deu 2:14 entire generation, that is, the men of war 1
1Kg 7: 1 Solomon . . and he finished his entire house. 1
2Kg 6:24 Ben-ha'dad king of Syria mustered his entire army 1
Jer 36:23 until the entire scroll was consumed in the fire 1
Tit 2:10 nor to pilfer, but to show entire and true fidelity 3
Tob 1:21 over the entire administration. 3
1Mc 3:40 so they departed with their entire force 3
3Mc 4:14 The entire race was to be registered 3

entire tribe 1. ἐθνηδόν
4Mc 2:19 their irrational slaughter of the entire tribe 1

entirely 1. κομιδῇ 2. πάντως
1Co 9:10 Does he not speak entirely for our sake? 2
4Mc 3: 1 This notion is entirely ridiculous 1

entitle 1. ἐπιβάλλω 2. καθήκω
Tob 3:17 because Tobias was entitled to possess her. 1
6:11 you are entitled to her and to her inheritance 1
12 because you . . are entitled to the inheritance. 2

entrails 1. כָּבֵד 2. קֶרֶב 3. ἔντερον 4. κοιλία
5. σπλάγχνον
Exd 29:13 shall take all the fat that covers the entrails 2
17 and wash its entrails and its legs, and put them 2
22 take . . the fat that covers the entrails 2
Lev 1: 9 its entrails and its legs he shall wash with water 2
13 the entrails and the legs he shall wash with water 2
3: 3 he shall offer the fat covering the entrails 2
3 offer . . all the fat that is on the entrails 2
9 the fat that covers the entrails, and all the fat 2
9 and all the fat that is on the entrails 2
14 shall offer . . the fat covering the entrails 2
14 offer . . all the fat that is on the entrails 2
4: 8 the fat that covers the entrails and all the fat 2
8 all the fat that is on the entrails 2
11 the bull . . with its head, its legs, its entrails 2
7: 3 the fat tail, the fat that covers the entrails 2
8:16 he took all the fat that was on the entrails 2
21 when the entrails and the legs were washed 2
25 he took . . all the fat that was on the entrails 2
9:14 he washed the entrails and the legs, and burned 2
19 that which covers the entrails, and the kidneys 4
Prv 7:23 till an arrow pierces its entrails; 1
2Mc 14:46 he tore out his entrails, took them with both hands 3
4Mc 5:30 gouge out my eyes and burn my entrails. 5
10: 8 drops of blood flowing from his entrails. 5
11:19 his entrails were burned through. 5

entrance 1. אִיתוֹן 2. בִּאָה 3. בּוֹא 4. בּוֹאֲכָה
5. דֶּרֶךְ מָבוֹא 6. לָבוֹא 7. לִפְנֵי 8. מָבוֹא 9. מוֹבָא
10. פֶּתַח 11. εἴσοδος 12. θύρα 13. introitus
Gen 38:14 she . . sat at the entrance to Enaim, which is 10
Num 4:26 screen for the entrance of the gate of the court 10
10: 3 at the entrance of the tent of meeting. 10
13:21 Zin to Rehob, near the entrance of Hamath. 6
16:18 they stood at the entrance of the tent of meeting 10
19 at the entrance of the tent of meeting. 10
50 to Moses at the entrance of the tent of meeting 10
34: 8 from Mount Hor . . to the entrance of Hamath 3
Jos 8:29 and cast it at the entrance of the gate of the city 10
13: 5 from Ba'al-gad . . to the entrance of Hamath 3
20: 4 stand at the entrance of the gate of the city 10
Jdg 3: 3 Ba'al-her'mon as far as the entrance of Hamath. 3
9:35 Ga'al . . stood in the entrance of the gate 10
40 many fell wounded, up to the entrance of the gate. 10
44 rushed forward and stood at the entrance 10
18:16 of war, stood by the entrance of the gate; 10
17 the priest stood by the entrance of the gate 10
1Sm 2:22 the women who served at the entrance to the tent 10
2Sm 10: 8 drew up in battle . . at the entrance of the gate; 10
11:23 but we drove them back to the entrance of the gate. 10
1Kg 6: 8 The entrance for the lowest story was 10
31 For the entrance to the inner sanctuary he made 10
33 he made for the entrance to the nave doorposts 10
8:65 from the entrance of Hamath to the Brook of Egypt 3
18:46 and ran before Ahab to the entrance of Jezreel. 4
19:13 went out and stood at the entrance of the cave. 10
22:10 the threshing floor at the entrance of the gate 10
2Kg 7: 3 there were . . lepers at the entrance to the gate; 10
10: 8 Lay them in two heaps at the entrance of the gate 10
11:16 she went through the horses' entrance 5
14:25 from the entrance of Hamath as far as the Sea 3
16:18 and the outer entrance for the king he removed 8
23: 8 that were at the entrance of the gate of Joshua 10
11 horses . . at the entrance to the house of the LORD 3
1Ch 4:39 They journeyed to the entrance of Gedor 8
5: 9 to the east as far as the entrance of the desert 3
9:19 keepers of the entrance. 8
21 at the entrance of the tent of meeting. 10
13: 5 from the Shihor of Egypt to the entrance of Hamath 6
19: 9 in battle array at the entrance of the city 10
2Ch 7: 8 the entrance of Hamath to the Brook of Egypt. 3
18: 9 threshing floor at the entrance of the gate 10
23:13 the king standing by his pillar at the entrance 8
15 she went into the entrance of the horse gate 8
33:14 wall . . for the entrance into the Fish Gate 3
Est 4: 2 he went up to the entrance of the king's gate 7
5: 1 king was . . opposite the entrance to the palace; 10
Ps 74: 5 At the upper entrance they hacked the wooden •
Prv 1:21 at the entrance of the city gates she speaks 10
8: 3 at the entrance of the portals she cries aloud 8
Jer 1:15 set his throne at the entrance of the gates 10
38:14 received him at the third entrance of the temple 8
43: 9 which is at the entrance to Pharaoh's palace 10
Ezk 8: 3 to the entrance of the gateway of the inner court 10
5 in the entrance, was this image of jealousy. 2
14 he brought me to the entrance of the north gate 10
27: 3 say to Tyre, who dwells at the entrance to the sea 8
40:15 From the front of the gate at the entrance 1
40 the vestibule at the entrance of the north gate 10
41: 2 And the breadth of the entrance was ten cubits; 10
2 the sidewalls of the entrance were five cubits 10
3 and measured the jambs of the entrance 10
3 and the breadth of the entrance, six cubits; 10
3 and the sidewalls of the entrance, seven cubits. 10
42: 9 Below these chambers was an entrance on the east 8
12 below the south chambers was an entrance 8
43:11 its arrangement, its exits and its entrances, 9
46: 3 people of the land shall worship at the entrance 10
19 Then he brought me through the entrance 8
47:15 by way of Hethlon to the entrance of Hamath 3
20 to a point opposite the entrance of Hamath. 3
48: 1 to the entrance of Hamath, as far as Hazar-e'non 3
Ams 6:14 from the entrance of Hamath to the Brook 3
2Pe 1:11 an entrance into the eternal kingdom of our Lord 11
2Es 4: 7 or which are the entrances of paradise?' ‡
7: 4 it has an entrance set in a narrow place 13
7 the entrance to it is narrow 13
12 so the entrances of this world were made narrow 13
13 the entrances of the greater world are broad 13
Wis 7: 6 there is for all mankind one entrance into life 11
Bel 1:13 they had made a hidden entrance 11
2Mc 2: 5 he sealed up the entrance. 12

entrance *See also* gain.

entrap in talk 1. ἀγρεύω
Mrk 12:13 to entrap him in his talk. 1

entreat 1. בִּקֵּשׁ מִלִּפְנֵי 2. חלה 3. חנן 4. עתר 5. פגע
6. פגע בְּ 7. δέω 8. ἱκετεύω 9. παραιτέομαι
10. παρακαλέω 11. deprecor 12. rogo
Gen 23: 8 and entreat for me Ephron the son of Zohar 5
Exd 8: 8 Pharaoh . . said, "Entreat the LORD to take away 4
9 Be pleased to command me when I am to entreat 4
9:28 Entreat the LORD; for there has been enough 4
10:17 entreat the LORD your God only to remove this 4
18 he went out from Pharaoh, and entreated the LORD. 4
Jdg 13: 8 Then Mano'ah entreated the LORD, and said, 4
Rut 1:16 Ruth said, "Entreat me not to leave you or to return 6
1Sm 13:12 and I have not entreated the favor of the LORD'; 2
1Kg 13: 6 the man of God entreated the LORD; 2
2Kg 1:13 and fell on his knees . . and entreated him 3
2Ch 33:12 he entreated the favor of the LORD his God 2
Est 4: 8 to make supplication to him and entreat him 1
Job 11:19 many will entreat your favor. 2
Ps 119:58 I entreat thy favor with all my heart; 2
Jer 15:11 So let it be, O LORD, if I have not entreated thee •
Dan 9:13 yet we have not entreated the favor of the LORD 2
Zec 7: 2 their men, to entreat the favor of the LORD 2
8:21 Let us go at once to entreat the favor of the LORD 2
22 to entreat the favor of the LORD. 2
Mal 1: 9 now entreat the favor of God 2
Lke 15:28 His father came out and entreated him 10
Act 9:38 the disciples . . sent two men to him entreating 10
2Co 6: 1 entreat you not to accept the grace of God 10
10: 1 I, Paul, myself entreat you 10
Php 4: 2 I entreat Eu-o'dia and I entreat Syn'tyche to agree 10
2 I entreat Eu-o'dia and I entreat Syn'tyche to agree 10
Heb 12:19 a voice whose words made the hearers entreat 9
2Es 1:28 Have I not entreated you as a father 12
28 as a father entreats his sons •
7:102or to entreat the Most High for them 11
10:37 Now therefore I entreat you to give your servant 11
Wis 13:18 for aid he entreats 8
Bar 2: 8 Yet we have not entreated the favor of the Lord 7
3Mc 1:16 entreated the supreme God 7
6:14 their parents entreat you with tears. 8

entreat favor 1. חלה 2. חלה פָּנִים
1Kg 13: 6 Entreat now the favor of the LORD your God 1
Jer 26:19 fear the LORD and entreat the favor of the LORD 2

entreaty 1. תַּחֲנוּן 2. δέησις 3. λιτανεία
Ezr 8:23 listened to our entreaty. •
Prv 18:23 poor use entreaties . . rich answer roughly. 1
1Mc 11:49 they cried out to the king with this entreaty 2
2Mc 3:20 they all made entreaty. 3
3Mc 5: 9 their entreaty ascended fervently to heaven. 3

entreaty *See also* grant, make, receive.

entrust 1. אמן 2. נתן 3. ἐμπιστεύω 4. παραδίδωμι
5. παραθήκη 6. παρακατατίθημι 7. παρατίθημι
8. πιστεύω 9. τίθημι 10. commendo 11. credo
Num12: 7 servant Moses; he is entrusted with all my house. 1
Jer 39:14 They entrusted him to Gedali'ah the son of Ahi'kam 2
Mat 25:14 entrusted to them his property; 4
Lke 16:11 who will entrust to you the true riches? 8
Rom 3: 2 the Jews are entrusted with the oracles of God. 8
1Co 9:17 I am entrusted with a commission. 8
2Co 5:19 entrusting to us the message 9
Gal 2: 7 entrusted with the gospel to the uncircumcised 8
7 had been entrusted with the gospel to the circumcised •
1Th 2: 4 entrusted with the gospel, so we speak 8
1Ti 1:11 with which I have been entrusted. 8
6:20 O Timothy, guard what has been entrusted to you. 5
2Ti 1:12 to guard until that Day what has been entrusted 5
14 guard the truth that has been entrusted to you 5
2: 2 entrust to faithful men 7
Tit 1: 3 the preaching with which I have been entrusted 8
1Pe 4:19 and entrust their souls to a faithful Creator. 7
2Es 2:37 Receive what the Lord has entrusted to you 10
5:17 Israel has been entrusted to you 11
Tob 10:12 See, I am entrusting my daughter to you 7
AEs 16: 5 who have been entrusted with the administration 8
Sir 50:24 May he entrust to us his mercy! 3
2Mc 3:22 keep what had been entrusted safe and secure 8
22 secure for those who had entrusted it 8
7:24 and entrust him with public affairs. 3
9:25 often entrusted and commended to most of you 6
10:13 which Philometor had entrusted to him 3
3Mc 3:21 the myriad affairs liberally entrusted to them 8

entry 1. פֶּתַח
Jer 19: 2 at the entry of the Potsherd Gate, and proclaim 1
26:10 took their seat in the entry of the New Gate 1
36:10 at the entry of the New Gate of the LORD'S house. 1

envelope 1. נקף 2. περιέχω
Lam 3: 5 he has besieged and enveloped me 1
Wis 18:14 For while gentle silence enveloped all things 2

enviable 1. μακαριστός
2Mc 7:24 he would make him rich and enviable 1

envious 1. קנא 2. ἀντίζηλος 3. βάσκανος 4. φθόνος
1Sm 2:32 look with envious eye on all the prosperity •
Ps 37: 1 be not envious of wrongdoers! 1
73: 3 For I was envious of the arrogant 1
Prv 24: 1 Be not envious of evil men, 1
19 be not envious of the wicked; 1
Sir 14: 3 man; and of what use is property to an envious man? 3
26: 6 when a wife is envious of a rival 2
3Mc 6: 7 who through envious slanders was cast down 4
envious *See also* make.

environs 1. κύκλος 2. ὅριον
1Mc 10:31 let Jerusalem and her environs . . be holy 2
89 Ekron and all its environs as his possession. 2
14:36 defile the environs of the sanctuary 1

envoy 1. לִיץ 2. מַלְאָךְ 3. צִיר 4. ἀνήρ 5. θεωρός 6. πρεσβευτής 7. πρέσβυς 8. πρεσβύτης
2Kg 20:12 sent envoys with letters and a present •
2Ch 32:31 matter of the envoys of the princes of Babylon 1
35:21 he sent envoys to him, saying, "What have we to do 2
Prv 13:17 but a faithful envoy brings healing. 3
Isa 30: 4 officials are at Zo'an and his envoys reach Ha'nes 2
33: 7 the envoys of peace weep bitterly. 2
39: 1 king of Babylon, sent envoys with letters •
57: 9 you sent your envoys far off 3
Jer 27: 3 the envoys who have come to Jerusalem 2
1Mc 11: 9 He sent envoys to Demetrius the king, saying, "Come 7
12: 4 to provide for the envoys safe conduct •
8 Onias welcomed the envoy with honor 4
23 command that our envoys report to you •
13:14 so he sent envoys to him and said 7
21 the men in the citadel kept sending envoys to Trypho 6
14:21 The envoys who were sent to our people 6
22 envoys of the Jews, have come to us 6
40 Romans had received the envoys of Simon with honor. 6
15:17 envoys of the Jews have come to us as our friends 6
2Mc 4:19 the vile Jason sent envoys 5
11:34 envoys of the Romans 8

envy 1. קנא 2. קִנְאָה 3. ζῆλος 4. ζηλόω 5. ὀφθαλμὸς πονηρός 6. φθονέω 7. φθόνος 8. zelo
Gen 26:14 that the Philistines envied him. 1
30: 1 Rachel . . envied her sister; she said to Jacob 1
Prv 3:31 Do not envy a man of violence 1
23:17 Let not your heart envy sinners 1
Ecc 4: 4 come from a man's envy of his neighbor. 2
9: 6 Their love and their hate and their envy 2
Ezk 31: 9 the trees of Eden envied it 1
35:11 according to the anger and envy which you showed 2
Mat 27:18 it was out of envy that they had delivered him up. 7
Mrk 7:22 envy, slander, pride, foolishness. 5
15:10 For he perceived that it was out of envy 7
Rom 1:29 Full of envy, murder, strife, deceit, malignity 7
Gal 5:21 envy, drunkenness, carousing, and the like 7
26 no envy of one another. 6
Php 1:15 Some indeed preach Christ from envy and rivalry 7
1Ti 6: 4 disputes about words, which produce envy 7
Tit 3: 3 passing our days in malice and envy 7
1Pe 2: 1 put away all . . insincerity and envy 7
2Es 2:28 The nations shall envy you 8
Wis 2:24 through the devil's envy death entered the world 7
6:23 travel in the company of sickly envy 7
23 for envy does not associate with wisdom. •
Sir 9:11 Do not envy the honors of a sinner 4
40: 5 there is anger and envy and trouble and unrest 3
45:18 Outsiders conspired against him, and envied him 4
1Mc 8:16 there is no envy or jealousy among them. 7
envy *See also* look.

enwrap 1. סָתַר
Job 22:14 Thick clouds enwrap him, so that he does not see 1

ephah 1. אֵיפָה
Exd 16:36 An omer is the tenth part of an ephah.) 1
Lev 5:11 bring . . a tenth of an ephah of fine flour 1
6:20 a tenth of an ephah of fine flour as a regular 1
14:10 a cereal offering of three tenths of an ephah •
21 a tenth of an ephah of fine flour mixed with oil •
19:36 just weights, a just ephah, and a just hin 1
23:13 two tenths of an ephah of fine flour mixed with oil •
17 bread . . made of two tenths of an ephah •
24: 5 two tenths of an ephah shall be in each cake •
Num 5:15 offering . . a tenth of an ephah of barley meal; 1
15: 4 offering of a tenth of an ephah of fine flour •
6 offering two tenths of an ephah of fine flour •
9 three tenths of an ephah of fine flour •
28: 5 also a tenth of an ephah of fine flour 1
9 two tenths of an ephah of fine flour •
12 three tenths of an ephah of fine flour •
20 three tenths of an ephah shall you offer •
28 three tenths of an ephah for each bull •
29: 3 three tenths of an ephah for the bull •
9 three tenths of an ephah for the bull •
14 three tenths of an ephah for each of the . . bulls •
Jdg 6:19 a kid, and unleavened cakes from an ephah of flour; 1
Rut 2:17 and it was about an ephah of barley. 1
1Sm 1:24 a . . bull, an ephah of flour, and a skin of wine; 1
17:17 Take . . an ephah of this parched grain 1
Isa 5:10 a homer of seed shall yield but an ephah. 1
Ezk 45:10 You shall have just balances, a just ephah 1
11 ephah and the bath shall be of the same measure 1
11 the ephah one tenth of a homer; 1
13 one sixth of an ephah from each homer of wheat 1
13 one sixth of an ephah from each homer of barley 1
24 he shall provide as a cereal offering an ephah 1
24 an ephah for each ram, and a hin of oil to each ephah 1
24 an ephah for each ram, and a hin of oil to each ephah 1
46: 5 cereal offering with the ram shall be an ephah 1
5 together with a hin of oil to each ephah. 1
7 as a cereal offering he shall provide an ephah 1
7 an ephah with the bull and an ephah with the ram 1
7 together with a hin of oil to each ephah. 1
11 bull shall be an ephah, and with a ram an ephah, 1
11 bull shall be an ephah, and with a ram an ephah, 1
11 together with a hin of oil to an ephah. 1
14 one sixth of an ephah, and one third of a hin of oil 1
Ams 8: 5 that we may make the ephah small 1
Zec 5: 6 He said, "This is the ephah that goes forth. 1
7 there was a woman sitting in the ephah! 1
8 he thrust her back into the ephah 1
9 lifted up the ephah between earth and heaven. 1
10 Where are they taking the ephah? 1
11 they will set the ephah down there on its base. •

ephod 1. אֵפוֹד
Exd 25: 7 for the ephod and for the breastpiece. 1
28: 4 they shall make: a breastpiece, an ephod, a robe 1
6 they shall make the ephod of gold, of blue 1
12 stones upon the shoulder-pieces of the ephod 1
15 like the work of the ephod you shall make it; 1
25 front to the shoulder-pieces of the ephod. 1
26 put them . . on its inside edge next to the ephod. 1
27 part of the two shoulder-pieces of the ephod 1
27 above the skilfully woven band of the ephod. 1
28 the skilfully woven band of the ephod 1
28 shall not come loose from the ephod. 1
31 you shall make the robe of the ephod all of blue. 1
29: 5 put on Aaron the coat and the robe of the ephod 1
5 put on Aaron . . the ephod, and the breastpiece 1
5 with the skilfully woven band of the ephod; 1
35: 9 for the ephod and for the breastpiece. 1
27 stones . . for the ephod and for the breastpiece 1
39: 2 he made the ephod of gold, blue and purple 1
4 They made for the ephod shoulder-pieces •
7 he set them on the shoulder-pieces of the ephod 1
8 breastpiece . . like the work of the ephod 1
18 in front to the shoulder-pieces of the ephod. 1
19 on its inside edge next to the ephod. 1
20 shoulder-pieces of the ephod, at its joining 1
20 above the skilfully woven band of the ephod. 1
21 its rings to the rings of the ephod with a lace 1
21 upon the skilfully woven band of the ephod 1
21 should not come loose from the ephod; 1
22 the robe of the ephod woven all of blue; 1
Lev 8: 7 put the ephod upon him, and girded him 1
7 skilfully woven band of the ephod, binding it 1
Jdg 8:27 Gideon made an ephod of it and put it in his city 1
17: 5 had a shrine, and he made an ephod and teraphim 1
18:14 in these houses there are an ephod, teraphim 1
17 took the graven image, the ephod, the teraphim 1
18 took the graven image, the ephod, the teraphim 1
20 he took the ephod, and the teraphim, and the graven 1
1Sm 2:18 Samuel was . . a boy girdled with a linen ephod. 1
28 go up . . to burn incense, to wear an ephod before me 1
14: 3 and Ahi'jah the son of Ahi'tub . . wearing an ephod. 1
21: 9 it is here wrapped in a cloth behind the ephod; 1
22:18 he killed . . persons who wore the linen ephod. 1
23: 6 Abi'athar . . came down with an ephod in his hand. 1
9 he said to Abi'athar . . "Bring the ephod here. 1
30: 7 David said to Abi'athar . . "Bring me the ephod. 1
7 Abi'athar brought the ephod to David. 1
2Sm 6:14 and David was girded with a linen ephod. 1
1Ch 15:27 and David wore a linen ephod. 1
Hos 3: 4 dwell many days . . without ephod or teraphim. 1

ephphatha 1. ἐφφαθά
Mrk 7:34 Eph'phatha," that is, "Be opened. 1

epileptic 1. σεληνιάζομαι
Mat 4:24 pains, demoniacs, epileptics, and paralytics 1
17:15 Lord, have mercy on my son, for he is an epileptic 1

episode 1. τὰ κατά
2Mc 3:40 This was the outcome of the episode 1

equal 1. אֱנוֹשׁ כְּעֶרְכִּי 2. דמה 3. כְּ 4. עַל פְּנֵי 5. ערך 6. εἷς 7. ἡλικιώτης 8. ἴσος 9. καθώς 10. ὡς
Deu 18: 8 They shall have equal portions to eat •
1Kg 6: 3 twenty cubits . . equal to the width of the house 4
2Ch 3: 4 twenty cubits . . equal to the width of the house; 4
Job 28:17 Gold and glass cannot equal it 5
Ps 55:13 you, my equal, my companion, my familiar friend. 1
Ezk 4: 5 390 days, equal to the number of the years •
31: 8 not rival it, nor the fir trees equal its boughs; 2
48: 8 in length equal to one of the tribal portions 3
Mat 20:12 you have made them equal to us 8
Joh 5:18 making himself equal with God. 8
1Co 3: 8 He who plants and he who waters are equal 6
Rev 21:16 its length and breadth and height are equal. 8
1Es 3:19 It makes equal the mind of the king and the orphan 6
Sir 6:11 In prosperity he will make himself your equal 10
7:28 what . . equals their gift to you? 9
2Mc 9:15 make, all of them, equal to citizens of Athens; 8
4Mc 11:14 I am their equal in mind. 7
13:21 they were born after an equal time of gestation 8
equal *See also* act, citizenship, make, part, seriousness, share, standing, treat.

equal to angel 1. ἰσάγγελος
Lke 20:36 they are equal to angels and are sons of God 1

equal to God 1. ἰσόθεος
2Mc 9:12 no mortal should think that he is equal to God. 1

equality 1. εἰμί ἴσος 2. ἰσότης
2Co 8:14 but that as a matter of equality 2
14 that there may be equality. 2
Php 2: 6 not count equality with God a thing to be grasped 1

equally 1. אִישׁ כְּאָח 2. ὁμοίως
Ezk 47:14 you shall divide it equally; 1
Wis 11:11 they were equally distressed 2
4Mc 5:21 for in either case the law is equally despised. 2

equip 1. ערך 2. ἐξαρτίζω 3. ἔχω 4. θωρακίζω 5. καθοπλίζω 6. καταρτίζω 7. καταρτισμός 8. κατασκευάζω 9. κοσμέω
1Ch 12:33 seasoned troops, equipped for battle 1
35 Of the Danites 28,600 men equipped for battle. 1
Eph 4:12 to equip the saints for the work of ministry 7
2Ti 3:17 equipped for every good work. 2
Heb 13:21 equip you with everything good 6
1Mc 6:43 one of the beasts was equipped with royal armor. 4
10: 6 to recruit troops, to equip them with arms 8
21 and equipped them with arms in abundance. 8
15: 3 have equipped warships 8
2Mc 10:18 well equipped to withstand a siege 3
3Mc 5:23 having equipped the beasts 5
38 Equip the elephants now once more 5
45 had been equipped with frightful devices 9
4Mc 11:22 equipped with nobility, will die with my brothers 5

equip for battle 1. חֲמֻשִׁים
Exd 13:18 Israel went up . . equipped for battle. 1

equipment 1. כְּלִי 2. ἑτοιμασία
Num 4:26 cords, and all the equipment for their service; 1
32 all their equipment and all their accessories; 1
1Sm 8:12 to make . . and the equipment of his chariots. 1
2Kg 7:15 way was littered with garments and equipment 1
2Ch 4:16 and all the equipment for these Huram-abi made 1
Eph 6:15 the equipment of the gospel of peace; 2

military equipment 1. σκεῦος
1Mc 15:26 silver and gold and much military equipment. 1

more equitable 1. ἐπιεικής
AEs 16: 9 judging . . with more equitable consideration 1

equity 1. אֱמֶת 2. יָשָׁר 3. מִישׁוֹר 4. מֵישָׁר 5. צְדָקָה
2Sm 8:15 David administered justice and equity to all 5
1Ch 18:14 David . . administered justice and equity 5
Ps 9: 8 he judges the peoples with equity. 4
45: 6 Your royal scepter is a scepter of equity; 3
67: 4 for thou dost judge the peoples with equity 3
75: 2 time which I appoint I will judge with equity. 4
96:10 he will judge the peoples with equity. 4
98: 9 will judge . . the peoples with equity. 4
99: 4 lover of justice, thou hast established equity; 4
Prv 1: 3 receive instruction in . . justice, and equity; 4
2: 9 Then you will understand . . justice and equity 4
29:14 If a king judges the poor with equity his throne 1
Isa 11: 4 and decide with equity for the meek of the earth; 3
Mic 3: 9 Israel, who abhor justice and pervert all equity 2

equivalent 1. כְּ 2. ἰσοδύναμος
Exd 22:17 he shall pay money equivalent to the marriage 1
4Mc 3:15 what was regarded as equivalent to blood. 2

eradicate 1. ἐκκόπτω
4Mc 3: 2 No one of us can eradicate that kind of desire 1
3 No one of us can eradicate anger from the mind 1
4 No one of us can eradicate malice 1

erect 1. נצב 2. עמד 3. עשה 4. קום 5. קוֹמְמִיּוּת 6. ἐγείρω 7. ἐπιτελέω 8. ἵστημι 9. κατορθόω 10. οἰκοδομέω 11. ὀρθός 12. συνίστημι 13. ὑψόω
Gen 33:20 There he erected an altar and called it 1
Exd 26:30 you shall erect the tabernacle according 4
40: 2 first month you shall erect the tabernacle 4
17 first month . . the tabernacle was erected. 4
18 Moses erected the tabernacle; he laid its bases 4

33 he erected the court round the tabernacle 4
Lev 26: 1 and erect no graven image or pillar 4
13 I have . . made you walk erect 5
1Kg 16:32 He erected an altar for Ba'al in the house of Ba'al 4
2Kg 21: 3 he erected altars for Ba'al, and made an Ashe'rah 4
23:15 the high place erected by Jerobo'am . . he pulled 3
2Ch 33: 3 erected altars to the 4
Ezr 2:68 freewill offerings . . to erect it on its site; 2
Isa 23:13 Chalde'ans . . They erected their siege towers 4
Ezk 43:18 when it is erected for offering burnt offerings 3
Heb 8: 5 when Moses was about to erect the tent 7
1Es 5:44 vowed that they would erect the house on its site 6
50 they erected the altar in its place 9
9:46 when he opened the law, they all stood erect 11
1Mc 1:54 they erected a desolating sacrilege 10
6: 7 the abomination which he had erected 10
12:36 erect a high barrier 13
13:28 He also erected seven pyramids 8
2Mc 15: 6 determined to erect a . . monument of victory 12

erect about 1. περιτίθημι
1Mc 13:29 erecting about them great columns 1

erection 1. ἔγερσις
1Es 5:62 the erection of the house of the Lord. 1

err 1. שׁגה 2. תעה 3. ὀλισθαίνω 4. πλανάω
Num15:22 if you err, and do not observe all these 1
1Sm 26:21 I . . played the fool, and have erred exceedingly. 1
Job 6:24 make me understand how I have erred. 1
19: 4 even if it be true that I have erred 1
Ps 58: 3 they err from their birth, speaking lies. 2
95:10 They are a people who err in heart 2
Prv 14:22 Do they not err that devise evil? 2
Isa 28: 7 with strong drink; they err in vision 1
29:24 those who err in spirit will come 2
35: 8 not pass over it, and fools shall not err therein. 2
Wis 14:22 Afterward it was not enough for them to err 4
Sir 28:26 Beware lest you err with your tongue 3

make err 1. תעה
Isa 63:17 O LORD, why dost thou make us err from thy ways 1

errand 1. דָּבָר
Gen 24:33 I will not eat until I have told my errand. 1
2Kg 9: 5 and he said, "I have an errand to you, O commander. 1

error 1. מְשׁוּגָה 2. שְׁגָגָה 3. שְׁגִיאָה 4. תָּהֳלָה 5. תּוֹעָה
6. שָׁלוּ (A) 7. ἀγνόημα 8. ἄγνοια 9. ἀμβλακία
10. πλάνη
Lev 5:18 the error which he committed unwittingly 2
Num15:25 they shall be forgiven; because it was an error 2
25 sin offering before the LORD, for their error. 2
26 whole population was involved in the error. 2
Job 4:18 his angels he charges with error; 4
19: 4 that I have erred, my error remains with myself. 1
Ps 19:12 But who can discern his errors? 3
Prv 12:28 but the way of error leads to death. •
Ecc 10: 5 an evil . . an error proceeding from the ruler: 2
Isa 32: 6 to utter error concerning the LORD 5
Dan 6: 4 faithful, and no error or fault was found in him. 6
Rom 1:27 receiving . . the due penalty for their error. 10
1Th 2: 3 does not spring from error or uncleanness 10
Heb 9: 7 for himself and for the errors of the people. 7
Jas 5:20 brings back a sinner from the error of his way 10
2Pe 2:18 escaped from those who live in error. 10
3:17 carried away with the error of lawless men 10
1Jn 4: 6 the spirit of truth and the spirit of error 10
Jde 1:11 and abandon themselves . . to Balaam's error 10
1Es 9:20 to give rams in expiation of their error. 8
Tob 5:13 They did not go astray in the error of our brethren 10
Wis 1:12 Do not invite death by the error of your life 10
12:24 For they went far astray on the paths of error 10
Sir 23: 2 That they may not spare me in my errors 7
12 all these errors will be far from the godly •
30:11 do not ignore his errors. •
1Mc 13:39 We pardon any errors and offenses committed 7
3Mc 2:19 Wipe away our sins and disperse our errors 9
error *See also* commit, sin.

unwitting error 1. ἀγνόημα
Jdt 5:20 if there is any unwitting error in this people 1

eruption 1. מִסְפַּחַה 2. סַפַּחַת
Lev 13: 2 When a man has . . a swelling or an eruption 2
6 it is only an eruption; and he shall wash 1
7 if the eruption spreads in the skin 1
8 if the eruption has spread in the skin 1
14:56 for a swelling or an eruption or a spot 2

escape 1. בוא 2. יצא 3. יצא מִתַּחַת 4. יתר 5. לוז
6. מַחֲלֹקֶת 7. מלט 8. נצל 9. סור 10. עבר 11. עלה
12. פלט 13. פָּלֵט 14. פָּלִיט 15. פְּלֵיטָה 16. שׁאר
17. שְׁאֵרִית 18. תּוֹצָאָה 19. ἀνανήφω 20. ἀπό
21. ἀποφεύγω 22. διασῴζω 23. διαφεύγω
24. ἐκφεύγω 25. ἐκφυγῆς 26. ἐξέρχομαι 27. μὴ ἔχω
28. παρέρχομαι 29. φεύγω 30. effugio 31. transmigro
Gen 7: 7 into the ark, to escape the waters of the flood. •
14:13 Then one who had escaped came 14
19:20 Let me escape there–is it not a little one?– 7
22 Make haste, escape there; for I can do nothing 7
32: 8 then the company which is left will escape. 15
Exd 1:10 lest they . . escape from the land. 11
Lev 26:37 stumble over one another, as if to escape a sword •
Deu 23:15 slave who has escaped from his master to you; 8
Jos 8:22 there was left none that survived or escaped. 14
Jdg 3:26 Ehud escaped while they delayed, and passed 7
26 the sculptured stones, and escaped to Se-i'rah. 7
29 strong, able-bodied men; not a man escaped. 7
1Sm 14:41 and Saul were taken, but the people escaped. 2
19:10 he eluded Saul . . And David fled, and escaped. 7
12 let David down . . and he fled away and escaped. 7
17 and let my enemy go, so that he has escaped? 7
18 Now David fled and escaped, and he came to Samuel 7
22: 1 David . . and escaped to the cave of Adullam; 7
20 Abi'athar, escaped and fled after David. 7
23:13 Saul was told that David had escaped from Kei'lah 7
28 therefore that place was called the Rock of Escape 6
27: 1 I should escape to the land of the Philistines; 7
1 I shall escape out of his hand. 7
30:17 not a man of them escaped, except 400 young men 7
2Sm 1: 3 he said . . "I have escaped from the camp of Israel. 7
15:14 else there will be no escape for us from Ab'salom; 15
1Kg 18:40 Seize the prophets . . let not one of them escape. 7
19:17 him who escapes from . . Haz'ael shall Jehu slay; 7
17 him who escapes from . . Jehu shall Eli'sha slay. 7
20:20 Ben-ha'dad . . escaped on a horse with horsemen. 7
2Kg 10:24 man who allows any . . to escape shall forfeit 7
25 Go in and slay them; let not a man escape. 2
13: 5 so that they escaped from the hand of the Syrians; 3
19:37 slew him . . and escaped into the land of Ar'arat. 7
1Ch 4:43 the remnant of the Amal'ekites that had escaped 15
2Ch 16: 7 the army of the king of Syria has escaped you. 7
20:24 bodies lying on the ground; none had escaped. 15
30: 6 remnant of you who have escaped from the hand 15
36:20 exile . . those who had escaped from the sword 17
Ezr 9:14 that there should be no remnant, nor any to escape? 15
15 left a remnant that has escaped, as at this day. 15
Neh 1: 2 Jews that survived, who had escaped exile 16
3 escaped exile are in great trouble and shame; 16
Est 4:13 Think not that . . you will escape any more 7
Job 1:15 I alone have escaped to tell you. 7
16 I alone have escaped to tell you. 7
17 I alone have escaped to tell you. 7
19 I alone have escaped to tell you. 7
15:30 he will not escape from darkness; 9
19:20 I have escaped by the skin of my teeth. 7
Ps 68:20 to God, the Lord, belongs escape from death. 18
88: 8 I am shut in so that I cannot escape; 2
124: 7 escaped as a bird from the snare of the fowlers 7
7 snare is broken, and we have escaped! 7
141:10 wicked . . into their own nets, while I escape. 10
Prv 3:21 let them not escape from your sight 5
4:21 Let them not escape from your sight; 5
12:13 but the righteous escapes from trouble. 2
19: 5 he who utters lies will not escape. 7
Ecc 7:26 he who pleases God escapes her 7
Isa 15: 9 a lion for those of Moab who escape 15
20: 6 we fled for help . . And we, how shall we escape?' 7
37:38 slew him . . and escaped into the land of Ar'arat. 7
Jer 11:11 evil upon them which they cannot escape; 2
25:35 nor escape for the lords of the flock. 15
26:21 he was afraid and fled and escaped to Egypt. 1
32: 4 Zedeki'ah king of Judah shall not escape 7
34: 3 You shall not escape from his hand 7
38:18 and you shall not escape from their hand. 7
23 you yourself shall not escape from their hand 7
41:15 But Ish'mael the son of Nethani'ah escaped 7
44:14 shall escape or survive or return to the land 14
28 And those who escape the sword shall return 14
46: 6 The swift cannot flee . . nor the warrior escape; 7
48: 8 come upon every city, and no city shall escape; 7
19 Ask him who flees and her who escapes; 7
50:28 they flee and escape from the land of Babylon 13
29 Encamp round about her; let no one escape. 15
51:50 You that have escaped from the sword, go, stand not 13
Lam 2:22 and on the day of . . none escaped or survived; 14
3: 7 He has walled me about so that I cannot escape; 2
Ezk 6: 8 have among the nations some who escape the sword 14
9 then those of you who escape will remember me 14
7:16 if any survivors escape 12
12:16 But I will let a few of them escape from the sword 14
15: 7 though they escape from the fire 2
17:15 Can a man escape who does such things? 7
15 Can he break the covenant and yet escape? 7
18 yet did all these things, he shall not escape. 7
33:21 a man who had escaped from Jerusalem came to me 14
Dan 11:42 land of Egypt shall not escape. 15
Jol 2: 3 desolate wilderness, and nothing escapes them. 15
32 and in Jerusalem there shall be those who escape 15
Ams 9: 1 not one of them shall escape. 13
Obd 1:17 in Mount Zion there shall be those that escape 15
Zec 2: 7 Ho! Escape to Zion 7
Mal 3:15 but when they put God to the test they escape. 7
Mat 23:33 how are you to escape being sentenced to hell? 29
Lke 21:36 may have strength to escape all these things 24
Joh 10:39 he escaped from their hands. 26
Act 16:27 supposing that the prisoners had escaped. 24
27:30 the sailors were seeking to escape from the ship 29
42 lest any should swim away and escape; 23
44 so it was that all escaped to land. 22
28: 1 After we had escaped 22
4 Though he has escaped from the sea 22
Rom 2: 3 you will escape the judgment of God? 24
2Co 11:33 escaped his hands. 24
1Th 5: 3 there will be no escape. 24
2Ti 2:26 they may escape from the snare of the devil 19
Heb 2: 3 how shall we escape 24
11:34 escaped the edge of the sword 29
12:25 if they did not escape when they refused him 24
25 much less shall we escape •
2Pe 1: 4 escape from the corruption that is in the world 21
2:18 escaped from those who live in error. 21
20 they have escaped the defilements of the world 21
2Es 4:42 makes haste to escape the pangs of birth 30
7:96 that they have now escaped what is corruptible 30
9: 7 and will be able to escape on account of his works 30
14:15 and hasten to escape from these times. 31
Tob 13: 2 there is no one who can escape his hand. 24
AEs 16: 4 they will escape the evil-hating justice of God 24
Wis 10: 6 he escaped the fire 29
15:19 escaped both the praise of God and his blessing 24
16:15 To escape from thy hand is impossible; 29
Sir 6:35 do not let wise proverbs escape you. 24
11:10 by fleeing you will not escape. 24
16:13 The sinner will not escape with his plunder 24
22:13 guard yourself from him to escape trouble 27
27:20 has escaped like a gazelle from a snare. 24
40: 6 like one who has escaped from the battle-front; 24
42:20 No thought escapes him 28
Sus 1:22 and if I do not, I shall not escape your hands. 24
1Mc 2:43 all who became fugitives to escape their troubles 20
4:26 Those of the foreigners who escaped 22
6:21 some of the garrison escaped from the siege 26
15:37 embarked on a ship and escaped to Orthosia. 29
2Mc 6:26 I shall not escape the hands of the Almighty. 24
7:31 you . . will certainly not escape the hands of God. 23
35 You have not yet escaped the judgment 24
12:35 Gorgias escaped and reached Marisa. 23
3Mc 4:19 had been bribed to contrive a means of escape 25
5:13 since they had escaped the appointed hour 23
6:29 since they now had escaped death. 24
4Mc 9:32 You will not escape, most abominable tyrant 24
escape *See also* allow, seek, way.

escape notice 1. λανθάνω
Act 26:26 none of these things has escaped his notice 1
Wis 1: 8 no one . . will escape notice 1

escort 1. בוא 2. εἰσάγω 3. παραπομπή 4. προπέμπω
5. προπομπή
Ps 45:14 her virgin companions, her escort, in her train. 1
1Es 8:51 foot soldiers and horsemen and an escort 5
Tob 8: 1 they escorted Tobias in to her. 2
Jdt 10:15 some of us will escort you and hand you over to him. 4
1Mc 9:37 from Nadabath with a large escort. 3
escort *See also* give.

escort over 1. שׁלח
2Sm 19:31 went on with the king . . to escort him over the Jordan. 1

especially 1. וְ 2. καί 3. μάλα 4. μάλιστα 5. μᾶλλον
6. πολύς 7. ὑπεραγόντως
Jos 2: 1 saying, "Go, view the land, especially Jericho. 1
Act 25:26 especially before you, King Agrippa 4
26: 3 you are especially familiar with all customs 4
1Co 14: 1 especially that you may prophesy. 5
Gal 6:10 especially to those who are of the household 4
Php 4:22 especially those of Caesar's household. 4
1Ti 4:10 especially of those who believe. 4
5: 8 not provide . . especially for his own family 4
17 especially those who labor in preaching 4
Tit 1:10 especially the circumcision party; 4
Phm 1:16 especially to me but how much more to you 4
2Pe 2:10 especially those who indulge in the lust 4
3Jn 1: 5 you render any service . . especially to strangers 2
Sir 0: 1 devoting himself especially to the reading 6
2Mc 7:20 The mother was especially admirable 7
10:32 especially well garrisoned 3
3Mc 5: 3 who were especially hostile toward the Jews. 4
4Mc 15: 4 Especially is this true of mothers 4

essential 1. ἀναγκαῖος 2. ἀρχή
Sir 29:21 The essentials for life are water and bread 2
2Mc 4:23 to complete the records of essential business. 1
4Mc 1: 2 the subject is essential to everyone 1

establish 1. אמן 2. בנה 3. חוק 4. יסד 5. יְסוֹד 6. יצג
7. כון 8. סמך 9. עזז 10. עמד 11. קום 12. שׂום
13. קום (A) 14. תקן (A) 15. ἀποκατάστασις
16. βεβαιόω 17. ἑτοιμάω 18. ἵστημι 19. καθίστημι
20. κρατέω 21. οἰκίζω 22. οἰκοδομέω 23. ποιέω
24. στερεόω 25. στηρίζω 26. συνίστημι 27. συντελέω

28. ὑπέρ 29. φέρω 30. aestimo 31. confirmo
32. perficio
Gen 6:18 I will establish my covenant with you; 11
9: 9 Behold, I establish my covenant with you 11
11 I establish my covenant with you 11
17 sign of the covenant which I have established 11
17: 7 I will establish my covenant between me and you 11
19 Isaac. I will establish my covenant with him 11
21 I will establish my covenant with Isaac 11
Exd 6: 4 I also established my covenant with them 11
15:17 O LORD, which thy hands have established. 7
Num21:27 be built, let the city of Sihon be established. 7
30:13 Any vow . . her husband may establish 11
14 then he establishes all her vows 11
14 he has established them, because he said nothing 11
Deu 28: 9 LORD will establish you as a people holy 11
29:13 that he may establish you this day as his people 11
32: 6 father, who . . made you and established you? 7
1Sm 1:23 wait . . only, may the LORD establish his word. 11
3:20 Samuel was established as a prophet of the LORD. 1
13:13 the LORD would have established your kingdom 7
20:31 you nor your kingdom shall be established. 7
24:20 kingdom . . shall be established in your hand. 11
2Sm 5:12 the LORD had established him king over Israel 7
7:12 I will raise . . and I will establish his kingdom. 7
13 and I will establish the throne of his kingdom 7
16 your throne shall be established for ever. 7
24 thou didst establish for thyself thy people 7
26 house of thy servant David will be established 7
1Kg 2: 4 the LORD may establish his word which he spoke 11
12 father; and his kingdom was firmly established. 7
24 as the LORD lives, who has established me 7
45 the throne of David shall be established before 7
46 the kingdom was established in the hand 7
6:12 if you . . then I will establish my word with you 11
9: 5 I will establish your royal throne over Israel 11
15: 4 gave him a lamp . . and establishing Jerusalem; 10
20:34 establish bazaars for yourself in Damascus 12
2Kg 23:24 that he might establish the words of the law 11
1Ch 9:22 David and Samuel the seer established them 4
14: 2 the LORD had established him king over Israel 7
17:11 and I will establish his kingdom. 7
12 and I will establish his throne for ever. 7
14 and his throne shall be established for ever 7
23 let the word which . . be established for ever 1
24 name will be established and magnified for ever 1
24 David will be established before thee. 7
22:10 I will establish his royal throne in Israel 7
24:19 procedure established for them by Aaron •
28: 7 I will establish his kingdom for ever 7
2Ch 1: 1 Solomon . . established himself in his kingdom 3
7:18 then I will establish your royal throne 11
9: 8 loved Israel and would establish them for ever 10
12: 1 rule of Rehobo'am was established and was strong 7
13 Rehobo'am established himself in Jerusalem 3
17: 5 the LORD established the kingdom in his hand; 7
20:20 Believe . . and you will be established; 1
21: 4 When Jeho'ram . . was established 3
Neh 13:30 established the duties of the priests 10
Job 21: 8 Their children are established 7
22:28 it will be established for you 11
28:27 he established it, and searched it out. 7
38:33 Can you establish their rule on the earth? 12
Ps 7: 9 come to an end, but establish thou the righteous 7
8: 3 moon and the stars which thou hast established; 7
9: 7 he has established his throne for judgment; 7
24: 2 and established it upon the rivers. 7
30: 7 thou hadst established me as a strong mountain; 10
37:23 he establishes him in whose way he delights; 7
48: 8 city of our God, which God establishes for ever. 7
65: 6 by thy strength hast established the mountains 7
74:16 hast established the luminaries and the sun. 7
76: 2 His abode has been established in Salem •
9 when God arose to establish judgment to save all •
78: 5 He established a testimony in Jacob 11
87: 5 for the Most High himself will establish her. 7
89: 2 For thy steadfast love was established for ever 2
4 I will establish your descendants for ever 7
29 I will establish his line for ever 12
37 Like the moon it shall be established for ever; 7
90:17 establish thou the work of our hands upon us 7
17 yea, the work of our hands establish thou it. 7
93: 1 world is established; it shall never be moved; 7
2 thy throne is established from of old; 7
96:10 world is established, it shall never be moved; 7
99: 4 lover of justice, thou hast established equity; 7
102:28 their posterity . . established before thee. 7
103:19 LORD has established his throne in the heavens 7
107:36 hungry dwell, and they establish a city to live in; 7
111: 8 they are established for ever and ever 8
119:90 thou hast established the earth, and it stands 7
140:11 Let not the slanderer be established in the land; 7
148: 6 he established them for ever and ever; 10
Prv 3:19 by understanding he established the heavens; 7
8:27 When he established the heavens, I was there 7
28 when he established the fountains of the deep 9
10:25 but the righteous is established for ever. 5
12: 3 A man is not established by wickedness 7
16: 3 your plans will be established. 7
12 throne is established by righteousness. 7
19:21 purpose of the LORD that will be established. 11
20:18 Plans are established by counsel; 7
24: 3 house . . by understanding it is established; 7
25: 5 throne will be established in righteousness. 7
29:14 his throne will be established for ever. 7
30: 4 Who has established all the ends of the earth? 11
Isa 2: 2 the mountain . . shall be established 7
7: 9 surely you shall not be established.' 1
9: 7 over his kingdom, to establish it, and to uphold it 7
16: 5 a throne will be established in steadfast love 7
42: 4 be discouraged till he has established justice 12
45:18 he established it; he did not create it a chaos 7
49: 8 to establish the land, to apportion the desolate 11
54:14 In righteousness you shall be established; 7
62: 7 give him no rest until he establishes Jerusalem 7
Jer 10:12 who established the world by his wisdom 7
30:20 their congregation shall be established 7
33: 2 the LORD who formed it to establish it 7
25 If I have not established my covenant with day 12
51:15 who established the world by his wisdom 7
Ezk 16:60 establish with you an everlasting covenant. 11
62 I will establish my covenant with you 11
Dan 4:36 established in my kingdom, 14
6: 7 king should establish an ordinance and enforce 13
8 establish the interdict and sign the document 13
15 which the king establishes can be changed. 13
Ams 5:15 and love good, and establish justice in the gate; 6
Mic 4: 1 the house of the LORD shall be established 7
Hab 1:12 O Rock, hast established them for chastisement. 4
Act 3:21 until the time for establishing 15
Rom 10: 3 and seeking to establish their own 18
1Co 7:37 whoever is firmly established in his heart 18
2Co 1:21 it is God who establishes us with you in Christ 16
Col 2: 7 built up in him and established in the faith 16
1Th 3: 2 to establish you in your faith and to exhort you 25
13 so that he may establish your hearts unblamable 25
2Th 2:17 establish them in every good work and word. 25
Heb 8: 8 when I will establish a new covenant 27
9:16 the death . . must be established. 29
10: 9 in order to establish the second. 18
Jas 5: 8 Establish your hearts, for the coming of the Lord 25
1Pe 5:10 will . . restore, establish, and strengthen you. 25
2Pe 1:12 you know them and are established in the truth 25
2Es 2:15 establish their feet, because I have chosen you 31
6: 3 before the powers of movement were established 31
4 before the footstool of Zion was established 30
8:23 and whose truth is established for ever- ‡
52 goodness is established and wisdom perfected 32
10:27 there was an established city ‡
42 but an established city has appeared to you- ‡
44 whom you now behold as an established city ‡
Tob 1: 4 and established for all generations for ever. 22
Sir 17:12 He established with them an eternal covenant 18
24:10 so I was established in Zion. 25
31:11 His prosperity will be established 24
37:13 establish the counsel of your own heart 18
38:32 Without them a city cannot be established 21
40:19 establish a man's name 25
42:17 which the Lord the Almighty has established 24
44:20 he established the covenant in his flesh 18
45:24 a covenant of peace was established with him 18
25 A covenant was also established with David •
46:13 established the kingdom and anointed rulers 19
1Mc 1:16 Antiochus saw that his kingdom was established 17
8:17 sent them to Rome to establish friendship 18
20 sent us to you to establish alliance and peace 18
10:52 established my rule 20
54 let us establish friendship with one another; 18
14:11 He established peace in the land 23
18 alliance which they had established with Judas 18
26 established its freedom. 18
2Mc 4: 9 to establish by his authority a gymnasium 26
11 who went on the mission to establish friendship 28
13: 3 thought that he would be established in office. 19
14:15 who established his own people for ever 26
3Mc 3: 5 they were established in good repute among all men. 19
26 the government will be established 19
4Mc 5:25 we believe that the law was established by God 19
13:23 brotherly affection had been so established 19

firmly establish 1. διατηρέω 2. εὐσταθέω
Sir 28: 1 he will firmly establish his sins. 1
3Mc 7: 4 our government would never be firmly established 2

establishment 1. מלך
2Ch 36:20 establishment of the kingdom of Persia 1

estate 1. שָׂדֶה 2. ὕπαρξις
1Kg 2:26 Go to An'athoth, to your estate; for you deserve 1
Gal 4: 1 though he is the owner of all the estate; •
Jdt 8: 7 she maintained this estate. •
16:21 went to Bethulia, and remained on her estate 2
estate *See also* man.

former estate 1. קַדְמָה
Ezk 16:55 daughters shall return to their former estate; 1
55 daughters shall return to their former estate; 1
55 daughters shall return to your former estate. 1

low estate 1. שֵׁפֶל 2. ταπείνωσις 3. humilitas
Ps 136:23 It is he who remembered us in our low estate 1
Lke 1:48 he has regarded the low estate of his handmaiden. 2
2Es 9:45 and looked upon my low estate 3
Sir 11:12 he lifts him out of his low estate 2

regal estate 1. מְלוּכָה
Ezk 16:13 grew . . beautiful, and came to regal estate. 1

esteem 1. חשב 2. יקר 3. עַיִן 4. εὐδοκιμέω
5. ἡγέομαι 6. κρίνω 7. τιμή
1Sm 18:30 so that his name was highly esteemed. 2
2Sm 16:23 so was . . esteemed, both by David and by Ab'salom. •
Neh 6:16 afraid and fell greatly in their own esteem; 3
Isa 53: 3 he was despised, and we esteemed him not. 1
4 yet we esteemed him stricken, smitten by God 1
Rom 14: 5 One man esteems one day as better than another 6
5 while another man esteems all days alike. 6
1Th 5:13 to esteem them very highly in love 5
Sir 40:25 good counsel is esteemed more than both. 4
41:16 not everything is confidently esteemed 4
2Mc 9:21 I remember . . your esteem and good will 7

lightly esteem 1. קלל
1Sm 2:30 those who despise me shall be lightly esteemed. 1

least esteemed 1. ἐξουθενέω
1Co 6: 4 who are least esteemed by the church? 1

estrange 1. זור 2. פרד 3. ἀλλοιόω 4. ἀπαλλοτριόω
5. abalieno
Job 19:13 my acquaintances are wholly estranged from me. 1
Prv 18: 1 He who is estranged seeks pretexts to break out 2
Isa 1: 4 they are utterly estranged. 1
Ezk 14: 5 house of Israel, who are all estranged from me 1
Col 1:21 you, who once were estranged and hostile in mind 4
2Es 6: 5 the imaginations . . were estranged 5
Sir 11:34 will estrange you from your family. 4
1Mc 11:12 He was estranged from Alexander 3

become estranged 1. ἀλλοτριόω 2. ἐξαλλοτριόω
1Mc 11:53 he became estranged from Jonathan 1
12:10 so that we may not become estranged from you 2
15:27 and became estranged from him. 1

eternal 1. עַד 2. עוֹלָם 3. קֶדֶם 4. ἀΐδιος 5. αἰών
6. αἰώνιος 7. εἰς αἰῶνα 8. inmortalis 9. perpetuus
Gen 49:26 beyond the blessings of the eternal mountains •
Deu 33:27 The eternal God is your dwelling place 3
Ecc 12: 5 because man goes to his eternal home 2
Jer 20:11 Their eternal dishonor will never be forgotten. 2
Hab 3: 6 then the eternal mountains were scattered 1
Mat 18: 8 to be thrown into the eternal fire. 6
19:16 to have eternal life? 6
29 and inherit eternal life. 6
25:41 Depart from me, you cursed, into the eternal fire 6
46 they will go away into eternal punishment 6
46 but the righteous into eternal life. 6
Mrk 3:29 guilty of an eternal sin"- 6
10:17 what must I do to inherit eternal life? 6
30 in the age to come eternal life. 6
Lke 10:25 Teacher, what shall I do to inherit eternal life? 6
16: 9 receive you into the eternal habitations. 6
18:18 what shall I do to inherit eternal life? 6
30 in the age to come eternal life. 6
Joh 3:15 whoever believes in him may have eternal life. 6
16 should not perish but have eternal life. 6
36 He who believes in the Son has eternal life; 6
4:14 a spring of water welling up to eternal life. 6
36 and gathers fruit for eternal life 6
5:24 he who hears . . has eternal life 6
39 in them you have eternal life 6
6:27 the food which endures to eternal life 6
40 every one . . should have eternal life 6
47 he who believes has eternal life. 6
54 he who . . drinks my blood has eternal life 6
68 You have the words of eternal life; 6
10:28 I give them eternal life 6
12:25 will keep it for eternal life. 6
50 I know that his commandment is eternal life. 6
17: 2 to give eternal life to all 6
3 this is eternal life, that they know thee 6
Act 13:46 judge yourselves unworthy of eternal life 6
48 as many as were ordained to eternal life 6
Rom 1:20 namely, his eternal power and deity 4
2: 7 he will give eternal life; 6
5:21 to eternal life through Jesus Christ our Lord. 6
6:22 and its end, eternal life. 6
23 but the free gift of God is eternal life in Christ 6
16:26 according to the command of the eternal God 6
2Co 4:17 preparing for us an eternal weight of glory 6

18 the things that are unseen are eternal. 6
5: 1 not made with hands, eternal in the heavens. 6
Gal 6: 8 will from the Spirit reap eternal life. 6
Eph 3:11 This was according to the eternal purpose 5
2Th 1: 9 suffer the punishment of eternal destruction 6
2:16 gave us eternal comfort and good hope 6
1Ti 1:16 who were to believe in him for eternal life. 6
6:12 the eternal life to which you were called 6
16 To him be honor and eternal dominion. Amen. 6
2Ti 2:10 salvation . . with its eternal glory. 6
Tit 1: 2 in hope of eternal life 6
3: 7 become heirs in hope of eternal life. 6
Heb 5: 9 he became the source of eternal salvation 6
6: 2 resurrection of the dead, and eternal judgment. 6
9:12 thus securing an eternal redemption. 6
14 who through the eternal Spirit offered himself 6
15 may receive the promised eternal inheritance 6
13:20 by the blood of the eternal covenant 6
1Pe 5:10 who has called you to his eternal glory in Christ 6
2Pe 1:11 an entrance into the eternal kingdom of our Lord 6
1Jn 1: 2 and proclaim to you the eternal life 6
2:25 this is what he has promised us, eternal life. 6
3:15 no murderer has eternal life abiding in him. 6
5:11 the testimony, that God gave us eternal life 6
13 that you may know that you have eternal life. 6
20 This is the true God and eternal life. 6
Jde 1: 6 kept by him in eternal chains in the nether gloom 4
7 by undergoing a punishment of eternal fire. 6
21 the mercy of our Lord . . unto eternal life. 6
Rev 14: 6 another angel . . with an eternal gospel to proclaim 6
2Es 2:35 because the eternal light will shine upon you 9
7:119 if an eternal age has been promised to us 8
Tob 3: 6 to go to the eternal abode 6
Wis 7:26 For she is a reflection of eternal light 4
17: 2 exiles from eternal providence. 6
Sir 1:15 She made among men an eternal foundation 5
16:27 He arranged his works in an eternal order 7
17:12 He established with them an eternal covenant 5
30:17 and eternal rest than chronic sickness. 5
46:19 Before the time of his eternal sleep 5
Sus 1:42 O eternal God, who dost discern what is secret 6
2Mc 1:25 who alone art just and almighty and eternal 6
3Mc 7:16 the eternal Savior of Israel 6
4Mc 9: 9 deservedly undergo . . eternal torment by fire 6
10:15 by the eternal destruction of the tyrant 6
12:12 intense and eternal fire and tortures 6
13:15 the danger of eternal torment lying before those 6
15: 3 religion that preserves them for eternal life 6

eternal one 1. *αἰώνιος*
3Mc 6:12 you, O Eternal One, who have all might and all power 1

eternity 1. עַד 2. עוֹלָם 3. *ἀϊδιότης* 4. *αἰών*
5. saeculum
Ecc 3:11 also he has put eternity into man's mind 2
Isa 45:17 put to shame or confounded to all eternity. 1
57:15 the high and lofty One who inhabits eternity 1
2Pe 3:18 glory both now and to the day of eternity. Amen. 4
2Es 8:20 O Lord who inhabitest eternity 5
Tob 6:17 she was destined for you from eternity 4
Wis 2:23 made him in the image of his own eternity 3
Sir 1: 2 the days of eternity–who can count them? 4
4 prudent understanding from eternity. 4
18:10 so are a few years in the day of eternity. 4
24: 9 From eternity, in the beginning, he created me 4
9 for eternity I shall not cease to exist. 4
4Mc 17:18 and live through blessed eternity. 4

all eternity 1. עוֹלָם עַד
Isa 45:17 put to shame or confounded to all eternity. 1

ethnarch 1. *ἐθνάρχης*
1Mc 14:47 be commander and ethnarch of the Jews and priests 1
15: 1 Simon, the priest and ethnarch of the Jews 1
2 Simon the high priest and ethnarch 1

eunuch 1. אִישׁ סָרִיס 2. סָרִיס 3. *εὐνοῦχος*
2Kg 9:32 Two or three eunuchs looked out at him. 2
20:18 they shall be eunuchs in the palace of the king 2
Est 1:10 he commanded . . the seven eunuchs who served 2
12 at the king's command conveyed by the eunuchs. 2
15 Ahasu-e'rus conveyed by the eunuchs? 2
2: 3 Hegai the king's eunuch . . in charge of the women; 2
14 Sha-ash'gaz the king's eunuch who was in charge 2
15 Hegai the king's eunuch, who had charge 2
21 Bigthan and Teresh, two of the king's eunuchs 2
4: 4 Esther's maids and her eunuchs came and told her 2
5 called for Hathach, one of the king's eunuchs 2
6: 2 Bigthana and Teresh, two of the king's eunuchs 2
14 the king's eunuchs arrived and brought Haman 2
7: 9 one of the eunuchs in attendance on the king 2
Isa 39: 7 be eunuchs in the palace of the king of Babylon. 2
56: 3 let not the eunuch say, "Behold, I am a dry tree. 2
4 the LORD: "To the eunuchs who keep my sabbaths 2
Jer 29: 2 King Jeconi'ah, and the queen mother, the eunuchs 2
34:19 the eunuchs, the priests, and all the people 2
38: 7 When E'bed-mel'ech the Ethiopian, a eunuch 1
41:16 soldiers, women, children, and eunuchs 2
Dan 1: 7 chief of the eunuchs gave them names: Daniel 2
8 asked the chief of the eunuchs to allow him not 2
9 favor . . in the sight of the chief of the eunuchs; 2
10 chief of the eunuchs said to Daniel, "I fear lest my 2
11 said to the steward whom the chief of the eunuchs 2
18 chief of the eunuchs brought them in before 2
Mat 19:12 For there are eunuchs who have been so from birth 3
12 there are eunuchs who have been made eunuchs 3
12 who have made themselves eunuchs 3
Act 8:27 an Ethiopian, a eunuch, a minister of the Can'dace 3
34 the eunuch said to Philip 3
36 the eunuch said, "See, here is water! 3
38 Philip and the eunuch 3
39 the eunuch saw him no more 3
Jdt 12:11 the eunuch who had charge of his personal affairs 3
AEs 12: 1 Gabatha and Tharra, the two eunuchs of the king 3
3 Then the king examined the two eunuchs 3
6 because of the two eunuchs of the king. 3
Wis 3:14 Blessed also is the eunuch 3
Sir 20: 4 Like a eunuch's desire to violate a maiden 3
30:20 like a eunuch who embraces a maiden and groans. 3

eunuch *See also* make.

evacuate 1. *ἐξέρχομαι*
1Mc 6:49 they evacuated the city 1
61 the Jews evacuated the stronghold. 1

evade 1. סבב מִפְּנֵי
1Sm 18:11 But David evaded him twice. 1

evangelist 1. *εὐαγγελιστής*
Act 21: 8 we entered the house of Philip the evangelist 1
Eph 4:11 some prophets, some evangelists 1
2Ti 4: 5 do the work of an evangelist 1

even 1. אִם 2. אַף 3. אַף כִּי 4. גַּם 5. הֵן 6. וְ 7. כְּ
8. כַּאֲשֶׁר 9. כִּי 10. מִן 11. עַד 12. עֶרֶב 13. *αὐτός*
14. *γάρ* 15. *δέ* 16. *εἰ* 17. *ἔτι* 18. *ἕως*
19. *ἕως τοῦ ἐλθεῖν* 20. *καθώς* 21. *καί* 22. *καὶ ἄν*
23. *καὶ ἔτι* 24. *καίτοι* 25. *καὶ τοῦτο* 26. *μέχρι*
27. *μή γε* 28. *μηδέ* 29. *μήποτε* 30. *μόνον* 31. *νῦν*
32. *ὅμως* 33. *οὐδέ* 34. *προσέτι* 35. *τε* 36. *ὥσπερ*
37. certe 38. et 39. nec 40. neque
Gen 27:34 Bless me, even me also, O my father! •
38 Bless me, even me also, O my father. •
30: 3 upon my knees, and even I may have children 4
46:34 keepers of cattle from our youth even until now 6
49:27 wolf . . at even dividing the spoil. 12
Exd 2:19 An Egyptian . . even drew water for us 4
4: 9 If they will not believe even these two signs 4
7:23 he did not lay even this to heart. 4
11: 5 even to the first-born of the maidservant who is 11
30:21 it shall be a statute for ever to them, even to him •
Lev 21:11 shall not . . defile himself, even for his father 7
Num 4:20 look upon the holy things even for a moment 10
6: 4 not even the seeds or the skins. 6
9:19 Even when the cloud continued 6
14:19 forgiven this people, from Egypt even until now. •
45 defeated them and pursued them, even to Hormah. 11
Deu 2:22 settled in their stead even to this day. 6
9: 8 Even at Horeb you provoked the LORD to wrath 4
12:31 even burn their sons and their daughters 4
23: 2 even to the tenth generation none 4
3 even to the tenth generation none belonging 6
32:31 even our enemies themselves being judges. •
39 'See now that I, even I, am he, and there is no god •
Jos 13: 6 the inhabitants of . . even all the Sido'nians. •
Rut 1:12 even if I should have a husband this night 4
17 May the LORD . . if even death parts me from you. •
2: 7 she has . . without resting even for a moment. •
15 Let her glean even among the sheaves 4
1Sm 8: 8 from the day I brought them up . . even to this day 6
14:15 the garrison and even the raiders trembled; 4
21 Hebrews who had . . even they also turned to be 4
18: 4 and even his sword and his bow and his girdle. 11
21: 5 are holy, even when it is a common journey; •
2Sm 17: 9 even now he has hidden himself in one of the pits •
10 Then even the valiant man . . will utterly melt 4
13 until not even a pebble is to be found there. 4
18:12 Even if I felt in my hand the weight of 1,000 6
1Kg 1:30 as I swore to you . . even so will I do this day. 9
4:25 Judah and Israel . . from Dan even to Beer-sheba 6
7: 7 Hall of the Throne . . even the Hall of Judgment; •
9 of costly stones . . even from the foundation •
17:20 hast thou brought calamity even upon the widow 4
18:22 I, even I only, am left a prophet of the LORD; •
19:10 I, even I only, am left; and they seek my life •
14 I, even I only, am left; and they seek my life •
2Kg 16: 3 He even burned his son as an offering 4
18:12 his covenant, even all that Moses . . commanded; •
21:15 since the day their fathers . . even to this day. 6
1Ch 11: 2 In times past, even when Saul was king, it was you 4
28:20 for the LORD God, even my God, is with you. •
2Ch 1:11 and have not even asked long life, but have asked 4
2: 6 heaven, even highest heaven, cannot contain him? 6
15:16 Even Ma'acah, his mother, King Asa removed 4
16:12 yet even in his disease he did not seek the LORD 4
22: 5 He even followed their counsel 4
26: 8 his fame spread even to the border of Egypt •
28: 2 He even made molten images for the Ba'als; 4
Ezr 4: 5 even until the reign of Darius king of Persia. 6
10: 2 even now there is hope for Israel in spite •
Neh 5: 8 but you even sell your brethren that they may be 4
15 Even their servants lorded it over the people. 4
9:18 Even when they had made . . a molten calf and said 2
13:26 nevertheless foreign women made even him to sin. 4
Est 5: 3 It shall be . . even to the half of my kingdom. 11
6 Even to the half of my kingdom, it shall be 11
12 Even Queen Esther let no one come . . but myself. 2
7: 2 Even to the half of my kingdom, it shall be 11
8 Will he even assault the queen in my presence 4
Job 4:18 Even in his servants he puts no trust 5
5: 5 the hungry eat, and he takes it even out of thorns; •
6:10 I would even exult in pain unsparing; •
27 You would even cast lots over the fatherless 2
16:19 Even now, behold, my witness is in heaven 4
19:18 Even young children despise me; 4
23: 3 that I might come even to his seat! •
25: 5 Behold, even the moon is not bright 11
40: 8 Will you even put me in the wrong? 2
41: 9 he is laid low even at the sight of him. 4
Ps 19:10 desired are they than gold, even much fine gold; 6
23: 4 Even though I walk through the valley 4
33:22 love, O LORD, be upon us, even as we hope in thee. 8
41: 9 Even my bosom friend in whom I trusted 4
49:10 Yea, he shall see that even the wise die •
68:18 gifts among men, even among the rebellious 2
71:18 even to old age and gray hairs, O God, do not forsake 4
84: 3 Even the sparrow finds a home 4
90:10 or even by reason of strength fourscore; 1
105:30 with frogs, even in the chambers of their kings. •
109: 4 accuse me, even as I make prayer for them. 6
116:10 I kept my faith, even when I said •
139: 4 Even before a word is on my tongue, lo, O LORD 9
10 even there thy hand shall lead me 4
12 even the darkness is not dark to thee 4
Prv 8:19 My fruit is better than gold, even fine gold 10
14:13 Even in laughter the heart is sad 4
20 The poor is disliked even by his neighbor 4
16: 4 even the wicked for the day of trouble. 4
7 makes even his enemies to be at peace with him. 4
17:28 Even a fool who keeps silent is considered wise; 4
19:24 will not even bring it back to his mouth. 4
20:11 Even a child makes himself known by his acts 4
22:19 I have made them known to you today, even to you. 2
28: 9 even his prayer is an abomination. 4
Ecc 2:23 even in the night his mind does not rest. 4
3:16 the place of justice, even there was wickedness •
16 of righteousness, even there was wickedness. •
8:17 even though a wise man claims to know 4
10: 3 Even when the fool walks . . he lacks sense 4
20 Even in your thought, do not curse the king 4
11: 2 Give a portion to seven, or even to eight 4
Isa 1: 6 From the sole of the foot even to the head 6
15 even though you make many prayers 4
8: 8 overflow and pass on, reaching even to the neck; 11
23:12 over to Cyprus, even there you will have no rest. 4
25:12 cast to the ground, even to the dust. 11
32: 7 even when the plea of the needy is right. 6
33:23 even the lame will take the prey. 4
40:30 Even youths shall faint and be weary 6
46: 4 even to your old age I am He, and to gray hairs •
48:15 I, even I, have spoken and called him •
49:15 Even these may forget, yet I will not forget you. 4
25 Even the captives of the mighty shall be taken 4
57: 9 your envoys far off, and sent down even to Sheol. •
11 Have I not held my peace, even for a long time 6
Jer 2:33 even to wicked women you have taught your ways. 4
3:25 we and our fathers, from our youth even to this day; 6
5:18 But even in those days, says the LORD 4
8: 7 Even the stork in the heavens knows her times; 4
13 even the leaves are withered 6
11: 7 warning them persistently, even to this day 6
12: 6 even your brothers and the house of your father 4
6 even they have dealt treacherously with you; 4
16 even as they taught my people to swear by Ba'al •
14: 5 Even the hind in the field forsakes her newborn 4
22:25 even into the hand of Nebuchadrez'zar 6
23:11 even in my house I have found their wickedness 4
27 even as their fathers forgot my name for Ba'al? 8
25:14 great kings shall make slaves even of them; 4
28:14 I have given to him even the beasts of the field 4
36:25 even when Elna'than and Delai'ah and Gemari'ah 4
37:10 For even if you should defeat the whole army 4
44:10 have not humbled themselves even to this day 11
46:21 Even her hired soldiers in her midst 4
49:20 Even the little ones of the flock shall be †
51: 9 and has been lifted up even to the skies. •
Lam 4: 3 Even the jackals give the breast and suckle 4
Ezk 4: 1 and portray upon it a city, even Jerusalem; •
5: 8 therefore thus says the Lord GOD: Behold, I, even I 4
6: 3 Behold, I, even I, will bring a sword upon you •
11:15 even your brethren, your fellow exiles •
14:14 even if these three men, Noah, Daniel, and Job •
16 even if these three men were in it •
20 even if Noah, Daniel, and Job were in it, as I live •

16:29 and even with this you were not satisfied. 4
21:27 ruin I will make it; there shall not be even a trace 4
23:37 have even offered up to them for food the sons 4
40 They even sent for men to come from far 3
25:13 I will make it desolate; from Teman even to Dedan •
32: 6 I will drench the land even to the mountains •
34: 2 prophesy, and say to them, even to the shepherds •
36:12 I will let men walk upon you, even my people Israel; •
41:17 to the space above the door, even to the inner room 6
Dan 8:10 It grew great, even to the host of heaven; •
11 magnified . . even up to the Prince of the host; •
25 even rise up against the Prince of princes; •
11:15 shall not stand, or even his picked troops •
26 Even those who eat his rich food •
Hos 3: 1 even as the LORD loves the people of Israel •
4: 3 and even the fish of the sea are taken away. 4
5:14 I, even I, will rend and go away, I will carry off •
9:12 Even if they bring up children 9
16 Even though they bring forth, I will slay 4
Jol 1:18 even the flocks of sheep are dismayed. 4
20 Even the wild beasts cry to thee 4
2:12 Yet even now," says the LORD, "return to me 4
16 gather the children, even nursing infants. 6
29 Even upon the menservants and maidservants 4
Ams 4: 2 with hooks, even the last of you with fishhooks. 6
5:22 Even though you offer me your burnt offerings 9
Zec 8:20 yet come, even the inhabitants of many cities; 6
9: 1 of Aram, even as all the tribes of Israel; 6
11:16 of the fat ones, tearing off even their hoofs. 6
14:14 even Judah will fight against Jerusalem. 4
Mat 5:46 Do not even the tax collectors do the same? 21
47 than others? Do not even the Gentiles do the same? 21
6:29 even Solomon in all his glory was not arrayed 33
8:10 Truly, I say to you, not even in Israel have I found •
27 that even winds and sea obey him? 21
10:30 even the hairs of your head are all numbered. 21
42 even a cup of cold water 30
13:12 even what he has will be taken away. 21
15:27 She said, "Yes, Lord, yet even the dogs eat the crumbs 21
18:17 if he refuses to listen even to the church 21
20:28 even as the Son of man came not to be served 36
21:21 but even if you say to this mountain 22
32 even when you saw it, you did not afterward repent •
24:24 to lead astray, if possible, even the elect. 21
36 not even the angels of heaven, nor the Son 33
25:29 even what he has will be taken away. 21
26:38 My soul is very sorrowful, even to death •
27:14 he gave him no answer, not even to a single charge; 33
Mrk 1:27 he commands even the unclean spirits 21
2: 2 not even about the door 28
28 the Son of man is lord even of the sabbath. 21
3:20 so that they could not even eat. 28
4:25 from him who has not, even what he has will be taken 21
41 Who then is this, that even wind and sea obey him? 21
5: 3 even with a chain; 33
28 If I touch even his garments, I shall be made well. 22
6:23 I will give you, even half of my kingdom. 18
56 touch even the fringe of his garment 22
7:28 Yes, Lord; yet even the dogs under the table eat 21
37 he even makes the deaf hear and the dumb speak. 21
8:26 Do not even enter the village. 28
13:32 not even the angels in heaven, nor the Son 33
14:29 Even though they all fall away, I will not. 21
34 My soul is very sorrowful, even to death 18
59 Yet not even so did their testimony agree. 33
Lke 1:15 with the Holy Spirit, even from his mother's womb. 17
3: 9 Even now the axe is laid to the root of the trees; 21
6:29 do not withhold even your shirt. 21
32 even sinners love those who love them. 21
33 even sinners do the same. 21
34 Even sinners lend to sinners 21
36 Be merciful, even as your Father is merciful. 21
7: 9 not even in Israel have I found such faith. 33
49 Who is this, who even forgives sins? 21
8:18 even what he thinks that he has will be taken 21
25 he commands even wind and water, and they obey 21
10:11 'Even the dust of your town that clings to our feet 21
17 even the demons are subject to us in your name! 21
12: 7 Why, even the hairs of your head are all numbered. 21
27 even Solomon in all his glory was not arrayed 33
14:26 yes, and even his own life 21
18:11 or even like this tax collector. 21
13 would not even lift up his eyes to heaven 33
15 Now they were bringing even infants to him 21
19:26 even what he has will be taken away. 21
42 saying, "Would that even today you knew the things 21
20:37 that the dead are raised, even Moses showed 21
21:16 You will be delivered up even by parents 21
23: 5 from Galilee even to this place. 18
24:23 saying that they had even seen a vision of angels 21
Joh 1:27 even he who comes after me •
5:23 even as they honor the Father 20
7: 5 For even his brothers did not believe in him. 33
8:25 Even what I have told you from the beginning. 21
41 we have one Father, even God. •
11:22 even now I know that whatever you ask from God 21
12:13 even the King of Israel! 21
42 many even of the authorities believed in him 21
13:34 even as I have loved you 20
14:17 even the Spirit of truth •
15:26 even the Spirit of truth •
17:11 that they may be one, even as we are one. 20
14 not of the world, even as I am not of the world. 20
16 not of the world, even as I am not of the world. 20
21 they may all be one; even as thou, Father, art in me 20
22 that they may be one even as we are one 20
23 and hast loved them even as thou hast loved me. 20
Act 5:15 they even carried out the sick into the streets 21
39 You might even be found opposing God! 29
7: 5 not even a foot's length 33
44 even as he who spoke to Moses directed him 20
8:13 Even Simon himself believed 21
10:45 had been poured out even on the Gentiles. 21
17:28 as even some of your poets have said 21
19: 2 never even heard that there is a Holy Spirit. 16
27 she may even be deposed from her magnificence 21
21:13 am ready not only to be imprisoned but even to die 21
24: 6 He even tried to profane the temple 21
26:11 I persecuted them even to foreign cities. 21
Rom 3:12 no one does good, not even one. 18
5: 7 perhaps for a good man one will dare even to die. 21
14 even over those whose sins were not like 21
9:24 even us whom he has called, not from the Jews only 21
11:23 And even the others, if they do not persist 21
1Co 1: 6 even as the testimony to Christ was confirmed 20
28 even things that are not •
2:10 even the depths of God. 21
3: 2 even yet you are not ready 31
4: 3 I do not even judge myself. 33
5: 1 of a kind that is not found even among pagans 33
11 not even to eat with such a one. 28
6: 8 even your own brethren. 25
11: 2 even as I have delivered them to you. 20
13:12 even as I have been fully understood. 20
14: 7 If even lifeless instruments 32
34 be subordinate, as even the law says. 20
15:15 We are even found to be misrepresenting God 21
16: 6 stay with you or even spend the winter 21
2Co 4: 3 even if our gospel is veiled 21
5:16 even though we once regarded Christ 21
7: 5 For even when we came into Macedo'nia 21
8 For even if I made you sorry with my letter 21
10: 8 even if I boast a little too much of our authority 35
13 to reach even to you. 21
11: 6 Even if I am unskilled in speaking 21
14 even Satan disguises himself as an angel •
16 even if you do, accept me as a fool 27
12:11 even though I am nothing. 21
Gal 1: 8 even if we, or an angel from heaven, should preach 21
2: 3 even Titus, who was with me, was not compelled 33
5 we did not yield submission even for a moment 33
13 so that even Barnabas was carried away 21
16 even we have believed in Christ Jesus 21
3:15 no one annuls even a man's will, or adds to it 32
6:13 For even those who receive circumcision 33
Eph 1: 4 even as he chose us in him 20
2: 5 even when we were dead through our trespasses 21
5: 3 covetousness must not even be named among you 28
12 it is a shame even to speak of the things 21
Php 2: 8 became obedient unto death, even death on a cross 15
17 Even if I am to be poured as a libation 21
3:18 now tell you even with tears 21
21 even to subject all things to himself. 21
4:16 for even in Thessaloni'ca you sent me help once 21
2Th 3:10 even when we were with you 21
1Ti 5: 6 she . . is dead even while she lives. •
25 even when they are not, they cannot remain hidden. •
Phm 1:19 say nothing of your owing me even your own self. 21
21 knowing that you will do even more than I say. 21
Heb 7: 9 One might even say . . 21
15 This becomes even more evident 21
9: 1 Now even the first covenant had regulations 21
18 Hence even the first covenant was not ratified 33
11:11 even when she was past the age 21
19 God was able to raise men even from the dead 21
36 even chains and imprisonment. 17
Jas 2:19 Even the demons believe–and shudder. 21
1Pe 3:14 even if you do suffer for righteousness' sake 21
4: 6 the gospel was preached even to the dead 21
2Pe 2: 1 even denying the Master who bought them 21
Jde 1:23 hating even the garment spotted by the flesh. 21
Rev 2:13 you did not deny . . even in the days of An'tipas 21
27 even as I myself have received power 21
13:13 even making fire come down from heaven to earth 21
15 so that the image of the beast should even speak 21
1Es 1:49 Even the leaders of the people and of the priests 21
2:19 will even resist kings. 21
4:42 Ask what you wish, even beyond what is written •
8:80 Even in our bondage we were not forsaken 21
92 even now there is hope for Israel. 21
2Es 5:45 it might even now be able to support all of them 38
7:130or even myself who have spoken to them. 39
8:48 even in this respect you will be praiseworthy 38
57 they have even trampled upon his righteous ones 38
11: 6 not even one creature that was on the earth. 40
17 rule as long as you, or even half as long. 39
12: 5 and not even a little strength is left in me 39
16:27 to see another, or even to hear his voice. 37
Jdt 1:10 even beyond Tanis and Memphis 19
4:12 They even surrounded the altar with sackcloth 21
8:11 you have even sworn and pronounced this oath 21
15 even to destroy us in the presence of our enemies. 21
11: 2 even now, if your people . . had not slighted me •
14 even the people . . have been doing this 21
13:11 even as he has done this day! 21
15: 5 even beyond Damascus and its borders. •
AEs 16: 3 they even undertake to scheme 21
Wis 3:17 Even if they live long 35
7:15 the guide even of wisdom 21
11:20 Even apart from these 21
12: 8 even these thou didst spare 21
24 animals which even their enemies despised 21
13: 8 Yet again, not even they are to be excused; 33
14: 5 even to the smallest piece of wood 21
6 even in the beginning 21
18 even those who did not know the king 21
15: 2 For even if we sin we are thine, knowing thy power; 21
12 get money however one can, even by base means. 22
18 worship even the most hateful animals 21
19 even as animals they are not so beautiful 33
16:10 even by the teeth of venomous serpents 33
19 even in the midst of water 21
23 the fire . . even forgot its native power. 21
17: 4 not even the inner chamber . . protected them 33
9 For even if nothing disturbing frightened them 21
10 refusing to look even at the air 21
18:12 the living were not sufficient even to bury them 33
19: 1 God knew in advance even their future actions 21
20 Fire even in water retained its normal power •
Sir 0: 2 Not only this work, but even the law itself, 21
4:28 Strive even to death for the truth 18
7: 8 even for one you will not go unpunished. 14
10: 9 for even in life his bowels decay. •
12: 9 even his friend will separate from him. 21
13: 3 A rich man does wrong, and he even adds reproaches; 13
23:19 perceive even the hidden places. •
27:24 even the Lord will hate him. 21
43:30 he will surpass even that 23
46:20 Even after he had fallen asleep he prophesied 21
47: 7 he crushed their power even to this day. 18
LJr 1:11 and even give some of it to the harlots 21
19 even more than they light for themselves 21
24 even when they were being cast 33
40 Besides, even the Chaldeans . . dishonor them; 21
59 better even the door of a house 21
1Mc 1:28 Even the land shook for its inhabitants 21
37 they even defiled the sanctuary. 21
43 Many even from Israel 21
2:19 Even if all the nations . . obey him •
7:46 not even one of them was left. 33
2Mc 3: 3 even Seleucus, the king of Asia 21
4: 3 even murders were committed 21
47 if they had pleaded even before Scythians. 21
49 Therefore even the Tyrians . . provided 21
6:20 even for the natural love of life. •
23 and his excellent life even from childhood •
26 even if for the present 21
8:18 to strike down . . even the whole world. •
12:14 railing at them and even blaspheming 34
3Mc 1:11 not even members of their own nation were allowed 28
12 Even after the law had been read to him 35
12 Even if those men are deprived of this honor 21
20 nurses abandoned even newborn children 15
2: 4 among whom were even giants 21
3:27 old people or children or even infants 21
4: 4 even some of their enemies 21
16 are not able even to communicate 21
6: 6 you rescued unharmed, even to a hair 26
10 Even if our lives have become entangled 15
11 'Not even their god has rescued them.' 33
15 Not even . . in the land of their enemies 33
17 even the nearby valleys resounded with them 21
20 Even the king began to shudder bodily 21
24 even me, your benefactor, you . . deprive 13
7:16 those who had held fast to God even to death 26
4Mc 1:11 all people, even their torturers, marveled †
25 there exists even a malevolent tendency 21
2: 7 a glutton, or even a drunkard 21
10 the law prevails even over affection for parents 21
14 reason . . can prevail even over enmity 21
15 reason rules even the more violent emotions 21
16 for it is sovereign over even this. 21
3:18 bodily agonies even when they are extreme •
20 even Seleucus Nicanor, king of Asia 21
4:25 even to the point that . . 21
5:10 you will do something even more senseless 21
18 Even if, as you suppose, our law were not . . divine 24
18 not even so would it be right for us 33
30 not even if you gouge out my eyes 33
37 one who does not fear your violence even to death. 26
6:11 in fact . . he amazed even his torturers 21
21 and not protect our divine law even to death. 26
30 he resisted even to the very tortures of death 26
34 when it masters even external agonies 21
7: 8 in sufferings even to death. 26
16 an aged man despised tortures even to death 26

8: 1 even the very young . . have prevailed 21
2 these should be tortured even more cruelly. •
10 Even I, your enemy, have compassion for your youth 21
25 Not even the law itself would arbitrarily slay 33
9: 6 it would be even more fitting •
14: 9 Even now, we ourselves shudder as we hear •
11 mind of woman despised even more diverse agonies 21
14 Even unreasoning animals, like mankind 21
19 since even bees . . defend themselves 21
19 and defend it even to the death? 18
15:10 they obeyed her even to death 26
16:14 you have conquered even a tyrant 21
17:10 and enduring torture even to death. 26

even *See also* army, if, no, nor, than, unable, without.

even declare 1. superdico
2Es 7:23 they even declared that the Most High 1

even if 1. אַף 2. *ἐάν* 3. *καὶ ἄν*
Job 19: 4 even if it be true that I have erred 1
Mat 26:35 Even if I must die with you, I will not deny you. 3
Joh 8:14 Even if I do bear witness to myself 3
16 Yet even if I do judge, my judgment is true 2
Wis 4: 4 For even if they put forth boughs for a while 3
9: 6 for even if one is perfect among the sons of men 3
14: 4 even if a man lacks skill, he may put to sea. 3
Sir 3:13 even if he is lacking in understanding 3
12:11 Even if he humbles himself 2
14: 7 even if he does good, he does it unintentionally 3
16:11 Even if there is only one stiff-necked person 3
22:21 Even if you have drawn your sword 2
4Mc 10:18 he said, "Even if you remove my organ of speech 3

even more 1. יסף 2. *ἔτι* 3. *μᾶλλον* 4. *πολύς*
Isa 15: 9 yet I will bring upon Dibon even more 1
1Co 14: 5 to speak in tongues, but even more to prophesy 3
2Mc 9: 7 but was even more filled with arrogance 2
4Mc 11: 3 you will incur punishment . . for even more crimes. 4

even now 1. *ἤδη*
Mat 3:10 Even now the axe is laid to the root of the trees; 1

even push away 1. *προσαπωθέω*
Sir 13:21 he is even pushed away by friends. 1

even push down 1. *προσανατρέπω*
Sir 13:23 should he stumble, they even push him down. 1

even reproach 1. *προσεπιτιμάω*
Sir 13:22 If a humble man slips, they even reproach him 1

even so 1. כָּכָה 2. כֵּן 3. *καί* 4. *ναί* 5. *οὗτος* 6. et
1Kg 1:37 As the LORD has been . . even so may he be 2
Jer 13: 9 Even so will I spoil the pride of Judah 1
28:11 Even so will I break the yoke of Nebuchadnez'zar 1
Joh 20:21 As the Father has sent me, even so I send you. 3
Eph 5:28 Even so husbands should love their wives 5
1Th 4:14 even so, through Jesus, God will bring 5
Rev 1: 7 Behold, he is coming . . Even so. Amen. 4
2Es 5:48 Even so have I given the womb of the earth to those 6

even then 1. *οὗτος*
1Co 14:21 even then they will not listen to me 1

even though 1. אִלּוּ 2. גַּם 3. וְ 4. כִּי 5. *καί* 6. *καὶ ἄν* 7. *καίπερ*
2Ch 30:19 even though not according to the sanctuary's rules 3
Ps 119:23 Even though princes sit plotting against me 2
Ecc 4:14 even though he had gone from prison to the throne 4
6: 6 Even though he should live 1,000 years 1
Jer 2:11 changed its gods, even though they are no gods? 3
Joh 10:38 if I do them, even though you do not believe me 6
Rom 2:14 even though they do not have the law. •
1Mc 8: 4 even though the place was far distant from them. 5
4Mc 2: 8 even though he is a lover of money 6
12: 2 Even though the tyrant had been . . reproached 7
18:14 Even though you go through the fire 6

even to all 1. *ὅσος*
Rev 1: 2 bore witness . . even to all that he saw. 1

even to the thought of 1. *ὥστε*
Tob 3:10 even to the thought of hanging herself 1

even unto 1. *ἄχρι* 2. *μέχρι*
Rev 12:11 they loved not their lives even unto death. 1
4Mc 13: 1 seven brothers despised sufferings even unto death 2

even yet 1. עַד הַיּוֹם הַזֶּה
Jos 22:17 sin . . from which even yet we have not cleansed 1

evening 1. נטה 2. נֶשֶׁף 3. ערב 4. עֶרֶב 5. עֵת הָעֶרֶב 6. *δειλινός* 7. *ἑσπέρα* 8. *ὀψέ* 9. *ὀψία* 10. *ὄψιος* 11. nox 12. serus
Gen 1: 5 there was evening and there was morning, one day 4
8 And there was evening and there was morning 4
13 there was evening and there was morning 4
19 was evening and there was morning, a fourth day 4
23 there was evening and there was morning 4
31 behold, it was very good. And there was evening 4
8:11 the dove came back to him in the evening 4
19: 1 The two angels came to Sodom in the evening 4
24:11 the well of water at the time of evening 4
63 to meditate in the field in the evening; 4
29:23 in the evening he took his daughter Leah 4
30:16 When Jacob came from the field in the evening 4
Exd 12: 6 Israel shall kill their lambs in the evening. 4
18 on the fourteenth day of the month at evening 4
18 the twenty-first day of the month at evening. 4
16: 6 At evening you shall know that it was the LORD who 4
8 the LORD gives you in the evening flesh to eat 4
13 In the evening quails came up and covered 4
18:13 stood about Moses from morning till evening. 4
14 stand about you from morning till evening? 4
27:21 tend it from evening to morning before the LORD. 4
29:39 the other lamb you shall offer in the evening; 4
41 the other lamb you shall offer in the evening 4
30: 8 when Aaron sets up the lamps in the evening 4
Lev 6:20 in the morning and half in the evening 4
11:24 touches . . shall be unclean until the evening 4
25 shall . . be unclean until the evening 4
27 shall be unclean until the evening 4
28 shall . . be unclean until the evening 4
31 shall be unclean until the evening 4
32 it shall be unclean until the evening 4
39 he . . shall be unclean until the evening 4
40 he . . shall . . be unclean until the evening 4
40 he . . shall . . be unclean until the evening 4
14:46 he . . shall be unclean until the evening 4
15: 5 in water, and be unclean until the evening 4
6 bathe . . and be unclean until the evening 4
7 bathe . . and be unclean until the evening 4
8 bathe . . and be unclean until the evening 4
10 touches . . shall be unclean until the evening 4
10 bathe . . and be unclean until the evening 4
11 bathe . . and be unclean until the evening 4
16 shall bathe . . and be unclean until the evening 4
17 be washed . . and be unclean until the evening 4
18 bathe . . and be unclean until the evening 4
19 touches her shall be unclean until the evening 4
21 bathe . . and be unclean until the evening 4
22 bathe . . and be unclean until the evening 4
23 touches it he shall be unclean until the evening 4
27 bathe . . and be unclean until the evening 4
17:15 bathe . . and be unclean until the evening 4
22: 6 any such shall be unclean until the evening 4
23: 5 on the fourteenth day of the month in the evening 4
32 on the ninth day of the month beginning at evening 4
32 from evening to evening shall you keep 4
32 from evening to evening shall you keep 4
24: 3 keep it in order from evening to morning 4
Num 9: 3 fourteenth day of this month, in the evening 4
5 on the fourteenth day of the month, in the evening 4
11 month on the fourteenth day in the evening 4
15 at evening it was over the tabernacle 4
21 cloud remained from evening until morning; 4
19: 7 priest shall be unclean until evening. 4
8 shall be unclean until evening 4
10 he who gathers . . be unclean until evening. 4
19 at evening he shall be clean. 4
21 touches . . shall be unclean until evening. 4
22 touches it shall be unclean until evening. 4
28: 4 the other lamb you shall offer in the evening; 4
8 The other lamb you shall offer in the evening; 4
Deu 16: 4 sacrifice on the evening of the first day 4
6 passover . . in the evening at the going down 4
23:11 when evening comes on, he shall bathe himself 4
28:67 morning you shall say, 'Would it were evening!' 4
67 at evening you shall say, 'Would it were morning!' 4
Jos 5:10 the passover on the fourteenth day . . at evening 4
7: 6 upon his face before the ark . . until the evening 4
8:29 he hanged the king of Ai on a tree until evening; 5
10:26 And they hung upon the trees until evening; 4
Jdg 19: 9 now the day has waned toward evening; pray tarry 3
16 old man was coming from his work . . at evening; 4
20:23 and wept before the LORD until the evening; 4
26 fasted that day until evening, and offered burnt 4
21: 2 to Bethel, and sat there till evening before God 4
Rut 2:17 she gleaned in the field until evening; 4
1Sm 14:24 Cursed be the man who eats food until . . evening 4
17:16 came . . and took his stand, morning and evening. 3
20: 5 hide myself . . till the third day at evening. 4
30:17 from twilight until the evening of the next day; 4
2Sm 1:12 they mourned and wept and fasted until evening 4
11:13 in the evening he went out to lie on his couch 4
1Kg 17: 6 ravens brought . . bread and meat in the evening; 4
22:35 king was propped up . . until at evening he died; 4
2Kg 16:15 burnt offering, and the evening cereal offering 4
1Ch 16:40 continually morning and evening 4
23:30 and praising the LORD, and likewise at evening. 4
2Ch 2: 4 and for burnt offerings morning and evening 4
13:11 They offer . . every morning and every evening 4
11 that its lamps may burn every evening; 4
18:34 in his chariot facing the Syrians until evening; 4
31: 3 burnt offerings of morning and evening 4
Ezr 3: 3 offered . . burnt offerings morning and evening. 4
9: 4 sat appalled until the evening sacrifice. 4
5 at the evening sacrifice I rose from my fasting 4
Est 2:14 In the evening she went, and in the morning . . came 4
Job 4:20 Between morning and evening they are destroyed; 4
Ps 55:17 Evening and morning and at noon I utter 4
59: 6 Each evening they come back, howling like dogs 4
14 Each evening they come back, howling like dogs 4
65: 8 the morning and the evening to shout for joy. 4
90: 6 in the evening it fades and withers. 4
102:11 My days are like an evening shadow; 1
104:23 to his work and to his labor until the evening. 4
109:23 I am gone, like a shadow at evening; 1
141: 2 lifting up of my hands as an evening sacrifice! 4
Prv 7: 9 in the twilight, in the evening 4
Ecc 11: 6 sow . . and at evening withhold not your hand; 4
Isa 5:11 who tarry late into the evening till wine 2
17:14 At evening time, behold, terror! 4
Jer 6: 4 for the shadows of evening lengthen! 4
Ezk 12: 4 go forth yourself at evening in their sight 4
7 in the evening I dug through the wall 4
24:18 in the morning, and at evening my wife died. 4
33:22 the evening before the fugitive came; 4
46: 2 but the gate shall not be shut until evening. 4
Dan 8:14 said to him, "For 2,300 evenings and mornings; 4
26 vision of the evenings and the mornings 4
9:21 came . . at the time of the evening sacrifice. 4
Hab 1: 8 horses . . more fierce than the evening wolves; 4
Zep 2: 7 they shall lie down at evening. 4
3: 3 her judges are evening wolves 4
Zec 14: 7 for at evening time there shall be light. 4
Mat 8:16 That evening they brought to him many 10
14:15 When it was evening, the disciples came to him 10
23 When evening came, he was there alone 10
16: 2 When it is evening, you say, 'It will be fair weather; 10
20: 8 when evening came, the owner of the vineyard said 10
26:20 When it was evening 10
27:57 When it was evening, there came a rich man 10
Mrk 1:32 That evening, at sundown 10
4:35 On that day, when evening had come, he said to them 10
6:47 when evening came, the boat was out on the sea 10
11:19 when evening came they went out of the city. 8
13:35 in the evening, or at midnight, or at cockcrow 8
14:17 when it was evening he came with the twelve. 10
15:42 when evening had come 10
Lke 24:29 it is toward evening and the day is now far spent 7
Joh 6:16 When evening came 10
20:19 On the evening of that day 10
Act 4: 3 it was already evening 7
28:23 from morning till evening 7
1Es 5:50 burnt offerings . . morning and evening. 6
8:72 I sat . . until the evening sacrifice. 6
2Es 7:40 water or air, or darkness or evening or morning 12
10: 2 I remained quiet until evening of the second day 11
Tob 6: 1 they came at evening to the Tigris river 7
Jdt 9: 1 when that evening's incense was being offered 7
12: 9 until she ate her food toward evening. 7
13: 1 When evening came, his slaves quickly withdrew 9
Sir 18:26 From morning to evening conditions change 7
1Mc 9:13 the battle raged from morning till evening. 7
3Mc 5: 5 The servants . . went out in the evening 7
4Mc 3: 8 when evening fell, he came 7

evenly *See* applied.

event 1. *ἔκβασις* 2. *καιρός* 3. *λόγος*
Act 19:21 Now after these events •
Heb 11: 7 being warned by God concerning events as yet unseen •
1Es 1:24 The events of his reign have been recorded •
2Es 12: 9 and the last events of the times. •
Wis 11:14 at the end of the events they marveled at him 1
19:10 they still recalled the events of their sojourn •
1Mc 7:33 After these events Nicanor went up to Mount Zion 3
2Mc 4:17 a fact which later events will make clear. 2
3Mc 6:33 a great banquet to celebrate these events •

eventide *See* reach.

ever 1. יוֹם 2. כָּל הַיָּמִים 3. לְאֹרֶךְ יָמִים 4. לָנֶצַח 5. לָעַד 6. לְעוֹלָם 7. מְאֹד 8. נֵצַח 9. עַד 10. עֲדֵי עַד 11. עַד עוֹלָם 12. עוֹד 13. עוֹלָם 14. תָּמִיד 15. עָלַם (A) 16. *αἰών* 17. *αἰώνιος* 18. *ἄχρι αἰῶνος* 19. *δι' αἰῶνος* 20. *διὰ παντός* 21. *εἰς αἰῶνα* 22. *εἰς αἰῶνας* 23. *εἰς ἅπαντα χρόνον* 24. *εἰς πάντας αἰῶνας* 25. *εἰς πάντας τοὺς αἰῶνας* 26. *εἰς τὸ διηνεκές* 27. *εἰς τὸν αἰῶνα* 28. *εἰς τὸν αἰῶνα χρόνον* 29. *εἰς τοὺς αἰῶνας* 30. *ἐνδελεχής* 31. *ἕως αἰῶνος* 32. *ἕως τοῦ αἰῶνος* 33. *καθ' ἅπαν* 34. *ὅσος* 35. *οὐδέπω* 36. *οὔπω* 37. *οὗτος* 38. *πάντας αἰῶνας* 39. *ποτέ* 40. *ποτε καὶ ἄλλοτε* 41. *πώποτε* 42. *τὸν ἅπαντα χρόνον* 43. per saeculum 44. semper 45. umquam
Gen 3:22 of the tree of life, and eat, and live for ever"- 13
6: 3 My spirit shall not abide in man for ever 6
8:21 neither will I ever again destroy every living 12
13:15 to you and to your descendants for ever. 13
34:12 Ask of me ever so much as marriage present 7
43: 9 then let me bear the blame for ever; 2
Exd 3:15 this is my name for ever, and thus I am to be 6

5:22 O LORD . . Why didst thou ever send me? •
10:10 he said to them, "The LORD be with you, if ever I let •
11: 6 there has never been, nor ever shall be again. •
12:14 you shall observe it as an ordinance for ever. 13
17 observe this day . . as an ordinance for ever. 13
24 ordinance for you and for your sons for ever. 13
15:18 The LORD will reign for ever and ever. 13
18 The LORD will reign for ever and ever. 9
19: 9 may also believe you for ever. 13
22:26 If ever you take your neighbor's garment •
27:21 It shall be a statute for ever to be observed 13
30:21 it shall be a statute for ever to them, even to him 13
31:17 sign for ever between me and the people of Israel 13
32:13 this land . . and they shall inherit it for ever.' 13
Lev 6:18 as decreed for ever throughout your generations 13
22 offer it to the LORD as decreed for ever 13
10: 9 statute for ever throughout your generations 13
15 a due for ever; as the LORD has commanded 13
16:29 it shall be a statute to you for ever 13
31 shall afflict yourselves; it is a statute for ever 13
17: 7 This shall be a statute for ever to them 13
23:14 a statute for ever throughout your generations 13
21 it is a statute for ever in all your dwellings 13
31 statute for ever throughout your generations 13
41 it is a statute for ever throughout 13
24: 3 it shall be a statute for ever 13
8 set it in order . . as a covenant for ever 13
25:46 your sons . . to inherit as a possession for ever 13
Num18:19 it is a covenant of salt for ever before the LORD 13
22:30 I ever accustomed to do so to you?" And he said, "No. •
Deu 4:32 such a great thing as this has ever happened •
32 such a great thing as this . . was ever heard of. •
33 Did any people ever hear the voice of a god •
34 has any god ever attempted to go and take a nation •
40 land which the LORD your God gives you for ever. 2
5:29 go well with them . . their children for ever! 13
12:28 you and with your children after you for ever 13
13:16 a heap for ever, it shall not be built again. 13
15:17 he shall be your bondman for ever. 13
18: 5 stand and minister . . him and his sons for ever. 1
19: 9 loving the LORD . . by walking ever in his ways- 2
23: 3 none . . enter the assembly of the LORD for ever; 13
6 not seek their peace . . all your days for ever. 13
28:46 upon you . . and upon your descendants for ever. 13
29:29 revealed belong to us and to our children for ever 13
32:40 I lift up my hand . . and swear, As I live for ever 13
Jos 4: 7 stones shall be to . . Israel a memorial for ever. 11
24 that you may fear the LORD your God for ever. 2
8:28 burned Ai, and made it for ever a heap of ruins 13
14: 9 shall be an inheritance for you . . for ever 11
Jdg 11:25 Did he ever strive against Israel, or did he ever •
25 against Israel, or did he ever go to war with them? •
1Sm 1:22 presence of the LORD, and abide there for ever. 11
2:30 should go in and out before me for ever'; 11
32 shall not be an old man in your house for ever. 2
35 go in and out before my anointed for ever. 2
3:13 I am about to punish his house for ever 11
14 shall not be expiated by sacrifice . . for ever. 11
13:13 established your kingdom over Israel for ever. 11
20:15 not cut off your loyalty from my house for ever. 11
23 behold the LORD is between you and me for ever. 11
42 'The LORD shall be between me and you . . for ever.' 11
2Sm 2:26 Abner called . . "Shall the sword devour for ever? 8
3:28 I and my kingdom are for ever guiltless 11
7:13 establish the throne of his kingdom for ever. 11
16 kingdom shall be made sure for ever before me; 11
16 your throne shall be established for ever. 11
24 establish . . Israel to be thy people for ever; 11
25 confirm for ever the word which thou hast spoken 11
26 and thy name will be magnified for ever, saying 11
29 that it may continue for ever before thee; 13
29 the house of thy servant be blessed for ever. 13
16: 4 let me ever find favor in your sight, my lord •
22:51 love . . to David, and his descendants for ever. 11
1Kg 1:31 and said, "May my lord King David live for ever. 13
2:33 So shall their blood come back upon . . for ever; 13
45 of David shall be established . . for ever. 13
8:13 I have built . . a place for thee to dwell in for ever. 13
9: 3 consecrated . . and put my name there for ever; 13
5 establish your . . throne over Israel for ever 13
10: 9 Because the LORD loved Israel for ever 13
11:39 I will for this afflict . . but not for ever.' 2
12: 7 then they will be your servants for ever. 2
2Kg 5:27 cleave to you, and to your descendants for ever. 13
8:19 promised . . a lamp to him and to his sons for ever. 2
18:33 Has any of the gods . . ever delivered his land †
21: 7 In this house . . I will put my name for ever; 13
1Ch 15: 2 and to minister to him for ever. 13
16:15 He is mindful of his covenant for ever 13
34 for his steadfast love endures for ever! 13
41 for his steadfast love endures for ever. 13
17:12 and I will establish his throne for ever. 13
14 confirm him in my house and in my kingdom for ever 13
14 and his throne shall be established for ever 13
22 make thy people Israel to be thy people for ever; 13
23 let the word which . . be established for ever 13
24 name will be established and magnified for ever 13
27 that it may continue for ever before thee; 13
27 what thou, O LORD, hast blessed is blessed for ever 13
22:10 establish his royal throne in Israel for ever. 13
23:13 that he and his sons for ever should burn incense 13
13 and pronounce blessings in his name for ever. 13
25 and he dwells in Jerusalem for ever. 13
28: 4 chose me . . to be king over Israel for ever; 13
7 I will establish his kingdom for ever 13
8 an inheritance to your children . . for ever. 13
9 if you forsake him, he will cast you off for ever. 9
29:10 Blessed art thou, O LORD . . for ever and ever. 13
10 Blessed art thou, O LORD . . for ever and ever. 13
18 O LORD . . keep for ever such purposes 13
2Ch 2: 4 the LORD our God, as ordained for ever for Israel. 13
5:13 is good, for his steadfast love endures for ever 13
6: 2 a place for thee to dwell in for ever. 13
7: 3 is good, for his steadfast love endures for ever. 13
6 -for his steadfast love endures for ever- 13
16 this house that my name may be there for ever; 13
9: 8 loved Israel and would establish them for ever 13
10: 7 then they will be your servants for ever. 1
13: 5 gave the kingship over Israel for ever to David 13
20: 7 give it for ever to the descendants of Abraham 13
21 for his steadfast love endures for ever. 13
21: 7 to give a lamp to him and to his sons for ever. 2
30: 8 his sanctuary, which he has sanctified for ever 13
33: 4 In Jerusalem shall my name be for ever. 13
7 In this house . . I will put my name for ever; 13
Ezr 3:11 steadfast love endures for ever toward Israel. 13
9:12 an inheritance to your children for ever.' 13
Neh 2: 3 Let the king live for ever! Why should not my face 13
13: 1 no Ammonite . . ever enter the assembly of God; 11
Job 4: 7 Think now, who that was innocent ever perished? •
20 they perish for ever without any regarding it. 4
7:16 I loathe my life; I would not live for ever. 6
14:20 Thou prevailest for ever against him 4
19:24 they were graven in the rock for ever! 5
20: 7 he will perish for ever like his own dung; 4
23: 7 I should be acquitted for ever by my judge. 4
36: 7 with kings upon the throne he sets them for ever 4
37:20 Did a man ever wish that he would be swallowed up? •
41: 4 to take him for your servant for ever? 6
Ps 5:11 let them ever sing for joy; and do thou defend them 6
9: 5 blotted out their name for ever and ever. 6
5 blotted out their name for ever and ever. 9
7 the LORD sits enthroned for ever 6
18 the hope of the poor shall not perish for ever. 5
10:16 The LORD is king for ever and ever; 13
16 The LORD is king for ever and ever; 9
12: 7 protect us, guard us ever from this generation. 6
13: 1 How long, O LORD? Wilt thou forget me for ever? 8
18:50 to David and his descendants for ever. 11
19: 9 the fear of the LORD is clean, enduring for ever; 5
21: 4 gavest it to him, length of days for ever and ever. 13
4 gavest it to him, length of days for ever and ever. 9
6 Yea, thou dost make him most blessed for ever; 5
22:26 praise the LORD! May your hearts live for ever! 5
23: 6 I shall dwell in the house of the LORD for ever. 3
25:15 My eyes are ever toward the LORD 14
28: 9 be thou their shepherd, and carry them for ever. 11
29:10 LORD sits enthroned as king for ever. 13
30:12 O LORD my God, I will give thanks to thee for ever. 6
33:11 The counsel of the LORD stands for ever 6
37:18 their heritage will abide for ever; 6
26 He is ever giving liberally and lending 2
27 do good; so shall you abide for ever. 6
28 The righteous shall be preserved for ever 6
29 possess the land, and dwell upon it for ever. 5
38:17 For I am ready to fall, and my pain is ever with me. 14
40:11 let . . thy faithfulness ever preserve me! 14
41:12 set me in thy presence for ever. 6
44: 8 we will give thanks to thy name for ever. Selah 6
23 Awake! Do not cast us off for ever! 4
45: 2 therefore God has blessed you for ever. 6
6 Your divine throne endures for ever and ever. 13
6 Your divine throne endures for ever and ever. 9
17 the peoples will praise you for ever and ever. 6
17 the peoples will praise you for ever and ever. 9
48: 8 city of our God, which God establishes for ever. 11
14 that this is God, our God for ever and ever. 13
14 that this is God, our God for ever and ever. 9
14 He will be our guide for ever. 16
49: 9 that he should continue to live on for ever 4
11 Their graves are their homes for ever 6
51: 3 my transgressions, and my sin is ever before me. 14
52: 5 God will break you down for ever; 4
8 in the steadfast love of God for ever and ever. 13
8 in the steadfast love of God for ever and ever. 9
9 I will thank thee for ever, because thou hast done 6
61: 4 Let me dwell in thy tent for ever! 13
7 May he be enthroned for ever before God; 13
8 So will I ever sing praises to thy name 5
66: 7 who rules by his might for ever 13
68:16 yea, where the LORD will dwell for ever! 8
72:17 May his name endure for ever 6
19 Blessed be his glorious name for ever; 6
73:26 the strength of my heart and my portion for ever. 6
74: 1 O God, why dost thou cast us off for ever? 4
10 Is the enemy to revile thy name for ever? 4
19 do not forget the life of thy poor for ever. 4
75: 9 I will rejoice for ever, I will sing praises 6
77: 7 Will the Lord spurn for ever 6
8 Has his steadfast love for ever ceased? 4
78:69 like the earth, which he has founded for ever. 6
79: 5 How long, O LORD? Wilt thou be angry for ever? 8
13 thy people . . will give thanks to thee for ever; 13
81:15 their fate would last for ever. 13
83:17 Let them be put to shame and dismayed for ever; 10
84: 4 dwell in thy house, ever singing thy praise! Selah 12
85: 5 Wilt thou be angry with us for ever? 13
86:12 I will glorify thy name for ever. 13
89: 1 I will sing of thy steadfast love, O LORD, for ever; 13
2 For thy steadfast love was established for ever 13
4 I will establish your descendants for ever 13
28 My steadfast love I will keep for him for ever 13
29 I will establish his line for ever 9
36 His line shall endure for ever 13
37 Like the moon it shall be established for ever; 13
46 How long, O LORD? Wilt thou hide thyself for ever? 8
52 Blessed be the LORD for ever! Amen and Amen. 13
90: 2 ever thou hadst formed the earth and the world •
92: 7 they are doomed to destruction for ever 10
8 but thou, O LORD, art on high for ever. 13
14 they are ever full of sap and green •
100: 5 LORD is good; his steadfast love endures for ever 13
102:12 But thou, O LORD, art enthroned for ever; 13
103: 9 nor will he keep his anger for ever. 13
104:31 May the glory of the LORD endure for ever 13
105: 8 He is mindful of his covenant for ever 13
106: 1 for his steadfast love endures for ever! 13
31 from generation to generation for ever. 13
107: 1 for his steadfast love endures for ever! 13
110: 4 priest for ever after the order of Melchiz'edek. 13
111: 3 his righteousness endures for ever. 9
5 he is ever mindful of his covenant. 13
8 they are established for ever and ever 9
8 they are established for ever and ever 13
9 he has commanded his covenant for ever. 13
10 His praise endures for ever! 9
112: 3 his righteousness endures for ever. 9
6 righteous . . will be remembered for ever. 13
9 his righteousness endures for ever; 9
117: 2 faithfulness of the LORD endures for ever. 13
118: 1 he is good; his steadfast love endures for ever! 13
2 Israel say, "His steadfast love endures for ever. 13
3 Aaron say, "His steadfast love endures for ever. 13
4 His steadfast love endures for ever. 13
29 for his steadfast love endures for ever! 13
119:44 I will keep thy law continually, for ever and ever; 6
44 I will keep thy law continually, for ever and ever; 9
89 For ever, O LORD, thy word is firmly fixed 6
98 wiser than my enemies, for it is ever with me. 6
111Thy testimonies are my heritage for ever; 6
112to perform thy statutes for ever, to the end. 6
142Thy righteousness is righteous for ever 6
144Thy testimonies are righteous for ever; 6
152that thou hast founded them for ever. 6
160of thy righteous ordinances endures for ever. 6
125: 1 Zion, which cannot be moved, but abides for ever. 13
132:12 sons also for ever shall sit upon your throne. 10
14 This is my resting place for ever; 9
135:13 Thy name, O LORD, endures for ever, thy renown, 13
136: 1 for his steadfast love endures for ever. 13
2 for his steadfast love endures for ever. 13
3 for his steadfast love endures for ever; 13
4 for his steadfast love endures for ever; 13
5 for his steadfast love endures for ever; 13
6 for his steadfast love endures for ever; 13
7 for his steadfast love endures for ever; 13
8 for his steadfast love endures for ever; 13
9 for his steadfast love endures for ever; 13
10 for his steadfast love endures for ever; 13
11 for his steadfast love endures for ever; 13
12 for his steadfast love endures for ever; 13
13 for his steadfast love endures for ever; 13
14 for his steadfast love endures for ever; 13
15 for his steadfast love endures for ever; 13
16 for his steadfast love endures for ever; 13
17 for his steadfast love endures for ever; 13
18 for his steadfast love endures for ever; 13
19 for his steadfast love endures for ever; 13
20 for his steadfast love endures for ever; 13
21 for his steadfast love endures for ever; 13
22 for his steadfast love endures for ever. 13
23 for his steadfast love endures for ever; 13
24 for his steadfast love endures for ever; 13
25 for his steadfast love endures for ever. 13
26 for his steadfast love endures for ever. 13
138: 8 thy steadfast love, O LORD, endures for ever. 13
145: 1 God and King, and bless thy name for ever and ever. 13
1 God and King, and bless thy name for ever and ever. 9
2 bless thee, and praise thy name for ever and ever. 13
2 bless thee, and praise thy name for ever and ever. 9
21 all flesh bless his holy name for ever and ever. 13
21 all flesh bless his holy name for ever and ever. 9
146: 6 who keeps faith for ever; 13
10 The LORD will reign for ever, thy God, O Zion 13
148: 6 he established them for ever and ever; 9
6 he established them for ever and ever; 13
Prv 10:25 but the righteous is established for ever. 13

12:19 Truthful lips endure for ever 9
27:24 for riches do not last for ever; 13
29:14 his throne will be established for ever. 9
Ecc 1: 4 A generation . . but the earth remains for ever. 13
3:14 I know that whatever God does endures for ever; 13
9: 6 they have no more for ever any share in all that is 13
Isa 17: 2 Her cities will be deserted for ever; •
25: 8 He will swallow up death for ever 4
26: 4 Trust in the LORD for ever 10
28:28 No, he does not thresh it for ever; 4
30: 8 for the time to come as a witness for ever. 11
32:14 hill and the watchtower . . become dens for ever 11
17 the result . . quietness and trust for ever. 11
34:10 its smoke shall go up for ever. 6
10 none shall pass through it for ever and ever. 4
10 none shall pass through it for ever and ever. 8
17 they shall possess it for ever 11
40: 8 fades; but the word of our God will stand for ever. 6
47: 7 You said, "I shall be mistress for ever 6
51: 6 but my salvation will be for ever 6
8 but my deliverance will be for ever 6
57:16 For I will not contend for ever, nor will I always 6
60:15 make you majestic for ever, a joy from age to age. 13
21 they shall possess the land for ever 6
64: 9 O LORD, and remember not iniquity for ever. 5
65:18 and rejoice for ever in that which I create; 10
Jer 3: 5 will he be angry for ever 6
12 says the LORD; I will not be angry for ever. 6
6: 7 sickness and wounds are ever before me. 14
7: 7 land that I gave of old to your fathers for ever. 13
15:14 a fire is kindled which shall burn for ever. 13
17: 4 a fire is kindled which shall burn for ever. 11
25 and this city shall be inhabited for ever. 6
18:16 a horror, a thing to be hissed at for ever. 13
20:17 and her womb for ever great. 13
25: 5 to you and your fathers from of old and for ever; 11
31:36 cease from being a nation before me for ever. 2
40 uprooted or overthrown any more for ever. 6
32:39 that they may fear me for ever, for their own good 2
33:11 for his steadfast love endures for ever! 6
18 and to make sacrifices for ever. 2
35: 6 drink wine, neither you nor your sons for ever; 11
50:39 she shall be peopled no more for ever 4
51:62 it shall be desolate for ever. 13
Lam 3:31 For the Lord will not cast off for ever 13
4:17 Our eyes failed, ever watching vainly for help; 12
5:19 But thou, O LORD, dost reign for ever; 13
20 Why dost thou forget us for ever 4
Ezk 15: 5 it is charred, can it ever be used for anything! 12
16:16 the like has never been, nor ever shall be. •
27:32 Who was ever destroyed like Tyre •
36 to a dreadful end and shall be no more for ever. 11
28:19 to a dreadful end and shall be no more for ever. 11
36:11 and will do more good to you than ever before. •
37:25 children's children shall dwell there for ever; 11
25 David my servant shall be their prince for ever. 6
43: 7 in the midst of the people of Israel for ever. 6
9 I will dwell in their midst for ever. 6
Dan 2: 4 O king, live for ever! Tell your servants the dream 15
20 Blessed be the name of God for ever and ever. 15
20 Blessed be the name of God for ever and ever. 15
44 bring them to an end, and it shall stand for ever; 15
3: 9 O king, live for ever! 15
4:34 praised and honored him who lives for ever; 15
5:10 queen said, "O king, live for ever! 15
6: 6 said to him, "O King Darius, live for ever! 15
21 Then Daniel said to the king, "O king, live for ever 15
26 for he is the living God, enduring for ever; 15
7:18 possess the kingdom for ever, for ever and ever.' 15
18 possess the kingdom for ever, for ever and ever.' 15
18 possess the kingdom for ever, for ever and ever.' 15
12: 3 shine . . like the stars for ever and ever. 13
3 shine . . like the stars for ever and ever. 9
7 heard him swear by him who lives for ever 13
Hos 2:19 And I will betroth you to me for ever; 13
Jol 3:20 But Judah shall be inhabited for ever 13
Ams 1:11 tore perpetually, and he kept his wrath for ever. 8
Obd 1:10 and you shall be cut off for ever. 6
Jon 2: 6 to the land whose bars closed upon me for ever; 6
Mic 2: 9 you take away my glory for ever. 13
4: 5 in the name of the LORD our God for ever and ever. 13
5 in the name of the LORD our God for ever and ever. 9
7:18 He does not retain his anger for ever 5
Hab 1:17 and mercilessly slaying nations for ever? 14
Zep 2: 9 possessed by nettles . . and a waste for ever. 11
Zec 1: 5 And the prophets, do they live for ever? 6
Mal 1: 4 the people with whom the LORD is angry for ever. 11
Mat 21:19 May no fruit ever come from you again! 27
Mrk 11: 2 a colt . . on which no one has ever sat 36
14 May no one ever eat fruit from you again. 27
Lke 1:33 he will reign over the house of Jacob for ever; 29
55 to Abraham and to his posterity for ever. 27
Joh 1:18 No one has ever seen God; 41
4:29 Come, see a man who told me all that I ever did. 34
39 woman's testimony, "He told me all that I ever did. 34
6:51 if any one eats of this bread, he will live for ever; 27
58 he who eats this bread will live for ever. 27
8:35 The slave does not continue in the house for ever; 27
35 the son continues for ever. 27
12:34 the Christ remains for ever 27
14:16 to be with you for ever 27
19:41 a new tomb where no one had ever been laid. 35
Rom 1:25 the Creator, who is blessed for ever! Amen. 16
9: 5 God who is over all be blessed for ever. Amen. 16
11:10 and bend their backs for ever. 20
36 To him be glory for ever. Amen. 16
1Co 12: 3 no one speaking by the Spirit of God ever says •
2Co 9: 9 his righteousness endures for ever. 27
11:31 he who is blessed for ever 29
Gal 1: 5 to whom be the glory for ever and ever. Amen. 16
5 to whom be the glory for ever and ever. Amen. 16
Eph 3:21 to all generations, for ever and ever. Amen. 16
21 to all generations, for ever and ever. Amen. 16
5:29 For no man ever hates his own flesh 39
Php 4:20 To our God and Father be glory for ever and ever. 16
20 To our God and Father be glory for ever and ever. 16
1Ti 1:17 be honor and glory for ever and ever. Amen. 29
17 be honor and glory for ever and ever. Amen. 16
6:16 whom no man has ever seen or can see •
2Ti 4:18 To him be the glory for ever and ever. Amen. 29
18 To him be the glory for ever and ever. Amen. 16
Phm 1:15 you might have him back for ever 17
Heb 1: 5 For to what angel did God ever say, "Thou art my Son 39
8 Thy throne, O God, is for ever and ever 27
8 Thy throne, O God, is for ever and ever 16
13 to what angel has he ever said, "Sit at my right hand 39
5: 6 a priest for ever, after the order of Melchiz'edek. 27
6:20 having become a high priest for ever 27
7: 3 he continues a priest for ever. 26
13 from which no one has ever served at the altar. •
17 a priest for ever, after the order of Melchiz'edek. 27
21 'Thou art a priest for ever.' 27
24 because he continues for ever. 27
28 appoints a Son who has been made perfect for ever. 27
13: 8 is the same yesterday and today and for ever. 29
21 to whom be glory for ever and ever. Amen. 29
21 to whom be glory for ever and ever. Amen. 16
1Pe 1:25 but the word of the Lord abides for ever. 16
4:11 glory and dominion for ever and ever. Amen. 16
11 glory and dominion for ever and ever. Amen. 16
5:11 To him be the dominion for ever and ever. Amen. 16
11 To him be the dominion for ever and ever. Amen. 16
2Pe 1:21 no prophecy ever came by the impulse of man . 39
1Jn 2:17 but he who does the will of God abides for ever. 27
4:12 No man has ever seen God; 41
2Jn 1: 2 the truth which . . will be with us for ever 27
Jde 1:13 gloom of darkness has been reserved for ever. 21
25 before all time and now and for ever. Amen. 25
Rev 1: 6 to him be glory and dominion for ever and ever. 16
6 to him be glory and dominion for ever and ever. 16
4: 9 thanks to him . . who lives for ever and ever 16
9 thanks to him . . who lives for ever and ever 16
10 worship him who lives for ever and ever; 16
10 worship him who lives for ever and ever; 16
5:13 honor and glory and might for ever and ever! 16
13 honor and glory and might for ever and ever! 16
7:12 might be to our God for ever and ever! Amen. 16
12 might be to our God for ever and ever! Amen. 16
10: 6 swore by him who lives for ever and ever 16
6 swore by him who lives for ever and ever 16
11:15 Christ, and he shall reign for ever and ever. 16
15 Christ, and he shall reign for ever and ever. 16
14:11 smoke of their torment goes up for ever and ever; 16
11 smoke of their torment goes up for ever and ever; 16
15: 7 the wrath of God who lives for ever and ever; 16
7 the wrath of God who lives for ever and ever; 16
19: 3 The smoke from her goes up for ever and ever. 16
3 The smoke from her goes up for ever and ever. 16
20:10 be tormented day and night for ever and ever. 16
10 be tormented day and night for ever and ever. 16
22: 5 and they shall reign for ever and ever. 16
5 and they shall reign for ever and ever. 16
1Es 4:38 truth endures and is strong for ever 27
38 lives and prevails for ever and ever. 27
38 lives and prevails for ever and ever. 16
5:61 his glory are for ever upon all Israel. 27
8:72 all who were ever moved at the word of the Lord 39
85 do not seek ever to have peace with them 42
85 for an inheritance to your children for ever. 31
2Es 4: 8 neither did I ever ascend into heaven.' 45
7:80 ever grieving and sad, in seven ways. 44
8:23 and whose truth is established for ever ‡
9:31 you shall be glorified through it for ever.' 43
Tob 1: 4 and established for all generations for ever. 16
3: 2 thou dost render true and righteous judgment for ever. 27
11 blessed is thy holy and honored name for ever. 29
11 May all thy works praise thee for ever. 27
8: 5 and blessed by thy holy and glorious name for ever. 29
15 let . . thy chosen people bless thee for ever. 24
10: 7 have given up hope of ever seeing me again. •
11:14 blessed is thy name for ever 29
12:17 But praise God for ever. 27
18 Therefore praise him for ever. 27
13: 1 Blessed is God who lives for ever 29
4 he is our Father for ever. 24
10 to all generations for ever. 16
12 blessed for ever will be all who love you. 27
14 they will be made glad for ever. 27
18 Blessed is God, who has exalted you for ever.' 38
14: 5 for all generations for ever 16
Jdt 12:20 much more than he had ever drunk in any one day 41
15:10 May the Almighty Lord bless you for ever! 28
16:16 he who fears the Lord shall be great for ever. 20
17 they shall weep in pain for ever. 31
AEs 10:13 from generation to generation for ever 27
14:10 to magnify for ever a mortal king. 21
Wis 3: 8 the Lord will reign over them for ever. 29
4:18 and an outrage among the dead for ever 19
5:15 the righteous live for ever 27
6:21 honor wisdom, that you may reign for ever. 27
14:13 nor will they exist for ever. 27
Sir 1: 1 comes from the Lord and is with him for ever. 27
2:10 who ever trusted in the Lord and was put to shame? •
10 who ever persevered in the fear of the Lord •
10 who ever called upon him and was overlooked? •
18: 1 He who lives for ever created the whole universe; 27
20:26 his shame is ever with him. 30
37:26 his name will live for ever. 27
40:12 good faith will stand for ever. 27
17 almsgiving endures for ever. 27
41:13 a good name endures for ever. 21
42:23 All these things live and remain for ever 27
44:13 Their posterity will continue for ever 31
45:13 No outsider ever put them on 31
24 have the dignity of the priesthood for ever. 29
46: 3 Who before him ever stood so firm? •
47:11 took away his sins, and exalted his power for ever; 21
13 prepare a sanctuary to stand for ever. 27
Bar 3: 3 thou art enthroned for ever, and we are perishing 16
3 for ever, and we are perishing for ever. 16
13 God, you would be dwelling in peace for ever. 16
4: 1 She is . . the law that endures for ever 16
23 give you back to me with joy and gladness for ever 16
5: 1 put on for ever the beauty of the glory from God. 16
4 For your name will for ever be called by God 16
Aza 1: 3 thy name is glorified for ever. 29
29 to be praised and highly exalted for ever; 29
30 to be highly praised and highly exalted for ever. 29
31 to be extolled and highly glorified for ever. 29
32 to be praised and highly exalted for ever. 29
33 to be extolled and highly exalted for ever. 29
34 to be sung and glorified for ever. 29
35 sing praise to him and highly exalt him for ever. 29
36 sing praise to him and highly exalt him for ever. 29
37 sing praise to him and highly exalt him for ever. 29
38 sing praise to him and highly exalt him for ever. 29
39 sing praise to him and highly exalt him for ever. 29
40 sing praise to him and highly exalt him for ever. 29
41 sing praise to him and highly exalt him for ever. 29
42 sing praise to him and highly exalt him for ever. 29
43 sing praise to him and highly exalt him for ever. 29
44 sing praise to him and highly exalt him for ever. 29
45 sing praise to him and highly exalt him for ever. 29
46 sing praise to him and highly exalt him for ever. 29
47 sing praise to him and highly exalt him for ever. 29
48 sing praise to him and highly exalt him for ever. 29
49 sing praise to him and highly exalt him for ever. 29
50 sing praise to him and highly exalt him for ever. 29
51 sing praise to him and highly exalt him for ever. 29
52 highly exalt him for ever. 29
53 sing praise to him and highly exalt him for ever. 29
54 sing praise to him and highly exalt him for ever. 29
55 sing praise to him and highly exalt him for ever. 29
56 sing praise to him and highly exalt him for ever. 29
57 sing praise to him and highly exalt him for ever. 29
58 sing praise to him and highly exalt him for ever. 29
59 sing praise to him and highly exalt him for ever. 29
60 sing praise to him and highly exalt him for ever. 29
61 sing praise to him and highly exalt him for ever. 29
62 sing praise to him and highly exalt him for ever. 29
63 sing praise to him and highly exalt him for ever. 29
64 sing praise to him and highly exalt him for ever. 29
65 sing praise to him and highly exalt him for ever. 29
66 sing praise to him and highly exalt him for ever; 29
67 his mercy endures for ever. 27
68 his mercy endures for ever. 27
Man 1:13 Do not be angry with me for ever or lay up evil for me 27
15 thine is the glory for ever. Amen. 27
1Mc 2:57 inherited the throne of the kingdom for ever. 22
3: 7 his memory is blessed for ever. 32
4:24 he is good, for his mercy endures for ever. 27
8:11 as many as ever opposed them, they destroyed 39
23 May all go well . . at sea and on land for ever 27
11:36 from this time forth for ever. 23
14:41 Simon should be their . . high priest for ever 27
2Mc 8:14 before he ever met them •
10: 4 if they should ever sin 39
13:10 now if ever to help those who . . 40
14:15 who established his own people for ever 18
36 keep undefiled for ever this house 21
15:30 the man who was ever in body and soul the defender 33
4Mc 7: 4 No city . . ever held out as did that most holy man 37
18:24 to whom be glory for ever and ever. Amen. 16
24 to whom be glory for ever and ever. Amen. 16

ever *See also* abide, again, more, new, no, nothing, than, thirsty.

ever since 1. מִן 2. *ἀπό* 3. *ἀφ' ἧς* 4. *ἐκ*
Ezr 4: 2 sacrificing to him ever since the days 1
Rom 1:20 Ever since the creation of the world 2
2Pe 3: 4 For ever since the fathers fell asleep 3
1Es 5:69 ever since the days of Esarhaddon 2
Jdt 12:16 ever since the day he first saw her. 2
AEs 14: 5 Ever since I was born 4

ever yet 1. *οὔπω* 2. *πώποτε*
Lke 19:30 a colt . . on which no one has ever yet sat 2
23:53 where no one had ever yet been laid. 1

ever-flowing 1. אֵתָן 2. *ἀέναος*
Ps 74:15 thou didst dry up ever-flowing streams. 1
Ams 5:24 and righteousness like an ever-flowing stream. 1
Wis 11: 6 Instead of the fountain of an ever-flowing river 2

everflowing 1. *ἀέναος*
2Mc 7:36 our brothers . . have drunk of everflowing life 1

evergreen 1. רַעֲנָן
Hos 14: 8 I am like an evergreen cypress 1

evergreen oak 1. *πρῖνος*
Sus 1:58 He answered, "Under an evergreen oak. 1

everlasting 1. כָּל עוֹלָמִים 2. לָנֶצַח 3. עַד עוֹלָם 4. עוֹלָם 5. קֶדֶם 6. עָלַם (A) 7. *ἀέναος* 8. *ἀΐδιος* 9. *αἰών* 10. *αἰώνιος* 11. aeternitas 12. aeternus 13. perennis
Gen 9:16 it and remember the everlasting covenant 4
17: 7 their generations for an everlasting covenant 4
8 for an everlasting possession; 4
13 be in your flesh an everlasting covenant. 4
19 my covenant with him as an everlasting covenant 4
21:33 the name of the LORD, the Everlasting God. 4
48: 4 this land . . for an everlasting possession. 4
49:26 the bounties of the everlasting hills; 4
Lev 16:34 this shall be an everlasting statute for you 4
Deu 33:15 with the . . abundance of the everlasting hills 4
27 underneath are the everlasting arms. 4
2Sm 23: 5 For he has made with me an everlasting covenant 4
1Ch 16:17 as an everlasting covenant to Israel 4
36 God of Israel, from everlasting to everlasting! 4
36 God of Israel, from everlasting to everlasting! 4
Neh 9: 5 LORD . . from everlasting to everlasting. 4
5 LORD . . from everlasting to everlasting. 4
Ps 9: 6 The enemy have vanished in everlasting ruins; 2
41:13 God of Israel, from everlasting to everlasting! 4
13 God of Israel, from everlasting to everlasting! 4
76: 4 more majestic than the everlasting mountains. 10
78:66 he put them to everlasting shame. 4
90: 2 from everlasting to everlasting thou art God. 4
2 from everlasting to everlasting thou art God. 4
93: 2 thy throne . . of old; thou art from everlasting. 4
103:17 everlasting to everlasting upon those who fear 4
17 everlasting to everlasting upon those who fear 4
105:10 to Israel as an everlasting covenant 4
106:48 God of Israel, from everlasting to everlasting! 4
48 God of Israel, from everlasting to everlasting! 4
139:24 lead me in the way everlasting! 4
145:13 Thy kingdom is an everlasting kingdom 1
Isa 24: 5 violated . . broken the everlasting covenant. 4
26: 4 for ever, for the LORD GOD is an everlasting rock. 4
33:14 Who . . can dwell with everlasting burnings? 4
35:10 everlasting joy shall be upon their heads; 4
40:28 The LORD is the everlasting God 4
45:17 saved by the LORD with everlasting salvation; 4
51:11 everlasting joy shall be upon their heads; 4
54: 8 with everlasting love I will have compassion 4
55: 3 I will make with you an everlasting covenant 4
13 an everlasting sign which shall not be cut off. 4
56: 5 I will give them an everlasting name 4
60:19 but the LORD will be your everlasting light 4
20 for the LORD will be your everlasting light 4
61: 7 double portion; yours shall be everlasting joy. 4
8 I will make an everlasting covenant with them. 4
63:12 to make for himself an everlasting name 4
Jer 10:10 he is the living God and the everlasting King. 4
23:40 I will bring upon you everlasting reproach 4
25: 9 a horror, a hissing, and an everlasting reproach. 4
12 making the land an everlasting waste. 4
31: 3 I have loved you with an everlasting love; 4
32:40 I will make with them an everlasting covenant 4
49:33 become a haunt of jackals, an everlasting waste; 3
50: 5 join . . to the LORD in an everlasting covenant 4
Ezk 16:60 establish with you an everlasting covenant. 4
37:26 it shall be an everlasting covenant with them; 4
Dan 4: 3 His kingdom is an everlasting kingdom 6
34 for his dominion is an everlasting dominion 6
7:14 his dominion is an everlasting dominion 6
27 kingdom shall be an everlasting kingdom 6
9:24 bring in everlasting righteousness 4
12: 2 some to everlasting life, and some to shame 4
2 some to shame and everlasting contempt. 4
Hab 1:12 Art thou not from everlasting, O LORD my God 5
3: 6 the everlasting hills sank low. 4
2Es 2:11 to these others the everlasting habitations 12
34 he will give you everlasting rest 11
3:15 didst make with him an everlasting covenant 12
7:120 that an everlasting hope has been promised to us 13
Tob 1: 6 it is ordained . . by an everlasting decree 10
AEs 14: 5 for an everlasting inheritance 10
Wis 8:13 leave an everlasting remembrance 10
10:14 she gave him everlasting honor. 10
Sir 2: 9 for good things, for everlasting joy and mercy. 9
15: 6 will acquire an everlasting name. 9
39:20 From everlasting to everlasting 9
20 From everlasting to everlasting 9
42:21 he is from everlasting and to everlasting. 9
21 he is from everlasting and to everlasting. 9
43: 6 to make the times and to be an everlasting sign. 9
44:18 Everlasting covenants were made with him 9
45: 7 He made an everlasting covenant with him 9
15 it was an everlasting covenant for him 9
49:12 prepared for everlasting glory. 9
Bar 2:35 I will make an everlasting covenant with them 10
4: 8 You forgot the everlasting God 10
10 which the Everlasting brought upon them. 10
14 which the Everlasting brought upon them. 10
20 I will cry to the Everlasting all my days. 10
22 I have put my hope in the Everlasting to save you 10
22 mercy . . from your everlasting Savior. 10
24 and with the splendor of the Everlasting. 10
29 he . . will bring you everlasting joy 10
35 For fire will come upon her from the Everlasting 10
5: 2 the diadem of the glory of the Everlasting. 10
7 ordered that . . everlasting hills be made low 7
1Mc 2:51 receive great honor and an everlasting name. 10
54 the covenant of everlasting priesthood. 10
6:44 to win for himself an everlasting name. 10
2Mc 7: 9 an everlasting renewal of life 10
4Mc 10:15 by the everlasting life of the pious 8

everlasting *See also* father.

evermore 1. אֹרֶךְ יָמִים 2. לְעוֹלָם 3. נֵצַח 4. עַד עוֹלָם 5. עוֹלָם 6. תָּמִיד 7. *αἰών* 8. aeternitas
1Kg 2:33 there shall be peace from the LORD for evermore. 5
Ps 16:11 in thy right hand are pleasures for evermore. 3
35:27 be glad, and say evermore, "Great is the LORD 6
70: 4 May those who love thy salvation say evermore 6
93: 5 holiness befits thy house, O LORD, for evermore. 1
113: 2 LORD from this time forth and for evermore! 5
115:18 bless . . from this time forth and for evermore. 5
121: 8 from this time forth and for evermore. 5
125: 2 from this time forth and for evermore. 5
131: 3 hope . . from this time forth and for evermore. 5
133: 3 commanded the blessing, life for evermore. 5
Isa 9: 7 from this time forth and for evermore. 5
59:21 the LORD, from this time forth and for evermore. 4
Ezk 37:26 my sanctuary in the midst of them for evermore. 2
28 sanctuary is in the midst of them for evermore. 2
Mic 4: 7 reign . . from this time forth and for evermore. 4
Rom 16:27 to the only wise God be glory for evermore 7
Rev 1:18 I died, and behold I am alive for evermore 7
2Es 2:35 eternal light will shine upon you for evermore. 8

every 1. אֶחָד 2. אִישׁ 3. בֵּין 4. כֹּל 5. לְ 6. רֹאשׁ 7. כֹּל (A) 8. *ἅπας* 9. *ἕκαστος* 10. *ἕκαστος πάντων* 11. *κατά* 12. *ὅσος* 13. *πανταχοῦ* 14. *πάντοτε* 15. *πᾶς* 16. omnis 17. singuli 18. unusquisque
Gen 1:21 God created . . every living creature that moves 4
21 every winged bird according to its kind 4
26 dominion . . over every creeping thing 4
28 dominion . . over every living thing that moves 4
29 God said, "Behold, I have given you every plant 4
29 given . . every tree with seed in its fruit; 4
30 to every beast of the earth 4
30 beast of the earth, and to every bird of the air 4
30 I have given every green plant for food. 4
2: 9 God made to grow every tree that is pleasant 4
16 You may freely eat of every tree of the garden; 4
19 out of the ground the LORD God formed every beast 4
19 every beast of the field and every bird of the air 4
19 whatever the man called every living creature 4
20 names . . to every beast of the field; 4
6: 5 and that every imagination of the thoughts 4
19 of every living thing of all flesh 4
19 you shall bring two of every sort into the ark 4
20 kinds, of every creeping thing of the ground 4
20 two of every sort shall come in to you 4
21 take with you every sort of food that is eaten 4
7: 4 every living thing that I have made 4
14 they and every beast according to its kind 4
14 every creeping thing that creeps on the earth 4
14 and every bird according to its kind 4
14 according to its kind, every bird of every sort. 4
14 according to its kind, every bird of every sort. 4
21 that swarm upon the earth, and every man; 4
23 He blotted out every living thing 4
8:17 Bring forth with you every living thing that is 4
17 birds and animals and every creeping thing 4
19 every beast, every creeping thing, and every bird 4
19 every beast, every creeping thing, and every bird 4
19 every beast, every creeping thing, and every bird 4
20 Noah . . took of every clean animal 4
20 clean animal and of every clean bird 4
21 destroy every living creature as I have done. 4
9: 2 dread of you shall be upon every beast 4
2 of the earth, and upon every bird of the air 4
3 Every moving thing that lives shall be food 4
5 of every beast I will require it and of man; 4
5 of man; of every man's brother I will require •
10 with every living creature that is with you 4
10 the birds, the cattle, and every beast of the earth 4
12 me and you and every living creature that is 4
15 you and every living creature of all flesh; 4
16 covenant between God and every living creature 4
17:10 Every male among you shall be circumcised. 4
12 every male throughout your generations 4
23 every male among the men of Abraham's house 4
20:13 you must do me: at every place to which we come 4
30:32 removing from it every speckled and spotted 4
32 every speckled and spotted sheep 4
35 every lamb that was black, and put them in charge 4
32:16 the hand of his servants, every drove by itself •
34:15 you will become as we are and every male of you 4
22 that every male among us be circumcised as they 4
24 and every male was circumcised 4
41:48 he stored up in every city the food •
42:25 gave orders . . to replace every man's money •
35 emptied their sacks, behold, every man's bundle •
43:21 and there was every man's money in the mouth of his •
45: 1 and he cried, "Make every one go out from me. 4
46:34 for every shepherd is an abomination 4
Exd 1:22 commanded all his people, "Every son that is born 4
22 but you shall let every daughter live. 4
9:19 hail shall come down upon every man and beast 4
22 hail . . upon . . every plant of the field 4
25 the hail struck down every plant of the field 4
25 hail . . shattered every tree of the field. 4
10: 5 they shall eat every tree of yours which grows 4
12 that they may . . eat every plant in the land 4
11: 2 that they ask, every man of his neighbor and every •
2 that they ask . . every woman of her neighbor •
12: 3 they shall take every man a lamb according •
16 what every one must eat, that only may be prepared 4
44 every slave that is bought for money may eat of it 4
13:13 Every firstling of an ass you shall redeem 4
13 Every first-born of man among your sons you shall 4
16: 4 go out and gather a day's portion every day •
16 Gather of it, every man of you, as much as he can eat; •
18:22 every great matter they shall bring to you 4
20:24 in every place where I cause my name to be 4
22: 9 For every breach of trust, whether it is for ox 4
25: 2 from every man whose heart makes him willing 4
27:19 All the utensils of the tabernacle for every use 4
29:36 every day you shall offer a bull as a sin offering 5
30: 7 every morning when he dresses the lamps he shall •
31: 5 in carving wood, for work in every craft. 4
32:27 Put every man his sword on his side, and go •
27 go . . and slay every man his brother •
27 slay . . every man his companion, and every man •
27 slay . . every man his neighbor.' •
33: 8 all the people rose up, and every man stood 4
10 rise up and worship, every man at his tent door. •
35:10 let every able man among you come and make all 4
21 they came, every one whose heart stirred him 4
21 and every one whose spirit moved him 4
22 every man dedicating an offering of gold 4
23 every man with whom was found blue or purple 4
33 in carving wood, for work in every skilled craft. 4
35 He has filled them with ability to do every sort 4
36: 1 Bez'alel and Oho'liab and every able man in whom 4
2 called . . every able man in whose mind the LORD 4
3 bringing him freewill offerings every morning †
4 able men who were doing every sort of task 4
30 sixteen bases, under every frame two bases. 1
Lev 6:12 the priest shall burn wood on it every morning •
18 Every male among the children of Aaron may eat 4
23 Every cereal offering of a priest 4
29 Every male among the priests may eat of it 4
7: 6 Every male among the priests may eat of it 4
9 every cereal offering baked in the oven 4
10 every cereal offering, mixed with oil or dry 4
11:15 every raven according to its kind 4
26 Every animal which parts the hoof but is not 4
26 every one who touches them shall be unclean 4
34 drink which may be drunk from every such vessel 4
41 Every swarming thing that swarms upon the earth 4
46 law pertaining to . . every living creature 4
46 to . . every living creature that swarms 4
15: 4 Every bed on which he who has the discharge lies 4
12 every vessel of wood shall be rinsed in water 4
17 every garment and every skin on which the semen 4
17 every garment and every skin on which the semen 4
24 every bed on which he lies shall be unclean 4
26 Every bed on which she lies 4
17:14 For the life of every creature is the blood of it 4
14 for the life of every creature is its blood 4
15 every person that eats what dies of itself 4
20: 9 For every one who curses his father or his mother •
24: 8 Every sabbath day Aaron shall set it in order •
27:25 Every valuation shall be according 4
28 every devoted thing is most holy to the LORD 4

32 every tenth animal of all that pass under 4
Num 1: 2 the number of . . every male, head by head; 4
20 every male from twenty years old and upward 4
22 every male from twenty years old and upward 4
3:12 the Levites . . instead of every first-born 4
15 every male from a month old and upward you shall 4
5: 2 put out of the camp every leper 4
9 every offering, all the holy things of the people 4
10 every man's holy things shall be his; •
7: 3 wagon for every two of the leaders •
11:10 weeping . . every man at the door of his tent; •
14:34 for every day a year, you shall bear your iniquity •
16:17 let every one of you take his censer •
17 every one of you bring before the LORD his censer •
18 every man took his censer, and they put fire •
18: 9 This shall be yours . . every offering of theirs 4
9 This shall be yours . . every cereal offering 4
9 This shall be yours . . every sin offering 4
9 This shall be yours . . every guilt offering 4
10 every male may eat of it; it is holy to you. 4
14 Every devoted thing in Israel shall be yours. 4
21 To the Levites I have given every tithe in Israel 4
29 you shall present every offering due to the LORD 4
19:15 every open vessel . . is unclean. 4
26:54 every tribe shall be given its inheritance 2
62 23,000, every male from a month old and upward; 4
28:10 this is the burnt offering of every sabbath •
13 cereal offering for every lamb; 1
30: 4 then . . every pledge . . shall stand. 4
11 not oppose her; then . . every pledge 4
31: 7 warred against Mid'ian . . and slew every male. 4
17 therefore, kill every male among the little ones 4
17 kill every woman who has known man by lying 4
20 purify every garment, every article of skin 4
20 purify every garment, every article of skin 4
20 purify . . every article of wood. 4
30 take one drawn out of every 50, of the persons •
47 from . . Israel's half Moses took one of every fifty •
53 men of war had taken booty, every man for himself.) •
32:21 every armed man of you will pass over the Jordan 4
34:18 You shall take one leader of every tribe 4
36: 8 every daughter who possesses an inheritance 4
Deu 1:41 And every man of you girded on his weapons of war •
2:34 and utterly destroyed every city, men, women 4
3: 6 destroying every city, men, women, and children. 4
20 then you shall return every man to his possession •
11: 6 tents, and every living thing that followed them 4
24 Every place on which the sole of your foot treads 4
12: 2 upon the hills and under every green tree 4
8 every man doing whatever is right in his own eyes; •
13 do not offer . . at every place that you see; 4
31 for every abominable thing which the LORD hates 4
14: 6 Every animal that parts the hoof and has the hoof 4
14 every raven after its kind; 4
28 At the end of every three years you shall bring 4
15: 1 end of every seven years you shall grant a release. •
2 every creditor shall release what he has lent 4
16:17 every man shall give as he is able, according •
21: 5 by their word every dispute . . shall be settled. 4
5 by their word . . every assault shall be settled. 4
23: 9 you shall keep yourself from every evil thing. 4
24:16 every man shall be put to death for his own sin. •
28:61 Every sickness also, and every affliction 4
61 Every sickness also, and every affliction 4
31:10 At the end of every seven years, at the set time •
Jos 1: 3 Every place that . . I have given to you 4
10:28 he utterly destroyed every person in it 4
30 smote it with the . . sword, and every person in it; 4
32 and smote it . . and every person in it 4
35 every person in it he utterly destroyed that day 4
37 and its king and its towns, and every person in it; 4
37 and utterly destroyed it with every person in it. 4
39 utterly destroyed every person in it; 4
11:14 every man they smote with the edge of the sword 4
Jdg 5:30 dividing the spoil?-A maiden or two for every man; 6
7: 5 likewise every one that kneels down to drink. 4
21:11 every male and every woman that has lain 4
11 male and every woman that has lain with a male 4
1Sm 2:29 choicest parts of every offering of my people 4
4: 8 smote the Egyptians with every sort of plague 4
14:34 So every one of the people brought his ox with him 4
22: 2 every one who was in distress . . gathered to him; 4
2 in distress, and every one who was in debt 4
2 was in debt, and every one who was discontented 4
23:14 Saul sought him every day 4
2Sm 4: 9 who has redeemed my life out of every adversity 4
13: 9 Amnon said, "Send out every one from me. 4
9 Send out every one from me." So every one went out 4
15: 4 every man with a suit or cause might come to me 4
1Kg 1:29 who has redeemed my soul out of every adversity 4
10:22 Once every three years the fleet . . used to come 5
11:15 Jo'ab the commander . . slew every male in Edom 4
16 until he had cut off every male in Edom); 4
14:10 and will cut off from Jerobo'am every male •
23 built . . Ashe'rim on every high hill 4
23 on every high hill and under every green tree; 4
19:18 leave . . every mouth that has not kissed him. 4
21:21 I . . will cut off from Ahab every male, bond or free •
22:53 provoked the LORD . . to anger in every way 4

2Kg 3:19 you shall conquer every fortified city 4
19 conquer every . . and every choice city 4
19 and shall fell every good tree 4
19 and ruin every good piece of land with stones. 4
25 on every good piece of land every man threw 4
25 they stopped every spring of water 4
9: 8 I will cut off from Ahab every male . . in Israel. •
15:20 50 shekels of silver from every man 1
16: 4 and on the hills, and under every green tree. 4
17:10 set up . . pillars and Ashe'rim on every high hill 4
10 Ashe'rim on every . . and under every green tree; 4
13 the LORD warned Israel . . by every prophet 4
13 the LORD warned Israel and Judah by . . every seer 4
29 But every nation still made gods of its own •
29 every nation in the cities in which they dwelt; •
25: 9 every great house he burned down. 4
29 every day of his life he dined regularly 4
1Ch 9:25 were obliged to come in every seven days 5
27 and they had charge of opening it every morning. •
32 the showbread, to prepare it every sabbath. •
13: 1 with the commanders . . with every leader. 4
23:30 stand every morning, thanking and praising •
28: 9 LORD . . understands every plan and thought. 4
21 with you in all the work will be every willing man 4
2Ch 9:21 once every three years the ships of Tarshish 5
11: 4 Return every man to his home •
13:11 They offer . . every morning and every evening •
11 They offer . . every morning and every evening •
11 that its lamps may burn every evening; •
20:27 returned, every man of Judah and Jerusalem 4
23:10 every man with his weapon in his hand •
25: 4 but every man shall die for his own sin. •
22 every man fled to his home. •
28: 4 burned incense . . under every green tree. 4
24 made . . altars in every corner of Jerusalem. 4
25 In every city of Judah he made high places 4
31: 1 every man to his possession. •
19 portions to every male among the priests 4
21 every work that he undertook in the service 4
34:13 all who did work in every kind of service; †
Ezr 10:14 with them the elders and judges of every city •
Neh 4:22 Let every man and his servant pass the night •
5:13 So may God shake out every man from his house 4
18 every ten days skins of wine in abundance; 3
9:22 didst allot to them every corner; •
10:31 forego . . the exaction of every debt. 4
35 bring . . first fruits of all fruit of every tree 4
37 bring . . fruit of every tree, the wine and the oil 4
11:23 settled provision . . as every day required. 4
Est 1:22 he sent . . to every province in its own script •
22 sent . . to every people in its own language •
22 that every man be lord in his own house 4
2:11 And every day Mor'decai walked 4
3: 8 laws are different from those of every other 4
12 to every province in its own script •
12 to . . every people in its own language; •
14 be issued . . in every province by proclamation 4
4: 3 in every province . . there was great mourning 4
8: 9 an edict . . to every province in its own script †
11 allowed the Jews who were in every city to gather 4
13 was to be issued as a decree in every province 4
17 And in every province . . there was gladness 4
17 and in every city . . there was gladness and joy 4
9:27 they would . . at the time appointed every year 4
28 days . . kept throughout every generation 4
28 throughout every generation, in every family •
28 generation, in every family, province, and city †
Job 12:10 In his hand is the life of every living thing 4
28:10 his eye sees every precious thing. 4
37: 7 He seals up the hand of every man 4
39: 8 he searches after every green thing. 4
Ps 6: 6 every night I flood my bed with tears; 4
7:11 a God who has indignation every day. 4
39: 5 Surely every man stands as a mere breath! Selah 4
11 surely every man is a mere breath! Selah 4
50:10 For every beast of the forest is mine 4
54: 7 For thou hast delivered me from every trouble 4
73:14 been stricken, and chastened every morning. •
88: 9 Every day I call upon thee, O LORD; 4
104:11 they give drink to every beast of the field; 4
105:16 When he . . broke every staff of bread 4
118:11 They surrounded me, surrounded me on every side; •
119:101 I hold back my feet from every evil way 4
104 therefore I hate every false way. 4
128 I hate every false way. 4
145: 2 Every day I will bless thee, and praise thy name 4
16 satisfiest the desire of every living thing. 4
Prv 2: 9 Then you will understand . . every good path; 4
7:12 at every corner she lies in wait. 4
15: 3 The eyes of the LORD are in every place 4
20: 3 but every fool will be quarreling. 4
21: 2 Every way of a man is right in his own eyes 4
30: 5 Every word of God proves true; 4
Ecc 3: 1 and a time for every matter under heaven 4
17 for he has appointed a time for every matter 4
17 a time for every matter, and for every work. 4
5:19 Every man also to whom God has given wealth 4
8: 6 For every matter has its time and way 4
12:14 For God will bring every deed into judgment 4

14 bring . . into judgment, with every secret thing 4
Isa 2:15 against every high tower, and . . fortified wall; 4
15 high tower, and against every fortified wall; 4
4: 3 every one who has been recorded for life 4
7:23 every place where there used to be 1,000 vines 4
9: 5 For every boot of the tramping warrior in battle 4
5 every garment rolled in blood will be burned 4
17 and an evildoer, and every mouth speaks folly. 4
13: 7 hands . . be feeble, and every man's heart will melt 4
14 every man will turn to his own people •
14 and every man will flee to his own land. •
15: 2 On every head is baldness, every beard is shorn; 4
2 On every head is baldness, every beard is shorn; 4
19: 2 they will fight, every man against his brother •
2 and every man against his neighbor •
17 every one to whom it is mentioned will fear 4
22:24 every . . vessel, from the cups to all the flagons. 4
24:10 every house is shut up so that none can enter. 4
30:25 upon every lofty mountain and every high hill 4
25 upon every lofty mountain and every high hill 4
32 every stroke of the staff of punishment 4
40: 4 Every valley shall be lifted up 4
4 and every mountain and hill be made low; 4
41: 2 from the east whom victory meets at every step? •
44:23 O mountains, O forest, and every tree in it! 4
45:23 To me every knee shall bow 4
23 every knee shall bow, every tongue shall swear. 4
51:20 at the head of every street like an antelope 4
54:17 confute every tongue that rises against you 4
57: 5 lust among the oaks, under every green tree; 4
14 remove every obstruction from my people's way. •
58: 6 the oppressed go free, and to break every yoke? 4
Jer 1:15 every one shall set his throne at the entrance •
2:20 Yea, upon every high hill . . you bowed down 4
20 and under every green tree you bowed down 4
3: 6 how she went up on every high hill 4
6 on every high hill and under every green tree 4
13 favors among strangers under every green tree 4
4:29 every city takes to flight; they enter thickets; 4
9: 4 for every brother is a supplanter 4
4 and every neighbor goes about as a slanderer. 4
10:14 Every man is stupid and without knowledge; 4
14 every goldsmith is put to shame by his idols; 4
12: 4 and the grass of every field wither? 4
13:12 Every jar shall be filled with wine. 4
12 know that every jar will be filled with wine? 4
16:16 hunt them from every mountain and every hill 4
16 hunt them from every mountain and every hill 4
17: 2 and their Ashe'rim, beside every green tree •
10 to give to every man according to his ways •
19: 3 the ears of every one who hears of it will tingle. 4
22: 8 and every man will say to his neighbor •
29:26 charge in the house of the LORD over every madman 4
30: 6 then do I see every man with his hands on his loins 4
6 Why has every face turned pale? 4
31:25 and every languishing soul I will replenish. 4
43: 6 and every person whom Nebu'zarad'an . . had left 4
47: 2 and every inhabitant of the land shall wail. 4
4 from Tyre and Sidon every helper that remains. 4
48: 8 The destroyer shall come upon every city 4
37 For every head is shaved and every beard cut off; 4
37 For every head is shaved and every beard cut off; 4
49:17 every one who passes by it will be horrified 4
32 I will scatter to every wind those who cut 4
32 I will bring their calamity from every side 4
50:13 every one who passes by Babylon shall be 4
16 every one shall turn to his own people •
16 and every one shall flee to his own land. •
26 Come against her from every quarter; •
51: 6 the midst of Babylon, let every man save his life! •
17 Every man is stupid and without knowledge; 4
17 every goldsmith is put to shame by his idols; 4
28 deputies, and every land under their dominion. 4
31 that his city is taken on every side; •
45 Let every man save his life from the fierce anger •
52:13 every great house he burned down. 4
33 every day of his life he dined . . at the king's 4
Lam 2:19 who faint for hunger at the head of every street. 4
3:23 they are new every morning; •
4: 1 holy stones lie . . at the head of every street. 4
Ezk 1: 9 they went every one straight forward •
6:13 round about their altars, upon every high hill 4
13 on all the mountain tops, under every green tree 4
13 under every leafy oak, wherever they offered 4
8:12 in the dark, every man in his room of pictures? •
10:14 every one had four faces •
22 They went every one straight forward. •
12:14 toward every wind all who are round about him 4
22 days grow long, and every vision comes to nought 4
23 are at hand, and the fulfilment of every vision. 4
13:18 veils for the heads of persons of every stature 4
16:24 and made yourself a lofty place in every square; 4
25 at the head of every street you built your lofty 4
31 your vaulted chamber at the head of every street 4
31 and making your lofty place in every square. 4
44 Behold, every one who uses proverbs will use this 4
17:21 the survivors shall be scattered to every wind; 4
18:30 O house of Israel, every one according to his ways •
20: 7 every one of you, and do not defile yourselves •

8 they did not every man cast away the detestable •
39 Go serve every one of you his idols •
47 it shall devour every green tree in you 4
47 devour every green tree in you and every dry tree; 4
21: 7 When it comes, every heart will melt 4
7 all hands will be feeble, every spirit will faint 4
22: 6 every one according to his power, have been bent •
23: 7 all the idols of every one on whom she doted. 4
27:12 because of your great wealth of every kind; 4
18 goods, because of your great wealth of every kind; 4
28:13 every precious stone was your covering 4
29:18 every head was made bald and every shoulder was 4
18 was made bald and every shoulder was rubbed bare; 4
34: 6 over all the mountains and on every high hill; 4
38:20 every wall shall tumble to the ground. 4
21 every man's sword will be against his brother. •
39: 4 I will give you to birds of prey of every sort 4
17 Speak to the birds of every sort and to all beasts 4
41:18 Every cherub had two faces •
44:29 every devoted thing in Israel shall be theirs. 4
30 every offering of all kinds from all 4
45:15 one sheep from every flock of 200 •
47: 9 every living creature which swarms will live 4
12 they will bear fresh fruit every month •
Dan 1:20 every matter of wisdom and understanding 4
3: 5 hear the sound of . . every kind of music 7
7 heard the sound of . . every kind of music 7
10 made a decree, that every man who hears the sound 7
10 hears the sound of . . every kind of music 7
15 hear the sound of . . every kind of music 7
11:36 magnify himself above every god, 4
Hos 9:15 Every evil of theirs is in Gilgal; 4
13:15 strip his treasury of every precious thing. 4
Ams 2: 8 they lay themselves down beside every altar 4
4: 4 bring . . your tithes every three days; 5
8: 3 in every place they shall be cast out in silence. 4
8 and every one mourn who dwells in it 4
10 I will bring . . baldness on every head; 4
Obd 1: 9 every man from Mount Esau will be cut off •
Jon 3: 8 yea, let every one turn from his evil way •
Mic 4: 4 but they shall sit every man under his vine •
Nah 2: 9 of treasure, or wealth of every precious thing. 4
3:10 dashed in pieces at the head of every street; 4
Hab 1:10 They laugh at every fortress 4
Zep 3: 5 every morning he shows forth his justice †
Hag 2:14 and so with every work of their hands; 4
22 go down every one by the sword of his fellow. •
Zec 3:10 every one of you will invite his neighbor •
5: 3 every one who steals shall be cut off henceforth 4
3 every one who swears falsely shall be cut off 4
8:10 for I set every man against his fellow. 4
23 the nations of every tongue shall take hold 4
10: 1 to every one the vegetation in the field. •
4 of them the battle bow, out of them every ruler. 4
12: 4 I will strike every horse with panic 4
4 when I strike every horse of the peoples 4
13: 4 every prophet will be ashamed of his vision 2
14:16 Then every one that survives of all the nations 4
21 every pot in Jerusalem and Judah shall be sacred 4
Mal 1:11 in every place incense is offered to my name 4
2:17 By saying, "Every one who does evil is good 4
Mat 3:10 every tree therefore that does not bear good 15
4: 4 by bread alone, but by every word that proceeds 15
23 healing every disease and every infirmity 15
23 healing every disease and every infirmity 15
5:22 But I say to you that every one who is angry 15
28 I say to you that every one who looks at a woman 15
32 I say to you that every one who divorces his wife 15
7: 8 For every one who asks receives 15
17 So, every sound tree bears good fruit 15
19 Every tree that does not bear good fruit is cut 15
21 Not every one who says to me, 'Lord, Lord,' shall enter 15
24 Every one then who hears these words of mine 15
26 And every one who hears these words of mine 15
9:35 and healing every disease and every infirmity. 15
35 and healing every disease and every infirmity. 15
10: 1 and to heal every disease and every infirmity. 15
1 and to heal every disease and every infirmity. 15
32 So every one who acknowledges me before men 15
12:25 Every kingdom divided against itself 15
31 every sin and blasphemy will be forgiven men 15
36 will render account for every careless word 15
13:47 and gathered fish of every kind; 15
52 Therefore every scribe who has been trained 15
15:13 Every plant which my heavenly Father has 15
18:16 that every word may be confirmed 15
35 will do to every one of you •
Lke 2:23 Every male that opens the womb shall be called holy 15
41 Now his parents went to Jerusalem every year 11
3: 5 Every valley shall be filled 15
5 every mountain and hill shall be brought low 15
9 every tree . . that does not bear good fruit 15
4:13 when the devil had ended every temptation 15
37 reports of him went out into every place 15
40 he laid his hands on every one of them 9
5:17 who had come from every village of Galilee 15
10: 1 into every town and place 15
11: 4 we ourselves forgive every one who is indebted 15
10 every one who asks receives 15
17 Every kingdom divided against itself is laid waste 15
42 you tithe the mint and rue and every herb 15
12: 8 I tell you, every one who acknowledges me 15
10 every one who speaks a word against the Son of man 15
21:37 every day he was teaching in the temple •
Joh 1: 9 The true light that enlightens every man 15
2:10 said to him, "Every man serves the good wine first; 15
15: 2 Every branch of mine that bears no fruit 15
2 every branch that does bear fruit he prunes 15
Act 2: 5 devout men from every nation under heaven. 15
43 fear came upon every soul 15
3:23 every soul that does not listen to that prophet 15
5:42 every day in the temple and at home 15
10:35 in every nation any one who fears him 15
13:27 the prophets which are read every sabbath 15
14:23 they had appointed elders . . in every church 11
15:21 Moses has had in every city those who preach him 11
21 he is read every sabbath in the synagogues. 15
36 in every city where we proclaimed the word 15
17:17 he argued . . in the market place every day 15
26 he made from one every nation of men 15
18: 4 he argued in the synagogue every sabbath 15
20:23 the Holy Spirit testifies to me in every city 11
31 not cease . . to admonish every one with tears. 9
21:26 the offering presented for every one of them. 9
22:19 in every synagogue I imprisoned . . those who believed 11
Rom 2: 9 and distress for every human being who does evil 15
3: 2 Much in every way. 15
4 Let God be true though every man be false 15
19 so that every mouth may be stopped 15
13: 1 Let every person be subject to the governing 15
14:11 As I live, says the Lord, every knee shall bow to me 15
11 and every tongue shall give praise to God. 15
1Co 1: 2 all those who in every place call on the name 15
5 that in every way you were enriched in him 15
4:17 as I teach them everywhere in every church. 13
6:18 Every other sin which a man commits 15
9:25 Every athlete exercises self-control 15
11: 3 the head of every man is Christ 15
12: 6 the same God who inspires them all in every one. 15
15:24 after destroying every rule 15
24 destroying every rule and every authority 15
30 Why am I in peril every hour? 15
16: 2 On the first day of every week •
16 to every fellow worker and laborer. 15
2Co 4: 2 commend ourselves to every man's conscience 15
8 We are afflicted in every way 15
16 our inner nature is being renewed every day. †
6: 4 we commend ourselves in every way 15
7: 1 let us cleanse ourselves from every defilement 15
5 we were afflicted at every turn 15
11 At every point you have proved yourselves 15
9: 8 provide you with every blessing in abundance 15
8 provide in abundance for every good work. 15
11 You will be enriched in every way for great generosity 15
10: 5 every proud obstacle to the knowledge of God 15
5 take every thought captive to obey Christ 15
6 being ready to punish every disobedience 15
11: 6 in every way we have made this plain to you 15
Gal 3:10 it is written, "Cursed be every one 15
13 Cursed be every one who hangs on a tree"– 15
5: 3 to every man who receives circumcision 15
Eph 1: 3 blessed us . . with every spiritual blessing 15
21 and above every name that is named 15
3:15 every family in heaven and on earth is named 15
4:14 carried about with every wind of doctrine 15
15 we are to grow up in every way into him 15
16 every joint with which it is supplied 15
19 greedy to practice every kind of uncleanness. 15
Php 1: 4 always in every prayer of mine for you all 14
18 What then? Only that in every way 15
2: 9 the name which is above every name 15
10 at the name of Jesus every knee should bow 15
11 every tongue confess that Jesus Christ is Lord 15
4:19 my God will supply every need of yours 15
21 Greet every saint in Christ Jesus 15
Col 1:10 bearing fruit in every good work 15
23 been preached to every creature under heaven 15
28 warning every man and teaching every man 15
28 teaching every man in all wisdom 15
28 that we may present every man mature in Christ. 15
4: 6 you may know how you ought to answer every one. 9
1Th 5:22 abstain from every form of evil. 15
2Th 1: 3 the love of every one of you for one another 10
11 may fulfil every good resolve and work of faith 15
2: 4 exalts himself against every so-called god 15
17 establish them in every good work and word. 15
3:17 This is the mark in every letter of mine 15
1Ti 2: 2 godly and respectful in every way. 15
8 in every place the men should pray 15
3: 4 submissive and respectful in every way; 15
4: 8 godliness is of value in every way 15
5:10 and devoted herself to doing good in every way. 15
2Ti 3:17 equipped for every good work. 15
4:18 The Lord will rescue me from every evil 15
Tit 1: 5 appoint elders in every town as I directed you 11
2: 9 to give satisfaction in every respect 15
Heb 2: 2 every transgression or disobedience 15
17 had to be made like his brethren in every respect 15
3: 4 For every house is built by some one 15
13 exhort one another every day 9
4:15 one who in every respect has been tempted 15
5: 1 every high priest chosen from among men 15
8: 3 every high priest is appointed to offer gifts 15
9:19 when every commandment . . had been declared 15
10:11 every priest stands daily at his service 15
12: 1 Therefore . . let us also lay aside every weight 15
6 chastises every son whom he receives. 15
Jas 1:17 Every good endowment . . is from above 15
17 and every perfect gift is from above 15
19 Let every man be quick to hear, slow to speak 15
3: 7 For every kind of beast and bird, of reptile 15
16 there will be disorder and every vile practice. 15
1Pe 2:13 Be subject . . to every human institution 15
2Pe 1: 5 make every effort to supplement your faith 15
1Jn 4: 1 Beloved, do not believe every spirit 15
2 every spirit which confesses that Jesus Christ 15
3 every spirit which does not confess Jesus 15
5: 1 every one who loves the parent loves the child. 15
Rev 1: 7 he is coming . . and every eye will see him 15
5: 9 ransom men for God from every tribe and tongue 15
13 I heard every creature in heaven and on earth 15
6:14 every mountain and island was removed 15
7: 4 144,000 sealed, out of every tribe 15
9 multitude . . from every nation, from all tribes 15
17 and God will wipe away every tear from their eyes. 15
11: 6 and to smite the earth with every plague 15
13: 7 every tribe and people and tongue and nation 15
8 every one whose name has not been written 15
14: 6 to every nation and tribe and tongue and people; 15
16: 3 and every living thing died that was in the sea. 15
20 And every island fled away 15
18: 2 a haunt of every foul spirit 15
2 a haunt of every foul and hateful bird; 15
21: 4 he will wipe away every tear from their eyes 15
19 foundations . . were adorned with every jewel; 15
1Es 1:33 every one of the acts of Josiah 11
3:20 It turns every thought to feasting and mirth 15
4:15 Women gave birth to the king and to every people 15
52 to be offered on the altar every day 11
5:51 offered the proper sacrifices every day 11
6:30 regularly every year, without quibbling 11
33 Therefore may the Lord . . destroy every king 15
8:61 he delivered us from every enemy on the way 15
2Es 3: 8 every nation walked after its own will 18
5:23 O sovereign Lord, from every forest of the earth 16
34 for every hour I suffer agonies of heart 16
7:89 and withstood danger every hour 16
127 the contest which every man . . shall wage •
8: 6 every mortal who bears the likeness of a human 16
9:44 every hour and every day during those 30 years 17
44 every hour and every day during those 30 years 17
15: 4 For every unbeliever shall die in his unbelief. 16
6 For iniquity has spread throughout every land 16
40 shall pour out upon every high and lofty place 16
16:29 three or four olives may be left on every tree 17
50 who searches out every sin on earth. 16
Tob 4:18 Seek advice from every wise man 15
19 Bless the Lord God on every occasion 15
21 fear God and refrain from every sin 15
8:15 with every pure and holy blessing 15
10: 7 she went out every day to the road 11
12: 9 it will purge away every sin 15
Jdt 2: 3 every one who had not obeyed his command 15
8 every brook and river 15
18 also plenty of food for every man 15
4: 4 they sent to every district of Samaria 15
9 every man of Israel cried out to God 15
10 every resident alien and hired laborer 15
7:20 belonging to every inhabitant of Bethulia 15
9:14 cause thy whole nation and every tribe to know 15
11: 7 who had sent you to direct every living soul 15
17 every night your servant will go out 11
13: 3 as she did every day 11
14: 7 Blessed are you in every tent of Judah! 15
7 In every nation 15
11 every man took his weapons 15
15: 2 fled by every path across the plain 15
3 the men of Israel, every one that was a soldier 15
16:16 every sacrifice as a fragrant offering 15
AEs 11: 7 at their roaring every nation prepared for war 15
12 sought all day to understand it in every detail. 15
13: 4 have laws contrary to those of every nation 15
10 earth and every wonderful thing under heaven 15
14: 2 every part that she loved to adorn 15
16:11 the good will that we have for every nation 15
19 post . . this letter publicly in every place 15
24 Every city and country, without exception 15
Wis 6:16 meets them in every thought. 15
7:27 in every generation she passes into holy souls 11
29 excels every constellation of the stars. 15
13:14 and covering every blemish in it with paint; 15
14: 4 showing that thou canst save from every danger 15
27 the beginning and cause and end of every evil. 15
16: 8 it is thou who deliverest from every evil. 15
20 providing every pleasure 15
20 suited to every taste. 15
Sir 5: 9 Do not winnow with every wind 15

9 nor follow every path 15
6:35 Be ready to listen to every narrative 15
8:19 Do not reveal your thoughts to every one 15
11:29 Do not bring every man into your home 15
13:15 Every creature loves its like 15
15 every person his neighbor; 15
14:19 Every product decays and ceases to exist 15
15:19 he knows every deed of man. 15
16:14 He will make room for every act of mercy 15
17:17 He appointed a ruler for every nation 9
18:28 Every intelligent man knows wisdom 15
24: 6 in the whole earth, and in every people and nation 15
26:12 so will she sit in front of every post 15
29: 3 on every occasion you will find what you need. 15
30: 7 his feelings will be troubled at every cry. 15
31: 7 every fool will be taken captive by it. 15
13 Therefore it sheds tears from every face. 15
15 in every matter be thoughtful. 15
32:23 Guard yourself in every act 15
35: 9 With every gift show a cheerful face 15
36:22 surpasses every human desire. 15
37: 1 Every friend will say, "I too am a friend 15
7 Every counselor praises counsel 15
16 Reason is the beginning of every work 15
16 counsel precedes every undertaking. 15
28 not every person enjoys everything. 15
38:27 So too is every craftsman and master workman 15
39:33 he will supply every need in its hour. 15
40: 1 Much labor was created for every man 15
41:16 it is good to retain every kind of shame 15
23 will find favor with every man. 15
42:23 remain for ever for every need 15
43:20 it rests upon every pool of water 15
45:14 be wholly burned twice every day continually. 11
47:25 For they sought out every sort of wickedness 15
49: 1 it is sweet as honey to every mouth 15
16 Adam above every living being in the creation. 15
Bar 5: 7 every high mountain and the everlasting hills 15
8 The woods and every fragrant tree have shaded 15
LJr 1:61 the wind likewise blows in every land. 15
71 a thorn bush in a garden, on which every bird sits 15
Bel 1: 3 every day they spent on it twelve bushels 9
4 revered it and went every day to worship it 9
6 see how much he eats and drinks every day? 9
32 every day they had been given two human bodies *
1Mc 1:25 Israel mourned deeply in every community 15
27 Every bridegroom took up the lament 15
52 Many of the people, every one who forsook the law 15
53 drove Israel into hiding in every place of refuge 15
2:27 Let every one who is zealous for the law 15
41 fight against every man who comes to attack us 15
5:28 killed every male by the edge of the sword 15
35 he killed every male in it 15
51 He destroyed every male by the edge of the sword 15
12:11 remember you constantly on every occasion 15
13:20 kept marching along opposite him to every place 15
14:14 and did away with every lawless and wicked man. 15
35 He sought in every way to exalt his people. 15
15: 8 Every debt you owe to the royal treasury 15
2Mc 1:17 Blessed in every way be our God 15
25 who dost rescue Israel from every evil 15
9: 7 to torture every limb of his body. 15
11 he was tortured with pain every moment. 11
17 would visit every inhabited place 15
10: 8 should observe these days every year. 11
11: 3 to put up the high priesthood for sale every year. 11
15 every request . . which Maccabeus delivered 12
3Mc 1:13 when he entered every other temple 15
3:23 in every situation 9
24 they are ill-disposed toward us in every way 15
29 Every place detected sheltering a Jew 15
5:51 imploring the Ruler over every power 8
6: 1 had been adorned with every virtue 15
7: 7 every charge of whatever kind. 15
9 not man but the Ruler over every power 15
4Mc 2: 4 to rule . . also over every desire. 15
5: 2 to seize each and every Hebrew 9
8: 3 modest, noble, and accomplished in every way 15
5 Young men, I admire each and every one of you 9
9:14 though broken in every member 15
18: 1 obey this law and exercise piety in every way 15

every *See also* day, moment, morning, side, turn, way, year.

every kind 1. כֹּל

Ezk 38:21 I will summon every kind of terror against Gog 1

every man 1. אִישׁ 2. אִישׁ וְאִישׁ 3. כֹּל 4. כָּל הָאָדָם 5. ἕκαστος 6. unusquisque

Gen 16:12 his hand against every man 3
12 every man and every man's hand against him; 3
44:11 Then every man quickly lowered his sack 1
11 to the ground, and every man opened his sack. 1
13 rent their clothes, and every man loaded his ass 1
Exd 7:12 For every man cast down his rod, and they became 1
16:29 remain every man of you in his place, let no man go 1
35:24 every man with whom was found acacia wood 3
Num 1:26 every man able to go forth to war 3
28 every man able to go forth to war 3
30 every man able to go forth to war 3
32 every man able to go forth to war 3
34 every man able to go forth to war 3
36 every man able to go forth to war 3
38 every man able to go forth to war 3
40 every man able to go forth to war 3
42 every man able to go forth to war 3
45 every man able to go forth to war in Israel– 3
52 by their companies, every man by his own camp 1
52 by his own camp and every man by his own standard 1
32:27 every man who is armed for war, before the LORD 3
29 every man who is armed to battle before the LORD 3
Jos 6: 5 people shall go up every man straight before him. 1
20 people went up . . every man straight before him 1
24:28 sent the people . . every man to his inheritance. 1
Jdg 7: 7 and let all the others go every man to his home. 1
8 sent all the rest of Israel every man to his tent 1
21 stood every man in his place round about the camp 1
22 the LORD set every man's sword against his fellow 1
8:24 give me every man of you the earrings of his spoil. 1
25 every man cast in it the earrings of his spoil. 1
9:55 was dead, they departed every man to his home. 1
17: 6 every man did what was right in his own eyes. 1
21:24 departed . . every man to his tribe and family 1
24 they went out . . every man to his inheritance. 1
25 every man did what was right in his own eyes. 1
1Sm 4:10 was defeated, and they fled, every man to his home; 1
8:22 Samuel then said . . "Go every man to his city. 1
13: 2 the rest . . he sent home, every man to his tent. 1
14:20 behold, every man's sword was against his fellow 1
34 Let every man bring his ox or his sheep 1
25:13 David said to his men, "Every man gird on his sword! 1
13 And every man of them girded on his sword; 1
26:23 LORD rewards every man for his righteousness 1
27: 3 every man with his household, and David with his 1
2Sm 19: 8 Now Israel had fled every man to his own home. 1
20: 1 every man to his tents, O Israel! 1
22 and they dispersed . . every man to his home. 1
1Kg 4:25 dwelt in safety . . every man under his vine 1
12:24 Return every man to his home 1
22:36 Every man to his city, and every man to his country! 1
36 Every man to his city, and every man to his country! 1
2Kg 3:25 on every . . piece of land every man threw a stone 1
9:13 Then in haste every man of them took his garment 1
11:11 the guards stood, every man with his weapons 1
14: 6 but every man shall die for his own sin. 1
12 and every man fled to his home. 1
Est 1: 8 had given orders . . to do as every man desired. 2
Ecc 5:19 Every man also to whom God has given wealth 4
Isa 3: 5 oppress one another, every man his fellow 1
5 oppress . . his fellow and every man his neighbor; 1
Jer 23:36 for the burden is every man's own word 1
32:19 rewarding every man according to his ways 1
37:10 every man in his tent, they would rise up 1
49: 5 driven out, every man straight before him 1
Ezk 9: 2 every man with his weapon for slaughter 1
Mat 16:27 then he will repay every man for what he has done. 5
Joh 16:32 when you will be scattered, every man to his home 5
Rom 2: 6 will render to every man according to his works 5
1Co 4: 5 Then every man will receive his commendation 5
2Es 13:33 every man shall leave his own land 6
Jdt 14: 2 let every valiant man take his weapons and go out 5

every one 1. אֶחָד 2. אִישׁ 3. כֹּל 4. כָּל הָאָדָם 5. ἕκαστος 6. καθ' ἕν 7. κατ' ὄνομα 8. ὅσος 9. ὅστις 10. πᾶς 11. τις 12. omnis 13. omnis unusquisque 14. unusquisque

Gen 20:16 and before every one you are righted. 3
21: 6 every one who hears will laugh over me. 3
27:29 Cursed be every one who curses you *
29 blessed be every one who blesses you! *
30:33 Every one that is not speckled and spotted 3
35 every one that had white on it 3
Exd 30:14 Every one who is numbered in the census 3
31:14 every one who profanes it shall be put to death; *
33: 7 And every one who sought the LORD would go out 3
35:24 Every one who could make an offering of silver 3
36: 2 called . . every one whose heart stirred him up 3
38:26 for every one who was numbered in the census 3
Lev 11:26 every one who touches them shall be unclean 3
19: 3 Every one of you shall revere his mother 2
8 every one who eats it shall bear his iniquity *
Num 2:34 so they set out, every one in his family 2
4:30 number them, every one that can enter the service 3
35 every one that could enter the service, for work 3
39 every one that could enter the service for work 3
43 every one that could enter the service, for work 3
47 every one that could enter to do the work 3
5: 2 put out . . every one having a discharge 3
2 put out of the camp . . every one that is unclean 3
13: 2 send a man, every one a leader among them. 3
15:12 do with every one according to their number. 1
16: 3 all the congregation are holy, every one of them 3
17:13 Every one who comes near . . shall die. 3
18:11 every one who is clean in your house may eat of it. 3
13 every one who is clean in your house may eat of it. 3
19:14 every one who comes into the tent 3
14 every one who is in the tent, shall be unclean 3
21: 8 every one who is bitten when he sees it, shall live. 3
24: 9 Blessed be every one who blesses you *
9 cursed be every one who curses you. *
25: 5 Every one of you slay his men who have yoked 2
36: 7 every one of the people of Israel shall cleave 2
8 every one of the people of Israel may possess 2
Jos 22:14 chiefs . . every one of them the head of a family 2
Jdg 7: 5 Every one that laps the water with his tongue 3
8:18 As you are, so were they, every one of them; 1
9:49 every one of the people cut down his bundle 3
20:16 every one could sling a stone at a hair, and not 3
1Sm 2:36 every one who is left in your house shall come 3
3:11 two ears of every one that hears it will tingle. 3
13:20 every one of the Israelites went down 3
20:15 LORD cuts off every one of the enemies of David 2
22: 7 will the son of Jesse give every one of you fields 3
2Sm 2: 3 David brought up . . every one with his household; 2
18:17 and all Israel fled every one to his own home. 2
1Kg 9: 8 every one passing by it will be astonished 3
10:25 Every one of them brought his present 2
2Kg 18:31 then every one of you will eat of his own vine 2
31 eat of his . . vine, and every one of his own fig tree 2
31 every one of you will drink the water of his own 2
21:12 the ears of every one who hears of it will tingle. 3
23:35 from every one according to his assessment 2
2Ch 7:21 every one passing by will be astonished, and say 3
9:24 Every one of them brought his present *
30:17 the passover lamb for every one who was not clean 3
18 The good LORD pardon every one 3
31:19 portions . . to every one among the Levites 3
Ezr 1: 5 every one whose spirit God had stirred to go up 3
3: 5 offerings of every one who made a freewill 3
6:21 every one who had joined them and separated 3
Neh 11: 3 towns of Judah every one lived on his property 2
20 towns of Judah, every one in his inheritance. 2
Job 40:11 look on every one that is proud, and abase him. 3
12 Look on every one that is proud, and bring him low; 3
Ps 12: 2 Every one utters lies to his neighbor; 2
32: 6 let every one who is godly offer prayer to thee; 3
119:160 every one of thy righteous ordinances endures 3
128: 1 Blessed is every one who fears the LORD 3
135:18 Like them . . yea, every one who trusts in them! 3
139:16 thy book were written, every one of them, the days 3
Prv 16: 5 Every one who is arrogant is an abomination 3
19: 6 every one is a friend to a man who gives gifts. 3
21: 5 but every one who is hasty comes only to want. 3
Ecc 3:13 God's gift . . that every one should eat and drink 4
10: 3 and he says to every one that he is a fool. 3
Isa 1:23 Every one loves a bribe and runs after gifts. 3
4: 3 every one who has been recorded for life 3
7:22 every one that is left in the land will eat curds 3
9:17 for every one is godless and an evildoer 3
15: 3 in the squares every one wails and melts 3
16: 7 let Moab wail, let every one wail for Moab. 3
19:17 every one to whom it is mentioned will fear 3
30: 5 every one comes to shame through a people 3
31: 7 every one shall cast away his idols of silver 2
36:16 then every one of you will eat of his own vine 2
16 of his own vine, and every one of his own fig tree 2
16 every one . . will drink the water of his own 2
41: 6 Every one helps his neighbor 2
43: 7 every one who is called by my name 3
53: 6 astray; we have turned every one to his own way; 2
55: 1 Ho, every one who thirsts, come to the waters; 3
56: 6 his servants, every one who keeps the sabbath 3
Jer 5: 6 every one who goes out of them shall be torn 3
6:13 every one is greedy for unjust gain; 3
13 from prophet to priest, every one deals falsely. 3
8: 6 Every one turns to his own course 3
10 every one is greedy for unjust gain; 3
10 from prophet to priest every one deals falsely. 3
9: 4 Let every one beware of his neighbor 2
5 Every one deceives his neighbor 2
11: 8 every one walked in the stubbornness of his evil 2
16:12 every one of you follows his stubborn evil will 2
18:11 Return, every one from his evil way 2
12 every one act according to the stubbornness 2
16 Every one who passes by it is horrified 3
19: 8 every one who passes by it will be horrified 3
9 and every one shall eat the flesh of his neighbor 2
20: 7 I have become a laughingstock . . every one mocks me. 3
23:17 every one who stubbornly follows his own heart 3
35 Thus shall you say, every one to his neighbor 2
35 one to his neighbor and every one to his brother 2
25: 5 saying, 'Turn now, every one of you, 2
26: 3 they will listen, and every one turn from his evil 2
30:16 foes, every one of them, shall go into captivity; 3
31:30 But every one shall die for his own sin; 2
34: 9 that every one should set free his Hebrew slaves 2
10 covenant that every one would set free his slave 2
17 by proclaiming liberty, every one to his brother 2
35:15 Turn now every one of you from his evil way 2
36: 3 so that every one may turn from his evil way 2
7 and that every one will turn from his evil way 2
Ezk 7:16 all of them moaning, every one over his iniquity. 2
32:10 tremble every moment, every one for his own life 2
Dan 12: 1 every one whose name . . found written in the book. 3
Zep 1: 9 punish every one who leaps over the threshold 3
2:15 Every one who passes by her hisses 3
Mat 19:29 every one who has left houses or brothers 10

25:29 For to every one who has will more be given 10
Mrk 1:37 Every one is searching for you. 10
9:48 For every one will be salted with fire. 10
Lke 6:30 Give to every one who begs from you 10
40 every one . . will be like his teacher. 10
47 Every one who comes to me and hears my words 10
12:48 Every one to whom much is given 10
14:11 For every one who exalts himself will be humbled 10
16:16 every one enters it violently 10
18 Every one who divorces his wife 10
18:14 every one who exalts himself will be humbled 10
19:26 to every one who has will more be given 10
20:18 Every one who falls on that stone 10
Joh 3: 8 so it is with every one who is born of the Spirit. 10
20 For every one who does evil hates the light 10
4:13 Every one who drinks . . will thirst again 10
6:40 every one who sees the Son and believes in him 10
45 Every one who has heard . . comes to me 10
8:34 every one who commits sin is a slave to sin. 10
11:48 every one will believe in him 10
13:10 you are clean, but not every one of you. 10
18:37 Every one who is of the truth hears my voice. 10
19:12 every one who makes himself a king 10
21:25 were every one of them to be written 6
Act 2:38 Repent, and be baptized every one of you 5
39 every one whom the Lord our God calls to him. 8
3:26 in turning every one of you from your wickedness 5
10:43 every one who believes in him receives 10
11:29 every one according to his ability 5
13:39 by him every one that believes is freed 10
16:26 every one's fetters were unfastened. 10
Rom 1:16 it is the power of God for salvation to every one 10
2:10 and honor and peace for every one who does good 10
10: 4 that every one who has faith may be justified. 10
13 For, "every one who calls upon the name of the Lord 10
12: 3 I bid every one among you not to think of himself 10
14: 5 Let every one be fully convinced in his own mind. 5
1Co 7:17 Only, let every one lead the life 5
15:28 that God may be everything to every one. 10
Eph 4:25 let every one speak the truth with his neighbor 5
2Ti 2:19 every one who names the name of the Lord depart 10
24 kindly to every one, an apt teacher, forbearing 10
Heb 2: 9 he might taste death for every one. 10
5:13 every one who lives on milk 10
8:11 they shall not teach every one his fellow 5
11 shall not teach . . every one his brother, saying 5
1Jn 2:29 every one who does right is born of him. 10
3: 3 every one who thus hopes in him purifies himself 10
4 Every one who commits sin is guilty 10
5: 1 Every one who believes that Jesus is the Christ 10
3Jn 1:12 Deme'trius has testimony from every one 10
15 Greet the friends, every one of them. 7
Rev 1: 7 every one who pierced him; 9
6:15 every one, slave and free, hid in the caves 10
22:12 to repay every one for what he has done. 5
15 every one who loves and practices falsehood. 10
18 I warn every one who hears the words 10
1Es 3:21 makes every one talk in millions. 10
2Es 7:27 every one who has been delivered from the evils 12
75 as soon as every one of us yields up his soul 14
105 every one shall bear his own righteousness 13
9: 7 every one who will be saved 12
12:49 Now go, every one of you to his house 14
Jdt 1:12 all Judea, and every one in Egypt 10
2:25 and killed every one who resisted him 10
7: 4 and every one said to his neighbor 5
10:19 and every one said to his neighbor 5
13: 4 every one went out 10
16:21 every one returned home to his own inheritance 5
Wis 16:21 was changed to suit every one's liking. 11
Sir 16:14 every one will receive 10
22: 1 every one hisses at his disgrace. 10
33: 6 he neighs under every one who sits on him. 10
37:28 For not everything is good for every one 10
41:16 is confidently esteemed by every one. 10
1Mc 2:42 every one who offered himself willingly for the law. 10
10:33 every one of the Jews taken as a captive 10
2Mc 1:23 –the priests and every one 10
5:12 to cut down relentlessly every one they met •
10:35 and with savage fury cut down every one they met. •
12:40 under the tunic of every one of the dead 5
15:35 a clear and conspicuous sign to every one 10
3Mc 7: 8 We also have ordered each and every one to return 10
4Mc 7:17 Not every one has full command of his emotions 10
17 because not every one has prudent reason. 10
8: 9 will compel me to destroy each and every one of you 5

every people 1. עַם וָעָם
Est 8: 9 an edict . . to every people in its own language 1

every person 1. כֹּל
Lev 7:25 For every person who eats of the fat of an animal 1

every place 1. κατὰ τόπον
1Mc 12: 4 letters to the people in every place 1

every sort 1. כֹּל
2Ch 15: 6 God troubled them with every sort of distress. 1
Ezk 17:23 in the shade of its branches birds of every sort †

every way 1. δι' ὅλου 2. πᾶς
Act 17:22 in every way you are very religious. 2
1Mc 6:18 They were trying in every way to harm them 1

everybody 1. כֹּל
Prv 26:10 Like an archer who wounds everybody is he who 1

everyone 1. εἷς ἕκαστος 2. πανταχόθεν 3. πᾶς
4Mc 1: 2 the subject is essential to everyone 3
4:26 tried to compel everyone in the nation 1
13: 1 everyone must concede 2

everything 1. כֹּל 2. כֹּל דָּבָר 3. מְלֹא 4. ἅπας 5. ὃς ἐάν 6. ὅσος 7. πᾶς 8. πλήρωμα 9. omnis
Gen 1:25 and everything that creeps upon the ground 1
30 and to everything that creeps on the earth 1
30 to . . everything that has the breath of life •
31 God saw everything that he had made 1
6:17 everything that is on the earth shall die. 1
7: 8 of birds, and of everything that creeps 1
22 everything on the dry land in whose nostrils 1
8:19 everything that moves upon the earth, went forth 1
9: 2 upon everything that creeps on the ground 1
3 you the green plants, I give you everything. 1
14:20 And Abram gave him a tenth of everything. 1
32:23 the stream, and likewise everything that he had. •
39: 8 and he has put everything that he has in my hand; 1
Exd 9:25 The hail struck down everything that was 1
Lev 11: 9 Everything in the waters that has fins and scales 1
12 Everything in the waters that has not fins 1
35 everything upon which . . their carcass falls 1
15: 4 everything on which he sits shall be unclean 1
20 everything upon which she lies 1
20 everything also upon which she sits 1
26 everything on which she sits shall be unclean 1
Num 18:15 Everything that opens the womb of all flesh 1
29:40 Moses told the people of Israel everything 1
31:23 everything that can stand the fire 2
Deu 8: 3 man lives by everything that proceeds out 1
12:32 Everything that I command you you shall 2
20:14 cattle, and everything else in the city 1
Jos 4:10 in the . . Jordan, until everything was finished 2
1Sm 3:18 Samuel told him everything and hid nothing 2
2Sm 3:36 as everything that the king did pleased 1
15:36 by them you shall send to me everything you hear. 2
1Kg 14:26 of the king's house; he took away everything. 1
1Ch 16:32 let the field exult, and everything in it! 1
26:32 oversight . . for everything pertaining to God 2
2Ch 12: 9 he took away everything. 1
31: 5 brought in abundantly the tithe of everything. 1
Ezr 8:34 weight of everything was recorded. 1
Neh 13:30 Thus I cleansed them from everything foreign 1
Est 4:17 went . . and did everything as Esther had ordered 1
6:13 Haman told . . everything that had befallen him. 1
Job 28:24 and sees everything under the heavens. 1
41:34 He beholds everything that is high; 1
Ps 69:34 the seas and everything that moves therein. 1
74: 3 the enemy has destroyed everything 1
96:12 let the field exult, and everything in it! 1
138: 2 exalted above everything thy name and thy word. •
150: 6 Let everything that breathes praise the LORD! 1
Prv 13:16 In everything a prudent man acts with knowledge 1
14:15 The simple believes everything 2
16: 4 The LORD has made everything for its purpose 1
24:27 get everything ready for you in the field; •
27: 7 one who is hungry everything bitter is sweet. 1
Ecc 1:14 I have seen everything that is done under the sun; 1
3: 1 For everything there is a season 1
11 He has made everything beautiful in its time; 1
7:15 In my vain life I have seen everything; 1
9: 1 Everything before them is vanity 1
10:19 wine gladdens . . and money answers everything. 1
11: 5 do not know the work of God who makes everything. 1
Jer 1:17 and say to them everything that I command you. 1
25:13 against it, everything written in this book 1
44:17 But we will do everything that we have vowed 2
18 we have lacked everything 1
Ezk 21:10 despised the rod, my son, with everything of wood. 1
30:12 desolation upon the land and everything in it 3
47: 9 everything will live where the river goes. 1
Zep 1: 2 I will utterly sweep away everything 1
Mat 8:33 going into the city they told everything 7
18:26 and I will pay you everything.' 7
19:27 Lo, we have left everything and followed you 7
22: 4 everything is ready; come to the marriage feast.' 7
23:20 swears by it and by everything on it; 7
Mrk 4:11 for those outside everything is in parables; 7
34 to his own disciples he explained everything. 7
8:25 was restored, and saw everything clearly. 4
10:28 Lo, we have left everything and followed you. 7
11:11 when he had looked round at everything 7
12:44 out of her poverty has put in everything she had 7
Lke 2:39 when they had performed everything 7
5:11 they left everything and followed him. 7
28 he left everything, and rose and followed him. 7
9:43 they were all marveling at everything he did 7
11:41 behold, everything is clean for you. 7
15:14 when he had spent everything 7
18:31 everything that is written of the Son of man 7
24:44 everything written about me in the law of Moses 7
Joh 10:41 everything . . John said about this man was true 7
17: 7 everything that thou hast given me is from thee; 7
21:17 he said to him, "Lord, you know everything 7
Act 4:24 the earth and the sea and everything in them 7
32 they had everything in common. 7
10: 8 having related everything to them 4
13:39 freed from everything 7
17:24 The God who made the world and everything in it 7
25 gives to all men life and breath and everything. 7
24: 8 will be able to learn from him about everything 7
14 believing everything laid down by the law 7
Rom 8:28 We know that in everything God works for good 7
14:20 Everything is indeed clean 7
1Co 2:10 the Spirit searches everything, even the depths 7
10:26 For "the earth is the Lord's, and everything in it. 8
33 just as I try to please all men in everything I do 7
11: 2 because you remember me in everything 7
15:28 that God may be everything to every one. 7
2Co 2: 9 know whether you are obedient in everything. 7
6:10 having nothing, and yet possessing everything. 7
7:14 just as everything we said to you was true 7
8: 7 Now as you excel in everything 7
9: 8 so that you may always have enough of everything 7
Eph 5:20 always and for everything giving thanks 7
24 let wives also be subject in everything 7
6:21 Tych'icus . . will tell you everything. 7
Php 3: 8 Indeed I count everything as loss 7
4: 6 in everything by prayer and supplication 7
Col 1:18 that in everything he might be preeminent. 7
3:14 which binds everything together in perfect harmony. •
17 do everything in the name of the Lord Jesus 7
20 Children, obey your parents in everything 7
22 Slaves, obey in everything 7
1Th 1: 9 They will tell you of everything 7
5:21 test everything; hold fast what is good 7
1Ti 4: 4 For everything created by God is good 7
6:17 richly furnishes us with everything to enjoy. 7
2Ti 2: 7 will grant you understanding in everything. 7
10 Therefore I endure everything 7
Tit 2:10 in everything they may adorn the doctrine of God 7
Heb 2: 8 Now in putting everything in subjection to him 7
8 Now in putting everything in subjection to him 7
8 do not yet see everything in subjection to him. 7
7: 2 a tenth part of everything 7
8: 5 See that you make everything 7
9:22 almost everything is purified with blood 7
13:21 equip you with everything good 7
1Pe 4:11 in order that in everything God may be glorified 7
1Jn 2:27 as his anointing teaches you about everything 7
3:20 God is greater . . and he knows everything. 7
1Es 2: 9 their neighbors helped them with everything 7
4: 5 they bring everything to the king 7
5 whatever spoil they take and everything else. 7
22 bring everything and give it to women? 7
57 everything that Cyrus had ordered to be done 7
8:64 the weight of everything was recorded 7
2Es 3:26 in everything doing as Adam . . had done 9
6:39 and darkness and silence embraced everything; •
9: 5 everything that has occurred in the world 9
13: 3 everything under his gaze trembled 9
14:22 I will write everything that has happened 9
Tob 2:14 You seem to know everything! 7
4:14 Watch yourself, my son, in everything you do 7
5: 1 Father, I will do everything 7
12:20 Write in a book everything that has happened. 7
Jdt 4: 1 heard of everything . . Holofernes . . had done 7
8:25 In spite of everything let us give thanks 7
AEs 16: 4 God, who always sees everything. 7
Wis 18:13 For though they had disbelieved everything 7
19:22 in everything, O Lord, thou hast exalted 7
Sir 10:27 has an abundance of everything 7
15:18 he is mighty in power and sees everything; 7
18:27 A wise man is cautious in everything 7
19:15 do not believe everything you hear. 7
25:11 The fear of the Lord surpasses everything 7
31:14 Do not reach out your hand for everything you see 5
37:28 For not everything is good for every one 7
28 not every person enjoys everything. 7
39:21 everything has been created for its use. 7
41: 1 who is prosperous in everything 7
2 very old and distracted over everything 7
16 not everything is confidently esteemed 7
42:16 The sun looks down on everything with its light 7
Bel 1:15 ate and drank everything. 7
1Mc 1:48 abominable by everything unclean and profane 7
2Mc 7:28 see everything that is in them 7
10:23 success at arms in everything he undertook 7
11:14 them to settle everything on just terms 7
18 I have informed the king of everything 6
3Mc 2:25 who were strangers to everything just. 7
5:42 Phalaris in everything and filled with madness 7
6:40 provided with everything by the king 7
7: 9 in everything and inescapably as an antagonist 7
4Mc 14:13 which draws everything toward an emotion 7

everything else 1. λοιπός
3Mc 6:30 and everything else needed for a festival 1

everywhere 1. כֹּל 2. κατὰ πάντα 3. πανταχῇ
4. πανταχοῦ 5. πάντοθεν 6. πᾶς

Gen 13:10 the Jordan valley was well watered everywhere 1
Mrk 1:28 And at once his fame spread everywhere 4
16:20 they went forth and preached everywhere 4
Lke 9: 6 preaching the gospel and healing everywhere. 4
Act 17:30 now he commands all men everywhere to repent 4
21:28 This is the man who is teaching men everywhere 3
24: 3 in every way and everywhere we accept this 4
28:22 we know that everywhere it is spoken against. 4
1Co 4:17 as I teach them everywhere in every church. 4
Bar 5: 3 show your splendor everywhere under heaven. 6
2Mc 2:18 and will gather us from everywhere under heaven *
8: 7 talk of his valor spread everywhere. 3
3Mc 4: 2 everywhere their hearts were burning 5
7:12 everywhere in his kingdom 2

eviction 1. גְּרוּשָׁה

Ezk 45: 9 cease your evictions of my people, says the Lord 1

evidence 1. לְפִי 2. עֵד 3. פֶּה 4. ἔνδειγμα 5. ἐπί
6. μαρτύριον 7. στόμα 8. τεκμήριον 9. τρόπος

Exd 22:13 it is torn by beasts, let him bring it as evidence; 2
Num35:30 put to death on the evidence of witnesses; 1
Deu 17: 6 On the evidence of two witnesses or of three 3
6 not be put to death on the evidence of one witness. 3
19:15 only on the evidence of two witnesses, or of three 3
Mat 18:16 confirmed by the evidence of two or three 7
2Co 13: 1 by the evidence of two or three witnesses. 7
2Th 1: 5 is evidence of the righteous judgment of God 4
1Ti 5:19 except on the evidence of two or three witnesses. 5
Jas 5: 3 and their rust will be evidence against you 6
Wis 5:11 no evidence of its passage is found 8
10: 7 Evidence of their wickedness still remains 6
LJr 1:69 we have no evidence whatever that they are gods; 9

honest evidence 1. צֶדֶק

Prv 12:17 He who speaks the truth gives honest evidence 1

evident 1. δῆλος 2. κατάδηλος 3. πρόδηλος
4. φαίνω

Gal 3:11 Now it is evident that no man is justified 1
Heb 7:14 evident that our Lord was descended from Judah 3
15 This becomes even more evident 2
2Es 9: 5 the beginning is evident, and the end manifest; ‡
4Mc 1: 3 If, then, it is evident 4
2:15 It is evident that reason rules 4
3: 1 it is evident that reason rules 4

evident *See also* make.

evidently 1. γνώριμος

LJr 1:16 Therefore they evidently are not gods 1

evil 1. אָוֶן 2. רֹעַ 3. רַע 4. רָעָה 5. רעע 6. רֶשַׁע 7. שָׁוְא
8. ἀνόσιος 9. κακία 10. κακός 11. κακῶς
12. οὐκ ἀγαθός 13. πονηρία 14. πονηρός 15. σαπρός
16. φαῦλος 17. malignitas 18. malignus 19. malus

Gen 2: 9 and the tree of the knowledge of good and evil. 3
17 the tree of the knowledge of good and evil 3
3: 5 will be like God, knowing good and evil. 3
22 like one of us, knowing good and evil; 3
6: 5 of his heart was only evil continually. 3
8:21 man's heart is evil from his youth; 3
44: 4 say to them, 'Why have you returned evil for good? 4
34 I fear to see the evil that would come upon my 3
47: 9 few and evil have been the days of the years of my 3
48:16 the angel who has redeemed me from all evil, 3
50:15 Joseph will . . pay us back for all the evil 4
17 Forgive . . because they did evil to you.' 4
20 As for you, you meant evil against me; 4
Exd 5:19 The foremen . . saw that they were in evil plight 3
32:12 With evil intent did he bring them forth, to slay 4
12 repent of this evil against thy people. 4
14 LORD repented of the evil which he thought to do 4
22 you know the people, that they are set on evil. 3
33: 4 When the people heard these evil tidings 3
Lev 26: 6 I will remove evil beasts from the land 4
Num14:37 the men who brought up an evil report of the land 4
20: 5 to bring us to this evil place? It is no place 3
22:34 Now therefore, if it is evil in thy sight, I will go 3
32:13 generation that had done evil in the sight of the LORD 3
Deu 1:35 Not one of these men of this evil generation 3
39 children . . have no knowledge of good or evil 3
4:25 doing . . evil in the sight of the LORD your God 3
7:15 none of the evil diseases of Egypt . . will he inflict 3
9:18 in doing what was evil in the sight of the LORD 3
13: 5 So you shall purge the evil from the midst of you. 3
17: 2 does . . evil in the sight of the LORD your God 3
5 bring . . man or woman who has done this evil thing 3
7 So you shall purge the evil from the midst of you. 3
12 so you shall purge the evil from Israel. 3
19:19 you shall purge the evil from the midst of you. 3
20 never again commit any such evil among you. 3
21:21 so you shall purge the evil from your midst; 3
22:14 brings an evil name upon her, saying, 'I took 3
19 brought an evil name upon a virgin of Israel; 3
21 you shall purge the evil from the midst of you. 3
22 so you shall purge the evil from Israel. 3
24 so you shall purge the evil from the midst of you. 3
23: 9 you shall keep yourself from every evil thing. 3
24: 7 so you shall purge the evil from the midst of you. 3
28:20 on account of the evil of your doings 2
30:15 set before you . . life and good, death and evil. 3
31:17 many evils and troubles will come upon them 4
17 'Have not these evils come upon us because our God 4
18 on account of all the evil which they have done 4
21 when many evils and troubles have come upon them 4
29 in the days to come evil will befall you 4
29 will do what is evil in the sight of the LORD 3
32:23 I will heap evils upon them; I will spend my arrows 4
Jos 23:15 the LORD will bring upon you all the evil things 3
Jdg 2:11 Israel did what was evil in the sight of the LORD 3
15 the hand of the LORD was against them for evil 4
3: 7 Israel did what was evil in the sight of the LORD 3
12 again did what was evil in the sight of the LORD; 3
12 had done what was evil in the sight of the LORD. 3
4: 1 again did what was evil in the sight of the LORD 3
6: 1 Israel did what was evil in the sight of the LORD; 3
9:23 God sent an evil spirit between Abim'elech 4
10: 6 did what was evil in the sight of the LORD 3
13: 1 again did what was evil in the sight of the LORD; 3
20:13 put them to death, and put away evil from Israel. 4
1Sm 2:23 I hear of your evil dealings from all the people. 3
12:19 we have added to all our sins this evil 4
20 you have done all this evil, yet do not turn aside 4
15:19 and do what was evil in the sight of the LORD? 3
16:14 and an evil spirit from the LORD tormented him. 4
15 an evil spirit from God is tormenting you. 4
16 when the evil spirit from God is upon you 4
23 whenever the evil spirit from God was upon Saul •
23 Saul was . . well, and the evil spirit departed 4
17:28 know your presumption, and the evil of your heart; 2
18:10 an evil spirit from God rushed upon Saul 4
19: 9 Then an evil spirit from the LORD came upon Saul 4
20: 7 if he is angry, then know that evil is determined 4
9 determined . . that evil should come upon you 4
23: 9 David knew . . Saul was plotting evil against him; 4
24:17 good, whereas I have repaid you evil. 4
25:17 for evil is determined against our master 4
21 and he has returned me evil for good. 4
26 enemies and those who seek to do evil to my lord 4
28 evil shall not be found in you so long as you live. 4
39 has kept back his servant from evil; 4
2Sm 12: 9 you despised . . to do what is evil in his sight? 3
11 I will raise up evil against you out of your own 4
14:17 like the angel of God to discern good and evil. 3
15:14 lest he overtake us . . and bring down evil upon us 4
17:14 so that the LORD might bring evil upon Ab'salom. 4
18:32 and all who rise up against you for evil 4
19: 7 worse . . than all the evil that has come upon you 4
24:16 the LORD repented of the evil, and said 4
1Kg 2:44 You know . . all the evil that you did to David my 4
44 will bring back your evil upon your own head. 4
3: 9 that I may discern between good and evil; for who 3
9: 9 the LORD has brought all this evil upon them.' 4
11: 6 Solomon did what was evil in the sight of the LORD 3
13:33 Jerobo'am did not turn from his evil way 4
14:10 I will bring evil upon the house of Jerobo'am 4
22 Judah did what was evil in the sight of the LORD 3
15:26 He did what was evil in the sight of the LORD 3
34 He did what was evil in the sight of the LORD 3
16: 7 because of all the evil that he did 4
19 his sins . . doing evil in the sight of the LORD 3
25 Omri did what was evil in the sight of the LORD 3
30 Ahab . . did evil in the sight of the LORD 3
21:20 to do what is evil in the sight of the LORD. 3
21 Behold, I will bring evil upon you; 4
25 to do what was evil in the sight of the LORD 3
29 Because . . I will not bring the evil in his days; 4
29 I will bring the evil upon his house. 4
22: 8 never prophesies good concerning me, but evil. 3
18 would not prophesy good concerning me, but evil? 3
23 the LORD has spoken evil concerning you. 4
52 He did what was evil in the sight of the LORD 3
2Kg 3: 2 He did what was evil in the sight of the LORD 3
8:12 I know the evil that you will do to . . Israel; 4
18 And he did what was evil in the sight of the LORD. 3
27 and did what was evil in the sight of the LORD 3
13: 2 He did what was evil in the sight of the LORD 3
11 He also did what was evil in the sight of the LORD; 3
14:24 And he did what was evil in the sight of the LORD; 3
15: 9 And he did what was evil in the sight of the LORD 3
18 And he did what was evil in the sight of the LORD; 3
24 And he did what was evil in the sight of the LORD; 3
28 And he did what was evil in the sight of the LORD; 3
17: 2 And he did what was evil in the sight of the LORD 3
13 Turn from your evil ways and keep my . . statutes 3
17 and sold themselves to do evil in the sight 3
21: 2 And he did what was evil in the sight of the LORD 3
6 He did much evil in the sight of the LORD 3
9 to do more evil than the nations had done 3
12 bringing . . such evil that the ears of every one 4
15 they have done what is evil in my sight 3
16 they did what was evil in the sight of the LORD. 3
20 And he did what was evil in the sight of the LORD 3
22:16 I will bring evil upon this place and upon its 4
20 all the evil which I will bring upon this place.' 4
23:32 And he did what was evil in the sight of the LORD 3
37 And he did what was evil in the sight of the LORD 3
24: 9 And he did what was evil in the sight of the LORD 3
19 And he did what was evil in the sight of the LORD 3
1Ch 7:23 Beri'ah, because evil had befallen his house. 4
21:15 the LORD saw, and he repented of the evil; 4
2Ch 7:22 therefore he has brought all this evil upon them' 4
12:14 he did evil, for he did not set his heart to seek 3
18: 7 never prophecies good . . but always evil. 4
17 would not prophesy good concerning me, but evil? 3
22 the LORD has spoken evil concerning you. 4
20: 9 If evil comes upon us, the sword, judgment 4
21: 6 And he did what was evil in the sight of the LORD. 3
22: 4 He did what was evil in the sight of the LORD 3
29: 6 done what was evil in the sight of the LORD our God; 3
33: 2 He did what was evil in the sight of the LORD 3
6 He did much evil in the sight of the LORD 3
9 did more evil than the nations whom the LORD 3
22 He did what was evil in the sight of the LORD 3
34:24 I will bring evil upon this place 4
28 shall not see all the evil which I will bring 4
36: 5 did what was evil in the sight of the LORD his God. 3
9 He did what was evil in the sight of the LORD. 3
12 did what was evil in the sight of the LORD his God. 3
Ezr 9:13 after all that has come upon us for our evil deeds 3
Neh 6:13 could give me an evil name, in order to taunt me. 3
9:28 rest they did evil again before thee 3
13: 7 then discovered the evil that Eli'ashib had done 4
17 What is this evil thing which you are doing 3
18 did not our God bring all this evil on us 4
27 then listen to you and do all this great evil 4
Est 7: 7 for he saw that evil was determined against him 4
Job 1: 1 one who feared God, and turned away from evil. 3
8 man, who fears God and turns away from evil? 3
2: 3 man, who fears God and turns away from evil? 3
10 at the hand of God, and shall we not receive evil? 3
11 when Job's three friends heard of all this evil 4
5:19 in seven there shall no evil touch you. 3
15:35 They conceive mischief and bring forth evil 1
28:28 and to depart from evil is understanding.' 3
30:26 when I looked for good, evil came; 3
31:29 that hated me, or exulted when evil overtook him 3
42:11 all the evil that the LORD had brought upon him; 4
Ps 5: 4 evil may not sojourn with thee. 3
6: 8 Depart from me, all you workers of evil; 1
7: 4 if I have requited my friend with evil 3
9 O let the evil of the wicked come to an end 3
14 Behold, the wicked man conceives evil 1
15: 3 does no evil to his friend, nor takes up a reproach 4
21:11 If they plan evil against you 4
23: 4 I fear no evil; for thou art with me; 3
28: 3 the wicked, with those who are workers of evil 1
4 according to the evil of their deeds; 2
34:13 Keep your tongue from evil, and your lips 3
14 Depart from evil, and do good; seek peace 3
21 Evil shall slay the wicked; 4
35: 4 confounded who devise evil against me! 4
12 They requite me evil for good; my soul is forlorn. 4
36: 4 in a way that is not good; he spurns not evil. 3
37: 8 Fret not yourself, it tends only to evil. 5
19 they are not put to shame in evil times 4
27 Depart from evil, and do good; so shall you abide 3
38:20 Those who render me evil for good 4
40:12 For evils have encompassed me without number; 4
50:19 You give your mouth free rein for evil 4
51: 4 sinned, and done that which is evil in thy sight 3
52: 3 You love evil more than good 3
53: 4 Have those who work evil no understanding 1
54: 5 He will requite my enemies with evil; 3
56: 5 all their thoughts are against me for evil. 3
59: 2 deliver me from those who work evil, and save me 1
5 of those who treacherously plot evil. Selah 1
64: 5 They hold fast to their evil purpose; 3
90:15 as many years as we have seen evil. 4
91:10 no evil shall befall you 4
92:11 ears have heard the doom of my evil assailants. 5
97:10 The LORD loves those who hate evil; 3
101: 4 far from me; I will know nothing of evil. 3
109: 5 reward me evil for good, and hatred for my love. 4
20 of those who speak evil against my life! 3
112: 7 He is not afraid of evil tidings; his heart is firm 4
119:101 I hold back my feet from every evil way 3
121: 7 The LORD will keep you from all evil; 3
139:20 who lift themselves up against thee for evil! 7
140: 1 Deliver me, O LORD, from evil men; 3
11 let evil hunt down the violent man speedily! 3
141: 4 Incline not my heart to any evil 3
Prv 1:16 for their feet run to evil 3
33 will be at ease, without dread of evil. 4
2:12 delivering you from the way of evil 3
14 who rejoice in doing evil 3
14 who . . delight in the perversions of evil; 3
3: 7 fear the LORD, and turn away from evil. 3
29 Do not plan evil against your neighbor 4
4:27 turn your foot away from evil. 3
6:14 with perverted heart devises evil 3
18 feet that make haste to run to evil 4
24 to preserve you from the evil woman 3

8:13 The fear of the LORD is hatred of evil. 3
13 way of evil and perverted speech I hate. 3
11:19 but he who pursues evil will die. 4
27 but evil comes to him who searches for it. 4
12:20 Deceit is in the heart of those who devise evil 3
26 A righteous man turns away from evil •
13:19 turn away from evil is an abomination to fools. 3
14:16 A wise man is cautious and turns away from evil 3
19 The evil bow down before the good 3
22 Do they not err that devise evil? 3
15: 3 keeping watch on the evil and the good. 3
15 All the days of the afflicted are evil 3
16: 6 by the fear of the LORD a man avoids evil. 3
12 It is an abomination to kings to do evil 6
17 The highway of the upright turns aside from evil; 3
27 A worthless man plots evil 4
30 he who compresses his lips brings evil to pass. 4
17:13 If a man returns evil for good 4
13 evil will not depart from his house. 4
20: 8 throne of judgment winnows all evil with his eyes. 3
22 Do not say, "I will repay evil"; wait for the LORD 3
30 Blows that wound cleanse away evil; 3
21:10 The soul of the wicked desires evil; 3
24: 1 not envious of evil men, nor desire to be with them; 4
20 for the evil man has no future; 3
26:23 smooth lips with an evil heart. 3
28: 5 Evil men do not understand justice 3
10 misleads the upright into an evil way will fall 3
29: 6 An evil man is ensnared in his transgression 3
Ecc 2:21 This also is vanity and a great evil. 4
4: 3 and has not seen the evil deeds that are done 3
5: 1 for they do not know that they are doing evil. 3
13 There is a grievous evil which I have seen 4
16 This also is a grievous evil 4
6: 1 There is an evil which I have seen under the sun 4
8:11 sentence against an evil deed is not executed 4
11 the heart of the sons of men is fully set to do evil. 3
12 Though a sinner does evil 100 times 3
9: 2 to the good and the evil . . clean and the unclean 10
3 This is an evil in all that is done under the sun 3
3 also the hearts of men are full of evil 3
12 Like fish which are taken in an evil net 4
12 the sons of men are snared at an evil time 4
10: 5 There is an evil which I have seen under the sun 4
11: 2 for you know not what evil may happen on earth. 4
12: 1 in the days of . . youth, before the evil days come 4
13 with every secret thing, whether good or evil. 3
Isa 1:16 remove the evil of your doings from before my eyes 2
3: 9 For they have brought evil upon themselves. 4
5:20 Woe to those who call evil good and good evil 3
20 Woe to those who call evil good and good evil 3
7: 5 Remali'ah, has devised evil against you, saying 4
15 knows how to refuse the evil and choose the good. 3
16 For before the child knows how to refuse the evil 3
13:11 I will punish the world for its evil 4
29:20 all who watch to do evil shall be cut off 1
32: 7 The knaveries of the knave are evil; 3
33:15 who . . shuts his eyes from looking upon evil 3
47:11 evil shall come upon you 4
56: 2 and keeps his hand from doing any evil. 3
59: 7 Their feet run to evil, and they make haste 3
15 he who departs from evil makes himself a prey. 3
65:12 but you did what was evil in my eyes, 3
66: 4 but they did what was evil in my eyes 3
Jer 1:14 Out of the north evil shall break forth 4
2: 3 evil came upon them, says the LORD. 4
13 for my people have committed two evils 4
19 Know and see that it is evil and bitter for you 3
3: 5 but you have done all the evil that you could. 4
17 no more stubbornly follow their own evil heart. 3
4: 4 because of the evil of your doings. 2
6 stay not, for I bring evil from the north 4
14 How long shall your evil thoughts lodge within 1
15 from Dan and proclaims evil from Mount E'phraim. 1
5:12 He will do nothing; no evil will come upon us 4
6: 1 for evil looms out of the north 4
19 behold, I am bringing evil upon this people 4
7:24 and the stubbornness of their evil hearts 3
30 For the sons of Judah have done evil in my sight 3
8: 3 all the remnant that remains of this evil family 4
9: 3 for they proceed from evil to evil 4
3 for they proceed from evil to evil 4
11: 8 walked in the stubbornness of his evil heart. 3
11 I am bringing evil upon them 4
17 who planted you, has pronounced evil against you 4
17 because of the evil which the house of Israel 4
18 then thou didst show me their evil deeds. •
23 For I will bring evil upon the men of An'athoth 4
12:14 says the LORD concerning all my evil neighbors 3
13:10 This evil people, who refuse to hear my words 3
16:10 Why has the LORD pronounced all this great evil 4
12 every one of you follows his stubborn evil will 3
17:16 I have not pressed thee to send evil •
17 thou art my refuge in the day of evil. 4
18 bring upon them the day of evil; 4
18: 8 turns from its evil, I will repent of the evil 4
8 I will repent of the evil that I intended to do 4
10 and if it does evil in my sight 4
11 I am shaping evil against you and devising a plan 4
11 Return, every one from his evil way 4
12 according to the stubbornness of his evil heart. 3
20 Is evil a recompense for good? 4
19: 3 Behold, I am bringing such evil upon this place 4
15 all the evil that I have pronounced against it 4
21:10 For I have set my face against this city for evil 4
12 because of your evil doings. 2
23: 2 Behold, I will attend to you for your evil doings 2
10 Their course is evil, and their might is not right. 4
12 for I will bring evil upon them 4
17 they say, 'No evil shall come upon you. 4
22 they would have turned them from their evil way 3
22 their evil way, and from the evil of their doings. 2
25: 5 turn . . from his evil way and wrong doings 4
32 Behold, evil is going forth from nation to nation 4
26: 3 will listen, and every one turn from his evil way 4
3 that I may repent of the evil which I intend to do 4
3 to do to them because of their evil doings. 2
13 will repent of the evil which he has pronounced 4
19 did not the LORD repent of the evil 4
19 we are about to bring great evil upon ourselves. 4
29:11 says the LORD, plans for welfare and not for evil 4
32:23 thou hast made all this evil come upon them. 4
30 and the sons of Judah have done nothing but evil 3
32 because of all the evil of the sons of Israel 4
42 Just as I have brought all this great evil 4
35:15 Turn now every one of you from his evil way 4
17 all the evil that I have pronounced against them; 4
36: 3 will hear all the evil which I intend to do to them 4
3 so that every one may turn from his evil way 4
7 and that every one will turn from his evil way 4
31 all the evil that I have pronounced against them 4
39:16 words against this city for evil and not for good 4
40: 2 The LORD your God pronounced this evil 4
41:11 heard of all the evil which Ish'mael . . had done 4
42: 6 Whether it is good or evil, we will obey the voice 3
10 for I repent of the evil which I did to you. 4
17 from the evil which I will bring upon them. 4
44: 2 You have seen all the evil that I brought 4
7 Why do you commit this great evil 4
11 Behold, I will set my face against you for evil 4
17 had plenty of food, and prospered, and saw no evil. 4
22 The LORD could no longer bear your evil doings 2
23 that this evil has befallen you, as at this day. 4
27 I am watching over them for evil and not for good; 4
29 my words will surely stand against you for evil 4
45: 5 I am bringing evil upon all flesh, says the LORD; 4
48: 2 In Heshbon they planned evil against her 4
49:23 confounded, for they have heard evil tidings; 4
37 I will bring evil upon them, my fierce anger 4
51:24 for all the evil that they have done in Zion 4
60 all the evil that should come upon Babylon 4
64 because of the evil that I am bringing upon her. 4
52: 2 he did what was evil in the sight of the LORD 3
Lam 3:38 the mouth of the Most High that good and evil come? 4
Ezk 6: 9 for the evils which they have committed 4
10 not said in vain that I would do this evil to them. 4
11 say, Alas! because of all the evil abominations 4
14:21 sword, famine, evil beasts, and pestilence 4
22 you will be consoled for the evil 4
20:43 for all the evils that you have committed. 4
44 not according to your evil ways, nor according 3
33:11 turn back, turn back from your evil ways; 3
36: 3 you became the talk and evil gossip of the people; •
31 Then you will remember your evil ways 3
38:10 you will devise an evil scheme 4
Hos 7:15 yet they devise evil against me. 3
9:15 Every evil of theirs is in Gilgal; 4
Jol 2:13 in steadfast love, and repents of evil. 4
Ams 3: 6 Does evil befall a city, unless the LORD has done it? 4
5:13 keep silent . . for it is an evil time. 4
14 Seek good, and not evil, that you may live; 3
15 Hate evil, and love good, and establish justice 3
6: 3 O you who put far away the evil day, and bring near 3
9: 4 and I will set my eyes upon them for evil 4
10 who say, 'Evil shall not overtake or meet us.' 4
Jon 1: 7 know on whose account this evil has come upon us. 4
8 on whose account this evil has come upon us? 4
3: 8 yea, let every one turn from his evil way 4
10 what they did, how they turned from their evil way 4
10 God repented of the evil which he had said 4
4: 2 in steadfast love, and repentest of evil. 4
Mic 1:12 because evil has come down from the LORD 3
2: 1 devise wickedness and work evil upon their beds! 3
3 Behold, against this family I am devising evil 4
3 not walk haughtily, for it will be an evil time. 4
3: 2 you who hate the good and love the evil 4
11 No evil shall come upon us. 4
7: 3 Their hands are upon what is evil 3
Nah 1:11 one . . who plotted evil against the LORD 4
3:19 For upon whom has not come your unceasing evil? 4
Hab 1:13 Thou who art of purer eyes than to behold evil 3
2: 9 Woe to him who gets evil gain for his house 3
Zep 3:15 you shall fear evil no more. 3
Zec 1: 4 Return from your evil ways and from your evil 3
4 from your evil ways and from your evil deeds.' 3
7:10 none of you devise evil against his brother 4
8:17 do not devise evil in your hearts 4
Mal 1: 8 offer blind animals in sacrifice, is that no evil? 3
8 offer those that are lame or sick, is that no evil? 3
2:17 one who does evil is good in the sight of the LORD 3
Mat 5:11 utter all kinds of evil against you falsely 14
37 anything more than this comes from evil. 14
39 resist one who is evil. But if any one strikes you 14
45 he makes his sun rise on the evil and on the good 14
6:13 not into temptation, But deliver us from evil. 14
7:11 If you then, who are evil, know how to give good gifts 14
17 but the bad tree bears evil fruit. 14
18 A sound tree cannot bear evil fruit 14
9: 4 Why do you think evil in your hearts? 14
12:34 how can you speak good, when you are evil 14
35 and the evil man out of his evil treasure 14
35 and the evil man out of his evil treasure 14
35 out of his evil treasure brings forth evil. 14
39 An evil and adulterous generation 14
45 So shall it be also with this evil generation. 14
13:19 the evil one comes and snatches away what is sown 14
38 the weeds are the sons of the evil one 14
49 and separate the evil from the righteous 14
15:19 For out of the heart come evil thoughts, murder 14
16: 4 An evil and adulterous generation 14
27:23 he said, "Why, what evil has he done? 10
Mrk 7:21 out of the heart of man, come evil thoughts 10
15:14 Pilate said to them, "Why, what evil has he done? 10
Lke 6:22 and cast out your name as evil 14
45 the evil man out of his evil treasure produces evil; 14
45 the evil man out of his evil treasure produces evil; 14
45 the evil man out of his evil treasure produces evil; 14
7:21 diseases and plagues and evil spirits 14
8: 2 some women who had been healed of evil spirits 14
11:13 you then, who are evil, know how to give good gifts 14
29 This generation is an evil generation 14
23:22 Why, what evil has he done? 10
Joh 3:19 because their deeds were evil 14
20 For every one who does evil hates the light 16
5:29 those who have done evil 16
7: 7 because I testify of it that its works are evil. 14
Act 9:13 how much evil he has done 10
19:12 diseases left them and the evil spirits came out 14
13 pronounce . . over those who had evil spirits 14
15 the evil spirit answered them, "Jesus I know 14
16 the man in whom the evil spirit was leaped on them 14
23: 5 shall not speak evil of a ruler of your people.' 11
25:18 such evils as I supposed; 14
28:21 reported or spoken any evil about you. 14
Rom 1:29 all . . wickedness, evil, covetousness, malice. 13
30 haughty, boastful, inventors of evil 10
2: 9 and distress for every human being who does evil 10
3: 8 And why not do evil that good may come? 10
7:19 but the evil I do not want is what I do. 10
21 when I want to do right, evil lies close at hand. 10
12: 9 hate what is evil, hold fast to what is good; 14
17 Repay no one evil for evil 10
17 Repay no one evil for evil 10
21 Do not be overcome by evil 10
21 but overcome evil with good. 10
16:19 and guileless as to what is evil; 10
1Co 5: 8 the old leaven, the leaven of malice and evil 13
10: 6 not to desire evil as they did. 10
14:20 be babes in evil, but in thinking be mature. 9
2Co 5:10 so that each one may receive good or evil 16
Gal 1: 4 to deliver us from the present evil age 14
Eph 4:29 Let no evil talk come out of your mouths 15
5:16 because the days are evil. 14
6:13 that you may be able to withstand in the evil day 14
Php 3: 2 look out for the evil-workers 10
Col 1:21 doing evil deeds 14
3: 5 fornication, impurity, passion, evil desire 10
1Th 5:15 See that none of you repays evil for evil 10
15 See that none of you repays evil for evil 10
22 abstain from every form of evil. 14
2Th 3: 2 that we may be delivered from wicked and evil men; 14
3 he will strengthen you and guard you from evil. 14
1Ti 6:10 For the love of money is the root of all evils 10
2Ti 3:13 while evil men . . will go on from bad to worse 14
4:18 The Lord will rescue me from every evil 14
Tit 1:12 Cretans are always liars, evil beasts 10
2: 8 having nothing evil to say of us. 16
Heb 3:12 an evil, unbelieving heart 14
5:14 to distinguish good from evil. 10
10:22 our hearts sprinkled clean from an evil conscience 14
Jas 1:13 for God cannot be tempted with evil 10
2: 4 and become judges with evil thoughts? 14
3: 8 the tongue–a restless evil 10
4:16 All such boasting is evil. 14
1Pe 2:16 without using your freedom as a pretext for evil; 9
3: 9 Do not return evil for evil 10
9 Do not return evil for evil 10
10 let him keep his tongue from evil 10
11 let him turn away from evil and do right; 10
12 the face of the Lord is against those that do evil 10
1Jn 3:12 Because his own deeds were evil 14
3Jn 1:10 he is . . prating against me with evil words. 14
11 Beloved, do not imitate evil but imitate good. 10
Rev 16: 2 and foul and evil sores came upon the men 14
1Es 1:39 he did what was evil in the sight of the Lord. 14
44 He did what was evil in the sight of the Lord. 14
47 He also did what was evil in the sight of the Lord 14

8:86 has come about because of our evil deeds 14
2Es 1: 8 and hurl all evils upon them 19
34 and have done what is evil in my sight. 19
2: 3 and have done what is evil in my sight. 19
14 for I left out evil and created good 19
3:20 didst not take away from them their evil heart 18
21 For the first Adam, burdened with an evil heart 18
22 the law . . along with the evil root 17
22 good departed, and the evil remained. 17
26 for they also had the evil heart. 18
4: 4 and will teach you why the heart is evil. 18
28 For the evil about which you ask me has been sown 19
29 if the place where the evil has been sown 19
30 For a grain of evil seed was sown in Adam's heart 19
31 a grain of evil seed has produced. 19
33 Why are our years few and evil? 19
6:27 For evil shall be blotted out 19
7:12 they are few and evil, full of dangers 19
27 every one who has been delivered from the evils 19
48 For an evil heart has grown up in us 19
92 to overcome the evil thought which was formed 19
8:53 The root of evil is sealed up from you 19
12:43 the evils which have befallen us 19
13:38 with their evil thoughts and the torments 19
14:16 evils worse than those which you have now seen 19
17 the more shall evils be multiplied 19
15: 5 Behold," says the Lord, "I bring evils upon the world 19
49 I will send evils upon you, widowhood, poverty 19
Tob 3: 8 the evil demon Asmodeus had slain each of them 14
17 to bind Asmodeus the evil demon 14
6: 7 if a demon or evil spirit gives trouble to any one 14
12: 7 Do good, and evil will not overtake you. 10
Jdt 7:15 you will pay them back with evil 14
AEs 10: 9 the Lord has delivered us from all these evils 10
11: 9 they feared the evils that threatened them 10
Wis 3:12 Their wives are foolish, and their children evil; 14
4: 6 witnesses of evil against their parents 13
11 lest evil change his understanding 9
7:30 against wisdom evil does not prevail. 9
12:10 their origin was evil 14
14:22 they call such great evils peace. 10
27 the beginning and cause and end of every evil. 10
16: 8 it is thou who deliverest from every evil. 10
Sir 4:20 Observe the right time, and beware of evil 14
6: 4 An evil soul will destroy him who has it 14
7: 1 Do no evil, and evil will never befall you. 10
1 Do no evil, and evil will never befall you. 10
9: 1 do not teach her an evil lesson to your own hurt. 14
11:31 for he lies in wait, turning good into evil 10
33 Beware of a scoundrel, for he devises evil 14
12: 3 No good will come to the man who persists in evil 10
5 you will receive twice as much evil 10
13:24 poverty is evil in the opinion of the ungodly. 14
25 either for good or for evil. 10
14: 8 Evil is the man with a grudging eye 14
17: 7 showed them good and evil. 10
31 So flesh and blood devise evil. 14
18: 8 What is his good and what is his evil? 10
12 sees and recognizes that their end will be evil; 14
19: 6 for one who hates gossip evil is lessened. 9
25:16 rather . . than dwell with an evil wife. 14
23 a wounded heart are caused by an evil wife. 14
25 Allow . . no boldness of speech in an evil wife. 14
26: 7 An evil wife is an ox yoke which chafes 14
27:22 Whoever winks his eye plans evil deeds 10
27 If a man does evil, it will roll back upon him 14
28:21 its death is an evil death 14
31:10 had the power . . to do evil and did not do it? 10
33: 1 No evil will befall the man who fears the Lord 10
14 Good is the opposite of evil 10
27 idleness teaches much evil. 9
37: 3 O evil imagination 14
18 good and evil, life and death 10
39: 4 he tests the good and the evil among men. 10
27 just as they turn into evils for sinners. 10
41:11 the evil name of sinners will be blotted out. 12
42: 6 Where there is an evil wife, a seal is a good thing; 14
51:12 rescue me from an evil plight 14
Bar 1:21 what is evil in the sight of the Lord our God. 10
LJr 1:34 Whether one does evil to them or good 10
Man 1: 7 repentest over the evils of men. 9
10 have done what is evil in thy sight 10
13 Do not be angry with me for ever or lay up evil for me 10
1Mc 1: 9 they caused many evils on the earth. 10
11 many evils have come upon us. 10
15 sold themselves to do evil. 14
36 an evil adversary of Israel continually. 14
52 they did evil in the land; 10
2:30 because evils pressed heavily upon them. 10
6:12 now I remember the evils I did in Jerusalem 10
13 because of this . . these evils have come upon me; 10
7:23 Judas saw all the evil 9
11: 8 he kept devising evil designs against Alexander. 14
16:17 returned evil for good. 10
2Mc 1: 5 may he not forsake you in time of evil. 14
25 who dost rescue Israel from every evil 10
2:18 he has rescued us from great evils 10
4:47 Menelaus, the cause of all the evil, he acquitted 9
6: 3 utterly grievous was the onslaught of evil. 9
7:31 contrived all sorts of evil against the Hebrews 9
3Mc 1:16 to avert the violence of this evil design 11
2:12 rescued them from great evils 10
3:22 Since they incline constantly to evil 16
5: 8 avert with vengeance the evil plot against them 8
7: 9 if we devise any evil against them 14
4Mc 17: 2 frustrated his evil designs 10

evil *See also* art, bring, design, desire, device, devise, hatred, intent, make, nature, plight, plot, purpose, report, speak, work.

evil deed 1. facinus
2Es 1: 5 Go and declare to my people their evil deeds 1

do evil 1. רָעָה 2. רעע 3. ἀδικέω 4. κακοποιέω
Exd 5:22 O LORD, why hast thou done evil to this people? 2
23 since I came . . he has done evil to this people 2
23: 2 You shall not follow a multitude to do evil; 1
Lev 5: 4 a rash oath to do evil or to do good 2
1Kg 14: 9 you have done evil above all that were before you 2
16:25 and did more evil than all who were before him. 2
Prv 24: 8 plans to do evil will be called a mischief-maker. 2
Isa 1:16 remove the evil of your doings . . cease to do evil 2
Jer 4:22 They are skilled in doing evil 2
10: 5 Be not afraid of them, for they cannot do evil 2
13:23 you can do good who are accustomed to do evil. 2
38: 9 My lord the king, these men have done evil 2
Zec 8:14 As I purposed to do evil to you 2
3Jn 1:11 he who does evil has not seen God. 4
Rev 22:11 Let the evildoer still do evil 3
Sir 19:28 he will do evil when he finds an opportunity. 4

evil man 1. רַע 2. κακός
Job 35:12 does not answer, because of the pride of evil men. 1
Prv 4:14 do not walk in the way of evil men. 1
11:21 Be assured, an evil man will not go unpunished 1
12:13 evil man is ensnared by the transgression 1
17:11 An evil man seeks only rebellion 1
24:20 for the evil man has no future; 1
Ezk 30:12 and will sell the land into the hand of evil men; 1
Rev 2: 2 how you cannot bear evil men but have tested 2

more evil 1. πονηρός
Mat 12:45 seven other spirits more evil than himself 1
Lke 11:26 seven other spirits more evil than himself 1

most evil 1. malus
2Es 11:45 and your most evil little wings 1
45 and your most evil talons 1

evil one 1. πονηρός
Joh 17:15 that thou shouldst keep them from the evil one. 1
Eph 6:16 can quench all the flaming darts of the evil one. 1
1Jn 2:13 because you have overcome the evil one 1
14 and you have overcome the evil one. 1
3:12 and not be like Cain who was of the evil one 1
5:18 and the evil one does not touch him. 1
19 the whole world is in the power of the evil one. 1

evil thing 1. רָעָה 2. κακός 3. πονηρός
Ps 140: 2 who plan evil things in their heart 1
Prv 15:28 mouth of the wicked pours out evil things. 1
Mrk 7:23 All these evil things come from within 3
Lke 3:19 for all the evil things that Herod had done 3
16:25 Laz'arus in like manner evil things 2
Wis 15: 6 Lovers of evil things 2
Sir 39:25 just as evil things for sinners. 2
4Mc 6:14 destroying yourself through these evil things? 2

evil-doing 1. רָעָה 2. κακοπραγία
1Sm 25:39 returned the evil-doing of Nabal upon his own 1
Prv 14:32 The wicked is overthrown through his evil-doing 1
Ecc 7:15 a . . man who prolongs his life in his evil-doing. 1
Lam 1:22 Let all their evil-doing come before thee; 1
Wis 5:23 evil-doing will overturn the thrones of rulers. 2

evil-hating 1. μισοπόνηρος
AEs 16: 4 they will escape the evil-hating justice of God 1

evildoer 1. עשה רַע 2. עשה רָעָה 3. עשה רִשְׁעָה 4. פעל אָוֶן 5. רַע 6. רעע 7. ἀδικέω 8. ἐργάζομαι ἀνομίαν 9. ἐργατὴς τῆς ἀνομίας 10. κακὸν ποιέω 11. κακοῦργος 12. ποιὲω ἀνομίαν 13. πονηρεύω
2Sm 3:39 The LORD requite the evildoer according to his 2
Job 8:20 nor take the hand of evildoers. 6
34: 8 who goes in company with evildoers 4
22 deep darkness where evildoers may hide 4
Ps 5: 5 before thy eyes; thou hatest all evildoers. 4
10:15 Break thou the arm of the wicked and evildoer; 5
14: 4 all the evildoers who eat up my people 4
22:16 a company of evildoers encircle me; 6
26: 5 I hate the company of evildoers 6
27: 2 When evildoers assail me, uttering slanders 6
34:16 The face of the LORD is against evildoers 1
36:12 the evildoers lie prostrate, they are thrust down 4
64: 2 hide me . . from the scheming of evildoers 4
92: 7 though the wicked . . all evildoers flourish 4
9 all evildoers shall be scattered. 4
94: 4 arrogant words, they boast, all the evildoers. 4
16 Who stands up for me against evildoers? 4
101: 8 cutting off all the evildoers from the city 4
119:115 Depart from me, you evildoers 6
125: 5 who turn . . LORD will lead away with evildoers! 4
141: 9 Keep me . . from the snares of evildoers! 4
Prv 10:29 LORD is . . destruction to evildoers. 4
17: 4 An evildoer listens to wicked lips; 6
21:15 justice is done, it is . . dismay to evildoers. 4
24:19 Fret not yourself because of evildoers 6
Isa 1: 4 offspring of evildoers, sons who deal corruptly! 6
9:17 for every one is godless and an evildoer 6
14:20 May the descendants of evildoers nevermore be 6
31: 2 will arise against the house of the evildoers 6
Jer 20:13 the life of the needy from the hand of evildoers. 6
23:14 they strengthen the hands of evildoers 6
Hos 6: 8 Gilead is a city of evildoers 4
Mal 3:15 evildoers not only prosper 3
4: 1 the arrogant and all evildoers will be stubble; 3
Mat 7:23 'I never knew you; depart from me, you evildoers.' 8
13:41 all causes of sin and all evildoers 12
Joh 18:30 If this man were not an evildoer 10
Rev 22:11 Let the evildoer still do evil 7
AEs 14:19 save us from the hands of evildoers 13
16:15 we find that the Jews . . are not evildoers 11
1Mc 3: 6 all the evildoers were confounded 9

ewe 1. רָחֵל 2. שֶׂה
Gen 31:38 your ewes and your she-goats have not miscarried 1
32:14 200 ewes and twenty rams 1
Lev 22:28 whether the mother is a cow or a ewe 2
Sng 6: 6 Your teeth are like a flock of ewes 1

ewe *See also* shorn.

ewe lamb 1. כִּבְשָׂה
Gen 21:28 Abraham set seven ewe lambs of the flock apart. 1
29 What is the meaning of these seven ewe lambs 1
30 These seven ewe lambs you will take from my hand 1
Lev 14:10 and one ewe lamb a year old without blemish 1
Num 6:14 one ewe lamb a year old . . as a sin offering 1
2Sm 12: 3 the poor man had nothing but one little ewe lamb 1

ewe that has young 1. עול
Ps 78:71 from tending the ewes that had young 1

exact 1. יצא 2. נגשׂ 3. נשׁא 4. נשׁה 5. שׂוּם 6. ἐκζητέω 7. ποιέω 8. πράσσω
Exd 22:25 you shall not exact interest from him. 5
Deu 15: 2 he shall not exact it of his neighbor, his brother 2
3 Of a foreigner you may exact it 2
2Kg 15:20 Men'ahem exacted the money from Israel 1
23:35 He exacted the silver and the gold of the people 2
Neh 5: 7 exacting interest, each from his brother. 3
11 100th . . which you have been exacting 4
Job 11: 6 God exacts of you less than your guilt deserves. 4
Prv 29: 4 but one who exacts gifts ruins it. •
Tob 3: 5 are true in exacting penalty from me for my sins 7
Jdt 8:21 he will exact of us the penalty for its desecration. 6
1Mc 10:35 No one shall have authority to exact anything 8

exact (2)
2Kg 16:10 and its pattern, exact in all its details. •

exact *See* detail, sum.

exact a pledge 1. חבל
Job 22: 6 For you have exacted pledges of your brothers 1
Ezk 18:16 exacts no pledge, commits no robbery 1

exact a price for maintaining 1. ἐπιβάθρα
3Mc 2:31 the price to be exacted for maintaining the religion 1

exact tribute 1. φορολογέω
1Es 2:27 exacted tribute from Coelesyria and Phoenicia. 1

exaction 1. מַשָּׂאת 2. πλεονεξία
Neh 10:31 forego . . the exaction of every debt. •
Ams 5:11 the poor and take from him exactions of wheat 1
2Co 9: 5 ready not as an exaction but as a willing gift. 2

exactly 1. καί 2. κατευθικτέω 3. οὗτος
Act 27:25 it will be exactly as I have been told. 3
Sir 0: 2 not have exactly the same sense when translated 1
2Mc 14:43 in the heat of the struggle he did not hit exactly 2

more exactly 1. ἀκριβής
Act 23:15 you were going to determine his case more exactly 1

exactor 1. נגשׂ
Dan 11:20 one who shall send an exactor of tribute 1

exaggerate 1. προσλαμβάνω
Wis 17:11 it has always exaggerated the difficulties. 1

exalt 1. גבה 2. גדל 3. זְבַל 4. נשׂא 5. סלל 6. עלה 7. עֶלְיוֹן 8. רום 9. רום קֶרֶן 10. רמם 11. שׂגב 12. ἀνυψόω 13. δοξάζω 14. ἐξυψόω 15. ἐπαίρω 16. μεγαλύνω 17. μεγαλωσύνην δίδωμι 18. ὑπεραίρω

19. ὑψηλός 20. ὕψος 21. ὑψόω 22. ὕψωμα 23. effero 24. exalto
Exd 9:17 You are still exalting yourself against my 5
15: 2 this is . . my father's God, and I will exalt him. 8
Num16: 3 do you exalt yourselves above the assembly 4
24: 7 his kingdom shall be exalted. 4
Jos 3: 7 I will begin to exalt you in the sight of Israel 2
4:14 LORD exalted Joshua in the sight of all Israel; 2
1Sm 2: 1 my strength is exalted in the LORD. 8
7 poor and makes rich; he brings low, he also exalts. 8
10 LORD will . . and exalt the power of his anointed. 8
2Sm 5:12 had established him . . exalted his kingdom 4
22:47 and exalted be my God, the rock of my salvation 8
49 thou didst exalt me above my adversaries 8
1Kg 1: 5 Adoni'jah . . exalted himself, saying, "I will be 4
8:13 an exalted house, a place for thee to dwell 3
14: 7 Because I exalted you from among the people 8
16: 2 I exalted you out of the dust and made you leader 8
1Ch 14: 2 his kingdom was highly exalted 4
25: 5 according to the promise of God to exalt him; 9
29:11 O LORD, and thou art exalted as head above all. 4
2Ch 6: 2 I have built thee an exalted house 3
7:21 at this house, which is exalted, every one . . will 7
32:23 he was exalted in the sight of all nations 4
Neh 9: 5 thy glorious name which is exalted above all 8
Job 24:24 They are exalted a little while, and then are gone; 10
36: 7 he sets them for ever, and they are exalted. 1
22 Behold, God is exalted in his power; 11
Ps 12: 8 as vileness is exalted among the sons of men. 8
13: 2 How long shall my enemy be exalted over me? 8
18:46 exalted be the God of my salvation 8
48 yea, thou didst exalt me above my adversaries; 8
21:13 Be exalted, O LORD, in thy strength! 8
34: 3 let us exalt his name together! 8
37:34 he will exalt you to possess the land; 8
46:10 I am God. I am exalted among the nations 8
10 among the nations, I am exalted in the earth! 8
47: 9 of the earth belong to God; he is highly exalted! 6
57: 5 Be exalted, O God, above the heavens! 8
11 Be exalted, O God, above the heavens! 8
66: 7 let not the rebellious exalt themselves. Selah 8
75:10 the horns of the righteous shall be exalted. 8
89:17 by thy favor our horn is exalted. 8
19 I have exalted one chosen from the people. 8
24 in my name shall his horn be exalted. 8
42 Thou hast exalted the right hand of his foes; 8
92:10 thou hast exalted my horn like that of the wild ox; 8
97: 9 O LORD . . thou art exalted far above all gods. 6
99: 2 LORD . . is exalted over all the peoples. 8
108: 5 Be exalted, O God, above the heavens! 8
112: 9 his horn is exalted in honor. 8
118:16 the right hand of the LORD is exalted 8
138: 2 exalted above everything thy name and thy word. 8
148:13 name of the LORD, for his name alone is exalted; 11
Prv 4: 8 Prize her highly, and she will exalt you; 8
11:11 By the blessing of the upright a city is exalted 8
14:29 but he who has a hasty temper exalts folly. 8
34 Righteousness exalts a nation 8
30:32 If you have been foolish, exalting yourself 4
Isa 2:11 the LORD alone will be exalted in that day. 11
17 the LORD alone will be exalted in that day. 11
5:16 the LORD of hosts is exalted in justice 1
12: 4 make known . . proclaim that his name is exalted. 11
25: 1 my God; I will exalt thee, I will praise thy name; 8
30:18 he exalts himself to show mercy to you. 8
33: 5 The LORD is exalted, for he dwells on high; 11
10 now I will lift myself up; now I will be exalted. 4
52:13 prosper, he shall be exalted and lifted up 8
Lam 2:17 he has made . . and exalted the might of your foes. 8
Ezk 21:26 exalt that which is low, and abase that which is 1
29:15 and never again exalt itself above the nations; 4
Dan 11:12 multitude is taken, his heart shall be exalted 8
36 exalt himself and magnify himself 8
Hos 13: 1 he was exalted in Israel; but he incurred guilt 4
Zec 12: 7 Jerusalem may not be exalted over that of Judah. 2
Mat 11:23 you, Caper'na-um, will you be exalted to heaven? 21
23:12 whoever exalts himself will be humbled 21
12 whoever humbles himself will be exalted. 21
Lke 1:52 and exalted those of low degree; 21
10:15 you, Caper'na-um, will you be exalted to heaven? 21
14:11 For every one who exalts himself will be humbled 21
11 he who humbles himself will be exalted. 21
16:15 what is exalted among men 19
18:14 every one who exalts himself will be humbled 21
14 he who humbles himself will be exalted. 21
Act 2:33 Being therefore exalted at the right hand of God 21
5:31 God exalted him at his right hand as Leader 21
2Co 11: 7 abasing myself so that you might be exalted 21
2Th 2: 4 exalts himself against every so-called god 18
Heb 5: 5 did not exalt himself to be made a high priest 13
Jas 4:10 Humble yourselves . . and he will exalt you. 21
1Pe 1: 8 rejoice with unutterable and exalted joy. 13
5: 6 that in due time he may exalt you. 21
1Es 9:52 do not be sorrowful, for the Lord will exalt you. 13
2Es 2:43 but he was more exalted than they 24
8:20 who inhabitest eternity, whose eyes are exalted 23
Tob 12: 6 exalt him and give thanks to him 17
6 It is good to praise God and to exalt his name 21
13: 4 exalt him in the presence of all the living; 21
6 exalt the King of the ages. 21
7 I exalt my God; my soul exalts the King of heaven 21
7 I exalt my God; my soul exalts the King of heaven *
18 Blessed is God, who has exalted you for ever.' 21
14: 7 the Lord will exalt his people 21
Jdt 9: 7 they are exalted, with their horses and riders; 21
10: 8 Jerusalem may be exalted 22
16: 2 exalt him, and call upon his name. 21
8 to exalt the oppressed in Israel 20
AEs 11:11 the lowly were exalted 21
Wis 19:22 thou hast exalted and glorified thy people 16
Sir 1:19 he exalted the glory of those who held her fast. 12
30 Do not exalt yourself lest you fall 14
4:11 Wisdom exalts her sons and gives help 12
6: 2 not exalt yourself through your soul's counsel 15
7:11 there is One who abases and exalts. 12
11: 4 exalt yourself in the day that you are honored 15
15: 5 She will exalt him above his neighbors 21
32: 1 do not exalt yourself 15
33: 9 some of them he exalted and hallowed 12
12 some of them he blessed and exalted 12
43:30 exalt him as much as you can 21
30 When you exalt him, put forth all your strength 21
44:21 exalt his posterity like the stars 12
45: 6 He exalted Aaron, the brother of Moses 21
47: 5 to exalt the power of his people. 12
11 took away his sins, and exalted his power for ever; 12
50:22 who exalts our days from birth 21
1Mc 1: 3 he was exalted, and his heart was lifted up. 21
2:63 Today he will be exalted 15
8:13 they have been greatly exalted. 21
11:16 King Ptolemy was exalted. 21
26 he exalted him in the presence of all his friends 21
14:35 He sought in every way to exalt his people. 21
3Mc 2:21 scourged him who had exalted himself 15
6: 4 exalted with lawless insolence 15

exalt above 1. ὑψηλός
Heb 7:26 a high priest . . exalted above the heavens. 1

highly exalt 1. ὑπερυψόω
Php 2: 9 Therefore God has highly exalted him 1
Aza 1:29 to be praised and highly exalted for ever; 1
30 to be highly praised and highly exalted for ever. 1
32 to be praised and highly exalted for ever. 1
33 to be extolled and highly exalted for ever. 1
35 sing praise to him and highly exalt him for ever. 1
36 sing praise to him and highly exalt him for ever. 1
37 sing praise to him and highly exalt him for ever. 1
38 sing praise to him and highly exalt him for ever. 1
39 sing praise to him and highly exalt him for ever. 1
40 sing praise to him and highly exalt him for ever. 1
41 sing praise to him and highly exalt him for ever. 1
42 sing praise to him and highly exalt him for ever. 1
43 sing praise to him and highly exalt him for ever. 1
44 sing praise to him and highly exalt him for ever. 1
45 sing praise to him and highly exalt him for ever. 1
46 sing praise to him and highly exalt him for ever. 1
47 sing praise to him and highly exalt him for ever. 1
48 sing praise to him and highly exalt him for ever. 1
49 sing praise to him and highly exalt him for ever. 1
50 sing praise to him and highly exalt him for ever. 1
51 sing praise to him and highly exalt him for ever. 1
52 let it sing praise to him and highly exalt him 1
53 sing praise to him and highly exalt him for ever. 1
54 sing praise to him and highly exalt him for ever. 1
55 sing praise to him and highly exalt him for ever. 1
56 sing praise to him and highly exalt him for ever. 1
57 sing praise to him and highly exalt him for ever. 1
58 sing praise to him and highly exalt him for ever. 1
59 sing praise to him and highly exalt him for ever. 1
60 sing praise to him and highly exalt him for ever. 1
61 sing praise to him and highly exalt him for ever. 1
62 sing praise to him and highly exalt him for ever. 1
63 sing praise to him and highly exalt him for ever. 1
64 sing praise to him and highly exalt him for ever. 1
65 sing praise to him and highly exalt him for ever. 1
66 sing praise to him and highly exalt him for ever; 1

exaltation 1. ὕψος 2. ὕψωμα
Jas 1: 9 Let the lowly brother boast in his exaltation 1
Jdt 13: 4 for the exaltation of Jerusalem. 2
15: 9 You are the exaltation of Jerusalem 2
1Mc 1:40 her exaltation was turned into mourning. 1

examination 1. ἀνακρίνω 2. ἐξέτασις
Sus 1:48 condemned . . without examination 1
3Mc 7: 5 without any inquiry or examination 2

examination *See also* make.

examine 1. בור 2. בין 3. דרש 4. חקר 5. ראה 6. ἀνακρίνω 7. ἀνάκρισις 8. ἀνετάζω 9. δοκιμάζω 10. ἐξετάζω 11. ἐξετασμός 12. ἐπισκέπτομαι 13. ἐπισκοπή 14. πειράζω
Lev 13: 3 the priest shall examine the diseased spot 5
3 when the priest has examined him 5
5 the priest shall examine him on the seventh day 5
6 the priest shall examine him again 5
15 the priest shall examine the raw flesh 5
17 the priest shall examine him, and if the disease 5
21 if the priest examines it, and the hair on it 5
25 the priest shall examine it 5
26 if the priest examines it, and the hair in the spot 5
27 the priest shall examine him the seventh day 5
30 the priest shall examine the disease 5
31 if the priest examines the itching disease 5
32 the priest shall examine the disease 5
34 the priest shall examine the itch 5
36 then the priest shall examine him 5
43 Then the priest shall examine him 5
50 the priest shall examine the disease 5
51 he shall examine the disease on the seventh day 5
53 if the priest examines, and the disease has not 5
55 the priest shall examine the diseased thing 5
56 if the priest examines, and the disease is dim 5
14:36 before the priest goes to examine the disease 5
37 he shall examine the disease 5
Ezr 10:16 tenth month they sat down to examine the matter; 3
Prv 18:17 until the other comes and examines him. 4
Ecc 9: 1 But all this I laid to heart, examining it all 1
Jer 2:10 or send to Kedar and examine with care; 2
Lam 3:40 Let us test and examine our ways, and return 4
Lke 14:19 I go to examine them 9
23:14 after examining him before you 6
Act 4: 9 if we are being examined today 6
12:19 he examined the sentries 6
17:11 examining the scriptures daily 6
22:24 ordered him to be examined by scourging 8
29 those who were about to examine him withdrew 8
24: 8 By examining him yourself 6
25:26 after we have examined him 7
28:18 When they had examined me 6
1Co 9: 3 This is my defense to those who would examine me. 6
11:28 Let a man examine himself, and so eat of the bread 9
2Co 13: 5 Examine yourselves 14
Jdt 7: 7 examined the approaches to the city 12
AEs 12: 3 Then the king examined the two eunuchs 10
Wis 3:13 she will have fruit when God examines souls. 13
4: 6 when God examines them. 11
11:10 thou didst examine the ungodly 10
Sir 13:11 while he smiles he will be examining you. 10
18:20 Before judgment, examine yourself 10
Sus 1:51 Separate them . . and I will examine them. 6

strictly examine 1. scrutor
2Es 16:64 the Lord will strictly examine all their works 1

examine under torture 1. ἐξετάζω
Sir 23:10 continually examined under torture 1

example 1. γάρ 2. δεῖγμα 3. διά 4. ἴχνος 5. κατά 6. παράδειγμα 7. τύπος 8. ὑπογραμμός 9. ὑπόδειγμα 10. ὑποτύπωσις 11. item
Ecc 9:13 also seen this example of wisdom under the sun *
Joh 13:15 For I have given you an example 9
Rom 4:12 but also follow the example of the faith 4
Gal 3:15 To give a human example, brethren 5
Php 3:17 mark those who so live as you have an example in us 7
1Th 1: 7 you became an example to all the believers 7
2Th 3: 9 to give you in our conduct an example to imitate. 7
1Ti 1:16 an example to those who were to believe in him 10
4:12 set the believers an example in speech 7
Jas 5:10 As an example of suffering and patience 9
1Pe 2:21 Christ also suffered . . leaving you an example 8
5: 3 but being examples to the flock. 7
2Pe 2: 6 an example to those who were to be ungodly; 9
Jde 1: 7 serve as an example by undergoing a punishment 2
2Es 7: 6 Another example: There is a city 11
Sir 44:16 an example of repentance to all generations. 9
2Mc 6:10 For example, two women were brought in 1
28 leave to the young a noble example 9
31 leaving in his death an example of nobility 9
3Mc 2: 5 you made them an example 6
4Mc 1: 7 prove to you from many and various examples *
6:19 an example of the eating of defiling food. 6
12:16 not desert the excellent example of my brothers *
14:15 For example, among birds 1
18 by the example of unreasoning animals 3
17:23 proclaimed them to his soldiers as an example 9

example *See also* make.

set an example 1. ἐπιδείκνυμι
Jdt 8:24 let us set an example to our brethren 1

exasperate 1. φέρω πικρῶς
2Mc 7:39 being exasperated at his scorn. 1

exceed 1. רֹב 2. περισσεύω 3. πολύς
Ps 150: 2 praise him according to his exceeding greatness! 1
Mat 5:20 tell you, unless your righteousness exceeds 2
2Co 3: 9 the dispensation . . must far exceed it in splendor. 2
Rev 2:19 and that your latter works exceed the first. 3

exceeding 1. יַתִּיר (A)

Dan 2:31 This image, mighty and of exceeding brightness 1

exceeding *See also* joy.

exceedingly 1. אֱלֹהִים 2. בִּמְאֹד מְאֹד 3. גָּדוֹל 4. יֶתֶר 5. לְמַעְלָה 6. מְאֹד 7. עַד מְאֹד 8. רבה 9. רבה מְאֹד 10. יַתִּיר (A) 11. שַׂגִּיא (A) 12. *εὖ μάλα* 13. *περισσῶς* 14. *σφόδρα* 15. valde

Gen 17: 2 you, and will multiply you exceedingly. 6
6 I will make you exceedingly fruitful; 6
20 make him fruitful and multiply him exceedingly; 6
27:34 with an exceedingly great and bitter cry 7
30:43 Thus the man grew exceedingly rich 6
47:27 were fruitful and multiplied exceedingly. 6
Exd 1: 7 they multiplied and grew exceedingly strong; 2
Num14: 7 The land . . is an exceedingly good land. 6
Rut 1:13 it is exceedingly bitter to me for your sake 6
1Sm 26:21 I . . played the fool, and have erred exceedingly. 9
2Kg 10: 4 they were exceedingly afraid, and said, "Behold 6
1Ch 22: 5 for the LORD must be exceedingly magnificent 5
2Ch 1: 1 was with him and made him exceedingly great. 5
16: 8 a huge army with exceedingly many chariots 8
36:14 likewise were exceedingly unfaithful 8
Job 3:22 who rejoice exceedingly, and are glad †
Ps 119:96 thy commandment is exceedingly broad. 6
167 thy testimonies; I love them exceedingly. 6
Prv 30:24 Four things . . are exceedingly wise •
Isa 47: 6 on the aged you made your yoke exceedingly heavy. 6
64: 9 Be not exceedingly angry, O LORD 7
Lam 5:22 Art thou exceedingly angry with us? 7
Ezk 9: 9 The guilt of . . Judah is exceedingly great; 2
16:13 You grew exceedingly beautiful 2
37:10 upon their feet, an exceedingly great host. 6
Dan 6:23 Then the king was exceedingly glad 11
7: 7 terrible and dreadful and exceedingly strong; 10
19 exceedingly terrible, with its teeth of iron 10
8: 8 Then the he-goat magnified himself exceedingly; 7
9 grew exceedingly great toward the south, 4
11:25 war with an exceedingly great and mighty army; 7
Jol 2:11 his army, for his host is exceedingly great; 6
Jon 1:10 Then the men were exceedingly afraid 3
16 Then the men feared the LORD exceedingly 3
3: 3 Now Nin'eveh was an exceedingly great city 1
4: 1 it displeased Jonah exceedingly 3
6 Jonah was exceedingly glad 3
Zec 1:14 I am exceedingly jealous for Jerusalem 3
Mat 2:10 star, they rejoiced exceedingly with great joy; 14
Mrk 10:26 they were exceedingly astonished, and said 13
2Es 10:25 behold, her face suddenly shone exceedingly 15
12: 3 and the earth was exceedingly terrified 15
Jdt 2:28 those . . feared him exceedingly 14
Sir 43:11 exceedingly beautiful in its brightness. 14
47:24 Their sins became exceedingly many 14
2Mc 8:30 got possession of some exceedingly high strongholds 12

exceedingly *See also* afraid, great, sorry.

excel 1. גדל 2. יֵשׁ יִתְרוֹן לְ 3. יִתְרוֹן 4. *διαφέρω* 5. *περισσεύω* 6. *ὑπέρ* 7. *ὑπεράγω* 8. *φθάνω*

1Kg 10:23 King Solomon excelled all the kings of the earth 1
2Ch 9:22 King Solomon excelled all the kings of the earth 1
Ecc 2:13 wisdom excels folly as light excels darkness. 2
13 wisdom excels folly as light excels darkness. 3
1Co 14:12 strive to excel in building up the church. 5
2Co 8: 7 Now as you excel in everything 5
7 see that you excel in this gracious work also. 5
AEs 13: 3 Haman, who excels among us in sound judgment 4
Wis 7:29 excels every constellation of the stars. 6
Sir 33:16 by the blessing of the Lord I excelled 8
22 Excel in all that you do 7

excellence 1. *ἀρετή* 2. *καλλονή* 3. *σπουδαιότης*

Php 4: 8 whatever is gracious, if there is any excellence 1
2Pe 1: 3 called us to his own glory and excellence 1
Sir 6:15 no scales can measure his excellence. 2
31:23 their testimony to his excellence 2
2Mc 15:12 trained . . in all that belongs to excellence 1
3Mc 1: 9 impressed by its excellence and its beauty 3

excellent 1. גדל 2. יַתִּיר (A) 3. *ἀγαθός* 4. *ἀριστεία* 5. *διαφέρω* 6. *διάφορος* 7. *καλός*

Isa 28:29 wonderful in counsel, and excellent in wisdom. 1
Dan 5:12 excellent spirit, knowledge, and understanding 2
14 light and understanding and excellent wisdom 2
6: 3 because an excellent spirit was in him; 2
Rom 2:18 know his will and approve what is excellent 5
Php 1:10 so that you may approve what is excellent 5
Tit 3: 8 these are excellent and profitable to men. 7
Heb 8: 6 which is as much more excellent than the old as . . 6
Tob 4:11 charity is an excellent offering 3
Sir 14:25 will lodge in an excellent lodging place; 3
2Mc 1:35 he exchanged many excellent gifts. 6
6:23 and his excellent life even from childhood 7
4Mc 12:16 not desert the excellent example of my brothers 4

excellent *See also* leadership.

more excellent 1. *διάφορος* 2. *καθ' ὑπερβολήν*

1Co 12:31 I will show you a still more excellent way. 2
Heb 1: 4 the name . . is more excellent than theirs. 1

most excellent 1. *καλός* 2. *κράτιστος*

Lke 1: 3 it seemed good to me . . most excellent Theoph'ilus 2
Act 24: 2 by your provision, most excellent Felix 2
26:25 Paul said, "I am not mad, most excellent Festus 2
AEs 16:16 directed . . in the most excellent order. 1

excellently 1. חַיִל

Prv 31:29 Many women have done excellently 1

except 1. אִם 2. אֶפֶס 3. בִּלְתִּי 4. זוּלָה 5. כִּי 6. כִּי אִם 7. לְבַד מִן 8. מִבַּלְעֲדֵי 9. מִלְּבַד 10. רַק 11. לָהֵן (A) 12. *ἀλλά* 13. *ἀλλ' ἤ* 14. *ἐὰν μή* 15. *εἰ μή* 16. *ἐκτός* 17. *ἐκτὸς εἰ μή* 18. *ἐξουσία* 19. *ἕτερον ἤ* 20. *ἤ* 21. *μή* 22. *οὐ* 23. *παρεκτός* 24. *πάρεξ* 25. *πλήν* 26. *χωρίς* 27. nisi

Gen 39: 9 he kept back anything from me except yourself 6
Lev 21: 2 except for his nearest of kin, his mother 6
Num14:30 except Caleb the son of Jephun'neh and Joshua 6
26:65 not left a man . . except Caleb . . and Joshua 6
32:12 none except Caleb . . and Joshua the son of Nun 3
35:33 except by the blood of him who shed it. 1
Deu 1:36 except Caleb the son of Jephun'neh; he shall see it 4
Jos 11:13 none . . did Israel burn, except Hazor only; 4
19 There was not a city that . . except the Hivites 3
1Sm 18:25 no marriage present except 100 foreskins 5
30:17 not a man of them escaped, except 400 young men 6
22 not give them any . . except that each man may lead 6
2Sm 22:32 For who is God . . ? And who is a rock, except our God? 8
1Kg 8: 9 nothing in the ark except the two tables of stone 10
15: 5 what was right . . except in the matter of Uri'ah 10
17: 1 neither dew nor rain . . except by my word. 6
2Kg 4: 2 has nothing in the house, except a jar of oil. 6
24:14 none remained, except the poorest people 4
2Ch 2: 6 except as a place to burn incense before him? 6
5:10 was nothing in the ark except the two tables 10
21:17 so that no son was left to him except Jeho'ahaz 6
23: 6 except the priests and ministering Levites; 6
31:16 except those enrolled by genealogy 9
Est 2:15 asked for nothing except what Hegai . . advised. 6
4:11 are to be put to death, except the one to whom 7
Ps 18:31 who is a rock, except our God?- 4
Jer 44:14 they shall not return, except some fugitives. 6
Dan 2:11 none can show it to the king except the gods 11
3:28 serve and worship any god except their own God. 11
6: 7 to any god or man . . except to you, O king 11
12 god or man within 30 days except to you, O king 11
10:21 none who contends . . except Michael 6
Ams 9: 8 except that I will not utterly destroy the house 2
Mat 5:13 no longer good for anything except to be thrown out 15
32 his wife, except on the ground of unchastity 23
11:27 and no one knows the Son except the Father 15
27 and no one knows the Father except the Son 15
12:39 except the sign of the prophet Jonah. 15
13:57 is not without honor except in his own country 15
16: 4 except the sign of Jonah 15
19: 9 except for unchastity 21
Mrk 4:22 there is nothing hid, except to be made manifest; 14
22 nor is anything secret, except to come to light. 15
5:37 he allowed no one to follow him except Peter 15
6: 4 without honor, except in his own country 15
5 except that he laid his hands upon a few sick 15
8 nothing for their journey except a staff 15
Lke 8:51 except Peter and John and James 15
10:22 no one knows who the Son is except the Father 15
22 who the Father is except the Son 15
11:29 no sign . . except the sign of Jonah. 15
17:18 Was no one found . . except this foreigner? 15
Joh 3:27 except what is given him from heaven. 14
6:46 except him who is from God 15
13:10 does not need to wash, except for his feet 15
Act 8: 1 except the apostles. 25
11:19 speaking the word to none except Jews. 15
17:21 nothing except telling or hearing something 19
20:23 except that the Holy Spirit testifies to me 25
24:21 except this one thing which I cried out 20
26:29 might become such as I am–except for these chains. 23
Rom 13: 1 For there is no authority except from God 18
8 Owe no one anything, except to love one another; 15
15:18 except what Christ has wrought through me 22
1Co 1:14 baptized none of you except Crispus and Ga'ius; 15
2: 2 except Jesus Christ and him crucified. 15
11 except the spirit of the man which is in him 15
11 except the Spirit of God. 15
12: 3 except by the Holy Spirit. 15
15:27 he is excepted who put all things under him. 16
2Co 12: 5 I will not boast, except of my weaknesses. 15
13 except that I myself did not burden you 15
Gal 1:19 except James the Lord's brother. 15
6:14 far be it from me to glory except in the cross 15
Php 4:15 in giving and receiving except you only; 15
1Ti 5:19 except on the evidence of two or three witnesses. 17
Rev 2:17 which no one knows except him who receives it.' 15
14: 3 No one could learn that song except the 144,000 15
2Es 5:38 except he whose dwelling is not with men? 27
11:23 except the three heads that were at rest 27
13:52 except in the time of his day. 27
Tob 1:20 nothing was left to me except my wife Anna 25
6:14 he harms no one except those who approach her. 25
Jdt 6: 2 Who is God except Nebuchadnezzar? 15
8: 6 except the day before the sabbath 26
AEs 14:18 except in thee, O Lord God of Abraham. 25
Sir 22:14 what is its name except "Fool"? 13
49: 4 Except David and Hezekiah and Josiah 24
Sus 1:16 And no one was there except the two elders 25
1Mc 11:38 except the foreign troops 25
70 not one of them was left except Mattathias 25

except *See also* nothing.

except perhaps 1. *εἰ μήτι ἄν*

1Co 7: 5 except perhaps by agreement 1

without exception 1. *σύνολος*

AEs 16:24 Every city and country, without exception 1

excess 1. *μέθη* 2. *πολύς*

Tob 4:15 Do not drink wine to excess 1
Sir 31:29 Wine drunk to excess is bitterness of soul 2

excess *See also* number.

excessive 1. *περισσότερος*

2Co 2: 7 or he may be overwhelmed by excessive sorrow. 1

exchange 1. בְּ 2. מור 3. נתן 4. תַּחַת 5. תְּמוּרָה 6. *ἀλλάσσω* 7. *λαμβάνω καὶ μεταδίδωμι* 8. *μεταλαμβάνω* 9. *μεταλλάσσω* 10. *πέμπω ἀλλήλοις* 11. *περί*

Gen 47:16 I will give you food in exchange for your cattle 1
17 Joseph gave them food in exchange for the horses 1
17 food in exchange for all their cattle that year. 1
Lev 27:10 shall not . . exchange it, a good for a bad 2
10 if he makes any exchange of beast for beast •
10 that for which it is exchanged shall be holy 5
33 neither shall he exchange it; and if he exchanges 2
33 if he exchanges it . . it shall not be redeemed 2
33 then both it and that for which it is exchanged 5
Rut 4: 7 custom . . concerning redeeming and exchanging 5
Job 28:17 nor can it be exchanged for jewels of fine gold. 5
Ps 106:20 exchanged the glory of God for the image of an ox 2
Isa 43: 3 Ethiopia and Seba in exchange for you. 4
4 I give . . peoples in exchange for your life. 4
Ezk 27:12 iron, tin, and lead they exchanged for your wares. 3
13 they exchanged the persons of men 3
14 Beth-togar'mah exchanged for your wares horses 3
16 they exchanged for your wares emeralds, purple 3
17 they exchanged for your merchandise wheat 3
19 wine from Uzal they exchanged for your wares; 3
22 exchanged for your wares the best of all kinds 3
48:14 They shall not sell or exchange any of it; 2
Rom 1:23 exchanged the glory of the immortal God 6
25 they exchanged the truth about God for a lie 9
26 exchanged natural relations for unnatural 9
Rev 11:10 rejoice . . make merry and exchange presents 10
Sir 7:18 Do not exchange a friend for money 6
2Mc 1:35 he exchanged many excellent gifts. 7
3Mc 2:32 by paying money in exchange for life 11
4: 6 young women . . exchanged joy for wailing 8

exchange *See also* make, take.

exchange for life 1. *ἀντίψυχω*

4Mc 6:29 take my life in exchange for theirs. 1

excite 1. *ἔκθυμος* 2. *ἐντήκω* 3. *θροέω*

2Th 2: 2 not to be quickly shaken in mind or excited 3
2Mc 14:27 The king became excited 1
4Mc 8:26 Why does such contentiousness excite us 2

great excitement 1. *συνδρομή*

Jdt 10:18 There was great excitement in the whole camp 1

exclaim 1. *ἀναφωνέω* 2. *εἶπον*

Lke 1:42 she exclaimed with a loud cry, "Blessed are you 1
Tob 7: 7 he blessed him and exclaimed 2

exclude 1. גזר 2. מוֹצָא 3. *ἀφορίζω* 4. *ἐκκλείω* 5. *ἔργω* 6. *χωρίζω*

2Ch 26:21 for he was excluded from the house of the LORD. 1
Ezk 44: 5 those who are to be excluded from the sanctuary. 2
Lke 6:22 when they exclude you and revile you 3
Rom 3:27 what becomes of our boasting? It is excluded. 4
1Es 5:39 they were excluded from serving as priests. 6
3Mc 3:18 excluded us from entering 5

exclude as unclean 1. גאל

Ezr 2:62 were excluded from the priesthood as unclean; 1
Neh 7:64 were excluded from the priesthood as unclean; 1

exclusion

2Th 1: 9 and exclusion from the presence of the Lord •

excrement 1. צֵאָה
Deu 23:13 turn back and cover up your excrement. 1

excruciatingly *See* painful.

excuse 1. ἀπολογέομαι 2. παραιτέομαι 3. πρόφασις 4. συγγινώσκω 5. συγγνωμονέω 6. συγγνωστός
Lke 14:18 I pray you, have me excused.' 2
19 I pray you, have me excused.' 2
Joh 15:22 now they have no excuse for their sin. 3
Rom 2:15 thoughts accuse or perhaps excuse them 1
Wis 13: 8 Yet again, not even they are to be excused; 6
4Mc 5:13 it will excuse you from any transgression 5
8:22 Also, divine justice will excuse us 4

excuse *See also* make.

no excuse 1. ἀναπολόγητος
Rom 2: 1 Therefore you have no excuse, O man 1

without excuse 1. ἀναπολόγητος
Rom 1:20 So they are without excuse; 1

execration 1. אָלָה
Num 5:21 then . . LORD make you an execration and an oath 1
27 shall become an execration among her people. 1
Jer 42:18 You shall become an execration, a horror, a curse 1
44:12 they shall become an execration, a horror, a curse 1

execute 1. חשב 2. נתן 3. עשה 4. עבד (A) 5. ἔκδικος 6. ποιέω 7. ποῖος
Exd 12:12 on all the gods of Egypt I will execute judgments 3
Num 5:30 the priest shall execute upon her all this law. 3
31: 3 Arm men . . to execute the LORD'S vengeance 2
33: 4 upon their gods . . LORD executed judgments. 3
Deu 10:18 executes justice for the fatherless 3
33:21 with Israel he executed the commands and just 3
1Kg 10: 9 he has made you king, that you may execute justice 3
2Ch 2:14 and to do . . engraving and execute any design 1
9: 8 you may execute justice and righteousness. 3
24:24 Thus they executed judgment on Jo'ash. 3
Ezr 7:26 let judgment be strictly executed upon him 4
Est 9: 1 command and edict were about to be executed 3
Ps 9:16 has made himself known, he has executed judgment; 3
99: 4 executed justice and righteousness in Jacob. 3
140:12 LORD . . executes justice for the needy. *
146: 7 who executes justice for the oppressed; 3
149: 9 to execute on them the judgment written! 3
Ecc 8:11 Because sentence . . is not executed speedily 3
Isa 13: 3 have summoned my mighty men to execute my anger *
Jer 7: 5 if you truly execute justice one with another 3
23: 5 and shall execute justice and righteousness 3
20 the LORD will not turn back until he has executed 3
30:24 until he has executed and accomplished 3
33:15 and he shall execute justice and righteousness 3
Ezk 5: 8 I will execute judgments in the midst of you 3
10 and I will execute judgments on you 3
15 when I execute judgments on you in anger and fury 3
11: 9 and execute judgments upon you. 3
12 nor executed my ordinances, but have acted 3
16:41 burn your houses and execute judgments upon you 3
18: 8 executes true justice between man and man 3
20:24 because they had not executed my ordinances 3
23:10 when judgment had been executed upon her. 3
25:11 I will execute judgments upon Moab. 3
17 I will execute great vengeance upon them 3
28:22 when I execute judgments in her 3
26 shall dwell securely, when I execute judgments 3
30:14 and will execute acts of judgment upon Thebes. 3
19 Thus I will execute acts of judgment upon Egypt. 3
39:21 shall see my judgment which I have executed, 3
45: 9 and execute justice and righteousness; 3
Hos 11: 9 I will not execute my fierce anger 3
Jol 2:11 he that executes his word is powerful. 3
Mic 5:15 And in anger and wrath I will execute vengeance 3
7: 9 until he pleads my cause and executes judgment 3
Joh 5:27 has given him authority to execute judgment 6
Rom 9:28 Lord will execute his sentence upon the earth 6
13: 4 to execute his wrath on the wrongdoer. 5
Jde 1:15 to execute judgment on all, and to convict all 6
Jdt 2:12 what I have spoken my hand will execute. 6
Sir 20: 4 a man who executes judgments by violence. 7
35:17 and executes judgment. 6
Aza 1: 5 Thou hast executed true judgments 6

execute judgment 1. דין 2. פקד 3. שפט
2Ch 20:12 our God, wilt thou not execute judgment upon them? 3
22: 8 executing judgment upon the house of Ahab 3
Ps 75: 7 it is God who executes judgment, putting down one 3
110: 6 He will execute judgment among the nations 1
Isa 66:16 For by fire will the LORD execute judgment 3
Jer 51:52 when I will execute judgment upon her images 2

execute justice 1. דין
Jer 21:12 says the LORD: "'Execute justice in the morning 1

execute vengeance 1. נקם
Lev 26:25 that shall execute vengeance for the covenant 1

execution *See* lead, put.

executioner 1. פְּקֻדָּה 2. δήμιος
Ezk 9: 1 Draw near, you executioners of the city 1
2Mc 5: 8 abhorred as the executioner of his country 2

exempt 1. נָקִי 2. ἀφίημι
1Kg 15:22 Asa made a proclamation . . none was exempt 1
1Mc 10:29 and exempt all the Jews from payment of tribute 2

exercise 1. ποιέω
Rev 13: 5 allowed to exercise authority for . . months; 1
12 exercises all the authority of the first beast 1
3Mc 3:18 they were spared the exercise of our power *

exercise authority 1. רדה 2. δυναστεύω
2Ch 8:10 chief officers . . who exercised authority 1
AEs 16: 7 those who exercise authority unworthily 2

exercise authority over 1. κατεξουσιάζω
Mat 20:25 their great men exercise authority over them. 1
Mrk 10:42 their great men exercise authority over them. 1

exercise dominion 1. רדה
Num24:19 By Jacob shall dominion be exercised 1

exercise lordship over 1. κυριεύω
Lke 22:25 The kings . . exercise lordship over them 1

exercise piety 1. εὐσεβέω
4Mc 18: 1 obey this law and exercise piety in every way 1

exercise right of redemption 1. גאל
Lev 25:33 does not exercise his right of redemption 1

exercise self-control 1. ἐγκρατεύομαι
1Co 7: 9 if they cannot exercise self-control 1
9:25 Every athlete exercises self-control 1

exert 1. ἐπιτείνω 2. προσφέρω
Wis 16:24 exerts itself to punish the unrighteous 1
3Mc 3:10 to exert more earnest efforts for their assistance. 2

exert pressure 1. ἰσχύω
Sir 29: 6 If the lender exert pressure 1

exertion 1. τρέχω
Rom 9:16 So it depends not upon man's will or exertion 1

exhaust 1. כשל 2. פגר 3. ἐκλείπω 4. ἐκλύω 5. κάμνω 6. παρεκλείπω
1Sm 30:10 who were too exhausted to cross the brook Besor. 2
21 men, who had been too exhausted to follow David 2
Isa 40:30 and young men shall fall exhausted; 1
Jdt 11:12 Since their food supply is exhausted 6
1Mc 3:29 saw that the money in the treasury was exhausted 3
10:82 for the cavalry was exhausted 4
4Mc 3: 8 he came, sweating and quite exhausted 5

exhaustion 1. defatigatio
2Es 5:35 and the exhaustion of the people of Israel? 1

exhaustive 1. ἐξεργαστικός
2Mc 2:31 to forego exhaustive treatment. 1

exhibit 1. ἀποδείκνυμι 2. πρόδηλον ποιέω
1Co 4: 9 I think that God has exhibited us apostles 1
2Mc 14:39 wishing to exhibit the enmity which he had 2
3Mc 5:31 have exhibited . . a full and firm loyalty 1

exhort 1. παρακαλέω 2. προσπαρακαλέω 3. προτρέπω
Act 2:40 he testified with many other words and exhorted 1
11:23 he exhorted them all to remain faithful to the Lord 1
14:22 exhorting them to continue in the faith 1
15:32 exhorted the brethren with many words 1
16:40 they exhorted them and departed. 1
20: 1 and having exhorted them took leave of them 1
Rom 12: 8 he who exhorts, in his exhortation; 1
1Th 2:11 we exhorted each one of you 1
3: 2 to establish you in your faith and to exhort you 1
4: 1 we beseech and exhort you in the Lord Jesus 1
10 we exhort you, brethren, to do so more and more 1
5:14 we exhort you, brethren, admonish the idlers 1
2Th 3:12 Now such persons we command and exhort 1
1Ti 5: 1 exhort him as you would a father 1
2Ti 4: 2 convince, rebuke, and exhort 1
Tit 2:15 exhort and reprove with all authority 1
Heb 3:13 exhort one another every day 1
1Pe 5: 1 So I exhort the elders among you, as a fellow elder 1
12 I have written briefly to you, exhorting 1
2Mc 2: 3 with other similar words he exhorted them 1
8:16 exhorted them not to be frightened by the enemy 1
12:31 exhorted them to be well disposed to their race 2
42 the noble Judas exhorted the people 1
13:12 exhorted them and ordered them to stand ready. 1
14 exhorting his men to fight nobly to the death 1
15: 8 he exhorted his men not to fear the attack 1
3Mc 1: 4 exhorted them to defend themselves 1
4Mc 8: 5 I also exhort you to yield to me 1
17 Since the king has summoned and exhorted us 1
12: 7 when his mother had exhorted him 3

exhortation 1. παρακαλέω 2. παράκλησις 3. παρηγορία
Lke 3:18 So, with many other exhortations, he preached 1
Act 13:15 Brethren, if you have any word of exhortation 2
15:31 they rejoiced at the exhortation. 2
Rom 12: 8 he who exhorts, in his exhortation; 2
Heb 12: 5 the exhortation which addresses you as sons 2
13:22 bear with my word of exhortation 2
4Mc 6: 1 the exhortations of the tyrant 3

exile 1. גּוֹלָה 2. גלה 3. גָּלוּת 4. שְׁבִי 5. שלח 6. בֶּן גָּלוּת (A) 7. αἰχμαλωσία 8. ἀποικία 9. ἀποικισμός 10. μετάγω 11. ξένος 12. παρεπίδημος 13. παροικία 14. πάροικος 15. φυγάς 16. transmigratio
2Sm 15:19 you are a foreigner . . an exile from your home. 2
2Kg 17:23 Israel was exiled from their own land to Assyria 2
25:27 And in the 37th year of the exile of Jehoi'achin 3
1Ch 5:22 And they dwelt in their place until the exile. 1
6:15 Jehoz'adak went into exile when the LORD sent *
Ezr 1:11 when the exiles were brought up from Babylonia 1
2: 1 captivity of those exiles whom Nebuchadnez'zar 1
4: 1 adversaries . . heard that the returned exiles 1
6:16 Levites, and the rest of the returned exiles 6
19 returned exiles kept the passover. 1
20 passover lamb for all the returned exiles 1
21 people of Israel who had returned from exile 1
8:35 come from captivity, the returned exiles 1
9: 4 faithlessness of the returned exiles 1
10: 6 mourning over the faithlessness of the exiles. 1
7 proclamation . . to all the returned exiles 1
8 banned from the congregation of the exiles. 1
16 Then the returned exiles did so. 1
Neh 1: 2 Jews that survived, who had escaped exile 4
3 who escaped exile are in great trouble and shame; 4
7: 6 came up out of the captivity of those exiles 1
Isa 20: 4 Egyptians captives and the Ethiopians exiles 3
27: 8 by exile thou didst contend with them; 5
45:13 he shall build my city and set my exiles free 3
49:21 I was bereaved and barren, exiled and put away 2
Jer 24: 5 I will regard as good the exiles from Judah 3
28: 4 and all the exiles from Judah who went to Babylon 3
6 of the house of the LORD, and all the exiles. 1
29: 1 to the elders of the exiles, and to the priests 1
4 to all the exiles whom I have sent into exile 1
16 your kinsmen who did not go out with you into exile 1
20 all you exiles whom I sent away from Jerusalem 1
22 be used by all the exiles from Judah in Babylon 3
28 Your exile will be long; *
31 Send to all the exiles, saying, 'Thus says the LORD 1
40: 1 captives . . who were being exiled to Babylon. 2
46:19 Prepare yourselves baggage for exile 1
48: 7 and Chemosh shall go forth into exile 1
11 nor has he gone into exile; so his taste remains 1
49: 3 For Milcom shall go into exile, with his priests 1
Lam 4:22 he will keep you in exile no longer; 2
Ezk 1: 1 as I was among the exiles by the river Chebar 1
2 the fifth year of the exile of King Jehoi'achin 3
3:11 go, get you to the exiles, to your people 1
15 I came to the exiles at Tel-abib 1
11:15 even your brethren, your fellow exiles 7
24 by the Spirit of God into Chalde'a, to the exiles. 1
25 I told the exiles all the things that the LORD had 1
12: 3 prepare for yourself an exile's baggage 1
4 bring out your baggage . . as baggage for exile; 1
4 in their sight, as men do who must go into exile. 1
7 brought out my baggage . . as baggage for exile 1
11 they shall go into exile, into captivity. 1
25: 3 over the house of Judah when it went into exile; 1
33:21 In the twelfth year of our exile 3
40: 1 In the 25th year of our exile 3
Dan 2:25 I have found among the exiles from Judah a man 6
5:13 You are that Daniel, one of the exiles of Judah 6
6:13 That Daniel, who is one of the exiles from Judah 6
Ams 1: 6 because they carried into exile a whole people 3
15 their king shall go into exile, he and his princes 1
Obd 1:20 exiles in Halah who are of the people of Israel 3
20 the exiles of Jerusalem who are in Sephar'ad 3
Zec 6:10 Take from the exiles Heldai, Tobi'jah, and Jedai'ah 1
14: 2 half of the city shall go into exile 1
Act 7:29 and became an exile in the land of Mid'ian 14
Heb 11:13 they were strangers and exiles on the earth. 12
1Pe 1: 1 To the exiles of the Dispersion 12
17 throughout the time of your exile. 13
2:11 I beseech you as aliens and exiles to abstain 12
1Es 2:15 the returning exiles from Babylon to Jerusalem. 7
2Es 5:17 entrusted to you in the land of their exile? 16
Wis 17: 2 exiles from eternal providence. 15
Bar 2:30 land of their exile they will come to themselves 9
32 they will praise me in the land of their exile 9
3: 7 we will praise thee in our exile, for we have put 8
8 today in our exile where thou hast scattered us 8
2Mc 1:33 the exiled priests had hidden the fire 10
5: 9 he . . died in exile 11

3Mc 6:10 have become entangled in impieties in our exile 8
exile *See also* carry, drive, go, send, take.

exist 1. εἰμί 2. ἔνειμι 3. κεῖμαι 4. separo 5. sum
Rom 4:17 calls into existence the things that do not exist 1
13: 1 those that exist have been instituted by God. 1
1Co 8: 6 from whom are all things and for whom we exist •
6 through whom we exist. •
Heb 2:10 for whom and by whom all things exist •
11: 6 must believe that he exists 1
Jas 3:16 For where jealousy and selfish ambition exist •
2Pe 3: 5 by the word of God heavens existed long ago 1
6 the world that then existed was deluged with water •
7 the heavens and earth that now exist •
Rev 4:11 and by thy will they existed and were created. 1
1Es 4:17 men cannot exist without women. 1
2Es 4: 9 and without which you cannot exist 4
23 and the written covenants no longer exist; 5
7:23 that the Most High does not exist 5
8: 7 For thou alone dost exist 5
35 and among those who have existed there is no one ‡
9:18 when I was preparing for those who now exist 5
18 and no one opposed me then, for no one existed; 5
Wis 1:14 For he created all things that they might exist 1
2: 6 let us enjoy the good things that exist 1
7:17 he who gave me unerring knowledge of what exists 1
8: 6 who more than she is fashioner of what exists? 1
11:24 For thou lovest all things that exist 1
13: 1 they were unable . . to know him who exists 1
14:13 neither have they existed from the beginning 1
13 nor will they exist for ever. 1
Sir 16:26 existed from the beginning by his creation •
17:28 From the dead, as from one who does not exist 1
1Mc 3:29 laws that had existed from the earliest days. 1
2Mc 4:11 He set aside the existing royal concessions 3
4Mc 1:25 there exists even a malevolent tendency 2
exist *See also* cease.

existence 1. βίος 2. γένεσις 3. εἰμί 4. ζωή
Rom 4:17 calls into existence the things that do not exist 3
Wis 7: 5 has had a different beginning of existence; 2
15:12 he considered our existence an idle game 4
Sir 40:29 his existence cannot be considered as life 1
existence *See also* keep.

no existence 1. οὐδείς
1Co 8: 4 we know that "an idol has no real existence 1

thing that exists 1. εἰμί
2Mc 7:28 God did not make them out of things that existed. 1

exit 1. מוֹצָא 2. תּוֹצָאָה 3. exitus
Ezk 42:11 with the same exits and arrangements and doors. 1
43:11 its arrangement, its exits and its entrances, 1
48:30 These shall be the exits of the city 2
2Es 4: 7 or which are the exits of hell 3

exodus 1. ἔξοδος
Heb 11:22 made mention of the exodus of the Israelites 1

exorcist 1. ἐξορκιστής
Act 19:13 Then some of the itinerant Jewish exorcists 1

expand 1. ἐπιτείνω
4Mc 13:25 expanded their goodwill and harmony 1

expanse 1. רַחַב 2. locus
Job 38:18 Have you comprehended the expanse of the earth? 1
2Es 7: 3 There is a sea set in a wide expanse 2

expect 1. יחל 2. שִׂים פָּנִים עַל 3. ἀπροσδοκήτως 4. δοκέω 5. δόξα 6. ἐκδέχομαι 7. ἐλπίζω 8. προσδέχομαι 9. προσδοκάω 10. προσδοκία 11. ὑπολαμβάνω 12. ὑπονοέω 13. ὡς 14. spero
1Kg 2:15 and that all Israel fully expected me to reign; 2
Ezk 13: 6 yet they expect him to fulfil their word. 1
Mat 24:44 Son of man is coming at an hour you do not expect. 4
50 on a day when he does not expect him 9
Lke 12:46 on a day when he does not expect him 9
Act 3: 5 expecting to receive something from them. 9
10:24 Cornelius was expecting them 9
12:11 from all that the Jewish people were expecting. 10
28: 6 They waited, expecting him to swell up 9
1Co 16:11 I am expecting him with the brethren. 6
2Co 8: 5 this, not as we expected 7
2Es 5: 6 whom those who dwell on earth do not expect 14
7:117 in sorrow now and expect punishment after death? 14
Tob 8:16 It has not happened to me as I expected 12
Jdt 8:14 how do you expect to search out God •
Wis 12:22 when we are judged we may expect mercy. 9
14:29 swear wicked oaths and expect to suffer no harm. 8
18: 7 were expected by thy people. 8
2Mc 8:11 not expecting the judgment from the Almighty 8
12:37 when they were not expecting it 3
44 if he were not expecting that . . 9
3Mc 2:31 they expected to enhance their reputation 13
3: 8 expected that matters would change; 11
6:30 they had expected to meet their destruction. 5

expect in return 1. ἀπελπίζω
Lke 6:35 do good, and lend, expecting nothing in return 1

expectation 1. תּוֹחֶלֶת 2. תִּקְוָה 3. προσδοκάω 4. προσδοκία
Prv 10:28 expectation of the wicked comes to nought. 2
11: 7 expectation of the godless comes to nought. 1
23 the expectation of the wicked in wrath. 2
Lam 3:18 Gone is . . and my expectation from the LORD. 1
Lke 3:15 As the people were in expectation 3
Wis 17:13 the inner expectation of help, being weak 4
3Mc 5:41 in a tumult because of its expectation 4

eager expectation 1. ἀποκαραδοκία
Php 1:20 as it is my eager expectation and hope 1

beyond all expectations 1. παραδόξως
4Mc 4:14 having been preserved beyond all expectations 1

expedient 1. συμφέρω
Mat 19:10 it is not expedient to marry. 1
Joh 11:50 you do not understand that it is expedient 1
18:14 expedient that one man should die for the people. 1

expedition 1. יצא 2. ἐπιστρατεία 3. ἔφοδος
1Sm 23:13 When Saul was told . . he gave up the expedition. 1
1Mc 9:68 his plan and his expedition had been in vain. 3
3Mc 3:14 When our expedition took place in Asia 2
expedition *See also* go, make.

expell 1. גרשׁ 2. ἀλλοτριόω 3. ἐκβάλλω
1Kg 2:27 Solomon expelled Abi'athar from being priest 1
1Es 9: 4 the men themselves expelled from the multitude 2
1Mc 13:47 he expelled them from the city 3
50 he expelled them from there 3

expend 1. κατατίθημι
2Mc 4:19 to expend it for another purpose. 1

expense 1. מִן 2. δαπάνη 3. δαπάνημα 4. δέω 5. ἐπί 6. μίσθωμα 7. ὀψώνιον 8. συμβολή 9. σύνταξις
2Sm 19:42 Have we eaten at all at the king's expense? 1
Act 21:24 pay their expenses, so that they may share 5
28:30 he lived there two whole years at his own expense 6
1Co 9: 7 Who serves as a soldier at his own expense? 7
Tob 5:14 expenses for yourself as for my son? 4
Sir 18:32 lest you become impoverished by its expense. 8
1Mc 3:30 such funds as he had before for his expenses 2
10:39 to meet the necessary expenses of the sanctuary. 2
2Mc 3: 3 all the expenses connected with the service 3
9:16 the expenses incurred for the sacrifices 9

public expense 1. δημοτελής
3Mc 4: 1 a feast at public expense was arranged 1

very expensive 1. βαρύτιμος
Mat 26: 7 alabaster flask of very expensive ointment 1

experience 1. ידע 2. ראה 3. γίνομαι 4. ἐνεργέω 5. λαμβάνω 6. πάσχω 7. πεῖρα 8. πειράζω 9. πειράω 10. περιπίπτω 11. πολύπειρος 12. συγγυμνασία 13. pertranseo
Deu 1:13 Choose wise, understanding, and experienced men 1
15 heads of your tribes, wise and experienced men 1
Jdg 3: 1 Israel who had no experience of any war in Canaan; 1
Ecc 1:16 and my mind has had great experience of wisdom 2
2Co 1: 6 which you experience when you patiently endure 4
8 the affliction we experienced in Asia 3
Gal 3: 4 Did you experience so many things in vain? 6
1Pe 5: 9 the same experience of suffering is required •
2Es 4:23 about those things which we daily experience 13
7:14 the difficult and vain experiences •
Wis 2:24 those who belong to his party experience it. 8
8:18 in the experience of her company, understanding 12
12:26 will experience the deserved judgment of God. 8
18:20 experience of death touched also the righteous 7
19: 5 might experience an incredible journey 8
Sir 21:22 a man of experience 11
34:12 have escaped because of these experiences. •
36:20 a man of experience will pay him back. 11
2Mc 8: 9 a man of experience in military service. 9
3Mc 5: 5 would experience its final destruction. 5
6:33 the unexpected rescue which he had experienced. 3
4Mc 1:24 a man will see if he reflects on this experience 10
experience *See also* much.

rich experience 1. πολυπειρία
Sir 25: 6 Rich experience is the crown of the aged 1

wide experience 1. πολυπειρία
Wis 8: 8 if any one longs for wide experience 1
experienced *See* warrior.

expert 1. בין 2. למד 3. ערך 4. רבה 5. ἐπίσταμαι 6. ἰσχύς
Gen 21:20 the lad . . became an expert with the bow. 4
1Ch 5:18 valiant men, who . . drew the bow, expert in war 2
12: 8 warriors, expert with shield and spear 3
Sng 3: 8 all girt with swords and expert in war 2
Isa 3: 3 the skilful magician and the expert in charms. 1
Sir 45:12 a distinction to be prized, the work of an expert 6
Bar 3:26 giants . . great in stature, expert in war. 5

expert in war 1. אִישׁ מִלְחָמָה
2Sm 17: 8 Besides, your father is expert in war; 1

expiate 1. כפר
1Sm 3:14 iniquity . . shall not be expiated by sacrifice 1
Isa 27: 9 by this the guilt of Jacob will be expiated 1
47:11 which you will not be able to expiate; 1

expiation 1. חַטָּאת 2. ἱλασμός 3. ἱλαστήριον 4. ὑπέρ
Num 8: 7 sprinkle the water of expiation upon them 1
Rom 3:25 whom God put forward as an expiation by his blood 3
1Jn 2: 2 he is the expiation for our sins 2
4:10 sent his Son to be the expiation for our sins. 2
1Es 9:20 to give rams in expiation of their error. 4
4Mc 17:22 through . . their death as an expiation 3
expiation *See also* make.

make expiation 1. כפר
Num35:33 no expiation can be made for the land 1

expire 1. גוע 2. מלא 3. ἀποψύχω 4. λιποθυμέω 5. πληρόω 6. συντελέω
1Sm 18:26 Before the time had expired 2
Job 3:11 die at birth, come forth from the womb and expire? 1
Tob 10: 1 when the days for the journey had expired 5
7 until the fourteen days . . had expired 6
4Mc 6:26 burned to his very bones and about to expire 4
15:18 nor when the third expired; 3

explain 1. באר 2. בין 3. דבר בְּאָזְנַיִם 4. נגד 5. חוה (A) 6. ἀπαγγέλλω 7. δηλόω 8. διανοίγω 9. διασαφέω 10. ἐκτίθημι 11. ἐμφυσιόω 12. ἐπιλογίζομαι 13. ἐπιλύω 14. λέγω 15. ὑποδείκνυμι 16. φράζω 17. adaperio 18. enarro 19. expono 20. interpretor 21. ostendo
Gen 41:24 there was no one who could explain it to me. 4
Deu 1: 5 Moses undertook to explain this law, saying 1
Jos 20: 4 stand . . and explain his case to the elders 3
1Kg 10: 3 nothing . . which he could not explain to her. 4
2Ch 9: 2 nothing . . which he could not explain to her. 4
Est 4: 8 show it to Esther and explain it to her 4
Isa 28: 9 and to whom will he explain the message? 2
Dan 5:12 interpret dreams, explain riddles, 5
Mat 13:36 Explain to us the parable of the weeds 9
15:15 Peter said to him, "Explain the parable to us. 16
Mrk 4:34 to his own disciples he explained everything. 13
Act 11: 4 Peter began and explained to them in order 10
17: 3 explaining and proving that it was necessary 8
Heb 5:11 have much to say which is hard to explain 14
1Es 3:16 they shall explain their statements 7
17 Explain to us what you have written 6
9:48 at the same time explaining what was read. 11
2Es 5:37 and then I will explain to you the travail 21
10:32 I saw, and still see, what I am unable to explain. 18
12:12 it was not explained to him as I now explain 20
12 as I now explain or have explained it to you. 20
12 as I now explain or have explained it to you. 20
13:21 I will also explain to you the things 17
51 I said, "O sovereign Lord, explain this to me 21
56 and explain weighty and wondrous matters to you. 19
Tob 4: 2 explain to him about the money before I die? 15
20 now let me explain to you about the ten talents 15
7:10 let me explain the true situation to you. 15
2Mc 3:10 The high priest explained 15
4Mc 3: 6 Now this can be explained more clearly 12

explanation
2Es 7:51 hear the explanation for this. •
explanation *See also* give.

exploit 1. ἐμπορεύομαι 2. ἐργάζομαι ἐν
2Pe 2: 3 they will exploit you with false words 1
Sir 13: 4 A rich man will exploit you if you can be of use 2

explore 1. חפר 2. חקר 3. scrutino
Deu 1:22 that they may explore the land for us, and bring us 1
Jdg 18: 2 sent . . to spy out the land and to explore it; 2
2 they said to them, "Go and explore the land. 2
Jer 31:37 foundations of the earth below can be explored 2
2Es 13:52 Just as no one can explore or know 3

export 1. יצא
1Kg 10:29 they were exported to all the kings 1
2Ch 1:17 exported to all the kings of the Hittites 1

expose 1. גלה 2. מַחְשֹׂף 3. נתן 4. ἀσχημοσύνη 5. δίδωμι 6. διέρχομαι 7. ἔκθεσις 8. ἐκτίθημι 9. ἐλέγχω 10. ποιέω ἔκθετα 11. πρόκειμαι
Gen 30:37 in them, exposing the white of the rods. 2
Exd 20:26 that your nakedness be not exposed on it.' 1
Prv 26:26 his wickedness will be exposed in the assembly. 1
Lam 2:14 they have not exposed your iniquity to restore 1
Ezk 28:17 I exposed you before kings 3
Joh 3:20 lest his deeds should be exposed. 9
Act 7:19 forced our fathers to expose their infants 10
21 when he was exposed 8
Eph 5:11 but instead expose them. 9
13 when anything is exposed by the light 9
Rev 16:15 that he may not go naked and be seen exposed!") 4
Wis 11:14 been cast out and exposed 7
18: 5 one child had been exposed and rescued 8
Sir 28:19 who has not been exposed to its anger 6
1Mc 14:29 exposed themselves to danger 5
4Mc 15:15 the flesh of the head . . exposed like masks. 11

publicly expose 1. ἀπελέγχω 2. θεατρίζω
Heb 10:33 sometimes being publicly exposed to abuse 2
2Mc 4:33 he publicly exposed them 1

exposure 1. γυμνότης
2Co 11:27 often without food, in cold and exposure. 1

expound 1. ἐκτίθημι 2. ἐκφαίνω
Act 18:26 they took him and expounded to him the way of God 1
28:23 he expounded the matter to them 1
Sir 38:33 they cannot expound discipline or judgment 2

express 1. גלה 2. ἔχω 3. ἠθολογέω 4. λέγω 5. λόγος
Prv 18: 2 but only in expressing his opinion. 1
Sir 0: 2 For what was originally expressed in Hebrew 4
2 differ not a little as originally expressed. 4
34:11 I understand more than I can express. 5
3Mc 6:41 magnanimously expressing his concern 2
4Mc 15: 4 In what manner might I express 3
18: 6 expressed also these principles to her children 4

express disapproval 1. נוא
Num30: 5 if her father expresses disapproval to her 1
8 if . . her husband . . expresses disapproval 1

express pride 1. καυχάομαι
2Co 7:14 For if I have expressed to him some pride in you 1

expression 1. צְלֵם (A) 2. λέξις 3. λόγος 4. πρόσωπον
Dan 3:19 expression of his face was changed against 1
Sir 12:18 whisper much, and change his expression. 4
27: 6 the expression of a thought 3
2Mc 2:31 be allowed to strive for brevity of expression 2

expressly 1. בְּשֵׁם 2. נקב 3. ῥητῶς
1Ch 12:31 were expressly named to come and make David king. 1
16:41 the rest of those chosen and expressly named 1
41 the rest of those chosen and expressly named 2
1Ti 4: 1 Now the Spirit expressly says 3

expulsion 1. ἐξαποστολής
3Mc 4: 4 the most miserable expulsion of these people. 1

extend 1. אֶל פָּנִים 2. אֹרֶךְ 3. היה 4. יסף 5. יצא 6. משך 7. נטה 8. פרש 9. תאר 10. ἐκτείνω 11. πλατύνω 12. πλεονάζω 13. προτείνω
Gen 10:19 the Canaanites extended from Sidon *
30 The territory in which they lived extended 3
Exd 27: 5 the net shall extend halfway down the altar. 3
38: 4 network of bronze, under its ledge, extending *
Num21:13 extends from the boundary of the Amorites; 5
15 slope . . valleys that extends to the seat of Ar 7
34: 9 then the boundary shall extend to Ziphron 5
Jos 13:30 Their region extended from Mahana'im 3
15: 9 boundary extends from the top of the mountain 9
2Ch 3:11 The wings . . together extended twenty cubits 2
13 wings of these cherubim extended twenty cubits; 8
Ezr 7:28 extended . . his steadfast love before the king 7
9: 9 but has extended to us his steadfast love 7
Ps 36: 5 Thy steadfast love, O LORD, extends to the heavens *
109:12 Let there be none to extend kindness to him 6
Isa 11:11 the Lord will extend his hand yet a second time 4
66:12 I will extend prosperity to her like a river 7
Jer 25:33 shall extend from one end of the earth 3
Ezk 45: 7 extending from the western to the eastern *
48: 1 and extending from the east side to the west, 3
21 Extending from the 25,000 cubits of the holy 1
2Co 4:15 so that as grace extends to more and more people 12
Sir 4:31 Let not your hand be extended to receive 10
1Mc 3: 3 He extended the glory of his people 11
14: 6 He extended the borders of his nation 11
3Mc 2: 1 and extending his hands with calm dignity 13

extend far 1. רחק
Mic 7:11 In that day the boundary shall be far extended. 1

extent 1. גְּבוּל סָבִיב
Ezk 45: 1 it shall be holy throughout its whole extent. 1
extent *See also* such.

all the extent 1. πέρας
AEs 13: 2 open to travel throughout all its extent 1

full extent 1. גְּבוּלָה
Num34: 2 an inheritance, the land of Canaan in its full extent 1

exterminate 1. בער 2. חרם 3. שמד 4. συνεκτρίβω
Jos 11:20 and should receive no mercy but be exterminated 3
1Kg 22:46 the male cult prostitutes . . he exterminated 1
1Ch 4:41 and exterminated them to this day 2
Dan 11:44 to exterminate and utterly destroy many. 3
Wis 11:19 not only could their damage exterminate men 4

external 1. ἔξωθεν
4Mc 6:34 when it masters even external agonies 1

extinct 1. זעך
Job 17: 1 My spirit is broken, my days are extinct 1

extinction
2Pe 2: 6 he condemned them to extinction *

extinguish 1. דעך 2. ἀποσβέσις 3. καταπαύω 4. σβέννυμι 5. extinguo
Isa 43:17 they are extinguished, quenched like a wick 1
2Es 7:61 burn hotly, and are extinguished. 5
Wis 2: 3 When it is extinguished 4
Sir 3:30 Water extinguishes a blazing fire 2
10:17 extinguished the memory of them from the earth. 3

extol 1. זכר 2. ידה 3. רום 4. שגא 5. שבח 6. רום (A) 7. ἀνυψόω 8. δοκέω 9. μεγαλύνω 10. ὑπερυμνητός
2Sm 22:50 For this I will extol thee, O LORD 2
Job 36:24 to extol his work, of which men have sung. 4
Ps 18:49 For this I will extol thee, O LORD 2
30: 1 I will extol thee, O LORD, for thou hast drawn me up 3
66:17 he was extolled with my tongue. 3
89:16 who . . extol thy righteousness. *
99: 5 Extol the LORD our God; worship at his footstool! 3
9 Extol the LORD our God, and worship at his holy 3
107:32 let them extol him in the congregation 3
117: 1 Extol him, all peoples! 5
118:28 thou art my God, I will extol thee. 3
145: 1 I will extol thee, my God and King, and bless 3
Sng 1: 4 we will extol your love more than wine; 1
Dan 4:37 Now I, Nebuchadnez'zar, praise and extol and honor 6
Act 10:46 speaking in tongues and extolling God 9
19:17 the name of the Lord Jesus was extolled. 9
Sir 13:23 they extol to the clouds what he says 7
43:31 who can extol him as he is? 9
Aza 1:31 to be extolled and highly glorified for ever. 10
33 to be extolled and highly exalted for ever. 10
2Mc 4:24 extolled him with an air of authority 8

extort 1. עשק
Ezk 22:29 and have extorted from the sojourner 1

extortion 1. עֹשֶׁק 2. ἁρπαγή
Ps 62:10 Put no confidence in extortion 1
Ezk 18:18 his father, because he practiced extortion 1
22: 7 the sojourner suffers extortion in your midst; 1
12 and make gain of your neighbors by extortion; 1
29 The people of the land have practiced extortion 1
Mat 23:25 inside they are full of extortion and rapacity. 2
Lke 11:39 inside you are full of extortion and wickedness. 2
extortion *See also* practice.

extortioner 1. ἅρπαξ
Lke 18:11 extortioners, unjust, adulterers 1

extraordinary 1. οὐ τυγχάνω 2. παρεδόξασεν
Act 19:11 did extraordinary miracles by the hands of Paul 1
Sir 10:13 brought upon them extraordinary afflictions 2
extraordinary *See also* bring, degree.

extreme 1. קָצֶה 2. ἀκμή 3. καθ᾽ ὑπερβολήν 4. κατὰ βάθους 5. μέγας 6. ὑπερβάλλω
Jos 15:21 The cities . . of Judah in the extreme South 1
2Co 8: 2 their extreme poverty 4
2Mc 4:13 There was such an extreme of Hellenization 2
7:42 eating of sacrifices and the extreme tortures. 6
3Mc 7:22 restored it to them with extreme fear 5
4Mc 3:18 bodily agonies even when they are extreme 3
extreme *See also* end.

extremely 1. μάλιστα 2. περισσοτέρως
Gal 1:14 so extremely zealous was I for the traditions 2
4Mc 3:10 the king was extremely thirsty 1
12: 9 Extremely pleased by the boy's declaration 1

extremity 1. קָצֶה
Num22:36 at the city . . at the extremity of the boundary. 1

exult 1. גיל 2. סלד 3. עור 4. עָלֵז 5. עלז 6. עלץ 7. רִנָּה 8. שׂושׂ 9. ἀγαλλιάομαι 10. ἀγαλλιάω 11. γαυρόω 12. exulto 13. triumpho
1Sm 2: 1 My heart exults in the LORD; 6
2Sm 1:20 lest the daughters of the uncircumcised exult. 5
1Ch 16:32 let the field exult, and everything in it! 6
Job 6:10 I would even exult in pain unsparing; 2
20: 5 that the exulting of the wicked is short 7
31:29 that hated me, or exulted when evil overtook him 3
39:21 He paws in the valley, and exults in his strength; 8
Ps 5:11 that those who love thy name may exult in thee. 6
9: 2 I will be glad and exult in thee, I will sing praise 6
21: 1 in thy help how greatly he exults! 1
25: 2 let not my enemies exult over me. 6
28: 7 so I am helped, and my heart exults 5
35: 9 in the LORD, exulting in his deliverance. 8
68: 3 righteous be joyful; let them exult before God; 6
4 his name is the LORD, exult before him! 5
89:16 who exult in thy name all the day 1
94: 3 O LORD . . how long shall the wicked exult? 5
96:12 let the field exult, and everything in it! 5
149: 5 Let the faithful exult in glory; 5
Sng 1: 4 We will exult and rejoice in you; 1
Isa 5:14 go down, her throng and he who exults in her. 4
23:12 You will no more exult, O . . daughter of Sidon; 5
29:19 men shall exult in the Holy One of Israel. 1
49:13 Sing for joy, O heavens, and exult, O earth; 1
61:10 rejoice in the LORD, my soul shall exult in my God; 1
Jer 11:15 flesh avert your doom? Can you then exult? 5
50:11 Though you rejoice, though you exult 5
Hos 9: 1 Rejoice not, O Israel! Exult not like the peoples; 1
Hab 1:15 he rejoices and exults. 1
Zep 3:14 Rejoice and exult with all your heart 5
17 he will exult over you with loud singing 1
Zec 10: 7 their hearts shall exult in the LORD. 1
Rev 19: 7 Let us rejoice and exult and give him the glory 10
2Es 1:16 You have not exulted in my name 13
15:53 exulting and clapping your hands 12
3Mc 2:17 exult in the arrogance of their tongue, saying 9
6: 5 Sennacherib exulting in his countless forces 11

exultant 1. עַלִּיז
Isa 22: 2 you who are full of shoutings . . exultant town? 1
23: 7 exultant city whose origin is from days of old 1
Zep 2:15 This is the exultant city that dwelt secure 1

exultant one 1. עַלִּיז
Zep 3:11 from your midst your proudly exultant ones 1

exultation 1. עלז 2. εὐφραίνω 3. καύχημα
Ps 60: 6 With exultation I will divide up Shechem 1
108: 7 With exultation I will divide up Shechem 1
Wis 14:28 For their worshipers either rave in exultation 2
Sir 1:11 The fear of the Lord is glory and exultation 3

exulting one 1. עַלִּיז
Isa 13: 3 execute my anger, my proudly exulting ones. 1

eye 1. עַיִן 2. פָּנִים 3. עַיִן (A) 4. ἐναντίον 5. ὄμμα 6. ὅρασις 7. ὀφθαλμός 8. ὄψις 9. πρόσωπον 10. τρῆμα 11. τρυμαλιά 12. τρύπημα 13. ὑπέρ 14. oculus
Gen 3: 5 you eat of it your eyes will be opened 1
6 that it was a delight to the eyes 1
7 the eyes of both were opened 1
6: 8 Noah found favor in the eyes of the LORD. 1
13:10 Lot lifted up his eyes, and saw that the Jordan 1
14 Lift up your eyes, and look from the place 1
18: 2 He lifted up his eyes and looked, and behold 1
20:16 your vindication in the eyes of all who are 1
21:19 Then God opened her eyes, and she saw a well 1
22: 4 Abraham lifted up his eyes and saw the place afar 1
13 Abraham lifted up his eyes and looked 1
24:63 and he lifted up his eyes and looked 1
64 Rebekah lifted up her eyes, and when she saw Isaac 1
27: 1 When Isaac was old and his eyes were dim 1
29:17 Leah's eyes were weak, but Rachel was beautiful 1
30:41 rods in the runnels before the eyes of the flock 1
31:10 the flock I lifted up my eyes, and saw in a dream 1
12 he said, 'Lift up your eyes and see, all the goats 1
40 by night, and my sleep fled from my eyes. 1
33: 1 Jacob lifted up his eyes and looked 1
5 when Esau raised his eyes and saw the women 1
34:11 Let me find favor in your eyes 1
39: 7 his master's wife cast her eyes upon Joseph 1
42:24 from them and bound him before their eyes. 1
43:29 he lifted up his eyes, and saw his brother 1
44:21 to me, that I may set my eyes upon him.' 1
45:12 now your eyes see, and the eyes of my brother 1
12 and the eyes of my brother Benjamin see 1
46: 4 and Joseph's hand shall close your eyes. 1
47:15 Give us food; why should we die before your eyes? *
19 Why should we die before your eyes 1
48:10 Now the eyes of Israel were dim with age 1
49:12 his eyes shall be red with wine 1
50: 4 If now I have found favor in your eyes, speak 1
Exd 8:26 abominable to the Egyptians before their eyes 1

13: 9 as a memorial between your eyes, that the law 1
16 shall be as . . frontlets between your eyes; 1
14:10 the people of Israel lifted up their eyes 1
15:26 If you . . do that which is right in his eyes 1
20:20 that the fear of him may be before your eyes 2
21:24 eye for eye, tooth for tooth, hand for hand 1
24 eye for eye, tooth for tooth, hand for hand 1
26 When a man strikes the eye of his slave 1
26 he shall let the slave go free for the eye's sake. 1
Lev 4:13 the thing is hidden from the eyes of the assembly 1
13: 5 if in his eyes the disease is checked 1
37 if in his eyes the itch is checked 1
20: 4 if the people of the land do at all hide their eyes 1
24:20 fracture for fracture, eye for eye 1
20 fracture for fracture, eye for eye 1
26:16 consumption, and fever that waste the eyes 1
Num 5:13 it is hidden from the eyes of her husband 1
10:31 you will serve as eyes for us. 1
15:39 not to follow after . . your own eyes 1
16:14 Will you put out the eyes of these men? 1
20: 8 tell the rock before their eyes to yield 1
12 did not . . sanctify me in the eyes of the people 1
22:31 Then the LORD opened the eyes of Balaam, 1
24: 2 Balaam lifted up his eyes, and saw Israel 1
3 oracle of the man whose eye is opened 1
4 falling down, but having his eyes uncovered 1
15 the oracle of the man whose eye is opened 1
16 falling down, but having his eyes uncovered 1
27:14 to sanctify me at the waters before their eyes. 1
33:55 be as pricks in your eyes and thorns in your sides 1
Deu 1:30 just as he did for you in Egypt before your eyes 1
3:21 eyes have seen all that the LORD your God has done 1
27 lift up your eyes westward and northward 1
27 lift up your eyes . . and behold it with your eyes; 1
4: 3 Your eyes have seen what the LORD did 1
9 forget the things which your eyes have seen 1
19 beware lest you lift up your eyes to heaven 1
34 LORD . . did for you in Egypt before your eyes? 1
6: 8 they shall be as frontlets between your eyes. 1
22 LORD showed signs . . before our eyes; 1
7:16 your eye shall not pity them; neither shall you 1
19 great trials which your eyes saw, the signs 1
9:17 cast them . . and broke them before your eyes. 1
10:21 great . . things which your eyes have seen. 1
11: 7 for your eyes have seen all the great work 1
12 eyes of the LORD your God are always upon it 1
18 they shall be as frontlets between your eyes. 1
12: 8 every man doing whatever is right in his own eyes; 1
13: 8 nor shall your eye pity him, nor shall you spare 1
15: 9 your eye be hostile to your poor brother 1
16:19 bribe blinds the eyes of the wise and subverts 1
19:13 Your eye shall not pity him, but you shall purge 1
21 You eye shall not pity; it shall be life for life 1
21 life for life, eye for eye, tooth for tooth 1
21 life for life, eye for eye, tooth for tooth 1
21: 7 neither did our eyes see it shed. 1
24: 1 if then she finds no favor in his eyes 1
25:12 cut off her hand; your eye shall have no pity. 1
28:31 Your ox shall be slain before your eyes 1
32 while your eyes look on and fail with longing 1
34 driven mad by the sight which your eyes shall see. 1
65 LORD will give you there . . failing eyes 1
67 because of . . sights which your eyes shall see. 1
29: 2 LORD did before your eyes in the land of Egypt 1
3 great trials which your eyes saw 1
4 LORD has not given you . . eyes to see, or ears 1
32:10 cared for him, he kept him as the apple of his eye. 1
34: 4 I have let you see it with your eyes 1
7 his eye was not dim, nor his natural force abated. 1
Jos 5:13 When Joshua . . he lifted up his eyes and looked 1
23:13 a scourge on your sides, and thorns in your eyes 1
24: 7 and your eyes saw what I did to Egypt; 1
Jdg 16:21 Philistines seized him and gouged out his eyes 1
28 that I may be avenged . . for one of my two eyes. 1
17: 6 every man did what was right in his own eyes. 1
19:17 he lifted up his eyes, and saw the wayfarer 1
21:25 every man did what was right in his own eyes. 1
Rut 2: 9 Let your eyes be upon the field 1
10 Why have I found favor in your eyes 1
1Sm 1:18 Let your maidservant find favor in your eyes. 1
2:32 look with envious eye on all the prosperity •
33 spared to weep out his eyes and grieve his heart; 1
4:15 and his eyes were set, so that he could not see. 1
6:13 when they lifted up their eyes and saw the ark 1
11: 2 condition . . that I gouge out all your right eyes 1
12: 3 have I taken a bribe to blind my eyes with it? 1
16 which the LORD will do before your eyes. 1
14:27 his hand to his mouth; and his eyes became bright. 1
29 my eyes have become bright, because I tasted 1
15:17 Though you are little in your own eyes, are you not 1
16:12 Now he was ruddy, and had beautiful eyes, and was 1
18: 9 Saul eyed David from that day on. 1
20: 3 knows well that I have found favor in your eyes; 1
29 if I have found favor in your eyes, let me get away 1
24:10 Lo, this day your eyes have seen how the LORD gave 1
25: 8 let my young men find favor in your eyes; 1
26:21 my life was precious in your eyes this day; 1
27: 5 If I have found favor in your eyes, let a place be 1
2Sm 6:20 uncovering himself today before the eyes 1
22 and I will be abased in your eyes; 1
7:19 yet this was a small thing in thy eyes, O Lord GOD; 1
12:11 and I will take your wives before your eyes 1
13:34 young man who kept the watch lifted up his eyes 1
15:25 If I find favor in the eyes of the LORD 1
18:24 when he lifted up his eyes and looked, he saw a man 1
22:28 thy eyes are upon the haughty to bring them down. 1
24: 3 while the eyes of my lord the king still see it; 1
1Kg 1:20 the eyes of all Israel are upon you, to tell them 1
48 to sit on my throne this day, my own eyes seeing it.' 1
8:29 thy eyes may be open . . toward this house 1
52 Let thy eyes be open to the supplication 1
9: 3 my eyes and my heart will be there for all time. 1
10: 7 until I came and my own eyes had seen it; 1
11:38 do what is right in my eyes by keeping my statutes 1
14: 4 his eyes were dim because of his age. 1
8 doing only that which was right in my eyes 1
15: 5 David did what was right in the eyes of the LORD 1
11 Asa did what was right in the eyes of the LORD 1
20:38 with a bandage over his eyes. 1
41 made haste to take the bandage away from his eyes; 1
2Kg 4:34 putting . . his eyes upon his eyes, and his hands 1
34 putting . . his eyes upon his eyes, and his hands 1
35 child sneezed . . and the child opened his eyes. 1
6:17 O LORD, I pray thee, open his eyes that he may see. 1
17 LORD opened the eyes of the young man, and he saw; 1
20 LORD, open the eyes of these men, that they may see. 1
20 So the LORD opened their eyes, and they saw; 1
7: 2 You shall see it with your own eyes, but . . not eat 1
19 You shall see it with your own eyes, but . . not eat 1
9:30 she painted her eyes, and adorned her head 1
10: 5 do whatever is good in your eyes. 1
30 done well in carrying out what is right in my eyes 1
12: 2 Jeho'ash did what was right in the eyes of the LORD 1
14: 3 And he did what was right in the eyes of the LORD 1
15: 3 he did what was right in the eyes of the LORD 1
34 And he did what was right in the eyes of the LORD 1
16: 2 he did not do what was right in the eyes of the LORD 1
18: 3 And he did what was right in the eyes of the LORD 1
19:16 open thy eyes, O LORD, and see; and hear the words 1
22 Against whom . . and haughtily lifted your eyes? 1
22: 2 And he did what was right in the eyes of the LORD 1
20 and your eyes shall not see all the evil 1
25: 7 They slew the sons of Zedeki'ah before his eyes 1
7 slew the sons . . and put out the eyes of Zedeki'ah 1
1Ch 13: 4 the thing was right in the eyes of all the people. 1
17:17 this was a small thing in thy eyes, O God; 1
21:16 David lifted his eyes and saw the angel 1
2Ch 6:20 that thy eyes may be open day and night toward 1
40 Now, O my God, let thy eyes be open and thy ears 1
7:15 Now my eyes will be open and my ears attentive 1
16 my eyes and my heart will be there for all time. 1
9: 6 did not believe . . until my own eyes had seen it; 1
14: 2 what was good and right in the eyes of the LORD 1
16: 9 the eyes of the LORD run to and fro 1
20:12 do not know what to do, but our eyes are upon thee. 1
24: 2 Jo'ash did what was right in the eyes of the LORD 1
25: 2 he did what was right in the eyes of the LORD 1
26: 4 he did what was right in the eyes of the LORD 1
27: 2 he did what was right in the eyes of the LORD 1
28: 1 he did not do what was right in the eyes of the LORD 1
29: 2 he did what was right in the eyes of the LORD 1
8 as you see with your own eyes. 1
34: 2 He did what was right in the eyes of the LORD 1
28 your eyes shall not see all the evil which I will 1
Ezr 5: 5 eye of their God was upon the elders of the Jews 3
9: 8 that our God may brighten our eyes and grant us 1
Neh 1: 6 let thy ear be attentive, and thy eyes open 1
Est 2:15 Esther found favor in the eyes of all who saw her. 1
8: 5 and if . . I be pleasing in his eyes 1
Job 3:10 nor hide trouble from my eyes. 1
4:16 A form was before my eyes; 1
7: 7 my eye will never again see good. 1
8 The eye of him who sees me will behold me no more; 1
8 while thy eyes are upon me, I shall be gone. 1
10: 4 Hast thou eyes of flesh? Dost thou see as man sees? 1
18 Would that I had died before any eye had seen me 1
11: 4 My doctrine is pure, and I am clean in God's eyes.' 1
20 But the eyes of the wicked will fail; 1
13: 1 Lo, my eye has seen all this 1
14: 3 dost thou open thy eyes upon such a one 1
15:12 why do your eyes flash 1
16: 9 my adversary sharpens his eyes against me. 1
20 My friends scorn me; my eye pours out tears to God 1
17: 2 my eye dwells on their provocation. 1
5 the eyes of his children will fail. 1
7 My eye has grown dim from grief 1
19:15 I have become an alien in their eyes. 1
27 my eyes shall behold, and not another. 1
20: 9 The eye which saw him will see him no more 1
21: 8 and their offspring before their eyes. 1
20 Let their own eyes see their destruction 1
24:15 The eye of the adulterer also waits 1
15 waits for the twilight, saying, 'No eye will see 1
23 his eyes are upon their ways. 1
27:19 he opens his eyes, and his wealth is gone. 1
28: 7 the falcon's eye has not seen it. 1
10 his eye sees every precious thing. 1
21 It is hid from the eyes of all living 1
29:11 when the eye saw, it approved; 1
15 I was eyes to the blind, and feet to the lame. 1
31: 1 I have made a covenant with my eyes; 1
7 from the way, and my heart has gone after my eyes 1
16 or have caused the eyes of the widow to fail 1
32: 1 because he was righteous in his own eyes. 1
34:21 For his eyes are upon the ways of a man 1
36: 7 He does not withdraw his eyes from the righteous 1
39:29 he spies out the prey; his eyes behold it afar off. 1
41:18 his eyes are like the eyelids of the dawn. 1
42: 5 by the hearing of the ear, but now my eye sees thee; 1
Ps 5: 5 The boastful may not stand before thy eyes; 1
6: 7 My eye wastes away because of grief, it grows weak 1
10: 8 His eyes stealthily watch for the hapless 1
11: 4 his eyes behold, his eyelids test 1
13: 3 lighten my eyes, lest I sleep the sleep of death; 1
15: 4 in whose eyes a reprobate is despised 1
17: 2 my vindication come! Let thy eyes see the right! 1
8 Keep me as the apple of the eye; 1
11 they set their eyes to cast me to the ground. 1
18:27 but the haughty eyes thou dost bring down. 1
19: 8 the LORD is pure, enlightening the eyes; 1
25:15 My eyes are ever toward the LORD 1
26: 3 For thy steadfast love is before my eyes 1
31: 9 my eye is wasted from grief 1
32: 8 I will counsel you with my eye upon you. 1
33:18 Behold, the eye of the LORD is on those who fear him 1
34:15 The eyes of the LORD are toward the righteous 1
35:19 those wink the eye who hate me without cause. 1
21 they say, "Aha, Aha! our eyes have seen it! 1
36: 1 there is no fear of God before his eyes. 1
2 For he flatters himself in his own eyes 1
38:10 the light of my eyes–it also has gone from me. 1
54: 7 my eye has looked in triumph on my enemies. 1
66: 7 for ever, whose eyes keep watch on the nations– 1
69: 3 My eyes grow dim with waiting for my God. 1
23 Let their eyes be darkened 1
73: 7 Their eyes swell out with fatness 1
79:10 be known among the nations before our eyes! 1
88: 9 my eye grows dim through sorrow. 1
91: 8 only look with your eyes and see the recompense 1
92:11 My eyes have seen the downfall of my enemies 1
94: 9 He who formed the eye, does he not see? 1
101: 3 not set before my eyes anything that is base. 1
115: 5 They have . . eyes, but do not see. 1
116: 8 For thou hast delivered my . . eyes from tears 1
118:23 This . . LORD's doing; it is marvelous in our eyes. 1
119:18 Open my eyes, that I may behold wondrous things 1
37 Turn my eyes from looking at vanities; 1
82 My eyes fail with watching for thy promise; 1
123 My eyes fail with watching for thy salvation 1
136 My eyes shed streams of tears 1
148 My eyes are awake before the watches of the night 1
121: 1 I lift up my eyes to the hills. 1
123: 1 To thee I lift up my eyes, O thou who art enthroned 1
2 eyes of servants look to the hand of their master 1
2 as the eyes of a maid to the hand of her mistress 1
2 so our eyes look to the LORD our God 1
131: 1 O LORD, my . . eyes are not raised too high; 1
132: 4 not give sleep to my eyes or slumber to my eyelids 1
135:16 they have eyes, but they see not 1
139:16 Thy eyes beheld my unformed substance; 1
141: 8 my eyes are toward thee, O LORD God; 1
145:15 The eyes of all look to thee, and thou gives them 1
146: 8 the LORD opens the eyes of the blind. •
Prv 3: 7 Be not wise in your own eyes; 1
4:25 Let your eyes look directly forward 1
5:21 For a man's ways are before the eyes of the LORD 1
6: 4 Give your eyes no sleep 1
13 winks with his eyes, scrapes with his feet 1
17 haughty eyes, a lying tongue 1
7: 2 keep my teachings as the apple of your eye; 1
10:10 He who winks the eye causes trouble 1
26 Like vinegar to the teeth, and smoke to the eyes 1
12:15 The way of a fool is right in his own eyes 1
15: 3 The eyes of the LORD are in every place 1
30 The light of the eyes rejoices the heart 1
16: 2 All the ways of a man are pure in his own eyes 1
30 He who winks his eyes plans perverse things 1
17: 8 magic stone in the eyes of him who gives it; 1
24 but the eyes of a fool are on the ends of the earth. 1
20: 8 throne of judgment winnows all evil with his eyes. 1
12 hearing ear and the seeing eye, the LORD has made 1
13 open your eyes, and you will have plenty of bread. 1
21: 2 Every way of a man is right in his own eyes 1
4 Haughty eyes and a proud heart 1
10 his neighbor finds no mercy in his eyes. 1
22: 9 He who has a bountiful eye will be blessed 1
12 The eyes of the LORD keep watch over knowledge 1
23: 5 When your eyes light upon it, it is gone; 1
26 My son . . let your eyes observe my ways. 1
29 has wounds without cause? Who has redness of eyes? 1
33 Your eyes will see strange things 1
25: 7 What your eyes have seen 1
26: 5 lest he be wise in his own eyes. 1
12 Do you see a man who is wise in his own eyes? 1
16 sluggard is wiser in his own eyes than seven men 1
27:20 never satisfied are the eyes of man. 1
28:11 A rich man is wise in his own eyes, but a poor man 1

27 but he who hides his eyes will get many a curse. 1
29:13 LORD gives light to the eyes of both. 1
30:12 There are those who are pure in their own eyes 1
13 There are those-how lofty are their eyes 1
17 eye that mocks a father and scorns to obey 1
Ecc 1: 8 the eye is not satisfied with seeing 1
2:10 whatever my eyes desired I did not keep from them; 1
14 The wise man has his eyes in his head 1
4: 8 and his eyes are never satisfied with riches 1
5:11 and what gain . . but to see them with his eyes? 1
6: 9 Better is the sight of the eyes 1
8:16 how neither day nor night one's eyes see sleep; 1
11: 7 and it is pleasant for the eyes to behold the sun. 1
9 walk in the ways of . . and the sight of your eyes. 1
Sng 1:15 behold, you are beautiful; your eyes are doves. 1
4: 1 Your eyes are doves behind your veil. 1
9 ravished my heart with a glance of your eyes 1
5:12 His eyes are like doves beside springs of water 1
6: 5 Turn away your eyes from me, for they disturb me- 1
7: 4 Your eyes are pools in Heshbon, by the gate 1
8:10 I was in his eyes as one who brings peace. 1
Isa 1:15 When you spread . . your hands, I will hide my eyes 1
16 remove the evil of your doings from before my eyes 1
3:16 haughty . . glancing wantonly with their eyes 1
5:15 and the eyes of the haughty are humbled. 1
21 Woe to those who are wise in their own eyes 1
6: 5 for my eyes have seen the King, the LORD of hosts! 1
10 shut their eyes; lest they see with their eyes 1
10 shut their eyes; lest they see with their eyes 1
11: 3 He shall not judge by what his eyes see 1
13:16 infants . . be dashed in pieces before their eyes; 1
18 no mercy . . their eyes will not pity children. 1
17: 7 and their eyes will look to the Holy One of Israel; 1
29:10 and has closed your eyes, the prophets 1
18 out of . . darkness the eyes of the blind shall see. 1
30:20 but your eyes shall see your Teacher. 1
32: 3 Then the eyes of those who see will not be closed 1
33:15 who . . shuts his eyes from looking upon evil 1
17 Your eyes will see the king in his beauty; 1
20 Your eyes will see Jerusalem, a quiet habitation 1
35: 5 Then the eyes of the blind shall be opened 1
37:17 open thy eyes, O LORD, and see; 1
23 your voice and haughtily lifted your eyes? 1
38:14 My eyes are weary with looking upward. 1
40:26 Lift up your eyes on high and see 1
42: 7 to open the eyes that are blind 1
43: 4 Because you are precious in my eyes, and honored 1
8 the people who are blind, yet have eyes 1
44:18 for he has shut their eyes, so that they cannot see 1
49: 5 for I am honored in the eyes of the LORD 1
18 Lift up your eyes round about and see; 1
51: 6 Lift up your eyes to the heavens 1
52: 8 eye to eye they see the return of the LORD to Zion. 1
8 eye to eye they see the return of the LORD to Zion. 1
10 his holy arm before the eyes of all the nations; 1
59:10 we grope like those who have no eyes; 1
60: 4 Lift up your eyes round about, and see; 1
64: 4 no eye has seen a God besides thee 1
65:12 but you did what was evil in my eyes, 1
16 troubles are forgotten and are hid from my eyes. 1
66: 4 but they did what was evil in my eyes 1
Jer 3: 2 Lift up your eyes to the bare heights, and see! 1
4:30 that you enlarge your eyes with paint? 1
5: 3 O LORD, do not thy eyes look for truth? 1
21 senseless people, who have eyes, but see not 1
7:11 this house . . become a den of robbers in your eyes? 1
9: 1 head were waters, and my eyes a fountain of tears 1
18 that our eyes may run down with tears 1
13:17 my eyes will weep bitterly 1
20 Lift up your eyes and see those who come 1
14: 6 their eyes fail because there is no herbage. 1
17 Let my eyes run down with tears night and day 1
16: 9 make to cease from this place, before your eyes 1
17 For my eyes are upon all their ways; 1
17 nor is their iniquity concealed from my eyes. 1
22:17 have eyes and heart only for your dishonest gain 1
24: 6 I will set my eyes upon them for good 1
29:21 and he shall slay them before your eyes. 1
31:16 your voice from weeping, and your eyes from tears; 1
32: 4 speak with him face to face and see him eye to eye; 1
4 speak with him face to face and see him eye to eye; 1
19 whose eyes are open to all the ways of men 1
34: 3 you shall see the king of Babylon eye to eye 1
3 you shall see the king of Babylon eye to eye 1
15 repented and did what was right in my eyes 1
39: 6 the sons of Zedeki'ah at Riblah before his eyes; 1
7 He put out the eyes of Zedeki'ah 1
42: 2 for we are left but a few of many, as your eyes see us 1
51:24 I will requite . . Chalde'a before your very eyes 1
52:10 slew the sons of Zedeki'ah before his eyes 1
11 He put out the eyes of Zedeki'ah, and bound him 1
Lam 1:16 For these things I weep; my eyes flow with tears; 1
2: 4 and he has slain all the pride of our eyes 1
11 My eyes are spent with weeping; 1
18 Give yourself no rest, your eyes no respite! 1
3:48 my eyes flow with rivers of tears 1
49 My eyes will flow without ceasing 1
51 my eyes cause me grief at the fate 1
4:17 Our eyes failed, ever watching vainly for help; 1
5:17 for these things our eyes have grown dim 1
Ezk 1:18 and their rims were full of eyes round about. 1
5:11 my eye will not spare, and I will have no pity. 1
6: 9 and blinded their eyes which turn wantonly 1
7: 4 And my eye will not spare you, nor will I have pity; 1
9 And my eye will not spare, nor will I have pity; 1
8: 5 Then he said to me, "Son of man, lift up your eyes now 1
5 So I lifted up my eyes toward the north, and behold 1
18 my eye will not spare, nor will I have pity; 1
9: 5 and smite; your eye shall not spare 1
10 As for me, my eye will not spare, nor will I have pity 1
10: 2 And he went in before my eyes. 1
12 the wheels were full of eyes round about 1
12: 2 rebellious house, who have eyes to see, but see not 1
12 that he may not see the land with his eyes. 1
16: 5 No eye pitied you, to do any of these things to you 1
18: 6 or lift up his eyes to the idols of . . Israel 1
12 lifts up his eyes to the idols 1
15 or lift up his eyes to the idols . . of Israel 1
20: 7 the detestable things your eyes feast 1
8 the detestable things their eyes feasted 1
17 my eye spared them, and I did not destroy them 1
24 their eyes were set on their fathers' idols. 1
21: 6 sigh with . . bitter grief before their eyes. 1
23:27 you shall not lift up your eyes to the Egyptians 1
40 For them you bathed yourself, painted your eyes 1
24:16 I am about to take the delight of your eyes away 1
21 the pride of your power, the delight of your eyes 1
25 delight of their eyes and their heart's desire 1
28:17 exposed you before kings, to feast their eyes •
33:25 and lift up your eyes to your idols, 1
36:23 I vindicate my holiness before their eyes. 1
37:20 are in your hand before their eyes 1
38:16 I vindicate my holiness before their eyes. 1
23 and make myself known in the eyes of many 1
40: 4 the man said to me, "Son of man, look with your eyes 1
44: 5 see with your eyes, and hear with your ears 1
Dan 4:34 Nebuchadnez'zar, lifted my eyes to heaven 3
7: 8 horn were eyes like the eyes of a man, and a mouth 3
8 horn were eyes like the eyes of a man, and a mouth 3
20 had eyes and a mouth that spoke great things 3
8: 3 I raised my eyes and saw, and behold 1
5 goat had a conspicuous horn between his eyes. 1
21 great horn between his eyes is the first king. 1
9:18 open thy eyes and behold our desolations 1
10: 5 I lifted up my eyes and looked, and behold, a man 1
6 his eyes like flaming torches, his arms and legs 1
Hos 13:14 Compassion is hid from my eyes. 1
Jol 1:16 Is not the food cut off before our eyes 1
Ams 9: 4 and I will set my eyes upon them for evil 1
8 the eyes of the Lord GOD are upon the . . kingdom 1
Mic 4:11 and let our eyes gaze upon Zion. 1
7:10 My eyes will gloat over her; 1
Hab 1:13 Thou who art of purer eyes than to behold evil 1
Zep 3:20 when I restore your fortunes before your eyes 1
Zec 1:18 I lifted my eyes and saw, and behold, four horns! 1
2: 1 I lifted my eyes and saw, and behold, a man 1
8 he who touches you touches the apple of his eye. 1
4:10 These seven are the eyes of the LORD 1
5: 1 Again I lifted my eyes and saw 1
5 Lift your eyes, and see what this is that goes 1
9 Then I lifted my eyes and saw, and behold, 1
6: 1 again I lifted my eyes and saw 1
9: 8 for now I see with my own eyes. 1
11:17 May the sword smite his arm and his right eye! 1
17 wholly withered, his right eye utterly blinded! 1
12: 4 But upon the house of Judah I will open my eyes 1
14:12 their eyes shall rot in their sockets 1
Mal 1: 5 Your own eyes shall see this, and you shall say 1
Mat 5:29 If your right eye causes you to sin, pluck it out 7
38 heard that it was said, 'An eye for an eye and a tooth 7
38 Let him have an eye for an eye and a tooth for a tooth.' 7
6:22 The eye is the lamp of the body. So, if your eye 7
22 So, if your eye is sound, your whole body will be 7
23 if your eye is not sound, your whole body will be 7
7: 3 do you see the speck that is in your brother's eye 7
3 but do not notice the log that is in your own eye? 7
4 'Let me take the speck out of your eye,' 7
4 when there is the log in your own eye? 7
5 hypocrite, first take the log out of your own eye 7
5 to take the speck out of your brother's eye. 7
9:29 Then he touched their eyes, saying 7
30 their eyes were opened 7
13:15 and their eyes they have closed 7
15 lest they should perceive with their eyes 7
16 blessed are your eyes, for they see 7
17: 8 when they lifted up their eyes, they saw no one 7
18: 9 if your eye causes you to sin, pluck it out 7
9 with two eyes to be thrown into the hell of fire 7
19:24 for a camel to go through the eye of a needle 12
20:33 They said to him, "Lord, let our eyes be opened. 7
34 Jesus in pity touched their eyes 5
21:42 it is marvelous in our eyes'? 7
26:43 their eyes were heavy. 7
Mrk 8:18 Having eyes do you not see 7
23 when he had spit on his eyes 5
25 Then again he laid his hands upon his eyes 7
9:46 if your eye causes you to sin, pluck it out 7
46 with two eyes to be thrown into hell 7
10:25 a camel to go through the eye of a needle 11
12:11 it is marvelous in our eyes'? 7
14:40 their eyes were very heavy 7
Lke 2:30 for mine eyes have seen thy salvation 7
4:20 the eyes of all in the synagogue were fixed on him. 7
6:20 he lifted up his eyes on his disciples 7
41 do you see the speck that is in your brother's eye 7
41 do not notice the log that is in your own eye? 7
42 let me take out the speck that is in your eye 7
42 you . . do not see the log that is in your own eye 7
42 hypocrite, first take the log out of your own eye 7
42 take out the speck that is in your brother's eye. 7
10:23 Blessed are the eyes which see what you see! 7
11:34 Your eye is the lamp of your body 7
34 when your eye is sound 7
16:23 he lifted up his eyes, and saw Abraham far off 7
18:13 would not even lift up his eyes to heaven 7
25 to go through the eye of a needle 10
19:42 now they are hid from your eyes. 7
24:16 their eyes were kept from recognizing him. 7
31 their eyes were opened and they recognized him; 7
Joh 4:35 I tell you, lift up your eyes, and see how the fields 7
6: 5 Lifting up his eyes . . Jesus said 7
9: 6 and anointed the man's eyes with the clay 7
10 They said to him, "Then how were your eyes opened? 7
11 made clay and anointed my eyes and said to me 7
14 when Jesus made the clay and opened his eyes. 7
15 he said to them, "He put clay on my eyes, 7
17 since he has opened your eyes 7
21 nor do we know who opened his eyes 7
26 How did he open your eyes? 7
30 and yet he opened my eyes. 7
32 that any one opened the eyes of a man born blind. 7
10:21 Can a demon open the eyes of the blind? 7
11:37 he who opened the eyes of the blind man 7
41 Jesus lifted up his eyes and said, "Father 7
12:40 has blinded their eyes and hardened their heart 7
40 lest they should see with their eyes 7
17: 1 he lifted up his eyes to heaven and said 7
Act 9: 8 when his eyes were opened, he could see nothing 7
18 something like scales fell from his eyes 7
40 she opened her eyes 7
26:18 to open their eyes 7
28:27 their eyes they have closed 7
27 lest they should perceive with their eyes 7
Rom 3:18 There is no fear of God before their eyes. 7
11: 8 eyes that should not see and ears that should not 7
10 their eyes be darkened so that they cannot see 7
1Co 2: 9 What no eye has seen, nor ear heard 7
12:16 Because I am not an eye, I do not belong to the body 7
17 If the whole body were an eye 7
21 The eye cannot say to the hand, "I have no need 7
15:52 in a moment, in the twinkling of an eye 7
2Co 10: 7 Look at what is before your eyes 9
Gal 3: 1 before whose eyes 7
4:15 plucked out your eyes and given them to me. 7
Eph 1:18 having the eyes of your hearts enlightened 7
Heb 4:13 the eyes of him with whom we have to do. 7
1Pe 3:12 For the eyes of the Lord are upon the righteous 7
2Pe 2:14 They have eyes full of adultery 7
1Jn 1: 1 That . . which we have seen with our eyes 7
2:11 because the darkness has blinded his eyes. 7
16 the lust of the flesh and the lust of the eyes 7
Rev 1: 7 he is coming . . and every eye will see him 7
14 his eyes were like a flame of fire 7
2:18 the Son of God, who has eyes like a flame of fire 7
3:18 salve to anoint your eyes, that you may see. 7
4: 6 creatures, full of eyes in front and behind 7
8 creatures . . full of eyes all around and within 7
5: 6 a Lamb . . with seven horns and . . seven eyes 7
7:17 and God will wipe away every tear from their eyes. 7
19:12 His eyes are like a flame of fire 7
21: 4 he will wipe away every tear from their eyes 7
2Es 1:37 though they do not see me with bodily eyes 14
8:20 who inhabitest eternity, whose eyes are exalted 14
9:38 I lifted up my eyes and saw a woman on my right ‡
10:55 as far as it is possible for your eyes to see it 14
Tob 2:10 their fresh droppings fell into my open eyes 7
10 white films formed on my eyes 7
3:12 I have turned my eyes and my face toward thee. 7
17 to scale away the white films of Tobit's eyes •
4: 7 do not let your eye begrudge the gift 7
16 let your eye begrudge the gift when you made it. 7
5:20 your eyes will see him. 7
6: 8 anoint . . a man who has white films in his eyes 7
10: 5 you who are the light of my eyes? 7
11: 7 I know, Tobias, that your father will open his eyes. 7
8 You therefore must anoint his eyes with the gall; 7
11 he sprinkled the gall upon his father's eyes 7
12 when his eyes began to smart he rubbed them 7
13 scaled off from the corners of his eyes. 7
Jdt 2:11 if they refuse, your eye shall not spare 7
7:27 witness the death of our babes before our eyes 7
8:22 and a reproach in the eyes of those who acquire us. 4
10: 4 to entice the eyes of all men who might see her. 7
14 she was in their eyes marvelously beautiful 4
16: 9 Her sandal ravished his eyes 7
AEs 13:15 the eyes of our foes are upon us to annihilate us •
18 their death was before their eyes. 7

16: 9 judging what comes before our eyes 8
Wis 3: 2 In the eyes of the foolish 7
11:18 flash terrible sparks from their eyes; 5
15:15 these have neither the use of their eyes to see 5
Sir 4: 1 do not keep needy eyes waiting. 7
5 Do not avert your eye from the needy 7
9: 8 Turn away your eyes from a shapely woman 7
10:20 worthy of honor in his eyes. 7
11:12 the eyes of the Lord look upon him for his good 7
12:16 an enemy will weep with his eyes 7
14: 8 Evil is the man with a grudging eye 7
9 A greedy man's eye is not satisfied with a portion 7
10 A stingy man's eye begrudges bread 7
15:19 his eyes are on those who fear him 7
16: 5 Many such things my eye has seen 7
17: 6 He made for them tongue and eyes 7
8 He set his eye upon their hearts 7
13 Their eyes saw his glorious majesty 7
15 they will not be hid from his eyes. 7
19 his eyes are continually upon their ways. 7
18:18 the gift of a grudging man makes the eyes dim. 7
20:14 he has many eyes instead of one. 7
29 Presents and gifts blind the eyes of the wise; 7
22:19 A man who pricks an eye will make tears fall 7
23: 4 do not give me haughty eyes 7
19 His fear is confined to the eyes of men 7
19 the eyes of the Lord 7
26: 9 A wife's harlotry shows in her lustful eyes 7
11 Be on guard against her impudent eye 7
27: 1 whoever seeks to get rich will avert his eyes. 7
22 Whoever winks his eye plans evil deeds 7
30:20 he sees with his eyes and groans 7
31:13 Remember that a greedy eye is a bad thing 7
13 What has been created more greedy than the eye? 7
34:16 The eyes of the Lord are upon those who love him 7
17 He lifts up the soul and gives light to the eyes 7
20 Like one who kills a son before his father's eyes
38:28 his eyes are on the pattern of the object 7
39:19 nothing can be hid from his eyes. 7
40:22 The eye desires grace and beauty 7
43: 4 with bright beams it blinds the eyes. 7
18 The eye marvels at the beauty of its whiteness 7
45:12 the delight of the eyes, richly adorned. 7
51:27 See with your eyes that I have labored little 7
Bar 1:12 he will give light to our eyes, and we shall live 7
2:17 open thy eyes, O Lord, and see; for the dead who are 7
18 and feeble, and the eyes that are failing 7
3:14 where there is light for the eyes, and peace. 7
LJr 1:17 Their eyes are full of the dust 7
Sus 1: 9 and turned away their eyes from looking to Heaven 7
1Mc 6:10 Sleep departs from my eyes 7
9:39 They raised their eyes and looked 7
11:51 So the Jews gained glory in the eyes of the king 4
2Mc 3:36 which he had seen with his own eyes. 8
8:17 keeping before their eyes the lawless outrage 7
12:42 they had seen with their own eyes 8
3Mc 4: 4 the common object of pity before their eyes 7
10 with their eyes in total darkness 7
5:33 his eyes wavered and his face fell. 6
47 with invulnerable heart and with his own eyes 7
4Mc 4: 1 unable to injure Onias in the eyes of the nation 13
5:30 not even if you gouge out my eyes 5
6: 6 yet while the old man's eyes were raised to heaven 7
26 he lifted up his eyes to God and said 5
15:19 you looked at the eyes of each one in his tortures 7
18:21 pierced the pupils of their eyes 5

eye *See also* apple, fix, look.

eye fixed 1. נבט
Ps 119: 6 having my eyes fixed on all thy commandments. 1

one eye 1. *μονόφθαλμος*
Mat 18: 9 it is better for you to enter life with one eye 1
* Mrk 9:46 to enter the kingdom of God with one eye 1

under the eye 1. נֹכַח
Jdg 18: 6 The journey . . is under the eye of the LORD. 1

eye-service 1. *ὀφθαλμοδουλία*
Eph 6: 6 not in the way of eye-service, as men-pleasers 1

eyebrow 1. גַּב עַיִן
Lev 14: 9 shall shave off his beard and his eyebrows 1

eyelash 1. עַפְעַף
Prv 6:25 do not let her capture you with her eyelashes; 1

eyelid 1. עַפְעַף 2. שְׁמֻרָה 3. *βλέφαρον*
Job 3: 9 nor see the eyelids of the morning; 1
16:16 on my eyelids is deep darkness; 1
41:18 his eyes are like the eyelids of the dawn. 1
Ps 11: 4 his eyes behold, his eyelids test 1
77: 4 Thou dost hold my eyelids from closing; 2
132: 4 not give sleep to my eyes or slumber to my eyelids 1
Prv 6: 4 Give . . your eyelids no slumber; 1
30:13 There are those–how . . high their eyelids lift! 1
Jer 9:18 with tears, and our eyelids gush with water. 1
Sir 26: 9 she is known by her eyelids. 3

before the eyes 1. *ἐνώπιον*
Bel 1:42 they were devoured immediately before his eyes. 1

eyeservice 1. *ὀφθαλμοδουλία*
Col 3:22 not with eyeservice, as men-pleasers 1

eyesight 1. עַיִן
1Sm 3: 2 Eli, whose eyesight had begun to grow dim 1

eyewitness 1. *αὐτόπτης* 2. *ἐπόπτης*
Lke 1: 2 who from the beginning were eyewitnesses 1
2Pe 1:16 but we were eyewitnesses of his majesty. 2

F

fabric 1. *κτίσμα*

Sir 38:34 they keep stable the fabric of the world 1

blue fabric 1. תְּכֵלֶת

2Ch 2: 7 to work in . . purple, crimson, and blue fabrics 1
14 to work in . . purple, blue, and crimson fabrics 1
3:14 veil of blue and purple and crimson fabrics 1

crimson fabric 1. כַּרְמִיל

2Ch 2: 7 to work in . . purple, crimson, and blue fabrics 1
14 to work in . . purple, blue, and crimson fabrics 1
3:14 veil of blue and purple and crimson fabrics 1

purple fabric 1. אַרְגָּמָן 2. אַרְגְּוָן (A)

2Ch 2: 7 to work in . . purple, crimson, and blue fabrics 2
14 to work in . . purple, blue, and crimson fabrics 1
3:14 veil of blue and purple and crimson fabrics 1

face 1. אֶל 2. אֶל פָּנִים 3. אַף 4. לִפְנֵי 5. מִנֶּגֶד 6. מַרְאֶה 7. נֶגֶד 8. נֹכַח 9. עַיִן 10. פֶּה 11. פנה 12. פָּנִים 13. פָּנִים דֶּרֶךְ 14. פָּנִים לְ 15. ראה 16. אֲנַף (A) 17. *ἀντοφθαλμέω* 18. *ἀπέναντι* 19. *ἔναντι* 20. *ἐξ ἐναντίας* 21. *ἐπί* 22. *θεωρέω* 23. *κατὰ πρόσωπον* 24. *ὁράω* 25. *ὄψις* 26. *πρός* 27. *πρόσωπον* 28. *στόμα* 29. coram 30. facies 31. vultus

Gen 1: 2 and darkness was upon the face of the deep 12
2 Spirit . . was moving over the face of the waters 12
29 plant . . which is upon the face of all the earth 12
2: 6 and watered the whole face of the ground– 12
3:19 In the sweat of your face you shall eat bread 3
4:14 and from thy face I shall be hidden; 12
6: 1 men began to multiply on the face of the ground 12
7 whom I have created from the face of the ground 12
7: 3 kind alive upon the face of all the earth. 12
4 will blot out from the face of the ground. 12
18 the ark floated on the face of the waters. 12
23 living thing that was upon the face of the ground 12
8: 8 waters had subsided from the face of the ground; 12
9 were still on the face of the whole earth. 12
13 behold, the face of the ground was dry. 12
9:23 their faces were turned away, and they did not see 12
11: 4 abroad upon the face of the whole earth. 12
8 from there over the face of all the earth 12
9 them abroad over the face of all the earth. 12
17: 3 Then Abram fell on his face; and God said to him 12
17 Then Abraham fell on his face and laughed 12
19: 1 and bowed himself with his face to the earth 3
30:40 set the faces of the flocks toward the striped 12
31:21 and set his face toward the hill country 12
32:20 and afterwards I shall see his face; 12
30 saying, "For I have seen God face to face 12
30 saying, "For I have seen God face to face 12
33:10 for truly to see your face is like seeing the face 12
10 to see your face is like seeing the face of God 12
38:15 be a harlot, for she had covered her face. 12
40: 7 Why are your faces downcast today? 12
42: 6 before him with their faces to the ground. 3
43: 3 You shall not see my face, unless your brother is 12
5 You shall not see my face, unless your brother is 12
31 Then he washed his face and came out; 12
44:23 you shall see my face no more.' 12
26 cannot see the man's face unless our youngest 12
46:30 Now let me die, since I have seen your face 12
48:11 I had not thought to see your face; 12
12 he bowed himself with his face to the earth. 3
50: 1 Joseph fell on his father's face, and wept over him 12
Exd 3: 6 And Moses hid his face, for he was afraid to look 12
10: 5 they shall cover the face of the land 9
15 For they covered the face of the whole land 9
28 never see my face again; for in the day you see my 12
28 for in the day you see my face you shall die. 12
29 I will not see your face again. 12
16:14 there was on the face of the wilderness 12
25:20 with their wings, their faces one to another; 12
20 mercy seat shall the faces of the cherubim be. 12
32:12 to consume them from the face of the earth'? 12
33:11 Thus the LORD used to speak to Moses face to face 12
11 Thus the LORD used to speak to Moses face to face 12
16 other people that are upon the face of the earth? 12
20 But," he said, "you cannot see my face; 12
23 my back; but my face shall not be seen. 12
34:29 Moses did not know that the skin of his face shone 12
30 Moses, behold, the skin of his face shone 12
33 speaking with them, he put a veil on his face; 12
35 the people of Israel saw the face of Moses 12
35 saw . . that the skin of Moses' face shone; 12
35 and Moses would put the veil upon his face again 12
37: 9 their wings, with their faces one to another; 12
9 mercy seat were the faces of the cherubim. 12
Lev 9:24 they shouted, and fell on their faces 12
17:10 I will set my face against that person who eats 12
19:32 You shall . . honor the face of an old man 12
20: 3 I myself will set my face against that man 12
5 then I will set my face against that man 12
6 I will set my face against that person 12
21:18 a man blind or lame, or one who has a mutilated face •
26:17 I will set my face against you 12
Num 2: 2 they shall encamp facing the tent of meeting 5
6:25 The LORD make his face to shine upon you 12
11:31 about two cubits above the face of the earth. 12
12: 3 than all men that were on the face of the earth. 12
14 If her father had but spit in her face 12
14: 5 Moses and Aaron fell on their faces before all 12
14 for thou, O LORD, art seen face to face, and thy cloud 9
14 for thou, O LORD, art seen face to face, and thy cloud 9
16: 4 When Moses heard it, he fell on his face; 12
22 they fell on their faces, and said, "O God, the God 12
45 And they fell on their faces. 12
20: 6 Moses and Aaron went . . and fell on their faces. 12
22: 5 cover the face of the earth, and they are dwelling 9
11 a people . . covers the face of the earth; now come 9
31 he bowed his head, and fell on his face. 3
24: 1 Balaam . . set his face toward the wilderness. 12
Deu 1:17 you shall not be afraid of the face of man 12
5: 4 LORD spoke with you face to face at the mountain 12
4 LORD spoke with you face to face at the mountain 12
6:15 destroy you from off the face of the earth. 12
7: 6 out of all the people . . on the face of the earth. 12
10 and requites to their face those who hate him 12
10 not be slack . . he will requite him to his face. 12
14: 2 out of all the peoples . . on the face of the earth. 12
25: 9 pull his sandal off his foot, and spit in his face 12
28:31 ass . . violently taken away before your face 12
31:17 I will forsake them and hide my face from them 12
18 surely hide my face in that day on account of all 12
32:20 said, 'I will hide my face from them, I will see 12
34:10 like Moses, whom the LORD knew face to face 12
10 like Moses, whom the LORD knew face to face 12
Jos 5:14 And Joshua fell on his face to the earth 12
7: 6 and fell to the earth upon his face before the ark 12
10 Arise, why have you thus fallen upon your face? 12
15: 2 of the Salt Sea, from the bay that faces southward; 11
Jdg 6:22 now I have seen the angel of the LORD face to face. 12
22 now I have seen the angel of the LORD face to face. 12
13:20 and they fell on their faces to the ground. 12
Rut 2:10 she fell on her face, bowing to the ground, and said 12
1Sm 17:49 and he fell on his face to the ground. 12
20:15 LORD cuts off every . . from the face of the earth 12
41 David rose . . and fell on his face to the ground 3
24: 8 David bowed with his face to the earth 3
25:23 and fell before David on her face, and bowed 12
41 And she rose and bowed with her face to the ground 3
28:14 Saul . . bowed with his face to the ground 3
2Sm 2:22 How . . could I lift up my face to your brother Jo'ab? 12
3:13 you shall not see my face, unless you first bring 12
13 bring Michal . . when you come to see my face. 12
9: 6 came . . and fell on his face and did obeisance. 12
14: 4 she fell on her face to the ground 3
7 name nor remnant upon the face of the earth. 12
22 And Jo'ab fell on his face to the ground 12
33 and bowed himself on his face to the ground 3
18: 8 The battle spread over the face of . . the country; 12
28 bowed before the king with his face to the earth 3
19: 4 The king covered his face, and the king cried 12
5 covered with shame the faces of . . your servants 12
21: 1 and David sought the face of the LORD. 12
24:20 and did obeisance . . with his face to the ground. 3
1Kg 1:23 before the king, with his face to the ground. 3
31 bowed with her face to the ground, and did 3
7:25 twelve oxen, three facing north, three facing 11
25 twelve oxen . . three facing west, three facing 11
25 twelve oxen . . three facing south, and three 11
25 twelve oxen . . south, and three facing east; 11
13:34 and to destroy it from the face of the earth. 12
18: 7 Obadi'ah recognized him, and fell on his face 12
39 when . . the people saw it, they fell on their faces; 12
42 he bowed . . and put his face between his knees. 12
19:13 Eli'jah . . wrapped his face in his mantle 12
21: 4 he lay down on his bed, and turned away his face 12
22:35 the king was propped up . . facing the Syrians 8
2Kg 4:29 and lay my staff upon the face of the child. 12
31 and laid the staff upon the face of the child 12
8:15 dipped it in water and spread it over his face 12
9:32 he lifted up his face to the window, and said 12
37 shall be as dung upon the face of the field 12
12:17 Haz'ael set his face to go up against Jerusalem 12
14: 8 saying, "Come let us look one another in the face. 12
20: 2 Hezeki'ah turned his face to the wall, and prayed 12
1Ch 12: 8 whose faces were like the faces of lions 12
8 whose faces were like the faces of lions 12
21:16 clothed in sackcloth, fell upon their faces. 12
21 did obeisance to David with his face to the ground 3
2Ch 3:13 cherubim stood on their feet, facing the nave. 14
4: 4 It stood upon twelve oxen, three facing north 11
4 It stood upon twelve oxen . . three facing west 11
4 It stood upon twelve oxen . . three facing south 11
4 stood upon twelve oxen . . and three facing east; 11
6:42 do not turn away the face of thy anointed one! 12
7: 3 they bowed down with their faces to the earth 3
14 if my people . . and pray and seek my face 12
18:34 in his chariot facing the Syrians until evening; 8
20:18 bowed his head with his face to the ground 3
25:17 Come, let us look one another in the face. 12
29: 6 turned away their faces from the habitation 12
30: 9 will not turn away his face from you, if you return 12
32:21 returned with shame of face to his own land. 12
Ezr 9: 6 O my God, I am ashamed and blush to lift my face 12
Neh 2: 2 Why is your face sad, seeing you are not sick? 12
3 Why should not my face be sad, when the city 12
8: 3 read from it facing the square before the Water 4
6 worshiped the LORD . . faces to the ground. 3
Est 1:14 the seven princes of . . who saw the king's face 12
7: 8 As the words left . . they covered Haman's face. 12
9:26 because of . . and of what they had faced in this 15
Job 1:11 he will curse thee to thy face. 12
2: 5 he will curse thee to thy face. 12
4:15 A spirit glided past my face; 12
6:28 look at me; for I will not lie to your face. 12
9:24 he covers the faces of its judges– 12
11:15 then you will lift up your face without blemish; 12
13:15 yet I will defend my ways to his face. 12
20 I will not hide myself from thy face 12
24 Why dost thou hide thy face 12
15:27 because he has covered his face with his fat 12
16: 8 risen up against me, it testifies to my face. 12
16 My face is red with weeping 12
21:31 Who declares his way to his face 12
22:26 in the Almighty, and lift up your face to God. 12
23:17 by darkness, and thick darkness covers my face. 12
24:15 No eye will see me'; and he disguises his face. 12
18 swiftly carried away upon the face of the waters; 12
26: 9 He covers the face of the moon 12

10 described a circle upon the face of the waters 12
31:23 I could not have faced his majesty. •
34:29 When he hides his face, who can behold him 12
37:12 on the face of the habitable world. 12
38:30 the face of the deep is frozen. 12
40:13 bind their faces in the world below. 12
41:14 Who can open the doors of his face? 12
Ps 10:11 he has hidden his face, he will never see it. 12
11: 7 the upright shall behold his face. 12
13: 1 How long wilt thou hide thy face from me? 12
17:15 for me, I shall behold thy face in righteousness; 12
21:12 you will aim at their faces with your bows. 12
22:24 he has not hid his face from him, but has heard 12
24: 6 who seek him, who seek the face of the God of Jacob. 12
27: 8 Thou hast said, "Seek ye my face. 12
8 My heart says to thee, "Thy face, LORD, do I seek. 12
9 Hide not thy face from me. 12
30: 7 thou didst hide thy face, I was dismayed. 12
31:16 Let thy face shine on thy servant; 12
34: 5 be radiant; so your faces shall never be ashamed. 12
16 The face of the LORD is against evildoers 12
42: 2 When shall I come and behold the face of God? 12
44:15 shame has covered my face 12
24 Why dost thou hide thy face? 12
51: 9 Hide thy face from my sins 12
67: 1 and bless us and make his face to shine upon us 12
69: 7 shame has covered my face. 12
17 Hide not thy face from thy servant; 12
80: 3 let thy face shine, that we may be saved! 12
7 let thy face shine, that we may be saved! 12
19 let thy face shine, that we may be saved! 12
83:16 Fill their faces with shame, that they may seek 12
84: 9 look upon the face of thine anointed! 12
88:14 Why dost thou hide thy face from me? 12
102: 2 not hide thy face from me in the day of my distress! 12
104:15 oil to make his face shine 12
29 When thou hidest thy face, they are dismayed; 12
30 thou renewest the face of the ground. 12
119:135 Make thy face shine upon thy servant, and teach me 12
132:10 do not turn away the face of thy anointed one. 12
143: 7 Hide not thy face from me, lest I be like those 12
Prv 7:13 with impudent face she says to him 12
8:27 when he drew a circle on the face of the deep 12
16:15 In the light of a king's face there is life 12
17:24 understanding sets his face toward wisdom 12
21:29 A wicked man puts on a bold face 12
27:19 As in water face answers to face, so the mind of man 12
19 As in water face answers to face, so the mind of man 12
Ecc 8: 1 A man's wisdom makes his face shine 12
Sng 2:14 let me see your face, let me hear your voice 6
14 your voice is sweet, and your face is comely. 6
Isa 3:15 by crushing . . by grinding the face of the poor? 12
6: 2 each had six wings: with two he covered his face 12
8:17 LORD . . hiding his face from the house of Jacob 12
21 curse . . their God, and turn their faces upward; •
13: 8 look aghast . . their faces will be aflame. 12
14:21 and fill the face of the world with cities. 12
23:17 kingdoms of the world upon the face of the earth. 12
25: 8 the Lord GOD will wipe away tears from all faces 12
29:22 no more shall his face grow pale. 12
38: 2 Then Hezeki'ah turned his face to the wall 12
49:23 their faces to the ground they shall bow down 3
50: 6 I hid not my face from shame and spitting. 12
7 therefore I have set my face like a flint 12
53: 3 from whom men hide their faces he was despised 12
54: 8 In . . wrath for a moment I hid my face from you 12
57:17 angry, I smote him, I hid my face and was angry; •
59: 2 hid his face from you so that he does not hear. 12
64: 7 hast hid thy face from us, and hast delivered us 12
65: 3 a people who provoke me to my face continually 12
Jer 1:13 I see a boiling pot, facing away from the north. 12
2:27 turned their back to me, and not their face. 12
5: 3 They have made their faces harder than rock; 12
13:26 I myself will lift up your skirts over your face 12
17:16 that which came out of my lips was before thy face. 12
18:17 I will show them my back, not my face 12
21:10 For I have set my face against this city for evil 12
25:26 kingdoms . . which are on the face of the earth. 12
28:16 I will remove you from the face of the earth. 12
30: 6 Why has every face turned pale? 12
32: 4 and shall speak with him face to face 10
4 and shall speak with him face to face 10
33 have turned to me their back and not their face; 12
33: 5 for I have hidden my face from this city 12
34: 3 see . . eye to eye and speak with him face to face; 10
3 see . . eye to eye and speak with him face to face; 10
42:15 If you set your faces to enter Egypt 12
17 All the men who set their faces to go to Egypt 12
44:11 Behold, I will set my face against you for evil 12
12 the remnant of Judah who have set their faces 12
50: 5 the way to Zion, with faces turned toward it 12
51:51 dishonor has covered our face 12
Lam 1: 8 yea, she herself groans, and turns her face away. •
2: 3 withdrawn . . right hand in the face of the enemy; 12
Ezk 1: 6 but each had four faces 12
8 And the four had their faces and their wings thus 12
10 As for the likeness of their faces 12
10 each had the face of a man in front; 12
10 the four had the face of a lion on the right side 12
10 the four had the face of an ox on the left side 12
10 and the four had the face of an eagle at the back. 12
11 Such were their faces. 12
28 And when I saw it, I fell upon my face 12
3: 8 I have made your face hard against their faces 12
8 I have made your face hard against their faces 12
23 and I fell on my face. 12
4: 3 set your face toward it 12
7 you shall set your face toward the siege 12
6: 2 set your face toward the mountains of Israel 12
7:18 horror covers them; shame is upon all faces 12
22 I will turn my face from them 12
8: 3 gateway of the inner court that faces north 11
16 their faces toward the east, worshiping the sun 12
9: 2 direction of the upper gate, which faces north 11
8 I fell upon my face, and cried, "Ah Lord GOD! 12
10:11 but in whatever direction the front wheel faced 11
14 every one had four faces 12
14 faces: the first face was the face of the cherub 12
14 faces: the first face was the face of the cherub 12
14 and the second face was the face of a man 12
14 and the second face was the face of a man 12
14 and the third the face of a lion 12
14 and the fourth the face of an eagle. 12
21 Each had four faces, and each four wings 12
22 as for the likeness of their faces 12
22 the very faces whose appearance I had seen 12
11: 1 gate of the house of the LORD, which faces east. 11
13 fell down upon my face, and cried with a loud voice 12
12: 6 you shall cover your face, that you may not see 12
12 he shall cover his face, that he may not see 12
13:17 son of man, set your face against the daughters 12
14: 3 and set . . their iniquity before their faces; 12
4 stumbling block of his iniquity before his face 12
6 turn away your faces from all your abominations. 12
7 stumbling block of his iniquity before his face 12
8 I will set my face against that man 12
15: 7 I am the LORD, when I set my face against them. 12
7 I will set my face against them; 12
20:35 I will enter into judgment with you face to face. 12
35 I will enter into judgment with you face to face. 12
46 Son of man, set your face toward the south 12
47 all faces from south to north shall be scorched 12
21: 2 Son of man, set your face toward Jerusalem 12
25: 2 Son of man, set your face toward the Ammonites 12
27:35 are horribly afraid, their faces are convulsed. 12
28:21 Son of man, set your face toward Sidon 12
29: 2 set your face against Pharaoh king of Egypt 12
34: 6 were scattered over all the face of the earth 12
35: 2 Son of man, set your face against Mount Se'ir 12
38: 2 set your face toward Gog, of the land of Magog 12
20 all the men that are upon the face of the earth 12
39:14 bury those remaining upon the face of the land 12
23 I hid my face from them and gave them into the hand 12
24 and hid my face from them. 12
29 I will not hide my face any more from them 12
40: 6 Then he went into the gateway facing east 12
20 there was a gate which faced toward the north 12
22 as those of the gate which faced toward the east; 12
31 Its vestibule faced the outer court 1
34 Its vestibule faced the outer court •
37 Its vestibule faced the outer court •
44 one at the side of the north gate facing south 13
44 at the side of the south gate facing north. 13
45 chamber which faces south is for the priests 13
46 the chamber which faces north is for the priests 13
41:12 The building that was facing the temple yard 2
15 the length of the building facing the yard 2
18 Every cherub had two faces 12
19 face of a man toward the palm tree on the one side 12
19 the face of a young lion toward the palm tree 12
42: 3 facing the pavement which belonged to the outer 7
15 he led me out by the gate which faced east 12
43: 1 he brought me to the gate, the gate facing east. 11
3 I fell upon my face. 12
4 LORD entered the temple by the gate facing east 12
17 The steps of the altar shall face east. 11
44: 1 the sanctuary, which faces east; and it was shut. 11
4 I fell upon my face. 12
46: 1 The gate of the inner court that faces east 11
12 the gate facing east shall be opened for him 11
47: 1 temple toward the east (for the temple faced east); 12
2 to the outer gate, that faces toward the east 11
Dan 2:46 Then King Nebuchadnez'zar fell upon his face 16
3:19 expression of his face was changed against 16
8: 5 he-goat came . . across the face of the whole earth 12
17 came, I was frightened and fell upon my face. 12
18 fell into a deep sleep with my face to the ground; 12
9: 3 Then I turned my face to the Lord God, seeking him 12
7 but to us confusion of face, as at this day 12
8 To us, O Lord, belongs confusion of face 12
17 cause thy face to shine upon thy sanctuary 12
10: 6 his face like the appearance of lightning 12
9 I fell on my face in a deep sleep with my face 12
9 deep sleep with my face to the ground. 12
15 turned my face toward the ground and was dumb. 12
11:17 set his face to come with the strength 12
18 shall turn his face to the coastlands 12
19 shall turn his face back toward the fortresses 12
Hos 2: 2 that she put away her harlotry from her face 12
5: 5 The pride of Israel testifies to his face; 12
15 they acknowledge their guilt and seek my face 12
7: 2 Now their deeds . . they are before my face. 12
10: 7 perish, like a chip on the face of the waters. 12
Jol 2: 6 peoples are in anguish, all faces grow pale. 12
Mic 3: 4 he will hide his face from them at that time 12
Nah 2:10 anguish is on all loins, all faces grow pale! 12
3: 5 and will lift up your skirts over your face; 12
Zep 1: 2 sweep away everything from the face of the earth 12
3 I will cut off mankind from the face of the earth 12
Zec 5: 3 that goes out over the face of the whole land; 12
Mal 2: 3 will rebuke . . and spread dung upon your faces 12
Mat 6:16 the hypocrites, for they disfigure their faces 27
17 when you fast, anoint your head and wash your face 27
11:10 'Behold, I send my messenger before thy face 27
17: 2 and his face shone like the sun 27
6 they fell on their faces 27
18:10 the face of my Father who is in heaven. 27
26:39 going a little farther he fell on his face 27
67 Then they spat in his face, and struck him 27
Mrk 1: 2 Behold, I send my messenger before thy face 27
14:65 to cover his face, and to strike him, saying to him 27
15:39 when the centurion, who stood facing him, saw 20
Lke 5:12 he fell on his face and besought him 27
7:27 Behold, I send my messenger before thy face 27
9:51 he set his face to go to Jerusalem. 27
53 because his face was set toward Jerusalem. 27
17:16 he fell on his face at Jesus' feet 27
21:35 all who dwell upon the face of the whole earth; 27
24: 5 bowed their faces to the ground 27
Joh 11:44 his face wrapped with a cloth 25
Act 6:15 his face was like the face of an angel. 27
15 his face was like the face of an angel. 27
17:26 to live on all the face of the earth 27
20:25 all you . . will see my face no more. 27
38 that they should see his face no more 27
27:15 the ship was caught and could not face the wind 17
1Co 13:12 now we see in a mirror dimly, but then face to face. 27
12 now we see in a mirror dimly, but then face to face. 27
14:25 and so, falling on his face, he will worship God 27
2Co 3: 7 Israelites could not look at Moses' face 27
13 not like Moses, who put a veil over his face 27
18 we all, with unveiled face 27
4: 6 the glory of God in the face of Christ. 27
11:20 if a man . . puts on airs, or strikes you in the face. 27
Gal 2:11 I opposed him to his face 27
Php 4:12 I have learned the secret of facing plenty and hunger •
Col 2: 1 for all who have not seen my face 27
1Th 2: 2 in the face of great opposition. •
Jas 1:23 a man who observes his natural face in a mirror; 27
1Pe 3:12 the face of the Lord is against those that do evil 27
2Jn 1:12 I hope to . . talk with you face to face 28
12 I hope to . . talk with you face to face 28
3Jn 1:14 and we will talk together face to face. 28
14 and we will talk together face to face. 28
Rev 1:16 face was like the sun shining in full strength 25
4: 7 the third living creature with the face of a man 27
6:16 and hide us from the face of him who is seated 27
7:11 they fell on their faces before the throne 27
9: 7 their faces were like human faces 27
7 their faces were like human faces 27
10: 1 his face was like the sun, and his legs like 27
11:16 elders . . fell on their faces and worshiped God 27
22: 4 they shall see his face 27
1Es 4:24 he faces lions, and he walks in darkness 22
58 he lifted up his face to heaven toward Jerusalem 27
8:74 I am ashamed and confounded before thy face. 27
2Es 1:31 When you offer oblations to me, I will turn my face 30
4:11 When I heard this, I fell on my face ‡
5:16 Where have you been? And why is your face sad? 31
7:97 how their face is to shine like the sun 31
98 for they hasten to behold the face of him 31
125 the faces of those who practiced self-control 30
125 but our faces shall be blacker than darkness? 30
10:25 behold, her face suddenly shone exceedingly 30
12: 7 if my prayer has indeed come up before thy face 30
13: 3 wherever he turned his face to look 31
38 will reproach them to their face 29
15:54 Trick out the beauty of your face! 31
16:50 and shall accuse her to her face 30
Tob 2: 9 my face was uncovered. 27
3: 6 do not turn thy face away from me. 27
12 I have turned my eyes and my face toward thee. 27
4: 4 she faced many dangers for you 24
7 Do not turn your face away from any poor man 27
7 the face of God will not be turned away from you. 27
12:16 they fell upon their faces, for they were afraid. 27
13: 6 he will turn to you and will not hide his face 27
Jdt 2: 7 will cover the whole face of the earth 27
19 cover the whole face of the earth to the west 27
4: 6 Betomesthaim, which faces Esdraelon 18
6: 3 destroy them from the face of the earth 27
5 you shall not see my face again from this day 27
19 the faces of those who are consecrated to thee. 27
7: 3 from Bethulia to Cyamon, which faces Esdraelon. 18
4 These men will now lick up the face of the whole land 27
18 covered the whole face of the land 27

8: 7 had a very lovely face 25
9: 1 Then Judith fell upon her face 27
10: 7 and noted how her face was altered 27
14 heard her words, and observed her face 27
23 they all marveled at the beauty of her face 27
11:21 either for beauty of face or wisdom of speech! 27
13:16 was my face that tricked him to his destruction 27
14: 6 he fell down on his face and his spirit failed him. 27
16: 8 She anointed her face with ointment 27
AEs 15: 7 Lifting his face, flushed with splendor 27
Wis 4:20 will convict them to their face. 20
10: 5 in the face of his compassion for his child. 21
17: 4 dismal phantoms with gloomy faces appeared. 27
Sir 4: 4 nor turn your face away from the poor. 27
13:26 The mark of a happy heart is a cheerful face 27
14: 8 he averts his face and disregards people. 27
18:24 moment of vengeance when he turns away his face. 27
19:27 He hides his face and pretends not to hear 27
29 a sensible man is known by his face 27
25:17 darkens her face like that of a bear. 27
23 A dejected mind, a gloomy face, and a wounded heart 27
26: 4 at all times his face is cheerful. 27
17 so is a beautiful face on a stately figure. 27
31:13 Therefore it sheds tears from every face. 27
34: 3 the likeness of a face confronting a face. 27
3 the likeness of a face confronting a face. 27
35: 9 With every gift show a cheerful face 27
37: 5 in the face of battle take up the shield. 19
38: 8 from him health is upon the face of the earth. 27
50:17 fell to the ground upon their faces 27
Bar 1:15 confusion of face, as at this day, to us, to the men 27
2: 6 confusion of face to us and our fathers 27
LJr 1:13 their faces are wiped 27
21 when their faces have been blackened 27
Aza 1:18 we fear thee and seek thy face. 27
1Mc 4:40 They fell face down on the ground 27
55 All the people fell on their faces and worshiped 27
61 a stronghold that faced Idumea. 23
7: 3 Do not let me see their faces! 27
13:13 Simon encamped in Adida, facing the plain. 23
2Mc 3:16 his face and the change in his color 25
7: 6 which bore witness against the people to their faces 27
3Mc 2: 1 the high priest Simon, facing the sanctuary 20
5:33 his eyes wavered and his face fell. 27
6:15 and have not turned your face from us 27
18 revealed his holy face 27
4Mc 6:11 with his face bathed in sweat 27
24 he was so courageous in the face of the afflictions 26
14: 1 they encouraged them to face the torture 21

face about 1. סבב פָּנִים
1Kg 8:14 king faced about, and blessed all the assembly 1
2Ch 6: 3 king faced about, and blessed all the assembly 1

face downward 1. לִפְנֵי
1Sm 5: 3 Dagon had fallen face downward on the ground 1
4 Dagon had fallen face downward . . before the ark 1

face one another 1. ראה פָּנִים
2Kg 14:11 he and Amazi'ah . . faced one another in battle 1
2Ch 25:21 he and Amazi'ah king of Judah faced one another 1

face to face 1. ἐξ ἐναντίας 2. κατὰ πρόσωπον 3. πρόσωπον
Act 25:16 before the accused met the accusers face to face 2
2Co 10: 1 who am humble when face to face with you 2
1Th 2:17 we endeavored . . to see you face to face; 3
3:10 we may see you face to face 3
Sir 31: 6 their destruction has met them face to face. 2
45: 5 gave him the commandments face to face 2
1Mc 7:28 I shall come . . to see you face to face in peace. 3
11:68 they themselves met him face to face. 1

facet 1. עַיִן
Zec 3: 9 upon a single stone with seven facets 1

fact 1. בְּ 2. ἀσφαλής 3. γάρ 4. γέ τοι 5. καίπερ 6. καίτοι 7. νυνί 8. ὅτι 9. πρᾶγμα 10. σαφής
1Sm 24:11 by the fact that I cut off the skirt 1
Mat 16: 8 why do you discuss among yourselves the fact that 8
Mrk 8:17 Why do you discuss the fact that you have no bread? •
Act 13:34 as for the fact that he raised him from the dead 8
21:34 as he could not learn the facts 2
1Co 15:20 in fact Christ has been raised from the dead 7
2Pe 3: 5 They deliberately ignore this fact •
8 do not ignore this one fact, beloved •
Sus 1:48 condemned . . without learning the facts? 10
2Mc 3: 8 in fact to carry out the king's purpose. 9
4:17 a fact which later events will make clear. •
6:13 In fact, not to let the impious alone for long 3
13:25 in fact they were so angry 3
3Mc 5:32 In fact you would have been deprived of life 5
4Mc 2: 6 In fact, since the law has told us not to covet 6
6:11 in fact . . he amazed even his torturers 4
13: 3 in fact it was not so. 7
17:20 the fact that . . our enemies did not rule •
fact *See also* if, misrepresent.

faction 1. αἵρεσις
1Co 11:19 for there must be factions among you 1

factious 1. αἱρετικός 2. ἐριθεία
Rom 2: 8 those who are factious and do not obey the truth 2
Tit 3:10 As for a man who is factious 1

factor
4Mc 15:11 though so many factors influenced the mother •

faculty 1. αἰσθητήριον
Heb 5:14 their faculties trained by practice 1

fade 1. אמל 2. בלל 3. כלה 4. מלל 5. נבל 6. קפץ 7. ἀλλοιόω 8. καταργέω
Job 7: 9 As the cloud fades and vanishes 3
24:24 they wither and fade like the mallow; 6
Ps 37: 2 For they will soon fade like the grass, and wither 4
90: 6 in the evening it fades and withers. 4
Isa 28: 1 to the fading flower of its glorious beauty 5
4 the fading flower of its glorious beauty 5
40: 7 The grass withers, the flower fades 5
8 The grass withers, the flower fades; 5
64: 6 We all fade like a leaf, and our iniquities, 2
Nah 1: 4 the bloom of Lebanon fades. 1
2Co 3: 7 because of its brightness, fading as this was 8
13 see the end of the fading splendor. 8
1Mc 1:26 the beauty of women faded. 7

fade away 1. καταργέω 2. μαραίνω
2Co 3:11 For if what faded away came with splendor 1
Jas 1:11 So will the rich man fade away 2

fail 1. אבד 2. אזל 3. אַיִן 4. געל 5. חדל 6. חסר 7. יבש 8. יצא 9. כהה 10. כזב 11. כחש 12. כלה 13. כִּלָּיוֹן 14. כרת 15. כשל 16. לֹא אמן 17. נפל 18. נשת 19. עבר 20. עדר 21. עזב 22. פרר 23. רפה 24. תמם 25. שָׁלוּ (A) 26. ἀδιάπτωτος 27. ἀδόκιμος 28. ἀνέκλειπτος 29. ἀνίημι 30. ἀσθενέω 31. ἀσθένημα 32. διαπίπτω 33. διασφάλλω 34. ἐγκαταλείπω 35. ἐκλείπω 36. ἐκλύω 37. ἐκπίπτω 38. ἐλασσόω 39. ἐπιλείπω 40. καταλύω 41. μή 42. ὀλιγοψύχω 43. οὐ 44. πίπτω 45. πταίω 46. ὑστερέω 47. deficio 48. excedo 49. lapsus 50. vanus facio
Gen 42:28 At this their hearts failed them 8
Deu 4:31 LORD . . will not fail you or destroy you 23
28:32 eyes . . fail with longing for them all the day; 12
65 LORD will give you there . . failing eyes 13
31: 6 LORD . . will not fail you or forsake you. 23
8 LORD . . will not fail you or forsake you; 23
Jos 1: 5 be with you; I will not fail you or forsake you. 23
21:45 Not one of all the good promises . . had failed; 17
23:14 not one thing has failed of all the good things 17
14 all have come . . not one of them has failed. 17
1Sm 17:32 Let no man's heart fail because of him; 17
20: 5 and I should not fail to sit at table with the king; •
2Sm 4: 1 his courage failed, and all Israel was dismayed. 23
1Kg 2: 4 there shall not fail you a man on the throne 14
8:25 There shall never fail you a man before me to sit 14
56 not one word has failed of all his good promise 17
9: 5 There shall not fail you a man upon the throne 14
17:14 not be spent, and the cruse of oil shall not fail 6
16 neither did the cruse of oil fail 6
1Ch 28:20 He will not fail you or forsake you, 23
2Ch 6:16 'There shall never fail you a man before me to sit 14
7:18 'There shall not fail you a man to rule Israel.' 14
Ezr 6: 9 let that be given to them day by day without fail 25
Neh 4:10 The strength of the burden-bearers is failing 15
Est 9:27 that without fail they would keep these two days 19
Job 11:20 But the eyes of the wicked will fail; 12
14:11 As waters fail from a lake, and a river wastes away 2
17: 5 the eyes of his children will fail. 12
19:14 My kinsfolk and my close friends have failed me; 5
21:10 Their bull breeds without fail; their cow calves 4
Ps 31:10 my strength fails because of my misery 15
38:10 My heart throbs, my strength fails me; 21
40:12 my heart fails me. 21
73:26 My flesh and my heart may fail 12
119:82 My eyes fail with watching for thy promise; 12
123 My eyes fail with watching for thy salvation 12
143: 7 Make haste to answer me, O LORD! My spirit fails! 12
Prv 22: 8 rod of his fury will fail. 12
Ecc 12: 5 grasshopper drags itself along and desire fails; 22
Sng 5: 6 My soul failed me when he spoke. 8
Isa 15: 6 the grass is withered, the new growth fails 12
32:10 the vintage will fail, the fruit harvest will not 12
42: 4 He will not fail or be discouraged 9
44:12 he becomes hungry and his strength fails 3
51:14 go down to the Pit, neither shall his bread fail. 6
58:11 like a spring of water, whose waters fail not. 10
Jer 4: 9 courage shall fail both king and princes; 1
14: 6 their eyes fail because there is no herbage. 12
15:18 like a deceitful brook, like waters that fail? 16
51:30 strength has failed, they have become women; 18
Lam 4:17 Our eyes failed, ever watching vainly for help; 12
Ezk 47:12 leaves will not wither nor their fruit fail 24
Dan 11:14 order to fulfil the vision; but they shall fail. 15
Hos 9: 2 and the new wine shall fail them. 11
Jol 1:10 because the grain is destroyed, the wine fails 7
12 and gladness fails from the sons of men. 7
17 are ruined because the grain has failed. 7
Hab 2: 4 he whose soul is not upright in him shall fail •
3:17 Though . . the produce of the olive fail 11
Zep 3: 5 each dawn he does not fail; 20
Mat 16:11 How is it that you fail to perceive 43
Lke 12:33 with a treasure in the heavens that does not fail 28
16: 9 so that when it fails they may receive you 35
22:32 I have prayed for you that your faith may not fail; 35
23:45 while the sun's light failed 35
Joh 2: 3 When the wine failed, the mother of Jesus said 46
Act 5:38 if this plan . . is of men, it will fail; 40
Rom 9: 6 But it is not as though the word of God had failed. 37
11: 7 Israel failed to obtain what it sought. 43
15: 1 ought to bear with the failings of the weak 31
2Co 13: 6 I hope you will find out that we have not failed. 27
7 though we may seem to have failed. 27
Heb 4: 6 failed to enter because of disobedience 43
11:32 time would fail me to tell of Gideon, Barak, Samson 39
13: 5 he has said, "I will never fail you nor forsake you. 29
Jas 2:10 whoever . . fails in one point has become guilty 45
4:17 knows what is right to do and fails to do it 41
2Es 2:32 and my grace will not fail. 47
3:29 And my heart failed me 48
5:53 the time of old age, when the womb is failing.' 47
7:120 but we have miserably failed? 50
8:17 I see the failings of us who dwell in the land 49
15:13 because their seed shall fail 47
Jdt 6: 9 I have spoken and none of my words shall fail. 32
7:19 their courage failed 42
14: 6 he fell down on his face and his spirit failed him. 36
Wis 3:15 the root of understanding does not fail. 26
13: 9 how did they fail to find sooner the Lord 43
19:21 Flames . . failed to consume the flesh 43
Sir 2: 8 trust in him, and your reward will not fail; 45
7:34 Do not fail those who weep 46
17:24 encourages those whose endurance is failing. 35
31 Yet its light fails 35
19: 1 will fail little by little. 44
29:14 will fail him. 34
34: 7 those who put their hope in them have failed. 37
37:12 who will sorrow with you if you fail. 45
40:14 likewise transgressors will utterly fail. 35
41: 2 one who is in need and is failing in strength 38
Bar 2:18 and feeble, and the eyes that are failing 35
LJr 1:49 How then can one fail to see 43
52 Who then can fail to know that they are not gods? •
1Mc 6:22 How long will you fail to do justice 43
11:49 their courage failed 30
3Mc 5:12 he quite failed in his lawless purpose 33
4Mc 13: 5 How then can one fail to confess 43
fail *See also* likely.

cause to fail 1. כלה 2. כשל
Job 31:16 or have caused the eyes of the widow to fail 1
Lam 1:14 he caused my strength to fail; the Lord gave me 2

fail to achieve 1. ἀποπίπτω
Jdt 11: 6 my lord will not fail to achieve his purposes. 1

fail to bear 1. שכל
Mal 3:11 your vine in the field shall not fail to bear 1

fail to fulfill 1. παρέρχομαι
AEs 10: 5 none of them has failed to be fulfilled. 1

fail to know 1. ἀγνοέω
Wis 15:11 because he failed to know the one who formed him 1

fail to meet the test 1. ἀδόκιμος
2Co 13: 5 unless indeed you fail to meet the test! 1

fail to obtain 1. ὑστερέω
Heb 12:15 no one fail to obtain the grace of God 1

fail to reach 1. ὑστερέω
Heb 4: 1 lest any . . be judged to have failed to reach it. 1

fail to share 1. ἄμοιρος
Wis 2: 9 Let none of us fail to share in our revelry 1

fail utterly 1. excedo
2Es 4: 2 Your understanding has utterly failed 1

without fail
Jos 3:10 he will without fail drive out . . the Canaanites †

failure 1. אַיִן 2. ἥττημα 3. σφάλλω
Ps 144:14 suffering no mischance or failure in bearing; 1
Rom 11:12 if their failure means riches for the Gentiles 2
Wis 10: 8 their failures could never go unnoticed. 3

faint 1. דָּוֶה 2. דַּוָּי 3. חלה 4. יעף 5. יָעֵף 6. כהה 7. כֵּהֶה 8. כלה 9. כמה 10. מסס 11. עטף 12. עיף

13. עִיף 14. עלף 15. פוג 16. רכך 17. רפה
18. ἀποψύχω 19. ἐκλείπω 20. ἔκλυσις 21. ἐκλύω
22. ἐν ἐκλύσει 23. ὀλιγοψύχω 24. παρίημι 25. deficio

Gen 45:26 And his heart fainted, for he did not believe 15
Deu 20: 3 let not your heart faint; do not fear, or tremble 16
25:18 attacked you . . when you were faint and weary 13
Jdg 8: 4 300 men who were with him, faint yet pursuing. 13
5 for they are faint, and I am pursuing after Zebah 13
15 we should give bread to your men who are faint?' 5
1Sm 14:28 And the people were faint. 4
31 And the people were very faint; 4
2Sm 16: 2 the wine for those who faint in the wilderness 4
Job 19:27 not another. My heart faints within me! 8
Ps 61: 2 I call to thee, when my heart is faint. 11
63: 1 my flesh faints for thee, as in a dry and weary land 9
77: 3 I moan; I meditate, and my spirit faints. 11
84: 2 soul longs, yea, faints for the courts of the LORD; 8
102: 0 when he is faint and pours out his complaint 11
107: 5 hungry and thirsty, their soul fainted within 11
142: 3 When my spirit is faint, thou knowest my way! 11
143: 4 Therefore my spirit faints within me; 11
Prv 24:10 If you faint in the day of adversity 17
Isa 1: 5 The whole head is sick, and the whole heart faint. 2
7: 4 do not fear, and do not let your heart be faint 16
29: 8 dreams he is drinking and awakes faint 13
40:28 He does not faint or grow weary 4
29 He gives power to the faint 4
30 Even youths shall faint and be weary 4
31 not be weary, they shall walk and not faint. 4
44:12 strength fails, he drinks no water and is faint. 4
51:20 Your sons have fainted, they lie at the head 14
57:10 you found new life . . and so you were not faint. 3
61: 3 the mantle of praise instead of a faint spirit; 7
Jer 4:31 Woe is me! I am fainting before murderers. 12
51:46 Let not your heart faint, and be not fearful 16
Lam 1:13 he has left me stunned, faint all the day long. 1
22 for my groans are many and my heart is faint. 2
2:11 infants and babes faint in the streets 11
12 as they faint like wounded men in the streets 11
19 children, who faint for hunger . . every street. 11
Ezk 21: 7 all hands will be feeble, every spirit will faint 6
31:15 the trees of the field shall faint because of it. 14
Ams 8:13 the young men shall faint for thirst. 14
Jon 2: 7 my soul fainted within me, I remembered the LORD; 11
4: 8 he was faint; and he asked that he might die 14
Nah 2:10 Hearts faint and knees tremble 10
Mat 15:32 lest they faint on the way. 21
Mrk 8: 3 they will faint on the way 21
Lke 21:26 men fainting with fear and with foreboding 18
2Es 5:14 and my soul was so troubled that it fainted. 25
Jdt 7:22 the women and young men fainted from thirst 19
8: 9 because they were faint for lack of water 23
31 we will no longer be faint. 19
AEs 15: 7 the queen faltered, and turned pale and faint 22
15 as she was speaking, she fell fainting. 20
Sir 2:13 Woe to the faint heart, for it has no trust! 24
1Mc 3:17 we are faint, for we have eaten nothing today. 21
2Mc 3:24 became faint with terror. 20

faint *See also* make.

become faint 1. ἀσθενέω 2. ἐκλύω

1Mc 1:26 maidens and young men became faint 1
9: 8 He became faint, but he said to those who were left 2

fainthearted 1. מוג 2. רַךְ הַלֵּב 3. δειλός
4. δειλόψυχος 5. ὀλιγόψυχος 6. ὀλιγοψυχέω

Deu 20: 8 What man . . is fearful and fainthearted? 2
Jos 2:24 all the inhabitants of the land are fainthearted 1
1Th 5:14 encourage the fainthearted, help the weak 5
Sir 4: 9 do not be fainthearted in judging a case. 6
7:10 Do not be fainthearted in your prayer 6
1Mc 3:56 were planting vineyards, or were fainthearted 3
4Mc 16: 5 If this woman . . had been fainthearted 4

faintness 1. מֹרֶךְ

Lev 26:36 I will send faintness into their hearts 1

fair 1. חֵן 2. טוב 3. טוֹב 4. יפה 5. יָפֶה 6. יְפִי
7. שִׁפְרָה 8. תִּפְאָרָה 9. שַׁפִּיר (A) 10. καλός

Gen 6: 2 that the daughters of men were fair; 3
24:16 The maiden was very fair to look upon 3
26: 7 of Rebekah"; because she was fair to look upon. 3
Num24: 5 how fair are your tents, O Jacob 2
Jdg 15: 2 Is not her younger sister fairer than she? 3
1Kg 20: 3 your fairest wives and children also are mine.' 3
Est 1:11 to show . . her beauty; for she was fair to behold 3
Job 26:13 By his wind the heavens were made fair; 7
42:15 there were no women so fair as Job's daughters; 5
Ps 45: 2 You are the fairest of the sons of men; 4
Prv 1: 9 for they are a fair garland for your head 1
4: 9 She will place on your head a fair garland; 1
Sng 1: 8 If you do not know, O fairest among women 5
4: 7 You are all fair, my love; there is no flaw in you. 5
5: 9 What is your beloved . . O fairest among women? 5
6: 1 has your beloved gone, O fairest among women? 5
10 that looks forth like the dawn, fair as the moon 5
7: 6 How fair and pleasant you are, O loved one 4
Jer 11:16 A green olive tree, fair with goodly fruit'; 5
Ezk 16:17 You also took your fair jewels of my gold 8
39 and take your fair jewels, and leave you naked 8
31: 3 a cedar . . with fair branches and forest shade 5
Dan 4:12 Its leaves were fair and its fruit abundant 9
21 whose leaves were fair and its fruit abundant 9
Hos 10:11 and I spared her fair neck; 3
Ams 8:13 the fair virgins and the young men shall faint 5
Zec 9:17 Yea, how good and how fair it shall be! 6
Mat 15:26 It is not fair to take the children's bread 10

fair *See also* weather, word.

fair one 1. יָפָה

Sng 2:10 Arise, my love, my fair one, and come away; 1
13 Arise, my love, my fair one, and come away. 1

fairly 1. ἰσότης

Col 4: 1 Masters, treat your slaves justly and fairly 1

faith 1. אֱמוּנָה 2. אמן 3. אָמֵן 4. אֱמֶת 5. ἐμπιστεύω
6. πιστεύω 7. πίστις 8. πιστός 9. fides

Job 39:12 Do you have faith in him that he will return 2
Ps 78:22 because they had no faith in God 2
106:24 land, having no faith in his promise. 2
146: 6 who keeps faith for ever; 4
Isa 26: 2 righteous nation which keeps faith may enter 3
Hab 2: 4 but the righteous shall live by his faith. 1
Mat 8:10 not even in Israel have I found such faith. 7
9: 2 and when Jesus saw their faith he said 7
22 Take heart, daughter; your faith has made you 7
29 According to your faith be it done to you. 7
15:28 Jesus answered her, "O woman, great is your faith! 7
17:20 if you have faith as a grain of mustard seed 7
21:21 if you have faith and never doubt 7
22 you will receive, if you have faith. 6
23:23 justice and mercy and faith 7
Mrk 2: 5 when Jesus saw their faith 7
4:40 Why are you afraid? Have you no faith? 7
5:34 Daughter, your faith has made you well 7
10:52 Go your way; your faith has made you well 7
11:22 Jesus answered them, "Have faith in God. 7
Lke 5:20 when he saw their faith he said 7
7: 9 not even in Israel have I found such faith. 7
50 Your faith has saved you; go in peace. 7
8:25 He said to them, "Where is your faith? 7
48 Daughter, your faith has made you well 7
17: 5 The apostles said to the Lord, "Increase our faith! 7
6 If you had faith as a grain of mustard seed 7
19 Rise and go your way; your faith has made you well. 7
18: 8 will he find faith on earth? 7
42 Receive your sight; your faith has made you well. 7
22:32 I have prayed for you that your faith may not fail; 7
Act 3:16 by faith in his name 7
16 the faith which is through Jesus 7
6: 5 Stephen, a man full of faith and of the Holy Spirit 7
7 the priests were obedient to the faith. 7
11:24 a good man, full of the Holy Spirit and of faith. 7
13: 8 to turn away the proconsul from the faith. 7
14: 9 and seeing that he had faith to be made well 7
22 exhorting them to continue in the faith 7
27 how he had opened a door of faith to the Gentiles. 7
15: 9 cleansed their hearts by faith. 7
16: 5 So the churches were strengthened in the faith 7
20:21 faith in our Lord Jesus Christ. 7
24:24 and heard him speak upon faith in Christ Jesus. 7
26:18 among those who are sanctified by faith in me.' 7
27:25 I have faith in God 6
Rom 1: 5 to bring about the obedience of faith 7
8 your faith is proclaimed in all the world. 7
12 mutually encouraged by each other's faith 7
16 for salvation to every one who has faith 6
17 revealed through faith for faith; 7
17 revealed through faith for faith; 7
17 He who through faith is righteous shall live. 7
3:22 the righteousness of God through faith in Jesus 7
25 expiation by his blood, to be received by faith. 7
26 and that he justifies him who has faith in Jesus. 7
27 No, but on the principle of faith. 7
28 man is justified by faith apart from works of law. 7
30 the circumcised on the ground of their faith 7
30 and the uncircumcised through their faith. 7
31 Do we then overthrow the law by this faith? 7
4: 5 his faith is reckoned as righteousness. 7
9 faith was reckoned to Abraham as righteousness. 7
11 righteousness which he had by faith 7
12 the faith which our father Abraham had 7
13 but through the righteousness of faith. 7
14 If . . faith is null and the promise is void. 7
16 That is why it depends on faith 7
16 but also to those who share the faith of Abraham 7
19 He did not weaken in faith 7
20 but he grew strong in his faith as he gave glory 7
22 his faith was "reckoned to him as righteousness. •
5: 1 since we are justified by faith, we have peace 7
9:30 attained it . . righteousness through faith; 7
32 Why? Because they did not pursue it through faith 7
10: 4 that every one who has faith may be justified. 6
6 But the righteousness based on faith says 7
8 (that is, the word of faith which we preach); 7
17 So faith comes from what is heard 7
11:20 but you stand fast only through faith. 7
12: 3 the measure of faith which God has assigned him. 7
6 if prophecy, in proportion to our faith; 7
14: 1 As for the man who is weak in faith, welcome him 7
22 The faith . . keep between yourself and God; 7
23 because he does not act from faith; 7
23 for whatever does not proceed from faith is sin. 7
16:26 to bring about the obedience of faith– 7
1Co 2: 5 your faith might not rest in the wisdom of men 7
12: 9 to another faith by the same Spirit 7
13: 2 if I have all faith, so as to remove mountains 7
13 So faith, hope, love abide, these three 7
15:14 and your faith is in vain. 7
17 your faith is futile 7
16:13 Be watchful, stand firm in your faith 7
2Co 1:24 Not that we lord it over your faith 7
24 for you stand firm in your faith. 7
4:13 the same spirit of faith as he had who wrote 7
5: 7 for we walk by faith, not by sight. 7
8: 7 in faith, in utterance, in knowledge 7
10:15 our hope is that as your faith increases 7
13: 5 to see whether you are holding to your faith. 7
Gal 1:23 now preaching the faith he once tried to destroy 7
2:16 through faith in Jesus Christ 7
16 in order to be justified by faith in Christ 6
20 the life I now live in the flesh I live by faith 7
3: 2 by works of the law, or by hearing with faith? 7
5 by works of the law, or by hearing with faith? 7
7 it is men of faith who are the sons of Abraham. 7
8 God would justify the Gentiles by faith 7
9 who are men of faith are blessed with Abraham 7
9 blessed with Abraham who had faith. 8
11 He who through faith is righteous shall live"; 7
12 the law does not rest on faith 7
14 receive the promise of the Spirit through faith 7
22 what was promised to faith in Jesus Christ 7
23 Now before faith came 7
23 until faith should be revealed. 7
24 we might be justified by faith. 7
25 now that faith has come 7
26 you are all sons of God, through faith. 7
5: 5 For through the Spirit, by faith, we wait 7
6 faith working through love. 7
6:10 to those who are of the household of faith. 7
Eph 1:15 have heard of your faith in the Lord Jesus 7
2: 8 For by grace you have been saved through faith; 7
3:12 confidence of access through our faith in him. 7
17 Christ may dwell in your hearts through faith; 7
4: 5 one Lord, one faith, one baptism 7
13 until we all attain to the unity of the faith 7
6:16 besides all these, taking the shield of faith 7
23 Peace be to the brethren, and love with faith 7
Php 1:25 for your progress and joy in the faith 7
27 striving side by side for the faith of the gospel 7
2:17 upon the sacrificial offering of your faith 7
3: 9 that which is through faith in Christ 7
9 righteousness from God that depends on faith 7
Col 1: 4 we have heard of your faith in Christ Jesus 7
23 you continue in the faith, stable and steadfast 7
2: 5 the firmness of your faith in Christ. 7
7 built up in him and established in the faith 7
12 through faith in the working of God 7
1Th 1: 3 work of faith and labor of love 7
8 your faith in God has gone forth everywhere 7
3: 2 to establish you in your faith and to exhort you 7
5 I sent that I might know your faith 7
6 good news of your faith and love 7
7 comforted about you through your faith; 7
10 supply what is lacking in your faith? 7
5: 8 put on the breastplate of faith and love 7
2Th 1: 3 because your faith is growing abundantly 7
4 your steadfastness and faith 7
11 may fulfil every . . work of faith by his power 7
3: 2 not all have faith. 7
1Ti 1: 2 To Timothy, my true child in the faith 7
4 rather than the divine training that is in faith; 7
5 a good conscience and sincere faith. 7
14 the faith and love that are in Christ Jesus. 7
19 holding faith and a good conscience 7
19 certain persons . . made shipwreck of . . faith 7
2: 7 a teacher of the Gentiles in faith and truth. 7
15 if she continues in faith and love and holiness 7
3: 9 they must hold the mystery of the faith 7
13 great confidence in the faith which is in Christ 7
4: 1 in later times some will depart from the faith 7
6 nourished on the words of the faith 7
12 an example in speech and conduct, in love, in faith 7
5: 8 he has disowned the faith 7
6:10 some have wandered away from the faith 7
11 aim at righteousness, godliness, faith, love 7
12 Fight the good fight of the faith 7
21 some have missed the mark as regards the faith. 7
2Ti 1: 5 I am reminded of your sincere faith 7
5 a faith that dwelt first in your grandmother •
13 in the faith and love which are in Christ Jesus; 7
2:18 They are upsetting the faith of some. 7

22 aim at righteousness, faith, love, and peace 7
3: 8 men of corrupt mind and counterfeit faith; 7
10 my aim in life, my faith, my patience, my love 7
15 through faith in Christ Jesus. 7
4: 7 I have finished the race, I have kept the faith. 7
Tit 1: 1 to further the faith of God's elect 7
4 To Titus, my true child in a common faith 7
13 that they may be sound in the faith 7
2: 2 sound in faith, in love, and in steadfastness. 7
3:15 Greet those who love us in the faith 7
Phm 1: 5 the faith which you have toward the Lord Jesus 7
6 the sharing of your faith 7
Heb 4: 2 because it did not meet with faith in the hearers. 7
6: 1 foundation . . of faith toward God 7
12 through faith and patience 7
10:22 in full assurance of faith 7
38 my righteous one shall live by faith 7
39 those who have faith and keep their souls. 7
11: 1 Now faith is the assurance of things hoped for 7
3 By faith we understand . . 7
4 By faith . . a more acceptable sacrifice 7
4 through his faith he is still speaking. •
5 By faith Enoch was taken up 7
6 without faith it is impossible to please him. 7
7 By faith Noah . . took heed 7
7 the righteousness which comes by faith. 7
8 By faith Abraham obeyed 7
9 By faith he sojourned in the land of promise 7
11 By faith Sarah . . received power to conceive 7
13 These all died in faith 7
17 By faith Abraham . . offered up Isaac 7
20 By faith Isaac invoked future blessings 7
21 By faith Jacob . . blessed . . the sons of Joseph 7
22 By faith Joseph . . made mention of the exodus 7
23 By faith Moses . . was hid for three months 7
24 By faith Moses . . refused to be called the son 7
27 By faith he left Egypt 7
28 By faith he kept the Passover 7
29 By faith the people crossed the Red Sea 7
30 By faith the walls of Jericho fell down 7
31 By faith Rahab the harlot did not perish 7
33 who through faith conquered kingdoms 7
39 all these, though well attested by their faith 7
12: 2 Jesus the pioneer and perfecter of our faith 7
13: 7 imitate their faith. 7
Jas 1: 3 testing of your faith produces steadfastness. 7
6 let him ask in faith, with no doubting 7
2: 1 as you hold the faith of our Lord Jesus Christ 7
5 be rich in faith and heirs of the kingdom 7
14 if a man says he has faith but has not works? 7
14 Can his faith save him? 7
17 So faith by itself, if it has no works, is dead. 7
18 some one will say, "You have faith and I have works. 7
18 Show me your faith apart from your works 7
18 and I by my works will show you my faith. 7
20 that faith apart from works is barren? 7
22 You see that faith was active . . with his works 7
22 and faith was completed by works 7
24 justified by works and not by faith alone. 7
26 so faith apart from works is dead. 7
5:15 the prayer of faith will save the sick man 7
1Pe 1: 5 who by God's power are guarded through faith 7
7 the genuineness of your faith . . may redound 7
9 As the outcome of your faith you obtain 7
21 so that your faith and hope are in God. 7
5: 9 Resist him, firm in your faith 7
2Pe 1: 1 obtained a faith of equal standing with ours 7
5 to supplement your faith with virtue 7
1Jn 5: 4 the victory that overcomes the world, our faith. 7
Jde 1: 3 appealing to you to contend for the faith 7
20 build yourselves up on your most holy faith; 7
Rev 2:13 you hold fast my name and you did not deny my faith 7
19 'I know your works, your love and faith and service 7
13:10 a call for the endurance and faith of the saints. 7
14:12 the commandments of God and the faith of Jesus. 7
2Es 5: 1 and the land shall be barren of faith. 9
6: 5 before those who stored up treasures of faith 9
9: 7 on account of the faith by which he has believed 9
13:23 who have works and have faith in the Almighty. 9
Sir 4:16 If he has faith in her he will obtain her 5
40:12 good faith will stand for ever. 7
1Mc 10:27 now continue still to keep faith with us 7
4Mc 15:24 disregarded all these because of faith in God. 7
16:22 You too must have the same faith in God 7
17: 2 showed the courage of your faith! 7

faith *See also* breach, break, commit, keep, man.

good faith 1. אֱמֶת
Jdg 9:15 If in good faith you are anointing me king over 1
16 if you acted in good faith and honor when you made 1
19 if you then have acted in good faith and honor 1

little faith 1. ὀλιγοπιστία 2. ὀλιγόπιστος
Mat 6:30 he not much more clothe you, O men of little faith? 2
8:26 Why are you afraid, O men of little faith? 2
14:31 O man of little faith, why did you doubt? 2
17:20 He said to them, "Because of your little faith. 1

faithful 1. אֵמוּן 2. אֱמוּנָה 3. אמן 4. אֱמֶת 5. בֶּאֱמוּנָה 6. חָסִיד 7. כֵּן 8. אמן (A) 9. πιστός
Deu 7: 9 LORD . . the faithful God who keeps covenant 3
Jdg 5:15 with Deb'orah, and Is'sachar faithful to Barak; 7
1Sm 2:35 And I will raise up for myself a faithful priest 3
22:14 And who among all . . is so faithful as David 3
2Sm 20:19 those who are peaceable and faithful in Israel; 3
2Ch 31:18 for they were faithful in keeping themselves holy. 5
20 he did what was good and right and faithful 4
Neh 7: 2 more faithful and God-fearing man than many. 4
9: 8 thou didst find his heart faithful before thee 3
13:13 appointed . . for they were counted faithful; 3
Ps 12: 1 for the faithful have vanished 3
31: 5 thou hast redeemed me, O LORD, faithful God. 4
23 The LORD preserves the faithful 3
69:13 With thy faithful help 4
78: 8 whose spirit was not faithful to God. 3
101: 6 I will look with favor on the faithful in the land 3
111: 7 The works of his hands are faithful and just; 4
145:13 The LORD is faithful in all his words 3
149: 1 song, his praise in the assembly of the faithful! 6
5 Let the faithful exult in glory; 6
Prv 13:17 but a faithful envoy brings healing. 1
14: 5 A faithful witness does not lie 1
20: 6 but a faithful man who can find? 1
25:13 Like the cold of snow . . is a faithful messenger 3
27: 6 Faithful are the wounds of a friend; 3
28:20 A faithful man will abound with blessings 2
Isa 1:21 How the faithful city has become a harlot 3
26 the city of righteousness, the faithful city. 3
25: 1 plans formed of old, faithful and sure. 2
49: 7 the LORD, who is faithful, the Holy One of Israel 3
Jer 42: 5 May the LORD be a true and faithful witness 3
Dan 6: 4 because he was faithful, and no error or fault 8
Hos 11:12 Judah . . is faithful to the Holy One. 3
Zec 8: 3 Jerusalem shall be called the faithful city 4
Mat 24:45 Who then is the faithful and wise servant 9
25:21 Well done, good and faithful servant 9
21 you have been faithful over a little 9
23 Well done, good and faithful servant 9
23 you have been faithful over a little 9
Lke 12:42 Who then is the faithful and wise steward 9
16:10 He who is faithful in a very little 9
10 is faithful also in much 9
11 not been faithful in the unrighteous mammon 9
12 if you have not been faithful 9
19:17 Because you have been faithful in a very little 9
Act 16:15 If you have judged me to be faithful to the Lord 9
1Co 1: 9 God is faithful, by whom you were called 9
4:17 my beloved and faithful child in the Lord 9
10:13 God is faithful, and he will not let you be tempted 9
2Co 1:18 As surely as God is faithful 9
Eph 1: 1 the saints who are also faithful in Christ Jesus 9
6:21 faithful minister in the Lord 9
Col 1: 2 To the saints and faithful brethren in Christ 9
7 He is a faithful minister of Christ on our behalf 9
4: 7 he is a beloved brother and faithful minister 9
9 Ones'imus, the faithful and beloved brother 9
1Th 5:24 He who calls you is faithful, and he will do it. 9
2Th 3: 3 the Lord is faithful 9
1Ti 1:12 because he judged me faithful 9
3:11 temperate, faithful in all things. 9
2Ti 2: 2 entrust to faithful men 9
13 if we are faithless, he remains faithful 9
Heb 2:17 become a merciful and faithful high priest 9
3: 2 He was faithful to him who appointed him 9
2 just as Moses also was faithful in God's house. •
5 Now Moses was faithful in all God's house 9
6 Christ was faithful over God's house as a son •
10:23 he who promised is faithful; 9
11:11 since she considered him faithful 9
1Pe 4:19 and entrust their souls to a faithful Creator. 9
5:12 Silva'nus, a faithful brother as I regard him 9
1Jn 1: 9 he is faithful and just, and will forgive our sins 9
Rev 1: 5 and from Jesus Christ the faithful witness 9
2:10 Be faithful unto death 9
3:14 words of the Amen, the faithful and true witness 9
17:14 those with him are called the . . faithful 9
19:11 He who sat upon it is called Faithful and True 9
Wis 3: 9 the faithful will abide with him in love 9
Sir 1:14 she is created with the faithful in the womb. 9
6:14 A faithful friend is a sturdy shelter 9
15 nothing so precious as a faithful friend 9
16 A faithful friend is an elixir of life 9
44:20 when he was tested he was found faithful. 9
48:22 who was great and faithful in his vision. 9
1Mc 2:52 Was not Abraham found faithful when tested 9
7: 8 was faithful to the king. 9
2Mc 1: 2 Isaac and Jacob, his faithful servants. 9
3Mc 2:11 indeed you are faithful and true. 9
4Mc 7:15 whom the faithful seal of death has perfected! 9

faithful man 1. πιστός
1Mc 3:13 a body of faithful men who stayed with him 1

more faithful 1. πιστός
Sir 37:13 no one is more faithful to you than it is. 1

faithful one 1. חָסִיד 2. ὁ πιστός
1Sm 2: 9 He will guard the feet of his faithful ones; 1
Ps 50: 5 Gather to me my faithful ones, who made a covenant 1
89:19 thou didst speak in a vision to thy faithful one 1
149: 9 This is glory for all his faithful ones. 1
Rev 2:13 the days of An'tipas my witness, my faithful one 2

remain faithful 1. προσμένω
Act 11:23 he exhorted them all to remain faithful to the Lord 1

faithfully 1. אֱמוּנָה 2. אֱמֶת 3. בֶּאֱמוּנָה 4. בֶּאֱמֶת 5. לֶאֱמֶת 6. ἀραρότως 7. ἐν πίστει 8. πίστις
Jos 2:14 we will deal kindly and faithfully with you 2
1Sm 12:24 and serve him faithfully with all your heart; 4
2Ch 31:12 they faithfully brought in the contributions 3
15 faithfully assisting him in the cities 3
34:12 the men did the work faithfully. 3
Neh 9:33 dealt faithfully and we have acted wickedly; 2
Prv 12:22 but those who act faithfully are his delight. 1
Isa 42: 3 he will faithfully bring forth justice. 5
61: 8 I will faithfully give them their recompense 4
Jer 23:28 let him who has my word speak my word faithfully. 2
Sir 15:15 to act faithfully is a matter of your own choice. 8
3Mc 5: 4 Hermon . . proceeded faithfully to carry out the orders. 6
6:25 those who faithfully have held the fortresses 7

faithfulness 1. אֱמוּנָה 2. אֹמֶן 3. אֱמֶת 4. חֶסֶד 5. πίστις 6. fides
Gen 24:27 love and his faithfulness toward my master. 3
32:10 the steadfast love and all the faithfulness 3
Exd 34: 6 in steadfast love and faithfulness 3
Deu 32: 4 God of faithfulness and without iniquity, just 1
20 children in whom is no faithfulness. 2
Jos 24:14 and serve him in sincerity and in faithfulness; 3
1Sm 26:23 for his righteousness and his faithfulness; 1
2Sm 2: 6 the LORD show steadfast love and faithfulness 3
15:20 the LORD show steadfast love and faithfulness 3
1Kg 2: 4 to walk before me in faithfulness with all their 3
3: 6 before thee in faithfulness, in righteousness 3
2Kg 20: 3 walked . . in faithfulness and with a whole heart 3
2Ch 19: 9 in the fear of the LORD, in faithfulness 1
Ps 25:10 of the LORD are steadfast love and faithfulness 3
26: 3 I walk in faithfulness to thee. 3
30: 9 Will it tell of thy faithfulness? 3
33: 4 all his work is done in faithfulness. 1
36: 5 the heavens, thy faithfulness to the clouds. 1
40:10 I have spoken of thy faithfulness 1
10 thy faithfulness from the great congregation. 3
11 let . . thy faithfulness ever preserve me! 3
54: 5 in thy faithfulness put an end to them. 3
57: 3 his steadfast love and his faithfulness! 3
10 to the heavens, thy faithfulness to the clouds. 3
61: 7 steadfast love and faithfulness watch over him! 3
71:22 praise thee with the harp for thy faithfulness 3
85:10 Steadfast love and faithfulness will meet; 3
11 Faithfulness will spring up from the ground 3
86:15 abounding in steadfast love and faithfulness. 3
88:11 or thy faithfulness in Abaddon? 1
89: 1 proclaim thy faithfulness to all generations. 1
2 thy faithfulness is firm as the heavens. 1
5 thy faithfulness in the assembly of the holy ones! 1
8 O LORD, with thy faithfulness round about thee? 1
14 steadfast love and faithfulness go before thee. 3
24 faithfulness and my steadfast love . . be 1
33 but I will not . . be false to my faithfulness. 1
49 by thy faithfulness thou didst swear to David? 1
91: 4 his faithfulness is a shield and buckler. 3
92: 2 to declare . . thy faithfulness by night 1
98: 3 remembered his . . faithfulness to the house 1
100: 5 his faithfulness to all generations. 1
108: 4 thy faithfulness reaches to the clouds. 3
111: 8 performed with faithfulness and uprightness. 3
115: 1 the sake of thy steadfast love and thy faithfulness! 3
117: 2 faithfulness of the LORD endures for ever. 3
119:30 I have chosen the way of faithfulness 1
75 that in faithfulness thou hast afflicted me. 1
90 Thy faithfulness endures to all generations; 1
138 in righteousness and in all faithfulness. 1
138: 2 for thy steadfast love and thy faithfulness; 3
143: 1 faithfulness answer me, in thy righteousness! 1
Prv 3: 3 Let not loyalty and faithfulness forsake you; 3
14:22 who devise good meet loyalty and faithfulness. 3
16: 6 By loyalty and faithfulness iniquity is atoned 3
20:28 Loyalty and faithfulness preserve the king 3
Isa 11: 5 and faithfulness the girdle of his loins. 1
16: 5 a throne . . and on it will sit in faithfulness 3
38: 3 how I have walked before thee in faithfulness 3
18 to the pit cannot hope for thy faithfulness. 3
19 makes known to the children thy faithfulness. 3
Jer 31: 3 I have continued my faithfulness to you. 4
32:41 I will plant them in this land in faithfulness 3
Lam 3:23 new every morning; great is thy faithfulness. 1
Hos 2:20 I will betroth you to me in faithfulness; 1
4: 1 There is no faithfulness or kindness 3
Mic 7:20 Thou wilt show faithfulness to Jacob 3
Zec 8: 8 God, in faithfulness and in righteousness. 3
Rom 3: 3 Does their faithlessness nullify the faithfulness 5

Gal 5:22 patience, kindness, goodness, faithfulness 5
2Es 6:28 faithfulness shall flourish 6
7:34 and faithfulness shall grow strong. 6
Wis 3:14 shown him for his faithfulness 5
Sir 45: 4 He sanctified him through faithfulness 5
46:15 By his faithfulness he was proved to be a prophet 5
1Mc 14:35 The people saw Simon's faithfulness 5

faithfulness *See also* act.

faithless 1. בגד 2. בְּגְדוֹת 3. מעל 4. מַעַל 5. מְשׁוּבָה 6. שׁוֹבֵב 7. שׁוֹבָב 8. ἀπιστέω 9. ἄπιστος 10. ἀσύνθετος 11. apostata

2Ch 28:19 Ahaz . . had been faithless to the LORD. 3
22 distress he became yet more faithless 3
29:19 discarded in his reign when he was faithless 4
30: 7 faithless to the LORD God of their fathers 3
Ps 119:158 I look at the faithless with disgust 1
Prv 13:15 but the way of the faithless is their ruin. 1
21:18 faithless for the upright. 1
22:12 but he overthrows the words of the faithless. 1
23:28 increases the faithless among men. 1
Jer 3:11 Faithless Israel has shown herself less guilty 5
12 Return, faithless Israel, says the LORD. 5
14 Return, O faithless children, says the LORD; 7
20 Surely, as a faithless wife leaves her husband 1
20 have you been faithless to me, O house of Israel 1
22 Return, O faithless sons 7
5:11 Israel and . . Judah have been utterly faithless to me 1
31:22 How long will you waver, O faithless daughter? 6
49: 4 you boast of your valleys, O faithless daughter 6
Zep 3: 4 Her prophets are wanton, faithless men; 2
Mal 2:10 Why then are we faithless to one another 1
11 Judah has been faithless 1
14 the wife . . to whom you have been faithless 1
15 let none be faithless to the wife of his youth. 1
16 take heed to yourselves and do not be faithless. 1
Mat 17:17 O faithless and perverse generation 9
Mrk 9:19 he answered them, "O faithless generation 9
Lke 9:41 O faithless and perverse generation 9
Joh 20:27 do not be faithless, but believing. 9
Rom 1:31 foolish, faithless, heartless, ruthless. 10
2Ti 2:13 if we are faithless, he remains faithful 8
Rev 21: 8 as for the cowardly, the faithless, the polluted 9
2Es 15:25 Depart, you faithless children! 11

faithless man 1. בגד

Prv 25:19 Trust in a faithless man in time of trouble 1
Hab 1:13 why dost thou look on faithless men 1

faithless one 1. מְשׁוּבָה

Jer 3: 6 Have you seen what she did, that faithless one 1
8 for all the adulteries of that faithless one 1

faithlessly 1. מַעַל

Ezk 14:13 a land sins against me by acting faithlessly 1
15: 8 desolate, because they have acted faithlessly 1

faithlessly *See also* deal.

act faithlessly 1. מעל

Ezk 14:13 a land sins against me by acting faithlessly 1
15: 8 desolate, because they have acted faithlessly 1

faithlessness 1. זְנוּת 2. מַעַל 3. מְשׁוּבָה 4. ἀπιστία

Num 14:33 children . . suffer for your faithlessness 1
2Ch 33:19 all his sin and his faithlessness, and the sites 2
Ezr 9: 2 in this faithlessness the hand of the officials 2
4 because of the faithlessness of the . . exiles 2
10: 6 mourning over the faithlessness of the exiles. 2
Jer 3:22 faithless sons, I will heal your faithlessness. 3
Hos 14: 4 I will heal their faithlessness; 3
Rom 3: 3 Does their faithlessness nullify the faithfulness 4
Wis 14:25 theft and deceit, corruption, faithlessness 4

falcon 1. אַיָּה

Lev 11:14 the kite, the falcon according to its kind 1
Job 28: 7 the falcon's eye has not seen it. 1

fall 1. אנה 2. דְּחִי 3. הוא 4. היה 5. חול 6. יצא 7. ירד 8. כרע 9. כשל 10. כִּשָּׁלוֹן 11. מוט 12. מִכְשׁוֹל 13. מַפֶּלֶת 14. מרט 15. נבל 16. נטש 17. נכה 18. נפל 19. נתך 20. עלה 21. פשט 22. צֶלַע 23. שחה 24. נפל (A) 25. ἀποπίπτω 26. ἄπταιστος 27. βάλλω 28. βρέχω 29. γίνομαι 30. εἰμί 31. ἐκπίπτω 32. ἐμπίπτω 33. ἐπάγω 34. ἐπιβάλλω 35. ἐπιπίπτω 36. ἔρχομαι 37. καταβαίνω 38. κατάγω 39. καταπίπτω 40. κατέρχομαι 41. κλίνω 42. πίπτω 43. προπίπτω 44. πρόσκομμα 45. προσπίπτω 46. πταίω 47. πτῶμα 48. πτῶσις 49. συμπίπτω 50. ὑετός 51. ὑποπίπτω 52. cado 53. casus 54. concido 55. incido

Gen 4: 5 Cain was very angry, and his countenance fell. 18
6 angry, and why has your countenance fallen? 18
7:12 rain fell upon the earth 40 days and 40 nights. 4
14:10 Sodom and Gomor'rah fled, some fell into them 18
15:12 a deep sleep fell on Abram; 18
12 and lo, a dread and great darkness fell upon him. 18
17: 3 Then Abram fell on his face; and God said to him 18
17 Then Abraham fell on his face and laughed 18
33: 4 embraced him, and fell on his neck and kissed him 18
35: 5 as they journeyed, a terror from God fell upon 4
43:18 he may seek occasion against us and fall upon us 18
44:14 and they fell before him to the ground. 18
45:14 Then he fell upon his brother Benjamin's neck 18
46:29 and fell on his neck, and wept on his neck 18
49:17 that his rider falls backward. 18
50: 1 Joseph fell on his father's face, and wept over him 18
Exd 9: 3 the hand of the LORD will fall with a very severe 4
15:16 Terror and dread fall upon them; 18
21:13 but God let him fall into his hand 1
33 a pit . . and an ox or an ass falls into it 18
32:28 there fell of the people that day about three 18
Lev 9:24 they shouted, and fell on their faces 18
11:32 anything upon which any of them falls 18
33 if any of them falls into any earthen vessel 18
35 everything upon which . . their carcass falls 18
37 if any part of their carcass falls upon the seed 18
38 if . . any part of their carcass falls on it 18
13:40 If a man's hair has fallen from his head, he is bald 14
41 if a man's hair has fallen from his forehead 14
16: 9 the goat on which the lot fell for the LORD 20
10 the goat on which the lot fell for Aza'zel 20
26: 7 they shall fall before you by the sword 18
8 your enemies shall fall before you by the sword 18
36 sword, and they shall fall when none pursues 18
Num 11: 9 When the dew fell upon the camp in the night 7
9 When the dew fell . . the manna fell with it. 7
31 quails . . and let them fall beside the camp 16
14: 3 LORD bring us into this land, to fall by the sword? 18
5 Moses and Aaron fell on their faces before all 18
29 your dead bodies shall fall in this wilderness; 18
32 your dead bodies shall fall in this wilderness. 18
43 shall fall by the sword; because you have turned 18
16: 4 When Moses heard it, he fell on his face; 18
22 they fell on their faces, and said, "O God, the God 18
45 And they fell on their faces. 18
20: 6 Moses and Aaron went . . and fell on their faces. 18
22:31 he bowed his head, and fell on his face. 23
33:54 wherever the lot falls to any man, that shall be his 6
34: 2 Canaan (this is the land that shall fall to you 18
Deu 20:20 siegeworks against the city . . until it falls. 7
22: 8 may not bring the guilt . . if any one fall from it. 18
Jos 2: 9 I know . . that the fear of you has fallen upon us 18
5:14 And Joshua fell on his face to the earth 18
7: 6 and fell to the earth upon his face before the ark 18
10 Arise, why have you thus fallen upon your face? 18
8:24 all of them . . had fallen by the edge of the sword 18
25 And all who fell that day . . were 12,000 18
11: 7 Joshua came suddenly . . and fell upon them. 18
17: 5 there fell to Manas'seh ten portions, besides 18
18:11 the territory . . fell between the tribe of Judah 6
21:10 which went . . since the lot fell to them first. 4
22:20 wrath fell upon all the congregation of Israel? 4
Jdg 4:16 the army of Sis'era fell by the edge of the sword; 18
5:27 He sank, he fell, he lay still at her feet; 18
27 at her feet he sank, he fell; where he sank 18
27 at her feet . . where he sank, there he fell dead. 18
7:13 the tent, and struck it so that it fell, and turned 18
8:10 there had fallen 120,000 men who drew the sword. 18
9:40 many fell wounded, up to the entrance of the gate. 18
12: 6 there fell at that time 42,000 of the E'phraimites 18
13:20 and they fell on their faces to the ground. 18
15:18 shall I now die of thirst, and fall into the hands 18
16:30 and the house fell upon the lords and upon all 18
18: 1 until then no inheritance . . had fallen to them. 18
20:44 18,000 men of Benjamin fell, all of them men 18
46 all who fell that day of Benjamin were 25,000 men 18
Rut 2:10 she fell on her face, bowing to the ground, and said 18
1Sm 3:19 and let none of his words fall to the ground. 18
4:10 there fell of Israel 30,000 foot soldiers. 18
5: 3 Dagon had fallen face downward . . before the ark 18
4 Dagon had fallen face downward . . before the ark 18
11: 7 Then the dread of the LORD fell upon the people 18
14:13 they fell before Jonathan, and his armor-bearer 18
45 shall not one hair of his head fall to the ground; 18
17:49 and he fell on his face to the ground. 18
52 the wounded . . fell on the way from Sha-ara'im 18
20:41 David rose . . and fell on his face to the ground 18
25:23 and fell before David on her face, and bowed 18
24 She fell at his feet and said, "Upon me alone 18
26:12 a deep sleep from the LORD had fallen upon them. 18
20 Now therefore, let not my blood fall to the earth 18
28:20 Saul fell at once full length upon the ground 18
31: 1 Israel fled . . and fell slain on Mount Gilbo'a. 18
4 Saul took his own sword, and fell upon it. 18
5 armor-bearer . . also fell upon his sword, and died 18
8 Saul and his three sons fallen on Mount Gilbo'a. 18
2Sm 1: 2 he fell to the ground and did obeisance. 18
4 many of the people also have fallen and are dead; 18
10 I was sure . . he could not live after he had fallen; 18
12 mourned . . because they had fallen by the sword. 18
19 How are the mighty fallen! 18
25 How are the mighty fallen in the midst 18
27 How are the mighty fallen, and the weapons of war 18
2:23 and he fell there, and died where he was. 18
23 to the place where As'ahel had fallen and died 18
3:29 May it fall upon the head of Jo'ab 5
34 as one falls before the wicked you have fallen. 18
34 as one falls before the wicked you have fallen. 18
38 a prince and a great man has fallen this day 18
4: 4 as she fled in her haste, he fell, and became lame. 18
9: 6 came . . and fell on his face and did obeisance. 18
11:17 and some of the servants of David . . fell. 18
14: 4 she fell on her face to the ground 18
11 not one hair of your son shall fall to the ground. 18
22 And Jo'ab fell on his face to the ground 18
17: 9 when some of the people fall at the first attack 18
12 light upon him as the dew falls on the ground; 18
21:10 until rain fell upon them from the heavens; 19
22 they fell by the hand of David and by the hand 18
22:39 so that they did not rise; they fell under my feet. 18
23:20 slew a lion in a pit on a day when snow had fallen. •
24:14 let us fall into the hand of the LORD 18
14 but let me not fall into the hand of man. 18
1Kg 1:52 If . . not one of his hairs shall fall to the earth; 18
18: 7 Obadi'ah recognized him, and fell on his face 18
38 the fire of the LORD fell, and consumed 18
39 when . . the people saw it, they fell on their faces; 18
20:30 the wall fell upon 27,000 men that were left. 18
22:20 'Who will entice Ahab, that he may go up and fall 18
2Kg 1: 2 Ahazi'ah fell through the lattice 18
13 captain . . went up, and came and fell on his knees 8
2:13 the mantle of Eli'jah that had fallen from him 18
14 the mantle of Eli'jah that had fallen from him 18
4:37 She came and fell at his feet, bowing to the ground; 18
6: 5 felling a log, his axe head fell into the water; 18
6 Then the man of God said, "Where did it fall? 18
10:10 there shall fall to the earth nothing of the word 18
14:10 why should you provoke trouble so that you fall 18
1Ch 5:10 the Hagrites, who fell by their hand; 18
22 For many fell slain, because the war was of God. 18
10: 1 men of Israel . . fell slain on Mount Gilbo'a. 18
4 Saul took his own sword, and fell upon it. 18
5 he also fell upon his sword, and died. 18
8 found Saul and his sons fallen on Mount Gilbo'a. 18
11:22 slew a lion in a pit on a day when snow had fallen. •
20: 8 they fell by the hand of David and by the hand 18
21:13 let me fall into the hand of the LORD 18
13 but let me not fall into the hand of man. 18
14 and there fell 70,000 men of Israel. 18
16 clothed in sackcloth, fell upon their faces. 18
24: 7 The first lot fell to Jehoi'arib 6
25: 9 The first lot fell for Asaph to Joseph; 6
26:14 The lot for the east fell to Shelemi'ah. 18
2Ch 13:17 there fell slain of Israel 500,000 picked men. 18
14:13 the Ethiopians fell until none remained alive; 18
17:10 the fear of the LORD fell upon all the kingdoms 4
18:19 that he(Ahab) may go up and fall at Ramoth-gilead?' 18
25:13 fell upon the cities of Judah 21
19 so that you fall, you and Judah with you? 18
29: 9 For lo, our fathers have fallen by the sword 18
Ezr 9: 5 fell upon my knees and spread out my hands 8
Neh 6:16 afraid and fell greatly in their own esteem; 18
Est 6:13 If Mor'decai, before whom you have begun to fall, 18
13 not prevail . . but will surely fall before him. 18
7: 8 Haman was falling on the couch where Esther was; 18
8: 3 she fell at his feet and besought him with tears 18
17 for the fear of the Jews had fallen upon them. 18
9: 2 for the fear of them had fallen upon all peoples. 18
3 for the fear of Mor'decai had fallen upon them. 18
Job 1:16 another, and said, "The fire of God fell from heaven 18
19 it fell upon the young people, and they are dead; 18
20 shaved his head, and fell upon the ground 18
4:13 of the night, when deep sleep falls on men 18
13:11 terrify you, and the dread of him fall upon you? 18
14:18 the mountain falls and crumbles away 18
30:30 My skin turns black and falls from me •
31:22 then let my shoulder blade fall from my shoulder 18
33:15 the night, when deep sleep falls upon men 18
37: 6 For to the snow he says, 'Fall on the earth'; 3
Ps 5:10 O God; let them fall by their own counsels; 18
7:15 falls into the hole which he has made. 18
10:10 is crushed, sinks down, and falls by his might. 18
16: 6 The lines have fallen for me in pleasant places; 18
18:38 were not able to rise; they fell under my feet. 18
20: 8 They will collapse and fall; but we shall rise 18
27: 2 foes, they shall stumble and fall. 18
35: 8 let them fall therein to ruin! 18
37:24 though he fall, he shall not be cast headlong 18
38:17 For I am ready to fall, and my pain is ever with me. 22
45: 5 the peoples fall under you. 18
55: 4 the terrors of death have fallen upon me. 18
56:13 my soul from death, yea, my feet from falling 2
57: 6 but they have fallen into it themselves. 18
69: 9 of those who insult thee have fallen on me. 18
72: 6 May he be like rain that falls on the mown grass 7
78:28 he let them fall in the midst of their camp 18
64 Their priests fell by the sword 18
82: 7 die like men, and fall like any prince. 18
91: 7 1,000 may fall at your side 18
105:38 for dread of them had fallen upon it. 18
118:13 I was pushed hard, so that I was falling 18
119:56 This blessing has fallen to me 4
133: 3 dew of Hermon, which falls on the mountains 7
140:10 Let burning coals fall upon them! 11

141:10 Let the wicked together fall into their own nets 18
144:15 Happy the people to whom such blessings fall! *
145:14 The LORD upholds all who are falling 18
Prv 11: 5 but the wicked falls by his own wickedness. 18
14 Where there is no guidance, a people falls; 18
14:35 but his wrath falls on one who acts shamefully. 4
16:18 haughty spirit before a fall. 10
17:20 one with a perverse tongue falls into calamity. 18
22:14 he with whom the LORD is angry will fall into it. 18
24:16 righteous man falls seven times, and rises again; 18
17 Do not rejoice when your enemy falls 18
26:27 He who digs a pit will fall into it 18
28:10 misleads the upright . . fall into his own pit; 18
14 hardens his heart will fall into calamity. 18
18 who is perverse in his ways will fall into a pit. 18
Ecc 4:10 For if they fall, one will lift up his fellow; 18
10 but woe to him who is alone when he falls 18
9:12 at an evil time, when it suddenly falls upon them. 18
10: 8 He who digs a pit will fall into it; 18
11: 3 and if a tree falls to the south or to the north 18
3 the place where the tree falls, there it will lie. 18
Isa 3: 8 For Jerusalem has stumbled, and Judah has fallen; 18
25 Your men shall fall by the sword . . in battle. 18
8:15 stumble thereon; they shall fall and be broken; 18
9:10 The bricks have fallen, but we will build 18
10: 4 among the prisoners or fall among the slain. 18
34 and Lebanon with its majestic trees will fall. 18
13:15 and whoever is caught will fall by the sword. 18
14:12 How you are fallen from heaven, O Day Star 18
16: 9 upon your fruit . . the battle shout has fallen. 18
21: 9 And he answered, "Fallen, fallen is Babylon; 18
9 And he answered, "Fallen, fallen is Babylon; 18
22:25 the peg . . will be cut down and fall 18
24:18 He who flees . . shall fall into the pit; 18
20 upon it, and it falls, and will not rise again. 18
26:18 and the inhabitants of the world have not fallen. 18
19 on the land of the shades thou wilt let it fall. 18
28:13 that they may go, and fall backward, and be broken 9
30:25 day of the great slaughter, when the towers fall. 18
31: 3 will stumble, and he who is helped will fall 18
8 the Assyrian shall fall by a sword, not of man; 18
34: 4 host shall fall, as leaves fall from the vine 15
4 host shall fall, as leaves fall from the vine 15
4 like leaves falling from the fig tree. 15
7 Wild oxen shall fall with them 7
40:30 and young men shall fall exhausted; 9
47:11 disaster shall fall upon you 18
54:15 whoever stirs up strife with you shall fall 18
59:14 for truth has fallen in the public squares 9
Jer 6:15 Therefore they shall fall among those who fall; 18
15 Therefore they shall fall among those who fall; 18
8: 4 says the LORD: When men fall, do they not rise again? 18
12 Therefore they shall fall among the fallen; 18
12 Therefore they shall fall among the fallen; 18
9:22 men shall fall like dung upon the open field 18
20: 4 They shall fall by the sword of their enemies 18
10 all my familiar friends, watching for my fall. 22
23:12 into which they shall be driven and fall; 18
25:27 Drink, be drunk and vomit, fall and rise no more 18
34 and you shall fall like choice rams. 18
39:18 you shall not fall by the sword; 18
44:12 in the land of Egypt they shall fall; 18
46: 6 by the river Euphra'tes they have . . fallen. 18
12 they have both fallen together. 18
16 Your multitude stumbled and fell, and they said 18
48:32 upon . . your vintage the destroyer has fallen. 18
44 who flees from the terror shall fall into the pit 18
49:21 At . . their fall the earth shall tremble; 18
26 Therefore her young men shall fall in her squares 18
50:15 she has surrendered; her bulwarks have fallen 18
30 her young men shall fall in her squares 18
32 The proud one shall stumble and fall 18
51: 8 Suddenly Babylon has fallen and been broken; 18
44 the wall of Babylon has fallen. 18
47 and all her slain shall fall in the midst of her. 18
49 Babylon must fall for the slain of Israel 18
49 as for Babylon have fallen the slain of all 18
Lam 1: 7 When her people fell into the hand of the foe 18
9 her fall is terrible, she has no comforter. 7
2:21 maidens and . . young men have fallen by the sword; 18
5:16 The crown has fallen from our head; 18
Ezk 1:28 And when I saw it, I fell upon my face 18
3:23 and I fell on my face. 18
5:12 a third . . shall fall by the sword round about you; 18
6: 7 And the slain shall fall in the midst of you 18
11 for they shall fall by the sword, by famine 18
12 he that is near shall fall by the sword; 18
8: 1 the hand of the Lord GOD fell there upon me. 18
9: 8 I fell upon my face, and cried, "Ah Lord GOD! 18
11: 5 Spirit of the LORD fell upon me, and he said to me 18
10 You shall fall by the sword; 18
13:11 who daub it with whitewash that it shall fall! 18
11 be a deluge of rain, great hailstones will fall 18
12 when the wall falls, will it not be said to you 18
14 when it falls, you shall perish in the midst of it; 18
17:21 all the pick of his troops shall fall by the sword 18
21:15 hearts may melt, and many fall at all their gates. 12
23:25 your survivors shall fall by the sword. 18
24:21 whom you left behind shall fall by the sword. 18
25:13 Teman even to Dedan they shall fall by the sword. 18
26:11 your mighty pillars will fall to the ground. 7
15 at the sound of your fall, when the wounded groan 13
18 Now the isles tremble on the day of your fall; 13
28:23 the slain shall fall in the midst of her 18
29: 5 you shall fall upon the open field 18
30: 4 shall be in Ethiopia, when the slain fall in Egypt 18
5 shall fall with them by the sword. 18
6 says the LORD: Those who support Egypt shall fall 18
6 to Syene they shall fall within her by the sword 18
17 On and of Pibe'seth shall fall by the sword; 18
25 but the arms of Pharaoh shall fall; 18
31:12 in all the valleys its branches will fall 18
16 make the nations quake at the sound of its fall 13
32:20 They shall fall amid those who are slain 18
22 all of them slain, fallen by the sword; 18
23 all of them slain, fallen by the sword 18
24 all of them slain, fallen by the sword 18
27 they do not lie with the fallen mighty men of old 18
33:12 wickedness of the wicked, he shall not fall by it 9
21 came to me and said, "The city has fallen. 17
27 are in the waste places shall fall by the sword; 18
35: 8 those slain with the sword shall fall. 18
38:20 the cliffs shall fall 18
39: 4 You shall fall upon the mountains of Israel 18
5 You shall fall in the open field; for I have spoken 18
23 they all fell by the sword. 18
43: 3 I fell upon my face. 18
44: 4 I fell upon my face. 18
47:14 this land shall fall to you as your inheritance. 18
Dan 2:46 Then King Nebuchadnez'zar fell upon his face 24
3:23 fell bound into the burning fiery furnace. 24
4:31 there fell a voice from heaven, "O King 24
7:20 other horn . . before which three of them fell 24
8:17 came, I was frightened and fell upon my face. 18
10: 7 but a great trembling fell upon them 18
9 I fell on my face in a deep sleep with my face *
11:19 shall stumble and fall, and shall not be found. 18
33 though they shall fall by sword and flame 9
34 When they fall, they shall receive a little help. 9
35 some of those who are wise shall fall 9
41 tens of thousands shall fall, but these 9
Hos 7: 7 All their kings have fallen; 18
16 their princes shall fall by the sword 18
10: 8 and to the hills, Fall upon us. 18
13:16 they shall fall by the sword 18
Ams 3: 5 Does a bird fall in a snare on the earth 18
14 altar shall be cut off and fall to the ground. 18
5: 2 Fallen, no more to rise, is the virgin Israel; 18
7:17 sons and your daughters shall fall by the sword 18
8:14 they shall fall, and never rise again. 18
9: 9 a sieve, but no pebble shall fall upon the earth. 18
11 I will raise up the booth of David that is fallen 18
Jon 1: 7 So they cast lots, and the lot fell upon Jonah. 18
Mic 7: 8 when I fall, I shall rise; 18
Nah 3:12 if shaken they fall into the mouth of the eater. 18
Zec 11: 2 Wail, O cypress, for the cedar has fallen 18
2 for the thick forest has been felled! 7
14:13 a great panic from the LORD shall fall on them 4
15 plague like this plague shall fall on the horses 4
Mat 2:11 his mother, and they fell down and worshiped him. 42
7:25 rain fell, and the floods came, and the winds blew 37
25 it did not fall, because it had been founded 42
27 rain fell, and the floods came, and the wind blew 37
27 and it fell; and great was the fall of it. 42
27 and it fell; and great was the fall of it. 48
10:29 And not one of them will fall to the ground 42
12:11 it falls into a pit on the sabbath 32
13: 4 as he sowed, some seeds fell along the path 42
5 Other seeds fell on rocky ground 42
7 Other seeds fell upon thorns 42
8 Other seeds fell on good soil 42
15:14 both will fall into a pit. 42
27 crumbs that fall from their master's table. 42
17: 6 they fell on their faces 42
15 for often he falls into the fire 42
18:26 So the servant fell on his knees, imploring him 42
24:29 the stars will fall from heaven 42
26:39 going a little farther he fell on his face 42
Mrk 4: 4 as he sowed, some seed fell along the path 42
5 Other seed fell on rocky ground 42
7 Other seed fell among thorns 42
8 other seeds fell into good soil 42
5:22 seeing him, he fell at his feet 42
9:20 he fell on the ground and rolled about 42
13:25 the stars will be falling from heaven 42
14:35 going a little farther, he fell on the ground 42
Lke 2:34 this child is set for the fall and rising of many 48
5:12 he fell on his face and besought him 42
6:49 immediately it fell 49
8: 5 as he sowed, some fell along the path 42
6 some fell on the rock 39
7 some fell among thorns 42
8 some fell into good soil and grew 42
14 as for what fell among the thorns 42
41 falling at Jesus' feet he besought him to come 42
10:18 I saw Satan fall like lightning from heaven. 42
11:17 a divided household falls. 42
13: 4 the tower in Silo'am fell and killed them 42
14: 5 a son or an ox that has fallen into a well 42
15:12 give me the share of property that falls to me 34
16:21 fed with what fell from the rich man's table; 42
17:16 he fell on his face at Jesus' feet 42
20:18 Every one who falls on that stone 42
18 when it falls on any one it will crush him. 42
21:24 they will fall by the edge of the sword 42
23:30 they will begin to say to the mountains, 'Fall on us'; 42
Joh 11:32 Mary . . fell at his feet, saying to him, "Lord 42
12:24 a grain of wheat falls into the earth and dies 42
18: 6 they drew back and fell to the ground. 42
Act 1:18 falling headlong he burst open in the middle 29
26 the lot fell on Matthi'as 42
8:16 for it had not yet fallen on any of them 35
9: 4 he fell to the ground and heard a voice saying 42
18 something like scales fell from his eyes 25
37 In those days she fell sick and died 29
10:44 the Holy Spirit fell on all who heard the word. 35
11:15 As I began to speak, the Holy Spirit fell on them 35
13:11 Immediately mist and darkness fell upon him 42
15:16 rebuild the dwelling of David, which has fallen 42
20: 9 he fell down from the third story 42
22: 7 I fell to the ground and heard a voice saying to me 42
17 praying in the temple, I fell into a trance 29
26:14 when we had all fallen to the ground 39
Rom 2: 2 judgment . . falls upon those who do such things 30
11:11 I ask, have they stumbled so as to fall? By no means! 42
22 severity toward those who have fallen 42
14: 4 before his own master that he stands or falls. 42
20 but it is wrong for any one to make others fall 44
15: 3 The reproaches . . fell on me. 35
1Co 10: 8 and 23,000 fell in a single day. 42
12 thinks that he stands take heed lest he fall. 42
14:25 and so, falling on his face, he will worship God 42
1Ti 3: 6 fall into the condemnation of the devil; 32
6: 9 those who desire to be rich fall into temptation 32
Heb 3:17 who sinned, whose bodies fell in the wilderness 42
4:11 no one fall by the same sort of disobedience. 42
6: 7 drunk the rain that often falls upon it 36
Jas 1:11 its flower falls, and its beauty perishes 31
5:12 that you may not fall under condemnation. 42
1Pe 1:24 The grass withers, and the flower falls 31
2Pe 1:10 for if you do this you will never fall; 46
Jde 1:24 Now to him who is able to keep you from falling 26
Rev 1:17 When I saw him, I fell at his feet as though dead. 42
2: 5 Remember then from what you have fallen 42
6:13 the stars of the sky fell to the earth 42
16 Fall on us and hide us from the face of him 42
7:11 they fell on their faces before the throne 42
8: 7 fire, mixed with blood, which fell on the earth; 27
10 great star fell from heaven, blazing like a torch 42
10 star fell . . and it fell on a third of the rivers 42
9: 1 and I saw a star fallen from heaven to earth 42
11: 6 shut the sky, that no rain may fall during the days 28
11 and great fear fell on those who saw them. 35
13 great earthquake, and a tenth of the city fell; 42
16 elders . . fell on their faces and worshiped God 42
14: 8 Fallen, fallen is Babylon the great 42
8 Fallen, fallen is Babylon the great 42
16:19 and the cities of the nations fell 42
17:10 seven kings, five of whom have fallen 42
18: 2 Fallen, fallen is Babylon the great! 42
2 Fallen, fallen is Babylon the great! 42
1Es 9:47 fell to the ground and worshiped the Lord. 45
2Es 4:11 When I heard this, I fell on my face 52
5: 5 and the stars shall fall. ‡
7:118 the fall was not yours alone, but ours also 53
12:18 it shall be in danger of falling 52
18 nevertheless it shall not fall then 52
28 he also shall fall by the sword in the last days. 52
13:11 and fell on the onrushing multitude 54
23 will himself protect those who fall into peril 55
15:57 and you shall fall by the sword 52
57 all your people . . shall fall by the sword. 52
Tob 12:16 they fell upon their faces, for they were afraid. 42
Jdt 6: 6 you shall fall among their wounded 42
7:11 not a man of your army will fall. 42
9: 1 Then Judith fell upon her face 42
14: 6 he fell down on his face and his spirit failed him. 42
7 when they raised him up he fell at Judith's feet 45
16: 7 did not fall by the hands of the young men 51
AEs 15:15 as she was speaking, she fell fainting. 42
Wis 6: 5 severe judgment falls on those in high places. 29
7: 3 fell upon the kindred earth 39
11:20 men could fall at a single breath 42
22 drop of morning dew that falls upon the ground. 40
13:16 he takes thought for it, that it may not fall 39
16:11 lest they should fall into deep forgetfulness 32
18:23 when the dead had already fallen on one another 42
Sir 1:30 Do not exalt yourself lest you fall 42
2: 7 turn not aside, lest you fall. 42
3:31 at the moment of his falling he will find support. 48
13:21 when a humble man falls, he is even pushed away 42
15: 4 He will lean on her and will not fall 41
18:19 before you fall ill, take care of your health. *
22:27 that it may keep me from falling 42
23: 1 let me not fall because of them! 42
3 then I will not fall before my adversaries 42
24 punishment will fall on her children. 30

27:26 He who digs a pit will fall into it 32
29 Those who rejoice in the fall of the godly 48
28:18 Many have fallen by the edge of the sword 42
18 not so many as have fallen because of the tongue. 42
23 who forsake the Lord will fall into its power 32
26 lest you fall before him who lies in wait. 42
29:19 The sinner who has fallen into suretyship 32
19 will fall into lawsuits. 32
20 take heed to yourself lest you fall. 32
34:16 a defense against falling. 48
38:15 may he fall into the care of a physician. 32
16 My son, let your tears fall for the dead 38
43:18 the mind is amazed at its falling. 50
49:13 he raised for us the walls that had fallen 42
50:17 fell to the ground upon their faces 42
Bar 4:31 afflicted you and rejoiced at your fall. 48
33 rejoiced at your fall and was glad for your ruin 48
LJr 1:27 lest they fall to the ground 42
Sus 1:23 I choose not to do it and to fall into your hands 32
1Mc 1: 5 After this he fell sick 42
18 many were wounded and fell. 42
3:11 Many were wounded and fell, and the rest fled. 42
24 800 of them fell 42
4:15 all those in the rear fell by the sword 42
15 3,000 of them fell. 42
34 there fell of the army of Lysias 5,000 men 42
34 they fell in action. 42
40 They fell face down on the ground 42
55 All the people fell on their faces and worshiped 42
5:12 many of us have fallen 42
22 as many as 3,000 of the Gentiles fell 42
34 As many as 8,000 of them fell that day. 42
54 because not one of them had fallen 42
60 as many as 2,000 . . fell that day. 42
67 On that day some priests . . fell in battle 42
6:42 600 men of the king's army fell. 42
46 it fell to the ground upon him and he died. 42
7:32 About 500 men of the army of Nicanor fell 42
38 let them fall by the sword 42
43 he himself was the first to fall in the battle. 42
44 When his army saw that Nicanor had fallen 42
46 so that they all fell by the sword 42
8:10 Many of them were wounded and fell 42
9: 1 Nicanor and his army had fallen in battle 42
17 many on both sides were wounded and fell. 42
18 Judas also fell, and the rest fled. 42
21 How is the mighty fallen, the savior of Israel! 42
40 Many were wounded and fell 42
49 about 1,000 of Bacchides' men fell that day. 42
10:50 Demetrius fell on that day. 42
85 The number of those who fell by the sword 42
11:74 As many as 3,000 of the foreigners fell 42
12:37 part of the wall . . had fallen 42
13:22 that night a very heavy snow fell 30
16: 8 many of them were wounded and fell 42
10 about 2,000 of them fell 42
2Mc 3: 6 to fall under the control of the king. 42
27 When he suddenly fell to the ground 42
7: 3 The king fell into a rage 29
38 which has justly fallen on our whole nation. 33
9: 7 so it came about that he fell out of his chariot 42
7 the fall was so hard as to torture every limb 47
10: 4 they fell prostrate and besought the Lord 42
4 they might never again fall into such misfortunes 42
26 Falling upon the steps before the altar 45
12:34 it happened that a few of the Jews fell. 42
39 went to take up the bodies of the fallen 43
40 this was why these men had fallen. 42
42 because of the sin of those who had fallen. 43
44 those who had fallen would rise again 43
13:11 fall into the hands of the blasphemous Gentiles. 29
14:42 rather than to fall into the hands of sinners 29
44 he fell in the middle of the empty space. 36
3Mc 5:33 his eyes wavered and his face fell. •
4Mc 2:14 and helps raise up what has fallen. 42
3: 8 when evening fell, he came 29
6: 7 though he fell to the ground 42
8 to make him get up again after he fell. 42
15:20 corpses fallen on other corpses 42

fall *See also* countenance, droppings, shadow, snow.

fall among 1. ἐμπίπτω 2. περιπίπτω
Lke 10:30 he fell among robbers 2
36 the man who fell among the robbers? 1

fall asleep 1. ישן 2. ἀφυπνόω 3. κοιμάω 4. ὑπνόω
Gen 41: 5 he fell asleep and dreamed a second time; 1
Mat 27:52 saints who had fallen asleep were raised 3
Lke 8:23 as they sailed he fell asleep 2
Joh 11:11 Our friend Laz'arus has fallen asleep 3
12 Lord, if he has fallen asleep, he will recover. 3
Act 7:60 when he had said this, he fell asleep. 3
13:36 David . . fell asleep, and was laid with his fathers 3
1Co 15: 6 though some have fallen asleep. 3
18 Then those also who have fallen asleep in Christ 3
20 first fruits of those who have fallen asleep. 3
1Th 4:14 bring with him those who have fallen asleep. 3
15 shall not precede those who have fallen asleep. 3
2Pe 3: 4 For ever since the fathers fell asleep 3
Sir 46:20 Even after he had fallen asleep he prophesied 4
2Mc 12:45 that is laid up for those who fall asleep in godliness 3

fall away 1. נפל 2. סוג 3. סֵט 4. ἀφίστημι 5. ἐκπίπτω 6. σκανδαλίζω
Num 5:21 when the LORD makes your thigh fall away 1
22 make your body swell and your thigh fall away.' 1
27 body shall swell, and her thigh shall fall away 1
Ps 53: 3 They have all fallen away; 2
101: 3 I hate the work of those who fall away; 3
Mat 13:21 persecution arises . . immediately he falls away. 6
24:10 then many will fall away, and betray one another 6
26:31 You will all fall away because of me this night 6
33 Though they all fall away because of you 6
33 I will never fall away. 6
Mrk 4:17 immediately they fall away. 6
14:27 Jesus said to them, "You will all fall away 6
29 Even though they all fall away, I will not. 6
Lke 8:13 and in time of temptation fall away. 4
Joh 16: 1 to keep you from falling away. 6
Gal 5: 4 you have fallen away from grace. 5
Heb 3:12 leading you to fall away from the living God. 4

fall back 1. πάλιν
Rom 8:15 the spirit of slavery to fall back into fear 1

fall by lot 1. λαγχάνω
Lke 1: 9 it fell to him by lot to enter the temple 1

cause to fall 1. מטר 2. מצא 3. נפל 4. κατάγω 5. σκανδαλίζω
Gen 2:21 God caused a deep sleep to fall upon the man 3
Exd 9:18 I will cause very heavy hail to fall, such as never 1
2Kg 19: 7 I will cause him to fall by the sword 3
Jer 19: 7 and will cause their people to fall by the sword 3
Ezk 32:12 I will cause your multitude to fall by the swords 3
Zec 11: 6 Lo, I will cause men to fall 2
1Co 8:13 lest I cause my brother to fall. 5
Sir 35:15 cries out against him who has caused them to fall? 4

cause to fall away 1. ἀποβάλλω
Tob 11: 8 and will cause the white films to fall away 1

cause to fall upon 1. ἐπιβάλλω
Sir 36: 2 cause the fear of thee to fall upon . . 1

fall down 1. בטח 2. כשל 3. נפל 4. סגד 5. שחה 6. נפל (A) 7. καταπίπτω 8. πίπτω 9. προσπίπτω 10. cado
Gen 50:18 His brothers also came and fell down before him 3
Num24: 4 falling down, but having his eyes uncovered 3
16 falling down, but having his eyes uncovered 3
Deu 22: 4 brother's ass or his ox fallen down by the way 3
Jos 6: 5 and the wall of the city will fall down flat 3
20 raised a great shout, and the wall fell down flat 3
Jdg 19:26 the woman came and fell down at the door 3
2Sm 2:16 And each caught . . so they fell down together. 3
19:18 Shim'e-i the son of Gera fell down before the king 3
2Ch 20:18 fell down before the LORD, worshiping the LORD. 3
Ps 72:11 May all kings fall down before him 5
107:12 they fell down, with none to help. 2
Isa 44:15 makes it a graven image and falls down before it. 4
17 his idol; and falls down to it and worships it; 4
19 Shall I fall down before a block of wood? 4
46: 6 makes . . a god; then they fall down and worship! 4
Jer 12: 5 And if in a safe land you fall down 1
51: 4 They shall fall down slain 3
Ezk 11:13 Benai'ah died. Then I fell down upon my face 3
Dan 3: 5 fall down and worship the golden image 6
6 whoever does not fall down and worship shall 6
7 all . . fell down and worshiped the golden image 6
10 fall down and worship the golden image; 6
11 not fall down and worship shall be cast 6
15 fall down and worship the image which I have made 6
11:26 army . . swept away, and many shall fall down slain 3
Mat 4: 9 you, if you will fall down and worship me. 8
18:29 So his fellow servant fell down and besought him 8
Mrk 7:25 heard of him, and came and fell down at his feet. 9
Lke 5: 8 he fell down at Jesus' knees, saying 9
Act 5: 5 he fell down and died 8
10 Immediately she fell down at his feet and died. 8
10:25 and fell down at his feet and worshiped him. 8
28: 6 to swell up or suddenly fall down dead 7
Heb 11:30 By faith the walls of Jericho fell down 8
Rev 4:10 the 24 elders fall down before him 8
5: 8 the 24 elders fell down before the Lamb 8
14 and the elders fell down and worshiped. 8
19: 4 living creatures fell down and worshiped God 8
10 Then I fell down at his feet to worship him 8
22: 8 I fell down to worship at the feet of the angel 8
2Es 10: 1 when my son entered . . he fell down and died. 10
Jdt 6:18 Then the people fell down and worshiped God 8
7:22 and fell down in the streets of the city 8
Wis 17:16 whoever was there fell down 7
4Mc 4:11 Then Apollonius fell down half dead 7

fall down before 1. προσπίπτω
Mrk 3:11 they fell down before him and cried out 1
5:33 But the woman . . fell down before him 1
Lke 8:28 he cried out and fell down before him 1
47 and falling down before him declared 1
Act 16:29 he fell down before Paul and Silas 1

fall from the sky 1. διοπετής
Act 19:35 and of the sacred stone that fell from the sky? 1

fall headlong 1. πρηνής
3Mc 6:23 and saw them all fallen headlong to destruction 1

fall helpless 1. רפה
Jer 6:24 We have heard the report . . our hands fall helpless; 1
50:43 heard the report . . and his hands fell helpless; 1

fall ill 1. ἀρρωστέω
Sir 18:21 Before falling ill, humble yourself 1

fall in love 1. φιλέω
Tob 6:17 he fell in love with her 1

fall into 1. γίνομαι 2. ἐμπίπτω 3. ἐπιπίπτω
Lke 6:39 Will they not both fall into a pit? 2
Act 10:10 while they were preparing it, he fell into a trance 1
1Ti 3: 7 fall into reproach and the snare of the devil. 2
Heb 10:31 to fall into the hands of the living God. 2
Tob 14:10 Nadab fell into the trap and perished. 2
Sir 2:18 Let us fall into the hands of the Lord 2
8: 1 lest you fall into his hands. 2
9: 3 lest you fall into her snares. 2
2Mc 7:39 The king fell into a rage 1
3Mc 5:49 falling into one another's arms 3

fall into a deep sleep 1. רדם
Dan 8:18 fell into a deep sleep with my face to the ground; 1

fall into disuse 1. עבר
Est 9:28 Purim . . never fall into disuse among the Jews 1

fall into harlotry 1. זנה
Lev 19:29 lest the land fall into harlotry 1

fall into idolatry 1. ἐκπορνεύω
Sir 46:11 those whose hearts did not fall into idolatry 1

fall into the hand 1. ἐμπίπτω
2Mc 12:24 Timothy himself fell into the hands of . . 1

make fall 1. נפל 2. κατάγω 3. σκανδαλίζω 4. σκάνδαλον
1Sm 18:25 Now Saul thought to make David fall by the hand 1
Ps 73:18 thou dost make them fall to ruin. 1
106:26 swore . . would make them fall in the wilderness 1
Isa 37: 7 I will make him fall by the sword in his own land.' 1
Jer 15: 8 I have made anguish and terror fall upon them 1
Ezk 30:22 I will make the sword fall from his hand. 1
Rom 9:33 make men stumble, a rock that will make them fall; 4
2Co 11:29 Who is made to fall, and I am not indignant? 3
1Pe 2: 8 a rock that will make them fall 4
Sir 22:19 A man who pricks an eye will make tears fall 2

make fall back 1. שוב
Jdg 9:57 made all the wickedness of . . Shechem fall back 1

fall off 1. ἐκπίπτω 2. περιρέω
Act 12: 7 the chains fell off his hands. 1
4Mc 9:20 pieces of flesh were falling off the axles 2

fall out 1. נפל
2Sm 20: 8 with a sword . . and as he went forward it fell out. 1

fall over 1. נפל
1Sm 4:18 Eli fell over backward from his seat by the side 1

fall short 1. ὑστερέω
Rom 3:23 all have sinned and fall short of the glory of God 1

fall sick 1. חלה
1Sm 30:13 left me . . because I fell sick three days ago. 1
1Kg 14: 1 Abi'jah the son of Jerobo'am fell sick. 1
2Kg 13:14 Now when Eli'sha had fallen sick with the illness 1

fall to one's lot 1. λαγχάνω
Wis 8:19 a good soul fell to my lot; 1

fall upon 1. בוא 2. היה 3. נפל 4. פגע 5. פגשׁ 6. ἐπιβάλλω 7. ἐπιπίπτω 8. ὑποτίθημι
Exd 5: 3 lest he fall upon us with pestilence 4
12:13 no plague shall fall upon you to destroy you 2
Jdg 8:21 Rise yourself, and fall upon us; for as the man is 4
15:12 Swear to me that you will not fall upon me 4
18:25 heard among us, lest angry fellows fall upon you 4
1Sm 22:17 put forth their hand to fall upon the priests 4
18 king said . . "You turn and fall upon the priests. 4
18 And Do'eg . . turned and fell upon the priests 4
2Sm 1:15 David called . . and said, "Go, fall upon him. 4

Job 1:15 the Sabe'ans fell upon them and took them 3
Ezk 38:11 I will fall upon the quiet people who dwell 1
Hos 13: 8 will fall upon them like a bear robbed of her cubs 5
Lke 1:12 Zechari'ah was troubled . . and fear fell upon him. 7
Act 19:17 and fear fell upon them all 7
Jdt 2:28 fear and terror of him fell upon all the people 7
11:11 death will fall upon them 7
15: 5 with one accord they fell upon the enemy 7
6 The rest . . fell upon the Assyrian camp 7
1Mc 1:30 he suddenly fell upon the city 7
3:25 terror fell upon the Gentiles round about them. 7
4: 2 to fall upon the camp of the Jews 6
7:18 fear and dread of them fell upon all the people 7
12:26 to fall upon the Jews by night. 7
2Mc 14:41 Being surrounded, Razis fell upon his own sword 8

fall upon rear 1. זנב
Jos 10:19 pursue your enemies, fall upon their rear 1

fallen *See* grape.

falling *See* cause.

fallow *See* lie, ground.

false 1. בגד 2. בָּגוֹד 3. הֶבֶל 4. זנה 5. חלק 6. כָּזָב 7. כחש 8. לֹא כֵּן 9. מעל 10. מִרְמָה 11. שָׁוְא 12. שקר 13. שֶׁקֶר 14. *πλαστός* 15. *ψευδής* 16. *ψεύδομαι* 17. *ψεῦδος* 18. *ψεύστης*
Exd 20:16 You shall not bear false witness against 13
23: 1 You shall not utter a false report. 11
7 Keep far from a false charge, and do not slay 13
Deu 5:20 'Neither shall you bear false witness 11
19:18 if the witness is a false witness and has accused 13
2Ch 26:16 For he was false to the LORD his God 9
Job 31:28 for I should have been false to God above. 7
36: 4 For truly my words are not false; 13
Ps 24: 4 who does not lift up his soul to what is false 11
26: 4 I do not sit with false men 11
27:12 for false witnesses have risen against me 13
44:17 forgotten thee, or been false to thy covenant. 12
73:27 dost put an end to those who are false to thee. 4
89:33 but I will not . . be false to my faithfulness. 12
119:29 Put false ways far from me; 13
104 therefore I hate every false way. 13
128 I hate every false way. 13
Prv 6:19 a false witness who breathes out lies 13
11: 1 A false balance is an abomination to the LORD 10
12:17 but a false witness utters deceit. 13
14: 5 but a false witness breathes out lies. 13
17: 7 still less is false speech to a prince. 13
19: 5 A false witness will not go unpunished 13
9 A false witness will not go unpunished 13
20:23 false scales are not good. 10
21:28 A false witness will perish 6
25:18 who bears false witness against his neighbor 13
Isa 16: 6 the pride of Moab . . his boasts are false. 8
Jer 3: 7 and her false sister Judah saw it. 2
8 yet her false sister Judah did not fear 1
10 Yet . . her false sister Judah did not return to me 2
11 shown herself less guilty than false Judah. 1
8: 8 the false pen of the scribes has made it into a lie. 13
10: 3 for the customs of the peoples are false. 3
14 images are false, and there is no breath in them. 13
37:14 And Jeremiah said, "It is false; I am not deserting 13
48:30 his boasts are false, his deeds are false. 8
30 his boasts are false, his deeds are false. 8
51:17 images are false, and there is no breath in them. 13
Lam 2:14 have seen for you false and deceptive visions; 11
14 have seen for you oracles false and misleading. 11
Ezk 12:24 For there shall be no more any false vision 11
21:23 But to them it will seem like a false divination; 11
29 while they see for you false visions 11
22:28 seeing false visions and divining lies for them 11
Hos 10: 2 Their heart is false; 5
12: 7 A trader, in whose hands are false balances 10
Ams 8: 5 and deal deceitfully with false balances 10
Zec 8:17 love no false oath, for all these things I hate 13
10: 2 the dreamers tell false dreams 11
Act 6:13 and set up false witnesses who said 15
Rom 3: 4 Let God be true though every man be false 18
2Th 2:11 to make them believe what is false 17
Jas 3:14 do not boast and be false to the truth. 16
2Pe 2: 3 they will exploit you with false words 14
Rev 2: 2 tested those . . and found them to be false; 15
Tob 3: 6 because I have heard false reproaches 15
Jdt 11: 5 I will tell nothing false to my lord this night. 17
AEs 16: 6 the false trickery of their evil natures 15
Wis 10:14 Those who accused him she showed to be false 15
Sir 34: 1 A man of no understanding has vain and false hopes 15
36:19 so an intelligent mind detects false words. 15
LJr 1: 8 they are false and cannot speak. 15
44 Whatever is done for them is false 15
50 it will afterward be known that they are false. 15
59 better . . than to be these false gods 15
59 better . . than these false gods. 15
59 better . . than these false gods. 15
Sus 1:43 these men have borne false witness against me. 15
49 these men have borne false witness against her. 15
2Mc 5: 5 When a false rumor arose that Antiochus was dead 15

false *See also* Christ, accusation, apostle, brother, god, idol, play, prophet, prove, teacher, testimony, witness.

become false 1. הבל
2Kg 17:15 They went after false idols, and became false 1

something false 1. *ψευδής*
Sir 34: 4 from something false what will be true? 1

falsehood 1. דְּבַר שֶׁקֶר 2. כָּזָב 3. מעל 4. עַוְלָה 5. שָׁוְא 6. שֶׁקֶר 7. *ἀδικία* 8. *ψεῦδος* 9. *ψεῦσμα* 10. mendacium
Job 21:34 nothing left of your answers but falsehood. 3
27: 4 my lips will not speak falsehood 4
31: 5 If I have walked with falsehood 5
Ps 62: 4 They take pleasure in falsehood. 2
119:86 they persecute me with falsehood; help me! 6
163 I hate and abhor falsehood, but I love thy law. 6
144: 8 whose right hand is a right hand of falsehood. 6
11 whose right hand is a right hand of falsehood. 6
Prv 13: 5 A righteous man hates falsehood 1
29:12 ruler listens to falsehood, all his officials 1
30: 8 Remove far from me falsehood and lying; 5
Isa 5:18 those who draw iniquity with cords of falsehood 5
28:15 and in falsehood we have taken shelter"; 6
Jer 9: 3 falsehood and not truth has grown strong 6
Ezk 13: 6 They have spoken falsehood and divined a lie; 5
Hos 12: 1 they multiply falsehood and violence; 2
Joh 7:18 in him there is no falsehood. 7
Rom 3: 7 But if through my falsehood God's truthfulness 9
Eph 4:25 Therefore, putting away falsehood 8
Rev 21:27 any one who practices abomination or falsehood 8
22:15 every one who loves and practices falsehood. 8
2Es 14:18 and falsehood shall come near 10
Jdt 5: 5 No falsehood shall come from your servant's mouth. 8

falsely 1. בַּשֶּׁקֶר 2. לַשֶּׁקֶר 3. עַוְלָה 4. שֶׁקֶר 5. *ψεύδομαι*
Lev 6: 3 lied about it, swearing falsely- 4
5 or anything about which he has sworn falsely 4
19:12 you shall not swear by my name falsely 4
Deu 19:18 if the witness . . accused his brother falsely 4
Job 13: 7 Will you speak falsely for God 3
Jer 5: 2 As the LORD lives," yet they swear falsely. 2
31 the prophets prophesy falsely 1
6:13 from prophet to priest, every one deals falsely. 4
7: 9 steal, murder, commit adultery, swear falsely 2
8:10 from prophet to priest every one deals falsely. 4
20: 6 friends, to whom you have prophesied falsely. 1
27:15 but they are prophesying falsely in my name 2
40:16 for you are speaking falsely of Ish'mael. 4
Ezk 13:22 you have disheartened the righteous falsely 4
Hos 7: 1 for they deal falsely, the thief breaks 4
Zec 5: 3 every one who swears falsely shall be cut off *
4 the house of him who swears falsely by my name; 2
Mal 3: 5 against those who swear falsely 2
Mat 5:11 evil against you falsely on my account. 5

falsely *See also* call, deal, speak, swear.

falter 1. *ἐκκλίνω* 2. *πίπτω*
AEs 15: 7 the queen faltered, and turned pale and faint 2
Sir 12:15 if you falter, he will not stand by you. 1

fame 1. זֵכֶר 2. שֵׁם 3. שֵׁמַע 4. שֹׁמַע 5. *ἀκοή* 6. *διαφημίζω* 7. *ὄνομα*
Num 14:15 then the nations who have heard thy fame will say 3
Deu 26:19 praise and in fame and in honor 2
Jos 6:27 was with Joshua; and his fame was in all the land. 4
1Kg 4:31 wiser than . . and his fame was in all the nations 2
10: 1 the queen of Sheba heard of the fame of Solomon 2
1Ch 14:17 the fame of David went out into all lands 2
22: 5 of fame and glory throughout all lands; 2
2Ch 9: 1 the queen of Sheba heard of the fame of Solomon 3
26: 8 his fame spread even to the border of Egypt 2
15 fame spread far, for he was marvelously helped 2
Est 9: 4 Mor'decai . . his fame spread throughout all 4
Ps 72:17 for ever, his fame continue as long as the sun! 2
145: 7 pour forth the fame of thy abundant goodness 1
Isa 66:19 that have not heard my fame or seen my glory; 3
Mat 4:24 So his fame spread throughout all Syria 5
9:31 But they went away and spread his fame 6
14: 1 the tetrarch heard about the fame of Jesus; 5
Mrk 1:28 And at once his fame spread everywhere 5
1Mc 3:26 His fame reached the king 7
8: 1 Now Judas heard of the fame of the Romans 7
12 as many as have heard of their fame 7

famed 1. *ἔνδοξος*
1Mc 6: 1 Elymais in Persia was a city famed for its wealth 1

familiar 1. ידע 2. *γνώστης* 3. *ἐμπειράω*
1Kg 9:27 seamen who were familiar with the sea 1
2Ch 8:18 ships and servants familiar with the sea 1
Act 26: 3 you are especially familiar with all customs 2
Tob 5: 6 I am familiar with the way 3

familiar *See also* friend.

family 1. אָב 2. אָח 3. אֶלֶף 4. בַּיִת 5. בֵּית אָב 6. זֶרַע 7. מִשְׁפָּחָה 8. *γένος* 9. *ἴδιος* 10. *οἱ αὐτοῦ* 11. *οἰκεῖος* 12. *οἶκος* 13. *οἱ παρά* 14. *πανοικία* 15. *πατριά* 16. *πάτριος* 17. *πατρίς* 18. *σπέρμα*
Gen 8:19 the earth, went forth by families out of the ark. 7
10: 5 language, by their families, in their nations. 7
18 Afterward the families of the Canaanites 7
20 These are the sons of Ham, by their families 7
31 These are the sons of Shem, by their families 7
32 These are the families of the sons of Noah 7
12: 3 by you all the families of the earth shall bless 7
28:14 all the families of the earth bless themselves. 7
34:19 Now he was the most honored of all his family. 4
36:40 the chiefs of Esau, according to their families 7
37: 2 This is the history of the family of Jacob. *
Exd 1:21 midwives feared God he gave them families. 4
6:14 Carmi; these are the families of Reuben. 7
15 these are the families of Simeon. 7
17 of Gershon: Libni and Shim'e-i, by their families. 7
19 These are the families of the Levites according 7
24 these are the families of the Ko'rahites. 7
25 heads . . of the Levites by their families. 7
12:21 Select lambs . . according to your families 7
Lev 20: 5 my face against that man and against his family 7
25:10 each of you shall return to his family 7
41 go back to his own family, and return 7
45 from . . their families that are with you 7
47 sells . . to a member of the stranger's family 7
49 near kinsman belonging to his family may redeem 7
Num 1: 2 census . . by families, by fathers' houses 7
18 registered . . by families, by fathers' houses 7
20 their generations, by their families 7
22 Simeon . . by their families, by their fathers' 7
24 by their families, by their fathers' houses 7
26 by their families, by their fathers' houses 7
28 by their families, by their fathers' houses 7
30 by their families, by their fathers' houses 7
32 E'phraim, their generations, by their families 7
34 by their families, by their fathers' houses 7
36 by their families, by their fathers' houses 7
38 by their families, by their fathers' houses 7
40 by their families, by their fathers' houses 7
42 by their families, by their fathers' houses 7
2:34 so they set out, every one in his family 7
3:15 by fathers' houses and by families; 7
18 names of the sons of Gershon by their families 7
19 the sons of Kohath by their families 7
20 the sons of Merar'i by their families 7
20 These are the families of the Levites 7
21 Of Gershon were the family of the Libnites 7
21 the Libnites and the family of the Shim'e-ites; 7
21 these were the families of the Gershonites. 7
23 The families of the Gershonites were to encamp 7
27 Of Kohath were the family of the Amramites 7
27 Of Kohath . . the family of the Izhar'ites 7
27 Of Kohath . . the family of the He'bronites 7
27 Of Kohath . . the family of the Uzzie'lites; 7
27 these are the families of the Ko'hathites. 7
29 The families of the sons of Kohath were to encamp 7
30 house of the families of the Ko'hathites. 7
33 Of Merar'i were the family of the Mahlites 7
33 Of Merar'i were . . the family of the Mushites 7
33 these are the families of Merar'i. 7
35 fathers' house of the families of Merar'i 7
39 Moses and Aaron numbered . . by families 7
4: 2 Take a census . . by their families 7
18 tribe of the families of the Ko'hathites 7
22 by their families and their fathers' houses; 7
24 the service of the families of the Gershonites 7
28 service of the families . . of the Gershonites 7
29 number them by their families 7
33 service of the families of the sons of Merar'i 7
34 by their families and their fathers' houses 7
36 their number by families was 2,750. 7
37 number of the families of the Ko'hathites 7
38 by their families and their fathers' houses 7
40 number by their families and their fathers' 7
41 number of the families of the sons of Gershon 7
42 The number of the families of the sons of Merar'i 7
42 by their families and their fathers' houses 7
44 their number by families was 3,200. 7
45 numbered of the families of the sons of Merar'i 7
46 by their families and their fathers' houses 7
11:10 people weeping throughout their families 7
25: 6 came and brought a Mid'ianite woman to his family 2
26: 5 of Hanoch, the family of the Ha'nochites; 7
5 of Pallu, the family of the Pal'luites; 7
6 of Hezron, the family of the Hez'ronites; 7
6 of Carmi, the family of the Carmites. 7
7 These are the families of the Reubenites; 7
12 The sons of Simeon according to their families 7
12 of Nem'uel, the family of the Nem'uelites; 7
12 of Jamin, the family of the Ja'minites; 7
12 of Jachin, the family of the Ja'chinites; 7
13 of Zerah, the family of the Zer'ahites; 7
13 of Sha'ul, the family of the Sha'ulites. 7
14 These are the families of the Simeonites, 22,200. 7
15 The sons of Gad according to their families 7

15 of Zephon, the family of the Ze'phonites; 7
15 of Haggi, the family of the Haggites; 7
15 of Shuni, the family of the Shunites; 7
16 of Ozni, the family of the Oznites; 7
16 of Eri, the family of the Erites; 7
17 of Ar'od, the family of the Ar'odites; 7
17 of Are'li, the family of the Are'lites. 7
18 These are the families of the sons of Gad 7
20 sons of Judah according to their families were 7
20 of Shelah, the family of the Shela'nites; 7
20 of Perez, the family of the Per'ezites; 7
20 of Zerah, the family of the Zer'ahites. 7
21 of Hezron, the family of the Hez'ronites; 7
21 of Hamul, the family of the Hamu'lites. 7
22 families of Judah according to their number 7
23 sons of Is'sachar according to their families 7
23 of Tola, the family of the To'laites; 7
23 of Puvah, the family of the Punites; 7
24 of Jashub, the family of the Jash'ubites; 7
24 of Shimron, the family of the Shim'ronites. 7
25 families of Is'sachar according to their number 7
26 The sons of Zeb'ulun, according to their families 7
26 of Sered, the family of the Ser'edites; 7
26 of Elon, the family of the E'lonites; 7
26 of Jahleel, the family of the Jah'leelites. 7
27 These are the families of the Zeb'ulunites 7
28 The sons of Joseph according to their families 7
29 of Machir, the family of the Ma'chirites; 7
29 of Gilead, the family of the Gileadites. 7
30 of Ie'zer, the family of the Ie'zerites; 7
30 of Helek, the family of the He'lekites; 7
31 of As'riel, the family of the As'rielites; 7
31 of Shechem, the family of the She'chemites; 7
32 of Shemi'da, the family of the Shemi'daites; 7
32 of Hepher, the family of the He'pherites. 7
34 These are the families of Manas'seh; 7
35 sons of E'phraim according to their families 7
35 of Shuthe'lah, the family of the Shuthe'lahites; 7
35 of Becher, the family of the Bech'erites; 7
35 of Tahan, the family of the Ta'hanites. 7
36 of Eran, the family of the E'ranites. 7
37 These are the families of the sons of E'phraim 7
37 sons of Joseph according to their families. 7
38 sons of Benjamin according to their families 7
38 of Bela, the family of the Be'la-ites; 7
38 of Ashbel, the family of the Ash'belites; 7
38 of Ahi'ram, the family of the Ahi'ramites; 7
39 of Shephu'pham, the family of the Shu'phamites; 7
39 of Hupham, the family of the Hu'phamites. 7
40 of Ard, the family of the Ard'ites; 7
40 of Na'aman, the family of the Na'amites. 7
41 sons of Benjamin according to their families; 7
42 sons of Dan according to their families 7
42 of Shuham, the family of the Shu'hamites. 7
42 families of Dan according to their families. 7
42 families of Dan according to their families. 7
43 All the families of the Shu'hamites 7
44 The sons of Asher according to their families 7
44 of Imnah, the family of the Imnites; 7
44 of Ishvi, the family of the Ishvites; 7
44 of Beri'ah, the family of the Beri'ites. 7
45 of Heber, the family of the He'berites; 7
45 of Mal'chi-el, the family of the Mal'chi-elites. 7
47 These are the families of the sons of Asher 7
48 sons of Naph'tali according to their families 7
48 of Jahzeel, the family of the Jah'zeelites; 7
48 of Guni, the family of the Gunites; 7
49 of Jezer, the family of the Je'zerites; 7
49 of Shillem, the family of the Shil'lemites. 7
50 families of Naph'tali according 7
50 Naph'tali according to their families; 7
57 numbered according to their families 7
57 of Gershon, the family of the Gershonites; 7
57 of Kohath, the family of the Ko'hathites; 7
57 of Merar'i, the family of the Merar'ites. 7
58 families of Levi: the family of the Libnites 7
58 families of Levi: the family of the Libnites 7
58 of Levi . . the family of the He'bronites 7
58 of Levi . . the family of the Mahlites 7
58 of Levi . . the family of the Mushites 7
58 of Levi . . the family of the Ko'rahites. 7
27: 1 from the families of Manas'seh the son of Joseph. 7
4 name of our father be taken away from his family 7
11 his kinsman that is next to him of his family 7
33:54 inherit . . by lot according to your families; 7
36: 1 heads . . of the families of the sons of Gilead 7
6 marry within the family of the tribe 7
8 shall be wife to one of the family of the tribe 7
12 married into the families of . . Manas'seh 7
12 inheritance remained in the tribe of the family 7
Deu 25: 5 wife . . shall not be married outside the family •
29:18 lest there be . . a man or woman or family or tribe 7
Jos 7:14 and the tribe . . shall come near by families; 7
14 the family which the LORD takes shall come near 7
17 and he brought near the families of Judah 7
17 and the family of the Zer'ahites was taken; 7
17 and he brought near the family of the Zer'ahites 7
13:15 Moses gave . . according to their families. 7
23 according to their families with their cities 7
24 Moses gave . . according to their families. 7
28 the inheritance . . according to their families 7
29 it was allotted . . according to their families. 7
31 were allotted . . according to their families. 7
15: 1 The lot for . . Judah according to their families 7
12 is the boundary . . according to their families. 7
20 inheritance . . according to their families. 7
16: 5 territory of the E'phraimites by their families 7
8 Such is the inheritance of . . by their families 7
17: 2 allotments were made . . by their families 7
2 descendants of Manas'seh . . by their families. 7
18:11 The lot . . of Benjamin according to its families 7
20 the inheritance . . according to its families 7
21 the cities . . according to their families 7
28 the inheritance . . according to its families. 7
19: 1 the tribe of Simeon, according to its families; 7
8 inheritance . . according to its families. 7
10 the tribe of Zeb'ulun, according to its families. 7
16 the tribe of Zeb'ulun, according to its families 7
17 tribe of Is'sachar, according to its families. 7
23 the tribe of Is'sachar, according to its families 7
24 the tribe of Asher according to its families. 7
31 of the tribe of Asher according to its families 7
32 tribe of Naph'tali, according to its families. 7
39 the tribe of Naph'tali according to its families 7
40 for the tribe of Dan, according to its families. 7
48 of the tribe of Dan, according to their families 7
21: 4 lot came out for the families of the Ko'hathites. 7
5 by lot from the families of the tribe of E'phraim 7
6 by lot from the families of the tribe of Is'sachar 7
7 The Merar'ites according to their families 7
10 descendants of Aaron, one of the families 7
20 to the Ko'hathite families of the Levites 7
26 of the families of the rest of the Ko'hathites 7
27 Gershonites, one of the families of the Levites 7
33 The cities of the several families 7
34 the rest of the Levites, the Merar'ite families 7
40 the cities of the several Merar'ite families 7
40 the remainder of the families of the Levites 7
22:14 ten chiefs, one from each of the tribal families 5
14 chiefs . . every one of them the head of a family 5
21 in answer to the heads of the families of Israel 3
30 the heads of the families of Israel who were 3
Jdg 1:25 sword, but they let the man and all his family go. 7
6:15 in Manas'seh, and I am the least in my family. 5
27 too afraid of his family and the men of the town 5
8:27 and it became a snare to Gideon and to his family. 4
35 not show kindness to the family of Jerrubba'al 4
9: 1 them and to the whole clan of his mother's family 5
16:31 brothers and all his family came down and took 5
17: 7 man of Bethlehem in Judah, of the family of Judah 7
18:19 or to be priest to a tribe and family in Israel? 7
21:24 departed . . every man to his tribe and family 7
Rut 2: 1 a man of wealth, of the family of Elim'elech 7
3 Bo'az, who was of the family of Elim'elech. 7
1Sm 9:21 is not my family the humblest of all the families 7
21 of all the families of the tribe of Benjamin? 7
10:21 He brought . . Benjamin near by its families 7
21 the family of the Matrites was taken by lot; 7
21 brought the family of the Matrites near man 7
18:18 Who am I, and . . my father's family in Israel 7
20: 6 there is a . . sacrifice there for all the family. 7
29 our family holds a sacrifice in the city 7
2Sm 14: 7 And now the whole family has risen against 7
16: 5 came out a man of the family of the house of Saul 7
2Kg 11: 1 she arose and destroyed all the royal family. 6
25:25 Ish'mael the son of . . of the royal family, came 6
1Ch 2:53 the families of Kir'iath-je'arim 7
55 families also of the scribes that dwelt at Jabez 7
4: 2 These were the families of the Zo'rathites. 7
8 Koz was the father of . . the families of Ahar'hel 7
21 families of the house of linen workers 7
27 nor did all their family multiply like the men 7
38 these . . were princes in their families 7
5: 7 his kinsmen by their families 7
6:19 families of the Levites according to their 7
54 sons of Aaron of the families of Ko'hathites 7
60 All their cities throughout their families 7
61 given by lot out of the family of the tribe 7
62 To the Gershomites according to their families 7
63 To the Merar'ites according to their families 7
66 some of the families of the sons of Kohath 7
70 for the rest of the families of the Ko'hathites. 7
7: 5 belonging to all the families of Is'sachar 7
16:28 Ascribe to the LORD, O families of the peoples 7
2Ch 19: 8 certain . . heads of families of Israel 1
22:10 destroyed all the royal family of . . Judah. 6
Ezr 2:68 Some of the heads of families, when they came 1
Neh 4:13 people according to their families 7
Est 9:28 throughout every generation, in every family 7
Job 31:34 the contempt of families terrified me 7
32: 2 of Bar'achel the Buzite, of the family of Ram 7
Ps 22:27 all the families of the nations shall worship 7
96: 7 Ascribe to the LORD, O families of the peoples 7
107:41 makes their families like flocks. 7
Jer 2: 4 and all the families of the house of Israel. 7
3:14 will take you, one from a city and two from a family 7
8: 3 all the remnant that remains of this evil family 7
31: 1 I will be the God of all the families of Israel 7
33:24 has rejected the two families which he chose'? 7
41: 1 son of Eli'shama, of the royal family 6
Ezk 43:19 to the Levitical priests of the family of Zadok 6
45:15 from the families of Israel. •
Ams 3: 1 against the whole family which I brought up out 7
2 have I known of all the families of the earth; 7
Mic 2: 3 Behold, against this family I am devising evil 7
Zec 12:12 The land shall mourn, each family by itself; 7
12 the family of the house of David by itself 7
12 the family of the house of Nathan by itself 7
13 the family of the house of Levi by itself 7
13 the family of the Shim'e-ites by itself 7
14 all the families that are left, each by itself 7
14:17 if any of the families of the earth do not go up 7
18 if the family of Egypt do not go up and present 7
Mrk 3:21 when his family heard it 13
Act 3:25 shall all the families of the earth be blessed.' 15
4: 6 and all who were of the high-priestly family. 8
7:13 Joseph's family became known to Pharaoh. 8
13:26 Brethren, sons of the family of Abraham 8
16:33 he was baptized at once, with all his family. 10
Rom 16:10 those who belong to the family of Aristobu'lus. •
11 those . . who belong to the family of Narcis'sus. •
Eph 3:15 every family in heaven and on earth is named 15
1Ti 5: 4 learn their religious duty to their own family 12
8 not provide . . especially for his own family 11
Tit 1:11 since they are upsetting whole families 12
1Es 1: 4 prepare yourselves by your families and kindred 15
2: 8 the heads of families of the tribes of Judah 15
5:44 Some of the heads of families 15
Tob 1: 9 I married Anna, a member of our family 16
5:10 to what tribe and family do you belong? Tell me. 17
11 Are you looking for a tribe and a family 16
13 because I tried to learn your tribe and family. 15
Jdt 8: 2 who belonged to her tribe and family 16
18 any tribe or family or people or city of ours 15
AEs 14: 5 I have heard in the tribe of my family 16
Sir 11:34 will estrange you from your family. 9
1Mc 1:61 their families and those who circumcised them; 12
5:62 they did not belong to the family of those men 18
12:21 are brethren and are of the family of Abraham. 8
2Mc 1:10 who is of the family of the anointed priests 8
3Mc 3:27 together with his family. 14
6: 8 restored unharmed to all his family. 11
4Mc 5: 4 He was a man of priestly family, learned in the law 8
15:25 nature, family, parental love 8

family and friends 1. ὁ παρά

Sus 1:33 her family and friends and all who saw her wept. 1

famine 1. כָּפָן 2. רָעָב 3. רְעָבוֹן 4. λιμός 5. fames

Gen 12:10 Now there was a famine in the land. 2
10 sojourn there, for the famine was severe 2
26: 1 Now there was a famine in the land 2
1 famine in the land, besides the former famine 2
41:27 east wind are also seven years of famine. 2
30 there will arise seven years of famine 2
30 land of Egypt; the famine will consume the land 2
31 by reason of that famine which will follow 2
36 a reserve . . against the seven years of famine 2
36 that the land may not perish through the famine. 2
50 Before the year of famine came 2
54 the seven years of famine began to come 2
54 There was famine in all lands; but in all the land 2
56 when the famine had spread over all the land 2
56 for the famine was severe in the land of Egypt. 2
57 to buy grain, because the famine was severe 2
42: 5 for the famine was in the land of Canaan. 2
19 carry grain for the famine of your households 3
33 and take grain for the famine of your households 3
43: 1 Now the famine was severe in the land. 2
45: 6 For the famine has been in the land 2
11 for there are yet five years of famine to come; 2
47: 4 for the famine is severe in the land of Canaan; 2
13 for the famine was very severe, so that the land 2
13 Canaan languished by reason of the famine. 2
20 because the famine was severe upon them. 2
Rut 1: 1 In the days when . . there was a famine in the land 2
2Sm 21: 1 Now there was a famine in the days of David 2
24:13 Shall three years of famine come . . in your land? 2
1Kg 8:37 famine in the land . . pestilence or blight 2
18: 2 Now the famine was severe in Sama'ria. 2
2Kg 4:38 Eli'sha came . . to Gilgal when there was a famine 2
6:25 there was a great famine in Sama'ria 2
7: 4 the famine is in the city, and we shall die there; 2
8: 1 the LORD has called for a famine, and it will come 2
25: 3 the famine was so severe in the city that 2
1Ch 21:12 either three years of famine; 2
2Ch 6:28 If there is famine in the land, if there is 2
20: 9 If evil comes upon us . . or pestilence, or famine 2
32:11 may give you over to die by famine and by thirst 2
Neh 5: 3 mortgaging . . to get grain because of the famine. 2
Job 5:20 In famine he will redeem you from death 2
22 At destruction and famine you shall laugh 1
Ps 33:19 soul from death, and keep them alive in famine. 2
37:19 in the days of famine they have abundance. 3
105:16 When he summoned a famine on the land 2
Isa 14:30 but I will kill your root with famine 2

51:19 devastation and destruction, famine and sword; 2
Jer 5:12 nor shall we see sword or famine. 2
11:22 sons and their daughters shall die by famine; 2
14:12 but I will consume them by the sword, by famine 2
13 shall not see the sword, nor shall you have famine 2
15 Sword and famine shall not come on this land 2
15 By . . famine those prophets shall be consumed. 2
16 victims of famine and sword, with none to bury 2
18 if I enter the city, behold, the diseases of famine! 2
15: 2 those who are for famine, to famine 2
2 those who are for famine, to famine 2
16: 4 They shall perish by the sword and by famine 2
18:21 Therefore deliver up their children to famine; 2
21: 7 who survive the pestilence, sword, and famine 2
9 die by the sword, by famine, and by pestilence; 2
24:10 will send sword, famine, and pestilence upon them 2
27: 8 with the sword, with famine, and with pestilence 2
13 die by the sword, by famine, and by pestilence 2
28: 8 prophesied war, famine, and pestilence 2
29:17 I am sending on them sword, famine, and pestilence 2
18 pursue them with sword, famine, and pestilence 2
32:24 because of sword and famine and pestilence 2
36 given . . by sword, by famine, and by pestilence 2
34:17 liberty to the sword, to pestilence, and to famine 2
38: 2 die by the sword, by famine, and by pestilence; 2
42:16 the famine of which you are afraid shall follow 2
17 die by the sword, by famine, and by pestilence; 2
22 know . . that you shall die by the sword, by famine 2
44:12 by the sword and by famine they shall be consumed; 2
12 they shall die by the sword and by famine; 2
13 with the sword, with famine, and with pestilence 2
18 been consumed by the sword and by famine. 2
27 shall be consumed by the sword and by famine 2
52: 6 the famine was so severe in the city 2
Lam 5:10 skin is hot . . with the burning heat of famine. 2
Ezk 5:12 and be consumed with famine in the midst of you; 2
16 I loose against you my deadly arrows of famine 2
16 when I bring more and more famine upon you 2
17 I will send famine and wild beasts against you 2
6:11 fall by the sword, by famine, and by pestilence. 2
12 he that is left . . shall die of famine. 2
7:15 pestilence and famine are within; 2
15 in the city famine and pestilence devour. 2
12:16 from the sword, from famine and pestilence 2
14:13 break its staff of bread and send famine upon it 2
21 sword, famine, evil beasts, and pestilence 2
36:29 and make it abundant and lay no famine upon you. 2
30 may never again suffer the disgrace of famine 2
Ams 8:11 when I will send a famine on the land; 2
11 not a famine of bread, nor a thirst for water 2
Mat 24: 7 there will be famines and earthquakes 4
Mrk 13: 8 there will be famines 4
Lke 4:25 when there came a great famine over all the land; 4
15:14 a great famine arose in that country 4
21:11 in various places famines and pestilences 4
Act 7:11 came a famine throughout all Egypt and Canaan 4
11:28 there would be a great famine over all the world; 4
Rom 8:35 or famine, or nakedness, or peril, or sword? 4
Rev 6: 8 power . . to kill with sword and with famine 4
18: 8 plagues . . pestilence and mourning and famine 4
2Es 15: 5 the sword and famine and death and destruction. 5
49 widowhood, poverty, famine, sword, and pestilence 5
16:18 the beginning of famine, when many shall perish; 5
19 Behold, famine and plague 5
21 earth–the sword, famine, and great confusion. 5
22 who live on the earth shall perish by famine 5
22 who survive the famine shall die by the sword. 5
34 and their husbands shall perish of famine. 5
46 in captivity and famine they will beget 5
Tob 4:13 because shiftlessness is the mother of famine. 4
Jdt 5:10 When a famine spread over Canaan 4
7:14 their wives and children will waste away with famine 4
Sir 39:29 Fire and hail and famine and pestilence 4
40: 9 calamities, famine and affliction and plague. 4
48: 2 He brought a famine upon them 4
Bar 2:25 by famine and sword and pestilence. 4
1Mc 6:54 because famine had prevailed over the rest 4
9:24 In those days a very great famine occurred 4
13:49 many of them perished from famine. 4

famish 1. עָיֵף 2. רזה 3. רעב
Gen 25:29 Esau came in from the field, and he was famished. 1
30 eat some of that red pottage, for I am famished! 1
41:55 land of Egypt was famished, the people cried 3
Zep 2:11 yea, he will famish all the gods of the earth 2

famous 1. אַדִּיר 2. שֵׁם 3. תְּהִלָּה 4. *ἔνδοξος* 5. *ἔπαινος* 6. *ἐπίσημος* 7. *μέγας σφόδρα* 8. *ὀνομαστός* 9. *περιβόητος*
1Ch 5:24 mighty warriors, famous men 2
12:30 men of valor, famous men in their fathers' houses. 2
Ps 136:18 slew famous kings 1
Jer 49:25 How the famous city is forsaken, the joyful city! 3
2Co 8:18 the brother who is famous among all the churches 5
Jdt 16:23 She became more and more famous 7
Sir 44: 1 Let us now praise famous men 4
Bar 3:26 The giants were born there, who were famous of old 8
2Mc 2:22 the temple famous throughout the world 9
3Mc 6: 1 famous among the priests of the country 6

famous *See also* make.

famous man 1. *δοξάζω*
Sir 48: 6 famous men from their beds; 1

fan 1. *διερεθίζω* 2. *ἐκφυσάω*
4Mc 5:32 fan the fire more vehemently! 2
9:19 while fanning the flames 1

fancy 1. נֶפֶשׁ 2. הַרְהֹר (A) 3. *φαντάζομαι*
Sng 6:12 my fancy set me in a chariot beside my prince. 1
Dan 4: 5 fancies and the visions of my head alarmed me. 2
Sir 34: 5 like a woman in travail the mind has fancies. 3

fang 1. מְתַלְּעוֹת
Job 29:17 I broke the fangs of the unrighteous 1
Ps 58: 6 tear out the fangs of the young lions, O LORD! 1
Jol 1: 6 it has the fangs of a lioness. 1

far 1. בּוֹאֲךָ 2. הָלְאָה 3. הֲלֹם 4. יסף 5. יַרְכָה 6. כְּכל 7. כל 8. לְכל 9. לְמֵרָחוֹק 10. מְאֹד 11. מֶרְחָק 12. סור 13. עַד 14. עַד לְ 15. עוֹד 16. קֵץ 17. קָצֶה 18. רַב 19. רחק 20. רָחֵק 21. רָחֹק 22. *ἀφίστημι* 23. *ἄχρι* 24. *ἕως* 25. *ἕως πρός* 26. *ἕως τοῦ ἐλθεῖν εἰς* 27. *καθό* 28. *μακράν* 29. *μακρός* 30. *μακρύνω* 31. *μᾶλλον* 32. *μέχρι* 33. *πολὺς μᾶλλον* 34. *πόρρω* 35. *τοσοῦτος* 36. longe 37. multus 38. quantum
Gen 10:19 in the direction of Gerar, as far as Gaza 13
19 Gomor'rah, Admah, and Zeboi'im, as far as Lasha. 13
13: 3 he journeyed on from the Negeb as far as Bethel 13
12 Lot dwelt . . and moved his tent as far as Sodom. 13
14: 6 in their Mount Se'ir as far as El-paran 13
14 of them, and went in pursuit as far as Dan. 13
Lev 13:12 from head to foot, so far as the priest can see 8
Num16: 3 You have gone too far! For all the congregation 18
7 You have gone too far, sons of Levi! 18
21:24 to the Jabbok, as far as to the Ammonites; 13
26 all his land out of his hand, as far as the Arnon. 13
30 posterity perished from Heshbon, as far as Dibon 13
33:49 from Beth-jes'himoth as far as Abel-shittim 13
Deu 1: 7 as far as the great river, the river Euphra'tes. 13
44 Amorites . . beat you down in Se'ir as far as Hormah. 13
2:23 for the Avvim, who lived in villages as far as Gaza 13
36 From Aro'er . . as far as Gilead, there was not 13
3:10 as far as Sal'ecah and Ed're-i, cities of the kingdom 13
14 as far as the border of the Gesh'urites 13
16 from Gilead as far as the valley of the Arnon 13
17 from Chin'nereth as far as the sea of the Arabah 13
4:48 as far as Mount Si'rion (that is, Hermon) 13
49 as far as the Sea of the Arabah, under the slopes 13
12:21 If the place . . is too far from you, then you may 19
14:24 because the place is too far from you 19
20:15 do to all the cities which are very far from you 21
29:22 foreigner who comes from a far land, would say 21
34: 1 LORD showed him all the land. Gilead as far as Dan 13
2 all the land of Judah as far as the Western Sea 13
3 Jericho the city of palm trees, as far as Zo'ar. 13
Jos 1: 4 From the wilderness . . as far as the great river 13
2: 7 the men pursued after them . . as far as the fords; 13
7: 5 chased them before the gate as far as Sheb'arim 13
9: 6 We have come from a far country . . make a covenant 21
9 From a very far country your servants have come 21
22 Why . . deceive us, saying, 'We are very far from you 21
10:10 and smote them as far as Aze'kah and Makke'dah. 13
11 LORD threw down great stones . . as far as Aze'kah 13
41 and all the country of Goshen, as far as Gibeon. 13
11: 8 smote them and chased them as far as Great Sidon 13
8 and eastward as far as the valley of Mizpeh; 13
17 from Mount Halak . . as far as Ba'al-gad 13
12: 2 from . . the valley as far as the river Jabbok 13
13: 9 and all the tableland of Med'eba as far as Dibon; 13
10 cities . . as far as the boundary of the Ammonites; 13
15: 1 to the wilderness of Zin at the farthest south. 17
16: 3 as far as the territory of Lower Beth-hor'on 13
5 boundary . . as far as Upper Beth-hor'on 13
17:18 clear it and possess it to its farthest borders; •
19: 8 round about these cities as far as Ba'alath-beer 13
10 its inheritance reached as far as Sarid; 13
28 Rehob, Hammon, Kanah, as far as Sidon the Great; 13
33 its boundary ran . . as far as Lakkum; 13
Jdg 3: 3 Ba'al-her'mon as far as the entrance of Hamath. 14
6: 4 destroy . . as far as the neighborhood of Gaza 13
7:22 army fled as far as Beth-shit'tah toward Zer'erah 13
22 Zer'erah as far as the border of A'bel-meho'lah 13
24 seize the waters . . as far as Beth-bar'ah 13
24 and they seized the waters as far as Beth-bar'ah 13
11:33 he smote them . . as far as Abel-keramim 13
18: 7 they were far from the Sido'nians and had no 21
28 was no deliverer because it was far from Sidon 21
19:11 When they were near Jebus, the day was far spent 10
20:43 from Nohah as far as opposite Gib'e-ah on the east. 13
1Sm 6:12 after them as far as the border of Beth-she'mesh 13
7:11 and smote them, as far as below Beth-car. 13
10: 3 go on from there further and come to the oak 2
15: 7 Hav'ilah as far as Shur, which is east of Egypt. 1
17:52 and pursued the Philistines as far as Gath 13
52 on the way from Sha-ara'im as far as Gath and Ekron. 13
27: 8 of the land . . as far as Shur, to the land of Egypt. 1
1Kg 4:12 A'bel-meho'lah, as far as the other side of Jok'meam; 13
8:41 when a foreigner . . comes from a far country 21
12:30 people went . . and to the other as far as Dan. 13
2Kg 2: 2 the LORD has sent me as far as Bethel. 13
7:15 So they went after them as far as the Jordan; 13
14:25 from the . . as far as the Sea of the Arabah 13
18: 8 He smote the Philistines as far as Gaza and its 13
19:23 I entered its farthest retreat, its densest 16
20:14 They have come from a far country, from Babylon. 21
1Ch 4:33 were round about these cities as far as Ba'al. 13
5: 8 who dwelt in Aro'er, as far as Nebo and Ba'al-me'on. 13
9 to the east as far as the entrance of the desert 13
11 in the land of Bashan as far as Sal'ecah 13
12:40 from as far as Is'sachar and Zeb'ulun and Naph'tali 13
17:16 house, that thou hast brought me thus far? 3
29: 2 I have provided . . so far as I was able 6
2Ch 6:32 when a foreigner . . comes from a far country 21
36 carried away captive to a land far or near; 21
12: 4 came as far as Jerusalem. 13
14: 9 came as far as Mare'shah. 13
13 pursued them as far as Gerar 13
26:15 fame spread far, for he was marvelously helped 9
30:10 couriers went . . as far as Zeb'ulun; 13
34: 6 as far as Naph'tali, in their ruins round about 13
Neh 1: 9 your dispersed be under the farthest skies 17
3: 1 consecrated it as far as the Tower of the Hundred 13
1 consecrated . . as far as the Tower of Hanan'el. 13
8 restored Jerusalem as far as the Broad Wall. 13
13 repaired . . the wall, as far as the Dung Gate. 13
15 as far as the stairs that go down from the City 13
27 another section . . as far as the wall of Ophel. 13
31 Malchi'jah . . repaired as far as the house 13
4:19 we are separated on the wall, far from one another. 21
5: 8 We, as far as we are able, have bought back •
Est 9:20 all the provinces of . . both near and far 21
Job 5: 4 His sons are far from safety 19
21:16 The counsel of the wicked is far from me. 19
22:18 but the counsel of the wicked is far from me. 19
28: 3 search out to the farthest bound the ore in gloom 7
38:11 and said, 'Thus far shall you come, and no farther 4
Ps 22: 1 Why art thou so far from helping me 21
11 Be not far from me, for trouble is near 19
35:22 O LORD; be not silent! O Lord, be not far from me! 19
38:21 forsake me, O LORD! O my God, be not far from me! 19
48: 2 joy of all the earth, Mount Zion, in the far north 5
65: 5 all the ends of the earth, and of the farthest seas; 21
71:12 O God, be not far from me; O my God, make haste 19
73:27 For lo, those who are far from thee shall perish; 20
97: 9 O LORD . . thou art exalted far above all gods. 10
101: 4 Perverseness of heart shall be far from me; 12
103:12 as far as the east is from the west 19
109:17 He did not like blessing; may it be far from him! 19
119:150 with evil purpose; they are far from thy law. 19
155 Salvation is far from the wicked 21
Prv 15:29 The LORD is far from the wicked 21
25:25 Like cold water . . good news from a far country. 11
31:10 good wife . . is far more precious than jewels. 21
Ecc 7:23 I said, "I will be wise"; but it was far from me. 21
24 That which is, is far off, and deep, very deep; 21
Isa 8: 9 give ear, all you far countries; gird yourselves 11
14:13 sit on the mount of assembly in the far north; 5
15: 4 cry out, their voice is heard as far as Jahaz; 13
18: 2 to a people feared near and far 2
7 from a people feared near and far 2
29:13 while their hearts are far from me 19
30:27 Behold, the name of the LORD comes from far 11
39: 3 have come to me from a far country, from Babylon. 21
46:11 the man of my counsel from a far country. 11
12 Hearken . . you who are far from deliverance 21
54:14 you shall be far from oppression 19
57:19 peace, to the far and to the near, says the LORD; 21
59: 9 Therefore justice is far from us 19
11 is none; for salvation, but it is far from us. 19
60: 4 your sons shall come from far, and your daughters 21
9 of Tarshish first, to bring your sons from far 21
Jer 12: 2 art near in their mouth and far from their heart. 21
25:26 all the kings of the north, far and near 21
31:39 the measuring line shall go out farther 15
40 and all the fields as far as the brook Kidron 13
48: 4 Moab is destroyed; a cry is heard as far as Zo'ar. •
24 all the cities of the land of Moab, far and near. 21
32 Your branches . . reached as far as Jazer; 13
34 as far as Jahaz they utter their voice 13
49:30 Flee, wander far away, dwell in the depths 10
Lam 1:16 eyes . . with tears; for a comforter is far from me 19
Ezk 10: 5 the cherubim was heard as far as the outer court 13
22: 5 Those who are near and those who are far from you 21
23:40 They even sent for men to come from far 11
29:10 to Syene, as far as the border of Ethiopia. 13
47:16 Damascus and Hamath), as far as Hazer-hatticon •
18 to the eastern sea and as far as Tamar. •
19 it shall run from Tamar as far as the waters 13
48: 1 to the entrance of Hamath, as far as Hazar-e'non •
Dan 11: 2 fourth shall be far richer than all of them; •
10 again shall carry the war as far as his fortress. 13
Obd 1:20 possess Phoenicia as far as Zar'ephath; 13

Zec 10: 9 yet in far countries they shall remember me 11
Mat 15: 8 but their heart is far from me; 34
24:27 lightning . . shines as far as the west 24
26:58 as far as the courtyard of the high priest 24
Mrk 1:19 And going on a little farther •
7: 6 their heart is far from me; 34
12:34 You are not far from the kingdom of God. 28
Lke 7: 6 When he was not far from the house 28
15:13 and took his journey into a far country 29
19:12 A nobleman went into a far country 28
24:50 Then he led them out as far as Bethany 25
Joh 21: 8 they were not far from the land 28
Act 11:19 those . . traveled as far as Phoeni'cia and Cyprus 24
13: 6 had gone through the whole island as far as Paphos 23
17:15 Those . . brought him as far as Athens; 24
27 Yet he is not far from each one of us 28
22:21 I will send you far away to the Gentiles.' 28
23:23 get ready . . to go as far as Caesare'a. 24
28:15 as far as the Forum of Ap'pius and Three Taverns 23
Rom 12:18 so far as it depends upon you, live peaceably †
15:19 from Jerusalem and as far round as Illyr'icum 32
2Co 3: 9 the dispensation . . must far exceed it in splendor. 33
Php 1:23 that is far better. 31
1Pe 4:13 in so far as you share Christ's sufferings 27
2Es 7:48 and removed us far from life 36
8:47 you come far short of being able to love 37
10:55 as far as it is possible for your eyes to see it 38
Jdt 1: 9 and beyond the Jordan as far as Jerusalem 24
10 as far as the borders of Ethiopia. 24
12 as far as the coasts of the two seas. 24
2:24 as far as the sea. 24
7: 3 spread out . . over Dothan as far as Balbaim 24
15: 5 and cut them down as far as Choba 24
AEs 16:11 far enjoyed the good will that we have 35
Wis 12:24 For they went far astray on the paths of error 29
Sir 9:13 Keep far from a man who has the power to kill 29
15: 8 She is far from men of pride 28
23:12 all these errors will be far from the godly 22
30:23 remove sorrow far from you 29
Bar 3:21 Their sons have strayed far from her way. 34
LJr 1:73 he will be far from reproach. 29
Sus 1:51 Separate them far from each other 28
1Mc 7:45 from Adasa as far as Gazara 26
8: 4 even though the place was far distant from them. 29
12 They have subdued kings far and near 28
23 may sword and enemy be far from them. 30
9:15 he pursued them as far as Mount Azotus. 24
11: 7 as far as the river called Eleutherus 24
8 as far as Seleucia by the sea 24
62 he passed through the country as far as Damascus. 24
73 as far as Kadesh, to their camp 24
12:33 and marched through the country as far as Askalon 24
3Mc 4: 7 as far as the place of embarkation. 32
7:18 to each as far as his own house. 24

far *See also* bound, drive, extend, get, go, keep, put, recess, remove, spent, thus, withdraw.

far above 1. ὑπεράνω

Eph 1:21 far above all rule and authority and power 1
4:10 who also ascended far above all the heavens 1

far and wide 1. הָלְאָה

Num16:37 scatter the fire far and wide. For they are holy 1

far away 1. רחק מֶרְחָק 2. עַד 3. רחק 4. רָחֹק 5. ἕως 6. πόρρωθεν

Jdg 4:11 his tent as far away as the oak in Za-anan'nim 2
Prv 27:10 neighbor . . near than a brother who is far away. 4
Isa 17:13 he will rebuke them, and they will flee far away 1
22: 3 were captured, though they had fled far away. 4
49:19 and those who swallowed you up will be far away. 3
Dan 9: 7 all Israel . . near and those that are far away 4
Wis 14:17 they imagined their appearance far away 6
1Mc 14:16 It was heard in Rome, and as far away as Sparta 5

far be it 1. חָלִילָה 2. ἵλεως 3. μὴ γίνομαι

Gen 18:25 Far be it from thee to do such a thing 1
25 Far be that from thee! 1
44: 7 Far be it from your servants that they should do 1
17 he said, "Far be it from me that I should do so! 1
Jos 22:29 Far be it from us that we should rebel 1
24:16 Far be it from us that we should forsake the LORD 1
1Sm 2:30 but now the LORD declares: 'Far be it from me; 1
12:23 far be it from me that I . . sin against the LORD 1
20: 9 And Jonathan said, "Far be it from you! 1
2Sm 20:20 Far be it from me, far be it, that I should swallow up 1
20 Far be it from me, far be it, that I should swallow up 1
23:17 Far be it from me, O LORD, that I should do this. 1
1Ch 11:19 Far be it from me before my God that I should do 1
Job 27: 5 Far be it from me to say that you are right; 1
34:10 far be it from God that he should do wickedness 1
Gal 6:14 far be it from me to glory except in the cross 3
1Mc 2:21 Far be it from us to desert the law 2
9:10 Far be it from us to do such a thing 3
13: 5 now, far be it from me to spare my life 3

far down 1. שפל

Ps 113: 6 who looks far down upon the heavens and the earth? 1

far from it 1. חָלִילָה

1Sm 14:45 Shall Jonathan die, who has wrought . . ? Far from it! 1
20: 2 he said to him, "Far from it! You shall not die. 1

go far 1. רחק

Jer 2: 5 that they went far from me 1
Ezk 11:15 have said, 'They have gone far from the LORD; 1
44:10 the Levites who went far from me, going astray 1

far greater 1. περισσοτέρως 2. superabundo

2Co 11:23 with far greater labors, far more imprisonments 1
2Es 4:50 so the quantity that passed was far greater 2

far in the interior 1. introrsus

2Es 14:33 your brethren are farther in the interior. 1

far more 1. περισσοτέρως 2. ὑπὲρ πάντα

2Co 11:23 with far greater labors, far more imprisonments 1
Eph 3:20 is able to do far more abundantly 2

far off 1. מֶרְחוֹק 2. רחק 3. רָחֹק 4. רחק מְאֹד 5. ἀπὸ μακρόθεν 6. μακράν 7. μακρόθεν

Exd 33: 7 outside the camp, far off from the camp; 2
Deu 13: 7 whether near you or far off from you 3
30:11 not too hard for you, neither is it far off. 3
Jos 3:16 the waters . . stood and rose up in a heap far off 4
1Kg 8:46 captive to the land of the enemy, far off or near; 3
Ps 22:19 But thou, O LORD, be not far off! 2
Isa 33:13 Hear, you who are far off, what I have done; 3
46:13 I bring near my deliverance, it is not far off 2
57: 9 you sent your envoys far off 1
Ezk 6:12 He that is far off shall die of pestilence; 3
12:27 and he prophesies of times far off. 3
Jol 3: 8 will sell them to the Sabe'ans, to a nation far off; 3
Zec 6:15 those who are far off shall come and help to build 3
Lke 16:23 and saw Abraham far off and Laz'arus in his bosom. 5
18:13 the tax collector, standing far off 7
Act 2:39 the promise is . . to all that are far off 6
Eph 2:13 you who once were far off 6
17 he came and preached peace to you who were far off 6
Rev 18:10 they will stand far off, in fear of her torment 5
15 merchants of these wares . . will stand far off 5
17 all whose trade is on the sea, stood far off 5
Sir 16:22 who will await them? For the covenant is far off. 6

far over 1. עֵבֶר

Deu 3:16 as far over as the river Jabbok, the boundary 1

far part 1. יַרְכָה

Jer 6:22 stirring from the farthest parts of the earth. 1
25:32 stirring from the farthest parts of the earth! 1
31: 8 gather them from the farthest parts of the earth 1
50:41 stirring from the farthest parts of the earth. 1

too far off 1. μακρὰν ἀφίστημι

Sir 27:20 Do not go after him, for he is too far off 1

far-off 1. רחק 2. πόρρω

Ps 56: 0 according to The Dove on Far-off Terebinths. 1
Sir 47:16 Your name reached to far-off islands, and you were 2

fare 1. דֶּרֶךְ 2. היה 3. עשׂה בְּ 4. שָׁלוֹם 5. γίνομαι 6. εἰμί 7. καταλύω

Gen 18:25 wicked, so that the righteous fare as the wicked! 2
30:29 and how your cattle have fared with me. 2
Deu 15:16 since he fares well with you •
Rut 3:16 she said, "How did you fare, my daughter? •
1Sm 17:18 See how your brothers fare, and bring some token 4
2Kg 7:13 those . . here will fare like the whole multitude •
Est 2:11 to learn how Esther was and how she fared. 3
Hag 1: 5 Consider how you have fared. 1
7 Consider how you have fared. 1
2:16 how did you fare? When one came to a heap of twenty 6
Rom 9:29 we would have fared like Sodom 5
Sir 6: 1 so fares the double-tongued sinner. •
47:12 rose up a wise son who fared amply because of him; 7

fare (2) 1. שָׂכָר

Jon 1: 3 he paid the fare, and went on board, 1

fare *See* how, scant.

fare well 1. ἔρρω

3Mc 3:13 I myself and our government are faring well. 1
7: 2 We ourselves and our children are faring well 1

farewell 1. ἔρρωσθε. 2. ῥώννυμι 3. ὑγιαίνω 4. χαίρω

Gen 31:28 to kiss my sons and my daughters farewell? •
Act 15:29 you will do well. Farewell 2
2Co 13:11 Finally, brethren, farewell 4
2Mc 11:21 Farewell. The 148th year, Dioscorinthius 24th. 2
33 Farewell. The 148th year, Xanthicus fifteenth. 2
38 Farewell. The 148th year, Xanthicus fifteenth. 3
3Mc 7: 9 as an antagonist to avenge such acts. Farewell. 1

farewell *See also* bid, say.

farm 1. ἀγρός 2. γεωργία

Mat 22: 5 went off, one to his farm, another to his business 1
2Mc 12: 1 the Jews went about their farming. 2

farm *See also* work.

farmer 1. אִכָּר 2. γεωργός 3. agricola 4. cultor

2Ch 26:10 he had farmers and vinedressers in the hills 1
Jer 14: 4 the farmers are ashamed, they cover their heads. 1
31:24 farmers and those who wander with their flocks. 1
51:23 with you I break in pieces the farmer and his team; 1
Ams 5:16 They shall call the farmers to mourning 1
2Ti 2: 6 It is the hard-working farmer 2
Jas 5: 7 farmer waits for the precious fruit of the earth 2
2Es 8:41 just as the farmer sows many seeds 3
43 For if the farmer's seed does not come up 3
44 hast thou also made him like the farmer's seed? 3
9:17 as is the farmer, so is the threshing floor. 3
15:13 Let the farmers that till the ground mourn 4
Wis 17:17 whether he was a farmer or a shepherd or a workman 2

farther 1. διΐστημι

Act 27:28 a little farther on they sounded again 1

fascination 1. βασκανία

Wis 4:12 the fascination of wickedness obscures what is good 1

fashion 1. יצר 2. כון 3. כָּזֶה 4. עצב 5. עשׂה 6. צור 7. ἀναπλάσσω 8. ἁρμόζω 9. διατυπόω 10. ἐμμελέτημα 11. κατασκευάζω 12. οὕτως 13. τρόπος 14. plasma 15. plasmo

Exd 32: 4 and fashioned it with a graving tool, and made 6
2Ch 32:15 deceive you or mislead you in this fashion 3
Job 10: 8 Thy hands fashioned and made me; 4
31:15 And did not one fashion us in the womb? 2
Ps 33:15 he who fashions the hearts of them all 1
119:73 Thy hands have made and fashioned me; 2
Isa 44:10 Who fashions a god or casts an image 1
12 The ironsmith fashions it and works it •
13 he fashions it with planes, and marks it 5
45: 9 Does the clay say to him who fashions it 1
54:17 no weapon that is fashioned against you shall 1
1Es 4:12 since he is to be obeyed in this fashion? 12
2Es 8: 8 the body which is now fashioned in the womb 15
11 that what has been fashioned may be nourished 15
14 with so great labor was fashioned by thy command 15
38 concern myself about the fashioning of those 14
Wis 13:10 gold and silver fashioned with skill 10
15: 7 he fashions out of the same clay 7
19: 6 whole creation in its nature was fashioned anew 9
3Mc 4:13 in precisely the same fashion as the others 13
4Mc 2:21 Now when God fashioned man 11
5:14 When the tyrant urged him in this fashion 13
151 1: 2 My hands made a harp, my fingers fashioned a lyre. 8

fashion *See also* Scythian.

worldly fashion 1. σάρξ

2Co 10: 2 who suspect us of acting in worldly fashion. 1

fashioner 1. τεχνῖτις

Wis 7:22 wisdom, the fashioner of all things, taught me 1
8: 6 who more than she is fashioner of what exists? 1

fast 1. אֶל מוֹסֵרִים

Job 38:38 into a mass and the clods cleave fast together? •
Prv 7:22 he follows her . . as a stag is caught fast 1
Rom 11:20 but you stand fast only through faith. •

fast (2) 1. נזר 2. צום 3. צוֹם 4. תַּעֲנִית 5. מָוֶת (A) 6. ἐκτένεια 7. νηστεία 8. νηστεύω 9. ieiuno

Jdg 20:26 the LORD, and fasted that day until evening 2
1Sm 7: 6 they gathered . . and fasted on that day, and said 2
31:13 and buried them . . and fasted seven days. 2
2Sm 1:12 they mourned and wept and fasted until evening 2
12:16 and David fasted, and went in and lay all night 2
21 You fasted and wept for the child while it was 2
22 While the child was still alive, I fasted and wept; 2
23 he is dead; why should I fast? Can I bring him back 2
1Kg 21: 9 Proclaim a fast, and set Naboth on high 3
12 they proclaimed a fast 3
27 rent his clothes . . fasted and lay in sackcloth 2
1Ch 10:12 they . . fasted seven days. 2
2Ch 20: 3 Jehosh'aphat . . proclaimed a fast 2
Ezr 8:21 Then I proclaimed a fast there, at the river Aha'va 3
23 we fasted and besought our God for this 2
9: 5 at the evening sacrifice I rose from my fasting 4
Neh 1: 4 I continued fasting and praying before the God 2
9: 1 assembled with fasting and in sackcloth 3
Est 4: 3 great mourning . . with fasting and weeping 3
16 I and my maids will also fast as you do. 2
9:31 with regard to their fasts and their lamenting. 3
Ps 35:13 I afflicted myself with fasting. 3
69:10 When I humbled my soul with fasting 3
109:24 My knees are weak through fasting; 2
Isa 58: 3 'Why have we fasted, and thou seest it not? 2
3 in the day of your fast you seek your own pleasure 3
4 you fast only to quarrel and to fight and to hit 2
4 Fasting like yours this day will not make 3

5 the fast that I choose, a day for a man to humble 3
5 you call this a fast, and a day acceptable 3
6 Is not this the fast that I choose 3
Jer 14:12 Though they fast, I will not hear their cry 2
36: 6 and on a fast day in the hearing of all the people 3
9 Jerusalem proclaimed a fast before the LORD. 3
Dan 6:18 went to his palace, and spent the night fasting; 5
9: 3 with fasting and sackcloth and ashes. 3
Jol 1:14 Sanctify a fast, call a solemn assembly. 3
2:12 with all your heart, with fasting, with weeping 3
15 Blow the trumpet in Zion; sanctify a fast; 3
Jon 3: 5 they proclaimed a fast, and put on sackcloth 3
Zec 7: 3 Should I mourn and fast in the fifth month 1
5 When you fasted and mourned in the fifth month 2
5 for these 70 years, was it for me that you fasted? 2
8:19 fast of the fourth month, and the fast of the fifth 3
19 fast of the fourth month, and the fast of the fifth 3
19 the fast of the seventh, and the fast of the tenth 3
19 the fast of the seventh, and the fast of the tenth 3
Mat 4: 2 And he fasted 40 days and 40 nights 8
6:16 when you fast, do not look dismal 8
16 their faces that their fasting may be seen 8
17 when you fast, anoint your head and wash your face 8
18 that your fasting may not be seen by men 8
9:14 Why do we and the Pharisees fast 8
14 Pharisees fast, but your disciples do not fast? 8
15 and then they will fast. 8
Mrk 2:18 John's disciples and the Pharisees were fasting; 8
18 the disciples of the Pharisees fast 8
18 your disciples do not fast? 8
19 Jesus said to them, "Can the wedding guests fast 8
19 they cannot fast. 8
20 then they will fast in that day. 8
Lke 2:37 worshiping with fasting and prayer 7
5:33 disciples of John fast often and offer prayers 8
34 Can you make wedding guests fast 8
35 then they will fast in those days. 8
18:12 I fast twice a week, I give tithes of all that I get.' 8
Act 13: 2 While they were worshiping the Lord and fasting 8
3 Then after fasting and praying 8
14:23 with prayer and fasting 7
27: 9 because the fast had already gone by 7
1Es 8:50 There I proclaimed a fast for the young men 7
73 Then I rose from my fast 7
2Es 5:13 and fast for seven days 9
20 I fasted seven days, mourning and weeping 9
6:31 will pray again and fast again for seven days 9
35 I wept again and fasted seven days as before 9
9:23 do not fast during them, however; 9
10: 4 but without ceasing mourn and fast until I die. 9
Tob 12: 8 Prayer is good when accompanied by fasting 7
Jdt 4: 9 they humbled themselves with much fasting. 6
13 the people fasted many days throughout Judea 8
8: 6 She fasted all the days of her widowhood 8
Sir 34:26 if a man fasts for his sins 8
Bar 1: 5 they wept, and fasted, and prayed before the Lord; 8
1Mc 3:47 They fasted that day 8
2Mc 13:12 fasting and lying prostrate for three days 7

fast *See* catch, freeze, hasten, hold, stand.

fast asleep 1. רדם

Jon 1: 5 Jonah . . had lain down, and was fast asleep. 1

hold fast 1. חזק

Gen 21:18 Arise, lift up the lad, and hold him fast 1
Jer 8: 5 They hold fast to deceit, they refuse to return. 1
50:33 all who took them captive have held them fast 1

fasten 1. חזק 2. יצק 3. כון 4. נתן 5. צמד 6. שׂום 7. תקע 8. *ἀσφαλίζω* 9. *δέω* 10. *ζώννυμι* 11. *καθάπτω* 12. *καταδέω* 13. *κρεμάννυμι* 14. *πήγνυμι* 15. *προσηλόω*

Exd 25:26 and fasten the rings to the four corners 4
28:37 you shall fasten it on the turban by a lace of blue; 6
37:13 rings of gold, and fastened the rings to the four 4
39:31 they tied to it a lace of blue, to fasten it 4
Num19:15 open vessel, which has no cover fastened upon it 12
1Sm 31:10 they fastened his body to the wall of Beth-shan. 7
2Sm 20: 8 a girdle with a sword . . fastened upon his loins 5
1Ch 10:10 and fastened his head in the temple of Dagon. 7
Ps 41: 8 They say, "A deadly thing has fastened upon him; 2
Isa 22:23 I will fasten him like a peg in a sure place 7
25 the peg that was fastened in a sure place 7
41: 7 They fasten it with nails 1
Jer 10: 4 they fasten it with hammer and nails 1
Ezk 40:43 hooks . . were fastened round about within. 3
Mat 18: 6 have a great millstone fastened round his neck 13
Act 16:24 fastened their feet in the stocks. 8
28: 3 a viper came out . . and fastened on his hand. 11
Jdt 16: 8 fastened her hair with a tiara 9
Wis 13:15 and fastens it there with iron. 8
Sir 14:24 will also fasten his tent peg to her walls; 14
1Mc 6:37 they were fastened upon each beast 10
3Mc 4: 9 some were fastened by the neck to the benches 15

fasten together 1. שׂרג

Lam 1:14 by his hand they were fastened together; 1

faster than

2Es 4:34 You do not hasten faster than the Most High †

fastness 1. מִסְגֶּרֶת 2. מְצוּדָה

2Sm 22:46 and came trembling out of their fastnesses. 1
Job 39:28 makes his home in the fastness of the rocky crag. 2
Ps 18:45 came trembling out of their fastnesses. 1

fat 1. בָּרִיא 2. בְּרִיא בָשָׂר 3. דֶּשֶׁן 4. חֵלֶב 5. יֹתֶרֶת 6. מַשְׁמָן 7. מִשְׁמָן 8. פֶּדֶר 9. שָׁמֵן 10. *λίπασμα* 11. *πιόνων* 12. *στέαρ* 13. *στῆρ*

Gen 41: 2 came up out of the Nile seven cows sleek and fat 2
4 thin cows ate up the seven sleek and fat cows. 1
18 seven cows, fat and sleek, came up out of the Nile 2
20 gaunt cows ate up the first seven fat cows 1
45:18 and you shall eat the fat of the land.' 4
Exd 23:18 shall not . . let the fat of my feast remain 4
29:13 shall take all the fat that covers the entrails 4
13 take . . the two kidneys with the fat 4
22 You shall also take the fat of the ram 4
22 take . . the fat that covers the entrails 4
22 the two kidneys with the fat that is on them 5
Lev 1: 8 lay the pieces, the head, and the fat, in order 8
12 cut it into pieces, with its head and its fat 8
3: 3 he shall offer the fat covering the entrails 4
3 offer . . all the fat that is on the entrails 4
4 the two kidneys with the fat that is on them 4
9 he shall offer its fat, the fat tail entire 4
9 the fat that covers the entrails, and all the fat 4
9 and all the fat that is on the entrails 4
10 the two kidneys with the fat that is on them 4
14 shall offer . . the fat covering the entrails 4
14 offer . . all the fat that is on the entrails 4
15 the two kidneys with the fat that is on them 4
16 All fat is the LORD'S 4
17 a statute . . that you eat neither fat nor blood 4
4: 8 all the fat of the bull of the sin offering 4
8 the fat that covers the entrails and all the fat 4
8 all the fat that is on the entrails 4
9 the two kidneys with the fat that is on them 4
19 all its fat he shall take from it and burn 4
26 all its fat he shall burn on the altar 4
26 like the fat of sacrifice of peace offerings 4
31 all its fat he shall remove 4
31 as the fat is removed from the peace offerings 4
35 all its fat he shall remove as the fat of the lamb 4
35 he shall remove as the fat of the lamb is removed 4
6:12 shall burn on it the fat of the peace offerings 4
7: 3 all its fat shall be offered, the fat tail 4
3 the fat tail, the fat that covers the entrails 4
4 the two kidneys with the fat that is on them 4
23 You shall eat no fat, of ox, or sheep, or goat 4
24 The fat of an animal that dies of itself 4
24 and the fat of one that is torn by beast 4
25 For every person who eats of the fat of an animal 4
30 he shall bring the fat with the breast 4
31 The priest shall burn the fat on the altar 4
33 blood of the peace offerings and the fat 4
8:16 he took all the fat that was on the entrails 4
16 he took . . the two kidneys with their fat 4
20 Moses burned the head and the pieces and the fat 8
25 Then he took the fat, and the fat tail, and all 4
25 he took . . all the fat that was on the entrails 4
25 he took . . the two kidneys with their fat 4
26 placed them on the fat and on the right thigh 4
9:10 the fat and the kidneys and the appendage 4
19 the fat of the ox and of the ram, the fat tail 4
20 they put the fat upon the breasts, and he burned 4
20 the breasts, and he burned the fat upon the altar 4
24 the burnt offering and the fat upon the altar 4
10:15 bring with the offerings by fire of the fat 4
16:25 the fat of the sin offering he shall burn 4
17: 6 and burn the fat for a pleasing odor to the LORD 4
Num18:17 shall burn their fat as an offering by fire 4
Deu 32:14 fat of lambs and rams, herds of Bashan and goats 4
38 who ate the fat of their sacrifices, and drank 4
Jdg 3:17 Eglon king of Moab. Now Eglon was a very fat man. 1
22 after the blade, and the fat closed over the blade 4
1Sm 2:15 before the fat was burned, the priest's servant 4
16 Let them burn the fat first, and then take 4
15:22 is better . . to hearken than the fat of rams. 4
2Sm 1:22 from the fat of the mighty, the bow . . turned not 4
1Kg 4:23 ten fat oxen, and twenty . . cattle 1
2Ch 7: 7 offered . . and the fat of the peace offerings 4
7 could not hold . . cereal offering and the fat. 4
29:35 there was the fat of the peace offerings 4
Neh 8:10 Go your way, eat the fat and drink sweet wine 6
Job 15:27 because he has covered his face with his fat 4
21:24 his body full of fat 4
Ps 63: 5 My soul is feasted as with marrow and fat 3
119:70 their heart is gross like fat 4
Isa 1:11 burnt offerings of rams and the fat of fed beasts; 4
17: 4 and the fat of his flesh will grow lean. 7
34: 6 it is sated with blood, it is gorged with fat 4
6 with the fat of the kidneys of rams. 4
7 and their soil made rich with fat. 4
43:24 or satisfied me with the fat of your sacrifices. 4
Ezk 34: 3 You eat the fat 4
14 on fat pasture they shall feed on the mountains 9
16 the fat and the strong I will watch over; 9
20 judge between the fat sheep and the lean sheep. 1
39:19 And you shall eat fat till you are filled, 4
44: 7 when you offer to me my food, the fat and the blood. 4
15 attend on me to offer me the fat and the blood 4
Dan 1:15 seen that they were . . fatter in flesh than all 1
Zec 11:16 but devours the flesh of the fat ones, tearing off 1
1Es 1:14 the priests were offering the fat until night 12
9:51 go your way, eat the fat and drink the sweet 10
Jdt 16:16 all fat for burnt offerings . . is a very little thing 12
Sir 47: 2 As the fat is selected from the peace offering 12
Aza 1:16 with tens of thousands of fat lambs; 11
Bel 1:27 Then Daniel took pitch, fat, and hair 13

fat *See also* grow, make, piece, portion, put, tail, wax.

become fat 1. שׁמן

Neh 9:25 filled and became fat, and delighted themselves 1

fat calf 1. *σιτιστός*

Mat 22: 4 my oxen and my fat calves are killed 1

gathered fat 1. פִּימָה

Job 15:27 with his fat, and gathered fat upon his loins 1

fat part 1. חֵלֶב

2Ch 35:14 busied in offering . . the fat parts until night; 1

fat thing 1. שֶׁמֶן

Isa 25: 6 will make for all peoples a feast of fat things 1
6 wine on the lees, of fat things full of marrow 1

fatal 1. *θανατηφόρος*

4Mc 8:26 Why does . . such a fatal stubbornness please us 1

fate 1. דֶּרֶךְ 2. מִקְרֶה 3. עֵת 4. פְּקֻדָּה 5. *ἀνάγκη* 6. *μόρος* 7. casus

Num16:29 or if they are visited by the fate of all men 4
Ps 49:13 the fate of those who have foolish confidence 1
81:15 their fate would last for ever. 3
Ecc 2:14 yet I perceived that one fate comes to all of them. 2
3:19 fate of the sons of men and . . of beasts is the same; 2
19 fate of . . men and the fate of beasts is the same; 2
9: 2 since one fate comes to all, to the righteous 2
3 This is an evil in all . . that one fate comes to all; 2
Jer 49:20 their fold shall be appalled at their fate. •
50:45 their fold shall be appalled at their fate. •
Lam 3:51 grief at the fate of all the maidens of my city. •
2Es 3:10 the same fate befell them: as death came upon Adam 7
Wis 17:17 he was seized, and endured the inescapable fate; 5
19: 4 the fate they deserved drew them on to this end 5
2Mc 9:28 a most pitiable fate 6
13: 7 By such a fate it came about that . . 6
3Mc 5: 8 rescue them from the fate now prepared for them. 6

fate *See also* leave.

father 1. אָב 2. ילד 3. אַב (A) 4. *γεννάω* 5. *θεός* 6. *πατήρ* 7. *πατριά* 8. *πατρικός* 9. *πάτριος* 10. *πατρίς* 11. *πρόγονος* 12. pater

Gen 2:24 Therefore a man leaves his father and his mother 1
4:18 and Irad was the father of Me-hu'ja-el 2
18 and Me-hu'ja-el the father of Me-thu'sha-el 2
18 and Me-thu'sha-el the father of Lamech. 2
20 Jabal; he was the father of those who dwell 1
21 Jubal; he was the father of all those who play 1
9:18 Ham was the father of Canaan. 1
22 Ham, the father of Canaan, saw the nakedness 1
22 Ham . . saw the nakedness of his father 1
23 covered the nakedness of their father; 1
23 they did not see their father's nakedness. 1
10:21 To Shem also, the father of all the children 1
11:27 Terah was the father of Abram, Nahor, and Haran; 2
27 Nahor, and Haran; and Haran was the father of Lot. 2
28 Haran died before his father Terah in the land 1
29 of Haran the father of Milcah and Iscah. 1
12: 1 and your father's house to the land 1
15:15 you shall go to your fathers in peace; 1
17: 4 you shall be the father of a multitude 1
5 Abraham; for I have made you the father 1
20 he shall be the father of twelve princes 2
19:31 Our father is old, and there is not a man on earth 1
32 Come, let us make our father drink wine 1
32 we may preserve offspring through our father. 1
33 they made their father drink wine that night; 1
33 they made their father drink wine that night; 1
34 Behold, I lay last night with my father; 1
34 we may preserve offspring through out father. 1
35 they made their father drink wine that night 1
36 of Lot were with child by their father. 1
37 Moab; he is the father of the Moabites to this day. 1
38 Ben-ammi; he is the father of the Ammonites 1
20:12 the daughter of my father but not the daughter 1
13 God caused me to wander from my father's house 1
22: 7 Isaac said to his father Abraham, "My father! 1
7 Isaac said to his father Abraham, "My father! 1
21 Buz his brother, Kemu'el the father of Aram 1
24: 7 LORD . . who took me from my father's house 1
23 Is there room in your father's house for us 1

38 you shall go to my father's house and to my kindred 1
40 my son from my kindred and from my father's house; 1
25: 3 Jokshan was the father of Sheba and Dedan. 2
19 Abraham was the father of Isaac 2
26: 3 oath which I swore to Abraham your father. 1
15 the wells which his father's servants had dug 1
15 had dug in the days of Abraham his father. 1
18 days of Abraham his father; for the Philistines 1
18 he gave them the names which his father had given 1
24 I am the God of Abraham your father; fear not 1
27: 6 I heard your father speak to your brother Esau 1
9 prepare from them savory food for your father 1
10 you shall bring it to your father to eat 1
12 Perhaps my father will feel me, and I shall seem 1
14 prepared savory food, such as his father loved. 1
18 he went in to his father, and said, "My father"; 1
18 and said, "My father"; and he said, "Here I am; 1
19 Jacob said to his father, "I am Esau 1
22 Jacob went near to Isaac his father 1
26 Then his father Isaac said to him, "Come near 1
30 gone out from the presence of Isaac his father 1
31 savory food, and brought it to his father. 1
31 he said to his father, "Let my father arise 1
31 Let my father arise, and eat of his son's game 1
32 His father Isaac said to him, "Who are you? 1
34 When Esau heard the words of his father, he cried 1
34 and said to his father, "Bless me, even me also 1
34 Bless me, even me also, O my father! 1
38 Esau said to his father, "Have you but one 1
38 Have you but one blessing, my father? Bless me 1
38 Bless me, even me also, O my father. 1
39 Then Isaac his father answered him 1
41 because of the blessing with which his father 1
41 days of mourning for my father are approaching; 1
28: 2 to the house of Bethu'el your mother's father 1
7 that Jacob had obeyed his father and his mother 1
8 Canaanite women did not please Isaac his father 1
13 I am the LORD, the God of Abraham your father 1
21 that I come again to my father's house in peace 1
29: 9 Rachel came with her father's sheep; 1
12 told Rachel that he was her father's kinsman 1
12 Rebekah's son; and she ran and told her father. 1
31: 1 Jacob has taken all that was our father's; 1
1 and from what was our father's he has gained 1
3 Return to the land of your fathers 1
5 said to them, "I see that your father does not 1
5 But the God of my father has been with me. 1
6 You know that I have served your father 1
7 yet your father has cheated me 1
9 Thus God has taken away the cattle of your father 1
14 inheritance left to us in our father's house? 1
16 God has taken away from our father belongs to us 1
18 to go to the land of Canaan to his father Isaac. 1
19 and Rachel stole her father's household gods. 1
29 but the God of your father spoke to me last night 1
30 you longed greatly for your father's house 1
35 she said to her father, "Let not my lord be angry 1
42 If the God of my father, the God of Abraham 1
53 God of Nahor, the God of their father 1
53 Jacob swore by the Fear of his father Isaac 1
32: 9 Jacob said, "O God of my father Abraham 1
9 God of my father Isaac, O LORD who didst say to me 1
33:19 from the sons of Hamor, Shechem's father 1
34: 4 Shechem spoke to his father Hamor, saying 1
6 Hamor the father of Shechem went out to Jacob 1
11 Shechem . . said to her father and to her 1
13 answered Shechem and his father Hamor 1
35:18 Ben-o'ni; but his father called his name Benjamin 1
22 Bilhah his father's concubine; and Israel heard 1
27 Jacob came to his father Isaac at Mamre 1
36: 9 descendants of Esau the father of the E'domites 1
24 as he pastured the asses of Zib'eon his father. 1
43 of Edom (that is, Esau, the father of Edom), according 1
37: 1 dwelt in the land of his father's sojournings 1
2 sons of Bilhah and Zilpah, his father's wives; 1
2 brought an ill report of them to their father. 1
4 brothers saw that their father loved him more 1
10 when he told it to his father and to his brothers 1
10 his father rebuked him, and said to him 1
11 but his father kept the saying in mind. 1
12 brothers went to pasture their father's flock 1
22 out of their hand, to restore him to his father. 1
32 robe with sleeves and brought it to their father 1
35 to my son, mourning." Thus his father wept for him 1
38:11 Remain a widow in your father's house 1
11 Tamar went and dwelt in her father's house. 1
41:51 all my hardship and all my father's house. 1
42:13 this day with our father, and one is no more. 1
29 When they came to Jacob their father in the land 1
32 we are twelve brothers, sons of our father; 1
32 this day with our father in the land of Canaan.' 1
35 and when they and their father saw their bundles 1
36 Jacob their father said to them 1
37 Reuben said to his father, "Slay my two sons if I do 1
43: 2 their father said to them, "Go again 1
7 questioned us . . saying, 'Is your father still 1
8 Judah said to Israel his father, "Send the lad 1
11 Then their father Israel said to them 1
23 your God and the God of your father must have put 1

27 Is your father well, the old man of whom you spoke? 1
28 They said, "Your servant our father is well 1
44:17 but as for you, go up in peace to your father. 1
19 'Have you a father, or a brother?' 1
20 we said to my lord, 'We have a father, an old man 1
20 We have a . . brother . . and his father loves him. 1
22 said to my lord, 'The lad cannot leave his father 1
22 he should leave his father, his father would die. 1
22 he should leave his father, his father would die. 1
24 When we went back to your servant my father 1
25 when our father said, 'Go again, buy us a little food 1
27 Then your servant my father said to us 1
30 when I come to your servant my father 1
31 your servant our father with sorrow to Sheol. 1
32 became surety for the lad to my father, saying 1
32 in the sight of my father all my life.' 1
34 For how can I go back to my father if the lad is not 1
34 see the evil that would come upon my father. 1
45: 3 I am Joseph; is my father still alive? 1
8 and he has made me a father to Pharaoh 1
9 Make haste and go up to my father and say to him 1
13 You must tell my father of all my splendor 1
13 Make haste and bring my father down here. 1
18 take your father and your households, and come 1
19 take wagons . . and bring your father, and come. 1
23 To his father he sent as follows: ten asses loaded 1
23 provision for his father on the journey. 1
25 to the land of Canaan to their father Jacob. 1
27 the spirit of their father Jacob revived; 1
46: 1 sacrifices to the God of his father Isaac. 1
3 Then he said, "I am God, the God of your father; 1
5 the sons of Israel carried Jacob their father 1
29 went up to meet Israel his father in Goshen; 1
31 Joseph said to his . . father's household, 1
31 say . . 'My brothers and my father's household 1
34 keepers of cattle . . both we and our fathers,' 1
47: 1 told Pharaoh, "My father and my brothers 1
3 servants are shepherds, as our fathers were. 1
5 said to Joseph, "Your father and your brothers 1
6 settle your father and your brothers in the best 1
7 Then Joseph brought in Jacob his father, 1
9 the life of my fathers in the days of their 1
11 Then Joseph settled his father and his brothers 1
12 Joseph provided his father, his brothers, 1
12 Joseph provided . . all his father's household 1
30 let me lie with my fathers; carry me out of Egypt 1
48: 1 Joseph was told, "Behold, your father is ill"; 1
9 Joseph said to his father, "They are my sons 1
15 The God before whom my fathers Abraham and Isaac 1
16 the name of my fathers Abraham and Isaac; 1
17 Joseph saw that his father laid his right hand 1
17 he took his father's hand, to remove it 1
18 Joseph said to his father, "Not so, my father; 1
18 Not so, my father; for this one is the first-born; 1
19 his father refused, and said, "I know, my son, 1
21 bring you again to the land of your fathers. 1
49: 2 Assemble . . and hearken to Israel your father. 1
4 because you went up to your father's bed; 1
8 your father's sons shall bow down before you. 1
25 by the God of your father who will help you 1
26 The blessings of your father are mighty 1
28 and this is what their father said to them 1
29 bury me with my fathers in the cave 1
50: 1 Joseph fell on his father's face, and wept over him 1
2 commanded . . to embalm his father. 1
5 My father made me swear, saying, 'I am about to die 1
5 let me . . bury my father; then I will return. 1
6 Pharaoh answered, "Go up, and bury your father 1
7 Joseph went up to bury his father; 1
8 as well as . . his father's household; 1
10 and he made a mourning for his father seven days. 1
14 After he had buried his father, Joseph returned 1
14 all who had gone up with him to bury his father. 1
15 Joseph's brothers saw that their father was dead 1
16 Joseph, saying, "Your father gave this command 1
17 the servants of the God of your father. 1
22 Joseph dwelt in Egypt, he and his father's house; 1
Exd 2:16 drew water . . to water their father's flock. 1
18 When they came to their father Reu'el 1
3: 6 I am the God of your father, the God of Abraham 1
13 The God of your fathers has sent me to you,' 1
15 Say this . . 'The LORD, the God of your fathers 1
16 LORD, the God of your fathers, the God of Abraham 1
4: 5 believe that the LORD, the God of their fathers 1
6:14 These are the heads of their fathers' houses 1
10: 6 as neither your fathers nor your grandfathers 1
12: 3 a lamb according to their fathers' houses 1
13: 5 which he swore to your fathers to give you 1
11 brings you . . as he swore to you and your fathers 1
15: 2 this is . . my father's God, and I will exalt him. 1
18: 4 for he said, "The God of my father was my help 1
20: 5 the iniquity of the fathers upon the children 1
12 Honor your father and your mother, that your days 1
21:15 Whoever strikes his father or his mother shall 1
17 Whoever curses his father or his mother shall be 1
22:17 If her father utterly refuses to give her to him 1
34: 7 visiting the iniquity of the fathers upon 1
40:15 anoint them, as you anointed their father 1
Lev 16:32 and consecrated as priest in his father's place 1

18: 7 shall not uncover the nakedness of your father 1
8 not uncover the nakedness of your father's wife 1
8 your father's wife; it is your father's nakedness 1
9 the daughter of your father or the daughter 1
11 the nakedness of your father's wife's daughter 1
11 father's wife's daughter, begotten by your father 1
12 not uncover the nakedness of your father's sister 1
12 she is your father's near kinswoman 1
14 uncover the nakedness of your father's brother 1
19: 3 one of you shall revere his mother and father 1
20: 9 For every one who curses his father or his mother 1
9 he has cursed his father or his mother, his blood 1
11 The man who lies with his father's wife 1
11 The man . . has uncovered his father's nakedness 1
17 If a man takes his sister, a daughter of his father 1
19 nakedness . . of your father's sister 1
21: 2 his nearest of kin, his mother, his father, his son 1
9 profanes her father; she shall be burned 1
11 shall not . . defile himself, even for his father 1
22:13 daughter . . returns to her father's house 1
13 she may eat of her father's food; yet no outsider 1
24:10 woman's son, whose father was an Egyptian *
25:41 return to the possession of his fathers 1
26:39 also because of the iniquities of their fathers 1
40 they confess . . the iniquity of their fathers 1
Num 1: 2 census . . by families, by fathers' houses 1
4 being the head of the house of his fathers. 1
18 registered . . by families, by fathers' houses 1
20 by their fathers' houses, according to the number 1
22 by their families, by their fathers' houses 1
24 by their families, by their fathers' houses 1
26 by their families, by their fathers' houses 1
28 by their families, by their fathers' houses 1
30 by their families, by their fathers' houses 1
32 by their families, by their fathers' houses 1
34 by their families, by their fathers' houses 1
36 by their families, by their fathers' houses 1
38 by their families, by their fathers' houses 1
40 by their families, by their fathers' houses 1
42 by their families, by their fathers' houses 1
44 twelve men, each representing his fathers' house. 1
45 by their fathers' houses, from twenty years old 1
2: 2 with the ensigns of their fathers' houses; 1
32 Israel as numbered by their fathers' houses; 1
34 they set out . . according to his fathers' house. 1
3: 4 in the lifetime of Aaron their father. 1
15 Number the sons of Levi, by fathers' houses 1
20 the Levites, by their fathers' houses. 1
24 as head of the fathers' house of the Gershonites. 1
30 Eli-za'phan . . head of the fathers' house 1
35 head of the fathers' house of the families 1
4: 2 Take a census . . by their . . fathers' houses 1
22 by their families and their fathers' houses; 1
29 number them by . . their fathers' houses; 1
34 by their families and their fathers' houses 1
38 by their families and their fathers' houses 1
40 number by . . families and their fathers' houses 1
42 by their families and their fathers' houses 1
46 by their families and their fathers' houses 1
6: 7 Neither for his father nor for his mother 1
7: 2 leaders of Israel, heads of their fathers' houses 1
11:12 land . . thou didst swear to give their fathers?' 1
12:14 If her father had but spit in her face 1
13: 2 each tribe of their fathers shall you send a man 1
14:18 visiting the iniquity of fathers upon children 1
23 land which I swore to give to their fathers; 1
17: 2 get from them rods, one for each fathers' house 1
2 leaders according to their fathers' houses 1
3 one rod for the head of each fathers' house. 1
6 according to their fathers' houses, twelve rods; 1
18: 1 You and your sons and your fathers' house with you 1
2 tribe of Levi, the tribe of your father 1
20:15 how our fathers went down to Egypt 1
15 Egyptians dealt harshly with us and our fathers; 1
25:14 Zimri the son of Salu, head of a fathers' house 1
15 Zur . . head of the people of a fathers' house 1
26: 2 Take a census . . by their fathers' houses 1
29 Machir was the father of Gilead; 2
55 names of the tribes of their fathers 1
58 Kohath was the father of Amram. 2
27: 3 Our father died in the wilderness; 1
4 Why should the name of our father be taken away 1
4 possession among our father's brethren. 1
7 an inheritance among their father's brethren 1
7 cause the inheritance of their father to pass 1
10 give his inheritance to his father's brothers. 1
11 if his father has no brothers, then you shall give 1
30: 3 vows a vow . . while within her father's house 1
4 her father hears of her vow and of her pledge 1
5 if her father expresses disapproval to her 1
5 forgive her, because her father opposed her. 1
16 statutes . . between a father and his daughter 1
16 while in her youth, within her father's house. 1
32: 8 Thus did your fathers when I sent them 1
14 behold, you have risen in your fathers' stead 1
33:54 according to the tribes of your fathers 1
34:14 tribe of the sons of Reuben by fathers' houses 1
14 tribe of the sons of Gad by their fathers' houses 1
36: 3 taken from the inheritance of our fathers 1

4 taken from the inheritance of . . our fathers. 1
6 within the family of the tribe of their father. 1
7 inheritance of the tribe of his fathers. 1
8 wife to one . . family of the tribe of her father 1
8 may possess the inheritance of his fathers. 1
12 in the tribe of the family of their father. 1
Deu 1: 8 land which the LORD swore to your fathers 1
11 May the LORD, the God of your fathers, make you 1
21 as the LORD, the God of your fathers, has told you; 1
35 good land which I swore to give to your fathers 1
4: 1 land which the LORD, the God of your fathers, gives 1
31 covenant with your fathers which he swore 1
37 loved your fathers and chose their descendants 1
5: 3 Not with our fathers did the LORD make 1
9 visiting the iniquity of the fathers 1
16 'Honor your father and your mother 1
6: 3 as the LORD, the God of your fathers, has promised 1
10 into the land which he swore to your fathers 1
18 land which the LORD swore to give to your fathers 1
23 land which he swore to give to our fathers. 1
7: 8 keeping the oath which he swore to your fathers 1
12 which he swore to your fathers to keep; 1
13 in the land which he swore to your fathers to give 1
8: 1 land . . the LORD swore to give to your fathers. 1
3 you did not know, nor did your fathers know; 1
16 manna which your fathers did not know 1
18 his covenant which he swore to your fathers 1
9: 5 word which the LORD swore to your fathers 1
10:11 land, which I swore to their fathers to give them.' 1
15 LORD set his heart in love upon your fathers 1
22 Your fathers went down to Egypt 70 persons; 1
11: 9 LORD swore to your fathers to give to them 1
21 land which the LORD swore to your fathers to give 1
12: 1 which the LORD, the God of your fathers, has given 1
13: 6 other gods,' which neither you nor your fathers 1
17 multiply you, as he swore to your fathers 1
19: 8 enlarges . . as he has sworn to your fathers 1
8 all the land . . he promised to give to your fathers– 1
21:13 shall remain in your house and bewail her father 1
18 son, who will not obey the voice of his father 1
19 his father and his mother shall take hold of him 1
22:15 then the father of the young woman and her mother 1
16 father of the young woman shall say to the elders 1
19 give them to the father of the young woman 1
21 bring . . to the door of her father's house 1
21 by playing the harlot in her father's house; 1
29 give to the father of the young woman 1
30 A man shall not take his father's wife 1
30 nor shall he uncover her who is his father's. 1
24:16 fathers . . not be put to death for the children 1
16 nor . . children be put to death for the fathers; 1
26: 3 land . . LORD swore to our fathers to give us.' 1
5 wandering Aramean was my father; 1
7 Then we cried to the LORD the God of our fathers 1
15 as thou didst swear to our fathers, a land flowing 1
27: 3 as the LORD, the God of your fathers, has promised 1
16 'Cursed . . who dishonors his father or his mother.' 1
20 'Cursed be he who lies with his father's wife 1
20 because he has uncovered her who is his father's.' 1
22 sister, whether the daughter of his father 1
28:11 land which the LORD swore to your fathers to give 1
36 neither you nor your fathers have known; 1
64 gods . . neither you nor your fathers have known. 1
29:13 as he swore to your fathers, to Abraham, to Isaac 1
25 covenant of the LORD, the God of their fathers 1
30: 5 into the land which your fathers possessed 1
5 more prosperous and numerous than your fathers. 1
9 as he took delight in your fathers 1
20 land which the LORD swore to your fathers 1
31: 7 land . . LORD has sworn to their fathers to give 1
16 Behold, you are about to sleep with your fathers; 1
20 land . . which I swore to give to their fathers 1
32: 6 Is not he your father, who created you, who made you 1
7 ask your father, and he will show you; your elders 1
17 new gods . . your fathers had never dreaded. 1
33: 9 who said of his father and mother, 'I regard . . not'; 1
Jos 1: 6 land which I swore to their fathers to give them. 1
2:12 you also will deal kindly with my father's house 1
13 and save alive my father and mother, my brothers 1
18 gather into your house your father and mother 1
18 your brothers, and all your father's household. 1
4:21 your children ask their fathers in time to come 1
5: 6 land which the LORD had sworn to their fathers 1
6:23 and brought out Rahab, and her father and mother 1
25 Rahab . . and her father's household, and all who 1
14: 1 and the heads of the fathers' houses of the tribes 1
15:13 Kir'iath-ar'ba . . (Arba was the father of Anak). 1
18 she urged him to ask her father for a field; 1
17: 1 Machir the first-born . . the father of Gilead 1
4 among the brethren of their father. 1
18: 3 the land, which the LORD, the God of your fathers 1
19:51 and Joshua . . and the heads of the fathers' houses 1
21: 1 the heads of the fathers' houses of the Levites 1
1 the heads of the fathers' houses of the tribes 1
11 Kir'iath-ar'ba (Arba being the father of Anak) 1
43 the land which he swore to give to their fathers; 1
44 LORD gave . . just as he has sworn to their fathers; 1
22:28 the copy of the altar . . which our fathers made 1
24: 2 Your fathers lived of old beyond the Euphra'tes 1
2 Your fathers . . Terah, the father of Abraham 1
3 I took your father Abraham from beyond the River 1
6 I brought your fathers out of Egypt, and you came 1
6 Egyptians pursued your fathers with chariots 1
14 put away the gods which your fathers served 1
15 the gods your fathers served in the region 1
17 LORD . . brought us and our fathers up 1
32 from the sons of Hamor the father of Shechem 1
Jdg 1:14 to him, she urged him to ask her father for a field; 1
2: 1 the land which I swore to give to your fathers. 1
10 were gathered to their fathers; and there arose 1
12 they forsook the LORD, the God of their fathers 1
17 from the way in which their fathers had walked 1
19 turned back and behaved worse than their fathers 1
20 my covenant which I commanded their fathers 1
22 to walk in the way of the LORD as their fathers did 1
3: 4 LORD, which he commanded their fathers by Moses. 1
6:13 wonderful deeds which our fathers recounted 1
25 Take your father's bull . . and pull down 1
25 pull down the altar of Ba'al which your father has 1
8:32 age, and was buried in the tomb of Jo'ash his father 1
9: 5 he went to his father's house at Ophrah, and slew 1
17 for my father fought for you, and risked his life 1
18 and you have risen up against my father's house 1
28 serve the men of Hamor the father of Shechem? 1
56 crime . . which he committed against his father 1
11: 1 of a harlot. Gilead was the father of Jephthah. 2
2 You shall not inherit in our father's house; 1
7 hate me, and drive me out of my father's house? 1
36 My father, if you have opened your mouth 1
37 she said to her father, "Let this thing be done 1
39 the end of two months, she returned to her father 1
14: 2 and told his father and mother, "I saw one 1
3 his father and mother said to him, "Is there not 1
3 But Samson said to his father, "Get her for me; 1
4 His father and mother did not know that it was 1
5 Samson went down with his father and mother 1
6 he did not tell his father or his mother what he 1
9 he came to his father and mother, and gave some 1
10 his father went down to the woman, 1
15 we burn you and your father's house with fire. 1
16 Behold, I have not told my father nor my mother 1
19 In hot anger he went back to his father's house. 1
15: 1 But her father would not allow him to go in. 1
2 her father said, "I really thought that you 1
6 came up, and burned her and her father with fire. 1
16:31 buried him . . in the tomb of Mano'ah his father. 1
17:10 be to me a father and a priest, and I will give you 1
18:19 and come with us, and be to us a father and a priest. 1
19: 2 she went . . to her father's house at Bethlehem 1
3 he came to her father's house; and when the girl's 1
3 and when the girl's father saw him, he came with joy 1
4 his father-in-law, the girl's father, made him stay 1
5 to go; but the girl's father said to his son-in-law 1
6 the girl's father said to the man, "Be pleased 1
8 the girl's father said, "Strengthen your heart 1
9 his father-in-law, the girl's father, said to him 1
21:22 when their fathers or their brothers come 1
Rut 2:11 you left your father and mother and . . land 1
4:17 They named him Obed; he was the father of Jesse 1
17 he was the father of Jesse, the father of David. 1
18 descendants of . . Perez was the father of Hezron 2
1Sm 2:25 would not listen to the voice of their father; 1
27 I revealed myself to the house of your father 1
28 I gave to the house of your father all my 1
30 your house and the house of your father should go 1
31 cut off . . and the strength of your father's house 1
9: 3 Now the asses of Kish, Saul's father, were lost. 1
5 lest my father cease to care about the asses 1
20 Is it not for you and for all your father's house? 1
10: 2 your father has ceased to care about the asses 1
12 And a man . . answered, "And who is their father? 1
12: 6 who . . brought your fathers up out of the land 1
7 deeds . . performed for you and for your fathers. 1
8 your fathers cried to the LORD and the LORD sent 1
8 who brought forth your fathers out of Egypt 1
14: 1 But he did not tell his father. 1
27 Jonathan had not heard his father charge 1
28 Your father . . charged the people with an oath 1
29 Jonathan said, "My father has troubled the land; 1
51 Kish was the father of Saul, and Ner the father 1
51 and Ner the father of Abner was the son of Abi'el. 1
17:15 went back and forth . . to feed his father's sheep 1
25 the king will . . make his father's house free 1
34 Your servant used to keep sheep for his father; 1
18: 2 not let him return to his father's house. 1
18 Who am I, and . . my father's family in Israel 1
19: 2 Saul my father seeks to kill you; 1
3 stand beside my father in the field where you are 1
3 and I will speak to my father about you; 1
4 Jonathan spoke well of David to Saul his father 1
20: 1 what is my sin before your father, that he seeks my 1
2 my father does nothing . . without disclosing it 1
2 and why should my father hide this from me? 1
3 Your father knows well that I have found favor 1
6 If your father misses me at all, then say 1
8 why should you bring me to your father? 1
9 it was determined by my father that evil should 1
10 tell me if your father answers you roughly? 1
12 When I have sounded my father, about this time 1
13 should it please my father to do you harm 1
13 the LORD be with you, as he has been with my father. 1
32 Jonathan answered Saul his father, "Why should he 1
33 Jonathan knew that his father was determined 1
34 for David, because his father had disgraced him. 1
22: 1 his brothers and all his father's house heard it 1
3 Pray let my father and my mother stay with you 1
11 summon Ahim'elech . . and all his father's house 1
15 to his servant or to all the house of my father; 1
16 You shall . . you and all your father's house. 1
22 death of all the persons of your father's house. 1
23:17 the hand of Saul my father shall not find you; 1
17 Saul my father also knows this. 1
24:11 See, my father, see the skirt of your robe in my hand; 1
21 not destroy my name out of my father's house. 1
2Sm 2:32 As'ahel, and buried him in the tomb of his father 1
3: 7 Why have you gone in to my father's concubine? 1
8 showing loyalty to the house of Saul your father 1
29 fall upon . . Jo'ab, and upon all his father's house; 1
6:21 before the LORD, who chose me above your father 1
7:12 you lie down with your fathers 1
14 I will be his father, and he shall be my son. 1
9: 7 kindness for the sake of your father Jonathan 1
7 I will restore . . all the land of Saul your father; 1
10: 2 I will . . as his father dealt loyally with me. 1
2 sent . . to console him concerning his father. 1
3 Do you think . . that he is honoring your father? 1
13: 5 when your father comes to see you, say to him 1
14: 9 On me be the guilt . . and on my father's house; 1
15:34 as I have been your father's servant in time past 1
16: 3 will give me back the kingdom of my father.' 1
19 As I have served your father, so I will serve you. 1
21 Go in to your father's concubines, whom he has left 1
21 you have made yourself odious to your father 1
22 and Ab'salom went in to his father's concubines 1
17: 8 You know . . your father and his men are mighty men 1
8 Besides, your father is expert in war; 1
10 all Israel knows that your father is a mighty man 1
23 he died, and was buried in the tomb of his father. 1
19:28 all my father's house were but men doomed to death 1
37 die . . near the grave of my father and my mother. 1
21:14 And they buried . . in the tomb of Kish his father; 1
24:17 be against me and against my father's house. 1
1Kg 1: 6 His father had never . . displeased him by asking 1
21 when my lord the king sleeps with his fathers 1
2:10 David slept with his fathers, and was buried 1
12 Solomon sat upon the throne of David his father; 1
24 me, and placed me on the throne of David my father 1
26 you bore the ark . . before David my father 1
26 you shared in all the affliction of my father. 1
31 thus take away from me and from my father's house 1
32 without the knowledge of my father David 1
44 all the evil that you did to David my father; 1
3: 3 LORD, walking in the statutes of David his father; 1
6 steadfast love to thy servant David my father 1
7 made thy servant king in place of David my father 1
14 walk in my ways . . as your father David walked 1
5: 1 they had anointed him king in place of his father; 1
3 David my father could not build a house 1
5 as the LORD said to David my father, 'Your son 1
6:12 my word . . which I spoke to David your father. 1
7:14 his father was a man of Tyre, a worker in bronze; 1
51 the things which David his father had dedicated 1
8: 1 the leaders of the fathers' houses of . . Israel 1
15 what he promised . . to David my father, saying 1
17 Now it was in the heart of David my father to build 1
18 the LORD said to David my father, 'Whereas 1
20 I have risen in the place of David my father 1
21 covenant . . which he made with our fathers 1
24 hast kept with thy servant David my father 1
25 keep with thy servant David my father what thou 1
26 thou hast spoken to thy servant David my father. 1
34 to the land which thou gavest to their fathers. 1
40 in the land which thou gavest to our fathers. 1
48 their land, which thou gavest to their fathers 1
53 thou didst bring our fathers out of Egypt, O Lord 1
57 LORD our God be with us, as he was with our fathers; 1
58 his ordinances, which he commanded our fathers. 1
9: 4 you . . walk before me, as David your father walked 1
5 as I promised David your father, saying 1
9 who brought their fathers out of . . Egypt 1
11: 4 true . . as was the heart of David his father. 1
6 follow the LORD, as David his father had done. 1
12 for the sake of David your father I will not do it 1
17 with certain E'domites of his father's servants 1
21 Hadad heard . . that David slept with his fathers 1
27 the breach of the city of David his father. 1
33 keeping my statutes . . as David his father did. 1
43 Solomon slept with his fathers, and was buried 1
43 and was buried in the city of David his father; 1
12: 4 Your father made our yoke heavy. 1
4 lighten the hard service of your father 1
6 old men, who had stood before Solomon his father 1
9 'Lighten the yoke that your father put upon us'? 1
10 'Your father made our yoke heavy 1
10 little finger is thicker than my father's loins. 1
11 my father laid upon you a heavy yoke, I will add 1
11 My father chastised you with whips, but I will 1

14 My father made your yoke heavy, but I will add 1
14 my father chastised you with whips, but I will 1
13:11 the words also . . they told to their father. 1
12 their father said to him, "Which way did he go? 1
22 body shall not come to the tomb of your fathers.' 1
14:15 this good land which he gave to their fathers 1
20 he slept with his fathers, and Nadab . . reigned 1
22 more than all that their fathers had done. 1
31 Rehobo'am slept with his fathers and was buried 1
31 Rehobo'am . . was buried with his fathers 1
15: 3 in all the sins which his father did before him; 1
3 wholly true . . as the heart of David his father. 1
8 Abi'jam slept with his fathers; 1
11 what was right . . as David his father had done. 1
12 removed all the idols that his fathers had made. 1
15 he brought . . the votive gifts of his father 1
19 a league . . as between my father and your father 1
19 a league . . as between my father and your father 1
24 Asa slept with his fathers, and was buried 1
24 was buried with his fathers in the city of David 1
24 and was buried . . in the city of David his father; 1
26 and walked in the way of his father, and in his sin 1
16: 6 Ba'asha slept with his fathers, and was buried 1
28 Omri slept with his fathers, and was buried 1
18:18 but you have, and your father's house, because you 1
19: 4 take . . my life; for I am no better than my fathers. 1
20 Let me kiss my father and my mother 1
20:34 The cities which my father took . . I will restore; 1
34 The cities which my father took from your father 1
34 you may establish . . as my father did in Sama'ria. 1
21: 3 I should give you the inheritance of my fathers. 1
4 will not give you the inheritance of my fathers. 1
22:40 So Ahab slept with his fathers; 1
43 He walked in all the way of Asa his father; 1
46 who remained in the days of his father Asa 1
50 Jehosh'aphat slept with his fathers 1
50 Jehosh'aphat . . was buried with his fathers 1
50 and was buried . . in the city of David his father; 1
52 walked in the way of his father, and . . his mother 1
53 in every way that his father had done. 1
2Kg 2:12 Eli'sha saw it and he cried, "My father, my father! 1
12 Eli'sha saw it and he cried, "My father, my father! 1
3: 2 He did what was evil . . though not like his father 1
2 the pillar of Ba'al which his father had made. 1
13 Go to the prophets of your father and . . mother. 1
4:18 he went out . . to his father among the reapers. 1
19 he said to his father, "Oh, my head, my head! 1
19 The father said to his servant, "Carry him *
5:13 My father, if the prophet had commanded you to do 1
6:21 My father, shall I slay them? Shall I slay them? 1
8:24 So Joram slept with his fathers, and was buried 1
24 Joram slept . . and was buried with his fathers 1
9:25 you and I rode side by side behind Ahab his father 1
28 and buried him in his tomb with his fathers 1
10: 3 the best . . and set him on his father's throne 1
35 Jehu slept with his fathers, and they buried him 1
12:18 and Jeho'ram and Ahazi'ah, his fathers, the kings 1
21 And they buried him with his fathers in the city 1
13: 9 So Jeho'ahaz slept with his fathers 1
13 So Jo'ash slept with his fathers, and Jerobo'am sat 1
14 My father, my father! The chariots of Israel 1
14 My father, my father! The chariots of Israel 1
25 he had taken from Jeho'ahaz his father in war. 1
14: 3 And he did . . yet not like David his father; 1
3 he did in all things as Jo'ash his father had done. 1
5 he killed . . who had slain the king his father. 1
6 The fathers shall not be put to death 1
6 or the children be put to death for the fathers; 1
16 Jeho'ash slept with his fathers, and was buried 1
20 and he was buried in Jerusalem with his fathers 1
21 and made him king instead of his father Amazi'ah. 1
22 after the king slept with his fathers. 1
29 And Jerobo'am slept with his fathers, the kings 1
15: 3 to all that his father Amazi'ah had done. 1
7 And Azari'ah slept with his fathers 1
7 buried him with his fathers in the city of David 1
9 he did what was evil . . as his fathers had done. 1
22 And Men'ahem slept with his fathers 1
34 to all that his father Uzzi'ah had done. 1
38 Jotham slept with his fathers, and was buried 1
38 Jotham slept . . and was buried with his fathers 1
38 and was buried . . in the city of David his father; 1
16: 2 he did not do . . as his father David had done 1
20 And Ahaz slept with his fathers, and was buried 1
20 was buried with his fathers in the city of David; 1
17:13 all the law which I commanded your fathers 1
14 they . . were stubborn, as their fathers had been 1
15 and his covenant that he made with their fathers 1
41 as their fathers did, so they do to this day. 1
18: 3 according to all that David his father had done. 1
19:12 nations which my fathers destroyed, Gozan, Haran 1
20: 5 Thus says the LORD, the God of David your father 1
17 which your fathers have stored up till this day 1
21 And Hezeki'ah slept with his fathers; 1
21: 3 places which Hezeki'ah his father had destroyed; 1
8 out of the land which I gave to their fathers 1
15 since the day their fathers came out of Egypt 1
18 Manas'seh slept with his fathers, and was buried 1
20 evil . . as Manas'seh his father had done. 1
21 He walked in all the way . . his father walked 1
21 and served the idols that his father served 1
22 he forsook the LORD, the God of his fathers 1
22: 2 and walked in all the way of David his father 1
13 our fathers have not obeyed the words of this 1
20 I will gather you to your fathers, and you shall be 1
23:30 and made him king in his father's stead. 1
32 did . . according to all that his fathers had done. 1
34 made . . king in the place of Josi'ah his father 1
37 he . . according to all that his fathers had done. 1
24: 6 So Jehoi'akim slept with his fathers 1
9 according to all that his father had done. 1
1Ch 1:10 Cush was the father of Nimrod; 2
11 Egypt was the father of Ludim, An'amim, Le'habim 2
13 Canaan was the father of Sidon his first-born 2
18 Arpach'shad was the father of Shelah; 2
18 and Shelah was the father of Eber. 2
20 Joktan was the father of Almo'dad, Sheleph 2
34 Abraham was the father of Isaac. 2
2:10 Ram was the father of Ammin'adab 2
10 Ammin'adab was the father of Nahshon, prince 2
11 Nahshon was the father of Salma, Salma of Bo'az 2
13 Jesse was the father of Eli'ab his first-born 2
17 the father of Ama'sa was Jether the Ish'maelite. 1
20 Hur was the father of Uri 2
20 and Uri was the father of Bez'alel. 2
21 the daughter of Machir the father of Gilead 1
22 Segub was the father of Ja'ir 2
23 descendants of Machir, the father of Gilead. 1
24 Eph'rathah, the wife of Hezron his father 1
24 she bore him Ashhur, the father of Teko'a. 1
36 Attai . . father of Nathan and Nathan of Zabad. 2
37 Zabad . . father of Ephlal, and Ephlal of Obed. 2
38 Obed was the father of Jehu, and Jehu of Azari'ah. 2
39 Azari'ah was the father of Helez 2
40 Ele-a'sah . . father of Sismai, and Sismai 2
41 Shallum . . father of Jekami'ah, and Jekami'ah 2
42 Mare'shah . . who was the father of Ziph. 1
44 Shema . . father of Raham, the father of Jor'ke-am; 2
44 Shema . . father of Raham, the father of Jor'ke-am; 1
44 and Rekem was the father of Sham'mai. 2
45 and Ma'on was the father of Bethzur. 1
46 and Haran was the father of Gazez. 2
49 She also bore Sha'aph the father of Madman'nah 1
49 She also bore . . Sheva the father of Machbe'nah 1
49 She also bore . . Sheva . . the father of Gib'e-a; 1
50 Shobal the father of Kir'iath-je'arim. 1
51 Salma, the father of Bethlehem 1
51 and Hareph the father of Beth-gader. 1
52 Shobal . . father of Kir'iath-je'arim had other 1
55 Hammath, the father of the house of Rechab. 1
4: 2 Re-ai'ah the son of Shobal was the father of Jahath 2
2 and Jahath was the father of Ahu'mai and Lahad. 2
4 Penu'el was the father of Gedor 1
4 and Ezer the father of Hushah. 1
4 Eph'rathah, the father of Bethlehem. 1
5 Ashhur, the father of Teko'a, had two wives 1
8 Koz was the father of Anub, Zobe'bah 2
11 Chelub . . was the father of Mehir 2
11 Mehir, who was the father of Eshton. 1
12 Eshton was the father of Bethra'pha, Pase'ah 2
12 Tehin'nah the father of Irna'hash. 1
14 Meo'nothai was the father of Ophrah; 2
14 Serai'ah was the father of Jo'ab 2
14 Jo'ab the father of Ge-har'ashim 1
17 Ishbah, the father of Eshtemo'a. 1
18 his Jewish wife bore Jered the father of Gedor 1
18 his Jewish wife bore . . Heber the father of Soco 1
18 wife bore . . Jeku'thiel the father of Zano'ah. 1
19 were the fathers of Kei'lah the Garmite 1
21 sons of Shelah . . Er the father of Lecah 1
21 La'adah the father of Mare'shah 1
38 and their fathers' houses increased greatly. 1
5: 1 but because he polluted his father's couch 1
13 kinsmen according to their fathers' houses 1
15 Ahi . . was chief in their fathers' houses; 1
24 These were the heads of their fathers' houses 1
24 heads of their fathers' houses. 1
25 transgressed against the God of their fathers 1
6: 4 Elea'zar was the father of Phin'ehas 2
11 Azari'ah . . father of Amari'ah, Amari'ah of Ahi'tub 2
19 the families . . according to their fathers. 1
7: 2 heads of their fathers' houses, namely of Tola 1
4 with them . . according to their fathers' houses 1
7 sons of Bela . . five, heads of fathers' houses 1
9 heads of their fathers' houses, mighty warriors 1
14 she bore Machir the father of Gilead. 1
22 E'phraim their father mourned many days 1
31 Mal'chi-el, who was the father of Bir'zaith. 1
32 Heber was the father of Japhlet, Shomer, Hotham 2
40 men of Asher, heads of fathers' houses, approved 1
8: 1 Benjamin was the father of Bela his first-born 2
7 Gera, that is, Heglam . . father of Uzza and Ahi'hud. 2
29 Je-i'el the father of Gibeon dwelt in Gibeon 1
32 Mikloth (he was the father of Shime'e-ah). 2
33 Ner was the father of Kish, Kish of Saul 2
34 Mer'ib-ba'al was the father of Micah. 2
36 Ahaz was the father of Jeho'addah; 2
36 Jeho'addah . . father of Al'emeth, Az'maveth 2
36 Zimri was the father of Moza. 2
37 Moza was the father of Bin'e-a; Raphah was his son 2
9: 9 according to their fathers' houses. 1
13 their kinsmen, heads of their fathers' houses 1
19 Shallum . . and his kinsmen of his fathers' house 1
19 as their fathers had been in charge of the camp 1
35 In Gibeon dwelt the father of Gibeon, Je-i'el 1
38 Mikloth was the father of Shim'e-am; 2
39 Ner was the father of Kish, Kish of Saul 2
40 Mer'ib-ba'al was the father of Micah. 2
42 Ahaz was the father of Jarah 2
42 and Zimri was the father of Moza. 2
43 Moza . . father of Bin'e-a; and Rephai'ah was his son 2
12:17 may the God of our fathers see and rebuke you. 1
28 and 22 commanders from his own father's house. 1
30 men of valor, famous men in their fathers' houses. 1
17:11 days are fulfilled to go to be with your fathers 1
13 I will be his father, and he shall be my son; 1
19: 2 for his father dealt loyally with me. 1
2 to console him concerning his father. 1
3 Do you think . . that he is honoring your father? 1
21:17 be against me and against my father's house; 1
22:10 He shall be my son, and I will be his father 1
23:11 they became a father's house in one reckoning 1
24 were the sons of Levi by their fathers' houses 1
24: 2 Nadab and Abi'hu died before their father 1
4 heads of fathers' houses of the sons of Elea'zar 1
6 one father's house being chosen for Elea'zar 1
19 established for them by Aaron their father 1
30 the Levites according to their fathers' houses. 1
25: 3 under the direction of their father Jedu'thun 1
6 all under the direction of their father 1
26: 6 who were rulers in their fathers' houses 1
10 not the first-born, his father made him chief 1
13 cast lots by fathers' houses, small and great 1
28: 4 and in the house of Judah my father's house 1
4 God of Israel chose me from all my father's house 1
4 and among my father's sons he took pleasure in me 1
6 chosen him to be my son, and I will be his father. 1
9 you, Solomon my son, know the God of your father 1
29:10 O LORD, the God of Israel our father 1
15 and sojourners, as all our fathers were; 1
18 God of Abraham, Isaac, and Israel, our fathers 1
20 blessed the LORD, the God of their fathers 1
23 sat . . as king instead of David his father; 1
2Ch 1: 8 great and steadfast love to David my father 1
9 thy promise to David my father be now fulfilled 1
2: 3 dealt with David my father and sent him cedar 1
7 workers . . whom David my father provided. 1
14 and his father was a man of Tyre. 1
14 the craftsmen of my lord, David your father. 1
17 census of them which David his father had taken; 1
3: 1 where the LORD had appeared to David his father 1
5: 1 the things which David his father had dedicated 1
6: 4 promised with his mouth to David my father 1
7 in the heart of David my father to build a house 1
8 the LORD said to David my father, 'Whereas it was 1
10 for I have risen in the place of David my father 1
15 who hast kept with thy servant David my father 1
16 O LORD . . keep with thy servant David my father 1
25 thou gavest to them and to their fathers. 1
31 in the land which thou gavest to our fathers. 1
38 their land, which thou gavest to their fathers 1
7:17 if you walk before me, as David your father walked 1
18 as I covenanted with David your father, saying 1
22 they forsook the LORD the God of their fathers 1
8:14 According to the ordinance of David his father 1
9:31 Solomon slept with his fathers, and was buried 1
31 was buried in the city of David his father; 1
10: 4 Your father made our yoke heavy. 1
4 lighten the hard service of your father 1
6 old men, who had stood before Solomon his father 1
9 'Lighten the yoke that your father put upon us'? 1
10 'Your father made our yoke heavy 1
10 little finger is thicker than my father's loins. 1
11 now, whereas my father laid upon you a heavy yoke 1
11 My father chastised you with whips 1
14 My father made your yoke heavy, but I will add to it; 1
14 my father chastised you with whips 1
11:16 sacrifice to the LORD, the God of their fathers. 1
12:16 Rehobo'am slept with his fathers 1
13:12 do not fight . . the LORD, the God of your fathers; 1
18 relied upon the LORD, the God of their fathers. 1
14: 1 Abi'jah slept with his fathers 1
4 to seek the LORD, the God of their fathers 1
15:12 to seek the LORD, the God of their fathers 1
18 he brought . . the votive gifts of his father 1
16: 3 a league . . as between my father and your father; 1
3 a league . . as between my father and your father; 1
13 Asa slept with his fathers 1
17: 2 cities . . which Asa his father had taken. 1
3 he walked in the earlier ways of his father; 1
4 sought the God of his father 1
14 This was the muster of them by fathers' houses 1
19: 4 back to the LORD, the God of their fathers. 1
20: 6 LORD, God of our fathers, art thou not God in heaven? 1
32 He walked in the way of Asa his father 1
33 not yet set . . upon the God of their fathers. 1
21: 1 Jehosh'aphat slept with his fathers 1

1 buried with his fathers in the city of David; 1
3 Their father gave them great gifts 1
4 Jeho'ram had ascended the throne of his father 1
10 he had forsaken the LORD, the God of his fathers. 1
12 Thus says the LORD, the God of David your father 1
12 in the ways of Jehosh'aphat your father 1
13 killed your brothers, of your father's house 1
19 like the fires made for his fathers. 1
22: 4 for after the death of his father 1
24:18 house of the LORD, the God of their fathers 1
22 Jehoi'ada, Zechari'ah's father, had shown him 1
24 forsaken the LORD, the God of their fathers. 1
25: 3 servants who had slain the king his father. 1
4 fathers . . not be put to death for the children 1
4 or the children be put to death for the fathers; 1
5 Amazi'ah . . set them by fathers' houses 1
28 buried with his fathers in the city of David. 1
26: 1 made him king instead of his father Amazi'ah. 1
2 after the king slept with his fathers. 1
4 all that his father Amazi'ah had done. 1
23 buried him with his fathers in the burial field 1
23 Uzzi'ah slept with his fathers, and they buried him 1
27: 2 all that his father Uzzi'ah had done 1
9 Jotham slept with his fathers 1
28: 1 not do what was right . . like his father David. 1
6 forsaken the LORD, the God of their fathers. 1
9 LORD, the God of your fathers, was angry with Judah 1
25 provoking to anger . . the God of his fathers. 1
27 Ahaz slept with his fathers, and they buried him 1
29: 2 according to all that David his father had done. 1
5 house of the LORD, the God of your fathers 1
6 For our fathers have been unfaithful 1
9 For lo, our fathers have fallen by the sword 1
30: 7 Do not be like your fathers and your brethren 1
7 faithless to the LORD God of their fathers 1
8 Do not now be stiff-necked as your fathers were 1
19 to seek God, the LORD the God of his fathers 1
22 LORD the God of their fathers. 1
31:17 priests was according to their fathers' houses; 1
32:13 Do you not know what I and my fathers have done 1
14 nations which my fathers utterly destroyed 1
15 able to deliver . . from the hand of my fathers. 1
33 Hezeki'ah slept with his fathers, and they buried 1
33: 3 which his father Hezeki'ah had broken down 1
8 land which I appointed for your fathers 1
12 humbled . . before the God of his fathers. 1
20 Manas'seh slept with his fathers and they buried 1
22 did what was evil . . as Manas'seh his father had 1
22 all the images that Manas'seh his father had made 1
23 as Manas'seh his father had humbled himself 1
34: 2 walked in the ways of David his father; 1
3 he began to seek the God of David his father; 1
21 our fathers have not kept the word of the LORD 1
28 Behold, I will gather you to your fathers 1
32 covenant of God, the God of their fathers. 1
33 following the LORD the God of their fathers. 1
35: 4 Prepare . . according to your fathers' houses 1
5 groupings of the fathers' houses of your brethren 1
5 a part of a father's house of the Levites. 1
12 groupings of the fathers' houses of the lay 1
24 died, and was buried in the tombs of his fathers. 1
36: 1 made him king in his father's stead in Jerusalem. 1
15 LORD, the God of their fathers, sent persistently 1
Ezr 2:59 not prove their fathers' houses or their descent 1
4:15 search . . book of the records of your fathers. 3
5:12 our fathers had angered the God of heaven 3
7:27 Blessed be the LORD, the God of our fathers 1
8:28 offering to the LORD, the God of your fathers. 1
9: 7 From the days of our fathers to this day 1
10:11 make confession to the LORD the God of your fathers 1
16 Ezra . . selected men, heads of fathers' houses 1
16 according to their fathers' houses 1
Neh 1: 6 Yea, I and my father's house have sinned. 1
2: 3 when the city, the place of my fathers' sepulchres 1
5 Judah, to the city of my fathers' sepulchres 1
7:61 but they could not prove their fathers' houses 1
8:13 day the heads of fathers' houses of all the people 1
9: 2 confessed . . the iniquities of their fathers. 1
9 didst see the affliction of our fathers in Egypt 1
10 they acted insolently against our fathers; •
16 they and our fathers acted presumptuously 1
23 land which thou hadst told their fathers 1
32 come upon . . our prophets, our fathers, and all 1
34 kings, our princes, our priests, and our fathers 1
36 land . . gavest to our fathers to enjoy its fruit 1
10:34 according to our fathers' houses, at times 1
12:10 Jeshua was the father of Joi'akim 2
10 Joi'akim the father of Eli'ashib 2
10 Eli'ashib the father of Joi'ada •
11 Joi'ada the father of Jonathan 2
11 Jonathan the father of Jad'du-a. 2
13:18 Did not your fathers act in this way 1
Est 2: 7 Esther . . for she had neither father nor mother; 1
7 and when her father and her mother died 1
4:14 but you and your father's house will perish. 1
Job 8: 8 consider what the fathers have found; 1
15:10 aged are among us, older than your father. 1
18 have told, and their fathers have not hidden 1
17:14 if I say to the pit, 'You are my father,' 1

29:16 I was a father to the poor 1
30: 1 whose fathers I would have disdained 1
31:18 for from his youth I reared him as a father 1
38:28 Has the rain a father 1
42:15 their father gave them inheritance 1
Ps 22: 4 In thee our fathers trusted; 1
27:10 For my father and my mother have forsaken me 1
39:12 passing guest, a sojourner, like all my fathers. 1
44: 1 our fathers have told us, what deeds thou didst 1
45:10 forget your people and your father's house; 1
16 Instead of your fathers shall be your sons; 1
49:19 he will go to the generation of his fathers 1
68: 5 Father of the fatherless and protector 1
78: 3 heard and known, that our fathers have told us. 1
5 a law . . which he commanded our fathers to teach 1
8 that they should not be like their fathers 1
12 In the sight of their fathers he wrought marvels 1
57 acted treacherously like their fathers; 1
89:26 my Father, my God, and the Rock of my salvation.' 1
95: 9 your fathers tested me, and put me to the proof 1
103:13 As a father pities his children 1
106: 6 Both we and our fathers have sinned; 1
7 Our fathers, when they were in Egypt 1
109:14 May the iniquity of his fathers be remembered 1
Prv 1: 8 Hear, my son, your father's instruction 1
3:12 as a father the son in whom he delights. 1
4: 1 Hear, O sons, a father's instruction 1
3 When I was a son with my father, tender 1
6:20 My son, keep your father's commandment 1
10: 1 A wise son makes a glad father 1
13: 1 A wise son hears his father's instruction 1
15: 5 A fool despises his father's instruction 1
20 A wise son makes a glad father 1
17: 6 glory of sons is their fathers. 1
21 A stupid son is a grief to a father; 2
21 father of a fool has no joy. 1
25 A foolish son is a grief to his father 1
19:13 A foolish son is ruin to his father 1
14 House and wealth are inherited from fathers 1
26 who does violence to his father and chases away 1
20:20 If one curses his father or his mother 1
22:28 ancient landmark which your fathers have set. 1
23:22 Hearken to your father who begot you 1
24 father of the righteous will greatly rejoice; 1
25 Let your father and mother be glad 1
27:10 friend, and your father's friend, do not forsake; 1
28: 7 but a companion of gluttons shames his father. 1
24 He who robs his father or his mother and says, "That 1
29: 3 He who loves wisdom makes his father glad 1
30:11 There are those who curse their fathers 1
17 eye that mocks a father and scorns to obey 1
Ecc 5:14 he is father of a son, but . . nothing in his hand. 2
Isa 3: 6 hold of his brother in the house of his father 1
7:17 upon your people and upon your father's house 1
8: 4 child knows how to cry 'My father' or 'My mother,' 1
14:21 because of the guilt of their fathers 1
22:21 he shall be a father to the inhabitants 1
23 become a throne of honor to his father's house. 1
24 hang on him the whole weight of his father's house 1
37:12 the nations which my fathers destroyed 1
38: 5 Thus says the LORD, the God of David your father 1
19 the father makes known to the children thy 1
39: 6 which your fathers have stored up till this day 1
43:27 Your first father sinned 1
45:10 who says to a father, 'What are you begetting?' 1
51: 2 Look to Abraham your father and to Sarah 1
58:14 feed you with the heritage of Jacob your father 1
63:16 art our Father, though Abraham does not know us 1
16 thou, O LORD, art our Father, our Redeemer 1
64: 8 Yet, O LORD, thou art our Father; we are the clay 1
11 Our holy . . house, where our fathers praised thee 1
65: 7 their iniquities and their fathers' iniquities 1
Jer 2: 5 What wrong did your fathers find in me 1
27 who say to a tree, 'You are my father,' 1
3: 4 My father, thou art the friend of my youth 1
18 the land that I gave your fathers for a heritage. 1
19 And I thought you would call me, My Father 1
24 has devoured all for which our fathers labored 1
25 we and our fathers, from our youth even to this day; 1
6:21 they shall stumble; fathers and sons together 1
7: 7 in the land that I gave of old to your fathers 1
14 the place which I gave to you and to your fathers 1
18 children gather wood, the fathers kindle fire 1
22 I did not speak to your fathers or command them 1
25 the day that your fathers came out of the land 1
26 They did worse than their fathers. 1
9:14 after the Ba'als, as their fathers taught them. 1
16 whom neither they nor their fathers have known; 1
11: 4 which I commanded your fathers 1
5 the oath which I swore to your fathers 1
7 For I solemnly warned your fathers 1
10 my covenant which I made with their fathers. 1
12: 6 even your brothers and the house of your father 1
13:14 one against another, fathers and sons together 1
14:20 We acknowledge . . the iniquity of our fathers 1
16: 3 and the fathers who begot them in this land 1
7 to drink for his father or his mother. 1
11 your fathers have forsaken me, says the LORD 1
12 because you have done worse than your fathers 1

13 which neither you nor your fathers have known 1
15 to their own land which I gave to their fathers. 1
19 Our fathers have inherited nought but lies 1
17:22 the sabbath day holy, as I commanded your fathers. 1
19: 4 neither they nor their fathers nor the kings 1
20:15 brought the news to my father, "A son is born to you 1
22:11 who reigned instead of Josi'ah his father 1
15 Did not your father eat and drink and do justice 1
23:27 even as their fathers forgot my name for Ba'al? 1
39 and the city which I gave to you and your fathers. 1
24:10 the land which I gave to them and their fathers. 1
25: 5 to you and your fathers from of old and for ever; 1
30: 3 the land which I gave to their fathers 1
31: 9 for I am a father to Israel 1
29 no longer say: 'The fathers have eaten sour grapes 1
32 the covenant which I made with their fathers 1
32:18 requite the guilt of fathers to their children 1
22 thou didst swear to their fathers to give them 1
34: 5 And as spices were burned for your fathers 1
13 I made a covenant with your fathers 1
14 But your fathers did not listen to me 1
35: 6 for Jon'adab the son of Rechab, our father 1
8 the voice of Jon'adab the son of Rechab, our father 1
10 done all that Jon'adab our father commanded us. 1
14 for they have obeyed their father's command. 1
15 the land which I gave to you and your fathers.' 1
16 have kept the command which their father gave 1
18 have obeyed the command of Jon'adab your father 1
44: 3 knew not, neither they, nor you, nor your fathers. 1
9 forgotten the wickedness of your fathers 1
10 which I set before you and before your fathers. 1
17 as we did, both we and our fathers 1
21 you and your fathers, your kings and your princes 1
47: 3 the fathers look not back to the children 1
50: 7 the LORD, the hope of their fathers. 1
Lam 5: 7 Our fathers sinned, and are no more; 1
Ezk 2: 3 their fathers have transgressed against me 1
5:10 fathers shall eat their sons in the midst of you 1
10 and sons shall eat their fathers; 1
16: 3 your father was an Amorite 1
45 mother was a Hittite and your father an Amorite. 1
18: 2 The fathers have eaten sour grapes 1
4 soul of the father as well as the soul of the son 1
14 who sees all the sins which his father has done 1
17 he shall not die for his father's iniquity; 1
18 his father, because he practiced extortion 1
19 the son suffer for the iniquity of the father? 1
20 shall not suffer for the iniquity of the father 1
20 nor the father suffer for the iniquity of the son; 1
20: 4 let them know the abominations of their fathers 1
18 Do not walk in the statutes of your fathers 1
24 their eyes were set on their fathers' idols. 1
27 In this again your fathers blasphemed me 1
30 after the manner of your fathers and go astray 1
36 As I entered into judgment with your fathers 1
42 country which I swore to give to your fathers. 1
22: 7 Father and mother are treated with contempt 1
10 In you men uncover their fathers' nakedness; 1
11 defiles his sister, his father's daughter. 1
36:28 dwell in the land which I gave to your fathers; 1
37:25 shall dwell in the land where your fathers dwelt 1
44:25 however, for father or mother, for son or daughter 1
47:14 I swore to give it to your fathers 1
Dan 2:23 O God of my fathers, I give thanks and praise 3
5: 2 Nebuchadnez'zar his father had taken 3
11 days of your father light and understanding 3
11 King Nebuchadnez'zar, your father, made him chief 3
13 exiles . . king my father brought from Judah. 3
18 Most High God gave Nebuchadnez'zar your father 3
9: 6 spoke . . to . . our fathers, and to all the people 1
8 our kings, to our princes, and to our fathers 1
16 sins, and for the iniquities of our fathers 1
11:24 neither his fathers nor his fathers' fathers 1
24 neither his fathers nor his fathers' fathers 1
24 neither his fathers nor his fathers' fathers 1
37 He shall give no heed to the gods of his fathers 1
38 god whom his fathers did not know he shall honor 1
Hos 9:10 in its first season, I saw your fathers. 1
Jol 1: 2 in your days, or in the days of your fathers? 1
Ams 2: 4 lies . . after which their fathers walked. 1
Mic 7: 6 for the son treats the father with contempt 1
20 hast sworn to our fathers from the days of old 1
Zec 1: 2 The LORD was very angry with your fathers. 1
4 Be not like your fathers 1
5 Your fathers, where are they? 1
6 did they not overtake your fathers? 1
8:14 when your fathers provoked me to wrath 1
13: 3 his father and mother who bore him will say to him 1
3 his father and mother who bore him will say to him 1
Mal 1: 6 A son honors his father, and a servant his master. 1
6 If then I am a father, where is my honor? 1
2:10 Have we not all one father? 1
10 profaning the covenant of our fathers? 1
3: 7 From the days of your fathers you have turned 1
4: 6 turn the hearts of fathers to their children 1
6 turn . . the hearts of children to their fathers 1
Mat 1: 2 Abraham was the father of Isaac 4
2 and Isaac the father of Jacob 4
2 and Jacob the father of Judah 4

3 Judah the father of Perez and Zerah by Tamar 4
3 Perez the father of Hezron 4
3 and Hezron the father of Ram 4
4 Ram the father of Ammin'adab 4
4 Ammin'adab the father of Nahshon 4
4 and Nahshon the father of Salmon 4
5 Salmon the father of Bo'az by Rahab 4
5 Bo'az the father of Obed by Ruth 4
5 and Obed the father of Jesse 4
6 Jesse the father of David the king. 4
6 And David was the father of Solomon by the wife 4
7 Solomon the father of Rehoboam 4
7 and Rehoboam the father of Abi'jah 4
7 and Abi'jah the father of Asa 4
8 Asa the father of Jehosh'aphat 4
8 and Jehosh'aphat the father of Joram 4
8 and Joram the father of Uzzi'ah 4
9 Uzzi'ah the father of Jotham 4
9 and Jotham the father of Ahaz 4
9 and Ahaz the father of Hezeki'ah 4
10 Hezeki'ah the father of Manas'seh 4
10 and Manas'seh the father of Amos 4
10 and Amos the father of Josi'ah 4
11 Josi'ah the father of Jechoni'ah and his brothers 4
12 Jechoni'ah was the father of She-al'ti-el 4
12 She-al'ti-el the father of Zerub'babel 4
13 Zerub'babel the father of Abi'ud 4
13 and Abi'ud the father of Eli'akim 4
13 and Eli'akim the father of Azor 4
14 Azor the father of Zadok 4
14 and Zadok the father of Achim 4
14 and Achim the father of Eli'ud 4
15 Eli'ud the father of Elea'zar 4
15 and Elea'zar the father of Matthan 4
15 Matthan, and Matthan the father of Jacob 4
16 Jacob the father of Joseph the husband of Mary 4
2:22 in place of his father Herod, he was afraid to go 6
3: 9 say to yourselves, 'We have Abraham as our father'; 6
4:21 in the boat with Zeb'edee their father, mending 6
22 the boat and their father, and followed him. 6
5:16 give glory to your Father who is in heaven. 6
45 be sons of your Father who is in heaven 6
48 be perfect, as your heavenly Father is perfect. 6
6: 1 no reward from your Father who is in heaven. 10
4 in secret; and your Father who sees in secret 6
6 shut the door and pray to your Father who is 6
6 Father who is in secret; and your Father who sees 6
8 like them, for your Father knows what you need 6
9 Pray then like this: Our Father who art in heaven 6
14 men their trespasses, your heavenly Father also 6
15 neither will your Father forgive 6
18 fasting may not be seen by men but by your Father 6
18 Father who is in secret; and your Father who sees 6
26 barns, and yet your heavenly Father feeds them. 6
32 these things; and your heavenly Father knows 6
7:11 how much more will your Father who is in heaven 6
21 he who does the will of my Father who is in heaven. 6
8:21 Lord, let me first go and bury my father. 6
10:20 the Spirit of your Father speaking through you. 6
21 and the father his child 6
29 fall to the ground without your Father's will. 6
32 I also will acknowledge before my Father 6
33 before my Father who is in heaven. 6
35 For I have come to set a man against his father 6
37 He who loves father or mother more than me 6
11:25 I thank thee, Father, Lord of heaven and earth 6
26 yea, Father, for such was thy gracious will. 6
27 All things have been delivered to me by my Father; 6
27 and no one knows the Son except the Father 6
27 and no one knows the Father except the Son 6
12:50 For whoever does the will of my Father in heaven 6
13:43 in the kingdom of their Father 6
15: 4 'Honor your father and your mother,' 6
4 'He who speaks evil of father or mother 6
5 you say, 'If any one tells his father or his mother 10
5 he need not honor his father.' 6
13 which my heavenly Father has not planted 6
16:17 but my Father who is in heaven. 6
27 come with his angels in the glory of his Father 6
18:10 the face of my Father who is in heaven. 6
14 So it is not the will of my Father who is in heaven 6
19 it will be done for them by my Father in heaven. 6
35 So also my heavenly Father will do 6
19: 5 said, 'For this reason a man shall leave his father 6
19 Honor your father and mother 6
29 brothers or sisters or father or mother 6
20:23 for whom it has been prepared by my Father. 6
21:31 Which of the two did the will of his father? 6
23: 9 call no man your father on earth 6
9 you have one Father, who is in heaven. 6
30 saying, 'If we had lived in the days of our fathers 6
32 Fill up, then, the measure of your fathers. 6
24:36 but the Father only. 6
25:34 Come, O blessed of my Father 6
26:29 new with you in my Father's kingdom. 6
39 My father, if it be possible, let this cup pass 6
42 My Father, if this cannot pass unless I drink it 6
53 Do you think that I cannot appeal to my Father 6
28:19 baptizing them in the name of the Father 6

Mrk 1:20 they left their father Zeb'edee in the boat 6
5:40 and took the child's father and mother 6
7:10 For Moses said, 'Honor your father and your mother'; 6
10 'He who speaks evil of father or mother 6
11 you say, 'If a man tells his father or his mother 10
12 to do anything for his father or mother 10
8:38 glory of his Father with the holy angels. 6
9:21 Jesus asked his father, "How long has he had this? 6
24 Immediately the father of the child cried out 6
10: 7 a man shall leave his father and mother 6
19 Do not defraud, Honor your father and mother.' 6
29 house or brothers or sisters or mother or father 6
11:10 kingdom of our father David that is coming 6
25 so that your Father also who is in heaven 6
13:12 the father his child 6
32 nor the Son, but only the Father. 6
14:36 Abba, Father, all things are possible to thee 6
15:21 the father of Alexander and Rufus 6
Lke 1:17 to turn the hearts of the fathers to the children 6
32 give to him the throne of his father David 6
55 as he spoke to our fathers 6
59 would have named him Zechari'ah after his father 6
62 And they made signs to his father 10
67 And his father Zechari'ah was filled 6
72 to perform the mercy promised to our fathers 6
73 the oath which he swore to our father Abraham 6
2:33 his father and his mother marveled 6
48 Behold, your father and I have been looking 6
49 you not know that I must be in my Father's house? 6
3: 8 'We have Abraham as our father' 6
6:23 for so their fathers did to the prophets. 6
26 for their fathers did to the false prophets. 6
36 Be merciful, even as your Father is merciful. 6
8:51 the father and mother of the child. 6
9:26 the glory of the Father and of the holy angels. 6
42 healed the boy and gave him back to his father 10
59 he said, "Lord, let me first go and bury my father. 6
10:21 I thank thee, Father, Lord of heaven and earth 6
21 yea, Father, for such was thy gracious will. 6
22 no one knows who the Son is except the Father 6
22 who the Father is except the Son 6
22 who the Father is except the Son 6
11: 2 he said to them, "When you pray, say: "Father 6
11 What father among you, if his son asks for a fish 6
13 how much more will the heavenly Father give 6
47 tombs of the prophets whom your fathers killed. 6
48 consent to the deeds of your fathers 6
12:30 your Father knows that you need them. 6
32 it is your Father's good pleasure 6
53 father against son and son against father 6
53 father against son and son against father 6
14:26 does not hate his own father and mother and wife 6
15:12 the younger of them said to his father, 'Father 6
12 the younger of them said to his father, 'Father 6
17 How many of my father's hired servants have bread 6
18 I will arise and go to my father 6
18 I will say to him, "Father, I have sinned 6
20 he arose and came to his father 6
20 his father saw him and had compassion 6
21 the son said to him, 'Father, I have sinned 6
22 the father said to his servants 6
27 your father has killed the fatted calf 6
28 His father came out and entreated him 6
29 he answered his father, 'Lo, these many years 10
16:24 he called out, 'Father Abraham, have mercy 6
27 he said, 'Then I beg you, father 6
27 he said, 'Then I beg you, father 6
30 he said, 'No, father Abraham 6
18:20 Honor your father and mother.' 6
22:29 I assign to you, as my Father assigned to me 6
42 Father, if thou art willing 6
23:34 Jesus said, "Father, forgive them 6
46 Then Jesus, crying with a loud voice, said, "Father 6
24:49 behold, I send the promise of my Father upon you; 6
Joh 1:14 glory as of the only Son from the Father. 6
18 the only Son, who is in the bosom of the Father 6
2:16 not make my Father's house a house of trade. 6
3:35 the Father loves the Son, and has given all things 6
4:12 Are you greater than our father Jacob 6
20 Our fathers worshiped on this mountain; 6
21 nor in Jerusalem will you worship the Father. 6
23 will worship the Father in spirit and truth 10
23 for such the Father seeks to worship him. 6
53 The father knew that was the hour when Jesus 6
5:17 Jesus answered them, "My Father is working still 6
18 also called God his Father 6
19 only what he sees the Father doing 6
20 For the Father loves the Son 6
21 as the Father raises the dead and gives them life 6
22 The Father judges no one 6
23 even as they honor the Father 6
23 does not honor the Father who sent him. 6
26 For as the Father has life in himself 6
36 the works which the Father has granted me 6
36 bear me witness that the Father has sent me. 6
37 the Father who sent me has himself borne witness 6
43 I have come in my Father's name 6
45 Do not think that I shall accuse you to the Father 6
6:27 for on him has God the Father set his seal. 6

31 Our fathers ate the manna in the wilderness 6
32 my Father gives you the true bread from heaven. 6
37 All that the Father gives me will come to me 6
40 this is the will of my Father 6
42 Jesus . . whose father and mother we know? 6
44 unless the Father who sent me draws him 6
45 who has heard and learned from the Father 6
46 Not that any one has seen the Father 6
46 he has seen the Father. 6
49 Your fathers ate the manna in the wilderness 6
57 As the living Father sent me 6
57 I live because of the Father 6
58 not such as the fathers ate and died 6
65 unless it is granted him by the Father. 6
7:22 not that it is from Moses, but from the fathers 6
8:18 the Father who sent me bears witness to me. 6
19 They said to him therefore, "Where is your Father? 6
19 You know neither me nor my Father; 6
19 if you knew me, you would know my Father also. 6
27 he spoke to them of the Father. 6
28 speak thus as the Father taught me. 6
38 I speak of what I have seen with my Father 10
38 you do what you have heard from your father. 6
39 They answered him, "Abraham is our father. 6
41 You do what your father did. 6
41 we have one Father, even God. 6
42 If God were your Father, you would love me 6
44 You are of your father the devil 6
44 your will is to do your father's desires 6
44 for he is a liar and the father of lies. 6
49 I honor my Father, and you dishonor me. 6
53 Are you greater than our father Abraham, who died? 6
54 it is my Father who glorifies me 6
56 Your father Abraham rejoiced 6
10:15 as the Father knows me and I know the Father 6
15 as the Father knows me and I know the Father 6
17 For this reason the Father loves me 6
18 this charge I have received from my Father. 6
25 The works that I do in my Father's name 6
29 My Father, who has given them to me 6
29 able to snatch them out of the Father's hand. 6
30 I and the Father are one. 6
32 I have shown you many good works from the Father; 6
36 do you say of him whom the Father consecrated 6
37 If I am not doing the works of my Father 6
38 the Father is in me and I am in the Father. 6
38 the Father is in me and I am in the Father. 6
11:41 Father, I thank thee that thou hast heard me. 6
12:26 if any one serves me, the Father will honor him. 6
27 'Father, save me from this hour'? 6
28 Father, glorify thy name. 6
49 the Father who sent me 6
50 I say as the Father has bidden me. 6
13: 1 to depart out of this world to the Father 6
3 the Father had given all things into his hands 6
14: 2 In my Father's house are many rooms 6
6 no one comes to the Father, but by me. 6
7 you had known me, you would have known my Father 6
8 Philip said to him, "Lord, show us the Father 6
9 He who has seen me has seen the Father 6
9 how can you say, 'Show us the Father'? 6
10 I am in the Father and the Father in me 10
10 the Father who dwells in me does his works. 6
10 I am in the Father and the Father in me 6
11 I am in the Father and the Father in me 10
11 I am in the Father and the Father in me 6
12 because I go to the Father. 6
13 that the Father may be glorified in the Son; 6
16 I will pray the Father 6
20 In that day you will know that I am in my Father 6
21 he who loves me will be loved by my Father 6
23 my Father will love him 6
24 the word . . is not mine but the Father's who sent me. 6
26 Holy Spirit, whom the Father will send in my name 6
28 because I go to the Father 6
28 the Father is greater than I. 6
31 I do as the Father has commanded me 6
31 so that the world may know that I love the Father. 6
15: 1 my Father is the vinedresser. 6
8 By this my Father is glorified 6
9 As the Father has loved me, so have I loved you; 6
10 just as I have kept my Father's commandments 6
15 all that I have heard from my Father 6
16 whatever you ask the Father in my name 6
23 He who hates me hates my Father also. 6
24 they have seen and hated both me and my Father. 6
26 whom I shall send to you from the Father 6
26 who proceeds from the Father 6
16: 3 because they have not known the Father, nor me. 6
10 because I go to the Father 6
15 All that the Father has is mine 6
17 'because I go to the Father'? 6
23 if you ask anything of the Father, he will give it 6
25 tell you plainly of the Father. 6
26 I do not say to you that I shall pray the Father 6
27 have believed that I came from the Father. 5
27 for the Father himself loves you 6
28 I came from the Father 6
28 I am leaving the world and going to the Father. 6

32 yet I am not alone, for the Father is with me. 6
17: 1 Father, the hour has come; glorify thy Son 6
5 now, Father, glorify thou me in thy own presence 6
11 Holy Father, keep them in thy name 6
21 they may all be one; even as thou, Father, art in me 6
24 Father, I desire that they also . . may be with me 6
25 O righteous Father, the world has not known thee 6
18:11 not drink the cup which the Father has given me? 6
20:17 for I have not yet ascended to the Father 6
17 I am ascending to my Father and your Father 6
17 I am ascending to my Father and your Father 6
21 As the Father has sent me, even so I send you. 6
Act 1: 4 to wait for the promise of the Father 6
7 which the Father has fixed by his own authority. 6
2:33 having received from the Father the promise 6
3:13 the God of our fathers 6
25 the covenant which God gave to your fathers 6
4:25 by the mouth of our father David, thy servant 6
5:30 God of our fathers raised Jesus whom you killed 6
7: 2 Stephen said: "Brethren and fathers, hear me. 6
2 The God of glory appeared to our father Abraham 10
4 after his father died, God removed him from there 6
11 our fathers could find no food. 6
12 he sent forth our fathers the first time. 6
14 Joseph sent and called to him Jacob his father 6
15 he died, himself and our fathers 6
19 forced our fathers to expose their infants 6
20 brought up for three months in his father's house; 6
32 I am the God of your fathers 6
38 spoke to him at Mount Sinai, and with our fathers; 6
39 Our fathers refused to obey him 6
44 Our fathers had the tent of witness 6
45 Our fathers in turn brought it in with Joshua 6
45 which God thrust out before our fathers 6
51 As your fathers did, so do you. 6
52 did not your fathers persecute 6
13:17 The God of this people Israel chose our fathers 6
32 what God promised to the fathers 6
36 was laid with his fathers, and saw corruption; 6
15:10 neither our fathers nor we have been able to bear? 6
16: 1 his father was a Greek. 6
3 they all knew that his father was a Greek. 6
22: 1 Brethren and fathers, hear the defense 6
14 God of our fathers appointed you to know his will 6
26: 6 hope in the promise made by God to our fathers 6
28: 8 It happened that the father of Publius lay sick 6
25 was right in saying to your fathers 6
Rom 1: 7 Grace to you and peace from God our Father 6
4:11 to make him the father of all who believe 6
12 likewise the father of the circumcised 6
12 the faith which our father Abraham had 6
16 Abraham, for he is the father of us all 6
17 I have made you the father of many nations 6
18 that he should become the father of many nations; 6
6: 4 raised from the dead by the glory of the Father 6
8:15 the spirit of sonship. When we cry, "Abba! Father! 6
15: 6 the God and Father of our Lord Jesus Christ. 6
1Co 1: 3 peace from God our Father and the Lord Jesus 6
4:15 you do not have many fathers 6
5: 1 a man is living with his father's wife. 6
8: 6 yet for us there is one God, the Father 6
10: 1 our fathers were all under the cloud 6
15:24 when he delivers the kingdom to God the Father 6
2Co 1: 2 Grace to you and peace from God our Father 6
3 Blessed be the God and Father of our Lord Jesus 6
3 Father of mercies and God of all comfort 6
6:18 I will be a father to you, and you shall be my sons 6
11:31 The God and Father of the Lord Jesus 6
Gal 1: 1 through Jesus Christ and God the Father 6
3 Grace to you and peace from God the Father 6
4 according to the will of our God and Father; 6
14 for the traditions of my fathers. 8
4: 2 until the date set by the father. 6
6 his Son into our hearts, crying, "Abba! Father! 6
Eph 1: 2 Grace to you and peace from God our Father 6
3 the God and Father of our Lord Jesus Christ 6
17 God of our Lord Jesus Christ, the Father of glory 6
2:18 both have access in one Spirit to the Father. 6
3:14 For this reason I bow my knees before the Father 6
4: 6 one God and Father of us all, who is above all 6
5:20 giving thanks . . to God the Father. 6
31 shall leave his father and mother 6
6: 2 Honor your father and mother 6
4 Fathers, do not provoke your children to anger 6
23 God the Father and the Lord Jesus Christ. 6
Php 1: 2 Grace to you and peace from God our Father 6
2:11 to the glory of God the Father. 6
22 how as a son with a father he has served with me 10
4:20 To our God and Father be glory for ever and ever. 10
Col 1: 2 Grace to you and peace from God our Father. 6
3 God, the Father of our Lord Jesus Christ 10
12 giving thanks to the Father 10
3:17 giving thanks to God the Father through him. 10
21 Fathers, do not provoke your children 6
1Th 1: 1 in God the Father and the Lord Jesus Christ 10
3 remembering before our God and Father your work 6
2:11 for you know how, like a father with his children 6
3:11 Now may our God and Father himself 6
13 unblamable in holiness before our God and Father 6

2Th 1: 1 God our Father and the Lord Jesus Christ 10
2 Grace to you and peace from God the Father 6
2:16 Jesus Christ himself, and God our Father 6
1Ti 1: 2 Grace, mercy, and peace from God the Father 6
5: 1 exhort him as you would a father 6
2Ti 1: 2 Grace, mercy, and peace from God the Father 6
3 as did my fathers 11
Tit 1: 4 Grace and peace from God the Father 6
Phm 1: 3 Grace to you and peace from God our Father 6
Heb 1: 1 God spoke of old to our fathers by the prophets; 6
5 Or again, "I will be to him a father 6
3: 9 where your fathers put me to the test 6
8: 9 like the covenant that I made with their fathers 6
12: 7 whom his father does not discipline? 6
9 we have had earthly fathers to discipline us 6
9 be subject to the Father of spirits and live? 10
Jas 1:17 coming down from the Father of lights 6
27 pure and undefiled before God and the Father 10
2:21 Was not Abraham our father justified by works 6
3: 9 With it we bless the Lord and Father 6
1Pe 1: 2 chosen and destined by God the Father 6
3 Blessed be the God and Father of our Lord Jesus 6
17 if you invoke as Father him who judges each one 6
2Pe 1:17 he received honor and glory from God the Father 6
3: 4 For ever since the fathers fell asleep 6
1Jn 1: 2 the eternal life which was with the Father 6
3 with the Father and with his Son Jesus Christ. 6
2: 1 we have an advocate with the Father, Jesus Christ 6
13 I am writing to you, fathers, because you know him 6
13 because you know the Father. 6
14 I write to you, fathers, because you know him 6
15 love for the Father is not in him. 6
16 is not of the Father but is of the world. 6
22 he who denies the Father and the Son. 6
23 No one who denies the Son has the Father. 6
23 He who confesses the Son has the Father also. 6
24 then you will abide in the Son and in the Father. 10
3: 1 See what love the Father has given us 6
4:14 Father has sent his Son as the Savior of the world 6
2Jn 1: 3 from God the Father and from Jesus Christ 6
3 and from Jesus Christ the Father's Son 6
4 just as we have been commanded by the Father. 6
9 he who abides . . has both the Father and the Son. 6
Jde 1: 1 To those who are called, beloved in God the Father 10
Rev 1: 6 made us a kingdom, priests to his God and Father 10
2:27 as I myself have received power from my Father; 6
3: 5 I will confess his name before my Father 6
21 and sat down with my Father on his throne. 6
14: 1 144,000 who had his name and his Father's name 6
1Es 1:31 was buried in the tomb of his fathers. 8
34 made him king in succession to Josiah his father. 6
50 the God of their fathers sent by his messenger 6
2:21 search may be made in the records of your fathers. 6
4:20 A man leaves his own father, who brought him up 6
21 with no thought of his father or his mother 6
25 loves . . more than his father or his mother. 6
60 I give thee thanks, O Lord of our fathers. 6
62 they praised the God of their fathers 6
5: 1 heads of fathers' houses were chosen to go up 7
6:15 when our fathers sinned against the Lord 6
8:58 vowed to the Lord, the Lord of our fathers. 6
76 from the times of our fathers 6
77 because of our sins and the sins of our fathers 6
9: 8 give glory to the Lord the God of our fathers 6
2Es 1:28 as a father entreats his sons 12
29 you should be my sons and I should be your father? 12
38 now, father, look with pride and see the people 12
2: 5 I call upon you, father, as a witness 12
4:23 the law of our fathers has been made of no effect 12
7:103 fathers for sons or sons for parents 12
104 Just as now a father does not send his son 12
104 or a son his father, or a master his servant 12
106 and Moses for our fathers who sinned in the desert 12
8:31 For we and our fathers have passed our lives 12
9:29 to our fathers in the wilderness 12
32 though our fathers received the law 12
14:29 At first our fathers dwelt as aliens in Egypt 12
31 you and your fathers committed iniquity 12
Tob 1: 8 as Deborah my father's mother had commanded me 6
8 I was left an orphan by my father. 6
2: 3 Father, one of our people has been strangled 6
3: 3 those which my fathers committed before thee. 6
5 for my sins and those of my fathers 6
7 was reproached by her father's maids 6
10 But she said, "I am the only child of my father 6
15 I did not stain my name or the name of my father 6
15 I am my father's only child 6
4:12 from among the descendants of your fathers 6
12 a foreign woman, who is not of your father's tribe 6
12 Noah, Abraham, Isaac, and Jacob, our fathers of old 6
5: 1 Father, I will do everything 6
7 Wait for me, and I shall tell my father. 6
8 So he went in and said to his father 6
16 his father said to him 6
6:12 I will speak to her father 6
14 Now I am the only son my father has 6
14 the lives of my father and mother 6
15 the words with which your father commanded you 6
7: 5 Tobias said, "He is my father. 6

13 take her with you to your father. 6
8: 5 Blessed art thou, O God of our fathers 6
21 return in safety to his father 6
9: 4 my father is counting the days 6
10: 1 Now his father Tobit was counting each day 6
7 my father and mother have given up hope 6
8 I will send messengers to your father 6
9 Tobias replied, "No, send me back to my father. 6
11: 2 Are you not aware . . of how you left your father? 6
6 caught sight of him coming, and said to his father 6
7 I know, Tobias, that your father will open his eyes. 6
11 and took hold of his father 6
11 he sprinkled the gall upon his father's eyes 6
11 saying, "Be of good cheer, father. 6
15 he reported to his father the great things 6
17 blessed are your father and your mother. 6
12: 2 He replied, "Father, it would do me no harm 6
13: 4 he is our Father for ever. 6
14:12 when Anna died he buried her with his father. 6
13 their property and that of his father Tobit. 6
Jdt 5: 7 would not follow the gods of their fathers 6
7:28 our sins and the sins of our fathers 6
28 our God, the Lord of our fathers 6
8: 3 they buried him with his fathers in the field 6
19 why our fathers were handed over to the sword 6
9: 2 O Lord God of my father Simeon 6
12 Hear, O hear me, God of my father 6
10: 8 May the God of our fathers grant you favor 6
AEs 13: 6 is our second father 6
14: 5 didst take . . our fathers 6
16:11 he was called our father 6
16 both for us and for our fathers 11
Wis 2:16 boasts that God is his father. 6
9: 1 O God of my fathers and Lord of mercy 6
12 shall be worthy of the throne of my father. 6
10: 1 protected the first-formed father of the world 6
11:10 thou didst test them as a father does in warning 6
12: 6 destroy by the hands of our fathers 6
21 to whose fathers thou gavest oaths 6
14: 3 thy providence, O Father, that steers its course 6
15 a father . . made an image of his child 6
18: 6 night was made known beforehand to our fathers 6
9 they were singing the praises of the fathers. 6
22 the oaths and covenants given to our fathers. 6
24 the glories of the fathers 6
Sir 0: 1 the prophets and the other books of our fathers, 9
3: 1 Listen to me your father, O children 6
2 the Lord honored the father above the children 6
3 Whoever honors his father atones for sins 6
5 Whoever honors his father will be gladdened 6
6 Whoever glorifies his father will have 6
8 Honor your father by word and deed 6
9 a father's blessing strengthens the houses 6
10 glorify yourself by dishonoring your father 6
10 your father's dishonor is no glory to you. 6
11 For a man's glory comes from honoring his father 6
12 O son, help your father in his old age 6
14 For kindness to a father will not be forgotten 6
16 Whoever forsakes his father is like a blasphemer 6
4:10 Be like a father to orphans 6
7:27 With all your heart honor your father 6
8: 9 they themselves learned from their fathers; 6
22: 3 the father of an undisciplined son 6
4 who acts shamefully brings grief to her father. 4
5 disgraces father and husband 6
23: 1 O Lord, Father and Ruler of my life 6
4 O Lord, Father and God of my life 6
14 Remember your father and mother 6
30: 4 The father may die, and yet he is not dead 6
34:20 Like one who kills a son before his father's eyes 6
41: 7 Children will blame an ungodly father 6
17 before your father or mother 6
42: 9 A daughter keeps her father secretly wakeful 6
44: 1 our fathers in their generations. 6
19 the great father of a multitude of nations 6
22 for the sake of Abraham his father. 6
47:23 Solomon rested with his fathers 6
48:10 to turn the heart of the father to the son 6
22 he held strongly to the ways of David his father 6
51:10 I appealed to the Lord, the Father of my lord 6
Bar 1:16 our priests and our prophets and our fathers 6
19 Lord brought our fathers out of the land of Egypt 6
20 he brought our fathers out of the land of Egypt 6
2: 6 confusion of face to us and our fathers 6
19 any righteous deeds of our fathers or our kings 6
21 remain in the land which I gave to your fathers. 6
24 bones of our kings and the bones of our fathers 6
33 for they will remember the ways of their fathers 6
34 fathers, to Abraham and to Isaac and to Jacob 6
3: 5 Remember not the iniquities of our fathers 6
7 iniquity of our fathers who sinned before thee. 6
8 punished for all the iniquities of our fathers 6
Aza 1: 3 Blessed art thou, O Lord, God of our fathers 6
5 Jerusalem, the holy city of our fathers 6
29 Blessed art thou, O Lord, God of our fathers 6
Bel 1: 1 When King Astyages was laid with his fathers 6
Man 1: 1 O Lord Almighty, God of our fathers, of Abraham 6
1Mc 2:19 departing each one from the religion of his fathers 6
20 will live by the covenant of our fathers. 6

50 give your lives for the covenant of our fathers. 6
51 Remember the deeds of the fathers 6
54 Phinehas our father 6
65 always listen to him; he shall be your father. 6
69 he blessed them, and was gathered to his fathers. 6
70 was buried in the tomb of his fathers at Modein. 6
3: 2 all who had joined his father helped him 6
4: 9 Remember how our fathers were saved 6
10 remember his covenant with our fathers 6
6:23 We were happy to serve your father 6
7: 2 he was entering the royal palace of his fathers 6
9:19 buried him in the tomb of their fathers at Modein 6
10:52 and have taken my seat on the throne of my fathers 6
55 you returned to the land of your fathers 6
67 came from Crete to the land of his fathers. 6
72 your fathers were twice put to flight 6
11: 9 you shall reign over your father's kingdom. 6
32 'King Demetrius to Lasthenes his father 6
38 the troops who had served his fathers hated him. 6
40 to become king in place of his father 6
13: 3 house of my father have done for the laws 6
25 buried him in Modein, the city of his fathers. 6
27 Simon built a monument over the tomb of his father 6
28 for his father and mother and four brothers. 6
14:26 the house of his father have stood firm 6
15: 3 gained control of the kingdom of our fathers 6
10 Antiochus set out and invaded the land of his fathers 6
33 but only the inheritance of our fathers 6
34 we are firmly holding the inheritance of our fathers. 6
16: 1 reported to Simon his father what Cendebeus 6
2 my brothers and the house of my father have fought 6
21 reported to John . . that his father . . perished 6
24 time that he became high priest after his father 6
2Mc 1:19 when our fathers were . . led captive to Persia 6
25 didst choose the fathers and consecrate them 6
4:11 secured through John the father of Eupolemus 6
6: 1 to forsake the laws of their fathers 9
7: 2 rather than transgress the laws of our fathers. 9
8 He replied in the language of his fathers 9
21 the language of their fathers 9
30 was given to our fathers through Moses. 6
37 give up body and life for the laws of our fathers 9
8:15 the covenants made with their fathers 6
9:23 my father . . appointed his successor 6
11:23 Now that our father has gone on to the gods 6
24 our father's change to Greek customs 6
12:37 In the language of their fathers 9
13: 9 those that had been done in his father's time. 6
14:37 for his good will was called father of the Jews. 6
15:29 in the language of their fathers. 9
3Mc 2:12 when our fathers were oppressed 6
5: 7 their merciful God and Father 6
6: 3 look upon the descendants of Abraham, O Father 6
8 Jonah . . you, Father, watched over 6
32 and took up the song of their fathers 9
7: 6 as a father does for his children 6
16 giving thanks to the one God of their fathers 6
4Mc 2:19 Why else did Jacob, our most wise father, censure 6
3:20 our fathers were enjoying profound peace 6
5:37 The fathers will receive me as pure 6
7: 1 the reason of our father Eleazar 6
5 our father Eleazar broke the maddening waves 6
9 You, father, strengthened our loyalty to the law 6
11 our father Aaron, armed with the censer 6
9:29 death for the religion of our fathers! 9
10: 2 the same father begot me and those who died 6
13:12 Remember . . the father 6
17 all the fathers will praise us. 6
19 bequeathed through the fathers 6
15: 4 have a deeper sympathy . . than do the fathers. 6
16:20 our father Abraham was zealous to sacrifice 6
17: 6 children were true descendants of father Abraham. 6
18: 7 and did not go outside my father's house 8
9 when these sons had grown up their father died 6
23 the chorus of the fathers 6
151 1: 1 and youngest in my father's house; 6
1 I tended my father's sheep. 6
4 and took me from my father's sheep 6

father *See also* become, brother, city, foster, house, inherit, sister, ways.

become father 1. ילד 2. *γεννάω*

Gen 5: 3 Adam . . became the father of a son in his own 1
4 The days of Adam after he became the father 1
6 he became the father of Enosh. 1
9 he became the father of Kenan. 1
12 he became the father of Ma-hal'alel. 1
15 Ma-hal'alel . . became the father of Jared. 1
18 Jared . . became the father of Enoch. 1
21 Enoch . . became the father of Methu'selah. 1
25 Methu'selah . . became the father of Lamech. 1
28 Lamech . . became the father of a son 1
32 Noah became the father of Shem, Ham, and Japheth. 1
10: 8 Cush became the father of Nimrod; 1
13 Egypt became the father of Ludim, An'amim 1
15 Canaan became the father of Sidon 1
24 Arpach'shad became the father of Shelah; 1
24 and Shelah became the father of Eber. 1
26 Joktan became the father of Almo'dad, Sheleph 1
11:10 he became the father of Arpach'shad 1
12 35 years, he became the father of Shelah; 1
14 Shelah . . became the father of Eber; 1
16 Eber . . became the father of Peleg; 1
18 Peleg . . became the father of Re'u; 1
20 Re'u . . became the father of Serug; 1
22 Serug . . became the father of Nahor; 1
24 Nahor . . became the father of Terah; 1
26 Terah . . became the father of Abram, Nahor, 1
22:23 Bethu'el became the father of Rebekah. 1
Act 7: 8 so Abraham became the father of Isaac 2
8 Isaac became the father of Jacob •
29 Mid'ian, where he became the father of two sons. 2
1Co 4:15 became your father in Christ Jesus 2
Phm 1:10 whose father I have become in my imprisonment. 2
Tob 1: 9 by her I became the father of Tobias. 2

everlasting father 1. אֲבִיעַד

Isa 9: 6 Counselor, Mighty God, Everlasting Father 1

first father 1. *προπάτωρ*

3Mc 2:21 the first Father of all, holy among the holy ones 1

without father 1. *ἀπάτωρ*

Heb 7: 3 He is without father or mother or genealogy 1

father-in-law 1. חָם 2. חֹתֵן 3. *πενθερός*

Gen 38:13 when Tamar was told, "Your father-in-law is going up 1
25 she sent word to her father-in-law 1
Exd 3: 1 keeping the flock of his father-in-law, Jethro 2
4:18 Moses went back to Jethro his father-in-law 2
18: 1 Jethro, the priest of Mid'ian, Moses' father-in-law 2
2 Jethro, Moses' father-in-law, had taken Zippo'rah 2
5 Jethro, Moses' father-in-law, came with his sons 2
6 Lo, your father-in-law Jethro is coming to you 2
7 Moses went out to meet his father-in-law 2
8 Moses told his father-in-law all . . the LORD had done 2
12 Jethro, Moses' father-in-law, offered a burnt 2
12 came . . to eat bread with Moses' father-in-law 2
14 When Moses' father-in-law saw all that he was doing 2
15 Moses said to his father-in-law, "Because 2
17 Moses' father-in-law said to him, "What you are doing 2
24 Moses gave heed to the voice of his father-in-law 2
27 Then Moses let his father-in-law depart 2
Num10:29 Moses said to Hobab . . Moses' father-in-law 2
Jdg 1:16 descendants of the Ken'ite, Moses' father-in-law 2
4:11 Hobab the father-in-law of Moses, and had pitched 2
19: 4 his father-in-law, the girl's father, made him stay 2
7 the man rose up to go, his father-in-law urged him 2
9 his father-in-law, the girl's father, said to him 2
1Sm 4:19 that her father-in-law and her husband were dead 1
21 and because of her father-in-law and her husband. 1
Joh 18:13 he was the father-in-law of Ca'iaphas 3
Tob 10: 8 his father-in-law said to him, "Stay with me 3
14:12 Tobias returned . . to Raguel his father-in-law. 3
1Mc 11: 2 since he was Alexander's father-in-law. 3

father-in-law and mother-in-law 1. *πενθερός*

Tob 10:12 Honor your father-in-law and your mother-in-law 1
14:13 his father-in-law and mother-in-law 1

become father-in-law 1. *ἐπιγαμβρεύω*

1Mc 10:56 I will become your father-in-law 1

fatherless 1. אֵין אָב 2. יָתוֹם 3. *ὀρφανός* 4. pupillus

Exd 22:24 become widows and your children fatherless. 2
Deu 10:18 executes justice for the fatherless 2
14:29 Levite . . the fatherless, and the widow 2
16:11 rejoice . . you and . . the fatherless, and the widow 2
14 rejoice . . you and . . the fatherless 2
24:17 not pervert the justice due to . . the fatherless 2
19 for the sojourner, the fatherless, and the widow; 2
20 for the sojourner, the fatherless, and the widow. 2
21 for the sojourner, the fatherless, and the widow. 2
26:12 giving it to the . . fatherless, and the widow 2
13 given it to the . . fatherless, and the widow 2
27:19 perverts the justice due to . . fatherless 2
Job 5:15 he saves the fatherless from their mouth •
6:27 You would even cast lots over the fatherless 2
22: 9 the arms of the fatherless were crushed. 2
24: 3 They drive away the ass of the fatherless; 2
29:12 the fatherless who had none to help him. 2
31:17 the fatherless has not eaten of it 2
21 if I have raised my hand against the fatherless 2
Ps 10:14 thou hast been the helper of the fatherless. 2
18 do justice to the fatherless and the oppressed 2
68: 5 Father of the fatherless and protector 2
82: 3 Give justice to the weak and the fatherless; 2
94: 6 widow . . sojourner, and murder the fatherless; 2
109: 9 his children be fatherless, and his wife a widow! 2
146: 9 LORD . . upholds the widow and the fatherless; 2
Prv 23:10 Do not . . enter the fields of the fatherless; 2
Isa 1:17 defend the fatherless, plead for the widow. 2
23 They do not defend the fatherless 2
9:17 no compassion on their fatherless and widows; 2
10: 2 that they may make the fatherless their prey! 2
Jer 5:28 they judge not . . the cause of the fatherless 2
7: 6 oppress the alien, the fatherless or the widow 2
22: 3 to the alien, the fatherless, and the widow 2
Lam 5: 3 We have become orphans, fatherless; 1
Ezk 22: 7 the fatherless and the widow are wronged in you. 2
Zec 7:10 do not oppress the widow, the fatherless 2
2Es 2:20 secure justice for the fatherless 4
Sir 35:14 not ignore the supplication of the fatherless 3

fatherless *See also* child.

fathom 1. *ἐξιχνιάζω* 2. *ὀργυιά*

Act 27:28 So they sounded and found twenty fathoms 2
28 they sounded again and found fifteen fathoms. 2
Sir 24:28 the last one has not fathomed her; 1

fatling 1. בְּרִיא 2. מֵחַ 3. מְרִיא 4. מִשְׁמָן

1Sm 15: 9 the best of . . and of the oxen and of the fatlings 4
2Sm 6:13 he sacrificed an ox and a fatling. 3
1Kg 1: 9 Adoni'jah sacrificed sheep, oxen, and fatlings 3
19 He has sacrificed oxen, fatlings, and sheep 3
25 and has sacrificed oxen, fatlings, and sheep 3
Ps 66:15 I will offer to thee burnt offerings of fatlings 2
Isa 5:17 fatlings and kids shall feed among the ruins. 2
11: 6 the calf and the lion and the fatling together 3
Ezk 34: 3 you slaughter the fatlings; 1
39:18 of bulls, all of them fatlings of Bashan. 3

fatness 1. דֶּשֶׁן 2. חֵלֶב 3. שֶׁמֶן

Gen 27:28 give you . . of the fatness of the earth 3
39 Behold, away from the fatness of the earth 3
Jdg 9: 9 Shall I leave my fatness, by which gods and men are 1
Job 36:16 what was set on your table was full of fatness. 1
Ps 65:11 the tracks of thy chariot drip with fatness. 1
73: 7 Their eyes swell out with fatness 2
Isa 55: 2 what is good, and delight yourselves in fatness. 1

fatted 1. אבס 2. מַרְבֵּק 3. *σιτευτός*

1Sm 28:24 Now the woman had a fatted calf in the house 2
1Kg 4:23 harts, gazelles, roebucks, and fatted fowl. 1
Prv 15:17 Better is . . than a fatted ox and hatred with it. 1
Jer 46:21 soldiers in her midst are like fatted calves; 2
Lke 15:23 bring the fatted calf and kill it 3
27 your father has killed the fatted calf 3
30 you killed for him the fatted calf!' 3

fatted *See also* beast.

fatten 1. ברא 2. *τρέφω*

1Sm 2:29 by fattening yourselves upon the choicest 1
Jas 5: 5 you have fattened your hearts 2

fault 1. חטא 2. חֵטְא 3. מְאוּמָה 4. עָוֹן 5. שחת (A) 6. *μωμάομαι* 7. *πλημμέλεια*

Gen 41: 9 said to Pharaoh, "I remember my faults today. 2
Exd 5:16 are beaten; but the fault is in your own people. 1
1Sm 29: 3 I have found no fault in him to this day. 3
2Sm 3: 8 you charge me . . with a fault concerning a woman. 4
Ps 59: 4 for no fault of mine, they run and make ready. 4
73:10 turn and praise them; and find no fault in them. •
Dan 6: 4 could find no ground for complaint or any fault 5
4 faithful, and no error or fault was found in him. 5
2Co 6: 3 so that no fault may be found with our ministry 6
Sir 38:10 Give up your faults and direct your hands aright 7

fault *See also* confess, find, tell.

hidden fault 1. סתר

Ps 19:12 Clear thou me from hidden faults. 1

faultfinder 1. יִסּוֹר 2. *φαντασιοκοπέω*

Job 40: 2 Shall a faultfinder contend with the Almighty? 1
Sir 4:30 nor be a faultfinder with your servants. 2

faultfinding 1. רִיב

Exd 17: 7 because of the faultfinding of the children 1

faultless 1. *ἄμεμπτος*

Heb 8: 7 For if that first covenant had been faultless 1

favor 1. דָּבָר 2. חֵן 3. חֲנִינָה 4. חנן 5. חֶסֶד 6. חפץ בְּ 7. טוֹב 8. יָד 9. יפע עַל 10. לְ 11. נֹעַם 12. פָּנִים 13. רָצוֹן 14. תְּחִנָּה 15. *ἀγαθός* 16. *εὐδοκέω* 17. *εὐδοκία* 18. *εὔνοια* 19. *θέλω* 20. *ἱκανῶς* 21. *πρόκριμα* 22. *πρόσωπον* 23. *ὑπέρ* 24. *χαρίζομαι* 25. *χάρις* 26. *χαριτόω* 27. gratia

Gen 6: 8 Noah found favor in the eyes of the LORD. 2
18: 3 said, "My lord, if I have found favor 2
19:19 your servant has found favor in your sight 2
21 I grant you this favor also 1
32: 5 in order that I may find favor in your sight.' 2
33: 8 To find favor in the sight of my lord. 2
10 No, I pray you, if I have found favor in your sight 2
15 Let me find favor in the sight of my lord. 2
34:11 Let me find favor in your eyes 2
39: 4 Joseph found favor in his sight and attended him 2
21 LORD . . gave him favor in the sight of the keeper 2
47:29 If now I have found favor in your sight, 2
50: 4 If now I have found favor in your eyes, speak 2
Exd 3:21 I will give this people favor in the sight 2
11: 3 the LORD gave the people favor in the sight 2
12:36 the LORD had given the people favor in the sight 2

33:12 you have also found favor in my sight.' 2
13 Now therefore, I pray thee, if I have found favor 2
13 that I may know thee and find favor in thy sight. 2
16 For how shall it be known that I have found favor 2
17 for you have found favor in my sight, and I know you 2
34: 9 he said, "If now I have found favor in thy sight 2
Num11:11 why have I not found favor in thy sight 2
15 kill me at once, if I find favor in thy sight 2
32: 5 they said, "If we have found favor in your sight 2
Deu 24: 1 if then she finds no favor in his eyes 2
33:16 with the . . favor of him that dwelt in the bush. 13
23 O Naph'tali, satisfied with favor, and full 13
Jdg 6:17 If now I have found favor with thee, then show me 2
Rut 2: 2 after him in whose sight I shall find favor. 2
10 Why have I found favor in your eyes 2
1Sm 1:18 Let your maidservant find favor in your eyes. 2
13:12 and I have not entreated the favor of the LORD'; 12
16:22 Let David . . for he has found favor in my sight. 2
20: 3 knows well that I have found favor in your eyes; 2
29 if I have found favor in your eyes, let me get away 2
25: 8 Therefore let my young men find favor 2
27: 5 If I have found favor in your eyes, let a place be 2
2Sm 14:22 I have found favor in your sight, my lord the king 2
15:25 If I find favor in the eyes of the LORD 2
16: 4 let me . . find favor in your sight, my lord the king. 2
20:11 Whoever favors Jo'ab, and whoever is for David 6
1Kg 11:19 Hadad found great favor in the sight of Pharaoh 2
2Ch 33:12 he entreated the favor of the LORD his God 12
Ezr 9: 8 favor has been shown by the LORD our God 14
Neh 13:22 Remember this also in my favor, O my God •
Est 2: 9 And the maiden pleased him and won his favor; 5
15 Esther found favor in the eyes of all who saw her. 2
17 and she found grace and favor in his sight 5
5: 2 when the king saw . . she found favor in his sight 2
8 If I have found favor in the sight of the king 2
7: 3 If I have found favor in your sight, O king 2
8: 5 and if I have found favor in his sight 2
Job 10: 3 favor the designs of the wicked? 9
11:19 many will entreat your favor. 12
Ps 5:12 thou dost cover him with favor as with a shield. 13
30: 5 for a moment, and his favor is for a lifetime. 13
7 By thy favor, O LORD, thou hadst established me 13
45:12 the people of Tyre will sue your favor with gifts 12
84:11 sun and shield; he bestows favor and honor. 2
86:17 Show me a sign of thy favor, that those who hate me 7
89:17 by thy favor our horn is exalted. 13
90:17 Let the favor of the Lord our God be upon us 11
102:13 time to favor her; the appointed time has come. 4
106: 4 me, O LORD, when thou showest favor to thy people; 13
119:58 I entreat thy favor with all my heart; 12
132: 1 Remember, O LORD, in David's favor 10
Prv 3: 4 you will find favor and good repute 2
34 but to the humble he shows favor. 2
8:35 he who finds me . . obtains favor from the LORD; 13
11:27 He who diligently seeks good seeks favor 13
12: 2 A good man obtains favor from the LORD 13
13:15 Good sense wins favor 2
14: 9 scorns the wicked, but the upright enjoy his favor. 13
35 A servant who deals wisely has the king's favor 13
16:15 favor . . the clouds that bring the spring rain. 13
18:22 finds a wife . . obtains favor from the LORD. 13
19:12 but his favor is like dew upon the grass. 13
22: 1 favor is better than silver or gold. 2
28:23 who rebukes a man will afterward find more favor 2
29:26 Many seek the favor of a ruler 12
Ecc 9:11 bread to the wise . . nor favor to the men of skill; 2
10:12 The words of a wise man's mouth win him favor 2
Isa 49: 8 the LORD: "In a time of favor I have answered you 13
60:10 I smote you, but in my favor I have had mercy on you. 13
61: 2 to proclaim the year of the LORD'S favor 13
Jer 3:13 and scattered your favors among strangers •
16:13 for I will show you no favor. 3
Ezk 27:21 the princes of Kedar were your favored dealers 8
Dan 1: 9 gave Daniel favor and compassion in the sight 5
9:13 have not entreated the favor of the LORD our God 12
Zec 7: 2 their men, to entreat the favor of the LORD 12
8:21 Let us go at once to entreat the favor of the LORD 12
22 to entreat the favor of the LORD. 12
Mal 1: 9 now entreat the favor of God 12
2:13 or accepts it with favor at your hand. 13
Lke 1:28 he came to her and said, "Hail, O favored one 26
30 you have found favor with God. 25
2:40 the favor of God was upon him. 25
52 increased . . in favor with God and man. 25
Act 2:47 having favor with all the people 25
7:10 favor and wisdom before Pharaoh, king of Egypt 25
46 who found favor in the sight of God 25
24:27 desiring to do the Jews a favor 25
25: 3 asking as a favor 25
9 Festus, wishing to do the Jews a favor, said to Paul 25
1Co 4: 6 puffed up in favor of one against another. 23
2Co 8: 4 begging us earnestly for the favor 25
1Ti 5:21 I charge you to keep these rules without favor 21
1Es 8: 4 he found favor before the king 25
80 brought us into favor with the kings 25
2Es 4:44 If I have found favor in your sight 27
5:56 if I have found favor in thy sight 27
6:11 if I have found favor in thy sight 27
7:75 If I have found favor in thy sight, O Lord 27
102If I have found favor in thy sight 27
104Since you have found favor in my sight 27
8:42 If I have found favor before thee, let me speak. 27
12: 7 if I have found favor in thy sight 27
14:22 If then I have found favor before thee 27
Tob 1:13 Then the Most High gave me favor 25
12:18 For I did not come as a favor on my part 25
Jdt 4:15 to look with favor upon the whole house of Israel. 15
8:23 For our slavery will not bring us into favor 25
10: 8 May the God of our fathers grant you favor 25
Wis 14:26 forgetfulness of favors, pollution of souls 25
Sir 3:18 so you will find favor in the sight of the Lord. 25
31 Whoever requites favors 25
4:21 there is a shame which is glory and favor. 25
8:14 the decision will favor him •
32:14 those who rise early to seek him will find favor. 17
41:23 will find favor with every man. 25
45: 1 found favor in the sight of all flesh 25
Bar 1:12 we shall . . find favor in their sight. 25
2: 8 Yet we have not entreated the favor of the Lord 22
14 deliver us, and grant us favor in the sight 25
1Mc 4:10 to see whether he will favor us 19
10:47 They favored Alexander 16
60 found favor with them. 25
11:24 he won his favor. 25
53 did not repay the favors which Jonathan had done 18
2Mc 1:35 with those persons whom the king favored 24
3Mc 1: 4 matters were turning out rather in favor of Antiochus 20
4Mc 11:12 they are splendid favors that you grant us 25

favor *See also* entreat, find, grow, look, receive, regard, remember, seek.

high favor 1. נשׂא פָּנִים
2Kg 5: 1 a great man with his master and in high favor 1

favor little 1. ἡττάομαι
2Co 12:13 less favored than the rest of the churches 1

show favor 1. חנן 2. נשׂא פָּנִים
Deu 28:50 who shall not . . show favor to the young 1
Isa 26:10 If favor is shown to the wicked, he does not learn 1
27:11 he that formed them will show them no favor. 1
Lam 4:16 no honor was shown . . no favor to the elders. 1
Mal 1: 8 will he be pleased with you or show you favor? 2
9 With such a gift from your hand, will he show favor 2

special favor 1. ἐκλεκτός
Wis 3:14 special favor will be shown him 1

favorable 1. טוֹב 2. רצה 3. שָׁלוֹם 4. κατά 5. συνεργέω
Gen 40:16 that the interpretation was favorable, he said 1
41:16 God will give Pharaoh a favorable answer. 3
1Kg 22:13 the words of the prophets . . are favorable 1
2Ch 18:12 words of the prophets . . favorable to the king; 1
Ps 77: 7 spurn for ever, and never again be favorable? 2
85: 1 LORD, thou wast favorable to thy land; 2
Ezk 16:52 have made judgment favorable to your sisters; •
1Mc 12: 1 Jonathan saw that the time was favorable for him 5
13:35 Demetrius the king sent him a favorable reply 4

most favorable 1. εὔκαιρος
3Mc 5:44 at the places . . most favorable for keeping guard. 1

favorably 1. טוֹב
1Kg 22:13 let your word be . . and speak favorably. 1
2Ch 18:12 and speak favorably. 1

favorably *See also* dispose.

favored man 1. נשׂא פָּנִים
Job 22: 8 the land, and the favored man dwelt in it. 1

favorite 1. רצה
Deu 33:24 be Asher; let him be the favorite of his brothers 1

fawn 1. אָמַר 2. עֹפֶר
Gen 49:21 a hind let loose, that bears comely fawns. 1
Sng 4: 5 Your two breasts are like two fawns 2
7: 3 breasts are like two fawns, twins of a gazelle. 2

fawning *See* come.

come fawning 1. כחשׁ
Deu 33:29 Your enemies shall come fawning to you; 1

fear 1. אֵימָה 2. אמר 3. גור 4. דְּאָגָה 5. היה יָרֵא 6. חֲרָדָה 7. חַת 8. ירא 9. יִרְאָה 10. מְגוֹרָה 11. מוֹרָא 12. מוֹרָה 13. מִפְּנֵי 14. ערץ 15. פחד 16. פַּחַד 17. פַּחְדָּה 18. פֶּן 19. דחל (A) 20. δειλιάω 21. δεῖμα 22. δέος 23. διά 24. διευλαβέομαι 25. ἔκφοβος 26. εὐλάβεια 27. εὐλαβέομαι 28. μή 29. τρόμος 30. ὕποπτος 31. φοβερός 32. φοβέω 33. φόβος 34. pavor 35. revereor 36. timeo 37. timor 38. vereor
Gen 9: 2 The fear of you and the dread of you 11
15: 1 Fear not, Abram, I am your shield; 8
20:11 There is no fear of God at all in this place 9
21:17 said to her, "What troubles you, Hagar? Fear not; 8
22:12 for now I know that you fear God 8
26: 7 She is my sister"; for he feared to say, "My wife 8
24 I am the God of Abraham your father; fear not 8
31:42 God of Abraham and the Fear of Isaac 16
53 Jacob swore by the Fear of his father Isaac 16
32:11 Deliver me . . from the hand of Esau, for I fear him 8
35:17 midwife said to her, "Fear not; for now you will 8
38:11 -for he feared that he would die, like his 2
42: 4 for he feared that harm might befall him. 2
18 Do this and you will live, for I fear God 8
44:34 I fear to see the evil that would come upon my 18
50:19 Joseph said to them, "Fear not, 8
21 do not fear; I will provide for you 8
Exd 1:17 the midwives feared God 8
21 because the midwives feared God 8
9:20 Then he who feared the word of the LORD among 8
30 I know that you do not yet fear the LORD God. 8
14:10 and they were in great fear. 8
13 Moses said to the people, "Fear not, stand firm 8
31 Israel saw . . and the people feared the LORD; 8
18:21 choose able men . . such as fear God 8
20:20 Moses said to the people, "Do not fear; for God has 8
20 that the fear of him may be before your eyes 9
Lev 19:14 but you shall fear your God: I am the LORD 8
32 you shall fear your God; I am the LORD 8
25:17 fear your God; for I am the LORD your God 8
36 fear your God; that your brother may live 8
43 You shall not rule . . but shall fear your God 8
Num14: 9 do not fear the people of the land 8
9 LORD is with us; do not fear them. 8
21:34 Do not fear him; for I have given him into your hand 8
Deu 1:21 take possession . . do not fear or be dismayed.' 8
2:25 put the dread and fear of you upon the peoples 9
3: 2 LORD said to me, 'Do not fear him; 8
22 You shall not fear them; for it is the LORD your God 8
4:10 that they may learn to fear me all the days 9
5:29 to fear me and to keep all my commandments 9
6: 2 that you may fear the LORD your God 8
13 shall fear the LORD your God; you shall serve him 8
24 LORD commanded us . . to fear the LORD our God 9
8: 6 by walking in his ways and by fearing him. 9
10:12 require . . but to fear the LORD your God, to walk 9
20 fear the LORD your God; you shall serve him 8
11:25 LORD . . will lay the fear of you and the dread 16
13: 4 shall walk after the LORD your God and fear him 8
11 all Israel shall hear, and fear, and never again do 8
14:23 may learn to fear the LORD your God always. 9
17:13 all the people shall hear, and fear, and not act 8
19 learn to fear the LORD his God, by keeping all 9
19:20 rest shall hear, and fear, and shall never again 8
20: 3 do not fear, or tremble, or be in dread of them; 8
21:21 all Israel shall hear, and fear. 8
25:18 how he attacked you . . and he did not fear God. 8
28:58 that you may fear this glorious and awful name 9
67 because of the dread which your heart shall fear 15
31: 6 Be strong . . do not fear or be in dread of them 8
8 not . . forsake you; do not fear or be dismayed. 8
12 may hear and learn to fear the LORD your God 8
13 may hear and learn to fear the LORD your God 9
32:27 had I not feared provocation by the enemy, lest 3
Jos 2: 9 I know . . that the fear of you has fallen upon us 1
4:24 that you may fear the LORD your God for ever. 8
8: 1 the LORD said to Joshua, "Do not fear or be dismayed; 8
9:24 we feared greatly for our lives because of you 8
10: 2 he feared greatly, because Gibeon was a great 8
8 And the LORD said to Joshua, "Do not fear them 8
22:24 we did it from fear . . your children might say 4
24:14 fear the LORD, and serve him in sincerity 8
Jdg 4:18 turn aside to me; have no fear." So he turned aside 8
6:23 Peace be to you; do not fear, you shall not die. 8
7:10 if you fear to go down, go down . . with Purah 8
9:21 fled . . for fear of Abim'elech his brother. 13
Rut 3:11 do not fear, I will do for you all that you ask 8
1Sm 4:20 said to her, "Fear not, for you have borne a son. 8
12:14 If you will fear the LORD and serve him 8
18 the people greatly feared the LORD and Samuel. 8
20 Fear not; you have done all this evil, yet do not 8
24 Only fear the LORD, and serve him faithfully 8
14:26 no man put . . for the people feared the oath. 8
15:24 I feared the people and obeyed their voice. 8
22:23 Stay with me, fear not; for he . . seeks your life; 8
23:17 Fear not; for the hand of Saul . . shall not find you; 8
28:13 The king said to her, "Have no fear; what do you see? 8
31: 4 armor-bearer would not; for he feared greatly. 8
2Sm 3:11 could not answer Abner . . because he feared him. 9
9: 7 Do not fear; for I will show you kindness 8
10:19 Syrians feared to help the Ammonites any more. 8
12:18 And the servants of David feared to tell him 8
13:28 then kill him. Fear not; have I not commanded you? 8
17:10 the valiant man . . will utterly melt with fear; •
23: 3 When one rules justly . . ruling in the fear of God 9
1Kg 1:50 Adoni'jah feared Solomon; and he arose, and went 8
51 Adoni'jah fears King Solomon; for, lo, he has laid 8
8:40 they may fear thee all the days 8
43 that all . . may know thy name and fear thee 9
17:13 Fear not; go and do as you have said; 8
2Kg 4: 1 you know that your servant feared the LORD 5
6:16 Fear not, for those . . with us are more than those 8
17: 7 Israel had sinned . . and had feared other gods 8
25 at the beginning . . they did not fear the LORD; 8

28 and taught them how they should fear the LORD. 8
32 They also feared the LORD 8
33 they feared the LORD but also served their own 8
34 They do not fear the LORD, and they do not follow 8
35 You shall not fear other gods or bow yourselves 8
36 you shall fear the LORD, who brought you out 8
37 You shall not fear other gods 8
38 You shall not fear other gods 8
39 but you shall fear the LORD your God, and he will 8
41 these nations feared the LORD and also served 8
1Ch 10: 4 armor-bearer would not; for he feared greatly. 8
14:17 LORD brought the fear of him upon all nations. 16
22:13 and of good courage. Fear not, be not dismayed. 8
28:20 Fear not, be not dismayed; for the LORD God 8
2Ch 6:31 that they may fear thee and walk in thy ways 8
33 that all . . may know thy name and fear thee, as do 9
14:14 for the fear of the LORD was upon them. 16
17:10 the fear of the LORD fell upon all the kingdoms 16
19: 7 Now then, let the fear of the LORD be upon you; 16
9 Thus you shall do in the fear of the LORD 9
20: 3 Then Jehosh'aphat feared, and set himself to seek 8
15 says the LORD . . 'Fear not, and be not dismayed 8
17 Fear not, and be not dismayed(O Judah); 8
29 fear of God came on all the kingdoms 16
26: 5 Zechari'ah, who instructed him in the fear of God; 9
Ezr 3: 3 set the altar in its place, for fear was upon them 1
Neh 1:11 thy servants who delight to fear thy name; 9
5: 9 Ought you not to walk in the fear of our God 9
15 I did not do so, because of the fear of God. 9
Est 8:17 for the fear of the Jews had fallen upon them. 16
9: 2 for the fear of them had fallen upon all peoples. 16
3 for the fear of Mor'decai had fallen upon them. 16
Job 1: 1 one who feared God, and turned away from evil. 8
8 a blameless and upright man, who fears God 8
9 answered the LORD, "Does Job fear God for nought? 8
2: 3 a blameless and upright man, who fears God 8
3:25 For the thing that I fear comes upon me 15
4: 6 Is not your fear of God your confidence 9
5:21 and shall not fear destruction when it comes. 8
22 shall not fear the beasts of the earth. 8
6:14 forsakes the fear of the Almighty. 9
9:35 Then I would speak without fear of him 8
11:15 you will be secure, and will not fear. 8
15: 4 But you are doing away with the fear of God 9
21: 9 Their houses are safe from fear 16
22: 4 Is it for your fear of him that he reproves you 9
25: 2 Dominion and fear are with God; 16
28:28 Behold, the fear of the Lord, that is wisdom; 9
33: 7 Behold, no fear of me need terrify you; 1
37:24 men fear him; he does not regard any who are wise 8
39:16 though her labor be in vain, yet she has no fear; 16
22 He laughs at fear, and is not dismayed; 16
41:33 there is not his like, a creature without fear. 7
Ps 2:11 Serve the LORD with fear, with trembling 9
5: 7 toward thy holy temple in the fear of thee. 9
9:20 Put them in fear, O LORD! 12
15: 4 but who honors those who fear the LORD; 8
19: 9 the fear of the LORD is clean, enduring for ever; 9
22:23 You who fear the LORD, praise him! 8
25 my vows I will pay before those who fear him. 8
23: 4 I fear no evil; for thou art with me; 8
25:12 Who is the man that fears the LORD? 8
14 friendship of the LORD is for those who fear him 8
27: 1 The LORD is . . my salvation; whom shall I fear? 8
3 a host encamp against me, my heart shall not fear; 8
31:19 which thou hast laid up for those who fear thee 8
33: 8 Let all the earth fear the LORD 8
18 Behold, the eye of the LORD is on those who fear him 8
34: 4 answered me, and delivered me from all my fears. 10
7 of the LORD encamps around those who fear him 8
9 O fear the LORD, you his saints 8
9 for those who fear him have no want! 8
11 listen to me, I will teach you the fear of the LORD. 9
36: 1 there is no fear of God before his eyes. 16
40: 3 a song of praise to our God. Many will see and fear 8
46: 2 we will not fear though the earth should change 8
49: 5 Why should I fear in times of trouble 8
52: 6 The righteous shall see, and fear, and shall laugh 8
55: 5 Fear and trembling come upon me 9
19 because they keep no law, and do not fear God. 8
56: 4 whose word I praise, in God I trust without a fear. 8
11 in God I trust without fear. What can man do to me? 8
60: 4 Thou hast set up a banner for those who fear thee 8
61: 5 given me the heritage of those who fear thy name. 8
64: 4 shooting at him suddenly and without fear. 8
9 Then all men will fear; 8
66:16 Come and hear, all you who fear God 8
67: 7 let all the ends of the earth fear him! 8
76: 8 the earth feared and was still 8
11 bring gifts to him who is to be feared 11
85: 9 his salvation is at hand for those who fear him 8
86:11 unite my heart to fear thy name. 9
89: 7 God feared in the council of the holy ones 14
90:11 thy wrath according to the fear of thee? 9
91: 5 You will not fear the terror of the night 8
96: 4 he is to be feared above all gods. 8
102:15 The nations will fear the name of the LORD 8
103:11 so . . his steadfast love toward those who fear 8
13 As a father . . so the LORD pities those who fear 8
17 everlasting to everlasting upon those who fear 8
111: 5 He provides food for those who fear him; 8
10 The fear of the LORD is the beginning of wisdom; 9
112: 1 Blessed is the man who fears the LORD 8
115:11 You who fear the LORD, trust in the LORD! 8
13 he will bless those who fear the LORD 8
118: 4 who fear the LORD say, "His steadfast love endures 8
6 With the LORD on my side I do not fear. 8
119:38 thy promise, which is for those who fear thee. 9
63 I am a companion of all who fear thee 8
74 Those who fear thee shall see me and rejoice 8
79 Let those who fear thee turn to me 8
120 My flesh trembles for fear of thee, and I am afraid 16
128: 1 Blessed is every one who fears the LORD 8
4 thus shall the man be blessed who fears the LORD. 8
130: 4 forgiveness with thee, that thou . . be feared. 8
135:20 You that fear the LORD, bless the LORD! 8
145:19 He fulfils the desire of all who fear him 8
147:11 the LORD takes pleasure in those who fear him 8
Prv 1: 7 fear of the LORD is the beginning of knowledge; 9
29 did not choose the fear of the LORD 9
2: 5 then you will understand the fear of the LORD 9
3: 7 fear the LORD, and turn away from evil. 8
8:13 The fear of the LORD is hatred of evil. 9
9:10 The fear of the LORD is the beginning of wisdom 9
10:27 The fear of the LORD prolongs life 9
14: 2 He who walks in uprightness fears the LORD 8
26 In the fear of the LORD one has strong confidence 9
27 The fear of the LORD is a fountain of life 9
15:16 Better is a little with the fear of the LORD 9
33 The fear of the LORD is instruction in wisdom 9
16: 6 by the fear of the LORD a man avoids evil. 9
19:23 The fear of the LORD leads to life; 9
22: 4 reward for humility and fear of the LORD is 9
23:17 but continue in the fear of the LORD all the day. 9
24:21 My son, fear the LORD and the king 8
28:14 Blessed is the man who fears the LORD always; 15
29:25 The fear of man lays a snare 6
31:30 but a woman who fears the LORD is to be praised. 9
Ecc 3:14 God . . in order that men should fear before him. 8
5: 7 empty words grow many: but do you fear God. 8
7:18 he who fears God shall come forth from them all. 8
8:12 I know that it will be well with those who fear God 8
12 it will be well . . because they fear before him; 8
13 because he does not fear before God. 8
12:13 Fear God, and keep his commandments; 8
Isa 7: 4 say to him, 'Take heed, be quiet, do not fear 8
25 you will not come there for fear of briers 9
8:12 do not fear what they fear, nor be in dread. 8
12 do not fear what they fear, nor be in dread. 11
13 let him be your fear, and let him be your dread. 11
11: 2 the spirit of knowledge and the fear of the LORD. 9
3 his delight shall be in the fear of the LORD. 9
18: 2 to a people feared near and far 8
7 from a people feared near and far 8
19:17 every one to whom it is mentioned will fear 15
25: 3 cities of ruthless nations will fear thee. 8
29:13 their fear of me is a commandment of men 8
33: 6 the fear of the LORD is his treasure. 9
35: 4 Be strong, fear not! Behold, your God will come 8
40: 9 herald of good tidings, lift it up, fear not; 8
41:10 fear not, for I am with you 8
13 it is I who say to you, "Fear not, I will help you. 8
14 Fear not, you worm Jacob, you men of Israel! 8
43: 1 Fear not, for I have redeemed you; 8
5 Fear not, for I am with you; 8
44: 2 Fear not, O Jacob my servant 8
8 Fear not, nor be afraid; 15
50:10 fears the LORD and obeys the voice of his servant 8
51: 7 fear not the reproach of men, and be not dismayed 8
13 and fear continually all the day 15
54: 4 Fear not, for you will not be ashamed; 8
14 be far from oppression, for you shall not fear; 8
57:11 Whom did you dread and fear, so that you lied 8
11 for a long time, and so you do not fear me? 8
59:19 they shall fear the name of the LORD from the west 8
63:17 and harden our heart, so that we fear thee not? 9
66: 4 and bring their fears upon them; 10
Jer 2:19 the fear of me is not in you, says the Lord GOD 17
3: 8 yet her false sister Judah did not fear 8
5:22 Do you not fear me? says the LORD; 8
24 Let us fear the LORD our God, who gives the rain 8
10: 7 Who would not fear thee, O King of the nations? 8
17: 8 and does not fear when heat comes 8
23: 4 and they shall fear no more, nor be dismayed 8
26:19 Did he not fear the LORD 8
30:10 Then fear not, O Jacob my servant, says the LORD 8
32:39 that they may fear me for ever, for their own good 9
40 and I will put the fear of me in their hearts 9
33: 9 they shall fear and tremble 15
35:11 for fear of the army of the Chalde'ans 13
42:11 Do not fear the king of Babylon 8
11 do not fear him, says the LORD, for I am with you 8
16 then the sword which you fear shall overtake you 8
44:10 nor have they feared, nor walked in my law 8
46:27 But fear not, O Jacob my servant, nor be dismayed 8
28 Fear not, O Jacob my servant, says the LORD 8
Lam 3:57 thou didst say, 'Do not fear!' 8
Ezk 3: 9 fear them not, nor be dismayed at their looks 8
11: 8 You have feared the sword; 8
18:14 and fears, and does not do likewise 8
30:13 I will put fear in the land of Egypt. 9
Dan 1:10 fear lest my lord the king, who appointed 8
5:19 all . . trembled and feared before him; 19
6:26 all my royal dominion men tremble and fear 19
10:12 Fear not, Daniel, for from the first day 8
19 O man greatly beloved, fear not, peace be with you; 8
Hos 3: 5 and they shall come in fear to the LORD 15
10: 3 We have no king, for we fear not the LORD 8
Jol 2:21 Fear not, O land; be glad and rejoice 8
22 Fear not, you beasts of the field 8
Ams 3: 8 The lion has roared; who will not fear? 8
Jon 1: 9 I fear the LORD, the God of heaven, 8
16 Then the men feared the LORD exceedingly 8
Mic 6: 9 and it is sound wisdom to fear thy name 8
7:17 and they shall fear because of thee. 8
Hab 3: 2 the report of thee, and thy work, O LORD, do I fear. 8
Zep 3: 7 I said, 'Surely she will fear me 8
15 you shall fear evil no more. 8
16 Do not fear, O Zion; let not your hands grow weak. 8
Hag 1:12 the people feared before the LORD. 8
2: 5 My Spirit abides among you; fear not. 8
Zec 8:13 Fear not, but let your hands be strong. 8
15 to the house of Judah; fear not. 8
Mal 1: 6 And if I am a master, where is my fear? 11
14 my name is feared among the nations. 8
2: 5 I gave them to him, that he might fear; and he feared 11
5 he feared me, he stood in awe of my name. 8
3: 5 and do not fear me, says the LORD of hosts. 8
16 those who feared the LORD spoke with one another; 8
16 who feared the LORD and thought on his name. 8
4: 2 for you who fear my name the sun of righteousness 8
Mat 1:20 son of David, do not fear to take Mary your wife 32
10:26 So have no fear of them; for nothing is covered 32
28 do not fear those who kill the body 32
28 rather fear him who can destroy both soul and body 32
31 Fear not, therefore; you are of more value 32
14: 5 he feared the people 32
26 And they cried out for fear. 33
27 Take heart, it is I; have no fear. 32
17: 7 Rise, and have no fear. 32
21:46 they feared the multitudes 32
28: 4 for fear of him the guards trembled 33
8 they departed quickly from the tomb with fear 33
Mrk 5:33 came in fear and trembling 32
36 Do not fear, only believe. 32
6:20 for Herod feared John . . and kept him safe 32
50 Take heart, it is I; have no fear. 32
11:18 they feared him 32
12:12 feared the multitude 32
Lke 1:12 Zechari'ah was troubled . . and fear fell upon him. 33
50 his mercy is on those who fear him 32
65 fear came on all their neighbors 33
2: 9 and they were filled with fear. 33
7:16 Fear seized them all; and they glorified God 33
8:37 they were seized with great fear 33
50 Jesus on hearing this answered him, "Do not fear; 32
12: 4 my friends, do not fear those who kill the body 32
5 I will warn you whom to fear 32
5 fear him who, after he has killed, has power to cast 32
5 yes, I tell you, fear him! 32
7 Fear not; you are of more value than many sparrows. 32
32 Fear not, little flock 32
18: 2 a judge who neither feared God nor regarded man; 32
4 Though I neither fear God nor regard man 32
20:19 they feared the people 32
21:26 men fainting with fear and with foreboding 33
22: 2 they feared the people. 32
23:40 the other rebuked him, saying, "Do you not fear God 32
Joh 7:13 Yet for fear of the Jews no one spoke openly 33
9:22 because they feared the Jews 32
12:15 Fear not, daughter of Zion 32
42 for fear of the Pharisees they did not confess it 23
19:38 but secretly, for fear of the Jews 33
20:19 the doors being shut . . for fear of the Jews 33
Act 2:43 fear came upon every soul 33
5: 5 great fear came upon all who heard of it. 33
11 great fear came upon the whole church 33
9:31 walking in the fear of the Lord 33
10: 2 a devout man who feared God 32
22 a centurion, an upright and God-fearing man 32
35 any one who fears him and does what is right 32
13:16 Men of Israel, and you that fear God, listen. 32
26 those among you that fear God 32
19:17 and fear fell upon them all 33
27:17 then, fearing that they should run on the Syr'tis 32
29 fearing that we might run on the rocks 32
Rom 3:18 There is no fear of God before their eyes. 33
8:15 the spirit of slavery to fall back into fear 33
13: 3 Would you have no fear of him who is in authority? 32
1Co 2: 3 in weakness and in much fear and trembling; 33
2Co 5:11 Therefore, knowing the fear of the Lord 33
7: 1 make holiness perfect in the fear of God. 33
5 fighting without and fear within. 33
15 fear and trembling with which you received him. 33
12:20 I fear that perhaps I may come and find you 32
21 I fear that when I come again my God may humble me •
Gal 2:12 fearing the circumcision party. 32

Eph 6: 5 with fear and trembling, in singleness of heart 33
Php 2:12 your own salvation with fear and trembling; 33
Col 3:22 in singleness of heart, fearing the Lord. 32
1Th 3: 5 for fear that somehow the tempter had tempted 28
1Ti 5:20 so that the rest may stand in fear. 33
Heb 2:15 through fear of death 33
4: 1 let us fear lest any of you be judged . . 32
12:21 Moses said, "I tremble with fear. 25
1Pe 1:17 conduct yourselves with fear 33
2:17 Honor all men. Love the brotherhood. Fear God. 32
3:14 Have no fear of them, nor be troubled 32
1Jn 4:18 There is no fear in love 33
18 but perfect love casts out fear. 33
18 For fear has to do with punishment 33
18 and he who fears is not perfected in love. 32
Jde 1:23 on some have mercy with fear 33
Rev 1:17 saying, "Fear not, I am the first and the last 32
2:10 Do not fear what you are about to suffer. 32
11:11 and great fear fell on those who saw them. 33
18 those who fear thy name, both small and great 32
14: 7 Fear God and give him glory 32
15: 4 Who shall not fear and glorify thy name, O Lord? 32
18:10 they will stand far off, in fear of her torment 33
15 in fear of her torment, weeping and mourning 33
19: 5 his servants, you who fear him, small and great. 32
1Es 4:28 Do not all lands fear to touch him? 27
2Es 2:17 Do not fear, mother of sons, for I have chosen you 36
7:79 and who have hated those who fear God 36
87 and shall wither with fear at seeing the glory 37
98 and shall be glad without fear 35
8:28 acknowledged that thou art to be feared. 37
10:38 and tell you about the things which you fear 36
12: 3 in great perplexity of mind and great fear 37
5 the great fear with which I have been terrified 37
13:13 Then in great fear I awoke 34
15: 3 Do not fear the plots against you 36
20 all the kings of the earth to fear me 38
29 so that all who hear them fear and tremble. 36
33 fear and trembling shall come upon their army 37
37 there shall be fear and great trembling 37
16:67 Behold, God is the judge, fear him! 36
70 insurrection against those who fear the Lord. 36
71 destroying those who continue to fear the Lord. 36
75 Do not fear or doubt, for God is your guide. 36
Tob 1:19 I left home in fear. 32
4:21 You have great wealth if you fear God 32
6:14 now I fear that I may die 32
14: 2 continued to fear the Lord God and to praise him. 32
6 the Gentiles will turn to fear the Lord God in truth 32
Jdt 2:28 fear and terror of him fell upon all the people 32
28 those . . feared him exceedingly 32
8: 8 she feared God with great devotion. 32
14: 3 Then fear will come over them, and they will flee 33
15: 2 Fear and trembling came over them 33
16:15 to those who fear thee 32
16 he who fears the Lord shall be great for ever. 32
AEs 11: 9 they feared the evils that threatened them 32
14:19 save me from my fear! 33
15: 5 her heart was frozen with fear. 33
13 my heart was shaken with fear at your glory. 33
Wis 5: 2 they will be shaken with dreadful fear 33
12:11 it was not through fear of any one 27
17: 8 promised to drive off the fears . . of a sick soul 21
8 were sick themselves with ridiculous fear. 26
12 fear is nothing but surrender of the helps 33
15 sudden and unexpected fear overwhelmed them. 33
18:17 unexpected fears assailed them; 33
25 To these the destroyer yielded, these he feared; 32
Sir 1: 8 There is One who is wise, greatly to be feared 31
11 The fear of the Lord is glory and exultation 33
12 The fear of the Lord delights the heart 33
13 With him who fears the Lord it will go well 33
14 To fear the Lord is the beginning of wisdom 32
16 To fear the Lord is wisdom's full measure 32
18 The fear of the Lord is the crown of wisdom 33
20 To fear the Lord is the root of wisdom 32
27 the fear of the Lord is wisdom and instruction 33
28 Do not disobey the fear of the Lord; 33
30 because you did not come in the fear of the Lord 33
2: 7 You who fear the Lord, wait for his mercy 32
8 You who fear the Lord, trust in him 32
9 you who fear the Lord, hope for good things 32
10 who ever persevered in the fear of the Lord 33
15 who fear the Lord will not disobey his words 32
16 Those who fear the Lord will seek his approval 32
17 who fear the Lord will prepare their hearts 32
4:17 she will bring fear and cowardice upon him 33
6:16 those who fear the Lord will find him. 32
17 Whoever fears the Lord directs his friendship 32
7:29 With all your soul fear the Lord 27
31 Fear the Lord and honor the priest 33
9:13 you will not be worried by the fear of death 33
16 let your glorying be in the fear of the Lord. 33
18 A babbler is feared in his city 31
10:19 Those who fear the Lord. 32
20 those who fear the Lord are worthy of honor 32
22 their glory is the fear of the Lord. 33
24 greater than the man who fears the Lord. 32
15: 1 The man who fears the Lord will do this 32
13 they are not loved by those who fear him. 32
19 his eyes are on those who fear him 32
16: 2 unless the fear of the Lord is in them. 33
17: 4 He placed the fear of them in all living beings 33
19:20 All wisdom is the fear of the Lord 33
21: 6 he that fears the Lord will repent in his heart. 32
11 wisdom is the fulfilment of the fear of the Lord. 33
22:18 will not stand firm against any fear. 33
23:18 no one sees me. Why should I fear? 27
19 His fear is confined to the eyes of men 33
27 nothing is better than the fear of the Lord 33
25: 6 their boast is the fear of the Lord. 33
10 no one superior to him who fears the Lord. 32
11 The fear of the Lord surpasses everything 33
26: 3 the blessings of the man who fears the Lord. 33
27: 3 zealous in the fear of the Lord 33
32:14 He who fears the Lord will accept his discipline 32
16 Those who fear the Lord will form true judgments 32
18 an insolent and proud man will not cower in fear. 33
33: 1 No evil will befall the man who fears the Lord 32
34:13 The spirit of those who fear the Lord will live 32
14 He who fears the Lord will not be timid 32
15 Blessed is the soul of the man who fears the Lord! 32
36: 2 the fear of thee to fall upon all the nations. 33
40: 2 Their perplexities and fear of heart 33
5 fear of death, and fury and strife 33
7 wonders that his fear came to nothing. 33
26 the fear of the Lord is better than both 33
26 There is no loss in the fear of the Lord 33
27 The fear of the Lord is like a garden of blessing 33
41: 3 Do not fear the sentence of death 27
45: 2 made him great in the fears of his enemies. 33
23 he was zealous in the fear of the Lord 33
Bar 3: 7 For thou hast put the fear of thee in our hearts 33
33 he . . called it, and it obeyed him in fear; 29
LJr 1: 4 inspire fear in the heathen. 33
5 to let fear for these gods possess you 33
16 so do not fear them. 32
23 they are not gods; so do not fear them. 32
29 do not fear them. 32
65 do not fear them. 32
69 therefore do not fear them. 32
Aza 1:18 we fear thee and seek thy face. 32
Sus 1: 2 and one who feared the Lord. 32
57 and they were intimate with you through fear; 32
1Mc 2:62 Do not fear the words of a sinner 32
3: 6 Lawless men shrank back for fear of him 33
25 Then Judas and his brothers began to be feared 33
30 He feared that he might not have such funds 27
4: 8 Do not fear their numbers 32
7:18 fear and dread of them fell upon all the people 33
8:12 as many as have heard . . have feared them 32
12:40 He feared that Jonathan might not permit him 27
52 and were in great fear 32
2Mc 3:30 was full of fear and disturbance 22
32 fearing that the king might get the notion 30
6:30 because I fear him. 33
7:29 Do not fear this butcher 32
8:16 not to fear the great multitude of Gentiles 27
9:29 fearing the son of Antiochus 24
12:22 terror and fear came over the enemy 33
15: 8 not to fear the attack of the Gentiles 20
18 their greatest and first fear 33
3Mc 2:23 fearing lest he should lose his life 32
23 panic-stricken in their exceedingly great fear. 33
7:22 restored it to them with extreme fear 33
4Mc 1: 4 namely anger, fear, and pain. 33
23 Fear precedes pain and sorrow comes after. 33
4:10 instilling in them great fear and trembling. 33
5:37 as one who does not fear your violence 32
8:12 to persuade them out of fear 33
19 should we not fear the instruments of torture 32
22 for fearing the king when we are under compulsion. 32
25 for fearing the instruments of torture. 32
13:14 Let us not fear him who thinks he is killing us 32
14: 8 youths . . encircled the sevenfold fear of tortures 33
15: 8 yet because of the fear of God 33

fear *See also* cower, fill, melt, overcome, protect, stand, tremble, turn.

godly fear 1. *εὐλάβεια*
Heb 5: 7 he was heard for his godly fear. 1

show fear 1. *δειλαίνω*
1Mc 5:41 if he shows fear 1

trembling fear 1. *ἔντρομος*
Wis 17:10 they perished in trembling fear 1

without fear 1. *ἀφόβως*
Lke 1:74 that we . . might serve him without fear 1
Php 1:14 bold to speak the word of God without fear. 1

fearful 1. ירא 2. מהר 3. פלא 4. *ἔκφοβος*
5. *μεγάλη σφόδρα* 6. *φοβερός* 7. timore plenus
Deu 20: 8 What man . . is fearful and fainthearted? 1
Jdg 7: 3 Whoever is fearful and trembling, let him return 1
Ps 139:14 praise thee, for thou art fearful and wonderful. *
Isa 35: 4 Say to those who are of a fearful heart, "Be strong 2
Jer 51:46 be not fearful at the report heard in the land 1
Dan 8:24 cause fearful destruction, and shall succeed 3
Heb 10:27 a fearful prospect of judgment, and a fury of fire 6
Rev 16:21 men cursed God . . so fearful was that plague. 5
2Es 10:26 she suddenly uttered a loud and fearful cry 7
1Mc 13: 2 the people were trembling and fearful 4

fearful *See also* aspect.

altogether fearful 1. *πάνδεινος*
4Mc 3:15 David . . considered it an altogether fearful danger 1

fearful thing 1. *φοβερός*
Heb 10:31 It is a fearful thing 1

fearfully 1. לְמַשְׁחִית 2. *δεινός*
Dan 10: 8 my radiant appearance was fearfully changed 1
4Mc 12: 2 had been fearfully reproached by the brothers 2

fearfulness 1. דְּאָגָה
Ezk 4:16 shall eat bread by weight and with fearfulness; 1
12:18 water with trembling and with fearfulness; 1
19 They shall eat their bread with fearfulness 1

feast 1. אכל 2. זֶבַח 3. חַג 4. טוֹב 5. כֵּרָה 6. מוֹעֵד
7. מִשְׁתֶּה 8. מִשְׁתֵּה יַיִן 9. רוה 10. שבע 11. שתה
12. לְחֵם (A) 13. *γάμος* 14. *δεῖπνον* 15. *δοχή*
16. *ἑορτή* 17. *εὐφραίνω* 18. *εὐφροσύνη* 19. *εὐωχέω*
20. *εὐωχία* 21. *ἡμέρα* 22. *θοῖνα* 23. *κωθωνίζομαι*
24. *συμβολοκοπέω* 25. *συμπόσιον* 26. convivium
27. festus
Gen 19: 3 and he made them a feast 7
21: 8 and Abraham made a great feast 7
26:30 he made them a feast, and they ate and drank. 7
29:22 all the men of the place, and made a feast. 7
40:20 Pharaoh's birthday, he made a feast for all his 7
Exd 10: 9 for we must hold a feast to the LORD. 3
12:14 and you shall keep it as a feast to the LORD; 3
17 you shall observe the feast of unleavened bread *
13: 6 seventh day there shall be a feast to the LORD. 3
23:15 You shall keep the feast of unleavened bread; 3
16 You shall keep the feast of harvest 3
16 You shall keep the feast of ingathering 3
18 shall not . . let the fat of my feast remain 3
32: 5 Tomorrow shall be a feast to the LORD. 3
34:18 The feast of unleavened bread you shall keep. 3
22 you shall observe the feast of weeks 3
22 the feast of ingathering at the year's end. 3
25 the sacrifice of the feast of the passover 3
Lev 23: 6 the feast of unleavened bread to the LORD 3
34 for seven days is the feast of booths to the LORD 3
39 you shall keep the feast of the LORD seven days 3
Num28:17 on the fifteenth day of this month is a feast; 3
29:12 you shall keep a feast to the LORD seven days; 3
Deu 16:10 Then you shall keep the feast of weeks to the LORD 3
13 You shall keep the feast of booths seven days 3
14 rejoice in your feast, you and your son 3
16 appear . . at the feast of unleavened bread 3
16 appear . . at . . the feast of weeks 3
16 appear . . at . . the feast of booths. 3
31:10 year of release, at the feast of booths 3
Jdg 14:10 down to the woman, and Samson made a feast there; 7
12 tell me . . within the seven days of the feast 7
17 wept . . the seven days that their feast lasted; 7
21:19 there is the yearly feast of the LORD at Shiloh 3
1Sm 25: 8 find favor in your eyes; for we come on a feast day. 4
36 lo, he was holding a feast in his house 7
36 he was holding a feast . . like the feast of a king. 7
2Sm 3:20 David made a feast for Abner and the men 7
1Kg 1:41 with him heard it as they finished feasting. 1
3:15 offerings, and made a feast for all his servants. 7
8: 2 assembled . . at the feast in the month Eth'anim 3
65 Solomon held the feast . . and all Israel with him 3
12:32 Jerobo'am appointed a feast on the fifteenth day 3
32 a feast . . like the feast that was in Judah 3
33 he ordained a feast for the people of Israel 3
2Kg 6:23 So he prepared for them a great feast; 5
2Ch 5: 3 assembled before the king at the feast which is 3
7: 8 Solomon held the feast for seven days 3
9 for they had kept . . and the feast seven days. 3
8:13 commandment . . for . . the three annual feasts- 6
13 annual feasts-the feast of unleavened bread 3
13 three annual feasts- . . the feast of weeks 3
13 annual feasts- . . and the feast of tabernacles. 3
30:13 came . . to keep the feast of unleavened bread 3
21 kept the feast of unleavened bread seven days 3
23 agreed together to keep the feast for another *
35:17 kept . . feast of unleavened bread seven days. 3
Ezr 3: 4 kept the feast of booths, as it is written 3
6:22 kept the feast of unleavened bread seven days 3
Neh 8:14 booths during the feast of the seventh month 3
18 kept the feast seven days; and on the eighth day 3
Est 7: 1 king and Haman went in to feast with . . Esther. 11
7 And the king rose from the feast in wrath 8
8:17 and joy among the Jews, a feast and a holiday. 7
9:17 they . . made that a day of feasting and gladness. 7
18 making that a day of feasting and gladness. 7
19 for gladness and feasting and holiday-making 7

22 should make them days of feasting and gladness 7
Job 1: 4 His sons used to go and hold a feast in the house 7
5 when the days of the feast had run their course 7
Ps 36: 8 They feast on the abundance of thy house 9
63: 5 My soul is feasted as with marrow and fat 10
69:22 let their sacrificial feasts be a trap. ‡
81: 3 new moon, at the full moon, on our feast day. 3
Prv 15:15 but a cheerful heart has a continual feast. 7
17: 1 quiet than a house full of feasting with strife. 2
Ecc 7: 2 than to go to the house of feasting; 7
10:16 and your princes feast in the morning! 1
17 and your princes feast at the proper time 1
Isa 5:12 harp, timbrel and flute and wine at their feasts; 7
25: 6 will make for all peoples a feast of fat things 7
6 a feast of wine on the lees, of fat things full 7
29: 1 Add year to year; let the feasts run their round. 3
30:29 a song as in the night when a holy feast is kept; 3
Jer 16: 8 You shall not go into the house of feasting 7
31:14 I will feast the soul of the priests 9
51:39 I will prepare them a feast and make them drunk 7
Lam 4: 5 who feasted on dainties perish in the street; 1
Ezk 20: 7 the detestable things your eyes feast •
8 the detestable things their eyes feasted •
28:17 exposed you before kings, to feast their eyes •
36:38 flock at Jerusalem during her appointed feasts •
39:17 gather from all sides to the sacrificial feast •
17 a great sacrificial feast upon the mountains •
19 sacrificial feast which I am preparing for you. •
44:24 laws and my statutes in all my appointed feasts •
45:17 and drink offerings, at the feasts, the new moons 3
21 you shall celebrate the feast of the passover 3
25 for the seven days of the feast, he shall make 3
46:11 At the feasts and the appointed seasons 3
Dan 5: 1 King Belshaz'zar made a great feast 12
Hos 2:11 And I will put an end to all her mirth, her feasts 3
13 I will punish her for the feast days of the Ba'als •
9: 5 and on the day of the feast of the LORD? 3
Ams 5:21 I hate, I despise your feasts, and I take no delight 3
8:10 I will turn your feasts into mourning 3
Nah 1:15 Keep your feasts, O Judah, fulfil your vows 3
Zec 8:19 of joy and gladness, and cheerful feasts; 6
14:16 to worship . . and to keep the feast of booths. 3
18 that do not go up to keep the feast of booths. 3
19 that do not go up to keep the feast of booths. 3
Mat 23: 6 they love the place of honor at feasts 14
26: 5 Not during the feast, lest there be a tumult 16
27:15 Now at the feast the governor was accustomed 16
Mrk 12:39 and the places of honor at feasts 14
14: 2 Not during the feast, lest there be a tumult 16
15: 6 Now at the feast he used to release for them one 16
Lke 2:41 every year at the feast of the Passover. 16
43 when the feast was ended, as they were returning 21
5:29 Levi made him a great feast in his house 15
14:13 when you give a feast, invite the poor, the maimed 15
16:19 and who feasted sumptuously every day. 17
20:46 and love . . the places of honor at feasts 14
22: 1 Now the feast of Unleavened Bread drew near 16
Joh 2:23 when he was in Jerusalem at the Passover feast 16
4:45 all that he had done in Jerusalem at the feast 16
45 for they too had gone to the feast. 16
5: 1 After this there was a feast of the Jews 16
6: 4 the Passover, the feast of the Jews, was at hand. 16
7: 2 Now the Jews' feast of Tabernacles was at hand. 16
8 Go to the feast yourselves 16
8 I am not going up to this feast 16
10 after his brothers had gone up to the feast 16
11 The Jews were looking for him at the feast 16
14 About the middle of the feast 16
37 On the last day of the feast, the great day 16
11:56 do you think? That he will not come to the feast? 16
12:12 a great crowd who had come to the feast heard 16
20 among those who went up to worship at the feast 16
13: 1 Now before the feast of the Passover 16
29 Buy what we need for the feast 16
1Es 1:19 kept . . the feast of unleavened bread 16
3:20 It turns every thought to feasting and mirth 20
4:63 they feasted, with music and rejoicing 23
5:51 They kept the feast of booths 16
52 at all the consecrated feasts. 16
7:14 kept the feast of unleavened bread seven days 16
2Es 1:31 for I have rejected your feast days, and new moons 27
2:38 Rise and stand, and see at the feast of the Lord 26
Tob 1: 6 I alone went often to Jerusalem for the feasts 16
2: 1 at the feast of Pentecost 16
6 Your feasts shall be turned into mourning 16
8:20 before the days of the feast were over 13
Jdt 1:16 there he and his forces rested and feasted 19
8: 6 the feasts and days of rejoicing 16
16:20 the people continued feasting in Jerusalem 17
AEs 13:17 turn our mourning into feasting 20
14:17 I have not honored the king's feast 25
Sir 13: 8 not to be humiliated in your feasting. 18
18:33 become a beggar by feasting with borrowed money 24
32: 1 If they make you master of the feast •
33: 8 he appointed the different seasons and feasts; 16
47:10 He gave beauty to the feasts 16
Bar 1:14 on the days of the feasts and at appointed seasons. 16
1Mc 1:39 her feasts were turned into mourning 16
45 to profane sabbaths and feasts 16
10:21 at the feast of tabernacles 16
34 all the feasts and sabbaths and new moons 16
34 the three days before a feast 16
34 the three after a feast 16
12:11 both in our feasts and on other appropriate days 16
2Mc 1: 9 now see that you keep the feast of booths 21
18 the feast of the fire given when . . •
6: 6 nor observe the feasts of his fathers 16
7 when the feast of Dionysus came 16
10: 6 not long before, during the feast of booths 16
12:31 the feast of weeks was close at hand. 16
32 After the feast called Pentecost •
3Mc 4: 1 a feast at public expense was arranged 20
16 organizing feasts in honor of all his idols 25
5: 3 he returned to his feasting, together with . . his friends 20
31 a rich feast for the savage beasts 22
6:35 the Jews . . passed the time in feasting 20
40 Then they feasted 19

feast *See also* day, hold, place, prepare, steward.

appointed feast 1. מוֹעֵד
Lev 23: 2 The appointed feasts of the LORD 1
2 my appointed feasts, are these 1
4 These are the appointed feasts of the LORD 1
37 These are the appointed feasts of the LORD 1
44 declared . . the appointed feasts of the LORD 1
Num10:10 at your appointed feasts, and at the beginnings 1
15: 3 freewill offering or at your appointed feasts 1
29:39 shall offer to the LORD at your appointed feasts 1
2Ch 2: 4 on the sabbaths . . and the appointed feasts 1
31: 3 burnt offerings for the . . appointed feasts 1
Ezr 3: 5 offerings . . all the appointed feasts of the LORD 1
Neh 10:33 sabbaths, the new moons, the appointed feasts 1
Isa 1:14 new moons and . . appointed feasts my soul hates; 1
33:20 Look upon Zion, the city of our appointed feasts! 1
Lam 1: 4 Zion mourn, for none come to the appointed feasts; 1
2: 6 brought to an end . . appointed feast and sabbath 1
7 a clamor . . as on the day of an appointed feast. 1
22 didst invite as to the day of an appointed feast 1
Ezk 45:17 all the appointed feasts of the house of Israel 1
46: 9 come before the LORD at the appointed feasts 1
Hos 2:11 put an end to . . all her appointed feasts. 1
12: 9 in tents, as in the days of the appointed feast. 1

funeral feast 1. *περίδειπνον*
LJr 1:32 as some do at a funeral feast for a man who has died. 1

keep a feast 1. חגג
Exd 12:14 and you shall keep it as a feast to the LORD; 1
23:14 in the year you shall keep a feast to me. 1
Lev 23:39 you shall keep the feast of the LORD seven days 1
41 You shall keep it as a feast to the LORD seven days 1
Deu 16:15 seven days you shall keep the feast to the LORD 1
Nah 1:15 Keep your feasts, O Judah, fulfil your vows 1

love feast 1. *ἀγάπη*
Jde 1:12 These are blemishes on your love feasts 1

marriage feast 1. *γάμος* 2. epulum
Mat 22: 2 to a king who gave a marriage feast for his son 1
3 those who were invited to the marriage feast; 1
4 everything is ready; come to the marriage feast.' 1
9 invite to the marriage feast as many as you find.' 1
25:10 went in with him to the marriage feast 1
Lke 12:36 to come home from the marriage feast 1
14: 8 When . . invited by any one to a marriage feast 1
2Es 9:47 I set a day for the marriage feast. 2

feast of booths 1. *σκηνοπηγία* 2. *σκήνωμα*
2Mc 1:18 you also may celebrate the feast of booths 1
10: 6 in the manner of the feast of booths 2

feast of weeks 1. שָׁבוּעַ
Num28:26 offering . . to the LORD at your feast of weeks 1

wedding feast 1. *γάμος*
Tob 8:19 After this he gave a wedding feast for them 1
20 until the 14 days of the wedding feast were ended 1
9: 2 and bring him to the wedding feast. 1
6 they both . . came to the wedding feast 1
10: 7 until the 14 days of the wedding feast had expired 1

sacrificial feasting 1. *σπλαγχνοφάγος*
Wis 12: 5 their sacrificial feasting on human flesh 1

feather 1. נוֹצָה
Lev 1:16 he shall take away its crop with the feathers 1
Dan 4:33 till his hair grew as long as eagles' feathers •

feathered 1. pinna
2Es 11: 1 an eagle that had twelve feathered wings 1

fed *See* beast.

fee for divination 1. קֶסֶם
Num22: 7 with the fees for divination in their hand; 1

feeble 1. אֻמְלָל 2. כרע 3. כשל 4. לֹא כַבִּיר 5. עטף 6. רפה 7. רִפָּיוֹן 8. *ἀσθενέω* 9. *κάμνω*
Gen 30:42 the feebler of the flock he did not lay them there 5
42 the feebler were Laban's, and the stronger 5
1Sm 2: 4 bows . . are broken, but the feeble gird on strength. 3
2Ch 28:15 carrying all the feeble among them on asses 3
Neh 4: 2 What are these feeble Jews doing? 1
Job 4: 4 you have made firm the feeble knees. 2
Isa 13: 7 Therefore all hands will be feeble 6
16:14 those who survive will be very few and feeble. 4
35: 3 weak hands, and make firm the feeble knees. 3
Jer 47: 3 back to the children, so feeble are their hands 7
Ezk 7:17 All hands are feeble, and all knees weak as water. 6
21: 7 heart will melt and all hands will be feeble 6
Zec 12: 8 so that the feeblest among them on that day shall 3
Bar 2:18 person . . that goes about bent over and feeble 8
4Mc 7:13 his muscles flabby, his sinews feeble 9

become feeble 1. רפה
Jer 49:24 Damascus has become feeble, she turned to flee 1

feed 1. אכל 2. בער 3. טרף 4. כול 5. רעה 6. זון (A) 7. טעם (A) 8. *βόσκω* 9. *δίδωμι εἰς στόμα* 10. *ποτίζω* 11. *τρέφω* 12. *χορτάζω* 13. *ψωμίζω* 14. cibo
Gen 30:31 I will again feed your flock and keep it 5
36 and Jacob fed the rest of Laban's flock. 5
41: 2 seven cows . . and they fed in the reed grass. 5
18 came up out of the Nile and fed in the reed grass; 5
Exd 16:32 bread with which I fed you in the wilderness 1
22: 5 beast loose and it feeds in another man's field 2
34: 3 let no flocks or herds feed before that mountain. 5
Deu 8: 3 let you hunger and fed you with manna 1
16 who fed you in the wilderness with manna 1
1Sm 17:15 went back and forth . . to feed his father's sheep 5
1Kg 17: 4 I have commanded the ravens to feed you there. 4
9 I have commanded a widow there to feed you. 4
18: 4 hid them . . and fed them with bread and water.) 4
13 I hid 100 men . . and fed them with bread and water? 4
22:27 and feed him with scant fare of bread and water 1
2Ch 18:26 in prison, and feed him with scant fare 1
Job 1:14 were plowing and the asses feeding beside them; 5
24:21 They feed on the barren childless woman 5
Ps 80: 5 Thou hast fed them with the bread of tears 1
13 all that move in the field feed on it. 5
81:16 I would feed you with the finest of the wheat 1
Prv 10:21 The lips of the righteous feed many 5
15:14 but the mouths of fools feed on folly. 5
30: 8 feed me with the food that is needful for me 3
Sng 4: 5 like two fawns . . that feed among the lilies. 5
Isa 5:17 fatlings and kids shall feed among the ruins. 1
11: 7 The cow and the bear shall feed; 5
14:30 the first-born of the poor will feed 5
40:11 He will feed his flock like a shepherd 5
44:20 He feeds on ashes; a deluded mind has led him 5
49: 9 They shall feed along the ways, on all bare 5
58:14 I will feed you with the heritage of Jacob 1
61: 5 Aliens shall stand and feed your flocks 5
65:25 The wolf and the lamb shall feed together 5
Jer 3:15 who will feed you with knowledge 5
9:15 Behold, I will feed this people with wormwood 1
23:15 Behold, I will feed them with wormwood 1
50:19 and he shall feed on Carmel and in Bashan 5
Ezk 16:19 I fed you with fine flour and oil and honey 1
34: 2 of Israel who have been feeding yourselves! 5
2 Should not shepherds feed the sheep? 5
3 but you do not feed the sheep. 5
8 but the shepherds have fed themselves 5
8 have fed themselves, and have not fed my sheep; 5
10 and put a stop to their feeding the sheep; 5
10 no longer shall the shepherds feed themselves. 5
13 I will feed them on the mountains of Israel 5
14 I will feed them with good pasture 5
14 on fat pasture they shall feed on the mountains 5
16 I will feed them in justice. 5
18 Is it not enough for you to feed on the good 5
23 shepherd, my servant David, and he shall feed them 5
23 he shall feed them and be their shepherd. 5
Dan 4:12 all flesh was fed from it. 6
5:21 fed grass like an ox, and his body was wet 7
Hos 4: 8 They feed on the sin of my people; 1
16 can the LORD now feed them like a lamb in a broad 5
9: 2 Threshing floor and winevat shall not feed them 5
11: 4 and I bent down to them and fed them. 1
13: 6 but when they had fed to the full, they were filled •
Jon 3: 7 let them not feed, or drink water 5
Mic 5: 4 he shall stand and feed his flock 5
7:14 let them feed in Bashan and Gilead 5
Mat 6:26 barns, and yet your heavenly Father feeds them. 11
8:30 a herd of swine was feeding at some distance 8
15:33 bread enough . . to feed so great a crowd? 12
25:37 Lord, when did we see thee hungry and feed thee 11
Mrk 5:11 herd of swine was feeding there on the hillside; 8
7:27 he said to her, "Let the children first be fed 12
8: 4 How can one feed these men with bread here 12
Lke 8:32 herd of swine was feeding there on the hillside; 8
12:24 yet God feeds them 11
15:15 who sent him into his fields to feed swine. 8

16 he would gladly have fed on the pods 12
16:21 fed with what fell from the rich man's table; 12
Joh 21:15 He said to him, "Feed my lambs. 8
17 Jesus said to him, "Feed my sheep. 8
Rom 12:20 No, "if your enemy is hungry, feed him; 13
1Co 3: 2 I fed you with milk, not solid food 10
2Es 16:68 and shall feed you what was sacrificed to idols. 14
Wis 16:23 in order that the righteous might be fed 11
26 it is not the production of crops that feeds man 11
Sir 15: 3 will feed him with the bread of understanding 13
Bel 1:27 made cakes, which he fed to the dragon 9

feed fire 1. καίω
Aza 1:23 servants . . did not cease feeding the furnace fires 1

feed to the full 1. שׂבע
Jer 5: 7 When I fed them to the full 1

feed upon 1. ἐμπίμπλημι
Sus 1:32 that they might feed upon her beauty. 1

feel 1. בין 2. ידע 3. מושׁ 4. מצא 5. משׁשׁ 6. αἰσθάνομαι 7. αἴσθησις 8. γινώσκω 9. διάνοια 10. ἔχω 11. ζηλόω 12. οἴομαι 13. σπλάγχνον 14. φρονέω 15. φρόνησις 16. χαίρω 17. ψηλάφησις 18. ψυχή 19. sentio
Gen 27:12 Perhaps my father will feel me, and I shall seem 5
21 Come near, that I may feel you, my son 3
22 went near to Isaac his father, who felt him 5
Exd 10:21 over the land of Egypt, a darkness to be felt. 3
Jdg 16:26 Let me feel the pillars on which the house rests 5
Ps 58: 9 Sooner than your pots can feel the heat of thorns 1
115: 7 have hands, but do not feel; feet, but do not walk; 3
Prv 23:35 they beat me, but I did not feel it. 2
Jer 10:18 bring distress on them, that they may feel it. 4
Mrk 5:29 she felt in her body that she was healed 8
2Co 7: 9 you felt a godly grief •
11: 2 I feel a divine jealousy for you 11
Gal 4:15 What has become of the satisfaction you felt? •
Php 1: 7 It is right for me to feel thus about you all 14
1Th 3: 9 which we feel for your sake before our God 16
1Es 3:21 It makes all hearts feel rich •
2Es 13: 4 as wax melts when it feels the fire. 19
Wis 15:15 nor fingers to feel 17
Sir 22:19 one who pricks the heart makes it show feeling. 7
29:17 one who does not feel grateful 9
28 things are hard to bear for a man who has feeling 15
30: 7 his feelings will be troubled at every cry. 13
31:15 Judge your neighbor's feelings by your own •
20 he rises early, and feels fit 18
LJr 1:24 when they were being cast, they had no feeling. 6
2Mc 7:24 Antiochus felt that . . 12
4Mc 15: 9 she felt a greater tenderness toward them. 10

feel a weight 1. שׁקל
2Sm 18:12 Even if I felt in my hand the weight of 1,000 1

feel about 1. משׁשׁ
Gen 31:34 Laban felt all about the tent, but did not find 1

feel after 1. ψηλαφάω
Act 17:27 in the hope that they might feel after him 1

feel anguish 1. חול
Jer 5: 3 Thou hast smitten them, but they felt no anguish; 1

feel emotion 1. συμπάθεια
4Mc 14:13 an emotion felt in her inmost parts. 1

feel pain 1. כאב
Job 14:22 He feels only the pain of his own body 1

feel remorse 1. κατανύσσομαι
Sir 20:21 when he rests he feels no remorse. 1

feel revulsion 1. βαρύνω
2Mc 9: 9 the whole army felt revulsion at his decay. 1

feel secure 1. בטח
Isa 47:10 You felt secure in your wickedness 1
Ams 6: 1 those who feel secure on the mountain of Sama'ria 1

feel strong compassion 1. κατοικτίρω
4Mc 12: 2 he felt strong compassion for this child 1

feel sure 1. πείθω
2Co 2: 3 I felt sure of all of you 1
Heb 6: 9 we feel sure of better things 1

feel through 1. משׁשׁ
Gen 31:37 Although you have felt through all my goods 1

inmost feelings 1. νεφρός
Wis 1: 6 because God is witness of his inmost feelings 1

feign 1. ὑποκρίνω
4Mc 6:17 out of cowardice we feign a role unbecoming to us! 1

feign mad 1. הלל
1Sm 21:13 changed his behavior . . and feigned himself mad 1

feign madness 1. שׁנה טַעַם
Ps 34: 0 when he feigned madness before Abimelech 1

fell 1. חטב 2. כרת 3. נפל 4. שׁחת 5. שַׁלֶּכֶת
Jdg 20:21 and felled to the ground . . 22,000 men 4
25 and felled to the ground 18,000 men 4
2Kg 3:19 and shall fell every good tree 3
25 and felled all the good trees; 3
6: 5 as one was felling a log, his axe head fell 3
19:23 I felled its tallest cedars, its choicest 2
Isa 6:13 whose stump remains standing when it is felled. 5
37:24 I felled its tallest cedars 2
Jer 46:22 against her with axes, like those who fell trees. 1

fellow 1. אָח 2. אֶחָד 3. אִישׁ 4. בֵּן 5. חָבֵר 6. רֵעַ 7. חֲבֵרָה (A) 8. ἀδελφός 9. ἀνήρ 10. ἄνθρωπος 11. ἴδιος 12. πολίτης
Gen 19: 9 Stand back!" And they said, "This fellow came 2
Exd 2:13 Why do you strike your fellow? 6
Deu 20: 8 go back . . lest the heart of his fellows melt 1
Jdg 7:22 against his fellow and against all the army; 6
9: 4 hired worthless and reckless fellows 3
11: 3 worthless fellows collected round Jephthah 3
18:25 heard among us, lest angry fellows fall upon you 3
19:22 the men of the city, base fellows, beset the house 3
20:13 give up the men, the base fellows in Gib'e-ah 4
Rut 3:11 my fellow townsmen know that you are a woman •
1Sm 14:20 behold, every man's sword was against his fellow 6
21:15 you have brought this fellow to play the madman •
15 Shall this fellow come into my house? •
25:21 in vain have I guarded all that this fellow has •
25 Let not my lord regard this ill-natured fellow 3
29: 4 how could this fellow reconcile himself •
30:22 base fellows among the men . . with David said 3
2Sm 16: 7 Begone . . you man of blood, you worthless fellow! 3
20: 1 there happened to be there a worthless fellow 3
1Kg 20:35 a certain man . . said to his fellow 6
22:27 Put this fellow in prison, and feed him •
2Kg 9: 2 and go in and bid him rise from among his fellows 1
11 he said to them, "You know the fellow and his talk. 3
2Ch 18:26 say, 'Thus says the king, Put this fellow in prison •
Ezr 3: 2 Then arose Jeshua . . with his fellow priests 1
6:20 for their fellow priests, and for themselves; 1
Ps 45: 7 with the oil of gladness above your fellows; 5
Ecc 4:10 For if they fall, one will lift up his fellow; 5
Isa 3: 5 oppress one another, every man his fellow 3
34:14 the satyr shall cry to his fellow; 6
44:11 Behold, all his fellows shall be put to shame 5
Jer 34:14 each of you must set free the fellow Hebrew 1
Ezk 11:15 even your brethren, your fellow exiles 3
Dan 7:20 horn . . which seemed greater than its fellows. 7
Hag 2:22 go down every one by the sword of his fellow. 1
Zec 8:10 for I set every man against his fellow. 6
14:13 each will lay hold on the hand of his fellow 6
Mat 26:61 said, "This fellow said, 'I am able to destroy •
Act 17: 5 taking some wicked fellows of the rabble 9
Heb 8:11 they shall not teach every one his fellow 12
1Es 5:48 Jeshua . . with his fellow priests 8
Sir 4:27 Do not subject yourself to a foolish fellow 10
13:23 they say, "Who is this fellow? •
2Mc 4:38 he dispatched the bloodthirsty fellow •
5: 6 kept . . slaughtering his fellow citizens 11
9:13 Then the abominable fellow made a vow to the Lord •
14: 8 I have regard also for my fellow citizens 11
3Mc 1:23 They shouted to their fellows to take arms •

fellow *See also* Jew, Levite, base, citizen, countryman, disciple, elder, foolhardy, heir, insolent, mad, pestilent, prisoner, servant, soldier, such, vulgar, worker, worthless.

fellowship 1. רֶגֶשׁ 2. κοινωνέω 3. κοινωνία 4. συναναστροφή
Ps 55:14 within God's house we walked in fellowship. 1
Act 2:42 the apostles' teaching and fellowship 3
1Co 1: 9 called into the fellowship of his Son, Jesus 3
2Co 6:14 what fellowship has light with darkness? 3
13:14 the fellowship of the Holy Spirit 3
Gal 2: 9 gave to me . . the right hand of fellowship 3
1Jn 1: 3 so that you may have fellowship with us 3
3 our fellowship is with the Father 3
6 If we say we have fellowship with him 3
7 we have fellowship with one another 3
Sir 13:17 What fellowship has a wolf with a lamb? 2
3Mc 2:33 depriving them of common fellowship and mutual 4

female 1. בַּת 2. נְקֵבָה 3. θῆλυς
Gen 1:27 in the image of God . . male and female he created 2
5: 2 Male and female he created them, and he blessed 2
6:19 they shall be male and female. 2
7: 3 birds of the air also, male and female 2
9 two and two, male and female, went into the ark 2
16 they that entered, male and female of all flesh 2
Lev 3: 1 an animal from the herd, male or female 2
6 an animal from the flock, male or female 2
4:28 his offering a goat, a female without blemish 2
32 he shall bring a female without blemish 2
5: 6 a female from the flock, a lamb or a goat 2
12: 5 if she bears a female child, then she shall be 2
7 for her who bears a child, either male or female 2
15:33 for any one, male or female, who has a discharge 2
27: 4 If the person is a female, your valuation shall be 2
5 twenty shekels, and for a female ten shekels 2
6 for a male five shekels of silver, and for a female 2
7 fifteen shekels, and for a female ten shekels 2
Num 5: 3 you shall put out both male and female 2
15:27 sins unwittingly, he shall offer a female goat 1
Mat 19: 4 made them male and female 3
Mrk 10: 6 'God made them male and female.' 3
Gal 3:28 there is neither male nor female 3

female *See also* barren, singer, slave.

fence 1. גָּדֵר 2. גְּדֵרָה 3. περιφράσσω 4. φραγμός 5. χάραξ
Ps 62: 3 all of you, like a leaning wall, a tottering fence? 1
Nah 3:17 like clouds of locusts settling on the fences 2
Sir 22:18 Fences set on a high place will not stand firm 5
28:24 See that you fence in your property with thorns 3
36:25 Where there is no fence 4

fertile 1. זֶרַע 2. טוב 3. pinguis
Jdg 18: 9 have seen the land, and behold, it is very fertile. 2
Ezk 17: 5 seed of the land and planted it in fertile soil; 1
2Es 1:21 I divided fertile lands among you 3

fertile *See also* land.

very fertile 1. בֶּן שֶׁמֶן
Isa 5: 1 My beloved had a vineyard on a very fertile hill. 1

fervent 1. ζέω 2. θερμαίνω
Act 18:25 fervent in spirit 1
Sir 38:17 your wailing fervent 2

more fervent 1. ποθεινός
4Mc 13:26 they rendered their brotherly love more fervent. 1

fervently 1. ἐκτενῶς
Jas 5:17 he prayed fervently †
3Mc 5: 9 their entreaty ascended fervently to heaven. 1

fervor 1. ἐκτένεια
Jdt 4: 9 cried out to God with great fervor 1

festal 1. חֲלִיפָה
Gen 45:22 To each and all of them he gave festal garments; 1
22 he gave . . five festal garments. 1
Jdg 14:12 30 linen garments and 30 festal garments; 1
13 give me 30 linen garments and 30 festal garments 1

festal *See also* celebration, garment, gathering, procession, robe, shout.

fester 1. מקק
Ps 38: 5 My wounds grow foul and fester 1

festival 1. הִלּוּל 2. חַג 3. מוֹעֵד 4. ἑορτή 5. εὐφροσύνη 6. εὐφρόσυνος 7. εὐωχία 8. πανηγυρισμός 9. συμποσία
Jdg 9:27 and trod them, and held festival, and went 1
2Ch 30:22 ate the food of the festival for seven days 3
Ezk 45:23 the seven days of the festival he shall provide 2
Zep 3:18 as on a day of festival. 4
Col 2:16 a festival or a new moon or a sabbath. 4
Tob 2: 1 which is the sacred festival of the seven weeks •
AEs 16:22 among your commemorative festivals 4
Wis 15:12 considered . . life a festival held for profit 8
3Mc 6:30 needed for a festival of seven days 7
36 observance of the aforesaid days as a festival 6
7:15 they kept the day as a joyful festival 5
20 at the site of the festival 9

festival *See also* celebrate, keep.

appointed festival 1. מוֹעֵד
Hos 9: 5 What will you do on the day of appointed festival 1

joyous festival 1. εὐφρόσυνος
3Mc 7:19 to observe . . as a joyous festival 1

marriage festival 1. γάμος
3Mc 4: 8 the remaining days of their marriage festival 1

festivity 1. εὐφροσύνη
Tob 2: 6 all your festivities into lamentation 1

great festivity 1. εὐφροσύνη
Tob 11:19 Tobias' marriage was celebrated . . with great festivity. 1

fetch 1. בוא 2. יצא 3. לקח 4. נשׂא 5. עבט
Gen 18: 5 while I fetch a morsel of bread 3
27: 9 Go to the flock, and fetch me two good kids 3
13 only obey my word, and go, fetch them to me. 3
45 then I will send, and fetch you from there. 3
Exd 2: 5 saw the basket . . and sent her maid to fetch it. 3
Deu 19:12 elders . . shall send and fetch him from there 3

24:10 shall not go into his house to fetch his pledge. 5
30: 4 from there he will fetch you; 3
1Sm 10:23 Then they ran and fetched him from there; 3
16:11 Send and fetch him; for we will not sit down till he 3
20:31 send and fetch him to me, for he shall surely die. 3
26:22 Let one of the young men come over and fetch it. 3
2Sm 14: 2 sent to Teko'a, and fetched from there a wise woman 3
2Ch 8:18 fetched . . 450 talents of gold 3
Est 5:10 and he sent and fetched his friends and his wife 1
Job 36: 3 I will fetch my knowledge from afar 4
Jer 26:23 they fetched Uri'ah from Egypt and brought him 2

fetter 1. אסר 2. זִק 3. כֶּבֶל 4. לִנְחֻשְׁתַּיִם נגש 5. נְחֹשֶׁת 6. *δεσμός* 7. *δέω* 8. *πέδη*

2Sm 3:34 hands were not bound, your feet were not fettered; 4
2Kg 25: 7 and bound him in fetters, and took him to Babylon. 5
2Ch 36: 6 bound him in fetters to take him to Babylon. 5
Job 36: 8 if they are bound in fetters and caught 2
Ps 105:18 His feet were hurt with fetters 3
149: 8 to bind . . their nobles with fetters of iron 3
Ecc 7:26 woman whose heart . . and whose hands are fetters; 1
Jer 39: 7 and bound him in fetters to take him to Babylon. 5
52:11 of Zedeki'ah, and bound him in fetters 5
Mrk 5: 4 he had often been bound with fetters and chains 8
4 the fetters he broke in pieces 8
Lke 8:29 bound with chains and fetters 8
Act 16:26 every one's fetters were unfastened. 6
Col 4:18 Remember my fetters. Grace be with you. 6
2Ti 2: 9 for which I am suffering and wearing fetters 6
9 the word of God is not fettered. 7
Sir 6:24 Put your feet into her fetters 8
29 Then her fetters will become . . protection 8
21:19 education is fetters on his feet 8
28:19 has not been bound with its fetters; 6
20 its fetters are fetters of bronze; 6
20 its fetters are fetters of bronze; 6
33:28 if he does not obey, make his fetters heavy. 8
Man 1:10 I am weighted down with many an iron fetter 6
1Mc 3:41 silver and gold in immense amounts, and fetters 8
3Mc 3:25 bound securely with iron fetters 6
4: 9 had their feet secured by unbreakable fetters 8
4Mc 12: 2 when he saw that he was already in fetters 6

bronze fetter 1. נְחֹשֶׁת

Jdg 16:21 down to Gaza, and bound him with bronze fetters; 1

fetter of bronze 1. נְחֹשֶׁת

2Ch 33:11 bound him with fetters of bronze 1

feud 1. רִיב

Jdg 12: 2 and my people had a great feud with the Ammonites; 1

fever 1. קַדַּחַת 2. *πυρετός*

Lev 26:16 consumption, and fever that waste the eyes 1
Deu 28:22 LORD will smite you with consumption . . fever 1
Mat 8:15 he touched her hand, and the fever left her 2
Mrk 1:31 the fever left her; and she served them. 2
Lke 4:38 Now Simon's mother-in-law was ill with a high fever 2
39 he stood over her and rebuked the fever 2
Joh 4:52 Yesterday at the seventh hour the fever left him. 2
Act 28: 8 lay sick with fever and dysentery 2

fever *See also* sick.

few 1. אֶחָד 2. אַנְשֵׁי מִסְפָּר 3. מִזְעָר 4. מִסְפָּר 5. מעט 6. מְעַט 7. מִצְעָר 8. מַת 9. קצר 10. *ἐλάττων* 11. *μικρός* 12. *ὀλίγος* 13. *ὀλιγοστός* 14. *οὐ πολύς* 15. modicus 16. paucus

Gen 11: 1 the whole earth had one language and few words. 1
29:20 and they seemed to him but a few days 1
34:30 my numbers are few, and if they gather †
47: 9 few and evil have been the days of the years of my 6
Lev 25:16 if the years are few you shall diminish the price 5
52 If there remain but a few years until the year 6
Num 9:20 cloud was a few days over the tabernacle 4
13:18 whether they are few or many 6
Deu 4:27 you will be left few in number among the nations 8
7: 7 for you were the fewest of all peoples; 6
26: 5 Egypt and sojourned there, few in number; 6
33: 6 Let Reuben live, and not die, nor let his men be few. 4
Jos 7: 3 Let not all the people go . . for they are but few. 6
1Sm 14: 6 hinder the LORD from saving by many or by few. 6
17:28 with whom have you left those few sheep 6
1Ch 16:19 they were few in number, and of little account 8
2Ch 24:24 the army of the Syrians had come with few men 7
30:11 Only a few men of Asher, of Manas'seh, *
Neh 2:12 Then I arose in the night, I and a few men with me; 6
7: 4 city . . large, but the people within it were few 6
Job 10:20 Are not the days of my life few? 6
14: 1 Man that is born of a woman is of few days 9
16:22 For when a few years have come I shall go 4
Ps 39: 5 Behold, thou hast made my days a few handbreadths *
105:12 When they were few in number, of little account 8
109: 8 May his days be few; may another seize his goods! 6
Ecc 2: 3 to do . . during the few days of their life. 4
5: 2 therefore let your words be few. 6
18 the few days of his life which God has given him 4
6:12 while he lives the few days of his vain life 4
9:14 There was a little city with few men in it; 6
12: 3 and the grinders cease because they are few 5
Isa 1: 9 If the LORD . . had not left us a few survivors 6
10: 7 to destroy, and to cut off nations not a few; 6
19 remnant of the trees of his forest will be so few 4
21:17 the remainder of the archers . . will be few; 5
24: 6 inhabitants . . scorched, and few men are left. 3
65:20 there be in it an infant that lives but a few days *
Jer 30:19 I will multiply them, and they shall not be few; 5
42: 2 for we are left but a few of many, as your eyes see us 6
Ezk 12:16 But I will let a few of them escape from the sword 2
Dan 11:20 within a few days he shall be broken 1
Mat 7:14 and those who find it are few. 12
9:37 but the laborers are few; 12
15:34 They said, "Seven, and a few small fish. 12
22:14 For many are called, but few are chosen. 12
Mrk 6: 5 he laid his hands upon a few sick people 12
8: 7 they had a few small fish; and having blessed them 12
Lke 10: 2 harvest is plentiful, but the laborers are few 12
13:23 Lord, will those who are saved be few? 12
Joh 2:12 and there they stayed for a few days. 14
Act 17: 4 not a few of the leading women. 12
12 with not a few Greek women of high standing 12
1Pe 3:20 ark, in which a few . . were saved through water. 12
Rev 3: 4 Yet you have still a few names in Sardis 12
2Es 2:13 pray that your days may be few 16
4:33 Why are our years few and evil? 15
7:12 they are few and evil, full of dangers 16
47 that the world to come will bring delight to few 16
48 not just a few of us but almost all 16
51 that the righteous are not many but few 16
52 If you have just a few precious stones 16
60 I will rejoice over the few who shall be saved 16
140 there would probably be left only very few 16
8: 1 but the world to come for the sake of few. 16
3 Many have been created, but few shall be saved. 16
62 but only to you and a few like you. 16
10:57 before the Most High, as but few have been. 16
Tob 4: 8 if few, do not be afraid to give 12
Sir 17: 2 He gave to men few days, a limited time *
18:10 so are a few years in the day of eternity. 12
32: 8 Speak concisely, say much in few words 12
43:32 we have seen but few of his works. 12
Bar 2:13 we are left, few in number, among the nations 12
1Mc 3:17 How can we, few as we are, fight 13
18 It is easy for many to be hemmed in by few 12
18 no difference between saving by many or by few. 12
6:54 Few men were left in the sanctuary 12
7: 1 sailed with a few men to a city by the sea 12
28 I shall come with a few men to see you 12
50 the land of Judah had rest for a few days. 12
9: 9 we are too few. 12
12:45 choose for yourself a few men to stay with you 12
15:10 so that there were few with Trypho. 12
2Mc 8: 6 and put to flight not a few of the enemy. 12
9 in command of no fewer than 20,000 Gentiles 10
10:17 killing no fewer than 20,000. 11
12:34 it happened that a few of the Jews fell. 12
14:30 he gathered not a few of his men 12
3Mc 3:23 they abominate those few among them 12

few *See also* take.

become few 1. *ἐσμικρύνθημεν*

Aza 1:14 For we, O Lord, have become fewer than any nation 1

few in number 1. מִסְפָּר 2. מְעַט 3. *ὀλίγος*

Deu 28:62 multitude, you shall be left few in number; 2
Jer 44:28 shall return . . to the land of Judah, few in number; 1
2Mc 2:21 though few in number 3

few men 1. *ὀλίγος*

2Mc 1:15 Antiochus had come with a few men 1

few things 1. *ὀλίγος*

Rev 2:14 But I have a few things against you 1
Sir 34:10 He that is inexperienced knows few things 1

too few 1. לִמְעַט 2. מעט

2Kg 4: 3 borrow vessels . . empty vessels and not too few. 2
2Ch 29:34 the priests were too few and could not flay all 1

very few 1. מְעַט מִזְעָר

Isa 16:14 those who survive will be very few and feeble. 1

very few in number 1. *ὀλιγοστός*

Sir 48:15 the people were left very few in number 1

fidelity 1. *πίστις*

Tit 2:10 nor to pilfer, but to show entire and true fidelity 1
AEs 13: 3 unchanging good will and steadfast fidelity 1
Sir 1:27 he delights in fidelity and meekness. 1

field 1. אֶרֶץ 2. חוּץ 3. חֵלֶק 4. חֶלְקָה 5. יָגֵב 6. שָׂדֶה 7. שָׂדַי 8. שְׁדֵמָה 9. בַּר (A) 10. *ἀγραυλέω* 11. *ἀγρός* 12. *γεώργιον* 13. *γῆ* 14. *κανών* 15. *πεδίον* 16. *χώρα* 17. *χωρίον* 18. ager 19. agrestis 20. campus

Gen 2: 5 when no plant of the field was yet in the earth 6
5 and no herb of the field had yet sprung up– 6
19 every beast of the field and every bird of the air 6
20 names . . to every beast of the field; 6
3:18 and you shall eat the plants of the field. 6
4: 8 Cain said to Abel . . "Let us go out to the field. 15
8 And when they were in the field 6
23: 9 the cave . . is at the end of his field. 6
11 No, my lord, hear me; I give you the field 6
13 I will give the price of the field; accept it 6
17 the field of Ephron in Mach-pe'lah 6
17 the field with the cave which was in it 6
17 all the trees that were in the field 6
19 the cave of the field of Mach-pe'lah east of Mamre 6
20 The field and the cave that is in it 6
24:63 Isaac went out to meditate in the field 6
65 Who is . . walking in the field to meet us? 6
25: 9 in the cave of Mach-pe'lah, in the field of Ephron 6
10 the field which Abraham purchased 6
27 Esau was a skilful hunter, a man of the field 6
29 Esau came in from the field, and he was famished. 6
27: 3 go out to the field, and hunt game for me 6
5 when Esau went to the field to hunt for game 6
27 the smell of a field which the LORD has blessed! 6
29: 2 As he looked, he saw a well in the field 6
30:14 Reuben went and found mandrakes in the field 6
16 When Jacob came from the field in the evening 6
31: 4 Jacob . . called Rachel and Leah into the field 6
34: 5 but his sons were with the cattle in the field 6
7 came in from the field when they heard of it; 6
28 whatever was in the city and in the field; 6
37: 7 behold, we were binding sheaves in the field 6
15 a man found him wandering in the fields; 6
39: 5 upon all that he had, in house and field. 6
41:48 in every city the food from the fields around it. 6
47:20 for all the Egyptians sold their fields 6
24 shall be your own, as seed for the field and as food 6
49:29 cave that is in the field of Ephron the Hittite 6
30 in the cave that is in the field at Mach-pe'lah 6
30 which Abraham bought with the field from Ephron 6
32 the field and the cave that is in it were 6
50:13 buried him in the cave of the field at Mach-pe'lah 6
13 the cave . . which Abraham bought with the field 6
Exd 1:14 bitter . . in all kinds of work in the field; 6
8:13 the frogs died . . out of the fields. 6
9: 3 upon your cattle which are in the field 6
19 get . . all that you have in the field 6
19 upon every man and beast that is in the field 6
21 left his slaves and his cattle in the field. 6
22 hail . . upon . . every plant of the field 6
25 hail struck down everything . . in the field 6
25 the hail struck down every plant of the field 6
25 hail . . shattered every tree of the field. 6
10: 5 eat every tree of yours which grows in the field 6
15 neither tree nor plant of the field, through all 6
16:25 today you will not find it in the field. 6
22: 5 When a man causes a field or vineyard to be grazed 6
5 beast loose and it feeds in another man's field 6
5 best in his own field and in his own vineyard. 6
6 standing grain or the field is consumed 6
31 flesh that is torn by beasts in the field; 6
23:16 fruits of your labor, of what you sow in the field. 6
16 gather in from the field the fruit of your labor. 6
Lev 14: 7 shall let the living bird go into the open field 6
53 go out of the city into the open field 6
17: 5 sacrifices which they slay in the open field 6
19: 9 you shall not reap your field to its very border 6
19 you shall not sow your field with two kinds of seed 6
23:22 you shall not reap your field to its very border 6
25: 3 Six years you shall sow your field 6
4 shall not sow your field or prune your vineyard 6
12 you shall eat what it yields out of the field 6
31 the houses . . shall be reckoned with the fields 6
34 the fields of common land belonging 6
26: 4 the trees of the field shall yield their fruit 6
27:17 If he dedicates his field from the year 6
18 if he dedicates his field after the jubilee 6
19 if he who dedicates the field wishes to redeem it 6
20 if he does not wish to redeem the field 6
20 sold the field to another man, it shall not be 6
21 the field, when it is released in the jubilee 6
21 holy . . as a field that has been devoted 6
22 If he dedicates to the LORD a field 6
24 In the year of jubilee the field shall return 6
28 no devoted thing . . of his inherited field 6
Num 16:14 given us inheritance of fields and vineyards. 6
19:16 Whoever in the open field touches one who is 6
20:17 We will not pass through field or vineyard 6
21:22 we will not turn aside into field or vineyard; 6
22: 4 as the ox licks up the grass of the field. 6
23 ass turned aside . . and went into the field; 6
23:14 he took him to the field of Zophim, to the top 6
Deu 5:21 not desire your neighbor's house, his field 6
11:15 he will give grass in your fields for your cattle 6
14:22 comes forth from the field year by year. 6
20:19 Are the trees in the field men that they should be 6
24:19 When you reap your harvest in your field 6
19 reap . . and have forgotten a sheaf in the field 6
28: 3 in the city, and blessed shall you be in the field. 6
16 in the city, and cursed shall you be in the field. 6
38 carry much seed into the field, and shall gather 6
32:13 he ate the produce of the field; 6

32 their vine comes from . . the field of Gomor'rah; 8
Jos 15:18 she urged him to ask her father for a field; 6
21:12 the fields . . and its villages had been given 6
Jdg 1:14 to him, she urged him to ask her father for a field; 6
5:18 Naph'tali too, on the heights of the field. 6
9:27 went out into the field, and gathered the grapes 6
32 go by night . . and lie in wait in the fields. 6
42 following day the men went out into the fields. 6
43 took his men . . and laid wait in the fields; 6
44 two companies rushed upon all who were in the fields 6
13: 9 came again to the woman as she sat in the field; 6
19:16 an old man was coming from his work in the field 6
Rut 2: 2 Let me go to the field, and glean among the . . grain 6
3 went and gleaned in the field after the reapers; 6
3 to come to the part of the field belonging to Bo'az 6
8 do not go to glean in another field or leave this 6
9 your eyes be upon the field . . they are reaping 6
17 she gleaned in the field until evening; 6
22 lest in another field you be molested. 6
4: 5 The day you buy the field from the hand of Na'omi 6
1Sm 4: 2 slew about 4,000 men on the field of battle. 6
6:14 The cart came into the field of Joshua 6
18 is a witness to this day in the field of Joshua 6
8:14 the best of your fields and vineyards and olive 6
11: 5 Saul was coming from the field behind the oxen; 6
14:15 there was a panic in the camp, in the field 6
17:44 birds of the air and to the beasts of the field. 6
19: 3 stand beside my father in the field where you are 6
20: 5 but let me go, that I may hide myself in the field 6
11 Come, let us go out into the field. 6
11 they both went out into the field. 6
24 David hid himself in the field; 6
35 In the morning Jonathan went out into the field 6
22: 7 give every one of you fields and vineyards 6
25:15 did not miss anything when we were in the fields 6
2Sm 11:23 The men . . and came out against us in the field; 6
14: 6 they quarreled with one another in the field; 6
30 See, Jo'ab's field is next to mine, and he has barley 4
30 Ab'salom's servants set the field on fire. 4
31 Why have your servants set my field on fire? 4
17: 8 like a bear robbed of her cubs in the field. 6
18: 6 the army went out into the field against Israel; 6
20:12 he carried Ama'sa . . into the field 6
21:10 or the beasts of the field by night. 6
1Kg 16: 4 and any one of his who dies in the field 6
2Kg 4:39 One . . went out into the field to gather herbs 6
8: 6 all the produce of the fields . . until now. 6
9:37 shall be as dung upon the face of the field 6
19:26 and have become like plants of the field 6
23: 4 outside Jerusalem in the fields of the Kidron 8
1Ch 6:56 fields of the city and its villages 6
16:32 let the field exult, and everything in it! 6
27:26 over those who did the work of the field 6
2Ch 26:23 buried him with his fathers in the burial field 6
31: 5 first fruits . . of all the produce of the field; 6
19 sons of Aaron . . in the fields of common land 6
Neh 5: 3 We are mortgaging our fields, our vineyards 6
4 king's tax upon our fields and our vineyards. 6
5 for other men have our fields and our vineyards. 6
11 Return . . their fields, their vineyards 6
11:25 as for the villages, with their fields 6
30 Lachish and its fields 6
12:44 gather . . according to the fields of the towns; 6
13:10 Levites . . had fled each to his field. 6
Job 5:10 upon the earth and sends waters upon the fields; 2
23 in league with the stones of the field 6
23 the beasts of the field shall be at peace with you. 6
24: 6 They gather their fodder in the field 6
Ps 8: 7 sheep and oxen, and also the beasts of the field 6
50:11 all that moves in the field is mine. 6
72:16 from the cities like the grass of the field! 1
78:12 in the land of Egypt, in the fields of Zo'an. 6
43 in Egypt, and his miracles in the fields of Zo'an. 6
80:13 all that move in the field feed on it. 7
96:12 let the field exult, and everything in it! 6
103:15 man . . flourishes like a flower of the field; 6
104:11 they give drink to every beast of the field; 6
107:37 sow fields, and plant vineyards 6
132: 6 in Eph'rathah, we found it in the fields of Ja'ar. 6
144:13 thousands and ten thousands in our fields; 2
Prv 8:26 before he had made the earth with its fields 2
23:10 Do not . . enter the fields of the fatherless; 6
24:27 get everything ready for you in the field; 6
30 I passed by the field of a sluggard 6
27:26 goats the price of a field; 6
31:16 She considers a field and buys it; 6
Ecc 5: 9 an advantage to a land with cultivated fields. 6
Sng 2: 7 by the gazelles or the hinds of the field 6
3: 5 by the gazelles or the hinds of the field 6
7:11 Come, my beloved, let us go forth into the fields 6
Isa 5: 8 who join house to house, who add field to field 6
8 who join house to house, who add field to field 6
16: 8 For the fields of Heshbon languish 8
32:12 Beat upon your breasts for the pleasant fields 6
37:27 and have become like plants of the field 6
40: 6 all its beauty is like the flower of the field. 6
55:12 the trees of the field shall clap their hands. 6
56: 9 All you beasts of the field, come to devour- 6

Jer 4:17 Like keepers of a field are they against her 6
6:12 turned over to others, their fields and wives 6
25 Go not forth into the field, nor walk on the road; 6
7:20 the trees of the field and the fruit of the ground; 6
8:10 I will give . . their fields to conquerors 6
9:22 men shall fall like dung upon the open field 6
12: 4 and the grass of every field wither? 6
13:27 your lewd harlotries, on the hills in the field. 6
14: 5 Even the hind in the field forsakes her newborn 6
18 If I go out into the field, behold, those slain 6
26:18 Zion shall be plowed as a field; 6
27: 6 I have given him also the beasts of the field 6
28:14 I have given to him even the beasts of the field 6
31:40 and all the fields as far as the brook Kidron 8
32: 7 to you and say, 'Buy my field which is at An'athoth 6
8 and said to me, 'Buy my field which is at An'athoth 6
9 And I bought the field at An'athoth from Han'amel 6
15 and fields and vineyards shall again be bought 6
25 Buy the field for money and get witnesses 6
43 Fields shall be bought in this land 6
44 Fields shall be bought for money 6
35: 9 We have no vineyard or field or seed; 6
39:10 gave them vineyards and fields at the same time. 5
41: 8 wheat, barley, oil, and honey hidden in the fields. 6
Lam 4: 9 stricken by want of the fruits of the field. 6
Ezk 7:15 he that is in the field dies by the sword; 6
16: 5 but you were cast out on the open field 6
7 and grow up like a plant of the field. 6
17:24 the trees of the field shall know that I the LORD 6
29: 5 you shall fall upon the open field 6
31: 6 beasts of the field brought forth their young; 6
13 will be all the beasts of the field. 6
15 the trees of the field shall faint because of it. 6
32: 4 on the ground, on the open field I will fling you 6
33:27 him that is in the open field I will give 6
34:27 the trees of the field shall yield their fruit 6
36:30 I will make . . the increase of the field abundant 6
38:20 the beasts of the field, and all creeping things 6
39: 5 You shall fall in the open field; for I have spoken 6
10 they will not need to take wood out of the field 6
17 to all beasts of the field, 'Assemble and come 6
Dan 2:38 given . . the beasts of the field, and the birds 6
4:12 beasts of the field found shade under it 9
15 amid the tender grass of the field. 9
21 under which beasts of the field found shade 9
23 iron and bronze, in the tender grass of the field; 9
23 let his lot be with the beasts of the field 9
25 dwelling shall be with the beasts of the field; 9
32 dwelling shall be with the beasts of the field; 9
Hos 2:12 and the beasts of the field shall devour them. 6
18 covenant on that day with the beasts of the field 6
4: 3 in it languish, and also the beasts of the field 6
5: 7 the new moon shall devour them with their fields. 3
10: 4 poisonous weeds in the furrows of the field. 6
12:11 like stone heaps on the furrows of the field. 6
Jol 1:10 The fields are laid waste, the ground mourns; 6
11 because the harvest of the field has perished. 6
12 all the trees of the field are withered; 6
19 and flame has burned all the trees of the field. 6
2:22 Fear not, you beasts of the field 6
Ams 4: 7 one field would be rained upon 4
7 and the field on which it did not rain withered; 4
Mic 2: 2 They covet fields, and seize them; 6
4 Among our captors he divides our fields. 6
3:12 because of you Zion shall be plowed as a field; 6
Hab 3:17 the olive fail and the fields yield no food 8
Zep 2:14 in the midst of her, all the beasts of the field; 13
Zec 10: 1 to every one the vegetation in the field. 6
Mal 3:11 your vine in the field shall not fail to bear 6
Mat 6:28 about clothing? Consider the lilies of the field 11
30 the grass of the field, which today is alive 11
13:24 to a man who sowed good seed in his field; 11
27 Sir, did you not sow good seed in your field? 11
31 which a man took and sowed in his field; 11
36 the parable of the weeds of the field. 11
38 the field is the world 11
44 treasure hidden in a field 11
44 sells all that he has and buys that field. 11
24:18 let him who is in the field not turn back 11
40 Then two men will be in the field 11
27: 7 and bought with them the potter's field 11
8 that field has been called the Field of Blood 11
8 has been called the Field of Blood to this day. 11
10 and they gave them for the potter's field 11
Mrk 11: 8 which they had cut from the fields. 11
13:16 let him who is in the field not turn back 11
Lke 2: 8 there were shepherds out in the field 10
12:28 the grass which is alive in the field today 11
14:18 The first said to him, 'I have bought a field 11
15:15 who sent him into his fields to feed swine. 11
25 Now his elder son was in the field 11
17: 7 say to him when he has come in from the field 11
31 likewise let him who is in the field not turn back. 11
Joh 4: 5 near the field that Jacob gave to his son Joseph. 17
35 see how the fields are already white for harvest 16
Act 1:18 bought a field with the reward of his wickedness; 17
19 so that the field was called . . Akel'dama 17
19 Akel'dama, that is, Field of Blood 17

4:37 sold a field which belonged to him 11
1Co 3: 9 For we are God's fellow workers; you are God's field 12
2Co 10:15 our field among you may be greatly enlarged 14
16 work already done in another's field. 14
Jas 5: 4 the wages of the laborers who mowed your fields 16
2Es 4:29 the field where the good has been sown 18
7:65 but let the beasts of the field be glad 19
9:17 As is the field, so is the seed 18
24 go into a field of flowers 20
24 and eat only of the flowers of the field 20
26 I went . . into the field which is called Ardat 20
26 and ate of the plants of the field 18
10: 3 and fled, and came to this field, as you see. 20
32 I did as you directed, and went out into the field 20
51 Therefore I told you to remain in the field 20
53 Therefore I told you to go into the field 18
12:51 I sat in the field seven days 20
51 and I ate only of the flowers of the field 18
13:57 Then I arose and walked in the field 20
14:37 we proceeded to the field, and remained there. 20
15:41 all the fields and all the streams may be filled 20
16:28 out of the field, two who have hidden themselves 18
32 and its fields shall be for briers 18
77 as a field is choked with underbrush 18
Jdt 2:27 burned all their fields 11
3: 3 all our wheat fields, and our flocks and herds 15
4: 5 since their fields had recently been harvested. 15
6: 4 their fields will be full of their dead 15
8: 3 men who were binding sheaves in the field 15
3 the field between Dothan and Balamon. 11
7 cattle, and fields 11
11: 7 the beasts of the field and the cattle 11
Sir 24:14 like a beautiful olive tree in the field 15
Bel 1:33 was going into the field to take it to the reapers. 15
1Mc 16:10 the towers that were in the fields of Azotus 11

cucumber field 1. מִקְשָׁה
Isa 1: 8 Zion is left . . like a lodge in a cucumber field 1
Jer 10: 5 idols are like scarecrows in a cucumber field 1

fruitful field 1. כַּרְמֶל
Isa 16:10 gladness are taken away from the fruitful field; 1
29:17 Lebanon shall be turned into a fruitful field 1
17 the fruitful field shall be regarded as a forest? 1
32:15 and the wilderness becomes a fruitful field 1
15 and the fruitful field is deemed a forest. 1
16 and righteousness abide in the fruitful field. 1

open field 1. שָׂדֶה
2Sm 11:11 Jo'ab and . . are camping in the open field; 1

fierce 1. אַכְזָר 2. זַעַם 3. חדד 4. חָרוֹן 5. חֳרִי 6. עַז 7. קשה 8. קָשֶׁה 9. *ἀκμή* 10. *ἀνήμερος* 11. *βαρύς* 12. *εὔτονος* 13. *θυμός* 14. *καρτερός* 15. *μέγας* 16. *χαλεπός*
Gen 49: 7 Cursed be their anger, for it is fierce; 6
Exd 32:12 Turn from thy fierce wrath, and repent of this 4
Num25: 4 that the fierce anger of the LORD may turn away 4
32:14 increase still more the fierce anger of the LORD 4
1Sm 20:34 And Jonathan rose from the table in fierce anger 5
28:18 carry out his fierce wrath against Am'alek 4
2Sm 2:17 And the battle was very fierce that day; 8
19:43 But the words of the men of Judah were fiercer 7
Ezr 10:14 till the fierce wrath of our God over this matter 4
Job 4:10 The roar of the lion, the voice of the fierce lion •
20:23 God will send his fierce anger into him 4
41:10 No one is so fierce that he dares to stir him up. 1
Ps 78:49 He let loose on them his fierce anger, wrath 4
Isa 7: 4 at the fierce anger of Rezin and Syria 5
13: 9 the LORD comes . . with wrath and fierce anger 4
13 the LORD of hosts in the day of his fierce anger. 4
19: 4 a fierce king will rule over them 6
27: 8 he removed them with his fierce blast 8
Jer 4: 8 the fierce anger of the LORD has not turned back 4
12:13 because of the fierce anger of the LORD. 4
25:37 because of the fierce anger of the LORD. 4
38 and because of his fierce anger. 4
30:24 The fierce anger of the LORD will not turn back 4
49:37 I will bring evil upon them, my fierce anger 4
51:45 Let every man save his life from the fierce anger 4
Lam 1:12 LORD inflicted on the day of his fierce anger. 4
2: 3 cut down in fierce anger all the might of Israel; 5
6 and in his fierce indignation has spurned king 2
Hos 11: 9 I will not execute my fierce anger 4
Jon 3: 9 God may yet repent and turn from his fierce anger 4
Hab 1: 8 horses . . more fierce than the evening wolves; 3
Zep 2: 2 there comes upon you the fierce anger of the LORD 4
Mat 8:28 so fierce that no one could pass that way. 16
Act 20:29 fierce wolves will come in among you 11
2Ti 3: 3 profligates, fierce, haters of good 10
Rev 16: 9 men were scorched by the fierce heat 15
AEs 15: 7 he looked at her in fierce anger 9
Sir 10:18 nor fierce anger for those born of women. 13
2Mc 10:29 When the battle became fierce 14
4Mc 7:10 O elder, fiercer than fire 12
16: 2 a woman has despised the fiercest tortures. 15

fierce *See also* anger, attack, wrath.

fierce man 1. עַז
Ps 59: 3 fierce men band themselves against me. 1

fiercely *See* attack, blow.

fierceness 1. חָרוֹן 2. רַעַשׁ
Deu 13:17 LORD may turn from the fierceness of his anger 1
2Kg 23:26 turn from the fierceness of his great wrath 1
Job 39:24 With fierceness and rage he swallows the ground; 2

fiery 1. אֵשׁ 2. שָׂרָף 3. נוּר (A) 4. διὰ πυρός 5. διάπυρος 6. ἐμπυριστής 7. πῦρ 8. πύρπνοος 9. πυρώδης 10. φλόξ
Num21: 6 LORD sent fiery serpents among the people 2
8 Make a fiery serpent, and set it on a pole; 2
Deu 8:15 wilderness, with its fiery serpents 2
Ps 78:14 with a cloud, and all the night with a fiery light. 1
Dan 3: 6 cast into a burning fiery furnace. 3
11 cast into a burning fiery furnace. 3
15 cast into a burning fiery furnace; 3
17 able to deliver us from the burning fiery furnace; 3
20 cast them into the burning fiery furnace. 3
21 cast into the burning fiery furnace. 3
23 fell bound into the burning fiery furnace. 3
26 near to the door of the burning fiery furnace 3
7: 9 throne was fiery flames, its wheels were burning 3
Wis 11:18 such as breathe out fiery breath 8
Sir 36: 9 be consumed in the fiery wrath 7
43: 4 it breathes out fiery vapors 9
Aza 1:26 and drove the fiery flame out of the furnace 7
66 the midst of the burning fiery furnace 10
3Mc 6: 6 moistening the fiery furnace with dew 5
4Mc 7:11 conquered the fiery angel 6
13: 5 who were not turned back by fiery agonies? 4
16: 3 the raging fiery furnace of Mishael 7
21 were hurled into the fiery furnace 7

fiery *See also* heat, ordeal, rage, shaft.

fifteen 1. חֲמֵשׁ עֶשְׂרֵה 2. δεκαπέντε
Gen 7:20 covering them fifteen cubits deep. 1
Exd 27:14 the gate shall be fifteen cubits, with three 1
15 the hangings shall be fifteen cubits 1
38:14 hangings . . were fifteen cubits, with three 1
15 by the gate . . were hangings of fifteen cubits 1
Lev 27: 7 then your valuation for a male shall be fifteen 1
2Sm 9:10 Now Ziba had fifteen sons and twenty servants. 1
19:17 Ziba . . with his fifteen sons and his twenty 1
1Kg 7: 3 upon the 45 pillars, fifteen in each row. 1
2Kg 14:17 Amazi'ah . . lived fifteen years after the death 1
20: 6 And I will add fifteen years to your life. 1
2Ch 25:25 Amazi'ah . . lived fifteen years after the death 1
Isa 38: 5 behold, I will add fifteen years to your life. 1
Hos 3: 2 So I bought her for fifteen shekels of silver 1
Act 27:28 they sounded again and found fifteen fathoms. 2
Gal 1:18 remained with him fifteen days. 2

fifteenth 1. חֲמֵשׁ עֶשְׂרֵה 2. πεντεκαιδέκατος
Exd 16: 1 on the fifteenth day of the second month 1
Lev 23: 6 on the fifteenth day of the same month 1
34 On the fifteenth day of this seventh month 1
39 On the fifteenth day of the seventh month 1
Num28:17 on the fifteenth day of this month is a feast; 1
29:12 On the fifteenth day of the seventh month 1
33: 3 set out . . the fifteenth day of the first month; 1
1Kg 12:32 a feast on the fifteenth day of the eighth month 1
33 on the fifteenth day in the eighth month 1
2Kg 14:23 In the fifteenth year of Amazi'ah the son of Jo'ash 1
1Ch 24:14 the fifteenth to Bilgah, the sixteenth to Immer 1
25:22 fifteenth, to Jer'emoth, his sons and his brethren 1
2Ch 15:10 in the third month of the fifteenth year 1
Est 9:18 gathered . . and rested on the fifteenth day 1
21 Adar and also the fifteenth day of the same 1
Ezk 32:17 on the fifteenth day of the month 1
45:25 seventh month, on the fifteenth day of the month 1
Lke 3: 1 In the fifteenth year of the reign of Tiber'ius 2
AEs 10:13 on the fourteenth and fifteenth of that month 2
1Mc 1:54 Now on the fifteenth day of Chislev 2
2Mc 11:33 Farewell. The 148th year, Xanthicus fifteenth. 2
38 Farewell. The 148th year, Xanthicus fifteenth. 2

fifth 1. חֲמִישִׁי 2. חָמֵשׁ 3. πέμπτος 4. quintus
Gen 1:23 evening and there was morning, a fifth day 1
30:17 she conceived and bore Jacob a fifth son. 1
Lev 19:25 But in the fifth year you may eat of their fruit 1
Num 7:36 On the fifth day Shelu'mi-el . . of Simeon 1
29:26 On the fifth day nine bulls, two rams, fourteen 1
33:38 died . . on the first day of the fifth month. 1
Jos 19:24 The fifth lot came out for the tribe of Asher 1
Jdg 19: 8 on the fifth day he arose early in the morning 1
2Sm 3: 4 and the fifth, Shephati'ah the son of Abi'tal; 1
1Kg 14:25 In the fifth year of King Rehobo'am 1
2Kg 8:16 In the fifth year of Joram the son of Ahab 2
25: 8 In the fifth month, on the seventh day of the month 1
1Ch 2:14 Nethan'el the fourth, Raddai the fifth 1
3: 3 the fifth Shephati'ah, by Abi'tal; 1
8: 2 Nohah the fourth, and Rapha the fifth. 1
12:10 Mishman'nah fourth, Jeremiah fifth 1
24: 9 the fifth to Malchi'jah, the sixth to Mij'amin 1
25:12 fifth to Nethani'ah, his sons and his brethren 1
26: 3 Elam the fifth, Jehoha'nan the sixth, Eli-e-ho-e'nai 1
4 O'bed-e'dom had sons . . Nethan'el the fifth 1
27: 8 The fifth commander . . was Shamhuth 1
8 commander, for the fifth month, was Shamhuth 1
2Ch 12: 2 In the fifth year of King Rehobo'am 1
Ezr 7: 8 came to Jerusalem in the fifth month 1
9 first day of the fifth month he came to Jerusalem 1
Neh 6: 5 Sanbal'lat for the fifth time sent his servant 1
Jer 1: 3 the captivity of Jerusalem in the fifth month. 1
28: 1 in the fifth month of the fourth year, Hanani'ah 1
36: 9 In the fifth year of Jehoi'akim the son of Josi'ah 1
52:12 In the fifth month, on the tenth day 1
Ezk 1: 1 in the fourth month, on the fifth day of the month 2
2 On the fifth day of the month (it was the fifth year 2
2 the fifth year of the exile of King Jehoi'achin 1
8: 1 in the sixth month, on the fifth day of the month 2
20: 1 In the seventh year, in the fifth month 1
33:21 in the tenth month, on the fifth day of the month 2
Zec 7: 3 Should I mourn and fast in the fifth month 1
5 When you fasted and mourned in the fifth month 1
8:19 fast of the fourth month, and the fast of the fifth 1
Rev 6: 9 When he opened the fifth seal, I saw 3
9: 1 And the fifth angel blew his trumpet, and I saw 3
16:10 The fifth angel poured his bowl on the throne 3
21:20 the fifth onyx, the sixth carnelian 3
1Es 8: 6 the fifth month (this was the king's seventh year); 3
6 arrived . . on the new moon of the fifth month 3
2Es 6:47 On the fifth day thou didst command 4
7:85 The fifth way, they shall see how the habitations 4
96 The fifth order, they rejoice 4
Bar 1: 2 in the fifth year, on the seventh day of the month 3
2Mc 7:15 Next they brought forward the fifth 3
10:35 at dawn of the fifth day 3
3Mc 6:38 was set for the fifth to the seventh of Epeiph 3
4Mc 11: 1 the fifth leaped up, saying 3

fifties *See* charge.

fifty 1. חֲמִשִּׁים 2. πεντήκοντα
Exd 18:21 rulers of thousands, of hundreds, of fifties 1
25 rulers of thousands, of hundreds, of fifties, 1
Deu 1:15 heads over you, commanders . . of fifties 1
1Sm 8:12 commanders of . . and commanders of fifties 1
1Kg 18: 4 took . . prophets and hid them by fifties in a cave 1
13 how I hid 100 men . . by fifties in a cave 1
2Kg 1:14 the two former captains . . with their fifties; 1
Mrk 6:40 sat down in groups, by hundreds and by fifties. 2

fig 1. פַּגָּה 2. תְּאֵנָה 3. σῦκον
Gen 3: 7 they sewed fig leaves together 2
Num13:23 they brought also some pomegranates and figs. 2
20: 5 It is no place for grain, or figs, or vines 2
2Kg 20: 7 Bring a cake of figs. And let them take and lay it 2
Neh 13:15 also wine, grapes, figs, and all kinds of burdens 2
Sng 2:13 The fig tree puts forth its figs 1
Isa 38:21 Now Isaiah had said, "Let them take a cake of figs 2
Jer 8:13 are no grapes on the vine, nor figs on the fig tree; 2
24: 1 showed me this vision: Behold, two baskets of figs 2
2 One basket had very good figs, like first-ripe 2
2 had very good figs, like first-ripe figs 2
2 but the other basket had very bad figs 2
3 I said, "Figs, the good figs very good 2
3 the good figs very good, and the bad figs very bad 2
3 the good figs very good, and the bad figs very bad *
5 Like these good figs, so I will regard as good 2
8 the bad figs which are so bad they cannot be eaten 2
29:17 I will make them like vile figs which are so bad 2
Mat 7:16 gathered from thorns, or figs from thistles? 3
Mrk 11:13 it was not the season for figs. 3
Lke 6:44 figs are not gathered from thorns 3
Jas 3:12 a fig tree . . yield olives, or a grapevine figs? 3

early fig 1. פַּג
Ezk 27:17 wheat, olives and early figs, honey, oil, and balm. 1

first-ripe fig 1. בִּכּוּרָה 2. בִּכּוּרִים
Isa 28: 4 will be like a first-ripe fig before the summer 1
Mic 7: 1 no first-ripe fig which my soul desires. 1
Nah 3:12 are like fig trees with first-ripe figs– 2

fig tree 1. תְּאֵנָה 2. συκῆ
Deu 8: 8 a land of . . vines and fig trees and pomegranates 1
Jdg 9:10 the trees said to the fig tree, 'Come you, and reign 1
11 fig tree said . . 'Shall I leave my sweetness 1
1Kg 4:25 every man under his vine and under his fig tree 1
2Kg 18:31 eat of his . . vine, and every one of his own fig tree 1
Ps 105:33 He smote their vines and fig trees 1
Prv 27:18 He who tends a fig tree will eat its fruit 1
Sng 2:13 The fig tree puts forth its figs 1
Isa 34: 4 like leaves falling from the fig tree. 1
36:16 of his own vine, and every one of his own fig tree 1
Jer 5:17 they shall eat up your vines and your fig trees; 1
8:13 are no grapes on the vine, nor figs on the fig tree; 1
Hos 2:12 And I will lay waste her vines and her fig trees 1
9:10 first fruit on the fig tree, in its first season 1
Jol 1: 7 and splintered my fig trees; 1
12 The vine withers, the fig tree languishes. 1
2:22 and fig tree and vine give their full yield. 1
Ams 4: 9 your fig trees and your olive trees the locust 1
Mic 4: 4 every man under his vine and under his fig tree 1
Nah 3:12 All your fortresses are like fig trees 1
Hab 3:17 Though the fig tree do not blossom 1
Hag 2:19 Do the vine, the fig tree, the pomegranate 1
Zec 3:10 under his vine and under his fig tree. 1
Mat 21:19 seeing a fig tree by the wayside he went to it 2
19 And the fig tree withered at once. 2
20 How did the fig tree wither at once? 2
21 not only do what has been done to the fig tree 2
24:32 From the fig tree learn its lesson 2
Mrk 11:13 seeing in the distance a fig tree in leaf 2
20 they saw the fig tree withered away to its roots. 2
21 The fig tree which you cursed has withered. 2
13:28 From the fig tree learn its lesson 2
Lke 13: 6 A man had a fig tree planted in his vineyard 2
7 I have come seeking fruit on this fig tree 2
21:29 Look at the fig tree, and all the trees; 2
Joh 1:48 when you were under the fig tree, I saw you. 2
50 Because I said to you, I saw you under the fig tree 2
Jas 3:12 Can a fig tree, my brethren, yield olives 2
Rev 6:13 as the fig tree sheds its winter fruit 2
1Mc 14:12 Each man sat under his vine and his fig tree 2

fight 1. לחם 2. מִלְחָמָה 3. מַצָּה 4. נכה 5. צבא 6. ἀγών 7. ἀγωνίζομαι 8. εἰς παράταξιν 9. ἐναγωνίζομαι 10. μάχη 11. μάχομαι 12. νομή 13. παλαίω 14. παρατάσσω 15. ποιέω 16. ποιέω μάχην 17. πολεμέω 18. πολεμέω τὸν πόλεμον 19. πόλεμος 20. στρατεύω 21. συμμαχέω 22. συνάπτω 23. συνίστημι 24. ὑπερμαχέω 25. pugna 26. pugno
Exd 1:10 lest they . . fight against us and escape 1
14:14 The LORD will fight for you 1
25 the LORD fights for them against the Egyptians. 1
17: 8 came Am'alek and fought with Israel at Reph'idim. 1
9 Choose for us men, and go out, fight with Am'alek; 1
10 So Joshua . . fought with Am'alek; 1
Num21: 1 he fought against Israel, and took some 1
23 came to Jahaz, and fought against Israel. 1
26 Sihon . . fought against the former king of Moab 1
22:11 curse them for me; perhaps I shall be able to fight 1
Deu 1:30 The LORD your God . . will himself fight for you 1
41 sinned against the LORD; we will go up and fight 1
42 Do not go up or fight, for I am not in the midst of you; 1
3:22 for it is the LORD your God who fights for you.' 1
20: 4 LORD . . fight for you against your enemies 1
10 When you draw near to a city to fight against it 1
Jos 8: 1 take all the fighting men with you, and arise 2
3 Joshua arose, and all the fighting men, to go up 2
11 And all the fighting men who were with him went up 2
9: 2 they gathered . . to fight Joshua and Israel. 1
10:14 for the LORD fought for Israel. 1
25 do to all your enemies against whom you fight. 1
29 Joshua passed on . . and fought against Libnah 1
42 the LORD God of Israel fought for Israel. 1
11: 5 and came and encamped . . to fight with Israel. 1
19:47 the Danites went up and fought against Leshem 1
23: 3 for it is the LORD your God who has fought for you. 1
10 since it is the LORD your God who fights for you 1
24: 8 they fought with you, and I gave them 1
9 Then Balak . . arose and fought against Israel; 1
11 and the men of Jericho fought against you 1
Jdg 1: 1 against the Canaanites, to fight against them? 1
3 that we may fight against the Canaanites; 1
5 upon Ado'ni-be'zek at Bezek, and fought against him 1
8 the men of Judah fought against Jerusalem 1
9 Judah went down to fight against the Canaanites 1
5:19 The kings came, they fought; then fought the kings 1
19 then fought the kings of Canaan, at Ta'anach 1
20 From heaven fought the stars, from their courses 1
20 from their courses they fought against Sis'era. 1
8: 1 not to call us when you went to fight with Mid'ian? 1
9:17 for my father fought for you, and risked his life 1
38 whom you despised? Go out now and fight with them. 1
39 Ga'al went out . . and fought with Abim'elech. 1
45 Abim'elech fought against the city all that day; 1
52 came to the tower, and fought against it, and drew 1
10: 9 crossed the Jordan to fight also against Judah 1
18 Who . . will begin to fight against the Ammonites? 1
11: 6 our leader, that we may fight with the Ammonites. 1
8 you may go with us and fight with the Ammonites 1
9 bring me home again to fight with the Ammonites 1
12 that you have come to me to fight against my land? 1
20 and encamped at Jahaz, and fought with Israel. 1
32 over to the Ammonites to fight against them; 1
12: 1 Why did you cross over to fight against 1
3 have you come up to me this day, to fight against me? 1
4 gathered all . . Gilead and fought with E'phraim; 1
1Sm 4: 9 to you; acquit yourselves like men and fight. 1
10 the Philistines fought, and Israel was defeated 1
8:20 and go out before us and fight our battles. 1
12: 9 and they fought against them. 1
13: 5 the Philistines mustered to fight with Israel 1
14:47 When Saul . . he fought against all his enemies 1
52 There was hard fighting . . all the days of Saul; 2
15:18 and fight against them until they are consumed. 1
17: 9 If he is able to fight with me and kill me 1

10 give me a man, that we may fight together. 1
19 in the valley . . fighting with the Philistines. 1
32 servant will go and fight with this Philistine. 1
33 You are not able to go . . to fight with him; 1
18:17 be valiant . . and fight the LORD's battles. 1
19: 8 David went out and fought with the Philistines 1
23: 1 the Philistines are fighting against Kei'lah 1
5 David and his men . . fought with the Philistines 1
25:28 my lord is fighting the battles of the LORD; 1
28: 1 gathered . . for war, to fight against Israel. 1
29: 8 go and fight against the enemies of my lord 1
31: 1 Now the Philistines fought against Israel; 1
2Sm 2:28 pursued . . no more, nor did they fight any more. 1
8:10 had fought against Hadade'zer and defeated him; 1
10:14 Jo'ab returned from fighting . . the Ammonites *
17 Syrians . . against David, and fought with him. 1
11:15 Set Uri'ah in the . . hardest fighting 2
17 the men of the city came out and fought with Jo'ab; 1
18 and told David all the news about the fighting; 2
19 telling all . . about the fighting to the king 2
20 he says . . 'Why did you go so near the city to fight? 1
12:26 Now Jo'ab fought against Rabbah of the Ammonites 1
27 Jo'ab . . said, "I have fought against Rabbah; 1
29 went to Rabbah, and fought against it and took it. 1
18: 6 the battle was fought in the forest of E'phraim. *
1Kg 12:21 to fight against the house of Israel 1
24 You shall not go up or fight against your kinsmen 1
20: 1 and besieged Sama'ria, and fought against it. 1
26 and went up to Aphek, to fight against Israel. 2
22:31 Fight with neither small nor great, but only 1
32 So they turned to fight against him; 1
2Kg 3:21 that the kings had come up to fight against them 1
9:15 when he fought with Haz'ael king of Syria.) 1
10: 3 and fight for your master's house. 1
12:17 Haz'ael . . went up and fought against Gath 1
13:12 the might with which he fought against Amazi'ah 1
17 For you shall fight the Syrians in Aphek until 4
14:15 acts of Jeho'ash . . and how he fought with Amazi'ah 1
28 acts of Jerobo'am . . and his might, how he fought 1
19: 8 and found the king . . fighting against Libnah; 1
1Ch 10: 1 Now the Philistines fought against Israel; 1
18:10 because he had fought against Hadade'zer 1
19:17 against the Syrians, they fought with him. 1
2Ch 11: 1 180,000 chosen warriors, to fight against Israel 1
4 shall not go up or fight against your brethren. 1
13:12 O sons of Israel, do not fight against the LORD 1
18:30 Fight with neither small nor great 1
31 So they turned to fight against him; 1
20:17 You will not need to fight in this battle; 1
29 LORD had fought against the enemies of Israel. 1
22: 6 when he fought against Haz'ael king of Syria. 1
27: 5 He fought with the king of the Ammonites 1
32: 2 Sennach'erib . . intended to fight against 2
8 the LORD . . to help us and to fight our battles. 1
35:20 Neco king of Egypt went up to fight at Car'chemish 1
22 disguised himself in order to fight with him. 1
Neh 4: 8 together to come and fight against Jerusalem 1
14 fight for your brethren, your sons 1
20 rally to us there. Our God will fight for us. 1
Ps 35: 1 fight against those who fight against me! 1
56: 2 for many fight against me proudly. 1
Isa 19: 2 they will fight, every man against his brother 1
20: 1 came to Ashdod and fought against it and took it,– 1
29: 7 all the nations that fight against Ariel 5
7 all that fight against her and her stronghold 5
8 the nations be that fight against Mount Zion. 5
30:32 with brandished arm he will fight with them. 1
31: 4 LORD . . will come down to fight upon Mount Zion 5
37: 8 the king of Assyria fighting against Libnah; 1
9 He has set out to fight against you. 1
58: 4 you fast only to quarrel and to fight and to hit 3
63:10 be their enemy, and himself fought against them. 1
Jer 1:19 They will fight against you; 1
15:20 they will fight against you 1
21: 4 you are fighting against the king of Babylon 1
5 I myself will fight against you 1
32: 5 though you fight against the Chalde'ans 1
24 the Chalde'ans who are fighting against it. 1
29 Chalde'ans who are fighting against this city 1
33: 5 The Chalde'ans are coming in to fight 1
34: 1 the peoples were fighting against Jerusalem 1
7 king of Babylon was fighting against Jerusalem 1
22 they will fight against it, and take it, and burn it 1
37: 8 And the Chalde'ans shall come back and fight 1
10 army of Chalde'ans who are fighting against you 1
41:12 and went to fight against Ish'mael 1
51:30 The warriors of Babylon have ceased fighting 1
Dan 10:20 return to fight against the prince of Persia; 1
11:11 come out and fight with the king of the north; 1
Zec 10: 5 they shall fight because the LORD is with them 1
14: 3 will go forth and fight against those nations 1
3 as when he fights on a day of battle. 1
14 even Judah will fight against Jerusalem. 1
Joh 18:36 my servants would fight 7
2Co 7: 5 fighting without and fear within. 10
1Ti 6:12 Fight the good fight of the faith 7
12 Fight the good fight of the faith 6
2Ti 4: 7 I have fought the good fight 7
7 I have fought the good fight 6
Jas 4: 1 and what causes fightings among you? 10
2 you . . cannot obtain; so you fight and wage war. 11
Rev 12: 7 Michael . . angels fighting against the dragon; 17
7 and the dragon and his angels fought 17
13: 4 Who is like the beast, and who can fight against it? 17
1Es 1:28 tried to fight with him 17
2Es 13: 8 all . . were much afraid, yet dared to fight. 26
11 multitude which was prepared to fight 26
15:15 and nation shall rise up to fight against nation 25
Jdt 7:11 Therefore, my lord, do not fight against them 17
AEs 11: 6 great dragons came forward, both ready to fight 13
7 to fight against the nation of the righteous 17
Sir 4:28 the Lord God will fight for you. 17
8:16 Do not fight with a wrathful man 16
29:13 will fight on your behalf against your enemy. 17
46: 6 he was fighting in the sight of the Lord 19
1Mc 1: 2 He fought many battles, conquered strongholds 23
2:40 refuse to fight with the Gentiles for our lives 17
41 fight against every man who comes to attack us 17
66 and fight the battle against the peoples. 17
3: 2 they gladly fought for Israel. 18
10 a large force . . to fight against Israel. 17
17 fight against so great and strong a multitude 17
21 we fight for our lives and our laws. 17
43 fight for our people and the sanctuary. 17
58 to fight with these Gentiles 17
4:18 stand now against our enemies and fight them 17
41 to fight against those in the citadel 17
5:21 fought many battles against the Gentiles 22
32 Fight today for your brethren! 17
35 fought against it and took it 17
39 ready to come and fight against you 19
50 he fought against the city 17
56 the heroic war they had fought. 15
65 fought the sons of Esau in the land to the south 17
6:31 many days they fought and built engines of war; 17
31 burned these with fire, and fought manfully. 17
37 four armed men who fought from there 17
52 fought for many days. 17
63 he fought against him 17
7:28 Let there be no fighting between me and you 10
8: 6 who went to fight against them 19
32 fight you on sea and on land.' 17
9: 8 We may be able to fight them 17
9 let us come back with our brethren and fight them; 17
30 to fight our battle. 17
44 Let us rise up now and fight for our lives 17
64 he fought against it for many days 17
68 They fought with Bacchides 17
10:15 the battles that . . his brothers had fought 15
76 So they fought against it 17
11:41 they kept fighting against Israel. 17
46 began to fight. 17
50 and make the Jews stop fighting against us 17
55 they fought against Demetrius 17
65 and fought against it for many days and hemmed it in. 17
12:41 with 40,000 picked fighting men 8
51 they would fight for their lives *
13: 9 Fight our battles 17
14:13 No one was left in the land to fight them 19
26 they have fought and repulsed Israel's enemies 17
32 then Simon rose up and fought for his nation 17
15:26 2,000 picked men, to fight for him 21
16: 2 have fought the wars of Israel from our youth 17
3 go out and fight for our nation 24
2Mc 1:12 those who fought against the holy city. 14
5:14 40,000 in hand-to-hand fighting 12
8:16 exhorted them . . to fight nobly 7
10:17 and beat off all who fought upon the wall 11
21 to fight against them. *
28 the other made rage their leader in the fight. 6
12:11 After a hard fight 10
36 his men had been fighting for a long time 11
13:14 exhorting his men to fight nobly to the death 7
15:27 fighting with their hands 7
3Mc 1: 4 When a bitter fight resulted 10
4Mc 9:24 Fight the sacred and noble battle for religion. 20
16:16 Fight zealously for our ancestral law. 9

fight *See also* join.

fight against 1. לחם 2. ἀντιπαρατάσσω 3. παρεμβάλλω 4. πολεμέω

2Sm 21:15 and they fought against the Philistines; 1
1Kg 20:23 let us fight against them in the plain 1
25 we will fight against them in the plain 1
2Kg 8:29 at Ramah, when he fought against Haz'ael 1
19: 9 Behold, he has set out to fight against you 1
Ps 35: 1 fight against those who fight against me! 1
1Es 2:26 this city from of old has fought against kings 2
AEs 14:13 to hate the man who is fighting against us 4
1Mc 6:57 the place against which we are fighting is strong 3
13:47 and stopped fighting against them 4

fight against God 1. θεομαχέω

2Mc 7:19 for having tried to fight against God! 1

fight at one's side 1. συμμαχέω

4Mc 3: 4 reason can fight at our side 1

fight hand to hand 1. ἐμπλέκω

2Mc 15:17 by fighting hand to hand with all courage 1

fight off 1. ἀμύνω

Wis 11: 3 and fought off their foes. 1

fight on the side 1. συμμαχέω 2. σύμμαχος

2Mc 10:16 after . . beseeching God to fight on their side 2
11:13 because the mighty God fought on their side 1

fight together 1. חרב

2Kg 3:23 the kings have surely fought together 1

fight with a beast 1. θηριομαχέω

1Co 15:32 I fought with beasts at Ephesus 1

fight with one another 1. נצה

Deu 25:11 When men fight with one another, and the wife 1

figs *See* cake.

figure 1. דְּמוּת 2. כְּלִי 3. מַשְׂכִּית 4. סֶמֶל 5. פִּתּוּחַ 6. תַּבְנִית 7. εἶδος 8. ἡλικία 9. τύπος

Lev 26: 1 you shall not set up a figured stone in your land 3
Deu 4:16 a graven image . . in the form of any figure 4
1Sm 6: 8 put in a box at its side the figures of gold 2
15 and the box . . in which were the golden figures 2
1Kg 6:29 with carved figures of cherubim and palm trees 5
2Ch 4: 3 were figures of gourds, for 30 cubits 1
Isa 44:13 he shapes it into the figure of a man 6
Act 7:43 the figures which you made to worship 9
2Es 13: 3 this wind made something like the figure of a man ‡
Wis 15: 4 a figure stained with varied colors 7
Sir 26:17 so is a beautiful face on a stately figure. 8

figure (2) 1. מְלִיצָה 2. παροιμία

Prv 1: 6 to understand a proverb and a figure 1
Joh 10: 6 This figure Jesus used with them 2
16:25 I have said this to you in figures 2
25 when I shall no longer speak to you in figures 2
29 now you are speaking plainly, not in any figure! 2

figured stone 1. מַשְׂכִּית

Num33:52 destroy all their figured stones 1

figurehead 1. παράσημος

Act 28:11 with the Twin Brothers as figurehead. 1

filigree *See* set, setting.

fill 1. מלא 2. סבא 3. שׂבע 4. שָׂבֵעַ 5. שֹׂבַע 6. שָׂבְעָה 7. שׁכר 8. מלא (A) 9. γεμίζω 10. δίδωμι 11. διεμπίμπλημι 12. ἐμπίμπλημι 13. ἐμπληθύνω 14. ἐπιπληρόω 15. καταμεστόω 16. κορέννυμι 17. μεστόω 18. παρίστημι 19. πίμπλημι 20. πληρόω 21. πλήρωσις 22. πλησμονή 23. ποιέω 24. συμπληρόω 25. τρέπω 26. χορτάζω 27. χόω 28. facio 29. impleo 30. repleo

Gen 1:22 and multiply and fill the waters in the seas 1
28 Be fruitful and multiply, and fill the earth 1
6:11 the earth was filled with violence. 1
13 for the earth is filled with violence 1
9: 1 Be fruitful and multiply, and fill the earth. 1
21:19 she went, and filled the skin with water 1
24:16 She went down to the spring, and filled her jar 1
26:15 Philistines had stopped and filled with earth 1
42:25 Joseph gave orders to fill their bags with grain 1
44: 1 Fill the men's sacks with food, as much as they can 1
Exd 1: 7 so that the land was filled with them. 1
2:16 they came . . and filled the troughs to water 1
8:21 and the houses of the Egyptians shall be filled 1
10: 6 they shall fill your houses, and the houses of all 1
15: 9 my desire shall have its fill of them. 1
16:12 in the morning you shall be filled with bread; 3
31: 3 I have filled him with the Spirit of God 1
35:31 he has filled him with the Spirit of God 1
35 He has filled them with ability to do every sort 1
40:34 the glory of the LORD filled the tabernacle. 1
35 the glory of the LORD filled the tabernacle. 1
Lev 9:17 the cereal offering, and filled his hand from it 1
25:19 you will eat your fill, and dwell in it securely 5
Num14:21 as all the earth shall be filled with the glory 1
Deu 6:11 houses full of good things, which you did not fill 1
14:29 shall come and eat and be filled; 3
23:24 neighbor's vineyard . . eat your fill of grapes 6
26:12 that they may eat within your towns and be filled 3
Jos 9:13 these wineskins were new when we filled them 1
Jdg 6:38 dew from the fleece to fill a bowl with water. 1
1Sm 16: 1 Fill your horn with oil, and go; I will send you 1
1Kg 8:10 a cloud filled the house of the LORD 1
11 glory of the LORD filled the house of the LORD. 1
18:33 Fill four jars with water, and pour it 1
35 the water . . filled the trench also with water. 1
20:27 but the Syrians filled the country. 1
2Kg 3:17 that stream-bed shall be filled with water 1
20 till the country was filled with water. 1
10:21 the house . . was filled from one end to the other. 1
21:16 he had filled Jerusalem from one end to another 1
23:14 and filled their places with the bones of men. 1

24: 4 for he filled Jerusalem with innocent blood 1
1Ch 16:32 Let the sea roar, and all that fills it 1
2Ch 5:13 the house of the LORD, was filled with a cloud. 1
14 for the glory of the LORD filled the house of God. 1
7: 1 and the glory of the LORD filled the temple. 1
2 the glory of the LORD filled the LORD's house. 1
16:14 They laid him on a bier which had been filled 1
Ezr 9:11 filled it from end to end with their uncleanness. 1
Neh 9:25 ate, and were filled and became fat, and delighted 3
Est 3: 5 And when Haman saw . . Haman was filled with fury. 1
5: 9 he was filled with wrath against Mor'decai. 1
Job 3:15 princes . . who filled their houses with silver. 1
8:21 He will yet fill your mouth with laughter 1
9:18 get my breath, but fills me with bitterness. 3
10:15 I am filled with disgrace 4
15: 2 fill himself with the east wind? 1
20:23 To fill his belly to the full God will send his 1
22:18 Yet he filled their houses with good things– 1
23: 4 and fill my mouth with arguments. 1
31:31 that has not been filled with his meat?' 3
41: 7 Can you fill his skin with harpoons 1
Ps 10: 7 His mouth is filled with cursing and deceit 1
17:14 May their belly be filled with what thou hast 1
38: 7 For my loins are filled with burning 1
48:10 Thy right hand is filled with victory; 1
51: 8 Fill me with joy and gladness; ‡
71: 8 My mouth is filled with thy praise 1
72:19 may his glory fill the whole earth! Amen and Amen! 1
78:29 they ate and were well filled 3
80: 9 it took deep root and filled the land. 1
81:10 Open your mouth wide, and I will fill it. 1
83:16 Fill their faces with shame, that they may seek 1
104:28 thy hand, they are filled with good things. 3
107: 9 the hungry he fills with good things. 1
110: 6 among the nations, filling them with corpses; 1
126: 2 Then our mouth was filled with laughter 1
129: 7 with which the reaper does not fill his hand 1
147:14 he fills you with the finest of the wheat. 3
Prv 1:13 we shall fill our houses with spoil; 1
3:10 then your barns will be filled with plenty 1
8:21 those who love me, and filling their treasuries. 1
12:21 but the wicked are filled with trouble. 1
14:14 perverse man . . filled with the fruit of his ways 3
24: 4 by knowledge the rooms are filled with all 1
30:22 fool when he is filled with food; 3
Ecc 1: 8 the eye is not . . nor the ear filled with hearing. 1
Isa 2: 7 Their land is filled with silver and gold 1
7 their land is filled with horses 1
8 Their land is filled with idols; 1
6: 1 saw the Lord . . and his train filled the temple. 1
4 and the house was filled with smoke. 1
8: 8 its outspread wings will fill the breadth 1
14:21 and fill the face of the world with cities. 1
21: 3 Therefore my loins are filled with anguish; 1
27: 6 fill the whole world with fruit. 1
33: 5 he will fill Zion with justice 1
56:12 let us fill ourselves with strong drink; 2
65:11 and fill cups of mixed wine for Destiny; 1
Jer 13:12 Every jar shall be filled with wine. 1
12 know that every jar will be filled with wine? 1
13 will fill with drunkenness all the inhabitants 1
15:17 for thou hadst filled me with indignation. 1
16:18 filled my inheritance with . . abominations. 1
19: 4 filled this place with the blood of innocents 1
23:24 Do I not fill heaven and earth? says the LORD. 1
33: 5 and to fill them with the dead bodies of men 1
41: 9 the son of Nethani'ah filled it with the slain. 1
47: 2 shall overflow the land and all that fills it 1
51:14 Surely I will fill you with men, as many as locusts 1
34 he has filled his belly with my delicacies 1
Lam 3:15 He has filled me with bitterness 3
30 let him give . . and be filled with insults. 3
Ezk 3: 3 eat this scroll . . and fill your stomach with it. 1
7:19 not satisfy . . or fill their stomachs with it. 1
8:17 that they should fill the land with violence 1
9: 7 and fill the courts with the slain. Go forth. 1
10: 2 fill your hands with burning coals 1
3 and a cloud filled the inner court. 1
4 and the house was filled with the cloud 1
11: 6 and have filled its streets with the slain. 1
23:33 you will be filled with drunkenness and sorrow. 1
24: 4 fill it with choice bones. 1
27:25 you were filled and heavily laden 1
28:16 In the abundance of your trade you were filled 1
30:11 against Egypt, and fill the land with the slain. 1
32: 5 and fill the valleys with your carcass. 1
15 when the land is stripped of all that fills it 1
35: 8 I will fill your mountains with the slain; 1
36:38 the waste cities be filled with flocks of men. 1
39:19 And you shall eat fat till you are filled, 6
20 And you shall be filled at my table with horses 3
43: 5 behold, the glory of the LORD filled the temple. 1
44: 4 glory of the LORD filled the temple of the LORD; 1
Dan 2:35 great mountain and filled the whole earth. 8
Hos 13: 6 but when they had fed to the full, they were filled 3
Mic 3: 8 But as for me, I am filled with power 1
Nah 2:12 he filled his cave with prey 1
Hab 2:14 For the earth will be filled with the knowledge 1
Zep 1: 9 who fill their master's house with violence 1
Hag 1: 6 you drink, but you never have your fill; 7
2: 7 I will fill this house with splendor 1
Mat 22:10 so the wedding hall was filled with guests. 19
27:48 ran and took a sponge, filled it with vinegar 19
Mrk 4:37 so that the boat was already filling. 9
15:36 filling a sponge full of vinegar, put it on a reed 9
Lke 1:15 he will be filled with the Holy Spirit 19
41 Elizabeth was filled with the Holy Spirit 19
53 he has filled the hungry with good things 12
67 Zechari'ah was filled with the Holy Spirit 19
2:40 grew and became strong, filled with wisdom; 20
3: 5 Every valley shall be filled 20
4:28 all in the synagogue were filled with wrath. 19
5: 7 they came and filled both the boats 19
26 they glorified God and were filled with awe 19
6:11 they were filled with fury 19
8:23 they were filling with water, and were in danger. 24
14:23 that my house may be filled. 9
Joh 2: 7 Jesus said to them, "Fill the jars with water. 9
7 And they filled them up to the brim. 9
6:13 filled twelve baskets with fragments 9
12: 3 the house was filled with the fragrance 20
16: 6 sorrow has filled your hearts. 20
Act 2: 2 it filled all the house where they were sitting. 20
4 they were all filled with the Holy Spirit 19
13 They are filled with new wine. 17
3:10 they were filled with wonder and amazement 19
4: 8 Then Peter, filled with the Holy Spirit, said 19
31 they were all filled with the Holy Spirit 19
5: 3 why has Satan filled your heart to lie 20
17 filled with jealousy 19
28 you have filled Jerusalem with your teaching 20
9:17 be filled with the Holy Spirit. 19
13: 9 filled with the Holy Spirit 19
45 they were filled with jealousy 19
52 the disciples were filled with joy 20
19:29 So the city was filled with the confusion; 19
Rom 1:29 They were filled with all manner of wickedness 20
15:13 May the God of hope fill you with all joy and peace 20
14 filled with all knowledge, and able to instruct 20
1Co 4: 8 Already you are filled! 16
2Co 7: 4 I have great pride in you; I am filled with comfort 20
Eph 1:23 the fulness of him who fills all in all. 20
3:19 you may be filled with all the fulness of God. 20
4:10 that he might fill all things.) 20
5:18 be filled with the Spirit 20
Php 1:11 filled with the fruits of righteousness 20
4:18 I have received full payment, and more; I am filled 20
Col 1: 9 you may be filled with the knowledge of his will 20
2Ti 1: 4 that I may be filled with joy. 20
Jas 2:16 Go in peace, be warmed and filled 26
Rev 8: 5 took the censer and filled it with fire 9
15: 8 and the temple was filled with smoke 9
1Es 8:83 they have filled it with their uncleanness. 12
2Es 2:19 by these I will fill your children with joy. 30
4:32 how great a threshing floor they will fill! 28
5:25 thou hast filled for thyself one river 30
15:41 be filled with the abundance of those waters. 29
Tob 8:18 he ordered his servants to fill in the grave. 27
Jdt 2: 8 till their wounded shall fill their valleys 20
8 every . . river shall be filled with their dead 20
7:21 did not have enough water to drink their fill 22
8:31 the Lord will send us rain to fill our cisterns 21
10: 5 and filled a bag with parched grain 20
Wis 1: 7 the Spirit of the Lord has filled the world 20
12:19 thou hast filled thy sons with good hope 23
18:16 and stood and filled all things with death 20
Sir 1:17 she fills their whole house with desirable 12
2:16 who love him will be filled with the law. 12
4:12 those who seek her early will be filled with joy. 12
16:29 filled it with his good things; 12
17: 7 filled them with knowledge and understanding 12
23:11 will be filled with iniquity 19
11 his house will be filled with calamities. 19
24:25 It fills men with wisdom, like the Pishon 19
31: 3 when he rests he fills himself with his dainties. 12
32:15 He who seeks the law will be filled with it 12
33:16 like a grape-gatherer I filled my wine press. 20
36:14 Fill Zion 19
39: 6 will be filled with the spirit of understanding; 12
12 I am filled, like the moon at the full. 20
47:15 you filled it with parables and riddles. 12
48:12 Elisha was filled with his spirit 12
Bar 3:32 earth . . filled it with four-footed creatures; 12
1Mc 4:32 Fill them with cowardice 10
2Mc 3:30 was filled with joy and gladness 14
4:37 grieved at heart and filled with pity 25
40 were becoming aroused and filled with anger 11
6: 4 the temple was filled with debauchery 14
7:21 Filled with a noble spirit 20
8:21 he filled them with good courage 18
9: 7 but was even more filled with arrogance 20
13:16 In the end they filled the camp with terror 20
3Mc 1:16 they filled the temple with cries and tears; 12
18 filled the streets with groans 12
4: 3 what streets were not filled with mourning 12
16 was greatly and continually filled with joy 20
5: 1 was filled with overpowering anger and wrath 17
10 until they had been filled 20
30 he was filled with an overpowering wrath 20
42 Phalaris in everything and filled with madness 13
46 filled with countless masses of people 15
47 he had filled his impious mind with a deep rage 9
6:19 filled them with confusion and terror 20

fill *See also* all, drink, eat, get, take.

fill out 1. מלא
Isa 65:20 or an old man who does not fill out his days 1

fill up 1. *ἀναπληρόω* 2. *πληρόω* 3. *προσαναπληρόω*
Mat 23:32 Fill up, then, the measure of your fathers. 2
1Th 2:16 so as always to fill up the measure of their sins. 1
Wis 19: 4 in order that they might fill up the punishment 3
Bar 5: 7 the valleys filled up, to make level ground 2

fill with awe 1. *φοβέω σφόδρα* 2. *φοβέω φόβον μέγαν*
Mat 17: 6 on their faces, and were filled with awe 1
27:54 they were filled with awe, and said 1
Mrk 4:41 And they were filled with awe 2

fill with delight 1. רוה
Prv 5:19 her affection fill you at all times with delight 1

fill with fear 1. ירא מְאֹד 2. *φοβέω φόβον μέγαν*
1Sm 28:20 Saul fell at once . . filled with fear 1
Lke 2: 9 and they were filled with fear. 2
Lke 2: 9 and they were filled with fear. 2

fill with people 1. *συνοικίζω*
Sir 16: 4 a city will be filled with people 1

fill with vain hope 1. הבל
Jer 23:16 who prophesy . . filling you with vain hopes; 1

filled with many spectators 1. *πολυάνδριον*
4Mc 15:20 the place filled with many spectators 1

fillet 1. חָשׁוּק
Exd 27:10 hooks . . and their fillets shall be of silver. 1
11 hooks . . and their fillets shall be of silver. 1
17 the pillars around the court shall be filleted 1
36:38 their capitals, and their fillets were of gold 1
38:10 the hooks of the pillars and their fillets were 1
11 but the hooks of the pillars and their fillets 1
12 the pillars and their fillets were of silver. 1
17 the pillars and their fillets were of silver; 1
17 pillars . . were filleted with silver. 1
19 their capitals and their fillets of silver. 1

fillet *See also* make.

fills *See* all.

film *See* white.

filth 1. נִדָּה 2. צֹאָה 3. שִׁקּוּץ 4. *βόλβιτον* 5. *σκύβαλον*
2Ch 29: 5 carry out the filth from the holy place. 1
Prv 30:12 own eyes but are not cleansed of their filth. 2
Isa 4: 4 washed away the filth of the daughters of Zion 2
Nah 3: 6 I will throw filth at you 3
Sir 22: 2 may be compared to the filth of dunghills 4
27: 4 so a man's filth remains in his thoughts. 5

filthiness 1. טֻמְאָה 2. צֹאָה 3. *αἰσχρότης* 4. *ῥυπαρία*
Isa 28: 8 full of vomit, no place is without filthiness. 2
Ezk 22:15 I will consume your filthiness out of you. 1
24:11 may burn, that its filthiness may be melted in it 1
13 you were not cleansed from your filthiness 1
Eph 5: 4 Let there be no filthiness, nor silly talk 3
Jas 1:21 put away all filthiness and rank growth 4

filthy 1. טֻמְאָה 2. נִידָה 3. צֹא 4. צֹאִי 5. *ἀρδαλόω* 6. *ῥυπαίνω* 7. *ῥυπαρός*
Lam 1: 8 sinned . . therefore she became filthy; 2
Ezk 24:13 Its rust is your filthy lewdness. 1
Zec 3: 3 Joshua was . . clothed with filthy garments. 3
4 Remove the filthy garments from him. 4
Rev 22:11 Let . . the filthy still be filthy 7
11 Let . . the filthy still be filthy 6
Sir 22: 1 The indolent may be compared to a filthy stone 5

filthy thing 1. נִדָּה
Lam 1:17 Jerusalem has become a filthy thing among them. 1

fin 1. סְנַפִּיר
Lev 11: 9 Everything in the waters that has fins and scales 1
10 anything in . . the rivers that has not fins 1
12 Everything in the waters that has not fins 1
Deu 14: 9 whatever has fins and scales you may eat. 1
10 does not have fins and scales you shall not eat; 1

final 1. קֵץ 2. *πέρας* 3. *συντέλεια*
Ezk 21:25 day has come, the time of your final punishment 1
29 day has come, the time of their final punishment. 1
35: 5 at the time of their final punishment; 1
Heb 6:16 disputes an oath is final for confirmation. 2

1Mc 3:42 to cause their final destruction. 3
3Mc 5: 5 would experience its final destruction. 2

finally 1. ἐξ ὑστέρου 2. ἐπ' ἐσχάτων 3. ἔσχατος 4. λοιπός 5. πέρας 6. τέλος

1Sm 10:21 finally he brought the . . Matrites near man *
Mrk 12: 6 finally he sent him to them, saying 3
2Co 13:11 Finally, brethren, farewell 4
Eph 6:10 Finally, be strong in the Lord 4
Php 3: 1 Finally, my brethren, rejoice in the Lord 4
4: 8 Finally, brethren, whatever is true 4
1Th 4: 1 Finally, brethren, we beseech and exhort you 4
2Th 3: 1 Finally, brethren, pray for us 4
1Pe 3: 8 Finally, all of you, have unity of spirit, sympathy 6
Wis 3:17 finally their old age will be without honor. 2
Sir 13: 7 and finally he will deride you 2
LJr 1:72 they will finally themselves be consumed 1
2Mc 5: 8 Finally he met a miserable end 5

find 1. היה 2. הִנֵּה 3. חֵקֶר 4. כון 5. מצא 6. נשׂא 7. ראה 8. ראה נֶפֶשׁ 9. שׁכח (A) 10. ἀνευρίσκω 11. εἰμί 12. ἐξευρίσκω 13. εὕρεμα 14. εὑρίσκω 15. ἐφίστημι 16. ἔχω 17. ζητέω 18. καταλαμβάνω 19. λαμβάνω 20. τυγχάνω 21. φαίνω 22. invenio

Gen 2:20 but for the man there was not found a helper fit 5
4:14 on the earth, and whoever finds me will slay me. 5
6: 8 Noah found favor in the eyes of the LORD. 5
8: 9 the dove found no place to set her foot 5
11: 2 as men migrated from the east, they found a plain 5
16: 7 The angel of the LORD found her by a spring 5
18: 3 said, "My lord, if I have found favor 5
26 the LORD said, "If I find at Sodom 50 righteous 5
28 I will not destroy it if I find 45 there. 5
29 Suppose 40 are found there. 5
30 Suppose 30 are found there. 5
30 He answered, "I will not do it, if I find 30 there. 5
31 Suppose twenty are found there. 5
32 Suppose ten are found there." He answered 5
19:19 your servant has found favor in your sight 5
26:19 servants . . found there a well of springing 5
32 they had dug, and said to him, "We have found water 5
27:20 How is it that you have found it so quickly, my son? 5
30:14 Reuben went and found mandrakes in the field 5
33 if found with me, shall be counted stolen. *
31:32 one with whom you find your gods shall not live. 5
33 he did not find them. And he went out of Leah's tent 5
34 felt all about the tent, but did not find them. 5
35 searched, but did not find the household gods. 5
37 what have you found of all your household goods? 5
32: 5 in order that I may find favor in your sight.' 5
33: 8 Jacob answered, "To find favor in the sight of my 5
10 No, I pray you, if I have found favor in your sight 5
15 Let me find favor in the sight of my lord. 5
34:11 Let me find favor in your eyes 5
36:24 Anah; he is the Anah who found the hot springs 5
37:15 a man found him wandering in the fields; 5
17 after his brothers, and found them at Dothan. 5
32 to their father, and said, "This we have found; see 5
38:20 from the woman's hand, he could not find her. 5
22 he returned . . and said, "I have not found her; 5
23 you see, I sent this kid, and you could not find her 5
39: 4 Joseph found favor in his sight and attended him 5
41:38 Pharaoh said to his servants, "Can we find such 5
44: 8 Behold, the money which we found in the mouth 5
9 With whomever of your servants it be found 5
10 he with whom it is found shall be my slave 5
12 and the cup was found in Benjamin's sack. 5
16 he also in whose hand the cup has been found. 5
17 Only the man in whose hand the cup was found 5
47:14 all the money that was found in the land of Egypt 5
29 If now I have found favor in your sight, 5
50: 4 If now I have found favor in your eyes, speak 5
Exd 5:11 get your straw wherever you can find it; 5
12:19 no leaven shall be found in your houses; 5
15:22 went . . in the wilderness and found no water. 5
16:25 today you will not find it in the field. 5
27 went out to gather, and they found none. 5
21:16 sells him or is found in possession of him 5
22: 2 If a thief is found breaking in, and is struck 5
4 If the stolen beast is found alive in his 5
7 if the thief is found, he shall pay double. 5
8 If the thief is not found, the owner of the house 5
33:12 you have also found favor in my sight.' 5
13 Now therefore, I pray thee, if I have found favor 5
13 that I may know thee and find favor in thy sight. 5
16 For how shall it be known that I have found favor 5
17 for you have found favor in my sight, and I know you 5
34: 9 he said, "If now I have found favor in thy sight 5
35:23 every man with whom was found blue or purple 5
24 man with whom was found acacia wood of any use 5
Lev 6: 3 or has found what was lost and lied about it 5
4 the lost thing which he found 5
25:26 and finds sufficient means to redeem it 5
Num11:11 why have I not found favor in thy sight 5
15 kill me at once, if I find favor in thy sight 5
15:32 found a man gathering sticks on the sabbath day. 5
33 those who found him gathering sticks 5
31:50 brought the LORD'S offering, what each man found 5
32: 5 they said, "If we have found favor in your sight 5
35:27 avenger of blood finds him outside the bounds 5
Deu 4:29 you will seek the LORD . . and you will find him 5
17: 2 If there is found among you, within . . your towns 5
18:10 not be found among you any one who burns his son 5
20:11 people who are found in it shall do forced labor 5
21: 1 any one is found slain, lying in the open country 5
22: 3 any lost thing . . which he loses and you find; 5
14 I did not find in her the tokens of virginity,' 5
17 I did not find . . the tokens of virginity. 5
20 tokens . . were not found in the young woman 5
22 man is found lying with the wife of another man 5
28 seizes her and lies with her, and they are found 5
24: 1 if then she finds no favor in his eyes 5
1 no favor . . because he has found some indecency 5
7 If a man is found stealing one of his brethren 5
32:10 He found him in a desert land, and in the howling 5
Jos 2:22 pursuers had made search . . and found nothing. 5
10:17 The five kings have been found, hidden in the cave 5
Jdg 5:30 Are they not finding and dividing the spoil? 5
6:17 If now I have found favor with thee, then show me 5
15:15 he found a fresh jawbone of an ass, and put out his 5
17: 8 departed . . to live where he could find a place; 5
9 and I am going to sojourn where I may find a place. 5
20:48 smote . . men and beasts and all that they found. 5
48 all the towns which they found they set on fire. 5
21:12 they found . . 400 young virgins 5
Rut 1: 9 The LORD grant that you may find a home, 5
2: 2 after him in whose sight I shall find favor. 5
10 Why have I found favor in your eyes 5
1Sm 1:18 Let your maidservant find favor in your eyes. 5
9: 4 they passed . . but they did not find them. 5
4 they passed through . . but did not find them. 5
13 As soon as you enter the city, you will find him 5
20 not set your mind on them, for they have been found. 5
10: 2 The asses which you went to seek are found 5
7 do whatever your hand finds to do, for God is 5
14 we saw they were not to be found, we went to Samuel. *
16 He told us plainly that the asses had been found. 5
21 But when they sought him, he could not be found. 5
12: 5 you have not found anything in my hand. 5
13:19 there was no smith to be found throughout all 5
22 neither sword nor spear found in the hand of any 5
14:30 of the spoil of their enemies which they found; 5
16:22 Let David . . for he has found favor in my sight. 5
20: 3 knows well that I have found favor in your eyes; 5
21 I will send the lad, saying, 'Go, find the arrows.' 5
29 if I have found favor in your eyes, let me get away 5
36 he said . . "Run and find the arrows which I shoot. 5
23:17 the hand of Saul my father shall not find you; 5
24:19 if a man finds his enemy, will he let him go away 5
25: 8 Therefore let my young men find favor 5
28 evil shall not be found in you so long as you live. 5
27: 5 If I have found favor in your eyes, let a place be 5
29: 3 I have found no fault in him to this day. 5
6 I have found nothing wrong in you 5
8 What have you found in your servant . . until now 5
30: 3 came to the city, they found it burned with fire 2
11 They found an Egyptian in the open country 5
31: 3 hard upon Saul, and the archers found him; 5
8 they found Saul and his three sons fallen 5
2Sm 7:27 therefore thy servant has found courage to pray 5
14:22 I have found favor in your sight, my lord the king 5
15:25 If I find favor in the eyes of the LORD 5
16: 4 let me . . find favor in your sight, my lord the king. 5
17:12 come upon him in some place where he is to be found 5
13 until not even a pebble is to be found there. 5
20 And when they had sought and could not find them 5
1Kg 1: 3 they sought . . and found Ab'ishag the Shu'nammite 5
52 but if wickedness is found in him, he shall die. 5
11:19 Hadad found great favor in the sight of Pharaoh 5
29 the prophet Ahi'jah . . found him on the road. 5
13:14 and found him sitting under an oak; 5
28 he went and found his body thrown in the road 5
14:13 in him there is found something pleasing 5
18: 5 we may find grass and save the horses and mules 5
10 take an oath . . that they had not found you. 5
12 when I come and tell Ahab and he cannot find you 5
19:19 departed . . and found Eli'sha the son of Shaphat 5
20:37 The he found another man, and said, "Strike me 5
21:20 said to Eli'jah, "Have you found me, O my enemy? 5
20 I have found you, because you have sold yourself 5
2Kg 2:17 three days they sought him but did not find him. 5
4:39 went out . . found a wild vine and gathered from it 5
9:35 they found no more of her than the skull 5
12:10 the money that was found in the house of the LORD. 5
18 and all the gold that was found in the treasuries 5
14:14 vessels that were found in the house of the LORD 5
16: 8 silver and gold . . found in the house of the LORD 5
17: 4 the king of Assyria found treachery in Hoshe'a; 5
18:15 the silver that was found in the house of the LORD 5
19: 8 returned, and found the king of Assyria fighting 5
20:13 his armory, all that was found in his storehouses; 5
22: 8 I have found the book of the law in the house 5
9 emptied out the money that was found in the house 5
13 the words of this book that has been found; 5
23: 2 the book . . which had been found in the house 5
24 book that Hilki'ah . . found in the house 5
25:19 men of the . . council who were found in the city; 5
19 and 60 men . . who were found in the city. 5
1Ch 4:40 where they found rich, good pasture 5
41 destroyed . . the Me-u'nim who were found there 5
10: 3 Saul, and the archers found him; 5
8 found Saul and his sons fallen on Mount Gilbo'a. 5
17:25 servant has found courage to pray before thee. 5
20: 2 he found that it weighed a talent of gold 5
24: 4 chief men were found among the sons of Elea'zar 5
26:31 men of great ability . . were found at Jazer 5
28: 9 If you seek him, he will be found by you; 5
2Ch 2:17 Solomon took a census . . and there were found 5
15: 2 If you seek him, he will be found by you 5
4 sought him, he was found by them. 5
15 he was found by them, and the LORD gave them rest 5
19: 3 Nevertheless some good is found in you 5
20:16 you will find them at the end of the valley 5
25 found cattle in great numbers, goods, clothing 5
21:17 possessions they found that belonged 5
25: 5 found that they were 300,000 picked men 5
24 the vessels that were found in the house of God 5
29:16 the uncleanness that they found in the temple 5
30: 9 find compassion with their captors, and return *
32: 4 kings of Assyria come and find much water? 5
34:14 Hilki'ah the priest found the book of the law 5
15 found the book of the law in the house of the LORD"; 5
17 the money that was found in the house of the LORD 5
21 words of the book that has been found; 5
30 book of the covenant which had been found 5
36: 8 what was found against him, 5
Ezr 2:62 not found there, and so they were excluded 5
4:15 You will find in the book of the records and learn 9
19 found that this city from of old has risen 9
6: 2 scroll was found on which this was written 9
7:16 with all the silver and gold which you shall find 9
8:15 I found there none of the sons of Levi. 5
10:18 found Ma-asei'ah, Elie'zer, Jarib, and Gedali'ah 5
Neh 5: 8 They were silent, and could not find a word to say. 5
7: 5 found the book of the genealogy of those who came 5
5 I found the book . . and I found written in it 5
64 it was not found there, so they were excluded 5
8:14 found it written in the law that the LORD 5
9: 8 thou didst find his heart faithful before thee 5
13: 1 found written that no Ammonite or Moabite 5
Est 2:15 Esther found favor in the eyes of all who saw her. 6
17 loved Esther . . and she found grace and favor 6
23 the affair was investigated and found to be 5
4:16 gather all the Jews to be found in Susa, and . . fast 5
5: 2 when the king saw . . she found favor in his sight 6
8 If I have found favor in the sight of the king 5
6: 2 it was found written how Mor'decai had told about 5
7: 3 If I have found favor in your sight, O king 5
8: 5 and if I have found favor in his sight 5
Job 3:22 and are glad, when they find the grave? 5
8: 8 consider what the fathers have found; 3
16:18 let my cry find no resting place. 1
17:10 I shall not find a wise man among you. 5
19:28 The root of the matter is found in him'; 5
20: 8 He will fly away like a dream, and not be found; 5
23: 3 Oh, that I knew where I might find him 5
28:12 But where shall wisdom be found? 5
13 it is not found in the land of the living. 5
32: 3 he was angry . . because they had found no answer 5
13 Beware lest you say, 'We have found wisdom; 5
33:10 Behold, he finds occasions against me 5
24 from going down into the Pit, I have found a ransom; 5
37:23 The Almighty–we cannot find him; he is great 5
Ps 10:15 seek out his wickedness till thou find none. 5
17: 3 testest me, thou wilt find no wickedness in me; 5
22: 2 I cry by day . . and by night, but find no rest. *
37:36 though I sought him, he could not be found. 5
55: 8 I would haste to find me a shelter from the raging *
69:20 for comforters, but I found none. 5
73:10 turn and praise them; and find no fault in them. *
84: 3 Even the sparrow finds a home 5
89:20 I have found David, my servant; 5
107: 4 finding no way to a city to dwell in; 5
119:162I rejoice . . like one who finds great spoil. 5
132: 5 until I find a place for the LORD, a dwelling place 5
6 in Eph'rathah, we found it in the fields of Ja'ar. 5
Prv 1:13 we shall find all precious goods 5
28 they will seek me diligently but will not find 5
2: 5 then you will . . find the knowledge of God. 5
3: 4 you will find favor and good repute 5
13 Happy is the man who finds wisdom 5
4:22 For they are life to him who finds them 5
7:15 to seek you eagerly, and I have found you. 5
8: 9 They are all . . right to those who find knowledge. 5
12 I, wisdom . . find knowledge and discretion. 5
17 those who seek me diligently find me. 5
35 For he who finds me finds life 5
35 For he who finds me finds life 5
10:13 lips of him who has understanding wisdom is found 5
18:22 He who finds a wife finds a good thing 5
22 He who finds a wife finds a good thing 5
20: 6 but a faithful man who can find? 5
21:21 who pursues . . kindness will find life and honor. 5
24:14 if you find it, there will be a future 5
25:16 If you have found honey, eat only enough for you 5
28:23 who rebukes a man will afterward find more favor 5

29:21 will in the end find him his heir. •
31:10 A good wife who can find? She is far more precious 5
Ecc 2:24 eat and drink, and find enjoyment in his toil. 8
5:18 eat and drink and find enjoyment in all the toil 7
7:26 I found more bitter than death the woman whose 5
27 Behold, this is what I found, says the Preacher 5
27 adding one thing to another to find the sum 5
28 mind has sought repeatedly, but I have not found. 5
28 One man among 1,000 I found 5
28 but a woman among all these I have not found. 5
29 this alone I found, that God made man upright 5
9:10 Whatever your hand finds to do, do it 5
15 But there was found in it a poor wise man 5
11: 1 for you will find it after many days. 5
12:10 The Preacher sought to find pleasing words 5
Sng 3: 1 I sought him, but found him not; 5
2 I sought him, but found him not. 5
3 The watchmen found me, as they went about 5
4 I found him whom my soul loves. 5
5: 6 I sought him, but found him not; 5
7 The watchmen found me, as they went about the city; 5
8 I adjure you . . if you find my beloved 5
Isa 10:14 My hand has found like a nest the wealth 5
13:15 Whoever is found will be thrust through 5
22: 3 All of you who were found were captured 5
30:14 not a sherd is found with which to take fire 5
34:14 alight, and find for herself a resting place. 5
35: 9 they shall not be found there 5
37: 8 Rab'shakeh . . found the king of Assyria fighting 5
39: 2 all that was found in his storehouses. 5
41:12 contend with you, but you shall not find them; 5
51: 3 joy and gladness will be found in her 5
55: 6 Seek the LORD while he may be found 5
57:10 you found new life for your strength 5
65: 1 was ready to be found by those who did not seek me. 5
8 As the wine is found in the cluster 5
Jer 2: 5 What wrong did your fathers find in me 5
24 in her month they will find her. 5
34 Also on your skirts is found the lifeblood 5
34 you did not find them breaking in. 5
5: 1 Search her squares to see if you can find a man 5
26 For wicked men are found among my people; 5
6:16 and walk in it, and find rest for your souls. 5
14: 3 they come to the cisterns, they find no water 5
15:16 Thy words were found, and I ate them 5
23:11 even in my house I have found their wickedness 5
29: 7 for in its welfare you will find your welfare. 1
13 You will seek me and find me; 5
14 I will be found by you, says the LORD 5
31: 2 The people who survived the sword found grace 5
45: 3 I am weary with my groaning, and I find no rest. 5
48:27 Was he found among thieves 5
50: 7 All who found them have devoured them 5
20 and sin in Judah, and none shall be found; 5
24 you did not know it; you were found and caught 5
52:25 of the king's council, who were found in the city; 5
25 men . . who were found in the midst of the city. 5
Lam 1: 3 now among the nations, but finds no resting place; 5
6 Her princes . . like harts that find no pasture; 5
Ezk 22:30 that I should not destroy it; but I found none. 5
26:21 you will never be found again, says the Lord GOD. 5
28:15 blameless . . till iniquity was found in you. 5
Dan 1:19 among them all none was found like Daniel 5
20 found them ten times better than all 5
2:25 I have found among the exiles from Judah a man 9
35 away, so that not a trace of them could be found. 9
5:11 like the wisdom of the gods, were found in him 9
12 excellent spirit . . were found in this Daniel 9
14 light and . . excellent wisdom are found in you. 9
27 weighed in the balances and found wanting; 9
6: 4 sought to find a ground for complaint against 9
4 could find no ground for complaint or any fault 9
4 faithful, and no error or fault was found in him. 9
5 not find any ground for complaint against 9
5 unless we find it in connection with the law 9
11 found Daniel making petition and supplication 9
22 because I was found blameless before him; 9
23 no kind of hurt was found upon him 9
11:19 shall stumble and fall, and shall not be found. 5
12: 1 every one whose name . . found written in the book. 5
Hos 2: 6 against her, so that she cannot find her paths. 5
7 and she shall seek them, but shall not find them. 5
5: 6 but they will not find him; he has withdrawn 5
9:10 Like grapes in the wilderness, I found Israel. 5
Ams 8:12 the word of the LORD, but they shall not find it. 5
Jon 1: 3 to Joppa and found a ship going to Tarshish; 5
Mic 1:13 in you were found the transgressions of Israel. 5
Hab 2:12 a town with blood, and founds a city on iniquity! 4
Zep 3:13 be found in their mouth a deceitful tongue. 5
Mal 2: 6 no wrong was found on his lips. 5
Mat 1:18 came together she was found to be with child 14
2: 8 for the child, and when you have found him bring me 14
7: 7 Ask, and it will be given you; seek, and you will find; 14
8 and he who seeks finds 14
14 and those who find it are few. 14
8:10 not even in Israel have I found such faith. 14
10:39 He who finds his life will lose it 14
39 he who loses his life for my sake will find it. 14
11:29 and you will find rest for your souls. 14
12:43 but he finds none. 14
44 when he comes he finds it empty, swept 14
13:44 which a man found and covered up 14
46 on finding one pearl of great value 14
16:25 whoever loses his life for my sake will find it. 14
17:27 when you open its mouth you will find a shekel; 14
18:13 if he finds it, truly, I say to you, he rejoices 14
20: 6 he went out and found others standing 14
21: 2 immediately you will find an ass tied 14
19 found nothing on it but leaves only 14
22: 9 invite to the marriage feast as many as you find.' 14
10 gathered all whom they found, both bad and good; 14
24:46 whom his master when he comes will find so doing. 14
26:40 he came to the disciples and found them sleeping; 14
43 again he came and found them sleeping 14
60 they found none 14
Mrk 1:37 they found him and said to him 14
7:30 she went home, and found the child lying in bed 14
11: 2 immediately as you enter it you will find a colt 14
4 they went away, and found a colt tied at the door 14
13 he went to see if he could find anything on it. 14
13 When he came to it, he found nothing but leaves 14
13:36 lest he come suddenly and find you asleep. 14
14:16 found it as he had told them 14
37 he came and found them sleeping 14
40 again he came and found them sleeping 14
55 they found none. 14
Lke 1:30 you have found favor with God. 14
2:12 you will find a babe wrapped in swaddling cloths 14
16 they went with haste, and found Mary and Joseph 10
45 when they did not find him 14
46 After three days they found him in the temple 14
4:17 found the place where it was written 14
5:19 finding no way to bring him 14
6: 7 that they might find an accusation against him. 14
7: 9 not even in Israel have I found such faith. 14
10 they found the slave well. 14
8:35 found the man from whom the demons had gone 14
9:36 when the voice had spoken, Jesus was found alone. 14
11: 9 seek, and you will find; knock, and it will be opened 14
10 he who seeks finds 14
24 finding none he says, 'I will return to my house 14
25 when he comes he finds it swept and put in order. 14
12:37 those servants whom the master finds awake 14
38 and finds them so, blessed are those servants! 14
43 his master when he comes will find so doing. 14
13: 6 he came seeking fruit on it and found none. 14
7 I find none 14
15: 4 go after the one which is lost, until he finds it? 14
5 when he has found it, he lays it on his shoulders 14
6 I have found my sheep which was lost.' 14
8 seek diligently until she finds it? 14
9 when she has found it 14
9 I have found the coin which I had lost.' 14
24 he was lost, and is found 14
32 he was lost, and is found.' 14
17:18 Was no one found to return and give praise to God 14
18: 8 will he find faith on earth? 14
19:30 where on entering you will find a colt tied 14
32 went away and found it as he had told them. 14
48 they did not find anything they could do 14
22:13 they went, and found it as he had told them 14
45 found them sleeping for sorrow. 14
23: 2 We found this man perverting our nation 14
4 I find no crime in this man. 14
14 behold, I did not find this man guilty 14
22 I have found in him no crime deserving death 14
24: 2 they found the stone rolled away from the tomb 14
3 when they went in they did not find the body. 14
23 did not find his body 14
24 and found it just as the women had said 14
33 they found the eleven gathered together 14
Joh 1:41 He first found his brother Simon, and said to him 14
41 We have found the Messiah" (which means Christ). 14
43 And he found Philip and said to him, "Follow me. 14
45 Philip found Nathan'a-el, and said to him 14
45 We have found him of whom Moses in the law . . wrote 14
2:14 In the temple he found those who were selling 14
5:14 Afterward, Jesus found him in the temple, and said 14
6:25 When they found him on the other side of the sea 14
7:34 you will seek me and you will not find me 14
35 that we shall not find him 14
36 'You will seek me and you will not find me,' 14
9:35 having found him he said 14
10: 9 and will go in and out and find pasture. 14
11:17 he found that Laz'arus had . . been in the tomb 14
12:14 Jesus found a young ass and sat upon it 14
18:38 I find no crime in him. 14
19: 4 that you may know that I find no crime in him. 14
6 for I find no crime in him. 14
21: 6 you will find some 14
Act 4:21 they let them go, finding no way to punish them 14
5:10 When the young men came in they found her dead 14
22 they did not find them in the prison 14
23 We found the prison securely locked 14
23 when we opened it we found no one inside. 14
39 You might even be found opposing God! 14
7:11 our fathers could find no food. 14
46 who found favor in the sight of God 14
46 find a habitation for the God of Jacob. 14
8:40 Philip was found at Azo'tus 14
9: 2 if he found any belonging to the Way, men or women 14
33 There he found a man named Aene'as 14
10:27 he went in and found many persons gathered; 14
11:26 when he had found him, he brought him to Antioch. 14
12:19 Herod had sought for him and could not find him 14
13:22 I have found in David the son of Jesse a man 14
17: 6 when they could not find them 14
23 I found also an altar with this inscription 14
27 feel after him and find him 14
18: 2 he found a Jew named Aq'uila, a native of Pontus 14
19: 1 There he found some disciples. 14
19 and found it came to 50,000 pieces of silver. 14
21: 2 having found a ship crossing to Phoeni'cia 14
23: 9 We find nothing wrong in this man. 14
29 I found that he was accused 14
24: 5 we have found this man a pestilent fellow 14
12 they did not find me disputing with any one 14
18 they found me purified in the temple 14
20 say what wrongdoing they found 14
25:25 I found that he had done nothing deserving death; 18
27: 6 There the centurion found a ship of Alexandria 14
28 So they sounded and found twenty fathoms 14
28 they sounded again and found fifteen fathoms. 14
28:14 There we found brethren 14
Rom 7: 8 But sin, finding opportunity in the commandment 19
11 For sin, finding opportunity in the commandment 19
21 I find it to be a law that when I want to do right 14
10:20 I have been found by those who did not seek me; 14
1Co 4: 2 that they be found trustworthy. 14
5: 1 of a kind that is not found even among pagans •
15:15 We are even found to be misrepresenting God 14
2Co 1:20 For all the promises of God find their Yes in him. •
2:13 because I did not find my brother Titus there 14
5: 3 so that by putting it on we may not be found naked. 14
8:22 and found earnest in many matters 11
9: 4 if some . . find that you are not ready 14
12:20 I may come and find you not what I wish 14
20 you may find me not what you wish 14
Gal 2:17 we ourselves were found to be sinners 14
Eph 5: 9 for the fruit of light is found in all that is good •
Php 2: 8 being found in human form he humbled himself 14
3: 9 be found in him 14
2Ti 1:17 he searched for me eagerly and found me– 14
18 may the Lord grant him to find mercy from the Lord 14
Heb 4:16 we may receive mercy and find grace 14
11: 5 he was not found, because God had taken him 14
12:17 he was rejected for he found no chance to repent 14
1Pe 2:22 no guile was found on his lips. 14
2Pe 3:14 be zealous to be found by him without spot 14
2Jn 1: 4 to find some of your children following the truth 14
Jde 1: 3 I found it necessary to write appealing to you 16
Rev 2: 2 tested those . . and found them to be false; 14
3: 2 not found your works perfect in the sight of God. 14
5: 4 that no one was found worthy to open the scroll 14
9: 6 in those days men will seek death and will not find it; 14
14: 5 in their mouth no lie was found 14
16:20 and no mountains were to be found; 14
18:14 lost to thee, never to be found again! 14
21 Babylon . . shall be found no more; 14
22 a craftsman . . shall be found in thee no more; 14
24 And in her was found the blood of prophets 14
20:11 and no place was found for them. 14
15 name was not found written in the book of life 14
1Es 2:22 will find . . what has been written about them 14
26 it has been found that . . 14
4:42 for you have been found to be the wisest 14
5:38 were not found registered 14
39 was sought in the register and was not found 14
6: 8 we found the elders of the Jews 18
22 if it is found that . . 14
23 a scroll was found in which this was recorded 14
8: 4 he found favor before the king 14
13 all the gold and silver that may be found 14
42 When I found there none of the sons of the priests 14
53 we found him very merciful 20
9:18 were brought in and found to have foreign wives 14
2Es 2:23 When you find any who are dead 22
3:34 it will be found which way the turn of the scale 22
36 Thou mayest indeed find individual men 22
36 but nations thou wilt not find. 22
4:44 If I have found favor in your sight 22
5: 9 salt waters shall be found in the sweet 22
10 it shall be sought by many but shall not be found 22
56 if I have found favor in thy sight 22
6:11 if I have found favor in thy sight 22
22 storehouses shall suddenly be found to be empty; 22
7:75 If I have found favor in thy sight, O Lord 22
102 If I have found favor in thy sight 22
104 Since you have found favor in my sight 22
106 How then do we find that first Abraham prayed 22
8:42 If I have found favor before thee, let me speak. 22
12: 7 if I have found favor in thy sight 22
13:48 who are found within my holy borders 22
14:22 If then I have found favor before thee 22
22 that men may be able to find the path 22
Tob 1:18 they were not found. 14
2: 2 whatever poor man of our brethren you may find 14

5: 3 Find a man to go with you 17
4 he found Raphael, who was an angel 14
8 I have found some one to go with me 14
8:13 went in, and found them both asleep. 14
Jdt 6:14 came down from their city and found him 15
10: 6 found Uzziah standing there with the elders 14
14: 3 will not find him 14
15 and found him thrown down on the platform dead 14
17 when he did not find her 14
AEs 16:14 he would find us undefended 19
15 we find that the Jews . . are not evildoers 14
Wis 1: 2 he is found by those who do not put him to the test 14
3: 5 God tested them and found them worthy of himself; 14
5:10 when it has passed no trace can be found 14
11 no evidence of its passage is found 14
11 afterward no sign of its coming is found there; 14
6:10 who have been taught them will find a defense. 14
12 is found by those who seek her. 14
14 he will find her sitting at his gates. 14
7:29 she is found to be superior 14
8:11 I shall be found keen in judgment 14
9:16 what is at hand we find with labor 14
13: 6 while seeking God and desiring to find him. 14
9 how did they fail to find sooner the Lord 14
16: 9 no healing was found for them 14
Sir 0: 3 I found opportunity for no little instruction. 14
3:18 so you will find favor in the sight of the Lord. 14
31 at the moment of his falling he will find support. 14
6:14 he that has found one has found a treasure. 14
14 he that has found one has found a treasure. 14
16 those who fear the Lord will find him. 14
18 until you are old you will keep finding wisdom. 14
28 For at last you will find the rest she gives 14
11:19 I have found rest, and now I shall enjoy my goods! 14
12:16 if he finds an opportunity 14
17 If calamity befalls you, you will find him there 14
15: 6 He will find gladness and a crown of rejoicing 14
18:17 Both are to be found in a gracious man. •
20 you will find forgiveness. 14
28 he praises the one who finds her. 14
19:28 he will do evil when he finds an opportunity. 14
20: 5 There is one who by keeping silent is found wise 14
21:16 delight will be found 14
22:13 avoid him and you will find rest 14
23:12 may it never be found in the inheritance of Jacob! 14
25: 3 how then can you find anything in your old age? 14
26:10 lest, when she finds liberty, she use it to her hurt. 14
27:16 he will never find a congenial friend. 14
28:16 Whoever pays heed to slander will not find rest 14
29: 3 on every occasion you will find what you need. 14
31: 8 Blessed is the rich man who is found blameless 14
32:14 those who rise early to seek him will find favor. 14
17 will find a decision according to his liking. 14
33:25 Set your slave to work, and you will find rest; 14
35:10 as generously as your hand has found. 13
38:33 they are not found using proverbs. 14
40:18 he who finds treasure is better off than both. 14
41:23 will find favor with every man. 14
44:17 Noah was found perfect and righteous 14
19 no one has been found like him in glory; 14
20 when he was tested he was found faithful. 14
45: 1 found favor in the sight of all flesh 14
51:16 I found for myself much instruction. 14
20 through purification I found her 14
26 it is to be found close by. 14
27 have labored little and found myself much rest. 14
Bar 1:12 we shall . . find favor in their sight. 14
3:15 Who has found her place? And who has entered her 14
30 Who has gone over the sea, and found her, and will 14
32 he who knows all things knows her, he found her 12
36 He found the whole way to knowledge, and gave her 12
Aza 1:15 to make an offering before thee or to find mercy. 14
Sus 1:14 a time when they could find her alone. 14
63 because nothing shameful was found in her. 14
Bel 1:12 if you do not find that Bel has eaten it all 14
1Mc 1:23 he took also the hidden treasures which he found. 14
56 The books of the law which they found 14
57 Where the book of the covenant was found 14
58 those found month after month in the cities. 14
2:46 that they found within the borders of Israel. 14
52 Was not Abraham found faithful when tested 14
63 tomorrow he will not be found 14
4: 5 he found no one there 14
5: 6 where he found a strong band and many people 14
6:63 He found Philip in control of the city 14
10:16 So he said, "Shall we find another such man? 14
60 found favor with them. 14
11:42 if I find an opportunity. 20
12:21 found in writing concerning the Spartans 14
2Mc 1:20 they had not found fire but thick liquid 14
2: 1 One finds in the records that . . 14
5 Jeremiah came and found a cave 14
6 could not find it. 14
5:25 then, finding the Jews not at work 19
8: 7 He found the nights most advantageous 19
12:18 They did not find Timothy in that region 18
40 they found sacred tokens of the idols of Jamnia 14
14: 5 he found an opportunity 19
10 impossible for the government to find peace. 20

4Mc 3:14 found the spring 10
4:23 if any . . should be found observing the ancestral law 21

find *See also* try.

find a dwelling 1. ישב
Ps 68:10 thy flock found a dwelling in it; 1

find a liar 1. כזב
Prv 30: 6 lest he rebuke you, and you be found a liar. 1

find a place 1. χωρέω
Joh 8:37 because my word finds no place in you. 1

find acceptance 1. רָצוֹן
Lev 23:11 wave the sheaf . . that you may find acceptance 1

find comfort 1. בלג
Job 10:20 Let me alone, that I may find a little comfort 1

find delight 1. שעע
Ps 119:47 for I find my delight in thy commandments 1

find ease 1. רגע
Deu 28:65 among these nations you shall find no ease 1

find enjoyment 1. שמח
Ecc 5:19 to accept his lot and find enjoyment in his toil– 1

find fault 1. ריב 2. αἰτιάομαι 3. μέμφομαι 4. μωμάομαι
Exd 17: 2 Therefore the people found fault with Moses 1
2 Why do you find fault with me? 1
Rom 9:19 Why does he still find fault? 3
2Co 6: 3 so that no fault may be found with our ministry 4
Heb 8: 8 For he finds fault with them when he says 3
Sir 11: 7 Do not find fault before you investigate 3
29: 5 will find fault with the time. 2

find favor 1. יטב
Neh 2: 5 if your servant has found favor in your sight 1

find mercy 1. חנן 2. רחם 3. ἐλεέω
Prv 21:10 his neighbor finds no mercy in his eyes. 1
Hos 14: 3 In thee the orphan finds mercy. 2
Tob 8: 7 Grant that I may find mercy 3

find out 1. חקר 2. ידע 3. מצא 4. γινώσκω 5. διαλαμβάνω 6. ἐξερευνάω 7. ἐξετάζω 8. ἐπιγινώσκω 9. ἐπισκέπτομαι
Gen 44:16 God has found out the guilt of your servants; 3
Num32:23 and be sure your sin will find you out 3
Jdg 14:12 if you can tell me what it is . . and find it out 3
18 my heifer, you would not have found out my riddle. 3
1Kg 7:47 the weight of the bronze was not found out. 1
Neh 13:10 I also found out that the portions of the Levites 2
Job 11: 7 Can you find out the deep things of God? 3
7 Can you find out the limit of the Almighty? 3
Ps 21: 8 Your hand will find out all your enemies; 3
8 your right hand will find out those who hate you. 3
36: 2 that his iniquity cannot be found out and hated. 3
Prv 10: 9 but he who perverts his ways will be found out. 2
28:11 man who has understanding will find him out. 1
Ecc 3:11 so that he cannot find out what God has done 3
7:14 man may not find out anything that will be after 3
24 is far off, and deep . . who can find it out? 3
8:17 man cannot find out the work that is done 3
17 he will not find it out; 3
17 though a wise man claims . . he cannot find it out. 3
Mat 10:11 find out who is worthy in it 7
Mrk 6:38 when they had found out, they said 4
Act 22:24 to find out why they shouted thus against him. 8
1Co 4:19 find out not the talk of these arrogant people 4
2Co 13: 6 I hope you will find out that we have not failed. 4
1Es 5:66 they came to find out what the sound . . meant. 8
Jdt 5:20 and we find out their offense 9
8:14 nor find out what a man is thinking 5
14 and find out his mind or comprehend his thought 8
34 Only, do not try to find out what I plan 6
Wis 2:19 that we may find out how gentle he is 4
1Mc 9:34 Bacchides found this out on the sabbath day 4
16:22 he had found out that they were seeking to destroy 8

find perfect 1. τελειόω
Sir 31:10 Who has been tested by it and been found perfect? 1

find pleasure 1. שמח
Ecc 2:10 for my heart found pleasure in all my toil 1

find protection 1. σκεπάζω
1Mc 11:16 Alexander fled into Arabia to find protection there 1

find refuge 1. חסה
Ps 91: 4 under his wings you will find refuge; 1
Prv 14:32 righteous finds refuge through his integrity. 1
Isa 14:32 in her the afflicted of his people find refuge. 1

find relief 1. רוח
Job 32:20 I must speak, that I may find relief; 1

find rest 1. נוח 2. προσαναπαύω
Ecc 6: 5 yet it finds rest rather than he. 1
Wis 8:16 When I enter my house, I shall find rest with her 2

find safety 1. ἀνασώζω
1Mc 6:53 those who found safety in Judea 1

find shade 1. דור (A) 2. טלל (A)
Dan 4:12 beasts of the field found shade under it 2
21 under which beasts of the field found shade 1

find strength 1. ἰσχύω
Sir 43:28 Where shall we find strength to praise him? 1

find the way 1. εὐοδόω
Sir 43:26 Because of him his messenger finds the way 1

find trustworthy 1. ἐμπιστεύω
Sir 36:16 let thy prophets be found trustworthy. 1

finding *See* hope.

finds *See* night.

fine 1. חֵלֶב 2. חֵלֶב כִּלְיוֹת 3. טוֹב 4. יֶתֶר 5. עָתִיק 6. פזז 7. רֹאשׁ 8. רֵאשִׁית 9. תִּפְאָרָה 10. טָב (A) 11. ἀγαθός 12. καθαρός 13. καλός 14. λαμπρός 15. χρηστός
Exd 30:23 Take the finest spices: of liquid myrrh 7
Deu 32:14 with the finest of the wheat–and of the blood 2
1Kg 10:18 throne, and overlaid it with the finest gold. 6
2Ch 3: 5 nave he lined . . and covered it with fine gold 3
8 with 600 talents of fine gold. 3
Ezr 8:27 two vessels of fine bright bronze as precious 3
Ps 81:16 I would feed you with the finest of the wheat 1
147:14 he fills you with the finest of the wheat. 1
Prv 17: 7 Fine speech is not becoming to a fool; 4
Isa 23:18 supply abundant food and fine clothing 5
Ezk 16:10 I swathed you in fine linen •
23:26 your clothes and take away your fine jewels. 9
27: 7 fine embroidered linen from Egypt was your sail •
Dan 2:32 head of this image was of fine gold 10
Ams 6: 6 and anoint themselves with the finest oils 8
Mat 13:45 like a merchant in search of fine pearls 13
Jas 2: 2 For if a man with gold rings and in fine clothing 14
3 to the one who wears the fine clothing 14
1Pe 3: 3 adorning . . and wearing of fine clothing •
1Es 8:57 twelve bronze vessels of fine bronze 15
Jdt 10: 5 a cake of dried fruit and fine bread 12
2Mc 3: 2 glorified the temple with the finest presents 11
9:16 he would adorn with the finest offerings 13

fine (2) 1. ענש 2. ἀργυρικὴ ζημία 3. ζημιόω
Exd 21:22 the one who hurt her shall be fined 1
Deu 22:19 they shall fine him 100 shekels of silver 1
Ams 2: 8 they drink the wine of those who have been fined. 1
1Es 1:36 fined the nation 100 talents of silver 3
8:24 either fine or imprisonment. 2

fine (3) 1. דַק 2. סֹלֶת
Gen 18: 6 Make ready quickly three measures of fine meal 2
Exd 16:14 there was . . a fine, flake-like thing 1
14 flake-like thing, fine as hoarfrost 1
Deu 9:21 grinding it . . until it was as fine as dust; 1

fine *See* beat, clothes, dust, flour, gold, impose, linen, meal, produce.

fine way 1. καλῶς
Mrk 7: 9 You have a fine way of rejecting the commandment 1

finely *See* work, wrought.

finery 1. תִּפְאָרָה 2. κόσμος
Isa 3:18 take away . . finery of the anklets, the headbands 1
Jdt 12:15 arrayed herself in all her woman's finery 2

finger 1. אֶצְבַּע 2. אֶצְבַּע (A) 3. δάκτυλος 4. χειρὸς δάκτυλος 5. χειρὸς δάκτυλος
Exd 8:19 said to Pharaoh, "This is the finger of God. 1
29:12 put it upon . . the altar with your finger 1
31:18 tables of stone, written with the finger of God. 1
Lev 4: 6 the priest shall dip his finger in the blood 1
17 the priest shall dip his finger in the blood 1
25 the blood . . with his finger and put it 1
30 take some of its blood with his finger 1
34 blood . . with his finger and put it on the horns 1
8:15 blood, and with his finger put it on the horns 1
9: 9 he dipped his finger in the blood 1
14:16 dip his right finger in the oil that is in his left 1
16 sprinkle some oil with his finger seven times 1
27 sprinkle with his right finger some of the oil 1
16:14 blood . . and sprinkle it with his finger 1
14 he shall sprinkle the blood with his finger 1
19 sprinkle . . with his finger seven times 1
Num19: 4 shall take some of her blood with his finger 1
Deu 9:10 tables of stone written with the finger of God; 1
2Sm 21:20 man of . . stature, who had six fingers on each hand 1
1Ch 20: 6 who had six fingers on each hand, and six toes 1
Ps 8: 3 When I look at thy heavens, the work of thy fingers 1
144: 1 LORD, my rock, who trains . . my fingers for battle; 1
Prv 6:13 scrapes with his feet, points with his finger 1

7: 3 bind them on your fingers 1
Sng 5: 5 my hands dripped . . my fingers with liquid myrrh 1
Isa 2: 8 hands, to what their own fingers have made. 1
17: 8 will not look to what their own fingers have made 1
58: 9 the pointing of the finger, and speaking 1
59: 3 with blood and your fingers with iniquity; 1
Jer 52:21 its thickness was four fingers 1
Dan 5: 5 fingers of a man's hand appeared and wrote 2
Mat 23: 4 will not move them with their finger. 3
Mrk 7:33 he put his fingers into his ears, and he spat 3
Lke 11:20 if it is by the finger of God that I cast out demons 3
46 not touch the burdens with one of your fingers. 3
16:24 send Laz'arus to dip the end of his finger in water 3
Joh 8: 6 Jesus . . wrote with his finger on the ground. 3
8 and wrote with his finger on the ground. •
20:25 place my finger in the mark of the nails 3
27 Then he said to Thomas, "Put your finger here 3
Wis 15:15 nor fingers to feel 5
4Mc 15:15 toes and fingers scattered on the ground 5
15 their toes and fingers scattered on the ground 4
151 1: 2 My hands made a harp, my fingers fashioned a lyre. 3

little finger 1. קָטֹן
1Kg 12:10 My little finger is thicker than my father's 1
2Ch 10:10 little finger is thicker than my father's loins. 1

fingernail 1. *ἄκρα δάκτυλου κορυφή*
4Mc 10: 7 scalped him with their fingernails 1

finish 1. בצע 2. כלא 3. כלה 4. ספן 5. שׁלם 6. תמם 7. תמם לְ 8. כלל (A) 9. צלל (A) 10. שׁיציא (A) 11. שׁלם (A) 12. *ἀνίστημι* 13. *γίνομαι* 14. *διανύω* 15. *ἐκτελέω* 16. *ἐπιτελέω* 17. *παύω* 18. *πληρόω* 19. *συντέλεια* 20. *συντελέω* 21. *τελειόω* 22. *τελέω* 23. finio 24. perficio
Gen 2: 1 Thus the heavens and the earth were finished 3
2 on the seventh day God finished his work 3
6:16 for the ark, and finish it to a cubit above; 3
17:22 When he had finished talking with him 3
18:33 when he had finished speaking to Abraham; 3
24:19 When she had finished giving him a drink 3
27:30 As soon as Isaac had finished blessing Jacob 3
49:33 When Jacob finished charging his sons 3
Exd 34:33 when Moses had finished speaking with them 3
39:32 tabernacle of the tent of meeting was finished; 3
40:33 So Moses finished the work. 3
Num 4:15 have finished covering the sanctuary 3
7: 1 Moses had finished setting up the tabernacle 3
16:31 as he finished speaking all these words 3
Deu 26:12 When you have finished paying all the tithe 3
31:24 When Moses had finished writing the words 3
30 Moses spoke . . this song until they were finished 6
32:45 Moses had finished speaking all these words 3
Jos 3:17 the nation finished passing over the Jordan 7
4: 1 When all . . had finished passing over the Jordan 7
10 stood in . . until everything was finished 6
11 when all the people had finished passing over 7
8:24 When Israel had finished slaughtering . . Ai 3
10:20 Joshua and . . Israel had finished slaying them 3
19:49 had finished distributing the . . inheritances 3
51 they finished dividing the land. 3
Jdg 3:18 when Ehud had finished presenting the tribute 3
15:17 When he had finished speaking, he threw away 3
Rut 2:21 till they have finished all my harvest.' 3
3: 3 until he has finished eating and drinking. 3
1Sm 10:13 When he had finished prophesying, he came 3
13:10 as he had finished offering the burnt offering 3
18: 1 When he had finished speaking to Saul 3
24:16 David had finished speaking these words to Saul 3
2Sm 6:18 when David had finished offering the burnt 3
11:19 When you have finished telling all the news 3
13:36 And as soon as he had finished speaking, behold 3
1Kg 1:41 with him heard it as they finished feasting. 3
3: 1 until he had finished building his own house 3
6: 9 So he built the house, and finished it; 3
14 So Solomon built the house, and finished it. 3
22 he overlaid . . until all the house was finished. 6
38 the house was finished in all its parts 3
7: 1 Solomon . . and he finished his entire house. 3
7 was finished with cedar from floor to rafters. 4
22 Thus the work of the pillars was finished. 6
40 Hiram finished all the work that he did 3
51 work . . on the house of the LORD was finished. 5
8:54 as Solomon finished offering all this prayer 3
9: 1 When Solomon had finished building the house 3
25 So he finished the house. 5
1Ch 16: 2 finished offering the burnt offerings 3
27:24 Jo'ab . . began to number, but did not finish; 3
28:20 service of the house of the LORD is finished. 3
2Ch 4:11 Huram finished the work that he did for King 3
5: 1 all the work that Solomon did . . was finished. 5
7:11 Thus Solomon finished the house of the LORD 3
8:16 from the day . . was laid until it was finished. 3
24:10 into the chest until they had finished. 3
14 when they had finished, they brought 3
29:17 sixteenth day of the first month they finished. 3
28 until the burnt offering was finished. 3
29 When the offering was finished, the king 3
34 Levites helped them, until the work was finished 3
31: 1 Now when all this was finished, all Israel 3
7 finished them in the seventh month. 3
Ezr 4:12 finishing the walls and repairing 8
13 if this city is rebuilt and the walls finished 8
16 if this city is rebuilt and its walls finished 8
5: 3 decree to . . finish this structure? 9
9 gave you a decree . . to finish this structure?' 9
11 which a great king of Israel built and finished. 8
16 been in building, and it is not yet finished.' 11
6:14 finished their building by command of the God 8
15 house was finished on the third day of the month 10
Neh 6:15 wall was finished . . in 52 days. 5
Isa 10:12 When the Lord has finished all his work 1
Jer 26: 8 And when Jeremiah had finished speaking 3
43: 1 Jeremiah finished speaking to all the people 3
51:63 When you finish reading this book 3
Ezk 42:15 Now when he had finished measuring the interior 3
43:23 When you have finished cleansing it 3
Dan 9:24 finish the transgression, to put an end to sin 2
Ams 7: 2 they had finished eating the grass of the land 3
Mat 7:28 And when Jesus finished these sayings 22
11: 1 when Jesus had finished instructing 22
13:53 when Jesus had finished these parables 22
19: 1 Now when Jesus had finished these sayings 22
26: 1 When Jesus had finished all these sayings 22
Lke 13:32 the third day I finish my course. 21
14:29 is not able to finish 15
30 began to build, and was not able to finish.' 15
Joh 19:28 knowing that all was now finished 22
30 he said, "It is finished 22
21:15 When they had finished breakfast •
Act 13:25 as John was finishing his course, he said 18
21: 7 When we had finished the voyage from Tyre 14
2Ti 4: 7 I have finished the race, I have kept the faith. 22
Heb 4: 3 although his works were finished 13
Rev 11: 7 when they have finished their testimony 22
1Es 2:19 Now if this city is built and the walls finished 20
24 if this city is built and its walls finished 12
4:55 until the day when the temple should be finished 16
6: 4 finishing all the other things? 16
4 the builders that are finishing these things? 16
14 it was finished. 16
28 until the house of the Lord is finished; 16
7: 5 the holy house was finished 20
2Es 7: 1 When I had finished speaking these words 23
14:25 until what you are about to write is finished. 23
26 when you have finished 24
Tob 8: 1 When they had finished eating 20
Jdt 2: 4 When he had finished setting forth his plan 20
5:22 When Achior had finished saying this 17
8:34 for I will not tell you until I have finished 22
14: 9 when she had finished 17
Sir 7:25 you will have finished a great task 22
18: 7 When a man has finished, he is just beginning 20
23:20 so it was also after it was finished. 20
38: 8 His works will never be finished 20
27 he is careful to finish his work. 22
28 He sets his heart on finishing his handiwork 19
30 he sets his heart to finish the glazing 20
50:14 Finishing the service at the altars 19
1Mc 2:23 When he had finished speaking these words 17
3:23 When he finished speaking 17
4:19 Just as Judas was finishing this speech 18
51 they finished all the work they had undertaken. 22
2Mc 15: 5 to take up arms and finish the king's business. 16

finish speaking 1. *σιγάω*
Act 15:13 After they finished speaking, James replied 1

finish up 1. כלה
Neh 4: 2 Will they finish up in a day? Will they revive 1

fir tree 1. בְּרוֹשׁ
Ps 104:17 stork has her home in the fir trees. 1
Ezk 27: 5 They made all your planks of fir trees from Senir; 1
31: 8 not rival it, nor the fir trees equal its boughs; 1

fire 1. אוּר 2. אֵשׁ 3. אִשֶּׁה 4. בְּעֵרָה 5. יצת 6. שְׂרֵפָה 7. אֶשָּׁא (A) 8. נוּר (A) 9. *διεγείρω* 10. *καυσόω* 11. *πῦρ* 12. *πυρά* 13. *πύργος* 14. *πύρινος* 15. *πυρόω* 16. *φῶς* 17. ignis
Gen 15:17 behold, a smoking fire pot and a flaming torch 2
19:24 rained on Sodom and Gomor'rah brimstone and fire 2
22: 6 he took in his hand the fire and the knife. 2
7 He said, "Behold, the fire and the wood; 2
Exd 3: 2 the LORD appeared to him in a flame of fire 2
9:23 thunder and hail, and fire ran down to the earth. 2
24 there was hail, a fire flashing continually 2
13:21 and by night in a pillar of fire to give them light 2
22 the pillar of fire by night did not depart 2
14:24 the LORD in the pillar of fire and of cloud looked 2
19:18 because the LORD descended upon it in fire; 2
22: 6 When fire breaks out and catches in thorns 2
6 he that kindled the fire shall make full 4
24:17 like a devouring fire on the top of the mountain 2
29:14 you shall burn with fire outside the camp; 2
34 then you shall burn the remainder with fire; 2
32:20 burnt it with fire, and ground it to powder 2
24 so they gave it to me, and I threw it into the fire 2
35: 3 you shall kindle no fire in all your habitations 2
40:38 and fire was in it by night, in the sight of all 2
Lev 1: 7 Aaron the priest shall put fire on the altar 2
7 and lay wood in order upon the fire 2
8 lay . . in order upon the wood that is on the fire 2
12 the wood that is on the fire upon the altar 2
17 burn it . . upon the wood that is on the fire 2
2:14 new grain from fresh ears, parched with fire 2
3: 5 burnt offering, which is upon the wood on the fire 2
4:12 and shall burn it on a fire of wood 2
6: 9 the fire of the altar shall be kept burning on it 2
10 ashes to which the fire has consumed the burnt 2
12 The fire on the altar shall be kept burning on it 2
13 Fire shall be kept burning upon the altar 2
30 sin offering . . it shall be burned with fire 2
7:17 on the third day shall be burned with fire 2
19 not be eaten; it shall be burned with fire 2
8:17 the bull . . he burned with fire outside the camp 2
32 the flesh and the bread you shall burn with fire 2
9:11 the skin he burned with fire outside the camp 2
24 fire came forth from before the LORD 2
10: 1 each took his censer, and put fire in it 2
1 and offered unholy fire before the LORD 2
2 fire came forth from the presence of the LORD 2
13:52 leprosy; it shall be burned in the fire 2
55 shall burn it in the fire, whether the leprous 2
57 shall burn with fire that in which is the disease 2
16:12 censer full of coals of fire from the altar 2
13 put the incense on the fire before the LORD 2
27 and their dung shall be burned with fire 2
18:21 of your children to devote them by fire to Molech •
19: 6 anything left over . . shall be burned with fire 2
20:14 they shall be burned with fire, both he 2
21: 9 she shall be burned with fire 2
22:27 it shall be acceptable as an offering by fire 3
Num 3: 4 they offered unholy fire before the LORD 2
6:18 put it on the fire which is under the sacrifice 2
9:15 over the tabernacle like the appearance of fire 2
16 continually . . appearance of fire by night. 2
11: 1 fire of the LORD burned among them, and consumed 2
2 Moses prayed to the LORD, and the fire abated. 2
3 Tab'erah, because the fire of the LORD burned 2
14:14 goest before . . in a pillar of fire by night. 2
16: 7 put fire in them and put incense upon them 2
18 took his censer, and they put fire in them 2
35 fire came forth from the LORD, and consumed 2
37 scatter the fire far and wide. For they are holy 2
46 censer, and put fire therein from off the altar 2
18: 9 most holy things, reserved from the fire; 2
21:28 For fire went forth from Heshbon 2
30 we laid waste until fire spread to Med'eba. 11
26:10 when the fire devoured 250 men; 2
61 when they offered unholy fire before the LORD. 2
31:10 cities . . encampments, they burned with fire 2
23 everything that can stand the fire 2
23 everything . . you shall pass through the fire 2
23 whatever cannot stand the fire, you shall pass 2
Deu 1:33 who went before you . . in fire by night 2
4:11 mountain burned with fire to the heart of heaven 2
12 LORD spoke to you out of the midst of the fire; 2
15 spoke to you at Horeb out of the midst of the fire 2
24 LORD your God is a devouring fire, a jealous God. 2
33 voice of a god speaking out of the midst of the fire 2
36 on earth he let you see his great fire 2
36 you heard his words out of the midst of the fire. 2
5: 4 LORD spoke . . out of the midst of the fire 2
5 for you were afraid because of the fire 2
22 mountain out of the midst of the fire, the cloud 2
23 while the mountain was burning with fire 2
24 heard his voice out of the midst of the fire; 2
25 For this great fire will consume us; 2
26 living God speaking out of the midst of fire 2
7: 5 you shall . . burn their graven images with fire. 2
25 graven images . . you shall burn with fire; 2
9: 3 he who goes over before you as a devouring fire 2
10 spoken with you . . out of the midst of the fire 2
15 mountain was burning with fire; 2
21 calf . . and burned it with fire and crushed it 2
10: 4 LORD had spoken to you . . out of the midst of the fire 2
12: 3 and burn their Ashe'rim with fire; 2
31 burn their sons and their daughters in the fire 2
13:16 burn the city and all its spoil with fire 2
18:16 me not . . see this great fire any more, lest I die.' 2
32:22 For a fire is kindled by my anger, and it burns 2
33: 2 he came . . with flaming fire at his right hand. 2
Jos 6:24 they burned the city with fire, and all within it; 2
7:15 And he who is taken . . shall be burned with fire 2
25 they burned them with fire, and stoned them 2
8: 8 you shall set the city on fire, doing as the LORD 2
19 and they made haste to set the city on fire. 2
11: 6 you shall . . burn their chariots with fire. 2
9 and burned their chariots with fire. 2
11 put to the sword . . and he burned Hazor with fire. 2
Jdg 1: 8 took it, and smote it . . and set the city on fire. 2
6:21 there sprang up fire from the rock and consumed 2
9:15 if not, let fire come out of the bramble and devour 2
20 let fire come out from Abim'elech, and devour 2

20 let fire come out from the citizens of Shechem 2
49 they set the stronghold on fire over them 2
52 near to the door of the tower to burn it with fire. 2
12: 1 We will burn your house over you with fire. 2
14:15 we burn you and your father's house with fire. 2
15: 6 came up, and burned her and her father with fire. 2
14 the ropes . . became as flax that has caught fire 2
16: 9 as a string of tow snaps when it touches the fire. 2
18:27 smote them . . and burned the city with fire. 2
20:48 all the towns which they found they set on fire. 2
1Sm 30: 1 They had overcome Ziklag, and burned it with fire 2
3 came to the city, they found it burned with fire 2
14 and we burned Ziklag with fire. 2
2Sm 14:30 See, Jo'ab's field . . go and set it on fire. 2
30 Ab'salom's servants set the field on fire. 2
31 Why have your servants set my field on fire? 2
22: 9 Smoke went . . devouring fire from his mouth; 2
13 Out of the brightness . . coals of fire flamed 2
23: 7 and they are utterly consumed with fire. 2
1Kg 9:16 gone up and captured Gezer and burnt it with fire 2
16:18 and burned the king's house . . with fire, and died 2
18:23 and lay it on the wood, but put no fire to it; 2
23 and lay it on the wood, and put no fire to it. 2
24 the God who answers by fire, he is God. 2
25 call on the name of your god, but put no fire to it. 2
38 the fire of the LORD fell, and consumed 2
19:12 and after the earthquake a fire 2
12 a fire, but the LORD was not in the fire; 2
12 and after the fire a still small voice. 2
2Kg 1:10 let fire come down from heaven and consume you 2
10 Then fire came down from heaven, and consumed him 2
12 let fire come down from heaven and consume you 2
12 Then the fire of God came down from heaven 2
14 fire came down from heaven, and consumed the two 2
2:11 a chariot of fire and horses . . separated the two 2
11 a chariot . . and horses of fire separated the two 2
6:17 mountain was full of horses and chariots of fire 2
17:31 Sephar'vites burned their children in the fire 2
19:18 and have cast their gods into the fire; 2
23:11 and he burned the chariots of the sun with fire. 2
1Ch 21:26 and he answered him with fire from heaven upon 2
2Ch 7: 1 ended his prayer, fire came down from heaven 2
3 all the children of Israel saw the fire come down 2
16:14 they made a very great fire in his honor. 6
21:19 His people made no fire in his honor 6
19 like the fires made for his fathers. 6
35:13 they roasted the passover lamb with fire 2
36:19 burned all its palaces with fire, and destroyed 2
Neh 1: 3 Jerusalem . . its gates are destroyed by fire. 2
2: 3 its gates have been destroyed by fire? 2
13 its gates which had been destroyed by fire. 2
9:12 by a pillar of fire in the night to light for them 2
19 nor the pillar of fire by night which lighted 2
Job 1:16 another, and said, "The fire of God fell from heaven 2
15:34 fire consumes the tents of bribery. 2
18: 5 the flame of his fire does not shine. 2
20:26 a fire not blown upon will devour him; 2
22:20 what they left the fire has consumed.' 2
28: 5 but underneath it is turned up as by fire. 2
31:12 that would be a fire which consumes unto Abaddon 2
41:19 Out of his mouth . . sparks of fire leap forth. 2
Ps 11: 6 he will rain coals of fire and brimstone; 2
18: 8 devouring fire from his mouth; glowing coals 2
12 there broke through his clouds . . coals of fire. 2
13 uttered his voice, hailstones and coals of fire. 2
21: 9 in his wrath; and fire will consume them. 2
29: 7 voice of the LORD flashes forth flames of fire. 2
39: 3 As I mused, the fire burned; 2
46: 9 he burns the chariots with fire! 2
50: 3 before him is a devouring fire 2
66:12 we went through fire and through water; 2
68: 2 as wax melts before fire, let the wicked perish 2
74: 7 They set thy sanctuary on fire; 2
78:21 a fire was kindled against Jacob 2
63 Fire devoured their young men, and their maidens 2
79: 5 Will thy jealous wrath burn like fire? 2
80:16 have burned it with fire, they have cut it down; 2
83:14 As fire consumes the forest 2
89:46 How long will thy wrath burn like fire? 2
97: 3 Fire goes before him, and burns up his 2
104: 4 who makest . . fire and flame thy ministers. 2
105:39 fire to give light by night. 2
106:18 Fire also broke out in their company; 2
118:12 they blazed like a fire of thorns; 2
148: 8 fire and hail, snow and frost, stormy wind 2
Prv 6:27 Can a man carry fire in his bosom 2
16:27 his speech is like a scorching fire. 2
26:20 For lack of wood the fire goes out; 2
21 As charcoal to hot embers and wood to fire, so is 2
30:16 fire which never says, "Enough. 2
Sng 8: 6 Its flashes are flashes of fire 2
Isa 1: 7 your cities are burned with fire; 2
4: 5 smoke and the shining of a flaming fire by night; 2
5:24 as the tongue of fire devours the stubble 2
9: 5 every garment . . burned as fuel for the fire. 2
18 wickedness burns like a fire, it consumes briers 2
19 burned, and the people are like fuel for the fire; 2
10:16 burning . . kindled, like the burning of fire. 2
17 The light of Israel will become a fire 2
26:11 Let the fire for thy adversaries consume them. 2
29: 6 tempest, and the flame of a devouring fire. 2
30:14 sherd . . with which to take fire from the hearth 2
27 and his tongue is like a devouring fire; 2
30 in furious anger and a flame of devouring fire 2
33 deep and wide, with fire and wood in abundance; 2
31: 9 says the LORD, whose fire is in Zion 1
33:11 your breath is a fire that will consume you. 2
12 like thorns cut down, that are burned in the fire. 2
14 Who among us can dwell with the devouring fire? 2
37:19 have cast their gods into the fire; 2
43: 2 when you walk through fire you shall not be 2
44:15 warms himself, he kindles a fire and bakes bread; •
16 Half of it he burns in the fire; 2
16 and says, "Aha, I am warm, I have seen the fire! 1
19 Half of it I burned in the fire 2
47:14 they are like stubble, the fire consumes them; 2
14 No coal for warming . . no fire to sit before! 1
50:11 all you who kindle a fire, who set brands alight! 2
11 Walk by the light of your fire 2
54:16 I . . created the smith who blows the fire of coals 2
64: 2 as when fire kindles brushwood 2
2 and the fire causes water to boil– 2
11 beautiful house . . has been burned by fire 2
65: 5 in my nostrils, a fire that burns all the day. 2
66:15 For behold, the LORD will come in fire 2
15 anger in fury, and his rebuke with flames of fire. 2
16 For by fire will the LORD execute judgment 2
24 worm . . not die, their fire shall not be quenched 2
Jer 4: 4 lest my wrath go forth like fire, and burn 2
5:14 behold, I am making my words in your mouth a fire 2
14 this people wood, and the fire shall devour them. •
6:29 the lead is consumed by the fire; 2
7:18 children gather wood, the fathers kindle fire 2
31 burn their sons and their daughters in the fire; 2
11:16 with the roar of a great tempest he will set fire 2
15:14 a fire is kindled which shall burn for ever. 2
17: 4 in my anger a fire is kindled 2
27 then I will kindle a fire in its gates 2
19: 5 to burn their sons in the fire as burnt offerings 2
20: 9 there is in my heart as it were a burning fire 2
21:10 king of Babylon, and he shall burn it with fire. 2
12 lest my wrath go forth like fire 2
14 I will kindle a fire in her forest 2
22: 7 choicest cedars, and cast them into the fire. 2
23:29 Is not my word like fire, says the LORD 2
29:22 Ahab, whom the king of Babylon roasted in the fire 2
32:29 shall come and set this city on fire, and burn it 2
34: 2 and he shall burn it with fire. 2
22 fight . . and take it, and burn it with fire. 2
36:22 there was a fire burning in the brazier 11
23 and throw them into the fire in the brazier 2
23 until the entire scroll was consumed in the fire 2
32 scroll which Jehoi'akim . . had burned in the fire; 2
37: 8 they shall take it and burn it with fire. 2
10 they would rise up and burn this city with fire. 2
38:17 and this city shall not be burned with fire 2
18 the Chalde'ans, and they shall burn it with fire 2
23 and this city shall be burned with fire. 2
43:12 He shall kindle a fire in the temples of the gods 2
13 the gods of Egypt he shall burn with fire. 2
48:45 for a fire has gone forth from Heshbon 2
49: 2 and its villages shall be burned with fire; 2
27 And I will kindle a fire in the wall of Damascus 2
50:32 I will kindle a fire in his cities 2
51:30 her dwellings are on fire, her bars are broken. 5
32 the bulwarks are burned with fire 2
58 and her high gates shall be burned with fire. 2
58 the nations weary themselves only for fire. 2
Lam 1:13 From on high he sent fire; into my bones . . descend; 2
2: 3 he has burned like a flaming fire in Jacob 2
4 he has poured out his fury like fire. 2
4:11 and he kindled a fire in Zion 2
Ezk 1: 4 and fire flashing forth continually 2
4 the midst of the fire, as it were gleaming bronze. 2
13 that looked like burning coals of fire 2
13 the fire was bright 2
13 and out of the fire went forth lightning. 2
27 gleaming bronze, like the appearance of fire 2
27 I saw as it were the appearance of fire 2
5: 2 A third part you shall burn in the fire •
4 you shall take some, and cast them into the fire 2
4 cast them into the fire, and burn them in the fire; 2
4 a fire will come forth into all . . of Israel. 2
8: 2 below what appeared to be his loins it was fire 2
10: 6 Take fire from between the whirling wheels 2
7 to the fire that was between the cherubim 2
15: 4 Lo, it is given to the fire for fuel; 2
4 when the fire has consumed both ends of it 2
5 when the fire has consumed it and it is charred 2
6 the forest, which I have given to the fire for fuel 2
7 though they escape from the fire 2
7 from the fire, the fire shall yet consume them; 2
16:21 delivered them up as an offering by fire to them? •
19:12 stem was withered; the fire consumed it. 2
14 And fire has gone out from its stem, has consumed 2
20:26 in making them offer by fire all their first-born •
31 offer your gifts and sacrifice your sons by fire 2
47 Behold, I will kindle a fire in you 2
21:31 I will blow upon you with the fire of my wrath; 2
32 You shall be fuel for the fire; 2
22:20 to blow the fire upon it in order to melt it; 2
21 and blow upon you with the fire of my wrath 2
31 I have consumed them with the fire of my wrath; 2
23:25 your survivors shall be devoured by fire. 2
24:10 Heap on the logs, kindle the fire, boil well 2
12 its thick rust does not go out of it by fire. 2
28:14 in the midst of the stones of fire you walked. 2
16 out from the midst of the stones of fire. 2
18 I brought forth fire from the midst of you; 2
30: 8 when I have set fire to Egypt, and all her helpers 2
14 Pathros a desolation, and will set fire to Zo'an 2
16 I will set fire to Egypt; 2
38:22 rains and hailstones, fire and brimstone. 2
39: 6 I will send fire on Magog 2
9 they will make fires of them for seven years; 2
10 for they will make their fires of the weapons; 2
Dan 3:22 flame of the fire slew those men who took 8
24 Did we not cast three men bound into the fire? 8
25 four men loose, walking in the midst of the fire 8
26 Shadrach . . and Abed'nego came out from the fire. 8
27 saw that the fire had not had any power 8
27 no smell of fire had come upon them. 8
7: 9 throne . . flames, its wheels were burning fire. 8
10 stream of fire issued and came forth from before 8
11 destroyed and given over to be burned with fire. 7
Hos 7: 4 a heated oven, whose baker ceases to stir the fire •
6 in the morning it blazes like a flaming fire. 2
8:14 but I will send a fire upon his cities 2
Jol 1:19 For fire has devoured the pastures 2
20 and fire has devoured the pastures 2
2: 3 Fire devours before them 2
5 like the crackling of a flame of fire devouring 2
30 portents . . blood and fire and columns of smoke. 2
Ams 1: 4 I will send a fire upon the house of Haz'ael 2
7 I will send a fire upon the wall of Gaza 2
10 I will send a fire upon the wall of Tyre 2
12 I will send a fire upon Teman 2
14 I will kindle a fire in the wall of Rabbah 2
2: 2 I will send a fire upon Moab, and it shall devour 2
5 I will send a fire upon Judah 2
5: 6 lest he break out like fire in the house of Joseph 2
7: 4 the Lord GOD was calling for a judgment by fire 2
Obd 1:18 The house of Jacob shall be a fire 2
Mic 1: 4 valleys will be cleft, like wax before the fire 2
7 all her hires shall be burned with fire 2
Nah 1: 6 His wrath is poured out like fire 2
3:13 fire has devoured your bars. 2
15 There will the fire devour you, the sword will cut 2
Hab 2:13 from the LORD . . that peoples labor only for fire 2
Zep 1:18 In the fire of his jealous wrath 2
3: 8 for in the fire of my jealous wrath 2
Zec 2: 5 For I will be to her a wall of fire round about 2
3: 2 Is not this a brand plucked from the fire? 2
9: 4 she shall be devoured by fire. 2
11: 1 O Lebanon, that the fire may devour your cedars! 2
13: 9 I will put this third into the fire 2
Mal 3: 2 he is like a refiner's fire and like fullers' soap 2
Mat 3:10 good fruit is cut down and thrown into the fire. 11
11 baptize you with the Holy Spirit and with fire. 11
12 the chaff he will burn with unquenchable fire. 11
5:22 You fool!' shall be liable to the hell of fire. 11
7:19 tree . . is cut down and thrown into the fire. 11
13:40 as the weeds are gathered and burned with fire 11
42 throw them into the furnace of fire 11
50 throw them into the furnace of fire 11
17:15 for often he falls into the fire 11
18: 8 to be thrown into the eternal fire. 11
9 with two eyes to be thrown into the hell of fire 11
25:41 Depart from me, you cursed, into the eternal fire 11
Mrk 9:22 often cast him into the fire and into the water 11
43 to go to hell, to the unquenchable fire. 11
47 the fire is not quenched. 11
48 For every one will be salted with fire. 11
14:54 warming himself at the fire. 16
Lke 3: 9 every tree . . is cut down and thrown into the fire. 11
16 baptize you with the Holy Spirit and with fire. 11
17 the chaff he will burn with unquenchable fire. 11
9:54 do you want us to bid fire come down from heaven 11
12:49 I came to cast fire upon the earth 11
17:29 fire and sulphur rained from heaven 11
22:55 when they had kindled a fire 11
Joh 15: 6 the branches are gathered, thrown into the fire 11
Act 2: 3 there appeared to them tongues as of fire 11
19 blood, and fire, and vapor of smoke; 11
7:30 in a flame of fire in a bush. 11
28: 2 they kindled a fire and welcomed us all 12
3 put them on the fire 12
5 He, however, shook off the creature into the fire 11
1Co 3:13 because it will be revealed with fire 11
13 fire will test what sort of work 11
15 but only as through fire. 11
2Th 1: 7 with his mighty angels in flaming fire 11
Heb 1: 7 Who makes . . his servants flames of fire. 11
10:27 a fearful prospect of judgment, and a fury of fire 11
11:34 quenched raging fire 11
12:18 a blazing fire, and darkness, and gloom 11
29 for our God is a consuming fire. 11

Jas 3: 5 How great a forest is set ablaze by a small fire! 11
6 And the tongue is a fire. 11
5: 3 their rust . . will eat your flesh like fire 11
1Pe 1: 7 gold which though perishable is tested by fire 11
2Pe 3: 7 and earth . . have been stored up for fire 11
10 and the elements will be dissolved with fire 10
12 and the elements will melt with fire! 10
Jde 1: 7 by undergoing a punishment of eternal fire. 11
23 save some, by snatching them out of the fire; 11
Rev 1:14 his eyes were like a flame of fire 11
2:18 the Son of God, who has eyes like a flame of fire 11
3:18 I counsel you to buy from me gold refined by fire 11
4: 5 before the throne burn seven torches of fire 11
8: 5 took the censer and filled it with fire 11
7 there followed hail and fire, mixed with blood 11
8 like a great mountain, burning with fire 11
9:17 fire and smoke . . issued from their mouths. 11
18 killed, by the fire and smoke and sulphur 11
10: 1 and his legs like pillars of fire. 11
11: 5 fire pours out from their mouth and consumes 11
13:13 even making fire come down from heaven to earth 11
14:10 he shall be tormented with fire and sulfur 11
18 the angel who has power over fire 11
15: 2 appeared to be a sea of glass mingled with fire 11
16: 8 and it was allowed to scorch men with fire; 11
17:16 and devour her flesh and burn her up with fire 11
18: 8 and she shall be burned with fire; 11
19:12 His eyes are like a flame of fire 11
20 These two were thrown alive into the lake of fire 11
20: 9 but fire came down from heaven and consumed them 11
10 thrown into the lake of fire and sulphur 11
14 Death and Hades were thrown into the lake of fire 11
14 This is the second death, the lake of fire; 11
15 he was thrown into the lake of fire. 11
21: 8 in the lake that burns with fire and sulphur 11
1Es 1:12 roasted the passover lamb with fire, as required; 11
55 burned their towers with fire 13
6:24 where they sacrifice with perpetual fire; 11
2Es 1:14 I provided light for you from a pillar of fire 17
23 I did not send fire upon you for your blasphemies 17
3:19 of fire and earthquake and wind and ice 17
4: 5 he said to me, "Go, weigh for me the weight of fire 17
9 asked you only about fire and wind and the day 17
16 for the fire came and consumed it; 17
50 and the fire is greater than the smoke 17
5: 8 and fire shall often break out 17
7: 7 there is fire on the right hand 17
8 that is, between the fire and the water 17
38 and there are fire and torments! 17
8: 8 is preserved in fire and water 17
22 they are changed to wind and fire ‡
13: 4 as wax melts when it feels the fire. 17
10 from his mouth as it were a stream of fire 17
11 the stream of fire and the flaming breath 17
27 as for your seeing wind and fire and a storm 17
38 (which was symbolized by the fire). 17
14:39 but its color was like fire. 17
15:23 a fire will go forth from his wrath 17
41 fire and hail and flying swords 17
61 and they shall be like fire to you. 17
62 they shall burn with fire all your forests 17
16: 4 A fire has been sent upon you 17
6 or quench a fire in the stubble 17
9 Fire will go forth from his wrath 17
15 The fire is kindled, and shall not be put out 17
53 for God will burn coals of fire on the head of him 17
73 as gold that is tested by fire. 17
77 It is shut off and given up to be consumed by fire. 17
Jdt 7: 5 when they had kindled fires on their towers 11
13:13 they kindled a fire for light 11
16:17 fire and worms he will give to their flesh 11
AEs 16:24 shall be destroyed in wrath with spear and fire. 11
Wis 10: 6 he escaped the fire 11
13: 2 either fire or wind or swift air 11
16:16 and utterly consumed by fire. 11
17 the fire had still greater effect 11
19 at another time . . it burned more intensely than fire 11
22 Snow and ice withstood fire without melting 11
22 the fire that blazed in the hail 11
23 whereas the fire . . forgot its native power. •
27 For what was not destroyed by fire was melted 11
17: 5 no power of fire was able to give light 11
6 a dreadful, self-kindled fire 12
19:20 Fire even in water retained its normal power 11
Sir 2: 5 For gold is tested in the fire 11
3:30 Water extinguishes a blazing fire 11
7:17 the punishment of the ungodly is fire and worms. 11
8: 3 nor heap wood on his fire. 11
10 lest you be burned in his flaming fire. 11
9: 8 by it passion is kindled like a fire. 11
11:32 From a spark of fire come many burning coals 11
15:16 He has placed before you fire and water 11
16: 6 In an assembly of sinners a fire will be kindled 11
21: 9 their end is a flame of fire. 11
22:24 vapor and smoke of the furnace precede the fire; 11
23:16 The soul heated like a burning fire 11
16 will never cease until the fire burns him up. 11
28:10 In proportion to the fuel for the fire 11
11 A hasty quarrel kindles fire 11
31:26 Fire and water prove the temper of steel •
38:28 the breath of the fire melts his flesh 11
39:26 water and fire and iron and salt and wheat flour 11
29 Fire and hail and famine and pestilence 11
40:30 in his stomach a fire is kindled. 11
43:21 withers the tender grass like fire. 11
45:19 to consume them in flaming fire. 11
48: 1 Then the prophet Elijah arose like a fire 11
3 also three times brought down fire. 11
9 You who were taken up by a whirlwind of fire 11
9 in a chariot with horses of fire; 14
50: 9 like fire and incense in the censer 11
51: 4 from choking fire on every side 12
4 from the midst of fire which I did not kindle 11
Bar 1: 2 took Jerusalem and burned it with fire. 11
4:35 For fire will come upon her from the Everlasting 11
LJr 1:55 When fire breaks out in a temple of wooden gods 11
63 the fire sent from above to consume mountains 11
Aza 1: 2 in the midst of the fire he opened his mouth 11
27 the fire did not touch them at all . . or trouble them. 11
44 Bless the Lord, fire and heat 11
66 from the midst of the fire he has delivered us. 11
1Mc 1:31 He plundered the city, burned it with fire 11
56 The books . . they tore to pieces and burned with fire. 11
5: 5 burned with fire their towers 11
28 he seized all its spoils and burned it with fire. 11
35 plundered it, and burned it with fire. 11
44 and burned the sacred precincts with fire 11
68 graven images of their gods he burned with fire; 11
6:31 burned these with fire, and fought manfully. 11
10:84 he burned with fire. 11
11:61 burned its suburbs with fire 11
12:28 they kindled fires in their camp and withdrew. 12
29 they saw the fires burning. 16
16:10 John burned it with fire 11
2Mc 1:18 the feast of the fire given when . . 11
19 took some of the fire of the altar 11
20 the priests who had hidden the fire 11
20 they had not found fire but thick liquid 11
22 a great fire blazed up, so that all marveled. 12
33 the exiled priests had hidden the fire 11
2: 1 to take some of the fire 11
10 fire came down from heaven 11
10 the fire came down 11
7: 5 to take him to the fire, still breathing 12
21 she fired her woman's reasoning with a man's 9
9: 7 breathing fire in his rage against the Jews 11
10: 3 striking fire out of flint 11
35 fired with anger because of the blasphemies 15
36 they kindled fires and burned the blasphemers 13
13: 8 against the altar whose fire and ashes were holy 11
14:41 they ordered that fire be brought 11
3Mc 2: 5 consumed with fire and sulphur the men of Sodom 11
29 are also to be branded on their bodies by fire 11
5:43 and rapidly level it . . with fire and spear 11
4Mc 5:32 fan the fire more vehemently! 11
6:24 the guards brought him to the fire. 11
7:10 O elder, fiercer than fire 11
12 though being consumed by the fire 11
9: 9 deservedly undergo . . eternal torment by fire 11
19 they spread fire under him 11
22 as though transformed by fire into immortality 11
10:14 a fire hot enough to make me play the coward. 11
11:26 Your fire is cold to us 11
12:12 intense and eternal fire and tortures 11
14: 9 in agonies of fire at that. 11
10 the power of fire is intense and swift 11
15:15 the flesh of her children consumed by fire 11
18:12 Hananiah, Azariah, and Mishael in the fire. 11
14 Even though you go through the fire 11
20 quenched fire with fire in his cruel caldrons 11
20 quenched fire with fire in his cruel caldrons 11

fire *See also* burn, catch, coal, color, consume, feed, heat, kindle, make, offer, offering, throw, try.

charcoal fire 1. *ἀνθρακιά*

Joh 18:18 the servants . . had made a charcoal fire 1
21: 9 they saw a charcoal fire there 1

flaming fire 1. *πυριφλεγής*

Wis 18: 3 thou didst provide a flaming pillar of fire 1

fire-breathing 1. *πυρόπνους*

3Mc 6:34 their fire-breathing boldness 1

fire-quenching 1. *σβεστικός*

Wis 19:20 water forgot its fire-quenching nature. 1

firebrand 1. אוּד 2. זֵק

Prv 26:18 madman who throws firebrands, arrows, and death 2
Isa 7: 4 these two smoldering stumps of firebrands 1

firepan 1. מַחְתָּה

Exd 27: 3 shovels and basins and forks and firepans; 1
38: 3 the basins, the forks, and the firepans 1
Num 4:14 utensils . . the firepans, the forks, the shovels 1
1Kg 7:50 basins, dishes . . and firepans, of pure gold; 1
2Kg 25:15 the firepans also, and the bowls. 1
2Ch 4:22 dishes for incense, and firepans, of pure gold; 1
Jer 52:19 also the small bowls, and the firepans 1

firm 1. כּוּן 2. *ἄκρος* 3. *ἀσφαλής* 4. *βέβαιος* 5. *στερεός* 6. *τόνος*

Ps 89: 2 thy faithfulness is firm as the heavens. 1
112: 7 his heart is firm, trusting in the LORD. 1
1Co 16:13 Be watchful, stand firm in your faith •
2Ti 2:19 God's firm foundation stands, bearing this seal 5
Heb 3:14 if only we hold our first confidence firm 4
1Pe 5: 9 Resist him, firm in your faith 5
Wis 4: 3 will strike a deep root or take a firm hold. 3
3Mc 5:31 a full and firm loyalty to my ancestors. 4
7: 7 the friendly and firm goodwill 4
4Mc 7: 5 in setting his mind firm like a jutting cliff 2
13 his body no longer tense and firm 6
17: 4 maintaining firm an enduring hope in God. 4

firm *See also* covenant, foundation, hold, make, stand.

firmament 1. רָקִיעַ 2. *στερέωμα* 3. firmamentum

Gen 1: 6 God said, "Let there be a firmament 1
7 God made the firmament and separated the waters 1
7 the waters which were under the firmament 1
7 from the waters which were above the firmament 1
8 God called the firmament Heaven. 1
14 there be lights in the firmament of the heavens 1
15 let them be lights in the firmament 1
17 God set them in the firmament of the heavens 1
20 the earth across the firmament of the heavens 1
Ps 19: 1 the firmament proclaims his handiwork. 1
150: 1 praise him in his mighty firmament! 1
Ezk 1:22 there was the likeness of a firmament, shining 1
23 under the firmament their wings were stretched 1
25 voice from above the firmament over their heads; 1
26 above the firmament over their heads there was 1
10: 1 behold, on the firmament that was over the heads 1
Dan 12: 3 shine like the brightness of the firmament; 1
2Es 4: 7 or how many streams are above the firmament 3
6: 4 the measures of the firmaments were named 3
20 the books shall be opened before the firmament 3
41 thou didst create the spirit of the firmament 3
Sir 43: 1 the clear firmament 2
8 shining forth in the firmament of heaven. 2
Aza 1:34 Blessed art thou in the firmament of heaven 2

firmly 1. חזק 2. מְאֹד 3. *βέβαιος* 4. *ἑδραῖος* 5. *σφόδρα*

1Kg 2:12 father; and his kingdom was firmly established. 2
2Kg 14: 5 as soon as the royal power was firmly in his hand 1
2Ch 25: 3 as soon as the royal power was firmly in his hand 1
1Co 7:37 whoever is firmly established in his heart 4
Jdt 14:10 he believed firmly in God, and was circumcised 5
3Mc 5:42 he firmly swore an irrevocable oath 3

firmly *See also* believe, bind, bond, cast, drive, establish, fix, hold, set.

act firmly 1. *ἐνισχύω*

3Mc 2:32 the majority acted firmly 1

firmness 1. נְצָבָה (A) 2. *στερέωμα*

Dan 2:41 some of the firmness of iron shall be in it 1
Col 2: 5 the firmness of your faith in Christ. 2

first 1. אֶחָד 2. אַחֵר 3. בְּכוֹר 4. בִּכּוּרִים 5. בְּרֹאשׁ 6. בָּרִאשֹׁנָה 7. בַּתְּחִלָּה 8. זֶה 9. חלל 10. יוֹם 11. כַּיּוֹם 12. לִפְנֵי 13. קֶדֶם 14. רֹאשׁ 15. רִאשׁוֹן 16. רֵאשִׁית 17. רִאשֹׁנִי 18. תְּחִלָּה 19. חַד (A) 20. קַדְמָי (A) 21. *ἀρχή* 22. *ἀρχηγός* 23. *εἷς* 24. *ἐν πρώτοις* 25. *πρότερον* 26. *πρότερος* 27. *πρωτογένημα* 28. *πρῶτον* 29. *πρῶτος* 30. initio 31. primus 32. principium 33. prior

Gen 2:11 The name of the first is Pishon; 1
8: 5 in the tenth month, on the first day of the month 1
13 In the 601st year, in the first month 15
13 the first day of the month, the waters were dried 1
9:20 Noah was the first tiller of the soil. 9
10: 8 he was the first on earth to be a mighty man. 9
13: 4 made an altar at the first; 15
25:25 The first came forth red, all his body like a hairy 15
31 Jacob said, "First sell me your birthright. 11
33 Jacob said, "Swear to me first. 11
28:19 but the name of the city was Luz at the first. 15
38:28 scarlet thread, saying, "This came out first. 15
41:20 gaunt cows ate up the first seven fat cows 15
Exd 4: 8 If they will not . . heed the first sign, they may 15
12: 2 it shall be the first month of the year for you. 15
15 on the first day you shall put away leaven 15
15 from the first day until the seventh day 15
16 On the first day you shall hold a holy assembly 15
18 In the first month, on the fourteenth day 15
13: 2 whatever is the first to open the womb 3
23:19 The first of the first fruits of your ground 16
26: 4 the outmost curtain in the first set; 1
24 joined at the top, at the first ring; 1
28:17 topaz, and carbuncle shall be the first row; 1
29:40 with the first lamb a tenth measure of fine flour 1
34: 1 Cut two tables of stone like the first; 15
1 the words that were on the first tables 15

4 Moses cut two tables of stone like the first; 15
26 The first of the first fruits of your ground 16
36:11 edge of the outmost curtain of the first set; 1
29 but joined at the top, at the first ring; 1
39:10 of sardius, topaz, and carbuncle was the first row; 1
40: 2 On the first day of the first month you shall 1
2 On the first day of the first month you shall 15
17 And in the first month in the second year 15
17 second year, on the first day of the month 1
Lev 4:21 burn it as he burned the first bull 15
5: 8 who shall offer first the one for the sin offering 15
9:15 offered it for sin, like the first sin offering 15
23: 5 the first month, on the fourteenth day of the month 15
7 On the first day you shall have a holy 15
24 In the seventh month, on the first day of the month 1
35 On the first day shall be a holy convocation 15
39 on the first day shall be a solemn rest 15
40 you shall take on the first day the fruit 15
Num 1: 1 on the first day of the second month 1
18 on the first day of the second month 1
2: 9 They shall set out first on the march. 15
7:12 offered his offering the first day was Nahshon 15
9: 1 in the first month of the second year after 15
5 they kept the passover in the first month 15
10:14 men of Judah set out first by their companies; 15
13:20 time was the season of the first ripe grapes. 4
15:20 first of your coarse meal you shall present 16
21 Of the first of your coarse meal you shall give 16
20: 1 into the wilderness of Zin in the first month 15
24:20 Am'alek was the first of the nations, but in the end 16
28:16 fourteenth day of the first month is the LORD'S 15
18 the first day there shall be a holy convocation 15
29: 1 On the first day of the seventh month 1
33: 3 They set out from Ram'eses in the first month 15
3 set out . . the fifteenth day of the first month; 15
38 died . . on the first day of the fifth month. 1
Deu 1: 3 40th year, on the first day of the eleventh month 1
10: 1 Hew two tables of stone like the first, and come up 15
2 write . . the words that were on the first tables 15
3 hewed two tables of stone like the first 15
4 wrote on the tables, as at the first writing 15
10 I stayed on the mountain, as at the first time 15
13: 9 your hand shall be first . . to put him to death 15
16: 4 sacrifice on the evening of the first day 15
9 count . . from the time you first put the sickle 9
17: 7 hand of the witnesses shall be first against him 15
18: 4 first of the fleece of your sheep, you shall give 16
26: 2 take some of the first of all the fruit 16
10 now I bring the first of the fruit of the ground 16
Jos 4:19 people came . . on the tenth day of the first month 15
8:33 as Moses . . had commanded at the first 15
21:10 which went . . since the lot fell to them first. 15
Jdg 1: 1 Who shall go up first for us against 7
18:29 but the name of the city was La'ish at the first. 15
20:18 Which of us shall go up first to battle against 7
18 And the LORD said, "Judah shall go up first. 7
22 place where they had formed it on the first day. 15
32 said, "They are routed before us, as at the first. 15
39 smitten down before us, as in the first battle 15
Rut 3:10 made this last kindness greater than the first 15
1Sm 2:16 Let them burn the fat first, and then take 10
14:14 that first slaughter . . was of about twenty men 15
35 it was the first altar that he built to the LORD. 9
2Sm 3:13 not see my face, unless you first bring Michal 12
17: 9 when some of the people fall at the first attack 18
19:20 I have come . . the first of all the house of Joseph 15
43 Were we not the first to speak of bringing back 15
21: 9 were put to death in the first days of harvest 15
1Kg 1:51 Let King Solomon swear to me first that he will 11
3:22 The first said, "No, the dead child is yours 8
27 Give the living child to the first woman, and by no •
17:13 do as you have said; but first make me a little cake 6
18:25 Choose . . one bull and prepare it first 15
20: 9 All that you first demanded . . I will do; 6
17 servants of the governors . . went out first. 6
22: 5 Inquire first for the word of the LORD. 11
1Ch 9: 2 the first to dwell again in their possessions 15
11: 6 Whoever shall smite the Jeb'usites first 15
6 Jo'ab . . went up first, so he became chief. 15
12:15 the men who crossed the Jordan in the first month 15
16: 7 David first appointed that thanksgiving be sung 14
24: 7 The first lot fell to Jehoi'arib 15
25: 9 The first lot fell for Asaph to Joseph; 15
27: 2 Jasho'beam . . in charge of the first division 15
2 charge of the first division in the first month; 15
3 of all the commanders . . for the first month. 15
29:29 acts of King David, from first to last, are written 15
2Ch 3:12 was joined to the wing of the first cherub. 2
9:29 the acts of Solomon, from the first to last 15
12:15 Now the acts of Rehobo'am, from first to last 15
16:11 The acts of Asa, from first to last, are written 15
18: 4 Inquire first for the word of the LORD. 11
20:34 rest of the acts . . from first to last 15
25:26 rest of the deeds of Amazi'ah, from first to last 15
26:22 the rest of the acts of Uzzi'ah, from first to last 15
28:26 his acts and all his ways, from first to last 15
29: 3 In the first year of his reign, in the first month 15
3 In the first year of his reign, in the first month 15
17 to sanctify on the first day of the first month 1
17 to sanctify on the first day of the first month 15
17 on the sixteenth day of the first month 15
35: 1 lamb on the fourteenth day of the first month. 15
27 his acts, first and last, behold, they are written 15
36:22 Now in the first year of Cyrus king of Persia 1
Ezr 1: 1 In the first year of Cyrus king of Persia 1
3: 6 From the first day of the seventh month 1
12 old men who had seen the first house 15
5:13 first year of Cyrus king of Babylon 19
6: 3 In the first year of Cyrus the king 19
19 On the fourteenth day of the first month 15
7: 9 first day of the first month he began to go up 1
9 first day of the first month he began to go up 15
9 first day of the fifth month he came to Jerusalem 1
8:31 twelfth day of the first month, to go to Jerusalem; 15
10:16 On the first day of the tenth month they sat down 1
17 by the first day of the first month they had come 1
17 by the first day of the first month they had come 15
Neh 7: 5 genealogy of those who came up at the first 15
8: 2 on the first day of the seventh month. 1
18 day by day, from the first day to the last day 15
10:37 bring the first of our coarse meal 16
Est 1:14 saw the king's face, and sat first in the kingdom 15
3: 7 In the first month, which is the month of Nisan 15
12 summoned on the thirteenth day of the first month 15
Job 15: 7 Are you the first man that was born? 15
40:19 He is the first of the works of God; 16
42:14 he called the name of the first Jemi'mah; 1
Prv 8:22 LORD created me . . the first of his acts of old. 13
23 Ages ago I was set up, at the first 14
26 first of the dust of the world. 14
18:17 He who states his case first seems right 15
Isa 1:26 I will restore your judges as at the first 15
41: 4 I, the LORD, the first, and with the last; I am He. 15
27 I first have declared it to Zion 15
43:27 Your first father sinned 15
44: 6 I am the first and I am the last; 15
48:12 I called! I am He, I am the first, and I am the last. 15
52: 4 My people went down at the first into Egypt 15
60: 9 the ships of Tarshish first, 15
Jer 7:12 in Shiloh, where I made my name dwell at first 15
25: 1 the first year of Nebuchadrez'zar king of Babylon 17
33: 7 and rebuild them as they were at first. 15
11 will restore the fortunes of the land as at first 15
36:28 the former words that were in the first scroll 15
50:17 First the king of Assyria devoured him 15
Ezk 10:14 faces: the first face was the face of the cherub 1
26: 1 In the eleventh year, on the first day of the month 1
29:17 in the first month, on the first day of the month 15
17 in the first month, on the first day of the month 1
30:20 In the eleventh year, in the first month 15
31: 1 in the third month, on the first day of the month 1
32: 1 in the twelfth month, on the first day of the month 1
17 In the twelfth year, in the first month 29
40:21 of the same size as those of the first gate; 15
44:30 the first of all the first fruits of all kinds, 16
30 give to the priests the first of your coarse meal 16
45:18 Thus says the Lord GOD: In the first month 15
18 In the first month, on the first day of the month 1
21 first month, on the fourteenth day of the month 15
Dan 1:21 Daniel . . until the first year of King Cyrus. 1
7: 1 In the first year of Belshaz'zar king of Babylon 19
4 The first was like a lion and had eagles' wings. 20
8 before which three of the first horns 20
8: 1 after that which appeared to me at the first. 18
21 great horn between his eyes is the first king. 15
9: 1 In the first year of Darius the son of Ahasu-e'rus 1
2 first year of his reign, I, Daniel, perceived 1
21 Gabriel, whom I had seen in the vision at the first 18
10: 4 On the 24th day of the first month 15
12 first day that you set your mind to understand 15
11: 1 as for me, in the first year of Darius the Mede 1
Hos 1: 2 When the LORD first spoke through Hose'a 18
2: 7 shall say, 'I will go and return to my first husband 15
Ams 6: 1 the notable men of the first of the nations 16
7 shall now be the first of those to go into exile 5
Hag 1: 1 in the sixth month, on the first day of the month 1
Zec 6: 2 The first chariot had red horses 15
12: 7 will give victory to the tents of Judah first 15
Mat 5:24 first be reconciled to your brother 28
6:33 seek first his kingdom and his righteousness 28
7: 5 hypocrite, first take the log out of your own eye 28
8:21 Lord, let me first go and bury my father. 28
10: 2 first, Simon, who is called Peter 29
12:29 unless he first binds the strong man 28
45 worse than the first 29
13:30 Gather the weeds first and bind them in bundles 28
17:10 the scribes say that first Eli'jah must come? 28
27 cast a hook, and take the first fish that comes up 28
19:30 many that are first will be last 29
30 first will be last, and the last first. 29
20: 8 beginning with the last, up to the first.' 29
10 Now when the first came 29
16 the last will be first, and the first last. 29
16 the last will be first, and the first last. 29
27 whoever would be first among you 29
21:28 he went to the first and said 29
31 They said, "The first." Jesus said to them 29
36 Again he sent other servants, more than the first; 29
22:25 the first married, and died 29
38 This is the great and first commandment. 29
23:26 first cleanse the inside of the cup 28
26:17 Now on the first day of Unleavened Bread 29
27:64 the last fraud will be worse than the first. 29
28: 1 toward the dawn of the first day of the week 23
Mrk 3:27 unless he first binds the strong man 28
4:28 The earth produces of itself, first the blade 28
7:27 he said to her, "Let the children first be fed 28
9:11 the scribes say that first Eli'jah must come 28
12 Eli'jah does come first to restore all things 28
35 If any one would be first, he must be last of all 29
10:31 many that are first will be last 29
31 first will be last, and the last first. 29
44 whoever would be first among you 29
12:20 There were seven brothers; the first took a wife 29
28 Which commandment is the first of all? 29
29 Jesus answered, "The first is, 'Hear, O Israel 29
13:10 gospel must first be preached to all nations. 28
14:12 on the first day of Unleavened Bread 29
16: 2 very early on the first day of the week 23
9 Now when he rose early on the first day of the week 29
9 he appeared first to Mary Magdalene 29
Lke 2: 2 This was the first enrollment 29
6:42 hypocrite, first take the log out of your own eye 28
9:59 he said, "Lord, let me first go and bury my father. 28
61 let me first say farewell to those at my home. 28
10: 5 Whatever house you enter, first say, 'Peace 28
11:26 the last state . . becomes worse than the first. 29
38 he did not first wash before dinner. 28
12: 1 he began to say to his disciples first 28
13:30 behold, some are last who will be first 29
30 some are first who will be last. 29
14:18 The first said to him, 'I have bought a field 29
28 does not first sit down and count the cost 28
31 what king . . will not sit down first and take counsel 28
16: 5 he said to the first, 'How much . . owe my master?' 29
17:25 first he must suffer many things and be rejected 28
19:16 The first came before him, saying, 'Lord 29
20:29 the first took a wife, and died without children; 29
21: 9 this must first take place 28
24: 1 on the first day of the week, at early dawn 23
Joh 1:41 He first found his brother Simon, and said to him 28
2:10 said to him, "Every man serves the good wine first; 28
11 This, the first of his signs, Jesus did at Cana 21
6:64 Jesus knew from the first 21
7:51 judge a man without first giving him a hearing 28
8: 7 Let him . . be the first to throw a stone at her. 29
10:40 to the place where John at first baptized 28
12:16 His disciples did not understand this at first; 28
18:13 First they led him to Annas 28
19:32 the soldiers came and broke the legs of the first 29
39 who had at first come to him by night 28
20: 1 Now on the first day of the week 23
4 outran Peter and reached the tomb first; 29
8 the other disciple, who reached the tomb first 29
19 the first day of the week 23
Act 1: 1 In the first book, O The-oph'ilus 28
3:26 sent him to you first, to bless you 28
7:12 he sent forth our fathers the first time. 28
12:10 they had passed the first and the second guard 29
13:46 the word of God should be spoken first to you. 28
15:14 how God first visited the Gentiles 28
20: 7 On the first day of the week 23
18 from the first day that I set foot in Asia 29
26:20 declared first to those at Damascus 28
23 by being the first to rise from the dead 29
27:43 to throw themselves overboard first 29
Rom 1: 8 First, I thank my God through Jesus Christ 28
16 to the Jew first and also to the Greek. 28
2: 9 the Jew first and also the Greek. 28
10 the Jew first and also the Greek. 28
10:19 First Moses says, "I will make you jealous of those 29
13:11 nearer to us now than when we first believed; •
1Co 11:18 in the first place, when you assemble as a church 28
12:28 God has appointed in the church first apostles 28
14:30 let the first be silent. 29
15: 3 For I delivered to you as of first importance 29
45 The first man Adam became a living being 29
46 it is not the spiritual which is first 28
47 The first man was from the earth, a man of dust 29
16: 2 On the first day of every week 23
2Co 1:15 I wanted to come to you first 25
8: 5 first they gave themselves to the Lord and to us 28
10:14 we were the first to come all the way to you •
Gal 4:13 preached the gospel to you at first; 25
Eph 6: 2 (this is the first commandment with a promise) 29
Php 1: 5 from the first day until now. 29
1Th 4:16 the dead in Christ will rise first; 28
2Th 2: 3 unless the rebellion comes first 28
1Ti 2: 1 First of all, then, I urge that . . 28
13 For Adam was formed first, then Eve; 29
3:10 let them also be tested first 28
5: 4 let them first learn their religious duty 28
12 having violated their first pledge. 29
2Ti 1: 5 a faith that dwelt first in your grandmother 28
2: 6 ought to have the first share of the crops. 28
4:16 At my first defense no one took my part 29
Heb 2: 3 It was declared at first by the Lord 21

3:14 if only we hold our first confidence firm 21
5:12 teach you . . the first principles of God's word. 21
7: 2 He is first . . king of righteousness 28
27 to offer sacrifices daily, first for his own sins 25
8: 7 For if that first covenant had been faultless 29
13 he treats the first as obsolete 29
9: 1 the first covenant had regulations for worship 29
15 the transgressions under the first covenant. 29
18 Hence even the first covenant was not ratified 29
10: 9 He abolishes the first 28
Jas 3:17 wisdom from above is first pure, then peaceable 28
2Pe 1:20 First of all you must understand this 28
2:20 last state has become worse for them than the first. 29
3: 3 First of all you must understand this 28
1Jn 4:19 We love, because he first loved us. 29
Rev 1:17 saying, "Fear not, I am the first and the last 29
2: 4 you have abandoned the love you had at first. 29
5 repent and do the works you did at first. 29
8 The words of the first and the last 29
19 and that your latter works exceed the first. 29
4: 1 the first voice, which I had heard speaking to me 29
7 the first living creature like a lion 28
8: 7 The first angel blew his trumpet 29
9:12 The first woe has passed; 23
13:12 exercises all the authority of the first beast 29
12 makes . . inhabitants worship the first beast 28
16: 2 first angel went and poured his bowl on the earth 29
20: 5 This is the first resurrection. 29
6 holy is he who shares in the first resurrection! 29
21: 1 first heaven and the first earth had passed away 29
1 first heaven and the first earth had passed away 29
19 adorned with every jewel; the first was jasper 29
22:13 I am the Alpha and the Omega, the first and the last 29
1Es 1: 1 the fourteenth day of the first month 29
2: 1 In the first year of Cyrus as king of the Persians 29
3:10 The first wrote, "Wine is strongest. 23
17 Then the first . . began and said 29
5: 6 in the month of Nisan, the first month. 29
47 in the square before the first gate 29
6:17 in the first year that Cyrus reigned 29
24 In the first year of the reign of Cyrus 29
7:10 the fourteenth day of the first month 29
8: 6 left Babylon on the new moon of the first month 29
61 on the twelfth day of the first month 29
9:17 the new moon of the first month. 29
2Es 2:23 give you the first place in my resurrection. 31
3:21 For the first Adam, burdened with an evil heart 31
5:42 for those who are first there is no haste. 33
6: 7 when will be the end of the first age 33
38 and didst say on the first day 31
7:30 as it was at the first beginnings 33
70 he first prepared the judgment 31
78 first of all it adores the glory of the Most High. 31
81 The first way, because they have scorned the law 31
91 First of all, they shall see with great joy 31
92 The first order, because they have striven 31
106 first Abraham prayed for the people of Sodom 31
116 I answered and said, "This is my first and last word 31
10:28 Where is the angel Uriel, who came to me at first? 32
29 the angel who had come to me at first came to me 32
11:14 so that it disappeared like the first. 33
27 this disappeared more quickly than the first. 33
12:33 first he will set them . . before his judgment 31
14:29 At first our fathers dwelt as aliens in Egypt 30
45 Make public the 24 books that you wrote first 33
Tob 4:12 First of all take a wife 28
Jdt 2: 1 on the 22nd day of the first month 29
8:29 Today is not the first time •
12:16 ever since the day he first saw her. •
AEs 11: 2 on the first day of Nisan 23
Wis 7: 3 my first sound was a cry, like that of all. 29
Sir 4:17 at first she will walk with him on tortuous paths 29
11: 7 first consider, and then reprove. 29
23:23 first of all, she has disobeyed the law of the Most High 29
31:17 first to stop eating, for the sake of good manners 29
37: 8 learn first what is his interest 29
45:20 he allotted to him the first of the first fruits 27
20 he prepared bread of first fruits in abundance; 29
51:20 I gained understanding with her from the first 21
1Mc 2:18 be the first to come and do what the king commands 29
5:40 If he crosses over to us first 26
43 Then he crossed over against them first 26
6: 2 the . . king who first reigned over the Greeks. 29
6 that Lysias had gone first with a strong force 24
7:13 Hasideans were first among the sons of Israel 29
43 he himself was the first to fall in the battle. 29
8:24 If war comes first to Rome 26
27 if war comes first to the nation of the Jews 26
9: 3 In the first month of the 152nd year 29
10:41 have not paid as they did in the first years 29
47 he had been the first to speak peaceable words 22
13:42 In the first year of Simon the great high priest 29
16: 6 so he crossed over first 29
2Mc 4:33 having first withdrawn to a place of sanctuary •
7: 7 After the first brother had died in this way 29
8 as the first brother had done. 29
8:23 then, leading the first division himself 29
11: 7 Maccabeus himself was the first to take up arms 29
12:22 when Judas' first division appeared 29
14: 8 first because I am genuinely concerned 28
15:18 their greatest and first fear 29
4Mc 1:30 Observe now first of all 28
6: 2 First they stripped the old man 29
8: 2 conspicuously defeated in his first attempt 29
17: 7 those who first beheld it •

first *See also* bring, contestant, convert, father, formed, fruit, hope, issue, like, month, open, ripe, season, shearing, son, speak, time.

act first 1. *προφθάνω*
1Mc 10: 4 for he said, "Let us act first to make peace with him 1

first man 1. *πρῶτος*
Sir 24:28 Just as the first man did not know her perfectly 1

first-born 1. בְּכוֹר 2. בְּכִירָה 3. בְּכֹרָה 4. פֶּטֶר רֶחֶם 5. *πρωτότοκος* 6. primogenitus
Gen 10:15 father of Sidon his first-born, and Heth 1
19:31 the first-born said to the younger 2
33 the first-born went in, and lay with her father; 2
34 on the next day, the first-born said to the younger 2
37 first-born bore a son, and called his name Moab; 2
22:21 Uz the first-born, Buz his brother 1
25:13 Neba'ioth, the first-born of Ish'mael; 1
27:19 Jacob said . . "I am Esau your first-born. 1
32 I am your son, your first-born, Esau. 1
29:26 to give the younger before the first-born. 2
35:23 sons of Leah: Reuben (Jacob's first-born) 1
36:15 The sons of El'iphaz the first-born of Esau 1
38: 6 Judah took a wife for Er his first-born 1
7 Er, Judah's first-born, was wicked in the sight 1
41:51 called the name of the first-born Manas'seh 1
43:33 the first-born according to his birthright 1
46: 8 Jacob and his sons. Reuben, Jacob's first-born 1
48:14 for Manas'seh was the first-born. 1
18 Not so, my father; for this one is the first-born; 1
49: 3 Reuben, you are my first-born, my might 1
Exd 4:22 Thus says the LORD, Israel is my first-born son 1
23 behold, I will slay your first-born son.' 1
6:14 the sons of Reuben, the first-born of Israel 1
11: 5 all the first-born in the land of Egypt shall die 1
5 all . . shall die, from the first-born of Pharaoh 1
5 even to the first-born of the maidservant who is 1
5 and all the first-born of the cattle. 1
12:12 I will smite all the first-born in the land 1
29 smote all the first-born in the land of Egypt 1
29 from the first-born of Pharaoh who sat on his 1
29 to the first-born of the captive . . in the dungeon 1
29 smote . . and all the first-born of the cattle. 1
13: 2 Consecrate to me all the first-born; 1
13 Every first-born of man among your sons you shall 1
15 slew all the first-born in the land of Egypt 1
15 LORD slew . . both the first-born of man 1
15 first-born of man and the first-born of cattle. 1
15 but all the first-born of my sons I redeem.' 1
22:29 The first-born of your sons you shall give to me. 1
34:20 All the first-born of your sons you shall redeem. 1
Num 1:20 The people of Reuben, Israel's first-born 1
3: 2 Nadab the first-born, and Abi'hu, Elea'zar 1
12 instead of every first-born that opens the womb 1
13 for all the first-born are mine; 1
13 I slew all the first-born in the land of Egypt 1
13 consecrated . . the first-born in Israel 1
40 Number all the first-born males of the people 1
41 instead of all the first-born among the people 1
42 all the first-born among the people of Israel 1
43 all the first-born males . . were 22,273. 1
45 all the first-born among the people of Israel 1
46 273 of the first-born of the people of Israel 1
50 from the first-born of the people of Israel 1
8:16 first-born of all the people of Israel 1
17 first-born among the people of Israel are mine 1
17 slew all the first-born in the land of Egypt 1
18 all the first-born among the people of Israel. 1
18:15 the first-born of man you shall redeem 1
26: 5 Reuben, the first-born of Israel; 1
33: 4 Egyptians were burying all their first-born 1
Deu 21:15 if the first-born son is hers that is disliked 1
16 son of the disliked, who is the first-born 1
17 acknowledge the first-born . . of the disliked 1
17 right of the first-born is his. 3
Jos 6:26 At the cost of his first-born 1
17: 1 Manas'seh, for he was the first-born of Joseph. 1
1 To Machir the first-born of Manas'seh, the father 1
Jdg 8:20 he said to Jether his first-born, "Rise, and slay 1
1Sm 8: 2 The name of his first-born son was Jo'el 1
14:49 the name of the first-born was Merab 2
17:13 sons who went . . were Eli'ab the first-born 1
2Sm 3: 2 sons were born . . his first-born was Amnon 1
1Kg 16:34 at the cost of Abi'ram his first-born 1
1Ch 1:13 Canaan was the father of Sidon his first-born 1
29 the first-born of Ish'mael, Neba'ioth; and Kedar 1
2: 3 Now Er, Judah's first-born, was wicked in the sight 1
13 Jesse was the father of Eli'ab his first-born 1
25 The sons of Jerah'meel, the first-born of Hezron 1
25 The sons of Jerah'meel . . Ram, his first-born 1
27 The sons of Ram, the first-born of Jerah'meel: Ma'az 1
42 sons of Caleb . . Mare'shah his first-born 1
50 sons of Hur the first-born of Eph'rathah 1
3: 1 sons of David . . the first-born Amnon, by Ahin'o-am 1
15 The sons of Josi'ah: Joha'nan the first-born 1
4: 4 the sons of Hur, the first-born of Eph'rathah 1
5: 1 The sons of Reuben the first-born of Israel 1
1 (for he was the first-born; 1
3 the sons of Reuben, the first-born of Israel 1
6:28 sons of Samuel: Jo'el his first-born . . Abi'jah. 1
8: 1 Benjamin was the father of Bela his first-born 1
30 His first-born son: Abdon, then Zur, Kish, Ba'al, Nadab 1
39 The sons of Eshek his brother: Ulam his first-born 1
9: 5 of the Shi'lonites: Asai'ah the first-born 1
31 Mattithi'ah . . the first-born of Shallum 1
36 first-born son Abdon, then Zur, Kish, Ba'al, Ner 1
26: 2 Meshelemi'ah had sons: Zechari'ah the first-born 1
4 O'bed-e'dom had sons: Shemai'ah the first-born 1
10 for though he was not the first-born 1
2Ch 21: 3 to Jeho'ram, because he was the first-born. 1
Neh 10:36 bring . . first-born of our sons and of our cattle 1
Job 18:13 the first-born of death consumes his limbs. 1
Ps 78:51 He smote all the first-born in Egypt 1
89:27 I will make him the first-born 1
105:36 He smote all the first-born in their land 1
135: 8 He it was who smote the first-born of Egypt 1
136:10 to him who smote the first-born of Egypt 1
Isa 14:30 the first-born of the poor will feed 1
Jer 31: 9 a father to Israel, and E'phraim is my first-born. 1
Ezk 20:26 in making them offer by fire all their first-born 4
Mic 6: 7 Shall I give my first-born for my transgression 1
Zec 12:10 over him, as one weeps over a first-born. 1
Lke 2: 7 she gave birth to her first-born son 5
Rom 8:29 he might be the first-born among many brethren. 5
Col 1:15 the first-born of all creation; 5
18 he is the beginning, the first-born from the dead 5
Heb 1: 6 when he brings the first-born into the world 5
11:28 the Destroyer of the first-born 5
12:23 to the assembly of the first-born 5
Rev 1: 5 Jesus Christ . . the first-born of the dead 5
2Es 6:58 thy people, whom thou hast called thy first-born 6
Tob 5:13 offered the first-born of our flocks 5
Wis 18:13 yet, when their first-born were destroyed 5
4Mc 15:18 When the first-born breathed his last 5

first-born *See also* son, treat.

first-ripe *See* fig.

firstling 1. בְּכוֹר 2. בכר 3. פֶּטֶר 4. פֶּטֶר שֶׁגֶר
Gen 4: 4 Abel brought of the firstlings of his flock 1
Exd 13:12 All the firstlings of your cattle that are males 4
13 Every firstling of an ass you shall redeem 3
34:19 All . . the firstlings of cow and sheep. 3
20 The firstling of an ass you shall redeem 3
Lev 27:26 a firstling of animals . . belongs to the LORD 1
26 which as a firstling belongs to the LORD 2
Num 3:41 instead of all the firstlings among the cattle 1
18:15 firstling of unclean beasts you shall redeem. 1
17 firstling of a cow . . you shall not redeem; 1
17 firstling of a sheep . . you shall not redeem; 1
17 firstling of a goat, you shall not redeem; 1
Deu 12: 6 bring . . the firstlings of your herd 1
17 not eat . . the firstlings of your herd 1
14:23 eat . . the firstlings of your herd and flock; 1
15:19 firstling males that are born of your herd 1
19 shall do no work with the firstling of your herd 1
19 nor shear the firstling of your flock. 1
33:17 His firstling bull has majesty 1
Neh 10:36 firstlings of our herds and of our flocks. 1

fish 1. דָּג 2. דָּגָה 3. *ἁλιεύω* 4. *ἔνυδρος* 5. *ἰχθύς* 6. *ὀψάριον* 7. *προσφάγιον* 8. piscis
Gen 1:26 let them have dominion over the fish of the sea 2
28 and have dominion over the fish of the sea 2
9: 2 ground and all the fish of the sea; 1
Exd 7:18 the fish in the Nile shall die, and the Nile shall 2
21 the fish in the Nile died; and the Nile became foul 2
Num 11: 5 We remember the fish we ate in Egypt for nothing 2
22 Or shall all the fish of the sea be gathered 1
Deu 4:18 likeness of any fish that is in the water 2
1Kg 4:33 beasts, and of birds, and of reptiles, and of fish. 1
2Ch 33:14 wall . . for the entrance into the Fish Gate 1
Neh 13:16 brought in fish and all kinds of wares and sold 1
Job 12: 8 the fish of the sea will declare to you. 1
41: 7 or his head with fishing spears? 1
Ps 8: 8 the birds of the air, and the fish of the sea 1
105:29 waters into blood, and caused their fish to die. 2
Ecc 9:12 Like fish which are taken in an evil net 1
Isa 50: 2 fish stink for lack of water, and die of thirst. 2
Ezk 29: 4 the fish of your streams stick to your scales; 2
4 fish of your streams which stick to your scales. 2
5 you and all the fish of your streams; 2
38:20 the fish of the sea, and the birds of the air 1
47: 9 there will be very many fish; 2
10 its fish will be of very many kinds 2
10 of very many kinds, like the fish of the Great Sea. 2
Hos 4: 3 and even the fish of the sea are taken away. 1
Jon 1:17 LORD appointed a great fish to swallow up Jonah; 1
17 Jonah was in the belly of the fish three days 1
2: 1 to the LORD his God from the belly of the fish 2
10 the LORD spoke to the fish, and it vomited out 1

Hab 1:14 For thou makest men like the fish of the sea 1
Zep 1: 3 away the birds of the air and the fish of the sea. 1
10 a cry will be heard from the Fish Gate 1
Mat 7:10 Or if he asks for a fish, will give him a serpent? 5
13:47 and gathered fish of every kind; *
14:17 We have only five loaves here and two fish. 5
19 and taking the five loaves and the two fish 5
15:36 he took the seven loaves and the fish 5
17:27 cast a hook, and take the first fish that comes up 5
Mrk 6:38 they said, "Five, and two fish. 5
41 taking the five loaves and the two fish 5
41 he divided the two fish among them all. 5
43 full of broken pieces and of the fish. 5
Lke 5: 6 they enclosed a great shoal of fish 5
9 the catch of fish which they had taken; 5
9:13 We have no more than five loaves and two fish 5
16 taking the five loaves and the two fish 5
11:11 What father among you, if his son asks for a fish 5
11 will instead of a fish give him a serpent; 5
24:42 They gave him a piece of broiled fish 5
Joh 6: 9 a lad here who has five barley loaves and two fish; 6
11 so also the fish, as much as they wanted. 6
21: 3 Simon Peter said to them, "I am going fishing. 3
5 Jesus said to them, "Children have you any fish? 7
6 not able to haul it in, for the quantity of fish. 5
8 dragging the net full of fish 5
9 a charcoal fire . . with fish lying on it, and bread. 6
10 Bring some of the fish that you have just caught. 6
11 hauled the net ashore, full of large fish, 153 5
13 and so with the fish. 6
1Co 15:39 another for birds, and another for fish. 5
2Es 5: 7 the sea of Sodom shall cast up fish 8
6:47 bring forth living creatures, birds, and fishes; 8
16:12 its waves and the fish also shall be troubled 8
Tob 6: 2 A fish leaped up from the river 5
3 the angel said to him, "Catch the fish. 5
3 the young man seized the fish 5
4 Then the angel said to him, "Cut open the fish 5
5 they roasted and ate the fish. 5
6 of what use is the . . heart and gall of the fish? 5
16 some of the heart and liver of the fish 5
8: 2 and put the heart and liver of the fish upon them 5
11: 4 take the gall of the fish with you 5
Wis 19:10 instead of fish the river spewed out . . frogs 4

small fish 1. *ἰχθύδιον*
Mat 15:34 They said, "Seven, and a few small fish. 1
Mrk 8: 7 they had a few small fish; and having blessed them 1

fisher 1. דַּיָּג 2. *ἁλιεύς*
Jer 16:16 I am sending for many fishers, says the LORD 1
Mat 4:19 me, and I will make you fishers of men. 2
Mrk 1:17 Follow me and I will make you become fishers of men. 2

fisherman 1. דַּיָּג 2. *ἁλιεύς*
Isa 19: 8 The fishermen will mourn and lament 1
Ezk 47:10 Fishermen will stand beside the sea; 1
Mat 4:18 a net into the sea; for they were fishermen. 2
Mrk 1:16 for they were fishermen. 2
Lke 5: 2 but the fishermen had gone out of them 2

fishhook 1. חַכָּה 2. סִיר דּוּגָה
Job 41: 1 Can you draw out Levi'athan with a fishhook 1
Ams 4: 2 with hooks, even the last of you with fishhooks. 2

fissure 1. *ἁρμός*
Sir 27: 2 driven firmly into a fissure between stones 1

fist 1. אֶגְרֹף 2. חֹפֶן 3. יָד
Exd 21:18 strikes the other with a stone or with his fist 1
Prv 30: 4 Who has gathered the wind in his fists? 2
Isa 10:32 he will shake his fist at the mount of . . Zion 3
58: 4 and to fight and to hit with wicked fist. 1
Zep 2:15 Every one who passes . . hisses and shakes his fist 3

fit 1. יצא 2. יָשָׁר 3. כון 4. כְּנֶגֶד 5. עשה 6. *ἄξιος* 7. *εὔθετος* 8. *κατά* 9. *μετά*
Gen 2:18 I will make him a helper fit for him. 4
20 there was not found a helper fit for him. 4
2Kg 10: 3 select the best and fittest of your master's sons 2
24:16 all of them strong and fit for war. 5
2Ch 25: 5 300,000 picked men, fit for war 1
26:11 Uzzi'ah had an army of soldiers, fit for war 1
Ps 11: 2 they have fitted their arrow to the string 3
Lke 9:62 fit for the kingdom of God. 7
14:35 is fit neither for the land nor for the dunghill; 7
Wis 1:16 because they are fit to belong to his party. 6
15: 6 and fit for such objects of hope 6
Sir 31:20 he rises early, and feels fit 9
36:24 a helper fit for him and a pillar of support. 8

fit the occasion 1. *χρεία*
Eph 4:29 good for edifying, as fits the occasion 1

fit together 1. שלב
Exd 26:17 two tenons in each frame, for fitting together; 1
36:22 Each frame had two tenons, for fitting together; 1

fitly 1. אֹפֶן 2. עַל מִלֵּאת
Prv 25:11 A word fitly spoken is like apples of gold 1
Sng 5:12 His eyes are like . . bathed in milk, fitly set. 2

fitting 1. יָפֶה 2. נָאוֶה 3. אֲרִיךְ (A) 4. *ἀνήκω* 5. *ἄξιος* 6. *ἐναρμόζω* 7. *ἑξῆς* 8. *ἔπειμι* 9. *ἐσθίω* 10. *ἐφαρμόζω* 11. *πρέπω* 12. *ὡραῖος*
Ezr 4:14 not fitting for us to witness the king's dishonor 3
Prv 19:10 It is not fitting for a fool to live in luxury 2
26: 1 so honor is not fitting for a fool. 2
Ecc 5:18 what I have seen to be good and to be fitting is 1
Mat 3:15 thus it is fitting for us to fulfil all righteousness. 11
Lke 15:32 It was fitting to make merry and be glad 9
Eph 5: 3 as is fitting among saints. 11
4 nor silly talk, nor levity, which are not fitting; 4
Col 3:18 as is fitting in the Lord. 4
2Th 1: 3 to give thanks . . brethren, as is fitting 5
Heb 2:10 was fitting that he . . should make . . perfect 11
7:26 fitting that we should have such a high priest 11
Sir 15: 9 is not fitting on the lips of a sinner 12
32: 3 it is fitting that you should 11
33:28 Set him to work, as is fitting for him 11
3Mc 1: 9 and did what was fitting for the holy place 7
7:13 When they had applauded him in fitting manner 11
4Mc 1:10 it is fitting for me to praise for their virtues 8
9:26 after fitting themselves with iron gauntlets 6
11:10 fitting iron clamps on them 10

more fitting 1. *δίκαιος*
4Mc 9: 6 it would be even more fitting 1

fittingly 1. *πρεπόντως*
2Mc 15:12 one who spoke fittingly 1

five 1. חָמֵשׁ 2. *πέντε* 3. quinque
Gen 14: 9 Ar'ioch king of Ella'sar, four kings against five. 1
18:28 Suppose five of the 50 righteous are lacking? 1
28 Wilt thou destroy the whole city for lack of five? 1
43:34 but Benjamin's portion was five times as much 1
45: 6 there are yet five years in which there will be 1
11 for there are yet five years of famine to come; 1
22 he gave . . five festal garments. 1
47: 2 he took five men and presented them to Pharaoh. 1
Exd 22: 1 he shall pay five oxen for an ox, and four sheep 1
26: 3 Five curtains shall be coupled to one another; 1
3 the other five curtains shall be coupled to one 1
9 you shall couple five curtains by themselves 1
26 five for the frames of the one side 1
27 five bars for the frames of the other side 1
27 five bars for the frames of the side 1
37 shall make for the screen five pillars of acacia 1
37 you shall cast five bases of bronze for them. 1
27: 1 altar . . five cubits long and five cubits broad; 1
1 altar . . five cubits long and five cubits broad; 1
18 the breadth 50, and the height five cubits 1
36:10 he coupled five curtains to one another 1
10 the other five curtains he coupled 1
16 He coupled five curtains by themselves 1
31 he made bars of acacia wood, five for the frames 1
32 five bars for the frames of the other side 1
32 and five bars for the frames of the tabernacle 1
38 its five pillars with their hooks. 1
38 of gold, but their five bases were of bronze. 1
38: 1 five cubits was its length, and five cubits its 1
1 and five cubits its breadth; it was square 1
18 it was twenty cubits long and five cubits high 1
Lev 26: 8 Five of you shall chase 100 1
27: 5 If the person is from five years old up to twenty 1
6 If the person is from a month old up to five years 1
6 your valuation shall be for a male five shekels 1
Num 3:47 you shall take five shekels apiece; 1
7:17 sacrifice of peace offerings . . five rams 1
17 peace offerings . . five male goats 1
17 peace offerings . . five male lambs a year old. 1
23 peace offerings . . five rams, five male goats 1
23 peace offerings . . five rams, five male goats 1
23 peace offerings . . five male lambs a year old. 1
29 peace offerings . . five rams, five male goats 1
29 peace offerings . . five rams, five male goats 1
29 peace offerings . . five male lambs a year old. 1
35 peace offerings . . five rams, five male goats 1
35 peace offerings . . five rams, five male goats 1
35 peace offerings . . five male lambs a year old. 1
41 peace offerings . . five rams, five male goats 1
41 peace offerings . . five rams, five male goats 1
41 peace offerings . . five male lambs a year old. 1
47 peace offerings . . five rams, five male goats 1
47 peace offerings . . five rams, five male goats 1
47 peace offerings . . five male lambs a year old. 1
53 peace offerings . . five rams, five male goats 1
53 peace offerings . . five rams, five male goats 1
53 peace offerings . . five male lambs a year old. 1
59 peace offerings . . five rams, five male goats 1
59 peace offerings . . five rams, five male goats 1
59 peace offerings . . five male lambs a year old. 1
65 peace offerings . . five rams, five male goats 1
65 peace offerings . . five rams, five male goats 1
65 peace offerings . . five male lambs a year old. 1
71 peace offering . . five rams, five male goats 1
71 peace offering . . five rams, five male goats 1
71 peace offerings . . five male lambs a year old. 1
77 peace offerings . . five rams, five male goats 1
77 peace offerings . . five rams, five male goats 1
77 peace offerings . . five male lambs a year old. 1
83 peace offerings . . five rams, five male goats 1
83 peace offerings . . five rams, five male goats 1
83 peace offerings . . five male lambs a year old. 1
11:19 You shall not eat one day, or two days, or five days 1
18:16 you shall fix at five shekels in silver 1
31: 8 Evi . . Hur, and Reba, the five kings of Mid'ian; 1
Jos 10: 5 Then the five kings of the Amorites . . gathered 1
16 These five kings fled, and hid themselves 1
17 The five kings have been found, hidden in the cave 1
22 and bring those five kings out to me from the cave. 1
23 and brought those five kings out to him 1
26 Joshua smote . . and he hung them on five trees. 1
13: 3 there are five rulers of the Philistines 1
Jdg 3: 3 nations: the five lords of the Philistines 1
18: 2 the Danites sent five able men from the whole 1
7 the five men departed, and came to La'ish 1
14 Then the five men . . said to their brethren 1
17 the five men who had gone to spy out the land went 1
1Sm 6: 4 Five golden tumors and five golden mice 1
4 Five golden tumors and five golden mice 1
16 when the five lords of the Philistines saw it 1
18 all the cities . . belonging to the five lords 1
17:40 and chose five smooth stones from the brook 1
21: 3 Give me five loaves of bread, or whatever is here. 1
25:18 two skins of wine, and five sheep ready dressed 1
18 five measures of parched grain, and 100 clusters 1
42 Ab'igail . . and her five maidens attended her; 1
2Sm 4: 4 He was five years old when the news . . came 1
21: 8 and the five sons of Merab the daughter of Saul 1
1Kg 6: 6 The lowest story was five cubits broad 1
10 He built . . each story five cubits high 1
24 Five cubits was the length of one wing 1
24 and five cubits . . the other wing of the cherub; 1
7:16 the height of the one capital was five cubits 1
16 the height of the other capital was five cubits. 1
23 ten cubits from brim to brim, and five cubits high 1
39 set the stands, five on the south side of the house 1
39 stands . . and five on the north side of the house; 1
49 lampstands . . five on the south side and five 1
49 lampstands . . south side and five on the north 1
2Kg 6:25 of a kab of dove's dung for five shekels of silver. 1
7:13 Let some men take five of the remaining horses 1
13:19 and said, "You should have struck five or six times; 1
25:19 took . . and five men of the king's council 1
1Ch 2: 4 Judah had five sons in all. 1
6 The sons of Zerah . . five in all. 1
3:20 Berechi'ah, Hasadi'ah, and Ju'shab-he'sed, five. 1
4:32 Etam, A'in, Rimmon, Tochen , and Ashan, five cities 1
7: 3 sons of Izrahi'ah . . five, all of them chief men; 1
7 Ezbon, Uzzi, Uz'ziel, Jer'imoth, and Iri, five 1
11:23 a man of great stature, five cubits tall. 1
2Ch 3:11 one wing of the one, of five cubits, touched 1
11 its other wing, of five cubits, touched the wing 1
12 cherub, one wing, of five cubits, touched the wall 1
12 the other wing, also of five cubits, was joined 1
15 with a capital of five cubits on the top of each. 1
4: 2 molten sea . . brim to brim, and five cubits high 1
6 made ten lavers . . and set five on the south side 1
6 ten lavers . . and set . . five on the north side. 1
7 set them in the temple, five on the south side 1
7 set them in the temple . . and five on the north. 1
8 placed them in the temple, five on the south side 1
8 placed them in the temple . . five on the north. 1
6:13 bronze platform five cubits long, five . . wide 1
13 bronze platform five . . long, five cubits wide 1
Isa 17: 6 four or five on the branches of a fruit tree 1
19:18 In that day there will be five cities in . . Egypt 1
30:17 at the threat of five you shall flee 1
Jer 52:22 the height of the one capital was five cubits; 1
Ezk 40: 7 and the space between the side rooms, five cubits; 1
30 25 cubits long and five cubits broad. 1
48 of the vestibule, five cubits on either side; 1
41: 2 the sidewalls of the entrance were five cubits 1
9 outer wall of the side chambers was five cubits; 1
9 platform which was left free was five cubits. ‡
11 that was left free was five cubits round about. 1
12 the wall of the building was five cubits thick 1
45:12 five shekels shall be five shekels 2
12 five shekels shall be five shekels 2
Mat 14:17 We have only five loaves here and two fish. 2
19 and taking the five loaves and the two fish 2
16: 9 Do you not remember the five loaves 2
25: 2 Five of them were foolish, and five were wise. 2
2 Five of them were foolish, and five were wise. 2
15 to one he gave five talents, to another two 2
16 He who had received the five talents went at once 2
16 he made five talents more. 2
20 he who had received the five talents came forward 2
20 bringing five talents more, saying 2
20 Master, you delivered to me five talents 2
20 here I have made five talents more.' 2
Mrk 6:38 they said, "Five, and two fish. 2
41 taking the five loaves and the two fish 2

8:19 I broke the five loaves for the 5,000 2
Lke 1:24 for five months she hid herself, saying 2
9:13 We have no more than five loaves and two fish 2
16 taking the five loaves and the two fish 2
12: 6 Are not five sparrows sold for two pennies? 2
52 in one house there will be five divided 2
14:19 another said, 'I have bought five yoke of oxen 2
16:28 for I have five brothers, so that he may warn them 2
19:18 Lord, your pound has made five pounds.' 2
19 he said . . 'And you are to be over five cities.' 2
Joh 4:18 for you have had five husbands 2
5: 2 a pool . . which has five porticoes. 2
6: 9 a lad here who has five barley loaves and two fish; 2
13 fragments from the five barley loaves 2
Act 20: 6 in five days we came to them at Tro'as 2
24: 1 after five days the high priest . . came down 2
1Co 14:19 I would rather speak five words with my mind . . than 2
Rev 9: 5 were allowed to torture them for five months 2
10 their power of hurting men for five months lies 2
17:10 seven kings, five of whom have fallen 2
2Es 14:24 these five, because they are trained to write 3
37 I took the five men, as he commanded me 3
42 the Most High gave understanding to the five men 3
Jdt 7:30 Let us hold out for five more days 2
8: 9 to surrender the city . . after five days 2
15 choose to help us within these five days 2
1Mc 2: 2 He had five sons, John surnamed Gaddi 2
2Mc 2:23 has been set forth by Jason of Cyrene in five volumes 2
10:29 five resplendent men on horses 2
11: 5 about five leagues from Jerusalem 2

five *See also* cities, times.

five cities 1. πεντάπολις
Wis 10: 6 the fire that descended on the Five Cities. 1

fix 1. חָק 2. כון 3. נצב 4. נתן 5. עמד 6. עָרַךְ 7. קום 8. ἀτενίζω 9. ἵστημι 10. στηρίζω 11. τίθημι 12. fundo
Gen 41:32 dream means that the thing is fixed by God 2
Num18:16 their redemption price . . you shall fix 6
Deu 32: 8 he fixed the bounds of the peoples according 3
2Kg 8:11 And he fixed his gaze and stared at him 5
Est 9:32 Queen Esther fixed these practices of Purim 7
Ps 74:17 Thou hast fixed all the bounds of the earth; 3
148: 6 he fixed their bounds which cannot be passed. 4
Ezk 45:14 as the fixed portion of oil, one tenth of a bath 1
Lke 4:20 the eyes of all in the synagogue were fixed on him. 8
16:26 between us and you a great chasm has been fixed 10
Act 1: 7 which the Father has fixed by his own authority. 11
17:31 he has fixed a day on which he will judge the world 9
2Es 16:56 At his word the stars were fixed 12

fix attention upon 1. ἐπέχω
Act 3: 5 he fixed his attention upon them 1

firmly fix 1. נטע 2. נצב 3. στηρίζω
Ps 119:89 O LORD, thy word is firmly fixed in the heavens. 2
Ecc 12:11 like nails firmly fixed are the . . sayings 1
Sir 22:16 so the mind firmly fixed on a reasonable counsel 3

fix one's eye 1. נבט
Ps 119:15 on thy precepts, and fix my eyes on thy ways. 1

fix thought 1. ἐνθυμέομαι
Wis 6:15 To fix one's thought on her is . . understanding 1

fixed *See* allowance, eye, order.

flabby 1. περιχαλάω
4Mc 7:13 his muscles flabby, his sinews feeble 1

flag 1. ὀκνηρός
Rom12:11 Never flag in zeal, be aglow with the Spirit 1

flagon 1. כְּלִי נֶבֶל 2. קְשָׂוָה
Exd 25:29 make . . its flagons and bowls with which to pour 2
37:16 bowls and flagons with which to pour libations. 2
Num 4: 7 flagons for the drink offering; 2
Isa 22:24 every . . vessel, from the cups to all the flagons. 1

flagrant 1. עצם
Jer 30:14 guilt is great, because your sins are flagrant. 1
15 guilt is great, because your sins are flagrant 1

flagstaff 1. תֹּרֶן
Isa 30:17 you shall flee, till you are left like a flagstaff 1

flail 1. דוש
Jdg 8: 7 I will flail your flesh with the thorns 1

flake-like 1. חספס
Exd 16:14 there was . . a fine, flake-like thing 1

flame 1. אֵשׁ 2. לַהַב 3. לֶהָבָה 4. להט 5. לַהַט 6. שָׁבִיב 7. שַׁלְהֶבֶת 8. שְׁבִיב (A) 9. πῦρ 10. πυρά 11. πυρόω 12. φλεγμονή 13. φλόξ 14. ardeo 15. flamma
Gen 3:24 a flaming sword which turned every way 5
15:17 behold, a smoking fire pot and a flaming torch 1
Exd 3: 2 the LORD appeared to him in a flame of fire 3
Num21:28 from Heshbon, flame from the city of Sihon. 3
Deu 33: 2 he came . . with flaming fire at his right hand. •
Jdg 13:20 the flame went up toward heaven from the altar 2
20 the angel . . ascended in the flame of the altar 2
Job 15:30 the flame will dry up his shoots 7
18: 5 the flame of his fire does not shine. 6
41:21 a flame comes forth from his mouth. 2
Ps 29: 7 voice of the LORD flashes forth flames of fire. 3
83:14 as the flame sets the mountains ablaze 3
104: 4 who makest . . fire and flame thy ministers. 4
106:18 flame burned up the wicked. 3
Isa 4: 5 smoke and the shining of a flaming fire by night; 3
5:24 and as dry grass sinks down in the flame 3
10:17 Israel will become a fire, and his Holy One a flame; 3
29: 6 tempest, and the flame of a devouring fire. 2
30:30 in furious anger and a flame of devouring fire 2
43: 2 and the flame shall not consume you. 3
47:14 deliver themselves from the power of the flame. 3
66:15 anger in fury, and his rebuke with flames of fire. 2
Jer 48:45 has gone forth . . a flame from the house of Sihon; 3
Lam 2: 3 he has burned like a flaming fire in Jacob 3
Ezk 20:47 the blazing flame shall not be quenched 7
Dan 3:22 flame of the fire slew those men who took 8
7: 9 throne was fiery flames, its wheels were burning 8
10: 6 his eyes like flaming torches, his arms and legs 1
11:33 though they shall fall by sword and flame 3
Hos 7: 6 in the morning it blazes like a flaming fire. 3
Jol 1:19 and flame has burned all the trees of the field. 3
2: 3 and behind them a flame burns. 3
5 like the crackling of a flame of fire devouring 2
Obd 1:18 shall be a fire, and the house of Joseph a flame 3
Nah 2: 3 The chariots flash like flame when mustered 1
Zec 12: 6 Judah . . like a flaming torch among sheaves; 1
Lke 16:24 I am in anguish in this flame.' 13
Act 7:30 in a flame of fire in a bush. 13
Eph 6:16 can quench all the flaming darts of the evil one. 11
2Th 1: 7 with his mighty angels in flaming fire 13
Heb 1: 7 Who makes . . his servants flames of fire. 13
Rev 1:14 his eyes were like a flame of fire 13
2:18 the Son of God, who has eyes like a flame of fire 13
19:12 His eyes are like a flame of fire 13
2Es 4:48 and behold, a flaming furnace passed by before me 14
48 and when the flame had gone by I looked, and behold 15
7:61 and are similar to a flame and smoke 15
13:10 and from his lips a flaming breath 15
11 the stream of fire and the flaming breath 15
38 (which were symbolized by the flames) 15
Wis 10:17 a starry flame through the night. 13
16:18 At one time the flame was restrained 13
17: 5 nor did the brilliant flames of the stars avail 13
19:21 Flames . . failed to consume the flesh 13
Sir 8:10 lest you be burned in his flaming fire. 13
21: 9 their end is a flame of fire. 13
28:22 they will not be burned in its flame. 13
45:19 to consume them in flaming fire. 13
Aza 1: 1 they walked about in the midst of the flames 13
24 the flame streamed out above the furnace 13
26 and drove the fiery flame out of the furnace 13
1Mc 2:59 believed and were saved from the flame. 13
6:39 the hills . . gleamed like flaming torches. 9
2Mc 1:32 When this was done, a flame blazed up 13
3Mc 6: 6 had voluntarily surrendered their lives to the flames 9
6 turning the flame against all their enemies. 13
4Mc 3:17 and quench the flames of frenzied desires; 12
9:19 while fanning the flames •
17: 1 she threw herself into the flames 10
18:14 the flame shall not consume you.' 13

flame forth 1. בער
2Sm 22: 9 glowing coals flamed forth from him. 1
13 coals of fire flamed forth. 1
Ps 18: 8 glowing coals flamed forth from him. 1

most vehement flame 1. שַׁלְהֶבֶתְיָה
Sng 8: 6 are flashes of fire, a most vehement flame. 1

flaming *See* fire, torch.

flank 1. כָּתֵף 2. ἐκ 3. κέρας 4. μέρος
Ezk 25: 9 therefore I will lay open the flank of Moab 1
1Mc 6:38 on the two flanks of the army 4
9:12 Flanked by the two companies 2
2Mc 15:20 the cavalry deployed on the flanks 3

flash 1. לַהַב 2. לֶהָבָה 3. נֹגַהּ 4. רום 5. רֶשֶׁף 6. ἀστράπτω 7. διαστράπτω 8. ἔκλαμψις 9. ἐπιφαίνω 10. fio 11. nitor
Job 15:12 why do your eyes flash 4
39:23 the flashing spear and the javelin. 1
Ps 76: 3 There he broke the flashing arrows, the shield 5
105:32 lightning that flashed through their land. 2
Sng 8: 6 Its flashes are flashes of fire 5
6 Its flashes are flashes of fire 5
Ezk 21:10 for slaughter, polished to flash like lightning! •
28 polished to glitter and to flash like lightning •
Nah 2: 3 The chariots flash like flame when mustered •
3: 3 Horsemen charging, flashing sword 1
Hab 3: 4 like the light, rays flashed from his hand; •
11 at the flash of thy glittering spear. 3
Lke 17:24 For as lightning flashes and lights up the sky 6
2Es 6: 2 and before the flashes of lightning shone 11
10:25 and her countenance flashed like lightning 10
Wis 11:18 flash terrible sparks from their eyes; 6
16:22 the fire that . . flashed in the showers of rain; 7
LJr 1:61 the lightning, when it flashes, is widely seen 9
2Mc 5: 3 the flash of golden trappings 8

flash about 1. περιαστράπτω
Act 9: 3 suddenly a light from heaven flashed about him. 1

flash continually 1. לקח
Exd 9:24 hail, a fire flashing continually in the midst 1

flash forth 1. בלג 2. ברק 3. הלל 4. חצב
Job 41:18 His sneezings flash forth light 3
Ps 18:14 he flashed forth lightnings, and routed them. •
29: 7 voice of the LORD flashes forth flames of fire. 4
144: 6 Flash forth the lightning and scatter them 2
Ams 5: 9 destruction flash forth against the strong 1

flash forth continually 1. לקח
Ezk 1: 4 and fire flashing forth continually 1

flash lightning 1. corusco
2Es 16:10 He will flash lightning 1

lightning flash 1. περιαστράπτω
4Mc 4:10 with lightning flashing from their weapons 1

flash of lightning 1. בָּזָק 2. ἀστραπή
Ezk 1:14 darted to and fro, like a flash of lightning. 1
Rev 4: 5 From the throne issue flashes of lightning 2
8: 5 flashes of lightning, and an earthquake. 2
11:19 flashes of lightning, voices, peals of thunder 2
16:18 flashes of lightning, voices, peals of thunder 2

flash on every side 1. הלך
Ps 77:17 thy arrows flashed on every side. 1

flask 1. בַּקְבּוּק 2. פַּךְ 3. ἀγγεῖον 4. ἀλάβαστρον 5. καψάκης
2Kg 9: 1 take this flask of oil in your hand, and go 2
3 Then take the flask of oil, and pour it on his head 2
Jer 19: 1 Thus said the LORD, "Go, buy a potter's earthen flask 1
10 you shall break the flask in the sight of the men 1
Mat 25: 4 the wise took flasks of oil with their lamps. 3
26: 7 with an alabaster flask •
Mrk 14: 3 she broke the flask and poured it over his head. 4
Jdt 10: 5 gave her maid a bottle of wine and a flask of oil 5

alabaster flask 1. ἀλάβαστρον
Mrk 14: 3 a woman came with an alabaster flask of ointment 1
Lke 7:37 a woman . . brought an alabaster flask of ointment 1

flat 1. תַּחַת
Jos 6: 5 and the wall of the city will fall down flat 1
20 raised a great shout, and the wall fell down flat 1

flat *See also* cake, lay.

flatter 1. חלק 2. חָלָק 3. חֲלַקָּה 4. כנה 5. פתה 6. θαυμάζω 7. κολακεύω
Job 32:22 I do not know how to flatter 4
Ps 5: 9 they flatter with their tongue. 1
12: 2 with flattering lips . . they speak. 3
3 May the LORD cut off all flattering lips 3
36: 2 For he flatters himself in his own eyes 1
78:36 they flattered him with their mouths; 5
Prv 26:28 flattering mouth works ruin. 2
28:23 more favor than he who flatters with his tongue. 1
29: 5 A man who flatters his neighbor spreads a net 1
Ezk 12:24 any false vision or flattering divination 2
Jde 1:16 boasters, flattering people to gain advantage. 6
1Es 4:31 if she loses her temper with him, he flatters her 7
Wis 14:17 they might flatter the absent one as though present. 7

flattering *See* word.

flattery 1. חֲלַקָּה 2. חֲלַקְלַקּוֹת 3. κολακεία
Dan 11:21 obtain the kingdom by flatteries. 2
32 shall seduce with flattery those who violate 1
34 many shall join themselves to them with flattery; 2
1Th 2: 5 never used either words of flattery, as you know 3

flattery *See also* use.

flaunt 1. גלה 2. פָּרַשׂ
Prv 13:16 but a fool flaunts his folly. 2
Ezk 23:18 harlotry so openly and flaunted her nakedness 1

flaw 1. מום
Sng 4: 7 You are all fair, my love; there is no flaw in you. 1

flawless 1. בַּר
Sng 6: 9 the darling . . flawless to her that bore her. 1

flax 1. פֵּשֶׁת 2. פִּשְׁתָּה
Exd 9:31 The flax and the barley were ruined 2
31 the barley was in the ear and the flax was in bud. 2
Jos 2: 6 and hid them with the stalks of flax 1

Jdg 15:14 the ropes . . became as flax that has caught fire 1
Prv 31:13 She seeks wool and flax, and works 1
Isa 19: 9 The workers in combed flax will be in despair 1
Ezk 40: 3 a line of flax and a measuring reed in his hand; 1
Hos 2: 5 give me . . my wool and my flax, my oil and my drink 1
9 and I will take away my wool and my flax 1

flay 1. פשט 2. ἐπισπάω

Lev 1: 6 he shall flay the burnt offering and cut it 1
2Ch 29:34 could not flay all the burnt offerings 1
35:11 while the Levites flayed the victims. 1
Mic 3: 3 of my people, and flay their skin from off them 1
4Mc 9:28 flayed all his flesh up to his chin 2

flea 1. פַּרְעֹשׁ

1Sm 24:14 whom do you pursue? After a dead dog! After a flea! 1

flee 1. ברח 2. בָּרִיחַ 3. הלך 4. מלט 5. מְנוּסָה 6. מרא 7. נדד 8. נוד 9. נוס 10. נדד (A) 11. נוד (A) 12. ἀποδιδράσκω 13. ἀποδράω 14. ἀποφεύγω 15. διαδιδράσκω 16. διαφεύγω 17. ἐκφεύγω 18. ἐν ταῖς ὁδοῖς 19. ἐξέρχομαι 20. καταφεύγω 21. συμφεύγω 22. φεύγω 23. φυγαδεύω 24. φυγάς 25. φυγὰς ἀπέρχομαι 26. φυγὰς οἴχομαι 27. fugio 28. in fugam

Gen 14:10 and as the kings of Sodom and Gomor'rah fled 9
10 into them, and the rest fled to the mountain. 9
16: 6 dealt harshly with her, and she fled from her. 1
8 She said, "I am fleeing from my mistress Sar'ai. 1
19:17 they said, "Flee for your life; 4
17 flee to the hills, lest you be consumed. 4
19 but I cannot flee to the hills 4
20 Behold, yonder city is near enough to flee to 9
27:43 arise, flee to Laban my brother in Haran 1
31:20 that he did not tell him that he intended to flee. 1
21 He fled with all that he had, and arose and crossed 1
22 told Laban on the third day that Jacob had fled 1
27 Why did you flee secretly, and cheat me 1
40 by night, and my sleep fled from my eyes. 7
35: 1 to you when you fled from your brother Esau. 1
7 to him when he fled from his brother. 1
39:12 in her hand, and fled and got out of the house. 9
13 in her hand, and had fled out of the house 9
15 he left his garment with me, and fled and got out 9
18 garment with me, and fled out of the house. 9
Exd 2:15 But Moses fled from Pharaoh, and stayed 1
4: 3 it became a serpent; and Moses fled from it. 9
14: 5 king . . was told that the people had fled 1
25 Egyptians said, "Let us flee from before Israel; 9
27 the Egyptians fled into it, and the LORD routed 9
21:13 appoint for you a place to which he may flee. 9
Lev 26:17 you shall flee when none pursues you 9
36 they shall flee as one flees from the sword 9
36 they shall flee as one flees from the sword 5
Num10:35 let them that hate thee flee before thee. 9
16:34 all Israel . . round about them fled at their cry; 9
24:11 Therefore now flee to your place; 1
35: 6 where you shall permit the manslayer to flee 9
11 manslayer who kills . . without intent may flee there. 9
15 any one who kills . . without intent may flee there. 9
25 to his city of refuge, to which he had fled 9
26 bounds of his city of refuge to which he fled 9
32 for him who has fled to his city of refuge 9
Deu 4:42 that the manslayer might flee there 9
42 fleeing to one of these cities he might save his life 9
19: 3 so that any manslayer can flee to them. 9
4 manslayer, who by fleeing there may save his life. 9
5 may flee to one of these cities and save his life; 9
11 man flees into one of these cities 9
28: 7 one way, and flee before you seven ways. 9
25 go out one way . . and flee seven ways before them; 9
Jos 7: 4 and they fled before the men of Ai 9
8: 5 when they come out . . we shall flee before them; 9
6 they will say, 'They are fleeing from us, as before.' 9
6 we will flee from them; 9
15 and fled in the direction of the wilderness. 9
20 and they had no power to flee this way or that 9
20 people that fled to the wilderness turned back 9
10:11 And as they fled before Israel 9
16 These five kings fled, and hid themselves 9
20: 3 that the manslayer . . may flee there; 9
4 He shall flee to one of these cities 9
6 to . . his own home, to the town from which he fled.' 9
9 who killed . . without intent could flee there 9
Jdg 1: 6 Ado'ni-be'zek fled; but they pursued him, and caught 9
7:21 and all the army ran; they cried out and fled. 9
22 and the army fled as far as Beth-shit'tah 9
8:12 Zebah and Zalmun'na fled; and he pursued them 9
9:21 Jotham ran away and fled, and went to Beer 1
40 Abim'elech chased him, and he fled before him; 9
51 tower . . and all the people of the city fled to it 9
11: 3 Jephthah fled from his brothers, and dwelt 1
20:32 Let us flee, and draw them away from the city 9
45 they turned and fled toward the wilderness 9
47 600 men turned and fled toward the wilderness 9
1Sm 4:10 Israel was defeated, and they fled 9
16 I fled from the battle today. 9
17 Israel has fled before the Philistines 9
14:22 all . . heard that the Philistines were fleeing 9
17:24 All . . Israel, when they saw the man, fled from him 9
51 When the Philistines saw that . . they fled. 9
19: 8 great slaughter . . so that they fled before him. 9
10 he eluded Saul . . And David fled, and escaped. 9
18 Now David fled and escaped, and he came to Samuel 1
20: 1 David fled from Nai'oth in Ramah, and came and said 1
21:10 And David rose and fled that day from Saul 1
22:17 knew that he fled, and did not disclose it to me. 1
20 Abi'athar, escaped and fled after David. 1
23: 6 When Abi'athar . . fled to David to Kei'lah 1
27: 4 when it was told Saul that David had fled to Gath 1
30:17 400 young men, who mounted camels and fled. 9
31: 1 the men of Israel fled before the Philistines 9
7 saw that the men of Israel had fled and that Saul 9
7 they forsook their cities and fled; 9
2Sm 1: 4 The people have fled from the battle 9
4: 3 the Be-er'othites fled to Gitta'im 1
4 and his nurse took him up, and fled; 9
4 as she fled in her haste, he fell, and became lame. 9
10:13 battle . . the Syrians; and they fled before him. 9
14 when the Ammonites saw that the Syrians fled 9
14 they likewise fled before Abi'shai 9
18 And the Syrians fled before Israel; 9
13:29 all . . arose, and each mounted his mule and fled. 9
34 But Ab'salom fled. 1
37 But Ab'salom fled, and went to Talmai 1
38 So Ab'salom fled, and went to Geshur 1
15:14 Arise, and let us flee; or . . there will be no escape 1
17: 2 and all the people who are with him will flee. 9
18: 3 For if we flee, they will not care about us. 9
17 and all Israel fled every one to his own home. 9
19: 3 who are ashamed when they flee in battle. 9
8 Now Israel had fled every man to his own home. 9
9 and now he has fled out of the land from Ab'salom. 1
23:11 and the men fled from the Philistines. 9
24:13 Or will you flee three months before your foes 9
1Kg 2: 7 met me when I fled from Ab'salom your brother. 1
28 Jo'ab fled to the tent of the LORD and caught hold 9
29 Jo'ab has fled to the tent of the LORD, and behold 9
11:17 but Hadad fled to Egypt 1
23 Rezon . . who had fled from his master Hadade'zer 1
40 Jerobo'am arose, and fled into Egypt, to Shishak 1
12: 2 in Egypt, whither he had fled from King Solomon) 1
18 King Rehobo'am made haste . . to flee to Jerusalem. 9
20:20 the Syrians fled and Israel pursued them 9
30 the rest fled into the city of Aphek; 9
30 Ben-ha'dad also fled, and entered an inner chamber 9
2Kg 3:24 rose and attacked . . till they fled before them; 9
7: 7 leaving the camp . . and fled for their lives. 9
8:21 smote the E'domites . . but his army fled home. 9
9: 3 Then open the door and flee; do not tarry. 9
10 Then he opened the door, and fled. 9
23 Joram reined about and fled, saying to Ahazi'ah 9
27 Ahazi'ah . . fled in the direction of Beth-haggan. 9
27 And he fled to Megid'do, and died there. 9
14:12 and every man fled to his home. 9
19 they made a conspiracy . . and he fled to Lachish. 9
25: 4 the king with all the men of war fled by night 19
1Ch 10: 1 men of Israel fled before the Philistines 9
7 saw that the army had fled 9
7 they forsook their cities and fled; 9
11:13 and the men fled from the Philistines. 9
19:14 and they fled before him. 9
15 when the Ammonites saw that the Syrians fled 9
15 the Ammonites . . likewise fled before Abi'shai 9
18 the Syrians fled before Israel; 9
2Ch 10: 2 in Egypt, whither he had fled from King Solomon) 1
18 to mount his chariot, to flee to Jerusalem. 9
13:16 The men of Israel fled before Judah 9
14:12 and the Ethiopians fled. 9
25:22 every man fled to his home. 9
27 made a conspiracy . . and he fled to Lachish. 9
Neh 6:11 I said, "Should such a man as I flee? 1
13:10 Levites . . had fled each to his field. 1
Job 14: 2 he flees like a shadow, and continues not. 1
20:24 He will flee from an iron weapon; 1
26:13 his hand pierced the fleeing serpent. 2
27:22 he flees from its power in headlong flight. 1
39:18 When she rouses herself to flee, she laughs 6
Ps 3: 0 David, when he fled from Absalom his son. 1
11: 1 can you say to me, "Flee like a bird to the mountains; 8
31:11 those who see me in the street flee from me. 7
57: 0 of David, when he fled from Saul, in the cave. 1
68: 1 let those who hate him flee before him! 9
12 The kings of the armies, they flee, they flee! 7
12 The kings of the armies, they flee, they flee! 7
104: 7 At thy rebuke they fled; 9
114: 3 The sea looked and fled, Jordan turned back. 9
5 What ails you, O sea, that you flee? 9
139: 7 Or whither shall I flee from thy presence? 1
Prv 28: 1 The wicked flee when no one pursues 9
Sng 2:17 Until the day breathes and the shadows flee 9
4: 6 Until the day breathes and the shadows flee 9
Isa 10: 3 To whom will you flee for help 9
29 Ramah trembles, Gib'e-ah of Saul has fled. 9
13:14 and every man will flee to his own land. 9
15: 5 his fugitives flee to Zo'ar 2
17:13 he will rebuke them, and they will flee far away 9
20: 6 to whom we fled for help to be delivered 9
21:15 For they have fled from the swords 7
22: 3 All your rulers have fled together 7
3 were captured, though they had fled far away. 1
24:18 He who flees at the sound of the terror shall fall 9
27: 1 will punish Leviathan the fleeing serpent 2
30:17 1,000 shall flee at the threat of one 9
17 at the threat of five you shall flee 9
31: 8 he shall flee from the sword 9
33: 3 At the thunderous noise peoples flee 7
38:15 All my sleep has fled because of the bitterness •
48:20 Go forth from Babylon, flee from Chalde'a 1
Jer 4:25 and all the birds of the air had fled. 7
9:10 and the beasts have fled and are gone. 7
26:21 he was afraid and fled and escaped to Egypt. 1
39: 4 they fled, going out of the city at night 1
46:15 Why has Apis fled? Why did not your bull stand? 22
21 yea, they have turned and fled together 9
48: 6 Flee! Save yourselves! Be like a wild ass 9
19 Ask him who flees and her who escapes; 9
44 He who flees from the terror shall fall 9
49: 8 Flee, turn back, dwell in the depths, O inhabitants 9
24 she turned to flee, and panic seized her; 9
30 Flee, wander far away, dwell in the depths 9
50: 8 Flee from the midst of Babylon 8
16 and every one shall flee to his own land. 9
28 they flee and escape from the land of Babylon 9
51: 6 Flee from the midst of Babylon 9
52: 7 the men of war fled and went out from the city 1
Lam 1: 6 they fled without strength before the pursuer. 3
Dan 4:14 let the beasts flee from under it 11
6:18 no diversions . . and sleep fled from him. 10
10: 7 fled to hide themselves. 1
Hos 12:12 (Jacob fled to the land of Aram 1
Ams 5:19 as if a man fled from a lion, and a bear met him; 9
Jon 1: 3 Jonah rose to flee to Tarshish 1
10 he was fleeing from the presence of the LORD 1
4: 2 That is why I made haste to flee to Tarshish; 1
Zec 2: 6 ho! Flee from the land of the north, says the LORD; 9
14: 5 you shall flee as you fled from the earthquake 9
5 you shall flee as you fled from the earthquake 9
Mat 2:13 take the child and his mother, and flee to Egypt 22
3: 7 Who warned you to flee from the wrath to come? 22
8:33 The herdsmen fled, and going into the city 22
10:23 flee to the next 22
24:16 let those who are in Judea flee to the mountains; 22
26:56 Then all the disciples forsook him and fled. 22
Mrk 5:14 The herdsmen fled 22
13:14 let those who are in Judea flee to the mountains; 22
14:50 they all forsook him, and fled. 22
16: 8 And they went out and fled from the tomb; 22
Lke 3: 7 Who warned you to flee from the wrath to come? 22
8:34 they fled, and told it in the city 22
21:21 let those who are in Judea flee to the mountains 22
Joh 10: 5 they will flee from him 22
12 leaves the sheep and flees 22
13 He flees because he is a hireling •
Act 7:29 At this retort Moses fled 22
14: 6 they learned of it and fled to Lystra and Derbe 20
Jas 4: 7 Resist the devil and he will flee from you. 22
Rev 12: 6 and the woman fled into the wilderness 22
2Es 2:36 Flee from the shadow of this age 27
8:53 hell has fled and corruption has been forgotten; ‡
10: 3 that I might be quiet, I got up in the night and fled 27
15:32 and shall turn and flee. 28
16:41 Let him that sells be like one who will flee 27
Tob 1:18 put to death any who came fleeing from Judea 22
21 they fled to the mountains of Ararat 22
8: 3 he fled to the remotest parts of Egypt 22
Jdt 5: 8 they fled to Mesopotamia 22
10:12 I am fleeing from them 12
11: 3 now tell me why you have fled from them 13
16 I fled from them 13
14: 3 they will flee before you 22
4 pursue them and cut them down as they flee. 18
15: 2 fled by every path across the plain 22
AEs 14: 1 Esther the queen . . fled to the Lord; 20
Wis 1: 5 a . . disciplined spirit will flee from deceit 22
10:10 When a righteous man fled 24
Sir 11:10 by fleeing you will not escape. 15
21: 2 Flee from sin as from a snake 22
22:22 in these cases any friend will flee. 14
LJr 1:55 their priests will flee and escape 22
68 they can flee to cover and help themselves. 17
1Mc 1:18 Ptolemy turned and fled before him 22
38 Because of them the residents of Jerusalem fled; 22
2:28 he and his sons fled to the hills 22
44 the survivors fled to the Gentiles for safety. 22
3:11 Many were wounded and fell, and the rest fled. 22
24 the rest fled into the land of the Philistines. 22
4: 5 because he said, "These men are fleeing from us. 22
14 The Gentiles were crushed and fled into the plain 22
22 they all fled into the land of the Philistines. 22
5: 9 they fled to the stronghold of Dathema 22
11 capture the stronghold to which we have fled 20
34 they fled before him 22
43 and fled into the sacred precincts at Carnaim. 22
6: 4 So he fled and in great grief departed from there 22
7:32 the rest fled into the city of David. 22

44 they threw down their arms and fled. 22
9:10 to do such a thing as to flee from them 22
18 Judas also fell, and the rest fled. 22
33 they fled into the wilderness of Tekoa 22
40 the rest fled to the mountain 22
10:12 the foreigners . . fled; 22
49 the army of Demetrius fled 22
64 they all fled. 22
73 where there is no stone or pebble, or place to flee. 22
82 they were overwhelmed by him and fled 22
83 They fled to Azotus and entered Beth-dagon 22
11:16 Alexander fled into Arabia to find protection there 22
46 But the king fled into the palace 22
55 he fled and was routed. 22
70 All the men with Jonathan fled 22
72 he . . routed them, and they fled. 22
73 When his men who were fleeing saw this 22
15:21 Therefore if any pestilent men have fled to you 16
16: 8 the rest fled into the stronghold. 22
10 They also fled into the towers 22
2Mc 5: 7 fled again into the country of the Ammonites. 25
8 fleeing from city to city 22
8:24 forced them all to flee. 22
33 who had fled into one little house 22
10:32 Timothy . . fled to a stronghold called Gazara 21
11:11 and forced all the rest to flee. 22
14:14 the Gentiles . . who had fled before Judas 23
4Mc 4: 1 he fled the country 26

flee *See also* turn.

flee away 1.ברח 2.הלך וְברח 3.נוד 4.נוד הלך 5.נום 6.*φεύγω*

Jdg 4:15 alighted from his chariot and fled away on foot. 5
17 Sis'era fled away on foot to the tent of Ja'el 5
1Sm 19:12 let David down . . and he fled away and escaped. 2
2Kg 7: 7 So they fled away in the twilight 5
Job 9:25 they flee away, they see no good. 1
Isa 17:11 yet the harvest will flee away in a day of grief 3
35:10 and sorrow and sighing shall flee away. 5
51:11 and sorrow and sighing shall flee away. 5
Jer 46: 6 The swift cannot flee away 5
50: 3 both man and beast shall flee away. 4
Ams 2:16 the mighty shall flee away naked in that day 5
7:12 O seer, go, flee away to the land of Judah 1
9: 1 not one of them shall flee away 5
Rev 16:20 And every island fled away 6
20:11 from his presence earth and sky fled away 6
Tob 6:17 Then the demon will smell it and flee away 6

flee for refuge 1.חסה 2.*καταφεύγω*

Ps 143: 9 I have fled to thee for refuge! 1
Heb 6:18 we who have fled for refuge 2

flee for safety 1.עוז

Isa 10:31 the inhabitants of Gebim flee for safety. 1
Jer 4: 6 Raise a standard toward Zion, flee for safety 1
6: 1 Flee for safety, O people of Benjamin 1

flee in haste 1.נוס

Jer 46: 5 warriors are beaten down, and have fled in haste; 1

make flee 1.ברח 2.נוס

Exd 9:20 made his slaves and his cattle flee into the houses 2
Job 41:28 The arrow cannot make him flee; 1

flee out 1.*ἐκφεύγω*

Act 19:16 they fled out of that house naked and wounded. 1

fleece 1.גֵּז 2.גִּזָּה

Deu 18: 4 first of the fleece of your sheep, you shall give 1
Jdg 6:37 I am laying a fleece of wool on the threshing 2
37 if there is dew on the fleece alone, and it is dry 2
38 rose early next morning and squeezed the fleece 2
38 he wrung enough dew from the fleece to fill a bowl 2
39 let me make trial only this once with the fleece 2
39 let it be dry only on the fleece, and on all 2
40 it was dry on the fleece only, and on all the ground 2
Job 31:20 if he was not warmed with the fleece of my sheep; 1

soft fleece 1.*κώδιον*

Jdt 12:15 the soft fleeces which she had received from Bagoas 1

fleet 1.אֳנִי 2.*στόλος*

1Kg 9:27 Hiram sent with the fleet his servants 1
10:11 the fleet of Hiram, which brought gold from Ophir 1
22 ships of Tarshish at sea with the fleet of Hiram. 1
1Mc 1:17 with a large fleet. 2
2Mc 12: 9 and set fire to the harbor and the fleet 2
14: 1 a strong army and a fleet 2
3Mc 7:17 the fleet waited for them . . for seven days. 2

fleet of ships 1.אֳנִי

1Kg 9:26 Solomon built a fleet of ships at E'zion-ge'ber 1
10:22 For the king had a fleet of ships of Tarshish 1
22 the fleet of ships of Tarshish used to come 1

fleeting 1.חָדֵל 2.נִדָּף 3.*βραχύς* 4.*πρόσκαιρος*

Ps 39: 4 let me know how fleeting my life is! 1
Prv 21: 6 fleeting vapor and a snare of death. 2
Heb 11:25 to enjoy the fleeting pleasures of sin. 4
Wis 16:27 when simply warmed by a fleeting ray of the sun 3

flesh 1.בָּשָׂר 2.לְחוּם 3.עֶרְוָה 4.שְׁאֵר 5.בְּשַׂר (A) 6.*κρέας* 7.*σαρκικός* 8.*σάρξ* 9.caro

Gen 2:21 his ribs and closed up its place with flesh; 1
23 of my bones and flesh of my flesh; 1
23 flesh of my flesh; she shall be called Woman 1
24 cleaves to his wife, and they become one flesh. 1
6: 3 abide in man for ever, for he is flesh 1
12 for all flesh had corrupted their way 1
13 I have determined to make an end of all flesh; 1
17 to destroy all flesh in which is the breath of life 1
19 of every living thing of all flesh 1
7:15 two and two of all flesh in which there 1
16 they that entered, male and female of all flesh 1
21 all flesh died that moved upon the earth 1
8:17 that is with you of all flesh-birds and animals 1
9: 4 Only you shall not eat flesh with its life 1
11 never again shall all flesh be cut off 1
15 you and every living creature of all flesh; 1
15 never again become a flood to destroy all flesh. 1
16 of all flesh that is upon the earth. 1
17 I have established between me and all flesh 1
17:11 be circumcised in the flesh of your foreskins 1
13 be in your flesh an everlasting covenant. 1
14 not circumcised in the flesh of his foreskin 1
23 he circumcised the flesh of their foreskins 1
24 was circumcised in the flesh of his foreskin. 1
25 was circumcised in the flesh of his foreskin. 1
29:14 Laban said . . "Surely you are my bone and flesh! 1
37:27 he is our brother, our own flesh. 1
40:19 and the birds will eat the flesh from you. 1
Exd 4: 7 it was restored like the rest of his flesh. 1
12: 8 They shall eat the flesh that night, roasted; 1
46 carry forth any of the flesh outside the house; 1
16: 8 the LORD gives you in the evening flesh to eat 1
12 twilight you shall eat flesh, and in the morning 1
21:28 its flesh shall not be eaten; 1
22:31 you shall not eat any flesh that is torn by beasts 1
28:42 linen breeches to cover their naked flesh; 1
42 linen breeches to cover their naked flesh; 3
29:14 the flesh of the bull, and its skin, and its dung 1
31 ram of ordination, and boil its flesh 1
32 Aaron and his sons shall eat the flesh of the ram 1
34 if any of the flesh for the ordination 1
Lev 4:11 the skin of the bull and all its flesh 1
6:27 Whatever touches its flesh shall be holy 1
7:15 the flesh of the sacrifice of his peace 1
17 what remains of the flesh of the sacrifice 1
18 If any of the flesh of the sacrifice of his peace 1
19 Flesh that touches any unclean thing shall not 1
19 All who are clean may eat flesh 1
20 the person who eats of the flesh of the sacrifice 1
21 eats of the flesh of the sacrifice of the LORD'S 1
8:17 the bull, and its skin, and its flesh, and its dung 1
31 Boil the flesh at the door of the tent of meeting 1
32 what remains of the flesh and the bread 1
9:11 The flesh and the skin he burned with fire 1
11: 8 Of their flesh you shall not eat 1
11 of their flesh you shall not eat 1
12: 3 the flesh of his foreskin shall be circumcised 1
13:10 if . . there is quick raw flesh in the swelling 1
14 when raw flesh appears . . he shall be unclean 1
15 the priest shall examine the raw flesh 1
15 raw flesh is unclean, for it is leprosy 1
16 if the raw flesh turns again and is changed 1
16:27 their skin and their flesh and their dung 1
17:11 For the life of the flesh is in the blood 1
16 if he does not wash them or bathe his flesh 1
19:26 You shall not eat any flesh with the blood in it •
28 You shall not make any cuttings in your flesh 1
21: 5 nor make any cuttings in their flesh 1
26:29 You shall eat the flesh of your sons 1
29 you shall eat the flesh of your daughters 1
Num12:12 as one dead, of whom the flesh is half consumed 1
16:22 said, "O God, the God of the spirits of all flesh 1
18:15 Everything that opens the womb of all flesh 1
18 their flesh shall be yours, as the breast 1
19: 5 her skin, her flesh . . shall be burned; 1
27:16 Let the LORD, the God of the spirits of all flesh 1
Deu 5:26 For who is there of all flesh, that has heard 1
12:15 slaughter and eat flesh within any of your towns 1
20 you say, 'I will eat flesh,' because you crave flesh 1
20 you say, 'I will eat flesh,' because you crave flesh 1
20 you may eat as much flesh as you desire. 1
23 you shall not eat the life with the flesh. 1
27 offer . . burnt offerings, the flesh and the blood 1
27 but the flesh you may eat. 1
14: 8 flesh you shall not eat, and their carcasses 1
16: 4 nor shall any of the flesh . . remain all night 1
28:53 eat the . . flesh of your sons and daughters 1
55 not give . . any of the flesh of his children whom 1
32:42 my arrows . . and my sword shall devour flesh 1
Jdg 6:21 fire . . consumed the flesh and the unleavened 1
8: 7 I will flail your flesh with the thorns 1
9: 2 Remember also that I am your bone and your flesh. 1
1Sm 17:44 I will give your flesh to the birds of the air 1
2Sm 5: 1 and said, "Behold, we are your bone and flesh. 1
19:12 You are my kinsmen, you are my bone and my flesh; 1
13 say to Ama'sa, 'Are you not my bone and my flesh? 1
1Kg 19:21 slew them, and boiled their flesh with the yokes 1
21:27 and put sackcloth upon his flesh, and fasted 1
2Kg 4:34 the flesh of the child became warm. 1
5:10 Go and wash . . and your flesh shall be restored 1
14 and his flesh was restored like the flesh 1
14 was restored like the flesh of a little child 1
9:36 the dogs shall eat the flesh of Jez'ebel; 1
1Ch 11: 1 and said, "Behold, we are your bone and flesh. 1
2Ch 32: 8 With him is an arm of flesh; but with us is the LORD 1
Neh 5: 5 Now our flesh is as the flesh of our brethren 1
5 Now our flesh is as the flesh of our brethren 1
Job 2: 5 touch his bone and his flesh, and he will curse 1
4:15 glided past my face; the hair of my flesh stood up. 1
6:12 or is my flesh bronze? 1
7: 5 My flesh is clothed with worms and dirt; 1
10: 4 Hast thou eyes of flesh? Dost thou see as man sees? 1
11 Thou didst clothe me with skin and flesh 1
13:14 I will take my flesh in my teeth 1
19:20 My bones cleave to my skin and to my flesh 1
22 Why are you not satisfied with my flesh? 1
26 thus destroyed, then from my flesh I shall see God 1
21: 6 I am dismayed, and shuddering seizes my flesh. 1
33:21 His flesh is so wasted away that it cannot be seen; 1
25 let his flesh become fresh with youth; 1
34:15 all flesh would perish together 1
41:23 The folds of his flesh cleave together 1
Ps 38: 3 There is no soundness in my flesh 1
7 there is no soundness in my flesh. 1
50:13 Do I eat the flesh of bulls, or drink the blood 1
56: 4 I trust without a fear. What can flesh do to me? 1
63: 1 my flesh faints for thee, as in a dry and weary land 1
65: 2 To thee shall all flesh come 1
73:26 My flesh and my heart may fail 4
78:27 he rained flesh upon them like dust 4
39 He remembered that they were but flesh 1
79: 2 flesh of thy saints to the beasts of the earth. 1
84: 2 my heart and flesh sing for joy to the living God. 1
102: 5 of my loud groaning my bones cleave to my flesh. 1
119:120 My flesh trembles for fear of thee, and I am afraid 1
136:25 he who gives food to all flesh 1
145:21 all flesh bless his holy name for ever and ever. 1
Prv 3: 8 It will be healing to your flesh •
4:22 healing to all his flesh. 1
5:11 when your flesh and body are consumed 1
14:30 A tranquil mind gives life to the flesh 1
Ecc 4: 5 The fool folds his hands, and eats his own flesh. 1
12:12 and much study is a weariness of the flesh. 1
Isa 9:20 not satisfied; each devours his neighbor's flesh 1
17: 4 and the fat of his flesh will grow lean. 1
22:13 behold . . eating flesh and drinking wine. 1
31: 3 their horses are flesh, and not spirit. 1
40: 5 be revealed, and all flesh shall see it together 1
6 All flesh is grass, and all its beauty 1
44:16 over the half he eats flesh, he roasts meat 1
19 on its coals, I roasted flesh and have eaten; 1
49:26 I will make your oppressors eat their own flesh 1
26 Then all flesh shall know that I am the LORD 1
58: 7 and not to hide yourself from your own flesh? 1
65: 4 who eat swine's flesh, and broth of abominable 1
66:16 execute judgment, and by his sword, upon all flesh; 1
17 following one in the midst, eating swine's flesh 1
23 all flesh shall come to worship before me 1
24 they shall be an abhorrence to all flesh. 1
Jer 7:21 to your sacrifices, and eat the flesh. 1
11:15 Can vows and sacrificial flesh avert your doom? 1
12:12 no flesh has peace. 1
17: 5 man who trusts in man and makes flesh his arm 1
19: 9 I will make them eat the flesh of their sons 1
9 and every one shall eat the flesh of his neighbor 1
25:31 he is entering into judgment with all flesh 1
32:27 Behold, I am the LORD, the God of all flesh; 1
45: 5 I am bringing evil upon all flesh, says the LORD; 1
Lam 3: 4 He has made my flesh and my skin waste away 1
Ezk 4:14 nor has foul flesh come into my mouth. 1
11: 3 this city is the caldron, and we are the flesh. 1
7 they are the flesh, and this city is the caldron; 1
11 nor shall you be the flesh in the midst of it; 1
19 I will take the stony heart out of their flesh 1
19 stony heart out . . and give them a heart of flesh 1
20:48 flesh shall see that I the LORD have kindled it; 1
21: 4 against all flesh from south to north; 1
5 all flesh shall know that I the LORD have drawn my 1
24:10 kindle the fire, boil well the flesh 1
32: 5 I will strew your flesh upon the mountains 1
33:25 says the Lord GOD: You eat flesh with the blood •
36:26 I will take out of your flesh the heart of stone 1
26 the heart of stone and give you a heart of flesh. 1
37: 6 and will cause flesh to come upon you 1
8 flesh had come upon them, and skin had covered 1
39:17 you shall eat flesh and drink blood. 1
18 You shall eat the flesh of the mighty 1
40:43 on the tables the flesh of the offering was to be 1
44: 7 foreigners, uncircumcised in heart and flesh 1
9 No foreigner, uncircumcised in heart and flesh 1
Dan 1:15 seen that they were . . fatter in flesh than all 1

2:11 gods, whose dwelling is not with flesh. 5
4:12 all flesh was fed from it. 5
7: 5 it was told, 'Arise, devour much flesh.' 5
Hos 8:13 they sacrifice flesh and eat it; 1
Jol 2:28 that I will pour out my spirit on all flesh; 1
Mic 3: 2 who tear . . their flesh from off their bones; 4
3 who eat the flesh of my people, and flay their skin 4
3 like meat in a kettle, like flesh in a caldron. 1
Zep 1:17 poured out like dust, and their flesh like dung. 2
Hag 2:12 'If one carries holy flesh in the skirt of his 1
Zec 2:13 Be silent, all flesh, before the LORD; 1
11: 9 that are left devour the flesh of one another. 1
16 but devours the flesh of the fat ones, tearing off 1
14:12 their flesh shall rot 1
21 take of them and boil the flesh of the sacrifice •
Mat 16:17 For flesh and blood has not revealed this to you 8
19: 5 and the two shall become one flesh'? 8
6 So they are no longer two but one flesh 8
26:41 the flesh is weak. 8
Mrk 10: 8 the two shall become one flesh 8
8 So they are no longer two but one flesh. 8
14:38 the flesh is weak. 8
Lke 3: 6 all flesh shall see the salvation of God. 8
24:39 a spirit has not flesh and bones 8
Joh 1:13 born, not of blood nor of the will of the flesh 8
14 And the Word became flesh and dwelt among us 8
3: 6 That which is born of the flesh is flesh 8
6 That which is born of the flesh is flesh 8
6:51 the bread which I shall give . . is my flesh. 8
52 How can this man give us his flesh to eat? 8
53 unless you eat the flesh of the Son of man 8
54 he who eats my flesh and drinks my blood 8
55 my flesh is food indeed, and my blood is drink 8
56 who eats my flesh and drinks my blood abides in me 8
63 the flesh is of no avail 8
8:15 You judge according to the flesh, I judge no one. 8
17: 2 since thou hast given him power over all flesh 8
Act 2:17 I will pour out my Spirit upon all flesh 8
26 moreover my flesh will dwell in hope. 8
31 nor did his flesh see corruption. 8
Rom 1: 3 descended from David according to the flesh 8
4: 1 Abraham, our forefather according to the flesh? 8
7: 5 While we were living in the flesh 8
18 nothing good dwells within me, that is, in my flesh 8
25 but with my flesh I serve the law of sin. 8
8: 3 what the law, weakened by the flesh, could not do 8
3 his own Son in the likeness of sinful flesh 8
3 he condemned sin in the flesh 8
4 in us, who walk not according to the flesh 8
5 For those who live according to the flesh 8
5 who . . set their minds on the things of the flesh 8
6 To set the mind on the flesh is death 8
7 the mind that is set on the flesh is hostile to God; 8
8 and those who are in the flesh cannot please God. 8
9 But you are not in the flesh, you are in the Spirit 8
12 So then, brethren, we are debtors, not to the flesh 8
12 not to the flesh, to live according to the flesh- 8
13 if you live according to the flesh you will die 8
9: 5 and of their race, according to the flesh 8
8 children of the flesh who are the children of God 8
13:14 and make no provision for the flesh 8
1Co 3: 3 for you are still of the flesh 7
3 of the flesh, and behaving like ordinary men? 7
5: 5 for the destruction of the flesh 8
6:16 as it is written, "The two shall become one flesh. 8
15:39 For not all flesh is alike 8
50 flesh and blood cannot inherit the kingdom 8
2Co 4:11 Jesus may be manifested in our mortal flesh. 8
12: 7 a thorn was given me in the flesh 8
Gal 1:16 I did not confer with flesh and blood 8
2:20 the life I now live in the flesh I live by faith 8
3: 3 are you now ending with the flesh? 8
4:23 the son of the slave was born according to the flesh 8
29 who was born according to the flesh persecuted 8
5:13 your freedom as an opportunity for the flesh 8
16 do not gratify the desires of the flesh 8
17 the desires of the flesh are against the Spirit 8
17 the desires of the Spirit are against the flesh; 8
19 Now the works of the flesh are plain 8
24 crucified the flesh with its passions 8
6: 8 For he who sows to his own flesh 8
8 will from the flesh reap corruption 8
12 those who want to make a good showing in the flesh 8
13 they may glory in your flesh. 8
Eph 2: 3 once lived in the passions of our flesh 8
11 at one time you Gentiles in the flesh 8
11 which is made in the flesh by hands- 8
15 by abolishing in his flesh the law 8
5:29 For no man ever hates his own flesh 8
31 the two shall become one flesh. 8
6:12 we are not contending against flesh and blood 8
Php 1:22 If it is to be life in the flesh 8
24 to remain in the flesh is more necessary 8
3: 3 put no confidence in the flesh. 8
4 reason for confidence in the flesh also 8
4 reason for confidence in the flesh also 8
Col 1:22 now reconciled in his body of flesh by his death 8
24 in my flesh I complete what is lacking 8
2:11 putting off the body of flesh 8
13 the uncircumcision of your flesh 8
23 in checking the indulgence of the flesh. 8
1Ti 3:16 He was manifested in the flesh 8
Phm 1:16 both in the flesh and in the Lord. 8
Heb 2:14 Since . . the children share in flesh and blood 8
5: 7 In the days of his flesh, Jesus offered up prayers 8
9:13 sanctifies for the purification of the flesh 8
10:20 through the curtain, that is, through his flesh 8
Jas 5: 3 their rust . . will eat your flesh like fire 8
1Pe 1:24 All flesh is like grass 8
2:11 to abstain from the passions of the flesh 7
3:18 Christ . . put to death in the flesh 8
4: 1 Since therefore Christ suffered in the flesh 8
1 whoever has suffered in the flesh 8
2 so as to live for the rest of the time in the flesh 8
6 that though judged in the flesh like men 8
2Pe 2:18 entice with licentious passions of the flesh 8
1Jn 2:16 the lust of the flesh and the lust of the eyes 8
4: 2 that Jesus Christ has come in the flesh is of God 8
2Jn 1: 7 the coming of Jesus Christ in the flesh; 8
Jde 1: 8 these men in their dreamings defile the flesh 8
23 hating even the garment spotted by the flesh. 8
Rev 17:16 and devour her flesh and burn her up with fire 8
19:18 to eat the flesh of kings, the flesh of captains 8
18 to eat the flesh of kings, the flesh of captains 8
18 to eat . . the flesh of mighty men 8
18 to eat . . the flesh of horses and their riders 8
18 and the flesh of all men, both free and slave 8
21 and all the birds were gorged with their flesh. 8
2Es 1:31 new moons, and circumcisions of the flesh. 9
15:58 shall eat their own flesh in hunger for bread 9
Jdt 16:17 fire and worms he will give to their flesh 8
Wis 7: 1 in the womb of a mother I was molded into flesh 8
12: 5 sacrificial feasting on human flesh and blood. 8
19:21 the flesh of perishable creatures that walked 8
Sir 1:10 She dwells with all flesh according to his gift 8
14:18 so are the generations of flesh and blood 8
17:31 So flesh and blood devise evil. 8
19:12 Like an arrow stuck in the flesh of the thigh 8
28: 5 If he himself, being flesh, maintains wrath 8
31: 1 Wakefulness over wealth wastes away one's flesh 8
38:28 the breath of the fire melts his flesh 8
39:19 The works of all flesh are before him 8
40: 8 With all flesh, both man and beast 8
41: 3 this is the decree from the Lord for all flesh 8
44:18 all flesh should not be blotted out by a flood. 8
20 he established the covenant in his flesh 8
45: 1 found favor in the sight of all flesh 8
Bar 2: 3 we should eat, one the flesh of his son and another 8
3 we should eat . . another the flesh of his daughter. 8
Bel 1: 5 and has dominion over all flesh. 8
1Mc 7:17 The flesh of thy saints and their blood 8
2Mc 6:18 forced to open his mouth to eat swine's flesh. 6
19 spitting out the flesh •
21 he was eating the flesh of the sacrificial meal 6
7: 1 to partake of unlawful swine's flesh. 6
9: 9 his flesh rotted away 8
4Mc 6: 6 his flesh was being torn by scourges 8
7:18 are able to control the passions of the flesh 8
9:17 Cut my limbs, burn my flesh, and twist my joints. 8
20 pieces of flesh were falling off the axles 8
28 flayed all his flesh up to his chin 8
10: 8 he saw his own flesh torn all around 8
15:15 She watched the flesh of her children consumed 8
15 the flesh of the head to the chin exposed 8
20 When you saw the flesh of children 8
20 the flesh . . burned upon the flesh of other children 8

flesh *See also* man, mutilate, piece.

raw flesh 1. מִחְיָה
Lev 13:24 when . . the raw flesh of the burn becomes a spot 1

torn flesh 1. טְרֵפָה
Nah 2:12 his cave with prey and his dens with torn flesh. 1

fleshpot 1. סִיר בָּשָׂר
Exd 16: 3 when we sat by the fleshpots and ate bread 1

flies *See* swarm.

flight 1. מָנוֹס 2. מְנוּסָה 3. נדד 4. τροπή 5. φεύγω 6. φυγή
Job 27:22 he flees from its power in headlong flight. •
Isa 10:31 Madme'nah is in flight, the inhabitants of Gebim flee 3
52:12 you shall not go in flight, for the LORD will go 2
Dan 9:21 Gabriel . . came to me in swift flight at the time •
Ams 2:14 Flight shall perish from the swift 1
Mat 24:20 Pray that your flight may not be in winter 6
Jdt 15: 3 Those . . also took to flight 6
1Mc 15:11 he came in his flight to Dor, which is by the sea; 5
2Mc 4:42 put them all to flight 6
11:12 Lysias himself escaped by disgraceful flight. 5
12:22 they rushed off in flight 6
37 put them to flight. 4

flight *See also* put, take, turn.

hurried flight 1. חִפָּזוֹן
Deu 16: 3 came out of the land of Egypt in hurried flight 1

rushing flight 1. ῥοῖζος
Wis 5:11 and pierced by the force of its rushing flight 1

fling 1. טול 2. צמת 3. ῥίπτω
Lam 3:53 they flung me alive into the pit and cast stones 2
Ezk 32: 4 on the ground, on the open field I will fling you 1
4Mc 12:19 he flung himself into the braziers 3

fling dust 1. עפר
2Sm 16:13 cursed . . and threw stones at him and flung dust. 1

flint 1. חַלָּמִישׁ 2. צַר 3. צֹר 4. λίθος
Exd 4:25 Then Zippo'rah took a flint and cut off her son's 3
Jos 5: 2 Make flint knives and circumcise the people 3
3 Joshua made flint knives, and circumcised 3
Ps 114: 8 who turns the . . flint into a spring of water. 1
Isa 5:28 their horses' hoofs seem like flint 2
50: 7 therefore I have set my face like a flint 1
Ezk 3: 9 harder than flint have I made your forehead; 3
2Mc 10: 3 striking fire out of flint 4

flinty 1. חַלָּמִישׁ 2. ἀκρότομος
Deu 8:15 who brought you water out of the flinty rock 1
32:13 made him suck . . oil out of the flinty rock. 1
Wis 11: 4 water was given them out of flinty rock 2

flinty rock 1. חַלָּמִישׁ
Job 28: 9 Man puts his hand to the flinty rock 1

flit 1. נוד
Prv 26: 2 Like a sparrow in its flitting, like a swallow 1

float 1. הלך
Gen 7:18 and the ark floated on the face of the waters. 1

make float 1. צוף
2Kg 6: 6 threw it in there, and made the iron float. 1

flock 1. חַיָּה 2. מִקְנֶה 3. מִקְנֶה צֹאן 4. מַרְעִית 5. עֵדֶר 6. עֵז 7. צֹאן 8. ἀγελαῖος 9. ἀγέλη 10. ἀγεληδόν 11. καταλύω 12. ποίμνη 13. ποίμνιον 14. πρόβατον 15. grex 16. pecus
Gen 4: 4 Abel brought of the firstlings of his flock 7
13: 5 Lot . . also had flocks and herds and tents 7
21:28 Abraham set seven ewe lambs of the flock apart. 7
24:35 he has become great; he has given him flocks 7
26:14 He had possessions of flocks and herds 7
27: 9 Go to the flock, and fetch me two good kids 7
29: 2 lo, three flocks of sheep lying beside it; 5
2 for out of that well the flocks were watered. 5
3 when all the flocks were gathered there 5
8 they said, "We cannot until all the flocks are 5
10 Jacob . . watered the flock of Laban his mother's 7
30:31 I will again feed your flock and keep it 7
32 let me pass through all your flock today 7
36 and Jacob fed the rest of Laban's flock. 7
38 set the rods . . in front of the flocks 7
38 troughs, where the flocks came to drink. 7
39 the flocks bred in front of the rods 7
39 the flocks brought forth striped, speckled 7
40 set the faces of the flocks toward the striped 7
40 striped and all the black in the flock of Laban; 7
40 and did not put them with Laban's flock. 7
41 Whenever the stronger of the flock were breeding 7
41 rods in the runnels before the eyes of the flock 7
42 the feebler of the flock he did not lay them there 7
43 exceedingly rich, and had large flocks 7
31: 4 Leah into the field where his flock was 7
8 be your wages,' then all the flock bore spotted; 7
8 your wages,' then all the flock bore striped. 7
10 In the mating season of the flock I lifted up 7
10 which leaped upon the flock were striped 7
12 the goats that leap upon the flock are striped 7
38 I have not eaten the rams of your flocks. 7
41 served you . . six years for your flock 7
43 are my children, the flocks are my flocks 7
43 are my children, the flocks are my flocks 7
32: 5 I have oxen, asses, flocks, menservants 7
7 he divided . . the flocks and herds and camels 7
33:13 knows . . that the flocks and herds giving suck 7
13 overdriven for one day, all the flocks will die. 7
34:28 they took their flocks and their herds 7
37: 2 Joseph . . was shepherding the flock 7
12 to pasture their father's flock near Shechem. 7
13 your brothers pasturing the flock at Shechem? •
14 it is well with your brothers, and with the flock; 7
16 tell me . . where they are pasturing the flock. •
38:17 He answered, "I will send you a kid from the flock. 7
45:10 your flocks, your herds, and all that you have; 7
46:32 and they have brought their flocks, 7
47: 1 my brothers, with their flocks and herds 7
4 for there is no pasture for your servants' flocks 7
17 the horses, the flocks, the herds, and the asses 7
50: 8 only . . their flocks, and their herds were left 7
Exd 2:16 drew water . . to water their father's flock. 7
17 Moses . . helped them, and watered their flock. 7
19 drew water for us and watered the flock. 7
3: 1 Moses was keeping the flock of his father-in-law 7

1 and he led his flock to the west side 7
9: 3 plague upon . . the herds, and the flocks. 7
10: 9 sons and daughters and with our flocks and herds 7
24 let your flocks and your herds remain behind. 7
12:32 Take your flocks and your herds, as you have said 7
38 and very many cattle, both flocks and herds. 7
34: 3 let no flocks or herds feed before that mountain. 7
Lev 1: 2 cattle from the herd or from the flock 7
10 If his gift for a burnt offering is from the flock 7
3: 6 his offering . . is an animal from the flock 7
5: 6 a female from the flock, a lamb or a goat 7
15 bring . . a ram without blemish out of the flock 7
18 priest a ram without blemish out of the flock 7
6: 6 a ram without blemish out of the flock 7
22:21 offers . . from the herd or from the flock 7
27:32 all the tithe of herds and flocks 7
Num11:22 Shall flocks and herds be slaughtered for them 7
15: 3 offer to the LORD from the herd or from the flock 7
31: 9 they took as booty all their cattle, their flocks 2
28 tribute . . of the asses and of the flocks; 7
30 one drawn out of every 50, of . . the flocks 7
32:16 We will build sheepfolds here for our flocks 2
26 Our little ones, our wives, our flocks, and all our 2
Deu 7:13 bless . . the young of your flock 7
8:13 when your herds and flocks multiply 7
12: 6 bring . . the firstlings of your . . flock; 7
17 not eat . . the firstlings of . . your flock 7
21 then you may kill any of your herd or your flock 7
14:23 eat . . the firstlings of your herd and flock; 7
15:14 furnish him liberally out of your flock 7
19 firstling males that are born of your . . flock 7
19 nor shear the firstling of your flock. 7
16: 2 sacrifice . . from the flock or the herd 7
28: 4 Blessed shall be . . the young of your flock. 7
18 Cursed shall be . . the young of your flock. 7
51 not leave you . . the young of your flock 7
32:14 Curds from the herd, and milk from the flock 7
Jdg 5:16 the sheepfolds, to hear the piping for the flocks? 5
1Sm 8:17 He will take the tenth of your flocks 7
17:34 when there came . . and took a lamb from the flock 5
30:20 David also captured all the flocks and herds; 7
2Sm 12: 2 The rich man had very many flocks and herds; 7
4 was unwilling to take one of his own flock or herd 7
1Ch 4:39 to seek pasture for their flocks 7
41 there was pasture there for their flocks. 7
27:30 Over the flocks was Jaziz the Hagrite. 7
2Ch 32:29 provided . . flocks and herds in abundance; 3
35: 7 contributed . . lambs and kids from the flock 6
Ezr 10:19 their guilt offering was a ram of the flock 7
Neh 10:36 firstlings of our herds and of our flocks. 7
Job 21:11 They send forth their little ones like a flock 7
24: 2 they seize flocks and pasture them. 5
30: 1 have disdained to set with the dogs of my flock. 7
Ps 65:13 the meadows clothe themselves with flocks 7
68:10 thy flock found a dwelling in it; 1
77:20 Thou didst lead thy people like a flock 7
78:48 to the hail, and their flocks to thunderbolts. 2
52 guided them in the wilderness like a flock. 5
79:13 Then we thy people, the flock of thy pasture 7
80: 1 Shepherd . . who leadest Joseph like a flock! 7
107:41 makes their families like flocks. 7
Prv 27:23 Know well the condition of your flocks 7
Ecc 2: 7 I had also great possessions of herds and flocks 7
Sng 1: 7 Tell me . . where you pasture your flock •
7 wanders beside the flocks of your companions? 5
8 follow in the tracks of the flock 7
4: 1 Your hair is like a flock of goats 5
2 Your teeth are like a flock of shorn ewes 5
6: 2 to the beds of spices, to pasture his flock •
3 he pastures his flock among the lilies. •
5 Your hair is like a flock of goats 5
6 Your teeth are like a flock of ewes 5
Isa 13:20 no shepherds will make their flocks lie down •
17: 2 they will be for flocks, which will lie down 5
32:14 a joy of wild asses, a pasture of flocks; 5
40:11 He will feed his flock like a shepherd 5
60: 7 All the flocks of Kedar shall be gathered to you 7
61: 5 Aliens shall stand and feed your flocks 7
63:11 up out of the sea the shepherds of his flock? 7
65:10 Sharon shall become a pasture for flocks 7
Jer 3:24 for which our fathers labored, their flocks 7
5:17 they shall eat up your flocks and your herds; 7
6: 3 Shepherds with . . flocks shall come against her; 5
10:21 and all their flock is scattered. 4
13:17 because the LORD'S flock has been taken captive. 5
20 Where is the flock that was given you 5
20 flock that was given you, your beautiful flock? 7
23: 2 You have scattered my flock 7
3 Then I will gather the remnant of my flock 7
25:34 and roll in ashes, you lords of the flock 7
35 nor escape for the lords of the flock. 7
36 and the wail of the lords of the flock! 7
31:10 and will keep him as a shepherd keeps his flock. 5
12 and over the young of the flock and the herd; 7
24 farmers and those who wander with their flocks. 5
33:12 shepherds resting their flocks. 7
13 flocks shall again pass under the hands 7
49:20 little ones of the flock shall be dragged away; 7
29 Their tents and their flocks shall be taken 7
50: 8 and be as he-goats before the flock. 7
45 little ones of their flock shall be dragged away; 7
51:23 I break in pieces the shepherd and his flock; 5
Ezk 24: 5 Take the choicest one of the flock 7
25: 5 the cities of the Ammonites a fold for flocks. 7
34:12 As a shepherd seeks out his flock 5
17 As for you, my flock, thus says the Lord GOD: Behold 7
22 I will save my flock, they shall no longer be a prey; 7
36:37 to do for them: to increase their men like a flock. 7
38 Like the flock for sacrifices 7
38 for sacrifices, like the flock at Jerusalem 7
38 the waste cities be filled with flocks of men. 7
43:23 and a ram from the flock without blemish. 7
25 a sin offering; also a bull and a ram from the flock 7
45:15 one sheep from every flock of 200 7
Hos 5: 6 With their flocks and herds they shall go to seek 7
Jol 1:18 even the flocks of sheep are dismayed. 5
Ams 6: 4 and eat lambs from the flock, and calves 7
7:15 the LORD took me from following the flock 7
Jon 3: 7 Let neither man nor beast, herd nor flock 7
Mic 2:12 like sheep in a fold, like a flock in its pasture 5
4: 8 O tower of the flock, hill of the daughter of Zion 5
5: 4 he shall stand and feed his flock •
8 like a young lion among the flocks of sheep 5
7:14 Shepherd . . the flock of thy inheritance 7
Hab 3:17 Though . . the flock be cut off from the fold 7
Zep 2: 6 meadows for shepherds and folds for flocks. 7
Zec 9:16 save them for they are the flock of his people; 7
10: 3 the LORD of hosts cares for his flock 5
11: 4 shepherd of the flock doomed to slaughter. 7
7 the shepherd of the flock doomed to be slain 7
17 to my worthless shepherd, who deserts the flock! 7
Mal 1:14 Cursed be the cheat who has a male in his flock 5
Mat 26:31 the sheep of the flock will be scattered.' 12
Lke 2: 8 keeping watch over their flock by night. 12
12:32 Fear not, little flock 13
Joh 10:16 there shall be one flock, one shepherd. 12
Act 20:28 Take heed to yourselves and to all the flock 13
29 fierce wolves . . not sparing the flock; 13
1Co 9: 7 Who tends a flock 12
1Pe 5: 2 Tend the flock of God that is your charge 13
3 but being examples to the flock. 13
2Es 5:18 like a shepherd who leaves his flock 15
26 from all the flocks that have been made 16
7:65 the four-footed beasts and the flocks rejoice! 16
15:10 my people is led like a flock to the slaughter 15
Tob 5:13 offered the first-born of our flocks •
7: 8 they killed a ram from the flock 14
Jdt 2:27 destroyed their flocks and herds 13
3: 3 all our wheat fields, and our flocks and herds 13
Sir 18:13 turns them back, as a shepherd his flock. 13
27: 9 Birds flock with their kind 11
47: 3 with bears as with lambs of the flock. 14
Bar 4:26 taken away like a flock carried off by the enemy. 13
2Mc 14:14 flocked to join Nicanor, thinking that . . 10
23 the flocks of people that had gathered. 8
4Mc 5: 4 one man, Eleazar by name, leader of the flock 9

flock *See also* pasture.

little flock 1. חָשִׂיף
1Kg 20:27 before them like two little flocks of goats 1

flock together 1. *συνίστημι*
3Mc 1:19 Those women . . flocked together in the city. 1

flog 1. מַהֲלֻמוֹת 2. נכה 3. *μαστιγόω*
Prv 17:26 to flog noble men is wrong. 2
18: 6 A fool's . . mouth invites a flogging. 1
19:29 flogging for the backs of fools. 1
Mat 10:17 and flog you in their synagogues 3

flood 1. מַבּוּל 2. מַי 3. נָהָר 4. נזל 5. שׁחה 6. שִׁבֹּלֶת 7. שִׁבֹּלֶת מַיִם 8. שֶׁטֶף 9. שִׁפְעָה 10. תְּהוֹם 11. *κατακλύζω* 12. *κατακλυσμός* 13. *κλύδων* 14. *πλήμμυρα* 15. *ποταμός* 16. *ὕδωρ* 17. *χύμα* 18. diluvium 19. multus
Gen 6:17 I will bring a flood of waters upon the earth 1
7: 6 Noah was 600 years old when the flood . . came 1
7 into the ark, to escape the waters of the flood. 1
10 the waters of the flood came upon the earth. 1
17 The flood continued 40 days upon the earth; 1
9:11 all flesh be cut off by the waters of a flood 1
11 shall there be a flood to destroy the earth. 1
15 never again become a flood to destroy all flesh. 1
28 After the flood Noah lived 350 years; 1
10: 1 Japheth; sons were born to them after the flood. 1
32 spread abroad on the earth after the flood. 1
11:10 father of Arpach'shad two years after the flood; 1
Exd 15: 5 The floods cover them; they went down 10
8 waters piled up, the floods stood up in a heap; 4
2Sm 5:20 The LORD has broken . . like a bursting flood. 2
Job 22:11 you cannot see, and a flood of water covers you. 9
27:20 Terrors overtake him like a flood; 2
38:34 to the clouds, that a flood of waters may cover you? 9
Ps 6: 6 every night I flood my bed with tears; 5
29:10 The LORD sits enthroned over the flood; 1
69: 2 into deep waters, and the flood sweeps over me. 6
15 Let not the flood sweep over me 7
88:17 They surround me like a flood all day long; 2
93: 3 floods have lifted up, O LORD 3
3 O LORD, the floods have lifted up their voice 3
3 floods lift up their roaring. 3
98: 8 Let the floods clap their hands; 3
124: 4 then the flood would have swept us away 2
Sng 8: 7 cannot quench love, neither can floods drown it. 3
Dan 9:26 Its end shall come with a flood and to the end 8
Jon 2: 3 heart of the seas, and the flood was round about me; 3
Nah 1: 8 with an overflowing flood he will make a full end 8
Mat 7:25 rain fell, and the floods came, and the winds blew 15
27 rain fell, and the floods came, and the wind blew 15
24:38 For as in those days before the flood 12
39 they did not know until the flood came 12
Lke 6:48 when a flood arose 14
17:27 the flood came and destroyed them all. 12
2Pe 2: 5 he brought a flood upon the world of the ungodly; 12
2Es 3: 9 thou didst bring the flood upon the inhabitants 18
10 as death came upon Adam, so the flood upon them. 18
15:41 hail and flying swords and floods of water 19
Wis 10: 4 When the earth was flooded because of him 11
18: 5 didst destroy them all together by a mighty flood. 16
Sir 21:13 will increase like a flood 12
39:22 drenches it like a flood. 12
40:10 on their account the flood came. 12
44:17 a remnant was left . . when the flood came. 12
18 all flesh should not be blotted out by a flood. 12
1Mc 6:11 into what a great flood I now am plunged! 13
2Mc 2:24 considering the flood of numbers involved 17
3Mc 2: 4 by bringing upon them a boundless flood. 16
4Mc 15:31 carrying the world in the universal flood 12
32 the flood of your emotions and the violent winds 12

flood *See also* sweep.

bursting flood 1. פֶּרֶץ מַיִם
1Ch 14:11 my enemies by my hand, like a bursting flood. 1

floor 1. אֶרֶץ 2. קַרְקַע 3. *ἔδαφος*
Num 5:17 dust that is on the floor of the tabernacle 2
Jdg 3:25 and there lay their lord dead on the floor. 1
1Kg 6:15 from the floor of the house to . . the ceiling 2
15 he covered the floor . . with boards of cypress. 2
16 boards of cedar from the floor to the rafters 2
30 The floor of the house he overlaid with gold 2
7: 7 was finished with cedar from floor to rafters. 2
Job 5:26 a shock of grain comes up to the threshing floor •
Ezk 41:16 round about, from the floor up to the windows 1
20 from the floor to above the door 1
Bel 1:19 Look at the floor 3

threshing floor 1. גֹּרֶן 2. גֹּרֶן דָּגָן 3. אִדַּר (A) 4. *ἅλων* 5. area
Gen 50:10 When they came to the threshing floor of Atad 1
11 saw the mourning on the threshing floor of Atad 1
Num15:20 as an offering from the threshing floor 1
18:27 it were the grain of the threshing floor 1
30 reckoned . . as produce of the threshing floor 1
Deu 15:14 liberally . . out of your threshing floor 1
16:13 ingathering from your threshing floor 1
Jdg 6:37 am laying a fleece of wool on the threshing floor; 1
Rut 3: 2 See, he is winnowing . . at the threshing floor. 1
3 and put on . . and go down to the threshing floor; 1
6 she went down to the threshing floor 1
14 that the woman came to the threshing floor. 1
1Sm 23: 1 and are robbing the threshing floors. 1
2Sm 6: 6 when they came to the threshing floor of Nacon 1
24:16 angel . . was by the threshing floor of Arau'nah 1
18 an altar . . on the threshing floor of Arau'nah 1
21 David said, "To buy the threshing floor of you 1
24 David bought the threshing floor and the oxen 1
1Kg 22:10 the threshing floor at the entrance of the gate 1
2Kg 6:27 From the threshing floor, or from the wine press? 1
1Ch 13: 9 when they came to the threshing floor of Chidon 1
21:15 standing by the threshing floor of Ornan 1
18 altar to the LORD on the threshing floor of Ornan 1
21 and went forth from the threshing floor 1
22 to Ornan, "Give me the site of the threshing floor 1
28 answered him at the threshing floor of Ornan 1
2Ch 3: 1 on the threshing floor of Ornan the Jeb'usite. 1
18: 9 sitting at the threshing floor at the entrance 1
Job 39:12 and bring your grain to your threshing floor? 1
Jer 51:33 daughter of Babylon is like a threshing floor 1
Dan 2:35 like the chaff of the summer threshing floors; 3
Hos 9: 1 a harlot's hire upon all threshing floors 2
2 Threshing floor and winevat shall not feed them 1
13: 3 the chaff that swirls from the threshing floor 1
Jol 2:24 The threshing floors shall be full of grain 1
Mic 4:12 gathered . . as sheaves to the threshing floor. 1
Mat 3:12 clear his threshing floor and gather his wheat 4
Lke 3:17 to clear his threshing floor 4
2Es 4:32 how great a threshing floor they will fill! 5
9:17 as is the farmer, so is the threshing floor. 5

flour 1. סֹלֶת 2. קֶמַח 3. *ἄλευρον* 4. *σεμίδαλις*
Jdg 6:19 a kid, and unleavened cakes from an ephah of flour; 2
1Sm 1:24 a . . bull, an ephah of flour, and a skin of wine; 2
28:24 killed it, and she took flour, and kneaded it 2
1Ch 23:29 the showbread, the flour for the cereal offering 1

Ezk 46:14 one third of a hin of oil to moisten the flour 1
Mat 13:33 in three measures of flour 3
Lke 13:21 took and hid in three measures of flour 3
Sir 39:26 iron and salt and wheat flour and milk and honey 4

fine flour 1. סֹלֶת 2. σεμίδαλις

Exd 29: 2 You shall make them of fine wheat flour. 1
40 a tenth measure of fine flour mingled 1
Lev 2: 1 his offering shall be of fine flour 1
2 he shall take from it a handful of the fine flour 1
4 it shall be unleavened cakes of fine flour 1
5 shall be of fine flour unleavened, mixed with oil 1
7 it shall be made of fine flour with oil 1
5:11 tenth of an ephah of fine flour for a sin offering 1
6:15 one shall take from it a handful of the fine flour 1
20 a tenth of an ephah of fine flour as a regular 1
7:12 cakes of fine flour well mixed with oil 1
14:10 an ephah of fine flour mixed with oil, and one log 1
21 a tenth of an ephah of fine flour mixed with oil 1
23:13 two tenths of an ephah of fine flour mixed with oil 1
17 they shall be of fine flour, they shall be baked 1
24: 5 you shall take fine flour, and bake twelve cakes 1
Num 6:15 cakes of fine flour mixed with oil 1
7:13 both of them full of fine flour mixed with oil 1
19 both of them full of fine flour mixed with oil 1
25 fine flour mixed with oil for a cereal offering; 1
31 fine flour mixed with oil for a cereal offering; 1
37 fine flour mixed with oil for a cereal offering; 1
43 fine flour mixed with oil for a cereal offering; 1
49 fine flour mixed with oil for a cereal offering; 1
55 fine flour mixed with oil for a cereal offering; 1
61 fine flour mixed with oil for a cereal offering; 1
67 fine flour mixed with oil for a cereal offering; 1
73 fine flour mixed with oil for a cereal offering; 1
79 fine flour mixed with oil for a cereal offering; 1
8: 8 cereal offering of fine flour mixed with oil 1
15: 4 offering of a tenth of an ephah of fine flour 1
6 offering two tenths of an ephah of fine flour 1
9 three tenths of an ephah of fine flour 1
28: 5 also a tenth of an ephah of fine flour 1
9 fine flour for a cereal offering, mixed with oil 1
12 fine flour for a cereal offering, mixed with oil 1
12 two tenths of fine flour for a cereal offering 1
13 tenth of fine flour mixed with oil as a cereal 1
20 cereal offering of fine flour mixed with oil; 1
28 cereal offering of fine flour mixed with oil 1
29: 3 cereal offering of fine flour mixed with oil 1
9 cereal offerings of fine flour mixed with oil 1
14 cereal offering of fine flour mixed with oil 1
1Kg 4:22 provision . . was 30 cors of fine flour 1
1Ch 9:29 also over the fine flour, the wine, the oil 1
Ezk 16:13 you ate fine flour and honey and oil. 1
19 I fed you with fine flour and oil and honey 1
Rev 18:13 wine, oil, fine flour and wheat, cattle and sheep 2
Sir 35: 2 He who returns a kindness offers fine flour 2
38:11 a memorial portion of fine flour 2
Bel 1: 3 they spent on it twelve bushels of fine flour 2

flourish 1. פרה 2. פרח 3. צוץ 4. שגא 5. θάλλω 6. floreo

Job 8:11 Can reeds flourish where there is no water? 4
Ps 72: 7 In his days may righteousness flourish 2
90: 6 in the morning it flourishes and is renewed; 3
92: 7 though the wicked . . all evildoers flourish 3
12 The righteous flourish like the palm tree 2
13 they flourish in the courts of our God. 2
103:15 man . . flourishes like a flower of the field; 3
Prv 11:28 righteous will flourish like a green leaf. 2
14:11 but the tent of the upright will flourish. 2
Isa 66:14 your bones shall flourish like the grass; 2
Hos 13:15 Though he may flourish as the reed plant 1
14: 7 they shall flourish as a garden; •
2Es 6:28 faithfulness shall flourish 6
Sir 14:18 Like flourishing leaves on a spreading tree 5

cause to flourish 1. ἀναθάλλω

Sir 11:22 quickly God causes his blessing to flourish. 1

make flourish 1. נוב 2. פרח 3. ἀναθάλλω

Ezk 17:24 and make the dry tree flourish. 2
Zec 9:17 Grain shall make the young men flourish 1
Sir 1:18 making peace and perfect health to flourish. 3

flout 1. סלה

Lam 1:15 Lord flouted all my mighty men in the midst of me; 1

flow 1. אָפִיק 2. הלך 3. זוב 4. יָבָל 5. יצא 6. יצק 7. ירד 8. מוג 9. מסס 10. מָקוֹר 11. נגר 12. נהר 13. נזל 14. נַחַל 15. סוח 16. צָפָה 17. שטף 18. ἀπορέω 19. ἐκπορεύομαι 20. ἐξέρχομαι 21. ζωή 22. καταρέω 23. ῥέω 24. ῥύσις 25. decurro 26. fluo

Gen 2:14 river is Tigris, which flows east of Assyria. 2
Exd 3: 8 to . . a land flowing with milk and honey 3
17 to . . a land flowing with milk and honey. 3
13: 5 to give you, a land flowing with milk and honey 3
33: 3 Go up to a land flowing with milk and honey; 3
Lev 12: 7 she shall be clean from the flow of her blood 10
20:24 a land flowing with milk and honey.' I am the LORD 3
Num13:27 flows with milk and honey, and this is its fruit. 3
14: 8 land which flows with milk and honey. 3
16:13 out of a land flowing with milk and honey 3
14 into a land flowing with milk and honey 3
24: 7 Water shall flow from his buckets 13
Deu 6: 3 in a land flowing with milk and honey. 3
11: 9 land flowing with milk and honey. 3
26: 9 gave us . . land flowing with milk and honey. 3
15 a land flowing with milk and honey.' 3
27: 3 land flowing with milk and honey, as the LORD 3
31:20 into the land flowing with milk and honey 3
Jos 3:13 the Jordan shall be stopped from flowing •
5: 6 a land flowing with milk and honey. 3
1Kg 22:35 blood . . flowed into the bottom of the chariot. 6
2Ch 32: 4 the brook that flowed through the land 17
Job 20:17 the streams flowing with honey and curds. 14
Ps 42: 1 As a hart longs for flowing streams 1
104:10 springs gush forth . . flow between the hills. 2
105:41 flowed through the desert like a river. 2
147:18 he makes his wind blow, and the waters flow. 13
Prv 4:23 for from it flow the springs of life. •
Ecc 1: 7 where the streams flow, there they flow again. 2
7 where the streams flow, there they flow again. 2
Isa 2: 2 and all the nations shall flow to it 12
8: 6 refused the waters of Shilo'ah that flow gently 2
34: 3 the mountains shall flow with their blood. 9
44: 4 like grass . . like willows by flowing streams. 4
Jer 11: 5 to give them a land flowing with milk and honey 3
32:22 to give them, a land flowing with milk and honey; 3
51:44 The nations shall no longer flow to him; 12
Lam 1:16 For these things I weep; my eyes flow with tears; 7
3:48 my eyes flow with rivers of tears 7
49 My eyes will flow without ceasing 11
Ezk 20: 6 a land flowing with milk and honey 3
15 had given them, a land flowing with milk and honey 3
23:15 with flowing turbans on their heads, all of them 15
32: 6 even to the mountains with your flowing blood; 16
47: 8 This water flows toward the eastern region 5
12 the water for them flows from the sanctuary. 5
Jol 3:18 and the hills shall flow with milk 2
18 the stream beds of Judah shall flow with water; 2
Ams 9:13 sweet wine, and all the hills shall flow with it. 8
Mic 4: 1 and peoples shall flow to it 12
Mrk 5:25 woman who had had a flow of blood for twelve years 24
Lke 8:43 woman who had had a flow of blood for twelve years 24
44 immediately her flow of blood ceased. 24
Joh 7:38 shall flow rivers of living water.' 23
Rev 14:20 and blood flowed from the wine press 20
22: 1 flowing from the throne of God and of the Lamb 19
2Es 1:20 so that waters flowed in abundance 26
2:19 springs flowing with milk and honey 26
6:24 so that for three hours they shall not flow. 25
Jdt 7:12 flows from the foot of the mountain– 19
Sir 24:31 and his counsel like a flowing spring. 21
46: 8 into a land flowing with milk and honey. 23
Bar 1:20 to give to us a land flowing with milk and honey. 23
4Mc 6: 6 his blood flowing 22
10: 8 drops of blood flowing from his entrails. 18

flow around 1. סבב

Gen 2:11 it . . flows around the whole land of Havilah 1
13 which flows around the whole land of Cush. 1

flow away 1. ῥύομαι

Wis 16:29 and flow away like waste water. 1

cause to flow down 1. ירד

Ps 78:16 caused waters to flow down like rivers. 1

flow down 1. ירד

Jos 3:16 and those flowing down toward the sea of Arabah 1
Ezk 47: 1 water was flowing down from below the south end 1

flow forth 1. יצא

Deu 8: 7 and springs, flowing forth in valleys and hills 1

make flow 1. נזל 2. ἄγω

Isa 48:21 he made water flow for them from the rock; 1
Ezk 31: 4 made it grow tall, making its rivers flow round 2

flow out 1. יצא

Gen 2:10 A river flowed out of Eden to water the garden 1
Zec 14: 8 living waters shall flow out from Jerusalem 1

wonted flow 1. אֵתָן

Exd 14:27 the sea returned to its wonted flow 1

flower 1. אֵב 2. נִצָּה 3. נִצָּן 4. פֶּרַח 5. צִיץ 6. צִיצָה 7. ἄνθος 8. flos

Exd 25:31 its cups, its capitals, and its flowers shall be 4
33 made like almonds, each with capital and flower 4
33 three cups . . each with capital and flower 4
34 four cups . . with their capitals and flowers 4
37:17 and its flowers were of one piece with it. 4
19 cups . . with capital and flower on one branch 4
19 cups . . with capital and flower, on the other 4
20 cups . . with their capitals and flowers 4
Num 8: 4 from its base to its flowers, it was hammered work; 4
1Kg 6:18 was carved in the form of gourds and open flowers; 5
29 of cherubim and palm trees and open flowers 5
32 of cherubim, palm trees, and open flowers; 5
35 carved cherubim and palm trees and open flowers; 5
7:26 made like the brim . . like the flower of a lily; 4
49 the flowers, the lamps, and the tongs, of gold; 4
2Ch 4: 5 brim was made . . like the flower of a lily; 4
21 flowers, the lamps, and the tongs, of purest gold; 4
Job 8:12 While yet in flower and not cut down, they wither 1
14: 2 He comes forth like a flower, and withers; 5
Ps 103:15 man . . flourishes like a flower of the field; 5
Sng 2:12 The flowers appear on the earth 3
Isa 18: 5 and the flower becomes a ripening grape 2
28: 1 to the fading flower of its glorious beauty 5
4 the fading flower of its glorious beauty 6
40: 6 all its beauty is like the flower of the field. 5
7 The grass withers, the flower fades 5
8 The grass withers, the flower fades; 5
Jas 1:10 like the flower of the grass he will pass away. 7
11 its flower falls, and its beauty perishes 7
1Pe 1:24 and all its glory like the flower of grass. 7
24 The grass withers, and the flower falls 7
2Es 5:24 from all the flowers of the world 8
36 and make the withered flowers bloom again for me; 8
6: 3 before the beautiful flowers were seen 8
44 and flowers of inimitable color 8
9:17 as are the flowers, so are the colors 8
24 go into a field of flowers 8
24 and eat only of the flowers of the field 8
24 and drink no wine, but eat only flowers 8
26 and there I sat among the flowers 8
12:51 and I ate only of the flowers of the field 8
15:50 the glory . . shall wither like a flower 8
Wis 2: 7 let no flower of spring pass by us. 7
3Mc 7:16 crowned with all sorts of very fragrant flowers 7

flowing *See* locks, stop, stream, water.

flush 1. πυρόω

AEs 15: 7 Lifting his face, flushed with splendor 1

flute 1. חָלִיל 2. נְחִילָה 3. αὐλός

1Sm 10: 5 prophets coming . . with harp, tambourine, flute 1
Ps 5: 0 To the choirmaster: for the flutes. 2
Isa 5:12 harp, timbrel and flute and wine at their feasts; 1
30:29 as when one sets out to the sound of the flute to go 1
Jer 48:36 Therefore my heart moans for Moab like a flute 1
36 my heart moans like a flute for the men 1
1Co 14: 7 instruments, such as the flute or the harp 3
1Es 5: 2 with the music of drums and flutes; 3
Sir 40:21 The flute and the harp make pleasant melody 3
1Mc 3:45 the flute and the harp ceased to play. 3

flute *See also* player.

flutter 1. נדד 2. רחף

Deu 32:11 Like an eagle that . . flutters over its young 2
Isa 16: 2 Like fluttering birds 1

fly 1. דאה 2. כָּנָף 3. עוף 4. עיט 5. πέτομαι 6. πορεύομαι 7. φεύγω 8. convolo 9. volo

Gen 1:20 and let birds fly above the earth 3
Deu 4:17 likeness of any winged bird that flies in the air 3
28:49 bring a nation . . as swift as the eagle flies 1
1Sm 14:32 the people flew upon the spoil, and took sheep 4
2Sm 22:11 He rode on a cherub, and flew . . upon the wings 3
Job 5: 7 man is born to trouble as the sparks fly upward. 3
Ps 18:10 He rode on a cherub, and flew; he came swiftly 3
91: 5 of the night, nor the arrow that flies by day 3
148:10 creeping things and flying birds! 2
Prv 23: 5 flying like an eagle toward heaven. 3
26: 2 in its flitting, like a swallow in its flying 3
Isa 6: 2 each had six wings . . and with two he flew. 3
6 flew one of the seraphim to me, having in his hand 3
14:29 and its fruit will be a flying serpent. 3
30: 6 the lion, the viper and the flying serpent 3
60: 8 Who are these that fly like a cloud, 3
Jer 48:40 Behold, one shall fly swiftly like an eagle 1
49:22 one shall mount up and fly swiftly like an eagle 1
Hab 1: 8 they fly like an eagle swift to devour. 3
Zec 5: 1 lifted my eyes and saw, and behold, a flying scroll! 3
2 What do you see?" I answered, "I see a flying scroll; 3
Rev 4: 7 the fourth living creature like a flying eagle. 5
8:13 heard an eagle crying . . as it flew in midheaven 5
9: 6 they will long to die, and death will fly from them. 7
12:14 might fly from the serpent into the wilderness 5
14: 6 Then I saw another angel flying in midheaven 5
19:17 he called to all the birds that fly in midheaven 5
2Es 11: 5 I looked, and behold, the eagle flew with his wings 9
13: 3 behold, that man flew with the clouds of heaven; 8
6 a great mountain, and flew up upon it. 9
15:41 fire and hail and flying swords 9
Wis 5:21 Shafts of lightning will fly with true aim 6

fly (2) 1. זְבוּב 2. עָרֹב 3. μυῖα

Exd 8:24 the land was ruined by reason of flies. 2
Ecc 10: 1 Dead flies make . . ointment give off an evil odor; 1
Isa 7:18 the fly which is at the sources of the streams 1
Wis 16: 9 were killed by the bites of locusts and flies 3

fly around 1. περιπέτομαι
4Mc 14:17 by flying in circles around them 1

fly away 1. נדד 2. נצא 3. עוף
Job 20: 8 He will fly away like a dream, and not be found; 3
Ps 55: 6 wings like a dove! I would fly away and be at rest; 3
90:10 they are soon gone, and we fly away. 3
Jer 48: 9 Give wings to Moab, for she would fly away; 2
Hos 9:11 E'phraim's glory shall fly away like a bird- 3
Nah 3:16 The locust spreads its wings and flies away. 3
17 when the sun rises, they fly away; 1

fly away together 1. facio conmigrationem
2Es 5: 6 and the birds shall fly away together; 1

fly down 1. καθίπταμαι
Sir 43:17 He scatters the snow like birds flying down 1

fly forth 1. ἐκπέτομαι
Sir 43:14 the clouds fly forth like birds. 1

fly through 1. διίπταμαι
Wis 5:11 when a bird flies through the air 1

flying *See* creature.

foal 1. בֵּן 2. עַיִר 3. υἱός
Gen 49:11 Binding his foal to the vine 2
Zec 9: 9 riding on an ass, on a colt the foal of an ass. 1
Mat 21: 5 on an ass, and on a colt, the foal of an ass. 3

foam 1. חמר 2. ἀφρίζω 3. ἀφρός
Ps 46: 3 though its waters roar and foam 1
75: 8 there is a cup, with foaming wine, well mixed; 1
Mrk 9:18 he foams and grinds his teeth and becomes rigid; 2
Lke 9:39 it convulses him till he foams, and shatters him 3

foam *See also* cast.

foam at the mouth 1. ἀφρίζω
Mrk 9:20 rolled about, foaming at the mouth. 1

fodder 1. בְּלִיל 2. χόρτασμα
Job 6: 5 when he has grass, or the ox low over his fodder? 1
24: 6 They gather their fodder in the field 1
Sir 33:24 Fodder and a stick and burdens for an ass 2
38:26 he is careful about fodder for the heifers. 2

foe 1. איב 2. אִישׁ צַר 3. צַר 4. צרר 5. שׂנא 6. ἐχθρός
Deu 30: 7 put all these curses upon your foes and enemies 1
2Sm 24:13 Or will you flee three months before your foes 3
1Ch 21:12 or three months of devastation by your foes 3
Est 7: 6 Esther said, "A foe and enemy! This wicked Haman! 2
9: 1 the Jews should get the mastery over their foes 5
Ps 3: 1 O LORD, how many are my foes! 3
6: 7 My eye . . it grows weak because of all my foes. 4
8: 2 thou hast founded a bulwark because of thy foes 4
10: 5 as for all his foes, he puffs at them. 4
13: 4 lest my foes rejoice because I am shaken. 3
25:19 Consider how many are my foes 1
27: 2 my adversaries and foes, they shall stumble 1
30: 1 and hast not let my foes rejoice over me. 1
35:19 those rejoice over me who are wrongfully my foes 1
38:19 Those who are my foes without cause are mighty 1
44: 5 Through thee we push down our foes; 3
7 thou hast saved us from our foes 3
10 Thou hast made us turn back from the foe; 3
60:11 O grant us help against the foe 3
12 it is he who will tread down our foes. 3
68:23 dogs may have their portion from the foe. 1
69:19 my foes are all known to thee. 4
72: 9 May his foes bow down before him, and his enemies •
74: 4 Thy foes have roared in the midst of thy holy place; 4
10 How long, O God, is the foe to scoff? 3
23 Do not forget the clamor of thy foes 4
78:42 or the day when he redeemed them from the foe; 3
61 his glory to the hand of the foe. 3
81:14 turn my hand against their foes. 3
89:23 I will crush his foes before him 3
42 Thou hast exalted the right hand of his foes; 3
105:24 LORD . . made them stronger than their foes. 3
106:10 he saved them from the hand of the foe 5
108:12 O grant us help against the foe 3
13 it is he who will tread down our foes. 3
110: 2 Rule in the midst of your foes! 1
119:139 consumes me, because my foes forget thy words. 3
136:24 rescued us from our foes, for his steadfast love 3
Isa 1:24 on my enemies, and avenge myself on my foes. 1
29: 5 the multitude of your foes shall be like . . dust •
42:13 he shows himself mighty against his foes. 1
Jer 30:16 be devoured, and all your foes, every one of them 3
46:10 a day of vengeance, to avenge himself on his foes. 3
Lam 1: 5 Her foes have become the head 3
5 children have gone . . captives before the foe. 3
7 When her people fell into the hand of the foe 3
7 When her people fell . . the foe gloated over her 3
17 Jacob that his neighbors should be his foes; 3
2: 4 bent his bow . . with his right hand set like a foe; 3
17 he has made . . and exalted the might of your foes. 3
4:12 did not believe . . that foe or enemy could enter 3
Nah 1: 9 he will not take vengeance twice on his foes. •
3:13 The gates of your land are wide open to your foes; 1
Zec 8:10 neither was there any safety from the foe 3
10: 5 mighty men in battle, trampling the foe in the mud •
Mat 10:36 a man's foes will be those of his own household. 6
Rev 11: 5 fire pours out . . and consumes their foes; 6
12 in the sight of their foes they went up to heaven 6
AEs 13:15 the eyes of our foes are upon us to annihilate us •
Wis 11: 3 and fought off their foes. 6
Sir 19: 8 With friend or foe do not report it 6
25: 7 a man who lives to see the downfall of his foes; 6
1Mc 2: 9 her youths by the sword of the foe. 6

merciless foe 1. אַכְזָרִי
Jer 30:14 of an enemy, the punishment of a merciless foe 1

foeman 1. לחם
Ps 56: 1 all day long foemen oppress me; 1

foil 1. ἀθετέω 2. κατακρατέω
Jdt 16: 6 the Lord Almighty has foiled them 1
3Mc 1: 6 Now that he had foiled the plot 2

fold 1. בִּצְרָה 2. גְּדֵרָה 3. גָּלִיל 4. חבק 5. חִבֻּק
6. מִכְלָה 7. מַפָּל 8. מַרְבֵּץ 9. נָוֶה 10. נָוָה 11. רֵבֶץ
12. αὐλή
Num 32:24 Build cities . . and folds for your sheep; 2
36 fortified cities, and folds for sheep. 2
1Kg 6:34 the two leaves of the one door were folding 3
34 the two leaves of the other door were folding. 3
Job 5:24 you shall inspect your fold and miss nothing. 10
41:23 The folds of his flesh cleave together 7
Ps 50: 9 bull from your house, nor he-goat from your folds. 6
Prv 6:10 slumber, a little folding of the hands to rest 5
24:33 slumber, a little folding of the hands to rest 5
Ecc 4: 5 The fool folds his hands, and eats his own flesh. 4
Jer 23: 3 and I will bring them back to their fold 10
25:30 he will roar mightily against his fold, and shout 10
37 and the peaceful folds are devastated 9
49:20 their fold shall be appalled at their fate. 10
50: 6 they have gone, they have forgotten their fold. 11
45 their fold shall be appalled at their fate. 10
Ezk 25: 5 the cities of the Ammonites a fold for flocks. 8
Mic 2:12 I will set them together like sheep in a fold 1
Hab 3:17 Though . . the flock be cut off from the fold 6
Zep 2: 6 meadows for shepherds and folds for flocks. 2
Joh 10:16 I have other sheep, that are not of this fold 12

foliage 1. פֹּארָה
Ezk 17: 6 brought forth branches and put forth foliage. 1

foreign folk 1. עֵרֶב
Jer 25:20 and all the foreign folk among them; 1

old folks 1. זָקֵן
Jer 6:11 shall be taken, the old folk and the very aged. 1

follow 1. אַחַר 2. אַחֲרֵי 3. אֶל 4. אֵלֶּה 5. בְּ
6. בוא אַחֲרֵי 7. בוא אַף אַחֲרֵי 8. בוא בְּרֶגֶל 9. בְּרֶגֶל
10. היה 11. היה אַחֲרֵי 12. הלך אַחַר 13. הלך אַחֲרֵי
14. הלך בְּ 15. הלך בְּרֶגֶל 16. זֶה 17. יצא 18. יצא אַחֲרֵי
19. משך 20. נגע 21. עלה אַחֲרֵי 22. עשׂה 23. עשׂה בְּ
24. רדף 25. רדף אַחֲרֵי 26. שֵׁנִי 27. תור 28. תכה
29. בְּנֵמָא (A) 30. ἀκολουθέω 31. ἀπέρχομαι ὀπίσω
32. γίνομαι 33. δεῦτε ὀπίσω 34. διαγωγή 35. διώκω
36. εἰμί 37. ἐκ 38. ἐκ τοῦ ὄπισθεν 39. ἐξακολουθέω
40. ἐπακολουθέω 41. ἔπειμι 42. ἐπέρχομαι 43. ἕπομαι
44. ἔχω 45. κατά 46. κατακολουθέω 47. λέγω
48. μετά 49. μετέπειτα 50. ὅδε 51. οἴχομαι
52. ὄπισθεν 53. ὀπίσω 54. ὀπίσω πορεύω 55. οὗτος
56. οὕτως 57. παρακολουθέω 58. παρέρχομαι
59. πείθω 60. περιπατέω 61. ποιέω 62. πορεύομαι
63. πορεύω ἐν 64. πορεύω ὀπίσω 65. στοιχέω
66. συνακολουθέω 67. συνέπομαι 68. τοιόσδε
69. τοιοῦτος 70. τρόπον τοῦτον 71. ὑπογράφω
72. ὑπόκειμαι 73. sequor 74. subsequor
Gen 24: 5 Perhaps the woman may not be willing to follow me 13
8 if the woman is not willing to follow you 13
39 'Perhaps the woman will not follow me.' 13
61 Rebekah . . followed the man; 13
32:19 instructed . . all who followed the droves 13
41:31 by reason of that famine which will follow 2
44: 4 Up, follow after the men; and when you overtake 24
45:23 To his father he sent as follows: ten asses loaded 16
47:18 they came to him the following year, and said 26
Exd 11: 8 saying, 'Get you out, and all the people who follow 9
14:28 host of Pharaoh that had followed them 6
21:22 a miscarriage, and yet no harm follows 10
23 If any harm follows, then you shall give life 10
23: 2 You shall not follow a multitude to do evil; 11
Lev 20: 5 all who follow him in playing the harlot 2
Num 14:24 Caleb, because he . . has followed me fully 2
43 you have turned back from following the LORD 2
15:39 not to follow after your own heart and your own 27
16:25 elders of Israel followed him. 13
32:11 because they have not wholly followed me; 2
12 they have wholly followed the LORD.' 2
15 For if you turn away from following him 2
Deu 1:36 because he has wholly followed the LORD!' 2
4: 3 destroyed . . men who followed the Ba'al of Pe'or; 13
7: 4 they would turn away your sons from following me 2
11: 6 tents, and every living thing that followed them 9
12:30 take heed that you be not ensnared to follow them 2
16:20 Justice, and only justice, you shall follow 24
18: 9 not learn to follow the abominable practices 22
33: 3 they followed in thy steps, receiving direction 28
Jos 3: 3 you shall set out from your place and follow it 13
6: 8 ark of the covenant of the LORD following them. 2
14: 8 yet I wholly followed the LORD my God. 2
9 you have wholly followed the LORD my God. 2
14 he wholly followed the LORD, the God of Israel. 2
16: 5 territory of the E'phraimites . . was as follows •
21: 3 gave . . the following cities and pasture lands 4
9 gave the following cities mentioned by name 4
22:16 in turning away this day from following the LORD 2
18 you must turn away . . from following the LORD? 2
23 an altar to turn away from following the LORD; 2
29 and turn away this day from following the LORD 2
Jdg 3:28 he said to them, "Follow after me; for the LORD has 24
4:14 from Mount Tabor with 10,000 men following him 2
5:14 set out thither into the valley, following you 2
6:34 the Abiez'rites were called out to follow him. 2
35 and they too were called out to follow him. 2
8: 5 give loaves of bread to the people who follow me; 9
9: 3 and their hearts inclined to follow Abim'elech 2
4 and reckless fellows, who followed him. 13
49 and following Abim'elech put it against 13
Rut 1:16 not to leave you or to return from following you; 2
1Sm 12:14 if both you and the king . . will follow the LORD 11
20 do not turn aside from following the LORD 2
13: 7 and all the people followed him trembling. 2
15:11 he has turned back from following me 2
17:13 sons of Jesse had followed Saul to the battle; 2
14 the three eldest followed Saul 13
24: 1 Saul returned from following the Philistines 2
25:27 be given to the young men who follow my lord. 15
30:21 men, who had been too exhausted to follow David 13
2Sm 2:10 But the house of Judah followed David. 11
19 he turned . . from following Abner. 2
21 As'ahel would not turn aside from following him. 2
22 Turn . . from following me; why should I smite you 2
3:31 And King David followed the bier. 13
7: 8 I took you from . . from following the sheep 1
11: 8 there followed him a present from the king. 18
15:18 the . . Gittites who had followed him from Gath 8
17: 9 slaughter among the people who follow Ab'salom.' 2
23 Ahith'ophel saw that the counsel was not followed 22
20: 2 Israel withdrew from David, and followed Sheba 21
11 and whoever is for David, let him follow Jo'ab. 2
14 the Bichrites assembled, and followed him in. 7
1Kg 1: 7 and they followed Adoni'jah and helped him. 2
9: 6 if you turn aside from following me 2
11: 6 Solomon . . did not wholly follow the LORD 2
12:20 There was none that followed the house of David 2
14: 8 David, who . . followed me with all his heart 13
16:21 half . . followed Tibni the son of Ginath 11
21 Tibni . . to make him king, and half followed Omri. 11
22 the people who followed Omri overcame 2
22 overcame the people who followed Tibni 2
18:18 forsaken . . the LORD and followed the Ba'als. 13
21 If the LORD is God, follow him; 13
21 If the LORD . . but if Ba'al, then follow him. 13
19:20 Let me kiss . . and then I will follow you. 13
21 he returned from following him, and took the yoke 2
20:10 suffice . . for all the people who follow me. 9
19 the servants . . and the army which followed 2
2Kg 3: 9 the army or for the beasts which followed them. 9
4:17 bore a son about that time the following spring •
30 So he arose and followed her. 13
5:21 So Geha'zi followed Na'aman. And when Na'aman 25
6:19 follow me, and I will bring you to . . whom you seek. 13
11:15 and slay with the sword any one who follows her. 6
13: 2 and followed the sins of Jerobo'am 12
17:15 they followed the nations that were round about 13
21 Jerobo'am drove Israel from following the LORD 2
34 they do not follow the statutes 23
18: 6 he did not depart from following him, but kept 2
1Ch 17: 7 from the pasture, from following the sheep 2
2Ch 22: 5 He even followed their counsel 14
23:14 any one who follows her is to be slain 6
34:33 they did not turn away from following the LORD 2
35: 4 following the directions of David king 5
36:14 following all the abominations of the nations; •
Ezr 2:59 following were those who came up from Tel-me'lah 4
4: 8 wrote . . to Ar-ta-xerx'es the king as follows- 29
5: 7 sent him a report, in which was written as follows •
Neh 4:23 nor the men of the guard who followed me, none of us •
7:61 following were those who came up from Tel-me'lah 4
12:38 I followed them . . to the Broad Wall •
Job 21:33 all men follow after him, and those who go before 19
34:27 because they turned aside from following him 2
Ps 23: 6 Surely goodness and mercy shall follow me 24
81:12 to follow their own counsels. 14
94:15 all the upright in heart will follow it. 2
Prv 7:22 All at once he follows her, as an ox goes 13

12:11 follows worthless pursuits has no sense. 24
28:19 follows worthless pursuits will have plenty 24
Sng 1: 8 follow in the tracks of the flock 17
Isa 45:14 they shall follow you; they shall come over 13
59:13 the LORD, and turning away from following our God 1
65: 2 way that is not good, following their own devices; 1
66:17 go into the gardens, following one in the midst 1
Jer 2: 2 how you followed me in the wilderness 13
3:17 no more stubbornly follow their own evil heart. 13
19 and would not turn from following me. 2
9:14 but have stubbornly followed their own hearts 13
13:10 who stubbornly follow their own heart 14
16:12 every one of you follows his stubborn evil will 13
18:12 That is in vain! We will follow our own plans 13
23:17 every one who stubbornly follows his own heart 14
Ezk 7:26 Disaster . . upon disaster, rumor follows rumor; 3
10:11 the others followed without turning 13
13: 3 foolish prophets who follow their own spirit 12
37:24 They shall follow my ordinances and be careful 14
Dan 9:10 not obeyed . . by following his laws, 14
11:43 Libyans . . Ethiopians . . follow in his train. •
Hos 4: 2 they break all bounds and murder follows murder. 20
Ams 7:15 the LORD took me from following the flock 2
Hab 3: 5 pestilence, and plague followed close behind. 17
Zep 1: 6 who have turned back from following the LORD 2
Mat 4:19 he said to them, "Follow me, and I will make you 33
20 Immediately they left their nets and followed 30
22 the boat and their father, and followed him. 30
25 And great crowds followed him from Galilee 30
8: 1 great crowds followed him; 30
10 he marveled, and said to those who followed him 30
19 Teacher, I will follow you wherever you go. 30
22 Jesus said to him, "Follow me, and leave the dead 30
23 he got into the boat, his disciples followed him. 30
9: 9 and he said to him, "Follow me. 30
9 Follow me." And he rose and followed him. 30
19 Jesus rose and followed him, with his disciples. 30
27 two blind men followed him, crying aloud 30
10:38 he who does not take his cross and follow me 30
12:15 And many followed him, and he healed them all 30
14:13 they followed him on foot from the towns. 30
16:24 take up his cross and follow me. 30
19: 2 large crowds followed him, and he healed them 30
21 and come, follow me. 30
27 Lo, we have left everything and followed you 30
28 you who have followed me 30
20:29 a great crowd followed him. 30
34 they received their sight and followed him. 30
21: 9 that followed him 30
26:58 Peter followed him at a distance 30
27:55 who had followed Jesus from Galilee 30
Mrk 1:17 Follow me and I will make you become fishers of men. 33
18 immediately they left their nets and followed 30
20 and followed him. 31
2:14 he said to him, "Follow me. 30
14 he rose and followed him. 30
15 there were many who followed him. 30
3: 7 a great multitude from Galilee followed 30
5:24 a great crowd followed him and thronged about 30
37 he allowed no one to follow him except Peter 66
6: 1 his disciples followed him. 30
8:34 take up his cross and follow me. 30
9:38 we forbade him, because he was not following us. 30
10:21 come, follow me. 30
28 Lo, we have left everything and followed you. 30
32 those who followed were afraid 30
52 received his sight and followed him on the way. 30
11: 9 and those who followed cried out 30
14:13 a jar of water will meet you; follow him 30
51 a young man followed him 66
54 Peter had followed him at a distance 30
15:41 who, when he was in Galilee, followed him 30
Lke 1: 3 having followed all things closely for some time past 57
5:11 they left everything and followed him. 30
27 he said to him, "Follow me. 30
28 he left everything, and rose and followed him. 30
7: 9 turned and said to the multitude that followed 30
9:11 When the crowds learned it, they followed him 30
23 take up his cross daily and follow me. 30
49 we forbade him, because he does not follow with us. 30
57 I will follow you wherever you go. 30
59 To another he said, "Follow me. 30
61 Another said, "I will follow you, Lord 30
13:33 today and tomorrow and the day following 44
17:23 Do not go, do not follow them. 35
18:22 come, follow me. 30
28 Lo, we have left our homes and followed you. 30
43 immediately he received his sight and followed 30
22:10 follow him into the house which he enters 30
39 the disciples followed him. 30
49 when those . . saw what would follow, they said 36
54 Peter followed at a distance; 30
23:27 followed him a great multitude of the people 30
49 the women who had followed him from Galilee 66
55 The women . . followed, and saw the tomb 46
Joh 1:37 heard him say this, and they followed Jesus. 30
38 Jesus turned, and saw them following, and said 30
40 two who heard John speak, and followed him 30
43 And he found Philip and said to him, "Follow me. 30
6: 2 a multitude followed him 30
8:12 he who follows me will not walk in darkness 30
10: 4 he goes before them, and the sheep follow him 30
5 A stranger they will not follow 30
27 I know them, and they follow me; 30
11:31 they followed her 30
12:26 If any one serves me, he must follow me 30
13:36 Where I am going you cannot follow me now 30
36 you shall follow afterward. 30
37 Peter said . . "Lord, why cannot I follow you now? 30
18:15 Simon Peter followed Jesus 30
20: 6 Simon Peter came, following him 30
21:19 after this he said to him, "Follow me. 30
20 following them the disciple whom Jesus loved 30
22 what is that to you? Follow me! 30
Act 5:36 all who followed him were dispersed 59
37 all who followed him were scattered. 59
7:26 on the following day he appeared to them 41
12: 8 Wrap your mantle around you and follow me. 30
9 he went out and followed him 30
13:43 many Jews . . followed Paul and Barnabas 30
15:23 with the following letter •
16:17 She followed Paul and us, crying 46
20:15 we came the following day opposite Chi'os 41
21:18 On the following day Paul went in with us to James; 41
36 the mob of the people followed, crying 30
23:11 The following night the Lord stood by him 41
Rom 4:12 but also follow the example of the faith 65
5:16 judgment following one trespass 37
16 the free gift following many trespasses brings 37
1Co 10: 4 from the supernatural Rock which followed them 30
11:17 in the following instructions I do not commend 55
Eph 2: 2 following the prince of the power of the air 45
3 following the desires of body and mind 61
1Ti 4: 6 the good doctrine which you have followed. 57
2Ti 1:13 Follow the pattern of the sound words 44
1Pe 2:21 an example, that you should follow in his steps. 40
2Pe 1:16 For we did not follow cleverly devised myths 39
2: 2 And many will follow their licentiousness 39
15 they have followed the way of Balaam 39
3: 3 scoffers . . following their own passions 62
2Jn 1: 4 to find some of your children following the truth 60
6 this is love, that we follow his commandments; 60
6 this is the commandment . . that you follow love 60
3Jn 1: 3 as indeed you do follow the truth. 60
4 to hear that my children follow the truth. 60
Jde 1:16 malcontents, following their own passions 62
18 scoffers, following their own ungodly passions 62
Rev 6: 8 its rider's name was Death, and Hades followed him; 30
8: 7 there followed hail and fire, mixed with blood 32
13: 3 the whole earth followed the beast with wonder. 53
14: 4 it is these who follow the Lamb wherever he goes; 30
8 Another angel, a second, followed, saying 30
9 And another angel, a third, followed them, saying 30
13 for their deeds follow them! 30
19:14 armies of heaven . . followed him on white horses 30
1Es 2:16 wrote him the following letter 71
25 the king, in reply to Rehum . . wrote as follows 71
5:36 The following are those who came up 55
38 the following had assumed the priesthood •
7: 1 following the orders of King Darius 46
8: 8 The following is a copy 72
2Es 6: 7 and the beginning of the age that follows? 73
9 Jacob is the beginning of the age that follows. 73
7:35 recompense shall follow 74
11:20 the wings that followed also rose up 73
Jdt 2:24 Then he followed the Euphrates 58
5: 7 because they would not follow the gods 30
9: 5 those that went before and those that followed; 49
15:13 while all the men of Israel followed 30
AEs 13: 5 perversely following a strange manner of life 34
15: 4 while the other followed carrying her train. 40
16: 1 The following is a copy of this letter 71
Sir 0: 1 the prophets and the others that followed them, 30
3 to the translation of the following book, 50
5: 2 Do not follow your inclination and strength 39
9 nor follow every path 63
18:30 Do not follow your base desires 54
46:10 might see that it is good to follow the Lord. 64
Bar 1:21 each followed the intent of his own wicked heart 51
Aza 1:17 may we wholly follow thee 52
18 now with all our heart we follow thee 39
1Mc 1:44 to follow customs strange to the land 64
2:17 the king's officers spoke to Mattathias as follows 47
5:43 the whole army followed him 52
6:23 to live by what he said and to follow his commands. 46
7:45 as they followed kept sounding the battle call 53
8:19 they entered the senate chamber and spoke as follows •
31 we have written to him as follows 47
9:16 they turned and followed close behind Judas 38
10:17 sent it to him, in the following words 55
25 he sent a message to them in the following words 55
51 with the following message 55
69 Then he sent the following message to Jonathan •
11:29 its contents were as follows 55
13:35 and wrote him a letter as follows 69
14:22 we have recorded in our public decrees, as follows 56
28 the following was proclaimed to us •
15: 2 its contents were as follows 70
15 letters . . in which the following was written 50
2Mc 2: 4 the tent and the ark should follow with him 66
6 Some of those who followed him 66
7:27 she spoke in their native tongue as follows 56
8:36 because they followed the laws ordained by him. 30
9:18 wrote to the Jews the following letter 71
27 For I am sure that he will follow my policy 57
11:27 To the nation the king's letter was as follows 68
15: 2 the Jews who were compelled to follow him said 67
3Mc 2: 1 the high priest Simon . . prayed as follows 69
26 many of his friends . . followed his will. 43
5: 2 on the following day to drug all the elephants 42
39 the officials . . remonstrated as follows 50
48 the following armed forces 67
6: 1 and prayed as follows 50
21 turned back upon the armed forces following 67
41 wrote the following letter for them 71
4Mc 1:22 desire precedes pleasure and delight follows 48
5:15 he began to address the people as follows 56
16: 5 she would have . . perhaps spoken as follows 55

follow a philosophy 1. φιλοσοφέω
4Mc 8: 1 by following a philosophy . . 1

follow after 1. רדף
Ps 38:20 are my adversaries because I follow after good. 1

follow close after 1. דבק
Gen 31:23 followed close after him into the hill country 1

follow corrupt practices 1. שחת
2Ch 27: 2 the people still followed corrupt practices. 1

follow hard 1. דבק 2. קרא
1Sm 14:22 they too followed hard after them in the battle. 1
Jer 4:20 Disaster follows hard on disaster 2
42:16 famine . . shall follow hard after you to Egypt; 1

follow out 1. κατακολουθέω
Jdt 11: 6 if you follow out the words of your maidservant 1

follow steadfastly 1. דבק בְּ
2Sm 20: 2 men of Judah followed their king steadfastly 1

follow steps 1. ἰχνεύω
Sir 51:15 from my youth I followed her steps. 1

follow the course 1. κατά
Eph 2: 2 following the course of this world 1

follow the path 1. תמך
Prv 5: 5 her steps follow the path to Sheol; 1

follow wholly 1. ἐπακολουθέω
Sir 46: 6 he wholly followed the Mighty One. 1

follower 1. ὁ σύν
2Mc 10: 1 Maccabeus and his followers 1

following *See* day.

following one 1. alius
2Es 10:59 So I slept that night and the following one 1

following thing 1. οὗτος
Sir 42: 1 Of the following things do not be ashamed 1

folly 1. אִוֶּלֶת 2. כֶּסֶל 3. מַשְׂכִּית 4. נְבָלָה 5. סֶכֶל 6. סִכְלוּת 7. ἀβουλία 8. ἀλογιστία 9. ἄνοια 10. ἀφροσύνη 11. μάταιος 12. ματαιότης 13. μωρία
Gen 34: 7 because he had wrought folly in Israel by lying 4
Deu 22:21 wrought folly in Israel by playing the harlot 4
1Sm 25:25 Nabal is his name, and folly is with him; 4
Job 42: 8 not to deal with you according to your folly; 4
Ps 69: 5 O God, thou knowest my folly; the wrongs I have done 1
73: 7 their hearts overflow with follies. 3
Prv 5:23 because of his great folly he is lost. 1
12:23 but fools proclaim their folly. 1
13:16 but a fool flaunts his folly. 1
14: 1 but folly with her own hands tears it down. 1
8 but the folly of fools is deceiving. 1
18 The simple acquire folly, but the prudent 1
24 but folly is the garland of fools. 1
29 but he who has a hasty temper exalts folly. 1
15: 2 but the mouths of fools pour out folly. 1
14 but the mouths of fools feed on folly. 1
21 Folly is a joy to him who has no sense 1
16:22 but folly is the chastisement of fools. 1
17:12 rather than a fool in his folly. 1
18:13 answer before he hears, it is his folly and shame. 1
19: 3 When a man's folly brings his way to ruin 1
22:15 Folly is bound up in the heart of a child 1
24: 9 The devising of folly is sin 1
26: 4 Answer not a fool according to his folly 1
5 Answer a fool according to his folly 1
11 dog . . to his vomit is a fool that repeats his folly. 1
27:22 yet his folly will not depart from him. 1
Ecc 1:17 to know wisdom and to know madness and folly. 6
2: 3 how to cheer my body . . and how to lay hold on folly 6

12 turned to consider wisdom and madness and folly; 6
13 wisdom excels folly as light excels darkness. 6
7:25 and to know the wickedness of folly 2
10: 1 so a little folly outweighs wisdom and honor. 6
6 folly is set in many high places 5
Isa 9:17 and an evildoer, and every mouth speaks folly. 4
32: 6 For the fool speaks folly 4
Jer 29:23 because they have committed folly in Israel 4
1Co 1:18 folly to those who are perishing 13
21 through the folly of what we preach to save 13
23 a stumbling block to Jews and folly to Gentiles 13
2:14 they are folly to him 13
3:19 For the wisdom of this world is folly with God. 13
2Ti 3: 9 their folly will be plain to all 9
2Pe 2:18 For, uttering loud boasts of folly, they entice 12
Wis 10: 8 also left for mankind a reminder of their folly 10
12:23 those who in folly of life lived unrighteously 10
Sir 8:15 through his folly you will perish with him. 10
20:31 Better is the man who hides his folly 13
34: 5 Divinations and omens and dreams are folly 11
41:15 Better is the man who hides his folly 13
47:20 they were grieved at your folly 10
23 ample in folly and lacking in understanding 10
Bar 3:28 no wisdom, they perished through their folly. 7
2Mc 4: 6 Simon would not stop his folly. 9
40 advanced in years and no less advanced in folly. 9
14: 8 through the folly of those whom I have mentioned 8
15:33 and hang up these rewards of his folly 9
3Mc 3:16 who never cease from their folly. 9
20 But we . . accommodated ourselves to their folly 9

wanton folly 1. נְבָלָה
2Sm 13:12 do not force me . . do not do this wanton folly. 1

fondle 1. צחק
Gen 26: 8 window and saw Isaac fondling Rebekah his wife. 1

food 1. אֲכִילָה 2. אכל 3. אֹכֶל 4. בּוּל 5. בַּר 6. בָּרוּת 7. בִּרְיָה 8. טֶרֶף 9. לֶחֶם 10. מַאֲכָל 11. מַכֹּלֶת 12. צַיִד 13. צֵידָה 14. שְׁאֵר 15. מָזוֹן (A) 16. ἄρτος 17. βορά 18. βρῶμα 19. βρῶσις 20. βρωτός 21. δαπάνημα 22. διατρέφω 23. διατροφή 24. ἔδεσμα 25. ἐπισιτισμός 26. ἐσθίω 27. ὄψον 28. ὀψοποίημα 29. τράπεζα 30. τροφή 31. τροφός 32. τρυφή 33. χόρτασμα 34. esca
Gen 1:29 seed in its fruit; you shall have them for food. 2
30 I have given every green plant for food. 2
2: 9 pleasant to the sight and good for food 10
3: 6 tree was good for food, and that it was a delight 10
6:21 take with you every sort of food that is eaten 10
21 it shall serve as food for you and for them. 2
9: 3 moving thing that lives shall be food for you; 2
24:33 Then food was set before him to eat; 16
39: 6 he had no concern for anything but the food 9
40:17 basket there were all sorts of baked food 10
41:35 let them gather all the food of these good years 3
35 the authority of Pharaoh for food in the cities 3
36 That food shall be a reserve for the land 3
48 he gathered up all the food of the seven years 3
48 and stored up food in the cities; 3
48 stored up in every city the food from the fields 3
42: 7 They said, "From the land of Canaan, to buy food. 3
10 lord, but to buy food have your servants come. 3
43: 2 Go again, buy us a little food. 3
4 with us, we will go down and buy you food; 3
20 my lord, we came down the first time to buy food; 3
22 brought other money down in our hand to buy food. 3
31 controlling himself he said, "Let food be served. 9
44: 1 Fill the men's sacks with food, as much as they can 3
25 when our father said, 'Go again, buy us a little food 3
47:12 provided . . household with food, 9
13 Now there was no food in all the land; 9
15 Give us food; why should we die before your eyes? 9
16 I will give you food in exchange for your cattle 16
17 Joseph gave them food in exchange for the horses 9
17 and he supplied them with food in exchange 9
19 Buy us and our land for food, and we with our land 9
24 as food for yourselves and your households 2
24 and as food for your little ones. 2
49:20 Asher's food shall be rich 9
Exd 21:10 he shall not diminish her food, her clothing 14
Lev 3:11 on he altar as food offered by fire to the LORD 9
16 as food offered by fire for a pleasing odor 9
11:34 Any food in it which may be eaten . . be unclean 3
19:23 When you . . plant all kinds of trees for food 10
22: 7 he may eat . . because such are his food 9
11 that are born in his house may eat of his food 9
13 she may eat of her father's food; yet no outsider 9
25: 6 The sabbath of the land shall provide food 2
7 in your land all its yield shall be for food 2
37 nor give him your food for profit 2
Num15:19 when you eat of the food of the land 9
21: 5 For there is no food and no water, and we loathe 9
5 no food and . . we loathe this worthless food. 9
28: 2 My offering, my food for my offerings by fire 9
24 offer daily . . the food of an offering by fire 9
Deu 2: 6 purchase food from them for money, 3
28 You shall sell me food for money, that I may eat 3
10:18 sojourner, giving him food and clothing. 9
20:20 trees which you know are not trees for food 10
28:26 dead body shall be food for all birds of the air 10
54 man . . grudge food to his brother, to the wife •
Jdg 13:16 If you detain me, I will not eat of your food; 9
Rut 1: 6 LORD had visited his people and given them food. 9
2:18 and gave her what food she had left over •
1Sm 14:24 Cursed be the man who eats food until . . evening 9
24 So none of the people tasted food. 9
28 'Cursed be the man who eats food this day.' 9
20:24 the new moon came, the king sat down to eat food. 9
34 Jonathan rose . . and ate no food the second day 9
2Sm 12:17 he would not, nor did he eat food with them. 9
20 when he asked, they set food before him, and he ate. 9
21 but when the child died, you arose and ate food. 9
13: 5 give me bread . . and prepare the food in my sight 7
7 Go to . . Amnon's house, and prepare food for him. 7
10 Bring the food into the chamber, that I may eat 7
1Kg 5: 9 meet my wishes by providing food for my 9
11 gave Hiram . . wheat as food for his household 11
10: 5 the food of his table 10
11:18 and assigned him . . food, and gave him land. 9
19: 8 and went in the strength of that food 40 days 1
21: 4 turned away his face, and would eat no food. 9
5 Why is your spirit so vexed that you eat no food? 9
2Kg 4: 8 a wealthy woman . . who urged him to eat some food. 9
8 whenever . . he would turn in there to eat food. 9
25: 3 there was no food for the people of the land. 9
1Ch 12:40 came bringing food on asses and on camels 9
2Ch 9: 4 the food of his table, the seating of his officials 10
11:11 and put . . in them, stores of food, oil, and wine. 10
30:22 people ate the food of the festival for seven •
Ezr 2:63 not to partake of the most holy food •
3: 7 gave . . food, drink, and oil to the Sido'nians 10
Neh 5:15 took from them food and wine 9
7:65 not to partake of the most holy food, until •
13:15 warned them on the day when they sold food. 12
Job 6: 7 they are as food that is loathsome to me. 9
12:11 the ear try words as the palate tastes food? 3
20:14 yet his food is turned in his stomach; 9
23 rain it upon him as his food. •
24: 5 in the wilderness as food for their children. 9
33:20 loathes bread, and his appetite dainty food. 10
34: 3 the ear tests words as the palate tastes food. 2
36:31 he judges peoples; he gives food in abundance. 3
38:41 cry to God, and wander about for lack of food? 3
40:20 For the mountains yield food for him 4
Ps 42: 3 My tears have been my food day and night 9
59:15 They roam about for food, and growl 2
69:21 They gave me poison for food 6
74:14 thou didst give him as food for the creatures 10
78:18 tested God in their heart by demanding the food 3
25 he sent them food in abundance. 13
30 while the food was still in their mouths 2
79: 2 thy servants to the birds of the air for food 10
104:14 that he may bring forth food from the earth 9
21 lions roar . . seeking their food from God. 2
27 to give them their food in due season. 2
107:18 they loathed any kind of food 3
111: 5 He provides food for those who fear him; 8
136:25 he who gives food to all flesh 9
145:15 thou gives them their food in due season. 2
146: 7 who gives food to the hungry. 9
147: 9 He gives to the beasts their food 9
Prv 6: 8 she prepares her food in summer 9
13:23 The fallow ground of the poor yields much food 3
23: 3 delicacies, for they are deceptive food. 9
27:27 there will be enough goats' milk for your food 9
27 goats' milk for . . the food of your household 9
28: 3 beating rain that leaves no food. 9
30: 8 feed me with the food that is needful for me 9
22 fool when he is filled with food; 9
25 yet they provide their food in the summer; 9
31:14 she brings her food from afar. 9
15 yet night and provides food for her household 8
Isa 23:18 her merchandise will supply abundant food 2
62: 8 your grain to be food for your enemies 10
65:25 and dust shall be the serpent's food. 9
Jer 5:17 They shall eat up your harvest and your food; 9
7:33 this people will be food for the birds of the air 10
16: 4 their dead bodies shall be food for the birds 10
19: 7 will give their dead bodies for food to the birds 10
34:20 Their dead bodies shall be food for the birds 10
40: 5 guard gave him an allowance of food and a present •
44:17 then we had plenty of food, and prospered 9
52: 6 there was no food for the people of the land. 9
Lam 1:11 they trade their treasures for food to revive 3
19 they sought food to revive their strength. 3
4: 4 the children beg for food, but no one gives to them. 9
10 their own children; they became their food 5
Ezk 4:10 the food which you eat shall be by weight 10
16:49 she and her daughters had pride, surfeit of food 9
23:37 have even offered up to them for food the sons 2
29: 5 to the birds of the air I have given you as food. 2
34: 5 they became food for all the wild beasts. 2
8 my sheep have become food for all the wild beasts 2
10 that they may not be food for them. 2
44: 7 when you offer to me my food, the fat and the blood. 9
47:12 there will grow all kinds of trees for food. 10
12 Their fruit will be for food 10
48:18 Its produce shall be food for the workers 9
Dan 1:10 king, who appointed your food and your drink 10
4:12 Its . . fruit abundant, and in it was food for all. 15
21 in which was food for all; under which beasts 15
Hos 9: 3 and they shall eat unclean food in Assyria. •
Jol 1:16 Is not the food cut off before our eyes 3
Hab 1:16 by them he lives in luxury, and his food is rich. 10
3:17 the olive fail and the fields yield no food 3
Hag 2:12 or pottage, or wine, or oil, or any kind of food 10
Mal 1: 7 By offering polluted food upon my altar. 9
12 polluted, and the food for it may be despised. 2
3:10 that there may be food in my house; 8
Mat 3: 4 waist; and his food was locusts and wild honey. 30
6:25 put on. Is not life more than food, and the body 30
10:10 for the laborer deserves his food. 30
14:15 into the villages and buy food for themselves. 18
24:45 to give them their food at the proper time? 30
25:35 for I was hungry and you gave me food 26
42 for I was hungry and you gave me no food 26
Mrk 7:19 Thus he declared all foods clean.) 18
Lke 3:11 he who has food, let him do likewise. 18
9:13 go and buy food for all these people. 18
12:23 life is more than food 30
Joh 4: 8 had gone away into the city to buy food. 30
32 I have food to eat of which you do not know. 19
33 Has any one brought him food? 26
34 My food is to do the will of him who sent me 18
6:27 Do not labor for the food which perishes 19
27 the food which endures to eternal life 19
55 my flesh is food indeed, and my blood is drink 19
Act 2:46 partook of food with glad and generous hearts 30
7:11 our fathers could find no food. 33
9:19 took food and was strengthened 30
14:17 satisfying your hearts with food and gladness. 30
16:34 and set food before them 29
23:14 an oath to taste no food till we have killed Paul. •
27:33 Paul urged them all to take some food, saying 30
34 Therefore I urge you to take some food 30
36 all were encouraged and ate some food themselves. 30
Rom 14:17 For the kingdom of God is not food and drink 19
20 Do not, for the sake of food, destroy the work 18
1Co 6:13 Food is meant for the stomach 18
13 the stomach for food 18
8: 8 Food will not commend us to God 18
13 if food is a cause of my brother's falling 18
9: 4 Do we not have the right to our food and drink? 26
10: 3 all ate the same supernatural food 18
2Co 9:10 supplies seed to the sower and bread for food 19
Col 2:16 in questions of food and drink 19
1Ti 4: 3 and enjoin abstinence from foods which God created 18
6: 8 if we have food and clothing 23
Heb 5:12 You need milk, not solid food 30
14 solid food is for the mature 30
9:10 deal only with food and drink 18
13: 9 strengthened . . not by foods 18
Jas 2:15 If a brother or sister is . . in lack of daily food 30
1Es 5:54 they gave money . . and food and drink 20
8:79 to give us food in the time of our servitude. 30
80 they have given us food 30
2Es 1:19 and gave you manna for food 34
9:34 the sea a ship, or any dish food or drink 34
12:51 and my food was of plants during those days. 34
Tob 1:10 my relatives ate the food of the Gentiles; 16
2: 2 Upon seeing the abundance of food I said to my son 27
5 I washed myself and ate my food in sorrow. 16
Jdt 2:18 also plenty of food for every man 25
4: 5 and stored up food in preparation for war 25
5:10 and lived there as long as they had food 22
12: 1 to set a table for her with some of his own food 28
9 until she ate her food toward evening. 30
13:10 who placed it in her food bag 18
Wis 13:12 to prepare his food 30
16: 3 when they desired food 30
20 thou didst give thy people food of angels 16
19:11 when desire led them to ask for luxurious food; 32
21 the crystalline, easily melted kind of heavenly food. 30
Sir 13: 7 He will shame you with his foods 18
29:22 sumptuous food in another man's house. 24
30:18 like offerings of food placed upon a grave. 18
25 will give heed to the food he eats. 18
31:21 If you are overstuffed with food 24
23 Men will praise the one who is liberal with food 16
24 complain of the one who is niggardly with food 16
36:18 The stomach will take any food 18
18 yet one food is better than another. 18
37:20 he will be destitute of all food 30
29 do not give yourself up to food; 24
40:29 He pollutes himself with another man's food 24
41: 1 still has the vigor to enjoy his food! 30
Bel 1:11 you yourself, O king, shall set forth the food 18
14 the king set forth the food for Bel 18
1Mc 1:35 they stored up arms and food 30
63 They chose to die rather than to be defiled by food 18
6:53 they had no food in storage 18
9:52 in them he put troops and stores of food. 18
13:21 to send them food. 30
33 he stored food in the strongholds. 18
14:10 He supplied the cities with food 18

2Mc 11:31 for the Jews to enjoy their own food and laws 21
3Mc 3: 4 they kept their separateness with respect to foods. 30
7 differences in worship and foods 31
6: 7 cast down . . to lions as food for wild beasts 17
4Mc 1:33 when we are attracted to forbidden foods 30
34 all sorts of foods that are forbidden to us 18
4:26 to eat defiling foods and to renounce Judaism. 31
food *See also* allowance, depend, eat, get, portion, provide, serving, supply, take.

food for birds 1. οἰωνόβρωτος
3Mc 6:34 would be destroyed and become food for birds 1

food offered to an idol 1. εἰδωλόθυτος
1Co 8: 1 Now concerning food offered to idols 1
4 Hence, as to the eating of food offered to idols 1
7 some . . eat food as really offered to an idol 1
10 not be encouraged . . to eat food offered to idols? 1
10:19 That food offered to idols is anything 1

rich food 1. פַּתְבַּג 2. פַּת בַּג
Dan 1: 5 daily portion of the rich food which the king ate 2
8 not defile himself with the king's rich food 1
13 youths who eat the king's rich food 1
15 than all the youths who ate the king's rich food. 1
16 steward took away their rich food and the wine 1
11:26 who eat his rich food shall be his undoing; 2

food sacrificed to an idol 1. εἰδωλόθυτος
Rev 2:14 that they might eat food sacrificed to idols 1
20 and to eat food sacrificed to idols. 1
4Mc 5: 2 to eat pork and food sacrificed to idols. 1

savory food 1. מַטְעַם
Gen 27: 4 prepare for me savory food, such as I love 1
7 'Bring me game, and prepare for me savory food 1
9 prepare from them savory food for your father 1
14 and his mother prepared savory food 1
17 she gave the savory food and the bread 1
31 He also prepared savory food, and brought it 1

solid food 1. βρῶμα
1Co 3: 2 I fed you with milk, not solid food 1

unclean food 1. κοινός
1Mc 1:62 and were resolved . . not to eat unclean food. 1

without food 1. ἀσιτία 2. ἄσιτος 3. ἐν νηστείαις
Act 27:21 As they had been long without food 1
33 you have continued in suspense and without food 2
2Co 11:27 in hunger and thirst, often without food 3

fool 1. אֱוִיל 2. אִוֶּלֶת 3. אִישׁ אֱוִיל 4. אִישׁ כְּסִיל 5. כְּסִיל 6. נָבָל 7. סָכָל 8. ἀφρός 9. ἄφρων 10. μωρός
2Sm 3:33 Should Abner die as a fool dies? 6
Job 5: 2 Surely vexation kills the fool 1
3 I have seen the fool taking root 1
Ps 14: 1 The fool says in his heart, "There is no God. 6
39: 8 Make me not the scorn of the fool! 6
49:10 the fool and the stupid alike must perish 5
53: 1 The fool says in his heart, "There is no God. 6
94: 8 Fools, when will you be wise? 5
Prv 1: 7 fools despise wisdom and instruction. 1
22 How long will . . fools hate knowledge? 5
32 complacence of fools destroys them; 5
3:35 wise will inherit honor, but fools get disgrace. 5
10: 8 but a prating fool will come to ruin. 1
14 but the babbling of a fool brings ruin near. 1
18 he who utters slander is a fool. 5
21 but fools die for lack of sense. 1
23 It is like sport to a fool to do wrong 5
11:29 fool will be servant to the wise. 1
12:15 The way of a fool is right in his own eyes 1
16 The vexation of a fool is known at once 1
23 but fools proclaim their folly. 5
13:16 but a fool flaunts his folly. 5
19 turn away from evil is an abomination to fools. 5
20 but the companion of fools will suffer harm. 5
14: 3 The talk of a fool is a rod for his back 1
7 Leave the presence of a fool, for there you do not 4
8 but the folly of fools is deceiving. 5
16 but a fool throws off restraint and is careless. 5
24 but folly is the garland of fools. 2
33 but it is not known in the heart of fools. 5
15: 2 but the mouths of fools pour out folly. 5
5 A fool despises his father's instruction 1
7 spread knowledge; not so the minds of fools. 5
14 but the mouths of fools feed on folly. 5
16:22 but folly is the chastisement of fools. 1
17: 7 Fine speech is not becoming to a fool; 6
10 than 100 blows into a fool. 5
12 rather than a fool in his folly. 5
16 Why should a fool have a price in his hand 5
21 father of a fool has no joy. 6
24 but the eyes of a fool are on the ends of the earth. 5
28 Even a fool who keeps silent is considered wise; 1
18: 2 A fool takes no pleasure in understanding 5
6 A fool's lips bring strife 5
7 A fool's mouth is his ruin 5
19: 1 than a man who is perverse in speech, and is a fool. 5
10 It is not fitting for a fool to live in luxury 5
29 flogging for the backs of fools. 5
20: 3 but every fool will be quarreling. 1
23: 9 Do not speak in the hearing of a fool 5
24: 7 Wisdom is too high for a fool; 1
26: 1 so honor is not fitting for a fool. 5
3 bridle for the ass, and a rod for the back of fools. 5
4 Answer not a fool according to his folly 5
5 Answer a fool according to his folly 5
6 He who sends a message by the hand of a fool 5
7 proverb in the mouth of fools. 5
8 one who binds . . is he who gives honor to a fool. 5
9 Like a thorn . . proverb in the mouth of fools. 5
10 he who hires a passing fool or drunkard. 5
11 dog . . to his vomit is a fool that repeats his folly. 5
12 There is more hope for a fool than for him. 5
27: 3 but a fool's provocation is heavier than both. 1
22 Crush a fool in a mortar with a pestle along 1
28:26 He who trusts in his own mind is a fool; 5
29: 9 If a wise man has an argument with a fool, the fool 3
9 fool only rages and laughs, and there is no quiet. •
11 A fool gives full vent to his anger 5
20 There is more hope for a fool than for him. 5
30:22 fool when he is filled with food; 6
Ecc 2:14 but the fool walks in darkness; 5
15 What befalls the fool will befall me also; 5
16 of the wise man as of the fool there is no enduring 5
16 How the wise man dies just like the fool! 5
19 who knows whether he will be a wise man or a fool? 7
4: 5 The fool folds his hands, and eats his own flesh. 5
5: 1 is better than to offer the sacrifice of fools; 5
3 dream comes . . and a fool's voice with many words. 5
4 do not delay . . for he has no pleasure in fools. 5
6: 8 what advantage has the wise man over the fool? 5
7: 4 but the heart of fools is in the house of mirth. 5
5 hear the rebuke . . than to hear the song of fools. 5
6 as the crackling . . so is the laughter of the fools; 5
9 for anger lodges in the bosom of fools. 5
17 Be not wicked overmuch, neither be a fool; 7
9:17 better than the shouting of a ruler among fools. 5
10: 2 but a fool's heart toward the left. 5
3 when the fool walks on the road, he lacks sense 7
3 and he says to every one that he is a fool. 7
12 but the lips of a fool consume him. 5
14 A fool multiplies words, though no man knows 7
15 The toil of a fool wearies him 5
Isa 32: 5 The fool will no more be called noble 6
6 For the fool speaks folly 6
35: 8 not pass over it, and fools shall not err therein. 1
Jer 17:11 and at his end he will be a fool. 6
Hos 9: 7 The prophet is a fool, the man of the spirit is mad 1
Mat 5:22 whoever says, 'You fool!' shall be liable to the hell 10
23:17 You blind fools! 10
Lke 11:40 You fools! Did not he who made the outside 9
12:20 God said to him, 'Fool! 9
1Co 3:18 let him become a fool that he may become wise. 10
4:10 We are fools for Christ's sake, but you are wise 10
2Co 11:16 even if you do, accept me as a fool 9
19 For you gladly bear with fools, being wise 9
12: 6 Though if I wish to boast, I shall not be a fool 9
11 I have been a fool! You forced me to it 9
Wis 5: 4 made a byword of reproach– we fools! 9
15: 5 whose appearance arouses yearning in fools 9
Sir 8:17 Do not consult with a fool 10
18:18 A fool is ungracious and abusive 10
19:11 With such a word a fool will suffer pangs 10
12 so is a word inside a fool. 10
23 there is a fool who merely lacks wisdom. 8
20: 7 a braggart and fool goes beyond the right moment. 8
13 the courtesies of fools are wasted. 10
14 A fool's gift will profit you nothing 9
16 A fool will say, "I have no friend 10
20 A proverb from a fool's lips will be rejected 10
21:14 The mind of a fool is like a broken jar 10
16 A fool's narration is like a burden on a journey 10
18 so is wisdom to a fool 10
20 A fool raises his voice when he laughs 10
22 The foot of a fool rushes into a house 10
26 The mind of fools is in their mouth 10
22: 7 He who teaches a fool 10
8 He who tells a story to a fool 10
11 weep for the fool, for he lacks intelligence 10
11 the life of the fool is worse than death. 10
12 for a fool or an ungodly man it lasts all his life. 10
14 what is its name except "Fool"? 10
18 so a timid heart with a fool's purpose 10
27:11 the fool changes like the moon. 8
13 The talk of fools is offensive 10
31: 7 every fool will be taken captive by it. 8
30 increases the anger of a fool to his injury 9
33: 5 The heart of a fool is like a cart wheel 10
34: 1 dreams give wings to fools. 9
Sus 1:48 Are you such fools, you sons of Israel? 10
fool *See also* deem, make, play.

wanton fool 1. נָבָל
2Sm 13:13 you would be as one of the wanton fools in Israel. 1

become a fool 1. μωραίνω
Rom 1:22 Claiming to be wise, they became fools 1

foolhardy fellow 1. τολμηρός
Sir 8:15 Do not travel on the road with a foolhardy fellow 1

foolish 1. אֱוִיל 2. כְּסִיל 3. כְּסִילוּת 4. כסל 5. נבל 6. נָבָל 7. סָכָל 8. ἀνόητος 9. ἄνοια 10. ἀσύνετος 11. ἄφρων 12. εὐήθης 13. ληρώδης 14. μάταιος 15. μωρός 16. φλύαρος 17. stultus 18. vanus
Deu 32: 6 requite . . you foolish and senseless people? 6
21 I will provoke them with a foolish nation. 6
Prv 9:13 A foolish woman is noisy; 3
10: 1 but a foolish son is a sorrow to his mother. 2
15:20 but a foolish man despises his mother. 2
17:25 A foolish son is a grief to his father 2
19:13 A foolish son is ruin to his father 2
21:20 but a foolish man devours it. 2
30:32 If you have been foolish, exalting yourself 5
Ecc 4:13 Better is a . . youth than an old and foolish king 2
Isa 19:11 The princes of Zo'an are utterly foolish; 1
Jer 4:22 For my people are foolish, they know me not; 1
5:21 Hear this, O foolish and senseless people 7
10: 8 They are both stupid and foolish; 4
Ezk 13: 3 says the Lord GOD, Woe to the foolish prophets 6
Mat 7:26 will be like a foolish man who built his house 15
25: 2 Five of them were foolish, and five were wise. 15
3 For when the foolish took their lamps 15
8 the foolish said to the wise 15
Rom 1:14 both to the wise and to the foolish 8
31 foolish, faithless, heartless, ruthless. 10
2:20 a corrector of the foolish, a teacher of children 11
10:19 with a foolish nation I will make you angry. 10
1Co 1:27 God chose what is foolish in the world 15
2Co 11:16 I repeat, let no one think me foolish 11
Gal 3: 1 O foolish Galatians! Who has bewitched you 8
3 Are you so foolish? 8
Eph 5:17 Therefore do not be foolish 11
Tit 3: 3 For we ourselves were once foolish, disobedient 8
1Pe 2:15 put to silence the ignorance of foolish men. 11
2Es 4:19 I answered and said, "Each has made a foolish plan 18
10: 6 You most foolish of women 17
Wis 1: 3 when his power is tested, it convicts the foolish; 11
5 and will rise and depart from foolish thoughts 10
3: 2 In the eyes of the foolish 11
12 Their wives are foolish, and their children evil; 11
11:15 In return for their foolish and wicked thoughts 10
12:24 they were deceived like foolish babes. 11
13: 1 were foolish by nature 14
14:11 a snare to the feet of the foolish. 11
19: 3 they reached another foolish decision 9
Sir 4:27 Do not subject yourself to a foolish fellow 15
15: 7 Foolish men will not obtain her 10
20:22 lose it because of his foolish look. 11
42: 8 instruct the stupid or foolish or the aged man 15
50:26 the foolish people that dwell in Shechem. 15
2Mc 2:32 it is foolish to lengthen the preface 12
12:44 superfluous and foolish to pray for the dead 13
4Mc 5:11 not awaken from your foolish philosophy 16
foolish *See also* confidence, make.

foolish man 1. כְּסִיל 2. ἀνόητος 3. ἄφρων
Prv 8: 5 O foolish men, pay attention. 1
Lke 24:25 he said to them, "O foolish men, and slow of heart 2
1Co 15:36 You foolish man! What you sow does not come to life 3
Sir 22:13 Do not talk much with a foolish man 3

most foolish 1. ἄφρων
Wis 15:14 most foolish, and more miserable than an infant 1

foolish woman 1. נָבָל
Job 2:10 You speak as one of the foolish women would 1

foolishly 1. אִוֶּלֶת 2. פתה 3. μωρός
Prv 14:17 A man of quick temper acts foolishly 1
20:19 do not associate with one who speaks foolishly. 2
Sir 16:23 a senseless and misguided man thinks foolishly. 3

do foolishly 1. יאל 2. סכל
Gen 31:28 Now you have done foolishly. 2
Num12:11 do not punish us because we have done foolishly 1
1Sm 13:13 Samuel said to Saul, "You have done foolishly; 2
2Sm 24:10 for I have done very foolishly. 2
1Ch 21: 8 for I have done very foolishly. 2
2Ch 16: 9 You have done foolishly in this; 2

foolishness 1. אִוֶּלֶת 2. סִכְלוּת 3. ἀφροσύνη 4. μωρός
Ps 38: 5 grow foul and fester because of my foolishness 1
Ecc 7:25 to know . . and the foolishness which is madness. 2
10:13 of the words of his mouth is foolishness 2
Mrk 7:22 envy, slander, pride, foolishness. 3
1Co 1:25 For the foolishness of God is wiser than men 4

2Co 11: 1 bear with me in a little foolishness 3
foolishness *See also* turn.

foot 1. כַּף רֶגֶל 2. מַרְגְּלוֹת 3. עַל הָאָרֶץ 4. פַּעַם 5. קַרְסֹל 6. רֶגֶל 7. רַגְלִי 8. תַּחַת 9. תַּחְתִּי 10. רְגַל (A) 11. *βάσις* 12. *θεμέλιον* 13. *πεζός* 14. *πούς* 15. *ῥίζα* 16. *ὑποδέω* 17. *ὑποπόδιον* 18. pes

Gen 8: 9 the dove found no place to set her foot 6
18: 4 Let a little water be brought, and wash your feet 6
19: 2 spend the night, and wash your feet; 6
24:32 gave . . water to wash his feet 6
32 his feet and the feet of the men who were with him. 6
41:44 lift up hand or foot in all the land of Egypt. 6
43:24 when . . they had washed their feet 6
49:10 nor the ruler's staff from between his feet 6
33 Jacob . . drew up his feet into the bed 6
Exd 3: 5 Do not come near; put off your shoes from your feet 6
4:25 her son's foreskin, and touched Moses' feet with it 6
12:11 sandals on your feet, and your staff in your hand; 6
37 about 600,000 men on foot, besides women 7
19:17 took their stand at the foot of the mountain. 9
21:24 tooth for tooth, hand for hand, foot for foot 6
24 tooth for tooth, hand for hand, foot for foot 6
24: 4 built an altar at the foot of the mountain 8
10 there was under his feet as it were a pavement 6
25:12 four rings . . and put them on its four feet 4
29:20 upon the great toes of their right feet 6
30:19 his sons wash their hands and their feet. 6
21 They shall wash their hands and their feet 6
32:19 broke them at the foot of the mountain. 8
40:31 his sons washed their hands and their feet; 6
Lev 8:23 right hand and on the great toe of his right foot 6
24 blood . . on the great toes of their right feet 6
11:21 may eat those which have legs above their feet 6
23 all other winged insects which have four feet 6
42 whatever has many feet, all the swarming things 6
13:12 the skin of the diseased person from head to foot 6
14:14 on the great toe of his right foot 6
17 and on the great toe of his right foot 6
25 on the great toe of his right foot 6
28 the great toe of his right foot 6
21:19 or a man who has an injured foot or an injured hand 6
Num 11:21 The people among whom I am number 600,000 on foot; 7
20:19 let me only pass through on foot, nothing more. 6
22:25 ass . . pressed Balaam's foot against the wall; 6
Deu 2: 5 not so much as for the sole of the foot to tread 6
28 only let me pass through on foot 6
4:11 came near and stood at the foot of the mountain 8
8: 4 your foot did not swell, these 40 years. 6
11:10 sowed your seed and watered it with your feet 6
24 place . . sole of your foot treads shall be yours; 6
19:21 tooth for tooth, hand for hand, foot for foot. 6
21 tooth for tooth, hand for hand, foot for foot. 6
25: 9 pull his sandal off his foot, and spit in his face 6
28:35 sole of your foot to the crown of your head. 6
56 who would not venture to set the sole of her foot 6
57 afterbirth that comes out from between her feet 6
65 there shall be no rest for the sole of your foot; 6
29: 5 your sandals have not worn off your feet; 6
32:35 for the time when their foot shall slip; 6
33:24 let him dip his foot in oil. 6
Jos 1: 3 Every place that the sole of your foot will tread 6
3:13 soles of the feet of the priests who bear the ark 6
15 the feet of the priests . . were dipped 6
4: 3 from the very place where the priests' feet stood 6
9 place where the feet of the priests . . had stood; 6
18 and the soles of the priests' feet were lifted up 6
5:15 Put off your shoes from your feet; 6
9: 5 with worn-out, patched sandals on their feet 6
10:24 put your feet upon the necks of these kings. 6
24 they came near, and put their feet on their necks. 6
12: 3 southward to the foot of the slopes of Pisgah; 8
14: 9 the land on which your foot has trodden shall be 6
Jdg 4:15 alighted from his chariot and fled away on foot. 6
17 Sis'era fled away on foot to the tent of Ja'el 6
5:27 He sank, he fell, he lay still at her feet; 6
27 at her feet he sank, he fell; where he sank 6
19:21 and they washed their feet, and ate and drank. 6
20: 2 of God, 400,000 men on foot that drew the sword. 7
Rut 3: 4 then, go and uncover his feet and lie down; 2
7 she came . . and uncovered his feet, and lay down. 2
8 and turned over, and behold, a woman lay at his feet! 2
14 she lay at his feet until the morning 2
1Sm 2: 9 He will guard the feet of his faithful ones; 6
14:13 Then Jonathan climbed up on his hands and feet 6
25:24 She fell at his feet and said, "Upon me alone 6
41 to wash the feet of the servants of my lord. 6
2Sm 2:18 Now As'ahel was as swift of foot as a wild gazelle; 6
3:34 hands were not bound, your feet were not fettered; 6
4: 4 had a son who was crippled in his feet. 6
12 they killed them, and cut off their hands and feet 6
9: 3 There is still a son . . he is crippled in his feet. 6
13 Now he was lame in both his feet. 6
11: 8 Go down to your house, and wash your feet. 6
14:25 from the sole of his foot to the crown of his head 6
19:24 he had neither dressed his feet, nor . . his beard 6
21:20 who had six fingers . . and six toes on each foot 6
22:10 and came down; thick darkness was under his feet. 6
34 He made my feet like hinds' feet, and set me secure 6
34 He made my feet like hinds' feet, and set me secure •
37 Thou didst give . . and my feet did not slip; 5
39 so that they did not rise; they fell under my feet. 6
1Kg 2: 5 about my loins, and upon the sandals on my feet. 6
5: 3 the LORD put them under the soles of his feet. 6
14: 6 when Ahi'jah heard the sound of her feet 6
12 When your feet enter the city, the child 6
15:23 But in his old age he was diseased in his feet. 6
2Kg 4:27 when she came . . she caught hold of his feet. 6
37 She came and fell at his feet, bowing to the ground; 6
6:32 Is not the sound of his master's feet behind him? 6
9:35 found . . the skull and the feet and the palms 6
13:21 he revived, and stood on his feet. 6
19:24 I dried up with the sole of my foot all the streams 4
21: 8 I will not cause the feet of Israel to wander 6
1Ch 20: 6 who had six fingers . . and six toes on each foot •
28: 2 Then King David rose to his feet and said 6
2Ch 3:13 cherubim stood on their feet, facing the nave. 6
16:12 Asa was diseased in his feet 6
33: 8 no more remove the foot of Israel from the land 6
Neh 9:21 not wear out and their feet did not swell. 6
Est 8: 3 she fell at his feet and besought him with tears 6
Job 2: 7 from the sole of his foot to the crown of his head. 6
12: 5 it is ready for those whose feet slip. 6
13:27 Thou puttest my feet in the stocks 6
27 thou settest a bound to the soles of my feet. 6
18: 8 For he is cast into a net by his own feet 6
23:11 My foot has held fast to his steps; 6
29:15 I was eyes to the blind, and feet to the lame. 6
31: 5 my foot has hastened to deceit; 6
33:11 he puts my feet in the stocks 6
39:15 forgetting that a foot may crush them 6
Ps 2:12 kiss his feet, lest he be angry, and you perish •
8: 6 thou hast put all things under his feet 6
9:15 in the net . . has their own foot been caught. 6
17: 5 held fast to thy paths, my feet have not slipped. 4
18: 9 thick darkness was under his feet. 6
33 He made my feet like hinds' feet 6
33 He made my feet like hinds' feet •
36 my feet did not slip. 5
38 were not able to rise; they fell under my feet. 6
22:16 they have pierced my hands and feet– 6
25:15 for he will pluck my feet out of the net. 6
26:12 My foot stands on level ground; 6
31: 8 thou hast set my feet in a broad place. 6
36:11 Let not the foot of arrogance come upon me 6
38:16 who boast against me when my foot slips! 6
40: 2 set my feet upon a rock, making my steps secure. 6
47: 3 peoples under us, and nations under our feet. 6
56:13 my soul from death, yea, my feet from falling 6
58:10 he will bathe his feet in the blood of the wicked. 4
66: 6 men passed through the river on foot. 6
9 us among the living, and has not let our feet slip. 6
68:23 that you may bathe your feet in blood 6
73: 2 But as for me, my feet had almost stumbled 6
91:12 lest you dash your foot against a stone. 6
94:18 When I thought, "My foot slips," thy steadfast love 6
105:18 His feet were hurt with fetters 6
115: 7 have hands, but do not feel; feet, but do not walk; 6
116: 8 thou hast delivered my . . feet from stumbling; 6
119:59 I turn my feet to thy testimonies; 6
101 I held back my feet from every evil way 6
105 Thy word is a lamp to my feet and a light to my path. 6
121: 3 He will not let your foot be moved 6
122: 2 feet . . standing within your gates, O Jerusalem! 6
140: 4 violent men, who have planned to trip up my feet. 4
Prv 1:15 my son . . hold back your foot from their paths; 6
16 for their feet run to evil 6
3:23 your foot will not stumble. 6
26 LORD . . will keep your foot from being caught. 6
4:26 Take heed to the path of your feet 6
27 turn your foot away from evil. 6
5: 5 Her feet go down to death; 6
6:13 winks with his eyes, scrapes with his feet 6
18 feet that make haste to run to evil 6
28 walk upon hot coals and his feet not be scorched? 6
7:11 her feet do not stay at home; 6
19: 2 he who makes haste with his feet misses his way. 6
25:17 Let your foot be seldom in your neighbor's house 6
19 like a bad tooth or a foot that slips. 6
26: 6 cuts off his own feet and drinks violence. 6
29: 5 flatters his neighbor spreads a net for his feet. 4
Ecc 10: 7 and princes walking on foot like slaves. 3
Sng 5: 3 I had bathed my feet, how could I soil them? 6
7: 1 How graceful are your feet in sandals 4
Isa 1: 6 From the sole of the foot even to the head 6
3:16 mincing along . . tinkling with their feet; 6
6: 2 each had six wings . . with two he covered his feet 6
7:20 shave . . the head and the hair of the feet 6
20: 2 Go . . and take off your shoes from your feet 6
23: 7 city . . whose feet carried her to settle afar? 6
26: 6 The foot tramples it, the feet of the poor 6
6 The foot tramples it, the feet of the poor 6
28: 3 of E'phraim will be trodden under foot; 6
32:20 who let the feet of the ox and the ass range free. 6
37:25 I dried up with the sole of my foot all the streams 4
41: 3 passes on safely, by paths his feet have not trod. 6
49:23 bow down to you, and lick the dust of your feet. 6
52: 7 are the feet of him who brings good tidings 6
58:13 If you turn back your foot from the sabbath 6
59: 7 Their feet run to evil, and they make haste 6
60:13 and I will make the place of my feet glorious. 6
14 all who despised you shall bow down at your feet; 1
Jer 2:25 Keep your feet from going unshod 6
12: 5 If you have raced with men on foot 6
13:16 before your feet stumble on the . . mountains 6
14:10 they have not restrained their feet; 6
18:22 dug a pit to take me, and laid snares for my feet. 6
38:22 now that your feet are sunk in the mire 6
Lam 1:13 he spread a net for my feet; he turned me back; 6
3:34 To crush under foot all the prisoners 6
Ezk 1: 7 soles of their feet were like the sole of a calf's 6
7 of their feet were like the sole of a calf's foot 6
2: 1 And he said to me, "Son of man, stand upon your feet 6
2 the Spirit entered into me and set me upon my feet; 6
3:24 the Spirit entered into me, and set me upon my feet; 6
6:11 Clap your hands, and stamp your foot, and say, Alas! 6
24:17 Bind on your turban, and put . . shoes on your feet; 6
23 shall be on your heads and your shoes on your feet; 6
25: 6 clapped your hands and stamped your feet 6
29:11 No foot of man shall pass through it 6
11 no foot of beast shall pass through it; 6
32: 2 trouble the waters with your feet 6
13 no foot of man shall trouble them any more 6
34:18 that you must tread down with your feet the rest 6
18 that you must foul the rest with your feet? 6
19 my sheep eat what you have trodden with your feet 6
19 and drink what you have fouled with your feet? 6
37:10 and they lived, and stood upon their feet 6
43: 7 of my throne and the place of the soles of my feet 6
Dan 2:33 its feet partly of iron and partly of clay. 10
34 smote the image on its feet of iron and clay 10
41 saw the feet and toes partly of potter's clay 10
42 toes of the feet were partly iron and partly clay 10
7: 4 made to stand upon two feet like a man; 10
7 stamped the residue with its feet. 10
19 pieces, and stamped the residue with its feet; 10
8:13 sanctuary and host to be trampled under foot? •
18 but he touched me and set me on my feet. •
Ams 2:15 and he who is swift of foot shall not save himself 6
Nah 1: 3 and the clouds are the dust of his feet. 6
15 the feet of him who brings good tidings 6
Hab 3:19 he makes my feet like hinds' feet, he makes me tread 6
19 he makes my feet like hinds' feet, he makes me tread •
Zec 14: 4 his feet shall stand on the Mount of Olives 6
12 flesh . . rot while they are still on their feet 6
Mal 4: 3 they will be ashes under the soles of your feet 6
Mat 4: 6 lest you strike your foot against a stone.' 14
7: 6 lest they trample them under foot and turn 14
10:14 shake off the dust from your feet as you leave 14
15:30 they put them at his feet, and he healed them 14
18: 8 if your hand or your foot causes you to sin 14
8 than with two hands or two feet 14
22:13 'Bind him hand and foot, and cast him into the outer 14
44 till I put thy enemies under thy feet'? 14
28: 9 took hold of his feet and worshiped him. 14
Mrk 5:22 seeing him, he fell at his feet 14
6:11 shake off the dust that is on your feet 14
7:25 heard of him, and came and fell down at his feet. 14
9:45 if your foot causes you to sin, cut it off 14
45 with two feet to be thrown into hell. 14
12:36 till I put thy enemies under thy feet.' 14
Lke 1:79 to guide our feet into the way of peace. 14
4:11 lest you strike your foot against a stone.' 14
7:38 standing behind him at his feet, weeping 14
38 she began to wet his feet with her tears 14
38 kissed his feet 14
44 you gave me no water for my feet 14
44 she has wet my feet with her tears 14
45 she has not ceased to kiss my feet. 14
46 she has anointed my feet with ointment. 14
8:35 sitting at the feet of Jesus 14
41 falling at Jesus' feet he besought him to come 14
9: 5 shake off the dust from your feet 14
10:11 'Even the dust of your town that clings to our feet 14
39 a sister called Mary, who sat at the Lord's feet 14
15:22 put a ring on his hand, and shoes on his feet; 14
17:16 he fell on his face at Jesus' feet 14
20:43 till I make thy enemies a stool for thy feet.' 14
24:39 See my hands and my feet, that it is I myself 14
Jch 11: 2 wiped his feet with her hair 14
32 Mary . . fell at his feet, saying to him, "Lord 14
44 his hands and feet bound with bandages 14
12: 3 anointed the feet of Jesus 14
3 wiped his feet with her hair 14
13: 5 began to wash the disciples' feet 14
6 Peter said to him, "Lord, do you wash my feet? 14
8 Peter said to him, "You shall never wash my feet. 14
9 Simon Peter said to him, "Lord, not my feet only 14
10 does not need to wash, except for his feet 14
12 When he had washed their feet 14
14 I . . your Lord and Teacher, have washed your feet 14
14 you also ought to wash one another's feet. 14
20:12 one at the head and one at the feet. 14
Act 2:35 till I make thy enemies a stool for thy feet.' 14
3: 7 his feet and ankles were made strong. 11
4:35 laid it at the apostles' feet 14

37 laid it at the apostles' feet. 14
5: 2 laid it at the apostles' feet. 14
9 the feet of those that have buried your husband 14
10 Immediately she fell down at his feet and died. 14
7: 5 not even a foot's length 14
33 Take off the shoes from your feet 14
58 at the feet of a young man named Saul. 14
10:25 and fell down at his feet and worshiped him. 14
13:25 the sandals of whose feet I am not worthy to untie.' 14
51 they shook off the dust from their feet against them 14
14: 8 there was a man sitting, who could not use his feet; 14
10 said in a loud voice, "Stand upright on your feet. 14
16:24 fastened their feet in the stocks. 14
21:11 bound his own feet and hands, and said 14
22: 3 but brought up in this city at the feet of Gama'li-el 14
26:16 rise and stand upon your feet 14
Rom 3:15 Their feet are swift to shed blood 14
10:15 How beautiful are the feet of those who preach 14
16:20 God . . will soon crush Satan under your feet. 14
1Co 12:15 If the foot should say, "Because I am not a hand 14
21 the head to the feet, "I have no need of you. 14
15:25 until he has put all his enemies under his feet. 14
27 all things in subjection under his feet. 14
Eph 1:22 he has put all things under his feet 14
6:15 having shod your feet 16
1Ti 5:10 washed the feet of the saints 14
Heb 1:13 till I make thy enemies a stool for thy feet"? 14
2: 8 everything in subjection under his feet 14
10:13 his enemies should be made a stool for his feet. 17
12:13 make straight paths for your feet 14
Jas 2: 3 Stand there," or "Sit at my feet 17
Rev 1:15 his feet were like burnished bronze 14
17 When I saw him, I fell at his feet as though dead. 14
2:18 and whose feet are like burnished bronze. 14
3: 9 make them come and bow down before your feet 14
10: 2 And he set his right foot on the sea 14
2 right foot on the sea, and his left foot on the land •
11:11 they stood up on their feet, and great fear fell 14
12: 1 clothed with the sun, with the moon under her feet 14
13: 2 the beast that I saw . . its feet were like a bear's 14
19:10 Then I fell down at his feet to worship him 14
22: 8 I fell down to worship at the feet of the angel 14
2Es 1:26 and your feet are swift to commit murder. 18
2:15 establish their feet, because I have chosen you 18
25 nourish your sons, and strengthen their feet. 18
5:15 held me and strengthened me and set me on my feet. 18
6:13 He answered and said to me, "Rise to your feet 18
17 When I heard this, I rose to my feet and listened 18
10:30 and set me on my feet, and said to me 18
14: 2 I said, "Here I am, Lord," and I rose to my feet. 18
Jdt 2: 7 cover . . the earth with the feet of my armies 14
6:13 left him lying at the foot of the hill 15
7:12 flows from the foot of the mountain- 15
10: 4 she put sandals on her feet, and put on her anklets 14
14: 7 when they raised him up he fell at Judith's feet 14
AEs 13:13 willing to kiss the soles of his feet 14
Wis 14:11 a snare to the feet of the foolish. 14
15:15 their feet are of no use for walking. 14
Sir 6:24 Put your feet into her fetters 14
36 let your foot wear out his doorstep. 14
21:19 education is fetters on his feet 14
22 The foot of a fool rushes into a house 14
25:20 A sandy ascent for the feet of the aged 14
26:18 so are beautiful feet with a steadfast heart. 14
38:29 turning the wheel with his feet 14
30 makes it pliable with his feet 14
40:25 Gold and silver make the foot stand sure 14
50:15 he poured it out at the foot of the altar 12
51:15 my foot entered upon the straight path 14
Bar 5: 6 For they went forth from you on foot 13
LJr 1:17 the dust raised by the feet of those who enter. 14
26 Having no feet, they are carried 14
1Mc 5:48 we will simply pass by on foot 14
3Mc 4: 9 had their feet secured by unbreakable fetters 14
5:42 mangled by the knees and feet of the beasts 14
4Mc 10: 5 they disjointed his hands and feet 14
14: 6 Just as the hands and feet are moved 14

foot *See also* cut, man, people, set, trample, tread.

foot soldier 1. אִישׁ רַגְלִי 2. רַגְלִי 3. ἀνήρ 4. πεζός

1Sm 4:10 there fell of Israel 30,000 foot soldiers. 2
2Sm 8: 4 David took . . 20,000 foot soldiers; 1
10: 6 the Syrians of Zobah, 20,000 foot soldiers 2
1Kg 20:29 Israel smote of the Syrians 100,000 foot soldiers 2
1Ch 18: 4 David took from him . . 20,000 foot soldiers; 1
19:18 David slew of the Syrians . . 40,000 foot soldiers 1
1Es 8:51 I was ashamed to ask the king for foot soldiers 4
Jdt 2: 5 120,000 foot soldiers and 12,000 cavalry. 4
7: 2 and the foot soldiers handling it 4
9: 7 they glory in the strength of their foot soldiers; 4
1Mc 6:30 100,000 foot soldiers 4
9: 4 went to Berea with 20,000 foot soldiers 3

under foot 1. תַּחַת

Isa 41: 2 that he tramples kings under foot; 1

foothold 1. מַעֲמָד

Ps 69: 2 I sink in deep mire, where there is no foothold; 1

footman 1. רַגְלִי

2Kg 13: 7 an army of . . and ten chariots and 10,000 footmen; 1

footprint 1. עָקֵב

Ps 77:19 yet thy footprints were unseen. 1

footstep 1. עָקֵב 2. פַּעַם 3. ἴχνος

Ps 85:13 make his footsteps a way. 2
89:51 which they mock the footsteps of thy anointed. 1
Bel 1:19 notice whose footsteps these are. 3
20 The king said, "I see the footsteps of men and women 3

footstool 1. הֲדֹם לְרַגְלַיִם 2. הֲדֹם רַגְלַיִם 3. כֶּבֶשׁ 4. ὑποπόδιον 5. scabillum

1Ch 28: 2 house . . and for the footstool of our God; 2
2Ch 9:18 The throne had six steps and a footstool of gold 3
Ps 99: 5 LORD our God; worship at his footstool! Holy is he! 2
110: 1 till I make your enemies your footstool. 1
132: 7 Let us go . . let us worship at his footstool! 2
Isa 66: 1 Heaven is my throne and the earth is my footstool; 2
Lam 2: 1 he has not remembered his footstool 2
Mat 5:35 or by the earth, for it is his footstool 4
Act 7:49 'Heaven is my throne, and earth my footstool 4
2Es 6: 4 before the footstool of Zion was established 5

forasmuch 1. אֲשֶׁר

1Sm 20:42 Go in peace, forasmuch as we have sworn both of us 1

forbear 1. חדל 2. ἀνεξίκακος 3. ἀνέχομαι 4. ἀνίημι 5. μακροθυμέω

1Kg 22: 6 Shall I go to battle . . or shall I forbear? 1
15 shall we go . . to battle, or shall we forbear? 1
2Ch 18: 5 battle against Ramoth-gilead, or shall I forbear? 1
14 go to Ramoth-gilead to battle, or shall I forbear? 1
Job 16: 6 if I forbear, how much of it leaves me? 1
Eph 4: 2 forbearing one another in love 3
6: 9 forbear threatening 4
Col 3:13 forbearing one another 3
2Ti 2:24 kindly to every one, an apt teacher, forbearing 2
2Pe 3: 9 The Lord . . is forbearing toward you 5

forbearance 1. אֶרֶךְ אַף 2. ἀνεξικακία 3. ἀνοχή 4. ἐπιείκεια 5. ἐπιεικής 6. μακροθυμία 7. συγγνώμη 8. φειδώ

Jer 15:15 In thy forbearance take me not away; 1
Rom 2: 4 presume upon . . his . . forbearance and patience? 3
3:25 in his divine forbearance he had passed over 3
2Co 6: 6 by purity, knowledge, forbearance, kindness 6
Php 4: 5 Let all men know your forbearance 5
2Pe 3:15 count the forbearance of our Lord as salvation. 6
Wis 2:19 and make trial of his forbearance. 2
12:18 with great forbearance thou dost govern us 8
Sir 3:13 show forbearance 7
Aza 1:19 deal with us in thy forbearance 4
2Mc 10: 4 might be disciplined by him with forbearance 4

forbid 1. חָלִילָה 2. כלא 3. לא צוה 4. עָרֵל 5. צוה 6. צוה לא 7. ἀθέμιτος 8. ἀπαγορεύω 9. ἀπεῖπον 10. ἀπείργω 11. διαστέλλω 12. κωλύω

Lev 19:23 three years it shall be forbidden to you 4
Num11:28 Joshua . . said, "My lord Moses, forbid them. 2
Deu 2:37 wherever the LORD our God forbade us. 5
4:23 anything which the LORD your God has forbidden 5
17: 3 worshipped them . . which I have forbidden 3
1Sm 24: 6 The LORD forbid that I . . do this thing to my lord 1
26:11 The LORD forbid that I should put forth my hand 1
1Kg 21: 3 The LORD forbid that I should give you 1
Lam 1:10 thou didst forbid to enter thy congregation. 6
Mrk 9:38 we forbade him, because he was not following us. 12
39 Jesus said, "Do not forbid him 12
Lke 9:49 we forbade him, because he does not follow with us. 12
50 Jesus said to him, "Do not forbid him 12
23: 2 forbidding us to give tribute to Caesar 12
Act 10:47 Can any one forbid water for baptizing 12
16: 6 forbidden by the Holy Spirit to speak the word 12
1Co 14:39 do not forbid speaking in tongues; 12
1Ti 4: 3 who forbid marriage 12
Jdt 11:12 all that God by his laws has forbidden them to eat. 11
1Mc 1:45 to forbid burnt offerings and sacrifices 12
2Mc 6: 5 which were forbidden by the laws. 7
12:40 which the law forbids the Jews to wear 10
4Mc 1:33 when we are attracted to forbidden foods 9
34 all sorts of foods that are forbidden to us 8
5:26 he has forbidden us to eat meats 12

forbidden *See* count.

force 1. אפק 2. זְרוֹעַ 3. חזק 4. חַיִל 5. יָד 6. כבש 7. מַאֲמָץ 8. מַחֲנֶה 9. מֶמְשָׁלָה 10. עַם 11. ענה 12. אֶדְרַע (A) 13. ἀγγαρεύω 14. ἄγω 15. ἀναγκάζω 16. βαρύς 17. βία 18. βιάζω 19. δύναμις 20. ἐκβιάζω 21. ἐνέργεια 22. ἰσχύω 23. κακόω 24. καταχράομαι 25. κράτος 26. ὄχλος 27. παράταξις 28. περί 29. πλῆθος 30. στρατιά 31. τάξις 32. χείρ

Gen 14:15 he divided his forces against them by night •
Num20:20 came out against them with . . a strong force. 5
Jos 8:13 So they stationed the forces 10
10: 5 the five kings . . gathered their forces, and went •
1Sm 2:16 must give it now; and if not, I will take it by force. 3
13:12 so I forced myself, and offered the . . offering. 1
28: 1 the Philistines gathered their forces for war 8
29: 1 Philistines gathered all their forces at Aphek; 8
2Sm 13:12 do not force me; for such a thing is not done 11
14 being stronger . . he forced her, and lay with her. 11
22 because he had forced his sister Tamar. 11
32 determined from the day he forced his sister 11
2Kg 11: 7 two . . which come on duty in force on the sabbath •
25:23 the captains of the forces in the open country 4
26 all the people . . and the captains of the forces 4
2Ch 17: 2 He placed forces in all the fortified cities 4
32: 9 besieging Lachish with all his forces 9
Ezr 4:23 and by force and power made them cease 12
Neh 5: 5 yet we are forcing our sons and our daughters 6
Job 20:22 all the force of misery will come upon him. 5
36:19 or all the force of your strength? 7
Jer 40: 7 the captains of the forces in the open country 4
13 the leaders of the forces in the open country 4
41:11 and all the leaders of the forces with him heard 4
13 Kare'ah and all the leaders of the forces with him 4
16 leaders of the forces with him took all the rest 4
42: 1 Then all the commanders of the forces 4
8 the commanders of the forces who were with him 4
43: 4 the commanders of the forces and all the people 4
5 commanders of the forces took all the remnant 4
46:22 for her enemies march in force 4
Ezk 34: 4 with force and harshness you have ruled them. 3
Dan 11:10 war and assemble a multitude of great forces 4
15 forces of the south shall not stand 2
31 Forces from him shall appear 2
Mat 5:41 if any one forces you to go one mile, go with him two 13
Act 7:19 forced our fathers to expose their infants 23
2Co 12:11 I have been a fool! You forced me to it 15
Heb 9:17 since it is not in force as long as . . 22
1Es 3:24 since it forces men to do these things 15
Jdt 1: 4 so that his armies could march out in force 19
6 Many nations joined the forces of the Chaldeans. 27
13 he led his forces against King Arphaxad 19
16 there he and his forces rested and feasted 19
6: 3 He will send his forces and will destroy them 25
7: 2 their force of men of war was 170,000 infantry 19
12 keep all the men in your forces with you 19
26 to the army of Holofernes and to all his forces 19
Wis 5:11 and pierced by the force of its rushing flight 17
14:19 skilfully forced the likeness to take more beautiful 20
18:22 not by strength of body, and not by force of arms 21
1Mc 1:17 So he invaded Egypt with a strong force 26
20 came to Jerusalem with a strong force. 26
29 he came to Jerusalem with a large force. 26
2:25 king's officer who was forcing them to sacrifice 15
3:10 a large force from Samaria 19
27 sent and gathered all the forces of his kingdom 19
28 and gave a year's pay to his forces 19
35 Lysias was to send a force against them 19
40 so they departed with their entire force 19
41 forces from Syria . . joined with them. 19
42 the forces were encamped in their territory. 19
4: 3 to attack the king's force in Emmaus 19
9 when Pharaoh with his forces pursued them. 19
16 Then Judas and his force turned back 19
18 Gorgias and his force are near us in the hills. 19
5:11 Timothy is leading their forces. 19
18 he left Joseph . . with the rest of the forces 19
32 he said to the men of his forces 19
38 it is a very large force. 19
40 Timothy said to the officers of his forces 19
50 So the men of the forces encamped 19
56 Azariah, the commanders of the forces 19
58 they issued orders to the men of the forces 19
6: 6 that Lysias had gone first with a strong force 19
28 all his friends, the commanders of his forces 19
29 mercenary forces came to him 19
30 The number of his forces 19
47 when the Jews saw . . the fierce attack of the forces 19
56 with the forces that had gone with the king 19
57 said to the king, to the commanders of the forces 19
63 took the city by force. 17
7:10 came with a large force into the land of Judah 19
11 they saw that they had come with a large force. 19
20 left with him a force to help him 19
27 So Nicanor came to Jerusalem with a large force 19
8: 2 had defeated them and forced them to pay tribute 14
9: 6 When they saw the huge number of the enemy forces 19
43 he came with a large force on the sabbath day 19
60 He started to come with a large force 19
63 he assembled all his forces 29
67 and went into battle with his forces 19
10:36 Let Jews be enrolled in the king's forces 19
36 that is due to all the forces of the king. 19
48 Now Alexander the king assembled large forces 19
69 he assembled a large force 19
71 If you now have confidence in your forces 19
82 Then Simon brought forward his force 19
11: 1 Then the king of Egypt gathered great forces 19
3 he stationed forces as a garrison in each city. 19
15 marched out and met him with a strong force 32

70 commanders of the forces of the army. 30
12:24 with a larger force than before 19
13:53 so he made him commander of all the forces 19
14: 1 Demetrius the king assembled his forces 19
32 he armed the men of his nation's forces 19
15:25 continually throwing his forces against it 32
16: 5 behold, a large force of infantry and horsemen 19
2Mc 1:13 a force that seemed irresistible 19
6:18 forced to open his mouth to eat swine's flesh. 15
8:24 forced them all to flee. 15
30 In encounters with the forces of Timothy 28
32 They killed the commander of Timothy's forces 28
9: 3 to Nicanor and the forces of Timothy. 28
10:19 a force sufficient to besiege them •
24 gathered a tremendous force of mercenaries 19
36 and let in the rest of the force 31
11:11 and forced all the rest to flee. 15
13: 2 Each of them had a Greek force of 110,000 infantry 19
15 with a picked force of the bravest young men •
14:41 were forcing the door of the courtyard 18
3Mc 1: 1 he gave orders to all his forces 19
2:28 Those who object to this are to be taken by force 17
4: 5 forced to march at a swift pace 24
11 communicate with the king's forces 19
5:47 he . . rushed out in full force along with the beasts 16
48 the following armed forces 19
6: 5 Sennacherib exulting in his countless forces 19
16 all the arrogance of his forces. 19
19 They opposed the forces of the enemy 19
21 turned back upon the armed forces following 19
4Mc 2: 8 he is forced to act contrary to his natural ways 18
4:10 going up with his armed forces to seize the money 30
11:25 to force us to eat defiling foods 18

force *See also* draw, join, labor, levy, march, take.

armed force 1. חַיִל 2. δύναμις
Est 8:11 annihilate any armed force . . that might attack 1
3Mc 5:29 the beasts and the armed forces were ready 2
44 they confidently posted the armed forces 2

force back 1. συνελαύνω
2Mc 5: 5 the troops upon the wall had been forced back 1

generative force 1. γένεσις
Wis 1:14 the generative forces of the world are wholesome 1

military force 1. στρατός
4Mc 4: 5 a very strong military force. 1

natural force 1. לֵחַ
Deu 34: 7 his eye was not dim, nor his natural force abated. 1

forceful 1. מרץ
Job 6:25 How forceful are honest words! 1

combined forces 1. σύμμικτος
Jdt 1:16 he and all his combined forces 1

forcibly 1. ἀνάγκη 2. ἐν ἰσχύι
1Mc 2:46 they forcibly circumcised 2
3Mc 5: 7 they were forcibly confined on every side 1

forcibly *See also* enter.

ford 1. מַעֲבָר 2. מַעְבָּרָה 3. עבר 4. עֲבָרָה
Gen 32:22 children, and crossed the ford of the Jabbok. 1
Jos 2: 7 the men pursued after them . . as far as the fords; 2
Jdg 3:28 they . . seized the fords of the Jordan 2
12: 5 the Gileadites took the fords of the Jordan 2
6 him and slew him at the fords of the Jordan. 2
1Sm 13: 7 people hid . . or crossed the fords of the Jordan 3
2Sm 15:28 See, I will wait at the fords of the wilderness 4
17:16 Do not lodge . . at the fords of the wilderness 4
19:18 and they crossed the ford to bring over the king's 4
Isa 16: 2 the daughters of Moab at the fords of the Arnon. 2
Jer 51:32 the fords have been seized 2

forebode 1. προσδοκία
Lke 21:26 foreboding of what is coming on the world 1

forefather 1. אָב רִאשׁוֹן 2. רִאשׁוֹן 3. πατήρ 4. πρόγονος 5. προπάτωρ
Lev 26:45 remember the covenant with their forefathers 2
Ps 79: 8 against us the iniquities of our forefathers; 2
Jer 11:10 back to the iniquities of their forefathers 1
Rom 4: 1 Abraham, our forefather according to the flesh? 5
9:10 conceived . . by one man, our forefather Isaac 3
11:28 beloved for the sake of their forefathers. 3
Tob 1: 4 the whole tribe of Naphtali my forefather 3
5 so did the house of Naphtali my forefather. 3
Jdt 8:25 who is putting us to the test as he did our forefathers. 3
4Mc 9: 2 we are obviously putting our forefathers to shame 4

forefront 1. פָּנִים
2Sm 11:15 Set Uri'ah in the forefront of the . . fighting 1

forego 1. נטשׁ 2. παραιτέω
Neh 10:31 forego the crops of the seventh year 1
2Mc 2:31 to forego exhaustive treatment. 2

forehead 1. בֵּין עֵינַיִם 2. גַּבַּחַת 3. מֵצַח 4. פֵּאָה 5. פְּאַת פָּנִים 6. μέτωπον
Exd 28:38 It shall be upon Aaron's forehead, and Aaron shall 3
38 it shall always be upon his forehead 3
Lev 13:41 hair has fallen from his forehead and temples 5
42 it is leprosy breaking out . . on his forehead 2
Num24:17 it shall crush the forehead of Moab 4
Deu 14: 1 not . . make any baldness on your foreheads 1
1Sm 17:49 and struck the Philistine on his forehead; 3
49 the stone sank into his forehead, and he fell 3
2Ch 26:19 leprosy broke out on his forehead 3
20 behold, he was leprous in his forehead! 3
Isa 48: 4 neck is an iron sinew and your forehead brass 3
Jer 48:45 it has destroyed the forehead of Moab 4
Ezk 3: 7 all the house of Israel are of a hard forehead 3
8 your forehead hard against their foreheads. 3
8 your forehead hard against their foreheads. 3
9 harder than flint have I made your forehead; 3
9: 4 and put a mark upon the foreheads of the men 3
Rev 7: 3 sealed the servants . . upon their foreheads. 6
9: 4 who have not the seal of God upon their foreheads; 6
13:16 to be marked on the right hand or the forehead 6
14: 1 his Father's name written on their foreheads. 6
9 receives a mark on his forehead or on his hand 6
17: 5 on her forehead was written a name of mystery 6
20: 4 and had not received its mark on their foreheads 6
22: 4 and his name shall be on their foreheads. 6

forehead *See also* baldness.

bald forehead 1. גַּבַּחַת
Lev 13:42 if there is on the bald head or the bald forehead 1
43 on his bald head or on his bald forehead 1

foreign 1. זוּר 2. נֵכָר 3. נָכְרִי 4. סָמֵךְ 5. ἀλλογενής 6. ἀλλότριος 7. ἀλλόφυλος 8. ἐκ τῶν ἀλλογενῶν 9. ἔξω 10. ξένος 11. οὐκ ἴδιος
Gen 35: 2 Put away the foreign gods that are among you 2
4 they gave to Jacob all the foreign gods 2
Exd 2:22 he said, "I have been a sojourner in a foreign land. 3
18: 3 he said, "I have been a sojourner in a foreign land") 3
21: 8 have no right to sell her to a foreign people 3
Deu 32:12 LORD alone . . there was no foreign god with him. 2
Jos 24:20 If you forsake the LORD and serve foreign gods 2
23 put away the foreign gods which are among you 2
Jdg 10:16 So they put away the foreign gods from among them 2
1Sm 7: 3 put away the foreign gods and the Ash'taroth 2
1Kg 11: 1 Now King Solomon loved many foreign women 3
8 so he did for all his foreign wives 3
2Kg 19:24 I dug wells and drank foreign waters 1
2Ch 14: 3 took away the foreign altars and the high places 2
33:15 he took away the foreign gods and the idol 2
Ezr 10: 2 married foreign women from the peoples 3
10 You have trespassed and married foreign women 3
11 separate yourselves . . from the foreign wives. 3
14 all in our cities who have taken foreign wives 3
17 end of all the men who had married foreign women. 3
18 sons . . who had married foreign women 3
44 All these had married foreign women 3
Neh 13:26 nevertheless foreign women made even him to sin. 3
27 against our God by marrying foreign women? 3
30 Thus I cleansed them from everything foreign 2
Ps 81: 9 you shall nct bow down to a foreign god. 2
137: 4 How shall we sing the LORD'S song in a foreign land? 2
Jer 5:19 As you have forsaken me and served foreign gods 2
8:19 graven images, and with their foreign idols? 2
Ezk 3: 5 For you are not sent to a people of foreign speech 4
6 not to many peoples of foreign speech 4
Dan 11:39 fortresses by the help of a foreign god; 2
Zep 1: 8 and all who array themselves in foreign attire. 3
Mal 2:11 and has married the daughter of a foreign god. 2
Act 17:18 He seems to be a preacher of foreign divinities 10
26:11 I persecuted them even to foreign cities. 9
Heb 11: 9 as in a foreign land 6
34 put foreign armies to flight. 6
1Es 8:92 have married foreign women 5
93 we will put away all our foreign wives 8
9: 7 broken the law and married foreign women 5
9 separate . . from your foreign wives. 5
12 those in our settlements who have foreign wives 5
17 the cases of the men who had foreign wives 5
18 were brought in and found to have foreign wives 5
36 All these had married foreign women 5
Tob 4:12 do not marry a foreign woman 6
Jdt 5:18 and were led away captive to a foreign country 11
6: 1 in the presence of all the foreign contingents 7
Sir 29:18 they have wandered among foreign nations. 6
36: 3 Lift up thy hand against foreign nations 6
39: 4 travel through the lands of foreign nations 6
49: 5 they gave . . their glory to a foreign nation 6
Bar 3:10 that you are growing old in a foreign country 6
1Mc 11:38 except the foreign troops 10
15:33 neither taken foreign land nor seized foreign property 6
3Mc 6: 3 perishing as foreigners in a foreign land. 10

foreign *See also* descent, folk, property, troop.

foreigner 1. אִישׁ נָכְרִי 2. בֶּן נֵכָר 3. זוּר 4. יֶלֶד נָכְרִי 5. נֵכָר 6. נָכְרִי 7. ἀλλογενής 8. ἀλλόφυλος 9. βάρβαρος 10. ἕτερος 11. ξένος
Gen 17:12 bought with your money from any foreigner 2
27 those bought with money from a foreigner 2
31:15 Are we not regarded by him as foreigners? 6
Exd 12:43 passover: no foreigner shall eat of it; 2
Lev 22:25 any such animals gotten from a foreigner 5
Deu 14:21 give it . . or you may sell it to a foreigner; 6
15: 3 Of a foreigner you may exact it 6
17:15 you may not put a foreigner over you 1
23:20 To a foreigner you may lend upon interest 6
29:22 foreigner who comes from a far land, would say 6
Jdg 19:12 the city of foreigners, who do not belong 6
Rut 2:10 you should take notice of me, when I am a foreigner? 6
2Sm 15:19 Go . . stay with the king; for you are a foreigner 6
22:45 Foreigners came cringing to me; 2
46 Foreigners lost heart, and came trembling out 2
1Kg 8:41 a foreigner, who is not of thy people Israel, comes 6
43 to all for which the foreigner calls to thee; 6
2Ch 6:32 a foreigner, who is not of thy people Israel, comes 6
33 to all for which the foreigner calls to thee; 6
Neh 9: 2 Israelites separated . . from all foreigners 2
Ps 18:44 they obeyed me; foreigners came cringing to me. 2
45 Foreigners lost heart, and came trembling 2
Prv 20:16 hold him . . when he gives surety for foreigners. 6
27:13 hold him . . when he gives surety for foreigners. •
Isa 2: 6 they strike hands with foreigners. 4
56: 3 the foreigner who has joined himself to the LORD 2
6 the foreigners who join themselves to the LORD 2
60:10 Foreigners shall build up your walls 2
61: 5 foreigners shall be your plowmen 2
62: 8 and foreigners shall not drink your wine 2
Ezk 7:21 I will give it into the hands of foreigners 3
11: 9 and give you into the hands of foreigners 3
28:10 of the uncircumcised by the hand of foreigners; 3
30:12 by the hand of foreigners; I, the LORD, have spoken. 3
31:12 Foreigners, the most terrible of the nations 3
44: 7 in admitting foreigners, uncircumcised 2
8 you have set foreigners to keep my charge •
9 No foreigner, uncircumcised in heart and flesh 2
9 of all the foreigners who are among the people 2
Obd 1:11 and foreigners entered his gates 6
Lke 17:18 Was no one found . . except this foreigner? 7
Act 17:21 Now all the Athenians and the foreigners 11
1Co 14:11 I shall be a foreigner to the speaker 9
11 the speaker a foreigner to me. 9
21 by the lips of foreigners 10
LJr 1: 5 take care not to become at all like the foreigners 8
1Mc 4:12 When the foreigners looked up 8
26 Those of the foreigners who escaped 8
10:12 Then the foreigners who were in the strongholds 7
11:68 the army of the foreigners met him in the plain; 8
74 As many as 3,000 of the foreigners fell 8
2Mc 10: 2 had been built in the public square by the foreigners 8
5 had been profaned by the foreigners 8
3Mc 6: 3 perishing as foreigners in a foreign land. 11

foreknow 1. προγινώσκω
Rom 8:29 For those whom he foreknew he also predestined 1
11: 2 not rejected his people whom he foreknew. 1

foreknowledge 1. προγινώσκω 2. πρόγνωσις
Act 2:23 the definite plan and foreknowledge of God 2
Jdt 9: 6 thy judgment is with foreknowledge. 2
11:19 For this has been told me, by my foreknowledge 2
Wis 8: 8 she has foreknowledge of signs and wonders 1

foreman 1. נגשׂ 2. שֹׁטֵר
Exd 5: 6 the taskmasters of the people and their foremen 2
10 the taskmasters and the foremen of the people 1
14 the foremen of the people of Israel 2
15 Then the foremen of the people of Israel came 2
19 The foremen of the people of Israel saw that they 2

foremost 1. רִאשׁוֹן 2. πρῶτος
Gen 32:17 He instructed the foremost, "When Esau my brother 1
2Sm 18:27 the running of the foremost is like . . Ahi'ma-az 1
Ezr 9: 2 officials and chief men has been foremost. 1
1Ti 1:15 I am the foremost of sinners; 2
16 in me, as the foremost 2

forenoon 1. בִּתְרוֹן
2Sm 2:29 and marching the whole forenoon they came 1

foreordain 1. provideo
2Es 7:74 because of the times which he has foreordained! 1

forerunner 1. πρόδρομος
Heb 6:20 Jesus has gone as a forerunner on our behalf 1
Wis 12: 8 didst send wasps as forerunners of thy army 1

foresail 1. ἀρτέμων
Act 27:40 then hoisting the foresail to the wind 1

foresee 1. προβλέπω 2. προοράω
Act 2:31 he foresaw and spoke of the resurrection 2
Gal 3: 8 the scripture, foreseeing that God would justify 2
Heb 11:40 since God had foreseen something better for us 1

foreskin 1. עָרְלָה
Gen 17:11 be circumcised in the flesh of your foreskins 1
14 not circumcised in the flesh of his foreskin 1
23 he circumcised the flesh of their foreskins 1
24 was circumcised in the flesh of his foreskin. 1
25 was circumcised in the flesh of his foreskin. 1
Exd 4:25 took a flint and cut off her son's foreskin 1
Lev 12: 3 the flesh of his foreskin shall be circumcised 1
Deu 10:16 Circumcise therefore the foreskin of your heart 1
1Sm 18:25 except 100 foreskins of the Philistines 1
27 and David brought their foreskins 1
2Sm 3:14 I betrothed at the price of 100 foreskins 1
Jer 4: 4 remove the foreskin of your hearts, O men of Judah 1

forest 1. חֹרֶשׁ 2. יַעַר 3. עֵץ 4. פַּרְדֵּס 5. שָׂדֶה 6. ὕλη 7. silva
Deu 19: 5 when a man goes into the forest with his neighbor 2
Jos 17:15 go up to the forest, and there clear ground 2
18 though it is a forest, you shall clear it 2
1Sm 14:25 And all the people came into the forest; 2
26 And when the people entered the forest, behold 2
22: 5 David . . went into the forest of Hereth. 2
2Sm 18: 6 the battle was fought in the forest of E'phraim. 2
8 forest devoured more people . . than the sword. 2
17 and threw him into a great pit in the forest 2
1Kg 7: 2 He built the House of the Forest of Lebanon; 2
10:17 put them in the House of the Forest of Lebanon. 2
21 the vessels of the House of the Forest of Lebanon 2
2Kg 19:23 its farthest retreat, its densest forest. 2
2Ch 9:16 put them in the House of the Forest of Lebanon. 2
20 vessels of the House of the Forest of Lebanon 2
Neh 2: 8 letter to Asaph, the keeper of the king's forest 4
Ps 29: 9 voice of the LORD . . strips the forests bare; 2
50:10 For every beast of the forest is mine 2
80:13 The boar from the forest ravages it 2
83:14 As fire consumes the forest 2
104:20 when all the beasts of the forest creep forth. 2
Ecc 2: 6 pools . . to water the forest of growing trees. 2
Isa 7: 2 as the trees of the forest shake before the wind. 3
9:18 it kindles the thickets of the forest 2
10:18 The glory of his forest and of his fruitful land 2
19 remnant of the trees of his forest will be so few 2
34 cut down the thickets of the forest with an axe 2
22: 8 looked to the weapons of the House of the Forest 2
29:17 the fruitful field shall be regarded as a forest? 2
32:15 and the fruitful field is deemed a forest. 2
19 the forest will utterly go down 2
37:24 I came to its remotest height, its densest forest 2
44:14 lets it grow strong among the trees of the forest; 2
23 O mountains, O forest, and every tree in it! 2
56: 9 come to devour-all you beasts in the forest. 2
Jer 5: 6 Therefore a lion from the forest shall slay them 2
10: 3 A tree from the forest is cut down 2
12: 8 has become to me like a lion in the forest 2
21:14 I will kindle a fire in her forest 2
46:23 They shall cut down her forest, says the LORD 2
Ezk 15: 2 branch which is among the trees of the forest? 2
6 wood of the vine among the trees of the forest 2
20:46 and prophesy against the forest land in the Negeb 2
47 say to the forest of the Negeb, Hear the word 2
31: 3 a cedar . . with fair branches and forest shade 1
4 its streams to all the trees of the forest. 5
5 it towered high above all the trees of the forest; 5
39:10 out of the field or cut down any out of the forests 2
Hos 2:12 I will make them a forest 2
Ams 3: 4 Does a lion roar in the forest, when he has no prey? 2
Mic 5: 8 like a lion among the beasts of the forest 2
7:14 dwell alone in a forest in the midst of a garden 2
Zec 11: 2 for the thick forest has been felled! 2
Jas 3: 5 How great a forest is set ablaze by a small fire! 6
2Es 4:13 I went into a forest of trees of the plain 7
14 that we may make for ourselves more forests.' 7
15 let us go up and subdue the forest of the plain 7
16 the plan of the forest was in vain 7
19 for the land is assigned to the forest 7
21 For as the land is assigned to the forest 7
5:23 O sovereign Lord, from every forest of the earth 7
9:21 and one plant out of a great forest. ‡
11:37 a creature . . was aroused out of the forest 7
12:31 the lion whom you saw rousing up out of the forest 7
15:30 shall go forth like wild boars of the forest 7
42 walls, mountains and hills, trees of the forests 7
62 they shall burn with fire all your forests 7
16: 6 Can one drive off a hungry lion in the forest 7

forestall 1. προφθάνω
Sir 19:27 where no one notices, he will forestall you. 1

foretell 1. דבר 2. προκαταγγέλλω 3. σημαίνω 4. praedico
2Kg 24:13 as the LORD had foretold. 1
Act 3:18 foretold by the mouth of all the prophets 2
11:28 stood up and foretold by the Spirit 3
2Es 6:25 whoever remains after all that I have foretold 4
7:26 when the signs which I have foretold to you 4
27 the evils that I have foretold 4

forever 1. εἰς ἅπαντα χρόνον
3Mc 5:43 quickly render it forever empty 1

for ever *See* ever.

forewarn 1. προεῖπον 2. προμηνύω
1Th 4: 6 as we solemnly forewarned you. 1
Wis 18:19 dreams which disturbed them forewarned them 2

forfeit 1. חטא 2. חרם 3. ζημιόω
2Kg 10:24 who allows any . . escape shall forfeit his life. †
Ezr 10: 8 by order . . all his property should be forfeited 2
Prv 20: 2 he who provokes him to anger forfeits his life. 1
Hab 2:10 you have forfeited your life. 1
Mat 16:26 if he gains the whole world and forfeits his life? 3
Mrk 8:36 to gain the whole world and forfeit his life? 3
Lke 9:25 loses or forfeits himself? 3

forfeit to the king 1. βασιλικός
1Es 6:32 his property should be forfeited to the king. 1

forfeit to the sanctuary 1. קדשׁ
Deu 22: 9 whole yield be forfeited to the sanctuary 1

forge 1. פעל
Isa 44:12 with hammers, and forges it with his strong arm; 1

forger 1. לטשׁ
Gen 4:22 Tubal-cain; he was the forger of all instruments 1

forget 1. נשׁה 2. שׁכח 3. שָׁכֵחַ 4. ἀμνησία 5. ἀμνηστία 6. ἐκλανθάνομαι 7. ἐπιλανθάνομαι 8. ἐπιλανθάνω 9. ἐπιλησμονή 10. λήθη λαμβάνω 11. οὐ μιμνήσκω 12. πέλομαι 13. ὑπεροράω 14. oblino 15. obliviscor
Gen 27:45 until . . he forgets what you have done to him; 2
40:23 butler did not remember Joseph, but forgot him. 2
41:30 and all the plenty will be forgotten 2
Deu 4: 9 take heed . . lest you forget the things 2
23 Take heed . . lest you forget the covenant 2
31 LORD . . will not . . forget the covenant 2
6:12 then take heed lest you forget the LORD 2
8:11 Take heed lest you forget the LORD your God, by not 2
14 then . . you forget the LORD your God, who brought 2
19 if you forget the LORD your God and go after 2
9: 7 Remember and do not forget how you provoked 2
24:19 reap . . and have forgotten a sheaf in the field 2
25:19 blot out the remembrance . . you shall not forget. 2
26:13 not transgressed . . neither have I forgotten 2
32:18 you forgot the God who gave you birth. 2
Jdg 3: 7 forgetting the LORD their God, and serving 2
1Sm 1:11 and remember me, and not forget thy maidservant 2
12: 9 they forgot the LORD their God; and he sold them 2
2Kg 17:38 and you shall not forget the covenant 2
Job 8:13 Such are the paths of all who forget God; 2
9:27 If I say, 'I will forget my complaint 2
11:16 You will forget your misery; 2
19:15 the guests in my house have forgotten me; 2
24:20 The squares of the town forget them; 2
28: 4 they are forgotten by travelers 2
39:15 forgetting that a foot may crush them 2
Ps 9:12 he does not forget the cry of the afflicted. 2
17 depart to Sheol, all the nations that forget God. 3
18 For the needy shall not always be forgotten 2
10:11 He thinks in his heart, "God has forgotten 2
12 O God, lift up thy hand; forget not the afflicted. 2
13: 1 How long, O LORD? Wilt thou forget me for ever? 2
42: 9 I say to God, my rock: "Why hast thou forgotten me? 2
44:17 though we have not forgotten thee, or been false 2
20 If we had forgotten the name of our God 2
24 dost thou forget our affliction and oppression? 2
45:10 forget your people and your father's house; 2
50:22 Mark this, then, you who forget God 2
59:11 Slay them not, lest my people forget; 2
74:19 do not forget the life of thy poor for ever. 2
23 Do not forget the clamor of thy foes 2
77: 9 Has God forgotten to be gracious? 2
78: 7 hope in God, and not forget the works of God 2
11 They forgot what he had done 2
102: 4 I forget to eat my bread. 2
103: 2 Bless the LORD . . forget not all his benefits 2
106:13 they soon forgot his works; 2
21 forgot God, their Savior, who had done great 2
119:16 I will not forget thy word. 2
61 the wicked ensnare me, I do not forget thy law. 2
83 yet I have not forgotten thy statutes. 2
93 I will never forget thy precepts; 2
109 continually, but I do not forget thy law. 2
139 consumes me, because my foes forget thy words. 2
141 yet I do not forget thy precepts. 2
153 deliver me, for I do not forget thy law. 2
176 for I do not forget thy commandments. 2
137: 5 If I forget you, O Jerusalem, let my right hand 2
Prv 2:17 who . . forgets the covenant of her God; 2
3: 1 My son, do not forget my teaching 2
4: 5 do not forget, and do not turn away from the words 2
31: 5 lest they drink and forget what has been decreed 2
7 let them drink and forget their poverty 2
Ecc 2:16 seeing . . all will have been long forgotten. 2
Isa 17:10 For you have forgotten the God of your salvation 2
23:15 Tyre will be forgotten for 70 years 2
16 Take a harp, go about the city, O forgotten harlot! 2
44:21 O Israel, you will not be forgotten by me. 1
49:14 But Zion said, ". . my Lord has forgotten me. 2
15 Can a woman forget her sucking child 2
15 Even these may forget, yet I will not forget you. 2
15 Even these may forget, yet I will not forget you. 2
51:13 and have forgotten the LORD, your Maker 2
54: 4 for you will forget the shame of your youth 2
65:11 forsake the LORD, who forget my holy mountain 3
16 because the former troubles are forgotten 2
Jer 2:32 Can a maiden forget her ornaments 2
32 people have forgotten me days without number. 2
3:21 they have forgotten the LORD their God. 2
13:25 says the LORD, because you have forgotten me 2
18:15 But my people have forgotten me 2
20:11 Their eternal dishonor will never be forgotten. 2
23:27 even as their fathers forgot my name for Ba'al? 2
40 perpetual shame, which shall not be forgotten. 2
30:14 All your lovers have forgotten you; 2
44: 9 Have you forgotten the wickedness 2
50: 5 covenant which will never be forgotten. 2
6 they have gone, they have forgotten their fold. 2
Lam 3:17 I have forgotten what happiness is; 1
5:20 Why dost thou forget us for ever 2
Ezk 22:12 you have forgotten me, says the Lord GOD. 2
23:35 says the Lord GOD: Because you have forgotten me 2
39:26 They shall forget their shame •
Hos 2:13 after her lovers, and forgot me, says the LORD. 2
4: 6 And since you have forgotten the law of your God 2
6 I also will forget your children. 2
8:14 For Israel has forgotten his Maker 2
13: 6 therefore they forgot me. 2
Ams 8: 7 Surely I will never forget any of their deeds. 2
Mic 6:10 Can I forget the treasures of wickedness •
Mat 16: 5 they had forgotten to bring any bread. 7
Mrk 8:14 Now they had forgotten to bring bread 7
Lke 12: 6 not one of them is forgotten before God. 7
Php 3:13 one thing I do, forgetting what lies behind 7
Heb 12: 5 have you forgotten the exhortation 6
Jas 1:24 and at once forgets what he was like. 7
25 being no hearer that forgets but a doer that acts 9
2Pe 1: 9 forgotten that he was cleansed from his old sins 10
1Es 3:20 forgets all sorrow and debt. 11
21 forgets kings and satraps 11
22 they forget to be friendly with friends 11
2Es 1: 6 for they have forgotten me 14
14 Yet you have forgotten me, says the Lord. 14
8:53 hell has fled and corruption has been forgotten; ‡
12:47 the Mighty One has not forgotten you 14
16:67 Cease from your sins, and forget your iniquities 15
Wis 2: 4 Our name will be forgotten in time 8
16:23 the fire . . even forgot its native power. 8
19: 4 made them forget what had happened 5
20 water forgot its fire-quenching nature. 8
Sir 3:14 For kindness to a father will not be forgotten 8
7:27 do not forget the birth pangs of your mother. 8
11:25 In the day of prosperity, adversity is forgotten 4
27 The misery of an hour makes one forget luxury 9
13:10 not remain at a distance, lest you be forgotten. 8
29:15 Do not forget all the kindness of your surety 8
35: 7 the memory of it will not be forgotten. 8
37: 6 Do not forget a friend in your heart 8
38:21 Do not forget, there is no coming back 8
44:10 whose righteous deeds have not been forgotten; 12
Bar 4: 8 You forgot the everlasting God 8
1Mc 1:49 so that they should forget the law 8
2Mc 2: 2 not to forget the commandments of the Lord 8
7:23 since you now forget yourselves 13
3Mc 6:20 he forgot his sullen insolence. 10
4Mc 18:18 he did not forget to teach you the song 8

make forget 1. נשׁה 2. שׁכח
Gen 41:51 God has made me to forget all my hardship 1
Job 39:17 because God has made her forget wisdom 1
Jer 23:27 who think to make my people forget my name 2

forgetful 1. ἐπιλανθάνω
Sir 23:14 lest you be forgetful in their presence 1

forgetfulness 1. נְשִׁיָּה 2. ἀμνηστία 3. λήθη
Ps 88:12 or thy saving help in the land of forgetfulness? 1
Wis 14:26 forgetfulness of favors, pollution of souls 2
16:11 lest they should fall into deep forgetfulness 3
17: 3 behind a dark curtain of forgetfulness 3
3Mc 5:28 forgetfulness of the things he had . . devised. 3
4Mc 1: 5 is it not sovereign over forgetfulness and ignorance? 3
2:24 does not control forgetfulness and ignorance 3

forgive 1. כסה 2. כפר 3. נשׂא 4. נשׂא לְ 5. סלח 6. סַלָּח 7. סְלִיחָה 8. ἀνίημι 9. ἀπολύω 10. ἀφίημι 11. ἐξιλασμός 12. χαρίζομαι
Gen 50:17 Forgive, I pray you, the transgression 3
17 And now, we pray you, forgive the transgression 3
Exd 10:17 Now therefore, forgive my sin, I pray you 3
32:32 now, if thou wilt forgive their sin-and if not, blot 3

34: 7 forgiving iniquity and transgression and sin 3
Lev 4:20 and they shall be forgiven 5
26 and he shall be forgiven 5
31 make atonement for him, and he shall be forgiven 5
35 and he shall be forgiven 5
5:10 which he has committed, and he shall be forgiven 5
13 atonement . . and he shall be forgiven 5
16 guilt offering, and he shall be forgiven 5
18 he shall be forgiven 5
6: 7 he shall be forgiven for any of the things 5
19:22 the sin which he has committed shall be forgiven 5
Num14:18 forgiving iniquity and transgression 3
19 according as thou hast forgiven this people 3
15:25 make atonement . . and they shall be forgiven; 5
26 all the congregation . . shall be forgiven 5
28 make atonement for him; and he shall be forgiven. 5
30: 5 the LORD will forgive her, because her father 5
8 LORD will forgive her. 5
12 made them void, and the LORD will forgive her. 5
Deu 21: 8 Forgive, O LORD, thy people Israel, whom thou hast 2
8 but let the guilt of blood be forgiven them.' 2
Jos 24:19 he will not forgive your transgressions 3
1Sm 25:28 Pray forgive the trespass of your handmaid; 4
1Kg 8:30 hearken . . and when thou hearest, forgive. 5
34 hear . . and forgive the sin of thy people Israel 5
36 hear . . and forgive the sin of thy servants 5
39 hear . . and forgive, and act, and render to each 5
50 forgive thy people who have sinned against thee 5
2Ch 6:21 hear thou . . and when thou hearest, forgive. 5
25 hear . . and forgive the sin of thy people Israel 5
27 then hear . . and forgive the sin of thy servants 5
30 hear thou . . and forgive, and render to each 5
39 hear thou . . and forgive thy people who have 5
7:14 hear from heaven, and will forgive their sin 5
Neh 9:17 But thou art a God ready to forgive 7
Ps 25:18 Consider . . my trouble, and forgive all my sins. 3
32: 1 Blessed is he whose transgression is forgiven 3
5 then thou didst forgive the guilt of my sin. 3
65: 3 our transgressions . . thou dost forgive them. 2
78:38 he, being compassionate, forgave their iniquity 2
79: 9 deliver us, and forgive our sins, for thy name's sake! 2
85: 2 Thou didst forgive the iniquity of thy people; 3
86: 5 For thou, O Lord, art good and forgiving 6
99: 8 forgiving God to them, but an avenger 3
103: 3 who forgives all your iniquity, who heals 5
Prv 17: 9 He who forgives an offense seeks love 1
Isa 2: 9 men are brought low–forgive them not! 2
6: 7 your guilt is taken away, and your sin forgiven. 2
22:14 iniquity will not be forgiven you till you die. 2
33:24 the people . . will be forgiven their iniquity. 3
Jer 18:23 Forgive not their iniquity 2
31:34 for I will forgive their iniquity 5
33: 8 and I will forgive all the guilt of their sin 5
36: 3 that I may forgive their iniquity and their sin. 5
Lam 3:42 We have . . rebelled, and thou hast not forgiven. 5
Ezk 16:63 shame, when I forgive you all that you have done 2
Dan 9:19 O LORD, hear; O LORD, forgive; 5
Hos 1: 6 no more have pity . . to forgive them at all. 3
Ams 7: 2 I said, "O Lord GOD, forgive, I beseech thee! 5
Mat 6:12 And forgive us our debts, As we also have forgiven 10
12 debts, As we also have forgiven our debtors; 10
14 For if you forgive men their trespasses 10
14 your heavenly Father also will forgive you; 10
15 if you do not forgive men their trespasses 10
15 neither will your Father forgive 10
9: 2 Take heart, my son; your sins are forgiven. 10
5 For which is easier, to say, 'Your sins are forgiven,' 10
6 man has authority on earth to forgive sins 10
12:31 every sin and blasphemy will be forgiven men 10
31 will not be forgiven. 10
32 will be forgiven 10
32 will not be forgiven 10
18:21 and I forgive him? 10
27 released him and forgave him the debt. 10
32 'You wicked servant! I forgave you all that debt 10
35 if you do not forgive your brother 10
Mrk 2: 5 My son, your sins are forgiven. 10
7 Who can forgive sins but God alone? 10
9 'Your sins are forgiven,' 10
10 Son of man has authority on earth to forgive sins"- 10
3:28 Truly, I say to you, all sins will be forgiven 10
4:12 lest they should turn again, and be forgiven. 10
11:25 whenever you stand praying, forgive 10
25 may forgive you your trespasses. 10
Lke 5:20 Man, your sins are forgiven you. 10
21 Who can forgive sins but God only? 10
23 Which is easier, to say, 'Your sins are forgiven you,' 10
24 authority on earth to forgive sins 10
6:37 forgive, and you will be forgiven; 9
37 forgive, and you will be forgiven; 9
7:42 When they could not pay, he forgave them both. 12
43 The one, I suppose, to whom he forgave more. 12
47 I tell you, her sins, which are many, are forgiven 10
47 he who is forgiven little, loves little. 10
48 he said to her, "Your sins are forgiven. 10
49 Who is this, who even forgives sins? 10
11: 4 forgive us our sins 10
4 we ourselves forgive every one who is indebted 10
12:10 every one . . will be forgiven 10
10 against the Holy Spirit will not be forgiven. 10
17: 3 if he repents, forgive him; 10
4 you must forgive him. 10
23:34 Jesus said, "Father, forgive them 10
Joh 20:23 If you forgive the sins of any, they are forgiven; 10
23 If you forgive the sins of any, they are forgiven; 10
Act 8:22 the intent of your heart may be forgiven you. 10
Rom 4: 7 those whose iniquities are forgiven 10
2Co 2: 7 so you should rather turn to forgive and comfort 12
10 Any one whom you forgive, I also forgive 12
10 Any one whom you forgive, I also forgive •
10 What I have forgiven, if I have forgiven anything 12
10 What I have forgiven, if I have forgiven anything 12
12:13 Forgive me this wrong! 12
Eph 4:32 forgiving one another, as God in Christ forgave 12
32 forgiving one another, as God in Christ forgave 12
Col 2:13 having forgiven us all our trespasses 12
3:13 forgiving each other 12
13 as the Lord has forgiven you 12
13 so you also must forgive. •
Jas 5:15 and if he has committed sins, he will be forgiven. 10
1Jn 1: 9 he is faithful and just, and will forgive our sins 10
2:12 because your sins are forgiven for his sake. 10
Sir 2:11 he forgives sins and saves in time of affliction. 10
5: 6 he will forgive the multitude of my sins 5
16:11 he is mighty to forgive, and he pours out wrath. 11
28: 2 Forgive your neighbor the wrong he has done 10
Man 1:13 I earnestly beseech thee, forgive me, O Lord 8
13 forgive me, O Lord, forgive me! 8

forgiveness 1. סְלִיחָה 2. *ἄφεσις* 3. *ἐξιλασμός*

Ps 130: 4 there is forgiveness with thee 1
Dan 9: 9 To the Lord our God belong mercy and forgiveness; 1
Mat 26:28 for many for the forgiveness of sins. 2
Mrk 1: 4 repentance for the forgiveness of sins. 2
3:29 never has forgiveness 2
Lke 1:77 in the forgiveness of their sins 2
3: 3 repentance for the forgiveness of sins. 2
24:47 repentance and forgiveness of sins 2
Act 2:38 for the forgiveness of your sins 2
5:31 repentance to Israel and forgiveness of sins. 2
10:43 receives forgiveness of sins through his name. 2
13:38 forgiveness of sins is proclaimed to you 2
26:18 they may receive forgiveness of sins 2
Eph 1: 7 the forgiveness of our trespasses 2
Col 1:14 we have redemption, the forgiveness of sins. 2
Heb 9:22 there is no forgiveness of sins. 2
10:18 Where there is forgiveness of these 2
Sir 17:29 How great is . . his forgiveness 3
18:12 he grants them forgiveness in abundance. 3
20 you will find forgiveness. 3
Man 1: 7 promised repentance and forgiveness 2

fork 1. מַזְלֵג 2. מִזְלָגָה 3. מִזְרֶה

Exd 27: 3 shovels and basins and forks and firepans; 2
38: 3 the pots, the shovels, the basins, the forks 2
Num 4:14 utensils . . the firepans, the forks, the shovels 2
1Sm 2:13 come . . with a three-pronged fork in his hand 1
14 all that the fork brought up the priest would 1
1Ch 28:17 pure gold for the forks, the basins, and the cups; 2
2Ch 4:16 pots, the shovels, the forks, and all the equipment 2
Isa 30:24 which has been winnowed with shovel and fork. 3

winnowing fork 1. מִזְרֶה 2. *πτύον*

Jer 15: 7 I have winnowed them with a winnowing fork 1
Mat 3:12 His winnowing fork is in his hand 2
Lke 3:17 His winnowing fork is in his hand 2

forlorn 1. אמל 2. שְׁכוֹל 3. *ἀπογινώσκω*

1Sm 2: 5 but she who has many children is forlorn. 1
Ps 35:12 They requite me evil for good; my soul is forlorn. 2
Jdt 9:11 upholder of the weak, protector of the forlorn 3

form 1. דְּמוּת 2. היה 3. חול 4. חשב 5. יצר 6. כון 7. מַרְאֶה 8. ערך 9. עשה 10. צוּרָה 11. צִיר 12. קנה 13. קֶצֶב 14. קרץ 15. שום 16. תֹּאַר 17. תַּבְנִית 18. תְּמוּנָה 19. *γίνομαι* 20. *ἐγκυλίω* 21. *εἶδος* 22. *εἰμί* 23. *εὑρίσκω* 24. *καταλαμβάνω* 25. *κατασκευάζω* 26. *μορφή* 27. *μορφόω* 28. *μόρφωσις* 29. *οἰκοδομέω* 30. *ὄνομα* 31. *πλάσσω* 32. *συνίστημι* 33. *σχῆμα* 34. *τάξις* 35. *τύπος* 36. do 37. fingo 38. planto 39. plasmatio 40. plasmo 41. species

Gen 2: 7 the LORD God formed man of dust from the ground 5
8 and there he put the man whom he had formed. 5
19 out of the ground the LORD God formed every beast 5
Exd 26:24 they shall form the two corners. 2
Num12: 8 beholds the form of the LORD. 18
22:36 city of Moab, on the boundary formed by the Arnon •
Deu 4:12 you heard the sound of words, but saw no form; 18
15 Since you saw no form on the day that the LORD 18
16 a graven image . . in the form of any figure 18
23 make a graven image in the form of anything 18
25 by making a graven image in the form of anything 18
31:21 I know the purposes . . they are already forming 9
Jos 17:10 Manas'seh's, with the sea forming its boundary; 2
18:14 boundary goes . . This forms the western side. •
19: 9 inheritance . . formed part of the territory •
Jdg 20:22 took courage, and again formed the battle line 8
22 place where they had formed it on the first day. 8
1Kg 6:25 cherubim had the same measure and the same form. 13
31 the lintel and the doorposts formed a pentagon. •
33 doorposts of olivewood, in the form of a square •
7:37 cast alike, of the same measure and the same form. 13
Job 1:17 The Chalde'ans formed three companies 15
4:16 A form was before my eyes; 18
33: 6 I too was formed from a piece of clay. 14
Ps 17:15 I shall be satisfied with beholding thy form. 18
49:14 they descend, and their form shall waste away; 11
90: 2 ever thou hadst formed the earth and the world 3
94: 9 He who formed the eye, does he not see? 5
95: 5 for his hands formed the dry land. 5
104:26 Leviathan which thou didst form to sport in it. 5
139:13 For thou didst form my inward parts 12
16 were written . . the days that were formed for me 5
Isa 25: 1 hast done wonderful things, plans formed of old •
27:11 he that formed them will show them no favor. 5
29:16 say of him who formed it, "He has no understanding"? 5
43: 1 created you, O Jacob, he who formed you, O Israel 5
7 whom I created for my glory, whom I formed 5
10 Before me no god was formed 5
21 the people whom I formed for myself 5
44: 2 LORD who made you, who formed you from the womb 5
21 I formed you, you are my servant; 5
24 your Redeemer, who formed you from the womb 5
45: 7 I form light and create darkness 5
18 (he is God!), who formed the earth and made it 5
18 not create it a chaos, he formed it to be inhabited 5
49: 5 who formed me from the womb to be his servant 5
52:14 and his form beyond that of the sons of men– 16
53: 2 he had no form or comeliness that we should look 16
Jer 1: 5 Before I formed you in the womb I knew you 5
10:16 for he is the one who formed all things 5
33: 2 the LORD who formed it to establish it 5
49:20 and the purposes which he has formed 4
30 and formed a purpose against you. 4
50:45 and the purposes which he has formed 4
51:19 for he is the one who formed all things 5
Ezk 1: 5 their appearance: they had the form of men 1
26 was a likeness as it were of a human form. 7
8: 2 Then I beheld, and, lo, a form 1
3 He put forth the form of a hand, and took me 17
10: 1 like a sapphire, in form resembling a throne. 1
8 have the form of a human hand under their wings. 17
16: 7 your breasts were formed, and your hair had grown; 6
43:11 its exits and its entrances, and its whole form; 10
Ams 4:13 he who forms the mountains, and creates the wind 5
7: 1 behold, he was forming locusts 5
Zec 12: 1 founded the earth and formed the spirit of man 5
Mrk 16:12 After this he appeared in another form to two 26
Lke 3:22 Holy Spirit descended upon him in bodily form 21
Joh 5:37 his form you have never seen; 21
1Co 7:31 the form of this world is passing away. 33
Gal 4:19 until Christ be formed in you! 27
Php 2: 6 who, though he was in the form of God, did not count 26
7 emptied himself, taking the form of a servant 26
8 being found in human form he humbled himself 33
1Th 5:22 abstain from every form of evil. 21
1Ti 2:13 For Adam was formed first, then Eve; 31
2Ti 3: 5 holding the form of religion 28
2Pe 3: 5 an earth formed out of water and by means of water 32
2Es 3: 4 when thou didst form the earth 38
6:46 to serve man, who was about to be formed. 40
7:92 the evil thought which was formed with them 40
94 witness which he who formed them bears 40
8: 8 the womb which thou has formed endures 39
44 man, who has been formed by thy hands 40
44 and for whose sake thou hast formed all things 40
10:42 you do not now see the form of a woman 41
13:41 they formed this plan for themselves 36
16:61 who formed man 37
Tob 2:10 white films formed on my eyes 19
Jdt 7:18 they formed a vast multitude. 22
16:14 it formed them 29
Wis 9: 2 by thy wisdom hast formed man, to have dominion 25
13: 4 how much more powerful is he who formed them. 25
14:19 forced the likeness to take more beautiful form •
15: 5 they desire the lifeless form of a dead image. 21
8 he forms a futile god from the same clay 31
11 because he failed to know the one who formed him 31
16 one whose spirit is borrowed formed them 31
16 no man can form a god which is like himself. 31
16:25 changed into all forms •
18: 1 did not see their forms 26
12 by the one form of death 30
Sir 32:16 Those who fear the Lord will form true judgments 23
37: 3 why were you formed to cover the land with deceit? 20
1Mc 10:23 gotten ahead of us in forming a friendship 24
2Mc 9:18 in the form of a supplication 34
3Mc 3: 8 the crowds that suddenly were forming 19
30 The letter was written in the above form. 35
6:32 they formed choruses 32
4Mc 15: 4 a wondrous likeness both of mind and of form. 26

form *See also* beauty.

form a boundary 1. גבל
Jos 18:20 Jordan forms its boundary on the eastern side. 1

form a chorus 1. *χορεύω*
4Mc 14: 8 so these youths, forming a chorus 1

form like 1. *ἀπεικάζω*
Wis 13:13 he forms it like the image of a man 1

form of gourd 1. פְּקָעִים
1Kg 6:18 was carved in the form of gourds and open flowers; 1

form of prestige 1. *δόξα*
2Mc 4:15 the highest value upon Greek forms of prestige. 1

form ranks 1. *διάταξις*
Jdt 1: 4 his infantry form their ranks- 1

true form 1. *εἰκών*
Heb 10: 1 instead of the true form of these realities 1

without form 1. תֹּהוּ
Gen 1: 2 The earth was without form and void 1

formation *See* drawn.

close formation 1. *συστρέφω*
1Mc 12:50 and kept marching in close formation 1

first formed 1. *πρωτόπλαστος*
Wis 7: 1 a descendant of the first-formed child of earth; 1
10: 1 Wisdom protected the first-formed father 1

thing formed 1. יֵצֶר
Isa 29:16 the thing formed say of him who formed it 1

former 1. לְפָנִים 2. קַדְמָה 3. קַדְמֹנִי 4. רִאשׁוֹן 5. *γίνομαι* 6. *δέ* 7. *ἔμπροσθεν* 8. *ποτέ* 9. *πρίν* 10. *προάγω* 11. *προγίνομαι* 12. *πρότερον* 13. *πρότερος* 14. *πρὸ τούτου* 15. *πρῶτος* 16. initium 17. primus 18. prior
Gen 26: 1 famine in the land, besides the former famine 4
Num 6:12 but the former time shall be void 4
21:26 Sihon . . fought against the former king of Moab 4
Deu 24: 4 then her former husband . . may not take her again 4
2Kg 1:14 fire . . consumed the two former captains 4
17:34 they do according to the former manner. 4
40 but they did according to their former manner. 4
1Ch 4:40 the former inhabitants there belonged to Ham. 1
Neh 5:15 former governors who were before me laid heavy 4
Ecc 7:10 Why were the former days better than these? 4
Isa 9: 1 In the former time he brought into contempt 4
61: 4 they shall raise up the former devastations; 4
65: 7 into . . bosom payment for their former doings. 4
16 because the former troubles are forgotten 4
Jer 34: 5 fathers, the former kings who were before you 4
36:28 scroll and write on it all the former words 4
Ezk 16:55 daughters shall return to their former estate; 2
55 daughters shall return to their former estate; 2
55 daughters shall return to your former estate. 2
36:11 you to be inhabited as in your former times, 2
38:17 Are you he of whom I spoke in former days 3
Dan 11:13 again raise a multitude, greater than the former; 4
Mic 4: 8 the former dominion shall come 4
Hag 2: 3 among you that saw this house in its former glory? 4
9 of this house shall be greater than the former 4
Zec 1: 4 fathers, to whom the former prophets cried out 4
7: 7 the LORD proclaimed by the former prophets? 4
12 by his Spirit through the former prophets. 4
8:11 the remnant of this people as in the former days 4
14:10 Gate of Benjamin to the place of the former gate 4
Mal 3: 4 as in the days of old and as in former years. 3
Rom 3:25 because . . he had passed over former sins; 11
Gal 1:13 For you have heard of my former life in Judaism 8
Eph 4:22 which belongs to your former manner of life 13
Php 1:17 the former proclaim Christ out of partisanship 6
Heb 7:18 On the one hand, a former commandment is set aside 10
23 The former priests were many in number 5
10:32 recall the former days 12
1Pe 1:14 the passions of your former ignorance 12
1Es 5:63 old men who had seen the former house 14
2Es 6:34 vain thoughts concerning the former times 18
7: 1 who had been sent to me on the former nights 17
12:18 but shall regain its former power. 16
Wis 19:15 punishment . . will come upon the former •
Sir 21: 1 Do so no more, but pray about your former sins. 15
41: 3 remember your former days and the end of life 15
1Mc 12: 3 sent us to renew the former friendship 13
16 sent them to Rome to renew our former friendship 12
2Mc 14:38 in former times 7
15: 8 to keep in mind the former times 11
3Mc 6: 4 the former ruler of this Egypt 9

former *See also* action, estate, state, time.

former limited 1. *προσυστέλλω*
3Mc 2:29 they shall . . be reduced to their former limited status. 1

former one 1. קַדְמָי (A) 2. *πρότερος* 3. *πρῶτος* 4. prior
Dan 7:24 different from the former ones, 1
2Es 11:18 and held the rule like the former ones 4
Tob 14: 5 though it will not be like the former one 3
1Mc 4:47 and built a new altar like the former one. 2

former thing 1. רִאשׁוֹן 2. *πρῶτος*
Ecc 1:11 There is no remembrance of former things 1
Isa 41:22 Tell us the former things, what they are 1
42: 9 Behold, the former things have come to pass 1
43: 9 can declare this, and show us the former things? 1
18 Remember not the former things 1
46: 9 remember the former things of old; for I am God 1
48: 3 The former things I declared of old 1
65:17 and the former things shall not be remembered 1
Rev 21: 4 for the former things have passed away. 2

formerly 1. בָּרִאשֹׁנָה 2. לְפָנִים 3. רִאשׁוֹן 4. תְּמוֹל שִׁלְשֹׁם 5. *ποτέ* 6. *προγίνομαι* 7. *πρότερον* 8. *τότε* 9. olim
Gen 40:13 cup in his hand as formerly, when you were his 3
Deu 2:10 Emim formerly lived there, a people great and many 2
12 The Horites also lived in Se'ir formerly 2
20 Reph'aim formerly lived there, but the Ammonites 2
Jos 11:10 Hazor formerly was the head of all those 2
14:15 Now the name of Hebron formerly was Kir'iath-ar'ba; 2
15:15 the name of Debir formerly was Kir'iath-se'pher. 2
Jdg 1:10 the name of Hebron was formerly Kir'iath-ar'ba); 2
11 The name of Debir was formerly Kir'iath-se'pher. 2
23 (Now the name of the city was formerly Luz.) 2
1Sm 9: 9 Formerly in Israel, when a man went to inquire 2
9 who is now . . prophet was formerly called a seer. 2
2Sm 7:10 men shall afflict them no more, as formerly 1
2Kg 13: 5 the people . . dwelt in their homes as formerly. 4
1Ch 17: 9 violent men shall waste them no more, as formerly 1
Joh 9:13 the man who had formerly been blind. 5
Gal 4: 8 Formerly, when you did not know God 8
1Ti 1:13 though I formerly blasphemed and persecuted 7
Phm 1:11 (Formerly he was useless to you 5
Heb 4: 6 those who formerly received the good news 7
7:21 Those who formerly became priests •
1Pe 3:20 who formerly did not obey 5
2Es 5: 2 and beyond what you heard of formerly. 9
1Mc 3:46 Israel formerly had a place of prayer in Mizpah. 7
9:72 the captives whom he had formerly taken 7
11:27 in as many other honors as he had formerly had 7
34 royal taxes which the king formerly received 7
39 formerly . . one of Alexander's supporters 7
14:33 where formerly the arms . . had been stored 7
34 Azotus, where the enemy formerly dwelt 7
15: 3 so that I may restore it as it formerly was 7
27 the agreements he formerly had made with Simon 7
2Mc 9:16 which he had formerly plundered 7
11:31 just as formerly 7
14: 3 who had formerly been high priest 6

formless 1. *ἄμορφος*
Wis 11:17 which created the world out of formless matter 1

fornication 1. *πορνεία*
Mat 15:19 evil thoughts, murder, adultery, fornication 1
Mrk 7:21 fornication, theft, murder, adultery 1
Joh 8:41 They said to him, "We were not born of fornication 1
Gal 5:19 fornication, impurity, licentiousness 1
Eph 5: 3 fornication and all impurity or covetousness 1
Col 3: 5 fornication, impurity, passion, evil desire 1
Rev 17: 2 and with the wine of whose fornication 1
4 and the impurities of her fornication; 1
19: 2 who corrupted the earth with her fornication 1
Wis 14:12 the beginning of fornication 1

fornication *See also* commit.

fornicator 1. *ἄνθρωπος πόρνος* 2. *πόρνος*
Eph 5: 5 no fornicator or impure man 2
Rev 21: 8 as for murderers, fornicators, sorcerers 2
22:15 Outside are the . . fornicators and murderers 2
Sir 23:17 To a fornicator all bread tastes sweet 1

forsake 1. אַלְמָן 2. חָפְשִׁי 3. מֵאַחֲרֵי 4. מַעַל 5. נטשׁ 6. עזב 7. רפה 8. *ἀπολείπω* 9. *ἀποστασία* 10. *ἀφίημι* 11. *ἀφίστημι* 12. *ἐγκαταλείπω* 13. *καταλείπω* 14. *μεταβαίνω ἀπό* 15. derelinquo
Gen 24:27 the LORD . . who has not forsaken his steadfast 6
Deu 12:19 Take heed that you do not forsake the Levite 6
14:27 not forsake the Levite who is within your towns 6
28:20 evil of your doings, because you have forsaken 6
29:25 because they forsook the covenant of the LORD 6
31: 6 LORD . . will not fail you or forsake you. 6
8 LORD . . will not fail you or forsake you; 6
16 people . . will forsake me and break my covenant 6
17 I will forsake them and hide my face from them 6
32:15 then he forsook God who made him 5
Jos 1: 5 be with you; I will not fail you or forsake you. 6
22: 3 you have not forsaken your brethren these many 6
24:16 Far be it from us that we should forsake the LORD 6
20 If you forsake the LORD and serve foreign gods 6
Jdg 2:12 they forsook the LORD, the God of their fathers 6
13 They forsook the LORD, and served the Ba'als 6
10: 6 they forsook the LORD, and did not serve him. 6
10 have sinned . . because we have forsaken our God 6
13 Yet you have forsaken me and served other gods; 6
Rut 2:20 kindness has not forsaken the living or the dead! 6
1Sm 8: 8 done to me . . forsaking me and serving other gods 6
12:10 We have sinned, because we have forsaken the LORD 6
31: 7 they forsook their cities and fled; 6
1Kg 6:13 I will . . and will not forsake my people Israel. 6
8:57 God be with us . . may he not leave us or forsake us; 5
9: 9 they forsook the LORD their God who brought 6
11:33 he has forsaken me, and worshiped Ash'toreth 6
12: 8 he forsook the counsel which the old men gave him 6
13 forsaking the counsel which the old men 6
18:18 you have forsaken the commandments of the LORD 6
19:10 the people of Israel have forsaken thy covenant 6
14 the people of Israel have forsaken thy covenant 6
2Kg 7: 7 fled . . in the twilight and forsook their tents 6
17:16 they forsook all the commandments of the LORD 6
21:22 he forsook the LORD . . and did not walk in the way 6
22:17 they have forsaken me and have burned incense 6
1Ch 10: 7 they forsook their cities and fled; 6
28: 9 if you forsake him, he will cast you off for ever. 6
20 He will not fail you or forsake you, 6
2Ch 7:19 and forsake my statutes and my commandments 6
22 they forsook the LORD the God of their fathers 6
10: 8 he forsook the counsel which the old men gave him 6
13 forsaking the counsel of the old men 6
12: 1 he forsook the law of the LORD, and all Israel 6
13:10 the LORD is our God, and we have not forsaken him. 6
11 we keep the charge . . but you have forsaken him. 6
15: 2 but if you forsake him, he will forsake you. 6
2 but if you forsake him, he will forsake you. 6
21:10 because he had forsaken the LORD 6
24:18 they forsook the house of the LORD 6
20 you have forsaken the LORD, he has forsaken you.' 6
20 you have forsaken the LORD, he has forsaken you.' 6
24 forsaken the LORD, the God of their fathers. 6
28: 6 because they had forsaken the LORD 6
29: 6 forsaken him, and have turned away their faces 6
34:25 forsaken me and . . burned incense to other gods 6
Ezr 8:22 power of his wrath is against all that forsake 6
9: 9 yet our God has not forsaken us in our bondage 6
10 For we have forsaken thy commandments 6
Neh 9:17 steadfast love, and didst not forsake them. 6
19 mercies didst not forsake them in the wilderness; 6
31 didst not make an end of them or forsake them; 6
13:11 Why is the house of God forsaken? 6
Job 6:14 forsakes the fear of the Almighty. 6
18: 4 in your anger, shall the earth be forsaken for you 6
Ps 9:10 O LORD, hast not forsaken those who seek thee. 6
22: 1 My God, my God, why hast thou forsaken me? 6
27: 9 Cast me not off, forsake me not, O God 6
10 For my father and my mother have forsaken me 6
37: 8 Refrain from anger, and forsake wrath! 6
25 yet I have not seen the righteous forsaken 6
28 he will not forsake his saints. 6
38:21 Do not forsake me, O LORD! O my God, be not far 6
71: 9 forsake me not when my strength is spent. 6
11 and say, "God has forsaken him; pursue and seize him 6
18 to old age and gray hairs, O God, do not forsake me 6
78:60 He forsook his dwelling at Shiloh, the tent 5
88: 5 like one forsaken among the dead 2
89:30 If his children forsake my law 6
94:14 For the LORD will not forsake his people; 5
119: 8 O forsake me not utterly! 6
53 because of the wicked, who forsake thy law. 6
87 but I have not forsaken thy precepts. 6
138: 8 Do not forsake the work of thy hands. 7
Prv 2:13 who forsake the paths of uprightness 6
17 who forsakes the companion of her youth 6
3: 3 Let not loyalty and faithfulness forsake you; 6
4: 2 good precepts: do not forsake my teaching. 6
6 Do not forsake her, and she will keep you; 6
6:20 My son . . forsake not your mother's teaching. 5
15:10 severe discipline for him who forsakes the way; 6
27:10 friend, and your father's friend, do not forsake; 6
28: 4 Those who forsake the law praise the wicked 6
13 confesses and forsakes them will obtain mercy. 6
Isa 1: 4 They have forsaken the LORD . . the Holy One 6
28 rebels . . and those who forsake the LORD 6
10:14 as men gather eggs that have been forsaken 6
27:10 a habitation deserted and forsaken 6
32:14 For the palace will be forsaken 5
41:17 I the God of Israel will not forsake them. 6
42:16 things I will do, and I will not forsake them. 6
49:14 But Zion said, "The LORD has forsaken me 6
54: 6 For the LORD has called you like a wife forsaken 6
7 For a brief moment I forsook you 6
55: 7 let the wicked forsake his way 6
58: 2 and did not forsake the ordinance of their God; 6
60:15 Whereas you have been forsaken and hated 6
62: 4 You shall no more be termed Forsaken 6
12 be called Sought out, a city not forsaken. 6
65:11 you who forsake the LORD, who forget my holy 6
Jer 1:16 for all their wickedness in forsaking me; 6
2:13 they have forsaken me 6
17 upon yourself by forsaking the LORD your God 6

19 and bitter for you to forsake the LORD your God; 6
4:29 cities are forsaken, and no man dwells in them. 6
5: 7 Your children have forsaken me 6
19 As you have forsaken me and served foreign gods 6
7:29 for the LORD has rejected and forsaken 5
9:13 the LORD says: "Because they have forsaken my law 6
12: 7 I have forsaken my house 6
14: 5 Even the hind in the field forsakes her newborn 6
16:11 your fathers have forsaken me, says the LORD 6
11 and have forsaken me and have not kept my law 6
17:13 all who forsake thee shall be put to shame; 6
13 for they have forsaken the LORD 6
19: 4 Because the people have forsaken me 6
22: 9 Because they forsook the covenant of the LORD 6
49:25 How the famous city is forsaken, the joyful city! 6
51: 5 and Judah have not been forsaken by their God 1
9 Forsake her, and let us go each to his own country; 6
Lam 5:20 why dost thou so long forsake us? 6
Ezk 8:12 For they say . . the LORD has forsaken the land. 6
9: 9 for they say, 'The LORD has forsaken the land 6
20: 8 nor did they forsake the idols of Egypt. 6
Dan 11:30 heed to those who forsake the holy covenant. 6
Hos 1: 2 commits great harlotry by forsaking the LORD. 3
4:10 they have forsaken the LORD to cherish harlotry. 6
9: 1 you have played the harlot, forsaking your God. 4
Ams 5: 2 forsaken on her land, with none to raise her up. 5
Jon 2: 8 to vain idols forsake their true loyalty. 6
Mat 23:38 Behold, your house is forsaken and desolate. 10
26:56 Then all the disciples forsook him and fled. 10
27:46 My God, my God, why hast thou forsaken me? 12
Mrk 14:50 they all forsook him, and fled. 10
15:34 My God, my God, why hast thou forsaken me? 12
Lke 13:35 Behold, your house is forsaken 10
Act 21:21 you teach all the Jews . . to forsake Moses 9
2Co 4: 9 persecuted, but not forsaken 12
Heb 13: 5 he has said, "I will never fail you nor forsake you. 12
2Pe 2:15 Forsaking the right way they have gone astray; 13
1Es 8:80 we were not forsaken by our Lord 12
2Es 1:25 Because you have forsaken me 15
25 I also will forsake you 15
27 It is not as though you had forsaken me 15
27 you have forsaken yourselves, says the Lord. •
2: 2 'Go, my children, because I am a widow and forsaken. 15
4 For I am a widow and forsaken 15
3:15 thou wouldst never forsake his descendants 15
5:18 that you may not forsake us 15
8:56 and forsook his ways. 15
10:32 I said, "Because you have forsaken me! 15
34 I said, "Speak, my lord; only do not forsake me 15
12:41 that you have forsaken us and sit in this place? 15
44 Therefore if you forsake us, how much better 15
48 neither forsaken you nor withdrawn from you 15
13:54 because you have forsaken your own ways 15
Jdt 7:30 he will not forsake us utterly. 12
Sir 2:10 persevered . . and was forsaken? 12
3:16 Whoever forsakes his father is like a blasphemer 12
4:19 If he goes astray she will forsake him 12
7:30 do not forsake his ministers. 12
9:10 Forsake not an old friend 12
10:12 his heart has forsaken his Maker. 11
13: 4 if you are in need he will forsake you. 13
7 Should he see you afterwards, he will forsake you 13
17:25 Turn to the Lord and forsake your sins 8
28:23 who forsake the Lord will fall into its power 13
35: 3 to forsake unrighteousness is atonement. 11
41: 8 who have forsaken the law of the Most High God! 12
48:15 they did not forsake their sins 11
49: 4 they forsook the law of the Most High 13
51:10 not to forsake me in the days of affliction 12
20 therefore I will not be forsaken. 12
Bar 3: 8 our fathers who forsook the Lord our God.' 11
12 You have forsaken the fountain of wisdom. 12
4: 1 and those who forsake her will die. 13
Bel 1:38 hast not forsaken those who love thee. 12
1Mc 1:38 her children forsook her. 12
52 Many of the people, every one who forsook the law 12
10:14 who had forsaken the law and the commandments 13
2Mc 1: 5 may he not forsake you in time of evil. 13
5:20 what was forsaken in the wrath of the Almighty 13
6: 1 to forsake the laws of their fathers 14
16 he does not forsake his own people. 12
7:16 do not think that God has forsaken our people. 13

forsaken place 1. עֲזוּבָה
Isa 6:12 forsaken places are many in the midst of the land. 1

fort 1. בִּירָנִית 2. מִבְצָר 3. *φρούριον*
2Ch 27: 4 built . . forts and towers on the wooded hills. 1
Nah 3:14 Draw water for the siege, strengthen your forts; 2
2Mc 10:33 they besieged the fort for four days. 3

forth 1. מִן 2. *ἔξω* 3. *φέρω*
Ps 113: 2 LORD from this time forth and for evermore! 1
115:18 we will bless the LORD from this time forth 1
121: 8 from this time forth and for evermore. 1
125: 2 from this time forth and for evermore. 1
131: 3 hope . . from this time forth and for evermore. 1
Isa 9: 7 with righteousness from this time forth •
48: 6 From this time forth I make you hear new things •
59:21 the LORD, from this time forth and for evermore. •
Mic 4: 7 reign . . from this time forth and for evermore. •
Joh 15: 6 he is cast forth as a branch and withers 2
Sir 24:15 I gave forth the aroma of spices •
1Mc 11:36 from this time forth for ever. •
2Mc 14:45 though his blood gushed forth 3

forth *See also* belch, blossom, break, bring, burst, call, carry, cast, come, creep, draw, drive, flame, flash, flow, fly, give, go, gush, lead, leap, look, march, pour, put, rush, sally, send, set, shine, shoot, show, sound, spread, spring, sprout, stand, stretch, word.

fortification 1. מִבְצָר 2. *ὀχύρωσις*
Isa 25:12 fortifications of his walls he will bring down 1
1Mc 10:11 to build the walls . . for better fortification 2

fortification *See also* strengthen.

fortified 1. מְצוּרָה
2Ch 11:10 fortified cities which are in Judah 1
23 Judah and Benjamin, in all the fortified cities; 1
12: 4 he took the fortified cities of Judah 1
21: 3 great gifts . . together with fortified cities 1

well fortified 1. מִבְצָר
Dan 11:15 siegeworks, and take a well-fortified city. 1

fortify 1. בנה 2. בָּצוּר 3. בצר 4. חזק 5. מִבְצָר 6. מָצוֹר 7. מְצוּרָה 8. *ἐνισχύω* 9. *ἐρυμνός* 10. *θωρακίζω* 11. *οἰκοδομέω* 12. *ὀχυρός* 13. *ὀχυρόω* 14. *περιφράσσω* 15. *στερεόω* 16. *τειχίζω*
Num13:28 cities are fortified and very large; and besides 3
32:17 little ones shall live in the fortified cities 5
36 Beth-nim'rah and Beth-har'an, fortified cities 5
Deu 1:28 the cities are great and fortified up to heaven; 3
3: 5 cities fortified with high walls, gates, and bars 3
9: 1 cities great and fortified up to heaven 3
28:52 besiege . . until your high and fortified walls 3
Jos 10:20 remnant . . entered into the fortified cities 5
14:12 Anakim were there, with great fortified cities 3
19:29 turns . . reaching to the fortified city of Tyre; 5
35 The fortified cities are Ziddim, Zer, Hammath 5
1Sm 6:18 both fortified cities and unwalled villages. 5
2Sm 20: 6 pursue him, lest he get himself fortified cities 3
1Kg 16:24 the hill of Sama'ria . . he fortified the hill 1
2Kg 3:19 you shall conquer every fortified city 5
10: 2 chariots and horses, fortified cities also 5
17: 9 their towns, from watchtower to fortified city; 5
18: 8 He smote . . from watchtower to fortified city. 5
13 against all the fortified cities of Judah 3
19:25 you . . turn fortified cities into heaps of ruins 3
2Ch 8: 5 fortified cities with walls, gates, and bars 6
14: 6 He built fortified cities in Judah 7
17: 2 He placed forces in all the fortified cities 3
19 king had placed in the fortified cities 5
19: 5 in the land in all the fortified cities of Judah 3
26: 9 built towers in Jerusalem . . and fortified 4
32: 1 encamped against the fortified cities 3
33:14 in all the fortified cities in Judah. 3
Neh 9:25 captured fortified cities and a rich land 3
Ps 60: 9 Who will bring me to the fortified city? 6
108:10 Who will bring me to the fortified city? 5
Isa 2:15 high tower, and against every fortified wall; 3
22:10 you broke down the houses to fortify the wall. 3
25: 2 made the city a heap, the fortified city a ruin; 3
27:10 For the fortified city is solitary 3
36: 1 came up against all the fortified cities 3
37:26 make fortified cities crash into heaps of ruins 2
Jer 1:18 And I, behold, I make you this day a fortified city 5
4: 5 Assemble, and let us go into the fortified cities!' 5
5:17 your fortified cities in which you trust 5
8:14 let us go into the fortified cities and perish 5
15:20 I will make you . . a fortified wall of bronze; 3
34: 7 these were the only fortified cities of Judah 5
51:53 and though she should fortify her strong height 3
Ezk 21:20 and to Judah and to Jerusalem the fortified. 3
36:35 ruined cities are now inhabited and fortified. 3
Hos 8:14 and Judah has multiplied fortified cities; 3
Zep 1:16 and battle cry against the fortified cities 3
Jdt 4: 5 fortified the villages on them 16
5: 1 fortified all the high hilltops 16
Sir 48:17 Hezekiah fortified his city 13
50: 1 in his time fortified the temple. 15
4 fortified the city to withstand a seige. 8
1Mc 1:19 the fortified cities in the land of Egypt 12
33 Then they fortified the city of David 11
4: 7 the camp of the Gentiles, strong and fortified 10
60 At that time they fortified Mount Zion 11
61 He also fortified Beth-zur 13
6:26 have fortified both the sanctuary and Beth-zur; 13
9:52 He also fortified the city of Beth-zur, and Gazara 13
62 they fortified it. 15
10:45 and fortifying it round about 13
12:38 he fortified it and installed gates with bolts. 13
13:10 he fortified it on every side. 13
14:33 He fortified the cities of Judea, and Beth-zur 13
34 He also fortified Joppa, which is by the sea 13
37 fortified it for the safety of the country 13
15:39 build up Kedron and fortify its gates 13
2Mc 11: 5 which was a fortified place 9
12:13 which was strongly fortified with earthworks 14
27 Ephron, a fortified city where Lysias dwelt 12
4Mc 13: 7 fortifying the harbor of religion 13

fortitude 1. *καρτερία*
4Mc 15:28 she remembered his fortitude. 1

fortress 1. בִּירָה 2. בִּירָנִית 3. בַּיִת 4. מִבְצָר 5. מָעוֹז 6. מְצָד 7. מְצוּדָה 8. מְצוּרָה 9. מִשְׂגָּב 10. *βαρύς* 11. *ὀχύρωμα* 12. *τόπος* 13. *φρούριον*
2Sm 22: 2 The LORD is my rock . . my fortress . . my deliverer 7
24: 7 and came to the fortress of Tyre 4
2Kg 8:12 you will set on fire their fortresses 4
2Ch 11:11 He made the fortresses strong 8
17:12 He built in Judah fortresses and store-cities 2
Neh 2: 8 beams for the gates of the fortress of the temple 1
Ps 18: 2 The LORD is my rock, and my fortress 7
31: 2 refuge for me, a strong fortress to save me! 3
3 Yea, thou art my rock and my fortress; 7
59: 9 praises to thee; for thou, O God, art my fortress. 9
16 thou hast been to me a fortress and a refuge 9
17 praises to thee, for thou, O God, art my fortress 9
62: 2 He only is my rock and my salvation, my fortress; 9
6 He only is my rock and my salvation, my fortress; 9
71: 3 Be thou to me a rock of refuge, a strong fortress 12
3 save me, for thou art my rock and my fortress. 7
91: 2 My refuge and my fortress; my God, in whom I trust. 7
144: 2 my rock and my fortress, my stronghold 7
Isa 17: 3 The fortress will disappear from E'phraim 4
33:16 his . . defense will be the fortresses of rocks; 6
34:13 nettles and thistles in its fortresses. 4
Jer 48: 1 the fortress is put to shame and broken down; 9
Dan 11: 7 enter the fortress of the king of the north 5
10 again shall carry the war as far as his fortress. 5
19 face . . toward the fortresses of his own land; 5
31 appear and profane the temple and fortress 5
38 honor the god of fortresses instead of these; 5
39 He shall deal with the strongest fortresses 4
Hos 10:14 and all your fortresses shall be destroyed 4
11: 6 and devour them in their fortresses. •
Ams 5: 9 so that destruction comes upon the fortress. 4
Nah 3:12 All your fortresses are like fig trees 4
Hab 1:10 They laugh at every fortress 4
1Es 6:23 the fortress which is in the country of Media 10
1Mc 9:50 the fortress in Jericho, and Emmaus 11
2Mc 13:19 Beth-zur, a strong fortress of the Jews 13
3Mc 6:25 have held the fortresses of our country? 11

strong fortress 1. *ὀχύρωμα*
1Mc 6:62 saw what a strong fortress the place was 1

fortunate 1. *μακάριος*
Act 26: 2 I think myself fortunate that it is before you 1

fortunate *See also* think.

fortune 1. גַּד 2. שְׁבִית
Deu 30: 3 LORD your God will restore your fortunes 2
Job 42:10 the LORD restored the fortunes of Job 2
Ps 14: 7 the LORD restores the fortunes of his people 2
53: 6 When God restores the fortunes of his people 2
85: 1 thou didst restore the fortunes of Jacob. 2
126: 1 When the LORD restored the fortunes of Zion 2
4 Restore our fortunes, O LORD 2
Isa 65:11 who set a table for Fortune and fill cups 1
Jer 29:14 and I will restore your fortunes and gather you 2
30: 3 when I will restore the fortunes of my people 2
18 I will restore the fortunes of the tents of Jacob 2
31:23 and in its cities, when I restore their fortunes 2
32:44 for I will restore their fortunes, says the LORD. 2
33: 7 I will restore the fortunes of Judah 2
7 the fortunes of Judah and the fortunes of Israel 2
11 will restore the fortunes of the land as at first 2
26 For I will restore their fortunes 2
48:47 Yet I will restore the fortunes of Moab 2
49: 6 I will restore the fortunes of the Ammonites 2
39 I will restore the fortunes of Elam, says the LORD. 2
Lam 2:14 exposed your iniquity to restore your fortunes 2
Ezk 16:53 I will restore their fortunes 2
53 both the fortunes of Sodom and her daughters 2
53 and the fortunes of Sama'ria and her daughters 2
53 restore your own fortunes in the midst of them 2
29:14 I will restore the fortunes of Egypt 2
39:25 Now I will restore the fortunes of Jacob 2
Hos 6:11 When I would restore the fortunes of my people 2
Jol 3: 1 when I restore the fortunes of Judah 2
Ams 9:14 I will restore the fortunes of my people Israel 2
Zep 2: 7 be mindful of them and restore their fortunes. 2
3:20 when I restore your fortunes before your eyes 2

fortune *See also* turn.

good fortune 1. גַּד 2. *εὐημερία* 3. *εὐοδία*
Gen 30:11 Good fortune!" so she called his name Gad. 1
Sir 20: 9 There may be good fortune for a man in adversity 3
3Mc 3:11 the king, boastful of his present good fortune 2

forum 1. *φόρον*
Act 28:15 as far as the Forum of Ap'pius and Three Taverns 1

forward 1. הַלְאָה 2. לְפָנִים 3. מַעַל 4. קֶדֶם
5. ἔμπροσθεν

Jdg 9:44 the company that was with him rushed forward •
1Sm 16:13 came mightily upon David from that day forward. 3
30:25 And from that day forward he made it a statute 3
Job 23: 8 Behold, I go forward, but he is not there; 4
Jer 7:24 and went backward and not forward. 2
Ezk 39: 2 I will turn you about and drive you forward •
22 I am the LORD their God, from that day forward. 1
1Es 5:58 the Levites, as one man pressing forward the work †
2Mc 7: 7 they brought forward the second for their sport •
18 After him they brought forward the sixth •
4Mc 8:12 instruments of torture to be brought forward 5

forward *See also* bring, come, directly, go, look, move, press, push, put, straight, strain.

foster father 1. אמן

Isa 49:23 Kings shall be your foster fathers 1

foul 1. מִרְפָּשׂ 2. פִּגּוּל 3. רפס 4. ἀκάθαρτος 5. κακός

Ezk 4:14 nor has foul flesh come into my mouth. 2
32: 2 the waters with your feet, and foul their rivers. 3
34:18 that you must foul the rest with your feet? 3
19 and drink what you have fouled with your feet? 1
Rev 16: 2 and foul and evil sores came upon the men 5
13 I saw . . three foul spirits like frogs; 4
18: 2 a haunt of every foul spirit 4
2 a haunt of every foul and hateful bird; 4

foul *See also* grow, play, smell, talk, weed.

become foul 1. באשׁ 2. זנח

Exd 7:18 and the Nile shall become foul 1
21 the fish in the Nile died; and the Nile became foul 1
16:20 the morning, and it bred worms and became foul; 1
24 it did not become foul, and there were no worms 1
Isa 19: 6 its canals will become foul 2

found 1. יסד 2. θεμελιόω 3. καθιδρύω 4. καταβάλλω
5. fundo

Exd 9:18 in Egypt from the day it was founded until now. 1
Ps 8: 2 thou hast founded a bulwark because of thy foes 1
24: 2 for he has founded it upon the seas 1
78:69 like the earth, which he has founded for ever. 1
87: 1 On the holy mount stands the city he founded; †
89:11 world and all that is in it, thou hast founded them. 1
119:152 that thou hast founded them for ever. 1
Prv 3:19 The LORD by wisdom founded the earth; 1
Isa 14:32 The LORD has founded Zion 1
Ams 9: 6 and founds his vault upon the earth; 1
Zec 12: 1 stretched out the heavens and founded the earth 1
Mat 7:25 because it had been founded on the rock. 2
Heb 1:10 Thou, Lord, didst found the earth in the beginning 2
2Es 16:59 and founded it upon the waters; 5
2Mc 2:13 he founded a library 4
4:12 with alacrity he founded a gymnasium 3

foundation 1. אָמָּה 2. יסד 3. יְסוֹד 4. מוּסָד 5. מוֹסָד
6. מוּסָדָה 7. מָכוֹן 8. מִסָּד 9. שֵׁת 10. אֹשׁ (A)
11. θεμέλιος 12. θεμελιόω 13. καταβολή
14. fundamentum

Deu 32:22 sets on fire the foundations of the mountains. 5
2Sm 22: 8 the foundations of the heavens trembled 5
16 the foundations of the world were laid bare 5
1Kg 7: 9 from the foundation to the coping 8
10 The foundation was of costly stones, huge stones 2
2Ch 23: 5 one third at the Gate of the Foundation; 3
Ezr 3: 6 foundation of the temple of the LORD was not yet •
4:12 walls and repairing the foundations. 10
5:16 came and laid the foundations of the house of God 10
Job 4:19 houses of clay, whose foundation is in the dust 3
22:16 their foundation was washed away. 3
Ps 11: 3 if the foundations are destroyed 9
18: 7 the foundations also of the mountains trembled 5
15 the foundations of the world were laid bare 5
82: 5 all the foundations of the earth are shaken. 5
89:14 justice are the foundation of thy throne; 7
97: 2 justice are the foundation of his throne. 7
104: 5 Thou didst set the earth on its foundations 7
137: 7 Rase it, rase it! Down to its foundations! 3
Prv 8:29 when he marked out the foundations of the earth 5
Isa 6: 4 the foundations of the thresholds shook 1
24:18 and the foundations of the earth tremble. 5
28:16 a precious cornerstone, of a sure foundation 4
40:21 understood from the foundations of the earth? 5
58:12 you shall raise up the foundations of many 5
Jer 31:37 foundations of the earth below can be explored 5
51:26 for a corner and no stone for a foundation 5
Lam 4:11 a fire in Zion, which consumed its foundations. 3
Ezk 13:14 so that its foundation will be laid bare; 3
30: 4 her foundations are torn down. 3
41: 8 the foundations of the side chambers measured 6
Mic 1: 6 down her stones . . and uncover her foundations. 3
6: 2 Hear . . you enduring foundations of the earth; 5
Hag 2:18 that the foundation of the LORD'S temple was laid •
Zec 4: 9 hands of Zerub'babel have laid the foundation •
8: 9 the foundation of the house of the LORD of hosts •
Mat 13:35 hidden since the foundation of the world. 13
25:34 from the foundation of the world; 13
Lke 6:48 who dug deep, and laid the foundation upon rock; 11
49 a house on the ground without a foundation; 11
11:50 blood . . shed from the foundation of the world 13
14:29 Otherwise, when he has laid a foundation 11
Joh 17:24 given me . . before the foundation of the world. 13
Act 16:26 so that the foundations . . were shaken 11
Rom 15:20 lest I build on another man's foundation 11
1Co 3:10 I laid a foundation 11
11 For no other foundation can any one lay 11
12 Now if any one builds on the foundation with gold 11
14 which any man has built on the foundation •
Eph 1: 4 chose us in him before the foundation of the world 13
2:20 built upon the foundation of the apostles 11
1Ti 6:19 laying up . . a good foundation for the future 11
2Ti 2:19 God's firm foundation stands, bearing this seal 11
Heb 4: 3 were finished from the foundation of the world. 13
6: 1 not laying again a foundation of repentance 11
9:26 since the foundation of the world 13
11:10 the city which has foundations 11
1Pe 1:20 destined before the foundation of the world 13
Rev 13: 8 written before the foundation of the world 13
17: 8 from the foundation of the world 13
21:14 And the wall of the city had twelve foundations 11
19 The foundations of the wall of the city 11
1Es 6:20 laid the foundations of the house of the Lord 11
2Es 6: 2 and before the foundations of paradise were laid 14
15 and the foundations of the earth will understand 14
10:27 and a place of huge foundations showed itself. 14
53 where there was no foundation of any building 14
15:12 Let Egypt mourn, and its foundations 14
23 and will consume the foundations of the earth 14
16:12 The earth and its foundations quake 14
15 until it consumes the foundations of the earth. 14
Jdt 1: 3 60 cubits wide at the foundations; 12
16:15 be shaken to their foundations with the waters; 11
Wis 4:19 shake them from the foundations 11
Sir 1:15 She made among men an eternal foundation 11
3: 9 a mother's curse uproots their foundations. 11
10:16 destroyed them to the foundations of the earth. 12
16:19 mountains . . and the foundations of the earth 11

foundation *See also* lay.

firm foundation 1. σύστασις

3Mc 2: 9 you made it a firm foundation 1

fountain 1. אָפִיק 2. מַבּוּעַ 3. מַעְיָן 4. מָקוֹר 5. עַיִן
6. πηγή 7. fons

Gen 7:11 the fountains of the great deep burst forth 3
8: 2 the fountains of the deep and the windows 3
Lev 20:18 he has made naked her fountain 4
18 and she has uncovered the fountain of her blood 4
Deu 8: 7 good land, a land of . . fountains and springs 5
33:28 Israel dwelt . . the fountain of Jacob alone 5
1Sm 29: 1 encamped by the fountain which is in Jezreel. 5
Ps 36: 9 with thee is the fountain of life; 4
68:26 Bless . . LORD, O you who are of Israel's fountain! 4
Prv 5:18 Let your fountain be blessed 4
8:28 when he established the fountains of the deep 5
10:11 The mouth of the righteous is a fountain of life 4
13:14 The teaching of the wise is a fountain of life 4
14:27 The fear of the LORD is a fountain of life 4
16:22 Wisdom is a fountain of life to him who has it 4
18: 4 fountain of wisdom is a gushing stream. 4
25:26 Like a muddied spring or a polluted fountain 4
Ecc 12: 6 or the pitcher is broken at the fountain 2
Sng 4:12 my bride, a garden locked, a fountain sealed. 3
15 a garden fountain, a well of living water 3
Isa 41:18 and fountains in the midst of the valleys; 3
Jer 2:13 have forsaken me, the fountain of living waters 4
9: 1 head were waters, and my eyes a fountain of tears 4
17:13 forsaken the LORD, the fountain of living water. 4
51:36 I will dry up her sea and make her fountain dry; 4
Ezk 34:13 on the mountains of Israel, by the fountains 1
Hos 13:15 and his fountain shall dry up 4
Jol 3:18 a fountain shall come forth from the house 3
Zec 13: 1 On that day there shall be a fountain 4
Rev 8:10 it fell . . on the fountains of water. 6
14: 7 who made . . the sea and the fountains of water 6
16: 4 into the rivers and the fountains of water 6
21: 6 I will give from the fountain of the water of life 6
2Es 6:24 the springs of the fountains shall stand still 7
14:47 the fountain of wisdom 7
Wis 11: 6 Instead of the fountain of an ever-flowing river 6
Bar 3:12 You have forsaken the fountain of wisdom. 6
4Mc 13:21 they drank milk from the same fountains 6

four 1. אַרְבַּע 2. אַרְבַּע (A) 3. τέσσαρες 4. τέταρτος
5. quattuor

Gen 2:10 there it divided and became four rivers. 1
14: 9 Ar'ioch king of Ella'sar, four kings against five. 1
Exd 22: 1 shall pay . . four sheep for a sheep. 1
25:12 you shall cast four rings of gold for it 1
12 four rings . . and put them on its four feet 1
26 you shall make for it four rings of gold 1
26 the rings to the four corners at its four legs. 1
26 the rings to the four corners at its four legs. 1
34 on the lampstand . . four cups made like almonds 1
26: 2 and the breadth of each curtain four cubits; 1
8 the breadth of each curtain four cubits; 1
32 you shall hang it upon four pillars of acacia 1
32 with hooks of gold, upon four bases of silver. 1
27: 2 you shall make horns for it on its four corners; 1
4 make four bronze rings at its four corners. 1
4 make four bronze rings at its four corners. 1
16 it shall have four pillars and . . four bases. 1
16 have four pillars and with them four bases. 1
28:17 you shall set in it four rows of stones. 1
36: 9 and the breadth of each curtain four cubits; 1
15 the breadth of each curtain four cubits; 1
36 for it he made four pillars of acacia 1
36 and he cast for them four bases of silver. 1
37: 3 he cast for it four rings of gold 1
3 four rings of gold for its four corners 1
13 He cast for it four rings of gold, and fastened 1
13 the rings to the four corners at its four legs. 1
13 the rings to the four corners at its four legs. 1
20 four cups made like almonds, with their capitals 1
38: 2 He made horns for it on its four corners; 1
5 He cast four rings on the four corners 1
5 four rings on the four corners of the bronze 1
19 their pillars were four; their four bases were 1
19 their pillars were four; their four bases were 1
39:10 they set in it four rows of stones. 1
Lev 11:20 All winged insects that go upon all fours are 1
21 Yet among the winged insects that go on all fours 1
23 all other winged insects which have four feet 1
27 among the animals that go on all fours 1
42 whatever goes on all fours 1
Num 7: 7 Two wagons and four oxen he gave to . . Gershon 1
8 four wagons and eight oxen he gave 1
Deu 3:11 its length, and four cubits its breadth 1
22:12 tassels on the four corners of your cloak 1
Jos 19: 7 four cities with their villages; 1
21:18 and Almon with its pasture lands–four cities. 1
22 Kib'za-im . . Beth-hor'on . . four cities; 1
24 Ai'jalon . . Gath-rim'mon . . four cities; 1
29 Jarmuth . . En-gan'nim . . four cities; 1
31 Helkath . . and Rehob . . four cities; 1
35 Dimnah . . Na'halal . . four cities; 1
37 Ked'emoth . . and Meph'a-ath . . four cities; 1
39 Heshbon . . Jazer . . four cities in all. 1
Jdg 9:34 laid wait against Shechem in four companies. 1
11:40 went . . to lament . . four days in the year. 1
19: 2 at Bethlehem . . and was there some four months. 1
20:47 and abode at the rock of Rimmon four months. 1
1Sm 27: 7 number of the days . . was a year and four months. 1
2Sm 15: 7 at the end of four years Ab'salom said to the king 3
21:22 These four were descended from the giants 1
1Kg 7:19 the capitals . . were of lily-work, four cubits. 1
27 each stand was four cubits long, four cubits wide 1
27 each stand was four cubits long, four cubits wide 1
30 stand had four bronze wheels and axles of bronze; 1
30 at the four corners were supports for a laver. 1
32 the four wheels were underneath the panels; 1
34 There were four supports at the four corners 1
34 four supports at the four corners of each stand; 1
38 each laver measured four cubits 1
18:33 Fill four jars with water, and pour it 1
2Kg 7: 3 Now there were four men who were lepers 1
1Ch 3: 5 born to him in Jerusalem . . four by Bath-shu'a 1
7: 1 Tola, Pu'ah, Jashub, and Shimron, four. 1
9:24 The gatekeepers were on the four sides 1
26 for the four chief gatekeepers, who were Levites 1
21:20 his four sons who were with him hid themselves. 1
23:10 These four were the sons of Shim'e-i. 1
12 of Kohath: Amram, Izhar, Hebron, and Uz'ziel, four. 1
26:17 on the north four each day, on the south four 1
17 north four each day, on the south four each day 1
18 for the parbar . . there were four at the road 1
Neh 6: 4 sent to me four times in this way and I answered 1
Job 1:19 and struck the four corners of the house 1
42:16 saw his sons, and his sons' sons, four generations. 1
Prv 30:15 never satisfied; four never say, "Enough 1
18 Three things . . four I do not understand 1
21 three things . . under four it cannot bear up 1
29 Three things . . four are stately in their stride 1
Isa 11:12 Judah from the four corners of the earth. 1
17: 6 four or five on the branches of a fruit tree 1
Jer 15: 3 will appoint over them four kinds of destroyers 1
36:23 As Jehu'di read three or four columns 1
49:36 I will bring upon Elam the four winds 1
36 the four winds from the four quarters of heaven; 1
52:21 its thickness was four fingers 1
Ezk 1: 5 came the likeness of four living creatures. 1
6 but each had four faces 1
6 had four faces, and each of them had four wings. 1
8 Under their wings on their four sides 1
8 And the four had their faces and their wings thus 1
10 the four had the face of a lion on the right side 1
10 the four had the face of an ox on the left side 1
10 and the four had the face of an eagle at the back. 1
15 a wheel . . one for each of the four of them. 1
16 and the four had the same likeness 1
17 they went in any of their four directions 1
18 The four wheels had rims and they had spokes; 1

7: 2 end has come upon the four corners of the land. 1
10: 9 I looked, and behold, there were four wheels 1
10 the four had the same likeness 1
11 they went in any of their four directions 1
12 the wheels that the four of them had. 1
14 every one had four faces 1
21 Each had four faces, and each four wings 1
21 Each had four faces, and each four wings 1
14:21 upon Jerusalem my four sore acts of judgment 1
37: 9 Come from the four winds, O breath 1
40:41 Four tables were on the inside 1
41 four tables on the outside of the side of the gate 1
42 there were also four tables of hewn stone 1
41: 5 and the breadth of the side chambers, four cubits 1
42:20 He measured it on the four sides. It had a wall 1
43:14 smaller ledge to the larger ledge, four cubits 1
15 the altar hearth, four cubits; 1
15 projecting upward, four horns, one cubit high. 1
20 its blood, and put it on the four horns of the altar 1
20 on the four corners of the ledge, and upon the rim 1
45:19 the four corners of the ledge of the altar 1
46:21 and led me to the four corners of the court; 1
22 the four corners of the court were small courts 1
22 the four were of the same size. 1
23 around each of the four courts was a row 1
Dan 1:17 As for these four youths, God gave them learning 1
3:25 But I see four men loose, walking in the midst 2
7: 2 four winds of heaven were stirring up the great 2
3 four great beasts came up out of the sea 2
6 leopard, with four wings of a bird on its back; 2
6 beast had four heads; and dominion was given to it. 2
17 four great beasts are four kings who shall arise 2
17 four kings who shall arise out of the earth. 2
8: 8 there came up four conspicuous horns 1
8 four . . horns toward the four winds of heaven. 1
22 in place of which four others arose 1
22 four kingdoms shall arise from his nation 1
11: 4 divided toward the four winds of heaven 1
Ams 1: 3 for four, I will not revoke the punishment; 1
6 For three transgressions of Gaza, and for four 1
9 For three transgressions of Tyre, and for four 1
11 For three transgressions of Edom, and for four 1
13 transgressions of the Ammonites, and for four 1
2: 1 For three transgressions of Moab, and for four 1
4 For three transgressions of Judah, and for four 1
6 For three transgressions of Israel, and for four 1
Zec 1:18 I lifted my eyes and saw, and behold, four horns! 1
20 Then the LORD showed me four smiths. 1
2: 6 I have spread you abroad as the four winds 1
6: 1 four chariots came out from between two 1
5 These are going forth to the four winds of heaven 1
Mat 24:31 they will gather his elect from the four winds 3
Mrk 2: 3 bringing to him a paralytic carried by four men. 3
13:27 gather his elect from the four winds 3
Joh 11:17 Laz'arus had already been in the tomb four days. 3
19:23 they took his garments and made four parts 3
Act 10:11 great sheet, let down by four corners upon the earth. 3
30 Cornelius said, "Four days ago, about this hour 4
11: 5 a great sheet, let down from heaven by four corners 3
12: 4 delivered him to four squads of soldiers 3
21: 9 four unmarried daughters, who prophesied. 3
23 We have four men who are under a vow; 3
27:29 they let out four anchors from the stern 3
Rev 4: 6 round the throne . . are four living creatures 3
8 four living creatures, each . . with six wings 3
5: 6 the throne and the four living creatures 3
8 four living creatures and the 24 elders 3
14 the four living creatures said, "Amen! 3
6: 1 and I heard one of the four living creatures say 3
6 a voice in the midst of the four living creatures 3
7: 1 After this I saw four angels standing 3
1 After this I saw four angels standing 3
1 angels . . holding back the four winds 3
2 he called with a loud voice to the four angels 3
11 round the elders and the four living creatures 3
9:13 a voice from the four horns of the golden altar 3
14 Release the four angels who are bound 3
15 So the four angels were released 3
14: 3 and before the four living creatures 3
15: 7 And one of the four living creatures gave 3
19: 4 four living creatures fell down and worshiped 3
20: 8 nations . . at the four corners of the earth 3
2Es 3:19 thy glory passed through the four gates 5
6:21 premature children at three and four months 5
11:24 but four remained in their place. 5
39 not the one that remains of the four beasts 5
12:21 four shall be kept for the time 5
13: 5 gathered together from the four winds of heaven 5
16:29 three or four olives may be left on every tree 5
31 in those days three or four shall be left by those 5
Jdt 8: 4 three years and four months. 3
Sir 37:18 four turns of fortune appear 3
1Mc 6:37 upon each were four armed men 3
11:57 set you over the four districts 3
13:28 for his father and mother and four brothers. 3
2Mc 10:33 they besieged the fort for four days. 3

four *See also* three.

four days 1. τεταρταῖος
Joh 11:39 for he has been dead four days 1

four months 1. τετράμηνος
Joh 4:35 'There are yet four months, then comes the harvest'? 1

four parts 1. τετραμερής
2Mc 8:21 then he divided his army into four parts. 1

four rows 1. τετράστιχος
Wis 18:24 engraved on the four rows of stones 1

four things 1. אַרְבַּע
Prv 30:24 Four things on earth are small 1

four-footed 1. τετράποδος 2. quadrupes
2Es 7:65 the four-footed beasts and the flocks rejoice! 2
Bar 3:32 earth . . filled it with four-footed creatures; 1

fourfold 1. אַרְבַּע 2. τετραπλοῦς
2Sm 12: 6 and he shall restore the lamb fourfold 1
Lke 19: 8 I restore it fourfold. 2

fourscore 1. שְׁמֹנִים
Ps 90:10 or even by reason of strength fourscore; 1

foursquare 1. רבע 2. τετράγωνος
Ezk 40:47 and 100cubits broad, foursquare; 1
Rev 21:16 The city lies foursquare 2

fourteen 1. אַרְבַּע עֶשְׂרֵה 2. δεκατέσσαρες 3. δέκα τέσσαρες
Gen 31:41 I served you fourteen years for your two 1
46:22 who were born to Jacob-fourteen persons in all. 1
Num29:13 burnt offering . . two rams, fourteen male lambs 1
15 a tenth for each of the fourteen lambs; 1
17 second day . . fourteen male lambs a year old 1
20 third day . . fourteen male lambs a year old 1
23 fourth day . . fourteen male lambs a year old 1
26 fifth day . . fourteen male lambs a year old 1
29 sixth day . . fourteen male lambs a year old 1
32 seventh day . . fourteen male lambs a year old 1
Jos 15:36 fourteen cities with their villages. 1
18:28 fourteen cities with their villages. 1
1Ch 25: 5 God had given Heman fourteen sons 1
2Ch 13:21 took fourteen wives, and had 22 sons 1
Ezk 40:48 the breadth of the gate was fourteen cubits; 3
43:17 square, fourteen cubits long by fourteen broad 1
17 square, fourteen cubits long by fourteen broad 1
Mat 1:17 Abraham to David were fourteen generations 2
17 deportation to Babylon fourteen generations 2
17 to Babylon to the Christ fourteen generations. 2
2Co 12: 2 who fourteen years ago was caught up 2
Gal 2: 1 Then after fourteen years I went up again 2
Tob 8:19 a wedding feast . . which lasted fourteen days. 3
20 until the fourteen days . . were ended 3
10: 7 until the fourteen days . . had expired 3

fourteenth 1. אַרְבַּע עֶשְׂרֵה 2. אַרְבַּע עֶשְׂרֵה (A) 3. τεσσαρεσκαίδεκα 4. τεσσαρεσκαιδέκατος
Gen 14: 5 In the fourteenth year Ched-or-lao'mer 1
Exd 12: 6 keep it until the fourteenth day of this month 1
18 on the fourteenth day of the month at evening 1
Lev 23: 5 the first month, on the fourteenth day of the month 1
Num 9: 3 fourteenth day of this month, in the evening 1
5 first month, on the fourteenth day of the month 1
11 In the second month on the fourteenth day 1
28:16 fourteenth day of the first month is the LORD'S 1
Jos 5:10 passover on the fourteenth day of the month 1
2Kg 18:13 In the fourteenth year of King Hezeki'ah 1
1Ch 24:13 to Huppah, the fourteenth to Jesheb'e-ab 1
25:21 to the fourteenth, Mattithi'ah, his sons 1
2Ch 30:15 killed the passover lamb on the fourteenth day 1
35: 1 lamb on the fourteenth day of the first month. 1
Ezr 6:19 On the fourteenth day of the first month 2
Est 9:15 The Jews . . gathered also on the fourteenth day 1
17 and on the fourteenth day they rested 1
18 on the thirteenth day and on the fourteenth 1
19 Jews of . . hold the fourteenth day of the month 1
21 keep the fourteenth day of the month Adar 1
Isa 36: 1 In the fourteenth year of King Hezeki'ah 1
Ezk 40: 1 fourteenth year after the city was conquered 1
45:21 first month, on the fourteenth day of the month 1
Act 27:27 When the fourteenth night had come 4
33 Today is the fourteenth day 4
1Es 1: 1 the fourteenth day of the first month 4
7:10 the fourteenth day of the first month 4
AEs 10:13 on the fourteenth and fifteenth of that month 4
13: 6 on the fourteenth day of the twelfth month 4
3Mc 6:40 until the fourteenth day 3

fourth 1. אַרְבַּע 2. רְבִיעִי 3. רֶבַע 4. רְבִיעִי (A) 5. τέταρτος 6. quartus
Gen 1:19 was evening and there was morning, a fourth day 2
2:14 And the fourth river is the Euphra'tes. 2
15:16 shall come back here in the fourth generation; 2
Exd 20: 5 to the third and the fourth generation 3
28:20 the fourth row a beryl, an onyx, and a jasper; 2
34: 7 to the third and the fourth generation. 3
39:13 the fourth row, a beryl, an onyx, and a jasper; 2
Lev 19:24 in the fourth year all their fruit shall be holy 2
Num 7:30 On the fourth day Eli'zur . . of the men of Reuben 2
14:18 upon the third and upon the fourth generation.' 3
29:23 On the fourth day ten bulls, two rams, fourteen 2
Deu 5: 9 children to the third and fourth generation 3
Jos 19:17 The fourth lot came out for Is'sachar 2
Jdg 14:15 On the fourth day they said to Samson's wife 5
19: 5 on the fourth day they arose early in the morning 2
2Sm 3: 4 and the fourth, Adoni'jah the son of Haggith; 2
1Kg 6: 1 in the fourth year of Solomon's reign over Israel 2
37 In the fourth year the foundation . . was laid 2
22:41 began to reign . . in the fourth year of Ahab 1
2Kg 10:30 your sons of the fourth generation shall sit 2
15:12 sit upon the throne . . to the fourth generation. 2
18: 9 In the fourth year of King Hezeki'ah 2
25: 3 On the ninth day of the fourth month the famine •
1Ch 2:14 Nethan'el the fourth, Raddai the fifth 2
3: 2 the fourth Adoni'jah, whose mother was Haggith; 2
15 sons of Josi'ah . . the fourth Shallum. 2
8: 2 Nohah the fourth, and Rapha the fifth. 2
12:10 Mishman'nah fourth, Jeremiah fifth 2
23:19 sons of Hebron . . and Jekame'am the fourth. 2
24: 8 the third to Harim, the fourth to Se-o'rim 2
23 sons of Hebron . . Jeka-me'am the fourth. 2
25:11 fourth to Izri, his sons and his brethren, twelve; 2
26: 2 Meshelemi'ah had sons . . Jath'ni-el the fourth 2
4 O'bed-e'dom had sons . . Sachar the fourth 2
11 Tebali'ah the third, Zechari'ah the fourth 2
27: 7 As'ahel the brother of Jo'ab was fourth 2
7 As'ahel . . was fourth, for the fourth month 2
2Ch 3: 2 the second month of the fourth year of his reign. 1
20:26 On the fourth day they assembled in the Valley 2
Ezr 8:33 On the fourth day, within the house of our God 2
Neh 9: 3 read from . . the law . . for a fourth of the day; 2
Jer 25: 1 in the fourth year of Jehoi'akim the son of Josi'ah 2
28: 1 in the fifth month of the fourth year, Hanani'ah 2
36: 1 In the fourth year of Jehoi'akim the son of Josi'ah 2
39: 2 in the fourth month, on the ninth day of the month 2
45: 1 in the fourth year of Jehoi'akim the son of Josi'ah 2
46: 2 defeated in the fourth year of Jehoi'akim 2
51:59 to Babylon, in the fourth year of his reign. 2
52: 6 On the ninth day of the fourth month the famine 2
Ezk 1: 1 In the 30th year, in the fourth month 2
10:14 and the fourth the face of an eagle. 2
Dan 2:40 there shall be a fourth kingdom, strong as iron 4
3:25 appearance of the fourth is like a son of the gods. 4
7: 7 behold, a fourth beast, terrible and dreadful 4
19 know the truth concerning the fourth beast 4
23 Thus he said: 'As for the fourth beast, there 4
23 beast, there shall be a fourth kingdom on earth 4
11: 2 fourth shall be far richer than all of them; 2
Zec 6: 3 the fourth chariot dappled gray horses. 2
7: 1 In the fourth year of King Darius 1
1 fourth day of the ninth month, which is Chislev. 1
8:19 fast of the fourth month, and the fast of the fifth 2
Mat 14:25 in the fourth watch of the night he came to them 5
Mrk 6:48 about the fourth watch of the night he came 5
Rev 4: 7 the fourth living creature like a flying eagle. 5
6: 7 When he opened the fourth seal, I heard the voice 5
7 I heard the voice of the fourth living creature 5
8:12 The fourth angel blew his trumpet 5
16: 8 The fourth angel poured his bowl on the sun 5
21:19 every jewel . . the fourth emerald 5
2Es 6:45 On the fourth day thou didst command 6
7:84 The fourth way, they shall consider the torment 6
95 The fourth order, they understand the rest 6
11:40 You, the fourth that has come, have conquered 6
12:11 the fourth kingdom which appeared in a vision 6
Jdt 12:10 On the fourth day Holofernes held a banquet 5
AEs 11: 1 In the fourth year of the reign of Ptolemy 5
Sir 26: 5 of a fourth I am frightened 5
2Mc 7:13 they maltreated and tortured the fourth 5
3Mc 6:38 the fourth of Epeiph 5
4Mc 10:12 they dragged in the fourth, saying 5

fourth *See also* generation.

fowl 1. בַּרְבֻּרִים 2. עוֹף 3. צִפּוֹר 4. ὄρνις
Lev 7:26 eat no blood . . whether of fowl or of animal 2
1Kg 4:23 harts, gazelles, roebucks, and fatted fowl. 1
Neh 5:18 fowls likewise were prepared for me 3
4Mc 1:34 when we crave seafood and fowl and animals 4

fowler 1. יָקוֹשׁ 2. יָקוּשׁ 3. יקשׁ
Ps 91: 3 he will deliver you from the snare of the fowler 2
124: 7 escaped as a bird from the snare of the fowlers; 3
Prv 6: 5 like a bird from the hand of the fowler. 2
Jer 5:26 they lurk like fowlers lying in wait. 2
Hos 9: 8 yet a fowler's snare is on all his ways 1

fox 1. שׁוּעָל 2. ἀλώπηξ
Jdg 15: 4 Samson . . caught 300 foxes, and took torches; 1
5 he let the foxes go into the standing grain •
Neh 4: 3 if a fox goes up on it he will break down 1
Sng 2:15 Catch us the foxes . . that spoil the vineyards 1
15 foxes, the little foxes, that spoil the vineyards 1
Ezk 13: 4 Your prophets have been like foxes among ruins 1

Mat 8:20 Jesus said to him, “Foxes have holes 2
Lke 9:58 Jesus said to him, “Foxes have holes 2
13:32 he said to them, “Go and tell that fox, ‘Behold 2

fracture 1. שֶׁבֶר
Lev 24:20 fracture for fracture, eye for eye 1
20 fracture for fracture, eye for eye 1

fragile 1. εὔθραστος
Wis 15:13 he makes from earthy matter fragile vessels 1

more fragile 1. σαθρός
Wis 14: 1 a piece of wood more fragile than 1

fragment 1. מְכִתָּה 2. רְסִיס 3. κλάσμα
Isa 30:14 among its fragments not a sherd is found 1
Ams 6:11 the great house shall be smitten into fragments 2
Joh 6:12 Gather up the fragments left over 3
13 filled twelve baskets with fragments 3

fragrance 1. בֹּשֶׂם 2. זֵכֶר 3. מֶרְקָח 4. רֵיחַ 5. ἀτμίς 6. ὀσμή 7. odoramentum
Sng 1:12 the king was . . my nard gave forth its fragrance. 4
2:13 vines are in blossom; they give forth fragrance. 4
4:10 and the fragrance of your oils than any spice! 4
16 my garden, let its fragrance be wafted abroad. 1
5:13 like beds of spices, yielding fragrance. 3
7:13 The mandrakes give forth fragrance 4
Hos 14: 6 and his fragrance like Lebanon. 4
7 their fragrance shall be like the wine 2
Joh 12: 3 was filled with the fragrance of the ointment. 6
2Co 2:14 spreads the fragrance of the knowledge of him 6
16 to one a fragrance from death to death 6
16 to the other a fragrance from life to life 6
2Es 6:44 and odors of inexpressible fragrance 7
Sir 24:15 like the fragrance of frankincense 5
39:14 send forth fragrance like frankincense 6
14 Scatter the fragrance, and sing a hymn of praise; 6

fragrance *See also* send.

fragrant 1. לְרֵיחַ 2. סַם 3. εὐωδία 4. ὀσμὴ εὐωδίας 5. odor
Exd 25: 6 anointing oil and for the fragrant incense 2
30: 7 Aaron shall burn fragrant incense on it; 2
31:11 anointing oil and the fragrant incense 2
35: 8 anointing oil and for the fragrant incense 2
15 the anointing oil and the fragrant incense 2
28 anointing oil, and for the fragrant incense. 2
37:29 made . . the pure fragrant incense, blended 2
39:38 the anointing oil and the fragrant incense 2
40:27 burnt fragrant incense upon it; as the LORD had 2
Lev 4: 7 on the horns of the altar of fragrant incense 2
Num 4:16 charge of . . the fragrant incense 2
Ps 45: 8 your robes are all fragrant with myrrh and aloes *
Sng 1: 3 your anointing oils are fragrant 1
Eph 5: 2 a fragrant offering and sacrifice to God. 4
Php 4:18 a fragrant offering, a sacrifice acceptable 3
2Es 2:12 The tree . . shall give them fragrant perfume 5
Jdt 16:16 every sacrifice as a fragrant offering 3
Bar 5: 8 The woods and every fragrant tree have shaded 3

fragrant *See also* powder.

very fragrant 1. εὐώδης
3Mc 5:45 the very fragrant draughts of wine 1
7:16 crowned with all sorts of very fragrant flowers 1

frail 1. רַךְ
Gen 33:13 to him, “My lord knows that the children are frail 1

frame 1. יצר 2. יֵצֶר 3. מִסְגֶּרֶת 4. סַף 5. עֹצֶם 6. עֵרֶךְ 7. צמד 8. קֶרֶשׁ 9. שְׁלַבִּים 10. שָׁקוּף 11. שֶׁקֶף 12. συνίστημι
Exd 25:25 shall make around it a frame a handbreadth wide 3
25 make . . a molding of gold around the frame. 3
27 Close to the frame the rings shall lie, as holders 3
26:15 you shall make upright frames 8
16 Ten cubits shall be the length of a frame 8
16 a cubit and a half the breadth of each frame. 8
17 There shall be two tenons in each frame 8
17 for all the frames of the tabernacle. 8
18 You shall make the frames for the tabernacle 8
18 twenty frames for the south side; 8
19 bases . . you shall make under the twenty frames 8
19 two bases under one frame for its two tenons 8
19 two bases under another frame for its two tenons; 8
20 the tabernacle, on the north side twenty frames 8
21 forty bases of silver, two bases under one frame 8
21 and two bases under another frame; 8
22 tabernacle westward you shall make six frames. 8
23 you shall make two frames for corners 8
25 there shall be eight frames, with their bases 8
25 two bases under one frame, and two bases 8
25 and two bases under another frame. 8
26 five for the frames of the one side 8
27 five bars for the frames of the other side 8
27 five bars for the frames of the side 8
28 The middle bar, halfway up the frames, shall pass 8
29 You shall overlay the frames with gold 8
35:11 its hooks and its frames, its bars, its pillars 8
36:20 he made the upright frames for the tabernacle 8
21 Ten cubits was the length of a frame 8
21 a cubit and a half the breadth of each frame. 8
22 Each frame had two tenons, for fitting together; 8
22 he did this for all the frames of the tabernacle. 8
23 The frames for the tabernacle he made thus 8
23 made thus: twenty frames for the south side; 8
24 he made 40 bases of silver under the twenty frames 8
24 two bases under one frame for its two tenons 8
24 bases under another frame for its two tenons. 8
25 on the north side, he made twenty frames 8
26 bases of silver, two bases under one frame 8
26 and two bases under another frame. 8
27 for . . the tabernacle westward he made six frames. 8
28 he made two frames for corners 8
30 There were eight frames with their bases 8
30 sixteen bases, under every frame two bases. 8
31 he made bars of acacia wood, five for the frames 8
32 five bars for the frames of the other side 8
32 and five bars for the frames of the tabernacle 8
33 from end to end halfway up the frames. 8
34 he overlaid the frames with gold 8
37:12 he made around it a frame a handbreadth wide 3
12 made a molding of gold around the frame. 3
14 Close to the frame were the rings, as holders 3
39:33 all its utensils, its hooks, its frames, its bars 8
40:18 laid its bases, and set up its frames, and put in its 8
Num 3:36 charge . . was to be the frames of the tabernacle 8
4:31 charged to carry . . frames of the tabernacle 8
1Kg 6: 4 he made . . windows with recessed frames. 10
7: 5 windows had square frames, and window was 11
28 and the panels were set in the frames 9
29 on the panels that were set in the frames were 9
29 Upon the frames, both above and below the lions 9
2Kg 16:17 King Ahaz cut off the frames of the stands 3
Job 41:12 or his mighty strength, or his goodly frame. 6
Ps 50:19 your tongue frames deceit. 7
94:20 wicked rulers . . who frame mischief by statute? 1
103:14 knows our frame; he remembers that we are dust. 2
139:15 frame was not hidden . . when I was being made 5
Ezk 41:16 all three had windows with recessed frames. 4
3Mc 2:26 he framed evil reports in the various localities; 12

carrying frame 1. מוֹט
Num 4:10 put it upon the carrying frame. 1
12 put them on the carrying frame. 1

window frame 1. שָׁקוּף
1Kg 7: 4 There were window frames in three rows 1

frankincense 1. לְבֹנָה 2. λίβανος 3. λιβανωτός
Exd 30:34 Take . . sweet spices with pure frankincense 1
Lev 2: 1 oil upon it, and put frankincense on it 1
2 fine flour and oil, with all of its frankincense 1
15 oil upon it, and lay frankincense on it 1
16 burn . . the oil with all of its frankincense 1
5:11 and shall put no frankincense on it 1
6:15 with its oil and all the frankincense 1
24: 7 you shall put pure frankincense with each row 1
Num 5:15 no oil upon it and put no frankincense on it 1
Neh 13: 5 previously put the . . frankincense 1
9 with the cereal offering and the frankincense. 1
Sng 3: 6 of smoke, perfumed with myrrh and frankincense 1
4: 6 mountain of myrrh and the hill of frankincense. 1
14 with all trees of frankincense, myrrh and aloes 1
Isa 43:23 or wearied you with frankincense. 1
60: 6 They shall bring gold and frankincense 1
66: 3 who makes a memorial offering of frankincense 1
Jer 6:20 To what purpose does frankincense come to me 1
17:26 sacrifices, cereal offerings and frankincense 1
Mat 2:11 they offered him gifts, gold and frankincense 2
Rev 18:13 cinnamon, spice, incense, myrrh, frankincense 2
Sir 24:15 like the fragrance of frankincense 2
39:14 send forth fragrance like frankincense 2
3Mc 5: 2 large handfuls of frankincense 3
10 satiated with frankincense 2

frankincense *See also* mix.

fraud 1. מִרְמָה 2. πλάνη 3. circumventio
Ps 55:11 and fraud do not depart from its market place. 1
Zep 1: 9 who fill their master’s house with . . fraud. 1
Mat 27:64 the last fraud will be worse than the first. 2
Jas 5: 4 the wages . . which you kept back by fraud, cry out; *
2Es 7:23 proposed to themselves wicked frauds 3

free 1. בְּלֹא 2. חפש 3. חָפְשִׁי 4. נקה 5. נָקִי 6. נשׂא ראשׁ 7. עבר 8. עזב 9. פטר 10. רוד 11. αἴρω 12. ἀπαλλάσσω 13. ἀπολύω 14. δικαιόω 15. ἐκτός 16. ἐλεύθερος 17. ἐλευθερόω 18. λύσις 19. λύω 20. μή 21. libero
Gen 24: 8 then you will be free from this oath of mine; 4
41 then you will be free from my oath 4
41 give her to you, you will be free from my oath.’ 5
Exd 21: 2 in the seventh he shall go out free, for nothing. 3
5 my children; I will not go out free,’ 3
26 he shall let the slave go free for the eye’s sake. 3
27 shall let the slave go free for the tooth’s sake. 3
Lev 19:20 shall not be put to death, because she was not free 2
Num 5:19 be free from this water of bitterness 4
28 she shall be free and shall conceive children. 4
31 The man shall be free from iniquity, but the woman 4
Deu 15:12 in the seventh year you shall let him go free 3
13 when you let him go free from you 3
18 not seem hard to you, when you let him go free 3
24: 5 newly married . . shall be free at home one year 5
32:36 sees . . there is none remaining, bond or free. 8
1Sm 17:25 the king will . . make his father’s house free 3
1Kg 14:10 cut off . . every male, both bond and free in Israel 8
21:21 I . . will cut off from Ahab every male, bond or free 8
2Kg 9: 8 cut off . . every male, bond or free, in Israel. 8
14:26 for there was none left, bond or free 8
25:27 Evil-mero’dach . . graciously freed Jehoi’achin 6
1Ch 9:33 the singers . . free from other service 9
Job 3:19 the slave is free from his master. 3
39: 5 Who has let the wild ass go free? 3
Ps 17: 1 Give ear to my prayer from lips free of deceit! 1
81: 6 your hands were freed from the basket. 7
Isa 58: 6 to let the oppressed go free 3
Jer 2:31 We are free, we will come no more to thee’? 10
34: 9 that every one should set free his Hebrew slaves 3
10 covenant that every one would set free his slave 3
11 the male and female slaves they had set free 3
14 you must set him free from your service. 3
16 whom you had set free according to their desire 3
Mat 17:26 Jesus said to him, “Then the sons are free. 16
Lke 13:12 Woman, you are freed from your infirmity. 13
Joh 8:33 How is it that you say, ‘You will be made free’? 16
36 if the Son makes you free, you will be free indeed. 16
Act 13:39 by him every one that believes is freed 14
39 you could not be freed by the law of Moses. 14
Rom 6: 7 For he who has died is freed from sin. 14
20 you were free in regard to righteousness. 16
7: 3 But if her husband dies she is free from that law 16
1Co 7:22 Likewise he who was free when called 16
27 Are you bound to a wife? Do not seek to be free. 18
27 Are you free from a wife? Do not seek marriage. 19
39 she is free to be married to whom she wishes 16
9: 1 Am I not free? Am I not an apostle? 16
19 For though I am free from all men 16
12:13 Jews or Greeks, slaves or free 16
Gal 3:28 there is neither slave nor free 16
4:26 Jerusalem above is free, and she is our mother. 16
Eph 6: 8 whether he is a slave or free. 16
Rev 1: 5 To him who . . freed us from our sins by his blood 19
6:15 every one, slave and free, hid in the caves 16
13:16 both rich and poor, both free and slave 16
19:18 and the flesh of all men, both free and slave 16
1Es 3:19 of the slave and the free, of the poor and the rich. 16
9:13 until we are freed from the wrath of the Lord 19
2Es 11:46 that the whole earth, freed from your violence 21
Jdt 16:23 She set her maid free 16
Wis 12: 2 that they may be freed from wickedness 12
Sir 13:24 Riches are good if they are free from sin 20
1Mc 2:11 no longer free, she has become a slave. 16
8:18 to free themselves from the yoke 11
10:29 now I free you 13
33 I set free without payment 16
2Mc 2:22 freed the city 17
4:47 who would have been freed uncondemned 13
9:14 he was now declaring to be free; 16
11:25 that this nation also be free from disturbance 15
3Mc 7:20 they departed unharmed, free, and overjoyed 16
4Mc 8: 2 any who ate . . should be freed after eating 13
12: 9 they freed him at once. 19
14: 2 more royal than kings and freer than the free! 16
2 more royal than kings and freer than the free! 16

free *See also* gift, go, leave, make, part, range, shake, will.

free from anxiety 1. ἀμέριμνος
1Co 7:32 I want you to be free from anxieties 1
Wis 7:23 sure, free from anxiety, all-powerful 1

free from care 1. ἀμέριμνος
Wis 6:15 he . . will soon be free from care 1

free from love of money 1. ἀφιλάργυρος
Heb 13: 5 Keep your life free from love of money 1

free from reproach 1. ἀνεπίλημπτος
1Ti 6:14 unstained and free from reproach 1

free from sin 1. ἀναμάρτητος
2Mc 12:42 to keep themselves free from sin 1

free from tax 1. ἀφίημι
1Mc 10:31 let Jerusalem . . be holy and free from tax. 1

free from tribute 1. ἀφορολόγητος
1Mc 11:28 to free Judea . . from tribute 1

free man 1. חֹר 2. ἐλεύθερος 3. liber
Ecc 10:17 Happy . . when your king is the son of free men 1
Col 3:11 barbarian, Scyth’ian, slave, free man 2
1Pe 2:16 Live as free men, yet without using your freedom 2

2Es 10:22 our free men have suffered abuse 3
Sir 10:25 Free men will be at the service of a wise servant 2

free of charge 1. ἀδάπανος
1Co 9:18 I may make the gospel free of charge 1

free of obligation 1. נָקִי
Num32:22 return and be free of obligation to the LORD 1

set free 1. מֶרְחָב 2. נתר 3. פדה 4. פתח 5. שׁלח 6. ἀναλύω 7. ἀπολύω 8. ἀφίημι 9. ἐλευθερόω
Ps 44: 2 afflict the peoples, but them thou didst set free; 5
69:18 Draw near to me, redeem me, set me free 3
102:20 to set free those who were doomed to die; 4
105:20 the ruler of the peoples set him free; 4
118: 5 LORD answered me and set me free. 1
146: 7 The LORD sets the prisoners free; 2
Isa 45:13 he shall build my city and set my exiles free 5
Jer 34: 9 that every one should set free his Hebrew slaves 5
10 covenant that every one would set free his slave 5
10 they obeyed and set them free. 5
11 the male and female slaves they had set free 5
14 each of you must set free the fellow Hebrew 5
14 you must set him free from your service. 5
16 whom you had set free according to their desire 5
Zec 9:11 set your captives free from the waterless pit. 5
Act 26:32 This man could have been set free 7
Rom 6:18 and, having been set free from sin 9
22 But now that you have been set free from sin 9
8: 2 has set me free from the law of sin and death. 9
21 because the creation itself will be set free 9
Gal 5: 1 For freedom Christ has set us free 9
Jdt 16:23 She set her maid free 8
Wis 16:14 nor set free the imprisoned soul. 6
2Mc 1:27 set free those who are slaves among the Gentiles 9
10:21 by setting their enemies free 7

free woman 1. ἐλεύθερος
Gal 4:22 one by a slave and one by a free woman. 1
23 the son of the free woman through promise. 1
30 not inherit with the son of the free woman. 1
31 not . . of the slave but of the free woman. 1

freedman 1. ἀπελεύθερος 2. λιβερτῖνος
Act 6: 9 the synagogue of the Freedman 2
1Co 7:22 a slave is a freedman of the Lord 1

freedom 1. חֻפְשָׁה 2. ἐλευθερία 3. ἐλεύθερος 4. libertas
Lev 19:20 a woman . . not yet ransomed or given her freedom 1
1Co 7:21 if you can gain your freedom 3
2Co 3:17 where the Spirit of the Lord is, there is freedom. 2
Gal 2: 4 who slipped in to spy out our freedom 2
5: 1 For freedom Christ has set us free 2
13 For you were called to freedom, brethren 2
13 only do not use your freedom as an opportunity 2
1Pe 2:16 without using your freedom as a pretext for evil; 2
2Pe 2:19 They promise them freedom 2
1Es 4:49 in the interest of their freedom 2
53 should have their freedom 2
2Es 7:101 They shall have freedom for seven days 4
8:56 For they also received freedom 4
9:11 scorned my law while they still had freedom 4
Sir 7:21 do not withhold from him his freedom. 2
1Mc 14:26 established its freedom. 2
15: 7 I grant freedom to Jerusalem and the sanctuary. 3
3Mc 3:28 will be awarded his freedom. 2

freely 1. נְדָבָה 2. βούλομαι 3. μετὰ παρρησίας 4. παρρησιάζομαι 5. πολύς
Gen 2:16 You may freely eat of every tree of the garden; †
Deu 15:10 You shall give to him freely, and your heart †
1Sm 14:30 if the people had eaten freely today of the spoil †
Hos 14: 4 I will love them freely, for my anger has turned 1
Mrk 1:45 he went out and began to talk freely about it 5
Act 26:26 to him I speak freely 4
1Es 8:10 who freely choose to do so, may go with you 2
3Mc 7:12 freely and without royal authority 3
freely *See also* bestow, distribute, drink, give, move, offer.

freewill 1. ἑκούσιος
Jdt 4:14 the vows and freewill offerings of the people. 1
freewill *See also* offering.

freeze 1. לכד 2. ἀποστενόω 3. πήγνυμι
Job 38:30 the face of the deep is frozen. 1
AEs 15: 5 her heart was frozen with fear. 2
Sir 43:19 when it freezes, it becomes pointed thorns. 3
20 ice freezes over the water 3

freeze fast 1. יצק
Job 37:10 the broad waters are frozen fast. 1
frenzied *See* desire, urge.

frenzy 1. ἐμμανής 2. οἶστρος
Wis 14:23 hold frenzied revels with strange customs 1
4Mc 2: 3 he nullified the frenzy of the passions. 2

frequent 1. פרץ 2. πολλάκις 3. πυκνός 4. συναναστρέφω
1Sm 3: 1 was rare . . there was no frequent vision. 1
2Co 11:26 on frequent journeys, in danger from rivers 2
1Ti 5:23 your stomach and your frequent ailments. 3
Sir 41: 5 they frequent the haunts of the ungodly. 4

more frequent 1. πυκνός
2Mc 8: 8 he was pushing ahead with more frequent successes 1

frequently 1. προσκαρτερέω 2. πυκνός
Sus 1: 6 These men were frequently at Joakim's house 1
3Mc 4:12 the Jews' compatriots . . frequently went out in secret 2
7: 3 frequently urging us with malicious intent 2

fresh 1. חָדָשׁ 2. טָרִי 3. כַּרְמֶל 4. לַח 5. רַעֲנָן 6. γλυκύς 7. θερμός 8. καινός 9. iterum
Gen 30:37 Then Jacob took fresh rods of poplar and almond 4
Lev 23:14 eat neither bread nor grain parched or fresh 3
Num 6: 3 shall not drink . . or eat grapes, fresh or dried. 4
Jdg 15:15 he found a fresh jawbone of an ass, and put out his 2
16: 7 bind me with seven fresh bowstrings which have 4
8 brought her seven fresh bowstrings which had 4
Job 10:17 thou dost bring fresh hosts against me. •
29:20 glory fresh with me, and my bow ever new in my hand 1
Ps 92:10 thou hast poured over me fresh oil. 5
Mat 9:17 but new wine is put into fresh wineskins 8
Mrk 2:22 new wine is for fresh skins. 8
Lke 5:38 new wine must be put into fresh wineskins. 8
Jas 3:11 from the same opening fresh water and brackish? 6
12 No more can salt water yield fresh. 6
2Es 15:59 you shall come and suffer fresh afflictions 9
Tob 2:10 their fresh droppings fell into my open eyes 7
fresh *See also* ear, keep, leaf, obtain, water.

become fresh 1. רטפש 2. רפא
Job 33:25 let his flesh become fresh with youth; 1
Ezk 47: 8 the water will become fresh. 2
9 that the waters of the sea may become fresh; 2
11 its swamps and marshes will not become fresh; 2

freshet 1. אָפִיק נַחַל
Job 6:15 as a torrent-bed, as freshets that pass away 1
freshly *See* plucked.

fret 1. חרה 2. προσοχθίζω
Ps 37: 1 Fret not yourself because of the wicked 1
7 fret not yourself over him who prospers 1
8 Fret not yourself, it tends only to evil. 1
Prv 24:19 Fret not yourself because of evildoers 1
Sir 6:25 do not fret under her bonds. 2

fretful 1. כַּעַס
Prv 21:19 than with a contentious and fretful woman. 1

friend 1. אהב 2. אִישׁ 3. אַלּוּף 4. מֵרֵעַ 5. נכר 6. פְּלֹנִי אַלְמֹנִי 7. רֵעַ 8. רֵעֶה 9. רצה 10. שָׁלוֹם 11. שׁלם 12. ἑταῖρος 13. εὐνοέω 14. ἴδιος 15. συνήθης 16. φιλιάζω 17. φίλος 18. amicus 19. fidus
Gen 38:12 he and his friend Hirah the Adullamite. 7
20 Judah sent the kid by his friend the Adullamite 7
Exd 33:11 Moses face to face, as a man speaks to his friend. 7
Deu 13: 6 If . . your friend who is as your own soul, entices 7
Jdg 5:31 O LORD! But thy friends be like the sun as he rises 1
Rut 4: 1 Bo'az said, "Turn aside, friend; sit down here"; 6
1Sm 30:26 sent part . . to his friends, the elders of Judah 7
2Sm 3: 8 of Saul . . to his brothers, and to his friends 4
13: 3 But Amnon had a friend, whose name was Jon'adab 7
15:37 So Hushai, David's friend, came into the city 8
16:16 And when Hushai the Archite, David's friend, came 8
17 Is this your loyalty to your friend? 7
17 Why did you not go with your friend? 7
1Kg 4: 5 Zabud . . was priest and king's friend; 8
16:11 leave him a . . male of his kinsmen or his friends. 7
1Ch 27:33 and Hushai the Archite was the king's friend. 7
2Ch 20: 7 to the descendants of Abraham thy friend? 1
Est 5:10 he . . fetched his friends and his wife Zeresh. 1
14 his wife Zeresh and all his friends said to him 1
6:13 Haman told his wife Zeresh and all his friends 1
Job 2:11 when Job's three friends heard of all this evil 7
6:14 He who withholds kindness from a friend 7
27 and bargain over your friend. 7
12: 4 I am a laughingstock to my friends; 7
16:20 My friends scorn me; my eye pours out tears to God 7
17: 5 He who informs against his friends to get a share 7
19:21 Have pity on me, have pity on me, O you my friends 7
24:17 are friends with the terrors of deep darkness. 5
32: 3 he was angry also at Job's three friends 7
35: 4 I will answer you and your friends with you. 7
42: 7 against you and against your two friends; 7
10 Job, when he had prayed for his friends; 7
Ps 7: 4 if I have requited my friend with evil 11
15: 3 does no evil to his friend, nor takes up a reproach 7
35:14 as though I grieved for my friend or my brother; 7
38:11 My friends and companions stand aloof 1
50:18 If you see a thief, you are a friend of his; 9
55:20 stretched out his hand against his friends 10
88:18 Thou hast caused lover and friend to shun me; 7
Prv 14:20 but the rich has many friends. 1
17: 9 but he who repeats a matter alienates a friend. 3
17 A friend loves at all times 7
18:24 There are friends who pretend to be friends 7
24 There are friends who pretend to be friends •
24 friend who sticks closer than a brother. 1
19: 4 Wealth brings many new friends 7
4 but a poor man is deserted by his friend. 7
6 every one is a friend to a man who gives gifts. 7
7 how much more do his friends go far from him! 4
22:11 loves purity . . will have the king as his friend. 7
27: 6 Faithful are the wounds of a friend; 1
10 friend, and your father's friend, do not forsake; 7
10 friend, and your father's friend, do not forsake; 7
Sng 5: 1 Eat, O friends, and drink: drink deeply, O lovers! 7
16 This is my beloved and this is my friend 7
Isa 41: 8 Israel . . the offspring of Abraham, my friend; 1
Jer 3: 4 My father, thou art the friend of my youth 3
6:21 together, neighbor and friend shall perish. 7
13:21 whom you yourself have taught to be friends 3
20: 4 a terror to yourself and to all your friends. 1
6 you shall be buried, you and all your friends 1
Lam 1: 2 all her friends have dealt treacherously 7
Obd 1: 7 your trusted friends have set a trap under you 2
Mic 7: 5 have no confidence in a friend; 3
Zec 3: 8 you and your friends who sit before you 7
13: 6 The wounds I received in the house of my friends. 1
Mat 5:25 Make friends quickly with your accuser 13
11:19 a friend of tax collectors and sinners! 17
20:13 Friend, I am doing you no wrong 12
22:12 and he said to him, 'Friend, how did you get in here 12
26:50 Jesus said to him, "Friend, why are you here? 12
Mrk 5:19 Go home to your friends •
Lke 7: 6 the centurion sent friends to him, saying to him 17
34 a friend of tax collectors and sinners!' 17
11: 5 Which of you who has a friend will go to him 17
5 go to him at midnight and say to him, 'Friend 17
6 a friend of mine has arrived on a journey 17
8 because he is his friend 17
12: 4 I tell you, my friends, do not fear those who kill 17
14:10 'Friend, go up higher' 17
12 do not invite your friends or your brothers 17
15: 6 he calls together his friends and his neighbors 17
9 she calls together her friends and neighbors 17
29 that I might make merry with my friends. 17
16: 9 make friends . . by means of unrighteous mammon 17
21:16 parents and brothers and kinsmen and friends 17
23:12 Herod and Pilate became friends with each other 17
Joh 3:29 friend of the bridegroom . . rejoices greatly 17
11:11 Our friend Laz'arus has fallen asleep 17
15:13 that a man lay down his life for his friends. 17
14 You are my friends if you do what I command you. 17
15 I have called you friends 17
19:12 you are not Caesar's friend 17
Act 4:23 they went to their friends 14
10:24 called together his kinsmen and close friends. 17
19:31 some of the A'si-archs also, who were friends of his 17
24:23 none of his friends should be prevented 14
27: 3 gave him leave to go to his friends 17
Jas 2:23 and he was called the friend of God. 17
4: 4 whoever wishes to be a friend of the world 17
3Jn 1:15 The friends greet you. Greet the friends 17
15 Greet the friends, every one of them. 17
1Es 3:22 they forget to be friendly with friends 17
8:11 I and the seven friends who are my counselors 17
13 gifts . . which I and my friends have vowed 17
26 his counselors and all his friends and nobles. 17
2Es 5: 9 and all friends shall conquer one another 18
6:24 At that time friends shall make war on friends 18
24 At that time friends shall make war on friends 18
7:103 or friends for those who are most dear. ‡
104 or a friend his dearest friend, to be ill or sleep 19
104 or a friend his dearest friend, to be ill or sleep •
AEs 16: 5 the persuasion of friends 17
Wis 1:16 summoned death; considering him a friend 17
7:27 makes them friends of God, and prophets; 17
Sir 6: 1 do not become an enemy instead of a friend 17
5 A pleasant voice multiplies friends 17
7 When you gain a friend, gain him through testing 17
8 a friend who is such at his own convenience 17
9 there is a friend who changes into an enemy 17
10 there is a friend who is a table companion 17
13 be on guard toward your friends. 17
14 A faithful friend is a sturdy shelter 17
15 nothing so precious as a faithful friend 17
16 A faithful friend is an elixir of life 17
7:12 nor do the like to a friend. 17
18 Do not exchange a friend for money 17
9:10 Forsake not an old friend 17
10 A new friend is like new wine 17
12: 8 A friend will not be known in prosperity 17
9 even his friend will separate from him. 17
13:21 When a rich man totters, he is steadied by friends 17
21 he is even pushed away by friends. 17
14:13 Do good to a friend before you die 17
19: 8 With friend or foe do not report it 17
13 Question a friend, perhaps he did not do it 17

15 Question a friend, for often it is slander 17
20:16 A fool will say, "I have no friend 17
23 A man may for shame make promises to a friend 17
22:20 one who reviles a friend 17
21 have drawn your sword against a friend 17
22 have opened your mouth against your friend 17
22 in these cases any friend will flee. 17
25 I will not be ashamed to protect a friend 17
27:16 he will never find a congenial friend. 17
17 Love your friend and keep faith with him 17
28: 9 a sinful man will disturb friends 17
29:10 for the sake of a brother or a friend 17
30: 3 will glory in him in the presence of friends. 17
6 one to repay the kindness of his friends. 17
33: 6 A stallion is like a mocking friend 17
19 To son or wife, to brother or friend 17
37: 1 Every friend will say, "I too am a friend 17
1 Every friend will say, "I too am a friend 16
1 some friends are friends only in name. 17
1 some friends are friends only in name. 17
2 when a companion and friend turns to enmity? 17
4 rejoice in the happiness of a friend 17
5 help a friend for their stomach's sake 17
6 Do not forget a friend in your heart 17
40:23 A friend or a companion never meets one amiss 17
41:18 of unjust dealing, before your partner or friend; 17
22 abusive words, before friends 17
42: 3 of dividing the inheritance of friends; 12
Bel 1: 2 was the most honored of his friends. 17
1Mc 2:18 you . . will be numbered among the friends of the king 17
39 When Mattathias and his friends learned of it 17
45 Mattathias and his friends went about 17
3:38 mighty men among the friends of the king 17
6:10 So he called all his friends and said to them 17
14 Then he called for Philip, one of his friends 17
28 He assembled all his friends 17
7: 6 his brothers have destroyed all your friends 17
8 the king chose Bacchides, one of the king's friends 17
15 We will not seek to injure you or your friends. 17
8:12 with their friends and those who rely on them 17
20 we may be enrolled as your allies and friends. 17
31 made your yoke heavy upon our friends and allies 17
9:26 They sought and searched for the friends of Judas 17
28 Then all the friends of Judas assembled and said 17
35 begged the Nabateans, who were his friends 17
39 the bridegroom came out with his friends 17
10:16 Come now, we will make him our friend and ally. 17
19 a mighty warrior and worthy to be our friend. 17
20 you are to be called the king's friend 17
60 he gave them and their friends silver and gold 17
65 and enrolled him among his chief friends 17
11:26 in the presence of all his friends. 17
27 to be regarded as one of his chief friends. 17
33 To the nation of the Jews, who are our friends 17
57 and make you one of the friends of the king. 17
12:14 annoy you and our other allies and friends 17
43 commended him to all his friends 17
43 commanded his friends and his troops to obey him 17
13:36 Simon, the high priest and friend of kings 17
14:39 he made him one of the king's friends 17
40 the Jews were addressed by the Romans as friends 17
15:17 envoys of the Jews have come to us as our friends 17
28 He sent to him Athenobius, one of his friends 17
32 So Athenobius the friend of the king came 17
2Mc 1:14 together with his friends 17
3:31 Quickly some of Heliodorus' friends asked Onias 15
7:24 he would take him for his friend 17
8: 9 one of the king's chief friends 17
10:13 he was accused before Eupator by the king's friends 17
11:14 constraining him to be their friend. 17
14:11 the rest of the king's friends 17
3Mc 2:23 both friends and bodyguards . . dragged him out 17
26 many of his friends . . followed his will. 17
3:10 some of their neighbors and friends 17
5: 3 those of his friends and of the army 17
19 with the corroboration of his friends 17
26 while the king was receiving his friends 17
29 Hermon and all the king's friends pointed out 17
34 The king's friends . . sullenly slipped away 17
44 the friends and officers departed with great joy 17
6:23 angrily threatened his friends, saying 17
7: 3 Certain of our friends 17
4Mc 2:13 It is sovereign over the relationship of friends 17
13 one rebukes friends when they act wickedly. •
12: 5 if you yield to persuasion you will be my friend 17
8 all his friends that are with him. 17

bosom friend 1. אִישׁ שָׁלוֹם
Ps 41: 9 Even my bosom friend in whom I trusted 1

close friend 1. אַלּוּף 2. ידע
Job 19:14 My kinsfolk and my close friends have failed me; 2
Prv 16:28 whisperer separates close friends. 1

familiar friend 1. אֱנוֹשׁ שָׁלוֹם 2. ידע
2Kg 10:11 all his great men, and his familiar friends 2
Ps 55:13 you, my equal, my companion, my familiar friend. 2
Jer 20:10 Let us denounce him!" say all my familiar friends 1

intimate friend 1. מוֹדָע 2. מַת סוֹד
Job 19:19 All my intimate friends abhor me 2
Prv 7: 4 call insight your intimate friend; 1

trusted friend 1. אִישׁ שָׁלוֹם
Jer 38:22 saying, 'Your trusted friends have deceived you 1

friendly 1. שָׁלֵם 2. εἰρηνικός 3. μετ' εἰρήνης 4. φιλιάζω 5. φίλος
Gen 34:21 These men are friendly with us; let them dwell 1
Heb 11:31 she had given friendly welcome to the spies. 3
1Es 3:22 they forget to be friendly with friends 4
1Mc 5:48 Judas sent them this friendly message 2
3Mc 7: 7 the friendly and firm goodwill 5

friends *See* family.

friendship 1. סוֹד 2. שָׁלוֹם 3. φιλία
1Ch 12:17 If you have come to me in friendship to help me 2
Job 29: 4 when the friendship of God was upon my tent; 1
Ps 25:14 friendship of the LORD is for those who fear him 1
Jas 4: 4 friendship with the world is enmity with God? 3
Wis 7:14 those who get it obtain friendship with God 3
8:18 in friendship with her, pure delight 3
Sir 6:17 directs his friendship aright 3
22:20 will break off the friendship. 3
21 a renewal of friendship is possible. •
25: 1 friendship between neighbors 3
27:18 destroyed the friendship of your neighbor. 3
1Mc 8: 1 they pledged friendship to those who came to them 3
12 they have kept friendship. 3
17 to Rome to establish friendship and alliance 3
10:20 to take our side and keep friendship with us. 3
23 gotten ahead of us in forming a friendship 3
26 have continued your friendship with us 3
54 let us establish friendship with one another 3
12: 1 to confirm and renew the friendship with them. 3
3 to renew the former friendship and alliance 3
8 a clear declaration of alliance and friendship. 3
10 renew our brotherhood and friendship with you 3
16 sent them to Rome to renew our former friendship 3
14:18 to renew with him the friendship and alliance 3
22 come to us to renew their friendship with us. 3
15:17 to renew our ancient friendship and alliance. 3
2Mc 4:11 who went on the mission to establish friendship 3
6:22 on account of his old friendship with them. 3
4Mc 8: 5 to yield to me and enjoy my friendship. 3

friendship *See also* make, pledge.

fright 1. ἐκφοβέω
Wis 11:19 the mere sight of them could kill by fright. 1

frighten 1. בעת 2. חפז 3. ירא 4. ערץ 5. דחל (A) 6. δειλόομαι 7. δέω 8. ἐκθαμβέω 9. ἐκφοβέω 10. ἔμφοβος 11. καταπλήσσω 12. πτύρω 13. φοβέω 14. paveo
Jos 1: 9 be not frightened, neither be dismayed; 4
2Ch 32:18 they shouted it . . to frighten and terrify them 3
Neh 6: 9 For they all wanted to frighten us, thinking 3
Job 13:25 Wilt thou frighten a driven leaf 4
18:11 Terrors frighten him on every side, and chase him 1
40:23 if the river is turbulent he is not frightened; 2
Dan 2:31 its appearance was frightening. 5
8:17 came, I was frightened and fell upon my face. 1
Lke 24: 5 as they were frightened 10
37 they were startled and frightened 10
Joh 6:19 They were frightened 13
2Co 10: 9 seem to be frightening you with letters. 9
Php 1:28 not frightened in anything by your opponents. 12
2Es 10:25 so that I was too frightened to approach her 14
Wis 17: 9 For even if nothing disturbing frightened them 13
Sir 26: 5 of a fourth I am frightened 7
30: 9 Pamper a child, and he will frighten you 8
1Mc 4:21 they were greatly frightened 6
9: 6 they were greatly frightened 13
2Mc 8:16 exhorted them not to be frightened by the enemy 11

frighten away 1. חרד
Deu 28:26 there shall be no one to frighten them away. 1
Jer 7:33 and none will frighten them away. 1

frightening *See* mien.

frightful 1. φοβερός
3Mc 5:45 had been equipped with frightful devices 1

fringe 1. κράσπεδον
Mat 9:20 touched the fringe of his garment; 1
14:36 they might only touch the fringe of his garment 1
23: 5 and their fringes long 1
Mrk 6:56 touch even the fringe of his garment 1
Lke 8:44 touched the fringe of his garment 1

fro 1. שׁוב
Ezk 1:14 And the living creatures darted to and fro 1
Zec 7:14 was desolate, so that no one went to and fro 1
9: 8 as a guard, so that none shall march to and fro; 1

fro *See also* go, move, run, rush, swing, to, toss.

frog 1. צְפַרְדֵּעַ 2. βάτραχος
Exd 8: 2 behold, I will plague all your country with frogs; 1
3 Nile shall swarm with frogs which shall come up 1
4 the frogs shall come up on you and on your people 1
5 cause frogs to come upon the land of Egypt!' 1
6 the frogs came up and covered the land of Egypt. 1
7 magicians . . and brought frogs upon the land 1
8 Entreat the LORD to take away the frogs from me 1
9 entreat . . that the frogs be destroyed from you 1
11 The frogs shall depart from you and your houses 1
12 and Moses cried to the LORD concerning the frogs 1
13 the frogs died out of the houses and courtyards 1
Ps 78:45 devoured them, and frogs, which destroyed them. 1
105:30 Their land swarmed with frogs 1
Rev 16:13 I saw . . three foul spirits like frogs; 2
Wis 19:10 the river spewed out vast numbers of frogs. 2

from *See* abstain, part.

frond of palm 1. φοῖνιξ
2Mc 10: 7 bearing . . also fronds of palm 1

front 1. אֶל 2. אֶל מוּל 3. אֶל מוּל פָּנִים 4. גַּבַּחַת 5. לְנֹכַח 6. לְפִי 7. לִפְנֵי 8. מוּל 9. מוּל פְּנֵי 10. מִחוּץ 11. מִמּוּל פְּנֵי 12. נֹכַח פָּנִים 13. עַל 14. עַל פְּנֵי 15. פָּנִים 16. קדם 17. קֶדֶם 18. ראשׁ 19. רִאשׁוֹן 20. לָקֳבֵל (A) 21. ἀπέναντι 22. ἔμπροσθεν 23. ἐμπρόσθιος 24. ἐναντίος 25. κατὰ πρόσωπον 26. κατέναντι 27. πρό 28. προάγω 29. πρόσωπον
Gen 18: 2 behold, three men stood in front of him. 13
30:38 set the rods . . in front of the flocks 5
39 the flocks bred in front of the rods 1
33: 2 he put the maids with their children in front 19
Exd 14: 2 turn back and encamp in front of Pi-ha-hi'roth 7
2 encamp . . in front of Ba'al-ze'phon; 7
9 at the sea, by Pi-ha-hi'roth, in front of Ba'al-ze'phon. 7
25:37 to give light upon the space in front of it. 15
26: 9 you shall double over at the front of the tent. 15
27:13 The breadth of the court on the front to the east 17
28:25 and so attach it in front to the shoulder-pieces 9
27 attach them in front to the lower part of the two 9
37 it shall be on the front of the turban. 9
38:13 for the front of the east, 50 cubits. 17
39:18 they attached it in front to the shoulder-pieces 3
20 and attached them in front to the lower part 11
Lev 4: 6 in front of the veil of the sanctuary 15
17 before the LORD in front of the veil 15
6:14 before the LORD, in front of the altar 15
8: 9 on the turban, in front, he set the golden plate 9
13:55 the leprous spot is on the back or on the front 4
16:14 sprinkle it . . on the front of the mercy seat 15
Num 8: 2 shall give light in front of the lampstand. 9
3 its lamps to give light in front of the lampstand 3
16:43 Moses and Aaron came to the front of the tent 15
19: 4 toward the front of the tent of meeting 12
Jos 8:33 Israel . . half of them in front of Mount Ger'izim 2
33 half . . and half of them in front of Mount Ebal 2
Jdg 18:21 putting . . and the goods in front of them. 7
1Sm 14: 5 one crag rose on the north in front of Michmash 8
5 and the other on the south in front of Geba. 8
17:41 with his shield-bearer in front of him. 7
24: 2 seek David . . in front of the Wildgoats' Rocks. 14
2Sm 10: 9 was set against him both in front and in the rear 15
1Kg 6: 3 The vestibule in front of the nave of the house 14
3 and ten cubits deep in front of the house. 14
17 the nave in front of the inner sanctuary 7
21 he drew chains . . in front of the inner sanctuary 7
7: 6 there was a porch in front with pillars 14
9 costly stones . . sawed with saws, back and front 10
2Kg 16:14 altar . . he removed from the front of the house 15
1Ch 19:10 the battle was set against him both in front 15
2Ch 3: 4 The vestibule in front of the nave of the house 15
15 In front of the house he made two pillars 7
17 He set up the pillars in front of the temple 14
13:13 thus his troops were in front of Judah 7
15: 8 altar . . in front of the vestibule of the house 7
Est 2:11 Mor'decai walked in front of the court 7
4: 6 open square of the city in front of the king's gate 7
Ps 68:25 the singers in front, the minstrels last 16
Prv 8: 3 beside the gates in front of the town 6
Ezk 1:10 each had the face of a man in front; •
2:10 and it had writing on the front and on the back 15
10:11 but in whatever direction the front wheel faced 18
40:15 From the front of the gate at the entrance 15
17 30 chambers fronted on the pavement. •
19 distance from the inner front of the lower gate 15
19 outer front of the inner court, 100 cubits. 15
47 and the altar was in front of the temple. 7
41:14 also the breadth of the east front of the temple 15
21 in front of the holy place was something 15
25 canopy of wood in front of the vestibule 15
42:11 with a passage in front of them; 15
44: 4 by way of the north gate to the front of the temple; 15
Dan 5: 1 drank wine in front of the 1,000. 20
Jol 2:20 drive . . his front into the eastern sea 15
Lke 18:39 those who were in front rebuked him 28
Act 14:13 whose temple was in front of the city 27
18:17 and beat him in front of the tribunal 22

Rev 4: 6 creatures, full of eyes in front and behind 22
Jdt 2:25 fronting toward Arabia. 25
3: 9 fronting the great ridge of Judea; 21
Sir 26:12 so will she sit in front of every post 26
40: 6 like one who has escaped from the battle-front; 29
1Mc 1:22 the gold decoration on the front of the temple 25
4:57 They decorated the front of the temple 25
9:45 For look! the battle is in front of us and behind us; 24
13:27 with polished stone at the front and back. 22
2Mc 3:25 struck at him with its front hoofs 23
3Mc 4:11 the hippodrome . . in front of the city 27

front of tent 1. *προσκήνιον*

Jdt 10:22 he came forward to the front of the tent 1

frontier 1. גְּבוּל 2. מוּל 3. קָצֶה 4. *ὅριον*

Deu 2:19 when you approach the frontier of the sons of Ammon 2
Jos 22:11 an altar at the frontier of the land of Canaan 2
2Kg 3:21 were called out, and were drawn up at the frontier. 1
Ezk 25: 9 the flank of Moab from the cities on its frontier 3
Jdt 15: 4 to all the frontiers of Israel 4

frontlet 1. טוֹטָפוֹת

Exd 13:16 shall be as . . frontlets between your eyes; 1
Deu 6: 8 they shall be as frontlets between your eyes. 1
11:18 they shall be as frontlets between your eyes. 1

frost 1. חֲנָמֵל 2. קִיטוֹר 3. קֶרַח 4. *εὔδιον* 5. *παγετός* 6. *πάχνη* 7. gelu

Ps 78:47 vines with hail, and their sycamores with frost. 1
148: 8 fire and hail, snow and frost, stormy wind 2
Jer 36:30 to the heat by day and the frost by night. 3
Zec 14: 6 that day there shall be neither cold nor frost. *
2Es 7:41 or summer or spring or heat or winter or frost 7
Wis 16:29 will melt like wintry frost 6
Sir 3:15 as frost in fair weather, your sins will melt away. 4
Bar 2:25 cast out to the heat of day and the frost of night. 5
Aza 1:50 Bless the Lord, frosts and snows 6

fruit 1. יְבוּל 2. יְגִיעַ 3. לֶחֶם 4. מַאֲכָל 5. נִיב 6. פְּרִי 7. קַיִץ 8. תְּבוּאָה 9. תְּנוּבָה 10. אֵב (A) 11. *γένημα* 12. *καρπός* 13. *ὀπώρα* 14. fructus

Gen 1:11 earth put forth . . fruit trees bearing fruit 6
11 earth put forth . . fruit trees bearing fruit 6
12 and trees bearing fruit in which is their seed 6
29 given . . every tree with seed in its fruit; 6
3: 2 may eat of the fruit of the trees of the garden; 6
3 God said, 'You shall not eat of the fruit of the tree 6
6 make one wise, she took of its fruit and ate; 6
12 The woman . . gave me fruit of the tree, and I ate. *
4: 3 Cain brought to the LORD an offering of the fruit 6
30: 2 withheld from you the fruit of the womb? 6
Exd 10:15 they ate . . all the fruit of the trees 6
23:16 gather in from the field the fruit of your labor. *
Lev 19:23 then you shall count their fruit as forbidden 6
24 in the fourth year all their fruit shall be holy 6
25 But in the fifth year you may eat of their fruit 6
23:40 you shall take . . fruit of goodly trees 6
25: 3 prune your vineyard, and gather in its fruit 8
19 The land will yield its fruit, and you will eat 6
21 that it will bring forth fruit for three years 8
26: 4 the trees of the field shall yield their fruit 6
20 the trees of the land shall not yield their fruit 6
27:30 seed of the land or of the fruit of the trees 6
Num13:20 bring some of the fruit of the land. 6
26 showed them the fruit of the land. 6
27 flows with milk and honey, and this is its fruit. 6
Deu 1:25 took in their hands some of the fruit of the land 6
7:13 also bless the fruit of your body and the fruit 6
13 also bless . . the fruit of your ground 6
11:17 no rain, and the land yield no fruit, and you perish 1
26: 2 take . . first of all the fruit of the ground 6
10 now I bring the first of the fruit of the ground 6
28: 4 Blessed shall be the fruit of your body 6
4 Blessed shall be . . the fruit of your ground 6
4 Blessed shall be . . the fruit of your beasts 6
11 make you abound in . . the fruit of your body 6
11 make you abound in . . the fruit of your cattle 6
11 make you abound in . . the fruit of your ground 6
18 Cursed shall be the fruit of your body 6
18 Cursed shall be . . the fruit of your ground 6
33 nation . . shall eat up the fruit of your ground 6
42 All your trees and the fruit of your ground 6
51 eat . . of your cattle and the fruit of your ground 6
30: 9 prosperous in . . the fruit of your body 6
9 prosperous in . . the fruit of your cattle 6
9 prosperous in . . the fruit of your ground; 6
33:14 with the choicest fruits of the sun 8
Jos 5:12 Israel . . ate of the fruit of the land of Canaan 8
24:13 you eat the fruit of vineyards and oliveyards *
Jdg 9:11 Shall I leave my sweetness and my good fruit 9
2Kg 19:29 sow . . and plant vineyards, and eat their fruit. 6
30 again take root downward, and bear fruit upward; 6
Neh 9:25 possession of . . orchards and fruit trees 4
36 fathers to enjoy its fruit and its good gifts 6
10:35 bring . . first fruits of all fruit of every tree 6
37 bring . . fruit of every tree, the wine and the oil 6
Ps 1: 3 a tree . . that yields its fruit in its season 6
72:16 may its fruit be like Lebanon; and may men blossom 6
78:46 the fruit of their labor to the locust. *
80:12 so that all who pass along the way pluck its fruit? *
104:13 earth is satisfied with the fruit of thy work. 6
105:35 which . . ate up the fruit of their ground. 6
44 took possession of the fruit of the peoples' toil *
109:11 may strangers plunder the fruits of his toil! *
127: 3 fruit of the womb a reward. 6
128: 2 You shall eat the fruit of the labor of your hands; *
148: 9 fruit trees and all cedars! 6
Prv 1:31 therefore they shall eat the fruit of their way 6
8:19 My fruit is better than gold, even fine gold 6
11:30 The fruit of the righteous is a tree of life 6
12:14 fruit of his words a man is satisfied with good 6
13: 2 From the fruit of his mouth a good man eats good 6
14:14 perverse man . . filled with the fruit of his ways *
14 good man with the fruit of his deeds. *
18:20 From the fruit of his mouth a man is satisfied; 6
21 those who love it will eat its fruits. 6
27:18 He who tends a fig tree will eat its fruit 6
31:16 fruit of her hands she plants a vineyard. 6
31 Give her of the fruit of her hands 6
Ecc 2: 5 and planted in them all kinds of fruit trees. 6
Sng 2: 3 and his fruit was sweet to my taste. 6
4:13 an orchard . . with all choicest fruits 6
16 come to his garden, and eat its choicest fruits. 6
8:11 bring for its fruit 1,000 pieces 6
12 and the keepers of the fruit 200. 6
Isa 3:10 for they shall eat the fruit of their deeds. 6
4: 2 the fruit of the land shall be the pride and glory 6
13:18 they will have no mercy on the fruit of the womb; 6
14:29 and its fruit will be a flying serpent. 6
16: 9 upon your fruit and your harvest the battle 7
27: 6 fill the whole world with fruit. 9
9 the full fruit of the removal of his sin 6
32:10 vintage . . fail, the fruit harvest will not come. *
37:30 and plant vineyards, and eat their fruit. 6
31 take root downward, and bear fruit upward; 6
53:11 he shall see the fruit of the travail of his soul *
57:18 creating for his mourners the fruit of the lips. 5
65:21 shall plant vineyards and eat their fruit. 6
Jer 2: 7 into a plentiful land to enjoy its fruits 6
6:19 upon this people, the fruit of their devices 6
7:20 the trees of the field and the fruit of the ground; 6
11:16 A green olive tree, fair with goodly fruit'; 6
19 Let us destroy the tree with its fruit 3
12: 2 they take root; they grow and bring forth fruit; 6
17: 8 for it does not cease to bear fruit. 6
10 according to the fruit of his doings. 6
21:14 punish you according to the fruit of your doings 6
31: 5 planters shall plant, and shall enjoy the fruit. *
32:19 and according to the fruit of his doings; 6
Lam 4: 9 stricken by want of the fruits of the field. 9
Ezk 17: 8 and bear fruit, and become a noble vine. 6
23 that it may bring forth boughs and bear fruit 6
19:12 east wind dried it up; its fruit was stripped off; 6
14 And fire . . has consumed its branches and fruit 6
23:29 and take away all the fruit of your labor 2
25: 4 they shall eat your fruit 6
34:27 the trees of the field shall yield their fruit 6
36: 8 and yield your fruit to my people Israel; 6
30 I will make the fruit of the tree and the increase 6
47:12 leaves will not wither nor their fruit fail 6
12 Their fruit will be for food 6
Dan 4:12 Its leaves were fair and its fruit abundant 10
14 strip off its leaves and scatter its fruit; 10
21 whose leaves were fair and its fruit abundant 10
Hos 9:16 their root is dried up, they shall bear no fruit. 6
10: 1 a luxuriant vine that yields its fruit. 6
1 The more his fruit increased 6
12 reap the fruit of steadfast love; 12
13 you have eaten the fruit of lies. 6
14: 2 and we will render the fruit of our lips. 12
8 from me comes your fruit. 6
Jol 2:22 the tree bears its fruit 6
Ams 2: 9 I destroyed his fruit above, and his roots 6
6:12 and the fruit of righteousness into wormwood 6
9:14 and they shall make gardens and eat their fruit. 6
Mic 6: 7 give . . the fruit of my body for the sin of my soul? 6
7:13 be desolate . . for the fruit of their doings. 6
Hab 3:17 fig tree do not blossom, nor fruit be on the vines 1
Zec 8:12 sowing of peace; the vine shall yield its fruit 6
Mal 3:11 that it will not destroy the fruits of your soil; 6
Mat 3: 8 Bear fruit that befits repentance 12
10 tree therefore that does not bear good fruit 12
7:16 You will know them by their fruits. 12
17 So, every sound tree bears good fruit 12
17 but the bad tree bears evil fruit. 12
18 A sound tree cannot bear evil fruit 12
18 nor can a bad tree bear good fruit. 12
19 Every tree that does not bear good fruit is cut 12
20 Thus you will know them by their fruits. 12
12:33 Either make the tree good, and its fruit good 12
33 or make the tree bad, and its fruit bad 12
33 for the tree is known by its fruit. 12
21:19 May no fruit ever come from you again! 12
34 When the season of fruit drew near 12
34 to get his fruit; 12
41 who will give him the fruits in their seasons. 12
43 given to a nation producing the fruits of it. 12
26:29 I shall not drink again of this fruit of the vine 11
Mrk 11:14 May no one ever eat fruit from you again. 12
12: 2 some of the fruit of the vineyard. 12
14:25 I shall not drink again of the fruit of the vine 11
Lke 1:42 blessed is the fruit of your womb! 12
3: 8 Bear fruits that befit repentance 12
9 every tree . . that does not bear good fruit 12
6:43 For no good tree bears bad fruit 12
43 nor again does a bad tree bear good fruit; 12
44 for each tree is known by its own fruit 12
8:14 their fruit does not mature. *
13: 6 he came seeking fruit on it and found none. 12
7 I have come seeking fruit on this fig tree 12
9 if it bears fruit next year, well and good 12
20:10 give him some of the fruit of the vineyard 12
22:18 I shall not drink of the fruit of the vine 11
Joh 4:36 and gathers fruit for eternal life 12
12:24 if it dies, it bears much fruit. 12
15: 2 Every branch of mine that bears no fruit 12
2 every branch that does bear fruit he prunes 12
2 he prunes, that it may bear more fruit. 12
4 As the branch cannot bear fruit by itself 12
5 he it is that bears much fruit 12
8 that you bear much fruit 12
16 that you should go and bear fruit 12
16 that your fruit should abide 12
1Co 9: 7 without eating any of its fruit 12
Gal 5:22 the fruit of the Spirit is love, joy, peace 12
Eph 5: 9 for the fruit of light is found in all that is good 12
Php 1:11 filled with the fruits of righteousness 12
4:17 I seek the fruit which increases to your credit. 12
Heb 12:11 it yields the peaceful fruit of righteousness 12
13:15 the fruit of lips that acknowledge his name. 12
Jas 3:17 wisdom . . is . . full of mercy and good fruits 12
5: 7 farmer waits for the precious fruit of the earth 12
18 and the earth brought forth its fruit. 12
Rev 18:14 The fruit for which thy soul longed has gone 13
22: 2 the tree of life with its twelve kinds of fruit 12
2 tree of life . . yielding its fruit each month; 12
2Es 2:18 twelve trees loaded with various fruits 14
3:20 so that thy law might bring forth fruit in them. 14
4:31 how much fruit of ungodliness 14
6:28 the truth, which has been so long without fruit 14
44 For immediately fruit came forth 14
7:13 and really yield the fruit of immortality. 14
123whose fruit remains unspoiled 14
8: 6 so that fruit may be produced 14
10 milk . . which is the fruit of the breasts 14
9:31 it shall bring forth fruit in you 14
32 yet the fruit of the law did not perish 14
10:12 for I have lost the fruit of my womb 14
14 the earth . . has . . given her fruit, that is, man 14
16:46 for strangers shall gather their fruits 14
Wis 3:13 she will have fruit when God examines souls. 12
15 For the fruit of good labors is renowned 12
4: 5 their fruit will be useless, not ripe enough to eat 12
10:10 and increased the fruit of his toil. *
Sir 1:16 she satisfies men with her fruits; 12
6: 3 will devour your leaves and destroy your fruit 12
14:15 leave the fruit of your labors to another *
23:25 her branches will not bear fruit. 12
24:17 blossoms became glorious and abundant fruit. 12
27: 6 The fruit discloses the cultivation of a tree 12
28:15 deprived them of the fruit of their toil. *
37:22 the fruits of his understanding 12
23 the fruits of his understanding 12
45:20 he prepared bread of first fruits in abundance; *
50:10 like an olive tree putting forth its fruit 12
1Mc 10:30 the half of the fruit of the trees 12
14: 8 the trees of the plains their fruit. 12

fruit *See also* bear, bring, cake, enjoy, offering, tree, use.

bitter fruit 1. לַעֲנָה

Deu 29:18 root bearing poisonous and bitter fruit 1

choice fruit 1. זִמְרָה 2. מֶגֶד

Gen 43:11 do this: take some of the choice fruits of the land 1
Sng 7:13 over . . are all choice fruits, new as well as old 2

first fruit 1. בִּכּוּרָה 2. בִּכּוּרִים 3. רֵאשִׁית 4. *ἀπαρχή* 5. *νέος* 6. *πρωτογένημα*

Gen 49: 3 you are . . the first fruits of my strength 3
Exd 23:16 harvest, of the first fruits of your labor 2
19 The first of the first fruits of your ground 2
34:22 observe . . the first fruits of wheat harvest 2
26 The first of the first fruits of your ground 2
Lev 2:12 As an offering of first fruits you may bring them 3
14 If you offer a cereal offering of first fruits 2
14 the cereal offering of your first fruits 2
23:10 you shall bring the sheaf of the first fruits 3
17 baked with leaven, as first fruits to the LORD 2
20 bread of the first fruits as a wave offering 2
Num18:12 the first fruits of what they give to the LORD 3
28:26 On the day of the first fruits, when you offer 2
Deu 18: 4 first fruits of your grain, of your wine 3
2Kg 4:42 bringing the man of God bread of the first fruits 2
2Ch 31: 5 gave in abundance the first fruits of grain, wine 3

Neh 10:35 bring the first fruits of our ground 2
35 bring . . first fruits of all fruit of every tree 2
12:44 stores, the contributions, the first fruits 3
13:31 I provided . . for the first fruits. 2
Prv 3: 9 Honor the LORD . . with the first fruits 3
Jer 2: 3 holy to the LORD, the first fruits of his harvest. 3
Ezk 44:30 the first of all the first fruits of all kinds, 2
Hos 9:10 first fruit on the fig tree, in its first season 1
Rom 8:23 we . . who have the first fruits of the Spirit 4
11:16 If the dough offered as first fruits is holy 4
1Co 15:20 first fruits of those who have fallen asleep. 4
23 each in his own order: Christ the first fruits 4
Jas 1:18 we should be a kind of first fruits 4
Rev 14: 4 redeemed from mankind as first fruits for God 4
Tob 1: 6 Taking the first fruits and the tithes of my produce 4
Jdt 11:13 decided to consume the first fruits of the grain 4
Sir 7:31 the first fruits, the guilt offering 4
31 the first fruits of the holy things. 4
24:25 like the Tigris at the time of the first fruits. 5
35: 8 do not stint the first fruits of your hands. 4
45:20 he allotted to him the first of the first fruits 4
50: 8 like roses in the days of the first fruits 5
1Mc 3:49 the first fruits and the tithes 6

first ripe fruit 1. בִּכּוּרִים
Num18:13 first ripe fruits of all that is in their land 1

fruit of a tree 1. ἀκρόδρυα
1Mc 11:34 the crops of the land and the fruit of the trees. 1

fruit of toil 1. יְגַע
Job 20:18 He will give back the fruit of his toil 1

poisonous fruit 1. רֹאשׁ
Deu 29:18 root bearing poisonous and bitter fruit 1

summer fruit 1. קַיִץ
2Sm 16: 1 bunches of raisins, 100 of summer fruits 1
2 bread and summer fruit for the young men to eat 1
Jer 40:10 as for you, gather wine and summer fruits and oil 1
12 they gathered wine and summer fruits 1
48:32 upon your summer fruits and your vintage 1
Ams 8: 1 GOD showed me: behold, a basket of summer fruit. 1
2 And I said, "A basket of summer fruit. 1
Mic 7: 1 as when the summer fruit has been gathered 1

winter fruit 1. ὄλυνθος
Rev 6:13 as the fig tree sheds its winter fruit 1

fruitful 1. כַּרְמֶל 2. פרה 3. פְּרִי 4. καρπός 5. καρποφόρος 6. pomifer
Gen 1:22 blessed them, saying, "Be fruitful and multiply 2
28 said to them, "Be fruitful and multiply 2
8:17 and be fruitful and multiply upon the earth. 2
9: 1 Be fruitful and multiply, and fill the earth. 2
7 be fruitful and multiply 2
26:22 and we shall be fruitful in the land. 2
35:11 I am God Almighty: be fruitful and multiply; 2
47:27 they gained possessions in it, and were fruitful 2
49:22 Joseph is a fruitful bough 2
22 Joseph is . . a fruitful bough by a spring; 2
Exd 1: 7 the descendants of Israel were fruitful 2
Ps 107:34 a fruitful land into a salty waste 3
37 sow . . plant . . , and get a fruitful yield. 3
128: 3 wife . . like a fruitful vine within your house; 2
Isa 32:12 for the pleasant fields, for the fruitful vine 2
Jer 23: 3 and they shall be fruitful and multiply. 2
48:33 been taken away from the fruitful land of Moab; 1
Ezk 19:10 by the water, fruitful and full of branches 2
36:11 and they shall increase and be fruitful; 2
Act 14:17 he . . gave you from heaven rains and fruitful seasons 5
Php 1:22 that means fruitful labor for me 4
2Es 15:62 all your forests and your fruitful trees. 6
fruitful *See also* field, land, make.

make fruitful 1. פרה
Gen 17: 6 I will make you exceedingly fruitful; 1
20 I will bless him and make him fruitful 1
28: 3 God Almighty bless you and make you fruitful 1
41:52 For God has made me fruitful in the land of my 1
48: 4 I will make you fruitful, and multiply you 1

fruitless 1. ἄκαρπος
Jde 1:12 fruitless trees in late autumn, twice dead 1
Wis 15: 4 nor the fruitless toil of painters 1
4Mc 16: 7 fruitless nurturings and wretched nursings! 1

frustrate 1. נוא 2. פרר 3. ἀκυρόω 4. διαψεύδω 5. καθυστερέω
Ezr 4: 5 hired counselors . . to frustrate their purpose 2
Neh 4:15 heard . . that God had frustrated their plan 2
Job 5:12 He frustrates the devices of the crafty 2
Ps 33:10 LORD . . he frustrates the plans of the peoples. 1
Isa 44:25 who frustrates the omens of liars 2
Sir 16:13 the patience of the godly will not be frustrated. 5
3Mc 5:12 completely frustrated in his inflexible plan. 4
4Mc 17: 2 frustrated his evil designs 3

frustrate a purpose 1. ἄπρακτος
Jdt 11:11 and his purpose frustrated 1

frustration 1. מְגְעֶרֶת
Deu 28:20 send upon you curses, confusion, and frustration 1

fry in a pan 1. τηγανίζω
2Mc 7: 5 to fry him in a pan 1

fuel 1. אכל 2. בער 3. מַאֲכֹלֶת 4. ὕλη
Isa 9: 5 every garment . . burned as fuel for the fire. 3
19 burned, and the people are like fuel for the fire; 3
40:16 Lebanon would not suffice for fuel 2
44:15 Then it becomes fuel for a man; 2
Ezk 15: 4 Lo, it is given to the fire for fuel; 1
6 the forest, which I have given to the fire for fuel 1
21:32 You shall be fuel for the fire; 1
Sir 28:10 In proportion to the fuel for the fire 4

fugitive 1. בָּרִיחַ 2. נדד 3. נוס 4. נוע 5. פָּלִיט 6. פָּלֵיט 7. αὐτομολέω 8. φυγάς
Gen 4:12 you shall be a fugitive and a wanderer 4
14 I shall be a fugitive and a wanderer on the earth 4
Num21:29 He has made his sons fugitives, and his daughters 6
Jdg 12: 4 You are fugitives of E'phraim, you Gileadites 5
5 when any of the fugitives of E'phraim said, "Let me 5
Prv 28:17 let him be a fugitive until death; let no one help 3
Isa 15: 5 his fugitives flee to Zo'ar 1
16: 3 hide the outcasts, betray not the fugitive; 2
21:14 bring water, meet the fugitive with bread 2
Jer 44:14 they shall not return, except some fugitives. 6
48:45 In the shadow of Heshbon fugitives stop 3
49: 5 with none to gather the fugitives. 2
Ezk 24:26 on that day a fugitive will come to you to report 5
27 your mouth will be opened to the fugitive 5
33:22 the evening before the fugitive came; 5
Obd 1:14 at the parting of . . ways to cut off his fugitives; 5
Jdt 16:12 were wounded like the children of fugitives 7
Wis 19: 3 pursued as fugitives 8
2Mc 4:26 was driven as a fugitive into the land of Ammon. 8

become a fugitive 1. φυγαδεύω
1Mc 2:43 all who became fugitives to escape their troubles 1

fulfil 1. אמן 2. בוא 3. גמר 4. היה 5. מלא 6. עמד 7. עשׂה 8. פלא 9. קום 10. שׁלם 11. יסף (A) 12. ἀναπληρόω 13. ἐγείρω 14. ἐκπληρόω 15. ἐκπλήρωσις 16. ἐπιτελέω 17. πίμπλημι 18. πληροφορέω 19. πληρόω 20. πλήρωμα 21. ποιέω 22. συντελέω 23. συντηρέω 24. τελειόω 25. τελευτή 26. τελέω 27. compleo 28. impleo
Gen 25:24 When her days to be delivered were fulfilled 5
26: 3 I will fulfil the oath which I swore 9
Exd 23:26 I will fulfil the number of your days. 5
Lev 22:21 of peace offerings to the LORD, to fulfil a vow 8
Num15: 3 to fulfil a vow or as a freewill offering 8
8 prepare a bull for . . a sacrifice, to fulfil a vow 8
23:19 Or has he spoken, and will he not fulfil it? 9
Jos 23:15 the good things . . have been fulfilled for you 2
1Sm 3:12 I will fulfil against Eli all that I have spoken 9
2Sm 7:12 When your days are fulfilled and you lie down 5
1Kg 2:27 expelled Abi'athar . . thus fulfilling the word 5
8:15 with his hand has fulfilled what he promised 5
20 the LORD has fulfilled his promise which he made; 9
24 and with thy hand hast fulfilled it this day. 5
12:15 brought about . . that he might fulfil his word 9
1Ch 17:11 days are fulfilled to go to be with your fathers 5
2Ch 1: 9 thy promise to David my father be now fulfilled 1
6: 4 LORD . . who with his hand has fulfilled 5
10 the LORD has fulfilled his promise which he made; 9
15 and with thy hand hast fulfilled it this day. 5
10:15 that the LORD might fulfil his word 9
36:21 to fulfil the word of the LORD by . . Jeremiah 5
21 it kept sabbath, to fulfil 70 years. 5
Neh 9: 8 fulfilled thy promise, for thou art righteous. 9
Est 5: 6 Even . . half of my kingdom, it shall be fulfilled. 7
8 to grant my petition and fulfil my request 7
7: 2 to . . half of my kingdom, it shall be fulfilled. 7
9:12 what . . is your request? It shall be fulfilled. 7
Job 39: 2 Can you number the months that they fulfil 5
Ps 20: 4 your heart's desire, and fulfil all your plans! 5
5 May the LORD fulfil all your petitions! 5
57: 2 to God who fulfils his purpose for me. 3
145:19 He fulfils the desire of all who fear him 7
148: 8 stormy wind fulfilling his command! 7
Prv 13:12 but a desire fulfilled is a tree of life. 2
19 A desire fulfilled is sweet to the soul; 4
Isa 44:28 my shepherd, and he shall fulfil all my purpose'; 10
Jer 29:10 I will fulfil to you my promise and bring you back 9
33:14 when I will fulfil the promise I made to the house 9
39:16 Behold, I will fulfil my words against this city 2
44:25 and have fulfilled it with your hands, saying 5
Ezk 13: 6 yet they expect him to fulfil their word. 9
21: 7 Behold, it comes and it will be fulfilled 4
Dan 4:33 word was fulfilled upon Nebuchadnez'zar. 11
11:14 lift themselves up in order to fulfil the vision; 6
Nah 1:15 Keep your feasts, O Judah, fulfil your vows 10
Mat 1:22 All this took place to fulfil what the Lord had 19
2:15 the death of Herod. This was to fulfil 25
17 Then was fulfilled what was spoken 19
23 spoken by the prophets might be fulfilled 19
3:15 thus it is fitting for us to fulfil all righteousness. 19
4:14 spoken by the prophet Isaiah might be fulfilled 19
5:17 have come not to abolish them but to fulfil them. 19
8:17 This was to fulfil what was spoken by the prophet 19
12:17 This was to fulfil what was spoken by the prophet 19
13:14 With them indeed is fulfilled the prophecy 12
35 This was to fulfil what was spoken by the prophet 19
21: 4 This took place to fulfil what was spoken 19
26:54 how then should the scriptures be fulfilled 19
56 scriptures of the prophets might be fulfilled. 19
27: 9 Then was fulfilled what had been spoken 19
Mrk 1:15 saying, "The time is fulfilled 19
14:49 let the scriptures be fulfilled. 19
Lke 1:20 which will be fulfilled in their time. 19
4:21 scripture has been fulfilled in your hearing. 19
21:22 to fulfil all that is written. 17
24 until the times of the Gentiles are fulfilled. 19
22:16 I tell you I shall not eat it until it is fulfilled 19
37 this scripture must be fulfilled in me 26
24:44 everything . . must be fulfilled. 19
Joh 12:38 that the word . . might be fulfilled 19
13:18 that the scripture may be fulfilled 19
15:25 to fulfil the word that is written in their law 19
17:12 that the scripture might be fulfilled. 19
13 they may have my joy fulfilled in themselves. 19
18: 9 This was to fulfil the word which he had spoken 19
32 to fulfil the word which Jesus had spoken 19
19:24 This was to fulfil the scripture 19
28 Jesus . . said (to fulfil the scripture), "I thirst. 24
36 that the scripture might be fulfilled 19
Act 1:16 Brethren, the scripture had to be fulfilled 19
3:18 that his Christ should suffer, he thus fulfilled. 19
12:25 when they had fulfilled their mission 19
13:27 fulfilled these by condemning him. 19
29 when they had fulfilled all that was written 26
33 this he has fulfilled to us their children 14
14:26 the work which they had fulfilled. 19
21:26 the days of purification would be fulfilled 15
Rom 8: 4 requirement of the law might be fulfilled in us 19
13: 8 he who loves his neighbor has fulfilled the law. 19
10 therefore love is the fulfilling of the law. 20
Gal 5:14 For the whole law is fulfilled in one word 19
6: 2 and so fulfil the law of Christ. 12
Col 4:17 See that you fulfil the ministry 19
2Th 1:11 may fulfil every good resolve and work of faith 19
2Ti 4: 5 fulfil your ministry. 18
Jas 2: 8 If you really fulfill the royal law 26
23 the scripture was fulfilled which says 19
Rev 10: 7 the mystery of God . . should be fulfilled. 26
17:17 until the words of God shall be fulfilled. 26
1Es 4:46 I pray therefore that you fulfil the vow 21
8:21 scrupulously fulfilled for the Most High God 16
2Es 2:40 who have fulfilled the law of the Lord. 27
4:37 or arouse them until that measure is fulfilled.' 28
Jdt 10: 8 grant you favor and fulfil your plans 24
Wis 4:13 he fulfilled long years; 19
Sir 32: 2 when you have fulfilled your duties 21
34: 8 the law will be fulfilled 22
36:15 fulfil the prophecies spoken in thy name. 13
1Mc 2:55 because he fulfilled the command 19
11:33 who . . fulfil their obligations to us 23
4Mc 12:14 by dying nobly fulfilled their service to God 19

fulfil purpose 1. גמר
Ps 138: 8 The LORD will fulfil his purpose for me; 1
fulfill *See* fail.
fulfilling *See* succeed.

fulfillment 1. ἐκπληρόω
3Mc 1:22 the fulfillment of his intended purpose. 1

fulfilment 1. דָּבָר 2. ἀναπληρόω 3. ποιέω 4. ποίησις 5. συντέλεια 6. τελείωσις 7. τέλος
Ps 119:123 for the fulfilment of thy righteous promise. •
Ezk 12:23 are at hand, and the fulfilment of every vision. 1
Lke 1:45 fulfilment of what was spoken to her 6
22:37 what is written about me has its fulfilment. 7
1Es 1:57 in fulfilment of the word of the Lord 2
4:46 the vow whose fulfilment you vowed 3
Sir 19:20 in all wisdom there is the fulfilment of the law. 4
21:11 wisdom is the fulfilment of the fear of the Lord. 5
fulfilment *See also* bring.

full 1. בְּ 2. בְּראשׁ 3. יוֹם 4. כון 5. כֹּל 6. כָּלָה 7. מִכְלוֹל 8. מלא 9. מָלֵא 10. מְלֹא 11. רֹאשׁ 12. רַב 13. שֹׂבַע 14. שָׂבֵעַ 15. שָׂבָע 16. שָׁלֵם 17. תֹּם 18. תָּמִים 19. אַדְרַזְדָּא (A) 20. אָסְפַּרְנָא (A) 21. מלא (A) 22. γέμω 23. ἐμπίμπλημι 24. μεστός 25. ὅλος 26. ὁλοσχερῆ 27. παντελής 28. πᾶς 29. πλήρης 30. πληρόω 31. πλήρωμα 32. πολύς 33. σπουδαῖος 34. συμφύω 35. τέλειος 36. frequens 37. plenus
Gen 14:10 Now the Valley of Siddim was full of bitumen pits; •
23: 9 For the full price let him give it to me 10

25: 8 an old man and full of years, and was gathered 14
35:29 gathered to his people, old and full of days; 14
41: 7 swallowed up the seven plump and full ears. 10
22 ears growing on one stalk, full and good; 10
Exd 16: 3 when we . . ate bread to the full; 15
8 LORD gives . . in the morning bread to the full 13
22: 6 the fire shall make full restitution. •
14 he shall make full restitution. •
Lev 6: 5 he shall restore it in full, and shall add a fifth 11
16:12 he shall take a censer full of coals of fire 10
23:15 seven full weeks shall they be 18
25:30 If it is not redeemed within a full year 8
26: 5 you shall eat your bread to the full, and dwell 15
27:17 it shall stand at your full valuation •
Num 5: 7 he shall make full restitution for his wrong 2
7:13 both of them full of fine flour mixed with oil 10
14 one golden dish of ten shekels, full of incense; 10
19 both of them full of fine flour mixed with oil 10
20 one golden dish of ten shekels, full of incense; 10
25 both of them full of fine flour mixed with oil 10
26 one golden dish of ten shekels, full of incense; 10
31 both of them full of fine flour mixed with oil 10
32 one golden dish of ten shekels, full of incense; 10
37 both of them full of fine flour mixed with oil 10
38 one golden dish of ten shekels, full of incense; 10
43 both of them full of fine flour mixed with oil 10
44 one golden dish of ten shekels, full of incense; 10
49 both of them full of fine flour mixed with oil 10
50 one golden dish of ten shekels, full of incense; 10
55 both of them full of fine flour mixed with oil 10
56 one golden dish of ten shekels, full of incense; 10
61 both of them full of fine flour mixed with oil 10
62 one golden dish of ten shekels, full of incense; 10
67 both of them full of fine flour mixed with oil 10
68 one golden dish of ten shekels, full of incense; 10
73 both of them full of fine flour mixed with oil 10
74 one golden dish of ten shekels, full of incense; 10
79 both of them full of fine flour mixed with oil 10
80 one golden dish of ten shekels, full of incense; 10
86 the twelve golden dishes, full of incense 10
22:18 were to give me his house full of silver and gold 10
24:13 should give me his house full of silver and gold 10
Deu 6:11 houses full of good things, which you did not fill 10
11 when you eat and are full 13
8:10 you shall eat and be full, and you shall bless 13
12 lest, when you have eaten and are full 13
11:15 for your cattle and you shall eat and be full. 13
21:13 shall remain in your house and bewail . . a full month; 3
25:15 full and just weight . . a full and just measure 16
15 full and just weight . . a full and just measure 16
31:20 when . . have eaten and are full and grown fat 13
33:23 O Naph'tali . . full of the blessing of the LORD 10
34: 9 Joshua . . was full of the spirit of wisdom 10
Jdg 16:27 the house was full of men and women; all the lords 10
Rut 1:21 I went away full, and the LORD has brought me back 10
2:12 and a full reward be given you by the LORD 16
1Sm 2: 5 Those who were full have hired themselves out 14
28:20 Saul fell at once full length upon the ground 10
2Sm 8: 2 two . . put to death, and one full line to be spared. 10
13:23 After two full years Ab'salom had sheepshearers 3
14:28 Ab'salom dwelt two full years in Jerusalem •
23:11 where there was a plot of ground full of lentils; 10
1Kg 7:14 he was full of wisdom, understanding, and skill 8
2Kg 3:16 'I will make this dry stream-bed full of pools.' †
4: 4 pour into all . . and when one is full, set it aside. 10
6 When the vessels were full, she said to her son 8
39 and gathered from it his lap full of wild gourds 10
6:17 mountain was full of horses and chariots of fire 10
9:24 Jehu drew his bow with his full strength 8
1Ch 11:13 There was a plot of ground full of barley 10
12:38 came . . with full intent to make David king 16
21:22 give it to me at its full price 10
24 to Ornan, "No, but I will buy it for the full price; 10
23: 1 When David was old and full of days 13
29:28 he died in a good old age, full of days, riches 14
2Ch 24:15 Jehoi'ada grew old and full of days, and died; 13
Ezr 6: 8 cost is to be paid . . in full and without delay 20
7:23 let it be done in full for the house of the God 19
Neh 9:25 possession of houses full of all good things 10
Est 9:29 Mor'decai the Jew gave full written authority 5
Job 7: 4 I am full of tossing till the dawn. 13
14: 1 born of a woman is of few days, and full of trouble. 14
20:11 His bones are full of youthful vigor 8
23 To fill his belly to the full God will send his 8
21:23 One dies in full prosperity, being wholly at ease 17
24 his body full of fat 8
32:18 For I am full of words 8
36:16 what was set on your table was full of fatness. 8
17 you are full of the judgment on the wicked; 8
42:17 Job died, an old man, and full of days. 14
Ps 26:10 whose right hands are full of bribes. 8
29: 4 voice of the LORD is full of majesty. 1
33: 5 earth is full of the steadfast love of the LORD. 8
65: 9 the river of God is full of water; 8
74:20 are full of the habitations of violence. 8
88: 3 For my soul is full of troubles 13
104:24 the earth is full of thy creatures. 8
111: 3 Full of honor and majesty is his work •
119:64 The earth, O LORD, is full of thy steadfast love; 8
127: 5 Happy is the man who has his quiver full of them! 8
144:13 garners be full, providing all manner of store; 10
Prv 4:18 shines brighter and brighter until full day. 4
17: 1 quiet than a house full of feasting with strife. 10
20:17 but afterward his mouth will be full of gravel. 8
29:11 A fool gives full vent to his anger 5
30: 9 lest I be full, and deny thee, and say, 13
Ecc 1: 7 All streams run to the sea, but the sea is not full; 10
4: 6 two hands full of toil and a striving after wind. 10
9: 3 also the hearts of men are full of evil 10
11: 3 If the clouds are full of rain 8
Isa 1:15 I will not listen; your hands are full of blood. 8
21 the faithful city . . she that was full of justice! 10
2: 6 rejected . . because they are full of diviners 8
6: 3 the whole earth is full of his glory. 10
11: 9 earth shall be full of the knowledge of the LORD 8
13:21 and its houses will be full of howling creatures; 8
15: 9 For the waters of Dibon are full of blood; 8
22: 2 you who are full of shoutings, tumultuous city 10
7 Your choicest valleys were full of chariots 10
27: 9 the full fruit of the removal of his sin 5
28: 8 For all tables are full of vomit 10
30:27 his lips are full of indignation 10
51:20 they are full of the wrath of the LORD 10
Jer 4:12 a wind too full for this comes for me. 10
5:27 Like a basket full of birds, their houses are full 10
27 their houses are full of treachery; 10
6:11 Therefore I am full of the wrath of the LORD; 10
12: 6 they are in full cry after you; believe them not 10
23:10 For the land is full of adulterers; 8
35: 5 set before the Re'chabites pitchers full of wine 10
46:12 and the earth is full of your cry; 8
51: 5 the land of the Chalde'ans is full of guilt 8
Lam 1: 1 How lonely sits the city that was full of people! 12
Ezk 1:18 and their rims were full of eyes round about. 10
7:23 Because the land is full of bloody crimes 8
23 the city is full of violence 8
9: 9 the land is full of blood 8
9 is full of blood, and the city full of injustice; 8
10: 4 the court was full of the brightness of the glory 8
12 the wheels were full of eyes round about 10
11:13 wilt thou make a full end of the remnant of Israel? •
16: 7 and became tall and arrived at full maidenhood; •
22: 5 will mock you, you infamous one, full of tumult. 12
23:12 warriors clothed in full armor, horsemen riding 7
28:12 You were the signet of perfection, full of wisdom 10
32: 6 the watercourses will be full of you. 8
37: 1 in the midst of the valley; it was full of bones. 10
38: 4 and horsemen, all of them clothed in full armor 7
41: 8 measured a full reed of six long cubits. 9
Dan 3:19 Then Nebuchadnez'zar was full of fury 21
8:23 transgressors have reached their full measure •
10: 3 ate no delicacies . . for the full three weeks. 8
Hos 13: 6 but when they had fed to the full, they were filled 13
Jol 2:24 The threshing floors shall be full of grain 8
3:13 Go in, tread, for the wine press is full. 8
Ams 2:13 as a cart full of sheaves presses down. 10
Mic 6:12 Your rich men are full of violence; 8
Nah 3: 1 Woe to the bloody city, all full of lies and booty 10
Hab 3: 3 and the earth was full of his praise. Selah 8
Zep 1:18 for a full, yea, sudden end he will make 6
Zec 8: 5 the city shall be full of boys and girls playing 8
9:15 their blood like wine, and be full like a bowl 8
Mal 3:10 Bring the full tithes into the storehouse 5
Mat 6:22 eye is sound, your whole body will be full of light; •
23 your whole body will be full of darkness. If •
13:48 when it was full, men drew it ashore and sat down 30
14:20 twelve baskets full of the broken pieces 29
15:37 seven baskets full of the broken pieces left 29
23:25 inside they are full of extortion and rapacity. 22
27 within they are full of dead men's bones 22
28 within you are full of hypocrisy and iniquity. 24
Mrk 4:28 then the ear, then the full grain in the ear. 29
6:43 took up twelve baskets full of broken pieces 31
8: 8 the broken pieces left over, seven baskets full. •
19 how many baskets full of broken pieces 29
20 how many baskets full of broken pieces 31
15:36 filling a sponge full of vinegar, put it on a reed •
Lke 4: 1 Jesus, full of the Holy Spirit, returned 29
5:12 there came a man full of leprosy 29
6:25 Woe to you that are full now, for you shall hunger. 23
11:39 inside you are full of extortion and wickedness. 22
Joh 1:14 Word . . dwelt among us, full of grace and truth; 29
3:29 therefore this joy of mine is now full. 30
15:11 that your joy may be full. 30
16:24 ask, and you will receive, that your joy may be full. 30
19:29 A bowl full of vinegar stood there 24
29 they put a sponge full of the vinegar on hyssop 24
21: 8 dragging the net full of fish •
11 hauled the net ashore, full of large fish, 153 24
Act 6: 3 full of the Spirit and of wisdom 29
5 Stephen, a man full of faith and of the Holy Spirit 29
8 Stephen, full of grace and power 29
7:55 he, full of the Holy Spirit, gazed into heaven 29
9:36 She was full of good works and acts of charity. 29
11:24 a good man, full of the Holy Spirit and of faith. 29
13:10 full of all deceit and villainy 29
Rom 1:29 Full of envy, murder, strife, deceit, malignity 24
3:14 Their mouth is full of curses and bitterness. 22
15:14 that you yourselves are full of goodness 24
Php 1:20 with full courage now as always 28
1Th 1: 5 in the Holy Spirit and with full conviction 32
1Ti 1:15 The saying is sure and worthy of full acceptance 28
4: 9 is sure and worthy of full acceptance. 28
Jas 1: 4 let steadfastness have its full effect 35
3: 8 the tongue . . full of deadly poison. 24
17 wisdom . . is . . full of mercy and good fruits 24
2Pe 2:14 They have eyes full of adultery 24
2Jn 1: 8 that you may not lose . . but may win a full reward 29
Rev 1:16 face was like the sun shining in full strength •
4: 6 creatures, full of eyes in front and behind 22
8 creatures . . full of eyes all around and within 22
5: 8 and with golden bowls full of incense 22
6:12 the full moon became like blood 25
15: 7 seven golden bowls full of the wrath of God 22
17: 3 beast which was full of blasphemous names 22
4 holding . . a golden cup full of abominations 22
21: 9 the seven bowls full of the seven last plagues 22
1Es 1:23 his heart was full of godliness. 29
2Es 2:40 Take again your full number, O Zion •
41 The number of your children . . is full 37
4:27 because this age is full of sadness 37
38 all of us also are full of ungodliness. 37
49 after this a cloud full of water passed before me 37
6:13 and you will hear a full, resounding voice. 37
22 full storehouses shall suddenly be . . empty; 37
7: 6 and it is full of all good things; 37
12 they are few and evil, full of dangers 37
25 and full things are for the full. 37
68 full of sins and burdened with transgressions. 37
112the full glory does not abide in it 36
12: 2 and their reign was brief and full of tumult. 37
30 the reign which was brief and full of tumult 37
14:39 and behold, a full cup was offered to me 37
39 it was full of something like water 37
15:34 very threatening, full of wrath and storm. 37
40 full of wrath and tempest 37
Tob 13: 6 give thanks to him with your full voice 25
Jdt 6: 4 their fields will be full of their dead 30
AEs 15: 6 clothed in the full array of his majesty 28
14 your countenance is full of grace. 24
Wis 2: 6 and make use of the creation to the full as in youth. 33
3: 4 their hope is full of immortality. 29
5:22 hailstones full of wrath will be hurled 29
11:18 or newly created unknown beasts full of rage 29
12:21 oaths and covenants full of good promises! •
13:13 a stick crooked and full of knots 34
Sir 1:30 your heart was full of deceit. 29
19:26 inwardly he is full of deceit. 29
32:20 Do not go on a path full of hazards •
42:16 the work of the Lord is full of his glory. 29
50: 6 like the moon when it is full; 29
18 in sweet and full-toned melody. 32
LJr 1:17 Their eyes are full of the dust 29
Sus 1:28 the two elders came, full of their wicked plot 29
2Mc 3: 6 the treasury . . was full of untold sums of money 22
30 was full of fear and disturbance 22
13: 5 a tower . . 50 cubits high, full of ashes 29
3Mc 5:31 a full and firm loyalty to my ancestors. 26
47 he . . rushed out in full force along with the beasts 28
6:31 full of joy they apportioned to celebrants 29
7:16 had received the full enjoyment of deliverance 27

full *See also* accord, account, armor, assurance, command, end, extent, feed, grown, inclusion, make, measure, moon, number, pay, payment, permission, reach, time, view, vigor, weight, well, year, yield.

become full 1. מלא

Lev 19:29 and the land become full of wickedness 1

full of branches 1. עָנֵף

Ezk 19:10 by the water, fruitful and full of branches 1

full of darkness 1. σκοτεινός

Lke 11:34 when it is not sound, your body is full of darkness. 1

full of idols 1. κατείδωλος

Act 17:16 as he saw that the city was full of idols. 1

full of light 1. φωτεινός

Lke 11:34 your whole body is full of light 1
36 If then your whole body is full of light 1

full of marrow 1. מחה

Isa 25: 6 wine on the lees, of fat things full of marrow 1

full of pain 1. מַכְאוֹב

Ecc 2:23 For all his days are full of pain 1

full of sap 1. דָּשֵׁן

Ps 92:14 they are ever full of sap and green 1

full of sores 1. ἑλκόω

Lke 16:20 a poor man named Laz'arus, full of sores 1

full of talk 1. שָׂפָה

Job 11: 2 a man full of talk be vindicated? 1

full of weariness 1. יָגֵעַ
Ecc 1: 8 All things are full of weariness; 1

full of wrath 1. עבר
Ps 78:21 when the LORD heard, he was full of wrath; 1
59 When God heard, he was full of wrath 1
89:38 thou art full of wrath against thy anointed. 1

full thing 1. plenus
2Es 7:25 and full things are for the full. 1

too full 1. מָלֵא
Jer 4:12 a wind too full for this comes for me. 1

fuller 1. כבס 2. γναφεύς
Mal 3: 2 he is like a refiner's fire and like fullers' soap 1
Mrk 9: 3 as no fuller on earth could bleach them. 2

fully 1. מלא 2. מָלֵא 3. εἰς 4. εἰς πᾶσαν 5. εἰς τὸ παντελές 6. ἕως τέλους 7. καλός 8. πανευχία 9. πᾶς 10. πλήρωμα 11. πολύς 12. προστίθημι 13. σαφῶς 14. τελείως 15. plenissime
Num14:24 Caleb, because he . . has followed me fully 1
Rut 2:11 All that you have done . . has been fully told me †
1Kg 2:15 and that all Israel fully expected me to reign; •
Ecc 8:11 the heart of the sons of men is fully set to do evil. 2
Lke 13:11 could not fully straighten herself. 5
2Co 1:13 I hope you will understand fully 6
Gal 4: 4 when the time had fully come 10
Col 1:10 fully pleasing to him 4
1Pe 1:13 set your hope fully upon the grace that is coming 14
Jde 1: 5 though you were once for all fully informed 9
1Es 6: 8 Let it be fully known to our lord the king 9
2Es 12: 8 that thou mayest fully comfort my soul. 15
Sir 18: 5 who can fully recount his mercies? 12
1Mc 9:42 when they had fully avenged the blood †
2Mc 4:33 When Onias became fully aware of these acts 13
14:20 When the terms had been fully considered 11
15:22 he slew fully 185,000 3
3Mc 3:24 fully convinced by these indications 7
4Mc 3:12 armed themselves fully 8
fully *See also* arm, assure, believe, come, convince, preach, proclaim, recount, ripe, teach, understand.

fulness 1. מלא 2. מְלֹא 3. מְלֵאָה 4. שֹׂבַע 5. πίμπλημι 6. πλῆθος 7. πλήρωμα
Num18:27 reckoned . . as the fulness of the wine press. 3
Deu 33:16 with the best gifts of the earth and its fulness 2
Job 20:22 In the fulness of his sufficiency he will be 1
Ps 16:11 in thy presence there is fulness of joy 4
24: 1 The earth is the LORD'S and the fulness thereof 2
Joh 1:16 And from his fulness have we all received, grace 7
Rom15:29 come in the fulness of the blessing of Christ. 7
Eph 1:10 as a plan for the fulness of time 7
23 the fulness of him who fills all in all. 7
3:19 you may be filled with all the fulness of God. 7
4:13 measure of the stature of the fulness of Christ; 7
Col 1:19 in him all the fulness of God was pleased to dwell 7
2: 9 in him the whole fulness of deity dwells bodily 7
Tob 12: 9 will have fulness of life; 5
Sir 33:11 In the fulness of his knowledge 6
fulness *See also* come.

fulness of harvest 1. מְלֵאָה
Exd 22:29 offer from the fulness of your harvest 1

function 1. πρᾶξις
Rom12: 4 and all the members do not have the same function 1

fund 1. ἀργύριον 2. διάφορος 3. χρῆμα
1Mc 3:30 He feared that he might not have such funds •
31 raise a large fund. 1
10:41 all the additional funds •
2Mc 3: 6 the amount of the funds could not be reckoned 2
14 went in to direct the inspection of these funds. •
4Mc 4: 3 there are deposited tens of thousands in private funds 3
6 to seize the private funds in the treasury. 3

funeral 1. κηδεία
2Mc 4:49 provided magnificently for their funeral. 1
5:10 he had no funeral of any sort 1
funeral *See also* dirge, feast, give.

furious 1. זַעַף 2. חֵמָה 3. חֵמָה (A) 4. קְצַף (A) 5. θυμός
Prv 6:34 For jealousy makes a man furious 2
Isa 30:30 in furious anger and a flame of devouring fire 1
34: 2 and furious against all their host 2
Ezk 5:15 anger and fury, and with furious chastisements 2
Dan 2:12 king was angry and very furious, and commanded 4
3:13 Then Nebuchadnez'zar in furious rage commanded 3
Mat 2:16 been tricked by the wise men, was in a furious rage †
1Mc 2:49 it is a time of ruin and furious anger. 5

furiously 1. בְּשִׁגָּעוֹן 2. θηριωδῶς 3. ῥύδην
2Kg 9:20 the driving of Jehu . . for he drives furiously. 1
2Mc 3:25 it rushed furiously at Heliodorus 3
12:15 his men . . rushed furiously upon the walls. 2

furlong 1. στάδιον
Mat 14:24 the boat by this time was many furlongs distant 1

furnace 1. כִּבְשָׁן 2. כּוּר 3. מוֹקֵד 4. עֲלִיל 5. תַּנּוּר 6. אַתּוּן (A) 7. κάμινος 8. χωνευτήριον 9. clibanus 10. fornax
Gen 19:28 land went up like the smoke of a furnace. 1
Deu 4:20 LORD . . brought you forth out of the iron furnace 2
1Kg 8:51 out of Egypt, from the midst of the iron furnace). 2
Ps 12: 6 silver refined in a furnace on the ground 4
102: 3 my bones burn like a furnace. 3
Prv 17: 3 for silver, and the furnace is for gold 2
27:21 crucible is for silver . . furnace is for gold 2
Isa 31: 9 the LORD . . whose furnace is in Jerusalem. 5
48:10 I have tried you in the furnace of affliction. 2
Jer 11: 4 out of the land of Egypt, from the iron furnace 2
Ezk 22:18 bronze and tin and iron and lead in the furnace 2
20 bronze and iron and lead and tin into a furnace 2
22 As silver is melted in a furnace, so you shall be 2
Dan 3: 6 cast into a burning fiery furnace. 6
11 cast into a burning fiery furnace. 6
15 cast into a burning fiery furnace; 6
17 able to deliver us from the burning fiery furnace; 6
19 ordered the furnace heated seven times more 6
20 cast them into the burning fiery furnace. 6
21 cast into the burning fiery furnace. 6
22 king's order was strict and the furnace very hot 6
23 fell bound into the burning fiery furnace. 6
26 near to the door of the burning fiery furnace 6
Mat 13:42 throw them into the furnace of fire 7
50 throw them into the furnace of fire 7
Rev 1:15 like burnished bronze, refined as in a furnace 7
9: 2 rose smoke like the smoke of a great furnace 7
2Es 4:48 and behold, a flaming furnace passed by before me 10
7:36 and the furnace of hell shall be disclosed 9
Wis 3: 6 like gold in the furnace he tried them 8
Sir 2: 5 acceptable men in the furnace of humiliation. 7
22:24 vapor and smoke of the furnace precede the fire; 7
38:28 he wastes away in the heat of the furnace; 7
30 he is careful to clean the furnace. 7
43: 4 A man tending a furnace works in burning heat 7
Aza 1:23 servants . . did not cease feeding the furnace fires 7
24 streamed out above the furnace 49 cubits 7
25 the Chaldeans whom it caught about the furnace. 7
26 came down into the furnace to be with Azariah 7
26 and drove the fiery flame out of the furnace 7
27 made the midst of the furnace like a . . wind 7
28 glorified and blessed God in the furnace, saying 7
66 the midst of the burning fiery furnace 7
3Mc 6: 6 moistening the fiery furnace with dew 7
4Mc 13: 9 who despised the same ordeal of the furnace. 7
16: 3 the raging fiery furnace of Mishael 7
21 were hurled into the fiery furnace 7

furnish 1. ענק 2. παρέχω 3. στρωννύω 4. τάσσω 5. χορηγέω 6. praesto
Deu 15:14 furnish him liberally out of your flock 1
Ezk 45:17 the prince's duty to furnish the burnt offerings •
Mrk 14:15 a large upper room furnished and ready 3
Lke 22:12 he will show you a large upper room furnished; 3
1Ti 6:17 richly furnishes us with everything to enjoy. 2
2Es 8: 8 and dost furnish it with members 6
Sir 44: 6 rich men furnished with resources 5
1Mc 14:10 furnished them with the means of defense 4

furnish with doors 1. θυρόω
1Mc 4:57 and furnished them with doors. 1

furnishing 1. כְּלִי
Exd 31: 7 all the furnishings of the tent 1
Num 1:50 carry the tabernacle and all its furnishings 1
50 over all its furnishings, and over all that 1
3: 8 all the furnishings of the tent of meeting 1
4:15 covering . . the furnishing of the sanctuary 1
7: 1 consecrated it, with all its furnishings 1
19:18 sprinkle it . . upon all the furnishings 1

furniture 1. כְּלִי 2. κατασκεύασμα
Exd 25: 9 the tabernacle, and of all its furniture 1
40: 9 and consecrate it and all its furniture; 1
1Ch 9:29 Others . . were appointed over the furniture 1
Neh 13: 8 threw all the household furniture of Tobi'ah 1
Jdt 15:11 his beds and his bowls and all his furniture 2

furrow 1. מַעֲנָה 2. תֶּלֶם 3. αὖλαξ
Job 31:38 its furrows have wept together; 2
39:10 Can you bind him in the furrow with ropes 2
Ps 65:10 Thou waterest its furrows abundantly 2
129: 3 plowers . . made long their furrows. 1
Hos 10: 4 poisonous weeds in the furrows of the field. 2
12:11 like stone heaps on the furrows of the field. 2
Sir 7: 3 My son, do not sow the furrows of injustice 3
38:26 He sets his heart on plowing furrows 3
furrow's *See* length.

further 1. יֹסֵף 2. עוֹד 3. עוֹד 4. פוּק 5. שׁוּב 6. ἐπὶ πλεῖον 7. ἔτι 8. κατά 9. οὐκέτι 10. πάλιν 11. περαιτέρω 12. πόρρω 13. προστίθημι 14. συνεργός 15. adhuc
Deu 20: 8 officers shall speak further to the people 1
2Sm 19:28 What further right have I, then, to cry to the king? 2
2Ch 34:16 Shaphan . . further reported to the king 2
Est 9:12 what further is your request? 2
Ps 140: 8 do not further his evil plot! Selah 4
Ezk 8:17 with violence, and provoke me further to anger? 5
Zec 1:15 they furthered the disaster. 3
Mrk 5:35 Why trouble the Teacher any further? 7
15: 5 Jesus made no further answer 9
Lke 22:71 they said, "What further testimony do we need? 7
24:28 He appeared to be going further 12
Act 4:17 it may spread no further among the people 6
19:39 if you seek anything further 11
24: 4 to detain you no further 6
Rom15:12 further Isaiah says, "The root of Jesse shall come 10
Tit 1: 1 to further the faith of God's elect 8
Heb 7:11 what further need would there have been 7
12:19 that no further messages be spoken to them 13
1Es 2:29 that such wicked proceedings go no further 6
2Es 7:102show further to me, thy servant 15
2Mc 2:20 further the wars against Antiochus Epiphanes 7
14: 5 an opportunity that furthered his mad purpose 14
further *See also* carry, clothe, go, proceed, threaten, tighten, work.

furthermore 1. וְ 2. עוֹד 3. προσέτι
Deu 4:21 Furthermore the LORD was angry with me 1
9:13 Furthermore the LORD said to me, 'I have seen 1
2Ch 17: 6 furthermore he took the high places 2
4Mc 14: 1 Furthermore, they encouraged them 3

fury 1. זַעַם 2. חֵמָא 3. חֵמָה 4. חָרוֹן 5. עֶבְרָה 6. קִנְאָה 7. חֱמָא (A) 8. ἄνοια 9. ἐμμαίνομαι 10. ζῆλος 11. θυμός 12. μηνίαμα
Gen 27:44 with him . . until your brother's fury turns away 3
Exd 15: 7 thou sendest forth thy fury, it consumes them 4
Lev 26:28 then I will walk contrary to you in fury 3
Deu 29:28 uprooted . . in anger and fury and great wrath 3
Est 3: 5 And when Haman saw . . Haman was filled with fury. 3
Ps 2: 5 in his wrath, and terrify them in his fury, saying 4
7: 6 lift thyself up against the fury of my enemies; 5
Prv 22: 8 rod of his fury will fail. 5
Isa 10: 5 Ah, Assyria, the rod of my anger, the staff of my fury! 1
42:13 like a man of war he stirs up his fury; 6
51:13 fear . . because of the fury of the oppressor 3
13 And where is the fury of the oppressor? 3
59:17 and wrapped himself in fury as a mantle. 6
66:15 like the stormwind, to render his anger in fury 3
Jer 21: 5 in anger, and in fury, and in great wrath. 3
Lam 2: 4 he has poured out his fury like fire. 3
Ezk 5:13 I will vent my fury upon them and satisfy myself; 3
13 in my jealousy, when I spend my fury upon them. 3
15 when I execute judgments on you in anger and fury 3
6:12 Thus I will spend my fury upon them. 3
16:42 will I satisfy my fury on you 3
19:12 But the vine was plucked up in fury 3
21:17 also will clap my hands, and I will satisfy my fury; 3
23:25 against you, that they may deal with you in fury. 3
24:13 till I have satisfied my fury upon you. 3
Dan 3:19 Then Nebuchadnez'zar was full of fury 7
11:44 shall go forth with great fury to exterminate 2
Hab 3:12 Thou didst bestride the earth in fury 1
Lke 6:11 they were filled with fury 8
Act 26:11 in raging fury against them 9
Rom 2: 8 for those . . there will be wrath and fury. 11
Heb 10:27 a fearful prospect of judgment, and a fury of fire 10
Rev 16:19 to make her drain the cup of the fury of his wrath. 11
19:15 of the fury of the wrath of God the Almighty. 11
Sir 40: 5 fear of death, and fury and strife 12
48:10 calm the wrath of God before it breaks out in fury 11
2Mc 10:35 and with savage fury cut down every one they met. 11

insolent fury 1. מַרְהֵבָה
Isa 14: 4 oppressor has ceased, the insolent fury ceased! 1

futile 1. λῆρος 2. μάταιος
1Co 3:20 the thoughts of the wise are futile. 2
15:17 your faith is futile 2
Tit 3: 9 they are unprofitable and futile. 2
1Pe 1:18 you were ransomed from the futile ways 2
Wis 15: 8 he forms a futile god from the same clay 2
4Mc 5:11 dispel your futile reasonings 1

become futile 1. ματαιόω
Rom 1:21 but they became futile in their thinking 1

futility 1. ματαιότης
Rom 8:20 for the creation was subjected to futility 1
Eph 4:17 in the futility of their minds; 1

future 1. אַחֲרִית 2. עוֹלָם 3. αἰών 4. ἀπὸ τοῦ νῦν 5. εἰμί 6. λοιπός 7. μέλλω 8. μετὰ ταῦτα 9. τὰ μετὰ ταῦτα
Gen 9:12 is with you, for all future generations 2

2Sm 7:19 and . . shown me future generations, O Lord GOD! *
1Ch 17:17 and hast shown me future generations, O LORD God! *
Prv 19:20 that you may gain wisdom for the future. 1
23:18 Surely there is a future, and your hope 1
24:14 if you find it, there will be a future 1
20 for the evil man has no future; 1
Jer 29:11 and not for evil, to give you a future and a hope. 1
31:17 There is hope for your future, says the LORD 1
Act 24:25 self-control and future judgment 7
1Co 3:22 the present or the future, all are yours; 7
1Ti 6:19 laying up . . a good foundation for the future 7
Heb 11:20 invoked future blessings on Jacob and Esau. 7
AEs 16: 8 For the future we will take care 9
Wis 19: 1 God knew in advance even their future actions 7
Sir 3:31 gives thought to the future 8
11:23 what prosperity could be mine in the future? 4
24 what calamity could happen to me in the future? 4
24:33 leave it to all future generations. 3
1Mc 15: 8 any such future debts shall be canceled for you 5
2Mc 11:19 I will endeavor for the future to help 6
12:31 well disposed to their race in the future also. 6
3Mc 2:31 their future association with the king. 5

future thing 1. sum

2Es 8:46 things that are future are for those 1

G

gad about 1. אזל 2. *περιέρχομαι*
Jer 2:36 How lightly you gad about, changing your way! 1
1Ti 5:13 gadding about from house to house 2

gadfly 1. קֶרֶץ
Jer 46:20 but a gadfly from the north has come upon her. 1

gaily deck 1. טלא
Ezk 16:16 and made for yourself gaily decked shrines 1

gain 1. בין 2. בֶּצַע 3. גדל 4. יְגִיעַ 5. ידע 6. יִתְרוֹן 7. יִתְרוֹן לְ 8. כִּשְׁרוֹן 9. לקח 10. מצא 11. סַחַר 12. עשה 13. קנה 14. רכש 15. שָׁלָל 16. תְּבוּאָה 17. זבן (A) 18. *γίνομαι* 19. *δίδωμι* 20. *ἐκδέχομαι* 21. *ἐκφαίνω* 22. *ἐργασία* 23. *ἐργολάβεια* 24. *εὑρίσκω* 25. *κερδαίνω* 26. *κέρδος* 27. *κτάομαι* 28. *λαμβάνω* 29. *μανθάνω* 30. *μισθός* 31. *ὄφελος* 32. *περιποιέω* 33. *ποιέω* 34. *πορισμός* 35. *συμφέρω* 36. *χάρις* 37. *ὠφελέω* 38. consummo
Gen 26:13 the man became rich, and gained more and more 3
31: 1 was our father's he has gained all this wealth. 12
18 drove away . . all his livestock which he had gained 14
46: 6 goods, which they had gained in the land of Canaan 14
1Sm 8: 3 not walk in his ways, but turned aside after gain; 2
Job 22: 3 is it gain to him if you make your ways blameless? 2
30: 2 could I gain from the strength of their hands •
Ps 119:36 my heart to thy testimonies, and not to gain! 2
Prv 3:14 gain from it is better than gain from silver 11
14 gain from it is better than gain from silver 11
4: 1 be attentive, that you may gain insight; 5
10: 2 Treasures gained by wickedness do not profit •
16 leads to life, the gain of the wicked to sin. 16
15:32 he who heeds admonition gains understanding. 13
16:31 A hoary head . . is gained in a righteous life. 10
19:25 man of understanding, and he will gain knowledge. 1
20:17 Bread gained by deceit is sweet to a man •
21:11 wise man is instructed, he gains knowledge. 9
31:11 he will have no lack of gain. 15
Ecc 1: 3 What does man gain by all the toil 7
2:11 and there was nothing to be gained under the sun. 6
3: 9 What gain has the worker from his toil? 6
5:10 nor he who loves wealth, with gain 16
11 and what gain has their owner but to see them 8
16 and what gain has he that he toiled for the wind 6
Isa 15: 7 Therefore the abundance they have gained 12
33:15 who despises the gain of oppressions 2
56:11 to their own way, each to his own gain, one and all. 2
Jer 2:18 And now what do you gain by going to Egypt •
18 Or what do you gain by going to Assyria •
20: 5 all its gains, all its prized belongings 4
48:36 therefore the riches they gained have perished. 12
Ezk 33:31 but their heart is set on their gain. 2
Dan 2: 8 I know . . that you are trying to gain time 17
Hos 12: 8 Ah, but I am rich, I have gained wealth for myself": 10
Mic 4:13 and shall devote their gain to the LORD 2
Hab 2: 9 Woe to him who gets evil gain for his house 2
Mat 15: 5 What you would have gained from me is given to God 37
16:26 if he gains the whole world and forfeits his life? 25
18:15 If he listens to you, you have gained your brother. 25
27:24 So when Pilate saw that he was gaining nothing 37
Mrk 7:11 What you would have gained from me is Corban' 37
8:36 what does it profit a man, to gain the whole world 25
Lke 9:25 what does it profit a man if he gains the whole world 25
17:33 Whoever seeks to gain his life will lose it 32
21:19 By your endurance you will gain your lives. 27
Act 16:16 brought her owners much gain by soothsaying. 22
19 her owners saw that their hope of gain was gone 22
1Co 7:21 if you can gain your freedom 18
13: 3 but have not love, I gain nothing. 37
15:32 What do I gain if, humanly speaking, I fought 31
2Co 12: 1 I must boast; there is nothing to be gained by it 35
Php 1:21 For to me to live is Christ, and to die is gain. 26
3: 7 whatever gain I had 26
8 in order that I may gain Christ 25
1Ti 3:13 gain a good standing for themselves 32
6: 6 is great gain in godliness with contentment; 34
Tit 1:11 teaching for base gain 26
2Pe 2:15 Balaam . . who loved gain from wrongdoing 30
Jde 1:11 and abandon themselves for the sake of gain 30
16 boasters, flattering people to gain advantage. 36
2Es 4:15 there also we may gain more territory 38
Wis 14: 2 it was desire for gain that planned that vessel 34
Sir 6: 7 When you gain a friend, gain him through testing 27
7 When you gain a friend, gain him through testing 27
33 If you love to listen you will gain knowledge 20
8: 8 because from them you will gain instruction 29
9 because from them you will gain understanding 29
19:25 people who distort kindness to gain a verdict. 21
22:23 Gain the trust of your neighbor in his poverty 27
25: 9 happy is he who has gained good sense 24
10 How great is he who has gained wisdom! 24
29:19 who has fallen into suretyship and pursues gain 23
34:23 what do they gain but toil? 37
25 what has he gained by his washing? 37
26 what has he gained by humbling himself? 37
51:20 I gained understanding with her from the first 27
21 therefore I have gained a good possession. 27
28 you will gain by it much gold. 27
1Mc 2:48 they never let the sinner gain the upper hand. 19
2Mc 10:17 they gained possession of the places 18
13:26 Lysias . . gained their good will 33
15:21 he gains the victory for those who deserve it. 32
3Mc 6: 5 had already gained control of the whole world 28
gain *See also* get, greedy, make, man, means, unjust.

gain admission secretly 1. *παρεισδύω*
Jde 1: 4 For admission has been secretly gained 1

gain an advantage 1. גבר
2Sm 11:23 The men gained an advantage over us, and came out 1

gain an advantage over 1. *πλεονεκτέω*
2Co 2:11 to keep Satan from gaining the advantage over us; 1

gain by trading 1. *διαπραγματεύομαι*
Lke 19:15 might know what they had gained by trading. 1

gain by violence 1. בֶּצַע
Prv 1:19 Such are the ways of all who get gain by violence; 1

gain control 1. *ἐπικρατέω* 2. *κατακρατέω* 3. *κρατέω* 4. *κυριεύω* 5. percontineo
2Es 11:32 this head gained control of the whole earth 5
1Mc 7:22 They gained control of the land of Judah 2
8: 4 how they had gained control of the whole region 2
10:52 and gained control of our country; 1
11: 8 King Ptolemy gained control of the coastal cities 4
49 the Jews had gained control of the city 2
56 Trypho . . gained control of Antioch. 2
15: 3 certain pestilent men have gained control 2
9 When we gain control of our kingdom 3
2Mc 5: 7 He did not gain control of the government 3

dishonest gain 1. בֶּצַע
Jer 22:17 have eyes and heart only for your dishonest gain 1
Ezk 22:13 I strike my hands together at the dishonest gain 1
27 destroying lives to get dishonest gain. 1

gain dominion over 1. dominor
2Es 3:28 Is that why she has gained dominion over Zion? 1

gain entrance 1. *παρεμπίπτω*
Wis 7:25 nothing defiled gains entrance into her. 1

gain full control 1. *κρατέω*
1Mc 14: 6 and gained full control of the country. 1

gain glory 1. *δοξάζομαι*
1Mc 11:51 So the Jews gained glory in the eyes of the king 1

gain ground 1. *εἰς προκοπὴν ἔρχομαι*
2Mc 8: 8 When Philip saw that the man was gaining ground 1

gain honor 1. *δοξάζομαι*
1Mc 2:64 by it you will gain honor. 1

gain in idleness 1. *ἄνεσις*
Wis 13:13 shapes it with skill gained in idleness 1

gain learning 1. *φιλομαθέω*
Sir 0: 3 those living abroad who wished to gain learning, 1

gain mastery 1. *ἐπιβαίνω*
Sir 9: 2 so that she gains mastery over your strength. 1

gain peace 1. *εἰρηνεύω*
4Mc 18: 4 Because of them the nation gained peace 1

gain possession 1. *κυριεύω*
1Mc 10:76 Jonathan gained possession of Joppa. 1

gain possessions 1. אחז
Gen 47:27 they gained possessions in it, and were fruitful 1

shameful gain 1. *αἰσχροκερδῶς*
1Pe 5: 2 Tend . . not for shameful gain but eagerly 1

unjust gain 1. בֶּצַע
Prv 15:27 He who is greedy for unjust gain makes trouble 1
28:16 who hates unjust gain will prolong his days. 1
Jer 6:13 every one is greedy for unjust gain; 1
8:10 every one is greedy for unjust gain; 1

gain wealth 1. *πλουτέω*
Rev 18:15 The merchants of these wares, who gained wealth 1

gain wisdom 1. חכם
Prv 19:20 that you may gain wisdom for the future. 1

galbanum 1. חֶלְבְּנָה 2. *χαλβάνη*
Exd 30:34 sweet spices, stacte, and onycha, and galbanum 1
Sir 24:15 like galbanum, onycha, and stacte 2

gale 1. *ἄνεμος μέγας*
Rev 6:13 sheds its winter fruit when shaken by a gale; 1

gall 1. מְרֹרָה 2. מְרֵרָה 3. ראֹשׁ 4. *χολή*
Job 16:13 he pours out my gall on the ground. 2
20:14 in his stomach; it is the gall of asps within him. 1
25 the glittering point comes out of his gall; 1
Lam 3:19 Remember my . . the wormwood and the gall! 3
Mat 27:34 they offered him wine to drink, mingled with gall; 4
Act 8:23 For I see that you are in the gall of bitterness 4
Tob 6: 4 take the heart and liver and gall 4
6 of what use is the . . heart and gall of the fish? 4
8 as for the gall 4
11: 4 take the gall of the fish with you 4
8 You therefore must anoint his eyes with the gall; 4
11 he sprinkled the gall upon his father's eyes 4

gallery 1. אַתִּיק
Ezk 42: 3 was gallery against gallery in three stories. 1
3 was gallery against gallery in three stories. 1
5 for the galleries took more away from them 1

galley 1. אֳנִי
Isa 33:21 a place . . where no galley with oars can go 1

gallop 1. דהר 2. דַּהֲרָה
Jdg 5:22 with the galloping, galloping of his steeds. 2

22 with the galloping, galloping of his steeds. 2
Nah 3: 2 galloping horse and bounding chariot! 1

gallows 1. עֵץ
Est 2:23 the men were both hanged on the gallows. 1
5:14 Let a gallows 50 cubits high be made 1
14 pleased Haman, and he had the gallows made. 1
6: 4 hanged on the gallows that he had prepared 1
7: 9 the gallows . . is standing in Haman's house 1
10 hanged Haman on the gallows . . he had prepared 1
8: 7 of Haman, and they have hanged him on the gallows 1
9:13 let the . . sons of Haman be hanged on the gallows. 1
25 he and his sons should be hanged on the gallows. 1

game 1. צַיִד 2. *βρῶμα θήρας*
Gen 25:28 Isaac loved Esau, because he ate of his game; 1
27: 3 go out to the field, and hunt game for me 1
5 to the field to hunt for game and bring it 1
7 'Bring me game, and prepare for me savory food 1
19 eat of my game, that you may bless me. 1
25 that I may eat of my son's game and bless you. 1
31 eat of his son's game, that you may bless me. 1
33 Who was it then that hunted game and brought it 1
Sir 36:19 As the palate tastes the kinds of game 2

game (2) 1. *ἀγών*
2Mc 4:18 the quadrennial games were being held at Tyre 1

idle game 1. *παίγνιον*
Wis 15:12 he considered our existence an idle game 1

gangrene 1. *γάγγραινα*
2Ti 2:17 their talk will eat its way like gangrene 1

gape 1. פער 2. *ἐγχάσκω*
Job 16:10 Men have gaped at me with their mouth 1
1Es 4:19 they let all those things go, and gape at her 2

garb 1. שִׂמְלָה
Deu 21:13 shall put off her captive's garb, and shall remain 1

garden 1. גַּן 2. גַּנָּה 3. *κῆπος* 4. *παράδεισος* 5. paradisus
Gen 2: 8 the LORD God planted a garden in Eden, in the east; 1
9 the tree of life also in the midst of the garden 1
10 A river flowed out of Eden to water the garden 1
15 put him in the garden of Eden to till it and keep it. 1
16 You may freely eat of every tree of the garden; 1
3: 1 You shall not eat of any tree of the garden'? 1
2 may eat of the fruit of the trees of the garden; 1
3 the tree which is in the midst of the garden 1
8 walking in the garden in the cool of the day 1
8 hid themselves . . among the trees of the garden. 1
10 the sound of thee in the garden, and I was afraid 1
23 God sent him forth from the garden of Eden 1
24 at the east of the garden of Eden 1
13:10 watered everywhere like the garden of the LORD 1
Num24: 6 like gardens beside a river 2
Deu 11:10 like a garden of vegetables; 1
1Kg 21: 2 Give . . that I may have it for a vegetable garden 1
2Kg 21:18 and was buried in the garden of his house 1
18 and was buried . . in the garden of Uzza; 1
26 And he was buried in his tomb in the garden of Uzza; 1
25: 4 by the way of the gate . . by the king's garden 1
Neh 3:15 wall of the Pool of Shelah of the king's garden 1
Est 1: 5 in the court of the garden of the king's palace. 2
7: 7 rose . . in wrath and went into the palace garden; 2
8 And the king returned from the palace garden 2
Job 8:16 his shoots spread over his garden. 2
Ecc 2: 5 I made myself gardens and parks 2
Sng 4:12 A garden locked is my sister, my bride 1
12 my bride, a garden locked, a fountain sealed. 1
15 a garden fountain, a well of living water 1
16 and come, O south wind! Blow upon my garden 1
16 Let my beloved come to his garden 1
5: 1 I come to my garden, my sister, my bride 1
6: 2 My beloved has gone down to his garden 1
2 gone down . . to pasture his flock in the gardens 1
8:13 O you who dwell in the gardens . . let me hear it. 1
Isa 1:29 blush for the gardens which you have chosen. 2
30 like an oak . . and like a garden without water. 2
51: 3 like Eden, her desert like the garden of the LORD; 1
58:11 you shall be like a watered garden, like a spring 1
61:11 as a garden causes what is sown in it to spring up 2
65: 3 sacrificing in gardens and burning incense 2
66:17 and purify themselves to go into the gardens 2
Jer 29: 5 plant gardens and eat their produce. 2
28 and plant gardens and eat their produce. 2
31:12 their life shall be like a watered garden 1
39: 4 by way of the king's garden through the gate 1
52: 7 a gate between the two walls, by the king's garden 1
Lam 2: 6 He has broken down his booth like that of a garden 1
Ezk 28:13 You were in Eden, the garden of God; 1
31: 8 The cedars in the garden of God could not rival it 1
8 no tree in the garden of God was like it in beauty. 1
9 trees . . envied it, that were in the garden of God. 1
36:35 desolate has become like the garden of Eden 1
Hos 14: 7 they shall flourish as a garden; •
Jol 2: 3 The land is like the garden of Eden before them 1
Ams 4: 9 I laid waste your gardens and your vineyards; 2
9:14 and they shall make gardens and eat their fruit. 2
Lke 13:19 which a man took and sowed in his garden 3
Joh 18: 1 where there was a garden 3
26 Did I not see you in the garden with him? 3
19:41 there was a garden, and in the garden a new tomb 3
41 there was a garden, and in the garden a new tomb 3
2Es 3: 6 And thou didst lead him into the garden 5
Sir 24:30 like a water channel into a garden. 4
40:17 Kindness is like a garden of blessings 4
27 The fear of the Lord is like a garden of blessing 4
LJr 1:71 like a thorn bush in a garden 3
Sus 1: 7 Susanna would go into her husband's garden 4
15 she went in . . and wished to bathe in the garden 4
17 and shut the garden doors so that I may bathe. 4
18 They did as she said, shut the garden doors 4
20 Look, the garden doors are shut, no one sees us 4
25 And one of them ran and opened the garden doors. 4
26 servants heard the shouting in the garden 4
36 As we were walking in the garden alone 4
36 shut the garden doors, and dismissed the maids. 4
38 We were in a corner of the garden 4

garden *See also* land, plot, spacious.

gardener 1. *κηπουρός*
Joh 20:15 Supposing him to be the gardener, she said to him 1

garland 1. לִוְיָה 2. פְּאֵר 3. *στέμμα* 4. *στέφανος* 5. *στέφος*
Prv 1: 9 for they are a fair garland for your head 1
4: 9 She will place on your head a fair garland; 1
14:24 but folly is the garland of fools. •
Isa 61: 3 in Zion–to give them a garland instead of ashes 2
10 as a bridegroom decks himself with a garland 2
Act 14:13 brought oxen and garlands to the gates 3
Jdt 3: 7 welcomed him with garlands and dances 4
15:13 bearing their arms and wearing garlands 4
Sir 50:12 with a garland of brethren around him 4
3Mc 4: 8 their necks encircled with ropes instead of garlands 5

garlic 1. שׁוּם
Num11: 5 We remember the . . onions, and the garlic; 1

garment 1. בֶּגֶד 2. כְּתֹנֶת 3. לְבוּשׁ 4. מַד 5. מְדוּ 6. שַׂלְמָה 7. שִׂמְלָה 8. שִׁית 9. תַּחְרָא 10. לְבוּשׁ (A) 11. *ἔνδυμα* 12. *ἱμάτιον* 13. *στολή* 14. *χιτών* 15. tunica
Gen 3:21 made for Adam and for his wife garments of skins 2
9:23 Then Shem and Japheth took a garment 7
27:15 Then Rebekah took the best garments of Esau 1
27 he smelled the smell of his garments, and blessed 1
35: 2 and purify yourselves, and change your garments 7
37:34 Then Jacob rent his garments, and put sackcloth 7
38:14 she put off her widow's garments, and put on a veil 1
19 she put on the garments of her widowhood. 1
39:12 caught him by his garment, saying, "Lie with me 1
12 But he left his garment in her hand, and fled 1
13 he had left his garment in her hand, and had fled 1
15 he left his garment with me, and fled and got out 1
16 Then she laid up his garment by her 1
18 he left his garment with me, and fled out 1
41:42 and arrayed him in garments of fine linen 1
45:22 To each and all of them he gave festal garments; 7
22 he gave . . five festal garments. 7
49:11 he washes his garments in wine 3
Exd 19:10 and let them wash their garments 7
14 the people; and they washed their garments. 7
22:26 ever you take your neighbor's garment in pledge 6
28: 2 you shall make holy garments for Aaron 1
3 that they make Aaron's garments to consecrate 1
4 These are the garments which they shall make 1
4 they shall make holy garments for Aaron 1
32 an opening . . like the opening in a garment 9
29: 5 you shall take the garments, and put on Aaron 1
21 sprinkle it upon Aaron and his garments 1
21 upon his sons and his sons' garments with him; 1
21 he and his garments shall be holy 1
21 his sons and his sons' garments with him. 1
29 The holy garments of Aaron shall be for his sons 1
31:10 finely worked garments, the holy garments 1
10 holy garments for Aaron the priest 1
10 Aaron the priest and the garments of his sons 1
35:19 the finely wrought garments for ministering 1
19 the holy garments for Aaron the priest 1
19 the garments of his sons, for their service 1
21 for all its service, and for the holy garments. 1
39: 1 they made finely wrought garments 1
1 they made the holy garments for Aaron; 1
23 it was like the opening in a garment 9
41 the finely worked garments for ministering 1
41 the holy garments for Aaron the priest 1
41 the garments of his sons to serve as priests. 1
40:13 put upon Aaron the holy garments 1
Lev 6:10 the priest shall put on his linen garment 4
11 Then he shall put off his garments 1
11 put on other garments, and carry forth the ashes 1
27 when any of its blood is sprinkled on a garment 1
8: 2 Take Aaron and his sons with him, and the garments 1
30 sprinkled it upon Aaron and his garments 1
30 upon his sons and his sons' garments 1
30 so he consecrated Aaron and his garments 1
30 his sons and his sons' garments with him 1
11:32 whether it is an article of wood or a garment 1
13:47 Where there is a leprous disease in a garment 1
47 disease . . whether a woolen or a linen garment 1
49 disease shows . . reddish in the garment 1
51 If the disease has spread in the garment, in warp 1
52 he shall burn the garment, whether diseased 1
53 the disease has not spread in the garment in warp 1
56 shall tear the spot out of the garment or the skin 1
57 then if it appears again in the garment, in warp 1
58 the garment, warp or woof, or anything of skin 1
59 This is the law for a leprous disease in a garment 1
14:55 for leprosy in a garment or in a house 1
15:17 every garment and every skin on which the semen 1
16: 4 these are the holy garments 1
23 shall put off the linen garments which he put 1
24 and put on his garments, and come forth 1
32 make atonement, wearing the holy linen garments 1
19:19 a garment of cloth made of two kinds of stuff 1
21:10 who has been consecrated to wear his garments 1
Num15:38 make tassels on the corners of their garments 1
20:26 strip Aaron of his garments, and put them upon 1
28 Moses stripped Aaron of his garments 1
31:20 purify every garment, every article of skin 1
Deu 22: 3 so you shall do with his garment . . with any lost thing 7
5 nor shall a man put on a woman's garment; 7
17 spread the garment before the elders of the city. 7
24:17 not . . take a widow's garment in pledge; 1
Jos 9:13 and these garments and shoes of ours are worn out 6
Jdg 8:25 And they spread a garment, and every man cast in it 7
26 the purple garments worn by the kings of Mid'ian 1
14:12 30 linen garments and 30 festal garments; 1
13 give me 30 linen garments and 30 festal garments 1
1Sm 27: 9 took . . the asses, the camels, and the garments 1
28: 8 disguised himself and put on other garments 1
2Sm 10: 4 and cut off their garments in the middle 5
13:31 arose, and rent his garments, and lay on the earth; 1
31 and all his servants . . rent their garments. 1
14: 2 be a mourner, and put on mourning garments; 1
20:12 carried Ama'sa . . and threw a garment over him. 1
1Kg 10:25 garments, myrrh, spices, horses, and mules 6
11:29 Now Ahi'jah had clad himself with a new garment; 6
30 Ahi'jah laid hold of the new garment 6
2Kg 1: 8 They answered him, "He wore a garment of haircloth •
5: 5 taking . . gold, and ten festal garments. 1
22 give them . . silver and two festal garments.' 1
23 talents of silver . . with two festal garments 1
26 to accept money and garments, olive orchards 1
7:15 way was littered with garments and equipment 1
9:13 every man . . took his garment, and put it under him 1
25:29 So Jehoi'achin put off his prison garments. 1
1Ch 19: 4 cut off their garments in the middle 5
2Ch 9:24 his present . . garments, myrrh, spices, horses 6
Ezr 2:69 gave to . . the work . . 100 priests' garments. 2
9: 3 When I heard this, I rent my garments and my mantle 1
5 I rose . . with my garments and my mantle rent 1
Neh 7:70 governor gave . . 530 priests' garments. 2
72 rest . . gave . . 67 priests' garments. 2
Est 4: 4 she sent garments to clothe Mor'decai 1
Job 13:28 rotten thing, like a garment that is moth-eaten. 1
30:18 With violence it seizes my garment; 3
37:17 you whose garments are hot when the earth is 1
38: 9 when I made clouds its garment 3
14 it is dyed like a garment. 3
41:13 Who can strip off his outer garment? 3
Ps 22:18 they divide my garments among them 1
73: 6 violence covers them as a garment. 8
102:26 they will all wear out like a garment. 1
104: 2 coverest thyself with light as with a garment 6
6 didst cover it with the deep as with a garment; 3
109:19 May it be like a garment which he wraps round him 1
Prv 20:16 Take a man's garment when he has given surety 1
25:20 like one who takes off a garment on a cold day 1
27:13 Take a man's garment when he has given surety 1
30: 4 Who has wrapped up the waters in a garment? 7
Ecc 9: 8 Let your garments be always white; 1
Sng 4:11 the scent of your garments is like . . Lebanon. 6
5: 3 I had put off my garment, how could I put it on? 2
Isa 9: 5 every garment rolled in blood will be burned 7
50: 9 Behold, all of them will wear out like a garment; 1
51: 6 like smoke, the earth will wear out like a garment 1
8 For the moth will eat them up like a garment 1
52: 1 put on your beautiful garments, O Jerusalem 1
59:17 he put on garments of vengeance for clothing 1
61:10 he has clothed me with the garments of salvation 1
63: 1 that comes . . in crimsoned garments from Bozrah 1
2 garments like his that treads in the wine press? 1
3 their lifeblood is sprinkled upon my garments 1
64: 6 all our righteous deeds are like a polluted garment. 1
Jer 36:24 was afraid, nor did they rend their garments. 1
52:33 Jehoi'achin put off his prison garments. 1
Lam 4:14 defiled . . none could touch their garments. 3
Ezk 16:16 You took some of your garments 1
18 you took your embroidered garments to cover 1
18: 7 and covers the naked with a garment 1

16 and covers the naked with a garment 1
26:16 and strip off their embroidered garments; 1
42:14 outer court without laying there the garments 1
14 they shall put on other garments before they go 1
44:17 they shall wear linen garments; 1
19 to the people, they shall put off the garments 1
19 they shall put on other garments 1
19 holiness to the people with their garments. 1
Dan 3:21 bound in their . . hats, and their other garments 10
Jol 2:13 and rend your hearts and not your garments. 1
Ams 2: 8 beside . . altar upon garments taken in pledge; 1
Hag 2:12 carries holy flesh in the skirt of his garment 1
Zec 3: 3 Joshua was . . clothed with filthy garments. 1
4 Remove the filthy garments from him. 1
5 turban on his head and clothed him with garments; 1
14:14 gold, silver, and garments in great abundance. 1
Mal 2:16 covering one's garment with violence 3
Mat 3: 4 Now John wore a garment of camel's hair 11
9:16 a piece of unshrunk cloth on an old garment 12
16 for the patch tears away from the garment 12
20 touched the fringe of his garment; 12
21 she said to herself, "If I only touch his garment 12
14:36 they might only touch the fringe of his garment 12
17: 2 and his garments became white as light. 12
21: 7 and put their garments on them 12
8 the crowd spread their garments on the road 12
22:11 he saw there a man who had no wedding garment; 11
12 how did you get in here without a wedding garment?' 11
27:35 they divided his garments among them by casting lots 12
Mrk 2:21 sews a piece of unshrunk cloth on an old garment; 12
5:27 touched his garment. 12
28 If I touch even his garments, I shall be made well. 12
30 Who touched my garments? 12
6:56 touch even the fringe of his garment 12
9: 3 garments became glistening, intensely white 12
11: 7 and threw their garments on it 12
8 many spread their garments on the road 12
14:63 the high priest tore his garments, and said 14
15:24 and divided his garments among them 12
Lke 5:36 No one tears a piece from a new garment 12
36 and puts it upon an old garment 12
8:44 touched the fringe of his garment 12
19:35 throwing their garments on the colt 12
36 they spread their garments on the road. 12
23:34 they cast lots to divide his garments. 12
Joh 13: 4 rose from supper, laid aside his garments 12
12 When he had . . and taken his garments 12
19:23 they took his garments and made four parts 12
24 They parted my garments among them 12
Act 7:58 the witnesses laid down their garments 12
9:39 tunics and other garments which Dorcas made 12
14:14 they tore their garments 12
16:22 the magistrates tore the garments off them 12
18: 6 he shook out his garments and said to them 12
22:20 keeping the garments of those who killed him.' 12
23 as they cried out and waved their garments 12
Heb 1:11 they will all grow old like a garment 12
Jas 5: 2 and your garments are moth-eaten. 12
Jde 1:23 hating even the garment spotted by the flesh. 14
Rev 3: 4 people who have not soiled their garments; 12
5 shall be clad thus in white garments 12
18 and white garments to clothe you 12
4: 4 elders, clad in white garments, with golden 12
16:15 keeping his garments that he may not go naked 12
1Es 4:54 the priests' garments 13
5:45 100 priests' garments. 13
8:71 I rent my garments and my holy mantle 12
73 with my garments and my holy mantle rent 12
2Es 2:39 have received glorious garments from the Lord. 15
Jdt 8: 5 wore the garments of her widowhood. 12
10: 3 and took off her widow's garments 12
14:16 groaned and shouted, and rent his garments. 12
AEs 14: 2 put on the garments of distress and mourning 12
15: 1 took off the garments in which she had worshiped 12
Sir 14:17 All living beings become old like a garment 12
42:13 for from garments comes the moth 12
45:10 with a holy garment, of gold and blue and purple 13
Bar 5: 1 Take off the garment of your sorrow 13
LJr 1:11 They deck their gods out with garments like men 11
1Mc 3:49 also brought the garments of the priesthood 12
5:14 other messengers, with their garments rent, came 12
10:21 So Jonathan put on the holy garments 13
62 The king gave orders to take off Jonathan's garments 13
11:71 Jonathan rent his garments 12
14: 9 youths donned the glories and garments of war. 13
2Mc 3:15 in their priestly garments 13
4:38 tore off his garments 14

choice garment 1. מַכְלָל
Ezk 27:24 These traded with you in choice garments 1

festal garment 1. חֲלִיפָה
Jdg 14:19 gave the festal garments to those who had told 1
2Kg 5: 5 taking with him . . gold, and 10 festal garments. 1
22 give them . . silver and two festal garments.' 1
23 tied up two talents . . with two festal garments 1

linen garment 1. סָדִין
Jdg 14:12 I will give you 30 linen garments and 30 festal 1
13 give me 30 linen garments and 30 festal garments 1
Isa 3:23 the garments of gauze, the linen garments 1

garment of gauze 1. גִּלָּיוֹן
Isa 3:23 the garments of gauze, the linen garments 1

soldier's garment 1. מַד לְבוּשׁ
2Sm 20: 8 Now Jo'ab was wearing a soldier's garment 1

garments *See* array.

garner 1. אסף 2. מָזוּ
Ps 144:13 garners be full, providing all manner of store; 2
Isa 62: 9 those who garner it shall eat it 1

garrison 1. מַצָּב 2. מַצָּבָה 3. נְצִיב 4. δύναμις 5. φρουρά 6. φρούριον
1Sm 10: 5 where there is a garrison of the Philistines; 3
13: 3 Jonathan defeated the garrison . . at Geba; 3
4 had defeated the garrison of the Philistines 3
23 And the garrison of the Philistines went out 1
14: 1 go . . to the Philistine garrison on yonder side. 1
4 sought to go over to the Philistine garrison 1
6 go over to the garrison of these uncircumcised; 1
11 both of them showed themselves to the garrison 1
12 And the men of the garrison hailed Jonathan 2
15 the garrison and even the raiders trembled; 1
2Sm 8: 6 Then David put garrisons in Aram of Damascus; 3
14 And he put garrisons in Edom; throughout all Edom 3
14 throughout all Edom he put garrisons 3
23:14 and the garrison of the Philistines was 1
1Ch 11:16 garrison of the Philistines was 3
18: 6 Then David put garrisons in Syria of Damascus; 5
13 he put garrisons in Edom; 3
2Ch 17: 2 set garrisons in the land of Judah 3
1Mc 4:61 he stationed a garrison there to hold it 4
6:21 some of the garrison escaped from the siege •
9:51 he placed garrisons in them to harass Israel. 5
10:75 Apollonius had a garrison in Joppa. 5
11: 3 he stationed forces as a garrison in each city. 5
66 set a garrison over it. 5
12:34 he stationed a garrison there to guard it. 5
36 so that its garrison could neither buy nor sell. •
14:33 he placed there a garrison of Jews. 5
2Mc 10:32 especially well garrisoned 6
12:18 in one place he had left a very strong garrison. 5
13:20 Judas sent in to the garrison whatever was necessary. •

garrison *See also* station.

garrulous 1. γλωσσώδης
Sir 25:20 such is a garrulous wife for a quiet husband. 1

gash 1. גדד 2. גְּדוּד
Jer 41: 5 their clothes torn, and their bodies gashed 1
47: 5 Anakim, how long will you gash yourselves? 1
48:37 upon all the hands are gashes 2
Hos 7:14 for grain and wine they gash themselves 1

gasp 1. נשׁם 2. στενοχωρέω
Isa 42:14 a woman in travail, I will gasp and pant. 1
4Mc 11:11 gasping for breath and in anguish of body 2

gasp for breath 1. יפח 2. ἐπασθμαίνω
Jer 4:31 cry of the daughter of Zion gasping for breath 1
4Mc 6:11 gasping heavily for breath 2

last gasp 1. ψυχουλκέομαι
3Mc 5:25 at their last gasp, since the time had run out 1

gate 1. דֶּלֶת 2. פֶּתַח 3. שַׁעַר 4. αὐλή 5. ἐπί 6. θύρα 7. πύλη 8. πυλών 9. porta
Gen 19: 1 and Lot was sitting in the gate of Sodom. 3
22:17 shall possess the gate of their enemies 3
23:10 of all who went in at the gate of his city 3
18 before all who went in at the gate of his city. 3
24:60 may your descendants possess the gate of those 3
28:17 house of God, and this is the gate of heaven. 3
34:20 and his son Shechem came to the gate of their city 3
24 all who went out of the gate of his city hearkened 3
24 all who went out of the gate of his city. 3
Exd 20:10 the sojourner who is within your gates; 3
27:14 The hangings for the one side of the gate shall be •
16 For the gate of the court there shall be a screen 3
32:26 then Moses stood in the gate of the camp, and said 3
27 go to and fro from gate to gate throughout 3
27 go to and fro from gate to gate throughout 3
35:17 its bases, and the screen for the gate of the court; 3
38:14 The hangings for one side of the gate were •
15 on this hand and that hand by the gate of the court 3
18 the screen for the gate of the court was 3
31 the court, and the bases of the gate of the court 3
39:40 its bases, and the screen for the gate of the court 3
40: 8 hang up the screen for the gate of the court. 3
33 set up the screen of the gate of the court. 3
Num 4:26 screen for the entrance of the gate of the court 2
Deu 3: 5 cities fortified with high walls, gates, and bars 1
5:14 or the sojourner who is within your gates 3
6: 9 you shall write them . . on your gates. 3
11:20 write them . . upon your gates 3
17: 5 then you shall bring forth to your gates 3
21:19 city at the gate of the place where he lives 3
22:15 tokens . . to the elders of the city in the gate; 3
24 shall bring them both out to the gate of that city 3
25: 7 brother's wife . . go up to the gate to the elders 3
Jos 2: 5 when the gate was to be closed, at dark, the men went 3
7 as the pursuers had gone out, the gate was shut. 3
6:26 at the cost of his . . son shall he set up its gates. 1
7: 5 chased them before the gate as far as Sheb'arim 3
8:29 and cast it at the entrance of the gate of the city 3
20: 4 stand at the entrance of the gate of the city 3
Jdg 5: 8 new gods were chosen, then war was in the gates. 3
11 down to the gates marched the people of the LORD. 3
9:35 Ga'al . . stood in the entrance of the gate 3
40 many fell wounded, up to the entrance of the gate. 3
44 and stood at the entrance of the gate of the city 3
16: 2 in wait for him all night at the gate of the city. 3
3 and took hold of the doors of the gate of the city 3
18:16 of war, stood by the entrance of the gate; 3
17 the priest stood by the entrance of the gate 3
Rut 4: 1 And Bo'az went up to the gate and sat down there; 3
10 not be cut off . . from the gate of his native place; 3
11 all the people who were at the gate, and the elders 3
1Sm 4:18 Eli fell . . from his seat by the side of the gate; 3
9:18 Then Saul approached Samuel in the gate, and said 3
17:52 pursued . . as far as Gath and the gates of Ekron 3
21:13 and made marks on the doors of the gate 3
23: 7 by entering a town that has gates and bars. 1
2Sm 3:27 Jo'ab took him aside into the midst of the gate 3
10: 8 drew up in battle . . at the entrance of the gate; 3
11:23 but we drove them back to the entrance of the gate. 3
15: 2 rise early and stand beside the way of the gate; 3
18: 4 the king stood at the side of the gate 3
24 Now David was sitting between the two gates; 3
24 and the watchman went up to the roof of the gate 3
26 and the watchman called to the gate and said 3
33 and went up to the chamber over the gate, and wept; 3
19: 8 Then the king arose, and took his seat in the gate. 3
8 Behold, the king is sitting in the gate"; 3
23:15 the well of Bethlehem which is by the gate! 3
16 out of the well of Bethlehem which was by the gate 3
1Kg 16:34 and set up its gates at the cost of . . Segub 1
17:10 when he came to the gate of the city, behold, a widow 2
22:10 at the entrance of the gate of Sama'ria; 2
2Kg 7: 1 meal shall be sold for . . at the gate of Sama'ria. 3
3 there were . . lepers at the entrance to the gate; 3
17 king had appointed . . to have charge of the gate; 3
17 people trod upon him in the gate, so that he died 3
18 about this time tomorrow in the gate of Sama'ria 3
20 the people trod upon him in the gate and he died. 3
9:31 as Jehu entered the gate, she said, "Is it peace 3
10: 8 Lay them in two heaps at the entrance of the gate 3
11: 6 another third being at the gate Sur and a third 3
6 and a third at the gate behind the guards) 3
19 marching through the gate of the guards 3
14:13 from the E'phraim Gate to the Corner Gate. 3
13 from the E'phraim Gate to the Corner Gate. 3
15:35 He built the upper gate of the house of the LORD. 3
23: 8 and he broke down the high places of the gates 3
8 that were at the entrance of the gate of Joshua 3
8 which were on one's left at the gate of the city. 3
25: 4 by the way of the gate between the two walls 3
1Ch 9:18 stationed hitherto in the king's gate 3
23 in charge of the gates of the house of the LORD 3
11:17 from the well of Bethlehem which is by the gate! 3
18 the well of Bethlehem which was by the gate 3
16:42 The sons of Jedu'thun were appointed to the gate. 3
22: 3 iron for nails for the doors of the gates 3
26:13 cast lots by fathers' houses . . for their gates. 3
16 the gate of Shal'lecheth on the road that goes up. 3
2Ch 8: 5 fortified cities with walls, gates, and bars 1
14 gatekeepers . . for the several gates; 3
14: 7 surround them with . . gates and bars; 1
18: 9 the entrance of the gate of Sama'ria; 2
23: 5 one third at the Gate of the Foundation; 3
15 the entrance of the horse gate of the king's house 3
19 gatekeepers at the gates of the house of the LORD 3
20 marching through the upper gate 3
24: 8 set it outside the gate of the house of the LORD. 3
25:23 from the E'phraim Gate to the Corner Gate. 3
23 from the E'phraim Gate to the Corner Gate. 3
26: 9 built towers in Jerusalem at the Corner Gate 3
9 built towers in Jerusalem . . at the Valley Gate 3
27: 3 He built the upper gate of the house of the LORD 3
31: 2 minister in the gates of the camp of the LORD 3
32: 6 in the square at the gate of the city 3
33:14 wall . . for the entrance into the Fish Gate 3
35:15 the gatekeepers were at each gate; 3
Neh 1: 3 Jerusalem . . its gates are destroyed by fire. 3
2: 3 its gates have been destroyed by fire? 3
8 give me timber to make beams for the gates 3
13 I inspected the walls . . and its gates 3
17 Jerusalem lies in ruins with its gates burned. 3
6: 1 I had not set up the doors in the gates) 3
7: 3 Let not the gates of Jerusalem be opened 3
11:19 brethren, who kept watch at the gates, were 172. 3
12:25 standing guard at the storehouses of the gates. 3
30 purified the people and the gates and the wall. 3
13:19 When it began to be dark at the gates of Jerusalem 3

19 I set some of my servants over the gates 3
22 purify themselves and come and guard the gates 3
Est 2:19 Mor'decai was sitting at the king's gate. 3
21 as Mor'decai was sitting at the king's gate 3
3: 2 the king's servants who were at the king's gate 3
3 the king's servants who were at the king's gate 3
4: 2 he went up to the entrance of the king's gate 3
2 no one might enter the king's gate clothed 3
6 open square of the city in front of the king's gate 3
5: 9 But when Haman saw Mor'decai in the king's gate 3
13 I see Mor'decai the Jew sitting at the king's gate. 3
6:10 to Mor'decai the Jew who sits at the king's gate. 3
12 Then Mor'decai returned to the king's gate. 3
Job 5: 4 far from safety, they are crushed in the gate 3
29: 7 When I went out to the gate of the city 3
31:21 because I saw help in the gate; 3
38:17 Have the gates of death been revealed to you 3
17 or have you seen the gates of deep darkness? 3
Ps 9:13 O thou who liftest me up from the gates of death 3
14 in the gates of the daughter of Zion I may rejoice 3
24: 7 Lift up your heads, O gates! 3
9 Lift up your heads, O gates! 3
69:12 I am the talk of those who sit in the gate 3
87: 2 LORD loves the gates of Zion more than all 3
100: 4 Enter his gates with thanksgiving, and his courts 3
107:18 drew near to the gates of death. 3
118:19 Open to me the gates of righteousness 3
20 This is the gate of the LORD; 3
122: 2 feet . . standing within your gates, O Jerusalem! 3
127: 5 when he speaks with his enemies in the gate. 3
147:13 For he strengthens the bars of your gates; 3
Prv 1:21 at the entrance of the city gates she speaks 3
8: 3 beside the gates in front of the town 3
34 who listens to me, watching daily at my gates 1
14:19 the wicked at the gates of the righteous. 3
22:22 Do not . . crush the afflicted at the gate; 3
24: 7 in the gate he does not open his mouth. 3
31:23 Her husband is known in the gates 3
31 let her works praise her in the gates. 3
Sng 7: 4 eyes are pools . . by the gate of Bath-rab'bim. 3
Isa 3:26 her gates shall lament and mourn; 2
13: 2 wave . . for them to enter the gates of the nobles. 2
14:31 Wail, O gate; cry, O city; melt in fear 3
22: 7 and the horsemen took their stand at the gates. 3
24:12 in the city, the gates are battered into ruins. 3
26: 2 Open the gates, that the righteous nation 3
28: 6 those who turn back the battle at the gate. 3
29:21 lay a snare for him who reproves in the gate 3
38:10 I am consigned to the gates of Sheol 3
45: 1 to open doors . . that gates may not be closed 3
54:12 pinnacles of agate, your gates of carbuncles 3
60:11 Your gates shall be open continually; 3
18 your walls Salvation, and your gates Praise. 3
62:10 Go through, go through the gates, prepare the way 3
Jer 1:15 at the entrance of the gates of Jerusalem 3
7: 2 Stand in the gate of the LORD'S house, and proclaim 3
2 all you men of Judah who enter these gates 3
14: 2 Judah mourns and her gates languish; 3
15: 7 I have winnowed them . . in the gates of the land; 3
17:19 Go and stand in the Benjamin Gate 3
19 they go out, and in all the gates of Jerusalem 3
20 of Jerusalem, who enter by these gates. 3
21 or bring it in by the gates of Jerusalem. 3
24 and bring in no burden by the gates of this city 3
25 then there shall enter by the gates of this city 3
27 and enter by the gates of Jerusalem 3
27 then I will kindle a fire in its gates 3
19: 2 at the entry of the Potsherd Gate, and proclaim 2
20: 2 the upper Benjamin Gate of the house of the LORD. 3
22: 2 and your people who enter these gates. 3
4 then there shall enter the gates of this house 3
19 and cast forth beyond the gates of Jerusalem. 3
26:10 took their seat in the entry of the New Gate 2
31:40 to the corner of the Horse Gate toward the east 3
36:10 at the entry of the New Gate of the LORD'S house. 3
37:13 When he was at the Benjamin Gate 3
38: 7 the king was sitting in the Benjamin Gate 3
39: 3 king of Babylon came and sat in the middle gate 3
4 garden through the gate between the two walls; 3
49:31 that has no gates or bars, that dwells alone. 1
51:58 and her high gates shall be burned with fire. 3
52: 7 went out from the city by night by the way of a gate 3
Lam 1: 4 all her gates are desolate, her priests groan; 3
2: 9 Her gates have sunk into the ground; 3
4:12 foe or enemy could enter the gates of Jerusalem. 3
Ezk 8: 5 behold, north of the altar gate, in the entrance 3
14 he brought me to the entrance of the north gate 3
9: 2 six men came from the direction of the upper gate 3
10:19 the door of the east gate of the house of the LORD; 3
11: 1 to the east gate of the house of the LORD 3
21:15 hearts may melt, and many fall at all their gates. 3
22 to set battering rams against the gates 3
26: 2 Aha, the gate of the peoples is broken 1
10 when he enters your gates as one enters a city 3
38:11 without walls, and having no bars or gates 1
40: 6 and measured the threshold of the gate 3
7 and the threshold of the gate by the vestibule 3
7 by the vestibule of the gate at the inner end 3
9 the vestibule of the gate was at the inner end. 3
10 three side rooms on either side of the east gate; 3
13 Then he measured the gate from the back of the one 3
15 From the front of the gate at the entrance 3
15 to the end of the inner vestibule of the gate 3
18 the pavement ran along the side of the gates 3
18 corresponding to the length of the gates; 3
19 distance from the inner front of the lower gate 3
20 there was a gate which faced toward the north 3
21 of the same size as those of the first gate; 3
22 as those of the gate which faced toward the east; 3
23 And opposite the gate on the north, as on the east 3
23 as on the east, was a gate to the inner court; 3
23 he measured from gate to gate, 100 cubits. 3
23 he measured from gate to gate, 100 cubits. 3
24 behold, there was a gate on the south; 3
27 there was a gate on the south of the inner court; 3
27 he measured from gate to gate toward the south 3
27 he measured from gate to gate toward the south 3
28 he brought me to the inner court by the south gate 3
28 he measured the south gate; it was of the same size 3
32 he measured the gate; it was of the same size 3
35 Then he brought me to the north gate 3
38 with its door in the vestibule of the gate 3
39 And in the vestibule of the gate were two tables 3
40 the entrance of the north gate were two tables; 2
40 on the other side of the vestibule of the gate 3
41 four tables on the outside of the side of the gate 3
44 one at the side of the north gate facing south 3
44 at the side of the south gate facing north. 3
48 the breadth of the gate was fourteen cubits; 3
48 the sidewalls of the gate were three cubits 6
42:15 he led me out by the gate which faced east 3
43: 1 Afterward he brought me to the gate 3
1 he brought me to the gate, the gate facing east. 3
4 glory of the LORD entered the temple by the gate 3
44: 1 me back to the outer gate of the sanctuary 3
2 And he said to me, "This gate shall remain shut; 3
3 he shall enter by way of the vestibule of the gate 3
4 he brought me by way of the north gate to the front 3
11 having oversight at the gates of the temple, 3
17 they enter the gates of the inner court, 3
17 they minister at the gates of the inner court, 3
45:19 and the posts of the gate of the inner court. 3
46: 1 The gate of the inner court that faces east 3
2 prince shall enter by the vestibule of the gate 3
2 and shall take his stand by the post of the gate. 3
2 he shall worship at the threshold of the gate. 3
2 but the gate shall not be shut until evening. 3
3 shall worship at the entrance of that gate 3
8 he shall go in by the vestibule of the gate 3
9 he who enters by the north gate to worship 3
9 by the north gate . . shall go out by the south gate; 3
9 he who enters by the south gate 3
9 by the south gate shall go out by the north gate 3
9 return by way of the gate by which he entered 3
12 the gate facing east shall be opened for him 3
12 after he has gone out the gate shall be shut. 3
19 the entrance, which was at the side of the gate 3
47: 2 Then he brought me out by way of the north gate 3
2 and led me round on the outside to the outer gate 3
48:31 three gates, the gate of Reuben, the gate of Judah 3
31 three gates, the gate of Reuben, the gate of Judah 3
31 three gates, the gate of Reuben, the gate of Judah 3
31 of Reuben, the gate of Judah, and the gate of Levi 3
31 gates of the city being named after the tribes 3
32 three gates, the gate of Joseph, the gate 3
32 gates, the gate of Joseph, the gate of Benjamin 3
32 gates, the gate of Joseph, the gate of Benjamin 3
32 the gate of Benjamin, and the gate of Dan. 3
33 three gates, the gate of Simeon, the gate 3
33 the gate of Simeon, the gate of Is'sachar 3
33 the gate of Is'sachar, and the gate of Zeb'ulun. 3
33 the gate of Is'sachar, and the gate of Zeb'ulun. 3
34 three gates, the gate of Gad, the gate of Asher 3
34 three gates, the gate of Gad, the gate of Asher 3
34 of Gad, the gate of Asher, and the gate of Naph'tali. 3
34 of Gad, the gate of Asher, and the gate of Naph'tali. 3
Hos 11: 6 consume the bars of their gates, and devour them •
Ams 5:10 They hate him who reproves in the gate 3
12 take a bribe, and turn aside the needy in the gate. 3
15 and love good, and establish justice in the gate; 3
Obd 1:11 and foreigners entered his gates 3
13 You should not have entered the gate of my people 3
Mic 1: 9 it has reached to the gate of my people 3
12 evil has come down . . to the gate of Jerusalem. 3
2:13 they will break through and pass the gate 3
Nah 2: 6 The river gates are opened 3
3:13 The gates of your land are wide open to your foes; 3
Zep 1:10 a cry will be heard from the Fish Gate 3
Zec 8:16 render in your gates judgments that are true 3
14:10 aloft upon its site from the Gate of Benjamin 3
10 Gate of Benjamin to the place of the former gate 3
10 the place of the former gate, to the Corner Gate 3
Mat 7:13 Enter by the narrow gate; for the gate is wide 7
13 for the gate is wide and the way is easy 7
14 For the gate is narrow and the way is hard 7
24:33 you know that he is near, at the very gates. 6
Mrk 13:29 you know that he is near, at the very gates. 6
Lke 7:12 As he drew near to the gate of the city 7
16:20 at his gate lay a poor man named Laz'arus 8
Act 3: 2 whom they laid daily at that gate of the temple 6
10 at the Beautiful Gate of the temple 7
9:24 were watching the gates day and night, to kill him; 7
10:17 stood before the gate 8
12:10 they came to the iron gate leading into the city. 7
14 in her joy she did not open the gate but ran 8
14 told that Peter was standing at the gate. 8
14:13 brought oxen and garlands to the gates 8
16:13 we went outside the gate to the riverside 7
21:30 at once the gates were shut. 6
Heb 13:12 Jesus also suffered outside the gate 7
Rev 21:12 It had a great, high wall, with twelve gates 8
12 and at the gates twelve angels 8
12 and on the gates the names of the twelve tribes •
13 on the east three gates, on the north three gates 8
13 on the east three gates, on the north three gates 8
13 on the south three gates 8
13 and on the west three gates. 8
15 to measure the city and its gates and walls. 8
21 And the twelve gates were twelve pearls 8
21 each of the gates made of a single pearl 8
25 and its gates shall never be shut by day- 8
22:14 that they may enter the city by the gates. 8
1Es 1:16 The gatekeepers were at each gate 8
5:47 in the square before the first gate 8
7: 9 the gatekeepers were at each gate. 8
9:38 the open square before the east gate of the temple; 8
41 in the open square before the gate of the temple 8
2Es 3:19 thy glory passed through the four gates 9
Tob 11:16 meet his daughter-in-law at the gate of Nineveh 7
Jdt 1: 3 at the gates he built towers 7
4 he made its gates, which were 70 cubits high 7
7:22 and in the passages through the gates 7
8:33 Stand at the city gate tonight 7
10: 6 Then they went out to the city gate of Bethulia 7
9 Order the gate of the city to be opened for me 7
9 they ordered the young men to open the gate •
13:10 came to its gates. 7
11 called out . . to the watchmen at the gates 7
11 Open, open the gate! God, our God, is still with us 7
12 they hurried down to the city gate 7
13 they opened the gate and admitted them 7
AEs 16:18 the man . . has been hanged at the gate of Susa 7
Wis 6:14 he will find her sitting at his gates. 7
16:13 lead men down to the gates of Hades and back again. 7
Sir 49:13 set up the gates and bars 7
LJr 1:18 just as the gates are shut on every side upon a man 4
1Mc 4:38 the altar profaned, and the gates burned 6
57 they restored the gates 7
5:22 He pursued them to the gate of Ptolemais 7
47 and blocked up the gates with stones. 7
9:50 with high walls and gates and bars. 7
10:75 the men of the city closed its gates •
76 the men . . became afraid and opened the gates •
11: 2 the people of the cities opened their gates to him •
12:38 he fortified it and installed gates with bolts. 6
48 the men of Ptolemais closed the gates and seized him 7
13:33 high towers and great walls and gates and bolts 7
15:39 build up Kedron and fortify its gates 7
2Mc 1: 8 burned the gate and shed innocent blood 8
3:19 Some of the maidens . . ran together to the gates 8
8:33 burned those who had set fire to the sacred gates 8
10:36 Others broke open the gates 7
3Mc 5:48 by the elephants going out at the gate 7
51 they stood now at the gates of death. 7
6:18 opened the heavenly gates 7
31 near to death, or rather, who stood at its gates 5
4Mc 3:13 Eluding the sentinels at the gates 7

gate *See also* keeper.

city gate 1. שַׁעַר

Lam 5:14 The old men have quit the city gate 1

city's gate 1. *χωρίον*

2Mc 12: 7 because the city's gates were closed, he withdrew 1

gatekeeper 1. שֹׁעֵר 2. שֹׁעֵר הַסִּפִּים 3. *θυρωρός*

2Kg 7:10 came and called to the gatekeepers of the city 1
11 Then the gatekeepers called out, and it was told 1
1Ch 9:17 gatekeepers . . Shallum, Akkub, Talmon, Ahi'man 1
18 the gatekeepers of the camp of the Levites. 1
21 Zechari'ah . . was gatekeeper at the entrance 1
22 chosen as gatekeepers at the thresholds, were 212 1
24 The gatekeepers were on the four sides 1
26 for the four chief gatekeepers, who were Levites 1
15:18 and the gatekeepers O'bed-e'dom and Je-i'el. 1
23 and Elka'nah were to be gatekeepers for the ark. 1
24 Jehi'ah also were to be gatekeepers for the ark. 1
16:38 O'bed-e'dom . . and Hosah were to be gatekeepers. 1
23: 5 4,000 gatekeepers 1
26: 1 As for the divisions of the gatekeepers 1
12 These divisions of the gatekeepers 1
19 These were the divisions of the gatekeepers 1
2Ch 8:14 appointed . . gatekeepers in their divisions 1
23: 4 one third shall be gatekeepers 2
19 He stationed the gatekeepers at the gates 1
34:13 Levites were . . officials, and gatekeepers. 1

35:15 the gatekeepers were at each gate; 1
Ezr 2:42 sons of the gatekeepers: the sons of Shallum 1
70 singers, the gatekeepers, and the temple servants 1
7: 7 singers and gatekeepers, and the temple 1
10:24 Of the gatekeepers: Shallum, Telem, and Uri. 1
Neh 7: 1 gatekeepers, the singers, and the Levites 1
45 gatekeepers: the sons of Shallum, the sons of Ater 1
73 gatekeepers, the singers, some of the people 1
10:28 gatekeepers, the singers, the temple servants 1
39 priests . . the gatekeepers and the singers. 1
11:19 gatekeepers, Akkub, Talmon and their brethren 1
12:25 gatekeepers standing guard at the storehouses 1
45 as did the singers and the gatekeepers 1
47 portions for the singers and the gatekeepers; 1
13: 5 given by commandment to the . . gatekeepers 1
Joh 10: 3 To him the gatekeeper opens 3
1Es 1:16 The gatekeepers were at each gate 3
5:28 The gatekeepers: the sons of Shallum 3
46 the temple singers, the gatekeepers 3
7: 9 the gatekeepers were at each gate. 3
8: 5 temple singers and gatekeepers 3
22 temple singers or gatekeepers 3
9:25 Of the gatekeepers: Shallum and Telem. 3

gateway 1. שַׁעַר 2. *προαύλιον* 3. *πυλών*

Ezk 8: 3 to the entrance of the gateway of the inner court 1
11: 1 at the door of the gateway there were 25 men; 1
40: 3 he was standing in the gateway. 1
6 Then he went into the gateway facing east 1
8 Then he measured the vestibule of the gateway 1
11 breadth of the opening of the gateway, ten cubits; 1
11 and the breadth of the gateway, thirteen cubits. 1
14 the vestibule of the gateway was the court. 1
16 the gateway had windows round about 1
Mrk 14:68 he went out into the gateway 2
Act 12:13 when he knocked at the door of the gateway 3

gather 1. אגר 2. אסף 3. אֹסֵף 4. ארה 5. בצר 6. דגר 7. חֲשְׁרָה 8. יעד 9. כנס 10. לקט 11. משך 12. סוֹד 13. סוּף 14. עשה 15. קבץ 16. קְבֻצָה 17. קהל 18. קוה 19. קצר 20. קשש 21. רכש 22. *ἀθροίζω* 23. *εἰμί* 24. *ἐκκλησία* 25. *ἐπίθεσις* 26. *ἐπισυνάγω* 27. *ἔρχομαι* 28. *λαμβάνω* 29. *προστίθημι* 30. *συλλέγω* 31. *συμπορεύομαι* 32. *συνάγω* 33. *συναθροίζω* 34. *συνέρχομαι* 35. *συντρέχω* 36. *συστρέφω* 37. *τρυγάω* 38. colligo 39. congrego 40. meto 41. vindemio

Gen 12: 5 possessions which they had gathered 21
25: 8 Abraham . . was gathered to his people. 2
17 died, and was gathered to his kindred. 2
29: 3 when all the flocks were gathered there 2
31:46 Jacob said to his kinsmen, "Gather stones 10
34:30 my numbers are few, and if they gather themselves 2
35:29 he died and was gathered to his people 2
41:35 let them gather all the food of these good years 15
49:29 I am to be gathered to my people; bury me with my 2
33 Jacob . . was gathered to his people. 2
Exd 16: 4 the people shall go out and gather a day's portion 10
5 it will be twice as much as they gather daily. 10
16 'Gather of it, every man of you 10
17 Israel did so; they gathered, some more, some less. 10
18 each gathered according to what he could eat. 10
21 Morning by morning they gathered it, each as much 10
22 the sixth day they gathered twice as much bread 10
26 Six days you shall gather it; but on the seventh 10
27 some of the people went out to gather 10
23:10 shall sow your land and gather in its yield; 2
16 end of the year, when you gather in from the field 2
Lev 19: 9 neither shall you gather the gleanings after 10
10 neither shall you gather the fallen grapes 10
23:22 nor shall you gather the gleanings 10
39 when you have gathered in the produce of the land 2
25: 3 prune your vineyard, and gather in its fruit 2
5 of your undressed vine you shall not gather 5
11 nor gather the grapes from the undressed vines 5
20 we may not sow or gather in our crop?' 2
26:25 if you gather within your cities I will send 2
Num10: 3 all the congregation shall gather themselves 8
4 leaders . . shall gather themselves to you. 8
11: 8 people went about and gathered it, and ground it 10
16 Gather for me 70 men of the elders of Israel 2
24 he gathered 70 men of the elders of the people 2
32 people rose . . and gathered the quails; 2
32 he who gathered least gathered ten homers; 2
15:32 found a man gathering sticks on the sabbath day. 20
33 those who found him gathering sticks 20
19:10 he who gathers the ashes of the heifer shall wash 2
20:10 Moses and Aaron gathered the assembly together 17
24 Aaron shall be gathered to his people; 2
26 Aaron shall be gathered to his people 2
21:16 LORD said to Moses, "Gather the people together 2
23 He gathered all his men together, and went out 2
27: 3 those who gathered themselves together 8
13 you also shall be gathered to your people 2
13 as your brother Aaron was gathered 2
31: 2 afterward you shall be gathered to your people. 2
Deu 4:10 Gather the people to me, that I may let them hear 17
11:14 that you may gather in your grain and your wine 2
13:16 You shall gather all its spoil into the midst 15
28:38 carry much seed . . and shall gather little in; 2
39 but you shall neither . . nor gather the grapes; 1
30: 3 gather you again from all the peoples 15
4 from there the LORD your God will gather you 15
32:50 die . . and be gathered to your people, as Aaron 2
50 died . . and was gathered to his people; 2
33: 5 when the heads of the people were gathered 2
Jos 2:18 you shall gather into your house your father 2
10: 5 the five kings . . gathered their forces, and went 2
6 all the kings of . . are gathered against us. 15
22:12 whole assembly of the people of Israel gathered 17
24: 1 Then Joshua gathered all . . Israel to Shechem 2
Jdg 2:10 generation also were gathered to their fathers; 2
3:13 He gathered to himself the Ammonites 2
4: 6 commands you, 'Go, gather your men at Mount Tabor 11
12: 4 Then Jephthah gathered all the men of Gilead 15
16:23 the lords of the Philistines gathered to offer 2
20:11 all the men of Israel gathered against the city 2
Rut 2: 7 Pray, let me glean and gather among the sheaves 2
1Sm 7: 5 Gather all Israel at Mizpah, and I will pray 15
6 they gathered at Mizpah, and drew water 15
7 that the people of Israel had gathered at Mizpah 15
17: 1 Philistines gathered their armies for battle; 2
1 and they were gathered at Socoh 2
2 And Saul and the men of Israel were gathered 2
22: 2 every one who was in distress . . gathered to him; 15
28: 1 the Philistines gathered their forces for war 15
4 Saul gathered all Israel, and they encamped 15
29: 1 Now the Philistines gathered all their forces 15
2Sm 3:21 I . . will gather all Israel to my lord the king 15
6: 1 David . . gathered all the chosen men of Israel 2
10:15 they gathered themselves together. 2
17:11 my counsel is that all Israel be gathered to you 2
21:13 they gathered the bones of those who were hanged. 2
22:12 He made . . thick clouds, a gathering of water. 7
23: 9 Philistines who were gathered there for battle 2
1Kg 11:24 he gathered men about him and became leader 15
17:10 a widow was there gathering sticks; 20
12 I am gathering a couple of sticks, that I may go 20
18:19 send and gather all Israel to me at Mount Carmel 15
2Kg 4:39 One . . went out into the field to gather herbs 10
39 went out . . found a wild vine and gathered from it 10
22:20 I will gather you to your fathers, and you shall be 2
20 and you shall be gathered to your grave in peace 2
23: 1 and all the elders . . were gathered to him. 2
1Ch 11:13 Philistines were gathered there for battle. 2
16:35 O God of our salvation, and gather and save us 15
2Ch 12: 5 had gathered at Jerusalem because of Shishak 2
13: 7 scoundrels gathered about him and defied 15
15: 9 he gathered all Judah and Benjamin 15
10 They were gathered at Jerusalem 15
23: 2 went about . . and gathered the Levites 15
24: 5 he gathered the priests and the Levites 15
5 gather from all Israel money to repair 15
29:15 They gathered their brethren 2
20 Hezeki'ah . . gathered the officials of the city 2
32: 4 A great many people were gathered 15
34:28 Behold, I will gather you to your fathers 2
28 you shall be gathered to your grave in peace 2
Ezr 3: 1 people gathered as one man to Jerusalem. 2
7:28 gathered leading men from Israel to go up 15
8:15 I gathered them to the river that runs to Aha'va 15
9: 4 gathered round me while I sat appalled 2
10: 1 great assembly . . gathered to him out of Israel; 15
Neh 1: 9 I will gather them thence and bring them 15
5:16 my servants were gathered there for the work. 15
8: 1 people gathered as one man into the square 2
12:44 gather . . portions required by the law 9
Est 2: 3 officers . . to gather all the beautiful young 15
8 many maidens were gathered in Susa the capital 15
4:16 gather all the Jews to be found in Susa, and . . fast 9
8:11 the Jews . . to gather and defend their lives 17
9: 2 the Jews gathered in their cities . . to lay hands 17
15 The Jews . . gathered also on the fourteenth day 17
16 Jews who . . also gathered to defend their lives 17
18 Jews . . in Susa gathered on the thirteenth day 17
Job 15:27 with his fat, and gathered fat upon his loins 14
24: 6 They gather their fodder in the field 19
34:14 gather to himself his breath 2
Ps 33: 7 He gathered the waters of the sea as in a bottle; 9
35:15 But at my stumbling they gathered in glee 2
39: 6 man heaps up, and knows not who will gather! 2
41: 6 empty words, while his heart gathers mischief; 15
47: 9 The princes of the peoples gather 2
50: 5 Gather to me my faithful ones, who made a covenant 2
102:22 when peoples gather together, and kingdoms 15
106:47 O LORD . . and gather us from among the nations 15
107: 3 gathered in from the lands, from the east 15
147: 2 LORD . . gathers the outcasts of Israel. 9
Prv 6: 8 gathers her sustenance in harvest. 1
10: 5 A son who gathers in summer is prudent 1
13:11 he who gathers little by little will increase 15
27:25 herbage of the mountains is gathered 2
28: 8 gathers it for him who is kind to the poor. 15
30: 4 Who has gathered the wind in his fists? 2
Ecc 2: 8 I also gathered for myself silver and gold 9
26 to the sinner he gives . . gathering and heaping 2
Sng 5: 1 I gather my myrrh with my spice, I eat my honeycomb 4
6: 2 to pasture his flock . . and to gather lilies. 10
Isa 10:14 as men gather eggs that have been forsaken 2
14 eggs . . forsaken so I have gathered all the earth; 2
11:12 outcasts . . and gather the dispersed of Judah 15
13:14 or like sheep with none to gather them 15
17: 5 as when the reaper gathers standing grain 2
24:22 They will be gathered together as prisoners 2
27:12 you will be gathered one by one 10
33: 4 spoil is gathered as the caterpillar gathers; 2
4 spoil is gathered as the caterpillar gathers; 3
34:15 lay and hatch and gather her young in her shadow; 6
15 yea, there shall the kites be gathered 15
16 and his Spirit has gathered them. 15
40:11 he will gather the lambs in his arms 15
43: 5 from the east, and from the west I will gather you; 15
9 Let all the nations gather together 15
49: 5 to him, and that Israel might be gathered to him 2
18 they all gather, they come to you. 15
54: 7 but with great compassion I will gather you. 15
56: 8 the Lord GOD, who gathers the outcasts of Israel 15
8 I will gather yet others to him 15
8 others to him besides those already gathered. 15
60: 7 All the flocks of Kedar shall be gathered to you 15
62: 9 those who gather it shall drink it in the courts 15
66:18 and I am coming to gather all nations and tongues; 15
Jer 3:17 and all nations shall gather to it 18
6:11 and upon the gatherings of young men, also; 12
7:18 children gather wood, the fathers kindle fire 10
8: 2 and they shall not be gathered or buried; 2
13 When I would gather them, says the LORD 13
9:22 sheaves after the reaper, and none shall gather 2
17:11 Like the partridge that gathers a brood 6
23: 3 Then I will gather the remnant of my flock 15
25:33 They shall not be lamented, or gathered, or buried; 2
26: 9 And all the people gathered about Jeremiah 17
29:14 and I will restore your fortunes and gather you 15
31: 8 gather them from the farthest parts of the earth 15
10 say, 'He who scattered Israel will gather him 15
32:37 Behold, I will gather them from all the countries 15
40:10 as for you, gather wine and summer fruits and oil 2
12 they gathered wine and summer fruits 2
15 all the Jews who are gathered about you 15
49: 5 with none to gather the fugitives. 15
Ezk 11:17 I will gather you from the peoples 15
16:37 therefore, behold, I will gather all your lovers 15
37 I will gather them against you from every side 15
20:34 and gather you out of the countries 15
41 and gather you out of the countries 15
22:19 I will gather you into the midst of Jerusalem. 15
20 As men gather silver and bronze and iron and lead 16
20 so I will gather you in my anger and in my wrath 15
21 I will gather you and blow upon you with the fire 9
28: 4 and have gathered gold and silver 14
25 When I gather the house of Israel 15
29: 5 you shall fall . . and not be gathered and buried. 2
13 I will gather the Egyptians from the peoples 15
34:13 and gather them from the countries 15
36:24 and gather you from all the countries 15
37:21 and will gather them from all sides 15
38: 8 the land where people were gathered 15
12 the people who were gathered from the nations 2
39:17 gather from all sides to the sacrificial feast 2
27 and gathered them from their enemies' lands 15
28 and then gathered them into their own land. 9
Hos 1:11 and the people of Israel shall be gathered 15
9: 6 Egypt shall gather them 15
10:10 and nations shall be gathered against them 2
Jol 1:14 Gather the elders and all the inhabitants 2
2:16 gather the people. Sanctify the congregation; 2
16 gather the children, even nursing infants. 2
3: 2 I will gather all the nations 15
11 nations round about, gather yourselves there. 15
Mic 1: 7 for from the hire of a harlot she gathered them 15
2:12 I will surely gather all of you, O Jacob 2
12 O Jacob, I will gather the remnant of Israel; 15
4: 6 and gather those who have been driven away 15
12 he has gathered them as sheaves to the threshing 15
7: 1 as when the summer fruit has been gathered 3
Nah 3:18 scattered on the mountains with none to gather 15
Hab 1: 9 They gather captives like sand. 2
15 he gathers them in his seine; 2
2: 5 He gathers for himself all nations 2
Zep 3: 8 For my decision is to gather nations 2
19 And I will save the lame and gather the outcast 15
Zec 10: 8 I will signal for them and gather them 15
10 and gather them from Assyria; 15
14: 2 For I will gather all the nations 2
Mat 3:12 clear his threshing floor and gather his wheat 32
6:26 they neither sow nor reap nor gather into barns 32
7:16 Are grapes gathered from thorns 30
12:30 and he who does not gather with me scatters. 32
13: 2 great crowds gathered about him 32
28 Then do you want us to go and gather them? 30
29 lest in gathering the weeds you root up the wheat 30
30 Gather the weeds first and bind them in bundles 30
30 but gather the wheat into my barn. 32
40 as the weeds are gathered and burned with fire 30
41 and they will gather out of his kingdom 30

47 and gathered fish of every kind; 32
16: 9 and how many baskets you gathered? 28
10 and how many baskets you gathered? 28
17:22 As they were gathering in Galilee 36
18:20 For where two or three are gathered in my name 32
22:10 gathered all whom they found, both bad and good; 32
23:37 as a hen gathers her brood under her wings 26
24:31 they will gather his elect from the four winds 26
25:24 gathering where you did not winnow; 32
26 gather where I have not winnowed? 32
32 Before him will be gathered all the nations 32
26: 3 the elders of the people gathered in the palace 32
57 where the scribes and the elders had gathered. 32
27:17 So when they had gathered, Pilate said to them 32
27 they gathered the whole battalion before him. 32
62 the chief priests and the Pharisees gathered 32
Mrk 2:13 and all the crowd gathered about him 27
4: 1 a very large crowd gathered about him 32
5:21 a great crowd gathered about him 32
8: 1 when again a great crowd had gathered 23
10: 1 crowds gathered to him again 31
13:27 gather his elect from the four winds 26
Lke 3:17 to gather the wheat into his granary 32
5:15 great multitudes gathered to hear 34
6:44 figs are not gathered from thorns 30
11:23 he who does not gather with me scatters. 32
13:34 as a hen gathers her brood under her wings *
15:13 the younger son gathered all he had 32
Joh 4:36 and gathers fruit for eternal life 32
11:47 the Pharisees gathered the council, and said 32
52 to gather into one the children of God 32
15: 6 the branches are gathered, thrown into the fire 32
Act 4:26 the rulers were gathered together 32
5:16 gathered from the towns around Jerusalem 34
10:27 he went in and found many persons gathered; 34
20: 8 in the upper chamber where we were gathered. 32
28: 3 Paul had gathered a bundle of sticks 36
17 when they had gathered, he said to them, "Brethren 34
2Co 8:15 He who gathered much had nothing over *
15 he who gathered little had no lack. *
Rev 14:18 and gather the clusters of the vine of the earth 37
19 the angel . . gathered the vintage of the earth 37
19:17 Come, gather for the great supper of God 32
19 kings . . with their armies gathered to make war 32
20: 8 Gog and Magog, to gather them for battle; 32
1Es 4:18 If men gather gold and silver 32
5:47 they gathered as one man in the square 32
8:27 I gathered men from Israel to go up with me. 32
9:38 the whole multitude gathered with one accord 32
2Es 1:30 I gathered you as a hen gathers her brood 38
30 as a hen gathers her brood under her wings *
5:36 and gather for me the scattered raindrops 38
7:95 being gathered into their chambers and guarded 39
101 and afterwards they shall be gathered 39
11: 2 and the clouds were gathered about him. 38
13:34 an innumerable multitude shall be gathered 38
39 him gather to himself another multitude 38
14:23 He answered me and said, "Go and gather the people 39
16:25 The trees shall bear fruit, and who will gather it? 41
30 or as when a vineyard is gathered 41
46 for strangers shall gather their fruits 40
Tob 13: 5 will gather us from all the nations 32
Jdt 14: 6 at the gathering of the people 24
15:12 Then all the women of Israel gathered to see her 35
16:22 died and was gathered to his people. 29
AEs 10: 8 gathered to destroy the name of the Jews. 26
Sir 21: 8 like one who gathers stones for his burial mound. 32
25: 3 You have gathered nothing in your youth 32
26: 5 The slander of a city, the gathering of a mob 24
36:11 Gather all the tribes of Jacob 32
47:18 you gathered gold like tin 32
Bar 4:37 they are coming, gathered from east and west 32
5: 5 see your children gathered from west and east 32
Sus 1:28 gathered at the house of her husband Joakim 34
1Mc 1: 4 He gathered a very strong army 32
2:69 he blessed them, and was gathered to his fathers. 29
3: 9 he gathered in those who were perishing. 32
13 Judas had gathered a large company 22
27 sent and gathered all the forces of his kingdom 32
5:37 Timothy gathered another army 32
38 All the Gentiles around us have gathered to him 26
64 Men gathered to them and praised them. 26
6:20 They gathered together and besieged the citadel 32
11: 1 Then the king of Egypt gathered great forces 22
60 all the army of Syria gathered to him as allies. 22
14: 7 He gathered a host of captives 32
30 was gathered to his people. 29
2Mc 2:18 and will gather us from everywhere under heaven 26
8: 1 so they gathered about 6,000 men. 32
10:21 he gathered the leaders of the people 32
24 gathered a tremendous force of mercenaries 32
11: 2 gathered about 80,000 men and all his cavalry 33
14:15 the gathering of the Gentiles 25
23 the flocks of people that had gathered. 32
30 he gathered not a few of his men 36
3Mc 1:21 the supplications of those gathered there 30
3: 1 all should promptly be gathered into one place 32
6:25 senselessly gathered here 22

gather a crowd 1. ὀχλοποιέω
Act 17: 5 they gathered a crowd, set the city in an uproar 1

gather about 1. סבב 2. ἐπισυνάγω 3. κυκλόω
Ps 7: 7 assembly of the peoples be gathered about thee; 1
Act 14:20 when the disciples gathered about him, he rose up 3
1Es 8:91 there gathered about him a very great throng 2
Jdt 7:23 all the people . . gathered about Uzziah 2

gather against 1. ἐπισυνάγω
2Mc 4:39 the populace gathered against Lysimachus 1

gather around 1. ἐπισυνάγω 2. περικυκλόω
Jdt 13:13 they . . gathered around them. 2
1Mc 11:55 All the troops . . gathered around him 1

gather grapes 1. בצר 2. vindemio
Deu 24:21 When you gather the grapes of your vineyard 1
Jdg 9:27 and gathered the grapes from their vineyards 1
2Es 16:43 like one who will not gather the grapes; 2

gather little 1. מעט
Exd 16:18 and he that gathered little had no lack; 1
Num11:32 he who gathered least gathered ten homers; 1

gather much 1. רבה
Exd 16:18 he that gathered much had nothing over 1

gather round 1. סבב 2. ἐπισυνάγω 3. κυκλόω 4. περιστροφή
Gen 37: 7 gathered round it, and bowed down to my sheaf. 1
Joh 10:24 the Jews gathered round him and said to him 3
1Es 8:72 gathered round me, as I mourned 2
Sir 50: 5 when the people gathered round him 4

gather straw 1. קשש
Exd 5: 7 let them go and gather straw for themselves. 1

gather stubble 1. קשש
Exd 5:12 scattered . . to gather stubble for straw. 1

gather the last grape 1. ἐπιρωγολογέομαι
4Mc 2: 9 nor gathers the last grapes from the vineyard 1

gather together 1. אסף 2. יעד 3. כנס 4. מִקְוֶה 5. צבר 6. קבץ 7. קהל 8. קוה 9. כנש (A) 10. ἀθροίζω 11. ἐπισυνάγω 12. συλλέγω 13. συναγελάζω 14. συνάγω 15. συναθροίζω 16. colligo 17. congrego
Gen 1: 9 Let the waters . . be gathered together 8
10 waters . . gathered together he called Seas 4
29: 7 time for the animals to be gathered together; 1
8 until all the flocks are gathered together 1
22 Laban gathered together all the men of the place 1
49: 1 Gather yourselves together, that I may tell you 1
Exd 3:16 Go and gather the elders of Israel together 1
4:29 went and gathered together all the elders 1
8:14 they gathered them together in heaps 5
32: 1 the people gathered themselves together 7
26 the sons of Levi gathered themselves together 1
Num10: 7 when the assembly is to be gathered together 7
11:22 fish of the sea be gathered together for them 1
14:35 that are gathered together against me 2
16:11 you and all your company have gathered together; 2
Jos 9: 2 they gathered together with one accord to fight 6
Jdg 9:47 was told that . . the people . . were gathered together. 6
11:20 so Sihon gathered all his people together 1
1Sm 5: 8 So they sent and gathered together all the lords 1
11 They sent . . and gathered together all the lords 1
8: 4 elders . . gathered together and came to Samuel 6
2Sm 2:25 the . . gathered themselves together 6
30 when he had gathered all the people together 6
10:17 when it was told . . he gathered all Israel together 1
12:28 Now, then, gather the rest of the people together 1
29 David gathered all the people together and went 1
23:11 The Philistines gathered together at Lehi 1
1Kg 10:26 Solomon gathered together chariots 1
18:20 Ahab sent . . and gathered the prophets together 6
20: 1 Ben-ha'dad . . gathered all his army together; 6
22: 6 king of Israel gathered the prophets together 6
1Ch 11: 1 all Israel gathered together to David at Hebron 6
15: 4 David gathered together the sons of Aaron 1
19:17 he gathered all Israel together 1
22: 2 David commanded to gather together the aliens 3
2Ch 1:14 Solomon gathered together chariots 1
18: 5 king of Israel gathered the prophets together 6
28:24 Ahaz gathered together the vessels of the house 1
32: 6 gathered them together to him in the square 6
34:29 king sent and gathered together all the elders 1
Neh 12:28 sons of the singers gathered together 1
13:11 gathered them together and set them 6
Est 2:19 virgins were gathered together the second time 6
Ps 35:15 in glee, they gathered together against me; 1
Ecc 3: 5 cast away . . and a time to gather stones together; 3
Isa 13: 4 an uproar . . of nations gathering together! 1
60: 4 they all gather together, they come to you; 6
Jer 8:14 Why do we sit still? Gather together 1
49:14 Gather yourselves together and come against 6
Dan 3:27 king's counselors gathered together 9
Zep 3:20 at the time when I gather you together 6
Mat 22:41 Now while the Pharisees were gathered together 14
23:37 I have gathered your children together 11
24:28 there the eagles will be gathered together. 14
Mrk 1:33 the whole city was gathered together 11
2: 2 And many were gathered together 14
7: 1 Now when the Pharisees gathered together to him 14
Lke 12: 1 when so many thousands . . had gathered together 11
13:34 would I have gathered your children together 11
17:37 there the eagles will be gathered together. 11
22:66 the assembly of the elders . . gathered together 14
24:33 they found the eleven gathered together 10
Act 4: 5 their rulers . . were gathered together 14
27 were gathered together . . both Herod and . . Pilate 14
31 the place in which they were gathered together 14
12:12 many were gathered together and were praying. 15
13:44 almost the whole city gathered together 14
14:27 they gathered the church together 14
15: 6 The apostles and the elders were gathered together 14
30 having gathered the congregation together 14
19:25 These he gathered together 15
20: 7 when we were gathered together to break bread 14
2Es 6: 3 hosts of angels were gathered together 16
42 to be gathered together in the seventh part 17
47 where the water had been gathered together 17
50 where the water had been gathered together 17
12:40 they all gathered together 17
13: 5 men were gathered together from the four winds 17
47 the multitude gathered together in peace. 16
49 the nations that are gathered together 16
14:27 I gathered all the people together, and said 17
Tob 13:13 they will be gathered together 14
Jdt 4: 3 all the people of Judea were newly gathered together 12
Sir 21: 9 like tow gathered together 14
1Mc 3:10 Apollonius gathered together Gentiles 14
5:45 Judas gathered together all the Israelites 14
10:61 group . . gathered together against him to accuse him 11
12:37 So they gathered together to build up the city; 14
13: 2 and gathering the people together 10
6 the nations have gathered together out of hatred 14
2Mc 1:27 Gather together our scattered people 11
2: 7 until God gathers his people together again 14
8:16 Maccabeus gathered his men together 14
3Mc 7: 3 friends . . persuaded us to gather together the Jews 15
4Mc 18:23 the sons . . are gathered together into the chorus 13

gather together again 1. ἐπισυναγωγή
2Mc 2: 7 until God gathers his people together again 1

gather together against 1. ἐπισυνάγω
1Mc 5: 9 Gentiles . . gathered together against the Israelites 1
10 The Gentiles . . have gathered together against us 1
15 against them had gathered together men 1

gather up 1. אסף 2. לקט 3. קבץ 4. συνάγω
Gen 41:48 he gathered up all the food of the seven years 3
47:14 Joseph gathered up all the money that was found 2
Num19: 9 clean shall gather up the ashes of the heifer 1
1Sm 20:38 Jonathan's lad gathered up the arrows 2
2Sm 14:14 like water spilt . . which cannot be gathered up 1
Ps 104:28 When thou givest to them, they gather it up; 2
Jer 10:17 Gather up your bundle from the ground 1
Hos 8:10 I will soon gather them up. 3
Joh 6:12 Gather up the fragments left over 4
13 they gathered them up and filled twelve baskets 4

gathered *See* fat.

grape gatherer 1. בצר 2. τρύγητος 3. τρυγών
Jer 6: 9 like a grape-gatherer pass your hand again over 1
49: 9 If grape-gatherers came to you 1
Obd 1: 5 If grape gatherers came to you 1
Sir 33:16 like one who gleans after the grape-gatherers 2
16 like a grape-gatherer I filled my wine press. 3

festal gathering 1. πανήγυρις
Heb 12:22 innumerable angels in festal gathering 1

gaunt 1. רַע 2. רַע מַרְאֶה 3. רַע תֹּאַר
Gen 41: 3 behold, seven other cows, gaunt and thin, came up 2
4 the gaunt and thin cows ate up the seven sleek 2
19 cows . . poor and very gaunt and thin 3
20 the thin and gaunt cows ate up the first seven 1
21 for they were still as gaunt as at the beginning. 1
27 The seven lean and gaunt cows that came up after 1

become gaunt 1. כחש
Ps 109:24 my body has become gaunt. 1

gauntlet 1. χείρ
4Mc 9:26 after fitting themselves with iron gauntlets 1

gauze *See* garment.

gay 1. εὐφροσύνη
Jdt 10: 3 arrayed herself in her gayest apparel 1

gaze 1. חזה 2. נבט 3. עַפְעַף 4. פָּנִים 5. ראה 6. שאה 7. שגח 8. ἀτενίζω 9. βλέπω 10. ἐπιβλέπω 11. θεωρέω 12. κατανοήσις 13. ὁράω 14. video

Gen 24:21 The man gazed at her in silence 6
Exd 19:21 to the LORD to gaze and many of them perish. 5
Jdg 5:28 the mother of Sis'era gazed through the lattice 10
2Kg 8:11 And he fixed his gaze and stared at him 4
Prv 4:25 your gaze be straight before you. 3
Sng 1: 6 Do not gaze at me because I am swarthy 5
2: 9 there he stands . . gazing in at the windows 7
Isa 47:13 who divide the heavens, who gaze at the stars 1
Mic 4:11 and let our eyes gaze upon Zion. 1
Hab 2:15 and makes them drunk, to gaze on their shame! 2
Lke 22:56 seeing him as he sat in the light and gazing at him 8
Act 1:10 while they were gazing into heaven as he went 8
6:15 gazing at him, all who sat in the council saw 8
7:55 he, full of the Holy Spirit, gazed into heaven 8
Rev 11: 9 men . . gaze at their dead bodies and refuse 9
1Es 4:31 the king would gaze at her with mouth agape 11
2Es 13: 3 everything under his gaze trembled 14
Wis 19: 8 after gazing on marvelous wonders. 11
Sir 41:21 gazing at another man's wife; 12
4Mc 15:19 gazing boldly at the same agonies 13

gaze *See also* direct.

gazelle 1. צְבָא 2. צְבִי 3. צְבִיָּה 4. *δορκάς*

Deu 12:15 as of the gazelle and as of the hart. 2
22 Just as the gazelle or the hart is eaten 2
14: 5 the hart, the gazelle, the roebuck, the wild goat 2
15:22 eat it, as though it were a gazelle or a hart. 2
2Sm 2:18 Now As'ahel was as swift of foot as a wild gazelle; 2
1Kg 4:23 sheep, besides harts, gazelles, roebucks 2
1Ch 12: 8 who were swift as gazelles upon the mountains 2
Prv 6: 5 save yourself like a gazelle from the hunter 2
Sng 2: 7 by the gazelles or the hinds of the field 1
9 My beloved is like a gazelle, or a young stag. 2
17 turn, my beloved, be like a gazelle 2
3: 5 I adjure you . . by the gazelles or the hinds 1
4: 5 breasts are like two fawns, twins of a gazelle 3
7: 3 breasts are like two fawns, twins of a gazelle. 3
8:14 Make haste . . and be like a gazelle or a young stag 2
Isa 13:14 like a hunted gazelle, or like sheep 2
Sir 27:20 has escaped like a gazelle from a snare. 4

gazingstock 1. רְאִי

Nah 3: 6 and make you a gazingstock. 1

gear 1. *σκεῦος*

Act 27:17 they lowered the gear, and so were driven. 1

gecko 1. אֲנָקָה

Lev 11:30 the gecko, the land crocodile, the lizard 1

gem 1. *λίθος*

Wis 7: 9 Neither did I liken to her any priceless gem 1

genealogical *See* record.

genealogy 1. יחשׂ 2. יַחַשׂ 3. תּוֹלֵדוֹת 4. *γενεαλογέω* 5. *γενεαλογία* 6. *γένεσις* 7. *γενικῆς γραφή*

Gen 10:32 the families . . according to their genealogies 3
1Ch 1:29 These are their genealogies: the first-born 3
26:31 of whatever genealogy or fathers' houses. 3
Ezr 8: 1 this is the genealogy of those who went up with me 1
Neh 7: 5 found the book of the genealogy of those who came 2
Mat 1: 1 The book of the genealogy of Jesus Christ 6
1Ti 1: 4 myths and endless genealogies 5
Tit 3: 9 avoid stupid controversies, genealogies 5
Heb 7: 6 this man who has not their genealogy 4
1Es 5:39 when the genealogy of these men was sought 7

genealogy *See also* enrol, enrollment, reckon.

without genealogy 1. *ἀγενεαλόγητος*

Heb 7: 3 He is without father or mother or genealogy 1

general 1. *ἄλλος* 2. *κοινός* 3. *μέγας* 4. *ὁμοθυμαδόν* 5. *πάνδημον* 6. *πᾶς*

Jdt 7:29 Then great and general lamentation arose 4
1Mc 13:37 we are ready to make a general peace with you 3
2Mc 3:18 to make a general supplication 5
9:21 to take thought for the general security of all. 2
3Mc 7:12 The king then . . granted them a general license 6
4Mc 13:22 both general education and our discipline 1

general (2) 1. שַׂר 2. *ἀρχιστράτηγος* 3. *στρατηγός* 4. *χιλίαρχος*

Jdg 4: 7 I will draw out Sis'era, the general of Jabin's army 1
Rev 6:15 and the generals and the rich and the strong 4
1Es 3: 2 all the satraps and generals and governors 3
14 satraps and generals and governors and prefects 3
4:47 all the treasurers and governors and generals 3
Jdt 2:14 and called together all the commanders, generals 3
4: 1 Holofernes, the general of Nebuchadnezzar 2
5: 1 Holofernes, the general of the Assyrian army 2
14:12 they went to the generals and the captains 3
1Mc 8:10 they sent a general against the Greeks 3
10:65 and made him general and governor of the province. 3
2Mc 8: 9 a general and a man of experience 3
9:19 Antiochus their king and general 3
3Mc 3:12 his generals and soldiers in Egypt 3
4: 4 the generals in the several cities 3
18 was impossible for all the generals in Egypt. 3
6:41 wrote . . to the generals in the cities 3
7: 1 Ptolemy Philopator to the generals in Egypt 3

chief general 1. *ἀρχιστράτηγος*

Jdt 2: 4 Holofernes, the chief general of his army 1

generation 1. דּוֹר 2. תּוֹלֵדוֹת 3. דָּר (A) 4. *γενεά* 5. *γένεσις*

Gen 2: 4 the generations of the heavens and the earth 2
5: 1 This is the book of the generations of Adam. 2
6: 9 These are the generations of Noah. 2
9 Noah was . . blameless in his generation; 1
7: 1 are righteous before me in this generation. 1
9:12 is with you, for all future generations 1
10: 1 These are the generations of the sons of Noah 2
15:16 shall come back here in the fourth generation; 1
17: 7 after you throughout their generations 1
9 after you throughout their generations. 1
12 every male throughout your generations 1
Exd 1: 6 Joseph died . . and all that generation. 1
3:15 to be remembered throughout all generations. 1
6:16 the sons of Levi according to their generations 2
19 Levites according to their generations. 2
12:14 throughout your generations you shall observe 1
17 observe this day, throughout your generations 1
42 Israel throughout their generations. 1
16:32 omer of it be kept throughout your generations 1
33 to be kept throughout your generations. 1
17:16 war with Am'alek from generation to generation. 1
16 war with Am'alek from generation to generation. 1
20: 5 to the third and the fourth generation •
27:21 observed throughout their generations 1
29:42 burnt offering throughout your generations 1
30: 8 before the LORD throughout your generations. 1
10 once in the year throughout your generations; 1
21 descendants throughout their generations. 1
31 anointing oil throughout your generations. 1
31:13 between me and you throughout your generations 1
16 throughout their generations, as a perpetual 1
34: 7 to the third and the fourth generation. •
40:15 priesthood throughout their generations. 1
Lev 3:17 statute throughout your generations 1
6:18 as decreed for ever throughout your generations 1
7:36 a perpetual due throughout their generations 1
10: 9 statute for ever throughout your generations 1
17: 7 statute . . throughout their generations 1
21:17 descendants throughout their generations 1
22: 3 your descendants throughout your generations 1
23:14 a statute for ever throughout your generations 1
21 it is a statute . . throughout your generations 1
31 statute for ever throughout your generations 1
41 a statute for ever throughout your generations 1
43 that your generations may know that I made 1
24: 3 a statute . . throughout your generations 1
25:30 to him who bought it, throughout his generations 1
Num 1:20 their generations, by their families 2
22 Of the people of Simeon, their generations 2
24 Of the people of Gad, their generations 2
26 Of the people of Judah, their generations 2
28 Of the people of Is'sachar, their generations 2
30 Of the people of Zeb'ulun, their generations 2
32 E'phraim, their generations, by their families 2
34 Of the people of Manas'seh, their generations 2
36 Of the people of Benjamin, their generations 2
38 Of the people of Dan, their generations 2
40 Of the people of Asher, their generations 2
42 Of the people of Naph'tali, their generations 2
3: 1 These are the generations of Aaron and Moses 2
10: 8 statute throughout your generations. 1
14:18 upon the third and upon the fourth generation.' •
15:14 among you throughout your generations 1
15 statute throughout your generations; 1
21 offering throughout your generations. 1
23 onward throughout your generations 1
38 make tassels . . throughout their generations 1
18:23 statute throughout your generations; 1
32:13 until all the generation . . was consumed. 1
35:29 throughout your generations 1
Deu 1:35 Not one of these men of this evil generation 1
2:14 entire generation, that is, the men of war 1
5: 9 children to the third and fourth generation •
7: 9 God who keeps covenant . . to 1,000 generations 1
23: 2 even to the tenth generation none 1
3 even to the tenth generation none belonging 1
8 children of the third generation that are born 1
29:22 generation to come, your children who rise up 1
32: 5 they are a perverse and crooked generation. 1
7 of old, consider the years of many generations; 1
20 for they are a perverse generation 1
Jos 22:27 between us and you, and . . the generations after 1
Jdg 2:10 all that generation also were gathered to their 1
10 there arose another generation after them 1
3: 2 that the generations of the people of Israel 1
2Sm 7:19 and . . shown me future generations, O Lord GOD! •
2Kg 10:30 your sons of the fourth generation shall sit •
15:12 sit upon the throne . . to the fourth generation. •
1Ch 5: 7 genealogy of their generations was reckoned 2
7: 2 mighty warriors of their generations 2
4 along with them, by their generations 2
9 according to their generations 2
8:28 according to their generations, chief men. 2
9: 9 their kinsmen according to their generations 2
34 according to their generations, leaders 2
16:15 the word that he commanded, for 1,000 generations 1
17:17 and hast shown me future generations, O LORD God! •
Est 9:28 days . . kept throughout every generation 1
Job 42:16 saw his sons, and his sons' sons, four generations. 1
Ps 10: 6 I shall not be moved; throughout all generations 1
12: 7 protect us, guard us ever from this generation. 1
14: 5 for God is with the generation of the righteous. 1
22:30 shall tell of the Lord to the coming generation 1
24: 6 Such is the generation of those who seek him 1
33:11 the thoughts of his heart to all generations. 1
45:17 name to be celebrated in all generations; 1
48:13 that you may tell the next generation 1
49:11 their dwelling places to all generations 1
19 he will go to the generation of his fathers 1
61: 6 the king; may his years endure to all generations! 1
71:18 thy might to all the generations to come. 4
72: 5 as long as the moon, throughout all generations! 1
73:15 been untrue to the generation of thy children. 1
78: 4 but tell to the coming generation 1
6 that the next generation might know them 1
8 fathers, a stubborn and rebellious generation 1
8 a generation whose heart was not steadfast 1
79:13 generation to generation we will recount 1
13 generation to generation we will recount 1
85: 5 Wilt thou prolong thy anger to all generations? 1
89: 1 proclaim thy faithfulness to all generations. 1
4 build your throne for all generations.'" Selah 1
90: 1 Lord . . our dwelling place in all generations. 1
95:10 40 years I loathed that generation and said 1
100: 5 his faithfulness to all generations. 1
102:12 thy name endures to all generations. 1
18 Let this be recorded for a generation to come 1
24 whose years endure throughout all generations! 1
105: 8 He is mindful . . for 1,000 generations 1
106:31 righteousness from generation to generation 1
31 righteousness from generation to generation 1
109:13 his name be blotted out in the second generation! 1
112: 2 generation of the upright will be blessed. 1
119:90 Thy faithfulness endures to all generations; 1
145: 4 One generation shall laud thy works to another 1
13 dominion endures throughout all generations. •
146:10 reign for ever, thy God, O Zion, to all generations. 1
Prv 27:24 does a crown endure to all generations? 1
Ecc 1: 4 A generation goes, and a generation comes 1
4 A generation goes, and a generation comes 1
Isa 13:20 inhabited or dwelt in for all generations; 1
34:10 generation to generation it shall lie waste; 1
10 generation to generation it shall lie waste; 1
17 from generation to generation they shall dwell 1
17 from generation to generation they shall dwell 1
41: 4 calling the generations from the beginning? 1
51: 8 for ever, and my salvation to all generations. 1
9 as in days of old, the generations of long ago. 1
53: 8 as for his generation, who considered that he was 1
58:12 raise up the foundations of many generations; 1
61: 4 the devastations of many generations. 1
Jer 2:31 And you, O generation, heed the word of the LORD. 1
7:29 and forsaken the generation of his wrath. 1
50:39 nor inhabited for all generations. 1
Lam 5:19 thy throne endures to all generations. 1
Dan 4: 3 his dominion is from generation to generation. 3
3 his dominion is from generation to generation. 3
34 kingdom endures from generation to generation; 3
34 kingdom endures from generation to generation; 3
Jol 1: 3 and their children another generation. 1
2: 2 through the years of all generations. 1
3:20 and Jerusalem to all generations. 1
Mat 1:17 So all the generations from Abraham to David 4
17 Abraham to David were fourteen generations 4
17 deportation to Babylon fourteen generations 4
17 to Babylon to the Christ fourteen generations. 4
11:16 to what shall I compare this generation? 4
12:39 An evil and adulterous generation 4
41 at the judgment with this generation 4
42 at the judgment with this generation 4
45 So shall it be also with this evil generation. 4
16: 4 An evil and adulterous generation 4
17:17 O faithless and perverse generation 4
23:36 all this will come upon this generation. 4
24:34 this generation will not pass away 4
Mrk 8:12 Why does this generation seek a sign? 4
12 no sign shall be given to this generation. 4
38 in this adulterous and sinful generation 4
9:19 he answered them, "O faithless generation 4
13:30 this generation will not pass away 4
Lke 1:48 all generations will call me blessed; 4
50 who fear him from generation to generation. 4
50 who fear him from generation to generation. 4
7:31 shall I compare the men of this generation 4
9:41 O faithless and perverse generation 4
11:29 This generation is an evil generation 4
29 This generation is an evil generation 4
30 so will the Son of man be to this generation. 4

31 arise . . with the men of this generation 4
32 arise at the judgment with this generation 4
50 the blood . . may be required of this generation 4
51 it shall be required of this generation. 4
16: 8 more shrewd in dealing with their own generation 4
17:25 be rejected by this generation. 4
21:32 this generation will not pass away 4
Act 2:40 Save yourselves from this crooked generation. 4
8:33 Who can describe his generation? 4
13:36 served the counsel of God in his own generation 4
14:16 In past generations he allowed all the nations 4
15:21 from early generations 4
Eph 3: 5 the sons of men in other generations 4
21 to all generations, for ever and ever. Amen. 4
Php 2:15 a crooked and perverse generation 4
Col 1:26 the mystery hidden for ages and generations 4
Heb 3:10 Therefore I was provoked with that generation 4
Jde 1:14 Enoch in the seventh generation from Adam *
Tob 1: 4 and established for all generations for ever. 4
13:10 to all generations for ever. 4
11 Generations of generations will give . . 4
11 Generations of generations will give . . 4
14: 5 for all generations for ever 4
Jdt 8:18 never in our generation 4
AEs 10:13 from generation to generation for ever 4
13 from generation to generation for ever 4
Wis 3:19 the end of an unrighteous generation 4
7:27 in every generation she passes into holy souls 4
14: 6 left to the world the seed of a new generation. 5
Sir 2:10 Consider the ancient generations and see 4
14:18 so are the generations of flesh and blood 4
16:27 their dominion for all generations 4
24:33 leave it to all future generations. 4
44: 1 our fathers in their generations. 5
7 all these were honored in their generations 4
14 their name lives to all generations. 4
16 an example of repentance to all generations. 4
45:26 endure throughout their generations. 4
LJr 1: 3 for a long time, up to seven generations 4
1Mc 2:51 deeds . . which they did in their generations 4
61 so observe, from generation to generation 4
61 so observe, from generation to generation 4

third generation 1. שִׁלֵּשׁ
Gen 50:23 saw E'phraim's children of the third generation 1

all generations 1. γενεὰ γενεῶν
Jdt 8:32 through all generations of our descendants. 1
Sir 39: 9 his name will live through all generations. 1

generative *See* force.

generosity 1. ἀγαθός 2. ἁπλότης
Mat 20:15 Or do you begrudge my generosity?' 1
2Co 9:11 You will be enriched in every way for great generosity 2
13 the generosity of your contribution for them 2

show generosity 1. φιλανθρωπέω
2Mc 13:23 and showed generosity to the holy place. 1

generous 1. חנן 2. נָדִיב 3. ἀγαθός 4. ἀνοίγω χεῖρας 5. ἀφελότης 6. κοινωνικός
Exd 35: 5 whoever is of a generous heart, let him bring 2
Ps 37:21 but the righteous is generous and gives; 1
Act 2:46 partook of food with glad and generous hearts 5
1Ti 6:18 be rich in good deeds, liberal and generous 6
Sir 14: 5 to whom will he be generous? 3
40:14 A generous man will be made glad 4

generous man 1. נָדִיב
Prv 19: 6 Many seek the favor of a generous man 1

generously 1. ἁπλῶς 2. εὐψύχως
Jas 1: 5 let him ask God, who gives to all men generously 1
3Mc 7:18 the king had generously provided all things to them 2

generously *See also* deal.

gentle 1. אַלּוּף 2. מַרְפֵּא 3. ἐπιεικής 4. ἤπιος 5. ἥσυχος 6. πρᾶος 7. πραΰς
Prv 15: 4 A gentle tongue is a tree of life 2
Jer 11:19 But I was like a gentle lamb led to the slaughter. 1
Mat 11:29 for I am gentle and lowly in heart 7
1Th 2: 7 we were gentle among you 4
1Ti 3: 3 no drunkard, not violent but gentle 3
Tit 3: 2 to be gentle, and to show perfect courtesy 3
Jas 3:17 wisdom from above is . . gentle, open to reason 3
1Pe 2:18 be submissive . . not only to the kind and gentle 3
3: 4 the imperishable jewel of a gentle and quiet spirit 7
Wis 18:14 For while gentle silence enveloped all things 5
2Mc 15:12 of modest bearing and gentle manner 6

gentle *See also* rain.

how gentle 1. ἐπιείκεια
Wis 2:19 that we may find out how gentle he is 1

gentleman 1. ἀνήρ
1Es 3:18 Gentlemen, how is wine the strongest? 1
24 Gentlemen, is not wine the strongest 1
4: 2 Gentlemen, are not men strongest 1
12 Gentlemen, why is not the king the strongest 1
14 Gentlemen, is not the king great 1
32 Gentlemen, why are not women strong 1
34 Gentlemen, are not women strong? 1

gentleness 1. ἐπιείκεια 2. πραϋπάθεια 3. πραΰτης
1Co 4:21 with love in a spirit of gentleness? 3
2Co 10: 1 by the meekness and gentleness of Christ 1
Gal 5:23 gentleness, self-control 3
6: 1 restore him in a spirit of gentleness 3
1Ti 6:11 faith, love, steadfastness, gentleness. 2
2Ti 2:25 correcting his opponents with gentleness 3
1Pe 3:15 yet do it with gentleness and reverence; 3
AEs 15: 8 God changed the spirit of the king to gentleness 3

gently 1. לְאַט 2. πραΰτης
Isa 8: 6 refused the waters of Shilo'ah that flow gently 1
Sir 4: 8 answer him peaceably and gently. 2

gently *See also* blow, deal, lead.

genuine 1. ἀνυπόκριτος 2. γνήσιος 3. δόκιμος
Rom 12: 9 Let love be genuine; hate what is evil 1
1Co 11:19 in order that those who are genuine among you 3
2Co 6: 6 kindness, the Holy Spirit, genuine love 1
8: 8 your love also is genuine. 2
AEs 11: 1 which they said was genuine *

genuinely 1. γνησίως
Php 2:20 who will be genuinely anxious for your welfare. 1
2Mc 14: 8 genuinely concerned for the interests . . king 1

genuineness 1. δοκίμιον
1Pe 1: 7 the genuineness of your faith . . may redound 1

gerah 1. גֵּרָה
Exd 30:13 (the shekel is twenty gerahs) 1
Lev 27:25 twenty gerahs shall make a shekel 1
Num 3:47 of the sanctuary, the shekel of twenty gerahs 1
18:16 shekel of the sanctuary, which is twenty gerahs. 1
Ezk 45:12 The shekel shall be twenty gerahs; 1

gestation
4Mc 13:21 they were born after an equal time of gestation *

get 1. בוא 2. היה 3. הלך 4. לקח 5. מצא 6. נשא 7. נתן 8. עוד 9. עלה 10. עשה 11. עשק 12. פוק 13. פַּעַל 14. קנה 15. קִנְיָן 16. שוב 17. תמך 18. ἀναλαμβάνω 19. ἀπέρχομαι 20. ἀποκομίζω 21. γίνομαι 22. εἰσδύω 23. εἰσέρχομαι 24. ἐκφέρω 25. ἐσθίω 26. εὑρίσκω 27. ἔχω 28. κομίζω 29. κρατέω 30. κτάομαι 31. κτῆσις 32. λαμβάνω 33. μετέχω 34. παραγίνομαι 35. τυγχάνω 36. ὑπάγω 37. adquiro
Gen 4: 1 I have gotten a man with the help of the LORD. 14
12: 5 and the persons that they had gotten in Haran; 10
34: 4 Get me this maiden for my wife. 4
Exd 5: 4 Get to your burdens. 3
11 Go yourselves, get your straw wherever you can 4
Lev 6: 4 he took by robbery, or what he got by oppression 11
22:25 offer . . animals gotten from a foreigner *
Num 11:13 Where am I to get meat to give to all this people? *
17: 2 get from them rods, one for each fathers' house 4
Deu 8:17 power and . . my hand have gotten me this wealth.' 10
18 LORD . . who gives you power to get wealth; 10
24:19 sheaf in the field, you shall not go back to get it 4
Jdg 5:19 they got no spoils of silver. 4
14: 2 at Timnah; now get her for me as my wife. 4
3 his father, "Get her for me; for she pleases me well. 4
2Sm 15: 1 Ab'salom got himself a chariot and horses 10
20: 6 pursue him, lest he get himself fortified cities 5
2Kg 5:20 I will run after him, and get something 4
6: 2 go to the Jordan and each of us get there a log 4
2Ch 24: 3 Jehoi'ada got for him two wives, and he had sons 6
Neh 5: 2 let us get grain, that we may eat and keep alive. 4
3 mortgaging . . to get grain because of the famine. 4
9:10 thou didst get thee a name, as it is to this day. 10
Job 9:18 he will not let me get my breath 16
17: 5 informs . . to get a share of their property *
28:15 It cannot be gotten for gold 7
31:25 because my hand had gotten much; 5
Ps 74: 2 thy congregation, which thou hast gotten of old 14
90:12 number our days that we may get a heart of wisdom. 1
107:37 sow . . plant . . and get a fruitful yield. 10
132: 3 I will not enter my house or get into my bed; 9
Prv 3:13 Happy is . . the man who gets understanding 12
35 wise will inherit honor, but fools get disgrace. *
4: 5 Get wisdom; get insight. 14
5 Get wisdom; get insight. 14
7 The beginning of wisdom is this: Get wisdom 14
7 wisdom, and whatever you get, 15
7 Get wisdom, and whatever you get, get insight. 14
6:33 Wounds and dishonor will he get 5
9: 7 He who corrects a scoffer gets himself abuse 4
11: 8 trouble, and the wicked gets into it instead. 1
16 A gracious woman gets honor 17
16 violent men get riches. 17
18 one who sows righteousness gets a sure reward. *
12:27 but the diligent man will get precious wealth. *
13: 4 The soul of the sluggard craves, and gets nothing *
11 Wealth hastily gotten will dwindle *
16:16 To get wisdom is better than gold; 14
16 to get understanding is to be chosen 14
19: 8 He who gets wisdom loves himself; 14
21: 6 The getting of treasures by a lying tongue 13
28:27 but he who hides his eyes will get many a curse. *
29:26 but from the LORD a man gets justice. *
Ecc 2: 8 I got singers, both men and women 10
Isa 56:12 Come," they say, "let us get wine 4
Jer 17:11 so is he who gets riches but not by right; 10
32:10 I signed the deed, sealed it, got witnesses 8
25 Buy the field for money and get witnesses 8
36:21 Then the king sent Jehu'di to get the scroll 4
Lam 5: 4 We must pay for . . the wood we get must be bought. *
9 We get our bread at the peril of our lives 1
Ezk 3: 4 Son of man, go, get you to the house of Israel 1
11 go, get you to the exiles, to your people 1
18:31 and get yourselves a new heart and a new spirit! 10
28: 4 by . . your understanding you have gotten wealth 10
29:18 army got anything from Tyre to pay for the labor 2
38:12 the people . . who have gotten cattle and goods 10
Mat 7: 2 you give will be the measure you get. †
13:54 Where did this man get this wisdom *
56 Where then did this man get all this? *
15:33 Where are we to get bread enough in the desert *
16:23 he turned and said to Peter, "Get behind me, Satan! 36
21:34 to get his fruit; 32
22:12 how did you get in here without a wedding garment?' 23
Mrk 6: 2 Where did this man get all this? *
8:33 Get behind me, Satan! 36
12: 2 to get from them some of the fruit 32
Lke 9:12 to lodge and get provisions 26
18:12 I fast twice a week, I give tithes of all that I get.' 30
Joh 4:11 where do you get that living water? 27
6: 7 buy enough bread for each of them to get a little 32
Rom 6:21 then what return did you get from the things 27
22 the return you get is sanctification 27
1Co 9: 7 without getting some of the milk? 25
2Ti 4:11 Get Mark and bring him with you 18
2Es 5:27 thou hast gotten for thyself one people 37
7:59 for he who has what is hard to get *
Tob 2:13 So I said to her, "Where did you get the kid? *
5: 3 go and get the money. 32
16 Then he said to Tobias, "Get ready for the journey 21
9: 2 go to Gabael at Rages in Media and get the money 28
Jdt 12: 3 where can we get more like it for you? 24
15: 7 the Israelites . . got a great amount of booty 29
Wis 7:14 those who get it obtain friendship with God 30
8:18 I went about seeking how to get her for myself. 32
Sir 29: 5 will kiss another's hands until he gets a loan 32
36:24 He who acquires a wife gets his best possession *
40: 6 He gets little or no rest *
51:25 Get these things for yourselves without money. 30
28 Get instruction with a large sum of silver 33
Bar 3:17 men trust, and there is no end to their getting; 31
1Mc 3:41 to the camp to get the sons of Israel for slaves. 32
5:48 Let us pass through your land to get to our land 19
6:46 He got under the elephant 22
13:17 he sent to get the money and the sons 32
2Mc 1:20 sent the descendants . . to get it *
2:15 send people to get them for you. 20
3:32 fearing that the king might get the notion 27
5: 7 in the end got only disgrace from his conspiracy 32
7:11 said nobly, "I got these from Heaven 30
8: 5 As soon as Maccabeus got his army organized 21
9: 4 When I get there 34
12:28 they got the city into their hands 32
13:13 and get possession of the city. 21
15: 7 he would get help from the Lord. 35

get *See also* scheme.

get a husband 1. בעל
Prv 30:23 an unloved woman when she gets a husband 1

get a living 1. ζάω
1Co 9:14 get their living by the gospel. 1

get a measure 1. μετρέω
Mrk 4:24 the measure you give will be the measure you get 1

get a possession 1. κτάομαι
Sir 24: 6 in every people . . I have gotten a possession 1

get ahead 1. προφθάνω
1Mc 10:23 Alexander has gotten ahead of us 1

get away 1. אסף 2. הלך 3. מלט 4. עלה 5. רמם 6. ἀναχωρέω 7. ἐκτοπίζω 8. ἐξέρχομαι
Exd 10:28 Then Pharaoh said to him, "Get away from me; 2
Num 16:24 Get away from about the dwelling of Korah, Dathan 4
27 got away from about the dwelling of Korah, Dathan 4
45 Get away from the midst of this congregation 5
1Sm 20:29 if I have found favor in your eyes, let me get away 3
23:26 and David was making haste to get away from Saul 2
Ps 104:22 get them away and lie down in their dens. 1
Lke 13:31 Get away from here, for Herod wants to kill you. 8

2Mc 5:27 Judas . . got away to the wilderness 6
8:13 those . . ran off and got away. 7

get back 1. שׁוב 2. κομίζω 3. προσδέχομαι
Lev 25:28 if he has not sufficient means to get it back 1
Sir 29: 6 he will hardly get back half 2
2Mc 3:38 for you will get him back thoroughly scourged 3
7:11 from him I hope to get them back again. 2
29 in God's mercy I may get you back again 2

get back measure 1. ἀντιμετρέω
Lke 6:38 measure you give will be the measure you get back 1

get control 1. κατακρατέω
1Mc 8: 3 to get control of the silver and gold mines there 1
16:13 he determined to get control of the country 1

get dishonest gain 1. בצע
Ezk 22:27 destroying lives to get dishonest gain. 1

get dominion 1. שׁלט
Ps 119:133 let no iniquity get dominion over me. 1

get down 1. ברך (A)
Dan 6:10 got down upon his knees three times a day 1

get drunk 1. μεθύσκω
Lke 12:45 to eat and drink and get drunk 1
Eph 5:18 do not get drunk with wine, for that is debauchery; 1
1Th 5: 7 those who get drunk are drunk at night. 1

get enjoyment 1. עלס
Job 20:18 of his trading he will get no enjoyment. 1

get enough 1. שׂבע
Lam 5: 6 We have given the hand . . to get bread enough. 1

get entangled 1. ἐμπλέκω
2Ti 2: 4 gets entangled in civilian pursuits 1

get far 1. προκόπτω
2Ti 3: 9 they will not get very far 1

get food 1. ἐσθίω
1Co 9:13 get their food from the temple 1

get gain 1. בצע 2. κερδαίνω
Prv 1:19 Such are the ways of all who get gain by violence; 1
Hab 2: 9 Woe to him who gets evil gain for his house 1
Jas 4:13 and spend a year there and trade and get gain"; 2

get glory 1. כבד
Exd 14: 4 I will get glory over Pharaoh and all his host; 1
17 I will get glory over Pharaoh and all his host 1
18 I have gotten glory over Pharaoh, his chariots 1

get hastily 1. בהל
Prv 20:21 An inheritance gotten hastily in the beginning 1

get hold 1. ἐγκρατής
Sir 6:27 when you get hold of her, do not let her go. 1

get into 1. בוא 2. ἀναβαίνω 3. ἐμβαίνω
2Kg 7:12 we shall take them alive and get into the city.' 1
Mat 8:23 when he got into the boat, his disciples followed 3
9: 1 And getting into a boat he crossed over 3
13: 2 so that he got into a boat and sat there 3
14:22 Then he made the disciples get into the boat 3
32 when they got into the boat, the wind ceased. 2
15:39 sending away the crowds, he got into the boat 3
Mrk 4: 1 so that he got into a boat and sat in it on the sea; 3
5:18 as he was getting into the boat 3
6:45 he made his disciples get into the boat 3
51 got into the boat with them and the wind ceased. 2
8:10 he got into the boat with his disciples 3
13 he left them, and getting into the boat again 3
Lke 5: 3 Getting into one of the boats, which was Simon's 3
8:22 One day he got into a boat with his disciples 3
37 so he got into the boat and returned. 3
Joh 6:17 got into a boat 3
24 they . . got into the boats and went to Caper'na-um 3
21: 3 They went out and got into the boat 3
1Es 1:31 he got into his second chariot 2

get into safe shelter 1. עוז
Exd 9:19 get your cattle . . into safe shelter 1

get mastery 1. שׁלט
Est 9: 1 enemies of . . hoped to get the mastery over them 1
1 the Jews should get the mastery over their foes 1

get money 1. πορίζω
Wis 15:12 he says one must get money however one can 1

get near 1. προσφέρω
Mrk 2: 4 when they could not get near him 1

get off 1. הלך
Zec 6: 7 were impatient to get off and patrol the earth. 1

get one's fill 1. שׂבע
Ps 59:15 for food, and growl if they do not get their fill. 1

get out 1. יצא 2. ἀποβαίνω 3. ἐξέρχομαι 4. καταβαίνω
Gen 19:14 Up, get out of this place; 1
39:12 he left . . and fled and got out of the house. 1
15 he left . . and fled and got out of the house. 1
40:14 make mention . . and so get me out of this house. 1
Exd 11: 8 'Get you out, and all the people who follow you.' 1
Mat 5:26 you will never get out till you have paid the last 3
14:29 He said, "Come." So Peter got out of the boat 4
Mrk 6:54 when they got out of the boat 3
Lke 12:59 I tell you, you will never get out 3
Joh 21: 9 When they got out on land, they saw a charcoal fire 2
Act 22:18 Make haste and get quickly out of Jerusalem 3
Jdt 7:13 to keep watch that not a man gets out of the city. 3

get possession 1. חצק 2. ירשׁ 3. ἐγκρατὴς γίνομαι 4. κατακρατέω
Ezk 33:24 was only one man, yet he got possession of the land; 2
Dan 11: 6 child, and he who got possession of her. 1
1Mc 11: 1 he tried to get possession of Alexander's kingdom 4
2Mc 8:30 and got possession of some . . strongholds 3

get praise 1. ידה
Ps 49:18 a man gets praise when he does well for himself 1

get profit 1. יעל
Job 21:15 what profit do we get if we pray to him? 1

get property 1. אחז
Gen 34:10 trade in it, and get property in it. 1

get ready 1. עתד 2. ἑτοιμάζω 3. εὐτρεπίζω 4. παρασκευάζω 5. τάσσω
Prv 24:27 get everything ready for you in the field; 1
Act 23:23 get ready 200 soldiers 2
1Co 14: 8 who will get ready for battle? 4
1Mc 5:27 the enemy are getting ready to attack 5
13:22 So Trypho got all his cavalry ready to go 2
4Mc 5:32 Therefore get your torture wheels ready 3

get relief 1. נוח
Est 9:16 and got relief from their enemies, 1
22 days . . the Jews got relief from their enemies 1

get rich 1. πληθύνω
Sir 27: 1 whoever seeks to get rich will avert his eyes. 1

get spoil 1. שׁסה
Ps 44:10 our enemies have gotten spoil. 1

get the better 1. ἀριστεύω 2. λαμβάνω
2Co 12:16 I was crafty . . and got the better of you by guile. 2
4Mc 2:18 is able to get the better of the emotions 1

get there ahead 1. προέρχομαι
Mrk 6:33 they ran . . and got there ahead of them. 1

get to attest 1. עוד
Isa 8: 2 I got reliable witnesses . . to attest for me 1

get under shelter 1. ὑποδύω
Jdt 6:13 However, they got under the shelter of the hill 1

get understanding 1. בין 2. לבב
Job 11:12 a stupid man will get understanding 2
Ps 119:104 Through thy precepts I get understanding; 1

get up 1. עלה 2. קום 3. ἀνίστημι 4. διανίστημι 5. ἐξανίστημι 6. surgo
Jdg 19:28 Get up, let us be going." But there was no answer. 2
2Sm 5: 8 get up the water shaft to attack the lame •
Isa 40: 9 Get you up to a high mountain, O Zion 1
Mrk 5:42 immediately the girl got up and walked 3
Lke 8:55 her spirit returned, and she got up at once 3
11: 7 I cannot get up and give you anything'? 3
8 though he will not get up and give him anything 3
Act 12: 7 woke him, saying, "Get up quickly. 3
2Es 10: 3 that I might be quiet, I got up in the night and fled 6
Tob 8: 4 Tobias got up from the bed and said, "Sister, get up 3
4 Tobias got up from the bed and said, "Sister, get up 3
Jdt 12:15 she got up and arrayed herself 4
Sir 8:11 Do not get up and leave an insolent fellow 5
31:21 get up in the middle of the meal 3

get up again 1. שׁוב 2. ἐξανίστημι
2Kg 4:35 Then he got up again, and walked once to and fro 1
4Mc 6: 8 to make him get up again after he fell. 2

get up early in the morning 1. ὀρθρεύω
Tob 9: 6 In the morning they both got up early 1

get victory 1. ישׁע
Ps 98: 1 hand and his holy arm have gotten him victory. 1

get warm 1. חמם
1Kg 1: 1 King David . . could not get warm. 1

get water 1. ὑδρεύω
Jdt 7:13 where all the people of Bethulia get their water 1

get word 1. μεταλαμβάνω
2Mc 11: 6 When Maccabeus and his men got word 1
13:23 he got word that . . 1

ghost 1. אוֹב 2. φάντασμα
Isa 29: 4 come from the ground like the voice of a ghost 1
Mat 14:26 they were terrified, saying, "It is a ghost! 2
Mrk 6:49 they thought it was a ghost, and cried out; 2

giant 1. רְפָאִים 2. γίγας 3. μέγας
2Sm 21:16 Ish'bi-be'nob, one of the descendants of the giants 1
18 Saph . . was one of the descendants of the giants. 1
20 and he also was descended from the giants. 1
22 These . . were descended from the giants in Gath; 1
1Ch 20: 4 who was one of the descendants of the giants; 1
6 and he also was descended from the giants. 1
8 These were descended from the giants in Gath; 1
Rev 20: 1 the key of the bottomless pit and a giant chain. 3
Jdt 16: 7 nor did tall giants set upon him 2
Wis 14: 6 when arrogant giants were perishing 2
Sir 16: 7 He was not propitiated for the ancient giants 2
47: 4 In his youth did he not kill a giant 2
Bar 3:26 The giants were born there, who were famous of old 2
1Mc 3: 3 Like a giant he put on his breastplate 2
3Mc 2: 4 among whom were even giants 2

gift 1. אֶשְׁכָּר 2. בְּרָכָה 3. מִנְחָה 4. מַשְׂאֵת 5. מַתָּן 6. מַתָּנָה 7. מַתַּת 8. נֵדֶה 9. נָדָן 10. נתן 11. קָרְבָּן 12. שֹׁחַד 13. שַׁי 14. שַׁלְמֹן 15. תְּרוּמָה 16. מַתָּן (A) 17. מַתְּנָה (A) 18. ἀποστολή 19. δίδωμι 20. δόμα 21. δόσις 22. δωρεά 23. δώρημα 24. δῶρον 25. ἐλεημοσύνη 26. εὐλογία 27. μὴ λαμβάνω 28. ξενία 29. τιμή 30. χάρις 31. χάρισμα
Gen 25: 6 to the sons of his concubines Abraham gave gifts 6
33:11 Accept, I pray you, my gift that is brought to you 2
34:12 as marriage present and gift, and I will give 5
Exd 28:38 the people of Israel hallow as their holy gifts; 6
Lev 1:10 If his gift for a burnt offering is from the flock 11
17: 4 to offer it as a gift to the LORD 11
23:38 besides your gifts, and besides all your votive 6
Num 6:14 he shall offer his gift to the LORD 11
8:19 given the Levites as a gift to Aaron and his sons 10
18: 6 Levites . . are a gift to you, given to the LORD 6
7 I give your priesthood as a gift, and any one else 6
11 This also is yours, the offering of their gift 5
29 Out of all the gifts to you 6
1Ch 26:27 From spoil won in battles they dedicated gifts •
2Ch 21: 3 Their father gave them great gifts 6
32:23 many brought gifts to the LORD to Jerusalem 3
Est 2:18 He also . . and gave gifts with royal liberality. 4
9:22 sending . . to one another and gifts to the poor. 6
Ps 45:12 the people of Tyre will sue your favor with gifts 3
68:18 receiving gifts among men 6
29 temple at Jerusalem kings bear gifts to thee. 13
72:10 may the kings of Sheba and Seba bring gifts! 1
76:11 let all around him bring gifts to him 13
Prv 6:35 nor be appeased though you multiply gifts. 12
18:16 A man's gift makes room for him and brings him 5
19: 6 every one is a friend to a man who gives gifts. 5
21:14 A gift in secret averts anger; 5
25:14 man who boasts of a gift he does not give. 7
29: 4 but one who exacts gifts ruins it. 15
Ecc 3:13 it is God's gift to man that every one should eat 7
5:19 to accept his lot and . . -this is the gift of God. 7
Isa 1:23 Every one loves a bribe and runs after gifts. 14
18: 7 gifts will be brought to the LORD of hosts 13
Ezk 16:33 Men give gifts to all harlots; 8
33 but you gave your gifts to all your lovers 9
20:26 I defiled them through their very gifts 6
31 you offer your gifts and sacrifice your sons 6
39 no more profane with your gifts and your idols. 6
40 contributions and the choicest of your gifts 4
46:16 If the prince makes a gift to any of his sons 6
17 if he makes a gift out of his inheritance 6
17 his sons may keep a gift from his inheritance. •
Dan 2: 6 receive . . gifts and rewards and great honor. 16
48 gave Daniel high honors and many great gifts 16
5:17 gifts be for yourself, and give your rewards 17
Mal 1: 9 With such a gift from your hand, will he show favor •
Mat 2:11 opening their treasures, they offered him gifts 24
5:23 So if you are offering your gift at the altar 24
24 leave your gift there before the altar and go; 24
24 your brother, and then come and offer your gift. 24
7:11 know how to give good gifts to your children 20
8: 4 and offer the gift that Moses commanded 24
23:18 if any one swears by the gift that is on the altar 24
19 which is greater, the gift or the altar 24
19 or the altar that makes the gift sacred? 24
Lke 11:13 know how to give good gifts to your children 20
21: 1 and saw the rich putting their gifts into the treasury; 24
Joh 4:10 Jesus answered her, "If you knew the gift of God 22

Act 2:38 you shall receive the gift of the Holy Spirit. 22
8:20 you could obtain the gift of God with money! 22
10:45 the gift of the Holy Spirit had been poured out 22
11:17 If then God gave the same gift to them 22
28:10 They presented many gifts to us 29
Rom 1:11 that I may impart to you some spiritual gift 31
3:24 they are justified by his grace as a gift 22
4: 4 his wages are not reckoned as a gift but as his due. 30
11:29 For the gifts and the call of God are 31
35 who has given a gift to him *
12: 6 Having gifts that differ according to the grace 31
1Co 2:14 does not receive the gifts of the Spirit of God *
4: 7 why do you boast as if it were not a gift? 27
12: 4 there are varieties of gifts, but the same Spirit; 31
9 to another gifts of healing by the one Spirit 31
30 Do all possess gifts of healing? 31
31 earnestly desire the higher gifts 31
16: 3 to carry your gift to Jerusalem. 30
2Co 9: 5 and arrange in advance for this gift 26
15 Thanks be to God for his inexpressible gift! 22
Eph 2: 8 this is not your own doing, it is the gift of God– 24
3: 7 according to the gift of God's grace 22
4: 7 us according to the measure of Christ's gift. 22
8 he gave gifts to men. 20
11 his gifts were that some should be apostles 19
Php 4:17 Not that I seek the gift 20
18 having received from Epaphrodi'tus the gifts you sent *
1Ti 4:14 Do not neglect the gift you have 31
2Ti 1: 6 Hence I remind you to rekindle the gift of God 31
Heb 2: 4 by gifts of the Holy Spirit *
5: 1 to offer gifts and sacrifices for sins. 24
6: 4 who have tasted the heavenly gift 22
8: 3 is appointed to offer gifts and sacrifices; 24
4 since there are priests who offer gifts 24
9: 9 gifts and sacrifices are offered 24
11: 4 God bearing witness by accepting his gifts 24
Jas 1:17 and every perfect gift is from above 23
1Pe 4:10 As each has received a gift, employ it 31
1Es 2: 7 with gifts and with horses and cattle 21
3: 5 Darius the king will give rich gifts 22
8:13 the gifts for the Lord of Israel 24
Tob 2:14 It was given to me as a gift in addition to my wages 24
4: 7 begrudge the gift when you make it 25
8 make your gift from them in proportion 25
16 let your eye begrudge the gift when you made it. 25
13:11 bearing gifts in their hands 24
11 gifts for the King of heaven 24
Jdt 16:18 freewill offerings, and their gifts. 20
Wis 7:14 the gifts that come from instruction. 22
8:21 it was a mark of insight to know whose gift she was 30
Sir 1:10 She dwells with all flesh according to his gift 21
4: 3 nor delay your gift to a beggar. 21
7: 9 He will consider the multitude of my gifts 24
28 what . . equals their gift to you? *
31 the gift of the shoulders 21
11:17 gift of the Lord endures for those who are godly 21
18:15 cause grief . . when you present a gift. 21
16 So a word is better than a gift. 21
17 Indeed, does not a word surpass a good gift? 20
18 the gift of a grudging man makes the eyes dim. 21
20:10 There is a gift that profits you nothing 21
10 there is a gift that brings a double return. 21
14 A fool's gift will profit you nothing 21
29 Presents and gifts blind the eyes of the wise; 24
26:14 A silent wife is a gift of the Lord 21
32:13 satisfies you with his good gifts. *
34:18 the gifts of the lawless are not acceptable. 23
35: 9 With every gift show a cheerful face 21
38: 2 he will receive a gift from the king. 20
41:21 taking away some one's portion or gift 21
LJr 1:27 gifts are placed before them 24
1Mc 2:18 honored with silver and gold and many gifts. 18
3:30 the gifts which he used to give 20
10:24 and promise them honor and gifts 20
28 grant you many immunities and give you gifts. 20
39 I have given as a gift to the sanctuary 20
54 will make gifts to you and to her 20
60 silver and gold and many gifts 20
11:24 gold and clothing and numerous other gifts 28
12:43 he gave him gifts 20
16:19 he might give them silver and gold and gifts; 20
2Mc 1:35 he exchanged many excellent gifts. *
15:16 Take this holy sword, a gift from God 24
3Mc 1: 7 by endowing their sacred enclosures with gifts 22
4Mc 5: 9 wrong to spurn the gifts of nature. 30

gift *See also* give, make.

bestowed gift 1. χαρίζομαι
1Co 2:12 understand the gifts bestowed on us by God. 1

choice gift 1. טוב 2. מֶגֶד
Gen 24:10 taking all sorts of choice gifts from his master; 1
Deu 33:13 with the choicest gifts of heaven above 2

costly gift 1. חֲמוּדָה
Dan 11:38 honor with . . precious stones and costly gifts. 1

dedicated gift 1. קדש 2. קֹדֶשׁ
1Ch 26:20 and the treasuries of the dedicated gifts 2
26 all the treasuries of the dedicated gifts 2
28 all dedicated gifts were in the care 1
28:12 and the treasuries for dedicated gifts; 2

free gift 1. δωρεά 2. δώρημα 3. χάρισμα
Rom 5:15 But the free gift is not like the trespass. 3
15 the free gift in the grace of that one man Jesus 1
16 the free gift is not like . . that one man's sin. 2
16 the free gift following many trespasses brings 3
17 who receive . . the free gift of righteousness 1
6:23 but the free gift of God is eternal life in Christ 3

good gift 1. טוב 2. מֶגֶד
Deu 33:16 with the best gifts of the earth and its fulness 2
Neh 9:36 fathers to enjoy its fruit and its good gifts 1

liberal gift 1. ἁδρότης
2Co 8:20 no one should blame us about this liberal gift 1

gift of welcome 1. ξενία
3Mc 1: 8 to bring him gifts of welcome 1

parting gift 1. שִׁלּוּחִים
Mic 1:14 you shall give parting gifts to Mo'resheth-gath; 1

special gift 1. χάρισμα
1Co 7: 7 each has his own special gift from God 1

spiritual gift 1. πνευματικός 2. χάρισμα
1Co 1: 7 you are not lacking in any spiritual gift 2
12: 1 Now concerning spiritual gifts, brethren 1
14: 1 earnestly desire the spiritual gifts 1

votive gift 1. קֹדֶשׁ
1Kg 15:15 he brought . . the votive gifts of his father 1
15 gifts of his father and his own votive gifts 1
2Kg 12:18 Jeho'ash king of Judah took all the votive gifts 1
18 king of Judah took all . . and his own votive gifts 1
2Ch 15:18 he brought . . the votive gifts of his father 1
18 he brought . . his own votive gifts 1

willing gift 1. εὐλογία
2Co 9: 5 ready not as an exaction but as a willing gift. 1

gird 1. אזר 2. אסר 3. אפד 4. אֲפֻדָּה 5. חָגוֹר 6. חגר
7. חזק 8. διαζώννυμι 9. ἐμπορπάομαι 10. ἐπιτίθημι
11. ἐπιτίθημι ἐπὶ τὰς ὀσφύας 12. ζώννυμι
13. περιζώννυμι 14. συζώννυμι 15. ὑποζώννυμι
16. praecingo
Exd 12:11 your loins girded, your sandals on your feet 6
28: 8 the skilfully woven band upon it, to gird it 4
29: 5 gird him with the skilfully woven band 3
9 you shall gird them with girdles and bind caps 6
39: 5 the skilfully woven band upon it, to gird it 4
Lev 8: 7 girded him with the girdle, and clothed him 6
7 girded him with the skilfully woven band 6
13 Moses . . girded them with girdles, and bound 6
16: 4 He shall . . be girded with the linen girdle 6
Deu 1:41 And every man of you girded on his weapons of war 6
Jdg 3:16 a sword . . and he girded it on his right thigh 6
1Sm 2: 4 bows . . are broken, but the feeble gird on strength. 1
17:39 And David girded his sword over his armor 6
25:13 David said to his men, "Every man gird on his sword! 6
13 And every man of them girded on his sword; 6
13 David also girded on his sword; 6
2Sm 3:31 Rend your clothes, and gird on sackcloth 6
6:14 and David was girded with a linen ephod. 6
21:16 Ish'bi-be'nob . . who was girded with a new sword 6
22:40 thou didst gird me with strength for the battle; 1
1Kg 20:11 Let not him that girds on his armor boast himself 6
32 they girded sackcloth on their loins 6
Neh 4:18 builders had his sword girded at his side 2
Ps 18:32 the God who girded me with strength 1
39 thou didst gird me with strength for the battle; 1
30:11 loosed my sackcloth and girded me with gladness 1
45: 3 Gird your sword upon your thigh, O mighty one 6
65: 6 the mountains, being girded with might; 1
12 the hills gird themselves with joy 6
76:10 the residue of wrath thou wilt gird upon thee. 6
93: 1 LORD is robed, he is girded with strength. 1
109:19 like a belt with which he daily girds himself! 6
Prv 31:17 She girds her loins with strength 6
Isa 8: 9 far countries; gird yourselves and be dismayed; 1
9 gird yourselves and be dismayed. 1
15: 3 in the streets they gird on sackcloth; 6
22:12 to baldness and girding with sackcloth; 6
32:11 make . . bare, and gird sackcloth upon your loins. 6
45: 5 am the LORD . . I gird you, though you do not know me 1
Jer 4: 8 For this gird you with sackcloth, lament and wail; 6
6:26 O daughter of my people, gird on sackcloth 6
49: 3 Gird yourselves with sackcloth, lament, and run 6
Ezk 7:18 They gird themselves with sackcloth 6
23:15 girded with belts on their loins 5
27:31 bald for you, and gird themselves with sackcloth 6
44:18 they shall not gird themselves with anything 6
Dan 10: 5 whose loins were girded with gold of Uphaz. 6
Jol 1: 8 Lament like a virgin girded with sackcloth 6
13 Gird on sackcloth and lament, O priests 6
Nah 2: 1 Man the ramparts; watch the road; gird your loins; 7
Lke 12:35 Let your loins be girded and your lamps burning 13
37 he will gird himself and have them sit at table 13
17: 8 gird yourself and serve me 13
Joh 13: 4 girded himself with a towel. 8
5 the towel with which he was girded. 8
21:18 when you were young, you girded yourself 12
18 another will gird you 12
Eph 6:14 having girded your loins with truth 13
Rev 15: 6 and their breasts girded with golden girdles. 13
2Es 16: 2 Gird yourselves with sackcloth and haircloth 16
Jdt 4:10 they all girded themselves with sackcloth. 11
14 with their loins girded with sackcloth 13
8: 5 girded sackcloth about her loins 10
1Mc 3: 3 he girded on his armor of war and waged battles 14
58 Judas said, "Gird yourselves and be valiant 13
2Mc 3:19 girded with sackcloth under their breasts 15
10:25 girded their loins with sackcloth 12
3Mc 7: 5 girding themselves with . . cruelty 9

gird up 1. אזר 2. חגר 3. שנס 4. ἀναζώννυμι
1Kg 18:46 he girded up his loins and ran before Ahab 3
2Kg 4:29 Gird up your loins, and take my staff . . and go. 2
9: 1 Gird up your loins, and take this flask of oil 2
Job 38: 3 Gird up your loins like a man, I will question you 1
40: 7 Gird up your loins like a man; I will question you 1
Jer 1:17 But you, gird up your loins; 1
1Pe 1:13 Therefore gird up your minds, be sober 4

gird upon 1. חגר
Ps 76:10 the residue of wrath thou wilt gird upon thee. 1

girding 1. מַחֲגֹרֶת
Isa 3:24 instead of a rich robe, a girding of sackcloth; 1

girdle 1. אַבְנֵט 2. אֵזוֹר 3. חָגוֹר 4. חֲגוֹרָה 5. חגר
6. ζώνη
Exd 28: 4 a coat of checker work, a turban, and a girdle; 1
39 make a girdle embroidered with needlework. 1
40 for Aaron's sons you shall make coats and girdles 1
29: 9 you shall gird them with girdles and bind caps 1
39:29 the girdle of fine twined linen and of blue 1
Lev 8: 7 girded him with the girdle, and clothed him 1
13 Moses . . girded them with girdles, and bound 1
16: 4 He shall . . be girded with the linen girdle 1
1Sm 2:18 Samuel was . . a boy girdled with a linen ephod. 5
18: 4 and even his sword and his bow and his girdle. 3
2Sm 18:11 to give you ten pieces of silver and a girdle. 4
20: 8 and over it was a girdle with a sword in its sheath 3
1Kg 2: 5 innocent blood upon the girdle about my loins 4
2Kg 1: 8 He wore . . with a girdle of leather 2
Prv 31:24 she delivers girdles to the merchant. 3
Isa 3:24 instead of a girdle, a rope; 4
11: 5 Righteousness shall be the girdle of his waist 2
5 and faithfulness the girdle of his loins. 2
22:21 clothe him . . and will bind your girdle on him 1
Mat 3: 4 hair, and a leather girdle around his waist; 6
Mrk 1: 6 a leather girdle around his waist 6
Act 21:11 coming to us he took Paul's girdle 6
11 bind the man who owns this girdle 6
Rev 1:13 and with a golden girdle round his breast; 6
15: 6 and their breasts girded with golden girdles. 6
Jdt 9: 2 had loosed the girdle of a virgin to defile her *

girdle round 1. περιεζωσμένον πρός
Rev 1:13 and with a golden girdle round his breast; 1

girl 1. אִשָּׁה 2. יַלְדָּה 3. נַעֲרָה 4. עַלְמָה 5. κοράσιον
6. παρθένος
Exd 2: 8 So the girl went and called the child's mother. 4
Num31:18 all the young girls who have not known man 1
Jdg 19: 3 and when the girl's father saw him, he came with joy 3
4 his father-in-law, the girl's father, made him stay 3
5 to go; but the girl's father said to his son-in-law 3
6 the girl's father said to the man, "Be pleased 3
8 the girl's father said, "Strengthen your heart 3
9 his father-in-law, the girl's father, said to him 3
Jol 3: 3 and have sold a girl for wine, and have drunk it. 2
Zec 8: 5 the city shall be full of boys and girls playing 2
Mat 9:24 he said, "Depart; for the girl is not dead 5
25 took her by the hand, and the girl arose. 5
14:11 and given to the girl 5
Mrk 5:42 immediately the girl got up and walked 5
6:22 and the king said to the girl 5
28 gave it to the girl 5
28 the girl gave it to her mother. 5
1Co 7:28 if a girl marries she does not sin 6
34 the unmarried woman or girl is anxious 6
Tob 6:12 The girl is also beautiful and sensible 5
13 the girl has been given to seven husbands 5
7:17 the girl began to weep *
LJr 1: 9 as they would for a girl who loves ornaments; 6

girl *See also* slave.

little girl 1. κοράσιον
Mrk 5:41 which means, "Little girl, I say to you, arise. 1

girt 1. אחז

Sng 3: 8 all girt with swords and expert in war 1

give 1. בוא 2. דבר 3. דָּבָר 4. היה 5. הפך 6. חזק 7. חלק 8. יהב 9. יסף 10. יעץ 11. ירה 12. ישב 13. יָשַׁר 14. מצא 15. מַתַּת 16. נגד 17. נגר 18. נכה 19. נקב 20. נתן 21. סגר 22. עבד 23. עוד 24. עמד 25. ענה 26. עשה 27. פרס 28. צוה 29. רום 30. שום 31. שוב 32. שית 33. שלח 34. יהב (A) 35. נתן (A) 36. פשר (A) 37. שום (A) 38. *ἀναδίδωμι* 39. *ἀποδίδωμι* 40. *γίνομαι* 41. *διατίθημι* 42. *δίδωμι* 43. *δόμα* 44. *δόσις* 45. *δωρέομαι* 46. *δῶρον* 47. *εἰμί* 48. *εἰμὶ παρά* 49. *εἰς* 50. *ἐκδίδωμι* 51. *ἐνδείκνυμι* 52. *ἐξιλασμός* 53. *ἐπιδίδωμι* 54. *καλέω* 55. *λέγω* 56. *μεταδίδωμι* 57. *μετρέω* 58. *παραδίδωμι* 59. *παρέχω* 60. *πιπράσκω* 61. *ποιέω* 62. *ποῖος* 63. *ποτίζω* 64. *προδίδωμι* 65. *πρός* 66. *ὑπάρχω πρός* 67. *ὑπό* 68. *χαρίζομαι* 69. *χείρ* 70. *ψωμίζω* 71. ago 72. do 73. dono 74. facio 75. mitto 76. percipio 77. sum 78. trado

Gen 1:29 God said, "Behold, I have given you every plant 20
30 I have given every green plant for food. *
3: 6 she also gave some to her husband, and he ate. 20
12 The woman whom thou gavest to be with me 20
12 The woman . . gave me fruit of the tree, and I ate. 20
9: 3 and as I gave you the green plants *
3 you the green plants, I give you everything. 20
12: 7 To your descendants I will give this land. 20
13:15 you see I will give to you and to your descendants 20
17 the breadth of the land, for I will give it to you. 20
14:20 And Abram gave him a tenth of everything. 20
21 Give me the persons, but take the goods 20
15: 2 Abram said, "O Lord GOD, what wilt thou give me 20
3 Behold, thou hast given me no offspring; 20
7 from Ur of the Chalde'ans, to give you this land 20
18 To your descendants I give this land 20
16: 3 Sar'ai . . gave her to Abram her husband 20
5 May the wrong done to me be on you! I gave my maid 20
17: 8 I will give to you, and to your descendants after 20
16 moreover I will give you a son by her; 20
18: 7 gave it to the servant, who hastened to prepare it 20
20:14 male and female slaves, and gave them to Abraham 20
16 Sarah he said, "Behold, I have given your brother 20
21:14 Abraham . . gave it to Hagar 20
27 took sheep and oxen and gave them to Abim'elech 20
23: 4 a sojourner among you; give me property among you 20
9 that he may give me the cave of Mach-pe'lah 20
9 full price let him give it to me in your presence 20
11 No, my lord, hear me; I give you the field 20
11 of my people I give it to you; bury your dead. 20
13 But if you will, hear me; I will give the price 20
24: 7 To your descendants I will give this land,' 20
32 Laban ungirded the camels, and gave him straw 20
35 he has become great; he has given him flocks 20
36 and to him he has given all that he has. 20
41 and if they will not give her to you 20
53 gold, and raiment, and gave them to Rebekah; 20
53 he also gave to her brother and to her mother 20
25: 5 Abraham gave all he had to Isaac. 20
6 to the sons of his concubines Abraham gave gifts 20
34 Then Jacob gave Esau bread and pottage 20
26: 3 to your descendants I will give all these lands 20
4 will give to your descendants all these lands; 20
27:17 she gave the savory food and the bread 20
28 May God give you of the dew of heaven 20
37 all his brothers I have given to him for servants 20
28: 4 May he give the blessing of Abraham to you 20
4 of your sojournings which God gave to Abraham! 20
13 the land on which you lie I will give to you 20
20 If God . . will give me bread to eat and clothing 20
22 of all that thou givest me I will give the tenth 20
29:19 Laban said, "It is better that I give her to you 20
19 you than that I should give her to any other man; 20
21 Then Jacob said to Laban, "Give me my wife 8
24 Laban gave his maid Zilpah to his daughter Leah 20
26 to give the younger before the first-born. 20
27 we will give you the other also in return 20
28 then Laban gave him his daughter Rachel to wife. 20
29 Laban gave his maid Bilhah to his daughter 20
33 I am hated, he has given me this son also"; 20
30: 1 said to Jacob, "Give me children, or I shall die! 8
4 she gave him her maid Bilhah as a wife; 20
6 God . . has also heard my voice and given me a son"; 20
9 she took her maid Zilpah and gave her to Jacob 20
14 Give me, I pray, some of your son's mandrakes. 20
18 Leah said, "God has given me my hire 20
18 my hire because I gave my maid to my husband"; 20
26 Give me my wives and my children for whom I have 20
26 for you know the service which I have given you. 22
28 name your wages, and I will give it. 20
31 He said, "What shall I give you? 20
31 You shall not give me anything; 20
31: 9 cattle of your father, and given them to me. 20
15 he has been using up the money given for us. *
34: 8 I pray you, give her to him in marriage. 20
9 Make marriages with us; give your daughters 20
11 and whatever you say to me I will give. 20
12 and I will give according as you say to me; 20
12 only give me the maiden to be my wife. 20
14 do this thing, to give our sister to one who is 20
16 Then we will give our daughters to you 20
21 marriage, and let us give them our daughters. 20
35: 4 they gave to Jacob all the foreign gods 20
12 The land which I gave to Abraham and Isaac I will 20
12 land . . I will give to you, and I will give the land 20
12 land . . I will give to you, and I will give the land 20
38: 9 lest he should give offspring to his brother. 20
14 she had not been given to him in marriage. 20
16 She said, "What will you give me 20
17 And she said, "Will you give me a pledge 20
18 He said, "What pledge shall I give you? 20
18 he gave them to her, and went in to her 20
26 inasmuch as I did not give her to my son Shelah. 20
39:21 LORD . . gave him favor in the sight of the keeper 20
41:45 and he gave him in marriage As'enath 20
42:25 money in his sack, and to give them provisions 20
27 opened his sack to give his ass provender 20
43:24 the men into Joseph's house, and given them water 20
24 when he had given their asses provender 20
45:18 and I will give you the best of the land of Egypt 20
21 and Joseph gave them wagons 20
21 Joseph . . gave them provisions 20
22 To each and all of them he gave festal garments; 20
22 but to Benjamin he gave 300 shekels of silver 20
46:18 the sons of Zilpah, whom Laban gave to Leah 20
25 Bilhah, whom Laban gave to Rachel his daughter 20
47:11 and gave them a possession in the land of Egypt 20
15 Give us food; why should we die before your eyes? 8
16 Joseph answered, "Give your cattle, 8
16 I will give you food in exchange for your cattle 20
17 Joseph gave them food in exchange for the horses 20
19 give us seed, that we may live, and not die 20
22 lived on the allowance which Pharaoh gave them; 20
24 at the harvests you shall give a fifth to Pharaoh 20
48: 4 and will give this land to your descendants 20
9 They are my sons, whom God has given me here. 20
22 I have given to you rather than to your brothers 20
Exd 1:21 midwives feared God he gave them families. 26
2: 9 nurse him for me, and I will give you your wages. 20
21 the man, and he gave Moses his daughter Zippo'rah. 20
3:21 I will give this people favor in the sight 20
5: 7 You shall no longer give the people straw to make 20
10 Thus says Pharaoh, 'I will not give you straw. 20
16 No straw is given to your servants, yet they say 20
18 Go now, and work; for no straw shall be given you 20
6: 4 covenant . . to give them the land of Canaan 20
8 the land which I swore to give to Abraham, to Isaac 20
8 I will give it to you for a possession. 20
11: 3 the LORD gave the people favor in the sight 20
12:25 when you come to the land which the LORD will give 20
36 the LORD had given the people favor in the sight 20
13: 5 which he swore to your fathers to give you 20
11 to the land . . and shall give it to you 20
16: 8 the LORD gives you in the evening flesh to eat 20
15 the bread which the LORD has given you to eat. 20
29 See! The LORD has given you the sabbath, therefore 20
29 on the sixth day he gives you bread for two days; 20
17: 2 the people . . said, "Give us water to drink. 20
20:12 the land which the LORD your God gives you. 20
21: 4 If his master gives him a wife and she bears him 20
23 harm follows, then you shall give life for life 20
30 then he shall give for the redemption of his life 20
32 the owner shall give to the master 30 shekels 20
34 he shall give money to its owner 31
22:17 If her father utterly refuses to give her to him 20
29 The first-born of your sons you shall give to me. 20
30 on the eighth day you shall give it to me. 20
24:12 I will give you the tables of stone, with the law 20
25:16 put . . the testimony which I shall give you. 20
21 you shall put the testimony that I shall give 20
30:12 each shall give a ransom for himself to the LORD 20
13 Each who is numbered in the census shall give 20
14 Every one . . shall give the LORD'S offering. 20
15 The rich shall not give more, and the poor shall *
15 give the LORD'S offering to make atonement 20
31: 6 I have given to all able men ability 20
18 gave to Moses, when he had made an end of speaking 20
32:13 this land . . I will give to your descendants 20
24 so they gave it to me, and I threw it into the fire 20
33: 1 saying, 'To your descendants I will give it.' 20
Lev 5:16 shall add a fifth to it and give it to the priest 20
6: 5 give it to him to whom it belongs 20
17 I have given it as their portion of my offerings 20
7:32 the right thigh you shall give to the priest 20
34 I . . have given them to Aaron the priest 20
36 the LORD commanded this to be given them 20
10:14 for they are given as your due and your sons' due 20
17 holy and has been given to you that you may bear 20
14:34 land of Canaan, which I give you for a possession 20
15:14 and give them to the priest 20
17:11 I have given it for you upon the altar 20
18:21 You shall not give any of your children to devote 20
23 neither shall any woman give herself to a beast 24
19:20 a woman . . not yet ransomed or given her freedom 20
20: 2 who gives any of his children to Molech 20
3 he has given one of his children to Molech 20
4 when he gives one of his children to Molech 20
24 I will give it to you to possess, a land flowing 20
22:14 he shall . . give the holy thing to the priest 20
23:10 When you come into the land which I give you 20
38 freewill offerings, which you give to the LORD 20
25: 2 When you come into the land which I give to you 20
37 nor give him your food for profit 20
38 to give you the land of Canaan, and to be your God 20
26: 4 then I will give you your rains in their season 20
6 I will give peace in the land 20
27: 9 all of such that any man gives to the LORD is holy 20
23 the man shall give the amount of the valuation 20
Num 3: 9 you shall give the Levites to Aaron and his sons; 20
9 they are wholly given to him from among 20
48 give the money by which the excess number of them 20
51 Moses gave the redemption money to Aaron 20
5: 7 giving it to him to whom he did the wrong. 20
10 whatever any man gives to the priest shall be his. 20
6:26 lift up his countenance . . and give you peace. 30
7: 5 Accept these . . and give them to the Levites 20
6 wagons and the oxen, and gave them to the Levites. 20
7 gave to the sons of Gershon 20
8 gave to the sons of Merar'i 20
9 to the sons of Kohath he gave none 20
8:16 wholly given to me from among the people 20
19 given the Levites as a gift to Aaron and his sons 20
10:29 place of which the LORD said, 'I will give it to you'; 20
11:12 land . . thou didst swear to give their fathers?' *
13 Where am I to get meat to give to all this people? 20
13 they weep . . and say, 'Give us meat, that we may eat.' 20
18 LORD will give you meat, and you shall eat. 20
21 thou hast said, 'I will give them meat 20
13: 2 Canaan, which I give to the people of Israel; 20
14: 8 he will bring us into this land and give it to us 20
16 into the land which he swore to give to them *
23 land which I swore to give to their fathers; *
15: 2 land you are to inhabit, which I give you 20
21 you shall give to the LORD an offering 20
16:14 nor given us inheritance of fields 20
17: 6 their leaders gave him rods, one for each leader 20
18: 6 Levites . . are a gift to you, given to the LORD 20
7 I give your priesthood as a gift, and any one else 20
8 have given you whatever is kept of the offerings 20
8 I have given them to you as a portion 20
11 I have given them to you 20
12 the first fruits of what they give to the LORD 20
12 the first fruits . . I give to you. 20
19 All the holy offerings . . I give to you 20
21 To the Levites I have given every tithe in Israel 20
24 I have given to the Levites for an inheritance; 20
26 When you take . . the tithe which I have given you 20
28 give the LORD'S offering to Aaron the priest. 20
29 giving the hallowed part from them.' *
19: 3 you shall give her to Elea'zar the priest 20
20:12 assembly into the land which I have given them. 20
21 Thus Edom refused to give Israel passage 20
24 land which I have given to the people of Israel 20
21: 2 If thou wilt indeed give this people into my hand 20
16 Gather the people . . and I will give them water. 20
34 Do not fear him; for I have given him into your hand 20
22: 7 came to Balaam, and gave him Balak's message. 2
18 Though Balak were to give me his house 20
24:13 'If Balak should give me his house full of silver 20
25:12 Behold, I give to him my covenant of peace; 20
26:54 every tribe shall be given its inheritance 20
62 no inheritance given to them among . . Israel. 20
27: 4 Give to us a possession among our father's 20
7 give them possession of an inheritance 20
9 then . . give his inheritance to his brothers. 20
10 give his inheritance to his father's brothers. 20
11 then you shall give his inheritance 20
12 land which I have given to the people of Israel. 20
31:29 give it to Elea'zar the priest as an offering 20
30 take . . and give them to the Levites 20
41 Moses gave the tribute . . to Elea'zar the priest 20
47 Moses . . gave them to the Levites who had charge 20
32: 5 let this land be given to your servants 20
7 going over into the land which the LORD has given 20
9 from going into the land which the LORD had given 20
11 I swore to give to Abraham, to Isaac, and to Jacob *
29 If . . then you shall give them the land of Gilead 20
33 Moses gave to them, to the sons of Gad 20
40 Moses gave Gilead to Machir the son of Manas'seh 20
33:53 for I have given the land to you to possess it. 20
54 a large tribe you shall give a large inheritance *
34:13 LORD has commanded to give to the nine tribes 20
35: 2 Command . . Israel, that they give to the Levites 20
2 you shall give to the Levites pasture lands 20
4 pasture lands . . you shall give to the Levites 20
6 cities which you give to the Levites shall be 20
6 in addition to them you shall give 42 cities 20
7 All the cities which you give to the Levites 20
8 as for the cities which you shall give 20
8 each . . shall give of its cities to the Levites. 20
13 cities . . you give shall be your six cities of refuge. 20
14 You shall give three cities beyond the Jordan 20
36: 2 my lord to give the land for inheritance by lot 20

2 give the inheritance of Zeloph'ehad our brother 20
Deu 1: 8 give to them and to their descendants after them.' 20
20 hill country . . which the LORD our God gives us. 20
25 'It is a good land which the LORD our God gives us.' 20
27 give us into the hand of the Amorites, to destroy us. 20
35 good land which I swore to give to your fathers 20
36 to him and to his children I will give the land 20
39 to them I will give it, and they shall possess it. 20
2: 5 for I will not give you any of their land 20
5 I have given Mount Se'ir to Esau as a possession. 20
9 not give you any of their land for a possession 20
9 have given Ar to the sons of Lot for a possession.' 20
12 their possession, which the LORD gave to them.) 20
19 not give you any of the land of the sons of Ammon 20
19 because I have given it to the sons of Lot 20
24 I have given into your hand Sihon the Amorite 20
28 You shall . . give me water for money, 20
29 into the land which the LORD our God gives to us.' 20
30 might give him into your hand, as at this day. 20
36 LORD our God gave all into our hands. 20
3: 2 I have given him and all his people and his land 20
3 LORD our God gave into our hand Og also, the king 20
12 I gave to the Reubenites and the Gadites 20
13 the rest . . I gave to the half-tribe of Manas'seh. 20
15 To Machir I gave Gilead 20
16 I gave the territory from Gilead 20
18 LORD your God has given you this land to possess; 20
19 shall remain in the cities which I have given you 20
20 which the LORD . . gives them beyond the Jordan; 20
20 man to his possession which I have given you.' 20
4: 1 possession of the land which the LORD . . gives 20
21 land which the LORD . . gives you for an inheritance. 20
38 to give you their land for an inheritance 20
40 land which the LORD your God gives you for ever. 20
5:16 in the land which the LORD your God gives you. 20
22 upon two tables of stone, and gave them to me. 20
31 do them in the land which I give them to possess.' 20
6:10 land which he swore to your fathers . . to give you 20
18 land which the LORD swore to give to your fathers •
23 that he might bring us in and give us the land 20
23 land which he swore to give to our fathers. •
7: 3 not . . giving your daughters to their sons 20
13 in the land which he swore to your fathers to give 20
24 he will give their kings into your hand 20
8: 1 land . . the LORD swore to give to your fathers. •
10 bless the LORD . . for the good land he has given 20
18 LORD . . who gives you power to get wealth; 20
9: 6 LORD . . not giving you this good land to possess 20
10 LORD gave me the two tables of stone written 20
11 at the end . . LORD gave me the two tables of stone 20
23 take possession of the land which I have given you 20
10: 4 wrote on the tables . . and the LORD gave them to me. 20
11 land, which I swore to their fathers to give them.' 20
18 sojourner, giving him food and clothing. 20
11: 9 LORD swore to your fathers to give to them 20
14 he will give the rain for your land in its season 20
15 he will give grass in your fields for your cattle 20
17 perish . . off the good land which the LORD gives 20
21 land which the LORD swore to your fathers to give 20
31 land which the LORD your God gives you; 20
12: 1 which the LORD . . has given you to possess 20
9 to the rest . . which the LORD your God gives you. 20
15 blessing of the LORD . . which he has given you; 20
21 herd or your flock, which the LORD has given you 20
13: 1 prophet arises . . gives you a sign or a wonder 20
12 which the LORD your God gives you to dwell there 20
14:21 may give it to the alien who is within your towns 20
15: 4 land which the LORD your God gives you 20
7 land which the LORD your God gives you 20
9 your eye be hostile . . and you give him nothing 20
10 You shall give to him freely, and your heart 20
10 heart shall not be grudging when you give to him; 20
14 as the LORD . . has blessed you, you shall give 20
16: 5 within any . . towns which the LORD your God gives 20
10 freewill offering . . which you shall give 20
17 every man shall give as he is able, according •
17 blessing of the LORD your God which he has given 20
18 in all your towns which the LORD your God gives 20
20 inherit the land which the LORD your God gives 20
17: 2 any of your towns which the LORD your God gives 20
11 according to the instructions which they give 11
14 come to the land which the LORD your God gives you 20
18: 3 give to the priest the shoulder 20
4 first of the fleece of your sheep, you shall give 20
9 come into the land which the LORD your God gives 20
19: 1 whose land the LORD your God gives you 20
2 land which the LORD . . gives you to possess. 20
8 gives you all the land which he promised to give 20
8 all the land . . he promised to give to your fathers- 20
10 land . . LORD . . gives you for an inheritance 20
14 land that the LORD your God gives you to possess 20
20:13 when the LORD your God gives it into your hand 20
14 spoil . . which the LORD your God has given you. 20
16 cities . . LORD . . gives you for an inheritance 20
21: 1 in the land . . LORD your God gives you to possess 20
10 LORD your God gives them into your hands 20
17 by giving him a double portion of all that he has 20
23 your land which the LORD your God gives you 20
22:16 I gave my daughter to this man to wife 20

19 give them to the father of the young woman 20
29 man who lay with her shall give to the father 20
24: 4 land . . LORD your God gives you for an inheritance. 20
15 you shall give him his hire on the day he earns it 20
25: 3 Forty stripes may be given him, but not more; 18
15 in the land which the LORD your God gives you. 20
19 land . . LORD your God gives you for an inheritance 20
26: 1 land . . LORD your God gives you for an inheritance 20
2 harvest from your land . . LORD your God gives 20
3 land . . LORD swore to our fathers to give us.' 20
9 brought us into this place and gave us this land 20
10 first of the fruit . . which thou, O LORD, has given 20
11 good which the LORD your God has given to you 20
12 giving it to the Levite, the sojourner 20
13 moreover I have given it to the Levite 20
15 bless . . the ground which thou hast given us 20
27: 2 Jordan to the land which the LORD your God gives 20
3 enter the land which the LORD your God gives you 20
28: 8 land which the LORD your God gives you. 20
11 land which the LORD swore to your fathers to give 20
12 to give the rain of your land in its season 20
31 your sheep shall be given to your enemies 20
32 sons . . shall be given to another people 20
52 all your land, which the LORD your God has given 20
53 sons and daughters . . LORD your God has given 20
55 not give to any of them any of the flesh 20
65 LORD will give you there a trembling heart 20
29: 4 LORD has not given you a mind to understand 20
8 gave it for an inheritance to the Reubenites 20
30:20 land . . LORD swore to your fathers . . , to give them. 20
31: 7 land . . LORD has sworn to their fathers to give 20
9 Moses . . gave it to the priests the sons of Levi 20
20 land . . which I swore to give to their fathers •
21 brought them into the land that I swore to give. •
23 Israel into the land which I swore to give them •
32:49 Canaan, which I give to the people of Israel 20
52 land which I give to the people of Israel. 20
33: 8 Give to Levi thy Thummim, and thy Urim to thy godly 42
34: 4 swore . . 'I will give it to your descendants.' 20
Jos 1: 2 the land which I am giving to them, to . . Israel. 20
3 Every place that . . I have given to you 20
6 land which I swore to their fathers to give them. 20
11 land . . the LORD your God gives you to possess. 20
13 LORD your God is . . and will give you this land. 20
14 the land which Moses gave you beyond the Jordan; 20
15 the land which the LORD your God is giving them; 20
15 land which Moses . . gave you beyond the Jordan 20
2: 9 I know that the LORD has given you the land 20
12 swear to me by the LORD . . and give me a sure sign 20
14 we will deal . . when the LORD gives us the land. 20
24 the LORD has given all the land into our hands; 20
5: 6 the land which the LORD had sworn . . to give us 20
6: 2 I have given into your hand Jericho, with its king 20
16 Shout; for the LORD has given you the city. 20
7: 7 to give us into the hands of the Amorites 20
19 give glory to the LORD . . and render praise to him; 30
8: 1 go up to Ai; see, I have given into your hand the king 20
7 for the LORD your God will give it into your hand. 20
18 toward Ai; for I will give it into your hand. 20
9:24 had commanded . . Moses to give you all the land 20
10: 8 for I have given them into your hands; 20
12 when the LORD gave the Amorites over to . . Israel; 20
19 the LORD your God has given them into your hand. 20
30 the LORD gave it also . . into the hand of Israel; 20
32 and the LORD gave Lachish into the hand of Israel 20
11: 8 And the LORD gave them into the hand of Israel 20
23 and Joshua gave it for an inheritance to Israel 20
12: 6 and Moses . . gave their land for a possession 20
7 and Joshua gave their land to the tribes 20
13: 8 their inheritance, which Moses gave them 20
8 as Moses the servant of the LORD gave them 20
14 To the tribe of Levi . . Moses gave no inheritance; 20
15 Moses gave an inheritance to the . . Reubenites 20
24 Moses gave an inheritance also to the . . Gadites 20
29 Moses gave an inheritance to . . Manas'seh; 20
33 to the tribe of Levi Moses gave no inheritance; 20
14: 3 Moses had given an inheritance to the . . tribes 20
3 but to the Levites he gave no inheritance 20
4 no portion was given to the Levites in the land 20
12 give me this hill country of which the LORD spoke 20
13 Joshua blessed him; and he gave Hebron to Caleb 20
15:13 he gave to Caleb the son of Jephun'neh a portion 20
16 Whoever . . to him will I give Achsah my daughter 20
17 and he gave him Achsah his daughter as wife. 20
19 Give me a present; since you . . give me also 20
19 since you have . . give me also springs of water. 20
19 Caleb gave her the upper springs and the lower 20
17: 4 LORD commanded Moses to give us an inheritance 20
4 he gave them an inheritance among the brethren 20
14 Why have you given me but one lot and one portion 20
18: 3 the land, which the LORD . . has given you? 20
7 which Moses the servant of the LORD gave them. 20
19:49 people of Israel gave an inheritance among them 20
50 they gave him the city which he asked 20
20: 4 shall take him into the city, and give him a place 20
21: 2 The LORD commanded . . that we be given cities 20
3 Israel gave to the Levites the following cities 20
8 These . . the people of Israel gave by lot 20
9 they gave the following cities mentioned 20

11 They gave them Kir'iath-ar'ba . . that is Hebron 20
12 But the fields . . had been given to Caleb 20
13 to the descendants of Aaron . . they gave Hebron 20
21 To them were given Shechem, the city of refuge 20
27 to the Gershonites . . were given . . two cities; •
34 the rest . . were given out of the tribe of Zeb'ulun •
43 the LORD gave to Israel all the land . . he swore 20
43 the land which he swore to give to their fathers; 20
44 LORD had given all . . enemies into their hands. 20
22: 4 which Moses . . gave you on the other side 20
7 Moses had given a possession in Bashan; 20
7 to the other half Joshua had given a possession 20
23:13 good land which the LORD your God has given you. 20
15 good land which the LORD your God has given you 20
16 from off the good land which he has given to you. 20
24: 3 and made his offspring many. I gave him Isaac; 20
4 and to Isaac I gave Jacob and Esau. 20
4 I gave Esau the hill country of Se'ir to possess 20
8 they fought with you, and I gave them 20
11 and I gave them into your hand. 20
13 I gave you a land on which you had not labored 20
33 Gib'e-ah . . had been given him in the hill country 20
Jdg 1: 2 behold, I have given the land into his hand. 20
4 LORD gave the Canaanites and the Per'izzites 20
12 I will give him Achsah my daughter as wife. 20
13 and he gave him Achsah his daughter as wife. 20
15 She said to him, "Give me a present; since you have 8
15 me in the . . Negeb, give me also springs of water. 20
15 Caleb gave her the upper springs and the lower 20
20 Hebron was given to Caleb, as Moses had said; 20
2: 1 the land which I swore to give to your fathers. •
23 he did not give them into the power of Joshua. 20
3: 6 their own daughters they gave to their sons; 20
10 to war, and the LORD gave Cu'shan-rishatha'im king 20
28 for the LORD has given your enemies the Moabites 20
4: 7 troops; and I will give him into your hand.' 20
14 which the LORD has given Sis'era into your hand. 20
5:25 He asked water and she gave him milk 20
29 make answer, nay, she gives answer to herself 31
6: 1 the LORD gave them into the hand of Mid'ian 20
9 drove them out before you, and gave you their land; 20
13 cast us off, and given us into the hand of Mid'ian. 20
7: 2 for me to give the Mid'ianites into their hand 20
7 and give the Mid'ianites into your hand; 20
9 the camp; for I have given it into your hand. 20
14 his hand God has given Mid'ian and all the host. 20
15 LORD has given the host of Mid'ian into your hand. 20
8: 3 God has given into your hands the princes 20
5 Pray, give loaves of bread to the people who 20
6 your hand, that we should give bread to your army? 20
7 LORD has given Zebah and Zalmun'na into my hand 20
15 that we should give bread to your men who are 20
24 give me every man of you the earrings of his spoil. 20
25 And they answered, "We will willingly give them. 20
9: 4 they gave him 70 pieces of silver out of the house 20
11: 9 the Ammonites, and the LORD gives them over to me 20
21 the LORD . . gave Sihon and all his people 20
30 If thou wilt give the Ammonites into my hand 20
32 them; and the LORD gave them into his hand. 20
12: 3 Ammonites, and the LORD gave them into my hand; 20
9 30 sons; and 30 daughters he gave in marriage 33
13: 1 and the LORD gave them into the hand 20
14: 9 father and mother, and gave some to them 20
12 I will give you 30 linen garments and 30 festal 20
13 you shall give me 30 linen garments 20
19 took their spoil and gave the festal garments 20
20 Samson's wife was given to his companion •
15: 2 you . . hated her; so I gave her to your companion. 20
6 taken his wife and given her to his companion. 20
12 bind you, that we may give you into the hands 20
13 will only bind you and give you into their hands; 20
16: 5 we will each give you 1,100 pieces of silver. 20
23 Our god has given Samson our enemy into our hand. 20
24 Our god has given our enemy into our hand 20
17: 4 took . . silver, and gave it to the silversmith 20
10 and I will give you ten pieces of silver a year 20
18:10 land is broad; yea, God has given it into your hands 20
20: 7 Israel, all of you, give your advice and counsel 8
28 Go up; for . . I will give them into your hand. 20
36 The men of Israel gave ground to Benjamin 20
21: 1 No one of us shall give his daughter in marriage 20
7 we will not give them any of our daughters 20
14 they gave them the women whom they had saved 20
18 Yet we cannot give them wives of our daughters. 20
18 sworn, "Cursed be he who gives a wife to Benjamin. 20
22 we did not take . . neither did you give them 20
Rut 1: 6 LORD had visited his people and given them food. 20
2:12 and a full reward be given you by the LORD 4
18 she also brought out and gave her what food she had 20
3:17 saying, "These six measures of barley he gave to me 20
4: 7 one drew off his sandal and gave it to the other 20
12 the children that the LORD will give you 20
13 he went in to her, and the LORD gave her conception 20
1Sm 1: 4 he would give portions to Penin'nah his wife 20
5 he would give Hannah only one portion 20
11 but wilt give to thy maidservant a son 20
11 I will give him to the LORD all the days of his life 20
2:10 The LORD will . . he will give strength to his king 20
15 Give meat for the priest to roast; 20

16 No, you must give it now; and if not, I will take it 20
20 The LORD give you children by this woman 30
28 I gave to . . your father all my offerings by fire 20
6: 5 make images . . and give glory to the God of Israel; 20
8: 6 when they said, "Give us a king to govern us. 20
14 take the best of . . and give them to his servants. 20
15 take the tenth . . and give it to his officers 20
9: 8 I have . . silver, and I will give it to the man of God 20
22 gave them a place at the head of those . . invited 20
23 Bring the portion I gave you, of which I said to you 20
10: 4 they will greet you and give you two loaves 20
9 When he turned . . God gave him another heart; 5
14:10 the LORD has given them into our hand. 20
12 the LORD has given them into the hand of Israel. 20
37 Wilt thou give them into the hand of Israel? 20
41 If this guilt is in me or in Jonathan . . give Urim; 72
41 if . . guilt is in thy people Israel, give Thummim. 8
15:28 and has given it to a neighbor of yours 20
17:10 give me a man, that we may fight together. 20
25 the king . . will give him his daughter 20
44 I will give your flesh to the birds of the air 20
46 I will give the dead bodies . . to the birds 20
47 is the LORD's and he will give you into our hand. 20
18: 4 of the robe . . and gave it to David, and his armor 20
17 Here is . . Merab; I will give her to you for a wife; 20
19 when Merab . . should have been given to David 20
19 she was given to A'driel . . for a wife. 20
21 Let me give her to him, that she may be a snare 20
27 And Saul gave him his daughter Michal for a wife. 20
20:40 And Jonathan gave his weapons to his lad, and said 20
21: 3 Give me five loaves of bread, or whatever is here. 20
6 the priest gave him the holy bread; 20
9 David said, "There is none like that; give it to me. 20
22: 7 will the son of Jesse give every one of you fields 20
10 inquired of the LORD . . and gave him provisions 20
10 gave him the sword of Goliath the Philistine. 20
13 you have given him bread and a sword 20
23: 4 I will give the Philistines into your hand. 20
7 And Saul said, "God has given him into my hand; 60
14 but God did not give him into his hand. 20
24: 4 I will give your enemy into your hand 20
10 the LORD gave you today into my hand in the cave; 20
25: 8 give whatever you have at hand to your servants 20
11 give it to men who come from I do not know where? 20
27 now let this present . . be given to the young men 20
44 Saul had given Michal his daughter . . to Palti 20
26: 8 God has given your enemy into your hand this day; 21
23 the LORD gave you into my hand today 20
27: 5 let a place be given me in one of the country towns 20
6 that day A'chish gave him Ziklag; 20
28:17 and given it to your neighbor, David. 20
19 the LORD will give Israel also . . into the hand 20
19 LORD will give the army of Israel . . into the hand 20
30:11 they gave him bread and he ate, they gave him water 20
12 they gave him a piece of a cake of figs 20
22 we will not give them any of the spoil . . we have 20
23 shall not do so . . with what the LORD has given us; 20
23 preserved us and given into our hand the band 20
2Sm 3: 8 I . . have not given you into the hand of David; 14
14 Give me my wife Michal, whom I betrothed 20
4:10 and slew him . . which was the reward I gave him 20
5:19 Shall I go up . . ? Wilt thou give them into my hand? 20
19 I will certainly give the Philistines 20
9: 9 I have given to your master's son. 20
12: 8 I gave you your master's house, and . . wives 20
8 gave you the house of Israel and of Judah; 20
11 take your wives . . and give them to your neighbor 20
14:13 For in giving this decision the king convicts 2
16: 8 the LORD has given the kingdom into the hand 20
20 Give your counsel; what shall we do? 8
23 the counsel which Ahith'ophel gave was 10
17: 7 the counsel . . Ahith'ophel has given is not good. 10
18:11 I would have been glad to give you ten pieces 20
21: 6 let seven of his sons be given to us 20
6 And the king said, "I will give them. 20
9 and he gave them into the hands of the Gib'eonites 20
22:36 Thou hast given me the shield of thy salvation 20
48 who gave me vengeance and brought down peoples 20
24: 9 Jo'ab gave the sum of the numbering . . to the king 20
23 All this, O king, Arau'nah gives to the king. 20
1Kg 2:17 to give me Ab'ishag the Shu'nammite as my wife. 20
21 Let Ab'ishag . . be given to Adoni'jah your brother 20
3: 5 by night; and God said, "Ask what I shall give you. 20
6 hast given him a son to sit on his throne this day. 20
9 Give thy servant . . an understanding mind 20
12 I give you a wise and discerning mind, so that none 20
13 I give you also what you have not asked, both 20
25 child in two, and give half to the one, and half 20
26 give her the living child, and by no means slay it. 20
27 Give the living child to the first woman, and by no 20
4:29 God gave Solomon wisdom and understanding 20
5: 7 the LORD . . who has given to David a wise son 20
11 Solomon gave Hiram . . wheat as food 20
11 Solomon gave this to Hiram year by year. 20
12 the LORD gave Solomon wisdom, as he promised him; 20
8:34 to the land which thou gavest to their fathers. 20
36 thou hast given to thy people as an inheritance. 20
40 in the land which thou gavest to our fathers. 20
46 art angry with them, and dost give them to an enemy 20

48 their land, which thou gavest to their fathers 20
56 the LORD who has given rest to his people Israel 20
9: 7 cut off . . from the land which I have given them; 20
11 Solomon gave to Hiram twenty cities in the land 20
12 to see the cities which Solomon had given him 20
13 kind of cities are these which you have given me 20
16 Pharaoh . . had given it as dowry to his daughter 20
10:10 she gave the king 120 talents of gold 20
10 which the queen of Sheba gave to King Solomon. 20
13 King Solomon gave to the queen of Sheba 20
13 what was given her by the bounty of King Solomon. 20
11:11 and will give it to your servant. 20
13 I will give one tribe to your son 20
18 to Pharaoh . . who gave him a house 20
18 and assigned him . . food, and gave him land. 20
19 he gave him in marriage the sister of his own wife 20
31 I am about to . . and will give you ten tribes 20
35 I will take the kingdom . . and will give it to you 20
36 Yet to his son I will give one tribe 20
38 I will be with you . . and I will give Israel to you. 20
12: 8 he forsook the counsel which the old men gave him 10
13 the counsel which the old men had given him 10
13: 3 he gave a sign the same day, saying, "This is the sign 20
5 the sign which the man of God had given 20
7 Come home with me . . and I will give you a reward. 20
8 If you give me half your house, I will not go 20
26 the LORD has given him to the lion, which has torn 20
14: 8 tore the kingdom away . . and gave it to you; 20
15 this good land which he gave to their fathers 20
15: 4 the LORD his God gave him a lamp in Jerusalem 20
18 Asa . . gave them into the hands of his servants; 20
17:19 he said to her, "Give me your son. 20
18: 9 you would give your servant into the hand of Ahab 20
23 Let two bulls be given to us; 20
26 they took the bull which was given them 20
19:21 boiled their flesh . . and gave it to the people 20
20:13 Behold, I will give it into your hand this day; 20
28 I will give all this great multitude 20
21: 2 Give me your vineyard, that I may have it 20
2 Give me . . and I will give you a better vineyard 20
2 I will give you its value in money. 20
3 I should give you the inheritance of my fathers. 20
4 he had said, "I will not give you the inheritance 20
6 Give me your vineyard for money; 20
6 or else . . I will give you another vineyard for it'; 20
6 and he answered, 'I will not give you my vineyard.' 20
7 I will give you the vineyard of Naboth 20
15 which he refused to give you for money; 20
22: 6 the Lord will give it into the hand of the king. 20
12 the LORD will give it into the hand of the king. 20
15 the LORD will give it into the hand of the king. 20
2Kg 3:10 called these three . . to give them into the hand 20
13 the LORD . . called these three kings to give them 20
18 he will also give the Moabites into your hand 20
4:42 Eli'sha said, "Give to the men, that they may eat. 20
43 Give them to the men, that they may eat 20
5: 1 by him the LORD had given victory to Syria. 20
17 let there be given . . two mules' burden of earth; 20
22 give them a talent of silver and two . . garments.' 20
6:28 woman said . . 'Give your son, that we may eat him 20
29 I said to her, 'Give your son, that we may eat him'; 20
8:19 he promised to give a lamp to him and to his sons 20
29 wounds which the Syrians had given him at Ramah 18
9:15 of the wounds which the Syrians had given him 18
10:15 Jehu said, "If it is, give me your hand. 20
15 So he gave him his hand. And Jehu took him up 20
24 allows any of those whom I give into your hands 1
11:12 put the crown upon him, and gave him the testimony; 20
12:11 they would give the money that was weighed out 20
14 that was given to the workmen who were repairing 20
13: 3 he gave them continually into the hand of Haz'ael 20
5 Therefore the LORD gave Israel a savior 20
14: 9 saying, 'Give your daughter to my son for a wife'; 20
15:12 the promise of the LORD which he gave to Jehu 2
19 Men'aham gave Pul 1,000 talents of silver 20
20 exacted . . to give to the king of Assyria. 20
17:15 covenant . . and the warnings which he gave them. 23
20 and gave them into the hand of spoilers 20
18:15 Hezeki'ah gave him all the silver that was found 20
16 stripped the gold from . . and gave it to the king 20
23 I will give you 2,000 horses 20
30 city will not be given into the hand of the king 20
19:10 that Jerusalem will not be given into the hand 20
21: 8 out of the land which I gave to their fathers 20
14 cast off . . and give them into the hand of their 20
22: 5 let it be given into the hand of the workmen 20
5 and let them give it to the workmen who are 20
8 Hilki'ah gave the book to Shaphan, and he read it. 20
10 Hilki'ah the priest has given me a book. 20
23:35 Jehoi'akim gave the silver and . . to Pharaoh 20
35 he taxed the land to give the money 20
35 He exacted . . to give it to Pharaoh Neco. 20
25:28 and gave him a seat above the seats of the kings 20
30 a regular allowance was given him by the king 20
1Ch 2:35 Sheshan gave his daughter in marriage to Jarha 20
5: 1 his birthright was given to the sons of Joseph 20
20 Hagrites and all . . were given into their hands 20
6:55 to them they gave Hebron in the land of Judah 20
56 they gave to Caleb the son of Jephun'neh. 20

57 To the sons of Aaron they gave the cities 20
61 the Ko'hathites were given by lot . . ten cities. •
64 the people of Israel gave the Levites the cities 20
65 They also gave them by lot . . these cities 20
67 They were given the cities of refuge 20
71 To the Gershomites were given •
14:10 Wilt thou give them into my hand? 20
10 Go up, and I will give them into your hand. 20
16:18 saying, "To you I will give the land of Canaan 20
21: 5 Jo'ab gave the sum of the numbering of the people 20
22 to Ornan, "Give me the site of the threshing floor 20
22 give it to me at its full price 20
23 see, I give the oxen for burnt offerings 20
23 the wheat for a cereal offering. I give it all. 20
22: 9 I will give peace and quiet to Israel in his days. 20
25: 5 God had given Heman fourteen sons 20
28: 5 of all my sons (for the LORD has given me many sons 20
11 David gave Solomon his son the plan 20
29: 3 I give it to the house of my God 20
7 They gave for the service of the house of God 20
8 precious stones gave them to the treasury 20
14 and of thy own have we given thee. 20
2Ch 1: 7 God . . said to him, "Ask what I shall give you. 20
10 Give me now wisdom and knowledge to go out 20
12 will also give you riches, possessions, and honor 20
2:10 give for your servants . . 20,000 cors 20
12 who has given King David a wise son 20
6:25 land . . thou gavest to them and to their 20
27 thy land, which thou hast given to thy people 20
31 in the land which thou gavest to our fathers. 20
36 art angry with them, and dost give them to an enemy 20
38 their land, which thou gavest to their fathers 20
7:20 pluck you up from the land which I have given you; 20
8: 2 rebuilt the cities which Huram had given to him 20
9: 9 Then she gave the king . . talents of gold 20
9 which the queen of Sheba gave to King Solomon. 20
12 King Solomon gave to the queen of Sheba 20
10: 8 he forsook the counsel which the old men gave him 10
11:23 he gave them abundant provisions 20
13: 5 LORD . . gave the kingship over Israel for ever 20
16 God gave them into their hand. 20
16: 8 relied on the LORD, he gave them into your hand. 20
18: 5 God will give it into the hand of the king. 20
11 LORD will give it into the hand of the king. 20
14 they will be given into your hand. 20
19: 6 the LORD; he is with you in giving judgment. 3
8 to give judgment for the LORD •
20: 7 give it for ever to the descendants of Abraham 20
21: 3 Their father gave them great gifts 20
3 but he gave the kingdom to Jeho'ram 20
7 promised to give a lamp to him and to his sons 20
23:11 put the crown upon him, and gave him the testimony; •
24:12 king and Jehoi'ada gave it to those who had charge 20
25: 9 100 talents which I have given to the army 20
9 The LORD is able to give you much more than this. 20
18 Give your daughter to my son for a wife 20
20 it was of God, in order that he might give them 20
27: 5 Ammonites gave him that year 100 talents 20
28: 5 LORD his God gave him into the hand of the king 20
5 also given into the hand of the king of Israel 20
9 was angry with Judah, he gave them into your hand 20
21 Ahaz . . gave tribute to the king of Assyria; 20
30:12 The hand of God was also upon Judah to give them 20
24 Hezeki'ah . . gave the assembly 1,000 bulls 29
24 princes gave the assembly 1,000 bulls and 10,000 29
31: 4 commanded the people . . to give the portion due 20
4 might give themselves to the law of the LORD. 6
32:11 may give you over to die by famine and by thirst 20
24 answered him and gave him a sign. 20
29 God had given him very great possessions. 20
33: 8 all the law . . given through Moses. •
34:10 workmen . . gave it for repairing . . the house. 20
11 They gave it to the carpenters and the builders 20
14 book of the law of the LORD given through Moses. •
15 Hilki'ah gave the book to Shaphan. 20
18 Hilki'ah the priest has given me a book. 20
35: 8 gave to the priests for the passover offerings 20
9 gave to the Levites for the passover offerings 29
36:17 he gave them all into his hand. 20
23 LORD . . has given me all the kingdoms 20
Ezr 1: 2 LORD . . has given me all the kingdoms 20
2:69 gave to the treasury of the work 61,000 darics 20
3: 7 gave money to the masons and the carpenters 20
5: 3 Who gave you a decree to build this house 37
9 'Who gave you a decree to build this house 37
12 gave them into the hand of Nebuchadnez'zar king 34
6: 9 whatever is needed . . let that be given to them 34
7: 6 law of Moses . . LORD the God of Israel had given; 20
11 letter . . Ar-ta-xerx'es gave to Ezra the priest 20
19 vessels that have been given you for the service 34
9: 7 been given into the hand of the kings of the lands 20
8 to give us a secure hold within his holy place 20
9 to give us protection in Judea and Jerusalem. 20
12 Therefore give not your daughters to their sons 20
13 hast given us such a remnant as this 20
Neh 2: 1 I took up the wine and gave it to the king. 20
7 let letters be given me to the governors 20
8 letter to Asaph . . that he may give me timber 20
9 governors . . and gave them the king's letter. 20

6:13 could give me an evil name, in order to taunt me. •
7:70 heads of fathers' houses gave to the work. 20
70 governor gave to the treasury 1,000 darics of gold 20
71 heads . . gave into the treasury of the work 20
72 rest of the people gave was 20,000 darics of gold 20
8: 1 law of Moses which the LORD had given to Israel. 28
8 gave the sense, so that the people understood 30
9: 7 the God who didst . . give him the name Abraham; 30
8 covenant to give to his descendants the land 20
13 give them right ordinances and true laws 20
15 give them bread from heaven for their hunger 20
15 possess the land which thou hadst sworn to give 20
20 Thou gavest thy good Spirit to instruct them 20
20 gavest them water for their thirst. 20
22 thou didst give them kingdoms and peoples 20
24 Canaanites, and didst give them into their hands 20
27 give them into the hand of their enemies 20
27 great mercies thou didst give them saviors 20
30 Therefore thou didst give them into the hand 20
34 not . . heeded . . warnings which thou didst give 23
35 great goodness which thou gavest them 20
36 land that thou gavest to our fathers to enjoy 20
10:29 God's law . . given by Moses the servant of God 20
30 not give our daughters to the peoples of the land 20
12:47 gave the daily portions for the singers 20
13: 5 which were given by commandment to the Levites •
10 portions of the Levites had not been given 20
25 You shall not give your daughters to their sons 20
Est 1: 3 gave a banquet for all his princes and servants 26
5 the king gave for all the people . . a banquet 26
9 Queen Vashti also gave a banquet for the women 26
19 let the king give her royal position to another 20
20 all women will give honor to their husbands 20
2: 3 let their ointments be given them. 20
13 she was given whatever she desired to take 20
18 the king gave a great banquet to all his princes 26
18 He also . . and gave gifts with royal liberality. 20
3:10 signet ring . . and gave it to Haman the Ag'agite 20
11 The money is given to you, the people also, 20
4: 8 Mor'decai also gave him a copy of the . . decree 20
5: 3 What is your request? It shall be given you, 20
7: 3 let my life be given me at my petition 20
8: 1 King Ahasu-e'rus gave . . Esther the house of Haman 20
2 his signet ring . . and gave it to Mor'decai. 20
7 Behold, I have given Esther the house of Haman 20
Job 1:21 the LORD gave, and the LORD has taken away; 20
2: 4 All that a man has he will give for his life. 20
3:20 Why is light given to him that is in misery 20
23 Why is light given to a man whose way is hid •
5:10 he gives rain upon the earth and sends waters 20
9:24 The earth is given into the hand of the wicked; 20
15:19 to whom alone the land was given 20
24:23 He gives them security, and they are supported; 20
28:25 When he gave to the wind its weight 26
31:37 I would give him an account of all my steps; 16
32:17 I also will give my answer; 25
35: 7 If you are righteous, what do you give to him; 20
10 Where is God my Maker, who gives songs in the night 20
36: 6 but gives the afflicted their right. 20
31 he judges peoples; he gives food in abundance. 20
37:10 By the breath of God ice is given 20
38:36 or given understanding to the mists? 20
39: 6 to whom I have given the steppe for his home 30
19 Do you give the horse his might? 20
41:11 Who has given to me, that I should repay him? •
42:10 the LORD gave Job twice as much as he had before. 9
11 each of them gave him a piece of money and a ring 20
15 their father gave them inheritance 20
Ps 18:35 Thou hast given me the shield of thy salvation 20
47 the God who gave me vengeance 20
21: 2 Thou hast given him his heart's desire 20
4 He asked life of thee; thou gavest it to him 20
29:11 May the LORD give strength to his people! 20
37: 4 he will give you the desires of your heart. 20
21 but the righteous is generous and gives; 20
40: 6 but thou hast given me an open ear. †
49: 7 or give to God the price of his life 20
51:16 were I to give a burnt offering, thou wouldst not 20
61: 5 given me the heritage of those who fear thy name. 20
66: 2 give to him glorious praise! 30
68: 6 God gives the desolate a home to dwell in; •
11 Lord gives the command; 20
35 God . . gives power and strength to his people. 20
69:21 They gave me poison for food 20
72: 1 Give the king thy justice, O God 20
15 Long may he live, may gold of Sheba be given to him! 20
74:14 thou didst give him as food for the creatures 20
78:20 Can he also give bread, or provide meat 20
24 manna to eat, and gave them the grain of heaven. 20
29 well filled, for he gave them what they craved. 1
46 He gave their crops to the caterpillar 20
79: 2 given the bodies of thy servants to the birds 20
85:12 Yea, the LORD will give what is good 20
86:16 give thy strength to thy servant 20
99: 7 testimonies, and the statutes that he gave them. 20
104:27 to give them their food in due season. 20
28 When thou givest to them, they gather it up; 20
105:11 saying, "To you I will give the land of Canaan 20
32 He gave them hail for rain 20
44 he gave them the lands of the nations; 20
106:15 he gave them what they asked 20
41 he gave them into the hand of the nations 20
111: 6 in giving them the heritage of the nations. 20
112: 9 has distributed freely, he has given to the poor; 20
113: 9 He gives the barren woman a home 12
115: 1 O LORD, not to us, but to thy name give glory 20
16 but the earth he has given to the sons of men. 20
120: 3 What shall be given to you? 20
124: 6 LORD, who has not given us as prey to their teeth! 20
127: 2 for he gives to his beloved sleep. 20
132: 4 not give sleep to my eyes or slumber to my eyelids 20
135:12 gave their land as a heritage 20
136:21 gave their land as a heritage 20
25 he who gives food to all flesh 20
144:10 who givest victory to kings, who rescuest David 20
145:15 thou givest them their food in due season. 20
146: 7 who gives food to the hungry. 20
147: 9 He gives to the beasts their food 20
16 He gives snow like wool; he scatters hoarfrost 20
Prv 1: 4 that prudence may be given to the simple 20
2: 6 For the LORD gives wisdom; 20
3: 2 abundant welfare will they give you. 9
28 Go, and come again, tomorrow I will give it"– 20
4: 2 for I give you good precepts 20
5: 9 lest you give your honor to others 20
6: 4 Give your eyes no sleep 20
31 he will give all the goods of his house. 20
9: 9 Give instruction to a wise man, and he will be 20
11:24 another withholds what he should give 13
12:17 He who speaks the truth gives honest evidence 16
14:30 A tranquil mind gives life to the flesh •
17: 8 magic stone in the eyes of him who gives it; •
18:13 If one gives answer before he hears 31
19: 6 every one is a friend to a man who gives gifts. •
21:26 but the righteous gives and does not hold back. 20
22:16 who . . gives to the rich, will only come to want. 20
21 that you may give a true answer to those who sent 31
24 Make no friendship with a man given to anger •
23: 2 put a knife . . if you are a man given to appetite. •
26 My son, give me your heart 20
24:26 He who gives a right answer kisses the lips. 31
25:14 man who boasts of a gift he does not give. •
26: 8 one who binds . . is he who gives honor to a fool. 20
27:23 give attention to your herds; 32
28:27 He who gives to the poor will not want 20
29:15 The rod and reproof give wisdom 20
17 give you rest; he will give delight to your heart. 20
22 man given to anger causes much transgression. •
30: 8 give me neither poverty nor riches; 20
15 The leech has two daughters; "Give, give," they cry. 8
15 The leech has two daughters; "Give, give," they cry. 8
31: 3 Give not your strength to women 20
6 Give strong drink to him who is perishing 20
31 Give her of the fruit of her hands 20
Ecc 1:13 it is an unhappy business that God has given 20
2:26 God gives wisdom and knowledge and joy; 20
26 to the sinner he gives the work of gathering 20
26 he gives . . only to give to one who pleases God. 20
3:10 the business that God has given to the sons of men 20
5:18 the few days of his life which God has given him 20
19 to whom God has given wealth and possessions 20
6: 2 to whom God gives wealth, possessions, and honor 20
8: 8 wickedness deliver those who are given to it. •
15 days of life which God gives him under the sun. 20
9: 9 vain life which he has given you under the sun 20
11: 2 Give a portion to seven, or even to eight 20
12: 7 and the spirit returns to God who gave it. 20
11 the . . sayings which are given by one Shepherd. 20
Sng 7:12 There I will give you my love. 20
Isa 7:14 Therefore the Lord himself will give you a sign. 20
22 because of the abundance of milk which they give 26
8:18 I and the children whom the LORD has given me 20
9: 6 For to us a child is born, to us a son is given; 20
16: 3 Give counsel, grant justice; 1
19:11 counselors of Pharaoh give stupid counsel. •
28: 7 err in vision, they stumble in giving judgment. •
29:11 When men give it to one who can read, saying 20
12 when they give the book to one who cannot read 20
30:20 though the Lord give you the bread of adversity 20
23 he will give rain for the seed with which you sow 20
33:16 his bread will be given him, his water will be sure. 20
35: 2 The glory of Lebanon shall be given to it 20
36: 8 I will give you 2,000 horses 20
15 not be given into the hand of the king of Assyria. 20
37:10 not be given into the hand of the king of Assyria. 20
40:29 He gives power to the faint 20
41:27 and I give to Jerusalem a herald of good tidings. 20
28 no counselor who, when I ask, gives an answer. 31
42: 5 who gives breath to the people upon it 20
6 I have given you as a covenant to the people 20
8 my glory I give to no other 20
12 Let them give glory to the LORD 30
43: 3 I give Egypt as your ransom 20
4 Because . . I love you, I give men in return for you 20
20 for I give water in the wilderness 20
45: 3 I will give you the treasures of darkness 20
47: 6 I gave them into your hand, you showed them no 20
48:11 My glory I will not give to another. 20
49: 6 I will give you as a light to the nations 20
8 I have kept you and given you as a covenant 20
50: 4 has given me the tongue of those who are taught 20
6 I gave my back to the smiters, and my cheeks 20
55:10 giving seed to the sower and bread to the eater 20
56: 5 I will give in my house and within my walls 20
5 I will give them an everlasting name 20
57:11 and did not remember me, did not give me a thought? 30
61: 3 in Zion–to give them a garland instead of ashes 20
8 I will faithfully give them their recompense 20
62: 2 a new name which the mouth of the LORD will give. 19
7 give him no rest until he establishes Jerusalem 20
8 I will not again give your grain to be food 20
Jer 3:15 I will give you shepherds after my own heart 20
19 and give you a pleasant land, a heritage 20
5:24 the LORD our God, who gives the rain in its season 20
7: 7 in the land that I gave of old to your fathers 20
14 the place which I gave to you and to your fathers 20
8:10 Therefore I will give their wives to others 20
13 and what I gave them has passed away from them. 20
11: 5 to give them a land flowing with milk and honey 20
12: 7 I have given the beloved of my soul into the hands 20
13:16 Give glory to the LORD your God 20
20 Where is the flock that was given you 20
14:13 but I will give you assured peace in this place. 20
22 Or can the heavens give showers? 20
15: 9 And the rest of them I will give to the sword 20
13 wealth and your treasures I will give as spoil 20
16:15 to their own land which I gave to their fathers. 20
17: 3 and all your treasures I will give for spoil 20
4 your hand from your heritage which I gave to you 20
10 to give to every man according to his ways 20
18:21 give them over to the power of the sword 17
19: 7 will give their dead bodies for food to the birds 20
20: 4 I will give all Judah into the hand of the king 20
5 Moreover, I will give all the wealth of the city 20
21: 7 Afterward, says the LORD, I will give Zedeki'ah 20
10 be given into the hand of the king of Babylon 20
22:13 for nothing, and does not give him his wages; 20
25 give you into the hand of those who seek your life 20
23:39 and the city which I gave to you and your fathers. 20
24: 7 I will give them a heart to know that I am the LORD; 20
10 destroyed from the land which I gave to them 20
25: 5 which the LORD has given to you and your fathers 20
27: 5 and I give it to whomever it seems right to me. 20
6 Now I have given all these lands into the hand 20
6 I have given him also the beasts of the field 20
28:14 I have given to him even the beasts of the field 20
29:11 and not for evil, to give you a future and a hope. 20
30: 3 the land which I gave to their fathers 20
31:35 says the LORD, who gives the sun for light by day 20
32: 3 I am giving this city into the hand of the king 20
4 shall surely be given into the hand of the king 20
12 and I gave the deed of purchase to Baruch 20
16 After I had given the deed of purchase to Baruch 20
22 thou gavest them this land 20
22 thou didst swear to their fathers to give them 20
24 the city is given into the hands of the Chalde'ans 20
25 the city is given into the hands of the Chalde'ans 20
28 giving this city into the hands of the Chalde'ans 20
36 It is given into the hand of the king of Babylon 20
39 I will give them one heart and one way 20
43 it is given into the hands of the Chalde'ans. 20
34: 2 I am giving this city into the hand of the king 20
20 I will give them into the hand of their enemies 20
21 I will give into the hand of their enemies 20
35:14 which Jon'adab the son of Rechab gave to his sons 28
15 you shall dwell in the land which I gave to you 20
16 have kept the command which their father gave 28
36:32 another scroll and gave it to Baruch the scribe 20
37:21 and a loaf of bread was given him daily 20
38: 3 This city shall surely be given into the hand 20
18 shall be given into the hand of the Chalde'ans 20
20 Jeremiah said, "You shall not be given to them. 20
39:10 and gave them vineyards and fields 20
17 and you shall not be given into the hand of the men 20
40: 5 So the captain of the guard gave him an allowance 20
43:11 giving to the pestilence those who are doomed •
44:20 all the people who had given him this answer 25
30 Behold, I will give Pharaoh Hophra king of Egypt 20
30 as I gave Zedeki'ah king of Judah into the hand 20
45: 5 but I will give you your life as a prize of war 20
48: 9 Give wings to Moab, for she would fly away; 20
52:32 and gave him a seat above the seats of the kings 20
34 a regular allowance was given him by the king 20
Lam 1:14 Lord gave me into the hands of those whom I cannot 20
2:18 Give yourself no rest, your eyes no respite! 20
3:30 let him give his cheek to the smiter 20
65 Thou wilt give them dullness of heart; 20
4: 3 Even the jackals give the breast and suckle 7
4 the children beg for food, but no one gives to them. 27
5: 6 We have given the hand to Egypt . . to get bread 20
Ezk 2: 8 open your mouth, and eat what I give you. 20
3: 3 Son of man, eat this scroll that I give you 20
7:21 I will give it into the hands of foreigners 20
11: 9 and give you into the hands of foreigners 20
15 to us this land is given for a possession. 20
17 I will give you the land of Israel. 20
19 I will give them one heart 20

19 stony heart out . . and give them a heart of flesh 20
15: 4 Lo, it is given to the fire for fuel; 20
6 the forest, which I have given to the fire for fuel 20
16:17 my gold and of my silver, which I had given you 20
19 Also my bread which I gave you 20
33 Men give gifts to all harlots; 20
33 but you gave your gifts to all your lovers 20
34 you gave hire, while no hire was given to you; 20
34 you gave hire, while no hire was given to you; 20
36 the blood of your children that you gave to them 20
39 And I will give you into the hand of your lovers 20
41 you shall also give hire no more. 20
61 and give them to you as daughters 20
17:15 that they might give him horses and a large army. 20
18 he gave his hand and yet did all these things 20
18: 7 commits no robbery, gives his bread to the hungry 20
16 but gives his bread to the hungry 20
20:11 I gave them my statutes 20
12 Moreover I gave them my sabbaths, as a sign 20
15 bring them into the land which I had given them 20
25 Moreover I gave them statutes that were not good 20
28 into the land which I swore to give them 20
42 country which I swore to give to your fathers. 20
21:11 the sword is given to be polished 20
11 sharpened and polished to be given into the hand 20
15 I have given the glittering sword; 20
27 whose right it is; and to him I will give it. 20
23:31 therefore I will give her cup into your hand. 20
25:10 I will give it along with the Ammonites 20
27:10 they gave you splendor. 20
28:25 their own land which I gave to my servant Jacob. 20
29: 5 to the birds of the air I have given you as food. 20
19 I will give the land of Egypt to Nebuchadrez'zar 20
20 I have given him the land of Egypt 20
31:11 I will give it into the hand of a mighty one 20
33:24 the land is surely given us to possess. 20
27 I will give to the beasts to be devoured; 20
35:12 are laid desolate, they are given us to devour. 20
36: 5 against all Edom, who gave my land to themselves 20
26 A new heart I will give you, and a new spirit 20
26 the heart of stone and give you a heart of flesh. 20
28 dwell in the land which I gave to your fathers; 20
37:25 in the land . . that I gave to my servant Jacob; 20
39: 4 I will give you to birds of prey of every sort 20
11 I will give to Gog a place for burial in Israel 20
23 and gave them into the hand of their adversaries 20
43:19 you shall give to the Levitical priests 20
44:28 you shall give them no possession in Israel; 20
30 you shall also give to the priests 20
45:16 the people of the land shall give this offering 42
46:11 with the lambs as much as one is able to give 15
47:14 I swore to give it to your fathers 20
Dan 1: 7 chief of the eunuchs gave them names: Daniel 30
9 God gave Daniel favor and compassion 20
12 us be given vegetables to eat and water to drink. 20
16 steward took away . . and gave them vegetables. 20
17 God gave them learning and skill in all letters 20
2:21 he gives wisdom to the wise and knowledge 34
23 for thou hast given me wisdom and strength 34
37 to whom the God of heaven has given the kingdom 34
38 into whose hand he has given, wherever they dwell 34
48 Then the king gave Daniel high honors 34
4:16 let a beast's mind be given to him; 34
17 kingdom of men, and gives it to whom he will 35
25 kingdom of men, and gives it to whom he will. 35
32 kingdom of men and gives it to whom he will. 35
5:16 heard that you can give interpretations 36
17 yourself, and give your rewards to another; 34
18 Most High God gave Nebuchadnez'zar your father 34
19 because of the greatness that he gave him 34
28 kingdom is . . given to the Medes and Persians. 34
6: 2 to whom these satraps should give account 34
7: 4 mind of a man was given to it. 34
6 beast had four heads; and dominion was given to it. 34
14 to him was given dominion and glory and kingdom 34
22 judgment . . given for the saints of the Most High 34
25 given into his hand for a time, two times, and half 34
27 given to the people of the saints of the Most High; 34
8:12 host was given over to it together 20
11:11 it shall be given into his hand. 20
17 give him the daughter of women to destroy 20
21 to whom royal majesty has not been given; 20
Hos 2: 5 my lovers, who give me my bread and my water 20
8 did not know that it was I who gave her the grain 20
12 These are my hire, which my lovers have given me.' 20
15 And there I will give her her vineyards 20
9:14 Give them, O LORD–what wilt thou give? 20
14 Give them, O LORD–what wilt thou give? 20
14 Give them a miscarrying womb and dry breasts. 20
13:10 those of whom you said, "Give me a king and princes"? 20
11 I have given you kings in my anger 20
Jol 2:22 and fig tree and vine give their full yield. 20
23 he has given the early rain for your vindication 20
30 I will give portents in the heavens 20
3: 3 and have given a boy for a harlot 20
Ams 4: 6 I gave you cleanness of teeth in all your cities 20
9:15 plucked up out of the land which I have given them 20
Mic 1:14 you shall give parting gifts to Mo'resheth-gath; 20
6: 7 Shall I give my first-born for my transgression 20

14 and what you save I will give to the sword. 20
Hag 2: 9 I will give prosperity, says the LORD of hosts.' 20
Zec 3: 7 I will give you the right of access 20
8:12 the ground shall give its increase 20
12 the heavens shall give their dew; 20
10: 1 who gives men showers of rain, to every one 20
11:12 If it seems right to you, give me my wages; 8
Mal 2: 2 will not lay it to heart to give glory to my name 20
5 covenant of life and peace, and I gave them to him 20
Mat 4: 9 All these I will give you, if you will fall down 42
5:31 let him give her a certificate of divorce.' 42
42 Give to him who begs from you, and do not refuse him 42
6: 2 Thus, when you give alms, sound no trumpet before 61
3 when you give alms, do not let your left hand know 61
11 Give us this day our daily bread; 42
7: 2 you will be judged, and the measure you give 57
6 Do not give dogs what is holy; and do not throw 42
7 Ask, and it will be given you; seek, and you will find; 42
9 asks him for bread, will give him a stone? 53
10 Or if he asks for a fish, will give him a serpent? 53
11 If you then, who are evil, know how to give good gifts 42
11 who is in heaven give good things to those who ask 42
9: 8 they glorified God, who had given such authority 42
10: 1 and gave them authority over unclean spirits 42
8 You received without paying, give without pay. 42
19 for what you are to say will be given to you 42
42 whoever gives to one of these little ones 63
12:39 but no sign shall be given to it 42
13:11 To you it has been given to know the secrets 42
11 but to them it has not been given. 42
12 For to him who has will more be given 42
14: 7 to give her whatever she might ask. 42
8 she said, "Give me the head of John the Baptist 42
9 he commanded it to be given; 42
11 and given to the girl 42
16 you give them something to eat. 42
19 broke and gave the loaves to the disciples 42
19 and the disciples gave them to the crowds. •
15: 5 What you would have gained from me is given to God 46
36 he broke them and gave them to the disciples 42
36 and the disciples gave them to the crowds. •
16: 4 but no sign shall be given to it 42
19 I will give you the keys of the kingdom of heaven 42
26 Or what shall a man give in return for his life? 42
17:27 take that and give it to them for me 42
19: 7 did Moses command one to give a certificate 42
11 but only those to whom it is given. 42
21 sell what you possess and give to the poor 42
20: 4 and whatever is right I will give you 42
14 I choose to give to this last as I give to you. 42
14 I choose to give to this last as I give to you. •
28 to give his life as a ransom for many. 42
21:23 who gave you this authority? 42
41 who will give him the fruits in their seasons. 39
43 given to a nation producing the fruits of it. 42
22: 2 to a king who gave a marriage feast for his son 61
24:29 the moon will not give its light 42
45 to give them their food at the proper time? 42
25: 8 'Give us some of your oil 42
15 to one he gave five talents, to another two 42
28 give it to him who has the ten talents. 42
29 For to every one who has will more be given 42
35 for I was hungry and you gave me food 42
42 for I was hungry and you gave me no food 42
26: 9 and given to the poor. 42
15 said, "What will you give me if I deliver him to you? 42
26 broke it, and gave it to the disciples and said 42
27 when he had given thanks he gave it to them, saying 42
48 Now the betrayer had given them a sign, saying 42
27:10 and they gave them for the potter's field 42
14 he gave him no answer, not even to a single charge; •
58 Then Pilate ordered it to be given to him. 39
28:12 counsel, they gave a sum of money to the soldiers 42
18 in heaven and on earth has been given to me. 42
Mrk 2:26 also gave it to those who were with him? 42
4:11 given the secret of the kingdom of God 42
24 the measure you give will be the measure you get 57
25 For to him who has will more be given 42
5:43 and told them to give her something to eat. 42
6: 2 What is the wisdom given to him? 42
7 and gave them authority over the unclean spirits. 42
21 when Herod on his birthday gave a banquet 61
23 he vowed . . "Whatever you ask me, I will give you 42
25 I want you to give me at once the head of John 42
28 gave it to the girl 42
28 the girl gave it to her mother. 42
37 he answered them, "You give them something to eat. 42
37 give it to them to eat? 42
41 broke the loaves, and gave them to the disciples 42
8: 6 he broke them and gave them to his disciples 42
12 no sign shall be given to this generation. 42
37 For what can a man give in return for his life? 42
10:21 go, sell what you have, and give to the poor 42
45 to give his life as a ransom for many. 42
11:28 who gave you this authority to do them? 42
12: 9 give the vineyard to others. 42
13:11 say whatever is given you in that hour 42
24 the moon will not give its light 42
14: 5 given to the poor 42

11 they were glad, and promised to give him money. 42
22 broke it, and gave it to them, and said, "Take 42
23 when he had given thanks he gave it to them 42
44 Now the betrayer had given them a sign, saying 42
Lke 1:32 the Lord God will give to him the throne 42
77 to give knowledge of salvation to his people 42
2:21 he was called Jesus, the name given by the angel 54
4: 6 I will give all this authority and their glory; 42
6 I give it to whom I will. 42
17 was given to him the book of the prophet Isaiah. 53
6: 4 also gave it to those with him? 42
30 Give to every one who begs from you 42
38 give, and it will be given to you 42
38 give, and it will be given to you 42
7:15 he gave him to his mother. 42
44 you gave me no water for my feet 42
45 You gave me no kiss 42
8:10 To you it has been given to know the secrets 42
18 to him who has will more be given 42
55 something should be given her to eat. 42
9: 1 gave them power and authority over all demons 42
13 he said to them, "You give them something to eat. 42
16 gave them to the disciples 42
10:19 have given you authority to tread upon serpents 42
35 gave them to the innkeeper, saying 42
11: 3 Give us each day our daily bread; 42
7 I cannot get up and give you anything'? 42
8 though he will not get up and give him anything 42
8 he will rise and give him whatever he needs. 42
9 I tell you, Ask, and it will be given you 42
11 will instead of a fish give him a serpent; 53
12 or if he asks for an egg, will give him a scorpion? 53
13 know how to give good gifts to your children 42
13 will the heavenly Father give the Holy Spirit 42
29 it seeks a sign, but no sign shall be given to it 42
41 give for alms those things which are within; 42
12:32 Father's good pleasure to give you the kingdom. 42
33 Sell your possessions, and give alms 42
42 to give them their portion of food 42
48 Every one to whom much is given 42
51 you think that I have come to give peace on earth? 42
14: 9 'Give place to this man,' 42
12 When you give a dinner or a banquet 61
13 when you give a feast, invite the poor, the maimed 61
16 A man once gave a great banquet, and invited many; 61
15:12 give me the share of property that falls to me 42
16 no one gave him anything. 42
29 yet you never gave me a kid, that I might make merry 42
16:12 who will give you that which is your own? 42
17:18 Was no one found to return and give praise to God 42
18:43 all the people, when they saw it, gave praise to God. 42
19: 8 the half of my goods I give to the poor 42
13 he gave them ten pounds 42
15 these servants, to whom he had given the money 42
24 give it to him who has the ten pounds.' 42
26 to every one who has will more be given 42
20: 2 who it is that gave you this authority. 42
10 give him some of the fruit of the vineyard 42
16 give the vineyard to others 42
22 Is it lawful for us to give tribute to Caesar 42
21:15 for I will give you a mouth and wisdom 42
22: 5 they were glad, and engaged to give him money. 42
19 when he had given thanks he broke it and gave it 42
19 This is my body which is given for you 42
23: 2 forbidding us to give tribute to Caesar 42
24:30 blessed, and broke it, and gave it to them. 53
42 They gave him a piece of broiled fish 53
Joh 1:12 he gave power to become children of God; 42
17 For the law was given through Moses; 42
3:16 God so loved the world that he gave his only Son 42
27 except what is given him from heaven. 42
34 for it is not by measure that he gives the Spirit; 42
35 and has given all things into his hand. 42
4: 5 near the field that Jacob gave to his son Joseph. 42
7 Jesus said to her, "Give me a drink. 42
10 who it is that is saying to you, 'Give me a drink,' 42
10 and he would have given you living water. 42
12 Jacob, who gave us the well, and drank from it 42
14 whoever drinks of the water that I shall give him 42
14 the water that I shall give him will become in him 42
15 Sir, give me this water, that I may not thirst 42
5:22 has given all judgment to the Son 42
27 has given him authority to execute judgment 42
6:27 which the Son of man will give to you 42
31 'He gave them bread from heaven to eat.' 42
32 was not Moses who gave you the bread from heaven; 42
32 my Father gives you the true bread from heaven. 42
33 gives life to the world. 42
34 They said to him, "Lord, give us this bread always. 42
37 All that the Father gives me will come to me 42
39 I should lose nothing of all that he has given me 42
51 bread which I shall give for the life of the world 42
52 How can this man give us his flesh to eat? 42
7:19 Did not Moses give you the law? 42
22 Moses gave you circumcision 42
39 as yet the Spirit had not been given 47
9:24 Give God the praise 42
10:28 I give them eternal life 42
29 My Father, who has given them to me 42

11:22 whatever you ask from God, God will give you. 42
57 the Pharisees had given orders 42
12: 5 sold for 300 denarii and given to the poor? 42
49 has himself given me commandment what to say 42
13: 3 the Father had given all things into his hands 42
15 For I have given you an example 42
26 I shall give this morsel when I have dipped it 42
26 when he had dipped the morsel, he gave it to Judas 42
29 that he should give something to the poor. 42
34 A new commandment I give to you 42
14:16 he will give you another Counselor, to be with you 42
27 Peace I leave with you; my peace I give to you 42
27 not as the world gives do I give to you 42
27 not as the world gives do I give to you 42
15:16 he may give it to you. 42
16:23 if you ask anything of the Father, he will give it 42
17: 2 since thou hast given him power over all flesh 42
2 to give eternal life to all 42
2 to all whom thou hast given him. 42
4 the work which thou gavest me to do; 42
6 the men whom thou gavest me out of the world 42
6 thou gavest them to me, and they have kept thy word. 42
7 everything that thou hast given me is from thee; 42
8 I have given them the words which thou gavest me 42
8 I have given them the words which thou gavest me 42
9 those whom thou hast given me, for they are thine; 42
11 keep them in thy name, which thou hast given me 42
12 which thou hast given me 42
14 I have given them thy word 42
22 The glory which thou hast given me 42
22 I have given to them 42
24 they also, whom thou hast given me 42
24 to behold my glory which thou hast given me 42
18: 9 Of those whom thou gavest me I lost not one. 42
11 not drink the cup which the Father has given me? 42
19: 9 But Jesus gave no answer. 42
11 unless it had been given you from above 42
21:13 Jesus came and took the bread and gave it to them 42
Act 2: 4 as the Spirit gave them utterance. 42
3: 6 I have no silver and gold, but I give you what I have; 42
16 the faith . . has given the man this perfect health 42
25 the covenant which God gave to your fathers 41
4:12 no other name under heaven given among men 42
33 the apostles gave their testimony 39
5:31 give repentance to Israel 42
32 whom God has given to those who obey him. 42
7: 5 yet he gave him no inheritance in it 42
5 promised to give it to him in possession 42
8 he gave him the covenant of circumcision 42
10 gave him favor and wisdom before Pharaoh 42
25 God was giving them deliverance by his hand 42
38 he received living oracles to give to us. 42
8:18 the Spirit was given 42
19 saying, "Give me also this power 42
9:41 he gave her his hand and lifted her up 42
10: 2 gave alms liberally to the people 61
11:17 If then God gave the same gift to them 42
17 the same gift to them as he gave to us •
12:23 because he did not give God the glory 42
13:20 he gave them judges until Samuel the prophet. 42
21 Then they asked for a king; and God gave them Saul 42
34 give you the holy and sure blessings of David.' 42
14:17 he . . gave you from heaven rains and fruitful seasons 42
15: 3 they gave great joy to all the brethren. 61
8 giving them the Holy Spirit just as he did to us; 42
17:25 since he himself gives to all men life and breath 42
31 of this he has given assurance to all men 59
19:40 no cause that we can give to justify this 39
20:32 give you the inheritance 42
35 'It is more blessed to give than to receive.' 42
24:26 he hoped that money would be given him by Paul 42
27:34 it will give you strength 66
Rom 2: 7 he will give eternal life; •
4:20 grew strong in his faith as he gave glory to God 42
5: 5 the Holy Spirit which has been given to us. 42
13 sin . . was in the world before the law was given •
8:32 will he not also give us all things with him? 68
11: 8 as it is written, "God gave them a spirit of stupor 42
35 given a gift to him that he might be repaid? 64
12: 3 by the grace given to me I bid every one among you 42
6 that differ according to the grace given to us 42
14:12 each of us shall give account of himself to God. 42
15: 8 to confirm the promises given to the patriarchs •
15 because of the grace given me by God 42
1Co 1: 4 because of the grace of God which was given you 42
3:10 According to the grace of God given to me 42
7: 3 husband should give to his wife her conjugal rights 39
25 I give my opinion as one who by the Lord's mercy 42
9:16 that gives me no ground for boasting 47
10:32 Give no offense to Jews or to Greeks 40
11:15 her hair is given to her for a covering. 42
12: 7 To each is given the manifestation of the Spirit 42
8 To one is given through the Spirit the utterance 42
24 giving the greater honor to the inferior part 42
14: 7 do not give distinct notes 42
8 if the bugle gives an indistinct sound 42
15:38 God gives it a body as he has chosen 42
57 thanks be to God, who gives us the victory 42
2Co 1:22 given us his Spirit in our hearts as a guarantee. 42
4: 6 to give the light of the knowledge of the glory 65
5: 5 who has given us the Spirit as a guarantee. 42
12 giving you cause to be proud of us 42
18 gave us the ministry of reconciliation; 42
8: 3 they gave according to their means, as I can testify •
5 first they gave themselves to the Lord and to us 42
10 in this matter I give my advice 42
24 So give proof, before the churches, of your love 51
9: 9 He scatters abroad, he gives to the poor 42
10: 8 which the Lord gave for building you up 42
12: 7 a thorn was given me in the flesh 42
13:10 which the Lord has given me for building up 42
Gal 1: 4 who gave himself for our sins 42
2: 9 when they perceived the grace that was given 42
9 gave to me and Barnabas the right hand 42
20 Son of God, who loved me and gave himself for me. 58
3:15 To give a human example, brethren 55
18 God gave it to Abraham by a promise. 68
21 if a law had been given which could make alive 42
22 might be given to those who believe. 42
4:15 plucked out your eyes and given them to me. 42
Eph 1:17 may give you a spirit of wisdom and of revelation 42
3: 2 the stewardship of God's grace that was given to me 42
7 which was given me by the working of his power. 42
8 To me . . this grace was given 42
4: 7 grace was given to each of us 42
8 he gave gifts to men. 42
27 give no opportunity to the devil. 42
28 that he may be able to give to those in need. 56
6:19 that utterance may be given me 42
Php 4:15 in giving and receiving except you only; 44
Col 1:25 the divine office which was given to me 42
1Th 4: 2 For you know what instructions we gave you 42
8 who gives his Holy Spirit to you. 42
2Th 2:16 who loved us and gave us eternal comfort 42
3: 9 to give you in our conduct an example to imitate. 42
16 Lord of peace himself give you peace at all times 42
1Ti 2: 6 who gave himself as a ransom for all 42
4:14 which was given you by prophetic utterance 42
5:14 give the enemy no occasion to revile us. 42
2Ti 1: 7 for God did not give us a spirit of timidity 42
9 the grace which he gave us in Christ Jesus ages ago 42
Tit 2:14 who gave himself for us to redeem us 42
Heb 2:13 again, "Here am I, and the children God has given me. 42
7: 4 Abraham . . gave him a tithe of the spoils. 42
13:17 as men who will have to give account 39
Jas 1: 5 let him ask God, who gives to all men generously 42
5 and it will be given him. 42
2:16 without giving them the things needed 42
4: 6 But he gives more grace; therefore it says 42
6 God . . gives grace to the humble. 42
5:18 Then he prayed again and the heaven gave rain 42
1Pe 1:21 who raised him from the dead and gave him glory 42
4: 5 give account to him who is ready to judge 39
5: 5 God . . gives grace to the humble. 42
2Pe 3:15 Paul wrote . . according to the wisdom given him 42
1Jn 3: 1 See what love the Father has given us 42
24 by the Spirit which he has given us. 42
4:13 because he has given us of his own Spirit. 42
5:11 the testimony, that God gave us eternal life 42
16 he will ask, and God will give him life 42
20 the Son of God . . has given us understanding 42
2Jn 1:10 do not receive him . . or give him any greeting; 55
Rev 1: 1 The revelation of Jesus Christ, which God gave 42
2:10 and I will give you the crown of life. 42
17 To him who conquers I will give some . . manna 42
17 and I will give him a white stone 42
21 I gave her time to repent, but she refuses 42
23 I will give to each of you as your works deserve. 42
26 I will give him power over the nations 42
28 I will give him the morning star. 42
4: 9 whenever the living creatures give glory 42
6: 2 its rider had a bow; and a crown was given to him 42
4 and he was given a great sword. 42
8 they were given power over a fourth of the earth 42
11 Then they were each given a white robe and told 42
7: 2 angels who had been given power to harm earth 42
8: 2 and seven trumpets were given to them. 42
3 given much incense to mingle with the prayers 42
9: 1 given the key of the shaft of the bottomless pit; 42
3 were given power like the power of scorpions 42
10: 9 angel and told him to give me the little scroll; 42
11: 1 Then I was given a measuring rod like a staff 42
2 for it is given over to the nations 42
13 terrified and gave glory to the God of heaven. 42
12:14 woman was given the two wings of the great eagle 42
13: 2 to it the dragon gave his power and his throne 42
4 for he had given his authority to the beast 42
5 And the beast was given a mouth 42
7 authority was given it over every tribe 42
15 allowed to give breath to the image of the beast 42
14: 7 Fear God and give him glory 42
15: 7 the four living creatures gave the seven angels 42
16: 6 and thou hast given them blood to drink. 42
9 and they did not repent and give him glory. 42
17:13 give over their power and authority to the beast; 42
17 and giving over their royal power to the beast 42
18: 7 give her a like measure of torment and mourning. 42
19: 7 Let us rejoice and exult and give him the glory 42
21: 6 To the thirsty I will give from the fountain 42
1Es 1: 6 the commandment . . which was given to Moses. 42
7 gave to the people who were present 30,000 lambs 45
7 these were given from the king's possessions 42
8 gave to the priests for the passover 2,600 sheep 42
9 gave the Levites for the passover 5,000 sheep 42
53 he gave them all into their hands. 58
2:11 he gave them to Mithridates his treasurer 58
12 by him they were given to Sheshbazzar 58
3: 1 Now King Darius gave a great banquet 61
5 Darius the king will give rich gifts 42
9 they will give him the writing 42
9 the victory shall be given 42
13 they took the writing and gave it to him 42
4:22 bring everything and give it to women? 42
42 we will give it to you 42
51 that twenty talents a year should be given 42
60 Blessed art thou, who hast given me wisdom 42
62 because he had given them release and permission 42
5:45 would give to the sacred treasury for the work 42
54 they gave money to the masons and the carpenters 42
6:29 a portion be scrupulously given to these men 42
8: 3 which was given by the God of Israel; 50
6 the prosperous journey which the Lord gave them. 42
14 together with what is given by the nation 45
17 which are given you for the use of the temple 42
19 they shall take care to give him 42
49 had given for the service of the Levites 42
55 the nobles and all Israel had given. 45
56 I weighed and gave to them 650 talents of silver 58
79 to give us food in the time of our servitude. 42
80 they have given us food 42
81 to give us a stronghold in Judea and Jerusalem. 42
82 which thou didst give by thy servants 42
87 give us such a root as this 42
9: 8 give glory to the Lord the God of our fathers •
20 to give rams in expiation of their error. 52
39 which had been given by the Lord God of Israel. 58
41 all the multitude gave attention to the law. 53
54 to give portions to those who had none 42
2Es 1:13 I gave you Moses as leader and Aaron as priest; 72
15 I gave you camps for your protection 72
19 and gave you manna for food 72
24 and will give them my name 72
35 I will give your houses to a people that will come 78
39 to them I will give as leaders Abraham, Isaac 72
2: 1 I gave them commandments through my servants 72
10 that I will give them the kingdom of Jerusalem 72
10 which I was going to give to Israel. 72
11 and will give to these others 72
12 The tree . . shall give them fragrant perfume 77
20 give to the needy, defend the orphan 72
23 give you the first place in my resurrection. 72
26 Not one of the servants whom I have given you 72
34 he will give you everlasting rest 72
37 be joyful, giving thanks to him 71
3: 5 it gave thee Adam, a lifeless body ‡
15 and thou gavest to him Isaac 72
15 and to Isaac thou gavest Jacob and Esau. 72
19 to give the law to the descendants of Jacob 72
5:27 thou hast given the law which is approved by all. 73
48 Even so have I given the womb of the earth to those 72
50 Since thou hast now given me the opportunity 72
6:51 thou didst give Behemoth one of the parts 72
52 to Leviathan thou didst give the seventh part 72
58 thy people . . have been given into their hands. 78
7: 9 If now that city is given to a man 72
78 leaves the body to return again to him who gave it 72
94 they kept the law which was given them in trust. 72
100 Will time therefore be given to the souls 72
135 because he would rather give than take away; 73
138 if he did not give out of his goodness 73
8: 5 for you have been given only a short time to live. 72
6 give us seed for our heart 72
24 and give ear to the petition of thy creature; 76
9:45 and considered my distress, and gave me a son 72
10:14 the earth . . has . . given her fruit, that is, man 72
24 and the Most High may give you rest 74
14:31 Then land was given to you for a possession 72
32 in due time he took from you what he had given. 73
42 the Most High gave understanding to the five men 72
46 in order to give them to the wise 78
15:20 to turn and repay what they have given them. 72
16:61 and gave him breath and life and understanding 75
Tob 1: 6 I would give these to the priests 42
7 I would give a tenth to the sons of Levi 42
8 I would give to those to whom it was my duty 42
13 Then the Most High gave me favor 42
17 I would give my bread to the hungry 42
2:14 It was given to me as a gift in addition to my wages 42
3: 4 thou gavest us over to plunder, captivity, and death; 42
8 because she had been given to seven husbands 42
17 to give Sarah the daughter of Raguel in marriage 42
4: 7 Give alms from your possessions 61
8 afraid to give according to the little you have. 61
16 Give all your surplus to charity 61
16 Give of your bread to the hungry 42
17 give none to sinners. 42
19 the Lord himself gives all good things 42

5: 3 Then Tobit gave him the receipt, and said to him 42
19 the life that is given to us by the Lord is enough 42
6:10 I will suggest that she be given to you in marriage 42
12 cannot give her to another man 42
13 the girl has been given to seven husbands 42
15 she will be given to you in marriage. 42
7:11 I have given my daughter to seven husbands 42
13 he gave her to Tobias to be his wife, saying 58
8: 6 gavest him Eve his wife as a helper and support. 42
19 After this he gave a wedding feast for them 61
9: 5 He gave him the receipt 42
5 gave them to him. 42
10: 2 there is no one to give him the money? 42
10 Raguel arose and gave him his wife Sarah 42
12: 2 to give him half of what I have brought back. 42
8 It is better to give alms than to treasure up gold. 61
13:11 Generations . . will give you joyful praise. 42
14: 2 He gave alms, and he continued to fear the Lord God 61
10 Ahikar gave alms and escaped the deathtrap 61
Jdt 3: 8 given to him to destroy all the gods of the land 42
6:21 gave a banquet for the elders 61
9: 2 gavest a sword to take revenge on the strangers 42
4 thou gavest their wives for a prey 42
9 give to me, a widow, the strength to do what I plan. 42
10: 5 gave her maid a bottle of wine and a flask of oil 42
13: 9 gave Holofernes' head to her maid 58
14:13 to come down against us to give battle 49
15:11 They gave Judith the tent of Holofernes 42
12 gave them to the women who were with her; 42
16:17 fire and worms he will give to their flesh 42
19 which the people had given her 42
19 the canopy . . she gave as a votive offering to the Lord. 42
AEs 14: 6 thou hast given us into the hands of our enemies 58
Wis 6: 3 For your dominion was given you from the Lord 42
7: 7 understanding was given me 42
17 he who gave me unerring knowledge of what exists 42
8: 9 knowing that she would give me good counsel •
21 would not possess wisdom unless God gave her 42
9: 4 give me the wisdom that sits by thy throne 42
17 unless thou hast given wisdom 42
10: 2 and gave him strength to rule all things. 42
10 gave him knowledge of angels 42
14 she gave him everlasting honor. 42
17 She gave holy men the reward of their labors 39
11: 4 water was given them out of flinty rock 42
7 thou gavest them abundant water unexpectedly 42
12: 9 give the ungodly into the hands of the righteous 42
10 thou gavest them a chance to repent 42
19 because thou givest repentance for sins. 42
21 to whose fathers thou gavest oaths 42
14: 3 because thou hast given it a path in the sea 42
16:20 thou didst give thy people food of angels 70
18: 4 the imperishable light of the law was to be given 42
22 the oaths and covenants given to our fathers. •
19:12 to give them relief, quails came up from the sea. 49
Sir 0: 1 many great teachings have been given to us 42
1:12 gives gladness and joy and long life. 42
4: 5 nor give a man occasion to curse you; 42
6:28 For at last you will find the rest she gives •
7:10 nor neglect to give alms. 61
25 give her to a man of understanding. 45
31 give him his portion, as is commanded you 42
33 Give graciously to all the living 43
8: 9 learn how to give an answer in time of need. 42
9: 2 Do not give yourself to a woman 42
6 Do not give yourself to harlots 42
11:33 lest he give you a lasting blemish. 42
12: 3 to him who does not give alms. 68
4 Give to the godly man, but do not help the sinner. 42
5 do not give to the ungodly 42
5 hold back his bread, and do not give it to him 42
7 Give to the good man, but do not help the sinner. 42
13: 6 he will smile at you and give you hope 42
14:13 reach out and give to him as much as you can. 42
16 Give, and take, and beguile yourself 42
15:17 whichever he chooses will be given to him. 42
20 he has not given any one permission to sin. 42
17: 2 He gave to men few days, a limited time 42
6 he gave them ears and a mind for thinking. 42
27 as do those who are alive and give thanks? 42
20:15 He gives little and upbraids much 42
23: 4 do not give me haughty eyes 42
24:15 I gave forth the aroma of spices 42
27:23 with your own words he will give offense. 42
29:15 he has given his life for you. 42
30:11 Give him no authority in his youth 42
21 Do not give yourself over to sorrow 42
33:13 to give them as he decides. 39
19 do not give power over yourself 42
19 do not give your property to another 42
34: 6 do not give your mind to them. 42
35: 2 he who gives alms sacrifices a thank offering. 62
10 Give to the Most High as he has given 42
10 Give to the Most High as he has given 44
37:21 for grace was not given him by the Lord 42
27 see what is bad for it and do not give it that. 42
38: 6 he gave skill to men 42
12 give the physician his place 42
20 Do not give your heart to sorrow; drive it away 42

41:19 surliness in receiving and giving 44
44:23 and gave him his inheritance 20
45: 5 gave him the commandments face to face 42
7 gave him the priesthood of the people 42
17 In his commandments he gave him authority 42
20 He added glory to Aaron and gave him a heritage 42
21 which he gave to him and his descendants. 42
46: 9 the Lord gave Caleb strength 42
47: 5 he gave him strength in his right hand 42
8 In all that he did he gave thanks to the Holy One 42
10 He gave beauty to the feasts 42
11 he gave him the covenant of kings 42
22 he gave a remnant to Jacob 42
23 gave Ephraim a sinful way. 42
49: 5 for they gave their power to others 42
50:23 May he give us gladness of heart 42
51:17 to him who gives wisdom I will give glory. 42
17 to him who gives wisdom I will give glory. 42
22 The Lord gave me a tongue as my reward 42
30 in God's time he will give you your reward. 42
Bar 1: 6 they collected money, each giving what he could; 69
12 And the Lord will give us strength 42
12 he will give light to our eyes, and we shall live 42
20 to give to us a land flowing with milk and honey. 42
2: 4 he gave them into subjection to all the kingdoms 42
21 remain in the land which I gave to your fathers. 42
31 I will give them a heart that obeys 42
34 land which I swore to give to their fathers •
35 remove . . from the land which I have given them. 42
3:27 God did not . . nor give them the way to knowledge; 42
36 gave her to Jacob his servant and to Israel whom 42
4: 3 Do not give your glory to another 42
LJr 1:11 give some of it to the harlots in the brothel. 42
28 give none to the poor or helpless. 56
35 they are not able to give either wealth or money; 42
53 they cannot . . give rain to men. 42
Aza 1: 9 hast given us into the hands of lawless enemies 58
20 give glory to thy name, O Lord! 42
Sus 1:50 and inform us, for God has given you that right. 42
Bel 1:22 and gave Bel over to Daniel 42
26 if you, O king, will give me permission 42
26 The king said, "I give you permission. 42
32 they had been given two human bodies and two sheep 42
32 these were not given to them now 42
1Mc 2:50 give your lives for the covenant of our fathers. 42
3:28 and gave a year's pay to his forces 42
30 the gifts which he used to give 42
4:30 didst give the camp of the Philistines 58
5:62 through whom deliverance was given to Israel. 42
6:15 He gave him the crown and his robe and the signet 42
44 So he gave his life to save his people 42
8: 7 pay a heavy tribute and give hostages 42
8 took from him and gave to Eumenes the king. 42
26 not give or supply grain, arms, money, or ships 42
28 to the enemy allies shall be given no grain, arms 42
10: 6 Demetrius gave him authority to recruit troops 42
8 had given him authority to recruit troops. 42
28 grant you many immunities and give you gifts. 42
32 give it to the high priest 42
36 let the maintenance be given them 42
39 I have given as a gift to the sanctuary 42
41 they shall give from now 42
54 give me now your daughter as my wife 42
60 he gave them and their friends silver and gold 42
89 it is the custom to give to the kinsmen of kings 42
89 He also gave him Ekron and all its environs 42
11: 9 I will give you in marriage my daughter 42
10 For I now regret that I gave him my daughter 42
12 gave her to Demetrius 42
37 let it be given to Jonathan 42
12: 4 the Romans gave them letters 42
25 he gave them no opportunity to invade 42
43 he gave him gifts 42
14: 8 the ground gave its increase 42
15:31 or else give me for them 500 talents of silver 42
35 for them we will give you 100 talents. 42
38 gave him troops of infantry and cavalry. 42
16:15 he gave them a great banquet, and hid men there. 61
19 so that he might give them silver and gold 42
2Mc 1: 3 May he give you all a heart to worship him 42
18 the feast of the fire given when . . •
2: 2 after giving them the law 42
4:30 because their cities had been given as a present 42
32 gave them to Andronicus 68
34 and gave him his right hand 42
7:14 cherish the hope that God gives 67
22 It was not I who gave you life and breath 68
30 was given to our fathers through Moses. 42
8:23 gave the watchword, "God's help 42
30 giving to those who had been tortured 61
10:38 gives them the victory. 42
11:26 and give them pledges of friendship 42
12:11 promising to give him cattle 42
13:15 He gave his men the watchword, "God's victory 38
22 gave pledges, received theirs, withdrew 42
14:19 to give and receive pledges of friendship. 42
15: 8 the victory which the Almighty would give them. 48
15 gave to Judas a golden sword 58
15 as he gave it he addressed him thus 42

33 said that he would give it piecemeal to the birds 42
3Mc 1: 4 promising to give them each two minas of gold 42
2:20 give us peace. 61
3: 2 a pretext being given by a report 42
5:15 he gave him an account of the situation. 61
17 he urged them to give themselves over to revelry 42
19 he had carried out completely the order given him •
4Mc 1:12 giving glory to the all-wise God. 42
2:23 To the mind he gave the law 42
13:13 who gave us our lives 42

give a brief summary 1. συντέμνω
2Mc 10:10 we . . will give a brief summary 1

give a charge 1. צוה
Jer 27: 4 Give them this charge for their masters 1
47: 7 can it be quiet, when the LORD has given it a charge? 1

give a coat 1. καταχρίω
Wis 13:14 giving it a coat of red paint 1

give a command 1. אמר 2. צוה 3. εἶπον 4. ἐντέλλω 5. παραγγέλλω
Gen 50:16 Your father gave this command before he died 2
1Ch 14:12 left their gods there, and David gave command 1
21:17 Was it not I who gave command to number the people 1
Jer 7:23 But this command I gave them, 'Obey my voice 2
2Th 3:10 we gave you this command 5
Wis 9: 8 Thou hast given command to build a temple 3
Sir 45: 3 He gave him commands for his people 4
1Mc 5:19 he gave them this command 4
42 and gave them this command 4
9:55 or give commands concerning his house. 4

give a commandment 1. ἐντέλλω
Sir 24: 8 the Creator of all things gave me a commandment 1

give a crown 1. στεφανόω
4Mc 17:15 and gave the crown to its own athletes. 1

give a funeral 1. θάπτω
Tob 14:11 Tobias gave him a magnificent funeral. 1
13 he gave . . magnificent funerals 1

give a gift 1. נשא
2Sm 19:42 Or has he given us any gift? 1

give a hearing 1. ἀκούω
Joh 7:51 judge a man without first giving him a hearing 1

give a marriage present 1. מהר
Exd 22:16 he shall give the marriage present for her 1

give a measure 1. μετρέω
Lke 6:38 measure you give will be the measure you get back 1

give a message 1. צוה 2. ἀναγγέλλω
Est 4:10 Esther spoke to Hathach and gave him a message 1
LJr 1: 1 to give them the message which God had commanded 2

give a name 1. קרא 2. καλέω
Gen 2:20 The man gave names to all cattle 1
26:18 he gave them the names which his father had given 1
18 the names which his father had given them. 1
Num32:38 gave other names to the cities which they built. 1
Rut 4:17 the women of the neighborhood gave him a name 1
Ps 147: 4 stars, he gives to all of them their names. 1
Wis 13:10 who give the name "gods" to the works of men's hands 2

give a parable 1. דמה
Hos 12:10 and through the prophets gave parables. 1

give a pledge 1. תקע כַּף
Prv 6: 1 if you have . . given your pledge for a stranger; 1
17:18 A man without sense gives a pledge, and becomes 1
22:26 Be not one of those who give pledges 1

give a reply 1. ἀποκρίνω
1Mc 15:33 Simon gave him this reply 1

give a report 1. ἀπαγγέλλω
Jdt 10:13 to give him a true report 1

give a resting place 1. καταπαύω
Sir 24:11 gave me a resting place 1

give a shout 1. רוע 2. βοάω
1Sm 4: 5 When the ark . . all Israel gave a mighty shout 1
1Mc 3:54 they sounded the trumpets and gave a loud shout. 2

give a tenth 1. עשר
Gen 28:22 give me I will give the tenth to thee. 1

give a tithe 1. ἀποδεκατόω
Lke 18:12 I fast twice a week, I give tithes of all that I get.' 1

give a warning 1. זהר
Ezk 3:18 and you give him no warning, nor speak to warn 1

give a wide place 1. רחב
2Sm 22:37 Thou didst give a wide place for my steps under me 1
Ps 18:36 Thou didst give a wide place for my steps under me 1

give aid 1. προΐστημι
Rom 12: 8 he who gives aid, with zeal; 1

almost give out 1. σπανίζω
Jdt 11:12 their water has almost given out 1

also give 1. προσδίδωμι
Tob 2:12 they also gave her a kid; 1

give an award 1. ἀθλοθετέω
4Mc 17:12 on that day virtue gave the awards 1

give an explanation 1. demonstro
2Es 10:37 to give your servant an explanation of this 1

give an inheritance 1. נחל 2. κατακληρονομέω
Deu 32: 8 Most High gave to the nations their inheritance 1
Ezk 46:18 he shall give his sons their inheritance 1
Sir 36:11 give them their inheritance 2
46: 1 that he might give Israel its inheritance. 2

give an interpretation 1. פתר
Gen 41:12 he interpreted . . giving an interpretation 1

give an oath 1. שבע 2. ὄμνυμι
2Sm 19:23 You shall not die." And the king gave him his oath. 1
1Mc 6:61 the king and the commanders gave them their oath 2

give an opportunity 1. παρέχω
4Mc 11:12 you give us an opportunity to show our endurance 1

give an oracle 1. נגד
Hos 4:12 and their staff gives them oracles. 1

give answer 1. ענה 2. ὑπακούω 3. respondeo
Gen 41:16 God will give Pharaoh a favorable answer. 1
Job 19:16 I call to my servant, but he gives me no answer; 1
Sng 3: 1 I called him, but he gave no answer. 2
5: 6 I sought him . . I called him, but he gave no answer 1
2Es 4: 9 and you have given me no answer about them! 3

give approval 1. συναινέω
3Mc 5:21 all . . joyfully with one accord gave their approval 1

give as a possession 1. נחל
Deu 19: 3 land which the LORD . . gives you as a possession 1

give as an inheritance 1. κατακληρονομέω
Act 13:19 he gave them their land as an inheritance 1

give assurance 1. ἵστημι
Sir 44:22 To Isaac also he gave the same assurance 1

give attention 1. בין 2. פקד 3. προσέχω
Job 32:12 I gave you my attention 1
Jer 27:22 until the day when I give attention to them 2
3Mc 2: 2 give attention to us who are suffering 3

give away 1. ψωμίζω
1Co 13: 3 If I give away all I have 1

give back 1. שוב 2. שלם 3. ἀνταποδίδωμι 4. ἀποδίδωμι 5. reddo
2Sm 16: 3 the house of Israel will give me back the kingdom 1
Job 20:10 his hands will give back his wealth. 1
18 He will give back the fruit of his toil 1
Ezk 33:15 gives back what he has taken by robbery 2
Lke 4:20 he closed the book, and gave it back to the attendant 4
9:42 healed the boy and gave him back to his father 4
2Es 4:42 these places hasten to give back those things 5
Sir 7:28 what can you give back to them 3
Bar 4:23 God will give you back to me with joy and gladness 4
2Mc 7:23 the Creator . . will . . give life and breath back to you 4
9:16 the holy vessels he would give back 4
14:46 to give them back to him again 4

give birth 1. חול 2. ילד 3. ἀποκυέω 4. γεννάω 5. τίκτω 6. pario
Deu 32:18 you forgot the God who gave you birth. 1
1Sm 4:19 was with child, about to give birth. 2
19 she bowed and gave birth; for her pains came 2
1Kg 3:17 I gave birth to a child while she was in the house. 2
18 after I was delivered, this woman also gave birth; 2
Job 38:29 who has given birth to the hoarfrost of heaven? 2
Isa 23: 4 I have neither travailed nor given birth 2
66: 7 Before she was in labor she gave birth; 2
Jer 2:27 and to a stone, 'You gave me birth.' 2
Lke 1:57 and she gave birth to a son. 4
2: 7 she gave birth to her first-born son 5
Jas 1:15 desire when it has conceived gives birth to sin; 5
1Es 4:15 Women gave birth to the king and to every people 4
2Es 6:21 women with child shall give birth 6
4Mc 15:17 who alone gave birth to such complete devotion! 3

give birth to many 1. πολύγονος
4Mc 15: 5 mothers are the weaker sex and give birth to many 1

give blessing 1. ברך
2Sm 13:25 but he would not go but gave him his blessing. 1

certainly give life 1. vivifico
2Es 5:45 wilt certainly give life at one time 1

give charge 1. פקד 2. צוה 3. ἐντέλλω 4. παραγγέλλω
Exd 6:13 the LORD . . gave them a charge to the people 2
1Kg 11:28 he gave him charge over all the forced labor 1
1Ch 22:12 that when he gives you charge over Israel 2
Neh 7: 2 I gave . . charge over Jerusalem 2
Job 34:13 Who gave him charge over the earth 1
Ps 91:11 For he will give his angels charge of you 2
Mat 4: 6 for it is written, 'He will give his angels charge 3
Lke 4:10 He will give his angels charge of you, to guard you,' 3
1Co 7:10 To the married I give charge, not I but the Lord 4

give command 1. צוה 2. προστάσσω
Exd 36: 6 So Moses gave command, and word was proclaimed 1
Num 32:28 Moses gave command concerning them to Elea'zar 1
Isa 23:11 the LORD has given command concerning Canaan 1
Jer 39:11 Nebuchadrez'zar king of Babylon gave command 1
1Es 1:52 he gave command to bring against them the kings 2

give commandment 1. צוה 2. ἐντέλλω
Exd 34:32 he gave them in commandment all 1
Num 15:23 from the day the the LORD gave commandment 1
Nah 1:14 The LORD has given commandment about you 1
Act 1: 2 after he had given commandment . . to the apostles 2
Sir 17:14 he gave commandment to each of them 2

give consent 1. συγκατατίθημι 2. συνευδοκέω
Sus 1:20 we are in love with you; so give your consent 1
2Mc 11:35 we also give consent. 2

give consolation 1. נחם
Zec 10: 2 tell false dreams, and give empty consolation. 1

give counsel 1. יעץ 2. βουλεύω 3. συμβουλεύω
Exd 18:19 Listen now to my voice; I will give you counsel 1
1Kg 1:12 Now therefore come, let me give you counsel 1
Ps 16: 7 I bless the LORD who gives me counsel; 1
Jer 38:15 if I give you counsel, you will not listen to me. 1
Ezk 11: 2 men who devise iniquity . . who give wicked counsel 1
Joh 18:14 It was Ca'iaphas who had given counsel to the Jews 3
Sir 37: 7 some give counsel in their own interest. 3
44: 3 giving counsel by their understanding 2

give courage 1. ἀνδρειόω 2. θαρσύνω
AEs 14:12 give me courage, O King of the gods 2
4Mc 15:23 devout reason, giving her heart a man's courage 1

give deliverance 1. ישע
Ps 72: 4 give deliverance to the needy 1

give directions 1. διατάσσω 2. ἐντέλλω
1Co 11:34 I will give directions when I come. 1
Heb 11:22 gave directions concerning his burial. 2

give divination 1. קסם
Ezk 13: 9 the prophets . . who give lying divinations; 1

give dominion 1. משל
Ps 8: 6 Thou hast given him dominion over the works 1

give drink 1. שקה 2. ποτίζω
Gen 21:19 filled the skin . . and gave the lad a drink. 1
24:18 let down her jar . . and gave him a drink. 1
19 When she had finished giving him a drink 1
46 Drink, and I will give your camels drink also.' 1
46 So I drank, and she gave the camels drink also. 1
Num 20: 8 give drink to the congregation and their cattle. 1
Jdg 4:19 she opened a skin of milk and gave him a drink 1
Ps 36: 8 thou givest them drink from the river of thy 1
78:15 and gave them drink abundantly as from the deep. 1
104:11 they give drink to every beast of the field; 1
Isa 43:20 in the desert, to give drink to my chosen people 1
Mat 25:35 I was thirsty and you gave me drink 2
37 when did we see thee . . thirsty and give thee drink? 2
42 I was thirsty and you gave me no drink 2
Rom 12:20 if he is thirsty, give him drink; 2

give ear 1. אזן 2. שמע 3. ἐνωτίζομαι
Deu 1:45 did not hearken to your voice or give ear to you 1
32: 1 Give ear, O heavens, and I will speak; 1
Jdg 5: 3 Hear, O kings; give ear, O princes; to the LORD I will 1
1Kg 8:52 Let thy eyes be open . . giving ear to them 2
Neh 9:30 thy prophets; yet they would not give ear. 1
Job 34: 2 give ear to me, you who know; 1
Ps 5: 1 Give ear to my words, O LORD; 1
17: 1 Give ear to my prayer from lips free of deceit! 1
39:12 Hear my prayer, O LORD, and give ear to my cry; 1
49: 1 Give ear, all inhabitants of the world 1
54: 2 O God; give ear to the words of my mouth. 1
55: 1 Give ear to my prayer, O God; and hide not thyself 1
19 God will give ear, and humble them 2
78: 1 Give ear, O my people, to my teaching; 1
80: 1 Give ear, O Shepherd of Israel 1
84: 8 give ear, O God of Jacob! Selah 1
86: 6 Give ear, O LORD, to my prayer; 1
140: 6 give ear to the voice of my supplications, O LORD! 1
141: 1 Give ear to my voice, when I call to thee! 1
143: 1 O LORD; give ear to my supplications! 1
Isa 1: 2 Hear, O heavens, and give ear, O earth; 1
10 Give ear to the teaching of our God . . Gomor'rah! 1
8: 9 give ear, all you far countries; gird yourselves 1
28:23 Give ear, and hear my voice; 1
32: 9 you complacent daughters, give ear to my speech. 1
42:23 Who among you will give ear to this 1
51: 4 Listen to me, my people, and give ear to me, my nation 1
Jer 13:15 Hear and give ear; be not proud 1
Jol 1: 2 give ear, all inhabitants of the land! 1
Act 2:14 let this be known to you, and give ear to my words. 3
Wis 6: 2 Give ear, you that rule over multitudes 3
Bar 3: 9 life, O Israel; give ear, and learn wisdom! 3

give encouragement 1. παρακαλέω
Act 20: 2 and had given them much encouragement 1

give escort 1. προπέμπω
1Es 4:47 give escort to him 1

give for a heritage 1. נחל
Jer 3:18 the land that I gave your fathers for a heritage. 1

give forth 1. נתן
Ps 77:17 the skies gave forth thunder; thy arrows flashed 1
Sng 1:12 the king was . . my nard gave forth its fragrance. 1
2:13 vines are in blossom; they give forth fragrance. 1
7:13 The mandrakes give forth fragrance 1
Hab 3:10 the deep gave forth its voice, it lifted its hands 1

give free rein 1. שלח
Ps 50:19 You give your mouth free rein for evil 1

give free utterance 1. עזב
Job 10: 1 I will give free utterance to my complaint; 1

give freely 1. פזר
Prv 11:24 One man gives freely, yet grows all the richer; 1

give full vent 1. כלה
Lam 4:11 The LORD gave full vent to his wrath 1

give gladness 1. שמח
Jer 31:13 comfort them, and give them gladness for sorrow. 1

give glory 1. כבד 2. δοξάζω 3. glorifico 4. honorifico
Isa 24:15 Therefore in the east give glory to the LORD; 1
Mat 5:16 give glory to your Father who is in heaven. 2
2Es 9:45 and we gave great glory to the Mighty One. 4
13:57 giving great glory and praise to the Most High 3

give good heed 1. φυλάσσω
Sir 32:22 give good heed to your paths. 1

give graciously 1. חנן
Gen 33: 5 The children whom God has graciously given 1

give great 1. גדל
2Sm 22:51 Great triumphs he gives to his king 1
Ps 18:50 Great triumphs he gives to his king 1

give greetings 1. ἀσπάζομαι
Col 4:15 Give my greetings to the brethren at La-odice'a 1

give grief 1. λυπέω
Sir 30: 9 play with him, and he will give you grief. 1

give growth 1. αὐξάνω
1Co 3: 6 Apol'los watered, but God gave the growth. 1
7 but only God who gives the growth. 1

give heed 1. אזן 2. בין 3. נתן לב 4. ענה 5. קשב 6. שום 7. שכל 8. שית לב 9. שמע 10. שמר 11. ἐπέχω 12. ἐπιμελέομαι 13. προσέχω 14. προσοχή 15. intendo 16. neglego
Gen 16:11 the LORD has given heed to your affliction. 9
Exd 15:26 If you . . give heed to his commandments 1
18:24 Moses gave heed to the voice of his father-in-law 9
23:21 Give heed to him and hearken to his voice 10
Deu 4: 1 give heed to the statutes and the ordinances 9
18:14 For these nations . . give heed to soothsayers 9
19 whoever will not give heed to my words which he 9
21:18 though they chastise him, will not give heed 9
Jdg 6:10 But you have not given heed to my voice. 9
1Sm 4:20 Fear not . . " But she did not answer or give heed. 8
2Ch 24:19 but they would not give heed. 1
33:10 The LORD spoke . . but they gave no heed. 5
Job 23: 6 No; he would give heed to me. 6
33:31 Give heed, O Job, listen to me; 5
Ps 5: 1 O LORD; give heed to my groaning. 2

66:19 he has given heed to the voice of my prayer. 5
101: 2 I will give heed to the way that is blameless. 7
107:43 Whoever is wise, let him give heed to these things; 10
142: 6 Give heed to my cry; for I am brought very low! 5
Prv 1:23 Give heed to my reproof; *
16:20 He who gives heed to the word will prosper 7
17: 4 liar gives heed to a mischievous tongue. 1
29:19 for though he understands, he will not give heed. 4
Ecc 7:21 Do not give heed to all the things that men say 3
Jer 6:17 saying, 'Give heed to the sound of the trumpet!' 5
17 But they said, 'We will not give heed.' 5
19 because they have not given heed to my words; 5
8: 6 I have given heed and listened 5
18:19 Give heed to me, O LORD, and hearken to my plea. 5
23:18 or who has given heed to his word and listened? 5
Dan 9:13 our iniquities and giving heed to thy truth. 7
19 O LORD, give heed and act 5
10:11 Daniel . . give heed to the words that I speak 2
11:30 turn back and give heed to those who forsake 2
37 He shall give no heed to the gods of his fathers 2
37 he shall not give heed to any other god 2
Hos 5: 1 Hear this, O priests! Give heed, O house of Israel! 5
Act 8: 6 the multitudes with one accord gave heed 13
10 all gave heed to him 13
11 they gave heed to him 13
16:14 to give heed to what was said by Paul. 13
1Ti 4: 1 giving heed to deceitful spirits 13
Tit 1:14 instead of giving heed to Jewish myths 13
2Es 7:99 who would not give heed shall suffer 16
9:30 and give heed to my words, O descendants of Jacob. 15
Wis 6:18 giving heed to her laws 14
8:12 when I speak they will give heed 13
Sir 4:15 whoever gives heed to her will dwell secure. 13
30:25 will give heed to the food he eats. 12
32:24 gives heed to the commandments 13
34: 2 so is he who gives heed to dreams. 11

give help 1. ישע 2. ἐπιλαμβάνω
Ps 108: 6 give help by thy right hand, and answer me! 1
Sir 4:11 gives help to those who seek her. 2

give high honor 1. רבה (A)
Dan 2:48 gave Daniel high honors and many great gifts 1

give in abundance 1. רבה 2. שבע
2Ch 31: 5 Israel gave in abundance the first fruits 1
Ps 105:40 gave them bread from heaven in abundance. 2

give in commandment 1. צוה
Exd 25:22 all that I will give you in commandment 1
Deu 1: 3 all that the LORD had given him in commandment 1

give in full number 1. מלא
1Sm 18:27 which were given in full number to the king 1

give in marriage 1. נתן לְאִישׁ 2. γαμίζω 3. γαμίσκω 4. ἐκδίδωμι 5. συνοικίζω
Jer 29: 6 and give your daughters in marriage 1
Mat 22:30 they neither marry nor are given in marriage 2
24:38 marrying and giving in marriage 2
Mrk 12:25 they neither marry nor are given in marriage 2
Lke 17:27 they were given in marriage 2
20:34 The sons of this age . . are given in marriage; 3
35 neither marry nor are given in marriage 2
1Es 8:84 do not give your daughters in marriage 5
Sir 7:25 Give a daughter in marriage 4
1Mc 10:58 Ptolemy gave him Cleopatra . . in marriage 4

give increase 1. יסף
Ps 115:14 May the LORD give you increase . . your children! 1

give information 1. ἐμφανίζω 2. μηνύω 3. προσαγγέλλω
Act 25:15 the chief priests . . gave information about him 1
2Mc 13:21 Rhodocus . . gave secret information to the enemy 3
3Mc 3:28 Any one willing to give information 2

give insight 1. בין
Sir 6:37 It is he who will give insight to your mind 1

give instruction 1. διαστέλλω 2. παρακαλέω
Act 15:24 although we gave them no instructions 1
Tit 1: 9 be able to give instruction in sound doctrine 2

give judgment 1. פְּלִילִיָּה 2. שפט 3. κρίνω τό κρίμα
Ps 9: 4 sat on the throne giving righteous judgment. 2
Isa 28: 7 err in vision, they stumble in giving judgment. 1
Mic 3:11 Its heads give judgment for a bribe 2
Rev 18:20 for God has given judgment for you against her! 3

give justice 1. צדק 2. שפט
2Sm 15: 4 might come to me, and I would give him justice. 1
Ps 82: 3 Give justice to the weak and the fatherless; 2

give large 1. רבה
Num26:54 a large tribe you shall give a large inheritance 1

give law 1. νομοθετέω
2Mc 3:15 who had given the law about deposits 1
4Mc 5:25 in giving us the law 1

give leave 1. ἐπιτρέπω
Mrk 5:13 So he gave them leave 1
Lke 8:32 So he gave them leave. 1
Joh 19:38 and Pilate gave him leave 1
Act 21:40 And when he had given him leave 1
27: 3 gave him leave to go to his friends 1

give less 1. מעט
Exd 30:15 and the poor shall not give less 1

give liberally 1. חנן
Ps 37:26 He is ever giving liberally and lending 1

give life 1. חיה 2. vivifico
Job 33: 4 the breath of the Almighty gives me life. 1
Ps 80:18 give us life, and we will call on thy name! 1
119:37 give me life in thy ways. 1
40 thy righteousness give me life! 1
50 in my affliction that thy promise gives me life. 1
93 thy precepts; for by them thou hast given me life. 1
107I am sorely afflicted; give me life, O LORD 1
154redeem me; give me life according to thy promise! 1
156O LORD; give me life according to thy justice. 1
2Es 8: 8 because thou dost give life to the body 2

give light 1. אור 2. הלל 3. ἐπιφαίνω 4. ἐπιφαύσκω 5. λάμπω 6. φαίνω 7. φωτίζω
Gen 1:15 in . . the heavens to give light upon the earth 1
17 God set them in . . the heavens to give light 1
Exd 13:21 give them light, that they might travel by day 1
25:37 to give light upon the space in front of it. 1
Num 8: 2 seven lamps shall give light in front 1
3 Aaron . . set up its lamps to give light in front *
Ps 105:39 fire to give light by night. 1
118:27 The LORD is God, and he has given us light. 1
119:130The unfolding of thy words gives light; 1
Prv 29:13 LORD gives light to the eyes of both. 1
Isa 13:10 their constellations will not give their light; 2
60:19 nor for brightness shall the moon give light 1
Ezk 32: 7 the moon shall not give its light. 1
Mat 5:15 and it gives light to all in the house. 5
Lke 1:79 to give light to those who sit in darkness 3
11:36 as when a lamp with its rays gives you light. 7
Eph 5:14 Christ shall give you light. 4
Wis 17: 5 no power of fire was able to give light 7
Sir 34:17 He lifts up the soul and gives light to the eyes 7
LJr 1:67 shine like the sun or give light like the moon. 7
1Mc 4:50 these gave light in the temple. 6

make give off 1. נבע
Ecc 10: 1 Dead flies make . . ointment give off an evil odor; 1

give more 1. προστίθημι
Tob 12: 1 he must also be given more. 1

give no ground for complaint 1. ἀνέγκλητος
3Mc 5:31 who give me no ground for complaint 1

give notice 1. διαγγέλλω 2. ἐμφανίζω
Act 21:26 to give notice when . . purification would be fulfilled 1
23:15 give notice now to the tribune to bring him down 2

give offense 1. προσκόπτω 2. σκανδαλίζω
Mat 17:27 However, not to give offense to them, go to the sea 2
Sir 31:17 do not be insatiable, lest you give offense. 1

give orders 1. אמר 2. יסד 3. צוה 4. διατάσσω 5. ἐντέλλω 6. ἐπινεύω 7. ἐπιτάσσω 8. κελεύω 9. παραγγέλλω 10. προστάσσω 11. συντάσσω 12. τίθημι
Gen 12:20 Pharaoh gave men orders concerning him; 3
42:25 Joseph gave orders to fill their bags with grain 3
2Sm 14: 8 Go . . and I will give orders concerning you. 3
18: 5 when the king gave orders to all the commanders 3
Neh 13: 9 I gave orders and they cleansed the chambers; 1
19 gave orders that they should not be opened until 1
Est 1: 8 the king had given orders . . to do as every man 2
6: 1 he gave orders to bring the book of . . deeds 1
9:25 he gave orders in writing that his wicked plot 1
Jer 37:21 King Zedeki'ah gave orders 3
Mat 8:18 he gave orders to go over to the other side. 8
Mrk 6:27 and gave orders to bring his head 7
Act 16:22 and gave orders to beat them with rods. 8
24:23 he gave orders to the centurion 4
1Es 8:10 I have given orders 10
Jdt 4: 8 Israelites did as Joakim . . had given order. 11
7:16 he gave orders to do as they had said. 11
1Mc 3:34 and gave him orders about all that he wanted done 5
6:57 So he quickly gave orders to depart 6
1M 6:62 and gave orders to tear down the wall all around. 5
1Mc 9:54 Alcimus gave orders to tear down the wall 7
10:62 The king gave orders to take off Jonathan's garments 10
11:23 he gave orders to continue the siege 8
14:48 they gave orders to inscribe this decree 12
2Mc 7: 3 and gave orders that pans and caldrons be heated. 10
9: 7 and giving orders to hasten the journey 8
12: 5 he gave orders to his men 9
15:10 he gave his orders 9
3Mc 1: 1 he gave orders to all his forces 9
3:25 Therefore we have given orders 10
5: 3 When he had given these orders 10
37 must I give you orders about these things? 10
4Mc 8: 3 When the tyrant had given these orders 4
10:17 Antiochus gave orders to cut out his tongue. 8

give out 1. δόσις 2. ἐκλείπω 3. λέγω
Act 5:36 Theu'das arose, giving himself out to be somebody 3
Sir 42: 7 make a record of all that you give out or take in. 1
3Mc 4:20 the paper and the pens . . had already given out. 2

give over 1. נגר 2. נתן 3. נתן בְּיָד 4. נתן לִפְנֵי 5. סגר 6. סכר 7. שלח 8. שמט 9. יהב (A) 10. δίδωμι 11. ἔκδοτον 12. ἐν χειρί 13. παραδίδωμι 14. προΐημι 15. do 16. trado
Num21: 3 the LORD . . gave over the Canaanites; 2
Deu 2:31 I have begun to give Sihon and his land over to you; 4
33 LORD our God gave him over to us; and we defeated 4
7: 2 when the LORD your God gives them over to you 4
16 peoples that the LORD . . will give over to you 2
23 LORD . . will give them over to you, and throw them 4
31: 5 LORD will give them over to you, and you shall do 2
Jos 11: 6 I will give over all of them, slain, to Israel; 2
Jdg 2:14 he gave them over to plunderers, who plundered 2
Ps 63:10 they shall be given over to the power of the sword 1
78:48 He gave over their cattle to the hail 5
50 but gave their lives over to the plague. 5
62 He gave his people over to the sword 5
81:12 I gave them over to their stubborn hearts 7
118:18 LORD . . has not given me over to death. 2
141: 6 given over to those who shall condemn them 8
Isa 19: 4 I will give over the Egyptians into the hand 6
34: 2 doomed them, has given them over for slaughter. 2
Jer 26:24 so that he was not given over to the people 3
Ezk 31:14 for they are all given over to death 2
35: 5 and gave over the people of Israel 1
Dan 7:11 destroyed and given over to be burned with fire. 9
8:13 giving over of the sanctuary 2
Act 7:42 God . . gave them over to worship the host of heaven 13
1Es 6:15 gave them over into the hands of Nebuchadnezzar 13
8:77 were given over to the kings of the earth 13
2Es 4:23 why Israel has been given over to the Gentiles 15
23 has been given over to godless tribes 15
5:28 why hast thou given over the one to the many 16
10:23 has been given over into the hands of those 16
Bel 1:22 and gave Bel over to Daniel 11
1Mc 2: 7 to dwell there when it was given over to the enemy 10
7 the sanctuary given over to aliens? 12
4Mc 18: 3 those who gave over their bodies in suffering 14

give peace 1. נוח
1Ch 22: 9 I will give him peace from all his enemies 1
18 has he not given you peace on every side? 1
23:25 the God of Israel, has given peace to his people; 1
2Ch 14: 6 no war in those years, for the LORD gave him peace. 1
7 he has given us peace on every side. 1

give permission 1. ἐπιχωρέω
2Mc 4: 9 if permission were given 1

give place 1. ἐξέρχομαι
Sir 29:27 Give place, stranger, to an honored person 1

give power 1. שלט 2. ἐκποιέω
Ecc 5:19 given wealth . . and power to enjoy them 1
6: 2 yet God does not give him power to enjoy them 1
Sir 18: 4 To none has he given power to proclaim his works; 2

give praise 1. הלל 2. ידה 3. αἰνέω 4. ἐξομολογέω 5. εὐλογέω 6. laudo
Ps 6: 5 in Sheol who can give thee praise? 2
135: 1 give praise, O servants of the LORD 1
Jer 31: 7 proclaim, give praise, and say, 'The LORD has saved 1
Rom 14:11 and every tongue shall give praise to God. 4
2Es 13:57 giving great glory and praise to the Most High 6
Tob 13:18 and will give praise, saying, 'Blessed is God 3
2Mc 8:27 giving great praise and thanks to the Lord 5

give provender 1. בלל
Jdg 19:21 he brought him . . and gave the asses provender; 1

give provocation 1. כעס
Hos 12:14 E'phraim has given bitter provocation; 1

give rebirth 1. ἀνατίκτω
4Mc 16:13 as though . . giving rebirth for immortality 1

give recognition 1. ἐπιγινώσκω
1Co 16:18 Give recognition to such men. 1

give reinforcement 1. συνεπισχύω
AEs 16:20 give them reinforcements 1

give repute 1. גדל
1Ch 29:25 LORD gave Solomon great repute in the sight 1

give respite 1. דמם 2. רפה 3. שׁקט
1Sm 11: 3 Give us seven days respite that we may send 2
Ps 94:13 to give him respite from days of trouble 3
Lam 2:18 Give yourself no rest, your eyes no respite! 1

give rest 1. נהל 2. נוח 3. רגע 4. ἀναπαύω 5. καταπαύω
Exd 33:14 will go with you, and I will give you rest. 2
Deu 3:20 until the LORD gives rest to your brethren 2
12:10 gives you rest from all your enemies round about 2
25:19 LORD . . given you rest from all your enemies 2
Jos 1:15 until the LORD gives rest to your brethren 2
21:44 And the LORD gave them rest on every side 2
22: 4 the LORD your God has given rest to your brethren 2
23: 1 the LORD had given rest to Israel from all their 2
2Sm 7: 1 the LORD had given him rest from all his enemies 2
11 and I will give you rest from all your enemies. 2
1Kg 5: 4 the LORD my God has given me rest on every side; 2
2Ch 15:15 the LORD gave them rest round about. 2
20:30 for his God gave him rest round about. 2
32:22 LORD . . gave them rest on every side. 1
Prv 29:17 Discipline your son, and he will give you rest; 2
Isa 14: 3 When the LORD has given you rest from your pain 2
28:12 This is rest; give rest to the weary; 2
63:14 the Spirit of the LORD gave them rest. 2
Jer 50:34 that he may give rest to the earth 3
Lam 5: 5 we are . . driven; we are weary, we are given no rest. 2
Mat 11:28 and I will give you rest. 4
Heb 4: 8 For if Joshua had given them rest 5
Sir 47:13 God gave him rest on every side 5

give revelation 1. ירה
Hab 2:19 dumb stone, Arise! Can this give revelation? 1

give room 1. רחב
Ps 4: 1 Thou hast given me room when I was in distress. 1

give sandals 1. נעל
2Ch 28:15 they clothed them, gave them sandals 1

give satisfaction 1. εὐάρεστος
Tit 2: 9 to give satisfaction in every respect 1

give sentence 1. שׁפט 2. ἐπικρίνω
1Sm 24:15 the LORD . . and give sentence between me and you 1
Lke 23:24 So Pilate gave sentence 2

give small 1. מעט
Num26:54 small tribe you shall give a small inheritance; 1
33:54 small tribe you shall give a small inheritance; 1

give some 1. μερίζω
2Mc 8:28 they gave some of the spoils to . . the widows 1

give stability 1. עמד
Prv 29: 4 By justice a king gives stability to the land 1

give still more 1. προστίθημι
Mrk 4:24 still more will be given you. 1

give strength 1. חזק 2. עזז 3. ἐνδυναμόω 4. κραταιόω
1Ch 29:12 to make great and to give strength to all. 1
Ecc 7:19 Wisdom gives strength . . more than ten rulers 2
1Ti 1:12 I thank him who has given me strength for this 3
2Ti 4:17 gave me strength to proclaim the message fully 3
Jdt 13: 7 Give me strength this day, O Lord God of Israel! 4

give strong support 1. חזק
1Ch 11:10 men, who gave him strong support in his kingdom 1

give success 1. צלח 2. εὐοδόω
Neh 1:11 give success to thy servant today, and grant him 1
Ps 118:25 O LORD, we beseech thee, give us success! 1
2Mc 10: 7 who had given success to the purifying 2

give suck 1. עול 2. θηλάζω 3. τρέφω
Gen 33:13 flocks and herds giving suck are a care to me; 1
Mat 24:19 those who give suck in those days! 2
Mrk 13:17 those who give suck in those days! 2
Lke 21:23 Alas . . for those who give suck in those days! 2
23:29 and the breasts that never gave suck!' 3

give support 1. סעד
Ps 20: 2 May he . . give you support from Zion! 1

give surety 1. ערב 2. תקע 3. ἐγγυάω
Job 17: 3 who is there that will give surety for me? 2
Prv 11:15 He who gives surety for a stranger will smart 1
20:16 garment when he has given surety for a stranger 1
16 hold him . . when he gives surety for foreigners. •
27:13 garment when he has given surety for a stranger 1
13 hold him . . when he gives surety for foreigners. •
Sir 8:13 Do not give surety beyond your means 3
13 if you give surety 3

give thanks 1. ידה 2. תּוֹדָה 3. ידא (A) 4. ἀνθομολογέω 5. ἐξομολογέω 6. εὐχαριστέω 7. εὐχαριστία 8. ὁμολογέω
1Ch 16: 8 O give thanks to the LORD, call on his name 1
34 O give thanks to the LORD, for he is good; 1
35 that we may give thanks to thy holy name 1
41 expressly named to give thanks to the LORD 1
2Ch 7: 3 bowed down . . and worshiped and gave thanks 1
6 instruments . . David made for giving thanks 1
20:21 Give thanks to the LORD, for his steadfast love 1
30:22 giving thanks to the LORD the God 1
31: 2 minister . . and to give thanks and praise. 1
Ezr 3:11 praising and giving thanks to the LORD 1
Neh 12:24 praise and to give thanks, 1
31 two great companies which gave thanks 2
38 other company of those who gave thanks went 2
40 both companies of those who gave thanks stood 2
Ps 7:17 I will give to the LORD the thanks due 1
9: 1 I will give thanks to the LORD with my whole heart; 1
28: 7 with my song I give thanks to him. 1
30: 4 O you his saints, and give thanks to his holy name. 1
12 O LORD my God, I will give thanks to thee for ever. 1
44: 8 we will give thanks to thy name for ever. Selah 1
54: 6 I will give thanks to thy name, O LORD, for it is good. 1
57: 9 I will give thanks to thee, O Lord 1
75: 1 We give thanks to thee, O God; we give thanks; 1
1 We give thanks to thee, O God; we give thanks; 1
79:13 thy people . . will give thanks to thee for ever; 1
86:12 I give thanks to thee, O Lord my God 1
92: 1 It is good to give thanks to the LORD 1
97:12 O you righteous, and give thanks to his holy name! 1
100: 4 Give thanks to him, bless his name! 1
105: 1 O give thanks to the LORD, call on his name 1
106: 1 O give thanks to the LORD, for he is good; 1
47 that we may give thanks to thy holy name 1
107: 1 O give thanks to the LORD, for he is good; 1
108: 3 give thanks to thee, O LORD, among the peoples 1
109:30 With my mouth I will give great thanks to the LORD; 1
111: 1 I will give thanks to the LORD with my whole heart 1
118: 1 O give thanks to the LORD, for he is good; 1
19 enter through them and give thanks to the LORD. 1
28 Thou art my God, and I will give thanks to thee; 1
29 O give thanks to the LORD, for he is good; 1
122: 4 for Israel, to give thanks to the name of the LORD. 1
136: 1 O give thanks to the LORD, for he is good 1
2 O give thanks to the God of gods 1
3 O give thanks to the Lord of lords 1
26 O give thanks to the God of heaven 1
138: 1 I give thee thanks, O LORD, with my whole heart; 1
2 give thanks to thy name for thy steadfast love 1
140:13 Surely the righteous . . give thanks to thy name; 1
142: 7 out of prison, that I may give thanks to thy name! 1
145:10 All thy works shall give thanks to thee, O LORD 1
Isa 12: 1 I will give thanks to thee, O LORD 1
4 you will say in that day: "Give thanks to the LORD 1
Jer 33:11 Give thanks to the LORD of hosts 1
Dan 2:23 O God of my fathers, I give thanks and praise 3
6:10 prayed and gave thanks before his God 3
Mat 15:36 having given thanks he broke them and gave them 6
26:27 when he had given thanks he gave it to them, saying 6
Mrk 8: 6 and having given thanks he broke them 6
14:23 when he had given thanks he gave it to them 6
Lke 2:38 coming up at that very hour she gave thanks to God 4
17:16 and he fell . . giving him thanks 6
22:17 he took a cup, and when he had given thanks he said 6
19 when he had given thanks he broke it and gave it 6
Joh 6:11 when he had given thanks 6
23 after the Lord had given thanks. 6
Act 27:35 giving thanks to God in the presence of all 6
Rom 1:21 they did not honor him as God or give thanks to him 6
14: 6 in honor of the Lord, since he gives thanks to God; 6
6 abstains in honor of the Lord and gives thanks to God. 6
16: 4 all the churches of the Gentiles give thanks; 6
1Co 1: 4 I give thanks to God always for you 6
10:30 because of that for which I give thanks? 6
11:24 when he had given thanks, he broke it, and said 6
14:17 For you may give thanks well enough 6
2Co 1:11 so that many will give thanks on our behalf 6
Eph 1:16 I do not cease to give thanks for you 6
5:20 always and for everything giving thanks 6
Col 1:12 giving thanks to the Father 6
3:17 giving thanks to God the Father through him. 6
1Th 1: 2 We give thanks to God always for you all 6
5:18 give thanks in all circumstances 6
2Th 1: 3 We are bound to give thanks to God always for you 6
2:13 we are bound to give thanks to God always for you 6
Rev 11:17 saying, "We give thanks to thee, Lord God Almighty 6
1Es 4:60 I give thee thanks, O Lord of our fathers. 8
5:61 they sang hymns, giving thanks to the Lord 8
Tob 11:17 Tobit gave thanks before them 5
12: 6 Praise God and give thanks to him 5
6 exalt him and give thanks to him 5
6 Do not be slow to give him thanks. 5
20 now give thanks to God 5
13: 6 give thanks to him with your full voice 5
6 I give him thanks in the land of my captivity 5
8 and give him thanks in Jerusalem. 5
10 Give thanks worthily to the Lord 5
14: 7 his people will give thanks to God 5
Jdt 8:25 In spite of everything let us give thanks 6
Wis 16:28 one must rise before the sun to give thee thanks 7
Sir 39: 6 give thanks to the Lord in prayer. 5
15 give thanks to him with praise 5
51: 1 I will give thanks to thee, O Lord and King 5
1 I give thanks to thy name 5
12 I will give thanks to thee and praise thee 5
Aza 1:67 Give thanks to the Lord, for he is good 5
68 sing praise to him and give thanks to him 5
3Mc 6:33 the king . . gave thanks to heaven unceasingly 4
7:16 joyfully and loudly giving thanks to the one God 6

give thought 1. עַיִן חוּם 2. עשׁת 3. μιμνήσκω
Gen 45:20 Give no thought to your goods 1
Jon 1: 6 Perhaps the god will give a thought to us 2
Sir 3:31 gives thought to the future 3
Bar 3:23 the way to wisdom, nor given thought to her paths. 3

give to 1. συντελέω
1Es 2:27 that the men in it were given to rebellion and war 1

give to carry 1. ἐπιτίθημι
Jdt 10: 5 and gave them to her to carry. 1

give to drink 1. גמא 2. שׁקה 3. ποτίζω 4. potiono
Gen 24:17 give me a little water to drink from your jar. 1
43 Pray give me a little water from your jar to drink 2
Jdg 4:19 he said to her, "Pray, give me a little water to drink; 2
1Sm 30:11 and he ate, they gave him water to drink 2
2Sm 23:15 O that some one would give me water to drink 2
1Ch 11:17 O that some one would give me water to drink 2
Job 22: 7 You have given no water to the weary to drink 2
Ps 60: 3 thou hast given us wine to drink that made us reel. 2
69:21 for my thirst they gave me vinegar to drink. 2
80: 5 given them tears to drink in full measure. 2
Prv 25:21 if he is thirsty, give him water to drink; 2
Sng 8: 2 I would give you spiced wine to drink 2
Jer 8:14 and has given us poisoned water to drink 2
9:15 and give them poisonous water to drink. 2
16: 7 any one give him the cup of consolation to drink 2
23:15 wormwood, and give them poisoned water to drink; 2
Mat 27:48 put it on a reed, and gave it to him to drink. 3
Mrk 9:41 whoever gives you a cup of water to drink 3
15:36 gave it to him to drink, saying, "Wait 3
2Es 14:38 and drink what I give you to drink. 4
Sir 15: 3 give him the water of wisdom to drink. 3

give to eat 1. אכל 2. ברה
Num11:18 Who will give us meat to eat? For it was well with us 1
2Sm 13: 5 Let my sister Tamar come and give me bread to eat 2
Prv 25:21 If your enemy is hungry, give him bread to eat; 1
Ezk 3: 2 I opened my mouth, and he gave me the scroll to eat. 1

give to God 1. δῶρον
Mrk 7:11 Corban' (that is, given to God)- 1

give to harlotry 1. זנה
Hos 4:18 drunkards, they give themselves to harlotry 1

give to inherit 1. ירשׁ 2. נחל
Deu 12:10 land which the LORD your God gives you to inherit 2
2Ch 20:11 possession, which thou hast given us to inherit. 1
Jer 12:14 heritage which I have given . . Israel to inherit 2

give to possess 1. ירשׁ
Jdg 11:24 what Chemosh your god gives you to possess? 1

give trouble 1. ὀχλέω
Tob 6: 7 if a demon or evil spirit gives trouble to any one 1

give understanding 1. בין
Ps 119:34 Give me understanding, that I may keep thy law 1
73 give me understanding that I may learn 1
125I am thy servant; give me understanding 1
144give me understanding that I may live. 1
169give me understanding according to thy word! 1

give up 1. חדל 2. יצא 3. נתן 4. סגר 5. עזב 6. עלה 7. ἀπαλλάσσω 8. ἀφίημι 9. ἀφίστημι 10. διαλλάσσω 11. δίδωμι 12. ἐγκαταλείπω 13. ἐκδίδωμι 14. ἐκχέω 15. καταλείπω 16. καταργέω 17. οὐκέτι 18. παραδίδωμι 19. πίπτω ἀπό 20. προδίδωμι 21. φεύγω 22. χαρίζομαι 23. mitto 24. reddo
Deu 23:14 to save you and to give up your enemies before you 3
15 not give up to his master a slave who has escaped 4
32:30 unless . . LORD had given them up? 4
Jos 20: 5 they shall not give up the slayer into his hand; 4
Jdg 20:13 give up the men . . that we may put them to death 3
1Sm 11: 3 no one to save us, we will give ourselves up to you. 2
10 Tomorrow we will give ourselves up to you 2
23:13 When Saul was told . . he gave up the expedition. 1
2Sm 2:27 surely the men would have given up the pursuit 6
14: 7 Give up the man who struck his brother 3
20:21 give up him alone, and I will withdraw 3
1Kg 14:16 he will give Israel up because of the sins 3
2Kg 24:12 Jehoi'achin the king of Judah gave himself up 2

Neh 4: 4 give them up to be plundered in a land where 3
Job 16:11 God gives me up to the ungodly 4
Ps 16:10 For thou dost not give me up to Sheol 5
27:12 Give me not up to the will of my adversaries; 3
41: 2 dost not give him up to the will of his enemies. 3
Isa 41: 2 He gives up nations before him 3
42:24 Who gave up Jacob to the spoiler 3
43: 6 I will say to the north, Give up 3
Ezk 15: 6 so will I give up the inhabitants of Jerusalem. 3
23: 8 She did not give up her harlotry 5
Dan 11: 6 shall be given up, and her attendants, her child 3
Hos 11: 8 How can I give you up, O E'phraim! 3
Mic 5: 3 he shall give them up until the time 3
Joh 19:30 he bowed his head and gave up his spirit. 18
Act 6: 2 that we should give up preaching the word of God 15
25:11 no one can give me up to them 22
16 not the custom of the Romans to give up any one 22
Rom 1:24 God gave them up in the lusts of their hearts 18
26 God gave them up to dishonorable passions. 18
27 the men . . gave up natural relations with women 8
28 God gave them up to a base mind 18
8:32 not spare his own Son but gave him up for us all 18
1Co 13:11 when I became a man, I gave up childish ways. 16
2Co 4:11 always being given up to death for Jesus' sake 18
Eph 4:19 have given themselves up to licentiousness 18
5: 2 Christ . . gave himself up for us 18
25 loved the church and gave himself up for her 18
Rev 9:20 nor give up worshiping demons and idols of gold *
20:13 And the sea gave up the dead in it 11
13 Death and Hades gave up the dead in them 11
1Es 4:50 the Idumeans should give up the villages 8
2Es 7:32 the earth shall give up those who are asleep in it 24
32 and the chambers shall give up the souls 24
8: 9 when the womb gives up again 24
16:77 It is shut off and given up to be consumed by fire. 23
Tob 10: 7 my father and mother have given up hope 17
Jdt 4:12 praying . . not to give up their infants as prey 11
7:13 and they will give up their city 13
9: 3 thou gavest up their rulers to be slain 11
Wis 12:20 opportunity to give up their wickedness 7
Sir 14: 2 has not given up his hope. 19
37:29 do not give yourself up to food; 14
38:10 Give up your faults and direct your hands aright 9
47:22 the Lord will never give up his mercy 15
Aza 1:11 For thy name's sake do not give us up utterly 18
1Mc 1:42 that each should give up his customs. 12
2Mc 6:27 Therefore, by manfully giving up my life now 10
7:37 I, like my brothers, give up body and life 20
3Mc 2:31 some . . readily gave themselves up 11
4Mc 8:19 and give up this vain opinion 21

give up all hope 1. ἀπελπίζω
2Mc 9:18 he gave up all hope for himself 1

give up to despair 1. יאשׁ
Ecc 2:20 I turned about and gave my heart up to despair 1

give vent 1. יצא 2. ἀναφέρω
Prv 29:11 A fool gives full vent to his anger 1
1Mc 2:24 He gave vent to righteous anger 2

give victory 1. ישׁע 2. βραβεύω
Deu 20: 4 fight for you . . to give you the victory.' 1
2Sm 8: 6 the LORD gave victory to David wherever he went. 1
14 the LORD gave victory to David wherever he went. 1
1Ch 18: 6 LORD gave victory to David wherever he went. 1
13 the LORD gave victory to David wherever he went. 1
Job 40:14 that your own right hand can give you victory. 1
Ps 20: 9 Give victory to the king, O LORD; 1
44: 3 nor did their own arm give them victory; 1
60: 5 give victory by thy right hand and answer us! 1
Zep 3:17 God . . a warrior who gives victory; 1
Zec 12: 7 the LORD will give victory to the tents of Judah 1
Wis 10:12 in his arduous contest she gave him the victory 2

give warning 1. זהר 2. עוד
Jer 6:10 To whom shall I speak and give warning 2
Ezk 3:17 you shall give them warning from me. 1
33: 7 you shall give them warning from me. 1

give way 1. מוט 2. מושׁ 3. שׁרא (A) 4. εἴκω 5. ἐπιδίδωμι 6. τρέπω
Prv 25:26 righteous man who gives way before the wicked. 1
Isa 22:25 the peg . . will give way; and it will be cut down 2
Dan 5: 6 limbs gave way, and his knees knocked together. 3
Act 27:15 we gave way to it and were driven. 5
3Mc 5:49 and giving way to lamentation and groans 6
4Mc 1: 6 so that one may not give way to them. 4

give way to insanity 1. μαίνομαι
4Mc 10:13 do not give way to the same insanity 1

give welcome 1. δέχομαι
Heb 11:31 she had given friendly welcome to the spies. 1

give willingly 1. נדב
1Ch 29: 9 rejoiced because these had given willingly 1

give wings 1. ἀναπτερόω
Sir 34: 1 dreams give wings to fools. 1

give wisdom 1. שׂכל
Dan 9:22 come out to give you wisdom and understanding. 1

give written 1. כתב
Est 9:29 Queen Esther . . gave full written authority 1

given *See* order.

given to anger 1. θυμώδης
Sir 28: 8 a man given to anger will kindle strife 1

given to swearing 1. πολύορκος
Sir 27:14 The talk of men given to swearing 1

giver 1. δότης 2. donator
2Co 9: 7 God loves a cheerful giver. 1
2Es 7:138 he is called giver, because if he did not give 2

giving of the law 1. νομοθεσία
Rom 9: 4 the covenants, the giving of the law, the worship 1

glad 1. גיל 2. טוב 3. יטב 4. עַל 5. שׂושׂ 6. שׂמח 7. שָׂמֵחַ 8. שִׂמְחָה 9. טאב (A) 10. ἀγαθός 11. ἀγαλλιάω 12. ἄσμενος 13. βούλομαι 14. εὐφραίνω 15. εὐφροσύνη 16. ἡδέως 17. θέλω 18. χαίρω 19. gaudeo 20. laetor
Exd 4:14 and when he sees you he will be glad in his heart. 6
Jdg 18:20 the priest's heart was glad; he took the ephod 3
1Sm 11: 9 When . . told the men of Jabesh, they were glad. 6
2Sm 18:11 I would have been glad to give you ten pieces 4
1Kg 8:66 joyful and glad of heart for all the goodness 2
1Ch 16:31 Let the heavens be glad, and let the earth rejoice 6
2Ch 7:10 sent the people away . . joyful and glad of heart 2
Est 5: 9 Haman went out that day joyful and glad of heart. 2
Job 3:22 who rejoice exceedingly, and are glad 5
22:19 The righteous see it and are glad; 6
Ps 9: 2 I will be glad and exult in thee, I will sing praise 6
14: 7 Jacob shall rejoice, Israel shall be glad. 6
16: 9 Therefore my heart is glad, and my soul rejoices; 6
31: 7 I will rejoice and be glad for thy steadfast love 6
32:11 Be glad in the LORD, and rejoice, O righteous 6
33:21 Yea, our heart is glad in him, because we trust 6
34: 2 let the afflicted hear and be glad. 6
35:27 be glad, and say evermore, "Great is the LORD 6
40:16 may all who seek thee rejoice and be glad in thee; 6
48:11 let Mount Zion be glad! 6
53: 6 Jacob will rejoice and Israel be glad. 6
67: 4 Let the nations be glad and sing for joy 6
69:32 Let the oppressed see it and be glad; 6
70: 4 May all who seek thee rejoice and be glad in thee! 6
90:14 that we may rejoice and be glad all our days. 6
96:11 Let the heavens be glad, and let the earth rejoice; 6
97: 1 LORD reigns; let . . the many coastlands be glad! 6
8 Zion hears and is glad, and the daughters of Judah 6
105:38 Egypt was glad when they departed 6
107:30 Then they were glad because they had quiet 6
42 The upright see it and are glad; 6
109:28 may thy servant be glad! 6
118:24 let us rejoice and be glad in it. 6
122: 1 I was glad when they said to me, "Let us go 6
126: 3 The LORD has done great things for us; we are glad. 7
149: 2 Let Israel be glad in his Maker 6
Prv 15:13 A glad heart makes a cheerful countenance 7
17: 5 who is glad at calamity will not go unpunished. 7
23:15 if your heart is wise, my heart too will be glad. 6
24 he who begets a wise son will be glad in him. 6
25 Let your father and mother be glad 6
24:17 let not your heart be glad when he stumbles; 1
Isa 25: 9 let us be glad and rejoice in his salvation. 6
35: 1 The wilderness and the dry land shall be glad 5
65:18 But be glad . . for ever in that which I create; 5
19 rejoice in Jerusalem, and be glad in my people; 5
66:10 Rejoice with Jerusalem, and be glad for her 1
Lam 1:21 enemies . . they are glad that thou hast done it. 5
4:21 Rejoice and be glad, O daughter of Edom 6
Dan 6:23 Then the king was exceedingly glad 9
Jol 2:21 Fear not, O land; be glad and rejoice 6
23 Be glad, O sons of Zion, and rejoice in the LORD 6
Jon 4: 6 Jonah was exceedingly glad 8
Zec 10: 7 their hearts shall be glad as with wine. 6
Mat 5:12 Rejoice and be glad, for your reward is great 11
Mrk 14:11 when they heard it they were glad 18
Lke 15:32 It was fitting to make merry and be glad 18
22: 5 they were glad, and engaged to give him money. 18
23: 8 When Herod saw Jesus, he was very glad 18
Joh 6:21 they were glad to take him into the boat 17
8:56 he saw it and was glad. 18
11:15 for your sake I am glad that I was not there 18
20:20 the disciples were glad when they saw the Lord. 18
Act 2:26 my heart was glad, and my tongue rejoiced; 14
46 partook of food with glad and generous hearts 11
11:23 When he came and saw the grace of God, he was glad; 18
13:48 they were glad and glorified the word of God; 18
2Co 13: 9 we are glad when we are weak and you are strong. 18
Php 2:17 I am glad and rejoice with you all. 18
18 you also should be glad and rejoice with me. 18
Phm 1:13 I would have been glad to keep him with me 13
1Pe 4:13 that you may also rejoice and be glad 11
2Es 7:65 but let the beasts of the field be glad 20
98 and shall be glad without fear 19
Tob 13:13 Rejoice and be glad for the sons of the righteous 11
Sir 26: 4 Whether rich or poor, his heart is glad 10
31:27 It has been created to make men glad. 15
Bar 3:34 the stars shone in their watches, and were glad; 14
4:33 rejoiced at your fall and was glad for your ruin 14
2Mc 6:30 in my soul I am glad to suffer these things 16
9:20 I am glad *
10:33 Then Maccabeus and his men were glad 12

glad *See also* make, shout, song.

gladden 1. שׂמח 2. εὐφραίνω 3. ἱλαρύνω 4. μακαρίζω
Ps 86: 4 Gladden the soul of thy servant, for to thee, O Lord 1
104:15 wine to gladden the heart of man 1
Ecc 10:19 Bread is . . for laughter, and wine gladdens life 1
Sir 3: 5 will be gladdened by his own children 2
4:18 come straight back to him and gladden him 2
25: 7 With nine thoughts I have gladdened my heart 4
36:22 A woman's beauty gladdens the countenance 3
40:20 Wine and music gladden the heart 2
2Mc 15:27 were greatly gladdened by God's manifestation. 2

gladly 1. ἀσμένως 2. ἐπιθυμέω 3. ἡδέως 4. μετ' εὐφροσύνης
Mrk 6:20 yet he heard him gladly. 3
12:37 the great throng heard him gladly. 3
Lke 15:16 he would gladly have fed on the pods 2
Act 21:17 the brethren received us gladly. 1
2Co 11:19 For you gladly bear with fools, being wise 3
12: 9 I will all the more gladly boast of my weaknesses 3
1Mc 3: 2 they gladly fought for Israel. 4
2Mc 2:27 we will gladly endure the uncomfortable toil 3
3Mc 3:15 gladly treating them well. 1
4Mc 10:20 Gladly, for the sake of God 3

gladly *See also* adopt.

most gladly 1. ἡδέως
2Co 12:15 most gladly spend and be spent for your souls 1

gladness 1. טוב 2. מָשׂוֹשׂ 3. שִׂמְחָה 4. שָׂשׂוֹן 5. ἀγαλλίαμα 6. ἀγαλλίασις 7. εὐφροσύνη 8. χαρά 9. χαρμόσυνος 10. laetitia
Num 10:10 On the day of your gladness also 3
Deu 28:47 did not serve . . with . . gladness of heart 1
1Ch 29:22 ate and drank . . that day with great gladness. 3
2Ch 29:30 sang praises with gladness, and they bowed down 3
30:21 kept the feast . . with great gladness 3
23 kept it for another seven days with gladness. 3
Neh 12:27 celebrate the dedication with gladness 3
Est 8:16 Jews had light and gladness and joy and honor. 3
17 there was gladness and joy among the Jews, a feast 3
9:17 they . . made that a day of feasting and gladness. 3
18 making that a day of feasting and gladness. 3
19 for gladness and feasting and holiday-making 3
22 turned for them from sorrow into gladness 3
22 should make them days of feasting and gladness 3
Ps 30:11 loosed my sackcloth and girded me with gladness 3
45: 7 with the oil of gladness above your fellows; 4
15 With joy and gladness they are led along 3
51: 8 Fill me with joy and gladness; 3
100: 2 Serve the LORD with gladness! 3
106: 5 that I may rejoice in the gladness of thy nation 3
Prv 10:28 The hope of the righteous ends in gladness 3
Sng 3:11 on the day of the gladness of his heart. 3
Isa 16:10 joy and gladness are taken away 3
22:13 behold, joy and gladness, slaying oxen 3
24:11 all joy . . the gladness of the earth is banished. 2
30:29 gladness of heart, as when one sets out 3
35:10 they shall obtain joy and gladness 3
51: 3 joy and gladness will be found in her 3
11 they shall obtain joy and gladness 3
61: 3 the oil of gladness instead of mourning 4
65:14 my servants shall sing for gladness of heart 1
Jer 7:34 the voice of mirth and the voice of gladness 3
16: 9 the voice of mirth and the voice of gladness 3
25:10 the voice of mirth and the voice of gladness 3
31: 7 Sing aloud with gladness for Jacob 3
33:11 the voice of mirth and the voice of gladness 3
48:33 Gladness and joy have been taken away 3
Jol 1:12 and gladness fails from the sons of men. 4
16 joy and gladness from the house of our God? 3
Zep 3:17 he will rejoice over you with gladness 3
Zec 8:19 to the house of Judah seasons of joy and gladness 3
Lke 1:14 you will have joy and gladness 6
Act 2:28 make me full of gladness with thy presence.' 7
14:17 satisfying your hearts with food and gladness. 7
Heb 1: 9 has anointed thee with the oil of gladness 6
2Es 1:37 whose children rejoice with gladness 10
2: 3 I brought you up with gladness 10
15 embrace your sons; bring them up with gladness 10
AEs 10:13 with an assembly and joy and gladness before God 7
Wis 8:16 no pain, but gladness and joy. 7
Sir 1:11 gladness and a crown of rejoicing. 7
12 gives gladness and joy and long life. 7

6:31 put her on like a crown of gladness. 5
15: 6 He will find gladness and a crown of rejoicing 7
30:16 there is no gladness above joy of heart. 7
22 Gladness of heart is the life of man 7
31:28 rejoicing of heart and gladness of soul. 7
35: 9 dedicate your tithe with gladness. 7
50:23 May he give us gladness of heart 7
Bar 2:23 the voice of mirth and the voice of gladness 9
3:34 They shone with gladness for him who made them. 7
4:23 God will give you back to me with joy and gladness 7
1Mc 4:56 and offered burnt offerings with gladness 7
58 There was very great gladness among the people 7
59 observed with gladness and joy for eight days 7
5:54 they went up to Mount Zion with gladness and joy 7
7:48 celebrated that day as a day of great gladness. 7
10:66 returned to Jerusalem in peace and gladness. 7
2Mc 3:30 was filled with joy and gladness 7
3Mc 4: 1 was arranged . . with shouts and gladness 8

gladness *See also* know, shout.

glamour 1. species
2Es 15:46 you, Asia, who share in the glamour of Babylon 1

glance
Sng 4: 9 ravished my heart with a glance of your eyes *

glance wantonly 1. שׂקר
Isa 3:16 haughty . . glancing wantonly with their eyes 1

glass 1. זְכוֹכִית 2. ὑάλινος 3. ὕαλος
Job 28:17 Gold and glass cannot equal it 1
Rev 4: 6 there is as it were a sea of glass, like crystal. 2
15: 2 appeared to be a sea of glass mingled with fire 2
2 standing beside the sea of glass 2
21:18 while the city was pure gold, clear as glass. 3
21 street . . was pure gold, transparent as glass. 3

glaze
Prv 26:23 Like the glaze covering an earthen vessel *

glazing 1. χρῖσμα
Sir 38:30 he sets his heart to finish the glazing 1

gleam 1. עַיִן 2. ראה 3. καταυγάζω 4. φωτίζω
Ezk 1:16 was like the gleaming of a chrysolite; 1
27 I saw as it were gleaming bronze 1
8: 2 of brightness, like gleaming bronze. 1
Dan 10: 6 arms and legs like the gleam of burnished bronze 1
Nah 2: 4 they gleam like torches 2
Sir 43: 9 a gleaming array in the heights of the Lord. 4
50: 7 like the rainbow gleaming in glorious clouds; 4
1Mc 6:39 the hills . . gleamed like flaming torches. 3

gleaming *See* bronze.

glean 1. לקט 2. לקשׁ 3. עוֹלֵלוֹת 4. עלל 5. ἐπικαρπολογέω 6. καλαμάομαι
Deu 24:21 gather . . you shall not glean it afterward; 4
Jdg 8: 2 Is not the gleaning of the grapes of E′phraim 4
Rut 2: 2 and glean among the ears of grain after him 1
3 she set forth and went and gleaned in the field 1
7 Pray, let me glean and gather among the sheaves 1
8 do not go to glean in another field or leave this 1
15 When she rose to glean, Bo′az instructed his . . men 1
15 Let her glean even among the sheaves 1
16 also pull out some . . and leave it for her to glean 1
17 she gleaned in the field until evening; 1
17 then she beat out what she had gleaned 1
18 she showed her mother-in-law what she had gleaned 1
19 Where did you glean today? 1
23 she kept close . . gleaning until the end 1
Job 24: 6 they glean the vineyard of the wicked man. 2
Isa 17: 5 as when one gleans the ears of grain in the Valley 1
24:13 as at the gleaning when the vintage is done. 3
Jer 6: 9 Glean thoroughly as a vine the remnant of Israel; 4
Mic 7: 1 as when the vintage has been gleaned 4
Sir 33:16 like one who gleans after the grape-gatherers 6
4Mc 2: 9 he neither gleans his harvest 5

gleanings 1. לֶקֶט 2. עוֹלֵלוֹת
Lev 19: 9 gather the gleanings after your harvest 1
23:22 nor . . gather the gleanings after your harvest 1
Isa 17: 6 Gleanings will be left in it, as when an olive tree 2
Jer 49: 9 came to you, would they not leave gleanings? 2
Obd 1: 5 gatherers . . would they not leave gleanings? 2

glee 1. שׂמחה
Ps 35:15 But at my stumbling they gathered in glee 1

glen 1. מְצֻלָה
Zec 1: 8 standing among the myrtle trees in the glen; 1

glide away 1. הלך
Jer 46:22 She makes a sound like a serpent gliding away; 1

glide over 1. דבב
Sng 7: 9 goes down smoothly, gliding over lips and teeth. 1

glide past 1. חלף
Job 4:15 A spirit glided past my face; 1

glisten 1. στίλβω
Mrk 9: 3 garments became glistening, intensely white 1

glitter 1. אִבְחָה 2. בָּרָק 3. στίλβω
Deu 32:41 if I whet my glittering sword, and my hand 2
Ezk 21:15 I have given the glittering sword; 1
28 polished to glitter and to flash like lightning *
Nah 3: 3 flashing sword and glittering spear 2
Hab 3:11 at the flash of thy glittering spear. 2
1Es 8:57 bronze vessels . . that glittered like gold. 3

glittering *See* point.

gloat 1. ראה
Ps 22:17 they stare and gloat over me; 1
Lam 1: 7 foe gloated over her, mocking at her downfall. 1
Obd 1:12 you should not have gloated over . . your brother 1
13 you should not have gloated over his disaster 1
Mic 7:10 My eyes will gloat over her; 1

gloom 1. אֹפֶל 2. אֹפֶל 3. אֲפֵלָה 4. חֹשֶׁךְ 5. מוּעָף 6. מָעוּף 7. עֵיפָה 8. עֲרָפֶל 9. צַלְמָוֶת 10. γνόφος 11. ζόφος
Deu 4:11 mountain . . wrapped in darkness, cloud, and gloom. 8
Job 3: 5 Let gloom and deep darkness claim it. 4
10:21 not return, to the land of gloom and deep darkness 4
22 the land of gloom and chaos 7
28: 3 the ore in gloom and deep darkness. 2
34:22 There is no gloom or deep darkness 4
Ps 107:10 Some sat in darkness and in gloom, prisoners 9
14 he brought them out of darkness and gloom 9
Isa 8:22 distress and darkness, the gloom of anguish; 6
9: 1 there will be no gloom for her . . in anguish. 5
29:18 out of their gloom . . the eyes of the blind 2
58:10 in the darkness and your gloom be as the noonday. 3
59: 9 and for brightness, but we walk in gloom. 3
Jer 13:16 while you look for light he turns it into gloom 9
Jol 2: 2 a day of darkness and gloom, a day of clouds 3
Ams 5:20 and not light, and gloom with no brightness in it? 1
Zep 1:15 a day of darkness and gloom, a day of clouds 3
Heb 12:18 a blazing fire, and darkness, and gloom 11
2Pe 2: 4 God . . committed them to pits of nether gloom 11
17 the nether gloom of darkness has been reserved. 11
AEs 11: 8 behold, a day of darkness and gloom 10

gloom *See also* clothe.

nether gloom 1. ζόφος
Jde 1: 6 kept by him in eternal chains in the nether gloom 1
13 the nether gloom of darkness has been reserved 1

gloomy 1. ἀμείδητος 2. σκυθρωπός
Wis 17: 4 dismal phantoms with gloomy faces appeared. 1
Sir 25:23 A dejected mind, a gloomy face, and a wounded heart 2

glorification 1. δόξα
1Co 2: 7 before the ages for our glorification. 1

glorify 1. כבד 2. פאר 3. δοξάζω 4. ἐνδοξάζομαι 5. παραδοξάζω 6. συνδοξάζω 7. glorifico 8. gloriosus
Lev 10: 3 before all the people I will be glorified.′ 1
Ps 22:23 all you sons of Jacob, glorify him, and stand in awe 1
50:15 I will deliver you, and you shall glorify me. 1
86: 9 before thee, O Lord, and shall glorify thy name. 1
12 I will glorify thy name for ever. 1
Isa 25: 3 Therefore strong peoples will glorify thee; 1
26:15 thou art glorified; thou hast enlarged 1
44:23 redeemed Jacob, and will be glorified in Israel. 2
49: 3 my servant, Israel, in whom I will be glorified. 2
55: 5 the Holy One of Israel, for he has glorified you. 2
60: 7 and I will glorify my glorious house. 2
9 Holy One of Israel, because he has glorified you. 2
21 the work of my hands, that I might be glorified. 2
61: 3 planting of the LORD, that he may be glorified. 2
66: 5 said, ′Let the LORD be glorified, 1
Mat 9: 8 they glorified God, who had given such authority 3
15:31 and they glorified the God of Israel. 3
Mrk 2:12 so that they were all amazed and glorified God 3
Lke 2:20 glorifying and praising God 3
4:15 being glorified by all. 3
5:25 and went home, glorifying God. 3
26 they glorified God and were filled with awe 3
7:16 Fear seized them all; and they glorified God 3
18:43 and followed him, glorifying God 3
Joh 7:39 because Jesus was not yet glorified. 3
8:54 If I glorify myself, my glory is nothing 3
54 it is my Father who glorifies me 3
11: 4 the Son of God may be glorified by means of it. 3
12:16 when Jesus was glorified, then they remembered 3
23 The hour . . for the Son of man to be glorified. 3
28 Father, glorify thy name. 3
28 I have glorified it, and I will glorify it again. 3
28 I have glorified it, and I will glorify it again. 3
13:31 Now is the Son of man glorified 3
31 in him God is glorified; 3
32 if God is glorified in him 3
32 God will also glorify him in himself 3
32 and glorify him at once. 3
14:13 that the Father may be glorified in the Son; 3
15: 8 By this my Father is glorified 3
16:14 He will glorify me, for he will take what is mine 3
17: 1 Father, the hour has come; glorify thy Son 3
1 glorify thy Son that the Son may glorify thee 3
4 I glorified thee on earth 3
5 now, Father, glorify thou me in thy own presence 3
10 I am glorified in them. 3
21:19 to show by what death he was to glorify God 3
Act 3:13 glorified his servant Jesus 3
11:18 they glorified God, saying 3
13:48 they were glad and glorified the word of God; 3
21:20 when they heard it, they glorified God 3
Rom 8:17 in order that we may also be glorified with him. 6
30 and those whom he justified he also glorified. 3
15: 6 together you may with one voice glorify the God 3
9 the Gentiles might glorify God for his mercy. 3
1Co 6:20 So glorify God in your body. 3
2Co 9:13 glorify God by your obedience 3
Gal 1:24 they glorified God because of me. 3
2Th 1:10 comes on that day to be glorified in his saints 4
12 that the name of our Lord Jesus may be glorified 4
1Pe 2:12 and glorify God on the day of visitation. 3
4:11 God may be glorified through Jesus Christ. 3
16 but under that name let him glorify God. 3
Rev 15: 4 Who shall not fear and glorify thy name, O Lord? 3
18: 7 As she glorified herself and played the wanton 3
1Es 8:25 to glorify his house which is in Jerusalem 3
81 glorified the temple of our Lord 3
2Es 7:98 to receive their reward when glorified. 8
9:31 you shall be glorified through it for ever.′ 7
AEs 14: 7 because we glorified their gods 3
Wis 8: 3 She glorifies her noble birth by living with God 3
18: 8 thou didst call us to thyself and glorify us. 3
19:22 thou hast exalted and glorified thy people 3
Sir 3: 4 whoever glorifies his mother 3
6 Whoever glorifies his father will have 3
10 glorify yourself by dishonoring your father 3
20 he is glorified by the humble. 3
10:26 glorify yourself at a time when you are in want. 3
28 My son, glorify yourself with humility 3
35: 8 Glorify the Lord generously 3
38: 6 he might be glorified in his marvelous works. 4
45: 3 the Lord glorified him in the presence of kings. 3
47: 6 they glorified him for his ten thousands 3
Aza 1: 3 thy name is glorified for ever. 3
28 praised and glorified and blessed God 3
34 to be sung and glorified for ever. 3
2Mc 3: 2 glorified the temple with the finest presents 3
3Mc 2: 9 when you had glorified it 5

highly glorify 1. ὑπερένδοξος
Aza 1:31 to be extolled and highly glorified for ever. 1

glorious 1. אַדִּיר 2. אדר 3. אור 4. הדר 5. כבד 6. כָּבוֹד 7. צְבִי 8. תִּפְאָרָה 9. ἀοίδιμος 10. δόξα 11. δοξάζω 12. εἰς δόξαν 13. ἔνδοξος 14. εὐπρέπεια 15. μεγαλομερής 16. μεγαλοπρέπεια 17. μεγαλοπρεπής 18. φιλότιμος 19. splendidus
Exd 15: 6 Thy right hand, O LORD, glorious in power 2
Deu 28:58 that you may fear this glorious and awful name 5
1Ch 29:13 thank thee, our God, and praise thy glorious name 8
Neh 9: 5 Blessed be thy glorious name which is exalted 6
Ps 66: 2 give to him glorious praise! 6
72:19 Blessed be his glorious name for ever; 6
76: 4 Glorious art thou 3
145: 5 On the glorious splendor of thy majesty 6
12 make known . . glorious splendor of thy kingdom. 6
Isa 3: 8 their deeds . . defying his glorious presence. 6
4: 2 the branch . . shall be beautiful and glorious 6
11:10 seek, and his dwellings shall be glorious. 6
60: 7 and I will glorify my glorious house. 8
63: 1 he that is glorious in his apparel 4
12 who caused his glorious arm to go at the right 8
14 to make for thyself a glorious name. 8
15 and see, from thy holy and glorious habitation. 8
Jer 14:21 do not dishonor thy glorious throne; 6
17:12 A glorious throne set on high from the beginning 6
48:17 mighty scepter is broken, the glorious staff. 8
Ezk 20: 6 milk and honey, the most glorious of all lands. 7
15 milk and honey, the most glorious of all lands 7
Dan 8: 9 toward the east, and toward the glorious land. 7
11:16 stand in the glorious land, and all of it 7
41 He shall come into the glorious land. 7
45 between the sea and the glorious holy mountain; 7
Zec 11: 2 for the glorious trees are ruined! 1
Mat 19:28 the Son of man shall sit on his glorious throne 10
25:31 then he will sit on his glorious throne. 10
Rom 8:21 the glorious liberty of the children of God. 10
Eph 1: 6 to the praise of his glorious grace 10
18 what are the riches of his glorious inheritance 10
Php 3:21 to be like his glorious body 10
Col 1:11 with all power, according to his glorious might 10
1Ti 1:11 in accordance with the glorious gospel 10
2Es 2:39 have received glorious garments from the Lord. 19
Tob 8: 5 and blessed by thy holy and glorious name for ever. 13

14: 5 will be rebuilt there with a glorious building 13
Jdt 9: 8 the tabernacle where thy glorious name rests 10
16:13 O Lord, thou are great and glorious 13
Wis 5:16 Therefore they will receive a glorious crown 14
18: 3 a harmless sun for their glorious wandering. 18
Sir 6:29 her collar a glorious robe. 10
31 You will wear her like a glorious robe 10
17:13 Their eyes saw his glorious majesty 10
24:16 my branches are glorious and graceful. 10
17 blossoms became glorious and abundant fruit. 10
27: 8 will attain it and wear it as a glorious robe. 10
43:12 It encircles the heaven with its glorious arc; 10
45: 7 put a glorious robe upon him. 10
46: 2 How glorious he was when he lifted his hands 11
47: 6 when the glorious diadem was bestowed upon him. 10
48: 4 How glorious you were, O Elijah 11
50: 5 How glorious he was 11
7 like the rainbow gleaming in glorious clouds; 10
11 When he put on his glorious robe 10
Aza 1:22 the only God, glorious over the whole world. 13
30 blessed is thy glorious, holy name 10
Man 1: 3 sealed it with thy terrible and glorious name; 13
5 for thy glorious splendor cannot be borne 16
1Mc 2: 9 her glorious vessels 10
2Mc 8:15 called them by his holy and glorious name. 17
3Mc 2:14 holy place . . dedicated to your glorious name. 10
5: 8 in a glorious manifestation rescue them 15
6:18 two glorious angels of fearful aspect 11
4Mc 7: 9 through your glorious endurance 12
10: 1 When he too had endured a glorious death 9

glorious *See also* make, power.

glorious deed 1. תְּהִלָּה
Exd 15:11 terrible in glorious deeds, doing wonders? 1
Ps 78: 4 but tell . . the glorious deeds of the LORD 1

most glorious 1. *μεγαλόδοξος*
3Mc 6:18 the most glorious, almighty, and true God 1

glorious one 1. *δόξα*
2Pe 2:10 they are not afraid to revile the glorious ones 1
Jde 1: 8 reject authority, and revile the glorious ones. 1

glorious thing 1. כבד 2. *ἔνδοξος*
Ps 87: 3 Glorious things are spoken of you, O city of God. 1
Lke 13:17 all the glorious things that were done by him 2
1Es 1:56 utterly destroyed all its glorious things. 2

gloriously 1. גֵּאוּת 2. *δόξα* 3. *ἐνδόξως* 4. splendide
Exd 15: 1 to the LORD, for he has triumphed gloriously; †
21 Sing to the LORD, for he has triumphed gloriously; †
Isa 12: 5 praises to the LORD, for he has done gloriously; 1
2Es 8:29 regard those who have gloriously taught thy law. 4
Tob 12: 7 gloriously to reveal the works of God 3
11 gloriously to reveal the works of God.' 3
2Mc 3:26 gloriously beautiful and splendidly dressed 2

most gloriously 1. *μεγαλοδόξως*
3Mc 6:39 the Lord of all most gloriously revealed his mercy 1

glory 1. אַדֶּרֶת 2. אמר 3. הֶדֶר 4. הָדָר 5. הֲדָרָה 6. הוד 7. הלל 8. יְקָר 9. כבד 10. כָּבוֹד 11. נֵצַח 12. צְבִי 13. שׁבח 14. תִּפְאָרָה 15. יְקָר (A) 16. *ἀγαλλιάω* 17. *γαυρίαμα* 18. *γαυριάω* 19. *δόξα* 20. *κατακαυχάομαι* 21. *καυχάομαι* 22. *καύχημα* 23. claritas 24. gloria 25. glorior 26. honos
Exd 16: 7 in the morning you shall see the glory of the LORD 10
10 the glory of the LORD appeared in the cloud. 10
24:16 The glory of the LORD settled on Mount Sinai 10
17 the appearance of the glory of the LORD was like 10
28: 2 make holy garments . . for glory and for beauty. 10
40 you shall make them for glory and beauty. 10
29:43 it shall be sanctified by my glory; 10
33:18 Moses said, "I pray thee, show me thy glory. 10
22 while my glory passes by I will put you in a cleft 10
40:34 the glory of the LORD filled the tabernacle. 10
35 the glory of the LORD filled the tabernacle. 10
Lev 9: 6 the glory of the LORD will appear to you 10
23 the glory of the LORD appeared to all the people 10
Num14:10 Then the glory of the LORD appeared at the tent 10
21 earth shall be filled with the glory of the LORD 10
22 none of the men who have seen my glory and my signs 10
16:19 glory of the LORD appeared to all 10
42 covered it, and the glory of the LORD appeared. 10
20: 6 And the glory of the LORD appeared to them 10
Deu 5:24 LORD our God has shown us his glory and greatness 10
Jos 7:19 give glory to the LORD . . and render praise to him; 10
Jdg 4: 9 which you are going will not lead to your glory 14
1Sm 4:21 The glory has departed from Israel! 10
22 And she said, "The glory has departed from Israel 10
6: 5 make images . . and give glory to the God of Israel; 10
15:29 the Glory of Israel will not lie or repent; 11
2Sm 1:19 Thy glory, O Israel, is slain upon thy high places! 12
1Kg 8:11 glory of the LORD filled the house of the LORD. 10
2Kg 14:10 Be content with your glory, and stay at home; 9
1Ch 16:10 Glory in his holy name; 7
24 Declare his glory among the nations 10
28 ascribe to the LORD glory and strength! 10
29 Ascribe to the LORD the glory due his name; 10
35 give thanks . . and glory in thy praise. 13
22: 5 of fame and glory throughout all lands; 14
29:11 Thine, O LORD, is . . the glory, and the victory 14
2Ch 5:14 for the glory of the LORD filled the house of God. 10
7: 1 and the glory of the LORD filled the temple. 10
2 the glory of the LORD filled the LORD's house. 10
3 saw . . and the glory of the LORD upon the temple 10
Est 1: 4 while he showed the riches of his royal glory 10
Job 19: 9 He has stripped from me my glory 10
29:20 glory fresh with me, and my bow ever new in my hand 10
40:10 clothe yourself with glory and splendor. 6
Ps 3: 3 my glory, and the lifter of my head. 10
8: 1 Thou whose glory above the heavens is chanted 6
5 and dost crown him with glory and honor. 10
19: 1 The heavens are telling the glory of God; 10
21: 5 His glory is great through thy help; 10
24: 7 that the King of glory may come in. 10
8 Who is the King of glory? The LORD 10
9 that the King of glory may come in. 10
10 Who is the King of glory? The LORD of hosts, he is 10
10 The LORD of hosts, he is the King of glory! Selah 10
26: 8 thy house, and the place where thy glory dwells. 10
29: 1 ascribe to the LORD glory and strength. 10
2 Ascribe to the LORD the glory of his name; 10
3 God of glory thunders, the LORD, upon many waters. 10
9 in his temple all cry, "Glory! 10
37:20 of the LORD are like the glory of the pastures 8
45: 3 O mighty one, in your glory and majesty! 6
49:16 rich, when the glory of his house increases. 10
17 his glory will not go down after him. 10
57: 5 Let thy glory be over all the earth! 10
11 Let thy glory be over all the earth! 10
63: 2 in the sanctuary, beholding thy power and glory. 10
11 all who swear by him shall glory; 7
64:10 Let all the upright in heart glory! 7
66: 2 sing the glory of his name; 10
71: 8 with thy praise, and with thy glory all the day. 14
72:19 may his glory fill the whole earth! Amen and Amen! 10
73:24 afterward thou wilt receive me to glory. 10
78:61 his glory to the hand of the foe. 14
79: 9 O God of our salvation, for the glory of thy name; 10
85: 9 that glory may dwell in our land. 10
89:17 For thou art the glory of their strength; 14
96: 3 Declare his glory among the nations 10
7 ascribe to the LORD glory and strength! 10
8 Acribe to the LORD the glory due his name; 10
97: 6 all the peoples behold his glory. 10
102:15 all the kings of the earth, thy glory. 10
16 For the LORD . . will appear in his glory; 10
104:31 May the glory of the LORD endure for ever 10
105: 3 Glory in his holy name; 7
106: 5 that I may glory with thy heritage. 7
20 exchanged the glory of God for the image of an ox 10
47 that we may . . glory in thy praise. 13
108: 5 Let thy glory be over all the earth! 10
113: 4 his glory above the heavens. 10
115: 1 O LORD, not to us, but to thy name give glory 10
138: 5 for great is the glory of the LORD. 10
145:11 They shall speak of the glory of thy kingdom 10
148:13 his glory is above earth and heaven. 6
149: 5 Let the faithful exult in glory; 10
9 This is glory for all his faithful ones. 4
Prv 14:28 In a multitude of people is the glory of a king 5
16:31 A hoary head is a crown of glory; 14
17: 6 glory of sons is their fathers. 14
19:11 it is his glory to overlook an offense. 14
20:29 The glory of young men is their strength 14
25: 2 It is the glory of God to conceal things 10
2 but the glory of kings is to search things out. 10
28:12 When the righteous triumph, there is great glory; 14
Isa 2:10 and hide . . and from the glory of his majesty. 4
19 of the LORD, and from the glory of his majesty 4
21 the terror . . and from the glory of his majesty 4
4: 2 the pride and glory of the survivors of Israel. 14
5 over all the glory . . a canopy and a pavilion. 10
6: 3 the whole earth is full of his glory. 10
8: 7 the king of Assyria and all his glory; 10
10:16 and under his glory a burning will be kindled 10
18 The glory of his forest and of his fruitful land 10
13:19 Babylon, the glory of kingdoms, the splendor 12
14:18 All the kings of the nations lie in glory 10
16:14 the glory of Moab will be brought into contempt 10
17: 3 Syria . . like the glory of the children of Israel 10
4 in that day the glory of Jacob will be brought low 10
21:16 year . . all the glory of Kedar will come to an end; 10
23: 9 has purposed it, to defile the pride of all glory 12
24:16 songs of praise, of glory to the Righteous One. 12
23 before his elders he will manifest his glory. 10
28: 5 the LORD of hosts will be a crown of glory 12
35: 2 The glory of Lebanon shall be given to it 10
2 They shall see the glory of the LORD 10
40: 5 And the glory of the LORD shall be revealed 10
41:16 in the Holy One of Israel you shall glory. 7
42: 8 my glory I give to no other 10
12 Let them give glory to the LORD 10
43: 7 whom I created for my glory, whom I formed 10
45:25 the offspring of Israel shall triumph and glory. 7
46:13 I will put salvation in Zion, for Israel my glory. 14
48:11 My glory I will not give to another. 10
58: 8 the glory of the LORD shall be your rear guard. 10
59:19 and his glory from the rising of the sun; 10
60: 1 and the glory of the LORD has risen upon you. 10
2 and his glory will be seen upon you. 10
13 The glory of Lebanon shall come to you 10
19 and your God will be your glory. 14
61: 6 the nations, and in their riches you shall glory. 2
62: 2 your vindication, and all the kings your glory; 10
66:11 with delight from the abundance of her glory. 10
18 and they shall come and shall see my glory 10
19 that have not heard my fame or seen my glory; 10
19 they shall declare my glory among the nations. 10
Jer 2:11 But my people have changed their glory 10
4: 2 and in him shall they glory. 7
9:23 Let not the wise man glory in his wisdom 7
23 let not the mighty man glory in his might 7
23 let not the rich man glory in his riches; 7
24 but let him who glories glory in this 7
24 but let him who glories glory in this 7
13:11 might be for me a people, a name, a praise, and a glory 14
16 Give glory to the LORD your God 10
33: 9 and a glory before all the nations of the earth 14
48:18 Come down from your glory, and sit on the parched 10
Lam 3:18 I say, "Gone is my glory, and my expectation 11
Ezk 1:28 the likeness of the glory of the LORD. 10
3:12 and as the glory of the LORD arose from its place 10
23 and, lo, the glory of the LORD stood there 10
23 the glory which I had seen by the river Chebar; 10
8: 4 behold, the glory of the God of Israel was there 10
9: 3 Now the glory of the God of Israel had gone up 10
10: 4 the glory of the LORD went up from the cherubim 10
4 full of the brightness of the glory of the LORD. 10
18 Then the glory of the LORD went forth 10
19 the glory of the God of Israel was over them. 10
11:22 and the glory of the God of Israel was over them. 10
23 And the glory of the LORD went up from the midst 10
24:25 from them their stronghold, their joy and glory 14
25: 9 on its frontier, the glory of the country 12
31:18 Whom are you thus like in glory and in greatness 10
39:21 I will set my glory among the nations; 10
43: 2 the glory of the God of Israel came from the east; 10
2 the earth shone with his glory. 10
4 glory of the LORD entered the temple by the gate 10
5 behold, the glory of the LORD filled the temple. 10
44: 4 glory of the LORD filled the temple of the LORD; 10
Dan 2:37 given the . . power, and the might, and the glory. 15
4:30 by my mighty power . . for the glory of my majesty? 15
36 glory of my kingdom, my majesty and splendor 15
5:18 kingship and greatness and glory and majesty; 15
20 deposed . . and his glory was taken from him; 15
7:14 to him was given dominion and glory and kingdom 15
11:20 exactor . . through the glory of the kingdom; 3
Hos 4: 7 I will change their glory into shame. 10
18 they love shame more than their glory. •
9:11 E'phraim's glory shall fly away like a bird– 10
10: 5 over its glory which has departed from it. 10
Mic 1:15 the glory of Israel shall come to Adullam. 10
2: 9 from their young children you take away my glory 4
Hab 2:14 with the knowledge of the glory of the LORD 10
16 will be sated with contempt instead of glory. 10
16 and shame will come upon your glory! 10
3: 3 His glory covered the heavens 6
Hag 2: 3 among you that saw this house in its former glory? 10
Zec 2: 5 says the LORD, and I will be the glory within her. 10
8 after his glory sent me to the nations 10
10:12 they shall glory in his name," says the LORD. 20
11: 3 of the shepherds, for their glory is despoiled! 1
12: 7 Judah first, that the glory of the house of David 14
7 the glory of the inhabitants of Jerusalem may 14
Mal 2: 2 will not lay it to heart to give glory to my name 10
Mat 4: 8 the kingdoms of the world and the glory of them; 19
6:29 Solomon in all his glory was not arrayed like one 19
16:27 come with his angels in the glory of his Father 19
24:30 with power and great glory; 19
25:31 When the Son of man comes in his glory 19
Mrk 8:38 when he comes in the glory of his Father 19
10:37 one at your left, in your glory. 19
13:26 coming in clouds with great power and glory. 19
Lke 2: 9 the glory of the Lord shone around them 19
14 Glory to God in the highest 19
32 for glory to thy people Israel. 19
4: 6 I will give all this authority and their glory; 19
9:26 when he comes in his glory 19
26 the glory of the Father and of the holy angels. •
31 who appeared in glory and spoke of his departure 19
32 when they wakened they saw his glory 19
12:27 even Solomon in all his glory was not arrayed 19
19:38 Peace in heaven and glory in the highest! 19
21:27 coming in a cloud with power and great glory. 19
24:26 suffer these things and enter into his glory? 19
Joh 1:14 we have beheld his glory, glory as of the only Son 19
14 glory as of the only Son from the Father. 19
2:11 Jesus did at Cana . . and manifested his glory; 19
5:41 I do not receive glory from men. 19
44 who receive glory from one another 19
44 do not seek the glory that comes from the only God?. 19
7:18 He . . seeks his own glory 19
18 he who seeks the glory of him who sent him is true 19

8:50 Yet I do not seek my own glory 19
54 If I glorify myself, my glory is nothing 19
11: 4 it is for the glory of God 19
40 if you would believe you would see the glory of God? 19
12:41 because he saw his glory and spoke of him. 19
17: 5 glory which I had . . before the world was made. 19
22 The glory which thou hast given me 19
24 to behold my glory which thou hast given me 19
Act 7: 2 The God of glory appeared to our father Abraham 19
55 saw the glory of God 19
12:23 because he did not give God the glory 19
Rom 1:23 exchanged the glory of the immortal God 19
2: 7 seek for glory and honor and immortality 19
10 glory and honor and peace for every one 19
3: 7 if . . God's truthfulness abounds to his glory 19
23 all have sinned and fall short of the glory of God 19
4:20 grew strong in his faith as he gave glory to God 19
5: 2 we rejoice in our hope of sharing the glory of God. 19
6: 4 raised from the dead by the glory of the Father 19
8:18 the glory that is to be revealed to us. 19
9: 4 to them belong the sonship, the glory 19
23 in order to make known the riches of his glory 19
23 which he has prepared beforehand for glory 19
11:36 To him be glory for ever. Amen. 19
15: 7 Welcome one another . . for the glory of God. 19
16:27 to the only wise God be glory for evermore 19
1Co 2: 8 they would not have crucified the Lord of glory. 19
10:31 do all to the glory of God. 19
11: 7 since he is the image and glory of God 19
7 woman is the glory of man. 19
15:40 the glory of the celestial is one 19
40 the glory of the terrestrial is another. *
41 one glory of the sun, and another glory of the moon 19
41 one glory of the sun, and another glory of the moon 19
41 another glory of the stars 19
41 star differs from star in glory. 19
43 It is sown in dishonor, it is raised in glory. 19
2Co 1:20 the Amen through him, to the glory of God. 19
3:18 beholding the glory of the Lord 19
18 from one degree of glory to another 19
4: 4 the light of the gospel of the glory of Christ 19
6 the light of the knowledge of the glory of God 19
15 increase thanksgiving, to the glory of God. 19
17 preparing for us an eternal weight of glory 19
8:19 for the glory of the Lord and to show our good will. 19
23 messengers of the churches, the glory of Christ. 19
Gal 1: 5 to whom be the glory for ever and ever. Amen. 19
6:13 they may glory in your flesh. 21
14 far be it from me to glory except in the cross 21
Eph 1:12 to live for the praise of his glory. 19
14 to the praise of his glory. 19
17 God of our Lord Jesus Christ, the Father of glory 19
3:13 what I am suffering for you, which is your glory. 19
16 according to the riches of his glory 19
21 to him be glory in the church and in Christ Jesus 19
Php 1:11 to the glory and praise of God. 19
2:11 to the glory of God the Father. 19
3: 3 worship God in spirit, and glory in Christ Jesus 21
19 glory in their shame 19
4:19 his riches in glory in Christ Jesus. 19
20 To our God and Father be glory for ever and ever. 19
Col 1:27 the riches of the glory of this mystery 19
27 which is Christ in you, the hope of glory. 19
3: 4 you also will appear with him in glory. 19
1Th 2: 6 nor did we seek glory from men 19
12 who calls you into his own kingdom and glory. 19
20 For you are our glory and joy. 19
2Th 1: 9 exclusion . . from the glory of his might 19
2:14 may obtain the glory of our Lord Jesus Christ. 19
1Ti 1:17 be honor and glory for ever and ever. Amen. 19
3:16 believed on in the world, taken up in glory. 19
2Ti 2:10 salvation . . with its eternal glory. 19
4:18 To him be the glory for ever and ever. Amen. 19
Tit 2:13 the appearing of the glory of our great God 19
Heb 1: 3 He reflects the glory of God 19
2: 7 thou hast crowned him with glory and honor 19
9 crowned with glory and honor 19
10 in bringing many sons to glory 19
3: 3 counted worthy of . . much more glory than Moses 19
9: 5 above it were the cherubim of glory 19
13:21 to whom be glory for ever and ever. Amen. 19
Jas 2: 1 our Lord Jesus Christ, the Lord of glory. 19
1Pe 1: 7 faith . . may redound to praise and glory 19
11 sufferings of Christ and the subsequent glory. 19
21 who raised him from the dead and gave him glory 19
24 and all its glory like the flower of grass. 19
4:11 To him belong glory and dominion 19
13 and be glad when his glory is revealed. 19
14 the spirit of glory and of God rests upon you. 19
5: 1 a partaker in the glory that is to be revealed. 19
4 you will obtain the unfading crown of glory. 19
10 who has called you to his eternal glory in Christ 19
2Pe 1: 3 called us to his own glory and excellence 19
17 he received honor and glory from God the Father 19
17 the voice was borne to him by the Majestic Glory 19
3:18 To him be the glory both now and to . . eternity. 19
Jde 1:24 present you . . before the presence of his glory 19
25 to the only God . . be glory, majesty, dominion 19
Rev 1: 6 to him be glory and dominion for ever and ever. 19
4: 9 creatures give glory and honor and thanks to him 19
11 Lord and God, to receive glory and honor and power 19
5:12 to receive . . honor and glory and blessing! 19
13 to the Lamb be blessing and honor and glory 19
7:12 Blessing and glory and wisdom and thanksgiving 19
11:13 terrified and gave glory to the God of heaven. 19
14: 7 Fear God and give him glory 19
15: 8 smoke from the glory of God and from his power 19
16: 9 and they did not repent and give him glory. 19
19: 1 Salvation and glory and power belong to our God 19
7 Let us rejoice and exult and give him the glory 19
21:11 having the glory of God 19
23 for the glory of God is its light 19
24 the kings of the earth shall bring their glory 19
26 the glory and the honor of the nations. 19
1Es 4:17 Women make men's clothes; they bring men glory 19
59 thine is the glory. I am thy servant. 19
5:61 because his goodness and his glory are for ever 19
9: 8 give glory to the Lord the God of our fathers 19
2Es 2:11 Moreover, I will take back to myself their glory 24
36 receive the joy of your glory 24
3:19 thy glory passed through the four gates 24
7:42 only the splendor of the glory of the Most High 23
60 they who have made my glory to prevail now 24
78 first of all it adores the glory of the Most High. 24
87 at seeing the glory of the Most High 24
91 with great joy the glory of him who receives them 24
95 and the glory which awaits them in the last days. 24
112the full glory does not abide in it 24
122that the glory of the Most High will defend those 24
8:21 and whose glory is beyond comprehension 24
30 who have always put their trust in thy glory. 24
51 the glory of those who are like yourself 24
9:37 does not perish but remains in its glory. 26
10:23 for she has now lost the seal of her glory 24
50 has shown you the brilliance of her glory 24
15:46 the glamour . . and the glory of her person- 24
47 to please and glory in your lovers 25
50 the glory of your power shall wither 24
60 and abolish a portion of your glory 24
63 and abolish the glory of your countenance. 24
16:12 and before the glory of his power. 24
53 I have not sinned before God and his glory. 24
Tob 3:16 in the presence of the glory of the great God. 19
12:15 the presence of the glory of the Holy One. 19
13:14 will rejoice for you upon seeing all your glory 19
Jdt 9: 7 they glory in the strength of their foot soldiers; 18
10: 8 the people of Israel may glory 17
15: 9 you are the great glory of Israel 17
AEs 13:14 not set the glory of man above the glory of God 19
14 not set the glory of man above the glory of God 19
14: 9 to quench thy altar and the glory of thy house 19
15:13 my heart was shaken with fear at your glory. 19
Wis 7:25 a pure emanation of the glory of the Almighty; 19
8:10 I shall have glory among the multitudes 19
9:10 from the throne of thy glory send her 19
11 guard me with her glory. 19
15: 9 he counts it his glory 19
18:24 the glories of the fathers 19
Sir 1:11 The fear of the Lord is glory and exultation 19
19 he exalted the glory of those who held her fast. 19
3:10 your father's dishonor is no glory to you. 19
11 For a man's glory comes from honoring his father 19
4:13 Whoever holds her fast will obtain glory 19
21 there is a shame which is glory and favor. 19
5:13 Glory and dishonor come from speaking 19
9:16 let your glorying be in the fear of the Lord. 22
10:22 their glory is the fear of the Lord. 22
14:27 will dwell in the midst of her glory. 19
17:13 their ears heard the glory of his voice. 19
20:11 There are losses because of glory 19
24: 1 will glory in the midst of her people. 21
2 in the presence of his host she will glory. 21
29: 6 instead of glory will repay him with dishonor. 19
30: 3 will glory in him in the presence of friends. 16
36:14 Fill . . thy temple with thy glory. 19
38:25 who glories in the shaft of a goad 21
39: 8 will glory in the law of the Lord's covenant. 21
40:27 covers a man better than any glory. 19
42:16 the work of the Lord is full of his glory. 19
17 the universe may stand firm in his glory. 19
25 who can have enough of beholding his glory? 19
43: 1 the appearance of heaven in a spectacle of glory. 19
9 The glory of the stars is the beauty of heaven 19
44: 2 The Lord apportioned to them great glory 19
7 were the glory of their times. 22
13 their glory will not be blotted out. 19
19 no one has been found like him in glory; 19
45: 2 He made him equal in glory to the holy ones 19
3 showed him part of his glory. 19
20 He added glory to Aaron and gave him a heritage 19
23 Phinehas the son of Eleazar is the third in glory 19
26 their glory may endure 19
47: 8 with ascriptions of glory 19
11 a throne of glory in Israel. 19
49: 5 they gave . . their glory to a foreign nation 19
8 It was Ezekiel who saw the vision of glory 19
12 prepared for everlasting glory. 19
50:20 to glory in his name; 21
51:17 to him who gives wisdom I will give glory. 19
Bar 2:17 will not ascribe glory or justice to the Lord 19
18 will ascribe to thee glory and righteousness 19
4: 3 Do not give your glory to another 19
24 salvation . . will come to you with great glory 19
37 they are . . rejoicing in the glory of God. 19
5: 1 put on for ever the beauty of the glory from God. 19
2 the diadem of the glory of the Everlasting. 19
4 Peace of righteousness and glory of godliness. 19
6 carried in glory, as on a royal throne. 19
7 so that Israel may walk safely in the glory of God 19
9 lead Israel with joy, in the light of his glory 19
Aza 1:20 give glory to thy name, O Lord! 19
31 Blessed art thou in the temple of thy holy glory 19
Man 1:15 thine is the glory for ever. Amen. 19
1Mc 1:40 Her dishonor now grew as great as her glory 19
2:12 our beauty, and our glory have been laid waste 19
3: 3 He extended the glory of his people 19
12:12 we rejoice in your glory. 19
14: 9 youths donned the glories and garments of war. 19
21 told us about your glory and honor 19
29 they brought great glory to their nation. 19
35 glory which he had resolved to win for his nation 19
15: 9 so that your glory will become manifest 19
2Mc 2: 8 the glory of the Lord and the cloud will appear 19
5:16 to enhance the glory and honor of the place. 19
20 was restored again in all its glory 19
14: 7 Therefore I have laid aside my ancestral glory 19
3Mc 2: 9 the glory of your great and honored name. 19
16 you graciously bestowed your glory upon your people 19
4Mc 1:12 giving glory to the all-wise God. 19
18:24 to whom be glory for ever and ever. Amen. 19

glory *See also* appear, bring, gain, get, give, love, manifest, receive.

cause to glory 1. *καύχημα*
Php 1:26 ample cause to glory in Christ Jesus 1

show glory 1. כבד
Ezk 39:13 on the day that I show my glory, says the Lord GOD. 1

glow 1. *αὐγή* 2. *ἐκκαίω*
Sir 28:12 If you blow on a spark, it will glow 2
2Mc 12: 9 the glow of the light was seen in Jerusalem 1

glowing *See* coal.

glue together 1. *συγκολλάω*
Sir 22: 7 like one who glues potsherds together 1

glutton 1. זלל 2. *ἄπληστος* 3. *γαστήρ* 4. *γαστρίμαργος* 5. *φάγος*
Deu 21:20 This our son . . is a glutton and a drunkard.' 1
Prv 23:21 drunkard and the glutton will come to poverty 1
28: 7 but a companion of gluttons shames his father. 1
Mat 11:19 and they say, 'Behold, a glutton and a drunkard 5
Lke 7:34 and you say, 'Behold, a glutton and a drunkard 5
Tit 1:12 are always liars, evil beasts, lazy gluttons. 3
Sir 31:20 nausea and colic are with the glutton. 2
4Mc 2: 7 habitually a solitary gormandizer, a glutton 4

gluttonous *See* eater.

gluttony 1. *ἀπληστία* 2. *γαστριμαργία* 3. *κοιλίας ὄρεξις* 4. *λαιμαργία* 5. *λιχνεία*
Sir 23: 6 Let neither gluttony nor lust overcome me 3
37:30 gluttony leads to nausea. 1
31 Many have died of gluttony 1
3Mc 6:36 not for drinking and gluttony 5
4Mc 1: 3 namely, gluttony and lust 2
27 gluttony, and solitary gormandizing. 4

gnash 1. חרק 2. *βρυγμός* 3. *γομφιάζω*
Job 16: 9 he has gnashed his teeth at me; 1
Ps 35:16 more and more, gnashing at me with their teeth. 1
37:12 The wicked . . gnashes his teeth at him; 1
112:10 wicked man . . gnashes his teeth and melts away; 1
Lam 2:16 your enemies . . they hiss, they gnash their teeth 1
Mat 8:12 there men will weep and gnash their teeth. 2
13:42 there men will weep and gnash their teeth. 2
50 there men will weep and gnash their teeth. 2
22:13 there men will weep and gnash their teeth.' 2
24:51 there men will weep and gnash their teeth. 2
25:30 there men will weep and gnash their teeth.' 2
Lke 13:28 There you will weep and gnash your teeth 2
Sir 30:10 in the end you will gnash your teeth. 3

gnashing of teeth 1. *βρυγμός*
Sir 51: 3 from the gnashings of teeth about to devour me 1

gnat 1. כֵּן 2. מוֹכֵן 3. *κώνωψ* 4. *σκνίψ*
Exd 8:16 that it may become gnats throughout all the land 1
17 and there came gnats on man and beast; 1
17 dust of the earth became gnats throughout all 1
18 tried by their secret arts to bring forth gnats 1
18 So there were gnats on man and beast. 1
Ps 105:31 flies, and gnats throughout their country. 1
Isa 51: 6 and they who dwell in it will die like gnats; 2
Mat 23:24 straining out a gnat and swallowing a camel! 3
Wis 19:10 how . . the earth brought forth gnats 4

gnaw 1. ערק 2. *μασάομαι*

Job 30: 3 they gnaw the dry and desolate ground; 1
17 the pain that gnaws me takes no rest. 1
Rev 16:10 men gnawed their tongues in anguish 2

gnaw a bone 1. עצם

Jer 50:17 king of Babylon has gnawed his bones. 1

go 1. אבד 2. אזל 3. אַיִן 4. אפס 5. ארח 6. אֲשׁוּר 7. בוא 8. גוז 9. גלה 10. דרך 11. דֶּרֶךְ 12. היה 13. הֲלִיכָה 14. הלך 15. חלף 16. יסף 17. יצא 18. ירד 19. כלה 20. לוה 21. מַהֲלָךְ 22. מוֹצָא 23. נגשׁ 24. נסע 25. סור 26. עבר 27. עזב 28. עלה 29. עשׂה 30. פתח 31. צעד 32. קום 33. קרב 34. ראה 35. רפה 36. שׁוב 37. שׁלח 38. שׂרה 39. תמם 40. אזל (A) 41. אתא (A) 42. הלך (A) 43. עבד (A) 44. עלל (A) 45. ἄγω 46. ἀκόλουθος 47. ἀναβαίνω 48. ἀναζεύγνυμι 49. ἀναλύω 50. ἀνίημι 51. ἄπειμι 52. ἀπέρχομαι 53. ἀποίχομαι 54. ἀπολύω 55. ἀποσπάω 56. ἀποτρέχω 57. ἄρχω 58. ἀφίημι 59. βαδίζω 60. γίνομαι 61. δεῦρο 62. διαγίνομαι 63. διαπορεύομαι 64. διεξίημι 65. διέρχομαι 66. ἐάω 67. εἰμί 68. εἰς 69. εἰσάγω 70. εἴσειμι 71. εἰσέρχομαι 72. εἰσπορεύομαι 73. ἐκπίπτω 74. ἐκπορεύω 75. ἐνεργέω 76. ἐξαφίημι 77. ἐξέρχομαι 78. ἐξέρχομαι καὶ εἰσέρχομαι 79. ἐπιβαίνω 80. ἐπιπορεύομαι 81. ἔρχομαι 82. ἐφίστημι 83. ἥκω 84. ἵημι 85. μεθίστημι 86. μέλλω 87. μεταβαίνω 88. ὁδός 89. οἴχομαι 90. παραγίνομαι 91. παραπορεύομαι 92. παρέρχομαι 93. παρίημι 94. περιπατέω 95. ποιέω 96. πορεία 97. πορεύω 98. προβαίνω 99. προέρχομαι 100. προκόπτω 101. προσέρχομαι 102. πρότερον 103. στέλλω 104. συμπορεύομαι 105. συνέρχομαι 106. ὑπάγω 107. φέρω 108. abeo 109. ambulo 110. contingo 111. eo 112. ingredior 113. introeo 114. pertranseo 115. praetereo 116. proficio 117. proficiscor 118. transeo 119. vado 120. venio

Gen 3:14 upon your belly you shall go 14
7: 1 Then the LORD said to Noah, "Go into the ark 7
7 wife and his sons' wives with him went into the ark 7
9 two and two, male and female, went into the ark 7
15 They went into the ark with Noah 7
16 of all flesh, went in as God had commanded him; 7
8: 7 sent forth a raven; and it went to and fro 17
10:11 From that land he went into Assyria 17
11:31 of the Chalde'ans to go into the land of Canaan; 14
12: 1 Now the LORD said to Abram, "Go from your country 14
4 Abram went, as the LORD had told him; 14
4 and Lot went with him. 14
5 and they set forth to go to the land of Canaan. 14
9 still going toward the Negeb. 24
19 Now then, here is your wife, take her, and be gone. 14
13: 5 Lot, who went with Abram, also had flocks and herds 14
14:11 all their provisions, and went their way; 14
24 the share of the men who went with me; 14
15:15 you shall go to your fathers in peace; 7
16: 2 me from bearing children; go in to my maid; 7
4 he went in to Hagar, and she conceived; 7
8 you come from and where are you going? 14
18:16 looked toward Sodom; and Abraham went with them 14
22 the men turned from there, and went toward Sodom; 14
33 the LORD went his way, when he had finished 14
19: 2 then you may rise up early and go on your way. 14
33 the first-born went in, and lay with her father; 7
34 then you go in and lie with him 7
21:15 When the water in the skin was gone 19
16 Then she went, and sat down over against him 14
19 well of water; and she went, and filled the skin 14
22: 2 and go to the land of Mori'ah 14
3 Abraham . . arose and went to the place 14
5 I and the lad will go yonder and worship 14
6 they went both of them together. 14
8 So they went both of them together. 14
13 and Abraham went and took the ram 14
19 they arose and went together to Beer-sheba; 14
23: 2 and Abraham went in to mourn for Sarah and to weep 7
10 the Hittites, of all who went in at the gate 7
18 before all who went in at the gate of his city. 7
24: 4 will go to my country and to my kindred 14
10 and he arose, and went to Mesopota'mia 14
30 Thus the man spoke to me," he went to the man; 7
38 you shall go to my father's house and to my kindred 14
42 if now thou wilt prosper the way which I go 14
51 Behold, Rebekah is before you, take her and go 14
55 at least ten days; after that she may go. 14
56 let me go that I may go to my master. 37
56 let me . . that I may go to my master. 14
58 Will you go with this man?" She said, "I will go. 14
58 Will you go with this man?" She said, "I will go. 14
61 thus the servant took Rebekah, and went his way. 14
25:22 why do I live?" So she went to inquire of the LORD. 14
34 and he ate and drank, and rose and went his way. 14
26: 1 And Isaac went to Gerar, to Abim'elech 14
26 Then Abim'elech went to him from Gerar 14
27: 5 when Esau went to the field to hunt for game 14
9 Go to the flock, and fetch me two good kids 14
13 only obey my word, and go, fetch them to me. 14
14 he went and took them and brought them 14
18 he went in to his father, and said, "My father"; 7
28: 2 Arise, go to Paddan-aram to the house of Bethu'el 14
5 Isaac sent Jacob away; and he went to Paddan-aram 14
7 Jacob had . . gone to Paddan-aram. 14
9 Esau went to Ish'mael and took to wife 14
10 Jacob left Beer-sheba, and went toward Haran. 14
15 I am with you and will keep you wherever you go 14
20 will keep me in this way that I go, and will give me 14
29: 7 water the sheep, and go, pasture them. 14
21 Give me my wife that I may go in to her 7
23 brought her to Jacob; and he went in to her. 7
30 Jacob went in to Rachel also, and he loved Rachel 7
30: 3 Then she said, "Here is my maid Bilhah; go in to her 7
4 Bilhah as a wife; and Jacob went in to her. 7
14 Reuben went and found mandrakes in the field 14
25 that I may go to my own home and country. 14
26 for whom I have served you, and let me go; 14
31:18 to go to the land of Canaan to his father Isaac. 7
19 Laban had gone to shear his sheep 14
33 Laban went into Jacob's tent, and into Leah's 7
32: 1 Jacob went on his way and the angels of God met him; 14
17 To whom do you belong? Where are you going? 14
20 appease him with the present that goes before me 14
26 Then he said, "Let me go, for the day is breaking. 37
26 I will not let you go, unless you bless me. 37
33: 3 He himself went on before them, bowing himself 26
12 Let us journey on our way, and I will go before you. 14
34:17 we will take our daughter, and we will be gone. 14
35: 3 God who . . has been with me wherever I have gone. 14
22 Reuben went and lay with Bilhah 14
36: 6 and he went into a land away from his brother 14
37:12 Now his brothers went to pasture their father's 14
14 he said to him, "Go now, see if it is well 14
17 away, for I heard them say, 'Let us go to Dothan.' 14
17 Joseph went after his brothers, and found them 14
30 The lad is gone; and I, where shall I go? 3
30 The lad is gone; and I, where shall I go? 7
38: 2 he married her and went in to her 7
8 Judah said to Onan, "Go in to your brother's wife 7
9 when he went in to his brother's wife he spilled 7
11 Tamar went and dwelt in her father's house. 14
18 he gave them to her, and went in to her 7
41:55 said to all the Egyptians, "Go to Joseph; 14
42:15 you shall not go from this place 17
19 and let the rest go and carry grain for the famine 14
33 take grain . . and go your way. 14
43: 8 Send the lad with me, and we will arise and go 14
44: 4 they had gone but a short distance from the city 17
26 If our youngest brother goes with us, then we will •
45:17 Do this: load your beasts and go back to the land 14
28 I will go and see him before I die. 14
47: 1 Joseph went in and told Pharaoh, 7
15 Give us food . . For our money is gone. 4
16 exchange for your cattle, if your money is gone. 4
48: 7 there was still some distance to go to Ephrath; 7
Exd 2: 1 Now a man from the house of Levi went and took 14
7 Shall I go and call you a nurse from the Hebrew 14
8 said to her, "Go." So the girl went and called 14
8 So the girl went and called the child's mother. 14
3:11 said to God, "Who am I that I should go to Pharaoh 14
16 Go and gather the elders of Israel together 14
18 you and the elders of Israel shall go to the king 7
18 and now, we pray you, let us go a three days' journey 14
19 king of Egypt will not let you go unless 14
20 after that he will let you go. 37
21 and when you go, you shall not go empty 14
21 and when you go, you shall not go empty 14
4:12 Now therefore go, and I will be with your mouth 14
18 Moses went back to Jethro his father-in-law 14
18 And Jethro said to Moses, "Go in peace. 14
21 so that he will not let the people go. 37
23 I say to you, "Let my son go that he may serve me"; 37
23 if you refuse to let him go, behold, I will slay 37
27 The LORD said to Aaron, "Go into the wilderness 14
27 So he went, and met him at the mountain of God 14
29 Then Moses and Aaron went and gathered together 14
5: 1 Afterward Moses and Aaron went to Pharaoh 7
1 Thus says the LORD . . 'Let my people go 37
2 that I should . . let Israel go? 37
2 and moreover I will not let Israel go. 37
3 let us go, we pray, a three days' journey 14
7 let them go and gather straw for themselves. 14
8 therefore they cry, "Let us go and offer sacrifice 14
11 Go yourselves, get your straw wherever you can 14
17 idle; therefore you say, 'Let us go and sacrifice 14
18 Go now, and work; for no straw shall be given you 14
6:11 Go in, tell Pharaoh king of Egypt to let the people 7
11 tell Pharaoh . . to let the people of Israel go 37
7: 2 shall tell Pharaoh to let the people of Israel go 37
10 So Moses and Aaron went to Pharaoh and did 7
14 Pharaoh . . refuses to let the people go. 37
15 Go to Pharaoh in the morning, as he is going out 14
16 LORD . . sent me to you, saying, "Let my people go 37
23 Pharaoh turned and went into his house 7
8: 1 LORD said to Moses, "Go in to Pharaoh and say to him 7
1 say to him, 'Thus says the LORD, "Let my people go 37
2 if you refuse to let them go, behold, I will plague 37
8 and I will let the people go to sacrifice 37
20 say to him, 'Thus says the LORD, "Let my people go 37
21 if you will not let my people go . . I will send swarms 37
25 Pharaoh . . said, "Go, sacrifice to your God within 14
27 We must go three days' journey 14
28 So Pharaoh said, "I will let you go, to sacrifice 37
29 deal falsely again by not letting the people go 37
32 Pharaoh . . and did not let the people go. 37
9: 1 Then the LORD said to Moses, "Go in to Pharaoh 7
1 Thus says the LORD . . "Let my people go 37
2 For if you refuse to let them go and still hold 37
10: 1 Then the LORD said to Moses, "Go in to Pharaoh; 7
3 Moses and Aaron went in to Pharaoh, and said to him 7
3 Let my people go, that they may serve me. 37
4 For if you refuse to let my people go, behold 37
7 Let the men go, that they may serve the LORD 37
8 Pharaoh; and he said to them, "Go, serve the LORD 14
8 Go, serve the LORD your God; but who are to go? 14
9 Moses said, "We will go with our young and our old; 14
9 we will go with our sons and daughters 14
10 if ever I let you and your little ones go! 37
11 No! Go, the men among you, and serve the LORD 14
20 he did not let the children of Israel go. 37
24 Pharaoh called Moses, and said, "Go, serve the LORD; 14
24 serve the LORD; your children also may go with you; 14
26 Our cattle also must go with us; 14
27 Pharaoh's heart, and he would not let them go. 37
11: 1 one plague more . . afterwards he will let you go 37
1 when he lets you go, he will drive you away 37
10 let the people of Israel go out of his land. 37
12:28 Then the people of Israel went and did so; 14
31 go, serve the LORD, as you have said. 14
32 flocks and your herds, as you have said, and be gone; 14
13:15 For when Pharaoh stubbornly refused to let us go 37
17 When Pharaoh let the people go, God did not lead 37
21 the LORD went before them by day in a pillar 14
14: 5 that we have let Israel go from serving us? 37
16 Israel may go on dry ground through the sea. 7
17 the Egyptians so that they shall go in after them 7
19 angel of God who went before the host of Israel 14
19 the angel . . moved and went behind them; 14
22 the people of Israel went into the midst 7
23 The Egyptians pursued, and went in after them 7
15:19 chariots and his horsemen went into the sea 7
22 they went into the wilderness of Shur; 17
22 they went three days in the wilderness 14
17: 5 take in your hand the rod . . and go. 14
18: 7 and they . . went into the tent. 7
23 all this people also will go to their place 7
27 and he went his way to his own country. 14
19:10 the LORD said to Moses, "Go to the people 14
21:26 he shall let the slave go free for the eye's sake. 37
27 shall let the slave go free for the tooth's sake. 37
23:23 When my angel goes before you, and brings you 14
24:14 whoever has a cause, let him go to them. 23
28:29 when he goes into the holy place, to bring them 7
30 when he goes in before the LORD; 7
35 shall be heard when he goes into the holy place 7
43 when they go into the tent of meeting 7
30:20 When they go into the tent of meeting, or when they 7
32: 1 said to him, "Up, make us gods, who shall go before us; 14
23 For they said to me, 'Make us gods, who shall go 14
34 now go, lead the people to the place of which I have 14
34 behold, my angel shall go before you. 14
33: 8 Moses, until he had gone into the tent. 7
14 he said, "My presence will go with you, and I will 14
15 If thy presence will not go with me, do not carry us 14
16 Is it not in thy going with us, so that we are 14
34: 9 let the Lord, I pray thee, go in the midst of us 14
12 inhabitants of the land whither you go 7
34 whenever Moses went in before the LORD to speak 7
35 until he went in to speak with him. 7
40:32 when they went into the tent of meeting 7
Lev 9:23 Moses and Aaron went into the tent of meeting 7
10: 9 no wine . . when you go into the tent of meeting 7
11:20 All winged insects that go upon all fours are 14
21 Yet among the winged insects that go on all fours 14
27 all that go on their paws, among the animals 14
27 among the animals that go on all fours 14
42 Whatever goes on its belly 14
42 whatever goes on all fours 14
14: 7 shall let the living bird go into the open field 37
36 before the priest goes to examine the disease 7
36 afterward the priest shall go in to see the house 7
44 then the priest shall go and look 7
53 he shall let the living bird go out of the city 37
16:22 he shall let the goat go in the wilderness 37
23 which he put on when he went into the holy place 7
26 he who lets the goat go to Aza'zel shall wash 37
19:16 You shall not go up and down as a slanderer 14
21:11 he shall not go in to any dead body, nor defile 7
24: 7 it may go with the bread as a memorial portion 12
Num 4: 5 Aaron and his sons shall go in and take down 7
19 Aaron and his sons shall go in and appoint them 7
20 they shall not go in to look upon the holy things 7
5: 8 restitution for wrong shall go to the LORD •

7:89 when Moses went into the tent of meeting to speak 7
8: 7 let them go with a razor over all their body 26
15 Levites shall go in to do service at the tent 7
22 Levites went in to do their service in the tent 7
24 shall go in to perform the work in the service 7
10: 9 go to war in your land against the adversary 7
30 he said to him, "I will not go; I will depart 14
32 if you go with us, whatever good the LORD will do 14
33 ark . . went before them three days' journey 24
13:32 The land, through which we have gone, to spy it out 26
14:14 thou goest before them, in a pillar of cloud by day 14
24 I will bring into the land into which he went 7
38 of those men who went to spy out the land. 14
16: 3 You have gone too far! For all the congregation *
7 You have gone too far, sons of Levi! *
25 Then Moses rose and went to Dathan and Abi'ram; 14
17: 8 morrow Moses went into the tent of the testimony; 7
20: 6 Moses . . went from the presence of the assembly 7
21:18 from the wilderness they went on to Mat'tanah *
22 we will go by the King's Highway, until we have 14
22:12 God said to Balaam, "You shall not go with them; 14
13 Go to your own land; for the LORD has refused 14
13 for the LORD has refused to let me go with you. 14
14 princes of Moab rose and went to Balak, and said 7
20 If the men have come to call you, rise, go with them; 14
21 Balaam . . went with the princes of Moab. 14
22 God's anger was kindled because he went; 14
23 ass turned aside . . and went into the field; 14
35 angel of the LORD said to Balaam, "Go with the men; 14
35 So Balaam went on with the princes of Balak. 14
39 Then Balaam went with Balak, and they came 14
23: 3 Stand beside your burnt offering, and I will go; 14
3 And he went to a bare height. 14
24: 1 he did not go, as at other times, to look for omens 14
14 now, behold, I am going to my people; 14
25 Then Balaam rose, and went back to his place; 14
25 Balak also went his way. 14
25: 8 went after the man of Israel into the inner room 7
31: 3 Arm men . . that they may go against Mid'ian 12
21 said to the men of war who had gone to battle 7
32: 6 your brethren go to the war while you sit here? 7
9 discouraged . . Israel from going into the land 7
20 take up arms to go before the LORD for war *
39 sons of Machir the son of Manas'seh went to Gilead 14
41 Ja'ir . . of Manas'seh went and took their villages 14
42 Nobah went and took Kenath and its villages 14
33: 8 went a three days' journey in the wilderness of Etham 14
34: 4 Ka'desh-bar'nea; then it shall go on to Ha'zar-ad'dar 17
Deu 1: 7 go to the hill country of the Amorites, and to all 7
8 go in and take possession of the land 7
19 went through all that great and terrible 14
30 LORD your God who goes before you will . . fight 14
31 LORD . . bore you, . . , in all the way that you went 14
33 who went before you in the way to seek you out 14
33 went . . to show you by what way you should go 14
37 angry . . and said, 'You also shall not go in there; 7
39 your children . . shall go in there 7
2: 7 knows your going through this great wilderness; 14
8 we went on, away from our brethren the sons of Esau 26
8 And we turned and went in the direction 26
27 pass through your land; I will go only by the road 14
4: 1 live, and go in and take possession of the land 7
34 has any god ever attempted to go and take a nation 7
5:30 Go and say to them, "Return to your tents. 14
6:14 You shall not go after other gods 14
18 that you may go in and take possession 7
8: 1 that you may . . go in and possess the land 7
19 forget . . and go after other gods and serve them 14
9: 1 to go in to dispossess nations greater 7
5 are you going in to possess their land; 7
10:11 Arise, go on your journey at the head of the people 14
11 that they may go in and possess the land 7
11: 8 and go in and take possession of the land 7
28 to go after other gods which you have not known. 14
31 pass over . . to go in to take possession of the land 7
12: 5 thither you shall go 7
26 take, and you shall go to the place which the LORD 7
29 cuts off . . nations whom you go in to dispossess 7
13: 2 if he says, 'Let us go after other gods,' 14
6 entices . . saying, 'Let us go and serve other gods,' 14
13 go and serve other gods,' which you have not known 14
14:25 go to the place which the LORD your God chooses 14
15:12 in the seventh year you shall let him go free 37
13 when you let him go free from you 37
13 you shall not let him go empty-handed; 37
18 not seem hard to you, when you let him go free 37
16: 7 morning you shall turn and go to your tents. 14
17: 3 gone and served other gods and worshipped them 14
19: 5 when a man goes into the forest with his neighbor 7
20: 4 LORD your God is he that goes with you, to fight 14
5 Let him go back to his house, lest he die 14
6 Let him go back to his house, lest he die 14
7 Let him go back to his house, lest he die 14
8 Let him go back to his house, lest the heart 14
21:13 after that you may go in to her, and be her husband 7
14 let her go where she will 37
22: 7 let the mother go, but the young you may take 37
13 takes a wife, and goes in to her, and then spurns her 7
23:10 not clean . . then he shall go outside the camp 17

24 When you go into your neighbor's vineyard 7
25 When you go into your neighbor's standing grain 7
24: 2 if she goes and becomes another man's wife 14
10 shall not go into his house to fetch his pledge. 7
25: 3 if one should go on to beat him with more stripes 16
5 husband's brother shall go in to her, and take her 7
26: 2 basket, and . . go to the place which the LORD 14
3 go to the priest who is in office at that time 7
28:14 do not turn . . to go after other gods to serve 14
41 not be yours; for they shall go into captivity. 14
29:18 turns . . to go and serve the gods of those nations; 14
26 went and served other gods and worshiped them 14
31: 6 for it is the LORD your God who goes with you; 14
7 for you shall go with this people into the land 7
8 LORD who goes before you; he will be with you 14
14 Moses and Joshua went and presented themselves 14
16 land, where they go to be among them 7
32:36 when he sees that their power is gone 2
52 you shall see . . but you shall not go there 7
Jos 1: 7 that you may have good success wherever you go. 14
9 for the LORD your God is with you wherever you go. 14
11 to go in to take possession of the land 7
16 and wherever you send us we will go. 14
2: 1 saying, "Go, view the land, especially Jericho. 14
1 And they went, and came into the house of a harlot 14
5 the men went out; where the men went I do not know; 14
16 Go into the hills, lest the pursuers meet you; 14
16 then afterward you may go your way. 14
22 They departed, and went into the hills 7
3: 4 follow it, that you may know the way you shall go 14
6 took up the ark . . and went before the people. 14
5:13 and Joshua went to him and said to him, "Are you 14
6: 9 And the armed men went before the priests 14
13 and the armed men went before them 14
23 the young men . . went in, and brought out Rahab 7
8: 9 and they went to the place of ambush 14
9: 4 and went and made ready provisions, and took 14
6 they went to Joshua in the camp at Gilgal, and said 14
11 Take provisions . . and go to meet them 14
10:24 the chiefs of the men of war who had gone with him 14
14:11 my strength . . for war, and for going and coming. 17
16: 1 allotment . . went from the Jordan by Jericho 17
2 then going from Bethel to Luz, it passes along 17
8 the boundary goes westward to the brook Kanah 14
17: 7 then the boundary goes along southward 14
9 boundary . . goes on the north side of the brook *
18: 3 be slack to go in and take possession of the land 7
8 charged those who went to write the description 14
9 So the men went and passed up and down in the land 14
15 and the boundary goes from there to Ephron 17
17 then it bends . . going on to En-she'mesh 17
17 going on to En-she'mesh, and thence goes 17
19:12 thence it goes to Dab'erath, then up to Japhi'a; 17
13 and going on to Rimmon it bends toward Ne'ah; 17
27 it goes to Beth-dagon, and touches Zeb'ulun *
34 boundary turns . . and goes from there to Hukkok 17
21:10 cities . . which went to the descendants of Aaron 12
22: 4 therefore turn and go to your home in the land 14
6 and they went to their homes. 14
9 parting . . to go to the land of Gilead 14
23:16 and go and serve other gods and bow down to them. 14
24:17 and preserved us in all the way that we went 14
Jdg 1: 3 I likewise will go with you into the territory 14
3 So Simeon went with him. 14
10 Judah went against the Canaanites who dwelt 14
11 they went against the inhabitants of Debir. 14
16 Arad; and they went and settled with the people. 14
17 Judah went with Simeon his brother 14
25 sword, but they let the man and all his family go. 37
26 the man went to the land of the Hittites and built 14
2: 6 the people of Israel went each to his 14
12 they went after other gods, from among the gods 14
19 worse than their fathers, going after other gods 14
3:13 and went and defeated Israel; and they took 14
22 the hilt also went in after the blade, and the fat 7
24 When he had gone, the servants came; 17
4: 6 commands you, 'Go, gather your men at Mount Tabor 14
8 Barak said to her, "If you will go with me, I will go; 14
8 Barak said to her, "If you will go with me, I will go; 14
8 but if you will not go with me, I will not go. 14
8 but if you will not go with me, I will not go. 14
9 she said, "I will surely go with you; nevertheless 14
9 the road on which you are going will not lead 14
9 Deb'orah arose, and went with Barak to Kedesh. 14
21 took a hammer in her hand, and went softly to him 7
22 So he went in to her tent; and there lay Sis'era dead 7
6:14 said, "Go in this might of yours and deliver Israel 14
19 So Gideon went into his house and prepared a kid 7
7: 4 he of whom I say to you, 'This man shall go with you,' 14
4 to you, 'This man shall go with you,' shall go with you; 14
4 to you, 'This man shall not go with you,' shall not go. 14
4 to you, 'This man shall not go with you,' shall not go. 14
7 and let all the others go every man to his home. 14
8: 1 not to call us when you went to fight with Mid'ian? 14
29 Jerubba'al . . went and dwelt in his own house. 14
9: 1 Abim'elech the son of Jerubba'al went to Shechem 14
5 he went to his father's house at Ophrah, and slew 7
6 Beth-millo, and they went and made Abim'elech king 14
7 he went and stood on the top of Mount Ger'izim 14

9 leave my fatness . . and go to sway over the trees?' 14
11 and my good fruit, and go to sway over the trees?' 14
13 cheers gods and men, and go to sway over the trees?' 14
21 Jotham . . fled, and went to Beer and dwelt there 14
27 festival, and went into the house of their god 7
32 go by night . . and lie in wait in the fields. 32
50 Then Abim'elech went to Thebez, and encamped 14
51 and they went to the roof of the tower. 28
10:14 Go and cry to the gods whom you have chosen; 14
11: 3 round Jephthah, and went raiding with him. 17
5 the elders of Gilead went to bring Jephthah 14
8 turned to you now, that you may go with us and fight 14
11 Jephthah went with the elders of Gilead 14
16 from Egypt, Israel went through the wilderness 14
37 let me alone two months, that I may go and wander 14
38 And he said, "Go." And he sent her away 14
40 daughters of Israel went year by year to lament 14
12: 1 Why . . and did not call us to go with you? 14
13:11 Mano'ah arose and went after his wife, and came 14
14: 3 all our people, that you must go to take a wife 14
9 out into his hands, and went on, eating as he went; 14
9 out into his hands, and went on, eating as he went; 14
15: 1 harvest, Samson went to visit his wife with a kid; *
1 and he said, "I will go in to my wife in the chamber. 7
1 But her father would not allow him to go in. 7
4 Samson went and caught 300 foxes 14
5 he let the foxes go into the standing grain 37
16: 1 Samson went to Gaza, and there he saw a harlot 14
1 and there he saw a harlot, and he went in to her. 7
17: 9 and I am going to sojourn where I may find a place. 14
18: 2 they said to them, "Go and explore the land. 14
6 Go in peace. The journey on which you go is under 14
6 The journey on which you go is under the eye 14
9 be slow to go, and enter in and possess the land. 14
10 When you go, you will come to an unsuspecting 7
14 the five men who had gone to spy out the country 14
17 five men who had gone to spy out the land went up 14
18 when these went into Micah's house and took 7
20 graven image, and went in the midst of the people. 7
24 take my gods . . and go away, and what have I left? 14
26 the Danites went their way; and when Micah saw 14
19: 2 she went away from him to her father's house 14
3 her husband arose and went after her, to speak 14
5 arose early in the morning, and he prepared to go; 14
5 with a morsel of bread, and after that you may go. 14
7 when the man rose up to go, his father-in-law urged 14
9 arise early . . for your journey, and go home. 14
14 So they passed on and went their way; and the sun 14
15 turned aside there, to go in and spend the night 7
15 he went in and sat down in the open square 7
17 said, "Where are you going? and whence do you come? 14
18 I went to Bethlehem in Judah; and I am going to my 14
18 I am going to my home; and nobody takes me into his 14
25 And as the dawn began to break, they let her go. 37
27 when he . . went out to go on his way, behold, there 14
28 Get up, let us be going." But there was no answer. 14
20: 8 We will not any of us go to his tent, and none of us 14
25 Benjamin went against them out of Gib'e-ah 17
21:10 Go and smite the inhabitants of Ja'besh-gil'ead 14
20 Go and lie in wait in the vineyards 14
21 and go to the land of Benjamin. 14
23 they went and returned to their inheritance 14
Rut 1: 1 a certain man . . went to sojourn in the country 14
7 and they went on the way to return to . . Judah. 14
8 Go, return each of you to her mother's house. 14
11 Turn back, my daughters, why will you go with me? 14
12 Turn back, my daughters, go your way, 14
16 where you go I will go, and where you lodge I will 14
16 where you go I will go, and where you lodge I will 14
18 Na'omi saw that she was determined to go with her 14
19 the two of them went on until they came 14
2: 2 Let me go to the field, and glean among the . . grain 14
2 And she said to her, "Go, my daughter. 14
3 she set forth and went and gleaned in the field 7
8 do not go to glean in another field or leave this 14
9 Let your eyes be upon . . and go after them. 14
9 when you are thirsty, go to the vessels and drink 14
3: 4 then, go and uncover his feet and lie down; 7
7 he went to lie down at the end of the heap of grain. 7
10 you have not gone after young men, whether poor 14
4:13 he went in to her, and the LORD gave her conception 7
1Sm 1: 7 it went on year by year; as often as she went 29
17 Go in peace, and the God of Israel grant 14
18 she said . . " Then the woman went her way and ate 14
2:11 Then Elka'nah went home to Ramah. 14
3: 5 lie down again." So he went and lay down. 14
6 Samuel arose and went to Eli, and said, "Here I am 14
8 And he arose and went to Eli, and said, "Here I am 14
9 Eli said to Samuel, "Go, lie down; and if he calls you 14
9 So Samuel went and lay down in his place. 14
4:16 And he said, "How did it go, my son? 12
6: 6 After he . . did not they let the people go 37
8 Then send it off, and let it go its way. 14
12 the cows went straight . . lowing as they went; 14
12 the lords . . went after them as far as the border 14
7:16 went on a circuit . . to Bethel, Gilgal, and Mizpah; 14
8:22 Samuel then said . . "Go every man to his city. 14
9: 3 Take . . and arise, go and look for the asses. 14
6 a man of God in this city . . Let us go there; 14

7 But if we go, what can we bring the man? 14
7 the bread in our sacks is gone, and there is no 2
9 when a man went to inquire of God, he said, "Come 14
9 he said, "Come, let us go to the seer"; 14
10 Well said; come, let us go." So they went to the city 14
10 they went to the city where the man of God was. 14
19 in the morning I will let you go and will tell you 37
10: 2 The asses which you went to seek are found 14
3 Then you shall go on from there further 15
14 Saul's uncle said to him . . "Where did you go? 14
14 when we saw they were not . . we went to Samuel. 7
26 Saul also went to his home at Gib'e-ah 14
26 Saul also went . . and with him went men of valor 14
11:14 let us go to Gilgal and there renew the kingdom. 14
15 all the people went to Gilgal . . made Saul king 14
14: 3 the people did not know that Jonathan had gone. 14
17 Saul said . . "Number and see who has gone from us. 14
18 the ark of God went at that time with the people *
20 Saul and all . . rallied and went into the battle; 7
46 and the Philistines went to their own place. 14
15: 3 Now go and smite Am'alek, and utterly destroy all 14
6 Go, depart, go down from among the Amal'ekites 14
18 Go, utterly destroy the sinners, the Amal'ekites 14
20 I have gone on the mission on which the LORD sent 14
34 Samuel went to Ramah; and Saul went up to his house 14
16: 1 Fill your horn with oil, and go; I will send you 14
2 How can I go? If Saul hears it, he will kill me. 14
13 And Samuel rose up, and went to Ramah. 14
17: 7 and his shield-bearer went before him. 14
13 the names of his three sons who went to the battle 14
20 David rose . . and took the provisions, and went 14
22 David left . . and went and greeted his brothers. 7
32 your servant will go and fight with this 14
33 You are not able to go against this Philistine 14
35 I went after him and smote him and delivered it 17
37 Saul said to David, "Go, and the LORD be with you! 14
39 David girded his . . and he tried in vain to go 14
39 I cannot go with these; for I am not used to them. 14
18:27 David arose and went . . and killed 200 14
19:17 Why have you deceived me thus, and let my enemy go 37
17 He said to me, 'Let me go; why should I kill you?' 37
18 And he and Samuel went and dwelt at Nai'oth. 14
22 he himself went to Ramah, and came to . . Secu; 14
23 And he went from there to Nai'oth in Ramah; 14
23 Spirit of God came . . and as he went he prophesied 14
20: 5 but let me go, that I may hide myself in the field 37
13 and send you away, that you may go in safety. 14
19 then go to the place where you hid yourself 7
21 I will send the lad, saying, 'Go, find the arrows.' 14
22 if I say . . then go; for the LORD has sent you away. 14
28 David . . asked leave of me to go to Bethlehem; *
29 he said, 'Let me go; for our family holds a sacrifice 37
40 Go and carry them to the city. 14
41 as soon as the lad had gone, David rose from beside 7
42 Go in peace, forasmuch as we have sworn both of us 14
21:10 David rose . . and went to A'chish the king of Gath. 7
22: 3 And David went from there to Mizpeh of Moab; 14
23: 2 Shall I go and attack these Philistines? 14
2 Go and attack the Philistines and save Kei'lah. 14
3 if we go to Kei'lah against the . . Philistines? 14
5 And David and his men went to Kei'lah, and fought 14
13 and they went wherever they could go. 14
13 and they went wherever they could go. 14
16 Jonathan . . rose, and went to David at Horesh 14
18 David remained at Horesh, and Jonathan went home. 14
22 Go, make yet more sure; know and see the place 14
23 I will go with you; and . . I will search him out 14
24 And they arose, and went to Ziph ahead of Saul. 14
25 And Saul and his men went to seek him. 14
26 Saul went on one side of the mountain 14
28 Saul . . went against the Philistines; 14
24: 2 Saul took . . and went to seek David and his men 14
3 a cave; and Saul went in to relieve himself. 7
7 Saul rose up and left . . and went upon his way. 14
19 if a man finds his enemy, will he let him go away 37
22 And David swore this to Saul. Then Saul went home; 14
25: 5 Go up to Carmel, and go to Nabal, and greet him 7
15 when . . in the fields, as long as we went with them; 14
19 Go on before me; behold, I come after you. 26
42 she went after the messengers of David 14
26: 7 David and Abi'shai went to the army by night; 7
11 but take now the spear . . and let us go. 14
19 driven me out . . saying, 'Go, serve other gods.' 14
25 David went his way, and Saul returned to his place. 14
28: 7 a medium, that I may go to her and inquire of her. 14
8 Saul . . went, he and two men with him; 14
22 you may have strength when you go on your way. 14
29: 7 go peaceably, that you . . not displease the lords 14
8 go and fight against the enemies of my lord 14
30: 2 but carried them off, and went their way. 14
10 But David went on with the pursuit *
22 fellows among the men who had gone with David 14
22 Because they did not go with us, we will not give 14
31:12 valiant men arose, and went all night 14
2Sm 1: 4 David said to him, "How did it go? Tell me. 12
15 David called . . and said, "Go, fall upon him. 23
2:19 as he went he turned neither to the right hand nor 14
29 Abner . . went all that night through the Arabah; 14
3: 7 Why have you gone in to my father's concubine? 7

16 But her husband went with her, weeping after her 14
16 Abner said to him, "Go, return"; and he returned. 14
19 then Abner went to tell David at Hebron 14
21 I will arise and go, and will gather all Israel 14
21 David sent Abner away; and he went in peace. 14
22 he had sent him away, and he had gone in peace. 14
23 Abner . . came to the king, and he has let him go 37
23 he has let him go, and he has gone in peace. 14
24 Jo'ab went to the king and said, 7
24 you have sent him away, so that he is gone? 14
4: 7 and went by the way of the Arabah all night 14
5: 6 And the king and his men went to Jerusalem 14
6: 2 David arose and went . . from Ba'ale-judah 14
4 with the ark of God; and Ahi'o went before the ark. 14
12 David went and brought up the ark of God 14
13 when those who bore the ark . . had gone six paces 31
7: 3 Go, do all that is in your heart; 14
5 Go and tell my servant David, 'Thus says the LORD 14
9 and I have been with you wherever you went 14
18 David went in and sat before the LORD, and said 7
23 Israel, whom God went to redeem to be his people 14
8: 3 he went to restore his power at the river 14
6 the LORD gave victory to David wherever he went. 14
14 the LORD gave victory to David wherever he went. 14
11:11 shall I then go to my house, to eat and to drink 7
22 the messenger went, and came and told David all 14
12:15 Then Nathan went to his house. 14
16 and went in and lay all night upon the ground. 7
20 he then went to his own house; 7
23 I shall go to him, but he will not return to me. 14
24 David comforted his wife . . and went in to her 7
29 David . . went to Rabbah 14
13: 7 Go to your brother Amnon's house, and prepare food 14
8 Tamar went to her brother Amnon's house 14
15 And Amnon said to her, "Arise, be gone. 14
19 and went away, crying aloud as she went. 14
24 the king and his servants go with your servant. 14
25 let us not all go, lest we be burdensome to you. 14
25 but he would not go but gave him his blessing. 14
26 If not, pray let my brother Amnon go with us. 14
26 the king said to him, "Why should he go with you? 14
27 until he let Amnon and all the king's sons go 37
37 But Ab'salom fled, and went to Talmai 14
38 So Ab'salom fled, and went to Geshur 14
14: 3 and go to the king, and speak thus to him. 7
8 Go to your house, and I will give orders 14
21 I grant this; go, bring back the young man Ab'salom. 14
23 So Jo'ab arose and went to Geshur 14
30 See, Jo'ab's field . . go and set it on fire. 14
31 Then Jo'ab arose and went to Ab'salom at his house 7
32 therefore let me go into the presence of the king; 34
33 Then Jo'ab went to the king, and told him; 7
15: 7 Pray let me go and pay my vow, which I have vowed 14
9 The king said to him, "Go in peace." So he arose 14
9 Go in peace." So he arose, and went to Hebron. 14
11 With Ab'salom went 200 men from Jerusalem 14
11 they went in their simplicity, and knew nothing. 14
13 The . . men of Israel have gone after Ab'salom. 12
14 go in haste, lest he overtake us quickly 14
19 Why do you also go with us? Go . . stay with the king; 14
20 make you wander . . seeing I go I know not where? 14
22 And David said to It'tai, "Go then, pass on. 14
30 David went up . . weeping as he went, barefoot 28
30 and they went up, weeping as they went. 28
33 If you go on with me, you will be a burden to me. 26
16:13 So David and his men went on the road 14
13 Shim'e-i went along . . and cursed as he went 14
17 Why did you not go with your friend? 14
21 Go in to your father's concubines, whom he has left 7
22 and Ab'salom went in to his father's concubines 7
17:11 my counsel . . and that you go to battle in person. 14
17 a maidservant used to go and tell them 14
17 tell them, and they would go and tell King David; 14
21 After they had gone, the men came up out of the well 14
21 the men came up . . and went and told King David. 14
23 saddled his ass, and went off home to his own city. 14
18: 9 the mule went under the . . branches of a great oak 7
9 while the mule that was under him went on. 26
21 Jo'ab said . . "Go, tell the king what you have seen. 14
24 and the watchman went up to the roof of the gate 14
33 and as he went, he said, "O my son Ab'salom, my son 14
19: 7 if you do not go, not a man will stay with you 17
25 Why did you not go with me, Mephib'osheth? 14
26 that I may ride upon it and go with the king.' 14
31 and he went on with the king to the Jordan 26
40 The king went on to Gilgal, and Chimham went 26
40 The king went on . . and Chimham went on with him; 26
20: 3 and provided for them, but did not go in to them. 7
5 Ama'sa went to summon Judah; but he delayed 14
13 all the people went on after Jo'ab to pursue Sheba 26
22 the woman went to all the people in her wisdom. 7
21:12 David went and took the bones of Saul 14
23:17 of the men who went at the risk of their lives? 14
24: 1 he incited David . . "Go, number Israel and Judah. 14
12 Go and say to David, 'Thus says the LORD 14
1Kg 1:13 Go in at once to King David, and say to him, 'Did you 7
15 So Bathshe'ba went to the king into his chamber 7
49 all the guests . . rose, and each went his own way. 14

50 he arose, and went, and caught hold of the horns 14
53 and Solomon said to him, "Go to your house. 14
2: 2 I am about to go the way of all the earth. Be strong 14
8 cursed me . . on the day when I went to Mahana'im; 14
19 Bathshe'ba went to King Solomon, to speak to him 7
26 Go to An'athoth, to your estate; for you deserve 14
29 sent Benai'ah . . saying, "Go, strike him down. 14
40 Shim'e-i arose . . and went to Gath to Achish 14
40 Shim'e-i went and brought his slaves from Gath. 14
41 Shim'e-i had gone from Jerusalem to Gath 14
42 the day you go forth and go to any place whatever 14
3: 4 the king went to Gibeon to sacrifice there 14
5: 9 rafts to go by sea to the place you direct *
8:66 and went to their homes joyful and glad of heart 14
9: 6 if you . . go and serve other gods and worship them 14
28 they went to Ophir, and brought from there gold 7
10:13 she turned and went back to her own land 14
16 600 shekels of gold went into each shield. 28
17 three minas of gold went into each shield; 28
11: 5 Solomon went after Ash'toreth the goddess 14
10 that he should not go after other gods; 14
21 Let me depart, that I may go to my own country. 14
22 you are now seeking to go to your own country 14
22 And he said to him, "Only let me go. 37
24 they went to Damascus and dwelt there 14
12: 1 Rehobo'am went to Shechem, for all Israel had come 14
24 they hearkened to . . the LORD, and went home again 14
30 the people went to the one at Bethel 14
13: 8 I will not go in with you. And I will not eat bread 7
10 he went another way, and did not return by the way 14
12 their father said to him, "Which way did he go? 14
12 the way which the man of God . . had gone. 14
14 he went after the man of God, and found him 14
16 he said, "I may not return with you, or go in with you; 7
24 as he went away a lion met him on the road 14
28 he went and found his body thrown in the road 14
14: 2 Arise, and disguise yourself . . go to Shiloh; 14
3 Take with you . . and go to him; 7
4 she arose, and went to Shiloh, and came to the house 14
7 Go, tell Jerobo'am, 'Thus says the LORD 14
9 and have gone and made for yourself other gods 14
12 Arise therefore, go to your house. 14
28 as the king went into the house of the LORD 7
15:19 sending to you a present . . go, break your league 14
16:18 he went into the citadel of the king's house 7
31 took for wife Jez'ebel . . and went and served Ba'al 14
17: 5 he went and did according to the word of the LORD; 14
5 he went and dwelt by the brook Cherith 14
9 Arise, go to Zar'ephath . . and dwell there. 14
10 So he arose and went to Zar'ephath; 14
11 as she was going to bring it, he called to her 14
12 I may go in and prepare it for myself and my son 7
13 Fear not; go and do as you have said; 7
15 she went and did as Eli'jah said; 14
18: 1 Go, show yourself to Ahab; and I will send rain 14
2 So Eli'jah went to show himself to Ahab. 14
5 Go through the land to all the springs of water 14
6 Ahab went in one direction by himself 14
6 Obadi'ah went in another direction by himself. 14
8 Go, tell your lord, 'Behold, Eli'jah is here.' 14
11 'Go, tell your lord, "Behold, Eli'jah is here."' 14
12 as soon as I have gone from you 14
14 'Go, tell your lord, "Behold, Eli'jah is here"'; 14
16 Obadi'ah went to meet Ahab, and told him; 14
16 Obadi'ah . . told him; and Ahab went to meet Eli'jah. 14
45 And Ahab rode and went to Jezreel. 14
19: 3 he was afraid, and he arose and went for his life 14
4 he . . went a day's journey into the wilderness 14
8 and went in the strength of that food 40 days 14
15 Go, return on your way to the wilderness 14
21 he arose and went after Eli'jah, and ministered 14
20:27 the people of Israel . . went against them; 14
32 girded sackcloth . . and went to the king 7
33 Then he said, "Go and bring him. 7
34 And Ahab said, "I will let you go on these terms. 37
34 So he made a covenant with him and let him go. 37
36 as soon as you have gone . . a lion shall kill you. 14
40 as your servant was busy . . he was gone. 3
42 you have let go . . the man whom I had devoted 37
42 your life shall go for his life, and your people 12
43 king . . went to his house resentful and sullen 14
21: 4 Ahab went into his house vexed and sullen 7
18 where he has gone to take possession. 18
26 He did very abominably in going after idols 14
22: 4 Will you go with me to battle at Ramoth-gilead? 14
6 Shall I go to battle against Ramoth-gilead 14
13 the messenger who went to summon Micai'ah said 14
15 Micai'ah, shall we go to Ramoth-gilead to battle 14
24 How did the Spirit . . go from me to speak to you? 26
30 I will disguise myself and go into battle, but you 7
30 king . . disguised himself and went into battle. 7
36 about sunset a cry went through the army 26
48 Jehosh'aphat made ships . . to go to Ophir for gold; 14
48 but they did not go, for the ships were wrecked 14
49 Let my servants go with your servants in the ships 14
2Kg 1: 2 Go, inquire of Ba'al-ze'bub, the god of Ekron, whether 14
3 that you are going to inquire of Ba'al-ze'bub 14
4 not come down from the bed to which you have gone 28
4 So Eli'jah went. 14

6 Go back to the king who sent you, and say to him 14
6 not come down from the bed to which you have gone 28
16 not come down from the bed to which you have gone 28
2: 6 So the two of them went on. 14
7 50 men of the sons of the prophets also went 14
11 as they still went on and talked, behold, a chariot 14
16 pray, let them go, and seek your master; 14
18 he said to them, "Did I not say to you, Do not go? 14
21 he went to the spring of water and threw salt in it 17
25 From there he went on to Mount Carmel 14
3: 7 he went and sent word to Jehosh'aphat 14
7 will you go with me to battle against Moab? 14
7 I will go; I am as you are, my people as your people 28
9 So the king of Israel went with the king of Judah 14
13 Go to the prophets of your father and . . mother. 14
24 slaughtering the Moabites as they went. 72
4: 3 Go outside, borrow vessels of all your neighbors 14
4 Then go in, and shut the door upon yourself 7
5 she went from him and shut the door upon 14
7 Go, sell the oil and pay your debts 14
8 One day Eli'sha went on to Shunem 26
10 so that whenever he comes to us, he can go in there. 25
23 he said, "Why will you go to him today? 14
29 Gird up your loins, and take my staff . . and go. 14
31 Geha'zi went on ahead and laid the staff 26
33 So he went in and shut the door . . and prayed 7
5: 4 Na'aman went in and told his lord, 7
5 Go now, and I will send a letter to the king 14
5 So he went, taking with him ten talents of silver 14
10 Go and wash in the Jordan seven times 14
19 He said to him, "Go in peace. 14
19 when Na'aman had gone from him a short distance 14
25 He went in, and stood before his master 7
25 And he said, "Your servant went nowhere. 14
26 Did I not go with you in spirit when the man turned 14
6: 2 Let us go to the Jordan and each of us get . . a log 14
2 Let us go to the Jordan . . " And he answered, "Go. 14
3 one . . said, "Be pleased to go with your servants. 14
3 go with your servants." And he answered, "I will go. 14
4 So he went with them. And when they came 14
13 Go and see where he is, that I may send and seize 14
22 they may eat and drink and go to their master. 14
23 he sent them away, and they went to their master. 14
7: 5 they arose . . to go to the camp of the Syrians; 7
8 they went into a tent, and ate and drank 7
8 carried off silver and . . and went and hid them; 14
8 carried off things from it, and went and hid them. 14
9 come, let us go and tell the king's household. 7
14 the king sent them . . saying, "Go and see. 14
15 So they went after them as far as the Jordan; 14
8: 2 she went with her household and sojourned 14
8 Take a present . . and go to meet the man of God 14
9 So Haz'ael went to meet him, and took a present 14
10 Go, say to him, 'You shall certainly recover'; 14
28 He went with Joram . . to make war against Haz'ael 14
9: 1 take this flask of oil . . and go to Ramoth-gilead. 14
2 and go in and bid him rise from among his fellows 7
4 the young man, the prophet, went to Ramoth-gilead. 14
15 out of the city to go and tell the news in Jezreel. 14
16 Jehu mounted his chariot, and went to Jezreel 14
18 So a man on horseback went to meet him, and said 14
21 set out, each in his chariot, and went to meet Jehu 17
34 Then he went in and ate and drank; and he said 7
35 when they went to bury her, they found 14
10:12 Then he set out and went to Sama'ria. 14
24 Then he went in to offer sacrifices 7
25 Go in and slay them; let not a man escape. 7
25 and went into the inner room of the house of Ba'al 14
11: 9 each brought his men who were to go off duty 7
13 When Athali'ah heard . . she went into the house 7
18 the people of the land went to the house of Ba'al 7
16:10 When King Ahaz went to Damascus to meet 14
17:15 They went after false idols, and became false 14
27 let him go and dwell there, and teach them the law 14
22:13 Go, inquire of the LORD for me, and for the people 14
14 So . . and Asai'ah went to meet Huldah the prophetess 14
23:29 King Josi'ah went to meet him; and Pharaoh Neco 14
25: 4 And they went in the direction of the Arabah. 14
26 all the people . . arose, and went to Egypt; 7
1Ch 2:21 Hezron went in to the daughter of Machir 7
24 Caleb went in to Eph'rathah, the wife of Hezron 81
4:42 some of them . . went to Mount Se'ir 14
6:15 Jehoz'adak went into exile when the LORD sent 14
7:23 E'phraim went in to his wife, and she conceived 7
11: 4 and all Israel went to Jerusalem, that is Jebus 14
12:20 As he went to Ziklag these men of Manas'seh 14
15:25 went to bring up the ark of the covenant 14
17: 4 Go and tell my servant David, 'Thus says the LORD 14
5 but I have gone from tent to tent 12
8 I have been with you wherever you went 14
11 days are fulfilled to go to be with your fathers 14
16 Then King David went in and sat before the LORD 7
21 Israel, whom God went to redeem to be his people 14
18: 3 as he went to set up his monument 14
6 LORD gave victory to David wherever he went. 14
13 the LORD gave victory to David wherever he went. 14
21: 2 Go, number Israel, from Beer-sheba to Dan 14
4 Jo'ab departed and went throughout all Israel 14
10 Go and say to David, 'Thus says the LORD 14

30 David could not go before it to inquire of God 14
27: 1 concerning the divisions that came and went 17
2Ch 1: 3 Solomon . . went to the high place . . at Gibeon; 14
6:41 now arise, O LORD God, and go to thy resting place •
7:19 turn aside . . and go and serve other gods 14
8: 3 Solomon went to Ma'math-zo'bah, and took it. 14
17 Then Solomon went to E'zion-ge'ber and Eloth 14
18 went to Ophir . . with the servants of Solomon 7
9:15 600 shekels of . . gold went into each shield. 28
16 300 shekels of gold went into each shield; 28
21 king's ships went to Tarshish with the servants 14
10: 1 Rehobo'am went to Shechem 14
11: 4 returned and did not go against Jerobo'am. 14
16: 3 go, break your league with Ba'asha king of Israel 14
18: 3 Will you go with me to Ramoth-gilead? 14
5 Shall we go to battle against Ramoth-gilead 14
12 messenger who went to summon Micai'ah said to him 14
14 Micai'ah, shall we go to Ramoth-gilead to battle 14
23 Spirit of the LORD go from me to speak to you? 26
24 see on that day when you go into an inner chamber 7
29 I will disguise myself and go into battle 7
29 and they went into battle. 7
19: 2 Because of this, wrath has gone out against you •
20:21 as they went before the army, and say 17
36 He joined him in building ships to go to Tarshish 14
37 ships . . were not able to go to Tarshish. 14
22: 5 went with Jeho'ram . . to make war against Haz'ael 14
7 come about through his going to visit Joram. 7
23: 8 men, who were to go off duty on the sabbath 7
12 she went into the house of the LORD to the people; 7
15 she went into the entrance of the horse gate 7
17 people went to the house of Ba'al, and tore it down; 7
25: 7 O king, do not let the army of Israel go with you 7
10 Amazi'ah discharged the army . . to go home 14
11 went to the Valley of Salt and smote 10,000 men 14
13 sent back, not letting them go with him to battle 14
26:17 Azari'ah the priest went in after him 7
29:15 and went in as the king had commanded 7
18 Then they went in to Hezeki'ah the king and said 7
30: 6 couriers went throughout all Israel and Judah 14
10 couriers went from city to city 26
34:21 Go, inquire of the LORD for me and for those who are 14
22 Hilki'ah . . went to Huldah the prophetess 14
Ezr 4:12 Jews who came up . . have gone to Jerusalem. 41
23 they went in haste to the Jews at Jerusalem 40
5: 8 went to the province of Judah, to the house 40
8 this work goes on diligently and prospers 43
15 Take these vessels, go and put them in the temple 40
7:13 freely offers to go to Jerusalem, may go with you. 42
13 freely offers to go to Jerusalem, may go with you. 42
8:31 twelfth day of the first month, to go to Jerusalem; 14
10: 6 Ezra . . went to the chamber of Jehoha'nan 14
Neh 2: 6 How long will you be gone, and when will you return 21
14 went on to the Fountain Gate and to the King's Pool; 26
16 officials did not know where I had gone 14
6:10 Now when I went into the house of Shemai'ah 7
11 man such as I could go into the temple and live? 7
11 I will not go in. 7
8:10 Go your way, eat the fat and drink sweet wine 14
12 all the people went their way to eat and drink 14
9:12 light for them the way in which they should go. 14
15 thou didst tell them to go in to possess the land 7
19 lighted for them the way by which they should go. 14
24 descendants went in and possessed the land 7
37 rich yield goes to the kings whom thou hast set •
12:31 two great companies which . . went in procession. •
31 One went to the right upon the wall to the Dung Gate; •
32 after them went Hoshai'ah and half of the princes 14
36 Ezra the scribe went before them. •
38 other company . . went to the left 14
13: 6 32nd year . . I went to the king. 7
Est 2:12 came for each maiden to go in to King Ahasu-e'rus 7
13 when the maiden went in to the king in this way 7
14 In the evening she went, and in the morning . . came 7
14 she did not go in to the king again, 7
15 the turn came for Esther . . to go in to the king 7
3:15 The couriers went in haste by order of the king 17
4: 5 to go to Mor'decai to learn what this was and why •
8 charge her to go to the king to make supplication 7
9 Hathach went and told Esther what Mor'decai had 7
11 if any . . goes to the king inside the inner court 7
16 Go, gather all the Jews . . and hold a fast 14
16 I will go to the king, though it is against the law; 7
5:10 Haman restrained himself, and went home; 7
14 then go merrily with the king to the dinner. 7
7: 1 king and Haman went in to feast with . . Esther. 7
7 rose . . in wrath and went into the palace garden; •
Job 1: 4 His sons used to go and hold a feast in the house 14
7: 8 while thy eyes are upon me, I shall be gone. 3
9:26 They go by like skiffs of reed, like an eagle 15
10:21 before I go whence I shall not return 14
16:22 I shall go the way whence I shall not return. 14
19:10 He breaks me down on every side, and I am gone 14
20:13 he is loath to let it go, and holds it in his mouth 27
21:33 those who go before him are innumerable. •
23: 8 Behold, I go forward, but he is not there; 14
24:24 They are exalted a little while, and then are gone; 3
27: 6 hold fast my righteousness, and will not let it go; 35
19 he opens his eyes, and his wealth is gone. 3

21 The east wind lifts him up and he is gone; 14
30: 2 could I gain from . . men whose vigor is gone? 1
31: 7 from the way, and my heart has gone after my eyes 14
34: 8 who goes in company with evildoers 5
23 a time for any man to go before God in judgment. 14
37: 3 Under the whole heaven he lets it go 38
8 Then the beasts go into their lairs, 7
38:35 that they may go and say to you, 'Here we are'? 14
39: 5 Who has let the wild ass go free? 37
41:19 Out of his mouth go flaming torches; 14
42: 8 go to my servant Job, and offer up for yourselves 14
9 went and did what the LORD had told them; 14
Ps 32: 8 instruct you and teach you the way you should go; 14
38:10 the light of my eyes-it also has gone from me. 3
42: 4 how I went with the throng, and led them 26
7 thy waves and thy billows have gone over me. 26
9 Why hast thou forgotten me? Why go I mourning 14
43: 2 why hast thou cast me off? Why go I mourning 14
4 Then I will go to the altar of God 7
49:19 he will go to the generation of his fathers 7
51: 0 came to him, after he had gone in to Bathsheba. 7
54: 0 when the Ziphites went and told Saul 7
63: 9 shall go down into the depths of the earth; 7
66:12 we went through fire and through water; 7
73:17 until I went into the sanctuary of God; 7
84: 6 As they go through the valley of Baca they make it 26
7 They go from strength to strength; 14
85:13 Righteousness will go before him 14
90:10 they are soon gone, and we fly away. 8
97: 3 Fire goes before him, and burns up his 14
103:16 for the wind passes over it, and it is gone 3
104:26 There go the ships, and Leviathan which thou 14
109:23 I am gone, like a shadow at evening; 14
122: 1 Let us go to the house of the LORD! 14
124: 5 then over us would have gone the raging waters. 26
132: 7 Let us go to his dwelling place; let us worship 7
8 Arise, O LORD, and go to thy resting place •
139: 7 Whither shall I go from thy Spirit? 14
143: 8 Teach me the way I should go, for to thee I lift up 14
Prv 2:19 none who go to her come back 7
3:28 Go, and come again, tomorrow I will give it"- 14
4:15 Avoid it; do not go on it; 26
5:10 lest . . your labors go to the house of an alien; •
6: 3 go, hasten, and importune your neighbor. 14
6 Go to the ant, O sluggard; 14
29 So is he who goes in to his neighbor's wife; 7
7:19 husband . . has gone on a long journey; 14
22 follows her, as an ox goes to the slaughter 7
14:15 but the prudent looks where he is going. 6
15:12 A scoffer . . will not go to the wise. 14
33 humility goes before honor. •
16:18 Pride goes before destruction •
18:12 but humility goes before honor. •
22: 3 but the simple go on, and suffer for it. 26
6 Train up a child in the way he should go •
24 nor go with a wrathful man 7
23: 5 When your eyes light upon it, it is gone; 3
30 those who go to try mixed wine. 7
27:10 do not go to your brother's house in the day 7
12 but the simple go on, and suffer for it. 26
25 When the grass is gone, and the new growth appears 9
Ecc 1: 4 A generation goes, and a generation comes 14
6 round and round goes the wind, and on its circuits 14
3:20 All go to one place . . and all turn to dust again. 14
4:14 even though he had gone from prison to the throne 17
5: 1 Guard your steps when you go to the house of God; 14
15 As he came from his mother's womb he shall go again 14
16 This also is . . evil: just as he came, so shall he go; 14
6: 4 For it comes into vanity and goes into darkness 14
6 though he should . . do not all go to the one place? 14
7: 2 It is better to go to the house of mourning 14
2 than to go to the house of feasting; 14
8: 3 go from his presence, do not delay 14
10 they used to go in and out of the holy place 7
15 enjoyment . . for this will go with him in his toil 20
9: 3 they live, and after that they go to the dead. •
7 Go, eat your bread with enjoyment, and drink 14
10 or wisdom in Sheol, to which you are going. 14
12: 5 because man goes to his eternal home 14
Sng 2:11 lo, the winter is past, the rain is over and gone. 14
3: 4 I held him, and would not let him go 35
5: 6 I opened . . but my beloved had turned and gone. 26
6: 1 Whither has your beloved gone, O fairest 14
Isa 3:16 mincing along as they go, tinkling with . . feet; 14
6: 8 who will go for us?" Then I said, "Here am I! Send me. 14
9 he said, "Go, and say to this people: 'Hear and hear 14
8: 3 I went to the prophetess, and she conceived 33
7 over all its channels and go over all its banks; 14
14:17 who did not let his prisoners go home?' 30
18: 2 Go, you swift messengers, to a nation 14
20: 2 Go, and loose the sackcloth from your loins 14
21: 6 Go, set a watchman, let him announce what he sees. 14
22:15 Come, go to this steward, to Shebna 7
28:13 that they may go, and fall backward, and be broken 14
30: 8 now, go, write it before them on a tablet 7
29 to go to the mountain of the LORD, to the Rock 7
33:21 a place . . where no galley with oars can go 14
38: 5 Go and say to Hezeki'ah, Thus says the LORD 14

45: 2 I will go before you and level the mountains 14
16 the makers of idols go in confusion together. 14
46: 2 but themselves go into captivity. 14
47: 5 go into darkness, O daughter of the Chalde'ans 7
48:17 your God . . who leads you in the way you should go. 14
52:12 you shall not go in flight, for the LORD will go 14
12 not go in flight, for the LORD will go before you 14
57:17 he went on backsliding in the way of his own 14
58: 6 to let the oppressed go free 37
8 your righteousness shall go before you 14
13 if you honor it, not going your own ways 29
59: 8 no one who goes in them knows peace. 10
66:17 and purify themselves to go into the gardens •
Jer 1: 7 for to all to whom I send you you shall go 14
2: 2 Go and proclaim in the hearing of Jerusalem 14
5 went far from me, and went after worthlessness 14
8 and went after things that do not profit. 14
18 And now what do you gain by going to Egypt 11
18 Or what do you gain by going to Assyria 11
23 am not defiled, I have not gone after the Ba'als'? 14
25 Keep your feet from going unshod •
25 I have loved strangers, and after them I will go.' 14
3: 1 If a man divorces his wife and she goes from him 14
8 but she too went and played the harlot. 14
12 Go, and proclaim these words toward the north 14
4: 5 Assemble, and let us go into the fortified cities!' 7
5: 5 I will go to the great, and will speak to them; 14
6:29 in vain the refining goes on †
7: 6 if you do not go after other gods to your own hurt 14
9 and go after other gods that you have not known 14
10 only to go on doing all these abominations? •
12 Go now to my place that was in Shiloh 14
24 and went backward and not forward. 12
8: 2 which they have gone after 14
14 let us go into the fortified cities and perish 7
9:10 and the beasts have fled and are gone. 14
14 and have gone after the Ba'als, as their fathers •
10:20 my children have gone from me, and they are not; 17
11:10 they have gone after other gods to serve them; 14
12 and the inhabitants of Jerusalem will go and cry 14
12: 9 Go, assemble all the wild beasts; 14
13: 1 Go and buy a linen waistcloth 14
4 and arise, go to the Euphra'tes, and hide it there 14
5 I went, and hid it by the Euphra'tes 14
6 the LORD said to me, "Arise, go to the Euphra'tes 14
7 Then I went to the Euphra'tes, and dug 14
10 and have gone after other gods to serve them 14
15: 1 Send them out of my sight, and let them go! 17
2 when they ask you, 'Where shall we go?' 17
6 says the LORD, you keep going backward; 14
16: 5 Do not enter the house of mourning, or go to lament 14
8 You shall not go into the house of feasting 7
11 and have gone after other gods and have served 14
17:19 Go and stand in the Benjamin Gate 14
18:15 and have gone into bypaths, not the highway 14
19: 1 Thus said the LORD, "Go, buy a potter's earthen flask 14
10 in the sight of the men who go with you 14
20: 6 who dwell in your house, shall go into captivity; 14
6 shall go into captivity; to Babylon you shall go; 7
22:22 and your lovers shall go into captivity; 14
25: 6 do not go after other gods to serve and worship 14
27:18 and in Jerusalem may not go to Babylon. 7
28: 4 and all the exiles from Judah who went to Babylon 7
11 But Jeremiah the prophet went his way. 14
13 Go, tell Hanani'ah, 'Thus says the LORD 14
30:16 foes, every one of them, shall go into captivity; 14
31:21 the highway, the road by which you went. 14
34: 2 Go and speak to Zedeki'ah king of Judah 14
3 and you shall go to Babylon. 7
35: 2 Go to the house of the Re'chabites 14
11 we said, 'Come, and let us go to Jerusalem 7
13 Go and say to the men of Judah 14
15 amend your doings, and do not go after other gods 14
36: 5 I am debarred from going to the house of the LORD; 7
6 you are to go, and on a fast day in the hearing of all 7
19 Go and hide, you and Jeremiah 14
20 they went into the court to the king 7
37: 4 was still going in and out among the people 7
12 from Jerusalem to go to the land of Benjamin 14
21 until all the bread of the city was gone. 39
38: 8 E'bed-mel'ech went from the king's house and said 17
11 E'bed-mel'ech took the men with him and went 7
39: 4 and they went toward the Arabah. 17
16 Go, and say to E'bed-mel'ech the Ethiopian 14
40: 1 the captain of the guard had let him go from Ramah 37
4 go wherever you think it good and right to go. 14
4 go wherever you think it good and right to go. 14
5 or go wherever you think it right to go. 14
5 or go wherever you think it right to go. 14
5 gave him an allowance . . and let him go. 37
6 Then Jeremiah went to Gedali'ah the son of Ahi'kam 7
8 they went to Gedali'ah at Mizpah 7
15 Let me go and slay Ish'mael the son of Nethani'ah 14
41:12 and went to fight against Ish'mael 14
14 came back, and went to Joha'nan the son of Kare'ah. 14
15 escaped . . and went to the Ammonites. 14
17 And they went and stayed at Geruth Chimham 14
17 near Bethlehem, intending to go to Egypt 7
42: 3 LORD your God may show us the way we should go 14
14 saying, 'No, we will go to the land of Egypt 7
15 set your faces to enter Egypt and go to live there 7
17 All the men who set their faces to go to Egypt 7
18 will be poured out on you when you go to Egypt. 7
19 said to you, O remnant of Judah, 'Do not go to Egypt. 7
22 in the place where you desire to go to live. 7
43: 2 not send you to say, 'Do not go to Egypt to live there'; 7
44: 3 they went to burn incense and serve other gods 14
45: 5 as a prize of war in all places to which you may go. 14
48:11 nor has he gone into exile; so his taste remains 14
49: 3 For Milcom shall go into exile, with his priests 14
50: 6 from mountain to hill they have gone 14
33 have held them fast, they refuse to let them go. 37
51: 9 Forsake her, and let us go each to his own country; 14
50 escaped from the sword, go, stand not still! 14
59 he went with Zedeki'ah king of Judah to Babylon 14
52: 7 And they went in the direction of the Arabah. 14
Lam 1:18 my maidens and . . men have gone into captivity. 14
3:18 I say, "Gone is my glory, and my expectation 1
Ezk 1: 9 they went every one straight forward 14
9 straight forward, without turning as they went. 14
12 And each went straight forward; 14
12 wherever the spirit would go, they went 14
12 wherever the spirit would go, they went 14
12 they went, without turning as they went. 14
17 When they went, they went in any of their four 14
17 they went in any of their four directions 14
17 four directions without turning as they went. 14
19 when the living creatures went, the wheels went 14
19 creatures went, the wheels went beside them; 14
20 Wherever the spirit would go, they went 14
20 Wherever the spirit would go, they went 14
21 When those went, these went; 14
21 When those went, these went; 14
24 when they went, I heard the sound of their wings 14
3: 1 and go, speak to the house of Israel. 14
4 Son of man, go, get you to the house of Israel 14
11 go, get you to the exiles, to your people 14
14 and I went in bitterness in the heat of my spirit 14
24 said to me, "Go, shut yourself within your house. 7
7:14 but none goes to battle, for my wrath is upon all 14
8: 9 he said to me, "Go in, and see the vile abominations 7
10 I went in and saw; and there, portrayed 7
9: 2 they went in and stood beside the bronze altar. 7
10: 2 Go in among the whirling wheels 7
2 And he went in before my eyes. 7
3 the south side of the house, when the man went in; 7
6 he went in and stood beside a wheel. 7
11 When they went, they went in any of their four 14
11 they went in any of their four directions 14
11 four directions without turning as they went 14
11 followed without turning as they went. 14
16 when the cherubim went, the wheels went beside 14
16 the cherubim went, the wheels went beside them; 14
22 They went every one straight forward. 14
11:16 in the countries where they have gone. 7
21 whose heart goes after their detestable things 14
12: 4 in their sight, as men do who must go into exile. 22
11 they shall go into exile, into captivity. 14
16 abominations among the nations where they go 7
20:16 for their heart went after their idols. 14
29 What is the high place to which you go? 7
37 and I will let you go in by number. 69
39 Go serve every one of you his idols 14
23:31 You have gone the way of your sister; 14
44 they have gone in to her, as men go in to a harlot. 7
44 they have gone in to her, as men go in to a harlot. 7
44 Thus they went in to Oho'lah and to Ohol'ibah 7
25: 3 over the house of Judah when it went into exile; 14
30:17 and the women shall go into captivity. 14
18 her daughters shall go into captivity. 14
31:12 the peoples of the earth will go from its shadow 18
35: 7 I will cut off from it all who come and go. 36
37:21 from the nations among which they have gone 14
38: 8 in the latter years you will go against the land 7
40: 6 Then he went into the gateway facing east 7
41: 3 Then he went into the inner room and measured 7
44:25 defile themselves by going near to a dead person; 7
27 on the day that he goes into the holy place 7
46: 8 he shall go in by the vestibule of the gate 7
10 When they go in, the prince shall go in with them; 7
10 When they go in, the prince shall go in with them; 7
47: 3 Going on eastward with a line in his hand 17
9 wherever the river goes every living creature 7
9 for this water goes there 7
9 everything will live where the river goes. 7
Dan 2:16 Daniel went in and besought the king to appoint 44
17 Then Daniel went to his house and made the matter 40
24 Therefore Daniel went in to Ar'ioch 44
24 Daniel . . went and said thus to him 40
6:10 went to his house where he had windows 44
18 king went to his palace, and spent the night 40
19 king arose and went in haste to the den of lions. 40
11: 4 plucked up and go to others besides these. •
12: 9 Go your way, Daniel, for the words are shut up 14
13 go your way till the end; and you shall rest 14
Hos 1: 2 the LORD said to Hose'a, "Go, take to yourself a wife 14
3 he went and took Gomer the daughter of Dibla'im 14
2: 5 For she said, 'I will go after my lovers 14
7 shall say, 'I will go and return to my first husband 14
13 and went after her lovers, and forgot me 14
3: 1 Go again, love a woman who is beloved of a paramour 14
5: 6 they shall go to seek the LORD 14
11 because he was determined to go after vanity. 14
13 then E'phraim went to Assyria 14
7:11 calling to Egypt, going to Assyria. 14
12 As they go, I will spread over them my net; 14
9: 6 For behold, they are going to Assyria; 14
11: 2 The more I called them, the more they went from me; 14
10 They shall go after the LORD 14
Jol 1:13 Go in, pass the night in sackcloth, O ministers 7
3:13 Go in, tread, for the wine press is full. 7
Ams 1:15 their king shall go into exile, he and his princes 14
6: 2 Calneh, and see; and thence go to Hamath the great; 14
7:12 Amazi'ah said to Amos, "O seer, go, flee away 14
15 LORD said to me, 'Go, prophesy to my people Israel.' 14
9: 4 they go into captivity before their enemies 14
Jon 1: 2 Arise, go to Nin'eveh, that great city 14
3 to Joppa and found a ship going to Tarshish; 7
3 he paid the fare, and went on board, 18
3 went on board, to go with them to Tarshish, 7
3: 2 Arise, go to Nin'eveh, that great city, and proclaim 14
3 Jonah arose and went to Nin'eveh 14
4 Jonah began to go into the city 7
4 began to go into the city, going a day's journey. •
4: 5 Then Jonah went out of the city and sat to the east 17
Mic 1: 8 will lament and wail; I will go stripped and naked; 14
2:10 Arise and go, for this is no place to rest; 14
4:10 you shall go to Babylon. 7
Nah 2: 5 officers are summoned, they stumble as they go 13
3:10 Yet she was carried away, she went into captivity; 14
14 go into the clay, tread the mortar 7
Hab 1:11 they sweep by like the wind and go on, guilty men 26
3: 5 Before him went pestilence 14
Zec 2: 2 Then I said, "Where are you going?" And he said to me 14
6: 6 with the black horses goes toward the north 17
6 the white ones go toward the west country 17
6 and the dappled ones go toward the south country. 17
7 he said, "Go, patrol the earth." So they patrolled 14
8 Behold, those who go toward the north country 17
10 and go the same day to the house of Josi'ah 7
7:14 was desolate, so that no one went to and fro 26
8:21 the inhabitants of one city shall go to another 14
21 Let us go at once to entreat the favor of the LORD 14
21 to seek the LORD of hosts; I am going. 14
23 hold of the robe of a Jew, saying, 'Let us go with you 14
14: 2 half of the city shall go into exile 17
Mat 2: 8 he sent them to Bethlehem, saying, "Go and search 97
9 When they had heard the king they went their way; 97
11 going into the house they saw the child with Mary 81
20 his mother, and go to the land of Israel, for those 97
21 his mother, and went to the land of Israel. 71
22 he was afraid to go there, and being warned 52
23 he went and dwelt in a city called Nazareth 81
4:13 leaving Nazareth he went and dwelt in Caper'na-um 81
21 going on from there he saw two other brothers 98
5:24 leave your gift there before the altar and go; 106
25 accuser, while you are going with him to court 88
30 members than that your whole body go into hell. 52
41 if any one forces you to go one mile, go with him two •
41 forces you to go one mile, go with him two miles. 106
8: 4 but go, show yourself to the priest 106
9 I say to one, 'Go,' and he goes, and to another, 'Come,' 97
9 I say to one, 'Go,' and he goes, and to another, 'Come,' 97
13 to the centurion Jesus said, "Go; be it done for you 106
19 Teacher, I will follow you wherever you go. 52
21 Lord, let me first go and bury my father. 52
25 they went and woke him, saying, "Save, Lord 101
32 he said to them, "Go." So they came out 106
32 Go." So they came out and went into the swine; 52
33 The herdsmen fled, and going into the city 52
9: 6 Rise, take up your bed and go home. 106
7 he rose and went home. 52
13 Go and learn what this means, 'I desire mercy 97
25 he went in and took her by the hand 71
26 the report of this went through all 77
10: 5 Go nowhere among the Gentiles 52
6 go rather to the lost sheep 97
7 preach as you go, saying 97
11: 1 he went on from there to teach and preach 87
4 Jesus answered them, "Go and tell John 97
12: 1 At that time Jesus went through the grainfields 97
9 And he went on from there, and entered 87
45 he goes and brings with him seven other spirits 97
13:28 Then do you want us to go and gather them? 52
36 Then he left the crowds and went into the house. 81
44 in his joy he goes and sells all that he has 106
46 went and sold all that he had and bought it. 52
14:12 and they went and told Jesus. 81
15 send the crowds away to go into the villages 52
15:29 Jesus went on from there 87
39 and went to the region of Magadan. 81
16:21 he must go to Jerusalem and suffer many things 52
17:27 However, not to give offense to them, go to the sea 97
18:12 and go in search of the one that went astray? 97
15 If your brother sins against you, go and tell him 106
30 He refused and went and put him in prison 52
31 they went and reported to their lord 81

19:15 he laid his hands on them and went away. 97
21 If you would be perfect, go, sell what you possess 106
24 for a camel to go through the eye of a needle 65
20: 4 to them he said, 'You go into the vineyard too 106
4 So they went. 52
7 He said to them, 'You go into the vineyard too.' 106
14 Take what belongs to you, and go 106
21: 2 saying to them, "Go into the village opposite you 97
6 The disciples went and did as Jesus had directed 97
19 seeing a fig tree by the wayside he went to it 81
28 he went to the first and said 101
28 'Son, go and work in the vineyard today.' 106
29 but afterward he repented and went. 52
30 he went to the second and said the same 101
30 he answered, 'I go, sir,' but did not go. •
30 he answered, 'I go, sir,' but did not go. 52
22: 9 Go therefore to the thoroughfares, and invite 97
15 Then the Pharisees went and took counsel 97
23:13 nor allow those who would enter to go in. 71
25: 1 went to meet the bridegroom. 77
9 go rather to the dealers and buy for yourselves.' 97
10 while they went to buy, the bridegroom came 81
10 those who were ready went in with him 71
16 He who had received the five talents went at once 97
18 he who had received the one talent went 52
25 so I was afraid, and I went and hid your talent 52
26:14 Judas Iscariot, went to the chief priests 97
18 Go into the city to a certain one, and say to him 106
24 The Son of man goes as it is written of him 106
36 Then Jesus went with them to a place 81
36 Sit here, while I go yonder and pray. 52
46 Rise, let us be going; see, my betrayer is at hand. 45
58 going inside he sat with the guards to see 71
75 he went out and wept bitterly. 77
27: 5 he departed; and he went and hanged himself. 52
53 went into the holy city and appeared to many. 71
58 He went to Pilate and asked for the body of Jesus. 101
64 lest his disciples go and steal him away 81
65 go, make it as secure as you can. 106
66 So they went and made the sepulchre secure 97
28: 1 the other Mary went to see the sepulchre. 81
7 Then go quickly and tell his disciples 97
10 go and tell my brethren to go to Galilee 106
10 go and tell my brethren to go to Galilee 52
11 While they were going 97
11 behold, some of the guard went into the city 81
16 Now the eleven disciples went to Galilee 97
19 Go therefore and make disciples of all nations 97
Mrk 1:19 And going on a little farther 98
38 he said to them, "Let us go on to the next towns 45
39 he went throughout all Galilee 81
44 go, show yourself to the priest 106
2:11 I say to you, rise, take up your pallet and go home. 106
23 he was going through the grainfields 91
3:19 Then he went home; 81
5:19 Go home to your friends 106
24 he went with him 52
34 go in peace, and be healed of your disease. 106
40 and went in where the child was. 72
6:27 He went and beheaded him in the prison 52
31 many were coming and going 106
33 Now many saw them going, and knew them 106
36 to go into the country and villages round about 52
37 we go and buy 200 denarii worth of bread 52
38 How many loaves have you? Go and see. 106
7:15 which by going into him can defile him 72
18 whatever goes into a man from outside 72
30 she went home, and found the child lying in bed 52
30 the child lying in bed, and the demon gone. 77
31 went through Sidon to the Sea of Galilee 81
8:10 went to the district of Dalmanu'tha. 81
27 Jesus went on with his disciples 77
9:30 They went on from there 77
43 with two hands to go to hell 52
10: 1 he left there and went to the region of Judea 81
21 go, sell what you have, and give to the poor 106
52 Go your way; your faith has made you well 106
11: 2 said to them, "Go into the village opposite you 106
6 and they let them go. 58
11 he entered Jerusalem, and went into the temple; •
13 he went to see if he could find anything on it. 81
14:10 went to the chief priests in order to betray him 52
12 Where will you have us go 52
13 Go into the city 106
16 the disciples set out and went to the city 81
21 For the Son of man goes as it is written of him 106
32 they went to a place which was called Gethsem'ane; 81
42 Rise, let us be going; see, my betrayer is at hand. 45
15:43 took courage and went to Pilate 71
16: 1 so that they might go and anoint him. 81
2 they went to the tomb when the sun had risen. 81
7 But go, tell his disciples and Peter that he is going 106
10 She went and told those who had been with him 97
15 Go into all the world and preach the gospel 97
Lke 1:23 he went to his home. 52
39 and went with haste into the hill country 97
2: 3 all went to be enrolled, each to his own city. 97
16 they went with haste, and found Mary and Joseph 81
41 Now his parents went to Jerusalem every year 97
44 they went a day's journey 81
3: 3 he went into all the region about the Jordan 81
4:16 he went to the synagogue, as his custom was 71
30 passing through the midst of them he went away. 97
42 he departed and went into a lonely place 97
5:14 tell no one; but "go and show yourself to the priest 52
24 I say to you, rise, take up your bed and go home. 97
25 and took up that on which he lay, and went home 52
7: 6 Jesus went with them 97
8 I say to one, 'Go,' and he goes 97
8 I say to one, 'Go,' and he goes 97
11 Soon afterward he went to a city called Na'in 97
11 his disciples and a great crowd went with him. 104
22 Go and tell John what you have seen and heard 97
24 When the messengers of John had gone 52
50 Your faith has saved you; go in peace. 97
8:14 as they go on their way 97
24 they went and woke him, saying, "Master, Master 101
35 found the man from whom the demons had gone 77
38 The man from whom the demons had gone begged 77
42 As he went, the people pressed round him. 106
48 your faith has made you well; go in peace. 97
9:12 Send the crowd away, to go into the villages 97
13 go and buy food for all these people. 97
51 he set his face to go to Jerusalem. 97
52 who went and entered a village of the Samaritans 97
56 And they went on to another village. 97
57 As they were going along the road, a man said to him 97
57 I will follow you wherever you go. 52
59 he said, "Lord, let me first go and bury my father. 52
60 as for you, go and proclaim the kingdom of God.". 52
10: 3 Go your way; behold, I send you out as lambs 106
7 do not go from house to house. 87
10 go into its streets and say 77
34 and went to him and bound up his wounds 101
37 Jesus said to him "Go and do likewise. 97
40 she went to him and said, "Lord, do you not care 82
11: 5 Which of you who has a friend will go to him 97
26 Then he goes and brings seven other spirits 97
37 so he went in and sat at table. 71
12:58 you go with your accuser before the magistrate 106
13:32 he said to them, "Go and tell that fox, 'Behold 97
14: 1 when he went to dine at the house of a ruler 81
4 he took him and healed him, and let him go. 54
10 go and sit in the lowest place 97
19 I go to examine them 97
31 what king, going to encounter another king in war 97
15: 4 go after the one which is lost, until he finds it? 97
15 So he went 97
18 I will arise and go to my father 97
28 he was angry and refused to go in 71
16:30 if some one goes to them from the dead 97
17:14 Go and show yourselves to the priests. 97
14 as they went they were cleansed. 106
23 Do not go, do not follow them. 52
18:36 hearing a multitude going by 63
19: 7 He has gone in to be the guest of . . a sinner 71
12 A nobleman went into a far country 97
28 when he had said this, he went on ahead 97
30 saying, "Go into the village opposite 106
21: 8 'The time is at hand!' Do not go after them. 97
22: 8 So Jesus sent Peter and John, saying, "Go 97
13 they went, and found it as he had told them 52
22 For the Son of man goes as it has been determined; 97
33 I am ready to go with you to prison and to death. 97
39 went, as was his custom, to the Mount of Olives; 97
23:52 This man went to Pilate 101
24: 1 at early dawn, they went to the tomb 81
3 when they went in they did not find the body. 71
13 two of them were going to a village named Emma'us 97
15 Jesus himself drew near and went with them. 104
24 Some of those who were with us went to the tomb 52
28 drew near to the village to which they were going 97
28 He appeared to be going further 97
29 So he went in to stay with them. 71
Joh 1:43 The next day Jesus decided to go to Galilee. 77
3: 8 you do not know whence it comes or whither it goes;106
22 After this Jesus . . went into the land of Judea; 81
26 here he is, baptizing, and all are going to him. 81
4:16 Go, call your husband, and come here. 106
45 for they too had gone to the feast. 81
47 he went and begged him to come down and heal 52
50 Jesus said to him, "Go; your son will live. 97
5: 7 while I am going another steps down before me. 81
6: 1 Jesus went to the other side of the Sea of Galilee 52
21 at the land to which they were going. 106
24 they . . got into the boats and went to Caper'na-um 81
68 Simon Peter answered . . "Lord, to whom shall we go? 52
7: 3 Leave here and go to Judea 106
8 Go to the feast yourselves 47
33 then I go to him who sent me; 106
35 Where does this man intend to go 97
35 Does he intend to go to the Dispersion 97
45 The officers then went back to the chief priests 81
50 Nicode'mus, who had gone to him before 81
53 They went each to his own house. 97
8: 1 Jesus went to the Mount of Olives. 97
11 go, and do not sin again. 97
14 I know whence I have come and whither I am going 106
14 do not know whence I come or whither I am going. 106
21 where I am going, you cannot come. 106
22 since he says, 'Where I am going, you cannot come'? 106
9: 7 saying to him, "Go, wash in the pool of Silo'am 106
7 So he went and washed and came back seeing. 52
11 'Go to Silo'am and wash'; so I went and washed 106
11 so I went and washed and received my sight. 52
10: 4 he goes before them, and the sheep follow him 97
9 and will go in and out and find pasture. 71
11: 7 Let us go into Judea again. 45
8 are you going there again? 106
11 I go to awake him out of sleep. 97
15 let us go to him. 45
16 Let us also go, that we may die with him. 45
28 went and called her sister Mary, saying quietly 52
29 when she heard it, she rose quickly and went 81
31 supposing that she was going to the tomb to weep 106
44 Jesus said to them, "Unbind him, and let him go. 106
46 some of them went to the Pharisees 52
48 If we let him go on thus 58
54 went from there to the country 52
12:19 look, the world has gone after him. 52
22 Philip went and told Andrew 81
22 Andrew went with Philip and they told Jesus. 81
35 does not know where he goes. 106
13: 3 he had come from God and was going to God 106
27 What you are going to do, do quickly. •
33 'Where I am going you cannot come.' 106
36 Simon Peter said to him, "Lord, where are you going?106
36 Where I am going you cannot follow me now 106
14: 2 I go to prepare a place for you? 97
3 when I go and prepare a place for you 97
4 you know the way where I am going. 106
5 Lord, we do not know where you are going 106
12 because I go to the Father. 97
28 because I go to the Father 97
31 Rise, let us go hence. 45
15:16 that you should go and bear fruit 106
16: 5 now I am going to him who sent me 106
5 yet none of you asks me, 'Where are you going?' 106
7 if I go, I will send him to you. 97
10 because I go to the Father 106
17 'because I go to the Father'? 106
28 I am leaving the world and going to the Father. 97
18: 3 went there with lanterns and torches 81
8 I am he; so, if you seek me, let these men go. 58
20: 2 went to Simon Peter and the other disciple 81
3 they went toward the tomb. 57
5 but he did not go in. 71
8 also went in, and he saw and believed; 71
17 go to my brethren and say to them 97
18 Mary Mag'dalene went and said to the disciples 81
21: 3 Simon Peter said to them, "I am going fishing. 106
3 They said to him, "We will go with you. 81
18 carry you where you do not wish to go. •
20 Lord, who is it that is going to betray you? •
Act 1:10 while they were gazing into heaven as he went 97
11 Jesus . . will come in the same way as you saw him go 97
21 the Lord Jesus went in and out among us 71
25 to go to his own place. 97
3: 3 Seeing Peter and John about to go into the temple 70
4:21 they let them go, finding no way to punish them 54
23 they went to their friends 81
5:20 Go and stand in the temple and speak to the people 97
26 captain with the officers went and brought them 52
40 and let them go. 54
7: 3 go into the land which I will show you.' 61
8:26 Rise and go toward the south 97
27 he rose and went 97
36 as they went along the road 97
39 went on his way rejoicing. 97
9: 1 Saul . . went to the high priest 101
11 Rise and go to the street called Straight 97
15 the Lord said to him, "Go 97
28 So he went in and out among them at Jerusalem 72
39 So Peter rose and went with them 105
10:27 he went in and found many persons gathered; 71
11: 3 saying, "Why did you go to uncircumcised men 71
12 the Spirit told me to go with them 105
25 Barnabas went to Tarsus to look for Saul; 77
12:12 When he realized this, he went to the house of Mary 81
17 Then he departed and went to another place. 97
13:51 and went to Ico'nium. 81
14:20 on the next day he went on with Barnabas to Derbe. 77
15:38 and had not gone with them to the work. 105
16: 7 they attempted to go into Bithyn'ia 97
10 immediately we sought to go on into Macedo'nia 77
16 As we were going to the place of prayer 97
19 her owners saw that their hope of gain was gone 77
35 sent the police, saying, "Let those men go. 54
36 The magistrates have sent to let you go 54
36 now therefore come out and go in peace. 97
17: 2 Paul went in, as was his custom 71
9 they let them go. 54
10 they went into the Jewish synagogue. 51
18: 1 After this he left Athens and went to Corinth. 81
6 From now on I will go to the Gentiles. 97
7 went to the house of a man named Titius Justus 71
19:21 resolved . . to . . go to Jerusalem, saying 97

30 Paul wished to go in among the crowd 71
20: 5 These went on and were waiting for us at Tro'as 99
22 now, behold, I am going to Jerusalem 97
25 among whom I have gone preaching the kingdom 65
21: 4 they told Paul not to go on to Jerusalem. 79
16 some of the disciples from Caesare'a went with us 105
18 On the following day Paul went in with us to James; 70
22:10 the Lord said to me, 'Rise, and go into Damascus 97
26 he went to the tribune and said to him 101
23:14 they went to the chief priests and elders, and said 101
15 as though you were going to determine his case 86
16 he went and entered the barracks and told Paul. 90
20 as though they were going to inquire . . about him 86
23 get ready . . to go as far as Caesare'a. 97
32 leaving the horsemen to go on with him. 52
24:25 Go away for the present 97
25: 4 he himself intended to go there shortly. 74
12 to Caesar you shall go. 97
20 I asked whether he wished to go to Jerusalem 97
27: 3 gave him leave to go to his friends 97
9 because the fast had already gone by 92
32 cut away the ropes of the boat, and let it go. 73
28:26 'Go to this people, and say, You shall indeed hear 97
Rom 15:24 I hope to see you in passing as I go to Spain 97
25 I am going to Jerusalem with aid for the saints. 97
28 I shall go on by way of you to Spain; 52
1Co 4: 6 learn by us not to go beyond what is written •
5:10 since then you would need to go out of the world. 77
10:27 you are disposed to go 97
16: 4 If it seems advisable that I should go also 97
6 may speed me on my journey, wherever I go. 97
2Co 2:13 So I took leave of them and went on to Macedo'nia. 77
8:17 he is going to you of his own accord. 77
9: 5 necessary to urge the brethren to go on to you 99
12: 1 go on to visions and revelations of the Lord. 81
18 I urged Titus to go, and sent the brother with him. •
Gal 1:21 I went into the regions of Syria and Cili'cia. 81
2: 9 we should go to the Gentiles •
Php 2:23 just as soon as I see how it will go with me; •
1Ti 1: 3 As I urged you when I was going to Macedonia 97
2Ti 3:13 impostors will go on from bad to worse 100
4:10 has deserted me and gone to Thessaloni'ca; 97
10 Crescens has gone to Galatia, Titus to Dalmatia. •
Heb 6: 1 let us . . go on to maturity 107
20 Jesus has gone as a forerunner on our behalf 71
9: 7 into the second only the high priest goes •
11: 8 he went out, not knowing where he was to go. 81
Jas 2:16 Go in peace, be warmed and filled 106
4:13 tomorrow we will go into such and such a town 97
1Pe 3:19 he went and preached to the spirits in prison 97
22 who has gone into heaven 97
1Jn 2:11 and does not know where he is going 106
Rev 5: 7 he went and took the scroll from the right hand 81
10: 8 Go, take the scroll which is open in the hand 106
9 So I went to the angel and told him to give me 52
13:10 If . . to be taken captive, to captivity he goes; 106
14: 4 it is these who follow the Lamb wherever he goes; 106
16: 1 Go and pour out on the earth the seven bowls 106
2 first angel went and poured his bowl on the earth 52
15 that he may not go naked and be seen exposed!") 94
17: 8 The beast . . is to ascend . . and go to perdition; 106
11 As for the beast . . it goes to perdition. 106
18:14 The fruit for which thy soul longed has gone 52
1Es 1:25 Pharaoh, king of Egypt, went to make war 81
2:18 have gone to Jerusalem 81
20 since the building of the temple is now going on 75
30 went in haste to Jerusalem 48
3: 3 Darius the king went to his bedroom 49
4: 4 if he sends them out against the enemy, they go 59
19 they let all those things go, and gape at her 58
61 he took the letters, and went to Babylon 77
6: 8 when we went to the country of Judea 90
10 These operations are going on rapidly 60
8:10 may go with you to Jerusalem. 104
14 rams and lambs and what goes with them 46
45 I told them to go to Iddo 81
9: 1 went from the court of the temple 97
2Es 1: 5 Go and declare to my people their evil deeds 119
2: 2 'Go, my children, because I am a widow and forsaken. 111
4 Go, my children, and ask for mercy from the Lord.' 111
10 which I was going to give to Israel. •
33 a command . . to go to Israel 111
48 Then the angel said to me, "Go, tell my people 119
4: 5 he said to me, "Go, weigh for me the weight of fire 119
13 I went into a forest of trees of the plain 117
14 Come, let us go and make war against the sea 111
40 Go and ask a woman who is with child 119
45 whether for us the greater part has gone by. 114
46 For I know what has gone by 114
48 and when the flame had gone by I looked, and behold 118
7:136 to those who are gone and to those yet to come 115
9:24 go into a field of flowers 111
26 I went, as he directed me, into the field 117
10:10 and behold, almost all go to perdition 109
13 the multitude that is now in it goes as it came'; 108
22 our Levites have gone into captivity 108
53 Therefore I told you to go into the field 120
55 go in and see the splendor and vastness 112
11:19 so it went with all the wings 110
12:49 Now go, every one of you to his house 111
50 the people went into the city, as I told them to do. 116
13:41 and go to a more distant region 117
43 they went in by the narrow passages 113
45 a long way to go, a journey of a year and a half •
14:20 For behold, I will go, as thou hast commanded me 108
23 He answered me and said, "Go and gather the people 119
27 Then I went as he commanded me 116
15:17 For a man will desire to go into a city 111
43 they shall go on steadily to Babylon 118
Tob 1: 3 who went with me into the land of the Assyrians 104
6 I alone went often to Jerusalem for the feasts 97
7 I would go and spend the proceeds 97
14 I used to go into Media 97
15 I could no longer go into Media. 97
19 went and informed the king about me 97
2: 2 Go and bring 59
7 I went and dug a grave and buried the body. 89
10 I went to physicians, but they did not help me. 97
10 took care of me until he went to Elymais. 97
3: 6 to go to the eternal abode 68
9 Why do you beat us? If they are dead, go with them! 59
4:15 let drunkenness go with you on your way. 97
5: 3 Find a man to go with you 104
3 go and get the money. 97
4 he went to look for a man 97
5 Can you go with me to Rages in Media? 97
6 The angel replied, "I will go with you 97
8 he said to him, "Go, and do not delay. 97
8 So he went in and said to his father 71
8 I have found some one to go with me 104
8 and whether he is a reliable man to go with you. 97
11 a man whom you will pay to go with your son 104
13 when we went together to Jerusalem to worship 97
16 Go with this man 97
17 as he goes in and out before us? 72
21 For a good angel will go with him 104
6:14 if I go in I will die as those before me did 71
17 You will save her, and she will go with you 97
8: 2 As he went he remembered the words of Raphael 97
9 Raguel arose and went and dug a grave 97
11 Then Raguel went into his house 81
13 went in, and found them both asleep. 71
9: 2 go to Gabael at Rages in Media and get the money 97
10: 5 Am I not distressed, my child, that I let you go 58
11: 6 so is the man who went with him! 97
15 his son went in rejoicing 71
16 Those who saw him as he went were amazed 97
12: 1 see to the wages of the man who went with you; 105
13 in order to go and lay out the dead 52
14: 4 Go to Media, my son 52
Jdt 2: 6 Go and attack the whole west country 77
10 You shall go 77
5: 9 go to the land of Canaan 97
6: 7 Now my slaves are going to take you back •
7:21 their cisterns were going dry •
8:18 as was done in days gone by- 102
35 Uzziah and the rulers said to her, "Go in peace 97
35 may the Lord God go before you •
36 went to their posts. 97
10:11 The women went straight on through the valley; 97
12 where are you going? 97
13 I will show him a way by which he can go 97
15 Go at once to his tent 101
19 if we let them go 58
12:11 Go now and persuade the Hebrew woman 97
12 it will be a disgrace if we let such a woman go 93
15 her maid went 101
13: 1 they went to bed, for they all were weary 53
10 as they were accustomed to go for prayer •
16 who has protected me in the way I went 97
14: 3 they will seize their arms and go into the camp 97
12 they went to the generals and the captains 81
14 Bagoas went in and knocked at the door of the tent 71
17 Then he went to the tent where Judith had stayed 71
16:21 Judith went to Bethulia 52
Wis 3: 3 their going from us to be their destruction 96
4: 2 they long for it when it has gone 52
15: 8 after a little while goes to the earth 97
Sir 6:27 when you get hold of her, do not let her go. 58
7: 8 even for one you will not go unpunished. 67
12:11 he humbles himself and goes about cringing 97
21: 5 The prayer of a poor man goes from his lips •
25:26 If she does not go as you direct 97
27:19 you have let your neighbor go 58
29:24 It is a miserable life to go from house to house •
31: 8 who does not go after gold. 97
32:20 Do not go on a path full of hazards 97
33:31 which way will you go to seek him? •
34:26 goes again and does the same things 97
41:10 so the ungodly go from curse to destruction. •
Bar 3:33 he who sends forth the light, and it goes, called it 97
4:19 Go, my children, go; for I have been left desolate. 59
19 Go, my children, go; for I have been left desolate. 59
Aza 1: 7 that it might go well with us. 60
Sus 1: 8 two . . used to see her . . going in and walking about 72
13 Let us go home, for it is mealtime. 97
15 she went in as before with only two maids 71
Bel 1: 4 revered it and went every day to worship it 97
10 the king went with Daniel into the temple of Bel. 81
11 Behold, we are going outside 56
13 through which they used to go in regularly 72
19 restrained the king from going in, and said 71
29 Going to the king, they said, "Hand Daniel over to us 81
33 was going into the field to take it to the reapers. 97
1Mc 1:11 Let us go and make a covenant with the Gentiles 97
13 some of the people eagerly went to the king 97
3:31 determined to go to Persia 97
39 to go into the land of Judah and destroy it 81
41 went to the camp to get the sons of Israel 81
45 not one of her children went in or out 72
46 So they assembled and went to Mizpah 81
4:26 went and reported to Lysias 90
5:17 Choose your men and go and rescue your brethren 97
17 I and Jonathan my brother will go to Gilead. 97
20 assigned to Simon to go to Galilee 97
21 so Simon went to Galilee 97
24 went three days' journey into the wilderness. 97
29 they went all the way to the stronghold of Dathema. 97
39 Judas went to meet them. 97
45 to go to the land of Judah. 81
46 they had to go through it. 97
57 let us go and make war on the Gentiles around us. 97
66 to go into the land of the Philistines 97
6: 5 the armies which had gone into the land of Judah 97
6 that Lysias had gone first with a strong force 97
22 They went to the king and said, "How long 97
36 wherever it went they went with it 97
36 wherever it went they went with it 97
56 with the forces that had gone with the king 97
7: 7 let him go and see all the ruin 97
36 the priests went in and stood before the altar 71
8: 6 who went to fight against them 97
19 They went to Rome, a very long journey 97
23 May all go well with the Romans 60
9: 2 They went by the road which leads to Gilgal 97
4 then they marched off and went to Berea 97
14 then all the stouthearted men went with him 105
29 no one like him to go against our enemies 78
47 he eluded him and went to the rear. •
59 they went and consulted with him. 97
65 he went with only a few men. 81
10:60 went with pomp to Ptolemais and met the two kings; 97
77 went to Azotus as though he were going farther 97
11: 2 and went to meet him •
7 Jonathan went with the king as far as the river 97
21 certain lawless men . . went to the king 97
24 for he went to the king at Ptolemais 97
39 So he went to Imalkue the Arab 97
12: 3 they went to Rome and entered the senate chamber 97
17 We have commanded them to go also to you 97
32 Then he broke camp and went to Damascus 81
13:20 to every place he went. 97
22 So Trypho got all his cavalry ready to go 81
22 he did not go because of the snow 81
22 He marched off and went into the land of Gilead. 81
14: 3 he went and defeated the army of Demetrius 97
15:25 he shut Trypho up and kept him from going out or in. 72
2Mc 3: 5 he went to Apollonius of Tarsus 81
14 he set a day and went in to direct the inspection 70
4:11 who went on the mission to establish friendship 95
31 the king went hastily to settle the trouble 84
5: 9 having embarked to go to the Lacedaemonians •
6:17 we must go on briefly with the story. 81
20 as men ought to go 101
28 he went at once to the rack. 81
7:19 do not think that you will go unpunished 67
8:20 when 8,000 in all went into the affair 81
11:23 Now that our father has gone on to the gods 85
26 and go on happily in the conduct of their own affairs. 62
12: 1 the Jews went about their farming. 60
10 When they had gone more than a mile from there 55
17 When they had gone 95 miles from there 55
24 he besought them to let him go in safety 76
25 they let him go 54
38 went to the city of Adullam 84
39 Judas and his men went to take up the bodies 81
13:25 went to Ptolemais 81
14: 4 went to King Demetrius in about the 151st year 83
26 went to Demetrius 83
31 he went to the great and holy temple 90
15:36 never to let this day go unobserved 66
3Mc 1: 4 went to the troops with wailing and tears 80
4:11 to those from the city going out into the country 103
5:18 After the party had been going on for some time 98
4Mc 3:13 went searching throughout the enemy camp 64
4: 8 Apollonius went on to the temple. 51
11:16 go on torturing! •
12:12 these throughout all time will never let you go. 50
14: 6 those holy youths . . agreed to go to death for its sake. •

go *See also* allow, left, mad, right.

go aboard 1. ἀναβαίνω 2. ἐπιβαίνω

Joh 21:11 Simon Peter went aboard and hauled the net ashore 1
Act 21: 2 we went aboard, and set sail. 2

go about 1. הלך 2. נקף 3. סבב 4. עשה 5. שוט 6. βαδίζω 7. διέρχομαι 8. κυκλόω 9. περιάγω 10. περιέρχομαι 11. περίημι 12. περιπατέω 13. περίπατος

Num11: 8 people went about and gathered it, and ground it 5
Deu 2: 1 for many days we went about Mount Se'ir. 3
3 You have been going about this mountain country 3
Jos 6:11 the ark . . to compass the city, going about it once; 2
1Kg 21:27 and lay in sackcloth, and went about dejectedly. 1
2Ch 17: 9 they went about through all the cities of Judah 3
23: 2 they went about through Judah 3
Job 24:10 They go about naked, without clothing; hungry 1
30:28 I go about blackened, but not by the sun; 1
Ps 26: 6 in innocence, and go about thy altar, O LORD 3
35:14 I went about as one who laments his mother 1
38: 6 all the day I go about mourning. 1
39: 6 Surely man goes about as a shadow! 1
Prv 6:12 wicked man . . goes about with crooked speech 1
11:13 who goes about as a talebearer reveals secrets 1
20:19 He who goes about gossiping reveals secrets; 1
Ecc 12: 5 and the mourners go about the streets; 3
Sng 3: 2 I will rise now and go about the city 3
3 watchmen found me, as they went about in the city. 3
5: 7 The watchmen found me, as they went about the city; 3
Isa 23:16 Take a harp, go about the city, O forgotten harlot! 3
Jer 6:28 They are . . rebellious, going about with slanders; 1
9: 4 and every neighbor goes about as a slanderer. 1
Dan 8:27 then I rose and went about the king's business; 4
Mic 2:11 If a man should go about and utter wind and lies 1
Mat 4:23 And he went about all Galilee teaching 9
9:35 Jesus went about all the cities and villages 9
Mrk 6: 6 he went about among the villages teaching. 9
12:38 who like to go about in long robes 12
Lke 20:46 the scribes, who like to go about in long robes 12
Joh 6:66 and no longer went about with him. 12
7: 1 After this Jesus went about in Galilee 12
1 he would not go about in Judea 12
11:54 Jesus therefore no longer went about openly 12
Act 8: 4 those . . went about preaching the word. 7
10:38 how he went about doing good 7
13:11 he went about seeking people to lead him 9
Heb 11:37 they went about in skins of sheep and goats 10
Wis 6:16 she goes about seeking those worthy of her 10
8:18 I went about seeking how to get her for myself. 11
Sir 9:13 you are going about on the city battlements. 12
10:27 one who goes about boasting, but lacks bread. 13
Bar 2:18 person . . that goes about bent over and feeble 6
1Mc 2:45 Mattathias and his friends went about 8

go abroad 1. διέρχομαι 2. ἐκπορεύομαι

Lke 5:15 the report went abroad concerning him 1
Rev 16:14 who go abroad to the kings of the whole world 2

go across 1. διέρχομαι

Mrk 4:35 Let us go across to the other side. 1
Lke 8:22 Let us go across to the other side of the lake. 1

go after 1. διώκω

Sir 27:20 Do not go after him, for he is too far off 1

go again 1. שוב 2. שוב ובוא

Gen 43: 2 Go again, buy us a little food. 1
13 also your brother, and arise, go again to the man; 1
44:25 when our father said, 'Go again, buy us a little food 1
Jos 20: 6 the slayer may go again to his own town and . . home 2
1Kg 18:43 And he said, "Go again seven times. 1

go against 1. חזק מִן

2Kg 3:26 Moab saw that the battle was going against him 1

go ahead 1. יסף עבר 2. προάγω 3. προέρχομαι 4. προλαμβάνω 5. προπορεύομαι

Num22:26 Then the angel of the LORD went ahead, and stood 1
Act 20:13 But going ahead to the ship, we set sail for Assos 3
1Co 11:21 in eating, each one goes ahead with his own meal 4
2Jn 1: 9 Any one who goes ahead and does not abide 2
Jdt 2:19 to go ahead of King Nebuchadnezzar 3
1Mc 9:11 the archers went ahead of the army 5

go along 1. הלך 2. συνεξέρχομαι 3. συνέρχομαι 4. transeo

Num20:17 we will go along the King's Highway 1
2Sm 16:13 Shim'e-i went along on the hillside opposite him 1
2Es 16:32 because no sheep will go along them. 4
Tob 11: 4 the dog went along behind them. 3
Jdt 2:20 Along with them went a mixed crowd 2

go and meet 1. ὑπαντάω

Joh 11:20 she went and met him, while Mary sat in the house. 1

go around 1. נקף 2. סבב 3. סָבִיב

Num21: 4 set out . . to go around the land of Edom; 2
Jos 6: 3 all the men of war going around the city once. 1
Jdg 11:18 went around the land of Edom and the land of Moab 2
2Sm 5:23 You shall not go up; go around to their rear 2
24: 6 came to Dan, and from Dan they went around to Sidon 3
1Ch 14:14 go around and come upon them 2
Ps 55:10 Day and night they go around it on its walls; 2

go ashore 1. ἐξέρχομαι

Mat 14:14 As he went ashore he saw a great throng 1
Mrk 6:34 As he went ashore he saw a great throng 1

go aside 1. סיג 2. פרד 3. ἀναχωρέω 4. ἀπέρχομαι

1Kg 18:27 he is a god; either he is musing, or he has gone aside 1
Hos 4:14 for the men themselves go aside with harlots 2
Act 4:15 commanded them to go aside out of the council 4
23:19 The tribune . . going aside asked him privately 3

go astray 1. זור 2. זנה 3. נדח 4. סוט 5. סור 6. שטה 7. שגג 8. תעה 9. ἀποπλανάω 10. πλανάω

Exd 23: 4 If you meet your enemy's ox or his ass going astray 8
Num 5:12 If any man's wife goes astray and acts 6
20 if you have gone astray 6
29 when a wife . . goes astray and defiles herself 6
Deu 22: 1 not see your brother's ox or his sheep go astray 3
Ps 14: 3 They have all gone astray, they are all alike 5
40: 4 to those who go astray after false gods! 4
58: 3 The wicked go astray from the womb 1
119:67 Before I was afflicted I went astray; 7
118dost spurn all who go astray from thy statutes; 7
176I have gone astray like a lost sheep; 8
Prv 10:17 but he who rejects reproof goes astray. 8
Isa 53: 6 All we like sheep have gone astray; 8
Jer 42:20 you have gone astray at the cost of your lives. 8
Ezk 20:30 and go astray after their detestable things? 2
44:10 going astray from me after their idols 8
10 after their idols when Israel went astray 8
15 when the people of Israel went astray from me 8
48:11 who kept my charge, who did not go astray 8
11 go astray when the people of Israel went astray 8
Mat 18:12 and one of them has gone astray 10
12 and go in search of the one that went astray? 10
13 more than over the 99 that never went astray. 10
Heb 3:10 They always go astray in their hearts 10
2Pe 2:15 Forsaking the right way they have gone astray; 10
Tob 5:13 They did not go astray in the error of our brethren 10
Wis 12:24 For they went far astray on the paths of error 10
13: 6 perhaps they go astray while seeking God 10
17: 1 therefore unintructed souls have gone astray. 10
Sir 4:19 If he goes astray she will forsake him 9
Bar 4:28 For just as you purposed to go astray from God 10

go away 1. אזל 2. הלך 3. יצא 4. נסע 5. עבר 6. עלה 7. ἀναλύω 8. ἀπέρχομαι 9. ἀποδημέω 10. ἐξέρχομαι 11. μεταίρω 12. οἴχομαι 13. πορεύω 14. ὑπάγω

Gen 4:16 Cain went away from the presence of the LORD 3
26:16 Abim'elech said to Isaac, "Go away from us; 2
31:30 now you have gone away because you longed 2
34:26 took Dinah out of Shechem's house, and went away. 3
37:17 the man said, "They have gone away 4
38:19 she arose and went away, and taking off her veil 2
Jdg 19:28 and the man rose up and went away to his home. 2
Rut 1:21 I went away full, and the LORD has brought me back 2
1Sm 15:27 As Samuel turned to go away, Saul laid hold upon 2
26:12 David took the spear and . . and they went away. 2
28:25 Then they rose and went away that night. 2
2Sm 13:19 and went away, crying aloud as she went. 2
17:18 so both of them went away quickly 2
1Kg 12: 5 said to them, "Depart . . " So the people went away. 2
2Kg 5:11 Na'aman was angry, and went away, saying, "Behold 2
12 So he turned and went away in a rage. 2
12:18 Then Haz'ael went away from Jerusalem. 6
2Ch 10: 5 So the people went away. 2
Est 4:17 Mor'decai then went away and did everything 5
Ps 34: 0 so that he drove him out, and he went away. 2
55:15 let them go away in terror into their graves. •
Prv 20:14 but when he goes away, then he boasts. 1
Jer 5:23 they have turned aside and gone away. 2
9: 2 that I might leave my people and go away from them! 2
22:10 but weep bitterly for him who goes away 2
11 and who went away from this place 3
43:12 he shall go away from there in peace. 3
Lam 1: 5 her children have gone away, captives 2
Hos 5:14 I, even I, will rend and go away, I will carry off 2
6: 4 Your love is . . like the dew that goes early away. 2
13: 3 they shall be . . like the dew that goes early away 2
Mat 9:31 But they went away and spread his fame 10
32 As they were going away, behold, a dumb demoniac 10
11: 7 As they went away, Jesus began to speak 13
13:25 sowed weeds among the wheat, and went away. 8
53 when Jesus had finished . . he went away 11
14:16 Jesus said, "They need not go away 8
15:21 Jesus went away from there and withdrew 10
19: 1 he went away from Galilee and entered 11
22 he went away sorrowful 8
22:22 they left him and went away. 8
24: 1 Jesus left the temple and was going away 10
25:15 Then he went away. 9
46 they will go away into eternal punishment 8
26:42 Again, for the second time, he went away and prayed 8
44 So, leaving them again, he went away 8
Mrk 5:20 he went away and began to proclaim 8
6: 1 He went away from there 10
32 they went away in the boat to a lonely place 8
7:24 he arose and went away to the region of Tyre 8
10:22 he went away sorrowful 8
11: 4 they went away, and found a colt tied at the door 8
12:12 so they left him and went away. 8
14:39 again he went away and prayed 8
Lke 2:15 When the angels went away from them into heaven 8
8:39 And he went away 8
11:53 As he went away from there 10
19:32 So those who were sent went away 8
22: 4 he went away 8
Joh 4: 8 For his disciples had gone away into the city 8
28 left her water jar, and went away into the city 8
5:15 The man went away and told the Jews 8
6:22 his disciples had gone away alone. 8
67 Do you also wish to go away? 14
8: 9 when they heard it, they went away, one by one 10
21 he said to them, "I go away, and you will seek me 14
10:40 He went away again across the Jordan 8
12:11 on account of him many of the Jews were going away 14
14:28 'I go away, and I will come to you.' 14
16: 7 it is to your advantage that I go away 8
7 if I do not go away, the Counselor will not come 8
Gal 1:17 I went away into Arabia 8
Jas 1:24 he observes himself and goes away 8
1Es 4:11 no one may go away to attend to his own affairs 8
2Mc 14:34 Having said this, he went away 8
3Mc 2:24 but went away uttering bitter threats. 7
4Mc 4:14 Apollonius . . went away to report to the king 12

go back 1. בוא 2. הלך 3. עלה 4. פרע 5. שוב 6. שוב וָבוֹא 7. ἀπέρχομαι

Gen 44:24 When we went back to your servant my father 3
33 let the lad go back with his brothers. 3
34 For how can I go back to my father if the lad is not 3
Exd 4:18 Moses went back to Jethro his father-in-law 5
18 Let me go back, I pray, to my kinsmen in Egypt 5
19 the LORD said to Moses in Mid'ian, "Go back to Egypt; 5
20 Moses . . went back to the land of Egypt; 5
21 the LORD said to Moses, "When you go back to Egypt 5
Lev 25:41 he and his children with him, and go back to his own 5
Num14: 3 would it not be better for us to go back to Egypt? 5
4 Let us choose a captain, and go back to Egypt. 5
22:34 if it is evil in thy sight, I will go back again. 5
Deu 24:19 forgotten a sheaf . . you shall not go back to get 5
Jos 22: 8 Go back to your homes with much wealth 5
Jdg 14:19 In hot anger he went back to his father's house. 3
18:26 he turned and went back to his home. 5
Rut 1:15 See, your sister-in-law has gone back to her people 5
3:17 for he said, 'You must not go back empty-handed 1
1Sm 1:19 they went back to their house at Ramah. 6
9: 5 Come, let us go back, lest my father cease to care 5
17:15 but David went back and forth from Saul 5
29: 7 go back now; and go peaceably 5
2Sm 15:19 Go back, and stay with the king; 5
20 Go back, and take your brethren with you; 5
27 Look, go back to the city in peace, you and Abi'athar 5
1Kg 13:19 he went back with him, and ate bread in his house 5
19:20 Go back again; for what have I done to you? 2
2Kg 2:13 went back and stood on the bank of the Jordan. 5
20: 9 shall the shadow go . . or go back 10 steps? 5
10 rather let the shadow go back ten steps. 5
2Ch 9:12 So she turned and went back to her own land 2
Jer 46:16 Arise, and let us go back to our own people 5
Ezk 24:14 I will do it; I will not go back, I will not spare 4
47: 7 As I went back, I saw upon the bank of the river 5
Mrk 16:13 they went back and told the rest 7
Joh 20:10 the disciples went back to their homes. 7
1Mc 7:20 then Bacchides went back to the king. 7

go backward 1. ἀναποδίζω

Sir 48:23 In his days the sun went backward 1

go before 1. קָדִים 2. קדם 3. προάγω 4. προέρχομαι 5. προπορεύομαι 6. πρότερος 7. sum 8. transeo

Ps 89:14 steadfast love and faithfulness go before thee. 2
Ezk 40:19 Then he went before me to the north 1
Hab 1: 9 terror of them goes before them. 1
Mat 2: 9 in the East went before them, till it came to rest 3
14:22 and go before him to the other side 3
21: 9 the crowds that went before him 3
31 go into the kingdom of God before you. 3
26:32 I will go before you to Galilee. 3
28: 7 behold, he is going before you to Galilee 3
Mrk 6:45 go before him to the other side, to Beth-sa'ida 3
11: 9 those who went before . . cried out 3
14:28 I will go before you to Galilee. 3
16: 7 he is going before you to Galilee; 3
Lke 1:17 he will go before him in the spirit 4
76 you will go before the Lord to prepare his ways 5
Act 7:40 saying to Aaron, 'Make for us gods to go before us 5
2Es 11:32 all the wings that had gone before. 7
40 all the beasts that have gone before 8
Jdt 9: 5 those that went before and those that followed; 6
15:13 she went before all the people in the dance 4
AEs 15: 7 the maid who went before her. 5

go beyond 1. יצא 2. עבר 3. ὑπερβαίνω
Num22:18 could not go beyond the command of the LORD 2
24:13 I would not be able to go beyond the word of the LORD 2
35:26 shall at any time go beyond the bounds of his city 1
Sir 20: 7 a braggart and fool goes beyond the right moment. 3

go by 1. עבר
Jer 46:17 king of Egypt, 'Noisy one who lets the hour go by.' 1

go by land 1. πεζεύω
Act 20:13 intending himself to go by land. 1

cause to go 1. הלך
Isa 63:12 who caused his glorious arm to go at the right 1

go deep 1. נחת
Prv 17:10 A rebuke goes deeper into a man of understanding 1

go down 1. בוא 2. היה 3. הלך 4. ירד 5. מָבוֹא 6. נחת 7. נְחַת 8. עבר 9. צנח 10. מַעַל (A) 11. ἀφικνέομαι 12. ἐπιδύω 13. καταβαίνω 14. κατέρχομαι 15. συγκαταβαίνω 16. descendo
Gen 11: 7 Come, let us go down, and . . confuse their language 4
12:10 So Abram went down to Egypt to sojourn there 4
15:12 As the sun was going down, a deep sleep fell 1
17 When the sun had gone down and it was dark 1
18:21 I will go down to see whether they have done 4
24:16 She went down to the spring, and filled her jar 4
45 and she went down to the spring, and drew. 4
26: 2 Do not go down to Egypt; dwell in the land of which I 4
37:35 No, I shall go down to Sheol to my son, mourning. 4
38: 1 Judah went down from his brothers 4
42: 2 grain in Egypt; go down and buy grain for us there 4
3 ten of Joseph's brothers went down to buy grain 4
38 he said, "My son shall not go down with you 4
43: 4 with us, we will go down and buy you food; 4
5 if you will not send him, we will not go down 4
15 and they arose and went down to Egypt 4
44:26 we said, 'We cannot go down. 4
26 If . . brother goes with us, then we will go down; 4
46: 3 do not be afraid to go down to Egypt; 4
4 I will go down with you to Egypt 4
Exd 15: 5 they went down into the depths like a stone. 4
17:12 were steady until the going down of the sun. 1
19:14 Moses went down from the mountain to the people 4
21 LORD said to Moses, "Go down and warn the people 4
24 Go down, and come up bringing Aaron with you; 4
25 So Moses went down to the people and told them. 4
22:26 restore it to him before the sun goes down; 1
32: 7 the LORD said to Moses, "Go down; for your people 4
15 Moses turned, and went down from the mountain 4
Num16:30 they go down alive into Sheol, then you shall know 4
33 they . . went down alive into Sheol; 4
20:15 how our fathers went down to Egypt 4
34:11 the boundary shall go down from Shepham to Riblah 4
11 boundary shall go down, and reach to the shoulder 4
12 boundary shall go down to the Jordan, and its end 4
Deu 9:12 LORD said to me, 'Arise, go down quickly from here; 4
10:22 Your fathers went down to Egypt 70 persons; 4
11:30 west of the road, toward the going down of the sun 5
16: 6 evening at the going down of the sun 1
24:13 when the sun goes down, you shall restore to him 1
15 hire . . day he earns it, before the sun goes down 1
26: 5 went down into Egypt and sojourned there 4
Jos 1: 4 to the Great Sea toward the going down of the sun 5
8:29 and at the going down of the sun Joshua commanded 1
10:11 they were going down the ascent of Beth-hor'on *
13 The sun stayed . . and did not hasten to go down 1
27 at the time of the going down of the sun 1
15:10 boundary . . goes down to Beth-she'mesh 4
16: 3 then it goes down westward to the territory 4
7 it goes down from Jan-o'ah to At'aroth 4
17: 9 Then the boundary went down to the brook Kanah. 4
18:13 then the boundary goes down to At'aroth-ad'dar 4
16 boundary goes down to the border of the mountain 4
16 and it then goes down the valley of Hinnom 4
17 then it goes down to the Stone of Bohan 4
18 and passing on . . it goes down to the Arabah; 4
24: 4 but Jacob and his children went down to Egypt. 4
Jdg 1: 9 men of Judah went down to fight . . the Canaanites 4
3:27 people of Israel went down with him from the hill 4
28 So they went down after him, and seized the fords 4
4:14 Barak went down from Mount Tabor with 10,000 men 4
21 drove the peg . . till it went down into the ground 9
7: 9 LORD said to him, "Arise, go down against the camp; 4
10 if you fear to go down, go down . . with Purah 4
10 if you fear . . go down to the camp with Purah 4
11 your hands shall be strengthened to go down 4
11 Then he went down with Purah his servant 4
14: 1 Samson went down to Timnah, and at Timnah he saw 4
5 Samson went down with his father and mother 4
7 he went down and talked with the woman; 4
10 And his father went down to the woman 4
18 to him on the seventh day before the sun went down 1
19 he went down to Ash'kelon and killed 30 men 4
15: 8 he went down and stayed in the cleft of the rock 4
11 men of Judah went down to the cleft of the rock 4
19:14 the sun went down on them near Gib'e-ah 1
Rut 3: 3 and put on . . and go down to the threshing floor; 4
6 she went down to the threshing floor 4
1Sm 9:27 they were going down to the outskirts of the city 4
10: 8 And you shall go down before me to Gilgal; 4
13:20 the Israelites went down to the Philistines 4
14:36 Let us go down after the Philistines by night 4
37 Shall I go down after the Philistines? 4
15: 6 Go, depart, go down from among the Amal'ekites 4
12 and turned, and passed on, and went down to Gilgal. 4
22: 1 when his brothers . . they went down there to him. 4
23: 4 go down to Kei'lah; for I will give . . into your hand. 4
8 Saul summoned all . . to war, to go down to Kei'lah 4
25 David was told; therefore he went down to the rock 4
25: 1 David . . went down to the wilderness of Paran. 4
26: 2 Saul arose and went down to the wilderness 4
6 Who will go down with me into the camp to Saul? 4
6 And Abi'shai said, "I will go down with you. 4
10 or he shall go down into battle and perish. 4
29: 4 he shall not go down with us to battle 4
30:24 For as his share is who goes down into the battle 4
2Sm 2:24 and as the sun was going down they came to the hill 1
3:35 if I taste bread or . . till the sun goes down! 1
5:17 David heard . . and went down to the stronghold. 4
11: 8 Go down to your house, and wash your feet. 4
9 Uri'ah slept . . and did not go down to his house. 4
10 they told David, "Uri'ah did not go down to his house 4
10 Why did you not go down to your house? 4
13 he went out . . but he did not go down to his house. 4
17:18 who had a well . . and they went down into it. 4
21:15 and David went down together with his servants 4
23:13 And three of the 30 chief men went down 4
20 He also went down and slew a lion in a pit 4
21 but Benai'ah went down to him with a staff 4
1Kg 1:25 he has gone down this day, and has sacrificed oxen 4
38 Zadok . . went down and caused Solomon to ride 4
2: 6 do not let his gray head go down to Sheol in peace. 4
18:44 Go up, say to Ahab, 'Prepare your chariot and go down 4
21:16 Ahab arose to go down to the vineyard of Naboth 4
18 Arise, go down to meet Ahab . . who is in Sama'ria; 4
2Kg 1:15 Go down with him; do not be afraid of him. 4
15 So he arose and went down with him to the king 4
2: 2 So they went down to Bethel. 4
3:12 and Jehosh'aphat and the king of Edom went down 4
5:14 he went down and dipped himself . . in the Jordan 4
6: 9 do not pass . . for the Syrians are going down there. 7
8:29 Ahazi'ah . . went down to see Joram the son of Ahab 4
12:20 house of Millo, on the way that goes down to Silla. 4
13:14 Jo'ash king of Israel went down to him, and wept 4
1Ch 11:15 Three of the 30 chief men went down to the rock 4
22 also went down and slew a lion in a pit 4
23 but Benai'ah went down to him with a staff 4
2Ch 18: 2 After some years he went down to Ahab in Sama'ria. 4
20:16 Tomorrow go down against them; 4
22: 6 Ahazi'ah . . went down to see Joram the son of Ahab 4
Neh 3:15 stairs that go down from the City of David. 4
Job 7: 9 he who goes down to Sheol does not come up; 4
17:16 Will it go down to the bars of Sheol? 4
21:13 and in peace they go down to Sheol. 6
33:24 Deliver him from going down into the Pit 4
28 has redeemed my soul from going down into the Pit 8
Ps 22:29 before him shall bow all who go down to the dust 4
28: 1 I become like those who go down to the Pit. 4
30: 3 from among those gone down to the Pit. 4
9 profit is there in my death, if I go down to the Pit? 4
49:17 his glory will not go down after him. 4
55:15 let them go down to Sheol alive; 4
88: 4 I am reckoned among those who go down to the Pit; 4
107:23 Some went down to the sea in ships, doing business 4
26 mounted up to heaven, they went down to the depths; 4
115:17 nor do any that go down into silence. 4
143: 7 lest I be like those who go down to the Pit. 4
Prv 1:12 like those who go down to the Pit; 4
5: 5 Her feet go down to death; 4
7:27 going down to the chambers of death. 4
18: 8 go down into the inner parts of the body. 4
23:31 sparkles in the cup and goes down smoothly. 3
26:22 go down into the inner parts of the body. 4
Ecc 1: 5 The sun rises and the sun goes down 1
3:21 and the spirit of the beast goes down to the earth? 4
Sng 6: 2 My beloved has gone down to his garden 4
11 I went down to the nut orchard 4
7: 9 like the best wine that goes down smoothly 3
Isa 5:14 nobility of Jerusalem and her multitude go down 4
14:19 pierced . . who go down to the stones of the Pit 4
30: 2 who set out to go down to Egypt 4
31: 1 Woe to those who go down to Egypt for help 4
32:19 the forest will utterly go down 4
38:18 those who go down to the pit cannot hope 4
51:14 he shall not die and go down to the Pit *
52: 4 My people went down at the first into Egypt 4
60:20 Your sun shall no more go down 1
63:14 Like cattle that go down into the valley 4
Jer 15: 9 her sun went down while it was yet day; 1
18: 2 Arise, and go down to the potter's house 4
3 I went down to the potter's house 4
22: 1 Go down to the house of the king of Judah 4
36:12 he went down to the king's house 4
48:15 and the choicest of his young men have gone down 4
50:27 all her bulls, let them go down to the slaughter. 4
Ezk 26:20 primeval ruins, with those who go down to the Pit 4
31: 7 for its roots went down to abundant waters. 2
14 among . . men, with those who go down to the Pit. 4
15 Thus says the Lord GOD: When it goes down to Sheol 4
16 down to Sheol with those who go down to the Pit; 4
17 They also shall go down to Sheol with it 4
32:18 to those who have gone down to the Pit 4
19 Go down, and be laid with the uncircumcised. 4
24 went down uncircumcised into the nether world 4
24 their shame with those who go down to the Pit. 4
25 bear their shame with those who go down to the Pit; 4
27 who went down to Sheol with their weapons of war 4
29 uncircumcised, with those who go down to the Pit. 4
30 all the Sido'nians, who have gone down in shame 4
30 their shame with those who go down to the Pit. 4
47: 8 the eastern region and goes down into the Arabah; 4
Dan 6:14 labored till the sun went down to rescue him. 10
Ams 6: 2 then go down to Gath of the Philistines. 4
Jon 1: 3 He went down to Joppa and found a ship 4
5 Jonah had gone down into the inner part 4
2: 6 I went down to the land whose bars closed upon me 4
Mic 3: 6 The sun shall go down upon the prophets 1
Hag 2:22 the horses and their riders shall go down 4
Mat 24:17 let him who is on the housetop not go down 13
Mrk 13:15 let him who is on the housetop not go down 13
Lke 2:51 he went down with them and came to Nazareth 13
4:31 he went down to Caper'na-um, a city of Galilee 14
10:30 A man was going down from Jerusalem to Jericho 13
31 Now by chance a priest was going down that road; 13
18:14 this man went down to his house justified 13
Joh 2:12 After this he went down to Caper'na-um 13
4:51 As he was going down, his servants met him 13
6:16 his disciples went down to the sea 13
Act 7:15 Jacob went down into Egypt 13
8: 5 Philip went down to a city of Sama'ria 14
26 the road that goes down from Jerusalem to Gaza. 13
38 both went down into the water 13
10:20 Rise and go down 13
21 Peter went down to the men and said, "I am the one 13
12:19 Then he went down from Judea to Caesare'a 14
13: 4 they went down to Seleu'cia 14
14:25 they went down to Attali'a; 14
15:30 when they were sent off, they went down to Antioch; 14
16: 8 so, passing by My'sia, they went down to Tro'as. 13
18:22 and then went down to Antioch. 13
20:10 Paul went down and bent over him 13
23:10 the tribune . . commanded the soldiers to go down 13
25: 5 let the men of authority among you go down with me 15
6 he went down to Caesare'a 13
7 the Jews who had gone down from Jerusalem 13
Eph 4:26 do not let the sun go down on your anger. 12
2Es 4: 8 I never went down into the deep 16
Tob 6: 2 Then the young man went down to wash himself. 13
14:10 as he himself went down into the darkness. 13
Jdt 2:27 Then he went down into the plain of Damascus 13
3: 6 Then he went down to the seacoast with his army 13
5:10 they went down to Egypt 13
8:32 a thing which will go down through all generations 11
10: 2 called her maid and went down into the house 13
10 watched her until she had gone down the mountain 13
14: 2 as if you were going down to the plain 13
2 only do not go down. 13
AEs 13: 7 may in one day go down in violence to Hades 14
Bar 3:19 They have vanished and gone down to Hades 13
1Mc 2:29 many . . went down to the wilderness to dwell there 13
31 men . . had gone down to the hiding places 13
16:14 he went down to Jericho with Mattathias and Judas 13

go dumbfounded 1. דמם
Ps 31:17 let them go dumbfounded to Sheol. 1

go early 1. שכם
Gen 19:27 Abraham went early in the morning to the place 1

go far 1. רחק 2. διοδεύω 3. προέρχομαι 4. προκόπτω
Jos 8: 4 do not go very far from the city 1
Prv 19: 7 how much more do his friends go far from him! 1
Mat 26:39 going a little farther he fell on his face 3
Mrk 14:35 going a little farther, he fell on the ground 3
Rom 13:12 the night is far gone, the day is at hand. 4
1Mc 10:77 went to Azotus as though he were going farther 2

go far away 1. רחק 2. prolongo
Exd 8:28 only you shall not go very far away. 1
2Es 14:18 For truth shall go farther away 2

go forth 1. הלך 2. יצא 3. מוֹצָא 4. נסע 5. נפק (A) 6. ἐξέρχομαι 7. ἔξοδος 8. exeo 9. procedo 10. proficio
Gen 8:16 Go forth from the ark, you and your wife 2
18 So Noah went forth, and his sons and his wife 2
19 the earth, went forth by families out of the ark. 2
9:18 The sons of Noah who went forth from the ark 2
11:31 and they went forth together from Ur 2
31:13 Now arise, go forth from this land, and return 2
Exd 11: 4 midnight I will go forth in the midst of Egypt; 2
12:31 and said, "Rise up, go forth from among my people 2
13: 4 This day you are to go forth, in the month of Abib. 2
14: 8 pursued the people . . as they went forth defiantly. 2

19: 1 Israel had gone forth out of the land of Egypt 2
Num 1: 3 all in Israel who are able to go forth to war 2
20 old and upward, all who were able to go forth to war 2
22 all who were able to go forth to war 2
24 people . . all who were able to go forth to war 2
26 every man able to go forth to war 2
28 every man able to go forth to war 2
30 every man able to go forth to war 2
32 every man able to go forth to war 2
34 every man able to go forth to war 2
36 every man able to go forth to war 2
38 every man able to go forth to war 2
40 every man able to go forth to war 2
42 every man able to go forth to war 2
45 every man able to go forth to war in Israel– 2
11:31 there went forth a wind from the LORD 4
16:46 for wrath has gone forth from the LORD, the plague 2
21:28 For fire went forth from Heshbon 2
26: 2 all in Israel who are able to go forth to war. 2
31:13 went forth to meet them outside the camp. 2
33: 1 when they went forth out of the land of Egypt 2
Deu 20: 1 When you go forth to war against your enemies 2
21:10 When you go forth to war against your enemies 2
23: 9 go forth against your enemies and are in camp 2
Jdg 5: 4 LORD, when thou didst go forth from Se'ir 2
9: 8 trees once went forth to anoint a king over them; 1
11:36 according to what has gone forth from your mouth 2
Rut 1:13 the hand of the LORD has gone forth against me. 2
1Sm 17:15 but David went back and forth from Saul 1
20 the host was going forth to the battle line 2
55 Saul saw David go forth against the Philistine 2
2Sm 11: 1 In . . the time when kings go forth to battle 2
13:39 spirit of the king longed to go forth to Ab'salom; 2
15:16 So the king went forth, and all his household 2
17 the king went forth, and all the people after him; 2
24:20 Arau'nah went forth, and did obeisance to the king 2
1Kg 2:36 dwell there, and do not go forth from there 2
37 on the day you go forth, and cross the brook Kidron 2
42 the day you go forth and go to any place whatever 2
19:11 he said, "Go forth, and stand upon the mount 2
22:22 he said, 'I will go forth, and will be a lying spirit 2
22 you shall succeed; go forth and do so.' 2
2Kg 8: 3 she went forth to appeal to the king for her house 2
18: 7 wherever he went forth, he prospered. 2
19:31 for out of Jerusalem shall go forth a remnant 2
35 And that night the angel of the LORD went forth 2
1Ch 20: 1 spring . . the time when kings go forth to battle 2
21:21 and went forth from the threshing floor 2
2Ch 18:21 he said, 'I will go forth, and will be a lying spirit 2
21 you shall succeed; go forth and do so.' 2
Est 1:19 let a royal order go forth from him 2
Job 1:12 Satan went forth from the presence of the LORD. 2
2: 7 Satan went forth from the presence of the LORD 2
24: 5 asses in the desert they go forth to their toil 2
39: 4 they go forth, and do not return to them. 2
Ps 60:10 Thou dost not go forth, O God, with our armies. 2
68: 7 O God, when thou didst go forth before thy people 2
104:23 Man goes forth to his work and to his labor 2
108:11 Thou dost not go forth, O God, with our armies. 2
114: 1 When Israel went forth from Egypt 2
126: 6 He that goes forth weeping, bearing the seed 1
Sng 3:11 Go forth, O daughters of Zion, and behold 2
7:11 Come, my beloved, let us go forth into the fields 2
Isa 2: 3 For out of Zion shall go forth the law 2
7: 3 the LORD said to Isaiah, "Go forth to meet Ahaz 2
37:32 for out of Jerusalem shall go forth a remnant 2
36 the angel of the LORD went forth 2
42:13 The LORD goes forth like a mighty man 2
45:23 from my mouth has gone forth in righteousness 2
48: 3 they went forth from my mouth 2
20 Go forth from Babylon, flee from Chalde'a 2
49:17 and those who laid you waste go forth from you. 2
51: 4 for a law will go forth from me, and my justice 2
5 draws near speedily, my salvation has gone forth 2
55:11 shall my word be that goes forth from my mouth; 2
62: 1 until her vindication goes forth as brightness 2
66:24 they shall go forth and look on the dead bodies 2
Jer 4: 4 lest my wrath go forth like fire, and burn 2
7 he has gone forth from his place 2
6:25 Go not forth into the field, nor walk on the road; 2
21:12 lest my wrath go forth like fire 2
23:15 ungodliness has gone forth into all the land. 2
19 Wrath has gone forth, a whirling tempest; 2
25:32 Behold, evil is going forth from nation to nation 2
30:23 Behold the storm of the LORD! Wrath has gone forth 2
31: 4 shall go forth in the dance of the merrymakers. 2
46: 9 Let the warriors go forth: men of Ethiopia and Put 2
48: 7 and Chemosh shall go forth into exile 2
45 for a fire has gone forth from Heshbon 2
Ezk 1:13 and out of the fire went forth lightning. 2
3:22 and he said to me, "Arise, go forth into the plain 2
23 So I arose and went forth into the plain; 2
9: 7 and fill the courts with the slain. Go forth. 2
7 they went forth, and smote in the city. 2
10:18 Then the glory of the LORD went forth 2
19 as they went forth, with the wheels beside them; 2
12: 4 and you shall go forth yourself at evening 2
7 I went forth in the dark, carrying my outfit 2
12 and shall go forth; he shall dig through the wall 2
16:14 your renown went forth among the nations 2
30: 9 that day swift messengers shall go forth from me 2
39: 9 Israel will go forth and make fires 2
Dan 2:13 decree went forth . . wise men were to be slain 5
9:23 At the beginning . . a word went forth 2
25 going forth of the word to restore and build 3
11:44 shall go forth with great fury to exterminate 2
Hos 6: 3 his going forth is sure as the dawn; 3
5 and my judgment goes forth as the light. 2
Ams 5: 3 The city that went forth 1,000 shall have 2
3 that which went forth 100 shall have ten 2
Mic 4: 2 For out of Zion shall go forth the law 2
10 for now you shall go forth from the city 2
Hab 1: 4 the law is slacked and justice never goes forth. 2
4 justice goes forth perverted. 2
3:13 wentest forth for the salvation of thy people 2
Zec 5: 5 see what this is that goes forth. 2
6 He said, "This is the ephah that goes forth. 2
6: 5 These are going forth to the four winds of heaven 2
9:14 and his arrow go forth like lightning; 2
14: 3 Then the LORD will go forth and fight 2
Mal 4: 2 You shall go forth leaping like calves 2
Mrk 5:30 perceiving in himself that power had gone forth 6
16:20 they went forth and preached everywhere 6
Lke 8:46 I perceive that power has gone forth from me. 6
Joh 18: 1 he went forth . . across the Kidron valley 6
1Th 1: 8 your faith in God has gone forth everywhere 6
Heb 13:13 Therefore let us go forth to him outside the camp 6
2Es 6:43 For thy word went forth 9
7:78 decree has gone forth from the Most High 10
15:23 a fire will go forth from his wrath 8
30 shall go forth like wild boars of the forest 8
16: 9 Fire will go forth from his wrath 8
Sir 5: 7 suddenly the wrath of the Lord will go forth 6
24:30 I went forth like a canal from a river 6
43: 2 making proclamation as it goes forth 7
Bar 5: 6 For they went forth from you on foot 6
1Mc 4:13 they went forth from their camp to battle 6
5:65 Then Judas and his brothers went forth 6
7:41 thy angel went forth and struck down 185,000 6
10:63 Go forth with him into the middle of the city 6
12:33 Simon also went forth 6

go forward 1. בוא 2. הלך 3. יצא 4. נסע 5. עבר 6. עלה

Exd 14:15 Tell the people of Israel to go forward. 4
Jos 6: 7 Go forward; march around the city 5
8 priests . . went forward, blowing the trumpets 5
2Sm 20: 8 with a sword . . and as he went forward it fell out. 3
2Kg 3:24 they went forward, slaughtering the Moabites 1
20: 9 shall the shadow go forward 10 steps, or go back 2
2Ch 24:13 the repairing went forward in their hands 6
Neh 4: 7 repairing of the walls . . was going forward 6

go free 1. שלח 2. ἀπολύω

Ezk 13:20 let the souls that you hunt go free like birds. 1
Sus 1:53 and letting the guilty go free 2

go further 1. προβαίνω

1Es 2:29 that such wicked proceedings go no further 1

go here and there 1. διέρχομαι

Act 9:32 Now as Peter went here and there among them all 1

go home 1. סבב 2. שוב 3. ἀπέρχομαι 4. καταπορεύομαι

2Kg 19:36 Sennach'erib . . departed, and went home 2
1Ch 16:43 and David went home to bless his household. 1
Isa 37:37 and went home and dwelt at Nin'eveh. 2
1Mc 12:45 and will turn round and go home 3
2Mc 11:30 those who go home by the 30th day of Xanthicus 4

go hungry 1. רעב

Prv 10: 3 The LORD does not let the righteous go hungry 1

go ill 1. רעע

Ps 106:32 it went ill with Moses on their account; 1

go in and out 1. הלך

1Sm 2:30 that your house . . should go in and out before me 1
35 he shall go in and out before my anointed 1

go in another direction 1. תאר

Jos 18:14 Then the boundary goes in another direction 1

go in pursuit 1. רדף

Gen 14:14 of them, and went in pursuit as far as Dan. 1

go in the other direction 1. שוב

Jos 19:12 it goes in the other direction eastward 1

go into 1. בוא 2. ἀναβαίνω 3. εἴσειμι 4. εἰσέρχομαι 5. εἰσπορεύομαι 6. ingredior

Gen 39:11 one day, when he went into the house to do his work 1
Jos 6:19 they shall go into the treasury of the LORD. 1
22 Go into the harlot's house, and bring . . the woman 1
Rut 1: 2 They went into the country of Moab and remained 1
2:18 And she took it up and went into the city; 1
3:15 then she went into the city. 1
1Sm 12: 8 When Jacob went into Egypt . . then your fathers 1
20:42 And he rose . . and Jonathan went into the city. 1
22: 5 depart, and go into the land of Judah. 1
5 David . . went into the forest of Hereth. 1
2Sm 12:20 he went into the house of the LORD, and worshiped; 1
1Kg 22:25 on that day when you go into an inner chamber 1
2Kg 5:18 when my master goes into the house of Rimmon 1
9: 6 So he arose, and went into the house; 1
10:23 Jehu went into the house of Ba'al with Jehon'adab 1
19: 1 and went into the house of the LORD. 1
2Ch 12:11 often as the king went into the house of the LORD 1
29:16 The priests went into the inner part of the house 1
Isa 37: 1 and went into the house of the LORD. 1
Ams 5:19 or went into the house and leaned with his hand 1
Mat 6: 6 when you pray, go into your room and shut the door 4
15:11 not what goes into the mouth defiles a man 4
17 Do you not see that whatever goes into the mouth 5
Mrk 1:21 And they went into Caper'na-um 5
Lke 7:36 he went into the Pharisee's house 4
Joh 20: 6 Simon Peter came . . and went into the tomb 4
Act 13:14 on the sabbath day they went into the synagogue 4
18:19 but he himself went into the synagogue 4
21:26 and went into the temple 3
Heb 9: 6 the priests go continually into the outer tent 3
2Es 10:17 Therefore go into the city to your husband. 6
18 I will not go into the city, but I will die here. 6
Jdt 14:15 he opened it and went into the bedchamber 4
Sus 1: 7 Susanna would go into her husband's garden 5
2Mc 5:12 to slay those who went into the house. 2

go into another country 1. ἀποδημέω

Mat 21:33 and went into another country. 1
Mrk 12: 1 and went into another country. 1
Lke 20: 9 and went into another country 1

go into battle 1. ἀναβαίνω

1Mc 9:67 and went into battle with his forces 1

go into captivity 1. גלה

Ezk 39:23 that the house of Israel went into captivity 1

go into exile 1. גלה

Isa 5:13 my people go into exile for want of knowledge; 1
Lam 1: 3 Judah has gone into exile because of affliction 1
Ezk 12: 3 and go into exile by day in their sight; 1
Ams 1: 5 and the people of Syria shall go into exile to Kir 1
5: 5 for Gilgal shall surely go into exile 1
6: 7 shall now be the first of those to go into exile 1
7:11 and Israel must go into exile away from his land 1
17 shall surely go into exile away from its land.' 1
Mic 1:16 for they shall go from you into exile. 1

go into hiding 1. συγκρύπτω

2Mc 14:30 and went into hiding from Nicanor. 1

go late 1. אחר

Ps 127: 2 in vain that you rise up early and go late to rest 1

let go 1. רפה

Prv 4:13 Keep hold of instruction, do not let go; 1

go like an exile 1. גלה

Ezk 12: 3 you shall go like an exile from your place 1

go limping 1. פסח

1Kg 18:21 How long will you go limping with two . . opinions? 1

make go astray 1. נדח

2Ch 21:11 into unfaithfulness, and made Judah go astray. 1

make go down 1. בוא

Ams 8: 9 I will make the sun go down at noon 1

make go out 1. יצא

Gen 45: 1 and he cried, "Make every one go out from me. 1

go near 1. בוא 2. נגש 3. קרב 4. προσάγω

Gen 27:22 Jacob went near to Isaac his father 2
Exd 19:15 Be ready . . do not go near a woman. 2
Num 6: 6 he shall not go near a dead body. 1
Deu 5:27 Go near, and hear all that the LORD our God will say; 3
2Sm 11:20 he says . . 'Why did you go so near the city to fight? 2
21 Why did you go so near the wall? 2
Prv 5: 8 do not go near the door of her house, 3
Ezk 42:14 they go near to that which is for the people. 3
Sir 12:13 Who will pity . . any who go near wild beasts? 4

go off 1. ἀπέρχομαι 2. ἐξέρχομαι

Mat 22: 5 But they made light of it and went off 1
Act 10:23 The next day he rose and went off with them 2
Rev 12:17 went off to make war on the rest of her offspring 1
LJr 1:58 and go off with this booty 1

go on a journey 1. נשא רַגְלַיִם 2. ἀποδημέω 3. ἀπόδημος 4. πορεύω

Gen 29: 1 Then Jacob went on his journey 1
Mat 25:14 For it will be as when a man going on a journey 2
Mrk 13:34 It is like a man going on a journey 3
Act 21: 5 we departed and went on our journey 4

go on an expedition 1. יצא
1Sm 21: 5 Of a truth . . as always when I go on an expedition; 1

go on board 1. ἐμβαίνω
Act 21: 6 we went on board the ship, and they returned home. 1

go on one's way 1. διαπορεύομαι 2. πορεύω
Lke 10:38 Now as they went on their way, he entered a village; 2
13:22 He went on his way through towns and villages 1
33 I must go on my way today and tomorrow 2
Tob 11: 1 After this Tobias went on his way 2

go on through 1. διωδεύω
Lke 8: 1 Soon afterward he went on through cities 1

go on travels 1. πλανάω
Sir 51:13 before I went on my travels 1

go on with 1. ἐπιτελέω
2Mc 3:23 Heliodorus went on with what had been decided. 1

go one's way 1. βαδίζω 2. οἴχομαι 3. πορεύω 4. ὑπάγω
Mrk 7:29 he said to her, "For this saying you may go your way; 4
Lke 17:19 Rise and go your way; your faith has made you well. 3
Joh 4:50 The man believed . . and went his way. 3
1Es 9:51 go your way, eat the fat and drink the sweet 1
54 Then they all went their way 2

go onward 1. נסע
Exd 40:36 the people of Israel would go onward; 1
37 then they did not go onward till the day 1

go out 1. אסר 2. הלך 3. יצא 4. כבה 5. מוֹצָא 6. נפק (A) 7. ἀπέρχομαι 8. ἀποβαίνω 9. δαπανάω 10. διεξέρχομαι 11. διέρχομαι 12. εἰμί 13. ἐκβαίνω 14. ἐκπορεύομαι 15. ἔξειμι 16. ἐξέρχομαι 17. πορεύω 18. σβέννυμι 19. exeo
Gen 4: 8 Cain said to Abel . . "Let us go out to the field. 11
14: 8 went out, and they joined battle 3
17 king of Sodom went out to meet him at the Valley 3
19: 6 Lot went out of the door to the men 3
14 Lot went out and said to his sons-in-law 3
24:11 evening, the time when women go out to draw water. 3
63 Isaac went out to meditate in the field 3
27: 3 go out to the field, and hunt game for me 3
30 when Jacob had scarcely gone out 3
30:16 Leah went out to meet him, and said 3
31:33 he did not find them. And he went out of Leah's tent 3
34: 1 Dinah . . went out to visit the women of the land; 3
6 Hamor the father of Shechem went out to Jacob 3
24 all who went out of the gate of his city hearkened 3
24 all who went out of the gate of his city. 3
41:45 Joseph went out over the land of Egypt. 3
46 Joseph went out from the presence of Pharaoh 3
47:10 Jacob . . went out from the presence of Pharaoh. 3
Exd 2:11 when Moses had grown up, he went out to his people 3
13 When he went out the next day, behold, two Hebrews 3
5:10 taskmasters . . went out and said to the people 3
7:15 Go to Pharaoh . . as he is going out to the water; 3
8:12 So Moses and Aaron went out from Pharaoh; 3
20 wait for Pharaoh, as he goes out to the water 3
29 Behold, I am going out from you and I will pray 3
30 So Moses went out from Pharaoh and prayed 3
9:29 As soon as I have gone out of the city, I will 3
33 So Moses went out of the city from Pharaoh 3
10: 6 Then he turned and went out from Pharaoh. 3
18 So he went out from Pharaoh, and entreated 3
11: 8 And after that I will go out. 3
8 And he went out from Pharaoh in hot anger. 3
12:22 and none of you shall go out of the door 3
41 hosts of the LORD went out from the land of Egypt. 3
15:20 and all the women went out after her 3
16: 4 the people shall go out and gather a day's portion 3
27 some of the people went out to gather 3
29 let no man go out of his place on the seventh day. 3
17: 9 Choose for us men, and go out, fight with Am'alek; 3
18: 7 Moses went out to meet his father-in-law 3
21: 2 in the seventh he shall go out free, for nothing. 3
3 If he comes in single, he shall go out single; 3
3 if . . married, then his wife shall go out with him. 3
4 be her master's and he shall go out alone. 3
5 I love . . I will not go out free,' 3
7 she shall not go out as the male slaves do. 3
11 she shall go out for nothing, without payment 3
25:32 shall be six branches going out of its sides 3
33 -so for the six branches going out of the lampstand; 3
35 the six branches going out from the lampstand. 3
33: 7 every one . . would go out to the tent of meeting 3
8 Whenever Moses went out to the tent 3
37:18 there were six branches going out of its sides 3
19 for the six branches going out of the lampstand. 3
21 each pair of the six branches going out of it. 3
Lev 6:12 kept burning on it, it shall not go out 4
13 upon the altar continually; it shall not go out 4
8:33 you shall not go out from the door of the tent 3
10: 7 do not go out from the door of the tent of meeting 3
14: 3 the priest shall go out of the camp, and the priest 3
38 then the priest shall go out of the house 3
16:18 Then he shall go out to the altar 3
21:12 neither shall he go out of the sanctuary 3
24:10 went out among the people of Israel 3
25:41 then he shall go out from you, he and his children 3
Num 11:24 Moses went out and told the people the words 3
26 they had not gone out to the tent 3
21:23 went out against Israel to the wilderness 3
22:36 Balak . . went out to meet him at the city of Moab 3
27:17 who shall go out before them 3
21 at his word they shall go out, and . . come 3
31:27 between the warriors who went out to battle 3
28 tribute from the men of war who went out to battle 3
36 half, the portion of those who had gone out to war 3
33: 3 Israel went out triumphantly in the sight of all 3
Deu 13:13 certain base fellows have gone out among you 3
15:16 I will not go out from you,' because he loves you 3
23:12 place outside the camp and you shall go out to it; 3
24: 5 newly married, he shall not go out with the army 3
28: 6 come in, and blessed shall you be when you go out. 3
19 come in, and cursed shall you be when you go out. 3
25 go out one way against them, and flee seven ways 3
31: 2 I am no longer able to go out and come in. 3
33:18 Rejoice, Zeb'ulun, in your going out; and Is'sachar 3
Jos 2: 5 the men went out; where the men went I do not know; 3
7 as the pursuers had gone out, the gate was shut. 3
19 If any one goes out of the doors of your house 3
6: 1 was shut up . . none went out, and none came in. 3
10 neither shall any word go out of your mouth 3
8:14 made haste and went out early to the descent 3
17 not a man left . . who did not go out after Israel; 3
15: 3 it goes out southward of the ascent of Akrab'bim 3
4 passes . . to Azmon, goes out by the Brook of Egypt 3
11 the boundary goes out to the shoulder of the hill 3
11 the boundary . . goes out to Jabneel; 3
Jdg 3:10 he judged Israel; he went out to war 3
19 all his attendants went out from his presence. 3
23 Then Ehud went out into the vestibule 3
4:14 Does not the LORD go out before you?" So Barak went 3
22 Ja'el went out to meet him, and said to him 3
5: 9 My heart goes out to the commanders of Israel •
9:27 they went out into the field, and gathered 3
35 Ga'al . . went out and stood in the entrance 3
38 whom you despised? Go out now and fight with them. 3
39 Ga'al went out at the head of the men of Shechem 3
42 following day the men went out into the fields. 3
16:20 I will go out as at other times, and shake myself 3
19:23 the man . . went out to them and said to them, "No 3
27 he opened the doors . . and went out to go on his way 3
20:14 to go out to battle against the people of Israel 3
20 the men of Israel went out to battle against 3
28 Shall we yet again go out to battle against our 3
31 the Benjaminites went out against the people 3
21:24 Israel departed . . and they went out from there 3
Rut 2:22 It is well . . that you go out with his maidens 3
1Sm 3: 3 the lamp of God had not yet gone out 4
4: 1 Now Israel went out to battle . . the Philistines; 3
7:11 the men of Israel went out of Mizpah and pursued 3
8:20 that our king may govern us and go out before us 3
9:26 Saul . . and Samuel went out into the street. 3
13:10 Samuel came; and Saul went out to meet him 3
23 garrison of the Philistines went out to the pass 3
18: 5 And David went out and was successful 3
13 and he went out and came in before the people. 3
16 for he went out and came in before them. 3
19: 3 and I will go out and stand beside my father 3
8 David went out and fought with the Philistines 3
20:11 Come, let us go out into the field. 3
11 they both went out into the field. 3
35 In the morning Jonathan went out into the field 3
24: 8 David also arose, and went out of the cave 3
25:37 in the morning, when the wine had gone out of Nabal 3
28: 1 you and your men are to go out with me in the army. 3
30:21 they went out to meet David and to meet the people 3
2Sm 2:12 Abner . . went out from Mahana'im to Gibeon. 3
13 Jo'ab . . and the servants of David, went out and met 3
3:25 and to know your going out and your coming in 5
5:24 the LORD has gone out before you to smite the army 3
11: 8 Uri'ah went out of the king's house 3
13 in the evening he went out to lie on his couch 3
13: 9 Send out every one from me." So every one went out 3
14: 1 that the king's heart went out to Ab'salom. •
18: 2 king said . . "I myself will also go out with you. 3
3 But the men said, "You shall not go out. 3
6 the army went out into the field against Israel; 3
19: 7 arise, go out and speak kindly to your servants; 3
20: 7 And there went out after Abi'shai, Jo'ab 3
7 they went out from Jerusalem to pursue Sheba 3
21:17 You shall no more go out with us to battle 3
24: 4 Jo'ab and . . went out from the presence of the king 3
7 and they went out to the Negeb of Judah 3
1Kg 2:46 and he went out and struck him down, and he died 3
3: 7 I do not know how to go out or come in. 3
8:44 thy people go out to battle against their enemy 3
11:29 at that time, when Jerobo'am went out of Jerusalem 3
12:25 and he went out from there and built Penu'el. 3
15:17 no one to go out or come in to Asa king of Judah. 3
19:13 Eli'jah . . went out and stood at the entrance 3
20:16 And they went out at noon 3
17 servants of the governors . . went out first. 3
19 these went out of the city, the servants 3
21 king of Israel went out, and captured the horses 3
31 put sackcloth on . . and go out to the king of Israel; 3
39 Your servant went out into the . . battle; 3
2Kg 4:18 he went out one day to his father 3
21 and shut the door upon him, and went out. 3
37 then she took up her son and went out. 3
39 One of them went out . . to gather herbs 3
5:27 So he went out from his presence a leper 3
6:15 servant . . rose early in the morning and went out 3
7:12 they have gone out of the camp to hide themselves 3
16 Then the people went out, and plundered the camp 3
10: 9 in the morning, when he went out, he stood, and said 3
11: 8 Be with the king when he goes out and . . comes in. 3
19:27 I know . . and your going out and coming in 3
20: 4 before Isaiah had gone out of the middle court 3
1Ch 12:17 David went out to meet them and said to them 3
14: 8 David heard of it and went out against them. 3
15 go out to battle; for God has gone out before you 3
15 God has gone out before you to smite the army 3
17 the fame of David went out into all lands 3
2Ch 1:10 wisdom and knowledge to go out and come 3
6:34 If thy people go out to battle against their 3
13: 3 Abi'jah went out to battle having an army 1
14:10 Asa went out to meet him 3
15: 2 he went out to meet Asa, and said to him, "Hear me, 3
5 there was no peace to him who went out 3
16: 1 that he might permit no one to go out or come 3
19: 2 Jehu the son of Hana'ni the seer went out 3
4 Jehosh'aphat . . went out again among the people 3
20:17 tomorrow go out against them 3
20 went out into the wilderness of Teko'a; 3
20 as they went out, Jehosh'aphat stood and said 3
22: 7 came there he went out with Jeho'ram to meet Jehu 3
23: 7 Be with the king . . when he goes out. 3
24: 5 Go out to the cities of Judah, and gather 3
26: 6 He went out and made war against the Philistines 3
18 Go out of the sanctuary; for you have done wrong 3
20 he himself hastened to go out 3
28: 9 he went out to meet the army that came to Sama'ria 3
31: 1 Israel who were present went out to the cities 3
35:20 Neco . . went up . . and Josi'ah went out against him 3
Neh 2:13 I went out by night by the Valley Gate 3
8:15 Go out to the hills and bring branches of olive 3
16 people went out and brought them and made booths 3
Est 4: 1 and went out into the midst of the city 3
6 Hathach went out to Mor'decai in the open square 3
5: 9 Haman went out that day joyful and glad of heart. 3
8:15 Mor'decai went out from . . the king in royal robes 3
Job 15:13 and let such words go out of your mouth? 3
29: 7 When I went out to the gate of the city 3
31:34 so that I kept silence, and did not go out of doors- 3
39:21 in his strength; he goes out to meet the weapons. 3
Ps 19: 4 yet their voice goes out through all the earth 3
41: 6 gathers mischief; when he goes out, he tells it 3
44: 9 abased us, and hast not gone out with our armies. 3
81: 5 when he went out over the land of Egypt. 3
121: 8 LORD will keep your going out and your coming 3
Prv 22:10 Drive out a scoffer, and strife will go out 3
26:20 For lack of wood the fire goes out; 4
31:18 Her lamp does not go out at night. 4
Ecc 8:10 they used to go in and out of the holy place 2
Isa 37:28 sitting down and your going out and coming in 3
52:11 depart, go out thence, touch no unclean thing; 3
11 go out from the midst of her, purify yourselves 3
12 For you shall not go out in haste 3
55:12 you shall go out in joy, and be led forth in peace; 3
Jer 5: 6 one who goes out of them shall be torn in pieces; 3
14:18 If I go out into the field, behold, those slain 3
17:19 the kings of Judah enter and by which they go out 3
19: 2 and go out to the valley of the son of Hinnom 3
21: 9 he who goes out and surrenders to the Chalde'ans 3
29:16 your kinsmen who did not go out with you into exile 3
31:39 the measuring line shall go out farther 3
37: 4 was still going in and out among the people 3
38: 2 but he who goes out to the Chalde'ans shall live; 3
39: 4 they fled, going out of the city at night 3
50: 8 and go out of the land of the Chalde'ans 3
51:45 Go out of the midst of her, my people! 3
52: 7 the men of war fled and went out from the city 3
Ezk 3:25 so that you cannot go out among the people; 3
10: 7 man clothed in linen, who took it and went out. 3
12: 5 Dig through the wall . . and go out through it. 10
12 shall dig through the wall and go out through it; 16
19:14 And fire has gone out from its stem, has consumed 3
21: 4 therefore my sword shall go out of its sheath 3
24: 6 rust is in it, and whose rust has not gone out of it! 3
12 its thick rust does not go out of it by fire. 3
36:20 yet they had to go out of his land. 3
42:14 they shall not go out of it into the outer court 3
44: 3 and shall go out by the same way. 3
19 they go out into the outer court to the people 3
46: 2 Then he shall go out, but the gate shall not be shut 3
8 he shall go out by the same way. 3
9 by the north gate . . shall go out by the south gate; 3
9 by the south gate shall go out by the north gate 3
9 but each shall go out straight ahead. 3
10 when they go out, he shall go out. 3

10 when they go out, he shall go out. 3
12 Then he shall go out, and after he has gone out 3
12 after he has gone out the gate shall be shut. 3
Dan 2:14 who had gone out to slay the wise men of Babylon; 6
Ams 4: 3 And you shall go out through the breaches 3
Mic 2:13 break through and pass the gate, going out by it. 3
Zec 5: 3 Then he said to me, "This is the curse that goes out 3
8:10 safety from the foe for him who went out or came in; 3
Mat 3: 5 Then went out to him Jerusalem and all Judea 14
11: 7 What did you go out into the wilderness to behold? 16
8 Why then did you go out? 16
9 Why then did you go out? To see a prophet? 16
12:14 the Pharisees went out and took counsel 16
43 When the unclean spirit has gone out of a man 16
13: 1 That same day Jesus went out of the house and sat 16
3 A sower went out to sow. 16
18:28 that same servant, as he went out 16
20: 1 a householder who went out early in the morning 16
3 going out about the third hour he saw others 16
5 Going out again about the sixth hour 16
6 about the eleventh hour he went out 16
29 as they went out of Jericho 14
21:17 leaving them, he went out of the city to Bethany 16
22:10 And those servants went out into the streets 16
24:26 if they say to you . . do not go out 16
25: 8 for our lamps are going out.' 18
26:30 they went out to the Mount of Olives. 16
71 when he went out to the porch, another maid saw him 16
27:32 As they went out, they came upon a man of Cyre'ne 16
Mrk 1: 5 there went out to him all the country of Judea 14
35 he rose and went out to a lonely place 16
45 he went out and began to talk freely about it 16
2:12 took up the pallet and went out before them all 16
13 He went out again beside the sea 16
3: 6 The Pharisees went out 16
21 they went out to seize him 16
4: 3 Listen! A sower went out to sow. 16
6:12 So they went out and preached 16
24 she went out, and said to her mother 16
11:11 he went out to Bethany with the twelve. 16
19 when evening came they went out of the city. 14
14:26 they went out to the Mount of Olives. 16
68 he went out into the gateway 16
16: 8 And they went out and fled from the tomb; 16
Lke 2: 1 a decree went out from Caesar Augustus 16
4:14 and a report concerning him went out 16
37 reports of him went out into every place 14
5: 2 but the fishermen had gone out of them 8
27 After this he went out, and saw a tax collector 16
6:12 In these days he went out to the mountain to pray; 16
7:24 What did you go out into the wilderness to behold? 16
25 What then did you go out to see? 16
26 What then did you go out to see? A prophet? 16
8: 2 Mary . . from whom seven demons had gone out 16
5 A sower went out to sow his seed 16
35 Then people went out to see what had happened 16
11:14 when the demon had gone out, the dumb man spoke 16
24 When the unclean spirit has gone out of a man 16
14:18 I must go out and see it 16
21 Go out quickly to the streets and lanes of the city 16
23 Go out to the highways and hedges 16
17:29 on the day when Lot went out from Sodom 16
21:37 at night he went out and lodged on the mount 16
22:62 he went out and wept bitterly. 16
Joh 4:30 They went out of the city and were coming to him. 16
8:59 Jesus hid himself, and went out of the temple. 16
11:31 the Jews . . saw Mary rise quickly and go out 16
12:13 and went out to meet him 16
13:30 he immediately went out; and it was night. 16
31 When he had gone out, Jesus said 16
18:16 the other disciple . . went out and spoke to the maid 16
29 Pilate went out to them and said 16
38 he went out to the Jews again 16
19: 4 Pilate went out again, and said to them 16
17 and he went out, bearing his own cross 16
21: 3 They went out and got into the boat 16
Act 9:28 So he went in and out among them at Jerusalem 14
12: 9 he went out and followed him 16
10 they went out and passed on through one street; 16
13:42 As they went out, the people begged 15
16:40 So they went out of the prison, and visited Lydia; 16
17:33 Paul went out from among them. 16
Rom 10:18 Their voice has gone out to all the earth 16
2Co 7:15 his heart goes out all the more to you 12
Heb 11: 8 when he was called to go out 16
8 he went out, not knowing where he was to go. 16
15 that land from which they had gone out 13
1Jn 2:19 They went out from us, but they were not of us; 16
19 but they went out, that it might be plain •
4: 1 many false prophets have gone out into the world 16
2Jn 1: 7 For many deceivers have gone out into the world 16
Rev 3:12 the temple of my God; never shall he go out of it 16
6: 2 and he went out conquering and to conquer. 16
1Es 1:25 Josiah went out against him. 16
4:23 A man takes his sword, and goes out to travel 14
58 When the young man went out 16
2Es 10:32 I did as you directed, and went out into the field 19
Tob 5:16 they both went out and departed 16
10: 7 she went out every day to the road 17
11:16 Then Tobit went out to meet his daughter-in-law 16
Jdt 8:33 I will go out with my maid 16
10: 6 Then they went out to the city gate of Bethulia 16
9 and I will go out 16
10 When they had done this, Judith went out 16
11:17 your servant will go out into the valley 16
18 then you shall go out with your whole army 16
12: 6 command that your servant be permitted to go out 16
7 and went out each night to the valley of Bethulia 14
13 Bagoas went out from the presence of Holofernes 16
13: 3 she said she would be going out for her prayers. 16
4 every one went out 7
9 after a moment she went out 16
10 Then the two of them went out together 16
14: 2 let every valiant man . . go out of the city 16
11 they went out in companies to the passes 16
Sus 1:14 when they went out, they parted from each other. 16
18 and went out by the side doors 16
19 When the maids had gone out, the two elders rose 16
Bel 1:14 When they had gone out 16
14 Then they went out, shut the door and sealed it 16
1Mc 3:11 When Judas learned of it, he went out to meet him 16
13 who stayed with him and went out to battle 14
16 Judas went out to meet him with a small company. 16
5:67 they went out to battle unwisely. 16
7:24 Judas went out into all the surrounding parts 16
24 going out into the country. 14
31 he went out to meet Judas in battle 16
35 he went out in great anger. 16
39 Now Nicanor went out from Jerusalem 16
9:65 while he went out into the country 16
12:41 Jonathan went out to meet him 16
13:49 men . . were prevented from going out to the country 14
15:25 he shut Trypho up and kept him from going out or in. 14
41 so that they might go out 14
16: 3 go out and fight for our nation 16
2Mc 1:32 it went out. 9
2: 4 he went out to the mountain 16
3Mc 4:12 the Jews' compatriots . . frequently went out in secret 14
5: 5 The servants . . went out in the evening 15
48 by the elephants going out at the gate 15
151 1: 6 I went out to meet the Philistine 16

go out early 1. שכם
Sng 7:12 let us go out early to the vineyards 1

go outside 1. ἐξέρχομαι 2. ὑπερβαίνω
Act 16:13 we went outside the gate to the riverside 1
4Mc 18: 7 and did not go outside my father's house 2

go over 1. בדל 2. ימה 3. נפל 4. עבר 5. ἀναχωρέω 6. ἀπέρχομαι 7. διαβαίνω 8. διέρχομαι 9. ἐπιπορεύομαι 10. μεταβαίνω 11. transeo
Gen 38:16 He went over to her at the road side, and said 2
Num32: 7 discourage . . Israel from going over into the land 4
Deu 2:13 'Now rise up, and go over the brook Zered.' 4
13 So we went over the brook Zered. 4
24 'Rise up . . and go over the valley of the Arnon; 4
29 until I go over the Jordan into the land 4
3:21 all the kingdoms into which you are going over. 4
25 Let me go over, I pray, and see the good land 4
27 for you shall not go over this Jordan. 4
28 for he shall go over at the head of this people 4
4:14 land which you are going over to possess. 4
22 I must die in this land, I must not go over the Jordan 4
22 but you shall go over and take possession 4
26 land . . you are going over the Jordan to possess; 4
6: 1 land to which you are going over, to possess it; 4
9: 3 he who goes over before you as a devouring fire 4
11: 8 the land which you are going over to possess 4
11 land which you are going over to possess is a land 4
12:10 when you go over the Jordan, and live in the land 4
30:13 'Who will go over the sea for us, and bring it to us 4
18 land . . going over the Jordan to enter and possess. 4
31: 2 said to me, 'You shall not go over this Jordan.' 4
3 LORD your God himself will go over before you; 4
3 Joshua will go over at your head, as the LORD 4
13 land . . you are going over the Jordan to possess. 4
32:47 land which you are going over the Jordan 4
34: 4 let you see it . . but you shall not go over there. 4
Jos 1: 2 arise, go over this Jordan you and all this people 4
24:11 And you went over the Jordan and came to Jericho 4
Jdg 12: 5 the fugitives of E'phraim said, "Let me go over 4
1Sm 14: 1 Come, let us go over to the Philistine garrison 4
4 In the pass, by which Jonathan sought to go over 4
6 Come, let us go over to the garrison of these 4
26:13 Then David went over to the other side 4
27: 2 David arose and went over, he and the 600 men 4
2Sm 16: 9 Why should . . ? Let me go over and take off his head. 4
17:20 They have gone over the brook of water. 4
21 Arise, and go quickly over the water; 4
19:36 Your servant will go a little way over the Jordan 4
37 here is . . Chimham; let him go over with my lord 4
38 the king answered, "Chimham shall go over with me 4
39 Then all the people went over the Jordan 4
39 all . . went over the Jordan, and the king went over; 4
2Kg 2: 8 the two of them could go over on dry ground. 4
14 water was parted . . and Eli'sha went over. 4
7: 4 come, let us go over to the camp of the Syrians; 3
1Ch 12: 8 From the Gadites there went over to David 1
Ps 38: 4 For my iniquities have gone over my head; 4
124: 4 torrent would have gone over us; 4
Isa 54: 9 waters of Noah should no more go over the earth 4
Mat 8:18 he gave orders to go over to the other side. 6
Lke 2:15 Let us go over to Bethlehem and see this thing 8
2Es 12: 2 And the two wings that had gone over to it arose 11
Bar 3:30 Who has gone over the sea, and found her, and will 7
LJr 1:62 God commands the clouds to go over the whole world 9
2Mc 6:24 Eleazar . . has gone over to an alien religion 10
10:13 and had gone over to Antiochus Epiphanes. 5

go over the boughs 1. פאר
Deu 24:20 you shall not go over the boughs again; 1

go quickly 1. רוץ 2. ἀποτρέχω
2Kg 4:22 Send . . that I may quickly go to the man of God 1
Sir 32:11 go home quickly and do not linger. 2

ready to go 1. חוש
Num32:17 take up arms, ready to go before the people of Israel 1

go round 1. נקף 2. סבב 3. ἐκκλίνω
Ecc 1: 6 wind blows . . south, and goes round to the north; 2
Isa 15: 8 For a cry has gone round the land of Moab; 1
1Mc 5:46 they could not go round it to the right or to the left; 3

go round about 1. נקף
Ps 48:12 Walk about Zion, go round about her 1

go straight 1. ישר
1Sm 6:12 cows went straight in the direction 1
Prv 9:15 who are going straight on their way 1

go thence 1. יצא
Jos 16: 6 and the boundary goes thence to the sea; 1

go through 1. בוא 2. עבר 3. פסג 4. שוט 5. διαπορεύομαι 6. διέρχομαι 7. εἰσέρχομαι
Gen 41:46 Joseph . . went through all the land of Egypt. 2
Lev 26: 6 the sword shall not go through your land 2
Jos 3: 2 the officers went through the camp 2
2Sm 24: 2 Go through all the tribes of Israel, from Dan 4
8 when they had gone through all the land, they came 4
2Kg 11:16 she went through the horses' entrance 1
Neh 9:11 went through the midst of the sea on dry land; 2
Ps 48:13 go through her citadels; that you may tell 3
Isa 62:10 Go through . . the gates, prepare the way 2
10 Go through, go through the gates, prepare the way 2
Ezk 9: 4 And the LORD said to him, "Go through the city 2
14:17 and say, Let a sword go through the land; 2
Mic 5: 8 which, when it goes through, treads down 2
Mrk 10:25 a camel to go through the eye of a needle 6
Lke 6: 1 while he was going through the grainfields 5
9: 6 they departed and went through the villages 6
18:25 to go through the eye of a needle 6
Act 13: 6 When they had gone through the whole island 6
15:41 he went through Syria and Cili'cia 6
16: 4 As they went on their way through the cities 5
6 they went through the region of Phry'gia and Galatia 6
18:23 he departed and went . . through the region of Galatia 6
20: 2 When he had gone through these parts 6
AEs 15: 6 When she had gone through all the doors 7
1Mc 3: 8 He went through the cities of Judah; 6
37 and went through the upper provinces. 5
6: 1 Antiochus was going through the upper provinces 5
4Mc 18:14 Even though you go through the fire 6

go through all 1. τελέω
Mat 10:23 you will not have gone through all the towns 1

go to and fro 1. עבר וָשׁוּב 2. שוט
Exd 32:27 go to and fro from gate to gate throughout 1
Job 1: 7 From going to and fro on the earth 2
2: 2 From going to and fro on the earth 2

go to bed 1. שכב
Job 27:19 He goes to bed rich, but will do so no more; 1

go to law 1. שפט 2. δικάζω 3. κρίνω
Isa 59: 4 no one goes to law honestly 1
1Co 6: 1 does he dare go to law before the unrighteous 3
6 brother goes to law against brother 3
Sir 8:14 Do not go to law against a judge 2

go to meet 1. συναντάω 2. ὑπαντάω
Joh 12:18 The reason why the crowd went to meet him 2
Sir 9: 3 Do not go to meet a loose woman 2
1Mc 11:64 He went to meet them 1

go to rest 1. ἀναπαύω
Sir 39:11 if he goes to rest, it is enough for him. 1

go to ruin 1. שחת
2Ch 34:11 buildings . . kings of Judah had let go to ruin. 1

go to see 1. προσέρχομαι
Act 18: 2 he went to see them; 1

go to sleep 1. κοιμάω
1Es 3: 3 went to sleep, and then awoke. 1
Tob 8: 9 Then they both went to sleep for the night. 1

go to war 1. לחם 2. צבא
Num31:42 separated from that of the men who had gone to war- 2
Jdg 11:25 against Israel, or did he ever go to war with them? 1

go unanswered 1. לֹא ענה
Job 11: 2 Should a multitude of words go unanswered 1

go unheard 1. ἀποκρύπτω
Wis 1:10 the sound of murmurings does not go unheard. 1

go unnoticed 1. λανθάνω
Wis 10: 8 their failures could never go unnoticed. 1

go unpunished 1. לֹא אשם 2. לֹא נקה 3. נקה
Prv 6:29 none who touches her will go unpunished. 3
11:21 Be assured, an evil man will not go unpunished 3
16: 5 be assured, he will not go unpunished. 3
17: 5 who is glad at calamity will not go unpunished. 3
19: 5 A false witness will not go unpunished 3
9 A false witness will not go unpunished 3
28:20 he who hastens to be rich will not go unpunished. 2
Jer 25:29 and shall you go unpunished? You shall not 3
29 You shall not go unpunished 3
49:12 will you go unpunished? You shall not 3
12 You shall not go unpunished, but you must drink. 3
Zec 11: 5 Those who buy them slay them and go unpunished; 1

go up 1. בוא 2. הלך 3. נגש 4. עלה 5. רום
6. ἀναβαίνω 7. ἀνάβασις 8. ἀνέρχομαι 9. ἀνίημι
10. ἀπαίρω 11. ἀπέρχομαι 12. ἐπιβαίνω
13. παραγίνομαι 14. προσάγω 15. προσαναβαίνω
16. προσέρχομαι 17. συναναβαίνω 18. ascendo
19. subeo
Gen 2: 6 a mist went up from the earth 4
13: 1 Abram went up from Egypt, he and his wife 4
17:22 talking with him, God went up from Abraham. 4
19:28 land went up like the smoke of a furnace. 4
30 Lot went up out of Zo'ar, and dwelt in the hills 4
26:23 From there he went up to Beer-sheba. 4
29:10 Jacob went up and rolled the stone from the well's 3
35: 1 God said to Jacob, "Arise, go up to Bethel 4
3 then let us arise and go up to Bethel 4
13 Then God went up from him in the place 4
38:12 when Judah was comforted, he went up to Timnah 4
13 father-in-law is going up to Timnah to shear 4
43:19 they went up to the steward of Joseph's house 3
44:17 but as for you, go up in peace to your father. 4
18 Then Judah went up to him and said, "O my lord 3
45: 9 Make haste and go up to my father and say to him 4
25 they went up out of Egypt, and came to the land 4
46:29 Joseph . . went up to meet Israel his father 4
31 I will go up and tell Pharaoh, and will say to him 4
49: 4 because you went up to your father's bed; 4
4 you defiled it-you went up to my couch! 4
9 from the prey, my son, you have gone up. 4
50: 5 Now therefore let me go up, I pray you, and bury my 4
6 Pharaoh answered, "Go up, and bury your father 4
7 Joseph went up to bury his father; 4
7 with him went up all the servants of Pharaoh 4
9 went up with him both chariots and horsemen; 4
14 all who had gone up with him to bury his father. 4
Exd 12:38 A mixed multitude also went up with them 4
13:18 Israel went up out of the land of Egypt equipped 4
16:14 when the dew had gone up, there was on the face 4
17:10 Aaron, and Hur went up to the top of the hill. 4
19: 3 Moses went up to God, and the LORD called to him 4
12 Take heed that you do not go up into the mountain 4
18 the smoke of it went up like the smoke of a kiln 4
20 LORD called Moses . . and Moses went up. 4
20:26 you shall not go up by steps to my altar 4
24: 9 Abi'hu, and 70 of the elders of Israel went up 4
13 Moses went up into the mountain of God. 4
15 Then Moses went up on the mountain, and the cloud 4
18 And Moses . . went up on the mountain. 4
32:30 I will go up to the LORD; 4
33: 1 Depart, go up hence, you and the people whom you 4
3 Go up to a land flowing with milk and honey; •
3 but I will not go up among you, lest I consume you 4
5 if for a single moment I should go up among you 4
34: 4 went up on Mount Sinai, as the LORD had commanded 4
24 when you go up to appear before the LORD your God 4
Num13:17 Go up into the Negeb yonder, and go up into the hill 4
17 into the Negeb . . and go up into the hill country 4
21 So they went up and spied out the land 4
22 They went up into the Negeb, and came to Hebron; 4
30 Caleb . . said, "Let us go up at once, and occupy it; 4
31 Then the men who had gone up with him said 4
31 We are not able to go up against the people; 4
14:40 went up to the heights of the hill country, saying 4
40 go up to the place which the LORD has promised; 4
42 Do not go up lest you be struck down before 4
44 presumed to go up to the heights of the hill 4
20:19 We will go up by the highway; and if we drink 4
27 they went up Mount Hor in the sight of all 4
21:33 Then they turned and went up by the way to Bashan; 4
27:12 Go up into this mountain to Ab'arim, and see 4
32: 9 For when they went up to the Valley of Eshcol 4
33:38 Aaron the priest went up Mount Hor at the command 4
Deu 1:21 go up, take possession, as the LORD . . has told you; 4
22 bring us word . . of the way by which we must go up 4
24 they turned and went up into the hill country 4
26 Yet you would not go up, but rebelled 4
28 Whither are we going up? 4
41 sinned against the LORD; we will go up and fight 4
41 thought it easy to go up into the hill country. 4
42 Do not go up or fight, for I am not in the midst of you; 4
43 presumptuous and went up into the hill country. 4
3: 1 Then we turned and went up the way to Bashan; 4
27 Go up to the top of Pisgah, and lift up your eyes 4
5: 5 you did not go up into the mountain. He said 4
9: 9 When I went up the mountain to receive the tables 4
23 Go up and take possession of the land 4
10: 3 went up the mountain with the two tables 4
17: 8 then you shall arise and go up to the place 4
25: 7 brother's wife . . go up to the gate to the elders 4
9 then his brother's wife shall go up to him 3
30:12 'Who will go up for us to heaven, and bring it to us 4
34: 1 Moses went up from the plains of Moab 4
Jos 6: 5 and the people shall go up . . before him 4
20 the people went up into the city, every man 4
7: 2 Joshua . . said to them, "Go up and spy out the land 4
2 And the men went up and spied out Ai. 4
3 Let not all the people go up . . they are but few. 4
3 about 2,000 or 3,000 men go up and attack Ai; 4
4 about 3,000 went up there from the people; 4
8: 1 take all the fighting men . . and arise, go up to Ai; 4
3 Joshua arose, and . . the fighting men, to go up to Ai; 4
10 Joshua . . went up, with the elders of Israel 4
11 And all the fighting men who were with him went up 4
20 behold, the smoke of the city went up to heaven; 4
21 saw . . that the smoke of the city went up 4
10: 5 and went up with all their armies and encamped 4
7 So Joshua went up from Gilgal 4
36 Joshua went up with all Israel from Eglon 4
14: 8 my brethren who went up with me 4
15: 3 along to Zin, and goes up south of Ka'desh-bar'nea 4
6 the boundary goes up to Beth-hoglah, and passes 4
6 and the boundary goes up to the stone of Bohan 4
7 and the boundary goes up to Debir from the Valley 4
8 then the boundary goes up by the valley of the son 4
8 and the boundary goes up to the top 4
15 And he went up from there against . . Debir; 4
16: 1 into the wilderness, going up from Jericho 4
17:15 go up to the forest, and there clear ground 4
18:12 boundary goes up the shoulder north of Jericho 4
19:11 its boundary goes up westward, and on to Mar'eal 4
47 the Danites went up and fought against Leshem 4
Jdg 1: 1 Who shall go up first for us against 4
2 The LORD said, "Judah shall go up; behold, I have 4
4 Judah went up and the LORD gave the Canaanites 4
16 went up with the people of Judah from the city 4
22 The house of Joseph also went up against Bethel; 4
2: 1 the angel of the LORD went up from Gilgal 4
4:10 and 10,000 men went up at his heels; 4
10 went up at his heels; and Deb'orah went up with him. 4
12 the son of Abin'o-am had gone up to Mount Tabor 4
6:35 and Naph'tali; and they went up to meet them. 4
8: 8 from there he went up to Penu'el, and spoke to them 4
11 Gideon went up . . and attacked the army; 4
9:48 Abim'elech went up to Mount Zalmon 4
13:20 the flame went up toward heaven from the altar 4
18: 9 They said, "Arise, and let us go up against them; 4
12 and went up and encamped at Kir'iath-je'arim 4
17 five men . . went up, and entered and took 4
20: 3 that the people of Israel had gone up to Mizpah. 4
9 we will do to Gib'e-ah: we will go up against it by lot •
18 Israel arose and went up to Bethel, and inquired 4
18 Which of us shall go up first to battle against 4
18 And the LORD said, "Judah shall go up first. •
23 people of Israel went up and wept before the LORD 4
23 And the LORD said, "Go up against them. 4
26 the whole army, went up and came to Bethel 4
28 Go up; for tomorrow I will give them into your hand. 4
30 Israel went up against the Benjaminites 4
31 in the highways, one of which goes up to Bethel 4
40 the whole of the city went up in smoke to heaven. 4
21:19 the highway that goes up from Bethel to Shechem 4
Rut 4: 1 And Bo'az went up to the gate and sat down there; 4
1Sm 1: 3 Now this man used to go up year by year 4
7 as often as she went up to the house of the LORD 4
21 Elka'nah and . . went up to offer to the LORD 4
22 Hannah did not go up, for she said to her husband 4
2:19 she went up . . to offer the yearly sacrifice. 4
28 to be my priest, to go up to my altar, to burn incense 4
5:12 and the cry of the city went up to heaven. 4
6: 9 if it goes up on the way to its own land 4
20 And to whom shall he go up away from us? 4
7: 7 the Philistines went up against Israel. 4
9:11 As they went up the hill to the city, 4
13 find him, before he goes up to the high place to eat; 4
13 Now go up, for you will meet him immediately. 4
14 they went up to the city. As they were entering 4
19 I am the seer; go up before me to the the high place 4
10: 3 three men going up to God at Bethel will meet you 4
11: 1 Nahash . . went up and besieged Ja'besh-gil'ead; 4
13:15 Samuel arose, and went up from Gilgal to Gib'e-ah 4
14: 9 will stand still . . and we will not go up to them. 4
10 But if they say, 'Come up to us,' then we will go up; 4
21 Hebrews who . . and who had gone up with them 4
46 Then Saul went up from pursuing the Philistines; 4
15:34 and Saul went up to his house in Gib'e-ah of Saul. 4
23:19 the Ziphites went up to Saul at Gib'e-ah, saying 4
29 David went up from there 4
24:22 but David and his men went up to the stronghold. 4
25: 5 Go up to Carmel, and go to Nabal, and greet him 4
13 and about 400 men went up after David 4
35 Go up in peace to your house; see, I have hearkened 4
27: 8 Now David and his men went up, and made raids 4
29: 9 He shall not go up with us to the battle. 4
11 But the Philistines went up to Jezreel. 4
2Sm 2: 1 Shall I go up into any of the cities of Judah? 4
1 And the LORD said to him, "Go up. 4
1 Go up." David said, "To which shall I go up? 4
2 David went up there, and his two wives also 4
5:17 all the Philistines went up in search of David; 4
19 Shall I go up against the Philistines? 4
19 Go up; for I will certainly give . . into your hand. 4
23 You shall not go up; go around to their rear 4
15:30 David went up the ascent of the Mount of Olives 4
30 and they went up, weeping as they went. 4
18:33 and went up to the chamber over the gate, and wept; 4
19:34 that I should go up with the king to Jerusalem? 4
22: 9 Smoke went up from his nostrils, and . . fire 4
24:18 Go up, rear an altar . . on the threshing floor 4
19 David went up at Gad's word, 4
1Kg 1:40 all the people went up after him, playing on pipes 4
45 they have gone up from there rejoicing 4
2:34 Benai'ah . . went up, and struck him down 4
6: 8 one went up by stairs to the middle story 4
9:16 Pharaoh . . had gone up and captured Gezer 4
24 Pharaoh's daughter went up from the city of David 4
11:15 Jo'ab the commander . . went up to bury the slain 4
12:24 You shall not go up or fight against your kinsmen 4
27 if this people go up to offer sacrifices 4
28 You have gone up to Jerusalem long enough. 4
33 He went up to the altar which he had made in Bethel 4
33 and went up to the altar to burn incense. 4
15:17 Ba'asha king of Israel went up against Judah 4
16:17 So Omri went up from Gib'bethon 4
18:41 Eli'jah said to Ahab, "Go up, eat and drink; 4
42 So Ahab went up to eat and to drink. 4
42 And Eli'jah went up to the top of Carmel; 4
43 he said . . "Go up now, look toward the sea. 4
43 he went up and looked, and said, "There is nothing. 4
44 Go up, say to Ahab, 'Prepare your chariot and go down 4
20: 1 and he went up and besieged Sama'ria 4
26 Ben-ha'dad mustered . . and went up to Aphek 4
22: 6 Go up; for the Lord will give it into the hand 4
12 Go up to Ramoth-gilead and triumph; 4
15 Go up and triumph; the LORD will give it 4
20 'Who will entice Ahab, that he may go up and fall 4
29 the king of Israel and Jehosh'aphat . . went up 4
2Kg 1: 3 Arise, go up to meet the messengers of the king 4
9 He went up to Eli'jah . . and said to him, "O man of God 4
11 And he went up and said to him, "O man of God 6
13 the third captain of 50 went up, and came 4
2:11 And Eli'jah went up by a whirlwind into heaven. 4
23 He went up from there to Bethel; 4
23 while he was going up on the way, some . . boys came 4
23 boys . . jeered at him, saying, "Go up, you baldhead! 4
23 saying, "Go up, you baldhead! Go up, you baldhead! 4
4:21 she went up and laid him on the bed of the man of God 4
34 Then he went up and lay upon the child 4
35 and went up, and stretched himself upon him; 4
6:24 Ben-ha'dad . . and went up, and besieged Sama'ria. 4
12:17 Haz'ael . . went up and fought against Gath 4
17 Haz'ael set his face to go up against Jerusalem 4
14:11 So Jeho'ash king of Israel went up 4
16:12 the king drew near to the altar, and went up on it 4
18:17 And they went up and came to Jerusalem. 4
25 Go up against this land, and destroy it.' 4
19:14 and Hezeki'ah went up to the house of the LORD 4
23 I have gone up the heights of the mountains 4
20: 5 you shall go up to the house of the LORD. 4
8 I . . go up to the house of the LORD on the third day? 4
22: 4 Go up to Hilki'ah the high priest 4
23: 2 And the king went up to the house of the LORD 4
29 Pharaoh Neco . . went up to the king of Assyria 4
1Ch 11: 6 Jo'ab . . went up first, so he became chief. 4
13: 6 David and all Israel went up to Ba'alah 4
14: 8 all the Philistines went up in search of David; 4
10 Shall I go up against the Philistines? 4
10 Go up, and I will give them into your hand. 4
11 And he went up to Ba'al-pera'zim 4
14 You shall not go up after them 4
21:18 David should go up and rear an altar to the LORD 4
19 David went up at Gad's word, which he had spoken 4
26:16 the gate of Shal'lecheth on the road that goes up. 4
2Ch 1: 6 Solomon went up there to the bronze altar 4

11: 4 shall not go up or fight against your brethren. 4
16: 1 Ba'asha king of Israel went up against Judah 4
18: 2 induced him to go up against Ramoth-gilead. 4
5 they said, "Go up; for God will give it into the hand 4
11 Go up to Ramoth-gilead and triumph; 4
14 And he answered, "Go up and triumph; 4
19 that he may go up and fall at Ramoth-gilead?' 4
28 went up to Ramoth-gilead. 4
25:21 Jo'ash king of Israel went up; 4
29:20 Hezeki'ah . . went up to the house of the LORD. 4
34:30 the king went up to the house of the LORD 4
35:20 Neco king of Egypt went up to fight at Car'chemish 4
36:23 may the LORD his God be with him. Let him go up. 4
Ezr 1: 3 let him go up to Jerusalem, which is in Judah 4
5 stirred to go up to rebuild the house of the LORD 4
7: 6 this Ezra went up from Babylonia. He was a scribe 4
7 there went up also to Jerusalem 4
9 go up from Babylonia, and on the first day 4
28 gathered leading men from Israel to go up 4
8: 1 this is the genealogy of those who went up with me 4
Neh 2:15 Then I went up in the night by the valley 4
4: 3 if a fox goes up on it he will break down 4
12:37 Fountain Gate they went up straight before 4
Est 4: 2 he went up to the entrance of the king's gate 1
Job 6:18 they go up into the waste, and perish. 4
Ps 18: 8 Smoke went up from his nostrils 4
47: 5 God has gone up with a shout 4
62: 9 men . . are a delusion; in the balances they go up; 4
74:23 the uproar of thy adversaries which goes up 4
122: 4 to which the tribes go up, the tribes of the LORD 4
Prv 26: 9 thorn that goes up into the hand of a drunkard 4
Isa 2: 3 Come, let us go up to the mountain of the LORD 4
5:24 as rottenness, and their blossom go up like dust; 4
7: 6 Let us go up against Judah and terrify it 4
10:27 He has gone up from Rimmon •
15: 2 Dibon has gone up to the high places to weep; 4
5 For at the ascent of Luhith they go up weeping; 4
21: 2 Go up, O Elam, lay siege, O Media; 4
22: 1 that you have gone up, all of you, to the housetops 4
34:10 its smoke shall go up for ever. 4
36:10 said to me, Go up against this land, and destroy it.' 4
37:14 and Hezeki'ah went up to the house of the LORD 4
24 I have gone up the heights of the mountains 4
38:22 sign that I shall go up to the house of the LORD 4
57: 7 and thither you went up to offer sacrifice. 4
8 bed, you have gone up to it, you have made it wide; 4
Jer 3: 6 how she went up on every high hill 2
4: 7 A lion has gone up from his thicket 4
5:10 Go up through her vine-rows and destroy 4
14: 2 and the cry of Jerusalem goes up. 4
22:20 Go up to Lebanon, and cry out, and lift up your voice 4
31: 6 Arise, and let us go up to Zion, to the LORD our God. 4
46:11 Go up to Gilead, and take balm, O virgin daughter 4
48: 5 For at the ascent of Luhith they go up weeping; 4
50:21 Go up against the land of Meratha'im 4
Ezk 8:11 and the smoke of the cloud of incense went up. 4
9: 3 Now the glory of the God of Israel had gone up 4
10: 4 the glory of the LORD went up from the cherubim 5
11:23 And the glory of the LORD went up from the midst 4
24 Then the vision that I had seen went up from me. 4
13: 5 You have not gone up into the breaches 4
38:11 say, 'I will go up against the land of unwalled 4
40: 6 into the gateway facing east, going up its steps 4
41: 7 thus one went up from the lowest story to the top 4
Hos 1:11 and they shall go up from the land 4
4:15 Enter not into Gilgal, nor go up to Beth-a'ven 4
8: 9 For they have gone up to Assyria 4
Ams 4:10 the stench of your camp go up into your nostrils; 4
Obd 1:21 Saviors shall go up to Mount Zion to rule 4
Mic 2:13 He who opens the breach will go up before them; 4
4: 2 Come, let us go up to the mountain of the LORD 4
Hag 1: 8 Go up to the hills and bring wood and build 4
Zec 14:16 shall go up year after year to worship the King 4
17 if any of the families of the earth do not go up 4
18 if the family of Egypt do not go up and present 4
18 nations that do not go up to keep the feast 4
19 that do not go up to keep the feast of booths. 4
Mat 3:16 he went up immediately from the water, and behold 6
5: 1 Seeing the crowds, he went up on the mountain 6
14:23 he went up on the mountain by himself to pray 6
15:29 he went up on the mountain, and sat down there. 6
17:24 the collectors . . went up to Peter and said 16
20:17 as Jesus was going up to Jerusalem 6
18 Behold, we are going up to Jerusalem 6
Mrk 3:13 And he went up on the mountain 6
6:46 he went up on the mountain to pray. 11
10:32 they were on the road, going up to Jerusalem 6
33 saying, "Behold, we are going up to Jerusalem; 6
14:45 he went up to him at once, and said, "Master! 16
Lke 2: 4 Joseph also went up from Galilee 6
42 they went up according to custom; 6
5:19 they went up on the roof 6
9:28 and went up on the mountain to pray. 6
14:10 'Friend, go up higher' 15
18:10 Two men went up into the temple to pray 6
31 Behold, we are going up to Jerusalem 6
19:28 he went on ahead, going up to Jerusalem. 6
Joh 2:13 and Jesus went up to Jerusalem. 6
5: 1 and Jesus went up to Jerusalem. 6

6: 3 Jesus went up on the mountain 8
7: 8 I am not going up to this feast 6
10 after his brothers had gone up to the feast 6
10 he also went up, not publicly but in private. 6
14 Jesus went up into the temple and taught. 6
11:55 many went up from the country to Jerusalem 6
12:20 among those who went up to worship at the feast 6
Act 1:13 they went up to the upper room 6
3: 1 Now Peter and John were going up to the temple 6
8:29 Go up and join this chariot. 16
10: 9 Peter went up on the housetop to pray 6
11: 2 when Peter went up to Jerusalem 6
15: 2 appointed to go up to Jerusalem to the apostles 6
18:22 he went up and greeted the church 6
20:11 when Paul had gone up and had broken bread 6
21:12 the people there begged him not to go up to Jerusalem 6
15 we made ready and went up to Jerusalem. 6
24:11 since I went up to worship at Jerusalem; 6
25: 1 he went up to Jerusalem from Caesare'a. 6
9 Do you wish to go up to Jerusalem 6
Gal 1:17 nor did I go up to Jerusalem 8
18 Then after three years I went up to Jerusalem 8
2: 1 I went up again to Jerusalem with Barnabas 6
2 I went up by revelation 6
Rev 11:12 they went up to heaven in a cloud. 6
14:11 smoke of their torment goes up for ever and ever; 6
19: 3 The smoke from her goes up for ever and ever. 6
1Es 2: 5 let him go up to Jerusalem, which is in Judea 6
8 go up to build the house in Jerusalem for the Lord; 6
4:47 all who were going up with him to build Jerusalem. 6
49 Jews who were going up from his kingdom to Judea 6
63 to go up and build Jerusalem and the temple 6
5: 1 heads of fathers' houses were chosen to go up 6
3 he made them go up with them. 17
4 These are the names of the men who went up 6
8:27 I gathered men from Israel to go up with me. 17
28 their groups, who went up with me from Babylon 6
2Es 4:15 let us go up and subdue the forest of the plain 18
15:44 then the dust and smoke shall go up to heaven 19
Jdt 2:22 and went up into the hill country 11
5:20 then we will go up and defeat them. 6
24 Therefore let us go up, Lord Holofernes 6
6:11 from the plain they went up into the hill country 10
7:13 We . . will go up to the tops of the nearby mountains 6
18 the sons of Ammon went up and encamped 6
32 they went up on the walls 11
13: 6 She went up to the post at the end of the bed 16
10 and went up the mountain to Bethulia 15
Sir 46: 9 he went up to the hill country 12
50:11 went up to the holy altar 7
Bar 3:29 Who has gone up into heaven, and taken her 6
1Mc 1:20 He went up against Israel and came to Jerusalem 6
3:15 a strong army . . went up with him to help him 6
4:36 let us go up to cleanse the sanctuary 6
37 they went up to Mount Zion. 6
5:31 the cry of the city went up to Heaven 6
54 they went up to Mount Zion with gladness and joy 6
6:48 The soldiers . . went up to Jerusalem against them 6
7:33 After these events Nicanor went up to Mount Zion 6
9: 8 Let us rise and go up against our enemies 6
38 and went up and hid under cover of the mountain. 6
13: 2 So he went up to Jerusalem 6
45 went up on the wall with their clothes rent 6
16: 1 John went up from Gazara and reported to Simon 6
2Mc 2: 4 to the mountain where Moses had gone up 6
6:19 he . . went up to the rack of his own accord 14
12:31 Then they went up to Jerusalem 13
3Mc 3:16 and went up to honor the temple 6
4Mc 4: 4 and went up to Seleucus to inform him 6
10 while Apollonius was going up 9

go up and down 1. הלך 2. הלך וְהלך
Jos 18: 4 that they may set out and go up and down the land 1
8 Go up and down and write a description of the land 2

go upward 1. עלה לְמָעְלָה
Ecc 3:21 Who knows whether the spirit of man goes upward 1

go wantonly 1. זנה
Num15:39 which you are inclined to go after wantonly. 1

go way 1. *πορεύω*
Tob 11: 4 they went their way 1

go well 1. טוֹב 2. טוב 3. יטב 4. *εὖ εἰμί* 5. *εὐοδόω*
Gen 12:13 Say you are my sister, that it may go well with me 3
Deu 4:40 it may go well with you, and with your children 3
5:16 that it may go well with you, in the land 3
29 it might go well with them and with their children 3
33 that you may live, and that it may go well with you 2
6: 3 that it may go well with you 3
18 do what is right . . that it may go well with you 3
12:25 all may go well with you and with your children 3
28 that it may go well with you and with your children 3
22: 7 may go well with you, and that you may live long. 3
Prv 11:10 goes well with the righteous, the city rejoices; 1
3Jn 1: 2 Beloved, I pray that all may go well with you 5
Sir 1:13 it will go well at the end 4

go wrong 1. פרר 2. *ἀχρειόω*
Prv 15:22 Without counsel plans go wrong 1
Rom 3:12 together they have gone wrong; 2

goad 1. דָּרְבָן 2. דָּרְבֹנָה 3. *κέντρον*
1Sm 13:21 a third of a shekel for . . setting the goads. 1
Ecc 12:11 The sayings of the wise are like goads 2
Act 26:14 It hurts you to kick against the goads.' 3
Sir 38:25 who glories in the shaft of a goad 3

goal 1. *σκοπός* 2. finis
Php 3:14 I press on toward the goal for the prize 1
2Es 5:40 the goal of the love 2

goat 1. יָעֵל 2. עֵז 3. עַתּוּד 4. צָפִיר 5. שֵׂה עִזִּים 6. שָׂעִיר 7. שְׂעִיר עִזִּים 8. *αἴγειος* 9. *αἴξ* 10. *ἐρίφιον* 11. *ἔριφος* 12. *τράγος*
Gen 30:32 the spotted and speckled among the goats; 2
33 not speckled and spotted among the goats 2
31:12 the goats that leap upon the flock are striped 3
37:31 they . . killed a goat, and dipped the robe 7
Exd 12: 5 you shall take it from the sheep or from the goats; 2
25: 4 scarlet stuff and fine twined linen, goats' hair 2
Lev 1:10 from the flock, from the sheep or goats 2
3:12 If his offering is a goat 2
4:23 as his offering a goat, a male without blemish 2
24 shall lay his hand upon the head of the goat 6
28 his offering a goat, a female without blemish 7
5: 6 a female from the flock, a lamb or a goat 7
7:23 You shall eat no fat, of ox, or sheep, or goat 2
9: 3 Take a male goat for a sin offering, and a calf 2
15 took the goat of the sin offering 6
10:16 inquired about the goat of the sin offering 6
16: 7 take the two goats, and set them before the LORD 6
8 Aaron shall cast lots upon the two goats 6
9 the goat on which the lot fell for the LORD 6
10 the goat on which the lot fell for Aza'zel 6
15 Then he shall kill the goat of the sin offering 6
18 the blood of the bull and of the blood of the goat 6
20 he shall present the live goat 6
21 both his hands upon the head of the live goat 6
21 he shall put them upon the head of the goat 6
22 The goat shall bear all their iniquities 6
22 he shall let the goat go in the wilderness 6
26 he who lets the goat go to Aza'zel shall wash 6
27 sin offering and the goat for the sin offering 6
17: 3 If any man . . kills an ox or a lamb or a goat 2
22:19 a male . . of the bulls or the sheep or the goats 2
27 When a bull or sheep or goat is born 2
Num15:27 sins unwittingly, he shall offer a female goat 2
18:17 firstling of a goat, you shall not redeem; 2
Deu 14: 4 animals you may eat: the ox, the sheep, the goat 5
32:14 fat of lambs and rams, herds of Bashan and goats 3
1Sm 19:13 and put a pillow of goats' hair at its head 2
16 with the pillow of goats' hair at its head. 2
25: 2 he had 3,000 sheep and 1,000 goats. 2
1Kg 20:27 before them like two little flocks of goats 2
Job 39: 1 Do you know when the mountain goats bring forth? 1
Ps 50:13 eat the flesh of bulls, or drink the blood of goats? 3
66:15 I will make an offering of bulls and goats. Selah 3
Prv 27:26 goats the price of a field; 3
27 there will be enough goats' milk for your food 2
Sng 4: 1 Your hair is like a flock of goats 2
6: 5 Your hair is like a flock of goats 2
Isa 34: 6 gorged with fat, with the blood of lambs and goats 3
Ezk 27:21 your favored dealers in lambs, rams, and goats; 3
39:18 of rams, of lambs, and of goats, of bulls, 3
43:25 you shall provide daily a goat for a sin offering; 6
Dan 8: 5 goat had a conspicuous horn between his eyes. 4
Mat 25:32 as a shepherd separates the sheep from the goats 11
33 the goats at the left. 10
Heb 9:12 taking not the blood of goats and calves 12
13 the blood of goats and bulls 12
19 he took the blood of calves and goats 12
10: 4 the blood of bulls and goats 12
11:37 they went about in skins of sheep and goats 8
Jdt 2:17 sheep and oxen and goats for provision; 9

goat *See also* wild.

he goat 1. עַתּוּד 2. צָפִיר 3. צְפִיר עִזִּים 4. צָפִיר שָׂעִיר 5. שָׂעִיר 6. שְׂעִיר עִזִּים 7. תַּיִשׁ 8. צְפִיר עִזִּין (A) 9. *τράγος* 10. *χίμαρος*
Gen 30:35 the he-goats that were striped and spotted 7
31:10 in a dream that the he-goats which leaped upon 1
32:14 200 she-goats and twenty he-goats 7
2Ch 17:11 Arabs also brought him . . 7,700 he-goats. 7
29:21 they brought . . seven lambs, and seven he-goats 3
23 the he-goats for the sin offering were brought 5
Ezr 6:17 sin offering for all Israel twelve he-goats 8
8:35 as a sin offering twelve he-goats; 2
Ps 50: 9 bull from your house, nor he-goat from your folds. 1
Prv 30:31 strutting cock, the he-goat, and a king striding 7
Isa 1:11 in the blood of bulls, or of lambs, or of he-goats. 1
Jer 50: 8 and be as he-goats before the flock. 1
51:40 lambs to the slaughter, like rams and he-goats. 1
Ezk 34:17 I judge between sheep and sheep, rams and he-goats 1
43:22 on the second day you shall offer a he-goat 6
45:23 and a he-goat daily for a sin offering. 6

Dan 8: 5 he-goat came from the west across the . . earth 3
8 Then the he-goat magnified himself exceedingly; 3
21 he-goat is the king of Greece; 4
1Es 7: 8 twelve he-goats for the sin of all Israel 10
8:66 72 lambs, and as a thank offering twelve he-goats 9

male goat 1. עַתּוּד 2. שָׂעִיר 3. שְׂעִיר עִזִּים

Lev 9: 3 Take a male goat for a sin offering, and a calf 2
16: 5 two male goats for a sin offering 3
23:19 you shall offer one male goat for a sin offering 3
Num 7:16 one male goat for a sin offering; 3
17 peace offerings . . five male goats 1
22 one male goat for a sin offering; 3
23 peace offerings . . five rams, five male goats 1
28 one male goat for a sin offering; 3
29 peace offerings . . five rams, five male goats 1
34 one male goat for a sin offering; 3
35 peace offerings . . five rams, five male goats 1
40 one male goat for a sin offering; 3
41 peace offerings . . five rams, five male goats 1
46 one male goat for a sin offering; 3
47 peace offerings . . five rams, five male goats 1
52 one male goat for a sin offering; 3
53 peace offerings . . five rams, five male goats 1
58 one male goat for a sin offering; 3
59 peace offerings . . five rams, five male goats 1
64 one male goat for a sin offering; 3
65 peace offerings . . five rams, five male goats 1
70 one male goat for a sin offering; 3
71 peace offering . . five rams, five male goats 1
76 one male goat for a sin offering; 3
77 peace offerings . . five rams, five male goats 1
82 one male goat for a sin offering; 3
83 peace offerings . . five rams, five male goats 1
87 twelve male goats for a sin offering; 3
88 peace offerings . . the male goats 60 1
15:24 and one male goat for a sin offering. 3
28:15 Also one male goat for a sin offering to the LORD; 3
22 also one male goat for a sin offering 2
30 with one male goat, to make atonement for you. 3
29: 5 one male goat for a sin offering, to make atonement 3
11 also one male goat for a sin offering 3
16 also one male goat for a sin offering 3
19 also one male goat for a sin offering 3
22 also one male goat for a sin offering 2
25 also one male goat for a sin offering 3
28 also one male goat for a sin offering; 2
31 also one male goat for a sin offering; 2
34 also one male goat for a sin offering; 2
38 also one male goat for a sin offering; 2

young goat 1. ἔριφος

Sir 47: 3 He played with lions as with young goats 1

goatskin 1. עוֹר תַּחַשׁ 2. תַּחַשׁ

Exd 25: 5 tanned rams' skins, goatskins, acacia wood 1
26:14 of tanned rams' skins and goatskins. 1
35: 7 tanned rams' skins, and goatskins; acacia wood 1
23 or goats' hair or tanned rams' skins or goatskins 1
36:19 of tanned rams' skins and goatskins. 1
39:34 the covering of tanned rams' skins and goatskins 2
Num 4: 6 then they shall put on it a covering of goatskin 1
8 and cover the same with a covering of goatskin 1
10 put it . . in a covering of goatskin 1
11 cover it with a covering of goatskin 1
12 cover them with a covering of goatskin, and put 1
14 they shall spread upon it a covering of goatskin 1
25 carry . . the covering of goatskin that is on top 2

goblet 1. כְּלִי

Est 1: 7 Drinks were served in golden goblets 1
7 in golden goblets, goblets of different kinds 1

god 1. אֵל 2. אֱלוֹהַּ 3. אֱלֹהִים 4. אֱלָהּ (A) 5. אֱלָהִים (A) 6. θεός 7. dius

Gen 31:30 father's house, but why did you steal my gods? 2
32 one with whom you find your gods shall not live. 3
35: 2 Put away the foreign gods that are among you 3
4 they gave to Jacob all the foreign gods 3
Exd 12:12 on all the gods of Egypt I will execute judgments 3
15:11 Who is like thee, O LORD, among the gods? 1
18:11 Now I know that the LORD is greater than all gods 3
20: 3 You shall have no other gods before me. 3
23 You shall not make gods of silver to be with me 3
23 nor shall you make for yourselves gods of gold. 3
22:20 Whoever sacrifices to any god, save to the LORD 3
23:13 make no mention of the names of other gods 3
24 you shall not bow down to their gods, nor serve 3
32 make no covenant with them or with their gods. 3
33 if you serve their gods, it will surely be a snare 3
32: 1 said to him, "Up, make us gods, who shall go before us; 3
4 they said, "These are your gods, O Israel, who 3
8 and said, 'These are your gods, O Israel, who brought 3
23 For they said to me, 'Make us gods, who shall go 3
31 they have made for themselves gods of gold. 3
34:14 for you shall worship no other god, for the LORD 1
15 and when they play the harlot after their gods 3
15 when they . . sacrifice to their gods 3
16 play the harlot after their gods and make 3
16 make your sons play the harlot after their gods. 3
17 You shall make for yourself no molten gods. 3
Lev 19: 4 Do not . . make for yourselves molten gods 3
Num25: 2 people to the sacrifices of their gods 3
2 people ate, and bowed down to their gods. 3
33: 4 upon their gods also the LORD executed 3
Deu 3:24 what god is there in heaven or on earth who can do 1
4: 7 has a god so near to it as the LORD our God is to us 3
28 there you will serve gods of wood and stone 3
33 Did any people ever hear the voice of a god 3
34 has any god ever attempted to go and take a nation 3
5: 7 You shall have no other gods before me. 3
6:14 You shall not go after other gods 3
14 other gods, of the gods of the peoples 3
7: 4 turn away your sons . . to serve other gods; 3
16 serve their gods, for that would be a snare to you. 3
25 The graven images of their gods you shall burn 3
8:19 forget . . and go after other gods and serve them 3
10:17 LORD your God is God of gods and Lord of lords 3
11:16 turn aside and serve other gods and worship 3
28 to go after other gods which you have not known. 3
12: 2 places where the nation . . served their gods 3
3 hew down the graven images of their gods 3
30 that you do not inquire about their gods, saying 3
30 How did these nations serve their gods?-that I 3
31 abominable thing . . they have done for their gods; 3
31 burn their sons . . in the fire to their gods. 3
13: 2 go after other gods,' which you have not known 3
6 entices . . saying, 'Let us go and serve other gods,' 3
7 gods of the people that are round about you 3
13 go and serve other gods,' which you have not known 3
17: 3 gone and served other gods and worshipped them 3
18:20 prophet . . who speaks in the name of other gods 3
20:18 which they have done in the service of their gods 3
28:14 do not turn . . to go after other gods to serve 3
36 shall serve other gods, of wood and stone. 3
64 there . . serve other gods, of wood and stone 3
29:18 turns . . to go and serve the gods of those nations; 3
26 went and served other gods and worshiped them 3
26 worshiped them, gods whom they had not known 3
30:17 drawn away to worship other gods and serve them 3
31:16 rise and play the harlot after the strange gods 3
18 evil . . because they have turned to other gods. 3
20 they will turn to other gods and serve them 3
32:12 LORD alone . . there was no foreign god with him. 1
17 They sacrificed to demons which were no gods 2
17 They sacrificed to . . gods they had never known 3
21 have stirred me to jealousy with what is no god; 1
37 'Where are their gods, the rock in which they took 3
39 I, even I, am he, and there is no god beside me; 3
Jos 23: 7 or make mention of the names of their gods 3
16 and go and serve other gods and bow down to them. 3
24: 2 and they served other gods. 3
14 put away the gods which your fathers served 3
15 the gods your fathers served in the region 3
15 the gods of the Amorites in whose land you dwell; 3
16 that we . . forsake the LORD, to serve other gods; 3
20 If you forsake the LORD and serve foreign gods 3
23 put away the foreign gods which are among you 3
Jdg 2: 3 their gods shall be a snare to you. 3
12 they went after other gods, from among the gods 3
12 from among the gods of the peoples who were round 3
17 played the harlot after other gods and bowed 3
19 worse than their fathers, going after other gods 3
3: 6 to their sons; and they served their gods. 3
5: 8 When new gods were chosen, then war was 3
6:10 not pay reverence to the gods of the Amorites 3
31 If he is a god, let him contend for himself 3
8:33 turned again . . and made Ba'al-be'rith their god. 3
9: 9 my fatness, by which gods and men are honored 3
13 Shall I leave my wine which cheers gods and men 3
27 festival, and went into the house of their god 3
10: 6 the Ash'taroth, the gods of Syria, the gods of Sidon 3
6 gods of Syria, the gods of Sidon, the gods of Moab 3
6 Syria, the gods of Sidon, the gods of Moab, the gods 3
6 Sidon, the gods of Moab, the gods of the Ammonites 3
6 the Ammonites, and the gods of the Philistines; 3
13 Yet you have forsaken me and served other gods; 3
14 Go and cry to the gods whom you have chosen; 3
16 So they put away the foreign gods from among them 3
11:24 what Chemosh your god gives you to possess? 3
16:23 to offer a great sacrifice to Dagon their god 3
23 Our god has given Samson our enemy into our hand. 3
24 when the people saw him, they praised their god; 3
24 Our god has given our enemy into our hand 3
18:24 You take my gods which I made, and the priest, and go 3
Rut 1:15 has gone back to her people and to her gods; 3
1Sm 4: 7 they said, "A god has come into the camp. 3
8 deliver us from the power of these mighty gods? 3
8 These are the gods who smote the Egyptians 3
5: 7 his hand is heavy upon us and upon Dagon our god. 3
6: 5 his hand from off you and your gods and your land. 3
7: 3 put away the foreign gods and the Ash'taroth 3
8: 8 done to me . . forsaking me and serving other gods 3
17:43 And the Philistine cursed David by his gods. 3
26:19 driven me out . . saying, 'Go, serve other gods.' 3
28:13 I see a god coming up out of the earth. 3
2Sm 7:23 by driving out . . a nation and its gods? 3
1Kg 9: 6 if you . . go and serve other gods and worship them 3
9 forsook the LORD . . and laid hold on other gods 3
11: 2 they will turn away your heart after their gods"; 3
4 his wives turned away his heart after other gods; 3
8 burned incense and sacrificed to their gods. 3
10 that he should not go after other gods; 3
33 Ash'toreth . . Chemosh the god of Moab, and Milcom 3
33 Chemosh . . and Milcom the god of the Ammonites 3
12:28 Behold your gods, O Israel, who brought you up 3
14: 9 made for yourself other gods, and molten images 3
18:24 you call on the name of your god 3
25 call on the name of your god, but put no fire to it. 3
27 Cry aloud, for he is a god; either he is musing 3
19: 2 So may the gods do to me, and more also, if I do not 3
20:10 The gods do so to me, and more also, if the dust 3
23 Their gods are gods of the hills 3
23 Their gods are gods of the hills 3
28 The LORD is a god of the hills but he is not a god 3
28 The LORD is . . not a god of the valleys 3
2Kg 1: 2 Go, inquire of Ba'al-ze'bub, the god of Ekron, whether 3
3 going to inquire of Ba'al-ze'bub, the god of Ekron?' 3
6 to inquire of Ba'al-ze'bub, the god of Ekron? 3
16 to inquire of Ba'al-ze'bub, the god of Ekron 3
5:17 will not . . sacrifice to any god but the LORD. 3
17: 7 Israel had sinned . . and had feared other gods 3
26 do not know the law of the god of the land; 3
26 they do not know the law of the god of the land. 3
27 and teach them the law of the god of the land. 3
29 But every nation still made gods of its own 3
31 and Anam'melech, the gods of Sephar-va'im. 2
33 feared the LORD but also served their own gods 3
35 You shall not fear other gods or bow yourselves 3
37 You shall not fear other gods 3
38 You shall not fear other gods 3
18:33 Has any of the gods . . ever delivered his land 3
34 Where are the gods of Hamath and Arpad? 3
34 Where are the gods of Sepharva'im, Hena, and Ivvah? 3
35 Who among all the gods . . have delivered their 3
19:12 Have the gods of the nations delivered them 3
18 and have cast their gods into the fire; 3
18 they were no gods, but the work of men's hands, wood 3
37 he was worshiping in the house of Nisroch his god 3
22:17 forsaken me and . . burned incense to other gods 3
1Ch 5:25 played the harlot after the gods of the peoples 3
10:10 they put his armor in the temple of their gods 3
14:12 left their gods there, and David gave command 3
16:25 he is to be held in awe above all gods. 3
26 For all the gods of the peoples are idols; 3
2Ch 2: 5 for our God is greater than all gods. 3
7:19 turn aside . . and go and serve other gods 3
22 forsook the LORD . . and laid hold on other gods 3
13: 8 golden calves which Jerobo'am made you for gods. 3
9 becomes a priest of what are no gods. 3
25:14 he brought the gods of the men of Se'ir 3
14 gods . . of Se'ir . . , and set them up as his gods 3
15 Why have you resorted to the gods of a people 3
20 because they had sought the gods of Edom. 3
28:23 For he sacrificed to the gods of Damascus 3
23 Because the gods of the kings of Syria helped 3
25 he made high places to burn incense to other gods 3
32:13 gods of the nations of those lands at all able 3
14 Who among all the gods . . was able to deliver 3
15 for no god of any nation or kingdom has been able 2
17 Like the gods . . who have not delivered 3
19 as they spoke of the gods of the peoples 3
21 And when he came into the house of his god 3
33:15 he took away the foreign gods and the idol 3
34:25 forsaken me and . . burned incense to other gods 3
Ezr 1: 7 carried . . and placed in the house of his gods. 3
Job 12: 6 are secure, who bring their god in their hand. 2
Ps 16: 4 who choose another god multiply their sorrows; •
44:20 or spread forth our hands to a strange god 1
58: 1 Do you indeed decree what is right, you gods? 1
77:13 What god is great like our God? 1
81: 9 There shall be no strange god among you; 1
9 you shall not bow down to a foreign god. 1
82: 1 in the midst of the gods he holds judgment 3
6 I say, "You are gods, sons of the Most High, all of you; 3
84: 7 God of gods will be seen in Zion. 3
86: 8 There is none like thee among the gods, O Lord 3
95: 3 For the LORD is . . a great King above all gods. 3
96: 4 he is to be feared above all gods. 3
5 For all the gods of the peoples are idols; 3
97: 7 all gods bow down before him. 3
9 O LORD . . thou art exalted far above all gods. 3
136: 2 O give thanks to the God of gods 3
138: 1 before the gods I sing thy praise; 3
Isa 17:10 you plant . . and set out slips of an alien god •
21: 9 her gods he has shattered to the ground. 3
36:18 Has any of the gods of the nations delivered 3
19 Where are the gods of Hamath and Arpad? 3
19 Where are the gods of Sepharva'im? 3
20 Who among all the gods of these countries 3
37:12 Have the gods of the nations delivered them 3
19 have cast their gods into the fire; 3
19 they were no gods, but the work of men's hands 3
38 he was worshiping in the house of Nisroch his god 3
41:23 that we may know that you are gods; 3
42:17 who say to molten images, "You are our gods. 3

43:10 Before me no god was formed 1
12 when there was no strange god among you; *
44: 6 first and I am the last; besides me there is no god. 3
10 Who fashions a god or casts an image 1
15 also he makes a god and worships it 1
17 the rest of it he makes into a god, his idol; 1
17 prays to it and says, "Deliver me, for thou art my god! 1
45:14 there is no other, no god besides him.' 3
20 and keep on praying to a god that cannot save. 1
21 there is no other god besides me 3
46: 6 hire a goldsmith, and he makes it into a god; 1
Jer 1:16 they have burned incense to other gods 3
2:11 Has a nation changed its gods 3
11 changed its gods, even though they are no gods? 3
28 where are your gods that you made for yourself? 3
28 for as many as your cities are your gods, O Judah. 3
5: 7 and have sworn by those who are no gods. 3
19 As you have forsaken me and served foreign gods 3
7: 6 if you do not go after other gods to your own hurt 3
9 and go after other gods that you have not known 3
18 they pour out drink offerings to other gods 3
10:11 gods who did not make the heavens and the earth 4
11:10 they have gone after other gods to serve them; 3
12 and cry to the gods to whom they burn incense 3
13 For your gods have become as many as your cities 3
13:10 and have gone after other gods to serve them 3
16:11 and have gone after other gods and have served 3
13 there you shall serve other gods day and night 3
20 Can man make for himself gods? Such are no gods! 3
20 Can man make for himself gods? Such are no gods! 3
19: 4 by burning incense in it to other gods 3
13 have been poured out to other gods 3
22: 9 and worshiped other gods and served them. 3
25: 6 do not go after other gods to serve and worship 3
32:29 offerings have been poured out to other gods 3
35:15 amend your doings, and do not go after other gods 3
43:12 He shall kindle a fire in the temples of the gods 3
13 the temples of the gods of Egypt he shall burn 3
44: 3 they went to burn incense and serve other gods 3
5 to turn . . and burn no incense to other gods. 3
8 burning incense to other gods 3
15 their wives had offered incense to other gods 3
46:25 and Pharaoh, and Egypt and her gods and her kings 3
48:35 in the high place and burns incense to his god. 3
Ezk 28: 2 you have said, 'I am a god, I sit in the seat 1
2 sit in the seat of the gods, in the heart of the seas 3
2 yet you are but a man, and no god 1
2 though you consider yourself as wise as a god 3
6 Because you consider yourself as wise as a god 3
9 Will you still say, 'I am a god,' 3
9 and no god, in the hands of those who wound you? 1
Dan 2:11 none can show it to the king except the gods 4
47 Truly, your God is God of gods and Lord of kings 4
3:12 not serve your gods or worship the golden image 4
14 not serve my gods or worship the golden image 4
15 god that will deliver you out of my hands? 4
18 not serve your gods or worship the golden image 4
25 appearance of the fourth is like a son of the gods. 4
28 serve and worship any god except their own God. 4
29 no other god who is able to deliver in this way. 4
4: 8 named Belteshaz'zar after the name of my god 4
8 Daniel . . in whom is the spirit of the holy gods- 4
9 know that the spirit of the holy gods is in you 4
18 for the spirit of the holy gods is in you. 4
5: 4 praised the gods of gold and silver, bronze, iron 5
11 man in whom is the spirit of the holy gods. 4
11 light . . and wisdom, like the wisdom of the gods 4
14 heard of you that the spirit of the holy gods 4
23 praised the gods of silver and gold, of bronze 4
6: 7 makes petition to any god or man for 30 days 4
12 petition to any god or man within 30 days 4
11: 8 carry off . . gods with their molten images 3
36 magnify himself above every god, 1
36 astonishing things against the God of gods. 1
37 He shall give no heed to the gods of his fathers 3
37 he shall not give heed to any other god 2
38 honor the god of fortresses instead of these; 2
38 god whom his fathers did not know he shall honor 2
39 fortresses by the help of a foreign god; 2
Hos 3: 1 they turn to other gods and love cakes of raisins. 3
Ams 5:26 Sakkuth your king, and Kaiwan your star-god 3
8:14 who swear . . and say, 'As thy god lives, O Dan,' 3
Jon 1: 5 mariners were afraid, and each cried to his god; 3
6 Arise, call upon your god! 3
6 Perhaps the god will give a thought to us 3
Mic 4: 5 all the peoples walk each in the name of its god 3
Nah 1:14 from the house of your gods I will cut off 3
Hab 1:11 guilty men, whose own might is their god! 2
Zep 2:11 yea, he will famish all the gods of the earth 3
Mal 2:11 and has married the daughter of a foreign god. 1
Joh 10:34 'I said, you are gods'? 6
35 If he called them gods to whom the word of God came 6
Act 7:40 saying to Aaron, 'Make for us gods to go before us 6
43 the star of the god Rephan 6
12:22 people shouted, "The voice of a god, and not of man! 6
14:11 The gods have come down to us in the likeness of men! 6
17:23 'To an unknown god.' 6
19:26 saying that gods made with hands are not gods. 6
26 saying that gods made with hands are not gods. 6
28: 6 changed their minds and said that he was a god. 6
1Co 8: 5 may be so-called gods in heaven or on earth 6
5 as indeed there are many "gods" and many "lords"- 6
2Co 4: 4 the god of this world has blinded the minds 6
Gal 4: 8 in bondage to beings that by nature are no gods; 6
Php 3:19 Their end is destruction, their god is the belly 6
2Th 2: 4 every so-called god or object of worship 6
2Es 1: 6 have offered sacrifices to strange gods. 7
Jdt 3: 8 given to him to destroy all the gods of the land 6
8 tongues and tribes should call upon him as god. 6
5: 7 would not follow the gods of their fathers 6
8 they drove them out from the presence of their gods 6
8:18 which worshiped gods made with hands 6
20 we know no other god but him 6
AEs 14: 7 because we glorified their gods 6
12 give me courage, O King of the gods 6
Wis 12:13 For neither is there any god besides thee 6
24 accepting as gods 6
27 creatures which they had thought to be gods 6
13: 2 the gods that rule the world. 6
3 If . . men assumed them to be gods 6
10 who give the name "gods" to the works of men's hands 6
14: 8 the perishable thing was named a god. 6
15 he now honored as a god 6
15: 8 he forms a futile god from the same clay 6
15 thought that all their heathen idols were gods 6
16 no man can form a god which is like himself. 6
Bar 1:21 by serving other gods and doing what is evil 6
LJr 1: 4 Now in Babylon you will see gods made of silver 6
5 to let fear for these gods possess you *
9 make crowns for the heads of their gods 6
10 secretly take gold and silver from their gods 6
11 They deck their gods out with garments like men *
11 these gods of silver and gold and wood 6
14 Like a local ruler the god holds a scepter *
16 Therefore they evidently are not gods 6
17 so are the gods of the heathen 6
19 though their gods can see none of them. *
23 they are not gods; so do not fear them. 6
27 because . . these gods are made to stand *
28 the sacrifices that are offered to these gods *
29 Since you know . . that they are not gods 6
30 For why should they be called gods? 6
30 serve meals for gods of silver and gold and wood; 6
32 They howl and shout before their gods as some do 6
33 The priests take some of the clothing of their gods 6
40 Why then must any one think that they are gods *
40 Why then must any one . . call them gods? 6
44 Why then must any one think that they are gods 6
44 Why then must any one . . call them gods? 6
46 how then can . . things . . made by them be gods? 6
48 where they can hide themselves and their gods. *
49 that these are not gods 6
51 they are not gods but the work of men's hands 6
52 Who then can fail to know that they are not gods? 6
55 the gods will be burnt in two like beams. *
55 When fire breaks out in a temple of wooden gods 6
56 must any one admit or think that they are gods? 6
59 better . . than to be these false gods 6
59 better . . than these false gods. 6
59 better . . than these false gods. 6
64 Therefore one must not think that they are gods 6
64 one must not think . . nor call them gods *
65 Since you know then that they are not gods 6
69 we have no evidence whatever that they are gods; 6
70 gods of wood, overlaid with gold and silver. 6
71 their gods of wood, overlaid with gold and silver 6
72 you will know that they are not gods 6
Aza 1:68 Bless him, all who worship the Lord, the God of gods 6
Bel 1:24 You cannot deny that this is a living god 6
1Mc 5:68 graven images of their gods he burned with fire; 6
2Mc 11:23 Now that our father has gone on to the gods 6
3Mc 3:14 by the gods' deliberate alliance with us in battle 6
6:11 'Not even their god has rescued them.' 6

god *See also* counterfeit.

false god 1. הֶבֶל 2. כָּזָב 3. שָׁוְא
Ps 40: 4 to those who go astray after false gods! 2
Jer 14:22 the false gods of the nations that can bring rain? 1
18:15 they burn incense to false gods; 3

household god 1. תְּרָפִים
Gen 31:19 and Rachel stole her father's household gods. 1
34 Rachel had taken the household gods 1
35 searched, but did not find the household gods. 1

new god 1. חָדָשׁ
Deu 32:17 sacrificed to . . new gods that had come in of late 1

strange god 1. זור
Deu 32:16 They stirred him to jealousy with strange gods; 1

without God 1. ἄθεος
Eph 2:12 having no hope and without God in the world. 1

goddess 1. אֱלֹהִים 2. θεά 3. θεός
1Kg 11: 5 Ash'toreth the goddess of the Sido'nians 1
33 Ash'toreth the goddess of the Sido'nians 1
Act 19:27 the temple of the great goddess Ar'temis 2
37 blasphemers of our goddess. 3

godless 1. אָוֶן 2. בְּלִיַּעַל 3. זֵד 4. חָנֵף 5. βέβηλος 6. impius
2Sm 23: 6 godless men are all like thorns . . thrown away; 2
Job 15:34 For the company of the godless is barren 4
17: 8 innocent stirs himself up against the godless. 4
20: 5 the joy of the godless but for a moment? 4
27: 8 what is the hope of the godless when God cuts him 4
34:30 that a godless man should not reign 4
36:13 The godless in heart cherish anger; 4
Ps 119:69 The godless besmear me with lies 3
78 Let the godless be put to shame 3
122 let not the godless oppress me. 3
Prv 11: 7 expectation of the godless comes to nought. 1
Isa 9:17 for every one is godless and an evildoer 4
10: 6 Against a godless nation I send him 4
33:14 in Zion . . trembling has seized the godless 4
1Ti 4: 7 Have nothing to do with godless . . myths 5
6:20 Avoid the godless chatter and contradictions 5
2Ti 2:16 Avoid such godless chatter 5
2Es 4:23 has been given over to godless tribes 6

godless man 1. זֵד 2. חָנֵף
Job 8:13 the hope of the godless man shall perish. 2
13:16 a godless man shall not come before him. 2
Ps 119:51 Godless men utterly deride me, but I do not turn 1
85 Godless men have dug pitfalls for me 1
Prv 11: 9 mouth the godless man would destroy his neighbor 2

godliness 1. εὐσέβεια 2. θεοσέβεια
1Ti 4: 7 Train yourself in godliness; 1
8 godliness is of value in every way 1
6: 3 the teaching which accords with godliness 1
5 imagining that godliness is a means of gain. 1
6 is great gain in godliness with contentment; 1
11 aim at righteousness, godliness, faith, love 1
Tit 1: 1 the truth which accords with godliness 1
2Pe 1: 3 all things that pertain to life and godliness 1
6 and steadfastness with godliness 1
7 and godliness with brotherly affection 1
3:11 in lives of holiness and godliness 1
1Es 1:23 his heart was full of godliness. 1
Wis 10:12 godliness is more powerful than anything. 1
Sir 1:25 godliness is an abomination to a sinner. 2
49: 3 he strengthened godliness. 1
Bar 5: 4 Peace of righteousness and glory of godliness. 2
2Mc 12:45 that is laid up for those who fall asleep in godliness 1
4Mc 7:22 to overcome the emotions through godliness? 2

godly 1. אֱלֹהִים 2. חָסִיד 3. εὐσέβεια 4. εὐσεβής 5. εὐσεβῶς 6. θεός 7. κατὰ θεόν
Ps 4: 3 But know that the LORD has set apart the godly 2
12: 1 Help, LORD; for there is no longer any that is godly; 2
32: 6 let every one who is godly offer prayer to thee; 2
52: 1 O mighty man, of mischief done against the godly? *
9 for it is good, in the presence of the godly. 2
86: 2 Preserve my life, for I am godly; 2
Mal 2:15 what does he desire? Godly offspring. 1
2Co 1:12 with holiness and godly sincerity 6
7: 9 you felt a godly grief 7
10 For godly grief produces a repentance 7
11 what earnestness this godly grief has produced 7
1Ti 2: 2 godly and respectful in every way. 3
Tit 2:12 to live sober, upright, and godly lives in this world 5
2Pe 2: 9 the Lord knows how to rescue the godly from trial 4
Sir 11:17 gift of the Lord endures for those who are godly 4
22 blessing of the Lord is the reward of the godly 4
16:13 the patience of the godly will not be frustrated. 4
23:12 all these errors will be far from the godly 4
27:29 Those who rejoice in the fall of the godly 4
28:22 It will not be master over the godly 4
33:14 so the sinner is the opposite of the godly. 4
37:12 stay constantly with a godly man 4
39:27 All these are for good to the godly 4
43:33 to the godly he has granted wisdom. 4
4Mc 10:10 because of our godly training and virtue 6

godly *See also* fear, life.

godly man 1. חָסִיד 2. εὐσεβέω 3. εὐσεβής
Mic 7: 2 The godly man has perished from the earth 1
Sir 12: 2 Do good to a godly man, and you will be repaid 2
4 Give to the godly man, but do not help the sinner. 2
13:17 No more has a sinner with a godly man. 3
27:11 The talk of the godly man is always wise 3

godly one 1. אִישׁ חָסִיד 2. חָסִיד
Deu 33: 8 Give to Levi . . and thy Urim to thy godly one 1
Ps 16:10 to Sheol, or let thy godly one see the Pit. 2

gold 1. בֶּצֶר 2. זָהָב 3. חָרוּץ 4. כֶּתֶם 5. סְגוֹר 6. פַּז 7. דְּהַב (A) 8. περίχρυσος 9. χρυσίον 10. χρυσός 11. χρυσοῦς 12. χρύσωμα 13. aurum
Gen 2:11 the whole land of Havilah, where there is gold; 2
12 the gold of that land is good; 2
13: 2 was very rich in cattle, in silver, and in gold. 2
24:22 the man took a gold ring weighing a half shekel 2

22 bracelets . . weighing ten gold shekels 2
35 given him flocks and herds, silver and gold 2
53 brought forth jewelry of silver and of gold 2
41:42 of fine linen, and put a gold chain about his neck; 2
44: 8 should we steal silver or gold from your lord's 2
Exd 3:22 ask of her . . jewelry of silver and of gold 2
11: 2 that they ask . . jewelry of silver and of gold. 2
12:35 asked . . jewelry of silver and of gold 2
20:23 nor shall you make for yourselves gods of gold. 2
25: 3 this is the offering . . gold, silver, and bronze 2
11 you shall overlay it with pure gold 2
11 make upon it a molding of gold round about. 2
12 you shall cast four rings of gold for it 2
13 make poles . . and overlay them with gold. 2
17 Then you shall make a mercy seat of pure gold; 2
18 you shall make two cherubim of gold; 2
24 You shall overlay it with pure gold 2
24 and make a molding of gold around it. 2
25 make . . a molding of gold around the frame. 2
26 you shall make for it four rings of gold 2
28 make the poles . . and overlay them with gold 2
29 of pure gold you shall make them. 2
31 you shall make a lampstand of pure gold. 2
36 one piece of hammered work of pure gold. 2
38 snuffers and their trays shall be of pure gold. 2
39 Of a talent of pure gold shall it be made, with all 2
26: 6 you shall make 50 clasps of gold 2
29 You shall overlay the frames with gold 2
29 shall make their rings of gold for holders 2
29 and you shall overlay the bars with gold. 2
32 four pillars of acacia overlaid with gold 2
32 acacia overlaid with gold, with hooks of gold 2
37 pillars of acacia, and overlay them with gold; 2
37 their hooks shall be of gold 2
28: 5 They shall receive gold, blue and purple 2
6 they shall make the ephod of gold, of blue 2
8 materials, of gold, blue and purple and scarlet 2
11 enclose them in settings of gold filigree. 2
13 you shall make settings of gold filigree 2
14 two chains of pure gold, twisted like cords; 2
15 of gold, blue and purple and scarlet stuff 2
20 they shall be set in gold filigree. 2
22 make . . twisted chains like cords, of pure gold; 2
23 shall make for the breastpiece two rings of gold 2
24 the two cords of gold in the two rings at the edges 2
26 you shall make two rings of gold, and put them 2
27 you shall make two rings of gold, and attach them 2
33 with bells of gold between them 2
36 you shall make a plate of pure gold, and engrave 2
30: 3 you shall overlay it with pure gold 2
3 make for it a molding of gold round about. 2
5 make the poles . . overlay them with gold. 2
31: 4 to work in gold, silver, and bronze 2
32: 2 Take off the rings of gold which are in the ears 2
3 people took off the rings of gold which were 2
4 he received the gold at their hand, and fashioned •
24 I said to them, 'Let any who have gold take it off'; 2
31 they have made for themselves gods of gold. 2
35: 5 bring the LORD'S offering: gold, silver, and bronze 2
22 rings and armlets, all sorts of gold objects 2
22 dedicating an offering of gold to the LORD. 2
32 to work in gold and silver and bronze 2
36:13 he made 50 clasps of gold 2
34 he overlaid the frames with gold 2
34 made their rings of gold for holders for the bars 2
34 and overlaid the bars with gold. 2
36 pillars of acacia, and overlaid them with gold; 2
36 their hooks were of gold, and he cast for them four 2
38 their capitals, and their fillets were of gold 2
37: 2 he overlaid it with pure gold within and without 2
2 and made a molding of gold around it. 2
3 he cast for it four rings of gold 2
4 made poles . . and overlaid them with gold 2
6 he made a mercy seat of pure gold; 2
7 he made two cherubim of hammered gold; 2
11 he overlaid it with pure gold, and made a molding 2
11 and made a molding of gold around it. 2
12 made a molding of gold around the frame. 2
13 He cast for it four rings of gold, and fastened 2
15 made the poles . . and overlaid them with gold. 2
16 he made the vessels of pure gold which were to be 2
17 He also made the lampstand of pure gold. 2
22 was one piece of hammered work of pure gold. 2
23 its snuffers and its trays of pure gold. 2
24 all its utensils of a talent of pure gold. 2
26 He overlaid it with pure gold, its top 2
26 and he made a molding of gold round about it 2
27 made two rings of gold on it under its molding 2
28 the poles . . and overlaid them with gold. 2
38:24 All the gold that was used for the work 2
24 the gold from the offering, was 29 talents 2
39: 2 he made the ephod of gold, blue and purple 2
3 gold leaf was hammered and cut into threads 2
5 of gold, blue and purple and scarlet stuff 2
6 enclosed in settings of gold filigree 2
8 of gold, blue and purple and scarlet stuff 2
13 they were enclosed in settings of gold filigree. 2
15 twisted chains like cords, of pure gold; 2
16 they made two settings of gold filigree 2
16 they made . . two gold rings, and put the two rings 2
17 they put the two cords of gold in the two rings 2
19 Then they made two rings of gold 2
20 they made two rings of gold, and attached them 2
25 They also made bells of pure gold 2
30 they made the plate of the holy crown of pure gold 2
Num 7:86 all the gold of the dishes being 120 shekels; 2
8: 4 lampstand, hammered work of gold; from its base 2
22:18 were to give me his house full of silver and gold 2
24:13 should give me his house full of silver and gold 2
31:22 only the gold, the silver, the bronze, the iron 2
50 LORD'S offering . . articles of gold 2
51 Moses and Elea'zar . . received from them the gold 2
52 all the gold of the offering that they offered 2
54 Moses and Elea'zar the priest received the gold 2
Deu 7:25 not covet the silver or the gold that is on them 2
8:13 when . . your silver and gold is multiplied 2
17:17 nor . . greatly multiply for himself silver and gold. 2
29:17 their idols of wood and stone, of silver and gold 2
Jos 6:19 all silver and gold, and vessels of . . are sacred 2
24 silver and gold, and the vessels of bronze 2
7:21 I saw . . and a bar of gold weighing 50 shekels 2
24 and the silver and the mantle and the bar of gold 2
22: 8 with very many cattle, with silver, gold, bronze 2
Jdg 8:26 the weight . . was 1,700 shekels of gold; 2
1Sm 6: 8 put in a box at its side the figures of gold 2
2Sm 1:24 who put ornaments of gold upon your apparel. 2
8: 7 David took the shields of gold . . carried 2
10 articles of silver, of gold, and of bronze; 2
11 with the silver and gold which he dedicated 2
12:30 the weight of it was a talent of gold, and in it was 2
21: 4 not a matter of silver or gold between us and Saul 2
1Kg 6:20 sanctuary . . and he overlaid it with pure gold. 2
21 Solomon overlaid the inside . . with pure gold 2
21 he drew chains of gold across, in front 2
21 the inner sanctuary, and overlaid it with gold. 2
22 he overlaid the whole house with gold 2
22 Also the whole altar . . he overlaid with gold. 2
28 And he overlaid the cherubim with gold. 2
30 The floor of the house he overlaid with gold 2
32 he overlaid them with gold, and spread gold 2
32 spread gold upon the cherubim and . . palm trees. 2
35 he overlaid them with gold evenly applied 2
7:49 the lampstands of pure gold, five on the south 2
49 the flowers, the lamps, and the tongs, of gold; 2
50 basins, dishes . . and firepans, of pure gold; 2
50 the sockets of gold, for the doors 2
51 Solomon brought in . . the silver, the gold 2
9:11 supplied . . cedar and cypress timber and gold 2
14 Hiram had sent to the king 120 talents of gold. 2
28 they went to Ophir, and brought from there gold 2
10: 2 with camels bearing spices, and very much gold 2
10 she gave the king 120 talents of gold 2
11 the fleet of Hiram, which brought gold from Ophir 2
14 the weight of gold that came to Solomon 2
14 weight of gold . . was 666 talents of gold 2
16 Solomon made . . large shields of beaten gold; 2
16 600 shekels of gold went into each shield. 2
17 he made 300 shields of beaten gold; 2
17 three minas of gold went into each shield; 2
18 throne, and overlaid it with the finest gold. 2
21 All King Solomon's drinking vessels were of gold 2
21 all the vessels of the House . . were of pure gold; 2
22 bringing gold, silver, ivory, apes, and peacocks. 2
25 his present, articles of silver and gold 2
12:28 king took counsel, and made two calves of gold. 2
14:26 He also took away all the shields of gold 2
15:15 his . . votive gifts, silver, and gold, and vessels. 2
18 Asa took all the silver and the gold 2
19 I am sending to you a present of silver and gold; 2
20: 3 Your silver and your gold are mine; 2
5 Deliver to me your silver and your gold 2
7 he sent to me . . for my silver and my gold 2
22:48 Jehosh'aphat made ships . . to go to Ophir for gold; 2
2Kg 5: 5 taking with him . . silver, 6,000 shekels of gold 2
7: 8 they carried off silver and gold and clothing 2
12:13 trumpets, or any vessels of gold, or of silver 2
18 and all the gold that was found in the treasuries 2
14:14 he seized all the gold and silver 2
16: 8 Ahaz . . took the silver and gold that was found 2
18:14 300 talents of silver and 30 talents of gold. 2
16 Hezeki'ah stripped the gold from the doors •
20:13 all his treasure house, the silver, the gold 2
23:33 a tribute of . . silver and a talent of gold. 2
35 gave the silver and the gold to Pharaoh 2
35 He exacted the silver and the gold of the people 2
24:13 all the vessels of gold in the temple of the LORD 2
25:15 What was of gold the captain . . took away as gold 2
15 What was of gold the captain . . took away as gold 2
1Ch 18: 7 David took the shields of gold 2
10 articles of gold, of silver, and of bronze; 2
11 the silver and gold which he had carried off 2
20: 2 he found that it weighed a talent of gold 2
21:25 David paid Ornan 600 shekels of gold by weight 2
22:14 for the house of the LORD 100,000 talents of gold 2
16 gold, silver, bronze, and iron. Arise and be doing! 2
28:14 the weight of gold for all golden vessels 2
15 weight of gold for each lampstand and its lamps 2
16 weight of gold for each table for the showbread 2
17 pure gold for the forks, the basins, and the cups; 2
18 for the altar of incense made of refined gold 2
29: 2 the gold for the things of gold 2
3 I have a treasure of my own of gold and silver 2
4 3,000 talents of gold, of the gold of Ophir 2
4 3,000 talents of gold, of the gold of Ophir 2
5 gold for the things of gold and silver 2
7 5,000 talents and 10,000 darics of gold 2
2Ch 1:15 king made silver and gold as common . . as stone 2
2: 7 now send me a man skilled to work in gold, silver 2
14 He is trained to work in gold, silver, bronze, iron 2
3: 4 He overlaid it on the inside with pure gold. 2
5 nave he lined . . and covered it with fine gold 2
6 The gold was gold of Parva'im. 2
6 The gold was gold of Parva'im. 2
7 he lined the house with gold-its beams 2
8 with 600 talents of fine gold. 2
9 weight . . one shekel to 50 shekels of gold. 2
9 And he overlaid the upper chambers with gold. 2
10 cherubim of wood and overlaid them with gold. 2
4: 8 And he made 100 basins of gold. 2
20 the lampstands and their lamps of pure gold 2
21 flowers, the lamps, and the tongs, of purest gold; 2
22 dishes for incense, and firepans, of pure gold; 2
22 the sockets of the temple . . were of gold. 2
5: 1 stored the silver, the gold, and all the vessels 2
8:18 there 450 talents of gold 2
9: 1 camels bearing spices and very much gold 2
9 she gave . . 120 talents of gold 2
10 the servants . . who brought gold from Ophir 2
13 weight of gold that came to Solomon in one year 2
13 weight of gold . . was 666 talents of gold 2
14 brought gold and silver to Solomon. 2
15 Solomon made 200 large shields of beaten gold; 2
15 600 shekels of . . gold went into each shield. 2
16 he made 300 shields of beaten gold; 2
16 300 shekels of gold went into each shield; 2
17 ivory throne, and overlaid it with pure gold. 2
18 The throne had six steps and a footstool of gold 2
20 All King Solomon's drinking vessels were of gold 2
20 all the vessels of the House . . were of pure gold; 2
21 ships . . used to come bringing gold, silver 2
24 his present, articles of silver and of gold 2
12: 9 He also took away the shields of gold 2
13:11 set out the showbread on the table of pure gold •
15:18 votive gifts, silver, and gold, and vessels. 2
16: 2 Then Asa took silver and gold from the treasures 2
3 behold, I am sending to you silver and gold; 2
21: 3 gifts, of silver, gold, and valuable possessions 2
24:14 vessels of gold and silver. 2
25:24 he seized all the gold and silver 2
32:27 made for himself treasuries for silver, for gold 2
36: 3 tribute of . . silver and a talent of gold. 2
Ezr 1: 4 be assisted . . with silver and gold, with goods 2
6 aided them with vessels of silver, with gold 2
9 number . . 1,000 basins of gold 2
10 30 bowls of gold, 2,410 bowls of silver 2
11 all the vessels of gold and of silver were 5,469. 2
2:69 gave to . . the work 61,000 darics of gold 2
5:14 gold and silver vessels of the house of God 7
6: 5 gold and silver vessels of the house of God 7
7:15 also to convey the silver and gold which the king 7
16 with all the silver and gold which you shall find 7
18 do with the rest of the silver and gold 7
8:25 weighed out . . silver and the gold and the vessels 2
26 silver vessels . . and 100 talents of gold 2
27 twenty bowls of gold worth 1,000 darics 2
27 fine bright bronze as precious as gold. 2
28 silver and the gold are a freewill offering 2
30 took over the weight of the silver and the gold 2
33 silver and the gold and the vessels were weighed 2
Neh 7:70 governor gave to the treasury 1,000 darics of gold 2
71 gave into the treasury . . 20,000 darics of gold 2
72 rest of the people gave was 20,000 darics of gold 2
Est 1: 6 and also couches of gold and silver 2
Job 3:15 or with princes who had gold 2
22:24 if you lay gold in the dust 1
24 gold of Ophir among the stones of the torrent bed •
25 if the Almighty is your gold 1
23:10 when he has tried me, I shall come forth as gold. 2
28: 1 a place for gold which they refine. 2
6 place of sapphires, and it has dust of gold. 2
15 It cannot be gotten for gold 5
16 It cannot be valued in the gold of Ophir 4
17 Gold and glass cannot equal it 2
31:24 If I have made gold my trust 2
42:11 gave him a piece of money and a ring of gold. 2
Ps 19:10 More to be desired are they than gold 2
45: 9 stands the queen in gold of Ophir. 4
13 decked in her chamber with gold-woven robes; 2
68:13 with silver, its pinions with green gold. 3
72:15 Long may he live, may gold of Sheba be given to him! 2
105:37 Then he led forth Israel with silver and gold 2
115: 4 idols are silver and gold, the work of men's hands. 2
119:72 better . . than thousands of gold and silver 2
127 Therefore I love thy commandments above gold 2
135:15 The idols of the nations are silver and gold 2
Prv 3:14 its profit better than gold. 3
8:10 Take . . knowledge rather than choice gold; 3

19 My fruit is better than gold, even fine gold 3
11:22 Like a gold ring in a swine's snout is a beautiful 2
16:16 To get wisdom is better than gold; 3
17: 3 for silver, and the furnace is for gold 2
20:15 There is gold, and abundance of costly stones; 2
22: 1 favor is better than silver or gold. 2
25:11 fitly spoken is like apples of gold in a setting 2
12 Like a gold ring or an ornament of gold 2
12 Like a gold ring or an ornament of gold 4
27:21 crucible is for silver . . furnace is for gold 2
Ecc 2: 8 I also gathered for myself silver and gold 2
Sng 1:11 We will make you ornaments of gold 2
3:10 He made its posts of silver, its back of gold 2
5:11 His head is the finest gold; 4
14 His arms are rounded gold, set with jewels. 2
15 His legs are alabaster . . set upon bases of gold. 6
Isa 2: 7 Their land is filled with silver and gold 2
20 of silver and their idols of gold, which they made 2
13:12 fine gold, and mankind than the gold of Ophir. 4
17 no regard for silver and do not delight in gold. 2
30:22 defile . . your gold-plated molten images. 2
31: 7 every one shall cast away . . his idols of gold 2
39: 2 his treasure house, the silver, the gold 2
40:19 The idol! . . a goldsmith overlays it with gold 2
46: 6 Those who lavish gold from the purse 2
60: 6 They shall bring gold and frankincense 2
9 sons from far, their silver and gold with them 2
17 Instead of bronze I will bring gold 2
Jer 4:30 that you deck yourself with ornaments of gold 2
10: 4 Men deck it with silver and gold; 2
9 silver . . from Tarshish, and gold from Uphaz. 2
52:19 What was of gold the captain of the guard took 2
19 gold the captain of the guard took away as gold 2
Lam 4: 1 How the gold has grown dim . . pure gold is changed! 2
Ezk 7:19 and their gold is like an unclean thing; 2
19 silver and gold are not able to deliver them 2
16:13 Thus you were decked with gold and silver; 2
17 You also took your fair jewels of my gold 2
27:22 spices, and all precious stones, and gold. 2
28: 4 gathered gold and silver into your treasuries; 2
13 and wrought in gold were your settings 2
38:13 to carry away silver and gold, to take away cattle 2
Dan 2:32 head of this image was of fine gold 7
35 iron, the clay, the bronze, the silver, and the gold 7
38 making you rule . . you are the head of gold. 7
45 broke in pieces the . . silver, and the gold. 7
3: 1 King Nebuchadnez'zar made an image of gold 7
5: 2 commanded that the vessels of gold and of silver 7
4 praised the gods of gold and silver, bronze, iron 7
7 purple, and have a chain of gold about his neck 7
16 purple, and have a chain of gold about your neck 7
23 praised the gods of silver and gold, of bronze 7
29 purple, a chain of gold was put about his neck 7
10: 5 whose loins were girded with gold of Uphaz. 4
11: 8 their precious vessels of silver and of gold; 2
38 honor with gold and silver, with precious stones 2
43 become ruler of the treasures of gold . . silver 2
Hos 2: 8 and who lavished upon her silver and gold 2
8: 4 With their silver and gold they made idols 2
Jol 3: 5 For you have taken my silver and my gold 2
Nah 2: 9 Plunder the silver, plunder the gold! 2
Hab 2:19 Behold, it is overlaid with gold and silver 2
Zep 1:18 Neither their silver nor their gold shall be 2
Hag 2: 8 the gold is mine, says the LORD of hosts. 2
Zec 4: 2 I said, "I see, and behold, a lampstand all of gold 2
6:11 Take from them silver and gold, and make a crown 2
9: 3 like dust, and gold like the dirt of the streets. 3
13: 9 refines silver, and test them as gold is tested. 2
14:14 shall be collected, gold, silver, and garments 2
Mal 3: 3 sons of Levi and refine them like gold and silver 2
Mat 2:11 they offered him gifts, gold and frankincense 10
10: 9 Take no gold, nor silver, nor copper in your belts 10
23:16 if any one swears by the gold of the temple 10
17 which is greater, the gold or the temple 10
17 or the temple that has made the gold sacred? 10
Act 3: 6 I have no silver and gold, but I give you what I have; 9
17:29 we ought not to think that the Deity is like gold 10
20:33 I coveted no one's silver or gold or apparel. 9
1Co 3:12 builds on the foundation with gold, silver 10
1Ti 2: 9 not with braided hair or gold or pearls 9
2Ti 2:20 there are not only vessels of gold and silver 11
Heb 9: 4 the ark . . covered on all sides with gold 9
Jas 5: 3 Your gold and silver have rusted 10
1Pe 1: 7 faith, more precious than gold 9
18 with perishable things such as silver or gold 9
3: 3 outward adorning with . . decoration of gold 9
Rev 3:18 I counsel you to buy from me gold refined by fire 9
9: 7 on their heads . . what looked like crowns of gold 10
20 demons and idols of gold and silver and bronze 11
17: 4 and bedecked with gold and jewels and pearls 9
18:12 cargo of gold, silver, jewels and pearls 10
16 bedecked with gold, with jewels, and with pearls! 9
21:15 And he who talked to me had a measuring rod of gold 11
18 while the city was pure gold, clear as glass. 9
21 and the street of the city was pure gold 9
1Es 1:36 100 talents of silver and a talent of gold. 9
2: 6 be helped by the men of his place with gold 9
9 with silver and gold, with horses and cattle 9
13 1,000 gold cups, 1,000 silver cups 11

13 29 silver censers, 30 gold bowls, 2,410 silver bowls 11
14 All the vessels were handed over, gold and silver 11
3: 6 clothed in purple, and drink from gold cups 12
6 sleep on a gold bed 10
4:18 If men gather gold and silver 9
19 all prefer her to gold or silver 9
5:45 1,000 minas of gold, 5,000 minas of silver 9
6:18 the holy vessels of gold and of silver 11
26 the holy vessels . . both of gold and of silver 11
8:13 all the gold and silver that may be found 9
14 both gold and silver for bulls and rams and lambs 9
16 to do with the gold and silver 9
55 I weighed out to them the silver and the gold 9
56 a 100 talents of gold 9
58 the silver and the gold are vowed to the Lord 9
60 the silver and the gold 9
62 the silver and the gold were weighed 9
2Es 7:55 Say to her, 'You produce gold and silver and brass 13
56 silver is more abundant than gold 13
8: 2 but only a little dust from which gold comes 13
16:73 as gold that is tested by fire. 13
Tob 12: 8 It is better to give alms than to treasure up gold. 9
13:16 her towers and battlements with pure gold. 9
Jdt 2:18 a huge amount of gold and silver 9
5: 9 settled, and prospered, with much gold and silver 9
8: 7 Manasseh had left her gold and silver 9
10:21 gold and emeralds and precious stones. 9
AEs 15: 6 all covered with gold and precious stones 10
Wis 3: 6 like gold in the furnace he tried them 10
7: 9 because all gold is but a little sand in her sight 10
13:10 gold and silver fashioned with skill 10
Sir 2: 5 For gold is tested in the fire 10
7:18 a real brother for the gold of Ophir. 9
19 her charm is worth more than gold. 9
8: 2 gold has ruined many 9
26:18 Like pillars of gold on a base of silver 11
28:24 lock up your silver and gold 9
29:11 it will profit you more than gold. 9
30:15 Health and soundness are better than all gold 9
31: 5 He who loves gold will not be justified 9
6 Many have come to ruin because of gold 9
8 who does not go after gold. 9
32: 5 A ruby seal in a setting of gold 11
6 A seal of emerald in a rich setting of gold 11
40:25 Gold and silver make the foot stand sure 9
41:12 longer than 1,000 great stores of gold. 9
45:10 with a holy garment, of gold and blue and purple 11
11 in a setting of gold, the work of a jeweler 9
12 with a gold crown upon his turban 11
47:18 you gathered gold like tin 9
50: 9 like a vessel of hammered gold 9
51:28 you will gain by it much gold. 10
Bar 3:17 who hoard up silver and gold, in which men trust 9
30 Who . . found her, and will buy her for pure gold? 9
LJr 1: 4 you will see gods made of silver and gold and wood 11
9 People take gold 9
10 secretly take gold and silver from their gods 9
11 these gods of silver and gold and wood 11
24 As for the gold which they wear for beauty 9
30 serve meals for gods of silver and gold and wood; 11
57 overlaid with silver and gold 8
58 strip them of their gold and silver 9
1Mc 1:22 the gold decoration on the front of the temple 11
23 the silver and the gold, and the costly vessels 9
2:18 honored with silver and gold and many gifts. 9
3:41 they took silver and gold in immense amounts 9
4:23 they seized much gold and silver 9
6: 1 a city famed for its wealth in silver and gold. 9
12 I seized all her vessels of silver and gold 11
39 the sun shone upon the shields of gold and brass 11
8: 3 to get control of the silver and gold mines there 9
10:60 he gave them and their friends silver and gold 9
11:24 taking silver and gold and clothing 9
58 dress in purple and wear a gold buckle. 11
13:37 received the gold crown and the palm branch 11
14:24 sent Numenius to Rome with a large gold shield 11
44 to be clothed in purple or put on a gold buckle. 11
15:18 have brought a gold shield weighing 1,000 minas. 11
26 silver and gold and much military equipment. 9
16:11 he had much silver and gold 9
19 so that he might give them silver and gold 9
2Mc 2: 2 upon seeing the gold and silver statues 11
3:11 400 talents of silver and 200 of gold 9
25 was seen to have armor and weapons of gold. 11
11: 8 brandishing weapons of gold. 11
14: 4 presenting to him a crown of gold and a palm 11
3Mc 1: 4 promising to give them each two minas of gold 9

gold *See also* bridle, cup, overlay, plate, ring, vessel, wear, worker.

fine gold 1. כֶּתֶם 2. פָּז

Job 28:17 nor can it be exchanged for jewels of fine gold. 2
31:24 gold my trust, or called fine gold my confidence; 1
Ps 19:10 desired are they than gold, even much fine gold; 2
21: 3 thou dost set a crown of fine gold upon his head. 2
119:127 thy commandments above gold, above fine gold. 2
Prv 8:19 My fruit is better than gold, even fine gold 2
Sng 5:11 His head is the finest gold; 2
Isa 13:12 I will make men more rare than fine gold 2
Lam 4: 2 sons of Zion, worth their weight in fine gold 2

like gold 1. χρυσοειδής

1Es 8:57 bronze vessels . . that glittered like gold. 1

pure gold 1. טָהוֹר 2. כֶּתֶם

Exd 39:37 the lampstand of pure gold and its lamps 1
Lev 24: 4 the lamps in order upon the lampstand of pure gold 1
6 set them . . upon the table of pure gold 1
Job 28:19 nor can it be valued in pure gold. 2
Lam 4: 1 gold has grown dim, how the pure gold is changed! 2

thing of gold 1. זָהָב

1Ch 29: 2 the gold for the things of gold 1
5 gold for the things of gold and silver 1

golden 1. זָהָב 2. דְּהַב (A) 3. διάχρυσος 4. χρυσός 5. χρυσοῦς 6. χρύσωμα

Exd 28:34 a golden bell and a pomegranate, a golden bell 1
34 a pomegranate, a golden bell and a pomegranate 1
30: 4 two golden rings shall you make for it; 1
39:38 the golden altar, the anointing oil 1
40: 5 you shall put the golden altar for incense 1
26 he put the golden altar in the tent of meeting 1
Lev 8: 9 on the turban, in front, he set the golden plate 1
Num 4:11 over the golden altar they shall spread a cloth 1
7:14 one golden dish of ten shekels, full of incense; 1
20 one golden dish of ten shekels, full of incense; 1
26 one golden dish of ten shekels, full of incense; 1
32 one golden dish of ten shekels, full of incense; 1
38 one golden dish of ten shekels, full of incense; 1
44 one golden dish of ten shekels, full of incense; 1
50 one golden dish of ten shekels, full of incense; 1
56 one golden dish of ten shekels, full of incense; 1
62 one golden dish of ten shekels, full of incense; 1
68 one golden dish of ten shekels, full of incense; 1
74 one golden dish of ten shekels, full of incense; 1
80 one golden dish of ten shekels, full of incense; 1
84 dedication offering . . twelve golden dishes 1
86 the twelve golden dishes, full of incense 1
Jdg 8:24 For they had golden earrings, because they were 1
26 weight of the golden earrings that he requested 1
1Sm 6: 4 Five golden tumors and five golden mice 1
4 Five golden tumors and five golden mice 1
11 the box with the golden mice and the . . tumors. 1
15 and the box . . in which were the golden figures 1
17 These are the golden tumors . . one for Ashdod 1
18 the golden mice, according to the number of all 1
1Kg 7:48 the golden altar, the golden table for the bread 1
48 the golden table for the bread of the Presence 1
2Kg 10:29 the golden calves that were in Bethel, and in Dan. 1
1Ch 28:14 for all golden vessels for each service 1
15 weight of the golden lampstands and their lamps 1
17 for the golden bowls and the weight of each; 1
18 his plan for the golden chariot of the cherubim 1
2Ch 4: 7 he made ten golden lampstands as prescribed 1
19 things . . in the house of God: the golden altar 1
13: 8 because you . . have with you the golden calves 1
11 care for the golden lampstand 1
Est 1: 7 Drinks were served in golden goblets 1
4:11 to whom the king holds out the golden scepter 1
5: 2 and he held out to Esther the golden scepter 1
8: 4 the king held out the golden scepter to Esther 1
15 robes of blue and white, with a great golden crown 1
Ecc 12: 6 or the golden bowl is broken 1
Jer 51: 7 Babylon was a golden cup in the LORD'S hand 1
Dan 3: 5 fall down and worship the golden image 2
7 all . . fell down and worshiped the golden image 2
10 fall down and worship the golden image; 2
12 not serve your gods or worship the golden image 2
14 not serve my gods or worship the golden image 2
18 not serve your gods or worship the golden image 2
5: 3 brought in the golden and silver vessels 2
Zec 4:12 trees, which are beside the two golden pipes 1
Heb 9: 4 having the golden altar of incense 5
4 which contained a golden urn holding the manna 5
Rev 1:12 and on turning I saw seven golden lampstands 5
13 and with a golden girdle round his breast; 5
20 seven stars . . and the seven golden lampstands 5
2: 1 who walks among the seven golden lampstands. 5
4: 4 elders . . with golden crowns upon their heads. 5
5: 8 and with golden bowls full of incense 5
8: 3 angel . . stood at the altar with a golden censer; 5
3 prayers of all the saints upon the golden altar 5
9:13 a voice from the four horns of the golden altar 4
14:14 like a son of man, with a golden crown on his head 5
15: 6 and their breasts girded with golden girdles. 5
7 seven golden bowls full of the wrath of God 5
17: 4 holding . . a golden cup full of abominations 5
1Es 8:57 twenty golden bowls, and twelve bronze vessels 6
AEs 15:11 Then he raised the golden scepter 5
Sir 6:30 Her yoke is a golden ornament 5
21:21 education is like a golden ornament 5
45: 9 with very many golden bells round about 5
1Mc 1:21 entered the sanctuary and took the golden altar 5
22 the bowls, the golden censers, the curtain 5
4:57 golden crowns and small shields 5

6: 2 golden shields, breastplates, and weapons 5
10:20 he sent him a purple robe and a golden crown 5
89 he sent to him a golden buckle 5
2Mc 5: 2 there appeared golden-clad horsemen 3
3 the flash of golden trappings 5
15:15 gave to Judas a golden sword 5

golden *See also* bridle, splendor.

goldsmith 1. צרף 2. צֹרְפִי 3. χρυσοχόος

Neh 3: 8 Uz'ziel the son of Harhai'ah, goldsmiths 1
31 Malchi'jah, one of the goldsmiths, repaired as far 2
32 goldsmiths and the merchants repaired. 1
Isa 40:19 The idol! . . a goldsmith overlays it with gold 1
41: 7 The craftsman encourages the goldsmith 1
46: 6 hire a goldsmith, and he makes it into a god; 1
Jer 10: 9 the work . . of the hands of the goldsmith; 1
14 every goldsmith is put to shame by his idols; 1
51:17 every goldsmith is put to shame by his idols; 1
LJr 1:45 They are made by carpenters and goldsmiths 3

gone *See* half.

all gone 1. תמם

1Kg 14:10 as a man burns up dung until it is all gone. 1

gong 1. χαλκός

1Co 13: 1 I am a noisy gong or a clanging cymbal. 1

good 1. בֶּצַע 2. הֵן 3. חַיִל 4. חֵלֶב 5. חֲמוּדָה 6. טוב 7. טוּב 8. טוֹב 9. טוֹבָה 10. יטב 11. יָפֶה 12. יתר 13. לָמָּה 14. מְאֹד 15. צלח 16. ראשׁ 17. רֵאשִׁית 18. שָׁלוֹם 19. טָב (A) 20. ἀγαθοεργέω 21. ἀγαθός 22. ἀγαθωσύνη 23. ἀρχή 24. βελτίων 25. βουλὴ ἀγαθή 26. διαφέρω 27. ἐπιτήδειος 28. εὖ 29. ἐφικτός 30. ἤδη 31. ἡδύς 32. ἰσχύω 33. καλός 34. καλῶς 35. κατά 36. κρείττων 37. μᾶλλον 38. πολὺ πλέον 39. πολύς 40. πρῶτος 41. συμφέρω 42. ὑπέρ 43. ὑπερέχω 44. χρηστός 45. χρηστότης 46. ὠφελέω 47. bonus 48. facilis 49. prosum

Gen 1: 4 God saw that the light was good 8
10 And God saw that it was good 8
12 And God saw that it was good 8
18 And God saw that it was good 8
21 And God saw that it was good 8
25 And God saw that it was good 8
31 behold, it was very good. And there was evening 8
2: 9 pleasant to the sight and good for food 8
9 and the tree of the knowledge of good and evil. 8
12 the gold of that land is good; 8
17 the tree of the knowledge of good and evil 8
18 the LORD God said, "It is not good that the man 8
3: 5 will be like God, knowing good and evil. 8
6 tree was good for food, and that it was a delight 8
22 like one of us, knowing good and evil; 8
15:15 you shall be buried in a good old age. 8
18: 7 took a calf, tender and good 8
24:50 from the LORD; we cannot speak to you bad or good. 8
25: 8 Abraham . . died in a good old age, an old man 8
26:29 we . . have done to you nothing but good 8
27: 9 Go to the flock, and fetch me two good kids 8
15 Then Rebekah took the best garments of Esau 5
46 of the land, what good will my life be to me?". 13
29:19 Laban said, "It is better that I give her to you 8
30:20 God has endowed me with a good dowry; 8
34 Laban said, "Good! Let it be as you have said. 2
31:24 say not a word to Jacob, either good or bad. 8
29 you speak to Jacob neither good nor bad.' 8
39: 6 Now Joseph was handsome and good-looking. 11
41: 5 and behold, seven ears of grain, plump and good 8
22 ears growing on one stalk, full and good; 8
24 the thin ears swallowed up the seven good ears. 8
26 The seven good cows are seven years 8
26 and the seven good ears are seven years; 8
35 let them gather all the food of these good years 8
44: 4 say to them, 'Why have you returned evil for good? 8
45:18 and I will give you the best of the land of Egypt 7
20 for the best of all the land of Egypt is yours.' 7
47: 6 settle your father and your brothers in the best 10
11 possession . . in the best of the land 10
49:15 he saw that a resting place was good 8
50:20 but God meant it for good, to bring it about 9
Exd 3: 8 bring them up . . to a good and broad land 8
14:12 For it would have been better for us to serve 8
18: 9 Jethro rejoiced for all the good which the LORD 8
17 What you are doing is not good. 8
22: 5 make restitution from the best in his own field 10
Lev 27:10 shall not . . exchange it, a good for a bad 8
10 a good for a bad, or a bad for a good 8
12 the priest shall value it as either good or bad 8
14 the priest shall value it as either good or bad 8
33 A man shall not inquire whether it is good or bad 8
Num10:29 for the LORD has promised good to Israel. 8
32 whatever good the LORD will do to us 8
13:19 whether the land that they dwell in is good or bad 8
14: 3 would it not be better for us to go back to Egypt? 8
7 The land . . is an exceedingly good land. 8
18:12 All the best of the oil, and all the best of the wine 4
12 All the best of the oil, and all the best of the wine 4
29 offering . . from all the best of them 4
30 When you have offered from it the best of it 4
32 bear no sin . . when you have offered the best 4
24:13 to do either good or bad of my own will; 8
36: 6 Let them marry whom they think best; 8
Deu 1:14 'The thing that you have spoken is good for us to do.' 8
23 The thing seemed good to me, and I took twelve men 10
25 'It is a good land which the LORD our God gives us.' 8
35 Not one . . shall see the good land which I swore 8
39 children . . have no knowledge of good or evil 8
2: 4 they will be afraid of you. So take good heed; 14
3:25 Let me . . see the good land beyond the Jordan 8
4:15 Therefore take good heed to yourselves. 14
21 swore . . that I should not enter the good land 8
22 go over and take possession of that good land. 8
6:18 do what is right and good in the sight of the LORD 8
18 that you may . . take possession of the good land 8
24 LORD commanded us . . for our good always 8
8: 7 LORD your God is bringing you into a good land 8
10 bless the LORD . . for the good land he has given 8
9: 6 LORD . . not giving you this good land to possess 8
10:13 which I command you this day for your good? 8
11:17 perish quickly off the good land which the LORD 8
12:28 do what is good and right in the sight of the LORD 8
23:16 where it pleases him best; you shall not oppress •
26:11 rejoice in all the good which the LORD your God 8
28:12 will open to you his good treasury the heavens 8
30:15 set before you . . life and good, death and evil. 8
33:21 He chose the best of the land for himself 17
Jos 9:25 do as it seems good and right in your sight to do 8
21:45 Not one of all the good promises . . had failed; 8
22: 5 Take good care to observe the commandment 14
23:11 Take good heed to yourselves, therefore, to love 14
13 till you perish from off this good land 8
14 of all the good things which the LORD . . promised 8
15 just as all the good things . . have been fulfilled 8
15 destroyed you from off this good land 8
16 you shall perish quickly from off the good land 8
Jdg 8: 2 the grapes of E'phraim better than the vintage 8
32 Gideon the son of Jo'ash died in a good old age 8
35 in return for all the good that he had done 8
9: 2 Which is better for you, that all 70 of the sons 8
11 Shall I leave my sweetness and my good fruit 8
10:15 have sinned; do to us whatever seems good to thee; 8
11:25 are you any better than Balak the son of Zippor 8
18:19 Is it better for you to be priest to the house 8
19:24 Ravish . . and do with them what seems good to you; 8
1Sm 1:23 Do what seems best to you, wait until you have 8
2:24 No, my sons; it is no good report that I hear 8
3:18 It is the LORD; let him do what seems good to him. 8
8:14 He will take the best of your fields 8
16 He will take . . and the best of your cattle 8
11:10 and you may do to us whatever seems good to you. 8
12:23 I will instruct you in the good and the right way. 8
14:36 And they said, "Do whatever seems good to you. 8
40 the people said to Saul, "Do what seems good to you. 8
15: 9 spared Agag, and the best of the sheep 10
9 the fatlings, and the lambs, and all that was good 8
15 people spared the best of the sheep and . . oxen 10
21 people took . . the best of the things devoted 17
22 Behold, to obey is better than sacrifice 8
28 given it to a neighbor . . who is better than you. 8
18: 5 And this was good in the sight of all the people 10
19: 4 and . . his deeds have been of good service to you; 8
20: 7 If he says, 'Good!' it will be well with your servant; 8
24: 4 you shall do to him as it shall seem good to you. 10
17 you have repaid me good . . I have repaid you evil. 8
19 LORD reward you with good for what you have done 8
25: 3 woman was of good understanding and beautiful 8
15 men were very good to us, and we suffered no harm 8
21 and he has returned me evil for good. 8
30 according to all the good that he has spoken 8
26:16 This thing that you have done is not good. 8
27: 1 there is nothing better for me than . . escape 8
2Sm 2: 6 I will do good to you because you have done this 8
3:13 And he said, "Good; I will make a covenant with you; 8
19 all that Israel and . . Benjamin thought good 8
10:12 and may the LORD do what seems good to him. 8
13:22 But Ab'salom spoke to Amnon neither good nor bad; 8
14:17 like the angel of God to discern good and evil. 8
32 It would be better for me to be there still. 8
15: 3 See, your claims are good and right; 8
26 here I am, let him do to me what seems good to him. 8
16:12 the LORD will repay me with good for this cursing 8
17: 7 the counsel . . Ahith'ophel has given is not good. 8
14 counsel of Hushai . . is better than the counsel 8
14 to defeat the good counsel of Ahith'ophel 8
18: 3 it is better that you send us help from the city. 8
4 king said . . "Whatever seems best to you I will do. 10
27 He is a good man, and comes with good tidings. 8
27 He is a good man, and comes with good tidings. 8
19:27 do therefore what seems good to you. 8
37 and do for him whatever seems good to you. 8
38 and I will do for him whatever seems good to you; 8
24:22 my lord . . take and offer up what seems good to him; 8
1Kg 2:32 slew . . two men more righteous and better 8
38 What you say is good; as my lord the king has said 8
42 And you said to me, 'What you say is good; I obey.' 8
3: 9 that I may discern between good and evil; for who 8
8:36 teach them the good way in which they should walk; 8
56 not one word has failed of all his good promise 8
12: 7 serve them, and speak good words to them 8
14:15 root up Israel out of this good land which he gave 8
19: 4 take . . my life; for I am no better than my fathers. 8
21: 2 Give me . . and I will give you a better vineyard 8
2 or, if it seems good to you, I will give you . . money. 8
22: 8 for he never prophesies good . . but evil. 8
18 that he would not prophesy good concerning me 8
2Kg 3:19 and shall fell every good tree 8
19 and ruin every good piece of land with stones. 8
25 on every good piece of land every man threw 8
25 and felled all the good trees; 8
5:12 rivers of Damascus, better than all the waters 8
10: 3 select the best and fittest of your master's sons 8
5 do whatever is good in your eyes. 8
20: 3 I have . . and have done what is good in thy sight. 8
19 The word of the LORD which you have spoken is good. 8
1Ch 4:40 where they found rich, good pasture 8
13: 2 If it seems good to you, and if it is the will 8
16:34 O give thanks to the LORD, for he is good; 8
19:13 and may the LORD do what seems good to him. 8
21:23 let my lord the king do what seems good to him; 8
28: 8 that you may possess this good land 8
29:28 he died in a good old age, full of days, riches 8
2Ch 5:13 For he is good, for his steadfast love endures 8
6:27 when thou dost teach them the good way 8
7: 3 For he is good, for his steadfast love endures 8
10: 7 If you will . . speak good words to them 8
12:12 moreover, conditions were good in Judah. 8
14: 2 Asa did what was good and right 8
18: 7 never prophesies good concerning me, but always 8
17 would not prophesy good concerning me, but evil? 8
19: 3 Nevertheless some good is found in you 8
21:13 brothers . . who were better than yourself; 8
24:16 because he had done good in Israel 8
30:18 The good LORD pardon every one 8
22 the Levites who showed good skill in the service 8
31:20 he did what was good and right and faithful 8
Ezr 3:11 For he is good, for his steadfast love endures 8
5:17 if it seem good to the king, let search be made 19
7: 9 for the good hand of his God was upon him. 8
8:18 by the good hand of our God upon us, they brought us 8
22 hand of our God is for good upon all that seek him 8
9:12 that you may be strong, and eat the good of the land 7
Neh 2: 8 for the good hand of my God was upon me. 8
18 hand of my God which had been upon me for good 8
18 strengthened their hands for the good work. 8
5: 9 I said, "The thing that you are doing is not good. 8
19 Remember for my good, O my God, all that I have done 8
9:13 give them . . good statutes and commandments. 8
20 Thou gavest thy good Spirit to instruct them 8
13:31 Remember me, O my God, for good. 8
Est 1:19 give . . to another who is better than she. 8
3:11 is given . . to do with them as it seems good to you. 8
Job 2:10 Shall we receive good at the hand of God 8
5:27 it is true. Hear, and know it for your good. •
7: 7 my eye will never again see good. 8
9:25 they flee away, they see no good. 8
10: 3 Does it seem good to thee to oppress 8
21:25 bitterness of soul, never having tasted of good. 8
22:18 Yet he filled their houses with good things– 8
21 be at peace; thereby good will come to you. 8
30:26 when I looked for good, evil came; 8
34: 4 let us determine among ourselves what is good. 8
Ps 4: 6 many who say, "O that we might see some good! 8
14: 1 there is none that does good. 8
3 there is none that does good, no, not one. 8
16: 2 Thou art my Lord; I have no good apart from thee. 9
25: 8 Good and upright is the LORD; 8
34: 8 O taste and see that the LORD is good! 8
12 covets many days, that he may enjoy good? 8
14 Depart from evil, and do good; seek peace 8
35:12 They requite me evil for good; my soul is forlorn. 8
36: 4 he sets himself in a way that is not good; 8
37: 3 Trust in the LORD, and do good; 8
16 Better is a little that the righteous has 8
27 Depart from evil, and do good; so shall you abide 8
38:20 Those who render me evil for good 8
20 are my adversaries because I follow after good. 8
52: 3 You love evil more than good 8
9 I will proclaim thy name, for it is good 8
53: 1 there is none that does good. 8
3 there is none that does good, no, not one. 8
54: 6 I will give thanks to thy name, O LORD, for it is good. 8
63: 3 Because thy steadfast love is better than life 8
69:16 Answer me, O LORD, for thy steadfast love is good; 8
73: 1 Truly God is good to the upright 8
28 for me it is good to be near God; 8
84:10 day in thy courts is better than 1,000 8
85:12 Yea, the LORD will give what is good 8
86: 5 For thou, O Lord, art good and forgiving 8
92: 1 It is good to give thanks to the LORD 8
100: 5 LORD is good; his steadfast love endures for ever 8
103: 5 who satisfies you with good as long as you live 8
106: 1 O give thanks to the LORD, for he is good; 8
107: 1 O give thanks to the LORD, for he is good; 8
109: 5 reward me evil for good, and hatred for my love. 8
21 because thy steadfast love is good, deliver me! 8

111:10 good understanding have all those who practice 8
118: 1 O give thanks to the LORD, for he is good; 8
8 It is better to take refuge in the LORD 8
9 better to take refuge in the LORD 8
29 O give thanks to the LORD, for he is good; 8
119:39 for thy ordinances are good. 8
66 Teach me good judgment and knowledge 7
68 Thou art good and doest good; 8
71 It is good for me that I was afflicted 8
72 The law of thy mouth is better to me 8
122Be surety for thy servant for good; 8
122: 9 I will seek your good. 8
125: 4 Do good, O LORD, to those who are good 8
133: 1 how good and pleasant it is when brothers dwell 8
135: 3 Praise the LORD, for the LORD is good; 8
136: 1 O give thanks to the LORD, for he is good 8
143:10 Let thy good spirit lead me on a level path! 8
145: 9 The LORD is good to all, and his compassion 8
147: 1 For it is good to sing praises to our God; 8
Prv 2: 9 Then you will understand . . every good path; 8
3: 4 you will find favor and good repute 8
14 gain from it is better than gain from silver •
14 its profit better than gold. 8
27 Do not withhold good from those to whom it is due 8
4: 2 for I give you good precepts 8
8:11 for wisdom is better than jewels 8
19 My fruit is better than gold, even fine gold 8
11:23 desire of the righteous ends only in good; 8
27 He who diligently seeks good seeks favor 8
12: 4 A good wife is the crown of her husband 3
9 Better is a man of humble standing who works 8
14 fruit of his words a man is satisfied with good 8
20 but those who plan good have joy. 18
25 but a good word makes him glad. 8
13: 2 From the fruit of his mouth a good man eats good •
2 From the fruit of his mouth a good man eats good 8
15 Good sense wins favor 8
14:14 good man with the fruit of his deeds. 8
19 The evil bow down before the good 8
22 who devise good meet loyalty and faithfulness. 8
15: 3 keeping watch on the evil and the good. 8
16 Better is a little with the fear of the LORD 8
17 Better is a dinner of herbs where love is 8
23 word in season, how good it is! 8
30 good news refreshes the bones. 8
16: 8 Better is a little with righteousness 8
16 To get wisdom is better than gold; 8
19 better to be of a lowly spirit with the poor 8
29 leads him in a way that is not good. 8
32 He who is slow to anger is better than the mighty 8
17: 1 Better is a dry morsel with quiet 8
13 If a man returns evil for good 8
22 A cheerful heart is a good medicine 10
26 To impose a fine on a righteous man is not good; 8
18: 5 It is not good to be partial to a wicked man 8
19: 1 Better is a poor man who walks in his integrity 8
2 It is not good for a man to be without knowledge 8
22 poor man is better than a liar. 8
20:23 false scales are not good. 8
21: 9 It is better to live in a corner of the housetop 8
19 It is better to live in a desert land 8
22: 1 good name . . be chosen rather than great riches •
1 favor is better than silver or gold. 8
24:13 My son, eat honey, for it is good 8
23 Partiality in judging is not good. 8
25 delight, and a good blessing will be upon them. 8
25: 7 for it is better to be told, "Come up here 8
24 better to live in a corner of the housetop 8
25 Like cold water . . good news from a far country. 8
27 It is not good to eat much honey 8
27: 5 Better is open rebuke than hidden love. 8
10 Better is a neighbor who is near than a brother 8
28: 6 Better is a poor man who walks in his integrity 8
21 To show partiality is not good; 8
31:10 A good wife who can find? She is far more precious 3
12 She does him good, and not harm 8
Ecc 2: 3 I might see what was good for the sons of men to do 8
24 There is nothing better for a man than that he 8
3:12 there is nothing better for them than to be happy 8
22 nothing better than that a man . . enjoy his work 8
4: 3 better than both is he who has not yet been 8
6 Better is a handful of quietness than two 8
9 Two are better than one . . they have a good reward 8
9 because they have a good reward for their toil. 8
13 Better is a poor and wise youth than an old 8
5: 5 It is better that you should not vow than that you 8
18 what I have seen to be good and to be fitting is 8
6: 6 Even though he should live . . yet enjoy no good 8
9 Better is the sight . . than the wandering 8
11 the more vanity, and what is man the better? 12
12 For who knows what is good for man 8
7: 1 A good name is better than precious ointment; 8
1 A good name is better than precious ointment; 8
2 It is better to go to the house of mourning 8
3 Sorrow is better than laughter 8
5 It is better for a man to hear the rebuke 8
8 Better is the end of a thing than its beginning; 8
8 and the patient in spirit is better 8
10 Why were the former days better than these? 8
11 Wisdom is good with an inheritance, an advantage 8
18 It is good that you should take hold of this 8
20 not a . . man on earth who does good and never sins. 8
9: 2 to the good and the evil . . clean and the unclean 8
4 for a living dog is better than a dead lion. 8
16 But I say that wisdom is better than might 8
17 the wise . . heard in quiet are better •
18 Wisdom is better than weapons of war 8
18 but one sinner destroys much good. 8
11: 6 do not know . . or whether both alike will be good. 8
12:14 with every secret thing, whether good or evil. 8
Sng 1: 2 For your love is better than wine 8
4:10 how much better is your love than wine 6
7: 9 and your kisses like the best wine that goes down 8
Isa 1:19 If . . obedient, you shall eat the good of the land; 7
5:20 Woe to those who call evil good and good evil 8
20 Woe to those who call evil good and good evil 8
7:15 knows how to refuse the evil and choose the good. 8
16 knows how to refuse the evil and choose the good 8
38: 3 and have done what is good in thy sight. 8
39: 8 word of the LORD which you have spoken is good. 8
41: 7 saying of the soldering, "It is good"; 8
52: 7 who publishes peace, who brings good tidings 8
55: 2 Hearken diligently to me, and eat what is good 8
56: 5 a monument and a name better than sons 8
65: 2 people, who walk in a way that is not good 8
Jer 5:25 and your sins have kept good from you. 8
6:16 ask for the ancient paths, where the good way is; 8
8:15 We looked for peace, but no good came 8
13: 7 waistcloth was spoiled; it was good for nothing. 15
10 like this waistcloth, which is good for nothing. 15
14:19 We looked for peace, but no good came; 8
15:11 O LORD, if I have not entreated thee for their good 8
17: 6 in the desert, and shall not see any good come. 8
18:10 I will repent of the good which I had intended 8
20 Is evil a recompense for good? 8
20 how I stood before thee to speak good for them 8
21:10 for evil and not for good, says the LORD 8
24: 2 One basket had very good figs, like first-ripe 8
3 the good figs very good, and the bad figs very bad 8
3 the good figs very good, and the bad figs very bad 8
5 Like these good figs, so I will regard as good 8
5 I will regard as good the exiles from Judah 8
6 I will set my eyes upon them for good 8
26:14 Do with me as seems good and right to you. 8
29:32 to see the good that I will do to my people 8
32:39 that they may fear me for ever, for their own good 8
39 and the good of their children after them. •
42 I will bring upon them all the good that I promise 8
33: 9 who shall hear of all the good that I do for them; 8
9 all the good and all the prosperity I provide 8
11 the LORD is good, for his steadfast love endures 8
39:16 words against this city for evil and not for good 8
40: 4 If it seems good to you to come with me to Babylon 8
4 go wherever you think it good and right to go. 8
42: 6 Whether it is good or evil, we will obey the voice 8
44:27 I am watching over them for evil and not for good; 8
Lam 3:25 The LORD is good to those who wait for him 8
26 It is good that one should wait quietly 8
27 It is good for a man that he bear the yoke 8
38 the mouth of the Most High that good and evil come? 8
Ezk 17: 8 he transplanted it to good soil 8
18:18 and did what is not good among his people 8
20:25 Moreover I gave them statutes that were not good 8
24: 4 put in it the pieces of flesh, all the good pieces 8
27:22 for your wares the best of all kinds of spices 16
31:16 the trees of Eden, the choice and best of Lebanon 8
34:14 I will feed them with good pasture 8
14 there they shall lie down in good grazing land 8
18 Is it not enough for you to feed on the good 8
36:31 your evil ways, and your deeds that were not good; 8
Dan 1:15 seen that they were better in appearance 8
3:15 fall down and worship the image . . well and good; •
Hos 2: 7 for it was better with me then than now.' 8
4:13 and terebinth, because their shade is good. 8
8: 3 Israel has spurned the good; 8
14: 2 Take away all iniquity; accept that which is good 8
Ams 5:14 Seek good, and not evil, that you may live; 8
15 Hate evil, and love good, and establish justice 8
6: 2 Are they better than these kingdoms? 8
9: 4 set my eyes upon them for evil and not for good. 8
Jon 4: 3 for it is better for me to die than to live. 8
8 It is better for me to die than to live. 8
Mic 1:12 inhabitants of Maroth wait anxiously for good 8
3: 2 you who hate the good and love the evil 8
6: 8 He has showed you, O man, what is good; 8
7: 4 The best of them is like a brier 8
Nah 1: 7 The LORD is good, a stronghold 8
3: 8 Are you better than Thebes that sat by the Nile 10
Zec 3: 8 who sit before you, for they are men of good omen •
9:17 Yea, how good and how fair it shall be! 7
Mal 2:17 one who does evil is good in the sight of the LORD 8
3:14 What is the good of our keeping his charge 1
Mat 3:10 tree therefore that does not bear good fruit 33
5:13 no longer good for anything except to be thrown out 32
16 that they may see your good works and give glory 33
45 he makes his sun rise on the evil and on the good 21
7:11 know how to give good gifts to your children 21
17 So, every sound tree bears good fruit 33
18 nor can a bad tree bear good fruit. 33
19 Every tree that does not bear good fruit is cut 33
12:12 So it is lawful to do good on the sabbath. 34
33 Either make the tree good, and its fruit good 33
33 Either make the tree good, and its fruit good 33
34 You brood of vipers! how can you speak good 21
35 The good man out of his good treasure 21
35 The good man out of his good treasure 21
35 out of his good treasure brings forth good 21
13: 8 Other seeds fell on good soil 33
23 As for what was sown on good soil 33
24 to a man who sowed good seed in his field; 33
27 Sir, did you not sow good seed in your field? 33
37 He who sows the good seed is the Son of man; 33
38 and the good seed means the sons of the kingdom 33
48 sat down and sorted the good into vessels 33
19:17 Why do you ask me about what is good? 21
17 One there is who is good 21
22:10 gathered all whom they found, both bad and good; 21
25:21 Well done, good and faithful servant 21
23 Well done, good and faithful servant 21
Mrk 3: 4 Is it lawful on the sabbath to do good or to do harm 21
4: 8 other seeds fell into good soil 33
20 those that were sown upon the good soil 33
5:26 no better but rather grew worse. 46
9:49 Salt is good 33
10:17 Good Teacher, what must I do 21
18 Why do you call me good? No one is good but God 21
18 Why do you call me good? No one is good but God 21
14: 7 whenever you will, you can do good to them; 28
Lke 3: 9 every tree . . that does not bear good fruit 33
5:39 for he says, 'The old is good.' 44
6:27 Love your enemies, do good to those who hate you 34
38 good measure, pressed down, shaken together 33
43 For no good tree bears bad fruit 33
43 nor again does a bad tree bear good fruit; 33
45 The good man out of the good treasure of his heart 21
45 The good man out of the good treasure of his heart 21
45 The good man . . produces good 21
8: 8 some fell into good soil and grew 21
15 as for that in the good soil 33
15 hold it fast in an honest and good heart 21
10:42 Mary has chosen the good portion 21
11:13 know how to give good gifts to your children 21
13: 9 if it bears fruit next year, well and good •
14:34 Salt is good 33
15:22 Bring quickly the best robe, and put it on him; 40
18:18 a ruler asked him, "Good Teacher, what shall I do 21
19 Why do you call me good? No one is good but God 21
19 Why do you call me good? No one is good but God 21
19:17 he said to him, 'Well done, good servant! 21
23:50 member of the council, a good and righteous man 21
Joh 1:46 Can anything good come out of Nazareth? 21
2:10 said to him, "Every man serves the good wine first; 33
10 but you have kept the good wine until now. 33
5:29 who have done good, to the resurrection of life 21
10:11 I am the good shepherd 33
11 The good shepherd lays down his life 33
14 I am the good shepherd 33
32 I have shown you many good works from the Father; 33
33 It is not for a good work that we stone you 33
Act 9:36 She was full of good works and acts of charity. 21
11:24 a good man, full of the Holy Spirit and of faith. 21
23: 1 I have lived before God in all good conscience 21
Rom 2:10 and honor and peace for every one who does good 21
3: 8 And why not do evil that good may come? 21
12 no one does good, not even one. 45
4:19 his own body, which was as good as dead 30
7:12 and the commandment is holy and just and good. 21
13 Did that which is good, then, bring death to me? 21
13 sin, working death in me through what is good 21
16 I agree that the law is good. 35
18 For I know that nothing good dwells within me 21
19 For I do not do the good I want, but the evil I do not 21
8:28 God works for good with those who love him 21
9:11 and had done nothing either good or bad 21
10:15 the feet of those who preach good news! 21
12: 2 what is good and acceptable and perfect. 21
9 hate what is evil, hold fast to what is good; 21
21 but overcome evil with good. 21
13: 3 For rulers are not a terror to good conduct 21
3 Then do what is good 21
4 for he is God's servant for your good. 21
14:16 do not let your good be spoken of as evil. 21
15: 2 let each of us please his neighbor for his good 21
16:19 I would have you wise as to what is good 21
1Co 5: 6 Your boasting is not good. Do you not know 33
7: 9 it is better to marry than to be aflame with passion. 36
10:24 Let no one seek his own good •
24 the good of his neighbor. •
11:17 it is not for the better but for the worse. 21
15:33 Bad company ruins good morals. 44
2Co 5:10 so that each one may receive good or evil 21
8:10 it is best for you now to complete 41
9: 8 provide in abundance for every good work. 21
11:23 Are they servants of Christ? I am a better one 42
Gal 4: 1 the heir . . is no better than a slave 26
18 it is always good to be made much 33
6:10 as we have opportunity, let us do good to all men 21

Eph 2:10 created in Christ Jesus for good works 21
4:29 only such as is good for edifying 21
5: 9 found in all that is good and right and true 22
6: 8 knowing that whatever good any one does 21
Php 1: 6 I am sure that he who began a good work in you 21
23 that is far better. 21
2: 3 count others better than yourselves. 43
Col 1:10 bearing fruit in every good work 21
1Th 5:15 always seek to do good to one another and to all. 21
21 test everything; hold fast what is good 33
2Th 1:11 may fulfil every good resolve and work of faith 22
2:16 gave us eternal comfort and good hope 21
17 establish them in every good work and word. 21
1Ti 1: 5 that issues from a pure heart and a good conscience 21
8 Now we know that the law is good 33
18 inspired by them you may wage the good warfare 33
19 holding faith and a good conscience 21
2: 3 This is good 33
10 by good deeds 21
3:13 gain a good standing for themselves 33
4: 4 For everything created by God is good 33
6 you will be a good minister of Christ Jesus 33
6 the good doctrine which you have followed. 33
5:10 she must be well attested for her good deeds 33
10 and devoted herself to doing good in every way. 21
25 also good deeds are conspicuous 33
6:12 Fight the good fight of the faith 33
12 you were called when you made the good confession 33
13 who . . before Pontius Pilate made the good confession 33
18 They are to do good, to be rich in good deeds 20
19 thus laying up for themselves a good foundation 33
2Ti 2: 3 as a good soldier of Christ Jesus. 33
21 ready for any good work. 21
3:17 equipped for every good work. 21
4: 7 I have fought the good fight 33
Tit 1:16 detestable, disobedient, unfit for any good deed. 21
2: 7 in all respects a model of good deeds 33
14 who are zealous for good deeds. 33
3: 8 may be careful to apply themselves to good deeds 33
14 learn to apply themselves to good deeds 33
Phm 1: 6 knowledge of all the good that is ours in Christ. 21
Heb 5:14 to distinguish good from evil. 33
7:19 on the other hand, a better hope is introduced 36
22 makes Jesus the surety of a better covenant. 36
8: 6 the covenant he mediates is better 36
6 since it is enacted on better promises. 36
9:23 purified . . with better sacrifices than these. 36
10:24 to stir up one another to love and good works 33
34 a better possession and an abiding one. 36
11:12 Therefore from one man, and him as good as dead *
16 as it is, they desire a better country 36
35 that they might rise again to a better life. 36
40 since God had foreseen something better for us 36
12:10 he disciplines us for our good 41
13:21 equip you with everything good 21
Jas 1:17 Every good endowment . . is from above 21
3:13 By his good life let him show his works 33
17 wisdom . . is . . full of mercy and good fruits 21
1Pe 2:12 Maintain good conduct among the Gentiles 33
12 they may see your good deeds and glorify God 33
3:10 He that would love life and see good days 21
16 those who revile your good behavior in Christ 21
17 For it is better to suffer for doing right 36
4:10 as good stewards of God's varied grace 33
2Pe 2:21 better for them never to have known the way 36
3Jn 1:11 Beloved, do not imitate evil but imitate good. 21
1Es 2:20 we think it best not to neglect such a matter 34
5:44 to the best of their ability. 35
2Es 1:18 It would have been better for us 47
2:14 for I left out evil and created good 47
25 Good nurse, nourish your sons 47
3:22 but what was good departed 47
28 Are the deeds of those . . any better? 47
31 Are the deeds of Babylon better than those of Zion? 47
4:12 better for us not to be here than to come here 47
29 the field where the good has been sown 47
7:63 it would have been better if the dust itself 47
66 For it is much better with them than with us 47
69 perhaps it would have been better for us. 47
82 because they cannot now make a good repentance 47
116 it would have been better if the earth had not 47
117 For what good is it to all that they live in sorrow 49
119 For what good is it to us 49
120 what good is it that an everlasting hope *
8:36 to those who have no store of good works. 47
12:44 how much better it would have been for us 47
45 For we are no better than those who died there. 47
13:20 Yet it is better to come into these things 48
Tob 2: 1 a good dinner was prepared for me 33
4: 9 you will be laying up a good treasure 21
5:13 of a good and noble lineage. 21
13 My brother, you come of good stock. 33
21 For a good angel will go with him 21
7: 7 Son of that good and noble man! 33
12 The merciful God will guide you both for the best. 33
8: 6 It is not good that the man should be alone 33
10:12 Let me hear a good report of you 33
12: 6 It is good to praise God and to exalt his name 21
7 It is good to guard the secret of a king 33

7 Do good, and evil will not overtake you. 21
8 Prayer is good when accompanied by fasting 21
8 is better than much with wrongdoing 21
11 It is good to guard the secret of a king 33
14: 4 will be scattered . . from the good land 21
Jdt 3: 4 deal with them in any way that seems good to you. 21
15:10 you have done great good to Israel 21
Wis 3:15 For the fruit of good labors is renowned 21
4: 1 Better than this is childlessness with virtue 21
5 not ripe enough to eat, and good for nothing. 27
12 the fascination of wickedness obscures what is good 33
8: 9 knowing that she would give me good counsel 21
19 a good soul fell to my lot; 21
20 rather, being good, I entered an undefiled body. 21
10: 8 not only . . hindered from recognizing the good 33
12:21 oaths and covenants full of good promises! 21
13: 3 know how much better than these is their Lord 24
14:26 confusion over what is good 21
15:17 he is better than the objects he worships 36
Sir 6:19 wait for her good harvest 21
7:13 the habit of lying serves no good. 21
19 Do not deprive yourself of a wise and good wife 21
10:27 Better is a man who works 21
11: 3 her product is the best of sweet things. 23
12 the eyes of the Lord look upon him for his good 21
31 for he lies in wait, turning good into evil 21
12: 2 Do good to a godly man, and you will be repaid 28
3 No good will come to the man who persists in evil 21
5 Do good to the humble 28
5 evil for all the good which you do to him. 21
13:24 Riches are good if they are free from sin 21
25 either for good or for evil. 21
14: 7 even if he does good, he does it unintentionally 28
13 Do good to a friend before you die 28
14 let not your share of desired good pass by you. 21
16: 3 one is better than 1,000 21
17: 7 showed them good and evil. 21
18: 8 What is his good and what is his evil? 21
16 So a word is better than a gift. 21
17 Indeed, does not a word surpass a good gift? 21
19:24 Better is the God-fearing man 21
20:16 there is no gratitude for my good deeds 21
18 better than a slip of the tongue 37
31 Better is the man who hides his folly 21
23:27 nothing is better than the fear of the Lord 21
26: 1 Happy is the husband of a good wife 21
3 A good wife is a great blessing 21
16 beauty of a good wife in her well-ordered home. 21
29:14 A good man will be surety for his neighbor 21
22 Better is the life of a poor man 21
30:15 Health and soundness are better than all gold 21
16 There is no wealth better than health of body 21
17 Death is better than a miserable life 21
25 A man of cheerful and good heart 21
32: 6 the melody of music with good wine. 31
13 satisfies you with his good gifts. 21
33: 7 Why is any day better than another 43
14 Good is the opposite of evil 21
21 For it is better that your children should ask 21
36:18 yet one food is better than another. 33
21 one daughter is better than another. 21
24 He who acquires a wife gets his best possession 17
37: 9 tell you, "Your way is good," and then stand aloof 33
18 good and evil, life and death 21
28 For not everything is good for every one 41
39: 4 he tests the good and the evil among men. 21
16 they are very good 33
27 All these are for good to the godly 21
33 The works of the Lord are all good 21
40:12 good faith will stand for ever. *
28 it is better to die than to beg. 21
41:13 The days of a good life are numbered 21
13 a good name endures for ever. 21
15 Better is the man who hides his folly 21
16 it is good to retain every kind of shame 33
42:14 Better is the wickedness of a man 21
46:10 might see that it is good to follow the Lord. 33
51:18 I was zealous for the good 21
21 therefore I have gained a good possession. 21
LJr 1:34 Whether one does evil to them or good 21
38 take pity on a widow or do good to an orphan. 28
59 it is better to be a king who shows his courage 21
64 either to decide a case or to do good to men. 28
68 The wild beasts are better than they are 21
73 Better therefore is a just man who has no idols 21
Aza 1:67 Give thanks to the Lord, for he is good 44
1Mc 3:59 It is better for us to die in battle 21
4:24 he is good, for his mercy endures for ever. 33
45 they thought it best to tear it down 25
8: 7 and surrender some of their best provinces 33
10:11 to build the walls . . for better fortification *
27 repay you with good for what you do for us. 21
11:33 we have determined to do good 21
13: 5 for I am not better than my brothers. 21
14: 4 He sought the good of his nation 21
16:17 returned evil for good. 21
2Mc 1: 1 brethren in Egypt, Greeting, and good peace. 21
4:37 the moderation and good conduct of the deceased; 39
45 already as good as beaten *

5: 4 the apparition might prove to have been a good omen. 21
9:22 I have good hope of recovering from my illness 39
11: 6 to send a good angel to save Israel. 21
14:30 did not spring from the best motives 21
15:12 a noble and good man 21
23 now, O Sovereign of the heavens, send a good angel 21
38 that was the best I could do. 29
3Mc 1: 2 took with him the best of the Ptolemaic arms 21
3:22 disdained what is good 33
26 in good order and in the best state. 21
4Mc 1: 8 I can demonstrate it best 38
2:23 temperate, just, good, and courageous. 21
4: 1 the noble and good man, Onias 21

good *See also* appearance, bring, cheer, child, clothes, conduct, counsel, courage, deed, faith, fortune, gift, hater, health, hope, judgment, looks, love, luck, make, manners, news, order, pleasure, presence, prove, purpose, reason, receive, repute, resolve, seat, sense, service, success, teach, think, tidings, time, way, while, will.

common good 1. *συμφέρω*

1Co 12: 7 To each is given . . the Spirit for the common good. 1
2Mc 11:15 Maccabeus, having regard for the common good 1

good courage 1. חזק

Num13:20 Be of good courage, and bring some 1

good deed 1. חֶסֶד 2. טוֹבָה 3. *ἀγαθοποιέω* 4. *ἀγαθός* 5. *εὐπραξία*

2Ch 32:32 rest of the acts of Hezeki'ah, and his good deeds 1
35:26 his good deeds according to what is written 1
Neh 6:19 Also they spoke of his good deeds in my presence 2
13:14 wipe not out my good deeds that I have done 1
Mat 19:16 Teacher, what good deed must I do 4
Tob 12:13 your good deed was not hidden from me 3
Sir 12: 1 you will be thanked for your good deeds. 4
18:15 My son, do not mix reproach with your good deeds 4
3Mc 3: 5 the good deeds of upright people 5

do good 1. יטב 2. יעל 3. *ἀγαθοποιέω* 4. *ἀγαθοποιός* 5. *ἀγαθουργέω* 6. *ἀγαθόω* 7. *εὐεργετέω* 8. *εὐποιΐα* 9. *χρήσιμος* 10. *ὠφελέω*

Gen 32: 9 Return to your country . . and I will do you good 1
12 thou didst say, 'I will do you good 1
Lev 5: 4 a rash oath to do evil or to do good 1
Num10:29 come with us, and we will do you good; for the LORD 1
32 whatever good the LORD will do to us 1
32 good the LORD will do . . same will we do to you. 1
Deu 8:16 humble you and test you, to do you good in the end. 1
28:63 as the LORD took delight in doing you good 1
Jos 24:20 and do you harm . . after having done you good. 1
Job 15: 3 or in words with which he can do no good? 2
24:21 and do no good to the widow. 1
Ps 36: 3 he has ceased to act wisely and do good. 1
51:18 Do good to Zion in thy good pleasure; 1
119:68 Thou art good and doest good; 1
125: 4 Do good, O LORD, to those who are good 1
Isa 1:17 learn to do good; seek justice 1
41:23 do good, or do harm, that we may be dismayed 1
Jer 4:22 but how to do good they know not. 1
10: 5 cannot do evil, neither is it in them to do good. 1
13:23 you can do good who are accustomed to do evil. 1
32:40 that I will not turn away from doing good to them; 1
41 I will rejoice in doing them good 1
Ezk 36:11 and will do more good to you than ever before. 1
Mic 2: 7 Do not my words do good to him who walks uprightly? 1
Zep 1:12 The LORD will not do good, nor will he do ill.' 1
Zec 8:15 so again have I purposed in these days to do good 1
Lke 6: 9 is it lawful on the sabbath to do good or to do harm 3
33 if you do good to those who do good to you 3
33 if you do good to those who do good to you 3
35 love your enemies, and do good, and lend 3
Act 10:38 how he went about doing good 7
14:17 he did good and gave you from heaven rains 5
1Ti 6:18 They are to do good, to be rich in good deeds 5
2Ti 2:14 avoid disputing about words, which does no good 9
Heb 13:16 Do not neglect to do good 8
3Jn 1:11 He who does good is of God; 4
Sir 38:21 you do the dead no good, and you injure yourself. 10
42:14 Better . . than a woman who does good 4
49: 9 did good to those who directed their ways aright. 6
2Mc 1: 2 May God do good to you 3

do one good 1. שוה

Est 5:13 this does me no good, so long as I see Mor'decai 1

good man 1. טוֹב 2. צַדִּיק 3. *ἀγαθός*

Ps 141: 5 Let a good man strike or rebuke me in kindness 2
Prv 2:20 you will walk in the way of good men 1
12: 2 A good man obtains favor from the LORD 1
13:22 A good man leaves an inheritance 1
Ecc 9: 2 As is the good man, so is the sinner; 1
Joh 7:12 While some said, "He is a good man 3
Rom 5: 7 perhaps for a good man one will dare even to die. 3
Jdt 11: 8 you are the one good man in the whole kingdom 3
Wis 18: 9 the holy children of good men offered sacrifices 3
Sir 12: 7 Give to the good man, but do not help the sinner. 3

good people 1. ἀγαθός
Sir 39:25 good things were created for good people 1

good place 1. טוֹב
Est 2: 9 advanced her . . to the best place in the harem. 1

seem good 1. יטב 2. ישר 3. יטב (A) 4. שפר (A)
5. δοκέω 6. κρίνω 7. φαίνω
Gen 41:37 This proposal seemed good to Pharaoh 1
Ezr 7:18 Whatever seems good to you and your brethren 3
Jer 18: 4 as it seemed good to the potter to do. 2
Dan 4: 2 seemed good to me to show the signs and wonders 4
Lke 1: 3 it seemed good to me also 5
Act 15:22 it seemed good to the apostles and the elders 5
25 it has seemed good to us, having come to one accord 5
28 For it has seemed good to the Holy Spirit and to us 5
1Es 2:21 if it seems good to you 7
8:94 as seems good to you 6
1Mc 15:20 it has seemed good to us to accept the shield from them 5

spiritual good 1. πνευματικός
1Co 9:11 If we have sown spiritual good among you 1

good thing 1. טוב 2. טוֹב 3. ἀγαθός 4. κρείττων
5. bonus
Gen 45:23 asses loaded with the good things of Egypt 1
Deu 6:11 houses full of good things, which you did not fill 1
2Sm 7:28 thou . . promised this good thing to thy servant; 2
1Ch 17:26 hast promised this good thing to thy servant; 2
Neh 9:25 possession of houses full of all good things 1
Job 22:18 Yet he filled their houses with good things- 2
Ps 34:10 but those who seek the LORD lack no good thing. 2
84:11 No good thing does the LORD withhold 2
104:28 thy hand, they are filled with good things. 2
107: 9 the hungry he fills with good things. 2
Prv 18:22 He who finds a wife finds a good thing 2
Ecc 6: 3 but he does not enjoy life's good things 2
8:15 man has no good thing under the sun but to eat 2
Isa 58:11 and satisfy your desire with good things •
Jer 2: 7 to enjoy its fruits and its good things. 1
Mat 7:11 will your Father . . give good things to those who ask 3
Lke 1:53 he has filled the hungry with good things 3
16:25 you in your lifetime received your good things 3
Gal 6: 6 share all good things with him who teaches. 3
Heb 6: 9 we feel sure of better things 4
9:11 a high priest of the good things that have come 3
10: 1 a shadow of the good things to come 3
1Es 8:85 may be strong and eat the good things of the land 3
2Es 7: 6 and it is full of all good things; 5
Tob 4:19 the Lord himself gives all good things 3
Jdt 15: 8 the good things which the Lord had done 3
Wis 2: 6 let us enjoy the good things that exist 3
7:11 All good things came to me along with her 3
13: 1 the good things that are seen 3
Sir 2: 9 you who fear the Lord, hope for good things 3
11:14 Good things and bad, life and death 3
16:29 filled it with his good things; 3
30:18 Good things poured out upon a mouth 3
39:25 good things were created for good people 3
42: 6 Where there is an evil wife, a seal is a good thing; 3
25 One confirms the good things of the other 3
1Mc 14: 9 they all talked together of good things 3
4Mc 12:11 you have received good things . . from God 3

goodly 1. הָדָר 2. חִין 3. טוֹב 4. שפר 5. תֹּאַר
Lev 23:40 you shall take . . fruit of goodly trees 1
Deu 3:25 see . . that goodly hill country, and Lebanon.' 3
6:10 great and goodly cities, which you did not build 3
8:12 when you . . have built goodly houses and live 3
Job 41:12 or his mighty strength, or his goodly frame. 2
Ps 16: 6 in pleasant places; yea, I have a goodly heritage. 4
21: 3 For thou dost meet him with goodly blessings; 3
45: 1 My heart overflows with a goodly theme; 3
Prv 28:10 blameless will have a goodly inheritance. 3
Jer 11:16 A green olive tree, fair with goodly fruit'; 5

goodly *See also* child.

goodness 1. טוב 2. טוֹב 3. טוֹבָה 4. ἀγαθός
5. ἀγαθότης 6. ἀγαθωσύνη 7. καλός 8. χρηστότης
9. bonitas
Exd 33:19 I will make all my goodness pass before you 1
1Kg 8:66 the goodness that the LORD had shown to David 2
2Ch 6:41 and let thy saints rejoice in thy goodness. 2
7:10 joyful and . . for the goodness that the LORD 2
Neh 9:25 delighted themselves in thy great goodness. 1
35 did not serve thee . . in thy great goodness 1
Ps 23: 6 Surely goodness and mercy shall follow me 2
25: 7 remember me, for thy goodness' sake, O LORD! 1
27:13 believe that I shall see the goodness of the LORD 1
31:19 O how abundant is thy goodness, which thou hast 1
65: 4 be satisfied with the goodness of thy house 1
68:10 goodness, O God, thou didst provide for the needy. 3
145: 7 pour forth the fame of thy abundant goodness 1
Isa 63: 7 and the great goodness to the house of Israel 1
Jer 31:12 shall be radiant over the goodness of the LORD 1
14 my people shall be satisfied with my goodness 1
Hos 3: 5 come . . to his goodness in the latter days. 1
Rom 15:14 that you yourselves are full of goodness 6
Gal 5:22 love, joy, peace, patience, kindness, goodness 6
Tit 3: 4 the goodness and loving kindness of God 8
Phm 1:14 your goodness might not be by compulsion 4
Heb 6: 5 have tasted the goodness of the word of God 7
1Es 5:61 because his goodness and his glory are for ever 8
2Es 7:138 if he did not give out of his goodness 9
8:36 righteousness and goodness will be declared 9
52 goodness is established and wisdom perfected 9
Wis 7:26 an image of his goodness. 5
12:22 we may meditate upon thy goodness when we judge 5
Sir 45:23 in the ready goodness of his soul 5
Man 1: 7 Thou, O Lord, according to thy great goodness 8
14 in me thou wilt manifest thy goodness 6

goodness *See also* know, lover, nobility.

goods 1. הוֹן 2. חַיִל 3. טוּב 4. טוֹב 5. כָּבוֹד 6. כְּלִי
7. מְלָאכָה 8. מַעֲשֶׂה 9. פְּקֻדָּה 10. קִנְיָן 11. רְכוּשׁ
12. שָׁלָל 13. נְכַס (A) 14. ἀγαθός 15. ἀποσκευή
16. βίος 17. κατέχω 18. σκευή 19. σκεῦος 20. σκῦλον
21. ὕπαρξις 22. ὑπάρχω 23. substantia
Gen 14:11 the enemy took all the goods of Sodom 11
12 in Sodom, and his goods, and departed. 11
16 Then he brought back all the goods 11
16 also brought back his kinsman Lot with his goods 11
21 but take the goods for yourself. 11
31:37 Although you have felt through all my goods 6
45:20 Give no thought to your goods 6
46: 6 They also took their cattle and their goods 11
Exd 22: 7 delivers to his neighbor money or goods to keep 6
8 he has put his hand to his neighbor's goods. 7
Num 16:32 men that belonged to Korah and all their goods. 11
31: 9 took as booty . . all their goods. 2
Jdg 18:21 little ones and the cattle and the goods in front 5
2Kg 8: 9 took a present . . all kinds of goods of Damascus 3
2Ch 20:25 found cattle in great numbers, goods, clothing 11
Ezr 1: 4 be assisted . . with goods and with beasts 11
6 aided them with . . goods, with beasts 11
7:26 whether . . for confiscation of his goods 13
8:21 ourselves, our children, and all our goods. 11
Est 3:13 to destroy . . and to plunder their goods. 12
8:11 to destroy, to slay . . and to plunder their goods 12
Ps 109: 8 May his days be few; may another seize his goods! 9
Prv 1:13 we shall find all precious goods 1
6:31 he will give all the goods of his house. 1
Ecc 5:11 When goods increase, they increase who eat them; 4
Jer 49:29 be taken, their curtains and all their goods; 6
Ezk 27:16 trafficked . . because of your abundant goods; 8
18 trafficked with you for your abundant goods 8
38:12 the people . . who have gotten cattle and goods 10
13 take away cattle and goods, to seize great spoil 10
Dan 11:24 scattering among them plunder, spoil, and goods. 11
Obd 1:13 you should not have looted his goods 2
Zep 1:13 Their goods shall be plundered 2
Mat 12:29 and plunder his goods 19
Mrk 3:27 enter a strong man's house and plunder his goods 18
Lke 6:30 of him who takes away your goods •
11:21 his goods are in peace; 22
12:18 there I will store all my grain and my goods. 14
19 Soul, you have ample goods laid up for many years; 14
16: 1 this man was wasting his goods. 22
17:31 who is on the housetop, with his goods in the house 18
19: 8 the half of my goods I give to the poor 22
Act 2:45 they sold their possessions and goods 21
1Co 7:30 those who buy as though they had no goods 17
1Jn 3:17 if any one has the world's goods 16
2Es 15:19 plunder their goods, because of hunger for bread 23
16:46 gather their fruits, and plunder their goods 23
72 For they shall destroy and plunder their goods 23
Sir 11:19 I have found rest, and now I shall enjoy my goods! 14
14: 4 others will live in luxury on his goods. 14
1Mc 5:13 captured their wives and children and goods 15
45 with their wives and children and goods 15
9:40 they took all their goods. 20

goods *See also* seller.

desirable goods 1. ἐπιθύμημα
Sir 1:17 fills their whole house with desirable goods 1

household goods 1. כְּלִי בַּיִת
Gen 31:37 what have you found of all your household goods? 1

goodwill 1. εὔνοια
3Mc 6:26 Who . . differed . . in their goodwill toward us 1
7: 7 the friendly and firm goodwill 1
4Mc 13:25 expanded their goodwill and harmony 1

gopher 1. גֹּפֶר
Gen 6:14 Make yourself an ark of gopher wood; 1

gore 1. נגח 2. נָגַח
Exd 21:28 When an ox gores a man or a woman to death 1
29 if the ox has been accustomed to gore in the past 2
31 If it gores a man's son or daughter, he shall be 1
32 If the ox gores a slave, male or female, the owner 1
36 the ox has been accustomed to gore in the past 2

gore (2) 1. ἰχώρων
4Mc 9:20 was being quenched by the drippings of gore 1

gorge 1. דשן 2. פַּחַת 3. שׂבע 4. χορτάζω
Isa 34: 6 it is sated with blood, it is gorged with fat 1
Jer 48:28 that nests in the sides of the mouth of a gorge. 2
Ezk 32: 4 I will gorge the beasts of the whole earth 3
Rev 19:21 and all the birds were gorged with their flesh. 4

gorgeous 1. λαμπρός
Lke 23:11 then, arraying him in gorgeous apparel 1

gorgeously 1. ἔνδοξος
Lke 7:25 Behold, those who are gorgeously appareled 1

solitary gormandizer 1. μονοφάγος
4Mc 2: 7 habitually a solitary gormandizer, a glutton 1

solitary gormandizing 1. μονοφαγία
4Mc 1:27 gluttony, and solitary gormandizing. 1

gospel 1. εὐαγγέλιον
Mat 4:23 preaching the gospel of the kingdom and healing 1
9:35 preaching the gospel of the kingdom, and healing 1
24:14 this gospel of the kingdom will be preached 1
26:13 wherever this gospel is preached 1
Mrk 1: 1 The beginning of the Gospel of Jesus Christ 1
14 preaching the gospel of God 1
15 repent, and believe in the gospel. 1
8:35 loses his life for my sake and the gospel's 1
10:29 for my sake and for the gospel 1
13:10 gospel must first be preached to all nations. 1
14: 9 the gospel is preached in the whole world 1
16:15 Go into all the world and preach the gospel 1
Act 15: 7 the Gentiles should hear the word of the gospel 1
20:24 testify to the gospel of the grace of God. 1
Rom 1: 1 Paul . . set apart for the gospel of God 1
3 the gospel concerning his Son •
9 I serve with my spirit in the gospel of his Son 1
16 For I am not ashamed of the gospel 1
2:16 when, according to my gospel, God judges 1
10:16 But they have not all obeyed the gospel; 1
11:28 As regards the gospel they are enemies of God 1
15:16 in the priestly service of the gospel of God 1
19 I have fully preached the gospel of Christ 1
16:25 to strengthen you according to my gospel 1
1Co 4:15 your father in Christ Jesus through the gospel. 1
9:12 an obstacle in the way of the gospel of Christ. 1
14 those who proclaim the gospel 1
14 get their living by the gospel. 1
18 I may make the gospel free of charge 1
18 making full use of my right in the gospel. 1
23 I do it all for the sake of the gospel 1
2Co 2:12 to preach the gospel of Christ 1
4: 3 even if our gospel is veiled 1
4 the light of the gospel of the glory of Christ 1
8:18 for his preaching of the gospel; 1
9:13 acknowledging the gospel of Christ 1
10:14 all the way to you with the gospel of Christ. 1
11: 4 if you accept a different gospel 1
7 because I preached God's gospel without cost 1
Gal 1: 6 turning to a different gospel- 1
7 not that there is another gospel •
7 want to pervert the gospel of Christ. 1
11 the gospel which was preached by me is not man's 1
11 the gospel . . is not man's gospel. •
2: 2 the gospel which I preach among the Gentiles 1
5 the truth of the gospel might be preserved 1
7 entrusted with the gospel to the uncircumcised 1
7 had been entrusted with the gospel to the circumcised •
14 straightforward about the truth of the gospel 1
Eph 1:13 the word of truth, the gospel of your salvation 1
3: 6 partakers . . through the gospel. 1
7 Of this gospel I was made a minister •
6:15 the equipment of the gospel of peace; 1
19 to proclaim the mystery of the gospel 1
Php 1: 5 thankful for your partnership in the gospel 1
7 in the defense and confirmation of the gospel. 1
12 really served to advance the gospel 1
16 I am put here for the defense of the gospel; 1
27 manner of life be worthy of the gospel of Christ 1
27 striving side by side for the faith of the gospel 1
2:22 he has served with me in the gospel. 1
4: 3 labored side by side with me in the gospel 1
15 in the beginning of the gospel 1
Col 1: 5 in the word of the truth, the gospel 1
23 not shifting from the hope of the gospel 1
1Th 1: 5 for our gospel came to you not only in word 1
2: 2 to declare to you the gospel of God 1
4 entrusted with the gospel, so we speak 1
8 ready to share with you not only the gospel of God 1
9 while we preached to you the gospel of God. 1
3: 2 brother and God's servant in the gospel of Christ 1
2Th 1: 8 who do not obey the gospel of our Lord Jesus. 1
2:14 To this he called you through our gospel 1
1Ti 1:11 in accordance with the glorious gospel 1
2Ti 1: 8 share in suffering for the gospel 1
10 brought life . . to light through the gospel. 1
11 For this gospel I was appointed a preacher 1
2: 8 descended from David, as preached in my gospel 1
9 the gospel for which I am suffering •

Phm 1:13 during my imprisonment for the gospel; 1
1Pe 4:17 the end of those who do not obey the gospel of God? 1
Rev 14: 6 another angel . . with an eternal gospel to proclaim 1

gospel *See also* preach.

gossip 1. דִּבָּה 2. רָכִיל 3. θρυλέω 4. λαλιά 5. φλύαρος 6. ψιθυρισμός 7. ψιθυριστής
Prv 20:19 He who goes about gossiping reveals secrets; 2
Ezk 36: 3 you became the talk and evil gossip of the people; 1
Rom 1:29 Full of envy, murder . . they are gossips 7
2Co 12:20 anger, selfishness, slander, gossip, conceit 6
1Ti 5:13 not only idlers but gossips and busybodies 5
Sir 19: 6 for one who hates gossip evil is lessened. 4
3Mc 3: 7 they gossiped about the differences in worship 3

gouge out 1. נקר 2. ἐκκόπτω
Jdg 16:21 Philistines seized him and gouged out his eyes 1
1Sm 11: 2 condition . . that I gouge out all your right eyes 1
4Mc 5:30 not even if you gouge out my eyes 2

gourd 1. פְּקָעִים 2. פַּקֻּעָה
1Kg 7:24 Under its brim were gourds, for 30 cubits 1
24 the gourds were in two rows, cast with it 1
2Kg 4:39 and gathered from it his lap full of wild gourds 2
2Ch 4: 3 were figures of gourds, for 30 cubits *
3 gourds were in two rows, cast with it when it was *

gourd *See also* form.

govern 1. חבשׁ 2. עשה מְלוּכָה 3. שׁפט 4. διακυβερνάω 5. διοικέω 6. ἡγεμονία 7. κρατέω 8. κρίνω 9. κυβερνάω 10. ποιμαίνω 11. πολιτεύω 12. ὑπερέχω 13. guberno
1Sm 8: 5 a king to govern us like all the nations. 3
6 when they said, "Give us a king to govern us. 3
20 that our king may govern us and go out before us 3
1Kg 3: 9 an understanding mind to govern thy people 3
9 for who is able to govern this thy great people? 3
21: 7 Do you now govern Israel? Arise, and eat bread 2
2Kg 15: 5 was over the household, governing the people 3
2Ch 26:21 Jotham . . governing the people of the land. 3
Job 34:17 Shall one who hates justice govern? 1
Prv 8:16 by me princes rule, and nobles govern the earth. 7
Mat 2: 6 a ruler who will govern my people Israel.' 10
Rom 13: 1 be subject to the governing authorities. 12
2Es 13:58 because he governs the times 13
AEs 16:15 are governed by most righteous laws 11
Wis 3: 8 They will govern nations and rule over peoples 8
8:14 I shall govern peoples 5
12:18 with great forbearance thou dost govern us 5
Sus 1: 5 elders . . , who were supposed to govern the people. 9
3Mc 6: 2 governing all creation with mercy 4
4Mc 6:33 we properly attribute to it the power to govern. 6

govern a life 1. πολιτεύω
4Mc 5:16 persuaded to govern our lives by the divine law 1

govern well 1. εὐκοσμέω
1Mc 8:15 concerning the people, to govern them well. 1

government 1. מִשְׂרָה 2. ἀρχή 3. ἐξουσία 4. πρᾶγμα
Isa 9: 6 the government will be upon his shoulder 1
7 Of the increase of his government and of peace 1
AEs 13: 5 this people . . is ill-disposed to our government 4
7 leave our government completely secure 4
Sir 10: 4 The government of the earth 3
1Mc 6:56 he was trying to seize control of the government. 4
2Mc 3:38 any enemy or plotter against your government 4
4: 2 to designate as a plotter against the government 4
21 had become hostile to his government 4
5: 7 He did not gain control of the government 2
8: 8 for aid to the king's government. 4
9:24 they would know to whom the government was left. 4
10:11 to have charge of the government 4
11: 1 who was in charge of the government 4
19 maintain your good will toward the government 4
13: 2 who had charge of the government 4
23 who had been left in charge of the government 4
14:10 impossible for the government to find peace. 4
26 Nicanor was disloyal to the government 4
3Mc 3: 7 hostile and greatly opposed to his government. 4
13 I myself and our government are faring well. 4
26 the government will be established 4
6:28 granted . . stability to our government. 4
7: 1 all in authority in his government 4
4 our government would never be . . established 4
11 the king's government. 4
4Mc 4: 3 because I am loyal to the king's government 4
8: 7 have positions of authority in my government 4
12: 5 a leader in the government of the kingdom. 4

government *See also* alter, loyal.

government official 1. χρεία
1Mc 10:41 which the government officials have not paid 1

governor 1. משׁל 2. נָגִיד 3. פֶּחָה 4. שַׂר 5. שַׁלִּיט 6. תִּרְשָׁתָא 7. אֲפָרְסְכָיֵא (A) 8. אֲפָרְסַתְכָיֵא (A) 9. פֶּחָה (A) 10. ἐθνάρχης 11. εἰμὶ ἐπί 12. ἔπαρχος 13. ἐπικρατέω 14. ἐπιστάτης 15. ἡγεμονεύω 16. ἡγεμών 17. ἡγέομαι 18. κυριεύω 19. προστάτης 20. σατράπης 21. στρατηγός 22. τοπαρχής
Gen 42: 6 Now Joseph was governor over the land; 5
1Kg 10:15 which came . . from the governors of the land. 3
20:14 the servants of the governors of the districts. 4
15 the servants of the governors of the districts 4
17 The servants of the governors of the districts 4
19 the servants of the governors of the districts 4
22:26 take him back to Amon the governor of the city 4
2Kg 23: 8 of the gate of Joshua the governor of the city 4
25:22 he appointed Gedali'ah the son of . . governor. *
23 the king . . had appointed Gedali'ah governor *
2Ch 9:14 kings of Arabia and the governors of the land 3
18:25 take him back to Amon the governor of the city 4
19:11 Zebedi'ah . . the governor of the house of Judah 2
23:20 he took . . the governors of the people 1
34: 8 he sent . . Ma-asei'ah the governor of the city 4
Ezr 2:63 governor told them that they were not to partake 6
4: 9 their associates, the judges, the governors 8
5: 3 Tat'tenai the governor of the province Beyond 9
6 Tat'tenai the governor of the province 9
6 associates the governors . . in the province 7
14 Shesh-baz'zar, whom he had made governor; 9
6: 6 therefore, Tat'tenai, governor of the province 9
6 associates the governors . . in the province 7
7 let the governor of the Jews and the elders 9
13 Tat'tenai, the governor of the province 9
8:36 king's commissions . . to the governors 3
Neh 2: 7 governors of the province Beyond the River 3
9 Then I came to the governors of the province 3
3: 7 who were under the jurisdiction of the governor 3
5:14 appointed . . governor in the land of Judah 3
14 neither . . ate the food allowance of the governor. 3
15 former governors who were before me laid heavy 3
18 not demand the food allowance of the governor 3
7: 2 I gave . . Hanani'ah the governor of the castle 4
65 governor told them that they were not to partake 6
70 governor gave to the treasury 1,000 darics of gold 6
8: 9 Nehemi'ah, who was the governor 6
10: 1 Nehemi'ah the governor, the son of Hacali'ah 6
12:26 days of Nehemi'ah the governor and of Ezra 3
Est 1: 3 and the nobles and governors of the provinces 4
3:12 to the king's satraps and to the governors over 3
8: 9 to the satraps and the governors and the princes 3
9: 3 the princes . . and the satraps and the governors 3
Jer 40: 5 whom the king of Babylon appointed governor *
7 Gedali'ah the son of Ahi'kam governor in the land *
11 appointed Gedali'ah . . as governor over them *
41: 2 whom the king of Babylon had appointed governor *
18 whom the king of Babylon had made governor *
51:23 I break in pieces governors and commanders. 3
28 the Medes, with their governors and deputies 3
57 her wise men, her governors, her commanders 3
Ezk 23: 6 governors and commanders, all of them desirable 3
12 Assyrians, governors and commanders, warriors 3
23 desirable young men, governors and commanders 3
Dan 3: 2 assemble the . . governors, the counselors 9
3 Then the satraps, the prefects, and the governors 9
27 satraps, the prefects, the governors 9
6: 7 presidents . . the counselors and the governors 9
Hag 1: 1 to Zerub'babel . . governor of Judah, 3
14 Zerub'babel . . governor of Judah 3
2: 2 Speak now to Zerub'babel . . governor of Judah 3
21 Speak to Zerub'babel, governor of Judah, saying 3
Mal 1: 8 Present that to your governor; will he be pleased 3
Mat 10:18 you will be dragged before governors and kings 16
27: 2 delivered him to Pilate the governor. 16
11 Now Jesus stood before the governor 16
11 the governor asked him 16
14 so that the governor wondered greatly. 16
15 the governor was accustomed to release 16
21 The governor again said to them 16
27 Then the soldiers of the governor took Jesus 16
28:14 if this comes to the governor's ears 16
Mrk 13: 9 stand before governors and kings for my sake 16
Lke 2: 2 when Quirin'ius was governor of Syria. 15
3: 1 Pontius Pilate being governor of Judea 15
20:20 authority and jurisdiction of the governor. 16
21:12 you will be brought before kings and governors 16
Act 7:10 who made him governor over Egypt 17
23:24 and bring him safely to Felix the governor. 16
26 to his Excellency the governor Felix, greeting. 16
33 delivered the letter to the governor 16
24: 1 They laid before the governor their case 16
10 when the governor had motioned to him to speak 16
26:30 Then the king rose, and the governor and Berni'ce 16
2Co 11:32 the governor under King Ar'etas guarded the city 10
1Pe 2:14 or to governors as sent by him to punish 16
1Es 2:12 given to Sheshbazzar the governor of Judea. 19
3: 2 all the satraps and generals and governors 22
14 satraps and generals and governors and prefects 22
4:47 all the treasurers and governors and generals 22
48 he wrote letters to all the governors 22
49 no officer or satrap or governor or treasurer 22
6: 3 Sisinnes the governor of Syria and Phoenicia 12
7 Sisinnes the governor of Syria and Phoenicia 12
18 delivered to . . Sheshbazzar the governor 12
27 Sisinnes the governor of Syria and Phoenicia 12
27 the servant of the Lord and governor of Judea 12
29 Zerubbabel the governor 12
7: 1 Sisinnes the governor of Coelesyria 12
8:67 the governors of Coelesyria and Phoenicia 12
Jdt 5: 2 all the governors of the coastland 20
AEs 13: 1 to the governors under them 22
1Mc 7: 8 governor of the province Beyond the River 18
10:69 Apollonius the governor of Coelesyria 11
11:59 Simon his brother he made governor 21
14:42 that he should be governor over them 21
16:11 appointed governor over the plain of Jericho 21
2Mc 3: 5 who at that time was governor of Coelesyria 21
4: 4 governor of Coelesyria and Phoenicia 21
5:22 he left governors to afflict the people 14
8: 8 he wrote to Ptolemy, the governor of Coelesyria 21
10:11 to be chief governor of Coelesyria and Phoenicia. 21
14 When Gorgias became governor of the region 21
12: 2 some of the governors in various places 21
2 these Nicanor the governor of Cyprus †
32 Gorgias, the governor of Idumea. 21
13:24 governor from Ptolemais to Gerar 21
14:12 appointed him governor of Judea, and sent him off 21
3Mc 2: 3 the creator of all things and the governor of all 13
4Mc 2:22 as a sacred governor over them all. 16
4: 2 he came to Apollonius, governor of Syria 21
7:16 devout reason is governor of the emotions. 16

governor of the province 1. μεριδάρχη
1Mc 10:65 and made him general and governor of the province. 1

gown 1. λινοῦς
Jdt 16: 8 and put on a linen gown to deceive him. 1

grace 1. חֵן 2. נֹעַם 3. χάρις 4. χάρισμα 5. gratia
Est 2:17 and she found grace and favor in his sight 1
Ps 45: 2 grace is poured upon your lips; 1
Jer 31: 2 The people who survived the sword found grace 1
Zec 4: 7 the top stone amid shouts of 'Grace, grace to it! 1
7 the top stone amid shouts of 'Grace, grace to it! 1
11: 7 staffs; one I named Grace, the other I named Union. 2
10 I took my staff Grace, and I broke it 2
Joh 1:14 Word . . dwelt among us, full of grace and truth; 3
16 have we all received, grace upon grace. 3
16 have we all received, grace upon grace. 3
17 grace and truth came through Jesus Christ. 3
Act 4:33 great grace was upon them all. 3
6: 8 Stephen, full of grace and power 3
11:23 When he came and saw the grace of God, he was glad; 3
13:43 urged them to continue in the grace of God. 3
14: 3 who bore witness to the word of his grace 3
26 where they had been commended to the grace of God 3
15:11 saved through the grace of the Lord Jesus 3
40 commended . . to the grace of the Lord. 3
18:27 helped those who through grace had believed 3
20:24 testify to the gospel of the grace of God. 3
32 I commend you . . to the word of his grace 3
Rom 1: 5 we have received grace and apostleship 3
7 Grace to you and peace from God our Father 3
3:24 they are justified by his grace as a gift 3
4:16 in order that the promise may rest on grace 3
5: 2 we have obtained access to this grace 3
15 the grace of God . . abounded for many. 3
15 the free gift in the grace of that one man Jesus 3
17 those who receive the abundance of grace 3
20 where sin increased, grace abounded all the more 3
21 grace also might reign through righteousness 3
6: 1 Are we to continue in sin that grace may abound? 3
14 since you are not under law but under grace. 3
15 because we are not under law but under grace? 3
11: 5 there is a remnant, chosen by grace. 3
6 But if it is by grace, it is no longer on the basis 3
6 otherwise grace would no longer be grace. 3
6 otherwise grace would no longer be grace. 3
12: 3 For by the grace given to me I bid every one 3
6 gifts that differ according to the grace given 4
15:15 because of the grace given me by God 3
16:20 The grace of our Lord Jesus Christ be with you. 3
1Co 1: 3 Grace to you and peace from God our Father 3
4 because of the grace of God which was given you 3
3:10 According to the grace of God given to me 3
15:10 by the grace of God I am what I am 3
10 his grace toward me was not in vain 3
10 though it was not I, but the grace of God 3
16:23 The grace of the Lord Jesus be with you. 3
2Co 1: 2 Grace to you and peace from God our Father 3
12 not by earthly wisdom but by the grace of God. 3
4:15 so that as grace extends to more and more people 3
6: 1 not to accept the grace of God in vain. 3
8: 1 the grace of God which has been shown 3
9 For you know the grace of our Lord Jesus Christ 3
9:14 because of the surpassing grace of God in you. 3
12: 9 he said to me, "My grace is sufficient for you 3
13:14 The grace of the Lord Jesus Christ 3
Gal 1: 3 Grace to you and peace from God the Father 3
6 who called you in the grace of Christ 3
15 called me through his grace 3
2: 9 when they perceived the grace that was given 3

21 I do not nullify the grace of God 3
5: 4 you have fallen away from grace. 3
6:18 The grace of our Lord Jesus Christ 3
Eph 1: 2 Grace to you and peace from God our Father 3
6 to the praise of his glorious grace 3
7 according to the riches of his grace 3
2: 5 (by grace you have been saved) 3
7 might show the immeasurable riches of his grace 3
8 For by grace you have been saved through faith; 3
3: 2 the stewardship of God's grace that was given to me 3
7 according to the gift of God's grace 3
8 To me . . this grace was given 3
4: 7 grace was given to each of us 3
29 that it may impart grace to those who hear. 3
6:24 Grace be with all who love our Lord Jesus Christ 3
Php 1: 2 Grace to you and peace from God our Father 3
7 you are all partakers with me of grace 3
4:23 grace of the Lord Jesus Christ 3
Col 1: 2 Grace to you and peace from God our Father. 3
6 heard and understood the grace of God in truth 3
4:18 Remember my fetters. Grace be with you. 3
1Th 1: 1 Grace to you and peace. 3
5:28 The grace of our Lord Jesus Christ be with you. 3
2Th 1: 2 Grace to you and peace from God the Father 3
12 according to the grace of our God 3
2:16 eternal comfort and good hope through grace 3
3:18 The grace of our Lord Jesus Christ be with you 3
1Ti 1: 2 Grace, mercy, and peace from God the Father 3
14 the grace of our Lord overflowed for me 3
6:21 Grace be with you. 3
2Ti 1: 2 Grace, mercy, and peace from God the Father 3
9 the grace which he gave us in Christ Jesus ages ago 3
2: 1 be strong in the grace that is in Christ Jesus 3
4:22 The Lord be with your spirit. Grace be with you. 3
Tit 1: 4 Grace and peace from God the Father 3
2:11 the grace of God has appeared 3
3: 7 that we might be justified by his grace 3
15 Grace be with you all. 3
Phm 1: 3 Grace to you and peace from God our Father 3
25 The grace of the Lord Jesus Christ 3
Heb 2: 9 that by the grace of God he might taste death 3
4:16 with confidence draw near to the throne of grace 3
16 we may receive mercy and find grace 3
10:29 outraged the Spirit of grace 3
12:15 no one fail to obtain the grace of God 3
13: 9 is well that the heart be strengthened by grace 3
25 Grace be with all of you. Amen. 3
Jas 4: 6 But he gives more grace; therefore it says 3
6 God . . gives grace to the humble. 3
1Pe 1: 2 May grace and peace be multiplied to you. 3
10 The prophets who prophesied of the grace 3
13 set your hope fully upon the grace that is coming 3
3: 7 since you are joint heirs of the grace of life 3
4:10 as good stewards of God's varied grace 3
5: 5 God . . gives grace to the humble. 3
10 the God of all grace, who has called you 3
12 and declaring that this is the true grace of God; 3
2Pe 1: 2 May grace and peace be multiplied to you 3
3:18 grow in the grace and knowledge of our Lord 3
2Jn 1: 3 Grace, mercy, and peace will be with us, from God 3
Jde 1: 4 ungodly persons who pervert the grace of our God 3
Rev 1: 4 Grace to you and peace from him who is and who was 3
2Es 2:32 and my grace will not fail. 5
AEs 15:14 your countenance is full of grace. 3
Wis 3: 9 because grace and mercy are upon his elect 3
4:15 God's grace and mercy are with his elect 3
Sir 37:21 for grace was not given him by the Lord 3
40:22 The eye desires grace and beauty 3

graceful 1. חֵן 2. טוֹב חֵן 3. יפה 4. χάρις

Prv 5:19 lovely hind, a graceful doe. 1
Sng 7: 1 How graceful are your feet in sandals 3
Nah 3: 4 the harlot, graceful and of deadly charms 2
Sir 24:16 my branches are glorious and graceful. 4

gracefulness 1. εὐσχημοσύνη

4Mc 6: 2 the gracefulness of his piety. 1

gracious 1. חֵן 2. חַנּוּן 3. חנן 4. חָסִיד 5. טוֹב 6. נָעִים 7. ἐν χάριτι 8. εὐαπάντητος 9. εὔλαλος 10. εὔφημος 11. ἵλεως 12. φιλάνθρωπος 13. χάρις 14. χαριτόομαι 15. miserator 16. misereor

Gen 43:29 God be gracious to you, my son! 3
Exd 33:19 I will be gracious to whom I will be gracious 3
19 I will be gracious to whom I will be gracious 3
34: 6 a God merciful and gracious, slow to anger 2
Num 6:25 LORD make his face to shine . . and be gracious 3
Rut 2:13 Then she said, "You are most gracious to me, my lord 1
2Sm 12:22 Who knows whether the LORD will be gracious to me 3
2Kg 13:23 the LORD was gracious to them and had compassion 3
2Ch 30: 9 For the LORD your God is gracious and merciful 2
Neh 9:17 God ready to forgive, gracious and merciful 2
31 for thou art a gracious and merciful God. 2
Job 33:24 he is gracious to him, and says, 'Deliver him 3
Ps 4: 1 Be gracious to me, and hear my prayer. 3
6: 2 Be gracious to me, O LORD, for I am languishing; 3
9:13 Be gracious to me, O LORD! Behold what I suffer 3
25:16 Turn thou to me, and be gracious to me; 3
26:11 redeem me, and be gracious to me. 3
27: 7 Hear, O LORD, when I cry aloud, be gracious to me 3
30:10 Hear, O LORD, and be gracious to me! 3
31: 9 Be gracious to me, O LORD, for I am in distress; 3
41: 4 As for me, I said, "O LORD, be gracious to me; 3
10 do thou, O LORD, be gracious to me, and raise me up 3
56: 1 Be gracious to me, O God, for men trample upon me; 3
67: 1 May God be gracious to us and bless us 3
77: 9 Has God forgotten to be gracious? 3
86: 3 be gracious to me, O Lord 3
15 O Lord, art a God merciful and gracious 2
103: 8 The LORD is merciful and gracious 2
111: 4 LORD is gracious and merciful. 2
112: 4 LORD is gracious, merciful, and righteous. 2
116: 5 Gracious is the LORD, and righteous; 2
119:58 be gracious to me according to thy promise. 3
132 Turn to me and be gracious to me, as is thy wont 3
135: 3 sing to his name, for he is gracious! 6
145: 8 The LORD is gracious and merciful 2
13 LORD is . . gracious in all his deeds. 4
147: 1 for he is gracious, and a song of praise is seemly. 6
Prv 11:16 A gracious woman gets honor 1
22:11 purity of heart, and whose speech is gracious 1
Isa 30:18 Therefore the LORD waits to be gracious to you; 3
19 He will surely be gracious to you at the sound 3
33: 2 O LORD, be gracious to us; we wait for thee. 3
Jol 2:13 for he is gracious and merciful, slow to anger 2
Ams 5:15 God of hosts, will be gracious to the remnant 3
Jon 4: 2 for I knew that thou art a gracious God 2
Zec 1:13 gracious and comforting words to the angel 5
Mal 1: 9 that he may be gracious to us. 3
Lke 4:22 wondered at the gracious words 13
Php 4: 8 whatever is gracious, if there is any excellence 10
Col 4: 6 Let your speech always be gracious 7
1Es 8:10 In accordance with my gracious decision 12
2Es 7:133 gracious, because he is gracious to those 15
133 gracious, because he is gracious to those 16
Sir 6: 5 a gracious tongue multiplies courtesies. 9
18:17 Both are to be found in a gracious man. 14
2Mc 2:22 with great kindness became gracious to them– 11
10:26 they besought him to be gracious to them 11
14: 9 the gracious kindness which you show to all. 8

gracious *See also* will, work.

graciously 1. חנן 2. εὐμενῶς 3. χάρις

Jdg 21:22 Grant them graciously to us; because we did not 1
2Kg 25:27 Evil-mero'dach . . graciously freed Jehoi'achin *
Ps 119:29 graciously teach me thy law! 1
29 graciously teach me thy law! *
Prv 26:25 when he speaks graciously, believe him not 1
Wis 6:16 she graciously appears to them in their paths 2
Sir 7:33 Give graciously to all the living 3

graciously *See also* bestow, deal, give.

more graciously 1. κρείττων

Heb 12:24 that speaks more graciously than the blood of Abel. 1

graft 1. ἐγκεντρίζω

Rom 11:17 a wild olive shoot, were grafted in their place 1
19 were broken off so that I might be grafted in. 1
23 even the others . . will be grafted in 1
23 for God has the power to graft them in again. 1

graft into 1. ἐγκεντρίζω

Rom 11:24 grafted . . into a cultivated olive tree 1
24 branches be grafted back into their own olive 1

grain 1. בַּר 2. דָּגָן 3. זֶרַע 4. לֶחֶם 5. מָעָה 6. רִיפָה 7. שִׁבֹּלֶת 8. שֶׁבֶר 9. καρπός 10. κόκκος 11. σιτία 12. σῖτος 13. σπορά 14. σπόρος 15. ψῆφος 16. frumentum 17. granum

Gen 27:28 of the earth, and plenty of grain and wine. 2
37 and with grain and wine I have sustained him. 2
41:35 let them . . lay up grain under the authority 1
49 Joseph stored up grain in great abundance 1
42: 1 When Jacob learned that there was grain in Egypt 8
2 I have heard that there is grain in Egypt; 8
3 brothers went down to buy grain in Egypt. 1
19 carry grain for the famine of your households 8
25 Joseph gave orders to fill their bags with grain 1
26 Then they loaded their asses with their grain 8
33 and take grain for the famine of your households *
43: 2 when they had eaten the grain which they had 8
44: 2 put my cup . . with his money for the grain. 8
45:23 sent . . ten she-asses loaded with grain, bread 1
47:14 money . . for the grain which they bought; 8
Num 18:12 all the best of the wine and of the grain 2
27 it were the grain of the threshing floor 2
20: 5 It is no place for grain, or figs, or vines 3
Deu 7:13 also bless . . grain and your wine and your oil 2
11:14 gather in your grain and your wine and your oil. 2
12:17 not eat . . the tithe of your grain or of your wine 2
14:23 you shall eat the tithe of your grain, of your wine 2
18: 4 first fruits of your grain, of your wine 2
25: 4 not muzzle an ox when it treads out the grain. *
28:51 who also shall not leave you grain, wine, or oil 2
33:28 Israel dwelt . . in a land of grain and wine; 2
Rut 3: 7 he went to lie down at the end of the heap of grain. *
1Sm 8:15 take the tenth of your grain and . . vineyards 3
2Sm 17:19 spread a covering . . and scattered grain upon it; 6
2Kg 18:32 a land like your own land, a land of grain and wine 2
2Ch 31: 5 gave in abundance the first fruits of grain, wine 2
32:28 storehouses also for the yield of grain, wine 2
Neh 5: 2 let us get grain, that we may eat and keep alive. 2
3 mortgaging . . to get grain because of the famine. 2
10 Moreover I . . lending them money and grain. 2
11 Return . . 100th of money, grain, wine, and oil 2
10:31 if the peoples . . bring in wares or any grain 8
39 bring the contribution of grain, wine, and oil 2
13: 5 previously put the . . tithes of grain, wine, and oil 2
12 Judah brought the tithe of the grain, wine, and oil 2
15 bringing in heaps of grain and loading them *
Job 24:24 they are cut off like the heads of grain. 7
39:12 and bring your grain to your threshing floor? 3
Ps 4: 7 than they have when their grain and wine abound. 2
65: 9 thou providest their grain 2
13 the valleys deck themselves with grain 1
72:16 May there be abundance of grain in the land; 1
78:24 manna to eat, and gave them the grain of heaven. 2
Prv 11:26 The people curse him who holds back grain 1
14: 4 Where there are no oxen, there is no grain; 1
Isa 23: 3 your revenue was the grain of Shihor 3
27:12 the LORD will thresh out the grain 7
30:23 will give . . grain, the produce of the ground 4
36:17 like your own land, a land of grain and wine 2
48:19 the sand, and your descendants like its grains; 5
62: 8 I will not again give your grain to be food 2
Jer 31:12 over the grain, the wine, and the oil 2
50:26 pile her up like heaps of grain, and destroy her *
Ezk 36:29 I will summon the grain and make it abundant 2
Hos 2: 8 did not know that it was I who gave her the grain 2
9 Therefore I will take back my grain in its time 2
22 and the earth shall answer the grain, the wine 2
7:14 for grain and wine they gash themselves 2
Jol 1:10 because the grain is destroyed, the wine fails 2
17 are ruined because the grain has failed. 2
2:19 Behold, I am sending to you grain, wine, and oil 2
24 The threshing floors shall be full of grain 1
Ams 8: 5 will the new moon be over, that we may sell grain? 8
Hag 1:11 upon the grain, the new wine, the oil 2
Zec 9:17 Grain shall make the young men flourish 2
Mat 13: 8 and brought forth grain 9
26 when the plants came up and bore grain 9
31 The kingdom of heaven is like a grain of mustard 10
17:20 if you have faith as a grain of mustard seed 10
Mrk 4: 7 it yielded no grain. 9
8 seeds fell into good soil and brought forth grain 9
28 then the ear, then the full grain in the ear. 12
29 when the grain is ripe 9
31 It is like a grain of mustard seed 10
Lke 12:18 there I will store all my grain and my goods. 12
13:19 It is like a grain of mustard seed which a man took 10
17: 6 If you had faith as a grain of mustard seed 10
Joh 12:24 unless a grain of wheat falls into the earth 10
Act 7:12 when Jacob heard that there was grain in Egypt 11
1Co 15:37 perhaps of wheat or of some other grain. *
2Es 4:30 For a grain of evil seed was sown in Adam's heart 17
31 a grain of evil seed has produced. 17
15:42 and grass of the meadows, and their grain. 16
Jdt 11:13 decided to consume the first fruits of the grain 12
Sir 18:10 Like . . a grain of sand 15
40:22 the green shoots of grain more than both. 14
1Mc 8:26 not give or supply grain, arms, money, or ships 12
28 shall be given no grain, arms, money, or ships 12
10:30 instead of collecting the third of the grain 13

grain *See also* bread, buy, ear, head, shock, standing, tread.

crushed grain 1. גֶּרֶשׂ 2. רִיפָה

Lev 2:16 burn . . part of the crushed grain and of the oil 1
Prv 27:22 fool in a mortar . . along with crushed grain 2

new grain 1. חָדָשׁ 2. כַּרְמֶל

Lev 2:14 offer . . crushed new grain from fresh ears 2
23:16 a cereal offering of new grain to the LORD 1
Num 28:26 cereal offering of new grain to the LORD 1

grain of sand 1. ἄμμος

Heb 11:12 the innumerable grains of sand by the seashore. 1

parched grain 1. קלה 2. קָלִי 3. ἄλφιτον

Lev 23:14 eat neither bread nor grain parched or fresh 2
Jos 5:11 they ate . . unleavened cakes and parched grain. 1
Rut 2:14 she sat . . and he passed to her parched grain; 2
1Sm 17:17 Take . . an ephah of this parched grain 2
25:18 five measures of parched grain, and 100 clusters 2
2Sm 17:28 brought . . wheat, barley, meal, parched grain 2
Jdt 10: 5 and filled a bag with parched grain 3

stacked grain 1. גָּדִישׁ

Exd 22: 6 fire breaks out . . so that the stacked grain 1

grainfield 1. σπόριμος

Mat 12: 1 At that time Jesus went through the grainfields 1
Mrk 2:23 he was going through the grainfields 1
Lke 6: 1 while he was going through the grainfields 1

granary 1.מַאֲבוּס 2.מַמְּגֻרוֹת 3.ἀποθήκη
Jer 50:26 open her granaries; pile her up like heaps 1
Jol 1:17 the granaries are ruined 2
Mat 3:12 and gather his wheat into the granary 3
Lke 3:17 to gather the wheat into his granary 3

grandchild 1.בֵּן 2.בֶּן בֵּן
Gen 31:55 Laban arose, and kissed his grandchildren 1
Prv 17: 6 Grandchildren are the crown of the aged 2

grandchildren 1.ἔκγονος
1Ti 5: 4 If a widow has children or grandchildren 1

granddaughter 1.בַּת
2Kg 8:26 was Athali'ah; she was a granddaughter of Omri 1
2Ch 22: 2 Athali'ah, the granddaughter of Omri. 1

grandeur 1.μεγαλεῖος
Sir 17:10 to proclaim the grandeur of his works. 1

grandfather 1.אֲבִי אָב 2.πάππος
Exd 10: 6 your fathers nor your grandfathers have seen 1
Sir 0: 1 my grandfather Jesus, after devoting himself 2

grandmother 1.μάμμη
2Ti 1: 5 dwelt first in your grandmother Lo'is 1
4Mc 16: 9 have the happiness of being called grandmother. 1

grandson 1.בֵּן 2.בֶּן בֵּן 3.υἱός
Gen 11:31 son of Haran, his grandson, and Sar'ai 2
Jdg 8:22 Rule over us, you and your son and your grandson 2
12:14 He had 40 sons and 30 grandsons, who rode 2
1Ch 8:40 bowmen, having many sons and grandsons, 150. 2
2Ch 22: 9 He is the grandson of Jehosh'aphat 1
Jer 27: 7 shall serve him and his son and his grandson 2
Tob 14: 3 he called his son and grandsons 3

grant 1.בוא 2.גמל 3.יהב 4.נשא 5.נתן 6.עשה 7.רִשְׁיוֹן 8.שׂוּם 9.ἀπονέμω 10.ἀφίημι 11.γίνομαι 12.δίδωμι 13.δωρέομαι 14.εἰμί 15.εἰς 16.ἐπιτάσσω 17.λαμβάνω 18.ὁμολογέω 19.παρέχω 20.ποιέω 21.συγχωρέω 22.τίθημι 23.χαρίζομαι 24.do 25.permitto
Gen 19:21 He said to him, "Behold, I grant you this favor 4
43:14 may God Almighty grant you mercy before the man 5
Lev 25:24 you shall grant a redemption of the land 5
Deu 15: 1 end of every seven years you shall grant a release. 6
Jdg 15:18 Thou hast granted this great deliverance 5
21:22 Grant them graciously to us; because we did not •
Rut 1: 9 The LORD grant that you may find a home, 5
1Sm 1:17 Go . . and the God of Israel grant your petition 5
27 I prayed; and the LORD has granted me my petition 5
2Sm 14:21 I grant this; go, bring back the young man Ab'salom. 6
22 the king has granted the request of his servant. 6
1Kg 1:48 who has granted one of my offspring to sit on my 5
8:36 forgive . . and grant rain upon thy land 5
50 grant them compassion in the sight of those who 5
1Ch 4:10 And God granted what he asked. 1
22:12 LORD grant you discretion and understanding 5
29:19 Grant to Solomon my son that with a whole heart 5
2Ch 1:12 wisdom and knowledge are granted to you. 5
6:27 forgive the sin . . and grant rain upon thy land 5
12: 7 but I will grant them some deliverance 5
Ezr 3: 7 according to the grant which they had from Cyrus 7
7: 6 king granted him all that he asked 5
9: 8 grant us a little reviving in our bondage. 5
9 grant us some reviving to set up the house of our God 5
Neh 1:11 grant him mercy in the sight of this man. 5
2: 8 king granted me what I asked, for the good hand 5
Est 2:18 granted a remission of taxes to the provinces 6
5: 6 What is your petition? It shall be granted you. 5
8 and if it please the king to grant my petition 5
7: 2 What is your petition . . ? It shall be granted you. 5
9:12 It shall be granted you. 5
Job 6: 8 and that God would grant my desire; 5
10:12 Thou hast granted me life and steadfast love; 6
13:20 Only grant two things to me, then I will not hide 6
Ps 20: 4 May he grant you your heart's desire 5
60:11 O grant us help against the foe 3
85: 7 O LORD, and grant us thy salvation. 5
108:12 O grant us help against the foe 3
140: 8 Grant not, O LORD, the desires of the wicked; 5
Prv 10:24 but the desire of the righteous will be granted. 5
Isa 16: 3 Give counsel, grant justice; 6
61: 3 to grant to those who mourn in Zion– 8
63: 7 according to all that the LORD has granted us 2
7 which he has granted them according to his mercy 2
Jer 42:12 I will grant you mercy 5
Mat 20:23 is not mine to grant 12
Mrk 6:22 Ask me for whatever you wish, and I will grant it. 12
10:37 Grant us to sit, one at your right hand 12
40 is not mine to grant 12
15:45 he granted the body to Joseph. 13
Lke 1:43 why is this granted me •
74 to grant us that we, being delivered 12
23:24 their demand should be granted. 11
Joh 5:26 he has granted the Son also to have life in himself 12
36 which the Father has granted me to accomplish 12
6:65 unless it is granted him by the Father. 12
Act 3:14 asked for a murderer to be granted to you 23
4:29 grant to thy servants to speak thy word 12
7:17 which God had granted to Abraham 18
11:18 God has granted repentance unto life. 12
14: 3 granting signs . . to be done by their hands. 12
27:24 lo, God has granted you all those who sail with you.' 23
Rom 15: 5 May the God . . grant you to live in such harmony 12
2Co 1:11 the blessing granted us 15
12:16 granting that I myself did not burden you 14
Eph 3:16 he may grant you to be strengthened with might 12
Php 1:29 granted to you that for the sake of Christ 23
2Th 1: 7 to grant rest with us to you who are afflicted •
2Ti 1:16 May the Lord grant mercy 12
18 may the Lord grant him to find mercy from the Lord 12
2: 7 the Lord will grant you understanding 12
25 God may perhaps grant that . . 12
Phm 1:22 through your prayers to be granted to you. 23
2Pe 1: 3 His divine power has granted to us all things 13
4 he has granted to us his precious . . promises 13
Rev 2: 7 To him who conquers I will grant to eat of the tree 12
3:21 I will grant him to sit with me on my throne 12
11: 3 I will grant my two witnesses power to prophesy 12
19: 8 it was granted her to be clothed with fine linen 12
2Es 5: 4 if the Most High grants that you live 24
8: 6 O Lord who are over us, grant to thy servant 25
Tob 7:18 the Lord of heaven and earth grant you joy 12
8: 7 Grant that I may find mercy 16
10:12 grant me to see your children by my daughter 12
Jdt 10: 8 May the God of our fathers grant you favor 12
13:20 May God grant this to be a perpetual honor to you 20
Wis 7:15 May God grant that I speak with judgment 12
12:20 granting them time and opportunity 12
Sir 6:37 your desire for wisdom will be granted. 12
17: 2 granted them authority 12
4 granted them dominion over beasts and birds. •
24 Yet to those who repent he grants a return 12
26: 3 granted among the blessings of the man who fears 12
34:17 he grants healing, life, and blessing. 12
43:33 to the godly he has granted wisdom. 12
45:26 May the Lord grant you wisdom in your heart 12
50:23 grant that peace may be in our days in Israel •
Bar 2:14 for thy own sake deliver us, and grant us favor 12
1Mc 10:28 grant you many immunities and give you gifts. 10
40 I also grant 15,000 shekels of silver 12
11:34 we have granted release from the royal taxes •
36 not one of these grants shall be canceled •
50 Grant us peace 12
58 and granted him the right to drink from gold cups 12
66 Then they asked him to grant them terms of peace 17
13:34 a request to grant relief to the country 20
14:46 agreed to grant Simon the right 22
15: 5 the kings before me have granted you 10
7 I grant freedom to Jerusalem and the sanctuary. •
2Mc 3:31 to grant life 23
33 for his sake the Lord has granted you your life. 23
11:15 the king granted every request 21
35 what Lysias the kinsman of the king has granted 21
12:11 to grant them pledges of friendship 12
3Mc 3:16 we had granted very great revenues to the temples 9
5:11 is bestowed by him who grants it 23
6:28 has granted an unimpeded and notable stability 19
7:12 The king then . . granted them a general license 12
4Mc 5: 8 Why, when nature has granted it to us 23
11:12 they are splendid favors that you grant us 23

grant *See also* make.

grant a request at once 1.συναινέω
3Mc 6:41 The king granted their request at once 1

grant entreaty 1.עתר
1Ch 5:20 God . . granted their entreaty 1

grant in abundance 1.πληθύνω
Sir 18:12 he grants them forgiveness in abundance. 1

grant petition 1.נשא פָּנִים
1Sm 25:35 and I have granted your petition. 1

grant prayer 1.עתר
Gen 25:21 and the LORD granted his prayer 1

grant release 1.ἀφίημι 2.ἐπαρκέω
1Mc 11:35 from all these we shall grant them release. 2
13:37 to grant you release from tribute. 1

grant success 1.קרה לִפְנֵי 2.εὐοδόω
Gen 24:12 O LORD . . grant me success today, I pray thee 1
27:20 Because the LORD your God granted me success. 1
Sir 38:14 grant them success in diagnosis and in healing 2

grape 1.בֹּסֶר 2.עֵנָב 3.תִּירוֹשׁ 4.σταφυλή 5.acinus 6.uva
Gen 40:10 and the clusters ripened into grapes. 2
11 I took the grapes and pressed them into Pharaoh's 2
49:11 he washes . . his vesture in the blood of grapes; 2
Lev 25: 5 grapes of your undressed vine you shall not 2
11 nor gather the grapes from the undressed vines •
Num 6: 3 shall not drink any juice of grapes or eat grapes 2
3 shall not drink . . or eat grapes, fresh or dried. 2
13:23 branch with a single cluster of grapes 2
Deu 23:24 neighbor's vineyard . . eat your fill of grapes 2
28:39 but you shall neither . . nor gather the grapes; •
32:14 of the blood of the grape you drank wine. 2
32 their grapes are grapes of poison 2
32 their grapes are grapes of poison 2
Jdg 8: 2 Is not the gleaning of the grapes of E'phraim •
Neh 13:15 also wine, grapes, figs, and all kinds of burdens 2
Sng 7:12 see . . whether the grape blossoms have opened •
Isa 5: 2 he looked for it to yield grapes 2
4 When I looked for it to yield grapes 2
18: 5 and the flower becomes a ripening grape 1
Jer 8:13 there are no grapes on the vine 2
25:30 and shout, like those who tread grapes •
Hos 9:10 Like grapes in the wilderness, I found Israel. 2
Ams 9:13 and the treader of grapes him who sows the seed; 2
Mic 6:15 you shall tread grapes, but not drink wine. 3
Mat 7:16 Are grapes gathered from thorns 4
Lke 6:44 nor are grapes picked from a bramble bush. 4
Rev 14:18 gather the clusters . . for its grapes are ripe. 4
2Es 9:21 and saved for myself one grape out of a cluster 5
22 but let my grape and my plant be saved 5
16:26 The grapes shall ripen, and who will tread them? 6
Sir 39:26 milk and honey, the blood of the grape, and oil 4
50:15 poured a libation of the blood of the grape 4
51:15 From blossom to ripening grape 4
1Mc 6:34 the juice of grapes and mulberries 4

grape *See also* cluster, gather, gatherer.

fallen grape 1.פֶּרֶט
Lev 19:10 neither shall you gather the fallen grapes 1

ripe grape 1.עֵנָב
Num 13:20 time was the season of the first ripe grapes. 1

unripe grape 1.בֹּסֶר
Job 15:33 He will shake off his unripe grape, like the vine 1

wild grape 1.בְּאֻשִׁים
Isa 5: 2 to yield grapes, but it yielded wild grapes. 1
4 to yield grapes, why did it yield wild grapes? 1

sour grapes 1.בֹּסֶר
Jer 31:29 no longer say: 'The fathers have eaten sour grapes 1
30 each man who eats sour grapes 1
Ezk 18: 2 The fathers have eaten sour grapes 1

grapevine 1.גֶּפֶן הַיַּיִן 2.ἄμπελος
Num 6: 4 eat nothing that is produced by the grapevine 1
Jas 3:12 a fig tree . . yield olives, or a grapevine figs? 2

grapple 1.διαμαχίζομαι
Sir 51:19 My soul grappled with wisdom 1

grasp 1.חזק 2.כַּף 3.לפת 4.קרא 5.תפשׂ 6.γινώσκω 7.δράσσομαι 8.λαμβάνω 9.teneo
Jdg 16:29 Samson grasped the two middle pillars 3
Ps 71: 4 from the grasp of the unjust and cruel man. 2
Prv 27:16 or to grasp oil in his right hand. 4
Isa 45: 1 to Cyrus, whose right hand I have grasped 1
Jer 15:21 and redeem you from the grasp of the ruthless. 2
Ezk 29: 7 when they grasped you with the hand, you broke 5
Lke 18:34 they did not grasp what was said. 6
2Es 10:30 he grasped my right hand and strengthened me 9
Sir 26: 7 taking hold of her is like grasping a scorpion. 7
2Mc 12:35 grasping his cloak 8

thing to grasp 1.ἁρπαγμός
Php 2: 6 not count equality with God a thing to be grasped 1

grass 1.דושׁ 2.דֶּשֶׁא 3.חָצִיר 4.יֶרֶק 5.עֵשֶׂב 6.עֵשֶׂב(A) 7.χόρτος 8.faenum
Num 22: 4 as the ox licks up the grass of the field. 4
Deu 11:15 he will give grass in your fields for your cattle 5
29:23 growing nothing, where no grass can sprout 5
2Sm 23: 4 rain that makes grass to sprout from the earth. 2
1Kg 18: 5 we may find grass and save the horses and mules 3
2Kg 19:26 have become like plants . . and like tender grass 2
26 like tender grass, like grass on the housetops; 3
Job 5:25 your offspring as the grass of the earth. 5
6: 5 Does the wild ass bray when he has grass 2
38:27 to make the ground put forth grass? 2
40:15 Behold, Be'hemoth . . he eats grass like an ox. 3
Ps 37: 2 For they will soon fade like the grass, and wither 3
58: 7 like grass let them be trodden down and wither. •
72:16 from the cities like the grass of the field! 5
90: 5 dream, like grass which is renewed in the morning 3
92: 7 though the wicked sprout like grass 5
102: 4 My heart is smitten like grass, and withered; 5
11 I wither away like grass. 5
103:15 As for man, his days are like grass; 3
104:14 Thou dost cause the grass to grow for the cattle 3
106:20 God for the image of an ox that eats grass. 5
129: 6 Let them be like the grass on the housetops 3
147: 8 he makes grass grow upon the hills. 3
Prv 19:12 but his favor is like dew upon the grass. 5

27:25 When the grass is gone, and the new growth appears 3
Isa 15: 6 the grass is withered, the new growth fails 3
35: 7 the grass shall become reeds and rushes. 3
37:27 like tender grass, like grass on the housetops 2
27 like tender grass, like grass on the housetops 2
40: 6 All flesh is grass, and all its beauty 3
7 The grass withers, the flower fades 3
7 The grass withers . . surely the people is grass. 3
8 The grass withers, the flower fades; 3
44: 4 They shall spring up like grass amid waters 3
51:12 who dies, of the son of man who is made like grass 3
66:14 your bones shall flourish like the grass; 2
Jer 12: 4 and the grass of every field wither? 5
14: 5 forsakes her . . calf because there is no grass. 2
50:11 though you are wanton as a heifer at grass 1
Dan 4:15 lot be with the beasts in the grass of the earth; 6
25 made to eat grass like an ox, and you shall be wet 6
32 shall be made to eat grass like an ox; 6
33 driven from among men, and ate grass like an ox 6
5:21 fed grass like an ox, and his body was wet 6
Ams 7: 2 they had finished eating the grass of the land 5
Mic 5: 7 dew from the LORD, like showers upon the grass 5
Mat 6:30 But if God so clothes the grass of the field 7
14:19 he ordered the crowds to sit down on the grass 7
Mrk 6:39 to sit down by companies upon the green grass. 7
Lke 12:28 if God so clothes the grass 7
Joh 6:10 Now there was much grass in the place 7
Jas 1:10 like the flower of the grass he will pass away. 7
11 the sun rises . . and withers the grass 7
1Pe 1:24 All flesh is like grass 7
24 and all its glory like the flower of grass. 7
24 The grass withers, and the flower falls 7
Rev 8: 7 and all green grass was burnt up. 7
9: 4 they were told not to harm the grass of the earth 7
2Es 9:27 after seven days, as I lay on the grass 8
15:42 and grass of the meadows, and their grain. 8
Sir 40:16 will be plucked up before any grass. 7

dry grass 1. חֲשַׁשׁ
Isa 5:24 and as dry grass sinks down in the flame 1

mown grass 1. גֵּז
Ps 72: 6 May he be like rain that falls on the mown grass 1

reed grass 1. אָחוּ
Gen 41: 2 seven cows . . and they fed in the reed grass. 1
18 came up out of the Nile and fed in the reed grass; 1

tender grass 1. דֶּשֶׁא 2. יֶרֶק 3. דִּתְאָ(A) 4. χλόη
Deu 32: 2 as the dew, as the gentle rain upon the tender grass 1
Isa 37:27 like plants of the field and like tender grass 2
Dan 4:15 amid the tender grass of the field. 3
23 iron and bronze, in the tender grass of the field; 3
Sir 43:21 withers the tender grass like fire. 4

grasshopper 1. אַרְבֶּה 2. חָגָב
Lev 11:22 may eat . . the grasshopper according to its kind 2
Num13:33 we seemed to ourselves like grasshoppers 2
Ecc 12: 5 grasshopper drags itself along and desire fails; 2
Isa 40:22 and its inhabitants are like grasshoppers; 2
Nah 3:15 multiply like the grasshopper! 1
17 Your princes are like grasshoppers 1

grassy 1. χλοηφόρος
Wis 19: 7 a grassy plain out of the raging waves 1

grateful 1. ἀχάριστος 2. χάρις
Heb 12:28 Therefore let us be grateful 2
Sir 29:17 one who does not feel grateful 1
2Mc 3:33 Be very grateful to Onias the high priest 2

gratify 1. εἰς 2. τελέω
Rom13:14 make no provision for the flesh, to gratify its desires. 1
Gal 5:16 do not gratify the desires of the flesh. 2

grating 1. מִכְבָּר
Exd 27: 4 You shall also make for it a grating 1
35:16 with its grating of bronze, its poles, and all its 1
38: 4 he made for the altar a grating, a network 1
5 four corners of the bronze grating as holders 1
30 the bronze altar and the bronze grating for it 1
39:39 the bronze altar, and its grating of bronze 1

gratitude 1. εὐχαριστία 2. χάρις 3. gratia
Act 24: 3 we accept this with all gratitude. 1
2Es 1:37 I call to witness the gratitude of the people 3
Sir 20:16 there is no gratitude for my good deeds 2
37:11 with a grudging man about gratitude 1
2Mc 2:27 However, to secure the gratitude of many 1

grave 1. קֶבֶר 2. קְבֻרָה 3. שְׁאוֹל 4. αἴδης 5. μνημεῖον 6. τάφος 7. τόπος 8. sepulchrum
Gen 35:20 Jacob set up a pillar upon her grave; 2
Exd 14:11 Is it because there are no graves in Egypt 1
Num19:16 Whoever . . touches . . a bone of a man, or a grave 1
18 upon him who touched the . . dead, or the grave; 1
2Sm 3:32 and the king . . wept at the grave of Abner; 1
19:37 die . . near the grave of my father and my mother. 1
1Kg 13:30 he laid the body in his own grave; 1
31 bury me in the grave in which the man of God is 1
14:13 he only of Jerobo'am shall come to the grave 1
2Kg 13:21 and the man was cast into the grave of Eli'sha; 1
22:20 and you shall be gathered to your grave in peace 1
23: 6 cast . . upon the graves of the common people. 1
2Ch 34: 4 made dust of them and strewed it over the graves 1
28 you shall be gathered to your grave in peace 1
Job 3:22 and are glad, when they find the grave? 1
5:26 You shall come to your grave in ripe old age 1
10:19 carried from the womb to the grave. 1
17: 1 my days are extinct, the grave is ready for me. 1
21:32 When he is borne to the grave 1
Ps 49:11 Their graves are their homes for ever 6
14 straight to the grave they descend •
55:15 let them go away in terror into their graves. •
88: 5 like the slain that lie in the grave 1
11 Is thy steadfast love declared in the grave 1
Sng 8: 6 love is strong . . jealousy is cruel as the grave. 3
Isa 53: 9 they made his grave with the wicked 1
Jer 20:17 so my mother would have been my grave 1
Ezk 32:22 all her company, their graves round about her 1
23 whose graves are set in the uttermost parts 1
23 the Pit, and her company is round about her grave; 2
24 Elam . . and all her multitude about her grave; 2
25 all her multitude, their graves round about her 1
26 their multitude, their graves round about them 1
37:12 says the Lord GOD: Behold, I will open your graves 1
12 open your graves, and raise you from your graves 1
13 know that I am the LORD, when I open your graves 1
13 and raise you from your graves, O my people. 1
Nah 1:14 I will make your grave, for you are vile. 1
Lke 11:44 you are like graves which are not seen 5
Rom 3:13 Their throat is an open grave 6
2Es 2:23 commit them to the grave and mark it 8
5:35 Or why did not my mother's womb become my grave 8
Tob 3:10 I shall bring his old age down in sorrow to the grave. 4
4: 4 bury her beside me in the same grave. 6
17 Place your bread on the grave of the righteous 6
6:14 and bring . . to the grave in sorrow on my account 6
8: 9 Raguel arose and went and dug a grave 6
18 he ordered his servants to fill in the grave. 6
Wis 19: 3 were lamenting at the graves of their dead 6
Sir 30:18 like offerings of food placed upon a grave. 6
Bar 2:24 bones . . would be brought out of their graves; 7

grave (2) 1. כבד 2. μέγας
Gen 18:20 is great and their sin is very grave 1
2Mc 1:11 Having been saved by God out of grave dangers 2

grave (3) 1. חקק 2. חרת
Exd 32:16 the writing of God, graven upon the tables. 2
Isa 49:16 Behold, I have graven you on the palms of my hands; 1

grave *See* dig.

gravel 1. חָצָץ
Prv 20:17 but afterward his mouth will be full of gravel. 1
Lam 3:16 He has made my teeth grind on gravel 1

graven 1. חצב 2. γλυπτός
Job 19:24 they were graven in the rock for ever! 1
Wis 14:16 graven images were worshiped. 2
15:13 fragile vessels and graven images. 2

graving tool 1. חֶרֶט
Exd 32: 4 and fashioned it with a graving tool, and made 1

gravity 1. σεμνότης
Tit 2: 7 in your teaching show integrity, gravity 1

gray 1. שׂיב 2. שֵׂיבָה
1Sm 12: 2 I am old and gray, and behold, my sons are with you; 1
1Kg 2: 6 do not let his gray head go down to Sheol in peace. 2
9 you shall bring his gray head down with blood 2
Zec 6: 3 the fourth chariot dappled gray horses. •

gray *See also* hair, haired.

graze 1. רעה
Isa 5:17 Then shall the lambs graze as in their pasture 1
27:10 there the calf grazes, there he lies down 1
30:23 your cattle will graze in large pastures; 1

cause to graze over 1. בער
Exd 22: 5 causes a field or vineyard to be grazed over 1

grazing *See* land.

great 1. גָּבֹהַּ 2. גבר 3. גָּדוֹל 4. גדול 5. גדל 6. גְּדֶל 7. הָרָה 8. כָּבֵד 9. כַּבִּיר 10. לְמַעְלָה 11. לָרֹב 12. מְאֹד 13. מִדָּה 14. עָצוּם 15. עצם 16. רַב 17. רֹב 18. רבה 19. רום 20. רַע 21. שגה 22. שַׂגִּיא 23. גְּלָל(A) 24. רַב(A) 25. שַׂגִּיא(A) 26. ἀγαθός 27. βαρύς 28. ἡλίκος 29. ἱκανός 30. ἰσχυρός 31. κράτος 32. λίαν 33. μεγαλεῖος 34. μεγαλύνω 35. μεγάλως 36. μέγας 37. μεγιστάνων 38. μεγιστάω 39. ὀνικός 40. πᾶς 41. περισσότερος 42. περισσῶς 43. πλῆθος 44. πολύς 45. προβαίνω 46. πῶς μᾶλλον 47. σφόδρα 48. τηλικοῦτος 49. τοσοῦτος 50. amplus 51. celsus 52. copiosus 53. gemo 54. magnus 55. multiplico 56. multitudo 57. multus 58. non modicus 59. tantus 60. valde
Gen 1:16 God made the two great lights 3
16 two great lights, the greater light to rule 3
21 God created the great sea monsters 3
4:13 My punishment is greater than I can bear. 3
6: 5 the wickedness of man was great in the earth 16
7:11 the fountains of the great deep burst forth 16
10:12 Nin'eveh and Calah; that is the great city. 3
12: 2 make of you a great nation, and I will bless you 3
17 Pharaoh and his house with great plagues 3
13: 6 for their possessions were so great 16
13 were wicked, great sinners against the LORD. 12
15: 1 I am your shield; your reward shall be very great. 18
12 and lo, a dread and great darkness fell upon him. 3
14 they shall come out with great possessions. 3
18 of Egypt to the great river, the river Euphra'tes 3
17:20 princes, and I will make him a great nation. 3
18:18 Abraham shall become a great and mighty nation 3
20 Sodom and Gomor'rah is great and their sin 18
19:11 the men . . both small and great 3
20: 9 brought on me and my kingdom a great sin? 3
21: 8 and Abraham made a great feast 3
18 for I will make him a great nation. 3
26:14 He had . . a great household 16
27:34 with an exceedingly great and bitter cry 3
36: 7 For their possessions were too great for them 16
39: 9 he is not greater in this house than I am; 3
9 how then can I do this great wickedness, and sin 3
41:29 There will come seven years of great plenty 3
40 the throne will I be greater than you. 5
49 Joseph stored up grain in great abundance 12
46: 3 for I will there make of you a great nation. 3
48:19 and he also shall be great; nevertheless his 5
19 his younger brother shall be greater than he 5
50: 9 horsemen; it was a very great company. 8
10 lamented there with a very great and sorrowful 3
Exd 3: 3 I will turn aside and see this great sight 3
6: 6 redeem you . . with great acts of judgment 3
7: 4 out of . . Egypt by great acts of judgment. 3
8:24 there came great swarms of flies into the house 8
11: 3 Moreover, the man Moses was very great in the land 3
6 there shall be a great cry throughout all 3
12:30 and there was a great cry in Egypt 3
14:10 and they were in great fear. 12
31 Israel saw the great work which the LORD did 3
18:11 Now I know that the LORD is greater than all gods 3
22 every great matter they shall bring to you 3
32:10 but of you I will make a great nation. 3
11 brought forth . . with great power 3
21 that you have brought a great sin upon them? 3
30 You have sinned a great sin. And now I will go up 3
31 said, "Alas, this people have sinned a great sin; 3
Lev 19:15 not be partial to the poor or defer to the great 3
Num11:33 LORD smote the people with a very great plague. 16
14:12 you a nation greater and mightier than they. 3
17 let the power of the LORD be as great as thou hast 5
22: 3 Moab was in great dread of the people 12
17 for I will surely do you great honor 12
32: 1 sons of Gad had a very great multitude of cattle; 14
34: 6 you shall have the Great Sea and its coast 3
7 from the Great Sea you shall mark out your line 3
Deu 1: 7 as far as the great river, the river Euphra'tes. 3
17 you shall hear the small and the great alike; 3
19 through all that great and terrible wilderness 3
28 The people are greater and taller than we; 3
28 the cities are great and fortified up to heaven; 3
2: 7 knows your going through this great wilderness; 3
10 Emim . . a people great and many, and tall 3
21 a people great and many, and tall as the Anakim; 3
4: 6 great nation is a wise and understanding people.' 3
7 what great nation is there that has a god so near 3
8 what great nation is there, that has statutes 3
32 ask . . whether such a great thing as this 3
34 by . . an outstretched arm, and by great terrors 3
36 on earth he let you see his great fire 3
37 brought you out of Egypt . . by his great power 3
38 driving out . . nations greater and mightier 3
5:25 For this great fire will consume us; 3
6:10 great and goodly cities, which you did not build 3
22 showed signs and wonders, great and grievous 3
7: 1 Jeb'usites, seven nations greater and mightier 16
17 These nations are greater than I; how can I 16
19 great trials which your eyes saw, the signs 3
21 in the midst of you, a great and terrible God. 3
23 over to you, and throw them into great confusion 3
8:15 led you through the great and terrible wilderness 3
9: 1 nations greater and mightier than yourselves 3
1 cities great and fortified up to heaven 3
2 people great and tall, the sons of the Anakim 3
14 nation mightier and greater than they.' 16
29 whom thou didst bring out by thy great power 3
10:17 great, the mighty, and the terrible God 3
11: 7 all the great work of the LORD which he did. 3
23 nations greater and mightier than yourselves. 3
18:16 me not . . see this great fire any more, lest I die.' 3
26: 5 became a nation, great, mighty, and populous. 3

8 with great terror, with signs and wonders; 3
29: 3 great trials which your eyes saw 3
3 your eyes saw, the signs, and those great wonders; 3
24 What means the heat of this great anger?' 3
28 uprooted . . in anger and fury and great wrath 3
Jos 1: 4 as far as the great river, the river Euphra'tes 3
4 all the land of the Hittites to the Great Sea 3
6: 5 all the people shall shout with a great shout; 3
20 As soon as the . . the people raised a great shout 3
7: 9 what wilt thou do for thy great name? 3
26 And they raised over him a great heap of stones 3
8:29 and raised over it a great heap of stones 3
9: 1 the lowland all along the coast of the Great Sea 3
10: 2 Gibeon was a great city, like . . the royal cities 3
2 it was greater than Ai, and all its men were mighty. 3
10 who slew them with a great slaughter at Gibeon 3
11 the LORD threw down great stones from heaven 3
18 Roll great stones against the mouth of the cave 3
20 slaying them with a very great slaughter 3
27 set great stones against the mouth of the cave 3
11: 4 they came out, with all their troops, a great host 16
8 smote them and chased them as far as Great Sidon 16
14:12 Anakim were there, with great fortified cities 3
15 this Arba was the greatest man among the Anakim. 3
15:12 And the west boundary was the Great Sea with its 3
47 to . . and the Great Sea with its coast-line. 3
17:17 You are a numerous people, and have great power; 3
19:28 Rehob, Hammon, Kanah, as far as Sidon the Great; 16
22:10 an altar by the Jordan, an altar of great size. 3
23: 4 from the Jordan to the Great Sea in the west. 3
9 driven out before you great and strong nations; 3
24:17 and who did those great signs in our sight 3
26 and he took a great stone, and set it up there 3
Jdg 2: 7 all the great work which the LORD had done 3
5:15 there were great searchings of heart 3
16 there were great searchings of heart. 3
11:33 he smote them . . with a very great slaughter. 3
12: 2 and my people had a great feud with the Ammonites; 12
15: 8 he smote them hip and thigh with great slaughter; 3
18 Thou hast granted this great deliverance 3
16: 5 see wherein his great strength lies 3
6 Please tell me wherein your great strength lies 3
15 not told me wherein your great strength lies. 3
23 gathered to offer a great sacrifice to Dagon 3
20:38 when they made a great cloud of smoke rise up out *
21: 5 they had taken a great oath concerning him who 3
1Sm 1:16 speaking out of my great anxiety and vexation. 17
2:17 the sin . . was very great in the sight of the LORD; 3
4: 6 What does this great shouting . . mean? 3
10 and there was a very great slaughter 3
17 has also been a great slaughter among the people; 3
5: 9 LORD was against . . causing a very great panic 3
6: 9 if . . then it is he who has done us this great harm; 3
14 A great stone was there; 3
15 took down the . . and set them upon the great stone; 3
18 The great stone, beside which they set . . the ark 3
19 the LORD had made a great slaughter 3
12:16 see this great thing, which the LORD will do 3
17 shall know and see that your wickedness is great 16
22 not cast away his people, for his great name's sake 3
14:20 and there was very great confusion. 3
30 now the slaughter . . has not been great. 18
33 roll a great stone to me here. 3
45 who has wrought this great victory in Israel? 3
15:22 Has the LORD as great delight in . . as in obeying *
17:25 the king will enrich with great riches 3
18:15 And when Saul saw that he had great success 12
19: 5 the LORD wrought a great victory for all Israel. 3
8 and made a great slaughter among them 3
22 went to Ramah, and came to the great well . . in Secu; 3
20: 2 my father does nothing either great or small 3
23: 5 fought . . and made a great slaughter among them. 3
26:13 stood afar off . . with a great space between them; 16
28:15 Saul answered, "I am in great distress; 12
30: 2 taken . . all who were in it, both small and great; 3
16 because of all the great spoil they had taken 3
19 Nothing was missing, whether small or great 3
2Sm 5:10 And David became greater and greater 3
10 And David became greater and greater †
7: 9 and I will make for you a great name 3
22 Therefore thou art great, O LORD God; 5
12:30 brought forth the spoil . . a very great amount. 18
13:15 Then Amnon hated her with very great hatred; 3
15 the hatred . . was greater than the love 3
16 wrong in sending me . . is greater than the other 3
18: 7 and the slaughter there was great on that day 3
9 mule went under the thick branches of a great oak 3
17 they took Ab'salom, and threw him into a great pit 3
17 raised over him a very great heap of stones; 3
29 When Jo'ab sent your servant, I saw a great tumult 3
20: 8 they were at the great stone which is in Gibeon 3
23:10 and the LORD wrought a great victory that day; 3
12 and the LORD wrought a great victory. 3
20 was a valiant man . . a doer of great deeds; 16
24:14 I am in great distress, let us fall into the hand 12
14 into the hand of the LORD, for his mercy is great; 16
1Kg 1:40 playing on pipes, and rejoicing with great joy 3
3: 4 to Gibeon . . for that was the great high place; 3
6 Thou hast shown great and steadfast love to thy 3
6 hast kept for him this great and steadfast love 3
8 a great people, that cannot be numbered 16
9 for who is able to govern this thy great people? 8
4:13 60 great cities with walls and bronze bars); 3
5: 7 given . . a wise son to be over this great people. 16
17 they quarried out great, costly stones 3
7: 9 court of the house of the LORD to the great court. 3
12 The great court had three courses of hewn stone 3
8:42 hear of thy great name, and thy mighty hand 3
65 and all Israel with him, a great assembly 3
10: 2 She came to Jerusalem with a very great retinue 8
10 gold, and a very great quantity of spices 18
11 brought from Ophir a very great amount of almug 18
18 The king also made a great ivory throne 3
11:19 Hadad found great favor in the sight of Pharaoh 12
18:32 trench . . as great as would contain two measures *
45 heavens grew black . . and there was a great rain. 3
19: 7 eat, else the journey will be too great for you. 16
11 a great and strong wind rent the mountains 3
20:13 Have you seen all this great multitude? 3
21 and killed the Syrians with a great slaughter. 3
28 give all this great multitude into your hand 3
22:31 Fight with neither small nor great, but only 3
2Kg 3:27 And there came great wrath upon Israel; 3
4:38 Set on the great pot, and boil pottage 3
5: 1 Na'aman . . was a great man with his master 3
13 prophet had commanded you to do some great thing 3
6:14 he sent . . horses and chariots and a great army; 8
23 So he prepared for them a great feast; 3
25 there was a great famine in Sama'ria 3
7: 6 chariots, and of horses, the sound of a great army 3
8:13 What is . . that he should do this great thing? 3
10:19 I have a great sacrifice to offer to Ba'al; 3
16:15 Upon the great altar burn the morning burnt offering 3
17:21 Jerobo'am . . and made them commit great sin. 3
36 brought you out . . with great power 3
18:17 and the Rab'shakeh with a great army from Lachish 8
19 Thus says the great king, the king of Assyria 3
28 Hear the word of the great king 3
22:13 Go, inquire . . for great is the wrath of the LORD 3
23: 2 all the people, both small and great; 3
26 turn from the fierceness of his great wrath 3
25: 9 every great house he burned down. 3
26 all the people, both small and great . . arose 3
1Ch 11:14 and the LORD saved them by a great victory. 3
22 a valiant man of Kabzeel, a doer of great deeds; 16
12:14 the lesser over 100 and the greater over 1,000. 3
22 until there was a great army, like an army of God. 3
16:25 For great is the LORD, and greatly to be praised 3
20: 2 the spoil of the city, a very great amount. 18
21:13 Then David said to Gad, "I am in great distress; 12
13 the hand of the LORD, for his mercy is very great; 16
22: 8 have shed much blood and have waged great wars; 3
25: 8 they cast lots for their duties, small and great 3
26:13 they cast lots . . small and great alike 3
29: 1 young and inexperienced, and the work is great; 3
22 ate and drank . . that day with great gladness. 3
25 LORD gave Solomon great repute in the sight 10
2Ch 1: 8 Thou hast shown great and steadfast love 3
10 who can rule this thy people, that is so great? 3
2: 5 The house which I am to build will be great 3
5 house . . will be great, for our God is greater 3
9 house I am to build will be great and wonderful. 3
4: 9 made the court of the priests, and the great court 3
6:32 from a far country for the sake of thy great name 3
7: 8 all Israel with him, a very great congregation 3
9: 1 having a very great retinue and camels 8
17 The king also made a great ivory throne 3
13:17 Abij'ah . . slew them with a great slaughter; 16
15: 5 great disturbances afflicted 16
16:14 they made a very great fire in his honor. 3
17: 5 Jehosh'aphat; and he had great riches and honor. 17
13 he had great stores in the cities of Judah. 16
18: 1 Now Jehosh'aphat had great riches and honor; 11
30 Fight with neither small nor great 3
20: 2 great multitude is coming against you from Edom 16
12 we are powerless against this great multitude 16
15 be not dismayed at this great multitude; 16
21: 3 Their father gave them great gifts 16
14 LORD will bring a great plague on your people 3
19 bowels came out . . and he died in great agony. 20
24:24 LORD delivered into their hand a very great army 11
26:15 engines . . to shoot arrows and great stones. 3
28: 5 Israel, who defeated him with great slaughter. 3
13 For our guilt is already great 16
30:13 many people came . . a very great assembly. 11
21 kept the feast . . with great gladness 3
26 there was great joy in Jerusalem 3
32: 4 A great many people were gathered *
7 for there is one greater with us than with him. 16
27 Hezeki'ah had very great riches and honor; 18
29 God had given him very great possessions. 16
34:21 great is the wrath of the LORD that is poured out 3
30 all the people both great and small; 3
36:18 vessels of the house of God, great and small 3
Ezr 3:11 all the people shouted with a great shout 3
13 for the people shouted with a great shout 3
4:10 nations whom the great and noble Osnap'par 16
5: 8 went to . . Judah, to the house of the great God. 24
11 which a great king of Israel built and finished. 24
6: 4 with three courses of great stones 23
9: 7 to this day we have been in great guilt; 3
13 for our evil deeds and for our great guilt 3
10: 1 very great assembly of men, women, and children 16
Neh 1: 3 escaped exile are in great trouble and shame; 3
5 O LORD God of heaven, the great and terrible God 3
10 people . . thou hast redeemed by thy great power 3
3:27 section opposite the great projecting tower 3
4:14 Remember the Lord, who is great and terrible 3
19 The work is great and widely spread 18
5: 1 Now there arose a great outcry of the people 3
7 And I held a great assembly against them 3
6: 3 I am doing a great work and I cannot come down. 3
8: 6 Ezra blessed the Lord, the great God; 3
12 send portions and to make great rejoicing 3
17 And there was very great rejoicing. 3
9:18 when they . . had committed great blasphemies 3
19 thou in thy great mercies didst not forsake them 16
25 delighted themselves in thy great goodness. 3
26 disobedient . . committed great blasphemies. 3
27 according to thy great mercies thou didst give 16
31 in thy great mercies thou didst not make an end 16
32 our God, the great and mighty and terrible God 3
35 did not serve thee . . in thy great goodness 16
37 we are in great distress. 3
12:31 appointed two great companies which gave 3
43 offered great sacrifices that day and rejoiced 3
43 God had made them rejoice with great joy; 3
13:27 then listen to you and do all this great evil 3
Est 1: 5 all . . in Susa the capital, both great and small 3
2:18 the king gave a great banquet to all his princes 3
4: 3 there was great mourning among the Jews 3
8:15 robes of blue and white, with a great golden crown 3
9: 4 For Mor'decai was great in the king's house 3
10: 3 and he was great among the Jews and popular 3
Job 1: 3 this man was the greatest of all the people 3
19 behold, a great wind came across the wilderness 3
2:13 for they saw that his suffering was very great. 5
3:19 The small and the great are there 3
8: 2 and the words of your mouth be a great wind? 9
7 your latter days will be very great. 21
22: 5 Is not your wickedness great? 16
31:25 if I have rejoiced because my wealth was great 16
34 because I stood in great fear of the multitude 16
33:12 I will answer you. God is greater than man. 18
36:26 Behold, God is great, and we know him not; 22
37:23 he is great in power and justice 22
38:21 the number of your days is great! 16
39:11 you depend on him because his strength is great 16
Ps 12: 3 cut off . . the tongue that makes great boasts 3
19:11 in keeping them there is great reward. 16
13 and innocent of great transgression. 16
21: 5 His glory is great through thy help; 3
22:25 thee comes my praise in the great congregation; 16
25:11 O LORD, pardon my guilt, for it is great. 16
26:12 in the great congregation I will bless the LORD. *
32: 6 rush of great waters, they shall not reach him. 16
33:16 A king is not saved by his great army; 16
16 a warrior is not delivered by his great strength. 16
17 by its great might it cannot save. 17
35:18 Then I will thank thee in the great congregation; 16
27 be glad, and say evermore, "Great is the LORD 5
36: 6 thy judgments are like the great deep; 16
40: 9 news of deliverance in the great congregation; 16
10 thy faithfulness from the great congregation. 16
16 say continually, "Great is the LORD! 5
47: 2 is terrible, a great king over all the earth. 3
48: 1 Great is the LORD and greatly to be praised 3
2 Zion, in the far north, the city of the great King. 16
53: 5 There they are, in great terror †
57:10 For thy steadfast love is great to the heavens 3
66: 3 So great is thy power that thy enemies cringe 17
68:11 great is the host of those who bore the tidings 16
70: 4 who love thy salvation say evermore, "God is great! 5
76: 1 In Judah God is known, his name is great in Israel. 3
77:13 What god is great like our God? 3
19 thy path through the great waters; 16
79:11 according to thy great power preserve 6
86:10 For thou art great and doest wondrous things 3
13 For great is thy steadfast love toward me; 3
89: 7 great and terrible above all that are round 16
92: 5 How great are thy works, O LORD! 5
95: 3 For the LORD is a great God, and a great King 3
3 For the LORD is . . a great King above all gods. 3
96: 4 For great is the LORD, and greatly to be praised; 3
99: 2 The LORD is great in Zion; 3
3 praise thy great and terrible name! Holy is he! 3
103:11 so great is his steadfast love toward those who 2
104: 1 O LORD my God, thou art very great! 5
25 Yonder is the sea, great and wide, which teems 3
25 living things both small and great. 3
107:23 doing business on the great waters; 16
108: 4 thy steadfast love is great above the heavens 3
109:30 With my mouth I will give great thanks to the LORD; 12
111: 2 Great are the works of the LORD 3
115:13 bless . . who fear the LORD, both small and great. 3
117: 2 For great is his steadfast love toward us; 2
119:156 Great is thy mercy, O LORD; 16

162 I rejoice . . like one who finds great spoil. 16
165 Great peace have those who love thy law; 16
135: 5 For I know that the LORD is great 3
136: 4 to him who alone does great wonders 3
7 to him who made the great lights 3
17 to him who smote the great kings 3
138: 5 for great is the glory of the LORD. 3
145: 3 Great is the LORD, and greatly to be praised 3
147: 5 Great is our LORD, and abundant in power; 3
Prv 5:23 because of his great folly he is lost. 17
13: 7 another pretends to be poor, yet has great wealth. 16
14:29 He who is slow to anger has great understanding 16
15:16 Better . . than great treasure and trouble with it. 16
16: 8 Better . . than great revenues with injustice. 17
19:19 A man of great wrath will pay the penalty; 5
22: 1 good name . . be chosen rather than great riches 16
25: 6 Do not . . stand in the place of the great; 3
28:12 When the righteous triumph, there is great glory; 16
Ecc 1:16 I have acquired great wisdom, surpassing all 5
16 and my mind has had great experience of wisdom 18
2: 7 I had also great possessions of herds and flocks 18
21 This also is vanity and a great evil. 16
9:13 I have also seen this . . and it seemed great to me. 3
14 and a great king came against it and besieged it 3
14 and besieged it, building great siegeworks 3
10: 4 deference will make amends for great offenses. 3
12: 9 and arranging proverbs with great care. 18
Isa 9: 2 who walked in darkness have seen a great light; 3
10:10 images were greater than those of Jerusalem •
33 the great in height will be hewn down 19
12: 6 for great in your midst is the Holy One of Israel. 3
13: 4 a tumult on the mountains as of a great multitude! 16
16:14 contempt, in spite of all his great multitude 16
27: 1 the LORD with his hard and great and strong sword 3
13 in that day a great trumpet will be blown 3
29: 6 with earthquake and great noise, with whirlwind 3
30:25 in the day of the great slaughter 16
32: 2 like the shade of a great rock in a weary land. 8
34: 6 LORD has . . a great slaughter in the land of Edom. 3
36: 2 to King Hezeki'ah at Jerusalem, with a great army. 8
4 Thus says the great king, the king of Assyria 3
13 Hear the words of the great king 3
38:17 for my welfare that I had great bitterness; •
47: 9 and the great power of your enchantments. 12
51:10 didst dry up the sea, the waters of the great deep; 16
53:12 I will divide him a portion with the great 16
54: 7 but with great compassion I will gather you. 3
13 and great shall be the prosperity of your sons. 16
56:12 will be like this day, great beyond measure. 3
63: 7 and the great goodness to the house of Israel 16
Jer 4: 6 evil from the north, and great destruction. 3
5: 5 I will go to the great, and will speak to them; 3
6 their apostasies are great. 15
6: 1 for evil looms . . and great destruction. 3
13 For from the least to the greatest of them 3
22 a great nation is stirring 3
8:10 the least to the greatest every one is greedy 3
10: 6 There is none like thee, O LORD; thou art great 3
6 thou art great, and thy name is great in might. 3
22 Hark, a rumor! Behold, it comes!–a great commotion 3
11:16 with the roar of a great tempest he will set fire 3
13: 9 pride of Judah and the great pride of Jerusalem. 16
14:17 my people is smitten with a great wound 3
16: 6 Both great and small shall die in this land; 3
10 Why has the LORD pronounced all this great evil 3
20:17 and her womb for ever great. 7
21: 5 in anger, and in fury, and in great wrath. 3
6 they shall die of a great pestilence. 3
22: 8 Why has the LORD dealt thus with this great city? 3
14 who says, 'I will build myself a great house 13
25:14 many nations and great kings shall make slaves 3
32 and a great tempest is stirring 3
26:19 we are about to bring great evil upon ourselves. 3
27: 5 I who by my great power and my outstretched arm 3
7 and great kings shall make him their slave. 3
28: 8 against many countries and great kingdoms. 3
30: 7 Alas! that day is so great there is none like it; 3
14 because your guilt is great, because your sins 17
15 pain is incurable. Because your guilt is great 17
31: 8 a great company, they shall return here. 3
34 know me, from the least of them to the greatest 3
32:17 made the heavens and the earth by thy great power 3
18 O great and mighty God whose name is the LORD 3
19 great in counsel and mighty in deed; 3
21 hand and outstretched arm, and with great terror; 3
37 in my anger and my wrath and in great indignation; 3
42 Just as I have brought all this great evil 3
33: 3 and will tell you great and hidden things 3
36: 7 for great is the anger and wrath 3
40:12 wine and summer fruits in great abundance. 12
41:12 They came upon him at the great pool 16
42: 1 all the people from the least to the greatest 3
8 and all the people from the least to the greatest 3
44: 7 Why do you commit this great evil 3
12 from the least to the greatest, they shall die 3
15 and all the women who stood by, a great assembly 3
26 I have sworn by my great name, says the LORD 3
48: 3 'Desolation and great destruction!' 3
50: 9 against Babylon a company of great nations 3
22 battle is in the land, and great destruction! 3
51:54 from Babylon! The noise of great destruction 3
52:13 every great house he burned down. 3
Lam 1: 1 a widow . . she that was great among the nations! 16
3:23 new every morning; great is thy faithfulness. 16
4: 6 chastisement . . greater than the punishment 5
Ezk 1: 4 wind came out of the north, and a great cloud 3
3:12 I heard behind me the sound of a great earthquake; 3
13 wheels . . that sounded like a great earthquake. 3
8: 6 see what they are doing, the great abominations 3
6 you will see still greater abominations. 3
13 You will see still greater abominations 3
15 You will see still greater abominations 3
9: 9 The guilt of . . Judah is exceedingly great; 3
13:11 be a deluge of rain, great hailstones will fall •
13 and great hailstones in wrath to destroy it. •
17: 3 A great eagle with great wings and long pinions 3
3 A great eagle with great wings and long pinions 3
7 there was another great eagle with great wings 3
7 there was another great eagle with great wings 3
17 Pharaoh with his mighty army and great company 16
21:14 it is the sword for the great slaughter 3
25:17 I will execute great vengeance upon them 3
26:19 the deep over you, and the great waters cover you 16
27:12 because of your great wealth of every kind; 17
18 goods, because of your great wealth of every kind; 17
28: 5 by your great wisdom in trade you have increased 17
29: 3 Pharaoh king of Egypt, the great dragon that lies 3
30:16 fire to Egypt; Pelusium shall be in great agony; †
31: 3 and of great height, its top among the clouds. 1
6 under its shadow dwelt all great nations. 16
36:23 I will vindicate the holiness of my great name 3
37:10 upon their feet, an exceedingly great host. 3
38: 4 a great company, all of them with buckler 16
13 take away cattle and goods, to seize great spoil 3
15 riding on horses, a great host, a mighty army; 3
19 shall be a great shaking in the land of Israel; 3
39:17 a great sacrificial feast upon the mountains 3
47:10 of very many kinds, like the fish of the Great Sea. 3
15 from the Great Sea by way of Hethlon 3
19 thence along the Brook of Egypt to the Great Sea. 3
20 the Great Sea shall be the boundary to a point 3
48:28 thence along the Brook of Egypt to the Great Sea. 3
Dan 2: 6 receive . . gifts and rewards and great honor. 25
10 no great and powerful king has asked such a thing 24
31 You saw, O king, and behold, a great image. 25
35 stone . . became a great mountain and filled 24
45 great God has made known to the king what shall be 24
48 gave Daniel high honors and many great gifts 24
4: 3 How great are his signs, how mighty his wonders! 24
10 midst of the earth; and its height was great. 25
30 great Babylon, which I have built by my mighty 24
5: 1 King Belshaz'zar made a great feast 24
7: 2 four winds . . were stirring up the great sea. 24
3 four great beasts came up out of the sea 24
7 great iron teeth; it devoured and broke in pieces 24
11 looked . . because of the sound of the great words 24
17 four great beasts are four kings who shall arise 24
20 horn . . which seemed greater than its fellows. 24
8: 8 when he was strong, the great horn was broken 3
21 great horn between his eyes is the first king. 3
24 His power shall be great, and he shall cause 15
9: 4 O Lord, the great and terrible God 3
12 by bringing upon us a great calamity; 3
18 but on the ground of thy great mercy. 16
10: 1 word was true, and it was a great conflict. 3
4 as I was standing on the bank of the great river 3
7 but a great trembling fell upon them 3
8 I was left alone and saw this great vision 3
11: 3 rule with great dominion and do according 16
5 his dominion shall be a great dominion. 16
10 war and assemble a multitude of great forces 16
11 raise a great multitude, but it shall be given 16
13 again raise a multitude, greater than the former; 16
13 come on with a great army and abundant supplies. 3
25 against the king of the south with a great army; 3
25 war with an exceedingly great and mighty army; 3
28 he shall return to his land with great substance 3
44 shall go forth with great fury to exterminate 3
12: 1 Michael, the great prince who has charge 3
Hos 1: 2 for the land commits great harlotry †
11 for great shall be the day of Jezreel. 3
5:13 went to Assyria, and sent to the great king. •
9: 7 because of your great iniquity 17
7 because of your . . great hatred. 16
10: 6 carried to Assyria, as tribute to the great king. •
15 done to you . . because of your great wickedness. †
Jol 2: 2 upon the mountains a great and powerful people; 16
11 his army, for his host is exceedingly great; 16
11 For the day of the LORD is great and very terrible; 3
25 my great army, which I sent among you. 3
31 before the great and terrible day of the LORD 3
3:13 The vats overflow, for their wickedness is great. 16
Ams 3: 9 of Sama'ria, and see the great tumults within her 16
15 the great houses shall come to an end 16
5:12 your transgressions, and how great are your sins 14
6: 2 Calneh, and see; and thence go to Hamath the great; 16
2 is their territory greater than your territory 16
11 the great house shall be smitten into fragments 3
7: 4 and it devoured the great deep 16
Jon 1: 2 Arise, go to Nin'eveh, that great city 3
4 the LORD hurled a great wind upon the sea 3
12 this great tempest has come upon you. 3
17 LORD appointed a great fish to swallow up Jonah; 3
3: 2 Arise, go to Nin'eveh, that great city, and proclaim 3
3 Now Nin'eveh was an exceedingly great city 3
5 from the greatest of them to the least of them. 3
4:11 And should not I pity Nin'eveh, that great city 3
Mic 5: 4 for now he shall be great to the ends of the earth. 5
Nah 1: 3 The LORD is slow to anger and of great might 5
Zep 1:14 The great day of the LORD is near 3
Hag 2: 9 latter splendor of this house shall be greater 3
Zec 4: 7 What are you, O great mountain? 3
7:12 great wrath came from the LORD of hosts. 3
8: 2 I am jealous for Zion with great jealousy 3
2 I am jealous for her with great wrath. 3
12:11 the mourning in Jerusalem will be as great 5
14:13 a great panic from the LORD shall fall on them 16
14 gold, silver, and garments in great abundance. 12
Mal 1: 5 Great is the LORD, beyond the border of Israel! 5
11 my name is great among the nations, says the LORD 3
11 my name is great among the nations, says the LORD 3
14 I am a great King, says the LORD of hosts 3
4: 5 before the great and terrible day of the LORD 3
Mat 2:10 star, they rejoiced exceedingly with great joy; 36
4:16 the people who sat in darkness have seen a great 36
25 And great crowds followed him from Galilee 44
5:12 for your reward is great in heaven, for so men 44
19 shall be called great in the kingdom of heaven. 36
35 for it is the city of the great King. 36
7:27 and it fell; and great was the fall of it. 36
8: 1 great crowds followed him; 44
18 Now when Jesus saw great crowds around him •
24 behold, there arose a great storm on the sea 36
26 and there was a great calm. 36
11:11 has risen no one greater than John the Baptist 36
11 least in the kingdom of heaven is greater than he. 36
12: 6 something greater than the temple is here. 36
41 behold, something greater than Jonah is here. 44
42 behold, something greater than Solomon is here. 44
13: 2 great crowds gathered about him 44
32 when it has grown it is the greatest of shrubs 36
14:14 As he went ashore he saw a great throng 44
15:28 Jesus answered her, "O woman, great is your faith! 36
30 great crowds came to him 44
33 bread enough . . to feed so great a crowd? 49
18: 1 Who is the greatest in the kingdom of heaven? 36
4 he is the greatest in the kingdom of heaven. 36
6 have a great millstone fastened round his neck 39
19:22 for he had great possessions. 44
20:26 whoever would be great among you 36
29 a great crowd followed him. 44
22:36 Teacher, which is the great commandment 36
38 This is the great and first commandment. 36
23:11 He who is greatest among you 36
17 which is greater, the gold or the temple 36
19 which is greater, the gift or the altar 36
24:21 For then there will be a great tribulation 36
24 false prophets will arise and show great signs 36
30 with power and great glory; 44
26:47 with him a great crowd with swords and clubs 44
27:60 rolled a great stone to the door of the tomb 36
28: 2 behold, there was a great earthquake 36
8 with fear and great joy 36
Mrk 1:35 in the morning, a great while before day, he rose 32
3: 7 a great multitude from Galilee followed 44
8 from about Tyre and Sidon a great multitude 44
4:32 becomes the greatest of all shrubs 36
37 a great storm of wind arose 36
39 the wind ceased, and there was a great calm. 36
5:11 Now a great herd of swine was feeding there 36
21 a great crowd gathered about him 44
24 a great crowd followed him and thronged about 44
6:34 As he went ashore he saw a great throng 44
8: 1 when again a great crowd had gathered 44
9:14 they saw a great crowd about them 44
34 who was the greatest. 36
10:22 he had great possessions. 44
43 whoever would be great among you 36
46 his disciples and a great multitude 29
12:31 no other commandment greater than these. 36
37 the great throng heard him gladly. 44
40 They will receive the greater condemnation. 41
13: 2 Do you see these great buildings? 36
26 coming in clouds with great power and glory. 44
Lke 1:15 for he will be great before the Lord 36
32 He will be great 36
58 the Lord had shown great mercy to her 34
2:10 behold, I bring you good news of a great joy 36
36 she was of a great age 45
4:25 when there came a great famine over all the land; 36
5: 6 they enclosed a great shoal of fish 44
15 great multitudes gathered to hear 44
29 Levi made him a great feast in his house 36
6:17 with a great crowd of his disciples 44
17 a great multitude of people from all Judea 44
23 for behold, your reward is great in heaven 44
35 your reward will be great 44

49 the ruin of that house was great. 36
7:11 his disciples and a great crowd went with him. 44
16 A great prophet has arisen among us! 36
28 none is greater than John 36
28 who is least in the kingdom of God is greater than he. 36
8: 4 And when a great crowd came together 44
37 they were seized with great fear 36
9:37 a great crowd met him. 44
46 which of them was the greatest. 36
48 who is least among you all is the one who is great. 36
11:31 behold, something greater than Solomon is here. 44
32 behold, something greater than Jonah is here. 44
14:16 A man once gave a great banquet, and invited many; 36
25 Now great multitudes accompanied him 44
15:14 a great famine arose in that country 30
16:26 between us and you a great chasm has been fixed 36
20:47 They will receive the greater condemnation. 41
21:11 there will be great earthquakes 36
11 terrors and great signs from heaven. 36
23 great distress shall be upon the earth 36
27 coming in a cloud with power and great glory. 44
22:24 which of them was to be regarded as the greatest. 36
26 the greatest among you become as the youngest 36
27 which is the greater 36
23:27 followed him a great multitude of the people 44
24:52 they returned to Jerusalem with great joy, 36
Joh 4:12 Are you greater than our father Jacob 36
5:20 greater works than these will he show him 36
36 the testimony . . is greater than that of John 36
7:37 On the last day of the feast, the great day 36
8:53 Are you greater than our father Abraham, who died? 36
10:29 My Father . . is greater than all 36
12: 9 When the great crowd of the Jews learned 44
12 a great crowd who had come to the feast heard 44
13:16 a servant is not greater than his master 36
16 nor is he who is sent greater than he who sent him. 36
14:12 greater works than these will he do 36
28 the Father is greater than I. 36
15:13 Greater love has no man than this 36
20 'A servant is not greater than his master.' 36
19:11 who delivered me to you has the greater sin. 36
Act 2:20 the great and manifest day. 36
4:33 with great power 36
33 great grace was upon them all. 36
5: 5 great fear came upon all who heard of it. 36
11 great fear came upon the whole church 36
6: 7 a great many of the priests 44
8 did great wonders and signs among the people. 36
7:11 there came a famine . . and great affliction 36
8: 1 a great persecution arose against the church 36
2 made great lamentation over him. 36
9 saying that he himself was somebody great. 36
10 all gave heed . . from the least to the greatest 36
10 that power of God which is called Great. 36
13 seeing signs and great miracles performed 36
10:11 something descending, like a great sheet 36
11: 5 like a great sheet 36
21 a great number that believed turned to the Lord. 44
28 there would be a great famine over all the world; 36
14: 1 so spoke that a great company believed 44
15: 3 they gave great joy to all the brethren. 36
28 no greater burden than these necessary things 44
16:26 suddenly there was a great earthquake 36
17: 4 as did a great many of the devout Greeks 44
19:27 the temple of the great goddess Ar'temis 36
28 Great is Ar'temis of the Ephesians! 36
34 Great is Ar'temis of the Ephesians! 36
35 the city . . is temple keeper of the great Ar'temis 36
21:40 when there was a great hush 44
22: 6 a great light from heaven suddenly shone about me 29
23: 9 Then a great clamor arose 36
25:23 Agrippa and Berni'ce came with great pomp 44
26:22 I stand here testifying both to small and great 36
24 your great learning is turning you mad. 44
Rom 6:19 to impurity and to greater and greater iniquity †
9: 2 great sorrow and unceasing anguish in my heart. 36
1Co 12:23 we invest with the greater honor 41
23 treated with greater modesty 41
24 giving the greater honor to the inferior part 41
13:13 but the greatest of these is love. 36
14: 5 He who prophesies is greater than he who speaks 36
2Co 3: 8 the Spirit be attended with greater splendor? 46
6: 4 through great endurance, in afflictions 44
7: 4 I have great confidence in you 44
4 I have great pride in you; I am filled with comfort 44
8:22 because of his great confidence in you. 44
9:11 You will be enriched in every way for great generosity 40
Eph 1:19 according to the working of his great might 31
2: 4 out of the great love with which he loved us 44
1Th 2: 2 in the face of great opposition. 44
17 we endeavored . . with great desire to see you 44
1Ti 3:13 great confidence in the faith which is in Christ 44
16 Great indeed . . is the mystery of our religion 36
6: 6 is great gain in godliness with contentment; 36
2Ti 2:20 In a great house 36
4:14 Alexander the coppersmith did me great harm 44
Tit 2:13 glory of our great God and Savior Jesus Christ 36
Heb 4:14 Since then we have a great high priest 36
6:13 since he had no one greater by whom to swear 36
16 Men indeed swear by a greater than themselves 36
8:11 from the least of them to the greatest. 36
9:11 then through the greater and more perfect tent 36
10:21 since we have a great priest over the house of God 36
35 your confidence, which has a great reward. 36
11:26 greater wealth than the treasures of Egypt 36
12: 1 surrounded by so great a cloud of witnesses 49
13:20 our Lord Jesus, the great shepherd of the sheep 36
Jas 3: 1 we . . shall be judged with greater strictness. 36
4 Look at the ships also; though they are so great 48
5 How great a forest is set ablaze by a small fire! 28
5:16 The prayer of a righteous man has great power 44
1Pe 1: 3 By his great mercy we have been born anew 44
2Pe 2:11 angels, though greater in might and power 36
1Jn 3:20 for God is greater than our hearts 36
4: 4 greater than he who is in the world. 36
5: 9 testimony of men, the testimony of God is greater; 36
3Jn 1: 4 No greater joy can I have than this 36
Jde 1: 6 kept . . until the judgment of the great day; 36
Rev 2:22 I will throw into great tribulation 36
6: 4 and he was given a great sword. 36
12 I looked, and behold, there was a great earthquake; 36
17 for the great day of their wrath has come 36
7: 9 a great multitude which no man could number 44
14 they who have come out of the great tribulation; 36
8: 8 something like a great mountain, burning 36
10 great star fell from heaven, blazing like a torch 36
9: 2 rose smoke like the smoke of a great furnace 36
14 angels . . bound at the great river Euphra'tes. 36
11: 8 the great city which is allegorically called 36
11 and great fear fell on those who saw them. 36
13 And at that hour there was a great earthquake 36
17 hast taken thy great power and begun to reign. 36
18 those who fear thy name, both small and great 36
12: 1 a great portent appeared in heaven, a woman 36
3 great red dragon, with seven heads and ten horns 36
9 And the great dragon was thrown down 36
12 for the devil has come down to you in great wrath 36
14 woman was given the two wings of the great eagle 36
13: 2 dragon gave his power . . and great authority. 36
13 It works great signs, even making fire come down 36
16 all, both small and great, both rich and poor 36
14: 8 Fallen, fallen is Babylon the great 36
19 into the great wine press of the wrath of God; 36
15: 1 another portent in heaven, great and wonderful 36
3 Great and wonderful are thy deeds, O Lord God 36
16:14 to assemble them for battle on the great day 36
18 a great earthquake such as had never been 36
18 so great was that earthquake. 36
19 The great city was split into three parts 36
19 and God remembered great Babylon 36
21 great hailstones . . dropped on men from heaven 36
17: 1 I will show you the judgment of the great harlot 36
5 Babylon the great, mother of harlots 36
18 And the woman that you saw is the great city 36
18: 1 I saw another angel . . having great authority; 36
2 Fallen, fallen is Babylon the great! 36
10 alas! thou great city, thou mighty city, Babylon! 36
16 Alas, alas, for the great city 36
18 What city was like the great city? 36
19 Alas, alas, for the great city 36
21 angel took up a stone like a great millstone 36
21 So shall Babylon the great city be thrown down 36
19: 1 a loud voice of a great multitude in heaven 36
2 judged the great harlot who corrupted the earth 36
5 his servants, you who fear him, small and great. 36
6 what seemed to be the voice of a great multitude 44
17 Come, gather for the great supper of God 36
18 and the flesh of all men . . both small and great. 36
20:11 I saw a great white throne and him who sat upon it; 36
12 dead, great and small, standing before the throne 36
21:10 he carried me away to a great, high mountain 36
12 It had a great, high wall, with twelve gates 36
1Es 1:54 all the holy vessels of the Lord, great and small 36
3: 1 Now King Darius gave a great banquet 36
5 give rich gifts and great honors of victory. 36
4:14 is not the king great, and are not men many 36
28 Is not the king great in his power? 36
35 Is he not great who does these things? 36
35 Is he not great who does these things? 36
41 Great is truth, and strongest of all! 36
5:62 sounded trumpets and shouted with a great shout 36
6: 9 building . . a great new house for the Lord 36
14 a king of Israel who was great and strong 36
8: 7 For Ezra possessed great knowledge 44
76 we are in great sin to this day. 36
86 because of our evil deeds and our great sins 36
91 there gathered about him a very great throng 44
91 there was great weeping among the multitude. 36
9: 2 he was mourning over the great iniquities 36
11 the multitude is great and it is winter 44
54 to make great rejoicing; 35
2Es 1:14 and did great wonders among you 54
2:42 I, Ezra, saw on Mount Zion a great multitude 54
43 In their midst was a young man of great stature 51
3:16 and Jacob became a great multitude. 54
4:32 how great a threshing floor they will fill! 54
45 whether for us the greater part has gone by. 57
50 and the fire is greater than the smoke 50
5: 1 shall be seized with great terror 57
7:12 and involved in great hardships. 54
13 the entrances of the greater world are broad 54
91 they shall see with great joy the glory of him 57
92 because they have striven with great effort 57
98 The seventh order, which is greater than all 54
8:14 with so great labor was fashioned by thy command 59
49 in order to receive the greatest glory. 57
50 because they have walked in great pride. 57
9:16 as a wave is greater than a drop of water. 55
21 I saw and spared some with great difficulty 60
21 and one plant out of a great forest. 57
45 and we gave great glory to the Mighty One. 60
10:11 she who lost so great a multitude 54
24 Therefore shake off your great sadness 57
11:29 for it was greater than the other two heads. 54
12: 3 Then I awoke in great perplexity of mind 57
3 in great perplexity of mind and great fear 54
5 because of the great fear 57
18 great struggles shall arise 58
40 from the least to the greatest 54
13: 6 he carved out for himself a great mountain 54
11 the flaming breath and the great storm 56
13 Then in great fear I awoke 56
19 they shall see great dangers and much distress 54
57 giving great glory and praise to the Most High 57
15:19 and because of great tribulation. 57
30 and with great power they shall come 54
31 if they combine in great power and turn to pursue 54
37 there shall be fear and great trembling 57
40 great and mighty clouds 54
16:21 earth–the sword, famine, and great confusion. 54
26 For in all places there shall be great solitude; 57
38 Just as a woman . . has great pains about her womb 53
68 behold, the burning wrath of a great multitude 52
70 there shall be a great insurrection 57
Tob 3: 6 great is the sorrow within me 44
16 in the presence of the glory of the great God. 36
4:13 For in pride there is ruin and great confusion; 44
13 in shiftlessness there is loss and great want 36
21 You have great wealth if you fear God 44
5:12 I am Azarias the son of the great Ananias 36
13 the sons of the great Shemaiah 36
8:16 thou hast treated us according to thy great mercy. 44
12:22 confessed the great and wonderful works of God 36
13:15 Let my soul praise God the great King. 36
Jdt 1: 1 the great city of Nineveh 36
5 the great plain which is on the borders of Ragae. 36
8 Upper Galilee and the great Plain of Esdraelon 36
2: 5 Thus says the Great King 36
3: 2 the servants of Nebuchadnezzar, the Great King 36
9 fronting the great ridge of Judea; 36
4: 9 cried out to God with great fervor 36
5:10 there they became a great multitude 44
10 so great that they could not be counted. •
7: 2 a very great multitude. 44
18 supply trains spread out in great number 44
24 you have done us a great injury 36
29 Then great and general lamentation arose 36
8: 8 she feared God with great devotion. 47
19 they suffered a great catastrophe 36
12:16 he was moved with great desire to possess her 47
20 drank a great quantity of wine 47
13: 4 no one, either small or great, was left 36
13 They all ran together, both small and great 36
14: 9 the people raised a great shout 36
15: 5 outflanked them with great slaughter 36
9 you are the great glory of Israel 36
9 you are the great pride of our nation! 36
10 you have done great good to Israel •
16:13 O Lord, thou are great and glorious 36
16 he who fears the Lord shall be great for ever. 36
AEs 10: 9 God has done great signs and wonders 36
11: 2 the reign of Artaxerxes the Great 36
3 a great man, serving in the court of the king. 36
6 behold, two great dragons came forward 36
8 affliction and great tumult upon the earth! 36
10 there came a great river, with abundant water; 36
13: 1 The Great King, Artaxerxes . . writes thus 36
16: 1 The Great King, Artaxerxes 36
Wis 3: 5 they will receive great good 36
5: 1 righteous man will stand with great confidence 44
6: 7 because he himself made both small and great 36
11:21 it is always in thy power to show great strength 35
12:18 with great forbearance thou dost govern us 44
14:22 they live in great strife due to ignorance 36
16:17 the fire had still greater effect 44
17: 1 Great are thy judgments and hard to describe; 36
Sir 0: 1 many great teachings have been given to us 36
3 using . . great watchfulness and skill 44
3:20 For great is the might of the Lord 36
5: 6 Do not say, "His mercy is great 44
15 In great and small matters do not act amiss 36
7:25 you will have finished a great task 36
10:24 greater than the man who fears the Lord. 36
11: 1 will seat him among the great. 37
15:18 For great is the wisdom of the Lord 44
16:12 As great as his mercy, so great is also his reproof; 44
12 As great as his mercy, so great is also his reproof; 44

17:29 How great is the mercy of the Lord 36
18: 9 The number of a man's days is great 44
32 Do not revel in great luxury 36
24:29 and her counsel deeper than the great abyss. 36
25:10 How great is he who has gained wisdom! 36
22 There is wrath and impudence and great disgrace 36
26: 3 A good wife is a great blessing 26
8 There is great anger when a wife is drunken 36
31:12 Are you seated at the table of a great man? 4
32: 9 Among the great do not act as their equal 38
33:18 Hear me, you who are great among the people 38
39: 6 If the great Lord is willing 36
11 he will leave a name greater than 1,000 *
41:12 longer than 1,000 great stores of gold. 36
42:11 put you to shame before the great multitude. 44
43: 5 Great is the Lord who made it 36
28 he is greater than all his works. 36
29 Terrible is the Lord and very great 36
32 Many things greater than these lie hidden 36
44: 2 The Lord apportioned to them great glory 44
19 the great father of a multitude of nations 36
46: 1 He became . . a great savior of God's elect 36
6 the great Lord answered him 36
48:22 who was great and faithful in his vision. 36
50:16 they made a great noise 36
Bar 1: 4 in the hearing of all the people, small and great 36
2:11 with great power and outstretched arm 36
27 all thy kindness and in all thy great compassion 36
29 this very great multitude will surely turn 36
3:24 O Israel, how great is the house of God! And how vast 36
25 It is great and has no bounds; it is high 36
4: 9 God has brought great sorrow upon me; 36
24 salvation . . will come to you with great glory 36
Sus 1:31 Now Susanna was a woman of great refinement 47
64 Daniel had a great reputation among the people. 36
Bel 1:18 You are great, O Bel; and with you there is no deceit 36
23 a great dragon, which the Babylonians revered. 36
41 Thou art great, O Lord God of Daniel 36
Man 1: 7 Thou, O Lord, according to thy great goodness 43
14 thou wilt save me in thy great mercy 44
1Mc 1:24 spoke with great arrogance. 36
33 fortified . . with a great strong wall 36
35 became a great snare. 36
40 Her dishonor now grew as great as her glory *
64 very great wrath came upon Israel. 36
2:17 You are a leader, honored and great in this city 36
51 receive great honor and an everlasting name. 36
58 Elijah because of great zeal for the law †
70 Israel mourned for him with great lamentation. 36
3:17 fight against so great and strong a multitude 49
20 come against us in great pride and lawlessness 43
4:23 and cloth dyed blue and sea purple, and great riches. 36
25 Thus Israel had a great deliverance that day. 36
39 mourned with great lamentation 36
58 There was very great gladness among the people 36
5:16 a great assembly was called 36
23 led them to Judea with great rejoicing. 36
45 the small and the great 36
61 Thus the people suffered a great rout 36
6: 4 So he fled and in great grief departed from there 36
11 into what a great flood I now am plunged! 36
7: 8 a great man in the kingdom 36
19 killed them and threw them into a great pit. 36
22 did great damage in Israel. 36
35 he went out in great anger. 36
48 celebrated that day as a day of great gladness. 36
8: 4 inflicted great disaster upon them 36
6 They also defeated Antiochus the Great, king of Asia 36
9:20 all Israel made great lamentation for him 36
24 In those days a very great famine occurred 36
27 Thus there was great distress in Israel 36
37 sons of Jambri are celebrating a great wedding 36
37 a daughter of one of the great nobles of Canaan 36
56 Alcimus died at that time in great agony. 36
10:37 stationed in the great strongholds of the king 36
46 because they remembered the great wrongs 36
58 celebrated her wedding . . with great pomp 36
86 came out to meet him with great pomp. 36
11: 1 Then the king of Egypt gathered great forces 44
12:49 into Galilee and the Great Plain 36
52 and were in great fear 47
13:17 lest he arouse great hostility among the people 36
26 All Israel bewailed him with great lamentation 36
29 erecting about them great columns 36
32 he brought great calamity upon the land. 36
33 with high towers and great walls and gates 36
42 In the first year of Simon the great high priest 36
44 a great tumult arose in the city. 36
51 because a great enemy had been crushed 36
14:11 Israel rejoiced with great joy. 36
27 the third year of Simon the great high priest 36
28 in Asaramel, in the great assembly of the priests 36
29 they brought great glory to their nation. 36
32 He spent great sums of his own money 44
36 do great damage to its purity. 36
15: 9 we will bestow great honor upon you 36
29 you have done great damage in the land 36
32 when he saw . . his great magnificence 29
35 they were causing great damage among the people 36
16:15 he gave them a great banquet, and hid men there. 36
17 So he committed an act of great treachery 36
2Mc 1:22 a great fire blazed up, so that all marveled. 36
2:18 he has rescued us from great evils 36
19 the purification of the great temple 36
22 with great kindness became gracious to them– 40
3:21 the high priest in his great anguish. 35
24 caused so great a manifestation 36
28 with a great retinue and all his bodyguard 44
5: 6 success . . is the greatest misfortune 36
20 when the great Lord became reconciled. 36
26 and killed great numbers of people. 29
6:13 is a sign of great kindness. 36
8:27 giving great praise and thanks to the Lord 42
10:38 who shows great kindness to Israel 35
12:15 calling upon the great Sovereign of the world 36
24 With great guile he besought them to let him go 44
27 great stores of war engines and missiles 44
14:13 as high priest of the greatest temple. 36
31 he went to the great and holy temple 36
15:18 their greatest and first fear 36
3Mc 2: 9 the glory of your great and honored name. 36
12 rescued them from great evils 36
13 because of our many and great sins 36
3:15 clemency and great benevolence 44
5:10 been filled with a great abundance of wine 44
23 began to move them along in the great colonnade. 36
6:17 they raised great cries to heaven 36
33 after convening a great banquet 27
7: 2 the great God guiding our affairs 36
21 They also possessed greater prestige 44
22 God perfectly performed great deeds 33
4Mc 4:10 instilling in them great fear and trembling. 44
5:20 in matters either small or great 36
11:23 I myself will bring a great avenger upon you 36
13:15 for great is the struggle of the soul 36
15: 9 she felt a greater tenderness toward them. 36

great *See also* ability, affliction, amount, army, body, care, compassion, congregation, delight, excitement, festivity, give, grow, honor, joy, length, make, millstone, misery, multitude, number, pain, population, power, quantity, refinement, stature, store, such, terror, toe, value, variety, while, wickedness.

become great 1. גדל 2. הלך וְגָדוֹל
Gen 19:13 the outcry . . has become great before the LORD 1
24:35 he has become great; he has given him flocks 1
1Ch 11: 9 David became greater and greater 2
Ecc 2: 9 I became great and surpassed all 1
Jer 5:27 therefore they have become great and rich 1

great deed 1. גָּדוֹל
Deu 34:12 all the great and terrible deeds which Moses 1

do a great thing 1. גדל
1Sm 12:24 consider what great things he has done for you. 1

exceedingly great 1. *ὑπερβάλλω*
3Mc 2:23 panic-stricken in their exceedingly great fear. 1

how great 1. *πηλίκος* 2. *πόσος* 3. *τίς* 4. qualis
Mat 6:23 you is darkness, how great is the darkness! 2
Col 1:27 how great . . are the riches . . of this mystery 3
Heb 7: 4 See how great he is! 1
2Es 2:48 tell my people how great and many are the wonders 4
4Mc 15:22 How great and how many torments 1

great in stature 1. *εὐμεγέθης*
Bar 3:26 giants . . great in stature, expert in war. 1

great lizard 1. צָב
Lev 11:29 the mouse, the great lizard according to its kind 1

make great 1. גדל
Gen 12: 2 I will bless you, and make your name great 1
Ezk 24: 9 I also will make the pile great. 1

great man 1. גָּדוֹל 2. *μέγας* 3. *μεγιστάν* 4. *μεγιστάω*
2Sm 3:38 a prince and a great man has fallen this day 1
2Kg 10: 6 king's sons . . were with the great men of the city 1
11 Jehu slew all that remained . . all his great men 1
Prv 18:16 A man's gift . . brings him before great men. 1
Mic 7: 3 the great man utters the evil desire of his soul; 1
Nah 3:10 and all her great men were bound in chains. 1
Mat 20:25 their great men exercise authority over them. 2
Mrk 10:42 their great men exercise authority over them. 2
Rev 6:15 Then the kings of the earth and the great men 3
18:23 thy merchants were the great men of the earth 3
Sir 4: 7 bow your head low to a great man. 3
8: 8 learn how to serve great men. 3
20:27 a sensible man will please great men. 4
28 whoever pleases great men 4
23:14 when you sit among great men 4
28:14 overturned the houses of great men. 3
38: 3 in the presence of great men he is admired. 4
39: 4 serve among great men and appear before rulers; 3
1Mc 7: 8 a great man in the kingdom 2

great one 1. גָּדוֹל
2Sm 7: 9 like the name of the great ones of the earth. 1
1Ch 17: 8 like the name of the great ones of the earth. 1

great owl 1. יַנְשׁוּף
Deu 14:16 the little owl and the great owl, the water hen 1

show great 1. גדל
Gen 19:19 and you have shown me great kindness 1

such great 1. *τηλικοῦτος* 2. *τοσοῦτος* 3. tantus
Heb 2: 3 if we neglect such a great salvation 1
2Es 1: 9 on whom I have bestowed such great benefits? 3
Wis 12:20 thou didst punish with such great care and indulgence 2
14:22 they call such great evils peace. 2
4Mc 16: 4 so many and such great emotions 1

great thing 1. גָּדוֹל 2. גְּדוּלָּה 3. גדל 4. רַב (A) 5. *μεγαλεῖος* 6. *μέγας* 7. *ὅσος* 8. magnus
Deu 10:21 done for you these great and terrible things 1
2Sm 7:23 and doing for them great and terrible things 2
2Kg 8: 4 Tell me all the great things . . Eli'sha has done. 1
1Ch 17:19 in making known all these great things. 2
21 making . . a name for great and terrible things 2
Job 5: 9 who does great things and unsearchable 1
9:10 who does great things beyond understanding 1
37: 5 he does great things which we cannot 1
Ps 71:19 Thou who hast done great things, O God 1
106:21 Savior, who had done great things in Egypt 1
126: 2 The LORD has done great things for them. 3
3 The LORD has done great things for us; we are glad. 3
131: 1 I do not occupy myself with things too great 1
Jer 45: 5 And do you seek great things for yourself? 1
Dan 7: 8 eyes of a man, and a mouth speaking great things. 4
20 had eyes and a mouth that spoke great things 4
Jol 2:20 for he has done great things. 3
21 rejoice, for the LORD has done great things! 3
Lke 1:49 for he who is mighty has done great things for me 6
Joh 1:50 You shall see greater things than these. 6
Jas 3: 5 the tongue . . boasts of great things. 6
2Es 5:13 you shall hear yet greater things than these. 8
6:31 I will again declare to you greater things 8
Tob 11:15 he reported . . the great things that had happened 5
Sir 50:22 who in every way does great things 6
1Mc 6:27 they will do still greater things 6
13: 3 what great things I and my brothers . . have done 7

too great 1. *πολύς*
AEs 16: 2 the too great kindness of their benefactors 1
Sir 3:23 matters too great for human understanding 1

very great 1. אֱלֹהִים 2. *μέγας* 3. *πολύς*
1Sm 14:15 earth quaked; and it became a very great panic. 1
2Pe 1: 4 his precious and very great promises 2
Wis 18: 1 for thy holy ones there was very great light. 2
2Mc 3:35 and made very great vows to the Savior of his life 2
3Mc 3:16 we had granted very great revenues to the temples 3

greater *See* far.

greater than 1. super
2Es 11:32 and it had greater power over the world than all 1

greatly 1. גָּדוֹל 2. לָרֹב 3. מְאֹד 4. רַב 5. רבה 6. שַׂגִּיא (A) 7. *εἰς περισσείαν* 8. *ἐπὶ πολὺ σφόδρα* 9. *λίαν* 10. *μάλιστα* 11. *μεγάλως* 12. *μέγας* 13. *μέγα τι* 14. *μέγεθος* 15. *πολύς* 16. *σφόδρα* 17. valde
Gen 3:16 I will greatly multiply your pain †
7:18 The waters prevailed and increased greatly 3
16:10 I will so greatly multiply your descendants †
24:35 The LORD has greatly blessed my master 3
31:30 you longed greatly for your father's house †
32: 7 Then Jacob was greatly afraid and distressed; 3
Exd 19:18 and the whole mountain quaked greatly. 3
Num14:39 people mourned greatly. 3
Deu 6: 3 that you may multiply greatly, as the LORD 3
17:17 nor . . greatly multiply for himself silver and gold. 3
Jos 9:24 we feared greatly for our lives because of you 3
10: 2 he feared greatly, because Gibeon was a great 3
1Sm 11: 6 and his anger was greatly kindled. 3
15 Saul and all the men of Israel rejoiced greatly. 3
12:18 the people greatly feared the LORD and Samuel. 3
16:21 Saul loved him greatly, and he became his 3
17:11 they were dismayed and greatly afraid. 3
20:19 And on the third day you will be greatly missed; 3
28: 5 he was afraid, and his heart trembled greatly. 3
30: 6 And David was greatly distressed; 3
31: 4 armor-bearer would not; for he feared greatly. 3
2Sm 10: 5 meet them, for the men were greatly ashamed. 3
12: 5 Then David's anger was greatly kindled 3
24:10 I have sinned greatly in what I have done. 3
1Kg 5: 7 When Hiram heard . . he rejoiced greatly, and said 3
18: 3 Now Obadi'ah revered the LORD greatly; 3
1Ch 4:38 and their fathers' houses increased greatly. 2
10: 4 armor-bearer would not; for he feared greatly. 3
16:25 For great is the LORD, and greatly to be praised 3
19: 5 for the men were greatly ashamed. 3

21: 8 I have sinned greatly in that I have done this 3
29: 9 David the king also rejoiced greatly. 1
2Ch 33:12 humbled himself greatly before the God 3
Ezr 10:13 we have greatly transgressed in this matter. 5
Neh 2:10 displeased them greatly that some one 1
4: 1 Sanbal'lat . . was angry and greatly enraged 5
6:16 afraid and fell greatly in their own esteem; 3
Job 35:15 he does not greatly heed transgression 3
Ps 21: 1 in thy help how greatly he exults! 3
48: 1 Great is the LORD and greatly to be praised 3
62: 2 I shall not be greatly moved. 4
65: 9 and waterest it, thou greatly enrichest it; 4
96: 4 For great is the LORD, and greatly to be praised; 3
107:38 By his blessing they multiply greatly; 3
112: 1 who greatly delights in his commandments! 3
116:10 even when I said, "I am greatly afflicted"; 3
145: 3 Great is the LORD, and greatly to be praised 3
Prv 23:24 father of the righteous will greatly rejoice; †
Isa 61:10 I will greatly rejoice in the LORD †
Jer 3: 1 Would not that land be greatly polluted? †
20:11 They will be greatly shamed 3
Ezk 20:13 and my sabbaths they greatly profaned. 3
Dan 5: 9 Then King Belshaz'zar was greatly alarmed 6
7:28 As for me, Daniel, my thoughts greatly alarmed me 6
Zec 9: 9 Rejoice greatly, O daughter of Zion! 3
Mat 17:23 And they were greatly distressed. 16
18:31 they were greatly distressed 16
19:25 they were greatly astonished, saying 16
27:14 so that the governor wondered greatly. 9
Joh 3:29 friend of the bridegroom . . rejoices greatly †
Act 6: 7 the number of the disciples multiplied greatly 16
18:27 greatly helped those who . . had believed 15
2Co 10:15 our field among you may be greatly enlarged 7
Php 4:10 I rejoice in the Lord greatly 11
2Jn 1: 4 I rejoiced greatly to find some of your children 9
3Jn 1: 3 For I greatly rejoiced 9
Rev 17: 6 When I saw her I marveled greatly. 12
2Es 3: 3 My spirit was greatly agitated 17
5:33 Are you greatly disturbed in mind over Israel? 17
6:14 where you are standing is greatly shaken †
37 For my spirit was greatly aroused 17
9:41 I am greatly embittered in spirit 17
45 And I rejoiced greatly over him 17
10:39 and mourned greatly over Zion. 17
Tob 9: 4 if I delay long he will be greatly distressed. 9
10: 3 he was greatly distressed. 9
Jdt 4: 2 they were therefore very greatly terrified 16
6:20 they consoled Achior, and praised him greatly. 16
7: 4 they were greatly terrified 16
32 they were greatly depressed in the city. 15
10: 7 they greatly admired her beauty, and said to her 8
13:17 All the people were greatly astonished 16
14:19 rent their tunics and were greatly dismayed 16
15: 6 plundered it, and were greatly enriched. 16
Sir 1: 8 There is One who is wise, greatly to be feared 16
7:17 Humble yourself greatly 16
11: 6 Many rulers have been greatly disgraced 16
25: 2 I am greatly offended at their life 16
42:22 How greatly to be desired are all his works •
Bar 2:18 the person that is greatly distressed, that goes 14
Sus 1:27 the servants were greatly ashamed 16
1Mc 2:14 Mattathias . . put on sackcloth, and mourned greatly. 16
3:27 he was greatly angered †
31 He was greatly perplexed in mind 16
4:21 they were greatly frightened 16
5:63 his brothers were greatly honored in all Israel 16
7:48 The people rejoiced greatly 16
8:13 they have been greatly exalted. 16
9: 6 they were greatly frightened 16
68 They distressed him greatly 16
69 So he was greatly enraged at the lawless men †
10: 8 They were greatly alarmed when they heard 12
46 how he had greatly oppressed them. 16
68 he was greatly grieved and returned to Antioch. 16
11:53 but oppressed him greatly. 16
15:36 the king was greatly angered. 12
16:22 When he heard this, he was greatly shocked 16
2Mc 1:11 we thank him greatly for taking our side 11
8:32 one who had greatly troubled the Jews. 15
15:27 were greatly gladdened by God's manifestation. 11
3Mc 3: 7 hostile and greatly opposed to his government. 13
4:16 The king was greatly . . filled with joy 13
4Mc 4:22 the people of Jerusalem . . rejoiced greatly 10

greatly *See also* amaze, beloved, distress, increase, please, respect, sin, trouble, troubled.

how greatly 1. *ἡλίκος*

Col 2: 1 For I want you to know how greatly I strive for you 1

greatness 1. גָּדוֹל 2. גְּדוּלָּה 3. גֹּדֶל 4. מַרְבִּית 5. רֹב 6. רְבוּ (A) 7. רְבוּ (A) 8. *μεγαλωσύνη* 9. *μέγεθος* 10. *πλῆθος*

Exd 15: 7 In the greatness of thy majesty 5
16 because of the greatness of thy arm, they are 1
Num14:19 according to the greatness of thy steadfast love 3
Deu 3:24 show . . thy greatness and thy mighty hand; 3
5:24 LORD our God has shown us his glory and greatness 3
9:26 whom thou hast redeemed through thy greatness 3
11: 2 consider . . his greatness, his mighty hand 3
32: 3 Ascribe greatness to our God! 3
2Sm 7:21 thou hast wrought all this greatness 2
1Ch 17:19 thou hast wrought all this greatness 2
29:11 Thine, O LORD, is the greatness, and the power 2
2Ch 9: 6 half the greatness of your wisdom was not told me; 4
Neh 13:22 according to the greatness of thy steadfast love. 5
Job 23: 6 he contend with me in the greatness of his power? 5
36:18 let not the greatness of the ransom turn you 5
Ps 145: 3 his greatness is unsearchable. 2
6 I will declare thy greatness. 2
150: 2 praise him according to his exceeding greatness! 3
Isa 40:26 by the greatness of his might 5
63: 1 marching in the greatness of his strength? 5
Jer 13:22 it is for the greatness of your iniquity 5
Ezk 31: 2 Whom are you like in your greatness? 3
7 It was beautiful in its greatness 3
18 Whom are you thus like in glory and in greatness 3
Dan 4:22 Your greatness has grown and reaches to heaven 7
36 still more greatness was added to me. 6
5:18 kingship and greatness and glory and majesty; 7
19 because of the greatness that he gave him 7
7:27 dominion and the greatness of the kingdoms 7
Eph 1:19 what is the immeasurable greatness of his power 9
1Es 4:46 this befits your greatness 8
Tob 13: 4 Make his greatness known there 8
Wis 6: 7 nor show deference to greatness 9
13: 5 from the greatness and beauty of created things 9
Sir 51: 3 in the greatness of thy mercy and of thy name 10
1Mc 9:22 the brave deeds that he did, and his greatness 8

show greatness 1. גדל

Ezk 38:23 I will show my greatness and my holiness 1

greave 1. מִצְחָה

1Sm 17: 6 And he had greaves of bronze upon his legs 1

greed 1. בֶּטֶן 2. נֶפֶשׁ 3. *πλεονέκτης* 4. *πλεονεξία*

Job 20:20 Because his greed knew no rest 1
Ezk 16:27 and delivered you to the greed of your enemies 2
Hab 2: 5 His greed is as wide as Sheol; 2
1Co 5:11 if he is guilty of immorality or greed 3
1Th 2: 5 or a cloak for greed, as God is witness; 4
2Pe 2: 3 in their greed they will exploit you 4
14 They have hearts trained in greed. 4

greedily

Ps 57: 4 I lie in the midst of lions that greedily devour •

greedily *See also* chew.

greedy 1. בצע 2. נשׂא נֶפֶשׁ 3. *ἀνοίγω φάρυγγα* 4. *ἐπιθυμέω* 5. *πλεονέκτης* 6. *πλεονεξία* 7. *πονηρός* 8. *φειδωλός*

Prv 15:27 He who is greedy for unjust gain makes trouble 1
Jer 6:13 every one is greedy for unjust gain; 1
8:10 every one is greedy for unjust gain; 1
Hos 4: 8 they are greedy for their iniquity. 2
1Co 5:10 the greedy and robbers, or idolaters 5
6:10 nor thieves, nor the greedy, nor drunkards 5
Eph 4:19 greedy to practice every kind of uncleanness. 6
Sir 31:12 Do not be greedy at it, and do not say 3
13 Remember that a greedy eye is a bad thing 7
1Mc 4:17 he said to the people, "Do not be greedy for plunder 4
4Mc 2: 9 If one is greedy 8

greedy for gain 1. *αἰσχροκερδής*

1Ti 3: 8 not addicted to much wine, not greedy for gain; 1
Tit 1: 7 a drunkard or violent or greedy for gain 1

greedy man 1. רְחַב נֶפֶשׁ 2. *πλεονεκτέω*

Prv 28:25 A greedy man stirs up strife 1
Sir 14: 9 A greedy man's eye is not satisfied with a portion 2

more greedy 1. *πονηρός*

Sir 31:13 What has been created more greedy than the eye? 1

green 1. דשׁא 2. דֶּשֶׁא 3. חַי 4. יֶרֶק 5. יְרַקְרַק 6. לַח 7. רַעֲנָן 8. *ὑγρός* 9. *χλωρός*

Gen 1:30 I have given every green plant for food. 4
9: 3 and as I gave you the green plants 4
Deu 12: 2 upon the hills and under every green tree 7
1Kg 14:23 on every high hill and under every green tree; 7
2Kg 16: 4 and on the hills, and under every green tree. 7
17:10 Ashe'rim on every . . and under every green tree; 7
2Ch 28: 4 burned incense . . under every green tree. 7
Job 15:32 his branch will not be green. 7
Ps 23: 2 he makes me lie down in green pastures. 2
37: 2 like the grass, and wither like the green herb. 4
52: 8 I am like a green olive tree in the house of God. 7
58: 9 feel the heat of thorns, whether green or ablaze 3
68:13 with silver, its pinions with green gold. 5
92:14 they are ever full of sap and green 7
Sng 1:16 Our couch is green; 7
Isa 57: 5 lust among the oaks, under every green tree; 7
Jer 2:20 and under every green tree you bowed down 7
3: 6 on every high hill and under every green tree 7
13 favors among strangers under every green tree 7
11:16 The LORD once called you, 'A green olive tree 7
17: 2 and their Ashe'rim, beside every green tree 7
8 for its leaves remain green 7
Ezk 6:13 on all the mountain tops, under every green tree 7
17:24 dry up the green tree, and make the dry tree 6
20:47 it shall devour every green tree in you 6
Jol 2:22 for the pastures of the wilderness are green; 1
Mrk 6:39 to sit down by companies upon the green grass. 9
Lke 23:31 if they do this when the wood is green 8
Rev 8: 7 and all green grass was burnt up. 9

green *See also* growth, leaf, shoot.

green thing 1. יָרוֹק 2. יֶרֶק

Exd 10:15 not a green thing remained, neither tree nor 2
Job 39: 8 he searches after every green thing. 1

greenish 1. יְרַקְרַק

Lev 13:49 if the disease shows greenish or reddish 1
14:37 walls of the house with greenish or reddish spots 1

greet 1. ברך 2. שׁאל לְשָׁלוֹם 3. *αἱρετίζω* 4. *ἀσπάζομαι* 5. *λαλέω εἰρήνην* 6. *λέγω χαίρω*

1Sm 10: 4 they will greet you and give you two loaves 2
17:22 David left . . and went and greeted his brothers. 2
25: 5 go to Nabal, and greet him in my name. 2
2Sm 8:10 To'i sent his son Joram to King David, to greet him 2
2Kg 10:15 he greeted him, and said to him, "Is your heart true 1
1Ch 18:10 he sent his son Hador'am to King David, to greet him 2
Isa 14: 9 when you come, it rouses the shades to greet you •
Mrk 9:15 greatly amazed, and ran up to him and greeted him. 4
Lke 1:40 greeted Elizabeth. 4
Act 18:22 he went up and greeted the church 4
21: 7 we greeted the brethren 4
19 After greeting them 4
Rom16: 3 Greet Prisca and Aq'uila, my fellow workers 4
5 greet also the church in their house. •
5 Greet my beloved Epae'netus 4
6 Greet Mary, who has worked hard among you. 4
7 Greet Androni'cus and Ju'nias, my kinsmen 4
8 Greet Amplia'tus, my beloved in the Lord. 4
9 Greet Urba'nus, our fellow worker in Christ 4
10 Greet Apel'les, who is approved in Christ. 4
10 Greet those who belong to . . Aristobu'lus. 4
11 Greet my kinsman Hero'dion. 4
11 Greet those in the Lord who belong to the family 4
12 Greet those workers in the Lord 4
12 Greet the beloved Persis, who has worked hard 4
13 Greet Rufus, eminent in the Lord 4
14 Greet Asyn'critus, Phlegon, Hermes, Pat'robas 4
15 Greet Philol'ogus, Julia, Nereus and his sister 4
16 Greet one another with a holy kiss. 4
16 All the churches of Christ greet you. 4
21 Timothy, my fellow worker, greets you; 4
22 I Tertius . . greet you in the Lord. 4
23 Ga'ius, who is host to me . . greets you. 4
23 Eras'tus . . and our brother Quartus, greet you. 4
1Co 16:20 Greet one another with a holy kiss. 4
2Co 13:12 Greet one another with a holy kiss 4
13 All the saints greet you. 4
Php 4:21 Greet every saint in Christ Jesus 4
21 The brethren who are with me greet you. 4
22 All the saints greet you 4
Col 4:10 Aristar'chus my fellow prisoner greets you 4
12 Ep'aphras . . greets you 4
14 Luke the beloved physician and Demas greet you. 4
1Th 5:26 Greet all the brethren with a holy kiss. 4
2Ti 4:19 Greet Prisca and Aq'uila 4
Tit 3:15 Greet those who love us in the faith 4
Heb 11:13 having seen it and greeted it from afar 4
13:24 Greet all your leaders and all the saints 4
1Pe 5:14 Greet one another with the kiss of love. 4
2Jn 1:11 for he who greets him shares his wicked work. 6
13 The children of your elect sister greet you. 4
3Jn 1:15 The friends greet you. Greet the friends 4
15 Greet the friends, every one of them. 4
Tob 5: 9 he entered and they greeted each other. 4
7: 1 Sarah met them and greeted them 3
Jdt 15: 8 to see Judith and to greet her. 5
Sir 41:20 of silence, before those who greet you 4
1Mc 7:29 they greeted one another peaceably 4
33 came out . . to greet him peaceably 4
11: 6 they greeted one another 4
12:17 greet you and deliver to you this letter from us 4
3Mc 1: 8 sent some of their . . elders to greet him 4

greeting 1. שְׁלָם (A) 2. *ἀσπασμός* 3. *χαίρω*

Ezr 4:11 Your servants . . send greeting. And now •
17 To Rehum . . and Shim'shai . . , greeting. And now 1
Lke 1:29 considered . . what sort of greeting this might be. 2
41 when Elizabeth heard the greeting of Mary 2
44 when the voice of your greeting came to my ears 2
Act 15:23 to the brethren . . greeting. 3
23:26 to his Excellency the governor Felix, greeting. 3
1Co 16:21 I, Paul, write this greeting with my own hand. 2
Col 4:18 I, Paul, write this greeting with my own hand. 2
2Th 3:17 I, Paul, write this greeting with my own hand 2
Jas 1: 1 To the twelve tribes . . Greeting. 3
2Jn 1:10 do not receive him . . or give him any greeting; 3
1Es 6: 8 To King Darius, greeting 3

8: 9 Artaxerxes to Ezra . . , greeting. 3
Tob 7: 1 They returned her greeting •
AEs 16: 1 to the rulers of the provinces . . greeting. 3
1Mc 10:18 Alexander to his brother Jonathan, greeting. 3
25 Demetrius to the nation of the Jews, greeting. 3
11:30 to the nation of the Jews, greeting. 3
32 Demetrius to Lasthenes his father, greeting. 3
12: 6 to their brethren the Spartans, greeting. 3
20 Arius . . to Onias the high priest, greeting. 3
13:36 to the elders and nation of the Jews, greeting. 3
14:20 to Simon the high priest . . greeting. 3
15: 2 to the nation of the Jews, greeting. 3
16 Lucius . . to King Ptolemy, greeting. 3
2Mc 1: 1 brethren in Egypt, Greeting, and good peace. 3
10 to the Jews in Egypt, Greeting, and good health. 3
11:16 Lysias to the people of the Jews, greeting 3
22 King Antiochus to his brother Lysias, greeting. 3
27 King Antiochus . . to the other Jews, greeting. 3
34 to the people of the Jews, greeting. 3
3Mc 3:12 greetings and good health. 3
7: 1 greetings and good health. 3

greetings *See* give, send.

griddle 1. מַחֲבַת
Lev 2: 5 a cereal offering baked on a griddle 1
6:21 It shall be made with oil on a griddle 1
7: 9 all that is prepared on a pan or a griddle 1

grief 1. חלה 2. חֳלִי 3. יָגוֹן 4. כַּעַס 5. כַּעַשׂ 6. לְאֶרֶץ 7. תּוּגָה 8. ἄλγος 9. λυπέω 10. λύπη 11. ὀδυνάω 12. πένθος 13. περίλυπος 14. doleo 15. tristitia
Job 17: 7 My eye has grown dim from grief 5
Ps 6: 7 My eye wastes away because of grief, it grows weak 4
31: 9 my eye is wasted from grief 4
77:10 It is my grief that the right hand of the Most High 1
Prv 14:13 end of joy is grief. 7
17:21 A stupid son is a grief to a father; 7
25 A foolish son is a grief to his father 4
Ecc 5:17 and spent all his days in darkness and grief 12
Isa 17:11 flee away in a day of grief and incurable pain. 1
53: 3 a man of sorrows, and acquainted with grief; 2
4 he has borne our griefs and carried our sorrows; 2
Jer 8:18 My grief is beyond healing, my heart is sick 3
Lam 2:11 soul is in tumult; my heart is poured out in grief 6
2Co 7: 9 you felt a godly grief 9
10 For godly grief produces a repentance 10
10 worldly grief produces death. 10
11 what earnestness this godly grief has produced 9
1Es 8:71 sat down in anxiety and grief. 13
2Es 5:34 but because of my grief I have spoken 14
7:131 there shall not be grief at their destruction 15
Tob 3: 1 Then in my grief I wept, and I prayed in anguish 9
Wis 8: 9 counsel and encouragement in cares and grief. 10
11:12 for a twofold grief possessed them 10
14:15 consumed with grief at an untimely bereavement •
Sir 18:15 nor cause grief by your words 10
22: 4 who acts shamefully brings grief to her father. 10
26: 6 There is grief of heart and sorrow 8
36:20 A perverse mind will cause grief 10
37: 2 Is it not a grief to the death 10
Bar 4:34 her insolence will be turned to grief. 12
1Mc 6: 4 So he fled and in great grief departed from there 10
8 He took to his bed and became sick from grief 10
9 because deep grief continually gripped him 10
13 I am perishing of deep grief in a strange land. 10
4Mc 18: 9 did not have the grief of bereavement. 11

grief *See also* cause, give, put, strike.

bitter grief 1. מְרִירוּת
Ezk 21: 6 sigh with breaking heart and bitter grief 1

cause grief 1. יגה 2. עלל 3. ἐπιλυπέω
Lam 3:32 though he cause grief, he will have compassion 1
51 my eyes cause me grief at the fate 2
3Mc 7: 9 or cause them any grief at all 3

deep grief 1. tristitia contristo
2Es 10: 7 is in deep grief and great affliction. 1

grief-stricken 1. περίλυπος
1Es 8:72 I sat grief-stricken 1

grievance 1. πρᾶγμα
1Co 6: 1 When one of you has a grievance against a brother 1

grieve 1. אבל 2. אָגֵם 3. ארב 4. חלה 5. יגה 6. עגם 7. עצב 8. βαρύνω 9. δεινάζω 10. δυσφόρως 11. δυσφόρως φέρω 12. ἐπιλυπέω 13. κατανύσσομαι 14. λυπέω 15. ὀδυνάω 16. συλλυπέω 17. χαλεπαίνω 18. contristo 19. doleo
Gen 6: 6 the earth, and it grieved him to his heart. 7
1Sm 2:33 spared to weep out his eyes and grieve his heart; 3
15:35 did not see Saul . . but Samuel grieved over Saul. 1
16: 1 How long will you grieve over Saul 1
20: 3 'Let not Jonathan know this, lest he be grieved.' 7
34 and ate no food . . for he was grieved for David 7
2Sm 19: 2 people heard . . "The king is grieving for his son. 7
Neh 8:10 not be grieved, for the joy of the LORD 7
11 Be quiet, for this day is holy; do not be grieved. 7
Job 30:25 Was not my soul grieved for the poor? 6
Ps 35:14 as though I grieved for my friend or my brother; •
78:40 in the wilderness and grieved him in the desert! 7
Isa 19:10 and all who work for hire will be grieved. 2
54: 6 like a wife forsaken and grieved in spirit 7
63:10 But they rebelled and grieved his holy Spirit; 7
Lam 3:33 he does not willingly afflict or grieve . . men. 5
Ams 6: 6 but are not grieved over the ruin of Joseph! 4
Mrk 3: 5 grieved at their hardness of heart 16
Joh 21:17 Peter was grieved 14
2Co 7: 8 I see that that letter grieved you 14
9 As it is, I rejoice, not because you were grieved 14
9 because you were grieved into repenting 14
Eph 4:30 do not grieve the Holy Spirit of God 14
1Th 4:13 that you may not grieve as others do 14
1Es 1:24 how they grieved the Lord deeply 14
2Es 7:61 I will not grieve over the multitude of those 18
80 ever grieving and sad, in seven ways. 19
8:15 about thy people, for whom I am grieved 19
9:38 and was deeply grieved at heart 19
40 and why are you grieved at heart? 19
10:11 or you who are grieving for one? 19
50 seeing that you are sincerely grieved 18
Tob 3:10 she was deeply grieved 14
4: 3 do what is pleasing to her, and do not grieve her. 14
10:12 do nothing to grieve her. 14
13:14 those who grieved over all your afflictions 14
Wis 14:24 or grieve one another by adultery 15
Sir 3:12 do not grieve him as long as he lives; 14
4: 2 Do not grieve the one who is hungry 14
21:24 a discreet man is grieved by the disgrace. 8
26:28 At two things my heart is grieved 14
30: 5 when he died he was not grieved; 14
47:20 they were grieved at your folly 13
Bar 4: 8 and you grieved Jerusalem, who reared you. 14
33 so she will be grieved at her own desolation. 14
1Mc 10:22 he was grieved and said 14
68 he was greatly grieved and returned to Antioch. 14
14:16 they were deeply grieved. 14
2Mc 4:35 grieved and displeased at the unjust murder 9
37 Therefore Antiochus was grieved at heart 12
14:28 he was troubled and grieved 11
3Mc 3: 8 being grieved at the situation 10
4Mc 16:12 nor did she grieve as they were dying 14
22 have the same faith in God and not be grieved. 17

grievous 1. חלה 2. כָּבֵד 3. מרץ 4. רַע 5. βαρύς 6. δυσχερής 7. ἐπίπονος 8. μοχθηρός 9. χαλεπός 10. malus 11. molestus
Gen 41:31 will follow, for it will be very grievous. 2
50:11 they said, "This is a grievous mourning 2
Deu 6:22 showed signs and wonders, great and grievous 4
28:35 LORD will smite you . . with grievous boils 4
59 bring . . sicknesses grievous and lasting. 4
1Kg 2: 8 Shim'e-i . . who cursed me with a grievous curse 3
Ecc 2:17 what is done under the sun was grievous to me; 4
5:13 There is a grievous evil which I have seen 1
16 This also is a grievous evil 1
Jer 10:19 Woe is me because of my hurt! My wound is grievous. 1
14:17 with a great wound, with a very grievous blow. 1
30:12 hurt is incurable, and your wound is grievous. 1
Mic 2:10 that destroys with a grievous destruction. 3
Nah 3:19 no assuaging your hurt, your wound is grievous 1
2Es 5:21 the thoughts of my heart were very grievous to me 11
11:40 and over all the earth with grievous oppression; 10
Wis 3:19 the end . . is grievous. 9
Sir 27:15 their abuse is grievous to hear. 8
2Mc 6: 3 Harsh and utterly grievous 6
3Mc 5:47 the grievous and pitiful destruction 7
6: 5 speaking grievous words with boasting 5

more grievous 1. χαλεπός
4Mc 9: 4 to be more grievous than death itself. 1
16: 8 the more grievous anxieties of your upbringing. 1

most grievous 1. molestus
2Es 14:15 the thoughts that are most grievous to you 1

grievously 1. δεινός
Lam 1: 8 Jerusalem sinned grievously •
Ezk 25:12 has grievously offended in taking vengeance †
Zec 12: 3 who lift it shall grievously hurt themselves. †
Sir 38:16 as one who is suffering grievously 1

grievously *See also* hurt, suffer.

grind 1. טחן 2. טַחֲנָה 3. נשא 4. קוֹל 5. ἀλήθω 6. βρύχω 7. τρίζω
Exd 32:20 burnt it with fire, and ground it to powder 1
Num 11: 8 ground it in mills or beat it in mortars 1
Deu 9:21 burned . . and crushed it, grinding it very small 1
Jdg 16:21 fetters; and he ground at the mill in the prison. 1
Job 31:10 then let my wife grind for another 1
Ecc 12: 4 when the sound of the grinding is low 2
Isa 3:15 by crushing . . by grinding the face of the poor? 1
47: 2 Take the millstones and grind meal 1
Jer 25:10 the grinding of the millstones and the light 4
Lam 5:13 Young men are compelled to grind at the mill; 3
Mat 24:41 Two women will be grinding at the mill 5
Mrk 9:18 he foams and grinds his teeth and becomes rigid; 7
Lke 17:35 There will be two women grinding together 5
Act 7:54 they ground their teeth against him. 6

make grind 1. גרס
Lam 3:16 He has made my teeth grind on gravel 1

grinder 1. טחן
Ecc 12: 3 and the grinders cease because they are few 1

grip 1. ἐπί
1Mc 6: 9 because deep grief continually gripped him 1

groan 1. אנח 2. אֲנָחָה 3. אנק 4. אֲנָקָה 5. הָגִיג 6. נאק 7. נְאָקָה 8. נהם 9. שׁאג 10. שְׁאָגָה 11. γόος 12. καταστενάζω 13. στεναγμός 14. στενάζω 15. gemitus 16. gemo
Exd 2:23 people of Israel groaned under their bondage 1
24 God heard their groaning, and God remembered 7
6: 5 I have heard the groaning of the people of Israel 7
Jdg 2:18 moved to pity by their groaning because of those 7
Job 3:24 my groanings are poured out like water. 10
24:12 From out of the city the dying groan 6
Ps 5: 1 O LORD; give heed to my groaning. 5
12: 5 because the needy groan, I will now arise 4
22: 1 far from helping me, from the words of my groaning? 10
32: 3 my body wasted away through my groaning all day 10
38: 8 I groan because of the tumult of my heart. 9
79:11 Let the groans of the prisoners come before thee; 4
102:20 to hear the groans of the prisoners 4
Prv 5:11 at the end of your life you groan 8
29: 2 but when the wicked rule, the people groan. 1
Jer 22:23 how you will groan when pangs come upon you 12
51:52 through all her land the wounded shall groan. 3
Lam 1: 4 all her gates are desolate, her priests groan; 1
8 yea, she herself groans, and turns her face away. 1
11 All her people groan as they search for bread; 1
21 Hear how I groan; there is none to comfort me. 1
22 for my groans are many and my heart is faint. 2
Ezk 9: 4 men who sigh and groan over all the abominations 3
24:23 in your iniquities and groan to one another. 8
26:15 at the sound of your fall, when the wounded groan 3
30:24 break the arms of Pharaoh, and he will groan 6
Jol 1:18 How the beasts groan! 1
Mic 4:10 Writhe and groan, O daughter of Zion •
Mal 2:13 with tears, with weeping and groaning because he 4
Act 7:34 heard their groaning 13
Rom 8:23 groan inwardly as we wait for adoption as sons 14
2Co 5: 2 Here indeed we groan 14
2Es 1:19 I pitied your groanings 15
16:39 and the world will groan, and pains will seize it 16
Jdt 14:16 cried out with a loud voice and wept and groaned 13
Wis 5: 3 in anguish of spirit they will groan, and say 14
11:12 groaning at the memory of what had occurred. 13
Sir 30:20 he sees with his eyes and groans 14
20 like a eunuch who embraces a maiden and groans. 14
1Mc 1:26 rulers and elders groaned 14
3Mc 1:18 filled . . with groans and lamentations. 13
4: 2 groaned because of the unexpected destruction 13
5:49 and giving way to lamentation and groans 11
6:34 groaned as they . . were overcome by disgrace 12
4Mc 9:21 the courageous youth . . did not groan 14

groan aloud 1. ἀναστενάζω
2Mc 6:30 he groaned aloud and said 1

groan together 1. συστενάζω
Rom 8:22 creation has been groaning in travail together 1

groaning 1. אֲנָחָה
Job 23: 2 his hand is heavy in spite of my groaning. 1
Ps 102: 5 Because of my loud groaning my bones cleave 1
Jer 45: 3 I am weary with my groaning, and I find no rest. 1

grope 1. גשש 2. מצא 3. משש
Gen 19:11 so that they wearied themselves groping 2
Deu 28:29 grope at noonday, as the blind grope in darkness 3
29 grope at noonday, as the blind grope in darkness 3
Job 5:14 and grope at noonday as in the night. 3
12:25 They grope in the dark without light; 3
Isa 59:10 We grope for the wall like the blind 1
10 we grope like those who have no eyes; 1

gross 1. טפש
Ps 119:70 their heart is gross like fat 1

ground 1. אֲדָמָה 2. אֶרֶץ 3. חָרִישׁ 4. מוֹצָא 5. מָקוֹם 6. עָפָר 7. פָּנִים 8. שָׂדֶה 9. אֲרַע (A) 10. γῆ 11. ἔδαφος 12. πεδίον 13. πρηνής 14. χαμαί 15. terra
Gen 1:25 and everything that creeps upon the ground 1
2: 5 and there was no man to till the ground; 1
6 and watered the whole face of the ground– 1
7 the LORD God formed man of dust from the ground 1
9 out of the ground the LORD God made to grow 1
19 out of the ground the LORD God formed every beast 1
3:17 cursed is the ground because of you; 1

19 you shall eat bread till you return to the ground 1
23 sent him forth . . to till the ground 1
4: 2 keeper of sheep, and Cain a tiller of the ground. 1
3 LORD an offering of the fruit of the ground, 1
10 brother's blood is crying to me from the ground. 1
11 now you are cursed from the ground 1
12 When you till the ground, it shall no longer yield 1
14 thou hast driven me this day away from the ground; 1
5:29 called his name Noah, saying, "Out of the ground 1
6: 1 men began to multiply on the face of the ground 1
7 whom I have created from the face of the ground 1
20 kinds, of every creeping thing of the ground 1
7: 4 will blot out from the face of the ground. 1
8 of everything that creeps on the ground 1
23 living thing that was upon the face of the ground 1
8: 8 waters had subsided from the face of the ground; 1
13 behold, the face of the ground was dry. 1
21 I will never again curse the ground 1
9: 2 upon everything that creeps on the ground 1
19:25 overthrew . . what grew on the ground. 1
33: 3 bowing himself to the ground seven times 2
37:10 to bow ourselves to the ground before you? 2
38: 9 he spilled the semen on the ground 2
42: 6 before him with their faces to the ground. 2
43:26 and bowed down to him to the ground. 2
44:11 every man quickly lowered his sack to the ground 2
14 and they fell before him to the ground. 2
Exd 3: 5 place on which you are standing is holy ground. 1
4: 3 he said, "Cast it to the ground." So he cast it 2
3 So he cast it on the ground, and it became a serpent; 2
8:21 and also the ground on which they stand. 1
16:14 fine as hoarfrost on the ground. 2
23:19 first fruits of your ground you shall bring 1
34:26 The first of the first fruits of your ground 1
Lev 20:25 or by anything with which the ground teems 1
Num16:30 ground opens its mouth, and swallows them up 1
31 the ground under them split asunder; 1
Deu 4:18 likeness of anything that creeps on the ground 1
7:13 also bless . . the fruit of your ground 1
15:23 blood . . pour it out on the ground like water. 2
22: 6 come upon a bird's nest, in any tree or on the ground 2
26: 2 take . . first of all the fruit of the ground 1
10 now I bring the first of the fruit of the ground 1
15 bless . . the ground which thou hast given us 1
28: 4 Blessed shall be . . the fruit of your ground 1
11 make you abound in . . the fruit of your ground 1
18 Cursed shall be . . the fruit of your ground 1
33 nation . . shall eat up the fruit of your ground 1
42 All your trees and the fruit of your ground 1
51 eat . . of your cattle and the fruit of your ground 1
56 not venture to set . . her foot upon the ground 2
30: 9 prosperous in . . the fruit of your ground; 1
Jos 24:32 buried at Shechem, in the portion of ground 8
Jdg 4:21 into his temple, till it went down into the ground 2
6:37 if there is dew . . and it is dry on all the ground 2
39 the fleece, and on all the ground let there be dew. 2
40 fleece only, and on all the ground there was dew. 2
13:20 and they fell on their faces to the ground. 2
20:21 and felled to the ground . . 22,000 men 2
25 and felled to the ground 18,000 men 2
36 The men of Israel gave ground to Benjamin 5
Rut 2:10 she fell on her face, bowing to the ground, and said 2
1Sm 3:19 and let none of his words fall to the ground. 2
5: 3 Dagon had fallen face downward on the ground 2
4 Dagon had fallen face downward on the ground 2
8:12 some to plow his ground and to reap his harvest 3
14:25 people came . . and there was honey on the ground. 8
32 took sheep and . . and slew them on the ground; 2
45 shall not one hair of his head fall to the ground; 2
17:49 and he fell on his face to the ground. 2
20:41 David . . fell on his face to the ground, and bowed 2
25:23 and fell before David . . and bowed to the ground. 2
41 And she rose and bowed with her face to the ground 2
26: 7 with his spear stuck in the ground at his head; 2
28:14 Saul . . bowed with his face to the ground 2
20 Saul fell at once full length upon the ground 2
2Sm 1: 2 he fell to the ground and did obeisance. 2
2:22 Turn aside . . why should I smite you to the ground? 2
8: 2 measured . . making them lie down on the ground; 2
12:16 and went in and lay all night upon the ground. 2
17 stood beside him, to raise him from the ground; 2
14: 4 she fell on her face to the ground 2
11 not one hair of your son shall fall to the ground. 2
14 we are like water spilt on the ground 2
22 And Jo'ab fell on his face to the ground 2
33 and bowed himself on his face to the ground 2
17:12 light upon him as the dew falls on the ground; 1
18:11 Why . . did you not strike him there to the ground? 2
20:10 Jo'ab struck . . and shed his bowels to the ground 2
23:11 where there was a plot of ground full of lentils; 8
24:20 and did obeisance . . with his face to the ground. 2
1Kg 1:23 before the king, with his face to the ground. 2
31 bowed with her face to the ground, and did 2
2Kg 2:15 they came . . and bowed to the ground before him. 2
4:37 She came and fell at his feet, bowing to the ground; 2
9:25 Take him up, and cast him on the plot of ground 8
26 I will requite you on this plot of ground.' •
26 take him up and cast him on the plot of ground •
13:18 he said to the king . . "Strike the ground with them"; 2
1Ch 11:13 There was a plot of ground full of barley 8
21:21 did obeisance to David with his face to the ground 2
2Ch 4:17 in the clay ground between Succoth and Zer'edah. 1
20:18 bowed his head with his face to the ground 2
24 behold, they were dead bodies lying on the ground; 2
Neh 8: 6 worshiped the LORD . . faces to the ground. 2
10:35 bring the first fruits of our ground 1
37 bring to the Levites the tithes from our ground 1
Job 1:20 fell upon the ground, and worshiped. 2
2:13 they sat with him on the ground seven days 2
5: 6 nor does trouble sprout from the ground; 1
14: 8 and its stump die in the ground 6
16:13 he pours out my gall on the ground. 2
18:10 A rope is hid for him in the ground 2
38:27 to make the ground put forth grass? 4
39:14 her eggs . . and lets them be warmed on the ground 6
24 With fierceness and rage he swallows the ground; 2
Ps 7: 5 let him trample my life to the ground 2
12: 6 silver refined in a furnace on the ground 2
17:11 they set their eyes to cast me to the ground. 2
44:25 our body cleaves to the ground. 2
74: 7 to the ground they desecrated the dwelling 2
80: 9 Thou didst clear the ground for it; •
83:10 who became dung for the ground. 1
85:11 Faithfulness will spring up from the ground 2
89:44 Thou hast . . cast his throne to the ground. 2
104:30 thou renewest the face of the ground. 1
105:35 which . . ate up the fruit of their ground. 1
143: 3 enemy . . has crushed my life to the ground; 2
147: 6 LORD . . casts the wicked to the ground. 2
Prv 24:31 ground was covered with nettles 7
Isa 2:19 enter the caves . . and the holes of the ground 6
3:26 mourn; ravaged, she shall sit upon the ground. 2
14:12 How you are cut down to the ground 2
21: 9 her gods he has shattered to the ground. 2
25:12 cast to the ground, even to the dust. 2
26: 5 He lays it low, lays it low to the ground 2
28:24 does he continually open and harrow his ground? 1
29: 4 your voice shall come from the ground 2
30:23 rain for the seed with which you sow the ground 1
23 the produce of the ground, which will be rich 1
24 the oxen and the asses that till the ground 1
47: 1 sit on the ground without a throne, O daughter 2
49:23 their faces to the ground they shall bow down 2
51:23 and you have made your back like the ground 2
53: 2 a young plant, and like a root out of dry ground; 2
Jer 7:20 the trees of the field and the fruit of the ground; 1
8: 2 be as dung on the surface of the ground. 1
10:17 Gather up your bundle from the ground 2
14: 2 her people lament on the ground 2
4 Because of the ground which is dismayed 1
16: 4 shall be as dung on the surface of the ground. 1
25:33 they shall be dung on the surface of the ground. 1
51:58 Babylon shall be leveled to the ground †
Lam 2: 2 brought . . to the ground in dishonor the kingdom 2
9 Her gates have sunk into the ground; 2
10 The elders of . . Zion sit on the ground in silence; 2
10 maidens . . have bowed their heads to the ground. 2
Ezk 13:14 and bring it down to the ground 2
19:12 was plucked up in fury, cast down to the ground; 2
24: 7 not pour it upon the ground to cover it with dust. 2
26:11 your mighty pillars will fall to the ground. 2
16 they will sit upon the ground 2
28:17 I cast you to the ground; 2
32: 4 I will cast you on the ground 2
38:20 and all creeping things that creep on the ground 1
20 every wall shall tumble to the ground. 2
42: 6 the upper chambers were set back from the ground 2
43:14 from the base on the ground to the lower ledge 2
Dan 7: 4 lifted up from the ground and made to stand 9
8: 5 he-goat came . . without touching the ground; 2
7 cast him down to the ground and trampled upon him; 2
10 host of the stars it cast down to the ground 2
12 truth was cast down to the ground 2
18 fell into a deep sleep with my face to the ground; 2
10: 9 deep sleep with my face to the ground. 2
15 turned my face toward the ground and was dumb. 2
Hos 2:18 of the air, and the creeping things of the ground; 1
Jol 1:10 The fields are laid waste, the ground mourns; 1
Ams 3: 5 Does a snare spring up from the ground 1
14 altar shall be cut off and fall to the ground. 2
9: 8 I will destroy it from the surface of the ground; 1
Obd 1: 3 Who will bring me down to the ground? 2
Hag 1:11 upon what the ground brings forth, upon men 1
Zec 8:12 the ground shall give its increase 1
Mat 10:29 And not one of them will fall to the ground 10
15:35 commanding the crowd to sit down on the ground 10
25:18 dug in the ground and hid his master's money. 10
25 I went and hid your talent in the ground 10
Mrk 4:26 as if a man should scatter seed upon the ground 10
31 which, when sown upon the ground, is the smallest 10
8: 6 he commanded the crowd to sit down on the ground; 10
9:20 he fell on the ground and rolled about 10
14:35 going a little farther, he fell on the ground 10
Lke 6:49 a house on the ground without a foundation; 10
13: 7 Cut it down; why should it use up the ground?' 10
24: 5 bowed their faces to the ground 10
Joh 8: 6 Jesus . . wrote with his finger on the ground. 10
8 and wrote with his finger on the ground. 10
9: 6 As he said this, he spat on the ground 14
18: 6 they drew back and fell to the ground. 14
Act 7:33 the place where you are standing is holy ground. 10
9: 4 he fell to the ground and heard a voice saying 10
8 Saul arose from the ground 10
22: 7 I fell to the ground and heard a voice saying to me 11
26:14 when we had all fallen to the ground 10
1Es 9:47 fell to the ground and worshiped the Lord. 10
2Es 8:41 the farmer sows many seeds upon the ground 15
9:34 when the ground has received seed 15
15:13 Let the farmers that till the ground mourn 15
Jdt 5:18 the temple of their God was razed to the ground 11
16: 5 dash my infants to the ground 11
Wis 4:19 he will dash them speechless to the ground 13
11:22 drop of morning dew that falls upon the ground. 10
Sir 11: 5 Many kings have had to sit on the ground 11
33:10 All men are from the ground 11
50:17 fell to the ground upon their faces 10
Bar 5: 7 the valleys filled up, to make level ground 10
LJr 1:27 lest they fall to the ground 10
1Mc 4:40 They fell face down on the ground 10
6:46 it fell to the ground upon him and he died. 10
14: 8 the ground gave its increase 10
2Mc 3:27 When he suddenly fell to the ground 10
14:33 I will level this precinct of God to the ground 12
3Mc 2:22 he lay helpless on the ground 11
5:43 by burning to the ground the temple 13
6: 7 Daniel . . was cast down into the ground to lions 10
4Mc 6: 7 though he fell to the ground 11
15:15 their toes and fingers scattered on the ground 10

ground (2) 1. עַל 2. διά 3. εἰς 4. ἐκ 5. θεμελιόω 6. λόγος 7. ὅτι 8. πρηνής 9. χαμαί

Dan 9:18 before thee on the ground of our righteousness 1
18 but on the ground of thy great mercy. 1
Mat 5:32 his wife, except on the ground of unchastity 6
Rom 3:30 the circumcised on the ground of their faith 4
1Co 9:15 deprive me of my ground for boasting. •
16 that gives me no ground for boasting •
10:25 without . . question on the ground of conscience. 2
27 without . . question on the ground of conscience. 2
Eph 3:17 being rooted and grounded in love 5
1Ti 6: 2 on the ground that they are brethren 7
Jdt 12:15 and spread on the ground for her . . the soft fleeces 9
14:18 For look, here is Holofernes lying on the ground 9
Sir 31:10 Let it be for him a ground for boasting 3
3Mc 5:50 they prostrated themselves . . on the ground 8

ground *See* clear, dash, gain, lie, occupy, strew.

clay ground 1. מַעֲבֶה

1Kg 7:46 in the clay ground between Succoth and Zarethan. 1

desolate ground 1. מְשׁוֹאָה

Job 30: 3 they gnaw the dry and desolate ground; 1

dry ground 1. חָרָבָה 2. יַבָּשָׁה 3. צִיָּה

Exd 4: 9 take some water . . and pour it upon the dry ground; 2
9 water . . will become blood upon the dry ground. 2
14:16 Israel may go on dry ground through the sea. 2
22 went into the midst of the sea on dry ground 2
29 the people of Israel walked on dry ground 2
15:19 Israel walked on dry ground in the midst 2
Jos 3:17 while all Israel were passing over on dry ground 1
17 stood on dry ground in the midst of the Jordan 1
4:18 soles of the . . feet were lifted up on dry ground 1
22 'Israel passed over this Jordan on dry ground.' 2
2Kg 2: 8 the two of them could go over on dry ground. 1
Job 30: 3 they gnaw the dry and desolate ground; 3
Isa 44: 3 For I will pour . . streams on the dry ground; 2

fallow ground 1. נִיר

Prv 13:23 The fallow ground of the poor yields much food 1
Jer 4: 3 Break up your fallow ground 1
Hos 10:12 break up your fallow ground 1

ground for complaint 1. עִלָּה (A)

Dan 6: 4 sought to find a ground for complaint against 1
4 could find no ground for complaint or any fault 1
5 not find any ground for complaint against 1

level ground 1. מִישׁוֹר

Ps 26:12 My foot stands on level ground; 1
Isa 42:16 turn . . the rough places into level ground. 1

parched ground 1. צָמָא

Jer 48:18 Come down . . and sit on the parched ground 1

rocky ground 1. πετρώδης

Mat 13: 5 Other seeds fell on rocky ground 1
20 As for what was sown on rocky ground 1
Mrk 4: 5 Other seed fell on rocky ground 1
16 the ones sown upon rocky ground 1

stony ground 1. λιθώδεσις

Sir 32:20 do not stumble over stony ground. 1

thirsty ground 1. צִמָּאוֹן

Deu 8:15 thirsty ground where there was no water 1

Ps 107:33 turns . . springs of water into thirsty ground 1
Isa 35: 7 a pool, and the thirsty ground springs of water; 1

uneven ground 1. עָקֹב
Isa 40: 4 the uneven ground shall become level 1

group 1. *μεριδαρχία* 2. *πρασιά* 3. *συναγωγή*
Mrk 6:40 So they sat down in groups 2
1Es 5: 4 over their groups 1
8:28 their groups, who went up with me from Babylon 1
1Mc 7:12 Then a group of scribes appeared in a body 3
10:61 A group of pestilent men from Israel, lawless men •

group *See also* choral.

group about 1. *περιέχω*
4Mc 8: 4 grouped about their mother as if in a chorus 1

grouping 1. מִפְלַגָּה 2. פְּלֻגָּה 3. *μεριδαρχία*
2Ch 35: 5 according to the groupings of the fathers' 2
12 groupings of the fathers' houses of the lay 1
1Es 1: 5 groupings of the fathers' houses of you Levites 3
11 the grouping of the fathers' houses 3

sacred grove 1. *ἄλσος*
Jdt 3: 8 and cut down their sacred groves 1

thick grove 1. silva
2Es 16:28 in thick groves and clefts in the rocks. 1

grow 1. גאה 2. גבהּ 3. גדל 4. דגה 5. היה 6. הלך 7. יסף 8. יצא 9. סָפִיחַ 10. עלה 11. פרה 12. צֶאֱצָא 13. צמח 14. צֶמַח 15. קבץ 16. שגה 17. רבה (A) 18. שגא (A) 19. *αὐξάνω* 20. *αὔξω* 21. *γίνομαι* 22. *εἰμί* 23. *ἐπιφύω* 24. *ἔρχομαι* 25. *μηκύνω* 26. *οἰκίζω* 27. *πληθύνω* 28. *συμφύω* 29. *τροφή* 30. *φύω* 31. cresco 32. habeo 33. nascor
Gen 19:25 overthrew . . what grew on the ground. 14
21: 8 the child grew, and was weaned; 3
41: 5 plump and good, were growing on one stalk. 10
22 saw in my dream seven ears growing on one stalk 10
48:16 let them grow into a multitude in the midst 4
Exd 2:10 the child grew, and she brought him 3
10: 5 eat every tree of yours which grows in the field 13
19:19 sound of the trumpet grew louder, Moses spoke 6
Lev 13:37 if . . itch is checked, black hair has grown in it 13
25: 5 What grows of itself . . you shall not reap 9
11 neither sow, nor reap what grows of itself 9
Deu 29:23 burnt-out waste, unsown, and growing nothing 13
Jdg 13:24 Samson; and the boy grew, and the LORD blessed him. 3
16:22 the hair of his head began to grow again 13
Rut 1:13 would you therefore wait till they were grown? 3
1Sm 2:21 the boy Samuel grew in the presence of the LORD. 3
3:19 And Samuel grew, and the LORD was with him 3
2Sm 10: 5 Remain at Jericho until your beards have grown 13
15:12 And the conspiracy grew strong 5
2Kg 4:18 When the child had grown, he went out one day 3
19:29 this year you shall eat what grows of itself 9
1Ch 19: 5 Remain at Jericho until your beards have grown 13
Ezr 4:22 why should damage grow to the hurt of the king? 18
Job 8:11 Can papyrus grow where there is no marsh? 1
17: 9 he that has clean hands grows stronger 7
31: 8 let what grows for me be rooted out. 12
40 let thorns grow instead of wheat 8
Ps 92:12 The righteous . . grow like a cedar in Lebanon. 16
Prv 11:24 One man gives freely, yet grows all the richer; 7
Ecc 2: 6 pools . . to water the forest of growing trees. 13
Isa 11: 1 of Jesse, and a branch shall grow out of his roots. 11
37:30 this year eat what grows of itself 9
Jer 12: 2 they take root; they grow and bring forth fruit; 6
Ezk 16: 7 your breasts were formed, and your hair had grown; 13
17:10 wither away on the bed where it grew? 14
31:14 in order that no trees by the waters may grow 2
47:12 there will grow all kinds of trees for food. 10
Dan 4:11 tree grew and became strong, and its top reached 17
20 tree you saw, which grew and became strong 17
22 it is you, O king, who have grown and become strong 17
22 Your greatness has grown and reaches to heaven 17
Jol 2: 6 peoples are in anguish, all faces grow pale. 15
Jon 1:11 For the sea grew more and more tempestuous. 6
13 for the sea grew more and more tempestuous 6
Nah 2:10 anguish is on all loins, all faces grow pale! 15
Mat 6:28 how they grow; they neither toil nor spin; 19
13:32 when it has grown it is the greatest of shrubs 19
Mrk 4:27 the seed should sprout and grow 25
5:26 no better but rather grew worse. 24
6:35 when it grew late, his disciples came to him 21
Lke 1:80 the child grew and became strong in spirit 19
2:40 And the child grew and became strong 19
8: 7 and the thorns grew with it and choked it. 28
8 some fell into good soil and grew 30
12:27 Consider the lilies, how they grow 19
13:19 it grew and became a tree 19
Act 7:17 the people grew and multiplied in Egypt 19
12:24 the word of God grew and multiplied. 19
19:20 the word of the Lord grew and prevailed 19
Eph 2:21 grows into a holy temple in the Lord; 20
Col 1: 6 it is bearing fruit and growing 19
2:19 grows with a growth that is from God. 20
Heb 11:24 Moses, when he was grown up 21
2Pe 3:18 grow in the grace and knowledge of our Lord 19
2Es 2:19 mighty mountains on which roses and lilies grow; 32
7:64 now the mind grows with us 31
71 for you have said that the mind grows with us. 31
11: 3 out of his wings there grew opposing wings 33
Sir 10: 3 a city will grow 26
39:13 bud like a rose growing by a stream of water; 30
Aza 1:54 Bless the Lord, all things that grow on the earth 30
1Mc 1:40 Her dishonor now grew as great as her glory 27
2Mc 4:50 remained in office, growing in wickedness 23
5:27 they continued to live on what grew wild 29
4Mc 1:28 two plants growing from the body and the soul 22
13:20 growing from the same blood 19
22 they grow stronger from this common nurture 20

grow abundantly 1. *ὑπεραυξάνω*
2Th 1: 3 because your faith is growing abundantly 1

grow beautiful 1. יפה
Ezk 16:13 You grew exceedingly beautiful 1

grow black 1. קדר
1Kg 18:45 the heavens grew black with clouds and wind 1

cause to grow 1. צמח
Ps 104:14 Thou dost cause the grass to grow for the cattle 1

grow cold 1. *ψύχω*
Mat 24:12 most men's love will grow cold. 1

grow dim 1. דאב 2. חשך 3. כהה 4. כֵּהָה 5. כלה 6. עמם
1Sm 3: 2 Eli, whose eyesight had begun to grow dim 4
Job 17: 7 My eye has grown dim from grief 3
Ps 69: 3 My eyes grow dim with waiting for my God. 5
88: 9 my eye grows dim through sorrow. 1
Lam 4: 1 How the gold has grown dim . . pure gold is changed! 6
5:17 for these things our eyes have grown dim 2

grow drowsy 1. *νυστάζω*
2Sm 4: 6 the doorkeeper . . but she grew drowsy and slept; 1

grow dull 1. *παχύνω*
Mat 13:15 For this people's heart has grown dull 1
Act 28:27 this people's heart has grown dull 1

grow fat 1. דשן 2. שמן
Deu 31:20 when . . have eaten and are full and grown fat 1
Jer 5:28 they have grown fat and sleek. 2

grow foul 1. באש
Ps 38: 5 My wounds grow foul and fester 1

grow great 1. גדל
2Ch 17:12 Jehosh'aphat grew steadily greater. 1
Dan 8: 9 little horn, which grew exceedingly great 1
10 It grew great, even to the host of heaven; 1

grow hot 1. חמם 2. עלה
Exd 16:21 but when the sun grew hot, it melted. 1
1Kg 22:35 the battle grew hot . . and the king was propped up 2
2Ch 18:34 the battle grew hot that day 2

grow in favor 1. טוב
1Sm 2:26 continued to grow both in stature and in favor 1

grow in stature 1. גדל
1Sm 2:26 the boy Samuel continued to grow both in stature 1

grow large 1. רבה
Ezk 31: 5 its boughs grew large and its branches long 1

grow lean 1. רזה
Isa 17: 4 and the fat of his flesh will grow lean. 1

grow long 1. ארך 2. גדל 3. שלח 4. רבה (A)
Num 6: 5 shall let the locks of hair of his head grow long. 2
Ezk 12:22 days grow long, and every vision comes to nought 1
31: 5 its boughs grew large and its branches long 1
44:20 shave their heads or let their locks grow long; 3
Dan 4:33 till his hair grew as long as eagles' feathers 4

make grow 1. גדל 2. סוג 3. צמח
Gen 2: 9 God made to grow every tree that is pleasant 3
Ps 147: 8 he makes grass grow upon the hills. 3
Isa 17:11 you make them grow on the day that you plant them 2
Jon 4:10 which you did not labor, nor did you make it grow 1

make grow tall 1. רום
Ezk 31: 4 waters nourished it, the deep made it grow tall 1

grow many 1. רבה
Ecc 5: 7 For when dreams increase, empty words grow many 1

grow mighty 1. גבר 2. חזק
2Ch 13:21 Abi'jah grew mighty. And he took fourteen wives 2
Job 21: 7 the wicked live, reach old age, and grow mighty 1

grow more and more 1. הלך
Est 9: 4 the man Mor'decai grew more and more powerful. 1

grow numerous 1. רבה
Deu 7:22 lest the wild beasts grow too numerous for you. 1

grow old 1. בלה 2. זקן 3. ישן 4. *γηράσκω* 5. *παλαιόω* 6. senesco
Gen 18:12 After I have grown old, and my husband is old 1
Deu 4:25 When you . . have grown old in the land 3
2Ch 24:15 Jehoi'ada grew old and full of days, and died; 2
Job 14: 8 Though its root grow old in the earth 2
Lke 12:33 purses that do not grow old 5
Heb 1:11 they will all grow old like a garment 5
8:13 what is becoming obsolete and growing old 4
2Es 14:10 and the times begin to grow old. 6
Tob 14: 3 When he had grown very old 4
3 behold, I have grown old 4
13 He grew old with honor 4
Jdt 16:23 and grew old in her husband's house 4
Sir 8: 6 some of us are growing old. 4
11:20 grow old in your work. 5
Bar 3:10 that you are growing old in a foreign country 5
1Mc 16: 3 now I have grown old 4

grow old together 1. *συγκαταγηρασκω*
Tob 8: 7 Grant that I . . may grow old together with her. 1

grow out 1. יצא
1Kg 4:33 cedar . . to the hyssop that grows out of the wall; 1

grow over 1. עלה
Isa 34:13 Thorns shall grow over its strongholds 1

grow pale 1. חור
Isa 29:22 no more shall his face grow pale. 1

grow proud 1. גבה
2Ch 26:16 when he was strong he grew proud 1

grow rich 1. נשׂג יָד 2. פרק 3. *πλουτέω*
Gen 30:43 Thus the man grew exceedingly rich 2
Lev 25:49 if he grows rich he may redeem himself 1
Rev 18: 3 grown rich with the wealth of her wantonness. 3
19 all who had ships at sea grew rich by her wealth! 3

grow strong 1. אמץ 2. חזק 3. עצם 4. *ἐνδυναμόω* 5. *ἐνισχύω* 6. *ἐπισχύω* 7. *ἰσχύω* 8. *κρατύνω* 9. convalesco
Exd 1: 7 they multiplied and grew exceedingly strong; 3
20 the people multiplied and grew very strong. 3
Jos 17:13 when the people of Israel grew strong 2
Jdg 1:28 When Israel grew strong, they put the Canaanites 2
2Sm 3: 1 and David grew stronger and stronger 2
Isa 44:14 carpenter . . lets it grow strong among the trees 1
Jer 9: 3 falsehood and not truth has grown strong 5
Rom 4:20 but he grew strong in his faith as he gave glory 4
2Es 7:34 and faithfulness shall grow strong. 9
Wis 14:16 the ungodly custom, grown strong with time 8
1Mc 2:64 be courageous and grow strong in the law 7
6: 6 that the Jews had grown strong from the arms 6
7:25 Judas and those with him had grown strong 5

grow strong against 1. supervalesco
2Es 15:16 growing strong against one another 1

grow tall 1. *ἀνυψόω*
Sir 24:13 I grew tall like a cedar in Lebanon 1
14 I grew tall like a palm tree in En-ge'di 1
14 like a plane tree I grew tall. 1

grow thick 1. עבה
Deu 32:15 waxed fat, you grew thick, you became sleek; 1

grow tired 1. *κοπιάω*
1Mc 10:81 the enemy's horses grew tired. 1

grow together 1. *συναυξάνω*
Mat 13:30 Let both grow together until the harvest 1

grow up 1. גדל 2. עלה 3. צמח 4. קום 5. רבה 6. שׁלף 7. *ἀναβαίνω* 8. *αὐξάνω* 9. *ἐνήλιξ* 10. *πληθύνω* 11. *φύω* 12. coadulesco 13. cresco 14. incresco
Gen 21:20 God was with the lad, and he grew up; 1
25:27 When the boys grew up, Esau was a skilful hunter 1
38:11 Remain a widow . . till Shelah my son grows up 1
14 for she saw that Shelah was grown up 1
Exd 2:11 when Moses had grown up, he went out to his people 1
Jdg 11: 2 when his wife's sons grew up, they thrust Jephthah 1
2Sm 12: 3 And he brought it up, and it grew up with him 1
1Kg 12: 8 the young men who had grown up with him 1
10 the young men who had grown up with him said 1

2Ch 10: 8 who had grown up with him and stood before him. 1
10 the young men who had grown up with him said 1
Job 39: 4 they grow up in the open; they go forth 5
Ps 129: 6 like the grass . . which withers before it grows up 6
Isa 5: 6 not be . . hoed, and briers and thorns shall grow up; 2
32:13 soil of my people growing up in thorns and briers; 2
53: 2 For he grew up before him like a young plant 2
Ezk 7:11 Violence has grown up into a rod of wickedness; 4
16: 7 and grow up like a plant of the field. 10
7 And you grew up and became tall 5
Hos 10: 8 Thorn and thistle shall grow up on their altars; 2
Zec 6:12 for he shall grow up in his place 3
Mat 13: 7 and the thorns grew up and choked them. 7
Mrk 4: 7 the thorns grew up and choked it 7
8 brought forth grain, growing up and increasing 7
32 yet when it is sown it grows up 7
Lke 8: 6 as it grew up, it withered away 11
Eph 4:15 we are to grow up in every way into him 8
1Pe 2: 2 that by it you may grow up to salvation; 8
2Es 4:10 the things with which you have grown up; 12
7:48 For an evil heart has grown up in us 14
9:47 when he grew up and I came to take a wife for him 13
4Mc 18: 9 when these sons had grown up their father died 9

grow very short 1. *συστέλλω*

1Co 7:29 the appointed time has grown very short 1

grow wanton against 1. *καταστρηνιάω*

1Ti 5:11 when they grow wanton against Christ 1

grow warm and tender 1. כמר

Hos 11: 8 my compassion grows warm and tender. 1

grow weak 1. עתק 2. רפה 3. *ἐκλείπω*

Ps 6: 7 My eye . . it grows weak because of all my foes. 1
Zep 3:16 Do not fear, O Zion; let not your hands grow weak. 2
1Mc 6:57 We daily grow weaker, our food supply is scant 3

grow weary 1. יגע 2. יעף 3. כָּבֵד 4. *ἐγκακέω* 5. *ἐκλύω* 6. *κοπιάω*

Exd 17:12 Moses' hands grew weary; so they took a stone 3
2Sm 21:15 and they fought against . . and David grew weary. 2
Isa 40:28 He does not faint or grow weary 1
Gal 6: 9 let us not grow weary in well-doing 4
Heb 12: 3 you may not grow weary or fainthearted. 5
Rev 2: 3 and you have not grown weary. 6
Sir 16:27 they neither hunger nor grow weary 6
43:30 put forth all your strength, and do not grow weary 6

grow worse 1. עכר

Ps 39: 2 I held my peace to no avail; my distress grew worse 1

growl 1. הגה 2. המה 3. חרץ 4. לון 5. נהם 6. נער 7. *γρύζω*

Exd 11: 7 against . . Israel . . not a dog shall growl; 3
Ps 59:15 for food, and growl if they do not get their fill. 4
Prv 19:12 A king's wrath is like the growling of a lion 2
20: 2 dread wrath of a king is like the growling of a lion; 2
Isa 5:29 they growl and seize their prey, they carry it off 5
30 They will growl over it on that day 5
31: 4 As a lion or a young lion growls over his prey 1
59:11 We all growl like bears, 2
Jer 51:38 they shall growl like lions' whelps. 6
Jdt 11:19 not a dog will so much as open its mouth to growl 7

grown 1. קום

2Kg 19:26 like tender grass . . blighted before it is grown? 1
Isa 37:27 like grass . . blighted before it is grown. 1

full grown 1. גדל 2. *ἀποτελέω*

Ps 144:12 our sons in their youth be like plants full grown 1
Jas 1:15 sin when it is full-grown brings forth death. 2

growth 1. צָמַח 2. *αὔξησις*

Ps 65:10 with showers, and blessing its growth. 1
Eph 4:16 makes bodily growth and upbuilds itself in love. 2
Col 2:19 grows with a growth that is from God. 2

growth *See also* give, rank.

green growth 1. *χλωρός*

Rev 9: 4 not to harm . . any green growth or any tree 1

latter growth 1. לֶקֶשׁ

Ams 7: 1 beginning of the shooting up of the latter growth 1
1 the latter growth after the king's mowings. 1

new growth 1. דֶּשֶׁא

Prv 27:25 When the grass is gone, and the new growth appears 1
Isa 15: 6 the grass is withered, the new growth fails 1

rank growth 1. *περισσεία*

Jas 1:21 all filthiness and rank growth of wickedness 1

grudge 1. רעע 2. רעע עַיִן 3. *βασκαίνω* 4. *ἐνέχω*

Deu 15:10 give . . and your heart shall not be grudging 1
28:54 man . . grudge food to his brother, to the wife 2
56 woman . . will grudge to the husband of her bosom 2
Mrk 6:19 Hero'di-as had a grudge against him 4
Sir 14: 6 meaner than the man who is grudging to himself 3
8 Evil is the man with a grudging eye 3

grudging man 1. *βάσκανος*

Sir 18:18 the gift of a grudging man makes the eyes dim. 1
37:11 with a grudging man about gratitude 1

without grudging 1. *ἀφθόνως*

Wis 7:13 I impart without grudging 1

grumble 1. *γογγύζω* 2. *γογγυσμός* 3. *στενάζω*

Mat 20:11 they grumbled at the householder 1
1Co 10:10 nor grumble, as some of them did 1
Php 2:14 Do all things without grumbling or questioning 2
Jas 5: 9 Do not grumble, brethren, against one another 3
Sir 10:25 a man of understanding will not grumble. 1

grumbler 1. *γογγυστής*

Jde 1:16 These are grumblers, malcontents 1

guarantee 1. *ἀρραβών* 2. *βέβαιος*

Rom 4:16 and be guaranteed to all his descendants– 2
2Co 1:22 given us his Spirit in our hearts as a guarantee. 1
5: 5 who has given us the Spirit as a guarantee. 1
Eph 1:14 which is the guarantee of our inheritance 1

guard 1. טַבָּח 2. מַטָּרָה 3. מִצָּבָה 4. מִשְׁמָר 5. מִשְׁמֶרֶת 6. נצר 7. סָבִיב 8. רוץ 9. שמר 10. שקד 11. טַבָּח (A) 12. *διαφυλάσσω* 13. *δορυφόρος* 14. *κουστωδία* 15. *κρύπτω* 16. *παρεμβολή* 17. *προσέχω* 18. *σωματοφύλαξ* 19. *τηρέω* 20. *τήρησις* 21. *ὑπασπιστής* 22. *ὑπηρέτης* 23. *φρουρά* 24. *φρουρέω* 25. *φυλακή* 26. *φυλάσσω* 27. conservo

Gen 3:24 a flaming sword . . to guard the way to the tree 9
37:36 officer of Pharaoh, the captain of the guard. 1
39: 1 the captain of the guard, an Egyptian 1
40: 3 in the house of the captain of the guard 1
4 The captain of the guard charged Joseph 1
41:10 put me . . in the house of the captain of the guard 1
12 with us, a servant of the captain of the guard; 1
Exd 23:20 angel before you, to guard you on the way 9
Jos 10:18 the cave, and set men by it to guard them; 9
1Sm 2: 9 He will guard the feet of his faithful ones; 9
22:17 the king said to the guard who stood about him 8
25:21 in vain have I guarded all that this fellow has 9
1Kg 14:27 committed them to the . . officers of the guard 8
28 the guard bore them and brought them back 8
2Kg 9:14 Joram . . had been on guard at Ramoth-gilead 9
10:25 Jehu said to the guard and to the officers, "Go 8
25 the guard and the officers cast them out 8
11: 4 the captains of the Carites and of the guards 8
5 who come off . . and guard the king's house 9
6 and a third at the gate behind the guards) 8
6 a third . . shall guard the palace; 9
7 which come on . . and guard the house of the LORD 9
11 the guards stood, every man with his weapons 8
13 heard the noise of the guard and of the people 8
19 he took the captains, the Carites, the guards 8
19 marching through the gate of the guards 8
12: 9 the priests who guarded the threshold put in it 9
25:10 the army . . who were with the captain of the guard 1
11 Nebu'zarad'an the captain of the guard carried 1
12 the captain of the guard left some of . . to be 1
15 gold the captain of the guard took away as gold 1
18 the captain of the guard took Serai'ah 1
20 Nebu'zarad'an the captain of the guard took them 1
1Ch 9:23 were in charge of the gates . . as guards. 5
2Ch 12:10 to the hands of the officers of the guard 8
11 guard came and bore them, and brought them back 8
23:10 he set all the people as a guard for the king 7
Ezr 8:29 Guard them and keep them until you weigh them 10
Neh 3:25 upper house of the king at the court of the guard. 2
4: 9 set a guard as a protection against them day 4
22 may be a guard for us by night and may labor by day. 4
23 neither I . . nor my servants nor the men of the guard 4
7: 3 still standing guard let them shut and bar •
3 Appoint guards from among the inhabitants 5
12:25 gatekeepers standing guard at the storehouses 4
13:22 purify themselves and come and guard the gates 9
Est 2:21 Bigthan and Teresh . . who guarded the threshold 9
6: 2 two . . eunuchs, who guarded the threshold 9
Job 7:12 a sea monster, that thou settest a guard over me? 4
Ps 12: 7 protect us, guard us ever from this generation. 6
25:20 Oh guard my life, and deliver me; 9
39: 1 I said, "I will guard my ways, that I may not sin 9
91:11 charge of you to guard you in all your ways. 9
119: 9 way pure? By guarding it according to thy word. 9
140: 4 Guard me, O LORD, from the hands of the wicked; 9
141: 3 Set a guard over my mouth, O LORD 9
Prv 2: 8 guarding the paths of justice 6
11 understanding will guard you; 6
4: 6 love her, and she will guard you. 6
13 guard her, for she is your life. 6
5: 2 that . . your lips may guard knowledge. 6
13: 3 He who guards his mouth preserves his life; 6
6 Righteousness guards him whose way is upright 6
16:17 he who guards his way preserves his life. 6
22: 5 he who guards himself will keep far from them. 9
27:18 he who guards his master will be honored. 9
Ecc 5: 1 Guard your steps when you go to the house of God; 9
Isa 27: 3 Lest any one harm it, I guard it night and day; 6
Jer 32: 2 in the court of the guard which was in the palace 2
8 my cousin came to me in the court of the guard 2
12 Jews who were sitting in the court of the guard. 2
33: 1 while he was still shut up in the court of the guard 2
37:21 committed Jeremiah to the court of the guard; 2
21 Jeremiah remained in the court of the guard. 2
38: 6 cistern . . which was in the court of the guard 2
13 And Jeremiah remained in the court of the guard. 2
28 Jeremiah remained in the court of the guard 2
39: 9 Then Nebu'zarad'an, the captain of the guard 1
10 Nebu'zarad'an, the captain of the guard, 1
11 Nebu'zarad'an, the captain of the guard, saying 1
13 Nebu'zarad'an the captain of the guard 1
14 and took Jeremiah from the court of the guard. 2
15 while he was shut up in the court of the guard 2
40: 1 the captain of the guard had let him go from Ramah 1
2 The captain of the guard took Jeremiah and said 1
5 So the captain of the guard gave him an allowance 1
41:10 Nebu'zarad'an, the captain of the guard 1
43: 6 Nebu'zarad'an the captain of the guard had left 1
52:14 Chalde'ans, who were with the captain of the guard 1
15 Nebu'zarad'an the captain of the guard 1
16 Nebu'zarad'an the captain of the guard left some 1
19 What was of gold the captain of the guard took 1
24 And the captain of the guard took Serai'ah 1
26 Nebu'zarad'an the captain of the guard took them 1
30 Nebu'zarad'an the captain of the guard 1
Ezk 38: 7 and be a guard for them. 4
Dan 2:14 Ar'ioch, the captain of the king's guard 11
Mic 7: 5 guard the doors of your mouth from her who lies 9
Zec 9: 8 Then I will encamp at my house as a guard 3
Mal 2: 7 For the lips of a priest should guard knowledge 9
Mat 5:25 the judge to the guard, and you be put in prison; 22
26:58 he sat with the guards to see the end. 22
27:66 by sealing the stone and setting a guard. 14
28: 4 for fear of him the guards trembled 19
11 behold, some of the guard went into the city 14
Mrk 14:54 he was sitting with the guards 22
65 the guards received him with blows. 22
Lke 4:10 He will give his angels charge of you, to guard you,' 12
11:21 a strong man, fully armed, guards his own palace 26
Joh 17:12 I have guarded them, and none of them is lost 26
Act 12: 4 four squads of soldiers to guard him 26
6 sentries . . were guarding the prison; 19
10 they had passed the first and the second guard 25
23:35 to be guarded in Herod's praetorium. 26
28:16 with the soldier that guarded him. 26
2Co 11:32 the governor under King Ar'etas guarded the city 24
2Th 3: 3 he will strengthen you and guard you from evil. 26
1Ti 6:20 O Timothy, guard what has been entrusted to you. 26
2Ti 1:12 I am sure that he is able to guard until that Day 26
14 guard the truth that has been entrusted to you 26
1Pe 1: 5 who by God's power are guarded through faith 24
1Es 4:56 should be provided for all who guarded the city 24
8:59 Be watchful and on guard until you deliver them 26
2Es 7:85 are guarded by angels in profound quiet. 27
95 and guarded by angels in profound quiet 27
Tob 12: 7 It is good to guard the secret of a king 15
11 It is good to guard the secret of a king 15
Jdt 7: 5 they remained on guard all that night. 26
7 seized them and set guards of soldiers over them 16
12: 7 Holofernes commanded his guards not to hinder 18
Wis 9:11 guard me with her glory. 26
Sir 6:13 be on guard toward your friends. 17
12:11 watch yourself, and be on your guard against him; 26
18:27 in days of sin he guards against wrongdoing. 17
22:13 guard yourself from him to escape trouble 26
27 O that a guard were set over my mouth 25
26:11 Be on guard against her impudent eye 26
32:23 Guard yourself in every act 9
34:16 a guard against stumbling 25
40:29 guards against that. 26
LJr 1:70 a scarecrow . . that guards nothing 26
1Mc 5:18 he left Joseph . . in Judea to guard it; 20
6:50 stationed a guard there to hold it. 23
9:53 put them under guard in the citadel at Jerusalem. 25
10:32 station in it men of his own choice to guard it. 26
12:34 he stationed a garrison there to guard it. 26
13:12 Jonathan was with him under guard. 25
14: 3 took him to Arsaces, who put him under guard. 25
4Mc 3:12 When his guards complained bitterly 21
5: 2 ordered the guards to seize . . every Hebrew 13
6: 1 the guards who were standing by dragged him 13
8 One of the cruel guards rushed at him 13
23 you, guards of the tyrant, why do you delay? 13
24 the guards brought him to the fire. •
8:13 when the guards had placed before them wheels 13
9:11 Then . . the guards brought forward the eldest 21
16 when the guards said 13
26 the guards brought in the next eldest 13
11: 9 the guards bound him 13
27 it is not the guards of the tyrant 13
17: 1 Some of the guards said 13

18: 7 I guarded the rib from which woman was made. 26
guard *See also* keep, off, soldier.

guard a right 1. iustifico
2Es 2:20 Guard the rights of the widow 1

guard of soldier 1. κουστωδία
Mat 27:65 Pilate said to them, "You have a guard of soldiers; 1

praetorian guard 1. πραιτώριον
Php 1:13 throughout the whole praetorian guard 1

rear guard 1. אסף 2. עָקֵב
Num10:25 Dan, acting as the rear guard of all the camps 1
Jos 6: 9 and the rear guard came after the ark 1
13 and the rear guard came after the ark of the LORD 1
8:13 and its rear guard west of the city. 2
Isa 52:12 and the God of Israel will be your rear guard. 1
58: 8 the glory of the LORD shall be your rear guard. 1

under guard 1. מִשְׁמֶרֶת 2. ἀσφαλῶς
2Sm 20: 3 took the ten . . and put them in a house under guard 1
Mrk 14:44 seize him and lead him away under guard. 2

guardian 1. אמן 2. סכן 3. ἐπίσκοπος 4. ἐπίτροπος
2Kg 10: 1 sent . . and to the guardians of the sons of Ahab 1
5 together with the elders and the guardians 1
Ezk 28:14 With an anointed guardian cherub I placed you; 2
16 the guardian cherub drove you out from the midst 2
Gal 4: 2 he is under guardians and trustees 4
1Pe 2:25 the Shepherd and Guardian of your souls. 3
2Mc 11: 1 Lysias, the king's guardian and kinsman 4
13: 2 with him Lysias, his guardian 4
14: 2 Antiochus and his guardian Lysias. 4

guardian of the law 1. νομοφύλαξ
4Mc 15:32 O guardian of the law 1

guardroom 1. רוץ 2. תָּא הָרָצִים
1Kg 14:28 the guard . . and brought them back to the guardroom. 2
2Ch 12:11 and brought them back to the guardroom. 1

guess 1. εἰκάζω
Wis 9:16 We can hardly guess at what is on earth 1

guest 1. גור 2. קרא 3. ἀνάκειμαι 4. καταλύτης 5. καταλύω 6. κλητός 7. ξενίζω 8. ξένος 9. συμπόσιον 10. συνανάκειμαι 11. υἱός
1Sm 9:24 it was kept . . that you might eat with the guests. •
2Sm 15:11 200 men from Jerusalem who were invited guests •
1Kg 1:41 Adoni'jah and all the guests who were with him 2
49 all the guests of Adoni'jah trembled, and rose 2
Job 19:15 the guests in my house have forgotten me; 1
Prv 9:18 that her guests are in the depths of Sheol. 2
Zep 1: 7 the LORD has . . consecrated his guests. 2
Mat 9:15 Jesus said to them, "Can the wedding guests mourn 11
14: 9 because of his oaths and his guests 10
22:10 so the wedding hall was filled with guests. 3
11 But when the king came in to look at the guests 3
Mrk 2:19 Jesus said to them, "Can the wedding guests fast 11
6:22 she pleased Herod and his guests 10
26 because of his oaths and his guests 3
Lke 5:34 Can you make wedding guests fast 11
19: 7 to be the guest of a man who is a sinner. 5
Act 10:23 So he called them in to be his guests 7
Wis 5:14 the remembrance of a guest who stays but a day 4
19:14 these made slaves of guests 8
3Mc 5:14 seeing that the guests were assembled 6
36 king . . urged the guests to return to . . celebrating. 9

become a guest 1. ἐπιξενόομαι
AEs 16:10 having become our guest 1

passing guest 1. גֵּר
Ps 39:12 I am thy passing guest, a sojourner 1

guest room 1. κατάλυμα 2. ξενία
Mrk 14:14 'The Teacher says, Where is my guest room 1
Lke 22:11 Where is the guest room 1
Phm 1:22 At the same time, prepare a guest room for me 2

guidance 1. תַּחְבֻּלָה 2. ἀφήγημα
Job 37:12 They turn round and round by his guidance 1
Prv 11:14 Where there is no guidance, a people falls; 1
4Mc 14: 6 moved in harmony with the guidance of the mind 2
guidance *See also* seek.

wise guidance 1. תַּחְבֻּלָה
Prv 20:18 by wise guidance wage war. 1
24: 6 for by wise guidance you can wage your war 1

guide 1. דרך 2. נהג 3. נהל 4. נחה 5. ἄγω 6. εὐοδόω 7. ἡγεμών 8. κατευθύνω 9. κυβερνάω 10. μετάγω 11. ὁδηγέω 12. ὁδηγός 13. παιδαγωγός 14. dispono 15. dux
Exd 15:13 thou hast guided them by thy strength 3
Job 31:18 from his mother's womb I guided him 4
38:32 or can you guide the Bear with its children? 4
Ps 31: 3 for thy name's sake lead me and guide me 3
48:14 He will be our guide for ever. 2
67: 4 with equity and guide the nations upon earth. 4
73:24 Thou dost guide me with thy counsel 4
78:52 guided them in the wilderness like a flock. 2
72 tended them, and guided them with skilful hand. 4
Prv 11: 3 The integrity of the upright guides them 4
Ecc 2: 3 my mind still guiding me with wisdom 2
Isa 42:16 in paths . . they have not known I will guide them. 1
49:10 and by springs of water will guide them. 3
51:18 none to guide her among all the sons she has borne 3
58:11 And the LORD will guide you continually 4
Mat 15:14 Let them alone; they are blind guides 12
23:16 Woe to you, blind guides, who say 12
24 You blind guides, straining out a gnat 12
Lke 1:79 to guide our feet into the way of peace. 8
Joh 16:13 he will guide you into all the truth 11
Act 1:16 Judas who was guide to those who arrested Jesus. 12
8:31 he said, "How can I, unless some one guides me? 11
Rom 2:19 if you are sure that you are a guide to the blind 12
1Co 4:15 For though you have countless guides in Christ 13
Jas 3: 3 we guide their whole bodies. 10
4 they are guided by a very small rudder 10
Rev 7:17 and he will guide them to springs of living water; 11
2Es 8:11 and afterwards thou wilt guide him in thy mercy. 14
16:75 Do not fear or doubt, for God is your guide. 15
Tob 7:12 The merciful God will guide you both for the best. 6
Jdt 13:18 guided you to strike the head of the leader 8
Wis 7:15 the guide even of wisdom 12
9:11 she will guide me wisely in my actions 11
10:10 she guided him on straight paths 11
17 she guided them along a marvelous way 11
14: 6 guided by thy hand 9
18: 3 a guide for thy people's unknown journey 12
1Mc 4: 2 Men from the citadel were his guides. 12
6:15 that he might guide Antiochus his son 5
2Mc 5:15 guided by Menelaus, who had become a traitor 12
3Mc 7: 2 the great God guiding our affairs 8
4Mc 1:30 For reason is the guide of the virtues 7

guidepost 1. תַּמְרוּר
Jer 31:21 make yourself guideposts; 1

guile 1. מִרְמָה 2. מַשָּׁאוֹן 3. שֶׁקֶר 4. γοητεία 5. δόλος
Gen 27:35 he said, "Your brother came with guile 1
Ps 119:78 shame, because they have subverted me with guile; 3
Prv 26:26 though his hatred be covered with guile 2
Joh 1:47 Behold, an Israelite indeed, in whom is no guile! 5
2Co 12:16 I was crafty . . and got the better of you by guile. 5
1Th 2: 3 nor is it made with guile; 5
1Pe 2: 1 So put away all malice and all guile 5
22 no guile was found on his lips. 5
3:10 let him keep . . his lips from speaking guile; 5
Wis 4:11 lest . . guile deceive his soul. 5
2Mc 12:24 With great guile he besought them to let him go 4

without guile 1. ἀδόλως
Wis 7:13 I learned without guile 1

guileless 1. ἀκέραιος
Rom16:19 and guileless as to what is evil; 1

guilt 1. אָשָׁם 2. אַשְׁמָה 3. עָוֹן 4. רָעָה 5. ἁμαρτία 6. iniquitas
Gen 26:10 and you would have brought guilt upon us. 1
44:16 God has found out the guilt of your servants; 3
Exd 28:38 Aaron shall take upon himself any guilt 3
43 lest they bring guilt upon themselves and die. 3
Lev 22:16 so cause them to bear iniquity and guilt 2
Deu 19:13 purge the guilt of innocent blood from Israel •
21: 8 set not the guilt of innocent blood in the midst •
8 but let the guilt of blood be forgiven them.' •
9 purge the guilt of innocent blood •
1Sm 14:41 If this guilt is in me or in Jonathan my son, O LORD 6
41 if this guilt is in thy people . . give Thummim. 6
20: 1 What have I done? What is my guilt? 3
8 But if there is guilt in me, slay me yourself; 3
25:24 Upon me alone, my lord, be the guilt; 3
26:18 For what have I done? What guilt is on my hands? 4
2Sm 14: 9 On me be the guilt, my lord the king 3
32 if there is guilt in me, let him kill me.' 3
22:24 I was blameless . . and I kept myself from guilt. 3
1Kg 2:31 take away . . the guilt for the blood which Jo'ab •
1Ch 21: 3 Why should he bring guilt upon Israel? 2
2Ch 24:18 wrath came upon Judah . . for this their guilt. 2
28:13 in addition to our present sins and guilt. 2
13 For our guilt is already great 2
Ezr 9: 6 our guilt has mounted up to the heavens. 2
7 to this day we have been in great guilt; 2
13 for our evil deeds and for our great guilt 2
15 Behold, we are before thee in our guilt 2
10:10 so increased the guilt of Israel. 2
19 offering was a ram of the flock for their guilt. 2
Neh 4: 5 Do not cover their guilt, and let not their sin 3
Job 11: 6 God exacts of you less than your guilt deserves. 3
Ps 18:23 I kept myself from guilt. 3
25:11 O LORD, pardon my guilt, for it is great. 3
32: 5 then thou didst forgive the guilt of my sin. 3
Isa 6: 7 your guilt is taken away, and your sin forgiven. 3
14:21 because of the guilt of their fathers 3
27: 9 by this the guilt of Jacob will be expiated 3
Jer 2:22 the stain of your guilt is still before me 3
3:13 Only acknowledge your guilt, that you rebelled 3
30:14 because your guilt is great, because your sins 3
15 pain is incurable. Because your guilt is great 3
32:18 requite the guilt of fathers to their children 3
33: 8 from all the guilt of their sin against me 3
8 and I will forgive all the guilt of their sin 3
51: 5 the land of the Chalde'ans is full of guilt 1
Ezk 9: 9 The guilt of the house of Israel and Judah is 3
16:49 Behold, this was the guilt of your sister Sodom 3
21:23 but he brings their guilt to remembrance 3
24 you have made your guilt to be remembered 3
Hos 5: 5 E'phraim shall stumble in his guilt; 3
12: 8 can never offset the guilt he has incurred. 3
Zec 3: 9 I will remove the guilt of this land 3
Joh 9:41 If you were blind, you would have no guilt 5
41 now that you say, 'We see,' your guilt remains. 5
Wis 1: 6 not free a blasphemer from the guilt of his words; •
guilt *See also* acknowledge, bear, bring, incur, offering, suffer.

guilt of blood 1. דָּם
Deu 22: 8 may not bring the guilt of blood upon your house 1

guilt of bloodshed 1. דָּם
Deu 19:10 so the guilt of bloodshed be upon you. 1
guiltiness *See* blood.

guiltless 1. נקה 2. נָקִי 3. ἁγνός 4. ἀναίτιος 5. ἀνέγκλητος
Jos 2:17 We will be guiltless with respect to this oath 2
19 blood shall be upon . . and we shall be guiltless; 2
20 we shall be guiltless with respect to your oath 2
1Sm 26: 9 Do not destroy him; for who can . . and be guiltless? 1
2Sm 3:28 I and my kingdom are . . guiltless before the LORD 2
14: 9 let the king and his throne be guiltless. 2
Jer 2:34 is found the lifeblood of guiltless poor; 2
Mat 12: 5 profane the sabbath, and are guiltless? 4
7 you would not have condemned the guiltless. 4
1Co 1: 8 guiltless in the day of our Lord Jesus Christ. 5
2Co 7:11 proved yourselves guiltless in the matter. 3
guiltless *See also* hold.

guilty 1. אשם 2. וָזָר 3. מַעַל 4. עָוֹן 5. רשע 6. רָשָׁע 7. αἴτιος 8. ἁμαρτάνω 9. ἔνοχος 10. ποιέω
Gen 42:21 In truth we are guilty concerning our brother 1
Lev 4:13 has commanded not to be done and are guilty 1
22 has commanded not to be done, and is guilty 1
27 has commanded not to be done, and is guilty 1
5: 2 he has become unclean, he shall be guilty 1
3 when he comes to know it he shall be guilty 1
4 he shall in any of these be guilty 1
5 When a man is guilty in any of these, he shall 1
17 though he does not know it, yet he is guilty 1
19 It is a guilt offering; he is guilty 1
Num 5: 6 When a man or woman . . that person is guilty 1
14:18 but he will by no means clear the guilty 4
35:27 he shall not be guilty of blood. •
31 for the life of a murderer, who is guilty of death;. 6
Deu 25: 1 innocent and condemning the guilty 6
Jdg 21:22 did you give . . else you would now be guilty. 1
2Sm 19:19 Let not my lord hold me guilty or remember how 4
1Kg 8:32 condemning the guilty by bringing his conduct 6
2Ch 6:23 requiting the guilty by bringing his conduct 6
Job 10: 7 although thou knowest that I am not guilty 5
Ps 109: 7 When he is tried, let him come forth guilty; 6
Prv 21: 8 The way of the guilty is crooked 2
Isa 5:23 who acquit the guilty for a bribe 6
Jer 50: 7 and their enemies have said, 'We are not guilty 1
Ezk 18:24 the treachery of which he is guilty and the sin 3
35: 6 because you are guilty of blood 8
Mrk 3:29 guilty of an eternal sin" 9
Lke 23:14 guilty of any of your charges against him; 7
1Co 5:11 if he is guilty of immorality or greed •
11:27 be guilty of profaning the body and blood of the Lord. 9
Jas 2:10 whoever . . fails in one point has become guilty 9
1Jn 3: 4 one who commits sin is guilty of lawlessness; 10
Sus 1:53 and letting the guilty go free 7
2Mc 13: 6 any man guilty of sacrilege 9
guilty *See also* clear, declare, hold.

become guilty 1. אשׁם
Lev 6: 4 when one has sinned and become guilty 1
7 which one may do and thereby become guilty 1
Jer 2: 3 All who ate of it became guilty; 1
Ezk 22: 4 You have become guilty by the blood 1
Hos 4:15 O Israel, let not Judah become guilty. 1

guilty man 1. אשׁם 2. רָשָׁע
Deu 25: 2 then if the guilty man deserves to be beaten 2
Hab 1:11 guilty men, whose own might is their god! 1

show less guilty 1. צדק
Jer 3:11 Faithless Israel has shown herself less guilty 1

guilty way 1. אָשָׁם

Ps 68:21 hairy crown of him who walks in his guilty ways. 1

gull *See* sea.

gully 1. עָרוּץ

Job 30: 6 In the gullies of the torrents they must dwell 1

gum 1. נְכֹאת

Gen 37:25 with their camels bearing gum, balm, and myrrh 1
43:11 a little honey, gum, myrrh, pistachio nuts 1

gush 1. נבע 2. נזל 3. κρουνηδόν

Prv 18: 4 fountain of wisdom is a gushing stream. 1
Jer 9:18 with tears, and our eyelids gush with water. 2
2Mc 14:45 though his blood gushed forth 3

gush forth 1. זוב

Ps 105:41 He opened the rock, and water gushed forth; 1

make gush forth 1. שלח

Ps 104:10 Thou makest springs gush forth in the valleys; 1

gush out 1. זוב 2. שפך 3. ἐκχέω

1Kg 18:28 cut themselves . . until the blood gushed out 2
Ps 78:20 He smote the rock so that water gushed out 1
Isa 48:21 he cleft the rock and the water gushed out. 1
Act 1:18 all his bowels gushed out. 3

gymnasium 1. γυμνάσιον

1Mc 1:14 So they built a gymnasium in Jerusalem 1
2Mc 4: 9 to establish by his authority a gymnasium 1
12 with alacrity he founded a gymnasium 1
4Mc 4:20 not only was a gymnasium constructed 1

H

habit 1. ἐθισμός 2. ἔθος 3. ἐνδελεχισμός 4. ἦθος
Heb 10:25 as is the habit of some 2
Sir 7:13 the habit of lying serves no good. 3
23:14 be deemed a fool on account of your habits 1
4Mc 1:29 so tames the jungle of habits and emotions. 4
13:27 virtuous habits had augmented the affection 4

habitable 1. ישב 2. οἰκητός
Exd 16:35 forty years, till they came to a habitable land; 1
3Mc 4: 3 or what habitable place at all 2

habitable world 1. תֵּבֵל אֶרֶץ
Job 37:12 on the face of the habitable world. 1

habitation 1. זְבֻל 2. מוֹשָׁב 3. מָעוֹן 4. מְעֹנָה 5. מִשְׁכָּן 6. נָוֶה 7. נָוָה 8. שׁכן 9. ἔπαυλις 10. κατασκήνωσις 11. κατοικία 12. οἶκος 13. σκηνή 14. σκήνωμα 15. σκήνωσις 16. habitaculum 17. inhabitatio 18. tabernaculum
Exd 35: 3 you shall kindle no fire in all your habitations 2
Lev 13:46 dwell alone in a habitation outside the camp 2
Deu 26:15 Look down from thy holy habitation, from heaven 3
2Sm 15:25 he will . . let me see both it and his habitation; 7
2Ch 29: 6 turned away . . from the habitation of the LORD 5
30:27 their prayer came to his holy habitation 3
Job 8: 6 and reward you with a rightful habitation. 7
18:15 brimstone is scattered upon his habitation. 7
Ps 26: 8 O LORD, I love the habitation of thy house 3
46: 4 city of God, the holy habitation of the Most High. 5
68: 5 Father . . is God in his holy habitation. 3
74:20 are full of the habitations of violence. 6
78:28 let them fall . . all around their habitations. 5
79: 7 devoured Jacob, and laid waste his habitation. 7
91: 9 have made . . Most High your habitation 3
104:12 birds of the air have their habitation; 8
132:13 chosen Zion; he has desired it for his habitation 2
Isa 22:16 carve a habitation for yourself in the rock? 5
27:10 a habitation deserted and forsaken 7
32:18 My people will abide in a peaceful habitation 7
33:20 Your eyes will see Jerusalem, a quiet habitation 7
54: 2 curtains of your habitations be stretched out; 5
63:15 and see, from thy holy and glorious habitation. 1
Jer 10:25 and have laid waste his habitation. 7
21:13 or who shall enter our habitations? 4
25:30 and from his holy habitation utter his voice; 3
31:23 LORD bless you, O habitation of righteousness 7
33:12 there shall again be habitations of shepherds 7
50: 7 sinned against the LORD, their true habitation 7
Lam 2: 2 has destroyed . . all the habitations of Jacob; 6
Ezk 6:14 and waste, throughout all their habitations 2
Hab 1: 6 who march . . to seize habitations not their own. 5
3:11 The sun and moon stood still in their habitation 1
Lke 16: 9 receive you into the eternal habitations. 13
Act 1:20 Let his habitation become desolate 9
7:46 find a habitation for the God of Jacob. 14
17:26 the boundaries of their habitation 11
2Es 2:11 to these others the everlasting habitations 18
7:80 such spirits shall not enter into habitations 17
85 how the habitations of the others are guarded 16
101 they shall be gathered in their habitations. 16
121 safe and healthful habitations 16
Wis 9: 8 an altar in the city of thy habitation 10
Sir 44: 6 living peaceably in their habitations– 11
Bar 2:16 O Lord, look down from thy holy habitation 12
2Mc 14:35 a temple for thy habitation among us; 15

habitation *See also* make.

habitual 1. ἐνδελεχίζω
Sir 20:25 A thief is preferable to a habitual liar 1

habitually 1. ἦθος 2. συνεθίζω
Sir 23: 9 do not habitually utter the name of the Holy One; 2
4Mc 2: 7 habitually a solitary gormandizer, a glutton 1

hack
Ps 74: 5 they hacked the wooden trellis with axes. •

night hag 1. לִילִית
Isa 34:14 yea, there shall the night hag alight 1

haggard 1. דַּל
2Sm 13: 4 why are you so haggard morning after morning? 1

hail 1. בָּרָד 2. χάλαζα 3. grando
Exd 9:18 I will cause very heavy hail to fall, such as never 1
19 for the hail shall come down upon every man 1
22 that there may be hail in all the land of Egypt 1
23 the LORD sent thunder and hail, and fire ran down 1
23 the LORD rained hail upon the land of Egypt; 1
24 there was hail, a fire flashing continually 1
24 flashing continually in the midst of the hail 1
24 there was . . very heavy hail, such as had never 1
25 The hail struck down everything that was 1
25 the hail struck down every plant of the field 1
26 in the land of Goshen . . there was no hail. 1
28 there has been enough of this thunder and hail 1
29 there will be no more hail, that you may know that 1
33 the thunder and the hail ceased, and the rain 1
34 the rain and the hail and the thunder had ceased 1
10: 5 they shall eat what is left to you after the hail 1
12 that they may . . eat . . all that the hail has left. 1
15 they ate all . . which the hail had left; 1
Job 38:22 have you seen the storehouses of the hail 1
Ps 78:47 He destroyed their vines with hail 1
48 He gave over their cattle to the hail 1
105:32 He gave them hail for rain 1
148: 8 fire and hail, snow and frost, stormy wind 1
Isa 28: 2 like a storm of hail, a destroying tempest 1
17 hail will sweep away the refuge of lies 1
Hag 2:17 I smote you . . with blight and mildew and hail; 1
Rev 8: 7 there followed hail and fire, mixed with blood 2
11:19 peals of thunder, an earthquake, and heavy hail. 2
16:21 till men cursed God for the plague of the hail 2
2Es 7:41 winter or frost or cold or hail or rain or dew 3
15:13 by blight and hail and by a terrible tempest. 3
41 fire and hail and flying swords 3
Wis 16:16 unusual rains and hail and relentless storms 2
22 the fire that blazed in the hail 2
Sir 39:29 Fire and hail and famine and pestilence 2

hail (2) 1. ענה 2. χαίρω
1Sm 14:12 the men . . hailed Jonathan and his armor-bearer 1
Mat 26:49 he came up to Jesus at once and said, "Hail, Master! 2
27:29 they mocked him, saying, "Hail, King of the Jews! 2
28: 9 behold, Jesus met them and said, "Hail! 2
Mrk 15:18 they began to salute him, "Hail, King of the Jews! 2
Lke 1:28 he came to her and said, "Hail, O favored one 2
Joh 19: 3 they came up to him, saying, "Hail, King of the Jews! 2

hailstone 1. אֶבֶן אֶלְגָּבִישׁ 2. אֶבֶן בָּרָד 3. בָּרָד 4. λίθος χαλάζης 5. χάλαζα
Jos 10:11 were more who died because of the hailstones 2
Ps 18:12 there broke through his clouds hailstones 3
13 uttered his voice, hailstones and coals of fire. 3
Isa 30:30 with a cloudburst and tempest and hailstones. 2
Ezk 13:11 be a deluge of rain, great hailstones will fall 1
13 and great hailstones in wrath to destroy it. 1
38:22 torrential rains and hailstones 1
Rev 16:21 great hailstones . . dropped on men from heaven 5
Wis 5:22 hailstones full of wrath will be hurled 5
Sir 43:15 the hailstones are broken in pieces. 4
46: 6 hailstones of mighty power 4

hair 1. נֵזֶר 2. שֵׂעָר 3. שַׂעֲרָה 4. שְׂעַר (A) 5. θρίξ 6. κεφαλή 7. κόμη 8. τρίχωμα 9. coma
Lev 10: 6 Do not let the hair of your heads hang loose •
13: 3 if the hair in the diseased spot has turned white 2
4 if . . the hair in it has not turned white 2
10 swelling . . which has turned the hair white 2
20 if . . its hair has turned white, then the priest 2
21 if . . the hair on it is not white 2
25 if the hair in the spot has turned white 2
26 if . . the hair in the spot is not white 2
30 if . . the hair in it is yellow and thin 2
31 if . . there is no black hair in it 2
32 if . . there is in it no yellow hair 2
36 the priest need not seek for the yellow hair 2
37 if . . itch is checked, black hair has grown in it 2
40 If a man's hair has fallen from his head, he is bald •
41 if a man's hair has fallen from his forehead •
45 shall . . let the hair of his head hang loose •
14: 8 shave off all his hair, and bathe himself in water 2
9 he shall shave all his hair off his head 2
9 his beard and his eyebrows, all his hair 2
19:27 You shall not round off the hair on your temples •
21:10 shall not let the hair of his head hang loose •
Num 6: 5 shall let the locks of hair of his head grow long. 2
18 shall take the hair from his consecrated head 2
Jdg 16:22 the hair of his head began to grow again 2
20:16 could sling a stone at a hair, and not miss. 3
1Sm 14:45 shall not one hair of his head fall to the ground; 3
19:13 and put a pillow of goats' hair at its head •
16 with the pillow of goats' hair at its head. •
2Sm 14:11 not one hair of your son shall fall to the ground. 3
26 he weighed the hair of his head, 200 shekels 2
1Kg 1:52 If . . not one of his hairs shall fall to the earth; 3
Ezr 9: 3 pulled hair from my head and beard 2
Job 4:15 glided past my face; the hair of my flesh stood up. 3
Ps 40:12 they are more than the hairs of my head; 3
69: 4 More in number than the hairs of my head 3
Sng 4: 1 Your hair is like a flock of goats 2
6: 5 Your hair is like a flock of goats 2
Isa 7:20 shave . . the head and the hair of the feet 2
Jer 7:29 Cut off your hair and cast it away; 1
9:26 in the desert that cut the corners of their hair; •
25:23 Buz, and all who cut the corners of their hair; •
49:32 those who cut the corners of their hair •
Ezk 5: 1 take balances for weighing, and divide the hair. •
16: 7 your breasts were formed, and your hair had grown; 2
23:34 and pluck out your hair, and tear your breasts; •
44:20 they shall only trim the hair of their heads. •
Dan 3:27 hair of their heads was not singed 4
4:33 till his hair grew as long as eagles' feathers 4
7: 9 as snow, and the hair of his head like pure wool; 4
Mic 1:16 Make yourselves bald and cut off your hair •
Mat 3: 4 a garment of camel's hair, and a leather girdle 5
5:36 head, for you cannot make one hair white or black. 5
10:30 even the hairs of your head are all numbered. 5
Mrk 1: 6 Now John was clothed in camel's hair 5
Lke 7:38 wiped them with the hair of her head 5
44 wiped them with her hair. 5
12: 7 Why, even the hairs of your head are all numbered. 5
21:18 not a hair of your head will perish. 5
Joh 11: 2 wiped his feet with her hair 5
12: 3 wiped his feet with her hair 5
Act 18:18 At Cen'chre-ae he cut his hair, for he had a vow. 6
27:34 since not a hair is to perish from the head of any 5
1Co 11:15 her hair is given to her for a covering. 7
1Pe 3: 3 outward adorning with braiding of hair 5
Rev 1:14 his head and his hair were white as white wool 5
9: 8 their hair like women's hair, and their teeth like 5
8 their hair like women's hair, and their teeth like 5
1Es 8:71 pulled out hair from my head and beard 8
2Es 1: 8 Pull out the hair of your head 9
Jdt 10: 3 and combed her hair and put on a tiara 5
13: 7 and took hold of the hair of his head 7
16: 8 fastened her hair with a tiara 5
AEs 14: 2 she covered with her tangled hair. 5
Sir 27:14 makes one's hair stand on end 5
Bel 1:27 took pitch, fat, and hair, and boiled them together 5
36 lifted him by his hair and set him down in Babylon 7
2Mc 7: 7 They tore off the skin of his head with the hair 5
3Mc 1:18 sprinkled their hair with dust 7

4: 6 their myrrh-perfumed hair sprinkled with ashes 7
6: 6 you rescued unharmed, even to a hair 5

hair *See also* braided, cut, goat's, pull, shave, unbind, wear.

goat's hair 1. עֵז
Exd 26: 7 You shall also make curtains of goats' hair 1
35: 6 scarlet stuff and fine twined linen; goats' hair 1
23 scarlet stuff or fine linen or goats' hair 1
26 women . . with ability spun the goats' hair. 1
36:14 He also made curtains of goats' hair for a tent 1
Num31:20 purify . . all work of goats' hair 1

gray hair 1. שֵׂיבָה 2. πολιά
Gen 42:38 you would bring down my gray hairs with sorrow 1
44:29 you will bring down my gray hairs in sorrow 1
31 bring down the gray hairs of your servant 1
Deu 32:25 the sucking child with the man of gray hairs. 1
Ps 71:18 to old age and gray hairs, O God, do not forsake me 1
Prv 20:29 beauty of old men is their gray hair. 1
Isa 46: 4 I am He, and to gray hairs I will carry you. 1
Hos 7: 9 gray hairs are sprinkled upon him 1
Wis 2:10 nor regard the gray hairs of the aged. 2
4: 9 understanding is gray hair for men 2
2Mc 6:23 gray hairs . . he had reached with distinction 2
15:13 distinguished by his gray hair and dignity 2
4Mc 5: 7 for I respect your age and your gray hairs. 2
7:15 O man of blessed age and of venerable gray hair 2

long hair 1. κομάω
1Co 11:15 if a woman has long hair, it is her pride 1

well-set hair 1. מַעֲשֶׂה מִקְשֶׁה
Isa 3:24 instead of well-set hair, baldness; 1

haircloth 1. שֵׂעָר 2. cilicium
2Kg 1: 8 They answered him, "He wore a garment of haircloth 1
2Es 16: 2 Gird yourselves with sackcloth and haircloth 2

gray haired 1. שִׂיב
Job 15:10 Both the gray-haired and the aged are among us 1

gray haired man 1. πολιά
Sir 25: 4 judgment in gray-haired men 1

long haired 1. פֶּרַע
Deu 32:42 from the long-haired heads of the enemy.' 1

hairy 1. שֵׂעָר 2. שָׂעִר
Gen 25:25 came forth red, all his body like a hairy mantle; 1
27:11 Behold, my brother Esau is a hairy man 2
23 his hands were hairy like his brother Esau's 2
Ps 68:21 hairy crown of him who walks in his guilty ways. 1
Zec 13: 4 not put on a hairy mantle in order to deceive 1

half 1. בֶּתֶר 2. חֵצִי 3. מֶחֱצָה 4. מַחֲצִית 5. מִשְׁנֶה 6. פֶּלַח 7. פְּלַג (A) 8. ἥμισυς 9. dimidium 10. dimidius 11. medius
Gen 15:10 in two, and laid each half over against the other; 1
Exd 24: 6 Moses took half of the blood and put it in basins 2
6 and half of the blood he threw against the altar. 2
25:10 two cubits and a half shall be its length 2
10 a cubit and a half its breadth 2
10 and a cubit and a half its height. 2
17 two cubits and a half shall be its length 2
17 and a cubit and a half its breadth. 2
23 and a cubit and a half its height. 2
26:12 the half curtain that remains, shall hang over 2
16 a cubit and a half the breadth of each frame. 2
30:13 Each . . shall give this: half a shekel according 4
13 half a shekel as an offering to the LORD. 4
15 shall not give less, than the half shekel 4
36:21 a cubit and a half the breadth of each frame. 2
37: 1 two cubits and a half was its length 2
1 a cubit and a half its breadth, and a cubit 2
1 its breadth, and a cubit and a half its height. 2
6 two cubits and a half was its length 2
6 its length, and a cubit and a half its breadth. 2
10 its breadth, and a cubit and a half its height; 2
38:26 a beka a head (that is, half a shekel, by the shekel 4
Lev 6:20 fine flour . . half of it in the morning 4
20 in the morning and half in the evening 4
Num12:12 as one dead, of whom the flesh is half consumed 2
15: 9 fine flour, mixed with half a hin of oil 2
10 offer for the drink offering half a hin of wine 2
28:14 offerings shall be half a hin of wine for a bull 2
31:29 take it from their half, and give it to Elea'zar 4
30 from the people of Israel's half you shall take 4
36 half, the portion of those who had gone out to war 3
42 From the people of Israel's half, which Moses 4
43 now the congregation's half was 337,500 sheep 3
47 from the people of Israel's half Moses took 4
32:33 to the half-tribe of Manas'seh the son of Joseph 2
34:13 to give to the nine tribes and to the half-tribe 2
14 also the half-tribe of Manas'seh; 2
15 two tribes and the half-tribe have received 2
Deu 3:12 half the hill country of Gilead with its cities; 2
13 the rest . . I gave to the half-tribe of Manas'seh. 2
15:18 at half the cost of a hired servant he has served 5
29: 8 inheritance to . . half-tribe of the Manas'sites. 2
Jos 1:12 the Gadites, and the half-tribe of Manas'seh 2
4:12 and the sons of Gad and the half-tribe of Manas'seh 2
8:33 Israel . . half of them in front of Mount Ger'izim 2
33 half . . and half of them in front of Mount Ebal 2
12: 2 ruled from . . as far as.., that is, half of Gilead 2
5 ruled over . . and over half of Gilead 2
6 and the Gadites and the half-tribe of Manas'seh. 2
13: 7 the nine tribes and half the tribe of Manas'seh. 2
8 With the other half of the tribe of Manas'seh 8
25 and half the land of the Ammonites, to Aro'er 2
29 Moses gave . . to the half-tribe of Manas'seh; 2
29 was allotted to the half-tribe of the Manas'sites 2
31 and half Gilead, and Ash'taroth, and Ed're-i 2
31 were allotted . . for the half of the Machirites 2
18: 7 and Gad and Reuben and half the tribe of Manas'seh 2
21: 5 the tribe of Dan and the half-tribe of Manas'seh 2
6 and from the half-tribe of Manas'seh in Bashan 2
25 and out of the half-tribe of Manas'seh, Ta'anach 4
27 were given out of the half-tribe of Manas'seh 2
22: 1 and the Gadites, and the half-tribe of Manas'seh 2
7 Now to the one half of . . Manas'seh Moses had given 2
7 to the other half Joshua had given a possession 2
9 the Gadites and the half-tribe of Manas'seh 2
10 the Gadites and the half-tribe of Manas'seh built 2
11 and the half-tribe of Manas'seh have built 2
13 and the Gadites and the half-tribe of Manas'seh 2
15 to . . the Gadites, and the half-tribe of Manas'seh 2
21 the Gadites, and the half-tribe of Manas'seh said 2
1Sm 14:14 twenty men within . . half a furrow's length 2
2Sm 10: 4 and shaved off half the beard of each, and cut off 2
18: 3 If half of us die, they will not care about us. 2
19:40 all . . of Judah, and also half the people of Israel 2
1Kg 3:25 child in two, and give half to the one, and half 2
25 two, and give half to the one, and half to the other. 2
7:31 its opening was round . . a cubit and a half deep. 2
32 and the height of a wheel was a cubit and a half. 2
35 on the top . . was a round band half a cubit high; 2
10: 7 and behold, the half was not told me; 2
13: 8 If you give me half your house, I will not go 2
16: 9 Zimri, commander of half his chariots, conspired 4
21 half of the people followed Tibni. 2
21 Tibni . . to make him king, and half followed Omri. 2
1Ch 2:52 other sons: Haro'eh, half of the Menu'hoth. 2
54 sons of Salma . . half of the Man'aha'thites 2
5:18 the half-tribe of Manas'seh had valiant men 2
23 the half-tribe of Manas'seh dwelt in the land 2
26 them away . . and the half-tribe of Manas'seh 2
6:61 out of the half-tribe, the half of Manas'seh 4
61 out of the half-tribe, the half of Manas'seh 2
70 out of the half-tribe of Manas'seh, Aner 4
71 were given out of the half-tribe of Manas'seh 2
12:31 Of the half-tribe of Manas'seh 18,000 2
37 and Gadites and the half-tribe of Manas'seh 2
26:32 the Gadites, and the half-tribe of the Manas'sites 2
27:20 for the half-tribe of Manas'seh, Jo'el the son 2
21 for the half-tribe of Manas'seh in Gilead, 2
2Ch 9: 6 half the greatness of your wisdom was not told me; 2
Neh 3: 9 ruler of half the district of Jerusalem 2
12 ruler of half the district of Jerusalem 2
16 ruler of half the district of Beth-zur 2
17 Hashabi'ah, ruler of half the district of Kei'lah 2
18 Bav'vai . . ruler of half the district of Kei'lah; 2
4: 6 wall was joined together to half its height. 2
16 half of my servants worked on construction 2
16 half held the spears, shields, bows 2
21 half of them held the spears from the break 2
12:32 went Hoshai'ah and half of the princes of Judah 2
38 I followed them with half of the people 2
40 house of God, and I and half of the officials 2
13:24 half of their children spoke the language 2
Est 5: 3 It shall be . . even to the half of my kingdom. 2
6 Even to the half of my kingdom, it shall be 2
7: 2 Even to the half of my kingdom, it shall be 2
Sng 4: 3 Your cheeks are like halves of a pomegranate 6
6: 7 Your cheeks are like halves of a pomegranate 6
Isa 44:16 Half of it he burns in the fire; 2
16 over the half he eats flesh, he roasts meat 2
19 Half of it I burned in the fire 2
Ezk 16:51 Sama'ria has not committed half your sins; 2
40:42 a cubit and a half long, and a cubit and a half broad 2
42 a cubit and a half long, and a cubit and a half broad 2
43:17 with a rim around it half a cubit broad 2
Dan 7:25 into his hand for a time, two times, and half a time 7
9:27 for half of the week he shall cause sacrifice 2
12: 7 would be for a time, two times, and half a time; 2
Zec 14: 2 half of the city shall go into exile 2
4 one half of the Mount shall withdraw northward 2
4 northward, and the other half southward. 2
8 from Jerusalem, half of them to the eastern sea 2
8 eastern sea and half of them to the western sea; 2
Mrk 6:23 I will give you, even half of my kingdom. 8
Lke 19: 8 the half of my goods I give to the poor 8
Rev 11: 9 For three days and a half men from the peoples 8
11 after the three and a half days a breath of life 8
12:14 be nourished for a time, and times, and half a time. 8
2Es 13:45 a long way to go, a journey of a year and a half 10
14:12 as well as half of the tenth part 9
12 besides half of the tenth part. 11
Tob 8:21 then he should take half of Raguel's property 8
10:10 half of his property in slaves, cattle, and money. 8
12: 2 to give him half of what I have brought back. 8
5 Take half of all that you two have brought back. 8
Sir 29: 6 he will hardly get back half 8
1Mc 3:34 he turned over to Lysias half of his troops 8
37 the king took the remaining half of his troops 8
10:30 the half of the fruit of the trees 8

half *See also* live.

half an hour 1. ἡμίωρον
Rev 8: 1 silence in heaven for about half an hour. 1

half as long 1. dimidium
2Es 11:17 rule as long as you, or even half as long. 1

half as much 1. מַחֲצִית
Exd 30:23 of sweet-smelling cinnamon half as much 1

half dead 1. ἡμιθανής 2. ἡμίθνητος
Lke 10:30 and departed, leaving him half dead. 1
Wis 18:18 one here and another there, hurled down half dead 2
4Mc 4:11 Then Apollonius fell down half dead 1

half gone 1. μεσάζω
Wis 18:14 and night in its swift course was now half gone 1

half shekel 1. בֶּקַע
Gen 24:22 the man took a gold ring weighing a half shekel 1

half-shekel 1. δίδραχμον
Mat 17:24 the collectors of the half-shekel tax 1

halfway 1. חֲצִי
Exd 27: 5 the net shall extend halfway down the altar. 1
38: 4 a grating . . extending halfway down. 1

halfway up 1. בְּתוֹךְ
Exd 26:28 The middle bar, halfway up the frames, shall pass 1
36:33 from end to end halfway up the frames. 1

hall 1. בַּיִת אוּלָם 2. בַּיִת 3. לִשְׁכָּה 4. בַּיִת (A) 5. σχολή
1Sm 9:22 Samuel took . . and brought them into the hall 3
1Kg 7: 6 he made the Hall of Pillars; its length was 50 cubits 1
7 he made the Hall of the Throne 1
7 Hall of the Throne . . even the Hall of Judgment; 1
8 own house . . in the other court back of the hall 1
8 Solomon also made a house like this hall 1
Est 5: 1 in the inner court . . opposite the king's hall. 2
Dan 5:10 queen . . came into the banqueting hall; 4
Act 19: 9 and argued daily in the hall of Tyran'nus. 5

audience hall 1. ἀκροατήριον
Act 25:23 and they entered the audience hall 1

banquet hall 1. συμπόσιον
1Mc 16:16 and rushed in against Simon in the banquet hall 1

wedding hall 1. νυμφών
Mat 22:10 so the wedding hall was filled with guests. 1

hallow 1. קדשׁ 2. ἁγιάζω 3. μεθ' ἁγιότητος
Gen 2: 3 God blessed the seventh day and hallowed it 1
Exd 20:11 LORD blessed the sabbath day and hallowed it. 1
28:38 the people of Israel hallow as their holy gifts; 1
Lev 16:19 cleanse it and hallow it from the uncleannesses 1
22:32 I will be hallowed among the people of Israel 1
25:10 you shall hallow the 50th year, and proclaim 1
2Ch 36:14 house . . which he had hallowed in Jerusalem. 1
Ezk 20:20 hallow my sabbaths that they may be a sign 1
Mat 6: 9 Father who art in heaven, Hallowed be thy name. 2
Lke 11: 2 hallowed be thy name. Thy kingdom come. 2
1Es 1:49 which had been hallowed in Jerusalem. 2
Sir 33: 9 some of them he exalted and hallowed 2
2Mc 15: 2 honored and hallowed above other days 3

hallowed part 1. מִקְדָּשׁ
Num18:29 giving the hallowed part from them.' 1

hallowed thing 1. קֹדֶשׁ
Lev 12: 4 she shall not touch any hallowed thing 1

halt 1. בצע 2. עמד 3. ἐφ' ἑαυτοῦ εἰμί
2Sm 15:17 and they halted at the last house. 2
2Kg 5: 9 Na'aman . . halted at the door of Eli'sha's house. 2
Isa 10:32 This very day he will halt at Nob 2
Jol 2: 8 burst through the weapons and are not halted. 1
Nah 2: 8 Halt! Halt!" they cry; but none turns back. 2
8 Halt! Halt!" they cry; but none turns back. 2
2Mc 10:27 when they came near to the enemy they halted. 3

halt *See also* come.

hammer 1. כֵּילַפּוֹת 2. מַפֵּץ 3. מַקֶּבֶת 4. מִקְשָׁה 5. פַּטִּישׁ 6. רִקּוּעַ 7. רקע 8. ὁλοσφύρητος 9. σφῦρα
Exd 37: 7 he made two cherubim of hammered gold; 4
39: 3 gold leaf was hammered and cut into threads 7
Num16:38 into hammered plates as a covering for the altar 6

Jdg 4:21 a tent peg, and took a hammer in her hand 3
1Kg 6: 7 hammer nor axe nor any tool of iron was heard 3
Ps 74: 6 wood they broke down with hatchets and hammers. 1
Isa 41: 7 he who smooths with the hammer him who strikes 5
44:12 he shapes it with hammers, and forges it 3
Jer 10: 4 they fasten it with hammer and nails 3
23:29 and like a hammer which breaks the rock in pieces? 5
50:23 How the hammer of the whole earth is cut down 5
51:20 You are my hammer and weapon of war 2
Sir 38:28 he inclines his ear to the sound of the hammer 9
50: 9 like a vessel of hammered gold 8

hammer out 1. רקע
Num16:39 were hammered out as a covering for the altar 1

hammered *See* work.

hamper 1. צרר
Prv 4:12 When you walk, your step will not be hampered; 1

hamstring 1. עקר
Gen 49: 6 and in their wantonness they hamstring oxen. 1
Jos 11: 6 you shall hamstring their horses 1
9 Joshua . . hamstrung their horses 1
2Sm 8: 4 and David hamstrung all the chariot horses 1
1Ch 18: 4 David hamstrung all the chariot horses 1

hand 1. היה 2. חֹפֶן 3. יָד 4. כַּף 5. כַּף יָד 6. לָבוֹא 7. מצא יָד 8. מִקְּרֹב 9. קרב 10. יַד (A) 11. *αὐτόχειρ* 12. *ἐγγίζω* 13. *ἐγγύς* 14. *ἐπί* 15. *μέν* 16. *παραδίδωμι* 17. *πούς* 18. *πρόκειμαι* 19. *ὑπό* 20. *ὑποχείριος* 21. *χείρ* 22. *χειροπέδη* 23. adpropinquo 24. adsum 25. manus

Gen 3:22 good and evil; and now, lest he put forth his hand 3
4:11 to receive your brother's blood from your hand. 3
5:29 from our work and from the toil of our hands. 3
8: 9 he put forth his hand and took her 3
9: 2 into your hand they are delivered. 3
14:20 who has delivered your enemies into your hand! 3
16:12 his hand against every man 3
12 every man and every man's hand against him; 3
19:10 the men put forth their hands 3
16 the men seized him and his wife . . by the hand 3
20: 5 the innocence of my hands I have done this 4
21:18 hold him fast with your hand; 3
30 These seven ewe lambs you will take from my hand 3
22: 6 he took in his hand the fire and the knife. 3
10 Then Abraham put forth his hand 3
12 He said, "Do not lay your hand on the lad 3
24: 2 servant . . "Put your hand under my thigh 3
9 the servant put his hand under the thigh 3
18 and she quickly let down her jar upon her hand 3
25:26 his hand had taken hold of Esau's heel; 3
27:16 the skins of the kids she put upon his hands 3
17 had prepared, into the hand of her son Jacob. 3
22 Jacob's voice, but the hands are the hands of Esau 3
22 Jacob's voice, but the hands are the hands of Esau 3
23 his hands were hairy like his brother Esau's 3
23 his brother Esau's hands; so he blessed him. 3
31:39 of my hand you required it 3
42 God saw my affliction and the labor of my hands 4
32:11 Deliver me . . from the hand of my brother 3
11 Deliver me . . from the hand of Esau, for I fear him 3
16 These he delivered into the hand of his servants 3
33:10 in your sight, then accept my present from my hand; 3
37:21 he delivered him out of their hands, saying 3
22 in the wilderness, but lay no hand upon him 3
22 -that he might rescue him out of their hand 3
27 and let not our hand be upon him 3
38:18 your cord, and your staff that is in your hand. 3
20 to receive the pledge from the woman's hand 3
28 when she was in labor, one put out a hand; 3
28 took and bound on his hand a scarlet thread 3
29 drew back his hand, behold, his brother came out 3
30 came out with the scarlet thread upon his hand; 3
39: 3 caused all that he did to prosper in his hands. 3
8 and he has put everything that he has in my hand; 3
12 But he left his garment in her hand, and fled 3
13 he had left his garment in her hand, and had fled 3
40:11 Pharaoh's cup was in my hand; and I took the grapes 3
11 and placed the cup in Pharaoh's hand. 4
13 and you shall place Pharaoh's cup in his hand 3
21 and he placed the cup in Pharaoh's hand; 4
41:42 Then Pharaoh took his signet ring from his hand 3
42 from his hand and put it on Joseph's hand 3
44 no man shall lift up hand or foot in all the land 3
42:37 put him in my hands, and I will bring him back 3
43: 9 I will be surety for him; of my hand 3
22 brought other money down in our hand to buy food. 3
44:16 he also in whose hand the cup has been found. 3
17 the man in whose hand the cup was found shall be my 3
46: 4 and Joseph's hand shall close your eyes. 3
47:29 put your hand under my thigh, and promise to deal 3
48:14 his right hand . . crossing his hands 3
17 his father laid his right hand upon the head 3
17 he took his father's hand, to remove it 3
22 which I took from the hand of the Amorites 3
49: 8 your hand shall be on the neck of your enemies; 3
24 were made agile by the hands of the Mighty One 3
Exd 2:19 delivered us out of the hand of the shepherds 3
3: 8 deliver them out of the hand of the Egyptians 3
19 not let you go unless compelled by a mighty hand. 3
20 So I will stretch out my hand and smite Egypt 3
4: 2 What is that in your hand?" He said, "A rod. 3
4 the LORD said to Moses, "Put out your hand, and take 3
4 it by the tail"- so he put out his hand and caught it 3
4 caught it, and it became a rod in his hand- 4
6 LORD said to him, "Put your hand into your bosom. 3
6 your bosom." And he put his hand into his bosom; 3
6 he took it out, behold, his hand was leprous 3
7 Then God said, "Put your hand back into your bosom. 3
7 So he put his hand back into his bosom; 3
17 you shall take in your hand this rod 3
20 and in his hand Moses took the rod of God. 3
5:21 you . . put a sword in their hand to kill us. 3
6: 1 for with a strong hand he will send them out 3
1 yea, with a strong hand he will drive them out 3
7: 4 then I will lay my hand upon Egypt and bring forth 3
5 when I stretch forth my hand upon Egypt and bring 3
15 Go . . take in your hand the rod which was turned 3
17 strike . . the Nile with the rod that is in my hand 3
19 stretch out your hand over the waters of Egypt 3
8: 5 Say to Aaron, 'Stretch out your hand with your rod 3
6 So Aaron stretched out his hand over the waters 3
17 Aaron stretched out his hand with his rod 3
9: 3 the hand of the LORD will fall with a very severe 3
15 For by now I could have put forth my hand 3
22 Moses, "Stretch forth your hand toward heaven 3
29 I will stretch out my hands to the LORD; 4
33 Moses . . stretched out his hands to the LORD; 4
10:12 Stretch out your hand over the land of Egypt 3
21 Stretch out your hand toward heaven that there 3
22 So Moses stretched out his hand toward heaven 3
12:11 sandals on your feet, and your staff in your hand; 3
13: 3 for by strength of hand the LORD brought you out 3
9 a sign on your hand and as a memorial between 3
9 for with a strong hand the LORD has brought you 3
14 By strength of hand the LORD brought us out 3
16 It shall be as a mark on your hand or frontlets 3
16 strong hand the LORD brought us out of Egypt. 3
14:16 stretch out your hand over the sea and divide it 3
21 Then Moses stretched out his hand over the sea; 3
26 Stretch out your hand over the sea, that the water 3
27 So Moses stretched forth his hand over the sea 3
30 saved . . from the hand of the Egyptians; 3
15: 9 I will draw my sword, my hand shall destroy them.' 3
17 O LORD, which thy hands have established. 3
20 Miriam . . took a timbrel in her hand; 3
16: 3 that we had died by the hand of the LORD in the land 3
17: 5 and take in your hand the rod with which you 3
9 I will stand . . with the rod of God in my hand. 3
11 Moses held up his hand, Israel prevailed; 3
11 whenever he lowered his hand, Am'alek prevailed. 3
12 Moses' hands grew weary; so they took a stone 3
12 and Aaron and Hur held up his hands, one on one side 3
12 so his hands were steady until the going down 3
16 saying, "A hand upon the banner of the LORD! 3
18: 9 delivered them out of the hand of the Egyptians. 3
10 delivered you out of the hand of the Egyptians 3
10 delivered you . . out of the hand of Pharaoh. 3
11 people from under the hand of the Egyptians 3
19:13 no hand shall touch him, but he shall be stoned 3
21:13 God let him fall into his hand, then I will appoint 3
20 slave dies under his hand, he shall be punished. 3
24 tooth for tooth, hand for hand, foot for foot 3
24 tooth for tooth, hand for hand, foot for foot 3
22: 8 he has put his hand to his neighbor's goods. 3
11 has not put his hand to his neighbor's property; 3
23: 1 You shall not join hands with a wicked man 3
31 inhabitants of the land into your hand 3
24:11 he did not lay his hand on the chief men 3
29:10 his sons shall lay their hands upon the head 3
15 Aaron and his sons shall lay their hands upon 3
19 shall lay their hands upon the head of the ram 3
20 upon the thumbs of their right hands 3
24 you shall put all these in the hands of Aaron 4
24 the hands of Aaron and in the hands of his sons 4
25 Then you shall take them from their hands 3
30:19 his sons wash their hands and their feet. 3
21 They shall wash their hands and their feet 3
32: 4 he received the gold at their hand, and fashioned 3
11 with great power and with a mighty hand? 3
15 with the two tables of the testimony in his hands 3
19 he threw the tables out of his hands and broke 3
33:22 I will cover you with my hand until I have passed 4
23 then I will take away my hand, and you shall see 4
34: 4 and took in his hand two tables of stone. 3
29 with the two tables of the testimony in his hand 3
35:25 women . . spun with their hands, and brought 3
38:15 on this hand and that hand by the gate of the court •
15 on this hand and that hand by the gate of the court •
40:31 his sons washed their hands and their feet; 3
Lev 1: 4 he shall lay his hand upon the head of the burnt 3
3: 2 he shall lay his hand upon the head 3
8 laying his hand upon the head of his offering 3
13 lay his hand upon its head, and kill it 3
4: 4 lay his hand on the head of the bull 3
15 shall lay their hands upon the head of the bull 3
24 shall lay his hand upon the head of the goat 3
29 he shall lay his hand on the head 3
33 lay his hand upon the head of the sin offering 3
7:30 he shall bring with his own hands the offerings 3
8:14 Aaron and his sons laid their hands upon the head 3
18 Aaron and his sons laid their hands on the head 3
22 Aaron and his sons laid their hands on the head 3
23 on the thumb of his right hand and on the great toe 3
24 blood . . on the thumbs of their right hands 3
27 he put all these in the hands of Aaron 4
27 hands of Aaron and in the hands of his sons 4
28 Then Moses took them from their hands, and burned 4
9:17 the cereal offering, and filled his hand from it 4
22 Then Aaron lifted up his hands toward the people 3
14:14 on the thumb of his right hand, and on the great toe 3
15 pour it into the palm of his own left hand •
16 the oil that is in his left hand, and sprinkle some 4
17 some of the oil that remains in his hand 4
17 the thumb of his right hand, and on the great toe 3
18 the rest of the oil that is in the priest's hand 4
25 on the thumb of his right hand, and on the great toe 3
26 some of the oil into the palm of his own left hand •
27 oil that is in his left hand seven times 4
28 the oil that is in his hand on the tip of the right 4
28 on the thumb of his right hand, and the great toe 3
29 the rest of the oil that is in the priest's hand 4
15:11 touches without having rinsed his hands in water 3
16:21 Aaron shall lay both his hands upon the head 3
21 by the hand of a man who is in readiness 3
21:19 or a man who has an injured foot or an injured hand 3
24:14 all who heard him lay their hands upon his head 3
25:28 then what he sold shall remain in the hand of him 3
26:25 you shall be delivered into the hand of the enemy 3
Num 4:33 under the hand of Ith'amar the son of Aaron 3
5:18 in her hands the cereal offering of remembrance 4
18 in his hand the priest shall have the water 3
25 offering of jealousy out of the woman's hand 3
6:19 shall put them upon the hands of the Nazirite 4
8:10 Israel shall lay their hands upon the Levites 3
12 Then the Levites shall lay their hands upon 3
11:23 LORD said to Moses, "Is the LORD'S hand shortened? 3
15:30 person who does anything with a high hand 3
20:11 Moses lifted up his hand and struck the rock 3
21: 2 If thou wilt indeed give this people into my hand 3
26 taken all his land out of his hand 3
34 Do not fear him; for I have given him into your hand 3
22: 7 with the fees for divination in their hand; 3
23 angel . . with a drawn sword in his hand; 3
29 I wish I had a sword in my hand, for then I would kill 3
31 saw the angel . . with his drawn sword in his hand; 3
24:10 Balak . . struck his hands together; 4
25: 7 Phin'ehas . . took a spear in his hand 3
27:18 Take Joshua . . and lay your hand upon him; 3
23 he laid his hands upon him, and commissioned him 3
31: 6 with . . the trumpets for the alarm in his hand. 3
35:17 if he struck him down with a stone in the hand 3
18 struck him down with a weapon of wood in the hand 3
21 or in enmity struck him down with his hand 3
25 manslayer from the hand of the avenger of blood 3
Deu 1:25 took in their hands some of the fruit of the land 3
27 give us into the hand of the Amorites, to destroy us. 3
2: 7 LORD . . blessed you in all the work of your hands; 3
15 For indeed the hand of the LORD was against them 3
24 I have given into your hand Sihon the Amorite 3
30 might give him into your hand, as at this day. 3
3: 2 given . . into your hand; and you shall do to him 3
3 LORD our God gave into our hand Og also, the king 3
8 took the land . . out of the hand of the two kings 3
24 show . . thy greatness and thy mighty hand; 3
4:28 gods of wood and stone, the work of men's hands 3
34 by a mighty hand and an outstretched arm 3
5:15 with a mighty hand and an outstretched arm; 3
6: 8 you shall bind them as a sign upon your hand 3
21 LORD brought us out of Egypt with a mighty hand; 3
7: 8 the LORD has brought you out with a mighty hand 3
8 redeemed you . . from the hand of Pharaoh 3
19 saw, the . . mighty hand, and the outstretched arm 3
24 he will give their kings into your hand 3
8:17 My power and the might of my hand have gotten me 3
9:15 two tables of the covenant were in my two hands. 3
17 two tables, and cast them out of my two hands 3
26 brought out of Egypt with a mighty hand. 3
10: 3 up the mountain with the two tables in my hand. 3
11: 2 consider . . mighty hand and his outstretched arm 3
18 you shall bind them as a sign upon your hand 3
13: 9 your hand shall be first . . to put him to death 3
9 afterwards the hand of all the people. 3
17 None . . shall cleave to your hand; that the LORD 3
14:25 money, and bind up the money in your hand, and go 3
29 bless . . all the work of your hands that you do. 3
15: 3 your hand shall release. 3
7 not . . shut your hand against your poor brother 3
8 open your hand to him, and lend him sufficient 3
11 You shall open wide your hand to your brother 3
16:10 tribute of a freewill offering from your hand 3
15 LORD . . will bless . . all the work of your hands 3

17: 7 hand of the witnesses shall be first against him 3
7 death, and afterward the hand of all the people. 3
19: 5 his hand swings the axe to cut down a tree 3
21 tooth for tooth, hand for hand, foot for foot. 3
21 tooth for tooth, hand for hand, foot for foot. 3
20:13 when the LORD your God gives it into your hand 3
21: 6 elders . . wash their hands over the heifer 3
7 Our hands did not shed this blood, neither did our 3
10 LORD your God gives them into your hands 3
23:25 grain, you may pluck the ears with your hand 3
24: 1 bill of divorce and puts it in her hand and sends 3
3 bill of divorce and puts it in her hand 3
19 LORD . . bless you in all the work of your hands. 3
25:11 husband from the hand of him who is beating him 3
11 puts out her hand and seizes him by the private 3
12 cut off her hand; your eye shall have no pity. 4
26: 4 priest shall take the basket from your hand 3
8 LORD brought us out of Egypt with a mighty hand 3
27:15 image . . a thing made by the hands of a craftsman 3
28:12 to bless all the work of your hands; 3
32 not be in the power of your hand to prevent it. 3
30: 9 make . . prosperous in all the work of your hand 3
31:29 him to anger through the work of your hands. 3
32:27 Our hand is triumphant, the LORD has not wrought 3
35 day of their calamity is at hand, and their doom 9
39 there is none that can deliver out of my hand. 3
40 For I lift up my hand to heaven, and swear, As I live 3
41 if . . my hand takes hold on judgment 3
33: 3 all those consecrated to him were in his hand; 3
7 With thy hands contend for him, and be a help 3
11 Bless, O LORD . . and accept the work of his hands; 3
34: 9 for Moses had laid his hands upon him; 3
Jos 2:19 but if a hand is laid upon any one who is with you 3
24 the LORD has given all the land into our hands; 3
4:24 all . . may know that the hand of the LORD is mighty; 3
5:13 stood before him with his drawn sword in his hand; 3
6: 2 I have given into your hand Jericho, with its king 3
7: 7 to give us into the hands of the Amorites 3
8: 1 I have given into your hand the king of Ai 3
7 for the LORD your God will give it into your hand. 3
18 Stretch out the javelin that is in your hand 3
18 toward Ai; for I will give it into your hand. 3
18 Joshua stretched out the javelin . . in his hand 3
19 as soon as he had stretched out his hand, they ran 3
26 Joshua did not draw back his hand . . until he had 3
9:11 Take provisions in your hand for the journey 3
25 we are in your hand: do as it seems good and right 3
26 and delivered them out of the hand of the people 3
10: 6 Do not relax your hand from your servants; 3
8 for I have given them into your hands; 3
19 the LORD your God has given them into your hand. 3
30 gave it also and its king into the hand of Israel; 3
32 and the LORD gave Lachish into the hand of Israel 3
11: 8 And the LORD gave them into the hand of Israel 3
20: 5 they shall not give up the slayer into his hand; 3
9 not die by the hand of the avenger of blood 3
21:44 LORD had given all . . enemies into their hands. 3
22:31 saved . . Israel from the hand of the LORD. 3
24: 8 and I gave them into your hand 3
10 he blessed you; so I delivered you out of his hand. 3
11 and I gave them into your hand. 3
Jdg 1: 2 behold, I have given the land into his hand. 3
4 LORD gave . . into their hand; and they defeated 3
35 the hand of the house of Joseph rested heavily 3
2:15 the hand of the LORD was against them for evil 3
18 he saved them from the hand of their enemies 3
3: 8 he sold them into the hand of Cu'shan-rishatha'im 3
10 king of Mesopota'mia into his hand; and his hand 3
10 and his hand prevailed over Cu'shan-rishatha'im. 3
21 Ehud reached with his left hand, took the sword 3
28 LORD has given . . the Moabites into your hand. 3
30 was subdued that day under the hand of Israel. 3
4: 2 sold them into the hand of Jabin king of Canaan 3
7 troops; and I will give him into your hand.' 3
9 LORD will sell Sis'era into the hand of a woman. 3
14 which the LORD has given Sis'era into your hand. 3
21 took a hammer in her hand, and went softly to him 3
24 the hand of the people of Israel bore harder 3
5:26 She put her hand to the tent peg and her right hand 3
6: 1 the LORD gave them into the hand of Mid'ian 3
2 And the hand of Mid'ian prevailed over Israel; 3
9 I delivered you from the hand of the Egyptians 3
9 delivered . . from the hand of all who oppressed 3
13 cast us off, and given us into the hand of Mid'ian. 4
14 Go . . and deliver Israel from the hand of Mid'ian; 4
21 tip of the staff that was in his hand, and touched 3
36 said to God, "If thou wilt deliver Israel by my hand 3
37 know that thou wilt deliver Israel by my hand 3
7: 2 for me to give the Mid'ianites into their hand 3
2 against me, saying, 'My own hand has delivered me.' 3
6 that lapped, putting their hands to their mouths 3
7 and give the Mid'ianites into your hand; 3
8 he took the jars of the people from their hands 3
9 the camp; for I have given it into your hand. 3
11 your hands shall be strengthened to go down 3
14 Israel; into his hand God has given Mid'ian and all 3
15 LORD has given the host of Mid'ian into your hand. 3
16 and put trumpets into the hands of all of them 3
19 and smashed the jars that were in their hands. 3
20 the jars, holding in their left hands the torches 3
20 and in their right hands the trumpets to blow; 3
8: 3 God has given into your hands the princes 3
6 Are Zebah and Zalmun'na already in your hand 5
7 LORD has given Zebah and Zalmun'na into my hand 3
15 Are Zebah and Zalmun'na already in your hand 5
22 you have delivered us out of the hand of Mid'ian. 3
34 rescued them from the hand of all their enemies 3
9:17 his life, and rescued you from the hand of Mid'ian; 3
24 who strengthened his hands to slay his brothers. 3
29 Would that this people were under my hand! 3
48 Abim'elech took an axe in his hand, and cut down 3
10: 7 he sold them into the hand of the Philistines 3
7 sold them . . and into the hand of the Ammonites 3
12 cried to me, and I delivered you out of their hand. 3
11:21 LORD . . gave Sihon . . into the hand of Israel 3
30 If thou wilt give the Ammonites into my hand 3
32 them; and the LORD gave them into his hand. 3
12: 2 you did not deliver me from their hand. 3
3 I took my life in my hand, and crossed over 4
3 and the LORD gave them into my hand; 3
13: 1 gave them into the hand of the Philistines 3
5 to deliver . . from the hand of the Philistines. 3
23 have accepted . . a cereal offering at our hands 3
14: 6 as one tears a kid; and he had nothing in his hand. 3
9 He scraped it out into his hands, and went on 4
15:12 give you into the hands of the Philistines. 3
13 will only bind you and give you into their hands; 3
14 caught fire, and his bonds melted off his hands. 3
15 of an ass, and put out his hand and seized it 3
17 he threw away the jawbone out of his hand; 3
18 great deliverance by the hand of thy servant; 3
18 and fall into the hands of the uncircumcised? 3
16:18 came up . . and brought the money in their hands. 3
23 Our god has given Samson our enemy into our hand. 3
24 Our god has given our enemy into our hand 3
26 Samson said to the lad who held him by the hand 3
17: 3 I consecrate the silver to the LORD from my hand 3
18:10 land is broad; yea, God has given it into your hands 3
19 Keep quiet, put your hand upon your mouth, and come 3
19:27 at the door . . with her hands on the threshold. 3
20:28 Go up; for . . I will give them into your hand. 3
Rut 1:13 the hand of the LORD has gone forth against me. 3
4: 5 The day you buy the field from the hand of Na'omi 3
9 bought from the hand of Na'omi all that belonged 3
1Sm 2:13 come . . with a three-pronged fork in his hand 3
5: 4 head of Dagon and both his hands were . . cut off 5
6 The hand of the LORD was heavy upon the people 3
7 his hand is heavy upon us and upon Dagon our god. 3
9 the hand of the LORD was against the city 3
11 The hand of God was very heavy there; 3
6: 3 why his hand does not turn away from you. 3
5 lighten his hand from off you and your gods 3
9 we shall know that it is not his hand that struck us 3
7: 3 deliver you out of the hand of the Philistines. 3
8 he may save us from the hand of the Philistines. 3
13 the hand of the LORD was against the Philistines 3
14 rescued . . from the hand of the Philistines. 3
9:16 save my people from the hand of the Philistines; 3
10: 1 you will save them from the hand of their enemies 21
4 bread, which you shall accept from their hand. 3
7 do whatever your hand finds to do, for God is 3
18 I delivered you from the hand of the Egyptians 3
18 delivered . . from the hand of all the kingdoms 3
11: 7 sent them . . by the hand of the messengers 3
12: 3 from whose hand have I taken a bribe 3
4 or oppressed us or taken . . from any man's hand. 3
5 you have not found anything in my hand. 3
9 and he sold them into the hand of Sis'era 3
9 he sold them . . into the hand of the Philistines 3
9 he sold them . . into the hand of the king of Moab; 3
10 deliver us out of the hand of our enemies 3
11 and delivered you out of the hand of your enemies 3
15 the hand of the LORD will be against you 3
13:22 nor spear found in the hand of any of the people 3
14:10 the LORD has given them into our hand. 3
12 the LORD has given them into the hand of Israel. 3
13 Then Jonathan climbed up on his hands and feet 3
19 and Saul said to the priest, "Withdraw your hand. 3
26 honey was . . but no man put his hand to his mouth; 3
27 so he put forth the tip of the staff . . in his hand 3
27 and dipped it in . . and put his hand to his mouth; 3
37 Wilt thou give them into the hand of Israel? 3
43 with the tip of the staff that was in my hand; 3
48 Israel out of the hands of those who plundered 3
16:23 David took the lyre and played it with his hand; 3
17:37 deliver me from the hand of this Philistine. 3
40 Then he took his staff in his hand 3
40 his sling was in his hand, and he drew near 3
46 This day the LORD will deliver you into my hand 3
47 is the LORD's and he will give you into our hand. 3
49 David put his hand in his bag and took out a stone 3
50 there was no sword in the hand of David. 3
57 with the head of the Philistine in his hand. 3
18:10 Saul had his spear in his hand; 3
17 Let not my hand be upon him, but . . the Philistines 3
17 but let the hand of the Philistines be upon him. 3
21 the hand of the Philistines may be against him. 3
25 make David fall by the hand of the Philistines. 3
19: 5 for he took his life in his hand and he slew 4
9 as he sat in his house with his spear in his hand; 3
20:19 where you hid . . when the matter was in hand •
21: 3 what have you at hand? Give me five loaves of bread 3
4 I have no common bread at hand, but . . holy bread; 3
8 And have you not here a spear or a sword at hand? 3
13 and feigned himself mad in their hands 3
22: 6 Saul was sitting . . with his spear in his hand 3
17 their hand also is with David, and they knew 3
17 servants . . would not put forth their hand 3
23: 4 I will give the Philistines into your hand. 3
6 Abi'athar . . came down with an ephod in his hand. 3
7 And Saul said, "God has given him into my hand; 3
11 Will the men of Kei'lah surrender me into his hand? 3
12 surrender me and my men into the hand of Saul? 3
14 but God did not give him into his hand. 3
16 Jonathan . . and strengthened his hand in God. 3
17 the hand of Saul my father shall not find you; 3
20 our part . . to surrender him into the king's hand. 3
24: 4 I will give your enemy into your hand 3
6 do this thing . . to put forth my hand against him 3
10 the LORD gave you today into my hand in the cave; 3
10 I said, 'I will not put forth my hand against my lord; 3
11 See, my father, see the skirt of your robe in my hand; 3
11 see that there is no wrong or treason in my hands. 3
12 the LORD . . but my hand shall not be against you. 3
13 but my hand shall not be against you. 3
15 and plead my cause, and deliver me from your hand. 3
18 not kill me when the LORD put me into your hands. 3
20 kingdom . . shall be established in your hand. 3
25: 8 give whatever you have at hand to your servants 7
26 and from taking vengeance with your own hand 3
33 and from avenging myself with my own hand! 3
35 received from her hand what she had brought him; 3
39 the insult I received at the hand of Nabal 3
26: 8 God has given your enemy into your hand this day; 3
9 put forth his hand against the LORD's anointed 3
11 put forth my hand against the LORD's anointed; 3
18 For what have I done? What guilt is on my hands? 3
23 the LORD gave you into my hand today 3
23 put forth my hand against the LORD's anointed. 3
27: 1 I shall now perish one day by the hand of Saul; 3
1 I shall escape out of his hand. 3
28:17 the LORD has torn the kingdom out of your hand 3
19 give Israel . . into the hand of the Philistines; 3
19 Israel also . . into the hand of the Philistines. 3
21 I have taken my life in my hand, and have hearkened 4
30:15 kill me, or deliver me into the hands of my master 3
23 preserved us and given into our hand the band 3
2Sm 1:14 to put forth your hand to destroy the . . anointed? 3
2: 7 Now . . let your hands be strong, and be valiant; 3
3: 8 I . . have not given you into the hand of David; 3
12 my hand shall be with you to bring over all Israel 3
18 By the hand of . . David I will save my people 3
18 save . . Israel from the hand of the Philistines 3
18 save . . and from the hand of all their enemies. 3
34 Your hands were not bound 3
4:11 shall I not now require his blood at your hand 3
12 they killed them, and cut off their hands and feet 3
5:19 Shall I go up . . ? Wilt thou give them into my hand? 3
19 I will . . give the Philistines into your hand. 3
6: 6 Uzzah put out his hand to the ark . . and took hold •
7 because he put forth his hand to the ark; •
8: 1 David took . . out of the hand of the Philistines. 3
11:14 David wrote . . and sent it by the hand of Uri'ah. 3
12: 7 and I delivered you out of the hand of Saul; 3
13: 5 that I may see it, and eat it from her hand.' 3
6 let my sister . . that I may eat from her hand. 3
10 Bring the food . . that I may eat from your hand. 3
19 she laid her hand on her head, and went away, crying 3
14:16 and deliver his servant from the hand of the man 4
19 Is the hand of Jo'ab with you in all this? 3
15: 5 he would put out his hand, and take hold of him 3
16: 8 has given the kingdom into the hand of your son 3
21 hands of all . . with you will be strengthened. 3
18:12 Even if I felt in my hand the weight of 1,000 4
12 would not put forth my hand against the king's son; 3
14 he took three darts in his hand, and thrust them 4
28 the men who raised their hand against my lord 3
19: 9 The king delivered us from the hand of our 4
9 and saved us from the hand of the Philistines; 4
20: 9 Jo'ab took Ama'sa by the beard with his right hand 3
10 did not observe the sword which was in Jo'ab's hand; 3
21 a man . . has lifted up his hand against King David; 3
21: 9 and he gave them into the hands of the Gib'eonites 3
20 man of . . stature, who had six fingers on each hand 3
22 fell by the hand of David and . . his servants. 3
22 fell by . . David and by the hand of his servants. 3
22: 1 delivered him from the hand of all his enemies 4
1 hand of all his enemies, and from the hand of Saul. 4
21 according to the cleanness of my hands he 3
35 He trains my hands for war, so that my arms can bend 3
23: 6 thorns . . for they cannot be taken with the hand; 3
10 struck . . Philistines until his hand was weary 3
10 hand was weary, and his hand cleaved to the sword; 3
21 The Egyptian had a spear in his hand; 3

21 and snatched the spear out of the Egyptian's hand 3
24:14 let us fall into the hand of the LORD 3
14 but let me not fall into the hand of man. 3
16 when the angel stretched forth his hand 3
16 and said . . "It is enough; now stay your hand. 3
17 Let thy hand, I pray thee, be against me 3
1Kg 2:46 kingdom was established in the hand of Solomon. 3
8:15 with his hand has fulfilled what he promised 3
22 and spread forth his hands toward heaven; 4
24 and with thy hand hast fulfilled it this day. 3
38 and stretching out his hands toward this house; 4
42 hear of thy great name, and thy mighty hand 3
54 knelt with hands outstretched toward heaven; 4
11:12 I will tear it out of the hand of your son. 3
26 Jerobo'am . . lifted up his hand against the king. 3
27 why he lifted up his hand against the king. 3
31 to tear the kingdom from the hand of Solomon 3
34 I will not take the whole kingdom out of his hand; 3
35 I will take the kingdom out of his son's hand 3
13: 4 Jerobo'am stretched out his hand from the altar 3
4 And his hand, which he stretched out . . dried up 3
6 pray for me, that my hand may be restored to me. 3
6 the king's hand was restored to him 3
14:27 and committed them to the hands of the officers 3
15:18 Asa . . gave them into the hands of his servants; 3
16: 7 provoking him to anger with the work of his hands 3
17:11 Bring me a morsel of bread in your hand. 3
18: 9 you would give your servant into the hand of Ahab 3
44 a little cloud like a man's hand is rising 4
46 the hand of the LORD was on Eli'jah; 3
20: 6 and lay hands on whatever pleases them 3
13 Behold, I will give it into your hand this day; 3
28 give all this great multitude into your hand 3
42 you have let go out of your hand the man whom I had 3
22: 3 do not take it out of the hand of the king of Syria? 3
6 the Lord will give it into the hand of the king. 3
12 the LORD will give it into the hand of the king. 3
15 the LORD will give it into the hand of the king. 3
2Kg 3:10 to give them into the hand of Moab. 3
11 Eli'sha . . poured water on the hands of Eli'jah. 3
13 to give them into the hand of Moab. 3
18 he will also give the Moabites into your hand 3
4:29 take my staff in your hand and go. 3
34 eyes upon his eyes, and his hands upon his hands; 4
34 eyes upon his eyes, and his hands upon his hands; 4
5:11 wave his hand over the place, and cure the leper. 3
20 in not accepting from his hand what he brought. 3
24 he took them from their hand, and put them 3
6: 7 Take it up." So he reached out his hand and took it. 3
7: 2 the captain on whose hand the king leaned said 3
17 appointed the captain on whose hand he leaned 3
9: 1 take this flask of oil in your hand, and go 3
35 the skull and the feet and the palms of her hands. 3
10:15 Jehu said, "If it is, give me your hand. 3
15 So he gave him his hand. And Jehu took him up 3
24 allows any of those whom I give into your hands 3
11: 8 surround . . each with his weapons in his hand; 3
11 every man with his weapons in his hand 3
12 and they clapped their hands, and said, "Long live 4
16 So they laid hands on her; 3
12:11 give the money . . into the hands of the workmen 3
15 the men into whose hand they delivered the money 3
13: 3 he gave them continually into the hand of Haz'ael 3
3 gave them . . and into the hand of Ben-ha'dad 3
5 so that they escaped from the hand of the Syrians; 3
16 And Eli'sha laid his hands upon the king's hands. 3
16 And Eli'sha laid his hands upon the king's hands. 3
14: 5 as soon as the royal power was firmly in his hand 3
27 so he saved them by the hand of Jerobo'am the son 3
16: 7 and rescue me from the hand of the king of Syria 4
7 rescue me . . from the hand of the king of Israel 4
17: 7 out of . . Egypt from under the hand of Pharaoh 3
20 and gave them into the hand of spoilers 3
39 deliver you out of the hand of all your enemies. 3
18:21 will pierce the hand of any man who leans on it. 4
29 he will not be able to deliver you out of my hand. 3
30 not be given into the hand of the king of Assyria.' 3
33 his land out of the hand of the king of Assyria? 3
34 Have they delivered Sama'ria out of my hand? 3
35 have delivered their countries out of my hand 3
35 the LORD should deliver Jerusalem out of my hand?' 3
19:10 not be given into the hand of the king of Assyria. 3
14 received . . from the hand of the messengers 3
18 no gods, but the work of men's hands, wood and stone; 3
19 O LORD . . save us, I beseech thee, from his hand 3
20: 6 deliver . . out of the hand of the king of Assyria 4
21:14 and give them into the hand of their enemies 3
22: 2 did not turn aside to the right hand or to the left. •
5 let it be given into the hand of the workmen 3
7 for the money which is delivered into their hand 3
9 have delivered it into the hand of the workmen 3
17 provoke me . . with all the work of their hands 3
1Ch 4:10 saying, "Oh . . that thy hand might be with me 3
5:10 the Hagrites, who fell by their hand; 3
20 Hagrites and all . . were given into their hands 3
6:15 into exile by the hand of Nebuchadnez'zar. 3
11:23 Egyptian had in his hand a spear 3
23 and snatched the spear out of the Egyptian's hand 3

12:17 although there is no wrong in my hands 4
13: 9 Uzzah put out his hand to hold the ark 3
10 smote him because he put forth his hand to the ark; 3
14:10 Wilt thou give them into my hand? 3
10 Go up, and I will give them into your hand. 3
11 God has broken through my enemies by my hand 3
18: 1 its villages out of the hand of the Philistines. 3
20: 6 who had six fingers on each hand, and six toes •
8 they fell by the hand of David and by the hand 3
8 they fell by . . the hand of his servants. 3
21:13 let me fall into the hand of the LORD 3
13 but let me not fall into the hand of man. 3
15 It is enough; now stay your hand. 3
16 and in his hand a drawn sword stretched out 3
17 thy hand, I pray thee, O LORD my God, be against me 3
22:18 the inhabitants of the land into my hand; 3
28:19 clear by the writing from the hand of the LORD 3
29:12 In thy hand are power and might; 3
12 In thy hand are power and might; 3
16 all this abundance . . comes from thy hand 3
2Ch 6: 4 LORD . . who with his hand has fulfilled 3
12 before the altar . . and spread forth his hands. 4
13 and spread forth his hands toward heaven; 4
15 and with thy hand hast fulfilled it this day. 3
29 and stretching out his hands toward this house; 4
32 comes . . for the sake of . . thy mighty hand 3
12: 5 I have abandoned you to the hand of Shishak.' 3
7 by the hand of Shishak. 3
10 committed them to the hands of the officers 3
13: 8 kingdom . . in the hand of the sons of David 3
16 God gave them into their hand. 3
15: 7 But you, take courage! Do not let your hands be weak 3
16: 8 relied on the LORD, he gave them into your hand. 3
17: 5 the LORD established the kingdom in his hand; 3
18: 5 God will give it into the hand of the king. 3
11 LORD will give it into the hand of the king. 3
14 they will be given into your hand. 3
20: 6 In thy hand are power and nmight 3
23: 7 each with his weapons in his hand; 3
10 every man with his weapon in his hand 3
15 laid hands on her; and she went into the entrance 3
24:13 the repairing went forward in their hands 3
24 LORD delivered into their hand a very great army 3
25: 3 as soon as the royal power was firmly in his hand •
15 not deliver their own people from your hand? 3
20 give them into the hand of their enemies 3
26:19 Now he had a censer in his hand to burn incense 3
28: 5 gave him into the hand of the king of Syria 3
5 also given into the hand of the king of Israel 3
9 was angry with Judah, he gave them into your hand 3
29:23 they laid their hands upon them 3
30: 6 escaped from the hand of the kings of Assyria. 4
12 The hand of God was also upon Judah to give them 3
16 they received from the hand of the Levites. 3
32:11 deliver us from the hand of the king of Assyria"? 4
13 at all able to deliver their lands out of my hand? 3
14 was able to deliver his people from my hand 3
14 God should be able to deliver you from my hand? 3
15 able to deliver his people from my hand 3
15 able to deliver . . from the hand of my fathers. 3
15 How . . will your God deliver you out of my hand!' 3
17 have not delivered their people from my hands 3
17 God . . will not deliver his people from my hand. 3
19 gods . . which are the work of men's hands. 3
22 LORD saved . . from the hand of Sennach'erib 3
22 LORD saved . . from the hand of all his enemies; 3
34:17 delivered it into the hand of the overseers 3
25 provoke me . . with all the works of their hands 3
36:17 he gave them all into his hand. 3
Ezr 5: 8 goes on diligently and prospers in their hands. 10
12 gave them into the hand of Nebuchadnez'zar king 10
6:12 any . . people that shall put forth a hand 10
7: 6 for the hand of the LORD his God was upon him. 3
9 for the good hand of his God was upon him. 3
14 law of your God, which is in your hand 10
25 wisdom of your God which is in your hand 10
28 hand of the LORD my God was upon me 3
8:18 by the good hand of our God upon us, they brought us 3
22 hand of our God is for good upon all that seek him 3
26 I weighed out into their hand 650 talents 3
31 hand of our God was upon us, and he delivered us 3
31 delivered us from the hand of the enemy 4
33 weighed into the hands of Mer'emoth the priest 3
9: 2 hand of the officials and chief men 3
5 fell . . and spread out my hands to the LORD my God 4
7 been given into the hand of the kings of the lands 3
Neh 1:10 redeemed by thy great power and by thy strong hand. 3
2: 8 for the good hand of my God was upon me. 3
18 I told them of the hand of my God which had been 3
18 strengthened their hands for the good work. 3
4:17 each with one hand labored on the work 3
23 each kept his weapon in his hand. •
6: 5 sent his servant . . with an open letter in his hand. 3
9 Their hands will drop from the work 3
9 But now, O God, strengthen thou my hands. 3
8: 6 answered, "Amen, Amen," lifting up their hands; 3
9:24 Canaanites, and didst give them into their hands 3
27 give them into the hand of their enemies 3

27 saved them from the hand of their enemies. 3
28 abandon them to the hand of their enemies 3
30 into the hand of the peoples of the lands. 3
11:24 Pethahi'ah . . at the king's hand in all matters 3
13:21 If you do so again I will lay hands on you. 3
Est 2:21 angry and sought to lay hands on King Ahasu-e'rus. 3
3: 6 But he disdained to lay hands on Mor'decai alone. 3
9 I will pay . . into the hands of those who have 3
10 took his . . ring from his hand and gave it to Haman 3
5: 2 held . . the golden scepter that was in his hand. 3
6: 2 who had sought to lay hands upon King Ahasu-e'rus. 3
8: 7 hanged . . because he would lay hands on the Jews. 3
9: 2 Jews gathered . . to lay hands on such as sought 3
10 but they laid no hand on the plunder. 3
15 but they laid no hands on the plunder. 3
16 but they laid no hands on the plunder. 3
Job 1:10 Thou hast blessed the work of his hands 3
11 put forth thy hand now, and touch all that he has 3
12 only upon himself do not put forth your hand. 3
2: 5 But put forth thy hand now, and touch his bone 3
10 Shall we receive good at the hand of God 21
4: 3 you have strengthened the weak hands. 3
5:12 that their hands achieve no success. 3
15 the needy from the hand of the mighty. 3
18 he smites, but his hands heal. 3
6: 9 that he would let loose his hand and cut me off! 3
23 Or, 'Deliver me from the adversary's hand'? 3
23 Or, 'Ransom me from the hand of oppressors'? 3
8:20 nor take the hand of evildoers. 3
9:24 The earth is given into the hand of the wicked; 3
30 If I wash myself . . and cleanse my hands with lye 4
33 no umpire . . who might lay his hand upon us both. 3
10: 3 to oppress, to despise the work of thy hands 4
7 there is none to deliver out of thy hand? 3
8 Thy hands fashioned and made me; 3
11:13 you will stretch out your hands toward him. 4
14 If iniquity is in your hand, put it far away 3
12: 6 are secure, who bring their god in their hand. 3
9 not know that the hand of the LORD has done this? 3
10 In his hand is the life of every living thing 3
13:14 and put my life in my hand. 4
21 withdraw thy hand far from me 4
14:15 thou wouldest long for the work of thy hands. 3
15:23 He knows that a day of darkness is ready at his hand; 3
25 he has stretched forth his hand against God 3
16:11 casts me into the hands of the wicked. 3
17 although there is no violence in my hands 4
17: 9 he that has clean hands grows stronger 3
19:21 for the hand of God has touched me! 3
20:10 his hands will give back his wealth. 3
21: 5 be appalled, and lay your hand upon your mouth. 3
16 Behold, is not their prosperity in their hand? 3
22:30 delivered through the cleanness of your hands. 4
23: 2 his hand is heavy in spite of my groaning. 3
26:13 his hand pierced the fleeing serpent. 3
27:11 I will teach you concerning the hand of God; 3
23 It claps its hands at him, and hisses at him 4
28: 9 Man puts his hand to the flinty rock 3
29: 9 from talking, and laid their hand on their mouth; 4
20 glory fresh with me, and my bow ever new in my hand 3
30: 2 could I gain from the strength of their hands 3
21 with the might of thy hand thou dost persecute 3
24 not one in a heap of ruins stretch out his hand 3
31: 7 if any spot has cleaved to my hands; 4
21 if I have raised my hand against the fatherless 3
25 because my hand had gotten much; 3
27 enticed, and my mouth has kissed my hand; 3
34:19 for they are all the work of his hands? 3
20 the mighty are taken away by no human hand. 3
37 he claps his hands among us •
35: 7 what does he receive from your hand? 3
36:32 He covers his hands with the lightning 4
37: 7 He seals up the hand of every man 3
40: 4 shall I answer thee? I lay my hand on my mouth. 3
41: 8 Lay hands on him; think of the battle; 4
Ps 7: 3 if I have done this, if there is wrong in my hands 4
8: 6 given him dominion over the works of thy hands; 3
9:16 wicked are snared in the work of their own hands. 4
10:12 Arise, O LORD; O God, lift up thy hand; 3
14 vexation, that thou mayst take it into thy hands; 3
17:14 by thy hand, O LORD, from men whose portion 3
18: 0 delivered him from the hand of all his enemies 4
0 hand of all his enemies, and from the hand of Saul. 3
20 according to the cleanness of my hands 3
24 the cleanness of my hands in his sight. 3
34 He trains my hands for war 3
21: 8 Your hand will find out all your enemies; 3
22:16 they have pierced my hands and feet- 3
24: 4 He who has clean hands and a pure heart 4
26: 6 I wash my hands in innocence 4
10 men in whose hands are evil devices 3
28: 2 I lift up my hands toward thy most holy 3
4 requite . . according to the work of their hands; 3
5 the works of the LORD, or the work of his hands 3
31: 5 Into thy hand I commit my spirit; 3
8 hast not delivered me into the hand of the enemy; 3
15 My times are in thy hand; 3
15 deliver me from the hand of my enemies 3

32: 4 For day and night thy hand was heavy upon me; 3
36:11 nor the hand of the wicked drive me away. 3
37:24 for the LORD is the stay of his hand. 3
38: 2 thy hand has come down on me. 3
39:10 I am spent by the blows of thy hand. 3
44: 2 with thy own hand didst drive out the nations 3
20 or spread forth our hands to a strange god 4
47: 1 Clap your hands, all peoples! Shout to God 4
55:20 My companion stretched out his hand 3
58: 2 your hands deal out violence on earth. 3
63: 4 I will lift up my hands and call on thy name. 4
68:31 Ethiopia hasten to stretch out her hands to God. 3
71: 4 Rescue me, O my God, from the hand of the wicked 3
73:13 my heart clean and washed my hands in innocence. 4
23 thou dost hold my right hand. 3
74:11 Why dost thou hold back thy hand 3
75: 8 For in the hand of the LORD there is a cup 3
76: 5 all the men of war were unable to use their hands. 3
77: 2 my hand is stretched out without wearying; 3
20 like a flock by the hand of Moses and Aaron. 3
78:61 his glory to the hand of the foe. 3
72 tended them, and guided them with skilful hand. 4
80:17 But let thy hand be upon the man of thy right hand 3
81: 6 your hands were freed from the basket. 4
14 turn my hand against their foes. 3
82: 4 deliver them from the hand of the wicked. 3
85: 9 Surely his salvation is at hand 9
88: 5 no more, for they are cut off from thy hand. 3
9 I spread out my hands to thee. 4
89:13 strong is thy hand, high thy right hand. 3
21 so that my hand shall ever abide with him 3
25 I will set his hand on the sea 3
44 Thou hast removed the scepter from his hand •
90:17 establish thou the work of our hands upon us 3
17 yea, the work of our hands establish thou it. 3
91:12 On their hands they will bear you up 4
92: 4 at the works of thy hands I sing for joy. 3
95: 4 In his hand are the depths of the earth; 3
5 for his hands formed the dry land. 3
7 people of his pasture, and the sheep of his hand. 3
97:10 delivers them from the hand of the wicked. 3
98: 8 Let the floods clap their hands; 4
102:25 heavens are the work of thy hands. 3
104:28 when thou openest thy hand, they are filled 3
106:10 he saved them from the hand of the foe 3
26 Therefore he raised his hand and swore to them 3
41 he gave them into the hand of the nations 3
109:27 Let them know that this is thy hand; 3
111: 7 The works of his hands are faithful and just; 3
115: 4 idols are silver and gold, the work of men's hands. 3
7 have hands, but do not feel; feet, but do not walk; 3
119:73 Thy hands have made and fashioned me; 3
109I hold my life in my hand continually 4
173Let thy hand be ready to help me 3
121: 5 LORD is your shade on your right hand. 3
123: 2 eyes of servants look to the hand of their master 3
2 as the eyes of a maid to the hand of her mistress 3
125: 3 righteous put forth their hands to do wrong. 3
127: 4 Like arrows in the hand of a warrior are the sons 3
128: 2 You shall eat the fruit of the labor of your hands; 4
129: 7 with which the reaper does not fill his hand 4
134: 2 Lift up your hands to the holy place, and bless 3
135:15 idols . . silver and gold, the work of men's hands. 3
136:12 with a strong hand and an outstretched arm 3
138: 7 stretch out thy hand against the wrath of my 3
8 Do not forsake the work of thy hands. 3
139: 5 layest thy hand upon me. 4
10 even there thy hand shall lead me 3
140: 4 Guard me, O LORD, from the hands of the wicked; 3
141: 2 lifting up of my hands as an evening sacrifice! 4
143: 5 I muse on what thy hands have wrought. 3
6 I stretch out my hands to thee; my soul thirsts 3
144: 1 LORD, my rock, who trains my hands for war 3
7 Stretch forth thy hand from on high 3
7 rescue me and deliver me from . . hand of aliens 3
11 deliver me from the hand of aliens 3
145:16 Thou openest thy hand, thou satisfiest 3
149: 6 Let . . two-edged swords in their hands 3
Prv 1:24 stretched out my hand and no one has heeded 3
6: 5 like a bird from the hand of the fowler. 3
10 a little folding of the hands to rest 3
17 hands that shed innocent blood 3
10: 4 A slack hand causes poverty 4
4 but the hand of the diligent makes rich. 3
12:14 and the work of a man's hand comes back to him. 3
24 The hand of the diligent will rule 3
14: 1 but folly with her own hands tears it down. 3
17:16 fool have a price in his hand to buy wisdom 3
19:24 The sluggard buries his hand in the dish 3
21: 1 heart is a stream of water in the hand of the LORD; 3
25 kills him for his hands refuse to labor. 3
24:33 slumber, a little folding of the hands to rest 3
26: 6 He who sends a message by the hand of a fool 3
9 thorn that goes up into the hand of a drunkard 3
15 The sluggard buries his hand in the dish; 3
30:28 lizards you can take in your hands 3
32 put your hand on your mouth. 3
31:13 She . . works with willing hands. 4
16 fruit of her hands she plants a vineyard. 4
19 She puts her hands to the distaff 3
19 her hands hold the spindle. 4
20 She opens her hand to the poor 4
20 She . . reaches out her hands to the needy. 3
31 Give her of the fruit of her hands 3
Ecc 2:11 Then I considered all that my hands had done 3
24 This also, I saw, is from the hand of God; 3
4: 5 The fool folds his hands, and eats his own flesh. 3
6 two hands full of toil and a striving after wind. 2
5: 6 why should God . . destroy the work of your hands? 3
14 he is father . . but he has nothing in his hand. 3
15 nothing . . which he may carry away in his hand. 3
7:18 hold of this, and from that withhold not your hand; 3
26 woman whose heart . . and whose hands are fetters; 3
9: 1 the wise and their deeds are in the hand of God; 3
10 Whatever your hand finds to do, do it 3
11: 6 sow . . and at evening withhold not your hand; 3
Sng 5: 4 My beloved put his hand to the latch 3
5 I arose to open . . and my hands dripped with myrrh 3
7: 1 thighs are like jewels, the work of a master hand. 3
Isa 1:15 When you spread forth your hands, I will hide 4
15 I will not listen; your hands are full of blood. 3
25 I will turn my hand against you 3
2: 8 the work of their hands, to what their own fingers 3
3:11 what his hands have done shall be done to him. 3
5:12 the deeds of the LORD, or see the work of his hands. 3
25 he stretched out his hand against them and smote 3
25 turned away and his hand is stretched out still. 3
6: 6 the seraphim . . having in his hand a burning coal 3
8:11 spoke thus to me with his strong hand upon me 3
9:12 For all this . . his hand is stretched out still. 3
17 turned away and his hand is stretched out still. 3
21 turned away and his hand is stretched out still. 3
10: 4 turned away and his hand is stretched out still. 3
10 my hand has reached to the kingdoms of the idols 3
13 he says: "By the strength of my hand I have done it 3
14 My hand has found like a nest the wealth 3
11: 8 weaned child . . put his hand on the adder's den. 3
11 the Lord will extend his hand yet a second time 3
14 shall put forth their hand against Edom and Moab 3
15 wave his hand over the River with his scorching 3
13: 2 wave the hand for them to enter the gates 3
7 Therefore all hands will be feeble 3
22 its time is close at hand and its days 6
14:26 the hand . . stretched out over all the nations. 3
27 His hand is stretched out, and who will turn it back? 3
17: 8 regard for the altars, the work of their hands 3
19: 4 the Egyptians into the hand of a hard master; 3
16 tremble with fear before the hand which the LORD 3
25 Blessed be . . and Assyria the work of my hands 3
22:21 and will commit your authority to his hand; 3
23:11 He has stretched out his hand over the sea 3
25:10 the hand of the LORD will rest on this mountain 3
11 he will spread out his hands in the midst of it 3
11 as a swimmer spreads his hands out to swim; •
11 his pride together with the skill of his hands. 3
26:11 O LORD, thy hand is lifted up, but they see it not 3
28: 4 he eats it up as soon as it is in his hand. 4
29:23 For when he sees his children, the work of my hands 3
31: 3 When the LORD stretches out his hand 3
7 idols . . your hands have sinfully made for you. 3
33:15 who shakes his hands, lest they hold a bribe 4
34:17 his hand . . portioned it out to them with the line; 3
35: 3 Strengthen the weak hands 3
36: 6 will pierce the hand of any man who leans on it. 4
15 not be given into the hand of the king of Assyria. 3
18 his land out of the hand of the king of Assyria? 3
19 Have they delivered Sama'ria out of my hand? 3
20 have delivered their countries out of my hand 3
20 the LORD should deliver Jerusalem out of my hand?' 3
37:10 not be given into the hand of the king of Assyria. 3
14 the letter from the hand of the messengers 3
19 they were no gods, but the work of men's hands 3
20 now, O LORD our God, save us from his hand 3
38: 6 this city out of the hand of the king of Assyria 4
40: 2 from the LORD'S hand double for all her sins. 3
41:20 that the hand of the LORD has done this 3
42: 6 I have taken you by the hand and kept you; 3
43:13 there is none who can deliver from my hand; 3
44: 5 and another will write on his hand, 'The LORD'S,' 3
45:11 or command me concerning the work of my hands? 3
12 it was my hands that stretched out the heavens 3
47: 6 I gave them into your hand, you showed them no 3
48:13 My hand laid the foundation of the earth 3
49: 2 in the shadow of his hand he hid me; 3
16 Behold, I have graven you on the palms of my hands; •
22 Behold, I will lift up my hand to the nations 3
50: 2 Is my hand shortened, that it cannot redeem? 3
11 have from my hand: you shall lie down in torment. 3
51:16 in your mouth, and hid you in the shadow of my hand 3
17 drunk at the hand of the LORD the cup of his wrath 3
18 none to take her by the hand among all the sons 3
22 I have taken from your hand the cup of staggering; 3
23 I will put it into the hand of your tormentors 3
53:10 the will of the LORD shall prosper in his hand; 3
55:12 the trees of the field shall clap their hands. 4
56: 2 and keeps his hand from doing any evil. 3
59: 1 Behold, the LORD'S hand is not shortened 3
3 For your hands are defiled with blood 4
6 and deeds of violence are in their hands. 4
60:21 the shoot of my planting, the work of my hands 3
62: 3 shall be a crown of beauty in the hand of the LORD 3
3 and a royal diadem in the hand of your God. 4
64: 7 delivered us into the hand of our iniquities. 3
8 art our potter; we are all the work of thy hand. 3
65: 2 I spread out my hands all the day to a rebellious 3
22 chosen shall long enjoy the work of their hands. 3
66: 2 All these things my hand has made 3
14 that the hand of the LORD is with his servants 3
Jer 1: 9 the LORD put forth his hand and touched my mouth; 3
16 and worshiped the works of their own hands. 3
2:37 you will come away with your hands upon your head 3
4:31 gasping for breath, stretching out her hands 4
6: 9 pass your hand again over its branches. 3
12 for I will stretch out my hand 3
24 heard the report of it, our hands fall helpless; 3
10: 3 and worked with an axe by the hands of a craftsman. 3
9 the work . . of the hands of the goldsmith; 3
11:21 Do not prophesy . . or you will die by our hand 3
12: 7 beloved of my soul into the hands of her enemies. 4
15: 6 I have stretched out my hand against you 3
17 I sat alone, because thy hand was upon me 3
21 I will deliver you out of the hand of the wicked 3
17: 4 You shall loosen your hand from your heritage •
18: 4 vessel . . of clay was spoiled in the potter's hand 3
6 Behold, like the clay in the potter's hand 3
6 so are you in my hand, O house of Israel. 3
19: 7 and by the hand of those who seek their life. 3
20: 4 all Judah into the hand of the king of Babylon; 3
5 the kings of Judah into the hand of their enemies 3
13 the life of the needy from the hand of evildoers. 3
21: 4 the weapons of war which are in your hands 3
5 will fight against you with outstretched hand 3
7 into the hand of Nebuchadrez'zar king of Babylon 3
7 and into the hand of their enemies 3
7 into the hand of those who seek their lives. 3
10 be given into the hand of the king of Babylon 3
12 and deliver from the hand of the oppressor 3
22: 3 and deliver from the hand of the oppressor 3
24 Coni'ah . . were the signet ring on my right hand 3
25 give you into the hand of those who seek your life 3
25 into the hand of those of whom you are afraid 3
25 into the hand of Nebuchadrez'zar king of Babylon 3
25 and into the hand of the Chalde'ans 3
23:14 they strengthen the hands of evildoers 3
23 Am I a God at hand, says the LORD 8
25: 6 provoke me to anger with the work of your hands. 3
7 provoke me to anger with the work of your hands 3
14 their deeds and the work of their hands. 3
15 Take from my hand this cup of the wine of wrath 3
17 I took the cup from the LORD'S hand 3
28 if they refuse to accept the cup from your hand 3
26:14 But as for me, behold, I am in your hands. 3
24 the hand of Ahi'kam the son of Shaphan 3
27: 3 and the king of Sidon by the hand of the envoys 3
6 all these lands into the hand of Nebuchadnez'zar 3
8 until I have consumed it by his hand. 3
29: 3 was sent by the hand of Ela'sah the son of Shaphan 3
21 deliver them into the hand of Nebuchadrez'zar 3
30: 6 then do I see every man with his hands on his loins 3
31:11 has redeemed him from hands too strong for him. 3
32 when I took them by the hand to bring them out 3
32: 3 this city into the hand of the king of Babylon 3
4 shall not escape out of the hand of the Chalde'ans 3
4 be given into the hand of the king of Babylon 3
21 with a strong hand and outstretched arm 3
24 the city is given into the hands of the Chalde'ans 3
25 the city is given into the hands of the Chalde'ans 3
28 giving this city into the hands of the Chalde'ans 3
28 into the hand of Nebuchadrez'zar king of Babylon 3
30 to anger by the work of their hands, says the LORD. 3
36 It is given into the hand of the king of Babylon 3
43 it is given into the hands of the Chalde'ans. 3
33:13 flocks shall again pass under the hands 3
34: 2 this city into the hand of the king of Babylon 3
3 You shall not escape from his hand 3
3 surely be captured and delivered into his hand; 3
20 I will give them into the hand of their enemies 3
20 and into the hand of those who seek their lives. 3
21 I will give into the hand of their enemies 3
21 and into the hand of those who seek their lives 3
21 into the hand of the army of the king of Babylon 3
36:14 to say to Baruch, "Take in your hand the scroll 3
14 took the scroll in his hand and came to them. 3
37:17 You shall be delivered into the hand of the king 3
38: 3 into the hand of the army of the king of Babylon 3
4 for he is weakening the hands of the soldiers 3
4 weakening . . the hands of all the people 3
5 King Zedeki'ah said, "Behold, he is in your hands; 3
16 or deliver you into the hand of these men 3
18 shall be given into the hand of the Chalde'ans 3
18 and you shall not escape from their hand. 3
23 you yourself shall not escape from their hand 3
39:17 and you shall not be given into the hand of the men 3
40: 4 release you today from the chains on your hands. 3

42:11 to save you and to deliver you from his hand. 3
43: 3 to deliver us into the hand of the Chalde'ans 3
9 Take in your hands large stones, and hide them 3
44: 8 provoke me to anger with the works of your hands 3
25 and have fulfilled it with your hands, saying 3
30 Hophra king of Egypt into the hand of his enemies 3
30 and into the hand of those who seek his life 3
30 into the hand of Nebuchadrez'zar king of Babylon 3
46:24 she shall be delivered into the hand of a people 3
26 I will deliver them into the hand of those 3
26 into the hand of Nebuchadrez'zar king of Babylon 3
47: 3 back to the children, so feeble are their hands 3
48:16 The calamity of Moab is near at hand 6
37 upon all the hands are gashes 3
50:43 report of them, and his hands fell helpless; 3
51: 7 Babylon was a golden cup in the LORD'S hand 3
25 I will stretch out my hand against you 3
Lam 1: 7 When her people fell into the hand of the foe 3
10 The enemy has stretched out his hands over all 3
14 by his hand they were fastened together; 3
14 Lord gave me into the hands of those whom I cannot 3
17 Zion stretches out her hands 3
2: 7 he has delivered into the hand of the enemy 3
8 he restrained not his hand from destroying; 3
15 All who pass along the way clap their hands at you; 4
19 Lift your hands to him for . . your children 4
3: 3 against me he turns his hand again and again 3
41 Let us lift up our hearts and hands to God 4
64 requite . . according to the work of their hands. 3
4: 2 reckoned as . . pots, the work of a potter's hands! 3
6 overthrown in a moment, no hand being laid on it. 3
10 The hands of compassionate women have boiled 3
5: 6 We have given the hand to Egypt . . to get bread 3
8 there is none to deliver us from their hand. 3
12 Princes are hung up by their hands; 3
Ezk 1: 3 and the hand of the LORD was upon him there. 3
8 Under their wings . . they had human hands. 3
2: 9 I looked, behold, a hand was stretched out to me 3
3:14 the hand of the LORD being strong upon me; 3
18 but his blood I will require at your hand. 3
20 but his blood I will require at your hand. 3
22 the hand of the LORD was there upon me; 3
6:11 Clap your hands, and stamp your foot, and say, Alas! 4
14 I will stretch out my hand against them 3
7:17 All hands are feeble, and all knees weak as water. 3
21 I will give it into the hands of foreigners 3
27 the hands of the people of the land are palsied 3
8: 1 the hand of the Lord GOD fell there upon me. 3
3 He put forth the form of a hand, and took me 3
11 Each had his censer in his hand 3
9: 1 each with his destroying weapon in his hand. 3
2 man with his weapon for slaughter in his hand 3
10: 2 fill your hands with burning coals 2
7 a cherub stretched forth his hand 3
7 put it into the hands of the man clothed in linen 2
8 have the form of a human hand under their wings. 3
21 and underneath . . the semblance of human hands. 3
11: 9 and give you into the hands of foreigners 3
12: 7 I dug through the wall with my own hands; 3
23 But say to them, The days are at hand 9
13: 9 My hand will be against the prophets 3
21 and deliver my people out of your hand 3
21 they shall be no more in your hand as prey; 3
23 I will deliver my people out of your hand. 3
14: 9 I will stretch out my hand against him 3
13 I stretch out my hand against it 3
16:27 I stretched out my hand against you 3
39 And I will give you into the hand of your lovers 3
17:18 he gave his hand and yet did all these things 3
18: 8 withholds his hand from iniquity 3
17 withholds his hand from iniquity 3
20:22 But I withheld my hand 3
33 says the Lord GOD, surely with a mighty hand 3
34 with a mighty hand and an outstretched arm 3
21: 7 heart will melt and all hands will be feeble 3
11 polished to be given into the hand of the slayer. 3
14 clap your hands and let the sword come down twice 4
17 I also will clap my hands 4
31 I will deliver you into the hands of brutal men 3
22:13 I strike my hands together at the dishonest gain 4
14 your courage endure, or can your hands be strong 3
23: 9 I delivered her into the hands of her lovers 3
9 into the hands of the Assyrians 3
28 deliver you into the hands of those whom you hate 3
28 hands of those from whom you turned in disgust; 3
31 therefore I will give her cup into your hand. 3
37 and blood is upon their hands; 3
42 they put bracelets upon the hands of the women 3
45 are adulteresses, and blood is upon their hands. 3
25: 6 Because you have clapped your hands 3
7 behold, I have stretched out my hand against you 3
13 I will stretch out my hand against Edom 3
14 vengeance upon Edom by the hand of my people 3
16 Behold, I will stretch out my hand 3
28: 9 and no god, in the hands of those who wound you? 3
10 of the uncircumcised by the hand of foreigners; 3
29: 7 when they grasped you with the hand, you broke 4
30:10 by the hand of Nebuchadrez'zar king of Babylon. 3
12 and will sell the land into the hand of evil men; 3
12 by the hand of foreigners; I, the LORD, have spoken. 3
22 I will make the sword fall from his hand. 3
24 and put my sword in his hand; 3
25 I put my sword into the hand of the king of Babylon 3
31:11 I will give it into the hand of a mighty one 3
33: 6 his blood I will require at the watchman's hand. 3
8 but his blood I will require at your hand. 3
22 Now the hand of the LORD had been upon me 3
34:10 I will require my sheep at their hand 3
27 deliver them from the hand of those who enslaved 3
35: 3 I will stretch out my hand against you 3
37: 1 hand of the LORD was upon me, and he brought me 3
17 that they may become one in your hand. 3
19 stick of Joseph (which is in the hand of E phraim) 3
19 that they may be one in my hand. 3
20 the sticks on which you write are in your hand 3
39: 3 then I will strike your bow from your left hand 3
3 make your arrows drop out of your right hand. 3
21 and my hand which I have laid on them. 3
23 and gave them into the hand of their adversaries 3
40: 1 on that very day, the hand of the LORD was upon me 3
3 a line of flax and a measuring reed in his hand; 3
5 the length of the measuring reed in the man's hand 3
47: 3 Going on eastward with a line in his hand 3
Dan 2:34 As you looked, a stone was cut out by no human hand 10
38 into whose hand he has given, wherever they dwell 10
45 stone was cut from a mountain by no human hand 10
3:15 god that will deliver you out of my hands? 10
17 God . . will deliver us out of your hand, O king. 10
4:35 can stay his hand or say to him, "What doest thou? 10
5: 5 fingers of a man's hand appeared and wrote 10
5 king saw the hand as it wrote. 10
23 but the God in whose hand is your breath 10
24 Then from his presence the hand was sent 10
7:25 given into his hand for a time, two times, and half 10
8:25 cunning . . make deceit prosper under his hand 3
25 but, by no human hand, he shall be broken. 3
9:15 out of the land of Egypt with a mighty hand 3
10:10 behold, a hand touched me and set me trembling 3
10 set me trembling on my hands and knees. 5
11:11 it shall be given into his hand. 3
41 these shall be delivered out of his hand: Edom 3
42 stretch out his hand against the countries 3
Hos 2:10 and no one shall rescue her out of my hand. 3
7: 5 he stretched out his hand with mockers. 3
12: 7 A trader, in whose hands are false balances 3
14: 3 will say no more, 'Our God,' to the work of our hands. 3
Jol 3: 8 your daughters into the hand of the sons of Judah 3
Ams 1: 8 I will turn my hand against Ekron; 3
5:19 and leaned with his hand against the wall 3
7: 7 the Lord . . with a plumb line in his hand. 3
9: 2 dig into Sheol, from there shall my hand take them; 3
Jon 3: 8 from the violence which is in his hands. 4
Mic 2: 1 because it is in the power of their hand. 3
4:10 will redeem you from the hand of your enemies. 4
5: 9 Your hand shall be lifted up over 3
12 I will cut off sorceries from your hand 3
13 shall bow down no more to the work of your hands; 3
7: 3 Their hands are upon what is evil 4
4 now their confusion is at hand. 1
16 they shall lay their hands on their mouths; 3
Nah 3:19 hear the news of you clap their hands over you. 4
Hab 3: 4 like the light, rays flashed from his hand; 3
10 gave forth its voice, it lifted its hands on high. 3
Zep 1: 4 I will stretch out my hand against Judah 3
: 7 For the day of the LORD is at hand; 9
2:13 he will stretch out his hand against the north 3
3:16 Do not fear, O Zion; let not your hands grow weak. 3
Hag 2:14 and so with every work of their hands; 3
Zec 2: 1 behold, a man with a measuring line in his hand! 3
9 Behold, I will shake my hand over them 3
4: 9 hands of Zerub'babel have laid the foundation 3
9 his hands shall also comple te it. 3
10 shall see the plummet in the hand of Zerub'babel. 3
8: 4 each with staff in hand for very age. 3
9 says the LORD of hosts: "Let your hands be strong 3
13 Fear not, but let your hands be strong. 3
11: 6 men to fall each into the hand of his shepherd 3
6 of his shepherd, and each into the hand of his king; 3
6 I will deliver none from their hand. 3
13: 7 I will turn my hand against the little ones. 3
14:13 each will lay hold on the hand of his fellow 3
13 the hand of the one will be raised against 3
13 will be raised against the hand of the other; 3
Mal 1: 9 With such a gift from your hand, will he show favor 3
10 I will not accept an offering from your hand. 3
13 Shall I accept that from your hand? says the LORD. 3
2:13 or accepts it with favor at your hand. 3
Mat 3: 2 Repent, for the kingdom of heaven is at hand. 12
12 winnowing fork is in his hand, and he will clear 21
4: 6 charge of you,' and 'On their hands they will bear 21
17 Repent, for the kingdom of heaven is at hand. 12
5:30 And if your right hand causes you to sin, cut it off 21
8: 3 And he stretched out his hand and touched him 21
15 he touched her hand, and the fever left her 21
9:18 but come and lay your hand on her 21
25 he went in and took her by the hand 21
10: 7 'The kingdom of heaven is at hand.' 12
12:10 behold, there was a man with a withered hand 21
13 Then he said to the man, "Stretch out your hand. 21
49 stretching out his hand toward his disciples 21
14:31 Jesus immediately reached out his hand 21
15: 2 For they do not wash their hands when they eat. 21
20 to eat with unwashed hands does not defile a man. 21
17:12 So also the Son of man will suffer at their hands. 19
22 Son of man is to be delivered into the hands of men 21
18: 8 if your hand or your foot causes you to sin 21
8 than with two hands or two feet 21
19:13 that he might lay his hands on them and pray 21
15 he laid his hands on them and went away. 21
22:13 'Bind him hand and foot, and cast him into the outer 21
26:18 The Teacher says, My time is at hand 13
23 He who has dipped his hand in the dish with me 21
45 Behold, the hour is at hand 12
45 Son of man is betrayed into the hands of sinners. 21
46 Rise, let us be going; see, my betrayer is at hand. 12
50 came up and laid hands on Jesus and seized him. 21
51 Jesus stretched out his hand and drew his sword 21
27:24 took water and washed his hands before the crowd 21
Mrk 1:15 the kingdom of God is at hand 12
31 he came and took her by the hand and lifted her up 21
41 Moved with pity, he stretched out his hand 21
3: 1 a man was there who had a withered hand. 21
3 he said to the man who had the withered hand 21
5 said to the man, "Stretch out your hand. 21
5 He stretched it out, and his hand was restored. 21
5:23 Come and lay your hands on her 21
41 Taking her by the hand he said . . , "Tal'itha cu'mi"; 21
6: 2 What mighty works are wrought by his hands! 21
5 he laid his hands upon a few sick people 21
7: 2 ate with hands defiled, that is, unwashed. 21
3 do not eat unless they wash their hands 21
5 but eat with hands defiled? 21
13 through your tradition which you hand on. 16
32 they besought him to lay his hand upon him. 21
8:23 he took the blind man by the hand 21
23 and laid his hands upon him 21
25 Then again he laid his hands upon his eyes 21
9:27 Jesus took him by the hand and lifted him up 21
31 delivered into the hands of men 21
43 if your hand causes you to sin, cut it off 21
43 with two hands to go to hell 21
10:16 laying his hands upon them. 21
14:41 Son of man is betrayed into the hands of sinners. 21
42 Rise, let us be going; see, my betrayer is at hand. 12
46 they laid hands on him and seized him. 21
16:18 they will lay their hands on the sick 21
Lke 1:66 the hand of the Lord was with him. 21
71 saved . . from the hand of all who hate us 21
74 delivered from the hand of our enemies 21
3:17 His winnowing fork is in his hand 21
4:11 'On their hands they will bear you up 21
40 he laid his hands on every one of them 21
5:13 he stretched out his hand, and touched him, saying 21
6: 1 rubbing them in their hands. 21
6 a man was there whose right hand was withered. 21
8 he said to the man who had the withered hand 21
10 said to him, "Stretch out your hand. 21
10 he did so, and his hand was restored. 21
8:54 taking her by the hand he called, saying, "Child 21
9:44 to be delivered into the hands of men. 21
62 No one who puts his hand to the plow 21
13:13 he laid his hands upon her 21
15:22 put a ring on his hand, and shoes on his feet; 21
20:19 tried to lay hands on him at that very hour 21
21: 8 'The time is at hand!' Do not go after them. 12
12 before all this they will lay their hands on you 21
22:21 behold the hand of him who betrays me 21
53 you did not lay hands on me 21
23:46 Father, into thy hands I commit my spirit! 21
24: 7 must be delivered into the hands of sinful men 21
39 See my hands and my feet, that it is I myself 21
50 and lifting up his hands he blessed them. 21
Joh 2:13 The Passover of the Jews was at hand 13
3:35 and has given all things into his hand. 21
6: 4 the Passover, the feast of the Jews, was at hand. 13
7: 2 Now the Jews' feast of Tabernacles was at hand. 13
30 no one laid hands on him 21
44 but no one laid hands on him. 21
10:28 no one shall snatch them out of my hand. 21
29 is able to snatch them out of the Father's hand. 21
39 he escaped from their hands. 21
11:44 his hands and feet bound with bandages 21
55 Now the Passover of the Jews was at hand 13
13: 3 the Father had given all things into his hands 21
9 not my feet only but also my hands and my head! 21
20:20 he showed them his hands and his side 21
25 Unless I see in his hands the print of the nails 21
25 place my hand in his side 21
27 Put your finger here, and see my hands 21
27 and put out your hand, and place it in my side 21
21:18 when you are old, you will stretch out your hands 21
Act 2:23 and killed by the hands of lawless men. 21
3: 7 he took him by the right hand and raised him up; 21
4:28 whatever thy hand and thy plan had predestined 21

30 while thou stretchest out thy hand to heal 21
5:12 done . . by the hands of the apostles 21
6: 6 they prayed and laid their hands upon them. 21
7:25 God was giving them deliverance by his hand 21
35 by the hand of the angel 21
41 rejoiced in the works of their hands. 21
50 Did not my hand make all these things?' 21
8:17 Then they laid their hands on them 21
18 through the laying on of the apostles' hands 21
19 any one on whom I lay my hands 21
9:12 Anani'as come in and lay his hands on him 21
17 laying his hands on him he said, "Brother Saul 21
41 he gave her his hand and lifted her up 21
11:21 the hand of the Lord was with them 21
30 by the hand of Barnabas and Saul. 21
12: 1 Herod the king laid violent hands upon some 21
7 the chains fell off his hands. 21
11 and rescued me from the hand of Herod 21
17 motioning to them with his hand to be silent 21
13: 3 they laid their hands on them and sent them off. 21
11 now, behold, the hand of the Lord is upon you 21
16 So Paul stood up, and motioning with his hand said 21
14: 3 granting . . wonders to be done by their hands. 21
17:25 nor is he served by human hands 21
19: 6 when Paul had laid his hands upon them 21
11 did extraordinary miracles by the hands of Paul 21
26 saying that gods made with hands are not gods. 21
33 Alexander motioned with his hand 21
20:34 these hands ministered to my necessities 21
21:11 deliver him into the hands of the Gentiles.' 21
11 bound his own feet and hands, and said 21
27 stirred up all the crowd, and laid hands on him 21
40 motioned with his hand to the people 21
23:19 The tribune took him by the hand 21
26: 1 Paul stretched out his hand and made his defense 21
27:19 they cast out with their own hands the tackle 11
28: 3 a viper came out . . and fastened on his hand. 21
4 saw the creature hanging from his hand 21
8 putting his hands on him healed him. 21
17 from Jerusalem into the hands of the Romans. 21
Rom 10:21 All day long I have held out my hands 21
13:12 the night is far gone, the day is at hand. 12
1Co 4:12 we labor, working with our own hands 21
12:15 Because I am not a hand, I do not belong to the body 21
21 The eye cannot say to the hand, "I have no need 21
16:21 I, Paul, write this greeting with my own hand. 21
2Co 11:24 received at the hands of the Jews the forty lashes 19
33 escaped his hands. 21
Gal 6:11 I am writing to you with my own hand. 21
Eph 4:28 let him labor, doing honest work with his hands 21
Php 4: 5 The Lord is at hand. 13
Col 4:18 I, Paul, write this greeting with my own hand. 21
1Th 4:11 to work with your hands, as we charged you; 21
2Th 3:17 I, Paul, write this greeting with my own hand 21
1Ti 2: 8 lifting holy hands without anger or quarreling; 21
4:14 the council of elders laid their hands upon you 21
5:22 Do not be hasty in the laying on of hands 21
2Ti 1: 6 within you through the laying on of my hands; 21
Phm 1:19 I, Paul, write this with my own hand, I will repay 21
Heb 1:10 the heavens are the work of thy hands; 21
6: 2 the laying on of hands 21
7:18 On the one hand, a former commandment is set aside 15
8: 9 on the day when I took them by the hand 21
10:31 to fall into the hands of the living God. 21
12:12 Therefore lift your drooping hands 21
Jas 4: 8 Cleanse your hands, you sinners 21
5: 8 for the coming of the Lord is at hand. 12
1Pe 4: 7 The end of all things is at hand; 12
5: 6 under the mighty hand of God 21
1Jn 1: 1 we have looked upon and touched with our hands 21
Rev 1:16 in his right hand he held seven stars 21
6: 5 and its rider had a balance in his hand; 21
7: 9 in white robes, with palm branches in their hands 21
8: 4 rose . . from the hand of the angel before God. 21
9:20 did not repent of the works of their hands 21
10: 2 He had a little scroll open in his hand. 21
5 the angel . . lifted up his right hand to heaven 21
8 the scroll which is open in the hand of the angel 21
10 took the little scroll from the hand of the angel 21
13:16 to be marked on the right hand or the forehead 21
14: 9 receives a mark on his forehead or on his hand 21
14 crown on his head, and a sharp sickle in his hand. 21
15: 2 standing . . with harps of God in their hands. •
17: 4 holding in her hand a golden cup 21
20: 1 holding in his hand the key of the bottomless pit 21
4 its mark on their foreheads or their hands. 21
1Es 1:53 he gave them all into their hands. 21
6:10 the work is prospering in their hands 21
15 gave them over into the hands of Nebuchadnezzar 21
33 stretch out their hands to hinder . . that house 21
7:15 to strengthen their hands 21
8:47 by the mighty hand of our Lord 21
61 by the mighty hand of our Lord 21
73 stretching forth my hands to the Lord 21
9:47 they lifted up their hands, and fell to the ground 21
2Es 1:26 for you have defiled your hands with blood 25
2:29 My hands will cover you 25
46 and puts palms in their hands? 25

3: 5 Yet he was the workmanship of thy hands 25
27 deliver the city into the hands of thy enemies. 25
5:30 they should be punished at thy own hands. 25
6: 8 Jacob's hand held Esau's heel from the beginning. 25
10 For the beginning of a man is his hand 25
10 between the heel and the hand 25
58 thy people . . have been given into their hands. 25
8: 7 we are a work of thy hands, as thou hast declared. 25
44 man, who has been formed by thy hands 25
10:23 has been given over into the hands of those 25
13: 9 he neither lifted his hand nor held a spear 25
36 the mountain carved out without hands. 25
15:11 I will bring them out with a mighty hand 25
15 with swords in their hands. 25
53 exulting and clapping your hands 25
16: 2 for your destruction is at hand. 23
74 Behold, the days of tribulation are at hand 24
Tob 5:17 Is he not the staff of our hands 21
7:13 taking her by the hand he gave her to Tobias 21
13: 2 there is no one who can escape his hand. 21
11 bearing gifts in their hands 21
Jdt 2:12 what I have spoken my hand will execute. 21
7:25 God has sold us into their hands 21
8:33 the Lord will deliver Israel by my hand. 21
9:10 crush their arrogance by the hand of a woman. 21
11:13 to touch these things with their hands. 21
22 to lend strength to our hands 21
12: 4 the Lord carries out by my hand 21
13: 4 look in this hour upon the work of my hands 21
14 has destroyed our enemies by my hand 21
15 Lord has struck him down by the hand of a woman. 21
14: 6 in the hand of one of the men 21
15:12 she took branches in her hands 21
16: 3 he has delivered me out of the hands of my pursuers 21
6 has foiled them by the hand of a woman. 21
7 did not fall by the hands of the young men •
AEs 12: 2 preparing to lay hands upon Artaxerxes the king; 21
14: 4 for my danger is in my hand. 21
6 thou hast given us into the hands of our enemies 21
14 save us by thy hand, and help me, who am alone 21
19 save us from the hands of evildoers 21
16: 7 the more ancient records which we hand on 16
7 investigation of matters close at hand. 17
Wis 1:12 nor bring on destruction by the works of your hands; 21
2:18 deliver him from the hand of his adversaries. 21
3: 1 the souls of the righteous are in the hand of God 21
14 the eunuch whose hands have done no lawless deed 21
5:16 a beautiful diadem from the hand of the Lord 21
7:11 in her hands uncounted wealth. 21
16 For both we and our words are in his hand 21
8:12 they will put their hands on their mouths. 21
18 in the labors of her hands, unfailing wealth 21
9:16 what is at hand we find with labor 21
10:20 and praised with one accord thy defending hand 21
11: 1 the hand of a holy prophet. 21
17 thy all-powerful hand, which created the world 21
12: 6 destroy by the hands of our fathers 21
9 give the ungodly into the hands of the righteous 20
13:10 who give the name "gods" to the works of men's hands 21
10 a useless stone, the work of an ancient hand. 21
19 a thing whose hands have no strength. 21
19 money-making and work and success with his hands 21
14: 6 guided by thy hand 21
15 and handed on to his dependents secret rites 16
15:17 what he makes with lawless hands is dead 21
16:15 To escape from thy hand is impossible; 21
19: 8 those protected by thy hand 21
Sir 2:12 Woe to timid hearts and to slack hands 21
18 Let us fall into the hands of the Lord 21
18 not into the hands of men 21
4: 9 Deliver . . from the hand of the wrongdoer 21
31 Let not your hand be extended to receive 21
5:12 if not, put your hand on your mouth. 21
7:32 Stretch forth your hand to the poor 21
8: 1 lest you fall into his hands. 21
16 where no help is at hand, he will strike you down. •
10: 4 government . . is in the hands of the Lord 21
5 The success of a man is in the hands of the Lord 21
12:18 he will shake his head, and clap his hands 21
15:16 stretch out your hand for whichever you wish. 21
21:19 like manacles on his right hand. 22
22: 2 any one that picks it up will shake it off his hand. 21
25:23 Drooping hands and weak knees 21
27:19 as you allow a bird to escape from your hand 21
29: 1 he that strengthens him with his hand 21
5 A man will kiss another's hands 21
26 if you have anything at hand, let me have it to eat. 21
31:14 Do not reach out your hand for everything you see 21
18 do not reach out your hand before they do. 21
33:13 As clay in the hand of the potter 21
13 so men are in the hand of him who made them 21
21 you should look to the hand of you sons. 21
25 leave his hands idle, and he will seek liberty. 21
35: 8 do not stint the first fruits of your hands. 21
10 as generously as your hand has found. 21
36: 3 Lift up thy hand against foreign nations 21
6 make thy hand and thy right arm glorious. 21

38:10 Give up your faults and direct your hands aright 21
13 when success lies in the hands of physicians 21
31 All these rely upon their hands 21
42: 6 where there are many hands, lock things up. 21
43:12 the hands of the Most High have stretched it out. 21
46: 2 How glorious he was when he lifted his hands 21
4 Was not the sun held back by his hand? 21
47: 4 when he lifted his hand with a stone in the sling 21
48:18 he lifted up his hand against Zion 21
19 their hands trembled 21
20 spreading forth their hands toward him 21
20 delivered them by the hand of Isaiah. 21
49:11 He was like a signet on the right hand 21
50:12 received . . from the hands of the priests 21
13 with the Lord's offering in their hands 21
15 he reached out his hand to the cup 21
20 lifted up his hands over the whole congregation 21
51: 3 from the hand of those who sought my life 21
8 dost save them from the hand of their enemies. 21
19 I spread out my hands to the heavens 21
Bar 2:11 out of the land of Egypt with a mighty hand 21
4:18 deliver you from the hand of your enemies. 21
21 deliver you from the power and hand of the enemy. 21
LJr 1:51 they are not gods but the work of men's hands 21
Aza 1: 9 hast given us into the hands of lawless enemies 21
66 saved us from the hand of death 21
Sus 1:22 and if I do not, I shall not escape your hands. 21
23 I choose not to do it and to fall into your hands 21
34 two elders . . laid their hands upon her head. 21
1Mc 2:47 the work prospered in their hands. 21
48 rescued the law out of the hands of the Gentiles 21
3: 6 deliverance prospered by his hand. 21
4:30 by the hand of thy servant David 21
30 didst give . . into the hands of Jonathan 21
31 hem in this army by the hand of thy people Israel 21
5:12 Now then come and rescue us from their hands 21
50 the city was delivered into his hands. 21
6:25 they stretched out their hands 21
7:35 delivered into my hands this time 21
9:46 delivered from the hands of our enemies. 21
47 Jonathan stretched out his hand to strike Bacchides 21
12: 9 the holy books which are in our hands 21
27 to keep their arms at hand 14
39 to raise his hand against Antiochus the king. 21
42 he was afraid to raise his hand against him. 21
14:31 lay hands on their sanctuary 21
36 in his days things prospered in his hands 21
16: 2 things have prospered in our hands 21
2Mc 3:20 holding up their hands to heaven 21
5:16 He took the holy vessels with his polluted hands 21
16 swept away with profane hands the votive offerings 21
6:26 I shall not escape the hands of the Almighty. 21
7:10 and courageously stretched forth his hands 21
14 One cannot but choose to die at the hands of men 19
31 you . . will certainly not escape the hands of God. 21
34 when you raise your hand 21
12:28 they got the city into their hands 20
13:11 and not to let . . fall into the hands of the . . Gentiles 20
14:34 Then the priests stretched forth their hands 21
42 rather than to fall into the hands of sinners 20
46 he tore out his entrails, took them with both hands 21
15:12 was praying with outstretched hands 21
21 Maccabeus . . stretched out his hands toward heaven 21
27 fighting with their hands 21
3Mc 2: 1 and extending his hands with calm dignity 21
8 when they had seen works of your hands 21
5: 5 and bound the hands of the wretched people 21
13 to show the might of his all-powerful hand 21
25 stretched their hands toward heaven 21
46 and urged the king on to the matter at hand. 18
6:10 rescue us from the hand of the enemy 21
7:10 their own hands . . should receive the punishment •
4Mc 4:11 Apollonius . . stretched out his hands toward heaven 21
9:11 bound his hands and arms with thongs on each side. 21
28 tore out his sinews with the iron hands 21
10: 5 they disjointed his hands and feet 21
13:12 by whose hand Isaac would have submitted 21
14: 6 Just as the hands and feet are moved 21
15:20 severed hands upon hands 21
20 severed hands upon hands 21
16:20 when Isaac saw his father's hand wielding a sword 21
17:19 All who are consecrated are under your hands. 21
151 1: 2 My hands made a harp, my fingers fashioned a lyre. 21

hand *See also* close, fight, hollow, lead, left, lie, make, people, strike, turn.

into the hand 1. לִפְנֵי

Deu 2:36 LORD our God gave all into our hands. 1

other hand 1. אוֹ 2. δέ

2Sm 18:13 On the other hand, if I had dealt treacherously 1
1Co 14: 3 On the other hand, he who prophesies speaks to men 2
Heb 7:19 on the other hand, a better hope is introduced 2

hand over 1. מגן 2. נתן 3. נתן עַל יַד 4. *διακομίζω* 5. *δίδωμι* 6. *παραδίδωμι* 7. *παραχωρέω* 8. trado

Deu 19:12 hand him over to the avenger of blood 2

2Kg 12: 7 take no more money . . but hand it over 2
Est 6: 9 let the robes and the horse be handed over to one 3
Jer 38:19 lest I be handed over to them and they abuse me. 2
Ezk 25: 4 I am handing you over to the people of the East 2
7 and will hand you over as spoil to the nations; 2
Hos 11: 8 How can I hand you over, O Israel! 1
Mat 5:25 lest your accuser hand you over to the judge 6
Lke 12:58 lest . . the judge hand you over to the officer 6
Joh 18:30 we would not have handed him over. 6
35 the chief priests have handed you over to me 6
36 that I might not be handed over to the Jews 6
19:16 he handed him over to them to be crucified. 6
1Es 2:14 All the vessels were handed over, gold and silver 4
2Es 15:26 he will hand them over to death and slaughter. 8
56 and will hand you over to adversities. 8
Jdt 2: 7 and will hand them over to be plundered by my troops 5
11 you shall hand them over to slaughter 5
6:10 and hand him over to the men of Israel. 6
8:19 why our fathers were handed over to the sword 5
10:12 are about to be handed over to you to be devoured. 5
15 some of us will escort you and hand you over to him. 6
11:15 they will be handed over to you to be destroyed. 5
Sir 4:19 hand him over to his ruin. 6
11: 6 illustrious men have been handed over to others. 6
Bar 4: 6 you were handed over to your enemies 6
Bel 1:29 Going to the king, they said, "Hand Daniel over to us 6
30 under compulsion he handed Daniel over to them. 6
1Mc 11:40 and insistently urged him to hand Antiochus over 6
12:34 they were ready to hand over the stronghold 6
45 I will hand it over to you 6
15:21 hand them over to Simon the high priest 6
30 hand over the cities which you have seized 6
2Mc 8:11 and promising to hand over 90 slaves for a talent 7
10: 4 and not be handed over to blasphemous . . nations 6
14:31 and commanded them to hand the man over. 6
33 If you do not hand Judas over to me as a prisoner 6

right hand 1. יָמִין 2. ימן 3. δεξιός 4. dexter
Gen 13: 9 take the right hand, then I will go to the left. 1
24:49 I may turn to the right hand or to the left. 1
48:13 E'phraim in his right hand toward Israel's left 1
13 Manas'seh . . toward Israel's right hand 1
14 Israel stretched out his right hand and laid it 1
18 the first-born; put your right hand upon his head. 1
Exd 14:22 on their right hand and on their left. 1
29 on their right hand and on their left. 1
15: 6 Thy right hand, O LORD, glorious in power 1
6 thy right hand, O LORD, shatters the enemy. 1
12 Thou didst stretch out thy right hand 1
Num20:17 not turn aside to the right hand or to the left 1
Deu 5:32 not turn aside to the right hand or to the left. 1
17:11 not turn . . either to the right hand or to the left. 1
20 not turn . . either to the right hand or to the left; 1
28:14 do not turn . . to the right hand or to the left 1
33: 2 he came . . with flaming fire at his right hand. 1
Jos 1: 7 turn not from it to the right hand or to the left 1
23: 6 turning . . neither to the right hand nor to the left 1
Jdg 5:26 She put . . her right hand to the workmen's mallet; 1
16:29 he leaned . . upon them, his right hand on the one 1
2Sm 2:19 turned neither to the right hand nor to the left 1
21 Turn aside to your right hand or to your left 1
16: 6 mighty men were on his right hand and on his left. 1
1Kg 22:19 host of heaven standing . . on his right hand 1
1Ch 6:39 his brother Asaph, who stood on his right hand 1
12: 2 with either the right or the left hand; 2
2Ch 18:18 all the host of heaven standing on his right hand 1
Neh 8: 4 beside him stood . . Ma-asei'ah on his right hand; 1
Job 23: 9 I turn to the right hand, but I cannot see him. 1
30:12 On my right hand the rabble rise, 1
40:14 that your own right hand can give you victory. 1
Ps 16: 8 he is at my right hand, I shall not be moved. 1
11 in thy right hand are pleasures for evermore. 1
17: 7 those who seek refuge . . at thy right hand. 1
18:35 thy right hand supported me, and thy help made me 1
20: 6 with mighty victories by his right hand. 1
21: 8 your right hand will find out those who hate you. 1
26:10 whose right hands are full of bribes. 1
44: 3 thy right hand, and thy arm, and the light of thy 1
45: 4 let your right hand teach you dread deeds! 1
9 at your right hand stands the queen in gold 1
48:10 Thy right hand is filled with victory; 1
60: 5 give victory by thy right hand and answer us! 1
63: 8 My soul clings to thee; thy right hand upholds me. 1
74:11 why dost thou keep thy right hand in thy bosom? 1
77:10 the right hand of the Most High has changed. 1
78:54 the mountain which his right hand had won. 1
80:15 the stock which thy right hand planted. 1
17 But let thy hand be upon the man of thy right hand 1
89:13 strong is thy hand, high thy right hand. 1
25 I will set . . his right hand on the rivers. 1
42 Thou hast exalted the right hand of his foes; 1
91: 7 fall at your side, 10,000 at your right hand; 1
98: 1 right hand and his holy arm have gotten him 1
108: 6 give help by thy right hand, and answer me! 1
109:31 For he stands at the right hand of the needy 1
110: 1 Sit at my right hand, till I make your enemies 1
5 The Lord is at your right hand; 1
118:15 The right hand of the LORD does valiantly 1
16 the right hand of the LORD is exalted 1
16 the right hand of the LORD does valiantly! 1
137: 5 forget you, O Jerusalem, let my right hand wither! 1
138: 7 thy right hand delivers me. 1
139:10 even there . . thy right hand shall hold me. 1
144: 8 whose right hand is . . of falsehood. 1
8 whose . . is a right hand of falsehood. 1
11 whose right hand is . . of falsehood. 1
11 whose . . is a right hand of falsehood. 1
Prv 3:16 Long life is in her right hand; 1
27:16 or to grasp oil in his right hand. 1
Sng 2: 6 O . . that his right hand embraced me! 1
8: 3 O that . . and that his right hand embraced me! 1
Isa 41:10 I will uphold you with my victorious right hand. 1
13 For I, the LORD your God, hold your right hand; 1
44:20 or say, "Is there not a lie in my right hand? 1
45: 1 to Cyrus, whose right hand I have grasped 1
48:13 and my right hand spread out the heavens; 1
62: 8 has sworn by his right hand and by his mighty arm 1
63:12 his glorious arm to go at the right hand of Moses 1
Lam 2: 3 he has withdrawn from them his right hand 1
4 bent his bow . . with his right hand set like a foe; 1
Ezk 21:22 Into his right hand comes the lot for Jerusalem 1
Dan 12: 7 his right hand and his left hand toward heaven; 1
Jon 4:11 who do not know their right hand from their left 1
Hab 2:16 The cup in the LORD'S right hand will come around 1
Zec 3: 1 Satan standing at his right hand to accuse him. 1
Mat 6: 3 your left hand know what your right hand is doing 3
20:21 one at your right hand and one at your left 3
23 to sit at my right hand and at my left 3
22:44 'The Lord said to my Lord, Sit at my right hand 3
25:33 he will place the sheep at his right hand 3
34 Then the King will say to those at his right hand 3
26:64 the Son of man seated at the right hand of Power 3
27:29 and put a reed in his right hand 3
Mrk 10:37 one at your right hand and one at your left 3
40 to sit at my right hand or at my left 3
12:36 The Lord said to my Lord, Sit at my right hand 3
14:62 the Son of man seated at the right hand of Power 3
16:19 Jesus . . sat down at the right hand of God. 3
Lke 20:42 The Lord said to my Lord, Sit at my right hand 3
22:69 seated at the right hand of the power of God. 3
Act 2:25 he is at my right hand that I may not be shaken; 3
33 Being therefore exalted at the right hand of God 3
34 The Lord said to my Lord, Sit at my right hand 3
5:31 God exalted him at his right hand as Leader 3
7:55 Jesus standing at the right hand of God; 3
56 the Son of man standing at the right hand of God. 3
Rom 8:34 Christ Jesus . . who is at the right hand of God 3
2Co 6: 7 for the right hand and for the left; 3
Gal 2: 9 gave to me . . the right hand of fellowship 3
Eph 1:20 made him sit at his right hand 3
Col 3: 1 where Christ is, seated at the right hand of God. 3
Heb 1: 3 he sat down at the right hand of the Majesty on high 3
13 to what angel has he ever said, "Sit at my right hand 3
8: 1 one who is seated at the right hand of the throne 3
10:12 he sat down at the right hand of God 3
12: 2 seated at the right hand of the throne of God. 3
1Pe 3:22 who . . is at the right hand of God 3
Rev 1:17 But he laid his right hand upon me, saying, "Fear not 3
20 the seven stars which you saw in my right hand 3
2: 1 him who holds the seven stars in his right hand 3
5: 1 And I saw in the right hand of him who was seated 3
7 he went and took the scroll from the right hand 3
1Es 4:29 she would sit at the king's right hand 3
9:43 Baalsamus on his right hand 3
2Es 3: 6 into the garden which thy right hand had planted 4
7: 7 there is fire on the right hand 4
10:30 he grasped my right hand and strengthened me 4
15:22 My right hand will not spare the sinners 4
16:13 For his right hand that bends the bow is strong 4
Wis 5:16 because with his right hand he will cover them 3
Sir 47: 5 he gave him strength in his right hand 3
LJr 1:15 It has a dagger in its right hand, and has an axe 3
1Mc 2:22 to the right hand or to the left. 3
7:47 the right hand which he so arrogantly stretched out 3
2Mc 4:34 and gave him his right hand 3
14:33 he stretched out his right hand 3
15:15 Jeremiah stretched out his right hand 3

upper hand 1. κέρας
1Mc 2:48 they never let the sinner gain the upper hand. 1

hand-to-hand 1. ἐν χειρῶν νομαῖς
2Mc 5:14 40,000 in hand-to-hand fighting 1

handbag 1. חָרִיט
Isa 3:22 the mantles, the cloaks, and the handbags; 1

handbreadth 1. טֶפַח 2. טפח
Exd 25:25 shall make around it a frame a handbreadth wide 2
37:12 he made around it a frame a handbreadth wide 2
1Kg 7:26 Its thickness was a handbreadth; and its brim 1
2Ch 4: 5 Its thickness was a handbreadth; and its brim was 1
Ps 39: 5 Behold, thou hast made my days a few handbreadths 1
Ezk 40: 5 long cubits, each being a cubit and a handbreadth 2
43 And hooks, a handbreadth long, were fastened 2
43:13 cubits (the cubit being a cubit and a handbreadth 2

handful 1. חֹפֶן 2. כַּף 3. מְלֹא חָפְנַיִם 4. מְלֹא כַּף 5. מְלֹא קֹמֶץ 6. קֹמֶץ 7. שֹׁעַל 8. δράκος
Exd 9: 8 to Moses and Aaron, "Take handfuls of ashes 3
Lev 2: 2 he shall take from it a handful of the fine flour 5
5:12 a handful of it as its memorial portion 5
6:15 one shall take from it a handful of the fine flour 6
16:12 and two handfuls of sweet incense beaten small 1
1Kg 17:12 nothing baked, only a handful of meal in a jar 2
20:10 dust . . shall suffice for handfuls for all 7
Ecc 4: 6 Better is a handful of quietness than two 4
Ezk 13:19 for handfuls of barley and for pieces of bread 7
3Mc 5: 2 large handfuls of frankincense 8
handful *See also* take.

handiwork 1. מַעֲשֵׂה יָדַיִם 2. ἔργον
Ps 19: 1 the firmament proclaims his handiwork. 1
Sir 38:28 intent upon his handiwork in iron 2
28 He sets his heart on finishing his handiwork 2

handkerchief 1. σουδάριον
Act 19:12 so that handkerchiefs . . were carried away 1

handle 1. אחז 2. דרך 3. יָד 4. כַּף 5. עֵץ 6. עשה 7. תפש 8. תפש בַּכָּף 9. ἀπαντάω 10. ἅπτω 11. ἐν 12. κράτος 13. ψηλαφάω
Deu 19: 5 head slips from the handle and strikes 5
2Ch 25: 5 fit for war, able to handle spear and shield. 1
Sng 5: 5 my hands dripped . . upon the handles of the bolt. 4
Isa 45: 9 Does the clay say . . 'Your work has no handles'? 3
Jer 2: 8 Those who handle the law did not know me; 7
46: 9 men of Ethiopia and Put who handle the shield 7
9 men of Lud, skilled in handling the bow. 2
50:16 one who handles the sickle in time of harvest; 7
Ezk 21:11 given to be polished, that it may be handled; 8
23: 3 and their virgin bosoms handled. 6
8 had lain with her and handled her virgin bosom 6
21 when the Egyptians handled your bosom 6
27:29 from their ships come all that handle the oar. 7
Ams 2:15 he who handles the bow shall not stand 7
Lke 24:39 handle me, and see 13
Col 2:21 Do not handle, Do not taste, Do not touch 10
Jdt 7: 2 and the foot soldiers handling it 11
Sir 38:25 How can he become wise who handles the plow 12
2Mc 7:39 handled him worse than the others 9
handle *See also* easy.

rightly handle 1. ὀρθοτομέω
2Ti 2:15 rightly handling the word of truth. 1

handmaid 1. אָמָה 2. שִׁפְחָה 3. δούλη 4. ancilla
1Sm 25:24 pray let your handmaid speak in your ears 1
24 and hear the words of your handmaid. 1
25 your handmaid did not see the young men of my lord 1
28 Pray forgive the trespass of your handmaid; 1
31 when the LORD . . then remember your handmaid. 1
41 your handmaid is a servant to wash the feet 1
28:21 Behold, your handmaid has hearkened to you; 2
22 Now therefore, you also hearken to your handmaid; 2
2Sm 14: 6 your handmaid had two sons, and they quarreled 2
7 whole family has risen against your handmaid 2
12 Pray let your handmaid speak a word to my lord 2
15 your handmaid thought, 'I will speak to the king; 2
17 And your handmaid thought, 'The word of my lord 2
19 put . . these words in the mouth of your handmaid. 2
Ps 86:16 save the son of thy handmaid. 1
116:16 O LORD, I . . thy servant, the son of thy handmaid. 1
Lke 1:38 Mary said, "Behold, I am the handmaid of the Lord 3
2Es 9:45 after 30 years God heard your handmaid 4

handmaiden 1. δούλη
Lke 1:48 he has regarded the low estate of his handmaiden. 1

handpike 1. מַקֵּל יָד
Ezk 39: 9 bucklers, bows and arrows, handpikes and spears 1

into the hands 1. לִפְנֵי
Deu 2:36 LORD our God gave all into our hands. 1

handsome 1. טוֹב 2. טוֹב רֳאִי 3. טוֹב תֹּאַר 4. יְפֵה תֹאַר 5. מַרְאֶה 6. καλός
Gen 39: 6 Now Joseph was handsome and good-looking. 4
1Sm 9: 2 a son whose name was Saul, a handsome young man. 1
2 There was not a man . . more handsome than he; 1
16:12 Now he . . had beautiful eyes, and was handsome. 2
2Sm 23:21 And he slew an Egyptian, a handsome man. 5
1Kg 1: 6 He was also a very handsome man; and he was born 3
4Mc 8: 3 seven brothers–handsome, modest, noble 6
151 1: 5 My brothers were handsome and tall 6
handsome *See also* appearance.

hang 1. דלל 2. חנק 3. יקע 4. נתן 5. סרח 6. תלא 7. תלה 8. ἀπάγχω 9. ἐκδέω 10. κρεμάννυμι 11. κρεμάω 12. περίκειμαι 13. σταυρόω
Gen 40:19 your head–from you!–and hang you on a tree; 7
22 but he hanged the chief baker 7
41:13 to my office, and the baker was hanged. 7
Exd 26:12 shall hang over the back of the tabernacle. 5

13 the curtains of the tent shall hang over 5
32 you shall hang it upon four pillars of acacia 4
33 you shall hang the veil from the clasps, and bring 4
Num25: 4 hang them in the sun before the LORD 3
Deu 21:22 if a man . . put to death, and you hang him on a tree 7
28:66 your life shall hang in doubt before you; 7
Jos 8:29 he hanged the king of Ai on a tree until evening; 7
10:26 Joshua smote . . and he hung them on five trees. 7
26 And they hung upon the trees until evening; 7
2Sm 4:12 killed them . . and hanged them beside the pool 7
17:23 And he set his house in order, and hanged himself; 2
18:10 Behold, I saw Ab'salom hanging in an oak. 7
21: 9 they hanged them on the mountain before the LORD 3
12 Beth-shan, where the Philistines had hanged them 6
13 they gathered the bones of those who were hanged. 3
Est 2:23 the men were both hanged on the gallows. 7
5:14 tell the king to have Mor'decai hanged upon it; 7
6: 4 speak to the king about having Mor'decai hanged 7
7:10 And the king said, "Hang him on that. 7
10 Hang him on that." So they hanged Haman 7
8: 7 of Haman, and they have hanged him on the gallows 7
9:13 let the . . sons of Haman be hanged on the gallows. 7
14 and the ten sons of Haman were hanged. 7
25 he and his sons should be hanged on the gallows. 7
Job 26: 7 over the void, and hangs the earth upon nothing. 7
28: 4 they hang afar from men, they swing to and fro. 1
Sng 4: 4 for an arsenal, whereon hang 1,000 bucklers 7
Isa 22:24 hang on him the whole weight of his father's house 7
Ezk 15: 3 Do men take a peg from it to hang any vessel on? 7
27:10 men of war; they hung the shield and helmet in you; 7
11 they hung their shields upon your walls 7
Mat 27: 5 he departed; and he went and hanged himself. 8
Mrk 9:42 if a great millstone were hung round his neck 12
Lke 23:39 the criminals who were hanged railed at him 10
Act 5:30 whom you killed by hanging him on a tree. 11
10:39 They put him to death by hanging him on a tree; 11
28: 4 saw the creature hanging from his hand 10
Gal 3:13 Cursed be every one who hangs on a tree"– 10
1Es 6:32 he should be hanged upon it 10
Tob 3:10 even to the thought of hanging herself 8
Jdt 13: 6 and took down his sword that hung there. •
14: 1 hang it upon the parapet of your wall. 11
11 they hung the head of Holofernes on the wall 11
AEs 16:18 the man . . has been hanged at the gate of Susa 13
1Mc 1:61 they hung the infants from their mothers' necks. 11
2Mc 6:10 with their babies hung at their breasts 11
15:35 he hung Nicanor's head from the citadel 9

hang loose 1. נטש 2. פרע
Lev 10: 6 Do not let the hair of your heads hang loose 2
13:45 shall . . let the hair of his head hang loose 2
21:10 shall not let the hair of his head hang loose 2
Isa 33:23 Your tackle hangs loose; 1

hang round 1. περίκειμαι
Lke 17: 2 if a millstone were hung round his neck 1

hang up 1. יקע 2. נתן 3. תלה 4. ἐκπετάζω 5. κρεμάω
Exd 40: 8 hang up the screen for the gate of the court. 2
2Sm 21: 6 that we may hang them up before the LORD at Gibeon 1
Ps 137: 2 On the willows there we hung up our lyres 3
Lam 5:12 Princes are hung up by their hands; 3
1Mc 4:51 and hung up the curtains 4
2Mc 15:33 and hang up these rewards of his folly 5

hang upon 1. ἐκκρεμάννυμι
Lke 19:48 all the people hung upon his words. 1

hang useless 1. דלה
Prv 26: 7 Like a lame man's legs, which hang useless 1

hanged man 1. תלה
Deu 21:23 hanged man is accursed by God; 1

hanging 1. בַּיִת 2. קֶלַע
Exd 27: 9 the court shall have hangings of fine twined 2
11 there shall be hangings 100 cubits long 2
12 there shall be hangings for 50 cubits 2
14 The hangings for the one side of the gate 2
15 the hangings shall be fifteen cubits 2
18 with hangings of fine twined linen and bases •
35:17 the hangings of the court, its pillars 2
38: 9 for the south side the hangings of the court 2
12 for the west side were hangings of 50 cubits 2
14 The hangings for one side of the gate 2
15 by the gate . . were hangings of fifteen cubits 2
16 All the hangings round about the court 2
18 corresponding to the hangings of the court. 2
39:40 the hangings of the court, its pillars 2
Num 3:26 the hangings of the court, the screen for the door 2
4:26 the hangings of the court, and the screen 2
2Kg 23: 7 where the women wove hangings for the Ashe'rah. 1
hanging *See also* leave.

blue hanging 1. תְּכֵלֶת
Est 1: 6 white cotton curtains and blue hangings 1

hapless 1. חֵלְכָה
Ps 10: 8 His eyes stealthily watch for the hapless 1
10 The hapless is crushed, sinks down, and falls 1
14 the hapless commits himself to thee; 1

happen 1. היה 2. מצא 3. נגע 4. קרא 5. קרה 6. ἀποβαίνω 7. γίνομαι 8. εἰμί 9. κατά 10. συμβαίνω 11. συντελέω 12. τυγχάνω 13. contingo 14. facio 15. patior 16. sum
Gen 38: 1 It happened at that time that Judah went down 1
Deu 4:32 such a great thing as this has ever happened 1
Jdg 19:30 Such a thing has never happened or been seen 1
Rut 2: 3 she happened to come to the part of the field •
1Sm 4: 7 nothing like this has happened before. 1
6: 9 not his hand . . it happened to us by chance. 1
2Sm 1: 6 By chance I happened to be on Mount Gilbo'a; 5
11: 2 It happened, late one afternoon . . that he saw 1
20: 1 there happened to be there a worthless fellow 4
1Kg 2:39 it happened . . that two of Shim'e-i's slaves ran 1
14: 3 he will tell you what shall happen to the child. 1
2Kg 7:20 so it happened to him, for the people trod upon him 1
Neh 1: 1 Now it happened in the month of Chislev 1
Est 4: 7 Mor'decai told him all that had happened to him 5
Ecc 1:11 any remembrance of later things yet to happen 1
8:14 men to whom it happens according to the deeds 3
14 men to whom it happens according to the deeds 3
9:11 but time and chance happen to them all. 5
11: 2 for you know not what evil may happen on earth. 1
Isa 20: 6 what has happened to those in whom we hoped •
23:15 it will happen to Tyre as in the song of the harlot 1
41:22 Let them bring them, and tell us what is to happen. 5
Jer 5:30 An . . and horrible thing has happened in the land 1
6:18 know, O congregation, what will happen to them. •
41: 3 the Chalde'an soldiers who happened to be there. 2
48:19 Ask him who flees . . say, 'What has happened?' 1
Ezk 20:32 What is in your mind shall never happen 1
Jol 1: 2 Has such a thing happened in your days 1
Mic 6: 5 and what happened from Shittim to Gilgal •
Mat 8:33 they told everything, and what had happened •
16:22 God forbid, Lord! This shall never happen to you. 8
Mrk 5:14 people came to see what it was that had happened. 7
16 those who had seen it told what had happened 7
10:32 he began to tell them what was to happen to him 10
13:18 Pray that it may not happen in winter. 7
Lke 2:15 this thing that has happened 7
8:34 When the herdsmen saw what had happened 7
35 Then people went out to see what had happened 7
56 he charged them to tell no one what had happened. 7
9:18 Now it happened that as he was praying alone 7
12:54 and so it happens. 7
55 'There will be scorching heat'; and it happens. 7
23:31 what will happen when it is dry? 7
24:14 about all these things that had happened. 10
18 who does not know the things that have happened 7
21 it is now the third day since this happened. 7
35 Then they told what had happened on the road •
Act 3:10 amazement at what had happened to him. 10
4:21 all men praised God for what had happened. 7
5: 7 his wife came in, not knowing what had happened. 7
10:16 This happened three times 7
11:10 This happened three times 7
28: 8 It happened that the father of Publius lay sick 7
1Co 10:11 Now these things happened to them as a warning 10
Php 1:12 what has happened to me 9
1Pe 4:12 as though something strange were happening 10
2Pe 2:22 It has happened to them according to the true proverb 10
1Es 1:25 it happened that Pharaoh . . went to make war 10
8:86 all that has happened to us 10
2Es 9:34 when it happens that what was sown . . 16
42 I said to her, "What has happened to you? Tell me. 15
10: 1 it happened that when my son entered 14
6 do you not see our mourning, and what has happened 13
49 you began to console her for what had happened. 13
13:20 and not to see what shall happen in the last days. 13
14:16 those which you have now seen happen 13
22 write everything that has happened in the world 14
Tob 3: 7 it also happened that Sarah . . was reproached 10
8:16 It has not happened to me as I expected 7
11:15 great things that had happened to him in Media. 7
12:20 Write in a book everything that has happened. 11
14: 8 what the prophet Jonah said will surely happen. 8
Jdt 6:16 Uzziah asked him what had happened. 10
8:26 what happened to Jacob in Mesopotamia in Syria 7
15: 1 they were amazed at what had happened. 7
5 they were told what had happened 7
Wis 2:17 let us test what will happen at the end of his life; •
19: 4 made them forget what had happened 10
Sir 5: 4 Do not say, "I sinned, and what happened to me? 7
22:26 if some harm should happen to me because of him 10
37: 9 then stand aloof to see what will happen to you. 10
Sus 1:26 rushed in . . to see what had happened to her. 10
1Mc 4:20 the smoke . . showed what had happened. 7
26 reported to Lysias all that had happened. 10
27 things had not happened . . as he had intended 7
5:25 told them all that had happened 10
2Mc 4:30 it happened that . . 10
32 other vessels, as it happened, he had sold to Tyre 12
5: 2 it happened that . . 10
11 When news of what had happened reached the king 7
18 if it had not happened that . . 10
7: 1 It happened also that . . 10
18 Therefore astounding things have happened. 7
9: 1 About that time, as it happened 12
3 news came to him of what had happened to Nicanor 7
24 if anything unexpected happened 6
25 and waiting to see what will happen. 6
10: 5 It happened that . . 10
21 When word of what had happened came to Maccabeus 7
11: 1 being vexed at what had happened 7
12:34 it happened that a few of the Jews fell. 10
42 they had seen . . what had happened 7
13:17 This happened, just as day was dawning 7
3Mc 1: 8 to congratulate him on what had happened 10
15 since this has happened," the king said 7
4:12 when this had happened 7
4Mc 4:14 went away to report to the king what had happened 10
14: 9 they not only saw what was happening •
happen *See also* calamity.

cause to happen 1. מצא
Job 37:13 for his land, or for love, he causes it to happen. 1

thing that happens 1. γίνομαι
3Mc 7: 8 the irrational things that have happened. 1

happily 1. ἡδέως
2Mc 11:26 and go on happily in the conduct of their own affairs. 1

happiness 1. טוֹב 2. εὐφροσύνη 3. μακαρισθήσομαι
Lam 3:17 I have forgotten what happiness is; 1
Tob 8:17 in health and happiness and mercy. 2
Sir 37: 4 rejoice in the happiness of a friend 2
4Mc 16: 9 have the happiness of being called grandmother. 3

happy 1. אֶשֶׁר 2. אשר 3. טוב 4. שמח 5. שָׂמֵחַ 6. ἀγαθός 7. ἐν ἀγαθοῖς 8. εὐδοκέω 9. ἱλαρός 10. μακάριος
Gen 30:13 Happy am I! For the women will call me happy 2
Deu 24: 5 year, to be happy with his wife whom he has taken. 4
33:29 Happy are you, O Israel! Who is like you, a people 1
1Kg 4:20 Judah and Israel . . ate and drank and were happy. 5
10: 8 Happy are your wives! 1
8 Happy are these your servants 1
2Ch 9: 7 Happy are your wives! Happy are . . your servants 1
7 Happy are your wives! Happy are . . your servants 1
Job 5:17 Behold, happy is the man whom God reproves; 1
Ps 34: 8 Happy is the man who takes refuge in him! 1
127: 5 Happy is the man who has his quiver full of them! 1
128: 2 you shall be happy, and it shall be well with you. 1
137: 8 Happy shall he be who requites you with what you 1
9 Happy shall he be who takes your little ones 1
144:15 Happy the people to whom such blessings fall! 1
15 Happy the people whose God is the LORD! 1
146: 5 Happy is he whose help is the God of Jacob 1
Prv 3:13 Happy is the man who finds wisdom 1
8:32 happy are those who keep my ways. 1
34 Happy is the man who listens to me 1
14:21 but happy is he who is kind to the poor. 1
16:20 happy is he who trusts in the LORD. 1
Ecc 3:12 nothing better . . than to be happy and enjoy 4
10:17 Happy are you, O land, when your king is the son 1
Isa 32:20 Happy are you who sow beside all waters 1
Lam 4: 9 Happier were the victims . . than the victims 3
Rom 14:22 happy is he who has no reason to judge himself 10
1Co 7:40 she is happier if she remains as she is 10
AEs 15: 5 she looked happy, as if beloved 9
Sir 13:26 The mark of a happy heart is a cheerful face 7
14:14 Do not deprive yourself of a happy day 6
25: 8 happy is he who lives with an intelligent wife 10
9 happy is he who has gained good sense 10
26: 1 Happy is the husband of a good wife 10
28:19 Happy is the man who is protected from it 10
Bar 4: 4 Happy are we, O Israel, for we know what is pleasing 10
1Mc 6:23 We were happy to serve your father 8
10:55 Happy was the day on which you returned 6
happy *See also* call, count, make.

happy man 1. μακάριος
4Mc 18: 9 A happy man was he 1

harass 1. צור 2. צרר 3. γυμνάζω 4. ἐχθραίνω 5. κατασείω 6. κολαφίζω 7. σκύλλω
Num25:17 Harass the Mid'ianites, and smite them; 2
18 for they have harassed you with their wiles 2
Deu 2: 9 'Do not harass Moab or contend with them in battle 1
19 sons of Ammon, do not harass them or contend 1
Isa 11:13 and those who harass Judah shall be cut off; 2
13 and Judah shall not harass E'phraim. 2
Mat 9:36 because they were harassed and helpless 7
2Co 12: 7 a messenger of Satan, to harass me 6
1Mc 6:38 to harass the enemy 5
9:51 he placed garrisons in them to harass Israel. 4
2Mc 10:15 the Idumeans . . were harassing the Jews 3

harass sorely 1. שׂטם
Gen 49:23 The archers . . harassed him sorely; 1

harbor 1. שִׂית 2. λιμήν 3. συντηρέω

Prv 26:24 He who hates . . harbors deceit in his heart; 1
Act 27:12 because the harbor was not suitable to winter in 2
12 they could reach Phoenix, a harbor of Crete 2
1Es 5:55 convey them in rafts to the harbor of Joppa 2
Sir 28: 3 Does a man harbor anger against another 3
1Mc 14: 5 To crown all his honors he took Joppa for a harbor 2
2Mc 12: 6 He set fire to the harbor by night 2
9 and set fire to the harbor and the fleet 2
14: 1 Demetrius . . had sailed into the harbor of Tripolis 2
4Mc 13: 6 just as towers jutting out over harbors 2
7 fortifying the harbor of religion 2

hard 1. גָּדוֹל 2. גַּלְמוּד 3. חָזָק 4. יצק 5. כָּבֵד 6. מְאֹד 7. פלא 8. קשה 9. קָשֶׁה 10. רַב 11. δεινῶς 12. δυσερμήνευτος 13. δύσκολος 14. δυσκόλως 15. δυσχερής 16. θλίβω 17. καρτερός 18. καταπονίνημι 19. περισσότερος 20. πολύς 21. σκληρός 22. σκληρότης 23. σφόδρα 24. difficile

Gen 18:14 Is anything too hard for the LORD? 7
19: 9 Then they pressed hard against the man Lot 6
35:16 Rachel travailed, and she had hard labor. 8
17 when she was in her hard labor, the midwife said 8
Exd 1:14 made their lives bitter with hard service 9
18:26 hard cases they brought to Moses 9
Deu 1:17 case that is too hard for you, you shall bring to me 8
15:18 not seem hard to you, when you let him go free 8
26: 6 Egyptians . . laid upon us hard bondage. 9
30:11 this commandment . . is not too hard for you 7
Jdg 20:34 came against Gib'e-ah . . and the battle was hard; 5
1Sm 14:52 There was hard fighting . . all the days of Saul; 3
2Sm 3:39 these men the sons of Zeru'iah are too hard for me. 9
11:15 Set Uri'ah in the . . hardest fighting 3
1Kg 12: 4 lighten the hard service of your father 9
2Kg 2:10 he said, "You have asked a hard thing; 8
2Ch 10: 4 lighten the hard service of your father 9
Job 30: 3 Through want and hard hunger they gnaw 2
25 Did not I weep for him whose day was hard? 9
37:18 spread out the skies, hard as a molten mirror? 3
41:24 His heart is hard as a stone 4
24 hard as a stone, hard as the nether millstone. 4
Ps 118:13 I was pushed hard, so that I was falling †
Isa 14: 3 hard service with which you were made to serve 9
19: 4 the Egyptians into the hand of a hard master; 9
27: 1 the LORD with his hard and great and strong sword 9
Jer 32:17 Nothing is too hard for thee 7
27 is anything too hard for me? 7
Lam 1: 3 exile because of affliction and hard servitude; 10
Ezk 3: 5 a people of foreign speech and a hard language 5
6 peoples of foreign speech and a hard language 5
7 all the house of Israel are of a hard forehead 3
8 I have made your face hard against their faces 3
8 your forehead hard against their foreheads. 3
9 harder than flint have I made your forehead; 3
29:18 Babylon made his army labor hard against Tyre; 1
Jon 1:13 the men rowed hard to bring the ship back to land •
Mat 7:14 For the gate is narrow and the way is hard 16
19:23 it will be hard for a rich man to enter 14
25:24 Master, I knew you to be a hard man 21
Mrk 10:23 How hard it will be for those who have riches 14
24 how hard it is to enter the kingdom of God! 13
Lke 11:53 the Pharisees began to press him hard 11
18:24 How hard it is for those who have riches to enter 14
Joh 6:60 This is a hard saying; who can listen to it? 21
Rom 2: 5 by your hard and impenitent heart 22
16: 6 Greet Mary, who has worked hard among you. 20
12 beloved Persis, who has worked hard in the Lord. 20
1Co 15:10 On the contrary, I worked harder than any of them 19
Col 4:13 I bear him witness that he has worked hard for you 20
Heb 5:11 have much to say which is hard to explain 12
10:32 you endured a hard struggle with sufferings 20
2Es 7:59 for he who has what is hard to get 24
Wis 11: 4 slaking of thirst from hard stone. 21
Bel 1:30 The king saw that they were pressing him hard 23
2Mc 9: 7 the fall was so hard as to torture every limb 15
12:11 After a hard fight 17
3Mc 4:14 the hard labor . . briefly mentioned before 18

hard *See also* drive, follow, labor, press, pursue, question, service.

become hard 1. חבא

Job 38:30 The waters become hard like stone 1

make hard 1. חזק

Jer 5: 3 They have made their faces harder than rock; 1

hard thing 1. קָשָׁה

Ps 60: 3 Thou hast made thy people suffer hard things; 1

hard to bear 1. βαρύς 2. δυσβάστακτος

Mat 23: 4 They bind heavy burdens, hard to bear 1
Lke 11:46 you load men with burdens hard to bear 2
Sir 29:28 things are hard to bear for a man who has feeling 1

hard to besiege 1. δυσπολιόρκητος

2Mc 12:21 that place was hard to besiege and difficult of access 1

hard to describe 1. δυσδιήγητος

Wis 17: 1 Great are thy judgments and hard to describe; 1

hard to understand 1. δυσνόητος

2Pe 3:16 There are some things in them hard to understand 1

too hard 1. ὑπεραίρω

Sir 48:13 Nothing was too hard for him 1

hard-pressed 1. περίστημι

2Mc 14: 9 to take thought for . . our hard-pressed nation 1

hard-working 1. κοπιάω

2Ti 2: 6 It is the hard-working farmer 1

harden 1. אמץ 2. חזק 3. כבד 4. קשה 5. קשח 6. רגע 7. תקף (A) 8. πωρόω 9. πώρωσις 10. σκληρύνω

Exd 4:21 but I will harden his heart, so that he will not let 2
7: 3 I will harden Pharaoh's heart 4
13 Still Pharaoh's heart was hardened 2
14 LORD said to Moses, "Pharaoh's heart is hardened 3
22 so Pharaoh's heart remained hardened 2
8:15 he hardened his heart, and would not listen 3
19 But Pharaoh's heart was hardened, and he would not 2
32 Pharaoh hardened his heart this time also 3
9: 7 But the heart of Pharaoh was hardened 3
12 the LORD hardened the heart of Pharaoh 2
34 he sinned yet again, and hardened his heart 3
35 the heart of Pharaoh was hardened, and he did not 2
10: 1 I have hardened his heart and the heart of his 3
20 the LORD hardened Pharaoh's heart, and he did not 2
27 the LORD hardened Pharaoh's heart, and he would 2
11:10 the LORD hardened Pharaoh's heart 2
14: 4 I will harden Pharaoh's heart, and he will pursue 2
8 the LORD hardened the heart of Pharaoh 2
17 I will harden the hearts of the Egyptians 2
Deu 2:30 for the LORD your God hardened his spirit 4
15: 7 not harden your heart or shut your hand 1
Jos 11:20 For it was the LORD's doing to harden their hearts 2
1Sm 6: 6 harden your hearts as the Egyptians and Pharaoh 3
6 Egyptians and Pharaoh hardened their hearts? 3
2Ch 36:13 hardened his heart against turning to the LORD 1
Job 7: 5 my skin hardens, then breaks out afresh. 6
9: 4 who has hardened himself against him 4
Ps 95: 8 Harden not your hearts, as at Mer'ibah, as on the day 4
Prv 28:14 hardens his heart will fall into calamity. 4
Isa 63:17 and harden our heart, so that we fear thee not? 5
Dan 5:20 heart was lifted up and his spirit was hardened 7
Mrk 6:52 their hearts were hardened. 8
8:17 Are your hearts hardened? 8
Joh 12:40 has blinded their eyes and hardened their heart 8
Rom 9:18 and he hardens the heart of whomever he wills. 10
11: 7 The elect obtained it, but the rest were hardened 8
25 a hardening has come upon part of Israel 9
2Co 3:14 their minds were hardened 8
Heb 3: 8 do not harden your hearts as in the rebellion 10
13 hardened by the deceitfulness of sin. 10
15 do not harden your hearts as in the rebellion. 10
4: 7 do not harden your hearts. 10
1Es 1:48 he stiffened his neck and hardened his heart •

harder *See* harder.

harder and harder 1. הלך וְקָשָׁה

Jdg 4:24 W:QF$FH#Israel bore harder and harder on Jabin the king 1

hardly 1. μόγις 2. μόλις

Lke 9:39 shatters him, and will hardly leave him. 1
Rom 5: 7 Why, one will hardly die for a righteous man 2
Wis 9:16 We can hardly guess at what is on earth 2
Sir 26:29 A merchant can hardly keep from wrongdoing 2
29: 6 he will hardly get back half 2

hardness 1. עֹז 2. πώρωσις

Ecc 8: 1 and the hardness of his countenance is changed. 1
Mrk 3: 5 grieved at their hardness of heart 2
Eph 4:18 due to their hardness of heart; 2

hardness of heart 1. σκληροκαρδία

Mat 19: 8 For your hardness of heart Moses allowed you 1
Mrk 10: 5 For your hardness of heart he wrote 1
16:14 for their unbelief and hardness of heart 1

hardship 1. עָמָל 2. תְּלָאָה 3. ἀνάγκη 4. μόχθος 5. labor

Gen 41:51 God has made me to forget all my hardship 1
Exd 18: 8 all the hardship that had come upon them 2
Neh 9:32 let not all the hardship seem little to thee 2
2Co 6: 4 in afflictions, hardships, calamities 3
11:27 in toil and hardship 4
12:10 I am content with weaknesses, insults, hardships 3
2Es 7:12 and involved in great hardships. 5

hardship *See also* endure.

hare 1. אַרְנֶבֶת

Lev 11: 6 the hare, because it chews the cud but does not 1
Deu 14: 7 not eat . . the camel, the hare, and the rock badger 1

harem 1. בֵּית נָשִׁים

Est 2: 3 gather all . . young virgins to the harem in Susa 1
9 advanced her . . to the best place in the harem. 1
11 walked in front of the court of the harem 1
13 take with her from the harem to the king's palace. 1
14 to the second harem in custody of Sha-ash'gaz 1

hark 1. הִנֵּה 2. קוֹל 3. ἰδού

Ps 118:15 Hark, glad songs of victory in the tents 2
Sng 5: 2 Hark! my beloved is knocking. 2
Isa 13: 4 Hark, a tumult on the mountains 2
4 Hark, an uproar of kingdoms, of nations gathering 2
52: 8 Hark, your watchmen lift up their voice 2
66: 6 Hark, an uproar from the city! 2
Jer 8:19 Hark, the cry of the daughter of my people 1
10:22 Hark, a rumor! Behold, it comes!–a great commotion 2
25:36 Hark, the cry of the shepherds 2
48: 3 Hark! a cry from Horona'im, 'Desolation 2
50:28 Hark! they flee and escape from the land 2
51:54 Hark! a cry from Babylon! 2
Zec 11: 3 Hark, the wail of the shepherds, for their glory 2
3 Hark, the roar of the lions, for the jungle 2
Act 5: 9 Hark, the feet . . are at the door 3

harlot 1. זוֹנָה 2. זנה 3. קְדֵשָׁה 4. אִשָּׁה זוֹנָה 4. ἑταίρα 5. πόρνη 6. fornicaria

Gen 34:31 they said, "Should he treat our sister as a harlot? 2
38:15 When Judah saw her, he thought her to be a harlot 2
21 Where is the harlot who was at Enaim 3
21 And they said, "No harlot has been here. 3
22 men of the place say, 'No harlot has been here.' 3
Lev 21: 7 They shall not marry a harlot or a woman who has 2
14 a woman who has been defiled, or a harlot 2
Deu 23:18 not bring the hire of a harlot, or the wages of a dog 2
Jos 2: 1 into the house of a harlot whose name was Rahab 1
6:17 Rahab the harlot and . . in her house shall live 2
22 Go into the harlot's house, and bring . . the woman 1
25 But Rahab the harlot, and . . Joshua saved alive; 2
Jdg 11: 1 a mighty warrior, but he was the son of a harlot. 1
16: 1 Samson went to Gaza, and there he saw a harlot 1
1Kg 3:16 two harlots came to the king, and stood before 1
22:38 and the harlots washed themselves in it 2
Prv 6:26 for a harlot may be hired for a loaf of bread 1
7:10 dressed as a harlot, wily of heart. 2
23:27 For a harlot is a deep pit; 2
29: 3 one who keeps company with harlots squanders 2
Isa 1:21 How the faithful city has become a harlot 2
23:15 it will happen to Tyre as in the song of the harlot 2
16 Take a harp, go about the city, O forgotten harlot! 2
57: 3 offspring of the adulterer and the harlot. 2
Jer 2:20 you bowed down as a harlot. 2
3: 3 you have a harlot's brow, you refuse to be ashamed. 1
5: 7 and trooped to the houses of harlots. 2
Ezk 16:30 did all these things, the deeds of a brazen harlot; 1
31 were not like a harlot, because you scorned hire. 2
33 Men give gifts to all harlots; 2
35 Wherefore, O harlot, hear the word of the LORD 2
23:44 they have gone in to her, as men go in to a harlot. 1
Hos 4:14 for the men themselves go aside with harlots 2
Jol 3: 3 and have given a boy for a harlot 2
Ams 7:17 Your wife shall be a harlot in the city 2
Mic 1: 7 for from the hire of a harlot she gathered them 2
7 and to the hire of a harlot they shall return. 2
Nah 3: 4 all for the countless harlotries of the harlot 2
Mat 21:31 the tax collectors and the harlots 5
32 the tax collectors and the harlots believed him; 5
Lke 15:30 who has devoured your living with harlots 5
Heb 11:31 By faith Rahab the harlot did not perish 5
Jas 2:25 was not also Rahab the harlot justified by works 5
Rev 17: 1 I will show you the judgment of the great harlot 5
5 Babylon the great, mother of harlots 5
15 waters that you saw, where the harlot is seated 5
16 they and the beast will hate the harlot; 5
19: 2 judged the great harlot who corrupted the earth 5
2Es 15:48 You have imitated that hateful harlot •
55 The reward of a harlot is in your bosom 6
16:49 a . . virtuous woman abhors a harlot 6
Sir 9: 6 Do not give yourself to harlots 5
19: 2 the man who consorts with harlots 5
41:20 looking at a woman who is a harlot 4
LJr 1:11 give some of it to the harlots in the brothel. 5
2Mc 6: 4 the Gentiles, who dallied with harlots 4

harlot *See also* make, play, solicit.

harlot's hire 1. אֶתְנָן

Hos 9: 1 You have loved a harlot's hire 1

harlotry 1. זְנוּנִים 2. זְנוּת 3. תַּזְנוּת 4. πορνεία 5. fornicatio

Gen 38:24 moreover she is with child by harlotry. 1
2Kg 9:22 the harlotries and the sorceries of your mother 1
Jer 3: 2 have polluted the land with your vile harlotry. 2
9 Because harlotry was so light to her 2
13:27 adulteries and neighings, your lewd harlotries 2
Ezk 16:15 and lavished your harlotries on any passer-by. 3
20 Were your harlotries so small a matter 3
22 in all your abominations and your harlotries 3
25 to any passer-by, and multiplying your harlotry. 3

26 multiplying your harlotry, to provoke me 3
29 You multiplied your harlotry 3
33 come to you from every side for your harlotries. 3
34 different from other women in your harlotries; 3
36 your nakedness uncovered in your harlotries 3
23: 7 She bestowed her harlotries upon them 3
8 She did not give up her harlotry 3
11 in her doting and in her harlotry, which was worse 3
14 she carried her harlotry further; 3
18 When she carried on her harlotry so openly 3
19 Yet she increased her harlotry 3
27 your harlotry brought from the land of Egypt; 2
29 nakedness of your harlotry shall be uncovered. 1
29 Your lewdness and your harlotry 3
35 consequences of your lewdness and harlotry. 3
43 commit adultery when they practice harlotry 3
43: 7 neither they, nor their kings, by their harlotry 2
Hos 1: 2 Go, take to yourself a wife of harlotry 1
2 a wife of harlotry and have children of harlotry 1
2: 2 that she put away her harlotry from her face 1
4 no pity, because they are children of harlotry. 1
4:10 they have forsaken the LORD to cherish harlotry. 2
12 For a spirit of harlotry has led them astray 1
5: 4 For the spirit of harlotry is within them 1
6:10 E'phraim's harlotry is there, Israel is defiled. 2
Nah 3: 4 all for the countless harlotries of the harlot 1
4 who betrays nations with her harlotries 1
2Es 15:47 you have decked out your daughters in harlotry 5
Sir 23:23 she has committed adultery through harlotry 4
26: 9 A wife's harlotry shows in her lustful eyes 4

harlotry *See also* commit, fall, give, practice.

harm 1. אָסוֹן 2. דְּבַר רַע 3. פקד 4. רַע 5. רָעָה 6. רעע
7. שׂנא (A) 8. *ἀδικέω* 9. *κακός* 10. *κακόω* 11. *κατά*
12. *πράσσω κακόν* 13. iniuste

Gen 26:29 that you will do us no harm, just as we have not 5
31: 7 but God did not permit him to harm me. 6
29 It is in my power to do you harm; 4
52 pass over . . this pillar to me, for harm. 5
42: 4 for he feared that harm might befall him. 1
38 If harm should befall him on the journey 1
44:29 If . . harm befalls him, you will bring down my 1
Exd 21:22 a miscarriage, and yet no harm follows 1
23 If any harm follows, then you shall give life 1
Num16:15 I have not harmed one of them. 6
35:23 he was not his enemy, and did not seek his harm; 5
1Sm 6: 9 if . . then it is he who has done us this great harm; 5
20:13 should it please my father to do you harm 5
2Sm 12:18 how then can we . . ? He may do himself some harm. 5
2Kg 4:41 And there was no harm in the pot. 2
1Ch 4:10 saying, "Oh . . that thou wouldst keep me from harm 5
Neh 6: 2 But they intended to do me harm. 5
Prv 3:30 Do not contend . . when he has done you no harm. 5
19:23 he will not be visited by harm. 4
31:12 She does him good, and not harm 4
Ecc 8: 5 He who obeys a command will meet no harm 4
Isa 27: 3 Lest any one harm it, I guard it night and day; 3
Jer 25: 7 with the work of your hands to your own harm. 4
38: 4 not seeking the welfare . . but their harm. 5
39:12 Take him, look after him well and do him no harm 4
Dan 3:27 mantles were not harmed, and no smell of fire 7
Hab 2: 9 nest on high, to be safe from the reach of harm! 4
Act 16:28 Paul cried with a loud voice, "Do not harm yourself 12
18:10 no man shall attack you to harm you 10
28: 5 shook off the creature . . and suffered no harm. 9
2Ti 4:14 Alexander the coppersmith did me great harm 9
1Pe 3:13 Now who is there to harm you if you are zealous 10
Rev 6: 6 but do not harm oil and wine! 8
7: 2 angels who had been given power to harm earth 8
3 Do not harm the earth or the sea or the trees 8
9: 4 they were told not to harm the grass of the earth 8
11: 5 if any one would harm them, fire pours out 8
5 if any one would harm them, thus he is doomed 8
2Es 7:115or to harm him who is victorious. ‡
12:41 and what harm have we done you 13
Tob 6:14 he harms no one except those who approach her. 8
AEs 13: 5 doing all the harm they can 9
Sir 4:22 Do not show partiality, to your own harm 11
22:26 if some harm should happen to me because of him 9
36: 9 may those who harm thy people meet destruction. 10
Aza 1:20 Let all who do harm to thy servants be put to shame; 9
1Mc 6:18 They were trying in every way to harm them 9
7:14 he will not harm us. 8
9:71 he would not try to harm him as long as he lived. 9
15:19 should not seek their harm or make war against them 9

harm *See also* suffer.

do harm 1. כלם 2. רעע 3. *βλάπτω* 4. *κακοποιέω*
5. *καταβλάπτω* 6. noceo

Jos 24:20 then he will turn and do you harm, and consume you 2
1Sm 25: 7 and we did them no harm, and they missed nothing 1
26:21 return, my son David, for I will no more do you harm 2
2Sm 20: 6 Now Sheba . . will do us more harm than Ab'salom; 2
1Ch 16:22 Touch not my anointed ones, do my prophets no harm! 2
Ps 105:15 Touch not my anointed ones, do my prophets no harm! 2
Isa 41:23 do good, or do harm, that we may be dismayed 2
Jer 25: 6 Then I will do you no harm. 2
Mrk 3: 4 Is it lawful on the sabbath to do good or to do harm 4
Lke 4:35 he came out of him, having done him no harm. 3
6: 9 is it lawful on the sabbath to do good or to do harm 4
2Es 11:42 the walls of those who did you no harm. 6
Tob 12: 2 it would do me no harm to give him half 3
1Mc 5:48 No one will do you harm 4
3Mc 7: 8 with no one in any place doing them harm at all 5

harmful 1. *πολέμιος* 2. nocivus

2Es 15: 6 their harmful deeds have reached their limit. 2
2Mc 15:39 For just as it is harmful to drink wine alone 1

harmless 1. *ἀβλαβής*

Wis 18: 3 a harmless sun for their glorious wandering. 1

harmonious 1. *εὐάρμοστος*

4Mc 14: 3 O sacred and harmonious concord 1

harmony 1. *αὐτός* 2. *ὁμόνοια* 3. *συμφωνέω*
4. *συμφώνως*

Rom 12:16 Live in harmony with one another; 1
15: 5 to live in such harmony with one another 1
Col 3:14 which binds everything together in perfect harmony. •
4Mc 3:21 a revolution against the public harmony 2
13:25 expanded their goodwill and harmony 2
14: 6 moved in harmony with the guidance of the mind 4
7 O most holy seven, brothers in harmony! 3

harmony *See also* live, man.

harness 1. אסר 2. רתם

Jer 46: 4 Harness the horses; mount, O horsemen! 1
Mic 1:13 Harness the steeds to the chariots 2

special harness 1. *μηχανή*

1Mc 6:37 were fastened upon each beast by special harness 1

harp 1. כְּלִי נֵבֶל 2. כִּנּוֹר 3. נֵבֶל 4. פְּסַנְטֵרִין (A)
5. *κιθάρα* 6. *κινύρα* 7. *ὄργανον* 8. *ψαλτήριον*
9. psalterium

1Sm 10: 5 prophets coming . . with harp, tambourine, flute 3
2Sm 6: 5 making merry . . with songs and lyres and harps 3
1Kg 10:12 king made . . lyres also and harps for the singers; 3
1Ch 13: 8 making merry . . with . . harps and tambourines 3
15:16 on harps and lyres and cymbals, to raise sounds 3
20 were to play harps according to Al'amoth; 3
28 and made loud music on harps and lyres. 3
16: 5 and Je-i'el, who were to play harps and lyres; 3
25: 1 prophesy with . . with harps, and with cymbals. 3
6 with cymbals, harps, and lyres for the service 3
2Ch 5:12 arrayed in fine linen, with cymbals, harps 3
9:11 algum wood steps . . lyres also and harps 3
20:28 to Jerusalem with harps and lyres and trumpets 3
29:25 Levites . . with cymbals, harps, and lyres 3
Neh 12:27 celebrate . . with cymbals, harps, and lyres. 3
Ps 33: 2 make melody to him with the harp of ten strings! 3
57: 8 Awake, my soul! Awake, O harp and lyre! 3
71:22 I will also praise thee with the harp 1
81: 2 sound the timbrel, the sweet lyre with the harp. 3
92: 3 to the music of the lute and the harp 3
108: 2 Awake, O harp and lyre! I will awake the dawn! 3
144: 9 upon a ten-stringed harp I will play to thee 3
150: 3 praise him with lute and harp! 2
Isa 5:12 They have lyre and harp, timbrel and flute 3
14:11 brought down to Sheol, the sound of your harps; 3
23:16 Take a harp, go about the city, O forgotten harlot! 2
Dan 3: 5 hear the sound of the . . harp, bagpipe 4
7 heard the sound of . . harp, bagpipe 4
10 hears the sound of . . harp, bagpipe 4
15 hear the sound of . . harp, bagpipe, and every kind 4
Ams 5:23 to the melody of your harps I will not listen. 3
6: 5 who sing idle songs to the sound of the harp 3
1Co 14: 7 instruments, such as the flute or the harp 5
Rev 5: 8 fell down before the Lamb, each holding a harp 5
14: 2 like the sound of harpers playing on their harps 5
15: 2 standing . . with harps of God in their hands. 5
2Es 10:22 our harp has been laid low 9
Wis 19:18 on a harp the notes vary the nature of the rhythm 8
Sir 40:21 The flute and the harp make pleasant melody 8
1Mc 3:45 the flute and the harp ceased to play. 6
4:54 it was dedicated with songs and harps and lutes 5
13:51 with harps and cymbals 6
151 1: 2 My hands made a harp, my fingers fashioned a lyre. 7

harpoon 1. שֻׂכָּה

Job 41: 7 Can you fill his skin with harpoons 1

harrow 1. שׂדד

Job 39:10 or will he harrow the valleys after you? 1
Isa 28:24 does he continually open and harrow his ground? 1
Hos 10:11 Judah must plow, Jacob must harrow for himself. 1

harsh 1. עָצָב 2. *ἀπηνή* 3. *πικραίνω* 4. *πικρία*
5. *τραχύς* 6. *χαλεπός*

Prv 15: 1 but a harsh word stirs up anger. 1
Col 3:19 do not be harsh with them. 3
Wis 17:19 the harsh crash of rocks hurled down 2
Sir 6:20 She seems very harsh to the uninstructed 5
2Mc 6: 3 Harsh and utterly grievous 6
3Mc 4: 4 with such a harsh and ruthless spirit 4

harsh *See also* treatment.

harsh thing 1. *σκληρός*

Jde 1:15 harsh things which ungodly sinners have spoken 1

harshly 1. קָשֶׁה

1Kg 12:13 the king answered the people harshly 1
2Ch 10:13 the king answered them harshly 1

harshly *See also* deal, treat.

harshness 1. פֶּרֶךְ

Lev 25:43 You shall not rule over him with harshness 1
46 not rule, one over another, with harshness 1
53 he shall not rule with harshness over him 1
Ezk 34: 4 with force and harshness you have ruled them. 1

hart 1. אַיָּל

Deu 12:15 as of the gazelle and as of the hart. 1
22 Just as the gazelle or the hart is eaten 1
14: 5 the hart, the gazelle, the roebuck, the wild goat 1
15:22 eat it, as though it were a gazelle or a hart. 1
1Kg 4:23 sheep, besides harts, gazelles, roebucks 1
Ps 42: 1 As a hart longs for flowing streams 1
Isa 35: 6 then shall the lame man leap like a hart 1
Lam 1: 6 Her princes have become like harts 1

harvest 1. אָסִף 2. בוא 3. קָצִיר 4. קצר 5. תְּבוּאָה
6. *ἀμητός* 7. *γένημα* 8. *θερίζω* 9. *θερισμός*
10. *θημωνιά* 11. *καρπός* 12. destrictio
13. fructus areae

Gen 8:22 While the earth remains, seedtime and harvest 3
30:14 In the days of wheat harvest Reuben went 3
45: 6 there will be neither plowing nor harvest. 3
47:24 at the harvests you shall give a fifth to Pharaoh 5
Exd 23:16 You shall keep the feast of harvest 3
34:21 in plowing time and in harvest you shall rest. 3
22 observe . . the first fruits of wheat harvest 3
Lev 19: 9 When you reap the harvest of your land 3
9 gather the gleanings after your harvest 3
23:10 When you . . reap its harvest, you shall bring 3
10 the sheaf of the first fruits of your harvest 3
22 when you reap the harvest of your land 3
22 nor . . gather the gleanings after your harvest 3
25: 5 What grows of itself in your harvest 3
Deu 24:19 When you reap your harvest in your field 3
26: 2 fruit . . which you harvest from your land 2
Jos 3:15 overflows . . throughout the time of harvest 3
Jdg 15: 1 at the time of wheat harvest, Samson went to visit 3
Rut 1:22 they came . . at the beginning of barley harvest. 3
2:21 till they have finished all my harvest.' 3
23 until the end of the barley and wheat harvests; 3
1Sm 6:13 Beth-she'mesh were reaping their wheat harvest 3
8:12 some to plow his ground and to reap his harvest 3
12:17 Is it not wheat harvest today? I will call upon 3
2Sm 21: 9 were put to death in the first days of harvest 3
9 at the beginning of barley harvest. 3
10 spread it . . from the beginning of harvest until 3
Job 5: 5 His harvest the hungry eat 3
Prv 6: 8 gathers her sustenance in harvest. 3
10: 5 but a son who sleeps in harvest brings shame. 3
20: 4 he will seek at harvest and have nothing. 3
25:13 Like the cold of snow in the time of harvest 3
26: 1 Like snow in summer or rain in harvest 3
Isa 9: 3 rejoice before thee as with joy at the harvest 3
16: 9 upon your fruit and your harvest the battle 3
17: 5 gathers . . grain and his arm harvests the ears 4
11 yet the harvest will flee away in a day of grief 3
18: 4 like a cloud of dew in the heat of harvest. 3
5 For before the harvest, when the blossom is over 3
23: 3 your revenue was . . the harvest of the Nile; 3
32:10 vintage . . fail, the fruit harvest will not come. 1
Jer 2: 3 holy to the LORD, the first fruits of his harvest. 5
5:17 They shall eat up your harvest and your food; 3
24 keeps . . the weeks appointed for the harvest.' 3
8:20 The harvest is past, the summer is ended 3
12:13 They shall be ashamed of their harvests 5
50:16 one who handles the sickle in time of harvest; 3
51:33 and the time of her harvest will come. 3
Hos 6:11 For you also, O Judah, a harvest is appointed. 3
Jol 1:11 because the harvest of the field has perished. 3
3:13 Put in the sickle, for the harvest is ripe. 3
Ams 4: 7 when there were yet three months to the harvest; 3
Hag 1: 6 You have sown much, and harvested little; 2
Mat 9:37 The harvest is plentiful 9
38 pray therefore the Lord of the harvest 9
38 to send out laborers into his harvest. 9
13:30 Let both grow together until the harvest 9
30 at harvest time I will tell the reapers 9
39 the harvest is the close of the age 9
Mrk 4:29 because the harvest has come. 9
Lke 10: 2 harvest is plentiful, but the laborers are few 9
2 pray therefore the Lord of the harvest 9
2 to send out laborers into his harvest. 9
Joh 4:35 'There are yet four months, then comes the harvest'? 9

35 see how the fields are already white for harvest 9
Rom 1:13 in order that I may reap some harvest among you 11
2Co 9:10 increase the harvest of your righteousness. 7
Jas 3:18 the harvest of righteousness is sown in peace 11
Rev 14:15 for the harvest of the earth is fully ripe. 9
2Es 4:28 sown, but the harvest of it has not yet come. 12
35 And when will come the harvest of our reward? 13
Jdt 2:27 he went down . . during the wheat harvest 9
4: 5 since their fields had recently been harvested. 8
8: 2 died during the barley harvest. 9
Sir 6:19 wait for her good harvest 11
20:28 will heap up his harvest 10
24:26 like the Jordan at harvest time. 9
4Mc 2: 9 he neither gleans his harvest 6

harvest *See also* fulness, reap, time.

harvester 1. θερίζω
Jas 5: 4 cries of the harvesters have reached the ears 1

haste 1. בהל 2. דחף 3. חוש 4. חפז 5. חִפָּזוֹן 6. מהר 7. בְּהִילוּ (A) 8. בהל (A) 9. σπεύδω 10. σπουδή 11. enim 12. velocitas
Exd 10:16 Then Pharaoh called Moses and Aaron in haste 6
12:11 you shall eat it in haste. 5
33 urgent . . to send them out of the land in haste; 6
Jos 4:10 The people passed over in haste; 6
Jdg 13:10 the woman ran in haste and told her husband 6
2Sm 4: 4 as she fled in her haste, he fell, and became lame. 4
15:14 go in haste, lest he overtake us quickly 6
2Kg 7:15 the Syrians had thrown away in their haste. 4
9:13 Then in haste every man of them took his garment 6
Ezr 4:23 they went in haste to the Jews at Jerusalem 7
Est 3:15 The couriers went in haste by order of the king 2
6:14 eunuchs arrived and brought Haman in haste 1
8:14 the couriers . . rode out in haste 1
Job 20: 2 answer me, because of my haste within me. 3
Ps 55: 8 I would haste to find me a shelter from the raging 3
Isa 28:16 'He who believes will not be in haste.' 3
52:12 For you shall not go out in haste 5
Dan 2:25 brought in Daniel before the king in haste 8
3:24 King . . was astonished and rose up in haste. 8
6:19 king arose and went in haste to the den of lions. 8
Mrk 6:25 she came immediately with haste to the king 10
Lke 1:39 and went with haste into the hill country 10
2:16 they went with haste, and found Mary and Joseph 9
1Es 2:30 went in haste to Jerusalem 10
2Es 4:34 for your haste is for yourself 11
5:42 for those who are first there is no haste. 12
Sus 1:50 Then all the people returned in haste. 10
1Mc 6:63 Then he departed with haste 10
3Mc 4:15 bitter haste and zealous intentness 10

haste *See also* flee, make, require.

hasten 1. אוץ 2. בהל 3. דחף 4. חוש 5. מהר 6. עוש 7. פוח 8. שאף 9. ἐποξύνω 10. κατασπεύδω 11. ὁρμάω 12. σπεύδω 13. ταχύνω 14. φθάνω 15. festino
Gen 18: 6 Abraham hastened into the tent to Sarah, and said 5
7 gave it to the servant, who hastened to prepare it 5
Jos 10:13 The sun stayed . . and did not hasten to go down 1
1Sm 4:14 Then the man hastened and came and told Eli. 5
2Ch 24: 5 see that you hasten the matter. 5
5 But the Levites did not hasten it. 5
26:20 he himself hastened to go out 3
Job 31: 5 my foot has hastened to deceit; 4
Ps 22:19 be not far off! O thou my help, hasten to my aid! 4
70: 5 I am poor and needy; hasten to me, O God! 4
119:60 I hasten . . to keep thy commandments. 4
Prv 6: 3 go, hasten, and importune your neighbor. •
28:20 he who hastens to be rich will not go unpunished. 1
22 A miserly man hastens after wealth 2
Ecc 1: 5 and hastens to the place where it rises. 8
Isa 60:22 I am the LORD; in its time I will hasten it. 4
Jer 48:16 and his affliction hastens apace. 5
Jol 3:11 Hasten and come, all you nations round about 6
Nah 2: 5 they hasten to the wall, the mantelet is set up. 5
Hab 2: 3 it hastens to the end–it will not lie. 7
Act 20:16 he was hastening to be at Jerusalem 12
2Pe 3:12 and hastening the coming of the day of God 12
2Es 4:34 You do not hasten faster than the Most High 15
34 but the Highest hastens on behalf of many. •
42 these places hasten to give back those things 15
7:98 for they hasten to behold the face of him 15
14:15 and hasten to escape from these times. 15
18 the eagle . . is already hastening to come. 15
Wis 6:13 She hastens to make herself known 14
Sir 36: 8 Hasten the day, and remember the appointed time 12
43: 5 at his command it hastens on its course. 10
1Mc 2:35 Then the enemy hastened to attack them. 13
13:10 hastened to complete the walls of Jerusalem 13
2Mc 4:14 hastened to take part in the . . proceedings 12
9: 7 and giving orders to hasten the journey 9
14 which he was hastening to level to the ground 12
12:20 hastened after Timothy 11
29 they hastened to Scythopolis 11
32 they hastened against Gorgias 11
4Mc 14: 5 hastened to death by torture 12

hasten fast 1. מַהֵר מְאֹד
Zep 1:14 day of the LORD is near, near and hastening fast; 1

hasten off 1. ἀνατρέχω
2Mc 9:25 when I hastened off to the upper provinces 1

hasten swiftly 1. festino
2Es 4:26 because the age is hastening swiftly to its end. 1

hasten to stretch out 1. רוץ
Ps 68:31 Ethiopia hasten to stretch out her hands to God. 1

hastily 1. מַהֵר 2. מְהֵרָה 3. επισπουδάζω 4. μετὰ σπουδῆς 5. ταχύς
Jdg 9:54 Then he called hastily to the young man 2
Prv 13:11 Wealth hastily gotten will dwindle 3
25: 8 do not hastily bring into court; 1
Wis 19: 2 and hastily sent them forth 4
Sir 6: 7 do not trust him hastily. 5
2Mc 4:31 the king went hastily to settle the trouble 5

hastily *See also* get.

bring hastily 1. רוץ
Gen 41:14 called Joseph, and they brought him hastily out 1

hasty 1. אוץ 2. מהר 3. קְצַר 4. κατασπεύδω 5. σπεύδω 6. ταχέως 7. propero
Prv 14:29 but he who has a hasty temper exalts folly. 3
21: 5 but every one who is hasty comes only to want. 1
29:20 Do you see a man who is hasty in his words? 1
Ecc 5: 2 let your heart be hasty to utter a word before God 2
Hab 1: 6 the Chalde'ans, that bitter and hasty nation 2
1Ti 5:22 Do not be hasty in the laying on of hands 6
2Es 6:34 lest you be hasty concerning the last times.' 7
Sir 2: 2 do not be hasty in time of calamity. 5
28:11 A hasty quarrel kindles fire 4

hasty *See also* judgment.

hat 1. כַּרְבְּלָא (A)
Dan 3:21 bound in their mantles, their tunics, their hats 1

hatch 1. בקע 2. ילד 3. ἀποτίκτω
Isa 34:15 There shall the owl nest and lay and hatch 1
59: 5 They hatch adders' eggs, they weave 1
5 and from one which is crushed a viper is hatched. 1
Jer 17:11 that gathers a brood which she did not hatch 2
4Mc 14:16 hatch the nestlings and ward off the intruder. 3

hatchet 1. כַּשִּׁיל
Ps 74: 6 its carved wood they broke down with hatchets 1

hate 1. שטם 2. שנא 3. שִׂנְאָה 4. שנא (A) 5. ἀποστυγέω 6. ἐχθραίνω 7. μισέω 8. μισητός 9. μῖσος 10. στυγέω 11. odi
Gen 24:60 possess the gate of those who hate them! 2
26:27 you come to me, seeing that you hate me 2
27:41 Now Esau hated Jacob because of the blessing 1
29:31 When the LORD saw that Leah was hated 2
33 Because the LORD has heard that I am hated 2
37: 4 they hated him, and could not speak peaceably 2
5 to his brothers they only hated him the more. 2
8 they hated him yet more for his dreams 2
50:15 It may be that Joseph will hate us and pay us back 1
Exd 18:21 who are trustworthy and who hate a bribe; 2
20: 5 the fourth generation of those who hate me 2
23: 5 If you see the ass of one who hates you lying under 2
Lev 19:17 You shall not hate your brother in your heart 2
26:17 those who hate you shall rule over you 2
Num10:35 let them that hate thee flee before thee. 2
Deu 1:27 'Because the LORD hated us he has brought us forth 3
5: 9 third and fourth generation of those who hate me 2
7:10 and requites to their face those who hate him 2
10 he will not be slack with him who hates him 2
15 he will lay them upon all who hate you. 2
9:28 because he hated them, he has brought them out 3
12:31 for every abominable thing which the LORD hates 2
16:22 not set up a pillar which the LORD your God hates. 2
19:11 if any man hates his neighbor, and lies in wait 2
32:41 I . . will requite those who hate me. 2
33:11 crush the loins of . . those that hate him 2
Jdg 11: 7 Did you not hate me, and drive me out of my father's 2
14:16 You only hate me, you do not love me; you have put 2
15: 2 I really thought that you utterly hated her; 2
2Sm 5: 8 lame and the blind, who are hated by David's soul. 2
13:15 Then Amnon hated her with very great hatred; 2
15 the hatred with which he hated her was greater 2
22 Ab'salom hated Amnon, because he had forced 2
19: 6 you love those who hate you and hate those who 2
6 love . . who hate you and hate those who love you. 2
22:18 He delivered me from . . those who hated me; 2
41 those who hated me, and I destroyed them. 2
1Kg 22: 8 Micai'ah . . but I hate him, for he never prophesies 2
2Ch 1:11 not asked . . or the life of those who hate you 2
18: 7 I hate him, for he never prophesies good 2
19: 2 Should you . . love those who hate the LORD? 2
Est 9: 5 and did as they pleased to those who hated them. 2
16 slew 75,000 of those who hated them 2
Job 8:22 Those who hate you will be clothed with shame 2
16: 9 He has torn me in his wrath, and hated me; 1
31:29 If I have rejoiced at the ruin of him that hated me 2
34:17 Shall one who hates justice govern? 2
Ps 5: 5 before thy eyes; thou hatest all evildoers. 2
9:13 Behold what I suffer from those who hate me 2
11: 5 his soul hates him that loves violence. 2
18:17 strong enemy, and from those who hated me; 2
40 those who hated me I destroyed. 2
21: 8 your right hand will find out those who hate you. 2
25:19 foes, and with what violent hatred they hate me. 2
26: 5 I hate the company of evildoers 2
31: 6 Thou hatest those who pay regard to vain idols; 2
34:21 those who hate the righteous will be condemned. 2
35:19 those wink the eye who hate me without cause. 2
36: 2 that his iniquity cannot be found out and hated. 2
38:19 many are those who hate me wrongfully. 2
41: 7 All who hate me whisper together about me; 2
44: 7 hast put to confusion those who hate us. 2
45: 7 you love righteousness and hate wickedness. 2
50:17 For you hate discipline 2
68: 1 let those who hate him flee before him! 2
69: 4 More . . are those who hate me without cause; 2
81:15 Those who hate the LORD would cringe toward him 2
83: 2 those who hate thee have raised their heads. 2
86:17 that those who hate me may see and be put to shame 2
89:23 I will . . strike down those who hate him. 2
97:10 The LORD loves those who hate evil; •
101: 3 I hate the work of those who fall away; 2
105:25 He turned their hearts to hate his people 2
106:41 so that those who hated them ruled over them. 2
109: 3 They beset me with words of hate 3
118: 7 I shall look in triumph on those who hate me. 2
119:104 therefore I hate every false way. 2
113 I hate double-minded men, but I love the law. 2
128 I hate every false way. 2
163 I hate and abhor falsehood, but I love thy law. 2
120: 6 long . . my dwelling among those who hate peace. 2
129: 5 who hate Zion be put to shame and turned backward! 2
139:21 Do I not hate them that hate thee, O LORD? 2
21 Do I not hate them that hate thee, O LORD? 2
22 I hate them with perfect hatred; 2
Prv 1:22 How long will . . fools hate knowledge? 2
29 Because they hated knowledge 2
5:12 you say, "How I hated discipline 2
6:16 There are six things which the LORD hates 2
8:13 way of evil and perverted speech I hate. 2
36 all who hate me love death. 2
9: 8 Do not reprove a scoffer, or he will hate you; 2
11:15 but he who hates suretyship is secure. 2
12: 1 but he who hates reproof is stupid. 2
13: 5 A righteous man hates falsehood 2
24 He who spares the rod hates his son 2
15:10 he who hates reproof will die. 2
27 but he who hates bribes will live. 2
19: 7 All a poor man's brothers hate him; 2
25:17 lest he become weary of you and hate you. 2
26:24 He who hates, dissembles with his lips 2
28 A lying tongue hates its victims 2
28:16 who hates unjust gain will prolong his days. 2
29:10 Bloodthirsty men hate one who is blameless 2
24 The partner of a thief hates his own life; 2
Ecc 2:17 I hated life, because . . was grievous to me; 2
18 I hated all my toil in which I had toiled 2
3: 8 a time to love, and a time to hate; 2
9: 1 whether it is love or hate man does not know. 3
6 Their love and their hate and their envy 3
Isa 1:14 Your new moons and your . . feasts my soul hates; 2
60:15 Whereas you have been forsaken and hated 2
61: 8 I the LORD love justice, I hate robbery and wrong; 2
66: 5 Your brethren who hate you and cast you out 2
Jer 12: 8 her voice against me; therefore I hate her. 2
44: 4 Oh, do not do this abominable thing that I hate! 2
Ezk 23:28 deliver you into the hands of those whom you hate 2
Dan 4:19 My lord, may the dream be for those who hate you 4
Hos 9:15 in Gilgal; there I began to hate them. 2
Ams 5:10 They hate him who reproves in the gate 2
15 Hate evil, and love good, and establish justice 2
21 I hate, I despise your feasts, and I take no delight 2
6: 8 the pride of Jacob, and hate his strongholds; 2
Mic 3: 2 you who hate the good and love the evil 2
Zec 8:17 for all these things I hate, says the LORD. 2
Mal 1: 3 I have hated Esau; I have laid waste his hill 2
2:16 For I hate divorce, says the LORD the God of Israel 2
Mat 5:43 love your neighbor and hate your enemy.' 7
6:24 for either he will hate the one and love the other 7
10:22 you will be hated by all for my name's sake 7
24: 9 hated by all nations for my name's sake. 7
10 betray one another, and hate one another. 7
Mrk 13:13 you will be hated by all for my name's sake 7
Lke 1:71 saved . . from the hand of all who hate us 7
6:22 Blessed are you when men hate you 7
27 Love your enemies, do good to those who hate you 7
14:26 does not hate his own father and mother and wife 7

16:13 either he will hate the one and love the other 7
19:14 his citizens hated him 7
21:17 you will be hated by all for my name's sake. 7
Joh 3:20 For every one who does evil hates the light 7
7: 7 The world cannot hate you, but it hates me 7
7 The world cannot hate you, but it hates me 7
12:25 he who hates his life in this world will keep it 7
15:18 If the world hates you, know that it has hated me 7
18 know that it has hated me before it hated you. 7
18 know that it has hated me before it hated you. 7
19 therefore the world hates you. 7
23 He who hates me hates my Father also. 7
23 He who hates me hates my Father also. 7
24 they have seen and hated both me and my Father. 7
25 'They hated me without a cause.' 7
17:14 the world has hated them 7
Rom 7:15 but I do the very thing I hate. 7
9:13 As it is written, "Jacob I loved, but Esau I hated. 7
12: 9 hate what is evil, hold fast to what is good; 5
Eph 5:29 For no man ever hates his own flesh 7
Tit 3: 3 hated by men and hating one another; 7
Heb 1: 9 loved righteousness and hated lawlessness; 7
1Jn 2: 9 and hates his brother is in the darkness still. 7
11 he who hates his brother is in the darkness 7
3:13 Do not wonder, brethren, that the world hates you. 7
15 Any one who hates his brother is a murderer 7
4:20 If any one says, "I love God," and hates his brother 7
Jde 1:23 hating even the garment spotted by the flesh. 7
Rev 2: 6 you hate the works of the Nicola'itans 7
6 works of the Nicola'itans, which I also hate. 7
17:16 they and the beast will hate the harlot; 7
2Es 7:79 and who have hated those who fear God- 11
10:23 into the hands of those that hate us. 11
11:42 you have hated those who tell the truth 11
Tob 4:15 what you hate, do not do to any one 7
13:12 Cursed are all who hate you 7
Jdt 5:17 the God who hates iniquity is with them. 7
AEs 14:13 to hate the man who is fighting against us 9
15 I hate the splendor of the wicked 7
Wis 11:24 if thou hadst hated it. 7
12: 4 thou didst hate for their detestable practices 7
Sir 7:15 Do not hate toilsome labor, or farm work 7
9:18 the man who is reckless in speech will be hated. 7
12: 6 For the Most High also hates sinners 7
15:11 for he will not do what he hates. 7
13 The Lord hates all abominations 7
17:26 hate abominations intensely. 7
19: 6 for one who hates gossip evil is lessened. 7
9 when the time comes he will hate you. 7
20: 8 whoever usurps the right to speak will be hated. 7
21: 6 Whoever hates reproof 7
28 is hated in his neighborhood. 7
25: 2 My soul hates three kinds of men 7
14 Any attack, but not an attack from those who hate! 7
27:24 I have hated many things 7
24 even the Lord will hate him. 7
31:16 do not chew greedily, lest you be hated. 7
33: 2 A wise man will not hate the law 7
37:20 A man skilled in words may be hated 8
42: 9 if married, lest she be hated; 7
1Mc 7:26 Nicanor . . who hated and detested Israel 7
9:29 to deal with those of our nation who hate us. 6
11:21 certain lawless men who hated their nation 7
38 the troops who had served his fathers hated him. 6
2Mc 5: 8 hated as a rebel against the laws 10

hate insolence 1. μίσυβρις
3Mc 6: 9 now, you who hate insolence . . reveal yourself 1

really hate 1. odi
2Es 5:30 If thou dost really hate thy people 1

hated by a man 1. στυγητός
Tit 3: 3 hated by men and hating one another; 1

hateful 1. ἀπεχθάνομαι 2. μισέω 3. μισητός 4. στυγνός 5. odibilis 6. odiosus
Rev 18: 2 a haunt of every foul and hateful bird; 2
2Es 15:48 You have imitated that hateful harlot 5
60 as they pass they shall wreck the hateful city 6
Wis 14: 9 equally hateful to God 3
17: 5 avail to illumine that hateful night. 4
Sir 10: 7 Arrogance is hateful before the Lord 3
20:15 such a one is a hateful man. 3
3Mc 3: 4 For this reason they appeared hateful to some; 1

most hateful 1. αἰσχρός 2. ἐχθρός
AEs 16:24 most hateful for all time to beasts and birds. 2
Wis 15:18 worship even the most hateful animals 2
Aza 1: 9 the hands of lawless enemies, most hateful rebels 2
3Mc 3:27 with the most hateful torments 1
4Mc 5:27 which are most hateful to us. 2

hater of God 1. θεοστυγής
Rom 1:30 slanderers, haters of God, insolent, haughty 1

hater of good 1. ἀφιλάγαθος
2Ti 3: 3 profligates, fierce, haters of good 1

hater of mankind 1. μισάνθρωπος
4Mc 11: 4 Hater of virtue, hater of mankind 1

hater of virtue 1. μισάρετος
4Mc 11: 4 Hater of virtue, hater of mankind 1

hatred 1. מַשְׂטֵמָה 2. שׂנא 3. שִׂנְאָה 4. ἔχθρα 5. ἐχθρός 6. μισέω
Num35:20 if he stabbed him from hatred, or hurled at him 3
2Sm 13:15 Then Amnon hated her with very great hatred; 3
15 the hatred . . was greater than the love 3
Ps 25:19 foes, and with what violent hatred they hate me. 3
109: 5 reward me evil for good, and hatred for my love. 3
139:22 I hate them with perfect hatred; 3
Prv 8:13 The fear of the LORD is hatred of evil. 2
10:12 Hatred stirs up strife 3
18 He who conceals hatred has lying lips 3
15:17 Better is . . than a fatted ox and hatred with it. 3
26:26 though his hatred be covered with guile 3
Ezk 23:29 they shall deal with you in hatred 3
35:11 showed because of your hatred against them; 3
Hos 9: 7 because of your . . great hatred. 1
8 and hatred in the house of his God. 1
1Mc 11:40 the hatred which the troops of Demetrius had 5
13: 6 the nations have gathered together out of hatred 4
2Mc 4: 3 When his hatred progressed to such a degree 5
4Mc 9: 3 in your hatred for us 6

hatred of strangers 1. μισοξενία
Wis 19:13 practiced a more bitter hatred of strangers. 1

hatred of wickedness 1. μισοπονηρία
2Mc 3: 1 because of . . his hatred of wickedness 1

show hatred of crime 1. μισοπονηρέω
2Mc 4:49 showing their hatred of the crime 1

show hatred of evil 1. μισοπονηρέω
2Mc 8: 4 to show his hatred of evil. 1

haughtily 1. גַּאֲוָה 2. מָרוֹם 3. רוֹמָה
2Kg 19:22 Against whom . . and haughtily lifted your eyes? 2
Ps 31:23 but abundantly requites him who acts haughtily. 1
Isa 37:23 your voice and haughtily lifted your eyes? 2
Mic 2: 3 and you shall not walk haughtily 3

haughtiness 1. גַּאֲוָה 2. גַּבְהוּת 3. רוּם
Isa 2:17 the haughtiness of man shall be humbled 2
13:11 and lay low the haughtiness of the ruthless. 1
Jer 48:29 his arrogance, and the haughtiness of his heart. 3

haughty 1. גבה 2. גָּבֹהַּ 3. גֹּבַהּ 4. גַּבְהוּת 5. רוּם 6. רוּם 7. רַם 8. μέγας 9. μετεωρισμός 10. ὑπερήφανος 11. ὑψηλὰ φρονέω 12. ὑψηλοφρονέω
2Sm 22:28 thy eyes are upon the haughty to bring them down. 6
Ps 18:27 but the haughty eyes thou dost bring down. 7
101: 5 man of haughty looks and arrogant heart 2
138: 6 but the haughty he knows from afar. 2
Prv 6:17 haughty eyes, a lying tongue 7
16:18 haughty spirit before a fall. 3
18:12 Before destruction a man's heart is haughty 1
21: 4 Haughty eyes and a proud heart 5
Isa 2:11 The haughty looks of man shall be brought low 4
3:16 haughty and walk with outstretched necks 1
5:15 and the eyes of the haughty are humbled. 2
Ezk 16:50 They were haughty, and did abominable things 1
Zep 3:11 shall no longer be haughty in my holy mountain. 1
Rom 1:30 slanderers, haters of God, insolent, haughty 10
12:16 do not be haughty, but associate with the lowly; 11
1Ti 6:17 charge them not to be haughty 12
Rev 13: 5 a mouth uttering haughty and blasphemous words 8
Sir 23: 4 do not give me haughty eyes 9
3Mc 1:27 not to overlook this unlawful and haughty deed. 10

haughty *See also* pride.

haughty man 1. יָהִיר
Prv 21:24 Scoffer" is the name of the proud, haughty man 1

haul 1. ἕλκω
Joh 21: 6 now they were not able to haul it• 1
11 hauled the net ashore, full of large fish, 153 1

haul up 1. ἀνάγω
Ezk 32: 3 I will haul you up in my dragnet. 1

haunt 1. מָעוֹן 2. נָוֶה 3. רֶגֶל 4. παροικία 5. φυλακή 6. regio
1Sm 23:22 know and see the place where his haunt is 3
Isa 34:13 It shall be the haunt of jackals 2
35: 7 the haunt of jackals shall become a swamp 2
Jer 49:33 Hazor shall become a haunt of jackals 1
51:37 become a heap of ruins, the haunt of jackals 1
Rev 18: 2 a haunt of every foul spirit 5
2 a haunt of every foul and hateful bird; 5
2Es 5: 8 the wild beasts shall roam beyond their haunts 6
Sir 41: 5 they frequent the haunts of the ungodly. 4

haven 1. חוֹף 2. מָבוֹא 3. מָחוֹז 4. λιμήν 5. portus
Gen 49:13 he shall become a haven for ships 1
Ps 107:30 brought them to their desired haven. 3
Isa 23: 1 for Tyre is laid waste, without house or haven! 2
2Es 12:42 and like a haven for a ship saved from a storm. 5
4Mc 7: 3 he sailed into the haven of immortal victory. 4

havoc *See* make.

hawk 1. נֵץ 2. קָאָת
Lev 11:16 the sea gull, the hawk according to its kind 1
Deu 14:15 the ostrich, the nighthawk, the sea gull, the hawk 1
Job 39:26 Is it by your wisdom that the hawk soars 1
Isa 34:11 But the hawk and the porcupine shall possess it 2

hay 1. χόρτος
1Co 3:12 with gold, silver, precious stones, wood, hay, straw- 1

hazard 1. ἀντίπτωμα
Sir 32:20 Do not go on a path full of hazards 1

head 1. אַף 2. בַּרְזֶל 3. גֻּלְגֹּלֶת 4. לֶהָבָה 5. לִפְנֵי 6. מְרַאֲשׁוֹת 7. מַרְאֶשֶׁת 8. נצב 9. נָשִׂיא 10. פָּנִים 11. צֶמַח 12. קָדְקֹד 13. ראשׁ 14. שַׂר 15. רֵאשׁ (A) 16. ἄκρος 17. ἀρχηγός 18. ἀρχίφυλος 19. ἡγέομαι 20. κεφαλή 21. προηγέομαι 22. προκαθηγέομαι 23. προκάθημαι 24. προτομή 25. caput
Gen 3:15 her seed; he shall bruise your head 13
40:13 will lift up your head and restore you 13
16 there were three cake baskets on my head 13
17 eating it out of the basket on my head. 13
19 three days Pharaoh will lift up your head 13
20 his servants, and lifted up the head of the chief 13
20 chief butler and the head of the chief baker 13
47:31 Israel bowed himself upon the head of his bed. 13
48:14 right hand and laid it upon the head of E'phraim 13
14 and his left hand upon the head of Manas'seh 13
17 laid his right hand upon the head of E'phraim 13
17 to remove it from E'phraim's head to Manas'seh's 13
17 from E'phraim's head to Manas'seh's head. 13
18 the first-born; put your right hand upon his head. 13
49:26 may they be on the head of Joseph, and on the brow 13
Exd 6:14 These are the heads of their fathers' houses 13
25 These are the heads of the fathers' houses 13
12: 9 but roasted, its head with its legs and its inner 13
18:25 Moses . . made them heads over the people 13
28:32 It shall have in it an opening for the head 13
29: 6 you shall set the turban on his head 13
7 and pour it on his head and anoint him. 13
10 shall lay their hands upon the head of the bull 13
15 shall lay their hands upon the head of the ram 13
17 and put them with its pieces and its head 13
19 shall lay their hands upon the head of the ram 13
38:26 a beka a head (that is, half a shekel, by the shekel 3
Lev 1: 4 lay his hand upon the head of the burnt offering 13
8 lay the pieces, the head, and the fat, in order 13
12 he shall cut it into pieces, with its head 13
15 wring off its head, and burn it on the altar 13
3: 2 shall lay his hand upon the head of his offering 13
8 laying his hand upon the head of his offering 13
13 lay his hand upon its head, and kill it 13
4: 4 lay his hand on the head of the bull 13
11 the bull . . with its head, its legs, its entrails 13
15 shall lay their hands upon the head of the bull 13
24 shall lay his hand upon the head of the goat 13
29 lay his hand on the head of the sin offering 13
33 lay his hand upon the head of the sin offering 13
5: 8 he shall wring its head from its neck 13
8: 9 he set the turban upon his head, and on the turban 13
12 poured some of the anointing oil on Aaron's head 13
14 their hands upon the head of the bull 13
18 laid their hands on the head of the ram 13
20 Moses burned the head and the pieces and the fat 13
22 laid their hands on the head of the ram 13
9:13 delivered the burnt offering . . and the head 13
10: 6 Do not let the hair of your heads hang loose 13
13:12 the skin of the diseased person from head to foot 13
29 woman has a disease on the head or the beard 13
30 it is an itch, a leprosy of the head or the beard 13
40 If a man's hair has fallen from his head, he is bald 13
44 he is unclean . . his disease is on his head 13
45 shall . . let the hair of his head hang loose 13
14: 9 he shall shave all his hair off his head 13
18 oil . . he shall put on the head of him who is to be 13
29 shall put on the head of him who is to be cleansed 13
16:21 both his hands upon the head of the live goat 13
21 he shall put them upon the head of the goat 13
21: 5 They shall not make tonsures upon their heads 13
10 upon whose head the anointing oil is poured 13
10 shall not let the hair of his head hang loose 13
24:14 all who heard him lay their hands upon his head 13
Num 1: 4 each man being the head of the house 13
16 These were . . the heads of the clans of Israel. 13
3:24 with Eli'asaph . . as head of the fathers' house 9
30 Eli-za'phan . . head of the fathers' house 9
35 head of the fathers' house of the families 9

5:18 priest . . unbind the hair of the woman's head 13
6: 5 no razor shall come upon his head; 13
5 shall let the locks of hair of his head grow long. 13
7 because his separation to God is upon his head. 13
9 he defiles his consecrated head 13
9 shall shave his head on the day of his cleansing; 13
11 And he shall consecrate his head that same day. 13
18 Nazirite shall shave his consecrated head 13
18 shall take the hair from his consecrated head 13
7: 2 leaders of Israel, heads of their fathers' houses 13
8:12 shall lay their hands upon the heads of the bulls; 13
10: 4 leaders, the heads of the tribes of Israel 13
13: 3 men who were heads of the people of Israel. 13
17: 3 one rod for the head of each fathers' house. 13
22:31 he bowed his head, and fell on his face. *
25:14 Zimri the son of Salu, head of a fathers' house 9
15 Zur . . head of the people of a fathers' house 13
30: 1 Moses said to the heads of the tribes 13
31:26 you and Elea'zar the priest and the heads 13
32:28 command . . to the heads of the fathers' houses 13
36: 1 The heads of the fathers' houses of the families 13
1 leaders, the heads of the fathers' houses 13
Deu 1:13 men . . and I will appoint them as your heads.' 13
15 So I took the heads of your tribes 13
15 set them as heads over you, commanders 13
3:28 for he shall go over at the head of this people 10
5:23 all the heads of your tribes, and your elders; 13
10:11 Arise, go on your journey at the head of the people 10
19: 5 head slips from the handle and strikes 2
20: 9 commanders . . appointed at the head of the people. 13
21:12 she shall shave her head and pare her nails. 13
28:13 LORD will make you the head, and not the tail; 13
23 heavens over your head shall be brass 13
44 he shall be the head, and you shall be the tail. 13
29:10 heads of your tribes, your elders 13
31: 3 Joshua will go over at your head, as the LORD 10
32:42 from the long-haired heads of the enemy.' 13
33: 5 when the heads of the people were gathered 13
16 Let these come upon the head of Joseph 13
21 he came to the heads of the people, with Israel 13
Jos 2:19 If any one goes . . his blood shall be upon his head 13
19 if a hand is laid . . his blood shall be on our head. 13
7: 6 and they put dust upon their heads. 13
11:10 for Hazor . . was the head of all those kingdoms. 13
14: 1 and the heads of the fathers' houses of the tribes 13
19:51 and Joshua . . and the heads of the fathers' houses 13
21: 1 the heads of the fathers' houses of the Levites 13
1 came . . and to the heads of the fathers' houses 13
22:14 chiefs . . every one of them the head of a family 13
21 in answer to the heads of the families of Israel 13
30 the heads of the families of Israel who were 13
23: 2 summoned all Israel, their elders and heads 13
24: 1 and summoned the elders, the heads, the judges 13
Jdg 3:27 went down with him . . having him at their head. 5
5:26 she crushed his head, she shattered and pierced 13
7:25 they brought the heads of Oreb and Zeeb to Gideon 13
8:28 and they lifted up their heads no more. 13
9:39 Ga'al went out at the head of the men of Shechem 5
53 threw an upper millstone upon Abim'elech's head 13
57 the wickedness . . fall back upon their heads 13
10:18 He shall be head over all the inhabitants 13
11: 8 be our head over all the inhabitants of Gilead. 13
9 the LORD gives them over to me, I will be your head. 13
11 and the people made him head and leader over them; 13
13: 5 bear a son. No razor shall come upon his head 13
16:13 If you weave the seven locks of my head 13
14 took the seven locks of his head and wove them *
17 A razor has never come upon my head; for I have been 13
19 and had him shave off the seven locks of his head. 13
22 the hair of his head began to grow again 13
1Sm 1:11 to the LORD . . and no razor shall touch his head. 13
4:12 his clothes rent and with earth upon his head. 13
5: 4 the head of Dagon and . . his hands were lying cut 13
9:22 gave them a place at the head of those . . invited 13
10: 1 Samuel took a vial of oil and poured it on his head 13
14:45 shall not one hair of his head fall to the ground; 13
15:17 are you not the head of the tribes of Israel? 13
17: 5 He had a helmet of bronze on his head 13
7 and his spear's head weighed 600 shekels of iron; 4
38 he put a helmet of bronze on his head 13
46 and I will strike you down, and cut off your head; 13
51 took his sword . . and cut off his head with it. 13
54 David took the head of the Philistine 13
57 with the head of the Philistine in his hand. 13
19:13 and put a pillow of goats' hair at its head 6
16 with the pillow of goats' hair at its head. 6
20 the prophets . . and Samuel standing as head 8
25:39 returned the evil . . of Nabal upon his own head. 13
26: 7 with his spear stuck in the ground at his head; 6
11 but take now the spear that is at his head 6
12 took the spear and the jar . . from Saul's head; 6
16 and the jar of water that was at his head. 6
29: 4 Would it not be with the heads of the men here? 13
31: 9 they cut off his head, and stripped off his armor 13
2Sm 1: 2 with his clothes rent and earth upon his head. 13
10 I took the crown which was on his head 13
16 David said to him, "Your blood be upon your head; 13
2:16 And each caught his opponent by the head 13
3: 8 Am I a dog's head of Judah? This day I keep showing 13
29 May it fall upon the head of Jo'ab 13
4: 7 They took his head, and went by the . . Arabah 13
8 and brought the head of Ish-bo'sheth to David 13
8 Here is the head of Ish-bo'sheth, the son of Saul 13
12 they took the head of Ish-bo'sheth, and buried it 13
10:16 they came to Helam, with Shobach . . at their head. 5
12:30 And he took the crown of their king from his head; 13
30 the crown . . and it was placed on David's head. 13
13:19 Tamar put ashes on her head, and rent the long robe 13
19 she laid her hand on her head, and went away, crying 13
14:25 from the sole of his foot to the crown of his head *
26 And when he cut the hair of his head 13
26 he weighed the hair of his head, 200 shekels 13
15:30 weeping . . barefoot and with his head covered; 13
30 the people who were with him covered their heads 13
32 with his coat rent and earth upon his head. 13
16: 9 Why should . . ? Let me go over and take off his head. 13
18: 9 Ab'salom was . . and his head caught fast in the oak 13
20:21 his head shall be thrown to you over the wall. 13
22 they cut off the head of Sheba the son of Bichri 13
22:44 thou didst keep me as the head of the nations; 13
1Kg 2: 6 do not let his gray head go down to Sheol in peace. *
9 you shall bring his gray head down with blood *
32 bring back his bloody deeds upon his own head 13
33 blood come back upon the head of Jo'ab and upon 13
33 head of Jo'ab and upon the head of his descendants 13
37 shall die; your blood shall be upon your own head. 13
44 will bring back your evil upon your own head. 13
8: 1 the elders . . and all the heads of the tribes 13
32 by bringing his conduct upon his own head 13
10:19 at the back of the throne was a calf's head 13
19: 6 there was at his head a cake baked on hot stones 7
20:31 sackcloth on our loins and ropes upon our heads 13
32 girded sackcloth . . and put ropes on their heads 13
2Kg 4:19 he said to his father, "Oh, my head, my head! 13
19 he said to his father, "Oh, my head, my head! 13
6:25 an ass's head was sold for 80 shekels of silver 13
31 if the head of Eli'sha . . remains on his shoulders 13
32 see how this murderer has sent to take off my head? 13
9: 3 Then take the flask of oil, and pour it on his head 13
6 and the young man poured the oil on his head 13
30 she painted her eyes, and adorned her head 13
10: 6 take the heads of your master's sons, and come to me 13
7 slew them . . and put their heads in baskets 13
8 They have brought the heads of the king's sons 13
19:21 she wags her head behind you–the daughter 13
1Ch 5:24 These were the heads of their fathers' houses 13
24 heads of their fathers' houses. 13
7: 2 sons of Tola . . heads of their fathers' houses 13
7 sons of Bela . . five, heads of fathers' houses 13
9 heads of their fathers' houses, mighty warriors 13
11 according to the heads of their fathers' houses 13
40 men of Asher, heads of fathers' houses, approved 13
8: 6 heads of fathers' houses of the inhabitants 13
10 These were his sons, heads of fathers' houses. 13
13 Beri'ah and Shema . . heads of fathers' houses 13
28 These were the heads of fathers' houses 13
9: 9 All these were heads of fathers' houses 13
13 their kinsmen, heads of their fathers' houses 13
33 the heads of fathers' houses of the Levites 13
34 heads of fathers' houses of the Levites 13
10: 9 they stripped him and took his head and his armor 13
10 and fastened his head in the temple of Dagon. 3
12:19 At peril to our heads he will desert to his master 13
15:12 the heads of the fathers' houses of the Levites; 13
19:16 the commander of the army . . at their head. 10
20: 2 David took the crown of their king from his head; 13
2 the crown . . was placed on David's head. 13
23: 9 the heads of the fathers' houses of Ladan. 13
24 heads of fathers' houses as they were registered 13
24: 4 under sixteen heads of fathers' houses 13
6 the heads of the fathers' houses of the priests 13
31 These also, the head of each father's house and his 13
31 heads of fathers' houses of the priests 13
26:21 heads of the fathers' houses belonging to Ladan 13
26 and the heads of the fathers' houses 13
32 2,700 men of ability, heads of fathers' houses 13
27: 1 heads of fathers' houses, the commanders 13
29: 6 heads of fathers' houses made their freewill 14
11 O LORD, and thou art exalted as head above all. 13
2Ch 1: 2 to all the leaders . . heads of fathers' houses. 13
5: 2 assembled the . . and all the heads of the tribes 13
6:23 guilty by bringing his conduct upon his own head 13
13:12 Behold, God is with us at our head 13
19: 8 certain . . heads of families of Israel 13
20:18 Then Jehosh'aphat bowed his head 1
27 Jehosh'aphat at their head 13
23: 2 the heads of fathers' houses of Israel 13
26:12 heads of fathers' houses of mighty men of valor 13
Ezr 1: 5 Then rose up the heads of the fathers' houses 13
2:68 Some of the heads of families, when they came 13
3:12 many of the . . heads of fathers' houses, old men 13
4: 2 Zerub'babel and the heads of fathers' houses 13
3 rest of the heads of fathers' houses in Israel 13
5:10 write down the names of the men at their head. 15
8: 1 These are the heads of their fathers' houses 13
29 Levites and the heads of fathers' houses 14
9: 3 pulled hair from my head and beard 13
6 our iniquities have risen higher than our heads 13
10:16 Ezra . . selected men, heads of fathers' houses 13
Neh 4: 4 turn back their taunt upon their own heads 13
7:70 Now some of the heads of fathers' houses gave 13
71 some of the heads of fathers' houses gave 13
8:13 day the heads of fathers' houses of all the people 13
9: 1 assembled . . with earth upon their heads. *
11:13 his brethren, heads of fathers' houses, 245; 13
12:12 days . . were priests, heads of fathers' houses 13
22 there were recorded the heads of fathers' houses; 13
23 sons of Levi, heads of fathers' houses 13
Est 2:17 set the royal crown on her head and made her queen 13
6: 8 and on whose head a royal crown is set; 13
12 Haman . . mourning and with his head covered. 13
9:25 his wicked plot . . should come upon his own head 13
Job 1:20 Job arose, and rent his robe, and shaved his head 13
2:12 sprinkled dust upon their heads toward heaven. 13
10:15 If I am righteous, I cannot lift up my head 13
16: 4 together against you, and shake my head at you. 13
19: 9 my glory, and taken the crown from my head. 13
20: 6 to the heavens, and his head reach to the clouds 13
24:24 they are cut off like the heads of grain. 13
29: 3 when his lamp shone upon my head 13
41: 7 or his head with fishing spears? 13
Ps 3: 3 my glory, and the lifter of my head. 13
7:16 His mischief returns upon his own head 13
18:43 thou didst make me the head of the nations; 13
21: 3 thou dost set a crown of fine gold upon his head. 13
22: 7 they make mouths at me, they wag their heads; 13
23: 5 thou anointest my head with oil, my cup overflows. 13
24: 7 Lift up your heads, O gates! 13
9 Lift up your heads, O gates! 13
27: 6 now my head shall be lifted up above my enemies 13
35:13 I prayed with head bowed on my bosom †
38: 4 For my iniquities have gone over my head; 13
40:12 they are more than the hairs of my head; 13
64: 8 all who see them will wag their heads. *
66:12 thou didst let men ride over our heads; 13
68:21 But God will shatter the heads of his enemies 13
69: 4 More in number than the hairs of my head 13
74:13 thou didst break the heads of the dragons 13
14 Thou didst crush the heads of Leviathan 13
83: 2 those who hate thee have raised their heads. 13
109:25 my accusers; when they see me, they wag their heads. 13
110: 7 therefore he will lift up his head. 13
118:22 rejected has become the head of the corner. 13
133: 2 It is like the precious oil upon the head 13
140: 7 thou hast covered my head in the day of battle. 13
9 Those who surround me lift up their head 13
141: 5 but let the oil of the wicked never anoint my head; 13
Prv 1: 9 for they are a fair garland for your head 13
4: 9 She will place on your head a fair garland; 13
10: 6 Blessings are on the head of the righteous 13
11:26 but a blessing is on the head of him who sells it. 13
25:22 for you will heap coals of fire on his head 13
Ecc 2:14 The wise man has his eyes in his head 13
9: 8 let not oil be lacking on your head. 13
Sng 2: 6 O that his left hand were under my head 13
5: 2 my head is wet with dew, my locks with the drops 13
11 His head is the finest gold; 13
7: 5 Your head crowns you like Carmel 13
8: 3 O that his left hand were under my head 13
Isa 1: 5 The whole head is sick, and the whole heart faint. 13
6 From the sole of the foot even to the head 13
3:17 smite with a scab the heads of the daughters 12
7: 8 For the head of Syria is Damascus 13
8 the head of Damascus is Rezin. 13
9 the head of E'phraim is Sama'ria 13
9 the head of Sama'ria is the son of Remali'ah. 13
20 shave . . the head and the hair of the feet 13
9:14 So the LORD cut off from Israel head and tail 13
15 the elder and honored man is the head 13
15: 2 On every head is baldness, every beard is shorn; 13
19:15 nothing for Egypt which head or tail . . may do. 13
28: 1 on the head of the rich valley of those overcome 13
4 beauty, which is on the head of the rich valley 13
29:10 and covered your heads, the seers. 13
35:10 everlasting joy shall be upon their heads; 13
37:22 she wags her head behind you– 13
51:11 everlasting joy shall be upon their heads; 13
20 at the head of every street like an antelope 13
58: 5 Is it to bow down his head like a rush 13
59:17 and a helmet of salvation upon his head; 13
Jer 2:37 you will come away with your hands upon your head 13
9: 1 O that my head were waters, and my eyes a fountain 13
13:18 beautiful crown has come down from your head. 20
21 What will you say when they set as head over you 13
14: 3 ashamed and confounded and cover their heads. 13
4 the farmers are ashamed, they cover their heads. 13
18:16 Every one who passes by it . . shakes his head. 13
23:19 it will burst upon the head of the wicked. 13
30:23 it will burst upon the head of the wicked. 13
48:27 whenever you spoke of him you wagged your head? *
37 For every head is shaved and every beard cut off; 13
52:31 lifted up the head of Jehoi'achin king of Judah 13
Lam 1: 5 foes have become the head, her enemies prosper 13
2:10 cast dust on their heads and put on sackcloth; 13
10 the maidens of Jerusalem have bowed their heads 13
15 they hiss and wag their heads at the daughter 13
19 who faint for hunger at the head of every street. 13

3:54 water closed over my head; I said, 'I am lost.' 13
4: 1 holy stones lie . . at the head of every street. 13
5:16 The crown has fallen from our head; 13
Ezk 1:22 Over the heads of the living creatures there was 13
22 firmament . . spread out above their heads. 13
25 voice from above the firmament over their heads; 13
26 above the firmament over their heads there was 13
5: 1 razor and pass it over your head and your beard; 13
7:18 shame . . and baldness on all their heads. 13
8: 3 the form of a hand, and took me by a lock of my head; 13
9:10 but I will requite their deeds upon their heads. 13
10: 1 firmament . . over the heads of the cherubim 13
11:21 I will requit their deeds upon their own heads 13
13:18 and make veils for the heads of persons 13
16:12 and a beautiful crown upon your head. 13
25 at the head of every street you built your lofty 13
31 your vaulted chamber at the head of every street 13
43 behold, I will requite your deeds upon your head 13
17:19 which he broke, I will requite upon his head. 13
21:19 a signpost, make it at the head of the way to a city; 13
: at the head of the two ways, to use divination; 13
22:31 their way have I requited upon their heads 13
23:15 with flowing turbans on their heads, all of them 13
42 and beautiful crowns upon their heads. 13
24:23 Your turbans shall be on your heads 13
27:30 They cast dust on their heads and wallow in ashes; 13
29:18 every head was made bald and every shoulder was 13
32:27 whose swords were laid under their heads 13
33: 4 his blood shall be upon his own head. 13
44:18 They shall have linen turbans upon their heads 13
20 They shall not shave their heads 13
20 they shall only trim the hair of their heads. 13
Dan 1:10 So you would endanger my head with the king. 13
2:28 Your dream and the visions of your head as you lay 15
32 head of this image was of fine gold 15
38 making you rule . . you are the head of gold. 15
3:27 hair of their heads was not singed 15
4: 5 fancies and the visions of my head alarmed me. 15
10 visions of my head as I lay in bed were these 15
13 I saw in the visions of my head as I lay in bed 15
7: 1 Daniel had a dream and visions of his head 15
6 beast had four heads; and dominion was given to it. 15
9 as snow, and the hair of his head like pure wool; 15
15 visions of my head alarmed me. 15
20 concerning the ten horns that were on its head 15
Hos 1:11 and they shall appoint for themselves one head; 13
8: 7 The standing grain has no heads 11
Jol 3: 4 will requite your deed upon your own head 13
7 and I will requite your deed upon your own head. 13
Ams 8:10 I will bring . . baldness on every head; 13
9: 1 and shatter them on the heads of all the people; 13
Obd 1:15 your deeds shall return on your own head. 13
Jon 2: 5 round about me; weeds were wrapped about my head 13
4: 6 that it might be a shade over his head 13
8 the sun beat upon the head of Jonah 13
Mic 2:13 will pass on before them, the LORD at their head. 13
3: 1 And I said: Hear, you heads of Jacob 13
9 Hear this, you heads of the house of Jacob 13
11 Its heads give judgment for a bribe 13
Nah 3:10 dashed in pieces at the head of every street; 13
Hab 3:13 Thou didst crush the head of the wicked 13
14 pierce with thy shafts the head of his warriors 13
Zec 1:21 scattered Judah, so that no man raised his head; 13
3: 5 I said, "Let them put a clean turban on his head. 13
5 they put a clean turban on his head 13
6:11 make a crown, and set it upon the head of Joshua 13
12: 8 like God, like the angel of the LORD, at their head. 10
Mat 5:36 do not swear by your head, for you cannot make one 20
6:17 when you fast, anoint your head and wash your face 20
8:20 but the Son of man has nowhere to lay his head. 20
10:30 even the hairs of your head are all numbered. 20
14: 8 she said, "Give me the head of John the Baptist 20
11 his head was brought on a platter 20
21:42 has become the head of the corner 20
26: 7 she poured it on his head 20
27:29 plaiting a crown of thorns they put it on his head 20
30 took the reed and struck him on the head. 20
37 over his head they put the charge against him 20
39 who passed by derided him, wagging their heads 20
Mrk 6:24 she said, "The head of John the baptizer. 20
25 I want you to give me at once the head of John 20
27 and gave orders to bring his head 20
28 brought his head on a platter 20
12:10 has become the head of the corner; 20
14: 3 she broke the flask and poured it over his head. 20
15:19 they struck his head with a reed, and spat upon him 20
29 wagging their heads, and saying, "Aha! 20
Lke 7:38 wiped them with the hair of her head 20
46 You did not anoint my head with oil 20
9:58 the Son of man has nowhere to lay his head. 20
12: 7 Why, even the hairs of your head are all numbered. 20
20:17 has become the head of the corner'? 20
21:18 not a hair of your head will perish. 20
28 look up and raise your heads 20
Joh 13: 9 not my feet only but also my hands and my head! 20
19: 2 put it on his head, and arrayed him in a purple robe; 20
30 he bowed his head and gave up his spirit. 20
20: 7 the napkin, which had been on his head 20
12 one at the head and one at the feet. 20

Act 4:11 which has become the head of the corner. 20
18: 6 Your blood be upon your heads! I am innocent 20
21:24 so that they may shave their heads 20
27:34 since not a hair is to perish from the head of any 20
Rom 12:20 you will heap burning coals upon his head. 20
1Co 11: 3 the head of every man is Christ 20
3 the head of a woman is her husband 20
3 the head of Christ is God. 20
4 who prays or prophesies with his head covered 20
4 with his head covered dishonors his head 20
5 who prays or prophesies with her head unveiled 20
5 with her head unveiled dishonors her head 20
5 it is the same as if her head were shaven. •
7 For a man ought not to cover his head 20
10 That is why a woman ought to have a veil on her head 20
13 for a woman to pray to God with her head uncovered? •
12:21 the head to the feet, "I have no need of you. 20
Eph 1:22 has made him the head over all things 20
4:15 to grow up in every way into him who is the head 20
5:23 For the husband is the head of the wife as Christ 20
23 as Christ is the head of the church 20
Col 1:18 He is the head of the body, the church 20
2:10 the head of all rule and authority. 20
19 not holding fast to the Head 20
Heb 11:21 bowing in worship over the head of his staff. 16
1Pe 2: 7 stone . . has become the head of the corner 20
Rev 1:14 his head and his hair were white as white wool 20
4: 4 elders . . with golden crowns upon their heads. 20
9: 7 on their heads were what looked like crowns 20
17 and the heads of the horses were like lions' heads 20
17 and the heads of the horses were like lions' heads 20
19 their tails are like serpents, with heads 20
10: 1 mighty angel . . with a rainbow over his head 20
12: 1 and on her head a crown of twelve stars; 20
3 great red dragon, with seven heads and ten horns 20
3 and ten horns, and seven diadems upon his heads. 20
13: 1 I saw a beast . . with ten horns and seven heads 20
1 and a blasphemous name upon its heads. 20
3 One of its heads seemed to have a mortal wound 20
14:14 like a son of man, with a golden crown on his head 20
17: 3 and it had seven heads and ten horns. 20
7 and of the beast with seven heads and ten horns 20
9 the seven heads are seven mountains 20
18:19 And they threw dust on their heads, as they wept 20
19:12 and on his head are many diadems; 20
1Es 2: 8 the heads of families of the tribes of Judah 18
4:30 take the crown from the king's head 20
5: 1 heads of fathers' houses were chosen to go up 17
44 Some of the heads of families 19
63 heads of fathers' houses 23
68 Jeshua and the heads of the fathers' houses 19
70 Jeshua and the heads of the fathers' houses 19
6:12 the names of those who are at their head. 22
8:59 the heads of the fathers' houses of Israel 19
71 pulled out hair from my head and beard 20
75 For our sins have risen higher than our heads 20
2Es 1: 8 Pull out the hair of your head 25
2:43 and on the head of each of them he placed a crown 25
9:38 and there were ashes on her head. 25
11: 1 had twelve feathered wings and three heads. 25
4 his heads were at rest; the middle head was larger 25
4 the middle head was larger than the other heads 25
4 the middle head was larger than the other heads 25
9 let the heads be reserved for the last. 25
10 and behold, the voice did not come from his heads 25
23 except the three heads that were at rest 25
24 and remained under the head 25
29 behold, one of the heads that were at rest 25
29 for it was greater than the other two heads. 25
30 I saw how it allied the two heads with itself 25
31 the head turned with those that were with it 25
32 this head gained control of the whole earth 25
33 the middle head also suddenly disappeared 25
34 the two heads remained 25
35 the head on the right side devoured the one 25
45 and your malicious heads 25
12: 2 behold, the remaining head disappeared 25
17 coming not from the eagle's heads 25
22 As for your seeing three heads at rest 25
24 therefore they are called the heads of the eagle. 25
26 your seeing that the large head disappeared 25
29 to the head which was on the right side 25
16:53 coals of fire on the head of him who says 25
Jdt 4:11 and put ashes on their heads 20
8:22 he will bring upon our heads among the Gentiles 20
9: 1 and put ashes on her head 20
9 send thy wrath upon their heads 20
13: 6 above Holofernes' head 20
7 and took hold of the hair of his head 20
9 gave Holofernes' head to her maid 20
15 Then she took the head out of the bag and showed it 20
15 here is the head of Holofernes 20
18 to strike the head of the leader of our enemies. 20
14: 1 take this head and hang it upon the parapet 20
6 when he came and saw the head of Holofernes 20
11 they hung the head of Holofernes on the wall 20
15 with his head cut off and missing. 20
18 his head is not on him! 20
AEs 14: 2 she covered her head with ashes and dung 20

16 which is upon my head 20
15: 7 collapsed upon the head of the maid 20
Wis 18:24 thy majesty on the diadem upon his head. 20
Sir 4: 7 bow your head low to a great man. 20
11: 1 The wisdom of a humble man will lift up his head 20
13 raises up his head, so that many are amazed at him. 20
12:18 he will shake his head, and clap his hands 20
13: 7 will forsake you, and shake his head at you. 20
17:23 will bring their recompense on their heads. 20
20:11 raised their heads from humble circumstances. 20
27:25 throws it on his own head 20
36:10 Crush the heads of the rulers of the enemy, who say 20
38: 3 The skill of the physician lifts up his head 20
44:23 he made to rest upon the head of Jacob 20
Bar 5: 2 put on your head the diadem 20
LJr 1: 9 make crowns for the heads of their gods 20
22 birds light on their bodies and heads 20
31 their heads and beards shaved 20
31 their heads uncovered. 20
Sus 1:34 two elders . . laid their hands upon her head. 20
55 Very well! You have lied against your own head 20
59 You also have lied against your own head 20
Bel 1:36 angel of the Lord took him by the crown of his head 20
1Mc 3:47 and sprinkled ashes on their heads 20
6:35 with brass helmets on their heads 20
7:47 they cut off Nicanor's head 20
11:13 Thus he put two crowns upon his head 20
17 Zabdiel the Arab cut off the head of Alexander 20
71 put dust on his head, and prayed. 20
2Mc 1:16 and dismembered them and cut off their heads 20
7: 7 They tore off the skin of his head with the hair 20
10:25 his men sprinkled dust upon their heads 20
11: 8 there . . a horseman appeared at their head 21
14:15 they sprinkled dust upon their heads •
15:30 ordered them to cut off Nicanor's head and arm 20
32 He showed them the vile Nicanor's head 20
35 he hung Nicanor's head from the citadel 24
4Mc 15:15 the flesh of the head to the chin exposed 20
20 scalped heads upon heads 20
20 scalped heads upon heads 20

head *See also* bow, crown, wound.

axe head 1. בַּרְזֶל
2Kg 6: 5 felling a log, his axe head fell into the water; 1

bald head 1. קָרַחַת
Lev 13:42 if there is on the bald head or the bald forehead 1
42 it is leprosy breaking out on his bald head 1
43 swelling is reddish-white on his bald head 1

head by head 1. לְגֻלְגְּלוֹת
Num 1: 2 the number of . . every male, head by head; 1
18 twenty years old and upward, head by head 1
20 according to the number of names, head by head 1
22 according to the number of names, head by head 1

hoary head 1. שֵׂיבָה
Lev 19:32 You shall rise up before the hoary head 1
Prv 16:31 A hoary head is a crown of glory; 1

head of grain 1. *στάχυς* 2. spica
Mat 12: 1 they began to pluck heads of grain and to eat. 1
Mrk 2:23 his disciples began to pluck heads of grain. 1
Lke 6: 1 his disciples plucked and ate some heads of grain 1
2Es 4:32 When heads of grain without number are sown 2

under the head 1. מְרַאֲשׁוֹת
Gen 28:11 he put it under his head and lay down in that place 1
18 he took the stone which he had put under his head 1

headband 1. שְׁבִים
Isa 3:18 finery of . . the headbands, and the crescents; 1

headdress 1. פְּאֵר
Isa 3:20 the headdresses, the armlets, the sashes 1

headlong 1. *πρηνής*
Job 27:22 he flees from its power in headlong flight. †
Act 1:18 falling headlong he burst open in the middle 1
headlong *See also* cast, fall, hurl, plunge, throw.

headstrong 1. *ἀδιάτρεπτος*
Sir 26:10 Keep strict watch over a headstrong daughter 1
42:11 Keep strict watch over a headstrong daughter 1
headway *See* make.

heal 1. אֲרוּכָה 2. גהה 3. חיה 4. נתן רְפָאָה 5. רפא
6. רְפאוּת 7. *διασῴζω* 8. *θεραπεύω* 9. *ἰάομαι* 10. *ἴασις*
11. *ποιέω ὑγιῆ* 12. *ὑγιής* 13. *ὑγιὴς γίνομαι* 14. curo
Gen 20:17 Abraham prayed to God; and God healed Abim'elech 5
17 God healed Abim'elech, and also healed his wife 5
Exd 21:19 and shall have him thoroughly healed. 5
Lev 13:18 when there is . . a boil that has healed 5
37 the itch is healed, he is clean 5
14: 3 Then, if the leprous disease is healed in the leper 5
48 the house clean, for the disease is healed 5
Num12:13 Moses cried . . "Heal her, O God, I beseech thee. 5
Deu 28:27 smite you . . of which you cannot be healed. 5

35 grievous boils of which you cannot be healed 5
32:39 I kill and I make alive; I wound and I heal; 5
Jos 5: 8 remained . . in the camp till they were healed. 3
1Sm 6: 3 Then you will be healed, and it will be known to you 5
2Kg 8:29 Joram returned to be healed . . of the wounds 5
9:15 King Joram had returned to be healed in Jezreel 5
20: 5 I have seen your tears; behold, I will heal you; 5
8 What shall be the sign that the LORD will heal me 5
2Ch 7:14 will forgive their sin and heal their land. 5
22: 6 he returned to be healed in Jezreel of the wounds 5
30:20 the LORD heard Hezeki'ah, and healed the people. 5
Job 5:18 he smites, but his hands heal. 5
Ps 6: 2 O LORD, heal me, for my bones are troubled. 5
30: 2 I cried to thee for help, and thou hast healed me. 5
41: 3 thou healest all his infirmities. †
4 heal me, for I have sinned against thee! 5
103: 3 who forgives . . who heals all your diseases 5
107:20 he sent forth his word, and healed them 5
147: 3 He heals the brokenhearted, and binds up 5
Prv 3: 8 It will be healing to your flesh 6
Ecc 3: 3 a time to kill, and a time to heal; 5
Isa 6:10 lest they see . . and turn and be healed. 5
19:22 the LORD will smite Egypt, smiting and healing 5
22 he will heed their supplications and heal them. 5
30:26 and heals the wounds inflicted by his blow. 5
53: 5 made us whole, and with his stripes we are healed. 5
57:18 I have seen his ways, but I will heal him; 5
19 Peace . . says the LORD; and I will heal him. 5
58: 8 and your healing shall spring up speedily; 1
Jer 3:22 faithless sons, I will heal your faithlessness. 5
6:14 They have healed the wound of my people lightly 5
8:11 They have healed the wound of my people lightly 5
15:18 my wound incurable, refusing to be healed? 5
17:14 Heal me, O LORD, and I shall be healed; 5
14 Heal me, O LORD, and I shall be healed; 5
30:17 and your wounds I will heal, says the LORD 5
33: 6 and I will heal them and reveal to them abundance 5
51: 8 Take balm for her pain; perhaps she may be healed. 5
9 We would have healed Babylon 5
9 have healed Babylon, but she was not healed. 5
Ezk 30:21 bound up, to heal it by binding it with a bandage 4
34: 4 the sick you have not healed 5
Hos 5:13 But he is not able to cure you or heal your wound. 2
6: 1 for he has torn, that he may heal us; 5
7: 1 when I would heal Israel 5
11: 3 but they did not know that I healed them. 5
14: 4 I will heal their faithlessness; 5
Zec 11:16 or seek the wandering, or heal the maimed 5
Mat 4:24 paralytics, and he healed them. 8
8: 7 he said to him, "I will come and heal him. 8
8 say the word, and my servant will be healed. 9
13 And the servant was healed at that very moment. 9
16 and healed all who were sick. 8
10: 1 and to heal every disease and every infirmity. 8
8 Heal the sick, raise the dead, cleanse lepers 8
12:10 they asked him, "Is it lawful to heal on the sabbath? 8
15 And many followed him, and he healed them all 8
22 he healed him, so that the dumb man spoke and saw. 8
13:15 and turn for me to heal them.' 9
14:14 and healed their sick. 8
15:28 And her daughter was healed instantly. 9
30 they put them at his feet, and he healed them 8
17:16 and they could not heal him. 8
19: 2 and he healed them there. 8
21:14 lame came to him in the temple, and he healed them. 8
Mrk 1:34 healed many who were sick with various diseases 8
3: 2 whether he would heal him on the sabbath 8
10 he had healed many 8
5:29 she felt in her body that she was healed 9
34 go in peace, and be healed of your disease. 12
6: 5 and healed them. 8
13 and healed them. 8
Lke 4:23 Physician, heal yourself 8
40 and healed them. 8
5:15 to be healed of their infirmities. 8
17 the power of the Lord was with him to heal. 9
6: 7 to see whether he would heal on the sabbath 8
17 to be healed of their diseases 9
19 for power came forth from him and healed them all. 9
7: 3 asking him to come and heal his slave. 7
7 But say the word, and let my servant be healed. 9
8: 2 some women who had been healed of evil spirits 8
43 and could not be healed by any one 8
47 how she had been immediately healed. 9
9: 2 to preach the kingdom of God and to heal. 9
42 healed the boy and gave him back to his father 9
10: 9 heal the sick in it and say to them 8
13:14 Jesus had healed on the sabbath 8
14 come on those days and be healed 8
14: 3 Is it lawful to heal on the sabbath, or not? 8
4 he took him and healed him, and let him go. 9
17:15 Then one of them, when he saw that he was healed 9
22:51 he touched his ear and healed him. 9
Joh 4:47 went and begged him to come down and heal his son 9
5: 6 he said to him, "Do you want to be healed? 13
9 at once the man was healed 12
11 he answered them, "The man who healed me said 11
13 the man who had been healed did not know 9
15 it was Jesus who had healed him. 11
12:40 turn for me to heal them. 9
Act 4:14 seeing the man that had been healed 8
30 while thou stretchest out thy hand to heal 10
5:16 they were all healed. 8
8: 7 many who were paralyzed or lame were healed. 8
9:34 Peter said to him, "Aene'as, Jesus Christ heals you; 9
28: 8 putting his hands on him healed him. 9
27 turn for me to heal them.' 9
Heb 12:13 not be put out of joint but rather be healed. 9
Jas 5:16 and pray for one another, that you may be healed. 9
1Pe 2:24 By his wounds you have been healed. 9
Rev 13: 3 but its mortal wound was healed 8
12 the first beast, whose mortal wound was healed. 8
2Es 7:104 to be ill or sleep or eat or be healed in his stead 14
Tob 3:17 Raphael was sent to heal the two of them 9
12: 3 he also healed you. 8
14 now God sent me to heal you 9
Wis 16:10 thy mercy came to their help and healed them. 9
12 it was thy word, O Lord, which heals all men. 9
Sir 38: 7 By them he heals and takes away pain; 8
9 pray to the Lord, and he will heal you. 9
43:22 A mist quickly heals all things 10

healer 1. חבש 2. רפא 3. *ἴαμα*
Exd 15:26 for I am the LORD, your healer. 2
Isa 3: 7 he will speak out, saying: "I will not be a healer; 1
1Co 12:28 then workers of miracles, then healers, helpers 3

healing 1. מַרְפֵּא 2. תְּעָלָה 3. תְּרוּפָה 4. *θεραπεία* 5. *θεραπεύω* 6. *ἴαμα* 7. *ἰάομαι* 8. *ἴασις* 9. medella
Prv 4:22 healing to all his flesh. 1
6:15 in a moment he will be broken beyond healing. 1
29: 1 suddenly be broken beyond healing. 1
Jer 8:15 for a time of healing, but behold, terror. 1
18 My grief is beyond healing, my heart is sick •
14:19 smitten us so that there is no healing for us? 1
19 for a time of healing, but behold, terror. 1
30:13 no medicine for your wound, no healing for you. 2
33: 6 Behold, I will bring to it health and healing 1
46:11 there is no healing for you. 2
Ezk 47:12 will be for food, and their leaves for healing. 3
Mal 4: 2 sun of . . shall rise, with healing in its wings. 1
Mat 4:23 preaching the gospel of the kingdom and healing 5
9:35 and healing every disease and every infirmity. 5
Lke 9: 6 preaching the gospel and healing everywhere. 5
11 cured those who had need of healing. 4
Act 4:22 man on whom this sign of healing was performed 8
10:38 healing all that were oppressed by the devil 7
1Co 12: 9 to another gifts of healing by the one Spirit 6
30 Do all possess gifts of healing? 6
Rev 22: 2 leaves . . were for the healing of the nations. 4
2Es 7:123 in which are abundance and healing 9
Wis 16: 9 no healing was found for them 6
Sir 3:28 The affliction of the proud has no healing 8
21: 3 there is no healing for its wound. 8
28: 3 yet seek for healing from the Lord? 8
34:17 he grants healing, life, and blessing. 8
38: 2 for healing comes from the Most High 8
14 grant them success in diagnosis and in healing 8
healing *See also* bring.

health 1. אֲרוּכָה 2. מַרְפֵּא 3. שָׁלוֹם 4. *εἰρήνη* 5. *ὑγιαίνω* 6. *ὑγίεια*
Ps 38: 3 there is no health in my bones because of my sin. 3
Prv 16:24 sweetness to the soul and health to the body. 2
Jer 8:22 the health of the daughter of my people 1
30:17 For I will restore health to you 1
33: 6 Behold, I will bring to it health and healing 1
3Jn 1: 2 I pray . . that you may be in health; 5
Tob 8:17 in health and happiness and mercy. 6
Wis 7:10 I loved her more than health and beauty 6
13:18 For health he appeals to a thing that is weak 6
Sir 1:18 making peace and perfect health to flourish. 6
30:15 Health and soundness are better than all gold 6
16 There is no wealth better than health of body 6
38: 8 from him health is upon the face of the earth. 4
health *See also* take, wish.

good health 1. *ῥώννυμι* 2. *ὑγιαίνω*
Tob 7: 4 he asked them, "Is he in good health? 2
5 They replied, "He is alive and in good health. 2
2Mc 1:10 to the Jews in Egypt, Greeting, and good health. 2
11:28 We also are in good health. 2
3Mc 3:12 greetings and good health. 1
7: 1 greetings and good health. 1

perfect health 1. *ὁλοκληρία*
Act 3:16 the faith . . has given the man this perfect health 1

healthful 1. securitas
2Es 7:121 safe and healthful habitations 1

healthy 1. *ὑγίεια*
Sir 31:20 Healthy sleep depends on moderate eating 1

heap 1. אסף 2. גַּל 3. חֲמוֹר 4. חֹמֶר 5. חתה 6. כֹּבֶד 7. כנס 8. מְעִי 9. נֵד 10. עִי 11. עֲרֵמָה 12. צִבֻּר 13. רבה 14. תֵּל 15. *ἐπιστοιβάζω* 16. *θημωνιά* 17. *κολλάω* 18. *πίμπλημι* 19. *προστίθημι* 20. *σωρεύω* 21. *σωρηδόν* 22. *σωρός* 23. agger
Gen 31:46 and they took stones, and made a heap; 2
46 made a heap; and they ate there by the heap. 2
48 This heap is a witness between you and me today. 2
51 See this heap and the pillar, which I have set 2
52 This heap is a witness, and the pillar is a witness 2
52 I will not pass over this heap to you 2
52 I will not pass over this heap to you 2
Exd 8:14 they gathered them together in heaps 4
15: 8 waters piled up, the floods stood up in a heap; 9
Deu 13:16 it shall be a heap for ever, it shall not be built 14
32:23 I will heap evils upon them; I will spend my arrows 1
Jos 3:13 the waters . . from above shall stand in one heap. 9
16 the waters . . stood and rose up in a heap far off 9
7:26 And they raised over him a great heap of stones 2
8:28 burned Ai, and made it for ever a heap of ruins 14
29 and raised over it a great heap of stones 2
Jdg 15:16 With the jawbone of an ass, heaps upon heaps 3
16 With the jawbone of an ass, heaps upon heaps 3
Rut 3: 7 he went to lie down at the end of the heap of grain. 11
2Sm 18:17 raised over him a very great heap of stones; 2
2Kg 10: 8 Lay them in two heaps at the entrance of the gate 12
19:25 you . . turn fortified cities into heaps of ruins 2
2Ch 31: 6 laid them in heaps. 11
7 In the third month they began to pile up the heaps 11
8 Hezeki'ah and the princes came and saw the heaps 11
9 Hezeki'ah questioned . . about the heaps. 11
Neh 4: 2 revive the stones out of the heaps of rubbish 11
13:15 bringing in heaps of grain and loading them 11
Ps 78:13 and made the waters stand like a heap. 9
Prv 25:22 for you will heap coals of fire on his head 5
Ecc 2:26 to the sinner he gives . . gathering and heaping 7
Sng 7: 2 belly is a heap of wheat, encircled with lilies. 11
Isa 17: 1 cease to be a city, and will become a heap of ruins. 8
25: 2 For thou hast made the city a heap 2
37:26 make fortified cities crash into heaps of ruins 2
Jer 9: 6 Heaping oppression upon oppression •
50:26 pile her up like heaps of grain, and destroy her 11
Ezk 24:10 Heap on the logs, kindle the fire, boil well 13
Mic 1: 6 I will make Sama'ria a heap in the open country 10
Nah 3: 3 hosts of slain, heaps of corpses, dead bodies 6
Hag 2:16 When one came to a heap of twenty measures 11
Rom 12:20 you will heap burning coals upon his head. 20
Rev 18: 5 for her sins are heaped high as heaven 17
2Es 2: 9 lies in lumps of pitch and heaps of ashes 23
Wis 18:23 the dead had already fallen on one another in heaps 21
Sir 3:27 the sinner will heap sin upon sin. 19
8: 3 nor heap wood on his fire. 15
37:24 A wise man will have praise heaped upon him 18
39:17 At his word the waters stood in a heap 16
1Mc 11: 4 they had piled them in heaps along his route. 16
4Mc 9:20 the heap of coals was being quenched 22
heap *See also* ash, stone.

heap of ruins 1. גַּל 2. מַכְשֵׁלָה 3. עִי
Job 15:28 which were destined to become heaps of ruins; 1
30:24 not one in a heap of ruins stretch out his hand 3
Isa 3: 6 this heap of ruins shall be under your rule"; 2
Jer 9:11 I will make Jerusalem a heap of ruins 1
26:18 Jerusalem shall become a heap of ruins 3
51:37 Babylon shall become a heap of ruins 1
Mic 3:12 Jerusalem shall become a heap of ruins 3

heap up 1. צבר 2. רבה 3. *ἀνυψόω*
Job 27:16 Though he heap up silver like dust 1
Ps 39: 6 man heaps up, and knows not who will gather! 1
Hab 1:10 for they heap up earth and take it. 1
2: 6 Woe to him who heaps up what is not his own 2
Zec 9: 3 heaped up silver like dust, and gold like the dirt 1
Sir 20:28 will heap up his harvest 3

heap up empty phrases 1. *βατταλογέω*
Mat 6: 7 in praying do not heap up empty phrases 1

hear 1. אזן 2. אֹזֶן 3. בוא 4. מִשְׁמָע 5. ענה 6. קול 7. שְׁמוּעָה 8. שמע 9. שֵׁמַע 10. שמע אֹזֶן 11. שמע (A) 12. *ἀκοή* 13. *ἀκοὴ ὠτίων* 14. *ἀκουστός* 15. *ἀκούω* 16. *ἀκροάομαι* 17. *ἀκρόασις* 18. *ἀναγγέλλω* 19. *γινώσκω* 20. *διακούω* 21. *εἰσακούω* 22. *ἐπακούω* 23. *λόγος* 24. *μεταλαμβάνω* 25. *ναί* 26. *οὖς* 27. audio 28. evidens 29. exaudio 30. suscipio
Gen 3: 8 they heard the sound of the LORD God walking 8
10 he said, "I heard the sound of thee in the garden 8
4:23 wives: "Adah and Zillah, hear my voice; 8
14:14 When Abram heard that his kinsman had been taken 8
17:20 As for Ish'mael, I have heard you; 8
21: 6 every one who hears will laugh over me. 8
17 God heard the voice of the lad; 8
17 Fear not; for God has heard the voice of the lad 8
26 tell me, and I have not heard of it until today. 8
23: 6 Hear us, my lord; you are a mighty prince among us. 8
8 I should bury my dead out of my sight, hear me 8
10 answered Abraham in the hearing of the Hittites 2
11 No, my lord, hear me; I give you the field 8
13 he said to Ephron in the hearing of the people 2
13 But if you will, hear me; I will give the price 8

16 which he had named in the hearing of the Hittites 2
24:30 when he heard the words of Rebekah his sister 8
52 When Abraham's servant heard their words 8
27: 6 Rebekah said to her son Jacob, "I heard your father 8
34 When Esau heard the words of his father, he cried 8
29:13 When Laban heard the tidings of Jacob 8
33 Because the LORD has heard that I am hated 8
30: 6 God . . has also heard my voice and given me a son"; 8
31: 1 Jacob heard that the sons of Laban were saying 8
34: 5 Now Jacob heard that he had defiled his daughter 8
7 came in from the field when they heard of it; 8
35:22 his father's concubine; and Israel heard of it. 8
37: 6 Hear this dream which I have dreamed 8
17 away, for I heard them say, 'Let us go to Dothan.' 8
21 when Reuben heard it, he delivered him out 8
39:15 when he heard that I lifted up my voice and cried 8
19 When his master heard the words which his wife 8
41:15 I have heard it said of you that when you hear 8
15 when you hear a dream you can interpret it. 8
42: 2 he said, "Behold, I have heard that there is grain 8
43:25 for they heard that they should eat bread there. 8
45: 2 he wept aloud, so that the Egyptians heard it 8
2 and the household of Pharaoh heard it. 8
16 When the report was heard in Pharaoh's house 8
49: 2 Assemble and hear, O sons of Jacob 8
Exd 2:15 When Pharaoh heard of it, he sought to kill Moses. 8
24 God heard their groaning, and God remembered 8
3: 7 I have seen . . and have heard their cry 8
4:31 and when they heard that the LORD had visited 8
6: 5 I have heard the groaning of the people of Israel 8
10: 2 that you may tell in the hearing of your son 2
11: 2 Speak now in the hearing of the people 2
15:14 The peoples have heard, they tremble; 8
16: 7 the LORD, because he has heard your murmurings 8
8 because the LORD has heard your murmurings 8
9 LORD, for he has heard your murmurings.' 8
12 I have heard the murmurings of the people 8
18: 1 Jethro . . heard of all that God had done 8
19: 9 that the people may hear when I speak with you 8
20:19 said to Moses, "You speak to us, and we will hear; 8
22:23 cry out to me, I will surely hear their cry; 8
27 cries to me, I will hear, for I am compassionate. 8
23:13 nor let such be heard out of your mouth. 8
24: 7 and read it in the hearing of the people; 2
28:35 its sound shall be heard when he goes 8
32:17 When Joshua heard the noise of the people 8
18 of defeat, but the sound of singing that I hear. 8
33: 4 When the people heard these evil tidings 8
Lev 5: 1 any one sins in that he hears a public adjuration 8
10:20 when Moses heard that, he was content 8
24:14 all who heard him lay their hands upon his head 8
Num 7:89 Moses . . heard the voice speaking to him 8
9: 8 Wait, that I may hear what the LORD will command 8
11: 1 people complained in the hearing of the LORD 2
1 when the LORD heard it, his anger was kindled 8
10 Moses heard the people weeping throughout 8
18 you have wept in the hearing of the LORD, saying 2
12: 2 And the LORD heard it. 8
6 said, "Hear my words: If there is a prophet among you 8
14:13 Then the Egyptians will hear of it 8
14 They have heard that thou, O LORD, art in the midst 8
15 then the nations who have heard thy fame will say 8
27 heard the murmurings of the people of Israel 8
28 'what you have said in my hearing I will do to you 2
16: 4 When Moses heard it, he fell on his face; 8
8 Moses said to Korah, "Hear now, you sons of Levi 8
20:10 Hear now, you rebels; shall we bring forth water 8
16 when we cried to the LORD, he heard our voice 8
21: 1 Canaanite . . heard that Israel was coming 8
22:36 When Balak heard that Balaam had come 8
23:18 Rise, Balak, and hear; hearken to me, O son of Zippor 8
24: 4 oracle of him who hears the words of God 8
16 the oracle of him who hears the words of God 8
30: 4 her father hears of her vow and of her pledge 8
5 disapproval to her on the day that he hears of it 8
7 her husband hears of it, and says nothing to her 8
7 says nothing to her on the day that he hears; 8
11 her husband heard of it, and said nothing to her 8
12 makes them null and void on the day that he hears 8
14 he said nothing to her on the day that he heard 8
15 if he makes them null and void after he has heard 8
33:40 heard of the coming of the people of Israel. 8
Deu 1:16 'Hear the cases between your brethren, and judge 8
17 you shall hear the small and the great alike; 8
17 you shall bring to me, and I will hear it.' 8
34 heard your words, and was angered, and he swore 8
2:25 hear the report of you and shall tremble 8
4: 6 peoples, who, when they hear all these statutes 8
10 that I may let them hear my words, so that they 8
12 you heard the sound of words, but saw no form; 8
28 gods . . that neither see, nor hear, nor eat, nor smell. 8
32 such a great thing as this . . was ever heard of. 8
33 Did any people ever hear the voice of a god 8
33 any people ever hear . . as you have heard 8
36 Out of heaven he let you hear his voice 8
36 you heard his words out of the midst of the fire. 8
5: 1 Hear, O Israel, the statutes and the ordinances 8
1 which I speak in your hearing this day 2
23 heard the voice out of the midst of the darkness 8
24 heard his voice out of the midst of the fire; 8
25 if we hear the voice of the LORD our God any more 8
26 heard the voice of the living God speaking 8
27 Go near, and hear all that the LORD our God will say; 8
27 speak to us . . we will hear and do it.' 8
28 LORD heard your words, when you spoke to me; 8
28 'I have heard the words of this people 8
6: 3 Hear therefore, O Israel, and be careful to do them; 8
4 Hear, O Israel: The LORD our God is one LORD; 8
9: 1 Hear, O Israel; you are to pass over the Jordan 8
2 sons of the Anakim . . of whom you have heard it said 8
13:11 all Israel shall hear, and fear, and never again do 8
12 If you hear in one of your cities, which the LORD 8
17: 4 told you and you hear of it; then you shall inquire 8
13 all the people shall hear, and fear, and not act 8
18:16 'Let me not hear again the voice of the LORD my God 8
19:20 rest shall hear, and fear, and shall never again 8
20: 3 say to them, 'Hear, O Israel, you draw near this day 8
21:21 all Israel shall hear, and fear. 8
26: 7 LORD heard our voice, and saw our affliction 8
27: 9 Keep silence and hear, O Israel 8
29: 4 LORD has not given you . . ears to hear. 8
19 when he hears the words of this sworn covenant 8
30:12 bring it to us, that we may hear it and do it?' 8
13 bring it to us, that we may hear it and do it?' 8
17 if your heart turns away, and you will not hear 8
31:11 read this law before all Israel in their hearing. 2
12 may hear and learn to fear the LORD your God 8
13 may hear and learn to fear the LORD your God 8
32: 1 let the earth hear the words of my mouth. 8
44 recited . . song in the hearing of the people 2
33: 7 Hear, O LORD, the voice of Judah, and bring him 8
Jos 2:10 For we have heard how the LORD dried up the water 8
11 And as soon as we heard it, our hearts melted 8
3: 9 Come . . and hear the words of the LORD your God. 8
5: 1 When all the kings . . heard that the LORD had 8
6: 5 as soon as you hear the sound of the trumpet 8
10 You shall not shout or let your voice be heard 8
20 soon as the people heard the sound of the trumpet 8
7: 9 all the inhabitants of the land will hear of it 8
9: 1 When all the kings . . heard of this 8
3 Gibeon heard what Joshua had done to Jericho 8
9 we have heard a report of him, and all that he did 8
16 they heard that they were their neighbors 8
10: 1 When Ado'ni-ze'dek . . heard how Joshua had taken Ai 8
11: 1 When Jabin king of Hazor heard of this, he sent 8
14:12 you heard on that day how the Anakim were there 8
22:11 And the people of Israel heard say 8
12 when the people of Israel heard of it 8
30 Phin'ehas . . heard the words that the Reubenites 8
24:27 it has heard all the words of the LORD 8
Jdg 5: 3 Hear, O kings; give ear, O princes; to the LORD I will 8
16 the sheepfolds, to hear the piping for the flocks? 8
7:11 you shall hear what they say, and afterward 8
15 When Gideon heard the telling of the dream 8
9:30 When Zebul . . heard the words of Ga'al the son 8
46 the people of the Tower of Shechem heard of it 8
14:13 Put your riddle, that we may hear it. 8
18:25 Do not let your voice be heard among us, lest angry 8
20: 3 Now the Benjaminites heard that the people 8
Rut 1: 6 she had heard . . the LORD had visited his people 8
1Sm 1:13 only her lips moved, and her voice was not heard; 8
2:22 Eli . . heard all that his sons were doing 8
23 I hear of your evil dealings from all the people. 8
24 report that I hear the people . . spreading 8
3: 9 you shall say, 'Speak, LORD, for thy servant hears.' 8
10 And Samuel said, "Speak, for thy servant hears. 8
11 two ears of every one that hears it will tingle. 8
4: 6 the Philistines heard the noise of the shouting 8
14 When Eli heard the sound of the outcry, he said 8
19 heard the tidings that the ark . . was captured 8
7: 7 the Philistines heard . . Israel had gathered 8
7 when . . Israel heard of it they were afraid 8
8:21 when Samuel had heard all the words of the people 8
11: 6 came . . upon Saul when he heard these words 8
13: 3 Jonathan . . and the Philistines heard of it. 8
3 blew the trumpet . . saying, "Let the Hebrews hear. 8
4 Israel heard . . Saul had defeated the garrison 8
14:22 all . . heard that the Philistines were fleeing 8
27 Jonathan had not heard his father charge 8
15:14 What then is . . the lowing of oxen which I hear? 8
16: 2 How can I go? If Saul hears it, he will kill me. 8
17:11 all Israel heard these words of the Philistine 8
23 spoke the same words . . And David heard him. 8
28 Now Eli'ab . . heard when he spoke to the men; 8
31 When the words which David spoke were heard 8
22: 1 his brothers and all his father's house heard it 8
6 Now Saul heard that David was discovered 8
7 Saul said . . "Hear now, you Benjaminites; 8
12 Saul said, "Hear now, son of Ahi'tub. 8
23:10 thy servant has surely heard that Saul seeks 8
11 Will Saul come down, as thy servant has heard? 8
25 And when Saul heard that, he pursued after David 8
25: 4 David heard . . Nabal was shearing his sheep. 8
7 I hear that you have shearers; 8
24 and hear the words of your handmaid. 8
39 When David heard that Nabal was dead, he said 8
26:19 let my lord . . hear the words of his servant. 8
31:11 Ja'besh-gil'ead heard what the Philistines had 8
2Sm 3:28 Afterward, when David heard of it, he said 8
4: 1 Saul's son . . heard that Abner had died at Hebron 8
5:17 Philistines heard . . David had been anointed 8
17 David heard . . and went down to the stronghold. 8
24 when you hear the sound of marching in the tops 8
7:22 according to all . . we have heard with our ears. 8
8: 9 To'i . . heard that David had defeated the whole 8
10: 7 when David heard of it, he sent Jo'ab 8
11:26 the wife . . heard that Uri'ah her husband was dead 8
13:21 When King David heard of all these things 8
14:16 For the king will hear, and deliver his servant 8
15: 3 there is no man deputed by the king to hear you. 8
10 As soon as you hear the sound of the trumpet 8
35 whatever you hear . . tell it to Zadok 8
36 by them you shall send to me everything you hear. 8
16:21 all Israel will hear that you have made yourself 8
17: 5 Call Hushai . . and let us hear what he has to say. 8
9 when some . . fall.., whoever hears it will say 8
18: 5 all the people heard when the king gave orders 8
12 in our hearing the king commanded you 2
19: 2 the people heard that day, "The king is grieving 8
20:16 a wise woman called . . "Hear! Hear! Tell Jo'ab, 'Come 8
16 a wise woman called . . "Hear! Hear! Tell Jo'ab, 'Come 8
22: 7 From his temple he heard my voice, and my cry came 8
45 as soon as they heard of me, they obeyed me. 10
1Kg 1:11 Have you not heard that Adoni'jah . . has become 8
41 Adoni'jah and all . . with him heard it as they 8
41 when Jo'ab heard the sound of the trumpet, he said 8
45 an uproar. This is the noise that you have heard. 8
3:28 all Israel heard of the judgment which the king 8
4:34 men came . . to hear the wisdom of Solomon 8
34 kings of the earth, who had heard of his wisdom. 8
5: 1 when he heard that they had anointed him king 8
7 When Hiram heard the words of Solomon 8
8 I have heard the message which you have sent to me; 8
6: 7 axe nor any tool of iron was heard in the temple 8
8:30 hear thou in heaven thy dwelling place; 8
30 hearken . . and when thou hearest, forgive. 8
32 hear thou in heaven, and act, and judge 8
34 hear thou in heaven, and forgive the sin 8
36 hear thou in heaven, and forgive the sin 8
39 hear thou in heaven . . and forgive, and act 8
42 they shall hear of thy great name, and thy mighty 8
43 hear thou in heaven thy dwelling place 8
45 hear thou in heaven their prayer 8
49 hear thou in heaven . . and maintain their cause 8
9: 3 I have heard your prayer and your supplication 8
10: 1 the queen of Sheba heard of the fame of Solomon 8
6 The report was true which I heard in my own land 8
7 prosperity surpass the report which I heard. 8
8 who . . stand before you and hear your wisdom! 8
24 whole earth sought . . Solomon to hear his wisdom 8
11:21 Hadad heard . . that David slept with his fathers 8
12: 2 when Jerobo'am the son of Nebat heard of it 8
20 when all Israel heard that Jerobo'am had returned 8
13: 4 when the king heard the saying of the man of God 8
26 when the prophet . . heard of it, he said 8
14: 6 when Ahi'jah heard the sound of her feet 8
15:21 when Ba'asha heard of it, he stopped building 8
16:16 the troops . . heard it said, "Zimri has conspired 8
19:13 when Eli'jah heard it, he wrapped his face in his 8
20:12 When Ben-ha'dad heard this message . . he said 8
31 we have heard that the kings . . are merciful 8
21:15 As soon as Jez'ebel heard . . Jea'ebel said to Ahab 8
16 as soon as Ahab heard . . Ahab arose to go down 8
27 when Ahab heard those words, he rent his clothes 8
22:19 Therefore hear the word of the LORD: I saw the LORD 8
28 And he said, "Hear, all you peoples! 8
2Kg 3:21 the Moabites heard that the kings had come up 8
5: 8 Eli'sha . . heard that the king of Israel had rent 8
6:30 When the king heard . . he rent his clothes 8
7: 1 Hear the word of the LORD: thus says the LORD 8
10 there was no one to be seen or heard there, nothing *
9:30 When Jehu came to Jezreel, Jez'ebel heard of it; 8
11:13 Athali'ah heard the noise of the guard 8
18:26 do not speak . . within the hearing of the people 2
28 Hear the word of the great king 8
19: 1 When King Hezeki'ah heard it, he rent his clothes 8
4 the LORD . . heard all the words of the Rab'shakeh 8
4 the words which the LORD your God has heard; 8
6 be afraid because of the words . . you have heard 8
7 he shall hear a rumor and return to his own land; 8
8 for he heard that the king had left Lachish. 8
9 when the king heard concerning Tirha'kah king 8
11 you have heard what the kings . . have done to all 8
16 Incline thy ear, O LORD, and hear; open thy eyes 8
16 hear the words of Sennach'erib, which he has sent 8
20 Your prayer to me . . I have heard. 8
25 Have you not heard that I determined it long ago? 8
20: 5 I have heard your prayer, I have seen your tears; 8
12 for he heard that Hezeki'ah had been sick. 8
16 Isaiah said to Hezeki'ah, "Hear the word of the LORD 8
21:12 the ears of every one who hears of it will tingle. 8
22:11 the king heard the words of the book of the law 8
18 Regarding the words which you have heard 8
19 you heard how I spoke against this place 8
19 because your heart was . . I also have heard you 8
23: 2 he read in their hearing all the words of the book 2
25:23 heard that the king of Babylon had appointed 8

1Ch 10:11 heard all that the Philistines had done to Saul 8
14: 8 Philistines heard that David had been anointed 8
8 David heard of it and went out against them. 8
15 when you hear the sound of marching 8
17:20 all that we have heard with our ears. 8
18: 9 To'u king of Hamath heard that David had defeated 8
19: 8 When David heard of it, he sent Jo'ab 8
28: 2 and said: "Hear me, my brethren and my people. 8
8 and in the hearing of our God 2
2Ch 6:21 yea, hear thou from heaven thy dwelling place; 8
21 hear thou . . and when thou hearest, forgive. 8
23 then hear thou from heaven, and act, and judge 8
25 hear thou . . and forgive the sin of thy people 8
27 then hear thou in heaven, and forgive the sin 8
30 then hear thou from heaven thy dwelling place 8
33 hear thou from heaven . . and do according to all 8
35 then hear thou from heaven their prayer 8
39 then hear thou from heaven their prayer 8
7:12 I have heard your prayer, and have chosen this 8
14 then I will hear from heaven, and will forgive 8
9: 1 the queen of Sheba heard of the fame of Solomon 8
5 The report was true which I heard in my own land 8
6 you surpass the report which I heard. 8
7 servants, who continually . . hear your wisdom! 8
23 sought . . Solomon to hear his wisdom 8
10: 2 when Jerobo'am the son of Nebat heard of it 8
13: 4 Abi'jah . . said, "Hear me, O Jerobo'am and all Israel! 8
15: 2 Hear me, Asa, and all Judah and Benjamin 8
8 When Asa heard these words . . he took courage 8
16: 5 when Ba'asha heard of it 8
18:18 Micai'ah said, "Therefore hear the word of the LORD 8
27 Micai'ah . . said, "Hear, all you peoples! 8
20: 9 cry to thee . . and thou wilt hear and save.' 8
20 Hear me, Judah and inhabitants of Jerusalem! 8
29 when they heard that the LORD had fought against 8
23:12 When Athali'ah heard the noise of the people 8
28:11 Now hear me, and send back the captives 8
29: 5 Hear me, Levites! Now sanctify yourselves 8
30:20 the LORD heard Hezeki'ah, and healed the people. 8
27 their voice was heard 8
33:13 God . . heard his supplication and brought him 8
34:19 When the king heard the words of the law 8
26 Regarding the words which you have heard 8
27 humbled yourself . . when you heard his words 8
27 I also have heard you, says the LORD 8
30 read in their hearing all the words of the book 2
Ezr 3:13 with a great shout, and the sound was heard afar. 8
4: 1 adversaries . . heard that the returned exiles 8
9: 3 When I heard this, I rent my garments and my mantle 8
Neh 1: 4 When I heard these words I sat down and wept 8
6 to hear the prayer of thy servant which I now pray 8
2:10 when Sanbal'lat . . and Tobi'ah . . , heard this 8
19 when Sanbal'lat . . and Geshem the Arab heard 8
4: 1 Sanbal'lat heard that we were building the wall 8
4 Hear, O our God, for we are despised; 8
7 when Sanbal'lat . . heard that the repairing 8
15 When our enemies heard that it was known to us 8
20 place where you hear the sound of the trumpet 8
5: 6 I was very angry when I heard their outcry 8
6:16 when all our enemies heard of it, all the nations 8
8: 2 men . . and all who could hear with understanding 8
9 people wept when they heard the words of the law. 8
9: 9 thou didst . . hear their cry at the Red Sea 8
27 cried . . and thou didst hear them from heaven; 8
28 cried to thee thou didst hear from heaven 8
12:43 joy of Jerusalem was heard afar off. 8
13: 1 book of Moses in the hearing of the people; 2
3 When the people heard the law, they separated 8
Est 1:18 ladies . . who have heard of the queen's behavior 8
Job 2:11 when Job's three friends heard of all this evil 8
3: 7 let no joyful cry be heard in it. 3
18 they hear not the voice of the taskmaster. 8
4:16 there was silence, then I heard a voice 8
5:27 it is true. Hear, and know it for your good. 8
13: 1 my ear has heard and understood it. 8
6 Hear now my reasoning 8
15:17 I will show you, hear me; 8
16: 2 I have heard many such things; 8
20: 3 I hear censure which insults me 8
22:27 You will make your prayer to him, and he will hear 8
26:14 how small a whisper do we hear of him! 8
27: 9 Will God hear his cry, when trouble comes upon him? 8
28:22 Abaddon and Death say, 'We have heard a rumor of it 8
29:11 When the ear heard, it called me blessed 8
31:35 Oh, that I had one to hear me! 8
33: 1 now, hear my speech, O Job, and listen 8
8 Surely, you have spoken in my hearing 2
8 I have heard the sound of your words. 8
34: 2 Hear my words, you wise men 8
10 Therefore, hear me, you men of understanding 8
16 If you have understanding, hear this; 8
28 he heard the cry of the afflicted– 8
34 the wise man who hears me will say 8
35:13 Surely God does not hear an empty cry 8
37: 4 the lightnings when his voice is heard. 8
14 Hear this, O Job; stop and consider the wondrous 1
39: 7 he hears not the shouts of the driver. 8
42: 4 'Hear, and I will speak; I will question you 8
5 I had heard of thee by the hearing of the ear 8

5 I had heard of thee by the hearing of the ear 9
Ps 4: 1 Be gracious to me, and hear my prayer. 8
3 the LORD hears when I call to him. 8
5: 3 O LORD, in the morning thou dost hear my voice; 8
6: 8 for the LORD has heard the sound of my weeping. 8
9 The LORD has heard my supplication; 8
10:17 O LORD, thou wilt hear the desire of the meek; 8
17: 1 Hear a just cause, O LORD; attend to my cry! 8
6 O God; incline thy ear to me, hear my words. 8
18: 6 From his temple he heard my voice, and my cry to him 8
44 As soon as they heard of me they obeyed me; 9
19: 3 nor are there words; their voice is not heard; 8
22:24 but has heard, when he cried to him. 8
27: 7 Hear, O LORD, when I cry aloud, be gracious to me 8
28: 2 Hear the voice of my supplication, as I cry to thee 8
6 for he has heard the voice of my supplications. 8
30:10 Hear, O LORD, and be gracious to me! 8
31:13 Yea, I hear the whispering of many– 8
22 But thou didst hear my supplications 8
34: 2 let the afflicted hear and be glad. 8
6 This poor man cried, and the LORD heard him 8
17 When the righteous cry for help, the LORD hears 8
38:13 I am like a deaf man, I do not hear 8
14 Yea, I am like a man who does not hear 8
39:12 Hear my prayer, O LORD, and give ear to my cry; 8
40: 1 the LORD; he inclined to me and heard my cry. 8
44: 1 We have heard with our ears, O God 8
45:10 Hear, O daughter, consider, and incline your ear; 8
48: 8 As we have heard, so have we seen in the city 8
49: 1 Hear this, all peoples! Give ear, all inhabitants 8
50: 7 Hear, O my people, and I will speak 8
54: 2 Hear my prayer, O God; 8
55:17 my complaint and moan, and he will hear my voice. 8
58: 5 so that it does not hear the voice of charmers 8
59: 7 for "Who," they think, "will hear us? 8
61: 1 Hear my cry, O God, listen to my prayer; 8
5 For thou, O God, hast heard my vows 8
62:11 Once God has spoken; twice have I heard this 8
64: 1 Hear my voice, O God, in my complaint; 8
65: 2 O thou who hearest prayer! 8
66: 8 O peoples, let the sound of his praise be heard 8
16 Come and hear, all you who fear God 8
69:33 For the LORD hears the needy, and does not despise 8
77: 1 I cry aloud to God, aloud to God, that he may hear me. 1
78: 3 things that we have heard and known 8
21 when the LORD heard, he was full of wrath; 8
59 When God heard, he was full of wrath 8
81: 5 I hear a voice I had not known 8
8 Hear, O my people, while I admonish you! 8
84: 8 O LORD God of hosts, hear my prayer; 8
85: 8 Let me hear what God the LORD will speak 8
92:11 ears have heard the doom of my evil assailants. 8
94: 9 He who planted the ear, does he not hear? 8
97: 8 Zion hears and is glad, and the daughters of Judah 8
102: 1 Hear my prayer, O LORD; let my cry come to thee! 8
20 to hear the groans of the prisoners 8
106:44 regarded their distress, when he heard their cry. 8
115: 6 have ears, but do not hear; noses, but do not smell. 8
116: 1 has heard my voice and my supplications. 8
119:149 Hear my voice in thy steadfast love; 8
130: 2 Lord, hear my voice! Let thy ears be attentive 8
132: 6 heard of it in Eph'rathah, we found it in the fields 8
135:17 they have ears, but they hear not 1
138: 4 for they have heard the words of thy mouth; 8
143: 1 Hear my prayer, O LORD; give ear 8
8 Let me hear in the morning of thy steadfast love 8
145:19 all who fear him, he also hears their cry, and saves 8
Prv 1: 5 wise man also may hear and increase in learning 8
8 Hear, my son, your father's instruction 8
4: 1 Hear, O sons, a father's instruction 8
10 Hear, my son, and accept my words 8
8: 6 Hear, for I will speak noble things 8
33 Hear instruction and be wise, and do not neglect 8
13: 1 A wise son hears his father's instruction •
15:29 but he hears the prayer of the righteous. 8
18:13 If one gives answer before he hears 8
19:27 Cease, my son, to hear instructions only to stray 8
20:12 hearing ear and the seeing eye, the LORD has made 8
21:13 himself cry out and not be heard. 5
28 but the word of a man who hears will endure. 8
22:17 Incline your ear, and hear the words of the wise 8
23: 9 Do not speak in the hearing of a fool 2
19 Hear, my son, and be wise, and direct your mind 8
25:10 lest he who hears you bring shame upon you 8
28: 9 If one turns away his ear from hearing the law 8
29:24 hears the curse, but discloses nothing. 8
Ecc 1: 8 the eye is not . . nor the ear filled with hearing. 8
7: 5 better for a man to hear the rebuke of the wise 8
5 hear the rebuke . . than to hear the song of fools. 8
21 lest you hear your servant cursing you; 8
9:17 words of the wise heard in quiet are better 8
12:13 The end of the matter; all has been heard. 8
Sng 2:12 the voice of the turtledove is heard in our land. 8
14 let me see your face, let me hear your voice 8
8:13 are listening for your voice; let me hear it. 8
Isa 1: 2 Hear, O heavens, and give ear, O earth; 8
10 Hear the word of the LORD, you rulers of Sodom! 8
5: 9 The LORD of hosts has sworn in my hearing 2
6: 8 I heard the voice of the Lord saying, "Whom shall I 8

9 Hear and hear, but do not understand; 8
9 Hear and hear, but do not understand; 8
10 lest they see . . and hear with their ears 8
7:13 he said, "Hear then, O house of David! 8
11: 3 what his eyes see, or decide by what his ears hear; 4
15: 4 cry out, their voice is heard as far as Jahaz; 8
16: 6 have heard of the pride of Moab, how proud he was; 8
18: 3 a signal . . look! When a trumpet is blown, hear! 8
21: 3 I am bowed down so that I cannot hear 8
10 what I have heard from the LORD of hosts 8
24:16 From the ends of the earth we hear songs of praise 8
28:12 and this is repose"; yet they would not hear. 8
14 Therefore hear the word of the LORD, you scoffers 8
22 for I have heard a decree of destruction 8
23 Give ear, and hear my voice; 8
23 hear my voice; hearken, and hear my speech. 8
29:18 In that day the deaf shall hear the words of a book 8
30: 9 who will not hear the instruction of the LORD; 8
19 of your cry; when he hears it, he will answer you. 8
21 your ears shall hear a word behind you 8
32: 3 and the ears of those who hear will hearken. 8
9 Rise up, you women who are at ease, hear my voice; 8
33:13 Hear, you who are far off, what I have done; 8
15 who stops his ears from hearing of bloodshed 8
34: 1 Draw near, O nations, to hear, and hearken 8
36:11 within the hearing of the people . . on the wall. 2
13 Hear the words of the great king 8
37: 1 When King Hezeki'ah heard it, he rent his clothes 8
4 may be . . God heard the words of the Rab'shakeh 8
4 words which the LORD your God has heard; 8
6 afraid because of the words that you have heard 8
7 put a spirit in him, so that he shall hear a rumor 8
8 for he had heard that the king had left Lachish. 8
9 Now the king heard concerning Tirha'kah king 8
9 when he heard it, he sent messengers to Hezeki'ah 8
11 Behold, you have heard what the kings of Assyria 8
17 Incline thy ear, O LORD, and hear; 8
17 hear all the words of Sennach'erib 8
26 Have you not heard that I determined it long ago? 8
38: 5 I have heard your prayer, I have seen your tears; 8
39: 1 he heard that he had been sick and had recovered. 8
5 Isaiah said to Hezeki'ah, "Hear the word of the LORD 8
40:21 Have you not known? Have you not heard? 8
28 Have you not known? Have you not heard? 8
41:26 none who proclaimed, none who heard your words. 8
42:18 Hear, you deaf; and look, you blind, that you may see! 8
20 his ears are open, but he does not hear. 8
43: 9 and let them hear and say, It is true. 8
44: 1 But now hear, O Jacob my servant 8
47: 8 Now therefore hear this, you lover of pleasures 8
48: 1 Hear this, O house of Jacob, who are called 8
6 You have heard; now see all this; 8
7 before today you have never heard of them 8
8 You have never heard, you have never known 8
14 Assemble, all of you, and hear! 8
16 Draw near to me, hear this: from the beginning 8
50: 4 he wakens my ear to hear as those who are taught. 8
51:21 Therefore hear this, you who are afflicted 8
52:15 that which they have not heard they shall 8
53: 1 Who has believed what we have heard? 7
55: 3 come to me; hear, that your soul may live; 8
59: 1 cannot save, or his ear dull, that it cannot hear; 8
2 hid his face from you so that he does not hear. 8
60:18 Violence shall no more be heard in your land 8
64: 4 of old no one has heard or perceived by the ear 8
65:19 no more shall be heard in it the sound of weeping 8
24 while they are yet speaking I will hear. 8
66: 5 Hear the word of the LORD, 8
8 Who has heard such a thing? 8
19 that have not heard my fame or seen my glory; 8
Jer 2: 2 Go and proclaim in the hearing of Jerusalem 2
4 Hear the word of the LORD, O house of Jacob 8
3:21 A voice on the bare heights is heard 8
4:19 I hear the sound of the trumpet, the alarm of war. 8
21 I see . . and hear the sound of the trumpet? 8
31 For I heard a cry as of a woman in travail 8
5:21 Hear this, O foolish and senseless people 8
21 have eyes, but see not, who have ears, but hear not. 8
6: 7 violence and destruction are heard within her; 8
10 To whom . . give warning, that they may hear? 8
18 hear, O nations, and know, O congregation 8
19 Hear, O earth; behold, I am bringing evil 8
24 We have heard the report of it 8
7: 2 and say, Hear the word of the LORD 8
16 and do not intercede with me, for I do not hear you. 8
8:16 The snorting of their horses is heard from Dan; 8
9:10 and the lowing of cattle is not heard; 8
19 For a sound of wailing is heard from Zion 8
20 Hear, O women, the word of the LORD 8
10: 1 Hear the word which the LORD speaks to you 8
11: 2 Hear the words of this covenant 8
6 Hear the words of this covenant and do them. 8
10 their forefathers, who refused to hear my words; 8
13:10 This evil people, who refuse to hear my words 8
15 Hear and give ear; be not proud 8
14:12 Though they fast, I will not hear their cry 8
17:20 say: 'Hear the word of the LORD, you kings of Judah 8
23 stiffened their neck, that they might not hear 8
18: 2 and there I will let you hear my words. 8

13 among the nations, who has heard the like of this? 8
22 May a cry be heard from their houses 8
19: 3 You shall say, 'Hear the word of the LORD 8
3 the ears of every one who hears of it will tingle. 8
15 stiffened their neck, refusing to hear my words. 8
20: 1 heard Jeremiah prophesying these things. 8
10 I hear many whispering. Terror is on every side! 8
16 let him hear a cry in the morning 8
21:11 to . . Judah say, 'Hear the word of the LORD 8
22: 2 and say, 'Hear the word of the LORD, O King of Judah 8
29 O land, land, land, hear the word of the LORD! 8
23:18 of the LORD to perceive and to hear his word 8
25 I have heard what the prophets have said 8
25: 4 neither listened nor inclined your ears to hear 8
26: 7 the people heard Jeremiah speaking these words 8
10 When the princes of Judah heard these things 8
11 as you have heard with your own ears. 8
12 to prophesy . . all the words you have heard. 8
21 his warriors and all the princes, heard his words 8
21 but when Uri'ah heard of it, he was afraid and fled 8
28: 7 Yet hear now this word which I speak 8
7 hear now this word which I speak in your hearing 2
7 and in the hearing of all the people. 2
29:12 come and pray to me, and I will hear you. 8
20 Hear the word of the LORD, all you exiles 8
29 read this letter in the hearing of Jeremiah 2
30: 5 Thus says the LORD: We have heard a cry of panic 8
31:10 Hear the word of the LORD, O nations, and declare it 8
15 Thus says the LORD: "A voice is heard in Ramah 8
18 I have heard E'phraim bemoaning 8
33: 9 who shall hear of all the good that I do for them; 8
10 there shall be heard again 8
34: 4 Yet hear the word of the LORD, O Zedeki'ah 8
36: 3 It may be that the house of Judah will hear 8
6 and on a fast day in the hearing of all the people 2
6 shall read them also in the hearing of all the men 2
10 Then, in the hearing of all the people, Baruch read 2
11 heard all the words of the LORD from the scroll 8
13 Micai'ah told them all the words that he had heard 8
13 read the scroll in the hearing of the people. 2
14 scroll that you read in the hearing of the people 2
16 When they heard all the words, they turned 8
24 nor any of his servants who heard all these words 8
31 but they would not hear. 8
37: 5 who were besieging Jerusalem heard news of them 8
20 Now hear, I pray you, O my lord the king 8
38: 1 and Pashhur the son of Malchi'ah heard the words 8
7 When E'bed-mel'ech the Ethiopian . . heard that 8
25 If the princes hear that I have spoken with you 8
40: 7 men heard that the king of Babylon had appointed 8
11 heard that the king of Babylon had left a remnant 8
41:11 and all the leaders of the forces with him heard 8
42: 4 Jeremiah the prophet said to them, "I have heard 8
14 shall not see war, or hear the sound of the trumpet 8
15 then hear the word of the LORD, O remnant of Judah. 8
44:24 Hear the word of the LORD, all you of Judah 8
26 Therefore hear the word of the LORD 8
46:12 The nations have heard of your shame 8
48: 4 Moab is destroyed; a cry is heard as far as Zo'ar. 8
5 they have heard the cry of destruction. 8
29 have heard of the pride of Moab–he is very proud 8
49:14 I have heard tidings from the LORD 8
20 Therefore hear the plan which the LORD has made 8
21 their cry shall be heard at the Red Sea. 8
23 confounded, for they have heard evil tidings; 8
50:43 The king of Babylon heard the report of them 8
45 Therefore hear the plan which the LORD has made 8
46 and her cry shall be heard among the nations. 8
51:46 be not fearful at the report heard in the land 8
51 We are put to shame, for we have heard reproach; 8
Lam 1:18 but hear, all you peoples, and behold my suffering; 8
21 Hear how I groan; there is none to comfort me. 8
21 All my enemies have heard of my trouble; 8
3:56 thou didst hear my plea, 'Do not close thine ear 8
61 Thou hast heard their taunts, O LORD 8
Ezk 1:24 when they went, I heard the sound of their wings 8
28 and I heard the voice of one speaking. 8
2: 2 and I heard him speaking to me. 8
5 whether they hear or refuse to hear 8
5 whether they hear or refuse to hear •
7 speak . . whether they hear or refuse to hear; 8
7 speak . . whether they hear or refuse to hear; •
8 But you, son of man, hear what I say to you; 8
3:10 receive in your heart, and hear with your ears. 8
11 whether they hear or refuse to hear. 8
11 whether they hear or refuse to hear. •
12 I heard behind me the sound of a great earthquake; 8
17 whenever you hear a word from my mouth 8
27 he that will hear, let him hear; 8
27 he that will hear, let him hear; 8
27 and he that will refuse to hear, let him refuse; •
6: 3 You mountains of Israel, hear the word of the Lord 8
8:18 though they cry . . I will not hear them. 8
9: 5 to the others he said in my hearing, "Pass through 2
10: 5 the cherubim was heard as far as the outer court 8
13 were called in my hearing the whirling wheels. 2
12: 2 who have ears to hear, but hear not; 8
2 who have ears to hear, but hear not; 8
13: 2 prophesy and say . . 'Hear the word of the LORD!' 8
16:35 Wherefore, O harlot, hear the word of the LORD 8
18:25 Hear now, O house of Israel: Is my way not just? 8
19: 9 no more be heard upon the mountains of Israel. 8
20:47 Hear the word of the LORD: Thus says the Lord GOD 8
25: 3 Say to the Ammonites, Hear the word of the Lord GOD 8
26:13 the sound of your lyres shall be heard no more. 8
33: 4 then if any one who hears the sound of the trumpet 8
5 He heard the sound of the trumpet 8
7 whenever you hear a word from my mouth 8
30 Come, and hear what the word is that comes forth 8
31 they hear what you say but they will not do it; 8
32 for they hear what you say, but they will not do it. 8
34: 7 you shepherds, hear the word of the LORD 8
9 you shepherds, hear the word of the LORD 8
35:12 And you shall know that I, the LORD, have heard all 8
13 and multiplied your words against me; I heard it. 8
36: 1 O mountains of Israel, hear the word of the LORD. 8
4 O mountains of Israel, hear the word of the Lord 8
15 I will not let you hear any more the reproach 8
37: 4 say to them, O dry bones, hear the word of the LORD. 8
40: 4 look with your eyes, and hear with your ears, 8
43: 6 I heard one speaking to me out of the temple; 8
44: 5 see with your eyes, and hear with your ears 8
Dan 3: 5 hear the sound of the horn, pipe, lyre, trigon 11
7 Therefore, as soon as all the peoples heard 11
10 made a decree, that every man who hears the sound 11
15 hear the sound of the horn, pipe, lyre, trigon 11
5:14 heard of you that the spirit of the holy gods 11
16 heard that you can give interpretations 11
23 gods . . which do not see or hear or know 11
6:14 Then the king, when he heard these words, 11
8:13 Then I heard a holy one speaking; 8
16 I heard a man's voice between the banks of the U'lai 8
9:18 O my God, incline thy ear and hear; open thy eyes 8
19 O LORD, hear; O LORD, forgive; 8
10: 9 Then I heard the sound of his words; 8
9 when I heard the sound of his words, I fell 8
12 from the first day . . your words have been heard 8
12: 7 heard him swear by him who lives for ever 8
8 I heard, but I did not understand. 8
Hos 4: 1 Hear the word of the LORD, O people of Israel; 8
5: 1 Hear this, O priests! Give heed, O house of Israel! 8
Jol 1: 2 Hear this, you aged men 8
Ams 3: 1 Hear this word that the LORD has spoken against 8
13 Hear, and testify against the house of Jacob 8
4: 1 Hear this word, you cows of Bashan 8
5: 1 Hear this word which I take up over you 8
7:16 Now therefore hear the word of the LORD. 8
8: 4 Hear this, you who trample upon the needy 8
11 but of hearing the words of the LORD. 8
Obd 1: 1 We have heard tidings from the LORD 8
Jon 2: 2 of Sheol I cried, and thou didst hear my voice. 8
Mic 1: 2 Hear, you peoples, all of you; 8
3: 1 Hear, you heads of Jacob and rulers of the house 8
9 Hear this, you heads of the house of Jacob 8
6: 1 Hear what the LORD says: Arise, plead your case 8
1 and let the hills hear your voice. 8
2 Hear, you mountains, the controversy of the LORD 8
9 Hear, O tribe and assembly of the city! 8
7: 7 my God will hear me. 8
Nah 2:13 voice of your messengers shall no more be heard. 8
3:19 All who hear the news of you clap their hands 8
Hab 1: 2 how long shall I cry . . and thou wilt not hear? 8
3: 2 O LORD, I have heard the report of thee, and thy work 8
16 I hear, and my body trembles, my lips quiver 8
Zep 1:10 a cry will be heard from the Fish Gate 6
2: 8 I have heard the taunts of Moab 8
Zec 1: 4 But they did not hear or heed me, says the LORD. 8
3: 8 Hear now, O Joshua the high priest 8
7:11 stopped their ears that they might not hear. 8
12 lest they should hear the law and the words 8
13 As I called, and they would not hear, so they called 8
13 they called, and I would not hear," says the LORD 8
8: 9 who in these days have been hearing these words 8
23 for we have heard that God is with you. 8
Mal 3:16 the LORD heeded and heard them 8
Mat 2: 3 When Herod the king heard this, he was troubled 15
9 When they had heard the king they went their way; 15
18 A voice was heard in Ramah, wailing and loud 15
22 when he heard that Archela'us reigned over Judea 15
4:12 Now when he heard that John had been arrested 15
5:21 You have heard that it was said to the men of old 15
27 You have heard that it was said, 'You shall not 15
33 Again you have heard that it was said to the men 15
38 You have heard that it was said, 'An eye for an eye 15
43 You have heard that it was said, 'You shall love 15
6: 7 that they will be heard for their many words. 21
7:24 Every one then who hears these words of mine 15
26 And every one who hears these words of mine 15
8:10 When Jesus heard him, he marveled 15
9:12 But when he heard it, he said 15
10:27 what you hear whispered, proclaim 15
11: 2 when John heard in prison about the deeds 15
4 Go and tell John what you hear and see 15
5 lame walk, lepers are cleansed and the deaf hear 15
15 He who has ears to hear, let him hear. 15
15 He who has ears to hear, let him hear. 15
12:19 nor will any one hear his voice in the streets; 15
24 when the Pharisees heard it they said 15
42 to hear the wisdom of Solomon 15
13: 9 He who has ears, let him hear. 15
13 and hearing they do not hear 15
13 hearing they do not hear, nor do they understand. 15
14 You shall indeed hear but never understand 15
15 and their ears are heavy of hearing 15
15 and hear with their ears 15
16 and your ears, for they hear. 15
17 and to hear what you hear, and did not hear it. 15
17 and to hear what you hear, and did not hear it. 15
17 and to hear what you hear, and did not hear it. 15
18 Hear then the parable of the sower. 15
19 When any one hears the word of the kingdom 15
20 this is he who hears the word 15
22 this is he who hears the word 15
23 this is he who hears the word 15
43 He who has ears, let him hear. 15
14: 1 At that time Herod the tetrarch heard 15
13 when Jesus heard this, he withdrew from there 15
13 But when the crowds heard it 15
15:10 Hear and understand 15
12 when they heard this saying? 15
17: 6 When the disciples heard this 15
19:22 When the young man heard this he went away 15
25 When the disciples heard this 15
20:24 when the ten heard it 15
30 when they heard that Jesus was passing by 15
21:16 they said to him, "Do you hear what these are saying? 15
33 Hear another parable 15
45 priests and the Pharisees heard his parables 15
22:22 When they heard it, they marveled 15
33 when the crowd heard it 15
34 when the Pharisees heard 15
24: 6 you will hear of wars and rumors of wars 15
26:65 You have now heard his blasphemy. 15
27:13 hear how many things they testify against you? 15
47 some of the bystanders hearing it said 15
Mrk 2:17 when Jesus heard it, he said to them 15
3: 8 a great multitude, hearing all that he did, came 15
21 when his family heard it 15
4: 9 he said, "He who has ears to hear, let him hear. 15
9 he said, "He who has ears to hear, let him hear. 15
12 and may indeed hear but not understand 15
15 when they hear, Satan immediately comes 15
16 who, when they hear the word, immediately receive 15
18 they are those who hear the word 15
20 the ones who hear the word and accept it 15
23 If any man has ears to hear, let him hear. 15
23 If any man has ears to hear, let him hear. 15
24 he said to them, "Take heed what you hear 15
33 as they were able to hear it; 15
5:27 She had heard the reports about Jesus 15
6: 2 many who heard him were astonished, saying 15
11 they refuse to hear you 15
14 King Herod heard of it; 15
16 when Herod heard of it he said 15
20 When he heard him, he was much perplexed 15
20 yet he heard him gladly. 15
29 When his disciples heard of it 15
55 to any place where they heard he was. 15
7:14 Hear me, all of you, and understand 15
25 heard of him, and came and fell down at his feet. 15
37 he even makes the deaf hear and the dumb speak. 15
8:18 having ears do you not hear 15
10:41 when the ten heard it, they began to be indignant 15
47 when he heard that it was Jesus of Nazareth 15
11:14 his disciples heard it. 15
18 the chief priests and the scribes heard it 15
12:28 heard them disputing with one another 15
29 Jesus answered, "The first is, 'Hear, O Israel 15
37 the great throng heard him gladly. 15
13: 7 when you hear of wars and rumors of wars 15
14:11 when they heard it they were glad 15
58 We heard him say, 'I will destroy this temple 15
64 You have heard his blasphemy. 15
15:35 some of the bystanders hearing it said, "Behold 15
16:11 when they heard that he was alive 15
Lke 1:13 for your prayer is heard 21
41 when Elizabeth heard the greeting of Mary 15
58 her neighbors and kinsfolk heard 15
66 all who heard them laid them up in their hearts 15
2:18 all who heard it wondered 15
20 for all they had heard and seen 15
47 all who heard him were amazed 15
4:21 scripture has been fulfilled in your hearing. 26
23 what we have heard you did at Caper'na-um, do here 15
28 When they heard this 15
5: 1 people pressed upon him to hear the word of God 15
15 great multitudes gathered to hear 15
6:17 who came to hear him 15
27 I say to you that hear, Love your enemies 15
47 who comes to me and hears my words and does them 15
49 he who hears and does not do them 15
7: 1 all his sayings in the hearing of the people 12
3 When he heard of Jesus 15
9 When Jesus heard this he marveled at him 15
22 Go and tell John what you have seen and heard 15
22 lepers are cleansed, and the deaf hear 15
29 (When they heard this 15

8: 8 He who has ears to hear, let him hear. 15
8 He who has ears to hear, let him hear. 15
10 hearing they may not understand. 15
12 The ones along the path are those who have heard; 15
13 who, when they hear the word, receive it with joy 15
14 they are those who hear 15
15 they are those who, hearing the word, hold it fast 15
18 Take heed then how you hear 15
21 those who hear the word of God and do it. 15
50 Jesus on hearing this answered him, "Do not fear; 15
9: 7 Now Herod the tetrarch heard of all that was done 15
9 who is this about whom I hear such things? 15
10:16 He who hears you hears me 15
16 He who hears you hears me 15
24 and to hear what you hear, and did not hear it. 15
24 and to hear what you hear, and did not hear it. 15
24 and to hear what you hear, and did not hear it. 15
11:28 Blessed rather are those who hear the word of God 15
31 to hear the wisdom of Solomon 15
12: 3 have said in the dark shall be heard in the light 15
14:15 When one of those who sat at table with him heard 15
35 He who has ears to hear, let him hear. 15
35 He who has ears to hear, let him hear. 15
15: 1 sinners were all drawing near to hear him. 15
25 he heard music and dancing. 15
16: 2 What is this that I hear about you? 15
14 The Pharisees, who were lovers of money, heard all 15
29 let them hear them.' 15
31 If they do not hear Moses and the prophets 15
18: 6 Hear what the unrighteous judge says. 15
22 when Jesus heard it, he said to him, "One thing 15
23 when he heard this he became sad 15
26 Those who heard it said, "Then who can be saved? 15
36 hearing a multitude going by 15
19:11 As they heard these things 15
20:16 When they heard this, they said, "God forbid! 15
45 in the hearing of all the people 15
21: 9 when you hear of wars and tumults 15
38 came to him in the temple to hear him. 15
22:71 We have heard it ourselves from his own lips. 15
23: 6 When Pilate heard this 15
8 desired to see him, because he had heard about him 15
Joh 1:37 The two disciples heard him say this 15
40 One of the two who heard John speak . . was Andrew 15
3: 8 The wind blows . . and you hear the sound of it 15
29 the friend . . who stands and hears him, rejoices 15
32 He bears witness to what he has seen and heard 15
4: 1 when the Lord knew that the Pharisees had heard 15
42 for we have heard for ourselves 15
47 heard that Jesus had come from Judea to Galilee 15
5:24 he who hears my word and believes him who sent me 15
25 when the dead will hear the voice of the Son of God 15
25 those who hear will live. 15
28 all who are in the tombs will hear his voice. 15
30 as I hear, I judge; and my judgment is just 15
37 His voice you have never heard 15
6:45 Every one who has heard and learned 15
60 Many of his disciples, when they heard it, said 15
7:32 The Pharisees heard the crowd thus muttering 15
40 When they heard these words 15
8: 9 when they heard it, they went away, one by one 15
26 I declare to the world what I have heard from him. 15
38 you do what you have heard from your father. 15
40 has told you the truth which I heard from God 15
43 It is because you cannot bear to hear my word. 15
47 He who is of God hears the words of God 15
47 the reason why you do not hear them is 15
9:27 Why do you want to hear it again? 15
32 Never since the world began has it been heard 15
35 Jesus heard that they had cast him out 15
40 the Pharisees near him heard this, and they said 15
10: 3 the sheep hear his voice 15
27 My sheep hear my voice, and I know them 15
11: 4 when Jesus heard it he said 15
6 when he heard that he was ill 15
20 When Martha heard that Jesus was coming 15
29 when she heard it, she rose quickly and went 15
41 Father, I thank thee that thou hast heard me. 15
42 I knew that thou hearest me always 15
12:12 a great crowd who had come to the feast heard 15
18 they heard he had done this sign. 15
29 The crowd standing by heard it and said 15
34 crowd answered him, "We have heard from the law 15
47 If any one hears my sayings and does not keep them 15
14:24 the word which you hear is not mine 15
28 You heard me say to you, 'I go away 15
15:15 all that I have heard from my Father 15
16:13 whatever he hears he will speak 15
18:21 Ask those who have heard me, what I said to them; 15
37 Every one who is of the truth hears my voice. 15
19: 8 When Pilate heard these words 15
13 When Pilate heard these words 15
21: 7 When Simon Peter heard that it was the Lord 15
Act 1: 4 which, he said, "you heard from me 15
2: 6 each one heard them speaking in his own language. 15
8 how is it that we hear 15
11 we hear them telling in our own tongues 15
22 Men of Israel, hear these words 15
33 he has poured out this which you see and hear. 15
37 when they heard this they were cut to the heart 15
4: 4 many of those who heard the word believed 15
20 cannot but speak of what we have seen and heard. 15
24 when they heard it 15
5: 5 When Anani'as heard these words 15
5 great fear came upon all who heard of it. 15
11 upon all who heard of these things. 15
21 when they heard this 15
24 when . . the chief priests heard these words 15
33 When they heard this they were enraged 15
6:11 We have heard him speak blasphemous words 15
14 we have heard him say 15
7: 2 Stephen said: "Brethren and fathers, hear me. 15
12 when Jacob heard that there was grain in Egypt 15
34 heard their groaning 15
54 when they heard these things they were enraged 15
8: 6 when they heard him and saw the signs which he did. 15
14 Now when the apostles at Jerusalem heard 15
30 Philip ran to him, and heard him reading Isaiah 15
9: 4 he fell to the ground and heard a voice saying 15
7 hearing the voice but seeing no one. 15
13 I have heard from many about this man 15
21 all who heard him were amazed, and said 15
38 hearing that Peter was there 15
10:22 to hear what you have to say. 15
31 saying, 'Cornelius, your prayer has been heard 21
33 hear all that you have been commanded by the Lord 15
44 the Holy Spirit fell on all who heard the word. 15
46 For they heard them speaking in tongues 15
11: 1 heard that the Gentiles also had received 15
7 I heard a voice saying to me, 'Rise, Peter 15
18 When they heard this they were silenced 15
13: 7 sought to hear the word of God. 15
44 gathered together to hear the word of God. 15
48 when the Gentiles heard this, they were glad 15
14:14 when the apostles Barnabas and Paul heard of it 15
15: 7 the Gentiles should hear the word of the gospel 15
24 Since we have heard 15
16:14 One who heard us was a woman named Lydia 15
38 were afraid when they heard 15
17: 8 were disturbed when they heard this. 15
21 telling or hearing something new. 15
32 when they heard of the resurrection of the dead 15
32 others said, "We will hear you again about this. 15
18: 8 many of the Corinthians hearing Paul believed 15
26 when Priscilla and Aq'uila heard him 15
19: 2 never even heard that there is a Holy Spirit. 15
5 On hearing this, they were baptized 15
10 the residents of Asia heard the word of the Lord 15
26 you see and hear 15
28 When they heard this they were enraged 15
21:12 When we heard this 15
20 when they heard it, they glorified God 15
22 They will certainly hear that you have come. 15
22: 1 hear the defense which I now make before you. 15
2 when they heard 15
7 I fell to the ground and heard a voice saying to me 15
9 did not hear the voice of the one who was speaking 15
14 see the Just One and to hear a voice from his mouth; 15
15 a witness . . of what you have seen and heard. 15
26 When the centurion heard that 15
23:16 Now the son of Paul's sister heard of their ambush; 15
35 I will hear you when your accusers arrive. 20
24: 4 I beg you in your kindness to hear us briefly. 15
24 and heard him speak upon faith in Christ Jesus. 15
25:22 I should like to hear the man myself. 15
22 Tomorrow," said he, "you shall hear him. 15
26:14 heard a voice saying to me in the Hebrew language 15
29 not only you but also all who hear me this day 15
28:15 the brethren there, when they heard of us, came 15
22 we desire to hear from you what your views are 15
26 You shall indeed hear but never understand 15
27 their ears are heavy of hearing 15
27 hear with their ears 15
Rom 10:14 to believe in him of whom they have never heard? 15
14 And how are they to hear without a preacher? 15
16 Lord, who has believed what he has heard from us? 12
17 So faith comes from what is heard 12
17 what is heard comes by the preaching of Christ. 12
18 But I ask, have they not heard? Indeed they have; 15
11: 8 eyes . . not see and ears that should not hear 15
15:21 shall understand who have never heard of him. 15
1Co 2: 9 What no eye has seen, nor ear heard 15
11:18 I hear that there are divisions among you 15
12:17 where would be the hearing 12
2Co 12: 4 he heard things that cannot be told 15
6 he sees in me or hears from me. 15
Gal 1:13 For you have heard of my former life in Judaism 15
23 they only heard it said 15
3: 2 by works of the law, or by hearing with faith? 12
5 by works of the law, or by hearing with faith? 12
4:21 do you not hear the law? 15
Eph 1:13 you also, who have heard the word of truth 15
15 because I have heard of your faith in the Lord 15
3: 2 assuming that you have heard of the stewardship 15
4:21 assuming that you have heard about him 15
29 that it may impart grace to those who hear. 15
Php 1:27 I may hear of you that you stand firm in one spirit 15
30 which you saw and now hear to be mine. 15
2:26 distressed because you heard that he was ill. 15
4: 9 What you have learned and received and heard 15
Col 1: 4 we have heard of your faith in Christ Jesus 15
6 from the day you heard and understood 15
9 from the day we heard of it 15
23 the gospel which you heard 15
1Th 2:13 the word of God which you heard from us 12
2Th 3:11 we hear that some of you are living in idleness 15
2Ti 1:13 the sound words which you have heard from me 15
2: 2 what you have heard from me 15
4:17 all the Gentiles might hear it 15
Phm 1: 5 because I hear of your love 15
Heb 2: 1 pay the closer attention to what we have heard 15
3 it was attested to us by those who heard him 15
3: 7 Today, when you hear his voice 15
15 while it is said, "Today, when you hear his voice 15
16 Who were they that heard and yet were rebellious? 15
4: 2 the message which they heard did not benefit 12
7 Today, when you hear his voice 15
5: 7 he was heard for his godly fear. 21
11 since you have become dull of hearing. 12
Jas 1:19 Let every man be quick to hear, slow to speak 15
5:11 You have heard of the steadfastness of Job 15
2Pe 1:18 we heard this voice borne from heaven 15
2: 8 what that righteous man saw and heard 12
1Jn 1: 1 That . . from the beginning, which we have heard 15
3 that which we have seen and heard we proclaim 15
5 the message we have heard from him and proclaim 15
2: 7 old commandment is the word which you have heard 15
18 and as you have heard that antichrist is coming 15
24 Let what you heard from the beginning abide 15
24 what you heard from the beginning abides in you 15
3:11 message which you have heard from the beginning 15
4: 3 antichrist, of which you heard that it was coming 15
5:14 if we ask anything according to his will he hears 15
15 if we know that he hears us in whatever we ask 15
2Jn 1: 6 as you have heard from the beginning 15
3Jn 1: 4 to hear that my children follow the truth. 15
Rev 1: 3 and blessed are those who hear, and who keep 15
10 and I heard behind me a loud voice like a trumpet 15
2: 7 He who has an ear, let him hear what the Spirit says 15
11 He who has an ear, let him hear what the Spirit says 15
17 He who has an ear, let him hear what the Spirit says 15
29 He who has an ear, let him hear what the Spirit says 15
3: 3 Remember then what you received and heard; 15
6 He who has an ear, let him hear what the Spirit says 15
13 He who has an ear, let him hear what the Spirit says 15
20 if any one hears my voice and opens the door 15
22 He who has an ear, let him hear what the Spirit says 15
4: 1 the first voice, which I had heard speaking to me 15
5:11 Then I looked, and I heard around the throne 15
13 I heard every creature in heaven and on earth 15
6: 1 and I heard one of the four living creatures say 15
3 I heard the second living creature say, "Come! 15
5 I heard the third living creature say, "Come! 15
6 I heard what seemed to be a voice in the midst 15
7 I heard the voice of the fourth living creature 15
7: 4 I heard the number of the sealed 15
8:13 I heard an eagle crying with a loud voice 15
9:13 I heard a voice from the four horns of the . . altar 15
16 number of the troops . . I heard their number. 15
20 idols . . which cannot either see or hear or walk; 15
10: 4 I was about to write, but I heard a voice 15
8 voice which I had heard from heaven spoke to me 15
11:12 Then they heard a loud voice from heaven saying 15
12:10 And I heard a loud voice in heaven, saying 15
13: 9 If any one has an ear, let him hear 15
14: 2 I heard a voice from heaven 15
2 the voice I heard was like the sound of harpers 15
13 And I heard a voice from heaven saying, "Write this 15
16: 1 Then I heard a loud voice from the temple 15
5 And I heard the angel of water say 15
7 I heard the altar cry, "Yea, Lord God the Almighty 15
18: 4 Then I heard another voice from heaven saying 15
22 sound of harpers . . shall be heard in thee no more 15
22 the millstone shall be heard in thee no more; 15
23 the voice . . shall be heard in thee no more; 15
19: 1 After this I heard what seemed to be a loud voice 15
6 Then I heard what seemed to be the voice 15
21: 3 I heard a loud voice from the throne saying 15
22: 8 I John am he who heard and saw these things. 15
8 when I heard and saw them, I fell down to worship 15
17 And let him who hears say, "Come. 15
18 I warn every one who hears the words 15
1Es 5:65 that the people could not hear the trumpets 15
65 the sound was heard afar; 15
66 when the enemies of . . Judah . . heard it 15
8:71 As soon as I heard these things 15
9:40 for . . all the priests to hear the law 15
50 now they were all weeping as they heard the law- 15
2Es 1:35 who without having heard me will believe 27
2:34 I say to you, O nations that hear and understand 27
4:11 When I heard this, I fell on my face 28
5: 2 and beyond what you heard of formerly. 27
7 and all shall hear his voice. 27
13 you shall hear yet greater things than these. 27
19 He heard what I said and left me. 27
6:13 and you will hear a full, resounding voice. 27
17 When I heard this, I rose to my feet and listened 27

23 when all hear it 27
7:51 hear the explanation for this. 27
8:18 I have heard of the swiftness of the judgment 27
19 Therefore hear my voice, and understand my words 27
24 hear, O Lord, the prayer of thy servant 29
9:30 thou didst say, 'Hear me, O Israel 27
45 after 30 years God heard your handmaid 29
10:35 and I have heard what I do not understand. 27
56 you will hear as much as your ears can hear. 27
56 you will hear as much as your ears can hear. 27
11:16 Hear me, you who have ruled the earth all this time; 27
36 Then I heard a voice saying to me, "Look before you 27
37 I heard how he uttered a man's voice to the eagle 27
12:17 As for your hearing a voice that spoke 27
31 and as for all his words that you have heard 27
40 When all the people heard that the seven days 27
13: 4 all who heard his voice melted as wax melts 27
14 and hast deemed me worthy to have my prayer heard 30
33 when all the nations hear his voice 27
14: 8 the interpretations that you have heard; 27
28 Hear these words, O Israel 27
15:29 so that all who hear them fear and tremble. 27
16:27 to see another, or even to hear his voice. 27
40 Hear my words, O my people; prepare for battle 27
74 Hear, my elect," says the Lord. 27
Tob 3: 6 because I have heard false reproaches 15
10 When she heard these things 15
13 Command . . that I hear reproach no more. 15
15 command . . that I hear reproach no more. 15
16 The prayer of both was heard 21
6:13 I have heard that . . 15
17 When Tobias heard these things, he fell in love 15
7: 7 When he heard that Tobit had lost his sight 15
10:12 Let me hear a good report of you 15
14:15 he heard of the destruction of Nineveh 15
Jdt 4: 1 heard of everything . . Holofernes . . had done 15
13 the Lord heard their prayers 21
5: 1 When Holofernes . . heard 18
5 Let my lord now hear a word 15
7: 9 Let our lord hear a word 15
8: 1 At that time Judith heard about these things 15
9 When Judith heard the wicked words 15
9 when she heard all that Uzziah said to them 15
17 he will hear our voice, if it pleases him. 21
9: 4 O God, my God, hear me also, a widow. 21
12 Hear, O hear me, God of my father 25
12 Hear, O hear me, God of my father 25
12 King of all thy creation, hear my prayer! 21
10:14 When the men heard her words 15
11: 8 For we have heard of your wisdom and skill 15
9 we have heard his words 15
16 as many as shall hear about them. 15
13:12 When the men of her city heard her voice 15
14: 7 those who hear your name will be alarmed. 15
19 When the leaders of the Assyrian army heard this 15
15: 1 When the men in the tents heard it 15
5 when the Israelites heard it 15
AEs 13:17 Hear my prayer, and have mercy 22
14: 5 I have heard in the tribe of my family 15
19 hear the voice of the despairing 21
Wis 1:10 because a jealous ear hears all things 16
8:15 be afraid of me when they hear of me 15
11:13 when they heard 15
15:15 nor ears with which to hear 15
18: 1 Their enemies heard their voices 15
Sir 3: 5 when he prays he will be heard. 21
4: 6 his Creator will hear his prayer. 22
5:11 Be quick to hear, and be deliberate in answering. 17
11: 8 Do not answer before you have heard 15
16: 5 my ear has heard things more striking 15
17:13 their ears heard the glory of his voice. 15
19: 9 for some one has heard you and watched you 15
10 Have you heard a word? Let it die with you. 15
15 do not believe everything you hear. 23
21:15 when a reveler hears it, he dislikes it 15
15 When a man of understanding hears a wise saying 15
22:26 whoever hears of it will beware of him. 15
27: 7 Do not praise a man before you hear him reason *
15 their abuse is grievous to hear. 12
29:25 besides this you will hear bitter words 15
33: 4 Prepare what to say, and thus you will be heard; 15
18 Hear me, you who are great among the people 15
41:23 repeating and telling what you hear 12
43:24 we marvel at what we hear. 13
45: 9 to make their ringing heard in the temple 14
46:17 made his voice heard with a mighty sound; 14
48: 7 who heard rebuke at Sinai 15
20 the Holy One quickly heard them from heaven 22
50:16 heard for remembrance before the Most High. 14
51:11 My prayer was heard 21
Bar 1: 3 Baruch read the words of this book in the hearing 26
3 in the hearing of all the people who came to hear 26
3 of all the people who came to hear the book *
4 in the hearing of the mighty men and the princes 26
4 and in the hearing of the elders 26
4 in the hearing of all the people, small and great 26
2:14 Hear, O Lord, our prayer and our supplication 21
16 Incline thy ear, O Lord, and hear; 15
31 give them a heart that obeys and ears that hear; 15
3: 2 Hear, O Lord, and have mercy, for we have sinned 15
4 O Lord Almighty, God of Israel, hear now the prayer 15
9 Hear the commandments of life, O Israel; give ear 15
22 She has not been heard of in Canaan, nor seen 15
Sus 1:26 When the household servants heard the shouting 15
44 The Lord heard her cry. 21
Bel 1:28 When the Babylonians heard it 15
1Mc 3:13 Seron, the commander of the Syrian army, heard 15
27 When king Antiochus heard these reports 15
41 traders of the region heard what was said to them 15
4: 3 Judas heard of it 15
27 When he heard it 15
5: 1 When the Gentiles round about heard 15
16 When Judas and the people heard these messages 15
56 Joseph . . heard of their brave deeds 15
63 wherever their name was heard. 15
6: 1 when he heard 15
8 When the king heard this news, he was astounded 15
28 The king was enraged when he heard this 15
41 All who heard the noise made by their multitude 15
55 Then Lysias heard 15
8: 1 Now Judas heard of the fame of the Romans 15
12 as many as have heard of their fame 15
9: 1 When Demetrius heard 15
33 his brother and all who were with him heard of it 19
43 When Bacchides heard of this 15
10: 2 When Demetrius the king heard of it 15
7 read the letter in the hearing of all the people 26
8 They were greatly alarmed when they heard 15
15 Now Alexander the king heard of all the promises 15
19 We have heard about you 15
22 When Demetrius heard of these things 15
26 we have heard of it and rejoiced. 15
46 When Jonathan and the people heard these words 15
68 When Alexander the king heard of it 15
74 When Jonathan heard the words of Apollonius 15
77 When Apollonius heard of it 15
88 When Alexander the king heard of these things 15
11:15 Alexander heard of it 15
22 When he heard this he was angry 15
22 as soon as he heard it he set out 15
23 When Jonathan heard this 15
63 Then Jonathan heard 15
12:24 Now Jonathan heard 15
28 When the enemy heard 15
34 for he had heard 15
13: 1 Simon heard 15
7 when they heard these words 15
14: 2 When Arsaces the king of Persia and Media heard 15
16 It was heard in Rome, and as far away as Sparta 15
17 When they heard 15
25 When the people heard these things they said 15
40 heard that the Jews were addressed by the Romans 15
16:22 When he heard this, he was greatly shocked 15
2Mc 1: 5 May he hear your prayers and be reconciled to you 22
8 We besought the Lord and we were heard 21
10:13 He heard himself called a traitor at every turn 15
11:24 We have heard that . . 15
12: 5 Judas heard of the cruelty visited on his countrymen 24
13:10 when Judas heard of this 24
14:15 When the Jews heard of Nicanor's coming 15
18 hearing of the valor of Judas and his men 15
15: 1 When Nicanor heard 24
3Mc 2:21 having heard the lawful supplication 21
4:12 the king, hearing that . . 15
5:35 Then the Jews, upon hearing what the king had said 15
48 and heard the loud and tumultuous noise 15
6:23 when he heard the shouting 15
4Mc 4:22 he heard that a rumor of his death had spread 15
8:15 when they had heard the inducements 15
9:27 they heard this noble decision. 15
10:17 When he heard this 15
18 God hears also those who are mute. 15
14: 9 as we hear of the tribulations of these young men; 15
9 yes, not only heard the direct word of threat 15
151 1: 3 The Lord himself; it is he who hears. 21

hear *See also* come, pretend.

hear before 1. προακούω
Col 1: 5 you have heard before in the word of the truth 1

cause to hear 1. שמע
Isa 30:30 the LORD will cause his majestic voice to be heard 1
Jer 49: 2 when I will cause the battle cry to be heard 1

make hear 1. שמע 2. ἀκουτίζω 3. do
2Kg 7: 6 the Lord had made the army . . hear the sound 1
2Ch 5:13 to make themselves heard in unison in praise 1
Isa 42: 2 lift up his voice, or make it heard in the street; 1
48: 6 From this time forth I make you hear new things 1
58: 4 Fasting . . will not make your voice to be heard 1
4 will not make your voice to be heard on high. 1
2Es 5: 7 one . . shall make his voice heard by night 3
Sir 45: 5 He made him hear his voice 2

hear no more 1. שבת מפני
Isa 30:11 let us hear no more of the Holy One of Israel. 1

surely hear 1. audio
2Es 6:32 because your voice has surely been heard 1

hearer 1. ἀκουστός 2. ἀκούω 3. ἀκροατής
Rom 2:13 it is not the hearers of the law who are righteous 3
1Ti 4:16 you will save both yourself and your hearers. 2
2Ti 2:14 which does no good, but only ruins the hearers. 2
Heb 4: 2 because it did not meet with faith in the hearers. 2
12:19 a voice whose words made the hearers entreat 2
Jas 1:22 But be doers of the word, and not hearers only 3
23 For if any one is a hearer of the word and not a doer 3
25 being no hearer that forgets but a doer that acts 3
Wis 1: 6 a hearer of his tongue. 1
4Mc 15:21 attract the attention of their hearers 2

hearing *See* give.

hearken 1. אזן 2. קשב 3. שמע 4. שמע בקול
5. ἀκούω 6. εἰσακούω 7. ἐνωτίζομαι
Gen 4:23 hearken to what I say: I have slain a man 1
16: 2 And Abram hearkened to the voice of Sar'ai. 3
30:17 God hearkened to Leah, and she conceived and bore 3
22 God remembered Rachel . . hearkened to her 3
34:24 all . . hearkened to Hamor and his son Shechem; 3
49: 2 Assemble . . and hearken to Israel your father. 3
Exd 3:18 they will hearken to your voice; and you 3
15:26 saying, "If you will diligently hearken 3
23:21 Give heed to him and hearken to his voice 3
22 if you hearken attentively to his voice and do 3
Lev 26:14 if you will not hearken to me 3
18 if in spite of this you will not hearken to me 3
21 if you . . will not hearken to me 3
27 if in spite of this you will not hearken to me 3
Num14:22 have not hearkened to my voice 3
21: 3 LORD hearkened to the voice of Israel, and gave 3
23:18 Rise, Balak, and hear; hearken to me, O son of Zippor 1
Deu 1:43 I spoke to you, and you would not hearken; 3
45 LORD did not hearken to your voice or give ear 3
3:26 LORD was angry . . and would not hearken to me; 3
7:12 because you hearken to these ordinances 3
9:19 But the LORD hearkened to me that time also. 3
10:10 LORD hearkened to me that time also; 3
23: 5 LORD your God would not hearken to Balaam; 3
Jos 5: 6 they did not hearken to the voice of the LORD; 3
10:14 when the LORD hearkened to the voice of a man; 3
1Sm 8: 7 Hearken to the . . people in all that they say 3
9 hearken to their voice; only, you shall . . warn 3
22 Hearken to their voice, and make them a king. 3
12: 1 I have hearkened to your voice 3
14 fear . . and serve him and hearken to his voice 3
15 if you will not hearken to the voice of the LORD 3
15: 1 now therefore hearken to the words of the LORD. 3
22 is better . . to hearken than the fat of rams. 2
19: 6 And Saul hearkened to the voice of Jonathan; 3
25:35 I have hearkened to your voice 3
28:21 Behold, your handmaid has hearkened to you; 3
21 I . . have hearkened to what you have said to me. 3
22 Now therefore, you also hearken to your handmaid; 4
23 urged him; and he hearkened to their words. 3
1Kg 8:28 have regard . . hearkening to the cry 3
29 thou mayest hearken to the prayer 3
30 hearken thou to the supplication of thy servant 3
11:38 if you will hearken to all that I command you 3
12:15 So the king did not hearken to the people; 3
16 all Israel saw that the king did not hearken 3
24 they hearkened to the word of the LORD 3
15:20 Ben-ha'dad hearkened to King Asa 3
17:22 the LORD hearkened to the voice of Eli'jah; 3
20:25 And he hearkened to their voice, and did so. 3
2Kg 13: 4 Jeho'ahaz besought . . and the LORD hearkened 3
16: 9 And the king of Assyria hearkened to him; 3
2Ch 6:19 hearkening to the cry and to the prayer 3
20 that thou mayest hearken to the prayer 3
21 hearken thou to the supplications of thy 3
10:15 the king did not hearken to the people; 3
16 Israel saw that the king did not hearken to them 3
11: 4 So they hearkened to the word of the LORD 3
16: 4 Ben-ha'dad hearkened to King Asa 3
20:15 Hearken, all Judah and inhabitants of Jerusalem 2
24:17 then the king hearkened to them. 3
Job 36:11 If they hearken and serve him 3
12 if they do not hearken, they perish by the sword 3
37: 2 Hearken to the thunder of his voice 3
Ps 5: 2 Hearken to the sound of my cry, my King and my God 2
86: 6 hearken to my cry of supplication. 2
95: 7 O that today you would hearken to his voice! 3
103:20 do his word, hearkening to the voice of his word! 3
Prv 23:22 Hearken to your father who begot you 3
Isa 10:30 O daughter of Gallim! Hearken, O La'ishah! 2
28:23 hear my voice; hearken, and hear my speech. 2
32: 3 and the ears of those who hear will hearken. 2
34: 1 Draw near, O nations, to hear, and hearken 2
46: 3 Hearken to me, O house of Jacob 3
12 Hearken to me, you stubborn of heart 3
48:12 Hearken to me, O Jacob, and Israel, whom I called! 3
18 O that you had hearkened to my commandments! 2
49: 1 O coastlands, and hearken, you peoples from afar. 2
51: 1 Hearken to me, you who pursue deliverance 3
7 Hearken to me, you who know righteousness 3

55: 2 Hearken diligently to me, and eat what is good 3
Jer 18:19 Give heed to me, O LORD, and hearken to my plea. 3
Dan 1:14 hearkened to them in this matter, and tested them 3
9:17 hearken to the prayer of thy servant 3
Hos 5: 1 Hearken, O house of the king! 1
9:17 because they have not hearkened to him; 3
Mic 1: 2 hearken, O earth, and all that is in it; 2
Zec 7:11 But they refused to hearken 2
Sir 33:18 you leaders of the congregation, hearken. 7
36:17 Hearken, O Lord, to the prayer of thy servants 6
Bar 4: 9 and she said: "Hearken, you neighbors of Zion 5
2Mc 8: 3 to hearken to the blood that cried out to him 6

heart 1. בֶּטֶן 2. חֵלֶב 3. כָּבֵד 4. כִּלְיָה 5. לֵב 6. לֵבָב 7. לִבָּה 8. מֵעֶה 9. מָתְנַיִם 10. נֶפֶשׁ 11. קֶרֶב 12. רַחֲמִים 13. לֵב (A) 14. διάνοια 15. ἑαυτοῦ 16. καρδία 17. κοιλία 18. νεφρός 19. νοῦς 20. σπλάγχνον 21. στέρνον 22. ψυχή 23. ψυχικῶς 24. animus 25. cor 26. renes

Gen 6: 5 the thoughts of his heart was only evil 5
6 the earth, and it grieved him to his heart. 5
8:21 the LORD said in his heart, "I will never again 5
21 for the imagination of man's heart is evil 5
20: 5 In the integrity of my heart . . I have done this. 6
6 you have done this in the integrity of your heart 6
24:45 Before I had done speaking in my heart 5
42:28 At this their hearts failed them 5
43:30 Joseph made haste, for his heart yearned for his 12
45:26 And his heart fainted, for he did not believe 5
Exd 4:14 and when he sees you he will be glad in his heart. 5
21 but I will harden his heart, so that he will not let 5
7: 3 I will harden Pharaoh's heart 5
13 Still Pharaoh's heart was hardened 5
14 LORD said to Moses, "Pharaoh's heart is hardened 5
22 so Pharaoh's heart remained hardened 5
23 he did not lay even this to heart. 5
8:15 he hardened his heart, and would not listen 5
19 But Pharaoh's heart was hardened, and he would not 5
32 Pharaoh hardened his heart this time also 5
9: 7 But the heart of Pharaoh was hardened 5
12 the LORD hardened the heart of Pharaoh 5
14 send all my plagues upon your heart 5
34 he sinned yet again, and hardened his heart 5
35 the heart of Pharaoh was hardened, and he did not 5
10: 1 I have hardened his heart and the heart of his 5
1 I have hardened his heart and the heart of his 5
20 the LORD hardened Pharaoh's heart, and he did not 5
27 the LORD hardened Pharaoh's heart, and he would 5
11:10 the LORD hardened Pharaoh's heart 5
14: 4 I will harden Pharaoh's heart, and he will pursue 5
8 the LORD hardened the heart of Pharaoh 5
17 I will harden the hearts of the Egyptians 5
15: 8 the deeps congealed in the heart of the sea. 5
23: 9 you know the heart of a stranger 10
25: 2 from every man whose heart makes him willing 5
28:29 names . . upon his heart, when he goes 5
30 they shall be upon Aaron's heart, when he goes 5
30 the judgment . . upon his heart before the LORD 5
35: 5 whoever is of a generous heart, let him bring 5
21 they came, every one whose heart stirred him 5
22 all who were of a willing heart brought brooches 5
26 all the women whose hearts were moved 5
29 the people . . whose heart moved them to bring 5
36: 2 called . . every one whose heart stirred him up 5
Lev 19:17 You shall not hate your brother in your heart 6
26:36 I will send faintness into their hearts 6
41 if then their uncircumcised heart is humbled 6
Num 15:39 not to follow after your own heart and your own 6
32: 7 you discourage the heart of the people of Israel 5
9 discouraged the heart of the people of Israel 5
Deu 1:28 Our brethren have made our hearts melt, saying 6
2:30 the LORD your God . . made his heart obstinate 6
4: 9 depart from your heart all the days of your life; 6
11 mountain burned with fire to the heart of heaven 5
29 if you search after him with all your heart 6
39 know therefore this day, and lay it to your heart 6
6: 5 shall love the LORD your God with all your heart 6
6 these words . . shall be upon your heart; 6
7:17 If you say in your heart, 'These nations 6
8: 2 testing you to know what was in your heart 6
5 Know then in your heart that, as a man disciplines 6
14 then your heart be lifted up, and you forget 6
17 Beware lest you say in your heart, 'My power 6
9: 4 Do not say in your heart, after the LORD your God 6
5 Not because of . . the uprightness of your heart 6
10:12 to serve the LORD your God with all your heart 6
15 LORD set his heart in love upon your fathers *
16 Circumcise therefore the foreskin of your heart 6
11:13 to serve him with all your heart and . . soul 6
16 lest your heart be deceived, and you turn aside 6
18 lay up these words of mine in your heart 6
13: 3 whether you love the LORD . . with all your heart 6
15: 7 not harden your heart or shut your hand 6
9 be a base thought in your heart, and you say 6
10 give . . and your heart shall not be grudging 6
17:17 not multiply wives . . lest his heart turn away; 6
20 his heart may not be lifted up above his brethren 6
18:21 if you say in your heart, 'How may we know the word 6
20: 3 let not your heart faint; do not fear, or tremble 6
8 go back . . lest the heart of his fellows melt 6
8 lest the heart of his fellows melt as his heart.' 6
24:15 (for he is poor, and sets his heart upon it); 10
26:16 do . . with all your heart and with all your soul. 6
28:47 did not serve . . with . . gladness of heart 6
65 LORD will give you there a trembling heart 5
67 because of the dread which your heart shall fear 6
29:18 heart turns away this day from the LORD our God 6
19 one who . . blesses himself in his heart, saying 5
19 though I walk in the stubbornness of my heart.' 5
30: 2 obey . . with all your heart and with all your soul; 6
6 LORD your God will circumcise your heart 6
6 God will circumcise . . the heart of your offspring 6
6 love the LORD your God with all your heart 6
10 turn to the LORD your God with all your heart 6
14 very near you . . in your mouth and in your heart 6
17 if your heart turns away, and you will not hear 6
32:46 Lay to heart all the words which I enjoin upon you 6
Jos 2:11 And as soon as we heard it, our hearts melted 6
5: 1 their heart melted, and there was no . . spirit 6
7: 5 And the hearts of the people melted, and became 6
11:20 For it was the LORD's doing to harden their hearts 5
14: 7 and I brought him word again as it was in my heart. 6
8 my brethren . . made the heart of the people melt; 5
22: 5 and to serve him with all your heart and . . soul. 6
23:14 you know in your hearts and souls, all of you 6
24:23 put away . . and incline your heart to the LORD 6
Jdg 5: 9 My heart goes out to the commanders of Israel 5
15 there were great searchings of heart 5
16 there were great searchings of heart. 5
9: 3 and their hearts inclined to follow Abim'elech 5
16:15 you say, 'I love you,' when your heart is not with me? 5
25 when their hearts were merry, they said, "Call 5
18:20 the priest's heart was glad; he took the ephod 5
19: 5 Strengthen your heart with a morsel of bread 5
6 spend the night, and let your heart be merry. 5
8 Strengthen your heart, and tarry until the day 6
9 lodge here and let your heart be merry; 6
22 As they were making their hearts merry, behold 5
Rut 3: 7 Bo'az had eaten and drunk, and his heart was merry 5
1Sm 1: 8 And why do you not eat? And why is your heart sad? 6
13 Hannah was speaking in her heart; 5
2: 1 My heart exults in the LORD; 5
33 spared to weep out his eyes and grieve his heart; 10
35 do according to what is in my heart and in my mind; 6
4:13 for his heart trembled for the ark of God. 5
6: 6 harden your hearts as the Egyptians and Pharaoh 6
6 Egyptians and Pharaoh hardened their hearts? 5
7: 3 you are returning to the LORD with all your heart 6
3 put away . . and direct your heart to the LORD 6
10: 9 When he turned . . God gave him another heart; 5
26 went men of valor whose hearts God had touched. 5
12:20 but serve the LORD with all your heart; 6
24 and serve him faithfully with all your heart; 6
13:14 the LORD has sought out a man after his own heart; 6
16: 7 man looks on . . but the LORD looks on the heart. 6
17:28 know your presumption, and the evil of your heart; 6
32 Let no man's heart fail because of him; 5
21:12 And David took these words to heart 6
23:20 according to all your heart's desire to come down 10
24: 5 David's heart smote him, because he had cut off 5
25:36 And Nabal's heart was merry within him 5
37 his wife told him . . and his heart died within him 5
27: 1 David said in his heart, "I shall now perish one day 5
28: 5 he was afraid, and his heart trembled greatly. 5
2Sm 3:21 you may reign over all that your heart desires. 10
6:16 and she despised him in her heart. 5
7: 3 Go, do all that is in your heart; 6
21 of thy promise, and according to thy own heart 6
13:20 he is your brother; do not take this to heart. 5
28 Mark when Amnon's heart is merry with wine 5
33 let . . the king so take it to heart as to suppose 5
14: 1 Jo'ab . . perceived that the king's heart went out 5
15: 6 so Ab'salom stole the hearts of the men of Israel. 5
13 The hearts of the men . . have gone after Ab'salom. 5
17:10 valiant . . whose heart is like the heart of a lion 5
10 valiant . . whose heart is like the heart of a lion 5
18:14 and thrust them into the heart of Ab'salom 5
19:14 he swayed the heart of all the men of Judah as one 6
24:10 But David's heart smote him after he had numbered 5
1Kg 2: 4 in faithfulness with all their heart 6
44 You know in your own heart all the evil that you 6
3: 6 and in uprightness of heart toward thee; and thou 6
26 to the king, because her heart yearned for her son 12
8:17 Now it was in the heart of David my father to build 6
18 it was in your heart to build a house for my name 6
18 Whereas . . you did well that it was in your heart; 6
23 who walk before thee with all their heart; 5
38 each knowing the affliction of his own heart 6
39 render to each whose heart thou knowest 6
39 knowest the hearts of all the children of men); 6
47 if they lay it to heart . . and repent 5
48 repent . . and with all their heart 10
58 incline our hearts to him, to walk in all his ways 6
61 Let your heart . . be wholly true to the LORD 6
66 joyful and glad of heart for all the goodness 5
9: 3 my eyes and my heart will be there for all time. 5
4 walk . . with integrity of heart and uprightness 6
11: 2 they will turn away your heart after their gods"; 6
3 and his wives turned away his heart. 5
4 his wives turned away his heart after other gods; 6
4 his heart was not wholly true to the LORD his God 6
4 true . . as was the heart of David his father. 6
9 his heart had turned away from the LORD 6
12:26 Jerobo'am said in his heart 5
27 the heart of this people will turn again 5
33 in the month which he had devised of his own heart; 5
14: 8 David, who . . followed me with all his heart 6
15: 3 his heart was not wholly true to the LORD his God 6
3 wholly true . . as the heart of David his father. 6
14 the heart of Asa was wholly true to the LORD 6
18:37 and that thou hast turned their hearts back. 5
21: 7 Arise, and eat . . and let your heart be cheerful; 5
2Kg 9:24 shot Joram . . so that the arrow pierced his heart 5
10:15 Is your heart true to my heart as mine is to yours? 6
15 Is your heart true to my heart as mine is to yours? 6
30 have done . . according to all that was in my heart 6
31 walk in the law of the LORD . . with all his heart; 6
12: 4 the money which a man's heart prompts him to bring 5
14:10 and your heart has lifted you up. 5
20: 3 walked . . in faithfulness and with a whole heart 6
22:19 your heart was penitent, and you humbled 6
23: 3 to keep his . . with all his heart and all his soul 5
25 turned to the LORD with all his heart and with all 6
1Ch 12:17 to help me, my heart will be knit to you; 6
15:29 Michal . . despised him in her heart. 5
16:10 let the hearts of those who seek the LORD rejoice! 5
17: 2 Do all that is in your heart, for God is with you. 6
19 O LORD, and according to thy own heart 5
22: 7 My son, I had it in my heart to build a house 6
19 set your mind and heart to seek the LORD your God. 6
28: 2 I had it in my heart to build a house of rest 6
9 serve him with a whole heart 5
9 LORD searches all hearts, and understands every 6
29: 9 with a whole heart they had offered freely 5
17 I know, my God, that thou triest the heart 6
17 in the uprightness of my heart I have freely 6
18 such purposes and . . in the hearts of thy people 6
18 thy people, and direct their hearts toward thee. 6
19 Grant to Solomon my son that with a whole heart 6
2Ch 1:11 Because this was in your heart 6
6: 7 Now it was in the heart of David my father to build 6
8 it was in your heart to build a house for my name 6
8 you did well that it was in your heart; 6
14 who walk before thee with all their heart; 5
30 render to each whose heart thou knowest 6
30 only, knowest the hearts of the children of men); 6
37 yet if they lay it to heart in the land 6
38 if they repent . . mind and with all their heart 5
7:10 sent the people away . . joyful and glad of heart 5
16 my eyes and my heart will be there for all time. 5
11:16 those who had set their hearts to seek the LORD 6
12:14 for he did not set his heart to seek the LORD. 5
15:12 to seek the LORD . . with all their heart 6
15 for they had sworn with all their heart 6
17 the heart of Asa was blameless all his days. 6
16: 9 in behalf of those whose heart is blameless 6
17: 6 His heart was courageous in the ways of the LORD; 5
19: 3 have set your heart to seek God. 6
9 in faithfulness, and with your whole heart 6
20:33 people had not yet set their hearts upon the God 6
22: 9 who sought the LORD with all his heart. 6
25: 2 yet not with a blameless heart. 6
19 your heart has lifted you up in boastfulness. 5
29:10 it is in my heart to make a covenant with the LORD 6
31 of a willing heart brought burnt offerings. 5
34 for the Levites were more upright in heart 6
30:12 to give them one heart to do what the king 6
19 who sets his heart to seek God, the LORD 6
31:21 every work . . he did with all his heart, and prospered. 6
32:25 did not make return . . for his heart was proud 5
26 humbled himself for the pride of his heart 5
31 to try . . and to know all that was in his heart. 6
34:27 because your heart was penitent and you humbled 6
31 to keep . . with all his heart and all his soul 6
36:13 hardened his heart against turning to the LORD 6
Ezr 6:22 LORD . . turned the heart of the king of Assyria 5
7:10 Ezra had set his heart to study the law of the LORD 6
27 such a thing as this into the heart of the king 5
Neh 2: 2 This is nothing else but sadness of the heart. 5
12 my God had put into my heart to do for Jerusalem. 5
9: 8 thou didst find his heart faithful before thee 6
Est 1:10 when the heart of the king was merry with wine 5
5: 9 Haman went out that day joyful and glad of heart. 5
Job 1: 5 sons have sinned, and cursed God in their hearts. 6
9: 4 He is wise in heart, and mighty in strength 6
10:13 Yet these things thou didst hide in thy heart; 6
11:13 If you set your heart aright 5
15:12 Why does your heart carry you away 5
35 their heart prepares deceit. 1
17:11 my plans are broken off, the desires of my heart. 6
19:27 not another. My heart faints within me! 4
22:22 lay up his words in your heart. 6
23:16 God has made my heart faint; 5
27: 6 my heart does not reproach me for any of my days. 6
29:13 I caused the widow's heart to sing for joy. 5
30:27 My heart is in turmoil, and is never still; 8

31: 7 from the way, and my heart has gone after my eyes 5
9 If my heart has been enticed to a woman 5
27 my heart has been secretly enticed 5
32:19 Behold, my heart is like wine that has no vent; 1
33: 3 My words declare the uprightness of my heart 5
36:13 The godless in heart cherish anger; 5
37: 1 At this also my heart trembles, and leaps out 5
41:24 His heart is hard as a stone 5
Ps 4: 4 commune with your own hearts on your beds 6
7 Thou hast put more joy in my heart than they have 5
5: 9 their heart is destruction 11
7: 9 thou who triest the minds and hearts 4
10 with God, who saves the upright in heart. 5
9: 1 I will give thanks to the LORD with my whole heart; 5
10: 3 For the wicked boasts of the desires of his heart 10
6 He thinks in his heart, "I shall not be moved; 5
11 He thinks in his heart, "God has forgotten 5
13 does the wicked renounce God, and say in his heart 5
17 of the meek; thou wilt strengthen their heart 5
11: 2 to shoot in the dark at the upright in heart; 5
12: 2 with . . a double heart they speak. 5
13: 2 in my soul, and have sorrow in my heart all the day? 6
5 my heart shall rejoice in thy salvation. 5
14: 1 The fool says in his heart, "There is no God. 5
15: 2 what is right, and speaks truth from his heart; 6
16: 7 in the night also my heart instructs me. 4
9 Therefore my heart is glad, and my soul rejoices; 5
17: 3 If thou triest my heart, if thou visitest me 5
10 They close their hearts to pity; 2
19: 8 the precepts . . are right, rejoicing the heart; 5
14 Let . . the meditation of my heart be acceptable 5
20: 4 May he grant you your heart's desire 6
21: 2 Thou hast given him his heart's desire 5
22:14 all my bones are out of joint; my heart is like wax 5
26 praise the LORD! May your hearts live for ever! 6
24: 4 He who has clean hands and a pure heart 6
25:17 Relieve the troubles of my heart 6
26: 2 O LORD, and try me; test my heart and my mind. 5
27: 3 a host encamp against me, my heart shall not fear; 5
8 My heart says to thee, "Thy face, LORD, do I seek. 5
14 be strong, and let your heart take courage; 5
28: 3 while mischief is in their hearts. 6
7 in him my heart trusts; so I am helped 5
7 so I am helped, and my heart exults 5
31:24 Be strong, and let your heart take courage 6
32:11 shout for joy, all you upright in heart! 5
33:11 the thoughts of his heart to all generations. 5
15 he who fashions the hearts of them all 5
21 Yea, our heart is glad in him, because we trust 5
36: 1 speaks to the wicked deep in his heart; 5
10 thy salvation to the upright of heart! 5
37: 4 he will give you the desires of your heart. 5
15 their sword shall enter their own heart 5
31 The law of his God is in his heart; 5
38: 8 I groan because of the tumult of my heart. 5
10 My heart throbs, my strength fails me; 5
39: 3 my heart became hot within me. 5
40: 8 O my God; thy law is within my heart. 8
10 I have not hid thy saving help within my heart 5
12 my heart fails me. 5
41: 6 empty words, while his heart gathers mischief; 5
44:18 Our heart has not turned back 5
21 For he knows the secrets of the heart. 5
45: 1 My heart overflows with a goodly theme; 5
5 are sharp in the heart of the king's enemies; 5
46: 2 though the mountains shake in the heart of the sea; 5
49: 3 meditation of my heart shall be understanding. 5
51:10 Create in me a clean heart, O God 5
17 a . . contrite heart, O God, thou wilt not despise. 5
53: 1 The fool says in his heart, "There is no God. 5
55: 4 My heart is in anguish within me 5
21 was smoother than butter, yet war was in his heart; 5
57: 7 My heart is steadfast, O God, my heart is steadfast! 5
7 My heart is steadfast, O God, my heart is steadfast! 5
58: 2 Nay, in your hearts you devise wrongs; 5
61: 2 I call to thee, when my heart is faint. 5
62: 8 O people; pour out your heart before him; 6
10 if riches increase, set not your heart on them. 5
64: 6 For the inward mind and heart of a man are deep! 5
10 Let all the upright in heart glory! 5
66:18 If I had cherished iniquity in my heart 5
69:20 Insults have broken my heart 5
32 you who seek God, let your hearts revive. 6
73: 1 to the upright, to those who are pure in heart. 6
7 their hearts overflow with follies. 6
13 All in vain have I kept my heart clean 6
21 when I was pricked in heart 4
26 My flesh and my heart may fail 6
26 God is the strength of my heart and my portion 6
77: 6 I commune with my heart in the night; 6
78: 8 a generation whose heart was not steadfast 5
18 tested God in their heart by demanding the food 6
37 Their heart was not steadfast toward him; 5
72 With upright heart he tended them 6
81:12 I gave them over to their stubborn hearts 5
84: 2 my heart and flesh sing for joy to the living God. 5
5 in whose heart are the highways to Zion. 6
85: 8 saints, to those who turn to him in their hearts. 16
86:11 unite my heart to fear thy name. 6
12 I give thanks to thee . . with my whole heart 6
90:12 number our days that we may get a heart of wisdom. 6
94:15 all the upright in heart will follow it. 5
19 cares of my heart are many, thy consolations 11
95: 8 Harden not your hearts, as at Mer'ibah, as on the day 6
10 They are a people who err in heart 6
97:11 Light dawns . . and joy for the upright in heart. 5
101: 2 walk with integrity of heart within my house; 6
4 Perverseness of heart shall be far from me; 6
5 man of haughty looks and arrogant heart 6
102: 4 My heart is smitten like grass, and withered; 5
104:15 wine to gladden the heart of man 6
15 bread to strengthen man's heart. 6
105: 3 let the hearts of those who seek the LORD rejoice! 5
25 He turned their hearts to hate his people 5
107:12 Their hearts were bowed down with hard labor; 5
108: 1 My heart is steadfast, O God, my heart is steadfast! 5
1 My heart is steadfast, O God, my heart is steadfast! •
109:22 poor and needy, and my heart is stricken within 5
111: 1 I will give thanks to the LORD with my whole heart 6
112: 7 his heart is firm, trusting in the LORD. 5
8 His heart is steady, he will not be afraid 5
119: 2 Blessed . . who seek him with their whole heart 5
7 I will praise thee with an upright heart 6
10 With my whole heart I seek thee; let me not wander 5
11 I have laid up thy word in my heart 5
34 keep thy law and observe it with my whole heart. 5
36 Incline my heart to thy testimonies 5
58 I entreat thy favor with all my heart; 5
69 with my whole heart I keep thy precepts; 5
70 their heart is gross like fat 5
80 May my heart be blameless in thy statutes 5
111 testimonies . . yea, they are the joy of my heart. 5
112 I incline my heart to perform thy statutes 5
145 With my whole heart I cry; answer me, O LORD! 5
161 my heart stands in awe of thy words. 5
125: 4 to those who are upright in their hearts! 5
131: 1 O LORD, my heart is not lifted up, my eyes are not 5
138: 1 I give thee thanks, O LORD, with my whole heart; 5
139:23 Search me, O God, and know my heart! 6
140: 2 who plan evil things in their heart 5
141: 4 Incline not my heart to any evil 5
143: 4 my heart within me is appalled. 5
Prv 2: 2 inclining your heart to understanding; 5
10 for wisdom will come into your heart 5
3: 1 but let your heart keep my commandments; 5
3 write them on the tablet of your heart. 5
5 Trust in the LORD with all your heart 5
4: 4 Let your heart hold fast my words; 5
21 keep them within your heart. 6
23 Keep your heart with all vigilance; 5
5:12 you say, "How . . my heart despised reproof! 5
6:14 with perverted heart devises evil 5
18 a heart that devises wicked plans 5
21 Bind them upon your heart always; 5
25 Do not desire her beauty in your heart 6
7: 3 write them on the tablet of your heart. 5
10 dressed as a harlot, wily of heart. 5
25 Let not your heart turn aside to her ways 5
10: 8 The wise of heart will heed commandments 5
12:20 Deceit is in the heart of those who devise evil 5
25 Anxiety in a man's heart weighs him down 5
13:12 Hope deferred makes the heart sick 5
14:10 The heart knows its own bitterness 5
13 Even in laughter the heart is sad 5
33 but it is not known in the heart of fools. 11
15:11 how much more the hearts of men! 5
13 A glad heart makes a cheerful countenance 5
13 but by sorrow of heart the spirit is broken. 5
15 but a cheerful heart has a continual feast. 5
30 The light of the eyes rejoices the heart 5
16:21 The wise of heart is called a man of discernment 5
17: 3 furnace is for gold, and the LORD tries hearts. 5
22 A cheerful heart is a good medicine 5
18:12 Before destruction a man's heart is haughty 5
19: 3 way to ruin, his heart rages against the LORD. 5
18 do not set your heart on his destruction. 10
20: 9 Who can say, "I have made my heart clean; 5
21: 1 The king's heart is a stream of water in the hand 5
2 but the LORD weighs the heart. 5
4 Haughty eyes and a proud heart 5
22:11 He who loves purity of heart, and whose speech 5
15 Folly is bound up in the heart of a child 5
23: 7 Eat and drink!" . . but his heart is not with you. 5
15 if your heart is wise, my heart too will be glad. 5
15 if your heart is wise, my heart too will be glad. 5
17 Let not your heart envy sinners 5
26 My son, give me your heart 5
24:12 does not he who weighs the heart perceive it? 5
17 let not your heart be glad when he stumbles; 5
25:20 He who sings songs to a heavy heart is like one who 5
26:23 smooth lips with an evil heart. 5
24 He who hates . . harbors deceit in his heart; 11
25 for there are seven abominations in his heart; 5
27: 9 Oil and perfume make the heart glad 5
11 Be wise, my son, and make my heart glad 5
28:14 hardens his heart will fall into calamity. 5
29:17 give you rest; he will give delight to your heart. 10
31:11 The heart of her husband trusts in her 5
Ecc 2:10 I kept my heart from no pleasure 5
10 for my heart found pleasure in all my toil 5
20 I turned about and gave my heart up to despair 5
3:17 I said in my heart, God will judge the righteous 5
18 I said in my heart with regard to . . men that God is 5
5: 2 Be not rash . . nor let your heart be hasty to utter 5
20 God keeps him occupied with joy in his heart. 5
7: 2 end of all men, and the living will lay it to heart. 5
3 by sadness of countenance the heart is made glad. 5
4 The heart of the wise is in the house of mourning; 5
4 but the heart of fools is in the house of mirth. 5
22 your heart knows that many times you have 5
26 the woman whose heart is snares and nets 5
8:11 the heart of the sons of men is fully set to do evil. 5
9: 1 But all this I laid to heart, examining it all 5
3 also the hearts of men are full of evil 5
3 and madness is in their hearts while they live 6
7 Go, eat . . and drink your wine with a merry heart; 5
10: 2 A wise man's heart inclines him toward the right 5
2 but a fool's heart toward the left. 5
11: 9 let your heart cheer you in the days of your youth; 5
9 walk in the ways of your heart and . . of your eyes. 5
Sng 3:11 on the day of the gladness of his heart. 5
5: 2 I slept, but my heart was awake. 5
4 and my heart was thrilled within me. 8
8: 6 Set me as a seal upon your heart . . upon your arm; 5
Isa 1: 5 The whole head is sick, and the whole heart faint. 6
6:10 Make the heart of this people fat 5
10 lest they . . understand with their hearts 6
7: 2 his heart and the heart of his people shook 6
2 his heart and the heart of his people shook 6
4 do not fear, and do not let your heart be faint 6
9: 9 who say in pride and in arrogance of heart 6
13: 7 hands . . be feeble, and every man's heart will melt 6
14:13 You said in your heart, 'I will ascend to heaven; 6
15: 5 My heart cries out for Moab; his fugitives flee 5
16:11 soul moans . . for Moab, and my heart for Kir-he'res. 11
19: 1 the heart of the Egyptians will melt within 6
29:13 while their hearts are far from me 5
30:29 gladness of heart, as when one sets out 6
35: 4 Say to those who are of a fearful heart, "Be strong 5
38: 3 in faithfulness and with a whole heart 5
42:25 it burned him, but he did not take it to heart. 5
46:12 Hearken to me, you stubborn of heart 5
47: 7 that you did not lay these things to heart 5
8 say in your heart, "I am, and there is no one 6
10 led you astray, and you said in your heart 5
49:21 will say in your heart: 'Who has borne me these? 6
51: 7 the people in whose heart is my law; 5
57: 1 righteous . . perishes, and no one lays it to heart; 5
15 and to revive the heart of the contrite. 5
17 went on backsliding in the way of his own heart. 5
59:13 and uttering from the heart lying words. 5
60: 5 be radiant, your heart shall thrill and rejoice; 6
63: 4 For the day of vengeance was in my heart 5
15 The yearning of thy heart and thy compassion 8
17 and harden our heart, so that we fear thee not? 5
65:14 my servants shall sing for gladness of heart 5
14 but you shall cry out for pain of heart 5
66:14 You shall see, and your heart shall rejoice; 5
Jer 3:10 Judah did not return to me with her whole heart 5
15 I will give you shepherds after my own heart 5
17 no more stubbornly follow their own evil heart. 5
4: 4 remove the foreskin of your hearts, O men of Judah 6
14 O Jerusalem, wash your heart from wickedness 5
18 it is bitter; it has reached your very heart. 5
19 the walls of my heart! My heart is beating wildly; 5
19 the walls of my heart! My heart is beating wildly; 5
5:23 this people has a stubborn and rebellious heart; 5
24 They do not say in their hearts, 'Let us fear 6
7:24 and the stubbornness of their evil hearts 5
8:18 beyond healing, my heart is sick within me. 5
21 For the wound of . . my people is my heart wounded •
9: 8 but in his heart he plans an ambush for him. 11
14 but have stubbornly followed their own hearts 5
26 the house of Israel is uncircumcised in heart. 5
11: 8 walked in the stubbornness of his evil heart. 5
20 who triest the heart and the mind 5
12: 2 art near in their mouth and far from their heart. 4
11 land is made desolate, but no man lays it to heart. 5
13:10 who stubbornly follow their own heart 5
22 And if you say in your heart 6
15: 1 yet my heart would not turn toward this people. 10
16 became to me a joy and the delight of my heart; 6
17: 1 it is engraved on the tablet of their heart 5
5 whose heart turns away from the LORD. 5
9 The heart is deceitful above all things 5
10 I the LORD search the mind and try the heart 5
18:12 according to the stubbornness of his evil heart. 5
20: 9 there is in my heart as it were a burning fire 5
12 O LORD . . who seest the heart and the mind 5
22:17 have eyes and heart only for your dishonest gain 5
23: 9 My heart is broken within me, all my bones shake; 5
17 every one who stubbornly follows his own heart 5
26 shall there be lies in the heart of the prophets 5
26 and who prophesy the deceit of their own heart 5
24: 7 I will give them a heart to know that I am the LORD; 5
7 they shall return to me with their whole heart. 5
29:13 when you seek me with all your heart 6

31:20 Therefore my heart yearns for him; 8
33 and I will write it upon their hearts; 5
32:39 I will give them one heart and one way 5
40 and I will put the fear of me in their hearts 6
41 faithfulness, with all my heart and all my soul. 5
48:29 his arrogance, and the haughtiness of his heart. 5
36 Therefore my heart moans for Moab like a flute 5
36 my heart moans like a flute for the men 5
41 The heart of the warriors of Moab 5
41 shall be in that day like the heart of a woman 5
49:16 has deceived you, and the pride of your heart 5
22 heart of the warriors of Edom shall be in that day 5
22 like the heart of a woman in her pangs. 5
51:46 Let not your heart faint 6
Lam 1:20 my soul is in tumult, my heart is wrung within me 5
22 for my groans are many and my heart is faint. 5
2:11 soul is in tumult; my heart is poured out in grief 3
19 Pour out your heart like water before 5
3:13 He drove into my heart the arrows of his quiver; 4
41 Let us lift up our hearts and hands to God 6
65 Thou wilt give them dullness of heart; 5
5:15 The joy of our hearts has ceased; 5
17 For this our heart has become sick 5
Ezk 3: 7 are of a hard forehead and of a stubborn heart. 5
10 that I shall speak to you receive in your heart 6
6: 9 when I have broken their wanton heart 5
11:19 I will give them one heart 5
19 I will take the stony heart out of their flesh 5
19 stony heart out . . and give them a heart of flesh 5
21 whose heart goes after their detestable things 5
14: 3 men have taken their idols into their hearts 5
4 Any man . . who takes his idols into his heart 5
5 I may lay hold of the hearts of the house of Israel 5
7 taking his idols into his heart 5
16:30 How lovesick is your heart, says the Lord GOD 7
18:31 and get yourselves a new heart and a new spirit! 5
20:16 for their heart went after their idols. 5
21: 6 sigh with breaking heart and bitter grief 9
7 When it comes, every heart will melt 5
15 that their hearts may melt, and many fall 5
24:25 delight of their eyes and their heart's desire 10
25:15 and took vengeance with malice of heart 10
27: 4 Your borders are in the heart of the seas; 5
25 and heavily laden in the heart of the seas. 5
26 wind has wrecked you in the heart of the seas. 5
27 you . . sink into the heart of the seas 5
28: 2 says the Lord GOD: "Because your heart is proud 5
2 sit in the seat of the gods, in the heart of the seas 5
5 your heart has become proud in your wealth 6
8 the death of the slain in the heart of the seas. 5
17 Your heart was proud because of your beauty; 5
31:10 its heart was proud of its height 6
32: 9 I will trouble the hearts of many peoples 5
33:31 but their heart is set on their gain. 5
36:26 A new heart I will give you, and a new spirit 5
26 I will take out of your flesh the heart of stone 5
26 the heart of stone and give you a heart of flesh. 5
44: 7 foreigners, uncircumcised in heart and flesh 5
9 No foreigner, uncircumcised in heart and flesh 5
Dan 5:20 heart was lifted up and his spirit was hardened 13
22 his son, Belshaz'zar, have not humbled your heart 13
11:12 multitude is taken, his heart shall be exalted 6
28 heart shall be set against the holy covenant. 6
Hos 7: 6 For like an oven their hearts burn with intrigue; 5
14 They do not cry to me from the heart 5
10: 2 Their heart is false; 5
11: 8 My heart recoils within me, my compassion grows 5
13: 6 and their heart was lifted up; 5
Jol 2:12 says the LORD, "return to me with all your heart 6
13 and rend your hearts and not your garments. 6
Ams 2:16 stout of heart among the mighty shall flee away 5
Obd 1: 3 The pride of your heart has deceived you 5
3 whose dwelling is high, who say in your heart 5
Jon 2: 3 cast me into the deep, into the heart of the seas 6
Nah 2:10 Hearts faint and knees tremble 5
Zep 1:12 who say in their hearts, 'The LORD will not do good 6
3:14 Rejoice and exult with all your heart 5
Zec 7:10 devise evil against his brother in your heart. 6
12 They made their hearts like adamant 5
8:17 do not devise evil in your hearts 6
10: 7 their hearts shall be glad as with wine. 5
7 their hearts shall exult in the LORD. 5
Mal 2: 2 will not lay it to heart to give glory to my name 5
2 cursed them, because you do not lay it to heart. 5
4: 6 turn the hearts of fathers to their children 5
6 turn . . the hearts of children to their fathers 5
Mat 5: 8 are the pure in heart, for they shall see God. 16
28 committed adultery with her in his heart. 16
6:21 treasure is, there will your heart be also. 16
9: 4 Why do you think evil in your hearts? 16
11:29 for I am gentle and lowly in heart 16
12:34 For out of the abundance of the heart 16
40 three nights in the heart of the earth. 16
13:15 For this people's heart has grown dull 16
15 and understand with their heart 16
19 and snatches away what is sown in his heart 16
15: 8 but their heart is far from me; 16
18 comes out of the mouth proceeds from the heart 16
19 For out of the heart come evil thoughts, murder 16
18:35 do not forgive your brother from your heart. 16
22:37 love the Lord your God with all your heart 16
Mrk 2: 6 questioning in their hearts 16
8 Why do you question thus in your hearts? 16
3: 5 grieved at their hardness of heart 16
6:52 their hearts were hardened. 16
7: 6 their heart is far from me; 16
19 since it enters, not his heart but his stomach 16
21 out of the heart of man, come evil thoughts 16
8:17 Are your hearts hardened? 16
11:23 does not doubt in his heart 16
12:30 shall love the Lord your God with all your heart 16
33 to love him with all the heart 16
Lke 1:17 to turn the hearts of the fathers to the children 16
51 in the imagination of their hearts 16
66 all who heard them laid them up in their hearts 16
2:19 pondering them in her heart. 16
35 thoughts out of many hearts may be revealed. 16
51 his mother kept all these things in her heart. 16
3:15 all men questioned in their hearts concerning John 16
5:22 Why do you question in your hearts? 16
6:45 The good man out of the good treasure of his heart 16
45 out of the abundance of the heart 16
8:12 takes away the word from their hearts 16
15 hold it fast in an honest and good heart 16
9:47 Jesus perceived the thought of their hearts 16
10:27 shall love the Lord your God with all your heart 16
12:34 there will your heart be also. 16
16:15 God knows your hearts 16
21:34 lest your hearts be weighed down 16
24:25 slow of heart to believe 16
32 Did not our hearts burn within us 16
38 why do questionings rise in your hearts? 16
Joh 7:38 'Out of his heart shall flow rivers 17
12:40 has blinded their eyes and hardened their heart 16
40 perceive with their heart 16
13: 2 the heart of Judas Iscariot, Simon's son 16
14: 1 Let not your hearts be troubled; believe in God 16
27 Let not your hearts be troubled 16
16: 6 sorrow has filled your hearts. 16
22 our hearts will rejoice 16
Act 2:26 my heart was glad, and my tongue rejoiced; 16
37 when they heard this they were cut to the heart 16
46 partook of food with glad and generous hearts 16
4:32 who believed were of one heart and soul 16
5: 3 why has Satan filled your heart to lie 16
4 you have contrived this deed in your heart 16
7:23 it came into his heart to visit his brethren 16
39 in their hearts they turned to Egypt 16
51 uncircumcised in heart and ears 16
8:21 your heart is not right before God. 16
22 the intent of your heart may be forgiven you. 16
13:22 a man after my heart, who will do all my will.' 16
14:17 satisfying your hearts with food and gladness. 16
15: 9 cleansed their hearts by faith. 16
16:14 opened her heart to give heed to what was said 16
21:13 What are you doing, weeping and breaking my heart? 16
28:27 this people's heart has grown dull 16
27 understand with their heart 16
Rom 1:24 God gave them up in the lusts of their hearts 16
2: 5 by your hard and impenitent heart 16
15 what the law requires is written on their hearts 16
29 and real circumcision is a matter of the heart 16
5: 5 God's love has been poured into our hearts 16
6:17 you . . have become obedient from the heart 16
8:27 he who searches the hearts of men knows 16
9: 2 great sorrow and unceasing anguish in my heart. 16
18 and he hardens the heart of whomever he wills. •
10: 1 Brethren, my heart's desire and prayer to God 16
6 Do not say in your heart, "Who will ascend 16
8 The word is near you, on your lips and in your heart 16
9 and believe in your heart that God raised him 16
10 man believes with his heart and so is justified 16
16:18 they deceive the hearts of the simple-minded. 16
1Co 2: 9 nor the heart of man conceived 16
4: 5 and will disclose the purposes of the heart. 16
7:37 whoever is firmly established in his heart 16
37 determined this in his heart 16
14:25 the secrets of his heart are disclosed 16
2Co 1:22 given us his Spirit in our hearts as a guarantee. 16
2: 4 much affliction and anguish of heart 16
3: 2 written on your hearts, to be known and read by all 16
3 but on tablets of human hearts. 16
4: 6 who has shone in our hearts 16
5:12 on a man's position and not on his heart. 16
6:11 our heart is wide. 16
13 widen your hearts also. •
7: 3 I said before that you are in our hearts 16
15 his heart goes out all the more to you 20
8:16 earnest care for you into the heart of Titus. 16
Gal 4: 6 his Son into our hearts, crying, "Abba! Father! 16
Eph 1:18 having the eyes of your hearts enlightened 16
3:17 Christ may dwell in your hearts through faith; 16
4:18 due to their hardness of heart; 16
5:19 making melody to the Lord with all your heart 16
6: 5 with fear and trembling, in singleness of heart 16
6 doing the will of God from the heart 22
22 that he may encourage your hearts. 16
Php 1: 7 because I hold you in my heart 16
4: 7 keep your hearts and your minds in Christ Jesus. 16
Col 2: 2 that their hearts may be encouraged 16
3:15 let the peace of Christ rule in your hearts 16
16 sing . . with thankfulness in your hearts to God. 16
22 in singleness of heart, fearing the Lord. 16
4: 8 he may encourage your hearts 16
1Th 2: 4 to please God who tests our hearts. 16
17 in person not in heart 16
3:13 so that he may establish your hearts unblamable 16
2Th 2:17 comfort your hearts and establish them 16
3: 5 May the Lord direct your hearts to the love of God 16
1Ti 1: 5 that issues from a pure heart and a good conscience 16
6:10 pierced their hearts with many pangs. 15
2Ti 2:22 those who call upon the Lord from a pure heart. 16
Phm 1: 7 the hearts of the saints have been refreshed 20
20 Refresh my heart in Christ. 20
Heb 3: 8 do not harden your hearts as in the rebellion 16
10 They always go astray in their hearts 16
12 an evil, unbelieving heart 16
15 do not harden your hearts as in the rebellion. 16
4: 7 do not harden your hearts. 16
12 the thoughts and intentions of the heart. 16
8:10 write them on their hearts 16
10:16 I will put my laws on their hearts 16
22 let us draw near with a true heart 16
22 our hearts sprinkled clean from an evil conscience 16
13: 9 is well that the heart be strengthened by grace 16
Jas 1:26 If any one . . deceives his heart 16
3:14 if you have . . selfish ambition in your hearts 16
4: 8 purify your hearts, you men of double mind. 16
5: 5 you have fattened your hearts 16
8 Establish your hearts, for the coming of the Lord 16
1Pe 1:22 love one another earnestly from the heart. 16
3: 4 let it be the hidden person of the heart 16
15 in your hearts reverence Christ as Lord. 16
2Pe 1:19 and the morning star rises in your hearts. 16
2:14 They have hearts trained in greed. 16
1Jn 3:17 sees . . in need, yet closes his heart against him 20
19 and reassure our hearts before him 16
20 whenever our hearts condemn us; 16
20 for God is greater than our hearts 16
21 Beloved, if our hearts do not condemn us 16
Rev 2:23 that I am he who searches mind and heart 16
17:17 for God has put it into their hearts 16
18: 7 Since in her heart she says, 'A queen I sit 16
1Es 1:23 his heart was full of godliness. 16
48 he stiffened his neck and hardened his heart 16
2: 9 from many whose hearts were stirred. 19
3:21 It makes all hearts feel rich 16
8:25 who put this into the heart of the king 16
2Es 3: 1 and my thoughts welled up in my heart 25
20 didst not take away from them their evil heart 25
21 For the first Adam, burdened with an evil heart 25
22 the law was in the people's heart 25
26 for they also had the evil heart. 25
28 Then I said in my heart 25
29 And my heart failed me 25
4: 4 and will teach you why the heart is evil. 25
7 How many dwellings are in the heart of the sea 25
30 For a grain of evil seed was sown in Adam's heart 25
5:21 the thoughts of my heart were very grievous to me 25
34 for every hour I suffer agonies of heart 26
6:26 the heart of the earth's inhabitants 25
36 on the eighth night my heart was troubled 25
7:48 For an evil heart has grown up in us 25
8: 4 and drink wisdom, O my heart! ‡
6 give us seed for our heart 25
58 said in their hearts that there is not God 25
9:27 my heart was troubled again as it was before. 25
36 as well as our heart which received it; 25
38 When I said these things in my heart 25
38 and was deeply grieved at heart 24
40 and why are you grieved at heart? 24
10:25 and my heart was terrified ‡
55 do not let your heart be terrified 25
12:38 whose hearts you know are able to comprehend 25
13: 3 a man come up out of the heart of the sea ‡
25 a man come up from the heart of the sea 25
51 the man coming up from the heart of the sea? 25
14: 8 Lay up in your heart the signs 25
25 you shall come here, and I will light in your heart 25
34 rule over your minds and discipline your hearts 25
40 my heart poured forth understanding 25
16:54 their thoughts and their hearts. 25
61 and put a heart in the midst of his body 25
63 and what you think in your hearts! 25
Tob 1:12 because I remembered God with all my heart. 22
4:13 in your heart do not disdain your brethren 16
6: 4 take the heart and liver and gall 16
6 of what use is the . . heart and gall of the fish? 16
7 He replied, "As for the heart and liver 16
16 some of the heart and liver of the fish 16
8: 2 and put the heart and liver of the fish upon them 16
13: 6 with all your heart and with all your soul 16
Jdt 6: 9 hope in your heart that they will not be taken 16
8:14 You cannot plumb the depths of the human heart 16
27 to search their hearts 16
28 has been spoken out of a true heart 16
29 your heart's disposition is right. 16

10:16 do not be afraid in your heart 16
11: 1 do not be afraid in your heart 16
12:16 Holofernes' heart was ravished with her 16
13: 4 Then Judith . . said in her heart 16
19 will never depart from the hearts of men 16
AEs 14:13 turn his heart to hate 16
15: 5 her heart was frozen with fear. 16
13 my heart was shaken with fear at your glory. 16
Wis 1: 1 seek him with sincerity of heart; 16
6 a true observer of his heart 16
2: 2 a spark kindled by the beating of our hearts. 16
4:15 nor take such a thing to heart 14
8:21 with my whole heart I said 16
15:10 His heart is ashes, his hope is cheaper than dirt 16
Sir 1:12 The fear of the Lord delights the heart 16
30 your heart was full of deceit. 16
2: 2 Set your heart right and be steadfast 16
12 Woe to timid hearts and to slack hands 16
13 Woe to the faint heart, for it has no trust! 16
17 who fear the Lord will prepare their hearts 16
5: 2 walking according to the desires of your heart. 16
7:27 With all your heart honor your father 16
9: 9 lest your heart turn aside to her 22
10:12 his heart has forsaken his Maker. 16
13:25 A man's heart changes his countenance 16
26 The mark of a happy heart is a cheerful face 16
14: 2 Blessed is he whose heart does not condemn him 22
17: 8 He set his eye upon their hearts 16
21: 6 he that fears the Lord will repent in his heart. 16
22:18 so a timid heart with a fool's purpose 16
19 one who pricks the heart makes it show feeling. 16
25: 7 With nine thoughts I have gladdened my heart 16
13 Any wound, but not a wound of the heart! 16
23 A dejected mind, a gloomy face, and a wounded heart 16
26: 4 Whether rich or poor, his heart is glad 16
5 Of three things my heart is afraid 16
6 There is grief of heart and sorrow 16
18 so are beautiful feet with a steadfast heart. 21
28 At two things my heart is grieved 16
30:16 there is no gladness above joy of heart. 16
22 Gladness of heart is the life of man 16
23 Delight your soul and comfort your heart 16
25 A man of cheerful and good heart 16
31:26 so wine tests hearts in the strife of the proud. 16
28 rejoicing of heart and gladness of soul. 16
33: 5 The heart of a fool is like a cart wheel 20
37: 6 Do not forget a friend in your heart 22
13 establish the counsel of your own heart 16
17 As a clue to changes of heart 16
38:10 cleanse your heart from all sin. 16
18 sorrow of heart saps one's strength. 16
19 the life of the poor man weighs down his heart. 16
20 Do not give your heart to sorrow; drive it away 16
26 He sets his heart on plowing furrows 16
27 he sets his heart on painting a lifelike image 16
28 He sets his heart on finishing his handiwork 16
30 he sets his heart to finish the glazing 16
39: 5 will set his heart to rise early to seek the Lord 16
35 now sing praise with all your heart and voice 16
40: 2 Their perplexities and fear of heart 16
20 Wine and music gladden the heart 16
26 Riches and strength lift up the heart 16
42:18 He searches out the abyss, and the hearts of men 16
45:26 May the Lord grant you wisdom in your heart 16
46:11 those whose hearts did not fall into idolatry 16
47: 8 he sang praise with all his heart 16
48:10 to turn the heart of the father to the son 16
19 their hearts were shaken 16
49: 3 He set his heart upon the Lord 16
50:23 May he give us gladness of heart 16
27 who out of his heart poured forth wisdom. 16
28 he who lays them to heart will become wise. 16
51:15 my heart delighted in her 16
21 My heart was stirred to seek her 17
Bar 1:21 each followed the intent of his own wicked heart 16
2: 8 from the thoughts of his wicked heart. 16
31 give them a heart that obeys and ears that hear; 16
3: 7 For thou hast put the fear of thee in our hearts 16
7 we have put away from our hearts all the iniquity 16
LJr 1: 6 say in your heart, "It is thou, O Lord 14
20 men say their hearts have melted 16
Aza 1:16 with a contrite heart and a humble spirit 22
18 now with all our heart we follow thee 16
65 you who are holy and humble in heart 16
Sus 1:35 for her heart trusted in the Lord. 16
56 and lust has perverted your heart. 16
Man 1:11 now I bend the knee of my heart 16
1Mc 1: 3 he was exalted, and his heart was lifted up. 16
62 and were resolved in their hearts *
2:24 burned with zeal and his heart was stirred 18
12:28 they were afraid and were terrified at heart 16
16:13 His heart was lifted up 16
2Mc 1: 3 May he give you all a heart to worship him 16
3 a strong heart and a willing spirit. 16
4 May he open your heart to his law 16
2: 3 the law should not depart from their hearts. 16
3:16 to be wounded at heart 14
17 the pain lodged in his heart. 16
4:37 Therefore Antiochus was grieved at heart 23
11: 9 were strengthened in heart 22
15:27 praying to God in their hearts 16
3Mc 4: 2 everywhere their hearts were burning 16
5:47 with invulnerable heart and with his own eyes 16
4Mc 7:18 as many as attend to religion with a whole heart 16
13:13 Let us with all our hearts consecrate ourselves 16
15:23 devout reason, giving her heart a man's courage 20
29 carried away the prize . . in your heart! 20

heart *See also* desire, hardness, know, lose, open, ravish, set, take.

secret heart 1. סתם
Ps 51: 6 therefore teach me wisdom in my secret heart. 1

tender heart 1. *εὔσπλαγχνος*
1Pe 3: 8 have . . a tender heart and a humble mind. 1

very heart 1. *σπλάγχνον*
Phm 1:12 sending him back to you, sending my very heart. 1

hearth 1. בשל 2. יקד 3. מוֹקְדָה 4. *ἐσχάρα*
Lev 6: 9 The burnt offering shall be on the hearth 3
Isa 30:14 sherd . . with which to take fire from the hearth 2
Ezk 46:23 with hearths made at the bottom of the rows 1
Sir 50:12 as he stood by the hearth of the altar 4

hearth *See also* altar.

altar hearth 1. אֲרִאֵיל
Ezk 43:15 the altar hearth, four cubits; 1
15 from the altar hearth projecting upward 1
16 The altar hearth shall be square 1

heartily 1. *ἐκ ψυχῆς*
Col 3:23 Whatever your task, work heartily 1

heartless 1. *ἄστοργος*
Rom 1:31 foolish, faithless, heartless, ruthless. 1

hearty 1. *πολύς*
1Co 16:19 send you hearty greetings in the Lord. 1
2Mc 9:19 Antiochus . . sends hearty greetings 1

heat 1. אֵוַת נֶפֶשׁ 2. בער 3. זרב 4. חֹם 5. חֵמָה 6. חַמָּה 7. חֹרֶב 8. חֵרָבוֹן 9. חֲרוֹן 10. חֳרִי 11. אזא (A) 12. *ἐκπυρόω* 13. *θέρμη* 14. *θερμός* 15. *θερμότης* 16. *καῦμα* 17. *καύσων* 18. *σπουδή* 19. aestus 20. ardor
Gen 8:22 cold and heat, summer and winter, day and night 4
18: 1 the door of his tent in the heat of the day. 4
31:40 Thus I was; by day the heat consumed me 7
Deu 29:24 What means the heat of this great anger?' 10
1Sm 11:11 cut down the Ammonites until the heat of the day; 4
2Sm 4: 5 about the heat of the day they came to the house 4
Job 6:17 In time of heat they disappear; 3
24:19 Drought and heat snatch away the snow waters; 4
30:30 My skin turns black . . and my bones burn with heat. 7
Ps 19: 6 there is nothing hid from its heat. 6
32: 4 my strength was dried up as by the heat of summer. 8
58: 9 Sooner than your pots can feel the heat of thorns *
Isa 4: 6 for a shade by day from the heat, and for a refuge 7
18: 4 from my dwelling like clear heat in sunshine 4
4 like a cloud of dew in the heat of harvest. 4
25: 4 shelter from the storm and a shade from the heat 7
5 like heat in a dry place. 7
5 as heat by the shade of a cloud 7
42:25 he poured upon him the heat of his anger 5
Jer 2:24 a wild ass . . in her heat sniffing the wind! 1
17: 8 and does not fear when heat comes 4
36:30 his dead body shall be cast out to the heat by day 7
Ezk 3:14 and I went in bitterness in the heat of my spirit 5
Dan 3:19 ordered the furnace heated seven times more 11
19 seven times more than it was wont to be heated. 11
Hos 7: 4 they are like a heated oven 2
5 the princes became sick with the heat of wine; 5
Nah 1: 6 Who can endure the heat of his anger? 9
Zep 3: 8 upon them my indignation, all the heat of my anger; 9
Act 28: 3 when a viper came out because of the heat 13
Rev 16: 9 men were scorched by the fierce heat 16
2Es 1:20 Because of the heat I covered you 19
7:41 or summer or spring or heat or winter or frost 19
15:50 when the heat rises that is sent upon you. 20
Wis 2: 4 mist that is..overcome by its heat. 15
Sir 14:27 he will be sheltered by her from the heat 16
23:16 The soul heated like a burning fire 14
38:28 he wastes away in the heat of the furnace; 14
43:22 when the dew appears, it refreshes from the heat. 17
Bar 2:25 cast out to the heat of day and the frost of night. 16
Aza 1:44 Bless the Lord, fire and heat 16
2Mc 7: 3 and gave orders that pans and caldrons be heated. 12
4 These were heated immediately 12
14:43 in the heat of the struggle he did not hit exactly 18

burning heat 1. זַלְעָפָה 2. רֶשֶׁף 3. *καῦμα* 4. *καύσων*
Deu 32:24 devoured with burning heat and poisonous 2
Lam 5:10 skin is hot . . with the burning heat of famine. 1
Jdt 8: 3 he was overcome by the burning heat 4
Sir 43: 3 who can withstand its burning heat? 3
4 A man tending a furnace works in burning heat 3

fiery heat 1. חַרְחֻר
Deu 28:22 smite you with . . inflammation, and fiery heat 1

heat in the fire 1. *πυρόω*
4Mc 11:19 sharp spits that had been heated in the fire 1

scorching heat 1. *καῦμα* 2. *καύσων*
Mat 20:12 the burden of the day and the scorching heat.' 2
Lke 12:55 'There will be scorching heat'; and it happens. 2
Jas 1:11 For the sun rises with its scorching heat 2
Rev 7:16 sun shall not strike them, nor any scorching heat 1
Sir 18:16 Does not the dew assuage the scorching heat? 2

summer heat 1. *καίω*
Aza 1:45 Bless the Lord, winter cold and summer heat 1

heathen 1. גּוֹי 2. *ἀλλοεθνής* 3. *ἐθνικός* 4. *ἔθνος*
Ps 79: 1 O God, the heathen have come into thy inheritance; 1
1Co 12: 2 You know that when you were heathen 4
1Th 4: 5 like heathen who do not know God; 4
3Jn 1: 7 they . . have accepted nothing from the heathen 3
Wis 14:11 a visitation also upon the heathen idols 4
15:15 thought that all their heathen idols were gods 4
LJr 1: 4 inspire fear in the heathen. 4
17 so are the gods of the heathen *
3Mc 4: 6 were torn by the harsh treatment of the heathen. 2

heathen *See also* cult.

heaven 1. מְעָלָה 2. מָרוֹם 3. שָׁמַיִם 4. שְׁמַיִן (A) 5. *ἐπουράνιος* 6. *οὐράνιος* 7. *οὐρανόθεν* 8. *οὐρανός* 9. *ὕψος* 10. caelum
Gen 1: 1 God created the heavens and the earth 3
8 God called the firmament Heaven. 3
9 Let the waters under the heavens be gathered 3
14 there be lights in the firmament of the heavens 3
15 in the firmament of the heavens to give light 3
17 God set them in the firmament of the heavens 3
20 the earth across the firmament of the heavens 3
2: 1 Thus the heavens and the earth were finished 3
4 the generations of the heavens and the earth 3
4 the LORD God made the earth and the heavens 3
6:17 from under heaven; everything that is 3
7:11 and the windows of the heavens were opened. 3
19 mountains under the whole heaven were covered; 3
8: 2 and the windows of the heavens were closed 3
2 the rain from the heavens was restrained 3
11: 4 a city, and a tower with its top in the heavens 3
14:19 by God Most High, maker of heaven and earth; 3
22 LORD God Most High, maker of heaven and earth 3
15: 5 Look toward heaven, and number the stars 3
19:24 fire from the LORD out of heaven; 3
21:17 and the angel of God called to Hagar from heaven 3
22:11 the angel of the LORD called to him from heaven 3
15 called to Abraham a second time from heaven 3
17 multiply your descendants as the stars of heaven 3
24: 3 LORD, the God of heaven and of the earth 3
7 The LORD, the God of heaven, who took me 3
26: 4 descendants as the stars of heaven 3
27:28 May God give you of the dew of heaven 3
39 and away from the dew of heaven on high. 3
28:12 and the top of it reached to heaven; 3
17 house of God, and this is the gate of heaven. 3
49:25 will bless you with blessings of heaven above 3
Exd 9: 8 Take handfuls of ashes . . throw them toward heaven 3
10 and Moses threw them toward heaven, and it became 3
22 Moses, "Stretch forth your hand toward heaven 3
23 Moses stretched forth his rod toward heaven; 3
10:21 Stretch out your hand toward heaven that there 3
22 So Moses stretched out his hand toward heaven 3
16: 4 Behold, I will rain bread from heaven for you; 3
17:14 remembrance of Am'alek from under heaven. 3
20: 4 likeness of anything that is in heaven above 3
11 for in six days the LORD made heaven and earth 3
22 that I have talked with you from heaven. 3
24:10 like the very heaven for clearness. 3
31:17 in six days the LORD made heaven and earth 3
32:13 your descendants as the stars of heaven 3
Lev 26:19 I will make your heavens like iron 3
Deu 1:10 you are . . as the stars of heaven for multitude. 3
28 the cities are great and fortified up to heaven; 3
2:25 peoples that are under the whole of heaven 3
3:24 what god is there in heaven or on earth who can do 3
4:11 mountain burned with fire to the heart of heaven 3
19 beware lest you lift up your eyes to heaven 3
19 sun and . . the stars, all the host of heaven 3
19 all the peoples under the whole heaven. 3
26 I call heaven and earth to witness against you 3
32 ask from one end of heaven to the other 3
36 Out of heaven he let you hear his voice 3
39 know . . that the LORD is God in heaven above 3
5: 8 any likeness of anything that is in heaven above 3
7:24 shall make their name perish from under heaven; 3
9: 1 cities great and fortified up to heaven 3
14 I may . . blot out their name from under heaven; 3
10:14 Behold, to the LORD your God belong heaven 3
14 to the LORD . . belong . . the heaven of heavens 3
14 to the LORD . . belong . . the heaven of heavens 3
22 made you as the stars of heaven for multitude. 3

11:11 which drinks water by the rain from heaven 3
17 he shut up the heavens, so that there be no rain 3
21 as long as the heavens are above the earth. 3
17: 3 worshipped . . moon or any of the host of heaven 3
25:19 remembrance of Am'alek from under heaven; 3
26:15 Look down from thy holy habitation, from heaven 3
28:12 will open to you his good treasury the heavens 3
23 heavens over your head shall be brass 3
24 from heaven it shall come down upon you until 3
62 you were as the stars of heaven for multitude 3
29:20 LORD would blot out his name from under heaven. 3
30: 4 outcasts are in the uttermost parts of heaven 3
12 is not in heaven, that you should say, 'Who will go up 3
12 'Who will go up for us to heaven, and bring it to us 3
19 I call heaven and earth to witness against you 3
31:28 call heaven and earth to witness against them. 3
32: 1 Give ear, O heavens, and I will speak; 3
40 For I lift up my hand to heaven, and swear, As I live 3
33:13 with the choicest gifts of heaven above 3
26 who rides through the heavens to your help 3
28 yea, his heavens drop down dew. 3
Jos 2:11 is God in heaven above and on earth beneath. 3
8:20 behold, the smoke of the city went up to heaven; 3
10:11 the LORD threw down great stones from heaven 3
13 The sun stayed in the midst of heaven 3
Jdg 5: 4 the earth trembled, and the heavens dropped 3
20 From heaven fought the stars, from their courses 3
13:20 the flame went up toward heaven from the altar 3
20:40 the whole of the city went up in smoke to heaven. 3
1Sm 2:10 against them he will thunder in heaven. 3
5:12 and the cry of the city went up to heaven. 3
2Sm 18: 9 and he was left hanging between heaven and earth 3
21:10 until rain fell upon them from the heavens; 3
22: 8 foundations of the heavens trembled and quaked 3
10 He bowed the heavens, and came down; 3
14 The LORD thundered from heaven 3
1Kg 8:12 The LORD has set the sun in the heavens 8
22 and spread forth his hands toward heaven; 3
23 God like thee, in heaven above or on earth beneath 3
27 heaven and the highest heaven cannot contain 3
30 hear thou in heaven thy dwelling place; 3
32 hear thou in heaven, and act, and judge 3
34 hear thou in heaven, and forgive the sin 3
35 When heaven is shut up and there is no rain 3
36 hear thou in heaven, and forgive the sin 3
39 hear . . in heaven thy dwelling place, and forgive 3
43 hear thou in heaven thy dwelling place 3
45 hear thou in heaven their prayer 3
49 hear thou in heaven thy dwelling place 3
54 knelt with hands outstretched toward heaven; 3
18:45 the heavens grew black with clouds and wind 3
22:19 the LORD sitting . . and all the host of heaven 3
2Kg 1:10 let fire come down from heaven and consume you 3
10 Then fire came down from heaven, and consumed him 3
12 let fire come down from heaven and consume you 3
12 Then the fire of God came down from heaven 3
14 fire came down from heaven, and consumed the two 3
2: 1 about to take Eli'jah up to heaven by a whirlwind 3
11 And Eli'jah went up by a whirlwind into heaven. 3
7: 2 If the LORD . . should make windows in heaven 3
19 If the LORD . . should make windows in heaven 3
14:27 blot out the name of Israel from under heaven 3
17:16 and worshiped all the host of heaven, and served 3
19:15 O LORD . . thou hast made heaven and earth. 3
21: 3 and worshiped all the host of heaven, and served 3
5 And he built altars for all the host of heaven 3
23: 4 Ba'al, for Ashe'rah, and for all the host of heaven; 3
5 constellations, and all the host of the heavens. 3
1Ch 16:26 are idols; but the LORD made the heavens. 3
31 Let the heavens be glad, and let the earth rejoice 3
21:16 of the LORD standing between earth and heaven 3
26 and he answered him with fire from heaven upon 3
27:23 to make Israel as many as the stars of heaven. 3
29:11 all . . in the heavens and in the earth is thine; 3
2Ch 2: 6 since heaven . . cannot contain him? 3
6 heaven, even highest heaven, cannot contain him? 3
12 LORD . . who made heaven and earth 3
6:13 and spread forth his hands toward heaven; 3
14 there is no God like thee, in heaven or on earth 3
18 heaven and the highest heaven cannot contain 3
18 heaven and the highest heaven cannot contain 3
21 yea, hear thou from heaven thy dwelling place; 3
23 then hear thou from heaven, and act, and judge 3
25 then hear thou from heaven, and forgive the sin 3
26 When heaven is shut up and there is no rain 3
27 then hear thou in heaven, and forgive the sin 3
30 then hear thou from heaven thy dwelling place 3
33 hear thou from heaven . . and do according to all 3
35 then hear thou from heaven their prayer 3
39 then hear thou from heaven their prayer 3
7: 1 ended his prayer, fire came down from heaven 3
13 When I shut up the heavens so that there is no rain 3
14 then I will hear from heaven, and will forgive 3
18:18 all the host of heaven standing on his right hand 3
20: 6 LORD, God of our fathers, art thou not God in heaven? 3
28: 9 in a rage which has reached up to heaven. 3
30:27 came to his holy habitation in heaven. 3
32:20 prayed because of this and cried to heaven. 3
33: 3 worshiped all the host of heaven, and served them. 3
5 he built altars for all the host of heaven 3
36:23 LORD, the God of heaven, has given me all 3
Ezr 1: 2 LORD, the God of heaven, has given me all 3
5:11 'We are the servants of the God of heaven and earth 4
12 our fathers had angered the God of heaven 4
6: 9 burnt offerings to the God of heaven 4
10 offer pleasing sacrifices to the God of heaven 4
7:12 Ezra . . scribe of the law of the God of heaven. 4
21 Ezra . . scribe of the law of the God of heaven 4
23 Whatever is commanded by the God of heaven 4
23 be done in full for the house of the God of heaven 4
9: 6 our guilt has mounted up to the heavens. 3
Neh 1: 4 fasting and praying before the God of heaven. 3
5 I said, "O LORD God of heaven, the great and terrible 3
2: 4 I prayed to the God of heaven. 3
20 The God of heaven will make us prosper 3
9: 6 thou hast made heaven, the heaven of heavens 3
6 thou hast made heaven, the heaven of heavens 3
6 thou hast made heaven, the heaven of heavens 3
6 host of heaven worships thee. 3
13 Thou didst . . speak with them from heaven 3
15 give them bread from heaven for their hunger 3
23 descendants as the stars of heaven 3
27 cried . . and thou didst hear them from heaven; 3
28 cried to thee thou didst hear from heaven 3
Job 1:16 another, and said, "The fire of God fell from heaven 3
2:12 sprinkled dust upon their heads toward heaven. 3
9: 8 who alone stretched out the heavens 3
11: 8 It is higher than heaven–what can you do? 3
14:12 till the heavens are no more he will not awake 3
15:15 the heavens are not clean in his sight; 3
16:19 Even now, behold, my witness is in heaven 3
20: 6 Though his height mount up to the heavens 3
27 The heavens will reveal his iniquity 3
22:12 Is not God high in the heavens? 3
14 he walks on the vault of heaven.' 3
26:11 The pillars of heaven tremble, and are astounded 3
13 By his wind the heavens were made fair; 3
28:24 and sees everything under the heavens. 3
35: 5 Look at the heavens, and see; and behold the clouds 3
37: 3 Under the whole heaven he lets it go 3
38:29 who has given birth to the hoarfrost of heaven? 3
33 Do you know the ordinances of the heavens? 3
37 Or who can tilt the waterskins of the heavens 3
41:11 Whatever is under the whole heaven is mine. 3
Ps 2: 4 He who sits in the heavens laughs; 3
8: 1 Thou whose glory above the heavens is chanted 3
3 When I look at thy heavens, the work of thy fingers 3
11: 4 in his holy temple, the LORD'S throne is in heaven; 3
14: 2 The LORD looks down from heaven 3
18: 9 He bowed the heavens, and came down; 3
13 The LORD also thundered in the heavens 3
19: 1 The heavens are telling the glory of God; 3
6 Its rising is from the end of the heavens 3
20: 6 he will answer him from his holy heaven 3
33: 6 By the word of the LORD the heavens were made 3
13 The LORD looks down from heaven, he sees all 3
36: 5 Thy steadfast love, O LORD, extends to the heavens 3
50: 4 He calls to the heavens above and to the earth 3
6 The heavens declare his righteousness 3
53: 2 God looks down from heaven upon the sons of men 3
57: 3 He will send from heaven and save me 3
5 Be exalted, O God, above the heavens! 3
10 For thy steadfast love is great to the heavens 3
11 Be exalted, O God, above the heavens! 3
68: 8 earth quaked, the heavens poured down rain 3
33 him who rides in the heavens, the ancient heavens; 3
33 him who rides in the heavens, the ancient heavens; 3
69:34 Let heaven and earth praise him 3
73: 9 They set their mouths against the heavens 3
25 Whom have I in heaven but thee? 3
76: 8 From the heavens thou didst utter judgment; 3
78:23 he commanded . . and opened the doors of heaven; 3
24 manna to eat, and gave them the grain of heaven. 3
26 He caused the east wind to blow in the heavens 3
69 He built his sanctuary like the high heavens •
80:14 Look down from heaven, and see; 3
89: 2 thy faithfulness is firm as the heavens. 3
5 Let the heavens praise thy wonders, O LORD 3
11 The heavens are thine, the earth also is thine; 3
29 his throne as the days of the heavens. 3
96: 5 but the LORD made the heavens. 3
11 Let the heavens be glad, and let the earth rejoice; 3
97: 6 The heavens proclaim his righteousness; 3
102:19 from heaven the LORD looked at the earth 3
25 heavens are the work of thy hands. 3
103:11 For as the heavens are high above the earth 3
19 LORD has established his throne in the heavens 3
104: 2 who hast stretched out the heavens like a tent 3
105:40 gave them bread from heaven in abundance. 3
107:26 mounted up to heaven, they went down to the depths; 3
108: 4 thy steadfast love is great above the heavens 3
5 Be exalted, O God, above the heavens! 3
113: 4 his glory above the heavens. 3
6 who looks far down upon the heavens and the earth? 3
115: 3 Our God is in the heavens; 3
15 blessed by the LORD, who made heaven and earth! 3
16 The heavens are the LORD's heavens 3
16 The heavens are the LORD's heavens 3
119:89 O LORD, thy word is firmly fixed in the heavens. 3
121: 2 help . . from the LORD, who made heaven and earth. 3
123: 1 O thou who art enthroned in the heavens! 3
124: 8 LORD, who made heaven and earth. 3
134: 3 LORD bless . . he who made heaven and earth! 3
135: 6 in heaven and on earth, in the seas and all deeps. 3
136: 5 to him who by understanding made the heavens 3
26 O give thanks to the God of heaven 3
139: 8 If I ascend to heaven, thou art there! 3
144: 5 Bow thy heavens, O LORD, and come down! 3
146: 6 who made heaven and earth, the sea, and all that 3
147: 8 He covers the heavens with clouds 3
148: 1 Praise the LORD from the heavens, praise him 3
4 Praise him, you highest heavens 3
4 Praise him, you . . waters above the heavens! 3
13 his glory is above earth and heaven. 3
Prv 3:19 by understanding he established the heavens; 3
8:27 When he established the heavens, I was there 3
23: 5 flying like an eagle toward heaven. 3
25: 3 As the heaven for height, and the earth for depth 3
30: 4 Who has ascended to heaven and come down? 3
Ecc 1:13 to seek . . by wisdom all that is done under heaven; 3
2: 3 for . . men to do under heaven during the few days 3
3: 1 and a time for every matter under heaven 3
5: 2 for God is in heaven, and you upon earth; 3
Isa 1: 2 Hear, O heavens, and give ear, O earth; 3
7:11 a sign . . let it be deep as Sheol or high as heaven. 1
13: 5 come from a distant land . . the end of the heavens 3
10 For the stars of the heavens 3
13 Therefore I will make the heavens tremble 3
14:12 How you are fallen from heaven, O Day Star 3
13 You said in your heart, 'I will ascend to heaven; 3
24: 4 the heavens languish together with the earth. 2
18 For the windows of heaven are opened 2
21 that day the LORD will punish the host of heaven 2
21 punish the host of heaven, in heaven 2
34: 4 All the host of heaven shall rot away 3
5 For my sword has drunk its fill in the heavens; 3
37:16 thou hast made heaven and earth. 3
40:12 Who has . . marked off the heavens with a span 3
22 who stretches out the heavens like a curtain 3
42: 5 Thus says God, the LORD, who created the heavens 3
44:23 Sing, O heavens, for the LORD has done it; 3
24 the LORD . . who stretched out the heavens alone 3
45: 8 Shower, O heavens, from above, and let the skies 3
12 it was my hands that stretched out the heavens 3
18 says the LORD, who created the heavens (he is God!) 3
47:13 let them . . save you, those who divide the heavens 3
48:13 and my right hand spread out the heavens; 3
49:13 Sing for joy, O heavens, and exult, O earth; 3
50: 3 I clothe the heavens with blackness 3
51: 6 Lift up your eyes to the heavens 3
6 for the heavens will vanish like smoke 3
13 your Maker, who stretched out the heavens 3
16 stretching out the heavens and laying 3
55: 9 For as the heavens are higher than the earth 3
10 For as the rain and the snow come down from heaven 3
63:15 Look down from heaven and see 3
64: 1 that thou wouldst rend the heavens and come down 3
65:17 For behold, I create new heavens and a new earth; 3
66: 1 Heaven is my throne and the earth is my footstool; 3
22 the new heavens and the new earth 3
Jer 2:12 Be appalled, O heavens, at this, be shocked 3
4:23 and to the heavens, and they had no light. 3
28 earth shall mourn, and the heavens above be black; 3
7:18 knead dough, to make cakes for the queen of heaven; 3
8: 2 and all the host of heaven, which they have loved 3
7 Even the stork in the heavens knows her times; 3
10: 2 nor be dismayed at the signs of the heavens 3
11 gods who did not make the heavens and the earth 4
11 from the earth and from under the heavens. 3
12 his understanding stretched out the heavens. 3
13 there is a tumult of waters in the heavens 3
14:22 Or can the heavens give showers? 3
19:13 incense has been burned to all the host of heaven 3
23:24 Do I not fill heaven and earth? says the LORD. 3
31:37 If the heavens above can be measured 3
32:17 'Ah Lord GOD! It is thou who hast made the heavens 3
33:22 As the host of heaven cannot be numbered 3
25 and night and the ordinances of heaven and earth 3
44:17 we have vowed, burn incense to the queen of heaven 3
18 left off burning incense to the queen of heaven 3
19 When we burned incense to the queen of heaven 3
25 to burn incense to the queen of heaven 3
49:36 the four winds from the four quarters of heaven; 3
51: 9 for her judgment has reached up to heaven 3
15 by his understanding stretched out the heavens. 3
16 there is a tumult of waters in the heavens 3
48 the heavens and the earth, and all that is in them 3
53 Though Babylon should mount up to heaven 3
Lam 2: 1 has cast down from heaven to earth the splendor 3
3:41 lift up our hearts and hands to God in heaven 3
50 until the LORD from heaven looks down and sees; 3
66 and destroy them from under thy heavens, O LORD. 3
4:19 were swifter than the vultures in the heavens; 3
Ezk 1: 1 the heavens were opened, and I saw visions of God. 3
8: 3 the Spirit lifted me up between earth and heaven 3
32: 7 When I blot you out, I will cover the heavens 3
8 bright lights of heaven will I make dark over you 3

Dan 2:18 told them to seek mercy of the God of heaven 4
19 Then Daniel blessed the God of heaven. 4
28 there is a God in heaven who reveals mysteries 4
37 to whom the God of heaven has given the kingdom 4
44 God of heaven will set up a kingdom 4
4:11 tree grew . . and its top reached to heaven 4
13 a watcher, a holy one, came down from heaven. 4
15 Let him be wet with the dew of heaven; 4
20 grew . . so that its top reached to heaven 4
22 Your greatness has grown and reaches to heaven 4
23 holy one, coming down from heaven and saying, 4
23 let him be wet with the dew of heaven; 4
25 wet with the dew of heaven, 4
26 from the time that you know that Heaven rules. 4
31 there fell a voice from heaven, "O King 4
33 body was wet with the dew of heaven 4
34 Nebuchadnez'zar, lifted my eyes to heaven 4
35 does according to his will in the host of heaven 4
37 praise and extol and honor the King of heaven; 4
5:21 body was wet with the dew of heaven 4
23 lifted up yourself against the Lord of heaven; 4
6:27 works signs and wonders in heaven and on earth 4
7: 2 four winds of heaven were stirring up the great 4
13 clouds of heaven there came one like a son of man 4
27 kingdoms under the whole heaven shall be given 4
8: 8 four . . horns toward the four winds of heaven. 3
10 It grew great, even to the host of heaven; 3
9:12 under the whole heaven there has not been done 3
11: 4 divided toward the four winds of heaven 3
12: 7 his right hand and his left hand toward heaven; 3
Hos 2:21 that day, says the LORD, I will answer the heavens 3
Jol 2:10 earth quakes before them, the heavens tremble. 3
30 I will give portents in the heavens 3
3:16 and the heavens and the earth shake. 3
Ams 9: 2 though they climb up to heaven 3
6 who builds his upper chambers in the heavens 3
Jon 1: 9 I fear the LORD, the God of heaven, 3
Nah 3:16 merchants more than the stars of the heavens. 3
Hab 3: 3 His glory covered the heavens 3
Zep 1: 5 bow down on the roofs to the host of the heavens; 3
Hag 1:10 the heavens above you have withheld the dew 3
2: 6 I will shake the heavens and the earth and the sea 3
21 I am about to shake the heavens and the earth 3
Zec 2: 6 as the four winds of the heavens, says the LORD. 3
5: 9 lifted up the ephah between earth and heaven. 3
6: 5 These are going forth to the four winds of heaven 3
8:12 the heavens shall give their dew; 3
12: 1 Thus says the LORD, who stretched out the heavens 3
Mal 3:10 if I will not open the windows of heaven for you 3
Mat 3: 2 Repent, for the kingdom of heaven is at hand. 8
16 behold, the heavens were opened and he saw 8
17 a voice from heaven, saying, "This is my beloved Son 8
4:17 Repent, for the kingdom of heaven is at hand. 8
5: 3 spirit, for theirs is the kingdom of heaven. 8
10 for theirs is the kingdom of heaven. 8
12 reward is great in heaven, for so men persecuted 8
16 give glory to your Father who is in heaven. 8
18 For truly, I say to you, till heaven and earth pass 8
19 so, shall be called least in the kingdom of heaven; 8
19 shall be called great in the kingdom of heaven. 8
20 you will never enter the kingdom of heaven. 8
34 at all, either by heaven, for it is the throne of God 8
45 Father who is in heaven; for he makes his sun rise 8
6: 1 no reward from your Father who is in heaven. 8
9 Father who art in heaven, Hallowed be thy name. 8
10 come. Thy will be done, On earth as it is in heaven. 8
20 lay up for yourselves treasures in heaven 8
7:11 how much more will your Father who is in heaven 8
21 shall enter the kingdom of heaven 8
21 he who does the will of my Father who is in heaven. 8
8:11 Abraham, Isaac, and Jacob in the kingdom of heaven 8
10: 7 'The kingdom of heaven is at hand.' 8
32 before my Father who is in heaven; 8
33 before my Father who is in heaven. 8
11:11 yet he who is least in the kingdom of heaven 8
12 the kingdom of heaven has suffered violence 8
23 you, Caper'na-um, will you be exalted to heaven? 8
25 I thank thee, Father, Lord of heaven and earth 8
12:50 For whoever does the will of my Father in heaven 8
13:11 to know the secrets of the kingdom of heaven 8
24 The kingdom of heaven may be compared to a man 8
31 The kingdom of heaven is like a grain of mustard 8
33 The kingdom of heaven is like leaven 8
44 The kingdom of heaven is like treasure 8
45 Again, the kingdom of heaven is like a merchant 8
47 Again, the kingdom of heaven is like a net 8
52 trained for the kingdom of heaven 8
14:19 he looked up to heaven, and blessed, and broke 8
16: 1 they asked him to show them a sign from heaven. 8
17 but my Father who is in heaven. 8
19 I will give you the keys of the kingdom of heaven 8
19 shall be bound in heaven 8
19 shall be loosed in heaven. 8
18: 1 Who is the greatest in the kingdom of heaven? 8
3 you will never enter the kingdom of heaven. 8
4 he is the greatest in the kingdom of heaven. 8
10 in heaven their angels always behold the face 8
10 the face of my Father who is in heaven. 8
14 So it is not the will of my Father who is in heaven 8
18 shall be bound in heaven 8
18 loose on earth shall be loosed in heaven. 8
19 it will be done for them by my Father in heaven. 8
23 Therefore the kingdom of heaven may be compared 8
19:12 for the sake of the kingdom of heaven 8
14 for to such belongs the kingdom of heaven. 8
21 you will have treasure in heaven 8
23 to enter the kingdom of heaven. 8
20: 1 For the kingdom of heaven is like a householder 8
21:25 From heaven or from men? 8
25 If we say, 'From heaven,' he will say to us 8
22: 2 The kingdom of heaven may be compared to a king 8
30 but are like angels in heaven. 8
23: 9 you have one Father, who is in heaven. 6
13 you shut the kingdom of heaven against men 8
22 he who swears by heaven 8
24:29 the stars will fall from heaven 8
29 the powers of the heavens will be shaken; 8
30 the sign of the Son of man in heaven 8
30 see the Son of man coming on the clouds of heaven 8
31 from one end of heaven to the other. 8
35 Heaven and earth will pass away 8
36 not even the angels of heaven, nor the Son 8
25: 1 Then the kingdom of heaven shall be compared 8
26:64 coming on the clouds of heaven. 8
28: 2 an angel of the Lord descended from heaven 8
18 All authority in heaven and on earth 8
Mrk 1:10 he saw the heavens opened and the Spirit descending 8
11 a voice came from heaven, "Thou art my beloved Son; 8
6:41 he looked up to heaven 8
7:34 looking up to heaven, he sighed, and said 8
8:11 seeking from him a sign from heaven, to test him. 8
10:21 you will have treasure in heaven 8
11:25 Father . . who is in heaven may forgive you 8
30 Was the baptism of John from heaven or from men? 8
31 If we say, 'From heaven,' he will say 8
12:25 are like angels in heaven. 8
13:25 the powers in the heavens will be shaken. 8
25 the powers in the heavens will be shaken. 8
27 from the ends of the earth to the ends of heaven. 8
31 Heaven and earth will pass away 8
32 not even the angels in heaven, nor the Son 8
14:62 coming with the clouds of heaven. 8
16:19 Jesus . . was taken up into heaven 8
Lke 2:15 When the angels went away from them into heaven 8
3:21 the heaven was opened 8
22 a voice came from heaven 8
4:25 the heaven was shut up three years and six months 8
6:23 for behold, your reward is great in heaven 8
9:16 he looked up to heaven, and blessed and broke them 8
54 do you want us to bid fire come down from heaven 8
10:15 you, Caper'na-um, will you be exalted to heaven? 8
18 I saw Satan fall like lightning from heaven. 8
20 rejoice that your names are written in heaven. 8
21 I thank thee, Father, Lord of heaven and earth 8
11:16 others . . sought from him a sign from heaven. 8
12:33 with a treasure in the heavens that does not fail 8
15: 7 more joy in heaven over one sinner who repents 8
18 I have sinned against heaven and before you; 8
21 I have sinned against heaven and before you 8
16:17 it is easier for heaven and earth to pass away 8
17:29 fire and sulphur rained from heaven 8
18:13 would not even lift up his eyes to heaven 8
22 you will have treasure in heaven 8
19:38 Peace in heaven and glory in the highest! 8
20: 4 Was the baptism of John from heaven or from men? 8
5 If we say, 'From heaven,' he will say 8
21:11 terrors and great signs from heaven. 8
26 the powers of the heavens will be shaken. 8
33 Heaven and earth will pass away 8
24:51 and was carried up into heaven. 8
Joh 1:32 I saw the Spirit descend as a dove from heaven 8
51 truly, I say to you, you will see heaven opened 8
3:13 No one has ascended into heaven but he who 8
13 but he who descended from heaven, the Son of man. 8
27 except what is given him from heaven. 8
31 he who comes from heaven is above all. 8
6:31 'He gave them bread from heaven to eat.' 8
32 was not Moses who gave you the bread from heaven; 8
32 my Father gives you the true bread from heaven. 8
33 bread of God is that which comes down from heaven 8
38 I have come down from heaven, not to do my own will 8
41 I am the bread which came down from heaven. 8
42 does he now say, 'I have come down from heaven'? 8
50 This is the bread which comes down from heaven 8
51 I am the living bread which came down from heaven; 8
58 This is the bread which came down from heaven 8
12:28 Then a voice came from heaven 8
17: 1 he lifted up his eyes to heaven and said 8
Act 1:10 while they were gazing into heaven as he went 8
11 why do you stand looking into heaven? 8
11 who was taken up from you into heaven 8
11 in the same way as you saw him go into heaven. 8
2: 2 suddenly a sound came from heaven 8
5 devout men from every nation under heaven. 8
19 I will show wonders in the heaven above 8
34 David did not ascend into the heavens 8
3:21 whom heaven must receive 8
4:12 no other name under heaven given among men 8
24 the heaven and the earth and the sea 8
7:42 God . . gave them over to worship the host of heaven 8
49 'Heaven is my throne, and earth my footstool 8
55 he, full of the Holy Spirit, gazed into heaven 8
56 he said, "Behold, I see the heavens opened 8
9: 3 suddenly a light from heaven flashed about him. 8
10:11 saw the heaven opened, and something descending 8
16 the thing was taken up at once to heaven. 8
11: 5 a great sheet, let down from heaven by four corners 8
9 the voice answered a second time from heaven 8
10 all was drawn up again into heaven. 8
14:15 a living God who made the heaven and the earth 8
17 he . . gave you from heaven rains and fruitful seasons 7
17:24 being Lord of heaven and earth 8
22: 6 a great light from heaven suddenly shone about me 8
26:13 a light from heaven, brighter than the sun 7
Rom 1:18 For the wrath of God is revealed from heaven 8
10: 6 say in your heart, "Who will ascend into heaven? 8
1Co 8: 5 may be so-called gods in heaven or on earth 8
15:47 the second man is from heaven. 8
48 as is the man of heaven 5
48 so are those who are of heaven. 5
49 we shall also bear the image of the man of heaven. 5
2Co 5: 1 not made with hands, eternal in the heavens. 8
12: 2 a man in Christ . . caught up to the third heaven 8
Gal 1: 8 even if we, or an angel from heaven, should preach 8
Eph 1:10 things in heaven and things on earth. 8
3:15 every family in heaven and on earth is named 8
4:10 who also ascended far above all the heavens 8
6: 9 he who is both their Master and yours is in heaven 8
Php 2:10 in heaven and on earth and under the earth 5
3:20 our commonwealth is in heaven 8
Col 1: 5 because of the hope laid up for you in heaven 8
16 in heaven and on earth, visible and invisible 8
20 all things, whether on earth or in heaven 8
23 been preached to every creature under heaven 8
4: 1 knowing that you also have a Master in heaven. 8
1Th 1:10 to wait for his Son from heaven 8
4:16 For the Lord himself will descend from heaven 8
2Th 1: 7 when the Lord Jesus is revealed from heaven 8
Heb 1:10 the heavens are the work of thy hands; 8
4:14 high priest who has passed through the heavens 8
7:26 a high priest . . exalted above the heavens. 8
8: 1 right hand of the throne of the Majesty in heaven 8
9:24 into heaven itself 8
11:12 as many as the stars of heaven 8
12:23 who are enrolled in heaven 8
25 if we reject him who warns from heaven. 8
26 shake not only the earth but also the heaven. 8
Jas 5:12 do not swear, either by heaven or by earth 8
18 Then he prayed again and the heaven gave rain 8
1Pe 1: 4 inheritance which is . . kept in heaven for you 8
12 through the Holy Spirit sent from heaven 8
3:22 who has gone into heaven 8
2Pe 1:18 we heard this voice borne from heaven 8
3: 5 by the word of God heavens existed long ago 8
7 the heavens and earth that now exist 8
10 then the heavens will pass away with a loud noise 8
12 the heavens will be kindled and dissolved 8
13 we wait for new heavens and a new earth 8
Rev 3:12 city . . which comes down from my God out of heaven 8
4: 1 After this I looked, and lo, in heaven an open door! 8
2 I was in the Spirit, and lo, a throne stood in heaven 8
5: 3 no one in heaven or on earth or under the earth 8
13 I heard every creature in heaven and on earth 8
8: 1 silence in heaven for about half an hour. 8
10 great star fell from heaven, blazing like a torch 8
9: 1 and I saw a star fallen from heaven to earth 8
10: 1 coming down from heaven, wrapped in a cloud 8
4 but I heard a voice from heaven saying 8
5 the angel . . lifted up his right hand to heaven 8
6 who created heaven and what is in it 8
8 Then the voice which I had heard from heaven 8
11:12 Then they heard a loud voice from heaven saying 8
12 Then they heard a loud voice from heaven saying 8
13 terrified and gave glory to the God of heaven. 8
15 and there were loud voices in heaven, saying 8
19 Then God's temple in heaven was opened 8
12: 1 a great portent appeared in heaven, a woman 8
3 another portent appeared in heaven; 8
4 His tail swept down a third of the stars of heaven 8
7 Now war arose in heaven, Michael and his angels 8
8 there was no longer any place for them in heaven. 8
10 And I heard a loud voice in heaven, saying 8
12 Rejoice then, O heaven and you that dwell therein! 8
13: 6 his dwelling, that is, those who dwell in heaven. 8
13 even making fire come down from heaven to earth 8
14: 2 I heard a voice from heaven 8
7 and worship him who made heaven and earth 8
13 And I heard a voice from heaven saying, "Write this 8
17 another angel came out of the temple in heaven 8
15: 1 Then I saw another portent in heaven 8
5 temple of the tent of witness in heaven was opened 8
16:11 cursed the God of heaven for their pain and sores 8
21 great hailstones . . dropped on men from heaven 8
18: 1 I saw another angel coming down from heaven 8
4 Then I heard another voice from heaven saying 8
5 for her sins are heaped high as heaven 8
20 O heaven, O saints and apostles and prophets 8

19: 1 a great multitude in heaven, crying, "Hallelujah! 8
11 Then I saw heaven opened, and behold, a white horse! 8
14 And the armies of heaven . . followed him 8
20: 1 Then I saw an angel coming down from heaven 8
9 but fire came down from heaven and consumed them 8
21: 1 Then I saw a new heaven and a new earth; 8
1 first heaven and the first earth had passed away 8
2 new Jerusalem, coming down out of heaven from God 8
10 Jerusalem coming down out of heaven from God 8
1Es 4:34 The earth is vast, and heaven is high 8
34 it makes the circuit of the heavens 8
36 heaven blesses her 8
46 vowed to the King of heaven with your own lips. 8
58 he lifted up his face to heaven toward Jerusalem 8
58 praised the King of heaven, saying 8
6:13 the Lord who created the heaven and the earth. 8
15 the Lord of Israel who is in heaven 6
8:75 our mistakes have mounted up to heaven 8
2Es 2:14 Call, O call heaven and earth to witness 10
3:18 Thou didst bend down the heavens 10
4: 8 neither did I ever ascend into heaven.' 10
21 he who is above the heavens 10
21 what is above the height of the heavens. 10
6:38 'Let heaven and earth be made,' 10
11: 2 and all the winds of heaven blew upon him 10
6 I saw how all things under heaven were subjected 10
13: 3 behold, that man flew with the clouds of heaven; 10
5 gathered together from the four winds of heaven 10
15:44 then the dust and smoke shall go up to heaven 10
16:55 Let the heaven be made," and it was made. 10
59 who has spread out the heaven like an arch 10
Tob 5:16 God who dwells in heaven will prosper your way 8
7:18 the Lord of heaven and earth grant you joy 8
8: 5 the heavens and all thy creatures bless thee. 8
10:11 The God of heaven will prosper you, my children 8
12 The Lord of heaven bring you back safely 8
13: 7 I exalt my God; my soul exalts the King of heaven 8
11 gifts for the King of heaven 8
Jdt 5: 8 they worshiped the God of heaven 8
6:19 O Lord God of heaven, behold their arrogance 8
7:28 We call to witness against you heaven and earth 8
9:12 Lord of heaven and earth, Creator of the waters 8
11:17 serves the God of heaven day and night 8
13:18 who created the heavens and the earth 8
AEs 13:10 For thou hast made heaven and earth 8
10 earth and every wonderful thing under heaven 8
Wis 9:10 Send her forth from the holy heavens 8
16 who has traced out what is in the heavens? 8
13: 2 the luminaries of heaven 8
16:20 supply them from heaven with bread ready to eat 8
18:15 thy all-powerful word leaped from heaven 8
16 and touched heaven while standing on the earth. 8
Sir 1: 3 The height of heaven, the breadth of the earth 8
16:18 Behold, heaven and the highest heaven 8
17:32 He marshals the host of the height of heaven 8
24: 5 I have made the circuit of the vault of heaven 8
43: 1 the appearance of heaven in a spectacle of glory. 8
8 shining forth in the firmament of heaven. 8
9 The glory of the stars is the beauty of heaven 8
12 It encircles the heaven with its glorious arc; 8
45:15 for his descendants all the days of heaven 8
46:17 Then the Lord thundered from heaven 8
48: 3 By the word of the Lord he shut up the heavens 8
20 the Holy One quickly heard them from heaven 8
51:19 I spread out my hands to the heavens 9
Bar 1:11 days on earth may be like the days of heaven. 8
2: 2 Under the whole heaven there has not been done 8
3:29 Who has gone up into heaven, and taken her 8
5: 3 show your splendor everywhere under heaven. 8
LJr 1:54 they are like crows between heaven and earth. 8
67 show signs in the heavens and among the nations 8
Aza 1:13 as many as the stars of heaven 8
34 Blessed art thou in the firmament of heaven 8
36 Bless the Lord, you heavens 8
38 Bless the Lord, all waters above the heaven 8
41 Bless the Lord, stars of heaven 8
Sus 1: 9 and turned away their eyes from looking to Heaven 8
35 she, weeping, looked up toward heaven 8
Bel 1: 5 the living God, who created heaven and earth 8
Man 1: 2 thou who hast made heaven and earth 8
9 am unworthy to look up and see the height of heaven 8
15 all the host of heaven sings thy praise 8
1Mc 2:37 heaven and earth testify for us 8
58 Elijah . . was taken up into heaven. 8
3:18 in the sight of Heaven there is no difference 8
19 strength comes from Heaven. 8
50 they cried aloud to Heaven, saying 8
60 as his will in heaven may be, so he will do. 8
4:10 now let us cry to Heaven 8
24 they sang hymns and praises to Heaven 8
40 and cried out to Heaven. 8
55 blessed Heaven, who had prospered them. 8
5:31 cry of the city went up to Heaven with trumpets 8
9:46 Cry out now to Heaven that you may be delivered 8
12:15 have the help which comes from Heaven for our aid 8
16: 3 may the help which comes from Heaven be with you. 8
2Mc 2:10 fire came down from heaven 8
18 and will gather us from everywhere under heaven 8
21 the appearances which came from heaven 8
3:15 called toward heaven upon him 8
20 holding up their hands to heaven 8
34 you, who have been scourged by heaven 8
39 he who has his dwelling in heaven 5
7:11 said nobly, "I got these from Heaven 8
28 to look at the heaven and the earth 8
34 raise your hand against the children of heaven. 6
8:20 by the help that came to them from heaven 8
9: 4 the judgment of heaven rode with him! 8
10 he could touch the stars of heaven. 6
20 As my hope is in heaven 8
10:29 there appeared to the enemy from heaven 8
14:34 stretched forth their hands toward heaven 8
15: 3 asked if there were a sovereign in heaven 8
4 the living Lord himself, the Sovereign in heaven 8
8 when help had come to them from heaven 8
21 Maccabeus . . stretched out his hands toward heaven 8
23 now, O Sovereign of the heavens, send a good angel 8
34 they all, looking to heaven, blessed the Lord 8
3Mc 2: 2 Lord, Lord, king of the heavens 8
15 your dwelling, the heaven of heavens 8
15 your dwelling, the heaven of heavens 8
4:21 who was aiding the Jews from heaven. 8
5: 9 their entreaty ascended fervently to heaven. 8
25 stretched their hands toward heaven 8
50 help which they had received before from heaven 8
6:17 they raised great cries to heaven 8
28 the sons of the almighty and living God of heaven 5
33 the king . . gave thanks to heaven unceasingly 8
7: 6 the God of heaven surely defends the Jews 5
4Mc 4:10 angels on horseback . . appeared from heaven 7
11 Apollonius . . stretched out his hands toward heaven 8
6: 6 yet while the old man's eyes were raised to heaven 8
17: 5 The moon in heaven, with the stars 8
5 and are firmly set in heaven with them. 8

high heaven 1. מָרוֹם 2. שְׁמֵי הַשָּׁמַיִם
3. *οὐρανὸς τοῦ οὐρανοῦ*
1Kg 8:27 and the highest heaven cannot contain thee; 2
Job 25: 2 with God; he makes peace in his high heaven. 1
Ps 71:19 thy righteousness, O God, reach the high heavens. 1
Sir 16:18 Behold, heaven and the highest heaven 3

heavenly 1. *ἀμβρόσιος* 2. *ἀπ' οὐρανοῦ* 3. *ἐξ οὐρανοῦ*
4. *ἐπουράνιος* 5. *οὐράνιος* 6. caelestis
Mat 5:48 be perfect, as your heavenly Father is perfect. 5
6:14 men their trespasses, your heavenly Father also 5
26 barns, and yet your heavenly Father feeds them. 5
32 these things; and your heavenly Father knows 5
15:13 Every plant which my heavenly Father has 5
18:35 So also my heavenly Father will do 5
Lke 2:13 with the angel a multitude of the heavenly host 5
11:13 how much more will the heavenly Father give 3
Act 26:19 I was not disobedient to the heavenly vision 5
2Co 5: 2 long to put on our heavenly dwelling 3
2Ti 4:18 save me for his heavenly kingdom 4
Heb 3: 1 holy brethren, who share in a heavenly call 4
6: 4 who have tasted the heavenly gift 4
8: 5 a copy and shadow of the heavenly sanctuary 4
11:16 a better country, that is, a heavenly one 4
12:22 the heavenly Jerusalem 4
2Es 2:37 to him who has called you to heavenly kingdoms. 6
Wis 19:21 the crystalline, easily melted kind of heavenly food. 1
Sir 43: 1 The pride of the heavenly heights •
2Mc 11:10 having their heavenly ally 2
3Mc 6:18 opened the heavenly gates 5
4Mc 4:11 and propitiate the wrath of the heavenly army. 5
9:15 enemy of heavenly justice, savage of mind 5
11: 3 incur punishment from the heavenly justice 5
heavenly *See also* being.

heavenly place 1. *ἐπουράνιος*
Eph 1: 3 who has blessed us . . in the heavenly places 1
20 sit at his right hand in the heavenly places 1
2: 6 made us sit with him in the heavenly places 1
3:10 powers in the heavenly places. 1
6:12 the spiritual hosts . . in the heavenly places. 1

heavenly thing 1. *ἐπουράνιος* 2. *οὐρανός*
Joh 3:12 how can you believe if I tell you heavenly things? 1
Heb 9:23 the copies of the heavenly things 2
23 but the heavenly things themselves 1

heavily 1. כְּבֵדֻת 2. *μέρος* 3. *στερεόω* 4. *σφοδρός*
Exd 14:25 wheels so that they drove heavily; 1
Sir 39:28 in their anger they scourge heavily 3
2Mc 15:18 Their concern for wives . . lay upon them less heavily 2
4Mc 6:11 gasping heavily for breath 4
heavily *See also* breathe, laden, press, rest.

heavy 1. כבד 2. כָּבֵד 3. כֹּבֶד 4. מַעֲמָסָה 5. סבל
6. קשה 7. קָשֶׁה 8. רַע 9. *βαρέω* 10. *βαρέως*
11. *βαρύνω* 12. *βαρύς* 13. *ἰσχυρός* 14. *μέγας*
15. *δλκή* 16. *πολύς* 17. *χαλεπός* 18. copiosus
19. multus
Exd 9:18 I will cause very heavy hail to fall, such as never 2
24 there was . . very heavy hail, such as had never 2
18:18 for the thing is too heavy for you; you are not able 2
Num 11:14 burden is too heavy for me. 2
1Sm 4:18 neck was broken . . for he was an old man, and heavy. 2
5: 6 The hand of the LORD was heavy upon the people 1
7 his hand is heavy upon us and upon Dagon our god. 6
11 The hand of God was very heavy there; 1
2Sm 14:26 he used to cut it; when it was heavy on him, he cut it 2
1Kg 12: 4 lighten . . his heavy yoke upon us 2
11 my father laid upon you a heavy yoke, I will add 2
14: 6 I am charged with heavy tidings for you. 7
2Ch 10: 4 lighten the hard service . . and his heavy yoke 2
11 now, whereas my father laid upon you a heavy yoke 2
Neh 5:18 servitude was heavy upon this people. 1
Job 6: 3 then it would be heavier than the sand of the sea; 1
23: 2 his hand is heavy in spite of my groaning. 1
33: 7 my pressure will not be heavy upon you. 1
Ps 32: 4 For day and night thy hand was heavy upon me; 1
38: 4 they weigh like a burden too heavy for me. 2
144:14 may our cattle be heavy with young 5
Prv 25:20 He who sings songs to a heavy heart is like one who 8
27: 3 A stone is heavy, and sand is weighty 3
3 but a fool's provocation is heavier than both. 2
Lam 3: 7 he has put heavy chains on me; 1
Zec 12: 3 On that day I will make Jerusalem a heavy stone 4
Mat 13:15 and their ears are heavy of hearing 10
26:43 their eyes were heavy. 9
Lke 9:32 were heavy with sleep 9
Act 28:27 their ears are heavy of hearing 10
Rev 11:19 peals of thunder, an earthquake, and heavy hail. 14
16:21 great hailstones, heavy as a hundred-weight •
2Es 4:49 and poured down a heavy and violent rain 19
15:35 shall pour out a heavy tempest upon the earth 18
38 heavy storm clouds shall be stirred up 18
Wis 17:21 over those men alone heavy night was spread 12
21 still heavier than darkness 12
Sir 6:21 will weigh him down like a heavy testing stone 13
22:14 What is heavier than lead? 11
29:13 more than a heavy spear 15
40: 1 a heavy yoke is upon the sons of Adam 12
1Mc 5: 3 He dealt them a heavy blow and humbled them 14
34 he dealt them a heavy blow 14
8: 7 decreed that he . . should pay a heavy tribute 14
13:22 that night a very heavy snow fell 16
2Mc 4:16 For this reason heavy disaster overtook them 17
heavy *See also* burden, laden, lay, lie, make, rain.

very heavy 1. *καταβαρύνω*
Mrk 14:40 their eyes were very heavy 1

hedge 1. גְּדֵרָה 2. מְשֻׂכָּה 3. סוך 4. *φραγμός*
Job 3:23 a man whose way is hid, whom God has hedged in? 3
Isa 5: 5 I will remove its hedge, and it shall be devoured; 2
Jer 49: 3 lament, and run to and fro among the hedges! 1
Mat 21:33 set a hedge around it, and dug a wine press in it 4
Mrk 12: 1 and set a hedge around it 4
Lke 14:23 Go out to the highways and hedges 4
hedge *See also* put.

thorn hedge 1. מְסוּכָה
Mic 7: 4 the most upright of them a thorn hedge. 1

hedge up 1. שׂוך
Hos 2: 6 Therefore I will hedge up her way with thorns; 1

hedgehog 1. קִפֹּד
Isa 14:23 I will make it a possession of the hedgehog 1
Zep 2:14 the vulture and the hedgehog shall lodge in her 1

heed 1. בין 2. ידע 3. לקח 4. קשב 5. קָשַׁב 6. ראה
7. שמע 8. שמר 9. טְעֵם (A) 10. *ἀκούω* 11. *ἐντρέπω*
12. *προσέχω*
Gen 37:27 our own flesh." And his brothers heeded him. 7
Exd 4: 8 If they will not . . heed the first sign, they may 7
9 will not . . heed your voice, you shall take some 7
5: 2 Who is the LORD, that I should heed his voice 7
Deu 12:28 Be careful to heed all these words 7
18:15 raise up for you a prophet . . him you shall heed- 7
Jdg 11:28 the king . . did not heed the message of Jephthah 7
1Kg 18:29 there was no voice; no one answered, no one heeded. 5
20: 8 all the people said to him, "Do not heed or consent. 7
Neh 9:34 not kept thy law or heeded thy commandments 4
Job 30:20 I stand, and thou dost not heed me. 1
35:15 he does not greatly heed transgression 2
Prv 1:24 stretched out my hand and no one has heeded 4
10: 8 The wise of heart will heed commandments 3
17 He who heeds instruction is on the path to life 8
13:18 but he who heeds reproof is honored. 8
15: 5 but he who heeds admonition is prudent. 8
31 He whose ear heeds wholesome admonition 7
32 he who heeds admonition gains understanding. 7
Ecc 9:16 poor man's wisdom . . and his words are not heeded. 7
Jer 2:31 And you, O generation, heed the word of the LORD. 6
11: 3 Cursed be the man who does not heed the words 7
18:18 let us not heed any of his words. 4
22: 5 if you will not heed these words, I swear by myself 7
26: 5 to heed the words of my servants the prophets 7
5 I send to you urgently, though you have not heeded 7
29:19 because they did not heed my words, says the LORD 7

Dan 3:12 men, O king, pay no heed to you; they do not serve 9
6:13 pays no heed to you, O king, or the interdict 9
Zec 1: 4 But they did not hear or heed me, says the LORD. 4
Mal 3:16 the LORD heeded and heard them 4
Joh 10: 8 the sheep did not heed them. 10
16 they will heed my voice 10
1Es 1:28 did not heed the words of Jeremiah the prophet 12
47 did not heed the words 11
Sir 23:27 to heed the commandments of the Lord. 12
35: 1 he who heeds the commandments 12
Bar 1:18 have not heeded the voice of the Lord our God 10
19 we have been negligent, in not heeding his voice. 10
21 We did not heed the voice of the Lord our God 10
2: 5 we sinned . . in not heeding his voice. 10
3: 4 who did not heed the voice of the Lord their God 10
1Mc 2:68 heed what the law commands. 12
8:16 they all heed the one man 10

heed *See also* give, pay, take.

heed a supplication 1. עתר
2Sm 21:14 And . . God heeded supplications for the land. 1
24:25 So the LORD heeded supplications for the land 1
Isa 19:22 he will heed their supplications and heal them. 1

heed a warning 1. *νουθετέω*
Wis 12:26 who have not heeded the warning of light rebukes 1

heed an appeal 1. *παρακαλέω*
2Co 13:11 Mend your ways, heed my appeal 1

heedless
Prv 13:10 By insolence the heedless make strife •

heedlessly 1. *ἀπρονοήτως*
3Mc 1:14 someone heedlessly said that it was wrong 1

heel 1. עָקֵב 2. רֶגֶל 3. *πτέρνα* 4. calcaneum
Gen 3:15 head, and you shall bruise his heel. 1
25:26 his hand had taken hold of Esau's heel; 1
49:17 a viper . . that bites the horse's heels 1
19 raid Gad, but he shall raid at their heels. 1
Jdg 4:10 10,000 men went up at his heels; and Deb'orah 2
5:15 into the valley they rushed forth at his heels. 2
Job 18: 9 A trap seizes him by the heel, a snare lays hold 1
11 frighten him . . and chase him at his heels. 2
Ps 41: 9 bosom friend . . has lifted his heel against me. 1
Joh 13:18 who ate my bread has lifted his heel against me.' 3
2Es 6: 8 Jacob's hand held Esau's heel from the beginning. 4
10 and the end of a man is his heel ‡
10 between the heel and the hand 4
Sir 12:17 he will trip you by the heel; 3

heel *See also* take.

heifer 1. עֶגְלָה 2. עֶגְלַת בָּקָר 3. פָּרָה 4. *δάμαλις*
Gen 15: 9 He said to him, "Bring me a heifer three years old 1
Num19: 2 to bring you a red heifer without defect 3
5 heifer shall be burned in his sight; 3
6 into the midst of the burning of the heifer. 3
8 He who burns the heifer shall wash his clothes •
9 clean shall gather up the ashes of the heifer 3
10 he who gathers the ashes of the heifer shall wash 3
Deu 21: 3 elders of the city . . shall take a heifer 2
4 elders of that city shall bring the heifer down 1
4 break the heifer's neck there in the valley. 1
6 elders . . wash their hands over the heifer 1
Jdg 14:18 If you had not plowed with my heifer, you would not 1
1Sm 16: 2 And the LORD said, "Take a heifer with you, and say 2
Jer 46:20 A beautiful heifer is Egypt 1
50:11 though you are wanton as a heifer at grass 1
Hos 4:16 Like a stubborn heifer, Israel is stubborn; 3
10:11 a trained heifer that loved to thresh 1
Heb 9:13 the ashes of a heifer 4
Sir 38:26 he is careful about fodder for the heifers. 4

height 1. בָּמָה 2. גַּב 3. גָּבֹהַּ 4. גֹּבַהּ 5. מָרוֹם 6. קוֹמָה
7. רֹאשׁ 8. רוּם 9. רָמָה 10. שִׂיא 11. תָּוֶךְ 12. תּוֹעָפָה
13. רוּם (A) 14. *ὄρος* 15. *τέλος* 16. *ὑψηλός*
17. *ὕψιστος* 18. *ὕψος* 19. *ὕψωμα* 20. altitudo
21. eminens
Gen 6:15 its breadth 50 cubits, and its height 30 cubits. 6
Exd 25:10 and a cubit and a half its height. 6
23 and a cubit and a half its height. 6
27: 1 the altar . . its height shall be three cubits. 6
18 the breadth 50, and the height five cubits 6
30: 2 and two cubits shall be its height; 6
37: 1 its breadth, and a cubit and a half its height. 6
10 its breadth, and a cubit and a half its height; 6
25 it was square, and two cubits was its height; 6
38: 1 it was square, and three cubits was its height. 6
Num14:40 went up to the heights of the hill country, saying 7
44 go up to the heights of the hill country 7
21:28 the lords of the heights of the Arnon. 1
Jdg 5:18 Naph'tali too, on the heights of the field. 5
1Sm 16: 7 Do not look on . . or on the height of his stature 3
17: 4 whose height was six cubits and a span. 4
22: 6 at Gib'e-ah, under the tamarisk tree on the height 9
2Sm 22:34 made my feet . . and set me secure on the heights. 1
1Kg 6:26 The height of one cherub was ten cubits, and so was 6
7: 2 its breadth 50 cubits, and its height 30 cubits 6
15 Eighteen cubits was the height of one pillar 6
16 the height of the one capital was five cubits 6
16 the height of the other capital was five cubits. 6
32 and the height of a wheel was a cubit and a half. 6
2Kg 19:23 I have gone up the heights of the mountains 5
25:17 The height of the one pillar was eighteen cubits 6
17 the height of the capital was three cubits; 6
2Ch 3: 4 its height was 120 cubits. 4
Ezr 6: 3 height shall be 60 cubits and its breadth 13
Neh 4: 6 wall was joined together to half its height. •
Job 20: 6 Though his height mount up to the heavens 10
Ps 18:33 like hinds' feet, and set me secure on the heights. 1
95: 4 heights of the mountains are his also. 12
102:19 that he looked down from his holy height 5
148: 1 LORD from the heavens, praise him in the heights! 5
Prv 8: 2 On the heights beside the way 5
25: 3 As the heaven for height, and the earth for depth 8
Isa 10:33 the great in height will be hewn down 6
14:14 I will ascend above the heights of the clouds 1
16: 3 make your shade like night at the height of noon; 11
22:16 tomb for yourself, you who hew a tomb on the height 5
26: 5 he has brought low the inhabitants of the height 5
33:16 he will dwell on the heights; 5
37:24 I have gone up the heights of the mountains 5
24 I came to its remotest height, its densest forest 5
58:14 I will make you ride upon the heights of the earth; 1
Jer 26:18 and the mountain of the house a wooded height. 1
31:12 shall come and sing aloud on the height of Zion 5
49:16 you . . who hold the height of the hill. 5
51:53 and though she should fortify her strong height 5
52:21 the height of the one pillar was eighteen cubits 6
22 the height of the one capital was five cubits; 6
Ezk 17:23 on the mountain height of Israel will I plant it 5
19:11 seen in its height with the mass of its branches. 4
20:40 my holy mountain, the mountain height of Israel 5
31: 3 and of great height, its top among the clouds. 6
10 its heart was proud of its height 6
14 no trees by the waters may grow to lofty height 6
14 that drink water may reach up to them in height; 4
34:14 upon the mountain heights of Israel 5
36: 2 The ancient heights have become our possession, 1
40: 5 of the wall, one reed; and the height, one reed. 6
43:13 this shall be the height of the altar 2
Dan 3: 1 image of gold, whose height was 60 cubits 13
4:10 midst of the earth; and its height was great. 13
Ams 2: 9 whose height was like the height of the cedars 4
9 whose height was like the height of the cedars 4
4:13 and treads on the heights of the earth- the LORD 1
Mic 3:12 and the mountain of the house a wooded height. 1
Rom 8:39 nor height, nor depth, nor anything else 19
Eph 3:18 the breadth and length and height and depth 18
Rev 21:16 its length and breadth and height are equal. 18
1Es 6:25 its height to be 60 cubits 18
2Es 4:21 what is above the height of the heavens. 20
6: 4 before the heights of the air were lifted up 20
16:60 to send rivers from the heights to water the earth; 21
Jdt 7:10 the height of the mountains where they live 18
Sir 1: 3 The height of heaven, the breadth of the earth 18
17:32 He marshals the host of the height of heaven 18
24:13 like a cypress on the heights of Hermon. 14
26:16 Like the sun rising in the heights of the Lord 17
43: 1 The pride of the heavenly heights 18
9 a gleaming array in the heights of the Lord. 17
Bar 5: 5 stand upon the height and look toward the east 16
Man 1: 9 am unworthy to look up and see the height of heaven 18
2Mc 6:15 when our sins have reached their height. 15

height *See also* raise, throw.

bare height 1. שְׁפִי
Num23: 3 And he went to a bare height. 1
Isa 41:18 I will open rivers on the bare heights 1
49: 9 on all bare heights shall be their pasture; 1
Jer 3: 2 Lift up your eyes to the bare heights, and see! 1
21 A voice on the bare heights is heard 1
4:11 A hot wind from the bare heights in the desert 1
7:29 raise a lamentation on the bare heights 1
12:12 Upon all the bare heights in the desert 1
14: 6 The wild asses stand on the bare heights 1

heighten 1. *ἀνυψόω*
Sir 28:10 he will heighten his wrath. 1

heinous *See* crime.

heir 1. בֶּן מֶשֶׁק 2. ירשׁ 3. מָנוֹן 4. *κληρονομέω*
5. *κληρονόμος* 6. *συγκληρονόμος* 7. heres
Gen 15: 2 heir of my house is Elie'zer of Damascus? 1
3 and a slave born in my house will be my heir. 2
4 This man shall not be your heir; 2
4 your own son shall be your heir. 2
21:10 for the son of this slave woman shall not be heir 2
2Sm 14: 7 and so they would destroy the heir also. 2
Prv 29:21 pampers his servant . . end find him his heir. 3
Jer 49: 1 says the LORD: "Has Israel no sons? Has he no heir? 2
Mat 21:38 This is the heir 5
Mrk 12: 7 'This is the heir; come, let us kill him 5
Lke 20:14 This is the heir; let us kill him 5
Rom 4:14 If it is the adherents of the law who are . . heirs 5
8:17 if children, then heirs, heirs of God 5
17 heirs of God and fellow heirs with Christ 5
Gal 3:29 Abraham's offspring, heirs according to promise. 5
4: 1 I mean that the heir, as long as he is a child 5
7 if a son then an heir. 5
Tit 3: 7 become heirs in hope of eternal life. 5
Heb 1: 2 a Son, whom he appointed the heir of all things 5
6:17 the heirs of the promise 5
11: 7 became an heir of the righteousness 5
9 heirs with him of the same promise. 6
Jas 2: 5 heirs of the kingdom which he has promised 5
2Es 7: 9 how will the heir receive his inheritance 7
Tob 3:15 he has no child to be his heir 4
Sir 23:22 provides an heir by a stranger. 5

fellow heir 1. *συγκληρονόμος*
Rom 8:17 heirs of God and fellow heirs with Christ 1
Eph 3: 6 that is, how the Gentiles are fellow heirs 1

joint heirs 1. *συγκληρονόμος*
1Pe 3: 7 since you are joint heirs of the grace of life 1

hell 1. *γέεννα* 2. gehenna 3. infernus
Mat 5:22 You fool!' shall be liable to the hell of fire. 1
29 than that your whole body be thrown into hell. 1
30 members than that your whole body go into hell. 1
10:28 who can destroy both soul and body in hell. 1
18: 9 with two eyes to be thrown into the hell of fire 1
23:15 twice as much a child of hell as yourselves. 1
33 how are you to escape being sentenced to hell? 1
Mrk 9:43 with two hands to go to hell 1
45 with two feet to be thrown into hell. 1
46 with two eyes to be thrown into hell 1
Lke 12: 5 who . . has power to cast into hell 1
Jas 3: 6 and set on fire by hell. 1
2Es 4: 7 or which are the exits of hell ‡
8 nor as yet into hell 3
7:36 and the furnace of hell shall be disclosed 2
8:53 hell has fled and corruption has been forgotten; ‡

hell *See also* cast.

helmet 1. כּוֹבַע 2. מָעוֹז רֹאשׁ 3. קוֹבַע 4. *κόρυς*
5. *περικεφαλαία*
1Sm 17: 5 He had a helmet of bronze on his head 1
38 he put a helmet of bronze on his head 3
2Ch 26:14 Uzzi'ah prepared . . helmets, coats of mail, bows 1
Ps 60: 7 E'phraim is my helmet; Judah is my scepter. 2
108: 8 E'phraim is my helmet; Judah my scepter. 2
Isa 59:17 and a helmet of salvation upon his head; 1
Jer 46: 4 Take your stations with your helmets 1
Ezk 23:24 on every side with buckler, shield, and helmet 3
27:10 men of war; they hung the shield and helmet in you; 1
38: 5 are with them, all of them with shield and helmet; 1
Eph 6:17 take the helmet of salvation 5
1Th 5: 8 for a helmet the hope of salvation. 5
Wis 5:18 wear impartial justice as a helmet; 4
1Mc 6:35 with brass helmets on their heads 5

help 1. אֱיָלוּת 2. היה יָד אֵת 3. היה לִישׁוּעָה 4. חזק
5. יעל 6. יְשׁוּעָה 7. ישׁע 8. יֵשַׁע 9. יִתְרוֹן 10. נשׂא
11. עדר 12. עזר 13. עֵזֶר 14. עֶזְרָה 15. עֲנָוָה 16. פקד
17. תמך 18. תְּשׁוּעָה 19. סעד (A) 20. *ἀκούσιος*
21. *ἀντέχω* 22. *ἀντιλαμβάνω* 23. *ἀντίλημψις*
24. *ἀντίληψις* 25. *βοάω* 26. *βοήθεια* 27. *βοηθέω*
28. *βοήθημα* 29. *βοηθός* 30. *εἰς τὴν χρείαν* 31. *ἐν*
32. *ἐπιβοηθέω* 33. *ἐπικουρία* 34. *ἐπιχορηγία* 35. *μετά*
36. *παραίτιος* 37. *παρίστημι* 38. *σκέπη*
39. *συλλαμβάνω* 40. *συμβάλλω* 41. *συμμαχέω*
42. *συμποιέω* 43. *συμπονέω* 44. *συναντιλαμβάνομαι*
45. *συνυπουργέω* 46. *χρησίμος εἰμί* 47. *ὠφελέω*
48. adiutorium
Gen 4: 1 I have gotten a man with the help of the LORD. •
49:25 by the God of your father who will help you 12
Exd 2:17 but Moses stood up and helped them, and watered 7
18: 4 for he said, "The God of father was my help 13
23: 5 you shall help him to lift it up. •
Num 1:44 Moses . . numbered with the help of the leaders •
Deu 22: 4 you shall help him to lift them up again. •
28:29 there shall be no one to help you. 7
31 there shall be no one to help you. 7
32:38 Let them rise up and help you, let them 12
33: 7 be a help against his adversaries. 13
26 who rides through the heavens to your help 13
29 LORD, the shield of your help, and the sword 13
Jos 1:14 pass over armed before your brethren and . . help 12
10: 4 Come up to me, and help me, and let us smite Gibeon; 12
6 come up to us quickly, and save us, and help us; 12
33 Then Horam king of Gezer came up to help Lachish; 12
Jdg 4: 3 the people of Israel cried to the LORD for help; •
5:23 because they came not to the help of the LORD 14
23 came not . . to the help of the LORD against 14
1Sm 7:12 Ebene'zer; for he said, " . . the LORD has helped us. 12
2Sm 8: 5 Syrians . . came to help Hadade'zer king of Zobah 12
10:11 too strong for me, then you shall help me; 3
11 if the Ammonites . . then I will come and help you. 7
19 Syrians feared to help the Ammonites any more. 7

14: 4 and did obeisance, and said, "Help, O king. 7
18: 3 it is better that you send us help from the city. 12
22:36 Thou hast given . . and thy help made me great 15
23: 5 cause to prosper all my help and my desire? 8
1Kg 1: 7 and they followed Adoni'jah and helped him. 12
20:16 they went out . . he and the 32 kings who helped him. 12
2Kg 6:26 a woman cried out . . saying, "Help, my lord, O king! 7
27 If the LORD will not help you, whence shall I help 7
27 the LORD will not help you, whence shall I help you? 7
14:26 none left . . and there was none to help Israel. 12
15:19 help him to confirm his hold of the royal power. 2
1Ch 12: 1 were among the mighty men who helped him in war. 12
17 If you have come to me in friendship to help me 12
18 peace to you . . For your God helps you. 12
19 Yet he did not help them, for the rulers 12
21 They helped David against the band of raiders; 12
22 men kept coming to David to help him 12
33 to help David with singleness of purpose. 11
15:26 God helped the Levites who were carrying 12
18: 5 Syrians of Damascus came to help Hadade'zer 12
19:12 too strong for me, then you shall help me; 18
12 are too strong for you, then I will help you. 7
19 Syrians were not willing to help the Ammonites 7
22:17 leaders of Israel to help Solomon his son, saying 12
24: 3 With the help of Zadok of the sons of Elea'zar •
2Ch 14:11 O LORD, there is none like thee to help 12
11 Help us, O LORD our God, for we rely on thee 12
16:12 but sought help from physicians. •
18:31 Jehosh'aphat cried out, and the LORD helped him. 12
19: 2 Should you help the wicked 12
20: 4 Judah assembled to seek help from the LORD; •
23 they all helped to destroy one another. 12
25: 8 for God has power to help or to cast down. 12
26: 7 God helped him against the Philistines 12
13 an army . . to help the king against the enemy. 12
15 fame spread far, for he was marvelously helped 12
28:16 King Ahaz sent to the king of Assyria for help. 12
21 gave tribute . . but it did not help him. 14
23 Because the gods of the kings of Syria helped 12
23 I will sacrifice to them that they may help me. 12
29:34 their brethren the Levites helped them 4
32: 3 his officers and his mighty men . . helped him. 12
8 the LORD . . to help us and to fight our battles. 12
Ezr 5: 2 with them were the prophets of God, helping them. 19
Neh 5: 5 but it is not in our power to help it, for other men •
8: 7 helped the people to understand the law •
Est 9: 3 governors and . . officials also helped the Jews 10
Job 6:13 In truth I have no help in me 14
26: 2 How you have helped him who has no power! 12
4 With whose help have you uttered words •
29:12 the fatherless who had none to help him. 12
31:21 because I saw help in the gate; 14
Ps 3: 2 are saying of me, there is no help for him in God. 6
12: 1 Help, LORD; for there is no longer any that is godly; 7
18:35 hand supported me, and thy help made me great 15
20: 2 May he send you help from the sanctuary 13
6 Now I know that the LORD will help his anointed; 7
21: 1 in thy help how greatly he exults! 6
5 His glory is great through thy help; 6
22: 1 Why art thou so far from helping me 6
11 trouble is near and there is none to help. 12
19 be not far off! O thou my help, hasten to my aid! 1
27: 9 thou who hast been my help. Cast me not off 14
28: 7 so I am helped, and my heart exults 12
33:20 soul waits for the LORD; he is our help and shield. 13
35: 2 Take hold of shield . . and rise for my help! 14
37:40 The LORD helps them and delivers them; 12
38:22 Make haste to help me, O Lord, my salvation! 14
40:13 deliver me! O LORD, make haste to help me! 14
17 Thou art my help and my deliverer; do not tarry 14
42: 5 Hope in God; for I shall again praise him, my help 6
11 I shall again praise him, my help and my God. 6
43: 5 for I shall again praise him, my help and my God. 6
46: 1 God . . a very present help in trouble. 14
5 God will help her right early. 12
59: 4 Rouse thyself, come to my help, and see! •
60:11 O grant us help against the foe 14
11 help against the foe, for vain is the help of man! 18
63: 7 thou hast been my help 14
69:13 With thy faithful help 8
70: 1 O LORD, make haste to help me! 14
5 Thou art my help and my deliverer 13
71:12 be not far from me; O my God, make haste to help me! 14
79: 9 Help us, O God of our salvation 12
86:17 LORD, hast helped me and comforted me. 12
94:17 If the LORD had not been my help, my soul would 14
106: 4 help me when thou deliverest them; 16
107:12 they fell down, with none to help. 12
108:12 O grant us help against the foe 14
12 grant us help . . for vain is the help of man! 18
109:26 Help me, O LORD my God! 12
115: 9 He is their help and their shield. 13
10 He is their help and their shield. 13
11 He is their help and their shield. 13
118: 7 The LORD is on my side to help me; 12
13 pushed hard . . falling, but the LORD helped me. 12
119:86 they persecute me with falsehood; help me! 12
173Let thy hand be ready to help me 12
175let thy ordinances help me. 12

121: 1 From whence does my help come? 13
2 My help comes from the LORD, who made heaven 13
124: 8 help is in the name of the LORD, who made heaven 13
146: 3 Put not your trust in . . whom there is no help. 18
5 Happy is he whose help is the God of Jacob 13
Prv 18:19 A brother helped is like a strong city 27
20:22 wait for the LORD, and he will help you. 7
28:17 let him be a fugitive until death; let no one help 17
Ecc 10:10 but wisdom helps one to succeed. 9
Isa 10: 3 To whom will you flee for help 14
20: 6 to whom we fled for help to be delivered 14
30: 5 that brings neither help nor profit 13
7 For Egypt's help is worthless and empty 12
31: 1 Woe to those who go down to Egypt for help 14
3 will stumble, and he who is helped will fall 12
41: 6 Every one helps his neighbor 12
10 I will strengthen you, I will help you 12
13 it is I who say to you, "Fear not, I will help you. 12
14 I will help you, says the LORD; 12
44: 2 who formed you from the womb and will help you 12
49: 8 in a day of salvation I have helped you; 12
50: 7 For the Lord GOD helps me; 12
9 Behold, the Lord GOD helps me; 12
57:12 and your doings, but they will not help you. 5
63: 5 I looked, but there was no one to help; 12
Jer 37: 7 Behold, Pharoah's army which came to help you 14
Lam 1: 7 her people fell . . and there was none to help her 12
4:17 Our eyes failed, ever watching vainly for help; 14
Ezk 17:17 will not help him in war, when mounds are cast up •
Dan 10:13 but Michael, one of the chief princes, came to help 12
11:34 When they fall, they shall receive a little help. 13
39 fortresses by the help of a foreign god; •
45 yet he shall come to his end, with none to help him. 12
Hos 12: 6 by the help of your God, return, hold fast to love •
13: 9 I will destroy you, O Israel; who can help you? 13
Zec 6:15 those who are far off shall come and help to build •
Mat 15:25 Lord, help me. 27
Mrk 9:22 if you can do anything, have pity on us and help us. 27
24 cried out and said, "I believe; help my unbelief! 27
Lke 1:54 He has helped his servant Israel 22
5: 7 beckoned . . to come and help them 39
10:40 Tell her then to help me. 44
Act 16: 9 Come over to Macedo'nia and help us. 27
18:27 greatly helped those who . . had believed 40
20:35 by so toiling one must help the weak 22
21:28 crying out, "Men of Israel, help! 27
26:22 To this day I have had the help that comes from God 33
Rom 8:26 Likewise the Spirit helps us in our weakness; 44
16: 2 and help her in whatever she may require from you 37
2Co 1:11 You also must help us by prayer 45
6: 2 helped you on the day of salvation. 27
Php 1:19 the help of the Spirit of Jesus Christ 34
4: 3 I ask you also, true yokefellow, help these women 39
16 for even in Thessaloni'ca you sent me help once 30
1Th 5:14 encourage the fainthearted, help the weak 21
Tit 3:14 so as to help cases of urgent need •
Heb 2:18 he is able to help those who are tempted. 27
4:16 find grace to help in time of need. 26
1Es 2: 6 let each man, wherever he may live, be helped 27
9 their neighbors helped them with everything 25
4:48 to help him build the city. 35
6: 2 with the help of the prophets of the Lord 27
28 full effort be made to help the men 42
8:27 I was encouraged by the help of the Lord my God 24
2Es 2:18 I will send you help 48
Tob 2:10 I went to physicians, but they did not help me. 47
Jdt 6:21 they called on the God of Israel for help. 26
7:25 For now we have no one to help us 29
31 if these days pass by, and no help comes for us 26
8:11 unless the Lord turns and helps us 26
15 if he does not choose to help us 27
17 Therefore . . let us call upon him to help us 26
9: 4 and called on thee for help 29
13: 5 For now is the time to help thy inheritance 22
AEs 14: 3 help me, who am alone and have no helper but thee 27
14 save us by thy hand, and help me, who am alone 27
Wis 2:18 he will help him 22
13:16 because he knows that it cannot help itself 27
16 it is only an image and has need of help. 26
17:12 surrender of the helps that come from reason; 28
13 the inner expectation of help, being weak •
19:22 thou hast not neglected to help them at all times •
Sir 0: 1 those who love learning should be able to help 46
2: 6 Trust in him, and he will help you 22
3:12 O son, help your father in his old age 22
8:16 where no help is at hand, he will strike you down. 26
11:12 There is another who is slow and needs help 23
12: 4 Give to the godly man, but do not help the sinner. 22
7 Give to the good man, but do not help the sinner. 22
17 while pretending to help you, he will trip you 29
24:22 those who work with my help will not sin. 31
25:18 he cannot help sighing bitterly. 20
29: 4 cause trouble to those who help them. 27
9 Help a poor man for the commandment's sake 22
37: 5 help a friend for their stomach's sake 43
40:24 Brothers and help are for a time of trouble 26
26 with it there is no need to seek for help. 26
51: 7 there was no one to help me 29
Bar 4:17 But I, how can I help you? 27

LJr 1:58 they will not be able to help themselves. 27
68 they can flee to cover and help themselves. 47
1Mc 3: 2 all who had joined his father helped him 27
15 a strong army . . went up with him to help him 27
53 if thou dost not help us? 27
5:39 They also have hired Arabs to help them 26
7: 7 let him punish them and all who help them. 32
20 left with him a force to help him 27
8:13 Those whom they wish to help and to make kings 27
32 If now they appeal again for help against you •
10:24 that I may have their help. 26
72 who the others are that are helping us 27
74 Simon his brother met him to help him. 26
11:43 you will do well to send me men who will help me 41
12:15 have the help which comes from Heaven for our aid 26
14: 1 marched into Media to secure help 26
16: 3 may the help which comes from Heaven be with you. 26
2Mc 8:19 when help came to their ancestors 24
20 by the help that came to them from heaven 26
23 gave the watchword, "God's help 26
35 having been humbled with the help of the Lord 26
11:19 to help promote your welfare. 36
12:11 won the victory, by the help of God 26
11 to help his people in all other ways. 47
13:10 now if ever to help those who . . 32
13 march out and decide the matter by the help of God 26
17 because the Lord's help protected him. 38
15: 7 he would get help from the Lord. 24
8 when help had come to them from heaven 28
35 sign to every one of the help of the Lord. 26
3Mc 2:12 you helped them in their humiliation 27
33 They remained resolutely hopeful of obtaining help 24
3: 8 The Greeks . . were not strong enough to help them 27
5:25 implored the supreme God to help them again 27
50 considered the help which they had received 23
4Mc 3: 3 reason can help to deal with anger. 27
14:17 they do what they can to help their young 27

help *See also* call, come, cry, give, receive, unable, withhold.

mutual help 1. εὐχρηστία

3Mc 2:33 depriving them of . . fellowship and mutual help. 1

no help 1. ἀβοηθησία

Sir 51:10 the time when there is no help against the proud. 1

help raise up 1. συνεγείρω

4Mc 2:14 and helps raise up what has fallen. 1

righteous help 1. צְדָקָה

Ps 71:24 my tongue will talk of thy righteous help 1

saving help 1. צְדָקָה

Ps 40:10 I have not hid thy saving help within my heart 1
88:12 or thy saving help in the land of forgetfulness? 1

without help 1. solus

2Es 3: 4 and that without help 1

helper 1. עוֹר 2. עֵזֶר 3. עֶזְרָה 4. ἀντιλήπτωρ
5. ἀντίληψις 6. βοηθέω 7. βοηθός 8. διακονέω
9. προστάτις 10. adiutorium

Gen 2:18 be alone; I will make him a helper fit for him. 2
20 but for the man there was not found a helper fit 2
1Ch 12:18 Peace, peace to you, and peace to your helpers! 1
Job 9:13 beneath him bowed the helpers of Rahab. 1
Ps 10:14 thou hast been the helper of the fatherless. 1
30:10 be gracious to me! O LORD, be thou my helper! 1
54: 4 Behold, God is my helper; 1
72:12 he delivers . . the poor and him who has no helper. 1
Isa 31: 2 against the helpers of those who work iniquity. 3
3 the helper will stumble, and he who is helped will 1
Jer 47: 4 from Tyre and Sidon every helper that remains. 1
Ezk 12:14 round about him, his helpers and all his troops; 7
30: 8 set fire to Egypt, and all her helpers are broken. 1
32:21 chiefs shall speak of them, with their helpers 1
Nah 3: 9 Put and the Libyans were her helpers. 3
Act 19:22 having sent into Macedo'nia two of his helpers 8
Rom 16: 2 she has been a helper of many and of myself 9
1Co 12:28 then workers of miracles, then healers, helpers 5
Heb 13: 6 The Lord is my helper, I will not be afraid 7
2Es 16:33 because they have no helpers. 10
Tob 8: 6 gavest him Eve his wife as a helper and support. 7
6 let us make a helper for him like himself.' 7
Jdt 9:11 thou art God of the lowly, helper of the oppressed 7
AEs 14: 3 help me, who am alone and have no helper but thee 7
14 am alone and have no helper but thee, O Lord. •
Sir 13:22 If a rich man slips, his helpers are many 4
36:24 a helper fit for him and a pillar of support. 7
51: 2 thou hast been my protector and helper 7
2 Before those who stood by thou wast my helper 7
1Mc 12:53 they said, "They have no leader or helper 6

helpful 1. συμφέρω

1Co 6:12 not all things are helpful 1
10:23 not all things are helpful 1

helpless 1. אֶפּוּנָה 2. ἀβοήθητος 3. ἀδύνατος
4. ἄπρακτος 5. ἄχρηστος 6. ῥίπτω

Ps 88:15 I suffer thy terrors; I am helpless. 1
Mat 9:36 because they were harassed and helpless 6
Wis 12: 6 these parents who murder helpless lives 2
LJr 1:28 give none to the poor or helpless. 3
2Mc 7: 5 When he was utterly helpless 5
3Mc 2:22 he lay helpless on the ground 4

helpless *See also* fall.

helplessness 1. ἀδυναμία
3Mc 2:13 overtaken by helplessness. 1

hem 1. צמת 2. στενός 3. συγκλείω 4. συνέχω
Job 23:17 for I am hemmed in by darkness, and thick darkness 1
Lke 19:43 surround you, and hem you in on every side 4
Sus 1:22 I am hemmed in on every side. 2
1Mc 3:18 It is easy for many to be hemmed in by few 3
4:31 So do thou hem in this army 3
6:18 kept hemming Israel in around the sanctuary. 3
11:65 and fought against it for many days and hemmed it in. 3

hemorrhage 1. αἱμορροέω 2. πηγή
Mat 9:20 a woman who had suffered from a hemorrhage 1
Mrk 5:29 immediately the hemorrhage ceased 2

hen 1. ὄρνις 2. gallina
Mat 23:37 as a hen gathers her brood under her wings 1
Lke 13:34 as a hen gathers her brood under her wings 1
2Es 1:30 as a hen gathers her brood under her wings 2

hen *See also* water.

hence 1. מִזֶּה 2. עַל כֵּן 3. δι' ἣν αἰτίαν 4. ἐντεῦθεν 5. καί 6. ὅθεν 7. οὖν 8. ὥστε
Exd 11: 1 afterwards he will let you go hence; 1
33: 1 Depart, go up hence, you and the people whom you 1
1Sm 19:24 Hence it is said, "Is Saul also among the prophets? 2
Ezk 12:27 The vision that he sees is for many days hence *
42: 6 hence the upper chambers were set back 2
Dan 8:26 vision, for it pertains to many days hence. *
Joh 14:31 Rise, let us go hence. 4
1Co 8: 4 Hence, as to the eating of food offered to idols 7
2Ti 1: 6 Hence I remind you to rekindle the gift of God 3
Heb 8: 3 hence it is necessary for this priest also . . 6
9:18 Hence even the first covenant was not ratified 6
11:19 hence, figuratively speaking, he did receive him 6
13: 6 Hence we can confidently say 8
1Es 4:22 Hence you must realize that women rule over you! 4
Jdt 5: 8 hence they drove them out 5

hence *See also* take.

henceforth 1. וְעַתָּה 2. יסף 3. כָּל הַיָּמִים 4. מִזֶּה 5. מִיּוֹם 6. עוֹד 7. ἀπ' ἄρτι 8. ἀπὸ τοῦ νῦν 9. ἐπέκεινα 10. λοιπός 11. νῦν 12. amodo 13. residuus
Num18:22 henceforth the people of Israel shall not come 6
Jdg 2:21 I will not henceforth drive out before them any 2
2Sm 19:13 commander of my army henceforth in place 3
1Kg 14:14 And henceforth the LORD will smite Israel *
2Kg 2:21 henceforth neither death nor miscarriage 6
5:17 henceforth your servant will not offer 6
Isa 43:13 I am God, and also henceforth I am He; 5
Ezk 48:35 the name of the city henceforth shall be 5
Zec 5: 3 every one who steals shall be cut off henceforth 4
3 shall be cut off henceforth according to it. 4
Mal 3:15 Henceforth we deem the arrogant blessed; 1
Lke 1:48 behold, henceforth all generations will call me 8
5:10 henceforth you will be catching men. 8
12:52 henceforth in one house there will be five 8
Joh 14: 7 henceforth you know him and have seen him. 7
Gal 6:17 Henceforth let no man trouble me 10
2Ti 4: 8 Henceforth there is laid up for me . . 10
Rev 14:13 the dead who die in the Lord henceforth. 7
2Es 7:99 This is the order . . as henceforth is announced 12
14: 9 and henceforth you shall live with my Son 13
1Mc 10:30 I release them from this day and henceforth 9
11:35 the other payments henceforth due to us 8
15: 8 canceled . . from henceforth and for all time. 11

henna 1. כֹּפֶר
Sng 4:13 with all choicest fruits, henna with nard 1

henna blossom 1. כֹּפֶר
Sng 1:14 My beloved is to me a cluster of henna blossoms 1

herald 1. כָּרוֹז (A) 2. κῆρυξ
Dan 3: 4 herald proclaimed aloud, "You are commanded 1
2Pe 2: 5 preserved Noah, a herald of righteousness 2
Sir 20:15 he opens his mouth like a herald 2
4Mc 6: 4 while a herald opposite him cried out 2

herald of good tidings 1. בשׂר
Isa 40: 9 to a high mountain, O Zion, herald of good tidings 1
9 Jerusalem, herald of good tidings, lift it up 1
41:27 and I give to Jerusalem a herald of good tidings. 1

herb 1. אוֹרָה 2. דֶּשֶׁא 3. יֶרֶק 4. עֵשֶׂב 5. βοτάνη 6. λάχανον
Gen 2: 5 and no herb of the field had yet sprung up– 4
Deu 32: 2 speech distil . . as the showers upon the herb. 4
2Kg 4:39 One . . went out into the field to gather herbs 1
Ps 37: 2 like the grass, and wither like the green herb. 2
Prv 15:17 Better is a dinner of herbs where love is 3
Lke 11:42 you tithe mint and rue and every herb 6
Wis 16:12 For neither herb nor poultice cured them 5

bitter herb 1. מְרֹר
Exd 12: 8 with unleavened bread and bitter herbs 1
Num 9:11 eat it with unleavened bread and bitter herbs. 1

herbage 1. עֵשֶׂב
Prv 27:25 herbage of the mountains is gathered 1
Isa 42:15 mountains and hills, and dry up all their herbage; 1
Jer 14: 6 their eyes fail because there is no herbage. 1

herd 1. בֵּן 2. בָּקָר 3. הָמוֹן 4. מִקְנֶה 5. עֵדָה 6. עֵדֶר 7. צֹאן 8. רעה 9. שׁוֹר 10. שׁמר 11. ἀγέλη 12. βουκόλιον
Gen 13: 5 Lot . . also had flocks and herds and tents 2
18: 7 Abraham ran to the herd, and took a calf 2
24:35 given him flocks and herds, silver and gold 2
26:14 He had possessions of flocks and herds 2
32: 7 he divided . . the flocks and herds and camels 2
33:13 knows . . that the flocks and herds giving suck 2
34:28 they took their flocks and their herds 2
45:10 your flocks, your herds, and all that you have; 2
46:32 brought . . their herds, and all that they have.' 2
47: 1 my brothers, with their flocks and herds 2
17 the horses, the flocks, the herds, and the asses 7
18 and the herds of cattle are my lord's; 4
50: 8 only . . their flocks, and their herds were left 2
Exd 9: 3 plague upon . . the herds, and the flocks. 2
10: 9 sons and daughters and with our flocks and herds 2
24 let your flocks and your herds remain behind. 2
12:32 Take your flocks and your herds, as you have said 2
38 and very many cattle, both flocks and herds. 2
34: 3 let no flocks or herds feed before that mountain. 2
Lev 1: 2 cattle from the herd or from the flock 2
3 If his offering is a burnt offering from the herd 2
3: 1 if he offers an animal from the herd 2
22:21 offers . . from the herd or from the flock 2
27:32 all the tithe of herds and flocks 2
Num11:22 Shall flocks and herds be slaughtered for them 2
15: 3 offer to the LORD from the herd or from the flock 2
Deu 8:13 when your herds and flocks multiply 2
12: 6 bring . . the firstlings of your herd 2
17 not eat . . the firstlings of your herd 2
21 then you may kill any of your herd or your flock 2
14:23 eat . . the firstlings of your herd and flock; 2
15:19 firstling males that are born of your herd 2
19 shall do no work with the firstling of your herd 9
16: 2 sacrifice . . from the flock or the herd 2
32:14 Curds from the herd, and milk from the flock 2
14 fat of lambs and rams, herds of Bashan and goats 1
1Sm 30:20 David also captured all the flocks and herds; 2
2Sm 12: 2 The rich man had very many flocks and herds; 2
4 was unwilling to take one of his own flock or herd 2
17:29 brought . . sheep and cheese from the herd 2
1Ch 27:29 Over the herds that pastured in Sharon was 2
29 over the herds in the valleys was Shaphat the son 2
2Ch 26:10 he had large herds, both in the Shephe'lah 4
32:29 provided . . flocks and herds in abundance; 2
Neh 10:36 firstlings of our herds and of our flocks. 2
Ps 68:30 herd of bulls with the calves of the peoples. 5
Prv 27:23 give attention to your herds; 6
Ecc 2: 7 I had also great possessions of herds and flocks 2
Isa 65:10 the Valley of Achor a place for herds to lie down 2
Jer 3:24 and their herds, their sons and their daughters. 2
5:17 they shall eat up your flocks and your herds; 2
31:12 and over the young of the flock and the herd; 2
49:32 become booty, their herds of cattle a spoil. 3
Hos 5: 6 With their flocks and herds they shall go to seek 2
12: 1 E'phraim herds the wind, and pursues the east wind 8
12 and for a wife he herded sheep.) 10
Jol 1:18 The herds of cattle are perplexed 6
Jon 3: 7 Let neither man nor beast, herd nor flock 2
Hab 3:17 Though . . there be no herd in the stalls 2
Zep 2:14 Herds shall lie down in the midst of her 6
Mat 8:30 a herd of swine was feeding at some distance 11
31 cast us out, send us away into the herd of swine. 11
32 behold, the whole herd rushed down the steep bank 11
Mrk 5:11 Now a great herd of swine was feeding there 11
13 and the herd, numbering about 2,000 11
Lke 8:32 Now a large herd of swine was feeding there 11
33 the herd rushed down the steep bank into the lake 11
Jdt 2:27 destroyed their flocks and herds 12
3: 3 all our wheat fields, and our flocks and herds 12

herdsman 1. בּוֹקֵר 2. רעה 3. βόσκω
Gen 13: 7 strife between the herdsmen of Abram's cattle 2
7 Abram's cattle and the herdsmen of Lot's cattle. 2
8 and between your herdsmen and my herdsmen; 2
8 and between your herdsmen and my herdsmen; 2
26:20 the herdsmen of Gerar quarreled with Isaac's 2
20 herdsmen . . quarreled with Isaac's herdsmen 2
1Sm 21: 7 Do'eg the E'domite, the chief of Saul's herdsmen. 2
Ams 7:14 I am a herdsman, and a dresser of sycamore trees 1
Mat 8:33 The herdsmen fled, and going into the city 3
Mrk 5:14 The herdsmen fled,and told it in the city 3
Lke 8:34 When the herdsmen saw what had happened 3

herdsman *See also* staff.

here 1. אַיִן 2. אֵל 3. אֵלֶּה 4. אֲשֶׁר 5. בָּה 6. בָּזֶה 7. הֵא 8. הֲלֹם 9. הֵם 10. הֵנָּה 11. הִנֵּה 12. זֶה 13. כֹּה 14. מצא 15. עַד הֵנָּה 16. פֹּה 17. ראה 18. שָׁם 19. כֹּה (A) 20. ἄλλος 21. αὐτόθι 22. αὐτοῦ 23. δεῦρο 24. εἰς τὸ μέσον 25. ἐνθάδε 26. ἔνθεν 27. ἐνταῦθα 28. ἐντεῦθεν 29. ἕτοιμος 30. ἰδού 31. καί 32. ὅπου 33. ὁράω 34. οὗτος 35. πάρειμι 36. προχαλάω 37. ὧδε 38. adsum 39. ecce 40. hic 41. huc
Gen 12:19 Now then, here is your wife, take her, and be gone. 11
15:16 shall come back here in the fourth generation; 10
19:12 the men said to Lot, "Have you any one else here? 16
15 two daughters who are here, lest you be consumed 14
21:23 now therefore swear to me here by God 10
22: 1 Abraham!" And he said, "Here am I. 11
5 Stay here with the ass; I and the lad will go 16
7 My father!" And he said, "Here am I, my son. 11
11 Abraham, Abraham!" And he said, "Here am I. 11
27: 1 said to him, "My son"; and he answered, "Here I am. 11
18 and he said, "Here I am; who are you, my son? 11
30: 3 Then she said, "Here is my maid Bilhah; go in to her 11
31:11 in the dream, 'Jacob,' and I said, 'Here I am!' 11
37 Set it here before my kinsmen and your kinsmen 13
37:13 And he said to him, "Here I am. 11
19 They said . . "Here comes this dreamer. 11
22 cast him into this pit here in the wilderness 4
38:21 And they said, "No harlot has been here. 6
22 men of the place say, 'No harlot has been here.' 6
40:15 and here also I have done nothing 16
42:15 place unless your youngest brother comes here. 10
28 has been put back; here it is in the mouth of my sack 11
45: 5 do not be distressed . . because you sold me here; 10
8 it was not you who sent me here, but God; 10
13 Make haste and bring my father down here. 10
46: 2 said, "Jacob, Jacob." And he said, "Here am I. 11
47:23 Now here is seed for you, and you shall sow 7
48: 9 They are my sons, whom God has given me here. 6
50:25 and you shall carry up my bones from here. 12
Exd 3: 4 Moses, Moses!" And he said, "Here am I. 11
13:19 you must carry my bones with you from here. 12
24:14 Tarry here for us, until we come to you again; 12
33:15 do not carry us up from here. 12
Num14:40 See, we are here, we will go up to the place 11
20: 4 that we should die here, both we and our cattle? 18
16 here we are in Kadesh, a city on the edge 11
22: 8 Lodge here this night, and I will bring back word 16
19 Pray, now, tarry here this night also 6
23: 1 said to Balak, "Build for me here seven altars 6
1 provide for me here seven bulls and seven rams. 6
15 Stand here beside your burnt offering 13
29 Build for me here seven altars 6
29 provide for me here seven bulls and seven rams. 6
32: 6 your brethren go to the war while you sit here? 16
16 We will build sheepfolds here for our flocks 16
Deu 5: 3 who are all of us here alive this day. 16
31 But you, stand here by me, and I will tell you 16
9:12 LORD said to me, 'Arise, go down quickly from here; 12
12: 8 according to all that we are doing here this day 16
20:15 which are not cities of the nations here. *
29:15 but with him who is not here with us this day 16
15 with him who stands here with us this day 16
Jos 2: 2 certain men of Israel have come here tonight 10
4: 3 Take twelve stones from here out of the . . Jordan 12
9:12 Here is our bread; it was still warm when we took it 12
17: 9 The cities here . . belong to E'phraim. 3
18: 6 describe . . and bring the description here to me; 10
6 I will cast lots for you here before the LORD 16
8 I will cast lots for you here before the LORD 16
23: 7 be mixed with these nations left here among you *
12 the remnant of these nations left here among you *
Jdg 4:20 if any man . . asks you, 'Is any one here?' say, No. 16
6:18 Do not depart from here . . until I come to thee 12
26 an altar . . on the top of the stronghold here 12
14:15 Have you invited us here to impoverish us? *
16: 2 The Gazites were told, "Samson has come here 10
18: 3 said to him, "Who brought you here? What are you 8
3 doing in the place? What is your business here? 16
19: 9 lodge here and let your heart be merry 16
24 here are my virgin daughter and his concubine; 11
20: 7 all of you, give your advice and counsel here. 8
Rut 2:14 Come here, and eat some bread, and dip your morsel 8
4: 1 Bo'az said, "Turn aside, friend; sit down here 16
2 he took ten men . . and said, "Sit down here 16
4 Buy it in the presence of those sitting here *
1Sm 1:26 the woman who was standing here in your presence 6
3: 4 called, "Samuel! Samuel!" and he said, "Here I am! 11
5 ran to Eli, and said, "Here I am, for you called me. 11
6 went to Eli, and said, "Here I am, for you called me. 11
8 went to Eli, and said, "Here I am, for you called me. 11
16 and said, "Samuel, my son." And he said, "Here I am. 11
4: 3 bring the ark of the covenant . . here from Shiloh 2
9: 8 Here, I have with me the fourth part of a shekel 11
11 and said to them, "Is the seer here? 6
17 LORD told him, "Here is the man of whom I spoke 11

27 stop here yourself for a while, that I may •
12: 3 Here I am; testify against me before the LORD 11
14:33 roll a great stone to me here. 27
34 bring his ox or . . sheep, and slay them here, and eat; 6
43 I tasted a little honey . . here I am, I will die. 11
15:32 Bring here to me Agag the king of the Amal'ekites. •
16:11 And Samuel said to Jesse, "Are all your sons here? •
11 we will not sit down till he comes here. 16
18:17 Here is my elder daughter Merab; I will give her 11
21: 3 Give me five loaves of bread, or whatever is here. 14
8 And have you not here a spear or a sword 16
9 sword of Goliath . . is here wrapped in a cloth 11
9 take it, for there is none but that here. 6
22:12 Hear now . . " And he answered, "Here I am, my lord. 11
23: 3 Behold, we are afraid here in Judah 16
24: 4 Here is the day of which the LORD said to you 11
26:22 And David made answer, "Here is the spear, O king! 11
29: 3 What are these Hebrews doing here? •
4 Would it not be with the heads of the men here? 9
30:26 Here is a present for you from the spoil 11
2Sm 1: 7 saw me, and called to me. And I answered, 'Here I am.' 11
10 I took . . and I have brought them here to my lord. 10
4: 8 Here is the head of Ish-bo'sheth, the son of Saul 11
5: 6 who said to David, "You will not come in here 10
6 who said . . thinking, "David cannot come in here. 10
11:12 Remain here today also, and tomorrow I will let 6
14:32 Come here, that I may send you to the king 10
15:26 here I am, let him do to me what seems good to him. 11
18:30 And the king said, "Turn aside, and stand here. 13
19:37 But here is your servant Chimham; let him go over 11
20: 4 Call the men of Judah . . and be here yourself. 16
16 Hear! Tell Jo'ab, 'Come here, that I may speak to you.' 15
24:22 here are the oxen for the burnt offering 17
1Kg 1:23 they told the king, "Here is Nathan the prophet. 11
2:30 But he said, "No, I will die here. 16
17: 3 Depart from here and turn eastward 12
18: 8 Go, tell your lord, 'Behold, Eli'jah is here.' •
10 when they would say, 'He is not here,' 1
11 'Go, tell your lord, "Behold, Eli'hah is here."' •
14 'Go, tell your lord, "Behold, Eli'jah is here"'; •
19: 9 What are you doing here, Eli'jah? 16
13 What are you doing here, Eli'jah? 16
20:40 your servant was busy here and there 10
22: 7 Is there not here another prophet of the LORD 16
2Kg 2: 2 said to Eli'sha, "Tarry here, I pray you 16
4 said to him, "Eli'sha, tarry here, I pray you 16
6 said to him, "Tarry here, I pray you 16
3:11 Is there no prophet of the LORD here 16
11 Eli'sha the son of Shaphat is here 16
7: 3 Why do we sit here till we die? 16
4 and if we sit here, we die also. 16
13 those who are left here will fare like the whole 5
8: 5 O king, here is the woman, and here is her son 12
7 when it was told him, "The man of God has come here 15
10:23 there is no servant of the LORD here among you 16
1Ch 11: 5 said to David, "You will not come in here. 10
22: 1 David said, "Here shall be the house of the LORD God 12
1 and here the altar of burnt offering for Israel. 12
29:17 I have seen thy people, who are present here 16
2Ch 18: 6 Is there not here another prophet of the LORD 16
28:13 said . . "You shall not bring the captives in here 10
Ezr 4: 2 king of Assyria who brought us here. 16
Job 31:35 Here is my signature! let the Almighty answer me! 10
38:11 and here shall your proud waves be stayed 16
35 that they may go and say to you, 'Here we are'? 11
Ps 132:14 here I will dwell, for I have desired it. 16
Prv 9: 4 Whoever is simple, let him turn in here! 10
16 Whoever is simple, let him turn in here! 10
25: 7 for it is better to be told, "Come up here 10
Isa 6: 8 who will go for us?" Then I said, "Here am I! Send me. 11
21: 9 And, behold, here come riders, horsemen in pairs! 12
22:16 What have you to do here 16
16 and whom have you here 16
16 that you have hewn here a tomb for yourself 16
28:10 line upon line, here a little, there a little. 18
13 line upon line, here a little, there a little; 18
52: 5 therefore what have I here, says the LORD 16
58: 9 you shall cry, and he will say, Here I am. 11
65: 1 here am I," to a nation that did not call on my name. 11
Jer 22:11 away from this place: "He shall return here no more 18
31: 8 a great company, they shall return here. 10
38:10 Take three men with you from here 12
Ezk 8: 6 the house of Israel are committing here 16
9 abominations that they are committing here. 16
17 the abominations which they commit here 16
40: 4 you were brought here in order that I might show 10
Dan 3:26 servants of . . God, come forth, and come here! •
4: 9 here is the dream which I saw; •
7:28 Here is the end of the matter. 19
Zec 3: 7 of access among those who are standing here. •
Mat 8:29 Have you come here to torment us 37
12: 6 something greater than the temple is here. 37
41 something greater than Jonah is here. 37
42 something greater than Solomon is here. 37
49 he said, "Here are my mother and my brothers! 30
14: 8 she said, "Give me the head . . here on a platter. 37
17 We have only five loaves here and two fish. 37
18 And he said, "Bring them here to me. 37
16:28 some standing here who will not taste death 37
17: 4 Lord, it is well that we are here 37
4 if you wish, I will make three booths here, 37
17 Jesus answered . . Bring him here to me. 37
20 this mountain, 'Move from here to there,' and it will 26
20: 6 Why do you stand here idle all day? 37
22:12 how did you get in here without a wedding garment 37
24: 2 there will not be left here one stone 37
23 if any one says to you 'Lo, here is the Christ!' 37
25:20 here I have made five talents more.' 33
22 here I have made two talents more.' 33
25 Here you have what is yours.' 33
26:36 Sit here, while I go yonder and pray. 22
38 remain here, and watch with me. 37
50 Jesus said to him, "Friend, why are you here? 35
28: 6 He is not here; for he has risen, as he said. 37
Mrk 3: 3 Come here. 24
34 he said, "Here are my mother and my brothers! 33
6: 3 are not his sisters here with us? 37
8: 4 feed these men with bread here in the desert? 37
9: 1 some standing here who will not taste death 37
5 Master, it is well that we are here 37
11: 3 and will send it back here immediately. 37
13: 2 There will not be left here one stone 37
21 one says to you, 'Look, here is the Christ!' 37
14:32 to his disciples, "Sit here, while I pray. 37
34 soul is very sorrowful . . remain here, and watch. 37
16: 6 He has risen, he is not here 37
Lke 4: 9 throw yourself down from here; 28
23 you did . . do here also in your own country. 37
6: 8 Come and stand here." And he rose and stood there. 24
9:12 for we are here in a lonely place. 37
27 some standing here who will not taste death 22
33 Master, it is well that we are here 37
41 Jesus answered . . Bring your son here. 37
11:31 behold, something greater than Solomon is here. 37
32 behold, something greater than Jonah is here. 37
13:31 Get away from here, for Herod wants to kill you. 28
15:17 have bread . . but I perish here with hunger! 37
16:25 now he is conforted here, and you are in anguish. 37
26 in order that those who would pass from here 26
17:21 nor will they say, 'Lo, here it is!' 37
23 will say to you, 'Lo, there!' or 'Lo, here!' 37
19:20 'Lord, here is your pound 30
27 bring them here and slay them before me 37
30 untie it and bring it here. •
21: 6 there shall not be left here one stone upon another •
22:38 they said, "Look, Lord, here are two swords. 37
24:41 Have you anything here to eat? 25
Joh 3:26 to whom you bore witness, here he is, baptizing 33
4:15 I may not thirst, nor come here to draw. 25
16 Go, call your husband, and come here. 25
6: 9 a lad here who has five barley loaves 37
25 Rabbi, when did you come here? 37
7: 3 Leave here and go to Judea 28
6 your time is always here. 29
26 here he is, speaking openly, and they say nothing 33
11:21 Lord, if you had been here 37
28 The Teacher is here and is calling for you. 35
32 Lord, if you had been here 37
20:27 Put your finger here, and see my hands 37
Act 5:28 yet here you have filled Jerusalem 30
8:36 the eunuch said, "See, here is water! •
9:10 he said, "Here I am, Lord. 30
14 here he has authority from the chief priests 37
21 And he has come here for this purpose 37
16:28 Do not harm yourself, for we are all here 25
17: 6 These men . . have come here also. 25
19:37 you have brought these men here •
24:19 they ought to be here before you 35
25:17 When therefore they came together here 25
24 petitioned me, both at Jerusalem and here 25
26: 6 now I stand here on trial for hope in the promise •
22 I stand here testifying both to small and great •
2Co 12:14 Here for the third time I am ready to come to you. 30
Php 1:16 I am put here for the defense of the gospel; •
Col 3:11 Here there cannot be Greek and Jew 32
4: 9 everything that has taken place here. 37
Heb 2:13 again, "Here am I, and the children God has given me. 30
7: 8 Here tithes are received by mortal men 37
13:14 For here we have no lasting city 37
Jas 2: 3 you . . say, "Have a seat here, please 37
Rev 13:10 must he be slain. Here is a call for the endurance 37
14:12 Here is a call for the endurance of the saints 37
1Es 5:69 Esarhaddon . . who brought us here. 27
6:20 after coming here •
34 done with all diligence as here prescribed. 34
2Es 3:29 when I came here 41
4:12 better for us not to be here than to come here 38
35 'How long are we to remain here? ‡
7:38 here are delight and rest 40
10: 4 I intend not to return to the city, but to stay here 40
18 I will not go into the city, but I will die here. 40
58 tomorrow night you shall remain here. 40
12:39 wait here seven days more, so that you may be shown 40
14: 2 I said, "Here I am, Lord," and I rose to my feet. 39
25 you shall come here, and I will light in your heart 40
33 now you are here 40
Tob 2: 8 here he is burying the dead again! 33
7:11 Tobias said, "I will eat nothing here 37
13 Here she is; take her according to the law of Moses 33
11:15 here I see my son Tobias! 33
14: 1 Here Tobit ended his words of praise. 31
Jdt 3:10 here he camped between Geba and Scythopolis 31
9: 6 'Lo, we are here' 35
12: 3 none of your people is here with us. •
13:15 here is the head of Holofernes •
15 here is the canopy beneath which he lay 30
14:18 For look, here is Holofernes lying on the ground •
Wis 18:18 one here and another there, hurled down half dead 20
Bar 3:34 he called them, and they said, "Here we are! 35
2Mc 1: 6 We are now praying for you here. 37
14: 7 and have now come here 23
33 I will build here a splendid temple to Dionysus. 27
15:37 So I too will here end my story. 21
39 here will be the end. 27
3Mc 3:21 our amnesty toward their compatriots here •
6:25 taken each man . . and senselessly gathered here 25
4Mc 4: 3 I have come here because I am loyal •
10:19 See, here is my tongue; cut it off 36
17: 9 Here lie buried an aged priest and an aged woman 27

here *See also* bring, come, write.

here and there 1. *ἄλλως καὶ ἄλλως*
3Mc 1:20 nurses abandoned . . newborn children here and there 1

here present 1. *πάρειμι*
Act 10:33 we are all here present in the sight of God 1

hereafter 1. אַחַר 2. לְאָחוֹר 3. אַחֲרֵי דְנָה (A) 4. *ἀπ᾽ ἄρτι* 5. *εἰς μετέπειτα χρόνον* 6. *μετὰ τοῦτο* 7. amodo 8. iterum
Isa 41:23 Tell us what is to come hereafter, that we may know 2
Ezk 20:39 now and hereafter, if you will not listen to me; 1
Dan 2:29 in bed came thoughts of what would be hereafter 3
45 made known to the king what shall be hereafter. 3
Mat 26:64 hereafter you will see the Son of man 4
Rev 1:19 what is and what is to take place hereafter. 6
2Es 7:99 those who would not . . shall suffer hereafter. 7
14:16 evils worse . . shall be done hereafter. 8
20 who will warn those who will be born hereafter? 8
AEs 13: 7 completely secure and untroubled hereafter. 5
16:23 both now and hereafter it may mean salvation 6
Wis 2: 2 hereafter we shall be as though we had never been; 6

hereafter *See also* live.

hereby 1. בְּזֹה
Num16:28 Hereby you shall know that the LORD has sent me 1
Jos 3:10 Hereby you shall know that . . God is among you 1

herein *See* written.

heresy 1. *αἵρεσις*
2Pe 2: 1 secretly bring in destructive heresies 1

heretofore 1. גַּם מִתְּמוֹל גַּם מִשִּׁלְשֹׁם 2. תְּמוֹל שִׁלְשֹׁם
Exd 4:10 I am not eloquent, either heretofore or since 1
5: 7 no longer give the people . . as heretofore; 2
8 bricks which they made heretofore you shall lay 2

herewith 1. *ἰδού*
Bar 1:10 Herewith we send you money; so buy with the money 1

heritage 1. יְרֻשָּׁה 2. נַחֲלָה 3. *κληρονομέω* 4. *κληρονομία* 5. *μερίς*
Deu 9:26 O Lord GOD, destroy not thy people and thy heritage 2
29 For they are thy people and thy heritage 2
32: 9 LORD'S portion . . Jacob his allotted heritage 2
Jos 18: 7 for the priesthood of the LORD is their heritage; 2
1Sm 10: 1 has anointed you to be prince over his heritage. 2
26:19 I should have no share in the heritage of the LORD 2
2Sm 14:16 destroy me and my son . . from the heritage of God.' 2
20:19 why will you swallow up the heritage of the LORD? 2
21: 3 that you may bless the heritage of the LORD? 2
1Kg 8:51 they are thy people, and thy heritage 2
53 separate them . . to be thy heritage 2
2Kg 21:14 I will cast off the remnant of my heritage 2
Job 20:29 the heritage decreed for him by God. 2
27:13 the heritage which oppressors receive 2
31: 2 my heritage from the Almighty on high? 2
Ps 2: 8 I will make the nations your heritage 2
16: 6 in pleasant places; yea, I have a goodly heritage. 2
28: 9 O save thy people, and bless thy heritage; 2
33:12 the people whom he has chosen as his heritage! 2
37:18 their heritage will abide for ever; 2
47: 4 He chose our heritage for us, the pride of Jacob 2
61: 5 given me the heritage of those who fear thy name. 1
68: 9 thou didst restore thy heritage as it languished; 2
74: 2 redeemed to be the tribe of thy heritage! 2
78:62 and vented his wrath on his heritage. 2
94: 5 O LORD, and afflict thy heritage. 2
14 For the LORD . . will not abandon his heritage; 2
106: 5 that I may glory with thy heritage. 2
40 LORD . . abhorred his heritage; 2
111: 6 in giving them the heritage of the nations. 2
119:111 Thy testimonies are my heritage for ever; 2
127: 3 Lo, sons are a heritage from the LORD 2
135:12 gave their land as a heritage 2

12 as a heritage, a heritage to his people Israel. 2
136:21 gave their land as a heritage 2
22 a heritage to Israel his servant 2
Isa 19:25 Blessed be Egypt . . and Israel my heritage. 2
47: 6 was angry with my people, I profaned my heritage; 2
49: 8 to apportion the desolate heritages; 2
54:17 This is the heritage of the servants of the LORD 2
58:14 I will feed you with the heritage of Jacob 2
63:17 of thy servants, the tribes of thy heritage. 2
Jer 2: 7 and made my heritage an abomination. 2
3:19 a heritage most beauteous of all nations. 2
12: 7 I have abandoned my heritage; 2
8 My heritage has become to me like a lion 2
9 Is my heritage to me like a speckled bird of prey? 2
14 all my evil neighbors who touch the heritage 2
15 and I will bring them again each to his heritage 2
17: 4 You shall loosen your hand from your heritage 2
50:11 though you exult, O plunderers of my heritage 2
Jol 2:17 and make not thy heritage a reproach, 2
3: 2 on account of my people and my heritage Israel 2
Mal 1: 3 and left his heritage to jackals of the desert. 2
Rev 21: 7 He who conquers shall have this heritage 3
Sir 45:20 He added glory to Aaron and gave him a heritage 4
25 the heritage of the king is from son to son only 4
25 so the heritage of Aaron is for his descendants. 4
2Mc 14:15 always upholds his own heritage 5

heritage *See also* give.

hero 1. גִּבּוֹר
Isa 5:22 Woe to those who are heroes at drinking wine 1
Jer 48:14 do you say, 'We are heroes and mighty men of war'? 1

heroic
1Mc 5:56 the heroic war they had fought. *

heron 1. אֲנָפָה
Lev 11:19 the stork, the heron according to its kind 1
Deu 14:18 stork, the heron, after their kinds; 1

hesitate 1. חשך 2. ὀκνέω 3. φείδομαι
Job 30:10 they do not hesitate to spit at the sight of me. 1
Tob 12:13 did not hesitate to rise and leave your dinner 2
Sir 13:12 he will not hesitate to injure or to imprison. 3

hesitation 1. διακρίνω
Act 10:20 go down, and accompany them without hesitation; 1

hew 1. גָּזִית 2. חטב 3. חצב 4. פסל 5. λαξεύω 6. λατομέω 7. ξυστός
Deu 6:11 cisterns hewn out, which you did not hew 3
10: 1 Hew two tables of stone like the first, and come up 4
3 I made an ark . . and hewed two tables of stone 4
29:11 both he who hews your wood and he who draws 2
1Kg 7: 9 were made of costly stones, hewn according 1
11 costly stones, hewn according to measurement 1
Isa 10:15 the axe vaunt itself over him who hews with it 3
22:16 that you have hewn here a tomb for yourself 3
16 you who hew a tomb on the height 3
51: 1 look to the rock from which you were hewn 3
Ezk 40:42 there were also four tables of hewn stone 1
Hos 6: 5 Therefore I have hewn them by the prophets 3
Mat 27:60 his own new tomb, which he had hewn in the rock; 6
Mrk 15:46 a tomb which had been hewn out of the rock 6
1Es 6: 9 of hewn stone 7
25 with three courses of hewn stone 7
Jdt 1: 2 hewn stones three cubits thick 5

hew away 1. סור תיז
Isa 18: 5 and the spreading branches he will hew away. 1

hew down 1. גדע 2. כרת 3. גדד (A)
Deu 7: 5 you shall . . hew down their Ashe'rim 1
12: 3 hew down the graven images of their gods 1
2Ch 14: 3 hewed down the Ashe'rim 1
31: 1 all Israel . . hewed down the Ashe'rim 1
34: 4 hewed down the incense altars which stood 1
7 hewed down all the incense altars throughout 1
Isa 10:33 the great in height will be hewn down 1
Jer 6: 6 thus says the LORD of hosts: "Hew down her trees; 2
Dan 4:14 'Hew down the tree and cut off its branches 3
23 'Hew down the tree and destroy it, 3

hew in pieces 1. שסף
1Sm 15:33 And Samuel hewed Agag in pieces before the LORD 1

hew out 1. חצב 2. כרה
Gen 50: 5 in my tomb which I hewed out for myself in the land 2
Deu 6:11 cisterns hewn out, which you did not hew 1
2Ch 16:14 in the tomb which he had hewn out for himself 2
26:10 he built towers . . and hewed out many cisterns 1
Neh 9:25 possession of . . cisterns hewn out, vineyards 1
Isa 5: 2 planted it . . and hewed out a wine vat in it; 1
Jer 2:13 and hewed out cisterns for themselves 1

hewer 1. חטב 2. חצב 3. כרת
Jos 9:21 they became hewers of wood and drawers of water 1
23 be slaves, hewers of wood and drawers of water 1
27 made them that day hewers of wood and drawers 1
1Kg 5:15 Solomon also had . . and 80,000 hewers of stone 2
2Ch 2:10 give for your servants, the hewers who cut timber 1
Isa 14: 8 you were laid low, no hewer comes up against us.' 3

do hewing 1. פסל
1Kg 5:18 did the hewing and prepared the timber 1

hewn *See* stone.

hid *See* treasure.

hidden *See* fault, keep, store, trap, treasure.

remain hidden 1. κρύπτω
1Ti 5:25 good deeds . . they cannot remain hidden. 1

hidden thing 1. בצר 2. נצר 3. ἀπόκρυφος 4. κρυπτός 5. κρύπτω 6. abscondo
Isa 48: 6 hidden things which you have not known. 2
Jer 33: 3 and will tell you great and hidden things 1
1Co 4: 5 who will bring to light the things now hidden 4
2Es 16:62 and searches out hidden things in hidden places. 6
Sir 42:19 he reveals the tracks of hidden things. 3
48:25 the hidden things before they came to pass. 3
2Mc 12:41 who reveals the things that are hidden; 5

hide 1. חבא 2. חבה 3. חפש 4. טמן 5. כחד 6. כנף 7. כסה 8. מַסְתֵּר 9. מִסְתָּר 10. נוס 11. ספן 12. סתר 13. עלם 14. עמם 15. צפן 16. תַּעֲלֻמָה 17. ἀποκρύπτω 18. ἀπόκρυφος 19. ἀφανής 20. ἐγκρύπτω 21. καλύπτω 22. κατακρύπτω 23. κρυπτός 24. κρύπτω 25. κρυφός 26. κρύψις 27. λανθάνω 28. περικρύπτω 29. συγκαλύπτω 30. συγκρύπτω 31. συναποκρύπτω 32. abscondo 33. occulo 34. subduco
Gen 3: 8 and the man and his wife hid themselves 1
10 afraid, because I was naked; and I hid myself. 1
4:14 and from thy face I shall be hidden; 12
18:17 The LORD said, "Shall I hide from Abraham 7
35: 4 and Jacob hid them under the oak which was near 4
47:18 We will not hide from my lord that our money 5
Exd 2: 2 he was a goodly child, she hid him three months. 15
3 when she could hide him no longer she took for him 15
12 he killed the Egyptian and hid him in the sand. 4
3: 6 And Moses hid his face, for he was afraid to look 12
Lev 4:13 the thing is hidden from the eyes of the assembly 13
5: 2 it is hidden from him, and he has become unclean 13
3 becomes unclean, and it is hidden from him 13
4 and it is hidden from him, when he comes to know it 13
20: 4 if the people of the land do at all hide their eyes 13
Num 5:13 it is hidden from the eyes of her husband 13
Deu 7:20 until those who are left and hide themselves 12
31:17 I will forsake them and hide my face from them 12
18 I will surely hide my face in that day 12
32:20 said, 'I will hide my face from them, I will see 12
33:19 they suck . . the hidden treasures of the sand. 11
Jos 2: 4 the woman had taken the two men and hidden them; 15
6 and hid them with the stalks of flax 4
16 Go . . and hide yourselves there three days 1
6:17 because she hid the messengers that we sent. 1
25 she hid the messengers whom Joshua sent to spy 1
7:19 tell . . what you have done; do not hide it from me. 5
21 they are hidden in the earth inside my tent 4
22 it was hidden in his tent with the silver 4
10:16 fled, and hid themselves in the cave at Makke'dah. 1
17 The five kings have been found, hidden in the cave 1
27 into the cave where they had hidden themselves 1
Jdg 6:11 in the wine press, to hide it from the Mid'ianites. 10
9: 5 Jotham . . was left, for he hid himself. 1
1Sm 3:17 What was it that he told you? Do not hide it from me. 5
17 May God do so . . if you hide anything from me 5
18 Samuel told him . . and hid nothing from him. 5
10:22 Behold, he has hidden himself among the baggage. 1
13: 6 the people hid themselves in caves and in holes 1
14:11 the holes where they have hid themselves. 1
22 men . . who had hid themselves in the hill country 1
19: 2 stay in a secret place and hide yourself; 1
20: 2 and why should my father hide this from me? 12
5 but let me go, that I may hide myself in the field 12
19 then go to the place where you hid yourself 12
24 David hid himself in the field; 12
23:19 Does not David hide among us in the strongholds 12
23 note . . all the lurking places where he hides 1
26: 1 Is not David hiding himself on . . Hachi'lah 12
2Sm 14:18 Do not hide from me anything I ask you. 5
17: 9 even now he has hidden himself in one of the pits 1
18:13 (and there is nothing hidden from the king) 5
1Kg 10: 3 there was nothing hidden from the king 13
17: 3 Depart . . and hide yourself by the brook Cherith 12
18: 4 took . . prophets and hid them by fifties in a cave 1
13 how I hid 100 men of the LORD's prophets 1
22:25 on that day when you go . . to hide yourself. 2
2Kg 4:27 the LORD has hidden it from me, and has not told me. 13
6:29 'Give your son . . '; but she has hidden her son. 1
7: 8 carried off silver and . . and went and hid them; 4
8 carried off things from it, and went and hid them. 4
12 to hide themselves in the open country 2
11: 2 she hid him from Athali'ah, so that he was not slain; 12
3 he remained . . hid in the house of the LORD, while 1
1Ch 21:20 his four sons who were with him hid themselves. 1
2Ch 9: 2 there was nothing hidden from Solomon 13
18:24 you go into an inner chamber to hide yourself. 1
22: 9 Ahazi'ah . . captured while hiding in Sama'ria 1
11 Jeho-shab'e-ath . . hid him from Athali'ah 12
12 remained with them . . hid in the house of God 1
Job 3:10 nor hide trouble from my eyes. 12
16 Or why was I not as a hidden untimely birth 4
23 Why is light given to a man whose way is hid 12
5:21 You shall be hid from the scourge of the tongue 1
6:16 dark with ice, and where the snow hides itself. 13
10:13 Yet these things thou didst hide in thy heart; 15
13:20 I will not hide myself from thy face 12
24 Why dost thou hide thy face 12
14:13 Oh that thou wouldest hide me in Sheol 15
15:18 have told, and their fathers have not hidden 5
18:10 A rope is hid for him in the ground 4
20:12 in his mouth, though he hides it under his tongue 5
24: 4 the poor of the earth all hide themselves. 1
28:11 the thing that is hid he brings forth to light. 16
21 It is hid from the eyes of all living 13
31:33 from men, by hiding my iniquity in my bosom 4
34:22 deep darkness where evildoers may hide 12
29 When he hides his face, who can behold him 12
40:13 Hide them all in the dust together; 4
42: 3 this that hides counsel without knowledge? 13
Ps 9:15 in the net which they hid has their own foot been 4
10: 1 Why dost thou hide thyself in times of trouble? 13
11 he has hidden his face, he will never see it. 12
13: 1 How long wilt thou hide thy face from me? 12
17: 8 hide me in the shadow of thy wings 12
19: 6 there is nothing hid from its heat. 12
22:24 he has not hid his face from him, but has heard 12
27: 5 he will hide me in his shelter 15
9 Hide not thy face from me. 12
30: 7 thou didst hide thy face, I was dismayed. 12
31: 4 take me out of the net which is hidden for me 4
20 In the covert of thy presence thou hidest them 12
32: 5 I acknowledged my sin to thee, and I did not hide 7
35: 7 For without cause they hid their net for me; 4
8 let the net which they hid ensnare them; 4
38: 9 my sighing is not hidden from thee. 12
40:10 I have not hid thy saving help within my heart 7
44:24 Why dost thou hide thy face? 12
51: 9 Hide thy face from my sins 13
54: 0 went and told Saul, "David is in hiding among us. 12
55: 1 O God; and hide not thyself from my supplication! 13
12 insolently with me–then I could hide from him. 12
64: 2 hide me from the secret plots of the wicked 12
69: 5 the wrongs I have done are not hidden from thee. 5
17 Hide not thy face from thy servant; 12
78: 4 We will not hide them from their children 5
88:14 Why dost thou hide thy face from me? 12
89:46 How long, O LORD? Wilt thou hide thyself for ever? 12
102: 2 not hide thy face from me in the day of my distress! 12
104:29 When thou hidest thy face, they are dismayed; 12
119:19 hide not thy commandments from me! 12
139:15 frame was not hidden . . when I was being made 5
140: 5 Arrogant men have hidden a trap for me 4
142: 3 path where I walk they have hidden a trap for me. 4
143: 7 Hide not thy face from me, lest I be like those 12
Prv 22: 3 A prudent man sees danger and hides himself; 12
27: 5 Better is open rebuke than hidden love. 12
12 A prudent man sees danger and hides himself; 12
28:12 but when the wicked rise, men hide themselves. 3
27 but he who hides his eyes will get many a curse. 13
28 When the wicked rise, men hide themselves 12
Isa 1:15 When you spread . . your hands, I will hide my eyes 13
2:10 hide in the dust from . . the terror of the LORD 4
3: 9 like Sodom, they do not hide it. Woe to them! 5
8:17 I will wait for the LORD, who is hiding his face 12
16: 3 hide the outcasts, betray not the fugitive; 12
26:20 hide yourselves for a little while 2
29:14 discernment of . . discerning men shall be hid. 12
15 those who hide deep from the LORD their counsel 12
30:20 yet your Teacher will not hide himself any more 6
40:27 My way is hid from the LORD 12
42:22 trapped in holes and hidden in prisons; 1
45:15 Truly, thou art a God who hidest thyself 12
49: 2 in the shadow of his hand he hid me; 1
50: 6 I hid not my face from shame and spitting. 12
51:16 in your mouth, and hid you in the shadow of my hand 7
53: 3 from whom men hide their faces he was despised 8
54: 8 In . . wrath for a moment I hid my face from you 12
57:17 angry, I smote him, I hid my face and was angry; 13
58: 7 and not to hide yourself from your own flesh? 13
59: 2 your sins have hid his face from you 12
64: 7 thou hast hid thy face from us, 12
65:16 troubles are forgotten and are hid from my eyes. 12
Jer 13: 4 and hide it there in a cleft of the rock. 4
5 I went, and hid it by the Euphra'tes 4
6 waistcloth which I commanded you to hide there. 4
7 waistcloth from the place where I had hidden it. 4
16:17 they are not hid from me, nor is their iniquity 12
23:24 Can a man hide himself in secret places 12
33: 5 for I have hidden my face from this city 12
36:19 Go and hide, you and Jeremiah 12
26 but the LORD hid them. 12
38:14 I will ask you a question; hide nothing from me. 5
25 what the king said to you; hide nothing from us 5

43: 9 and hide them in the mortar in the pavement 4
10 his throne above these stones which I have hid 4
Lam 3:10 He is . . a bear lying in wait, like a lion in hiding; 9
Ezk 28: 3 wiser than Daniel; no secret is hidden from you; 14
39:23 I hid my face from them and gave them into the hand 12
24 and hid my face from them. 12
29 I will not hide my face any more from them 12
Dan 10: 7 fled to hide themselves. 1
Hos 5: 3 I know E'phraim, and Israel is not hid from me; 5
13:14 Compassion is hid from my eyes. 12
Ams 9: 3 Though they hide themselves on the top of Carmel 1
3 they hide from my sight at the bottom of the sea 12
Mic 3: 4 he will hide his face from them at that time 12
Zep 2: 3 perhaps you may be hidden on the day of the wrath 12
Mat 5:14 A city set on a hill cannot be hid. 24
10:26 or hidden that will not be known. 23
11:25 that thou hast hidden these things from the wise 24
13:33 leaven which a woman took and hid 20
35 I will utter what has been hidden 24
44 treasure hidden in a field 24
25:18 dug in the ground and hid his master's money. 24
25 I went and hid your talent in the ground 24
Mrk 4:22 there is nothing hid, except to be made manifest; 23
7:24 yet he could not be hid. 27
Lke 1:24 for five months she hid herself, saying 28
8:17 nothing is hid that shall not be made manifest 23
47 when the woman saw that she was not hidden 27
10:21 hidden these things from the wise 17
12: 2 or hidden that will not be known. 23
13:21 It is like leaven which a woman took and hid 20
18:34 this saying was hid from them 24
19:42 now they are hid from your eyes. 24
Joh 8:59 Jesus hid himself, and went out of the temple. 24
12:36 he departed and hid himself from them. 24
1Co 2: 7 we impart a secret and hidden wisdom of God 17
Eph 3: 9 plan of the mystery hidden for ages in God 17
Col 1:26 the mystery hidden for ages and generations 17
2: 3 in whom are hid all the treasures of wisdom 18
3: 3 your life is hid with Christ in God. 24
Heb 4:13 before him no creature is hidden 19
11:23 Moses, when he was born, was hid for three months 24
1Pe 3: 4 let it be the hidden person of the heart 23
Rev 2:17 I will give some of the hidden manna 24
6:15 every one, slave and free, hid in the caves 24
16 hide us from . . him who is seated on the throne 24
2Es 5: 1 and the way of truth shall be hidden 32
9 then shall reason hide itself 32
7:26 the land which now is hidden shall be disclosed. 34
8:53 illness is banished from you, and death is hidden; 32
12:37 and put it in a hidden place; 32
16:28 out of the field, two who have hidden themselves 32
62 and searches out hidden things in hidden places. 32
63 Woe to those who sin and want to hide their sins! 33
66 Or how will you hide your sins before God 32
Tob 1:19 so I hid myself 24
12:13 your good deed was not hidden from me 27
13: 6 he will turn to you and will not hide his face 24
Wis 6:22 I will hide no secrets from you 17
7:13 I do not hide her wealth 17
Sir 1:24 He will hide his words until the right moment 26
3:22 you do not need what is hidden. 24
4:23 do not hide your wisdom. •
6:12 will hide himself from your presence. 24
12: 8 nor will an enemy be hidden in adversity. 24
16:17 Do not say, "I shall be hidden from the Lord 24
17:15 they will not be hid from his eyes. 24
20 Their iniquities are not hidden from him 24
19:27 He hides his face and pretends not to hear 30
20:30 Hidden wisdom and unseen treasure 24
31 Better is the man who hides his folly 17
31 Better . . than the man who hides his wisdom. 17
22:25 I will not hide from him; 24
23:18 Darkness surrounds me, and the walls hide me 21
19 perceive even the hidden places. 18
26: 8 she will not hide her shame. 29
37:10 hide your counsel 24
39: 3 he will seek out the hidden meanings of proverbs 18
19 nothing can be hid from his eyes. 24
41:14 hidden wisdom and unseen treasure 24
15 Better is the man who hides his folly 17
15 Better . . than the man who hides his wisdom. 17
42:20 not one word is hidden from him. 24
43:32 Many things greater than these lie hidden 18
LJr 1:48 where they can hide themselves and their gods. 31
Sus 1:16 who had hid themselves and were watching her. 24
18 did not see the elders, because they were hidden. 24
37 Then a young man, who had been hidden, came to her 24
Bel 1:13 they had made a hidden entrance 24
1Mc 1:23 he took also the hidden treasures which he found. 18
53 they drove Israel into hiding 25
9:38 and went up and hid under cover of the mountain. 24
16:15 he gave them a great banquet, and hid men there. 20
2Mc 1:19 secretly hid it in the hollow of a dry cistern 22
20 the priests who had hidden the fire 17
33 the exiled priests had hidden the fire 24
10:37 They killed Timothy, who was hidden in a cistern 17

hide away 1. סתר
Isa 49: 2 a polished arrow, in his quiver he hid me away. 1

hiding *See* go.

hiding place 1. מַחֲבֵא 2. מִסְתָּר 3. סֵתֶר 4. κρυφός 5. latibulum
Ps 10: 8 in hiding places he murders the innocent. 2
32: 7 Thou art a hiding place for me, thou preservest me 3
119:114 Thou art my hiding place and my shield; 3
Isa 32: 2 Each will be like a hiding place from the wind 1
Jer 49:10 I have uncovered his hiding places 2
2Es 2:31 out of the hiding places of the earth 5
1Mc 2:31 had gone down to the hiding places in the wilderness. 4
36 or block up their hiding places 4
41 die as our brethren died in their hiding places. 4

hie 1. הלך
Sng 4: 6 I will hie me to the mountain of myrrh 1

high 1. בֶּן אִישׁ 2. גבה 3. גָּבֹהַּ 4. גָּבַהּ 5. גָּדוֹל 6. לְמַעְלָה 7. מֵעַל 8. מַעַל 9. מַעְלָה 10. מָרוֹם 11. מִשְׂגָּב 12. נשׂא 13. עַל 14. עֶלְיוֹן 15. קוֹמָה 16. רֹאשׁ 17. רַב 18. רום 19. רוּם 20. שגב 21. ἀνώτερος 22. ἀστεῖος 23. ἄχρι 24. βάθος 25. ἐπὶ μετεώρου 26. μέγας 27. μετέωρος 28. ὑπεράνω 29. ὑψηλός 30. ὕψιστος 31. ὕψος 32. altus 33. excelsus 34. usque
Gen 7:19 all the high mountains under the whole heaven 3
27:39 and away from the dew of heaven on high. 7
29: 7 He said, "Behold, it is still high day 5
Exd 38:18 it was twenty cubits long and five cubits high 15
Num 15:30 person who does anything with a high hand 18
24: 7 his king shall be higher than Agag 18
35:25 live in it until the death of the high priest 5
28 city of refuge until the death of the high priest; 5
28 but after the death of the high priest 5
32 may return . . before the death of the high priest. •
Deu 2:36 there was not a city too high for us; the LORD 20
3: 5 cities fortified with high walls, gates, and bars 3
12: 2 served their gods, upon the high mountains 18
26:19 that he will set you high above all nations 14
28: 1 LORD . . will set you high above all the nations 14
43 sojourner . . mount above you higher and higher; 8
43 sojourner . . mount above you higher and higher; 9
52 besiege . . until your high and fortified walls 3
Jos 20: 6 remain . . until the death of him who is high priest 5
2Sm 22:17 He reached from on high, he took me, he drew me out 10
23: 1 the oracle of the man who was raised on high 13
1Kg 4: 2 these were his high officials: Azari'ah the son •
6: 2 The house . . twenty cubits wide, and 30 cubits high. 15
10 He built . . each story five cubits high 15
20 long, twenty cubits wide, and twenty cubits high; 15
23 he made two cherubim . . each ten cubits high. 15
7:23 ten cubits from brim to brim, and five cubits high 15
27 long, four cubits wide, and three cubits high. 15
35 on the top . . was a round band half a cubit high; 15
14:23 built . . Ashe'rim on every high hill 3
21: 9 and set Naboth on high among the people; 16
12 they proclaimed a fast, and set Naboth on high 16
2Kg 12:10 the king's secretary and the high priest came up 5
17:10 set up . . pillars and Ashe'rim on every high hill 3
22: 4 Go up to Hilki'ah the high priest 5
8 And Hilki'ah the high priest said to Shaphan 5
23: 4 And the king commanded Hilki'ah the high priest 5
2Ch 2: 6 heaven, even highest heaven, cannot contain him? •
3:15 he made two pillars 35 cubits high 31
4: 1 made an altar of bronze . . and ten cubits high. 15
2 molten sea . . brim to brim, and five cubits high 15
6:13 bronze platform . . wide, and three cubits high 15
18 heaven and the highest heaven cannot contain •
34: 9 came to Hilki'ah the high priest and delivered 5
Ezr 9: 6 our iniquities have risen higher than our heads 6
Neh 3: 1 Then Eli'ashib the high priest rose up 5
20 door of the house of Eli'ashib the high priest. 5
13:28 Jehoi'ada, the son of Eli'ashib the high priest 5
Est 1:20 will give honor to their husbands, high and low. 5
5:14 Let a gallows 50 cubits high be made 3
7: 9 gallows . . in Haman's house, 50 cubits high. 3
Job 5:11 he sets on high those who are lowly 10
11: 8 It is higher than heaven–what can you do? 4
16:19 in heaven, and he that vouches for me is on high. 10
21:22 seeing that he judges those that are on high? 18
22:12 Is not God high in the heavens? 4
12 See the highest stars, how lofty they are! 16
31: 2 my heritage from the Almighty on high? 10
35: 5 behold the clouds, which are higher than you. 2
41:34 He beholds everything that is high; 3
Ps 7: 7 and over it take thy seat on high. 10
10: 5 thy judgments are on high, out of his sight; 10
18:16 He reached from on high, he took me, he drew me out 10
44:12 for a trifle, demanding no high price for them. †
49: 2 both low and high, rich and poor together! 1
61: 2 Lead thou me to the rock that is higher than I; 18
75: 5 do not lift up your horn on high 10
78:69 He built his sanctuary like the high heavens 18
89:13 strong is thy hand, high thy right hand. 18
27 make him . . highest of the kings of the earth. 14
92: 8 but thou, O LORD, art on high for ever. 10
93: 4 LORD on high is mighty! 10
103:11 For as the heavens are high above the earth 2
104:18 The high mountains are for the wild goats; 3
113: 4 The LORD is high above all nations 18
5 Who is like the LORD our God, who is seated on high 2
137: 6 if I do not set Jerusalem above my highest joy! 16
138: 6 For though the LORD is high, he regards the lowly; 18
139: 6 too wonderful for me; it is high, I cannot attain 20
144: 7 Stretch forth thy hand from on high 10
148: 4 Praise him, you highest heavens •
Prv 18:11 like a high wall protecting him. 20
24: 7 Wisdom is too high for a fool; 18
30:13 There are those . . how high their eyelids lift! 18
19 way of a ship on the high seas, and the way of a man •
Ecc 5: 8 for the high official is watched by a higher 3
12: 5 they are afraid also of what is high 3
Isa 2: 2 be established as the highest of the mountains 16
12 has a day . . against all that is lifted up and high; •
14 against all the high mountains, and . . hills; 18
15 against every high tower, and . . fortified wall; 3
6: 1 the Lord sitting upon a throne, high and lifted up; 18
7:11 a sign . . let it be deep as Sheol or high as heaven. 2
25:12 the high fortifications of his walls 11
30:13 iniquity . . like a break in a high wall 20
25 upon every lofty mountain and every high hill 12
32:15 until the Spirit is poured upon us from on high 10
33: 5 The LORD is exalted, for he dwells on high; 10
40: 9 Get you up to a high mountain, O Zion 3
26 Lift up your eyes on high and see 10
52:13 exalted and lifted up, and shall be very high. 2
55: 9 For as the heavens are higher than the earth 2
9 are my ways higher than your ways 2
57: 7 Upon a high . . mountain you have set your bed 3
15 the high and lofty One who inhabits eternity 18
15 I dwell in the high and holy place 10
58: 4 will not make your voice to be heard on high. 10
Jer 2:20 Yea, upon every high hill . . you bowed down 3
3: 6 how she went up on every high hill 3
17: 2 beside every green tree, and on the high hills 3
12 A glorious throne set on high from the beginning 10
25:30 The LORD will roar from on high 10
51:58 and her high gates shall be burned with fire. 3
Lam 1:13 From on high he sent fire; into my bones . . descend; 10
Ezk 6:13 round about their altars, upon every high hill 18
17:22 will plant it upon a high and lofty mountain; 3
24 shall know that I the LORD bring low the high tree 3
20:28 wherever they saw any high hill or any leafy tree 18
21:26 which is low, and abase that which is high. 3
27:26 rowers have brought you out into the high seas. 17
31: 5 it towered high above all the trees of the forest; 15
10 thus says the Lord GOD: Because it towered high 15
34: 6 over all the mountains and on every high hill; 18
40: 2 and set me down upon a very high mountain 3
42 a cubit and a half broad, and one cubit high 4
41:22 an altar of wood, three cubits high 3
43:13 its base shall be one cubit high 24
15 projecting upward, four horns, one cubit high. 28
Dan 8: 3 both horns were high, but one was higher 3
3 one was higher than the other, and the higher one 3
Obd 1: 3 whose dwelling is high, who say in your heart 10
Mic 4: 1 be established as the highest of the mountains 16
6: 6 and bow myself before God on high? 10
Hab 2: 9 evil gain for his house, to set his nest on high 10
3:10 gave forth its voice, it lifted its hands on high. 19
Hag 1: 1 to Joshua the son of Jehoz'adak, the high priest 5
12 Joshua the son of Jehoz'adak, the high priest 5
14 Joshua the son of Jehoz'adak, the high priest 5
2: 2 to Joshua the son of Jehoz'adak, the high priest 5
4 O Joshua, son of Jehoz'adak, the high priest; 5
Zec 3: 1 Then he showed me Joshua the high priest 5
8 Hear now, O Joshua the high priest 5
6:11 of Joshua, the son of Jehoz'adak, the high priest; 5
Mat 4: 8 Again, the devil took him to a very high mountain 29
17: 1 and led them up a high mountain apart. 29
21: 9 Hosanna in the highest! 30
Mrk 9: 2 led them up a high mountain apart by themselves; 29
11:10 Hosanna in the highest! 30
Lke 1:78 when the day shall dawn upon us from on high 31
2:14 Glory to God in the highest 30
4:38 Now Simon's mother-in-law was ill with a high fever 26
14:10 'Friend, go up higher' 21
19:38 Peace in heaven and glory in the highest! 30
24:49 until you are clothed with power from on high. 31
Joh 19:31 (for that sabbath was a high day) 26
1Co 12:31 earnestly desire the higher gifts 26
Eph 4: 8 When he ascended on high he led a host of captives 31
Heb 1: 3 he sat down at the right hand of the Majesty on high 29
Rev 14:20 blood flowed . . as high as a horse's bridle 23
18: 5 for her sins are heaped high as heaven 23
21:10 he carried me away to a great, high mountain 29
12 It had a great, high wall, with twelve gates 29
1Es 4:34 The earth is vast, and heaven is high 29
2Es 4:34 but the Highest hastens on behalf of many. 33
15:35 be blood from the sword as high as a horse's belly 34
40 shall pour out upon every high and lofty place 32
Jdt 1: 2 he made the walls 70 cubits high 31

3 he built towers 100 cubits high •
4 he made its gates, which were 70 cubits high 31
4: 5 and immediately seized all the high hilltops 29
6 Joakim, the high priest 26
8 Joakim the high priest 26
14 Joakim the high priest 26
5: 1 fortified all the high hilltops 29
7: 4 neither the high mountains nor the valleys 29
15: 8 Then Joakim the high priest . . came to witness 26
Wis 9:17 and sent thy holy Spirit from on high? 30
Sir 16:17 who from on high will remember me? 31
22:18 Fences set on a high place will not stand firm 27
24: 4 I dwelt in high places 29
37:14 seven watchmen sitting high on a watchtower. 25
43: 8 an instrument of the hosts on high 31
50: 1 the pride of his people was Simon the high priest 26
2 laid the foundations for the high double walls 31
2 high retaining walls for the temple enclosure. 29
Bar 3:25 has no bounds; it is high and immeasurable. 29
5: 7 every high mountain and the everlasting hills 29
1Mc 4:60 they fortified Mount Zion with high walls 29
6: 7 had surrounded the sanctuary with high walls 29
40 the king's army was spread out on the high hills 29
9:50 with high walls and gates and bars. 29
12:36 erect a high barrier 26
13:33 with high towers and great walls and gates 29
14:20 to Simon the high priest and to the elders 26
39 and paid him high honors. 26
15: 2 King Antiochus to Simon the high priest 26
2Mc 6:23 making a high resolve, worthy of his years 22
8:30 got possession of some exceedingly high strongholds 29
9: 8 he could weigh the high mountains in a balance 31
13: 5 there is a tower in that place, 50 cubits high •
4Mc 1: 2 it includes the praise of the highest virtue 26
5: 1 sitting in state . . on a certain high place 29

high *See also* bough, build, favor, heaven, honor, make, mount, office, official, position, praise, priest, priesthood, priestly, raise, rank, rise, set, standing, value.

most high 1. עֶלְיוֹן 2. עִלָּי (A) 3. עֶלְיוֹן (A) 4. *πανυπέρτατος* 5. ὕψιστος 6. altus

Gen 14:18 he was priest of God Most High. 1
19 Blessed be Abram by God Most High, maker of heaven 1
20 blessed be God Most High 1
22 I have sworn to the LORD God Most High 1
Num24:16 and knows the knowledge of the Most High 1
Deu 32: 8 Most High gave to the nations their inheritance 1
2Sm 22:14 and the Most High uttered his voice. 1
Ps 7:17 sing praise to the name of the LORD, the Most High. 1
9: 2 I will sing praise to thy name, O Most High. 1
18:13 the Most High uttered his voice 1
21: 7 through the steadfast love of the Most High 1
46: 4 city of God, the holy habitation of the Most High. 1
47: 2 the LORD, the Most High, is terrible, a great king 1
50:14 pay your vows to the Most High; 1
57: 2 I cry to God Most High, to God who fulfils 1
73:11 can God know? Is there knowledge in the Most High? 1
77:10 the right hand of the Most High has changed. 1
78:17 rebelling against the Most High in the desert. 1
35 was their rock, the Most High God their redeemer. 1
56 they tested and rebelled against the Most High 1
82: 6 I say, "You are gods, sons of the Most High, all of you; 1
83:18 LORD, art the Most High over all the earth. 1
87: 5 for the Most High himself will establish her. 1
91: 1 He who dwells in the shelter of the Most High 1
9 have made . . Most High your habitation 1
92: 1 good to . . sing praises to thy name, O Most High; 1
97: 9 For thou, O LORD, art most high over all the earth; 1
106: 7 rebelled against the Most High at the Red Sea. •
107:11 spurned the counsel of the Most High. 1
Isa 14:14 ascend . . I will make myself like the Most High.' 1
Lam 3:35 to turn aside . . in the presence of the Most High 1
38 from the mouth of the Most High that good and evil 1
Dan 3:26 servants of the Most High God, come forth 2
4: 2 signs . . Most High God has wrought toward me. 2
17 know that the Most High rules the kingdom of men 2
24 decree of the Most High, which has come upon my 2
25 know that the Most High rules the kingdom of men 2
32 Most High rules the kingdom of men 2
34 blessed the Most High, and praised and honored 2
5:18 O king, the Most High God gave Nebuchadnez'zar 2
21 knew . . Most High God rules the kingdom of men 2
7:18 saints of the Most High shall receive 3
22 judgment . . given for the saints of the Most High 3
25 He shall speak words against the Most High 2
25 shall wear out the saints of the Most High 3
27 given to the people of the saints of the Most High; 3
Mrk 5: 7 Jesus, Son of the Most High God? 5
Lke 1:32 He . . will be called the Son of the Most High 5
35 the power of the Most High will overshadow you; 5
76 you . . will be called the prophet of the Most High 5
6:35 you will be sons of the Most High 5
8:28 Jesus, Son of the Most High God 5
Act 7:48 Yet the Most High does not dwell in houses 5
16:17 These men are servants of the Most High God 5
1Es 2: 3 The Lord of Israel, the Lord Most High 5
6:31 libations may be made to the Most High God 5
8:19 reader of the law of the Most High God 5
21 scrupulously fulfilled for the Most High God 5
9:46 Ezra blessed the Lord God Most High 5
2Es 3: 3 I began to speak anxious words to the Most High 6
4: 2 you can comprehend the way of the Most High? 6
11 can your mind comprehend the way of the Most High? 6
34 You do not hasten faster than the Most High 6
5: 4 if the Most High grants that you live 6
22 to speak words in the presence of the Most High. 6
34 I strive to understand the way of the Most High 6
6:32 has surely been heard before the Most High 6
36 I began to speak in the presence of the Most High. 6
7:19 or wiser than the Most High! 6
23 that the Most High does not exist 6
33 the Most High shall be revealed 6
37 Then the Most High will say to the nations 6
42 only the splendor of the glory of the Most High 6
50 the Most High has made not one world but two. 6
70 When the Most High made the world 6
74 the Most High has been patient with those 6
77 a treasure of works laid up with the Most High 6
78 decree has gone forth from the Most High 6
78 first of all it adores the glory of the Most High. 6
79 and have not kept the way of the Most High 6
81 they have scorned the law of the Most High. 6
83 who have trusted the covenants of the Most High. 6
87 at seeing the glory of the Most High 6
88 who have kept the ways of the Most High 6
89 they laboriously served the Most High 6
102 or to entreat the Most High for them 6
122 that the glory of the Most High will defend those 6
132 that the Most High is now called merciful 6
8: 1 The Most High made this world for the sake of many 6
48 you will be praiseworthy before the Most High 6
56 but they despised the Most High 6
59 For the Most High did not intend 6
9: 2 when the Most High is about to visit the world 6
4 of these that the Most High spoke 6
6 also are the times of the Most High 6
25 pray to the Most High continually 6
28 I began to speak before the Most High, and said 6
44 I besought the Most High, night and day. 6
10:24 and the Most High may give you rest 6
38 the Most High has revealed many secrets to you. 6
50 now the Most High, seeing that you are . . grieved 6
52 the Most High would reveal these things to you. 6
54 the city of the Most High was to be revealed. 6
57 you have been called before the Most High 6
59 the Most High will show you 6
59 what the Most High will do to those 6
11:38 The Most High says to you 6
43 your insolence has come up before the Most High 6
44 the Most High has looked upon his times 6
12: 4 because you search out the ways of the Most High. 6
6 Therefore I will now beseech the Most High 6
23 the Most High will raise up three kings 6
30 whom the Most High has kept for the eagle's end 6
32 whom the Most High has kept until the end of days 6
36 worthy to learn this secret of the Most High. 6
39 whatever it pleases the Most High to show you. 6
47 for the Most High has you in remembrance 6
13:13 and I besought the Most High, and said 6
26 whom the Most High has been keeping for many ages 6
29 when the Most High will deliver those 6
44 For at that time the Most High performed signs 6
47 the Most High will stop the channels of the river 6
56 for there is a reward laid up with the Most High. 6
57 giving great glory and praise to the Most High 6
14:31 the ways which the Most High commanded you. 6
42 the Most High gave understanding to the five men 6
45 the Most High spoke to me, saying, "Make public 6
Tob 1: 4 the temple of the dwelling of the Most High 5
13 Then the Most High gave me favor 5
4:11 in the presence of the Most High. 5
Jdt 13:18 you are blessed by the Most High God 5
AEs 16:16 sons of the Most High, the most mighty living God 5
Wis 5:15 the Most High takes care of them. 5
6: 3 and your sovereignty from the Most High 5
Sir 4:10 you will then be like a son of the Most High 5
7: 9 when I make an offering to the Most High God 5
15 which were created by the Most High. 5
9:15 your discussion be about the law of the Most High. 5
12: 2 if not by him, certainly by the Most High. 5
6 For the Most High also hates sinners 5
17:26 Return to the Most High 5
27 Who will sing praises to the Most High in Hades 5
19:17 let the law of the Most High take its course. 5
23:18 The Most High will not take notice of my sins. 5
23 first of all, she has disobeyed the law of the Most High 5
24: 2 In the assembly of the Most High 5
3 I came forth from the mouth of the Most High 5
23 is the book of the covenant of the Most High God 5
28: 7 remember the covenant of the Most High 5
29:11 according to the commandments of the Most High 5
33:15 Look upon all the works of the Most High 5
34: 6 sent from the Most High as a visitation 5
19 The Most High is not pleased with the offerings 5
35: 6 its pleasing odor rises before the Most High. 5
10 Give to the Most High as he has given 5
17 he will not desist until the Most High visits him 5
37:15 besides all this pray to the Most High 5
38: 2 for healing comes from the Most High 5
39: 1 the study of the law of the Most High 5
5 will make supplication before the Most High 5
41: 4 can you reject the good pleasure of the Most High? 5
8 who have forsaken the law of the Most High God! 5
42: 2 of the law of the Most High and his covenant 5
18 the Most High knows all that may be known 5
43: 2 a marvelous instrument, the work of the Most High. 5
12 the hands of the Most High have stretched it out. 5
44:20 he kept the law of the Most High 5
46: 5 He called upon the Most High, the Mighty One 5
47: 5 For he appealed to the Lord, the Most High 5
48: 5 by the word of the Most High; 5
49: 4 they forsook the law of the Most High 5
50: 7 the sun shining upon the temple of the Most High 5
14 the offering to the Most High, the Almighty 5
15 a pleasing odor to the Most High, the King of all. 5
16 heard for remembrance before the Most High. 5
17 to worship their Lord, the Almighty, God Most High. 5
19 the people besought the Lord Most High in prayer 5
21 to receive the blessing from the Most High. 5
Man 1: 7 thou art the Lord Most High, of great compassion 5
2Mc 3:31 asked Onias to call upon the Most High 5
3Mc 1:20 they crowded together at the most high temple. 4
6: 2 Almighty God Most High 5
7: 9 the Most High God 5

high one 1. גָּבֹהַּ

Ecc 5: 8 and there are yet higher ones over them. 1
Dan 8: 3 higher one came up last. 1

high place 1. בָּמָה 2. גַּף מְרוֹם 3. מָרוֹם 4. *βωμός* 5. *ὑπερέχω*

Lev 26:30 I will destroy your high places 1
Num33:52 demolish all their high places; 1
Deu 32:13 He made him ride on the high places of the earth 1
33:29 shall tread upon their high places. 1
1Sm 9:12 people have a sacrifice today on the high place. 1
13 find him, before he goes up to the high place to eat; 1
14 Samuel coming . . on his way up to the high place. 1
19 I am the seer; go up before me to the high place 1
25 they came down from the high place into the city 1
10: 5 band of prophets coming down from the high place 1
13 finished prophesying, he came to the high place. 1
2Sm 1:19 Thy glory, O Israel, is slain upon thy high places! 1
25 Jonathan lies slain upon thy high places. 1
1Kg 3: 2 The people were sacrificing at the high places 1
3 he sacrificed . . at the high places. 1
4 to Gibeon . . for that was the great high place; 1
11: 7 Solomon built a high place for Chemosh 1
12:31 He also made houses on high places 1
32 placed in Bethel the priests of the high places 1
13: 2 sacrifice . . the priests of the high places 1
32 and against all the houses of the high places 1
33 Jerobo'am . . made priests for the high places 1
33 he consecrated to be priests of the high places. 1
14:23 they also built for themselves high places 1
15:14 the high places were not taken away. 1
22:43 yet the high places were not taken away 1
43 people . . and burned incense on the high places. 1
2Kg 12: 3 the high places were not taken away; 1
3 sacrifice and burn incense on the high places. 1
14: 4 But the high places were not removed; 1
4 people still sacrificed . . on the high places. 1
15: 4 the high places were not taken away; 1
4 still sacrificed and . . on the high places. 1
35 Nevertheless the high places were not removed; 1
35 and burned incense on the high places. 1
16: 4 And he . . and burned incense on the high places 1
17: 9 They built for themselves high places 1
11 there they burned incense on all the high places 1
29 and put them in the shrines of the high places 1
32 appointed . . as priests of the high places 1
32 sacrificed . . in the shrines of the high places. 1
18: 4 He removed the high places, and broke the pillars 1
22 high places and altars Hezeki'ah has removed 1
21: 3 he rebuilt the high places which . . had destroyed; 1
23: 5 had ordained to burn incense in the high places 1
8 and defiled the high places where the priests 1
8 and he broke down the high places of the gates 1
9 the priests of the high places did not come up 1
13 And the king defiled the high places 1
15 at Bethel, the high place erected by Jerobo'am 1
15 that altar with the high place he pulled down 1
19 all the shrines also of the high places 1
20 And he slew all the priests of the high places 1
1Ch 16:39 tabernacle of the LORD in the high place 1
21:29 were at that time in the high place at Gibeon; 1
2Ch 1: 3 Solomon . . went to the high place . . at Gibeon; 1
13 Solomon came from the high place at Gibeon 1
11:15 he appointed his own priests for the high places 1
14: 3 took away the foreign altars and the high places 1
5 took out of . . Judah the high places 1
15:17 the high places were not taken out of Israel. 1
17: 6 high places and the Ashe'rim out of Judah. 1

20:33 The high places, however, were not taken away; 1
21:11 he made high places in the hill country of Judah 1
28: 4 burned incense on the high places . . the hills 1
25 he made high places to burn incense to other gods 1
31: 1 all Israel . . broke down the high places 1
32:12 this same Hezeki'ah taken away his high places 1
33: 3 For he rebuilt the high places which his father 1
17 people still sacrificed at the high places 1
19 sites on which he built high places and set up 1
34: 3 purge Judah and Jerusalem of the high places 1
Ps 78:58 provoked him to anger with their high places; 1
Prv 9: 3 to call from the highest places in the town 2
14 she takes a seat on the high places of the town 3
Ecc 10: 6 folly is set in many high places 3
Isa 15: 2 Dibon has gone up to the high places to weep; 1
16:12 when he wearies himself upon the high place 1
36: 7 high places and altars Hezeki'ah has removed 1
Jer 7:31 And they have built the high place of Topheth 4
19: 5 and have built the high places of Ba'al 1
32:35 They built the high places of Ba'al in the valley 1
48:35 him who offers sacrifice in the high place 1
Ezk 6: 3 and I will destroy your high places. 1
6 your cities . . waste and your high places ruined 1
20:29 What is the high place to which you go? 1
Hos 10: 8 The high places of Aven, the sin of Israel 1
Ams 7: 9 the high places of Isaac shall be made desolate 1
Mic 1: 3 and tread upon the high places of the earth. 1
Hab 3:19 he makes me tread upon my high places. 1
Wis 6: 5 severe judgment falls on those in high places. 5

higher *See* build.

higher than 1. ὑπέρ
1Es 8:75 For our sins have risen higher than our heads 1

highland
2Es 15:58 who are in the mountains and highlands ‡

highly 1. לְמַעְלָה 2. מְאֹד
1Sm 18:30 so that his name was highly esteemed. 2
1Ch 14: 2 his kingdom was highly exalted 1
Ps 47: 9 of the earth belong to God; he is highly exalted! 2

highly *See also* exalt, glorify, necessary, praise, prize, think.

highly man 1. περισσεύω
Sir 19:24 Better . . than the highly prudent man 1

very highly 1. ὑπερεκπερισσοῦ
1Th 5:13 to esteem them very highly in love 1

highway 1. דֶּרֶךְ 2. דֶּרֶךְ סלל 3. מְסִלָּה 4. מַסְלוּל וָדֶרֶךְ 5. ὁδός 6. platea
Num20:17 we will go along the King's Highway 1
19 We will go up by the highway; and if we drink 3
21:22 we will go by the King's Highway, until we have 1
Jdg 20:31 kill some . . in the highways, one of which goes up 3
32 and draw them away from the city to the highways. 3
45 5,000 men of them were cut down in the highways 3
21:19 east of the highway that goes up from Bethel 3
1Sm 6:12 the cows went straight . . along one highway 3
2Sm 20:12 Ama'sa lay wallowing in his blood in the highway. 3
12 he carried Ama'sa out of the highway 3
13 When he was taken out of the highway 3
2Kg 18:17 which is on the highway to the Fuller's Field. 3
Ps 84: 5 in whose heart are the highways to Zion. 3
Prv 15:19 but the path of the upright is a level highway. •
16:17 The highway of the upright turns aside from evil; 3
Isa 7: 3 upper pool on the highway to the Fuller's Field 3
11:16 there will be a highway from Assyria 3
19:23 there will be a highway from Egypt to Assyria 3
33: 8 highways lie waste, the wayfaring man ceases. 3
35: 8 a highway shall be there, and it shall be called 4
36: 2 upper pool on the highway to the Fuller's Field. 3
40: 3 make straight in the desert a highway for our God. 3
49:11 and my highways shall be raised up. 3
59: 7 and destruction are in their highways. 3
62:10 build up, build up the highway, clear it of stones 3
Jer 18:15 and have gone into bypaths, not the highway 2
31:21 consider well the highway 3
Lke 14:23 Go out to the highways and hedges 5
2Es 1:13 and made safe highways for you 6
Tob 1:15 under him the highways were unsafe 5
1Mc 5: 4 ambushed them on the highways. 5
15:41 go out and make raids along the highways of Judea 5

hill 1. גִּבְעָה 2. הַר 3. מַעֲלֶה 4. עֹפֶל 5. קֶרֶן 6. βουνός 7. θίς 8. ὀρεινή 9. ὄρος 10. collis
Gen 19:17 flee to the hills, lest you be consumed. 2
19 but I cannot flee to the hills 2
30 Lot went up out of Zo'ar, and dwelt in the hills 2
49:26 the bounties of the everlasting hills; 1
Exd 17: 9 tomorrow I will stand on top of the hill 1
10 Aaron, and Hur went up to the top of the hill. 1
Num23: 9 mountains I see him, from the hills I behold him; 1
Deu 8: 7 a land . . flowing forth in valleys and hills 2
9 a land . . out of whose hills you can dig copper. 2
11:11 land of hills and valleys, which drinks water 2
12: 2 upon the hills and under every green tree 1
33:15 with the . . abundance of the everlasting hills 1
Jos 2:16 Go into the hills, lest the pursuers meet you; 2
22 They departed, and went into the hills 2
23 Then the two men came down again from the hills 2
13:19 and Zer'eth-sha'har on the hill of the valley 2
15:11 out to the shoulder of the hill north of Ekron •
Jdg 7: 1 camp . . was north of them, by the hill of Moreh 1
16: 3 carried them to the top of the hill that is before 2
1Sm 7: 1 brought it to the house of Abin'adab on the hill; 1
9:11 As they went up the hill to the city, they met young 3
23:19 in the strongholds . . on the hill of Hachi'lah 1
26: 1 Is not David hiding . . on the hill of Hachi'lah 1
3 Saul encamped on the hill of Hachi'lah 1
2Sm 2:24 as the sun was . . they came to the hill of Ammah 1
25 and took their stand on the top of a hill. 1
6: 3 out of the house of Abin'adab which was on the hill; 1
1Kg 14:23 built . . Ashe'rim on every high hill 1
16:24 He bought the hill of Sama'ria from Shemer 2
24 the hill of Sama'ria . . he fortified the hill 2
24 Sama'ria, after . . Shemer, the owner of the hill. 2
20:23 Their gods are gods of the hills 2
28 The LORD is a god of the hills but he is not a god 2
2Kg 1: 9 to Eli'jah, who was sitting on the top of a hill 2
5:24 when he came to the hill, he took them 4
16: 4 the high places, and on the hills, and under every 1
17:10 set up . . pillars and Ashe'rim on every high hill 1
2Ch 26:10 he had farmers and vinedressers in the hills 2
28: 4 burned incense on the high places . . the hills 1
Neh 8:15 Go out to the hills and bring branches of olive 2
Job 15: 7 Or were you brought forth before the hills? 1
Ps 2: 6 I have set my king on Zion, my holy hill. 2
3: 4 to the LORD, and he answers me from his holy hill. 2
15: 1 Who shall dwell on thy holy hill? 2
24: 3 Who shall ascend the hill of the LORD? 2
43: 3 let them lead me, let them bring me to thy holy hill 2
50:10 is mine, the cattle on 1,000 hills. 2
65:12 the hills gird themselves with joy 1
72: 3 for the people, and the hills, in righteousness! 1
98: 8 let the hills sing for joy together 2
104:10 springs gush forth . . flow between the hills. 2
114: 4 skipped like rams, the hills like lambs. 1
6 skip like rams? O hills, like lambs? 1
121: 1 I lift up my eyes to the hills. 2
147: 8 he makes grass grow upon the hills. 2
148: 9 Mountains and all hills 1
Prv 8:25 before the hills, I was brought forth; 1
Sng 2: 8 he comes, leaping . . bounding over the hills. 1
4: 6 mountain of myrrh and the hill of frankincense. 1
Isa 2: 2 mountains, and shall be raised above the hills; 1
14 high mountains, and against all the lofty hills; 1
5: 1 My beloved had a vineyard on a very fertile hill. 5
7:25 all the hills which used to be hoed with a hoe 2
10:32 the daughter of Zion, the hill of Jerusalem. 1
13: 2 On a bare hill raise a signal, cry aloud to them; 2
30:17 like a flagstaff . . like a signal on a hill. 1
25 upon every lofty mountain and every high hill 1
31: 4 to fight upon Mount Zion and upon its hill. 1
32:14 hill and the watchtower . . become dens for ever 4
40: 4 and every mountain and hill be made low; 1
12 mountains in scales and the hills in a balance? 1
41:15 and you shall make the hills like chaff; 1
42:15 I will lay waste mountains and hills 1
54:10 mountains may depart and the hills be removed 1
55:12 the mountains and the hills before you shall 1
65: 7 upon the mountains and reviled me upon the hills 1
Jer 2:20 Yea, upon every high hill . . you bowed down 1
3: 6 how she went up on every high hill 2
23 Truly the hills are a delusion 1
4:24 and all the hills moved to and fro. 1
13:27 your lewd harlotries, on the hills in the field. 1
16:16 hunt them from every mountain and every hill 1
17: 2 beside every green tree, and on the high hills 1
31: 6 will call in the hill country of E'phraim: 2
23 O habitation of righteousness, O holy hill! 2
39 shall go out farther, straight to the hill Gareb 1
49:16 you . . who hold the height of the hill. 1
50: 6 from mountain to hill they have gone 1
19 shall be satisfied on the hills of E'phraim 2
Ezk 6: 3 says the Lord GOD to the mountains and the hills 1
13 round about their altars, upon every high hill 1
20:28 wherever they saw any high hill or any leafy tree 1
34: 6 over all the mountains and on every high hill; 1
26 and the places round about my hill a blessing; 1
35: 8 on your hills and in your valleys 1
36: 4 says the Lord GOD to the mountains and the hills 1
6 and say to the mountains and hills, to the ravines 1
Dan 9:16 turn away from thy city Jerusalem, thy holy hill; 2
20 before the LORD my God for the holy hill of my God; 2
Hos 4:13 and make offerings upon the hills 1
10: 8 and to the hills, Fall upon us. 1
Jol 3:18 and the hills shall flow with milk 1
Ams 9:13 sweet wine, and all the hills shall flow with it. 1
Mic 4: 1 and shall be raised up above the hills; 1
8 O tower of the flock, hill of the daughter of Zion 4
6: 1 and let the hills hear your voice. 1
Nah 1: 5 The mountains quake before him, the hills melt; 1
Hab 3: 6 the everlasting hills sank low. 1
Zep 1:10 Second Quarter, a loud crash from the hills. 1
Hag 1: 8 Go up to the hills and bring wood and build 2
11 called for a drought upon the land and the hills 2
Mal 1: 3 I have laid waste his hill country 2
Mat 5:14 A city set on a hill cannot be hid. 9
Lke 3: 5 every mountain and hill shall be brought low 6
4:29 led him to the brow of the hill 9
23:30 to the hills, 'Cover us.' 6
2Es 15:42 destroy cities and walls, mountains and hills 10
Jdt 4: 7 to seize the passes up into the hills 8
5: 1 had closed the passes in the hills 8
6:12 ran out of the city to the top of the hill 9
13 However, they got under the shelter of the hill 9
13 left him lying at the foot of the hill 9
7: 4 the hills will bear their weight. 6
15: 3 had camped in the hills around Bethulia 8
16: 4 their cavalry covered the hills. 6
Bar 5: 7 ordered that . . everlasting hills be made low 7
Aza 1:53 Bless the Lord, mountains and hills 6
1Mc 2:28 he and his sons fled to the hills 9
4: 5 so he looked for them in the hills 9
18 Gorgias and his force are near us in the hills. 9
19 a detachment appeared, coming out of the hills. 9
46 in a convenient place on the temple hill 9
6:39 the hills were ablaze with them 9
48 the king's army was spread out on the high hills 9
13:52 the temple hill alongside the citadel 9
16:20 Jerusalem and the temple hill. 9

hill *See also* country.

wooded hill 1. חֹרֶשׁ
2Ch 27: 4 built . . forts and towers on the wooded hills. 1

hillside 1. צֶלַע הָהָר 2. ὄρος
2Sm 16:13 Shim'e-i went along on the hillside opposite him 1
Mrk 5:11 herd of swine was feeding there on the hillside; 2
Lke 8:32 herd of swine was feeding there on the hillside; 2

hilltop 1. κορυφὴ ὄρους 2. ὑψηλός
Jdt 2:24 destroyed all the hilltop cities 2
3: 6 and stationed garrisons in the hilltop cities 2
4: 5 and immediately seized all the high hilltops 1
5: 1 fortified all the high hilltops 1

hilt 1. נִצָּב
Jdg 3:22 the hilt also went in after the blade, and the fat 1

hin 1. הִין
Exd 29:40 a fourth of a hin of beaten oil, and a fourth of a hin 1
40 a fourth of a hin of wine for a libation. 1
30:24 of olive oil a hin; 1
Lev 19:36 just weights, a just ephah, and a just hin 1
23:13 with it shall be of wine, a fourth of a hin 1
Num15: 4 fine flour, mixed with a fourth of a hin of oil; 1
5 wine for the drink offering, a fourth of a hin 1
6 fine flour mixed with a third of a hin of oil; 1
7 drink . . you shall offer a third of a hin of wine 1
9 fine flour, mixed with half a hin of oil 1
10 offer for the drink offering half a hin of wine 1
28: 5 cereal offering, mixed with a fourth of a hin 1
7 offering shall be a fourth of a hin for each lamb; 1
14 offerings shall be half a hin of wine for a bull 1
14 drink offerings . . a third of a hin for a ram 1
14 drink offerings . . a fourth of a hin for a lamb; 1
Ezk 4:11 shall drink by measure, the sixth part of a hin; 1
45:24 an ephah for each ram, and a hin of oil to each ephah 1
46: 5 together with a hin of oil to each ephah. 1
7 together with a hin of oil to each ephah. 1
11 together with a hin of oil to an ephah. 1
14 one third of a hin of oil to moisten the flour 1

hind 1. אַיָּלָה
Gen 49:21 Naph'tali is a hind let loose 1
2Sm 22:34 He made my feet like hinds' feet, and set me secure 1
Job 39: 1 Do you observe the calving of the hinds? 1
Ps 18:33 He made my feet like hinds' feet 1
22: 0 according to The Hind of the Dawn. A Psalm 1
Prv 5:19 lovely hind, a graceful doe. 1
Sng 2: 7 by the gazelles or the hinds of the field 1
3: 5 by the gazelles or the hinds of the field 1
Jer 14: 5 Even the hind in the field forsakes her newborn 1
Hab 3:19 he makes my feet like hinds' feet, he makes me tread 1

hinder 1. גרע 2. מנע 3. מַעְצוֹר 4. שׁוּב 5. βλάπτω 6. διακωλύω 7. ἐγκόπτω 8. ἐμποδίζω 9. ἐμποδιστικός 10. ἔργω 11. κωλυτικός 12. κωλύω 13. prohibeo
Gen 23: 6 sepulchre, or hinder you from burying your dead. •
Num22:16 Let nothing hinder you from coming to me; 2
1Sm 14: 6 nothing can hinder the LORD from saving 3
Job 9:12 Behold, he snatches away; who can hinder him? 4
11:10 and calls to judgment, who can hinder him? 4
15: 4 and hindering meditation before God. 1
Isa 43:13 I am God . . I work and who can hinder it? 4
Mat 19:14 do not hinder them 12
Mrk 10:14 Let the children come to me, do not hinder them 12
Lke 11:52 you hindered those who were entering. 12
18:16 Let the children come to me, and do not hinder them; 12
Rom15:22 I have so often been hindered from coming to you. 7
Gal 5: 7 who hindered you from obeying the truth? 7
1Th 2:16 by hindering us from speaking to the Gentiles 12
18 but Satan hindered us. 7

1Pe 3: 7 in order that your prayers may not be hindered. 7
1Es 2:30 began to hinder the builders 12
5:72 hindered their building; 10
6:33 stretch out their hands to hinder . . that house 12
2Es 3: 8 and thou didst not hinder them. 13
Jdt 12: 7 not to hinder her 6
Wis 10: 8 not only . . hindered from recognizing the good 5
Sir 18:22 Let nothing hinder you from paying a vow 8
1Mc 9:55 and his work was hindered 8
3Mc 3: 2 a report that they hindered others 12
4Mc 1: 3 those emotions that hinder self-control 11
4 the emotions that hinder one from justice 9
2: 6 the emotions that hinder one from justice. 11

hinder part 1. אָחוֹר
1Kg 7:25 and all their hinder parts were inward. 1
2Ch 4: 4 oxen . . and all their hinder parts were inward. 1

hindrance 1. *σκάνδαλον*
Mat 16:23 You are a hindrance to me 1

hindrance in the way 1. *σκάνδαλον*
Rom 14:13 block or hindrance in the way of a brother. 1

hinge 1. צִיר
Prv 26:14 As a door turns on its hinges, so does a sluggard 1

hip 1. מִפְשָׂעָה 2. נָשֶׁה 3. צַד 4. שׁוֹק 5. שֵׁת
Gen 32:32 the Israelites do not eat the sinew of the hip 2
32 hollow of Jacob's thigh on the sinew of the hip. 2
Jdg 15: 8 he smote them hip and thigh with great slaughter; 4
2Sm 10: 4 cut off . . garments in the middle, at their hips 5
1Ch 19: 4 cut off their garments . . at their hips 1
Isa 66:12 you shall suck, you shall be carried upon her hip 3

hippodrome 1. *ἱππόδρομος*
3Mc 4:11 they should be enclosed in the hippodrome 1
5:46 crowding their way into the hippodrome 1
6:16 the king arrived at the hippodrome 1

hire 1. אֶתְנָה 2. אֶתְנַן 3. מְחִיר 4. סכר 5. שָׂכִיר
6. שכר 7. שֶׂכֶר 8. שָׂכָר 9. תנה 10. *μισθόω*
Gen 30:16 You must come in to me; for I have hired you with my 6
18 Leah said, "God has given me my hire 8
Exd 22:15 if it was hired, it came for its hire. 5
15 if it was . . it came for its hire. 8
Deu 23: 4 hired against you Balaam . . to curse you. 6
18 not bring the hire of a harlot, or the wages of a dog 2
24:15 you shall give him his hire on the day he earns it 8
Jdg 9: 4 Abim'elech hired worthless and reckless 6
18: 4 he has hired me, and I have become his priest. 6
2Sm 10: 6 Ammonites . . hired the Syrians of Beth-re'hob 6
2Kg 7: 6 the king of Israel has hired against us the kings 6
1Ch 19: 6 of silver to hire chariots and horsemen 6
7 They hired 32,000 chariots and the king of Ma'acah 6
2Ch 24:12 hired masons and carpenters to restore 6
25: 6 hired . . 100,000 mighty men of valor from Israel 6
Ezr 4: 5 hired counselors against them to frustrate 4
Neh 6:12 because Tobi'ah and Sanbal'lat had hired him. 6
13 For this purpose he was hired, 6
13: 2 hired Balaam against them to curse them 6
Prv 6:26 for a harlot may be hired for a loaf of bread •
26:10 he who hires a passing fool or drunkard. 6
Isa 7:20 a razor which is hired beyond the River 5
19:10 and all who work for hire will be grieved. 7
23:17 she will return to her hire, and will play 2
18 her hire will be dedicated to the LORD; 2
46: 6 hire a goldsmith, and he makes it into a god; 6
Jer 46:21 Even her hired soldiers in her midst 5
Ezk 16:31 were not like a harlot, because you scorned hire. 2
34 you gave hire, while no hire was given to you; 2
34 you gave hire, while no hire was given to you; 2
41 you shall also give hire no more. 2
Hos 2:12 her fig trees, of which she said, 'These are my hire 1
8: 9 E'phraim has hired lovers. 9
10 Though they hire allies among the nations 9
Mic 1: 7 all her hires shall be burned with fire 2
7 for from the hire of a harlot she gathered them 2
7 and to the hire of a harlot they shall return. 2
3:11 its priests teach for hire 3
Mat 20: 1 to hire laborers for his vineyard. 10
7 They said to him, 'Because no one has hired us.' 10
9 when those hired about the eleventh hour came •
1Mc 5:39 They also have hired Arabs to help them 10
hire *See also* harlot's.

hire a laborer 1. *μισθωτός*
Jdt 4:10 every resident alien and hired laborer 1

hire out 1. שׂכר
1Sm 2: 5 Those who were full have hired themselves out 1
hired *See* laborer, servant.

hired man 1. *μίσθιος*
Sir 37:11 with a man hired for a year 1

hireling 1. שָׂכִיר 2. *μισθωτός*
Job 7: 1 are not his days like the days of a hireling? 1
2 like a hireling who looks for his wages 1
14: 6 that he may enjoy, like a hireling, his day. 1
Isa 16:14 In three years, like the years of a hireling 1
21:16 a year, according to the years of a hireling 1
Mal 3: 5 those who oppress the hireling in his wages 1
Joh 10:12 He who is a hireling and not a shepherd 2
13 He flees because he is a hireling 2
Jdt 6: 2 who are you, Achior, and you hirelings of Ephraim 2
5 you, Achior, you Ammonite hireling 2

hiss 1. שׁרק 2. שְׁרֵקָה 3. *ἐκσυρίζω* 4. *συρισμός*
5. sibilatus
1Kg 9: 8 every one . . will be astonished, and will hiss; 1
Job 27:23 hands at him, and hisses at him from its place. 1
Jer 19: 8 and will hiss because of all its disasters. 1
25: 9 a horror, a hissing, and an everlasting reproach. 2
18 a desolation and a waste, a hissing and a curse 2
29:18 to be a curse, a terror, a hissing, and a reproach 2
49:17 and will hiss because of all its disasters. 1
50:13 be appalled, and hiss because of all her wounds. 1
51:37 the haunt of jackals, a horror and a hissing 2
Lam 2:15 they hiss and wag their heads at the daughter 1
16 your enemies . . they hiss, they gnash their teeth 1
Ezk 27:36 The merchants among the peoples hiss at you; 1
Mic 6:16 you a desolation, and your inhabitants a hissing; 2
Zep 2:15 Every one who passes by her hisses 1
2Es 15:29 their hissing shall spread over the earth 5
Wis 17: 9 the hissing of serpents 4
Sir 22: 1 every one hisses at his disgrace. 3

thing to hiss at 1. שְׁרִיקָה 2. שְׁרֵקָה
Jer 18:16 a horror, a thing to be hissed at for ever. 1
19: 8 make this city a horror, a thing to be hissed at; 2
hissing *See* object.

original historian 1. *ἱστορία ἀρχηγέτης*
2Mc 2:30 It is the duty of the original historian 1

history 1. דָּבָר 2. תּוֹלְדוֹת 3. *ἱστορέω* 4. *ἱστορία*
Gen 37: 2 This is the history of the family of Jacob. 2
2Ch 9:29 are they not written in the history of Nathan 1
1Es 1:33 the book of the histories of the kings of Judea; 3
2Mc 2:24 who wish to enter upon the narratives of history 4
32 while cutting short the history itself. 4
4Mc 17: 7 to paint the history of your piety as an artist 4

hit 1. נכה 2. *πληγή*
Isa 58: 4 and to fight and to hit with wicked fist. 1
2Mc 14:43 in the heat of the struggle he did not hit exactly 2

hitch up 1. *ζεύγνυμι*
Jdt 15:11 and loaded her mule and hitched up her carts 1

hither 1. הֲלֹם 2. הֵנָּה 3. *ἔνθεν* 4. *ὧδε*
Jos 3: 9 Come hither, and hear the words of the LORD 2
1Sm 10:22 they inquired again . . "Did the man come hither? 1
14:16 the multitude was surging hither and thither. 3
18 Saul said to Ahi'jah, "Bring hither the ark of God. •
36 the priest said, "Let us draw near hither to God. 1
38 Come hither, all you leaders of the people; 1
Isa 57: 3 But you, draw near hither, sons of the sorceress 2
Rev 4: 1 the first voice . . said, "Come up hither 4
11:12 voice from heaven saying to them, "Come up hither! 4

hitherto 1. עַד הֵנָּה 2. עַד כֹּה 3. תְּמוֹל שִׁלְשֹׁם
4. *ἕως ἄρτι*
Exd 5:14 not done all your task . . as hitherto? 3
Jos 17:14 I am . . since hitherto the LORD has blessed me? 2
1Sm 7:12 for he said, "Hitherto the LORD has helped us. 1
1Ch 9:18 stationed hitherto in the king's gate 1
12:29 the majority had hitherto kept their allegiance 1
Joh 16:24 Hitherto you have asked nothing in my name 4
1Co 8: 7 through being hitherto accustomed to idols 4

hive 1. *νοσσιά*
4Mc 14:19 sting those who approach their hive 1

ho 1. הוֹי
Isa 29: 1 Ho Ariel, Ariel, the city where David encamped! 1
55: 1 Ho, every one who thirsts, come to the waters; 1
Ezk 34: 2 Ho, shepherds of Israel who have been feeding 1
Zec 2: 6 Ho! ho! Flee from the land of the north 1
6 Ho! ho! Flee from the land of the north 1
7 Ho! Escape to Zion 1

hoard 1. חסן 2. מַטְמוֹן
Isa 23:18 it will not be stored or hoarded 1
45: 3 I will give you . . the hoards in secret places 2

hoard up 1. *θησαυρίζω*
Bar 3:17 who hoard up silver and gold, in which men trust 1

hoarfrost 1. כְּפוֹר 2. *πάχνη*
Exd 16:14 fine as hoarfrost on the ground. 1
Job 38:29 who has given birth to the hoarfrost of heaven? 1
Ps 147:16 he scatters hoarfrost like ashes. 1
Wis 5:14 like a light hoarfrost driven away by a storm 2
Sir 43:19 He pours the hoarfrost upon the earth like salt 2

hoary 1. שֵׂיבָה
Job 41:32 one would think the deep to be hoary. 1
hoary *See also* head.

hock 1. suffrago
2Es 15:36 a man's thigh and a camel's hock. 1

hoe 1. מַעְדֵּר 2. עדר
Isa 5: 6 not be pruned or hoed, and briers and thorns 2
7:25 all the hills which used to be hoed with a hoe 2
25 all the hills which used to be hoed with a hoe 1

hoist 1. *ἐπαίρω*
Act 27:40 then hoisting the foresail to the wind 1

hoist up 1. *αἴρω*
Act 27:17 after hoisting it up 1

hold 1. אחז 2. בְּיַד 3. היה 4. חזק 5. חצק 6. חשב
7. כול 8. מנע 9. נחל 10. נתן 11. עשה 12. תמך
13. תפש 14. דבק (A) 15. *ἄγω* 16. *ἀντιβάλλω*
17. *ἅπτω* 18. *βάσις* 19. *γίνομαι* 20. *διακρατέω*
21. *διατηρέω* 22. *δίδωμι* 23. *ἐγκρατής*
24. *ἐγκρατὴς γίνομαι* 25. *εἰμί* 26. *ἐν* 27. *ἐπιμένω*
28. *ἔχω* 29. *κατέχω* 30. *κρατέω* 31. *λέγω*
32. *λογίζομαι* 33. *νομίζω* 34. *ποιέω* 35. *προσφέρω*
36. *συνέχω* 37. *τηρέω* 38. *χωρέω* 39. capio 40. sum
41. sustineo 42. teneo
Exd 9: 2 refuse to let them go and still hold them 5
10: 9 for we must hold a feast to the LORD. •
12:16 On the first day you shall hold a holy assembly •
Lev 19:20 an inquiry shall be held 3
23:21 you shall hold a holy convocation 3
36 the eighth day you shall hold a holy convocation 3
Deu 19:14 inheritance which you will hold in the land 9
Jos 8: 4 do not go . . but hold yourselves all in readiness; 3
Jdg 7:20 the jars, holding in their left hands the torches 4
9:27 and trod them, and held festival, and went 11
16:26 Samson said to the lad who held him by the hand 5
Rut 3:15 she held it, and he measured out six . . of barley 1
1Sm 20:29 our family holds a sacrifice in the city •
25:36 lo, he was holding a feast in his house †
2Sm 3:29 is leprous, or who holds a spindle, or who is slain 5
19:19 Let not my lord hold me guilty or remember how 6
1Kg 7:26 it held 2,000 baths. 7
38 he made ten lavers . . each laver held 40 baths 7
8:65 Solomon held the feast . . and all Israel with him 11
2Kg 15:19 help him to confirm his hold of the royal power. 2
1Ch 13: 9 Uzzah put out his hand to hold the ark 1
2Ch 4: 5 it held over 3,000 baths. 5
7: 7 bronze altar Solomon had made could not hold 7
8 Solomon held the feast for seven days 11
9 on the eighth day they held a solemn assembly; 11
11:12 strong. So he held Judah and Benjamin. •
Neh 4:16 half held the spears, shields, bows 4
17 one hand . . and with the other held his weapon. 4
21 half of them held the spears from the break 4
5: 7 And I held a great assembly against them 10
16 I also held to the work on this wall 4
Est 9:19 Jews . . hold the fourteenth day . . as a day for 11
Job 1: 4 His sons used to go and hold a feast in the house 11
17: 9 Yet the righteous holds to his way 1
20:13 he is loath to let it go, and holds it in his mouth 8
Ps 16: 5 my chosen portion and my cup; thou holdest my lot. 12
73:23 thou dost hold my right hand. 1
77: 4 Thou dost hold my eyelids from closing; 1
119:109 I hold my life in my hand continually •
139:10 even there . . thy right hand shall hold me. 1
Prv 31:19 her hands hold the spindle. 12
Sng 3: 4 I held him, and would not let him go 1
Isa 33:15 who shakes his hands, lest they hold a bribe 12
41:13 For I, the LORD your God, hold your right hand; 5
Jer 2:13 broken cisterns, that can hold no water. 7
6:11 the wrath of the LORD; I am weary of holding it in. 7
20: 9 and I am weary with holding it in, and I cannot. 7
46:10 Lord GOD of hosts holds a sacrifice in the north •
48:26 in his vomit, and he too shall be held in derision. 3
49:16 you . . who hold the height of the hill. 13
Dan 2:43 not hold together, just as iron does not mix 14
Ams 1: 5 and him that holds the scepter from Beth-eden; 12
8 and him that holds the scepter from Ash'kelon; 12
Mal 2: 4 that my covenant with Levi may hold, says the LORD 3
Mat 14: 5 because they held him to be a prophet. 28
21:26 for all hold that John was a prophet. 28
46 because they held him to be a prophet. 28
Mrk 3: 6 immediately held counsel with the Hero'di-ans 22
11:32 for all held that John was a real prophet. 28
15: 1 the whole council held a consultation 34
Lke 22:63 Now the men who were holding Jesus mocked him 36
24:17 What is this conversation which you are holding 16
Joh 2: 6 jars . . each holding twenty or 30 gallons. 38
4:37 For here the saying holds true, 'One sows 25
19:29 held it to his mouth. 35
20:17 Jesus said to her, "Do not hold me 17
Act 2:24 it was not possible for him to be held by it. 30
25:21 I commanded him to be held 37
Rom 3:19 the whole world may be held accountable to God. 19

28 For we hold that a man is justified by faith 32
2Co 13: 5 to see whether you are holding to your faith. 26
Php 1: 7 because I hold you in my heart 28
2Th 2:15 hold to the traditions which you were taught 30
1Ti 1:19 holding faith and a good conscience 28
3: 9 they must hold the mystery of the faith 28
4: 8 as it holds promise for the present life 28
16 Take heed . . to your teaching; hold to that 27
2Ti 2:18 holding that the resurrection is past already. 31
3: 5 holding the form of religion 28
Heb 7:24 he holds his priesthood permanently 28
9: 4 which contained a golden urn holding the manna 28
Jas 2: 1 show no partiality as you hold the faith 28
1Pe 4: 8 hold unfailing your love for one another 28
Rev 1:16 in his right hand he held seven stars 28
2: 1 him who holds the seven stars in his right hand 30
14 some there who hold the teaching of Balaam 30
15 some who hold the teaching of the Nicola'itans. 30
24 you in Thyati'ra, who do not hold this teaching 28
5: 8 fell down before the Lamb, each holding a harp 28
17: 4 holding in her hand a golden cup 28
19:10 your brethren who hold the testimony of Jesus. 28
20: 1 holding in his hand the key of the bottomless pit 28
1Es 4:50 the villages of the Jews which they held; 20
2Es 2:43 And I was held spellbound. 42
5:15 the angel who had come and talked with me held me 42
44 neither can the world hold at one time those 41
6: 8 Jacob's hand held Esau's heel from the beginning. 42
50 the seventh part . . could not hold them both. 39
11:18 and held the rule like the former ones 42
21 others of them rose up, but did not hold the rule. 42
25 to set themselves up and hold the rule. 42
40 have held sway over the world with much terror 42
13: 9 he neither lifted his hand nor held a spear 42
28 as for his not holding a spear or weapon of war 42
16:69 shall be held in derision and contempt 40
Jdt 2:10 hold them for me till the day of their punishment. 21
12:10 Holofernes held a banquet for his slave only 34
Wis 4: 3 will strike a deep root or take a firm hold. 18
5: 4 This is the man whom we once held in derision 28
14:23 hold frenzied revels with strange customs 15
17: 4 the inner chamber that held them protected them 29
Sir 15: 1 he who holds to the law will obtain wisdom. 23
21:14 it will hold no knowledge. 30
LJr 1:14 Like a local ruler the god holds a scepter 28
Sus 1:39 but we could not hold the man, for he was too strong 24
1Mc 3:45 the sons of aliens held the citadel 26
4:61 he stationed a garrison there to hold it 37
6:50 stationed a guard there to hold it. 37
13:15 in connection with the offices he held 28
15: 7 strongholds which you have built and now hold 30
2Mc 4:18 the quadrennial games were being held at Tyre 15
27 Menelaus held the office 30
12:24 because he held the parents of most of them 28
14:22 they held the proper conference. 34
3Mc 6:25 those who faithfully have held the fortresses 30
7:21 being held in honor and awe •
22 those who held any restored it 28
4Mc 1:10 the honor in which they are held. •
4: 1 who then held the high priesthood for life 28
5:18 Even if . . we had wrongly held it to be divine 33
15:26 this mother held two ballots 30

hold *See also* catch, fast, get, keep, lay, seize, take.

hold a fast 1.צום
Est 4:16 hold a fast on my behalf, and neither eat nor drink 1

hold a feast 1.חגג
Exd 5: 1 Let my people go, that they may hold a feast to me 1

hold a vain opinion 1.*κενοδοξέω*
4Mc 5:10 by holding a vain opinion concerning the truth 1

hold against 1.*ἵστημι*
Act 7:60 Lord, do not hold this sin against them. 1

hold an assembly 1.קשש
Zep 2: 1 Come together and hold assembly 1

hold back 1.גרע 2.חשך 3.כלא 4.מנע 5.שוב 6.*ἀνακόπτω* 7.*ἐμποδίζω* 8.*κρατέω*
Num24:11 but the LORD has held you back from honor. 4
Ps 74:11 Why dost thou hold back thy hand 5
119:101 I hold back my feet from every evil way 3
Prv 1:15 my son . . hold back your foot from their paths; 4
11:26 The people curse him who holds back grain 4
21:26 but the righteous gives and does not hold back. 2
24:11 hold back those . . stumbling to the slaughter. 2
Isa 38:17 thou hast held back my life from the pit •
54: 2 hold not back, lengthen your cords 2
Jer 26: 2 all the words . . do not hold back a word. 1
Rev 7: 1 angels . . holding back the four winds 8
Wis 18:23 he intervened and held back the wrath 6
Sir 12: 5 hold back his bread, and do not give it to him 7
46: 4 Was not the sun held back by his hand? 7
4Mc 13: 6 towers . . hold back the threatening waves 6

hold captive 1.אסר 2.שבה 3.*κατέχω*
Ps 106:46 pitied by all those who held them captive. 2
Sng 7: 5 a king is held captive in the tresses. 1
Rom 7: 6 dead to that which held us captive 3

hold control 1.*κατακρατέω*
1Mc 15:28 You hold control of Joppa and Gazara 1

hold dear 1.רצה
Ps 102:14 For thy servants hold her stones dear 1

hold fast 1.אחז 2.דבק 3.דָּבֵק 4.חזק 5.חצק 6.לחץ 7.שמר 8.תמך 9.*ἐπέχω* 10.*ἔχω* 11.*κατέχω* 12.*κολλάω* 13.*κρατέω* 14.*κράτος*
Deu 4: 4 you who held fast to the LORD . . are all alive 3
2Kg 6:32 shut the door, and hold the door fast against him. 6
18: 6 For he held fast to the LORD; he did not depart 2
Job 2: 3 He still holds fast his integrity 5
9 Do you still hold fast your integrity? 5
23:11 My foot has held fast to his steps; 1
27: 6 I hold fast my righteousness 4
Ps 17: 5 My steps have held fast to thy paths 8
64: 5 They hold fast to their evil purpose; 4
Prv 3:18 those who hold her fast are called happy. 8
4: 4 Let your heart hold fast my words; 8
Isa 56: 2 and the son of man who holds it fast 4
4 who choose . . and hold fast my covenant 4
6 does not profane it, and holds fast my covenant- 4
Hos 12: 6 return, hold fast to love and justice 7
Mrk 7: 8 and hold fast the tradition of men. 13
Lke 8:15 they are those who, hearing the word, hold it fast 11
Rom 12: 9 hate what is evil, hold fast to what is good; 12
1Co 15: 2 by which you are saved, if you hold it fast 11
Php 2:16 holding fast the word of life 9
Col 2:19 not holding fast to the Head 13
1Th 5:21 test everything; hold fast what is good 11
Heb 3: 6 we are his house if we hold fast our confidence 11
4:14 let us hold fast our confession. 13
10:23 Let us hold fast the confession of our hope 11
Rev 2:13 you hold fast my name and you did not deny my faith 13
25 only hold fast what you have, until I come. 13
3:11 I am coming soon; hold fast what you have 14
Sir 1:19 he exalted the glory of those who held her fast. 13
4:13 Whoever holds her fast will obtain glory 14
25:11 to whom shall be likened the one who holds it fast? 14
Bar 4: 1 All who hold her fast will live 13
3Mc 7:16 those who had held fast to God even to death 10
4Mc 11:27 therefore, unconquered, we hold fast to reason. 10

hold firm 1.חזק 2.*ἀντέχω* 3.*κατέχω* 4.*ὑποφέρω*
Isa 33:23 it cannot hold the mast firm in its place 1
Tit 1: 9 he must hold firm to the sure word as taught 2
Heb 3:14 if only we hold our first confidence firm 3
4Mc 17: 3 you held firm and unswerving 4

firmly hold 1.*ἀντέχω*
1Mc 15:34 we are firmly holding the inheritance of our fathers. 1

hold for profit 1.*ἐπικερδής*
Wis 15:12 considered . . life a festival held for profit 1

hold guiltless 1.נקה 2.*δικαιόω*
Exd 20: 7 the LORD will not hold him guiltless 1
Deu 5:11 for the LORD will not hold him guiltless 1
1Kg 2: 9 hold him not guiltless, for you are a wise man; you 1
Sir 9:12 remember that they will not be held guiltless 2

hold guilty 1.אשם
Prv 30:10 lest he curse you, and you be held guilty. 1

hold head high in defiance 1.*ὑψαυχενέω*
3Mc 3:19 who hold their heads high in defiance 1

hold in awe 1.ירא
1Ch 16:25 he is to be held in awe above all gods. 1

hold in bondage 1.עבד
Exd 6: 5 people . . whom the Egyptians hold in bondage 1

hold in derision 1.לעג 2.לַעַג
Ps 59: 8 thou dost hold all the nations in derision. 1
Ezk 23:32 you shall be laughed at and held in derision 2

hold in high honor 1.*μεγαλύνω*
Act 5:13 the people held them in high honor. 1

hold in honor 1.כבד 2.*ἔνδοξος* 3.*τίμιος*
1Sm 9: 6 a man of God . . and he is a man that is held in honor; 1
2Sm 6:22 by the maids . . by them I shall be held in honor. 1
Act 5:34 Gama'li-el . . held in honor by all the people 3
1Co 4:10 You are held in honor, but we in disrepute. 2
Heb 13: 4 Let marriage be held in honor among all 3
AEs 11:11 the lowly . . consumed those held in honor 2

hold in pledge 1.חבל
Prv 20:16 hold him in pledge when he gives surety 1
27:13 hold him in pledge when he gives surety 1

hold in power 1.*καταδυναστεύω*
Wis 17: 2 they held the holy nation in their power 1

hold innocent 1.נקה
Job 9:28 for I know thou wilt not hold me innocent. 1

hold judgment 1.שפט
Ps 82: 1 in the midst of the gods he holds judgment 1

hold of account 1.*λογίζομαι*
Wis 3:17 they will be held of no account 1

hold one's peace 1.דמם 2.חרש 3.חשה
Gen 34: 5 so Jacob held his peace until they came. 2
Lev 10: 3 And Aaron held his peace 1
1Sm 10:27 they despised him . . But he held his peace. 2
2Sm 13:20 Has Amnon . . been with you? Now hold your peace 2
2Kg 2: 3 And he said, "Yes, I know it; hold your peace. 3
5 he answered, "Yes, I know it; hold your peace. 3
Est 7: 4 If we had been sold . . I would have held my peace; 3
Ps 39: 2 I was dumb and silent, I held my peace to no avail; 3
12 give ear to my cry; hold not thy peace at my tears! 2
83: 1 do not hold thy peace or be still, O God! 2
Isa 42:14 For a long time I have held my peace 3
57:11 Have I not held my peace, even for a long time 3

hold one's tongue 1.*σιωπάω*
Sir 32: 8 be as one who knows and yet holds his tongue. 1

hold out 1.אחז 2.ישט 3.*ἀντέχω* 4.*διακαρτερέω* 5.*ἐκπετάννυμι*
Rut 3:15 Bring the mantle you are wearing and hold it out. 1
Est 4:11 the one to whom the king holds out the . . scepter 2
5: 2 and he held out to Esther the golden scepter 2
8: 4 the king held out the golden scepter to Esther 2
Rom 10:21 All day long I have held out my hands 5
Jdt 7:30 Let us hold out for five more days 4
4Mc 7: 4 No city . . ever held out as did that most holy man 3

hold over till the next day 1.*αὐλίζομαι*
Tob 4:14 Do not hold over till the next day the wages 1

hold quietly 1.שבח
Prv 29:11 but a wise man quietly holds it back. 1

hold ready 1.*ἑτοιμάζω*
Rev 9:15 angels . . who had been held ready for the hour 1

hold safe 1.צפן
Ps 31:20 thou holdest them safe under thy shelter 1

secure hold 1.יָתֵד
Ezr 9: 8 to give us a secure hold within his holy place 1

hold strongly 1.*ἐνισχύω*
Sir 48:22 he held strongly to the ways of David his father 1

hold sway 1.teneo
2Es 12:15 the second . . shall hold sway for a longer time 1

hold sweet 1.מתק
Ps 55:14 We used to hold sweet converse together; 1

hold together 1.*συγκεῖμαι* 2.*συνέχω* 3.*συνίστημι*
Col 1:17 in him all things hold together. 3
Wis 1: 7 that which holds all things together 2
Sir 43:26 by his word all things hold together. 1

hold true 1.*στοιχέω*
Php 3:16 Only let us hold true to what we have attained. 1

hold unclean 1.טמא
Lev 20:25 which I have set apart for you to hold unclean 1

hold up 1.סעד 2.רום 3.תמך 4.*προτείνω*
Exd 17:11 Whenever Moses held up his hand, Israel 2
12 and Aaron and Hur held up his hands, one on one side 3
Ps 94:18 foot slips," thy steadfast love, O LORD, held me up. 1
119:117 Hold me up, that I may be safe 1
2Mc 3:20 holding up their hands to heaven 4

hold up to contempt 1.*παραδειγματίζω*
Heb 6: 6 crucify . . and hold him up to contempt. 1

hold water 1.מִקְוֶה
Lev 11:36 a spring or a cistern holding water shall be 1

holder 1.בַּיִת
Exd 25:27 the rings shall lie, as holders for the poles 1
26:29 rings of gold for holders for the bars; 1
30: 4 holders for poles with which to carry it. 1
36:34 made their rings of gold for holders for the bars 1
37:14 Close to the frame were the rings, as holders 1
27 two rings . . as holders for the poles 1
38: 5 four rings . . as holders for the poles; 1

holding 1.אֲחֻזָּה
2Ch 11:14 left their common lands and their holdings 1

thing that holds 1. susceptor
2Es 9:35 the things that held them remain 1

hole 1. חוֹחַ 2. חֹר 3. חֻר 4. מְחִלָּה 5. נקב 6. שַׁחַת 7. ὀπή 8. φωλεός
Deu 23:13 when you sit down outside, you shall dig a hole *
1Sm 13: 6 the people hid themselves in caves and in holes 1
14:11 coming out of the holes where they have hid 2
2Kg 12: 9 took a chest, and bored a hole in the lid of it 2
Job 30: 6 must dwell, in holes of the earth and of the rocks. 2
Ps 7:15 falls into the hole which he has made. 6
Isa 2:19 enter the caves . . and the holes of the ground 4
11: 8 sucking child . . play over the hole of the asp 2
42:22 they are all of them trapped in holes and hidden 3
Ezk 8: 7 when I looked, behold, there was a hole in the wall. 2
Hag 1: 6 earns wages to put them into a bag with holes. 5
Mat 8:20 Jesus said to him, "Foxes have holes 8
Lke 9:58 Jesus said to him, "Foxes have holes 8
4Mc 14:16 building . . in holes and tops of trees 7

holiday 1. יוֹם טוֹב
Est 8:17 and joy among the Jews, a feast and a holiday. 1
9:22 and from mourning into a holiday; 1

holiday-making 1. יוֹם טוֹב
Est 9:19 for gladness and feasting and holiday-making 1

holies *See* holy.

holiness 1. קֹדֶשׁ 2. ἁγίασμα 3. ἁγιασμός 4. ἁγιαστία 5. ἅγιος 6. ἁγιότης 7. ἁγιωσύνη 8. ὁσιότης 9. ὅσιως
Exd 15:11 majestic in holiness, terrible in glorious 1
Ps 89:35 Once for all I have sworn by my holiness; 1
93: 5 holiness befits thy house, O LORD, for evermore. 1
Ams 4: 2 The Lord GOD has sworn by his holiness 1
Lke 1:75 in holiness and righteousness before him 8
Rom 1: 4 in power according to the Spirit of holiness 7
2Co 1:12 with holiness and godly sincerity 6
7: 1 make holiness perfect in the fear of God. 7
Eph 4:24 in true righteousness and holiness. 8
1Th 3:13 unblamable in holiness before our God and Father 7
4: 4 take a wife for himself in holiness and honor 3
7 not called us for uncleanness, but in holiness. 3
1Ti 2:15 in faith and love and holiness, with modesty. 3
Heb 12:10 we may share his holiness. 6
14 the holiness without which no one will see . . 3
2Pe 3:11 in lives of holiness and godliness 5
Wis 2:22 nor hope for the wages of holiness 8
5:19 he will take holiness as an invincible shield 8
6:10 who observe holy things in holiness 9
9: 3 rule the world in holiness and righteousness 8
14:30 through contempt for holiness. 8
Sir 45:12 inscribed like a signet with "Holiness 2
2Mc 3:12 had trusted in the holiness of the place 7
14:36 now, O holy One, Lord of all holiness 3
4Mc 7: 9 did not abandon the holiness which you praised 4

holiness *See also* befit, communicate, manifest, vindicate.

show holiness 1. קדשׁ
Ezk 38:23 I will show my greatness and my holiness 1

hollow 1. כַּף 2. נבב 3. κοιλότης 4. κοίλωμα
Gen 32:25 he touched the hollow of his thigh; 1
32 the hip which is upon the hollow of the thigh 1
32 because he touched the hollow of Jacob's thigh 1
Exd 27: 8 You shall make it hollow, with boards; 2
38: 7 he made it hollow, with boards. 2
1Sm 25:29 he shall sling out as from the hollow of a sling. 1
Jer 52:21 thickness was four fingers, and it was hollow. 2
Wis 17:19 an echo thrown back from a hollow of the mountains 3
2Mc 1:19 secretly hid it in the hollow of a dry cistern 4

hollow of hand 1. שֹׁעַל
Isa 40:12 has measured the waters in the hollow of his hand 1

hollow place 1. מַכְתֵּשׁ
Jdg 15:19 God split open the hollow place that is at Lehi 1

holm tree 1. תִּרְזָה
Isa 44:14 he chooses a holm tree or an oak and lets it grow 1

holy 1. קָדוֹשׁ 2. קדשׁ 3. קֹדֶשׁ 4. קַדִּישׁ (A) 5. ἁγίασμα 6. ἁγιασμός 7. ἅγιος 8. ἁγνός 9. ἱερός 10. ὅσιος 11. ὁσίως 12. σεμνός 13. sancio
Exd 3: 5 place on which you are standing is holy ground. 3
12:16 On the first day you shall hold a holy assembly 3
16 and on the seventh day a holy assembly; 3
15:13 guided them by thy strength to thy holy abode. 3
16:23 Tomorrow is a day of solemn rest, a holy sabbath 3
19: 6 be to me a kingdom of priests and a holy nation. 3
26:33 separate . . the holy place from the most holy. 3
28: 2 you shall make holy garments for Aaron 3
4 they shall make holy garments for Aaron 3
36 engrave on it . . 'Holy to the LORD.' 3
38 the people of Israel hallow as their holy gifts; 3
29: 6 put the holy crown upon the turban. 3
21 he and his garments shall be holy 3
29 The holy garments of Aaron shall be for his sons 3
31 and boil its flesh in a holy place; 1
33 shall not eat of them, because they are holy. 3
34 it shall not be eaten, because it is holy. 3
37 consecrate it, and the altar shall be most holy; 3
30:10 it is most holy to the LORD. 3
25 a holy anointing oil it shall be. 3
29 consecrate them, that they may be most holy; 3
31 This shall be my holy anointing oil throughout 3
32 it is holy, and it shall be holy to you. 3
32 it is holy, and it shall be holy to you. 3
35 incense . . seasoned with salt, pure and holy; 3
36 it shall be for you most holy. 3
37 it shall be for you holy to the LORD. 3
31:10 holy garments for Aaron the priest 3
14 keep the sabbath, because it is holy for you; 3
15 sabbath of solemn rest, holy to the LORD; 3
35: 2 on the seventh day you shall have a holy sabbath 3
19 garments for ministering in the holy place 3
21 for all its service, and for the holy garments. 3
37:29 He made the holy anointing oil also, and the pure 3
39: 1 they made the holy garments for Aaron; 3
30 they made the plate of the holy crown of pure gold 3
30 the engraving of a signet, "Holy to the LORD. 3
41 garments for ministering in the holy place 3
40: 9 all its furniture; and it shall become holy. 3
10 and the altar shall be most holy. 3
13 put upon Aaron the holy garments 3
Lev 2: 3 it is a most holy part of the offerings by fire 3
10 it is a most holy part of the offering by fire 3
6:16 it shall be eaten unleavened in a holy place 1
25 be killed before the LORD; it is most holy 3
26 in a holy place it shall be eaten, in the court 1
27 Whatever touches its flesh shall be holy 3
27 on which it was sprinkled in a holy place 1
29 the priests may eat of it; it is most holy 3
7: 1 law of the guilt offering. It is most holy 3
6 it shall be eaten in a holy place; it is most holy 3
6 it shall be eaten in a holy place; it is most holy 3
8: 9 the holy crown, as the LORD commanded Moses 3
10:10 You are to distinguish between the holy 3
12 unleavened beside the altar, for it is most holy 3
13 you shall eat it in a holy place 1
11:44 consecrate yourselves therefore and be holy 3
44 consecrate . . and be holy, for I am holy 3
45 you shall therefore be holy, for I am holy 3
45 you shall therefore be holy, for I am holy 3
14:13 in the place . . in the holy place 3
13 belongs to the priest; it is most holy 3
16: 4 He shall put on the holy linen coat 3
4 these are the holy garments 3
24 he shall bathe his body in water in a holy place 3
32 make atonement, wearing the holy linen garments 3
19: 2 You shall be holy; for I the LORD your God am holy 1
2 You shall be holy; for I the LORD your God am holy 3
24 in the fourth year all their fruit shall be holy 3
20: 3 defiling my sanctuary and profaning my holy name 3
7 Consecrate yourselves therefore, and be holy 1
26 You shall be holy to me; for I the LORD am holy 1
26 You shall be holy to me; for I the LORD am holy 3
21: 6 They shall be holy to their God, and not profane 1
6 therefore they shall be holy 3
7 for the priest is holy to his God 1
8 he shall be holy to you; for I the LORD, who sanctify 1
8 for I the LORD, who sanctify you, am holy 3
22 He may eat the bread . . both of the most holy 3
22: 2 may not profane my holy name: I am the LORD 3
32 you shall not profane my holy name 3
23: 2 you shall proclaim as holy convocations 3
3 a sabbath of solemn rest, a holy convocation 3
4 These are . . the holy convocations 3
7 the first day you shall have a holy convocation 3
8 on the seventh day is a holy convocation 3
20 they shall be holy to the LORD for the priest 3
21 you shall hold a holy convocation 3
24 you shall observe . . a holy convocation 3
27 it shall be for you a time of holy convocation 3
35 On the first day shall be a holy convocation 3
36 the eighth day you shall hold a holy convocation 3
37 you shall proclaim as times of holy convocation 3
24: 9 they shall eat it in a holy place 3
25:12 For it is a jubilee; it shall be holy to you 3
27: 9 all of such that any man gives to the LORD is holy 3
10 that for which it is exchanged shall be holy 3
14 dedicates his house to be holy to the LORD 3
21 field . . shall be holy to the LORD 3
28 every devoted thing is most holy to the LORD 3
30 All the tithe of the land . . is holy to the LORD 3
32 All the tithe . . shall be holy to the LORD 3
33 it . . shall be holy; it shall not be redeemed 3
Num 5:17 shall take holy water in an earthen vessel 1
6: 5 until the time is completed . . he shall be holy; 1
8 days of his separation he is holy to the LORD. 1
15:40 do all my commandments, and be holy to your God. 1
16: 3 For all the congregation are holy, every one 1
5 In the morning the LORD will show who . . is holy 3
37 scatter the fire far and wide. For they are holy 2
38 before the LORD; therefore they are holy. 3
18: 9 shall be most holy to you and to your sons. 3
10 In a most holy place shall you eat of it; 3
10 every male may eat of it; it is holy to you. 3
17 you shall not redeem; they are holy. 3
19 All the holy offerings which the people 3
28:18 the first day there shall be a holy convocation 3
25 seventh day you shall have a holy convocation; 3
26 you shall have a holy convocation; 3
29: 1 first day . . you shall have a holy convocation; 3
7 tenth day . . you shall have a holy convocation 3
12 fifteenth . . you shall have a holy convocation; 3
35:25 high priest who was anointed with the holy oil. 3
Deu 7: 6 For you are a people holy to the LORD your God; 3
14: 2 For you are a people holy to the LORD your God 3
21 for you are a people holy to the LORD your God. 3
23:14 holy . . not see anything indecent among 3
26:15 Look down from thy holy habitation, from heaven 3
19 you shall be a people holy to the LORD your God 1
28: 9 establish you as a people holy to himself 3
Jos 5:15 Put off . . for the place where you stand is holy. 3
24:19 You cannot serve the LORD; for he is a holy God; 1
1Sm 2: 2 There is none holy like the LORD 3
6:20 Who is able to stand before the LORD, this holy God? 3
21: 4 I have no common bread . . but there is holy bread; 3
5 the vessels of the young men are holy 3
5 how much more today will their vessels be holy? 3
6 the priest gave him the holy bread; 3
1Kg 8: 4 and all the holy vessels that were in the tent; 3
2Kg 4: 9 I perceive that this is a holy man of God 3
1Ch 9:29 were appointed . . over all the holy utensils 3
16:10 Glory in his holy name; 3
29 Worship the LORD in holy array; 3
35 that we may give thanks to thy holy name 3
22:19 so that the ark . . and the holy vessels of God 3
23:13 was set apart to consecrate the most holy things 3
28 the care of . . the cleansing of all that is holy 3
29: 3 to all that I have provided for the holy house 3
16 for building thee a house for thy holy name 3
2Ch 3: 8 And he made the most holy place; 3
10 In the most holy place he made two cherubim 3
5: 5 brought up . . and all the holy vessels that were 3
8:11 places to which the ark . . has come are holy. 3
20:21 to sing to the LORD and praise him in holy array 3
23: 6 they may enter, for they are holy 3
30:27 their prayer came to his holy habitation 3
31:18 for they were faithful in keeping themselves holy. 3
35: 3 said to the Levites . . who were holy to the LORD 1
3 Put the holy ark in the house which Solomon 3
Ezr 2:63 not to partake of the most holy food 3
8:28 You are holy to the LORD, and the vessels are holy; 3
28 You are holy to the LORD, and the vessels are holy; 3
9: 2 holy race has mixed itself with the peoples 3
8 to give us a secure hold within his holy place 3
Neh 7:65 not to partake of the most holy food, until 3
8: 9 This day is holy to the LORD your God; 1
10 for this day is holy to our Lord; 1
11 Be quiet, for this day is holy; do not be grieved. 1
9:14 thou didst make known to them thy holy sabbath 3
10:31 not buy from them on the sabbath or on a holy day; 3
11: 1 one out of ten to live in Jerusalem the holy city 3
18 All the Levites in the holy city were 284. 3
Job 5: 1 To which of the holy ones will you turn? 1
Ps 2: 6 I have set my king on Zion, my holy hill. 3
3: 4 to the LORD, and he answers me from his holy hill. 3
5: 7 I will worship toward thy holy temple 3
11: 4 The LORD is in his holy temple 3
15: 1 Who shall dwell on thy holy hill? 3
20: 6 he will answer him from his holy heaven 3
22: 3 Yet thou art holy, enthroned on the praises 3
24: 3 And who shall stand in his holy place? 3
28: 2 lift up my hands toward thy most holy sanctuary. 3
29: 2 worship the LORD in holy array. 3
30: 4 O you his saints, and give thanks to his holy name. 3
33:21 glad in him, because we trust in his holy name. 3
43: 3 let them lead me, let them bring me to thy holy hill 3
46: 4 city of God, the holy habitation of the Most High. 3
47: 8 God sits on his holy throne. 3
48: 1 His holy mountain 3
51:11 take not thy holy Spirit from me. 3
65: 4 the goodness of thy house, thy holy temple! 3
68: 5 Father . . is God in his holy habitation. 3
77:13 Thy way, O God, is holy. 3
78:54 he brought them to his holy land, to the mountain 3
79: 1 heathen . . have defiled thy holy temple; 3
87: 1 On the holy mount stands the city he founded; 3
89:20 with my holy oil I have anointed him; 3
96: 9 Worship the LORD in holy array; 3
97:12 O you righteous, and give thanks to his holy name! 3
98: 1 right hand and his holy arm have gotten him 3
99: 3 praise thy great and terrible name! Holy is he! 3
5 LORD our God; worship at his footstool! Holy is he! 3
9 LORD our God, and worship at his holy mountain; 3
9 Extol the LORD . . for the LORD our God is holy! 3
102:19 that he looked down from his holy height 3
103: 1 all that is within me, bless his holy name! 3
105: 3 Glory in his holy name; 3
42 For he remembered his holy promise, and Abraham 3
106:47 that we may give thanks to thy holy name 3
110: 3 day you lead your host upon the holy mountains. 3
111: 9 Holy and terrible is his name! 3

138: 2 I bow down toward thy holy temple and give thanks 3
145:21 all flesh bless his holy name for ever and ever. 3
Prv 20:25 It is a snare for a man to say rashly, "It is holy 3
Ecc 8:10 they used to go in and out of the holy place 3
Isa 4: 3 he who is left . . will be called holy 3
5:16 the Holy God shows himself holy in righteousness 3
6: 3 Holy, holy, holy is the LORD of hosts; 3
3 Holy, holy, holy is the LORD of hosts; 3
3 Holy, holy, holy is the LORD of hosts; 3
13 The holy seed is its stump. 3
11: 9 shall not hurt or destroy in all my holy mountain; 3
27:13 worship . . on the holy mountain at Jerusalem. 3
35: 8 a highway . . and it shall be called the Holy Way; 3
40:25 that I should be like him? says the Holy One. 3
48: 2 For they call themselves after the holy city 3
52: 1 beautiful garments, O Jerusalem, the holy city; 3
10 The LORD has bared his holy arm before the eyes 3
56: 7 these I will bring to my holy mountain 3
57:13 the land, and shall inherit my holy mountain. 3
15 One who inhabits eternity, whose name is Holy 3
58:13 from doing your pleasure on my holy day 3
13 a delight and the holy day of the LORD honorable; 3
62:12 And they shall be called The holy people 3
63:10 But they rebelled and grieved his holy Spirit; 3
11 he who put in the midst of them his holy Spirit 3
15 and see, from thy holy and glorious habitation. 3
18 Thy holy people possessed thy sanctuary 3
64:10 Thy holy cities have become a wilderness 3
11 Our holy and beautiful house, 3
65:11 forsake the LORD, who forget my holy mountain 3
25 shall not hurt or destroy in all my holy mountain 3
66:20 upon dromedaries, to my holy mountain Jerusalem 3
Jer 2: 3 Israel was holy to the LORD, the first fruits 3
23: 9 because of the LORD and because of his holy words. 3
25:30 and from his holy habitation utter his voice; 3
31:23 O habitation of righteousness, O holy hill! 3
Lam 4: 1 holy stones lie scattered at . . every street. 3
Ezk 20:39 but my holy name you shall no more profane 3
40 my holy mountain, the mountain height of Israel 3
22:26 no distinction between the holy and the common 3
28:14 you were on the holy mountain of God; 3
36:20 whereever they came, they profaned my holy name 3
21 I had concern for my holy name 3
22 I am about to act, but for the sake of my holy name 3
39: 7 my holy name I will make known in the midst of my 3
7 I will not let my holy name be profaned any more; 3
25 I will be jealous for my holy name. 3
42:13 opposite the yard are the holy chambers 3
13 the priests . . shall eat the most holy offerings; 3
13 there they shall put the most holy offerings 3
13 and the guilt offering, for the place is holy. 1
14 for these are holy; they shall put on other 3
20 a separation between the holy and the common. 3
43: 7 house of Israel shall no more defile my holy name 3
8 They have defiled my holy name 3
12 upon the top of the mountain shall be most holy. 3
44:19 ministering, and lay them in the holy chambers; 3
23 the difference between the holy and the common 3
45: 1 a portion of the land as a holy district 3
1 it shall be holy throughout its whole extent. 3
3 in the holy district you shall measure •
6 the portion set apart as the holy district 3
7 the holy district and the property of the city 3
7 the holy district and the property of the city 3
46:19 north row of the holy chambers for the priests; 3
48:10 shall be the allotments of the holy portion 3
12 portion from the holy portion of the land •
14 portion of the land, for it is holy to the LORD. 3
18 of the length alongside the holy portion 3
18 it shall be alongside the holy portion. 3
20 the holy portion together with the property 3
21 What remains on both sides of the holy portion 3
21 from the 25,000 cubits of the holy portion •
21 The holy portion with the sanctuary 3
Dan 4: 8 Daniel . . in whom is the spirit of the holy gods– 4
9 know that the spirit of the holy gods is in you 4
18 for the spirit of the holy gods is in you. 4
5:11 man in whom is the spirit of the holy gods. 4
14 heard of you that the spirit of the holy gods 4
8:13 Then I heard a holy one speaking; 3
13 another holy one said to the one that spoke 3
9:16 turn away from thy city Jerusalem, thy holy hill; 3
20 before the LORD my God for the holy hill of my God; 3
24 concerning your people and your holy city 3
24 to anoint a most holy place. 3
11:28 heart shall be set against the holy covenant. 3
30 take action against the holy covenant. 3
30 heed to those who forsake the holy covenant. 3
45 between the sea and the glorious holy mountain; 3
12: 7 shattering of the power of the holy people 3
Jol 2: 1 sound the alarm on my holy mountain! 3
3:17 LORD your God, who dwell in Zion, my holy mountain. 3
17 And Jerusalem shall be holy 3
Ams 2: 7 the same maiden, so that my holy name is profaned; 3
Obd 1:16 For as you have drunk upon my holy mountain 3
17 Mount Zion . . and it shall be holy; 3
Jon 2: 4 how shall I again look upon thy holy temple? 3
7 my prayer came to thee, into thy holy temple. 3
Mic 1: 2 against you, the Lord from his holy temple. 3
Hab 2:20 But the LORD is in his holy temple; 3
Zep 3:11 shall no longer be haughty in my holy mountain. 3
Hag 2:12 'If one carries holy flesh in the skirt of his 3
Zec 2:12 inherit Judah as his portion in the holy land 3
13 he has roused himself from his holy dwelling. 3
8: 3 of the LORD of hosts, the holy mountain. 3
14: 5 God will come, and all the holy ones with him. 1
20 on the bells of the horses, "Holy to the LORD. 3
Mat 1:18 found to be with child of the Holy Spirit; 7
20 is conceived in her is of the Holy Spirit; 7
3:11 baptize you with the Holy Spirit and with fire. 7
4: 5 Then the devil took him to the holy city, and set 7
7: 6 Do not give dogs what is holy; and do not throw 7
12:32 but whoever speaks against the Holy Spirit 7
24:15 the prophet Daniel, standing in the holy place 7
27:53 went into the holy city and appeared to many. 7
28:19 Father and of the Son and of the Holy Spirit 7
Mrk 1: 8 he will baptize you with the Holy Spirit 7
3:29 whoever blasphemes against the Holy Spirit 7
6:20 knowing that he was a righteous and holy man 7
8:38 glory of his Father with the holy angels. 7
12:36 himself, inspired by the Holy Spirit, declared 7
13:11 it is not you who speak, but the Holy Spirit. 7
Lke 1:15 he will be filled with the Holy Spirit 7
35 The Holy Spirit will come upon you 7
35 the child to be born will be called holy, the Son of God 7
41 Elizabeth was filled with the Holy Spirit 7
49 holy is his name. 7
67 Zechari'ah was filled with the Holy Spirit 7
70 the mouth of his holy prophets from of old 7
72 to remember his holy covenant 7
2:23 shall be called holy to the Lord") 7
25 the Holy Spirit was upon him. 7
26 it had been revealed to him by the Holy Spirit 7
3:16 baptize you with the Holy Spirit and with fire. 7
22 Holy Spirit descended upon him in bodily form 7
4: 1 Jesus, full of the Holy Spirit, returned 7
9:26 the glory of the Father and of the holy angels. 7
10:21 In that same hour he rejoiced in the Holy Spirit 7
11:13 will the heavenly Father give the Holy Spirit 7
12:10 he who blasphemes against the Holy Spirit 7
12 the Holy Spirit will teach you in that very hour 7
Joh 1:33 this is he who baptizes with the Holy Spirit.' 7
11:48 and destroy both our holy place and our nation. •
14:26 the Counselor, the Holy Spirit 7
17:11 Holy Father, keep them in thy name 7
20:22 Receive the Holy Spirit. 7
Act 1: 2 had given commandment through the Holy Spirit 7
5 you shall be baptized with the Holy Spirit. 7
8 when the Holy Spirit has come upon you 7
16 which the Holy Spirit spoke beforehand 7
2: 4 they were all filled with the Holy Spirit 7
33 the promise of the Holy Spirit 7
38 you shall receive the gift of the Holy Spirit. 7
3:14 you denied the Holy and Righteous One 7
21 the mouth of his holy prophets from of old. 7
4: 8 Then Peter, filled with the Holy Spirit, said 7
25 who . . didst say by the Holy Spirit 7
27 gathered together against thy holy servant 7
30 through the name of thy holy servant Jesus. 7
31 they were all filled with the Holy Spirit 7
5: 3 filled your heart to lie to the Holy Spirit 7
32 so is the Holy Spirit 7
6: 5 Stephen, a man full of faith and of the Holy Spirit 7
13 to speak words against this holy place and the law; 7
7:33 the place where you are standing is holy ground. 7
51 you always resist the Holy Spirit 7
55 he, full of the Holy Spirit, gazed into heaven 7
8:15 they might receive the Holy Spirit; 7
17 they received the Holy Spirit. 7
19 may receive the Holy Spirit. 7
9:17 be filled with the Holy Spirit. 7
31 in the comfort of the Holy Spirit 7
10:22 was directed by a holy angel to send for you 7
38 anointed Jesus of Nazareth with the Holy Spirit 7
44 the Holy Spirit fell on all who heard the word. 7
45 the gift of the Holy Spirit had been poured out 7
47 who have received the Holy Spirit just as we have? 7
11:15 As I began to speak, the Holy Spirit fell on them 7
16 you shall be baptized with the Holy Spirit.' 7
24 a good man, full of the Holy Spirit and of faith. 7
13: 2 the Holy Spirit said, "Set apart for me Barnabas 7
4 being sent out by the Holy Spirit 7
9 filled with the Holy Spirit 7
34 give you the holy and sure blessings of David.' 10
52 filled with joy and with the Holy Spirit. 7
15: 8 giving them the Holy Spirit just as he did to us; 7
28 For it has seemed good to the Holy Spirit and to us 7
16: 6 forbidden by the Holy Spirit to speak the word 7
19: 2 he said to them, "Did you receive the Holy Spirit 7
2 never even heard that there is a Holy Spirit. 7
6 the Holy Spirit came on them 7
20:23 except that the Holy Spirit testifies to me 7
28 in which the Holy Spirit has made you overseers 7
21:11 Thus says the Holy Spirit 7
28 he has defiled this holy place. 7
28:25 The Holy Spirit was right in saying 7
Rom 1: 2 through his prophets in the holy scriptures 7
5: 5 poured into our hearts through the Holy Spirit 7
7:12 So the law is holy, and the commandment is holy 7
12 and the commandment is holy and just and good. 7
9: 1 my conscience bears me witness in the Holy Spirit 7
11:16 If the dough offered as first fruits is holy 7
16 and if the root is holy, so are the branches. 7
12: 1 as a living sacrifice, holy and acceptable to God 7
14:17 and peace and joy in the Holy Spirit; 7
15:13 by the power of the Holy Spirit you may abound 7
16 be acceptable, sanctified by the Holy Spirit. 7
19 by the power of the Holy Spirit •
16:16 Greet one another with a holy kiss. 7
1Co 3:17 God's temple is holy, and that temple you are. 7
6:19 a temple of the Holy Spirit within you 7
7:14 as it is they are holy. 7
34 how to be holy in body and spirit 7
12: 3 except by the Holy Spirit. 7
16:20 Greet one another with a holy kiss. 7
2Co 6: 6 kindness, the Holy Spirit, genuine love 7
13:12 Greet one another with a holy kiss 7
14 the fellowship of the Holy Spirit 7
Eph 1: 4 that we should be holy and blameless before him. 7
13 were sealed with the promised Holy Spirit 7
2:21 grows into a holy temple in the Lord; 7
3: 5 been revealed to his holy apostles and prophets 7
4:30 do not grieve the Holy Spirit of God 7
5:27 that she might be holy and without blemish. 7
Col 1:22 in order to present you holy . . before him 7
3:12 as God's chosen ones, holy and beloved 7
1Th 1: 5 also in power and in the Holy Spirit 7
6 with joy inspired by the Holy Spirit; 7
2:10 how holy and righteous and blameless 11
4: 8 who gives his Holy Spirit to you. 7
5:26 Greet all the brethren with a holy kiss. 7
1Ti 2: 8 lifting holy hands without anger or quarreling; 10
2Ti 1: 9 who saved us and called us with a holy calling 7
14 the Holy Spirit who dwells within us. 7
Tit 1: 8 upright, holy, and self-controlled; 10
3: 5 renewal in the Holy Spirit 7
Heb 2: 4 by gifts of the Holy Spirit 7
3: 1 Therefore, holy brethren . . consider Jesus 7
7 Therefore, as the Holy Spirit says 7
6: 4 have become partakers of the Holy Spirit 7
7:26 such a high priest, holy, blameless, unstained 10
9: 3 a tent called the Holy of Holies 7
3 a tent called the Holy of Holies 7
8 By this the Holy Spirit indicates 7
10:15 the Holy Spirit also bears witness to us 7
1Pe 1:12 through the Holy Spirit sent from heaven 7
15 as he who called you is holy, be holy yourselves 7
15 be holy yourselves in all your conduct; 7
16 it is written, "You shall be holy, for I am holy. 7
16 it is written, "You shall be holy, for I am holy. 7
2: 5 like living stones . . be a holy priesthood 7
9 you are . . a holy nation, God's own people 7
3: 5 holy women who hoped in God used to adorn 7
2Pe 1:18 for we were with him on the holy mountain. 7
21 men moved by the Holy Spirit spoke from God. 7
2:21 the holy commandment delivered to them. 7
3: 2 remember the predictions of the holy prophets 7
Jde 1:14 Behold, the Lord came with his holy myriads 7
20 pray in the Holy Spirit; 7
Rev 4: 8 sing, "Holy, holy, holy, is the Lord God Almighty 7
8 sing, "Holy, holy, holy, is the Lord God Almighty 7
8 sing, "Holy, holy, holy, is the Lord God Almighty 7
6:10 O Sovereign Lord, holy and true, how long before 7
11: 2 they will trample over the holy city for 42 months. 7
14:10 tormented . . in the presence of the holy angels 7
15: 4 O Lord? For thou alone art holy. 10
20: 6 holy is he who shares in the first resurrection! 7
21: 2 I saw the holy city, new Jerusalem, coming down 7
10 and showed me the holy city Jerusalem 7
22:11 Let . . the holy still be holy. 7
11 Let . . the holy still be holy. 7
19 God will take away his share . . in the holy city 7
1Es 1: 3 put the holy ark of the Lord in the house 7
41 Nebuchadnezzar also took some holy vessels 9
45 the holy vessels of the Lord 9
53 slew . . with the sword around their holy temple 7
54 all the holy vessels of the Lord, great and small 9
2:10 also brought out the holy vessels of the Lord 9
6:18 the holy vessels of gold and of silver 9
26 the holy vessels of the house of the Lord 9
7: 2 supervised the holy work with very great care 9
3 the holy work prospered 9
5 the holy house was finished 7
8:17 deliver the holy vessels of the Lord 9
55 the holy vessels of the house of our Lord 9
58 I said to them, "You are holy to the Lord 7
58 the vessels are holy 7
70 the holy race has been mixed 7
71 I rent my garments and my holy mantle 9
73 with my garments and my holy mantle rent 9
78 to leave to us a root and a name in thy holy place 5
9:50 This day is holy to the Lord 7
52 for the day is holy to the Lord 7
53 This day is holy; do not be sorrowful. 7
2Es 13:48 who are found within my holy borders 13
14:22 send the Holy Spirit into me 13
Tob 3:11 blessed is thy holy and honored name for ever. 7

8: 5 and blessed by thy holy and glorious name for ever. 7
15 with every pure and holy blessing 7
11:14 blessed are all thy holy angels. 7
12:15 I am Raphael, one of the seven holy angels 7
13: 9 O Jerusalem, the holy city, he will afflict you 7
Wis 1: 5 a holy and disciplined spirit 7
7:22 a spirit that is intelligent, holy, unique 7
27 in every generation she passes into holy souls 10
9: 8 a temple on thy holy mountain 7
8 a copy of the holy tent which thou didst prepare 7
10 Send her forth from the holy heavens 7
17 and sent thy holy Spirit from on high? 7
10:15 A holy people and blameless race 10
20 they sang hymns, O Lord, to thy holy name 7
11: 1 the hand of a holy prophet. 7
12: 3 Those who dwelt of old in thy holy land 7
17: 2 they held the holy nation in their power 7
18: 9 the holy children of good men offered sacrifices 10
Sir 17:10 they will praise his holy name 6
24:10 In the holy tabernacle I ministered before him 7
26:17 Like the shining lamp on the holy lampstand 7
39:13 Listen to me, O you holy sons 10
24 To the holy his ways are straight 10
45:10 with a holy garment, of gold and blue and purple 7
15 ordained him, and anointed him with holy oil 7
47:10 while they praised God's holy name 7
49:12 raised a temple holy to the Lord 7
50:11 went up to the holy altar 7
Bar 2:16 O Lord, look down from thy holy habitation 7
Aza 1: 5 Jerusalem, the holy city of our fathers 7
30 blessed is thy glorious, holy name 7
31 Blessed art thou in the temple of thy holy glory 7
65 you who are holy and humble in heart 10
Sus 1:45 God aroused the holy spirit of a young lad 7
1Mc 1:15 abandoned the holy covenant 7
63 to profane the holy covenant 7
2: 7 the ruin of my people, the ruin of the holy city 7
12 behold, our holy place, our beauty, and our glory 7
4:49 They made new holy vessels 7
10:21 So Jonathan put on the holy garments 7
31 let Jerusalem . . be holy and free from tax. 7
11:37 a conspicuous place on the holy mountain.' 7
12: 9 since we have as encouragement the holy books 7
2Mc 1: 7 the holy land and the kingdom 7
12 those who fought against the holy city. 7
29 Plant thy people in thy holy place, as Moses said. 7
2:18 into his holy place 7
3: 1 While the holy city was inhabited 7
18 the holy place was . . brought into contempt. •
4:48 the city and the villages and the holy vessels 9
5:16 He took the holy vessels with his polluted hands 9
17 therefore he was disregarding the holy place. •
19 the nation for the sake of the holy place •
25 waited until the holy sabbath day 7
6:23 moreover according to the holy God-given law 7
28 for the revered and holy laws 7
30 It is clear to the Lord in his holy knowledge 7
8:15 called them by his holy and glorious name. 12
17 against the holy place 7
23 to read aloud from the holy book 9
9:14 the holy city 7
16 the holy sanctuary 7
16 the holy vessels he would give back 9
10: 7 the purifying of his own holy place. •
12:45 it was a holy and pious thought 10
13: 8 against the altar whose fire and ashes were holy 8
10 the law and their country and the holy temple 7
23 and showed generosity to the holy place. •
14: 3 to have access again to the holy altar 7
31 he went to the great and holy temple 7
36 now, O holy One, Lord of all holiness 7
15:14 prays much for the people and the holy city 7
16 Take this holy sword, a gift from God 7
24 blasphemers who come against thy holy people 7
32 the holy house of the Almighty; 7
3Mc 1: 9 and did what was fitting for the holy place •
23 created a considerable disturbance in the holy place •
2: 2 holy among the holy ones, the only ruler, almighty 7
6 who had enslaved your holy people Israel. 7
13 see now, O holy King 7
14 undertakes to violate the holy place 7
21 the first Father of all, holy among the holy ones 7
5:13 Then the Jews . . praised their holy God 7
6: 1 directed . . to cease calling upon the holy God 7
5 Sennacherib . . was lifted up against your holy city 7
18 revealed his holy face 7
29 the Jews . . praised their holy God and Savior 7
7:10 who had willfully transgressed against the holy God 7
4Mc 4: 9 to shield the holy place 9
12 would praise the blessedness of the holy place 9
6:30 the holy man died nobly in his tortures 9
13: 8 For they constituted a holy chorus of religion 9
14: 6 those holy youths . . agreed to go to death for its sake. 9

holy *See also* inscribe, keep, make, offering, portion, regard, revere.

become holy 1. קדשׁ

Exd 29:37 whatever touches the altar shall become holy. 1
30:29 whatever touches them will become holy. 1
Lev 6:18 whoever touches them shall become holy 1
Hag 2:12 does it become holy?'" The priests answered, "No 1

holy man 1. *ἅγιος* 2. *ὅσιος*

Wis 10:17 She gave holy men the reward of their labors 2
Sir 45: 6 a holy man like him, of the tribe of Levi. 1

most holy 1. *ἅγιος* 2. *πανάγιος* 3. *σεμνός*

Jde 1:20 build yourselves up on your most holy faith; 1
2Mc 5:15 to enter the most holy temple in all the world 1
6:11 in view of their regard for that most holy day. 3
4Mc 14: 7 O most holy seven, brothers in harmony! 2

most holy man 1. *πανάγιος*

4Mc 7: 4 No city . . ever held out as did that most holy man 1

holy of holies 1. *ναός*

3Mc 1:10 and conceived a desire to enter the holy of holies. 1

holy one 1. קָדוֹשׁ 2. קֹדֶשׁ 3. קַדִּישׁ (A) 4. *ἅγιος* 5. *ὅσιος*

Num16: 7 man whom the LORD chooses shall be the holy one. 1
Deu 33: 2 he came from the ten thousands of holy ones 2
2Kg 19:22 Against the Holy One of Israel! 1
Job 5: 1 To which of the holy ones will you turn? 1
6:10 for I have not denied the words of the Holy One. 1
15:15 Behold, God puts no trust in his holy ones 1
Ps 71:22 sing praises to thee . . O Holy One of Israel. 1
78:41 and provoked the Holy One of Israel. 1
89: 5 thy faithfulness in the assembly of the holy ones! 1
7 God feared in the council of the holy ones 1
18 our king to the Holy One of Israel. 1
106:16 Moses and Aaron, the holy one of the LORD 1
Prv 9:10 knowledge of the Holy One is insight. 1
30: 3 not learned . . nor have I knowledge of the Holy One. 1
Isa 1: 4 they have despised the Holy One of Israel 1
5:19 the purpose of the Holy One of Israel draw near 1
24 have despised the word of the Holy One of Israel. 1
10:17 Israel will become a fire, and his Holy One a flame; 1
20 but will lean upon the LORD, the Holy One of Israel 1
12: 6 for great in your midst is the Holy One of Israel. 1
17: 7 and their eyes will look to the Holy One of Israel; 1
29:19 men shall exult in the Holy One of Israel. 1
23 they will sanctify the Holy One of Jacob 1
30:11 let us hear no more of the Holy One of Israel. 1
12 Therefore thus says the Holy One of Israel 1
15 For thus said the Lord GOD, the Holy One of Israel 1
31: 1 but do not look to the Holy One of Israel 1
37:23 Against whom . . ? Against the Holy One of Israel! 1
41:14 your Redeemer is the Holy One of Israel. 1
16 in the Holy One of Israel you shall glory. 1
20 the Holy One of Israel has created it. 1
43: 3 For I am the LORD your God, the Holy One 1
14 the LORD, your Redeemer, the Holy One of Israel 1
15 I am the LORD, your Holy One, the Creator 1
45:11 the LORD, the Holy One of Israel, and his Maker 1
47: 4 Our Redeemer . . is the Holy One of Israel. 1
48:17 the LORD, your Redeemer, the Holy One of Israel 1
49: 7 the LORD, the Redeemer of Israel and his Holy One 1
7 the LORD, who is faithful, the Holy One of Israel 1
54: 5 and the Holy One of Israel is your Redeemer 1
55: 5 the LORD your God, and of the Holy One of Israel 1
60: 9 for the Holy One of Israel, because he has 1
14 of the LORD, the Zion of the Holy One of Israel. 1
Jer 50:29 she has . . defied the LORD, the Holy One of Israel. 1
51: 5 is full of guilt against the Holy One of Israel. 1
Ezk 39: 7 know that I am the LORD, the Holy One in Israel. 1
Dan 4:13 a watcher, a holy one, came down from heaven. 3
17 decision by the word of the holy ones 3
23 king saw a watcher, a holy one, coming down 3
Hos 11: 9 for I am God and not man, the Holy One in your midst 1
12 Judah . . is faithful to the Holy One. 1
Hab 1:12 from everlasting, O LORD my God, my Holy One? 1
3: 3 came from Teman . . the Holy One from Mount Paran. 1
Zec 14: 5 God will come, and all the holy ones with him. 1
Mrk 1:24 I know who you are, the Holy One of God. 4
Lke 4:34 I know who you are, the Holy One of God. 4
Joh 6:69 . . come to know, that you are the Holy One of God 4
Act 2:27 nor let thy Holy One see corruption. 5
13:35 Thou wilt not let thy Holy One see corruption. 5
1Jn 2:20 you have been anointed by the Holy One 4
Rev 3: 7 'The words of the holy one, the true one 4
16: 5 thou who art and wast, O Holy One. 5
Tob 12:12 I brought a reminder . . before the Holy One 4
15 the presence of the glory of the Holy One. 4
Wis 3: 9 he watches over his holy ones. •
4:15 he watches over his holy ones. 5
18: 1 for thy holy ones there was very great light. 5
2 thy holy ones . . were doing them no injury •
5 had resolved to kill the babes of thy holy ones 5
Sir 4:14 Those who serve her will minister to the Holy One; 4
23: 9 do not habitually utter the name of the Holy One; 4
42:17 The Lord has not enabled his holy ones to recount 4
43:10 At the command of the Holy One 4
45: 2 He made him equal in glory to the holy ones 4
47: 8 In all that he did he gave thanks to the Holy One 4
48:20 the Holy One quickly heard them from heaven 4
Bar 4:22 joy has come to me from the Holy One 4
37 they are coming . . , at the word of the Holy One 4
5: 5 gathered . . at the word of the Holy One 4
Aza 1:12 Isaac thy servant and Israel thy holy one 4
3Mc 2: 2 holy among the holy ones, the only ruler, almighty 4
21 the first Father of all, holy among the holy ones 4

holy place 1. מוֹעֵד 2. מִקְדָּשׁ 3. קָדוֹשׁ 4. קֹדֶשׁ 5. *ἅγιος*

Exd 26:33 the veil shall separate for you the holy place 4
34 the ark . . in the most holy place. 4
28:29 when he goes into the holy place, to bring them 4
35 when he goes into the holy place before the LORD 4
43 come near the altar to minister in the holy place; 4
29:30 when he comes . . to minister in the holy place. 4
31:11 oil and the fragrant incense for the holy place. 4
35:19 garments for ministering in the holy place 4
39: 1 garments, for ministering in the holy place; 4
41 garments for ministering in the holy place 4
Lev 6:30 blood . . to make atonement in the holy place 4
16: 2 come . . into the holy place within the veil 4
3 thus shall Aaron come into the holy place 4
16 thus he shall make atonement for the holy place 4
17 he enters to make atonement in the holy place 4
20 made an end of atoning for the holy place 4
23 which he put on when he went into the holy place 4
27 brought in to make atonement in the holy place 4
Num28: 7 in the holy place you shall pour out 4
1Kg 6:16 as an inner sanctuary, as the most holy place. 4
7:50 innermost part . . the most holy place 4
8: 6 the inner sanctuary . . in the most holy place 4
8 from the holy place before the inner sanctuary; 4
10 when the priests came out of the holy place 4
1Ch 6:49 for all the work of the most holy place 4
2Ch 4:22 for the inner doors to the most holy place 4
5: 7 inner sanctuary . . in the most holy place 4
9 ends of the poles were seen from the holy place 4
11 Now when the priests came out of the holy place 4
29: 5 carry out the filth from the holy place. 4
7 in the holy place to the God of Israel. 4
35: 5 stand in the holy place according 4
Ps 68:17 Lord came from Sinai into the holy place. 4
74: 4 Thy foes have roared in the midst of thy holy place; 1
134: 2 hands to the holy place, and bless the LORD! 4
Isa 57:15 I dwell in the high and holy place 3
Jer 51:51 come into the holy places of the LORD'S house.' 2
Ezk 7:24 their holy places shall be profaned. 2
41: 4 And he said to me, This is the most holy place. 4
21 in front of the holy place was something 4
23 nave and the holy place had each a double door. 4
42:14 When the priests enter the holy place 4
44:27 on the day that he goes into the holy place 4
27 the inner court, to minister in the holy place 4
45: 3 shall be the sanctuary, the most holy place. 4
4 it shall be . . a holy place for the sanctuary. 2
48:12 a most holy place, adjoining the territory 4
Dan 9:24 to anoint a most holy place. 4
Heb 9: 2 it is called the Holy Place. 5
12 he entered once for all into the Holy Place 5
25 as the high priest enters the Holy Place yearly 5

show oneself holy 1. קדשׁ

Lev 10: 3 I will show myself holy among those who are near me 1
Num20:13 LORD . . showed himself holy among them. 1
Isa 5:16 the Holy God shows himself holy in righteousness 1

holy thing 1. מִקְדָּשׁ 2. קֹדֶשׁ 3. *ἅγιος* 4. *ὅσιος* 5. sancio

Lev 5:15 sins . . in any of the holy thing of the LORD 2
16 for what he has done amiss in the holy thing 2
6:17 it is a thing most holy, like the sin offering 2
10:17 since it is a thing most holy and has been given 2
19: 8 because he has profaned a holy thing of the LORD 2
21:22 He may eat the bread . . of the holy things 2
22: 2 keep away from the holy things of the people 2
3 If any one . . approaches the holy things 2
4 may eat of the holy things until he is clean 2
6 the person . . shall not eat of the holy things 2
7 afterward he may eat of the holy things 2
10 An outsider shall not eat of a holy thing 2
10 a hired servant shall not eat of a holy thing 2
12 not eat of the offering of the holy things 2
14 if a man eats of a holy thing unwittingly 2
14 and give the holy thing to the priest 2
15 The priests shall not profane the holy things 2
16 to bear iniquity . . by eating their holy thing 2
27:23 on that day as a holy thing to the LORD 2
Num 4: 4 in the tent of meeting: the most holy things. 2
15 must not touch the holy things, lest they die. 2
19 when they come near to the most holy things 2
20 they shall not go in to look upon the holy things 2
5: 9 all the holy things of the people of Israel 2
10 every man's holy things shall be his; 2
7: 9 charged with the care of the holy things 2
10:21 Ko'hathites set out, carrying the holy things 1
18: 9 This shall be yours of the most holy things 2
32 shall not profane the holy things of . . Israel 2
Deu 12:26 the holy things which are due from you 2
2Kg 12: 4 All the money of the holy things which is brought 2

1Ch 23:13 was set apart to consecrate the most holy things 2
Neh 10:33 holy things, and the sin offerings to make 2
Ezk 22: 8 You have despised my holy things 2
26 and have profaned my holy things; 2
44: 8 And you have not kept charge of my holy things; 2
1Es 5:40 told them not to share in the holy things 3
2Es 10:22 our holy things have been polluted 5
Wis 6:10 who observe holy things in holiness 4
Sir 7:31 the first fruits of the holy things. 2

holy-minded 1. ἱερόψυχος
4Mc 17: 4 Take courage, therefore, O holy-minded mother 1

homage 1. προσκυνέω
Mrk 15:19 they knelt down in homage to him. 1

do homage 1. סגד (A)
Dan 2:46 fell upon his face, and did homage to Daniel 1

home 1. אֹהֶל 2. בַּיִת 3. מָנוֹחַ 4. מָנוּחַ 5. מָקוֹם 6. רֵבֶץ
7. ἀναστρέφω 8. αὐτός 9. εἰς τὸν οἶκον 10. ἐνδημέω
11. ἴδιος 12. μόνος 13. νοσσιά 14. οἰκητήριον
15. οἰκία 16. οἶκος
Gen 30:25 that I may go to my own home and country. 5
31:55 then he departed and returned home. 5
39:16 his garment by her until his master came home 2
43:26 When Joseph came home, they brought 2
Exd 9:19 in the field and is not brought home 2
Lev 18: 9 whether born at home or born abroad 2
Num32:18 We will not return to our homes until 2
Deu 21:12 then you shall bring her home to your house •
22: 2 bring it home to your house, and it shall be •
24: 5 newly married . . shall be free at home one year 2
Jos 20: 6 slayer may go again to his . . town and his own home 2
22: 4 therefore turn and go to your home in the land 1
6 and they went to their homes. 1
7 Joshua sent them away to their homes and blessed 1
8 Go back to your homes with much wealth 1
9 the Reubenites and the Gadites . . returned home •
Jdg 7: 3 is fearful and trembling, let him return home.' •
7 and let all the others go every man to his home. 5
9:55 was dead, they departed every man to his home. 5
11: 9 If you bring me home again to fight •
34 Then Jephthah came to his home at Mizpah; 2
18:15 the house of the young Levite, at the home of Micah 2
22 When they were a good way from the home of Micah 2
26 he turned and went back to his home. 2
19: 9 arise early . . for your journey, and go home. 1
18 and I am going to my home; and nobody takes me 2
28 and the man rose up and went away to his home. 5
Rut 1: 9 The LORD grant that you . . find a home, each of you 4
3: 1 should I not seek a home for you, that it may be well 3
1Sm 2:11 Then Elka'nah went home to Ramah. 2
20 so then they would return to their home. 5
4:10 was defeated, and they fled, every man to his home; 1
6: 7 yoke the cows . . but take their calves home 2
10 two milch cows . . and shut up their calves at home 2
7:17 he would come back to Ramah, for his home was there 2
10:25 sent all the people away, each one to his home. 2
26 Saul also went to his home at Gib'e-ah 2
18: 6 As they were coming home, when David returned •
23:18 David remained . . and Jonathan went home. 2
24:22 And David swore this to Saul. Then Saul went home; 2
2Sm 13: 7 Then David sent home to Tamar, saying, "Go 2
15:19 you are a foreigner . . an exile from your home. 5
17:23 saddled his ass, and went off home to his own city. 2
18:17 and all Israel fled every one to his own home. 1
19: 8 Now Israel had fled every man to his own home. 1
30 since my lord the king has come safely home. 2
39 and he returned to his own home. 5
20:22 and they dispersed . . every man to his home. 1
1Kg 5:14 a month in Lebanon and two months at home; 2
8:66 and went to their homes joyful and glad of heart 1
12:24 Return every man to his home 2
24 they hearkened to . . the LORD, and went home again 2
13: 7 Come home with me, and refresh yourself 2
15 he said to him, "Come home with me and eat bread. 2
22:17 let each return to his home in peace.' 2
2Kg 8:21 smote the E'domites . . but his army fled home. 1
13: 5 and the people of Israel dwelt in their homes 1
14:10 Be content with your glory, and stay at home; 2
12 and every man fled to his home. 1
2Ch 7:10 he sent the people away to their homes, joyful 1
11: 4 Return every man to his home 2
18:16 let each return to his home in peace.' 2
25:10 Amazi'ah discharged the army . . to go home 5
10 returned home in fierce anger. 5
19 now stay at home; why should you provoke trouble 2
22 every man fled to his home. 1
Neh 4:14 fight for your . . wives, and your homes. 2
Est 5:10 Haman restrained himself, and went home; 2
Job 38:20 that you may discern the paths to its home? 2
39: 6 to whom I have given the steppe for his home 2
Ps 49:11 Their graves are their homes for ever 2
14 form shall waste away; Sheol shall be their home. •
68: 6 God gives the desolate a home to dwell in; 2
12 women at home divide the spoil 2
84: 3 Even the sparrow finds a home 2
104:17 stork has her home in the fir trees. 2
113: 9 He gives the barren woman a home 2
126: 6 come home with shouts of joy •
Prv 7:11 her feet do not stay at home; 2
19 For my husband is not at home; 2
20 at full moon he will come home. 2
24:15 do not violence to his home; 6
27: 8 from its nest, is a man who strays from his home. 5
30:26 yet they make their homes in the rocks; 2
Ecc 12: 5 because man goes to his eternal home 2
Isa 14:17 who did not let his prisoners go home?' 2
Jer 39:14 son of Shaphan, that he should take him home. 2
Lam 5: 2 turned over to strangers, our homes to aliens. 2
Ezk 36: 8 my people Israel; for they will soon come home. •
37:12 I will bring you home into the land of Israel. •
Hos 11:11 I will return them to their homes, says the LORD. 2
Hag 1: 9 when you brought it home, I blew it away. 2
Mat 8: 6 my servant is lying paralyzed at home 15
9: 6 Rise, take up your bed and go home. 16
7 he rose and went home. 16
17:25 when he came home, Jesus spoke to him first, saying 15
Mrk 2: 1 it was reported that he was at home. 16
11 I say to you, rise, take up your pallet and go home. 9
3:19 Then he went home; 16
5:19 Go home to your friends 9
7:30 she went home, and found the child lying in bed 9
8: 3 if I send them away hungry to their homes 16
26 he sent him away to his home, saying 16
13:34 when he leaves home 15
Lke 1:23 he went to his home. 16
56 returned to her home. 16
5:24 I say to you, rise, take up your bed and go home. 16
25 and went home, glorifying God. 16
8:39 Return to your home 16
9:61 let me first say farewell to those at my home. 16
15: 6 when he comes home, he calls together his friends 9
18:28 Lo, we have left our homes and followed you. 11
23:48 all . . returned home beating their breasts. •
Joh 1:11 He came to his own home •
14:23 we will come to him and make our home with him. 12
16:32 when you will be scattered, every man to his home 11
19:27 the disciple took her to his own home. •
20:10 the disciples went back to their homes. 8
Act 2:46 breaking bread in their homes 16
5:42 every day in the temple and at home 16
21: 6 we went on board the ship, and they returned home. 11
1Co 11:34 if any one is hungry, let him eat at home 16
14:35 let them ask their husbands at home 16
2Co 5: 6 we know that while we are at home in the body 10
8 be away from the body and at home with the Lord. 10
9 So whether we are at home or away 10
1Es 5:47 the sons of Israel were each in his own home •
Tob 2: 1 When I arrived home 16
Jdt 7:32 The women and children he sent home 16
8: 4 Judith had lived at home as a widow 16
Sir 4:30 Do not be like a lion in your home 16
11:29 Do not bring every man into your home 16
26:16 beauty of a good wife in her well-ordered home. 15
32:11 go home quickly and do not linger. 16
36:26 So who will trust a man that has no home 13
39: 3 be at home with the obscurities of parables 7
Sus 1:13 Let us go home, for it is mealtime. 16
52 your sins have now come home •
1Mc 3:56 each should return to his home 16
12:45 Dismiss them now to their homes 16
2Mc 11: 2 He intended to make the city a home for Greeks 14
3Mc 4:18 some still residing in their homes 15
5:21 each departed to his own home. 16
6:25 Who . . has taken each man from his home 15
27 Send them back to their homes in peace 11
37 asking for dismissal to their homes. 11
7: 8 every one to return to his own home 11

home *See also* bring, come, go, leave, make, receive, return, send, take.

homeborn 1. אֶזְרָח 2. יְלִיד בַּיִת
Jos 8:33 And all Israel, sojourner as well as homeborn 1
Jer 2:14 Is Israel a slave? Is he a homeborn servant? 2

homeland 1. πατρίς
Heb 11:14 they are seeking a homeland. 1
4Mc 17:21 and the homeland purified 1
18: 4 by reviving observance of the law in the homeland 1

homeless 1. מָרוּד 2. ἀστατέω
Isa 58: 7 and bring the homeless poor into your house; 1
1Co 4:11 we are ill-clad and buffeted and homeless 2

homer 1. חֹמֶר
Lev 27:16 a sowing of a homer of barley shall be valued 1
Num11:32 he who gathered least gathered ten homers; 1
Isa 5:10 a homer of seed shall yield but an ephah. 1
Ezk 45:11 the bath containing one tenth of a homer 1
11 the ephah one tenth of a homer; 1
11 the homer shall be the standard measure. 1
13 one sixth of an ephah from each homer of wheat 1
13 one sixth of an ephah from each homer of barley 1
14 the cor, like the homer, contains ten baths 1
Hos 3: 2 bought her for . . a homer and a lethech of barley. 1

homicide 1. דָּם
Deu 17: 8 between one kind of homicide and another 1

honest 1. ישר 2. יֹשֶׁר 3. ἀγαθός 4. καλός
1Sm 29: 6 As the LORD lives, you have been honest 1
Job 6:25 How forceful are honest words! 2
Lke 8:15 hold it fast in an honest and good heart 4
Eph 4:28 let him labor, doing honest work with his hands 3
Tit 3: 1 to be obedient, to be ready for any honest work 3

honest *See also* evidence.

honest man 1. כֵּן
Gen 42:11 we are honest men, your servants are not spies. 1
19 if you are honest men, let one . . remain confined 1
31 we said to him, 'We are honest men, we are not spies 1
33 By this I shall know that you are honest men 1
34 know that you are not spies but honest men 1

honestly 1. אֱמוּנָה 2. בֶּאֱמוּנָה
2Kg 12:15 they did not ask . . for they dealt honestly. 2
22: 7 no accounting shall . . for they deal honestly. 2
Isa 59: 4 no one goes to law honestly 1

honesty 1. צְדָקָה
Gen 30:33 my honesty will answer for me later, when you 1

honey 1. דְּבַשׁ 2. נֹפֶת 3. μέλι 4. mel
Gen 43:11 a present, a little balm and a little honey 1
Exd 3: 8 to . . a land flowing with milk and honey 1
17 to . . a land flowing with milk and honey. 1
13: 5 to give you, a land flowing with milk and honey 1
16:31 taste of it was like wafers made with honey. 1
33: 3 Go up to a land flowing with milk and honey; 1
Lev 2:11 no leaven nor any honey as an offering by fire 1
20:24 a land flowing with milk and honey.' I am the LORD 1
Num13:27 flows with milk and honey, and this is its fruit. 1
14: 8 land which flows with milk and honey. 1
16:13 out of a land flowing with milk and honey 1
14 into a land flowing with milk and honey 1
Deu 6: 3 in a land flowing with milk and honey. 1
8: 8 a land of olive trees and honey 1
11: 9 land flowing with milk and honey. 1
26: 9 gave us . . land flowing with milk and honey. 1
15 a land flowing with milk and honey.' 1
27: 3 land flowing with milk and honey, as the LORD 1
31:20 into the land flowing with milk and honey 1
32:13 he made him suck honey out of the rock, and oil 1
Jos 5: 6 a land flowing with milk and honey. 1
Jdg 14: 8 a swarm of bees in the body of the lion, and honey. 1
9 that he had taken the honey from the carcass 1
18 What is sweeter than honey? What is stronger 1
1Sm 14:25 people came . . and there was honey on the ground. 1
26 the honey was dropping, but no man put his hand 1
29 because I tasted a little of this honey. 1
43 I tasted a little honey with the tip of the staff 1
2Sm 17:29 brought . . honey and curds and sheep and cheese 1
1Kg 14: 3 Take . . ten loaves, some cakes, and a jar of honey 1
2Kg 18:32 and vineyards, a land of olive trees and honey 1
2Ch 31: 5 gave in abundance the first fruits of . . honey 1
Job 20:17 the streams flowing with honey and curds. 1
Ps 19:10 sweeter also than honey and drippings 1
81:16 with honey from the rock I would satisfy you. 1
119:103 words to my taste, sweeter than honey to my mouth! 1
Prv 5: 3 For the lips of a loose woman drip honey 2
24:13 My son, eat honey, for it is good 1
25:16 If you have found honey, eat only enough for you 1
27 It is not good to eat much honey 1
27: 7 He who is sated loathes honey 2
Sng 4:11 honey and milk are under your tongue; 1
5: 1 I eat my honeycomb with my honey, I drink my wine 1
Isa 7:15 He shall eat curds and honey 1
22 one . . left in the land will eat curds and honey. 1
Jer 11: 5 to give them a land flowing with milk and honey 1
32:22 to give them, a land flowing with milk and honey; 1
41: 8 we have stores of wheat, barley, oil, and honey 1
Ezk 3: 3 I ate it; and it was in my mouth as sweet as honey. 1
16:13 you ate fine flour and honey and oil. 1
19 I fed you with fine flour and oil and honey 1
20: 6 a land flowing with milk and honey 1
15 had given them, a land flowing with milk and honey 1
27:17 wheat, olives and early figs, honey, oil, and balm. 1
Mat 3: 4 waist; and his food was locusts and wild honey. 3
Mrk 1: 6 ate locusts and wild honey. 3
Rev 10: 9 bitter . . but sweet as honey in your mouth. 3
10 it was sweet as honey in my mouth 3
2Es 2:19 springs flowing with milk and honey 4
Sir 24:20 For the remembrance of me is sweeter than honey 3
39:26 iron and salt and wheat flour and milk and honey 3
46: 8 into a land flowing with milk and honey. 3
49: 1 it is sweet as honey to every mouth 3
Bar 1:20 to give to us a land flowing with milk and honey. 3

honeycomb 1. יַעַר 2. יַעְרַת דְּבַשׁ 3. צוּף 4. צוּף דְּבַשׁ
5. μέλιτος κηρίον
1Sm 14:27 tip of the staff . . and dipped it in the honeycomb 2

Ps 19:10 than honey and drippings of the honeycomb. 3
Prv 16:24 Pleasant words are like a honeycomb 4
Sng 5: 1 I eat my honeycomb with my honey, I drink my wine 1
Sir 24:20 and my inheritance sweeter than the honeycomb. 5

honeycomb *See also* drippings, make.

honor 1. גְּדוּלָּה 2. גדל 3. הדר 4. הָדָר 5. הוד 6. זבל 7. יְקָר 8. כבד 9. כָּבוֹד 10. נְדִיבָה 11. עשה יְקָר 12. שֵׁם 13. תָּמִים 14. תִּפְאָרָה 15. הדר (A) 16. יְקָר (A) 17. αὐξάνω 18. δόξα 19. δοξάζω 20. ἔνδοξος 21. ἐνδόξως 22. ἔντιμον ἔχω 23. ἔντιμος 24. ἐντίμως 25. ἐπί 26. ἐπιδόξως 27. εὔκλεια 28. θαυμάζω 29. κρίσις 30. μεγαλύνω 31. προσκυνέω 32. τιμάω 33. τιμή 34. τίμιος 35. ὕψος 36. nomino

Gen 30:20 now my husband will honor me 6
34:19 Now he was the most honored of all his family. 8
Exd 20:12 Honor your father and your mother, that your days 8
Lev 19:32 You shall . . honor the face of an old man 3
Num22:17 for I will surely do you great honor 8
37 did you not come to me? Am I not able to honor you? 8
24:11 I said, 'I will certainly honor you,' 8
11 but the LORD has held you back from honor. 9
Deu 5:16 'Honor your father and your mother 8
26:19 praise and in fame and in honor 14
Jdg 9: 9 my fatness, by which gods and men are honored 8
16 if you acted in good faith and honor when you made 13
19 if you then have acted in good faith and honor 13
13:17 when your words come true, we may honor you? 8
1Sm 2: 8 to make them sit . . and inherit a seat of honor. 9
29 Why then . . and honor your sons above me 8
30 those who honor me I will honor 8
30 those who honor me I will honor 8
15:30 yet honor me now before the elders of my people 8
22:14 the king's son-in-law . . and honored in your house? 8
2Sm 6:20 How the king of Israel honored himself today 8
10: 3 Do you think . . that he is honoring your father? 8
1Kg 3:13 what you have not asked, both riches and honor 9
1Ch 16:27 Honor and majesty are before him; 5
17:18 can David say to thee for honoring thy servant? 9
19: 3 Do you think . . that he is honoring your father? 8
29:12 riches and honor come from thee, and thou rulest 9
28 in a good old age, full of days, riches, and honor 9
2Ch 1:11 you have not asked possessions, wealth, honor 9
12 will also give you riches, possessions, and honor 9
16:14 they made a very great fire in his honor. •
17: 5 Jehosh'aphat; and he had great riches and honor. 9
18: 1 Now Jehosh'aphat had great riches and honor; 9
21:19 His people made no fire in his honor •
26:18 it will bring you no honor from the LORD God. 9
32:27 Hezeki'ah had very great riches and honor; 9
33 all Judah . . did him honor at his death. 9
Est 1:20 all women will give honor to their husbands 7
5:11 promotions with which the king had honored him 2
6: 3 What honor or dignity has been bestowed 7
6 be done to the man whom the king delights to honor? 7
6 Whom would the king delight to honor more than me? 11
7 For the man whom the king delights to honor 7
9 array the man whom the king delights to honor 7
9 done to the man whom the king delights to honor.' 7
11 done to the man whom the king delights to honor. 7
8:16 Jews had light and gladness and joy and honor. 7
Job 30:15 my honor is pursued as by the wind 10
Ps 4: 2 O men, how long shall my honor suffer shame? 9
8: 5 and dost crown him with glory and honor. 4
15: 4 but who honors those who fear the LORD; 8
50:23 brings thanksgiving as his sacrifice honors me; 8
62: 7 On God rests my deliverance and my honor; 9
71:21 Thou wilt increase my honor, and comfort me 1
84:11 sun and shield; he bestows favor and honor. 9
91:15 in trouble, I will rescue him and honor him. 8
96: 6 Honor and majesty are before him; 5
104: 1 Thou art clothed with honor and majesty 5
111: 3 Full of honor and majesty is his work 5
112: 9 his horn is exalted in honor. 9
Prv 3: 9 Honor the LORD with your substance 8
16 in her left hand are riches and honor. 9
35 wise will inherit honor, but fools get disgrace. 9
4: 8 she will honor you if you embrace her. 8
5: 9 lest you give your honor to others 5
8:18 Riches and honor are with me 9
11:16 A gracious woman gets honor 9
13:18 but he who heeds reproof is honored. 8
14:31 but he who is kind to the needy honors him. 8
15:33 humility goes before honor. 9
18:12 but humility goes before honor. 9
20: 3 It is an honor for a man to keep aloof from strife; 9
21:21 who pursues . . kindness will find life and honor. 9
22: 4 reward . . is riches and honor and life. 9
26: 1 so honor is not fitting for a fool. 9
8 one who binds . . is he who gives honor to a fool. 9
27:18 he who guards his master will be honored. 8
29:23 but he who is lowly in spirit will obtain honor. 9
Ecc 6: 2 to whom God gives wealth, possessions, and honor 9
10: 1 so a little folly outweighs wisdom and honor. 9
Isa 5:13 their honored men are dying of hunger 9
22:23 become a throne of honor to his father's house. 9
23: 8 whose traders were the honored of the earth? 8
9 to dishonor all the honored of the earth. 8
29:13 honor me with their lips, while their hearts are 8
43: 4 Because you are precious in my eyes, and honored 8
20 The wild beasts will honor me 8
23 or honored me with you sacrifices. 8
49: 5 for I am honored in the eyes of the LORD 8
58:13 if you honor it, not going your own ways 8
Lam 1: 8 all who honored her despise her 8
Ezk 39:13 it will redound to their honor 12
Dan 2: 6 receive . . gifts and rewards and great honor. 16
4:34 praised and honored him who lives for ever; 15
37 Now I, Nebuchadnez'zar, praise and extol and honor 15
5:23 whose are all your ways, you have not honored. 15
11:38 honor the god of fortresses instead of these; 8
38 shall honor with gold and silver, 8
39 acknowledge him he shall magnify with honor. 9
Zec 6:13 and shall bear royal honor, and shall sit and rule 5
Mal 1: 6 A son honors his father, and a servant his master. 8
6 If then I am a father, where is my honor? 9
Mat 15: 4 'Honor your father and your mother,' 32
5 he need not honor his father.' 32
8 'This people honors me with their lips 32
19:19 Honor your father and mother 32
Mrk 7: 6 This people honors me with their lips 32
10 For Moses said, 'Honor your father and your mother'; 32
10:19 Do not defraud, Honor your father and mother.' 32
Lke 14:10 then you will be honored in the presence of all 18
18:20 Honor your father and mother.' 32
Joh 4:44 that a prophet has no honor in his own country. 33
5:23 that all may honor the Son 32
23 even as they honor the Father 32
23 He who does not honor the Son 32
23 does not honor the Father who sent him. 32
8:49 I honor my Father, and you dishonor me. 32
12:26 if any one serves me, the Father will honor him. 32
Rom 1:21 they did not honor him as God or give thanks to him 19
2: 7 seek for glory and honor and immortality 18
10 and honor and peace for every one who does good 33
12:10 outdo one another in showing honor. 33
13: 7 honor to whom honor is due. 33
7 honor to whom honor is due. 33
14: 6 He . . observes it in honor of the Lord. •
6 He also who eats, eats in honor of the Lord •
6 he who abstains, abstains in honor of the Lord •
1Co 12:23 we invest with the greater honor 33
24 giving the greater honor to the inferior part 33
26 if one member is honored, all rejoice together. 19
2Co 6: 8 in honor and dishonor 18
Eph 6: 2 Honor your father and mother 32
Php 1:20 Christ will be honored in my body 30
2:29 receive him in the Lord . . and honor such men 22
1Th 4: 4 take a wife for himself in holiness and honor 33
1Ti 1:17 be honor and glory for ever and ever. Amen. 33
5: 3 Honor widows who are real widows. 32
17 be considered worthy of double honor 33
6: 1 regard their masters as worthy of all honor 33
16 To him be honor and eternal dominion. Amen. 33
Heb 2: 7 thou hast crowned him with glory and honor 33
9 crowned with glory and honor 33
3: 3 the builder of a house has more honor than the house. 33
5: 4 one does not take the honor upon himself 33
1Pe 1: 7 and honor at the revelation of Jesus Christ. 33
2:17 Honor all men. Love the brotherhood. Fear God. 32
17 Fear God. Honor the emperor. 32
3: 7 bestowing honor on the woman as the weaker sex 33
2Pe 1:17 he received honor and glory from God the Father 33
Rev 4: 9 creatures give glory and honor and thanks to him 33
11 Lord and God, to receive glory and honor and power 33
5:12 to receive . . honor and glory and blessing! 33
13 to the Lamb be blessing and honor and glory 33
7:12 honor and power and might be to our God for ever 33
21:26 the glory and the honor of the nations. 33
1Es 8: 4 the king showed him honor 18
26 who honored me in the sight of the king 32
67 these officials honored the people 19
9:45 he had the place of honor 26
2Es 7:60 and through them my name has now been honored. 36
Tob 3:11 blessed is thy holy and honored name for ever. 23
4: 3 Honor her all the days of your life 32
10:12 Honor your father-in-law and your mother-in-law 32
14:13 He grew old with honor 24
Jdt 12:13 come to my lord and be honored in his presence 19
13:20 May God grant this to be a perpetual honor to you 33
16:21 was honored in her time 20
AEs 14:17 I have not honored the king's feast 19
16: 2 The more often they are honored 32
Wis 4: 8 For old age is not honored for length of time 34
6:21 honor wisdom, that you may reign for ever. 32
8:10 and honor in the presence of the elders 18
10:14 she gave him everlasting honor. 18
14:15 he now honored as a god 32
17 men could not honor monarchs in their presence 32
17 a visible image of the king whom they honored 32
20 shortly before they had honored as a man. 32
Sir 2: 3 that you may be honored at the end of your life. 17
3: 2 the Lord honored the father above the children 19
3 Whoever honors his father atones for sins 33
5 Whoever honors his father will be gladdened 33
8 Honor your father by word and deed 32
11 For a man's glory comes from honoring his father 33
7: 4 nor the seat of honor from the king. 18
27 With all your heart honor your father 19
29 fear the Lord, and honor his priests. 28
31 Fear the Lord and honor the priest 19
9:11 Do not envy the honors of a sinner 18
10: 5 confers his honor upon the person of the scribe. 18
23 nor is it proper to honor a sinful man. 19
24 the ruler will be honored 19
28 ascribe to yourself honor 33
29 who will honor the man that dishonors his own life? 19
30 A poor man is honored for his knowledge 19
30 while a rich man is honored for his wealth. 19
31 A man honored in poverty, how much more in wealth! 19
11: 4 exalt yourself in the day that you are honored 18
24:12 I took root in an honored people 19
29:27 Give place, stranger, to an honored person 18
33:22 bring no stain upon your honor. 18
38: 1 Honor the physician with the honor due him 32
1 Honor the physician with the honor due him 33
16 Lay out his body with the honor due him 29
44: 7 all these were honored in their generations 19
46:12 the name of those who have been honored 19
47:20 You put stain upon your honor 18
49:16 Shem and Seth were honored among men 19
Bel 1: 2 was the most honored of his friends. 20
1Mc 1:39 her honor into contempt. 33
2:17 You are a leader, honored and great in this city 20
18 your sons will be honored with silver and gold 19
51 receive great honor and an everlasting name. 18
5:63 his brothers were greatly honored in all Israel 19
7:26 the king sent Nicanor, one of his honored princes 20
9:10 and leave no cause to question our honor. 18
10: 3 sent Jonathan a letter . . to honor him; 30
24 and promise them honor and gifts 35
64 when his accusers saw the honor that was paid him 18
65 Thus the king honored him 19
88 he honored Jonathan still more; 19
11:27 in as many other honors as he had formerly had 34
12: 8 Onias welcomed the envoy with honor 21
43 So he received him with honor 21
14: 4 as was the honor shown him, all his days. 18
5 To crown all his honors he took Joppa for a harbor 18
21 told us about your glory and honor 33
23 to receive these men with honor 21
39 and paid him high honors. 18
40 Romans had received the envoys of Simon with honor. 21
15: 9 we will bestow great honor upon you 18
2Mc 3: 2 the kings themselves honored the place 32
12 which is honored throughout the whole world. 32
4:15 disdaining the honors prized by their fathers 18
5:16 to enhance the glory and honor of the place. 33
6: 7 to walk in the procession in honor of Dionysus •
19 welcoming death with honor 27
13:23 honored the sanctuary 32
3Mc 1:12 Even if those men are deprived of this honor 33
2: 9 the glory of your great and honored name. 23
3:16 to honor the temple of those wicked people 32
17 honor it with magnificent . . offerings 32
4:16 organizing feasts in honor of all his idols 25
7:21 being held in honor and awe 18
4Mc 1:10 the honor in which they are held. 33
5:12 honoring my humane advice? 31
35 nor will I reject you, honored priesthood 34
11: 6 these deeds deserve honors, not tortures. 33
17: 5 who . . stand in honor before God 23
20 These . . are honored, not only with this honor 32
20 These . . are honored, not only with this honor 33

honor *See also* bestow, come, gain, give, hold, lady, pay, place, seat, thirst, unworthy, win, worthy.

honor above other 1. προτιμάω

2Mc 15: 2 has honored and hallowed above other days 1

great honor 1. ἔνδοξος

AEs 12: 6 was in great honor with the king 1

high honor 1. גְּדוּלָּה

Est 10: 2 the full account of the high honor of Mor'decai 1

honor of victory 1. ἐπινίκιος

1Es 3: 5 give rich gifts and great honors of victory. 1

show honor 1. נשא פָּנִים

Lam 4:16 no honor was shown to the priests 1

without honor 1. ἄδοξος 2. ἄτιμος

Mat 13:57 A prophet is not without honor 2
Mrk 6: 4 Jesus said to them, "A prophet is not without honor 2
Wis 3:17 finally their old age will be without honor. 2
5: 4 his end was without honor. 2
1Mc 2: 8 Her temple has become like a man without honor; 1

honorable 1. כבד 2. שׁוֹעַ 3. ἀγαθός 4. καλός 5. σεμνός

Num22:15 princes, more in number and more honorable 1
1Ch 4: 9 Jabez was more honorable than his brothers; 1
Isa 3: 5 insolent . . the base fellow to the honorable. 1

32: 5 nor the knave said to be honorable. 2
58:13 a delight and the holy day of the LORD honorable; 1
2Co 8:21 we aim at what is honorable 4
Php 4: 8 whatever is honorable, whatever is just 5
Jas 2: 7 Is it not they who blaspheme that honorable name 4
2Mc 7:20 admirable and worthy of honorable memory 3
4Mc 5:36 shall not stain the honorable mouth of my old age 5

less honorable 1. ἄτιμος
1Co 12:23 those parts of the body which we think less honorable 1

honorable man 1. δοξάζω
Sir 25: 5 understanding and counsel in honorable men! 1

honorably 1. ἀμέμπτως 2. ἀστείως 3. καλῶς
Heb 13:18 desiring to act honorably in all things. 3
AEs 13: 4 which we honorably intend 1
2Mc 12:43 In doing this he acted very well and honorably 2

honored *See* much.

make honored 1. כבד
Jer 30:19 I will make them honored 1

honored man 1. כבד 2. נשׂא פָּנִים
Isa 9:15 the elder and honored man is the head 2
Nah 3:10 for her honored men lots were cast 1

most honored 1. ἔνδοξος
Sus 1: 4 because he was the most honored of them all. 1
1Mc 1: 6 So he summoned his most honored officers 1

honored one 1. ἔντιμος
3Mc 6:13 O honored One, who have power to save 1

hoof 1. עָקֵב 2. פרס 3. פַּרְסָה 4. ὁπλή
Exd 10:26 Our cattle . . not a hoof shall be left behind 3
Lev 11: 3 Whatever parts the hoof and is cloven-footed 3
4 chew the cud or part the hoof, you shall not eat 3
4 chews the cud but does not part the hoof 3
5 it chews the cud but does not part the hoof 3
6 chews the cud but does not part the hoof 3
7 because it parts the hoof and is cloven-footed 3
26 Every animal which parts the hoof but is not 3
Deu 14: 6 Every animal that parts the hoof and has the hoof 3
6 Every animal that . . has the hoof cloven in two 3
7 of those that chew the cud or have the hoof cloven 3
7 because they chew the cud but do not part the hoof 3
8 parts the hoof but does not chew the cud 3
Jdg 5:22 loud beat the horses' hoofs with the galloping 1
Ps 69:31 more than an ox or a bull with horns and hoofs. 2
Isa 5:28 their horses' hoofs seem like flint 3
Jer 47: 3 At the noise of the stamping of the hoofs 3
Ezk 26:11 With the hoofs of his horses he will trample 3
32:13 nor shall the hoofs of beasts trouble them. 3
Mic 4:13 I will make your horn iron and your hoofs bronze; 3
Zec 11:16 of the fat ones, tearing off even their hoofs. 3
2Mc 3:25 struck at him with its front hoofs 4

hoofbeat 1. פַּעַם
Jdg 5:28 Why tarry the hoofbeats of his chariots?' 1

hook 1. וָו 2. חוֹחַ 3. חַח 4. חַכָּה 5. צִנָּה 6. קֶרֶס 7. שְׁפַתַּיִם 8. ἄγκιστρον 9. ὄνυξ 10. τροχαντήρ
Exd 26:32 acacia overlaid with gold, with hooks of gold 1
37 their hooks shall be of gold 1
27:10 the hooks of the pillars and their fillets 1
11 the hooks of the pillars and their fillets shall 1
17 their hooks shall be of silver 1
35:11 its hooks and its frames, its bars, its pillars 6
36:36 their hooks were of gold, and he cast for them four 1
38 its five pillars with their hooks. 1
38:10 the hooks of the pillars and their fillets were 1
11 but the hooks of the pillars and their fillets 1
12 hooks of the pillars and their fillets were 1
17 the hooks of the pillars . . were of silver; 1
19 four bases were of bronze, their hooks of silver 1
28 he made hooks for the pillars 1
39:33 all its utensils, its hooks, its frames, its bars 6
2Kg 19:28 I will put my hook in your nose and my bit 3
2Ch 33:11 who took Manas'seh with hooks and bound him 2
Job 40:24 Can one take him with hooks, or pierce his nose •
41: 2 rope in his nose, or pierce his jaw with a hook? 2
Isa 19: 8 mourn and lament, all who cast hook in the Nile; 4
37:29 I will put my hook in your nose 3
Ezk 19: 4 they brought him with hooks to the land of Egypt. 3
9 With hooks they put him in a cage, and brought him 3
29: 4 I will put hooks in your jaws 3
38: 4 I will turn you about, and put hooks into your jaws 3
40:43 And hooks, a handbreadth long, were fastened 7
Ams 4: 2 when they shall take you away with hooks 5
Hab 1:15 He brings all of them up with a hook 4
Mat 17:27 go to the sea and cast a hook 8
4Mc 8:13 rack and hooks and catapults and caldrons 10
9:26 with iron gauntlets having sharp hooks 9

pruning hook 1. מַזְמֵרָה
Isa 2: 4 plowshares, and their spears into pruning hooks; 1
18: 5 he will cut off the shoots with pruning hooks 1
Jol 3:10 into swords, and your pruning hooks into spears; 1
Mic 4: 3 shall beat . . their spears into pruning hooks; 1

hoopoe 1. דּוּכִיפַת
Lev 11:19 the stork . . the hoopoe and the bat 1
Deu 14:18 stork, the heron . . the hoopoe and the bat. 1

hoot 1. שׁיר
Zep 2:14 the owl shall hoot in the window 1

hope 1. בִּטָּחוֹן 2. יחל 3. כֶּסֶל 4. מַבָּט 5. מִבְטָח 6. מִקְוֶה 7. קוה 8. שׂבר 9. שֵׂבֶר 10. תּוֹחֶלֶת 11. תִּקְוָה 12. εἰ ἄρα γε 13. ἐλπίζω 14. ἐλπίς 15. ἔχω ἐλπίδα 16. spero 17. spes
Rut 1:12 If I should say I have hope, even . . have a husband 11
Ezr 10: 2 there is hope for Israel in spite of this. 6
Est 9: 1 enemies of the Jews hoped to get the mastery over 8
Job 3: 9 let it hope for light, but have none 7
4: 6 and the integrity of your ways your hope? 11
5:16 poor have hope, and injustice shuts her mouth. 11
6:19 of Tema look, the travelers of Sheba hope. 7
7: 6 and come to their end without hope. 11
8:13 the hope of the godless man shall perish. 11
11:18 you will have confidence, because there is hope; 11
20 their hope is to breathe their last. 11
13:15 Behold, he will slay me; I have no hope; 2
14: 7 For there is hope for a tree, if it be cut down 11
19 so thou destroyest the hope of man. 11
17:15 where then is my hope? Who will see my hope? 11
15 where then is my hope? Who will see my hope? 11
19:10 I am gone, and my hope has he pulled up like a tree. 11
27: 8 what is the hope of the godless when God cuts him 11
41: 9 Behold, the hope of a man is disappointed; 10
Ps 9:18 the hope of the poor shall not perish for ever. 11
33:18 on those who hope in his steadfast love 2
22 love, O LORD, be upon us, even as we hope in thee. 2
39: 7 now, Lord, for what do I wait? My hope is in thee. 10
42: 5 Hope in God; for I shall again praise him, my help 2
11 Hope in God; for I shall again praise him 2
43: 5 why are you disquieted within me? Hope in God; 2
62: 5 my soul waits in silence, for my hope is from him. 11
65: 5 God . . who art the hope of all the ends of the earth 5
69: 6 Let not those who hope in thee be put to shame 7
71: 5 For thou, O Lord, art my hope 11
14 I will hope continually, and will praise thee yet 2
78: 7 that they should set their hope in God 3
119:43 my hope is in thy ordinances. 2
74 rejoice, because I have hoped in thy word. 2
81 I hope in thy word. 2
114 I hope in thy word. 2
116 let me not be put to shame in my hope! 9
147 I . . cry for help; I hope in thy words. 2
166 I hope for thy salvation, O LORD 8
130: 5 for the LORD, my soul waits, and in his word I hope; 2
7 O Israel, hope in the LORD! 2
131: 3 O Israel, hope in the LORD from this time forth 2
146: 5 Happy is he whose . . hope is in the LORD his God 9
147:11 pleasure . . who hope in his steadfast love. 2
Prv 10:28 The hope of the righteous ends in gladness 10
11: 7 When the wicked dies, his hope perishes 11
13:12 Hope deferred makes the heart sick 10
19:18 Discipline your son while there is hope; 11
23:18 your hope will not be cut off. 11
24:14 if you find it . . your hope will not be cut off. 11
26:12 There is more hope for a fool than for him. 11
29:20 There is more hope for a fool than for him. 11
Ecc 9: 4 But he who is joined with all the living has hope 1
Isa 8:17 for the LORD . . and I will hope in him. 7
20: 5 confounded because of Ethiopia their hope 4
6 what has happened to those in whom we hoped 4
38:18 to the pit cannot hope for thy faithfulness. 8
51: 5 coastlands wait for me, and for my arm they hope. 2
Jer 14: 8 O thou hope of Israel, its savior 6
17:13 O LORD, the hope of Israel 6
29:11 and not for evil, to give you a future and a hope. 11
31:17 There is hope for your future, says the LORD 11
50: 7 the LORD, the hope of their fathers. 6
Lam 3:21 But this I call to mind, and therefore I have hope 2
24 therefore I will hope in him. 2
29 his mouth in the dust-there may yet be hope; 11
Ezk 19: 5 saw that she was baffled, that her hope was lost 11
37:11 our hope is lost; we are clean cut off 11
Hos 2:15 and make the Valley of Achor a door of hope. 11
Zec 9: 5 Ekron also, because its hopes are confounded. 4
12 Return to your stronghold, O prisoners of hope; 11
Mat 12:21 in his name will the Gentiles hope. 13
Lke 6:34 if you lend to those from whom you hope to receive 13
23: 8 he was hoping to see some sign done by him. 13
24:21 we had hoped that he was the one to redeem Israel. 13
Act 2:26 moreover my flesh will dwell in hope. 14
16:19 her owners saw that their hope of gain was gone 14
17:27 in the hope that they might feel after him 12
23: 6 the hope and the resurrection of the dead 14
24:15 having a hope in God which these . . accept 14
26 he hoped that money would be given him by Paul 13
26: 6 here on trial for hope in the promise made by God 14
7 to which our twelve tribes hope to attain 13
7 for this hope I am accused by Jews, O king! 14
27:20 all hope of our being saved was . . abandoned. 14
28:20 since it is because of the hope of Israel 14
Rom 4:18 In hope he believed against hope 14
18 In hope he believed against hope 14
5: 2 we rejoice in our hope of sharing the glory of God. 14
4 and character produces hope 14
5 and hope does not disappoint us 14
8:20 by the will of him who subjected it in hope; 14
24 For in this hope we were saved. 14
24 Now hope that is seen is not hope. 14
24 Now hope that is seen is not hope. 14
24 For who hopes for what he sees? 14
25 if we hope for what we do not see, we wait for it 13
12:12 Rejoice in your hope, be patient in tribulation 14
15: 4 by steadfastness . . we might have hope. 14
12 in him shall the Gentiles hope. 13
13 May the God of hope fill you with all joy and peace 14
13 of the Holy Spirit you may abound in hope. 14
24 I hope to see you in passing as I go to Spain 13
1Co 9:10 because the plowman should plow in hope 14
10 the thresher thresh in hope of a share in the crop. 14
13: 7 hopes all things, endures all things. 13
13 So faith, hope, love abide, these three 14
15:19 If for this life only we have hoped in Christ 13
16: 7 I hope to spend some time with you 13
2Co 1: 7 Our hope for you is unshaken 14
13 I hope you will understand fully 13
3:12 Since we have such a hope, we are very bold 14
5:11 I hope it is known also to your conscience. 13
10:15 our hope is that as your faith increases 14
13: 6 I hope you will find out that we have not failed. 13
Gal 5: 5 we wait for the hope of righteousness. 14
Eph 1:18 know what is the hope to which he has called you 14
2:12 having no hope and without God in the world. 14
4: 4 just as you were called to the one hope 14
Php 1:20 as it is my eager expectation and hope 14
2:19 I hope in the Lord Jesus to send Timothy to you 13
23 I hope therefore to send him 13
Col 1: 5 because of the hope laid up for you in heaven 14
23 not shifting from the hope of the gospel 14
27 which is Christ in you, the hope of glory. 14
1Th 1: 3 steadfastness of hope in our Lord Jesus Christ. 14
2:19 For what is our hope or joy or crown of boasting 14
4:13 you may not grieve as others do who have no hope 14
5: 8 for a helmet the hope of salvation. 14
2Th 2:16 eternal comfort and good hope through grace 14
1Ti 1: 1 God our Savior and of Christ Jesus our hope 14
3:14 I hope to come to you soon 13
6:17 nor to set their hopes on uncertain riches 13
Tit 1: 2 in hope of eternal life 14
2:13 awaiting our blessed hope 14
3: 7 become heirs in hope of eternal life. 14
Phm 1:22 I am hoping . . to be granted to you. 13
Heb 3: 6 hold fast our confidence and pride in our hope. 14
6:11 the full assurance of hope until the end 14
18 to seize the hope set before us. 14
19 a hope that enters into the inner shrine •
7:19 on the other hand, a better hope is introduced 14
10:23 Let us hold fast the confession of our hope 14
1Pe 1: 3 we have been born anew to a living hope 14
21 so that your faith and hope are in God. 14
3: 5 women who hoped in God used to adorn themselves 13
15 calls you to account for the hope that is in you 14
1Jn 3: 3 every one who thus hopes in him purifies himself 15
2Jn 1:12 I hope to come to see you and talk with you 13
3Jn 1:14 I hope to see you soon 13
1Es 8:92 even now there is hope for Israel. 14
2Es 5:12 at that time men shall hope but not obtain 16
7:18 while hoping for easier ones 16
120 that an everlasting hope has been promised to us 17
11:46 and may hope for the judgment and mercy of him 16
Tob 10: 7 have given up hope of ever seeing me again. 13
Jdt 6: 9 hope in your heart that they will not be taken 13
8:20 therefore we hope that he will not disdain us 13
13:19 Your hope will never depart 14
Wis 2:22 nor hope for the wages of holiness 13
3: 4 their hope is full of immortality. 14
11 Their hope is vain 14
18 If they die young, they will have no hope 14
5:14 Because the hope of the ungodly man is like chaff 14
13:10 miserable, with their hopes set on dead things 14
14: 6 the hope of the world took refuge on a raft 14
15: 6 and fit for such objects of hope 14
10 His heart is ashes, his hope is cheaper than dirt 14
16:29 the hope of an ungrateful man 14
Sir 2: 6 make your ways straight, and hope in him. 13
9 you who fear the Lord, hope for good things 13
13: 6 he will smile at you and give you hope 14
14: 2 has not given up his hope. 14
34: 1 A man of no understanding has vain and false hopes 14
13 their hope is in him who saves them. 14
14 nor play the coward, for he is his hope. 14
49:10 delivered them with confident hope. 14
Sus 1:60 blessed God, who saves those who hope in him. 13
2Mc 2:18 we have hope in God 13
3:29 deprived of any hope of recovery 14
7:11 from him I hope to get them back again. 13
14 cherish the hope that God gives 14
20 because of her hope in the Lord. 14

34 and puffed up by uncertain hopes 14
9:20 As my hope is in heaven 14
22 I have good hope of recovering from my illness 14
4Mc 17: 4 maintaining firm an enduring hope in God. 14

hope *See also* fill, give, put, set.

hope first 1. προελπίζω
Eph 1:12 we who first hoped in Christ 1

good hope 1. εὔελπις
Wis 12:19 thou hast filled thy sons with good hope 1

make hope 1. יחל
Ps 119:49 thy word . . in which thou hast made me hope. 1

hope of finding 1. τυγχάνω
2Mc 5: 9 in hope of finding protection 1

vain hope 1. כזב 2. שֶׁקֶר
Ps 33:17 The war horse is a vain hope for victory 2
116:11 I said . . "Men are all a vain hope. 1

without hope 1. ἀπελπίζω
Jdt 9:11 savior of those without hope. 1
Sir 27:21 whoever has betrayed secrets is without hope. 1

thing hoped 1. ἐλπίζω
Heb 11: 1 Now faith is the assurance of things hoped for 1

resolutely hopeful 1. εὔελπις
3Mc 2:33 They remained resolutely hopeful of obtaining help 1

hopeless 1. יאשׁ
Isa 57:10 but you did not say, "It is hopeless"; 1
Jer 2:25 It is hopeless, for I have loved strangers 1

hopelessly 1. εἰς τέλος
Sir 12:11 will know that it was not hopelessly tarnished. 1

hopper 1. יֶלֶק
Jol 2:25 the hopper, the destroyer, and the cutter 1

hopping *See* locust.

horde 1. אֲגַף 2. הָמוֹן 3. קָהָל 4. πλῆθος
Num22: 4 horde will now lick up all that is round about us 3
2Ch 32: 7 king of Assyria and all the horde that is with him; 2
Ezk 38: 6 Gomer and all his hordes; 1
6 with all his hordes–many peoples are with you. 1
9 and all your hordes, and many peoples with you. 1
22 rain upon him and his hordes and the many peoples 1
39: 4 all your hordes and the peoples that are with you; 1
2Mc 2:21 pursued the barbarian hordes 4

horn 1. קרן 2. קֶרֶן 3. שׁוֹפָר 4. תּוֹעָפָה 5. קֶרֶן (A) 6. κέρας
Gen 22:13 a ram, caught in a thicket by his horns; 2
Exd 27: 2 you shall make horns for it on its four corners; 2
2 its horns shall be of one piece with it 2
29:12 the blood . . put it upon the horns of the altar 2
30: 2 its horns shall be of one piece with it. 2
3 its top and its sides round about and its horns; 2
10 Aaron shall make atonement upon its horns 2
37:25 its horns were of one piece with it. 2
26 top, and its sides round about, and its horns; 2
38: 2 He made horns for it on its four corners; 2
2 its horns were of one piece with it 2
Lev 4: 7 some of the blood on the horns of the altar 2
18 the blood on the horns of the altar 2
25 put it on the horns of the altar of burnt offering 2
30 put it on the horns of the altar of burnt offering 2
34 put it on the horns of the altar of burnt offering 2
8:15 put it on the horns of the altar round about 2
9: 9 in the blood and put it on the horns of the altar 2
16:18 blood . . and put it on the horns of the altar 2
Num23:22 they have as it were the horns of the wild ox. 4
24: 8 he has as it were the horns of the wild ox 4
Deu 33:17 his horns are the horns of a wild ox; 2
17 his horns are the horns of a wild ox; 2
Jos 6: 5 when they make a long blast with the ram's horn 2
1Sm 16: 1 Fill your horn with oil, and go; I will send you 2
13 Then Samuel took the horn of oil, and anointed him 2
2Sm 6:15 with shouting, and with the sound of the horn. 3
22: 3 my God . . my shield and the horn of my salvation 2
1Kg 1:39 There Zadok . . took the horn of oil from the tent 2
50 went, and caught hold of the horns of the altar. 2
51 he has laid hold of the horns of the altar, saying 2
2:28 LORD and caught hold of the horns of the altar. 2
22:11 Zedeki'ah . . made for himself horns of iron 2
1Ch 15:28 the sound of the horn, trumpets, and cymbals 3
2Ch 15:14 took oath to the LORD . . with horns. 3
18:10 Zedeki'ah . . made for himself horns of iron 2
Ps 18: 2 my shield, and the horn of my salvation 2
22:21 my afflicted soul from the horns of the wild oxen! 2
69:31 more than an ox or a bull with horns and hoofs. 1
75: 4 and to the wicked, "Do not lift up your horn; 2
5 do not lift up your horn on high 2
10 All the horns of the wicked he will cut off 2
10 the horns of the righteous shall be exalted. 2
89:17 by thy favor our horn is exalted. 2
24 in my name shall his horn be exalted. 2
92:10 thou hast exalted my horn like that of the wild ox; 2
98: 6 With trumpets and the sound of the horn 3
112: 9 his horn is exalted in honor. 2
118:27 up to the horns of the altar! 2
132:17 There I will make a horn to sprout for David; 2
148:14 He has raised up a horn for his people 2
Jer 17: 1 of their heart, and on the horns of their altars 2
48:25 The horn of Moab is cut off, and his arm is broken 2
Ezk 29:21 On that day I will cause a horn to spring forth 2
34:21 and thrust at all the weak with your horns 2
43:15 projecting upward, four horns, one cubit high. 2
20 its blood, and put it on the four horns of the altar 2
Dan 3: 5 hear the sound of the horn, pipe, lyre, trigon 5
7 heard the sound of the horn, pipe, lyre, trigon 5
10 hears the sound of the horn, pipe, lyre, trigon 5
15 hear the sound of the horn, pipe, lyre, trigon 5
7: 7 It was different . . and it had ten horns. 5
8 I considered the horns, and behold, there came up 5
8 came up among them another horn, a little one 5
8 before which three of the first horns 5
8 horn were eyes like the eyes of a man, and a mouth 5
11 great words which the horn was speaking. 5
20 concerning the ten horns that were on its head 5
20 other horn which came up and before which three •
20 horn which had eyes and a mouth that spoke great 5
21 horn made war with the saints, and prevailed over 5
24 As for the ten horns, out of this kingdom 5
8: 3 It had two horns; and both horns were high, 2
3 both horns were high, but one was higher 2
5 goat had a conspicuous horn between his eyes. 2
6 He came to the ram with the two horns 2
7 struck the ram and broke his two horns; 2
8 when he was strong, the great horn was broken 2
8 there came up four conspicuous horns •
9 Out of one of them came forth a little horn 2
12 horn acted and prospered. •
20 As for the ram which you saw with the two horns 2
21 great horn between his eyes is the first king. 2
22 As for the horn that was broken, •
Hos 5: 8 Blow the horn in Gib'e-ah, the trumpet in Ramah. 3
Ams 3:14 and the horns of the altar shall be cut off 2
Mic 4:13 I will make your horn iron and your hoofs bronze; 2
Zec 1:18 I lifted my eyes and saw, and behold, four horns! 2
19 These are the horns which have scattered Judah 2
21 These are the horns which scattered Judah 2
21 to cast down the horns of the nations who lifted 2
21 the nations who lifted up their horns 2
Lke 1:69 and has raised up a horn of salvation for us 6
Rev 5: 6 a Lamb . . with seven horns and . . seven eyes 6
9:13 a voice from the four horns of the golden altar 6
12: 3 great red dragon, with seven heads and ten horns 6
13: 1 I saw a beast . . with ten horns and seven heads 6
1 a beast . . with ten diadems upon its horns 6
11 it had two horns like a lamb 6
17: 3 and it had seven heads and ten horns. 6
7 and of the beast with seven heads and ten horns 6
12 And the ten horns that you saw are ten kings 6
16 And the ten horns that you saw, they and the beast 6
Jdt 9: 8 to cast down the horn of thy altar with the sword. 6

horn *See also* ram's.

hornet 1. צִרְעָה
Exd 23:28 I will send hornets before you, which shall drive 1
Deu 7:20 LORD your God will send hornets among them 1
Jos 24:12 I sent the hornet before you, which drove them out 1

horrible thing 1. שַׁעֲרוּרָה 2. שַׁעֲרוּרִיָּה
Jer 5:30 An . . and horrible thing has happened in the land 1
18:13 virgin Israel has done a very horrible thing. 2
23:14 have seen a horrible thing: they commit adultery 1
Hos 6:10 In . . Israel I have seen a horrible thing; 2

horribly
Ezk 27:35 their kings are horribly afraid †

horrify 1. שׁמם
Jer 18:16 Every one who passes by it is horrified 1
19: 8 every one who passes by it will be horrified 1
49:17 every one who passes by it will be horrified 1
Ezk 20:26 that I might horrify them; 1

horror 1. זַעֲוָה 2. מְחִתָּה 3. מְשַׁמָּה 4. פַּלָּצוּת 5. שַׂעַר 6. שַׁמָּה 7. תִּפְלֶצֶת
Deu 28:25 be a horror to all the kingdoms of the earth. 1
37 you shall become a horror, a proverb, and a byword 6
Job 18:20 horror seizes them of the east. 5
Ps 31:11 a horror to my neighbors, an object of dread •
55: 5 come upon me, and horror overwhelms me. 4
Isa 21: 4 My mind reels, horror has appalled me; 4
Jer 15: 4 I will make them a horror to all the kingdoms 1
18:16 making their land a horror, a thing to be hissed 6
19: 8 And I will make this city a horror 6
24: 9 I will make them a horror to all the kingdoms 1
25: 9 and make them a horror, a hissing 6
29:18 them a horror to all the kingdoms of the earth 1
34:17 I will make you a horror to all the kingdoms 1
42:18 You shall become an execration, a horror, a curse 6
44:12 they shall become an execration, a horror, a curse 6
48:39 Moab has become a derision and a horror to all 2
49:13 says the LORD, that Bozrah shall become a horror 6
16 The horror you inspire has deceived you 7
17 Edom shall become a horror; 6
50:23 How Babylon has become a horror among the nations! 6
51:37 the haunt of jackals, a horror and a hissing 6
41 How Babylon has become a horror among the nations! 6
43 Her cities have become a horror, a land of drought 6
Ezk 5:15 a warning and a horror, to the nations round about 3
7:18 horror covers them; shame is upon all faces 4
23:33 A cup of horror and desolation 6

horror *See also* object.

thing of horror 1. תּוֹעֵבָה
Ps 88: 8 thou hast made me a thing of horror to them. 1

horror-stricken 1. horreo
2Es 15:37 who see that wrath shall be horror-stricken 1

horse 1. סוּס 2. פָּרָשׁ 3. ἵππος 4. equus
Gen 47:17 Joseph gave them food in exchange for the horses 1
49:17 a viper . . that bites the horse's heels 1
Exd 9: 3 plague upon . . the horses, the asses, the camels 1
14: 9 all Pharaoh's horses and chariots and his 1
23 Pharaoh's horses, his chariots, and his horsemen. 1
15: 1 the horse and his rider he has thrown into the sea. 1
19 For when the horses of Pharaoh with his chariots 1
21 the horse and his rider he has thrown 1
Deu 11: 4 did to . . their horses and to their chariots; 1
17:16 Only he must not multiply horses for himself 1
16 in order to multiply horses 1
20: 1 see horses and chariots and an army larger 1
Jos 11: 4 they came . . with very many horses and chariots. 1
6 you shall hamstring their horses 1
9 Joshua . . hamstrung their horses 1
Jdg 5:22 loud beat the horses' hoofs with the galloping 1
2Sm 15: 1 Ab'salom got himself a chariot and horses 1
1Kg 4:26 Solomon also had 40,000 stalls of horses 1
28 and straw for the horses . . they brought 1
10:25 garments, myrrh, spices, horses, and mules 1
28 Solomon's import of horses was from Egypt and Ku'e 1
29 could be imported . . a horse for 150; 1
18: 5 find grass and save the horses and mules alive 1
20: 1 32 kings were with him, and horses and chariots; 1
20 Ben-ha'dad . . escaped on a horse with horsemen. 1
21 went out, and captured the horses and chariots 1
25 horse for horse, and chariot for chariot; 1
25 horse for horse, and chariot for chariot; 1
22: 4 I am as you are . . my horses as your horses. 1
4 I am as you are . . my horses as your horses. 1
2Kg 2:11 a chariot . . and horses of fire separated the two 1
3: 7 I am as you are . . my horses as your horses. 1
7 I am as you are . . my horses as your horses. 1
5: 9 So Na'aman came with his horses and chariots 1
6:14 he sent . . horses and chariots and a great army; 1
15 an army with horses and chariots was round about 1
17 mountain was full of horses and chariots of fire 1
7: 6 the sound of chariots, and of horses . . of a great 1
7 and forsook their tents, their horses 1
10 there was no one . . nothing but the horses tied 1
13 Let some men take five of the remaining horses 1
9:33 her blood spattered on the wall and on the horses 1
10: 2 there are with you chariots and horses 1
11:16 she went through the horses' entrance 1
14:20 they brought him upon horses; and he was buried 1
18:23 I will give you 2,000 horses 1
23:11 he removed the horses . . dedicated to the sun 1
2Ch 1:16 Solomon's import of horses was from Egypt and Ku'e 1
17 imported . . a horse for 150; 1
9:24 his present . . myrrh, spices, horses, and mules 1
25 Solomon had 4,000 stalls for horses and chariots 1
28 horses were imported for Solomon from Egypt 1
23:15 the entrance of the horse gate of the king's house 1
25:28 they brought him upon horses; and he was buried 1
Ezr 2:66 Their horses were 736, their mules were 245 1
Neh 7:68 Their horses were 736, their mules 245 3
Est 6: 8 and the horse which the king has ridden 1
9 let the robes and the horse be handed over to one 1
10 take the robes and the horse, as you have said 1
11 Haman took the robes and the horse 1
Job 39:18 she laughs at the horse and his rider. 1
19 Do you give the horse his might? 1
Ps 20: 7 Some boast of chariots, and some of horses; 1
32: 9 Be not like a horse or a mule 1
33:17 The war horse is a vain hope for victory 1
76: 6 O God of Jacob, both rider and horse lay stunned. 1
147:10 His delight is not in the strength of the horse 1
Prv 21:31 The horse is made ready for the day of battle 1
26: 3 A whip for the horse, a bridle for the ass, and a rod 1
Ecc 10: 7 I have seen slaves on horses, and princes walking 1
Isa 2: 7 their land is filled with horses 1
5:28 their horses' hoofs seem like flint 1
28:28 he drives his cart wheel over it with his horses 2
30:16 you said, "No! We will speed upon horses 1
31: 1 who go down to Egypt for help and rely on horses 1
3 their horses are flesh, and not spirit. 1

36: 8 I will give you 2,000 horses 1
43:17 who brings forth chariot and horse 1
63:13 Like a horse in the desert, they did not stumble. 1
66:20 offering to the LORD, upon horses, and in chariots 1
Jer 4:13 his horses are swifter than eagles 1
6:23 they ride upon horses, set in array 1
8: 6 like a horse plunging headlong into battle. 1
16 The snorting of their horses is heard from Dan; 1
12: 5 how will you compete with horses? 1
17:25 kings . . riding in chariots and on horses 1
22: 4 riding in chariots and on horses 1
31:40 to the corner of the Horse Gate toward the east 1
46: 4 Harness the horses; mount, O horsemen! 1
9 Advance, O horses, and rage, O chariots! 1
50:37 A sword upon her horses and upon her chariots 1
42 they ride upon horses, arrayed as a man for battle 1
51:21 with you I break in pieces the horse and his rider; 1
27 bring up horses like bristling locusts. 1
Ezk 17:15 that they might give him horses and a large army. 1
23: 6 desirable young men, horsemen riding on horses. 1
12 clothed in full armor, horsemen riding on horses 1
20 and whose issue was like that of horses. 1
23 and warriors, all of them riding on horses. 1
26: 7 with horses and chariots, and with horsemen 1
10 His horses will be so many that their dust will 1
11 With the hoofs of his horses he will trample 1
27:14 Beth-togar'mah exchanged for your wares horses 1
38: 4 all your army, horses and horsemen, all of them 1
15 peoples with you, all of them riding on horses 1
39:20 And you shall be filled at my table with horses 1
Hos 1: 7 nor by war, nor by horses, nor by horsemen. 1
14: 3 we will not ride upon horses; 1
Jol 2: 4 appearance is like the appearance of horses 1
Ams 2:15 nor shall he who rides the horse save his life; 1
4:10 I carried away your horses; 1
6:12 Do horses run upon rocks? Does one plow the sea 1
Mic 5:10 I will cut off your horses from among you 1
Nah 3: 2 galloping horse and bounding chariot! 1
Hab 1: 8 Their horses are swifter than leopards 1
3: 8 when thou didst ride upon thy horses 1
15 Thou didst trample the sea with thy horses 1
Hag 2:22 the horses and their riders shall go down 1
Zec 1: 8 behold, a man riding upon a red horse! 1
8 behind him were red, sorrel, and white horses. 1
6: 2 The first chariot had red horses 1
2 chariot had red horses, the second black horses 1
3 the third white horses, and the fourth chariot 1
3 the fourth chariot dappled gray horses. 1
6 The chariot with the black horses goes toward 1
9:10 from E'phraim and the war horse from Jerusalem; 1
10: 5 they shall confound the riders on horses. 1
12: 4 I will strike every horse with panic 1
4 when I strike every horse of the peoples 1
14:15 plague like this plague shall fall on the horses 1
20 shall be inscribed on the bells of the horses 1
Jas 3: 3 If we put bits into the mouths of horses 3
Rev 6: 2 I saw . . a white horse, and its rider had a bow; 3
4 And out came another horse, bright red; 3
5 And I saw, and behold, a black horse, and its rider 3
8 a pale horse, and its rider's name was Death 3
9: 7 the locusts were like horses arrayed for battle; 3
9 like the noise of many chariots with horses 3
17 this was how I saw the horses in my vision 3
17 and the heads of the horses were like lions' heads 3
19 For the power of the horses is in their mouths 3
14:20 blood flowed . . as high as a horse's bridle 3
18:13 cattle and sheep, horses and chariots, and slaves 3
19:11 Then I saw heaven opened, and behold, a white horse! 3
14 armies of heaven . . followed him on white horses 3
18 to eat . . the flesh of horses and their riders 3
19 to make war against him who sits upon the horse 3
21 the sword of him who sits upon the horse 3
1Es 2: 7 with gifts and with horses and cattle 3
9 with silver and gold, with horses and cattle 3
5:43 435 camels, and 7,036 horses 3
2Es 15:35 be blood from the sword as high as a horse's belly 4
Jdt 9: 7 they are exalted, with their horses and riders; 3
Wis 19: 9 they ranged like horses 3
Sir 30: 8 A horse that is untamed turns out to be stubborn 3
48: 9 in a chariot with horses of fire; 3
1Mc 10:81 the enemy's horses grew tired. 3
2Mc 3:25 a magnificently caparisoned horse 3
10:29 on horses with golden bridles 3

chariot horse 1. רֶכֶב
2Sm 8: 4 and David hamstrung all the chariot horses 1
1Ch 18: 4 David hamstrung all the chariot horses 1

swift horse 1. רֶכֶשׁ
Est 8:10 sent by mounted couriers riding on swift horses 1
14 the couriers, mounted on their swift horses 1

war horse 1. פָּרָשׁ
Ezk 27:14 exchanged for your wares horses, war horses 1
Jol 2: 4 and like war horses they run. 1

horseback 1. סוּס 2. *ἔφιππος* 3. *ἱππεύς*
Est 6: 9 and let him conduct the man on horseback 1
Jdt 2:15 together with 12,000 archers on horseback 3
2Mc 12:35 who was on horseback and was a strong man 2
4Mc 4:10 angels on horseback . . appeared from heaven 2
horseback *See also* man.

horseman 1. בַּעַל פָּרָשׁ 2. פָּרָשׁ 3. רַכָּב 4. רכב סוס 5. *ἔφιππος* 6. *ἱππεύς* 7. *ἵππος*
Gen 50: 9 went up with him both chariots and horsemen; 2
Exd 14: 9 chariots and his horsemen and his army 2
17 all his host, his chariots, and his horsemen. 2
18 Pharaoh, his chariots, and his horsemen. 2
23 Pharaoh's horses, his chariots, and his horsemen. 2
26 upon their chariots, and upon their horsemen. 2
28 covered the chariots and the horsemen and all 2
15:19 Pharaoh with his chariots and his horsemen went 2
Jos 24: 6 pursued . . with chariots and horsemen 2
1Sm 8:11 appoint them to . . and to be his horsemen 2
13: 5 30,000 chariots, 6,000 horsemen, and troops 2
2Sm 1: 6 chariots and the horsemen were close upon him. 1
8: 4 David took from him 1,700 horsemen 2
10:18 David slew of the Syrians . . 40,000 horsemen 2
1Kg 1: 5 he prepared for himself chariots and horsemen 2
4:26 Solomon also had . . 12,000 horsemen. 2
9:19 for his chariots, and the cities for his horsemen 2
22 his chariot commanders and his horsemen. 2
10:26 Solomon gathered . . chariots and horsemen; 2
26 he had 1,400 chariots and 12,000 horsemen 2
20:20 Ben-ha'dad . . escaped on a horse with horsemen. 2
2Kg 2:12 father! the chariots of Israel and its horsemen! 2
9:17 Joram said, "Take a horseman, and send to meet them 3
19 he sent out a second horseman, who came . . and said 4
13: 7 an army of more than 50 horsemen and ten chariots 2
14 father! The chariots of Israel and its horsemen! 2
18:24 you rely on Egypt for chariots and for horsemen? 2
1Ch 18: 4 David took from him . . 7,000 horsemen 2
19: 6 of silver to hire chariots and horsemen 2
2Ch 1:14 gathered together chariots and horsemen; 2
14 chariots and 12,000 horsemen 2
8: 6 for his chariots, and the cities for his horsemen 2
9 commanders of his chariots, and his horsemen. 2
9:25 had . . horses and chariots, and 12,000 horsemen 2
12: 3 with 1,200 chariots and 60,000 horsemen. 2
16: 8 a huge army with exceedingly many . . horsemen? 2
Ezr 8:22 ask the king for a band of soldiers and horsemen 2
Neh 2: 9 sent with me officers of the army and horsemen. 2
Isa 21: 7 When he sees riders, horsemen in pairs 2
9 And, behold, here come riders, horsemen in pairs! 2
22: 6 Elam bore the quiver with chariots and horsemen 2
7 and the horsemen took their stand at the gates. 2
31: 1 and in horsemen because they are very strong 2
36: 9 you rely on Egypt for chariots and for horsemen? 2
Jer 4:29 At the noise of horseman and archer 2
46: 4 Harness the horses; mount, O horsemen! 2
Ezk 23: 6 desirable young men, horsemen riding on horses. 2
12 clothed in full armor, horsemen riding on horses 2
26: 7 with horses and chariots, and with horsemen 2
10 walls will shake at the noise of the horsemen 2
38: 4 all your army, horses and horsemen, all of them 2
Dan 11:40 with chariots and horsemen, and with many ships; 2
Hos 1: 7 nor by war, nor by horses, nor by horsemen. 2
Nah 3: 3 Horsemen charging, flashing sword 2
Hab 1: 8 their horsemen press proudly on. 2
8 Yea, their horsemen come from afar; 2
Act 23:23 200 soldiers with 70 horsemen 6
32 leaving the horsemen to go on with him. 6
1Es 2:30 with horsemen and a multitude in battle array 7
5: 2 Darius sent with them 1,000 horsemen 6
8:51 foot soldiers and horsemen and an escort 6
Jdt 2:19 chariots and horsemen 6
1Mc 6:30 20,000 horsemen 6
35 500 picked horsemen 7
38 The rest of the horsemen were stationed 7
15:41 stationed there horsemen and troops 6
16: 4 20,000 warriors and horsemen 6
5 behold, a large force of infantry and horsemen 6
7 and placed the horsemen in the midst of the infantry 6
2Mc 5: 2 there appeared golden-clad horsemen 6
3 troops of horsemen drawn up 7
10:31 20,500 were slaughtered, besides 600 horsemen. 6
11: 8 there . . a horseman appeared at their head 5
11 slew . . 1,600 horsemen 6
12:10 not less than 5,000 Arabs with 500 horsemen 6
35 one of the Thracian horsemen bore down upon him 6

hospitable 1. *φιλόξενος*
1Ti 3: 2 dignified, hospitable, an apt teacher 1
Tit 1: 8 but hospitable, a lover of goodness 1

hospitably 1. *φιλοφρόνως*
Act 28: 7 who received us and entertained us hospitably 1

hospitality 1. *φιλοξενία*
Rom 12:13 practice hospitality. 1
hospitality *See also* practice.

show hospitality 1. *ξενοδοχέω*
1Ti 5:10 has brought up children, shown hospitality 1

show hospitality to a stranger 1. *φιλοξενία*
Heb 13: 2 Do not neglect to show hospitality to strangers 1

host 1. חַיִל 2. מַחֲנֶה 3. עַם 4. צָבָא 5. קָהָל 6. רֹב 7. חַיִל (A) 8. *δύναμις* 9. *παρεμβολή* 10. *πλῆθος* 11. *πολύς* 12. *σαβαώθ* 13. *στρατιά* 14. exercitus 15. militia
Gen 2: 1 earth were finished, and all the host of them. 4
Exd 6:26 from the land of Egypt by their hosts. 4
7: 4 then I will . . bring forth my hosts, my people 4
12:17 I brought your hosts out of the land of Egypt 4
41 all the hosts of the LORD went out from the land 4
51 Israel out of the land of Egypt by their hosts. 4
14: 4 I will get glory over Pharaoh and all his host; 1
17 I will get glory over Pharaoh and all his host 1
19 angel of God who went before the host of Israel 2
20 between the host of Egypt and the host of Israel. 2
20 between the host of Egypt and the host of Israel. 2
24 looked down upon the host of the Egyptians 2
24 discomfited the host of the Egyptians 2
28 covered . . all the host of Pharaoh that had 1
15: 4 Pharaoh's chariots and his host he cast 1
Num 2: 4 his host as numbered being 74,600 4
6 his host as numbered being 54,400. 4
8 his host as numbered being 57,400. 4
11 his host as numbered being 46,500. 4
13 his host as numbered being 59,300 4
15 his host as numbered being 45,650 4
19 his host as numbered being 40,500 4
21 his host as numbered being 32,200 4
23 his host as numbered being 35,400 4
26 his host as numbered being 62,700 4
28 his host as numbered being 41,500 4
30 his host as numbered being 53,400 4
10:14 over their host was Nahshon . . of Ammin'adab. 4
15 over the host of the tribe of the men of Is'sachar 4
16 over the host of the tribe of the men of Zeb'ulun 4
18 over their host was Eli'zur the son of Shed'eur. 4
19 over the host of the tribe of the men of Simeon 4
20 over the host of the tribe of the men of Gad 4
22 over their host was Eli'shama the son of Ammi'hud. 4
23 over the host of the tribe of the men of Manas'seh 4
24 over the host of the tribe of the men of Benjamin 4
25 over their host was Ahie'zer . . of Ammishad'dai. 4
26 over the host of the tribe of the men of Asher 4
27 over the host of the tribe of the men of Naph'tali 4
28 the people of Israel according to their hosts 4
33: 1 went forth out of the land of Egypt by their hosts 4
Deu 4:19 sun and . . the stars, all the host of heaven 4
17: 3 worshipped . . moon or any of the host of heaven 4
Jos 11: 4 they came out, with all their troops, a great host 3
Jdg 7:14 his hand God has given Mid'ian and all the host. 2
15 LORD has given the host of Mid'ian into your hand. 2
1Sm 1: 3 to worship and to sacrifice to the LORD of hosts 4
11 O LORD of hosts, if thou wilt . . then I will give him 4
4: 4 the ark of the covenant of the LORD of hosts 4
15: 2 Thus says the LORD of hosts, 'I will punish 4
17:20 the host was going forth to the battle line 1
45 but I come to you in the name of the LORD of hosts 4
46 the dead bodies of the host of the Philistines 2
2Sm 5:10 for the LORD, the God of hosts, was with him. 4
6: 2 which is called by the name of the LORD of hosts 4
18 he blessed . . in the name of the LORD of hosts 4
7: 8 Thus says the LORD of hosts, I took you 4
26 saying, 'The LORD of hosts is God over Israel,' 4
27 thou, O LORD of hosts, the God of Israel, hast made 4
10: 7 he sent Jo'ab and all the host of the mighty men. 4
1Kg 18:15 As the LORD of hosts lives . . I will surely show 4
19:10 very jealous for the LORD, the God of hosts; 4
14 very jealous for the LORD, the God of hosts; 4
22:19 the LORD sitting . . and all the host of heaven 4
2Kg 3:14 As the LORD of hosts lives, whom I serve, were it not 4
17:16 and worshiped all the host of heaven, and served 4
21: 3 and worshiped all the host of heaven, and served 4
5 And he built altars for all the host of heaven 4
23: 4 Ba'al, for Ashe'rah, and for all the host of heaven; 4
5 constellations, and all the host of the heavens. 4
1Ch 11: 9 and greater, for the LORD of hosts was with him. 4
17: 7 Thus says the LORD of hosts 4
24 LORD of hosts, the God of Israel, is Israel's God 4
2Ch 18:18 all the host of heaven standing on his right hand 4
33: 3 worshiped all the host of heaven, and served them. 4
5 he built altars for all the host of heaven 4
Neh 9: 6 thou hast made heaven . . with all their host 4
6 host of heaven worships thee. 4
Job 10:17 thou dost bring fresh hosts against me.
Ps 24:10 The LORD of hosts, he is the King of glory! Selah 4
27: 3 Though a host encamp against me 2
33: 6 all their host by the breath of his mouth. 4
46: 7 The LORD of hosts is with us; 4
11 The LORD of hosts is with us; 4
48: 8 so have we seen in the city of the LORD of hosts 4
59: 5 Thou, LORD God of hosts, art God of Israel. 4
68:11 great is the host of those who bore the tidings 4
69: 6 be put to shame through me, O Lord GOD of hosts; 4
80: 4 O LORD God of hosts, how long wilt thou be angry 4
7 Restore us, O God of hosts; let thy face shine 4
14 Turn again, O God of hosts! Look down from heaven 4

19 Restore us, O LORD God of hosts! let thy face shine 4
84: 1 How lovely is thy dwelling place, O LORD of hosts! 4
3 at thy altars, O LORD of hosts, my King and my God. 4
8 O LORD God of hosts, hear my prayer; 4
12 O LORD of hosts, blessed is the man who trusts 4
89: 8 LORD God of hosts, who is mighty as thou art, O LORD 4
103:21 Bless the LORD, all his hosts, his ministers 4
110: 3 day you lead your host upon the holy mountains. 1
136:15 overthrew Pharaoh and his host in the Red Sea 1
148: 2 Praise him, all his angels, praise him, all his host! 4
Isa 1: 9 If the LORD of hosts had not left . . survivors 4
24 Therefore the Lord says, the LORD of hosts 4
2:12 the LORD of hosts has a day against all . . proud 4
3: 1 the LORD of hosts, is taking away from Jerusalem 4
15 What do you mean . . ?" says the Lord GOD of hosts. 4
5: 7 For the vineyard of the LORD of hosts is . . Israel 4
9 The LORD of hosts has sworn in my hearing 4
16 the LORD of hosts is exalted in justice 4
24 they have rejected the law of the LORD of hosts 4
6: 3 Holy, holy, holy is the LORD of hosts; 4
5 for my eyes have seen the King, the LORD of hosts! 4
8:13 the LORD of hosts, him you shall regard as holy; 4
18 are signs . . from the LORD of hosts 4
9: 7 The zeal of the LORD of hosts will do this. 4
13 did not turn . . nor seek the LORD of hosts. 4
19 wrath of the LORD of hosts the land is burned 4
10:16 the LORD of hosts, will send wasting sickness 4
23 For the Lord, the LORD of hosts, will make a full end 4
24 Therefore thus says the Lord, the LORD of hosts 4
26 the LORD of hosts will wield against them 4
33 Behold . . the LORD of hosts will lop the boughs 4
13: 4 The LORD of hosts is mustering a host for battle. 4
4 The LORD of hosts is mustering a host for battle. 4
13 tremble . . at the wrath of the LORD of hosts 4
14:22 I will rise up against them," says the LORD of hosts 4
23 I will sweep it . . says the LORD of hosts. 4
24 The LORD of hosts has sworn: "As I have planned 4
27 For the LORD of hosts has purposed 4
17: 3 of the children of Israel, says the LORD of hosts. 4
18: 7 to the LORD of hosts from a people tall and smooth 4
7 Zion, the place of the name of the LORD of hosts. 4
19: 4 rule over them, says the Lord, the LORD of hosts. 4
12 what the LORD of hosts has purposed against 4
16 the hand . . the LORD of hosts shakes over them. 4
17 the purpose which the LORD of hosts has purposed 4
18 swear allegiance to the LORD of hosts. 4
20 It will be a sign and a witness to the LORD of hosts 4
25 whom the LORD of hosts has blessed, saying 4
21:10 what I have heard from the LORD of hosts 4
22: 5 For the Lord GOD of hosts has a day of tumult 4
12 Lord GOD of hosts called to weeping and mourning 4
14 The LORD of hosts has revealed himself in my ears 4
14 till you die." says the Lord GOD of hosts. 4
15 Thus says the Lord GOD of hosts, "Come, go to this 4
25 In that day, says the LORD of hosts 4
23: 9 The LORD of hosts has purposed it 4
24:21 that day the LORD will punish the host of heaven 4
23 for the LORD of hosts will reign on Mount Zion 4
25: 6 the LORD of hosts will make for all peoples 4
28: 5 the LORD of hosts will be a crown of glory 4
22 destruction from the Lord GOD of hosts 4
29 This also comes from the LORD of hosts; 4
29: 6 be visited by the LORD of hosts with thunder 4
31: 4 the LORD of hosts will come down to fight 4
5 the LORD of hosts will protect Jerusalem; 4
34: 2 and furious against all their host 4
4 All the host of heaven shall rot away 4
4 host shall fall, as leaves fall from the vine 4
37:16 O LORD of hosts, God of Israel, who art enthroned 4
32 zeal of the LORD of hosts will accomplish this. 4
39: 5 Hear the word of the LORD of hosts 4
40:26 He who brings out their host by number 4
44: 6 King of Israel and his Redeemer, the LORD of hosts 4
45:12 the heavens, and I commanded all their host. 4
13 not for price or reward," says the LORD of hosts. 4
47: 4 Our Redeemer-the LORD of hosts is his name 4
48: 2 God of Israel; the LORD of hosts is his name. 4
51:15 that its waves roar-the LORD of hosts is his name 4
54: 5 is your husband, the LORD of hosts is his name; 4
Jer 2:19 says the Lord GOD of hosts. 4
5:14 Therefore thus says the LORD, the God of hosts 4
6: 6 thus says the LORD of hosts: "Hew down her trees; 4
9 Thus says the LORD of hosts 4
7: 3 Thus says the LORD of hosts, the God of Israel 4
21 Thus says the LORD of hosts, the God of Israel 4
8: 2 and all the host of heaven, which they have loved 4
3 where I have driven them, says the LORD of hosts. 4
9: 7 Therefore thus says the LORD of hosts: "Behold 4
15 Therefore thus says the LORD of hosts 4
17 Thus says the LORD of hosts: "Consider, and call 4
10:16 the LORD of hosts is his name. 4
11:17 The LORD of hosts, who planted you 4
20 But, O LORD of hosts, who judgest righteously 4
22 therefore thus says the LORD of hosts: "Behold 4
15:16 for I am called by thy name, O LORD, God of hosts. 4
16: 9 For thus says the LORD of hosts, the God of Israel 4
19: 3 Thus says the LORD of hosts, the God of Israel 4
11 and shall say to them, 'Thus says the LORD of hosts 4
13 incense has been burned to all the host of heaven 4

15 Thus says the LORD of hosts, the God of Israel 4
20:12 O LORD of hosts, who triest the righteous 4
23:15 Therefore thus says the LORD of hosts 4
16 Thus says the LORD of hosts 4
36 words of the living God, the LORD of hosts, our God. 4
25: 8 Therefore thus says the LORD of hosts: 4
27 you shall say to them, 'Thus says the LORD of hosts 4
28 you shall say to them, 'Thus says the LORD of hosts 4
29 inhabitants of the earth, says the LORD of hosts. 4
32 Thus says the LORD of hosts 4
26:18 Thus says the LORD of hosts, Zion shall be plowed 4
27: 4 Thus says the LORD of hosts, the God of Israel 4
18 then let them intercede with the LORD of hosts 4
19 For thus says the LORD of hosts 4
21 thus says the LORD of hosts, the God of Israel 4
28: 2 Thus says the LORD of hosts, the God of Israel 4
14 For thus says the LORD of hosts, the God of Israel 4
29: 4 Thus says the LORD of hosts, the God of Israel 4
8 For thus says the LORD of hosts, the God of Israel 4
17 Thus says the LORD of hosts, Behold 4
21 Thus says the LORD of hosts, the God of Israel 4
25 Thus says the LORD of hosts, the God of Israel 4
30: 8 come to pass in that day, says the LORD of hosts 4
31:23 Thus says the LORD of hosts, the God of Israel 4
35 the LORD of hosts is his name 4
32:14 Thus says the LORD of hosts, the God of Israel 4
15 For thus says the LORD of hosts, the God of Israel 4
18 mighty God whose name is the LORD of hosts 4
33:11 Give thanks to the LORD of hosts 4
12 Thus says the LORD of hosts 4
22 As the host of heaven cannot be numbered 4
35:13 Thus says the LORD of hosts, the God of Israel 4
17 Therefore, thus says the LORD, the God of hosts 4
18 Thus says the LORD of hosts, the God of Israel 4
19 therefore thus says the LORD of hosts 4
38:17 Thus says the LORD, the God of hosts 4
39:16 Thus says the LORD of hosts, the God of Israel 4
42:15 Thus says the LORD of hosts, the God of Israel 4
18 For thus says the LORD of hosts, the God of Israel 4
43:10 Thus says the LORD of hosts, the God of Israel 4
44: 2 Thus says the LORD of hosts, the God of Israel 4
7 thus says the LORD God of hosts, the God of Israel 4
11 thus says the LORD of hosts, the God of Israel 4
25 Thus says the LORD of hosts, the God of Israel 4
46:10 That day is the day of the Lord GOD of hosts 4
10 Lord GOD of hosts holds a sacrifice in the north 4
18 says the King, whose name is the LORD of hosts 4
25 The LORD of hosts, the God of Israel, said: "Behold 4
48: 1 Concerning Moab. Thus says the LORD of hosts 4
15 says the King, whose name is the LORD of hosts. 4
49: 5 bring terror upon you, says the Lord GOD of hosts 4
7 Concerning Edom. Thus says the LORD of hosts 4
26 destroyed in that day, says the LORD of hosts. 4
35 says the LORD of hosts: "Behold, I will break the bow 4
50:18 Therefore, thus says the LORD of hosts 4
25 for the Lord GOD of hosts has a work to do 4
31 against you, O proud one, says the Lord GOD of hosts; 4
33 Thus says the LORD of hosts: The people of Israel 4
34 Redeemer is strong; the LORD of hosts is his name. 4
51: 3 utterly destroy all her host. 4
5 not been forsaken by their God, the LORD of hosts; 4
14 The LORD of hosts has sworn by himself 4
19 the LORD of hosts is his name. 4
33 For thus says the LORD of hosts, the God of Israel 4
57 says the King, whose name is the LORD of hosts. 4
58 Thus says the LORD of hosts 4
Ezk 1:24 a sound of tumult like the sound of a host; 2
16:40 They shall bring up a host against you 5
23:24 with chariots and wagons and a host of peoples; 5
46 Bring up a host against them 5
47 the host shall stone them and dispatch them 5
26: 7 with horsemen and a host of many soldiers. 5
32: 3 throw my net over you with a host of many peoples; 5
37:10 upon their feet, an exceedingly great host. 1
38: 7 all the hosts that are assembled about you 5
13 you assembled your hosts to carry off plunder 5
15 riding on horses, a great host, a mighty army; 5
Dan 4:35 does according to his will in the host of heaven 7
8:10 It grew great, even to the host of heaven; 4
10 some of the host of the stars it cast down 4
11 magnified . . even up to the Prince of the host; 4
12 host was given over to it together 4
13 sanctuary and host to be trampled under foot? 4
Hos 12: 5 the LORD the God of hosts, the LORD is his name 4
Jol 2:11 his army, for his host is exceedingly great; 2
Ams 3:13 Jacob," says the Lord GOD, the God of hosts 4
4:13 of the earth- the LORD, the God of hosts, is his name! 4
5:14 the LORD, the God of hosts, will be with you 4
15 that the LORD, the God of hosts, will be gracious 4
16 LORD, the God of hosts, the Lord: "In all the squares 4
27 says the LORD, whose name is the God of hosts. 4
6: 8 says the LORD, the God of hosts): "I abhor the pride 4
14 O house of Israel," says the LORD, the God of hosts; 4
9: 5 The Lord, GOD of hosts, he who touches the earth 4
Mic 4: 4 for the mouth of the LORD of hosts has spoken. 4
Nah 2:13 Behold, I am against you, says the LORD of hosts 4
3: 3 hosts of slain, heaps of corpses, dead bodies 6
5 Behold, I am against you, says the LORD of hosts 4
Hab 2:13 from the LORD of hosts that peoples labor only 4

Zep 1: 5 bow down on the roofs to the host of the heavens; 4
2: 9 Therefore, as I live," says the LORD of hosts 4
10 boasted against the people of the LORD of hosts. 4
Hag 1: 2 Thus says the LORD of hosts: This people say 4
5 Now therefore thus says the LORD of hosts 4
7 Thus says the LORD of hosts: Consider how you have 4
9 Why? says the LORD of hosts. Because of my house 4
14 the house of the LORD of hosts, their God 4
2: 4 work, for I am with you, says the LORD of hosts 4
6 For thus says the LORD of hosts 4
7 this house with splendor, says the LORD of hosts. 4
8 the gold is mine, says the LORD of hosts. 4
9 greater than the former, says the LORD of hosts; 4
9 I will give prosperity, says the LORD of hosts.' 4
11 Thus says the LORD of hosts: Ask the priests 4
23 On that day, says the LORD of hosts, I will take you 4
23 for I have chosen you, says the LORD of hosts. 4
Zec 1: 3 Therefore say to them, Thus says the LORD of hosts 4
3 Return to me, says the LORD of hosts 4
3 and I will return to you, says the LORD of hosts. 4
4 Thus says the LORD of hosts, Return from your evil 4
6 As the LORD of hosts purposed to deal with us 4
12 O LORD of hosts, how long wilt thou have no mercy 4
14 Thus says the LORD of hosts: I am exceedingly 4
16 house shall be built in it, says the LORD of hosts 4
17 Cry again, Thus says the LORD of hosts 4
2: 8 thus said the LORD of hosts, after his glory sent 4
9 you will know that the LORD of hosts has sent me. 4
11 you shall know that the LORD of hosts has sent me 4
3: 7 Thus says the LORD of hosts: If you will walk 4
9 says the LORD of hosts, and I will remove the guilt 4
10 In that day, says the LORD of hosts 4
4: 6 by my Spirit, says the LORD of hosts. 4
9 know that the LORD of hosts has sent me to you. 4
5: 4 I will send it forth, says the LORD of hosts 4
6:12 say to him, 'Thus says the LORD of hosts 4
15 you shall know that the LORD of hosts has sent me 4
7: 3 the house of the LORD of hosts and the prophets 4
4 Then the word of the LORD of hosts came to me; 4
9 says the LORD of hosts, Render true judgments 4
12 law and the words which the LORD of hosts had sent 4
12 great wrath came from the LORD of hosts. 4
13 I would not hear," says the LORD of hosts 4
8: 1 the word of the LORD of hosts came to me, saying 4
2 Thus says the LORD of hosts: I am jealous for Zion 4
3 the mountain of the LORD of hosts, the holy 4
4 Thus says the LORD of hosts: Old men and old women 4
6 Thus says the LORD of hosts: If it is marvelous 4
6 marvelous in my sight, says the LORD of hosts? 4
7 Thus says the LORD of hosts: Behold, I will save 4
9 says the LORD of hosts: "Let your hands be strong 4
9 the foundation of the house of the LORD of hosts 4
11 as in the former days, says the LORD of hosts. 4
14 For thus says the LORD of hosts: "As I purposed to do 4
14 I did not relent, says the LORD of hosts 4
18 the word of the LORD of hosts came to me, saying 4
19 Thus says the LORD of hosts: The fast of the fourth 4
20 says the LORD of hosts: Peoples shall yet come 4
21 to seek the LORD of hosts; I am going. 4
22 shall come to seek the LORD of hosts in Jerusalem 4
23 Thus says the LORD of hosts: In those days ten men 4
9:15 The LORD of hosts will protect them 4
10: 3 the LORD of hosts cares for his flock 4
12: 5 strength through the LORD of hosts, their God. 4
13: 2 says the LORD of hosts, I will cut off the names 4
7 who stands next to me," says the LORD of hosts. 4
14:16 to worship the King, the LORD of hosts 4
17 Jerusalem to worship the King, the LORD of hosts 4
21 and Judah shall be sacred to the LORD of hosts 4
21 in the house of the LORD of hosts on that day. 4
Mal 1: 4 the LORD of hosts says, "They may build 4
6 says the LORD of hosts to you, O priests, 4
8 or show you favor? says the LORD of hosts. 4
9 show favor to any of you? says the LORD of hosts. 4
10 I have no pleasure in you, says the LORD of hosts 4
11 great among the nations, says the LORD of hosts. 4
13 you say, and you sniff at me, says the LORD of hosts. 4
14 I am a great King, says the LORD of hosts 4
2: 2 to give glory to my name, says the LORD of hosts 4
4 with Levi may hold, says the LORD of hosts. 4
7 for he is the messenger of the LORD of hosts. 4
8 the covenant of Levi, says the LORD of hosts 4
12 or to bring an offering to the LORD of hosts! 4
16 garment with violence, says the LORD of hosts. 4
3: 1 behold, he is coming, says the LORD of hosts. 4
5 and do not fear me, says the LORD of hosts. 4
7 I will return to you, says the LORD of hosts. 4
10 thereby put me to the test, says the LORD of hosts 4
11 shall not fail to bear, says the LORD of hosts. 4
12 a land of delight, says the LORD of hosts. 4
14 walking as in mourning before the LORD of hosts? 4
17 They shall be mine, says the LORD of hosts 4
4: 1 shall burn them up, says the LORD of hosts 4
3 on the day when I act, says the LORD of hosts. 4
Lke 2:13 with the angel a multitude of the heavenly host 13
Act 7:42 God . . gave them over to worship the host of heaven 13
Rom 9:29 If the Lord of hosts had not left us children 12
Jas 5: 4 reached the ears of the Lord of hosts. 12
1Es 9:46 God Most High, the God of hosts, the Almighty; 12

2Es 6: 3 before the innumerable hosts of angels 15
8:21 before whom the hosts of angels stand trembling 14
Sir 17:32 He marshals the host of the height of heaven 8
24: 2 in the presence of his host she will glory. 8
43: 8 an instrument of the hosts on high 9
Man 1:15 all the host of heaven sings thy praise 8
1Mc 3: 3 waged battles, protecting the host by his sword. 9
14: 7 He gathered a host of captives 11
15: 3 and have recruited a host of mercenary troops 10
2Mc 15:21 perceiving the hosts that were before him 10

host (2) 1. καλέω 2. ξένος
Lke 14:10 so that when your host comes he may say to you 1
Rom 16:23 Ga'ius, who is host to me and to the whole church 2

host *See* play.

mighty host 1. עָצוּם
Prv 7:26 yea, all her slain are a mighty host. 1

spiritual host 1. πνευματικός
Eph 6:12 against the spiritual hosts of wickedness 1

hostage 1. בֵּן תַּעֲרֻבָה 2. ὅμηρα 3. ὅμηρος
2Kg 14:14 he seized . . also hostages, and he returned 1
2Ch 25:24 seized . . hostages, and he returned to Sama'ria. 1
1Mc 1:10 he had been a hostage in Rome 2
8: 7 pay a heavy tribute and give hostages 3
9:53 sons of the leading men of the land as hostages 3
10: 6 he commanded that the hostages . . be released 3
9 released the hostages to Jonathan 3
11:62 took the sons of their rulers as hostages 3
13:16 two of his sons as hostages 3

hostile 1. רעע 2. ἀλλότριος 3. ἀπεχθῶς 4. δυσμενής 5. δυσμενῶς ἔχω 6. ἐναντιόω 7. ἐχθρός
Deu 15: 9 your eye be hostile to your poor brother 1
Rom 8: 7 the mind that is set on the flesh is hostile to God; 7
Col 1:21 you, who once were estranged and hostile in mind 7
AEs 13: 4 there is scattered a certain hostile people 4
7 those who have long been and are now hostile 4
Wis 19:15 their hostile reception of the aliens; 3
2Mc 4:21 had become hostile to his government 2
14:11 who were hostile to Judas 5
3Mc 3: 1 but was . . hostile toward those in the countryside 6
2 a hostile rumor was circulated 4
7 hostile and greatly opposed to his government. 4
5: 3 who were especially hostile toward the Jews. 3

become hostile 1. ἀλλοτριόω 2. ἐπανίστημι
Jdt 5:11 the king of Egypt became hostile to them 2
1Mc 6:24 and became hostile to us 1

hostility 1. ἀντιλογία 2. ἔχθρα
Eph 2:14 has broken down the dividing wall of hostility 2
16 thereby bringing the hostility to an end. 2
Heb 12: 3 who endured . . such hostility against himself 1
1Mc 13:17 lest he arouse great hostility among the people 2

hot 1. אַף 2. חַם 3. חֹם 4. חמם 5. חרה 6. חָרוֹן 7. חֳרִי 8. כמר 9. צַח 10. אזא (A) 11. ζεστός
Exd 11: 8 And he went out from Pharaoh in hot anger. 7
Deu 19: 6 lest the avenger of blood in hot anger pursue 4
Jdg 14:19 In hot anger he went back to his father's house. 5
1Sm 11: 9 Tomorrow, by the time the sun is hot, you shall have 3
21: 6 replaced by hot bread on the day it is taken away. 2
Neh 7: 3 not the gates . . be opened until the sun is hot; 3
Job 6:17 when it is hot, they vanish from their place. 3
37:17 you whose garments are hot when the earth is 2
Ps 85: 3 thou didst turn from thy hot anger. 6
Jer 4:11 A hot wind from the bare heights in the desert 9
Lam 4:11 full vent to his wrath, he poured out his hot anger; 6
5:10 Our skin is hot as an oven with . . heat of famine. 8
Ezk 24:11 that it may become hot, and its copper may burn 4
36: 5 my hot jealousy against the rest of the nations 1
Dan 3:22 king's order was strict and the furnace very hot 10
Hos 7: 7 All of them are hot as an oven 4
Zec 10: 3 My anger is hot against the shepherds 5
Rev 3:15 'I know your works: you are neither cold nor hot. 11
15 Would that you were cold or hot! 11
16 you are lukewarm, and neither cold nor hot 11

hot *See also* burn, coal, displeasure, ember, grow, indignation, iron, spring, stone, temper, tempered, wind.

become hot 1. חמם
Ps 39: 3 my heart became hot within me. 1

hot enough 1. καυστικός
4Mc 10:14 he said to them, "You do not have a fire hot enough 1

intensely hot 1. λάβρος πυρί
4Mc 16: 3 nor was the . . furnace . . so intensely hot 1

very hot 1. καῦμα
Sus 1:15 and wished to bathe in the garden, for it was very hot. 1

hotly 1. מְאֹד
Num 11:10 anger of the LORD blazed hotly 1

hotly *See also* burn, pursue.

hour 1. מוֹעֵד 2. καιρός 3. ὥρα 4. hora
Jer 46:17 king of Egypt, 'Noisy one who lets the hour go by.' 1
Mat 10:19 to say will be given to you in that hour; 3
20: 3 going out about the third hour he saw others 3
5 Going out again about the sixth hour •
5 the sixth hour and the ninth hour 3
6 about the eleventh hour he went out •
9 when those hired about the eleventh hour came •
12 saying, 'These last worked only one hour 3
24:36 of that day and hour no one knows 3
44 Son of man is coming at an hour you do not expect. 3
50 at an hour he does not know 3
25:13 you know neither the day nor the hour. 3
26:40 So, could you not watch with me one hour? 3
45 Behold, the hour is at hand 3
55 At that hour Jesus said to the crowds 3
27:45 Now from the sixth hour there was darkness 3
45 over all the land until the ninth hour. 3
46 about the ninth hour Jesus cried 3
Mrk 6:35 This is a lonely place, and the hour is now late; 3
13:11 say whatever is given you in that hour 3
32 of that day or that hour no one knows 3
14:35 if it were possible, the hour might pass from him. 3
37 Simon, are you asleep? Could you not watch one hour? 3
41 It is enough; the hour has come 3
15:25 it was the third hour, when they crucified him. 3
33 when the sixth hour had come 3
33 over the whole land until the ninth hour. 3
34 at the ninth hour Jesus cried with a loud voice 3
Lke 1:10 praying outside at the hour of incense 3
2:38 coming up at that very hour she gave thanks to God 3
7:21 In that hour he cured many of diseases 3
10:21 In that same hour he rejoiced in the Holy Spirit 3
12:12 the Holy Spirit will teach you in that very hour 3
39 at what hour the thief was coming 3
40 the Son of man is coming at an unexpected hour. 3
46 at an hour he does not know 3
13:31 At that very hour some Pharisees came, and said 3
20:19 tried to lay hands on him at that very hour 3
22:14 when the hour came, he sat at table 3
53 this is your hour, and the power of darkness. 3
59 after an interval of about an hour 3
23:44 It was now about the sixth hour 3
44 darkness over the whole land until the ninth hour 3
24:33 rose that same hour and returned to Jerusalem; 3
Joh 1:39 they stayed . . for it was about the tenth hour. 3
2: 4 Jesus said to her . . My hour has not yet come. 3
4: 6 It was about the sixth hour. 3
21 the hour is coming when neither on this mountain 3
23 But the hour is coming, and now is 3
52 So he asked them the hour when he began to mend 3
52 Yesterday at the seventh hour the fever left him. 3
53 knew that was the hour when Jesus had said to him 3
5:25 Truly, truly, I say to you, the hour is coming 3
28 the hour is coming when all . . will hear 3
7:30 because his hour had not yet come. 3
8:20 because his hour had not yet come. 3
11: 9 Are there not twelve hours in the day? 3
12:23 Jesus answered them, "The hour has come 3
27 'Father, save me from this hour'? 3
27 No, for this purpose I have come to this hour. 3
13: 1 when Jesus knew that his hour had come to depart 3
16: 2 indeed, the hour is coming 3
4 you, that when their hour comes you may remember 3
21 because her hour has come 3
25 the hour is coming 3
32 The hour is coming, indeed it has come 3
17: 1 Father, the hour has come; glorify thy Son 3
19:14 it was about the sixth hour 3
27 from that hour the disciple took her 3
Act 2:15 since it is only the third hour of the day; 3
3: 1 going up . . at the hour of prayer, the ninth hour. 3
1 going up . . at the hour of prayer, the ninth hour. •
5: 7 After an interval of about three hours 3
10: 3 About the ninth hour of the day 3
9 about the sixth hour. 3
30 Cornelius said, "Four days ago, about this hour 3
30 I was keeping the ninth hour of prayer in my house; •
16:18 it came out that very hour. 3
33 he took them the same hour of the night 3
19:34 for about two hours they all . . cried out 3
22:13 in that very hour I received my sight and saw him. 3
23:23 At the third hour of the night get ready 3
Rom 13:11 Besides this you know what hour it is 2
1Co 4:11 To the present hour we hunger and thirst 3
15:30 Why am I in peril every hour? 3
1Jn 2:18 Children, it is the last hour; 3
18 therefore we know that it is the last hour. 3
Rev 3: 3 you will not know at what hour I will come upon you 3
10 I will keep you from the hour of trial 3
9:15 angels . . who had been held ready for the hour 3
11:13 And at that hour there was a great earthquake 3
14: 7 Fear God . . for the hour of his judgment has come; 3
15 reap, for the hour to reap has come 3
17:12 receive authority as kings for one hour 3
18:10 Babylon! In one hour has thy judgment come. 3
17 In one hour all this wealth has been laid waste. 3
19 In one hour she has been laid waste. 3
2Es 5:34 for every hour I suffer agonies of heart 4
6:24 so that for three hours they shall not flow. 4
7:89 and withstood danger every hour 4
9:44 every hour and every day during those 30 years 4
14:26 tomorrow at this hour you shall begin to write. 4
16:38 about her womb for two or three hours beforehand 4
Jdt 13: 4 look in this hour upon the work of my hands 3
AEs 10:11 came to the hour and moment and day of decision 3
Sir 11:27 The misery of an hour makes one forget luxury 3
18:20 in the hour of visitation 3
33:23 in the hour of death 2
39:33 he will supply every need in its hour. 3
2Mc 8:25 obliged to return because the hour was late. 3
3Mc 2:19 reveal your mercy at this hour. 3
5:13 since they had escaped the appointed hour 3
14 since it was nearly the middle of the tenth hour 3
15 the hour of the banquet was already slipping by 2

hour *See also* half.

appointed hour 1. מוֹעֵד
1Sm 9:24 it was kept for you until the hour appointed 1

house 1. בַּיִת 2. זֶרַע 3. בַּיִת (A) 4. ἔσω 5. ἴδιος 6. οἴκησις 7. οἰκία 8. οἰκοδομέω 9. οἰκοδομή 10. οἰκοδόμος 11. οἶκος 12. οἶκος 13. domus
Gen 12: 1 and your father's house to the land 1
15 And the woman was taken into Pharaoh's house. 1
17 the LORD afflicted Pharaoh and his house 1
14:14 his trained men, born in his house, 318 of them 1
15: 2 heir of my house is Elie'zer of Damascus? 1
3 and a slave born in my house will be my heir. 1
17:12 your generations, whether born in your house 1
13 both he that is born in your house 1
23 all the slaves born in his house 1
23 every male among the men of Abraham's house 1
27 all the men of his house, those born in the house 1
27 all the men of his house, those born in the house 1
19: 2 I pray you, to your servant's house 1
3 they turned aside to him and entered his house; 1
4 to the last man, surrounded the house; 1
10 brought Lot into the house to them 1
11 the men who were at the door of the house 1
20:13 God caused me to wander from my father's house 1
18 the wombs of the house of Abim'elech 1
24: 2 to his servant, the oldest of his house 1
7 LORD . . who took me from my father's house 1
23 Is there room in your father's house for us 1
27 the way to the house of my master's kinsmen. 1
31 For I have prepared the house and a place 1
32 the man came into the house; and Laban ungirded 1
38 you shall go to my father's house and to my kindred 1
40 my son from my kindred and from my father's house; 1
27:15 garments . . which were with her in the house 1
28: 2 Arise, go to Paddan-aram to the house of Bethu'el 1
17 This is none other than the house of God 1
21 that I come again to my father's house in peace 1
22 stone . . shall be God's house; 1
29:13 kissed him, and brought him to his house. 1
31:14 inheritance left to us in our father's house? 1
30 you longed greatly for your father's house 1
41 These twenty years I have been in your house; 1
33:17 journeyed to Succoth, and built himself a house 1
34:26 took Dinah out of Shechem's house, and went away. 1
29 all that was in the houses, they captured 1
38:11 Remain a widow in your father's house 1
11 Tamar went and dwelt in her father's house. 1
39: 2 he was in the house of his master the Egyptian 1
4 and he made him overseer of his house and put him 1
5 he made him overseer in his house and over all 1
5 blessed the Egyptian's house for Joseph's sake; 1
5 upon all that he had, in house and field. 1
8 has no concern about anything in the house 1
9 he is not greater in this house than I am; 1
11 one day, when he went into the house to do his work 1
11 none of the men of the house was there in the house 1
11 none of the men of the house was there in the house 1
12 in her hand, and fled and got out of the house. •
13 in her hand, and had fled out of the house •
15 he left . . and fled and got out of the house. •
18 garment with me, and fled out of the house. •
40: 3 he put them in custody in the house of the captain 1
7 with him in custody in his master's house 1
14 make mention . . and so get me out of this house. 1
41:10 put me . . in the house of the captain of the guard 1
40 you shall be over my house, and all my people shall 1
51 all my hardship and all my father's house. 1
43:16 to the steward of his house, "Bring the men 1
16 the men into the house, and slaughter an animal 1
17 and brought the men to Joseph's house. 1
18 they were brought to Joseph's house 1
19 they went up to the steward of Joseph's house 1
19 spoke with him at the door of the house 1
24 the men into Joseph's house, and given them water 1
26 they brought into the house to him the present 1
44: 1 Then he commanded the steward of his house 1
8 steal silver or gold from your lord's house? 1
14 Judah and his brothers came to Joseph's house 1
45: 8 has made me . . lord of all his house 1

16 When the report was heard in Pharaoh's house 1
46:27 the persons of the house of Jacob, that came 1
47:14 Joseph brought the money into Pharaoh's house. 1
50:22 Joseph dwelt in Egypt, he and his father's house; 1
Exd 2: 1 Now a man from the house of Levi went and took 1
3:22 shall ask . . of her who sojourns in her house 1
6:14 These are the heads of their fathers' houses 1
7:23 Pharaoh turned and went into his house 1
8: 3 frogs which shall come up into your house 1
3 come up . . into the houses of your servants 1
9 frogs be destroyed from you and your houses 1
11 The frogs shall depart from you and your houses 1
13 the frogs died out of the houses and courtyards 1
21 flies . . on . . your people, and into your houses; 1
21 and the houses of the Egyptians shall be filled 1
24 great swarms of flies into the house of Pharaoh 1
24 house of Pharaoh and into his servants' houses 1
9:20 made his slaves and his cattle flee into the houses 1
10: 6 they shall fill your houses, and the houses of all 1
6 fill . . the houses of all your servants 1
12: 3 a lamb according to their fathers' houses 1
4 neighbor next to his house shall take according 1
7 two doorposts and the lintel of the houses 1
13 a sign . . upon the houses where you are; 1
15 you shall put away leaven out of your houses 1
19 no leaven shall be found in your houses; 1
22 go out of the door of his house until the morning. 1
23 destroyer to enter your houses to slay you. 1
27 for he passed over the houses of the people 1
27 slew the Egyptians but spared our houses.' 1
30 for there was not a house where one was not dead. 1
46 In one house shall it be eaten; 1
46 carry forth any of the flesh outside the house; 1
13: 3 came out from Egypt, out of the house of bondage 1
14 LORD brought us out . . from the house of bondage. 1
16:31 Now the house of Israel called its name manna; 1
19: 3 Thus you shall say to the house of Jacob, and tell 1
20: 2 brought you . . out of the house of bondage. 1
17 You shall not covet your neighbor's house; 1
22: 7 If . . it is stolen out of the man's house 1
8 the owner of the house shall come near to God 1
23:19 shall bring into the house of the LORD your God. 1
34:26 you shall bring to the house of the LORD your God. 1
40:38 by night, in the sight of all the house of Israel. 1
Lev 10: 6 but your brethren, the whole house of Israel 1
14:34 in a house in the land of your possession 1
35 then he who owns the house shall come and tell 1
35 seems to me to be some sort of disease in my house 1
36 priest shall command that they empty the house 1
36 lest all that is in the house be declared unclean 1
36 afterward the priest shall go in to see the house 1
37 if the disease is in the walls of the house 1
38 then the priest shall go out of the house 1
38 go out . . to the door of the house 1
38 go out . . and shut up the house seven days 1
39 the disease has spread in the walls of the house 1
41 cause the inside of the house to be scraped 1
42 shall take other plaster and plaster the house 1
43 If the disease breaks out again in the house 1
43 he has taken out the stones and scraped the house 1
44 if the disease has spread in the house 1
44 it is a malignant leprosy in the house 1
45 he shall break down the house, its stones 1
45 timber and all the plaster of the house 1
46 he who enters the house while it is shut up 1
47 lies down in the house shall wash his clothes 1
47 he who eats in the house shall wash his clothes 1
48 and the disease has not spread in the house 1
48 in the house after the house was plastered 1
48 then the priest shall pronounce the house clean 1
49 for the cleansing of the house he shall take two 1
51 and sprinkle the house seven times 1
52 Thus he shall cleanse the house with the blood 1
53 he shall make atonement for the house 1
55 for leprosy in a garment or in a house 1
16: 6 make atonement for himself and for his house 1
11 make atonement for himself and for his house 1
17 has made atonement for himself and for his house 1
17: 3 If any man of the house of Israel kills an ox 1
8 Any man of the house of Israel 1
10 If any man of the house of Israel 1
22:11 that are born in his house may eat of his food 1
13 daughter . . returns to her father's house 1
18 When any one of the house of Israel . . presents 1
25:29 If a man sells a dwelling house in a walled city 1
30 then the house that is in the walled city 1
31 the houses of the villages which have no wall 1
32 the houses in the cities of their possession 1
33 then the house that was sold in a city 1
33 for the houses in the cities of the Levites are 1
27:14 When a man dedicates his house to be holy 1
15 if he who dedicates it wishes to redeem his house 1
Num 1: 2 census . . by families, by fathers' houses 1
4 being the head of the house of his fathers. 1
18 registered . . by families, by fathers' houses 1
20 by their fathers' houses, according to the number 1
22 by their families, by their fathers' houses 1
24 by their families, by their fathers' houses 1
26 by their families, by their fathers' houses 1
28 by their families, by their fathers' houses 1
30 by their families, by their fathers' houses 1
32 by their families, by their fathers' houses 1
34 by their families, by their fathers' houses 1
36 by their families, by their fathers' houses 1
38 by their families, by their fathers' houses 1
40 by their families, by their fathers' houses 1
42 by their families, by their fathers' houses 1
44 twelve men, each representing his fathers' house. 1
45 by their fathers' houses, from twenty years old 1
2: 2 with the ensigns of their fathers' houses; 1
32 Israel as numbered by their fathers' houses; 1
34 they set out . . according to his fathers' house. 1
3:15 Number the sons of Levi, by fathers' houses 1
20 the Levites, by their fathers' houses. 1
24 as head of the fathers' house of the Gershonites. 1
30 Eli-za'phan . . head of the fathers' house 1
35 head of the fathers' house of the families 1
4: 2 Take a census . . by their . . fathers' houses 1
22 by their families and their fathers' houses; 1
29 number them by . . their fathers' houses; 1
34 by their families and their fathers' houses 1
38 by their families and their fathers' houses 1
40 number by . . families and their fathers' houses 1
42 by their families and their fathers' houses 1
46 by their families and their fathers' houses 1
7: 2 leaders of Israel, heads of their fathers' houses 1
12: 7 servant Moses; he is entrusted with all my house. 1
17: 2 get from them rods, one for each fathers' house 1
2 leaders according to their fathers' houses 1
3 one rod for the head of each fathers' house. 1
6 according to their fathers' houses, twelve rods; 1
8 rod of Aaron for the house of Levi had sprouted 1
18: 1 You and your sons and your fathers' house with you 1
11 every one who is clean in your house may eat of it. 1
13 every one who is clean in your house may eat of it. 1
20:29 all the house of Israel wept for Aaron 30 days 1
22:18 were to give me his house full of silver and gold 1
24:13 should give me his house full of silver and gold 1
25:14 Zimri the son of Salu, head of a fathers' house 1
15 Zur . . head of the people of a fathers' house 1
26: 2 Take a census . . by their fathers' houses 1
30: 3 vows a vow . . while within her father's house 1
10 if she vowed in her husband's house 1
16 while in her youth, within her father's house. 1
34:14 tribe of the sons of Reuben by fathers' houses 1
14 tribe of the sons of Gad by their fathers' houses 1
Deu 5: 6 who brought you out of . . the house of bondage. 1
21 not desire your neighbor's house, his field 1
6: 7 shall talk of them when you sit in your house 1
9 shall write them on the doorposts of your house 1
11 houses full of good things, which you did not fill 1
12 LORD, who brought you . . out of the house of bondage. 1
7: 8 LORD . . redeemed you from the house of bondage 1
26 not bring an abominable thing into your house 1
8:12 when you . . have built goodly houses and live 1
14 LORD . . brought you . . , out of the house of bondage 1
11:19 talking of them when you are sitting in your house 1
20 write them upon the doorposts of your house 1
13: 5 LORD . . redeemed you out of the house of bondage 1
10 LORD . . brought you . . out of the house of bondage. 1
19: 1 dwell in their cities and in their houses 1
20: 5 What man is there that has built a new house 1
5 Let him go back to his house, lest he die 1
6 Let him go back to his house, lest he die 1
7 Let him go back to his house, lest he die 1
8 go back to his house, lest the heart of his fellows 1
21:12 then you shall bring her home to your house 1
13 shall remain in your house and bewail . . a full month; 1
22: 2 bring it home to your house, and it shall be 1
8 When you build a new house, you shall make 1
8 may not bring the guilt of blood upon your house 1
21 bring . . to the door of her father's house 1
21 by playing the harlot in her father's house; 1
23:18 not bring . . into the house of the LORD your God 1
24: 1 sends her out of his house, and she departs 1
1 sends her out . . and she departs out of his house 1
3 dislikes her . . and sends her out of his house 1
10 shall not go into his house to fetch his pledge. 1
25: 9 man who does not build up his brother's house.' 1
10 the name of his house shall be called in Israel 1
10 The house of him that had his sandal pulled off. 1
14 not have in your house two kinds of measures 1
26:11 good . . LORD . . given to you and to your house 1
13 I have removed the sacred portion out of my house 1
28:30 shall build a house, and you shall not dwell in it; 1
Jos 2: 1 And they went, and came into the house of a harlot 1
3 men that have come to you, who entered your house; 1
12 you also will deal kindly with my father's house 1
15 her house was built into the city wall 1
18 you shall gather into your house your father 1
19 If any one goes out of the doors of your house 1
19 is laid upon any one who is with you in the house 1
6:17 and all who are with her in her house shall live 1
22 Go into the harlot's house, and bring . . the woman 1
24 put into the treasury of the house of the LORD. 1
9:12 when we took it from our houses as our food 1
23 and drawers of water for the house of my God. 1
14: 1 and the heads of the fathers' houses of the tribes •
17:17 to the house of Joseph, to E'phraim and Manas'seh 1
18: 5 and the house of Joseph in their territory 1
19:51 heads of the fathers' houses of the tribes •
21: 1 the heads of the fathers' houses of the Levites •
1 the heads of the fathers' houses of the tribes •
45 which the LORD had made to the house of Israel 1
24:15 but as for me and my house, we will serve the LORD. 1
17 up from . . Egypt, out of the house of bondage 1
Jdg 1:22 The house of Joseph also went up against Bethel; 1
23 And the house of Joseph sent to spy out Bethel. 1
35 the hand of the house of Joseph rested heavily 1
4:17 king of Hazor and the house of Heber the Ken'ite. 1
6: 8 I . . brought you out of the house of bondage; 1
19 So Gideon went into his house and prepared a kid •
8:29 Jerubba'al . . went and dwelt in his own house. 1
9: 4 pieces of silver out of the house of Ba'al-be'rith 1
5 he went to his father's house at Ophrah, and slew 1
16 you have dealt well with Jerubba'al and his house 1
18 and you have risen up against my father's house 1
19 honor with Jerubba'al and with his house this day 1
27 festival, and went into the house of their god 1
46 the stronghold of the house of El-be'rith. 1
10: 9 Benjamin and against the house of E'phraim; 1
11: 2 You shall not inherit in our father's house; 1
7 hate me, and drive me out of my father's house? 1
31 comes forth from the doors of my house to meet me 1
12: 1 We will burn your house over you with fire. 1
14:15 we burn you and your father's house with fire. 1
19 In hot anger he went back to his father's house. 1
16:26 Let me feel the pillars on which the house rests 1
27 the house was full of men and women; all the lords 1
29 two middle pillars upon which the house rested 1
30 bowed with all his might; and the house fell upon 1
17: 4 a molten image; and it was in the house of Micah. 1
8 hill country of E'phraim to the house of Micah. 1
12 became his priest, and was in the house of Micah. 1
18: 2 they came to . . E'phraim, to the house of Micah 1
3 When they were by the house of Micah 1
13 they passed on . . and came to the house of Micah. 1
14 Do you know that in these houses there are 1
15 and came to the house of the young Levite 1
18 when these went into Micah's house and took 1
19 be priest to the house of one man, or to be priest 1
22 the men who were in the houses near Micah's house 1
22 the men who were in the houses near Micah's house 1
31 he made, as long as the house of God was at Shiloh. 1
19: 2 she went . . to her father's house at Bethlehem 1
3 he came to her father's house; and when the girl's 1
15 no man took them into his house to spend 1
18 to my home; and nobody takes me into his house. 1
21 he brought him into his house, and gave the asses 1
22 the men . . beset the house round about, beating 1
22 they said to the old man, the master of the house 1
22 Bring out the man who came into your house, that we 1
23 the man, the master of the house, went out to them 1
23 this man has come into my house, do not do this vile 1
26 woman . . fell down at the door of the man's house 1
27 he opened the doors of the house and went out to go 1
27 lying at the door of the house, with her hands 1
29 when he entered his house, he took a knife 1
20: 5 rose against me, and beset the house round about 1
8 his tent, and none of us will return to his house. 1
Rut 1: 8 Go, return each of you to her mother's house. 1
9 find a home, each of you in the house of her husband! 1
4:11 the woman, who is coming into your house 1
11 who together built up the house of Israel. 1
12 and may your house be like the house of Perez 1
12 and may your house be like the house of Perez 1
1Sm 1: 7 as often as she went up to the house of the LORD 1
19 they went back to their house at Ramah. 1
21 the man Elka'nah and all his house went up to offer 1
24 she brought him to the house of the LORD at Shiloh; 1
2:27 I revealed myself to the house of your father 1
27 were in Egypt subject to the house of Pharaoh. 1
28 I gave to the house of your father all my 1
30 I promised that your house . . should go in and out 1
30 your house and the house of your father should go 1
31 cut off . . and the strength of your father's house 1
31 there will not be an old man in your house. 1
32 shall not be an old man in your house for ever. 1
33 the increase of your house shall die by the sword 1
35 and I will build him a sure house, and he shall go 1
36 every one who is left in your house shall come 1
3:12 all that I have spoken concerning his house 1
13 I am about to punish his house for ever 1
14 I swear to the house of Eli that the iniquity 1
14 the iniquity of Eli's house shall not be expiated 1
15 then he opened the doors of the house of the LORD. 1
5: 2 the ark . . and brought it into the house of Dagon 1
5 priests . . and all who enter the house of Dagon 1
7: 1 brought it to the house of Abin'adab on the hill; 1
2 all the house of Israel lamented after the LORD. 1
3 Then Samuel said to all the house of Israel 1
9:18 and said, "Tell me where is the house of the seer? 1
20 Is it not for you and for all your father's house? 1
15:34 and Saul went up to his house in Gib'e-ah of Saul. 1
17:25 the king will . . make his father's house free 1
18: 2 not let him return to his father's house. 1
10 and he raved within his house 1

19: 9 as he sat in his house with his spear in his hand; 1
11 Saul sent messengers to David's house to watch 1
20:15 and do not cut off your loyalty from my house 1
16 of Jonathan be cut off from the house of David. 1
21:15 Shall this fellow come into my house? 1
22: 1 his brothers and all his father's house heard it 1
11 summon Ahim'elech . . and all his father's house 1
14 the king's son-in-law . . and honored in your house? 1
15 to his servant or to all the house of my father; 1
16 You shall . . you and all your father's house. 1
22 death of all the persons of your father's house. 1
24:21 not destroy my name out of my father's house. 1
25: 1 they buried him in his house at Ramah. 1
6 Peace be to you, and peace be to your house 1
17 against our master and against all this house 1
28 the LORD will certainly make my lord a sure house 1
35 Go up in peace to your house; see, I have hearkened 1
36 lo, he was holding a feast in his house 1
28:24 Now the woman had a fatted calf in the house 1
2Sm 1:12 for the people . . and for the house of Israel 1
2: 4 anointed David king over the house of Judah. 1
7 and the house of Judah has anointed me king 1
10 But the house of Judah followed David. 1
11 David was king in Hebron over the house of Judah 1
3: 1 a long war between the house of Saul and . . David; 1
1 between the house of Saul and the house of David; 1
1 the house of Saul became weaker and weaker. 1
6 was war between the house of Saul and . . of David 1
6 between the house of Saul and the house of David 1
6 Abner was making himself strong in the house 1
8 showing loyalty to the house of Saul your father 1
10 to transfer the kingdom from the house of Saul 1
19 Israel and the whole house of Benjamin thought 1
29 fall upon . . Jo'ab, and upon all his father's house; 1
29 may the house of Jo'ab never be without one who has 1
4: 5 they came to the house of Ish-bo'sheth, as he was 1
6 the doorkeeper of the house had been cleaning 12
7 When they came into the house, as he lay on his bed 1
11 slain a righteous man in his . . house upon his bed 1
5: 8 blind and the lame shall not come into the house. 1
11 carpenters and masons who built David a house. 1
6: 3 and brought it out of the house of Abin'adab 1
5 David and all the house of Israel were . . merry 1
10 took it . . to the house of O'bed-e'dom the Gittite. 1
11 ark . . remained in the house of O'bed-e'dom 1
12 brought up the ark . . from the house of O'bed-e'dom 1
15 the house of Israel brought up the ark 1
19 Then all the people departed, each to his house. 1
21 chose me above your father, and . . all his house 1
7: 1 Now when the king dwelt in his house, and the LORD 1
2 I dwell in a house of cedar, but the ark 1
5 Would you build me a house to dwell in? 1
6 I have not dwelt in a house since . . I brought up 1
7 saying, "Why have you not built me a house of cedar? 1
11 declares . . that the LORD will make you a house. 1
13 He shall build a house for my name 1
16 your house and your kingdom shall be made sure 1
18 Who am I . . and what is my house, that thou hast 1
19 thou hast spoken also of thy servant's house 1
25 thou hast spoken . . and concerning his house 1
26 and the house of . . David will be established 1
27 made this revelation . . 'I will build you a house'; 1
29 it please thee to bless the house of thy servant 1
29 with thy blessing shall the house . . be blessed 1
9: 1 Is there still any one left of the house of Saul 1
2 a servant of the house of Saul whose name was Ziba 1
3 Is there not still some one of the house of Saul 1
4 He is in the house of Machir the son of Am'miel 1
5 David . . brought him from the house of Machir 1
9 All that belonged to Saul and to all his house 1
12 all who dwelt in Ziba's house became 1
11: 2 and was walking upon the roof of the king's house 1
4 Then she returned to her house. 1
8 Go down to your house, and wash your feet. 1
8 Uri'ah went out of the king's house 1
9 Uri'ah slept at the door of the king's house 1
9 Uri'ah slept . . and did not go down to his house. 1
10 they told David, "Uri'ah did not go down to his house 1
10 Why did you not go down to your house? 1
11 shall I then go to my house, to eat and to drink 1
13 he went out . . but he did not go down to his house. 1
27 David sent and brought her to his house 1
12: 8 I gave you your master's house, and . . wives 1
8 gave you the house of Israel and of Judah; 1
10 the sword shall never depart from your house 1
11 raise up evil against you out of your own house; 1
15 Then Nathan went to his house. 1
17 And the elders of his house stood beside him 1
20 he went into the house of the LORD, and worshiped; 1
20 he then went to his own house; 1
13: 7 Go to your brother Amnon's house, and prepare food 1
8 Tamar went to . . Amnon's house, where he was lying 1
20 Tamar dwelt . . in her brother Ab'salom's house. 1
14: 8 Go to your house, and I will give orders 1
9 On me be the guilt . . and on my father's house; 1
24 the king said, "Let him dwell apart in his own house; 1
24 Ab'salom dwelt apart in his own house 1
31 Then Jo'ab arose and went to Ab'salom at his house 1
15:16 the king left ten concubines to keep the house. 1
17 and they halted at the last house. 1
35 whatever you hear from the king's house, tell it 1
16: 3 the house of Israel will give me back the kingdom 1
5 came out a man of the family of the house of Saul 1
8 has avenged . . all the blood of the house of Saul 1
21 concubines, whom he has left to keep the house; 1
17:18 went . . and came to the house of a man at Bahu'rim 1
20 Ab'salom's servants came to the woman at the house 1
23 And he set his house in order, and hanged himself; 1
19: 5 Then Jo'ab came into the house to the king, and said 1
11 be the last to bring the king back to his house 1
17 Ziba the servant of the house of Saul . . rushed 1
20 I have come . . the first of all the house of Joseph 1
28 all my father's house were but men doomed to death 1
20: 3 And David came to his house at Jerusalem; 1
3 concubines whom he had left to care for the house 1
3 took the ten . . and put them in a house under guard 1
21: 1 There is bloodguilt on Saul and on his house 1
4 not a matter of . . between us and Saul or his house; 1
23: 5 Yea, does not my house stand so with God? 1
24:17 be against me and against my father's house. 1
1Kg 1:53 and Solomon said to him, "Go to your house. 1
2:24 David my father, and who has made me a house, as he 1
27 word of the LORD . . concerning the house of Eli 1
31 thus take away from me and from my father's house 1
33 descendants, and to his house, and to his throne 1
34 he was buried in his own house in the wilderness. 1
36 Build yourself a house . . and dwell there, and do 1
3: 1 building his own house and the house of the LORD 1
1 building his own house and the house of the LORD 1
2 because no house had yet been built for the name 1
17 my lord, this woman and I dwell in the same house; 1
17 I gave birth to a child while she was in the house. 1
18 there was no one else with us in the house, only we 1
18 no one else . . only we two were in the house. 1
5: 3 David . . could not build a house for the name 1
5 I purpose to build a house for the name of the LORD 1
5 'Your son . . shall build the house for my name.' 1
17 in order to lay the foundation of the house 1
18 the timber and the stone to build the house. 1
6: 1 he began to build the house of the LORD. 1
2 The house which King Solomon built for the LORD 1
3 The vestibule in front of the nave of the house 1
3 twenty cubits . . equal to the width of the house 1
3 and ten cubits deep in front of the house. 1
4 he made for the house windows with recessed 1
5 built a structure against the wall of the house 1
5 running round the walls of the house 1
6 around the outside of the house he made offsets 1
6 not be inserted into the walls of the house. 1
7 When the house was built, it was with stone 1
8 entrance . . was on the south side of the house; 1
9 So he built the house, and finished it; 1
9 made the ceiling of the house of beams and planks 1
10 He built the structure against the whole house 1
10 it was joined to the house with timbers of cedar. 1
12 Concerning this house which you are building 1
14 So Solomon built the house, and finished it. 1
15 He lined the walls of the house on the inside 1
15 from the floor of the house to . . the ceiling 1
15 he covered the floor of the house with boards 1
16 He built . . the rear of the house with boards 1
17 The house, that is, the nave . . was 40 cubits 1
18 The cedar within the house was carved in the form 1
19 he prepared in the innermost part of the house 1
21 Solomon overlaid the inside of the house 1
22 he overlaid the whole house with gold 1
22 he overlaid . . until all the house was finished. 1
27 the cherubim in the innermost part of the house; 1
27 wings touched . . in the middle of the house. 1
29 He carved all the walls of the house round about 1
30 The floor of the house he overlaid with gold 1
37 the foundation of the house of the LORD was laid 1
38 the house was finished in all its parts 1
7: 1 Solomon was building his own house 1
1 Solomon . . and he finished his entire house. 1
2 He built the House of the Forest of Lebanon; 1
8 His own house . . was of like workmanship. 1
8 Solomon also made a house like this hall 1
9 from the court of the house of the LORD •
12 so had the inner court of the house of the LORD 1
12 inner court . . and the vestibule of the house. 1
39 set the stands, five on the south side of the house 1
39 stands . . and five on the north side of the house; 1
39 set the sea on the southeast corner of the house. 1
40 all the work that he did . . on the house of the LORD 1
45 all these vessels in the house of the LORD 1
48 made all the vessels . . in the house of the LORD 1
50 for the doors of the innermost part of the house 1
51 work that . . Solomon did on the house of the LORD 1
51 them in the treasuries of the house of the LORD. 1
8: 1 the leaders of the fathers' houses of . . Israel •
6 its place, in the inner sanctuary of the house 1
10 a cloud filled the house of the LORD 1
11 glory of the LORD filled the house of the LORD. 1
13 an exalted house, a place for thee to dwell 1
16 to build a house, that my name might be there; 1
17 to build a house for the name of the LORD 1
18 it was in your heart to build a house for my name 1
19 you shall not build the house, but your son 1
19 your son . . shall build the house for my name.' 1
20 I have built the house for the name of the LORD 1
27 how much less this house which I have built! 1
29 thy eyes may be open . . toward this house 1
31 swears his oath before thine altar in this house 1
33 pray and make supplication to thee in this house; 1
38 and stretching out his hands toward this house; 1
42 when he comes and prays toward this house 1
43 this house which I have built is called 1
44 pray . . toward . . the house which I have built 1
48 the city . . and the house which I have built 1
63 the king and . . dedicated the house of the LORD. 1
64 the court that was before the house of the LORD; 1
9: 1 finished building the house of the LORD 1
1 building . . and the king's house 1
3 consecrated this house which you have built 1
7 house which I have consecrated . . I will cast out 1
8 this house will become a heap of ruins; 1
8 the LORD done thus to this land and to this house?' 1
10 years, in which Solomon had built the two houses 1
10 Solomon had built . . the house of the LORD 1
10 Solomon had built . . and the king's house 1
15 forced labor . . to build the house of the LORD 1
15 to build the house of the LORD and his own house 1
24 went up from the city of David to her own house 1
25 So he finished the house. 1
10: 4 the wisdom of Solomon, the house that he had built 1
5 which he offered at the house of the LORD 1
12 king made . . supports for the house of the LORD 1
12 the king made . . supports . . for the king's house 1
17 put them in the House of the Forest of Lebanon. 1
21 the vessels of the House of the Forest of Lebanon 1
11:14 Hadad . . he was of the royal house in Edom. 2
18 gave him a house, and assigned him an allowance 1
20 his son, whom Tah'penes weaned in Pharaoh's house; 1
20 Genu'bath was in Pharaoh's house 1
28 over all the forced labor of the house of Joseph. 1
38 I will be with you, and will build you a sure house 1
12:16 Look now to your own house, David. 1
19 in rebellion against the house of David 1
20 There was none that followed the house of David 1
21 Rehobo'am . . assembled all the house of Judah 1
21 to fight against the house of Israel 1
23 Say to Rehobo'am . . and to all the house of Judah 1
26 the kingdom will turn back to the house of David; 1
27 go up to offer sacrifices in the house of the LORD 1
31 He also made houses on high places 1
13: 2 a son shall be born to the house of David, Josi'ah 1
8 If you give me half your house, I will not go 1
18 Bring him back with you into your house 1
19 he went back with him, and ate bread in his house 1
32 and against all the houses of the high places 1
34 this thing became sin to the house of Jerobo'am 1
14: 4 went to Shiloh, and came to the house of Ahi'jah. 1
8 tore the kingdom away from the house of David 1
10 I will bring evil upon the house of Jerobo'am 1
10 and will utterly consume the house of Jerobo'am 1
12 Arise therefore, go to your house. 1
13 something pleasing . . in the house of Jerobo'am. 1
14 who shall cut off the house of Jerobo'am today. 1
17 as she came to the threshold of the house 1
26 took away the treasures of the house of the LORD 1
26 he took away . . the treasures of the king's house; 1
27 the guard, who kept the door of the king's house. 1
28 as the king went into the house of the LORD 1
15:15 he brought into the house of the LORD the . . gifts 1
18 left in the treasures of the house of the LORD 1
18 left in . . and the treasures of the king's house 1
27 Ba'asha the son of Ahi'jah, of the house of Is'sachar 1
29 he killed all the house of Jerobo'am; 1
29 he left to the house of Jerobo'am not one •
16: 3 I will utterly sweep away Ba'asha and his house 1
3 I will make your house like the house of Jerobo'am 1
3 I will make your house like the house of Jerobo'am 1
7 came . . against Ba'asha and his house 1
7 in being like the house of Jerobo'am 1
9 drinking himself drunk in the house of Arza 1
11 he killed all the house of Ba'asha; 1
12 Thus Zimri destroyed all the house of Ba'asha 1
18 he went into the citadel of the king's house 1
18 Zimri . . burned the king's house over him 1
32 He erected an altar for Ba'al in the house of Ba'al 1
17:17 the son of the woman, the mistress of the house 1
23 down from the upper chamber into the house 1
18:18 but you have, and your father's house, because you 1
20: 6 they shall search your house 1
6 your house and the houses of your servants 1
31 the kings of the house of Israel are merciful 1
43 king . . went to his house resentful and sullen 1
21: 2 Give me . . because it is near my house; 1
4 Ahab went into his house vexed and sullen 1
22 I will make your house like the house of Jerobo'am 1
22 I will make your house like the house of Jerobo'am 1
22 I will make your house . . like the house of Ba'asha 1
29 I will bring the evil upon his house. 1
22:39 acts of Ahab . . and the ivory house which he built 1
2Kg 4: 2 Tell me; what have you in the house? 1
2 Your maidservant has nothing in the house 1

32 When Eli'sha came into the house, he saw the child 1
35 he got up . . and walked once to and fro in the house 1
5: 9 Na'aman . . halted at the door of Eli'sha's house. 1
18 goes into the house of Rimmon to worship there 1
18 when . . and I bow myself in the house of Rimmon 1
18 when I bow myself in the house of Rimmon 1
24 he took them . . and put them in the house; 1
6:32 Eli'sha was sitting in his house 1
8: 3 to appeal to the king for her house and her land. 1
5 appealed to the king for her house and her land. 1
18 he walked . . as the house of Ahab had done 1
27 He also walked in the way of the house of Ahab 1
27 did what was evil . . as the house of Ahab had done 1
27 for he was son-in-law to the house of Ahab. 1
9: 6 So he arose, and went into the house; 1
7 you shall strike down the house of Ahab 1
8 For the whole house of Ahab shall perish; 1
9 I will make the house of Ahab like . . of Jerobo'am 1
9 make the house of Ahab like the house of Jerobo'am 1
9 and like the house of Ba'asha the son of Ahi'jah. 1
10: 3 and fight for your master's house. 1
10 the LORD spoke concerning the house of Ahab; 1
11 Jehu slew all that remained of the house of Ahab 1
21 And they entered the house of Ba'al 1
21 they entered . . and the house of Ba'al was filled 1
23 Jehu went into the house of Ba'al with Jehon'adab 1
25 and went into the inner room of the house of Ba'al 1
26 the pillar that was in the house of Ba'al 1
27 they . . demolished the house of Ba'al 1
30 and have done to the house of Ahab according 1
11: 3 he remained . . hid in the house of the LORD, while 1
4 and had them come to him in the house of the LORD; 1
4 and put them under oath in the house of the LORD 1
5 who come off . . and guard the king's house 1
7 which come on . . and guard the house of the LORD 1
10 and shields . . which were in the house of the LORD; 1
11 from the south side of the house to the north side 1
11 from the south . . to the north side of the house 1
11 guards stood . . around the altar and the house. 1
13 she went into the house of the LORD to the people; 1
15 Let her not be slain in the house of the LORD. 1
16 through the horses' entrance to the king's house 1
18 the people of the land went to the house of Ba'al 1
18 posted watchmen over the house of the LORD. 1
19 brought the king down from the house of the LORD 1
19 marching through the gate . . to the king's house. 1
20 Athali'ah had been slain . . at the king's house. 1
12: 4 the money . . brought into the house of the LORD 1
4 prompts him to bring into the house of the LORD 1
5 repair the house wherever any need of repairs is 1
6 the priests had made no repairs on the house. 1
7 Why are you not repairing the house? 1
7 but hand it over for the repair of the house. 1
8 that they should not repair the house. 1
9 right side as one entered the house of the LORD; 1
9 the money . . brought into the house of the LORD. 1
10 the money that was found in the house of the LORD. 1
11 who had the oversight of the house of the LORD; 1
11 builders who worked upon the house of the LORD 1
12 stone for making repairs on the house of the LORD 1
12 and for any outlay upon the repairs of the house. 1
13 were not made for the house of the LORD basins 1
13 money that was brought into the house of the LORD 1
14 workmen who were repairing the house of the LORD 1
16 was not brought into the house of the LORD; it 1
18 found in the treasuries of the house of the LORD 1
18 in the treasuries of . . and of the king's house 1
20 a conspiracy, and slew Jo'ash in the house of Millo 1
13: 6 depart from the sins of the house of Jerobo'am 1
14:14 vessels that were found in the house of the LORD 1
14 and in the treasuries of the king's house 1
15: 5 he was a leper . . and he dwelt in a separate house. 1
25 slew him . . in the citadel of the king's house; 1
35 He built the upper gate of the house of the LORD. 1
16: 8 silver and gold . . found in the house of the LORD 1
8 found . . and in the treasures of the king's house 1
14 altar . . he removed from the front of the house 1
14 place between his altar and the house of the LORD 1
18 he removed from the house of the LORD 1
17:21 When he had torn Israel from the house of David 1
18:15 the silver that was found in the house of the LORD 1
15 and in the treasuries of the king's house. 1
19: 1 and went into the house of the LORD. 1
14 and Hezeki'ah went up to the house of the LORD 1
30 remnant of the house of Judah shall . . take root 1
37 he was worshiping in the house of Nisroch his god 1
20: 1 Set your house in order; for you shall die 1
5 you shall go up to the house of the LORD. 1
8 I . . go up to the house of the LORD on the third day? 1
13 and he showed them all his treasure house 1
13 there was nothing in his house or in all his realm 1
15 He said, "What have they seen in your house? 1
15 They have seen all that is in my house; 1
17 all that is in your house . . shall be carried 1
21: 4 And he built altars in the house of the LORD 1
5 the two courts of the house of the LORD. 1
7 the graven image . . he set in the house 1
7 In this house . . I will put my name for ever; 1
13 and the plummet of the house of Ahab; 1
18 and was buried in the garden of his house 1
23 the servants . . and killed the king in his house. 1
22: 3 the king sent Shaphan . . to the house of the LORD 1
4 the money . . brought into the house of the LORD 1
5 who have the oversight of the house of the LORD; 1
5 give it to the workmen . . at the house of the LORD 1
5 workmen who are at . . repairing the house 1
6 timber and quarried stone to repair the house. 1
8 found the book of the law in the house of the LORD. 1
9 emptied out the money that was found in the house 1
9 who have the oversight of the house of the LORD. 1
23: 2 And the king went up to the house of the LORD 1
2 which had been found in the house of the LORD. 1
6 brought . . the Ashe'rah from the house of the LORD 1
7 he broke down the houses of the . . prostitutes 1
7 the houses . . which were in the house of the LORD 1
11 horses . . at the entrance to the house of the LORD 1
12 had made in the two courts of the house of the LORD 1
24 the book . . found in the house of the LORD. 1
27 Jerusalem, and the house of which I said 1
24:13 all the treasures of the house of the LORD 1
13 and the treasures of the king's house 1
25: 9 burned the house of the LORD, and the king's house 1
9 the king's house and all the houses of Jerusalem; 1
9 the king's house and all the houses of Jerusalem; 1
9 every great house he burned down. 1
13 the pillars of bronze . . in the house of the LORD 1
13 the bronze sea that were in the house of the LORD 1
16 which Solomon had made for the house of the LORD 1
1Ch 2:55 Hammath, the father of the house of Rechab. 1
4:21 families of the house of linen workers 1
38 and their fathers' houses increased greatly. 1
5:13 kinsmen according to their fathers' houses 1
15 Ahi . . was chief in their fathers' houses; 1
24 These were the heads of their fathers' houses 1
24 heads of their fathers' houses. 1
6:10 in the house that Solomon built in Jerusalem 1
31 put in charge . . in the house of the LORD 1
32 until Solomon had built the house of the LORD 1
48 service of the tabernacle of the house of God. 1
7: 2 heads of their fathers' houses, namely of Tola 1
4 with them . . according to their fathers' houses 1
7 sons of Bela . . five, heads of fathers' houses 1
9 heads of their fathers' houses, mighty warriors 1
23 Beri'ah, because evil had befallen his house. 1
40 men of Asher, heads of fathers' houses, approved 1
9: 9 according to their fathers' houses. 1
11 Ahi'tub . . chief officer of the house of God; 1
13 their kinsmen, heads of their fathers' houses 1
13 for the work of the service of the house of God. 1
19 Shallum . . and his kinsmen of his fathers' house 1
23 in charge of the gates of the house of the LORD 1
23 the house of the LORD, that is, the house of the tent 1
26 chambers and the treasures of the house of God. 1
27 they lodged round about the house of God; 1
10: 6 he and his three sons and all his house died 1
12:28 and 22 commanders from his own father's house. 1
29 kept their allegiance to the house of Saul. 1
30 men of valor, famous men in their fathers' houses. 1
13: 7 upon a new cart, from the house of Abin'adab 1
13 took it aside to the house of O'bed-e'dom 1
14 with the household of O'bed-e'dom in his house 1
14: 1 masons and carpenters to build a house for him. 1
15: 1 built houses for himself in the city of David; 1
25 to bring up the ark . . from the house of O'bed-e'dom 1
16:43 Then all the people departed each to his house 1
17: 1 Now when David dwelt in his house 1
1 Behold, I dwell in a house of cedar 1
4 You shall not build me a house to dwell in. 1
5 not dwelt in a house since the day I led up Israel 1
6 saying, "Why have you not built me a house of cedar? 1
10 that the LORD will build you a house. 1
12 He shall build a house for me 1
14 confirm him in my house and in my kingdom for ever 1
16 said, "Who am I, O LORD God, and what is my house 1
17 O God; thou hast also spoken of thy servant's house 1
23 thou hast spoken . . and concerning his house 1
24 house of thy servant David will be established 1
25 revealed . . that thou wilt build a house for him; 1
27 please thee to bless the house of thy servant 1
21:17 be against me and against my father's house; 1
22: 1 David said, "Here shall be the house of the LORD God 1
2 dressed stones for building the house of God. 1
5 the house that is to be built for the LORD 1
6 charged him to build a house for the LORD 1
7 in my heart to build a house to the name of the LORD 1
8 you shall not build a house to my name 1
10 He shall build a house for my name. 1
11 may succeed in building the house of the LORD 1
14 I have provided for the house of the LORD 1
19 into a house built for the name of the LORD. 1
23: 4 have charge of the work in the house of the LORD 1
11 they became a father's house in one reckoning 1
24 were the sons of Levi by their fathers' houses 1
24 the work for the service of the house of the LORD. 1
28 for the service of the house of the LORD 1
28 and any work for the service of the house of God; 1
32 for the service of the house of the LORD. 1
24: 4 heads of fathers' houses of the sons of Elea'zar 1
6 one father's house being chosen for Elea'zar 1
19 duty . . to come into the house of the LORD 1
30 the Levites according to their fathers' houses. 1
25: 6 in the music in the house of the LORD 1
6 the music . . for the service of the house of God. 1
26: 6 who were rulers in their fathers' houses 1
12 ministering in the house of the LORD; 1
13 cast lots by fathers' houses, small and great 1
20 had charge of the treasuries of the house of God 1
22 of the treasuries of the house of the LORD. 1
27 for the maintenance of the house of the LORD. 1
28: 2 I had it in my heart to build a house of rest 1
3 God said to me, 'You may not build a house 1
4 God of Israel chose me from all my father's house 1
4 chose Judah as leader, and in the house of Judah 1
4 chose Judah as leader, and in the house of Judah 1
6 Solomon your son who shall build my house 1
10 has chosen you to build a house for the sanctuary; 1
11 the plan of . . and of its houses, its treasuries 1
12 for the courts of the house of the LORD 1
12 treasuries of the house of God 1
13 the work of the service in the house of the LORD; 1
13 vessels for the service in the house of the LORD 1
20 work for the service of the house of the LORD 1
21 for all the service of the house of God; 1
29: 2 I have provided for the house of my God 1
3 to all that I have provided for the holy house 1
3 because of my devotion to the house of my God 1
3 I give it to the house of my God 1
4 for overlaying the walls of the house 1
7 They gave for the service of the house of God 1
8 gave them to the treasury of the house of the LORD 1
16 for building thee a house for thy holy name 1
2Ch 2: 3 sent him cedar to build himself a house to dwell 1
4 I am about to build a house for the name of the LORD 1
5 The house which I am to build will be great 1
6 But who is able to build him a house 1
6 Who am I to build a house for him 1
9 house I am to build will be great and wonderful. 1
3: 1 Then Solomon began to build the house of the LORD 1
3 measurements for building the house of God 1
4 The vestibule in front of the nave of the house •
4 twenty cubits . . equal to the width of the house; 1
6 He adorned the house with . . precious stones. 1
7 he lined the house with gold–its beams 1
8 corresponding to the breadth of the house 1
11 one wing of . . touched the wall of the house 1
12 one wing . . touched the wall of the house 1
15 In front of the house he made two pillars 1
4:10 set the sea at the southeast corner of the house. 1
11 that he did for King Solomon on the house of God 1
16 for King Solomon for the house of the LORD. 1
19 all the things that were in the house of God 1
5: 1 work that Solomon did for the house of the LORD 1
1 stored . . in the treasuries of the house of God. 1
7 to its place, in the inner sanctuary of the house 1
13 house, the house of the LORD, was filled 1
13 the house of the LORD, was filled with a cloud. 1
14 for the glory of the LORD filled the house of God. 1
6: 2 I have built thee an exalted house 1
5 I chose no city . . in which to build a house 1
7 David . . to build a house for the name of the LORD 1
8 it was in your heart to build a house for my name 1
9 nevertheless you shall not build the house 1
9 your son . . shall build the house for my name.' 1
10 I have built the house for the name of the LORD 1
18 how much less this house which I have built! 1
20 eyes may be open day and night toward this house 1
22 swears his oath before thy altar in this house 1
24 pray and make supplication to thee in this house 1
29 and stretching out his hands toward this house; 1
32 when he comes and prays toward this house 1
33 may know that this house . . called by thy name. 1
34 pray . . toward . . the house which I have built 1
38 pray toward . . and the house which I built 1
7: 2 the priests could not enter the house of the LORD 1
2 the glory of the LORD filled the LORD's house. 1
5 king and . . people dedicated the house of God. 1
7 the court that was before the house of the LORD; 1
11 Thus Solomon finished the house of the LORD 1
11 Solomon finished . . and the king's house; 1
11 planned to do in the house of the LORD and in his 1
11 planned to do in the house . . and in his own house 1
12 chosen this place . . as a house of sacrifice. 1
16 For now I have chosen and consecrated this house 1
20 and this house . . I will cast out of my sight 1
21 at this house . . every one passing by will be 1
21 'Why has the LORD done thus to . . and to this house? 1
8: 1 in which Solomon had built the house of the LORD 1
1 had built the house of the LORD and his own house 1
11 from . . to the house which he had built for her 1
11 My wife shall not live in the house of David 1
16 foundation of the house of the LORD was laid 1
16 So the house of the LORD was completed. 1
9: 3 queen of Sheba had seen . . the house that he had 1
4 which he offered at the house of the LORD 1
11 algum wood steps for the house of the LORD 1
11 algum wood steps for . . the king's house 1
16 put them in the House of the Forest of Lebanon. 1

20 all the vessels of the House . . were of pure gold; 1
10:16 Look now to your own house, David. 1
19 been in rebellion against the house of David 1
11: 1 he assembled the house of Judah, and Benjamin 1
12: 9 took away the treasures of the house of the LORD 1
9 he took away . . the treasures of the king's house; 1
10 who kept the door of the king's house. 1
11 often as the king went into the house of the LORD 1
15: 8 the vestibule of the house of the LORD. *
18 he brought into the house of God the votive gifts 1
16: 2 from the treasures of the house of the LORD 1
2 from the treasures of . . the king's house 1
17:14 This was the muster of them by fathers' houses 1
19: 1 returned in safety to his house in Jerusalem. 1
11 Zebedi'ah . . the governor of the house of Judah 1
20: 5 Jehosh'aphat stood . . in the house of the LORD 1
9 we will stand before this house, and before thee 1
9 for thy name is in this house 1
28 to the house of the LORD. 1
21: 6 he walked . . as the house of Ahab had done; 1
7 Yet the LORD would not destroy the house of David 1
13 house of Ahab led Israel into unfaithfulness 1
13 killed your brothers, of your father's house 1
17 possessions . . belonged to the king's house 1
22: 3 He also walked in the ways of the house of Ahab 1
4 did what was evil . . as the house of Ahab had done; 1
7 LORD had anointed to destroy the house of Ahab. 1
8 executing judgment upon the house of Ahab 1
9 house of Ahazi'ah had no one able to rule 1
10 all the royal family of the house of Judah. 1
12 remained with them . . hid in the house of God 1
23: 3 made a covenant with the king in the house of God. 1
5 one third shall be at the king's house 1
5 shall be in the courts of the house of the LORD. 1
6 Let no one enter the house of the LORD 1
7 whoever enters the house shall be slain. 1
9 which were in the house of God; 1
10 from the south side of the house to the north side 1
10 from the south . . to the north side of the house 1
10 around the altar and the house. 1
12 she went into the house of the LORD to the people; 1
14 Do not slay her in the house of the LORD. 1
15 the entrance of the horse gate of the king's house 1
17 people went to the house of Ba'al, and tore it down; 1
18 posted watchmen for the house of the LORD 1
18 organized to be in charge of the house of the LORD 1
19 gatekeepers at the gates of the house of the LORD 1
20 brought the king down from the house of the LORD 1
20 through the upper gate to the king's house. 1
24: 4 Jo'ash decided to restore the house of the LORD. 1
5 money to repair the house of your God 1
7 had broken into the house of God; 1
7 all the dedicated things of the house of the LORD 1
8 set it outside the gate of the house of the LORD. 1
12 charge of the work of the house of the LORD 1
12 hired masons . . to restore the house of the LORD 1
12 workers . . to repair the house of the LORD. 1
13 they restored the house of God 1
14 made utensils for the house of the LORD 1
14 offered burnt offerings in the house of the LORD 1
16 done good in Israel, and toward God and his house. 1
18 they forsook the house of the LORD 1
21 with stones in the court of the house of the LORD. 1
27 the rebuilding of the house of God 1
25: 5 Amazi'ah . . set them by fathers' houses 1
24 the vessels that were found in the house of God 1
24 he seized also the treasuries of the king's house 1
26:19 the priests in the house of the LORD 1
21 being a leper dwelt in a separate house 1
21 for he was excluded from the house of the LORD. 1
27: 3 He built the upper gate of the house of the LORD 1
28:21 For Ahaz took from the house of the LORD 1
21 Ahaz took from . . the house of the king 1
24 gathered . . the vessels of the house of God 1
24 cut in pieces the vessels of the house of God 1
24 Ahaz . . shut up the doors of the house of the LORD; 1
29: 3 opened the doors of the house of the LORD 1
5 sanctify the house of the LORD, the God 1
15 went in . . to cleanse the house of the LORD. 1
16 went into the inner part of the house of the LORD 1
16 into the court of the house of the LORD; 1
17 eight days they sanctified the house of the LORD 1
18 We have cleansed all the house of the LORD 1
20 Hezeki'ah . . went up to the house of the LORD. 1
25 he stationed the Levites in the house of the LORD 1
31 bring sacrifices . . to the house of the LORD. 1
35 service of the house of the LORD was restored. 1
30: 1 come to the house of the LORD at Jerusalem, to keep 1
15 burnt offerings into the house of the LORD. 1
31:10 Azari'ah . . who was of the house of Zadok 1
10 contributions into the house of the LORD 1
11 to prepare chambers in the house of the LORD; 1
13 Azari'ah the chief officer of the house of God. 1
16 all who entered the house of the LORD as the duty 1
17 priests was according to their fathers' houses; 1
21 he undertook in the service of the house of God 1
32:21 And when he came into the house of his god 1
33: 4 he built altars in the house of the LORD 1
5 in the two courts of the house of the LORD. 1
7 the image of the idol . . he set in the house of God 1
7 In this house . . I will put my name for ever; 1
15 gods and the idol from the house of the LORD 1
15 built on the mountain of the house of the LORD 1
20 they buried him in his house; 1
24 servants conspired . . killed him in his house. 1
34: 8 when he had purged the land and the house 1
8 to repair the house of the LORD his God. 1
9 money that had been brought into the house of God 1
10 who had the oversight of the house of the LORD; 1
10 workmen who were working in the house of the LORD 1
10 gave it for repairing and restoring the house. 1
14 money . . brought into the house of the LORD 1
15 found the book of the law in the house of the LORD"; 1
17 the money that was found in the house of the LORD 1
30 the king went up to the house of the LORD 1
30 which had been found in the house of the LORD. 1
35: 2 in the service of the house of the LORD. 1
3 Put the holy ark in the house which Solomon 1
4 Prepare . . according to your fathers' houses 1
5 groupings of the fathers' houses of your brethren 1
5 a part of a father's house of the Levites. 1
8 the chief officers of the house of God 1
12 groupings of the fathers' houses of the lay 1
21 against the house with which I am at war; 1
36: 7 part of the vessels of the house of the LORD 1
10 precious vessels of the house of the LORD 1
14 polluted the house of the LORD which he had 1
17 with the sword in the house of their sanctuary 1
18 vessels of the house of God, great and small 1
18 treasures of the house of the LORD 1
19 burned the house of God, and broke down the wall 1
23 charged me to build him a house at Jerusalem 1
Ezr 1: 2 charged me to build him a house at Jerusalem 1
3 Jerusalem . . and rebuild the house of the LORD 1
4 besides freewill offerings for the house of God 1
5 stirred to go up to rebuild the house of the LORD 1
7 brought out the vessels of the house of the LORD 1
7 carried . . and placed in the house of his gods. 1
2:36 sons of Jedai'ah, of the house of Jeshua, 973. 1
59 not prove their fathers' houses or their descent 1
68 when they came to the house of the LORD 1
68 made freewill offerings for the house of God 1
3: 8 their coming to the house of God at Jerusalem 1
8 oversight of the work of the house of the LORD. 1
9 oversight of the workmen in the house of God 1
11 foundation of the house of the LORD was laid. 1
12 old men who had seen the first house 1
12 saw the foundation of this house being laid 1
4: 3 building a house to our God; but we alone 1
24 the work on the house of God which is in Jerusalem 3
5: 2 arose and began to rebuild the house of God 3
3 Who gave you a decree to build this house 3
8 went to . . Judah, to the house of the great God. 3
9 'Who gave you a decree to build this house 3
11 rebuilding the house . . built many years ago 3
12 destroyed this house and carried away 3
13 decree that this house of God should be rebuilt. 3
14 gold and silver vessels of the house of God 3
15 let the house of God be rebuilt on its site. 3
16 came and laid the foundations of the house of God 3
17 rebuilding of this house of God in Jerusalem. 3
6: 1 house of the archives where the documents 3
3 Concerning the house of God at Jerusalem 3
3 let the house be rebuilt, the place where 3
5 gold and silver vessels of the house of God 3
5 you shall put them in the house of God. 3
7 let the work on this house of God alone; 3
7 Jews rebuild this house of God on its site. 3
8 do . . for the rebuilding of this house of God; 3
11 beam shall be pulled out of his house 3
11 his house shall be made a dunghill. 3
12 put forth a hand . . to destroy this house of God 3
15 house was finished on the third day of the month 3
16 celebrated the dedication of this house of God 3
17 offered at the dedication of this house of God 3
22 aided them in the work of the house of God 1
7:16 vowed willingly for the house of their God 3
17 offer them upon the altar of the house of your God 3
19 given you for the service of the house of your God 3
20 else is required for the house of your God 3
23 be done in full for the house of the God of heaven 3
24 or other servants of this house of God. 3
27 to beautify the house of the LORD . . in Jerusalem 1
8:17 to send us ministers for the house of our God. 1
25 offering for the house of our God which the king 1
29 within the chambers of the house of the LORD. 1
30 to bring them to Jerusalem, to the house of our God. 1
33 On the fourth day, within the house of our God 1
36 aided the people and the house of God. 1
9: 9 grant us some reviving to set up the house of our God 1
10: 1 casting himself down before the house of God 1
6 Then Ezra withdrew from before the house of God 1
9 sat in the open square before the house of God 1
16 Ezra . . selected men, heads of fathers' houses 1
16 according to their fathers' houses 1
Neh 1: 6 Yea, I and my father's house have sinned. 1
2: 8 make beams . . for the house which I shall occupy. 1
3:10 Jedai'ah . . repaired opposite his house; 1
16 repaired to . . the house of the mighty men. 1
20 door of the house of Eli'ashib the high priest. 1
21 section from the door of the house of Eli'ashib 1
21 from . . to the end of the house of Eli'ashib. 1
23 Benjamin . . repaired opposite their house. 1
23 Azari'ah . . repaired beside his own house. 1
24 section, from the house of Azari'ah to the Angle 1
25 projecting from the upper house of the king 1
28 repaired, each one opposite his own house. 1
29 Zadok . . repaired opposite his own house. 1
31 as far as the house of the temple servants 1
4:16 leaders stood behind all the house of Judah 1
5: 3 mortgaging our . . vineyards, and our houses 1
11 Return . . olive orchards, and their houses 1
13 So may God shake out every man from his house 1
6:10 into the house of Shemai'ah the son of Delai'ah 1
10 Let us meet together in the house of God 1
7: 3 Appoint guards . . each opposite his own house. 1
4 people . . were few and no houses had been built. 1
39 sons of Jedai'ah, namely the house of Jeshua, 973. 1
61 but they could not prove their fathers' houses 1
8:16 made booths . . in the courts of the house of God 1
9:25 possession of houses full of all good things 1
10:32 third part . . for the service of the house of our God 1
33 for all the work of the house of our God. 1
34 offering, to bring it into the house of our God 1
34 according to our fathers' houses, at times 1
35 first fruits . . year by year, to the house of the LORD; 1
36 also to bring to the house of our God 1
36 priests who minister in the house of our God 1
37 priests, to the chambers of the house of our God; 1
38 tithes to the house of our God, to the chambers 1
39 We will not neglect the house of our God. 1
11:11 Merai'oth, son of Ahi'tub, ruler of the house of God 1
12 their brethren who did the work of the house, 822; 1
16 who were over the outside work of the house of God; 1
22 singers, over the work of the house of God. 1
12:37 above the house of David, to the Water Gate 1
40 both companies . . stood in the house of God 1
13: 4 chambers of the house of our God 1
7 chamber in the courts of the house of God. 1
9 brought back . . the vessels of the house of God 1
11 Why is the house of God forsaken? 1
14 good deeds that I have done for the house of my God 1
Est 1:22 that every man be lord in his own house 1
4:14 but you and your father's house will perish. 1
6:12 But Haman hurried to his house, mourning 1
7: 8 Will he even assault the queen . . in my own house? 1
9 the gallows . . is standing in Haman's house 1
8: 1 King Ahasu-e'rus gave . . Esther the house of Haman 1
2 And Esther set Mor'decai over the house of Haman. 1
7 Behold, I have given Esther the house of Haman 1
9: 4 For Mor'decai was great in the king's house 1
Job 1: 4 go and hold a feast in the house of each on his day; 1
10 Hast thou not put a hedge about him and his house 1
13 drinking wine in their eldest brother's house; 1
18 drinking wine in their eldest brother's house; 1
19 and struck the four corners of the house 1
3:15 princes . . who filled their houses with silver. 1
4:19 how much more those who dwell in houses of clay 1
7:10 he returns no more to his house 1
8:15 He leans against his house, but it does not stand; 1
15:28 in houses which no man should inhabit 1
17:13 If I look for Sheol as my house 1
19:15 the guests in my house have forgotten me; 1
20:19 he has seized a house which he did not build. 1
28 possessions of his house will be carried away 1
21: 9 Their houses are safe from fear 1
21 For what do they care for their houses after them 1
28 For you say, 'Where is the house of the prince? 1
22:18 Yet he filled their houses with good things– 1
24:16 In the dark they dig through houses; 1
27:18 The house which he builds is like a spider's web 1
30:23 death, and to the house appointed for all living. 1
42:11 ate bread with him in his house; 1
Ps 5: 7 I through . . steadfast love will enter thy house 1
23: 6 I shall dwell in the house of the LORD for ever. 1
26: 8 O LORD, I love the habitation of thy house 1
27: 4 that I may dwell in the house of the LORD 1
36: 8 They feast on the abundance of thy house 1
42: 4 led them in procession to the house of God 1
45:10 forget your people and your father's house; 1
49:16 rich, when the glory of his house increases. 1
50: 9 I will accept no bull from your house 1
52: 0 David has come to the house of Ahimelech. 1
8 I am like a green olive tree in the house of God. 1
55:14 within God's house we walked in fellowship. 1
59: 0 of David, when Saul sent men to watch his house 1
65: 4 be satisfied with the goodness of thy house 1
66:13 I will come into thy house with burnt offerings; 1
69: 9 For zeal for thy house has consumed me 1
84: 4 Blessed are those who dwell in thy house 1
10 rather be a doorkeeper in the house of my God than 1
92:13 They are planted in the house of the LORD 1
93: 5 holiness befits thy house, O LORD, for evermore. 1
98: 3 love and faithfulness to the house of Israel. 1
101: 2 walk with integrity of heart within my house; 1
7 no . . practices deceit shall dwell in my house; 1
105:21 he made him lord of his house, and ruler of all 1

112: 3 Wealth and riches are in his house; 1
114: 1 house of Jacob from a people of strange language 1
115:10 O house of Aaron, put your trust in the LORD! 1
12 he will bless the house of Israel; 1
12 house of Israel; he will bless the house of Aaron; 1
116:19 in the courts of the house of the LORD 1
118: 3 house of Aaron say, "His steadfast love endures 1
26 We bless you from the house of the LORD 1
119:54 have been my songs in the house of my pilgrimage. 1
122: 1 Let us go to the house of the LORD! 1
5 thrones of the house of David. 1
9 For the sake of the house of the LORD our God 1
127: 1 Unless the LORD builds the house, those who build 1
128: 3 wife . . like a fruitful vine within your house; 1
132: 3 I will not enter my house or get into my bed; 1
134: 1 who stand by night in the house of the LORD! 1
135: 2 you that stand in the house of the LORD 1
2 that stand in . . courts of the house of our God! 1
19 O house of Israel, bless the LORD! O house of Aaron 1
19 Israel . . O house of Aaron, bless the LORD! 1
20 O house of Levi, bless the LORD! 1
Prv 1:13 we shall fill our houses with spoil; 1
2:18 for her house sinks down to death 1
3:33 LORD'S curse is on the house of the wicked 1
5: 8 do not go near the door of her house; 1
10 lest . . your labors go to the house of an alien; 1
6:31 he will give all the goods of his house. 1
7: 6 For at the window of my house I have looked out 1
8 taking the road to her house 1
27 Her house is the way to Sheol 1
9: 1 Wisdom has built her house 1
14 She sits at the door of her house 1
12: 7 but the house of the righteous will stand. 1
14: 1 Wisdom builds her house 1
11 The house of the wicked will be destroyed 1
15: 6 house of the righteous there is much treasure 1
25 The LORD tears down the house of the proud 1
17: 1 quiet than a house full of feasting with strife. 1
13 evil will not depart from his house. 1
19:14 House and wealth are inherited from fathers 1
21: 9 than in a house shared with a contentious woman. 1
12 The righteous observes the house of the wicked; 1
24: 3 By wisdom a house is built 1
27 after that build your house. 1
25:17 Let your foot be seldom in your neighbor's house 1
24 than in a house shared with a contentious woman. 1
27:10 do not go to your brother's house in the day 1
Ecc 2: 4 I built houses and planted vineyards for myself; 1
7 and had slaves who were born in my house; 1
5: 1 Guard your steps when you go to the house of God; 1
7: 2 It is better to go to the house of mourning 1
2 than to go to the house of feasting; 1
4 The heart of the wise is in the house of mourning; 1
4 but the heart of fools is in the house of mirth. 1
10:18 and through indolence the house leaks. 1
12: 3 the day when the keepers of the house tremble 1
Sng 1:17 the beams of our house are cedar, our rafters are 1
2: 4 He brought me to the banqueting house 1
3: 4 until I had brought him into my mother's house 1
8: 2 lead you and bring you into the house of my mother 1
7 a man offered for love all the wealth of his house 1
Isa 2: 2 the mountain of the house of the LORD shall be 1
3 mountain of the LORD . . house of the God of Jacob; 1
5 O house of Jacob, come, let us walk in the light 1
6 thou hast rejected thy people, the house of Jacob 1
3: 6 hold of his brother in the house of his father 1
7 n my house there is neither bread nor mantle 1
14 the spoil of the poor is in your houses. 1
5: 7 the vineyard of the LORD . . is the house of Israel 1
8 who join house to house, who add field to field 1
8 who join house to house, who add field to field 1
9 many houses shall be desolate, large . . houses 1
9 beautiful houses, without inhabitant. *
6: 4 and the house was filled with smoke. 1
11 cities . . and houses without men 1
7: 2 the house of David was told, "Syria is in league 1
13 O house of David! Is it too little for you to weary men 1
17 upon your people and upon your father's house 1
8:14 a rock of stumbling to both houses of Israel 1
17 LORD . . hiding his face from the house of Jacob 1
10:20 of Israel and the survivors of the house of Jacob 1
13:16 before their eyes; their houses . . be plundered 1
21 and its houses will be full of howling creatures; 1
14: 1 aliens . . will cleave to the house of Jacob. 1
2 the house of Israel will possess them 1
22: 8 looked to the weapons of the House of the Forest 1
10 you counted the houses of Jerusalem 1
10 you broke down the houses to fortify the wall. 1
18 you shall die . . you shame of your master's house. 1
21 a father . . to the house of Judah. 1
22 on his shoulder the key of the house of David; 1
23 become a throne of honor to his father's house. 1
24 hang on him the whole weight of his father's house 1
23: 1 for Tyre is laid waste, without house or haven! 1
24:10 every house is shut up so that none can enter. 1
29:22 says the LORD . . concerning the house of Jacob 1
31: 2 will arise against the house of the evildoers 1
32:13 yea, for all the joyous houses in the joyful city. 1
37: 1 and went into the house of the LORD. 1
14 and Hezeki'ah went up to the house of the LORD 1
31 the surviving remnant of the house of Judah 1
38 he was worshiping in the house of Nisroch his god 1
38: 1 Set your house in order; for you shall die 1
20 all the days of our life, at the house of the LORD. 1
22 sign that I shall go up to the house of the LORD 1
39: 2 he showed them his treasure house 1
2 There was nothing in his house or in all his realm 1
4 He said, "What have they seen in your house? 1
4 They have seen all that is in my house; 1
6 the days are coming, when all that is in your house 1
44:13 with the beauty of a man, to dwell in a house. 1
46: 3 Hearken to me, O house of Jacob 1
3 all the remnant of the house of Israel 1
48: 1 Hear this, O house of Jacob, who are called 1
56: 5 I will give in my house and within my walls 1
7 and make them joyful in my house of prayer; 1
7 my house shall be called a house of prayer 1
7 be called a house of prayer for all peoples. 1
58: 1 declare . . to the house of Jacob their sins. 1
7 and bring the homeless poor into your house; 1
60: 7 and I will glorify my glorious house. 1
63: 7 and the great goodness to the house of Israel 1
64:11 Our holy and beautiful house, 1
65:21 They shall build houses and inhabit them; 1
66: 1 what is the house which you would build for me 1
20 in a clean vessel to the house of the LORD. 1
Jer 2: 4 Hear the word of the LORD, O house of Jacob 1
4 and all the families of the house of Israel. 1
26 the house of Israel shall be shamed 1
3:18 the house of Judah shall join the house of Israel 1
18 the house of Judah shall join the house of Israel 1
20 have you been faithless to me, O house of Israel 1
5: 7 and trooped to the houses of harlots. 1
11 For the house of Israel and the house of Judah 1
11 For the house of Israel and the house of Judah 1
15 upon you a nation from afar, O house of Israel 1
20 Declare this in the house of Jacob 1
27 their houses are full of treachery; 1
6:12 Their houses shall be turned over to others 1
7: 2 Stand in the gate of the LORD'S house, and proclaim 1
10 and then come and stand before me in this house 1
11 Has this house, which is called by my name 1
14 I will do to the house which is called by my name 1
30 in the house which is called by my name 1
9:26 the house of Israel is uncircumcised in heart. 1
10: 1 the LORD speaks to you, O house of Israel. 1
11:10 the house of Israel and the house of Judah have 1
10 and the house of Judah have broken my covenant 1
15 What right has my beloved in my house 1
17 because of the evil which the house of Israel 1
17 of Israel and the house of Judah have done 1
12: 6 even your brothers and the house of your father 1
7 I have forsaken my house 1
14 will pluck up the house of Judah from among them. 1
13:11 I made the whole house of Israel . . cling to me 1
11 I made . . the whole house of Judah cling to me 1
16: 5 says the LORD: Do not enter the house of mourning 1
8 You shall not go into the house of feasting 1
17:22 And do not carry a burden out of your houses 1
26 thank offerings to the house of the LORD. 1
18: 2 Arise, and go down to the potter's house 1
3 I went down to the potter's house 1
6 O house of Israel, can I not do with you as this 1
6 so are you in my hand, O house of Israel. 1
22 May a cry be heard from their houses 1
19:13 houses of Jerusalem and the houses of the kings 1
13 houses of Jerusalem and the houses of the kings 1
13 houses upon whose roofs incense has been burned 1
14 and he stood in the court of the LORD'S house 1
20: 1 who was chief officer in the house of the LORD 1
2 the upper Benjamin Gate of the house of the LORD. 1
6 And you, Pashhur, and all who dwell in your house 1
21:11 And to the house of the king of Judah say 1
12 O house of David! Thus says the LORD 1
22: 1 Go down to the house of the king of Judah 1
4 then there shall enter the gates of this house 1
5 that this house shall become a desolation. 1
6 For thus says the LORD concerning the house 1
13 to him who builds his house by unrighteousness 1
14 who says, 'I will build myself a great house 1
23: 8 and led the descendants of the house of Israel 1
11 even in my house I have found their wickedness 1
26: 2 Stand in the court of the LORD'S house, and speak 1
2 which come to worship in the house of the LORD 1
6 then I will make this house like Shiloh 1
7 speaking these words in the house of the LORD. 1
9 the LORD, saying, 'This house shall be like Shiloh 1
9 about Jeremiah in the house of the LORD. 1
10 they came up from the king's house 1
10 to the house of the LORD and took their seat 1
10 the entry of the New Gate of the house of the LORD. 1
12 The LORD sent me to prophesy against this house 1
18 and the mountain of the house a wooded height. 1
27:16 saying, 'Behold, the vessels of the LORD'S house 1
18 vessels which are left in the house of the LORD 1
18 in the house of the king of Judah, and in Jerusalem 1
21 vessels which are left in the house of the LORD 1
21 in the house of the king of Judah, and in Jerusalem 1
28: 1 Hanani'ah . . spoke to me in the house of the LORD 1
3 to this place all the vessels of the LORD'S house 1
5 people who were standing in the house of the LORD; 1
6 from Babylon the vessels of the house of the LORD 1
29: 5 Build houses and live in them; 1
26 to have charge in the house of the LORD 1
28 exile will be long; build houses and live in them 1
31:27 says the LORD, when I will sow the house of Israel 1
27 sow the house of Israel and the house of Judah 1
31 will make a new covenant with the house of Israel 1
31 with the house of Israel and the house of Judah 1
33 make with the house of Israel after those days 1
32:15 Houses and fields and vineyards shall again be 1
29 houses on whose roofs incense has been offered 1
34 in the house which is called by my name 1
33: 4 concerning the houses of this city 1
4 houses of the kings of Judah which were torn down 1
11 bring thank offerings to the house of the LORD 1
14 fulfil the promise I made to the house of Israel 1
14 the house of Israel and the house of Judah. 1
17 a man to sit on the throne of the house of Israel 1
34:13 out of the house of bondage, saying 1
15 before me in the house which is called by my name; 1
35: 2 Go to the house of the Re'chabites 1
2 and bring them to the house of the LORD 1
3 his sons, and the whole house of the Re'chabites. 1
4 I brought them to the house of the LORD 1
7 you shall not build a house; you shall not sow seed; 1
9 and not to build houses to dwell in. 1
18 to the house of the Re'chabites Jeremiah said 1
36: 3 It may be that the house of Judah will hear 1
5 I am debarred from going to the house of the LORD; 1
6 in the LORD'S house you shall read the words 1
8 the words of the LORD in the LORD'S house. 1
10 read . . from the scroll, in the house of the LORD 1
10 at the entry of the New Gate of the LORD'S house. 1
12 he went down to the king's house 1
22 the king was sitting in the winter house 1
37:15 in the house of Jonathan the secretary 1
17 The king questioned him secretly in his house 1
20 do not send me back to the house of Jonathan 1
38: 7 Ethiopian, a eunuch, who was in the king's house 1
8 E'bed-mel'ech went from the king's house and said 1
11 and went to the house of the king, to a wardrobe 1
17 and you and your house shall live. 1
22 Behold, all the women left in the house of the king 1
26 he would not send me back to the house of Jonathan 1
39: 8 The Chalde'ans burned the king's house 1
8 The Chalde'ans burned . . the house of the people 1
48:13 as the house of Israel was ashamed of Bethel 1
45 has gone forth . . a flame from the house of Sihon; 1
51:51 come into the holy places of the LORD'S house.' 1
52:13 he burned the house of the LORD 1
13 the king's house and all the houses of Jerusalem; 1
13 the king's house and all the houses of Jerusalem; 1
13 every great house he burned down. 1
17 of bronze that were in the house of the LORD 1
17 the bronze sea that were in the house of the LORD 1
20 the king had made for the house of the LORD 1
Lam 1:20 in the house it is like death. 1
2: 7 a clamor was raised in the house of the LORD 1
Ezk 2: 5 for they are a rebellious house 1
6 for they are a rebellious house. 1
7 for they are a rebellious house. 1
8 be not rebellious like that rebellious house; 1
3: 1 and go, speak to the house of Israel. 1
4 Son of man, go, get you to the house of Israel 1
5 not sent to a people . . but to the house of Israel 1
7 But the house of Israel will not listen to you; 1
7 all the house of Israel are of a hard forehead 1
9 for they are a rebellious house. 1
17 I have made you a watchman for the house of Israel; 1
24 said to me, "Go, shut yourself within your house. 1
26 for they are a rebellious house. 1
27 for they are a rebellious house. 1
4: 3 This is a sign for the house of Israel. 1
4 lay the punishment of the house of Israel upon 1
5 you bear the punishment of the house of Israel. 1
6 and bear the punishment of the house of Judah; 1
5: 4 will come forth into all the house of Israel. 1
6:11 all the evil abominations of the house of Israel; 1
7:24 the nations to take possession of their houses; 1
8: 1 on the fifth day of the month, as I sat in my house 1
6 the great abominations that the house of Israel 1
10 and all the idols of the house of Israel. 1
11 70 men of the elders of the house of Israel 1
12 what the elders of the house of Israel are doing 1
14 the north gate of the house of the LORD; 1
16 me into the inner court of the house of the LORD; 1
17 Is it too slight a thing for the house of Judah 1
9: 3 had gone up . . to the threshold of the house; 1
6 began with the elders who were before the house. 1
7 Then he said to them, "Defile the house 1
9 The guilt of the house of Israel and Judah is 1
10: 3 were standing on the south side of the house 1
4 from the cherubim to the threshold of the house; 1
4 and the house was filled with the cloud 1
18 went forth from the threshold of the house 1
19 the door of the east gate of the house of the LORD; 1

11: 1 to the east gate of the house of the LORD 1
3 who say, 'The time is not near to build houses; 1
5 Thus says the LORD: So you think, O house of Israel; 1
15 your fellow exiles, the whole house of Israel 1
12: 2 you dwell in the midst of a rebellious house 1
3 for they are a rebellious house. 1
3 though they are a rebellious house. 1
6 I have made you a sign for the house of Israel. 1
9 has not the house of Israel, the rebellious house 1
9 has not the house of Israel, the rebellious house 1
10 and all the house of Israel who are in it. 1
24 no . . divination within the house of Israel. 1
25 in your days, O rebellious house, I will speak 1
27 Son of man, behold, they of the house of Israel say 1
13: 5 or built up a wall for the house of Israel 1
9 enrolled in the register of the house of Israel 1
14: 4 Any man of the house of Israel who takes his idols 1
5 I may lay hold of the hearts of the house of Israel 1
6 Therefore say to the house of Israel 1
7 For any one of the house of Israel 1
11 that the house of Israel may go no more astray 1
16:41 they shall burn your houses 1
17: 2 speak an allegory to the house of Israel; 1
12 Say now to the rebellious house, Do you not know 1
18: 6 his eyes to the idols of the house of Israel 1
15 his eyes to the idols of the house of Israel 1
25 Hear now, O house of Israel: Is my way not just? 1
29 Yet the house of Israel says, 'The way of the Lord is 1
29 O house of Israel, are my ways not just? 1
30 Therefore I will judge you, O house of Israel 1
31 Why will you die, O house of Israel? 1
20: 5 I swore to the seed of the house of Jacob 1
13 But the house of Israel rebelled against me 1
27 Therefore, son of man, speak to the house of Israel 1
30 Wherefore say to the house of Israel 1
31 And shall I be inquired of by you, O house of Israel? 1
39 As for you, O house of Israel, thus says the Lord GOD 1
40 there all the house of Israel, all of them 1
44 your corrupt doings, O house of Israel 1
22:18 the house of Israel has become dross to me; 1
23:39 And lo, this is what they did in my house. 1
47 and burn up their houses. 1
24: 3 utter an allegory to the rebellious house 1
21 Say to the house of Israel, Thus says the Lord GOD 1
25: 3 over the house of Judah when it went into exile; 1
8 the house of Judah is like all the other nations 1
12 acted revengefully against the house of Judah 1
26:12 your walls and destroy your pleasant houses; 1
28:24 for the house of Israel there shall be no more 1
25 When I gather the house of Israel 1
26 they shall build houses and plant vineyards. 1
29: 6 have been a staff of reed to the house of Israel; 1
16 again be the reliance of the house of Israel 1
21 a horn to spring forth to the house of Israel 1
33: 7 I have made a watchman for the house of Israel; 1
10 And you, son of man, say to the house of Israel 1
11 for why will you die, O house of Israel? 1
20 O house of Israel, I will judge each of you 1
30 by the walls and at the doors of the houses 1
34:30 the house of Israel, are my people, says the Lord 1
35:15 over the inheritance of the house of Israel 1
36:10 men upon you, the whole house of Israel, all of it; 1
17 when the house of Israel dwelt in their own land 1
21 which the house of Israel caused to be profaned 1
22 Therefore say to the house of Israel 1
22 It is not for your sake, O house of Israel 1
32 and confounded for your ways, O house of Israel. 1
37 I will let the house of Israel ask me to do for them 1
37:11 these bones are the whole house of Israel. 1
16 all the house of Israel associated with him 1
39:12 the house of Israel will be burying them 1
22 The house of Israel shall know that I am the LORD 1
23 that the house of Israel went into captivity 1
25 and have mercy upon the whole house of Israel; 1
29 when I pour out my Spirit upon the house of Israel 1
40: 4 declare all that you see to the house of Israel. 1
43: 7 house of Israel shall no more defile my holy name 1
10 describe to the house of Israel the temple 1
44: 6 say to the rebellious house 1
6 to the rebellious house, to the house of Israel 1
6 O house of Israel, let there be an end 1
12 of iniquity to the house of Israel 1
22 a virgin of the stock of the house of Israel 1
30 that a blessing may rest on your house. 1
45: 4 it shall be a place for their houses 1
6 it shall belong to the whole house of Israel. 1
8 they shall let the house of Israel have the land 1
17 all the appointed feasts of the house of Israel 1
17 to make atonement for the house of Israel. 1
Dan 2: 5 torn . . and your houses shall be laid in ruins. 3
17 Then Daniel went to his house and made the matter 3
3:29 limb from limb, and their houses laid in ruins; 3
4: 4 Nebuchadnez'zar, was at ease in my house 3
5: 3 out of the temple, the house of God in Jerusalem; 3
23 vessels of his house have been brought in before 3
6:10 went to his house where he had windows 3
Hos 1: 4 a little while, and I will punish the house of Jehu 1
4 put an end to the kingdom of the house of Israel. 1
6 for I will no more have pity on the house of Israel 1
7 But I will have pity on the house of Judah 1
5: 1 Hear this, O priests! Give heed, O house of Israel! 1
1 Hearken, O house of the king! 1
12 I am . . like dry rot to the house of Judah. 1
14 and like a young lion to the house of Judah. 1
6:10 In the house of Israel I have seen a horrible 1
8: 1 for a vulture is over the house of the LORD 1
9: 4 it shall not come to the house of the LORD. 1
8 and hatred in the house of his God. 1
15 I will drive them out of my house. 1
10:15 Thus it shall be done to you, O house of Israel 1
11:12 and the house of Israel with deceit; 1
Jol 1: 9 offering are cut off from the house of the LORD. 1
13 are withheld from the house of your God. 1
14 Gather . . to the house of the LORD your God; 1
16 joy and gladness from the house of our God? 1
2: 9 they climb up into the houses 1
3:18 shall come forth from the house of the LORD 1
Ams 1: 4 I will send a fire upon the house of Haz'ael 1
2: 8 and in the house of their God they drink the wine 1
3:13 Hear, and testify against the house of Jacob 1
15 I will smite the winter house 1
15 smite the winter house with the summer house; 1
15 and the houses of ivory shall perish 1
15 the great houses shall come to an end 1
5: 1 take up over you in lamentation, O house of Israel 1
3 have ten left to the house of Israel. 1
4 thus says the LORD to the house of Israel 1
6 lest he break out like fire in the house of Joseph 1
11 you have built houses of hewn stone 1
19 or went into the house and leaned with his hand 1
25 40 years in the wilderness, O house of Israel? 1
6: 1 of the nations, to whom the house of Israel come! 1
9 if ten men remain in one house, they shall die. 1
10 take him up to bring the bones out of the house 1
10 to him who is in the innermost parts of the house 1
11 the great house shall be smitten into fragments 1
11 into fragments, and the little house into bits. 1
14 raise up against you a nation, O house of Israel 1
7: 9 and I will rise against the house of Jerobo'am 1
10 against you in the midst of the house of Israel; 1
16 and do not preach against the house of Isaac.' 1
9: 8 I will not utterly destroy the house of Jacob 1
9 shake the house of Israel among all the nations 1
Obd 1:17 the house of Jacob shall possess their own 1
18 The house of Jacob shall be a fire 1
18 shall be a fire, and the house of Joseph a flame 1
18 of Joseph a flame, and the house of Esau stubble; 1
18 there shall be no survivor to the house of Esau; 1
Mic 1: 5 this is . . for the sins of the house of Israel. 1
5 And what is the sin of the house of Judah? 12
14 the houses of Achzib shall be a deceitful thing 1
2: 2 and seize them; and houses, and take them away; 1
2 they oppress a man and his house 1
7 Should this be said, O house of Jacob? 1
9 people you drive out from their pleasant houses; 1
3: 1 Hear, you . . rulers of the house of Israel! 1
9 Hear this, you heads of the house of Jacob 1
9 Hear this, you . . rulers of the house of Israel 1
12 and the mountain of the house a wooded height. 1
4: 1 the mountain of the house of the LORD shall be 1
2 let us go up . . to the house of the God of Jacob; 1
6: 4 and redeemed you from the house of bondage; 1
10 of wickedness in the house of the wicked 1
16 have kept . . all the works of the house of Ahab; 1
7: 6 a man's enemies are the men of his own house. 1
Nah 1:14 from the house of your gods I will cut off 1
Hab 2: 9 Woe to him who gets evil gain for his house 1
10 You have devised shame to your house 1
Zep 1: 9 who fill their master's house with violence 1
13 and their houses laid waste. 1
13 Though they build houses, they shall not inhabit 1
2: 7 possession of the remnant of the house of Judah 1
7 and in the houses of Ash'kelon they shall lie down 1
Hag 1: 2 has not yet come to rebuild the house of the LORD. 1
4 yourselves to dwell in your paneled houses 1
4 while this house lies in ruins? 1
8 to the hills and bring wood and build the house 1
9 Because of my house that lies in ruins 1
9 you busy yourselves each with his own house. 1
14 they came and worked on the house of the LORD 1
2: 3 among you that saw this house in its former glory? 1
7 I will fill this house with splendor 1
9 latter splendor of this house shall be greater 1
Zec 1:16 my house shall be built in it, says the LORD 1
3: 7 and keep my charge, then you shall rule my house 1
4: 9 laid the foundation of this house; 1
5: 4 it shall enter the house of the thief 1
4 the house of him who swears falsely by my name; 1
4 it shall abide in his house and consume it 1
11 To the land of Shinar, to build a house for it; 1
6:10 and go the same day to the house of Josi'ah 1
7: 3 to ask the priests of the house of the LORD 1
8: 9 the foundation of the house of the LORD of hosts 1
13 O house of Judah and house of Israel, so will I save 1
13 house of Israel, so will I save you 1
15 to do good to Jerusalem and to the house of Judah; 1
19 shall be to the house of Judah seasons of joy 1
9: 8 Then I will encamp at my house as a guard 1
10: 3 cares for his flock, the house of Judah 1
6 I will strengthen the house of Judah 1
6 I will save the house of Joseph. 1
11:13 into the treasury in the house of the LORD. 1
12: 4 But upon the house of Judah I will open my eyes 1
7 Judah first, that the glory of the house of David 1
8 the house of David shall be like God 1
10 I will pour out on the house of David 1
12 the family of the house of David by itself 1
12 the family of the house of Nathan by itself 1
13 the family of the house of Levi by itself 1
13: 1 shall be a fountain opened for the house of David 1
6 The wounds I received in the house of my friends. 1
14: 2 the city shall be taken and the houses plundered 1
20 pots in the house of the LORD shall be as the bowls 1
21 in the house of the LORD of hosts on that day. 1
Mal 3:10 that there may be food in my house; 1
Mat 2:11 going into the house they saw the child with Mary 7
5:15 and it gives light to all in the house. 7
7:24 like a wise man who built his house upon the rock; 7
25 the winds blew and beat upon that house 7
26 a foolish man who built his house upon the sand; 7
27 the wind blew and beat against that house 7
8:14 when Jesus entered Peter's house 7
9:10 And as he sat at table in the house 7
23 when Jesus came to the ruler's house 7
28 When he entered the house, the blind men came 7
10: 6 to the lost sheep of the house of Israel. 12
12 As you enter the house, salute it. 7
13 if the house is worthy, let your peace come upon it; 7
14 as you leave that house or town. 7
11: 8 those who wear soft raiment are in kings' houses. 12
12: 4 how he entered the house of God and ate the bread 12
25 no city or house divided against itself 7
29 Or how can one enter a strong man's house 7
29 Then indeed he may plunder his house. 7
44 I will return to my house from which I came. 12
13: 1 went out of the house and sat beside the sea. 7
36 Then he left the crowds and went into the house. 7
57 in his own country and in his own house. 7
15:24 only to the lost sheep of the house of Israel. 12
19:29 every one who has left houses or brothers 7
21:13 'My house shall be called a house of prayer' 12
13 'My house shall be called a house of prayer' 12
23:38 Behold, your house is forsaken and desolate. 12
24:17 to take what is in his house; 7
43 would not have let his house be broken into. 7
26: 6 at Bethany in the house of Simon the leper 7
18 passover at your house with my disciples.' •
Mrk 1:29 entered the house of Simon and Andrew 7
2:15 as he sat at table in his house 7
26 how he entered the house of God 12
3:25 if a house is divided against itself 7
25 that house will not be able to stand. 7
27 enter a strong man's house and plunder his goods 7
27 then indeed he may plunder his house. 7
5:35 there came from the ruler's house •
38 When they came to the house 12
6: 4 among his own kin, and in his own house. 7
10 he said to them, "Where you enter a house, stay there 7
7:17 when he had entered the house, and left the people 12
24 he entered a house, and would not have any one know 7
9:28 when he had entered the house 12
33 when he was in the house he asked them 7
10:10 in the house the disciples asked him again 7
29 there is no one who has left house or brothers 7
30 houses and brothers and sisters and mothers 7
11:17 My house shall be called a house of prayer 12
17 My house shall be called a house of prayer 12
12:40 who devour widows' houses 7
13:15 let him . . not go down, nor enter his house 7
35 when the master of the house will come 7
14: 3 at Bethany in the house of Simon the leper 7
Lke 1:27 of the house of David 12
33 he will reign over the house of Jacob for ever; 12
40 she entered the house of Zechari'ah 12
69 in the house of his servant David 12
2: 4 because he was of the house and lineage of David 12
49 Did . . not know that I must be in my Father's house? •
4:38 left the synagogue, and entered Simon's house. 7
5:29 Levi made him a great feast in his house 7
6: 4 how he entered the house of God 12
48 he is like a man building a house, who dug deep 8
48 the stream broke against that house 7
49 like a man who built a house on the ground 8
49 the ruin of that house was great. 7
7: 6 When he was not far from the house 7
10 those who had been sent returned to the house 12
36 he went into the Pharisee's house 12
37 he was at table in the Pharisee's house 7
44 I entered your house 7
8:27 he lived not in a house but among the tombs. 7
41 he besought him to come to his house 12
49 a man from the ruler's house came and said •
51 when he came to the house 7
9: 4 whatever house you enter, stay there 7
10: 5 Whatever house you enter, first say, 'Peace 7
5 'Peace be to this house!' 7
7 remain in the same house, eating and drinking 7

7 do not go from house to house. 7
7 do not go from house to house. 7
38 Martha received him into her house. •
11:24 I will return to my house from which I came.' 12
12:39 he would not have left his house to be broken into. 12
52 in one house there will be five divided 12
13:35 Behold, your house is forsaken 12
14: 1 when he went to dine at the house of a ruler 12
23 that my house may be filled. 12
15: 8 does not light a lamp and sweep the house and seek 7
25 as he came and drew near to the house 7
16: 4 so that people may receive me into their houses 12
27 I beg you, father, to send him to my father's house 12
17:31 who is on the housetop, with his goods in the house 7
18:14 this man went down to his house justified 12
29 there is no man who has left house or wife 7
19: 5 I must stay at your house today. 12
9 Today salvation has come to this house 12
46 'My house shall be a house of prayer'; 12
46 'My house shall be a house of prayer'; 12
20:47 who devour widows' houses 7
22:10 follow him into the house which he enters 7
54 bringing him into the high priest's house 7
Joh 2:16 not make my Father's house a house of trade. 12
16 not make my Father's house a house of trade. 12
17 Zeal for thy house will consume me. 12
7:53 They went each to his own house. 12
8:35 The slave does not continue in the house for ever; 7
11:20 she went and met him, while Mary sat in the house. 12
31 the Jews who were with her in the house 7
12: 3 the house was filled with the fragrance 7
14: 2 In my Father's house are many rooms 7
18:28 they led Jesus from the house of Ca'iaphas •
20:26 his disciples were again in the house 4
Act 2: 2 it filled all the house where they were sitting. 12
36 Let all the house of Israel therefore know 12
4:34 as many as were possessors of lands or houses 7
7:20 brought up for three months in his father's house; 12
42 40 years in the wilderness, O house of Israel? 12
47 it was Solomon who built a house for him. 8
48 Most High does not dwell in houses made with hands •
49 What house will you build for me, says the Lord 12
9:11 inquire in the house of Judas for a man of Tarsus 7
17 So Anani'as departed and entered the house. 7
10: 6 Simon, a tanner, whose house is by the seaside. 7
17 having made inquiry for Simon's house 7
22 to send for you to come to his house 12
30 I was keeping the ninth hour of prayer in my house; 12
32 he is lodging in the house of Simon 7
11:11 three men arrived at the house in which we were 7
12 we entered the man's house. 12
13 the angel standing in his house and saying 12
12:12 When he realized this, he went to the house of Mary 7
16:15 come to my house and stay. 12
32 to him and to all that were in his house. 7
34 Then he brought them up into his house 12
17: 5 attacked the house of Jason 7
18: 7 went to the house of a man named Titius Justus 7
7 his house was next door to the synagogue. 7
19:16 they fled out of that house naked and wounded. 12
20:20 teaching you in public and from house to house 11
20 teaching you in public and from house to house 11
21: 8 we entered the house of Philip the evangelist 12
16 bringing us to the house of Mnason of Cyprus •
Rom 16: 5 greet also the church in their house. 12
1Co 11:22 What! Do you not have houses to eat and drink in? 7
16:19 together with the church in their house 12
2Co 5: 1 a house not made with hands 9
Col 4:15 to Nympha and the church in her house. 12
2Ti 2:20 In a great house 7
21 consecrated and useful to the master of the house •
Phm 1: 2 the church in your house 12
Heb 3: 2 just as Moses also was faithful in God's house. 12
3 the builder of a house has more honor than the house 12
3 builder of a house has more honor than the house. 12
4 For every house is built by some one 12
5 Now Moses was faithful in all God's house 12
6 Christ was faithful over God's house as a son 12
6 we are his house if we hold fast our confidence 12
8: 8 with the house of Israel 12
8 with the house of Judah; 12
10 with the house of Israel after those days 12
10:21 since we have a great priest over the house of God 12
1Pe 2: 5 be yourselves built into a spiritual house 8
2Jn 1:10 do not receive him into the house 7
1Es 1: 3 the house which Solomon . . had built; 12
55 they burned the house of the Lord 12
2: 4 commanded me to build him a house at Jerusalem 8
5 build the house of the Lord of Israel 8
8 go up to build the house in Jerusalem for the Lord; 12
5: 1 heads of fathers' houses were chosen to go up 12
5 of the house of David, of the lineage of Phares 12
44 vowed that they would erect the house on its site 12
58 the work on the house of God 12
62 the erection of the house of the Lord. 12
63 old men who had seen the former house 12
70 building the house for the Lord our God 8
6: 2 arose and began to build the house of the Lord 8
4 By whose order are you building this house 12

9 building . . a great new house for the Lord 12
11 At whose command are you building this house 8
14 the house was built many years ago 12
16 they pulled down the house, and burned it 12
17 Cyrus wrote that this house should be rebuilt. 8
18 taken out of the house in Jerusalem 12
20 laid the foundations of the house of the Lord 12
22 building of the house of the Lord in Jerusalem 9
24 the building of the house of the Lord in Jerusalem 12
26 the holy vessels of the house of the Lord 12
26 took out of the house in Jerusalem 12
26 should be restored to the house in Jerusalem 12
27 to build this house of the Lord on its site. 12
28 until the house of the Lord is finished; 12
32 a beam should be taken out of his house 5
33 to hinder or damage that house of the Lord 12
7: 5 the holy house was finished 12
8:25 to glorify his house which is in Jerusalem 12
46 to serve as priests in the house of our Lord. 12
55 the holy vessels of the house of our Lord 12
59 in the chambers of the house of our Lord. 12
62 delivered in the house of our Lord to Meremoth 12
79 to uncover a light for us in the house of the Lord 12
2Es 1: 7 out of the house of bondage? 13
33 Your house is desolate 13
35 I will give your houses to a people that will come 13
9:24 a field of flowers where no house has been built 13
10:51 remain in the field where no house had been built 13
12:46 do not be sorrowful, O house of Jacob; 13
49 Now go, every one of you to his house 13
14:13 Now therefore, set your house in order 13
15:18 the houses shall be destroyed 13
19 an assault upon their houses with the sword 13
49 to lay waste your houses 13
16:31 those who search their houses with the sword. 13
46 plunder their goods, and overthrow their houses 13
47 their houses and possessions, and their persons 13
72 and drive them out of their houses. 13
Tob 1: 4 deserted the house of Jerusalem. 12
5 so did the house of Naphtali my forefather. 12
3:17 Tobit returned and entered his house 12
7: 1 arrived at the house of Raguel 7
1 she brought them into the house. 7
8:11 Then Raguel went into his house 7
11: 3 run ahead of your wife and prepare the house. 7
14: 4 The house of God in it will be burned down 12
5 they will rebuild the house of God 12
5 the house of God will be rebuilt there 12
Jdt 4:15 to look with favor upon the whole house of Israel. 12
6:17 said so boastfully against the house of Israel. 12
21 Uzziah took him from the assembly to his own house 12
8: 5 She set up a tent for herself on the roof of her house 12
6 and days of rejoicing of the house of Israel. 12
9: 1 being offered in the house of God in Jerusalem 12
13 they have planned . . against thy consecrated house 12
13 the house possessed by thy children. 12
10: 2 the house where she lived on sabbaths 12
11: 7 Nebuchadnezzar and all his house. 12
23 shall live in the house of King Nebuchadnezzar 12
12:13 who serve in the house of Nebuchadnezzar. 12
13:14 not withdrawn his mercy from the house of Israel 12
14: 5 the man who despised the house of Israel 12
6 they summoned Achior from the house of Uzziah. 12
10 was circumcised, and joined the house of Israel 12
18 the house of King Nebuchadnezzar 12
16:23 and grew old in her husband's house 12
24 the house of Israel mourned for her seven days. 12
AEs 14: 9 to quench thy altar and the glory of thy house 12
Wis 8:16 When I enter my house, I shall find rest with her 12
Sir 1:17 fills their whole house with desirable goods 12
3: 9 strengthens the houses of the children 12
14:24 he who encamps near her house 12
21: 4 thus the house of the proud will be laid waste. 12
8 who builds his house with other people's money 10
18 Like a house that has vanished 12
22 The foot of a fool rushes into a house 7
23 A boor peers into the house from the door 7
23:11 the scourge will not leave his house 12
11 his house will be filled with calamities. 12
27: 3 his house will be quickly overthrown. 12
28:14 overturned the houses of great men. 7
29:21 clothing and a house to cover one's nakedness. 12
22 sumptuous food in another man's house. •
24 It is a miserable life to go from house to house 7
24 It is a miserable life to go from house to house 7
27 brother has come to stay with me; I need my house. 7
47:13 that he might build a house for his name 12
48:15 with rulers from the house of David. 12
49:12 in their days they built the house 12
50: 1 who in his life repaired the house 12
Bar 1: 8 Baruch took the vessels of the house of the Lord 12
14 make your confession in the house of the Lord 12
2:26 house which is called by thy name thou hast made 12
26 wickedness of the house of Israel and the house 12
26 the house of Israel and the house of Judah. 12
3:24 O Israel, how great is the house of God! And how vast 12
LJr 1:59 the door of a house that protects its contents 7
Sus 1: 4 and had a spacious garden adjoining his house; 12

6 These men were frequently at Joakim's house 7
28 gathered at the house of her husband Joakim •
1Mc 1:28 all the house of Jacob was clothed with shame. 12
31 and tore down its houses and its surrounding walls. 12
55 and burned incense at the doors of the houses 7
3:56 he said to those who were building houses 8
7:35 then if I return safely I will burn up this house. 12
37 didst choose this house to be called by thy name 12
37 a house of prayer and supplication. 12
9:55 or give commands concerning his house. 12
13: 3 my brothers and the house of my father 12
47 cleansed the houses in which the idols were 7
48 built in it a house for himself. 6
14:26 his brothers and the house of his father 12
16: 2 I and my brothers and the house of my father 12
2Mc 2:29 the master builder of a new house 7
3:18 People . . hurried out of their houses in crowds 7
5:12 to slay those who went into the house. 7
14:36 keep undefiled for ever this house 12
15:32 the holy house of the Almighty; 12
3Mc 1:20 some in houses and some in the streets 12
2:10 because you love the house of Israel 12
18 We have trampled down the house of the sanctuary 12
18 as offensive houses are trampled down.' 12
7:18 to each as far as his own house. 7
4Mc 18: 7 and did not go outside my father's house 12
151 1: 1 and youngest in my father's house; 12

house *See also* born, build, master.

house after house 1. κατὰ τοὺς οἴκους

Act 8: 3 and entering house after house 1

father's house 1. אָב 2. πατήρ 3. πατριά 4. πατρικός

Exd 6:25 heads of the fathers' houses of the Levites 1
Num31:26 heads of the fathers' houses of the congregation; 1
32:28 command . . to the heads of the fathers' houses 1
36: 1 The heads of the fathers' houses of the families 1
1 of the fathers' houses of the sons of Joseph •
1 leaders, the heads of the fathers' houses 1
1Ch 7:11 according to the heads of their fathers' houses 1
8: 6 heads of fathers' houses of the inhabitants 1
10 These were his sons, heads of fathers' houses. 1
13 heads of fathers' houses of the inhabitants 1
28 These were the heads of fathers' houses 1
9: 9 All these were heads of fathers' houses 1
33 the heads of fathers' houses of the Levites 1
34 heads of fathers' houses of the Levites 1
15:12 the heads of the fathers' houses of the Levites; 1
23: 9 the heads of the fathers' houses of Ladan. 1
24 heads of fathers' houses as they were registered 1
24: 6 the heads of the fathers' houses of the priests 1
31 These also, the head of each father's house 1
31 heads of fathers' houses of the priests 1
26:21 heads of the fathers' houses belonging to Ladan 1
26 and the heads of the fathers' houses 1
31 of whatever genealogy or fathers' houses. 1
32 2,700 men of ability, heads of fathers' houses 1
27: 1 heads of fathers' houses, the commanders 1
29: 6 heads of fathers' houses made their freewill 1
2Ch 1: 2 to all the leaders . . heads of fathers' houses. 1
5: 2 the heads . . the leaders of the fathers' houses 1
23: 2 the heads of fathers' houses of Israel 1
26:12 heads of fathers' houses of mighty men of valor 1
Ezr 1: 5 heads of the fathers' houses of Judah 1
3:12 many of the . . heads of fathers' houses 1
4: 2 Zerub'babel and the heads of fathers' houses 1
3 rest of the heads of fathers' houses in Israel 1
8: 1 These are the heads of their fathers' houses 1
29 Levites and the heads of fathers' houses 1
Neh 7:70 heads of fathers' houses gave to the work. 1
71 some of the heads of fathers' houses gave 1
8:13 day the heads of fathers' houses of all the people 1
11:13 his brethren, heads of fathers' houses, 245; 1
12:12 days . . were priests, heads of fathers' houses 1
22 were recorded the heads of fathers' houses; 1
23 sons of Levi, heads of fathers' houses 1
1Es 1: 5 groupings of the fathers' houses of you Levites 4
11 the grouping of the fathers' houses 2
5: 4 according to their fathers' houses in the tribes 3
37 not prove by their fathers' houses or lineage 3
63 heads of fathers' houses 3
68 Jeshua and the heads of the fathers' houses 3
70 the heads of the fathers' houses in Israel said 3
8:28 according to their fathers' houses 3
59 the heads of the fathers' houses of Israel 3
9:16 the leading men of their fathers' houses 3
Sir 42:10 become pregnant in her father's house 4

little house 1. οἰκίδιον

2Mc 8:33 who had fled into one little house 1

ruined house 1. οἰκόπεδον

Sir 49:13 rebuilt our ruined houses. 1

house to house 1. οἰκία

1Ti 5:13 gadding about from house to house 1

household 1. בַּיִת 2. עֲבֻדָּה 3. *θεραπεία* 4. *οἰκεῖος* 5. *οἰκετεία* 6. *οἰκία* 7. *οἰκιακός* 8. *οἶκος* 9. *ὁ περί* 10. domus

Gen 7: 1 Go into the ark, you and all your household 1
18:19 his children and his household after him 1
24:28 the maiden ran and told her mother's household 1
26:14 He had . . a great household 2
30:30 But now when shall I provide for my own household 1
34:30 I shall be destroyed, both I and my household. 1
35: 2 Jacob said to his household 1
36: 6 Esau took . . all the members of his household 1
39:14 she called to the men of her household and said 1
42:19 carry grain for the famine of your households 1
33 and take grain for the famine of your households 1
45: 2 wept aloud . . and the household of Pharaoh 1
11 lest you and your household, and all that you have 1
18 take your father and your households, and come 1
46:31 Joseph said to his . . father's household, 1
31 say . . 'My brothers and my father's household 1
47:12 Joseph provided . . all his father's household 1
24 as food for yourselves and your households 1
50: 4 Joseph spoke to the household of Pharaoh, saying 1
7 with him went up . . the elders of his household 1
8 as well as all the household of Joseph 1
8 as well as . . his father's household; 1
Exd 1: 1 sons of Israel . . each with his household 1
12: 3 take . . a lamb for a household; 1
4 if the household is too small for a lamb, then a man 1
Num16:32 with their households and all the men 1
18:31 may eat it in any place, you and your households; 1
Deu 6:22 signs . . against Pharaoh and all his household 1
11: 6 with their households, their tents 1
12: 7 rejoice, you and your households 1
14:26 eat . . and rejoice, you and your household. 1
15:16 because he loves you and your household 1
20 eat it, you and your household, before the LORD 1
Jos 2:18 your brothers, and all your father's household. 1
6:25 Rahab . . and her father's household, and all who 1
7:14 and the family . . shall come near by households; 1
14 the household which the LORD takes shall come 1
18 and he brought near his household man by man 1
Jdg 18:25 lose your life with the lives of your household. 1
1Sm 27: 3 every man with his household, and David with his 1
2Sm 2: 3 David brought up . . every one with his household; 1
6:11 LORD blessed O'bed-e'dom and all his household. 1
12 The LORD has blessed the household of O'bed-e'dom 1
20 David returned to bless his household. 1
15:16 king went forth, and all his household after him. 1
16: 2 The asses are for the king's household to ride on 1
19:18 to bring over the king's household, and to do his 1
41 and brought the king and his household over 1
1Kg 4: 7 provided food for the king and his household; 1
5: 9 meet my wishes by providing . . for my household. 1
11 gave Hiram . . wheat as food for his household 1
16: 9 Arza, who was over the household in Tirzah 1
17:15 she, and he, and her household ate for many days. 1
18: 3 Ahab called Obadi'ah, who was over the household. 1
2Kg 7: 9 come, let us go and tell the king's household. 1
11 and it was told within the king's household. 1
8: 1 Arise, and depart with your household 1
2 she went with her household and sojourned 1
15: 5 And Jotham the king's son was over the household 1
18:18 Eli'akim . . who was over the household 1
37 Eli'akim . . who was over the household, and Shebna 1
19: 2 he sent Eli'akim, who was over the household 1
1Ch 13:14 remained with the household of O'bed-e'dom 1
14 the LORD blessed the household of O'bed-e'dom 1
16:43 and David went home to bless his household. 1
2Ch 26:21 Jotham his son was over the king's household 1
Neh 13: 8 threw all the household furniture of Tobi'ah 1
Prv 11:29 He who troubles his household will inherit wind 1
15:27 unjust gain makes trouble for his household 1
27:27 goats' milk for . . the food of your household 1
31:15 yet night and provides food for her household 1
21 She is not afraid of snow for her household. 1
21 for all her household are clothed in scarlet. 1
27 She looks well to the ways of her household 1
Isa 22:15 this steward, to Shebna, who is over the household 1
36: 3 the son of Hilki'ah, who was over the household 1
22 the son of Hilki'ah, who was over the household 1
37: 2 he sent Eli'akim, who was over the household 1
Jer 23:34 I will punish that man and his household. 1
Mat 10:25 will they malign those of his household. 7
36 a man's foes will be those of his own household. 7
24:45 whom his master has set over his household 5
Lke 11:17 a divided household falls. 8
12:42 whom his master will set over his household 3
Joh 4:53 and he himself believed, and all his household. 6
Act 7:10 governor over Egypt and over all his household. 8
10: 2 devout man who feared God with all his household 8
11:14 you will be saved, you and all your household.' 8
16:15 when she was baptized, with her household 8
31 you will be saved, you and your household. 8
18: 8 Crispus . . together with all his household 8
1Co 1:16 I did baptize also the household of Steph'anas. 8
16:15 household of Steph'anas were the first converts 6
Gal 6:10 to those who are of the household of faith. 4
Php 4:22 especially those of Caesar's household. 6
1Ti 3: 4 He must manage his own household well 8
5 man does not know how to manage his own household 8
12 let them manage . . their households well; 8
15 how one ought to behave in the household of God 8
2Ti 1:16 grant mercy to the household of Onesiph'orus 8
3: 6 those who make their way into households 6
4:19 Greet . . the household of Onesiph'orus. 8
Heb 11: 7 an ark for the saving of his household 8
1Pe 4:17 for judgment to begin with the household of God; 8
2Es 3:11 one of them, Noah with his household 10
Bel 1:29 or else we will kill you and your household. 8
4Mc 2:19 censure the households of Simeon and Levi 9

household *See also* god, goods, member, rule, servant.

all the household 1. *πανοικεί* 2. *πανοικία*

Act 16:34 he rejoiced with all his household 1
AEs 16:18 the man . . with all his household 2

householder 1. *οἰκοδεσπότης*

Mat 13:27 the servants of the householder came and said 1
52 like a householder who brings out of his treasure 1
20: 1 For the kingdom of heaven is like a householder 1
11 they grumbled at the householder 1
21:33 There was a householder who planted a vineyard 1
24:43 know this, that if the householder had known 1
Mrk 14:14 wherever he enters, say to the householder 1
Lke 12:39 if the householder had known at what hour 1
13:25 When once the householder has risen up 1
14:21 the householder in anger said to his servant 1
22:11 tell the householder, 'The Teacher says to you 1

housetop 1. גַּג 2. חֲצִיר גַּגּוֹת 3. *δῶμα*

2Kg 19:26 like tender grass, like grass on the housetops; 1
Ps 102: 7 lie awake, I am like a lonely bird on the housetop. 1
129: 6 Let them be like the grass on the housetops 1
Prv 21: 9 It is better to live in a corner of the housetop 1
25:24 better to live in a corner of the housetop 1
Isa 15: 3 on the housetops and in the squares 1
22: 1 that you have gone up, all of you, to the housetops 1
37:27 like tender grass, like grass on the housetops 2
Jer 48:38 On all the housetops of Moab and in the squares 1
Mat 10:27 proclaim upon the housetops. 3
24:17 let him who is on the housetop not go down 3
Mrk 13:15 let him who is on the housetop not go down 3
Lke 12: 3 shall be proclaimed upon the housetops. 3
17:31 who is on the housetop, with his goods in the house 3
Act 10: 9 Peter went up on the housetop to pray 3

housetop *See also* build.

hover 1. volo

2Es 6:39 then the Spirit was hovering 1

how 1. אַי 2. אֵיךְ 3. אֵיכָה 4. אֵיכָכָה 5. אַךְ 6. אַף 7. אֲשֶׁר 8. אֵת אֲשֶׁר 9. אֵת כָּל אֲשֶׁר 10. בַּמָּה 11. הֵיךְ 12. הִנֵּה 13. וְ 14. כַּאֲשֶׁר 15. כִּי 16. מְאֹד 17. מַדּוּעַ 18. מָה 19. מַה דֶּרֶךְ 20. מָה זֶה 21. מִי 22. עַד 23. כְּמָה (A) 24. *ἐν τίνι* 25. *ἰδού* 26. *ἵνα* 27. *καθώς* 28. *κατά* 29. *κατὰ τί* 30. *ὃν τρόπον* 31. *ὁ περί* 32. *ὅπως* 33. *ὅς* 34. *ὅσος* 35. *ὅτι* 36. *οὕτως* 37. *πόθεν* 38. *πῶς* 39. *τίνα τρόπον* 40. *τίς* 41. *ὡς* 42. quam 43. quemadmodum 44. quis 45. quomodo

Gen 6:15 This is how you are to make it 7
15: 8 how am I to know that I shall possess it? 10
20: 9 What have you done to us? And how have I sinned 18
26: 9 Behold, she is your wife; how then could you say 2
27:20 How is it that you have found it so quickly 20
28:17 was afraid, and said, "How awesome is this place! 18
30:29 You yourself know how I have served you 7
29 and how your cattle have fared with me. 7
39: 9 how then can I do this great wickedness, and sin 2
44: 8 how then should we steal silver or gold 2
16 What shall we speak? Or how can we clear ourselves 18
34 For how can I go back to my father if the lad is not 2
Exd 2:18 father Reu'el, he said, "How is it that you have come 17
6:12 how then shall Pharaoh listen to me, who am a man 2
30 how then shall Pharaoh listen to me? 2
10: 2 tell . . how I have made sport of the Egyptians 7
18: 1 Jethro . . heard . . how the LORD had brought 15
8 Moses told . . how the LORD had delivered them. •
19: 4 You have seen . . how I bore you on eagles' wings 7
33:16 For how shall it be known that I have found favor 10
Num10:31 you know how we are to encamp in the wilderness •
20:15 how our fathers went down to Egypt 13
23: 8 How can I curse whom God has not cursed? 18
8 How can I denounce whom the LORD has not 18
24: 5 how fair are your tents, O Jacob 18
Deu 1:12 How can I bear alone the weight and burden of you 3
31 you have seen how the LORD your God bore you 7
4:10 how on the day that you stood before the LORD •
7:17 nations are greater than I; how can I dispossess 3
9: 7 how you provoked the LORD your God to wrath 8
11: 4 how he made the water of the Red Sea overflow them 7
4 how the LORD has destroyed them to this day; •
6 how the earth opened its mouth and swallowed 7
12:30 How did these nations serve their gods?-that I 3
18:21 How may we know the word which the LORD has not 3
25:18 how he attacked you on the way, when you were faint 7
29:16 You know how we dwelt in the land of Egypt 8
16 how we came through the midst of the nations 8
31:27 For I know how rebellious and stubborn you are; •
32:30 How should one chase 1,000, and two 3
Jos 2:10 For we have heard how the LORD dried up the water 7
9: 7 then how can we make a covenant with you? 2
10: 1 When Ado'ni-ze'dek . . heard how Joshua had taken Ai 15
1 and how the inhabitants of Gibeon had made peace 15
14:12 you heard on that day how the Anakim were there 15
Jdg 6:15 Pray, Lord, how can I deliver Israel? Behold, my clan 10
16: 6 and how you might be bound, that one could subdue 10
10 me lies; please tell me how you might be bound. 10
13 and told me lies; tell me how you might be bound. 10
15 How can you say, 'I love you,' when your heart is not 2
18: 7 saw the people . . how they dwelt in security •
7 and how they were far from the Sido'nians and had •
24 How then do you ask me, 'What ails you?' 20
20: 3 Tell us, how was this wickedness brought to pass? 3
Rut 2:11 and how you left your father and mother •
3:16 she said, "How did you fare, my daughter? 21
18 Wait . . until you learn how the matter turns out 2
1Sm 2:22 he heard all . . and how they lay with the women who 7
4:16 And he said, "How did it go, my son? 18
5: 7 the men of Ashdod saw how things were, they said 15
10:11 all . . saw how he prophesied with the prophets 12
27 But some . . said, "How can this man save us? 18
14:29 see how my eyes have become bright 15
38 and know and see how this sin has arisen today. 10
16: 2 How can I go? If Saul hears it, he will kill me. 2
24:10 have seen how the LORD gave you today into my hand 7
18 you have declared . . how you have dealt well 7
28: 9 what Saul has done, how he has cut off the mediums 7
29: 4 how could this fellow reconcile himself 10
2Sm 1: 4 David said to him, "How did it go? Tell me. 18
5 How do you know that Saul and . . Jonathan are dead? 2
14 How is it you were not afraid to put forth 2
19 How are the mighty fallen! 2
25 How are the mighty fallen in the midst 2
27 How are the mighty fallen, and the weapons of war 2
2:22 How then could I lift up my face to your brother 2
6: 9 said, "How can the ark of the LORD come to me? 2
20 How the king of Israel honored himself today 18
12:18 how then can we say to him the child is dead? 2
19:19 or remember how your servant did wrong 7
21: 3 What shall I do . . ? And how shall I make expiation 10
1Kg 2: 5 what Jo'ab . . did to me, how he dealt with the two 7
12: 6 How do you advise me to answer this people? 2
14:19 acts of Jerobo'am, how he warred and how he reigned 7
19 acts of Jerobo'am, how he warred and how he reigned 7
18:13 how I hid 100 men of the LORD's prophets 13
19: 1 told Jez'ebel . . how he had slain all the prophets 9
20: 7 Mark now, and see how this man is seeking trouble; 15
21:29 Have you seen how Ahab has humbled himself 15
22:24 How did the Spirit of the LORD go from me 1
45 acts of Jehosh'aphat . . and how he warred 7
2Kg 4:43 How am I to set this before 100 men? 18
5: 7 see how he is seeking a quarrel with me. 15
6:32 see how this murderer has sent to take off my head? 15
8: 5 telling . . how Eli'sha had restored the dead 8
9:25 remember . . how the LORD uttered this oracle 13
10: 4 two kings could not . . how then can we stand? 2
13: 4 he saw . . how the king of Syria oppressed them. 15
14:15 acts of Jeho'ash . . and how he fought with Amazi'ah 7
28 acts of Jerobo'am . . and his might, how he fought 7
28 he fought, and how he recovered . . Damascus 7
17:28 and taught them how they should fear the LORD. 2
18:24 How then can you repulse a single captain 2
20: 3 Remember . . how I have walked before thee 7
20 all his might, and how he made the pool 7
22:19 you heard how I spoke against this place 7
1Ch 13:12 he said, "How can I bring the ark of God home to me? 11
2Ch 10: 6 How do you advise me to answer this people? 2
33:19 his prayer, and how God received his entreaty •
Ezr 7:22 oil, and salt without prescribing how much. •
Neh 2:17 how Jerusalem lies in ruins with its gates 7
Est 2:11 Mor'decai walked . . to learn how Esther was •
11 to learn how Esther was and how she fared. •
5:11 and how he had advanced him above the princes 7
6: 2 it was found written how Mor'decai had told about 7
8: 6 how can I endure to see the calamity . . coming 4
6 how can I endure to see the destruction of my 4
Job 6:24 make me understand how I have erred. 18
25 How forceful are honest words! 18
9: 2 it is so: but how can a man be just before God? 18
14 How then can I answer him, choosing my words 6
19:28 If you say, 'How we will pursue him!' 18
21:34 How then will you comfort me with empty nothings? 2
22:12 See the highest stars, how lofty they are! 15
25: 4 How then can man be righteous before God? 18
4 How can he who is born of woman be clean? 18
26: 2 How you have helped him who has no power! 18
2 How you have saved the arm that has no strength! •
3 How you have counseled him who has no wisdom 18
14 how small a whisper do we hear of him! 18
31: 1 how then could I look upon a virgin? 18
35: 3 How am I better off than if I had sinned? 18
Ps 3: 1 O LORD, how many are my foes! 18
8: 1 our Lord, how majestic is thy name in all the earth! 18

9 our Lord, how majestic is thy name in all the earth! 18
11: 1 I take refuge; how can you say to me, "Flee 2
21: 1 in thy help how greatly he exults! 18
25:19 Consider how many are my foes 15
31:19 O how abundant is thy goodness, which thou hast 18
36: 7 How precious is thy steadfast love, O God! 18
39: 4 let me know how fleeting my life is! 18
42: 4 how I went with the throng, and led them 15
46: 8 how he has wrought desolations in the earth. 7
66: 3 Say to God, "How terrible are thy deeds! 18
73:11 they say, "How can God know? 3
16 when I thought how to understand this •
19 How they are destroyed in a moment 2
74:18 Remember this, O LORD, how the enemy scoffs •
22 remember how the impious scoff at thee all the day! •
84: 1 How lovely is thy dwelling place, O LORD of hosts! 18
89:50 Remember, O Lord, how thy servant is scorned; •
50 how I bear in my bosom the insults of the peoples •
92: 5 How great are thy works, O LORD! 18
104:24 O LORD, how manifold are thy works! 18
119: 9 How can a young man keep his way pure? 10
97 Oh, how I love thy law! It is my meditation 18
103 How sweet are thy words to my taste 18
159 Consider how I love thy precepts! 15
132: 2 how he swore to the LORD and vowed to the Mighty 7
133: 1 how good and pleasant it is when brothers dwell 18
137: 4 How shall we sing the LORD'S song in a foreign land? 2
7 how they said, "Rase it, rase it! •
139:17 How precious to me are thy thoughts, O God! 18
17 thy thoughts, O God! How vast is the sum of them! 18
Prv 1:22 How long, O simple ones, will you love being simple? 22
5:12 you say, "How I hated discipline 2
6: 9 How long will you lie there, O sluggard? 22
15:23 word in season, how good it is! 18
28 The mind of the righteous ponders how to answer •
20:24 how then can man understand his way? 18
30:13 There are those-how lofty are their eyes 18
13 There are those- . . how high their eyelids lift! 18
Ecc 2: 3 I searched . . how to cheer my body with wine •
3 how to cheer my body . . and how to lay hold on folly •
16 How the wise man dies just like the fool! 2
4:11 they are warm; but how can one be warm alone? 2
8: 7 for who can tell him how it will be? 14
16 to see . . how neither day nor night one's eyes see 15
9: 1 examining it all, how the righteous and the wise 7
11: 5 you do not know how the spirit comes to the bones 19
Sng 4:10 How sweet is your love, my sister, my bride! 18
5: 3 I had put off my garment, how could I put it on? 4
3 I had bathed my feet, how could I soil them? 4
7: 1 How graceful are your feet in sandals 18
6 How fair and pleasant you are, O loved one 18
Isa 1:21 How the faithful city has become a harlot 3
14: 4 How the oppressor has ceased 2
12 How you are fallen from heaven, O Day Star 2
12 How you are cut down to the ground 2
16: 6 have heard of the pride of Moab, how proud he was; 16
19:11 How can you say to Pharaoh, "I am a son of the wise 2
20: 6 we fled for help . . And we, how shall we escape?' 2
36: 9 How then can you repulse a single captain 2
38: 3 Remember . . how I have walked before thee 7
48:11 I do it, for how should my name be profaned? 2
52: 7 How beautiful upon the mountains are the feet 18
Jer 2: 2 how you followed me in the wilderness •
21 How then have you turned degenerate 2
23 How can you say, 'I am not defiled 2
33 How well you direct your course to seek lovers! 18
36 How lightly you gad about, changing your way! 18
3: 6 how she went up on every high hill •
19 I thought how I would set you among my sons 2
5: 7 How can I pardon you? 1
8: 8 How can you say, 'We are wise 3
9:19 How we are ruined! We are utterly shamed 2
12: 5 how will you compete with horses? 2
5 how will you do in the jungle of the Jordan? 2
18:20 how I stood before thee to speak good for them •
22:23 how you will groan when pangs come upon you 18
36:17 Tell us, how did you write all these words? 2
47: 7 How can it be quiet 2
48:14 How do you say, 'We are heroes and . . men of war'? 2
17 say, 'How the mighty scepter is broken 3
39 How it is broken! How they wail! How Moab has 2
39 How it is broken! How they wail! How Moab 2
39 they wail! How Moab has turned his back in shame! 2
49:25 How the famous city is forsaken, the joyful city! 2
50:23 How the hammer of the whole earth is cut down 2
23 How Babylon has become a horror among the nations! 2
51:41 How Babylon is taken 2
41 How Babylon has become a horror among the nations! 2
Lam 1: 1 How lonely sits the city that was full of people! 3
1 How like a widow has she become, she that was great •
21 Hear how I groan; there is none to comfort me. 15
2: 1 How the Lord in his anger has set . . Zion under 3
4: 1 How the gold has grown dim . . pure gold is changed! 3
1 gold has grown dim, how the pure gold is changed! •
2 sons of Zion . . how they are reckoned as earthen 3
Ezk 15: 2 how does the wood of the vine surpass any wood 18
16:30 How lovesick is your heart, says the Lord GOD 18
26:17 and say to you, 'How you have vanished from the seas 2
33:10 waste away because of them; how then can we live? 2
Dan 4: 3 How great are his signs, how mighty his wonders! 23
3 How great are his signs, how mighty his wonders! 23
10:17 How can my lord's servant talk with my lord? 11
Hos 11: 8 How can I give you up, O E'phraim! 2
8 How can I hand you over, O Israel! •
8 How can I make you like Admah! 2
8 How can I treat you like Zeboi'im! •
Jol 1:18 How the beasts groan! 18
Ams 7: 2 How can Jacob stand? He is so small! 21
5 How can Jacob stand? He is so small"! 21
Obd 1: 5 plunderers by night-how you have been destroyed! 2
6 How Esau has been pillaged 2
Jon 2: 4 how shall I again look upon thy holy temple? 5
3:10 what they did, how they turned from their evil way 15
Mic 2: 4 portion of my people; how he removes it from me! 2
Zep 2: 8 how they have taunted my people 7
Hag 1: 5 Consider how you have fared. •
7 Consider how you have fared. •
2: 3 How do you see it now? Is it not in your sight 18
16 how did you fare? When one came to a heap of twenty 40
Zec 9:17 Yea, how good and how fair it shall be! 18
17 Yea, how good and how fair it shall be! 18
Mal 1: 2 But you say, "How hast thou loved us? 10
6 You say, 'How have we despised thy name? 10
7 upon my altar. And you say, 'How have we polluted it? 10
2:17 Yet you say, "How have we wearied him? 10
3: 7 But you say, 'How shall we return?' 10
8 robbing me. But you say, 'How are we robbing thee?' 10
13 Yet you say, 'How have we spoken against thee?' 18
Mat 5:13 if salt has lost its taste, how shall its saltness 24
6:28 lilies of the field, how they grow; they neither 38
7: 4 Or how can you say to your brother 38
10:19 do not be anxious how you are to speak 38
12: 4 how he entered the house of God and ate the bread 38
5 read in the law how on the sabbath the priests 35
14 and took counsel against him, how to destroy him. 32
26 how then will his kingdom stand? 38
29 Or how can one enter a strong man's house 38
34 You brood of vipers! how can you speak good 38
13:27 How then has it weeds? 37
16:11 How is it that you fail to perceive 38
21:20 How did the fig tree wither at once? 38
22:12 how did you get in here without a wedding garment?' 38
15 and took counsel how to entangle him in his talk. 32
43 How is it then that David, inspired by the Spirit 38
45 If David thus calls him Lord, how is he his son? 38
23:33 how are you to escape being sentenced to hell? 38
26:54 how then should the scriptures be fulfilled 38
27:63 said, "Sir, we remember how that impostor said 35
Mrk 2:26 how he entered the house of God 38
3: 6 how to destroy him. 32
23 How can Satan cast out Satan? 38
4:13 How then will you understand all the parables? 38
27 he knows not how. 41
5:19 how he has had mercy on you. •
8: 4 How can one feed these men with bread here 37
9:12 how is it written of the Son of man 38
49 how will you season it 24
10:23 How hard it will be for those who have riches 38
24 how hard it is to enter the kingdom of God! 38
12:26 how God said to him, 'I am the God of Abraham 38
35 How can the scribes say that the Christ is the son 38
37 David himself calls him Lord; so how is he his son? 37
14: 1 how to arrest him by stealth, and kill him; 38
72 Peter remembered how Jesus had said to him 41
Lke 1:18 Zechari'ah said to the angel, "How shall I know this? 29
34 How shall this be, since I have no husband? 38
2:49 he said to them, "How is it that you sought me? 40
6: 4 how he entered the house of God 41
42 how can you say to your brother, 'Brother 38
8:18 Take heed then how you hear 38
36 told them how he . . was healed. 38
47 how she had been immediately healed. 41
10:26 What is written in the law? How do you read? 38
11:18 how will his kingdom stand 38
12:11 do not be anxious how or what you are to answer 38
27 Consider the lilies, how they grow 38
50 how I am constrained until it is accomplished! 38
14: 7 when he marked how they chose the places of honor 38
34 how shall its saltness be restored? 24
18:24 How hard it is for those who have riches to enter 38
20:41 How can they say that the Christ is David's son? 38
44 David thus calls him Lord; so how is he his son? 38
21: 5 how it was adorned with noble stones 35
14 not to meditate beforehand how to answer •
22: 2 the scribes were seeking how to put him to death; 38
4 how he might betray him to them. 38
61 how he had said to him, "Before the cock crows today 41
23:55 saw the tomb, and how his body was laid; 41
24: 6 Remember how he told you 41
20 how our chief priests . . delivered him up 32
35 how he was known to them 41
Joh 1:48 Nathan'a-el said to him, "How do you know me? 37
3: 4 How can a man be born when he is old? 38
9 Nicode'mus said to him, "How can this be? 38
12 how can you believe if I tell you heavenly things? 38
4: 9 How is it that you, a Jew, ask a drink of me 38
35 see how the fields are already white for harvest 35
5:44 How can you believe 38
47 how will you believe my words? 38
6: 5 How are we to buy bread, so that . . people may eat? 37
42 How does he . . say, 'I have come down from heaven'? 38
52 How can this man give us his flesh to eat? 38
7:15 The Jews marveled at it, saying, "How is it 38
8:33 How is it that you say, 'You will be made free'? 38
9:10 They said to him, "Then how were your eyes opened? 38
15 again asked him how he had received his sight. 38
16 How can a man who is a sinner do such signs? 38
19 How then does he now see? 38
21 how he now sees we do not know 38
26 How did he open your eyes? 38
11:36 the Jews said, "See how he loved him! 38
53 they took counsel how to put him to death. 26
12:34 How can you say . . the Son of man must be lifted up? 38
14: 5 how can we know the way? 38
9 how can you say, 'Show us the Father'? 38
22 Judas (not Iscariot) said to him, "Lord, how is it 40
18:22 Is that how you answer the high priest? 36
Act 2: 8 how is it that we hear 38
5: 4 How is it that you have contrived this deed 40
9 How is it that you have agreed together to tempt 40
8:31 he said, "How can I, unless some one guides me? 38
9:27 declared to them how . . he had seen the Lord 38
27 how at Damascus he had preached boldly 38
10:28 You yourselves know how unlawful it is for a Jew 41
38 how God anointed Jesus of Nazareth 41
38 how he went about doing good •
11:13 he told us how he had seen the angel standing 38
16 I remembered the word of the Lord, how he said 41
12:17 how the Lord had brought him out of the prison 38
14:27 how he had opened a door of faith to the Gentiles. 35
15:14 how God first visited the Gentiles 27
36 see how they are. 38
20:18 You yourselves know how I lived among you 38
20 how I did not shrink from declaring to you 41
35 the words of the Lord Jesus, how he said 35
25:20 Being at a loss how to investigate these questions •
Rom 3: 6 For then how could God judge the world? 38
4:10 How then was it reckoned to him? 38
6: 2 How can we who died to sin still live in it? 38
8:26 for we do not know how to pray as we ought 40
10:14 how are men to call upon him 38
14 And how are they to believe in him 38
14 And how are they to hear without a preacher? 38
15 And how can men preach unless they are sent? 38
15 How beautiful are the feet of those who preach 41
11: 2 of Eli'jah, how he pleads with God against Israel? 41
33 How unsearchable are his judgments 41
33 and how inscrutable his ways! •
13:11 how it is full time now for you to wake from sleep. 35
1Co 3:10 Let each man take care how he builds upon it. 38
4: 1 This is how one should regard us 36
7:16 Wife, how do you know 40
16 Husband, how do you know 40
32 how to please the Lord; 38
33 how to please his wife 38
34 how to be holy in body and spirit 26
34 how to please her husband. 38
14: 6 how shall I benefit you 40
7 how will any one know what is played? 38
9 how will any one know what is said 38
16 how can any one in the position of an outsider say 38
15:12 the dead, how can some of you say that there is no 38
35 some one will ask, "How are the dead raised? 38
Gal 1:13 how I persecuted the church of God violently 35
2:14 how can you compel the Gentiles to live like Jews? 38
4: 9 how can you turn back again to the weak 38
Eph 3: 3 how the mystery was made known to me 35
6 that is, how the Gentiles are fellow heirs •
5:15 Look carefully then how you walk 38
6:21 you also may know how I am and what I am doing 28
22 that you may know how we are 31
Php 1: 8 how I yearn for you all 41
2:22 how as a son with a father he has served with me 35
23 just as soon as I see how it will go with me; •
Col 4: 6 you may know how you ought to answer every one. 38
8 you may know how we are 31
1Th 1: 9 how you turned to God from idols 38
2:10 how holy and righteous and blameless 41
11 for you know how, like a father with his children 41
4: 1 as you learned from us how you ought to live 38
2Th 3: 7 you yourselves know how you ought to imitate us; 38
1Ti 3: 5 how can he care for God's church? 38
15 you may know how one ought to behave 38
2Ti 3:15 how . . you have been acquainted with . . 35
Heb 2: 3 how shall we escape 38
10:24 let us consider how to stir up one another to love •
Jas 3: 5 How great a forest is set ablaze by a small fire! 25
5:11 how the Lord is compassionate and merciful. 35
1Jn 3:17 how does God's love abide in him? 38
Rev 2: 2 how you cannot bear evil men but have tested 35
9:17 this was how I saw the horses in my vision 36
1Es 1:24 how they grieved the Lord deeply 33
3:18 Gentlemen, how is wine the strongest? 38
2Es 3:30 for I have seen how thou dost endure those who sin 45
31 shown to any one how thy way may be comprehended. 45
4:11 how then can your mind comprehend the way 45
11 And how can one who is already worn out •

32 how great a threshing floor they will fill! 42
5:39 and how can I speak concerning the things 45
45 I said, "How hast thou said to thy servant 45
7: 5 how can he come to the broad part 45
9 how will the heir receive his inheritance 45
53 I said, "Lord, how could that be? 45
73 how will they answer in the last times? 45
85 how the habitations of the others are guarded *
86 they shall see how some of them will pass over 43
97 how their face is to shine like the sun 45
97 how they are to be made like the light of the stars 45
106I answered and said, "How then do we find 45
9:13 be curious as to how the ungodly will be punished; 45
13 but inquire how the righteous will be saved 45
10:49 you saw her likeness, how she mourned for her son 45
11: 6 I saw how all things under heaven were subjected 45
30 I saw how it allied the two heads with itself 45
37 I heard how he uttered a man's voice to the eagle 45
12:41 How have we offended you 44
13:10 I saw only how he sent forth from his mouth 45
16:66 Or how will you hide your sins before God 45
Tob 2: 6 the prophecy of Amos, how he said 27
5: 2 how can I obtain the money 38
10: 8 they will inform him how things are with you. 28
11: 2 Are you not aware . . of how you left your father? 38
13:14 How blessed are those who love you! *
14:10 how he brought him from light into darkness 41
11 consider . . how righteousness delivers 40
Jdt 4: 1 how he had plundered . . all their temples; 30
5: 3 How large is their army *
8: 9 how he promised them under oath to surrender . . 41
14 how do you expect to search out God 38
26 how he tested Isaac 34
10: 7 and noted how her face was altered *
AEs 13: 3 how this might be accomplished 38
Wis 6:22 will tell you what wisdom is and how she came to be 38
8:18 I went about seeking how to get her for myself. 32
11: 8 how thou didst punish their enemies. 38
9 they learned how the ungodly were tormented 38
25 How would anything have endured 38
25 how would anything . . have been preserved? *
13: 9 how did they fail to find sooner the Lord 38
16: 4 how their enemies were being tormented. 38
19:10 how . . the earth brought forth gnats 38
Sir 8: 8 learn how to serve great men. *
9 learn how to give an answer in time of need. *
10: 9 How can he who is dust and ashes be proud? 40
13: 2 How can the clay pot associate 40
17:29 How great is the mercy of the Lord 41
25: 3 how then can you find anything in your old age? 38
5 How attractive is wisdom in the aged 41
10 How great is he who has gained wisdom! 41
31:19 How ample a little is for a well-disciplined man! 41
38:25 How can he become wise who handles the plow 40
41: 1 O death, how bitter is the reminder of you 41
2 O death, how welcome is your sentence *
4 how can you reject 40
42:22 How greatly to be desired are all his works 41
22 how sparkling they are to see! 41
46: 2 How glorious he was when he lifted his hands 41
47:14 How wise you became in your youth! 41
48: 4 How glorious you were, O Elijah 41
49:11 How shall we magnify Zerubbabel? 38
50: 4 He considered how to save his people from ruin *
5 How glorious he was 41
Bar 3:24 O Israel, how great is the house of God! And how vast 41
24 And how vast the territory that he possesses! 41
4:17 But I, how can I help you? 40
LJr 1:46 how then can . . things . . made by them be gods? 38
49 How then can one fail to see 38
Sus 1:57 This is how you both have been dealing 36
1Mc 3:17 How can we, few as we are, fight 40
53 How will we be able to withstand them 38
4: 9 Remember how our fathers were saved 41
35 how ready they were either to live or to die nobly 41
8: 2 how they had defeated them 35
4 how they had gained control of the whole region *
9:21 How is the mighty fallen, the savior of Israel! 38
10:46 how he had greatly oppressed them. *
14:25 How shall we thank Simon and his sons? 40
2Mc 6:28 a noble example of how to die a good death *
7:17 see how his mighty power will torture you 41
22 I do not know how you came into being in my womb 32
9:25 I understand how the princes . . keep watching *
10: 6 remembering how . . they had been wandering 41
13:26 how the king's attack and withdrawal turned out. 36
15:37 This . . is how matters turned out with Nicanor. 36
4Mc 1:33 Otherwise how is it that . . 37
2: 7 Otherwise how could it be 39
24 How is it then, one might say 38
9:29 How sweet is any kind of death 41
13: 5 How then can one fail to confess 38
14:13 Observe how complex is a mother's love 38
16: 6 O how wretched am I and many times unhappy! *

how *See also* gentle, great, greatly, know, long, many, much, often, prosper, show.

how do 1. לְשָׁלוֹם
2Sm 11: 7 David asked how Jo'ab was doing, and how the people 1

how fare 1. לְשָׁלוֹם
2Sm 11: 7 asked how Jo'ab was doing, and how the people fared 1

however 1. אַךְ 2. וְ 3. כִּי אִם 4. רַק 5. בְּרַם (A)
6. ἀλλά 7. ἄλλος 8. δέ 9. καί 10. μέν 11. ὅθεν
12. ὅμως 13. οὖν 14. πλήν 15. ὡς ἄν 16. nam 17. sed
Deu 12:15 However, you may slaughter and eat flesh 4
Jos 16:10 However they did not drive out the Canaanites 2
1Kg 2:15 expected me to reign; however the kingdom has 2
3: 2 sacrificing at the high places, however 4
11:13 However I will not tear away all the kingdom; 4
2Kg 17:40 However they would not listen 2
23: 9 However, the priests . . did not come up 1
2Ch 20:33 The high places, however, were not taken away; 1
Ezr 5:13 However in the first year of Cyrus king 5
Ezk 44:25 however, for father or mother, for son or daughter 3
Mat 17:27 However, not to give offense to them, go to the sea 8
Joh 6:23 However, boats from Tiber'i-as came near the place 7
Act 28: 5 He, however, shook off the creature into the fire 13
Rom 15:25 At present, however, I am going to Jerusalem 8
1Co 8: 7 However, not all possess this knowledge 6
12: 2 however you may have been moved. 15
Eph 5:33 however, let each one of you love his wife 14
2Es 9:23 do not fast during them, however; 17
37 the law, however, does not perish but remains 16
Tob 2:10 Ahikar, however, took care of me 8
Jdt 6:13 However, they got under the shelter of the hill *
Wis 15:12 he says one must get money however one can 11
2Mc 2:27 However, to secure the gratitude of many 12
4:19 who carried the money, however, thought best 9
5: 7 did not gain control of the government, however; 10
3Mc 2:31 Now some, however . . readily gave themselves up 10
3: 3 Jews, however, continued to maintain good will 8
5:10 Hermon, however . . presented himself 8
36 The king, however, reconvened the party 8

however *See also* much.

howl 1. הָמָה 2. יָלַל 3. ὀλολύζω 4. ὠρύομαι
Deu 32:10 found him . . in the howling waste of the wilderness; 2
Ps 59: 6 Each evening they come back, howling like dogs 1
14 Each evening they come back, howling like dogs 1
Jas 5: 1 weep and howl for the miseries that are coming 3
LJr 1:32 They howl and shout before their gods as some do 4

howling *See* creature.

hub 1. חִשֻּׁר
1Kg 7:33 rims, their spokes, and their hubs, were all cast. 1

huddle together 1. ספח
Job 30: 7 under the nettles they huddle together. 1

huge 1. גָּדוֹל 2. לָרֹב 3. גְּלָל (A) 4. πολύς 5. magnus
1Kg 7:10 huge stones, stones of eight and ten cubits. 1
2Ch 16: 8 the Ethiopians and the Libyans a huge army 2
Ezr 5: 8 It is being built with huge stones 3
2Es 10:27 and a place of huge foundations showed itself. 5
1Mc 9: 6 When they saw the huge number of the enemy forces 4

huge *See also* amount.

human 1. אָדָם 2. ἀνθρώπινος 3. ἄνθρωπος
4. σάρκινος 5. σάρξ 6. homo
Lev 5: 3 Or if he touches human uncleanness, of whatever 1
Job 34:20 the mighty are taken away by no human hand. *
Ezk 1: 8 Under their wings . . they had human hands. 1
26 was a likeness as it were of a human form. 1
4:12 cake, baking it in their sight on human dung. 1
15 let you have cow's dung instead of human dung 1
10: 8 have the form of a human hand under their wings. 1
21 and underneath . . the semblance of human hands. 1
Dan 2:34 As you looked, a stone was cut out by no human hand *
45 stone was cut from a mountain by no human hand *
8:25 but, by no human hand, he shall be broken. *
Act 17:25 nor is he served by human hands 2
Rom 2: 9 and distress for every human being who does evil 3
1Co 2:13 in words not taught by human wisdom 2
4: 3 I should be judged by you or by any human court 2
9: 8 Do I say this on human authority? 3
2Co 3: 3 but on tablets of human hearts. 4
5:16 we regard no one from a human point of view 5
16 once regarded Christ from a human point of view 5
Gal 3:15 To give a human example, brethren 3
Php 2: 8 being found in human form he humbled himself 3
Col 2: 8 according to human tradition 3
22 according to human precepts and doctrines 3
1Pe 2:13 Be subject . . to every human institution 2
4: 2 no longer by human passions but by the will of God 3
2Pe 2:16 a dumb ass spoke with human voice 3
Rev 9: 7 their faces were like human faces 3
13:18 number of the beast, for it is a human number 3
18:13 and chariots, and slaves, that is, human souls. 3
2Es 7:29 and all who draw human breath. 6
65 Let the human race lament 6
Jdt 8:14 You cannot plumb the depths of the human heart 3
Wis 12: 5 sacrificial feasting on human flesh and blood. 5
15: 4 the evil intent of human art misled us 3
Sir 3:23 matters too great for human understanding 3
10:19 What race is worthy of honor? The human race 3
19 What race is unworthy of honor? The human race. 3
36:22 surpasses every human desire. 3
Bel 1:32 they had been given two human bodies and two sheep *
3Mc 6:26 accepted willingly the worst of human dangers 3
4Mc 1:16 the knowledge of divine and human matters 2
17 we learn . . human affairs to our advantage. 2
4:13 had been overcome by human treachery 2
17:14 the world and the human race were the spectators. 3

human *See also* being, life, semblance, term.

human way 1. κατὰ ἄνθρωπον
Rom 3: 5 (I speak in a human way.) 1

humane 1. φιλάνθρωπος
Wis 7:23 beneficent, humane, steadfast, sure 1
4Mc 5:12 honoring my humane advice? 1

humankind 1. φύσις ἀνθρώπινος
Jas 3: 7 every kind . . has been tamed by humankind 1

humanly *See* speak.

humble 1. דכא 2. כנע 3. ענה 4. עָנָו 5. עָנִי 6. צָנוּעַ
7. צָעִיר 8. שׁחח 9. שׁפל 10. שָׁפָל 11. שׁפל (A)
12. πραΰς 13. συγκάμπτω 14. συστέλλω
15. ταπεινός 16. ταπεινόω 17. ταπείνωσις
18. humilio
Gen 34: 2 he seized her and lay with her and humbled her. 3
Exd 10: 3 will you refuse to humble yourself before me? 3
Lev 26:41 if then their uncircumcised heart is humbled 2
Deu 8: 2 that he might humble you, testing you to know 3
3 humbled you and let you hunger and fed you 3
16 that he might humble you and test you 3
1Sm 9:21 is not my family the humblest of all the families 7
2Sm 22:28 Thou dost deliver a humble people 5
1Kg 21:29 Have you seen how Ahab has humbled himself 2
29 Because he has humbled himself before me, I will 2
2Kg 22:19 and you humbled yourself before the LORD 2
2Ch 7:14 if my people . . humble themselves, and pray 2
12: 6 the princes . . and the king humbled themselves 2
7 When the LORD saw that they humbled themselves 2
7 They have humbled themselves; I will not destroy 2
12 when he humbled himself the wrath of the LORD 2
30:11 Only a few men of . . Zeb'ulun humbled themselves 2
32:26 Hezeki'ah humbled himself for the pride 2
33:12 humbled himself greatly before the God 2
19 before he humbled himself 2
23 he did not humble himself before the LORD 2
23 as Manas'seh his father had humbled himself 2
34:27 because . . you humbled yourself before God 2
27 you have humbled yourself before me 2
36:12 not humble himself before Jeremiah the prophet 2
Ezr 8:21 that we might humble ourselves before our God 3
Job 22:23 you return to the Almighty and humble yourself 16
30:11 Because God has loosed my cord and humbled me 3
Ps 18:27 For thou dost deliver a humble people; 5
25: 9 He leads the humble in what is right, and teaches 4
9 in what is right, and teaches the humble his way. 4
55:19 God will give ear, and humble them 3
69:10 When I humbled my soul with fasting 13
89:22 the wicked shall not humble him. 3
149: 4 pleasure . . adorns the humble with victory. 4
Prv 3:34 but to the humble he shows favor. 4
11: 2 but with the humble is wisdom. 6
Isa 2: 9 So man is humbled, and men are brought low– 8
11 brought low, and the pride of men shall be humbled; 8
17 the haughtiness of man shall be humbled 8
5:15 and the eyes of the haughty are humbled. 9
57:15 with him who is of a contrite and humble spirit 10
15 to revive the spirit of the humble 10
58: 3 Why have we humbled ourselves, and thou takest no 3
5 the fast . . a day for a man to humble himself? 3
66: 2 he that is humble and contrite in spirit 5
Jer 37:20 lord the king: let my humble plea come before you *
38:26 I made a humble plea to the king *
44:10 They have not humbled themselves . . to this day 1
Ezk 17:14 that the kingdom might be humble 10
22:10 they humble women who are unclean 3
Dan 5:22 his son, Belshaz'zar, have not humbled your heart 11
10:12 day that you . . humbled yourself before your God 3
Zep 2: 3 Seek the LORD, all you humble of the land 4
3:12 in the midst of you a people humble and lowly. 5
Zec 9: 9 victorious is he, humble and riding on an ass 5
Mat 18: 4 Whoever humbles himself like this child 17
21: 5 humble, and mounted on an ass 12
23:12 whoever exalts himself will be humbled 16
12 whoever humbles himself will be exalted. 17
Lke 14:11 For every one who exalts himself will be humbled 16
11 he who humbles himself will be exalted. 16
18:14 every one who exalts himself will be humbled 16
14 he who humbles himself will be exalted. 16
2Co 10: 1 who am humble when face to face with you 15
12:21 my God may humble me before you 16
Php 2: 8 being found in human form he humbled himself 16

Jas 4: 6 God .. gives grace to the humble. 15
10 Humble yourselves before the Lord 16
1Pe 5: 5 God .. gives grace to the humble. 15
6 Humble yourselves therefore under .. God 16
2Es 8:49 because you have humbled yourself 18
Tob 4:19 he humbles whomever he wishes. 16
Jdt 4: 9 they humbled themselves with much fasting. 16
5:11 humbled them and made slaves of them. 16
AEs 14: 2 she utterly humbled her body 16
Sir 2: 4 in changes that humble you be patient. 17
17 will humble themselves before him. 16
3:18 the more you must humble yourself 15
20 he is glorified by the humble. 15
7:17 Humble yourself greatly 16
10:15 has planted the humble in their place. 15
12: 5 Do good to the humble 15
11 Even if he humbles himself 16
18:21 Before falling ill, humble yourself 16
34:26 what has he gained by humbling himself? 16
35:17 The prayer of the humble pierces the clouds 15
40: 3 the one who is humbled in dust and ashes 16
Aza 1:16 with a contrite heart and a humble spirit 17
65 you who are holy and humble in heart 15
1Mc 5: 3 He dealt them a heavy blow and humbled them 14
12:15 our enemies were humbled. 16
14:14 He strengthened all the humble of his people 15
2Mc 8:35 having been humbled with the help of the Lord 16

humble *See also* circumstance, mind, standing.

humble man 1. ταπεινός
Sir 11: 1 The wisdom of a humble man will lift up his head 1
13:21 when a humble man falls, he is even pushed away 1
22 If a humble man slips, they even reproach him 1

humbled *See* lie.

humbly 1. צנה
Mic 6: 8 to love kindness, and to walk humbly with your God? 1

humiliate 1. ענה 2. καταισχύνω 3. ταπεινόω
Deu 21:14 since you have humiliated her. 1
1Co 11:22 humiliate those who have nothing 2
2Co 9: 4 we be humiliated 2
Sir 13: 8 not to be humiliated in your feasting. 3

humiliation 1. חֶרְפָּה 2. כְּלִמָּה 3. ταπείνωσις 4. humilitas
Job 19: 5 and make my humiliation an argument against me 1
Isa 30: 3 shelter in .. of Egypt to your humiliation. 2
Act 8:33 In his humiliation justice was denied him 3
Jas 1:10 and the rich in his humiliation 3
2Es 6:19 and when the humiliation of Zion is complete 4
12:48 on account of the humiliation of our sanctuary. 4
Jdt 6:19 and have pity on the humiliation of our people 3
Sir 2: 5 acceptable men in the furnace of humiliation. 3
1Mc 3:51 thy priests mourn in humiliation. 3
3Mc 2:12 you helped them in their humiliation 3

humility 1. עֲנָוָה 2. πραΰτης 3. ταπεινότης 4. ταπεινοφροσύνη
Prv 15:33 humility goes before honor. 1
18:12 but humility goes before honor. 1
22: 4 reward for humility and fear of the LORD is 1
Zep 2: 3 seek righteousness, seek humility; 1
Act 20:19 serving the Lord with all humility 4
Php 2: 3 in humility count others better 4
1Pe 5: 5 Clothe yourselves .. with humility 4
Sir 10:28 My son, glorify yourself with humility 2
13:20 Humility is an abomination to a proud man; 3
36:23 If kindness and humility mark her speech 2

hump 1. דַּבֶּשֶׁת
Isa 30: 6 and their treasures on the humps of camels 1

hunchback 1. גִּבֵּן
Lev 21:20 or a hunchback, or a dwarf, or a man with a defect 1

hundred 1. מֵאָה 2. ἑκατόν 3. ἑκατόνταρχος
Exd 18:21 rulers of thousands, of hundreds, of fifties 1
25 rulers of thousands, of hundreds, of fifties 1
Num31:14 officers of the army .. commanders of hundreds 1
48 the officers .. the captains of hundreds 1
52 offering .. from .. the commanders of hundreds 1
54 from the commanders of thousands and of hundreds 1
Deu 1:15 heads over you, commanders .. of hundreds 1
1Sm 22: 7 will he make you .. and commanders of hundreds 1
29: 2 were passing on by hundreds and by thousands 1
2Sm 18: 1 set over them .. and commanders of hundreds. 1
4 army marched out by hundreds and by thousands. 1
1Ch 13: 1 commanders of thousands and of hundreds 1
26:26 officers of the thousands and the hundreds 1
27: 1 commanders of thousands and hundreds 1
28: 1 of thousands, the commanders of hundreds 1
29: 6 the commanders of thousands and of hundreds 1
2Ch 1: 2 to the commanders of thousands and of hundreds 1
23: 1 into a compact with the commanders of hundreds 1
25: 5 under commanders of thousands and of hundreds 1
Mrk 6:40 sat down in groups, by hundreds and by fifties. 2
1Mc 3:55 in charge of thousands and hundreds 3

hundred-weight 1. ταλαντιαῖος
Rev 16:21 great hailstones, heavy as a hundred-weight 1

hundredfold 1. מֵאָה 2. ἑκατόν 3. ἑκατονταπλασίων
Gen 26:12 Isaac .. reaped in the same year a hundredfold. 1
Mat 13: 8 grain, some a hundredfold, some 60, some 30. 2
23 in one case a hundredfold, in another 60 2
19:29 for my name's sake, will receive a hundredfold 3
Mrk 4: 8 thirtyfold and sixtyfold and a hundredfold. 2
20 thirtyfold and sixtyfold and a hundredfold. 2
10:30 who will not receive a hundredfold now 3
Lke 8: 8 some .. grew, and yielded a hundredfold 3

hunger 1. יֶשַׁח 2. כָּפָן 3. נֶפֶשׁ 4. רעב 5. רָעֵב 6. λιμός 7. νηστεία 8. πεινάω 9. fames
Exd 16: 3 to kill this whole assembly with hunger. 5
Deu 8: 3 humbled you and let you hunger and fed you 4
28:48 serve your enemies .. in hunger and thirst 5
32:24 they shall be wasted with hunger, and devoured 5
1Sm 2: 5 but those who were hungry have ceased to hunger. •
Neh 9:15 give them bread from heaven for their hunger 5
Job 30: 3 Through want and hard hunger they gnaw 2
Isa 5:13 men are dying of hunger .. parched with thirst. 5
29: 8 awakes with his hunger not satisfied 3
49:10 they shall not hunger or thirst 4
Jer 38: 9 he will die there of hunger, for there is no bread 5
Lam 2:19 children, who faint for hunger .. every street. 5
4: 9 Happier .. than the victims of hunger 5
Ezk 7:19 they cannot satisfy their hunger 3
34:29 shall no more be consumed with hunger in the land 5
Hos 9: 4 for their bread shall be for their hunger only; 3
Mic 6:14 and there shall be hunger in your inward parts; 1
Mat 5: 6 Blessed are those who hunger and thirst 8
Lke 6:21 Blessed are you that hunger now 8
25 Woe to you that are full now, for you shall hunger. 8
15:17 I perish here with hunger! 6
Joh 6:35 he who comes to me shall not hunger 8
1Co 4:11 To the present hour we hunger and thirst 8
2Co 6: 5 imprisonments, tumults, labors, watching, hunger; 7
11:27 in hunger and thirst, often without food 6
Php 4:12 I have learned the secret of facing plenty and hunger 8
Rev 7:16 They shall hunger no more, neither thirst 8
2Es 15:19 plunder their goods, because of hunger for bread 9
57 Your children shall die of hunger 9
58 shall perish of hunger 9
58 shall eat their own flesh in hunger for bread 9
Sir 16:27 they neither hunger nor grow weary 8
18:25 In the time of plenty think of the time of hunger; 6
24:21 Those who eat me will hunger for more 8
Bar 2:18 person that hungers, will ascribe to thee glory 8

hunger *See also* suffer.

hunger-bitten 1. רָעֵב
Job 18:12 His strength is hunger-bitten 1

hungry 1. רעב 2. רָעֵב 3. νῆστις 4. πεινάω 5. πρόσπεινος 6. esurio
1Sm 2: 5 but those who were hungry have ceased to hunger. 2
2Sm 17:29 The people are hungry and weary and thirsty 2
2Kg 7:12 They know that we are hungry; therefore they have 2
Job 5: 5 His harvest the hungry eat 2
22: 7 you have withheld bread from the hungry. 2
24:10 hungry, they carry the sheaves; 2
Ps 50:12 If I were hungry, I would not tell you; 1
107: 5 hungry and thirsty, their soul fainted within 2
9 the hungry he fills with good things. 2
36 there he lets the hungry dwell 2
146: 7 who gives food to the hungry. 2
Prv 6:30 steals to satisfy his appetite when he is hungry? 1
25:21 If your enemy is hungry, give him bread to eat; 2
27: 7 one who is hungry everything bitter is sweet. 2
Isa 8:21 through the land, greatly distressed and hungry; 2
21 when they are hungry, they will be enraged 1
9:20 They snatch on the right, but are still hungry 1
32: 6 to leave the craving of the hungry unsatisfied 2
44:12 he becomes hungry and his strength fails 2
58: 7 Is it not to share your bread with the hungry 2
10 if you pour yourself out for the hungry 2
65:13 servants shall eat, but you shall be hungry; 1
Jer 42:14 or be hungry for bread, and we will dwell there, 1
Ezk 18: 7 commits no robbery, gives his bread to the hungry 2
16 but gives his bread to the hungry 2
Mat 4: 2 and 40 nights, and afterward he was hungry. 4
12: 1 his disciples were hungry 4
3 read what David did, when he was hungry 4
15:32 I am unwilling to send them away hungry 3
21:18 he was hungry. 4
25:35 for I was hungry and you gave me food 4
37 Lord, when did we see thee hungry and feed thee 4
42 for I was hungry and you gave me no food 4
44 Lord, when did we see thee hungry or thirsty 4
Mrk 2:25 when he was in need and was hungry 4
8: 3 if I send them away hungry to their homes 3
11:12 when they came from Bethany, he was hungry. 4
Lke 1:53 he has filled the hungry with good things 4
4: 2 when they were ended, he was hungry. 4
6: 3 what David did when he was hungry 4
Act 10:10 he became hungry and desired something to eat; 5
Rom 12:20 No, "if your enemy is hungry, feed him; 4
1Co 11:21 one is hungry and another is drunk. 4
34 if any one is hungry, let him eat at home 4
2Es 1:17 When you were hungry and thirsty 6
16: 6 Can one drive off a hungry lion in the forest 6
Tob 1:17 I would give my bread to the hungry 4
4:16 Give of your bread to the hungry 4
Sir 4: 2 Do not grieve the one who is hungry 4
1Mc 13:49 So they were very hungry 4

hungry *See also* go.

hungry man 1. רָעֵב
Isa 29: 8 As when a hungry man dreams he is eating 1

hunt 1. נדח 2. פזר 3. צדה 4. צוד 5. צַיִד 6. רדף 7. שׂוּם קֶנֶץ
Gen 27: 3 go out to the field, and hunt game for me 4
5 to the field to hunt for game and bring it 4
30 Esau his brother came in from his hunting. 5
33 Who was it then that hunted game and brought it 4
1Sm 24:11 though you hunt my life to take it. 3
26:20 like one who hunts a partridge in the mountains. 6
Job 10:16 if I lift myself up, thou dost hunt me like a lion 4
18: 2 How long will you hunt for words? 7
38:39 Can you hunt the prey for the lion 4
Isa 13:14 like a hunted gazelle, or like sheep 1
Jer 16:16 and they shall hunt them from every mountain 4
50:17 Israel is a hunted sheep driven away by lions. 2
Lam 3:52 I have been hunted like a bird by .. my enemies 4
Ezk 13:18 persons of every stature, in the hunt for souls! 4
20 your magic bands with which you hunt the souls 4
20 I will let the souls that you hunt go free 4
Mic 7: 2 and each hunts his brother with a net. 4

hunt down 1. צוד 2. διώκω
Ps 140:11 let evil hunt down the violent man speedily! 1
Ezk 13:18 Will you hunt down souls belonging to my people 1
1Mc 2:47 They hunted down the arrogant men 2

hunter 1. צַיִד 2. צַיָּד 3. ἰχνευτής
Gen 10: 9 He was a mighty hunter before the LORD; 2
9 Like Nimrod a mighty hunter before the LORD. 2
25:27 When the boys grew up, Esau was a skilful hunter 2
Prv 6: 5 save yourself like a gazelle from the hunter •
Jer 16:16 and afterwards I will send for many hunters 1
Sir 14:22 Pursue wisdom like a hunter 3

hunting *See* spear, take.

hurl 1. טול 2. נכה 3. שׁלך 4. ἀποσφενδονάω 5. βολή 6. ἐνσείω 7. ἐντινάσσω 8. ῥίπτω 9. proicio
Num35:20 if he stabbed him from hatred, or hurled at him 3
22 if he .. hurled anything on him without lying in wait 3
Job 27:22 It hurls at him without pity; 3
Jer 16:13 therefore I will hurl you out of this land 1
22:26 I will hurl you and the mother who bore you 1
28 and his children hurled and cast into a land 1
Jon 1: 4 the LORD hurled a great wind upon the sea 1
Zec 9: 4 her possessions and hurl her wealth into the sea 2
2Es 1: 8 and hurl all evils upon them 9
Wis 5:22 will be hurled as from a catapult 8
1Mc 2:36 they did not answer them or hurl a stone at them 7
2Mc 5: 3 hurling of missiles 5
11:11 They hurled themselves like lions against the enemy 7
14:46 and hurled them at the crowd 6
4Mc 16:21 were hurled into the fiery furnace 4

hurl away 1. טול
Isa 22:17 Behold, the LORD will hurl you away violently 1

hurl down 1. καταράσσω 2. καταρρίπτω 3. ῥίπτω
Wis 17:19 the harsh crash of rocks hurled down 2
18:18 one here and another there, hurled down half dead 3
Sir 46: 6 He hurled down war upon that nation 1

hurl headlong 1. κρημνίζω
2Mc 6:10 then hurled them down headlong from the wall. 1

hurl out 1. προΐημι
2Mc 10:34 and hurled out wicked words. 1

hurricane 1. סוּפָה
Ps 83:15 terrify them with thy hurricane! 1

hurried *See* flight.

hurry 1. דחף 2. מְהֵרָה 3. σπεύδω 4. σπουδάζω 5. ταχύς
1Sm 20:38 Jonathan called after the lad, "Hurry, make haste 2
Est 6:12 But Haman hurried to his house, mourning 1
Jdt 10:15 hurrying down to the presence of our lord 3
13:12 they hurried down to the city gate 4
2Mc 5:21 hurried away to Antioch 5
3Mc 7:10 immediately hurry to make their departure 4

hurry out 1. ἐκπηδάω
2Mc 3:18 People also hurried out of their houses 1
3Mc 1:17 those . . were agitated and hurried out 1

hurt 1. הרע 2. חלה 3. כאב 4. נגף 5. עכר 6. ענה 7. עצב 8. רַע 9. רָעָה 10. רעע 11. שׂרט 12. שׁבר 13. שֶׁבֶר 14. חבל (A) 15. חֲבָל (A) 16. נזק (A) 17. ἀδικέω 18. βλάπτω 19. ἐπί 20. κακόω 21. λυπέω 22. σκληρός 23. τιμωρία
Exd 21:22 men strive together, and hurt a woman with child 4
22 the one who hurt her shall be fined *
35 When one man's ox hurts another's, so that it dies 4
22:10 If . . it dies or is hurt or is driven away 12
14 If . . it is hurt or dies, the owner not being 12
1Sm 24: 9 men who say, 'Behold, David seeks your hurt'? 9
25:34 LORD . . who has restrained me from hurting you 1
1Ch 4:10 keep me from harm so that it might not hurt me! 7
Ezr 4:22 why should damage grow to the hurt of the king? 16
Est 9: 2 to lay hands on such as sought their hurt. 9
Ps 15: 4 who swears to his own hurt and does not change; 1
38:12 those who seek my hurt speak of ruin 9
40:14 let them be turned back . . who desire my hurt! 9
70: 2 brought to dishonor who desire my hurt! 9
71:13 disgrace may they be covered who seek my hurt. 9
24 to shame and disgraced who sought to do me hurt. 9
105:18 His feet were hurt with fetters 6
Prv 11:17 but a cruel man hurts himself. 5
23:35 They struck me," you will say, "but I was not hurt; 2
Ecc 5:13 riches were kept by their owner to his hurt 9
8: 9 while man lords it over man to his hurt. 8
10: 9 He who quarries stones is hurt by them; 7
Isa 11: 9 They shall not hurt . . in all my holy mountain; 10
30:26 when the LORD binds up the hurt of his people 13
65:25 They shall not hurt . . in all my holy mountain 10
Jer 7: 6 if you do not go after other gods to your own hurt 8
10:19 Woe is me because of my hurt! My wound is grievous. 13
30:12 For thus says the LORD: Your hurt is incurable 13
15 Why do you cry out over your hurt? 13
Ezk 28:24 no more a brier to prick or a thorn to hurt them 3
Dan 3:25 walking in the midst of the fire . . not hurt; 15
6:22 shut the lions' mouths, and they have not hurt me 14
23 no kind of hurt was found upon him 15
Nah 3:19 There is no assuaging your hurt 13
Zec 12: 3 who lift it shall grievously hurt themselves. 11
Mrk 16:18 if they drink any deadly thing, it will not hurt 18
Lke 10:19 nothing shall hurt you. 17
Act 26:14 It hurts you to kick against the goads.' 22
Rev 2:11 He . . shall not be hurt by the second death 17
9:10 power of hurting men . . lies in their tails. 17
Jdt 11: 1 I have never hurt any one 20
4 No one will hurt you, but all will treat you well 17
Sir 9: 1 do not teach her an evil lesson to your own hurt. 19
26:10 lest, when she finds liberty, she use it to her hurt. *
Aza 1:27 did not touch them at all or hurt or trouble them. 21
4Mc 5:10 you continue to despise me to your own hurt. 23

hurtful 1. נזק (A) 2. βλαβερός
Ezr 4:15 rebellious city, hurtful to kings and provinces 1
1Ti 6: 9 into many senseless and hurtful desires 2

husband 1. אָדוֹן 2. אִישׁ 3. בעל 4. בַּעַל 5. רֵעַ 6. ἀδελφός 7. ἀνήρ 8. αὐτός 9. συζεύγνυμι 10. maritus 11. vir
Gen 3: 6 she also gave some to her husband, and he ate. 2
16 yet your desire shall be for your husband 2
16: 3 gave her to Abram her husband as a wife. 2
18:12 After I have grown old, and my husband is old 1
29:32 surely now my husband will love me. 2
34 Now this time my husband will be joined to me 2
30:15 that you have taken away my husband? 2
18 my hire because I gave my maid to my husband"; 2
20 now my husband will honor me 2
Exd 21:22 according as the woman's husband shall lay upon 4
Lev 21: 3 (who is near to him because she has had no husband 2
4 He shall not defile himself as a husband 4
7 marry a woman divorced from her husband 2
Num 5:13 it is hidden from the eyes of her husband 2
19 while you were under your husband's authority 2
20 though you are under your husband's authority 2
20 some man other than your husband has lain with you 2
27 acted unfaithfully against her husband 2
29 when a wife, though under her husband's authority 2
30: 6 if she is married to a husband 2
7 her husband hears of it, and says nothing to her 2
8 if, on the day that her husband comes to hear of it 2
10 if she vowed in her husband's house 2
11 her husband heard of it, and said nothing to her 2
12 if her husband makes them null and void on the day 2
12 her vows . . her husband has made them void 2
13 Any vow . . her husband may establish 2
13 Any vow . . her husband may make void. 2
14 if her husband says nothing to her from day to day 2
Deu 21:13 after that you may go in to her, and be her husband 3
24: 3 latter husband dislikes her and writes her 2
3 the latter husband dies, who took her to be his wife 2
4 then her former husband . . may not take her again 4
25:11 near to rescue her husband from the hand of him 2
28:56 woman . . will grudge to the husband of her bosom 2
Jdg 13: 6 woman came and told her husband, "A man of God 2
9 field; but Mano'ah her husband was not with her. 2
10 the woman ran in haste and told her husband 2
14:15 Entice your husband to tell us what the riddle is 2
19: 3 her husband arose and went after her, to speak 2
20: 4 the Levite, the husband of the woman 2
Rut 1: 3 But Elim'elech, the husband of Na'omi, died 2
5 woman was bereft of her two sons and her husband. 2
9 find a home, each of you in the house of her husband! 2
11 yet sons . . that they may become your husbands? 2
12 go your way, for I am too old to have a husband. 2
12 even if I should have a husband this night 2
2: 1 Now Na'omi had a kinsman of her husband's 2
11 you have done . . since the death of your husband 2
1Sm 1: 8 Elka'nah, her husband, said to her, "Hannah, why 2
22 Hannah did not go up, for she said to her husband 2
23 Elka'nah her husband said . . "Do what seems best 2
2:19 she went up with her husband to offer the yearly 2
4:19 that her father-in-law and her husband were dead 2
21 and because of her father-in-law and her husband. 2
25:19 But she did not tell her husband Nabal. 2
2Sm 3:15 Ish-bo'sheth sent, and took her from her husband 2
16 But her husband went with her, weeping after her 2
11:26 the wife . . heard that Uri'ah her husband was dead 2
26 she made lamentation for her husband. 4
14: 5 answered, "Alas, I am a widow; my husband is dead. 2
7 and leave to my husband neither name nor remnant 2
17: 3 back to you as a bride comes home to her husband. 7
2Kg 4: 1 Your servant my husband is dead; 2
9 she said to her husband, "Behold now, I perceive 2
14 Well, she has no son, and her husband is old. 2
22 she called to her husband, and said, "Send me one 2
26 Is it well with you? Is it well with your husband? 2
Est 1:17 to look with contempt upon their husbands 4
20 all women will give honor to their husbands 4
Prv 7:19 For my husband is not at home; 2
12: 4 A good wife is the crown of her husband 4
31:11 The heart of her husband trusts in her 4
23 Her husband is known in the gates 4
28 her husband also, and he praises her; 4
Isa 54: 5 For your Maker is your husband, the LORD of hosts 3
Jer 3:20 Surely, as a faithless wife leaves her husband 5
6:11 both husband and wife shall be taken 2
31:32 though I was their husband, says the LORD. 3
44:19 was it without our husbands' approval 2
Ezk 16:32 who receives strangers instead of her husband! 2
45 mother, who loathed her husband and her children; 2
45 your sisters, who loathed their husbands 2
Hos 2: 2 for she is not my wife, and I am not her husband– 2
7 shall say, 'I will go and return to my first husband 2
16 says the LORD, you will call me, 'My husband,' 2
Ams 4: 1 who say to their husbands, 'Bring, that we may drink 1
Mat 1:16 Joseph the husband of Mary, of whom Jesus was born 7
19 her husband Joseph, being a just man 8
Mrk 10:12 if she divorces her husband and marries another 7
Lke 1:34 How shall this be, since I have no husband? 7
2:36 lived with her husband seven years 7
16:18 he who marries a woman divorced from her husband 7
Joh 4:16 Go, call your husband, and come here. 7
17 The woman answered him, "I have no husband. 7
17 You are right in saying, 'I have no husband'; 7
18 for you have had five husbands 7
18 and he whom you now have is not your husband; 7
Act 5: 9 the feet of those that have buried your husband 7
10 buried her beside her husband. 7
Rom 7: 2 a married woman is bound by law to her husband 7
2 but if her husband dies she is discharged 7
2 is discharged from the law concerning the husband 7
3 with another man while her husband is alive. 7
3 But if her husband dies she is free from that law 7
1Co 7: 2 and each woman her own husband. 7
3 husband should give to his wife her conjugal rights 7
3 likewise the wife to her husband. 7
4 but the husband does 7
4 the husband does not rule over his own body 7
10 the wife should not separate from her husband 7
11 or else be reconciled to her husband 7
11 the husband should not divorce his wife. 7
13 If any woman has a husband who is an unbeliever 7
14 For the unbelieving husband is consecrated 7
14 consecrated through her husband 6
16 whether you will save your husband 7
16 Husband, how do you know 7
34 how to please her husband. 7
39 A wife is bound to her husband as long as he lives. 7
39 If the husband dies 7
11: 3 the head of a woman is her husband 7
14:35 let them ask their husbands at home 7
2Co 11: 2 to present you as a pure bride to her one husband. 7
Eph 5:22 Wives, be subject to your husbands, as to the Lord. 7
23 For the husband is the head of the wife as Christ 7
24 be subject in everything to their husbands. 7
25 Husbands, love your wives 7
28 Even so husbands should love their wives 7
33 let the wife see that she respects her husband. 7
Col 3:18 Wives, be subject to your husbands 7
19 Husbands, love your wives 7
1Ti 3: 2 the husband of one wife, temperate, sensible 7
12 Let deacons be the husband of one wife 7
5: 9 having been the wife of one husband; 7
Tit 1: 6 if any man is blameless, the husband of one wife 7
2: 5 submissive to their husbands 7
1Pe 3: 1 wives, be submissive to your husbands 7
5 women . . were submissive to their husbands 7
7 husbands, live considerately with your wives 7
Rev 21: 2 prepared as a bride adorned for her husband; 7
2Es 9:43 though I lived with my husband 30 years. 10
45 I and my husband and all my neighbors 11
10:17 Therefore go into the city to your husband. 11
16:33 because they have no husbands 11
34 and their husbands shall perish of famine. 11
Tob 3: 8 because she had been given to seven husbands 7
8 Do you not know that you strangle your husbands? 7
15 Already seven husbands of mine are dead *
6:13 the girl has been given to seven husbands 7
7:11 I have given my daughter to seven husbands 7
Jdt 8: 2 Her husband Manasseh, who belonged to her tribe 7
7 her husband Manasseh had left her gold 7
10: 3 while her husband Manasseh was living. 7
16:22 after Manasseh her husband died 7
23 and grew old in her husband's house 7
23 buried her in the cave of her husband Manasseh 7
24 who were next of kin to her husband Manasseh 7
Sir 4:10 Be . . instead of a husband to their mother 7
22: 4 A sensible daughter obtains her husband 7
5 disgraces father and husband 7
23:22 it is with a woman who leaves her husband 7
23 committed an offense against her husband 7
25: 1 a wife and a husband who live in harmony. 7
18 Her husband takes his meals among the neighbors 7
20 such is a garrulous wife for a quiet husband. 7
22 when a wife supports her husband. 7
23 the wife who does not make her husband happy. 7
26: 1 Happy is the husband of a good wife 7
2 A loyal wife rejoices her husband 7
13 A wife's charm delights her husband 7
36:23 her husband is not like other men. 7
40:23 a wife with her husband is better than both. 7
42:10 having a husband, lest she prove unfaithful 7
Sus 1: 7 Susanna would go into her husband's garden 7
28 gathered at the house of her husband Joakim 7
63 so did Joakim her husband and all her kindred 7
3Mc 4: 8 Their husbands . . spent the remaining days 9
4Mc 18: 9 I remained with my husband 7

husband *See also* brother, get, love.

hush 1. הַס 2. חבא 3. חשה 4. παύω 5. σιγή
Job 29:10 the voice of the nobles was hushed 2
Ps 107:29 waves of the sea were hushed. 3
Isa 16:10 no treader . . the vintage shout is hushed. 4
Ams 6:10 Hush! We must not mention the name of the LORD. 1
Act 21:40 when there was a great hush 5

hut 1. מְלוּנָה
Isa 24:20 The earth staggers . . it sways like a hut; 1

hyena 1. אִי 2. ὕαινα
Isa 13:22 Hyenas will cry in its towers 1
34:14 wild beasts shall meet with hyenas 1
Jer 50:39 wild beasts shall dwell with hyenas in Babylon 1
Sir 13:18 What peace is there between a hyena and a dog? 2

hymn 1. ὕμνος 2. ψαλμός
1Co 14:26 When you come together, each one has a hymn 2
Eph 5:19 addressing one another in psalms and hymns 1
Col 3:16 sing psalms and hymns and spiritual songs 1
1Es 5:61 they sang hymns, giving thanks to the Lord 1
1Mc 4:33 let all who know thy name praise thee with hymns. 1
13:47 then entered it with hymns and praise. 1
51 with hymns and songs 1
2Mc 1:30 Then the priests sang the hymns. 1
10: 7 they offered hymns of thanksgiving to him 1
38 with hymns and thanksgivings 1
12:37 he raised the battle cry, with hymns 1
4Mc 10:21 has been melodious with divine hymns. 1

hymn *See also* sing.

hymn of praise 1. αἶνος
Sir 15: 9 A hymn of praise is not fitting on the lips 1
10 For a hymn of praise should be uttered in wisdom 1

hypocrisy 1. εἰρωνεία 2. ὑπόκρισις
Mat 23:28 within you are full of hypocrisy and iniquity. 2
Mrk 12:15 knowing their hypocrisy, he said to them 2
Lke 12: 1 the leaven of the Pharisees, which is hypocrisy. 2
2Mc 13: 3 and with utter hypocrisy urged Antiochus 1

hypocrite 1. ὑποκρίνω 2. ὑποκριτής
Mat 6: 2 no trumpet before you, as the hypocrites do 2
5 not be like the hypocrites; for they love to stand 2
16 you fast, do not look dismal, like the hypocrites 2
7: 5 hypocrite, first take the log out of your own eye 2
15: 7 You hypocrites! Well did Isaiah prophesy of you 2
22:18 Why put me to the test, you hypocrites? 2
23:13 woe to you, scribes and Pharisees, hypocrites! 2
15 Woe to you, scribes and Pharisees, hypocrites! 2

23 Woe to you, scribes and Pharisees, hypocrites! 2
25 Woe to you, scribes and Pharisees, hypocrites! 2
27 Woe to you, scribes and Pharisees, hypocrites! 2
29 Woe to you, scribes and Pharisees, hypocrites! 2
24:51 will punish him, and put him with the hypocrites; 2
Mrk 7: 6 Well did Isaiah prophesy of you hypocrites 2
Lke 6:42 hypocrite, first take the log out of your own eye 2
12:56 You hypocrites! You know how to interpret 2
13:15 Then the Lord answered him, "You hypocrites! 2
Sir 1:29 Be not a hypocrite in men's sight 1
32:15 the hypocrite will stumble at it. 1

hypocritical 1. *ὑποκρίνω*

Sir 33: 2 he who is hypocritical about it 1

hyssop 1. אֵזוֹב 2. *ὑσσώπος*

Exd 12:22 Take a bunch of hyssop and dip it in the blood 1
Lev 14: 4 take . . cedarwood and scarlet stuff and hyssop 1
6 take . . the scarlet stuff and the hyssop 1
49 with cedarwood and scarlet stuff and hyssop 1
51 cedarwood and the hyssop and the scarlet stuff 1
52 with the cedarwood and hyssop and scarlet stuff 1
Num19: 6 priest shall take cedarwood and hyssop 1
18 then a clean person shall take hyssop, and dip it 1
1Kg 4:33 from the cedar . . to the hyssop that grows out 1
Ps 51: 7 Purge me with hyssop, and I shall be clean; 1
Joh 19:29 they put a sponge full of the vinegar on hyssop 2
Heb 9:19 with water and scarlet wool and hyssop 2

I

I am 1. אֲנִי 2. אָנֹכִי 3. היה 4. הִנֵּנִי 5. הִנְנִי 6. ἐγώ 7. εἰμί

Gen 15: 1 Fear not, Abram, I am your shield; 2
7 he said . . "I am the LORD who brought you from Ur 2
17: 1 I am God Almighty; walk before me, and be blameless. 2
26:24 I am the God of Abraham your father; fear not 2
24 fear not, for I am with you and will bless you 2
28:13 I am the LORD, the God of Abraham your father 2
15 Behold, I am with you and will keep you 2
31:13 I am the God of Bethel, where you anointed a pillar 2
35:11 God said to him, "I am God Almighty 2
46: 3 Then he said, "I am God, the God of your father; 2
Exd 3: 6 he said, "I am the God of your father •
14 God said to Moses, "I AM WHO I AM. 3
14 God said to Moses, "I AM WHO I AM. 3
14 Say this . . 'I AM has sent me to you.' 3
6: 2 God said to Moses, "I am the LORD. •
6 Say therefore . . 'I am the LORD, and I will bring •
7 and you shall know that I am the LORD your God •
8 I am the LORD.' •
29 the LORD said to Moses, "I am the LORD; tell Pharaoh •
7: 5 the Egyptians shall know that I am the LORD •
17 By this you shall know that I am the LORD •
8:22 that you may know that I am the LORD in the midst •
10: 2 that you may know that I am the LORD. 1
12:12 I will execute judgments: I am the LORD. 2
14: 4 the Egyptians shall know that I am the LORD. 2
18 the Egyptians shall know that I am the LORD 2
15:26 for I am the LORD, your healer. 2
16:12 then you shall know that I am the LORD your God.' 2
20: 2 I am the LORD your God, who brought you out •
5 for I the LORD your God am a jealous God •
22:27 cries to me, I will hear, for I am compassionate. 2
29:46 they shall know that I am the LORD their God, who •
46 dwell among them; I am the LORD their God. 1
Lev 11:44 For I am the LORD your God: consecrate yourselves 2
44 consecrate . . and be holy, for I am holy 2
45 For I am the LORD who brought you up out of the land 2
45 you shall therefore be holy, for I am holy 2
18: 2 "Say to the people of Israel, I am the LORD your God 2
2 Say to the people of Israel, I am the LORD your God 2
4 I am the LORD your God 2
5 I am the LORD 2
6 I am the LORD 2
21 and so profane the name of your God: I am the LORD 2
30 I am the LORD your God 2
19: 2 You shall be holy; for I the LORD your God am holy 2
3 you shall keep my sabbaths: I am the LORD your God 2
4 I am LORD your God 2
10 I am the LORD your God 2
12 and so profane the name of your God: I am the LORD 2
14 but you shall fear your God: I am the LORD 2
16 I am the LORD 2
18 love your neighbor as yourself: I am the LORD 2
25 may yield more richly for you: I am the LORD your God 2
28 or tattoo any marks upon you: I am the LORD 2
30 reverence my sanctuary: I am the LORD 2
31 I am the LORD your God 2
32 you shall fear your God; I am the LORD 2
34 I am the LORD your God 2
36 I am the LORD your God, who brought you out 2
37 my ordinances, and do them: I am the LORD 2
20: 7 be holy; for I am the LORD your God 2
8 do them; I am the LORD who sanctify you 2
24 I am the LORD your God, who have separated you 2
26 You shall be holy to me; for I the LORD am holy 2
21: 8 for I the LORD, who sanctify you, am holy 2
12 I am the LORD 2
15 for I am the LORD who sanctify him 2
23 for I am the LORD who sanctify them 2
22: 2 may not profane my holy name: I am the LORD 2
3 shall be cut off from my presence; I am the LORD 2
8 I am the LORD.' 2
9 they profane it: I am the LORD who sanctify them 2
16 holy thing: for I am the LORD who sanctify them 2
30 I am the LORD 2
31 keep my commandments and do them: I am the LORD 2
32 I am the LORD who sanctify you 2
33 who brought you . . to be your God: I am the LORD 2
23:22 I am the LORD your God 2
43 I am the LORD your God 2
24:22 for I am the LORD your God 2
25:17 fear your God; for I am the LORD your God 2
38 I am the LORD your God, who brought you forth 2
55 out of the land of Egypt: I am the LORD your God 2
26: 1 to bow down to them, for I am the LORD your God 2
2 reverence my sanctuary: I am the LORD 2
13 I am the LORD your God, who brought you forth 2
44 for I am the LORD their God 2
45 that I might be their God: I am the LORD 2
Num 3:13 they shall be mine: I am the LORD. 2
41 you shall take the Levites for me–I am the LORD 2
45 Levites shall be mine: I am the LORD. 2
10:10 I am the LORD your God. 2
15:41 I am the LORD your God, who brought you out 2
41 I am the LORD your God. 2
18:20 I am your portion and your inheritance 2
Deu 5: 6 I am the LORD your God, who brought you out 2
9 for I the LORD your God am a jealous God 2
29: 6 that you may know that I am the LORD your God. 2
32:39 I, even I, am he, and there is no god beside me; 2
Jdg 6:10 I said to you, 'I am the LORD your God; you shall not 1
1Kg 11:31 I am about to tear the kingdom from the hand 5
20:13 I will . . and you shall know that I am the LORD. 2
28 and you shall know that I am the LORD.' 1
Ps 35: 3 Say to my soul, "I am your deliverance! 1
46:10 Be still, and know that I am God. 2
50: 7 I will testify against you. I am God, your God. 2
81:10 I am the LORD your God, who brought you up 2
Isa 27: 3 I, the LORD, am its keeper; every moment I water it 1
41: 4 I, the LORD, the first, and with the last; I am He. 2
10 fear not, for I am with you 2
10 be not dismayed, for I am your God; 2
42: 6 I am the LORD, I have called you in righteousness 2
8 I am the LORD, that is my name; 2
43: 3 For I am the LORD your God, the Holy One 2
5 Fear not, for I am with you; 2
10 know and believe me and understand that I am He. 2
11 I, I am the LORD, and besides me there is no savior. 2
13 I am God, and also henceforth I am He; 2
13 I am God, and also henceforth I am He; 2
15 I am the LORD, your Holy One, the Creator 2
25 I, I am He who blots out your transgressions 2
44: 6 I am the first and I am the last; 2
6 I am the first and I am the last; 2
24 I am the LORD, who made all things 2
45: 5 I am the LORD, and there is no other 2
6 I am the LORD, and there is no other. 2
7 I am the LORD, who do all these things. 2
18 I am the LORD, and there is no other. 2
22 Turn to me . . For I am God, and there is no other. 2
46: 4 even to your old age I am He, and to gray hairs 2
9 for I am God, and there is no other; 2
9 there is no other; I am God, and there is none like me •
48:12 I called! I am He, I am the first, and I am the last. 2
12 I called! I am He, I am the first, and I am the last. 2
12 I called! I am He, I am the first, and I am the last. 2
17 I am the LORD your God, who teaches you to profit 2
49:23 Then you will know that I am the LORD; 2
26 flesh shall know that I am the LORD your Savior 2
51:12 I, I am he that comforts you; 2
15 For I am the LORD your God, who stirs up the sea 2
52: 6 they shall know that it is I who speak; here am I. 4
58: 9 you shall cry, and he will say, Here I am. 5
60:16 and you shall know that I, the LORD, am your Savior 2
22 I am the LORD; in its time I will hasten it. 2
65: 1 I said, "Here am I, here am I," to a nation 4
1 here am I," to a nation that did not call on my name. 5
Jer 1: 8 for I am with you to deliver you, says the LORD. 1
19 shall not prevail against you, for I am with you 1
3:12 I will not look on you in anger, for I am merciful 1
9:24 that I am the LORD who practice steadfast love 1
15:20 they shall not prevail over you, for I am with you 1
21:13 I am against you, O inhabitant of the valley 5
23:23 Am I a God at hand, says the LORD 1
30 behold, I am against the prophets, says the LORD 5
31 Behold, I am against the prophets, says the LORD 5
32 I am against those who prophesy lying dreams 5
24: 7 I will give them a heart to know that I am the LORD 1
29:23 I am the one who knows, and I am witness 2
23 I am the one who knows, and I am witness •
30:11 For I am with you to save you, says the LORD; 2
31: 9 for I am a father to Israel 3
32:27 Behold, I am the LORD, the God of all flesh; 1
42:11 do not fear him, says the LORD, for I am with you 1
46:28 O Jacob my servant, says the LORD, for I am with you. 1
50:31 Behold, I am against you, O proud one, says the Lord 5
51:25 Behold, I am against you, O destroying mountain 5
Ezk 5: 8 says the Lord GOD: Behold, I, even I, am against you; 5
6: 7 and you shall know that I am the LORD. 1
10 And they shall know that I am the LORD; 1
13 And you shall know that I am the LORD 1
14 Then they will know that I am the LORD. 1
7: 4 Then you will know that I am the LORD. 1
9 Then you will know that I am the LORD, who smite. 1
27 and they shall know that I am the LORD. 2
11:10 and you shall know that I am the LORD. 1
12 you shall know that I am the LORD; 1
12:15 they shall know that I am the LORD 1
16 and may know that I am the LORD. 1
20 and you shall know that I am the LORD. 1
13: 9 you shall know that I am the Lord GOD. 1
14 you shall know that I am the LORD. 1
20 Behold, I am against your magic bands 5
21 prey; and you shall know that I am the LORD. 1
23 Then you will know that I am the LORD. 1
14: 8 you shall know that I am the LORD. 1
15: 7 you will know that I am the LORD, when I set my face 2
16:62 you shall know that I am the LORD 1
20: 5 I swore to them, saying, I am the LORD your God. 1
7 I am the LORD your God. 1
19 I the LORD am your God; walk in my statutes 1
20 that you may know that I the LORD am your God. 1
26 that they might know that I am the LORD. 1
38 Then you will know that I am the LORD. 1
42 And you shall know that I am the LORD 1
44 you shall know that I am the LORD 1
21: 3 I am against you, and will draw forth my sword 5
22:16 you shall know that I am the LORD. 1
23:49 you shall know that I am the Lord GOD. 1
24:16 I am about to take the delight of your eyes away 5
24 then you will know that I am the Lord GOD. 1
27 they will know that I am the LORD. 1
25: 5 Then you will know that I am the LORD. 1
7 Then you will know that I am the LORD. 1
11 Then they will know that I am the LORD. 1
17 Then they will know that I am the LORD 1
26: 3 says the Lord GOD: Behold, I am against you, O Tyre 5
6 Then they will know that I am the LORD. 1
28:22 says the Lord GOD: "Behold, I am against you, O Sidon 5
22 they shall know that I am the LORD when I execute 1
23 Then they will know that I am the LORD. 1
24 Then they will know that I am the Lord GOD. 1
26 Then they will know that I am the LORD their God. 1
29: 3 Behold, I am against you, Pharaoh king of Egypt 5
6 Egypt shall know that I am the LORD. 1
9 Then they will know that I am the LORD. 1
10 therefore, behold, I am against you 1
16 Then they will know that I am the Lord GOD. 1
21 Then they will know that I am the LORD. 1
30: 8 Then they will know that I am the LORD 1
19 Then they will know that I am the LORD. 1

22 Behold, I am against Pharaoh king of Egypt 5
25 they shall know that I am the LORD. 1
26 Then they will know that I am the LORD. 1
32:15 then they will know that I am the LORD. 1
33:29 Then they will know that I am the LORD 1
34:10 the Lord GOD, Behold, I am against the shepherds 5
27 they shall know that I am the LORD 1
30 shall know that I, the LORD their God, am with them 1
31 and I am your God, says the Lord GOD. 1
35: 3 Behold, I am against you, mount Se'ir 5
4 and you shall know that I am the LORD. 1
9 Then you will know that I am the LORD. 1
15 Then they will know that I am the LORD. 1
36: 9 For, behold, I am for you, and I will turn to you 5
11 Then you will know that I am the LORD. 1
22 I am about to act, but for the sake of my holy name 1
23 the nations will know that I am the LORD 1
38 Then they will know that I am the LORD. 1
37: 6 you shall know that I am the LORD. 1
13 you shall know that I am the LORD 1
19 Behold, I am about to take the stick of Joseph 1
38: 3 says the Lord GOD: Behold, I am against you, O Gog 5
23 Then they will know that I am the LORD. 1
39: 1 says the Lord GOD: Behold, I am against you, O Gog 5
6 they shall know that I am the LORD. 1
7 the nations shall know that I am the LORD 1
22 The house of Israel shall know that I am the LORD 1
28 Then they shall know that I am the LORD their God 1
44:28 have no inheritance; I am their inheritance: 1
28 no possession in Israel; I am their possession. 1
Dan 10:20 when I am through with him, lo, the prince of Greece 1
Hos 1: 9 for you are not my people and I am not your God. 3
5:12 Therefore I am like a moth to E'phraim 2
12 Therefore I am like a moth to E'phraim 2
11: 9 for I am God and not man, the Holy One in your midst 2
12: 9 I am the LORD your God from the land of Egypt; 2
13: 4 I am the LORD your God from the land of Egypt; 2
14: 8 I am like an evergreen cypress 2
Jol 2:27 You shall know that I am in the midst of Israel 2
27 I, the LORD, am your God 2
3:17 you shall know that I am the LORD your God 2
Hag 1:13 the LORD's message, "I am with you, says the LORD. 2
2: 4 work, for I am with you, says the LORD of hosts 1
21 I am about to shake the heavens and the earth 1
Zec 10: 6 for I am the LORD their God and I will answer them. 1
12: 2 "Lo, I am about to make Jerusalem a cup of reeling 2
2 Lo, I am about to make Jerusalem a cup of reeling 2
Mal 1: 6 If then I am a father, where is my honor? 1
6 And if I am a master, where is my fear? says the LORD 1
14 I am a great King, says the LORD of hosts 1
Mat 18:20 there am I in the midst of them. 7
22:32 'I am the God of Abraham, and the God of Isaac 7
Mrk 12:26 I am the God of Abraham, and the God of Isaac •
14:62 Jesus said, "I am; and you will see the Son of man 7
Joh 6:35 Jesus said to them, "I am the bread of life 7
41 I am the bread which came down from heaven. 7
48 I am the bread of life. 7
51 I am the living bread which came down from heaven; 7
7:36 'Where I am you cannot come'? 7
8:24 unless you believe that I am he. 7
58 before Abraham was, I am. 7
10: 7 I am the door of the sheep. 7
11 I am the good shepherd 7
14 I am the good shepherd 7
11:25 Jesus said to her, "I am the resurrection 7
12:26 where I am, there shall my servant be also 7
13:13 you are right, for so I am. 7
19 you may believe that I am he. 6
33 Little children, yet a little while I am with you. 7
14: 6 I am the way, and the truth, and the life 7
11 Believe me that I am in the Father •
15: 1 I am the true vine 7
5 I am the vine, you are the branches. 7
17:24 I desire that they . . may be with me where I am 7
Rev 1: 8 I am the Alpha and the Omega," says the Lord God 7

ibex 1. דִּישֹׁן
Deu 14: 5 the ibex, the antelope, and the mountain-sheep 1

ibis 1. יַנְשׁוּף
Lev 11:17 the owl, the cormorant, the ibis 1

ice 1. קֶרַח 2. κρύσταλλος 3. πάγος 4. gelu
Job 6:16 which are dark with ice, and where the snow hides 1
37:10 By the breath of God ice is given 1
38:29 From whose womb did the ice come forth 1
Ps 147:17 He casts forth his ice like morsels; 1
2Es 3:19 of fire and earthquake and wind and ice 4
Wis 16:22 Snow and ice withstood fire without melting 2
Sir 43:20 ice freezes over the water 2
Aza 1:49 Bless the Lord, ice and cold 3

idea 1. διανόημα 2. ἐπίνοια
Wis 14:12 the idea of making idols 2
Sir 32:18 A man of judgment will not overlook an idea 1
idea *See also* conceive.

idiot 1. ἄλογος
3Mc 5:40 as though we are idiots 1

idle 1. רְמִיָּה 2. רפה 3. ἀργέω 4. ἀργός 5. ἀτακτέω
Exd 5: 8 you shall by no means lessen it; for they are idle; 2
17 he said, "You are idle, you are idle; 2
17 he said, "You are idle, you are idle; 2
Prv 19:15 idle person will suffer hunger. 1
Mat 20: 3 he saw others standing idle in the market place; 4
6 he said to them, 'Why do you stand here idle all day? 4
2Th 3: 7 we were not idle when we were with you 5
2Pe 2: 3 from of old their condemnation has not been idle 3
Sir 33:25 leave his hands idle, and he will seek liberty. •
27 Put him to work, that he may not be idle 4
idle *See also* game, tale.

idleness 1. עַצְלוּת 2. ἀργία 3. ἀτάκτως
Prv 31:27 She . . does not eat the bread of idleness. 1
2Th 3: 6 any brother who is living in idleness 3
11 we hear that some of you are living in idleness 3
Sir 33:27 idleness teaches much evil. 2
idleness *See also* gain.

idler 1. ἀργός 2. ἄτακτος 3. ὀκνηρός
1Th 5:14 we exhort you, brethren, admonish the idlers 2
1Ti 5:13 Besides that, they learn to be idlers 1
13 not only idlers but gossips and busybodies 1
Sir 37:11 with an idler about any work 3

idly 1. דָּבָר
Isa 58:13 seeking your own pleasure, or talking idly; 1

idol 1. אָוֶן 2. אֵימָה 3. אֱלִיל 4. גִּלּוּל 5. הֶבֶל 6. סֶמֶל 7. עָצָב 8. עֹצֶב 9. פְּסִיל 10. פֶּסֶל 11. צִיר 12. εἰδώλιον 13. εἴδωλον 14. idolum
Lev 19: 4 Do not turn to idols or make for yourselves 3
26: 1 You shall make for yourselves no idols 3
30 dead bodies upon the dead bodies of your idols 4
Deu 29:17 have seen their detestable things, their idols 4
32:21 they have provoked me with their idols. 5
1Sm 31: 9 carry the good news to their idols and . . people. 7
2Sm 5:21 And the Philistines left their idols there 7
1Kg 15:12 removed all the idols that his fathers had made. 4
16:13 provoking the LORD . . to anger with their idols. 5
26 provoking the LORD . . to anger by their idols. 5
21:26 He did very abominably in going after idols 4
2Kg 17:12 they served idols, of which the LORD had said 4
21:11 and has made Judah also to sin with his idols; 4
21 and served the idols that his father served 4
23:24 teraphim and the idols and all the abominations 4
1Ch 10: 9 the good news to their idols and to the people. 7
16:26 For all the gods of the peoples are idols; 3
2Ch 24:18 served the Ashe'rim and the idols. 7
33: 7 the image of the idol . . he set in the house of God 6
15 he took away the foreign gods and the idol 6
Ps 31: 6 Thou hatest those who pay regard to vain idols; 5
96: 5 For all the gods of the peoples are idols; 3
106:36 served their idols, which became a snare to them. 7
38 whom they sacrificed to the idols of Canaan; 7
115: 4 idols are silver and gold, the work of men's hands. 7
135:15 The idols of the nations are silver and gold 7
Isa 2: 8 Their land is filled with idols; 3
18 the idols shall utterly pass away. 3
20 men will cast forth their idols of silver 3
20 of silver and their idols of gold, which they made 3
10:10 my hand has reached to the kingdoms of the idols 3
11 shall I not do to Jerusalem and her idols as I have 7
19: 1 the idols of Egypt will tremble at his presence 3
3 they will consult the idols and the sorcerers 3
31: 7 every one shall cast away his idols of silver 3
7 every one shall cast away . . his idols of gold 3
40:19 The idol! a workman casts it 10
44: 9 All who make idols are nothing 10
17 the rest of it he makes into a god, his idol; 10
45:16 the makers of idols go in confusion together. 11
20 no knowledge who carry about their wooden idols 10
46: 1 Nebo stoops, their idols are on beasts and cattle; 7
48: 5 lest you should say, 'My idol did them 8
57:13 let your collection of idols deliver you! •
66: 3 frankincense, like him who blesses an idol. 1
Jer 8:19 graven images, and with their foreign idols? 5
10: 5 idols are like scarecrows in a cucumber field •
8 the instruction of idols is but wood! 5
14 every goldsmith is put to shame by his idols; 10
50: 2 images are put to shame, her idols are dismayed. 4
38 it is a land of images, and they are mad over idols. 2
51:17 every goldsmith is put to shame by his idols; 10
Ezk 6: 4 I will cast down your slain before your idols. 4
5 lay . . the people of Israel before their idols; 4
6 your idols broken and destroyed 4
9 eyes which turn wantonly after their idols; 4
13 when their slain lie among their idols 4
13 they offered pleasing odor to all their idols. 4
8:10 and all the idols of the house of Israel. 4
14: 3 men have taken their idols into their hearts 4
4 Any man . . who takes his idols into his heart 4
4 because of the multitude of his idols 4
5 are all estranged from me through their idols. 4
6 Repent and turn away from your idols; 4
7 taking his idols into his heart 4
16:36 with your lovers, and because of all your idols 4
18: 6 or lift up his eyes to the idols of . . Israel 4
12 lifts up his eyes to the idols 4
15 or lift up his eyes to the idols . . of Israel 4
20: 7 do not defile yourselves with the idols of Egypt; 4
8 nor did they forsake the idols of Egypt. 4
16 for their heart went after their idols. 4
18 nor defile yourselves with their idols. 4
24 their eyes were set on their fathers' idols. 4
31 you defile yourselves with all your idols 4
39 Go serve every one of you his idols 4
39 no more profane with your gifts and your idols. 4
22: 3 and that makes idols to defile herself! 4
4 and defiled by the idols which you have made; 4
23: 7 defiled herself with all the idols of every one 4
30 and polluted yourself with their idols. 4
37 with their idols they have committed adultery; 4
39 their children in sacrifice to their idols 4
30:13 Thus says the Lord GOD: I will destroy the idols 4
33:25 and lift up your eyes to your idols, and shed blood; 4
36:18 for the idols with which they had defiled it. 4
25 from all your idols I will cleanse you. 4
37:23 with their idols and their detestable things 4
44:10 going astray from me after their idols 4
12 they ministered to them before their idols 4
Hos 4:17 E'phraim is joined to idols, let him alone. 7
8: 4 With their silver and gold they made idols 7
10: 6 and Israel shall be ashamed of his idol. •
11: 2 and burning incense to idols. 9
13: 2 idols skilfully made of their silver 7
14: 8 O E'phraim, what have I to do with idols? 7
Jon 2: 8 Those who pay regard to vain idols 5
Mic 1: 7 and all her idols I will lay waste; 7
Hab 2:18 What profit is an idol when its maker has shaped 10
18 in his own creation when he makes dumb idols! 3
Zec 13: 2 I will cut off the names of the idols from the land 7
Act 7:41 offered a sacrifice to the idol 13
15:20 abstain from the pollutions of idols 13
Rom 2:22 You who abhor idols, do you rob temples? 13
1Co 8: 4 we know that "an idol has no real existence 13
7 through being hitherto accustomed to idols 13
10:19 that an idol is anything? 13
12: 2 you were led astray to dumb idols 13
2Co 6:16 What agreement has the temple of God with idols? 13
1Th 1: 9 how you turned to God from idols 13
1Jn 5:21 Little children, keep yourselves from idols. 13
Rev 9:20 nor give up worshiping demons and idols of gold 13
2Es 16:68 and shall feed you what was sacrificed to idols. 14
Tob 14: 6 will bury their idols. 13
AEs 14: 8 have covenanted with their idols 13
10 the praise of vain idols •
Wis 14: 8 the idol made with hands is accursed •
11 a visitation also upon the heathen idols 13
12 the idea of making idols 13
27 the worship of idols not to be named 13
29 for because they trust in lifeless idols 13
30 devoting themselves to idols 13
15:15 thought that all their heathen idols were gods 13
Sir 30:19 Of what use to an idol is an offering of fruit? 13
LJr 1:63 these idols are not to be compared with them •
73 Better therefore is a just man who has no idols 13
Bel 1: 3 Now the Babylonians had an idol called Bel 13
5 Because I do not revere man-made idols 13
1Mc 1:43 sacrificed to idols and profaned the sabbath. 13
3:48 were consulting the images of their idols. 13
10:83 Beth-dagon, the temple of their idol 12
13:47 cleansed the houses in which the idols were 13
2Mc 12:40 they found sacred tokens of the idols of Jamnia 13
3Mc 4:16 organizing feasts in honor of all his idols 13
151 1: 6 the Philistine, and he cursed me by his idols. 13
idol *See also* food, full, sacrifice, shrine, temple, worship.

abominable idol 1. שִׁקּוּץ
2Ch 15: 8 put away the abominable idols from all the land 1

detestable idol 1. שִׁקּוּץ
Jer 16:18 with the carcasses of their detestable idols 1

false idol 1. הֶבֶל
2Kg 17:15 They went after false idols, and became false 1

worthless idol 1. אֱלִיל
Ps 97: 7 to shame, who make their boast in worthless idols; 1

idolater 1. εἰδωλολάτρης
1Co 5:10 the greedy and robbers, or idolaters 1
11 if he . . is an idolater, reviler, drunkard 1
6: 9 neither the immoral, nor idolaters 1
10: 7 Do not be idolaters as some of them were 1
Eph 5: 5 one who is covetous (that is, an idolater) 1

Rev 21: 8 as for . . sorcerers, idolaters, and all liars 1
22:15 Outside are the . . murderers and idolaters 1

idolatrous *See* priest.

idolatry 1. גִּלּוּל 2. זְנוּת 3. תְּרָפִים 4. *εἰδωλολατρία*

1Sm 15:23 and stubbornness is as iniquity and idolatry. 3
Ezk 23:49 shall bear the penalty for your sinful idolatry; 1
43: 9 Now let them put away their idolatry 2
Gal 5:20 idolatry, sorcery, enmity, strife, jealousy, anger 4
Col 3: 5 covetousness, which is idolatry. 4
1Pe 4: 3 living in . . carousing, and lawless idolatry. 4

idolatry *See also* fall.

if 1. אוֹ 2. אוּלַי 3. אִלּוּ 4. אֲשֶׁר 5. בְּ 6. הֵן 7. הִנֵּה 8. וְ 9. כְּ 10. כַּאֲשֶׁר 11. כִּי 12. לוּ 13. לָכֵן 14. דִּי (A) 15. הֵן (A) 16. *ἄν* 17. *δέ* 18. *ἐάν* 19. *ἐάνπερ* 20. *εἴπερ* 21. *εἶτα* 22. *ἐν* 23. *ἐπί* 24. *καθόσπερ* 25. *καί* 26. *καὶ ἄν* 27. *ὅς* 28. *ὅτι* 29. *ὡς* 30. et 31. si

Gen 4:15 If any one slays Cain, vengeance shall be taken 13
24 If Cain is avenged sevenfold 11
8: 8 to see if the waters had subsided from the face *
30:33 if found with me, shall be counted stolen. *
33:13 if they are overdriven for one day, all the flocks *
34:30 my numbers are few, and if they gather themselves *
37:26 What profit is it if we slay our brother 11
42:38 he only is left. If harm should befall him *
43:14 If I am bereaved of my children, I am bereaved. *
44:22 for if he should leave his father *
29 If you take this one also from me, and harm befalls 8
34 go back to my father if the lad is not with me? 8
Exd 1:10 if war befall us, they join our enemies and fight 11
3:13 Moses said to God, "If I come to the people of Israel 7
8:26 If we sacrifice offerings abominable 6
10:10 he said to them, "The LORD be with you, if ever I let *
12:15 if any one eats what is leavened . . that person 11
19 for if any one eats what is leavened 11
20:25 for if you wield your tool upon it you profane it. 11
21:13 if he did not lie in wait for him, but God let him 4
14 if a man willfully attacks another to kill him 11
31 If it gores a man's son or daughter, he shall be *
36 Or if it is known that the ox has been accustomed *
22: 1 If a man steals an ox or a sheep, and kills it 11
7 If a man delivers to his neighbor money or goods 11
10 If a man delivers to his neighbor an ass or an ox 11
14 If a man borrows anything of his neighbor, and it 11
16 If a man seduces a virgin who is not betrothed 11
27 And if he cries to me, I will hear, for I am 11
23: 4 If you meet your enemy's ox or his ass going astray 11
5 If you see the ass of one who hates you lying under 11
33 for if you serve their gods, it will surely be 11
33: 5 if for a single moment I should go up among you *
Lev 4: 2 Say to the people of Israel, If any one sins 11
23 if the sin which he has committed is made known *
5: 1 If any one sins in that he hears 11
2 Or if any one touches an unclean thing *
3 Or if he touches human uncleanness, of whatever 11
4 Or if any one utters with his lips a rash oath 11
15 If any one commits a breach of faith and sins 11
6: 2 If any one sins and commits a breach of faith 11
2 robbery, or if he has oppressed his neighbor *
7:21 if any one touches an unclean thing 11
10:19 If I had eaten the sin offering today 8
11:33 if any of them falls into any earthen vessel *
37 if any part of their carcass falls upon the seed 11
38 if water is put on the seed 11
39 if any animal of which you may eat dies 11
12: 2 Say to the people of Israel, If a woman conceives 11
13: 3 if the hair in the diseased spot has turned white *
5 if in his eyes the disease is checked *
6 if the diseased spot is dim and the disease has *
8 if the eruption has spread in the skin *
10 if there is a white swelling in the skin *
13 if the leprosy has covered all his body *
16 if the raw flesh turns again and is changed 11
17 the priest shall examine him, and if the disease *
20 if it appears deeper than the skin and its hair *
25 if the hair in the spot has turned white 7
30 if it appears deeper than the skin, and the hair 7
31 if the priest examines the itching disease 11
32 if the itch has not spread 7
34 if the itch has not spread in the skin 7
36 if the itch has spread in the skin 7
39 if the spots on the skin . . are of a dull white 7
40 If a man's hair has fallen from his head, he is bald 11
42 if there is on the bald head or the bald forehead 11
43 if the diseased swelling is reddish-white 7
49 if the disease shows greenish or reddish *
51 If the disease has spread in the garment, in warp 11
55 if the diseased spot has not changed color 7
14: 3 Then, if the leprous disease is healed in the leper 7
37 if the disease is in the walls of the house 7
37 if it appears to be deeper than the surface *
39 if the disease has spread in the walls 7
44 if the disease has spread in the house 7
15: 8 if he who has the discharge spits on one 11
16 if a man has an emission of semen, he shall bathe 11
18 If a man lies with a woman and has an emission 8
25 If a woman has a discharge of blood for many days 11
25 if she has a discharge beyond the time 11
17: 3 If any man of the house of Israel kills an ox *
10 If any man of the house of Israel *
19:20 If a man lies carnally with a woman who is a slave 11
20: 6 If a person turns to mediums and wizards 8
10 If a man commits adultery with the wife 8
12 If a man lies with his daughter-in-law, both of them 8
13 If a man lies with a male as with a woman 8
14 If a man takes a wife and her mother also 8
15 If a man lies with a beast, he shall be put to death 8
16 If a woman approaches any beast and lies with it 8
17 If a man takes his sister, a daughter of his father 8
18 If a man lies with a woman having her sickness 8
20 If a man lies with his uncle's wife 8
21 If a man takes his brother's wife, it is impurity 8
21: 9 if she profanes herself by playing the harlot 11
22: 3 If any one of all your descendants throughout *
11 if a priest buys a slave as his property for money 11
12 If a priest's daughter is married to an outsider 11
13 if a priest's daughter is a widow or divorced 11
14 if a man eats of a holy thing unwittingly 11
25:14 if you sell to your neighbor or buy 11
16 If the years are many you shall increase the price *
16 if the years are few you shall diminish the price *
20 if you say, 'What shall we eat in the seventh year 11
20 If you say, 'What shall we eat in the seventh year 11
25 If your brother becomes poor, and sells part 11
26 If a man has no one to redeem it 11
29 If a man sells a dwelling house in a walled city 11
33 if one of the Levites does not exercise his right 4
35 if your brother becomes poor 11
39 if your brother becomes poor beside you 11
47 If a stranger or sojourner with you becomes rich 11
49 if he grows rich he may redeem himself *
26:25 if you gather within your cities I will send *
37 stumble over one another, as if to escape a sword 9
40 if they confess their iniquity *
41 if then their uncircumcised heart is humbled *
Num 1:51 if any one else comes near, he shall be *
3:10 if any one else comes near, he shall be put to death. *
5:12 If any man's wife goes astray and acts 11
13 if a man lies with her carnally, and it is hidden *
14 or if the spirit of jealousy comes upon him *
14 or if the spirit of jealousy comes upon him *
20 if you have gone astray 11
20 if you have defiled yourself 11
6: 7 if they die, shall he make himself unclean; 5
9 if any man dies very suddenly beside him 11
9:10 If any man of you or of your descendants *
14 if a stranger sojourns among you 11
21 if it continued for a day and a night *
10:32 if you go with us, whatever good the LORD will do 11
12:14 If her father had but spit in her face 8
14:15 Now if thou dost kill this people as one man *
15:14 if a stranger is sojourning with you, or any one 11
22 if you err, and do not observe all these 11
16:29 or if they are visited by the fate of all men *
27: 8 If a man dies, and has no son 11
32:15 For if you turn away from following him *
35:18 Or if he struck him down with a weapon of wood *
30 If any one kills a person, the murderer shall *
36: 3 if they are married to any of the sons *
Deu 4:25 if you act corruptly by making a graven image 8
29 if you search after him with all your heart 11
6:25 if we are careful to do all this commandment 11
7:17 If you say in your heart, 'These nations 11
11:27 blessing, if you obey the commandments 4
12:21 If the place which the LORD your God will choose 11
13: 1 If a prophet arises among you, or a dreamer 11
2 if he says, 'Let us go after other gods,' *
6 If your brother . . entices you secretly, saying 11
12 If you hear in one of your cities, which the LORD 11
14 behold, if it be true and certain that *
18 if you obey the voice of the LORD your God, keeping 11
14:24 if the way is too long for you, so that you 11
15: 7 If there is among you a poor man 11
12 If your brother . . is sold to you, he shall serve 11
16 if he says to you, 'I will not go out from you,' 11
21 if it has any blemish, if it is lame or blind 11
21 if it has any blemish, if it is lame or blind *
17: 2 If there is found among you, within any 11
4 if it is true and certain that such an abominable 7
8 If any case arises requiring decision 11
18: 6 if a Levite comes from any of your towns 11
21 if you say in your heart, 'How may we know the word 11
22 if the word does not come to pass or come true 8
19: 4 If any one kills his neighbor unintentionally *
11 if any man hates his neighbor, and lies in wait 11
16 If a malicious witness rises against any man 11
18 if the witness is a false witness and has accused 7
21: 1 If in the land which the LORD your God gives you 11
15 If a man has two wives, the one loved and the other 11
15 if the first-born son is hers that is disliked *
18 If a man has a stubborn and rebellious son 11
22 if a man has committed a crime punishable 11
22: 2 if he is not near you, or if you do not know him *
6 If you chance to come upon a bird's nest, in any tree 11
8 may not bring the guilt . . if any one fall from it. 11
13 If a man takes a wife, and goes in to her 11
22 If a man is found lying with the wife 11
23 If there is a betrothed virgin, and a man meets her 11
28 If a man meets a virgin who is not betrothed 11
23:10 If there is among you any man who is not clean 11
22 if you refrain from vowing, it . . no sin in you. 11
24: 2 if she goes and becomes another man's wife *
3 the latter husband dies, who took her to be his wife 11
7 If a man is found stealing one of his brethren 11
7 if he treats him as a slave or sells him *
25: 1 If there is a dispute between men, and they come 11
3 if one should go on to beat him with more stripes *
5 If brothers dwell together, and one of them dies 11
8 if he persists, saying, 'I do not wish to take her,' *
28: 2 if you obey the voice of the LORD your God. 11
9 if you keep the commandments of the LORD your God 11
13 if you obey the commandments of the LORD your God 11
14 if you do not turn aside from any of the words *
30:10 if you obey the voice of the LORD your God, to keep 11
10 if you turn to the LORD . . with all your heart 11
16 If you obey the commandments of the LORD your God 18
32:29 If they were wise, they would understand this 12
Jos 2:19 If any one goes . . his blood shall be upon his head *
20: 5 if the avenger . . pursues him, they shall not give 11
22:18 if you rebel against the LORD . . he will be angry *
28 If this should be said to us . . we should say 11
23:16 if you transgress the covenant of the LORD 5
24:20 If you forsake the LORD . . then he will turn and do 11
Jdg 6:13 if the LORD is with us, why then has all this 8
8:19 if you had saved them alive, I would not slay you. 12
9:36 You see the shadow . . as if they were men. 9
11:36 father, if you have opened your mouth to the LORD *
13:23 If the LORD had meant to kill us, he would not have 12
Rut 1:12 If I should say I have hope, even . . have a husband 11
12 even if I should have a husband this night *
17 May the LORD . . if even death parts me from you. 11
1Sm 2:16 if the man said to him, "Let them burn the fat first *
9: 7 But if we go, what can we bring the man? *
12:14 and if both you and the king . . it will be well; *
14:30 How much better if the people had eaten freely 12
41 If this guilt is in me or in Jonathan . . give Urim; 31
41 if this guilt is in thy people . . give Thummim. 31
16: 2 How can I go? If Saul hears it, he will kill me. 8
17:35 if he arose against me, I caught him by his beard *
19: 3 and if I learn anything I will tell you. 8
20:10 Who will tell me if your father answers you 1
12 if he is well disposed . . shall I not then send *
13 the LORD do so . . if I do not disclose it to you *
23: 3 how much more then if we go to Kei'lah 11
24:19 if a man finds his enemy, will he let him go away 11
25:29 If men rise up . . the life of my lord shall be bound 8
2Sm 2:27 if you had not spoken, surely the men would have 11
3: 9 God do so . . if I do not accomplish for David 11
13:26 If not, pray let my brother Amnon go with us. 8
14:10 If any one says anything to you, bring him to me *
16:10 If he is cursing because . . who then shall say 11
23 was as if one consulted the oracle of God; 4
18:12 Even if I felt in my hand the weight of 1,000 12
13 if I had dealt . . then you..would have stood *
19: 6 if Ab'salom were alive . . then you would be 12
7 if you do not go, not a man will stay with you 11
20: 3 they were shut up . . living as if in widowhood. *
1Kg 2:23 God do so . . if this word does not cost Adoni'jah 11
8:31 If a man sins . . and is made to take an oath 4
33 When thy people . . if they turn again to thee 8
35 When . . if they pray toward this place *
37 If there is famine in the land 11
37 if there is pestilence or blight or mildew 11
37 if their enemy besieges them in . . their cities; 11
44 If thy people go out to battle 11
46 If they sin against thee 11
47 if they lay it to heart . . and repent 8
48 if they repent with all their mind 8
16:31 And as if it had been a light thing for him *
19: 2 if I do not make your life as the life of one of them 11
2Kg 4:29 If you meet any one, do not salute him; 11
29 and if any one salutes you, do not reply; 11
5:13 if the prophet had commanded . . some great thing *
17 If not . . let there be given to your servant 8
6:27 If the LORD will not help you, whence shall I help *
7: 2 If the LORD . . should make windows in heaven 7
9 if we are silent . . punishment will overtake us; 8
19 If the LORD himself should . . could such a thing *
10:15 Jehu said, "If it is, give me your hand. 8
18:22 if you say to me, "We rely on the LORD . . " is it not he 11
1Ch 13: 2 good to you, and if it is the will of the LORD our God *
2Ch 6:26 if they pray toward this place, and acknowledge 8
28 If there is famine in the land, if there is 11
28 if there is pestilence or blight or mildew 11
28 if their enemies besiege them in . . cities; 11
34 If thy people go out to battle against their 11
36 If they sin against thee . . and thou art angry 11
37 yet if they lay it to heart in the land *
38 if they repent with all their mind and . . heart 8
7:14 if my people . . humble themselves, and pray 8

30: 9 For if you return to the LORD 5
Ezr 4:13 if this city is rebuilt and the walls finished 6
16 if this city is rebuilt and its walls finished 6
5:17 if it seem good to the king, let search be made 15
6:11 I make a decree that if any one alters this edict 14
10: 8 that if any one did not come within three days *
Neh 1: 8 'If you are unfaithful, I will scatter you among *
9 if you return to me and keep my commandments *
10:31 if the peoples of the land bring in wares *
Est 4:11 if any man or woman goes . . there is but one law; *
16 I will go to the king . . and if I perish, I perish. 10
7: 4 If we had been sold . . I would have held my peace; 3
8: 5 and if the thing seem right before the king *
Job 4: 2 If one ventures a word with you *
21 If their tent-cord is plucked up within them *
7:20 If I sin, what do I do to thee, thou watcher of men? *
10:15 If I am righteous, I cannot lift up my head 8
16 if I lift myself up, thou dost hunt me like a lion *
12:14 If he tears down, none can rebuild; 6
14 if he shuts a man in, none can open. *
15 If he withholds the waters, they dry up; 6
15 if he sends them out, they overwhelm the land. 8
16: 4 I also could speak as you do, if you were in my place; 12
6 if I forbear, how much of it leaves me? *
17:13 Sheol as my house, if I spread my couch in darkness *
14 if I say to the pit, 'You are my father,' *
19:28 If you say, 'How we will pursue him!' 11
21:15 what profit do we get if we pray to him? 11
22: 3 pleasure to the Almighty if you are righteous 11
3 is it gain to him if you make your ways blameless? 11
23 if you remove unrighteousness far *
24 if you lay gold in the dust *
25 if the Almighty is your gold *
31: 7 if any spot has cleaved to my hands; *
20 if he was not warmed with the fleece of my sheep; *
35: 3 How am I better off than if I had sinned? *
6 if your transgressions are multiplied *
39:16 cruelly with her young, as if they were not hers; *
40:23 if the river is turbulent he is not frightened; *
Ps 11: 3 if the foundations are destroyed 11
14: 2 to see if there are any that act wisely *
17: 3 If thou triest my heart, if thou visitest me *
3 if thou visitest me by night, if thou testest me *
3 if thou visitest me by night, if thou testest me *
21:11 If they plan evil against you 11
11 if they devise mischief, they will not succeed. *
28: 1 lest, if thou be silent to me, I become like those *
30: 9 profit is there in my death, if I go down to the Pit? 5
53: 2 to see if there are any that are wise *
62:10 if riches increase, set not your heart on them. 11
139: 8 If I make my bed in Sheol, thou art there! *
9 If I take the wings of the morning and dwell *
11 If I say, "Let only darkness cover me *
18 If I would count them, they are more than the sand. *
Prv 4: 8 she will honor you if you embrace her. 11
6: 2 if you are snared in the utterance of your lips *
30 if he steals to satisfy his appetite 11
31 if he is caught, he will pay sevenfold; *
9:12 if you scoff, you alone will bear it. 8
11:31 If the righteous is requited on earth 6
17:13 If a man returns evil for good *
18:13 If one gives answer before he hears *
20:20 If one curses his father or his mother *
22:18 for it will be pleasant if you keep them within 11
18 pleasant . . if all of them are ready on your lips. *
23:13 if you beat him with a rod, he will not die. 11
14 If you beat him with the rod you will save *
24:10 If you faint in the day of adversity *
12 If you say, "Behold, we did not know this, 11
25:16 If you have found honey, eat only enough for you *
28: 9 If one turns away his ear from hearing the law *
17 If a man is burdened with the blood of another *
29: 9 If a wise man has an argument with a fool, the fool *
12 If a ruler listens to falsehood *
14 If a king judges the poor with equity his throne *
Sng 8: 1 If I met you outside, I would kiss you *
Isa 5:30 if one look to the land, behold, darkness *
10:15 As if a rod should wield him who lifts it *
15 or as if a staff should lift him who is not wood! *
26:10 If favor is shown to the wicked, he does not learn *
33:12 the peoples will be as if burned to lime *
36: 7 if you say to me, "We rely on the LORD our God 11
46: 7 If one cries to it, it does not answer or save him *
54:15 If any one stirs up strife, it is not from me; 6
58: 2 as if they were a nation that did righteousness *
10 if you pour yourself out for the hungry *
13 if you honor it, not going your own ways 8
Jer 2:10 see if there has been such a thing. 6
3: 1 If a man divorces his wife and she goes from him 6
4: 2 if you swear, 'As the LORD lives,' in truth, in justice *
7: 6 if you do not oppress the alien *
6 if you do not go after other gods to your own hurt *
12: 5 If you have raced with men on foot 11
5 And if in a safe land you fall down *
13:22 And if you say in your heart 11
18: 7 If at any time I declare concerning a nation *
8 if that nation, concerning which I have spoken *
9 And if at any time I declare concerning a nation *
10 and if it does evil in my sight *
20: 9 If I say, "I will not mention him *
25:28 if they refuse to accept the cup from your hand 11
27: 8 But if any nation or kingdom will not serve *
38:15 If I tell you, will you not be sure to put me to death? 11
15 if I give you counsel, you will not listen to me. 11
25 If the princes hear that I have spoken with you 11
40: 5 If you remain, then return to Gedali'ah ‡
49:12 If those who did not deserve to drink the cup 4
Ezk 3:18 If I say to the wicked, 'You shall surely die,' 5
19 But if you warn the wicked, and he does not turn 11
20 if a righteous man turns from his righteousness 5
21 if you warn the righteous man not to sin 11
7:16 if any survivors escape *
10:10 likeness, as if a wheel were within a wheel. 10
14: 9 if the prophet be deceived and speak a word *
14 even if these three men, Noah, Daniel, and Job *
15 If I cause wild beasts to pass through the land 12
16 even if these three men were in it *
17 Or if I bring a sword upon that land, and say *
19 Or if I send a pestilence into that land *
20 even if Noah, Daniel, and Job were in it, as I live *
22 Yet, if there should be left in it any survivors *
18: 5 If a man is righteous and does what is lawful 11
6 if he does not eat upon the mountains *
10 If he begets a son who is a robber 8
14 if this man begets a son who sees all the sins 7
21 But if a wicked man turns away from all his sins 11
33: 2 and say to them, If I bring the sword upon a land 11
3 if he sees the sword coming upon the land *
4 then if any one who hears the sound of the trumpet *
5 But if he had taken warning, he would have saved *
6 if the watchman sees the sword coming *
8 If I say to the wicked, O wicked man 5
9 if you warn the wicked to turn from his way 11
13 yet if he trusts in his righteousness *
14 if he turns from his sin and does what is lawful *
15 if the wicked restores the pledge *
46:16 If the prince makes a gift to any of his sons 11
17 if he makes a gift out of his inheritance 11
Dan 2: 5 if you do not make known to me the dream and its 15
6 if you show the dream and its interpretation 15
9 if you do not make the dream known to me 15
3:15 Now if you are ready when you hear the sound 15
15 if you do not worship, you shall immediately 15
17 If it be so, our God whom we serve is able to deliver 15
18 if not, be it known to you, O king 15
5:16 Now if you can read the writing and make known 15
Hos 8: 7 if it were to yield, aliens would devour it. 2
12:11 if in Gilgal they sacrifice bulls *
Ams 5:19 as if a man fled from a lion, and a bear met him; 10
Mic 2:11 If a man should go about and utter wind and lies 12
Hab 1: 5 a work . . that you would not believe if told. 11
3:14 rejoicing as if to devour the poor in secret. *
Hag 2:12 'If one carries holy flesh in the skirt of his 6
Zec 8: 6 If it is marvelous in the sight of the remnant 11
13: 3 if any one again appears as a prophet 11
6 if one asks . . , 'What are these wounds on your back?' *
14:17 if any of the families of the earth do not go up *
Mal 1: 4 If Edom says, "We are shattered but we will rebuild 11
Mat 4: 9 All these I will give you, if you will fall down 18
5:13 the earth; but if salt has lost its taste, how shall 18
23 So if you are offering your gift at the altar 18
39 resist one who is evil. But if any one strikes you *
40 and if any one would sue you and take your coat *
41 if any one forces you to go one mile, go with him two *
46 For if you love those who love you, what reward 18
47 And if you salute only your brethren, what more 18
6:14 For if you forgive men their trespasses 18
15 if you do not forgive men their trespasses 18
22 So, if your eye is sound, your whole body will be 18
23 if your eye is not sound, your whole body will be 18
7: 9 Or what man of you, if his son asks him for bread *
10 Or if he asks for a fish, will give him a serpent? *
8: 2 saying, "Lord, if you will, you can make me clean. 18
9:21 she said to herself, "If I only touch his garment 18
10:13 if the house is worthy, let your peace come upon it; 18
13 if it is not worthy, let your peace return to you. 18
14 if any one will not receive you or listen 16
12:11 said to them, "What man of you, if he has one sheep 27
15: 5 you say, 'If any one tells his father or his mother *
14 if a blind man leads a blind man, both will fall 18
16:26 if he gains the whole world and forfeits his life? 18
17:20 For truly I say to you, if you have faith as a grain 18
18:12 If a man has a 100 sheep 18
13 if he finds it, truly, I say to you, he rejoices 18
15 If your brother sins against you, go and tell him 18
15 If he listens to you, you have gained your brother. 18
16 if he does not listen, take one or two others along 18
17 If he refuses to listen to them 18
17 if he refuses to listen even to the church 18
19 Again I say to you, if two of you agree on earth 18
35 if you do not forgive your brother 18
21: 3 If any one says anything to you, you shall say, 'The 18
21 if you have faith and never doubt 18
21 but even if you say to this mountain 26
22 you will receive, if you have faith. *
24 and if you tell me the answer 18
25 If we say, 'From heaven,' he will say to us 18
26 if we say, 'From men,' we are afraid of the multitude; 18
22:24 If a man dies, having no children 18
23:16 If any one swears by the temple, it is nothing *
16 if any one swears by the gold of the temple *
18 If any one swears by the altar, it is nothing *
18 if any one swears by the gift that is on the altar *
24:23 Then if any one says to you, 'Lo, here is the Christ!' 18
26 So, if they say to you, 'Lo, he is in the wilderness,' 18
26 if they say, 'Lo, he is in the inner rooms' *
48 if that wicked servant says to himself 18
26:15 said, "What will you give me if I deliver him to you? 25
28:14 if this comes to the governor's ears 18
Mrk 1:40 If you will, you can make me clean. 18
3:24 If a kingdom is divided against itself 18
25 if a house is divided against itself 18
4:26 as if a man should scatter seed upon the ground 29
38 Teacher, do you not care if we perish? 28
5:28 If I touch even his garments, I shall be made well. 18
6:11 if any place will not receive you *
7:11 you say, 'If a man tells his father or his mother 18
8: 3 if I send them away hungry to their homes 18
9:43 if your hand causes you to sin, cut it off 18
45 if your foot causes you to sin, cut it off 18
46 if your eye causes you to sin, pluck it out 18
49 if the salt has lost its saltness 18
10:12 if she divorces her husband and marries another 18
11: 3 If any one says to you, 'Why are you doing this?' 18
31 If we say, 'From heaven,' he will say 18
12:19 if a man's brother dies and leaves a wife 18
13:21 then if any one says to you, 'Look, here is the Christ!' 18
14:31 If I must die with you, I will not deny you. 18
16:18 if they drink any deadly thing, it will not hurt 26
Lke 4: 7 If you, then, will worship me, it shall all be yours. 18
5:12 Lord, if you will, you can make me clean. 18
6:33 if you do good to those who do good to you 18
34 if you lend to those from whom you hope to receive 18
9:25 what does it profit a man if he gains the whole world *
10: 6 if a son of peace is there 18
11:11 What father among you, if his son asks for a fish *
12 or if he asks for an egg, will give him a scorpion? *
12:38 If he comes in the second watch, or in the third 26
45 if that servant says to himself 18
13: 9 if it bears fruit next year, well and good 26
14:34 if salt has lost its taste 18
15: 4 if he has lost one of them *
8 having ten silver coins, if she loses one coin 18
16:30 if some one goes to them from the dead 18
31 if some one should rise from the dead.' 18
17: 3 if your brother sins, rebuke him 18
3 if he repents, forgive him; 18
4 if he sins against you seven times in the day 18
19:31 If any one asks you, 'Why are you untying it?' 18
40 He answered, "I tell you, if these were silent 18
20: 5 If we say, 'From heaven,' he will say 18
6 if we say, 'From men,' all the people will stone us 18
28 Moses wrote for us that if a man's brother dies 18
22:67 he said to them, "If I tell you, you will not believe; 18
68 if I ask you, you will not answer. 18
Joh 3:12 how can you believe if I tell you heavenly things? 18
5:31 If I bear witness to myself 18
43 if another comes in his own name 18
6:51 if any one eats of this bread, he will live for ever; 18
62 what if you were to see the Son of man ascending 18
7: 4 if he seeks to be known openly 25
17 if any man's will is to do his will 18
37 If any one thirst, let him come to me and drink. 18
8:31 If you continue in my word 18
36 if the Son makes you free, you will be free indeed. 18
51 if any one keeps my word, he will never see death. 18
52 and you say, 'If any one keeps my word 18
54 If I glorify myself, my glory is nothing 18
55 If I said, I do not know him, I should be a liar 26
9:22 if any one should confess him to be Christ *
31 if any one is a worshiper of God and does his will 18
10: 9 if any one enters by me, he will be saved 18
11: 9 If any one walks in the day, he does not stumble 18
10 if any one walks in the night, he stumbles 18
40 if you would believe you would see the glory of God? 18
48 If we let him go on thus 18
57 if any one knew where he was 18
12:24 if it dies, it bears much fruit. 18
26 If any one serves me, he must follow me 18
26 If any one serves me, the Father will honor him. 18
47 If any one hears my sayings and does not keep them 18
13: 8 If I do not wash you, you have no part in me. 18
17 blessed are you if you do them. 18
35 if you have love for one another. 18
14:14 if you ask anything in my name, I will do it. 18
15 If you love me, you will keep my commandments. 18
23 If a man loves me, he will keep my word 18
15: 6 If a man does not abide in me 18
7 If you abide in me, and my words abide in you 18
10 If you keep my commandments 18
14 You are my friends if you do what I command you. 18
16: 7 if I do not go away, the Counselor will not come 18
7 if I go, I will send him to you. 18
23 if you ask anything of the Father, he will give it 16
19:12 the Jews cried out, "If you release this man 18
20:23 If you forgive the sins of any, they are forgiven; 16
23 if you retain the sins of any, they are retained. 16

21:22 If it is my will that he remain until I come 18
23 If it is my will that he remain until I come 18
Act 5:38 if this plan or this undertaking is of men 18
9: 2 if he found any belonging to the Way, men or women 18
13:41 if one declares it to you.' 18
15:29 If you keep yourselves from these •
18:21 I will return to you if God wills •
20:24 if only I may accomplish my course 29
26: 5 if they are willing to testify 18
Rom 2:19 if you are sure that you are a guide to the blind •
25 Circumcision . . is of value if you obey the law; 18
25 if you break the law, your circumcision becomes 18
26 if a man who is uncircumcised keeps the . . law 18
6:16 if you yield . . to any one as obedient slaves •
7: 2 but if her husband dies she is discharged 18
3 an adulteress if she lives with another man 18
3 But if her husband dies she is free from that law 18
3 and if she marries another man 18
9:32 but as if it were based on works. 29
10: 9 if you confess with your lips that Jesus is Lord 18
11:12 if their failure means riches for the Gentiles •
23 if they do not persist in their unbelief 18
12:20 No, "if your enemy is hungry, feed him; 18
20 if he is thirsty, give him drink; 18
13: 4 But if you do wrong, be afraid 18
14: 8 If we live, we live to the Lord 18
8 and if we die, we die to the Lord; 18
23 But he who has doubts is condemned, if he eats 18
1Co 4: 7 why do you boast as if it were not a gift? •
19 I will come to you soon, if the Lord wills 18
5: 3 as if present 29
11 if he is guilty of immorality or greed 18
6: 4 If then you have such cases 18
7:11 if she does, let her remain single 18
28 if you marry, you do not sin 18
28 if a girl marries she does not sin 18
36 if his passions are strong, and it has to be 18
39 If the husband dies 18
40 she is happier if she remains as she is 18
8: 8 We are no worse off if we do not eat 18
8 and no better off if we do. 18
10 For if any one sees you, a man of knowledge, at table 18
10 if his conscience is weak •
9:16 For if I preach the gospel 18
16 Woe to me if I do not preach the gospel! 18
10:28 if some one says to you 18
11: 5 it is the same as if her head were shaven. •
15 if a woman has long hair, it is her pride 18
12:15 If the foot should say, "Because I am not a hand 18
16 if the ear should say, "Because I am not an eye 18
13: 1 If I speak in the tongues of men and of angels 18
2 And if I have prophetic powers 18
2 if I have all faith, so as to remove mountains 18
3 If I give away all I have 26
3 if I deliver my body to be burned, but have not love 18
14: 6 Now, brethren, if I come to you speaking in tongues 18
7 If even lifeless instruments 18
8 if the bugle gives an indistinct sound 18
9 if you in a tongue utter speech 18
11 if I do not know the meaning of the language 18
14 For if I pray in a tongue, my spirit prays 18
16 Otherwise, if you bless with the spirit 18
23 If, therefore, the whole church assembles 18
24 if all prophesy 18
28 if there is no one to interpret 18
30 If a revelation is made to another sitting 18
16: 4 If it seems advisable that I should go also 18
7 some time with you, if the Lord permits. 18
2Co 5: 1 For we know that if the earthly tent we live 18
9: 4 lest if some Macedo'nians come with me and find 18
10: 8 even if I boast a little too much of our authority 18
11: 4 if you receive a different spirit •
4 if you accept a different gospel •
12: 6 Though if I wish to boast, I shall not be a fool 18
13: 2 if I come again I will not spare them– 18
Gal 1: 8 even if we, or an angel from heaven, should preach 18
5: 2 if you receive circumcision 18
6: 1 Brethren, if a man is overtaken in any trespass 18
9 if we do not lose heart. •
Col 2:20 you live as if you still belonged to the world 29
3:13 if one has a complaint against another 18
4:10 if he comes to you, receive him) 18
1Th 3: 8 for now we live, if you stand fast in the Lord. 18
1Ti 1: 8 if any one uses it lawfully 18
2:15 if she continues in faith and love and holiness 18
3:10 then if they prove themselves blameless •
15 if I am delayed 18
4: 4 if it is received with thanksgiving; •
6 If you put these . . before the brethren •
5: 9 if she is not less than 60 years of age •
6: 8 if we have food and clothing •
2Ti 2:21 If any one purifies himself from what is ignoble 18
Heb 2: 3 if we neglect such a great salvation •
3: 6 we are his house if we hold fast our confidence 18
6: 3 this we will do if God permits. 19
6 if they then commit apostasy •
8 if it bears thorns and thistles •
10: 2 If the worshipers had once been cleansed •
26 For if we sin deliberately •
38 if he shrinks back, my soul has no pleasure in him. 18
11:29 the people crossed the Red Sea as if on dry land 29
12:25 if we reject him who warns from heaven. •
13:23 with whom I shall see you if he comes soon. 18
Jas 2: 2 For if a man with gold rings and in fine clothing 18
14 if a man says he has faith but has not works? 18
15 If a brother or sister is ill-clad 18
17 So faith by itself, if it has no works, is dead. 18
4:15 If the Lord wills, we shall live 18
5:15 and if he has committed sins, he will be forgiven. 26
19 if any one among you wanders from the truth 18
1Pe 3: 6 you are now her children if you do right •
13 if you are zealous for what is right? 18
2Pe 1: 8 For if these things are yours and abound •
10 for if you do this you will never fall; •
2: 5 if he did not spare the ancient world 25
6 if by turning the cities . . to ashes 25
7 if he rescued the righteous Lot 25
1Jn 1: 6 If we say we have fellowship with him 18
7 if we walk in the light, as he is in the light 18
8 If we say we have no sin, we deceive ourselves 18
9 If we confess our sins, he is faithful and just 18
10 If we say we have not sinned, we make him a liar 18
2: 1 if any one does sin, we have an advocate 18
3 we know him, if we keep his commandments. 18
15 If any one loves the world 18
24 If what you heard from the beginning abides 18
29 If you know that he is righteous, you may be sure 18
3:17 if any one has the world's goods 16
21 Beloved, if our hearts do not condemn us 18
4:12 if we love one another, God abides in us 18
20 If any one says, "I love God," and hates his brother 18
5:14 if we ask anything according to his will he hears 18
15 if we know that he hears us in whatever we ask 18
16 If any one sees his brother committing . . sin 18
3Jn 1:10 So if I come, I will bring up what he is doing 18
Rev 3: 3 If you will not awake, I will come like a thief 18
20 if any one hears my voice and opens the door 18
22:18 if any one adds to them, God will add to him 18
19 if any one takes away from the words of the book 18
1Es 2:19 Now if this city is built and the walls finished 18
21 if it seems good to you 16
24 if this city is built and its walls finished 18
4: 4 If he tells them to make war on one another 18
4 if he sends them out against the enemy, they go 18
5 if they win the victory 18
7 If he tells them to kill, they kill 18
7 if he tells them to release, they release •
8 if he tells them to attack, they attack •
8 if he tells them to lay waste, they lay waste •
8 if he tells them to build, they build •
9 if he tells them to cut down, they cut down •
9 if he tells them to plant, they plant. •
18 If men gather gold and silver 18
31 If she smiles at him, he laughs 18
31 if she loses her temper with him, he flatters her 18
6:22 if it is found that . . 18
22 if it is approved by our lord the king •
32 if any should transgress . . 18
9: 4 if any did not meet there within two or three days 16
2Es 4: 4 If you can solve one of them for me 31
7 said to me, "If I had asked you, 'How many dwellings 31
18 If now you were a judge between them 31
26 If you are alive, you will see, and if you live long 31
26 and if you live long, you will often marvel 31
29 If therefore that which has been sown 31
29 if the place where the evil has been sown •
40 if . . her womb can keep the child within her 31
44 If I have found favor in your sight 31
44 and if it is possible, and if I am worthy 31
44 and if it is possible, and if I am worthy 31
5: 4 if the Most High grants that you live 31
13 and if you pray again, and weep as you do now 31
30 If thou dost really hate thy people 31
45 If therefore all creatures will live at one time •
46 If you bear ten children, why one after another?' 31
56 if I have found favor in thy sight 31
6:11 if I have found favor in thy sight 31
14 if the place where you are standing is . . shaken 31
31 If therefore you will pray again 31
59 If the world has indeed been created for us 31
7: 5 If any one, then, wishes to reach the sea 31
9 If now that city is given to a man 31
52 If you have just a few precious stones 31
62 if the mind is made out of the dust 31
63 better if the dust itself had not been born 30
69 if we were not to come into judgment after death 31
75 If I have found favor in thy sight, O Lord 31
79 if it is one of those who have shown scorn 31
102 If I have found favor in thy sight 31
111 If therefore the earth had not produced Adam, or else 31
116 better if the earth had not produced Adam, or else •
119 if an eternal age has been promised to us 31
128 that if he is defeated he shall suffer 31
128 if he is victorious he shall receive 31
137 for if he did not make them abound 31
138 if he did not give out of his goodness 31
139 if he did not pardon those who were created 31
8:14 If then thou wilt suddenly and quickly destroy 31
32 For if thou hast desired to have pity on us 31
42 If I have found favor before thee, let me speak. 31
43 For if the farmer's seed does not come up 31
43 or if it has been ruined by too much rain 31
9:23 if you will let seven days more pass 31
10:12 if you say to me, 'My lamentation 31
16 if you acknowledge the decree of God to be just 31
12: 7 if I have found favor in thy sight 31
7 if I have been accounted righteous before thee 31
7 if my prayer has indeed come up before thy face 31
44 Therefore if you forsake us, how much better 31
44 if we also had been consumed in the burning 31
14:22 If then I have found favor before thee 31
34 If you, then, will rule over your minds 31
15:31 if they combine in great power and turn to pursue 31
Tob 3:10 if I do this, it will be a disgrace to him 18
4: 6 For if you do what is true •
8 If you have many possessions 29
8 if few, do not be afraid to give 18
14 if you serve God you will receive payment 18
21 You have great wealth if you fear God 18
5:15 if you both return safe and sound 18
6: 7 if a demon or evil spirit gives trouble to any one 18
14 I am afraid that if I go in I will die †
9: 4 if I delay long he will be greatly distressed. 18
13: 6 If you turn to him with all your heart 18
Jdt 2:11 if they refuse, your eye shall not spare 23
7:31 if these days pass by, and no help comes for us 18
8:15 if he does not choose to help us 18
17 he will hear our voice, if it pleases him. 18
21 For if we are captured all Judea will be captured 22
10:19 if we let them go •
11: 6 if you follow out the words of your maidservant 18
23 if you do as you have said, your God shall be my God 18
12: 3 If your supply runs out, where can we get more 18
12 if we do not embrace her she will laugh at us. 18
14: 2 as if you were going down to the plain 29
5 sent him to us as if to his death. 29
AEs 13: 9 if it is thy will to save Israel. 22
15: 5 she looked happy, as if beloved 29
Wis 3:17 Even if they live long 18
18 If they die young, they will have no hope 18
11:24 if thou hadst hated it. •
15: 2 For even if we sin we are thine, knowing thy power; 18
Sir 1:26 If you desire wisdom, keep the commandments •
4: 6 if . . he calls down a curse upon you •
16 If he has faith in her he will obtain her 18
19 If he goes astray she will forsake him 18
6:12 if you are brought low he will turn against you 18
32 If you are willing, my son, you will be taught 18
32 if you apply yourself you will become clever. 18
33 If you love to listen you will gain knowledge 18
33 if you incline your ear you will become wise. 18
36 If you see an intelligent man, visit him early 18
7:26 If you have a wife who pleases you •
8:12 if you do lend anything, be as one who has lost it. 18
13 if you give surety 18
9:13 if you approach him, make no misstep 26
11:10 if you multiply activities 18
10 if you pursue you will not overtake 18
12: 1 If you do a kindness, know to whom you do it 18
11 Even if he humbles himself 18
15 if you falter, he will not stand by you. 18
16 if he finds an opportunity 18
17 If calamity befalls you, you will find him there 18
13: 4 A rich man will exploit you if you can be of use 18
4 if you are in need he will forsake you. 18
5 If you own something, he will live with you 18
22 If a rich man slips, his helpers are many •
22 If a humble man slips, they even reproach him •
24 Riches are good if they are free from sin •
14: 5 If a man is mean to himself •
15:15 If you will, you can keep the commandments 18
16: 2 If they multiply , do not rejoice in them 18
18: 9 is great if he reaches 100 years. •
31 If you allow your soul to take pleasure 18
19:28 if . . he is prevented from sinning 18
21: 2 for if you approach sin, it will bite you 18
22:22 If you have opened your mouth 18
23:11 if he offends, his sin remains on him 18
11 if he disregards it, he sins doubly 18
26:11 do not wonder if she sins against you. 18
27: 3 If a man is not steadfast and zealous 18
8 If you pursue justice, you will attain it 18
17 if you betray his secrets, do not run after him. 18
27 If a man does evil, it will roll back upon him •
28: 5 If he himself, being flesh, maintains wrath •
12 If you blow on a spark, it will glow 18
12 if you spit on it, it will be put out 18
29: 6 If the lender exert pressure 18
31:27 if you drink it in moderation 18
32: 1 If they make you master of the feast •
33:28 if he does not obey, make his fetters heavy. 26
31 If you ill-treat him, and he leaves and runs away 18
34:18 If one sacrifices •
25 If a man washes after touching a dead body •
26 if a man fasts for his sins •
37:12 who will sorrow with you if you fail. 18
39: 6 If the great Lord is willing 18

11 if he lives long 18
11 if he goes to rest, it is enough for him. 18
42: 9 if married, lest she be hated; *
50:29 For if he does them, he will be strong 18
Bar 2:22 But if you will not obey the voice of the Lord 18
29 If you will not obey my voice, this very great 18
LJr 1:27 If any one sets one of them upright 18
27 if it is tipped over, it cannot straighten itself; 18
35 if one makes a vow to them and does not keep it 18
Sus 1:22 For if I do this thing, it is death for me; 18
22 and if I do not, I shall not escape your hands. 18
54 Now then, if you really saw her, tell me this 20
Bel 1: 8 If you do not tell me who is eating these 18
9 if you prove that Bel is eating them 18
12 if you do not find that Bel has eaten it all 18
26 if you, O king, will give me permission *
1Mc 2:40 If we all do as our brethren have done 18
3:53 if thou dost not help us? 18
5:40 If he crosses over to us first 18
41 if he shows fear 18
7:35 then if I return safely I will burn up this house. 18
8:24 If war comes first to Rome 18
27 if war comes first to the nation of the Jews 18
30 If . . both parties shall determine to add 18
32 If now they appeal again for help against you 18
11:42 if I find an opportunity. 18
2Mc 2:15 if you have need of them 18
4: 9 if permission were given 18
46 taking the king aside . . as if for refreshment 29
7:24 if he would turn from the ways of his fathers *
9:24 if anything unexpected happened 18
10: 4 if they should ever sin 18
11:19 If you will maintain your good will 18
12:45 if he was looking to the splendid reward 21
14:33 If you do not hand Judas over to me as a prisoner 18
3Mc 1: 4 two minas of gold if they won the battle. *
2:10 if we should have reverses 18
30 if any of them prefer 18
3:24 if a sudden disorder should later arise *
7: 9 if we devise any evil against them 18
4Mc 1:24 a man will see if he reflects on this experience 18
2: 9 If one is greedy 26
4:12 if he were delivered *
5:30 not even if you gouge out my eyes *
6:21 if we should be despised by the tyrant as unmanly *
8: 4 grouped about their mother as if in a chorus 24
7 if you will renounce the ancestral tradition *
9 if by disobedience you rouse my anger 18
11 if you disobey, nothing remains for you but to die *
21 if we disobey we are dead! *
26 when we can live in peace if we obey the king? *
12: 5 if you yield to persuasion you will be my friend *
13:17 if we so die *
16:17 if . . you young men were to be terrified 17

if אִם

Gen 4:7^{2}; 13:9^{2}, 16; 15:5; 18:3, 21, 26, 28, 30; 20:7; 23:8, 13; 24:8, 41, 42, 49^{2}; 25:22; 27:46; 28:20; 30:27, 31; 31:8^{2}, 50^{2}; 32:8; 33:10; 34:17; 42:19, 37; 43:4, 5, 9, 11; 44:26, 32; 47:6, 16, 29; 50:4, Exd 1:16^{2}; 4:8, 9; 8:2, 21; 9:2; 10:4; 12:4; 13:13; 15:26; 18:23; 19:5; 20:25; 21:3^{2}, 4, 5, 8, 9, 10, 11, 19, 21, 23, 27, 29, 30, 32; 22:1, 2, 3, 4, 7, 8, 12, 13, 15^{2}, 17, 23, 25, 26; 23:22; 29:34; 32:32^{2}; 33:13, 15; 34:9, 20; 40:37, Lev 1:3, 10, 14; 2:5, 7, 14; 3:1^{2}, 6, 7, 12; 4:3, 13, 27, 32; 5:7, 11, 17; 6:28; 7:12, 16, 18; 12:5, 8; 13:4, 7, 12, 21, 22, 23, 26, 27, 28, 35, 37, 41, 53, 56, 57; 14:21, 43, 48; 15:24, 28; 17:16; 19:7; 20:4; 25:28, 30, 51, 52, 54; 26:3, 14, 15^{2}, 18, 21, 23, 27; 27:4, 5, 6, 7, 8, 9, 10, 11, 13, 15, 16, 17, 18, 19, 20^{2}, 22, 27^{2}, 31, 33, Num 5:8, 19^{2}, 27, 28; 10:4; 11:15^{2}; 12:6; 14:8; 15:24, 27; 16:29, 30; 19:12; 20:19; 21:2, 9; 22:20, 34; 24:13; 27:9, 10, 11; 30:5, 6, 8, 10, 12, 14, 15; 32:5, 20^{2}, 23, 29, 30; 33:55; 35:16, 17, 20, 22, 26, Deu 5:25; 8:19; 11:13, 22, 28; 15:5; 19:8; 20:11, 12; 21:14; 22:2, 20, 25; 24:1, 12; 25:2, 7; 28:1, 15, 58; 30:4, 17; 32:41, Jos 2:14, 19, 20; 17:15; 22:19, 22, 23; 23:12; 24:15, Jdg 4:8^{2}, 20; 6:17, 31, 36, 37; 7:10; 9:15^{2}, 16^{2}, 19, 20; 11:9, 30; 13:16^{2}; 14:12, 13; 15:7; 16:7, 11, 13, 17; 21:21, Rut 3:13^{2}; 4:4, 1Sm 1:11; 2:16, 25^{2}; 3:9, 17; 6:3, 9^{2}; 7:3; 11:3; 12:14, 15, 25; 14:9, 10; 17:9^{2}; 19:11; 20:6, 7^{2}, 8, 9, 14, 21, 22, 29; 21:4, 9; 23:23; 25:22; 26:19^{2}; 27:5, 2Sm 3:35; 10:11^{2}; 11:20^{2}; 12:8; 14:32; 15:8, 25, 26, 33, 34; 17:6, 13; 18:3^{2}, 25; 19:13, 1Kg 1:52^{2}; 2:4; 3:14; 6:12; 8:25; 9:4, 6; 11:38; 12:7, 27; 13:8; 18:21^{2}; 20:10, 18^{2}, 39; 21:2, 6; 22:28, 2Kg 1:10, 12; 2:10^{2}; 6:31; 7:4^{4}; 9:15; 10:6^{2}; 18:23; 20:19; 21:8, 1Ch 12:17^{2}; 13:2; 19:12^{2}; 22:13; 28:7, 9, 2Ch 6:16, 22, 24; 7:17, 19; 10:7; 15:2^{2}; 18:27; 20:9; 25:8; 30:9; 33:8, Neh 2:5^{2}, 7; 4:3; 13:21, Est 1:19; 3:9; 4:14; 5:4, 8^{2}; 6:13; 7:3^{2}; 8:5^{2}; 9:13, Job 8:4, 5, 6, 18; 9:3, 16, 19^{2}, 24, 27, 30; 10:14, 15; 11:10, 13, 14; 13:10; 14:7, 14; 16:6; 17:13; 19:5; 22:23; 24:25; 27:14; 31:5, 7, 9, 13, 16, 19, 20, 21, 24, 25, 26, 29, 31, 33, 38, 39; 33:5, 23, 32, 33; 34:14, 16, 32; 35:6, 7; 36:8, 11, 12; 38:4, 18, Ps 7:3^{2}, 4, 12; 4:20; 0:12, 18; 9:15; 6:18; 3:15; 1:8; 9:30, 31; 30:3; 32:12; 37:5, 6^{2}; 39:8, 24, Prv 1:10, 11; 2:1, 3, 4; 3:24; 4:12; 6:1; 9:12; 19:19; 22:27; 23:2, 15; 24:14; 25:21^{2}; 30:32, Ecc 4:10, 11; 5:8; 6:3; 10:4, 10, 11; 11:3^{2}, 8, Sng 1:8; 5:8; 8:7, 9, Isa 1:19, 20; 7:9; 21:12; 36:8; 58:9, 13, Jer 2:28; 4:1^{2}; 5:1; 7:5^{2}; 8:4; 12:16, 17; 13:17; 14:18^{2}; 15:11^{2}, 19^{2}; 17:24, 27; 22:4, 5; 23:22, 38; 26:4, 15; 27:18^{2}; 31:36, 37; 33:20, 25; 37:10; 38:17, 18, 21; 40:4^{2}; 42:5, 10, 13, 15; 49:9, Lam 1:12, Ezk 3:6; 20:39; 21:13; 43:11, Hos 9:12; 12:11, Jol 3:4, Ams 3:4; 6:9, Obd 1:5, Nah 3:12, Hab 2:3, Hag 2:13, Zec 3:7; 6:15; 11:12^{2}; 14:18, Mal 1:6^{2}; 2:2^{2}; 3:10

if εἰ

Gen 37:14, Exd 4:23, Num 22:33, Mat 4:3, 6; 5:29, 30; 6:23, 30; 7:11; 8:31; 9:17; 10:25; 11:14, 21, 23; 12:7, 26, 27, 28; 14:28; 16:24; 17:4; 18:8, 9; 19:10, 17, 21; 22:45; 23:30; 24:22, 24, 43; 26:24, 39, 42, 63; 27:40, 43, Mrk 2:21, 22; 3:26; 4:23; 8:34; 9:22, 23, 35, 42; 11:13, 25; 13:20, 22; 14:21, 35; 15:44, Lke 4:3, 9; 5:36, 37; 6:32; 7:39; 9:23; 10:6, 13; 11:13, 18, 19, 20, 36; 12:26, 28, 39; 13:9; 14:26, 32; 16:11, 12, 31; 17:2, 6; 19:8; 22:42, 67; 23:31, 35, 37, Joh 1:25; 3:12; 4:10; 5:46, 47; 7:4, 23; 8:19, 39, 42, 46; 9:33, 41; 10:24, 35, 37, 38; 11:12, 21, 32; 13:14, 17, 32; 14:2, 7, 28; 15:18, 19, 20^{2}, 22, 24; 18:8, 23^{2}, 30, 36; 20:15, Act 4:9; 5:39; 8:22; 11:17; 13:15; 16:15; 17:11; 18:14; 19:38, 39; 20:16; 23:9; 24:19; 25:5, 11^{2}; 26:32; 27:39, Rom 2:17; 3:3, 5, 7; 4:2, 14; 5:10, 15, 17; 6:5, 8; 7:7^{2}, 16, 20; 8:10, 11, 13^{2}, 17, 25, 31; 9:22, 29; 11:6, 12, 15, 16^{2}, 17, 18, 21, 24; 12:6, 7, 18; 14:15; 15:27, 1Co 2:8; 3:12, 14, 15, 17, 18; 4:7; 6:2; 7:9, 12, 13, 15, 21, 36; 8:2, 3, 13; 9:2, 11^{2}, 12, 17^{2}; 10:27, 30; 11:6^{2}, 16, 31, 34; 12:17^{2}, 19, 26^{2}; 14:27, 35, 37, 38; 15:2, 12, 13, 14, 15, 16, 17, 19, 29, 32^{2}, 44; 16:22, 2Co 1:6^{2}; 2:2, 5, 10; 3:7, 9, 11; 4:3; 5:13^{2}, 17; 7:8, 14; 8:12; 10:7; 11:4, 6, 15, 16, 20, 30; 12:15, Gal 1:9, 10; 2:14, 17, 18, 21; 3:4, 18, 21, 29; 4:7, 15; 5:11, 15, 18, 25; 6:3, Php 1:22; 2:1, 17; 3:4, 11, 15; 4:8, Col 2:20; 3:1, 2Th 3:10, 14, 1Ti 3:1, 5; 5:4, 8, 16; 6:3, 2Ti 2:11, 12^{2}, 13, Tit 1:6, Phm 1:17, 18, Heb 2:2; 4:8; 7:11; 8:4, 7; 9:13; 11:15; 12:8, 25, Jas 1:5, 23, 26; 2:8, 9, 11; 3:2, 3, 14; 4:11, 1Pe 1:17; 2:19, 20^{2}; 3:14, 17; 4:14, 16, 17, 18, 2Pe 2:4, 20, 1Jn 2:19; 4:11; 5:9, 2Jn 1:10, Rev 2:5, 16; 11:5^{2}; 13:9, 10^{2}; 14:9; 20:15, 1Es 2:5; 6:21, Tob 1:17, 18; 3:9, 15; 8:12; 13:6, Jdt 5:20, 21; 11:2; 12:12, Wis 2:17, 18; 6:21; 8:5, 6, 7, 8; 11:25; 12:20; 13:3, 4, 9; 17:9, Sir 2:1; 5:12^{2}; 7:22; 12:2; 16:11; 19:13, 14; 22:26; 23:11; 25:26; 29:6, 26; 31:18, 21; 32:7; 33:30, 31; 36:23, Bar 3:13, Sus 1:21, 1Mc 1:57; 2:19; 9:10; 10:71; 13:40; 15:21, 2Mc 3:38; 4:47; 5:18; 6:26; 7:33; 8:15; 9:20; 11:28; 12:44; 13:10; 15:3, 38, 3Mc 1:12; 6:10, 4Mc 1:3, 5; 2:20, 24; 4:17, 23; 5:3, 10, 13, 18, 19; 6:18, 20, 32; 7:16; 8:2, 16, 17; 9:6, 7, 27; 11:16; 12:4; 13:2; 14:17; 16:1, 5; 17:7

if at all 1. ἐάνπερ

2Mc 3:38 if he escapes at all 1

if even 1. καὶ ἄν

Heb 12:20 If even a beast touches the mountain 1

if in fact 1. εἰ

Rom 8: 9 if in fact the Spirit of God dwells in you. 1

if not 1. לוּלֵא 2. nisi

Gen 31:42 If the God of my father . . had not been on my side 1
43:10 for if we had not delayed, we would now have 1
Jdg 14:18 If you had not plowed with my heifer, you would not 1
Ps 94:17 If the LORD had not been my help, my soul would 1
119:92 If thy law had not been my delight 1
124: 1 If it had not been the LORD who was on our side 1
2 if it had not been the LORD who was on our side 1
Isa 1: 9 If the LORD . . had not left us a few survivors 1
2Es 15:53 If you had not always killed my chosen people 2

if only 1. ἐάνπερ

Heb 3:14 if only we hold our first confidence firm 1

if really 1. εἴπερ

Jdt 6: 9 If you really hope in your heart 1
Sus 1:54 Now then, if you really saw her, tell me this 1

ignoble 1. ἀκλεής 2. ἀτιμία

2Ti 2:20 some for noble use, some for ignoble. 2
21 If any one purifies himself from what is ignoble *
3Mc 4:12 to lament bitterly the ignoble misfortune 1

ignominiously 1. ἀκλεῶς

3Mc 6:34 was ignominiously quenched. 1

ignorance 1. פְּתִי 2. ἀγνόημα 3. ἄγνοια 4. ἀγνωσία 5. ἀπαιδευσία

Ezk 45:20 one who has sinned through error or ignorance; 1
Act 3:17 now, brethren, I know that you acted in ignorance 3
17:30 The times of ignorance God overlooked 3
Eph 4:18 because of the ignorance that is in them 3
1Pe 1:14 the passions of your former ignorance 3
2:15 put to silence the ignorance of foolish men. 4
Wis 14:22 they live in great strife due to ignorance 3
17:13 prefers ignorance of what causes the torment. 3
Sir 4:25 be mindful of your ignorance. 5
28: 7 overlook ignorance. 3
51:19 lamented my ignorance of her. 2
4Mc 1: 5 is it not sovereign over forgetfulness and ignorance? 3
2:24 does not control forgetfulness and ignorance 3

do in ignorance 1. ἀγνοέω

2Mc 11:31 what he may have done in ignorance. 1

ignorant 1. לֹא יָדַע 2. ἀγνοέω 3. ἀγνωσία 4. ἀμαθής 5. ἀπαίδευτος 6. ἀσύνετος

Ps 73:22 I was stupid and ignorant, I was like a beast 1
Rom 10: 3 For, being ignorant of the righteousness 2
2Co 1: 8 For we do not want you to be ignorant, brethren 2
2:11 for we are not ignorant of his designs. 2
1Th 4:13 we would not have you ignorant, brethren 2
Heb 5: 2 He can deal gently with the ignorant and wayward 2
2Pe 2:12 reviling in matters of which they are ignorant 2
3:16 which the ignorant and unstable twist 4
Wis 13: 1 all men who were ignorant of God 3
Sir 20:19 continually on the lips of the ignorant. 5
24 it is continually on the lips of the ignorant. 5
21:18 the knowledge of the ignorant 6
4Mc 13:19 not ignorant of the affection of brotherhood 2

ignorantly 1. ἀγνοέω

1Ti 1:13 because I had acted ignorantly in unbelief 1

ignore 1. כסה 2. לֹא ידע 3. פרע 4. λανθάνω 5. παρακούω 6. ὑπεροράω 7. non cognosco

Deu 33: 9 he disowned . . and ignored his children. 2
Prv 1:25 you have ignored all my counsel 3
12:16 but the prudent man ignores an insult. 1
13:18 Poverty . . come to him who ignores instruction 3
15:32 He who ignores instruction despises himself 3
Mrk 5:36 But ignoring what they said 5
2Pe 3: 5 They deliberately ignore this fact 4
8 do not ignore this one fact, beloved 4
2Es 7:23 and they ignored his ways! 7
Sir 30:11 do not ignore his errors. *
35:14 not ignore the supplication of the fatherless 6

ill 1. אָוֶן 2. חלה 3. רַע 4. ἀρρωστία 5. ἄρρωστος 6. ἀσθενέω 7. πονηρός 8. συνέχω

Gen 37: 2 and Joseph brought an ill report of them to their 3
48: 1 Joseph was told, "Behold, your father is ill"; 2
1Sm 25: 3 but the man was churlish and ill-behaved; 3
Prv 12:21 No ill befalls the righteous 1
Isa 3:11 Woe to the wicked! It shall be ill with him 3
Lke 4:38 Now Simon's mother-in-law was ill with a high fever 8
Joh 4:46 there was an official whose son was ill. 6
11: 1 Now a certain man was ill, Laz'arus of Bethany 6
2 It was Mary . . whose brother Laz'arus was ill. 6
3 Lord, he whom you love is ill. 6
6 when he heard that he was ill 6
1Co 11:30 many of you are weak and ill, and some have died 5
Php 2:26 distressed because you heard that he was ill. 6
27 Indeed he was ill, near to death 6
2Ti 4:20 Troph'imus I left ill at Mile'tus. 6
2Es 7:104 to be ill or sleep or eat or be healed in his stead ‡
Jdt 8: 8 No one spoke ill of her 7
Sir 18:19 before you fall ill, take care of your health. 4

ill *See also* deal, fall, go, make, pretend, repute, treat.

become ill 1. חלה

1Kg 17:17 After this the son of the woman . . became ill; 1

do ill 1. רשע 2. κακοποίησις

Zep 1:12 The LORD will not do good, nor will he do ill.' 1
3Mc 3: 2 by men who conspired to do them ill 2

ill will 1. δυσμένεια

2Mc 6:29 those . . now changed to ill will 1
12: 3 as though there were no ill will to the Jews; 1

ill-bred person 1. ἀπαίδευτος

Sir 8: 4 Do not jest with an ill-bred person 1

ill-clad 1. γυμνιτεύω 2. γυμνός

1Co 4:11 we are ill-clad and buffeted and homeless 1
Jas 2:15 If a brother or sister is ill-clad 2

ill-disposed 1. δυσνοέω

AEs 13: 5 this people . . is ill-disposed to our government 1
3Mc 3:24 they are ill-disposed toward us in every way 1

ill-mannered 1. ἀπαιδευσία

Sir 21:24 It is ill-mannered for a man to listen at a door 1

ill-natured 1. בְּלִיַּעַל 2. בֶּן בְּלִיַּעַל

1Sm 25:17 he is so ill-natured that one cannot speak to him. 2
25 Let not my lord regard this ill-natured fellow 1

ill-treat 1. ענה 2. κακουχέω 3. κακόω

Gen 31:50 If you ill-treat my daughters 1
Act 7: 6 who would enslave them and ill-treat them 3
Heb 11:37 destitute, afflicted, ill-treated– 2
13: 3 Remember . . those who are ill-treated 2
Sir 33:31 If you ill-treat him, and he leaves and runs away 3

ill-treatment 1. κάκωσις 2. συγκακουχέομαι

Act 7:34 I have surely seen the ill-treatment of my people 1
Heb 11:25 share ill-treatment with the people of God 2

ill-will 1. δυσμένεια

3Mc 3:19 By maintaining their manifest ill-will toward us 1
7: 4 the ill-will which these people had 1

illegitimate 1. νόθος

Wis 4: 3 none of their illegitimate seedlings 1

illegitimate *See also* child.

illness 1. חֳלִי 2. ἀρρώστημα 3. ἀσθένεια 4. infirmitas

1Kg 17:17 his illness was so severe that there was no 1
2Kg 13:14 Now when Eli'sha had fallen sick with the illness 1
Ps 41: 3 in his illness thou healest all his 1
Joh 11: 4 This illness is not unto death 3
2Es 8:53 illness is banished from you, and death is hidden; 4
Sir 10:10 A long illness baffles the physician 2
31: 2 a severe illness carries off sleep. 2
2Mc 9:21 I suffered an annoying illness 3
22 I have good hope of recovering from my illness 3

illumine 1. καταλάμπω 2. καταυγάζω

Wis 17: 5 avail to illumine that hateful night. 2
20 was illumined with brilliant light 1

illusion 1. מַהֲתַלָּה
Isa 30:10 speak to us smooth things, prophesy illusions 1

illustrious 1. *θαυμαστός*
1Es 4:29 the daughter of the illustrious Bartacus 1

illustrious man 1. *ἔνδοξος*
Sir 11: 6 illustrious men have been handed over to others. 1

image 1. אֱלִיל 2. מִפְלֶצֶת 3. נֶסֶךְ 4. סֶמֶל 5. עָצָב 6. פָּסִיל 7. פֶּסֶל 8. צֶלֶם 9. תַּבְנִית 10. תְּרָפִים 11. צְלֵם (A) 12. *εἰκών* 13. *ὁμοίωμα* 14. imago
Gen 1:26 Let us make man in our image, after our likeness 8
27 God created man in his own image 8
27 in the image of God he created him; male and female 8
5: 3 son in his own likeness, after his image 8
9: 6 for God made man in his own image. 8
Num33:52 destroy all their molten images 8
1Sm 6: 5 make images of your tumors and . . of your mice 8
5 make . . and images of your mice that ravage 8
11 box with . . mice and the images of their tumors. 8
19:13 Michal took an image and laid it on the bed 10
16 the image was in the bed, with the pillow 10
1Kg 15:13 Asa cut down her image and burned it at . . Kidron. 2
2Kg 11:18 his altars and his images they broke in pieces 8
2Ch 15:16 Asa cut down her image, crushed it, and burned it 2
23:17 his altars and his images they broke in pieces 8
33: 7 the image of the idol . . he set in the house of God 7
19 sites on which he . . set up . . the images 6
22 Amon sacrificed to all the images that Manas'seh 6
34: 7 beat the Ashe'rim and the images into powder 6
Ps 97: 7 All worshipers of images are put to shame 7
106:20 God for the image of an ox that eats grass. 9
Isa 10:11 her idols as I have done to Sama'ria and her images? 1
21: 9 all the images of her gods he has shattered 6
40:20 to set up an image that will not move. 7
44:10 Who fashions a god or casts an image 7
Jer 10:14 images are false, and there is no breath in them. 3
50: 2 Her images are put to shame 5
38 it is a land of images, and they are mad over idols. 6
51:17 images are false, and there is no breath in them. 3
47 when I will punish the images of Babylon; 6
52 when I will execute judgment upon her images 6
Ezk 7:20 they made their abominable images 8
8: 3 where was the seat of the image of jealousy 4
5 in the entrance, was this image of jealousy. 4
16:17 and made for yourself images of men 8
23:14 images of the Chalde'ans portrayed in vermilion 8
30:13 and put an end to the images, in Memphis; 1
Dan 2:31 You saw, O king, and behold, a great image. 11
31 This image, mighty and of exceeding brightness 11
32 head of this image was of fine gold 11
34 smote the image on its feet of iron and clay 11
35 stone that struck the image became a great 11
3: 1 King Nebuchadnez'zar made an image of gold 11
2 come to the dedication of the image 11
3 assembled for the dedication of the image 11
3 stood before the image that Nebuchadnez'zar 11
5 fall down and worship the golden image 11
7 all . . fell down and worshiped the golden image 11
10 fall down and worship the golden image; 11
12 not serve your gods or worship the golden image 11
14 not serve my gods or worship the golden image 11
15 fall down and worship the image which I have made 11
18 not serve your gods or worship the golden image 11
Ams 5:26 your images, which you made for yourselves; 8
Mic 1: 7 All her images shall be beaten to pieces 6
5:13 I will cut off your images and your pillars 6
Rom 1:23 for images resembling mortal man or birds 12
8:29 to be conformed to the image of his Son 12
1Co 11: 7 since he is the image and glory of God 12
15:49 Just as we have borne the image of the man of dust 12
49 we shall also bear the image of the man of heaven. 12
Col 1:15 He is the image of the invisible God 12
3:10 after the image of its creator. 12
Rev 13:14 bidding them to make an image for the beast 12
15 allowed to give breath to the image of the beast 12
15 so that the image of the beast should even speak 12
15 those who would not worship the image of the beast 12
14: 9 If any one worships the beast and its image 12
11 these worshipers of the beast and its image 12
15: 2 those who had conquered the beast and its image 12
16: 2 the mark of the beast and worshiped its image. 12
19:20 and those who worshiped its image. 12
20: 4 and who had not worshiped the beast or its image 12
2Es 8:44 and is called thy own image 14
Wis 2:23 made him in the image of his own eternity 12
7:26 an image of his goodness. 12
13:13 he forms it like the image of a man 12
16 it is only an image and has need of help. 12
14:15 a father . . made an image of his child 12
16 graven images were worshiped. •
17 made a visible image of the king 12
15: 5 they desire the lifeless form of a dead image. 12
13 fragile vessels and graven images. •
17:21 an image of the darkness 12
Sir 17: 3 made them in his own image. 12
1Mc 3:48 were consulting the images of their idols. 13

image *See also* bear.

abominable image 1. מִפְלֶצֶת
1Kg 15:13 she had an abominable image made for Ashe'rah; 1
2Ch 15:16 she had made an abominable image for Ashe'rah. 1

graven image 1. פָּסִיל 2. פֶּסֶל 3. *γλυπτός*
Exd 20: 4 You shall not make for yourself a graven image 2
Lev 26: 1 and erect no graven image or pillar 2
Deu 4:16 lest you act corruptly by making a graven image 2
23 make a graven image in the form of anything 2
25 by making a graven image in the form of anything 2
5: 8 You shall not make for yourself a graven image 2
7: 5 you shall . . burn their graven images with fire. 1
25 The graven images of their gods you shall burn 1
12: 3 hew down the graven images of their gods 1
27:15 'Cursed . . man who makes a graven or molten image 2
Jdg 17: 3 I consecrate the silver . . to make a graven image 2
4 who made it into a graven image and a molten image; 2
18:14 in these houses . . an ephod, teraphim, a graven image 2
17 took the graven image, the ephod, the teraphim 2
18 these went . . and took the graven image, the ephod 2
20 the ephod, and the teraphim, and the graven image 2
30 the Danites set up the graven image 2
31 they set up Micah's graven image which he made 2
2Kg 17:41 and also served their graven images; 1
21: 7 the graven image of Ashe'rah . . he set in the house 2
2Ch 34: 3 Ashe'rim, and the graven and the molten images. 1
4 broke in pieces . . graven and the molten images 1
Ps 78:58 moved him to jealousy with their graven images. 1
Isa 10:10 the idols whose graven images were greater 1
30:22 defile your silver-covered graven images 1
42: 8 give to no other, nor my praise to graven images. 1
17 utterly put to shame, who trust in graven images 2
44:15 makes it a graven image and falls down before it. 2
48: 5 my graven image and my molten image commanded 2
Jer 8:19 provoked me to anger with their graven images 1
Nah 1:14 cut off the graven image and the molten image. 2
1Mc 5:68 graven images of their gods he burned with fire; 3

lifelike image 1. *ζωγραφία*
Sir 38:27 he sets his heart on painting a lifelike image 1

metal image 1. מַסֵּכָה
Hab 2:18 its maker has shaped it, a metal image 1

molten image 1. מַסֵּכָה 2. נְסִיךְ 3. נֶסֶךְ
Deu 9:12 they have made themselves a molten image.' 1
27:15 'Cursed . . man who makes a graven or molten image 1
Jdg 17: 3 to make a graven image and a molten image; 1
4 who made it into a graven image and a molten image; 1
18:14 ephod, teraphim, a graven image, and a molten image 1
14 ephod, teraphim, a graven image, and a molten image? 1
17 took . . the ephod, the teraphim, and the molten image 1
18 took . . ephod, the teraphim, and the molten image 1
1Kg 14: 9 made for yourself other gods, and molten images 1
2Kg 17:16 made for themselves molten images of two calves; 1
2Ch 28: 2 He even made molten images for the Ba'als; 1
34: 3 Ashe'rim, and the graven and the molten images. 1
4 broke in pieces . . graven and the molten images 1
Ps 106:19 calf in Horeb and worshiped a molten image. 1
Isa 30:22 defile . . your gold-plated molten images. 1
41:29 their molten images are empty wind. 3
42:17 who say to molten images, "You are our gods. 1
48: 5 graven image and my molten image commanded them 3
5 graven image and my molten image commanded them.' 3
Dan 11: 8 carry off . . gods with their molten images 2
Hos 13: 2 and make for themselves molten images, idols 1
Nah 1:14 cut off the graven image and the molten image. 1

imagination 1. יֵצֶר 2. *διάνοια* 3. *ἐνθύμημα* 4. *ἐνθύμησις* 5. adinventio
Gen 6: 5 and that every imagination of the thoughts 1
8:21 for the imagination of man's heart is evil 1
Lke 1:51 in the imagination of their hearts 2
Act 17:29 by the art and imagination of man. 4
2Es 6: 5 before the imaginations of those who now sin 5
16:54 their imaginations and their thoughts 5
63 Surely he knows your imaginations 5
Sir 37: 3 O evil imagination 3

imagine 1. חשׁב 2. *ἀνατυπόω* 3. *δοκέω* 4. *μελετάω* 5. *νομίζω* 6. *οἴομαι* 7. puto
Ps 41: 7 they imagine the worst for me. 1
Act 4:25 the peoples imagine vain things? 4
1Co 8: 2 If any one imagines that he knows something 3
1Ti 6: 5 imagining that godliness is a means of gain. 5
2Es 16:21 men will imagine that peace is assured for them 7
Wis 14:17 they imagined their appearance far away 2
2Mc 5: 6 imagining that he was setting up trophies 3
9: 8 imagining . . he could weigh the high mountains 6

imitate 1. *ἐξομοιόω* 2. *μιμέομαι* 3. *συμμιμητής* 4. imitor
Php 3:17 Brethren, join in imitating me 3
2Th 3: 7 you yourselves know how you ought to imitate us; 2
9 to give you in our conduct an example to imitate. 2
Heb 13: 7 imitate their faith. 2
3Jn 1:11 Beloved, do not imitate evil but imitate good. 2
11 Beloved, do not imitate evil but imitate good. 2
2Es 15:48 You have imitated that hateful harlot 4
Wis 4: 2 When it is present, men imitate it 2
15: 9 and imitates workers in copper 2
2Mc 4:16 wished to imitate completely 1
4Mc 9:23 Imitate me, brothers," he said. 2
13: 9 let us imitate the three youths in Assyria 2

imitator 1. *μιμητής*
1Co 4:16 I urge you, then, be imitators of me. 1
11: 1 Be imitators of me, as I am of Christ. 1
Eph 5: 1 be imitators of God, as beloved children. 1
1Th 1: 6 you became imitators of us and of the Lord 1
2:14 you, brethren, became imitators of the churches 1
Heb 6:12 imitators of those who . . inherit the promises. 1

immeasurable 1. *ἀμέτρητος* 2. *ὑπερβάλλω*
Eph 1:19 what is the immeasurable greatness of his power 2
2: 7 might show the immeasurable riches of his grace 2
Bar 3:25 has no bounds; it is high and immeasurable. 1
Man 1: 6 yet immeasurable . . is thy promised mercy 1
3Mc 2: 9 created the boundless and immeasurable earth 1

immediately 1. יוֹם 2. בַּהּ שַׁעֲתָא (A) 3. *εὐθέως* 4. *εὐθύς* 5. *ἤδη* 6. *παραχρῆμα* 7. amodo 8. statim 9. subito
1Sm 9:13 Now go up, for you will meet him immediately. 1
Dan 3: 6 immediately be cast into a . . fiery furnace. 2
15 immediately be cast into a . . fiery furnace; 2
4:33 Immediately the word was fulfilled upon 2
5: 5 Immediately the fingers of a man's hand appeared 2
Mat 3:16 he went up immediately from the water, and behold 4
4:20 Immediately they left their nets and followed 3
22 Immediately they left the boat and their father 3
8: 3 And immediately his leprosy was cleansed. 3
13: 5 and immediately they sprang up 3
20 and immediately receives it with joy; 4
21 persecution arises . . immediately he falls away. 4
14:27 immediately he spoke to them, saying 4
31 Jesus immediately reached out his hand 3
20:34 immediately they received their sight 3
21: 2 immediately you will find an ass tied 3
3 he will send them immediately. 4
24:29 Immediately after the tribulation 3
26:74 immediately the cock crowed. 3
Mrk 1:10 immediately he saw the heavens opened 4
12 The Spirit immediately drove him out 4
18 immediately they left their nets and followed 4
20 immediately he called them 4
21 immediately on the sabbath 4
23 immediately there was in their synagogue a man 4
29 immediately he left the synagogue 4
30 immediately they told him of her. 4
42 immediately the leprosy left him 4
2: 8 immediately Jesus, perceiving in his spirit 4
12 he rose, and immediately took up the pallet 4
3: 6 immediately held counsel with the Hero'di-ans 4
4: 5 and immediately it sprang up 4
15 when they hear, Satan immediately comes 4
16 immediately receive it with joy; 4
17 immediately they fall away. 4
5:29 immediately the hemorrhage ceased 4
30 immediately turned about in the crowd, and said 4
42 immediately the girl got up and walked 4
42 immediately overcome with amazement. 4
6:25 she came immediately with haste to the king 4
27 immediately the king sent a soldier of the guard 4
45 Immediately he made his disciples 4
50 But immediately he spoke to them and said 4
54 immediately the people recognized him 4
7:25 immediately a woman 4
8:10 immediately he got into the boat 4
9:15 immediately all the crowd, when they saw him 4
20 immediately it convulsed the boy 4
24 Immediately the father of the child cried out 4
10:52 immediately he received his sight 4
11: 2 immediately as you enter it you will find a colt 4
3 will send it back here immediately.' 4
14:43 immediately, while he was still speaking 4
72 immediately the cock crowed a second time. 4
Lke 1:64 immediately his mouth was opened 6
4:39 immediately she rose and served them. 6
5:13 immediately the leprosy left him. 3
25 immediately he rose before them 6
6:49 immediately it fell 4
8:44 immediately her flow of blood ceased. 6
47 how she had been immediately healed. 6
13:13 immediately she was made straight 6
14: 5 will not immediately pull him out on a sabbath day? 3
18:43 immediately he received his sight and followed 6
19:11 the kingdom of God was to appear immediately. 6
22:60 immediately, while he was still speaking 6
Joh 6:21 immediately the boat was at the land 3
13:30 he immediately went out; and it was night. 4
Act 3: 7 immediately his feet . . were made strong. 6
5:10 Immediately she fell down at his feet and died. 6

9:18 immediately something like scales fell 3
20 immediately he proclaimed Jesus, saying 3
34 immediately he rose. 3
12:10 immediately the angel left him. 3
23 Immediately an angel of the Lord smote him 6
13:11 Immediately mist and darkness fell upon him 6
16:10 immediately we sought to go on into Macedo'nia 3
26 immediately all the doors were opened 6
17:10 The brethren immediately sent Paul and Silas away 3
14 Then the brethren immediately sent Paul off 3
1Es 1:30 immediately his servants took him out . . 3
2Es 3: 7 immediately thou didst appoint death for him 8
6:44 For immediately fruit came forth 9
7:80 shall immediately wander about in torments 7
Sus 1:55 and will immediately cut you in two. •
Bel 1:39 the angel of God immediately returned Habakkuk 6
42 they were devoured immediately before his eyes. 6
2Mc 4:34 then . . he immediately put him out of the way. 6
38 he immediately stripped off the purple robe 6
6:13 to punish them immediately 3
7: 4 These were heated immediately 6
8:11 he immediately sent to the cities on the seacoast 3
10:22 immediately captured the two towers. 6
14:12 he immediately chose Nicanor 3
16 they set out from there immediately 3
3Mc 4: 8 seeing death immediately before them. 5
7:10 the Jews did not immediately hurry 4
4Mc 10: 8 They immediately brought him to the wheel 4

immediately *See also* seize.

immense 1. *ἀνείκαστος*

3Mc 1:28 cry of the crowds resulted in an immense uproar; 1

immense *See also* amount.

imminent 1. *θλίβω*

1Mc 9: 7 the battle was imminent 1

act immoderately 1. *περισσεύω*

Sir 33:29 Do not act immoderately toward anybody 1

immoral 1. *πόρνος*

1Co 5:10 not at all meaning the immoral of this world 1
6: 9 neither the immoral, nor idolaters 1
Heb 12:16 that no one be immoral or irreligious like Esau 1
13: 4 God will judge the immoral and adulterous. 1

immoral man 1. *πορνεύω* 2. *πόρνος*

1Co 5: 9 not to associate with immoral men; 2
6:18 the immoral man sins against his own body. 1

immoral person 1. *πόρνος*

1Ti 1:10 immoral persons, sodomites, kidnapers, liars 1

immorality 1. *πορνεία* 2. *πορνεύω* 3. *πόρνος*

1Co 5: 1 there is immorality among you 1
11 if he is guilty of immorality or greed 3
6:13 is not meant for immorality, but for the Lord 1
18 Shun immorality 1
7: 2 because of the temptation to immorality 1
10: 8 We must not indulge in immorality as some of them 2
2Co 12:21 impurity, immorality, and licentiousness 1
Rev 2:21 but she refuses to repent of her immorality. 1
9:21 nor did they repent of . . their immorality 1
Tob 4:12 Beware, my son, of all immorality 1
Sir 41:17 Be ashamed of immorality 1

immorality *See also* practice.

act immorally 1. *ἐκπορνεύω*

Jde 1: 7 acted immorally and indulged in unnatural lust 1

immortal 1. *ἀθάνατος* 2. *ἄφθαρτος* 3. inmortalis

Rom 1:23 exchanged the glory of the immortal God 2
1Ti 1:17 the King of ages, immortal, invisible, the only God 2
2Es 2:45 and have put on the immortal 3
7:113and the beginning of the immortal age to come 3
Wis 1:15 For righteousness is immortal. 1
12: 1 For thy immortal spirit is in all things. 2
Sir 17:30 since a son of man is not immortal. 1
4Mc 7: 3 he sailed into the haven of immortal victory. 1
14: 6 as though moved by an immortal spirit of devotion 1
18:23 have received pure and immortal souls from God 1

immortality 1. *ἀθανασία* 2. *ἀφθαρσία* 3. inmortalis 4. inmortalitas

Rom 2: 7 seek for glory and honor and immortality 2
1Co 15:53 this mortal nature must put on immortality. 1
54 the mortal puts on immortality 1
1Ti 6:16 who alone has immortality 1
2Ti 1:10 brought life and immortality to light 2
2Es 7:13 and really yield the fruit of immortality. 4
96 they are to receive and enjoy in immortality. 3
8:54 the treasure of immortality is made manifest. 4
Wis 3: 4 their hope is full of immortality. 1
4: 1 in the memory of virtue is immortality 1
6:18 assurance of immortality 2
19 immortality brings one near to God; 2
8:13 Because of her I shall have immortality 1
17 in kinship with wisdom there is immortality 1
15: 3 to know thy power is the root of immortality. 1
4Mc 9:22 as though transformed by fire into immortality 2
14: 5 running the course toward immortality 1
16:13 as though . . giving rebirth for immortality 1
17:12 The prize was immortality in endless life. 2

immovable 1. בַּל מוט 2. בַּל צען 3. *ἀκίνητος* 4. *ἀμετακίνητος* 5. *ἀσάλευτος*

Job 41:23 firmly cast upon him and immovable. 1
Isa 33:20 an immovable tent, whose stakes will never be 2
Act 27:41 the bow stuck and remained immovable 5
1Co 15:58 my beloved brethren, be steadfast, immovable 4
3Mc 6:19 binding them with immovable shackles. 3

immunity 1. *ἀτέλεια* 2. *ἄφεμα*

1Mc 10:28 grant you many immunities and give you gifts. 2
34 let them all be days of immunity and release 1

impair 1. שׁחת 2. נזק (A)

Rut 4: 6 I cannot . . lest I impair my own inheritance. 1
Ezr 4:13 will not pay . . royal revenue will be impaired. 2

impale 1. מחא (A)

Ezr 6:11 he shall be impaled upon it, and his house 1

impart 1. *δίδωμι* 2. *ἐκφαίνω* 3. *λαλέω* 4. *μεταδίδωμι*

Rom 1:11 that I may impart to you some spiritual gift 4
1Co 2: 6 Yet among the mature we do impart wisdom 3
7 we impart a secret and hidden wisdom of God 3
13 we impart this in words 3
Eph 4:29 that it may impart grace to those who hear. 1
Wis 7:13 I impart without grudging 4
Sir 16:25 I will impart instruction by weight 2

impart understanding 1. בין

Ps 119:130it imparts understanding to the simple. 1

impartial 1. *ἀνυπόκριτος*

Wis 5:18 wear impartial justice as a helmet; 1

impartially 1. *ἀπροσωπολήμπτως*

1Pe 1:17 invoke . . him who judges each one impartially 1

act impartially 1. *ἰσονομέω*

4Mc 5:24 in all our dealings we act impartially 1

impassable 1. *ἄβατος*

AEs 16:24 It shall be made not only impassable for men 1

impatient 1. בקשׁ 2. לאה 3. קצר 4. קצר רוּחַ

Job 4: 5 now it has come to you, and you are impatient; 2
21: 4 Why should I not be impatient? 4
Mic 2: 7 Is the Spirit of the LORD impatient? 3
Zec 6: 7 When the steeds came out, they were impatient 1

become impatient 1. קצר נֶפֶשׁ

Num21: 4 the people became impatient on the way. 1
Zec 11: 8 But I became impatient with them 1

impediment in speech 1. *μογιλάλος*

Mrk 7:32 a man who . . had an impediment in his speech 1

impel 1. *προτρέπω*

Wis 14:18 Then the ambition of the craftsman impelled 1

impenetrable 1. לֹא חקר

Jer 46:23 cut down her forest . . though it is impenetrable 1

impenitent 1. *ἀμετανόητος*

Rom 2: 5 by your hard and impenitent heart 1

imperfect 1. *ἐκ μέρους*

1Co 13: 9 For our knowledge is imperfect 1
9 our prophecy is imperfect; 1
10 the perfect comes, the imperfect will pass away. 1

imperfectly 1. *ἀδυναμέω*

Sir 0: 2 to have rendered some phrases imperfectly. 1

imperishable 1. *ἀφθαρσία* 2. *ἄφθαρτος*

1Co 9:25 but we an imperishable. 2
15:50 the perishable inherit the imperishable. 1
52 the dead will be raised imperishable 2
53 perishable nature must put on the imperishable 1
54 When the perishable puts on the imperishable 1
1Pe 1: 4 to an inheritance which is imperishable 2
23 not of perishable seed but of imperishable 2
3: 4 the imperishable jewel of a gentle and quiet spirit 2
Wis 18: 4 the imperishable light of the law was to be given 2

impiety 1. *ἀσέβεια* 2. *δυσσέβεια*

1Es 1:42 about . . his uncleanness and impiety 2
2Mc 8:33 the proper recompense for their impiety. 2
3Mc 6:10 have become entangled in impieties in our exile 1
4Mc 6:19 become a pattern of impiety to the young 2
9:32 the threats that come from impiety 1
10:11 because of your impiety and bloodthirstiness 1

impious 1. נָבָל 2. *ἀνόσιος* 3. *ἀσεβής* 4. *δυσσεβέω* 5. *δυσσεβής*

Ps 74:18 an impious people reviles thy name. 1
22 remember how the impious scoff at thee all the day! 1
1Pe 4:18 where will the impious and sinner appear? 3
2Mc 3:11 the impious Simon had misrepresented the facts. 5
6:13 In fact, not to let the impious alone for long 4
3Mc 2: 2 an impious and profane man 2
3: 1 When the impious king comprehended this situation 5
24 these impious people behind our backs 5
5:47 he had filled his impious mind with a deep rage 5

most impious 1. *ἀσεβής*

4Mc 12:11 profane tyrant, most impious of all the wicked 1

impiously 1. inreligiose

Ps 35:16 they impiously mocked more and more •
2Es 15: 8 ungodly deeds which they impiously commit 1

impiously *See also* behave.

act impiously 1. *ἀσεβέω*

4Mc 9:15 as one who acts impiously 1

implacable 1. *ἄσπονδος*

2Ti 3: 3 inhuman, implacable, slanderers, profligates 1

implant 1. *ἔμφυτος* 2. *ἐντίθημι* 3. *ἐπιφυτεύω* 4. *φυτεύω*

Jas 1:21 receive with meekness the implanted word 1
3Mc 5:28 he had implanted in the king's mind a forgetfulness 2
4Mc 13:19 which was implanted in the mother's womb. 4
15: 6 she had implanted in herself tender love toward them 3

implement 1. כְּלִי

1Sm 8:12 appoint . . and to make his implements of war 1
Zec 11:15 Take . . the implements of a worthless shepherd. 1

implore 1. שחה 2. *δέομαι* 3. *ἱκετεύω* 4. *λέγω*

1Sm 2:36 shall come to implore him for a piece of silver 1
Mat 18:26 So the servant fell on his knees, imploring him 4
3Mc 5:25 implored the supreme God to help them again 2
51 imploring the Ruler over every power 3
4Mc 4: 9 While the priests . . were imploring God 3
16:13 she implored them and urged them on to death 3

imply 1. *εἰμί* 2. *φημί*

1Co 10:19 What do I imply then? 2
20 No, I imply that what pagans sacrifice •
Gal 3:20 Now an intermediary implies more than one 1

import 1. יצא 2. מוֹצָא 3. עלה וְיצא

1Kg 10:28 Solomon's import of horses was from Egypt and Ku'e 2
29 A chariot could be imported from Egypt 3
2Ch 1:16 Solomon's import of horses was from Egypt and Ku'e 2
17 imported a chariot from Egypt for 600 1
9:28 horses were imported for Solomon from Egypt 1

importance

1Co 15: 3 For I delivered to you as of first importance •

important 1. *ἐπίκαιρος*

2Mc 10:15 who had control of important strongholds 1

importune 1. רהב

Prv 6: 3 go, hasten, and importune your neighbor. 1

importunity 1. *ἀναίδεια*

Lke 11: 8 yet because of his importunity he will rise 1

impose 1. נתן 2. רמא (A) 3. *ἐπίκειμαι*

2Kg 18:14 whatever you impose on me I will bear. 1
Ezr 7:24 not be lawful to impose tribute, custom, or toll 2
Ezk 26:17 who imposed your terror on all the mainland! 1
Heb 9:10 imposed until the time of reformation. 3

impose a fine 1. ענשׁ

Prv 17:26 To impose a fine on a righteous man is not good; 1

impose upon 1. *ἐπιβάλλω*

1Es 8:22 no one has authority to impose any tax upon them. 1

impossible 1. בצר 2. פלא 3. *ἀδυνατέω* 4. *ἀδύνατος* 5. *ἀμήχανος*

Gen 11: 6 to do will now be impossible for them. 1
2Sm 13: 2 it seemed impossible to Amnon to do anything 2
Mat 17:20 and nothing will be impossible to you. 3
19:26 With men this is impossible 4
Mrk 10:27 With men it is impossible, but not with God 4
Lke 1:37 For with God nothing will be impossible. 3
18:27 impossible with men is possible with God. 4
Heb 6: 4 For it is impossible to restore to repentance 4
18 it is impossible that God should prove false 4
10: 4 it is impossible . . 4
11: 6 without faith it is impossible to please him. 4
Wis 16:15 To escape from thy hand is impossible; 4
2Mc 3:12 he said that it was utterly impossible 5
14:10 impossible for the government to find peace. 4
3Mc 4:18 the task was impossible for all the generals 4

impostor 1. γόης 2. πλάνος
Mat 27:63 said, "Sir, we remember how that impostor said 2
2Co 6: 8 We are treated as impostors, and yet are true; 2
2Ti 3:13 impostors will go on from bad to worse 1

impoverish 1. ירש 2. סכן
Jdg 14:15 Have you invited us here to impoverish us? 1
Isa 40:20 He who is impoverished chooses for an offering 2

become impoverished 1. προσδέω
Sir 18:32 lest you become impoverished by its expense. 1

utter an imprecation 1. κατεύχομαι
4Mc 12:19 After he had uttered these imprecations 1

impress 1. ἐναποσφραγίζω 2. καταπλήσσω
3Mc 1: 9 impressed by its excellence and its beauty 2
4Mc 15: 4 We impress upon the character of a small child 1

imprison 1. כלא 2. נתן בֵּית הָאֵסוּר 3. סגר 4. δεσμός 5. δέω 6. κατάκλειστος 7. παραλαμβάνω 8. φυλακίζω
Job 11:10 If he passes through, and imprisons 3
Jer 32: 3 For Zedeki'ah king of Judah had imprisoned him 1
37:15 at Jeremiah, and they beat him and imprisoned him 2
Act 21:13 am ready not only to be imprisoned but even to die 5
22:19 I imprisoned and beat those who believed in thee. 8
Wis 16:14 nor set free the imprisoned soul. 7
18: 4 deprived of light and imprisoned in darkness 8
4 those who had kept thy sons imprisoned 6
Sir 13:12 he will not hesitate to injure or to imprison. 4

imprisonment 1. אֱסוּר (A) 2. ἀπαγωγή 3. δεσμός 4. φυλακή
Ezr 7:26 whether for death . . or for imprisonment. 1
Act 20:23 imprisonment and afflictions await me. 3
23:29 nothing deserving death or imprisonment. 3
26:31 nothing to deserve death or imprisonment. 3
2Co 6: 5 beatings, imprisonments, tumults, labors 4
11:23 with far greater labors, far more imprisonments 4
Php 1: 7 both in my imprisonment and in the defense 3
13 my imprisonment is for Christ; 3
14 in the Lord because of my imprisonment 3
17 thinking to afflict me in my imprisonment. 3
Phm 1:10 whose father I have become in my imprisonment. 3
13 during my imprisonment for the gospel; 3
Heb 11:36 even chains and imprisonment. 4
1Es 8:24 either fine or imprisonment. 2

improper 1. καθήκω
Rom 1:28 to a base mind and to improper conduct. 1
3Mc 4:16 uttering improper words 1

improve 1. טוב 2. יטב
Hos 10: 1 as his country improved 1
1 he improved his pillars. 2

improvement 1. κατάρτισις
2Co 13: 9 What we pray for is your improvement. 1

impudence 1. ἀναίδεια
Sir 25:22 There is wrath and impudence and great disgrace 1

impudent 1. עז 2. קְשֵׁה פָנִים 3. ἀναιδής 4. θρασύς
Prv 7:13 with impudent face she says to him 1
Ezk 2: 4 The people also are impudent and stubborn 2
Sir 22: 5 An impudent daughter disgraces father 4
26:11 Be on guard against her impudent eye 3

impulse 1. ἐπιθυμία 2. θέλημα 3. κίνημα
2Ti 3: 6 swayed by various impulses 1
2Pe 1:21 no prophecy ever came by the impulse of man 2
4Mc 1:35 all the impulses of the body are bridled 3

one impulse 1. ὁμοθυμαδόν
Jdt 15: 2 with one impulse all rushed out and fled 1

impure 1. πορνεία
Rev 14: 8 drink the wine of her impure passion. 1
18: 3 drunk the wine of her impure passion 1

impure man 1. ἀκάθαρτος
Eph 5: 5 no fornicator or impure man 1

impurity 1. טָמֵא 2. נִדָּה 3. ἀκαθαρσία 4. ἀκάθαρτος
Lev 15:19 she shall be in her impurity for seven days 2
20 upon which she lies during her impurity 2
24 if any man lies with her, and her impurity is on him 2
25 not at the time of her impurity 2
25 has a discharge beyond the time of her impurity 2
25 the days of her impurity, she shall be unclean 1
26 shall be to her as the bed of her impurity 2
26 be unclean, as in the uncleanness of her impurity 2
33 also for her who is sick with her impurity 2
20:21 it is impurity; he has uncovered his brother's 2
Num19: 9 they shall be kept . . for the water for impurity 2
13 water for impurity was not thrown upon him 2
20 water for impurity has not been thrown upon him 2
21 He who sprinkles the water for impurity 2
21 he who touches the water for impurity shall be 2
31:23 also be purified with the water of impurity; 2
Ezk 18: 6 or approach a woman in her time of impurity 2
22:10 women who are unclean in their impurity. 2
36:17 like the uncleanness of a woman in her impurity. 2
Rom 1:24 God gave them up . . to impurity 3
6:19 as you once yielded your members to impurity 3
2Co 12:21 impurity, immorality, and licentiousness 3
Gal 5:19 fornication, impurity, licentiousness 3
Eph 5: 3 fornication and all impurity or covetousness 3
Col 3: 5 fornication, impurity, passion, evil desire 3
Rev 17: 4 and the impurities of her fornication; 4

impute 1. חשב 2. שׂוּם
Lev 17: 4 bloodguilt shall be imputed to that man 1
1Sm 22:15 Let not the king impute anything to his servant 2
Ps 32: 2 the man to whom the LORD imputes no iniquity 1

inability 1. οὐ δύναμαι
AEs 16: 3 in their inability to stand prosperity 1

inaccessible 1. ἄβατος
3Mc 5:43 by burning . . the temple inaccessible to him 1

inappropriate 1. καθήκω
2Mc 4:19 because that was inappropriate 1

inasmuch 1. כִּי עַל כֵּן 2. כְּפִי אֲשֶׁר 3. לְ 4. ἐπειδήπερ 5. ἐφ' ὅσον
Gen 38:26 more righteous than I, inasmuch as I did not give 1
2Sm 14:13 convicts himself, inasmuch as the king does not 3
Mal 2: 9 inasmuch as you have not kept my ways 2
Lke 1: 1 Inasmuch as many have undertaken to compile 4
Rom11:13 Inasmuch then as I am an apostle to the Gentiles 5

inborn 1. ἔμφυτος
Wis 12:10 evil and their wickedness inborn 1

incense 1. לְבֹנָה 2. מִקְטָר 3. קְטוֹרָה 4. קִטֵּר 5. קְטֹרֶת 6. נִיחוֹחַ (A) 7. θυμίαμα 8. λίβανος
Exd 25: 6 anointing oil and for the fragrant incense 5
29 you shall make its plates and dishes for incense •
30: 1 You shall make an altar to burn incense upon; 5
7 Aaron shall burn fragrant incense on it; 5
8 a perpetual incense before the LORD 5
9 You shall offer no unholy incense thereon 5
27 its utensils, and the altar of incense 5
35 make an incense blended as by the perfumer 5
37 the incense which you shall make 5
31: 8 pure lampstand . . and the altar of incense 5
11 anointing oil and the fragrant incense 5
35: 8 anointing oil and for the fragrant incense 5
15 the altar of incense, with its poles 5
15 the anointing oil and the fragrant incense 5
28 anointing oil, and for the fragrant incense. 5
37:16 its plates and dishes for incense, and its bowls •
25 He made the altar of incense of acacia wood; 5
29 made . . the pure fragrant incense, blended 5
39:38 the anointing oil and the fragrant incense 5
40: 5 you shall put the golden altar for incense 5
27 burnt fragrant incense upon it; as the LORD had 5
Lev 4: 7 on the horns of the altar of fragrant incense 5
10: 1 put fire in it, and laid incense on it 5
16:12 and two handfuls of sweet incense beaten small 5
13 put the incense on the fire before the LORD 5
13 the cloud of the incense may cover the mercy seat 5
Num 4:16 charge of . . the fragrant incense 5
7:14 one golden dish of ten shekels, full of incense; 5
20 one golden dish of ten shekels, full of incense; 5
26 one golden dish of ten shekels, full of incense; 5
32 one golden dish of ten shekels, full of incense; 5
38 one golden dish of ten shekels, full of incense; 5
44 one golden dish of ten shekels, full of incense; 5
50 one golden dish of ten shekels, full of incense; 5
56 one golden dish of ten shekels, full of incense; 5
62 one golden dish of ten shekels, full of incense; 5
68 one golden dish of ten shekels, full of incense; 5
74 one golden dish of ten shekels, full of incense; 5
80 one golden dish of ten shekels, full of incense; 5
86 the twelve golden dishes, full of incense 5
16: 7 put fire in them and put incense upon them 5
17 take his censer, and put incense upon it 5
18 took his censer, and . . laid incense upon them 5
35 consumed the 250 men offering the incense. 5
40 should draw near to burn incense before the LORD 5
46 Take your censer . . and lay incense on it 5
47 he put on the incense, and made atonement 5
Deu 33:10 they shall put incense before thee 3
1Kg 7:50 The cups, snuffers, basins, dishes for incense •
2Kg 25:14 the dishes for incense and all the vessels •
1Ch 6:49 made offering . . and upon the altar of incense 5
9:29 over . . the oil, the incense, and the spices. 1
28:18 for the altar of incense made of refined gold 5
2Ch 2: 4 burning of incense of sweet spices before him 5
4:22 dishes for incense, and firepans, of pure gold; •
13:11 offer to the LORD . . incense of sweet spices 5
24:14 utensils . . and dishes for incense, and vessels •
26:16 to burn incense on the altar of incense. 5
19 house of the LORD, by the altar of incense. 5
Ps 141: 2 Let my prayer be counted as incense before thee 5
Isa 1:13 incense is an abomination to me. 5
Jer 41: 5 bringing cereal offerings and incense 1
44:21 As for the incense that you burned in the cities 4
52:18 dishes for incense, and all the vessels of bronze •
19 and the lampstands, and the dishes for incense •
Ezk 8:11 and the smoke of the cloud of incense went up. 5
16:18 and set my oil and my incense before them. 5
23:41 on which you had placed my incense and my oil. 5
Dan 2:46 King . . commanded that an offering and incense 6
Mal 1:11 in every place incense is offered to my name 2
Lke 1:10 praying outside at the hour of incense 7
11 on the right side of the altar of incense. 7
Rev 5: 8 and with golden bowls full of incense 7
8: 3 given much incense to mingle with the prayers 7
4 the smoke of the incense rose with the prayers 7
18:13 cinnamon, spice, incense, myrrh, frankincense 7
Tob 6:16 you shall take live ashes of incense 7
8: 2 he took the live ashes of incense 7
Jdt 9: 1 when that evening's incense was being offered 7
Wis 18:21 prayer and propitiation by incense 7
Sir 45:16 incense and a pleasing odor 7
49: 1 like a blending of incense 7
50: 9 like fire and incense in the censer 8
Bar 1:10 burnt offerings and sin offerings and incense 8
Aza 1:15 sacrifice, or oblation, or incense 7
1Mc 4:49 the altar of incense, and the table 7
2Mc 2: 5 the tent and the ark and the altar of incense 7
10: 3 they burned incense and lighted lamps 7

incense (2) 1. חרה
Isa 41:11 Behold, all who are incensed against you 1
45:24 be ashamed, all who were incensed against him. 1

incense *See* altar, burn, dish, offer.

become incensed 1. ἀγανακτέω
Wis 12:27 when in their suffering they became incensed 1

incentive 1. παραμύθιον
Php 2: 1 any incentive of love 1

incessant 1. ἄληκτον
3Mc 4: 2 among the Jews there was incessant mourning 1

incest 1. תֶּבֶל
Lev 20:12 they have committed incest, their blood is upon 1

incident 1. οὗτος
2Mc 4:43 Charges were brought . . about this incident. 1

incite 1. סות 2. ἐπισείω 3. παροτρύνω 4. ταράσσω
2Sm 24: 1 and he incited David against them, saying, "Go 1
1Kg 21:25 like Ahab, whom Jez'ebel his wife incited. 1
1Ch 21: 1 Satan . . incited David to number Israel. 1
Act 13:50 the Jews incited the devout women of high standing 3
17:13 stirring up and inciting the crowds. 4
2Mc 4: 1 saying that it was he who had incited Heliodorus 2

inclination 1. διαβούλιον 2. ἦθος 3. ψυχή
Sir 5: 2 Do not follow your inclination and strength 3
15:14 he left him in the power of his own inclination. 1
4Mc 2:21 he planted in him emotions and inclinations 2

incline 1. נטה 2. קשב 3. ἐκνεύω 4. κλίνω 5. φιλοφρονέω 6. declino
Num15:39 which you are inclined to go after wantonly. •
Jos 24:23 put away . . and incline your heart to the LORD 1
Jdg 9: 3 and their hearts inclined to follow Abim'elech 1
1Sm 14: 7 Do all that your mind inclines to . . I am with you •
1Kg 8:58 that he may incline our hearts to him 1
2Kg 19:16 Incline thy ear, O LORD, and hear; open thy eyes 1
Ps 10:17 thou wilt incline thy ear 2
17: 6 O God; incline thy ear to me, hear my words. 1
31: 2 Incline thy ear to me, rescue me speedily! 1
40: 1 the LORD; he inclined to me and heard my cry. 1
45:10 Hear, O daughter, consider, and incline your ear; 1
49: 4 I will incline my ear to a proverb; 1
71: 2 incline thy ear to me, and save me! 1
78: 1 incline your ears to the words of my mouth! 1
86: 1 Incline thy ear, O LORD, and answer me 1
88: 2 prayer come before thee, incline thy ear to my cry! 1
102: 2 Incline thy ear to me; answer me speedily 1
116: 2 Because he inclined his ear to me 1
119:36 Incline my heart to thy testimonies 1
112I incline my heart to perform thy statutes 1
141: 4 Incline not my heart to any evil 1
Prv 2: 2 inclining your heart to understanding; 1
4:20 incline your ear to my sayings. 1
5: 1 incline your ear to my understanding; 1
13 I did not . . incline my ear to my instructors. 1
22:17 Incline your ear, and hear the words of the wise 1
Ecc 10: 2 A wise man's heart inclines him toward the right •
Isa 37:17 Incline thy ear, O LORD, and hear; 1
55: 3 Incline your ear, and come to me; 1
Jer 7:24 But they did not obey or incline their ear 1
26 yet they did not listen to me, or incline their ear 1

11: 8 Yet they did not obey or incline their ear 1
17:23 Yet they did not listen or incline their ear 1
25: 4 neither listened nor inclined your ears to hear 1
34:14 did not listen to me or incline their ears to me. 1
35:15 But you did not incline your ear or listen to me. 1
44: 5 But they did not listen or incline their ear 1
Dan 9:18 O my God, incline thy ear and hear; open thy eyes 1
2Es 3:34 which way the turn of the scale will incline. 6
Sir 4: 8 Incline your ear to the poor 4
6:33 if you incline your ear you will become wise. 4
38:28 he inclines his ear to the sound of the hammer 4
51:16 I inclined my ear a little and received her 4
Bar 2:16 Incline thy ear, O Lord, and hear; 4
2Mc 2:25 to make it easy for those . . inclined to memorize 5
3Mc 3:22 Since they incline constantly to evil 3

incline precipitously 1. ἀπόκρημνος
2Mc 13: 5 which . . inclines precipitously into the ashes. 1

include 1. היה 2. וְ 3. מֶלֶךְ 4. ἐν οἷς 5. καί
6. περιέχω
Gen 46:26 own offspring, not including Jacob's sons' wives 3
Jos 19:18 Its territory included Jezreel, Chesul'loth 1
25 Its territory included Helkath, Hali, Beten 1
41 included Zorah, Esh'ta-ol, Ir-she'mesh 1
Jdg 20: 1 people of Israel . . including the land of Gilead 2
1Ch 21: 6 not include Levi and Benjamin in the numbering •
Rom 1: 6 including yourselves who are called to belong 4
1Mc 3:13 including a body of faithful men 5
4Mc 1: 2 it includes the praise of the highest virtue 6

full inclusion 1. πλήρωμα
Rom 11:12 how much more will their full inclusion mean! 1

income 1. תְּבוּאָה 2. λόγος
Prv 15: 6 but trouble befalls the income of the wicked. 1
1Mc 10:42 from the income of the services of the temple 2

incompetent 1. ἀνάξιος
1Co 6: 2 are you incompetent to try trivial cases? 1

incomplete 1. λείπω
Sir 42:24 he has made nothing incomplete. 1

incomprehension 1. ἀγνωσία
3Mc 5:27 completely overcome by incomprehension 1

inconvenient 1. δύσχρηστος
Wis 2:12 because he is inconvenient to us 1

incorruptible 1. non corruptus
2Es 7:97 being incorruptible from then on. 1

incorruption 1. ἀφθαρσία 2. incorruptio
2Es 4:11 how can one . . understand incorruption? 2
Wis 2:23 for God created man for incorruption 1

increase 1. גדל 2. יְבוּל 3. יסף 4. מַרְבֶּה 5. מַרְבִּית
6. נוב 7. ספה 8. פרה 9. פרץ 10. רַב 11. רֹב 12. רבב
13. רבה 14. שׂגה 15. שֶׁגֶר 16. תְּבוּאָה 17. תְּנוּבָה
18. תַּרְבִּית 19. αὐξάνω 20. γένημα 21. ἐπαθροίζω
22. ἐπαύξω 23. περισσεύω 24. πλεονάζω
25. πληθύνω 26. προκόπτω 27. πρόσβασις
28. προστίθημι 29. cresco 30. incresco 31. multiplico
Gen 7:17 and the waters increased, and bore up the ark 13
18 The waters prevailed and increased greatly 13
30:30 you had little . . it has increased abundantly; 9
Exd 23:30 before you, until you are increased and possess 8
Lev 25:16 If the years are many you shall increase the price 13
36 Take no interest from him or increase 18
26: 4 the land shall yield its increase 2
20 your land shall not yield its increase 2
Num 32:14 to increase still more the fierce anger 7
Deu 7:13 bless . . the increase of your cattle 15
28: 4 Blessed shall be . . the increase of your cattle 15
18 Cursed shall be . . the increase of your cattle 15
51 not leave you . . the increase of your cattle 15
32:22 burns . . devours the earth and its increase 2
Jdg 9:29 to Abim'elech, 'Increase your army, and come out.' 13
1Sm 2:33 and all the increase of your house shall die 5
14:19 the tumult in the camp . . increased more and more; 10
2Sm 15:12 and the people with Ab'salom kept increasing. 10
1Ch 4:38 and their fathers' houses increased greatly. 9
Ezr 10:10 so increased the guilt of Israel. 3
Job 1:10 his possessions have increased in the land. 9
10:17 against me, and increase thy vexation toward me; 13
31:12 it would burn to the root all my increase. 16
Ps 49:16 rich, when the glory of his house increases. 13
62:10 if riches increase, set not your heart on them. 6
67: 6 The earth has yielded its increase; 2
71:21 Thou wilt increase my honor, and comfort me 13
73:12 always at ease, they increase in riches. 14
85:12 our land will yield its increase. 2
138: 3 my strength of soul thou didst increase. •
Prv 1: 5 wise man also may hear and increase in learning 3
9: 9 teach a righteous man . . increase in learning. 3
13:11 he who gathers little by little will increase 13
16:21 pleasant speech increases persuasiveness. 3
22:16 oppresses the poor to increase his own wealth 13
23:28 increases the faithless among men. 3
28: 8 augments his wealth by interest and increase 18
28 but when they perish, the righteous increase. 13
29:16 authority, transgression increases; 13
Ecc 1:18 he who increases knowledge increases sorrow. 3
18 he who increases knowledge increases sorrow. 3
5: 7 For when dreams increase, empty words grow many 11
11 When goods increase, they increase who eat them; 13
11 When goods increase, they increase who eat them; 12
Isa 9: 3 the nation, thou hast increased its joy; 1
7 Of the increase of his government and of peace 4
26:15 thou hast increased the nation, O LORD 3
15 O LORD, thou hast increased the nation; 3
40:29 to him who has no might he increases strength. 13
Jer 3:16 you have multiplied and increased in the land 8
Ezk 18: 8 does not lend at interest or take any increase 18
13 lends at interest, and takes increase; 18
17 takes no interest or increase 18
22:12 you take interest and increase and make gain 18
23:19 Yet she increased her harlotry 13
28: 5 in trade you have increased your wealth 13
34:27 and the earth shall yield its increase 2
36:11 and they shall increase and be fruitful; 13
30 I will make . . the increase of the field abundant 17
37 to do for them: to increase their men like a flock. 13
Dan 12: 4 run to and fro, and knowledge shall increase. 13
Hos 4: 7 The more they increased, the more they sinned 12
10: 1 The more his fruit increased 11
Nah 3:16 increased your merchants more than the stars 13
Zec 8:12 the ground shall give its increase 2
Mrk 4: 8 brought forth grain, growing up and increasing 19
Lke 2:52 Jesus increased in wisdom and in stature 26
11:29 When the crowds were increasing, he began to say 21
17: 5 The apostles said to the Lord, "Increase our faith! 28
Joh 3:30 He must increase, but I must decrease. 19
Act 6: 7 the word of God increased 19
16: 5 they increased in numbers daily. 23
Rom 5:20 Law came in, to increase the trespass; 24
20 where sin increased, grace abounded all the more 24
2Co 4:15 increase thanksgiving, to the glory of God. 23
9:10 increase the harvest of your righteousness. 19
10:15 our hope is that as your faith increases 19
Php 4:17 I seek the fruit which increases to your credit. 24
Col 1:10 increasing in the knowledge of God. 19
1Th 3:12 may the Lord make you increase and abound in love 24
2Th 1: 3 the love of every one . . is increasing. 24
1Es 9: 7 have increased the sin of Israel. 28
2Es 1: 6 the sins of their parents have increased in them 29
5: 2 unrighteousness shall be increased 31
10 and unrestraint shall increase on earth. 31
7:111 when corruption has increased 30
114 and righteousness has increased 29
14:40 and wisdom increased in my breast 30
Jdt 9: 7 the Assyrians are increased in their might 25
Wis 10:10 and increased the fruit of his toil. 25
Sir 18: 6 It is not possible to diminish or increase them 28
21:12 a cleverness which increases bitterness. 25
13 will increase like a flood 25
31:30 Drunkenness increases the anger of a fool 25
43: 8 increasing marvelously in its phases 19
Bar 2:34 I will increase them, and they will not 25
1Mc 3:42 Judas . . saw that misfortunes had increased 25
14: 8 the ground gave its increase 20
2Mc 4:13 and increase in the adoption of foreign ways 27
3Mc 2:25 he increased in his deeds of malice 22
increase *See also* give.

increase greatly 1. שׁרץ
Exd 1: 7 Israel were fruitful and increased greatly; 1

increase in number 1. πληθύνω
Act 6: 1 when the disciples were increasing in number 1

increase in strength 1. ἐνδυναμόω
Act 9:22 Saul increased all the more in strength 1

incredible 1. ἄπιστος 2. παράδοξος
Act 26: 8 Why is it thought incredible by any of you 1
Wis 19: 5 might experience an incredible journey 2

most incredible 1. παράδοξος
Wis 16:17 most incredible of all 1

incur 1. חָטָא 2. ἐμπίπτω 3. ἐν 4. ἐπάγω
5. ἐπιβάλλω 6. ἔχω 7. κερδαίνω 8. κληρονομέω
9. κομίζω 10. λαμβάνω 11. ὀφείλω
Exd 28:38 take upon himself any guilt incurred in the holy •
Prv 9: 7 he who reproves a wicked man incurs injury. •
Hos 12: 8 can never offset the guilt he has incurred. 1
Act 27:21 incurred this injury and loss. 7
Rom 13: 2 and those who resist will incur judgment. 10
1Ti 5:12 so they incur condemnation 6
Sir 6: 1 a bad name incurs shame and reproach 8
9: 5 lest you stumble and incur penalties for her. 3
23:16 a third incurs wrath 4
39:23 The nations will incur his wrath 8
2Mc 9:16 the expenses incurred for the sacrifices 5
3Mc 1: 3 incurred the vengeance meant for the king. 9
3:28 property of the one who incurs the punishment 2
4Mc 11: 3 by murdering me you will incur punishment 11

incur a penalty 1. ὀφείλω
Tob 6:12 without incurring the penalty of death 1

incur guilt 1. אשׁם 2. אַשְׁמָה
2Ch 19:10 that they may not incure guilt before the LORD 1
10 Thus you shall do, and you will not incur guilt. 1
33:23 but this Amon incurred guilt more and more. 2
Hos 13: 1 but he incurred guilt through Ba'al and died. 1

incur peril 1. periclitor
2Es 13:20 come into these things, though incurring peril 1

incurable 1. אֵין מַרְפֵּא 2. אנשׁ 3. ἀνίατος
4. οὐκ ἦν ἴασις
2Ch 21:18 in his bowels with an incurable disease. 1
Job 34: 6 I am counted a liar; my wound is incurable 2
Isa 17:11 flee away in a day of grief and incurable pain. 2
Jer 15:18 Why is my pain unceasing, my wound incurable 2
30:12 For thus says the LORD: Your hurt is incurable 2
15 Your pain is incurable. 2
Mic 1: 9 her wound is incurable; and it has come to Judah 2
Jdt 5:12 afflicted . . Egypt with incurable plagues 4
2Mc 9: 5 struck him an incurable and unseen blow 3

indebted 1. ὀφείλω
Lke 11: 4 we ourselves forgive every one who is indebted 1

indecency 1. עֶרְוַת דָּבָר
Deu 24: 1 no favor . . because he has found some indecency 1

indecent 1. עֶרְוָה
Deu 23:14 that he may not see anything indecent among you 1

indecision 1. inconstabilitio
2Es 15:33 and indecision upon their kings. 1

indeed 1. אַךְ 2. אָמְנָה 3. אָמְנָה 4. אָמְנָם 5. אַף 6. גַּם
7. הִנֵּה 8. ἀληθής 9. ἀληθῶς 10. ἀλλά 11. γάρ 12. δέ
13. δή 14. ἰδού 15. καθώς 16. καί 17. καὶ γάρ
18. καίτοι 19. μέν 20. μενοῦνγε 21. ναί 22. ὄντως
23. πλήν 24. ὥσπερ 25. certus 26. quidem
27. quoniam
Gen 18:13 'Shall I indeed bear a child, now that I am old?' 3
23 Wilt thou indeed destroy the righteous 5
20:12 Besides she is indeed my sister 2
22:17 I will indeed bless you †
37: 8 His brothers said to him, "Are you indeed to reign †
8 Or are you indeed to have dominion over us? †
10 mother and your brothers indeed come to bow •
40:15 For I was indeed stolen out of the land †
44:15 know that such a man as I can indeed divine? †
Num 12: 2 Has the LORD indeed spoken only through Moses? 1
21: 2 If thou wilt indeed give this people into my hand †
Deu 2:15 For indeed the hand of the LORD was against them 6
17:15 may indeed set as king over you him whom the LORD †
1Sm 1:11 if thou wilt indeed look on the affliction of thy †
2Sm 15: 8 the LORD will indeed bring me back to Jerusalem †
1Kg 8:27 But will God indeed dwell on the earth? 3
2Kg 14:10 You have indeed smitten Edom †
2Ch 6:18 will God dwell indeed with man on the earth? 3
Job 19: 5 If indeed you magnify yourselves against me 4
Ps 58: 1 Do you indeed decree what is right, you gods? 3
Jer 13:12 Do we not indeed know that every jar will be filled †
22: 4 For if you will indeed obey this word †
Ezk 28: 3 you are indeed wiser than Daniel; 7
Dan 11:18 indeed he shall turn his insolence back upon him. 23
Ams 2:11 Is it not indeed so, O people of Israel? 5
Mal 2: 2 indeed I have already cursed them 6
Mat 12:29 Then indeed he may plunder his house. 16
13:14 With them indeed is fulfilled the prophecy 16
14 You shall indeed hear but never understand †
14 and you shall indeed see but never perceive. †
23 he indeed bears fruit, and yields 13
34 indeed he said nothing to them 16
26:41 the spirit indeed is willing 19
Mrk 3:27 then indeed he may plunder his house. 16
4:12 so that they may indeed see but not perceive †
12 and may indeed hear but not understand †
14:38 the spirit indeed is willing 19
Lke 23:41 we indeed justly 19
24:34 who said, "The Lord has risen indeed 22
Joh 1:47 Behold, an Israelite indeed, in whom is no guile! 9
4:42 we know that this is indeed the Savior 9
6:14 they said, "This is indeed the prophet 9
55 my flesh is food indeed, and my blood is drink 8
55 my blood is drink indeed. 8
8:36 if the Son makes you free, you will be free indeed. 22
16: 2 indeed, the hour is coming 10
32 The hour is coming, indeed it has come 16
Act 17:28 For we are indeed his offspring.' 16
28:26 You shall indeed hear but never understand †
26 you shall indeed see but never perceive. †
Rom 2:25 Circumcision indeed is of value if you obey 19
5:13 sin indeed was in the world before the law 11

8: 7 it does not submit to God's law, indeed it cannot; 11
34 Christ Jesus . . who indeed intercedes for us? 16
9:25 As indeed he says in Hose'a 16
10:18 But I ask, have they not heard? Indeed they have; 20
14:20 Everything is indeed clean 19
15:27 and indeed they are in debt to them *
1Co 8: 5 as indeed there are many "gods" and many "lords"- 24
2Co 3:10 Indeed, in this case, what once had splendor 17
5: 2 Here indeed we groan 17
Gal 3:21 then righteousness would indeed be by the law. 22
Php 1:15 Some indeed preach Christ from envy and rivalry 19
2:27 Indeed he was ill, near to death 17
3: 8 Indeed I count everything as loss 20
4:10 you were indeed concerned for me 16
Col 1: 6 as indeed in the whole world it is bearing fruit 16
2:23 These have indeed an appearance of wisdom 19
3:15 to which indeed you were called in the one body. 16
1Th 4:10 indeed you do love all the brethren 11
1Ti 3:16 Great indeed . . is the mystery of our religion 16
6:19 take hold of the life which is life indeed. 22
2Ti 3:12 Indeed all . . will be persecuted 12
Phm 1:11 now he is indeed useful to you and to me.) *
Heb 6:16 Men indeed swear by a greater than themselves 11
7:28 Indeed, the law appoints men in their weakness 11
9:22 Indeed . . everything is purified with blood 16
12:21 Indeed, so terrifying was the sight 16
3Jn 1: 3 as indeed you do follow the truth. 15
Rev 14:13 Blessed indeed," says the Spirit 21
2Es 3:36 Thou mayest indeed find individual men 26
6:59 If the world has indeed been created for us *
8:38 For indeed I will not concern myself 27
12: 7 if my prayer has indeed come up before thy face 25
Sir 18:17 Indeed, does not a word surpass a good gift? 14
3Mc 1:29 because indeed all at that time preferred death 13
2:11 indeed you are faithful and true. 13
4Mc 7:13 Most amazing, indeed 18
17: 8 Indeed it would be proper 11

indeed *See also* since, unless.

independent 1. χωρίς
1Co 11:11 woman is not independent of man nor man of woman; 1

indestructible 1. ἀκατάλυτος
Heb 7:16 by the power of an indestructible life. 1

indicate 1. δηλόω 2. σημαίνω 3. ὑπαγορεύω 4. ὑπογράφω 5. ὑποδείκνυμι
Act 25:27 not to indicate the charges against him. 2
Heb 9: 8 By this the Holy Spirit indicates 1
12:27 indicates the removal of what is shaken 1
1Pe 1:11 indicated by the Spirit of Christ within them 1
1Es 6:30 as the priests in Jerusalem may indicate 3
AEs 13: 6 those indicated to you in the letters of Haman 2
1Mc 8:25 as the occasion may indicate to them. 4
27 as the occasion may indicate to them. 4
2Mc 11:17 and have asked about the matters indicated therein. 2
3Mc 5:26 indicating that what the king desired was ready 5

indication 1. τεκμήριον
3Mc 3:24 fully convinced by these indications 1

indictment 1. סֵפֶר 2. רִיב
Job 31:35 I had the indictment written by my adversary! 1
Jer 25:31 the LORD has an indictment against the nations; 2
Hos 12: 2 The LORD has an indictment against Judah 2

indignant 1. עצב 2. ἀγανακτέω 3. δυσφορέω 4. πυρόω
Gen 34: 7 the men were indignant and very angry, because he 1
Jer 3: 5 will he be indignant to the end?' *
Mat 20:24 they were indignant at the two brothers. 2
21:15 they were indignant; 2
26: 8 when the disciples saw it, they were indignant 2
Mrk 10:14 he was indignant, and said to them 2
41 they began to be indignant at James and John. 2
Lke 13:14 indignant because Jesus had healed 2
2Co 11:29 Who is made to fall, and I am not indignant? 4
Bel 1:28 they were very indignant 2
2Mc 13:25 The people of Ptolemais were indignant 3

become indignant 1. קצר נֶפֶשׁ
Jdg 10:16 he became indignant over the misery of Israel. 1

indignantly 1. ἀγανακτέω
Mrk 14: 4 there were some who said to themselves indignantly 1

indignantly *See also* protest.

indignation 1. אַף 2. זעם 3. זַעַם 4. זַעַף 5. כַּעַס 6. עֶבְרָה 7. קִנְאָה 8. קֶצֶף 9. ἀγανάκτησις 10. indignatio
Ps 7:11 a God who has indignation every day. 2
38: 3 in my flesh because of thy indignation; 3
69:24 Pour out thy indignation upon them 3
78:49 anger, wrath, indignation, and distress 3
85: 4 put away thy indignation toward us! 5
102:10 because of thy indignation and anger; 3
Isa 10:25 in a . . while my indignation will come to an end 3
13: 5 the LORD and the weapons of his indignation 3
30:27 his lips are full of indignation 3
66:14 and his indignation is against his enemies. 2
Jer 10:10 the nations cannot endure his indignation. 3
15:17 for thou hadst filled me with indignation. 3
32:37 in my anger and my wrath and in great indignation; 8
Lam 2: 6 and in his fierce indignation has spurned king 1
Ezk 21:31 I will pour out my indignation upon you; 3
22:24 or rained upon in the day of indignation. 3
31 I have poured out my indignation upon them; 3
23:25 I will direct my indignation against you 7
Dan 8:19 what . . be at the latter end of the indignation; 3
11:36 prosper till the indignation is accomplished; 3
Mic 7: 9 I will bear the indignation of the LORD 4
Nah 1: 6 Who can stand before his indignation? 3
Hab 3: 8 or thy indignation against the sea 6
Zep 3: 8 to pour out upon them my indignation 3
Zec 1:12 thou hast had indignation these 70 years? 2
2Co 7:11 what indignation, what alarm, what longing 9
2Es 8:23 whose indignation makes the mountains melt 10

hot indignation 1. זַלְעָפָה
Ps 119:53 Hot indignation seizes me because of the wicked 1

indiscriminate *See* eating.

indispensable 1. ἀναγκαῖος
1Co 12:22 which seem to be weaker are indispensable 1

indistinct 1. ἄδηλος
1Co 14: 8 if the bugle gives an indistinct sound 1

individual 1. גֻּלְגֹּלֶת 2. per nomina
1Ch 23:24 names of the individuals from twenty years old 1
2Es 3:36 Thou mayest indeed find individual men 2

individually 1. ἐκ μέρους 2. ἐξ ὀνόματος 3. ἴδιος 4. καθ' εἷς
Rom 12: 5 and individually members one of another. 4
1Co 12:11 who apportions to each one individually 3
27 individually members of it. 1
3Mc 4:14 to be registered individually 2

indolence 1. שִׁפְלוּת יָדַיִם
Ecc 10:18 and through indolence the house leaks. 1

indolent 1. ὀκνηρός
Sir 22: 1 The indolent may be compared to a filthy stone 1
2 The indolent may be compared to . . 1

indomitable 1. ἀδάμαστος
4Mc 15:13 nurture and indomitable suffering by mothers! 1

indoors *See* keep.

induce 1. סות 2. ἄγω
2Ch 18: 2 induced him to go up against Ramoth-gilead. 1
2Mc 4:12 he induced . . the young men to wear the Greek hat. 2

induce to change the mind 1. μετατίθημι
2Mc 4:46 Ptolemy . . induced the king to change his mind. 1

inducement 1. ἐπαγωγός
4Mc 8:15 when they had heard the inducements 1

indulge 1. ἀπέρχομαι ὀπίσω 2. πορεύω
1Co 10: 8 We must not indulge in immorality as some of them *
2Pe 2:10 indulge in the lust of defiling passion 2
Jde 1: 7 acted immorally and indulged in unnatural lust 1

indulgence 1. δίεσις 2. πλησμονή
Col 2:23 in checking the indulgence of the flesh. 2
Wis 12:20 didst punish with such great care and indulgence 1

sinful indulgence 1. intemperantia
2Es 7:114 sinful indulgence has come to an end 1

indulgent 1. συγγνώμη
Sir 0: 2 and to be indulgent in cases where, 1

show too indulgent 1. ἱλαρόω τὸ πρόσωπον
Sir 7:24 show yourself too indulgent with them 1

industrious 1. עשה מְלָאכָה 2. ἐντρεχής
1Kg 11:28 Solomon saw that the young man was industrious 1
Sir 31:22 In all your work be industrious 2

ineffective 1. οὐκ ἀργός
2Pe 1: 8 keep you from being ineffective or unfruitful 1

render ineffective 1. ἐκυρεύω
4Mc 7:14 he rendered the many-headed rack ineffective. 1

inescapable 1. δυσάλητος
Wis 17:17 he was seized, and endured the inescapable fate; 1

inescapably 1. ἀφεύκτως
3Mc 7: 9 in everything and inescapably as an antagonist 1

inexhaustible 1. investigabilis
2Es 9:19 unfailing table and an inexhaustible pasture 1

inexorable 1. ἀπαραίτητος
Wis 16: 4 inexorable want should come 1

inexperienced 1. רַךְ 2. οὐ πειράω
1Ch 22: 5 Solomon my son is young and inexperienced 1
29: 1 Solomon my son . . is young and inexperienced 1
Sir 34:10 He that is inexperienced knows few things 2

utterly inexperienced 1. ἄπειρος
Wis 13:18 a thing that is utterly inexperienced; 1

inexpressible 1. ἀνεκδιήγητος 2. investigabilis
2Co 9:15 Thanks be to God for his inexpressible gift! 1
2Es 6:44 and odors of inexpressible fragrance 2

infamous 1. δυσκλεής
3Mc 3:23 in accordance with their infamous way of life 1

infamous one 1. טְמֵאַת שֵׁם
Ezk 22: 5 will mock you, you infamous one, full of tumult. 1

infant 1. ינק 2. עוּל 3. עוֹלֵל 4. βρέφος 5. θηλάζω 6. νήπιος 7. ὑπομάσθιος 8. infans
1Sm 15: 3 kill both man and woman, infant and suckling, ox 3
Job 3:16 as infants that never see the light? 3
24: 9 and take in pledge the infant of the poor. *
Ps 8: 2 by the mouth of babes and infants 1
Isa 13:16 Their infants will be dashed in pieces 3
65:20 there be in it an infant that lives but a few days 2
Jer 44: 7 to cut off from you man and woman, infant and child 3
Lam 2:11 infants and babes faint in the streets 3
Lke 18:15 Now they were bringing even infants to him 4
Act 7:19 forced our fathers to expose their infants 4
2Es 5:49 For as an infant does not bring forth 8
6:21 Infants a year old shall speak with their voices 8
Jdt 4:12 praying . . not to give up their infants as prey 6
16: 5 dash my infants to the ground 5
Wis 15:14 most foolish, and more miserable than an infant 6
1Mc 1:61 they hung the infants from their mothers' necks. 4
2Mc 5:13 slaughter of virgins and infants. 6
3Mc 3:27 old people or children or even infants 7
6:14 The whole throng of infants and their parents 6
4Mc 4:25 women . . along with their infants 4

infant *See also* slay.

nursing infant 1. ינק שָׁדַיִם
Jol 2:16 gather the children, even nursing infants. 1

infantry 1. ἀνήρ 2. πεζικός 3. πεζός
Jdt 1: 4 his infantry form their ranks- 3
2:22 his infantry, cavalry, and chariots 3
7: 2 their force of men of war was 170,000 infantry 3
20 The whole Assyrian army, their infantry 3
1Mc 3:39 and sent with them 40,000 infantry 1
4: 1 Now Gorgias took 5,000 infantry 1
15:38 gave him troops of infantry and cavalry. 2
16: 5 behold, a large force of infantry and horsemen 2
7 and placed the horsemen in the midst of the infantry 3
2Mc 11: 4 but was elated with his ten thousands of infantry 3
12:20 120,000 infantry and 2,500 cavalry. 3
33 he came out with 3,000 infantry and 400 cavalry. 3
13: 2 Each of them had a Greek force of 110,000 infantry 3
3Mc 1: 1 all his forces, both infantry and cavalry 2

infantry *See also* battle, troop.

infantryman 1. ἀνήρ
1Mc 4:28 he mustered 60,000 picked infantrymen 1

infatuate 1. שגה
Prv 5:19 be infatuated always with her love. 1
20 Why . . be infatuated, my son, with a loose woman 1

infer 1. εἰκάζω
Wis 8: 8 and infers the things to come 1
19:18 inferred from the sight of what took place. 1

inferior 1. נפל 2. אֲרַע (A) 3. ἔλαττον 4. ὑστερέω
Job 12: 3 as well as you; I am not inferior to you. 1
13: 2 What you know, I also know; I am not inferior to you. 1
Dan 2:39 After you shall arise another kingdom inferior 2
2Co 11: 5 inferior to these superlative apostles. 4
12:11 inferior to these superlative apostles 4
Heb 7: 7 the inferior is blessed by the superior. 3

inferior man 1. ἀνάξιος
Sir 25: 8 he who has not served a man inferior to himself; 1

inferior part 1. ὑστερέω
1Co 12:24 giving the greater honor to the inferior part 1

infirmity 1. ἀσθένεια 2. μαλακία 3. infirmitas
Ps 41: 3 thou healest all his infirmities. †
Mat 4:23 healing every disease and every infirmity 2
8:17 He took our infirmities and bore our diseases. 1
9:35 and healing every disease and every infirmity. 2
10: 1 and to heal every disease and every infirmity. 2
Lke 5:15 to be healed of their infirmities. 1
8: 2 been healed of evil spirits and infirmities 1

13:11 had had a spirit of infirmity for eighteen years; 1
12 Woman, you are freed from your infirmity. 1
2Es 4:27 this age is full of sadness and infirmities. 3

inflame 1. דלק 2. חמם 3. περικαίω 4. πυρόω 5. συμφρύγω

Isa 5:11 who tarry late . . till wine inflames them! 1
Jer 51:39 While they are inflamed I will prepare them 2
2Mc 4:38 inflamed with anger 4
4Mc 3:11 tormented and inflamed him 5
16: 3 inflamed as she saw her seven sons tortured 3

inflame still more 1. προσπυρόω

2Mc 14:11 the rest . . quickly inflamed Demetrius still more. 1

inflammation 1. דַּלֶּקֶת

Deu 28:22 smite you with . . inflammation, and fiery heat 1

inflexible 1. ἀμετάθετος

3Mc 5: 1 the king, completely inflexible 1
12 completely frustrated in his inflexible plan. 1

inflict 1. יגה 2. שׂום 3. ἀποδίδωμι 4. διαδίδωμι 5. διατίθημι 6. δίδωμι 7. δοκιμάζω 8. εἰς 9. ἐπιρριπτέω 10. ἐπιφέρω 11. πατάσσω

Deu 7:15 of the evil diseases . . will he inflict upon you 2
Isa 30:26 and heals the wounds inflicted by his blow. •
Lam 1:12 like my sorrow . . which the LORD inflicted 1
Rom 3: 5 That God is unjust to inflict wrath on us? 10
2Th 1: 8 inflicting vengeance upon those 6
AEs 16:18 has speedily inflicted on him the punishment 3
Sir 12: 6 will inflict punishment on the ungodly. 3
48: 8 who anointed kings to inflict retribution 8
1Mc 8: 4 inflicted great disaster upon them 11
2Mc 3:26 inflicting many blows on him. 9
9:28 such as he had inflicted on others 5
3Mc 2: 6 inflicting many and varied punishments 7
27 He proposed to inflict public disgrace 4

inflict cruelty 1. רצץ

2Ch 16:10 Asa inflicted cruelties upon some of the people 1

inflict upon 1. ἐπιτίθημι

Act 16:23 when they had inflicted many blows upon them 1

infliction 1. συμφορά

2Mc 9: 6 with many and strange infliction. 1

influence 1. ἕλκω 2. παρορμάω

4Mc 12: 6 to influence her to persuade the surviving son 2
15:11 though so many factors influenced the mother 1

inform 1. נגד 2. ידע (A) 3. ἀναγγέλλω 4. ἀνακοινόω 5. ἀπαγγέλλω 6. γνωρίζω 7. δηλόω 8. διασαφέω 9. ἐμφανίζω 10. ἐνδείκτης 11. καταμηνύω 12. κατηχέω 13. λέγω 14. μηνύω 15. οἶδα 16. ὑποδείκνυμι 17. doceo

2Sm 15:28 until word comes from you to inform me. 1
Ezr 4:14 therefore we send and inform the king 2
Job 17: 5 He who informs against his friends to get a share 1
Lke 1: 4 the things of which you have been informed. 12
Act 23:22 Tell no one that you have informed me of this. 9
25: 2 informed him against Paul 9
1Co 10:28 out of consideration for the man who informed 14
Jde 1: 5 though you were once for all fully informed 15
1Es 6:12 in order that we might inform you in writing 6
8:22 You are also informed that . . 13
2Es 10:38 and I will inform you 17
Tob 1:19 went and informed the king about me 16
10: 8 they will inform him how things are with you. 7
AEs 12: 2 he informed the king concerning them. 16
Sir 37:14 a man's soul sometimes keeps him better informed 5
Sus 1:50 and inform us, for God has given you that right. 3
2Mc 3: 7 the money about which he had been informed 14
4: 1 who had informed about the money 10
11:18 I have informed the king of everything 8
29 Menelaus has informed us that . . 9
13: 4 when Lysias informed him 16
14:20 the leader had informed the people 4
4Mc 4: 4 to inform him of the rich treasure. 11

information 1. ידע (A)

1Sm 23:23 See . . and come back to me with sure information. •
Ezr 5:10 asked them their names, for your information 1

information *See also* give.

secret information 1. μυστήριον

2Mc 13:21 Rhodocus . . gave secret information to the enemy 1

become infuriated 1. ἐκχολάω

3Mc 3: 1 he became so infuriated 1

ingathering 1. אָסִיף

Exd 23:16 You shall keep the feast of ingathering 1
34:22 the feast of ingathering at the year's end. 1

ingathering *See also* make.

ingenious 1. ποικίλος 2. πολύπλοκος

4Mc 7: 4 besieged with many ingenious war machines 1
15:24 the ingenious and various rackings 2

inhabit 1. ישׁב 2. מוֹשָׁב 3. שׁכן 4. תֵּבֵל 5. κατοικέω 6. οἰκητός 7. habito 8. inhabito

Num 15: 2 When you come into the land you are to inhabit 2
Jdg 1:17 defeated the Canaanites who inhabited Zephath 1
11:21 land of the Amorites, who inhabited that country 1
Job 15:28 in houses which no man should inhabit 1
Ps 109:10 may they be driven out of the ruins they inhabit! •
Prv 2:21 For the upright will inhabit the land 3
8:31 rejoicing in his inhabited world 4
Isa 13:20 It will never be inhabited or dwelt 1
42:11 the villages that Kedar inhabits; 1
44:26 who says of Jerusalem, 'She shall be inhabited,' 1
45:18 not create it a chaos, he formed it to be inhabited 1
57:15 the high and lofty One who inhabits eternity 3
65:21 They shall build houses and inhabit them; 1
22 They shall not build and another inhabit; 1
Jer 17:25 and this city shall be inhabited for ever. 1
46:26 Egypt shall be inhabited as in the days of old 3
50:13 she shall not be inhabited 1
39 nor inhabited for all generations. 3
Ezk 12:20 And the inhabited cities shall be laid waste 1
26:19 waste, like the cities that are not inhabited 1
20 so that you will not be inhabited or have a place 1
35: 9 and your cities shall not be inhabited. 1
36:10 the cities shall be inhabited 1
35 ruined cities are now inhabited and fortified. 1
38:12 assail the waste places which are now inhabited 1
Jol 3:20 But Judah shall be inhabited for ever 1
Ams 9:14 rebuild the ruined cities and inhabit them; 1
Zep 1:13 they build houses, they shall not inhabit them; 1
Zec 2: 4 Jerusalem shall be inhabited as villages 1
7: 7 When Jerusalem was inhabited and in prosperity 1
7 the South and the lowland were inhabited 1
12: 6 Jerusalem shall still be inhabited in its place 1
14:11 it shall be inhabited 1
2Es 3:28 the deeds of those who inhabit Babylon 7
6:24 the earth and those who inhabit it 8
7:74 those who inhabit the world 8
137 the world with those who inhabit it 7
8:20 O Lord who inhabitest eternity 8
50 those who inhabit the world in the last times 8
Jdt 5: 3 What cities do they inhabit? 5
Bar 4:35 for a long time she will be inhabited by demons. 5
2Mc 3: 1 the holy city was inhabited in unbroken peace 5
9:17 would visit every inhabited place 6
12:13 and inhabited by all sorts of Gentiles 5
3Mc 3:15 not rule the nations inhabiting Coele-Syria 5

cause to inhabit 1. ישׁב

Ezk 36:11 I will cause you to be inhabited 1
33 I will cause the cities to be inhabited 1

inhabitant 1. ישׁב 2. שׁכן 3. שָׁכֵן 4. דור (A) 5. ἐγχώριος 6. ἐνοικέω 7. κατοικέω 8. ὁ ἐν 9. inhabitantes

Gen 19:25 overthrew . . all the inhabitants of the cities 1
34:30 odious to the inhabitants of the land 1
36:20 Se'ir the Horite, the inhabitants of the land 1
50:11 When the inhabitants of the land, the Canaanites 1
Exd 15:14 pangs . . on the inhabitants of Philistia. 1
15 all the inhabitants of Canaan have melted away. 1
23:31 for I will deliver the inhabitants of the land 1
34:12 a covenant with the inhabitants of the land 1
15 make a covenant with the inhabitants of the land 1
Lev 18:25 the land vomited out its inhabitants 1
25:10 proclaim liberty . . to all its inhabitants 1
Num 13:32 land . . is a land that devours its inhabitants; 1
14:14 they will tell the inhabitants of this land. 1
32:17 cities because of the inhabitants of the land. 1
33:52 drive out all the inhabitants of the land 1
55 if you do not drive out the inhabitants of the land 1
Deu 13:13 have drawn away the inhabitants of the city 1
15 surely put the inhabitants of that city 1
Jos 2: 9 all the inhabitants of the land melt away 1
24 moreover all the inhabitants of the land are 1
7: 9 Canaanites and all the inhabitants of the land 1
8:24 finished slaughtering all the inhabitants of Ai 1
26 he had . . destroyed all the inhabitants of Ai. 1
9: 3 the inhabitants of Gibeon heard what Joshua had 1
11 elders and all the inhabitants of our country 1
24 and to destroy all the inhabitants of the land 1
10: 1 and how the inhabitants of Gibeon had made peace 1
11:19 except the Hivites, the inhabitants of Gibeon; 1
13: 6 all the inhabitants of the hill country 1
15:15 he went up . . against the inhabitants of Debir; 1
63 But the Jeb'usites, the inhabitants of Jerusalem 1
17: 7 southward to the inhabitants of En-tap'puah. 1
11 and the inhabitants of Dor and its villages 1
11 and the inhabitants of En-dor and its villages 1
11 and the inhabitants of Ta'anach and its villages 1
11 and the inhabitants of Megid'do and its villages; 1
Jdg 1:11 they went against the inhabitants of Debir. 1
19 could not drive out the inhabitants of the plain 1
27 did not drive out the inhabitants of Beth-she'an •
27 not drive out . . or the inhabitants of Dor 1
27 drive out . . or the inhabitants of Ibleam 1
27 drive out . . or the inhabitants of Megid'do 1
30 did not drive out the inhabitants of Kitron 1
30 not drive out . . or the inhabitants of Na'halol; 1
31 Asher did not drive out the inhabitants of Acco 1
31 did not drive out . . or the inhabitants of Sidon 1
32 the Canaanites, the inhabitants of the land; 1
33 not drive out the inhabitants of Beth-she'mesh 1
33 drive out . . or the inhabitants of Beth-anath 1
33 the Canaanites, the inhabitants of the land; 1
33 not drive out the inhabitants of Beth-she'mesh 1
2: 2 no covenant with the inhabitants of this land; 1
5:23 Curse Meroz . . curse bitterly its inhabitants 1
10:18 be head over all the inhabitants of Gilead. 1
11: 8 be our head over all the inhabitants of Gilead. 1
20:15 besides the inhabitants of Gib'e-ah, who mustered 1
21: 9 not one of the inhabitants of Ja'besh-gil'ead 1
10 Go and smite the inhabitants of Ja'besh-gil'ead 1
12 found among the inhabitants of Ja'besh-gil'ead 1
1Sm 6:21 sent . . to the inhabitants of Kir'iath-je'arim 1
23: 5 David delivered the inhabitants of Kei'lah. 1
27: 8 were the inhabitants of the land from of old 1
31:11 when the inhabitants of Ja'besh-gil'ead heard 1
2Sm 5: 6 the Jeb'usites, the inhabitants of the land 1
2Kg 19:26 their inhabitants . . are dismayed 1
22:16 evil upon this place and upon its inhabitants 1
19 against this place, and against its inhabitants 1
23: 2 men of . . and all the inhabitants of Jerusalem 1
1Ch 4:23 the potters and inhabitants of Neta'im 1
40 the former inhabitants there belonged to Ham. 1
8: 6 of fathers' houses of the inhabitants of Geba 1
13 fathers' houses of the inhabitants of Ai'jalon 1
13 who put to flight the inhabitants of Gath 1
11: 4 the Jeb'usites were, the inhabitants of the land. 1
5 The inhabitants of Jebus said to David 1
22:18 he has delivered the inhabitants of the land 1
2Ch 15: 5 afflicted all the inhabitants of the lands. 1
20: 7 O our God, drive out the inhabitants of this land 1
15 Hearken, all Judah and inhabitants of Jerusalem 1
18 all Judah and the inhabitants of Jerusalem fell 1
20 Hear me, Judah and inhabitants of Jerusalem! 1
23 rose against the inhabitants of Mount Se'ir 1
23 they had made an end of the inhabitants of Se'ir 1
21:11 inhabitants of Jerusalem into unfaithfulness 1
13 led Judah and the inhabitants of Jerusalem 1
22: 1 inhabitants of Jerusalem made Ahazi'ah . . king 1
32:22 LORD saved . . the inhabitants of Jerusalem 1
26 both he and the inhabitants of Jerusalem 1
33 all Judah and the inhabitants of Jerusalem did 1
33: 9 Manas'seh seduced . . inhabitants of Jerusalem 1
34: 9 from the inhabitants of Jerusalem. 1
24 I will bring evil upon . . its inhabitants 1
27 words against this place and its inhabitants 1
28 evil . . I will bring upon . . its inhabitants.' 1
30 men of Judah and the inhabitants of Jerusalem 1
32 inhabitants of Jerusalem did according 1
35:18 by Josi'ah . . and the inhabitants of Jerusalem. 1
Ezr 4: 6 against the inhabitants of Judah and Jerusalem. 1
Neh 3:13 Hanun and the inhabitants of Zano'ah repaired 1
7: 3 guards from among the inhabitants of Jerusalem 1
9:24 subdue . . inhabitants of the land 1
Job 26: 5 tremble, the waters and their inhabitants. 2
Ps 33: 8 the inhabitants of the world stand in awe of him! 1
14 looks forth on all the inhabitants of the earth 1
49: 1 Give ear, all inhabitants of the world 1
75: 3 When the earth totters, and all its inhabitants 1
83: 7 Philistia with the inhabitants of Tyre; 1
107:34 because of the wickedness of its inhabitants. 1
Isa 5: 3 now, O inhabitants of Jerusalem and men of Judah 1
9 beautiful houses, without inhabitant. 1
6:11 said: "Until cities lie waste without inhabitant 1
8:14 snare to the inhabitants of Jerusalem. 1
9: 9 E'phraim and the inhabitants of Sama'ria 1
10:31 the inhabitants of Gebim flee for safety. 1
12: 6 Shout, and sing for joy, O inhabitant of Zion 1
18: 3 All you inhabitants of the world, you who dwell 1
20: 6 the inhabitants of this coastland will say 1
21:14 with bread, O inhabitants of the land of Tema. 1
22:21 a father to the inhabitants of Jerusalem 1
23: 2 Be still, O inhabitants of the coast 1
6 to Tarshish, wail, O inhabitants of the coast! 1
24: 1 twist its surface and scatter its inhabitants. 1
5 The earth lies polluted under its inhabitants; 1
6 and its inhabitants suffer for their guilt; 1
6 the inhabitants of the earth are scorched 1
17 the snare are upon you, O inhabitant of the earth! 1
26: 5 he has brought low the inhabitants of the height 1
9 the inhabitants of the world learn 1
18 and the inhabitants of the world have not fallen. 1
21 to punish the inhabitants of the earth 1
33:24 no inhabitant will say, "I am sick"; 3
37:27 while their inhabitants, shorn of strength 1
38:11 man no more among the inhabitants of the world. 1
40:22 and its inhabitants are like grasshoppers; 1
42:10 the coastlands and their inhabitants. 1
11 let the inhabitants of Sela sing for joy 1
49:19 you will be too narrow for your inhabitants 1
Jer 1:14 upon all the inhabitants of the land. 1

2:15 his cities are in ruins, without inhabitant. 1
4: 3 says . . to the inhabitants of Jerusalem •
4 O men of Judah and inhabitants of Jerusalem; 1
7 your cities will be ruins without inhabitant. 1
6:12 my hand against the inhabitants of the land 1
8: 1 and the bones of the inhabitants of Jerusalem 1
9:11 Judah a desolation, without inhabitant. 1
10:18 I am slinging out the inhabitants of the land 1
11: 2 men of Judah and the inhabitants of Jerusalem. 1
9 men of Judah and the inhabitants of Jerusalem. 1
12 and the inhabitants of Jerusalem will go and cry 1
13:13 will fill with drunkenness all the inhabitants 1
13 prophets, and all the inhabitants of Jerusalem. 1
17:20 all Judah, and all the inhabitants of Jerusalem 1
25 men of Judah and the inhabitants of Jerusalem; 1
18:11 men of Judah and the inhabitants of Jerusalem 1
19: 3 O kings of Judah and inhabitants of Jerusalem. 1
12 this place, says the LORD, and to its inhabitants 1
21: 6 I will smite the inhabitants of this city 1
13 I am against you, O inhabitant of the valley 1
22:23 O inhabitant of Lebanon, nested among the cedars 1
23:14 Sodom to me, and its inhabitants like Gomor'rah. 1
25: 2 Judah and all the inhabitants of Jerusalem 1
9 bring . . against this land and its inhabitants 1
29 sword against all the inhabitants of the earth 1
30 against all the inhabitants of the earth. 1
26: 9 this city shall be desolate, without inhabitant'? 1
15 blood . . upon this city and its inhabitants 1
32:32 men of Judah and the inhabitants of Jerusalem. 1
33:10 desolate, without man or inhabitant or beast 1
34:22 Judah a desolation without inhabitant. 1
35:13 men of Judah and the inhabitants of Jerusalem 1
17 on Judah and all the inhabitants of Jerusalem 1
36:31 upon them, and upon the inhabitants of Jerusalem 1
42:18 were poured out on the inhabitants of Jerusalem 1
44:22 and a waste and a curse, without inhabitant 1
46: 8 I will destroy cities and their inhabitants. 1
19 baggage for exile, O inhabitants of Egypt! 1
19 become a waste, a ruin, without inhabitant. 1
47: 2 and every inhabitant of the land shall wail. 1
48: 9 become a desolation, with no inhabitant in them. 1
18 sit on the parched ground, O inhabitant of Dibon! 1
19 Stand by the way and watch, O inhabitant of Aro'er! 1
28 dwell in the rock, O inhabitants of Moab! 1
43 pit, and snare are before you, O inhabitant of Moab! 1
49: 8 dwell in the depths, O inhabitants of Dedan! 1
20 purposes . . against the inhabitants of Teman 1
30 dwell in the depths, O inhabitants of Hazor! 1
50:21 Go up . . against the inhabitants of Pekod. 1
34 but unrest to the inhabitants of Babylon. 1
35 A sword . . upon the inhabitants of Babylon 1
51: 1 against the inhabitants of Chalde'a 1
12 spoke concerning the inhabitants of Babylon. 1
24 Babylon and all the inhabitants of Chalde'a 1
29 Babylon a desolation, without inhabitant. 1
35 be upon Babylon," let the inhabitant of Zion say. 1
35 My blood be upon the inhabitants of Chalde'a 1
37 a horror and a hissing, without inhabitant. 1
Lam 4:12 kings . . or any of the inhabitants of the world 1
Ezk 7: 7 Your doom has come to you, O inhabitant of the land; 1
11:15 of whom the inhabitants of Jerusalem have said 1
12:19 concerning the inhabitants of Jerusalem 1
15: 6 so will I give up the inhabitants of Jerusalem. 1
26:17 and your inhabitants, who imposed your terror 1
27: 8 inhabitants of Sidon and Arvad were your rowers; 1
35 the inhabitants of the coastlands are appalled 1
29: 6 Then all the inhabitants of Egypt shall know 1
33:24 Son of man, the inhabitants of these waste places 1
Dan 4:35 inhabitants of the earth are accounted 4
35 heaven and among the inhabitants of the earth; 4
9: 7 men of Judah, to the inhabitants of Jerusalem 1
Hos 4: 1 a controversy with the inhabitants of the land. 1
10: 5 The inhabitants of Sama'ria tremble 3
Jol 1: 2 give ear, all inhabitants of the land! 1
14 the elders and all the inhabitants of the land 1
2: 1 Let all the inhabitants of the land tremble 1
Ams 1: 5 cut off the inhabitants from the Valley of Aven 1
8 I will cut off the inhabitants from Ashdod 1
Mic 1:11 Pass on your way, inhabitants of Shaphir 1
11 the inhabitants of Za'anan do not come forth; 1
12 For the inhabitants of Maroth wait anxiously 1
13 Harness the steeds . . inhabitants of Lachish; 1
15 a conqueror upon you, inhabitants of Mare'shah; 1
6:12 your inhabitants speak lies 1
16 you a desolation, and your inhabitants a hissing; 1
7:13 will be desolate because of its inhabitants 1
Zep 1: 4 and against all the inhabitants of Jerusalem; 1
11 Wail, O inhabitants of the Mortar! 1
18 sudden end . . of all the inhabitants of the earth. 1
2: 5 Woe to you inhabitants of the seacoast 1
5 and I will destroy you till no inhabitant is left. 1
3: 6 desolate, without a man, without an inhabitant. 1
Zec 8:20 yet come, even the inhabitants of many cities; 1
21 the inhabitants of one city shall go to another 1
11: 6 For I will no longer have pity on the inhabitants 1
12: 5 The inhabitants of Jerusalem have strength 1
7 the glory of the inhabitants of Jerusalem may 1
8 the LORD will put a shield about the inhabitants 1
10 of David and the inhabitants of Jerusalem 1
13: 1 house of David and the inhabitants of Jerusalem 1
Act 1:19 known to all the inhabitants of Jerusalem 7
4:16 is manifest to all the inhabitants of Jerusalem 7
Rev 13:12 and makes the earth and its inhabitants worship 7
2Es 3: 9 the flood upon the inhabitants of the world 9
25 the inhabitants of the city transgressed 9
34 those of the inhabitants of the world 9
35 have the inhabitants of the earth not sinned 9
6:18 I draw near to visit the inhabitants of the earth 9
26 the heart of the earth's inhabitants 9
11:32 dominated its inhabitants 9
34 also ruled over the earth and its inhabitants. 9
12:24 its inhabitants more oppressively than all 9
14:17 evils be multiplied among its inhabitants. 9
20 and its inhabitants are without light. 9
15:40 to destroy all the earth and its inhabitants 9
Jdt 1:12 also all the inhabitants of the land of Moab 7
3: 4 Our cities also and their inhabitants 7
5:15 destroyed all the inhabitants of Heshbon †
7:20 belonging to every inhabitant of Bethulia 7
Sir 10: 2 so are all its inhabitants. 7
Bar 1:15 to the inhabitants of Jerusalem 7
2:23 land will be a desolation without inhabitants. 6
1Mc 1:28 Even the land shook for its inhabitants 7
6:12 I sent to destroy the inhabitants of Judah 7
11:18 killed by the inhabitants of the strongholds. 8
2Mc 9: 2 Anticchus was put to flight by the inhabitants 5

inhabited place 1. מוֹשָׁב
Ezk 34:13 in all the inhabited places of the country. 1

inherit 1. אֲחֻזָּה 2. היה אֶל 3. ירשׁ 4. נחל 5. נַחֲלָה
6. *κληρονομέω* 7. *κληρονομία* 8. *κληρονόμος*
9. heredito 10. possido
Exd 32:13 this land . . and they shall inherit it for ever.' 4
Lev 20:24 I have said to you, 'You shall inherit their land 3
25:46 your sons . . to inherit as a possession for ever 3
27:28 no devoted thing . . of his inherited field 1
Num26:55 according to the names . . they shall inherit. 4
32:18 Israel have inherited each his inheritance. 4
19 we will not inherit with them on the other side 4
33:54 You shall inherit the land by lot according 4
54 according to the tribes . . you shall inherit. 4
34:13 This is the land which you shall inherit by lot 4
35: 8 in proportion to the inheritance which it inherits 4
Deu 16:20 live and inherit the land which the LORD . . gives 3
Jdg 11: 2 You shall not inherit in our father's house; 4
2Kg 2: 9 let me inherit a double share of your spirit. 2
Ps 69:36 the children of his servants shall inherit it 4
Prv 3:35 wise will inherit honor, but fools get disgrace. 4
11:29 He who troubles his household will inherit wind 4
19:14 House and wealth are inherited from fathers 5
Isa 57:13 the land, and shall inherit my holy mountain. 3
65: 9 my chosen shall inherit it, 3
Jer 16:19 Our fathers have inherited nought but lies 4
Zec 2:12 the LORD will inherit Judah as his portion 4
Mat 5: 5 the meek, for they shall inherit the earth. 6
19:29 and inherit eternal life. 6
25:34 inherit the kingdom prepared for you 6
Mrk 10:17 what must I do to inherit eternal life? 6
Lke 10:25 Teacher, what shall I do to inherit eternal life? 6
18:18 what shall I do to inherit eternal life? 6
Rom 4:13 promise . . that they should inherit the world 8
1Co 6: 9 unrighteous will not inherit the kingdom of God? 6
10 inherit the kingdom of God. 6
15:50 flesh and blood cannot inherit the kingdom 6
50 the perishable inherit the imperishable. 6
Gal 4:30 the son of the slave shall not inherit 6
5:21 shall not inherit the kingdom of God. 6
Heb 6:12 imitators of those who . . inherit the promises. 6
12:17 when he desired to inherit the blessing 6
2Es 7:17 that the righteous shall inherit these things 9
96 and shall inherit what is to come 10
Tob 4:12 their posterity will inherit the land. 6
14:13 He inherited their property 6
Jdt 4:12 the cities they had inherited to be destroyed 7
Sir 10:11 he will inherit creeping things, and wild beasts 6
19: 3 Decay and worms will inherit him 6
37:26 will inherit confidence 6
1Mc 2:10 What nation has not inherited her palaces 6
57 inherited the throne of the kingdom for ever. 6

inherit *See also* give.

cause to inherit 1. נחל 2. *κατακληρονομέω*
Deu 1:38 for he shall cause Israel to inherit it. 1
Jos 1: 6 you shall cause this people to inherit the land 1
Sir 44:21 cause them to inherit from sea to sea 2

inherit from father 1. *πατροπαράδοτος*
1Pe 1:18 futile ways inherited from your fathers 1

make inherit 1. ירשׁ 2. נחל
1Sm 2: 8 to make them sit . . and inherit a seat of honor. 2
Job 13:26 and makest me inherit the iniquities of my youth. 1

inheritance 1. אֲחֻזָּה 2. יְרֻשָּׁה 3. נחל 4. נַחֲלָה
5. נַחֲלָה 6. *κληρονομέω* 7. *κληρονομία* 8. *κλῆρος*
9. *μερίς* 10. hereditas

Gen 31:14 Is there any portion or inheritance left to us 5
48: 6 name of their brothers in their inheritance. 5
Lev 27:16 part of the land which is his by inheritance 1
22 is not a part of his possession by inheritance 1
Num16:14 nor given us inheritance of fields 5
18:20 You shall have no inheritance in their land 3
20 I am your portion and your inheritance 5
21 given every tithe in Israel for an inheritance 5
23 they shall have no inheritance. 5
24 I have given to the Levites for an inheritance; 5
24 have no inheritance among the people of Israel. 5
26 take . . the tithe . . for your inheritance 5
26:53 land shall be divided for inheritance 5
54 a large tribe you shall give a large inheritance 5
54 small tribe you shall give a small inheritance; 5
54 every tribe shall be given its inheritance 5
56 Their inheritance shall be divided 5
62 because there was no inheritance given to them 5
27: 7 give them possession of an inheritance 5
7 cause the inheritance of their father to pass 5
8 cause his inheritance to pass to his daughter. 5
9 then . . give his inheritance to his brothers. 5
10 give his inheritance to his father's brothers. 5
11 then . . give his inheritance to his kinsman 5
32:18 Israel have inherited each his inheritance. 5
19 our inheritance has come to us on this side 5
32 possession of our inheritance shall remain 5
33:54 a large tribe you shall give a large inheritance 5
54 small tribe you shall give a small inheritance; 5
34: 2 fall to you for an inheritance, the land of Canaan 5
14 have received their inheritance 5
15 received their inheritance beyond the Jordan 5
35: 2 from the inheritance of their possession 5
8 in proportion to the inheritance which it inherits 5
36: 2 my lord to give the land for inheritance by lot 5
2 give the inheritance of Zeloph'ehad our brother 5
3 inheritance will be taken from the inheritance 5
3 taken from the inheritance of our fathers 5
3 added to the inheritance of the tribe 5
3 be taken away from the lot of our inheritance. 5
4 inheritance will be added to the inheritance 5
4 added to the inheritance of the tribe 5
4 their inheritance will be taken 5
4 taken from the inheritance of . . our fathers. 5
7 inheritance . . shall not be transferred 5
7 every one . . shall cleave to the inheritance 5
8 every daughter who possesses an inheritance 5
8 may possess the inheritance of his fathers. 5
9 no inheritance shall be transferred from one 5
9 tribe . . shall cleave to its own inheritance.' 5
12 their inheritance remained in the tribe 5
Deu 4:21 land which the LORD . . gives you for an inheritance. 5
38 to give you their land for an inheritance 5
10: 9 no portion or inheritance with his brothers; 5
9 LORD is his inheritance, as the LORD your God said 5
12: 9 not as yet come to the rest and to the inheritance 5
12 since he has no portion or inheritance with you. 5
14:27 Levite . . has no portion or inheritance with you. 5
29 Levite, because he has no portion or inheritance 5
15: 4 gives you for an inheritance to possess) 5
18: 1 Levi . . no portion or inheritance with Israel; 5
2 no inheritance among their brethren; the LORD 5
2 LORD is their inheritance, as he promised them. 5
19:10 land . . LORD . . gives you for an inheritance 5
14 inheritance which you will hold in the land 5
20:16 cities . . LORD . . gives you for an inheritance 5
21:23 land . . your God gives you for an inheritance. 5
24: 4 land . . LORD your God gives you for an inheritance. 5
25:19 LORD . . gives you for an inheritance to possess 5
26: 1 land . . LORD your God gives you for an inheritance 5
29: 8 gave it for an inheritance to the Reubenites 5
Jos 11:23 and Joshua gave it for an inheritance to Israel 5
13: 6 only allot the land to Israel for an inheritance 5
7 Now . . divide this land for an inheritance 5
8 and the Gadites received their inheritance 5
14 To the tribe of Levi . . Moses gave no inheritance; 5
14 the offerings by fire . . are their inheritance •
15 Moses gave an inheritance to the . . Reubenites •
23 This was the inheritance of the Reubenites 5
24 Moses gave an inheritance also to the . . Gadites •
28 This is the inheritance of the Gadites 5
29 Moses gave an inheritance to . . Manas'seh; •
32 These are the inheritances which Moses •
33 to the tribe of Levi Moses gave no inheritance; 5
33 the LORD God of Israel is their inheritance 5
14: 1 these are the inheritances . . Israel received •
2 Their inheritance was by lot 5
3 Moses had given an inheritance to the . . tribes 5
3 but to the Levites he gave no inheritance 5
9 the land . . shall be an inheritance for you 5
13 he gave Hebron to Caleb . . for an inheritance. 5
14 Hebron became the inheritance of Caleb 5
15:20 This is the inheritance of the tribe of . . Judah 5
16: 5 the boundary of their inheritance on the east was 5
8 the inheritance of the tribe of the E'phraimites 5
9 within the inheritance of the Manas'sites 5
17: 4 LORD commanded Moses to give us an inheritance 5
4 he gave them an inheritance among the brethren 5
6 daughters of Manas'seh received an inheritance 5

14 but one lot and one portion as an inheritance 5
18: 2 whose inheritance had not yet been apportioned. 5
4 writing . . it with a view to their inheritances 5
7 Manas'seh have received their inheritance 5
20 This is the inheritance of the tribe of Benjamin 5
28 This is the inheritance of the tribe of Benjamin 5
19: 1 and its inheritance was in the midst 5
1 in the midst of the inheritance of the tribe 5
2 it had for its inheritance Beer-sheba, Sheba 5
8 This was the inheritance of the tribe of Simeon 5
9 The inheritance of . . Simeon formed part 5
9 inheritance in the midst of their inheritance. 5
10 the territory of its inheritance reached as far 5
16 This is the inheritance of the tribe of Zeb'ulun 5
23 This is the inheritance of the tribe of Is'sachar 5
31 This is the inheritance of the tribe of Asher 5
39 This is the inheritance of the tribe of Naph'tali 5
41 territory of its inheritance included Zorah 5
48 This is the inheritance of the tribe of Dan 5
49 Israel gave an inheritance . . to Joshua the son 5
51 These are the inheritances . . distributed 5
21: 3 cities and pasture . . out of their inheritance. 5
23: 4 Behold, I have allotted to you as an inheritance 5
24:28 sent the people . . every man to his inheritance. 5
30 And they buried him in his own inheritance 5
32 it became an inheritance of the descendants 5
Jdg 2: 6 went each to his inheritance to take possession 5
9 the bounds of his inheritance in Tim'nath-he'res 5
18: 1 Danites was seeking . . an inheritance to dwell 5
1 until then no inheritance . . had fallen to them. 5
20: 6 all the country of the inheritance of Israel; 5
21:17 There must be an inheritance for the survivors 2
23 they went and returned to their inheritance 5
24 they went out . . every man to his inheritance. 5
Rut 4: 5 restore the name of the dead to his inheritance. 5
6 I cannot . . lest I impair my own inheritance. 5
10 to perpetuate the . . dead in his inheritance 5
2Sm 20: 1 and we have no inheritance in the son of Jesse; 5
1Kg 8:36 thou hast given to thy people as an inheritance. 5
12:16 We have no inheritance in the son of Jesse. 5
21: 3 I should give you the inheritance of my fathers. 5
4 will not give you the inheritance of my fathers. 5
1Ch 16:18 Canaan, as your portion for an inheritance. 5
2Ch 6:27 land . . given to thy people as an inheritance. 5
10:16 We have no inheritance in the son of Jesse. 5
Ezr 9:12 leave it for an inheritance to your children •
Neh 11:20 towns of Judah, every one in his inheritance. 5
Job 42:15 their father gave them inheritance 5
Ps 78:71 of Jacob his people, of Israel his inheritance. 5
79: 1 O God, the heathen have come into thy inheritance; 5
105:11 Canaan as your portion for an inheritance. 5
Prv 17: 2 share the inheritance as one of the brothers. 5
20:21 An inheritance gotten hastily in the beginning 5
28:10 blameless will have a goodly inheritance. 3
Ecc 7:11 Wisdom is good with an inheritance, an advantage 5
Jer 10:16 and Israel is the tribe of his inheritance; 5
16:18 filled my inheritance with . . abominations. 5
51:19 and Israel is the tribe of his inheritance; 5
Lam 5: 2 Our inheritance . . turned over to strangers 5
Ezk 35:15 As you rejoiced over the inheritance 5
36:12 you shall be their inheritance 5
44:28 They shall have no inheritance; 5
28 have no inheritance; I am their inheritance: 5
46:16 a gift to any of his sons out of his inheritance 5
16 to his sons, it is their property by inheritance. 5
17 out of his inheritance to one of his servants 5
17 his sons may keep a gift from his inheritance. 5
18 The prince shall not take any of the inheritance 5
47:14 this land shall fall to you as your inheritance. 5
22 You shall allot it as an inheritance 5
22 with you they shall be allotted an inheritance 5
23 there you shall assign him his inheritance 5
48:29 the land which you shall allot as an inheritance 5
Mic 2: 2 they oppress . . a man and his inheritance. 5
7:14 Shepherd . . the flock of thy inheritance 5
18 pardoning . . for the remnant of his inheritance? 5
Mat 21:38 let us kill him and have his inheritance.' 7
Mrk 12: 7 the inheritance will be ours.' 7
Lke 12:13 bid my brother divide the inheritance with me. 7
20:14 that the inheritance may be ours.' 7
Act 7: 5 yet he gave him no inheritance in it 7
20:32 give you the inheritance 7
Gal 3:18 For if the inheritance is by the law 7
Eph 1:14 which is the guarantee of our inheritance 7
18 what are the riches of his glorious inheritance 7
5: 5 has any inheritance in the kingdom of Christ 7
Col 1:12 the inheritance of the saints in light. 8
3:24 you will receive the inheritance as your reward; 7
Heb 9:15 may receive the promised eternal inheritance 7
11: 8 a place which he was to receive as an inheritance; 7
1Pe 1: 4 to an inheritance which is imperishable 7
2Es 6:59 why do we not possess our world as an inheritance? 10
7: 9 is given to a man for an inheritance 10
9 how will the heir receive his inheritance 10
8:16 about thy inheritance, for whom I lament 10
45 and have mercy on thy inheritance 10
Tob 6:11 you are entitled to her and to her inheritance 7
12 because you . . are entitled to the inheritance. 7
Jdt 8:22 the desolation of our inheritance 7
9:12 God of my father, God of the inheritance of Israel 7
13: 5 For now is the time to help thy inheritance 7
16:21 every one returned home to his own inheritance 7
AEs 10:12 God . . vindicated his inheritance. 7
13:15 the inheritance that has been thine 7
17 have mercy upon thy inheritance 8
14: 5 for an everlasting inheritance 7
9 to destroy thy inheritance 7
Sir 9: 6 lest you lose your inheritance. 7
22:23 that you may share with him in his inheritance. 7
23:12 may it never be found in the inheritance of Jacob! 7
24:12 the Lord, who is their inheritance. 7
20 and my inheritance sweeter than the honeycomb. 7
23 an inheritance for the congregations of Jacob. 7
33:23 distribute your inheritance. 7
41: 6 The inheritance of the children of sinners 7
42: 3 of dividing the inheritance of friends; 7
44:11 their inheritance to their children's children. 4
23 gave him his inheritance 4
45:22 in the land of the people he has no inheritance 6
22 Lord himself is his portion and inheritance. 7
46: 8 to bring them into their inheritance 7
9 his children obtained it for an inheritance; 7
1Mc 2:56 Caleb . . received an inheritance in the land. 7
6:24 they have seized our inheritances. 7
15:33 but only the inheritance of our fathers 7
34 we are firmly holding the inheritance of our fathers. 7
2Mc 2: 4 had seen the inheritance of God. 7
17 has returned the inheritance to all 7
4Mc 18: 3 deemed worthy to share in a divine inheritance. 9

inheritance *See also* assign, distribute, divide, give, leave, obtain, possession, receive, take.

inheritor 1. ירשׁ

Isa 65: 9 and from Judah inheritors of my mountains; 1

inhuman 1. *ἄστοργος*

2Ti 3: 3 inhuman, implacable, slanderers, profligates 1

inimitable 1. inimitabilis

2Es 6:44 and flowers of inimitable color 1

iniquitous 1. אָוֶן

Isa 10: 1 Woe to those who decree iniquitous decrees 1

iniquity 1. אָוֶן 2. עָוֶל 3. עַוְלָה 4. עָוֹן 5. פֶּשַׁע 6. רֶשַׁע 7. עֲוָיָה (A) 8. *ἀδίκημα* 9. *ἀδικία* 10. *ἄδικος* 11. *ἀνομία* 12. *κακία* 13. iniquitas 14. iniuste 15. iniustitia

Gen 15:16 for the iniquity of the Amorites is not yet 4
Exd 20: 5 visiting the iniquity of the fathers upon 4
34: 7 forgiving iniquity and transgression and sin 5
7 visiting the iniquity of the fathers upon 4
9 and pardon our iniquity and our sin 4
Lev 5: 1 yet does not speak, he shall bear his iniquity 4
17 he is guilty and shall bear his iniquity 4
7:18 he who eats of it shall bear his iniquity 4
10:17 you may bear the iniquity of the congregation 4
16:21 all the iniquities of the people of Israel 4
22 The goat shall bear all their iniquities 4
17:16 he shall bear his iniquity 4
18:25 became defiled, so that I punished its iniquity 4
19: 8 every one who eats it shall bear his iniquity 4
20:17 he shall bear his iniquity 4
19 they shall bear their iniquity 4
22:16 so cause them to bear iniquity and guilt 4
26:39 pine away . . because of their iniquity 4
39 also because of the iniquities of their fathers 4
40 if they confess their iniquity 4
40 they confess . . the iniquity of their fathers 4
41 if . . they make amends for their iniquity 4
43 they shall make amends for their iniquity 4
Num 5:15 bringing iniquity to remembrance. 4
31 The man shall be free from iniquity, but the woman 4
31 but the woman shall bear her iniquity. 4
14:18 forgiving iniquity and transgression 4
18 visiting the iniquity of fathers upon children 4
19 Pardon the iniquity of this people, I pray thee 4
34 you shall bear your iniquity, 40 years 4
15:31 utterly cut off; his iniquity shall be upon him. 4
18: 1 bear iniquity in connection with the sanctuary; 4
1 shall bear iniquity in connection 4
23 Levites . . shall bear their iniquity; 4
30:15 then he shall bear her iniquity. 4
Deu 5: 9 visiting the iniquity of the fathers 4
32: 4 God of faithfulness and without iniquity, just 2
Jos 22:20 And he did not perish alone for his iniquity. 4
1Sm 3:13 punish . . for ever, for the iniquity which he knew 4
14 the iniquity of Eli's house shall not be expiated 4
15:23 and stubbornness is as iniquity and idolatry. 1
2Sm 24:10 I pray thee, take away the iniquity of thy servant; 4
1Ch 21: 8 I pray thee, take away the iniquity of thy servant; 4
Ezr 9: 6 our iniquities have risen higher than our heads 4
7 for our iniquities we, our kings, and our priests 4
13 punished us less than our iniquities deserved 4
Neh 9: 2 confessed . . the iniquities of their fathers. 4
Job 4: 8 who plow iniquity and sow trouble reap the same. 1
7:21 thou not pardon . . and take away my iniquity? 4
10: 6 that thou dost seek out my iniquity 4
14 mark me, and dost not acquit me of my iniquity. 4
11:11 when he sees iniquity, will he not consider it? 1
14 If iniquity is in your hand, put it far away 1
13:23 How many are my iniquities and my sins? 4
26 and makest me inherit the iniquities of my youth. 4
14:17 thou wouldest cover over my iniquity. 4
15: 5 For your iniquity teaches your mouth 4
16 corrupt, a man who drinks iniquity like water! 3
20:27 The heavens will reveal his iniquity 4
21:19 God stores up their iniquity for their sons.' 1
22: 5 There is no end to your iniquities. 4
31: 3 and disaster the workers of iniquity? 1
11 would be an iniquity to be punished by the judges; 4
28 this also would be an iniquity to be punished 4
33 from men, by hiding my iniquity in my bosom 4
33: 9 I am pure, and there is no iniquity in me. 4
34:32 if I have done iniquity, I will do it no more 2
36:10 commands that they return from iniquity. 1
21 Take heed, do not turn to iniquity 1
33 who is jealous with anger against iniquity. 3
Ps 10: 7 under his tongue are mischief and iniquity. 1
32: 2 the man to whom the LORD imputes no iniquity 4
5 not hide my iniquity; I said, "I will confess 4
36: 2 that his iniquity cannot be found out and hated. 4
38: 4 For my iniquities have gone over my head; 4
18 I confess my iniquity, I am sorry for my sin. 4
40:12 iniquities have overtaken me, till I cannot see; 4
49: 5 the iniquity of my persecutors surrounds me 4
51: 2 Wash me thoroughly from my iniquity 4
5 Behold, I was brought forth in iniquity, and in sin 4
9 from my sins, and blot out all my iniquities. 4
53: 1 They are corrupt, doing abominable iniquity; 2
66:18 If I had cherished iniquity in my heart 1
78:38 he, being compassionate, forgave their iniquity 4
79: 8 against us the iniquities of our forefathers; 4
85: 2 Thou didst forgive the iniquity of thy people; 4
89:32 I will punish . . their iniquity with scourges; 4
90: 8 Thou hast set our iniquities before thee 4
94:23 He will bring back on them their iniquity 1
103: 3 who forgives all your iniquity, who heals 4
10 nor requite us according to our iniquities. 4
106:43 were brought low through their iniquity. 4
107:17 because of their iniquities suffered 4
109:14 May the iniquity of his fathers be remembered 4
119:133 let no iniquity get dominion over me. 1
130: 3 LORD . . mark iniquities, Lord, who could stand? 4
8 he will redeem Israel from all his iniquities. 4
141: 4 wicked . . in company with men who work iniquity; 1
Prv 5:22 The iniquities of the wicked ensnare him 4
16: 6 By loyalty and faithfulness iniquity is atoned 4
19:28 mouth of the wicked devours iniquity. 1
Isa 1: 4 Ah, sinful nation, a people laden with iniquity 4
13 I cannot endure iniquity and solemn assembly. 1
5:18 those who draw iniquity with cords of falsehood 4
13:11 I will punish . . the wicked for their iniquity; 4
22:14 Surely this iniquity will not be forgiven you 4
26:21 to punish . . the earth for their iniquity 4
30:13 this iniquity shall be to you like a break 4
31: 2 against the helpers of those who work iniquity. 1
32: 6 speaks folly, and his mind plots iniquity 1
33:24 the people . . will be forgiven their iniquity. 4
40: 2 warfare is ended, that her iniquity is pardoned 4
43:24 you have wearied me with your iniquities. 4
50: 1 Behold, for your iniquities you were sold 4
53: 5 he was bruised for our iniquities; 4
6 the LORD has laid on him the iniquity of us all. 4
11 and he shall bear their iniquities. 4
57:17 Because of the iniquity of his covetousness 4
59: 2 but your iniquities have made a separation 4
3 with blood and your fingers with iniquity; 4
4 conceive mischief and bring forth iniquity. 1
6 Their works are works of iniquity 1
7 their thoughts are thoughts of iniquity 1
12 and we know our iniquities 4
64: 6 and our iniquities, like the wind, take us away. 4
7 delivered us into the hand of our iniquities. 4
9 O LORD, and remember not iniquity for ever. 4
65: 7 their iniquities and their fathers' iniquities 4
7 their iniquities and their fathers' iniquities 4
Jer 5:25 Your iniquities have turned these away 4
11:10 back to the iniquities of their forefathers 4
13:22 it is for the greatness of your iniquity 4
14: 7 Though our iniquities testify against us 4
10 now he will remember their iniquity and punish 4
20 We acknowledge . . the iniquity of our fathers 4
16:10 What is our iniquity? What is the sin 4
17 nor is their iniquity concealed from my eyes. 4
18 And I will doubly recompense their iniquity 4
18:23 Forgive not their iniquity 4
25:12 punish . . for their iniquity, says the LORD 4
31:34 for I will forgive their iniquity 4
36: 3 that I may forgive their iniquity and their sin. 4
31 I will punish . . his servants for their iniquity; 4
50:20 says the LORD, iniquity shall be sought in Israel 4
Lam 2:14 exposed your iniquity to restore your fortunes 4
4:13 the sins . . and the iniquities of her priests 4
22 your iniquity, O daughter of Edom, he will punish 4
5: 7 fathers sinned . . and we bear their iniquities. 4
Ezk 3:18 that wicked man shall die in his iniquity; 4

19 from his wicked way, he shall die in his iniquity; 4
20 from his righteousness and commits iniquity 2
7:13 and because of his iniquity, none can maintain 4
16 all of them moaning, every one over his iniquity. 4
19 it was the stumbling block of their iniquity. 4
11: 2 these are the men who devise iniquity 1
14: 3 and set the stumbling block of their iniquity 4
4 and sets the stumbling block of his iniquity 4
7 stumbling block of his iniquity before his face 4
18: 8 withholds his hand from iniquity 2
17 withholds his hand from iniquity 9
17 he shall not die for his father's iniquity; 4
18 behold, he shall die for his iniquity. 4
19 the son suffer for the iniquity of the father? 4
20 shall not suffer for the iniquity of the father 4
20 nor the father suffer for the iniquity of the son; 4
24 and commits iniquity and does the same 2
26 When a righteous man . . commits iniquity 2
26 for the iniquity which he has committed 2
30 Repent and turn . . lest iniquity be your ruin. 4
24:23 you shall pine away in your iniquities and groan 4
28:15 blameless . . till iniquity was found in you. 3
18 By the multitude of your iniquities 4
29:16 the house of Israel, recalling their iniquity 4
33: 6 that man is taken away in his iniquity 4
8 that wicked man shall die in his iniquity 4
9 he shall die in his iniquity 4
13 in his righteousness and commits iniquity 2
13 in the iniquity that he has committed he shall 2
15 in the statutes of life, committing no iniquity; 2
18 and commits iniquity, he shall die for it. 2
36:31 you will loathe yourselves for your iniquities 4
33 I cleanse you from all your iniquities 4
39:23 Israel went into captivity for their iniquity 4
43:10 that they may be ashamed of their iniquities. 4
44:12 and became a stumbling block of iniquity 4
Dan 4:27 break off . . your iniquities by showing mercy 7
9:13 turning from our iniquities and giving heed 4
16 sins, and for the iniquities of our fathers 4
24 atone for iniquity, to bring in everlasting 4
Hos 4: 8 they are greedy for their iniquity. 4
8:13 Now he will remember their iniquity 4
9: 7 because of your great iniquity 4
9 he will remember their iniquity 4
10:10 they are chastised for their double iniquity. 4
13 You have plowed iniquity 6
12:11 If there is iniquity in Gilead 1
13:12 The iniquity of E'phraim is bound up 4
14: 1 for you have stumbled because of your iniquity. 4
2 say to him, "Take away all iniquity; 4
Ams 3: 2 I will punish you for all your iniquities. 4
Mic 7:18 Who is a God like thee, pardoning iniquity 4
19 he will tread our iniquities under foot. 4
Hab 2:12 a town with blood, and founds a city on iniquity! 3
Zec 3: 4 Behold, I have taken your iniquity away from you 4
5: 6 he said, "This is their iniquity in all the land. 9
Mal 2: 6 he turned many from iniquity. 4
Mat 23:28 within you are full of hypocrisy and iniquity. 11
Lke 13:27 depart from me, all you workers of iniquity!' 11
Act 8:23 in the bond of iniquity. 9
Rom 4: 7 those whose iniquities are forgiven 11
6:19 to impurity and to greater and greater iniquity 11
2Co 6:14 righteousness and iniquity 11
2Ti 2:19 depart from iniquity. 9
Tit 2:14 to redeem us from all iniquity 11
Heb 8:12 For I will be merciful toward their iniquities 9
Rev 18: 5 and God has remembered her iniquities. 9
1Es 8:70 the nobles have been sharing in this iniquity. 11
72 as I mourned over this iniquity 11
90 Behold, we are now before thee in our iniquities; 11
9: 2 he was mourning over the great iniquities 11
2Es 1: 5 iniquities which they have committed against me 13
3:13 when they were committing iniquity before thee 13
34 Now therefore weigh in a balance our iniquities 13
6:19 when I require from the doers of iniquity 14
19 when I require . . the penalty of their iniquity 15
7:68 who have been born are involved in iniquities 13
72 because . . they committed iniquity 13
126 For while we lived and committed iniquity 13
138 those who have committed iniquities 13
14:31 you and your fathers committed iniquity 13
15: 6 For iniquity has spread throughout every land 13
16:20 they will not turn from their iniquities 13
50 righteousness shall abhor iniquity 13
52 and iniquity will be removed from the earth 13
65 your own iniquities shall stand as . . accusers 13
67 Cease from your sins, and forget your iniquities 13
76 or your iniquities prevail over you. 13
77 and overwhelmed by their iniquities 13
Tob 13: 5 He will afflict us for our iniquities 9
Jdt 5:17 the God who hates iniquity is with them. 9
6: 5 said these words on the day of your iniquity 9
Sir 7: 6 lest you be unable to remove iniquity 9
17:20 Their iniquities are not hidden from him 9
26 turn away from iniquity 9
23:11 will be filled with iniquity 11
25:19 Any iniquity is insignificant 12
19 insignificant compared to a wife's iniquity 12
27:10 so does sin for the workers of iniquity. 10
41:18 of iniquity, before a congregation or the people; 11
49: 2 took away the abominations of iniquity. 11
Bar 3: 5 Remember not the iniquities of our fathers 9
7 we have put away from our hearts all the iniquity 9
8 punished for all the iniquities of our fathers 9
Sus 1: 5 Iniquity came forth from Babylon 11
Man 1: 9 because of the multitude of my iniquities. 9

iniquity *See also* commit, doer, punishment.

initiate 1. μύστης 2. μύστις 3. τελετή
Wis 8: 4 For she is an initiate in the knowledge of God 2
12: 5 initiates from the midst of a heathen cult 1
3Mc 2:30 who have been initiated into the mysteries 3

initiation 1. τελετή
Wis 14:15 handed on . . secret rites and initiations. 1
23 they kill children in their initiations 1

inject 1. ἐμβάλλω
Sir 28: 9 inject enmity among those who are at peace. 1

injure 1. חמס 2. שָׁבַר 3. βλάπτω 4. κακοποιέω 5. κακός 6. κακόω 7. κάκωσις 8. λυπέω 9. confringo 10. laedo
Lev 21:19 or a man who has an injured foot 2
19 or a man who has . . an injured hand 2
Prv 8:36 he who misses me injures himself; 1
Rom 14:15 If your brother is being injured by what you eat 8
2Es 2:21 care for the injured and the weak 9
11:42 afflicted the meek and injured the peaceable; 10
AEs 12: 6 he sought to injure Mordecai and his people 4
16: 3 They not only seek to injure our subjects 4
Sir 13:12 he will not hesitate to injure or to imprison. 7
38:21 you do the dead no good, and you injure yourself. 7
1Mc 7:15 We will not seek to injure you or your friends. 5
2Mc 12:22 often they were injured by their own men 3
4Mc 4: 1 unable to injure Onias in the eyes of the nation 6
9: 7 do not suppose that you can injure us by torturing us. 3

injure *See also* seek.

injury 1. מוּם 2. ἀδίκημα 3. ἀδικία 4. κακία 5. πρόσκομμα 6. συμφορά 7. ὕβρις
Prv 9: 7 he who reproves a wicked man incurs injury. 1
Act 27:10 the voyage will be with injury and much loss 7
21 incurred this injury and loss. 7
Jdt 7:24 you have done us a great injury 3
Sir 10: 6 Do not be angry with your neighbor for any injury 2
31:30 increases the anger of a fool to his injury 5
2Mc 9: 4 the injury done by those who had put him to flight; 4
14:40 by arresting him he would do them an injury. 6

do injury 1. βλάπτω 2. κάκωσις
Wis 18: 2 thy holy ones . . were doing them no injury 1
2Mc 3:39 and destroys those who come to do it injury. 2

injustice 1. לֹא מִשְׁפָּט 2. מַטֶּה 3. עָוֶל 4. עַוְלָה 5. ἀδικία
Lev 19:15 You shall do no injustice in judgment 3
Job 5:16 poor have hope, and injustice shuts her mouth. 4
Prv 13:23 but it is swept away through injustice. 1
16: 8 Better . . than great revenues with injustice. 1
22: 8 He who sows injustice will reap calamity 4
Jer 22:13 and his upper rooms by injustice; 1
Ezk 7:10 Your doom has come, injustice has blossomed 2
9: 9 is full of blood, and the city full of injustice; 2
Hos 10:13 you have reaped injustice 4
Rom 9:14 Is there injustice on God's part? By no means! 5
Sir 7: 3 My son, do not sow the furrows of injustice 5
10: 7 injustice is outrageous to both. 5
8 on account of injustice and insolence 5
14: 9 mean injustice withers the soul. 5
20:28 will atone for injustice. 5
40:12 All bribery and injustice will be blotted out 5
1Mc 9:23 all the doers of injustice appeared. 5
3Mc 2: 4 those who in the past committed injustice 5

ink 1. דְּיוֹ 2. μέλας
Jer 36:18 while I wrote them with ink on the scroll. 1
2Co 3: 3 written not with ink but with the Spirit 2
2Jn 1:12 I would rather not use paper and ink 2
3Jn 1:13 but I would rather not write with pen and ink; 2

inlay
Ezk 27: 6 deck of pines . . of Cyprus, inlaid with ivory. •

inmost 1. ἔσω
Rom 7:22 For I delight in the law of God, in my inmost self. 1

inmost *See also* feelings.

inmost part 1. σπλάγχνον
4Mc 14:13 an emotion felt in her inmost parts. 1

inn 1. κατάλυμα 2. πανδοχεῖον
Lke 2: 7 because there was no place for them in the inn. 1
10:34 and brought him to an inn, and took care of him. 2

innate 1. σύμφυτος 2. φύσις
3Mc 3:22 in their innate malice 1
4Mc 16: 3 her innate parental love 2

inner 1. מֵהַבַּיְתָה 2. עַד 3. פָּנִים 4. פְּנִימָה 5. פְּנִימִי 6. ἔνδοθεν 7. ἔσω 8. ἐσώτερος
1Kg 6:29 all the walls . . in the inner and outer rooms. 3
30 The floor . . in the inner and outer rooms. 3
36 built the inner court with three courses of hewn 5
7:12 so had the inner court of the house of the LORD 5
2Kg 10:25 and went into the inner room of the house of Ba'al 2
2Ch 4:22 for the inner doors to the most holy place 5
Est 4:11 if any . . goes to the king inside the inner court 5
5: 1 and stood in the inner court of the king's palace 5
Ezk 8: 3 to the entrance of the gateway of the inner court 5
16 he brought me into the inner court of the house 5
10: 3 and a cloud filled the inner court. 5
40: 9 the vestibule of the gate was at the inner end. 1
15 to the end of the inner vestibule of the gate 5
19 he measured the distance from the inner front •
19 outer front of the inner court, 100 cubits. 5
23 as on the east, was a gate to the inner court; 5
27 there was a gate on the south of the inner court; 5
28 he brought me to the inner court by the south gate 5
32 he brought me to the inner court on the east side 5
44 he brought me from without into the inner court 5
44 there were two chambers in the inner court 5
41: 3 Then he went into the inner room and measured 4
15 and the inner room and the outer vestibule 5
17 to the space above the door, even to the inner room 5
17 on all the walls round about in the inner room 5
42: 1 Then he led me out into the inner court 8
3 twenty cubits which belonged to the inner court 5
43: 5 lifted me up, and brought me into the inner court; 5
44:17 they enter the gates of the inner court, 5
17 they minister at the gates of the inner court, 5
21 shall drink wine, when he enters the inner court. 5
27 into the holy place, into the inner court 5
45:19 and the posts of the gate of the inner court. 5
46: 1 The gate of the inner court that faces east 5
Act 16:24 he put them into the inner prison 8
2Co 4:16 our inner nature is being renewed every day. 7
Eph 3:16 through his Spirit in the inner man 7
Heb 6:19 enters into the inner shrine behind the curtain 8
Wis 17:13 the inner expectation of help, being weak 6
1Mc 9:54 the wall of the inner court of the sanctuary 8
3Mc 3:17 we proposed to enter their inner temple •

inner *See also* basin, chamber, end, room, sanctuary.

inner part 1. חֶדֶר 2. יַרְכָה 3. פְּנִימָה 4. קֶרֶב
Exd 12: 9 its head with its legs and its inner parts. 4
Lev 10:18 brought into the inner part of the sanctuary 3
2Ch 29:16 The priests went into the inner part of the house 3
Prv 18: 8 go down into the inner parts of the body. 1
26:22 go down into the inner parts of the body. 1
Jon 1: 5 had gone down into the inner part of the ship 2

innermost 1. חֶדֶר 2. פְּנִימִי
1Kg 7:50 for the doors of the innermost part of the house 2
Prv 20:27 searching all his innermost parts. 1
30 strokes make clean the innermost parts. 1

innermost part 1. יַרְכָה 2. תָּוֶךְ
1Sm 24: 3 were sitting in the innermost parts of the cave. 1
1Kg 6:19 he prepared in the innermost part of the house 2
27 the cherubim in the innermost part of the house; 2
Ams 6:10 to him who is in the innermost parts of the house 1

innkeeper 1. πανδοχεύς
Lke 10:35 gave them to the innkeeper, saying 1

innocence 1. נִקָּיוֹן 2. ἁπλότης
Gen 20: 5 the innocence of my hands I have done this 1
Ps 26: 6 I wash my hands in innocence 1
73:13 my heart clean and washed my hands in innocence. 1
1Mc 2:37 for they said, "Let us all die in our innocence; 2
60 Daniel because of his innocence 2

innocent 1. נקה 2. נָקִי 3. נָקִיא 4. צַדִּיק 5. צדק 6. ἀθῷος 7. ἄκακος 8. ἀκέραιος 9. ἀναίτιος 10. ἀναμάρτητος 11. δίκαιος 12. καθαρός 13. innocuus 14. innoxius
Gen 20: 4 he said, "Lord, wilt thou slay an innocent people? 4
Exd 23: 7 do not slay the innocent and righteous 2
Deu 19:10 lest innocent blood be shed in your land 2
13 purge the guilt of innocent blood from Israel 2
21: 8 set not the guilt of innocent blood in the midst 2
9 purge the guilt of innocent blood 2
25: 1 acquitting the innocent and condemning 4
27:25 who takes a bribe to slay an innocent person.' 2
1Sm 19: 5 why then will you sin against innocent blood 2
2Kg 10: 9 You are innocent. It was I who conspired 4
21:16 Manas'seh shed very much innocent blood 2
24: 4 and also for the innocent blood that he had shed; 2
4 for he filled Jerusalem with innocent blood 2
Job 4: 7 Think now, who that was innocent ever perished? 2
9:15 Though I am innocent, I cannot answer him; 5
20 Though I am innocent, my own mouth would condemn 5

23 he mocks at the calamity of the innocent. 2
17: 8 innocent stirs himself up against the godless. 2
22:19 the innocent laugh them to scorn 2
27:17 the innocent will divide the silver. 2
34: 5 For Job has said, 'I am innocent 5
Ps 10: 8 in hiding places he murders the innocent. 2
15: 5 and does not take a bribe against the innocent. 2
19:13 Then I shall be blameless, and innocent 1
94:21 condemn the innocent to death. 2
106:38 poured out innocent blood, the blood of their 2
Prv 1:11 let us wantonly ambush the innocent; 2
6:17 hands that shed innocent blood 2
24:24 He who says to the wicked, "You are innocent 4
Isa 5:23 for a bribe, and deprive the innocent of his right! 4
59: 7 and they make haste to shed innocent blood; 2
Jer 2:35 I am innocent; surely his anger has turned from me.' 1
7: 6 or shed innocent blood in this place 2
19: 4 filled this place with the blood of innocents 2
22: 3 nor shed innocent blood in this place. 2
17 dishonest gain, for shedding innocent blood 2
26:15 you will bring innocent blood upon yourselves 2
Jol 3:19 they have shed innocent blood in their land. 3
Jon 1:14 this man's life, and lay not on us innocent blood; 3
Mat 10:16 so be wise as serpents and innocent as doves. 8
23:35 from the blood of innocent Abel 11
Lke 23:47 Certainly this man was innocent! 11
Act 18: 6 Your blood be upon your heads! I am innocent 12
20:26 I am innocent of the blood of all of you 12
Php 2:15 you may be blameless and innocent 8
2Es 15: 8 Behold, innocent and righteous blood cries out 14
9 all the innocent blood from among them. 13
22 those who shed innocent blood on earth. 13
Tob 3:14 I am innocent of any sin with man 12
Wis 4:12 roving desire perverts the innocent mind. 7
Sus 1:46 I am innocent of the blood of this woman. 12
62 Thus innocent blood was saved that day. 9
2Mc 1: 8 burned the gate and shed innocent blood 6
8: 4 the lawless destruction of the innocent babies 10

innocent *See also* declare, hold.

innocent man 1. אִישׁ נָקִי

Job 22:30 He delivers the innocent man; 1

innumerable 1. אֵין מִסְפָּר 2. ἀμέτρητον 3. ἀναρίθμητος 4. μυριάς 5. οὐκ ἦν ἀριθμός 6. innumerabilis 7. non numerus

Job 21:33 those who go before him are innumerable. 1
Ps 104:25 sea . . which teems with things innumerable 1
Heb 11:12 the innumerable grains of sand by the seashore. 3
12:22 innumerable angels in festal gathering 4
2Es 6: 3 before the innumerable hosts of angels 6
7:140 only very few of the innumerable multitude. 6
13: 5 and behold, an innumerable multitude of men 7
11 nothing was seen of the innumerable multitude 6
34 an innumerable multitude shall be gathered 6
Jdt 2:17 innumerable sheep and oxen and goats 5
3Mc 4:17 because of their innumerable multitude 2

inquire 1. בעה 2. בקר 3. בקש 4. דרש 5. שאל 6. διερευνάω 7. ἐξερευνάω 8. ἐραυνάω 9. ζητέω 10. πυνθάνομαι 11. inquiro 12. interrogo

Gen 25:22 why do I live?" So she went to inquire of the LORD. 4
43:27 he inquired about their welfare, and said 5
Exd 18:15 Because the people come to me to inquire of God; 4
Lev 27:33 A man shall not inquire whether it is good or bad 2
Num 27:21 inquire for him by the judgment of the Urim 5
Deu 12:30 that you do not inquire about their gods, saying 4
13:14 inquire and make search and ask diligently; 4
17: 4 then you shall inquire diligently 4
19:18 judges shall inquire diligently 4
Jdg 1: 1 the people of Israel inquired of the LORD 5
6:29 after they had made search and inquired 3
18: 5 Inquire of God, we pray thee, that we may know 5
20:18 Israel . . went up to Bethel, and inquired of God 5
23 they inquired of the LORD, "Shall we again draw 5
27 the people of Israel inquired of the LORD 5
1Sm 9: 9 when a man went to inquire of God, he said, "Come 4
10:22 they inquired again of the LORD, "Did the man come 5
14:37 Saul inquired of God, "Shall I go down 5
17:56 king said, "Inquire whose son the stripling is. 5
22:10 and he inquired of the LORD for him 5
13 and have inquired of God for him, so that he 5
15 the first time that I have inquired of God for him? 5
23: 2 David inquired of the LORD, "Shall I go and attack 5
4 Then David inquired of the LORD again. 5
28: 6 when Saul inquired of the LORD, the LORD did not 5
7 a medium, that I may go to her and inquire of her. 4
30: 8 And David inquired of the LORD, "Shall I pursue 5
2Sm 2: 1 David inquired of the LORD, "Shall I go up into any 5
5:19 And David inquired of the LORD, "Shall I go up 5
23 And when David inquired of the LORD, he said 5
11: 3 And David sent and inquired about the woman. 4
1Kg 14: 5 is coming to inquire of you concerning her son; 4
22: 5 Inquire first for the word of the LORD. 4
7 prophet of the LORD of whom we may inquire? 4
8 yet one man by whom we may inquire of the LORD 4
2Kg 1: 2 inquire of Ba'al-ze'bub . . whether I shall recover 4
3 that you are going to inquire of Ba'al-ze'bub 4
6 that you are sending to inquire of Ba'al-ze'bub 4
16 sent messengers to inquire of Ba'al-ze'bub 4
16 there is no God in Israel to inquire of his word? 4
3:11 through whom we may inquire of the LORD? 4
8: 8 go to meet . . and inquire of the LORD through him 4
16:15 the bronze altar shall be for me to inquire by. 2
22:13 Go, inquire of the LORD for me, and for the people 4
18 king of Judah, who sent you to inquire of the LORD 4
1Ch 14:10 David inquired of God, "Shall I go up against 5
14 when David again inquired of God, God said to him 5
21:30 David could not go before it to inquire of God 4
2Ch 18: 4 Inquire first for the word of the LORD. 4
6 prophet of the LORD of whom we may inquire? 4
7 yet one man by whom we may inquire of the LORD 4
34:21 Go, inquire of the LORD for me and for those who are 4
26 king of Judah, who sent you to inquire of the LORD 4
Job 8: 8 For inquire, I pray you, of bygone ages 5
Ps 27: 4 of the LORD, and to inquire in his temple. 2
Isa 21:12 If you will inquire, inquire; come back again. 1
12 If you will inquire, inquire; come back again. 1
Jer 10:21 are stupid, and do not inquire of the LORD; 4
21: 2 Inquire of the LORD for us 4
37: 7 king of Judah who sent you to me to inquire of me. 4
Ezk 14: 3 should I let myself be inquired of at all by them? 4
7 yet comes to a prophet to inquire for himself 4
20: 1 certain of the elders of Israel came to inquire 4
3 Is it to inquire of me that you come? 4
3 says the Lord GOD, I will not be inquired of by you. 4
31 And shall I be inquired of by you, O house of Israel? 4
31 says the Lord GOD, I will not be inquired of by you. 4
Dan 1:20 matter . . concerning which the king inquired 3
Hos 4:12 My people inquire of a thing of wood 5
Zep 1: 6 who do not seek the LORD or inquire of him. 4
Mat 2: 4 he inquired of them where the Christ was to be 10
Lke 1:62 inquiring what he would have him called. •
18:36 he inquired what this meant. 10
Act 4: 7 when they had set them in the midst, they inquired 10
9:11 inquire in the house of Judas for a man of Tarsus 9
21:33 He inquired who he was and what he had done. 10
23:20 to inquire somewhat more closely about him. 10
1Pe 1:10 searched and inquired about this salvation 7
11 they inquired what person or time was indicated 8
2Es 4:23 For I did not wish to inquire about the ways above 12
5:50 Then I inquired and said 12
8:51 inquire concerning the glory of those 11
9:13 but inquire how the righteous will be saved 11
AEs 12: 2 inquired into their purposes 7
Wis 6: 3 inquire into your plans. 6
1Mc 3:48 to inquire into those matters •
2Mc 3: 9 inquired whether this really was the situation. 10
3Mc 1:13 he inquired why 10
5:27 inquired what the matter was 10
4Mc 9:27 they inquired if he were willing to eat 10
11:13 When the tyrant inquired . . he said 10

inquire about 1. דרש

Lev 10:16 Now Moses diligently inquired about the goat 1
2Ch 32:31 sent to him to inquire about the sign 1

inquirer 1. דרש

Ezk 14:10 and the punishment of the inquirer shall be alike 1

inquiry 1. בִּקֹּרֶת 2. ἀνακρίσεως 3. ἐλεγμός 4. ἐξέτασις 5. ἔρευνα 6. ἐρώτημα 7. ζητέω

Lev 19:20 an inquiry shall be held 1
Wis 1: 9 inquiry will be made 4
6: 8 a strict inquiry is in store for the mighty. 5
Sir 33: 3 as dependable as an inquiry by means of Urim. 6
41: 4 there is no inquiry about it in Hades. 3
3Mc 7: 5 without any inquiry or examination 2
4Mc 1:13 Our inquiry, accordingly, is . . 7

inquiry *See also* make.

insanity 1. μανία

4Mc 10:13 give way to the same insanity as your brothers 1

insanity *See also* give.

insatiable 1. בִּלְתִּי שָׂבְעָה 2. ἀκατάπαυστος 3. ἀπληστεύομαι 4. οὐκ ἐμπίμπλημι

Ezk 16:28 with the Assyrians, because you were insatiable; 1
2Pe 2:14 eyes full of adultery, insatiable for sin. 2
Sir 12:16 his thirst for blood will be insatiable. 4
31:17 do not be insatiable, lest you give offense. 3

insatiable *See also* appetite.

inscribe 1. חקק 2. רשם 3. רשם (A) 4. ἀναγράφω 5. γράφω 6. ἐκτύπωμα 7. ἐπιγράφω 8. τίθημι

Job 19:23 Oh that they were inscribed in a book! 1
Isa 30: 8 inscribe it in a book 1
Dan 5:24 hand was sent, and this writing was inscribed. 3
25 writing that was inscribed: MENE, MENE, TEKEL 3
10:21 tell you what is inscribed in the book of truth 2
Zec 14:20 shall be inscribed on the bells of the horses •
Rev 19:12 he has a name inscribed which no one knows 5
16 and on his thigh he has a name inscribed 5
21:12 on the gates the names . . were inscribed; 7
Sir 45:12 inscribed like a signet with "Holiness 6
1Mc 14:48 they gave orders to inscribe this decree 8
4Mc 17: 8 to inscribe upon their tomb these words 4

inscribe as holy 1. ἀνιερόω

3Mc 7:20 Then, after inscribing them as holy on a pillar 1

inscribe below 1. ὑπογράφω

3Mc 2:30 he inscribed below 1

inscription 1. מִכְתָּב 2. פִּתּוּחַ 3. ἐπιγραφή 4. ἐπιγράφω 5. κολάπτω γραφήν

Exd 39:30 wrote upon it an inscription, like the engraving 1
Zec 3: 9 I will engrave its inscription, says the LORD 2
Mat 22:20 Whose likeness and inscription is this? 3
Mrk 12:16 Whose likeness and inscription is this? 3
15:26 the inscription of the charge against him read 3
Lke 20:24 Whose likeness and inscription has it? 3
23:38 There was also an inscription over him 3
Act 17:23 I found also an altar with this inscription 4
3Mc 2:27 he set up a stone . . with this inscription 5

inscrutable 1. ἀνεξιχνίαστος

Rom 11:33 and how inscrutable his ways! 1

insect 1. שֶׁקֶץ 2. שֶׁרֶץ

Lev 11:20 All winged insects that go upon all fours are 2
21 Yet among the winged insects that go on all fours 2
23 all other winged insects which have four feet 1
Deu 14:19 all winged insects are unclean for you; 2

insecurely 1. ἐπισφαλῶς

Wis 4: 4 standing insecurely 1

insert 1. אחז

1Kg 6: 6 beams should not be inserted into the walls 1

close inshore 1. ἆσσον

Act 27:13 sailed along Crete, close inshore. 1

inside 1. אֶל 2. בְּ 3. בַּיִת 4. בַּיְתָה 5. בְּתוֹךְ 6. מִבַּיִת 7. מִפֹּה 8. מִפְּנִים 9. מִפְּנִימָה 10. פְּנִימָה 11. εἰς 12. ἐντός 13. ἔσω 14. ἔσωθεν

Gen 6:14 in the ark, and cover it inside and out with pitch. 6
Exd 28:26 put them . . on its inside edge next to the ephod. 4
39:19 on its inside edge next to the ephod. 3
Lev 14:41 cause the inside of the house to be scraped 6
Jos 7:21 they are hidden in the earth inside my tent 5
Jdg 7:16 and empty jars, with torches inside the jars. 5
2Sm 6:17 its place, inside the tent which David . . pitched 5
1Kg 6:15 lined the walls . . on the inside with boards 3
15 he covered them on the inside with wood; 3
21 Solomon overlaid the inside of the house 8
2Kg 16:18 way . . which had been built inside the palace 2
1Ch 16: 1 brought the ark of God, and set it inside the tent 5
2Ch 3: 4 He overlaid it on the inside with pure gold. 9
Est 4:11 if any . . goes to the king inside the inner court 1
5: 1 was sitting on his . . throne inside the palace 2
Ezk 40:16 the vestibule had windows round about inside 10
22 its vestibule was on the inside. •
26 its vestibule was on the inside; •
41 Four tables were on the inside 7
46:23 On the inside, around each of the four courts •
Mat 23:25 inside they are full of extortion and rapacity. 14
26 first cleanse the inside of the cup 12
26:58 going inside he sat with the guards to see 13
Mrk 15:16 the soldiers led him away inside the palace 13
Lke 11:39 inside you are full of extortion and wickedness. 14
40 he who made the outside make the inside also? 14
Act 5:23 when we opened it we found no one inside. 13
1Co 5:12 Is it not those inside the church 13
Bel 1: 7 this is but clay inside and brass outside 14
2Mc 1:15 inside the wall of the sacred precinct 11

inside the circuit of the city 1. περίβολος

3Mc 4:11 claim to be inside the circuit of the city. 1

insight 1. בִּינָה 2. שכל 3. σύνεσις 4. φρόνησις

Job 34:35 his words are without insight. 2
Prv 1: 2 That men may . . understand words of insight 1
2: 3 yes, if you cry out for insight 1
3: 5 do not rely on your own insight. 1
4: 1 be attentive, that you may gain insight; 1
5 Get wisdom; get insight. 1
7 Get wisdom, and whatever you get, get insight. 1
7: 4 call insight your intimate friend; 1
8:14 I have insight, I have strength. 1
9: 6 walk in the way of insight. 1
10 knowledge of the Holy One is insight. 1
Eph 1: 9 he has made known to us in all wisdom and insight 4
3: 4 perceive my insight into the mystery of Christ 3
Wis 8:21 it was a mark of insight to know whose gift she was 4

insight *See also* give, man.

insignificant 1. ἄσημος 2. μικρός

Sir 25:19 insignificant compared to a wife's iniquity 2
3Mc 1: 3 a certain insignificant man 1

insincerely 1. νόθος
3Mc 3:17 accepted our presence . . insincerely by deed 1

act insincerely 1. συνυποκρίνομαι
Gal 2:13 with the rest of the Jews acted insincerely 1

insincerity 1. ὑπόκρισις
Gal 2:13 carried away by their insincerity. 1
1Pe 2: 1 put away all . . insincerity and envy 1

without insincerity 1. ἀνυπόκριτος
Jas 3:17 without uncertainty or insincerity. 1

insist 1. διαβεβαιόομαι 2. διϊσχυρίζομαι 3. εἶπον 4. ζητέω 5. θέλω
Lke 22:59 still another insisted, saying, "Certainly 2
Act 12:15 she insisted that it was 2
1Co 13: 5 Love does not insist on its own way 4
Col 2:18 insisting on self-abasement 5
Tit 3: 8 I desire you to insist on these things 1
Jdt 5:22 insisted that he must be put to death. 3
insistently *See* urge.

insolence 1. זָדוֹן 2. זַעַם 3. חֶרְפָּה 4. עֶבְרָה 5. ἀγαυρίαμα 6. ἀγερωχία 7. θράσος 8. θρασύς 9. ὕβρις 10. ὑπερηφανία 11. contumelia
Prv 13:10 By insolence the heedless make strife 1
Isa 16: 6 of his arrogance, his pride, and his insolence– 4
Jer 48:30 I know his insolence, says the LORD; 4
Dan 11:18 commander shall put an end to his insolence; 3
18 indeed he shall turn his insolence back upon him. 3
Hos 7:16 because of the insolence of their tongue. 2
2Es 11:43 your insolence has come up before the Most High 11
AEs 13:12 not in insolence or pride or for any love of glory 9
Wis 12:17 dost rebuke any insolence among those who know it 7
Sir 10: 6 do not attempt anything by acts of insolence. 9
8 on account of injustice and insolence 9
16: 8 whom he loathed on account of their insolence. 10
Bar 4:34 her insolence will be turned to grief. 5
2Mc 9: 7 Yet he did not in any way stop his insolence 6
3Mc 2: 3 have done anything in insolence and arrogance. 9
21 had exalted himself in insolence and audacity. 9
6: 4 exalted with lawless insolence 8
5 grievous words with boasting and insolence 8
12 the senseless insolence of the lawless 9
20 he forgot his sullen insolence. 7
insolence *See also* hate.

insolent 1. זֵד 2. יָעַז 3. לֵץ 4. עָתָק 5. רַהַב 6. ἐξυβρίζω 7. ὑβριστής
Ps 75: 5 or speak with insolent neck. 4
119:21 Thou dost rebuke the insolent, accursed ones 1
Isa 3: 5 the youth will be insolent to the elder 5
33:19 You will see no more the insolent people 2
Jer 43: 2 and all the insolent men said to Jeremiah 1
Rom 1:30 slanderers, haters of God, insolent, haughty 7
Sir 32:18 an insolent and proud man will not cower in fear. 3
35:18 till he takes away the multitude of the insolent 7
2Mc 1:28 who oppress and are insolent with pride. 6
insolent *See also* fury.

insolent fellow 1. ὑβριστός
Sir 8:11 Do not get up and leave an insolent fellow 1

insolent man 1. זֵד
Ps 54: 3 For insolent men have risen against me 1
86:14 O God, insolent men have risen up against me; 1

insolently 1. בְּחֶרְפָּה 2. עָתָק
Job 16:10 they have struck me insolently upon the cheek 1
Ps 31:18 the lying lips be dumb, which speak insolently 2
insolently *See also* deal.

act insolently 1. זִיד
Neh 9:10 for thou knewest that they acted insolently 1

most insolently 1. ἀναγώγως
2Mc 12:14 those . . behaved most insolently toward Judas 1

inspect 1. פָּקַד 2. שׂבר 3. ἐπίσκεψις 4. καταμανθάνω
Neh 2:13 I inspected the walls of Jerusalem 2
15 went up . . by the valley and inspected the wall; 2
Job 5:24 you shall inspect your fold and miss nothing. 1
1Es 8:41 I inspected them. 4
2Mc 5:18 whom Seleucus . . sent to inspect the treasury. 3

inspection 1. ἐπίσκεψις
2Mc 3:14 went in to direct the inspection of these funds. 1
inspection *See also* make.

inspector 1. ἐπισκοπός
1Mc 1:51 he appointed inspectors over all the people 1

inspiration 1. παράκλησις
2Mc 15:11 the inspiration of brave words 1

inspire 1. נתן 2. γίνομαι 3. δείκνυμι 4. ἐμπνέω 5. ἐμφυσιόω 6. ἐν 7. ἐνεργέω
Exd 35:34 he has inspired him to teach, both him and Oho'liab 1
Jer 49:16 The horror you inspire has deceived you •
Mat 22:43 How is it then that David, inspired by the Spirit •
Mrk 12:36 David himself, inspired by the Holy Spirit •
Lke 2:27 inspired by the Spirit he came into the temple; •
1Co 12: 6 the same God who inspires them all in every one. 7
11 All these are inspired by one and the same Spirit 7
Col 1:29 the energy which he mightily inspires within me. 7
1Th 1: 6 with joy inspired by the Holy Spirit; •
1Ti 1:18 inspired by them you may wage the good warfare 6
1Es 9:55 because they were inspired by the words 5
Wis 15:11 formed him and inspired him with an active soul 4
LJr 1: 4 inspire fear in the heathen. 3
1Mc 4:35 the boldness which inspired those of Judas 2

inspire terror 1. ערץ
Isa 47:12 able to succeed, perhaps you may inspire terror. 1
inspired *See* decision.

inspired by God 1. θεόπνευστος
2Ti 3:16 All scripture is inspired by God 1

instability 1. ἀσταθῆ
3Mc 5:39 wondering at his instability of mind 1

install 1. מִלֵּא יָד 2. ἐφίστημι
Jdg 17: 5 and installed one of his sons, who became his 1
12 Micah installed the Levite, and the young man 1
1Mc 12:38 he fortified it and installed gates with bolts. 2

instant 1. פִּתְאֹם 2. ῥοπή
Isa 29: 5 passing chaff. And in an instant, suddenly 1
30:13 whose crash comes suddenly, in an instant; 1
Wis 18:12 in one instant 2

instantly 1. ἀπὸ τῆς ὥρας 2. εὐθέως
Mat 9:22 well." And instantly the woman was made well. 1
15:28 And her daughter was healed instantly. 1
17:18 and the boy was cured instantly. 1
Act 22:29 withdrew from him instantly 2

instead 1. אַל 2. וְלֹא 3. מִן 4. עַל 5. תַּחַת 6. ἀλλά 7. ἀντί 8. ἀπό 9. δέ 10. καί 11. καὶ οὐχί 12. μᾶλλον 13. οὐ 14. πλήν
Gen 4:25 appointed for me another child instead of Abel 5
22:13 up as a burnt offering instead of his son. 5
44:33 let your servant . . remain instead of the lad 5
Num 3:12 the Levites . . instead of every first-born 5
41 Levites . . instead of all the first-born 5
41 instead of all the firstlings among the cattle 5
45 Take the Levites instead of all the first-born 5
45 cattle of the Levites instead of their cattle; 5
8:16 instead of all that open the womb, the first-born 5
18 taken the Levites instead of all the first-born 5
Jdg 15: 2 sister fairer than she? Pray take her instead. 5
2Sm 17:25 had set Ama'sa over the army instead of Jo'ab. 5
18:33 Would I had died instead of you, O Ab'salom, my son 5
2Kg 14:21 and made him king instead of his father Amazi'ah. 5
17:24 placed them in . . instead of the people of Israel; 5
1Ch 29:23 Solomon sat . . as king instead of David 5
2Ch 26: 1 made him king instead of his father Amazi'ah. 5
28:20 afflicted him instead of strengthening him. 2
Est 2: 4 let the maiden . . be queen instead of Vashti. 7
17 and made her queen instead of Vashti. 5
Job 31:40 let thorns grow instead of wheat 5
40 thorns . . and foul weeds instead of barley. 5
Ps 45:16 Instead of your fathers shall be your sons; 5
Prv 8:10 Take my instruction instead of silver 1
11: 8 trouble, and the wicked gets into it instead. 5
Isa 3:24 Instead of perfume there will be rottenness; 5
24 instead of a girdle, a rope; 5
24 instead of well-set hair, baldness; 5
24 instead of a rich robe, a girding of sackcloth; 5
24 instead of beauty, shame. 5
55:13 Instead of the thorn shall come up the cypress; 5
13 instead of the brier shall come up the myrtle; 5
60:17 Instead of bronze I will bring gold 5
17 and instead of iron I will bring silver; 5
17 instead of wood, bronze, instead of stones, iron. 5
17 instead of wood, bronze, instead of stones, iron. 5
61: 3 in Zion–to give them a garland instead of ashes 5
3 the oil of gladness instead of mourning 5
3 the mantle of praise instead of a faint spirit; 5
7 Instead of your shame you shall have a double 5
7 instead of dishonor you shall rejoice •
Jer 22:11 who reigned instead of Josi'ah his father 5
29:26 The LORD has made you priest instead of Jehoi'ada 5
37: 1 reigned instead of Coni'ah the son of Jehoi'akim. 5
Ezk 4:15 let you have cow's dung instead of human dung 5
16:32 who receives strangers instead of her husband! 5
36:34 shall be tilled, instead of being the desolation 5
Dan 8: 8 instead of it there came up four conspicuous 5
11:38 honor the god of fortresses instead of these; 4
Hab 2:16 will be sated with contempt instead of glory. 3
Mrk 15:11 to have him release for them Barab'bas instead. 12
Lke 11:11 will instead of a fish give him a serpent; 10
12:31 Instead, seek his kingdom 14
1Co 6: 1 instead of the saints? 11
Eph 5: 4 instead let there be thanksgiving. 12
11 but instead expose them. 12
Tit 1:14 instead of giving heed to Jewish myths •
Heb 10: 1 instead of the true form of these realities 13
Jas 4:15 Instead you ought to say, "If the Lord wills 7
1Es 4:39 instead of anything that is unrighteous 8
AEs 14: 2 instead of costly perfumes 7
16:21 instead of a day of destruction for them. 7
Wis 11: 6 Instead of the fountain of an ever-flowing river 7
16: 2 Instead of this punishment 7
20 Instead of these things 7
19:10 instead of producing animals . . brought forth gnats 7
10 instead of fish the river spewed out . . frogs 7
Sir 4:10 Be . . instead of a husband to their mother 7
6: 1 do not become an enemy instead of a friend 7
20:14 he has many eyes instead of one. 7
29: 6 instead of glory will repay him with dishonor. 7
1Mc 10:30 instead of collecting the third of the grain 7
3Mc 3: 7 instead they gossiped 9
4: 6 raising a lament instead of a wedding song 7
8 their necks encircled with ropes instead of garlands 7
8 lamentations instead of good cheer 7
5:31 I would have prepared them . . instead of the Jews 7
32 you . . instead of these 7
6:31 instead of a bitter and lamentable death 7
4Mc 13: 3 Instead, by reason . . they prevailed 6
15:12 Instead, the mother urged them on 6

instigate 1. ὑποβάλλω
Act 6:11 Then they secretly instigated men, who said 1

instill 1. ἐνίημι
4Mc 4:10 instilling in them great fear and trembling. 1

instinct 1. φυσικός 2. φυσικῶς
2Pe 2:12 like irrational animals, creatures of instinct 1
Jde 1:10 they know by instinct as irrational animals do 2

institute 1. ἵστημι 2. τάσσω
Rom 13: 1 those that exist have been instituted by God. 2
3Mc 6:36 instituted the observance of the . . days 1

institution 1. κτίσις
1Pe 2:13 Be subject . . to every human institution 1

instruct 1. בין 2. זהר 3. ידע 4. יסר 5. ירה 6. צוה 7. שׂכל 8. διατάσσω 9. ἐντέλλω 10. κατηχέω 11. νουθετέω 12. παιδεία 13. παιδεύω 14. σοφίζω 15. συμβιβάζω 16. χρηματίζω 17. commoneo 18. erudio 19. instruo
Gen 32: 4 instructing them, "Thus you shall say to my lord 6
17 He instructed the foremost, "When Esau my brother 6
19 He likewise instructed the second and the third 6
Rut 2:15 Bo'az instructed his young men, saying 6
1Sm 12:23 I will instruct you in the good and the right way. 5
2Sm 11:19 and he instructed the messenger, "When you have 6
2Kg 12: 2 because Jehoi'ada the priest instructed him. 5
2Ch 19:10 then you shall instruct them 2
26: 5 Zechari'ah, who instructed him in the fear of God; 1
Neh 9:20 Thou gavest thy good Spirit to instruct them 7
Job 4: 3 Behold, you have instructed many 4
Ps 16: 7 in the night also my heart instructs me. 4
25: 8 therefore he instructs sinners in the way. 5
12 Him will he instruct in the way that he should 5
32: 8 I will instruct you and teach you the way 7
105:22 to instruct his princes at his pleasure 13
Prv 21:11 wise man is instructed, he gains knowledge. 7
Isa 28:26 For he is instructed aright; his God teaches him. 4
40:13 or as his counselor has instructed him? 3
Jer 31:19 and after I was instructed, I smote upon my thigh; 3
38:27 he answered them as the king had instructed him. 6
Mat 11: 1 when Jesus had finished instructing 8
Act 7:22 instructed in all the wisdom of the Egyptians 13
18:25 He had been instructed in the way of the Lord; 10
Rom 2:18 because you are instructed in the law 10
15:14 and able to instruct one another. 11
1Co 2:16 so as to instruct him 15
14:19 in order to instruct others 10
2Ti 3:15 which are able to instruct you for salvation 14
Heb 8: 5 he was instructed by God, saying 16
2Es 5:32 and I will instruct you 19
7:49 I will instruct you 19
8:12 and instructed him in thy law 18
10:33 to me, "Stand up like a man, and I will instruct you. 17
14:13 and instruct those that are wise ‡
Wis 6:11 long for them, and you will be instructed. 13
25 Therefore be instructed by my words 13
Sir 37:23 A wise man will instruct his own people 13
42: 8 Do not be ashamed to instruct the stupid 12
8 Then you will be truly instructed 13
2Mc 2: 2 instructed those who were being deported 9
4Mc 5:24 it instructs us in justice 13

instruct well 1. παιδεύω
Sir 40:29 a man who is intelligent and well instructed 1

instruction 1. ירה 2. למד 3. לֶקַח 4. מוּסָר 5. תּוֹרָה 6. διατάσσω 7. διδασκαλία 8. διδαχή 9. ἐντολή 10. νουθεσία 11. παιδεία 12. παραγγελία 13. παραγγέλλω

Exd 24:12 which I have written for their instruction. 1
Deu 17:11 according to the instructions which they give 5
Job 22:22 Receive instruction from his mouth 5
36:10 He opens their ears to instruction, and commands 4
Ps 60: 0 A Miktam of David; for instruction; 2
Prv 1: 2 That men may know wisdom and instruction 4
3 receive instruction in wise dealing 4
7 fools despise wisdom and instruction. 4
8 Hear, my son, your father's instruction 4
4: 1 Hear, O sons, a father's instruction 4
13 Keep hold of instruction, do not let go; 4
8:10 Take my instruction instead of silver 4
33 Hear instruction and be wise, and do not neglect 4
9: 9 Give instruction to a wise man, and he will be •
10:17 He who heeds instruction is on the path to life 4
13: 1 A wise son hears his father's instruction 4
18 Poverty . . come to him who ignores instruction 4
15: 5 A fool despises his father's instruction 4
32 He who ignores instruction despises himself 4
33 The fear of the LORD is instruction in wisdom 4
19:20 Listen to advice and accept instruction 4
27 Cease, my son, to hear instructions only to stray 4
23:12 Apply your mind to instruction and your ear 4
23 buy wisdom, instruction, and understanding. 4
24:32 I looked and received instruction. 4
Isa 29:24 those who murmur will accept instruction. 3
30: 9 who will not hear the instruction of the LORD; 5
Jer 10: 8 the instruction of idols is but wood! 4
17:23 they might not hear and receive instruction. 4
32:33 they have not listened to receive instruction. 4
35:13 Will you not receive instruction and listen 4
Mal 2: 6 True instruction was in his mouth 5
7 men should seek instruction from his mouth 5
8 caused many to stumble by your instruction; 5
9 but have shown partiality in your instruction. 5
Act 23:31 according to their instructions, took Paul 6
Rom 15: 4 was written for our instruction 7
1Co 10:11 they were written down for our instruction 10
11:17 in the following instructions I do not commend 13
Eph 6: 4 in the discipline and instruction of the Lord. 10
Col 4:10 you have received instructions 9
1Th 4: 2 For you know what instructions we gave you 12
1Ti 3:14 I am writing these instructions to you •
4: 6 If you put these instructions before the brethren •
Heb 6: 2 instruction about ablutions 8
Wis 3:11 whoever despises wisdom and instruction 11
6:17 the most sincere desire for instruction 11
17 concern for instruction is love of her 11
7:14 the gifts that come from instruction. 11
Sir 0: 1 should praise Israel for instruction and wisdom; 11
1 write something pertaining to instruction 11
3 I found opportunity for no little instruction. 11
1:27 the fear of the Lord is wisdom and instruction 11
6:18 My son, from your youth up choose instruction 11
8: 8 because from them you will gain instruction 11
16:25 I will impart instruction by weight 11
23: 7 Listen . . to instruction concerning speech 11
24:27 It makes instruction shine forth like light 11
32 again make instruction shine forth like the dawn 11
34 for all who seek instruction. •
33: 4 bind together your instruction 11
17 all who seek instruction. 11
39: 8 He will reveal instruction in his teaching 11
41:14 My children, observe instruction and be at peace; 11
44: 4 wise in their words of instruction; 11
50:27 Instruction in understanding and knowledge 11
51:16 I found for myself much instruction. 11
26 let your souls receive instruction 11
28 Get instruction with a large sum of silver 11

instruction *See also* give.

instructor 1. למד 2. παιδευτής

Prv 5:13 I did not . . incline my ear to my instructors. 1
4Mc 9: 6 which our aged instructor also overcame. 2

instrument 1. חרשׁ 2. כְּלִי 3. ἀρθρέμβολον ὄργανον 4. ὅπλον 5. ὄργανον 6. σκεῦος 7. φωνὴν δίδωμι

Gen 4:22 the forger of all instruments of bronze 1
Num 35:16 if he struck him down with an instrument of iron 2
1Ch 15:16 who should play loudly on musical instruments 2
16:42 the music and instruments for sacred song. 2
23: 5 the instruments which I have made for praise. 2
2Ch 5:13 raised, with . . and other musical instruments 2
7: 6 Levites . . with the instruments for music 2
23:13 singers with their musical instruments 2
29:26 The Levites stood with the instruments of David 2
27 accompanied by the instruments of David 2
34:12 Levites . . skilful with instruments of music 2
Neh 12:36 musical instruments of David the man of God; 2
Ezk 33:32 and plays well on an instrument, for they hear •
40:42 on which the instruments were to be laid 2
Ams 6: 5 and like David invent . . instruments of music; 2
Act 9:15 he is a chosen instrument of mine to carry my name 6
Rom 6:13 your members . . as instruments of wickedness 4
13 members to God as instruments of righteousness 4
1Co 14: 7 If even lifeless instruments 7
Sir 43: 2 a marvelous instrument, the work of the Most High. 6
8 an instrument of the hosts on high 6
4Mc 6:25 maliciously contrived instruments 5
10: 5 disjointed . . with their instruments 3
7 they abandoned the instruments and scalped him 5

instrument *See also* stringed.

musical instrument 1. μουσικός

1Es 5:59 with musical instruments and trumpets 1

instrument of music 1. שָׁלִישׁ

1Sm 18: 6 with songs of joy, and with instruments of music. 1

instrument of torture 1. βασανιστήριον

4Mc 6: 1 dragged him . . to the instruments of torture. 1
8: 1 the most painful instruments of torture. 1
12 he ordered the instruments of torture 1
19 should we not fear the instruments of torture 1
25 for fearing the instruments of torture. 1

insubordinate 1. ἀνυπότακτος

Tit 1: 6 being profligate or insubordinate. 1

insubordinate man 1. ἀνυπότακτος

Tit 1:10 For there are many insubordinate men 1

insult 1. חרף 2. חֶרְפָּה 3. כְּלִמָּה 4. צחק 5. קָלוֹן 6. רִיב חֶרְפָּה 7. ἐμπαιγμός 8. λέγω ῥακά 9. λοιδορία 10. ὀνειδισμός 11. ὕβρις 12. ὑβριστής

Gen 39:14 See, he has brought among us a Hebrew to insult us; 4
17 Hebrew servant . . came in to me to insult me; 4
1Sm 25:39 avenged the insult I received at the hand 6
Job 20: 3 I hear censure which insults me 3
Ps 69: 9 the insults of those who insult thee 2
9 the insults of those who insult thee 1
20 Insults have broken my heart 2
89:50 how I bear in my bosom the insults of the peoples •
Prv 12:16 but the prudent man ignores an insult. 5
14:31 He who oppresses a poor man insults his Maker 1
17: 5 He who mocks the poor insults his Maker; 1
Lam 3:30 let him give . . and be filled with insults. 2
Mat 5:22 liable to judgment; whoever insults his brother 8
2Co 12:10 I am content with weaknesses, insults, hardships 11
1Ti 1:13 blasphemed and persecuted and insulted him 12
Wis 2:19 Let us test him with insult and torture 11
Sir 22:24 so insults precede bloodshed. 9
23:15 A man accustomed to use insulting words 10
3Mc 3:25 with insulting and harsh treatment 11
5:22 in devising all sorts of insults 7

insure 1. ἐπί

4Mc 9: 4 this pity of yours which insures our safety 1

insurrection 1. στάσις 2. exsurrectio

Mrk 15: 7 who had committed murder in the insurrection 1
Lke 23:19 an insurrection started in the city 1
25 for insurrection and murder . . they asked for 1
2Es 16:70 there shall be a great insurrection 2

intact 1. ἐν

Tob 9: 5 the money bags with their seals intact 1

integrity 1. תֹּם 2. תֻּמָּה 3. תָּמִים 4. ἀφθορία 5. εὐθύτης 6. καθαρός 7. ὁσιότης

Gen 20: 5 In the integrity of my heart . . I have done this. 1
6 you have done this in the integrity of your heart 1
1Kg 9: 4 walk . . with integrity of heart and uprightness 1
Job 2: 3 He still holds fast his integrity 2
9 Do you still hold fast your integrity? 2
4: 6 and the integrity of your ways your hope? 1
27: 5 till I die I will not put away my integrity from me. 2
31: 6 in a just balance, and let God know my integrity! 2
Ps 7: 8 according to the integrity that is in me. 1
25:21 May integrity and uprightness preserve me 1
26: 1 I have walked in my integrity, and I have trusted 1
11 But as for me, I walk in my integrity; 1
41:12 But thou hast upheld me because of my integrity 1
101: 2 walk with integrity of heart within my house; 1
Prv 2: 7 he is a shield to those who walk in integrity 1
10: 9 He who walks in integrity walks securely 1
11: 3 The integrity of the upright guides them 2
14:32 righteous finds refuge through his integrity. 7
19: 1 Better is a poor man who walks in his integrity 1
20: 7 A righteous man who walks in his integrity– 1
28: 6 Better is a poor man who walks in his integrity 1
18 He who walks in integrity will be delivered 3
Tit 2: 7 in your teaching show integrity, gravity 4
Sir 7: 6 thus put a blot on your integrity. 5
2Mc 7:40 he died in his integrity 6

integrity *See also* man.

intelligence 1. תְּבוּנָה 2. σύνεσις 3. συνετός

Exd 31: 3 filled him with . . ability and intelligence 1
35:31 filled . . with ability, with intelligence 1
36: 1 LORD has put ability and intelligence to know 1
Act 13: 7 Proconsul, Sergius Paulus, a man of intelligence 3
Sir 19:24 God-fearing man who lacks intelligence 2
22:11 weep for the fool, for he lacks intelligence 2

intelligence *See also* lack.

without intelligence 1. ἄνους

2Mc 11:13 he was not without intelligence 1

intelligent 1. בין 2. ἐπιστήμων 3. νοερός 4. σύνεσις 5. συνετός

Prv 17:28 when he closes his lips, he is deemed intelligent. 1
18:15 An intelligent mind acquires knowledge 1
Ecc 9:11 bread to the wise, nor riches to the intelligent 1
Wis 7:22 a spirit that is intelligent, holy, unique 3
23 intelligent and pure and most subtle. 3
Sir 7:21 Let your soul love an intelligent servant 5
10:23 is not right to despise an intelligent poor man 5
21:16 be found in the speech of the intelligent. 5
22:17 A mind settled on an intelligent thought 4
25: 8 happy is he who lives with an intelligent wife 5
26:28 intelligent men 5
36:19 so an intelligent mind detects false words. 5
40:29 a man who is intelligent and well instructed 2

intelligent man 1. συνετός

Sir 3:29 The mind of the intelligent man 1
6:36 If you see an intelligent man, visit him early 1
18:28 Every intelligent man knows wisdom 1
19: 2 Wine and women lead intelligent men astray 1

intelligently 1. ἐν συνέσει

Sir 14:20 the man . . who reasons intelligently. 1

intelligible 1. εὔσημος

1Co 14: 9 speech that is not intelligible 1

intend 1. אמר 2. דמה 3. הלך 4. חשׁב 5. פָּנִים ל 6. βουλεύω 7. βούλομαι 8. διά 9. διανοέω 10. δοκέω 11. ἐννοέω 12. θέλω 13. κατευθύνω 14. λογίζομαι 15. μέλλω 16. προτίθημι 17. στέλλω 18. ψυχή 19. ὡς 20. cogito 21. volo

Gen 31:20 that he did not tell him that he intended to flee. •
2Ch 11:22 for he intended to make him king. •
28:10 now you intend to subjugate the people of Judah 1
32: 2 Sennach'erib . . intended to fight against 5
Neh 6: 2 But they intended to do me harm. 4
6 that you and the Jews intend to rebel; 4
Isa 10: 7 does not so intend, and his mind does not so think; 2
Jer 18: 8 repent of the evil that I intended to do to it. 4
10 the good which I had intended to do to it. 1
26: 3 that I may repent of the evil which I intend to do 4
36: 3 will hear all the evil which I intend to do to them 4
41:17 near Bethlehem, intending to go to Egypt 3
Joh 7:35 Where does this man intend to go 15
35 Does he intend to go to the Dispersion 15
Act 5:28 you intend to bring this man's blood upon us. 7
12: 4 intending after the Passover to bring him out 7
20: 7 intending to depart on the morrow 15
13 intending to take Paul aboard there 15
13 intending himself to go by land. 15
25: 4 he himself intended to go there shortly. 15
Rom 1:13 that I have often intended to come to you 16
1Co 16: 5 for I intend to pass through Macedo'nia •
2Co 8:20 We intend that no one should blame us 17
2Pe 1:12 I intend always to remind you of these things 15
2Es 8:59 For the Most High did not intend 21
10: 4 now I intend not to return to the city 20
Jdt 9: 5 Yea, the things thou didst intend came to pass 11
8 they intend to defile thy sanctuary 6
AEs 13: 4 which we honorably intend 13
Sir 19:16 A person may make a slip without intending it. 18
1Mc 4:27 things had not happened . . as he had intended 12
11:63 intending to remove him from office. 7
15: 3 I intend to lay claim to the kingdom 7
4 and intend to make a landing in the country 7
2Mc 1:14 For under pretext of intending to marry her •
4:20 this money was intended by the sender for . . Hercules 8
7: 2 What do you intend to ask and learn from us? 15
10:24 He came on, intending to take Judea by storm. 19
11: 2 He intended to make the city a home for Greeks 14
12: 7 intending to come again 19
3Mc 1: 2 intending single-handed to kill him 19
22 the fulfillment of his intended purpose. 9
4Mc 11:16 if you intend to torture me 10

intense 1. ὀξύς 2. πυκνός

4Mc 12:12 intense and eternal fire and tortures 2
14:10 the power of fire is intense and swift 1

more intense 1. κακός

2Mc 9:28 having endured the more intense suffering 1

intensely 1. δύναμις 2. λίαν 3. σφόδρα

Mrk 9: 3 garments became glistening, intensely white 2
Wis 16:19 at another time . . it burned more intensely than fire 1
Sir 17:26 hate abominations intensely. 3

intensely *See also* hot.

intensify 1. ἐπίτασις 2. συναύξω
Wis 14:18 to intensify their worship. 1
2Mc 4: 4 was intensifying the malice of Simon. 2

intent 1. לֵבָב 2. מְזִמָּה 3. διάνοια 4. ἐπίνοια 5. πρόθυμος
Exd 32:12 With evil intent did he bring them forth, to slay *
1Ch 12:38 came . . with full intent to make David king 1
Jer 23:20 and accomplished the intents of his mind. 2
30:24 and accomplished the intents of his mind. 2
Act 8:22 the intent of your heart may be forgiven you. 4
Wis 15: 4 the evil intent of human art misled us 4
Bar 1:21 each followed the intent of his own wicked heart 3
2Mc 4:14 no longer intent upon their service at the altar 5

evil intent 1. זִמָּה
Prv 21:27 how much more when he brings it with evil intent. 1

malicious intent 1. κακοήθεια
3Mc 7: 3 frequently urging us with malicious intent 1

treacherous intent 1. δόλος
1Mc 7:30 Nicanor had come to him with treacherous intent 1

intent upon 1. καταμανθάνω
Sir 38:28 intent upon his handiwork in iron 1

without intent 1. בִּשְׁגָגָה
Num35:11 manslayer who kills any person without intent 1
15 that any one who kills any person without intent 1
Jos 20: 3 manslayer who kills any person without intent 1
9 who killed a person without intent could flee 1

intention 1. βουλή 2. ἔννοια
Heb 4:12 the thoughts and intentions of the heart. 2
2Mc 14: 5 the disposition and intentions of the Jews 1
intently *See* look, observe.

intentness 1. προσεδρείας
3Mc 4:15 bitter haste and zealous intentness 1

intercede 1. פגע 2. פלל 3. ἀξιόω 4. ἐντυγχάνω 5. ὑπερεντυγχάνω 6. excuso
1Sm 2:25 if a man sins against the LORD, who can intercede 2
Jer 7:16 and do not intercede with me, for I do not hear you. 1
27:18 then let them intercede with the LORD of hosts 1
Rom 8:26 the Spirit himself intercedes for us with sighs 5
27 because the Spirit intercedes for the saints 4
34 Christ Jesus . . who indeed intercedes for us? 4
2Es 7:102will be able to intercede for the ungodly 6
Tob 1:22 Ahikar interceded for me 3

intercession 1. ἔντευξις
1Ti 2: 1 supplications, prayers, intercessions 1
intercession *See also* make.

intercourse 1. πλησιάζω 2. συνουσιασμός
2Mc 6: 4 had intercourse with women 1
4Mc 2: 3 in his prime for intercourse 2

interdict 1. אֱסָר (A)
Dan 6: 7 ordinance and enforce an interdict 1
8 establish the interdict and sign the document 1
9 King Darius signed the document and interdict. 1
12 said before the king, concerning the interdict 1
12 O king! Did you not sign an interdict, 1
13 pays no heed to . . the interdict you have signed 1
15 no interdict or ordinance which the king 1

interest 1. ἀνήκω 2. εἰς 3. ὑπέρ 4. χρεία
1Co 7:34 his interests are divided *
Php 2: 4 Let each of you look not only to his own interests *
4 but also to the interests of others. *
21 They all look after their own interests *
1Es 4:49 in the interest of their freedom 3
Sir 37: 7 some give counsel in their own interest. 2
8 learn first what is his interest 4
2Mc 14: 8 concerned for the interests of the king 1

interest (2) 1. מַשָּׁא 2. נֶשֶׁךְ 3. τόκος
Exd 22:25 you shall not exact interest from him. 2
Lev 25:36 Take no interest from him or increase 2
37 You shall not lend him your money at interest 2
Deu 23:19 interest on money, interest on victuals 2
19 interest on money, interest on victuals 2
19 interest on anything that is lent for interest. 2
Neh 5: 7 exacting interest, each from his brother. 1
10 Let us leave off this interest. 1
Ps 15: 5 who does not put out his money at interest 2
Prv 28: 8 augments his wealth by interest and increase 2
Ezk 18: 8 does not lend at interest or take any increase 2
13 lends at interest, and takes increase; 2
17 takes no interest or increase 2
22:12 you take interest and increase and make gain 2
Mat 25:27 what was my own with interest. 3
Lke 19:23 I should have collected it with interest?' 3
4Mc 2: 8 to lend without interest to the needy 3
interest *See* lend.

interior 1. פְּנִימִי 2. ἐντός
Ezk 42:15 Now when he had finished measuring the interior 1
1Mc 4:48 the sanctuary and the interior of the temple 2
interior *See also* far.

interlace 1. שרך
Jer 2:23 a restive young camel interlacing her tracks 1

intermarry 1. חתן
Ezr 9:14 intermarry with the peoples who practice 1

intermediary 1. μεσίτης
Gal 3:19 ordained by angels through an intermediary. 1
20 Now an intermediary implies more than one 1

internal 1. τά ἔνδον
2Mc 9: 5 with sharp internal tortures 1

interpose 1. פלל 2. μεσιτεύω
Ps 106:30 Phin'ehas stood up and interposed, and the plague 1
Heb 6:17 he interposed with an oath 2

interpret 1. פתר 2. פשר (A) 3. διακρίνω 4. διερμηνεύω 5. δοκιμάζω 6. συγκρίνω
Gen 40: 8 dreams, and there is no one to interpret them. 1
22 as Joseph had interpreted to them. 1
41:12 and when we told him, he interpreted our dreams 1
13 as he interpreted to us, so it came to pass; 1
15 and there is no one who can interpret it; 1
15 when you hear a dream you can interpret it. 1
Dan 5:12 interpret dreams, explain riddles, 2
Mat 16: 3 You know how to interpret 3
3 but you cannot interpret the signs of the times. *
Lke 12:56 You know how to interpret the appearance 5
56 do you not know how to interpret the present time? 5
24:27 he interpreted to them in all the scriptures 4
1Co 2:13 interpreting spiritual truths to those 6
12:30 Do all speak with tongues? Do all interpret? 4
14: 5 unless some one interprets 4
13 should pray for the power to interpret. 4
27 each in turn; and let one interpret. 4
28 if there is no one to interpret 4

interpretation 1. פֵּשֶׁר 2. פתר 3. פִּתְרוֹן 4. שֶׁבֶר 5. פְּשַׁר (A) 6. ἐπίλυσις 7. ἑρμηνεία 8. absolutio 9. interpretatio
Gen 40: 8 Do not interpretations belong to God? 3
12 This is its interpretation: the three branches 3
16 chief baker saw that the interpretation was 2
18 Joseph answered, "This is its interpretation 3
Jdg 7:15 the telling of the dream and its interpretation 4
Ecc 8: 1 And who knows the interpretation of a thing? 1
Dan 2: 4 dream, and we will show the interpretation. 5
5 known to me the dream and its interpretation 5
6 if you show the dream and its interpretation 5
6 show me the dream and its interpretation. 5
7 dream, and we will show its interpretation. 5
9 know that you can show me its interpretation. 5
16 might show to the king the interpretation. 5
24 I will show the king the interpretation. 5
25 make known to the king the interpretation 5
26 dream that I have seen and its interpretation? 5
30 in order that the interpretation may be made known 5
36 now we will tell the king its interpretation. 5
45 dream is certain, and its interpretation sure. 5
4: 6 known to me the interpretation of the dream. 5
7 could not make known to me its interpretation. 5
9 dream which I saw; tell me its interpretation. 5
18 you, O Belteshaz'zar, declare the interpretation 5
18 not able to make known to me the interpretation 5
19 not the dream or the interpretation alarm you. 5
19 may . . its interpretation for your enemies! 5
24 this is the interpretation, O king: It is a decree 5
5: 7 this writing, and shows me its interpretation 5
8 make known to the king the interpretation. 5
12 called, and he will show the interpretation. 5
15 make known to me its interpretation; 5
15 could not show the interpretation of the matter. 5
16 heard that you can give interpretations 5
16 writing and make known to me its interpretation 5
17 king and make known to him the interpretation. 5
26 This is the interpretation of the matter: 5
7:16 known to me the interpretation of the things. 5
1Co 12:10 to another the interpretation of tongues. 7
14:26 a tongue, or an interpretation 7
2Pe 1:20 a matter of one's own interpretation 6
2Es 4:47 I will show you the interpretation of a parable. 8
10:43 this is the interpretation 8
12: 8 and show me, thy servant, the interpretation 9
10 the interpretation of this 9
16 the interpretation of the 12 wings which you saw. 9
17 this is the interpretation 9
19 this is the interpretation 9
22 this is the interpretation 9
30 this is the interpretation 9
35 and this is its interpretation. 9
13:15 show me also the interpretation of this dream. 9
21 I will tell you the interpretation of the vision 9
22 this is the interpretation 9
25 This is the interpretation of the vision 9
28 this is the interpretation 9
53 the interpretation of the dream which you saw. 9
14: 8 the interpretations that you have heard; 9
Sir 47:17 for your interpretations 7
interpretation *See also* give.

interpreter 1. ליץ
Gen 42:23 for there was an interpreter between them. 1

interrupt 1. ἐμποδίζω 2. παρεμβάλλω
Sir 11: 8 nor interrupt a speaker in the midst of his words. 2
32: 3 do not interrupt the music. 1

interval 1. διάστημα 2. διΐστημι
Lke 22:59 after an interval of about an hour 2
Act 5: 7 After an interval of about three hours 1
3Mc 4:17 the previously mentioned interval of time 1

intervene 1. פגע 2. μεταξὺ ἵστημι
Isa 59:16 wondered that there was no one to intervene; 1
Wis 18:23 he intervened and held back the wrath 2

intervention 1. ἐνέργεια
2Mc 3:29 speechless because of the divine intervention 1

interview 1. ἔντευξις
2Mc 4: 8 promising the king at an interview 1

intimate 1. ὁμιλέω
Sus 1:54 Under what tree did you see them being intimate 1
57 and they were intimate with you through fear; 1
58 did you catch them being intimate with each other? 1
intimate *See also* friend.

into
2Es 8: 5 not of your own will did you come into the world ‡
into *See also* break, breathe, bring, build, cast, come, crowd, down, enter, fall, get, go, graft, look, put, rush, sail, sink, subjection, take, throw, turn, way.

intolerable 1. ἀφόρητος βάρος
2Mc 9:10 Because of his intolerable stench 1

intricate 1. πολύπλοκος
AEs 16:13 with intricate craft and deceit 1
intricately *See* wrought.

intrigue 1. אֶרֶב 2. ἐπιχείρημα 3. cogitatio
Hos 7: 6 For like an oven their hearts burn with intrigue; 1
2Es 9: 3 tumult of peoples, intrigues of nations 3
Sir 9: 4 lest you be caught in her intrigues. 2

introduce 1. עשה 2. γίνομαι 3. ἐπεισαγωγή 4. καινίζω
2Kg 17: 8 which the kings of Israel had introduced. 1
19 the customs which Israel had introduced. 1
Act 24: 2 reforms are introduced on behalf of this nation 2
Heb 7:19 on the other hand, a better hope is introduced 3
2Mc 4:11 and introduced new customs contrary to the law. 4

intruder 1. προσίημι
4Mc 14:16 hatch the nestlings and ward off the intruder. 1
19 even bees . . defend themselves against intruders 1

invade 1. בוא 2. בוא אל 3. בקע 4. גוד 5. עלה 6. εἰσέρχομαι 7. εἴσοδος 8. ἐμβατεύω 9. ἔρχομαι εἰς 10. παραγίνομαι
2Kg 13:20 Moabites used to invade the land in the spring 1
17: 5 Then the king of Assyria invaded all the land 5
2Ch 20:10 whom thou wouldst not let Israel invade 1
21:17 they came up against Judah, and invaded it 3
27: 2 only he did not invade the temple of the LORD. 2
28:17 E'domites had again invaded and defeated Judah 1
32: 1 Sennach'erib king of Assyria came and invaded 1
Lam 1:10 yea, she has seen the nations invade her 1
Hab 3:16 day of trouble to come upon people who invade us. 4
Jdt 4: 7 since by them Judea could be invaded 7
1Mc 1:17 So he invaded Egypt with a strong force 6
4:35 enlisted mercenaries, to invade Judea again 10
12:25 no opportunity to invade his own country. 8
13: 1 invade the land of Judah and destroy it 9
12 with a large army to invade the land of Judah 9
20 Trypho came to invade the country and destroy it 8
14: 2 heard that Demetrius had invaded his territory 6
31 their enemies decided to invade their country 8
15:10 Antiochus set out and invaded the land of his fathers *
40 and invade Judea and take the people captive 8
2Mc 11: 5 Invading Judea, he approached Beth-zur 6

invalid 1. ἀσθενέω
Joh 5: 3 In these lay a multitude of invalids, blind, lame 1

invalidate 1. ἀκυρόω
4Mc 5:18 to invalidate our reputation for piety. 1

invasion 1. ἔφοδος
2Mc 5: 1 Antiochus made his second invasion of Egypt. 1
8:12 Word came . . concerning Nicanor's invasion 1

invent 1. ברא 2. חשׁב 3. מַחֲשָׁבָה
2Ch 26:15 he made engines, invented by skilful men 3
Neh 6: 8 for you are inventing them out of your own mind. 1
Ams 6: 5 and like David invent . . instruments of music; 2

invent wickedly 1. πονηρεύω
Sus 1:43 things that they have wickedly invented against me! 1

invention 1. εὕρεσις
Wis 14:12 the invention of them was the corruption of life 1

inventor 1. ἐφευρετής 2. καινουργός
Rom 1:30 haughty, boastful, inventors of evil 1
4Mc 11:23 you inventor of tortures 2

invest 1. נתן 2. βάλλω 3. περιτίθημι
Num27:20 You shall invest him with some of your authority 1
Mat 25:27 Then you ought to have invested my money 2
1Co 12:23 we invest with the greater honor 3

investigate 1. בקשׁ 2. δοκιμάζω 3. ἐξετάζω 4. ἐτάζω 5. ζήτησις 6. στοχάζομαι
Est 2:23 the affair was investigated and found to be 1
Act 25:20 Being at a loss how to investigate these questions 5
1Es 9:16 to investigate the matter. 4
Wis 13: 9 they could investigate the world 6
Sir 3:21 nor investigate what is beyond your power. 3
11: 7 Do not find fault before you investigate 3
2Mc 1:34 the king investigated the matter 2

investigation 1. חֵקֶר 2. ἐκζητέω
Job 34:24 He shatters the mighty without investigation 1
AEs 16: 7 investigation of matters close at hand. 2

inveterate 1. προκατασκιρρόομαι
3Mc 4: 1 inveterate enmity . . was now made evident 1

invincible 1. ἀκαταμάχητος 2. ἀνίκητος 3. ἀνυπέρβλητος
Jdt 16:13 wonderful in strength, invincible. 3
Wis 5:19 he will take holiness as an invincible shield 1
2Mc 11:13 realized that the Hebrews were invincible 2
3Mc 4:21 an act of the invincible providence of him 2
6:13 cower today in fear of your invincible might 2
4Mc 9:18 sons of the Hebrews alone are invincible 2
11:21 religious knowledge, O tyrant, is invincible. 2

inviolability 1. ἀσυλία
2Mc 3:12 the sanctity and inviolability of the temple 1

invisible 1. ἀόρατος
Col 1:15 He is the image of the invisible God 1
16 in heaven and on earth, visible and invisible 1
1Ti 1:17 the King of ages, immortal, invisible, the only God 1
Heb 11:27 he endured as seeing him who is invisible. 1
invisible *See also* nature.

invitation 1. κλῆσις
3Mc 5:14 the person who was in charge of the invitations 1
27 being struck by the unusual invitation to come out *

invite 1. קרא 2. ζηλόω 3. καλέω 4. καλέω εἰς τὴν κλῆσιν 5. παρακαλέω 6. προκαλέω 7. προσκαλέω 8. φωνέω
Exd 34:15 when . . one invites you, you eat of his sacrifice 1
Num25: 2 These invited the people to the sacrifices 1
Jos 24: 9 and he sent and invited Balaam . . to curse you 1
Jdg 14:15 Have you invited us here to impoverish us? 1
1Sm 9:13 afterward those eat who are invited. 1
22 a place at the head of those who had been invited 1
16: 3 invite Jesse to the sacrifice, and I will show you 1
5 and invited them to the sacrifice. 1
2Sm 11:13 And David invited him, and he ate . . and drank 1
13:23 and Ab'salom invited all the king's sons. 1
15:11 200 men from Jerusalem who were invited guests 1
1Kg 1: 9 En-ro'gel, and he invited all his brothers 1
10 but he did not invite Nathan . . or Benai'ah 1
19 and has invited all the sons of the king, Abi'athar 1
19 but Solomon your servant he has not invited. 1
25 and has invited all the king's sons, Jo'ab 1
26 and your servant Solomon, he has not invited. 1
Est 5:12 I am invited by her together with the king. 1
Job 1: 4 they would send and invite their three sisters 1
Prv 18: 6 A fool's . . mouth invites a flogging. 1
Lam 2:22 Thou didst invite . . my terrors on every side; 1
Zec 3:10 every one of you will invite his neighbor 1
Mat 22: 3 sent his servants to call those who were invited 3
4 Tell those who are invited 3
8 but those invited were not worthy. 3
9 invite to the marriage feast as many as you find.' 3
Lke 7:39 Now when the Pharisee who had invited him saw it 3
14: 7 Now he told a parable to those who were invited 3
8 you are invited by any one to a marriage feast 3
8 lest a more eminent man than you be invited by him; 3
9 he who invited you both will come and say to you 3
10 when you are invited 3
12 He said also to the man who had invited him 3
12 do not invite your friends or your brothers 8
13 when you give a feast, invite the poor, the maimed 3
16 A man once gave a great banquet, and invited many; 3
17 to say to those who had been invited, 'Come 3
24 none of those men who were invited shall taste 3
Joh 2: 2 Jesus also was invited to the marriage 3
Act 8:31 he invited Philip to come up and sit with him. 5
28:14 were invited to stay with them for seven days 5
1Co 10:27 If one of the unbelievers invites you to dinner 3
Rev 19: 9 those who are invited to the marriage supper 3
Tob 5: 9 Tobias invited him 3
Jdt 12:10 did not invite any of his officers. 4
Wis 1:12 Do not invite death by the error of your life 2
Sir 13: 9 When a powerful man invites you, be reserved 7
9 he will invite you the more often. 7
2Mc 8:11 inviting them to buy Jewish slaves 6
12: 3 they invited the Jews . . to embark . . on boats 5
14: 5 was invited by Demetrius to a meeting of the council 7
3Mc 5:26 Hermon arrived and invited him to come out 3
4Mc 3:19 The present occasion now invites us 3

invite in return 1. ἀντικαλέω
Lke 14:12 lest they also invite you in return 1

invocation 1. ἐπίκλησις
2Mc 15:26 with invocation to God and prayers. 1

invoke 1. זכר 2. קרא 3. ἐπικαλέω
2Sm 14:11 Pray let the king invoke the LORD your God 1
1Ch 16: 4 to invoke, to thank, and to praise the LORD 1
Jer 44:26 that my name shall no more be invoked by the mouth 2
Jas 2: 7 that honorable name which was invoked over you? 3
1Pe 1:17 if you invoke as Father him who judges each one 3

invoke a blessing 1. ברך 2. εὐλογέω
Ps 72:15 blessings invoked for him all the day! 1
Heb 11:20 invoked future blessings on Jacob and Esau. 2

invoke a curse 1. ἀναθεματίζω 2. κατατίθημι
Mat 26:74 he began to invoke a curse on himself and to swear 2
Mrk 14:71 he began to invoke a curse on himself and to swear 1

invoke the aid 1. ἐπικαλέω
AEs 15: 2 after invoking the aid of the all-seeing God 1

involve 1. ἐν 2. περιβάλλω 3. προσενέχω 4. commisceo 5. fulcio
Num15:26 whole population was involved in the error. *
Heb 9:16 For where a will is involved *
2Es 7:12 and involved in great hardships. 5
68 who have been born are involved in iniquities 4
AEs 16: 5 have been involved in irremediable calamities 2
Sir 23:13 it involves sinful speech. 1
2Mc 2:24 considering the flood of numbers involved *
5:18 they were involved in many sins 3

become involved 1. συμφύρω
Sir 12:14 becomes involved in his sins. 1

invulnerable 1. ἀπήμαντος 2. ἄτρωτος
Wis 7:22 distinct, invulnerable, loving the good, keen 1
2Mc 8:36 therefore the Jews were invulnerable 2

inward 1. אֶל הַפְּנִימִית 2. בַּיִת 3. בַּיְתָה 4. פְּנִימָה
2Sm 5: 9 built . . round about from the Millo inward. 2
1Kg 7:25 and all their hinder parts were inward. 2
2Ch 4: 4 oxen . . and all their hinder parts were inward. 3
Ezk 40:16 windows . . narrowing inwards into their jambs 4
42: 4 And before the chambers was a passage inward 1
inward *See also* being, mind.

inward part 1. כִּלְיָה 2. קֶרֶב
Ps 139:13 For thou didst form my inward parts 1
Mic 6:14 and there shall be hunger in your inward parts; 2

inwardly 1. בְּנֶפֶשׁ 2. בְּקֶרֶב 3. ἔσωθεν 4. τὰ ἐντός 5. ψυχή
Ps 62: 4 They bless . . but inwardly they curse. Selah 2
Prv 23: 7 for he is like one who is inwardly reckoning. 1
Mat 7:15 in sheep's clothing but inwardly are ravenous 3
Sir 19:26 inwardly he is full of deceit. 4
2Mc 5:11 raging inwardly, he left Egypt 5

iota 1. ἰῶτα
Mat 5:18 heaven and earth pass away, not an iota, not a dot 1

irksome 1. ὀκνηρός
Php 3: 1 To write the same things to you is not irksome 1

iron 1. בַּרְזֶל 2. פַּרְזֶל (A) 3. σίδηρος 4. σιδηροῦς 5. ferrum
Gen 4:22 forger of all instruments of bronze and iron. 1
Lev 26:19 I will make your heavens like iron 1
Num31:22 only . . the bronze, the iron, the tin, and the lead 1
35:16 if he struck him down with an instrument of iron 1
Deu 3:11 behold, his bedstead was a bedstead of iron; 1
4:20 LORD . . brought you forth out of the iron furnace 1
8: 9 a land whose stones are iron, and out of whose hills 1
28:23 earth under you shall be iron. 1
48 he will put a yoke of iron upon your neck, until 1
33:25 Your bars shall be iron and bronze; 1
Jos 6:19 silver and gold, and vessels of bronze and iron 1
24 and gold, and the vessels of bronze and of iron 1
17:16 yet all the Canaanites . . have chariots of iron 1
18 drive out . . though they have chariots of iron 1
22: 8 many cattle, with silver, gold, bronze, and iron 1
Jdg 1:19 of the plain, because they had chariots of iron. 1
4: 3 he had 900 chariots of iron 1
13 called out all his chariots, 900 chariots of iron 1
1Sm 17: 7 and his spear's head weighed 600 shekels of iron; 1
2Sm 12:31 to labor with saws and iron picks and iron axes 1
31 to labor with saws and iron picks and iron axes 1
23: 7 arms himself with iron and the shaft of a spear 1
1Kg 6: 7 hammer nor axe nor any tool of iron was heard 1
8:51 out of Egypt, from the midst of the iron furnace). 1
22:11 Zedeki'ah . . made for himself horns of iron 1
2Kg 6: 6 threw it in there, and made the iron float. 1
1Ch 20: 3 to labor with saws and iron picks and axes; 1
22: 3 David also provided great stores of iron 1
14 silver, and bronze and iron beyond weighing 1
16 gold, silver, bronze, and iron. Arise and be doing! 1
29: 2 the iron for the things of iron 1
7 bronze, and 100,000 talents of iron. 1
2Ch 2: 7 skilled to work in gold, silver, bronze, and iron 1
14 He is trained to work in gold, silver, bronze, iron 1
18:10 Zedeki'ah . . made for himself horns of iron 1
24:12 workers in iron and bronze to repair 1
Job 19:24 Oh that with an iron pen and lead they were graven 1
20:24 He will flee from an iron weapon; 1
28: 2 Iron is taken out of the earth 1
40:18 his limbs like bars of iron. 1
41:27 He counts iron as straw, and bronze as rotten 1
Ps 2: 9 You shall break them with a rod of iron 1
105:18 his neck was put in a collar of iron; 1
107:10 prisoners in affliction and in irons 1
16 cuts in two the bars of iron. 1
149: 8 to bind . . their nobles with fetters of iron 1
Prv 27:17 Iron sharpens iron, and one man sharpens 1
17 Iron sharpens iron, and one man sharpens 1
Ecc 10:10 If the iron is blunt, and one does not whet the edge 1
Isa 45: 2 doors of bronze and cut asunder the bars of iron 1
48: 4 are obstinate, and your neck is an iron sinew 1
60:17 and instead of iron I will bring silver; 1
17 instead of wood, bronze, instead of stones, iron. 1
Jer 1:18 a fortified city, an iron pillar, and bronze walls 1
6:28 they are bronze and iron 1
11: 4 out of the land of Egypt, from the iron furnace 1
15:12 Can one break iron, iron from the north, and bronze? 1
12 Can one break iron, iron from the north, and bronze? 1
17: 1 The sin of Judah is written with a pen of iron; 1
28:13 but I will make in their place bars of iron. 1
14 upon the neck of all these nations an iron yoke 1
Ezk 4: 3 take an iron plate, and place it as an iron wall 1
3 place it as an iron wall between you and the city; 1
22:18 bronze and tin and iron and lead in the furnace 1
20 As men gather silver and bronze and iron and lead 1
27:12 wealth of every kind; silver, iron, tin, and lead 1
19 wrought iron, cassia, and calamus were bartered 1
Dan 2:33 its legs of iron, its feet partly of iron 2
33 its feet partly of iron and partly of clay. 2
34 smote the image on its feet of iron and clay 2
35 iron, the clay, the bronze, the silver, and the gold 2
40 there shall be a fourth kingdom, strong as iron 2
40 iron breaks to pieces and shatters all things; 2
40 like iron which crushes, it shall break and crush 2
41 toes partly of potter's clay and partly of iron 2
41 some of the firmness of iron shall be in it 2
41 just as you saw iron mixed with the miry clay. 2
42 toes of the feet were partly iron and partly clay 2
43 As you saw the iron mixed with miry clay 2
43 not hold . . just as iron does not mix with clay. 2
45 broke in pieces the iron, the bronze, the clay 2
4:15 bound with a band of iron and bronze 2
23 bound with a band of iron and bronze 2
5: 4 praised the gods of . . bronze, iron 2
23 gods of . . bronze, iron, wood, and stone 2
7: 7 great iron teeth; it devoured and broke in pieces 2
19 with its teeth of iron and claws of bronze; 2
Ams 1: 3 threshed Gilead with threshing sledges of iron. 1
Mic 4:13 I will make your horn iron and your hoofs bronze; 1
Act 12:10 they came to the iron gate leading into the city. 4
Rev 2:27 he shall rule them with a rod of iron 4
9: 9 they had scales like iron breastplates 4
12: 5 one who is to rule all nations with a rod of iron 4
18:12 articles of costly wood, bronze, iron and marble 3
19:15 and he will rule them with a rod of iron; 4
2Es 7:55 and also iron and lead and clay; 5
56 and brass than silver, and iron than brass 5
56 and lead than iron, and clay than lead.' 5
Wis 13:15 and fastens it there with iron. 3

Sir 22:15 Sand, salt, and a piece of iron are easier to bear 3
28:20 for its yoke is a yoke of iron 4
38:28 intent upon his handiwork in iron 3
39:26 water and fire and iron and salt and wheat flour 3
48:17 he tunneled the sheer rock with iron 3
Man 1:10 I am weighted down with many an iron fetter 3
2Mc 11: 9 the wildest beasts or walls of iron. 4
3Mc 3:25 bound securely with iron fetters 4
4Mc 8:13 braziers and thumbscrews and iron claws 4
9:26 after fitting themselves with iron gauntlets 4
28 tore out his sinews with the iron hands 4
11:10 fitting iron clamps on them 4
14:19 as though with an iron dart sting 3
iron *See also* bond, kettle, make, tool.

hot iron 1. *καυτηρίος*
4Mc 15:22 her sons were tortured . . with the hot irons! 1

thing of iron 1. בַּרְזֶל
1Ch 29: 2 the iron for the things of iron 1

ironsmith 1. חָרַשׁ בַּרְזֶל
Isa 44:12 The ironsmith fashions it and works it 1

irrational 1. *ἀλόγιστος* 2. *ἄλογος* 3. *μὴ λογισμός* 4. *οὐ μετὰ εὐλογιστίας* 5. *παρὰ λόγον*
2Pe 2:12 like irrational animals, creatures of instinct 2
Jde 1:10 they know by instinct as irrational animals do 2
Wis 11:15 led them astray to worship irrational serpents 2
15 a multitude of irrational creatures 2
3Mc 7: 8 the irrational things that have happened. 5
4Mc 2:19 their irrational slaughter of the entire tribe 3
3:11 a certain irrational desire 1
5:22 as though living by it were irrational 4
6:18 For it would be irrational 1

irrationally 1. *ἀλόγιστος*
4Mc 6:14 so irrationally destroying yourself 1

irreligion 1. *ἀσέβεια*
Tit 2:12 training us to renounce irreligion 1

irreligious 1. *βέβηλος*
Heb 12:16 that no one be immoral or irreligious like Esau 1

irremediable 1. *ἀνήκεστος*
AEs 16: 5 have been involved in irremediable calamities 1

irreproachable 1. *ἀνέγκλητος*
Col 1:22 blameless and irreproachable before him 1

irresistible 1. *ἀκώλυτος* 2. *ἀνυπόστατος*
Wis 7:22 loving the good, keen, irresistible 1
Man 1: 5 wrath of thy threat to sinners is irresistible; 2
2Mc 1:13 a force that seemed irresistible 2

irresolute 1. רַךְ לֵבָב
2Ch 13: 7 when Rehobo'am was young and irresolute 1

show irreverence 1. *ἀσεβέω*
2Mc 4:17 to show irreverence to the divine laws 1

irrevocable 1. *ἀμεταμέλητος* 2. *ἀτελής*
Rom 11:29 the gifts and the call of God are irrevocable 1
3Mc 5:42 he firmly swore an irrevocable oath 2

irrigate 1. *μεταχέω*
4Mc 1:29 and ties up and waters and thoroughly irrigates 1

irritable 1. *παροξύνω*
1Co 13: 5 it is not irritable or resentful; 1

irritate 1. רעם
1Sm 1: 6 rival used to provoke her sorely, to irritate her 1

island 1. אִי 2. *νῆσος*
Isa 42:15 I will turn the rivers into islands 1
Act 13: 6 had gone through the whole island as far as Paphos 2
27:26 we shall have to run on some island. 2
28: 1 then learned that the island was called Malta. 2
7 lands belonging to the chief man of the island 2
9 the rest of the people on the island who had diseases 2
11 in a ship which had wintered in the island 2
Rev 1: 9 I John . . was on the island called Patmos 2
6:14 every mountain and island was removed 2
16:20 And every island fled away 2
Sir 43:23 planted islands in it. 2
47:16 Your name reached to far-off islands, and you were 2
1Mc 6:29 came to him . . from islands of the seas. 2
8:11 The remaining kingdoms and islands 2
11:38 recruited from the islands of the nations 2
15: 1 sent a letter from the islands of the sea to Simon 2

small island 1. *νησίον*
Act 27:16 a small island called Cauda 1

isle 1. אִי 2. *νῆσος*
Ps 72:10 of Tarshish and of the isles render him tribute 1
Isa 40:15 behold, he takes up the isles like fine dust. 1
Ezk 26:18 Now the isles tremble on the day of your fall; 1
18 yea, the isles that are in the sea are dismayed 1
1Mc 14: 5 opened a way to the isles of the sea. 2

isolate 1. *κατὰ μόνας*
1Mc 12:36 in order to isolate it 1

issue 1. אַחֲרִית 2. יצא 3. נתן 4. נגד (A) 5. שׂוּם (A) 6. *ἐκπίπτω* 7. *ἐκπορεύομαι* 8. *ἐξέρχομαι* 9. *τίθημι* 10. exeo
Ezr 5:17 see whether a decree was issued by Cyrus the king 5
6: 3 Cyrus . . issued a decree: Concerning the house 5
Est 3:14 A copy of the document was to be issued as a decree 3
15 and the decree was issued in Susa the capital. 3
4: 8 decree issued in Susa for their destruction 3
8:13 A copy . . was to be issued as a decree 3
14 and the decree was issued in Susa the capital. 3
9:14 a decree was issued in Susa, and . . were hanged. 3
Ezk 47: 1 water was issuing from below the threshold 2
Dan 7:10 stream of fire issued and came forth from before 4
12: 8 O my lord, what shall be the issue of these things? 1
1Ti 1: 5 that issues from a pure heart and a good conscience *
Rev 1:16 from his mouth issued a sharp two-edged sword 7
4: 5 From the throne issue flashes of lightning 7
9:17 and smoke and sulphur issued from their mouths. 7
18 smoke and sulphur issuing from their mouths. 7
16:13 I saw, issuing from the mouth of the dragon *
19:15 From his mouth issues a sharp sword 7
21 the sword that issues from his mouth; 8
2Es 13: 4 whenever his voice issued from his mouth 10
Sir 27:28 Mockery and abuse issue from the proud man *
2Mc 6: 8 At the suggestion of Ptolemy a decree was issued 6
4Mc 4:23 after he had plundered them he issued a decree 9

issue (2) 1. זִרְמָה 2. צְפִעָה 3. *αἰτία* 4. *κρίσις*
Isa 22:24 of his father's house, the offspring and issue 2
Ezk 23:20 and whose issue was like that of horses. 1
2Mc 4:28 on account of this issue. 3
14:18 Nicanor . . shrank from deciding the issue 4

issue an order 1. *ἐπιτάσσω* 2. *παραγγέλλω*
1Es 2:28 Therefore I have now issued orders 1
1Mc 5:58 they issued orders to the men of the forces 2

first issue 1. רֵאשִׁית
Deu 21:17 first issue of his strength; the right 1
Ps 78:51 first issue of their strength in the tents of Ham. 1
105:36 smote . . first issue of all their strength. 1

issue previously 1. *προϋποτάσσομαι*
3Mc 1: 2 that had been previously issued to him 1
it *See* far, used.

itch 1. גָּרָב 2. חֶרֶס 3. נֶתֶק 4. *κνήθω*
Lev 13:30 it is an itch, a leprosy of the head or the beard 3
31 if the priest examines the itching disease 3
31 shut up the person with the itching disease 3
32 if the itch has not spread 3
32 the itch appears to be no deeper than the skin 3
33 himself, but the itch he shall not shave 3
34 the priest shall examine the itch 3
34 if the itch has not spread in the skin 3
35 if the itch spreads in the skin 3
36 if the itch has spread in the skin 3
37 if in his eyes the itch is checked 3
37 the itch is healed, he is clean 3
14:54 law for any leprous disease: for an itch 3
22:22 Animals . . having a discharge or an itch 1
Deu 28:27 smite you with . . scurvy and the itch 2
2Ti 4: 3 having itching ears 4
itching *See* disease.

itinerant 1. *περιέρχομαι*
Act 19:13 Then some of the itinerant Jewish exorcists 1

ivory 1. שֵׁן 2. שֶׁנְהַבִּים 3. *ἐλεφάντινος*
1Kg 10:18 The king also made a great ivory throne 1
22 bringing gold, silver, ivory, apes, and peacocks. 2
22:39 acts of Ahab . . and the ivory house which he built 1
2Ch 9:17 The king also made a great ivory throne 1
21 (ships) bringing . . ivory, apes, and peacocks. 2
Ps 45: 8 From ivory palaces stringed instruments make 1
Sng 5:14 His body is ivory work 1
7: 4 Your neck is like an ivory tower. 1
Ezk 27: 6 deck of pines . . of Cyprus, inlaid with ivory. 1
15 brought you in payment ivory tusks and ebony. 1
Ams 3:15 and the houses of ivory shall perish 1
6: 4 Woe to those who lie upon beds of ivory 1
Rev 18:12 all kinds of scented wood, all articles of ivory 3
ivy *See* wreath, wreathed.

ivy-leaf 1. *κισσόφυλλον*
3Mc 2:29 the ivy-leaf symbol of Dionysus 1

J

jacinth 1. לֶשֶׁם 2. ὑάκινθος

Exd 28:19 the third row a jacinth, an agate, and an amethyst; 1
39:12 the third row, a jacinth, an agate, and an amethyst; 1
Rev 21:20 the tenth chrysoprase, the eleventh jacinth 2

jackal 1. שׁוּעָל 2. תַּן

Neh 2:13 went . . to the Jackal's Well and to the Dung Gate 2
Job 30:29 I am a brother of jackals, and a companion 2
Ps 44:19 shouldst have broken us in the place of jackals 2
63:10 they shall be prey for jackals. 1
Isa 13:22 Hyenas . . and jackals in the pleasant palaces; 2
34:13 It shall be the haunt of jackals 2
35: 7 the haunt of jackals shall become a swamp 2
43:20 will honor me, the jackals and the ostriches; 2
Jer 9:11 make Jerusalem a heap of ruins, a lair of jackals; 2
10:22 to make . . Judah a desolation, a lair of jackals. 2
14: 6 they pant for air like jackals; 2
49:33 Hazor shall become a haunt of jackals 2
51:37 become a heap of ruins, the haunt of jackals 2
Lam 4: 3 Even the jackals give the breast and suckle 2
5:18 Zion . . lies desolate; jackals prowl over it. 1
Mic 1: 8 I will make lamentation like the jackals 2
Mal 1: 3 and left his heritage to jackals of the desert. 2

jailer 1. βασανιστής 2. δεσμοφύλαξ

Mat 18:34 in anger his lord delivered him to the jailers 1
Act 16:23 charging the jailer to keep them safely. 2
27 When the jailer woke 2
36 the jailer reported the words to Paul, saying 2

jamb 1. אַיִל

Ezk 40: 9 and its jambs, two cubits; 1
10 the jambs on either side were of the same size. 1
16 windows . . narrowing inwards into their jambs 1
16 and on the jambs were palm trees. 1
21 its jambs and its vestibule were of the same size 1
24 he measured its jambs and its vestibule; 1
26 it had palm trees on its jambs, one on either side. 1
29 Its side rooms, its jambs, and its vestibule were 1
31 palm trees were on its jambs 1
33 Its side rooms, its jambs, and its vestibule were 1
34 it had palm trees on its jambs, one on either side; 1
36 Its side rooms, its jambs, and its vestibule were 1
37 it had palm trees on its jambs, one on either side; 1
48 and measured the jambs of the vestibule 1
49 were pillars beside the jambs on either side. 1
41: 1 he brought me to the nave, and measured the jambs; 1
1 six cubits was the breadth of the jambs. *
3 and measured the jambs of the entrance 1

jar 1. אָסוּךְ 2. בַּקְבּוּק 3. כַּד 4. נֵבֶל 5. צִנְצֶנֶת 6. צַפַּחַת 7. ἀγγεῖον 8. κεράμιον 9. ὑδρία

Gen 24:14 'Pray let down your jar that I may drink,' 3
16 She went down to the spring, and filled her jar 3
17 give me a little water to drink from your jar. 3
18 and she quickly let down her jar upon her hand 3
20 she quickly emptied her jar into the trough 3
43 Pray give me a little water from your jar to drink 3
45 She quickly let down her jar from her shoulder 3
46 She quickly let down her jar from her shoulder 3
Exd 16:33 Moses said to Aaron, "Take a jar, and put an omer 5
Jdg 7: 8 he took the jars of the people from their hands *
16 into the hands of all of them and empty jars 3
16 and empty jars, with torches inside the jars. 3
19 and smashed the jars that were in their hands. 3
20 companies blew the trumpets and broke the jars 3
1Sm 26:11 take now the spear . . and the jar of water 6
12 David took the spear and the jar of water 6
16 see where the king's spear is, and the jar of water 6
1Kg 14: 3 Take . . ten loaves, some cakes, and a jar of honey 2
17:12 nothing baked, only a handful of meal in a jar 3
14 The jar of meal shall not be spent, and the cruse 3
16 The jar of meal was not spent 3
18:33 Fill four jars with water, and pour it 3
19: 6 a cake baked on hot stones and a jar of water. 6
2Kg 4: 2 has nothing in the house, except a jar of oil. 1
Jer 13:12 Every jar shall be filled with wine. 4
12 know that every jar will be filled with wine? 4
48:12 empty his vessels, and break his jars in pieces. 4
Mrk 14:13 a man carrying a jar of water will meet you 8
Lke 22:10 a man carrying a jar of water will meet you 8
Joh 2: 6 Now six stone jars were standing there 9
7 Jesus said to them, "Fill the jars with water. 9
Sir 21:14 The mind of a fool is like a broken jar 7

water jar 1. כַּד 2. ὑδρία

Gen 24:15 came out with her water jar upon her shoulder. 1
45 came out with her water jar on her shoulder; 1
Joh 4:28 the woman left her water jar, and went away 2

jasper 1. יָהֲלֹם 2. יָשְׁפֵה 3. ἴασπις

Exd 28:20 the fourth row a beryl, an onyx, and a jasper; 2
39:13 the fourth row, a beryl, an onyx, and a jasper; 2
Ezk 28:13 carnelian, topaz, and jasper, chrysolite, beryl 1
Rev 4: 3 he . . appeared like jasper and carnelian 3
21:11 its radiance . . like a jasper, clear as crystal. 3
18 The wall was built of jasper 3
19 adorned with every jewel; the first was jasper 3

javelin 1. כִּידוֹן 2. סְגוֹר 3. שִׁרְיָה

Jos 8:18 Stretch out the javelin that is in your hand 1
18 Joshua stretched out the javelin . . in his hand 1
26 his hand, with which he stretched out the javelin 1
1Sm 17: 6 a javelin of bronze . . between his shoulders. 1
45 with a sword and with a spear and with a javelin; 1
Job 39:23 the flashing spear and the javelin. 1
41:26 not avail; nor the spear, the dart, or the javelin. 3
29 he laughs at the rattle of javelins. 1
Ps 35: 3 Draw the spear and javelin against my pursuers! 2

jaw 1. לְחִי 2. מַלְקוֹחַ

Job 41: 2 rope in his nose, or pierce his jaw with a hook? 1
Ps 22:15 my tongue cleaves to my jaws; 2
Isa 30:28 and to place on the jaws of the peoples a bridle 1
Ezk 29: 4 I will put hooks in your jaws 1
38: 4 I will turn you about, and put hooks into your jaws 1
Hos 11: 4 as one, who eases the yoke on their jaws 1

jawbone 1. לְחִי

Jdg 15:15 he found a fresh jawbone of an ass, and put out his 1
16 With the jawbone of an ass, heaps upon heaps 1
16 with the jawbone of an ass have I slain 1,000 men 1
17 he threw away the jawbone out of his hand; 1

jealous 1. קנא 2. קַנָּא 3. קִנְאָה 4. קַנּוֹא 5. ζῆλος 6. ζηλόω 7. ζήλωσις

Gen 37:11 his brothers were jealous of him 1
Exd 20: 5 for I the LORD your God am a jealous God 2
34:14 the LORD, whose name is Jealous, is a jealous God) 2
14 the LORD, whose name is Jealous, is a jealous God) 2
Num 5:14 he is jealous of his wife who has defiled herself; 1
14 and he is jealous of his wife, 1
30 when . . he is jealous of his wife; 1
11:29 Moses said to him, "Are you jealous for my sake? 1
25:11 he was jealous with my jealousy among them 1
13 because he was jealous for his God 1
Deu 4:24 LORD your God is a devouring fire, a jealous God. 2
5: 9 for I the LORD your God am a jealous God 2
6:15 LORD your God in the midst of you is a jealous God; 2
Jos 24:19 he is a holy God; he is a jealous God; 4
1Kg 19:10 He said, "I have been very jealous for the LORD 1
14 He said, "I have been very jealous for the LORD 1
Job 36:33 who is jealous with anger against iniquity. *
Ps 106:16 men in the camp were jealous of Moses and Aaron 1
Isa 11:13 E'phraim shall not be jealous of Judah 1
Ezk 36: 6 Behold, I speak in my jealous wrath 3
39:25 I will be jealous for my holy name. 1
Nah 1: 2 The LORD is a jealous God and avenging 4
Zec 1:14 I am exceedingly jealous for Jerusalem 1
8: 2 I am jealous for Zion with great jealousy 1
2 I am jealous for her with great wrath. 1
Act 7: 9 the patriarchs, jealous of Joseph 6
17: 5 the Jews were jealous 6
1Co 13: 4 love is not jealous or boastful; 6
Wis 1:10 because a jealous ear hears all things 7
Sir 9: 1 Do not be jealous of the wife of your bosom 5
37:10 those who are jealous of you 6

jealous *See also* make, wrath.

become jealous 1. קנא

Jol 2:18 Then the LORD became jealous for his land 1

jealously 1. πρὸς φθόνον

Jas 4: 5 He yearns jealously over the spirit 1

jealousy 1. קִנְאָה 2. ζῆλος

Num 5:14 or if the spirit of jealousy comes upon him 1
14 or if the spirit of jealousy comes upon him 1
15 it is a cereal offering of jealousy 1
18 which is the cereal offering of jealousy. 1
25 shall take the cereal offering of jealousy 1
29 This is the law in cases of jealousy, when a wife 1
30 or when the spirit of jealousy comes upon a man 1
25:11 he was jealous with my jealousy among them 1
11 not consume the people of Israel in my jealousy. 1
Deu 29:20 rather the anger of the LORD and his jealousy 1
Job 5: 2 kills the fool, and jealousy slays the simple. 1
Prv 6:34 For jealousy makes a man furious 1
27: 4 but who can stand before jealousy? 1
Sng 8: 6 love is strong . . jealousy is cruel as the grave. 1
Isa 11:13 The jealousy of E'phraim shall depart 1
Ezk 5:13 I, the LORD, have spoken in my jealousy 1
8: 3 where was the seat of the image of jealousy 1
5 in the entrance, was this image of jealousy. 1
16:38 bring upon you the blood of wrath and jealousy. 1
42 and my jealousy shall depart from you; 1
36: 5 my hot jealousy against the rest of the nations 1
38:19 in my jealousy and in my blazing wrath I declare 1
Zec 8: 2 I am jealous for Zion with great jealousy 1
Act 5:17 filled with jealousy 2
13:45 they were filled with jealousy 2
Rom 13:13 not in quarreling and jealousy. 2
1Co 3: 3 For while there is jealousy and strife among you 2
2Co 11: 2 I feel a divine jealousy for you 2
12:20 perhaps there may be quarreling, jealousy, anger 2
Gal 5:20 idolatry, sorcery, enmity, strife, jealousy, anger 2
Jas 3:14 if you have bitter jealousy . . in your hearts 2
16 For where jealousy and selfish ambition exist 2
Sir 30:24 Jealousy and anger shorten life 2
1Mc 8:16 there is no envy or jealousy among them. 2

jealousy *See also* move, provoke, stir.

jeer 1. קלס

2Kg 2:23 some small boys came out of the city and jeered 1

jeopard 1. חרף

Jdg 5:18 Zeb'ulun . . jeoparded their lives to the death; 1

jest 1. צחק 2. προσπαίζω

Gen 19:14 But he seemed to his sons-in-law to be jesting. 1
Sir 8: 4 Do not jest with an ill-bred person 2

jewel 1. אֶבֶן 2. חֲלִי 3. כְּלִי 4. עֲנָק 5. פְּנִינִים 6. תַּרְשִׁישׁ 7. λίθος 8. λίθος τίμιος

Job 28:17 nor can it be exchanged for jewels of fine gold. 3
Prv 3:15 She is more precious than jewels 5
8:11 for wisdom is better than jewels 5
20:15 but the lips of knowledge are a precious jewel. 3
31:10 good wife . . is far more precious than jewels. 5
Sng 4: 9 with a glance . . with one jewel of your necklace. 4
5:14 His arms are rounded gold, set with jewels. 6
7: 1 Your rounded thighs are like jewels 2
Isa 61:10 and as a bride adorns herself with her jewels. 3
Ezk 16:17 You also took your fair jewels of my gold 3

39 and take your fair jewels, and leave you naked 3
23:26 your clothes and take away your fine jewels. 3
Zec 9:16 like the jewels of a crown they shall shine 1
1Pe 3: 4 the imperishable jewel of a gentle and quiet spirit •
Rev 17: 4 and bedecked with gold and jewels and pearls 8
18:12 cargo of gold, silver, jewels and pearls 8
16 bedecked with gold, with jewels, and with pearls! 8
21:11 its radiance like a most rare jewel, like a jasper 7
19 foundations . . were adorned with every jewel; 8

jeweler 1. חָרַשׁ אֶבֶן 2. *λιθούργος*
Exd 28:11 As a jeweler engraves signets, so shall you 1
Sir 45:11 in a setting of gold, the work of a jeweler 2

jewelry 1. חֲלִיָה 2. כְּלִי
Gen 24:53 the servant brought forth jewelry of silver 2
Exd 3:22 ask of her neighbor . . jewelry of silver 2
11: 2 that they ask . . jewelry of silver and of gold. 2
12:35 asked . . jewelry of silver and of gold 2
Hos 2:13 and decked herself with her ring and jewelry 1
jewels *See* string.

join 1. אחז 2. אַחֲרֵי 3. בוא 4. דבק 5. דָּבֵק 6. דבק בְּ 7. היה עִם 8. הלך עַל 9. חבר 10. חזק 11. יחד 12. יַחְדָּו 13. יַחְדָּו תַּמִּים 14. יסף 15. לוה 16. לוה עַל 17. מַחְבֶּרֶת 18. נגע 19. נתן 20. עמד 21. ערך 22. קרב 23. שׁית 24. *ἀναστρέφω* 25. *γίνομαι* 26. *ἐπισυνάγω* 27. *ἔρχομαι πρός* 28. *ζευγίζω* 29. *κολλάω* 30. *μετά* 31. *παραγίνομαι* 32. *πῆγμα* 33. *ποιὲω ὁμοῦ* 34. *προσκληρόω* 35. *προσκλίνω* 36. *προσκολλάω* 37. *προστίθημι* 38. *συμμείγνυμι* 39. *συμμίσγω* 40. *συνάγω* 41. *συναθροίζω* 42. *συναντάω* 43. *συνάπτω* 44. *συνέρχομαι* 45. *συνεφίστημι* 46. *συνίστημι* 47. *συντρέχω*
Gen 14: 8 they joined battle in the Valley of Siddim 21
29:34 Now this time my husband will be joined to me 15
49: 6 O my spirit, be not joined to their company; 11
Exd 1:10 if war befall us, they join our enemies and fight 14
23: 1 You shall not join hands with a wicked man 23
26:24 be separate beneath, but joined at the top 13
28:27 at its joining above the skilfully woven band 17
36:29 they were separate beneath, but joined at the top 12
39: 4 shoulder-pieces, joined to it at its two edges. 9
20 its joining above the skilfully woven band 17
Num18: 2 that they may join you and minister to you 15
4 shall join you, and attend to the tent of meeting 15
Jos 23:12 turn back, and join the remnant of these nations 6
1Sm 13: 4 people were called out to join Saul at Gilgal. 2
1Kg 5: 6 my servants will join your servants, and I will 7
6:10 it was joined to the house with timbers of cedar. 1
20:29 on the seventh day the battle was joined; 22
2Kg 23: 3 and all the people joined in the covenant. 20
2Ch 3:12 other wing . . was joined to the wing of the first 5
20:35 Jehosh'aphat king of Judah joined with Ahazi'ah 9
36 He joined him in building ships to go to Tarshish 9
37 Because you have joined with Ahazi'ah 9
35:22 but joined battle in the plain of Megid'do. 3
Ezr 6:21 every one who had joined them and separated •
Neh 10:29 join with their brethren, their nobles, and enter 10
11:36 Levites in Judah were joined to Benjamin. •
Est 9:27 themselves and . . all who joined them 16
Job 41:17 They are joined one to another; 4
Ps 83: 8 Assyria also has joined them; 15
Ecc 9: 4 But he who is joined with all the living has hope 9
Isa 5: 8 Woe to those who join house to house 18
14: 1 aliens will join them and will cleave 15
20 You will not be joined with them in burial 11
56: 3 the foreigner who has joined himself to the LORD 15
6 the foreigners who join themselves to the LORD 15
Jer 3:18 the house of Judah shall join the house of Israel 8
50: 5 saying, 'Come, let us join ourselves to the LORD 15
Ezk 37:17 join them together into one stick 22
19 I will join with it the stick of Judah 19
Dan 11:34 many shall join themselves to them with flattery; 15
Hos 4:17 E'phraim is joined to idols, let him alone. 9
Zec 2:11 many nations shall join themselves to the LORD 15
Mat 19: 5 and be joined to his wife 29
Mrk 10: 7 be joined to his wife 36
Lke 15:15 joined himself to one of the citizens 29
Act 5:13 None of the rest dared join them 29
36 a number of men, about 400, joined him 35
8:29 Go up and join this chariot. 29
9:26 he attempted to join the disciples 29
16:22 The crowd joined in attacking them 45
17: 4 joined Paul and Silas 34
34 some men joined him and believed 29
1Co 6:16 who joins himself to a prostitute becomes one 29
Eph 5:31 be joined to his wife 36
Php 3:17 Brethren, join in imitating me 25
1Pe 4: 4 They are surprised that you do not now join them 47
1Es 1:29 He joined battle with him in the plain of Megiddo 46
5:50 joined them from the other peoples of the land. 26
7: 6 the rest . . who joined them 37
Jdt 1: 6 He was joined by all the people of the hill country 42
6 Many nations joined the forces of the Chaldeans. 44
11 refused to join him in the war 44
7: 1 all the allies who had joined him 31
12:11 to join us and eat and drink with us. 27
14:10 was circumcised, and joined the house of Israel 37
1Mc 1:15 They joined with the Gentiles 28
52 Many of the people . . joined them 41
2:43 joined them and reinforced them. 37
3: 2 all who had joined his father helped him 29
41 forces from Syria . . joined with them. 37
6:21 some of the ungodly Israelites joined them. 29
7:22 all who were troubling their people joined him. 40
39 the Syrian army joined him. 42
11:69 emerged from their places and joined battle. 43
73 returned to him and joined him in the pursuit 30
13:14 he was about to join battle with him 43
2Mc 13: 3 Menelaus also joined them 38
12 When they had all joined in the same petition 33
14:14 flocked to join Nicanor, thinking that . . 39
3Mc 2:30 to join those who have been initiated 24
4Mc 9:21 the ligaments joining his bones 32

join battle 1. *παρατάσσω* 2. *προσβάλλω* 3. *συμβάλλω* 4. *συνάπτω*
1Mc 15:14 the ships joined battle from the sea 4
2Mc 8:23 he joined battle with Nicanor. 3
10:28 the two armies joined battle 2
12:34 When they joined battle 1

join forces 1. חבר 2. יעד
Gen 14: 3 all these joined forces in the valley of Siddim 1
Jos 11: 5 And all these kings joined their forces, and came 2

join in a charge 1. *συνεπιτίθημι*
Act 24: 9 The Jews also joined in the charge 1

join in apostasy 1. *συναφίστημι*
Tob 1: 5 All the tribes that joined in apostasy 1

join together 1. חבר 2. קשׁר 3. *συζεύγνυμι* 4. *συναρμολογέω*
Exd 28: 7 that it may be joined together. 1
Neh 4: 6 wall was joined together to half its height. 2
Job 16: 4 I could join words together against you 1
Mat 19: 6 What therefore God has joined together 3
Mrk 10: 9 What therefore God has joined together 3
Eph 2:21 in whom the whole structure is joined together 4
4:16 the whole body, joined and knit together 4

join with to fight 1. *συνεκπολεμέω*
Wis 5:20 creation will join with him to fight 1

joint 1. *ἄρθρον* 2. *ἁρμός* 3. *ἁφή*
Eph 4:16 every joint with which it is supplied 3
Col 2:19 knit together through its joints and ligaments 3
Heb 4:12 the division . . of joints and marrow 2
4Mc 9:17 Cut my limbs, burn my flesh, and twist my joints. 1
joint *See also* heirs, put.

out of joint 1. פרד
Ps 22:14 all my bones are out of joint; my heart is like wax 1

joint-dislocator 1. *ἀρθρέμβολον*·
4Mc 8:13 wheels and joint-dislocators 1

joke 1. שׂחק
Prv 26:19 deceives his neighbor and says, "I am only joking! 1

jostle 1. דחק
Jol 2: 8 They do not jostle one another 1

journey 1. דֶּרֶךְ 2. הלך 3. מַהֲלָךְ 4. מַסָּע 5. נסע 6. עשׂה דֶּרֶךְ 7. שׁור 8. *ἀποδημέω* 9. *ἄφιξις* 10. *ὁδεύω* 11. *ὁδοιπορέω* 12. *ὁδοιπορία* 13. *ὁδός* 14. *πορεία* 15. *πορείαν ποιέω* 16. *πορεύομαι* 17. iter
Gen 12: 9 Abram journeyed on 5
13: 3 he journeyed on from the Negeb as far as Bethel 2
11 and Lot journeyed east; 5
20: 1 Abraham journeyed toward the territory 5
24:21 whether the LORD had prospered his journey 1
30:36 he set a distance of three days' journey 1
33:12 Let us journey on our way, and I will go before you. 5
17 Jacob journeyed to Succoth 5
35: 5 as they journeyed, a terror from God fell upon 5
16 Then they journeyed from Bethel; 5
21 Israel journeyed on, and pitched his tent beyond 5
42:25 to give them provisions for the journey. 1
38 befall him on the journey that you are to make 1
45:21 and gave them provisions for the journey. 1
23 provision for his father on the journey. 1
Exd 3:18 go a three days' journey into the wilderness 1
5: 3 a three days' journey into the wilderness 1
8:27 go three days' journey into the wilderness 1
12:37 the people of Israel journeyed from Ram'eses 5
40:36 Throughout all their journeys, whenever 5
38 For throughout all their journeys the cloud 5
Num 9:10 If any man of you . . is afar off on a journey 1
13 the man who is clean and is not on a journey, yet 1
10:33 set out . . three days' journey; 1
33 ark . . went before them three days' journey 1
11:31 about a day's journey on this side 1
31 about . . a day's journey on the other side 1
35 From . . the people journeyed to Haze'roth; 5
20:22 And they journeyed from Kadesh, 5
33: 8 went a three days' journey in the wilderness of Etham 1
Deu 1: 2 eleven days' journey from Horeb by the way •
40 as for you, turn, and journey into the wilderness 5
2: 1 we turned, and journeyed into the wilderness 5
10: 6 Israel journeyed from Be-er'oth Bene-ja'akan 5
7 From there they journeyed to Gud'godah 5
11 Arise, go on your journey at the head of the people 4
28:68 journey which I promised that you should never 1
Jos 9:11 Take provisions in your hand for the journey 1
12 when we took it . . as our food for the journey •
13 shoes . . are worn out from the very long journey. 1
Jdg 11:18 they journeyed through the wilderness, and went 2
17: 8 and as he journeyed, he came to the hill country 6
18: 5 may know whether the journey . . will succeed. 1
6 The journey on which you go is under the eye 1
19: 9 arise early in the morning for your journey 1
1Sm 9: 6 tell us about the journey on which we have set 1
21: 5 are holy, even when it is a common journey; 1
2Sm 11:10 David said . . "Have you not come from a journey? 1
1Kg 18:27 he has gone aside, or he is on a journey, or perhaps 1
19: 4 he . . went a day's journey into the wilderness 1
7 Arise and eat, else the journey will be too great 1
1Ch 4:39 They journeyed to the entrance of Gedor 2
Prv 7:19 husband . . has gone on a long journey; 1
Isa 57: 9 You journeyed to Molech with oil and multiplied 7
Jon 3: 3 great city, three days' journey in breadth. 3
4 began to go into the city, going a day's journey. 3
Mat 10:10 no bag for your journey, nor two tunics 13
Mrk 6: 8 charged them to take nothing for their journey 13
10:17 as he was setting out on his journey 13
Lke 2:44 they went a day's journey 13
9: 3 he said to them, "Take nothing for your journey 13
10:33 a Samaritan, as he journeyed, came to where he was; 10
11: 6 a friend of mine has arrived on a journey 13
13:22 teaching, and journeying toward Jerusalem. 15
15:13 and took his journey into a far country 8
Joh 4: 6 Jesus, wearied as he was with his journey, sat down 12
Act 1:12 is near Jerusalem, a sabbath day's journey away; 13
9: 3 Now as he journeyed he approached Damascus 16
10: 9 The next day, as they were on their journey 11
22: 5 I journeyed to Damascus 16
26:12 Thus I journeyed to Damascus 16
13 shining round me and those who journeyed with me. 16
2Co 11:26 on frequent journeys, in danger from rivers 12
3Jn 1: 6 You will do well to send them on their journey •
2Es 13:45 a long way to go, a journey of a year and a half 17
Tob 5:16 Then he said to Tobias, "Get ready for the journey 13
16 his son made the preparations for the journey. 13
21 his journey will be successful 13
7: 8 which you talked about on the journey 14
10: 1 when the days for the journey had expired 14
11: 1 because he had made his journey a success 13
Wis 18: 3 a guide for thy people's unknown journey 12
19: 5 might experience an incredible journey 12
Sir 21:16 A fool's narration is like a burden on a journey 13
1Mc 5:24 went three days' journey into the wilderness. 13
7:45 The Jews pursued them a day's journey 13
8:19 They went to Rome, a very long journey 13
2Mc 3: 8 Heliodorus at once set out on his journey 14
9: 4 until he completed the journey 14
7 and giving orders to hasten the journey 14
3Mc 7:18 provided all things . . for their journey 9
journey *See also* go, make, speed, take.

prosperous journey 1. *εὐοδία* 2. *ὁδοιπορία*
1Es 8: 6 the prosperous journey which the Lord gave them. 1
50 to seek from him a prosperous journey 1
Wis 13:18 for a prosperous journey 2

journey through 1. *διοδεύω*
Wis 5: 7 we journeyed through trackless deserts 1
11: 2 They journeyed through an uninhabited wilderness 1

joy 1. גיל 2. גִּיל 3. גִּילָה 4. חֶדְוָה 5. מָשׂוֹשׂ 6. רִנָּה 7. שׂושׂ 8. שׂמח 9. שִׂמְחָה 10. שָׂשׂוֹן 11. תְּרוּעָה 12. חֶדְוָה (A) 13. *ἀγαλλίαμα* 14. *ἀγαλλιάω* 15. *εὐφραίνω* 16. *εὐφροσύνη* 17. *ἡδονή* 18. *τέρψις* 19. *χαρά* 20. *χαρμονή* 21. *χαρμόσυνος* 22. exultatio 23. gaudium 24. iucunditas
Jdg 19: 3 girl's father saw him, he came with joy to meet him. 8
1Kg 1:40 playing on pipes, and rejoicing with great joy 9
1Ch 12:40 for there was joy in Israel. 9
15:16 on harps . . and cymbals, to raise sounds of joy. 9
16:27 strength and joy are in his place. 4
2Ch 20:27 returning to Jerusalem with joy 9
30:26 there was great joy in Jerusalem 9
Ezr 3:12 wept . . though many shouted aloud for joy; 9
6:16 celebrated the dedication of this house . . with joy. 12
22 kept the feast . . seven days with joy; 9

Neh 8:10 for the joy of the LORD is your strength. 4
12:43 God had made them rejoice with great joy; 9
43 joy of Jerusalem was heard afar off. 9
Est 8:16 Jews had light and gladness and joy and honor. 10
17 there was gladness and joy among the Jews, a feast 10
Job 8:19 Behold, this is the joy of his way; 5
20: 5 the joy of the godless but for a moment? 9
33:26 he comes into his presence with joy. 11
Ps 4: 7 Thou hast put more joy in my heart than they have 9
16:11 in thy presence there is fulness of joy 9
19: 5 like a strong man runs its course with joy. 7
21: 6 make him glad with the joy of thy presence. 9
30: 5 for the night, but joy comes with the morning. 6
45:15 With joy and gladness they are led along 2
48: 2 is the joy of all the earth, Mount Zion 5
51: 8 Fill me with joy and gladness; 10
12 Restore to me the joy of thy salvation 10
65:12 the hills gird themselves with joy 2
68: 3 exult before God; let them be jubilant with joy! 9
97:11 Light dawns . . and joy for the upright in heart. 9
105:43 he led forth his people with joy 10
119:111 testimonies . . yea, they are the joy of my heart. 10
137: 6 if I do not set Jerusalem above my highest joy! 9
Prv 12:20 but those who plan good have joy. 9
14:10 no stranger shares its joy. 9
13 end of joy is grief. 9
15:21 Folly is a joy to him who has no sense 9
23 To make an apt answer is a joy to a man 9
17:21 father of a fool has no joy. 8
21:15 When justice is done, it is a joy to the righteous 9
Ecc 2:26 God gives wisdom and knowledge and joy; 9
5:20 God keeps him occupied with joy in his heart. 9
Isa 9: 3 thou hast increased its joy; they rejoice 9
3 rejoice before thee as with joy at the harvest 9
12: 3 With joy you will draw water from the wells 10
16:10 joy and gladness are taken away 9
22:13 behold, joy and gladness, slaying oxen 10
24:11 for lack of wine; all joy has reached its eventide; 9
29:19 The meek shall obtain fresh joy in the LORD 9
32:14 dens for ever, a joy of wild asses 5
35: 2 blossom . . and rejoice with joy and singing. 3
10 everlasting joy shall be upon their heads; 9
10 they shall obtain joy and gladness 10
48:20 declare this with a shout of joy, proclaim it 6
51: 3 joy and gladness will be found in her 10
11 everlasting joy shall be upon their heads; 9
11 they shall obtain joy and gladness 10
55:12 you shall go out in joy, and be led forth in peace; 9
60:15 make you majestic for ever, a joy from age to age. 5
61: 7 double portion; yours shall be everlasting joy. 9
65:18 Jerusalem a rejoicing, and her people a joy. 5
66: 5 Let the LORD be glorified, that we may see your joy 9
10 rejoice with her in joy, all you who mourn over her; 5
Jer 15:16 thy words became to me a joy 10
31:13 I will turn their mourning into joy 10
33: 9 And this city shall be to me a name of joy, a praise 10
48:33 Gladness and joy have been taken away 2
Lam 2:15 the perfection of beauty, the joy of all the earth? 5
5:15 The joy of our hearts has ceased; 5
Ezk 24:25 from them their stronghold, their joy and glory 5
36: 5 with wholehearted joy and utter contempt 9
Jol 1:16 joy and gladness from the house of our God? 2
Hab 3:18 I will joy in the God of my salvation. 1
Zec 8:19 to the house of Judah seasons of joy and gladness 10
Mat 2:10 star, they rejoiced exceedingly with great joy; 19
13:20 and immediately receives it with joy; 19
44 in his joy he goes and sells all that he has 19
25:21 enter into the joy of your master.' 19
23 enter into the joy of your master.' 19
28: 8 with fear and great joy 19
Mrk 4:16 immediately receive it with joy; 19
Lke 1:14 you will have joy and gladness 19
44 the babe in my womb leaped for joy. 14
2:10 behold, I bring you good news of a great joy 19
8:13 who, when they hear the word, receive it with joy 19
10:17 The 70 returned with joy, saying, "Lord 19
15: 7 more joy in heaven over one sinner who repents 19
10 there is joy before the angels of God 19
24:41 while they still disbelieved for joy 19
52 they returned to Jerusalem with great joy, 19
Joh 3:29 therefore this joy of mine is now full. 19
15:11 that my joy may be in you 19
11 that your joy may be full. 19
16:20 your sorrow will turn into joy. 19
21 for joy that a child is born into the world. 19
22 no one will take your joy from you. 19
24 ask, and you will receive, that your joy may be full. 19
17:13 they may have my joy fulfilled in themselves. 19
Act 8: 8 there was much joy in that city. 19
12:14 in her joy she did not open the gate but ran 19
13:52 the disciples were filled with joy 19
15: 3 they gave great joy to all the brethren. 19
Rom 14:17 and peace and joy in the Holy Spirit; 19
15:13 May the God of hope fill you with all joy and peace 19
32 that by God's will I may come to you with joy 19
2Co 1:24 we work with you for your joy 19
2: 3 that my joy would be the joy of you all. 19
3 that my joy would be the joy of you all. •
7:13 we rejoiced still more at the joy of Titus 19
8: 2 their abundance of joy 19
Gal 5:22 love, joy, peace, patience, kindness, goodness 19
Php 1: 4 making my prayer with joy 19
25 for your progress and joy in the faith 19
2: 2 complete my joy by being of the same mind 19
29 So receive him in the Lord with all joy 19
4: 1 my joy and crown 19
Col 1:11 for all endurance and patience with joy 19
1Th 1: 6 with joy inspired by the Holy Spirit; 19
2:19 For what is our hope or joy or crown of boasting 19
20 For you are our glory and joy. 19
3: 9 all the joy which we feel for your sake 19
2Ti 1: 4 that I may be filled with joy. 19
Phm 1: 7 I have derived much joy and comfort from your love 19
Heb 12: 2 for the joy that was set before him 19
Jas 1: 2 Count it all joy, my brethren 19
4: 9 be turned to mourning and your joy to dejection. 19
1Pe 1: 8 rejoice with unutterable and exalted joy. 19
1Jn 1: 4 we are writing this that our joy may be complete. 19
2Jn 1:12 so that our joy may be complete. 19
3Jn 1: 4 No greater joy can I have than this 19
2Es 2:19 by these I will fill your children with joy. 23
36 receive the joy of your glory 24
7:91 they shall see with great joy the glory of him 22
131 joy over those to whom salvation is assured. 23
Tob 7:18 the Lord . . grant you joy in place of this sorrow 19
13:10 his tent may be raised for you again with joy. 19
Jdt 12:14 it will be a joy to me until the day of my death! 13
AEs 10:13 with an assembly and joy and gladness before God 19
14:18 no joy since the day that I was brought here 15
16:21 God . . has made this day to be a joy to his chosen 16
Wis 8:16 no pain, but gladness and joy. 19
Sir 1:12 gives gladness and joy and long life. 19
23 then joy will burst forth for him. 16
2: 9 for good things, for everlasting joy and mercy. 16
4:12 those who seek her early will be filled with joy. 16
6:28 she will be changed into joy for you. 16
30:16 there is no gladness above joy of heart. 19
Bar 4:11 With joy I nurtured them 16
22 joy has come to me from the Holy One 19
23 God will give you back to me with joy and gladness 21
29 he . . will bring you everlasting joy 16
36 see the joy that is coming to you from God! 16
5: 9 For God will lead Israel with joy 16
1Mc 3:45 Joy was taken from Jacob 18
4:59 observed with gladness and joy for eight days 19
5:54 they went up to Mount Zion with gladness and joy 19
14:11 Israel rejoiced with great joy. 16
2Mc 3:30 was filled with joy and gladness 19
15:28 they were returning with joy 19
3Mc 4: 6 young women . . exchanged joy for wailing 18
16 was greatly and continually filled with joy 19
6:31 full of joy they apportioned to celebrants 20
32 formed choruses as a sign of peaceful joy. 16
4Mc 9:31 the joys that come from virtue 17

joy *See also* leap, shout, sing, song.

exceeding joy 1. שִׂמְחַת גִּיל
Ps 43: 4 will go to the altar of God, to God my exceeding joy; 1

great joy 1. *περιχαρής*
3Mc 5:44 the friends and officers departed with great joy 1

malicious joy 1. *ἐπίχαρμα*
Jdt 4:12 to the malicious joy of the Gentiles. 1

joyful 1. בְּטוֹב 2. עַלִּיז 3. רְנָנָה 4. שמח 5. שָׂמֵחַ 6. שִׂמְחָה 7. *εὐφροσύνη* 8. *εὐφρόσυνος* 9. *μετὰ χαρᾶς* 10. *χαρά* 11. gaudeo 12. iucundo
Deu 16:15 bless . . so that you will be altogether joyful. 5
1Kg 8:66 and went to their homes joyful and glad of heart 5
2Ch 7:10 sent the people away . . joyful and glad of heart 5
Ezr 3:13 not distinguish the sound of the joyful shout 6
Est 5: 9 Haman went out that day joyful and glad of heart. 5
Ps 63: 5 my mouth praises thee with joyful lips 3
68: 3 righteous be joyful; let them exult before God; 4
Ecc 7:14 In the day of prosperity be joyful 1
Isa 32:13 yea, for all the joyous houses in the joyful city. 2
Jer 49:25 How the famous city is forsaken, the joyful city! ‡
1Es 5:64 while many came with trumpets and a joyful noise 10
2Es 2:37 be joyful, giving thanks to him 12
13:13 some of whom were joyful and some sorrowful 11
Jdt 14: 9 made a joyful noise in their city. 8
3Mc 5:17 make the present portion of the banquet joyful 7
7:15 they kept the day as a joyful festival 9

joyful *See also* cry, make, praise, shouting.

joyfully 1. שׂוּשׂ 2. *μετὰ χαρᾶς* 3. *μετ' εὐφροσύνης* 4. *χαίρω*
Isa 64: 5 meetest him that joyfully works righteousness 1
Lke 19: 6 came down, and received him joyfully. 4
Heb 10:34 you joyfully accepted the plundering 2
13:17 Let them do this joyfully, and not sadly 2
3Mc 5:21 readily and joyfully . . gave their approval 2
6:34 had joyfully registered them 2
7:13 shouted the Hallelujah and joyfully departed. 2
16 joyfully and loudly giving thanks to the one God 3

joyfulness 1. שִׂמְחָה 2. *εὐφροσύνη*
Deu 28:47 did not serve . . with joyfulness and gladness 1
3Mc 6:30 celebrate their rescue with all joyfulness 2

joyous 1. מָשׂוֹשׂ 2. שָׂמֵחַ 3. *ἱλαρός*
Ps 113: 9 making her the joyous mother of children. 2
Isa 32:13 yea, for all the joyous houses in the joyful city. 1
3Mc 6:35 to the accompaniment of joyous thanksgiving 3

joyous *See also* festival, song.

joyously 1. שִׂמְחָה
1Ch 29:17 thy people . . offering freely and joyously 1

joyously *See also* praise.

jubilant 1. עַלִּיז 2. שׂוּשׂ
Ps 68: 3 exult before God; let them be jubilant with joy! 2
Isa 24: 8 the noise of the jubilant has ceased 1

jubilee 1. יוֹבֵל
Lev 25:10 it shall be a jubilee for you 1
11 A jubilee shall that 50th year be to you 1
12 For it is a jubilee; it shall be holy to you 1
13 In this year of jubilee each of you shall return 1
15 years after the jubilee, you shall buy 1
28 remain . . until the year of jubilee 1
28 in the jubilee it shall be released 1
30 it shall not be released in the jubilee 1
31 they shall be released in the jubilee 1
33 the house . . shall be released in the jubilee 1
40 serve with you until the year of the jubilee 1
50 when he sold himself until the year of jubilee 1
52 but a few years until the year of jubilee 1
54 then he shall be released in the year of jubilee 1
27:17 dedicates his field from the year of jubilee 1
18 if he dedicates his field after the jubilee 1
18 years that remain until the year of jubilee 1
21 the field, when it is released in the jubilee 1
23 shall compute . . up to the year of jubilee 1
24 In the year of jubilee the field shall return 1
Num 36: 4 when the jubilee of the people of Israel comes 1

judge 1. דין 2. דַּיָּן 3. מִשְׁפָּט 4. עשה מִשְׁפָּט 5. פָּלִיל 6. פְּלִילִי 7. שפט 8. דין (A) 9. דַּיָּן (A) 10. *ἀκρίβεια* 11. *ἀνακρίνω* 12. *ἀπό* 13. *διακρίνω* 14. *δικάζω* 15. *δικαστής* 16. *δοκέω* 17. *ἡγέομαι* 18. *κατακρίνω* 19. *κρίνω* 20. *κρίσις* 21. *κριτής* 22. *λαμβάνω κρίμα* 23. *νοέω* 24. *συγκρίνω* 25. aestimo 26. habeo 27. iudex 28. iudico
Gen 16: 5 May the LORD judge between you and me! 7
18:25 Shall not the Judge of all the earth do right? 7
19: 9 came to sojourn, and he would play the judge! 7
30: 6 Then Rachel said, "God has judged me 1
31:53 God of their father, judge between us. 7
49:16 Dan shall judge his people as one of the tribes 1
Exd 2:14 Who made you a prince and a judge over us? 7
5:21 said to them, "The LORD look upon you and judge 7
18:13 On the morrow Moses sat to judge the people 7
22 let them judge the people at all times; 7
26 they judged the people at all times; 7
21:22 and he shall pay as the judges determine. 5
Lev 19:15 in righteousness shall you judge your neighbor 7
Num 25: 5 Moses said to the judges of Israel, "Every one 7
35:24 then the congregation shall judge 7
Deu 1:16 I charged your judges at that time, 'Hear the cases 7
16 'Hear the cases . . and judge righteously 7
16:18 appoint judges and officers in all your towns 7
18 judge the people with righteous judgment. 7
17: 9 to the judge who is in office in those days 7
12 acts presumptuously, by not obeying . . the judge 7
19:17 LORD, before the priests and the judges 7
18 judges shall inquire diligently 7
21: 2 your elders and your judges shall come forth 7
25: 1 come into court, and the judges decide between •
2 judge shall cause him to lie down and be beaten 7
32:31 even our enemies themselves being judges. 5
Jos 8:33 with their elders and officers and their judges 7
23: 2 elders and heads, their judges and officers 7
24: 1 the heads, the judges, and the officers of Israel; 7
Jdg 2:16 the LORD raised up judges, who saved them 7
17 yet they did not listen to their judges; 7
18 Whenever the LORD raised up judges for them 7
18 the LORD was with the judge, and he saved them 7
18 hand of their enemies all the days of the judge; 7
19 whenever the judge died, they turned back 7
3:10 of the LORD came upon him, and he judged Israel; 7
4: 4 Deb'orah . . was judging Israel at that time. 7
10: 2 And he judged Israel 23 years. Then he died 7
3 Ja'ir the Gileadite, who judged Israel 22 years. 7
11:27 the LORD, the Judge, decide this day between 7
12: 7 Jephthah judged Israel six years. 7
8 After him Ibzan of Bethlehem judged Israel. 7
9 And he judged Israel seven years. 7
11 After him Elon the Zeb'ulunite judged Israel; 7
11 Elon . . and he judged Israel ten years. 7
13 After him Abdon the son of Hillel . . judged Israel. 7
14 rode on 70 asses; and he judged Israel eight years. 7
15:20 he judged Israel in the days of the Philistines 7

16:31 He had judged Israel twenty years. 7
Rut 1: 1 In the days when the judges ruled 7
1Sm 2:10 The LORD will judge the ends of the earth; 1
4:18 Eli fell . . He had judged Israel 40 years. 7
7: 6 Samuel judged the people of Israel at Mizpah. 7
15 Samuel judged Israel all the days of his life. 7
16 and he judged Israel in all these places. 7
8: 1 Samuel . . made his sons judges over Israel. 7
2 Jo'el . . Abi'jah; they were judges in Beer-sheba. 7
24:12 May the LORD judge between me and you 7
15 May the LORD therefore be judge 2
2Sm 7: 7 did I speak a word with any of the judges of Israel •
11 that I appointed judges over my people Israel; 7
15: 4 Oh that I were judge in the land! 7
1Kg 8:32 hear . . and act, and judge thy servants 7
2Kg 23:22 since the days of the judges who judged Israel 7
22 since the days of the judges who judged Israel 7
1Ch 16:33 the LORD, for he comes to judge the earth. 7
17: 6 did I speak a word with any of the judges of Israel 7
10 I appointed judges over my people Israel; 7
23: 4 6,000 shall be officers and judges 7
26:29 outside duties . . as officers and judges. 7
2Ch 1: 2 to the judges, and to all the leaders in all Israel 7
6:23 hear thou . . and act, and judge thy servants 7
19: 5 He appointed judges in the land 7
6 said to the judges, "Consider what you do 7
6 you judge not for man but for the LORD; 7
Ezr 4: 9 rest of their associates, the judges 9
7:25 appoint magistrates and judges who may judge 9
25 judges who may judge all the people 8
10:14 with them the elders and judges of every city 7
Job 9:24 he covers the faces of its judges– 7
12:17 judges he makes fools. 7
21:22 seeing that he judges those that are on high? 7
22:13 Can he judge through the deep darkness? 7
23: 7 I should be acquitted for ever by my judge. 7
31:11 would be an iniquity to be punished by the judges; 5
28 an iniquity to be punished by the judges 6
36:31 For by these he judges peoples; 1
Ps 7: 8 The LORD judges the peoples; 1
8 judge me, O LORD, according to my righteousness 7
11 God is a righteous judge 7
9: 8 he judges the world with righteousness 7
8 he judges the peoples with equity. 1
19 let the nations be judged before thee! 7
50: 4 to the earth, that he may judge his people 1
6 his righteousness, for God himself is judge! 7
58: 1 you gods? Do you judge the sons of men uprightly? 7
11 surely there is a God who judges on earth. 7
67: 4 for thou dost judge the peoples with equity 7
72: 2 May he judge thy people with righteousness 1
75: 2 time which I appoint I will judge with equity. 7
82: 2 How long will you judge unjustly 7
8 Arise, O God, judge the earth; 7
94: 2 Rise up, O judge of the earth; 7
96:10 he will judge the peoples with equity. 1
13 for he comes, for he comes to judge the earth. 7
13 He will judge the world with righteousness 7
98: 9 before the LORD, for he comes to judge the earth. 7
9 will judge the world with righteousness 7
119:84 When wilt thou judge those who persecute me? 4
Prv 24:23 Partiality in judging is not good. 3
27:21 man is judged by his praise. •
29:14 If a king judges the poor with equity his throne 7
31: 9 Open your mouth, judge righteously 7
Ecc 3:17 God will judge the righteous and the wicked 7
Isa 1:26 I will restore your judges as at the first 7
2: 4 He shall judge between the nations 7
3: 2 the judge and the prophet, the diviner 7
13 to contend, he stands to judge his people. 1
5: 3 men of Judah, judge . . between me and my vineyard. 7
11: 3 He shall not judge by what his eyes see 7
4 with righteousness he shall judge the poor 7
16: 5 one who judges and seeks justice 7
33:22 For the LORD is our judge, the LORD is our ruler 7
Jer 5:28 they judge not with justice . . to make it prosper 1
11:20 But, O LORD of hosts, who judgest righteously 7
22:16 He judged the cause of the poor and needy; 1
Lam 3:59 Thou hast seen . . O LORD; judge thou my cause. 7
Ezk 7: 3 and will judge you according to your ways; 7
8 and judge you according to your ways; 7
27 according to their own judgments I will judge 7
11:10 I will judge you at the border of Israel; 7
11 I will judge you at the border of Israel; 7
16:38 And I will judge you as women who break wedlock 7
38 who break wedlock and shed blood are judged 3
18:30 Therefore I will judge you, O house of Israel 7
20: 4 Will you judge them, son of man, will you judge them? 7
4 Will you judge them, son of man, will you judge them? 7
21:30 in the land of your origin, I will judge you. 7
22: 2 And you, son of man, will you judge 7
2 will you judge, will you judge the bloody city? 7
23:24 judgment to them, and they shall judge you 7
36 Son of man, will you judge Oho'lah and Ohol'ibah? 7
24:14 according to . . your doings I will judge you 7
33:20 I will judge each of you according to his ways. 7
34:17 I judge between sheep and sheep, rams and he-goats 7
20 will judge between the fat sheep and the lean 7
22 I will judge between sheep and sheep. 7
35:11 make myself known among you, when I judge you. 7
36:19 with their conduct and their deeds I judged them. 7
44:24 they shall act as judges, and they shall judge it 3
24 they shall judge it according to my judgments. 7
Jol 3:12 for there I will sit to judge all the nations 7
Mic 4: 3 He shall judge between many peoples 7
7: 3 the prince and the judge ask for a bribe 7
Zep 3: 3 her judges are evening wolves 7
Mat 5:25 you over to the judge, and the judge to the guard 21
25 you over to the judge, and the judge to the guard 21
7: 1 Judge not, that you be not judged. 19
1 Judge not, that you be not judged. 19
2 you will be judged, and the measure you give 19
12:27 Therefore they shall be your judges. 21
19:28 judging the twelve tribes of Israel. 19
Lke 6:37 Judge not, and you will not be judged 19
37 Judge not, and you will not be judged 19
7:43 he said to him "You have judged rightly. 19
11:19 Therefore they shall be your judges. 21
12:14 Man, who made me a judge or divider over you? 21
57 why do you not judge for yourselves what is right? 19
58 lest he drag you to the judge 21
58 lest . . the judge hand you over to the officer 21
18: 2 He said, "In a certain city there was a judge 21
6 Hear what the unrighteous judge says. 21
22:30 judging the twelve tribes of Israel. 19
Joh 5:22 The Father judges no one 19
30 as I hear, I judge; and my judgment is just 19
7:24 Do not judge by appearances 19
24 judge with right judgment. 19
51 Does our law judge a man 19
8:15 You judge according to the flesh, I judge no one. 19
15 You judge according to the flesh, I judge no one. 19
16 Yet even if I do judge, my judgment is true 19
16 it is not I alone that judge, but I and he who sent me. •
26 I have much to say about you and much to judge 19
50 there is One who seeks it and he will be the judge. 19
12:47 I do not judge him 19
47 for I did not come to judge the world 19
48 He who rejects me . . has a judge 19
48 the word that I have spoken will be his judge 19
16:11 because the ruler of this world is judged. 19
18:31 judge him by your own law 19
Act 4:19 you must judge; 19
7: 7 I will judge the nation which they serve,' said God 19
27 Who made you a ruler and a judge over us? 15
35 Who made you a ruler and a judge? 15
10:42 judge of the living and the dead. 21
13:20 he gave them judges until Samuel the prophet. 21
46 judge yourselves unworthy of eternal life 19
16:15 If you have judged me to be faithful to the Lord 19
17:31 he has fixed a day on which he will judge the world 19
18:15 I refuse to be a judge of these things. 21
23: 3 Are you sitting to judge me according to the law 19
24:10 many years you have been judge over this nation 21
Rom 2: 1 you have no excuse . . when you judge another; 19
1 you, the judge, are doing the very same things. 18
3 when you judge those who do such things 19
12 all who have sinned . . will be judged by the law. 19
16 God judges the secrets of men by Christ Jesus. 19
3: 4 and prevail when thou art judged. 19
6 For then how could God judge the world? 19
14:22 happy is he who has no reason to judge himself 19
1Co 2:15 The spiritual man judges all things 11
15 is himself to be judged by no one. 11
4: 3 I should be judged by you or by any human court 11
3 I do not even judge myself. 11
4 It is the Lord who judges me. 11
5:12 For what have I to do with judging outsiders? 11
12 those inside the church whom you are to judge? 19
13 God judges those outside 19
6: 2 know that the saints will judge the world 19
2 if the world is to be judged by you 19
3 Do you not know that we are to judge angels? 19
10:15 I speak as to sensible men; judge for yourselves 19
11:13 Judge for yourselves; is it proper 19
31 we should not be judged. 19
32 when we are judged by the Lord, we are chastened 19
1Ti 1:12 because he judged me faithful 17
2Ti 4: 1 who is to judge the living and the dead 19
8 which the Lord, the righteous judge, will award 21
Heb 4: 1 lest any . . be judged to have failed to reach it. 16
10:30 And again, "The Lord will judge his people. 19
12:23 a judge who is God of all 21
13: 4 God will judge the immoral and adulterous. 19
Jas 2: 4 and become judges with evil thoughts? 21
12 those . . to be judged under the law of liberty. 19
3: 1 we . . shall be judged with greater strictness. 22
4:11 speaks evil against . . or judges his brother 19
11 speaks evil against the law and judges the law. 19
11 if you judge the law, you are not a doer of the law 19
11 you are not a doer of the law but a judge. 21
12 There is one lawgiver and judge 21
12 But who are you that you judge your neighbor? 19
5: 9 Do not grumble . . that you may not be judged; 19
9 behold, the Judge is standing at the doors. 21
1Pe 1:17 if you invoke as Father him who judges each one 19
2:23 but he trusted to him who judges justly. 19
4: 5 who is ready to judge the living and the dead. 19
6 that though judged in the flesh like men 19
Rev 6:10 how long before thou wilt judge and avenge 19
11:18 and the time for the dead to be judged 19
18: 8 for mighty is the Lord God who judges her. 19
19: 2 he has judged the great harlot 20
11 and in righteousness he judges and makes war. 19
20:12 dead were judged by what was written in the books 19
13 and all were judged by what they had done. 19
1Es 2:17 the other judges of their council in Coelesyria 21
3: 9 the three nobles of Persia judge to be wisest 19
8:23 appoint judges and justices to judge 21
23 appoint judges and justices to judge 14
9:13 with the elders and judges of each place 21
2Es 4:18 If now you were a judge between them 27
20 He answered me and said, "You have judged rightly 28
20 but why have you not judged so in your own case? 28
7:11 what had been made was judged. 28
19 he said to me, "You are not a better judge than God 27
57 Judge therefore which things are precious 25
87 and before whom they are to be judged 28
139judge, because if he did not pardon those 27
11:41 you have judged the earth, but not with truth; 28
12: 9 For thou hast judged me worthy to be shown the end 26
14:32 because he is a righteous judge 27
16:67 Behold, God is the judge, fear him! 27
Jdt 7:24 God be judge between you and us! 19
10:19 and admired the Israelites, judging them by her 12
AEs 16: 9 judging what comes before our eyes 13
Wis 6: 1 learn, O judges of the ends of the earth. 15
9: 7 to be judge over thy sons and daughters. 15
12 I shall judge thy people justly 13
11: 9 when judged in wrath. 19
12:10 judging them little by little 19
13 prove that thou hast not judged unjustly; 19
18 sovereign in strength dost judge with mildness 19
21 with what strictness thou hast judged thy sons 10
22 we may meditate upon thy goodness when we judge 19
22 when we are judged we may expect mercy. 19
15:18 when judged by their lack of intelligence; 24
Sir 4: 9 do not be fainthearted in judging a case. 19
15 He who obeys her will judge the nations 19
7: 6 Do not seek to become a judge 21
8:14 Do not go to law against a judge 21
10:24 The nobleman, and the judge, and the ruler 21
11: 9 nor sit with sinners when they judge a case. 20
16:12 he judges a man according to his deeds. 19
31:15 Judge your neighbor's feelings by your own 23
35:12 the Lord is the judge 21
19 till he judges the case of his people 19
38:33 They do not sit in the judge's seat 15
41:18 of a transgression, before a judge or magistrate; 21
45:26 to judge his people in righteousness 19
46:11 The judges also, with their respective names 21
14 By the law of the Lord he judged the congregation 19
Bar 2: 1 against our judges who judged Israel 15
1 against our judges who judged Israel 14
LJr 1:54 They cannot judge their own cause 13
Sus 1: 5 two elders . . were appointed as judges. 21
5 Iniquity came . . from elders who were judges 21
41 they were elders of the people and judges; 21
1Mc 2:55 Joshua . . became a judge in Israel. 21
7:42 judge him according to this wickedness. 19
9:73 Jonathan began to judge the people 19
2Mc 12: 6 calling upon God the righteous Judge 21
3Mc 2: 3 you judge those who have done anything 19

judge *See also* play, serve.

judge amiss 1. נכר

Deu 32:27 lest their adversaries should judge amiss, lest 1

righteous judge 1. *δικαιοκρίτης*

2Mc 12:41 the Lord, the righteous Judge 1

judge truly 1. *διακρίνω*

1Co 11:31 if we judged ourselves truly 1

judgment 1. דִּין 2. דַּעַת 3. טַעַם 4. מִשְׁפָּט 5. רִיב 6. שְׁפוֹט 7. שפט 8. שֶׁפֶט 9. דִּין (A) 10. *βουλή* 11. *γνώμη* 12. *δικαίωμα* 13. *δίκη* 14. *δοκέω* 15. *κρίμα* 16. *κρίνω* 17. *κρίσις* 18. iudicium

Exd 12:12 on all the gods of Egypt I will execute judgments 8
28:15 you shall make a breastpiece of judgment 4
29 names . . in the breastpiece of judgment upon 4
30 in the breastpiece of judgment you shall put 4
30 thus Aaron shall bear the judgment of the people 4
Lev 19:15 You shall do no injustice in judgment 4
35 You shall do no wrong in judgment 4
Num27:21 by the judgment of the Urim before the LORD; 4
33: 4 upon their gods . . LORD executed judgments. 8
35:12 stands before the congregation for judgment. 4
Deu 1:17 You shall not be partial in judgment; 4
17 not be afraid . . for the judgment is God's; 4
16:18 judge the people with righteous judgment. 4
32:41 if . . my hand takes hold on judgment 4
Jos 20: 6 has stood before the congregation for judgment 4
Jdg 4: 5 the people of Israel came up to her for judgment. 4
2Sm 15: 2 had a suit to come before the king for judgment 4
6 to all of Israel who came to the king for judgment; 4

1Kg 3:28 Israel heard of the judgment which the king had 4
7: 7 Hall of the Throne . . even the Hall of Judgment; 4
20:40 So shall your judgment be; you . . have decided it. 4
1Ch 16:12 the wonders he wrought, the judgments he uttered 4
14 LORD our God; his judgments are in all the earth. 4
2Ch 19: 6 the LORD; he is with you in giving judgment. 4
8 to give judgment for the LORD 4
20: 9 If evil comes upon us, the sword, judgment 6
24:24 Thus they executed judgment on Jo'ash. 8
Ezr 7:26 let judgment be strictly executed upon him 9
Est 1:13 toward all who were versed in law and judgment 1
Job 14: 3 such a one and bring him into judgment with thee? 4
19:29 that you may know there is a judgment. 1
22: 4 reproves you, and enters into judgment with you? 4
24: 1 are not times of judgment kept by the Almighty •
34:23 a time for any man to go before God in judgment. 4
36:17 you are full of the judgment on the wicked; 4
17 judgment and justice seize you. 1
Ps 1: 5 the wicked will not stand in the judgment 4
7: 6 awake, O my God; thou hast appointed a judgment. 4
9: 7 he has established his throne for judgment; 4
16 has made himself known, he has executed judgment; 4
10: 5 thy judgments are on high, out of his sight; 4
36: 6 thy judgments are like the great deep; 4
48:11 of Judah rejoice because of thy judgments! 4
51: 4 in thy sentence and blameless in thy judgment. 7
76: 8 From the heavens thou didst utter judgment; 1
9 when God arose to establish judgment to save all 4
97: 8 rejoice, because of thy judgments, O God. 4
105: 5 Remember . . the judgments he uttered 4
7 LORD our God; his judgments are in all the earth. 4
119:66 Teach me good judgment and knowledge 3
75 I know, O LORD, that thy judgments are right 4
120I am afraid of thy judgments. 4
137O LORD, and right are thy judgments. 4
122: 5 There thrones for judgment were set 4
143: 2 Enter not into judgment with thy servant; 4
149: 9 to execute on them the judgment written! 4
Prv 16:10 his mouth does not sin in judgment. 4
20: 8 A king who sits on the throne of judgment 1
Ecc 11: 9 know that . . God will bring you into judgment. 4
12:14 For God will bring every deed into judgment 4
Isa 3:14 The LORD enters into judgment with the elders 4
4: 4 cleansed . . by a spirit of judgment 4
26: 8 In the path of thy judgments, O LORD, we wait 4
9 For when thy judgments are in the earth 4
28: 6 a spirit of justice to him who sits in judgment 4
32: 4 The mind of the rash will have good judgment 2
34: 5 behold, it descends for judgment upon Edom 4
41: 1 let us together draw near for judgment. 4
53: 8 By oppression and judgment he was taken away; 4
54:17 tongue that rises against you in judgment. 4
58: 2 they ask of me righteous judgments 4
Jer 1:16 And I will utter my judgments against them 4
4:12 Now it is I who speak in judgment upon them. 4
48:21 Judgment has come upon the tableland, upon Holon 4
47 Thus far is the judgment on Moab. 4
51: 9 for her judgment has reached up to heaven 4
Ezk 5: 8 I will execute judgments in the midst of you 4
10 and I will execute judgments on you 8
15 when I execute judgments on you in anger and fury 8
7:27 according to their own judgments I will judge 4
11: 9 and execute judgments upon you. 8
14:21 upon Jerusalem my four sore acts of judgment 8
16:41 burn your houses and execute judgments upon you 8
23:10 when judgment had been executed upon her. 6
24 I will commit the judgment to them 4
24 shall judge you according to their judgments. 4
25:11 I will execute judgments upon Moab. 8
28:22 when I execute judgments in her 8
26 shall dwell securely, when I execute judgments 8
30:14 and will execute acts of judgment upon Thebes. 8
19 Thus I will execute acts of judgment upon Egypt. 8
39:21 all the nations shall see my judgment 4
44:24 they shall judge it according to my judgments. 4
Dan 7:10 court sat in judgment, and the books were opened. •
22 judgment . . given for the saints of the Most High 9
26 court shall sit in judgment, and his dominion •
Hos 5: 1 For the judgment pertains to you; 4
11 E'phraim is oppressed, crushed in judgment 4
6: 5 and my judgment goes forth as the light. 4
10: 4 so judgment springs up like poisonous weeds 4
Ams 7: 4 the Lord GOD was calling for a judgment by fire 5
Mic 7: 9 until he pleads my cause and executes judgment 4
Hab 1:12 O LORD, thou hast ordained them as a judgment; 4
Zep 3:15 LORD has taken away the judgments against you 4
Zec 7: 9 says the LORD of hosts, Render true judgments 4
8:16 render in your gates judgments that are true 4
Mal 3: 5 Then I will draw near to you for judgment; 4
Mat 5:21 whoever kills shall be liable to judgment.' 17
22 his brother shall be liable to judgment 17
7: 2 For with the judgment you pronounce 15
10:15 it shall be more tolerable on the day of judgment 17
11:22 it shall be more tolerable on the day of judgment 17
24 it shall be more tolerable on the day of judgment 17
12:36 on the day of judgment men will render account 17
41 The men of Nin'eveh will arise at the judgment 17
42 The queen of the South will arise at the judgment 17
26:66 What is your judgment? 14

Lke 10:14 it shall be more tolerable in the judgment for Tyre 17
11:31 The queen of the South will arise at the judgment 17
32 The men of Nin'eveh will arise at the judgment 17
Joh 3:19 And this is the judgment, that the light has come 17
5:22 has given all judgment to the Son 17
24 he does not come into judgment 17
27 has given him authority to execute judgment 17
29 to the resurrection of judgment. 17
30 as I hear, I judge; and my judgment is just 17
7:24 judge with right judgment. 17
8:16 Yet even if I do judge, my judgment is true 17
9:39 Jesus said, "For judgment I came into this world 15
12:31 Now is the judgment of this world 17
16: 8 concerning sin and righteousness and judgment 17
11 concerning judgment 17
Act 15:19 Therefore my judgment is 16
21:25 we have sent a letter with our judgment 16
24:25 self-control and future judgment 15
Rom 2: 2 the judgment of God rightly falls upon those 15
3 you will escape the judgment of God? 15
5:16 judgment following one trespass 15
11:33 How unsearchable are his judgments 15
13: 2 and those who resist will incur judgment. 15
1Co 1:10 be united in the same mind and the same judgment. 11
7:40 in my judgment she is happier 11
11:29 eats and drinks judgment upon himself. 15
Gal 5:10 he who is troubling you will bear his judgment 15
2Th 1: 5 is evidence of the righteous judgment of God 17
1Ti 5:24 are conspicuous, pointing to judgment 17
Heb 6: 2 resurrection of the dead, and eternal judgment. 15
9:27 after that comes judgment 17
10:27 a fearful prospect of judgment, and a fury of fire 17
Jas 2:13 For judgment is without mercy 17
13 yet mercy triumphs over judgment. 17
1Pe 4:17 For the time has come for judgment to begin 15
2Pe 2: 4 into hell . . to be kept until the judgment; 17
9 under punishment until the day of judgment 17
11 do not pronounce a reviling judgment upon them 17
3: 7 kept until the day of judgment and destruction 17
1Jn 4:17 we may have confidence for the day of judgment 17
Jde 1: 6 kept . . until the judgment of the great day; 17
9 not presume to pronounce a reviling judgment 17
15 to execute judgment on all, and to convict all 17
Rev 14: 7 Fear God . . for the hour of his judgment has come; 17
15: 4 for thy judgments have been revealed. 12
16: 5 Just art thou in these thy judgments 16
7 Lord God . . true and just are thy judgments! 17
17: 1 I will show you the judgment of the great harlot 15
18:10 Babylon! In one hour has thy judgment come. 17
19: 2 for his judgments are true and just; 17
20: 4 those to whom judgment was committed. 15
1Es 4:40 there is nothing unrighteous in her judgment. 17
8: 7 taught . . all the ordinances and judgments. 15
2Es 5:34 and to search out part of his judgment. 18
40 so you cannot discover my judgment 18
42 He said to me, "I shall liken my judgment to a circle; 18
43 that thou mightest show thy judgment the sooner? 18
7:33 shall be revealed upon the seat of judgment 18
34 only judgment shall remain, truth shall stand 18
38 Thus he will speak to them on the day of judgment- 18
44 This is my judgment and its prescribed order 18
60 also will be the judgment which I have promised; ‡
66 they do not look for a judgment 18
69 if we were not to come into judgment after death 18
70 he first prepared the judgment 18
70 the things that pertain to the judgment. 18
73 What, then, will they have to say in the judgment 18
102whether on the day of judgment the righteous 18
104The day of judgment is decisive 18
113the day of judgment will be the end of this age 18
115him who has been condemned in the judgment 18
8:18 the swiftness of the judgment that is to come. 18
38 or about their death, their judgment 18
61 Therefore my judgment is now drawing near; 18
11:46 and may hope for the judgment and mercy of him 18
12:34 the day of judgment, of which I spoke to you 18
14:35 For after death the judgment will come 18
Tob 3: 5 now thy many judgments are true 17
Jdt 9: 6 thy judgment is with foreknowledge. 17
16:17 in the day of judgment 17
Wis 6: 5 severe judgment falls on those in high places. 17
7:15 May God grant that I speak with judgment 11
8:11 I shall be found keen in judgment 17
9: 3 and pronounce judgment in uprightness of soul 17
5 with little understanding of judgment and laws; 17
12:12 will resist thy judgment 15
25 thou didst send thy judgment to mock them. 17
26 will experience the deserved judgment of God. 17
16:18 they were being pursued by the judgment of God; 17
17: 1 Great are thy judgments and hard to describe; 17
Sir 6:23 Listen, my son, and accept my judgment 11
17:12 showed them his judgments. 15
18:14 who are eager for his judgments. 15
20 Before judgment, examine yourself 17
20: 4 a man who executes judgments by violence. 15
21: 5 his judgment comes speedily. 15
25: 4 judgment in gray-haired men 17
32:16 Those who fear the Lord will form true judgments 15

18 A man of judgment will not overlook an idea 10
35:17 and executes judgment. 17
38:33 nor do they understand the sentence of judgment; 15
33 they cannot expound discipline or judgment 15
42: 2 of rendering judgment to acquit the ungodly; 15
43:13 speeds the lightnings of his judgment. 15
45: 5 to teach . . Israel his judgments. 15
10 with the oracle of judgment, Urim and Thummim; 17
17 gave him authority and statutes and judgments 15
48: 7 heard . . judgments of vengeance at Horeb; 15
Aza 1: 4 all thy judgments are truth. 17
5 Thou hast executed true judgments 15
8 thou hast done in true judgment. 17
Sus 1: 9 or remembering righteous judgments. 15
53 pronouncing unjust judgments 17
2Mc 2:29 such in my judgment is the case with us. 14
7:35 the judgment of the almighty, all-seeing God. 17
36 by the judgment of God 17
8:11 not expecting the judgment from the Almighty 13
9: 4 the judgment of heaven rode with him! 17
18 the judgment of God had justly come upon him 17
11:37 so that we may have your judgment. 11
3Mc 2:22 since he was smitten by a righteous judgment. 17
4Mc 9:32 the judgments of the divine wrath. 13

judgment *See also* act, bring, call, enter, execute, give, hold, make, pass, place, pronounce, seat.

good judgment 1. בִּין דַּעַת
Isa 32: 4 The mind of the rash will have good judgment 1

hasty judgment 1. *ὑπόλημψις*
Sir 3:24 For their hasty judgment has led many astray 1

rational judgment 1. *λογισμός* 2. *φρόνησις*
4Mc 1: 2 virtue–I mean, of course, rational judgment. 2
18 Now the kinds of wisdom are rational judgment 2
19 Rational judgment is supreme over all of these 2
30 rational judgment is sovereign over the emotions 1

render judgment 1. שׁפט 2. *κρίνω*
1Kg 3:28 of the judgment which the king had rendered; 1
Zec 7: 9 says the LORD of hosts, Render true judgments 1
8:16 render in your gates judgments that are true 1
Tob 3: 2 thou dost render true and righteous judgment 2

righteous judgment 1. *δικαιοκρισία*
Rom 2: 5 when God's righteous judgment will be revealed. 1

sober judgment 1. *σωφρονέω*
Rom 12: 3 but to think with sober judgment 1

sound judgment 1. תּוּשִׁיָּה 2. *σωφροσύνη*
Prv 18: 1 seeks . . to break out against all sound judgment. 1
AEs 13: 3 Haman, who excels among us in sound judgment 2

judicious *See* make.

juice 1. מִשְׁרָה 2. עָסִיס 3. *αἷμα*
Num 6: 3 shall not drink any juice of grapes or eat grapes 1
Sng 8: 2 spiced wine . . the juice of my pomegranates. 2
1Mc 6:34 They showed the elephants the juice of grapes 3

jungle 1. גָּאוֹן 2. *ὕλη*
Jer 12: 5 how will you do in the jungle of the Jordan? 1
49:19 Behold, like a lion coming up from the jungle 1
50:44 Behold, like a lion coming up from the jungle 1
Zec 11: 3 for the jungle of the Jordan is laid waste! 1
4Mc 1:29 so tames the jungle of habits and emotions. 2

jurisdiction 1. כְּסֵא 2. *ἐξουσία*
Neh 3: 7 who were under the jurisdiction of the governor 1
Lke 20:20 authority and jurisdiction of the governor. 2
23: 7 he belonged to Herod's jurisdiction 2

just 1. אַךְ 2. גַּם 3. כְּ 4. כַּאֲשֶׁר 5. כְּכֹל אֲשֶׁר 6. כָּל עֻמַּת שֶׁ 7. לְעֻמַּת 8. צדק 9. צֶדֶק 10. הֵא כְּדִי (A) 11. כָּל קֳבֵל דִּי (A) 12. *ἄρτι* 13. *δή* 14. *ἔτι* 15. *ἤδη* 16. *καθάπερ* 17. *καθός* 18. *καθ' ὅσον* 19. *καθόσπερ* 20. *καθότι* 21. *καθώς* 22. *καθώσπερ* 23. *καὶ οὕτως* 24. *κατά* 25. *νῦν* 26. *ὁμοίως* 27. *ὃν τρόπον* 28. *οὖν* 29. *οὗτος* 30. *οὕτως* 31. *ποτέ* 32. *τότε* 33. *ὡς* 34. *ὡς καί* 35. *ὥσπερ* 36. adhuc 37. quemadmodum 38. quomodo 39. sicut 40. ut 41. valde
Gen 26:29 just as we have not touched you 4
Lev 4:10 just as these are taken from the ox 4
Num 22:33 just now I would have slain you and let her live. 2
29:40 everything just as the LORD had commanded 3
Deu 1:30 just as he did for you in Egypt before your eyes 3
41 go up and fight, just as the LORD our God commanded 3
12:22 Just as the gazelle or the hart is eaten 1
18:16 just as you desired of the LORD your God at Horeb 5
Jos 1:17 Just as we obeyed Moses . . so we will obey you; 3
21:44 the LORD gave them rest . . just as he has sworn 5
23:15 just as all the good things . . have been fulfilled 4
Jdg 7:19 came . . when they had just set the watch; •
Rut 3: 6 went . . and did just as her mother-in-law had told 5
1Sm 9:12 He is; behold, he is just ahead of you. •

2Sm 15:37 just as Ab'salom was entering Jerusalem. *
1Ch 24:31 lots, just as their brethren the sons of Aaron 7
26:12 had duties, just as their brethren did 7
Est 2:20 Esther obeyed . . just as when she was brought up 4
6: 4 Haman had just entered the outer court *
Job 9: 2 it is so: but how can a man be just before God? 8
Prv 8:15 By me kings reign, and rulers decree what is just; 9
Ecc 5:16 just as he came, so shall he go; 6
Isa 66:20 just as the Israelites bring their cereal 4
Jer 3: 4 Have you not just now called to me, 'My father *
32:42 Just as I have brought all this great evil 4
Dan 2:41 just as you saw iron mixed with the miry clay. 11
43 not hold . . just as iron does not mix with clay. 10
45 just as you saw that a stone was cut 11
Mat 9:18 saying, "My daughter has just died 12
13:40 Just as the weeds are gathered 28
Mrk 4:36 they took him with them in the boat, just as he was. 33
Lke 1: 2 just as they were delivered to us by those 21
15: 7 Just so, I tell you, there will be more joy in heaven 29
10 Just so, I tell you, there is joy before the angels 29
24:24 and found it just as the women had said 21
Joh 15:10 just as I have kept my Father's commandments 21
21: 4 Just as day was breaking, Jesus stood on the beach; 15
10 Bring some of the fish that you have just caught. 25
Act 10:47 who have received the Holy Spirit just as we have? 33
11:15 fell on them just as on us at the beginning. 35
15: 8 giving them the Holy Spirit just as he did to us; 21
11 we shall be saved . . just as they will. 27
Rom 6:19 just as you once yielded your members 35
11:30 Just as you were once disobedient to God 35
1Co 9:18 Just this: that in my preaching *
10:33 just as I try to please all men in everything I do 21
12:12 For just as the body is one and has many members 16
15:49 Just as we have borne the image of the man of dust 21
16: 7 For I do not want to see you now just in passing *
2Co 7:14 just as everything we said to you was true *
Gal 2: 7 just as Peter had been entrusted 21
Eph 4: 4 just as you were called to the one hope 21
Col 2: 7 just as you were taught 21
1Th 2: 4 just as we have been approved by God 21
3: 4 just as it has come to pass, and as you know. 21
4: 1 just as you are doing, you do so more and more. 21
5:11 build one another up, just as you are doing. 21
Heb 3: 2 just as Moses also was faithful in God's house. 33
4: 2 For good news came to us just as to them 16
5: 4 he is called by God, just as Aaron was. 22
9:27 just as it is appointed for men to die once 18
2Pe 2: 1 just as there will be false teachers among you 34
1Jn 2:27 just as it has been taught you, abide in him. 21
3:23 love one another, just as he has commanded us. 21
2Jn 1: 4 just as we have been commanded by the Father. 21
Jde 1: 7 just as Sodom and Gomor'rah and the surrounding 33
1Es 5:69 For we obey your Lord just as you do 26
2Es 4:42 For just as a woman who is in travail makes haste 37
5:40 He said to me, "Just as you cannot do one 38
42 just as for those who are last 39
6: 6 just as the end shall come through me 40
7:48 not just a few of us but almost all *
52 If you have just a few precious stones 41
104 Just as now a father does not send his son 37
8: 2 Just as, when you ask the earth, it will tell you 38
41 just as the farmer sows many seeds 39
59 For just as the things which I have predicted 39
9: 5 just as with everything that has occurred 39
11:33 just as the wings had done. 39
13:52 Just as no one can explore or know 39
15:21 Just as they have done to my elect until this day 39
16:16 Just as an arrow shot by a mighty archer 38
38 Just as a woman with child, in the ninth month 37
49 Just as a respectable and virtuous woman abhors 38
52 For behold, just a little while 36
Tob 14: 5 just as the prophets said of it. 21
Jdt 2: 1 carrying out his revenge . . just as he said. 21
13 sure to carry them out just as I have ordered you; 20
10:16 tell him just what you have said 24
Wis 19:17 just as . . those at the door of the righteous man 35
Sir 18: 7 When a man has finished, he is just beginning 32
24:28 Just as the first man did not know her perfectly 23
39:23 just as he turns fresh water into salt. 33
24 just as they are obstacles to the wicked. 30
25 just as evil things for sinners. 30
27 just as they turn into evils for sinners. 30
Bar 4:28 For just as you purposed to go astray from God 35
33 For just as she rejoiced at your fall 35
LJr 1:17 For just as one's dish is useless when it is broken 35
18 just as the gates are shut on every side upon a man 35
27 placed before them just as before the dead. 35
1Mc 4:19 Just as Judas was finishing this speech 14
10:37 just as the king has commanded in the land of Judah 17
2Mc 2:10 Just as Moses prayed to the Lord 21
27 just as it is not easy . . 16
3:28 this man who had just entered the . . treasury *
5:18 just as Heliodorus was 12
9: 8 he who had just been thinking that . . 12
10:28 Just as dawn was breaking 12
11:31 their own food and laws, just as formerly 24
13:11 the people who had just begun to revive 12
17 This happened, just as day was dawning 15
15:39 For just as it is harmful to drink wine alone 16
3Mc 4: 6 who had just entered the bridal chamber 12
6:15 just as you have said 21
16 Just as Eleazar was ending his prayer 12
4Mc 1:14 We shall decide just what reason is 31
28 Just as pleasure and pain are two plants 16
2: 6 Just so it is with the emotions 35
16 just as it repels anger 35
3:21 just at that time certain men attempted a revolution 13
7:11 just as our father Aaron . . ran 35
8: 6 Just as I am able to punish those who disobey 35
13: 6 just as towers jutting out over harbors 19
14: 6 Just as the hands and feet are moved 19
7 just as the seven days of creation 19
15:31 Just as Noah's ark . . endured the waves 19

just (2) 1. מִשְׁפָּט 2. צַדִּיק 3. צדק 4. צֶדֶק 5. שָׁלֵם 6. תכן 7. דִּין (A) 8. δίκαιος 9. δικαίως 10. ἔνδικος

Lev 19:36 You shall have just balances, just weights 4
36 You shall have . . just weights 4
36 You shall have . . a just ephah 4
36 shall have . . a just hin 4
Deu 25:15 full and just weight . . a full and just measure 4
15 full and just weight . . a full and just measure 4
32: 4 A God . . without iniquity, just and right is he. 2
Ezr 9:15 O LORD the God of Israel, thou art just 2
Neh 9:33 thou hast been just in all that has come upon us 2
Job 9: 2 it is so: but how can a man be just before God? 3
27:17 he may pile it up, but the just will wear it 2
31: 6 Let me be weighed in a just balance 4
35: 2 Do you think this to be just? 1
Ps 9: 4 For thou hast maintained my just cause; 1
111: 7 The works of his hands are faithful and just; 1
119:121 I have done what is just and right; do not leave me 1
145:17 LORD is just in all his ways, and kind in all 2
Prv 8:15 By me kings reign, and rulers decree what is just; 4
11: 1 but a just weight is his delight. 5
12: 5 The thoughts of the righteous are just; 1
16:11 A just balance and scales are the LORD'S; 1
21: 7 because they refuse to do what is just. 1
Jer 46:28 I will chasten you in just measure 1
Ezk 18:25 Yet you say, 'The way of the Lord is not just.' 6
25 Hear now, O house of Israel: Is my way not just? 6
25 Is it not your ways that are not just? 6
29 Israel says, 'The way of the Lord is not just. 6
29 O house of Israel, are my ways not just? 6
29 Is it not your ways that are not just? 6
33:17 Yet your people say, 'The way of the Lord is not just 6
17 when it is their own way that is not just. 6
20 Yet you say, 'The way of the Lord is not just.' 6
45:10 You shall have just balances, a just ephah 4
10 You shall have just balances, a just ephah 4
10 just balances, a just ephah, and a just bath. 4
Dan 4:37 for all his works are right and his ways are just; 7
Mat 1:19 husband Joseph, being a just man and unwilling 8
5:45 and sends rain on the just and on the unjust. 8
Lke 1:17 the disobedient to the wisdom of the just 8
14:14 repaid at the resurrection of the just. 8
Joh 5:30 as I hear, I judge; and my judgment is just 8
Act 24:15 a resurrection of both the just and the unjust. 8
Rom 3: 8 Their condemnation is just. 10
7:12 and the commandment is holy and just and good. 8
Php 4: 8 whatever is honorable, whatever is just 8
2Th 1: 6 since indeed God deems it just 8
1Ti 1: 9 the law is not laid down for the just 8
Heb 2: 2 received a just retribution 10
1Jn 1: 9 he is faithful and just, and will forgive our sins 8
Rev 15: 3 Just and true are thy ways, O King of the ages! 8
16: 5 Just art thou in these thy judgments 8
7 Lord God . . true and just are thy judgments! 8
19: 2 for his judgments are true and just; 8
Tob 14: 9 be merciful and just 8
Wis 14:30 just penalties will overtake them on two counts 8
LJr 1:73 Better therefore is a just man who has no idols 8
Aza 1: 4 For thou art just in all that thou hast done to us 8
2Mc 1:24 awe-inspiring and strong and just and merciful 8
25 who alone art just and almighty and eternal 8
7:36 receive just punishment for your arrogance. 8
13: 8 this was eminently just 9
3Mc 2: 3 For you . . are a just Ruler 8
25 who were strangers to everything just. 8
4Mc 2:23 temperate, just, good, and courageous. 8
9:24 the just Providence of our ancestors 8

just *See* acknowledge, cause, decree, like, measure, now, outside, penalty, requirement, term, tortured.

just as soon 1. ὡς ἂν ἐξαυτῆς

Php 2:23 just as soon as I see how it will go with me; 1

just man 1. צַדִּיק 2. δίκαιος

Job 12: 4 me, a just and blameless man, am a laughingstock. 1
Heb 12:23 to the spirits of just men made perfect 2

just one 1. δίκαιος

Act 22:14 see the Just One and to hear a voice from his mouth 1

just then 1. הִנֵּה

2Sm 3:22 Just then the servants of David arrived 1

justice 1. דִּין 2. מִשְׁפָּט 3. פְּלִילָה 4. צֶדֶק 5. דְּחַבֵּר (A) 6. δίκαιος 7. δικαιοσύνη 8. δικαίωμα 9. δικαστής 10. δίκη 11. κρίμα 12. κρίσις

Gen 18:19 the LORD by doing righteousness and justice; 2
Exd 23: 6 You shall not pervert the justice due 2
Deu 10:18 executes justice for the fatherless 2
16:19 not pervert justice . . not show partiality; 2
20 Justice, and only justice, you shall follow 4
20 Justice, and only justice, you shall follow 4
24:17 not pervert the justice due to the sojourner 2
27:19 'Cursed be he who perverts the justice due 2
32: 4 his work is perfect; for all his ways are justice. 2
1Sm 8: 3 they took bribes and perverted justice. 2
2Sm 8:15 David administered justice and equity to all 2
1Kg 3:28 the wisdom of God was in him, to render justice. 2
10: 9 you may execute justice and righteousness. 2
1Ch 18:14 David . . administered justice and equity 2
2Ch 9: 8 you may execute justice and righteousness. 2
Job 8: 3 Does God pervert justice? 2
9:19 If it is a matter of justice, who can summon him? 2
19: 7 I call aloud, but there is no justice. 2
29:14 my justice was like a robe and a turban. 2
34:12 the Almighty will not pervert justice. 2
17 Shall one who hates justice govern? 2
36:17 judgment and justice seize you. 2
37:23 he is great in power and justice 2
Ps 33: 5 He loves righteousness and justice; 2
37:28 For the LORD loves justice; 2
30 utters wisdom, and his tongue speaks justice. 2
72: 1 Give the king thy justice, O God 2
2 with righteousness, and thy poor with justice! 2
89:14 Righteousness and justice are the foundation 2
94:15 for justice will return to the righteous 2
97: 2 righteousness and justice are the foundation 2
99: 4 Mighty King, lover of justice, thou hast 2
4 executed justice and righteousness in Jacob. 2
101: 1 sing of loyalty and of justice; to thee, O LORD 2
103: 6 LORD works vindication and justice for all 2
106: 3 Blessed are they who observe justice 2
112: 5 who conducts his affairs with justice. 2
119:149 O LORD, in thy justice preserve my life. 2
156 O LORD; give me life according to thy justice. 2
140:12 LORD . . executes justice for the needy. 2
146: 7 who executes justice for the oppressed; 2
Prv 1: 3 receive instruction in . . justice, and equity; 2
2: 8 guarding the paths of justice 2
9 Then you will understand . . justice and equity 2
8:20 I walk in . . the paths of justice 2
17:23 accepts a bribe . . to pervert the ways of justice. 2
18: 5 not good . . to deprive a righteous man of justice. 2
19:28 A worthless witness mocks at justice 2
21: 3 To do righteousness and justice is more 2
15 When justice is done, it is a joy to the righteous 2
28: 5 Evil men do not understand justice 2
29: 4 By justice a king gives stability to the land 2
26 but from the LORD a man gets justice. 2
Ecc 3:16 in the place of justice, even there was 2
5: 8 see . . justice and right violently taken away 2
Isa 1:17 seek justice, correct oppression; 2
21 the faithful city . . she that was full of justice! 2
27 Zion shall be redeemed by justice 2
5: 7 he looked for justice, but behold, bloodshed; 2
16 the LORD of hosts is exalted in justice 2
9: 7 establish it, and to uphold it with justice 2
10: 2 to turn aside the needy from justice and to rob 1
16: 3 Give counsel, grant justice; 3
5 one who judges and seeks justice 2
28: 6 a spirit of justice to him who sits in judgment 2
17 I will make justice the line 2
30:18 For the LORD is a God of justice; 2
32: 1 and princes will rule in justice. 2
16 Then justice will dwell in the wilderness 2
33: 5 fill Zion with justice and righteousness; 2
40:14 and who taught him the path of justice 2
42: 1 he will bring forth justice to the nations. 2
3 he will faithfully bring forth justice. 2
4 till he has established justice in the earth; 2
51: 4 from me, and my justice for a light to the peoples. 2
56: 1 says the LORD: "Keep justice, and do righteousness 2
59: 8 and there is no justice in their paths; 2
9 Therefore justice is far from us 2
11 we look for justice, but there is none; 2
14 Justice is turned back, 2
15 it displeased him that there was no justice. 2
61: 8 I the LORD love justice, I hate robbery and wrong; 2
Jer 4: 2 if you swear, 'As the LORD lives,' in truth, in justice 2
5: 1 find a man, one who does justice and seeks truth; 2
28 they judge not with justice . . to make it prosper 1
7: 5 if you truly execute justice one with another 2
9:24 the LORD who practice steadfast love, justice 2
21:12 says the LORD: "'Execute justice in the morning 2
22: 3 Thus says the LORD: Do justice and righteousness 2
15 Did not your father eat and drink and do justice 2
23: 5 and shall execute justice and righteousness 2
33:15 and he shall execute justice and righteousness 2
Ezk 18: 8 executes true justice between man and man 2
34:16 I will feed them in justice. 2
45: 9 and execute justice and righteousness; 2

Dan 3: 2 assemble the . . treasurers, the justices 5
3 counselors, the treasurers, the justices 5
Hos 2:19 betroth you to me . . in justice, in steadfast love 2
12: 6 return, hold fast to love and justice 2
Ams 5: 7 O you who turn justice to wormwood 2
15 and love good, and establish justice in the gate; 2
24 But let justice roll down like waters 2
6:12 But you have turned justice into poison 2
Mic 3: 1 Israel! Is it not for you to know justice? 2
8 and with justice and might, to declare to Jacob 2
9 Israel, who abhor justice and pervert all equity 2
6: 8 does the LORD require of you but to do justice 2
Hab 1: 4 the law is slacked and justice never goes forth. 2
4 justice goes forth perverted. 2
7 their justice and dignity proceed 2
Zep 3: 5 every morning he shows forth his justice 2
Mal 2:17 Or by asking, "Where is the God of justice? 2
Mat 12:18 he shall proclaim justice to the Gentiles. 12
20 till he brings justice to victory; 12
23:23 justice and mercy and faith 12
Lke 11:42 neglect justice and the love of God 12
Act 8:33 In his humiliation justice was denied him 12
24:25 as he argued about justice and self-control 7
28: 4 justice has not allowed him to live. 10
Rom 3: 5 our wickedness serves to show the justice of God 7
Heb 11:33 enforced justice, received promises 7
1Es 8:23 appoint judges and justices to judge 9
AEs 16: 4 they will escape the evil-hating justice of God 10
Wis 1: 8 justice, when it punishes, will not pass him by. 10
5:18 wear impartial justice as a helmet; 12
8: 7 self-control and prudence, justice and courage; 7
11:20 when pursued by justice 10
Sir 16:22 Who will announce his acts of justice? 7
27: 8 If you pursue justice, you will attain it 6
Bar 2:17 will not ascribe glory or justice to the Lord 8
Aza 1: 5 in truth and justice thou hast brought all this 12
1Mc 2:29 who were seeking righteousness and justice 11
6:22 How long will you fail to do justice 12
7:18 they said, "There is no truth or justice in them 12
14:35 because of the justice and loyalty 7
2Mc 4:34 with no regard for justice 6
8:13 were cowardly and distrustful of God's justice 10
10:12 Ptolemy . . took the lead in showing justice to the Jews 6
4Mc 1: 4 the emotions that hinder one from justice 7
6 opposed to justice, courage, and self-control 7
18 justice, courage, and self-control. 7
2: 6 the emotions that hinder one from justice. 7
4:13 by human treachery and not by divine justice. 10
21 The divine justice was angered by these acts 10
5:24 it instructs us in justice 7
8:14 whatever justice you revere will be merciful 10
22 Also, divine justice will excuse us 10
9: 9 undergo from the divine justice 10
15 enemy of heavenly justice, savage of mind 10
11: 3 incur punishment from the heavenly justice 10
12:12 justice has laid up for you . . eternal fire 10
18:22 divine justice pursued . . the accursed tyrant. 10

justice *See also* administer, execute, give, perversion, pervert, secure.

do justice 1. שׁפט 2. *κρίνω*

Ps 10:18 to do justice to the fatherless 1
Sir 35:17 does justice for the righteous 2

justification 1. *δικαιοσύνη* 2. *δικαίωμα* 3. *δικαίωσις*

Rom 4:25 and raised for our justification. 3
5:16 but the free gift . . brings justification. 2
Gal 2:21 if justification were through the law 1

justify 1. צדק 2. *δικαιοσύνη* 3. *δικαιόω* 4. *δικαίωσις* 5. *λόγος* 6. iustifico

Job 32: 2 He was angry at Job because he justified himself 1
33:32 answer me; speak, for I desire to justify you. 1
40: 8 Will you condemn me that you may be justified? 1
Ps 51: 4 so that thou art justified in thy sentence 1
Prv 17:15 He who justifies the wicked and he who condemns 1
Isa 43: 9 Let them bring their witnesses to justify them 1
Mat 11:19 Yet wisdom is justified by her deeds. 3
12:37 for by your words you will be justified 3
Lke 7:29 the people and the tax collectors justified God 3
35 Yet wisdom is justified by all her children. 3
10:29 he, desiring to justify himself, said to Jesus 3
16:15 You are those who justify yourselves before men 3
18:14 this man went down to his house justified 3
Act 19:40 to justify this commotion. 5
Rom 2:13 but the doers of the law who will be justified. 3
3: 4 That thou mayest be justified in thy words 3
20 For no human being will be justified in his sight 3
24 they are justified by his grace as a gift 3
26 and that he justifies him who has faith in Jesus. 3
28 man is justified by faith apart from works of law. 3
30 and he will justify the circumcised 3
4: 2 For if Abraham was justified by works 3
5 but trusts him who justifies the ungodly 3
5: 1 since we are justified by faith, we have peace 3
9 Since . . we are now justified by his blood 3
8:30 and those whom he called he also justified; 3
30 and those whom he justified he also glorified. 3
33 It is God who justifies; 3
10: 4 that every one who has faith may be justified. 2
10 man believes with his heart and so is justified 2
1Co 6:11 justified in the name of the Lord Jesus Christ 3
Gal 2:16 a man is not justified by works of the law 3
16 in order to be justified by faith in Christ 3
16 by works of the law shall no one be justified. 3
17 if, in our endeavor to be justified in Christ 3
3: 8 God would justify the Gentiles by faith 3
11 no man is justified before God by the law 3
24 we might be justified by faith. 3
5: 4 you who would be justified by the law 3
Tit 3: 7 that we might be justified by his grace 3
Jas 2:21 Was not Abraham our father justified by works 3
24 You see that a man is justified by works 3
25 was not also Rahab the harlot justified by works 3
2Es 4:18 which would you undertake to justify 6
Sir 1:22 Unrighteous anger cannot be justified 3
10:29 Who will justify the man 4
13:22 he speaks unseemly words, and they justify him 3
23:11 he will not be justified 3
31: 5 He who loves gold will not be justified 3

justly 1. צַדִּיק 2. צֶדֶק 3. *δίκαιος* 4. *δικαίως*

2Sm 23: 3 When one rules justly over men 1
Isa 59: 4 No one enters suit justly, 2
Lke 23:41 we indeed justly 4
Col 4: 1 Masters, treat your slaves justly and fairly 3
1Pe 2:23 but he trusted to him who judges justly. 4
Wis 9:12 I shall judge thy people justly 4
19:13 they justly suffered because of their wicked acts; 4
2Mc 7:38 which has justly fallen on our whole nation. 4
9: 6 that very justly 4
18 the judgment of God had justly come upon him 3
3Mc 7: 7 we justly have acquitted them 3

jut out 1. *προβλής*

4Mc 13: 6 just as towers jutting out over harbors 1

jutting *See* cliff.

K

kab 1. קַב
2Kg 6:25 and the fourth part of a kab of dove's dung for five 1

keel 1. τρόπις
Wis 5:10 nor track of its keel in the waves; 1

keen 1. ὀξύς
Wis 7:22 distinct, invulnerable, loving the good, keen 1
8:11 I shall be found keen in judgment 1

keep 1. אצל 2. גרע 3. היה 4. היה לְ 5. הלך 6. חגג 7. חדל 8. חשׂך 9. יסף 10. כלא 11. לקח 12. מנע 13. מִשְׁמֶרֶת 14. נטר 15. נפל 16. נצר 17. עבד 18. עצר 19. עֲצָרָה ל 20. עשׂה 21. צפן 22. קום 23. קרב 24. רעה 25. רָעָה בְּ 26. שׂום 27. שׁאר 28. שׁוה 29. שׁמר 30. נטר (A) 31. ἄγω 32. ἀπέχω 33. ἀποδίδωμι 34. ἀφίστημι 35. διάγω 36. διακρατέω 37. διατηρέω 38. διαφυλάσσω 39. εἰμί 40. εἰμί ἐν 41. εἰς μή 42. ἐμμένω 43. ἐξαιρέω 44. ἔργω 45. ἔτι 46. ἔχω 47. ἵνα μή 48. ἵστημι 49. καθίστημι 50. καρτερέω 51. κατά 52. καταλείπω 53. κατατίθημι 54. κατέχω 55. κρατέω 56. κωλύω 57. λαμβάνω 58. μή 59. μήποτε 60. οὐκ ἐάω 61. παύω 62. περὶ γίνομαι 63. περιποίησις 64. ποιέω 65. στέγω 66. συντηρέω 67. τελέω 68. τηρέω 69. τήρησις 70. τίθημι 71. φείδομαι 72. φρουρέω 73. φυλάσσω 74. conservo 75. custodio 76. detineo 77. observo 78. reservo 79. retineo 80. servo

Gen 2:15 put him in the garden of Eden to till it and keep it. 29
17: 9 to Abraham, "As for you, you shall keep my covenant 29
10 This is my covenant, which you shall keep 29
18:19 household after him to keep the way of the LORD 29
20: 6 it was I who kept you from sinning against me; 8
26: 5 Abraham . . kept my charge, my commandments 29
28:15 I am with you and will keep you wherever you go 29
20 If God will be with me, and will keep me in this way 29
29: 9 with her father's sheep; for she kept them. 24
30:31 I will again feed your flock and keep it 29
33: 9 my brother; keep what you have for yourself. 3
38:23 Judah replied, "Let her keep the things as her own 11
41:35 food in the cities, and let them keep it. 29
Exd 3: 1 Moses was keeping the flock of his father-in-law 24
12: 6 you shall keep it until the fourteenth day 13
25 when you come . . you shall keep this service. 29
42 is a night of watching kept to the LORD by all *
47 All the congregation of Israel shall keep it. 20
48 stranger . . would keep the passover to the LORD 20
48 be circumcised, then he may come near and keep it; 20
13: 5 you shall keep this service in this month. 17
10 You shall therefore keep this ordinance 29
15:26 If you . . keep all his statutes 29
16:23 left over lay by to be kept till the morning.' 13
28 How long do you refuse to keep my commandments 29
32 omer of it be kept throughout your generations 13
33 to be kept throughout your generations. 13
34 placed it before the testimony, to be kept. 13
19: 5 if you will obey my voice and keep my covenant 29
20: 6 those who love me and keep my commandments. 29
21:18 his fist and the man does not die but keeps his bed 15
29 its owner has been warned but has not kept it 29
36 if . . its owner has not kept it 29
22: 7 delivers to his neighbor money or goods to keep 29
10 an ass or an ox or a sheep or any beast to keep 29
23:15 You shall keep the feast of unleavened bread; 29
16 You shall keep the feast of harvest *
16 the field. You shall keep the feast *
31:13 'You shall keep my sabbaths, for this is a sign 29
14 keep the sabbath, because it is holy for you; 29
16 people of Israel shall keep the sabbath 29
34: 7 keeping steadfast love for thousands 16
18 The feast of unleavened bread you shall keep. 29
36: 3 They still kept bringing him freewill *

Lev 18: 4 You shall do my ordinances and keep my statutes 29
5 You shall therefore keep my statutes 29
26 you shall keep my statutes and my ordinances 29
30 keep my charge never to practice any of these 29
19: 3 you shall keep my sabbaths: I am the LORD your God 29
19 You shall keep my statutes 29
30 You shall keep my sabbaths 29
20: 8 Keep my statutes, and do them; I am the LORD 29
22 You shall therefore keep all my statutes 29
22: 9 They shall therefore keep my charge 29
31 So you shall keep my commandments and do them 29
23:41 you shall keep it in the seventh month 6
25:18 and keep my ordinances and perform them 29
26: 2 You shall keep my sabbaths and reverence my 29
Num 6:24 The LORD bless you and keep you 29
8:26 in the tent of meeting, to keep the charge 29
9: 2 Israel keep the passover at its appointed time. 20
3 you shall keep it at its appointed time; 20
3 statutes and . . ordinances you shall keep it. 20
4 Israel that they should keep the passover. 20
5 they kept the passover in the first month 20
6 that they could not keep the passover on that day; 20
7 why are we kept from offering the LORD'S offering 2
10 he shall still keep the passover to the LORD. 20
11 second month . . in the evening they shall keep 20
12 according to all the statute . . they shall keep 20
13 yet refrains from keeping the passover 20
14 stranger . . will keep the passover to the LORD 20
19 people of Israel kept the charge of the LORD 29
23 they kept the charge of the LORD 29
17:10 to be kept as a sign for the rebels 13
18: 8 have given you whatever is kept of the offerings 13
19: 9 shall be kept for the congregation of . . Israel 3
29:12 you shall keep a feast to the LORD seven days; 6
Deu 4: 2 may keep the commandments of the LORD your God 29
6 Keep them and do them; for that will be your wisdom 29
9 Only take heed, and keep your soul diligently 29
40 shall keep his statutes and his commandments 29
5:10 those who love me and keep my commandments. 29
15 LORD your God commanded you to keep the sabbath 20
29 to fear me and to keep all my commandments 29
6: 2 keeping all his statutes and his commandments 29
17 You shall diligently keep the commandments 29
7: 8 LORD loves you, and is keeping the oath 29
9 LORD . . the faithful God who keeps covenant 29
9 those who love him and keep his commandments 29
12 hearken to these ordinances, and keep and do them 29
12 LORD your God will keep with you the covenant 29
12 which he swore to your fathers to keep; *
8: 2 whether you would keep his commandments, or not. 29
6 shall keep the commandments of the LORD your God 29
11 by not keeping his commandments 29
10:13 keep the commandments and statutes of the LORD 29
11: 1 keep his charge, his statutes, his ordinances 29
8 You shall therefore keep all the commandment 29
13: 4 fear him, and keep his commandments and obey 29
18 keeping all his commandments which I command 29
16: 1 keep the passover to the LORD your God; 20
10 Then you shall keep the feast of weeks to the LORD 20
13 You shall keep the feast of booths seven days 20
17:19 fear the LORD . . keeping all the words of this law 29
19: 9 careful to keep all this commandment 20
23: 9 you shall keep yourself from every evil thing. 29
26:17 keep his statutes and his commandments 29
18 that you are to keep all his commandments 29
27: 1 Keep all the commandment which I command you 29
10 keeping his commandments and his statutes 29
28: 9 if you keep the commandments of the LORD your God 29
45 to keep his commandments and his statutes 29
30: 8 keep all his commandments which I command you 20
10 keeping his commandments and his statutes 29
16 obey . . by keeping his commandments 29
32:10 cared for him, he kept him as the apple of his eye. 16
33: 9 they observed thy word, and kept thy covenant. 16
Jos 5:10 they kept the passover on the fourteenth day 20

6:18 keep yourselves from the things devoted 29
22: 2 You have kept all that Moses . . commanded you 29
3 have been careful to keep the charge of the LORD 29
5 walk in all his ways, and to keep his commandments 29
23: 6 be . . steadfast to keep and do all that is written 29
Jdg 5: 6 ceased and travelers kept to the byways. 5
1Sm 9:24 Samuel said, "See, what was kept is set before you. 27
24 it was kept for you until the hour appointed 29
13:13 you have not kept the commandment of the LORD 29
14 you have not kept what the LORD commanded you. 29
16:11 the youngest, but behold, he is keeping the sheep. 25
17:34 Your servant used to keep sheep for his father; 24
21: 4 if . . young men have kept themselves from women. 29
5 women have been kept from us as always when I go 19
25:16 while we were with them keeping the sheep. 24
33 who have kept me this day from bloodguilt 10
2Sm 3: 8 I keep showing loyalty to the house of Saul *
15:12 and the people with Ab'salom kept increasing. 5
16 the king left ten concubines to keep the house. 29
16:21 concubines, whom he has left to keep the house; 29
22:22 For I have kept the ways of the LORD, and have not 29
24 I was blameless . . and I kept myself from guilt. 29
44 thou didst keep me as the head of the nations; 29
1Kg 2: 3 keep the charge of the LORD your God, walking 29
3 walking in his ways and keeping his statutes, his 29
43 Why then have you not kept your oath to the LORD 29
3: 6 thou hast kept for him this great and steadfast 29
14 my ways, keeping my statutes and my commandments 29
6:12 and keep all my commandments and walk in them 29
8:23 God like thee . . keeping covenant and showing 29
24 hast kept with . . what thou didst declare to him; 29
25 keep with thy servant . . what thou hast promised 29
58 walk in all his ways, and to keep his commandments 29
61 walking in . . and keeping his commandments 29
9: 4 and keeping my statutes and my ordinances 29
6 turn aside . . and do not keep my commandments 29
11:10 he did not keep what the LORD commanded. 29
11 you have not kept my covenant and my statutes 29
33 and keeping my statutes and my ordinances *
34 David . . kept my commandments and my statutes; 29
38 do what is right in my eyes by keeping my statutes 29
13:21 and have not kept the commandment which the LORD 29
14: 8 like my servant David, who kept my commandments 29
27 the guard, who kept the door of the king's house. 29
20:39 said, 'Keep this man; if by any means he be missing 29
2Kg 17:13 Turn . . and keep my commandments and my statutes 29
19 Judah also did not keep the commandments 29
18: 6 he did not depart . . but kept the commandments 29
23: 3 walk after the LORD and to keep his commandments 29
21 Keep the passover to the LORD your God 20
22 no such passover had been kept since the days 20
23 this passover was kept to the LORD in Jerusalem. 20
1Ch 4:10 saying, "Oh . . that thou wouldst keep me from harm 20
10:13 he did not keep the command of the LORD 29
12:22 men kept coming to David to help him *
29 kept their allegiance to the house of Saul. 29
22:12 over Israel you may keep the law of the LORD 29
23:32 they shall keep charge of the tent of meeting 29
28: 7 in keeping my commandments and my ordinance 20
29:18 O LORD . . keep for ever such purposes 29
19 with a whole heart he may keep thy commandments 29
2Ch 6:14 keeping covenant and showing steadfast love 29
15 who hast kept with thy servant David my father 29
16 O LORD . . keep with thy servant David my father 29
7: 9 kept the dedication of the altar seven days 20
17 and keeping my statutes and my ordinances 29
12:10 who kept the door of the king's house. 29
13:11 for we keep the charge of the LORD our God 29
14: 4 to keep the law and the commandment. 20
23: 6 all the people shall keep the charge of the LORD. 29
30: 1 to keep the passover to the LORD the God of Israel. 20
2 had taken counsel to keep the passover 20
3 could not keep it in its time because the priests 20
5 should come and keep the passover to the LORD 20
5 had not kept it in great numbers as prescribed. 20

13 came . . to keep the feast of unleavened bread 20
21 kept the feast of unleavened bread seven days 20
23 agreed together to keep the feast for another 20
23 kept it for another seven days with gladness. 20
34:21 our fathers have not kept the word of the LORD 29
31 walk after the LORD and to keep his commandments 29
35: 1 Josi'ah kept a passover to the LORD in Jerusalem; 20
16 to keep the passover and to offer burnt 20
17 people of Israel . . present kept the passover 20
18 No passover like it had been kept in Israel since 20
18 none . . kept such a passover as was kept 20
18 such a passover as was kept by Josi'ah 20
19 eighteenth year . . this passover was kept. 20
36:16 they kept mocking the messengers of God •
Ezr 3: 4 kept the feast of booths, as it is written 20
6:19 returned exiles kept the passover. 20
22 kept the feast of unleavened bread seven days 20
8:29 Guard them and keep them until you weigh them 29
Neh 1: 5 God who keeps covenant and steadfast love 29
5 those who love him and keep his commandments; 29
7 have not kept the commandments, the statutes 29
9 return to me and keep my commandments 29
4:23 each kept his weapon in his hand. •
8:18 kept the feast seven days; and on the eighth day 20
9:32 God, who keepest covenant and steadfast love 29
34 not kept thy law or heeded thy commandments 29
Est 3: 8 and they do not keep the king's laws 20
9:21 they should keep the fourteenth day of the month 20
27 that without fail they would keep these two days 20
28 that these days should be remembered and kept 20
Job 4: 2 Yet who can keep from speaking? 18
22:15 Will you keep to the old way which wicked men have 29
23:11 I have kept his way and have not turned aside. 29
24: 1 are not times of judgment kept by the Almighty 21
36:19 Will your cry avail to keep you from distress •
Ps 16: 8 I keep the LORD always before me; 28
17: 8 Keep me as the apple of the eye; 29
18:21 For I have kept the ways of the LORD 29
23 I kept myself from guilt. 29
19:11 in keeping them there is great reward. 29
25:10 faithfulness, for those who keep his covenant 16
32: 9 bit and bridle, else it will not keep with you. 23
34:13 Keep your tongue from evil, and your lips 16
20 He keeps all his bones; not one of them is broken. 29
37:34 Wait for the LORD, and keep to his way 29
50:18 you keep company with adulterers. †
55:19 because they keep no law, and do not fear God. †
66: 9 who has kept us among the living 26
74:11 why dost thou keep thy right hand in thy bosom? •
78: 7 the works of God, but keep his commandments; 16
10 They did not keep God's covenant, but refused 29
89:28 My steadfast love I will keep for him for ever 29
31 if they . . do not keep my commandments 29
99: 7 kept his testimonies, and the statutes 29
103:18 to those who keep his covenant and remember to do 29
105:45 to the end that they should keep his statutes 29
119: 2 Blessed are those who keep his testimonies 16
4 Thou hast commanded thy precepts to be kept 29
5 may be steadfast in keeping thy statutes! 29
22 for I have kept thy testimonies. 16
33 way of thy statutes; and I will keep it to the end. 16
34 Give me understanding, that I may keep thy law 16
44 I will keep thy law continually, for ever and ever; 29
55 I remember thy name . . O LORD, and keep thy law. 29
56 This blessing . . that I have kept thy precepts. 16
57 LORD is my portion; I promise to keep thy words. 29
60 I . . do not delay to keep thy commandments. 29
63 all who fear thee, of those who keep thy precepts. 29
67 I went astray; but now I keep thy word. 29
69 with my whole heart I keep thy precepts; 16
88 that I may keep the testimonies of thy mouth. 29
100 more than the aged, for I keep thy precepts. 16
101 from every evil way, in order to keep thy word. 29
115 that I may keep the commandments of my God. 16
129 are wonderful; therefore my soul keeps them. 16
134 Redeem me . . that I may keep thy precepts. 29
136 streams of tears, because men do not keep thy law. 29
145 answer me, O LORD! I will keep thy statutes. 16
158 because they do not keep thy commands. 29
167 My soul keeps thy testimonies; I love them 29
168 I keep thy precepts and testimonies 29
121: 3 he who keeps you will not slumber. 29
4 keeps Israel will neither slumber nor sleep. 29
7 The LORD will keep you from all evil; 29
7 LORD . . will keep your life. 29
8 LORD will keep your going out and your coming 29
132:12 If your sons keep my covenant and my testimonies 29
141: 9 Keep me from the trap which they have laid for me 29
146: 6 who keeps faith for ever; 29
Prv 2:20 keep to the paths of the righteous. 29
3: 1 but let your heart keep my commandments; 16
21 My son, keep sound wisdom and discretion; 16
26 LORD . . will keep your foot from being caught. 29
4: 4 keep my commandments, and live; 29
6 Do not forsake her, and she will keep you; 29
21 keep them within your heart. 29
23 Keep your heart with all vigilance; 16
5: 2 that you may keep discretion 29
6:20 My son, keep your father's commandment 16

7: 1 My son, keep my words 29
2 keep my commandments and live 29
2 keep my teachings as the apple of your eye; •
8:32 happy are those who keep my ways. 29
19: 8 he who keeps understanding will prosper. 29
16 He who keeps the commandment keeps his life; 29
16 He who keeps the commandment keeps his life; 29
21:23 He who keeps his mouth and his tongue keeps 29
23 keeps his mouth . . keeps himself out of trouble. 29
22:18 for it will be pleasant if you keep them within 29
28: 4 but those who keep the law strive against them. 29
7 He who keeps the law is a wise son 16
29:18 but blessed is he who keeps the law. 29
Ecc 2:10 whatever my eyes desired I did not keep from them; 1
10 I kept my heart from no pleasure 12
3: 6 a time to keep, and a time to cast away; 29
5:13 riches were kept by their owner to his hurt 29
8: 2 Keep the king's command 29
12:13 Fear God, and keep his commandments; 29
Sng 1: 6 but, my own vineyard I have not kept! 14
Isa 26: 2 righteous nation which keeps faith may enter 29
3 Thou dost keep him in perfect peace 16
33:23 it cannot . . keep the sail spread out. •
42: 6 I have taken you by the hand and kept you; 16
45:20 and keep on praying to a god that cannot save. •
49: 8 I have kept you and given you as a covenant 16
56: 1 says the LORD: "Keep justice, and do righteousness 29
2 who keeps the sabbath, not profaning it 29
2 and keeps his hand from doing any evil. 29
4 "To the eunuchs who keep my sabbaths 29
6 his servants, every one who keeps the sabbath 29
65: 5 who say, "Keep to yourself, do not come near me 23
Jer 2:25 Keep your feet from going unshod 12
5:24 keeps . . the weeks appointed for the harvest.' 29
25 and your sins have kept good from you. 12
8: 7 swallow, and crane keep the time of their coming; 29
15: 6 says the LORD, you keep going backward; •
16:11 and have forsaken me and have not kept my law 29
31:10 and will keep him as a shepherd keeps his flock. 29
10 and will keep him as a shepherd keeps his flock. •
16 Thus says the LORD: "Keep your voice from weeping 12
34:18 and did not keep the terms of the covenant 22
35:14 gave to his sons, to drink no wine, has been kept; 22
16 have kept the command which their father gave 22
18 and kept all his precepts 29
Lam 4:22 he will keep you in exile no longer; 9
Ezk 5: 7 not walked in my statutes or kept my ordinances 20
11:20 and keep my ordinances and obey them; 29
17:14 that by keeping his covenant it might stand. 29
18:21 and keeps all my statutes and does what is lawful 29
44: 8 And you have not kept charge of my holy things; 29
8 you have set foreigners to keep my charge 29
14 I will appoint them to keep charge of the temple 29
15 sons of Zadok, who kept the charge of my sanctuary 29
16 to minister to me, and they shall keep my charge. 29
24 They shall keep my laws and my statutes 29
46:17 his sons may keep a gift from his inheritance. 4
48:11 priests, the sons of Zadok, who kept my charge 29
Dan 7:28 but I kept the matter in my mind. 30
9: 4 God, who keepest covenant and steadfast love 29
4 those who love him and keep his commandments 29
14 Therefore the LORD has kept ready the calamity •
Ams 1:11 tore perpetually, and he kept his wrath for ever. 73
2: 4 and have not kept his statutes, but their lies 29
Mic 6:16 For you have kept the statutes of Omri 73
Nah 1: 2 the LORD . . keeps wrath for his enemies. 14
Hab 1:17 Is he then to keep on emptying his net •
Zec 3: 7 If you will walk in my ways and keep my charge 29
11:12 right to you, give me my wages; but if not, keep them. 7
14:16 to worship . . and to keep the feast of booths. 6
18 that do not go up to keep the feast of booths. 6
19 that do not go up to keep the feast of booths. 6
Mal 2: 9 inasmuch as you have not kept my ways 29
3: 7 aside from my statutes and have not kept them. 29
14 What is the good of our keeping his charge 29
Mat 19:17 If you would enter life, keep the commandments. 68
26:18 keep the passover at your house 64
28:14 we will satisfy him and keep you out of trouble. 64
Mrk 7: 9 in order to keep your tradition! 48
9:10 So they kept the matter to themselves 55
Lke 2: 8 keeping watch over their flock by night. 73
19 Mary kept all these things 66
51 his mother kept all these things in her heart. 37
4:42 and would have kept him from leaving them; 54
11:28 those who hear the word of God and keep it! 73
18: 3 a widow in that city who kept coming to him •
19:20 your pound, which I kept laid away in a napkin; 46
24:16 their eyes were kept from recognizing him. 55
Joh 2:10 but you have kept the good wine until now. 68
7:19 Yet none of you keeps the law. 64
8:51 if any one keeps my word, he will never see death. 68
52 and you say, 'If any one keeps my word 68
55 I do know him and I keep his word. 68
9:16 for he does not keep the sabbath 68
11:37 Could not he . . have kept this man from dying? 64
12: 7 let her keep it for the day of my burial. 68
25 will keep it for eternal life. 73
47 If any one hears my sayings and does not keep them 73
14:15 If you love me, you will keep my commandments. 68

21 He who has my commandments and keeps them 68
23 If a man loves me, he will keep my word 68
24 He who does not love me does not keep my words 68
15:10 If you keep my commandments 68
10 just as I have kept my Father's commandments 68
20 if they kept my word, they will keep yours also. 68
20 if they kept my word, they will keep yours also. 68
16: 1 to keep you from falling away. 47
17: 6 thou gavest them to me, and they have kept thy word. 68
11 Holy Father, keep them in thy name 68
12 While I was with them, I kept them in thy name 68
15 that thou shouldst keep them from the evil one. 68
Act 7:53 you who received the law . . and did not keep it. 73
10:30 I was keeping the ninth hour of prayer in my house; •
12: 5 So Peter was kept in prison 68
15: 5 to charge them to keep the law of Moses. 68
29 If you keep yourselves from these 37
16:23 charging the jailer to keep them safely. 68
22:20 keeping the garments of those who killed him.' 73
25: 4 Paul was being kept at Caesare'a 68
27:43 centurion . . kept them from carrying out . . purpose 56
Rom 2:26 if a man who is uncircumcised keeps the . . law 73
27 physically uncircumcised but keep the law 67
11: 4 I have kept for myself 7,000 men who have not bowed 52
14:22 The faith . . keep between yourself and God; 46
1Co 7:19 keeping the commandments of God. 69
37 to keep her as his betrothed, he will do well. 68
2Co 2:11 to keep Satan from gaining the advantage over us; 47
4: 4 to keep them from seeing the light of the gospel 41
10:13 keep to the limits God has apportioned us 51
12: 7 to harass me, to keep me from being too elated. 47
7 to harass me, to keep me from being too elated. 47
Gal 5: 3 he is bound to keep the whole law. 64
6:13 do not themselves keep the law 73
Php 4: 7 keep your hearts and your minds in Christ Jesus. 72
1Ti 2:12 she is to keep silent. 40
3: 4 keeping his children submissive 46
5:21 I charge you to keep these rules without favor 73
22 keep yourself pure. 68
6:14 I charge you to keep the commandment unstained 68
2Ti 4: 7 I have finished the race, I have kept the faith. 68
Phm 1:13 I would have been glad to keep him with me 54
Heb 10:39 those who have faith and keep their souls. 63
11:28 By faith he kept the Passover 64
13: 5 Keep your life free from love of money •
Jas 1:27 to keep oneself unstained from the world. 68
2:10 For whoever keeps the whole law 68
1Pe 1: 4 inheritance which is . . kept in heaven for you 68
3:10 let him keep his tongue from evil 61
16 keep your conscience clear 46
2Pe 1: 8 keep you from being ineffective or unfruitful 49
2: 4 into hell . . to be kept until the judgment; 68
9 and to keep the unrighteous under punishment 68
3: 7 kept until the day of judgment and destruction 68
1Jn 2: 3 we know him, if we keep his commandments. 68
5 but whoever keeps his word 68
3:22 we receive . . because we keep his commandments 68
24 All who keep his commandments abide in him 68
5: 3 the love of God, that we keep his commandments. 68
18 but He who was born of God keeps him 68
21 Little children, keep yourselves from idols. 73
Jde 1: 1 To those who are . . and kept for Jesus Christ 68
6 the angels that did not keep their own position 68
6 kept by him in eternal chains in the nether gloom 68
21 keep yourselves in the love of God; 68
24 Now to him who is able to keep you from falling 73
Rev 1: 3 who hear, and who keep what is written therein; 68
2:26 He who conquers and who keeps my works 68
3: 3 what you received . . keep that, and repent. 68
8 you have kept my word and have not denied my name 68
10 you have kept my word of patient endurance 68
10 I will keep you from the hour of trial 68
18 keep the shame of your nakedness from being seen 58
8:12 a third of the day was kept from shining 58
12:17 make war . . on those who keep the commandments 68
14:12 saints, those who keep the commandments of God 68
16:15 keeping his garments that he may not go naked 68
22: 7 Blessed is he who keeps the words of the prophecy 68
9 with those who keep the words of this book. 68
1Es 1: 1 Josiah kept the passover to his Lord 31
6 keep the passover according to the commandment 64
17 the passover was kept 31
19 the people of Israel . . kept the passover 31
20 No passover like it had been kept in Israel 31
21 none of the kings . . had kept such a passover 31
21 such a passover as was kept by Josiah 31
22 this passover was kept. 31
2:23 kept setting up blockades in it from of old 45
5:51 They kept the feast of booths 31
73 they were kept from building for two years 44
7:10 kept the passover on the fourteenth day 31
14 kept the feast of unleavened bread seven days 31
2Es 1:24 that they may keep my statutes. 75
2: 5 because they would not keep my covenant 80
3:35 what nation has kept thy commandments so well? 77
36 individual men who have kept thy commandments 80
4:40 her womb can keep the child within her any longer. 79
6:42 thou didst dry up and keep 74
52 thou hast kept them to be eaten by whom thou wilt 80

7:45 who are alive and keep thy commandments! 77
72 they did not keep them 80
75 we shall be kept in rest until those times come 74
79 and have not kept the way of the Most High 80
88 this is the order of those who have kept the ways 80
89 might keep the law of the Lawgiver perfectly. 75
94 that while they were alive they kept the law 80
8: 9 that which keeps and that which is kept 80
9 that which keeps and that which is kept 80
9 which is kept shall both be kept by thy keeping. 80
9 which is kept shall both be kept by thy keeping. ‡
27 who have kept thy covenants amid afflictions. 75
9:32 did not keep it, and did not observe the statutes; 80
33 they did not keep what had been sown in them. 75
10:15 Now, therefore, keep your sorrow to yourself 79
12:21 four shall be kept for the time 80
21 but two shall be kept until the end. 80
30 whom the Most High has kept for the eagle's end 74
32 whom the Most High has kept until the end of days 78
38 are able to comprehend and keep these secrets. 80
13:26 whom the Most High has been keeping for many ages 74
42 there at least they might keep their statutes 77
42 which they had not kept in their own land. 80
14: 4 Mount Sinai, where I kept him with me many days; 76
30 received the law of life, which they did not keep 75
31 and did not keep the ways 80
34 you shall be kept alive 74
46 but keep the 70 that were written last 74
16:76 You who keep my commandments and precepts 80
Tob 1:11 I kept myself from eating it 66
3: 5 because we did not keep thy commandments 64
15 for whom I should keep myself as wife. 66
4:10 keeps you from entering the darkness; 60
14: 9 keep the law and the commandments 68
Jdt 6:12 all the slingers kept them from coming up 36
7:12 keep all the men in your forces with you 38
11:10 keep it in your mind, for it is true 53
12: 1 where his silver dishes were kept 70
Wis 1:11 keep your tongue from slander 71
6: 4 you did not rule rightly, nor keep the law 73
18 love of her is the keeping of her laws 69
10: 5 kept him strong 73
14:16 Then the ungodly custom . . was kept as a law 73
24 they no longer keep . . their marriages pure 73
17:16 thus was kept shut up in a prison not made of iron; 72
18: 4 those who had kept thy sons imprisoned 73
19: 6 thy children might be kept unharmed. 73
Sir 1:26 If you desire wisdom, keep the commandments 37
2:15 those who love him will keep his ways 66
6:18 until you are old you will keep finding wisdom. •
26 keep her ways with all your might. 66
7:22 if they are profitable to you, keep them. 42
8:17 for he will not be able to keep a secret. 65
9:13 Keep far from a man who has the power to kill 32
11:21 trust in the Lord and keep at your toil 42
13:12 Cruel is he who does not keep words to himself 66
13 Keep words to yourself and be very watchful 66
15:15 If you will, you can keep the commandments 66
17:22 will keep a person's kindness 66
20: 2 will be kept from loss. 56
21:11 Whoever keeps the law controls his thoughts 73
22:27 that it may keep me from falling 58
26:29 A merchant can hardly keep from wrongdoing 43
27:22 no one can keep him from them. 34
29: 1 keeps the commandments. 68
32:23 for this is the keeping of the commandments. 69
35: 1 He who keeps the law makes many offerings 66
3 To keep from wickedness is pleasing to the Lord 34
42: 3 of keeping accounts with a partner •
9 A daughter keeps her father secretly wakeful •
44:20 he kept the law of the Most High 66
LJr 1:35 if one makes a vow to them and does not keep it 33
1Mc 1:58 They kept using violence against Israel •
2:53 Joseph . . kept the commandment 73
4:60 to keep the Gentiles from coming 59
5: 3 because they kept lying in wait for Israel •
53 Judas kept rallying the laggards •
6:18 Now the men in the citadel kept hemming Israel •
7:45 The Jews . . kept sounding the battle call •
8:12 they have kept friendship. 66
26 they shall keep their obligations 73
28 they shall keep these obligations 73
10:20 to take our side and keep friendship with us. 66
26 Since you have kept your agreement with us 66
27 now continue still to keep faith with us 66
11: 8 he kept devising evil designs against Alexander. •
25 lawless men . . kept making complaints against him •
41 they kept fighting against Israel. •
12:27 to keep their arms at hand 39
40 so he kept seeking to seize and kill him •
47 He kept with himself 3,000 men 52
50 and kept marching in close formation •
13:20 Simon . . kept marching along opposite him •
21 the men in the citadel kept sending envoys to Trypho •
15:25 he shut Trypho up and kept him from going out or in. •
2Mc 1: 9 now see that you keep the feast of booths 31
2:12 Likewise Solomon also kept the eight days. 31
16 Will you therefore please keep the days? 31
3:15 keep them safe for those who had deposited them. 38
22 keep what had been entrusted safe and secure 38
4:28 When Sostratus . . kept requesting payment •
5: 6 Jason kept relentlessly slaughtering •
6:11 their piety kept them from defending themselves 46
7:17 Keep on, and see 50
8:17 keeping before their eyes the lawless outrage 57
27 they kept the sabbath 62
10:14 and at every turn kept on warring against the Jews. •
30 they kept him from being wounded 38
12:38 they kept the sabbath there. 35
42 to keep themselves free from sin 66
14: 4 During that day he kept quiet. 46
24 he kept Judas always in his presence 46
36 keep undefiled for ever this house 37
15: 3 who had commanded the keeping of the sabbath day. 31
8 to keep in mind the former times 46
34 he who has kept his own place undefiled. 37
3Mc 3: 4 they kept their separateness with respect to foods. 64
7:15 they kept the day as a joyful festival 31
4Mc 5:29 concerning the keeping of the law 73
6: 7 he kept his reason upright and unswerving. 46
15:10 obeyed her . . in keeping the ordinances. 73

keep *See also* burning, sacrificing, searching, waiting, watching.

keep a genealogical record 1. יחש
1Ch 4:33 and they kept a genealogical record. 1

keep alert 1. ἀγρυπνέω
Eph 6:18 To that end keep alert with all perseverance 1

keep alive 1. חיה 2. חיא (A) 3. διαζάω
Gen 6:19 bring . . into the ark, to keep them alive with you; 1
20 shall come in to you, to keep them alive. 1
7: 3 male and female, to keep their kind alive 1
45: 7 sent me . . to keep alive for you many survivors. 1
50:20 people should be kept alive, as they are today. 1
20 people should be kept alive, as they are today. 1
Num 31:18 all the young girls . . keep alive for yourselves 1
Jos 14:10 And now . . the LORD has kept me alive, as he said 1
Neh 5: 2 let us get grain, that we may eat and keep alive. 1
Job 36: 6 He does not keep the wicked alive 1
Ps 22:29 he who cannot keep himself alive. 1
33:19 soul from death, and keep them alive in famine. 1
41: 2 the LORD protects him and keeps him alive; 1
Isa 7:21 a man will keep alive a young cow and two sheep; 1
Jer 49:11 your fatherless children, I will keep them alive; 1
11 your fatherless children, I will keep them alive; 1
Dan 5:19 he slew, and whom he would he kept alive; 2
2Mc 5:27 and kept himself and his companions alive 3

keep aloof 1. ישב 2. רחק
Job 30:10 They abhor me, they keep aloof from me; 2
Prv 20: 3 It is an honor for a man to keep aloof from strife; 1

keep anger 1. נטר
Ps 103: 9 nor will he keep his anger for ever. 1

keep awake 1. γρηγορέω
1Th 5: 6 let us keep awake and be sober. 1

keep away 1. נזר 2. רְחִיק (A) 3. ἀπέχω 4. ἀφίστημι 5. κωλύω 6. στέλλω
Lev 22: 2 keep away from the holy things of the people 1
Ezr 6: 6 Now therefore, Tat'tenai . . keep away; 2
Act 5:38 keep away from these men and let them alone 4
2Th 3: 6 keep away from any brother who . . 6
1Es 6:27 Darius commanded . . to keep away from the place 3
4Mc 14:17 If they are not able to keep him away 5

keep back 1. חשך 2. מנע 3. ἀφυστερέω 4. νοσφίζω
Gen 39: 9 nor has he kept back anything from me except 1
1Sm 25:39 has kept back his servant from evil; 1
Job 33:18 he keeps back his soul from the Pit 1
Ps 19:13 Keep back thy servant also from presumptuous 1
Jer 42: 4 I will tell you; I will keep nothing back from you. 2
48:10 and cursed is he who keeps back his sword 2
Act 5: 2 he kept back some of the proceeds 4
3 to keep back part of the proceeds of the land? 4
Jas 5: 4 the wages . . which you kept back by fraud, cry out; 3

keep charge 1. שמר
Num 1:53 the Levites shall keep charge of the tabernacle 1

keep clean 1. זכה
Ps 73:13 All in vain have I kept my heart clean 1

keep close 1. דבק
Rut 2: 8 do not go . . but keep close to my maidens. 1
21 You shall keep close by my servants 1
23 she kept close to the maidens of Bo'az 1

keep company 1. רעה
Prv 29: 3 one who keeps company with harlots squanders 1

keep count 1. ספר
Ps 56: 8 Thou hast kept count of my tossings; 1

keep faith 1. אמן 2. πιστόω
Ps 116:10 I kept my faith, even when I said 1
Sir 27:17 Love your friend and keep faith with him 2
29: 3 Confirm your word and keep faith with him 2

keep far 1. רחק 2. διαχωρίζω
Exd 23: 7 Keep far from a false charge, and do not slay 1
Prv 5: 8 Keep your way far from her 1
22: 5 he who guards himself will keep far from them. 1
Sir 6:13 Keep yourself far from your enemies 2

keep festival 1. חגג
Ps 42: 4 of thanksgiving, a multitude keeping festival. 1

keep fresh 1. קור 2. קרר
Jer 6: 7 As a well keeps its water fresh 1
7 she keeps fresh her wickedness; 2

keep guard 1. τήρησις
3Mc 5:44 at the places . . most favorable for keeping guard. 1

keep guard over 1. φυλάσσω
1Es 3: 4 who kept guard over the person of the king 1

keep hidden 1. כסה
Prv 11:13 trustworthy in spirit keeps a thing hidden. 1

keep hold 1. חזק
Prv 4:13 Keep hold of instruction, do not let go; 1

keep holy 1. קדש
Exd 20: 8 Remember the sabbath day, to keep it holy. 1
Deu 5:12 'Observe the sabbath day, to keep it holy 1
2Ch 31:18 for they were faithful in keeping themselves holy. 1
Neh 13:22 guard the gates, to keep the sabbath day holy. 1
Isa 30:29 a song as in the night when a holy feast is kept; 1
Jer 17:22 keep the sabbath day holy, as I commanded 1
24 but keep the sabbath day holy and do no work on it 1
27 do not listen to me, to keep the sabbath day holy 1
Ezk 44:24 they shall keep my sabbaths holy. 1

keep in custody 1. τηρέω
Act 24:23 he should be kept in custody 1
25:21 when Paul had appealed to be kept in custody 1

keep in existence 1. conservo
2Es 6:49 Then thou didst keep in existence 1

keep in mind 1. זכר 2. שמר
Gen 37:11 but his father kept the saying in mind. 2
Ps 78:42 They did not keep in mind his power 1

keep in order 1. ערך
Lev 24: 3 Aaron shall keep it in order from evening 1
4 He shall keep the lamps in order 1

keep in remembrance 1. זכר
2Sm 18:18 I have no son to keep my name in remembrance"; 1

keep in store 1. צפן
Hos 13:12 his sin is kept in store. 1

keep in suspense 1. ψυχὴν αἴρω
Joh 10:24 How long will you keep us in suspense? 1

keep indoors 1. κατάκλειστος
2Mc 3:19 Some of the maidens who were kept indoors 1

keep long 1. ישן
Lev 26:10 you shall eat old store long kept 1

keep occupied 1. ענה
Ecc 5:20 God keeps him occupied with joy in his heart. 1

keep outcast 1. נדח
2Sm 14:14 means not to keep his banished one an outcast. 1

keep pure 1. זכה
Ps 119: 9 How can a young man keep his way pure? 1

keep quiet 1. חרש 2. חשה
Jdg 16: 2 They kept quiet all night, saying, "Let us wait till 1
18:19 Keep quiet, put your hand upon your mouth, and come 1
1Kg 22: 3 Ramoth-gilead belongs to us, and we keep quiet 2

keep ready 1. כון 2. γρηγορέω
Ezk 38: 7 Be ready and keep ready, you and all the hosts 1
Bar 2: 9 And the Lord has kept the calamities ready 2

keep sabbath 1. שבת 2. σαββατίζω
Lev 23:32 evening to evening shall you keep your sabbath 1
25: 2 the land shall keep a sabbath to the LORD 1
2Ch 36:21 All the days that it lay desolate it kept sabbath 1
1Es 1:58 keep sabbath all the time of its desolation 2
2Mc 6: 6 A man could neither keep the sabbath 2

keep safe 1. בטח 2. ἀσφάλεια 3. ἀσφαλίζω 4. συντηρέω

Ps 22: 9 thou didst keep me safe upon my mother's breasts. 1
Mrk 6:20 for Herod feared John . . and kept him safe 4
1Es 8:51 to keep us safe from our adversaries; 2
Wis 4:17 and for what he kept him safe. 3
10:12 and kept him safe from those who lay in wait for him 3

keep sane 1. σωφρονέω
1Pe 4: 7 therefore keep sane and sober for your prayers. 1

keep secret 1. κρύπτω 2. σιγάω 3. abscondo
Rom 16:25 the mystery which was kept secret for long ages 2
2Es 14: 6 and these you shall keep secret.' 3
Sir 8:18 do nothing that is to be kept secret 1

keep separate 1. נזר
Lev 15:31 you shall keep the people of Israel separate 1

keep sheep 1. ποιμαίνω
Lke 17: 7 who has a servant plowing or keeping sheep 1
Jdt 8:26 while he was keeping the sheep of Laban 1

keep silence 1. דֳּמִי 2. דמם 3. הַס 4. חרשׁ 5. חשׁה 6. סכת 7. σιγάω
Deu 27: 9 Keep silence and hear, O Israel 6
Est 4:14 For if you keep silence at such a time as this 4
Job 29:21 waited, and kept silence for my counsel. 2
31:34 so that I kept silence, and did not go out of doors- 2
41:12 I will not keep silence concerning his limbs 4
Ps 50: 3 Our God comes, he does not keep silence 4
83: 1 O God, do not keep silence; do not hold thy peace 1
Ecc 3: 7 a time to keep silence, and a time to speak; 5
Hab 2:20 let all the earth keep silence before him. 3
Lke 9:36 they kept silence and told no one in those days 7
Act 15:12 all the assembly kept silence 7
1Co 14:28 let each of them keep silence in church 7
34 the women should keep silence in the churches. 7

keep silent 1. דמם 2. חרשׁ 3. חשׁה 4. σιγάω 5. σιωπάω
Job 13: 5 Oh that you would keep silent 2
Prv 17:28 Even a fool who keeps silent is considered wise; 2
Isa 62: 1 For Zion's sake I will not keep silent 3
64:12 Wilt thou keep silent, and afflict us sorely? 3
65: 6 it is written before me: "I will not keep silent 3
Jer 4:19 I cannot keep silent; for I hear the sound 2
Ams 5:13 he who is prudent will keep silent in such a time; 1
Sir 20: 1 there is a man who keeps silent but is wise. 5
5 There is one who by keeping silent is found wise 5
6 there is one who keeps silent because he has no answer 5
6 keeps silent because he knows when to speak. 5
1Mc 11: 5 the king kept silent. 4

keep sober 1. νήφω
1Pe 4: 7 therefore keep sane and sober for your prayers. 1

keep sound 1. ὁλόκληρος
1Th 5:23 may your spirit and soul and body be kept sound 1

keep stable 1. στηρίζω
Sir 38:34 they keep stable the fabric of the world 1

keep steady 1. כון 2. תכן
Ps 75: 3 it is I who keep steady its pillars. Selah 2
119:133 Keep steady my steps according to thy promise 1

keep still 1. חרשׁ
Isa 42:14 I have kept still and restrained myself; 1

keep straight 1. ישׁר
Prv 11: 5 righteousness . . keeps his way straight 1

keep strict 1. στερεόω
Sir 26:10 Keep strict watch over a headstrong daughter 1
42:11 Keep strict watch over a headstrong daughter 1

keep the door 1. θυρωρός
Joh 18:17 The maid who kept the door said to Peter 1
keep the door *See also* maid.

keep under guard 1. φυλάσσω
Lke 8:29 he was kept under guard, and bound with chains 1

keep under restraint 1. συγκλείω
Gal 3:23 kept under restraint until faith 1

keep up a war 1. πολεμοτροφέω
2Mc 10:15 and endeavored to keep up the war. 1
14: 6 Those . . are keeping up war and stirring up sedition 1

keep watch 1. נצר 2. צפה 3. שׁמר 4. שׁקד 5. ἀγρυπνέω 6. προσέχω 7. προφυλακή 8. τηρέω 9. φυλάσσω
1Sm 26:15 Why then have you not kept watch over your lord 3
16 you have not kept watch over your lord 3
2Sm 13:34 young man who kept the watch lifted up his eyes 2
Neh 11:19 brethren, who kept watch at the gates, were 172. 3
Job 14:16 thou wouldest not keep watch over my sin; 3
21:32 watch is kept over his tomb. 4
Ps 66: 7 for ever, whose eyes keep watch on the nations- 2
141: 3 O LORD, keep watch over the door of my lips! 1
Prv 15: 3 keeping watch on the evil and the good. 2
22:12 The eyes of the LORD keep watch over knowledge 1
24:12 Does not he who keeps watch over your soul know it 1
Heb 13:17 for they are keeping watch over your souls 5
1Es 4:11 they keep watch around him 8
Jdt 7:13 and camp there to keep watch 7
AEs 12: 1 two eunuchs . . who kept watch in the courtyard 9
Sir 1:29 keep watch over your lips. 6

keep watch over 1. נצר 2. τηρέω
Prv 22:12 The eyes of the LORD keep watch over knowledge 1
24:12 Does not he who keeps watch over your soul know it 1
Mat 27:36 then they sat down and kept watch over him there. 2
54 keeping watch over Jesus, saw the earthquake 2

keep well 1. ἔθω
Sir 37:14 a man's soul sometimes keeps him better informed 1

keep with a position 1. ἀξία
1Mc 10:54 gifts . . in keeping with your position. 1

keeper 1. אִישׁ 2. נטר 3. נצר 4. רעה 5. שַׂר 6. שׁמר 7. ἐπί 8. συντηρέω
Gen 4: 2 Abel was a keeper of sheep, and Cain a tiller 4
9 I do not know; am I my brother's keeper? 6
39:21 favor in the sight of the keeper of the prison. 5
22 the keeper of the prison committed to Joseph's 5
23 the keeper of the prison paid no heed to anything 5
46:32 shepherds, for they have been keepers of cattle; 1
34 Your servants have been keepers of cattle 1
1Sm 17:20 David rose . . and left the sheep with a keeper 6
22 left the . . in charge of the keeper of the baggage 6
2Kg 22: 4 the keepers of the threshold have collected 6
14 of Tikvah, son of Harhas, keeper of the wardrobe 6
23: 4 the priests . . and the keepers of the threshold 6
25:18 took . . and the three keepers of the threshold; 6
1Ch 9:19 keepers of the thresholds of the tent 6
19 keepers of the entrance. 6
2Ch 34: 9 money . . the Levites, the keepers of the threshold 6
22 Tokhath, son of Hasrah, keeper of the wardrobe 6
Neh 2: 8 letter to Asaph, the keeper of the king's forest 6
3:29 Shemai'ah . . the keeper of the East Gate 6
Ps 121: 5 The LORD is your keeper; the LORD is your shade 6
Ecc 12: 3 the day when the keepers of the house tremble 6
Sng 1: 6 they made me keeper of the vineyards; 2
8:11 he let out the vineyard to keepers; 2
12 and the keepers of the fruit 200. 2
Isa 27: 3 I, the LORD, am its keeper; every moment I water it 3
Jer 4:17 Like keepers of a field are they against her 6
35: 4 the son of Shallum, keeper of the threshold. 6
52:24 priest, and the three keepers of the threshold; 6
Tob 1:22 Now Ahikar was cupbearer, keeper of the signet 7
Sir 37:12 whom you know to be a keeper of the commandments 8

elephant keeper 1. ἐλεφαντάρχης
3Mc 5:45 the elephant keeper 1

keeper of elephants 1. ἐλεφαντάρχης
3Mc 5: 4 Hermon, keeper of the elephants 1

keeper of the gate 1. שַׁעַר
2Ch 31:14 Ko're . . keeper of the east gate 1

temple keeper 1. νεωκόρος
Act 19:35 the city . . is temple keeper of the great Ar'temis 1

kernel 1. κόκκος
1Co 15:37 a bare kernel 1

kettle 1. דוּד 2. סִיר
1Sm 2:14 thrust it into the pan, or kettle, or caldron, or pot; 1
Mic 3: 3 and chop them up like meat in a kettle 2

iron kettle 1. λεβής
Sir 13: 2 can the clay pot associate with the iron kettle? 1

key 1. מַפְתֵּחַ 2. ἐπίκαιρος 3. κλείς
Jdg 3:25 roof chamber, they took the key and opened them; 1
Isa 22:22 on his shoulder the key of the house of David; 1
Mat 16:19 I will give you the keys of the kingdom of heaven 3
Lke 11:52 you have taken away the key of knowledge 3
Rev 1:18 and I have the keys of Death and Hades. 3
3: 7 the holy one, the true one, who has the key of David 3
9: 1 given the key of the shaft of the bottomless pit; 3
20: 1 holding in his hand the key of the bottomless pit 3
2Mc 14:22 armed men in readiness at key places 2

kick 1. בעט 2. λακτίζω 3. λάξ τύπτω
Deu 32:15 Jesh'urun waxed fat, and kicked; 1
Act 26:14 It hurts you to kick against the goads.' 2
4Mc 6: 8 rushed at him and began to kick him in the side 3

kid 1. בֵּן עֵז 2. גְּדִי 3. גְּדִיָּה 4. גְּדִי עִזִּים 5. עֵז 6. ἐρίφιον 7. ἔριφος
Gen 27: 9 Go to the flock, and fetch me two good kids 4
16 the skins of the kids she put upon his hands 4
38:17 He answered, "I will send you a kid from the flock. 2
20 Judah sent the kid by his friend the Adullamite 4
23 you see, I sent this kid, and you could not find her 2
Exd 23:19 You shall not boil a kid in its mother's milk. 2
34:26 You shall not boil a kid in its mother's milk. 2
Num 15:11 be done . . for each of the male lambs or the kids. 5
Deu 14:21 You shall not boil a kid in its mother's milk. 2
Jdg 6:19 Gideon . . prepared a kid, and unleavened cakes 4
13:15 Pray, let us detain you, and prepare a kid for you. 4
19 So Mano'ah took the kid with the cereal offering 4
14: 6 him, and he tore the lion asunder as one tears a kid; 2
15: 1 harvest, Samson went to visit his wife with a kid; 4
1Sm 10: 3 three men . . one carrying three kids, another 2
16:20 Jesse took an ass . . and a skin of wine and a kid 4
2Ch 35: 7 contributed . . lambs and kids from the flock 1
8 for the passover offerings 2,600 lambs and kids •
9 for the passover offerings 5,000 lambs and kids •
Sng 1: 8 pasture your kids beside the shepherd's tents. 3
Isa 5:17 fatlings and kids shall feed among the ruins. •
11: 6 and the leopard shall lie down with the kid 2
Lke 15:29 yet you never gave me a kid, that I might make merry 6
1Es 1: 7 gave to the people . . 30,000 lambs and kids 7
Tob 2:12 they also gave her a kid; 7
13 So I said to her, "Where did you get the kid? 6

kidnaper 1. ἀνδραποδιστής
1Ti 1:10 immoral persons, sodomites, kidnapers, liars 1

kidney 1. כִּלְיָה
Exd 29:13 take . . the two kidneys with the fat 1
22 the two kidneys with the fat that is on them 1
Lev 3: 4 the two kidneys with the fat that is on them 1
4 which he shall take away with the kidneys 1
10 the two kidneys with the fat that is on them 1
10 which he shall take away with the kidneys 1
15 the two kidneys with the fat that is on them 1
15 which he shall take away with the kidneys 1
4: 9 the two kidneys with the fat that is on them 1
9 which he shall take away with the kidneys •
7: 4 the two kidneys with the fat that is on them 1
4 which he shall take away with the kidneys 1
8:16 he took . . the two kidneys with their fat 1
25 he took . . the two kidneys with their fat 1
9:10 the fat and the kidneys and the appendage 1
19 the kidneys, and the appendage of the liver 1
Job 16:13 He slashes open my kidneys, and does not spare 1
Isa 34: 6 with the fat of the kidneys of rams. 1

kill 1. הרג 2. זבח 3. חָלָל 4. טבח 5. מות 6. נכה 7. קטל 8. רצח 9. שׁחט 10. שְׁחִיטָה 11. ἀναίρεσις 12. ἀναιρέω 13. ἀποκτείνω 14. ἀπόλλυμι 15. διαχειρίζω 16. διόλλυμι 17. ἐπαναιρέω 18. ἐπιβάλλω 19. θανατόω 20. θύω 21. καταβάλλω 22. κατακόπτω 23. καταστρώννυμι 24. κατασφάζω 25. κτείνω 26. σφάζω 27. φθορά 28. φονεύω 29. χειρόω 30. consumo 31. interficio 32. occido
Gen 4: 8 rose up against his brother Abel, and killed him. 1
15 lest any who came upon him should kill him. 6
12:12 will say, 'This is his wife'; then they will kill me 1
20:11 and they will kill me because of my wife. 1
26: 7 lest the men of the place should kill me 1
27:41 then I will kill my brother Jacob. 1
42 Esau comforts himself by planning to kill you. 1
34:25 the city unawares, and killed all the males. 1
37:18 they conspired against him to kill him. 5
20 let us kill him and throw him into one of the pits; 1
31 they . . killed a goat, and dipped the robe 9
Exd 1:16 if it is a son, you shall kill him; 5
2:12 seeing no one he killed the Egyptian and hid him 6
14 Do you mean to kill me as you killed the Egyptian? 1
14 Do you mean to kill me as you killed the Egyptian? 1
15 When Pharaoh heard of it, he sought to kill Moses. 1
4:24 on the way the LORD met him and sought to kill him. 5
5:21 you . . put a sword in their hand to kill us. 1
12: 6 congregation of Israel shall kill their lambs 9
21 Select lambs . . kill the passover lamb. 9
16: 3 brought us out . . to kill this whole assembly 5
17: 3 up out of Egypt, to kill us and our children 5
20:13 You shall not kill. 8
21:14 if a man willfully attacks another to kill him 1
29 if . . it kills a man or a woman 5
22: 1 ox or a sheep, and kills it or sells it 4
24 my wrath will burn, and I will kill you 1
29:11 you shall kill the bull before the LORD 9
20 you shall kill the ram, and take part of its blood 9
Lev 1: 5 Then he shall kill the bull before the LORD 9
11 he shall kill it on the north side of the altar 9
3: 2 his offering and kill it at the door of the tent 9
8 upon the head of his offering and killing it 9
13 and kill it before the tent of meeting 9
4: 4 he shall . . kill the bull before the LORD 9
15 the bull shall be killed before the LORD 9
24 kill it in the place where they kill the burnt 9
24 in the place where they kill the burnt offering 9
29 and kill the sin offering in the place 9
33 kill it for a sin offering in the place 9
33 the place where they kill the burnt offering 9
6:25 In the place where the burnt offering is killed 9

25 shall the sin offering be killed before the LORD 9
7: 2 in the place where they kill the burnt offering 9
2 they shall kill the guilt offering 9
8:15 Moses killed it, and took the blood 9
19 Moses killed it, and threw the blood 9
23 Moses killed it, and took some of its blood 9
9: 8 Aaron . . killed the calf of the sin offering 9
12 he killed the burnt offering 9
15 the goat . . and killed it, and offered it for sin 9
18 He killed the ox also and the ram 9
14: 5 the priest shall command them to kill one 9
6 the bird that was killed over the running water 9
13 he shall kill the lamb in the place where 9
13 in the place where they kill the sin offering 9
19 And afterward he shall kill the burnt offering 9
25 he shall kill the lamb of the guilt offering 9
50 shall kill one of the birds in an earthen vessel 9
51 dip them in the blood of the bird that was killed 9
16:11 he shall kill the bull as a sin offering 9
15 Then he shall kill the goat of the sin offering 9
17: 3 If any man . . kills an ox or a lamb or a goat 9
3 If any man . . kills it outside the camp 9
20:15 and you shall kill the beast 1
16 you shall kill the woman and the beast 1
22:28 you shall not kill both her and her young 9
24:17 He who kills a man shall be put to death 6
18 He who kills a beast shall make it good 6
21 He who kills a beast shall make it good 6
21 he who kills a man shall be put to death 6
Num 11:15 If thou wilt deal thus with me, kill me at once 1
14:15 Now if thou dost kill this people as one man 5
16:13 brought us up . . to kill us in the wilderness 5
41 You have killed the people of the LORD. 5
22:29 sword in my hand, for then I would kill you. 1
31:17 therefore, kill every male among the little ones 1
17 kill every woman who has known man by lying 1
19 whoever of you has killed any person 1
35:11 manslayer who kills any person without intent 6
15 that any one who kills any person without intent 6
30 If any one kills a person, the murderer shall 6
Deu 4:42 who kills his neighbor unintentionally 8
5:17 You shall not kill. 8
12:21 then you may kill any of your herd or your flock 2
13: 9 you shall kill him; your hand shall be first 1
19: 4 If any one kills his neighbor unintentionally 6
21: 1 is found . . and it is not known who killed him 6
32:39 I kill and I make alive; I wound and I heal; 5
Jos 7: 5 the men of Ai killed about 36 men of them 6
9:18 But the people of Israel did not kill them 6
26 and delivered them . . and they did not kill them. 1
10:11 the men of Israel killed with the sword. 1
13:22 Balaam also . . Israel killed with the sword 1
20: 3 manslayer who kills any person without intent 6
5 he killed his neighbor unwittingly 6
9 who killed a person without intent could flee 6
Jdg 3:29 they killed at that time about 10,000 6
31 Shamgar . . who killed 600 of the Philistines 6
7:25 they killed Oreb at the rock of Oreb, and Zeeb they 1
25 and Zeeb they killed at the wine press of Zeeb 1
9:45 he took the city, and killed the people . . in it; 1
54 Draw your sword and kill me, lest men say of me 5
54 kill me, lest men say of me, 'A woman killed him.' 1
56 against his father in killing his 70 brothers; 1
13:23 If the LORD had meant to kill us, he would not have 5
14:19 to Ash'kelon and killed 30 men of the town 6
15:13 give you into their hands; we will not kill you. 5
16: 2 wait till . . morning; then we will kill him. 1
20: 5 they meant to kill me, and they ravished my 1
31 they began to smite and kill some of the people 3
39 Benjamin had begun to smite and kill about 3
1Sm 2: 6 The LORD kills and brings to life; 5
14:13 and his armor-bearer killed them after him; 5
15: 3 do not spare them, but kill both man and woman 5
16: 2 How can I go? If Saul hears it, he will kill me. 1
17: 9 If he is able to fight with me and kill me 6
9 but if I prevail against him and kill him 6
25 the man who kills him, the king will enrich 6
26 What . . for the man who kills this Philistine 6
27 So shall it be done to the man who kills him. 6
35 I caught him . . and smote him and killed him. 5
36 Your servant has killed both lions and bears; 6
50 David . . struck the Philistine, and killed him; 5
51 took his sword . . and killed him, and cut off his 5
18:27 David . . killed 200 of the Philistines; 6
19: 1 Saul spoke to . . that they should kill David. 5
2 Saul my father seeks to kill you; 5
5 sin against innocent blood by killing David 5
11 watch him, that he might kill him in the morning. 5
11 If you do not . . tomorrow you will be killed. 5
15 Bring him up to me in the bed, that I may kill him. 5
17 He said to me, 'Let me go; why should I kill you?' 5
21: 9 Goliath . . whom you killed in the valley of Elah 6
22:17 king said . . "Turn and kill the priests of the LORD; 5
18 Do'eg . . killed on that day 85 persons 5
21 that Saul had killed the priests of the LORD. 1
24:10 and some bade me kill you, but I spared you. 1
11 I cut off the skirt of your robe, and did not kill 1
18 you did not kill me when the LORD put me 1
25:11 my meat that I have killed for my shearers 4
28:24 had a fatted calf . . and she quickly killed it 2
30: 2 they killed no one, but carried them off 5
15 Swear . . that you will not kill me, or deliver me 5
2Sm 3:30 he had killed their brother As'ahel in the battle 5
4:12 they killed them, and cut off their hands and feet 1
11:21 Who killed Abim'elech the son of Jerub'besheth? 6
13:28 and when I say to you, 'Strike Amnon,' then kill him. 5
32 have killed all the young men the king's sons 5
14: 6 and one struck the other and killed him. 5
7 that we may kill him for the life of his brother 5
32 if there is guilt in me, let him kill me.' 5
18:15 surrounded . . and struck him, and killed him. 5
21:12 on the day the Philistines killed Saul on Gilbo'a; 6
16 And Ish'bi-be'nob . . thought to kill David. 6
17 and attacked the Philistine and killed him. 5
1Kg 2:34 Benai'ah . . struck him down and killed him; 5
11:40 Solomon sought therefore to kill Jerobo'am; 5
12:27 they will kill me and return to Rehobo'am 1
13:24 a lion met him on the road and killed him. 5
15:28 Ba'asha killed him in the third year of Asa 5
29 he killed all the house of Jerobo'am; 6
16:10 Zimri came in and struck him down and killed him 5
11 he killed all the house of Ba'asha; 6
16 Zimri has conspired, and he has killed the king"; 6
18: 9 give your servant into the hand of Ahab, to kill me? 5
12 when I come and tell Ahab . . he will kill me 1
13 when Jez'ebel killed the prophets of the LORD 1
14 'Go, tell your lord . . '; and he will kill me. 1
40 Eli'jah brought them . . and killed them there. 9
20:20 each killed his man; the Syrians fled 6
21 and killed the Syrians with a great slaughter. 6
36 as soon as you have gone . . a lion shall kill you. 6
36 as soon as he . . a lion met him and killed him. 6
21:19 Have you killed, and also taken possession?"' 8
2Kg 5: 7 Am I God, to kill and to make alive 5
7: 4 and if they kill us we shall but die. 5
14: 5 he killed his servants who had slain the king 6
7 He killed 10,000 E'domites in the Valley of Salt 6
15:10 and struck him down at Ibleam, and killed him 5
16: 9 king of Assyria marched . . and he killed Rezin. 5
17:25 the LORD sent lions . . which killed some of them. 1
26 they are killing them, because they do not know 5
21:23 the servants . . and killed the king in his house. 5
25:25 came . . and attacked and killed Gedali'ah 5
1Ch 19:18 and killed also Shophach the commander 5
2Ch 18: 2 Ahab killed an abundance of sheep and oxen 2
21:13 killed your brothers, of your father's house 1
22: 8 he killed them. 1
24:22 but killed his son 1
25: 3 he killed his servants who had slain the king 1
13 killed 3,000 people in them, and took much spoil. 6
29:22 they killed the bulls, and the priests received 9
22 killed the rams and their blood was thrown 9
22 killed the lambs and their blood was thrown 9
24 the priests killed them and made a sin offering 9
30:15 killed the passover lamb on the fourteenth day 9
17 Levites had to kill the passover lamb 10
33:24 servants conspired . . killed him in his house. 5
35: 1 killed the passover lamb on the fourteenth day 9
6 kill the passover lamb, and sanctify yourselves 9
11 killed the passover lamb 9
Ezr 6:20 killed the passover lamb for all the returned 9
Neh 4:11 till we come . . and kill them and stop the work. 1
6:10 for they are coming to kill you, at night 1
10 at night they are coming to kill you. 1
9:26 law behind their back and killed thy prophets 1
Job 5: 2 Surely vexation kills the fool 1
20:16 the tongue of a viper will kill him. 1
24:14 that he may kill the poor and needy; 7
Ps 59: 0 sent men to watch his house in order to kill him. 5
60: 0 when Joab on his return killed 12,000 6
Prv 1:32 For the simple are killed by their turning away 1
21:25 The desire of the sluggard kills him 5
Ecc 3: 3 a time to kill, and a time to heal; 1
Isa 14:30 but I will kill your root with famine 5
22:13 behold . . slaying oxen and killing sheep 9
66: 3 He who slaughters an ox is like him who kills a man; 6
Jer 20:17 because he did not kill me in the womb; 5
41: 2 and struck down . . with the sword, and killed him 5
8 Do not kill us, for we have stores of wheat, 5
8 he refrained and did not kill them 5
43: 3 that they may kill us or take us into exile 5
Hos 4: 2 there is swearing, lying, killing, stealing 8
Mat 2:16 he sent and killed all the male children 12
5:21 men of old, 'You shall not kill; and whoever kills 28
21 shall not kill; and whoever kills shall be liable 28
10:28 do not fear those who kill the body 13
28 kill the body but cannot kill the soul 13
16:21 and be killed, and on the third day be raised. 13
17:23 they will kill him, and he will be raised 13
19:18 And Jesus said, "You shall not kill 28
21:35 beat one, killed another, and stoned another. 13
38 let us kill him and have his inheritance.' 13
39 and killed him. 13
22: 4 my oxen and my fat calves are killed 20
6 treated them shamefully, and killed them. 13
23:34 some of whom you will kill and crucify 13
37 O Jerusalem, Jerusalem, killing the prophets 13
26: 4 in order to arrest Jesus by stealth and kill him. 13
Mrk 3: 4 to save life or to kill 13
6:19 wanted to kill him. But she could not 13
8:31 be killed, and after three days rise again. 13
9:31 they will kill him 13
31 when he is killed, after three days he will rise. 13
10:19 Do not kill, Do not commit adultery 28
34 scourge him, and kill him 13
12: 5 he sent another, and him they killed 13
5 some they beat and some they killed. 13
7 'This is the heir; come, let us kill him 13
8 they took him and killed him 13
14: 1 how to arrest him by stealth, and kill him; 13
Lke 9:22 be killed, and on the third day be raised. 13
11:47 tombs of the prophets whom your fathers killed. 13
48 they killed them, and you build their tombs. 13
49 some of whom they will kill and persecute,' 13
12: 4 my friends, do not fear those who kill the body 13
5 fear him who, after he has killed, has power to cast 13
13: 4 the tower in Silo'am fell and killed them 13
31 Get away from here, for Herod wants to kill you. 13
34 O Jerusalem, Jerusalem, killing the prophets 13
15:23 bring the fatted calf and kill it 20
27 your father has killed the fatted calf 20
30 you killed for him the fatted calf!' 20
18:20 Do not commit adultery, Do not kill, Do not steal 28
33 they will scourge him and kill him 13
20:14 This is the heir; let us kill him 13
15 they cast him out of the vineyard and killed him. 13
Joh 5:18 why the Jews sought all the more to kill him 13
7: 1 because the Jews sought to kill him. 13
19 Why do you seek to kill me? 13
20 Who is seeking to kill you? 13
25 Is not this the man whom they seek to kill? 13
8:22 Then said the Jews, "Will he kill himself 13
37 yet you seek to kill me 13
40 now you seek to kill me 13
10:10 thief comes only to steal and kill and destroy 20
16: 2 when whoever kills you will think . . 13
Act 2:23 this Jesus . . you crucified and killed 12
3:15 killed the Author of life 13
5:30 whom you killed by hanging him on a tree. 15
33 they were enraged and wanted to kill them. 12
7:28 Do you want to kill me as you killed the Egyptian 12
28 kill me as you killed the Egyptian yesterday?' 12
52 they killed those who announced beforehand 13
9:23 the Jews plotted to kill him 12
24 were watching the gates day and night, to kill him; 12
29 they were seeking to kill him. 12
10:13 there came a voice to him, "Rise, Peter; kill and eat. 20
11: 7 'Rise, Peter; kill and eat.' 20
12: 2 He killed James the brother of John 12
13:28 yet they asked Pilate to have him killed. 12
16:27 he drew his sword and was about to kill himself 12
21:31 as they were trying to kill him 13
22:20 keeping the garments of those who killed him.' 12
23:12 till they had killed Paul. 13
14 an oath to taste no food till we have killed Paul. 13
15 we are ready to kill him before he comes near. 12
21 till they have killed him 12
27 and was about to be killed by them 12
25: 3 planning an ambush to kill him on the way. 12
26:21 Jews seized me in the temple and tried to kill me. 15
27:42 The soldiers' plan was to kill the prisoners 13
Rom 7:11 sin . . deceived me and by it killed me. 13
8:36 For thy sake we are being killed all the day 19
11: 3 Lord, they have killed thy prophets 13
13: 9 You shall not kill, You shall not steal 28
2Co 3: 6 the written code kills, but the Spirit gives life. 13
6: 9 as punished, and yet not killed; 19
1Th 2:15 who killed both the Lord Jesus and the prophets 13
Jas 2:11 he . . said also, "Do not kill. 28
11 If you do not commit adultery but do kill 28
4: 2 You desire and do not have; so you kill. 28
5: 6 you have killed the righteous man; 28
2Pe 2:12 creatures . . born to be caught and killed 27
Rev 2:13 An'tipas . . who was killed among you 13
6: 8 power . . to kill with sword and with famine 13
11 who were to be killed as they themselves had been. 13
9: 5 allowed to torture . . but not to kill them 13
15 angels . . ready . . to kill a third of mankind. 13
18 By . . three plagues a third of mankind was killed 13
20 rest of mankind, who were not killed by . . plagues 13
11: 5 thus he is doomed to be killed. 13
7 make war upon them and conquer them and kill them 13
13 7,000 people were killed in the earthquake 13
1Es 1: 1 he killed the passover lamb 20
6 kill the passover lamb 20
4: 5 They kill and are killed 28
5 They kill and are killed 28
7 If he tells them to kill, they kill 13
7 If he tells them to kill, they kill 13
2Es 1:18 led us into this wilderness to kill us? 31
15:53 If you had not always killed my chosen people 32
16:34 Their bridegrooms shall be killed in war 30
Tob 1:21 before two of Sennacherib's sons killed him 13
7: 8 they killed a ram from the flock 20
Jdt 1:12 he would kill them by the sword 12
2:25 and killed every one who resisted him 22
11:12 they have planned to kill their cattle 18

16: 5 and kill my young men with the sword 12
Wis 11:19 the mere sight of them could kill by fright. 16
14:24 they either treacherously kill one another 12
16: 9 were killed by the bites of locusts and flies 13
14 A man in his wickedness kills another 13
18: 5 had resolved to kill the babes of thy holy ones 13
Sir 9:13 Keep far from a man who has the power to kill 28
34:20 Like one who kills a son before his father's eyes 20
47: 4 In his youth did he not kill a giant 13
Bel 1:29 or else we will kill you and your household. 13
1Mc 2: 9 Her babes have been killed in her streets 13
24 he ran and killed him upon the altar. 26
25 At the same time he killed the king's officer 13
37 you are killing us unjustly. 14
3:11 he defeated and killed him 13
5: 2 they began to kill and destroy among the people. 19
13 all our brethren . . have been killed 19
28 killed every male by the edge of the sword 13
35 he killed every male in it 13
6:45 he killed men right and left 19
46 stabbed it from beneath, and killed it 12
7: 4 So the army killed them 13
16 he seized 60 of them and killed them in one day 13
19 killed them and threw them into a great pit. 20
9: 2 they took it and killed many people. 14
32 he tried to kill him. 13
40 and began killing them 13
61 seized . . and killed them. 13
69 he killed many of them 13
11:10 he has tried to kill me. 13
18 killed by the inhabitants of the strongholds. 14
45 they wanted to kill the king. 12
47 they killed . . as many as 100,000 men. 13
12:40 so he kept seeking to seize and kill him 14
48 they killed with the sword. 13
13:23 When he approached Baskama, he killed Jonathan 13
31 he killed him 13
15:40 take the people captive and kill them. 28
16:16 they killed him and his two sons 13
21 he has sent men to kill you also. 13
22 he seized the men . . and killed them 13
2Mc 4:34 Therefore Menelaus . . urged him to kill Onias. 29
42 they wounded many of them, and killed some 21
42 the temple robber himself they killed 29
5:13 Then there was killing of young and old 11
26 and killed great numbers of people. 23
8:30 they killed more than 20,000 of them 12
32 They killed the commander of Timothy's forces 12
10:17 killing no fewer than 20,000. 12
37 They killed Timothy, who was hidden in a cistern 24
12:28 killed as many as 25,000 of those who were within 23
14:13 with orders to kill Judas and scatter his men 17
3Mc 1: 2 intending single-handed to kill him 25
4Mc 5: 3 were to be broken on the wheel and killed. 12
13:14 Let us not fear him who thinks he is killing us 13
18:19 'I kill and I make alive 13

kill a child 1. *τεκνοφόνος*
Wis 14:23 they kill children in their initiations 1

kiln 1. כִּבְשָׁן 2. *κάμινος*
Exd 9: 8 Take handfuls of ashes from the kiln 1
10 So they took ashes from the kiln, and stood before 1
19:18 the smoke of it went up like the smoke of a kiln 1
Sir 27: 5 The kiln tests the potter's vessels 2

kin 1. שְׁאֵר 2. *συγγενής*
Lev 21: 2 his nearest of kin, his mother, his father, his son 1
2Sm 19:42 Because the king is near of kin to us. •
Mrk 6: 4 among his own kin, and in his own house. 2
Jdt 16:24 all those who were next of kin to her husband •

kin *See also* near, next, part.

near kin 1. גאל 2. שְׁאֵר
Lev 20:19 for that is to make naked one's near kin 2
Rut 2:20 The man is a relative . . one of our nearest kin. 1

kind 1. אִישׁ 2. זֶרַע 3. מִין 4. מִשְׁפָּחָה 5. מִשְׁפָּט 6. תַּבְנִית 7. זַן (A) 8. כֹּל (A) 9. *ἄλλος μέν* 10. *γένος* 11. *εἶδος* 12. *ἰδέα* 13. *οἷος* 14. *ὅμοιος* 15. *οὗτος* 16. *ποικιλία* 17. *ποῖος* 18. *τίς* 19. *τοιοῦτος* 20. *τρόπος* 21. *φύσις*
Gen 1:11 each according to its kind, upon the earth 3
12 yielding seed according to their own kinds 3
12 their seed, each according to its kind 3
21 creature . . according to their kinds 3
21 every winged bird according to its kind 3
24 living creatures according to their kinds 3
24 beasts of the earth according to their kinds 3
25 beasts of the earth according to their kinds 3
25 the cattle according to their kinds 3
25 creeps upon the ground according to its kind 3
6:20 Of the birds according to their kinds 3
20 and of the animals according to their kinds 3
20 every creeping thing . . according to its kind 3
7: 3 male and female, to keep their kind alive 2
14 they and every beast according to its kind 3
14 all the cattle according to their kinds 3
14 that creeps on the earth according to its kind 3
14 and every bird according to its kind, 3
Exd 22: 9 for any kind of lost thing, of which one says •
Lev 11:14 the kite, the falcon according to its kind 3
15 every raven according to its kind 3
16 the sea gull, the hawk according to its kind 3
19 the stork, the heron according to its kind 3
22 you may eat: the locust according to its kind 3
22 may eat . . the bald locust according to its kind 3
22 may eat . . the cricket according to its kind 3
22 may eat . . the grasshopper according to its kind 3
29 the mouse, the great lizard according to its kind 3
19:23 When you . . plant all kinds of trees for food •
Deu 14:13 buzzard, the kite, after their kinds; 3
14 every raven after its kind; 3
15 ostrich . . the hawk, after their kinds; 3
18 stork, the heron, after their kinds; 3
17: 8 between one kind of homicide and another •
8 between . . one kind of legal right and another •
8 between . . one kind of assault and another •
25:13 not . . two kinds of weights, a large and a small. •
14 not . . two kinds of measures, a large and a small. •
27:21 'Cursed be he who lies with any kind of beast.' •
1Kg 9:13 Therefore he said, "What kind of cities are these •
2Kg 1: 7 What kind of man was he who came to meet you 5
8: 9 took a present . . all kinds of goods of Damascus •
1Ch 22:15 and all kinds of craftsmen without number •
28:21 willing man who has skill for any kind of service; •
2Ch 34:13 all who did work in every kind of service; †
Neh 13:15 also wine, grapes, figs, and all kinds of burdens •
16 brought in fish and all kinds of wares and sold •
20 merchants and sellers of all kinds of wares •
Est 1: 7 in golden goblets, goblets of different kinds •
Ecc 2: 5 and planted in them all kinds of fruit trees. •
Jer 15: 3 will appoint over them four kinds of destroyers 4
Ezk 8:10 round about, were all kinds of creeping things 6
27:12 because of your great wealth of every kind; •
18 goods, because of your great wealth of every kind; •
22 for your wares the best of all kinds of spices •
39:20 men and all kinds of warriors,' says the Lord GOD. 1
44:30 the first of all the first fruits of all kinds, •
30 offering of all kinds from all your offerings •
47:10 its fish will be of very many kinds 3
12 there will grow all kinds of trees for food. •
Dan 3: 5 hear the sound of . . every kind of music 7
7 heard the sound of . . every kind of music 7
10 hears the sound of . . every kind of music 7
15 hear the sound of . . every kind of music 7
6:23 no kind of hurt was found upon him 8
Hag 2:12 or pottage, or wine, or oil, or any kind of food •
Mat 5:11 and persecute you and utter all kinds of evil •
13:47 and gathered fish of every kind; 10
Mrk 9:29 This kind cannot be driven out by anything 10
Act 10:12 In it were all kinds of animals and reptiles •
Rom 7: 8 sin . . wrought in me all kinds of covetousness. •
1Co 5: 1 of a kind that is not found even among pagans 19
7: 7 one of one kind and one of another. 15
12:10 to another various kinds of tongues 10
28 speakers in various kinds of tongues. 10
15:35 With what kind of body do they come? 17
38 to each kind of seed its own body. •
39 there is one kind for men, another for animals 9
Eph 4:19 greedy to practice every kind of uncleanness. •
1Th 1: 5 You know what kind of men we proved to be •
Jas 1:18 we should be a kind of first fruits 18
3: 7 For every kind of beast and bird, of reptile 21
Rev 18:12 all kinds of scented wood, all articles of ivory •
22: 2 the tree of life with its twelve kinds of fruit •
Wis 19:11 Afterward they saw also a new kind of birds 10
21 the crystalline, easily melted kind of heavenly food. 10
Sir 16:30 with all kinds of living beings •
25: 2 My soul hates three kinds of men 11
27: 9 Birds flock with their kind 14
36:19 As the palate tastes the kinds of game •
41:16 it is good to retain every kind of shame •
43:25 all kinds of living things 16
50: 9 adorned with all kinds of precious stones; •
3Mc 7: 7 every charge of whatever kind. 20
16 praise and all kinds of melodious songs. †
4Mc 1:14 how many kinds of emotions there are 12
18 Now the kinds of wisdom are rational judgment 12
3: 2 No one of us can eradicate that kind of desire 13
9:29 How sweet is any kind of death 20

kind (2) 1. חנן 2. חֶסֶד 3. חָסִיד 4. טוֹב 5. *ἀγαθός* 6. *ἥμερος* 7. *καλῶς ποιέω* 8. *φιλάνθρωπος* 9. *χρηστεύομαι* 10. *χρηστός*
2Ch 10: 7 If you will be kind to this people and please them 4
Ps 145:17 LORD is just . . and kind in all his doings. 3
Prv 11:17 A man who is kind benefits himself 2
14:21 but happy is he who is kind to the poor. 1
31 but he who is kind to the needy honors him. 1
19:17 He who is kind to the poor lends to the LORD 1
28: 8 gathers it for him who is kind to the poor. 1
Lke 6:35 he is kind to the ungrateful and the selfish. 10
1Co 13: 4 Love is patient and kind 9
Eph 4:32 be kind to one another, tenderhearted 10
Php 4:14 Yet it was kind of you to share my trouble. 7
Tit 2: 5 to be sensible, chaste, domestic, kind 5
1Pe 2:18 be submissive . . not only to the kind and gentle 5
Wis 12:19 the righteous man must be kind 8
15: 1 thou, our God, art kind and true 10
1Mc 6:11 I was kind and beloved in my power.' 10
2Mc 1:24 who alone art King and art kind 10
12:30 kind treatment of them in times of misfortune 6

kind *See* all, any, different, every, treatment, two, various.

kind enough 1. *καλῶς ποιέω*
Act 10:33 you have been kind enough to come 1

kindle 1. בער 2. דלק 3. חרה 4. חרר 5. יצת 6. יקד 7. להט 8. קדח 9. שלק 10. שרף 11. *ἀνακαίω* 12. *ἀνάπτω* 13. *ἅπτω* 14. *ἐκκαίω* 15. *ἐξάπτω* 16. *καίω* 17. *περιάπτω* 18. *πυρόω* 19. incendo
Gen 30: 2 Jacob's anger was kindled against Rachel 3
39:19 his master heard . . his anger was kindled. 3
Exd 4:14 the anger of the LORD was kindled against Moses 3
22: 6 he that kindled the fire shall make full 1
35: 3 you shall kindle no fire in all your habitations 1
Lev 10: 6 bewail the burning which the LORD has kindled 10
Num11: 1 when the LORD heard it, his anger was kindled 3
33 anger of the LORD was kindled against the people 3
12: 9 anger of the LORD was kindled against them 3
22:22 God's anger was kindled because he went; 3
27 Balaam's anger was kindled, and he struck the ass 3
24:10 Balak's anger was kindled against Balaam 3
25: 3 anger of the LORD was kindled against Israel; 3
32:10 LORD'S anger was kindled on that day, and he swore 3
13 the LORD'S anger was kindled against Israel 3
Deu 6:15 anger of the LORD your God be kindled against you 3
7: 4 anger of the LORD would be kindled against you 3
11:17 anger of the LORD be kindled against you 3
29:27 anger of the LORD was kindled against this land 3
31:17 my anger will be kindled against them in that day 3
32:22 For a fire is kindled by my anger, and it burns 8
Jos 23:16 the anger of the LORD will be kindled against you 3
Jdg 2:14 the anger of the LORD was kindled against Israel 3
20 the anger of the LORD was kindled against Israel; 3
3: 8 the anger of the LORD was kindled against Israel 3
9:30 When Zebul . . heard . . his anger was kindled. 3
10: 7 the anger of the LORD was kindled against Israel 3
1Sm 11: 6 and his anger was greatly kindled. 3
17:28 and Eli'ab's anger was kindled against David 3
20:30 Then Saul's anger was kindled against Jonathan 3
2Sm 6: 7 the anger of the LORD was kindled against Uzzah; 3
12: 5 Then David's anger was greatly kindled 3
24: 1 the anger of the LORD was kindled against Israel 3
2Kg 13: 3 the anger of the LORD was kindled against Israel 3
22:13 the wrath of the LORD that is kindled against us 5
17 my wrath will be kindled against this place 5
23:26 by which his anger was kindled against Judah 3
1Ch 13:10 the anger of the LORD was kindled against Uzzah; 3
Job 19:11 He has kindled his wrath against me 3
41:21 His breath kindles coals, and a flame comes forth 7
42: 7 My wrath is kindled against you 3
Ps 2:12 for his wrath is quickly kindled. 1
78:21 a fire was kindled against Jacob 9
106:40 anger of the LORD was kindled against his people 3
124: 3 when their anger was kindled against us; 3
Prv 26:21 so is a quarrelsome man for kindling strife. 4
Isa 5:25 anger of the LORD was kindled against his people 3
9:18 it kindles the thickets of the forest 5
10:16 and under his glory a burning will be kindled 6
30:33 like a stream of brimstone, kindles it. 1
44:15 warms himself, he kindles a fire and bakes bread; 9
50:11 all you who kindle a fire, who set brands alight! 8
11 fire, and by the brands which you have kindled! 1
64: 2 as when fire kindles brushwood 8
Jer 7:18 children gather wood, the fathers kindle fire 1
15:14 a fire is kindled which shall burn for ever. 8
17: 4 in my anger a fire is kindled 8
27 then I will kindle a fire in its gates 5
21:14 I will kindle a fire in her forest 5
43:12 He shall kindle a fire in the temples of the gods 16
44: 6 poured forth and kindled in the cities of Judah 1
49:27 And I will kindle a fire in the wall of Damascus 5
50:32 I will kindle a fire in his cities 5
Lam 4:11 and he kindled a fire in Zion 5
Ezk 20:47 Behold, I will kindle a fire in you 5
48 flesh shall see that I the LORD have kindled it; 1
24:10 Heap on the logs, kindle the fire, boil well 2
Ams 1:14 I will kindle a fire in the wall of Rabbah 5
Lke 12:49 would that it were already kindled! 12
22:55 when they had kindled a fire 17
Act 28: 2 they kindled a fire and welcomed us all 13
2Pe 3:12 the heavens will be kindled and dissolved 18
2Es 15:23 and the sinners, like straw that is kindled. 19
16:15 The fire is kindled, and shall not be put out 19
68 the burning wrath . . is kindled over you 19
Jdt 7: 5 when they had kindled fires on their towers 11
13:13 they kindled a fire for light 13
Wis 2: 2 a spark kindled by the beating of our hearts. •
Sir 8:10 Do not kindle the coals of a sinner 14
9: 8 by it passion is kindled like a fire. 11
16: 6 In an assembly of sinners a fire will be kindled 14
6 in a disobedient nation wrath was kindled. 14

28: 8 a man given to anger will kindle strife 14
11 A hasty quarrel kindles fire 14
32:16 like a light they will kindle righteous deeds. 15
40:30 in his stomach a fire is kindled. 16
51: 4 from the midst of fire which I did not kindle 14
1Mc 12:28 they kindled fires in their camp and withdrew. 11
2Mc 10:36 they kindled fires and burned the blasphemers 12

kindle fire 1. אור
Mal 1:10 that you might not kindle fire upon my altar 1

kindliness 1. χρηστότης
AEs 16:10 quite devoid of our kindliness 1

kindly 1. חֶסֶד 2. טוֹבָה 3. עַל לֵב 4. ἀγαθός 5. ἤπιος 6. καλός 7. φιλανθρωπία 8. φιλάνθρωπος 9. φιλανθρώπως 10. φιλοφρόνως 11. χάρις
Jos 2:12 swear . . that as I have dealt kindly with you 1
12 you also will deal kindly with my father's house 1
14 we will deal kindly and faithfully with you 1
Jdg 19: 3 to speak kindly to her and bring her back. 3
Rut 1: 8 Go, return . . May the LORD deal kindly with you 1
2:13 you have . . spoken kindly to your maidservant 3
1Sm 20: 8 Therefore deal kindly with your servant 1
2Sm 19: 7 arise, go out and speak kindly to your servants; 3
2Kg 25:28 he spoke kindly to him, and gave him a seat 2
Jer 52:32 he spoke kindly to him, and gave him a seat 2
Act 27: 3 Julius treated Paul kindly 9
1Th 3: 6 and reported that you always remember us kindly 4
2Ti 2:24 kindly to every one, an apt teacher, forbearing 5
1Es 6: 5 Yet the elders of the Jews were dealt with kindly 11
Wis 1: 6 For wisdom is a kindly spirit 8
Sir 13: 6 speak to you kindly and say, "What do you need? 6
2Mc 3: 9 When he . . had been kindly welcomed 10
6:22 by doing this he might . . be treated kindly 7

kindly *See also* deal, manner.

kindness 1. חֶסֶד 2. ἐλεημοσύνη 3. ἔλεος 4. ἐπιείκεια 5. εὖ 6. εὐεργεσία 7. ἠπιότης 8. φιλανθρωπία 9. φιλανθρώπως 10. χάρις 11. χρηστοήθεια 12. χρηστός 13. χρηστότης
Gen 19:19 and you have shown me great kindness 1
20:13 I said to her, 'This is the kindness you must do me 1
40:14 and do me the kindness, I pray you, to make mention 1
Jdg 8:35 they did not show kindness to the family 1
Rut 2:20 Blessed be he . . whose kindness has not forsaken 1
3:10 made this last kindness greater than the first 1
1Sm 15: 6 you showed kindness to all the people of Israel 1
2Sm 9: 1 that I may show him kindness for Jonathan's sake? 1
3 that I may show the kindness of God to him? 1
7 Do not fear; for I will show you kindness 1
2Ch 24:22 Jo'ash the king did not remember the kindness 1
Job 6:14 He who withholds kindness from a friend 1
Ps 109:12 Let there be none to extend kindness to him 1
16 For he did not remember to show kindness 1
141: 5 Let a good man strike or rebuke me in kindness 1
Prv 21:21 He who pursues righteousness and kindness 1
31:26 teaching of kindness is on her tongue. 1
Hos 4: 1 There is no faithfulness or kindness 1
Mic 6: 8 but to do justice, and to love kindness 1
Zec 7: 9 Render true judgments, show kindness and mercy 1
Act 24: 4 I beg you in your kindness to hear us briefly. 4
28: 2 the natives showed us unusual kindness 8
Rom 2: 4 Or do you presume upon the riches of his kindness 13
4 God's kindness is meant to lead you to repentance? 12
11:22 Note then the kindness and the severity of God 13
22 but God's kindness to you, provided you continue 13
22 provided you continue in his kindness; 13
2Co 6: 6 by purity, knowledge, forbearance, kindness 13
Gal 5:22 love, joy, peace, patience, kindness, goodness 13
Eph 2: 7 in kindness toward us in Christ Jesus. 13
Col 3:12 compassion, kindness, lowliness, meekness 13
1Pe 2: 3 for you have tasted the kindness of the Lord. 12
AEs 13: 2 always acting reasonably and with kindness 7
16: 2 the too great kindness of their benefactors 13
Wis 16:11 become unresponsive to thy kindness. 6
24 in kindness relaxes 6
Sir 3:14 For kindness to a father will not be forgotten 2
7:33 withhold not kindness from the dead. 10
12: 1 If you do a kindness, know to whom you do it 5
17:22 will keep a person's kindness 10
19:25 people who distort kindness to gain a verdict. 10
29:15 Do not forget all the kindness of your surety 10
30: 6 one to repay the kindness of his friends. 10
35: 2 He who returns a kindness offers fine flour 10
36:23 If kindness and humility mark her speech 3
37:11 with a merciless man about kindness 11
40:17 Kindness is like a garden of blessings 10
Bar 2:27 all thy kindness and in all thy great compassion 4
Man 1:11 beseeching thee for thy kindness. 13
2Mc 2:22 with great kindness became gracious to them– 4
6:13 is a sign of great kindness. 6
9:27 treat you with moderation and kindness. 9
14: 9 the gracious kindness which you show to all. 8

loving kindness 1. φιλανθρωπία
Tit 3: 4 the goodness and loving kindness of God 1

kindred 1. מוֹלֶדֶת 2. מִשְׁפָּחָה 3. עַם 4. γένος 5. ὁμοιοπαθής 6. συγγένεια 7. συγγενής 8. φυλή
Gen 12: 1 Go from your country and your kindred 1
24: 4 will go to my country and to my kindred 1
38 you shall go to my father's house and to my kindred 2
40 my son from my kindred and from my father's house; 2
41 free from my oath, when you come to my kindred; 2
25:17 died, and was gathered to his kindred. 3
31: 3 land of your fathers and to your kindred 1
32: 9 Return to your country and to your kindred 1
43: 7 carefully about ourselves and our kindred 1
Num 10:30 I will depart to my own land and to my kindred. 1
Jos 6:23 and they brought all her kindred 2
Est 2:10 Esther had not made known her people or kindred 1
20 had not made known her kindred or her people 1
8: 6 can I endure to see the destruction of my kindred? 1
Lke 1:61 None of your kindred is called by this name. 6
Act 7: 3 Depart from your land and from your kindred 6
14 all his kindred, 75 souls; 6
1Es 1: 4 prepare yourselves by your families and kindred 8
10 stood according to kindred 8
7: 9 the Levites stood . . according to kindred 8
Jdt 16:24 her own nearest kindred. 4
Wis 7: 3 fell upon the kindred earth 5
Sus 1:30 And she came, with her parents . . and all her kindred 7
63 so did Joakim her husband and all her kindred 7
2Mc 5: 6 success at the cost of one's kindred 7

king 1. מלך 2. מֶלֶךְ 3. מֶלֶךְ (A) 4. βασιλεία 5. βασίλειος 6. βασιλεύς 7. βασιλεύω 8. βασιλικός 9. τύραννος 10. regnum 11. rex
Gen 14: 1 In the days of Am'raphel king of Shinar 2
1 Am'raphel king of Shinar, Ar'ioch king of Ella'sar 2
1 king of Ella'sar, Ched-or-lao'mer king of Elam 2
1 king of Elam, and Tidal king of Goi'im 2
2 these kings made war with Bera king of Sodom *
2 these kings made war with Bera king of Sodom 2
2 Bera king of Sodom, Birsha king of Gomor'rah 2
2 Shinab king of Admah, Sheme'ber king of Zeboi'im 2
2 Shinab king of Admah, Sheme'ber king of Zeboi'im 2
2 of Zeboi'im, and the king of Bela (that is, Zo'ar). 2
5 Ched-or-lao'mer and the kings who were with him 2
8 Then the king of Sodom, the king of Gomor'rah 2
8 Then the king of Sodom, the king of Gomor'rah 2
8 the king of Admah, the king of Zeboi'im 2
8 the king of Admah, the king of Zeboi'im 2
8 of Zeboi'im, and the king of Bela (that is, Zo'ar) 2
9 with Ched-or-lao'mer king of Elam 2
9 with Ched-or-lao'mer king of Elam 2
9 Tidal king of Goi'im, Am'raphel king of Shinar 2
9 Ar'ioch king of Ella'sar, four kings against five. 2
9 Ar'ioch king of Ella'sar, four kings against five. 2
10 and as the kings of Sodom and Gomor'rah fled 2
17 of Ched-or-lao'mer and the kings who were with him 2
17 king of Sodom went out to meet him at the Valley 2
17 of Shaveh (that is, the King's Valley). 2
18 Mel-chiz'edek king of Salem brought out bread 2
21 the king of Sodom said to Abram 2
22 Abram said to the king of Sodom 2
17: 6 and kings shall come forth from you. 2
16 she shall be a mother of nations; kings of peoples 2
20: 2 And Abim'elech king of Gerar sent and took Sarah. 2
26: 1 to Gerar, to Abim'elech king of the Philistines. 2
8 Abim'elech king of the Philistines looked out 2
35:11 come from you, and kings shall spring from you. 2
36:31 These are the kings who reigned in the land 2
31 before any king reigned over the Israelites. 2
39:20 the prison, the place where the king's prisoners 2
40: 1 after this, the butler of the king of Egypt 2
1 his baker offended their lord the king of Egypt. 2
5 the baker of the king of Egypt, who were confined 2
41:46 entered the service of Pharaoh king of Egypt. 2
Exd 1: 8 Now there arose a new king over Egypt 2
15 the king of Egypt said to the Hebrew midwives 2
17 did not do as the king of Egypt commanded them 2
18 the king of Egypt called the midwives, and said 2
2:23 the king of Egypt died. And the people of Israel 2
3:18 you . . shall go to the king of Egypt and say to him 2
19 I know that the king of Egypt will not let you go 2
5: 4 the king of Egypt said to them, "Moses and Aaron 2
6:11 Go in, tell Pharaoh king of Egypt to let . . Israel go 2
13 a charge . . to Pharaoh king of Egypt to bring 2
27 It was they who spoke to Pharaoh king of Egypt 2
29 I am the LORD; tell Pharaoh king of Egypt all that I 2
14: 5 When the king of Egypt was told that the people 2
8 king of Egypt and he pursued the people of Israel 2
Num 20:14 Moses sent messengers . . to the king of Edom 2
17 we will go along the King's Highway 2
21: 1 Canaanite, the king of Arad, who dwelt in the Negeb 2
21 sent messengers to Sihon king of the Amorites 2
22 we will go by the King's Highway, until we have 2
26 city of Sihon the king of the Amorites 2
26 Sihon . . fought against the former king of Moab 2
29 his sons fugitives . . to an Amorite king, Sihon. 2
33 Og the king of Bashan came out against them 2
34 do to him as you did to Sihon king of the Amorites 2
22: 4 So Balak . . who was king of Moab at that time 2
10 Balak the son of Zippor, king of Moab, has sent to me 2
23: 7 king of Moab from the eastern mountains 2
21 the shout of a king is among them. 2
24: 7 his king shall be higher than Agag 2
31: 8 slew the kings of Mid'ian with the rest of their 2
8 Evi . . Hur, and Reba, the five kings of Mid'ian; 2
32:33 gave . . the kingdom of Sihon king of the Amorites 2
33 Moses gave . . the kingdom of Og king of Bashan 2
33:40 Canaanite, the king of Arad, who dwelt in the Negeb 2
Deu 1: 4 defeated Sihon the king of the Amorites 2
4 defeated . . Og the king of Bashan, who lived 2
2:24 Sihon the Amorite, king of Heshbon, and his land; 2
26 sent messengers . . to Sihon the king of Heshbon 2
30 Sihon the king of Heshbon would not let us pass 2
3: 1 Og the king of Bashan came out against us 2
2 as you did to Sihon the king of the Amorites 2
3 gave into our hand Og also, the king of Bashan 2
6 as we did to Sihon the king of Heshbon, destroying 2
8 out of the hand of the two kings of the Amorites 2
11 For only Og the king of Bashan was left 2
21 that the LORD your God has done to these two kings; 2
4:46 in the land of Sihon the king of the Amorites, who 2
47 possession of . . the land of Og the king of Bashan 2
47 two kings of the Amorites, who lived to the east 2
7: 8 from the hand of Pharaoh king of Egypt. 2
24 he will give their kings into your hand 2
11: 3 which he did in Egypt to Pharaoh the king of Egypt 2
17:14 I will set a king over me, like all the nations 2
15 may indeed set as king over you him whom the LORD 2
15 your brethren you shall set as king over you; 2
28:36 LORD will bring you, and your king . . to a nation 2
29: 7 Sihon the king of Heshbon and Og the king 2
7 Sihon . . of Heshbon and Og the king of Bashan 2
31: 4 Sihon and Og, the kings of the Amorites 2
33: 5 Thus the LORD became king in Jesh'urun 2
Jos 2: 2 And it was told the king of Jericho, "Behold 2
3 Then the king of Jericho sent to Rahab, saying 2
10 and what you did to the two kings of the Amorites 2
5: 1 all the kings of the Amorites that were beyond 2
1 and all the kings of the Canaanites . . by the sea 2
6: 2 Jericho, with its king and mighty men of valor. 2
8: 1 given into your hand the king of Ai, and his people 2
2 and you shall do to Ai and its king as you did 2
2 shall do to Ai . . as you did to Jericho and its king; 2
14 when the king of Ai saw this he . . made haste 2
23 But the king of Ai they took alive, and brought him 2
29 he hanged the king of Ai on a tree until evening; 2
9: 1 When all the kings who were beyond the Jordan 2
10 all that he did to the two kings of the Amorites 2
10 to the two kings . . Sihon the king of Heshbon 2
10 Sihon the king of Heshbon, and Og king of Bashan 2
10: 1 When Ado'ni-ze'dek king of Jerusalem heard 2
1 doing to Ai and its king as he had done to Jericho 2
1 doing . . as he had done to Jericho and its king 2
3 Ado'ni-ze'dek king of Jerusalem sent to Hoham 2
3 Ado'ni-ze'dek . . sent to Hoham king of Hebron 2
3 to Hoham king of Hebron, to Piram king of Jarmuth 2
3 to Japhi'a king of Lachish, and to Debir . . of Eglon 2
3 Japhi'a king of Lachish, and to Debir king of Eglon 2
5 Then the five kings of the Amorites . . gathered 2
5 the king of Jerusalem, the king of Hebron, the king 2
5 the king of Jerusalem, the king of Hebron, the king 2
5 the king of Hebron, the king of Jarmuth, the king 2
5 of Jarmuth, the king of Lachish, and the king 2
5 the king of Lachish, and the king of Eglon 2
6 all the kings of the Amorites . . are gathered 2
16 These five kings fled, and hid themselves 2
17 The five kings have been found, hidden in the cave 2
22 and bring those five kings out to me from the cave. 2
23 and brought those five kings out to him 2
23 five kings . . the king of Jerusalem 2
23 king of Jerusalem, the king of Hebron 2
23 king of Hebron, the king of Jarmuth 2
23 king of Hebron, the king of Jarmuth 2
23 the king of Lachish, and the king of Eglon. 2
24 when they brought those kings out to Joshua 2
24 put your feet upon the necks of these kings. 2
28 Joshua took Makke'dah . . and smote it and its king 2
28 he did to the king of Makke'dah as he had done 2
28 he did to . . as he had done to the king of Jericho. 2
30 gave it also and its king into the hand of Israel; 2
30 he did to its king as he had done to the king 2
30 he did to . . as he had done to the king of Jericho. 2
33 Then Horam king of Gezer came up to help Lachish; 2
37 and smote it . . and its king and its towns 2
39 and he took it with its king and all its towns; 2
39 as he had done to Hebron and to Libnah and its king 2
39 as he had done . . so he did to Debir and to its king. 2
40 defeated the whole land . . and all their kings; 2
42 And Joshua took all these kings and their land 2
11: 1 When Jabin king of Hazor heard of this, he sent 2
1 When Jabin . . he sent to Jobab king of Madon 2
1 he sent to . . the king of Shimron 2
1 he sent to . . the king of Ach'shaph 2
2 he sent . . to the kings who were 2
5 And all these kings joined their forces, and came 2
10 and took Hazor, and smote its king with the sword; 2
12 all the cities of those kings . . Joshua took 2
12 all the cities . . and all their kings, Joshua took 2
17 And he took all their kings, and smote them 2

18 Joshua made war a long time with all those kings. 2
12: 1 Now these are the kings of the land 2
2 these are the kings . . Sihon king of the Amorites 2
4 and Og king of Bashan, one of the . . Reph'aim 2
5 Gilead to the boundary of Sihon king of Heshbon. 2
7 the kings of the land whom Joshua . . defeated 2
9 the king of Jericho, one, the king of Ai 2
9 the king of Ai, which is beside Bethel, one; 2
10 king of Jerusalem, one; the king of Hebron, one; 2
10 king of Jerusalem, one; the king of Hebron, one; 2
11 the king of Jarmuth, one; the king of Lachish, one; 2
11 the king of Jarmuth, one; the king of Lachish, one; 2
12 the king of Eglon, one; the king of Gezer, one; 2
12 the king of Eglon, one; the king of Gezer, one; 2
13 the king of Debir, one; the king of Geder, one; 2
13 the king of Debir, one; the king of Geder, one; 2
14 the king of Hormah, one; the king of Arad, one; 2
14 the king of Hormah, one; the king of Arad, one; 2
15 the king of Libnah, one; the king of Adullam, one; 2
15 the king of Libnah, one; the king of Adullam, one; 2
16 the king of Makke'dah, one; the king of Bethel, one; 2
16 the king of Makke'dah, one; the king of Bethel, one; 2
17 the king of Tap'puah, one; the king of Hepher, one; 2
17 the king of Tap'puah, one; the king of Hepher, one; 2
18 the king of Aphek, one; the king of Lashar'on, one; 2
18 the king of Aphek, one; the king of Lashar'on, one; 2
19 the king of Madon, one; the king of Hazor, one; 2
19 the king of Madon, one; the king of Hazor, one; 2
20 the king of Shim'ron-me'ron, one; 2
20 the king of Ach'shaph, one; 2
21 the king of Ta'anach, one; the king of Megid'do, one; 2
21 the king of Ta'anach, one; the king of Megid'do, one; 2
22 the king of Kedesh, one; the king of Jok'ne-am . . one; 2
22 of Kedesh, one; the king of Jok'ne-am in Carmel, one; 2
23 the king of Dor in Naphath-dor, one; 2
23 king of Dor . . one; the king of Goi'im in Galilee, one; 2
24 the king of Tirzah, one: in all, 31 kings. 2
24 the king of Tirzah, one: in all, 31 kings. 2
13:10 all the cities of Sihon king of the Amorites 2
21 and all the kingdom of Sihon king of the Amorites 2
27 the rest of the kingdom of Sihon king of Heshbon 2
30 all Bashan, the whole kingdom of Og king of Bashan 2
24: 9 Balak the son of Zippor, king of Moab, arose 2
12 drove them out . . the two kings of the Amorites; 2
Jdg 1: 7 70 kings with their thumbs and their great toes 2
3: 8 hand of Cu'shan-rishatha'im king of Mesopota'mia; 2
10 Cu'shan-rishatha'im king of Mesopota'mia into his 2
12 and the LORD strengthened Eglon the king of Moab 2
14 Israel served Eglon the king of Moab eighteen 2
15 sent tribute by him to Eglon the king of Moab. 2
17 he presented the tribute to Eglon king of Moab. 2
19 and said, "I have a secret message for you, O king. 2
4: 2 hand of Jabin king of Canaan, who reigned in Hazor; 2
17 there was peace between Jabin the king of Hazor 2
23 God subdued Jabin the king of Canaan before 2
24 harder and harder on Jabin the king of Canaan 2
24 until they destroyed Jabin king of Canaan. 2
5: 3 Hear, O kings; give ear, O princes; to the LORD I will 2
19 The kings came, they fought; then fought the kings 2
19 then fought the kings of Canaan, at Ta'anach 2
8: 5 after Zebah and Zalmun'na, the kings of Mid'ian. 2
12 took the two kings of Mid'ian, Zebah and Zalmun'na 2
18 every one . . they resembled the sons of a king. 2
26 the purple garments worn by the kings of Mid'ian 2
9: 6 they went and made Abim'elech king, by the oak 2
8 trees once went forth to anoint a king over them; 2
15 If . . you are anointing me king over you 2
11:12 sent messengers to the king of the Ammonites 2
13 the king of the Ammonites answered 2
14 sent messengers . . to the king of the Ammonites 2
17 Israel then sent messengers to the king of Edom 2
17 your land'; but the king of Edom would not listen. 2
17 And they sent also to the king of Moab, but he would 2
19 sent messengers to Sihon king of the Amorites 2
19 Sihon king of the Amorites, king of Heshbon 2
25 better than Balak the son of Zippor, king of Moab? 2
28 the king of the Ammonites did not heed 2
17: 6 there was no king in Israel; every man did what was 2
18: 1 In those days there was no king in Israel. 2
19: 1 In those days, when there was no king in Israel 2
21:25 In those days there was no king in Israel; 2
1Sm 2:10 The LORD will . . he will give strength to his king 2
8: 5 appoint for us a king to govern us like all 2
6 when they said, "Give us a king to govern us. 2
7 they have rejected me from being king over them. 1
9 and show them the ways of the king who shall reign 2
10 to the people who were asking a king from him. 2
11 These will be the ways of the king who will reign 2
18 in that day you will cry out because of your king 2
19 No! but we will have a king over us 2
20 that our king may govern us and go out before us 2
22 Hearken to their voice, and make them a king. 2
10:19 and you have said, 'No! but set a king over us.' 2
24 And all the people shouted, "Long live the king! 2
12: 1 I have hearkened . . and have made a king over you. 2
2 And now, behold, the king walks before you; 2
9 commander of the army of Jabin king of Hazor 6
9 he sold them . . into the hand of the king of Moab; 2
12 saw that Nahash the king of the Ammonites came 2
12 you said to me, 'No, but a king shall reign over us,' 2
12 you said . . when the LORD your God was your king. 2
13 And now behold the king whom you have chosen 2
13 behold, the LORD has set a king over you. 2
14 if both you and the king . . will follow the LORD 2
15 the LORD will be against you and your king. 6
17 wickedness . . in asking for a king. 2
19 added . . this evil, to ask for ourselves a king. 2
25 you shall be swept away, both you and your king. 2
14:47 against the kings of Zobah, and against 2
15: 1 sent me to anoint you king over his people Israel; 2
8 And he took Agag the king of the Amal'ekites alive 2
11 I repent that I have made Saul king; 2
17 The LORD anointed you king over Israel. 2
20 I have brought Agag the king of Am'alek 2
23 LORD . . has also rejected you from being king. 2
26 has rejected you from being king over Israel. 2
32 Bring here to me Agag the king of the Amal'ekites. 2
16: 1 I have rejected him from being king over Israel? 1
1 I have provided for myself a king among his sons. 2
17:25 the man who kills him, the king will enrich 2
55 As your soul lives, O king, I cannot tell. 2
56 And the king said, "Inquire whose son 2
18: 6 the women came . . to meet King Saul, with timbrels 2
18 Who am I . . that I should be son-in-law to the king? 2
22 the king has delight in you, and all his servants 2
22 now then become the king's son-in-law. 2
23 a little thing to become the king's son-in-law 2
25 The king desires no marriage present except 2
25 that he may be avenged of the king's enemies. 2
26 it pleased David well to be the king's son-in-law. 2
27 which were given in full number to the king 2
27 that he might become the king's son-in-law. 2
19: 4 Let not the king sin against his servant David; 2
20: 5 and I should not fail to sit at table with the king; 2
24 the new moon came, the king sat down to eat food. 2
25 The king sat upon his seat, as at other times 2
29 For this . . he has not come to the king's table. 2
21: 2 The king has charged me with a matter, and said 2
8 because the king's business required haste. 2
10 David rose . . and went to A'chish the king of Gath. 2
11 Is not this David the king of the land? 2
12 and was much afraid of A'chish the king of Gath. 2
22: 3 David went . . and he said to the king of Moab 2
4 he left them with the king of Moab, and they stayed 2
11 the king sent to summon Ahim'elech the priest 2
11 priests . . at Nob; and all of them came to the king. 2
14 Then Ahim'elech answered the king 2
14 David, who is the king's son-in-law, and captain over 2
15 Let not the king impute anything to his servant 2
16 And the king said, "You shall surely die, Ahim'elech 2
17 the king said to the guard who stood about him 2
17 But the servants of the king would not put forth 2
18 the king said to Do'eg, "You turn and fall upon 2
23:17 you shall be king over Israel 1
20 Now come down, O king 2
20 our part . . to surrender him into the king's hand. 2
24: 8 David . . called after Saul, "My lord the king! 2
14 After whom has the king of Israel come out? 2
20 now, behold, I know that you shall surely be king 1
25:36 he was holding a feast . . like the feast of a king. 2
26:14 Abner answered, "Who are you that calls to the king? 2
15 have you not kept watch over your lord the king 2
15 For one . . came in to destroy the king your lord. 2
16 see where the king's spear is, and the jar of water 2
17 And David said, "It is my voice, my lord, O king. 2
19 let my lord the king hear . . his servant. 2
20 the king of Israel has come out to seek my life 2
22 And David made answer, "Here is the spear, O king! 2
27: 2 went . . to A'chish the son of Ma'och, king of Gath. 2
6 Ziklag has belonged to the kings of Judah 2
28:13 The king said to her, "Have no fear; what do you see? 2
29: 3 this David, the servant of Saul, king of Israel 2
8 and fight against the enemies of my lord the king? 2
2Sm 2: 4 anointed David king over the house of Judah. 2
7 house of Judah has anointed me king over them. 2
11 David was king in Hebron . . seven years 2
3: 3 of Ma'acah the daughter of Talmai king of Geshur; 2
17 you have been seeking David as king over you. 2
21 I . . will gather all Israel to my lord the king 2
23 Abner . . came to the king, and he has let him go 2
24 Jo'ab went to the king and said 2
31 And King David followed the bier. 2
32 the king lifted up his voice and wept at the grave 2
33 And the king lamented for Abner, saying 2
36 as everything that the king did pleased 2
37 it had not been the king's will to slay Abner 2
38 the king said to his servants 2
39 And I am this day weak, though anointed king; 2
4: 8 And they said to the king, "Here is the head 2
8 the LORD has avenged my lord the king . . on Saul 2
5: 2 when Saul was king over us, it was you that led out 2
3 the elders . . came to the king at Hebron; 2
3 King David made a covenant with them at Hebron 2
3 and they anointed David king over Israel. 2
6 And the king and his men went to Jerusalem 2
11 And Hiram king of Tyre sent messengers to David 2
12 the LORD had established him king over Israel 2
17 that David had been anointed king over Israel 2
6:12 And it was told King David, "The LORD has blessed 2
16 Michal . . saw King David leaping and dancing 2
20 How the king of Israel honored himself today 2
7: 1 Now when the king dwelt in his house, and the LORD 2
2 the king said to Nathan the prophet 2
3 Nathan said to the king, "Go, do all . . in your heart; 2
18 Then King David went in and sat before the LORD 2
8: 3 Hadade'zer the son of Rehob, king of Zobah 2
5 Syrians . . came to help Hadade'zer king of Zobah 2
8 And from . . King David took very much bronze. 2
9 When To'i king of Hamath heard that David had 2
10 To'i sent his son Joram to King David, to greet him 2
11 these also King David dedicated to the LORD 2
12 of Hadade'zer the son of Rehob, king of Zobah. 2
9: 2 and the king said to him, "Are you Ziba? 2
3 And the king said, "Is there not still some one 2
3 Ziba said to the king, "There is still a son 2
4 The king said to him, "Where is he? 2
4 Ziba said to the king, "He is in the house of Machir 2
5 Then King David sent and brought him 2
9 Then the king called Ziba, Saul's servant 2
11 Then Ziba said to the king, "According to all 2
11 According to all that my lord the king commands 2
11 Mephib'osheth ate . . like one of the king's sons. 2
13 for he ate always at the king's table. 2
10: 1 After this the king of the Ammonites died 2
5 And the king said, "Remain at Jericho until 2
6 hired . . the king of Ma'acah with 1,000 men 2
19 all the kings . . saw that they had been defeated 2
11: 1 In . . the time when kings go forth to battle 2
2 and was walking upon the roof of the king's house 2
8 Uri'ah went out of the king's house 2
8 there followed him a present from the king. 2
9 Uri'ah slept at the door of the king's house 2
19 telling all . . about the fighting to the king 2
20 then, if the king's anger rises, and if he says to you 2
24 some of the king's servants are dead; 2
12: 7 I anointed you king over Israel, and I delivered 2
30 And he took the crown of their king from his head; 2
13: 4 O son of the king, why are you so haggard 2
6 when the king came to see him, Amnon said 2
6 when the king came to see him, Amnon said 2
13 speak to the king; for he will not withhold me 2
18 thus were the virgin daughters of the king clad 2
21 When King David heard of all these things 2
23 and Ab'salom invited all the king's sons. 2
24 And Ab'salom came to the king, and said, "Behold 2
24 pray let the king and his servants go 2
25 But the king said to Ab'salom, "No, my son 2
26 the king said to him, "Why should he go with you? 2
27 he let Amnon and all the king's sons go with him. 2
29 Then all the king's sons arose, and each . . fled. 2
30 Ab'salom has slain all the king's sons 2
31 Then the king arose, and rent his garments 2
32 have killed all the young men the king's sons 2
33 let not my lord the king so take it to heart 2
33 to suppose that all the king's sons are dead; 2
35 Jon'adab said to the king, "Behold, the king's sons 2
35 Jon'adab said . . "Behold, the king's sons have come; 2
36 the king's sons came, and lifted up their voice 2
36 the king also and all his servants wept 2
37 went to Talmai the son of Ammi'hud, king of Geshur. 2
39 the spirit of the king longed to go . . to Ab'salom; 2
14: 1 Jo'ab . . perceived that the king's heart went out 2
3 and go to the king, and speak thus to him. 2
4 When the woman of Teko'a came to the king 2
4 and did obeisance, and said, "Help, O king. 2
5 And the king said to her, "What is your trouble? 2
8 Then the king said to the woman, "Go to your house 2
9 And the woman of Teko'a said to the king 2
9 On me be the guilt, my lord the king 2
9 let the king and his throne be guiltless. 2
10 The king said, "If any one says anything to you 2
11 Pray let the king invoke the LORD your God 2
12 let your handmaid speak a word to my lord the king 2
13 giving this decision the king convicts himself 2
13 the king does not bring his banished one home 2
15 Now I have come to say this to my lord the king 2
15 your handmaid thought, 'I will speak to the king; 2
15 it may be that the king will perform the request 2
16 For the king will hear, and deliver his servant 2
17 The word of my lord the king will set me at rest'; 2
17 for my lord the king is like the angel of God 2
18 the king answered the woman, "Do not hide from me 2
18 And the woman said, "Let my lord the king speak. 2
19 The king said, "Is the hand of Jo'ab with you 2
19 As surely as you live, my lord the king, one cannot 2
19 from anything that my lord the king has said. 2
21 Then the king said to Jo'ab, "Behold now, I grant this; 2
22 Jo'ab . . and did obeisance, and blessed the king; 2
22 I have found favor in your sight, my lord the king 2
22 the king has granted the request of his servant. 2
24 the king said, "Let him dwell apart in his own house; 2
24 Ab'salom . . did not come into the king's presence. 2
26 200 shekels by the king's weight. 2
28 without coming into the king's presence. 2
29 Then Ab'salom sent for Jo'ab, to send him to the king; 2
32 Come here, that I may send you to the king 2
32 therefore let me go into the presence of the king; 2

33 Then Jo'ab went to the king, and told him; 2
33 he came to the king, and bowed himself on his face 2
33 bowed . . on his face to the ground before the king; 2
33 and the king kissed Ab'salom. 2
15: 2 had a suit to come before the king for judgment 2
3 there is no man deputed by the king to hear you. 2
6 to all of Israel who came to the king for judgment; 2
7 Ab'salom said to the king, "Pray let me go 2
9 The king said to him, "Go in peace." So he arose 2
10 As soon as . . then say, 'Ab'salom is king at Hebron!' 1
15 And the king's servants said to the king 2
15 And the king's servants said to the king 2
15 ready to do whatever my lord the king decides. 2
16 So the king went forth, and all his household 2
16 the king left ten concubines to keep the house. 2
17 the king went forth, and all the people after him; 2
18 all the 600 . . passed on before the king. 2
19 Then the king said to It'tai the Gittite 2
19 Go back, and stay with the king; 2
21 But It'tai answered the king, "As the LORD lives 2
21 As the LORD lives, and as my lord the king lives 2
21 wherever my lord the king shall be . . there also 2
23 and the king crossed the brook Kidron 2
25 Then the king said to Zadok, "Carry the ark of God 2
27 The king also said to Zadok the priest 2
34 and say to Ab'salom, 'I will be your servant, O king; 2
35 whatever you hear from the king's house, tell it 2
16: 2 the king said to Ziba, "Why have you brought these? 2
2 The asses are for the king's household to ride on 2
3 And the king said, "And where is your master's son? 2
3 Ziba said to the king, "Behold, he remains 2
4 Then the king said to Ziba 2
4 let me . . find favor in your sight, my lord the king. 2
5 When King David came to Bahu'rim, there came out 2
6 at David, and at all the servants of King David; 2
9 Then Abi'shai the son of Zeru'iah said to the king 2
9 Why should this dead dog curse my lord the king? 2
10 But the king said, "What have I to do with you 2
14 And the king, and all the people . . arrived weary 2
16 Long live the king! Long live the king! 2
16 Long live the king! Long live the king! 2
17: 2 I will strike down the king only 2
16 lest the king and all the people . . be swallowed 2
17 tell them, and they would go and tell King David; 2
21 the men came up . . and went and told King David. 2
18: 2 And the king said to the men, "I myself will also go 2
4 The king said to them, "Whatever seems best to you 2
4 the king stood at the side of the gate 2
5 And the king ordered Jo'ab and Abi'shai and It'tai 2
5 when the king gave orders to all the commanders 2
12 would not put forth my hand against the king's son; 2
12 the king commanded you and Abi'shai and It'tai 2
13 (and there is nothing hidden from the king) 2
18 set up . . the pillar which is in the King's Valley 2
19 Let me run, and carry tidings to the king 2
20 carry no tidings, because the king's son is dead. 2
21 Jo'ab said . . "Go, tell the king what you have seen. 2
25 And the watchman called out and told the king. 2
25 And the king said, "If he is alone, there are tidings 2
26 The king said, "He also brings tidings. 2
27 the king said, "He is a good man, and comes with good 2
28 Then Ahi'ma-az cried out to the king, "All is well. 2
28 bowed before the king with his face to the earth 2
28 who raised their hand against my lord the king. 2
29 And the king said, "Is it well with the young man 2
30 And the king said, "Turn aside, and stand here. 2
31 Cushite said, "Good tidings for my lord the king! 2
32 The king said to the Cushite, "Is it well 2
32 the enemies of my lord the king, and all who rise up 2
33 And the king was deeply moved, and went . . and wept; 2
19: 1 the king is weeping and mourning for Ab'salom. 2
2 people heard . . "The king is grieving for his son. 2
4 The king covered his face, and the king cried 2
4 and the king cried with a loud voice, "O my son 2
5 Then Jo'ab came into the house to the king, and said 2
8 Then the king arose, and took his seat in the gate. 2
8 Behold, the king is sitting in the gate"; 2
8 and all the people came before the king. 2
9 The king delivered us from the hand of our 2
10 why . . say nothing about bringing the king back? 2
11 And King David sent this message to Zadok 2
11 be the last to bring the king back to his house 2
11 when the word of all Israel has come to the king? 2
12 should you be the last to bring back the king?' 2
14 they sent word to the king, "Return, both you and all 2
15 So the king came back to the Jordan; and Judah came 2
15 came . . to meet the king and to bring the king over 2
15 Judah came . . to bring the king over the Jordan. 2
16 with the men of Judah to meet King David; 2
17 Ziba . . rushed down to the Jordan before the king 2
18 to bring over the king's household, and to do his 2
18 Shim'e-i the son of Gera fell down before the king 2
19 And Shim'e-i . . said to the king, "Let not my lord 2
19 on the day my lord the king left Jerusalem; 2
19 let not the king bear it in mind. 2
20 the first . . to come down to meet my lord the king. 2
22 do I not know that I am this day king over Israel? 2
23 And the king said to Shim'e-i, "You shall not die. 2
23 You shall not die." And the king gave him his oath. 2
24 And Mephib'osheth . . came down to meet the king; 2
24 from the day the king departed until . . he came 2
25 And when he came from Jerusalem to meet the king 2
25 he came . . the king said to him, "Why did you not 2
26 answered, "My lord, O king, my servant deceived me; 2
26 that I may ride upon it and go with the king.' 2
27 He . . slandered your servant to my lord the king. 2
27 But my lord the king is like the angel of God; 2
28 but men doomed to death before my lord the king; 2
28 What further right have I, then, to cry to the king? 2
29 And the king said to him, "Why speak any more 2
30 Mephib'osheth said to the king, "Oh, let him take it 2
30 since my lord the king has come safely home. 2
31 and he went on with the king to the Jordan 2
32 he had provided the king with food while he stayed 2
33 the king said to Barzil'lai, "Come over with me 2
34 But Barzil'lai said to the king, "How many years 2
34 that I should go up with the king to Jerusalem? 2
35 Why then . . be an added burden to my lord the king? 2
36 Your servant will go a little . . with the king. 2
36 should the king recompense me with such a reward? 2
37 let him go over with my lord the king; 2
38 the king answered, "Chimham shall go over with me 2
39 all . . went over the Jordan, and the king went over; 2
39 and the king kissed Barzil'lai and blessed him 2
40 The king went on to Gilgal, and Chimham went 2
40 all the people . . brought the king on his way. 2
41 all the men of Israel came to the king, and said 2
41 all . . Israel came to the king, and said to the king 2
41 and brought the king and his household over 2
42 Because the king is near of kin to us. 2
42 Have we eaten at all at the king's expense? 2
43 We have ten shares in the king, and in David also 2
43 the first to speak of bringing back our king? 2
20: 2 men of Judah followed their king steadfastly 2
3 the king took the ten concubines whom he had left 2
4 Then the king said to Ama'sa, "Call the men of Judah 2
21 a man . . has lifted up his hand against King David; 2
22 And Jo'ab returned to Jerusalem to the king. 2
21: 2 the king called the Gib'eonites. 2
5 They said to the king, "The man who consumed us 2
6 And the king said, "I will give them. 2
7 But the king spared Mephib'osheth 2
8 The king took the two sons of Rizpah 2
14 and they did all that the king commanded. 2
22:51 Great triumphs he gives to his king 2
24: 2 the king said to Jo'ab and the commanders 2
3 Jo'ab said to the king, "May the LORD your God add 2
3 while the eyes of my lord the king still see it; 2
3 why does my lord the king delight in this thing? 2
4 But the king's word prevailed against Jo'ab 2
4 Jo'ab and . . went out from the presence of the king 2
9 Jo'ab gave the sum of the numbering . . to the king 2
20 he saw the king and his servants coming 2
20 Arau'nah went forth, and did obeisance to the king 2
21 Why has my lord the king come to his servant? 2
22 Let my lord the king take and offer up what seems 2
23 All this, O king, Arau'nah gives to the king. 2
23 All this, O king, Arau'nah gives to the king. 2
23 And Arau'nah said to the king, "The LORD your God 2
24 But the king said to Arau'nah, "No, but I will buy it 2
1Kg 1: 1 King David was old and advanced in years; 2
2 Let a young maiden be sought for my lord the king 2
2 and let her wait upon the king, and be his nurse; let 2
2 in your bosom, that my lord the king may be warm. 2
3 found Ab'ishag . . and brought her to the king. 2
4 she became the king's nurse and ministered to him; 2
4 and ministered to him; but the king knew her not. 2
5 exalted himself, saying, "I will be king"; 1
9 and he invited all his brothers, the king's sons 2
13 Go in at once to King David, and say to him, 'Did you 2
13 Did you not, my lord the king, swear 2
13 sit upon my throne"? Why then is Adoni'jah king?' 1
14 while you are still speaking with the king, I also 2
15 So Bathshe'ba went to the king into his chamber 2
15 now the king was very old, and Ab'ishag 2
15 old, and Ab'ishag . . was ministering to the king. 2
16 Bathshe'ba bowed and did obeisance to the king 2
16 and the king said, "What do you desire? 2
18 And now, behold, Adoni'jah is king, although you, my 1
18 is king, although you, my lord the king, do not know 2
19 and has invited all the sons of the king, Abi'athar 2
20 now, my lord the king, the eyes of all Israel are 2
20 who shall sit on the throne of my lord the king 2
21 when my lord the king sleeps with his fathers 2
22 While she was still speaking with the king 2
23 they told the king, "Here is Nathan the prophet. 2
23 when he came in before the king, he bowed before 2
23 he bowed before the king, with his face 2
24 My lord the king, have you said, 'Adoni'jah shall 2
25 and has invited all the king's sons, Jo'ab 2
25 before him, and saying, 'Long live King Adoni'jah!' 2
27 this thing been brought about by my lord the king 2
27 who should sit on the throne of my lord the king 2
28 Then King David answered, "Call Bathshe'ba to me. 2
28 So she came into the king's presence, and stood 2
28 the king's presence, and stood before the king. 2
29 the king swore, saying, "As the LORD lives, who has 2
31 bowed . . and did obeisance to the king, and said 2
31 and said, "May my lord King David live for ever. 2
32 King David said, "Call to me Zadok the priest 2
32 Call to me . . " So they came before the king. 2
33 the king said to them, "Take with you the servants 2
34 there anoint him king over Israel; then blow 2
34 blow the trumpet, and say, 'Long live King Solomon 2
35 sit upon my throne; for he shall be king in my stead; 1
36 Benai'ah . . answered the king, "Amen! May the LORD 2
36 May the LORD, the God of my lord the king, say so. 2
37 As the LORD has been with my lord the king, even 2
37 greater than the throne of my lord King David. 2
38 and caused Solomon to ride on King David's mule 2
39 and all the people said, "Long live King Solomon! 2
43 No, for our lord King David has made Solomon king; 2
44 the king has sent with him Zadok the priest 2
44 they have caused him to ride on the king's mule; 2
45 Zadok . . and Nathan . . have anointed him king 2
47 the king's servants came to congratulate our 2
47 to congratulate our lord King David, saying, 'Your 2
47 And the king bowed himself upon the bed. 2
48 the king also said, 'Blessed be the LORD, the God 2
51 Adoni'jah fears King Solomon; for, lo, he has laid 2
51 Let King Solomon swear to me first that he will 2
53 King Solomon sent, and they brought him down 2
53 And he came and did obeisance to King Solomon; 2
2:17 ask King Solomon . . to give me Ab'ishag 2
18 said, "Very well; I will speak for you to the king. 2
19 Bathshe'ba went to King Solomon, to speak to him 2
19 the king rose to meet her, and bowed down to her; 2
19 and had a seat brought for the king's mother; 2
20 the king said to her, "Make your request, my mother; 2
22 King Solomon answered his mother, "And why do you 2
23 King Solomon swore by the LORD, saying, "God do 2
25 So King Solomon sent Benai'ah the son of Jehoi'ada; 2
26 to Abi'athar the priest the king said, "Go 2
29 when it was told King Solomon, "Jo'ab has fled 2
30 The king commands, 'Come forth.'" But he said, "No 2
30 Benai'ah brought the king word again, saying, "Thus 2
31 The king replied to him, "Do as he has said, strike 2
35 The king put Benai'ah . . over the army in place 2
35 the king put Zadok the priest in the place 2
36 the king sent and summoned Shim'e-i, and said to him 2
38 Shim'e-i said to the king, "What you say is good; 2
38 as my lord the king has said, so will your servant 2
39 ran away to Achish, son of Ma'acah, king of Gath. 2
42 the king sent and summoned Shim'e-i, and said to him 2
44 The king also said to Shim'e-i, "You know in your own 2
45 King Solomon shall be blessed, and the throne 2
46 the king commanded Benai'ah . . and he went out 2
3: 1 a marriage alliance with Pharaoh king of Egypt; 2
4 the king went to Gibeon to sacrifice there 2
13 no other king shall compare with you, all 2
16 two harlots came to the king, and stood before 2
22 child is mine." Thus they spoke before the king. 2
23 the king said, "The one says, 'This is my son that is 2
24 the king said, "Bring me a sword." So a sword was 2
24 So a sword was brought before the king. 2
25 the king said, "Divide the living child in two 2
26 the woman . . said to the king, because her heart 2
27 the king answered and said, "Give the living child 2
28 of the judgment which the king had rendered; 2
28 stood in awe of the king, because they perceived 2
4: 1 King Solomon was king over all Israel 2
1 King Solomon was king over all Israel 2
5 Zabud . . was priest and king's friend; 2
7 provided food for the king and his household; 2
19 Gilead, the country of Sihon king of the Amorites 2
19 Gilead, the country . . and of Og king of Bashan. 2
24 over all the kings west of the Euphra'tes; 2
27 officers supplied provisions for King Solomon 2
27 and for all who came to King Solomon's table, each 2
34 men came . . from all the kings of the earth, who 2
5: 1 Hiram king of Tyre sent his servants to Solomon 2
1 they had anointed him king in place of his father; 2
13 King Solomon raised a levy of forced labor 2
17 At the king's command, they quarried out 2
6: 2 The house which King Solomon built for the LORD 2
7:13 King Solomon sent and brought Hiram from Tyre. 2
14 He came to King Solomon, and did all his work. 2
40 Hiram finished . . that he did for King Solomon 2
45 vessels . . which Hiram made for King Solomon 2
46 In the plain of the Jordan the king cast them 2
51 all the work that King Solomon did on the house 2
8: 1 assembled . . before King Solomon in Jerusalem 2
2 all the men of Israel assembled to King Solomon 2
5 King Solomon and all the congregation of Israel 2
14 Then the king faced about, and blessed all 2
62 the king, and all Israel . . offered sacrifice 2
63 the king and all . . Israel dedicated the house 2
64 the king consecrated the middle of the court 2
66 they blessed the king, and went to their homes 2
9: 1 building . . and the king's house 2
10 Solomon had built . . and the king's house 2
11 Hiram king of Tyre had supplied Solomon 2
11 King Solomon gave to Hiram twenty cities 2
14 Hiram had sent to the king 120 talents of gold. 2
15 forced labor which King Solomon levied to build 2
16 Pharaoh king of Egypt had gone up and captured 2
26 King Solomon built a fleet of ships 2

28 and they brought it to King Solomon. 2
10: 3 there was nothing hidden from the king 2
6 she said to the king, "The report was true 2
9 he has made you king, that you may execute justice 2
10 she gave the king 120 talents of gold 2
10 which the queen of Sheba gave to King Solomon. 2
12 the king made of the almug wood supports 2
12 the king made . . supports . . for the king's house 2
13 King Solomon gave to the queen of Sheba 2
13 what was given her by the bounty of King Solomon. 2
15 which came . . from all the kings of Arabia 2
16 King Solomon made 200 large shields of beaten gold; 2
17 and the king put them in the House of the Forest 2
18 The king also made a great ivory throne 2
21 All King Solomon's drinking vessels were of gold 2
22 For the king had a fleet of ships of Tarshish 2
23 King Solomon excelled all the kings of the earth 2
23 King Solomon excelled all the kings of the earth 2
26 in the chariot cities and with the king 2
27 the king made silver as common . . as stone 2
28 the king's traders received them . . at a price. 2
29 so through the king's traders they were exported •
29 exported to all the kings of the Hittites 2
29 exported to all . . the kings of Syria. 2
11: 1 Now King Solomon loved many foreign women 2
18 They . . came to Egypt, to Pharaoh king of Egypt 2
23 fled from his master Hadade'zer king of Zobah. 2
26 Jerobo'am . . lifted up his hand against the king. 2
27 why he lifted up his hand against the king. 2
37 and you shall be king over Israel. 2
40 Jerobo'am . . fled . . to Shishak king of Egypt 2
12: 2 in Egypt, whither he had fled from King Solomon) 2
6 King Rehobo'am took counsel with the old men 2
12 and all the people came . . as the king said, "Come 2
13 the king answered the people harshly 2
15 So the king did not hearken to the people; 2
16 all Israel saw that the king did not hearken 2
16 the people answered the king, "What portion 2
18 Then King Rehobo'am sent Ador'am 2
18 King Rehobo'am made haste to mount his chariot 2
23 Say to Rehobo'am the son of Solomon, king of Judah 2
27 turn . . to their lord, to Rehobo'am king of Judah 2
27 kill me and return to Rehobo'am king of Judah. 2
28 the king took counsel, and made two calves 2
13: 4 when the king heard the saying of the man of God 2
6 the king said to the man of God, "Entreat now 2
6 the king's hand was restored to him 2
7 the king said to the man of God, "Come home with me 2
8 the man of God said to the king 2
11 the words also which he had spoken to the king 2
14: 2 said of me that I should be king over this people. 2
14 LORD will raise up for himself a king over Israel 2
19 Book of the Chronicles of the Kings of Israel. 2
25 In the fifth year of King Rehobo'am 2
25 Shishak king of Egypt came up against Jerusalem; 2
26 he took away . . the treasures of the king's house; 2
27 King Rehobo'am made . . shields of bronze 2
27 the guard, who kept the door of the king's house. 2
28 as the king went into the house of the LORD 2
29 the Book of the Chronicles of the Kings of Judah? 2
15: 1 in the . . year of King Jerobo'am the son of Nebat 2
7 the Book of the Chronicles of the Kings of Judah? 2
9 In the twentieth year of Jerobo'am king of Israel 2
16 was war between Asa and Ba'asha king of Israel 2
17 Ba'asha king of Israel went up against Judah 2
17 no one to go out or come in to Asa king of Judah. 2
18 left in . . and the treasures of the king's house 2
18 and King Asa sent them to Ben-ha'dad 2
18 Tabrim'mon, the son of He'zion, king of Syria 2
19 go, break your league with Ba'asha king of Israel 2
20 Ben-ha'dad hearkened to King Asa 2
22 King Asa made a proclamation to all Judah 2
22 King Asa built Geba of Benjamin and Mizpah. 2
23 the Book of the Chronicles of the Kings of Judah? 2
25 to reign . . in the second year of Asa king of Judah; 2
28 killed him in the third year of Asa king of Judah 2
29 as soon as he was king, he killed all the house 1
31 the Book of the Chronicles of the Kings of Israel? 2
32 war between Asa and Ba'asha king of Israel 2
33 In the third year of Asa king of Judah 2
16: 5 the Book of the Chronicles of the Kings of Israel? 2
8 In the 26th year of Asa king of Judah 2
10 in the 27th year of Asa king of Judah 2
14 the Book of the Chronicles of the Kings of Israel? 2
15 In the 27th year of Asa king of Judah 2
16 Zimri has conspired, and he has killed the king"; 2
18 he went into the citadel of the king's house 2
18 Zimri . . burned the king's house over him 2
20 the Book of the Chronicles of the Kings of Israel? 2
23 In the 31st year of Asa king of Judah 2
27 the Book of the Chronicles of the Kings of Israel? 2
29 In the 38th year of Asa king of Judah 2
31 the daughter of Ethba'al king of the Sido'nians 2
33 than all the kings of Israel who were before him. 2
19:15 you shall anoint Haz'ael to be king over Syria; 2
16 Jehu . . you shall anoint to be king over Israel; 2
20: 1 Ben-ha'dad the king of Syria gathered . . his army 2
1 32 kings were with him, and horses and chariots; 2
2 he sent messengers . . to Ahab king of Israel 2
4 the king of Israel answered, "As you say, my lord 2
4 As you say, my lord, O king, I am yours 2
7 the king of Israel called all the elders 2
9 Tell my lord the king, 'All that you first demanded 2
11 the king of Israel answered, "Tell him 2
12 as he was drinking with the kings in the booths 2
13 behold, a prophet came near to Ahab king of Israel 2
16 they went out . . he and the 32 kings who helped him. 2
20 Ben-ha'dad king of Syria escaped on a horse 2
21 the king of Israel went out, and captured 2
22 the prophet came near to the king of Israel 2
22 the king of Syria will come up against you. 2
23 the servants of the king of Syria said to him 2
24 do this: remove the kings, each from his post 2
28 a man of God came . . and said to the king of Israel 2
31 the kings of the house of Israel are merciful 2
31 kings of the house of Israel are merciful kings; 2
31 put sackcloth . . and go out to the king of Israel; 2
32 and went to the king of Israel and said 2
38 the prophet departed, and waited for the king 2
39 as the king passed, he cried to the king and said 2
39 as the king passed, he cried to the king and said 2
40 The king of Israel said to him 2
41 the king of Israel recognized him 2
43 the king of Israel went to his house resentful 2
21: 1 beside the palace of Ahab king of Sama'ria. 2
10 saying, 'You have cursed God and the king.' 2
13 saying, "Naboth cursed God and the king. 2
18 go . . to meet Ahab king of Israel, who is in Sama'ria; 2
22: 2 Jehosh'aphat the king of Judah came down 2
2 Jehosh'aphat . . came down to the king of Israel. 2
3 the king of Israel said to his servants 2
3 do not take it out of the hand of the king of Syria? 2
4 Jehosh'aphat said to the king of Israel, "I am as you 2
5 Jehosh'aphat said to the king of Israel 2
6 the king of Israel gathered the prophets 2
6 the Lord will give it into the hand of the king. 2
8 the king of Israel said to Jehosh'aphat, "There is 2
8 Jehosh'aphat said, "Let not the king say so. 2
9 the king of Israel summoned an officer and said 2
10 Now the king of Israel and Jehosh'aphat the king 2
10 and Jehosh'aphat the king of Judah were sitting 2
12 the LORD will give it into the hand of the king. 2
13 the words . . are favorable to the king; 2
15 when he had come to the king, the king said to him 2
15 when he had come to the king, the king said to him 2
15 the LORD will give it into the hand of the king. 2
16 the king said to him, "How many times shall I adjure 2
18 the king of Israel said to Jehosh'aphat 2
26 the king of Israel said, "Seize Micai'ah 2
26 take him back . . to Jo'ash the king's son; 2
27 'Thus says the king, "Put this fellow in prison 2
29 the king of Israel and Jehosh'aphat . . went up 2
29 king of Israel and Jehosh'aphat the king of Judah 2
30 the king of Israel said to Jehosh'aphat 2
30 the king of Israel disguised himself and went 2
31 the king of Syria had commanded the . . captains 2
31 small nor great, but only with the king of Israel. 2
32 they said, "It is surely the king of Israel. 2
33 captains . . saw that it was not the king of Israel 2
34 drew his bow . . and struck the king of Israel 2
35 the king was propped up in his chariot 2
37 So the king died, and was brought to Sama'ria; 2
37 and they buried the king in Sama'ria. 2
39 the Book of the Chronicles of the Kings of Israel? 2
41 in the fourth year of Ahab king of Israel. 2
44 made peace with the king of Israel. 2
45 the Book of the Chronicles of the Kings of Judah? 2
47 There was no king in Edom; a deputy was king. 2
47 There was no king in Edom; a deputy was king. 2
51 seventeenth year of Jehosh'aphat king of Judah 2
2Kg 1: 3 to meet the messengers of the king of Sama'ria 2
5 The messengers returned to the king •
6 Go back to the king who sent you, and say to him 2
9 the king sent to him a captain of 50 men •
9 O man of God, the king says, 'Come down.' 2
11 the king sent to him another captain of 50 men •
11 this is the king's order, 'Come down quickly!' 2
13 Again the king sent the captain of a third 50 •
15 So he arose and went down with him to the king 2
17 Jeho'ram the son of Jehosh'aphat, king of Judah 2
18 the Book of the Chronicles of the Kings of Israel? 2
3: 1 eighteenth year of Jehosh'aphat king of Judah 2
4 Now Mesha king of Moab was a sheep breeder; 2
4 he had to deliver annually to the king of Israel 2
5 the king of Moab rebelled against . . Israel. 2
5 Moab rebelled against the king of Israel. 2
6 King Jeho'ram marched out of Sama'ria at that time 2
7 went and sent word to Jehosh'aphat king of Judah 2
7 The king of Moab has rebelled against me; 2
9 So the king of Israel went with the king of Judah 2
9 So the king of Israel went with the king of Judah 2
9 king of Israel went with . . and the king of Edom. 2
10 Then the king of Israel said, "Alas! 2
10 The LORD has called these three kings to give 2
11 one of the king of Israel's servants answered 2
12 the king of Israel and Jehosh'aphat . . went down 2
12 and Jehosh'aphat and the king of Edom went down 2
13 Eli'sha said to the king of Israel 2
13 But the king of Israel said to him, "No; it is the LORD 2
13 No; it is the LORD who has called these three kings 2
14 I have regard for Jehosh'aphat the king of Judah 2
21 the Moabites heard that the kings had come up 2
23 the kings have surely fought together 2
26 When the king of Moab saw . . he took with him 2
26 to break through, opposite the king of Edom; 2
4:13 a word spoken . . to the king or to the commander 2
5: 1 Na'aman, commander of the army of the king of Syria 2
5 the king of Syria said, "Go now 2
5 I will send a letter to the king of Israel. 2
6 he brought the letter to the king of Israel 2
7 when the king of Israel read the letter 2
8 that the king of Israel had rent his clothes 2
8 when Eli'sha . . he sent to the king, saying, "Why 2
6: 8 the King of Syria was warring against Israel 2
9 the man of God sent word to the king of Israel 2
10 the king of Israel sent to the place 2
11 the mind of the king of Syria was . . troubled 2
11 show me who of us is for the king of Israel? 2
12 None, my lord, O king; but Eli'sha the prophet 2
12 Eli'sha . . tells the king of Israel the words 2
21 When the king of Israel saw them he said to Eli'sha 2
24 Ben-ha'dad king of Syria mustered his entire army 2
26 as the king of Israel was passing by upon the wall 2
26 cried out to him, saying, "Help, my lord, O king! 2
28 And the king asked her, "What is your trouble? 2
30 When the king heard . . he rent his clothes 2
32 the king had dispatched a man from his presence; •
33 the king came down to him and said, "This trouble is •
7: 2 the captain on whose hand the king leaned said 2
6 the king of Israel has hired against us the kings 2
6 Israel has hired . . the kings of the Hittites 2
6 Hittites and the kings of Egypt to come upon us. 2
9 come, let us go and tell the king's household. 2
11 and it was told within the king's household. 2
12 the king rose in the night, and said 2
14 the king sent them after the army of the Syrians 2
15 And the messengers returned, and told the king. 2
17 Now the king had appointed the captain 2
17 man of God . . said when the king came down to him. 2
18 when the man of God had said to the king 2
8: 3 she went forth to appeal to the king for her house 2
4 Now the king was talking with Geha'zi the servant 2
5 he was telling the king how Eli'sha had restored 2
5 the woman . . appealed to the king for her house 2
5 And Geha'zi said, "My lord, O king, here is the woman 2
6 And when the king asked the woman, she told him. 2
6 So the king appointed an official for her, saying 2
7 Ben-ha'dad the king of Syria was sick; 2
8 the king said to Haz'ael, "Take a present with you 2
9 Your son Ben-ha'dad king of Syria has sent me to you 2
13 LORD has shown me . . you are to be king over Syria. 2
16 of Joram the son of Ahab, king of Israel 2
16 Jeho'ram the son of Jehosh'aphat, king of Judah 2
18 he walked in the way of the kings of Israel 2
23 the Book of the Chronicles of the Kings of Judah? 2
25 year of Joram the son of Ahab, king of Israel 2
25 Ahazi'ah the son of Jeho'ram, king of Judah 2
26 she was a granddaughter of Omri king of Israel. 2
28 to make war against Haz'ael king of Syria 2
29 King Joram returned to be healed in Jezreel 2
29 when he fought against Haz'ael king of Syria. 2
29 Ahazi'ah the son of Jeho'ram king of Judah went 2
9: 3 'Thus says the LORD, I anoint you king over Israel.' 2
6 I anoint you king over the people of the LORD 2
12 Thus says the LORD, I anoint you king over Israel.' 2
13 blew the trumpet, and proclaimed, "Jehu is king. 1
14 been on guard . . against Haz'ael king of Syria; 2
15 King Joram had returned to be healed in Jezreel 2
15 when he fought with Haz'ael king of Syria.) 2
16 Ahazi'ah king of Judah had come . . to visit Joram. 2
18 and said, "Thus says the king, 'Is it peace?' 2
19 and said, "Thus the king has said, 'Is it peace?' 2
21 Joram king of Israel and Ahazi'ah . . set out 2
21 Then Joram . . and Ahazi'ah king of Judah set out 2
27 When Ahazi'ah the king of Judah saw this, he fled 2
34 and bury her; for she is a king's daughter. 2
10: 4 the two kings could not stand before him; 2
6 the king's sons . . were with the great men 2
7 they took the king's sons, and slew them 2
8 They have brought the heads of the king's sons 2
13 Jehu met the kinsmen of Ahazi'ah king of Judah 2
34 the Book of the Chronicles of the Kings of Israel? 2
11: 2 Jehosh'eba, the daughter of King Joram, sister 2
2 and stole him away from among the king's sons 2
4 and he showed them the king's son. 2
5 who come off . . and guard the king's house 2
8 shall surround the king 2
8 Be with the king when he goes out and when he comes 2
10 the spears and shields that had been King David's 2
12 he brought out the king's son, and put the crown 2
12 they clapped . . and said, "Long live the king! 2
14 there was the king standing by the pillar 2
14 the captains and the trumpeters beside the king 2
16 through the horses' entrance to the king's house 2
17 between the LORD and the king and people 2
17 and also between the king and the people. 2
19 brought the king down from the house of the LORD 2

19 marching through the gate . . to the king's house. 2
19 And he took his seat on the throne of the kings. 2
20 Athali'ah had been slain . . at the king's house. 2
12: 6 But by the 23rd year of King Jeho'ash 2
7 King Jeho'ash summoned Jehoi'ada . . and the other 2
10 the king's secretary and the high priest came up 2
17 Haz'ael king of Syria went up . . against Gath 2
18 Jeho'ash king of Judah took all the votive gifts 2
18 and Jeho'ram and Ahazi'ah . . the kings of Judah 2
18 in the treasuries of . . and of the king's house 2
18 took . . and sent these to Haz'ael king of Syria. 2
19 the Book of the Chronicles of the Kings of Judah? 2
13: 1 year of Jo'ash the son of Ahazi'ah, king of Judah 2
3 gave them . . into the hand of Haz'ael king of Syria 2
4 he saw . . how the king of Syria oppressed them. 2
7 the king of Syria had destroyed them 2
8 the Book of the Chronicles of the Kings of Israel? 2
10 In the 37th year of Jo'ash king of Judah 2
12 he fought against Amazi'ah king of Judah 2
12 the Book of the Chronicles of the Kings of Israel? 2
13 Jo'ash was buried . . with the kings of Israel. 2
14 Jo'ash king of Israel went down to him, and wept 2
16 Then he said to the king of Israel, "Draw the bow"; 2
16 And Eli'sha laid his hands upon the king's hands. 2
18 he said to the king of Israel, "Strike the ground 2
22 Now Haz'ael king of Syria oppressed Israel 2
24 Haz'ael king of Syria died . . his son became king 2
14: 1 In the second year of Jo'ash . . king of Israel 2
1 Amazi'ah . . king of Judah, began to reign. 2
5 he killed . . who had slain the king his father. 2
8 sent messengers to Jeho'ash . . king of Israel 2
9 Jeho'ash king of Israel sent word to Amazi'ah 2
9 Jeho'ash . . sent word to Amazi'ah king of Judah 2
11 Jeho'ash king of Israel went up, and he and Amazi'ah 2
11 he and Amazi'ah king of Judah faced one another 2
13 Jeho'ash king of Israel captured Amazi'ah 2
13 Jeho'ash . . captured Amazi'ah king of Judah 2
14 and in the treasuries of the king's house 2
15 and how he fought with Amazi'ah king of Judah 2
15 the Book of the Chronicles of the Kings of Israel? 2
16 was buried in Sama'ria with the kings of Israel; 2
17 Amazi'ah the son of Jo'ash, king of Judah, lived 2
17 death of Jeho'ash son of Jeho'ahaz, king of Israel. 2
18 the Book of the Chronicles of the Kings of Judah? 2
22 after the king slept with his fathers. 2
23 fifteenth year of Amazi'ah . . king of Judah 2
23 Jerobo'am the son of Jo'ash, king of Israel, began 2
28 the Book of the Chronicles of the Kings of Israel? 2
29 slept with his fathers, the kings of Israel 2
15: 1 In the 27th year of Jerobo'am king of Israel 2
1 Azari'ah the son of Amazi'ah, king of Judah, began 2
5 the LORD smote the king, so that he was a leper 2
5 And Jotham the king's son was over the household 2
6 the Book of the Chronicles of the Kings of Judah? 2
8 In the 38th year of Azari'ah king of Judah 2
11 Book of the Chronicles of the Kings of Israel. 2
13 in the 39th year of Uzzi'ah king of Judah 2
15 Book of the Chronicles of the Kings of Israel. 2
17 In the 39th year of Azari'ah the king of Judah 2
19 Pul the king of Assyria came against the land; 2
20 exacted . . to give to the king of Assyria. 2
20 the king of Assyria turned back, and did not stay 2
21 the Book of the Chronicles of the Kings of Israel? 2
23 In the 50th year of Azari'ah king of Judah 2
25 slew him . . in the citadel of the king's house; 2
26 Book of the Chronicles of the Kings of Israel. 2
27 In the 52nd year of Azari'ah king of Judah 2
29 In the days of Pekah king of Israel 2
29 Tig'lath-pile'ser king of Assyria came 2
31 Book of the Chronicles of the Kings of Israel. 2
32 In the second year of Pekah . . king of Israel 2
32 Jotham the son of Uzzi'ah, king of Judah, began 2
36 the Book of the Chronicles of the Kings of Judah? 2
37 send Rezin the king of Syria . . against Judah. 2
16: 1 Ahaz the son of Jotham, king of Judah, began 2
3 but he walked in the way of the kings of Israel. 2
5 Rezin king of Syria . . came up to wage war 2
5 Pekah the son of Remali'ah, king of Israel, came up 2
6 the king of Edom recovered Elath for Edom 2
7 Ahaz sent . . to Tig'lath-pile'ser king of Assyria 2
7 and rescue me from the hand of the king of Syria 2
7 rescue me . . from the hand of the king of Israel 2
8 found . . and in the treasures of the king's house 2
8 and sent a present to the king of Assyria. 2
9 And the king of Assyria hearkened to him; 2
9 the king of Assyria marched up against Damascus 2
10 When King Ahaz went to Damascus to meet 2
10 to meet Tig'lath-pile'ser king of Assyria 2
10 King Ahaz sent to Uri'ah . . a model of the altar 2
11 in accordance with all that King Ahaz had sent 2
11 Uri'ah . . made it, before King Ahaz arrived 2
12 And when the king came from Damascus 2
12 when the king came . . the king viewed the altar. 2
12 the king drew near to the altar, and went up on it 2
15 King Ahaz commanded Uri'ah the priest, saying 2
15 cereal offering, and the king's burnt offering, and his 2
16 Uri'ah the priest did . . as King Ahaz commanded. 2
17 King Ahaz cut off the frames of the stands 2
18 and the outer entrance for the king he removed 2
18 he removed . . because of the king of Assyria. 2
19 the Book of the Chronicles of the Kings of Judah? 2
17: 1 In the twelfth year of Ahaz king of Judah 2
2 not as the kings of Israel who were before him. 2
3 Against him came up Shalmane'ser king of Assyria; 2
4 the king of Assyria found treachery in Hoshe'a; 2
4 he had sent messengers to So, king of Egypt 2
4 and offered no tribute to the king of Assyria 2
4 the king of Assyria shut him up, and bound him 2
5 Then the king of Assyria invaded all the land 2
6 the king of Assyria captured Sama'ria 2
7 from under the hand of Pharaoh king of Egypt 2
8 which the kings of Israel had introduced. 2
24 the king of Assyria brought people from Babylon 2
26 So the king of Assyria was told 2
27 Then the king of Assyria commanded, "Send 2
18: 1 third year of Hoshe'a son of Elah, king of Israel 2
1 Hezeki'ah the son of Ahaz, king of Judah, began 2
5 was none like him among all the kings of Judah 2
7 He rebelled against the king of Assyria 2
9 In the fourth year of King Hezeki'ah 2
9 seventh year of Hoshe'a son of Elah, king of Israel 2
9 Shalmane'ser king of Assyria came up against 2
10 which was the ninth year of Hoshe'a king of Israel 2
11 The king of Assyria carried the Israelites away 2
13 In the fourteenth year of King Hezeki'ah 2
13 Sennach'erib king of Assyria came up against all 2
14 Hezeki'ah king of Judah sent to . . at Lachish 2
14 Hezeki'ah . . sent to the king of Assyria 2
14 And the king of Assyria required of Hezeki'ah 2
14 Assyria required of Hezeki'ah king of Judah 2
15 and in the treasuries of the king's house. 2
16 which Hezeki'ah king of Judah had overlaid 2
16 and gave it to the king of Assyria. 2
17 the king of Assyria sent the Tartan, the Rab'saris 2
17 Assyria sent . . from Lachish to King Hezeki'ah 2
18 when they called for the king, there came out 2
19 Thus says the great king, the king of Assyria 2
19 Thus says the great king, the king of Assyria 2
21 Such is Pharaoh king of Egypt to all who rely 2
23 make a wager with my master the king of Assyria 2
28 the word of the great king, the king of Assyria! 2
28 the word of the great king, the king of Assyria! 2
29 Thus says the king: 'Do not let Hezeki'ah deceive 2
30 not be given into the hand of the king of Assyria.' 2
31 thus says the king of Assyria: 'Make your peace 2
33 his land out of the hand of the king of Assyria? 2
36 for the king's command was, "Do not answer 2
19: 1 When King Hezeki'ah heard it, he rent his clothes 2
4 his master the king of Assyria has sent to mock 2
5 the servants of King Hezeki'ah came to Isaiah 2
6 the servants of the king of Assyria have reviled 2
8 found the king of Assyria fighting against 2
8 for he heard that the king had left Lachish. *
9 when the king heard concerning Tirha'kah king *
9 heard concerning Tirha'kah king of Ethiopia 2
10 Thus shall you speak to Hezeki'ah king of Judah 2
10 not be given into the hand of the king of Assyria. 2
11 what the kings of Assyria have done to all lands 2
13 Where is the king of Hamath, the king of Arpad 2
13 Where is the king of Hamath, the king of Arpad 2
13 king of Arpad, the king of the city of Sepharva'im 2
13 Sepharva'im, the king of Hena, or the king of Ivvah?' *
13 Sepharva'im, the king of Hena, or the king of Ivvah?' *
17 the kings of Assyria have laid waste the nations 2
20 prayer to me about Sennach'erib king of Assyria 2
32 says the LORD concerning the king of Assyria 2
36 Sennach'erib king of Assyria departed, and went 2
20: 6 deliver . . out of the hand of the king of Assyria 2
12 Mero'dach-bal'adan the son of . . king of Babylon 2
14 Isaiah . . came to King Hezeki'ah, and said to him 2
18 be eunuchs in the palace of the king of Babylon. 2
20 the Book of the Chronicles of the Kings of Judah? 2
21: 3 made an Ashe'rah, as Ahab king of Israel had done 2
11 Manas'seh king of Judah has committed these 2
17 the Book of the Chronicles of the Kings of Judah? 2
23 the servants . . and killed the king in his house. 2
24 all those who had conspired against King Amon 2
25 the Book of the Chronicles of the Kings of Judah? 2
22: 3 In the eighteenth year of King Josi'ah 2
3 the king sent Shaphan . . to the house of the LORD 2
9 Shaphan . . came to the king, and reported 2
9 And Shaphan . . and reported to the king 2
10 Then Shaphan the secretary told the king 2
10 And Shaphan read it before the king. 2
11 the king heard the words of the book of the law 2
12 the king commanded Hilki'ah . . and Ahi'kam 2
12 and Shaphan . . and Asai'ah the king's servant 2
16 of the book which the king of Judah has read. 2
18 But as to the king of Judah, who sent you to inquire 2
20 And they brought back word to the king. 2
23: 1 the king sent, and all . . were gathered to him. 2
2 And the king went up to the house of the LORD 2
3 the king stood by the pillar and made a covenant 2
4 And the king commanded Hilki'ah the high priest 2
5 priests whom the kings of Judah had ordained 2
11 that the kings of Judah had dedicated to the sun 2
12 altars . . which the kings of Judah had made 2
13 And the king defiled the high places 2
13 which Solomon the king of Israel had built 2
19 the shrines . . which kings of Israel had made 2
21 And the king commanded . . "Keep the passover 2
22 or during all the days of the kings of Israel 2
22 of the kings of Israel or of the kings of Judah; 2
23 but in the eighteenth year of King Josi'ah 2
25 there was no king like him, who turned to the LORD 2
28 the Book of the Chronicles of the Kings of Judah? 2
29 Neco king of Egypt went up to the king of Assyria 2
29 Pharaoh Neco . . went up to the king of Assyria 2
29 King Josi'ah went to meet him; and Pharaoh Neco 2
24: 1 Nebuchadnez'zar king of Babylon came up 2
5 the Book of the Chronicles of the Kings of Judah? 2
7 king of Egypt did not come again out of his land 2
7 the king of Babylon had taken all that belonged 2
7 had taken all that belonged to the king of Egypt 2
10 the servants of Nebuchadnez'zar king of Babylon 2
11 Nebuchadnez'zar king of Babylon came to the city 2
12 Jehoi'achin the king of Judah gave himself up 2
12 the king . . gave himself up to the king of Babylon 2
12 The king of Babylon took him prisoner 2
13 and the treasures of the king's house 2
13 vessels . . which Solomon king of Israel had made 2
15 he carried away . . the king's mother 2
15 the king's mother, the king's wives, his officials 2
16 the king of Babylon brought captive to Babylon 2
17 the king of Babylon made Mattani'ah . . king 2
20 Zedeki'ah rebelled against the king of Babylon. 2
25: 1 Nebuchadnez'zar king of Babylon came with all 2
2 till the eleventh year of King Zedeki'ah. 2
4 the king with all the men of war fled by night 6
4 by the way of the gate . . by the king's garden 2
5 But the army of the Chalde'ans pursued the king 2
6 Then they captured the king, and brought him up 2
6 and brought him up to the king of Babylon 2
8 was the nineteenth year of King Nebuchadnez'zar 2
8 year of . . Nebuchadnez'zar, king of Babylon 2
8 Nebu'zarad'an . . a servant of the king of Babylon 2
9 the king's house and all the houses of Jerusalem; 2
11 who had deserted to the king of Babylon 2
19 took . . and five men of the king's council 2
20 took them, and brought them to the king of Babylon 2
21 the king of Babylon smote . . and put them to death 2
22 whom Nebuchadnez'zar king of Babylon had left 2
23 the king of Babylon had appointed Gedali'ah 2
24 dwell in the land, and serve the king of Babylon 2
27 year of the exile of Jehoi'achin king of Judah 2
27 Evil-mero'dach king of Babylon . . freed 2
27 freed Jehoi'achin king of Judah from prison; 2
28 and gave him a seat above the seats of the kings 2
29 he dined regularly at the king's table; *
30 a regular allowance was given him by the king 2
1Ch 1:43 These are the kings who reigned in the land of Edom 2
43 the land of Edom before any king reigned over 2
3: 2 Ma'acah, the daughter of Talmai, king of Geshur; 2
4:23 they dwelt there with the king for his work. 2
41 in the days of Hezeki'ah, king of Judah 2
5: 6 Til'gath-pilne'ser king of Assyria 2
17 enrolled . . in the days of Jotham king of Judah 2
17 in the days of Jerobo'am king of Israel. 2
26 stirred up the spirit of Pul king of Assyria 2
26 the spirit of Til'gath-pilne'ser king of Assyria 2
9: 1 written in the Book of the Kings of Israel. 2
18 stationed hitherto in the king's gate 2
11: 2 In times past, even when Saul was king, it was you 2
3 the elders of Israel came to the king at Hebron; 2
3 they anointed David king over Israel 2
14: 1 Hiram king of Tyre sent messengers to David 2
2 the LORD had established him king over Israel 2
8 David had been anointed king over all Israel 2
15:29 Michal . . saw King David dancing 2
16:21 he rebuked kings on their account 2
17:16 Then King David went in and sat before the LORD 2
18: 3 David also defeated Hadade'zer king of Zobah 2
5 Syrians . . came to help Hadade'zer king of Zobah 2
9 To'u king of Hamath heard that David had defeated 2
9 the whole army of Hadade'zer, king of Zobah 2
10 he sent his son Hador'am to King David, to greet him 2
11 these also King David dedicated to the LORD 2
17 the chief officials in the service of the king. 2
19: 1 after this Nahash the king of the Ammonites died 2
5 the king said, "Remain at Jericho 2
7 chariots and the king of Ma'acah with his army 2
9 the kings who had come were by themselves 2
20: 1 spring . . the time when kings go forth to battle 2
2 David took the crown of their king from his head; 2
21: 3 my lord the king, all of them my lord's servants? 2
4 the king's word prevailed against Jo'ab. 2
6 for the king's command was abhorrent to Jo'ab. 2
23 Take it; and let my lord the king do what seems good 2
24 King David said to Ornan, "No, but I will buy it 2
24: 6 in the presence of the king, and the princes 2
31 in the presence of King David, Zadok, Ahim'elech 2
25: 2 who prophesied under the direction of the king. 2
5 All these were the sons of Heman the king's seer 2
6 and Heman were under the order of the king. 2
26:26 the dedicated gifts which David the king 2
30 of the LORD and for the service of the king. 2
32 King David appointed him and his brethren 2

32 oversight . . for the affairs of the king. 2
27: 1 officers who served the king in all matters 2
24 was not entered in the chronicles of King David. 2
25 Over the king's treasuries was Az'maveth the son 2
31 these were stewards of King David's property. 2
32 and Jehi'el . . attended the king's sons. 2
33 Ahith'ophel was the king's counselor 2
33 and Hushai the Archite was the king's friend. 2
34 Jo'ab was commander of the king's army. 2
28: 1 officers of the divisions that served the king 2
1 the property and cattle of the king and his sons 2
2 Then King David rose to his feet and said 2
4 chose me . . to be king over Israel for ever; 2
29: 1 David the king said to all the assembly 2
6 and the officers over the king's work. 2
9 David the king also rejoiced greatly. 2
20 the LORD, and did obeisance to the king. 2
23 Then Solomon sat on the throne of the LORD as king 2
24 the mighty men, and also all the sons of King David 2
24 pledged their allegiance to King Solomon. 2
25 such royal majesty as had not been on any king 2
29 acts of King David, from first to last, are written 2
2Ch 1:12 such as none of the kings had who were before you 2
14 stationed in . . and with the king in Jerusalem. 2
15 king made silver and gold as common . . as stone 2
16 and the king's traders received them from Ku'e 2
17 exported to all the kings of the Hittites 2
17 exported to . . and the kings of Syria. 2
2: 3 Solomon sent word to Huram the king of Tyre 2
11 Then Huram the king of Tyre answered in a letter 2
11 LORD loves his people he has made you king 2
12 who has given King David a wise son 2
4:11 finished the work that he did for King Solomon 2
16 Huram-abi made . . for King Solomon for the house 2
17 In the plain of the Jordan the king cast them 2
5: 3 all the men of Israel assembled before the king 2
6 King Solomon and all the congregation of Israel 2
6: 3 king faced about, and blessed all the assembly 2
7: 4 the king and all the people offered sacrifice 2
5 King Solomon offered as a sacrifice 2
5 So the king and all the people dedicated 2
6 instruments . . which King David had made 2
11 Solomon finished . . and the king's house; 2
8:10 these were the chief officers of King Solomon 2
11 not live in the house of David king of Israel 2
15 not turn aside from what the king had commanded 2
18 talents of gold and brought it to King Solomon. 2
9: 5 she said to the king, "The report was true 2
8 LORD . . who has . . set you on his throne as king 2
8 he has made you king over them, that you may 2
9 Then she gave the king . . talents of gold 2
9 which the queen of Sheba gave to King Solomon. 2
11 king made of the algum wood steps for the house 2
11 algum wood steps for . . the king's house 2
12 King Solomon gave to the queen of Sheba 2
12 besides what she had brought to the king. 2
14 kings of Arabia and the governors of the land 2
15 King Solomon made 200 large shields of . . gold; 2
16 king put them in the House . . of Lebanon. 2
17 The king also made a great ivory throne 2
20 All King Solomon's drinking vessels were of gold 2
21 king's ships went to Tarshish with the servants 2
22 King Solomon excelled all the kings of the earth 2
22 King Solomon excelled all the kings of the earth 2
23 all the kings of the earth sought . . Solomon 2
25 stationed . . with the king in Jerusalem. 2
26 he ruled over all the kings from the Euphra'tes 2
27 king made silver as common in Jerusalem as stone 2
10: 2 in Egypt, whither he had fled from King Solomon) 2
6 Then King Rehobo'am took counsel with the old men 2
12 as the king said, "Come to me again the third day. 2
13 the king answered them harshly 2
14 King Rehobo'am spoke to them *
15 the king did not hearken to the people; 2
16 Israel saw that the king did not hearken to them 2
16 the people answered the king 2
18 Then King Rehobo'am send Hador'am 2
18 King Rehobo'am made haste to mount his chariot 2
11: 3 Say to Rehobo'am the son of Solomon king of Judah 2
12: 2 In the fifth year of King Rehobo'am 2
2 Shishak king of Egypt came up against Jerusalem 2
6 the princes . . and the king humbled themselves 2
9 Shishak king of Egypt came up against Jerusalem; 2
9 he took away . . the treasures of the king's house; 2
10 King Rehobo'am made in their stead shields 2
10 who kept the door of the king's house. 2
11 often as the king went into the house of the LORD 2
13 King Rehobo'am established himself 2
13: 1 In the eighteenth year of King Jerobo'am 2
15:16 King Asa removed from being queen mother 2
16: 1 Ba'asha king of Israel went up against Judah 2
1 no one to go out or come in to Asa king of Judah. 2
2 from the treasures of . . the king's house 2
2 sent them to Ben-ha'dad king of Syria 2
3 go, break your league with Ba'asha king of Israel 2
4 Ben-ha'dad hearkened to King Asa 2
6 Then King Asa took all Judah 2
7 Hana'ni the seer came to Asa king of Judah 2
7 Because you relied on the king of Syria 2

7 the army of the king of Syria has escaped you. 2
11 the Book of the Kings of Judah and Israel. 2
17:19 These were in the service of the king 2
19 king had placed in the fortified cities 2
18: 3 Ahab king of Israel said to Jehosh'aphat 2
3 Ahab . . said to Jehosh'aphat king of Judah 2
4 Jehosh'aphat said to the king of Israel 2
5 king of Israel gathered the prophets together 2
5 God will give it into the hand of the king. 2
7 the king of Israel said to Jehosh'aphat 2
7 Jehosh'aphat said, "Let not the king say so. 2
8 the king of Israel summoned an officer and said 2
9 king of Israel and Jehosh'aphat the king of Judah 2
9 king of Israel and Jehosh'aphat the king of Judah 2
11 LORD will give it into the hand of the king. 2
12 words of the prophets . . favorable to the king; 2
14 when he had come to the king, the king said to him 2
14 when he had come to the king, the king said to him 2
15 king said to him, "How many times shall I adjure you 2
17 the king of Israel said to Jehosh'aphat 2
19 LORD said, 'Who will entice Ahab the king of Israel 2
25 the king of Israel said, "Seize Micai'ah 2
25 take him back . . to Jo'ash the king's son; 2
26 say, 'Thus says the king, Put this fellow in prison 2
28 king of Israel and Jehosh'aphat the king of Judah 2
28 king of Israel and Jehosh'aphat the king of Judah 2
29 the king of Israel said to Jehosh'aphat 2
29 king of Israel disguised himself; 2
30 Now the king of Syria had commanded the captains 2
30 Fight . . only with the king of Israel. 2
31 It is the king of Israel. 2
32 saw that it was not the king of Israel 2
33 struck the king of Israel between 2
34 king of Israel propped himself up in his chariot 2
19: 1 Jehosh'aphat the king of Judah returned 2
2 Jehu . . said to King Jehosh'aphat 2
11 Zebedi'ah . . in all the king's matters; 2
20:15 Hearken, all Judah . . and King Jehosh'aphat 2
34 are recorded in the Book of the Kings of Israel. 2
35 Jehosh'aphat king of Judah joined with Ahazi'ah 2
35 Ahazi'ah king of Israel, who did wickedly. 2
21: 2 sons of Jehosh'aphat king of Judah. 2
5 Jeho'ram was 32 . . when he became king 1
6 he walked in the way of the kings of Israel 2
12 not walked . . in the ways of Asa king of Judah 2
13 have walked in the way of the kings of Israel 2
17 possessions . . belonged to the king's house 2
20 but not in the tombs of the kings. 2
22: 1 the son of Jeho'ram king of Judah reigned. 2
5 went with Jeho'ram the son of Ahab king of Israel 2
5 to make war against Haz'ael king of Syria 2
6 when he fought against Haz'ael king of Syria. 2
6 Ahazi'ah the son of Jeho'ram king of Judah 2
11 Jeho-shab'e-ath, the daughter of the king 2
11 stole him away from among the king's sons 2
11 Jeho-shab'e-ath, the daughter of King Jeho'ram 2
23: 3 all the assembly made a covenant with the king 2
3 Behold, the king's son! Let him reign 2
5 one third shall be at the king's house 2
7 The Levites shall surround the king 2
7 Be with the king when he comes 2
9 spears and . . shields that had been King David's 2
10 he set all the people as a guard for the king 2
11 Then he brought out the king's son 2
11 anointed him, and they said, "Long live the king. 2
12 the people running and praising the king 2
13 there was the king standing by his pillar 2
13 captains and the trumpeters beside the king 2
15 the entrance of the horse gate of the king's house 2
16 a covenant between himself and . . the king 2
20 brought the king down from the house of the LORD 2
20 through the upper gate to the king's house. 2
20 And they set the king upon the royal throne 2
24: 6 king summoned Jehoi'ada the chief, and said to him 2
8 the king commanded, and they made a chest 2
11 chest was brought to the king's officers 2
11 king's secretary . . would come and empty 2
12 king and Jehoi'ada gave it to those who had charge 2
14 brought the rest of the money before the king 2
16 buried him in the city of David among the kings 2
17 princes of Judah . . did obeisance to the king; 2
17 then the king hearkened to them. 2
21 by command of the king they stoned him 2
22 Jo'ash the king did not remember the kindness 2
23 sent all their spoil to the king of Damascus. 2
25 they did not bury him in the tombs of the kings. 2
27 in the Commentary on the Book of the Kings. 2
25: 3 he killed his servants who had slain the king 2
7 O king, do not let the army of Israel go with you 2
16 as he was speaking the king said to him *
17 Amazi'ah king of Judah took counsel and sent 2
17 son of Jeho'ahaz, son of Jehu, king of Israel 2
18 Jo'ash the king of Israel sent word to Amazi'ah 2
18 Jo'ash . . sent word to Amazi'ah king of Judah 2
21 Jo'ash king of Israel went up; 2
21 he and Amazi'ah king of Judah faced one another 2
23 Jo'ash king of Israel captured Amazi'ah 2
23 Jo'ash . . captured Amazi'ah king of Judah 2
24 he seized also the treasuries of the king's house 2

25 Amazi'ah the son of Jo'ash king of Judah 2
25 Jo'ash the son of Jeho'ahaz, king of Israel. 2
26 are they not written in the Book of the Kings 2
26: 2 after the king slept with his fathers. 2
11 Hanani'ah, one of the king's commanders. 2
13 an army . . to help the king against the enemy. 2
18 they withstood King Uzzi'ah, and said to him 2
21 King Uzzi'ah was a leper to the day of his death 2
21 Jotham his son was over the king's household 2
23 in the burial field which belonged to the kings 2
27: 5 He fought with the king of the Ammonites 2
7 in the Book of the Kings of Israel and Judah. 2
28: 2 walked in the ways of the kings of Israel. 2
5 gave him into the hand of the king of Syria 2
5 also given into the hand of the king of Israel 2
7 Zichri . . slew Ma-asei'ah the king's son 2
7 Elka'nah the next in authority to the king. 2
16 King Ahaz sent to the king of Assyria for help. 2
16 King Ahaz sent to the king of Assyria for help. 6
19 brought Judah low because of Ahaz king of Israel 2
20 Til'gath-pilne'ser king of Assyria came against 2
21 Ahaz took from . . the house of the king 2
21 Ahaz . . gave tribute to the king of Assyria; 2
22 more faithless to the LORD–this same King Ahaz. 2
23 Because the gods of the kings of Syria helped 2
26 the Book of the Kings of Judah and Israel. 2
27 into the tombs of the kings of Israel. 2
29:15 and went in as the king had commanded 2
18 Then they went in to Hezeki'ah the king and said 2
19 utensils which King Ahaz discarded in his reign 2
20 Then Hezeki'ah the king rose early and gathered 2
23 he-goats . . brought to the king and the assembly 2
24 king commanded that the burnt offering 2
25 commandment of David and of Gad the king's seer 2
27 by the instruments of David king of Israel. 2
29 king and all who were present with him bowed 2
30 Hezeki'ah the king and the princes commanded 2
30: 2 For the king and his princes and all the assembly 2
4 the plan seemed right to the king 2
6 with letters from the king and his princes 2
6 as the king had commanded, saying 2
6 escaped from the hand of the kings of Assyria. 2
12 to give them one heart to do what the king 2
24 Hezeki'ah king of Judah gave the assembly 2
26 time of Solomon the son of David king of Israel 2
31: 3 The contribution of the king 2
13 by the appointment of Hezeki'ah the king 2
32: 1 Sennach'erib king of Assyria came and invaded 2
4 Why should the kings of Assyria come and find 2
7 Do not be . . dismayed before the king of Assyria 2
8 from the words of Hezeki'ah king of Judah. 2
9 After this Sennach'erib king of Assyria 2
9 to Jerusalem to Hezeki'ah king of Judah 2
10 Thus says Sennach'erib king of Assyria 2
11 deliver us from the hand of the king of Assyria"? 2
20 Hezeki'ah the king and Isaiah . . prayed 2
21 in the camp of the king of Assyria. 2
22 from the hand of Sennach'erib king of Assyria 2
23 precious things to Hezeki'ah king of Judah 2
32 in the Book of the Kings of Judah and Israel. 2
33:11 commanders of the army of the king of Assyria 2
18 the Chronicles of the Kings of Israel. 2
25 slew all . . who had conspired against King Amon; 2
34:11 buildings . . kings of Judah had let go to ruin. 2
16 Shaphan brought the book to the king 2
16 Shaphan . . further reported to the king 2
18 Then Shaphan the secretary told the king 2
18 Shaphan read it before the king. 2
19 When the king heard the words of the law 2
20 king commanded Hilki'ah, Ahi'kam the son 2
20 king commanded . . Asai'ah the king's servant 2
22 Hilki'ah and those whom the king had sent went 2
24 book which was read before the king of Judah. 2
26 to the king of Judah . . thus shall you say to him 2
28 they brought back word to the king. 2
29 king sent and gathered together all the elders 2
30 the king went up to the house of the LORD 2
31 the king stood in his place and made a covenant 2
35: 3 house which Solomon . . king of Israel, built; 2
4 the directions of David king of Israel 2
7 these were from the king's possession. 2
10 according to the king's command. 2
15 command of David . . and Jedu'thun the king's seer 2
16 according to the command of King Josi'ah. 2
18 none of the kings of Israel had kept such 2
20 Neco king of Egypt went up to fight at Car'chemish 2
21 What have we to do with each other, king of Judah? 2
23 the archers shot King Josi'ah; and the king said 2
23 king said to his servants, "Take me away 2
27 in the Book of the Kings of Israel and Judah. 2
36: 3 Then the king of Egypt deposed him in Jerusalem 2
4 the king of Egypt made Eli'akim his brother king 2
6 came up Nebuchadnez'zar king of Babylon 2
8 Book of the Kings of Israel and Judah; 2
10 King Nebuchadnez'zar sent and brought him 2
13 He also rebelled against King Nebuchadnez'zar 2
17 he brought up . . the king of the Chalde'ans 2
18 treasures of the king and of his princes 2
22 Now in the first year of Cyrus king of Persia 2

22 stirred up the spirit of Cyrus king of Persia 2
23 Thus says Cyrus king of Persia, 'The LORD, the God 2
Ezr 1: 1 In the first year of Cyrus king of Persia 2
1 LORD stirred up the spirit of Cyrus king of Persia 2
2 Thus says Cyrus king of Persia: The LORD 2
7 Cyrus the king also brought out the vessels 2
8 Cyrus king of Persia brought these out in charge 2
2: 1 exiles whom Nebuchadnez'zar the king of Babylon 2
3: 7 grant which they had from Cyrus king of Persia. 2
10 directions of David king of Israel; 2
4: 2 since the days of E'sar-had'don king of Assyria 2
3 as King Cyrus the king of Persia has commanded us. 2
3 as King Cyrus the king of Persia has commanded us. 2
5 days of Cyrus king of Persia, even until the reign 2
5 even until the reign of Darius king of Persia. 2
7 wrote to Ar-ta-xerx'es king of Persia; 2
8 wrote . . to Ar-ta-xerx'es the king as follows– 2
11 To Ar-ta-xerx'es the king: Your servants 2
12 be it known to the king that the Jews who came up 2
13 Now be it known to the king that, if this city 2
14 not fitting for us to witness the king's dishonor 2
14 therefore we send and inform the king 2
15 rebellious city, hurtful to kings and provinces 2
16 We make known to the king that, if this city 2
17 king sent an answer: "To Rehum the commander 2
19 city . . has risen against kings 3
20 mighty kings have been over Jerusalem, who ruled 2
22 why should damage grow to the hurt of the king? 2
23 the copy of King Ar-ta-xerx'es' letter was read 3
24 second year of the reign of Darius king of Persia 3
5: 6 copy of the letter . . sent to Darius the king; 3
7 written as follows: "To Darius the king, all peace. 3
8 Be it known to the king that we went 3
11 which a great king of Israel built and finished. 3
12 into the hand of Nebuchadnez'zar king of Babylon 3
13 first year of Cyrus king of Babylon 3
13 Cyrus the king made a decree that this house 3
14 Cyrus the king took out of the temple of Babylon 3
17 if it seem good to the king, let search be made 3
17 see whether a decree was issued by Cyrus the king 3
17 let the king send us his pleasure in this matter. 3
6: 1 Darius the king made a decree, and search was made 3
3 In the first year of Cyrus the king 3
3 Cyrus the king issued a decree: Concerning 3
10 may . . pray for the life of the king and his sons. 3
12 overthrow any king or people that shall put 3
13 according to the word sent by Darius the king 3
13 did . . what Darius the king had ordered. *
14 Cyrus and Darius and Ar-ta-xerx'es king of Persia; 3
15 in the sixth year of the reign of Darius the king. 3
22 LORD . . turned the heart of the king of Assyria 2
7: 1 in the reign of Ar-ta-xerx'es king of Persia 2
6 king granted him all that he asked 2
7 in the seventh year of Ar-ta-xerx'es the king 2
8 which was in the seventh year of the king 2
11 copy of the letter which King Ar-ta-xerx'es gave 2
12 Ar-ta-xerx'es, king of kings, to Ezra the priest 3
12 Ar-ta-xerx'es, king of kings, to Ezra the priest 3
14 sent by the king and his seven counselors 3
15 silver and gold . . the king and his counselors 3
20 may provide it out of the king's treasury. 3
21 I, Ar-ta-xerx'es the king, make a decree 3
23 lest his wrath be against the realm of the king 3
26 not obey the law of your God and the law of the king 3
27 such a thing as this into the heart of the king 2
28 extended . . his steadfast love before the king 2
28 before all the king's mighty officers. 2
8: 1 Babylonia, in the reign of Ar-ta-xerx'es the king 2
22 ashamed to ask the king for a band of soldiers 2
22 since we had told the king, "The hand of our God 2
25 offering . . which the king and his counselors 2
36 delivered the king's commissions to the king's 2
36 king's commissions to the king's satraps 2
9: 7 for our iniquities we, our kings, and our priests 2
7 been given into the hand of the kings of the lands 2
9 his steadfast love before the kings of Persia 2
Neh 1:11 Now I was cupbearer to the king. 2
2: 1 Nisan, in the twentieth year of King Ar-ta-xerx'es 2
1 I took up the wine and gave it to the king. 2
2 king said to me, "Why is your face sad 2
3 I said to the king, "Let the king live for ever! 2
3 Let the king live for ever! Why should not my face 2
4 king said to me, "For what do you make request? 2
5 I said to the king, "If it pleases the king 2
5 If it pleases the king, and if your servant 2
6 king said to me (the queen sitting beside him) 2
6 it pleased the king to send me; and I set him a time. 2
7 I said to the king, "If it pleases the king 2
7 If it pleases the king, let letters be given me 2
8 letter to Asaph, the keeper of the king's forest 2
8 king granted me what I asked, for the good hand 2
9 governors . . and gave them the king's letter. 2
9 Now the king had sent with me officers of the army 2
18 also of the words which the king had spoken to me. 2
19 Are you rebelling against the king? 2
3:15 wall of the Pool of Shelah of the king's garden 2
25 projecting from the upper house of the king 2
5: 4 We have borrowed money for the king's tax 2
14 to the 32nd year of Ar-ta-xerx'es the king 2
6: 6 wish to become their king 2
7 to proclaim . . 'There is a king in Judah.' 2
7 reported to the king according to these words. 2
7: 6 exiles whom Nebuchadnez'zar the king of Babylon 2
9:22 possession of the land of Sihon king of Heshbon 2
22 possession of . . the land of Og king of Bashan. 2
24 with their kings and the peoples of the land 2
32 come upon . . our kings, our princes, our priests 2
32 since the time of the kings of Assyria until 2
34 kings, our princes, our priests, and our fathers 2
37 rich yield goes to the kings whom thou hast set 2
11:23 there was a command from the king concerning 2
24 Pethahi'ah . . at the king's hand in all matters 2
13: 6 year of Ar-ta-xerx'es king of Babylon 2
6 32nd year . . I went to the king. 2
6 after some time I asked leave of the king 2
26 not Solomon king of Israel sin on account of such 2
26 Among the many nations there was no king like him 2
26 God made him king over all Israel; 2
Est 1: 2 when King Ahasu-e'rus sat on his . . throne in Susa 2
5 the king gave for all the people . . a banquet 2
5 in the court of the garden of the king's palace. 2
7 wine was . . according to the bounty of the king. 2
8 the king had given orders . . to do as every man 2
9 in the palace which belonged to King Ahasu-e'rus. 2
10 when the heart of the king was merry with wine 2
10 the seven eunuchs who served King Ahasu-e'rus 2
11 to bring Queen Vashti before the king 2
12 Vashti refused to come at the king's command 2
12 At this the king was enraged, and his anger burned 2
13 the king said to the wise men who knew the times– 2
13 this was the king's procedure toward all who 2
14 the seven princes of . . who saw the king's face 2
15 performed the command of King Ahasu-e'rus 2
16 said in presence of the king and the princes 2
16 Not only to the king has Queen Vashti done wrong 2
16 who are in all the provinces of King Ahasu-e'rus. 2
17 King Ahasu-e'rus commanded Queen Vashti 2
18 will be telling it to all the king's princes 2
19 If it please the king, let a royal order go forth 2
19 Vashti is to come no more before King Ahasu-e'rus 2
19 let the king give her royal position to another 2
20 when the decree made by the king is proclaimed 2
21 This advice pleased the king and the princes 2
21 and the king did as Memu'can proposed; 2
2: 1 when the anger of King Ahasu-e'rus had abated 2
2 Then the king's servants who attended him said 2
2 Let . . young virgins be sought out for the king. 2
3 And let the king appoint officers . . to gather 2
3 Hegai the king's eunuch . . in charge of the women; 2
4 let the maiden who pleases the king be queen 2
4 This pleased the king, and he did so. 2
6 carried away with Jeconi'ah king of Judah 2
6 Nebuchadnez'zar king of Babylon had carried 2
8 when the king's order and his edict were proclaimed 2
8 Esther also was taken into the king's palace 2
9 and with seven chosen maids from the king's 2
12 came for each maiden to go in to King Ahasu-e'rus 2
13 when the maiden went in to the king in this way 2
13 take with her from the harem to the king's palace. 2
14 Sha-ash'gaz the king's eunuch who was in charge 2
14 she did not go in to the king again, 2
14 the king delighted in her and she was summoned 2
15 the turn came for Esther . . to go in to the king 2
15 Hegai the king's eunuch, who had charge 2
16 And when Esther was taken to King Ahasu-e'rus 2
17 the king loved Esther more than all the women 2
18 the king gave a great banquet to all his princes 2
19 Mor'decai was sitting at the king's gate. 2
21 as Mor'decai was sitting at the king's gate 2
21 Bigthan and Teresh, two of the king's eunuchs 2
21 angry and sought to lay hands on King Ahasu-e'rus. 2
22 and Esther told the king in the name of Mor'decai. 2
23 recorded in . . the presence of the king. 2
3: 1 King Ahasu-e'rus promoted Haman the Ag'agite 2
2 all the king's servants . . did obeisance to Haman; 2
2 the king's servants who were at the king's gate 2
2 for the king had so commanded concerning him. 2
3 Then the king's servants . . said to Mor'decai 2
3 the king's servants who were at the king's gate 2
3 Why do you transgress the king's command? 2
7 of Nisan, in the twelfth year of King Ahasu-e'rus 2
8 Then Haman said to King Ahasu-e'rus 2
8 and they do not keep the king's laws 2
8 is not for the king's profit to tolerate them. 2
9 If it please the king, let it be decreed 2
9 of those who have charge of the king's business *
9 that they may put it into the king's treasuries. 2
10 the king took his signet ring from his hand 2
11 the king said to Haman, "The money is given to you 2
12 Then the king's secretaries were summoned 2
12 an edict . . was written to the king's satraps 2
12 it was written in the name of King Ahasu-e'rus 2
12 and sealed with the king's ring. 2
13 Letters were sent . . to all the king's provinces 2
15 The couriers went in haste by order of the king 2
15 And the king and Haman sat down to drink; 2
4: 2 he went up to the entrance of the king's gate 2
2 no one might enter the king's gate clothed 2
3 wherever the king's command and his decree came 2
5 called for Hathach, one of the king's eunuchs 2
6 open square of the city in front of the king's gate 2
7 had promised to pay into the king's treasuries 2
8 charge her to go to the king to make supplication 2
11 All the king's servants . . know that if any 2
11 and the people of the king's provinces know 2
11 if any . . goes to the king inside the inner court 2
11 the one to whom the king holds out the . . scepter 2
11 I have not been called to come in to the king these 2
13 Think not that in the king's palace you will 2
16 I will go to the king, though it is against the law; 2
5: 1 and stood in the inner court of the king's palace 2
1 in the inner court . . opposite the king's hall. 2
1 The king was sitting on his royal throne inside 2
2 the king saw Queen Esther standing in the court 2
3 And the king said to her, "What is it, Queen Esther? 2
4 If it please the king, let the king and Haman come 2
4 let the king and Haman come this day to a dinner 2
4 to a dinner that I have prepared for the king. *
5 Then said the king, "Bring Haman quickly 2
5 the king and Haman came to the dinner 2
6 the king said to Esther, "What is your petition? 2
8 If I have found favor in the sight of the king 2
8 and if it please the king to grant my petition 2
8 let the king and Haman come . . to the dinner 2
8 and tomorrow I will do as the king has said. 2
9 But when Haman saw Mor'decai in the king's gate 2
11 promotions with which the king had honored him 2
11 above the princes and the servants of the king. 2
12 let no one come with the king to the banquet 2
12 I am invited by her together with the king. 2
13 I see Mor'decai the Jew sitting at the king's gate. 2
14 tell the king to have Mor'decai hanged upon it; 2
14 then go merrily with the king to the dinner. 2
6: 1 On that night the king could not sleep; 2
1 chronicles, and they were read before the king. 2
2 Bigthana and Teresh, two of the king's eunuchs 2
2 who had sought to lay hands upon King Ahasu-e'rus. 2
3 And the king said, "What honor or dignity has been 2
3 The king's servants who attended him said 2
4 And the king said, "Who is in the court? 2
4 just entered the outer court of the king's palace 2
4 Haman had just entered . . to speak to the king 2
5 the king's servants told him, "Haman is there 2
5 And the king said, "Let him come in. 2
6 Haman came in, and the king said to him 2
6 be done to the man whom the king delights to honor? 2
6 Whom would the king delight to honor more than me? 2
7 Haman said to the king, "For the man whom the king 2
7 For the man whom the king delights to honor 2
8 royal robes . . which the king has worn 2
8 and the horse which the king has ridden 2
9 handed . . to one of the king's most noble princes; 2
9 array the man whom the king delights to honor 2
9 done to the man whom the king delights to honor.' 2
10 Then the king said to Haman, "Make haste 2
10 to Mor'decai the Jew who sits at the king's gate. 2
11 done to the man whom the king delights to honor. 2
12 Then Mor'decai returned to the king's gate. 2
14 the king's eunuchs arrived and brought Haman 2
7: 1 the king and Haman went in to feast 2
2 king again said to Esther, "What is your petition 2
3 If I have found favor in your sight, O king 2
3 If I have found favor . . and if it please the king 2
4 is not to be compared with the loss to the king. 2
5 King Ahasu-e'rus said to Queen Esther, "Who is he 2
6 Haman was in terror before the king and the queen. 2
7 And the king rose from the feast in wrath 2
7 evil was determined against him by the king. 2
8 And the king returned from the palace garden 2
8 and the king said, "Will he even assault the queen 2
8 As the words left the mouth of the king 2
9 one of the eunuchs in attendance on the king 2
9 prepared for Mor'decai, whose word saved the king 2
10 And the king said, "Hang him on that. 2
10 Then the anger of the king abated. 2
8: 1 King Ahasu-e'rus gave . . Esther the house of Haman 2
1 And Mor'decai came before the king 2
2 the king took off his signet ring . . and gave it 2
3 Then Esther spoke again to the king; 2
4 the king held out the golden scepter to Esther 2
4 and Esther rose and stood before the king. 2
5 If it please the king, and if I have found favor 2
5 and if the thing seem right before the king 2
5 the Jews who are in all the provinces of the king. 2
7 King Ahasu-e'rus said to . . Esther and to Mor'decai 2
8 write as you please . . in the name of the king 2
8 you may write . . and seal it with the king's ring; 2
8 an edict written in the name of the king 2
8 edict written . . and sealed with the king's ring 2
9 The king's secretaries were summoned 2
10 The writing was in the name of King Ahasu-e'rus 2
10 The writing was . . sealed with the king's ring 2
11 the king allowed the Jews . . to gather and defend 2
12 throughout all the provinces of King Ahasu-e'rus 2
14 rode out in haste, urged by the king's command; 2
15 Mor'decai went out from the presence of the king 2
17 wherever the king's command and his edict came 2

9: 1 when the king's command and edict were about 2
2 throughout all the provinces of King Ahasu-e'rus 2
4 For Mor'decai was great in the king's house 2
11 the number of . . was reported to the king. 2
12 And the king said to Queen Esther, "In Susa 2
12 have they done in the rest of the king's provinces! 2
13 If it please the king, let the Jews . . be allowed 2
14 the king commanded this to be done; 2
16 the other Jews who were in the king's provinces 2
20 who were in all the provinces of King Ahasu-e'rus 2
25 when Esther came before the king, he gave orders 2
10: 1 King Ahasu-e'rus laid tribute on the land 2
2 the high honor . . to which the king advanced him 2
2 the Chronicles of the kings of Media and Persia? 2
3 Mor'decai . . was next in rank to King Ahasu-e'rus 2
Job 3:14 with kings and counselors of the earth 2
12:18 He looses the bonds of kings 2
15:24 against him, like a king prepared for battle. 2
18:14 he trusted, and is brought to the king of terrors. 2
29:25 as chief, and I dwelt like a king among his troops 2
34:18 who says to a king, 'Worthless one,' 2
36: 7 with kings upon the throne he sets them for ever 2
41:34 he is king over all the sons of pride. 2
Ps 2: 2 The kings of the earth set themselves 2
6 I have set my king on Zion, my holy hill. 2
10 Now therefore, O kings, be wise; be warned, O rulers 2
5: 2 Hearken to the sound of my cry, my King and my God 2
10:16 The LORD is king for ever and ever; 2
18:50 Great triumphs he gives to his king 2
20: 9 Give victory to the king, O LORD; 2
21: 1 In thy strength the king rejoices, O LORD; 2
7 For the king trusts in the LORD; 2
24: 7 that the King of glory may come in. 2
8 Who is the King of glory? The LORD 2
9 that the King of glory may come in. 2
10 Who is the King of glory? The LORD of hosts, he is 2
10 The LORD of hosts, he is the King of glory! Selah 2
29:10 LORD sits enthroned as king for ever. 2
33:16 A king is not saved by his great army; 2
44: 4 Thou art my King and my God 2
45: 1 I address my verses to the king; 2
5 are sharp in the heart of the king's enemies; 2
9 daughters of kings are among your ladies 2
11 the king will desire your beauty. 2
14 in many-colored robes she is led to the king 2
15 led along as they enter the palace of the king. 2
47: 2 is terrible, a great king over all the earth. 2
6 Sing praises to our King, sing praises! 2
7 For God is the king of all the earth; 2
48: 2 Zion, in the far north, the city of the great King. 2
4 lo, the kings assembled, they came on together. 2
61: 6 Prolong the life of the king; may his years endure 2
63:11 the king shall rejoice in God; 2
68:12 The kings of the armies, they flee, they flee! 2
14 When the Almighty scattered kings there 2
24 processions of my God, my King, into the sanctuary- 2
29 temple at Jerusalem kings bear gifts to thee. 2
72: 1 Give the king thy justice, O God 2
10 May the kings of Tarshish . . render him tribute 2
10 may the kings of Sheba and Seba bring gifts! 2
11 May all kings fall down before him 2
74:12 Yet God my King is from of old, working salvation 2
76:12 who is terrible to the kings of the earth. 2
84: 3 at thy altars, O LORD of hosts, my King and my God. 2
89:18 our king to the Holy One of Israel. 2
27 make him . . highest of the kings of the earth. 2
95: 3 For the LORD is . . a great King above all gods. 2
98: 6 make a joyful noise before the King, the LORD! 2
99: 4 Mighty King, lover of justice, thou hast 2
102:15 all the kings of the earth, thy glory. 2
105:14 he rebuked kings on their account 2
20 The king sent and released him 2
30 with frogs, even in the chambers of their kings. 2
110: 5 shatter kings on the day of his wrath. 2
119:46 will also speak of thy testimonies before kings 2
135:10 who smote many nations and slew mighty kings 2
11 Sihon, king of the Amorites, and Og, king of Bashan 2
11 Sihon, king of the Amorites, and Og, king of Bashan 2
136:17 to him who smote the great kings 2
18 slew famous kings 2
19 Sihon, king of the Amorites 2
20 Og, king of Bashan, for his steadfast love endures 2
138: 4 kings of the earth shall praise thee, O LORD 2
144:10 who givest victory to kings, who rescuest David 2
145: 1 I will extol thee, my God and King, and bless 2
148:11 Kings of the earth and all peoples 2
149: 2 let the sons of Zion rejoice in their King! 2
8 to bind their kings with chains 2
Prv 1: 1 proverbs of Solomon, son of David, king of Israel 2
8:15 By me kings reign, and rulers decree what is just; 2
14:28 In a multitude of people is the glory of a king 2
35 A servant who deals wisely has the king's favor 2
16:10 Inspired decisions are on the lips of a king; 2
12 It is an abomination to kings to do evil 2
13 Righteous lips are the delight of a king 2
14 A king's wrath is a messenger of death 2
15 In the light of a king's face there is life 2
19:12 A king's wrath is like the growling of a lion 2
20: 2 dread wrath of a king is like the growling of a lion; 2
8 A king who sits on the throne of judgment 2
26 A wise king winnows the wicked 2
28 Loyalty and faithfulness preserve the king 2
21: 1 The king's heart is a stream of water in the hand 2
22:11 loves purity . . will have the king as his friend. 2
29 skilful in his work? he will stand before kings; 2
24:21 My son, fear the LORD and the king 2
25: 1 proverbs . . men of Hezeki'ah king of Judah copied. 2
2 but the glory of kings is to search things out. 2
3 so the mind of kings is unsearchable. 2
5 away the wicked from the presence of the king 2
6 not put yourself forward in the king's presence 2
29: 4 By justice a king gives stability to the land 2
14 If a king judges the poor with equity his throne 2
30:27 locusts have no king, yet all of them march in rank; 2
28 yet it is in kings' palaces. 2
31 he-goat, and a king striding before his people. 2
31: 1 The words of Lemuel, king of Massa 2
3 Give not your . . ways to those who destroy kings. 2
4 not for kings, O Lemuel, it is not for kings to drink 2
4 not for kings to drink wine, or for rulers 2
Ecc 1: 1 the Preacher, the son of David, king in Jerusalem. 2
12 I . . have been king over Israel in Jerusalem. 2
2: 8 and gold and the treasure of kings and provinces; 2
12 for what can the man do who comes after the king? 2
4:13 Better is a . . youth than an old and foolish king 2
5: 9 a king is an advantage to a land with . . fields. 2
8: 2 Keep the king's command 2
4 For the word of the king is supreme, and who may say 2
9:14 and a great king came against it and besieged it 2
10:16 Woe to you, O land, when your king is a child 2
17 Happy . . when your king is the son of free men 2
20 Even in your thought, do not curse the king 2
Sng 1: 4 The king has brought me into his chambers. 2
12 While the king was on his couch, my nard gave forth 2
3: 9 King Solomon made himself a palanquin 2
11 Go . . O daughters of Zion, and behold King Solomon 2
7: 5 a king is held captive in the tresses. 2
Isa 1: 1 Uzzi'ah, Jotham, Ahaz, and Hezeki'ah, kings of Judah 2
6: 1 In the year that King Uzzi'ah died I saw the Lord 2
5 for my eyes have seen the King, the LORD of hosts! 2
7: 1 Ahaz the son of Jotham, son of Uzzi'ah, king of Judah 2
1 In the days of Ahaz . . Rezin the king of Syria 2
1 Pekah the son of Remali'ah the king of Israel came 2
6 set up the son of Ta'be-el as king in the midst of it 2
16 the land before whose two kings you are in dread 2
17 departed from Judah–the king of Assyria. 2
20 shave with a razor . . –with the king of Assyria 2
8: 4 carried away before the king of Assyria. 2
7 the king of Assyria and all his glory; 2
21 enraged and will curse their king and their God 2
10: 8 for he says: "Are not my commanders all kings? 2
12 the arrogant boasting of the king of Assyria 2
14: 4 take up this taunt against the king of Babylon 2
9 their thrones all who were kings of the nations. 2
18 All the kings of the nations lie in glory 2
28 In the year that King Ahaz died came this oracle 2
19: 4 a fierce king will rule over them 2
11 I am a son of the wise, a son of ancient kings"? 2
20: 1 commander . . sent by Sargon the king of Assyria 2
4 so shall the king of Assyria lead away 2
6 for help to be delivered from the king of Assyria! 2
23:15 for 70 years, like the days of one king. 2
24:21 in heaven, and the kings of the earth, on the earth. 2
30:33 yea, for the king it is made ready 2
32: 1 Behold, a king will reign in righteousness 2
33:17 Your eyes will see the king in his beauty; 2
22 the LORD is our king; he will save us. 2
36: 1 In the fourteenth year of King Hezeki'ah 2
1 Sennach'erib king of Assyria came up against all 2
2 the king of Assyria sent the Rab'shakeh 2
2 from Lachish to King Hezeki'ah at Jerusalem 2
4 Thus says the great king, the king of Assyria 2
4 Thus says the great king, the king of Assyria 2
6 Such is Pharaoh king of Egypt to all who rely 2
8 make a wager with my master the king of Assyria 2
13 Hear the words of the great king 2
13 the words of the great king, the king of Assyria! 2
14 says the king: 'Do not let Hezeki'ah deceive you 2
15 not be given into the hand of the king of Assyria. 2
16 for thus says the king of Assyria 2
18 his land out of the hand of the king of Assyria? 2
21 for the king's command was, "Do not answer him. 2
37: 1 When King Hezeki'ah heard it, he rent his clothes 2
4 Rab'shakeh, whom his master the king of Assyria 2
5 the servants of King Hezeki'ah came to Isaiah 2
6 servants of the king of Assyria have reviled me. 2
8 Rab'shakeh . . found the king of Assyria fighting 2
8 for he had heard that the king had left Lachish. •
9 Now the king heard concerning Tirha'kah king •
9 heard concerning Tirha'kah king of Ethiopia 2
10 Thus shall you speak to Hezeki'ah king of Judah 2
10 not be given into the hand of the king of Assyria. 2
11 what the kings of Assyria have done to all lands 2
13 Where is the king of Hamath, the king of Arpad 2
13 Where is the king of Hamath, the king of Arpad 2
13 king of Arpad, the king of the city of Sepharva'im 2
13 the king of Hena, or the king of Ivvah?' •
13 the king of Hena, or the king of Ivvah?' •
18 kings of Assyria have laid waste all the nations 2
21 concerning Sennach'erib king of Assyria 2
33 says the LORD concerning the king of Assyria 2
37 Then Sennach'erib king of Assyria departed 2
38: 6 this city out of the hand of the king of Assyria 2
9 A writing of Hezeki'ah king of Judah 2
39: 1 the son of Bal'adan, king of Babylon, sent envoys 2
3 Then Isaiah the prophet came to King Hezeki'ah 2
7 be eunuchs in the palace of the king of Babylon. 2
41: 2 that he tramples kings under foot; 2
21 bring your proofs, says the King of Jacob. 2
43:15 your Holy One, the Creator of Israel, your King. 2
44: 6 says the LORD, the King of Israel and his Redeemer 2
45: 1 ungird the loins of kings, to open doors 2
49: 7 Kings shall see and arise; princes 2
23 Kings shall be your foster fathers 2
52:15 kings shall shut their mouths because of him; 2
60: 3 and kings to the brightness of your rising. 2
10 and their kings shall minister to you; 2
11 the nations, with their kings led in procession. 2
16 you shall suck the breast of kings; 2
62: 2 your vindication, and all the kings your glory; 2
Jer 1: 2 in the days of Josi'ah the son of Amon, king of Judah 2
3 days of Jehoi'akim the son of Josi'ah, king of Judah 2
3 year of Zedeki'ah, the son of Josi'ah, king of Judah 2
18 against the kings of Judah, its princes 2
2:26 they, their kings, their princes, their priests 2
3: 6 The LORD said to me in the days of King Josi'ah 2
4: 9 courage shall fail both king and princes; 2
8: 1 says the LORD, the bones of the kings of Judah 2
19 Is the LORD not in Zion? Is her King not in her? 2
10: 7 Who would not fear thee, O King of the nations? 2
10 he is the living God and the everlasting King. 2
13:13 the kings who sit on David's throne, the priests 2
18 Say to the king and the queen mother 2
15: 4 Manas'seh the son of Hezeki'ah, king of Judah 2
17:19 Benjamin Gate, by which the kings of Judah enter 2
20 say: 'Hear the word of the LORD, you kings of Judah 2
25 kings who sit on the throne of David 2
19: 3 O kings of Judah and inhabitants of Jerusalem. 2
4 their fathers nor the kings of Judah have known; 2
13 houses of Jerusalem and the houses of the kings 2
20: 4 all Judah into the hand of the king of Babylon; 2
5 and all the treasures of the kings of Judah 2
21: 1 when King Zedeki'ah sent to him Pashhur 2
2 Nebuchadrez'zar king of Babylon is making war 2
4 you are fighting against the king of Babylon 2
7 give Zedeki'ah king of Judah, and his servants 2
7 into the hand of Nebuchadrez'zar king of Babylon 2
10 be given into the hand of the king of Babylon 2
11 And to the house of the king of Judah say 2
22: 1 Go down to the house of the king of Judah 2
2 and say, 'Hear the word of the LORD, O King of Judah 2
4 kings who sit on the throne of David 2
6 concerning the house of the king of Judah 2
11 Shallum the son of Josi'ah, king of Judah 2
15 think you are a king because you compete in cedar? 1
18 Jehoi'akim the son of Josi'ah, king of Judah 2
24 though Coni'ah the son of Jehoi'akim, king of Judah 2
25 into the hand of Nebuchadrez'zar king of Babylon 2
23: 5 and he shall reign as king and deal wisely 2
24: 1 After Nebuchadrez'zar king of Babylon had taken 2
1 Jeconi'ah the son of Jehoi'akim, king of Judah 2
8 will I treat Zedeki'ah the king of Judah 2
25: 1 Jehoi'akim the son of Josi'ah, king of Judah 2
1 the first year of Nebuchadrez'zar king of Babylon 2
3 Josi'ah the son of Amon, king of Judah, to this day 2
9 and for Nebuchadrez'zar the king of Babylon 2
11 nations shall serve the king of Babylon 70 years. 2
12 I will punish the king of Babylon and that nation 2
14 many nations and great kings shall make slaves 2
18 its kings and princes, to make them a desolation 2
19 Pharoah king of Egypt, his servants, his princes 2
20 all the kings of the land of Uz 2
20 all the kings of the land of the Philistines 2
22 all the kings of Tyre, all the kings of Sidon 2
22 all the kings of Tyre, all the kings of Sidon 2
22 and the kings of the coastland across the sea; 2
24 all the kings of Arabia 2
24 and all the kings of the mixed tribes 2
25 all the kings of Zimri, all the kings of Elam 2
25 all the kings of Zimri, all the kings of Elam 2
25 all the kings of Elam, and all the kings of Media; 2
26 all the kings of the north, far and near 2
26 And after them the king of Babylon shall drink. 2
26: 1 Jehoi'akim the son of Josi'ah, king of Judah 2
10 they came up from the king's house 2
18 prophesied in the days of Hezeki'ah king of Judah 2
19 Did Hezeki'ah king of Judah 2
21 And when King Jehoi'akim, with all his warriors 2
21 the king sought to put him to death; 2
22 Then King Jehoi'akim sent to Egypt certain men 2
23 from Egypt and brought him to King Jehoi'akim 2
27: 1 Zedeki'ah the son of Josi'ah, king of Judah 2
3 Send word to the king of Edom, the king of Moab 2
3 Send word to the king of Edom, the king of Moab 2
3 the king of the sons of Ammon, the king of Tyre 2
3 the king of the sons of Ammon, the king of Tyre 2
3 and the king of Sidon by the hand of the envoys 2

3 come to Jerusalem to Zedeki'ah king of Judah. 2
6 Nebuchadnez'zar, the king of Babylon, my servant 2
7 and great kings shall make him their slave. 2
8 not serve this Nebuchadnez'zar king of Babylon 2
8 and put its neck under the yoke of the king 2
9 You shall not serve the king of Babylon. 2
11 under the yoke of the king of Babylon and serve 2
12 To Zedeki'ah king of Judah I spoke in like manner 2
12 under the yoke of the king of Babylon, 2
13 nation which will not serve the king of Babylon? 2
14 You shall not serve the king of Babylon, 2
17 Do not listen to them; serve the king of Babylon 2
18 in the house of the king of Judah, and in Jerusalem 2
20 Nebuchadnez'zar king of Babylon did not take 2
20 Jeconi'ah the son of Jehoi'akim, king of Judah 2
21 in the house of the king of Judah, and in Jerusalem 2
28: 1 beginning of the reign of Zedeki'ah king of Judah 2
2 I have broken the yoke of the king of Babylon. 2
3 which Nebuchadnez'zar king of Babylon took away 2
4 Jeconi'ah the son of Jehoi'akim, king of Judah 2
4 for I will break the yoke of the king of Babylon. 2
11 the yoke of Nebuchadnez'zar king of Babylon 2
14 servitude to Nebuchadnez'zar king of Babylon 2
29: 2 This was after King Jeconi'ah, and the queen 2
3 whom Zedeki'ah king of Judah sent to Babylon 2
3 to Babylon to Nebuchadnez'zar king of Babylon. 2
16 Thus says the LORD concerning the king 2
21 into the hand of Nebuchadrez'zar king of Babylon 2
22 Ahab, whom the king of Babylon roasted in the fire 2
30: 9 and David their king, whom I will raise up for them. 2
32: 1 in the tenth year of Zedeki'ah king of Judah 2
2 the king of Babylon was besieging Jerusalem 2
2 which was in the palace of the king of Judah. 2
3 For Zedeki'ah king of Judah had imprisoned him 2
3 this city into the hand of the king of Babylon 2
4 Zedeki'ah king of Judah shall not escape 2
4 be given into the hand of the king of Babylon 2
28 into the hand of Nebuchadrez'zar king of Babylon 2
32 their kings and their princes, their priests 2
36 It is given into the hand of the king of Babylon 2
33: 4 houses of the kings of Judah which were torn down 2
34: 1 when Nebuchadrez'zar king of Babylon 2
2 Go and speak to Zedeki'ah king of Judah 2
2 this city into the hand of the king of Babylon 2
3 you shall see the king of Babylon eye to eye 2
4 the word of the LORD, O Zedeki'ah king of Judah 2
5 fathers, the former kings who were before you 2
6 spoke all these words to Zedeki'ah king of Judah 2
7 when the army of the king of Babylon was fighting 2
8 after King Zedeki'ah had made a covenant 2
21 And Zedeki'ah king of Judah, and his princes 2
21 into the hand of the army of the king of Babylon 2
35: 1 Jehoi'akim the son of Josi'ah, king of Judah 2
11 when Nebuchadrez'zar king of Babylon came up 2
36: 1 Jehoi'akim the son of Josi'ah, king of Judah 2
9 Jehoi'akim the son of Josi'ah, king of Judah 2
12 he went down to the king's house 2
16 We must report all these words to the king. 2
20 they went into the court to the king 2
20 and they reported all the words to the king. 2
21 Then the king sent Jehu'di to get the scroll 2
21 and Jehu'di read it to the king and all the princes 2
21 all the princes who stood beside the king. 2
22 the king was sitting in the winter house 2
23 the king would cut them off with a penknife *
24 Yet neither the king, nor any of his servants 2
25 Gemari'ah urged the king not to burn the scroll 2
26 And the king commanded Jerah'meel the king's son 2
26 And the king commanded Jerah'meel the king's son 2
27 Now, after the king had burned the scroll 2
28 which Jehoi'akim the king of Judah has burned. 2
29 And concerning Jehoi'akim king of Judah 2
29 the king of Babylon will certainly come 2
30 the LORD concerning Jehoi'akim king of Judah 2
32 scroll which Jehoi'akim king of Judah had burned 2
37: 1 whom Nebuchadrez'zar king of Babylon made king 2
3 King Zedeki'ah sent Jehu'cal the son of Shelemi'ah 2
7 Thus shall you say to the king of Judah 2
17 King Zedeki'ah sent for him, and received him. 2
17 The king questioned him secretly in his house 2
17 You shall be delivered into the hand of the king 2
18 Jeremiah also said to King Zedeki'ah 2
19 The king of Babylon will not come against you 2
20 Now hear, I pray you, O my lord the king 2
21 King Zedeki'ah gave orders 2
38: 3 into the hand of the army of the king of Babylon 2
4 Then the princes said to the king 2
5 King Zedeki'ah said, "Behold, he is in your hands; 2
5 for the king can do nothing against you. 2
6 into the cistern of Malchi'ah, the king's son 2
7 Ethiopian, a eunuch, who was in the king's house 2
7 the king was sitting in the Benjamin Gate 2
8 E'bed-mel'ech went from the king's house and said 2
8 went from the king's house and said to the king 2
9 My lord the king, these men have done evil 2
10 Then the king commanded E'bed-mel'ech 2
11 and went to the house of the king, to a wardrobe 2
14 King Zedeki'ah sent for Jeremiah the prophet 2
14 The king said to Jeremiah 2
16 Then King Zedeki'ah swore secretly to Jeremiah 2
17 surrender to the princes of the king of Babylon 2
18 surrender to the princes of the king of Babylon 2
19 King Zedeki'ah said to Jeremiah 2
22 the women left in the house of the king of Judah 2
22 led out to the princes of the king of Babylon 2
23 but shall be seized by the king of Babylon; 2
25 and say to you, 'Tell us what you said to the king 2
25 you said to the king and what the king said to you; 2
26 I made a humble plea to the king 2
27 he answered them as the king had instructed him. 2
39: 1 In the ninth year of Zedeki'ah king of Judah 2
1 Nebuchadrez'zar king of Babylon and all his army 2
3 the princes of the king of Babylon came and sat 2
3 the rest of the officers of the king of Babylon. 2
4 Zedeki'ah king of Judah and all the soldiers saw 2
4 by way of the king's garden through the gate 2
5 up to Nebuchadrez'zar king of Babylon, at Riblah 2
6 The king of Babylon slew the sons of Zedeki'ah 2
6 the king of Babylon slew all the nobles of Judah. 2
8 The Chalde'ans burned the king's house 2
11 Nebuchadrez'zar king of Babylon gave command 2
13 all the chief officers of the king of Babylon 2
40: 5 whom the king of Babylon appointed governor 2
7 men heard that the king of Babylon had appointed 2
9 Dwell in the land, and serve the king of Babylon 2
11 heard that the king of Babylon had left a remnant 2
14 Do you know that Ba'alis the king of the Ammonites 2
41: 1 Ish'mael . . one of the chief officers of the king 2
2 whom the king of Babylon had appointed governor 2
9 was the large cistern which King Asa had made 2
9 made for defense against Ba'asha king of Israel; 2
10 king's daughters and all the people who were left 2
18 whom the king of Babylon had made governor 2
42:11 Do not fear the king of Babylon 2
43:10 and take Nebuchadrez'zar the king of Babylon 2
44: 9 the wickedness of the kings of Judah 2
17 our kings and our princes, in the cities of Judah 2
21 you and your fathers, your kings and your princes 2
30 Behold, I will give Pharaoh Hophra king of Egypt 2
30 as I gave Zedeki'ah king of Judah into the hand 2
30 into the hand of Nebuchadrez'zar king of Babylon 2
45: 1 Jehoi'akim the son of Josi'ah, king of Judah 2
46: 2 the army of Pharaoh Neco, king of Egypt 2
2 which Nebuchadrez'zar king of Babylon defeated 2
2 Jehoi'akim the son of Josi'ah, king of Judah 2
13 the coming of Nebuchadrez'zar king of Babylon 2
17 Call the name of Pharaoh, king of Egypt, 'Noisy one 2
18 As I live, says the King, whose name is the LORD 2
25 and Pharaoh, and Egypt and her gods and her kings 2
26 into the hand of Nebuchadrez'zar king of Babylon 2
48:15 men have gone down to slaughter, says the King 2
49:28 which Nebuchadrez'zar king of Babylon smote. 2
30 Nebuchadrez'zar king of Babylon has made a plan 2
34 of the reign of Zedeki'ah king of Judah. 2
38 and destroy their king and princes, says the LORD. 2
50:17 First the king of Assyria devoured him 2
17 now at last Nebuchadrez'zar king of Babylon 2
18 I am bringing punishment on the king of Babylon 2
18 as I punished the king of Assyria. 2
41 many kings are stirring from the farthest parts 2
43 The king of Babylon heard the report of them 2
51:11 stirred up the spirit of the kings of the Medes 2
28 the kings of the Medes, with their governors 2
31 to tell the king of Babylon that his city is taken 2
34 the king of Babylon has devoured me 2
57 a perpetual sleep and not wake, says the King 2
59 he went with Zedeki'ah king of Judah to Babylon 2
52: 3 Zedeki'ah rebelled against the king of Babylon. 2
4 king of Babylon came with all his army 2
5 till the eleventh year of King Zedeki'ah. 2
7 a gate between the two walls, by the king's garden 2
8 But the army of the Chalde'ans pursued the king 2
9 Then they captured the king 2
9 and brought him up to the king of Babylon 2
10 The king of Babylon slew the sons of Zedeki'ah 2
11 and the king of Babylon took him to Babylon 2
12 the nineteenth year of King Nebuchadrez'zar 2
12 Nebuchadrez'zar, king of Babylon–Nebu'zarad'an 2
12 the bodyguard who served the king of Babylon 2
13 the king's house and all the houses of Jerusalem; 2
15 who had deserted to the king of Babylon 2
20 and the stands, which Solomon the king had made 2
25 the men of war, and seven men of the king's council 2
26 and brought them to the king of Babylon at Riblah. 2
27 And the king of Babylon smote them 2
31 of the captivity of Jehoi'achin king of Judah 2
31 lifted up the head of Jehoi'achin king of Judah 2
31 lifted up the head of Jehoi'achin king of Judah 2
32 and gave him a seat above the seats of the kings 2
33 he dined regularly at the king's table; *
34 a regular allowance was given him by the king 2
Lam 2: 6 in . . indignation has spurned king and priest. 2
9 her king and princes are among the nations; 2
4:12 The kings of the earth did not believe . . that foe 2
Ezk 1: 2 the fifth year of the exile of King Jehoi'achin 2
7:27 The king mourns, the prince is wrapped in despair 2
17:12 Behold, the king of Babylon came to Jerusalem 2
12 to Jerusalem, and took her king and her princes 2
16 the place where the king dwells who made him king 2
19: 9 in a cage, and brought him to the king of Babylon; 2
20:33 and with wrath poured out, I will be king over you. 1
21:19 ways for the sword of the king of Babylon to come; 2
21 king of Babylon stands at the parting of the way 2
24: 2 The king of Babylon has laid siege to Jerusalem 2
26: 7 Nebuchadrez'zar king of Babylon, king of kings 2
7 Nebuchadrez'zar king of Babylon, king of kings 2
7 Nebuchadrez'zar king of Babylon, king of kings 2
27:33 you enriched the kings of the earth. 2
35 their kings are horribly afraid 2
28:12 raise a lamentation over the king of Tyre, and say 2
17 I exposed you before kings 2
29: 2 set your face against Pharaoh king of Egypt 2
3 Behold, I am against you, Pharaoh king of Egypt 2
18 Nebuchadrez'zar king of Babylon made his army 2
19 give . . Egypt to Nebuchadrez'zar king of Babylon; 2
30:10 by the hand of Nebuchadrez'zar king of Babylon. 2
21 I have broken the arm of Pharaoh king of Egypt; 2
22 Behold, I am against Pharaoh king of Egypt 2
24 I will strengthen the arms of the king of Babylon 2
25 I will strengthen the arms of the king of Babylon 2
25 I put my sword into the hand of the king of Babylon 2
31: 2 say to Pharaoh king of Egypt and to his multitude 2
32: 2 raise a lamentation over Pharaoh king of Egypt 2
10 their kings shall shudder because of you 2
11 sword of the king of Babylon shall come upon you. 2
29 Edom is there, her kings and all her princes 2
37:22 one king shall be king over them all; 2
22 one king shall be king over them all; 2
24 My servant David shall be king over them; 2
43: 7 neither they, nor their kings, by their harlotry 2
7 and by the dead bodies of their kings 2
9 and the dead bodies of their kings far from me 2
Dan 1: 5 king assigned them a daily portion of the rich 2
5 daily portion of the rich food which the king ate 2
5 end of that time . . were to stand before the king. 2
8 not defile himself with the king's rich food 2
10 fear lest my lord the king, who appointed 2
10 So you would endanger my head with the king. 2
13 youths who eat the king's rich food 2
15 than all the youths who ate the king's rich food. 2
18 king had commanded that they should be brought 2
19 king spoke with them, and among them all 2
19 therefore they stood before the king. 2
20 matter . . concerning which the king inquired 2
21 Daniel . . until the first year of King Cyrus. 2
2: 2 Then the king commanded that the magicians 2
2 summoned, to tell the king his dreams. 2
2 So they came in and stood before the king. 2
3 king said to them, "I had a dream, and my spirit 2
4 Then the Chalde'ans said to the king, "O king 2
4 O king, live for ever! Tell your servants the dream 3
5 king answered the Chalde'ans, "The word from me 3
7 Let the king tell his servants the dream 3
8 The king answered, "I know with certainty 3
10 Chalde'ans answered the king, "There is not a man 3
10 not a man on earth who can meet the king's demand; 3
10 no great and powerful king has asked such a thing 3
11 thing that the king asks is difficult 3
11 none can show it to the king except the gods 3
12 king was angry and very furious, and commanded 3
14 Ar'ioch, the captain of the king's guard 3
15 said to Ar'ioch, the king's captain 3
15 Why is the decree of the king so severe? 3
16 Daniel . . besought the king to appoint him a time 3
16 might show to the king the interpretation. 3
21 he removes kings and sets up kings; 3
21 he removes kings and sets up kings; 3
23 for thou hast made known to us the king's matter. 3
24 Ar'ioch, whom the king had appointed to destroy 3
24 bring me in before the king 3
24 I will show the king the interpretation. 3
25 brought in Daniel before the king in haste 3
25 found . . a man who can make known to the king 3
26 king said to Daniel, whose name was Belteshaz'zar 3
27 Daniel answered the king, "No wise men, enchanters 3
27 can show to the king the mystery 3
27 can show . . the mystery which the king has asked 3
28 made known to King Nebuchadnez'zar what will be 3
29 O king, as you lay in bed came thoughts 3
30 interpretation may be made known to the king 3
31 You saw, O king, and behold, a great image. 3
36 now we will tell the king its interpretation. 3
37 O king, the king of kings, to whom the God of heaven 3
37 O king, the king of kings, to whom the God of heaven 3
37 O king, the king of kings, to whom the God of heaven 3
44 days of those kings the God of heaven will set up 3
45 made known to the king what shall be hereafter. 3
46 Then King Nebuchadnez'zar fell upon his face 3
47 king said to Daniel, "Truly, your God is God of gods 3
47 Truly, your God is God of gods and Lord of kings 3
48 Then the king gave Daniel high honors 3
49 Daniel made request of the king, and he appointed 3
49 but Daniel remained at the king's court. 3
3: 1 King Nebuchadnez'zar made an image of gold 3
2 Then King Nebuchadnez'zar sent to assemble 3
2 image which King Nebuchadnez'zar had set up. 3
3 image that King Nebuchadnez'zar had set up; 3

5 golden image . . King Nebuchadnez'zar has set up; 3
7 golden image . . King Nebuchadnez'zar had set up. 3
9 said to King Nebuchadnez'zar, "O king 3
9 said to King Nebuchadnez'zar, "O king 3
10 You, O king, have made a decree 3
12 men, O king, pay no heed to you; they do not serve 3
13 Then they brought these men before the king. 3
16 Shadrach . . and Abed'nego answered the king 3
17 God . . will deliver us out of your hand, O king. 3
18 if not, be it known to you, O king 3
22 king's order was strict and the furnace very hot 3
24 King Nebuchadnez'zar was astonished and rose up 3
24 counselors . . answered the king, "True, O king. 3
24 counselors . . answered the king, "True, O king. 3
27 satraps . . and the king's counselors gathered 3
28 set at nought the king's command, and yielded up 3
30 king promoted Shadrach, Meshach, and Abed'nego 3
4: 1 King Nebuchadnez'zar to all peoples 3
18 This dream I, King Nebuchadnez'zar, saw. 3
19 king said, "Belteshaz'zar, let not the dream 3
22 it is you, O king, who have grown and become strong 3
23 whereas the king saw a watcher, a holy one 3
24 this is the interpretation, O king: It is a decree 3
24 decree . . which has come upon my lord the king 3
27 Therefore, O king, let my counsel be acceptable 3
28 All this came upon King Nebuchadnez'zar. 3
30 king said, "Is not this great Babylon, 3
31 While the words were still in the king's mouth 3
31 O King Nebuchadnez'zar, to you it is spoken 3
37 praise and extol and honor the King of heaven; 3
5: 1 King Belshaz'zar made a great feast 3
2 king and his lords, his wives, and his concubines 3
3 king and his lords, his wives, and his concubines 3
5 plaster of the wall of the king's palace 3
5 king saw the hand as it wrote. 3
6 Then the king's color changed, 3
7 king cried aloud to bring in the enchanters 3
7 king said to the wise men of Babylon, 3
8 Then all the king's wise men came 3
8 make known to the king the interpretation. 3
9 Then King Belshaz'zar was greatly alarmed 3
10 because of the words of the king and his lords 3
10 queen said, "O king, live for ever! 3
11 King Nebuchadnez'zar, your father, made him chief 3
12 this Daniel, whom the king named Belteshaz'zar. 3
13 Then Daniel was brought in before the king. 3
13 king said to Daniel, "You are that Daniel 3
13 exiles . . king my father brought from Judah. 3
17 Daniel answered before the king, "Let your gifts 3
17 nevertheless I will read the writing to the king 3
18 O king, the Most High God gave Nebuchadnez'zar 3
30 night Belshaz'zar the Chalde'an king was slain. 3
6: 2 account, so that the king might suffer no loss. 3
3 king planned to set him over the whole kingdom. 3
6 came by agreement to the king and said to him, 3
6 said to him, "O King Darius, live for ever! 3
7 agreed that the king should establish 3
7 to any god or man . . except to you, O king 3
8 Now, O king, establish the interdict 3
9 King Darius signed the document and interdict. 3
12 said before the king, concerning the interdict 3
12 O king! Did you not sign an interdict, 3
12 god or man within 30 days except to you, O king 3
12 king answered, "The thing stands fast, 3
13 Then they answered before the king, 3
13 pays no heed to you, O king, or the interdict 3
14 Then the king, when he heard these words, 3
15 men came by agreement to the king, and said 3
15 came by agreement to the king, and said to the king 3
15 Know, O king, that it is a law of the Medes 3
15 which the king establishes can be changed. 3
16 king commanded, and Daniel was brought 3
16 king said to Daniel, "May your God, 3
17 king sealed it with his own signet 3
18 king went to his palace, and spent the night 3
19 king arose and went in haste to the den of lions. 3
21 Then Daniel said to the king, "O king, live for ever 3
21 Then Daniel said to the king, "O king, live for ever 3
22 also before you, O king, I have done no wrong. 3
23 Then the king was exceedingly glad 3
24 king commanded, and those men who had accused 3
25 Then King Darius wrote to all the peoples 3
7: 1 In the first year of Belshaz'zar king of Babylon 3
17 four kings who shall arise out of the earth. 3
24 horns, out of this kingdom ten kings shall arise 3
24 different . . and shall put down three kings. 3
8: 1 third year of the reign of King Belshaz'zar 2
20 these are the kings of Media and Persia. 2
21 he-goat is the king of Greece; 2
21 great horn between his eyes is the first king. 2
23 king of bold countenance, one who understands 2
27 then I rose and went about the king's business; 2
9: 6 spoke in thy name to our kings, our princes 2
8 our kings, to our princes, and to our fathers 2
10: 1 In the third year of Cyrus king of Persia 2
11: 2 Behold, three more kings shall arise in Persia; 2
3 Then a mighty king shall arise, who shall rule 2
5 Then the king of the south shall be strong 2
6 daughter of the king of the south shall come 2
6 shall come to the king of the north to make peace; 2
7 enter the fortress of the king of the north 2
8 refrain from attacking the king of the north. 2
9 come into the realm of the king of the south 2
11 king of the south, moved with anger, shall come out 2
11 come out and fight with the king of the north; 2
13 king of the north shall again raise a multitude 2
14 many shall rise against the king of the south; 2
15 Then the king of the north shall come and throw up 2
25 against the king of the south with a great army; 2
25 king of the south shall wage war 2
27 two kings, their minds shall be bent on mischief; 2
36 king shall do according to his will; 2
40 time of the end the king of the south shall attack 2
40 king of the north shall rush upon him like 2
Hos 1: 1 Uzzi'ah, Jotham, Ahaz, and Hezeki'ah, kings of Judah 2
1 Jerobo'am the son of Jo'ash, king of Israel. 2
3: 4 shall dwell many days without king or prince 2
5 and seek the LORD their God, and David their king; 2
5: 1 Hearken, O house of the king! 2
13 went to Assyria, and sent to the great king. 2
7: 3 By their wickedness they make the king glad 2
5 On the day of our king the princes became sick 2
7 All their kings have fallen; 2
8:10 shall cease . . from anointing king and princes. 2
10: 3 We have no king, for we fear not the LORD 2
3 and a king, what could he do for us? 2
6 carried to Assyria, as tribute to the great king. 2
7 Sama'ria's king shall perish 2
15 the king of Israel shall be utterly cut off. 2
11: 5 and Assyria shall be their king 2
13:10 Where now is your king, to save you; 2
10 those of whom you said, "Give me a king and princes"? 2
11 I have given you kings in my anger 2
Ams 1: 1 in the days of Uzzi'ah king of Judah 2
1 Jerobo'am the son of Jo'ash, king of Israel 2
15 their king shall go into exile, he and his princes 2
2: 1 he burned to lime the bones of the king of Edom. 2
5:26 You shall take up Sakkuth your king, and Kaiwan 2
7: 1 was the latter growth after the king's mowings. 2
10 Amazi'ah . . sent to Jerobo'am king of Israel 2
13 never . . at Bethel, for it is the king's sanctuary 2
Jon 3: 6 Then tidings reached the king of Nin'eveh 2
7 By the decree of the king and his nobles 2
Mic 1: 1 Jotham, Ahaz, and Hezeki'ah, kings of Judah 2
14 be a deceitful thing to the kings of Israel. 2
2:13 Their king will pass on before them 2
4: 9 Now why do you cry aloud? Is there no king in you? 2
6: 5 remember what Balak king of Moab devised 2
Nah 3:18 Your shepherds are asleep, O king of Assyria; 2
Hab 1:10 At kings they scoff, and of rulers they make sport. 2
Zep 1: 1 days of Josi'ah the son of Amon, king of Judah. 2
8 I will punish the officials and the king's sons 2
3:15 The King of Israel, the LORD, is in your midst; 2
Hag 1: 1 In the second year of Darius the king 2
15 In the second year of Darius the king 2
Zec 7: 1 In the fourth year of King Darius 2
9: 5 The king shall perish from Gaza; 2
9 O daughter of Jerusalem! Lo, your king comes to you; 2
11: 6 of his shepherd, and each into the hand of his king; 2
14: 5 earthquake in the days of Uzzi'ah king of Judah. 2
9 the LORD will become king over all the earth; 2
10 the Tower of Han'anel to the king's wine presses. 2
16 shall go up year after year to worship the King 2
17 Jerusalem to worship the King, the LORD of hosts 2
Mal 1:14 I am a great King, says the LORD of hosts 2
Mat 1: 6 Jesse the father of David the king. 6
2: 1 Bethlehem of Judea in the days of Herod the king 6
2 Where is he who has been born king of the Jews? 6
3 When Herod the king heard this, he was troubled 6
9 When they had heard the king they went their way; 6
5:35 for it is the city of the great King. 6
10:18 you will be dragged before governors and kings 6
11: 8 those who wear soft raiment are in kings' houses. 6
14: 9 the king was sorry 6
17:25 From whom do kings of the earth take toll 6
18:23 a king who wished to settle accounts 4
21: 5 Behold, your king is coming to you 6
22: 2 The kingdom of heaven may be compared to a king 4
7 The king was angry, and he sent his troops 6
11 But when the king came in to look at the guests 6
13 the king said to the attendants, 'Bind him 6
25:34 Then the King will say to those at his right hand 6
40 the King will answer them, 'Truly, I say to you 6
27:11 Are you the King of the Jews? 6
29 they mocked him, saying, "Hail, King of the Jews! 6
37 This is Jesus the King of the Jews. 6
42 He is the King of Israel 6
Mrk 6:14 King Herod heard of it; 6
22 and the king said to the girl 6
25 she came immediately with haste to the king 6
26 And the king was exceedingly sorry; 6
27 immediately the king sent a soldier of the guard 6
13: 9 stand before governors and kings for my sake 6
15: 2 Pilate asked him, "Are you the King of the Jews? 6
9 you want me to release for you the King of the Jews? 6
12 do with the man whom you call the King of the Jews? 6
18 they began to salute him, "Hail, King of the Jews! 6
26 The King of the Jews. 6
32 Let the Christ, the King of Israel, come down now 6
Lke 1: 5 In the days of Herod, king of Judea 6
7:25 those who . . live in luxury are in kings' courts. 5
10:24 many prophets and kings desired to see 6
14:31 what king, going to encounter another king in war 6
31 what king, going to encounter another king in war 6
19:38 the King who comes in the name of the Lord 6
21:12 you will be brought before kings and governors 6
22:25 The kings . . exercise lordship over them 6
23: 2 saying that he himself is Christ a king. 6
3 Pilate asked him, "Are you the King of the Jews? 6
37 If you are the King of the Jews, save yourself! 6
38 This is the King of the Jews. 6
Joh 1:49 you are the Son of God! You are the King of Israel! 6
6:15 and take him by force to make him king 6
12:13 even the King of Israel! 6
15 behold, your king is coming, sitting on an ass's colt! 6
18:33 Are you the King of the Jews? 6
37 Pilate said to him, "So you are a king? 6
37 Jesus answered, "You say that I am a king 6
39 release for you the King of the Jews? 6
19: 3 they came up to him, saying, "Hail, King of the Jews! 6
12 every one who makes himself a king 6
14 He said to the Jews, "Behold your King! 6
15 Pilate said to them, "Shall I crucify your King? 6
15 We have no king but Caesar. 6
19 it read, "Jesus of Nazareth, the King of the Jews. 6
21 Do not write, 'The King of the Jews,' 6
21 but 'This man said, I am King of the Jews.' 6
Act 4:26 The kings of the earth set themselves in array 6
7:10 favor and wisdom before Pharaoh, king of Egypt 6
18 another king who had not known Joseph. 6
9:15 to carry my name before the Gentiles and kings 6
12: 1 Herod the king laid violent hands upon some 6
20 persuaded Blastus, the king's chamberlain 6
20 their country depended on the king's country for food. 8
13:21 Then they asked for a king; and God gave them Saul 6
22 he raised up David to be their king 6
17: 7 saying that there is another king, Jesus. 6
25:13 Agrippa the king and Berni'ce 6
14 Festus laid Paul's case before the king, saying 6
24 King Agrippa and all who are present with us 6
26 especially before you, King Agrippa 6
26: 2 I think myself fortunate . . King Agrippa 6
7 for this hope I am accused by Jews, O king! 6
13 At midday, O king, I saw on the way a light 6
19 Wherefore, O King Agrippa, I was not disobedient 6
26 the king knows about these things 6
27 King Agrippa, do you believe the prophets? 6
30 Then the king rose, and the governor and Berni'ce 6
2Co 11:32 the governor under King Ar'etas guarded the city 6
1Ti 1:17 the King of ages, immortal, invisible, the only God 6
2: 2 for kings and all who are in high positions 6
6:15 the King of kings and Lord of lords 6
15 the King of kings and Lord of lords 7
Heb 7: 1 For this Melchiz'edek, king of Salem 6
1 returning from the slaughter of the kings 6
2 He is first . . king of righteousness 6
2 then he is also king of Salem, that is, king of peace. 6
2 then he is also king of Salem, that is, king of peace. 6
11:23 they were not afraid of the king's edict. 6
27 not being afraid of the anger of the king 6
Rev 1: 5 Jesus Christ . . the ruler of kings on earth. 6
6:15 Then the kings of the earth and the great men 6
9:11 as king over them the angel of the bottomless pit; 6
10:11 many peoples and nations and tongues and kings. 6
15: 3 Just and true are thy ways, O King of the ages! 6
16:12 to prepare the way for the kings of the east. 6
14 who go abroad to the kings of the whole world 6
17: 2 kings of the earth have committed fornication 6
10 seven kings, five of whom have fallen 6
12 And the ten horns that you saw are ten kings 6
12 they are to receive authority as kings 6
14 Lamb . . for he is Lord of lords and King of kings 6
14 Lamb . . for he is Lord of lords and King of kings 6
18 which has dominion over the kings of the earth. 4
18: 3 kings of the earth have committed fornication 6
9 the kings of the earth . . will weep and wail 6
19:16 a name inscribed, King of kings and Lord of lords. 6
16 a name inscribed, King of kings and Lord of lords. 6
18 to eat the flesh of kings, the flesh of captains 6
19 And I saw the beast and the kings of the earth 6
21:24 the kings of the earth shall bring their glory 6
1Es 1: 3 Solomon the king, the son of David 6
5 the directions of David king of Israel 6
15 Eddinus, who represented the king. 6
18 according to the command of King Josiah. 6
21 none of the kings of Israel 6
25 Pharaoh, king of Egypt, went to make war 6
26 the king of Egypt sent word to him saying 6
26 What have we to do with each other, king of Judea? 6
29 the commanders came down against King Josiah. 6
30 the king said to his servants 6
33 the book of the histories of the kings of Judea; 6
33 recorded in the book of the kings of Israel 6
34 made him king in succession to Josiah his father. 6
35 Then the king of Egypt deposed him from reigning 6
37 the king of Egypt made Jehoiakim . . king 6
37 made Jehoiakim . . king of Judea and Jerusalem. 6

40 Nebuchadnezzar king of Babylon 6
42 written in the chronicles of the kings. 6
46 made Zedekiah king of Judea and Jerusalem. 6
48 though King Nebuchadnezzar had made him swear 6
52 bring against them the kings of the Chaldeans. 6
2: 1 In the first year of Cyrus as king of the Persians 7
2 the spirit of Cyrus king of the Persians 6
3 Thus says Cyrus king of the Persians 6
3 the Lord Most High, has made me king of the world 6
10 Cyrus the king also brought out the holy vessels 6
11 When Cyrus king of the Perians brought these out 6
16 in the time of Artaxerxes king of the Persians 6
17 To King Artaxerxes our lord 6
18 Now be it known to our lord the king 6
19 will even resist kings. 6
21 to speak to our lord the king 6
22 troubling both kings and other cities 6
24 we now make known to you, O lord and king 6
25 the king, in reply to Rehum . . wrote as follows 6
26 this city from of old has fought against kings 6
27 mighty and cruel kings ruled in Jerusalem 6
29 go no further to the annoyance of kings. 6
30 when the letter from King Artaxerxes was read 6
30 the reign of Darius king of the Persians. 4
3: 1 Now King Darius gave a great banquet 6
3 Darius the king went to his bedroom 6
4 who kept guard over the person of the king 6
5 Darius the king will give rich gifts 6
8 put them under the pillow of Darius the king 6
9 said, "When the king wakes 6
9 the king and the three nobles of Persia 6
11 The second wrote, "The king is strongest. 6
13 When the king awoke 6
19 It makes equal the mind of the king and the orphan 6
21 forgets kings and satraps 6
4: 1 who had spoken of the strength of the king 6
3 the king is stronger; he is their lord and master 6
5 do not disobey the king's command 6
5 they bring everything to the king 6
6 reap the harvest and bring some to the king 6
6 they compel one another to pay taxes to the king. 6
12 Gentlemen, why is not the king the strongest 6
14 Gentlemen, is not the king great 6
15 Women gave birth to the king and to every people 6
28 Is not the king great in his power? 6
29 Apame, the king's concubine 6
29 she would sit at the king's right hand 6
30 take the crown from the king's head 6
30 slap the king with her left hand. 6
31 the king would gaze at her with mouth agape 6
33 the king and the nobles looked at one another 6
37 Wine is unrighteous, the king is unrighteous 6
42 the king said to him, "Ask what you wish 6
43 he said to the king 6
43 in the day when you became king 5
46 now, O lord the king, this is what I ask and request 6
46 vowed to the King of heaven with your own lips. 6
47 Darius the king rose, and kissed him 6
58 praised the King of heaven, saying 6
5: 6 Darius the king of the Persians 6
7 Nebuchadnezzar king of Babylon 6
55 the decree . . from Cyrus king of the Persians. 6
60 according to . . David king of Israel 6
69 the days of Esarhaddon king of the Assyrians 6
71 as Cyrus the king of the Persians has commanded 6
73 as long as King Cyrus lived 6
6: 8 To King Darius, greeting 6
8 Let it be fully known to our lord the king 6
14 a king of Israel who was great and strong 6
15 the hands of Nebuchadnezzar king of Babylon 6
15 king of Babylon, king of the Chaldeans; 6
17 King Cyrus wrote that . . 6
18 these Cyrus the king took out again 6
21 Now therefore, if it seems wise, O king 6
21 of our lord the king that are in Babylon; 6
22 was done with the consent of King Cyrus 6
22 if it is approved by our lord the king 6
24 King Cyrus ordered the building of the house 6
25 paid from the treasury of Cyrus the king; 6
31 libations . . for the king and his children 6
33 Therefore may the Lord . . destroy every king 6
34 I, King Darius, have decreed that it be done 6
7: 1 following the orders of King Darius 6
4 Darius and Artaxerxes, kings of the Persians,. 6
5 in the sixth year of King Darius 6
15 had changed the will of the king of the Assyrians 6
8: 1 Artaxerxes the king of the Persians 6
4 the king showed him honor 6
4 found favor before the king in all his requests. •
6 the fifth month (this was the king's seventh year); 6
8 written commission from Artaxerxes the king 6
9 King Artaxerxes to Ezra the priest 6
19 I, Artaxerxes the king, have commanded 6
21 wrath may not come upon the kingdom of the king 4
25 who put this into the heart of the king 6
26 who honored me in the sight of the king 6
28 in the reign of Artaxerxes the king 4
51 I was ashamed to ask the king for foot soldiers 6
52 for we had said to the king 6
55 which the king himself . . had given. 6
67 they delivered the king's orders 6
77 our brethren and our kings and our priests 6
77 were given over to the kings of the earth 6
80 the kings of the Persians 6
2Es 1: 3 in the reign of Artaxerxes, king of the Persians. 11
10 For their sake I have overthrown many kings 11
12:14 12 kings shall reign in it, one after another. 11
20 Eight kings shall arise in it 11
23 the Most High will raise up three kings 10
26 one of the kings shall die in his bed •
13:40 in the days of King Hoshea 11
40 Shalmaneser the king of the Assyrians 11
15:16 in their might have no respect for their king 11
20 I call together all the kings of the earth 11
33 and indecision upon their kings. 11
Tob 1: 2 in the days of Shalmaneser, king of the Assyrians 6
18 if Sennacherib the king put to death 6
18 When the bodies were sought by the king 6
19 went and informed the king about me 6
12: 7 It is good to guard the secret of a king 6
11 It is good to guard the secret of a king 6
13: 6 exalt the King of the ages. 6
7 I exalt my God; my soul exalts the King of heaven 6
10 praise the King of the ages 6
11 gifts for the King of heaven 6
15 Let my soul praise God the great King. 6
Jdt 1: 2 he is the king who built walls about Ecbatana •
5 King Nebuchadnezzar made war 6
5 Nebuchadnezzar made war against King Arphaxad 6
7 Then Nebuchadnezzar king of the Assyrians sent 6
11 Nebuchadnezzar king of the Assyrians 6
13 he led his forces against King Arphaxad 6
2: 1 Nebuchadnezzar king of the Assyrians 6
4 Nebuchadnezzar king of the Assyrians 6
5 Thus says the Great King 6
19 to go ahead of King Nebuchadnezzar 6
3: 2 the servants of Nebuchadnezzar, the Great King 6
4: 1 Nebuchadnezzar the king of the Assyrians 6
5: 3 Who rules over them as king, leading their army? 6
11 the king of Egypt became hostile to them 6
6: 3 the king's servants will destroy them as one man. •
4 So says King Nebuchadnezzar 6
9:12 Creator of the waters, King of all thy creation 6
11: 1 Nebuchadnezzar, the king of all the earth. 6
4 the servants of my lord King Nebuchadnezzar. 6
7 Nebuchadnezzar the king of the whole earth 6
23 shall live in the house of King Nebuchadnezzar 6
14:18 the house of King Nebuchadnezzar 6
AEs 10: 6 Esther, whom the king married and made queen. 6
11: 3 a great man, serving in the court of the king. 6
4 Nebuchadnezzar king of Babylon 6
4 Jeconiah king of Judea 6
12: 1 Gabatha and Tharra, the two eunuchs of the king 6
2 preparing to lay hands upon Artaxerxes the king; 6
2 he informed the king concerning them. 6
3 Then the king examined the two eunuchs 6
4 The king made a permanent record of these things 6
5 the king ordered Mordecai to serve in the court 6
6 was in great honor with the king 6
6 because of the two eunuchs of the king. 6
13: 1 The Great King, Artaxerxes . . writes thus 6
4 disregard the ordinances of the kings 6
9 O Lord, Lord, King who rulest over all things 6
15 now, O Lord God and King, God of Abraham 6
14: 3 O my Lord, thou only art our King 6
10 to magnify for ever a mortal king. 6
12 give me courage, O King of the gods 6
17 I have not honored the king's feast 6
15: 6 she stood before the king 6
8 God changed the spirit of the king to gentleness 6
16 the king was agitated 6
16: 1 The Great King, Artaxerxes 6
Wis 6: 1 Listen therefore, O kings, and understand 6
24 a sensible king is the stability of his people. 6
7: 5 no king has had a different beginning 6
9: 7 Thou hast chosen me to be king of thy people 6
10:16 withstood dread kings with wonders and signs. 6
11:10 as a stern king does in condemnation. 6
12:14 nor can any king or monarch confront thee 6
14:17 a visible image of the king whom they honored 6
18 even those who did not know the king •
18:11 the common man suffered the same loss as the king; 6
Sir 7: 4 nor the seat of honor from the king. 6
5 nor display your wisdom before the king. 6
8: 2 and has perverted the minds of kings 6
10: 3 An undisciplined king will ruin his people 6
10 the king of today will die tomorrow. 6
11: 5 Many kings have had to sit on the ground 9
38: 2 he will receive a gift from the king. 6
45: 3 the Lord glorified him in the presence of kings. 6
25 the heritage of the king is from son to son only 6
46:20 he prophesied and revealed to the king his death 6
47:11 he gave him the covenant of kings 6
48: 6 who brought kings down to destruction 6
8 who anointed kings to inflict retribution 6
23 he lengthened the life of the king. 6
49: 4 the kings of Judah came to an end; 6
51: 1 I will give thanks to thee, O Lord and King 6
6 slander of an unrighteous tongue to the king 6
Bar 1: 3 Jeconiah the son of Jehoiakim, king of Judah 6
8 Zedekiah the son of Josiah, king of Judah 6
9 after Nebuchadnezzar king of Babylon had 6
11 Nebuchadnezzar king of Babylon 6
12 Nebuchadnezzar king of Babylon 6
16 to our kings and our princes and our priests 6
2: 1 against our kings and against our princes 6
19 any righteous deeds of our fathers or our kings 6
21 serve the king of Babylon, and you will remain 6
22 if you . . will not serve the king of Babylon 6
24 not obey thy voice, to serve the king of Babylon; 6
24 bones of our kings and the bones of our fathers 6
LJr 1: 1 taken to Babylon as captives by the king 6
2 Nebuchadnezzar, king of the Babylonians. 6
18 a man who has offended a king 6
34 They cannot set up a king or depose one. 6
51 It will be manifest to all the nations and kings 6
53 they cannot set up a king over a country 6
56 they can offer no resistance to a king or any enemies. 6
59 it is better to be a king who shows his courage 6
66 For they can neither curse nor bless kings; 6
Aza 1: 9 an unjust king, the most wicked in all the world. 6
23 the king's servants who threw them 6
Bel 1: 1 When King Astyages was laid with his fathers 6
2 Daniel was a companion of the king 6
4 The king revered it 6
5 the king said to him, "Why do you not worship Bel? 6
6 The king said to him 6
7 Do not be deceived, O king 6
8 Then the king was angry, and he called his priests 6
9 Daniel said to the king 6
10 the king went with Daniel into the temple of Bel. 6
11 you yourself, O king, shall set forth the food 6
14 the king set forth the food for Bel 6
14 in the presence of the king alone 6
14 shut the door and sealed it with the king's signet 6
16 Early in the morning the king rose and came 6
17 the king said, "Are the seals unbroken, Daniel? 6
17 He answered, "They are unbroken, O king. 6
18 the king looked at the table 6
19 restrained the king from going in, and said 6
20 The king said, "I see the footsteps of men and women 6
21 the king was enraged, and he seized the priests 6
22 Therefore the king put them to death 6
24 the king said to Daniel 6
26 if you, O king, will give me permission 6
26 The king said, "I give you permission. 6
28 conspired against the king, saying 6
28 The king has become a Jew; he has destroyed Bel 6
29 Going to the king, they said, "Hand Daniel over to us 6
30 The king saw that they were pressing him hard 6
40 the king came to mourn for Daniel 6
41 the king shouted with a loud voice •
1Mc 1: 1 defeated Darius, king of the Persians 6
1 he succeeded him as king 7
1 (He had previously become king of Greece.) 7
2 and put to death the kings of the earth. 6
10 Antiochus Epiphanes, son of Antiochus the king; 6
13 some of the people eagerly went to the king 6
18 He engaged Ptolemy king of Egypt in battle 6
29 the king sent . . a chief collector of tribute 6
41 Then the king wrote to his whole kingdom 6
43 the Gentiles accepted the command of the king. 6
44 the king sent letters by messengers to Jerusalem 6
50 does not obey the command of the king shall die 6
57 the decree of the king condemned him to death. 6
2:15 the king's officers . . came to the city of Modein 6
17 Then the king's officers spoke to Mattathias 6
18 be the first to come and do what the king commands 6
18 you . . will be numbered among the friends of the king 6
19 live under the rule of the king obey him 4
22 We will not obey the king's words 6
23 When he had finished speaking these words 6
25 At the same time he killed the king's officer 6
31 it was reported to the king's officers 6
31 it was reported to the king's officers 6
33 do what the king commands, and you will live. 6
34 nor will we do what the king commands 6
48 hands of the Gentiles and kings 6
3: 7 He embittered many kings 6
14 who scorn the king's command. 6
26 His fame reached the king 6
27 When king Antiochus heard these reports 6
30 give more lavishly than preceding kings. 6
32 He left Lysias . . in charge of the king's affairs 4
37 Then the king took the remaining half 6
38 mighty men among the friends of the king 6
39 destroy it, as the king had commanded. 6
42 what the king had commanded to do to the people 6
4: 3 to attack the king's force in Emmaus 6
27 nor had they turned out as the king had commanded 6
6: 1 King Antiochus was going through the . . provinces 6
2 Alexander, the son of Philip, the Macedonian king 6
8 When the king heard this news, he was astounded 6
15 guide Antiochus his son and bring him up to be king 7
16 Antiochus the king died there in the 149th year. 6
17 when Lysias learned that the king was dead 6
17 when Lysias learned that the king was dead 7

22 They went to the king and said, "How long 6
28 The king was enraged when he heard this 6
32 encamped . . opposite the camp of the king 6
33 Early in the morning the king rose 6
40 the king's army was spread out on the high hills 6
42 600 men of the king's army fell. 6
43 he supposed that the king was upon it. 6
48 The soldiers of the king's army went up to Jerusalem 6
48 the king encamped in Judea and at Mount Zion. 6
50 the king took Beth-zur and stationed a guard there 6
55 Philip, whom King Antiochus . . had appointed 6
55 to bring up Antiochus his son to be king 7
56 with the forces that had gone with the king 6
57 said to the king, to the commanders of the forces 6
60 The speech pleased the king and the commanders 6
61 the king and the commanders gave them their oath 6
62 when the king entered Mount Zion 6
7: 6 they brought to the king this accusation 6
7 the ruin . . brought . . upon the land of the king 6
8 the king chose Bacchides, one of the king's friends 6
8 the king chose Bacchides, one of the king's friends 6
8 chose Bacchides . . was faithful to the king 4
20 then Bacchides went back to the king. 6
25 returned to the king and brought wicked charges 6
26 the king sent Nicanor, one of his honored princes 6
33 burnt offering . . being offered for the king. 6
41 When the messengers from the king spoke 6
8: 4 They also subdued the kings who came against them 6
5 Philip, and Perseus king of the Macedonians 6
6 They also defeated Antiochus the Great, king of Asia 6
8 took from him and gave to Eumenes the king. 6
12 They have subdued kings far and near 6
13 Those whom they wish to help and to make kings 7
13 Those whom they wish to help . . they make kings 7
31 wrongs which King Demetrius is doing to them 6
9:57 he returned to the king, and the land of Judah 6
10: 2 When Demetrius the king heard of it 6
8 the king had given him authority to recruit 6
15 Now Alexander the king heard of all the promises 6
18 King Alexander to his brother Jonathan, greeting 6
20 you are to be called the king's friend 6
25 King Demetrius to the nation of the Jews, greeting 6
36 Let Jews be enrolled in the king's forces 6
36 that is due to all the forces of the king. 6
37 stationed in the great strongholds of the king 6
37 just as the king has commanded in the land of Judah 6
40 15,000 shekels of silver . . out of the king's revenues 6
44 be paid from the revenues of the king 6
45 also be paid from the revenues of the king. 6
48 Now Alexander the king assembled large forces 6
49 The two kings met in battle, and the army 6
51 sent ambassadors to Ptolemy king of Egypt 6
55 Ptolemy the king replied and said 6
58 Alexander the king met him 6
58 and celebrated . . with great pomp, as kings do. 6
59 Then Alexander the king wrote to Jonathan 6
60 went with pomp to Ptolemais and met the two kings; 6
61 the king paid no attention to them. 6
62 The king gave orders to take off Jonathan's garments 6
63 The king also seated him at his side 6
65 the king honored him and enrolled him 6
68 When Alexander the king heard of it 6
88 When Alexander the king heard of these things 6
89 it is the custom to give to the kinsmen of kings 6
11: 1 Then the king of Egypt gathered great forces 6
2 Alexander the king had commanded them 6
5 They also told the king what Jonathan had done 6
5 the king kept silent. 6
6 Jonathan met the king at Joppa with pomp 6
7 Jonathan went with the king as far as the river 6
8 King Ptolemy gained control of the coastal cities 6
9 He sent envoys to Demetrius the king, saying, "Come 6
14 Alexander the king was in Cilicia at that time 6
16 and King Ptolemy was exalted 6
18 But King Ptolemy died three days later 6
21 certain lawless men . . went to the king 6
24 for he went to the king at Ptolemais 6
26 the king treated him as his predecessors 6
28 Then Jonathan asked the king to free Judea 6
29 The king consented, and wrote a letter to Jonathan 6
30 King Demetrius to Jonathan his brother 6
32 'King Demetrius to Lasthenes his father 6
34 royal taxes which the king formerly received 6
38 Now when Demetrius the king saw 6
41 Jonathan sent to Demetrius the king the request 6
44 when they came to the king 6
44 the king rejoiced at their arrival. 6
45 they wanted to kill the king. 6
46 But the king fled into the palace 6
47 So the king called the Jews to his aid 6
48 they saved the king. 6
49 they cried out to the king with this entreaty 6
51 So the Jews gained glory in the eyes of the king 6
52 So Demetrius the king sat on the throne 6
57 and make you one of the friends of the king. 6
12: 7 Arius, who was king among you 7
13 the kings round about us have waged war against us. 6
20 Arius, king of the Spartans 6
39 to raise his hand against Antiochus the king. 6
13:31 Trypho dealt treacherously with the young king 6
34 sent them to Demetrius the king with a request 6
35 Demetrius the king sent him a favorable reply 6
36 King Demetrius to Simon, the high priest 6
36 Simon, the high priest and friend of kings 6
14: 1 Demetrius the king assembled his forces 6
2 When Arsaces the king of Persia and Media heard 6
13 the kings were crushed in those days. 6
38 King Demetrius confirmed him 6
39 he made him one of the king's friends •
15: 1 Antiochus, the son of Demetrius the king 6
2 King Antiochus to Simon the high priest 6
5 the kings before me have granted you 6
15 with letters to the kings and countries 6
16 Lucius, consul of the Romans, to King Ptolemy 6
19 have decided to write to the kings and countries 6
22 wrote the same thing to Demetrius the king 6
25 Antiochus the king besieged Dor anew 6
32 So Athenobius the friend of the king came 6
32 He reported to him the words of the king 6
36 returned in wrath to the king and reported to him 6
36 the king was greatly angered. 6
38 Then the king made Cendebeus commander-in-chief 6
39 the king pursued Trypho. 6
41 as the king had ordered him. 6
16:18 wrote a report . . and sent it to the king 6
2Mc 1:10 teacher of Ptolemy the king 6
11 for taking our side against the king. 6
20 having been commissioned by the king of Persia 6
24 who alone art King and art kind 6
33 it was reported to the king of the Persians 6
34 the king investigated the matter 6
35 with those persons whom the king favored 6
2:13 the books about the kings and prophets 6
13 letters of kings about votive offerings. 6
3: 2 the kings themselves honored the place 6
3 even Seleucus, the king of Asia 6
6 to fall under the control of the king. 6
7 When Apollonius met the king 6
7 The king chose Heliodorus 6
8 in fact to carry out the king's purpose. 6
13 because of the king's commands which he had 8
32 fearing that the king might get the notion 6
35 he marched off with his forces to the king. 6
37 When the king asked Heliodorus . . he replied 6
4: 5 he betook himself to the king 6
6 without the king's attention 8
8 promising the king at an interview 6
10 When the king assented and Jason came to office 6
18 the king was present 6
21 for the coronation of Philometor as king 6
23 to carry the money to the king 6
24 he, when presented to the king, extolled him 6
25 After receiving the king's orders he returned 8
27 any of the money promised to the king. 6
28 the two of them were summoned by the king 6
30 Antiochis, the king's concubine. 6
31 the king went hastily to settle the trouble 6
36 the king returned from the region of Cilicia 6
44 When the king came to Tyre 6
45 to win over the king. 6
46 taking the king aside into a colonnade •
46 Ptolemy . . induced the king to change his mind. 6
5:11 When news of what had happened reached the king 6
16 the votive offerings which other kings had made 6
18 whom Seleucus the king sent 6
6: 1 the king sent an Athenian senator 6
7 the monthly celebration of the king's birthday 6
21 which had been commanded by the king 6
7: 1 were being compelled by the king 6
3 The king fell into a rage 6
5 the king ordered them to take him to the fire •
9 the King of the universe will raise us up 6
12 As a result the king himself and those with him 6
16 he looked at the king, and said •
25 the king called the mother to him 6
30 I will not obey the king's command 6
39 The king fell into a rage 6
8: 8 for aid to the king's government. 6
9 one of the king's chief friends •
10 to make up for the king the tribute due to the Romans 6
9:19 Antiochus their king and general 6
25 I have appointed my son Antiochus to be king 6
10:13 he was accused before Eupator by the king's friends •
11: 1 Lysias, the king's guardian and kinsman 6
14 promising that he would persuade the king 6
15 the king granted every request 6
18 I have informed the king of everything 6
22 The king's letter ran thus 6
22 King Antiochus to his brother Lysias, greeting. 6
27 To the nation the king's letter was as follows 6
27 King Antiochus to the senate of the Jews 6
35 what Lysias the kinsman of the king has granted 6
36 which he decided are to be referred to the king 6
12: 1 Lysias returned to the king 6
13: 4 the King of kings aroused the anger of Antiochus 6
4 the King of kings aroused the anger of Antiochus 6
9 The king with barbarous arrogance was coming 6
13 before the king's army could enter Judea 6
15 he attacked the king's pavilion at night 8
18 The king . . tried strategy in attacking their positions. 6
22 The king negotiated a second time 6
26 how the king's attack and withdrawal turned out. 6
14: 4 went to King Demetrius in about the 151st year 6
8 concerned for the interests of the king 6
9 Since you are acquainted, O king, with the details 6
11 the rest of the king's friends •
27 The king became excited 6
29 Since it was not possible to oppose the king 6
15: 5 to take up arms and finish the king's business. 8
22 in the time of Hezekiah king of Judea 6
3Mc 1: 3 Dositheus . . had led the king away •
3 incurred the vengeance meant for the king. •
11 the king was by no means persuaded. •
15 since this has happened," the king said •
21 because of what the king was profanely plotting. •
25 the elders near the king 6
2: 2 Lord, Lord, king of the heavens 6
9 O King, when you had created the . . earth 6
13 see now, O holy King 6
26 intently observing the king's purpose 6
31 their future association with the king. 6
3: 1 When the impious king comprehended this situation •
7 loyal neither to the king nor to his authorities 6
11 the king, boastful of his present good fortune •
12 King Ptolemy Philopator to his generals 6
19 in defiance of kings and their own benefactors 6
4:11 the voyage was concluded as the king had decreed 6
11 communicate with the king's forces •
12 the king, hearing that . . •
16 The king was greatly . . filled with joy 6
17 the scribes declared to the king 6
5: 1 the king . . was filled with overpowering anger •
10 to report to the king about these preparations. 6
11 the Lord sent upon the king a portion of sleep 6
14 approached the king and nudged him. 6
16 The king . . returned to his drinking 6
18 the king summoned Hermon 6
20 the king . . said that the Jews were benefited •
21 When the king had spoken 6
26 while the king was receiving his friends 6
26 indicating that what the king desired was ready 6
28 he had implanted in the king's mind a forgetfulness •
29 Hermon and all the king's friends pointed out •
29 O king, according to your eager purpose. 6
34 The king's friends . . sullenly slipped away •
35 Then the Jews, upon hearing what the king had said 6
35 praised the manifest Lord God, King of kings 6
35 praised the manifest Lord God, King of kings 6
36 The king, however, reconvened the party 6
40 O king, how long will you try us 6
42 Upon this the king . . firmly swore an . . oath 6
46 and urged the king on to the matter at hand. 6
6: 2 King of great power 6
5 oppressive king of the Assyrians 6
16 the king arrived at the hippodrome 6
20 Even the king began to shudder bodily 6
22 Then the king's anger was turned to pity and tears 6
30 Then the king . . summoned the official 6
33 Likewise also the king 6
37 Then they petitioned the king 6
40 provided with everything by the king 6
41 The king granted their request at once 6
7: 1 King Ptolemy Philopator to the generals 6
10 they requested of the king 6
11 the king's government. 6
12 The king then . . granted them a general license •
18 the king had generously provided all things to them 6
20 at the king's command 6
4Mc 3: 6 the story of King David's thirst. 6
10 the king was extremely thirsty 6
12 because of the king's craving 6
12 respecting the king's desire 6
14 from it boldly brought the king a drink. 6
20 even Seleucus Nicanor, king of Asia 6
4: 3 because I am loyal to the king's government 6
3 belong to King Seleucus. 6
4 he praised Simon for his service to the king 6
6 He said that he had come with the king's authority 6
13 lest King Seleucus suppose 6
14 went away to report to the king what had happened 6
15 When King Seleucus died 6
17 he would pay the king 3,660 talents annually. •
18 the king appointed him high priest •
5: 4 one man . . was brought before the king •
36 You, O king, shall not stain the honorable mouth •
6: 4 Obey the king's commands! 6
13 some of the king's retinue came to him and said 6
7:10 O supreme king over the passions, Eleazar! 6
8:17 Since the king has summoned and exhorted us 6
22 for fearing the king when we are under compulsion. 6
26 when we can live in peace if we obey the king? 6
10:13 obey the king and save yourself. 6
12: 8 he said, "Let me loose, let me speak to the king 6
14: 2 O reason, more royal than kings 6

king *See also* forfeit, make, money, possession, proclaim, set, treasury, use.

become king 1. מלך 2. מַלְכוּת 3. βασιλεύω
1Kg 1:11 that Adoni'jah the son of Haggith has become king 1
16:22 so Tibni died, and Omri became king. 1
2Kg 1:17 Jeho'ram, his brother, became king in his stead 1
3: 1 Jeho'ram . . became king over Israel in Sama'ria 1
8:15 And Haz'ael became king in his stead. 1
17 He was 32 years old when became king 1
13:24 When Haz'ael . . died, Ben-ha'dad his son became king 1
24: 8 Jehoi'achin was 18 years old when he became king 1
18 Zedeki'ah was 21 years old when he became king 1
Prv 30:22 a slave when he becomes king 1
Jer 52: 1 Zedeki'ah 21 years old when he became king; 1
31 king of Babylon, in the year that he became king 2
Dan 9: 1 became king over the realm of the Chalde'ans- 1
1Co 4: 8 Without us you have become kings! 3
1Es 1:43 Jehoiachin his son became king in his stead 3
1Mc 1:16 he determined to become king of the land of Egypt 3
11:19 So Demetrius became king in the 167th year. 3
40 to become king in place of his father 3
12:39 Then Trypho attempted to become king in Asia 3
13:32 and became king in his place 3

king of all 1. παμβασιλεύς
Sir 50:15 a pleasing odor to the Most High, the King of all. 1

kingdom 1. מְלוּכָה 2. מַלְכוּת 3. מַמְלָכָה 4. מַמְלְכוּת 5. מַלְכוּ (A) 6. מַלְכוּת (A) 7. ἀρχή 8. βασιλεία 9. βασιλεύω 10. βασιλικός 11. ἐπικράτησις 12. regnum
Gen 10:10 The beginning of his kingdom was Ba'bel, Erech 3
20: 9 brought on me and my kingdom a great sin? 3
Exd 19: 6 be to me a kingdom of priests and a holy nation. 3
Num24: 7 his kingdom shall be exalted. 2
32:33 gave . . the kingdom of Sihon king of the Amorites 3
33 Moses gave . . the kingdom of Og king of Bashan 3
Deu 3: 4 region of Argob, the kingdom of Og in Bashan. 3
10 Sal'ecah and Ed're-i, cities of the kingdom of Og 3
13 rest of Gilead, and all Bashan, the kingdom of Og 3
21 so will the LORD do to all the kingdoms 3
17:18 when he sits on the throne of his kingdom, he shall 3
20 continue long in his kingdom, he and his children 3
28:25 be a horror to all the kingdoms of the earth. 3
Jos 11:10 for Hazor . . was the head of all those kingdoms. 3
13:12 all the kingdom of Og in Bashan 4
21 and all the kingdom of Sihon king of the Amorites 4
27 the rest of the kingdom of Sihon king of Heshbon 4
30 all Bashan, the whole kingdom of Og king of Bashan 4
31 the cities of the kingdom of Og in Bashan; 4
1Sm 10:16 about the matter of the kingdom . . he did not tell 1
18 delivered . . from the hand of all the kingdoms 3
11:14 let us go to Gilgal and there renew the kingdom. 1
13:13 the LORD would have established your kingdom 3
14 But now your kingdom shall not continue; 3
15:28 The LORD has torn the kingdom of Israel from you 4
18: 8 and what more can he have but the kingdom? 1
20:31 you nor your kingdom shall be established. 2
24:20 the kingdom of Israel shall be established 3
28:17 the LORD has torn the kingdom out of your hand 3
2Sm 3:10 to transfer the kingdom from the house of Saul 3
28 I and my kingdom are . . guiltless before the LORD 3
5:12 had established him . . exalted his kingdom 3
7:12 I will raise . . and I will establish his kingdom. 3
13 and I will establish the throne of his kingdom 3
16 your house and your kingdom shall be made sure 3
16: 3 will give me back the kingdom of my father.' 4
8 the LORD has given the kingdom into the hand 1
1Kg 2:12 father; and his kingdom was firmly established. 2
15 You know that the kingdom was mine, and that all 1
15 the kingdom has turned about and become my 1
22 Ask for him the kingdom also; for he is my elder 1
46 the kingdom was established in the hand 3
4:21 Solomon ruled over all the kingdoms 3
10:20 The like of it was never made in any kingdom. 3
11:11 Since . . I will surely tear the kingdom from you 3
13 However I will not tear away all the kingdom; 3
31 to tear the kingdom from the hand of Solomon 3
34 I will not take the whole kingdom out of his hand; 3
35 I will take the kingdom out of his son's hand 1
12:21 to restore the kingdom to Rehobo'am 1
26 the kingdom will turn back to the house of David; 3
14: 8 tore the kingdom away from the house of David 3
18:10 no nation or kingdom whither my lord has not sent 3
10 he would take an oath of the kingdom or nation 3
2Kg 19:15 God, thou alone, of all the kingdoms of the earth; 3
19 that all the kingdoms of the earth may know 3
1Ch 10:14 the LORD . . turned the kingdom over to David 1
11:10 men, who gave him strong support in his kingdom 2
12:23 to turn the kingdom of Saul over to him 2
14: 2 his kingdom was highly exalted 2
16:20 from one kingdom to another people 3
17:11 and I will establish his kingdom. 2
14 confirm him in my house and in my kingdom for ever 2
28: 5 throne of the kingdom of the LORD over Israel. 2
7 I will establish his kingdom for ever 2
29:11 thine is the kingdom, O LORD, and thou art exalted 3
30 and upon all the kingdoms of the countries. 3
2Ch 1: 1 Solomon . . established himself in his kingdom 2
9:19 The like of it was never made in any kingdom. 3
11: 1 to restore the kingdom to Rehobo'am. 3
17 They strengthened the kingdom of Judah 2
12: 8 service of the kingdoms of the countries. 3
13: 8 you think to withstand the kingdom of the LORD 3
14: 5 And the kingdom had rest under him. 3
17: 5 the LORD established the kingdom in his hand; 3
10 fell upon all the kingdoms of the lands 3
20: 6 not rule over all the kingdoms of the nations? 3
29 came on all the kingdoms of other countries 3
21: 3 but he gave the kingdom to Jeho'ram 3
22: 9 had no one able to rule the kingdom. 3
29:21 for a sin offering for the kingdom 3
32:15 for no god of any nation or kingdom has been able 3
33:13 brought him again to Jerusalem into his kingdom. 2
36:20 establishment of the kingdom of Persia 2
22 made a proclamation throughout all his kingdom 2
23 given me all the kingdoms of the earth 3
Ezr 1: 1 made a proclamation throughout all his kingdom 2
2 given me all the kingdoms of the earth 3
7:13 Israel or their priests or Levites in my kingdom 6
Neh 9:22 thou didst give them kingdoms and peoples 3
35 not serve thee in their kingdom, and in thy great 2
Est 1:14 saw the king's face, and sat first in the kingdom 2
20 is proclaimed throughout all his kingdom 2
2: 3 officers in all the provinces of his kingdom 2
3: 6 throughout the whole kingdom of Ahasu-e'rus. 2
8 There is . . in all the provinces of your kingdom; 2
4:14 have . . come to the kingdom for such a time as this? 2
5: 3 It shall be . . even to the half of my kingdom. 2
6 Even to the half of my kingdom, it shall be 2
7: 2 Even to the half of my kingdom, it shall be 2
9:30 to the 127 provinces of the kingdom of Ahasu-e'rus 2
Ps 46: 6 The nations rage, the kingdoms totter; 3
68:32 Sing to God, O kingdoms of the earth; sing praises 3
79: 6 on the kingdoms that do not call on thy name! 3
102:22 when peoples gather together, and kingdoms 3
103:19 his kingdom rules over all. 2
105:13 from one kingdom to another people 3
135:11 Sihon . . Og, . . , and all the kingdoms of Canaan 3
145:11 They shall speak of the glory of thy kingdom 2
12 make known . . glorious splendor of thy kingdom. 2
13 Thy kingdom is an everlasting kingdom 2
13 Thy kingdom is an everlasting kingdom 2
Ecc 4:14 though . . in his own kingdom had been born poor. 2
Isa 9: 7 upon the throne of David, and over his kingdom 3
10:10 my hand has reached to the kingdoms of the idols 3
13: 4 Hark, an uproar of kingdoms, of nations gathering 3
19 Babylon, the glory of kingdoms, the splendor 3
14:16 who made the earth tremble, who shook kingdoms 3
17: 3 from E'phraim, and the kingdom from Damascus; 3
19: 2 city against city, kingdom against kingdom; 3
2 city against city, kingdom against kingdom; 3
23:11 hand over the sea, he has shaken the kingdoms; 3
17 with all the kingdoms of the world upon the face 3
34:12 They shall name it No Kingdom There 1
37:16 the God . . of all the kingdoms of the earth; 3
20 that all the kingdoms of the earth may know that 3
47: 5 no more be called the mistress of kingdoms. 3
60:12 and kingdom that will not serve you shall perish; 3
Jer 1:10 set you this day over nations and over kingdoms 3
15 all the tribes of the kingdoms of the north 3
10: 7 in all their kingdoms there is none like thee. 2
15: 4 I will make them a horror to all the kingdoms 3
18: 7 If . . I declare concerning a nation or a kingdom 3
9 or a kingdom that I will build and plant it 3
24: 9 a horror to all the kingdoms of the earth 3
25:26 and all the kingdoms of the world 3
27: 8 But if any nation or kingdom will not serve 3
28: 8 against many countries and great kingdoms. 3
29:18 them a horror to all the kingdoms of the earth 3
34: 1 all his army and all the kingdoms of the earth 3
17 a horror to all the kingdoms of the earth. 3
49:28 Concerning Kedar and the kingdoms of Hazor 3
51:20 with you I destroy kingdoms; 3
27 war against her, summon against her the kingdoms 3
Lam 2: 2 has brought down . . the kingdom and its rulers. 3
Ezk 17:14 that the kingdom might be humble 3
29:14 there they shall be a lowly kingdom. 3
15 It shall be the most lowly of the kingdoms 3
37:22 and no longer divided into two kingdoms. 3
Dan 1:20 magicians . . that were in all his kingdom. 2
2:37 given the kingdom, the power, and the might 6
39 After you shall arise another kingdom inferior 5
39 arise . . yet a third kingdom of bronze 5
40 there shall be a fourth kingdom, strong as iron 5
41 partly of iron, it shall be a divided kingdom; 5
42 kingdom shall be partly strong and partly brittle. 6
44 God of heaven will set up a kingdom 5
44 It shall break in pieces all these kingdoms 5
4: 3 His kingdom is an everlasting kingdom 6
3 His kingdom is an everlasting kingdom 6
17 know that the Most High rules the kingdom of men 6
18 because all the wise men of my kingdom 6
25 know that the Most High rules the kingdom of men 6
26 your kingdom shall be sure for you 6
31 kingdom has departed from you 6
32 Most High rules the kingdom of men 6
34 kingdom endures from generation to generation; 6
36 glory of my kingdom, my majesty and splendor 6
36 established in my kingdom, 6
5: 7 shall be the third ruler in the kingdom. 6
11 There is in your kingdom a man 6
16 shall be the third ruler in the kingdom. 6
21 knew . . Most High God rules the kingdom of men 6
26 MENE, God has numbered the days of your kingdom 6
28 PERES, your kingdom is divided and given 6
29 that he should be the third ruler in the kingdom. 6
31 Darius the Mede received the kingdom, 6
6: 1 Darius to set over the kingdom 120 satraps 6
1 120 satraps, to be throughout the whole kingdom; 6
3 king planned to set him over the whole kingdom. 6
4 against Daniel with regard to the kingdom; 6
7 presidents of the kingdom, the prefects 6
26 his kingdom shall never be destroyed 6
7:14 to him was given dominion and glory and kingdom 5
14 his kingdom one that shall not be destroyed. 6
18 saints . . shall receive the kingdom 6
18 possess the kingdom for ever, for ever and ever.' 6
22 time came when the saints received the kingdom. 6
23 beast, there shall be a fourth kingdom on earth 5
23 kingdom . . different from all the kingdoms 5
24 horns, out of this kingdom ten kings shall arise 6
27 kingdom and the dominion and the greatness 6
27 dominion and the greatness of the kingdoms 5
27 kingdom shall be an everlasting kingdom 6
27 kingdom shall be an everlasting kingdom 6
8:22 four kingdoms shall arise from his nation 2
10:13 prince of the kingdom of Persia withstood me 2
13 left . . with the prince of the kingdom of Persia •
11: 2 shall stir up all against the kingdom of Greece. 2
4 kingdom shall be broken and divided 2
4 kingdom shall be plucked up and go to others 2
17 come with the strength of his whole kingdom 2
17 daughter of women to destroy the kingdom; •
20 exactor . . through the glory of the kingdom; 2
21 obtain the kingdom by flatteries. 2
Hos 1: 4 put an end to the kingdom of the house of Israel. 4
Ams 6: 2 Are they better than these kingdoms? 3
7:13 and it is a temple of the kingdom. 3
9: 8 eyes of the Lord GOD are upon the sinful kingdom 3
Obd 1:21 and the kingdom shall be the LORD'S. 1
Mic 4: 8 come, the kingdom of the daughter of Jerusalem. 3
Nah 3: 5 let nations look . . and kingdoms on your shame. 3
Zep 3: 8 to gather nations, to assemble kingdoms 3
Hag 2:22 to overthrow the throne of kingdoms; 3
22 am about to destroy the strength of the kingdoms 3
Mat 3: 2 Repent, for the kingdom of heaven is at hand. 8
4: 8 showed him all the kingdoms of the world 8
17 Repent, for the kingdom of heaven is at hand. 8
23 preaching the gospel of the kingdom and healing 8
5: 3 spirit, for theirs is the kingdom of heaven. 8
10 for theirs is the kingdom of heaven. 8
19 so, shall be called least in the kingdom of heaven; 8
19 shall be called great in the kingdom of heaven. 8
20 you will never enter the kingdom of heaven. 8
6:10 Thy kingdom come. Thy will be done, On earth as it 8
33 seek first his kingdom and his righteousness 8
7:21 shall enter the kingdom of heaven 8
8:11 Abraham, Isaac, and Jacob in the kingdom of heaven 8
12 while the sons of the kingdom will be thrown 8
9:35 preaching the gospel of the kingdom, and healing 8
10: 7 'The kingdom of heaven is at hand.' 8
11:11 yet he who is least in the kingdom of heaven 8
12 the kingdom of heaven has suffered violence 8
12:25 Every kingdom divided against itself 8
26 how then will his kingdom stand? 8
28 then the kingdom of God has come upon you. 8
13:11 to know the secrets of the kingdom of heaven 8
19 When any one hears the word of the kingdom 8
24 The kingdom of heaven may be compared to a man 8
31 The kingdom of heaven is like a grain of mustard 8
33 The kingdom of heaven is like leaven 8
38 and the good seed means the sons of the kingdom 8
41 and they will gather out of his kingdom 8
43 in the kingdom of their Father 8
44 The kingdom of heaven is like treasure 8
45 Again, the kingdom of heaven is like a merchant 8
47 Again, the kingdom of heaven is like a net 8
52 trained for the kingdom of heaven 8
16:19 I will give you the keys of the kingdom of heaven 8
28 see the Son of man coming in his kingdom. 8
18: 1 Who is the greatest in the kingdom of heaven? 8
3 you will never enter the kingdom of heaven. 8
4 he is the greatest in the kingdom of heaven. 8
23 Therefore the kingdom of heaven may be compared 8
19:12 for the sake of the kingdom of heaven 8
14 for to such belongs the kingdom of heaven. 8
23 to enter the kingdom of heaven. 8
24 than for a rich man to enter the kingdom of God. 8
20: 1 For the kingdom of heaven is like a householder 8
21 and one at your left, in your kingdom. 8
21:31 go into the kingdom of God before you. 8
43 the kingdom of God will be taken away from you 8
22: 2 The kingdom of heaven may be compared to a king 8
23:13 you shut the kingdom of heaven against men 8
24: 7 kingdom against kingdom 8
7 kingdom against kingdom 8
14 this gospel of the kingdom will be preached 8

25: 1 Then the kingdom of heaven shall be compared 8
34 inherit the kingdom prepared for you 8
26:29 new with you in my Father's kingdom. 8
Mrk 1:15 the kingdom of God is at hand 8
3:24 If a kingdom is divided against itself 8
24 that kingdom cannot stand. 8
4:11 given the secret of the kingdom of God 8
26 The kingdom of God is as if a man should scatter 8
30 With what can we compare the kingdom of God 8
6:23 I will give you, even half of my kingdom. 8
9: 1 the kingdom of God has come with power. 8
46 to enter the kingdom of God with one eye 8
10:14 to such belongs the kingdom of God. 8
15 receive the kingdom of God like a child 8
23 to enter the kingdom of God! 8
24 how hard it is to enter the kingdom of God! 8
25 than for a rich man to enter the kingdom of God. 8
11:10 Blessed is the kingdom of our father David 8
12:34 You are not far from the kingdom of God. 8
13: 8 kingdom against kingdom 8
8 kingdom against kingdom 8
14:25 when I drink it new in the kingdom of God. 8
15:43 who was also himself looking for the kingdom of God 8
Lke 1:33 of his kingdom there will be no end. 8
4: 5 showed him all the kingdoms of the world 8
43 I must preach the good news of the kingdom of God 8
6:20 yours is the kingdom of God. 8
7:28 he who is least in the kingdom of God is greater 8
8: 1 bringing the good news of the kingdom of God 8
10 given to know the secrets of the kingdom of God; 8
9: 2 he sent them out to preach the kingdom of God 8
11 spoke to them of the kingdom of God 8
27 before they see the kingdom of God. 8
60 as for you, go and proclaim the kingdom of God.". 8
62 fit for the kingdom of God. 8
10: 9 'The kingdom of God has come near to you.' 8
11 the kingdom of God has come near.' 8
11: 2 hallowed be thy name. Thy kingdom come. 8
17 Every kingdom divided against itself is laid waste 8
18 how will his kingdom stand 8
20 then the kingdom of God has come upon you. 8
12:31 Instead, seek his kingdom 8
32 Father's good pleasure to give you the kingdom. 8
13:18 He said therefore, "What is the kingdom of God like? 8
20 To what shall I compare the kingdom of God? 8
28 all the prophets in the kingdom of God 8
29 and sit at table in the kingdom of God. 8
14:15 he who shall eat bread in the kingdom of God! 8
16:16 the good news of the kingdom of God is preached 8
17:20 asked . . when the kingdom of God was coming 8
20 he answered them, "The kingdom of God is not coming 8
21 behold, the kingdom of God is in the midst of you. 8
18:16 to such belongs the kingdom of God. 8
17 whoever does not receive the kingdom of God 8
24 How hard it is . . to enter the kingdom of God! 8
25 for a rich man to enter the kingdom of God. 8
29 left house . . for the sake of the kingdom of God 8
19:11 the kingdom of God was to appear immediately. 8
12 to receive a kingdom and then return. 8
15 When he returned, having received the kingdom 8
21:10 kingdom against kingdom; 8
10 kingdom against kingdom; 8
31 you know that the kingdom of God is near. 8
22:16 until it is fulfilled in the kingdom of God. 8
18 until the kingdom of God comes. 8
29 I assign to you . . a kingdom 8
30 you may eat and drink at my table in my kingdom 8
23:42 remember me when you come into your kingdom. 8
51 he was looking for the kingdom of God. 8
Joh 3: 3 he cannot see the kingdom of God. 8
5 he cannot enter the kingdom of God. 8
Act 1: 3 speaking of the kingdom of God. 8
6 at this time restore the kingdom to Israel? 8
8:12 as he preached good news about the kingdom of God 8
14:22 saying that . . we must enter the kingdom of God. 8
19: 8 arguing and pleading about the kingdom of God; 8
20:25 among whom I have gone preaching the kingdom 8
28:23 testifying to the kingdom of God 8
31 preaching the kingdom of God 8
Rom 14:17 For the kingdom of God is not food and drink 8
1Co 4:20 For the kingdom of God does not consist in talk 8
6: 9 unrighteous will not inherit the kingdom of God? 8
10 inherit the kingdom of God. 8
15:24 when he delivers the kingdom to God the Father 8
50 cannot inherit the kingdom of God 8
Gal 5:21 shall not inherit the kingdom of God. 8
Eph 5: 5 has any inheritance in the kingdom of Christ 8
Col 1:13 transferred us to the kingdom of his beloved Son 8
4:11 fellow workers for the kingdom of God 8
1Th 2:12 who calls you into his own kingdom and glory. 8
2Th 1: 5 you may be made worthy of the kingdom of God 8
2Ti 4: 1 by his appearing and his kingdom 8
18 save me for his heavenly kingdom 8
Heb 1: 8 the scepter of thy kingdom. 8
11:33 who through faith conquered kingdoms 8
12:28 for receiving a kingdom that cannot be shaken 8
Jas 2: 5 heirs of the kingdom which he has promised 8
2Pe 1:11 an entrance into the eternal kingdom of our Lord 8
Rev 1: 6 made us a kingdom, priests to his God and Father 8
9 share with you in Jesus . . the kingdom 8
5:10 hast made them a kingdom and priests to our God 8
11:15 The kingdom of the world has become the kingdom 8
15 become the kingdom of our Lord and of his Christ •
12:10 salvation . . power and the kingdom of our God 8
16:10 the beast, and its kingdom was in darkness; 8
1Es 1:24 beyond any other people or kingdom 8
2: 2 made a proclamation throughout all his kingdom 8
4:49 Jews who were going up from his kingdom to Judea 8
8:21 wrath may not come upon the kingdom of the king 8
24 all who transgress . . the law of the kingdom 10
2Es 2:10 that I will give them the kingdom of Jerusalem 12
13 The kingdom is already prepared for you; watch! 12
35 Be ready for the rewards of the kingdom 12
37 to him who has called you to heavenly kingdoms. 12
12:11 the fourth kingdom which appeared in a vision 12
13 when a kingdom shall arise on earth 12
13 all the kingdoms that have been before it. 12
18 In the midst of the time of that kingdom 12
13:31 and kingdom against kingdom. 12
31 and kingdom against kingdom. 12
Tob 1:21 over all the accounts of his kingdom 8
13: 1 blessed is his kingdom. 8
Jdt 1:12 swore by his throne and kingdom 8
2:12 as I live, and by the power of my kingdom 8
11: 8 you are the one good man in the whole kingdom 8
AEs 13: 2 in order to make my kingdom peaceable 8
3 has attained the second place in the kingdom 8
5 so that our kingdom may not attain stability. 8
16: 8 we will take care to render our kingdom quiet 8
12 he undertook to deprive us of our kingdom 7
13 of Esther, the blameless partner of our kingdom 8
14 would transfer the kingdom of the Persians 11
16 who has directed the kingdom 8
Wis 6: 4 as servants of his kingdom 8
20 the desire for wisdom leads to a kingdom. 8
10:10 she showed him the kingdom of God 8
14 until she brought him the scepter of a kingdom 8
Sir 44: 3 There were those who ruled in their kingdoms 8
46:13 established the kingdom and anointed rulers 8
47:21 a disobedient kingdom arose out of Ephraim. 8
Bar 2: 4 he gave them into subjection to all the kingdoms 8
Aza 1:33 Blessed art thou upon the throne of thy kingdom 8
Bel 1: 1 Cyrus the Persian received his kingdom. 8
1Mc 1: 6 and divided his kingdom among them 8
10 the kingdom of the Greeks. 8
16 Antiochus saw that his kingdom was established 8
16 that he might reign over both kingdoms. 8
41 Then the king wrote to his whole kingdom 8
51 In such words he wrote to his whole kingdom 8
2:57 inherited the throne of the kingdom for ever. 8
3:14 and win honor in the kingdom 8
27 sent and gathered all the forces of his kingdom 8
6:14 and made him ruler over all his kingdom. 8
29 came to him from other kingdoms 8
57 affairs of the kingdom press urgently upon us. 8
7: 4 took his seat upon the throne of his kingdom. 8
8 a great man in the kingdom 8
8:11 The remaining kingdoms and islands 8
18 the kingdom of the Greeks was . . enslaving 8
10:33 into any part of my kingdom 8
34 all the Jews who are in my kingdom. 8
37 be put in positions of trust in the kingdom 8
43 and receive back all his property in my kingdom. 8
52 Since I have returned to my kingdom 8
53 we have taken our seat on the throne of his kingdom 8
55 and took your seat on the throne of their kingdom. 8
11: 1 he tried to get possession of Alexander's kingdom 8
1 and add it to his own kingdom. 8
9 you shall reign over your father's kingdom. 8
11 because he coveted his kingdom. 8
51 all the people in his kingdom 8
52 sat on the throne of his kingdom 8
15: 3 gained control of the kingdom of our fathers 8
3 I intend to lay claim to the kingdom 8
4 have devastated many cities in my kingdom 8
9 When we gain control of our kingdom 8
28 they are cities of my kingdom. 8
29 taken possession of many places in my kingdom. 8
2Mc 1: 7 the holy land and the kingdom 8
4: 7 Antiochus . . succeeded to the kingdom 8
9:25 the neighbors to my kingdom 8
10:11 This man, when he succeeded to the kingdom 8
11:23 the subjects of the kingdom be undisturbed 8
14: 6 will not let the kingdom attain tranquillity. 8
26 that conspirator against the kingdom, Judas 8
3Mc 6:24 secretly devising acts of no advantage to the kingdom. 8
7: 3 the Jews of the kingdom 8
12 everywhere in his kingdom 8
4Mc 2:23 will rule a kingdom that is temperate, just, good 9
12: 5 a leader in the government of the kingdom. 8
11 you have received . . also your kingdom from God 8

kingdom *See also* unify.

kingly 1. מַלְכוּ (A)

Dan 5:20 deposed from his kingly throne, 1

kingship 1. מְלוּכָה 2. מַמְלָכָה 3. מַלְכוּ (A) 4. *βασιλεία* 5. *βασίλειος*

1Sm 10:25 told . . the rights and duties of the kingship 1
14:47 When Saul had taken the kingship over Israel 1
2Ch 13: 5 LORD . . gave the kingship over Israel for ever 2
Dan 5:18 kingship and greatness and glory and majesty; 3
Joh 18:36 Jesus answered, "My kingship is not of this world; 4
36 if my kingship were of this world 4
36 my kingship is not from the world. 4
1Es 4:40 the strength and the kingship and the power 5
2Mc 2:17 the kingship and priesthood and consecration 5

kinsfolk 1. אָח 2. חַי 3. קָרֹב 4. *συγγενής*

1Sm 18:18 Who am I, and who are my kinsfolk, 2
2Ch 28: 8 took captive 200,000 of their kinsfolk, women, sons 1
11 send back the captives from your kinsfolk 1
15 brought them to their kinsfolk at Jericho 1
Job 19:14 My kinsfolk and my close friends have failed me; 3
Lke 1:58 her neighbors and kinsfolk heard 4
2:44 they sought him among their kinsfolk 4

kinship 1. *συγγένεια*

Wis 8:17 in kinship with wisdom there is immortality 1
2Mc 5: 9 because of their kinship. 1
4Mc 10: 3 the noble kinship that binds me to my brothers. 1

kinsman 1. אָח 2. אִישׁ אָח 3. גאל 4. דּוֹד 5. מֹדַעַת 6. מוֹדַע 7. עַם 8. קָרֹב 9. שְׁאֵר 10. *ἀδελφός* 11. *ἐκ γένους* 12. *συγγενής* 13. proximus

Gen 13: 8 my herdsmen; for we are kinsmen. 2
14:14 When Abram heard that his kinsman had been taken 1
16 also brought back his kinsman Lot with his goods 1
16:12 he shall dwell over against all his kinsmen. 1
24:27 the way to the house of my master's kinsmen. 1
48 the daughter of my master's kinsman for his son. 1
29:12 told Rachel that he was her father's kinsman 1
15 Laban said to Jacob, "Because you are my kinsman 1
31:23 he took his kinsmen with him and pursued him 1
25 Laban with his kinsmen encamped in the hill 1
32 In the presence of our kinsmen point out 1
37 Set it here before my kinsmen and your kinsmen 1
37 Set it here before my kinsmen and your kinsmen 1
46 Jacob said to his kinsmen, "Gather stones 1
54 mountain and called his kinsmen to eat bread; 1
Exd 4:18 Let me go back, I pray, to my kinsmen in Egypt 1
Num 5: 8 if the man has no kinsman to whom restitution 3
27:11 then . . give his inheritance to his kinsman 9
Jdg 5:14 following you, Benjamin, with your kinsmen; 7
9: 1 went to Shechem to his mother's kinsmen and said 1
3 his mother's kinsmen spoke all these words on his 1
18 made . . king . . , because he is your kinsman– 1
26 Ga'al . . moved into Shechem with his kinsmen; 1
31 Ga'al the son of Ebed and his kinsmen have come 1
41 Zebul drove out Ga'al and his kinsmen 1
14: 3 a woman among the daughters of your kinsmen 1
Rut 2: 1 Now Na'omi had a kinsman of her husband's 6
3: 2 Now is not Bo'az our kinsman 5
12 yet there is a kinsman nearer than I. 3
4: 3 land which belonged to our kinsman Elim'elech. 1
2Sm 19:12 You are my kinsmen, you are my bone and my flesh; 1
1Kg 12:24 You shall not go up or fight against your kinsmen 1
16:11 leave him a . . male of his kinsmen or his friends. 3
2Kg 10:13 Jehu met the kinsmen of Ahazi'ah . . and he said 1
13 We are the kinsmen of Ahazi'ah, and we came down 1
1Ch 5: 7 his kinsmen by their families 1
13 kinsmen according to their fathers' houses 1
7: 5 Their kinsmen belonging to . . Is'sachar 1
8:32 Now these also dwelt opposite their kinsmen. 1
32 dwelt . . in Jerusalem, with their kinsmen. 1
9: 6 Of the sons of Zerah: Jeu'el and their kinsmen, 690. 1
9 their kinsmen according to their generations 1
13 their kinsmen, heads of their fathers' houses 1
17 gatekeepers were . . Ahi'man, and their kinsmen 1
19 Shallum . . and his kinsmen of his fathers' house 1
25 their kinsmen who were in their villages 1
32 Also some of their kinsmen of the Ko'hathites 1
38 dwelt opposite their kinsmen in Jerusalem 1
38 with their kinsmen. 1
12: 2 they were Benjaminites, Saul's kinsmen. 1
29 Of the Benjaminites, the kinsmen of Saul, 3,000 1
32 and all their kinsmen under their command. 1
23:22 their kinsmen, the sons of Kish, married them. 1
2Ch 5:12 Levitical singers . . their sons and kinsmen 1
Ezr 3: 2 arose . . Zerub'babel . . with his kinsmen 1
9 Jeshua with his sons and his kinsmen, and Kad'mi-el 1
9 Hen'adad and the Levites, their sons and kinsmen. 1
8:18 Sherebi'ah with his sons and kinsmen, eighteen. 1
19 Hashabi'ah . . his kinsmen and their sons, twenty; 1
24 Sherebi'ah, Hashabi'ah, and ten of their kinsmen 1
Neh 12:36 kinsmen, Shemai'ah, Az'arel, Mil'alai, Gil'alai, Ma'ai 1
Ps 38:11 my kinsmen stand afar off. 8
Jer 7:15 as I cast out all your kinsmen, all the offspring 1
29:16 your kinsmen who did not go out with you into exile 1
51:35 The violence done to me and to my kinsmen 9
Ams 6:10 when a man's kinsman, he who burns him 4
Lke 14:12 your brothers or your kinsmen or rich neighbors 12
21:16 parents and brothers and kinsmen and friends 12
Joh 18:26 a kinsman of the man whose ear Peter had cut off 12

Act 10:24 called together his kinsmen and close friends. 12
Rom 9: 3 the sake of my brethren, my kinsmen by race. 12
16: 7 Greet Androni'cus and Ju'nias, my kinsmen 12
11 Greet my kinsman Hero'dion. 12
21 so do Lucius and Jason and Sosip'ater, my kinsmen. 12
1Es 3: 7 shall be called kinsman of Darius. 12
4:42 you shall sit next to me, and be called my kinsman. 12
5:48 Zerubbabel . . with his kinsmen 10
8:47 Sherebiah with his sons and kinsmen, eighteen; 10
54 ten of their kinsmen with them; 10
2Es 7:103 relatives for their kinsmen 13
Tob 3:15 he has . . no near kinsman or kinsman's son 10
15 he has . . no near kinsman or kinsman's son •
6:11 for you are her only eligible kinsman. 11
Sir 41:21 rejecting the appeal of a kinsman 12
1Mc 10:89 it is the custom to give to the kinsmen of kings 12
11:31 wrote concerning you to Lasthenes our kinsman 12
2Mc 8: 1 summoned their kinsmen 12
11: 1 Lysias, the king's guardian and kinsman 12
35 what Lysias the kinsman of the king has granted 12
12:39 to bring them back to lie with their kinsmen 12

near kinsman 1.גאל 2.שְׁאֵר בָּשָׂר
Lev 25:49 near kinsman belonging to his family may redeem 2
Rut 3:12 And now it is true that I am a near kinsman 1

kinswoman 1.שְׁאֵר 2.συγγενίς
Lev 18:17 they are your near kinswomen; it is wickedness 1
Lke 1:36 behold, your kinswoman Elizabeth in her old age 2

near kinswoman 1.שְׁאֵר אָב 2.שְׁאֵר אֵם
Lev 18:12 she is your father's near kinswoman 1
13 for she is your mother's near kinswoman 2

kiss 1.חֵךְ 2.נְשִׁיקָה 3.נשק 4.καταφιλέω 5.φιλέω 6.φίλημα
Gen 27:26 said to him, "Come near and kiss me, my son. 3
27 he came near and kissed him; and he smelled 3
29:11 Then Jacob kissed Rachel, and wept aloud. 3
13 to meet him, and embraced him and kissed him 3
31:28 why did you not permit me to kiss my sons 3
55 Laban arose, and kissed his grandchildren 3
33: 4 on his neck and kissed him, and they wept. 3
45:15 he kissed all his brothers and wept upon them; 3
48:10 and he kissed them and embraced them. 3
50: 1 Joseph . . wept over him, and kissed him. 3
Exd 4:27 met him at the mountain of God and kissed him. 3
18: 7 Moses . . did obeisance and kissed him; 3
Rut 1: 9 Then she kissed them, and they . . wept. 3
14 and Orpah kissed her mother-in-law, but Ruth clung 3
1Sm 10: 1 and poured it on his head, and kissed him and said 3
20:41 they kissed one another, and wept with one 3
2Sm 14:33 and the king kissed Ab'salom. 3
15: 5 put out his hand, and take hold of him, and kiss him. 3
19:39 and the king kissed Barzil'lai and blessed him 3
20: 9 And Jo'ab took Ama'sa by the beard . . to kiss him. 3
1Kg 19:18 leave . . every mouth that has not kissed him. 3
20 Let me kiss my father and my mother 3
Job 31:27 enticed, and my mouth has kissed my hand; 3
Ps 2:12 kiss his feet, lest he be angry, and you perish 3
Prv 7:13 She seizes him and kisses him 3
24:26 He who gives a right answer kisses the lips. 3
27: 6 profuse are the kisses of an enemy. 2
Sng 1: 2 you would kiss me with the kisses of your mouth! 3
2 you would kiss me with the kisses of your mouth! 2
7: 9 and your kisses like the best wine that goes down 1
8: 1 If I met you outside, I would kiss you 3
Hos 13: 2 Sacrifice to these, they say. Men kiss calves! 3
Mat 26:48 The one I shall kiss is the man; seize him. 5
49 he kissed him. 4
Mrk 14:44 The one I shall kiss is the man 5
45 said, "Master!" And he kissed him. 4
Lke 7:38 kissed his feet 4
45 You gave me no kiss 6
45 she has not ceased to kiss my feet. 4
15:20 ran and embraced him and kissed him. 4
22:47 He drew near to Jesus to kiss him; 5
48 would you betray the Son of man with a kiss? 6
Act 20:37 they all wept and embraced Paul and kissed him. 4
Rom 16:16 Greet one another with a holy kiss. 6
1Co 16:20 Greet one another with a holy kiss. 6
2Co 13:12 Greet one another with a holy kiss 6
1Th 5:26 Greet all the brethren with a holy kiss. 6
1Pe 5:14 Greet one another with the kiss of love. 6
1Es 4:47 Darius the king rose, and kissed him 4
Tob 7: 6 Then Raguel sprang up and kissed him and wept. 4
10:12 And he kissed her. 5
AEs 13:13 willing to kiss the soles of his feet 5
Sir 29: 5 A man will kiss another's hands 4
3Mc 5:49 they kissed each other, embracing relatives 4

kiss each other 1.נשק
Ps 85:10 righteousness and peace will kiss each other. 1

kitchen 1.בֵּית הַמְבַשְּׁלִים
Ezk 46:24 These are the kitchens where those who minister 1

kite 1.אַיָּה 2.דָּאָה 3.דַּיָּה
Lev 11:14 the kite, the falcon according to its kind 2
Deu 14:13 buzzard, the kite, after their kinds; 1
Isa 34:15 yea, there shall the kites be gathered 3

knave 1.כִּילַי
Isa 32: 5 nor the knave said to be honorable. 1
7 The knaveries of the knave are evil; 1

knavery 1.כֵּלַי
Isa 32: 7 The knaveries of the knave are evil; 1

knead 1.לוּשׁ 2.θλίβω
Gen 18: 6 measures of fine meal, knead it, and make cakes. 1
1Sm 28:24 she took flour, and kneaded it and baked . . bread 1
2Sm 13: 8 And she took dough, and kneaded it, and made cakes 1
Jer 7:18 and the women knead dough, to make cakes 1
Hos 7: 4 the kneading of the dough until it is leavened. 1
Wis 15: 7 when a potter kneads the soft earth 2

kneading *See* bowl, trough.

knee 1.בֶּרֶךְ 2.אַרְכֻבָּה (A) 3.בְּרַךְ (A) 4.γόνυ
5.προσκυνέω
Gen 30: 3 that she may bear upon my knees 1
48:12 Then Joseph removed them from his knees 1
50:23 children . . were born upon Joseph's knees. 1
Deu 28:35 LORD will smite you on the knees and on the legs 1
Jdg 16:19 She made him sleep upon her knees; and she called 1
1Kg 18:42 he bowed . . and put his face between his knees. 1
19:18 leave . . all the knees that have not bowed to Ba'al 1
2Kg 1:13 captain . . went up, and came and fell on his knees 1
2Ch 6:13 Then he knelt upon his knees in the presence 1
Ezr 9: 5 fell upon my knees and spread out my hands 1
Job 3:12 Why did the knees receive me? 1
4: 4 you have made firm the feeble knees. 1
Ps 109:24 My knees are weak through fasting; 1
Isa 35: 3 weak hands, and make firm the feeble knees. 1
45:23 To me every knee shall bow 1
66:12 carried upon her hip, and dandled upon her knees. 1
Ezk 7:17 All hands are feeble, and all knees weak as water. 1
21: 7 all knees will be weak as water. 1
Dan 5: 6 limbs gave way, and his knees knocked together. 2
6:10 got down upon his knees three times a day 3
10:10 hand . . set me trembling on my hands and knees. 1
Nah 2:10 Hearts faint and knees tremble 1
Mat 18:26 So the servant fell on his knees, imploring him 5
Lke 5: 8 he fell down at Jesus' knees, saying 4
Rom 11: 4 7,000 men who have not bowed the knee to Ba'al". 4
14:11 As I live, says the Lord, every knee shall bow to me 4
Eph 3:14 For this reason I bow my knees before the Father 4
Php 2:10 at the name of Jesus every knee should bow 4
Heb 12:12 and strengthen your weak knees 4
Sir 25:23 Drooping hands and weak knees 4
Man 1:11 now I bend the knee of my heart 4
3Mc 2: 1 bending his knees and extending his hands 4
5:42 mangled by the knees and feet of the beasts 4
4Mc 11:10 they tied him to it on his knees 4

knee *See also* bow.

knee-deep 1.בֶּרֶךְ
Ezk 47: 4 led me through the water; and it was knee-deep. 1

kneel 1.ברך 2.כרע 3.γονυπετέω 4.προσκυνέω
1Kg 8:54 where he had knelt with hands outstretched 2
2Ch 6:13 Then he knelt upon his knees in the presence 1
Ps 95: 6 bow down, let us kneel before the LORD, our Maker! 1
Mat 8: 2 behold, a leper came to him and knelt before him 4
9:18 behold, a ruler came in and knelt before him 4
15:25 she came and knelt before him, saying 4
17:14 a man came up to him and kneeling before him said 3
20:20 kneeling before him she asked him 4
27:29 kneeling before him they mocked him, saying 3
Mrk 1:40 kneeling said to him 3
10:17 a man ran up and knelt before him, and asked him 3
Jdt 14: 7 he fell at Judith's feet, and knelt before her 4

kneel down 1.כרע 2.κάμπτω τὰ γόνατα
3.τίθημι τὰ γόνατα
Jdg 7: 5 likewise every one that kneels down to drink. 1
6 the rest of the people knelt down to drink water. 1
Mrk 15:19 they knelt down in homage to him. 3
Lke 22:41 and knelt down and prayed 3
Act 7:60 he knelt down and cried with a loud voice 3
9:40 Peter . . knelt down and prayed 3
20:36 when he had spoken thus, he knelt down and prayed 3
21: 5 and kneeling down on the beach we prayed 3
1Es 8:73 kneeling down and stretching forth my hands 2

make kneel down 1.ברך
Gen 24:11 he made the camels kneel down outside the city 1

knife 1.חֶרֶב 2.מַאֲכֶלֶת 3.שַׂכִּין
Gen 22: 6 he took in his hand the fire and the knife. 2
10 put forth his hand, and took the knife to slay 2
Jos 5: 2 Make flint knives and circumcise the people 1
3 Joshua made flint knives, and circumcised 1
Jdg 19:29 he took a knife, and . . he divided her, limb by limb 2
Prv 23: 2 put a knife to your throat if you are a man 3
30:14 whose teeth are swords, whose teeth are knives 2

knit 1.יַחַד 2.קשר
1Sm 18: 1 the soul of Jonathan was knit to the soul of David 2
1Ch 12:17 to help me, my heart will be knit to you; 1

knit together 1.סכך 2.שׂרג 3.συμβιβάζω
Job 10:11 and knit me together with bones and sinews. 1
40:17 the sinews of his thighs are knit together. 2
Ps 139:13 thou didst knit me together in my mother's womb. 1
Eph 4:16 the whole body, joined and knit together 3
Col 2: 2 as they are knit together in love 3
19 nourished and knit together through its joints 3

knock 1.דפק 2.נקשׁ (A) 3.κρούω
Sng 5: 2 Hark! my beloved is knocking. 1
Dan 5: 6 limbs gave way, and his knees knocked together. 2
Mat 7: 7 knock, and it will be opened to you. 3
8 and to him who knocks it will be opened. 3
Lke 11: 9 seek, and you will find; knock, and it will be opened 3
10 to him who knocks it will be opened. 3
12:36 open to him at once when he comes and knocks. 3
13:25 begin to stand outside and to knock at the door 3
Act 12:13 when he knocked at the door of the gateway 3
16 Peter continued knocking 3
Rev 3:20 Behold, I stand at the door and knock; 3
Jdt 14:14 Bagoas went in and knocked at the door of the tent 3

knock out 1.נפל
Exd 21:27 If he knocks out the tooth of his slave 1

knot 1.ὄζος
Wis 13:13 a stick crooked and full of knots 1

know 1.דַּעַת 2.הֵנָּה 3.חשב 4.ידע 5.יעץ 6.נָגַד
7.נכר 8.ידע (A) 9.ἀγνοέω 10.ἀφικνέομαι
11.γινώσκω 12.γνωρίζω 13.γνώριμος
14.γνῶσιν ἔχω 15.γνῶσις 16.γνωστέος
17.γνωστός 18.γνωστὸς εἰμί 19.εἰδέω 20.εἴδησις
21.εἶδος 22.ἐκδικέω 23.ἐπιγινώσκω 24.ἐπίγνωσις
25.ἐπίσταμαι 26.ἐπιστάτης 27.καλέω 28.λέγω
29.μανθάνω 30.μηνύω 31.οἶδα 32.ὁράω
33.οὐκ ἀγνοέω 34.συνίημι 35.φαιδρός 36.φανερός
37.φανερόω 38.cognosco 39.ignoro 40.intellego
41.nescio 42.nosco 43.scio
Gen 3: 5 For God knows that when you eat of it 4
5 will be like God, knowing good and evil. 4
7 they knew that they were naked; 4
22 like one of us, knowing good and evil; 4
4: 1 Adam knew Eve his wife, and she conceived 4
9 I do not know; am I my brother's keeper? 4
17 Cain knew his wife, and she conceived 4
25 Adam knew his wife again, and she bore a son 4
8:11 Noah knew that the waters had subsided 4
9:24 knew what his youngest son had done to him 4
12:11 I know that you are a woman beautiful to behold; 4
15: 8 how am I to know that I shall possess it? 4
13 Know of a surety that your descendants will be 4
18:21 has come to me; and if not, I will know. 4
19: 5 Bring them out to us, that we may know them. 4
8 Behold, I have two daughters who have not known 4
33 he did not know when she lay down 4
35 he did not know when she lay down 4
20: 6 Yes, I know that you have done this 4
7 do not restore her, know that you shall surely die 4
21:26 Abim'elech said, "I do not know who has done this 4
22:12 for now I know that you fear God 4
24:14 By this I shall know that thou hast shown 4
16 fair to look upon, a virgin, whom no man had known. 4
27: 2 Behold, I am old; I do not know the day of my death. 4
21 feel you, my son, to know whether you are really •
28:16 LORD is in this place, and I did not know it. 4
29: 5 said to them, "Do you know Laban the son of Nahor? 4
5 the son of Nahor?" They said, "We know him. 4
30:26 for you know the service which I have given you. 4
29 You yourself know how I have served you 4
31: 6 You know that I have served your father 4
32 Jacob did not know that Rachel had stolen them. 4
33:13 to him, "My lord knows that the children are frail 4
38: 9 Onan knew that the offspring would not be his; 4
16 he did not know that she was his daughter-in-law. 4
41:21 had eaten them no one would have known that they 4
42: 7 Joseph saw his brothers, and knew them 7
8 Thus Joseph knew his brothers 7
8 his brothers, but they did not know him. 7
23 They did not know that Joseph understood them 4
33 By this I shall know that you are honest men 4
34 then I shall know that you are not spies 4
43: 7 could we in any way know that he would say 4
22 We do not know who put our money in our sacks. 4
44:15 Do you not know that such a man as I can indeed 4
27 said to us, 'You know that my wife bore me two sons; 4
46:30 seen your face and know that you are still alive. •
47: 6 and if you know any able men among them, 4
48:19 his father refused, and said, "I know, my son, 4
19 my son, I know; he also shall become a people 4

Exd 1: 8 a new king over Egypt, who did not know Joseph. 4
2: 4 stood . . to know what would be done to him. 4
14 Moses . . thought, "Surely the thing is known. 4
25 people of Israel, and God knew their condition. 4
3: 7 I have seen . . I know their sufferings 4
19 I know that the king of Egypt will not let you go 4
4:14 Aaron . . the Levite? I know that he can speak well; 4
5: 2 I do not know the LORD, and moreover I will not let 4
6: 7 and you shall know that I am the LORD your God 4
7: 5 the Egyptians shall know that I am the LORD 4
17 By this you shall know that I am the LORD 4
8:10 that you may know that there is no one like 4
22 that you may know that I am the LORD in the midst 4
9:14 that you may know that there is none like me in all 4
29 that you may know that the earth is the LORD'S. 4
30 I know that you do not yet fear the LORD God. 4
10: 2 that you may know that I am the LORD. 4
26 we do not know with what we must serve the LORD 4
11: 7 you may know that the LORD makes a distinction 4
14: 4 the Egyptians shall know that I am the LORD. 4
18 the Egyptians shall know that I am the LORD 4
16: 6 At evening you shall know that it was the LORD who 4
12 then you shall know that I am the LORD your God.' 4
15 For they did not know what it was. 4
18:11 Now I know that the LORD is greater than all gods 4
21:36 Or if it is known that the ox has been accustomed 4
23: 9 you know the heart of a stranger 4
29:46 they shall know that I am the LORD their God, who 4
31:13 that you may know that I, the LORD, sanctify you. 4
32: 1 we do not know what has become of him. 4
22 you know the people, that they are set on evil. 4
23 we do not know what has become of him.' 4
33: 5 that I may know what to do with you.' 4
12 Bring up this people'; but thou hast not let me know 4
12 I know you by name, and you have also found favor 4
13 that I may know thee and find favor in thy sight. 4
16 For how shall it be known that I have found favor 4
17 found favor in my sight, and I know you by name. 4
34:29 Moses did not know that the skin of his face shone 4
Lev 5:17 though he does not know it, yet he is guilty 4
23:43 that your generations may know that I made 4
Num10:31 you know how we are to encamp in the wilderness 4
11:16 whom you know to be the elders of the people 4
14:31 shall know the land which you have despised. 4
34 and you shall know my displeasure.' 4
16:28 Hereby you shall know that the LORD has sent me 4
30 then you shall know that these men have despised 4
20:14 You know all the adversity that has befallen us 4
22: 6 for I know that he whom you bless is blessed 4
19 that I may know what more the LORD will say to me. 4
34 I did not know that thou didst stand in the road 4
24:14 come, I will let you know what this people will do 5
16 him who . . knows the knowledge of the Most High 4
31:17 kill every woman who has known man by lying 4
18 young girls who have not known man by lying 4
35 women who had not known man by lying with him. 4
Deu 2: 7 knows your going through this great wilderness; 4
11 like the Anakim they were also known as Reph'idim 3
20 That also is known as a land of Reph'aim; 3
3:19 your cattle (I know that you have many cattle) 4
4:35 shown, that you might know that the LORD is God; 4
39 know therefore this day, and lay it to your heart 4
7: 9 Know therefore that the LORD your God is God 4
15 none of the evil diseases of Egypt, which you knew 4
8: 2 testing you to know what was in your heart 4
3 fed you with manna, which you did not know, nor 4
3 you did not know, nor did your fathers know; 4
5 Know then in your heart that, as a man disciplines 4
16 manna which your fathers did not know 4
9: 2 sons of the Anakim, whom you know, and of whom 4
3 Know therefore this day that he who goes over 4
6 Know therefore, that the LORD your God is not 4
24 rebellious . . from the day that I knew you. 4
11: 2 children who have not known or seen it) 4
28 to go after other gods which you have not known. 4
13: 2 go after other gods,' which you have not known 4
3 testing you, to know whether you love the LORD 4
6 gods,' . . neither you nor your fathers have known 4
13 go and serve other gods,' which you have not known 4
18:21 How may we know the word which the LORD has not 4
20:20 trees which you know are not trees for food 4
21: 1 is found . . and it is not known who killed him 4
22: 2 if he is not near you, or if you do not know him 4
28:33 A nation which you have not known shall eat up 4
36 neither you nor your fathers have known; 4
64 gods . . neither you nor your fathers have known. 4
29: 6 that you may know that I am the LORD your God. 4
16 You know how we dwelt in the land of Egypt 4
26 worshiped them, gods whom they had not known 4
31:13 their children, who have not known it, may hear 4
21 I know the purposes . . they are already forming 4
27 For I know how rebellious and stubborn you are; 4
29 For I know that after my death you will surely act 4
32:17 They sacrificed to . . gods they had never known 4
34: 6 no man knows the place of his burial to this day. 4
10 like Moses, whom the LORD knew face to face 4
Jos 2: 4 men came . . but I did not know where they came from; 4
5 the men went out; where the men went I do not know; 4
9 I know that the LORD has given you the land 4
3: 4 follow it, that you may know the way you shall go 4
7 they may know that, as I was . . so I will be with you. 4
10 you shall know that the living God is among you 4
4:22 then you shall let your children know 4
24 all . . may know that the hand of the LORD is mighty; 4
8:14 but he did not know that there was an ambush 4
14: 6 You know what the LORD said to Moses 4
22:22 God, the LORD! He knows; and let Israel itself know! 4
22 God, the LORD! He knows; and let Israel itself know! 4
31 Today we know that the LORD is in the midst of us 4
23:13 know assuredly that the LORD . . will not 4
14 you know in your hearts and souls, all of you 4
24:31 and had known all the work which the LORD did 4
Jdg 2:10 who did not know the LORD or the work which he had 4
3: 2 the people of Israel might know war, that he might 4
2 war to such at least as had not known it before. 4
4 testing of Israel, to know whether Israel would 4
6:37 if . . then I shall know that thou wilt deliver 4
11:39 She had never known a man. 4
13:16 For Mano'ah did not know that he was the angel 4
21 Mano'ah knew that he was the angel of the LORD. 4
14: 4 His father and mother did not know that it was 4
15:11 Do you not know that the Philistines are rulers 4
16: 9 the secret of his strength was not known. 4
20 And he did not know that the LORD had left him. 4
17:13 Now I know that the LORD will prosper me, because I 4
18: 5 Inquire . . that we may know whether the journey 4
14 Do you know that in these houses there are 4
19:22 Bring out the man . . that we may know him. 4
25 put her out . . and they knew her, and abused her 4
20:34 the Benjaminites did not know that disaster was 4
21:12 virgins who had not known man by lying with him; 4
Rut 2:11 and came to a people that you did not know before. 4
3:11 my . . townsmen know that you are a woman of worth. 4
14 he said, "Let it not be known that the woman came 4
4: 4 but if you will not, tell me, that I may know 4
1Sm 1:19 And Elka'nah knew Hannah his wife, and the LORD 4
3: 7 Now Samuel did not yet know the LORD 4
13 punish . . for ever, for the iniquity which he knew 4
20 all Israel . . knew that Samuel was established 4
6: 3 it will be known to you why his hand does not turn 4
9 we shall know that it is not his hand that struck us 4
10:11 all who knew him before saw how he prophesied 4
12:17 shall know and see that your wickedness is great 4
14: 3 the people did not know that Jonathan had gone. 4
38 and know and see how this sin has arisen today. 4
17:28 I know your presumption . . the evil of your heart; 4
46 that all . . may know that there is a God in Israel 4
47 all . . may know that the LORD saves not with sword 4
18:28 Saul saw and knew that the LORD was with David 4
20: 3 Your father knows well that I have found favor 4
3 'Let not Jonathan know this, lest he be grieved.' 4
7 if he is angry, then know that evil is determined 4
9 If I knew that . . would I not tell you? 4
30 do I not know that you have chosen the son of Jesse 4
33 Jonathan knew that his father was determined 4
39 But the lad knew nothing; 4
39 only Jonathan and David knew the matter. 4
21: 2 Let no one know anything of the matter 4
22: 3 let . . till I know what God will do for me. 4
15 your servant has known nothing of all this 4
17 hand also is with David, and they knew that he fled 4
22 I knew on that day, when Do'eg . . was there 4
23: 9 David knew that Saul was plotting . . against him; 4
17 Saul my father also knows this. 4
22 know and see the place where his haunt is 4
24:11 know and see that there is no wrong 4
20 now, behold, I know that you shall surely be king 4
25:11 give it to men who come from I do not know where? 4
17 know this and consider what you should do; 4
26:12 No man saw it, or knew it, nor did any awake; 4
28: 2 Very well, you shall know what your servant can 4
9 Surely you know what Saul has done 4
14 And Saul knew that it was Samuel, and he bowed 4
29: 9 I know that you are as blameless . . as an angel 4
2Sm 1: 5 How do you know that Saul and . . Jonathan are dead? 4
2:26 Do you not know that the end will be bitter? 4
3:25 You know that Abner the son of Ner came to deceive 4
25 to deceive you, and to know your going out 4
25 to deceive . . and to know all that you are doing. 4
26 they brought . . but David did not know about it. 4
38 Do you not know that a prince . . has fallen 4
7:20 For thou knowest thy servant, O Lord GOD! 4
11:16 the place where he knew there were valiant men. 4
20 Did you not know . . they would shoot from the wall? 4
12:22 Who knows whether the LORD will be gracious to me 4
14:20 the wisdom of the angel of God to know all things 4
22 Today your servant knows that I have found favor 4
15:11 they went in their simplicity, and knew nothing. 4
20 make you wander . . seeing I go I know not where? •
17: 8 You know that your father and his men are mighty 4
10 all Israel knows that your father is a mighty man 4
19 spread a covering . . and nothing was known of it. 4
18:29 I saw a great tumult, but I do not know what it was. 4
19:20 For your servant knows that I have sinned; 4
22 do I not know that I am this day king over Israel? 4
22:44 people whom I had not known served me. 4
24: 2 that I may know the number of the people. 4
1Kg 1: 4 and ministered to him; but the king knew her not. 4
11 become king and David our lord does not know it? 4
18 Adoni'jah is king, although you . . do not know it. 4
2: 5 you know also what Jo'ab . . did to me, how he dealt 4
9 are a wise man; you will know what you ought to do 4
15 You know that the kingdom was mine, and that all 4
37 on the day . . know for certain that you shall die; 4
42 Know for certain that on the day . . you shall die'? 4
44 You know in your own heart all the evil that you 4
5: 3 You know that David . . could not build a house 4
6 I will pay . . for you know that there is no one 4
8:38 each knowing the affliction of his own heart 4
39 render to each whose heart thou knowest 4
39 thou only, knowest the hearts of all the children 4
43 that all . . may know thy name and fear thee 4
43 they may know that this house . . is called 4
60 all the peoples . . may know that the LORD is God; 4
14: 2 disguise yourself, that it be not known that you 4
17:24 Now I know that you are a man of God 4
18:12 the Spirit . . will carry you whither I know not; 4
36 LORD . . let it be known this day that thou art God 4
37 that this people may know that thou, O LORD, art God 4
20:13 I will . . and you shall know that I am the LORD. 4
28 and you shall know that I am the LORD.' 4
22: 3 Do you know that Ramoth-gilead belongs to us 4
2Kg 2: 3 Do you know that today the LORD will take away 4
3 And he said, "Yes, I know it; hold your peace. 4
5 Do you know that today the LORD will take away 4
5 he answered, "Yes, I know it; hold your peace. 4
4: 1 you know that your servant feared the LORD 4
39 into the pot . . not knowing what they were. 4
5: 6 know that I have sent to you Na'aman my servant 2
8 Let him . . that he may know that there is a prophet 4
15 I know that there is no God . . but in Israel; 4
7:12 They know that we are hungry; therefore they have 4
8:12 I know the evil that you will do to . . Israel; 4
9:11 he said to them, "You know the fellow and his talk. 4
10:10 Know then that there shall fall to the earth 4
17:26 The nations which you . . do not know the law 4
26 they do not know the law of the god of the land. 4
19:19 that all . . may know that thou, O LORD, art God 4
27 I know your sitting down and your going out 4
1Ch 12:32 to know what Israel ought to do 4
17:18 For thou knowest thy servant. 4
21: 2 bring me a report, that I may know their number. 4
28: 9 you, Solomon my son, know the God of your father 4
29:17 I know, my God, that thou triest the heart 4
2Ch 2: 8 I know that your servants know how to cut timber 4
6:29 each knowing his own affliction, and . . sorrow 4
30 render to each whose heart thou knowest 4
30 (for thou, thou only, knowest the hearts . . of men); 4
33 that all . . may know thy name and fear thee, as do 4
33 may know that this house . . called by thy name. 4
12: 8 that they may know my service 4
13: 5 know that the LORD . . gave the kingship 4
20:12 do not know what to do, but our eyes are upon thee. 4
25:16 I know that God has determined to destroy you 4
32:13 Do you not know what I and my fathers have done 4
31 to try . . and to know all that was in his heart. 4
33:13 Then Manas'seh knew that the LORD was God. 4
Ezr 4:12 be it known to the king that the Jews who came up 8
13 Now be it known to the king that, if this city 8
5: 8 Be it known to the king that we went 8
7:25 all such as know the laws of your God; 8
25 those who do not know them, you shall teach. 8
Neh 2:16 officials did not know where I had gone 4
4:11 not know or see till we come into the midst of them 4
15 When our enemies heard that it was known to us 4
9:10 for thou knewest that they acted insolently 4
Est 1:13 the king said to the wise men who knew the times- 4
4:11 All . . know that if any man or woman goes 4
14 who knows whether you have not come 4
Job 5:24 You shall know that your tent is safe 4
25 You shall know also that your descendants shall 4
27 it is true. Hear, and know it for your good. 4
7:10 nor does his place know him any more. 7
8: 9 for we are but of yesterday, and know nothing 4
9: 2 Truly I know that it is so: but how can a man be just 4
5 he who removes mountains, and they know it not 4
28 for I know thou wilt not hold me innocent. 4
10: 2 let me know why thou dost contend against me. 4
7 although thou knowest that I am not guilty 4
13 I know that this was thy purpose. 4
11: 6 Know then that God exacts of you less 4
8 Deeper than Sheol-what can you know? 4
11 For he knows worthless men; when he sees iniquity 4
12: 3 Who does not know such things as these? •
9 not know that the hand of the LORD has done this? 4
13: 2 What you know, I also know; I am not inferior to you. 1
2 What you know, I also know; I am not inferior to you. 4
18 I know that I shall be vindicated. 4
14:21 His sons come to honor, and he does not know it; 4
15: 9 What do you know that we do not know? 4
9 What do you know that we do not know? 4
23 He knows that a day of darkness is ready at his hand; 4
18:21 such is the place of him who knows not God. 4
19: 6 know then that God has put me in the wrong 4
25 For I know that my Redeemer lives 4
29 the sword, that you may know there is a judgment. 4
20: 4 Do you not know this from of old 4

20 Because his greed knew no rest 4
21:19 recompense it to themselves, that they may know 4
27 Behold, I know your thoughts 4
22:13 Therefore you say, 'What does God know? 4
23: 3 Oh, that I knew where I might find him 4
10 But he knows the way that I take; 4
24: 1 why do those who know him never see his days? 4
16 shut themselves up; they do not know the light. 4
28: 7 That path no bird of prey knows 4
13 Man does not know the way to it 4
23 God understands . . and he knows its place. 4
29:16 I searched out the cause of him whom I did not know. 4
30:23 Yea, I know that thou wilt bring me to death 4
31: 6 in a just balance, and let God know my integrity! 4
33: 3 what my lips know they speak sincerely. 4
34: 2 give ear to me, you who know; 4
25 Thus, knowing their works, he overturns them 7
33 therefore declare what you know. 4
36:26 Behold, God is great, and we know him not; 4
37: 7 every man, that all men may know his work. 4
16 Do you know the balancings of the clouds 4
38: 5 its measurements–surely you know! 4
18 Declare, if you know all this. 4
21 You know, for you were born 4
33 Do you know the ordinances of the heavens? 4
39: 1 Do you know when the mountain goats bring forth? 4
2 do you know the time when they bring forth 4
42: 2 I know that thou canst do all things 4
3 things too wonderful for me, which I did not know. 4
11 who had known him before, and ate bread with him 4
Ps 1: 6 for the LORD knows the way of the righteous 4
4: 3 But know that the LORD has set apart the godly 4
9:10 those who know thy name put their trust in thee 4
20 O LORD! Let the nations know that they are but men! 4
18:43 people whom I had not known served me. 4
20: 6 Now I know that the LORD will help his anointed; 4
35:11 they ask me of things that I know not. 4
15 cripples whom I knew not slandered me 4
36:10 thy steadfast love to those who know thee 4
37:18 The LORD knows the days of the blameless 4
38: 9 Lord, all my longing is known to thee 6
39: 4 LORD, let me know my end 4
4 let me know how fleeting my life is! 4
6 man heaps up, and knows not who will gather! 4
40: 9 not restrained my lips, as thou knowest, O LORD. 4
41:11 By this I know that thou art pleased with me 4
44:21 For he knows the secrets of the heart. 4
46:10 Be still, and know that I am God. 4
50:11 I know all the birds of the air 4
51: 3 For I know my transgressions 4
56: 9 This I know, that God is for me. 4
59:13 that men may know that God rules over Jacob 4
67: 2 that thy way may be known upon earth 4
69: 5 O God, thou knowest my folly; the wrongs I have done 4
19 Thou knowest my reproach, and my shame 4
19 my foes are all known to thee. †
73:11 they say, "How can God know? 4
74: 9 there is none among us who knows how long. 4
76: 1 In Judah God is known, his name is great in Israel. 4
78: 3 things that we have heard and known 4
6 that the next generation might know them 4
79: 6 out thy anger on the nations that do not know thee 4
10 be known among the nations before our eyes! 4
81: 5 I hear a voice I had not known 4
83:18 them know that thou alone, whose name is the LORD 4
87: 4 Among those who know me I mention Rahab 4
88:12 Are thy wonders known in the darkness 4
89:15 Blessed are the people who know the festal shout 4
91:14 I will protect him, because he knows my name. 4
92: 6 The dull man cannot know 4
94:11 the LORD, knows the thoughts of man 4
100: 3 Know that the LORD is God! It is he that made us 4
101: 4 far from me; I will know nothing of evil. 4
103:14 knows our frame; he remembers that we are dust. 4
16 it is gone, and its place knows it no more. 7
104:19 sun knows its time for setting. 4
109:27 Let them know that this is thy hand; 4
119:75 I know, O LORD, that thy judgments are right 4
79 turn to me, that they may know thy testimonies. 4
125understanding, that I may know thy testimonies! 4
152Long have I known from thy testimonies 4
135: 5 For I know that the LORD is great 4
138: 6 but the haughty he knows from afar. 4
139: 1 O LORD, thou hast searched me and known me! 4
2 Thou knowest when I sit down and when I rise up; 4
4 lo, O LORD, thou knowest it altogether. 4
14 Thou knowest me right well; 4
23 Search me, O God, and know my heart! 4
23 Try me and know my thoughts! 4
140:12 I know that the LORD maintains the cause 4
142: 3 When my spirit is faint, thou knowest my way! 4
147:20 other nation; they do not know his ordinances. 4
Prv 1: 2 That men may know wisdom and instruction 4
4:19 they do not know over what they stumble. 4
5: 6 her ways wander, and she does not know it. 4
7:23 he does not know that it will cost him his life. 4
9:13 A foolish woman . . is wanton and knows no shame. 4
18 he does not know that the dead are there 4
10:32 lips of the righteous know what is acceptable 4
12:16 The vexation of a fool is known at once 4
14:10 The heart knows its own bitterness 4
33 but it is not known in the heart of fools. 4
24:12 If you say, "Behold, we did not know this, 4
12 Does not he who keeps watch over your soul know it 4
14 Know that wisdom is such to your soul; 4
22 who knows the ruin that will come from them both? 4
27: 1 for you do not know what a day may bring forth. 4
23 Know well the condition of your flocks 4
28:22 does not know that want will come upon him. 4
29: 7 A righteous man knows the rights of the poor; 4
30: 4 and what is his son's name? Surely you know! 4
31:23 Her husband is known in the gates 4
Ecc 1:17 I applied my mind to know wisdom and . . madness 4
17 to know wisdom and to know madness and folly. 4
2:19 who knows whether he will be a wise man or a fool? 4
3:12 I know that there is nothing better . . than to be 4
14 I know that whatever God does endures for ever; 4
21 Who knows whether the spirit of man goes upward 4
5: 1 for they do not know that they are doing evil. 4
6: 5 it has not seen the sun or known anything; 4
10 it is known what man is, and that he is not able 4
12 For who knows what is good for man 4
7:22 your heart knows that many times you have 4
25 to know and to search out and to seek wisdom 4
25 and to know the wickedness of folly 4
8: 1 And who knows the interpretation of a thing? 4
5 the mind of a wise man will know the time and way. 4
7 For he does not know what is to be, for who can tell 4
12 I know that it will be well with those who fear God 4
16 When I applied my mind to know wisdom 4
17 even though a wise man claims to know 4
9: 1 whether it is love or hate man does not know. 4
5 For the living know that they will die 4
5 For the living know . . but the dead know nothing 4
12 For man does not know his time. 4
10:14 no man knows what is to be, and who can tell him 4
15 that he does not know the way to the city. 4
11: 2 for you know not what evil may happen on earth. 4
5 you do not know how the spirit comes to the bones 4
5 you do not know the work of God who makes 4
6 you do not know which will prosper, this or that 4
9 know that . . God will bring you into judgment. 4
Sng 1: 8 If you do not know . . follow in the tracks 4
Isa 1: 3 The ox knows its owner, and the ass its . . crib; 4
3 The ox knows its owner . . but Israel does not know 4
5:19 draw near, and let it come, that we may know it! 4
9: 9 all the people will know, E'phraim 4
12: 5 let this be known in all the earth. 4
19:21 the Egyptians will know the LORD in that day 4
29:15 and who say, "Who sees us? Who knows us 4
37:20 the earth may know that thou alone art the LORD. 4
28 I know your sitting down and your going out 4
40:21 Have you not known? Have you not heard? 4
28 Have you not known? Have you not heard? 4
41:20 that men may see and know 4
22 consider them, that we may know their outcome; 4
23 that we may know that you are gods; 4
26 Who declared it . . that we might know 4
42:16 I will lead the blind in a way that they know not 4
16 in paths . . they have not known I will guide them. 4
43:10 that you may know and believe me and understand 4
44: 8 a God besides me? There is no Rock; I know not any. 4
9 their witnesses neither see nor know 4
18 They know not, nor do they discern; 4
45: 3 that you may know that it is I, the LORD 4
4 I surname you, though you do not know me. 4
5 am the LORD . . I gird you, though you do not know me 4
6 that men may know, from the rising of the sun 4
47: 8 sit as a widow or know the loss of children 4
11 come on you suddenly, of which you know nothing. 4
48: 4 Because I know that you are obstinate 4
6 hidden things which you have not known. 4
7 lest you should say, 'Behold, I knew them.' 4
8 You have never heard, you have never known 4
8 I knew that you would deal very treacherously 4
49:23 Then you will know that I am the LORD; 4
26 flesh shall know that I am the LORD your Savior 4
50: 7 and I know that I shall not be put to shame; 4
51: 7 Hearken to me, you who know righteousness 4
52: 6 Therefore my people shall know my name; 4
6 in that day they shall know that it is I who speak; •
55: 5 Behold, you shall call nations that you know not 4
5 and nations that knew you not shall run to you 4
58: 2 Yet they seek me daily and delight to know my ways 4
59: 8 The way of peace they know not 4
8 no one who goes in them knows peace. 4
12 and we know our iniquities 4
60:16 and you shall know that I, the LORD, am your Savior 4
61: 9 descendants shall be known among the nations 4
63:16 art our Father, though Abraham does not know us 4
66:14 it shall be known that the hand of the LORD 4
18 For I know their works and their thoughts 25
Jer 1: 5 Before I formed you in the womb I knew you 4
2: 8 Those who handle the law did not know me; 4
19 Know and see that it is evil and bitter for you 4
23 know what you have done 4
4:22 For my people are foolish, they know me not; 4
5: 4 for they do not know the way of the LORD 4
5 for they know the way of the LORD 4
15 a nation whose language you do not know 4
6:18 hear, O nations, and know, O congregation 4
27 that you may know and assay their ways. 4
7: 9 and go after other gods that you have not known 4
8: 7 Even the stork in the heavens knows her times; 4
7 but my people know not the ordinance of the LORD. 4
9: 3 they do not know me, says the LORD. 4
6 they refuse to know me, says the LORD. 4
16 whom neither they nor their fathers have known; 4
24 glory in this, that he understands and knows me 4
10:23 I know, O LORD, that the way of man is not in himself 4
25 thy wrath upon the nations that know thee not 4
11:18 The LORD made it known to me and I knew; 4
19 I did not know it was against me they devised 4
12: 3 But thou, O LORD, knowest me; thou seest me 4
13:12 Do we not indeed know that every jar will be filled 4
15:14 serve your enemies in a land which you do not know 4
15 O LORD, thou knowest; remember me and visit me 4
15 know that for thy sake I bear reproach. 4
16:13 which neither you nor your fathers have known 4
21 they shall know that my name is the LORD. 4
17: 4 serve your enemies in a land which you do not know 4
16 have I desired the day of disaster, thou knowest; 4
18:23 Yet, thou, O LORD, knowest all their plotting 4
19: 4 their fathers nor the kings of Judah have known; 4
22:16 Is not this to know me? says the LORD. 4
28 and cast into a land which they do not know? 4
24: 7 I will give them a heart to know that I am the LORD; 4
26:15 Only know for certain that if you put me to death 4
28: 9 then it will be known that the LORD has truly sent 4
29:11 For I know the plans I have for you, says the LORD 4
23 I am the one who knows, and I am witness 4
31:34 and each his brother, saying, 'Know the LORD,' 4
34 for they shall all know me 4
32: 8 Then I knew that this was the word of the LORD. 4
33: 3 and hidden things which you have not known. 4
36:19 and let no one know where you are. 4
38:24 said to Jeremiah, "Let no one know of these words 4
40:14 Do you know that Ba'alis the king of the Ammonites 4
15 Let me go and slay Ish'mael . . and no one will know 4
41: 4 after the murder of Gedali'ah, before any one knew 4
42:19 Know for a certainty that I have warned you 4
22 know for a certainty that you shall die 4
44: 3 and serve other gods that they knew not 4
15 all the men who knew that their wives had offered 4
28 shall know whose word will stand, mine or theirs. 4
29 that you may know that my words will surely stand 4
48:17 who are round about him, and all who know his name; 4
30 I know his insolence, says the LORD; 4
50:24 you were taken, O Babylon, and you did not know it; 4
Ezk 2: 5 they will know that there has been a prophet 4
5:13 they shall know that I, the LORD, have spoken 4
6: 7 and you shall know that I am the LORD. 4
10 And they shall know that I am the LORD; 4
13 And you shall know that I am the LORD 4
14 Then they will know that I am the LORD. 4
7: 4 Then you will know that I am the LORD. 4
9 Then you will know that I am the LORD, who smite. 4
27 and they shall know that I am the LORD. 4
10:20 and I knew that they were cherubim. 4
11: 5 I know the things that come into your mind. 4
10 and you shall know that I am the LORD. 4
12 you shall know that I am the LORD; 4
12:15 they shall know that I am the LORD 4
16 and may know that I am the LORD. 4
20 and you shall know that I am the LORD. 4
13: 9 you shall know that I am the Lord GOD. 4
14 you shall know that I am the LORD. 4
21 prey; and you shall know that I am the LORD. 4
23 Then you will know that I am the LORD. 4
14: 8 you shall know that I am the LORD. 4
23 you shall know that I have not done without cause 4
15: 7 you will know that I am the LORD, when I set my face 4
16:62 you shall know that I am the LORD 4
17:12 Do you not know what these things mean? 4
21 you shall know that I, the LORD, have spoken. 4
24 the trees of the field shall know that I the LORD 4
20: 4 let them know the abominations of their fathers 4
12 that they might know that I the LORD sanctify 4
20 that you may know that I the LORD am your God. 4
26 that they might know that I am the LORD. 4
38 Then you will know that I am the LORD. 4
42 And you shall know that I am the LORD 4
44 you shall know that I am the LORD 4
21: 5 shall know that I the LORD have drawn my sword out 4
22:16 you shall know that I am the LORD. 4
22 you shall know that I the LORD have poured out my 4
23:49 you shall know that I am the Lord GOD. 4
24:24 then you will know that I am the Lord GOD. 4
27 they will know that I am the LORD. 4
25: 5 Then you will know that I am the LORD. 4
7 Then you will know that I am the LORD. 4
11 Then they will know that I am the LORD. 4
14 they shall know my vengeance, says the Lord GOD. 4
17 Then they will know that I am the LORD 4
26: 6 Then they will know that I am the LORD. 4
28:19 All who know you among the peoples are appalled 4
22 they shall know that I am the LORD when I execute 4

23 Then they will know that I am the LORD. 4
24 Then they will know that I am the Lord GOD. 4
26 Then they will know that I am the LORD their God. 4
29: 6 Then all the inhabitants of Egypt shall know 4
9 Then they will know that I am the LORD. 4
16 Then they will know that I am the Lord GOD. 4
21 Then they will know that I am the LORD. 4
30: 8 Then they will know that I am the LORD 4
19 Then they will know that I am the LORD. 4
25 they shall know that I am the LORD. 4
26 Then they will know that I am the LORD. 4
32: 9 into the countries which you have not known. 4
15 then they will know that I am the LORD. 4
33:29 Then they will know that I am the LORD 4
33 then they will know that a prophet has been among 4
34:27 they shall know that I am the LORD 4
30 shall know that I, the LORD their God, am with them 4
35: 4 and you shall know that I am the LORD. 4
9 Then you will know that I am the LORD. 4
12 And you shall know that I, the LORD, have heard all 4
15 Then they will know that I am the LORD. 4
36:11 Then you will know that I am the LORD. 4
23 the nations will know that I am the LORD 4
32 says the Lord GOD; let that be known to you. 4
36 left round about you shall know that I, the LORD 4
38 Then they will know that I am the LORD. 4
37: 3 And I answered, "O Lord GOD, thou knowest. 4
6 you shall know that I am the LORD. 4
13 you shall know that I am the LORD 4
14 then you shall know that I, the LORD, have spoken 4
28 the nations will know that I the LORD sanctify 4
38:16 against my land, that the nations may know me 4
23 Then they will know that I am the LORD. 4
39: 6 they shall know that I am the LORD. 4
7 the nations shall know that I am the LORD 4
22 The house of Israel shall know that I am the LORD 4
23 the nations shall know that the house of Israel 4
28 Then they shall know that I am the LORD their God 4
Dan 2: 3 spirit is troubled to know the dream. 4
8 I know with certainty that you are trying to gain 8
9 know that you can show me its interpretation. 8
22 he knows what is in the darkness 8
30 that you may know the thoughts of your mind. 8
3:18 if not, be it known to you, O king 8
4: 9 because I know that the spirit of the holy gods 8
17 that the living may know that the Most High rules 8
25 till you know that the Most High rules 8
26 sure for you from the time that you know 8
5:21 until he knew that the Most High God rules 8
22 not humbled your heart, though you knew all this 8
23 gods . . which do not see or hear or know 8
6:10 Daniel knew that the document had been signed 8
15 Know, O king, that it is a law of the Medes 8
9:25 Know therefore and understand that 4
10:20 Then he said, "Do you know why I have come to you? 4
11:32 people who know their God shall stand firm 4
38 god whom his fathers did not know he shall honor 4
Hos 2: 8 did not know that it was I who gave her the grain 4
20 and you shall know the LORD. 4
5: 3 I know E'phraim, and Israel is not hid from me; 4
4 and they know not the LORD. 4
6: 3 Let us know, let us press on to know the LORD; 4
3 Let us know, let us press on to know the LORD; 4
7: 9 Aliens devour his strength, and he knows it not; 4
9 and he knows it not. 4
8: 2 To me they cry, My God, we Israel know thee. 4
9: 7 Israel shall know it. 4
11: 3 but they did not know that I healed them. 4
12 but Judah is still known by God, and is faithful •
13: 4 you know no God but me 4
5 It was I who knew you in the wilderness 4
14: 9 whoever is discerning, let him know them; 4
Jol 2:14 Who knows whether he will not turn and repent 4
27 You shall know that I am in the midst of Israel 4
3:17 you shall know that I am the LORD your God 4
Ams 3: 2 You only have I known of all the families 4
5:12 For I know how many are your transgressions 4
Jon 1: 7 lots, that we may know on whose account this evil 4
10 the men knew that he was fleeing 4
12 I know it is because of me that this great tempest 4
3: 9 Who knows, God may yet repent 4
4: 2 for I knew that thou art a gracious God 4
11 who do not know their right hand from their left 4
Mic 3: 1 Israel! Is it not for you to know justice? 4
4:12 But they do not know the thoughts of the LORD 4
6: 5 that you may know the saving acts of the LORD. 4
Nah 1: 7 he knows those who take refuge in him. 4
3:17 they fly away; no one knows where they are. 4
Zep 3: 5 but the unjust knows no shame. 4
Zec 2: 9 you will know that the LORD of hosts has sent me. 4
11 you shall know that the LORD of hosts has sent me 4
4: 5 Do you not know what these are?" I said, "No, my lord. 4
9 you will know that the LORD of hosts has sent me 4
13 He said to me, "Do you not know what these are? 4
6:15 you shall know that the LORD of hosts has sent me 4
7:14 among all the nations which they had not known. 4
11:11 watching me, knew that it was the word of the LORD. 4
14: 7 continuous day (it is known to the LORD) 4
Mal 2: 4 So shall you know that I have sent this command 4

Mat 1:25 knew her not until she had borne a son; 11
6: 3 your left hand know what your right hand is doing 11
8 like them, for your Father knows what you need 31
32 your heavenly Father knows that you need them 31
7:16 You will know them by their fruits. 23
20 Thus you will know them by their fruits. 23
23 And then will I declare to them, 'I never knew you; 11
9: 4 Jesus, knowing their thoughts, said 32
6 But that you may know 31
30 See that no one knows it. 11
10:26 or hidden that will not be known. 11
11:27 and no one knows the Son except the Father 23
27 and no one knows the Father except the Son 23
12: 7 if you had known what this means, 'I desire mercy 11
16 ordered them not to make him known. 35
25 Knowing their thoughts, he said to them 31
33 for the tree is known by its fruit. 11
13:11 To you it has been given to know the secrets 11
15:12 Do you know that the Pharisees were offended 31
16: 3 You know how to interpret 11
17:12 they did not know him 23
20:22 You do not know what you are asking 31
25 You know that the rulers of the Gentiles 31
21:27 So they answered Jesus, "We do not know. 31
22:16 Teacher, we know that you are true 31
29 because you know neither the scriptures 31
24:32 you know that summer is near. 11
33 you know that he is near, at the very gates. 11
36 of that day and hour no one knows 31
39 they did not know until the flood came 11
42 Watch therefore, for you do not know 31
43 know this, that if the householder had known 11
43 know this, that if the householder had known 11
50 at an hour he does not know 11
25:12 'Truly, I say to you, I do not know you.' 31
13 you know neither the day nor the hour. 31
24 Master, I knew you to be a hard man 11
26 You knew that I reap where I have not sowed 31
26: 2 You know that after two days 31
70 I do not know what you mean. 31
72 I do not know the man. 31
74 I do not know the man. 31
27:18 For he knew that it was out of envy 31
28: 5 Do not be afraid; for I know that you seek Jesus 31
Mrk 1:24 I know who you are, the Holy One of God. 31
34 because they knew him. 31
2:10 that you may know 31
3:12 he strictly ordered them not to make him known. 35
4:27 he knows not how. 31
5:33 the woman, knowing what had been done to her, came 31
43 he strictly charged them that no one should know 11
6:14 Jesus' name had become known 35
20 knowing that he was a righteous and holy man 31
33 Now many saw them going, and knew them 23
7:24 he entered a house, and would not have any one know 11
9: 6 For he did not know what to say 31
30 he would not have any one know it; 11
10:19 You know the commandments 31
38 You do not know what you are asking 31
42 You know that those who are supposed to rule 31
11:33 So they answered Jesus, "We do not know. 31
12:14 we know that you are true, and care for no man 31
15 knowing their hypocrisy, he said to them 31
24 know neither the scriptures nor the power of God? 31
13:28 you know that summer is near. 11
29 you know that he is near, at the very gates. 11
32 of that day or that hour no one knows 31
33 Take heed, watch; for you do not know 31
35 Watch therefore–for you do not know 31
14:40 they did not know what to answer him. 31
68 I neither know nor understand what you mean. 31
71 I do not know this man of whom you speak. 31
Lke 1: 4 that you may know the truth 23
18 Zechari'ah said to the angel, "How shall I know this? 11
2:43 His parents did not know it 11
49 not know that I must be in my Father's house? 31
4:34 I know who you are, the Holy One of God. 31
41 because they knew that he was the Christ. 31
5:24 you may know that the Son of man has authority 31
6: 8 he knew their thoughts 31
44 for each tree is known by its own fruit 11
7:39 known who and what sort of woman this is 11
8:10 To you it has been given to know the secrets 11
17 that shall not be known and come to light. 11
53 they laughed at him, knowing that she was dead. 31
9:33 not knowing what he said. 31
10:11 nevertheless know this 11
22 no one knows who the Son is except the Father 11
11:17 he, knowing their thoughts, said to them 31
44 men walk over them without knowing it. 31
12: 2 or hidden that will not be known. 11
30 your Father knows that you need them. 31
39 know this, that if the householder had known 11
39 if the householder had known at what hour 31
46 at an hour he does not know 11
47 that servant who knew his master's will 11
48 who did not know, and did what deserved a beating 11
13:25 'I do not know where you come from.' 31
27 he will say, 'I tell you, I do not know 31

16:15 God knows your hearts 11
18:20 You know the commandments 31
19:15 might know what they had gained by trading. 11
22 You knew that I was a severe man 31
42 saying, "Would that even today you knew the things 11
44 you did not know the time of your visitation. 11
20: 7 they did not know whence it was. 31
21 we know that you speak and teach rightly 31
21:20 then know that its desolation has come near. 11
30 know that the summer is already near. 11
31 you know that the kingdom of God is near. 11
22:34 until you three times deny that you know me. 31
57 he denied it, saying, "Woman, I do not know him. 31
60 Peter said, "Man, I do not know what you are saying. 31
23:34 forgive them; for they know not what they do 31
24:18 who does not know the things that have happened 11
35 he was known to them in the breaking of the bread. 11
Joh 1:10 yet the world knew him not. 11
26 but among you stands one whom you do not know 31
31 I myself did not know him; 31
33 I myself did not know him; 31
48 Nathan'a-el said to him, "How do you know me? 11
2: 9 and did not know where it came 31
9 (. . the servants who had drawn the water knew) 31
25 because he knew all men 11
25 for he himself knew what was in man. 11
3: 2 we know that you are a teacher come from God; 31
8 you do not know whence it comes or whither it goes; 31
11 Truly, truly, I say to you, we speak of what we know 31
4: 1 when the Lord knew that the Pharisees had heard 11
10 Jesus answered her, "If you knew the gift of God 31
22 You worship what you do not know; 31
22 we worship what we know 31
25 I know that Messiah is coming 31
32 I have food to eat of which you do not know. 31
42 we know that this is indeed the Savior 31
53 The father knew that was the hour when Jesus 11
5: 6 and knew that he had been lying there a long time 11
13 man who had been healed did not know who it was 31
32 I know that the testimony . . is true. 31
42 I know that you have not the love of God 11
6: 6 he himself knew what he would do. 31
42 Jesus . . whose father and mother we know? 31
61 knowing in himself that his disciples murmured 31
64 Jesus knew from the first 31
69 . . come to know, that you are the Holy One of God 11
7: 4 if he seeks to be known openly •
17 he shall know whether the teaching is from God 11
26 Can it be that the authorities really know 11
27 Yet we know where this man comes from; 31
27 no one will know where he comes from. 11
28 You know me, and you know where I come from? 31
28 You know me, and you know where I come from? 31
28 he who sent me is true, and him you do not know. 31
29 I know him, for I come from him, and he sent me. 31
49 this crowd, who do not know the law, are accursed. 11
8:14 my testimony is true, for I know whence I have come 31
14 do not know whence I come or whither I am going. 31
19 Jesus answered, "You know neither me nor my Father 31
19 if you knew me, you would know my Father also. 31
19 if you knew me, you would know my Father also. 31
28 then you will know that I am he 11
32 you will know the truth 11
37 I know that you are descendants of Abraham 31
52 Now we know that you have a demon 11
55 you have not known him; I know him 11
55 you have not known him; I know him 31
55 If I said, I do not know him, I should be a liar 31
55 I do know him and I keep his word. 31
9:12 They said . . "Where is he?" He said, "I do not know 31
20 His parents answered, "We know that this is our son 31
21 how he now sees we do not know 31
21 nor do we know who opened his eyes 31
24 we know that this man is a sinner. 31
25 He answered, "Whether he is a sinner, I do not know; 31
25 one thing I know, that though I was blind, now I see. 31
29 We know that God has spoken to Moses 31
29 we do not know where he comes from. 31
30 You do not know where he comes 31
31 We know that God does not listen to sinners 31
10: 4 the sheep follow him, for they know his voice. 31
5 for they do not know the voice of strangers. 31
14 I know my own and my own know me 11
14 I know my own and my own know me 11
15 as the Father knows me and I know the Father 11
15 as the Father knows me and I know the Father 11
27 My sheep hear my voice, and I know them 11
38 that you may know and understand 11
11:22 even now I know that whatever you ask from God 31
24 Martha said to him, "I know that he will rise again 31
42 I knew that thou hearest me always 31
49 You know nothing at all; 31
57 if any one knew where he was 11
57 he should let them know 30
12:35 does not know where he goes. 31
50 I know that his commandment is eternal life. 31
13: 1 when Jesus knew that his hour had come to depart 31
3 Jesus, knowing that . . 31
7 What I am doing you do not know now 31

11 For he knew who was to betray him 31
12 said to them, "Do you know what I have done to you? 11
17 If you know these things 31
18 I know whom I have chosen 31
28 no one at the table knew why he said this to him. 11
35 all men will know that you are my disciples 11
14: 4 you know the way where I am going. 31
5 Lord, we do not know where you are going 31
5 how can we know the way? 31
7 If you had known me, you would have known . . Father 11
7 If you had known me, you would have known 11
7 henceforth you know him and have seen him. 11
9 yet you do not know me, Philip? 11
17 because it neither sees him nor knows him 11
17 you know him, for he dwells with you 11
20 In that day you will know that I am in my Father 11
31 so that the world may know that I love the Father. 11
15:15 servant does not know what his master is doing; 31
18 If the world hates you, know that it has hated me 11
21 because they do not know him who sent me. 31
16: 3 because they have not known the Father, nor me. 11
18 We do not know what he means. 31
19 Jesus knew that they wanted to ask him 11
30 Now we know that you know all things 31
30 Now we know that you know all things 31
17: 3 this is eternal life, that they know thee 11
7 Now they know that everything . . is from thee; 11
8 and know in truth that I came from thee 11
23 so that the world may know that thou hast sent me 11
25 O righteous Father, the world has not known thee 11
25 I have known thee 11
25 these know that thou hast sent me. 11
18: 2 Now Judas, who betrayed him, also knew the place; 31
4 Jesus, knowing all that was to befall him 31
15 this disciple was known to the high priest 17
16 other disciple, who was known to the high priest 17
21 what I said to them; they know what I said. 31
19: 4 that you may know that I find no crime in him. 11
10 Do you not know that I have power to release you 31
28 knowing that all was now finished 31
35 he knows that he tells the truth 31
20: 2 we do not know where they have laid him. 31
9 for as yet they did not know the scripture 31
13 I do not know where they have laid him. 31
14 she did not know that it was Jesus. 31
21: 4 yet the disciples did not know that it was Jesus. 31
12 They knew it was the Lord. 31
15 He said to him, "Yes, Lord; you know that I love you. 31
16 He said to him, "Yes, Lord; you know that I love you. 31
17 he said to him, "Lord, you know everything 31
17 you know everything; you know that I love you 11
24 we know that his testimony is true. 31
Act 1: 7 not for you to know times or seasons 11
19 it became known to all the inhabitants 17
2:14 let this be known to you, and give ear to my words. 17
22 as you yourselves know– 31
30 knowing that God had sworn with an oath to him 31
36 Let all the house of Israel therefore know 11
3:16 this man . . whom you see and know 31
17 now, brethren, I know that you acted in ignorance 31
4:10 be it known to you all 17
5: 7 his wife came in, not knowing what had happened. 31
7:13 Joseph's family became known to Pharaoh. 35
18 another king who had not known Joseph. 31
40 we do not know what has become of him.' 31
9:30 when the brethren knew it 23
42 it became known throughout all Joppa 17
10: 1 what was known as the Italian Cohort 27
28 You yourselves know how unlawful it is for a Jew 25
36 You know the word which he sent to Israel 31
12: 9 not know that what was done by the angel was real 31
13:38 Let it be known to you therefore, brethren 17
15: 7 you know that in the early days God made choice 25
18 who has made these things known from of old.' 17
16: 3 they all knew that his father was a Greek. 31
17:19 May we know what this new teaching is 11
20 wish to know therefore what these things mean 11
18:25 though he knew only the baptism of John. 25
19:15 Jesus I know, and Paul I know; but who are you? 11
15 Jesus I know, and Paul I know; but who are you? 25
17 this became known to all residents of Ephesus 17
25 said, "Men, you know 25
32 most . . did not know why they had come together. 31
35 Men of Ephesus, what man . . does not know 11
20:18 You yourselves know how I lived among you 25
22 not knowing what shall befall me there; 31
25 now, behold, I know 31
29 I know that . . fierce wolves will come 31
34 You yourselves know 11
21:24 Thus all will know 11
37 he said, "Do you know Greek? 11
22:14 God of our fathers appointed you to know his will 11
19 I said, 'Lord, they themselves know 25
30 desiring to know . . why the Jews accused him 11
23: 5 I did not know, brethren, that he was the high priest; 31
28 desiring to know the charge 23
25:10 I have done no wrong, as you know very well. 23
26: 4 is known by all the Jews. 31
26 the king knows about these things 26

27 I know that you believe. 31
28:22 we know that everywhere it is spoken against. 17
28 Let it be known to you then that this salvation 17
Rom 1:13 I want you to know, brethren 33
19 For what can be known about God is plain to them 17
21 for although they knew God they did not honor him 11
32 Though they know God's decree 23
2: 2 We know that the judgment of God rightly falls 31
4 Do you not know that God's kindness is meant 9
18 know his will and approve what is excellent 11
3:17 the way of peace they do not know. 11
19 Now we know that whatever the law says 31
5: 3 knowing that suffering produces endurance 31
6: 3 Do you not know that 9
6 We know that our old self was crucified with him 11
9 For we know that Christ . . will never die again; 31
16 Do you not know that if you yield yourselves 31
7: 1 Do you not know, brethren 9
1 for I am speaking to those who know the law– 11
7 if it had not been . . I should not have known sin. 11
7 I should not have known what it is to covet 31
14 We know that the law is spiritual; but I am carnal 31
18 For I know that nothing good dwells within me 31
8:22 We know that . . creation has been groaning 31
26 for we do not know how to pray as we ought 31
27 knows what is the mind of the Spirit 31
28 We know that in everything God works for good 31
11: 2 Do you not know what the scripture says of Eli'jah 31
34 For who has known the mind of the Lord 11
13:11 Besides this you know what hour it is 31
14:14 I know and am persuaded in the Lord Jesus 31
15:29 I know that when I come to you 31
16:19 For while your obedience is known to all 10
1Co 1:16 I do not know whether I baptized any one else.) 31
21 the world did not know God through wisdom 11
2: 2 For I decided to know nothing among you 31
11 what person knows a man's thoughts 31
16 For who has known the mind of the Lord 11
3:16 Do you not know that you are God's temple 31
20 The Lord knows that the thoughts of the wise 11
5: 6 Your boasting is not good. Do you not know 31
6: 2 know that the saints will judge the world 31
3 Do you not know that we are to judge angels? 31
9 Do you not know 31
15 know that your bodies are members of Christ 31
16 Do you not know 31
19 Do you not know that your body is a temple 31
7:16 Wife, how do you know 31
16 Husband, how do you know 31
8: 1 we know that "all of us possess knowledge. 31
2 If any one imagines that he knows something 11
2 he does not yet know as he ought to know. 11
2 he does not yet know as he ought to know. 11
3 if one loves God, one is known by him. 11
4 we know that "an idol has no real existence 31
9:13 Do you not know that those who are employed 31
24 Do you not know that in a race 31
10: 1 I want you to know, brethren 9
12: 2 You know that when you were heathen 31
13:12 Now I know in part; then I shall understand fully 11
14: 7 how will any one know what is played? 11
9 how will any one know what is said 11
11 if I do not know the meaning of the language 31
16 when he does not know what you are saying? 31
35 If there is anything they desire to know 29
15:58 knowing that in the Lord 31
16:15 Now, brethren, you know that the household 31
2Co 1: 7 we know that as you share in our sufferings 31
2: 4 to let you know the abundant love that I have 11
9 know whether you are obedient in everything. 11
3: 2 to be known and read by all men; 11
4:14 knowing that he who raised the Lord Jesus 31
5: 1 For we know that if the earthly tent we live 31
6 we know that while we are at home in the body 31
11 Therefore, knowing the fear of the Lord 31
11 what we are is known to God 37
11 I hope it is known also to your conscience. 37
21 For our sake he made him to be sin who knew no sin 11
8: 9 For you know the grace of our Lord Jesus Christ 11
9: 2 for I know your readiness 31
11:11 why? Because I do not love you? God knows I do! 31
31 knows that I do not lie. 31
12: 2 I know a man in Christ 31
2 I do not know, God knows. 31
2 I do not know, God knows. 31
3 I know that this man was caught up 31
3 I do not know, God knows– 31
3 I do not know, God knows– 31
Gal 1:11 I would have you know, brethren 12
22 I was still not known by sight 9
2:16 yet who know that a man is not justified by works 31
4: 8 Formerly, when you did not know God 31
9 now that you have come to know God 11
9 rather to be known by God 11
13 you know it was because of a bodily ailment 31
Eph 1:18 know what is the hope to which he has called you 31
3:19 to know the love of Christ 11
6: 8 knowing that whatever good any one does 31
9 knowing that he . . is in heaven 31

21 you also may know how I am and what I am doing 31
22 that you may know how we are 11
Php 1:12 I want you to know, brethren 11
13 so that it has become known 36
16 knowing that I am put here 31
19 For I know that through your prayers 31
25 Convinced of this, I know that I shall remain 31
2:22 Timothy's worth you know 11
3: 8 the surpassing worth of knowing Christ Jesus 15
10 know him and the power of his resurrection 11
4: 5 Let all men know your forbearance 11
15 you Philippians yourselves know 31
Col 2: 1 For I want you to know how greatly I strive for you 31
3:24 knowing . . you will receive the inheritance 31
4: 1 knowing that you also have a Master in heaven. 31
6 you may know how you ought to answer every one. 31
8 you may know how we are 11
1Th 1: 4 For we know, brethren beloved by God 31
5 You know what kind of men we proved to be 31
2: 1 For you yourselves know, brethren 31
2 shamefully treated at Philip'pi, as you know 31
5 never used either words of flattery, as you know 31
11 for you know how, like a father with his children 31
3: 3 You yourselves know that this is to be our lot. 31
4 just as it has come to pass, and as you know. 31
5 I sent that I might know your faith 11
4: 2 For you know what instructions we gave you 31
5 like heathen who do not know God; 31
5: 2 you yourselves know well that the day of the Lord 31
2Th 1: 8 those who do not know God 31
2: 6 you know what is restraining him now 31
3: 7 you yourselves know how you ought to imitate us; 31
1Ti 1: 8 Now we know that the law is good 31
3:15 you may know how one ought to behave 31
4: 3 those who believe and know the truth. 23
6: 4 is puffed up with conceit, he knows nothing 25
2Ti 1:12 I am not ashamed, for I know whom I have believed 31
18 you well know all the service he rendered 11
2:19 The Lord knows those who are his 11
23 you know that they breed quarrels. 31
25 they will repent and come to know the truth 24
3:14 knowing from whom you learned it 31
Tit 1:16 They profess to know God 31
3:11 knowing that such a person is perverted 31
Phm 1:21 knowing that you will do even more than I say. 31
Heb 3:10 they have not known my ways.' 11
8:11 saying, 'Know the Lord,' for all shall know me 11
11 saying, 'Know the Lord,' for all shall know me 31
10:30 we know him who said, "Vengeance is mine 31
34 since you knew 11
11: 8 he went out, not knowing where he was to go. 25
12:17 you know that afterward . . he was rejected 31
Jas 1: 3 for you know that the testing of your faith 11
19 Know this, my beloved brethren. 31
3: 1 for you know that we who teach shall be judged 31
4: 4 Unfaithful creatures! Do you not know 31
14 whereas you do not know about tomorrow. 25
17 knows what is right to do and fails to do it 31
5:20 let him know that whoever brings back a sinner 11
1Pe 1:18 You know that you were ransomed 31
5: 9 knowing that the same experience of suffering 31
2Pe 1:12 you know them and are established in the truth 31
14 know that the putting off of my body will be soon 31
2:21 better for them never to have known the way 23
21 than after knowing it to turn back 23
1Jn 2: 3 by this we may be sure that we know him 11
4 He who says "I know him" but disobeys 11
11 and does not know where he is going 31
13 because you know him who is from the beginning 11
13 because you know the Father. 11
14 because you know him who is from the beginning 11
18 therefore we know that it is the last hour. 11
20 and you all know. 31
21 not because you do not know the truth 31
21 I write to you . . because you know it 31
21 and know that no lie is of the truth. 31
29 If you know that he is righteous, you may be sure 31
3: 1 The reason why the world does not know us 11
1 is that it did not know him. 11
2 we know that when he appears we shall be like him 31
5 You know that he appeared to take away sins 31
6 no one who sins has either seen him or known him. 11
14 We know that we have passed out of death into life 31
15 you know that no murderer has eternal life 31
16 By this we know love, that he laid down his life 11
19 By this we shall know that we are of the truth 11
20 God is greater . . and he knows everything. 11
24 And by this we know that he abides in us 11
4: 2 By this you know the Spirit of God 11
6 We are of God. Whoever knows God listens to us 11
6 By this we know the spirit of truth 11
7 and he who loves is born of God and knows God. 11
8 He who does not love does not know God; 11
13 By this we know that we abide in him and he in us 11
16 So we know and believe the love God has for us. 11
5: 2 By this we know that we love the children of God 11
13 that you may know that you have eternal life. 31
15 if we know that he hears us in whatever we ask 31
15 we know that we have obtained the requests 31

18 We know that any one born of God does not sin 31
19 We know that we are of God 31
20 we know that the Son of God has come 31
20 given us understanding, to know him who is true; 11
2Jn 1: 1 and not only I but also all who know the truth 11
3Jn 1: 2 I know that it is well with your soul. •
12 and you know my testimony is true. 31
Jde 1:10 by those things that they know by instinct 31
Rev 2: 2 I know your works, your toil and your patient 31
3 I know you are enduring patiently and bearing up •
9 'I know your tribulation and your poverty 31
13 'I know where you dwell, where Satan's throne is; 31
17 a new name . . which no one knows except him 31
19 'I know your works, your love and faith and service 31
23 And all the churches shall know that I am he 11
3: 1 I know your works; you have the name of being alive 31
3 you will not know at what hour I will come upon you 11
8 'I know your works. 31
8 I know that you have but little power •
15 'I know your works: you are neither cold nor hot. 31
17 not knowing that you are wretched, pitiable, poor 31
7:14 I said to him, "Sir, you know." And he said to me 31
12:12 because he knows that his time is short! 31
19:12 he has a name inscribed which no one knows 31
1Es 2:18 Now be it known to our lord the king 17
6: 8 Let it be fully known to our lord the king 17
8:23 all those who know the law of your God 25
23 those who do not know it you shall teach. 25
2Es 3:32 Or has another nation known thee besides Israel? 38
4:46 For I know what has gone by 43
46 but I do not know what is to come. 39
52 for I do not know. 41
5: 7 one whom the many do not know 42
17 Or do you not know 41
38 I said, "O sovereign Lord, who is able to know 43
6:16 for they know that their end must be changed. 43
7:64 because we perish and know it. 43
66 nor do they know of any torment or salvation 43
132I answered and said, "I know, O Lord 43
8:15 About all mankind thou knowest best 43
58 though knowing full well that they must die. 43
9: 2 then you will know that it is the very time 40
4 then you will know that it was of these 40
10:35 For I have seen what I did not know 43
52 for I knew that the Most High would reveal 43
12:38 whose hearts you know are able to comprehend 43
13:52 explore or know what is in the depths of the sea 43
14:21 so no one knows the things which have been done 43
22 in characters which they did not know 43
15:26 the Lord knows all who transgress against him; 42
16:54 Behold, the Lord knows all the works of men 38
56 and he knows the number of the stars. 42
63 Surely he knows your imaginations 42
Tob 2:10 I did not know 31
14 You seem to know everything! 17
3: 8 Do you not know that you strangle your husbands? 34
14 Thou knowest, O Lord, that I am innocent 11
5: 2 when I do not know the man? 11
5 Tobias did not know it 21
11 Tobit said to him, "I should like to know, my brother 23
13 I used to know Ananias and Jathan 23
6:12 I know that Raguel . . cannot give her 25
7: 4 he said to them, "Do you know our brother Tobit? 11
8:12 let us bury him without any one knowing about it. 11
11: 7 I know, Tobias, that your father will open his eyes. 25
13: 6 who knows if he will accept you 11
Jdt 8:13 but you will never know anything! 23
20 we know no other god but him 11
9: 7 know not that thou art the Lord 11
14 to know and understand that thou art God 24
AEs 13:12 Thou knowest all things; thou knowest, O Lord 11
12 thou knowest, O Lord, that it was not in insolence 31
14:15 thou knowest that I hate 31
16 Thou knowest my necessity 31
Wis 1: 7 and that . . knows what is said; 14
2: 1 no one has been known to return from Hades. 11
22 they did not know the secret purposes of God 11
4: 1 because it is known both by God and by men. 11
5: 7 the way of the Lord we have not known. 23
7:12 I did not know that she was their mother. 9
17 to know the structure of the world 31
8: 8 she knows the things of old 31
9 knowing that she would give me good counsel 31
21 it was a mark of insight to know whose gift she was 31
9: 9 With thee is wisdom, who knows thy works 31
11 For she knows and understands all things 31
12:17 dost rebuke any insolence among those who know it 31
27 him whom they had before refused to know. 31
13: 1 they were unable . . to know him who exists 31
3 let them know 11
9 for if they had the power to know so much 31
16 because he knows that it cannot help itself 31
14:18 even those who did not know the king 9
15: 2 For even if we sin we are thine, knowing thy power; 31
2 because we know that we are accounted thine. 31
3 For to know thee is complete righteousness 25
3 to know thy power is the root of immortality. 31
13 this man, more than all others, knows 31
16:16 the ungodly, refusing to know thee 31

18 seeing this they might know 31
22 they might know 11
28 to make it known that one must rise before the sun 17
Sir 1: 6 Her clever devices–who knows them? 11
4:24 For wisdom is known through speech 11
8:18 for you do not know what he will divulge. 11
9:11 for you do not know what his end will be. 31
13 Know that you are walking in the midst of snares 23
11:19 he does not know how much time will pass 31
28 a man will be known through his children. 11
12: 1 If you do a kindness, know to whom you do it 11
8 A friend will not be known in prosperity 22
11 will know that it was not hopelessly tarnished. 11
15:19 he knows every deed of man. 23
16:17 Among so many people I shall not be known 11
18:28 Every intelligent man knows wisdom 11
19:29 A man is known by his appearance 23
29 a sensible man is known by his face 23
20: 6 keeps silent because he knows when to speak. 19
21: 7 He who is mighty in speech is known from afar 17
23:20 it was known to him 11
24:28 Just as the first man did not know her perfectly 11
26: 9 she is known by her eyelids. 11
27:27 he will not know where it came from. 23
32: 8 be as one who knows and yet holds his tongue. 11
34: 9 An educated man knows many things 11
10 He that is inexperienced knows few things 31
36: 5 let them know thee, as we have known 23
5 let them know thee, as we have known 23
17 all who are on the earth will know 11
37:12 whom you know to be a keeper of the commandments 23
38: 5 in order that his power might be known? 11
42:18 the Most High knows all that may be known 11
18 the Most High knows all that may be known 20
46: 6 so that the nations might know his armament 15
Bar 2:15 earth may know that thou art the Lord our God 11
30 For I know that they will not obey me, for they are 11
31 they will know that I am the Lord their God. 11
3:31 No one knows the way to her, or is concerned about 11
32 he who knows all things knows her, he found her 31
32 he who knows all things knows her, he found her 11
4: 4 for we know what is pleasing to God. 18
LJr 1:23 From this you will know that they are not gods 11
29 Since you know . . that they are not gods 11
50 it will afterward be known that they are false. 11
52 Who then can fail to know that they are not gods? 16
65 Since you know then that they are not gods 11
72 you will know that they are not gods 11
Aza 1:22 Let them know that thou art the Lord, the only God 11
Sus 1:43 thou knowest that these men have borne false 25
Bel 1:35 I know nothing about the den. 11
Man 1:12 I have sinned, and I know my transgressions. 11
1Mc 2:65 I know that Simeon . . is wise in counsel 31
3:52 thou knowest what they plot against us. 31
4:11 Then all the Gentiles will know 11
33 let all who know thy name praise thee with hymns. 31
6:13 I know that it is because of this 11
11:31 so that you may know what it says. 31
12:29 his men did not know it until morning 11
13: 3 You yourselves know 31
3 you know also the wars and the difficulties •
17 Simon knew that they were speaking deceitfully 11
15:12 for he knew that troubles had converged upon him 31
2Mc 1:27 let the Gentiles know that thou art our God. 11
33 When this matter became known 35
7:22 I do not know how you came into being in my womb 31
9:24 they would know to whom the government was left. 19
11:26 that they may know our policy and be of good cheer 31
14:32 did not know where the man was whom he sought 11
15:21 he knew that it is not by arms 11
3Mc 1: 3 Dositheus, known as the son of Drimylus 28
3:14 as you yourselves know 31
7: 9 For you should know that . . 11
4Mc 5: 4 and known to many in the tyrant's court 13
25 we know that in the nature of things 31
6:27 You know, O God 31
7:22 knows that it is blessed to endure any suffering 32
10: 2 he shouted, "Do you not know 9
16:25 They knew also 32
18: 2 knowing that devout reason is master 11

know *See also* aim, demand, fail, want.

know a long time 1. προγινώσκω

Act 26: 5 They have known for a long time 1

know beforehand 1. προγινώσκω 2. προράω

2Pe 3:17 beloved, knowing this beforehand, beware 1
4Mc 4:25 though they had known beforehand 2

cause to know 1. ידע

Job 38:12 caused the dawn to know its place 1

come to know 1. ידע 2. ἐπιγινώσκω

Lev 5: 1 whether he has seen or come to know the matter 1
3 when he comes to know it he shall be guilty 1
4 and it is hidden from him, when he comes to know it 1
Jdt 5: 8 the God of heaven, the God they had come to know 2

know gladness 1. בלג

Ps 39:13 Look away from me, that I may know gladness 1

know how 1. ידע 2. οἶδα

Exd 36: 1 ability and intelligence to know how to do any 1
1Kg 3: 7 I am but a little child; I do not know how to go out 1
5: 6 who knows how to cut timber like the Sido′nians. 1
2Ch 2: 8 I know that your servants know how to cut timber 1
Job 32:22 I do not know how to flatter 1
37:15 Do you know how God lays his command upon them 1
Ecc 6: 8 the poor man . . who knows how to conduct himself 1
Isa 7:15 knows how to refuse the evil and choose the good. 1
16 For before the child knows how to refuse the evil 1
8: 4 for before the child knows how to cry 'My father' 1
50: 4 that I may know how to sustain with a word him that 1
Jer 1: 6 "Ah, Lord GOD! Behold, I do not know how to speak 1
4:22 but how to do good they know not. 1
6:15 they did not know how to blush. 1
8:12 they did not know how to blush. 1
Ams 3:10 They do not know how to do right," says the LORD 1
Mat 7:11 If you then, who are evil, know how to give good gifts 2
Lke 11:13 you then, who are evil, know how to give good gifts 2
12:56 You know how to interpret the appearance 2
56 why do you not know how to interpret the present 2
Php 4:12 I know how to be abased, and I know how to abound 2
12 I know how to be abased, and I know how to abound 2
1Th 4: 4 each one of you know how to take a wife for himself 2
1Ti 3: 5 does not know how to manage his own household 2
2Pe 2: 9 the Lord knows how to rescue the godly from trial 2

know in advance 1. προῖδα

Wis 19: 1 God knew in advance even their future actions 1

make know 1. ידע

Exd 18:16 I make them know the statutes of God 1
20 you shall . . make them know the way 1
Deu 8: 3 that he might make you know that man does not live 1
2Sm 7:21 wrought all this . . to make thy servant know it. 1
Job 13:23 Make me know my transgression and my sin. 1
Ps 25: 4 Make me . . know thy ways, . . ; teach me thy paths 1
Jer 16:21 Therefore, behold, I will make them know 1
21 I will make them know my power and my might 1

know no bounds 1. עבר

Jer 5:28 They know no bounds in deeds of wickedness 1

no one knows 1. ἀγνοέω

Wis 5:12 so that no one knows its pathway. 1

know nothing of goodness 1. ἀπειράγαθος

AEs 16: 4 the boasts of those who know nothing of goodness 1

know the heart 1. καρδιογνώστης

Act 1:24 Lord, who knowest the hearts of all men 1
15: 8 God who knows the heart bore witness to them 1

know the truth 1. יצב (A)

Dan 7:19 desired to know the truth concerning the fourth 1

without knowing 1. ἀγνοέω

Wis 18:19 not perish without knowing why they suffered. 1

knowledge 1. דֵּעַ 2. דֵּעָה 3. דַּעַת 4. ידע 5. מַדָּע 6. עַיִן 7. מַנְדַּע (A) 8. γινώσκω 9. γνῶσις 10. ἐπίγνωσις 11. ἐπιστήμη 12. οἶδα 13. ὁράω 14. σύνοιδα 15. scientia

Gen 2: 9 and the tree of the knowledge of good and evil. 3
17 the tree of the knowledge of good and evil 3
Exd 31: 3 with knowledge and all craftsmanship 3
35:31 with ability, with intelligence, with knowledge 3
Num15:24 done unwittingly without the knowledge 6
24:16 him who . . knows the knowledge of the Most High 3
Deu 1:39 children . . have no knowledge of good or evil 4
1Sm 2: 3 the LORD is a God of knowledge 2
1Kg 2:32 without the knowledge of my father David 4
2Ch 1:10 Give me now wisdom and knowledge to go out 5
11 have asked wisdom and knowledge for yourself 5
12 wisdom and knowledge are granted to you. 5
Neh 10:28 all who have knowledge and understanding 4
Job 15: 2 Should a wise man answer with windy knowledge 3
21:14 We do not desire the knowledge of thy ways. 3
22 Will any teach God knowledge 3
34:35 Job speaks without knowledge 3
35:16 he multiplies words without knowledge. 3
36: 3 I will fetch my knowledge from afar 1
4 one who is perfect in knowledge is with you. 2
12 perish by the sword, and die without knowledge. 3
37:16 works of him who is perfect in knowledge 1
38: 2 darkens counsel by words without knowledge? 3
42: 3 this that hides counsel without knowledge? 3
Ps 14: 4 Have they no knowledge, all the evildoers 4
19: 2 night to night declares knowledge. 3
71:15 for their number is past my knowledge. †
73:11 can God know? Is there knowledge in the Most High? 2
82: 5 They have neither knowledge nor understanding 4
94:10 He who teaches men knowledge 3
119:66 Teach me good judgment and knowledge 2
139: 6 Such knowledge is too wonderful for me; it is high 3

Prv 1: 4 knowledge and discretion to the youth- 3
7 fear of the LORD is the beginning of knowledge; 3
22 How long will . . fools hate knowledge? 3
29 Because they hated knowledge 3
2: 5 then you will . . find the knowledge of God. 3
6 from his mouth come knowledge and understanding; 3
10 knowledge will be pleasant to your soul; 3
3:20 by his knowledge the deeps broke forth 3
5: 2 that . . your lips may guard knowledge. 3
8: 9 They are all . . right to those who find knowledge. 3
10 Take . . knowledge rather than choice gold; 3
12 I, wisdom . . find knowledge and discretion. 3
9:10 knowledge of the Holy One is insight. 3
10:14 Wise men lay up knowledge 3
11: 9 but by knowledge the righteous are delivered. 3
12: 1 Whoever loves discipline loves knowledge 3
23 A prudent man conceals his knowledge 3
13:16 In everything a prudent man acts with knowledge 3
14: 6 but knowledge is easy for a man of understanding. 3
7 for there you do not meet words of knowledge. 3
18 but the prudent are crowned with knowledge. 3
15: 2 The tongue of the wise dispenses knowledge 3
7 The lips of the wise spread knowledge; 3
14 mind . . who has understanding seeks knowledge 3
17:27 He who restrains his words has knowledge 3
18:15 An intelligent mind acquires knowledge 3
15 the ear of the wise seeks knowledge. 3
19: 2 It is not good for a man to be without knowledge 3
25 man of understanding, and he will gain knowledge. 3
27 only to stray from the words of knowledge. 3
20:15 but the lips of knowledge are a precious jewel. 3
21:11 wise man is instructed, he gains knowledge. 3
22:12 The eyes of the LORD keep watch over knowledge 3
17 apply your mind to my knowledge; 3
20 30 sayings of admonition and knowledge 3
23:12 Apply . . your ear to words of knowledge. 3
24: 4 by knowledge the rooms are filled with all 3
5 man of knowledge than he who has strength; 3
28: 2 but with men of understanding and knowledge 4
29: 7 wicked man does not understand such knowledge. 3
30: 3 not learned . . nor have I knowledge of the Holy One. 3
Ecc 1:16 had great experience of wisdom and knowledge. 3
18 he who increases knowledge increases sorrow. 3
2:21 a man who has toiled with wisdom and knowledge 3
26 God gives wisdom and knowledge and joy; 3
7:12 the advantage of knowledge is that 3
9:10 there is no work or thought or knowledge 3
12: 9 the Preacher also taught the people knowledge 3
Isa 5:13 my people go into exile for want of knowledge; 3
11: 2 the spirit of knowledge and the fear of the LORD. 2
9 earth shall be full of the knowledge of the LORD 2
28: 9 Whom will he teach knowledge 2
33: 6 abundance of salvation, wisdom, and knowledge; 3
40:14 and taught him knowledge, and showed him the way 2
44:19 nor is there knowledge or discernment to say 2
25 wise men back, and makes their knowledge foolish 3
45:20 have no knowledge who carry about . . idols 4
47:10 your wisdom and your knowledge led you astray 3
53:11 by his knowledge shall the righteous one 3
56:10 are blind, they are all without knowledge; 4
Jer 3:15 who will feed you with knowledge 2
10:14 Every man is stupid and without knowledge; 2
14:18 trade through the land, and have no knowledge. 4
51:17 Every man is stupid and without knowledge; 2
Dan 2:21 knowledge to those who have understanding; 7
5:12 excellent spirit, knowledge, and understanding 7
12: 4 run to and fro, and knowledge shall increase. 3
Hos 4: 1 There is . . no knowledge of God in the land; 2
6 My people are destroyed for lack of knowledge; 3
6 because you have rejected knowledge 2
6: 6 knowledge of God, rather than burnt offerings. 2
8: 4 They set up princes, but without my knowledge. 4
Hab 2:14 with the knowledge of the glory of the LORD 4
Mal 2: 7 For the lips of a priest should guard knowledge 2
Lke 1:77 to give knowledge of salvation to his people 9
11:52 you have taken away the key of knowledge 9
Act 5: 2 and with his wife's knowledge 14
24:22 having a rather accurate knowledge of the Way 12
Rom 2:20 in the law the embodiment of knowledge and truth- 9
3:20 since through the law comes knowledge of sin. 10
11:33 the riches and wisdom and knowledge of God! 9
15:14 filled with all knowledge, and able to instruct 9
1Co 1: 5 with all speech and all knowledge- 9
8: 1 we know that "all of us possess knowledge. 9
1 Knowledge" puffs up, but love builds up. 9
7 However, not all possess this knowledge 9
10 For if any one sees you, a man of knowledge, at table 9
11 so by your knowledge this weak man is destroyed 9
12: 8 to another the utterance of knowledge 9
13: 2 and understand all mysteries and all knowledge 9
8 as for knowledge, it will pass away. 9
9 For our knowledge is imperfect 8
14: 6 unless I bring you some revelation or knowledge 9
2Co 2:14 spreads the fragrance of the knowledge of him 9
4: 6 the light of the knowledge of the glory of God 9
6: 6 by purity, knowledge, forbearance, kindness 9
8: 7 in faith, in utterance, in knowledge 9
10: 5 every proud obstacle to the knowledge of God 9
11: 6 I am not in knowledge 9
Eph 1:17 revelation in the knowledge of him 10
3:19 the love of Christ which surpasses knowledge 9
4:13 the knowledge of the Son of God 10
Php 1: 9 with knowledge and all discernment 10
Col 1: 9 you may be filled with the knowledge of his will 10
10 increasing in the knowledge of God. 10
2: 2 the knowledge of God's mystery, of Christ 10
3 all the treasures of wisdom and knowledge. 9
3:10 which is being renewed in knowledge 10
1Ti 2: 4 to come to the knowledge of the truth. 10
6:20 what is falsely called knowledge 9
2Ti 3: 7 can never arrive at a knowledge of the truth. 10
Tit 1: 1 knowledge of the truth 10
Phm 1: 6 may promote the knowledge of all the good 10
Heb 10:26 after receiving the knowledge of the truth 10
2Pe 1: 2 in the knowledge of God and of Jesus our Lord. 10
3 through the knowledge of him who called us 10
5 to supplement . . virtue with knowledge 9
6 and knowledge with self-control 9
8 in the knowledge of our Lord Jesus Christ. 10
2:20 knowledge of our Lord and Savior Jesus Christ 10
3:18 grow in the grace and knowledge of our Lord 9
1Es 8: 7 For Ezra possessed great knowledge 11
2Es 14:47 and the river of knowledge. 15
AEs 14:15 Thou hast knowledge of all things 9
Wis 2:13 He professes to have knowledge of God 9
6:22 make knowledge of her clear 9
7:17 he who gave me unerring knowledge of what exists 9
8: 4 For she is an initiate in the knowledge of God 11
10:10 gave him knowledge of angels 9
14:22 to err about the knowledge of God 9
18: 6 they might rejoice in sure knowledge 12
Sir 1:19 he rained down knowledge 11
6:33 If you love to listen you will gain knowledge •
10:30 A poor man is honored for his knowledge 11
16:24 Listen to me, my son, and acquire knowledge 11
25 declare knowledge accurately. 11
17: 7 filled them with knowledge and understanding 11
11 He bestowed knowledge upon them 11
19:22 the knowledge of wickedness is not wisdom 11
21:13 The knowledge of a wise man will increase 9
14 it will hold no knowledge. 9
18 the knowledge of the ignorant 9
32: 3 with accurate knowledge 11
33:11 In the fulness of his knowledge 11
39: 7 He will direct his counsel and knowledge aright 11
45: 5 the law of life and knowledge 11
50:27 Instruction in understanding and knowledge 11
Bar 3:20 they have not learned the way to knowledge 11
27 God did not . . nor give them the way to knowledge; 11
36 He found the whole way to knowledge, and gave her 11
2Mc 6:30 It is clear to the Lord in his holy knowledge 9
4Mc 1: 2 to everyone who is seeking knowledge 11
16 the knowledge of divine and human matters 9
5:35 honored priesthood and knowledge of the law. 11
11:21 religious knowledge, O tyrant, is invincible. 11
16:23 people who have religious knowledge 13

knowledge *See also* come, take.

no knowledge 1. ἀγνωσία

1Co 15:34 For some have no knowledge of God 1

sound knowledge 1. תּוּשִׁיָּה

Job 26: 3 and plentifully declared sound knowledge! 1

known *See* make.

become known 1. ידע 2. γινώσκω

Lev 4:14 the sin which they have committed becomes known 1
Act 9:24 their plot became known to Saul 2
Sir 6:27 she will become known to you 2
46:15 he became known as a trustworthy seer. 2
1Mc 6: 3 his plan became known to the men of the city 2
7: 3 when this act became known to him, he said 2
30 It became known to Judas 2
8:10 this became known to them 2
9:60 unable to do it, because their plan became known. 2

well known 1. שֵׁם 2. ἐπιγινώσκω

Num16: 2 250 . . chosen from the assembly, well-known men; 1
2Co 6: 9 as unknown, and yet well known 2

L

labor 1. און 2. יְגִיעַ 3. יְגִיעַ כַּפַּיִם 4. יגע 5. ילד 6. מְלָאכָה 7. מַעֲשֶׂה 8. עבד 9. עֲבֹדָה 10. עמל 11. עֶצֶב 12. עשׂה 13. שׂדר (A) 14. ἀσχολία 15. διάγω 16. ἐργάζομαι 17. ἐργασία 18. ἔργον 19. κοπή 20. κοπιάω 21. κόπος 22. λατρεία ἔργων 23. μόχθος 24. πονέω 25. πόνος 26. φιλοπονία 27. labor 28. laboro

Gen 31:42 God saw my affliction and the labor of my hands 2
35:16 Rachel travailed, and she had hard labor. 5
17 when she was in her hard labor, the midwife said 5
38:28 when she was in labor, one put out a hand; 5
Exd 5: 9 work . . that they may labor at it 12
20: 9 Six days you shall labor, and do all your work; 8
23:16 harvest, of the first fruits of your labor 7
16 gather in from the field the fruit of your labor. 7
Deu 5:13 Six days you shall labor, and do all your work; 8
28:33 nation . . eat up the fruit . . of all your labors; 2
Jos 24:13 I gave you a land on which you had not labored 4
2Sm 12:31 brought forth the people . . and set them to labor •
1Ch 20: 3 to labor with saws and iron picks and axes; •
2Ch 24:13 those who were engaged in the work labored 12
Neh 4:17 each with one hand labored on the work 12
21 we labored at the work, and half of them held 12
22 may be a guard for us by night and may labor by day. 6
5:13 So may God shake out every man . . from his labor 2
Job 9:29 I shall be condemned; why then do I labor in vain? 4
39:11 will you leave to him your labor? 2
16 though her labor be in vain, yet she has no fear; 2
Ps 78:46 the fruit of their labor to the locust. 2
104:23 to his work and to his labor until the evening. 9
127: 1 those who build it labor in vain. 10
128: 2 You shall eat the fruit of the labor of your hands; 2
Prv 5:10 lest . . your labors go to the house of an alien; 11
21:25 kills him for his hands refuse to labor. 12
Ecc 2:20 gave my heart up . . over all the toil of my labors 10
Isa 22: 4 do not labor to comfort me for the destruction 1
47:12 your many sorceries, with which you have labored 4
15 Such to you are those with whom you have labored 4
49: 4 But I said, "I have labored in vain 4
55: 2 and your labor for that which does not satisfy? 2
62: 8 not drink your wine for which you have labored; 4
65:23 They shall not labor in vain, or bear children 4
Jer 3:24 has devoured all for which our fathers labored 2
51:58 The peoples labor for nought 4
Ezk 23:29 and take away all the fruit of your labor •
29:18 army got anything from Tyre to pay for the labor 9
20 Egypt as his recompense for which he labored 8
Dan 6:14 labored till the sun went down to rescue him. 13
Jon 4:10 You pity the plant, for which you did not labor 10
Hab 2:13 from the LORD . . that peoples labor only for fire 4
Hag 1:11 upon men and cattle, and upon all their labors. 3
Mat 11:28 Come to me, all who labor and are heavy laden 20
Joh 4:38 I sent you to reap that for which you did not labor; 20
38 others have labored, and you have entered 20
38 and you have entered into their labor. 21
6:27 Do not labor for the food which perishes 16
1Co 3: 8 shall receive his wages according to his labor. 21
4:12 we labor, working with our own hands 20
15:58 in the Lord your labor is not in vain. 21
2Co 6: 5 beatings, imprisonments, tumults, labors 21
10:15 We do not boast beyond limit, in other men's labors; 21
11:23 with far greater labors, far more imprisonments 21
Gal 4:11 I am afraid I have labored over you in vain. 20
Eph 4:28 rather let him labor 20
Php 1:22 that means fruitful labor for me 18
2:16 I did not run in vain or labor in vain. 20
1Th 1: 3 work of faith and labor of love 21
2: 9 For you remember our labor and toil, brethren 21
3: 5 our labor would be in vain. 21
5:12 respect those who labor among you 20
2Th 3: 8 with toil and labor we worked night and day 23
1Ti 5:17 especially those who labor in preaching 20
Heb 4:10 ceases from his labors as God did from his. 18
Rev 14:13 that they may rest from their labors 21
1Es 4:22 Do you not labor and toil 24
2Es 3:33 and their labor has borne no fruit 27
5:12 shall labor but their ways shall not prosper. 28
8:14 with so great labor was fashioned by thy command 27
9:22 because with much labor I have perfected them. 27
16:45 Because those who labor, labor in vain; 28
45 Because those who labor, labor in vain; 28
Wis 3:11 their labors are unprofitable 21
15 For the fruit of good labors is renowned 25
5: 1 those who make light of his labors. 25
8: 7 her labors are virtues 25
18 in the labors of her hands, unfailing wealth 25
9:16 what is at hand we find with labor 25
10:10 she prospered him in his labors 23
17 She gave holy men the reward of their labors 19
Sir 0: 3 I should myself devote some pains and labor 26
7:15 Do not hate toilsome labor, or farm work 17
14:15 leave the fruit of your labors to another 25
16:27 they do not cease from their labors. 18
24:34 Observe that I have not labored for myself alone 20
33:17 I have not labored for myself alone 20
38:27 labors by night as well as by day 15
40: 1 Much labor was created for every man 14
51:27 See with your eyes that I have labored little 20
Bar 3:18 are anxious, whose labors are beyond measure? 18
3Mc 4:14 the hard labor . . briefly mentioned before 22

labor (2) 1. חול

Isa 66: 7 Before she was in labor she gave birth; 1
8 as Zion was in labor she brought forth her sons. 1

diligent labor 1. φιλοπονέω

Sir 0: 2 despite our diligent labor in translating, 1

forced labor 1. מַס 2. סֵבֶל

Gen 49:15 and became a slave at forced labor. 1
Deu 20:11 people who are found in it shall do forced labor 1
Jos 16:10 but have become slaves to do forced labor. 1
17:13 they put the Canaanites to forced labor 1
Jdg 1:28 they put the Canaanites to forced labor, but did 1
30 dwelt . . and became subject to forced labor. 1
33 and of Beth-anath became subject to forced labor 1
35 them, and they became subject to forced labor. 1
2Sm 20:24 and Ador'am was in charge of the forced labor; 1
1Kg 4: 6 Adoni'ram . . was in charge of the forced labor. 1
5:13 King Solomon raised a levy of forced labor 1
9:15 the forced labor which King Solomon levied 1
11:28 over all the forced labor of the house of Joseph. 2
12:18 Ador'am, who was taskmaster over the forced labor 1
2Ch 10:18 Hador'am . . taskmaster over the forced labor 1
Prv 12:24 while the slothful will be put to forced labor. 1
Isa 31: 8 and his young men shall be put to forced labor. 1

hard labor 1. עָמָל

Ps 107:12 Their hearts were bowed down with hard labor; 1

make labor 1. עבד

Ezk 29:18 king of Babylon made his army labor hard 1

labor side by side 1. συναθλέω

Php 4: 3 they have labored side by side with me 1

woman in labor 1. ילד 2. τίκτω

Jer 30: 6 with his hands on his loins like a woman in labor? 1
Sir 19:11 suffer pangs like a woman in labor with a child. 2

laborer 1. עבד 2. ἐργάτης 3. κοπιάω

Ecc 5:12 Sweet is the sleep of a laborer 1
Mat 9:37 but the laborers are few; 2
38 to send out laborers into his harvest. 2
10:10 for the laborer deserves his food. 2
20: 1 to hire laborers for his vineyard. 2
2 After agreeing with the laborers 2
8 Call the laborers and pay them their wages 2
Lke 10: 2 harvest is plentiful, but the laborers are few 2
2 to send out laborers into his harvest. 2
7 the laborer deserves his wages 2
1Co 16:16 to every fellow worker and laborer. 3
1Ti 5:18 The laborer deserves his wages. 2
Jas 5: 4 the wages of the laborers who mowed your fields 2

hired laborer 1. μίσθιος

Sir 7:20 a hired laborer who devotes himself to you. 1

laborious 1. עֲבֹדָה

Lev 23: 7 convocation; you shall do no laborious work 1
8 convocation; you shall do no laborious work 1
21 you shall do no laborious work: it is a statute 1
25 You shall do no laborious work 1
35 convocation; you shall do no laborious work 1
36 solemn assembly; you shall do no laborious work 1
Num29:35 solemn assembly: you shall do no laborious work. 1

laboriously 1. ἐπίμοχθος 2. labor

2Es 7:89 they laboriously served the Most High 2
Wis 15: 7 and laboriously molds each vessel for our service 1

lace 1. פְּתִיל

Exd 28:28 the ephod with a lace of blue, that it may lie upon 1
37 you shall fasten it on the turban by a lace of blue; 1
39:21 rings of the ephod with a lace of blue 1
31 they tied to it a lace of blue, to fasten it 1

lack 1. אַיִן 2. אֶפֶס 3. בְּ 4. בְּלִי 5. חדל 6. חסר 7. חָסֵר 8. חֹסֶר 9. חֶסְרוֹן 10. כרת 11. מַחְסוֹר 12. עדר 13. פקד 14. ἄνευ 15. ἀπολείπω 16. ἄπορος 17. ἐκλείπω 18. ἐλασσόω 19. ἐλαττονέω 20. ἐλαττόω 21. ἐλάττωμα 22. ἐλλιπής 23. ἡττάω 24. λείπω 25. μὴ πάρειμι 26. σπάνις 27. στερέω 28. ὑστερέω 29. ὑστέρημα 30. ὕστερος

Gen 18:28 Suppose five of the 50 righteous are lacking? 6
28 Wilt thou destroy the whole city for lack of five? 3
Exd 16:18 and he that gathered little had no lack; 6
Deu 2: 7 LORD . . been with you; you have lacked nothing.' 6
8: 9 a land . . in which you will lack nothing 6
Jdg 18: 7 dwelt in security . . lacking nothing that is •
10 where there is no lack of anything that is 11
19:19 with your servants; there is no lack of anything. 11
21: 3 there . . be today one tribe lacking in Israel? 13
1Sm 21:15 Do I lack madmen, that you have brought this 7
2Sm 3:29 or who is slain by the sword, or who lacks bread! 7
1Kg 11:22 Pharaoh said to him, "What have you lacked with me 6
Neh 9:21 sustain them . . and they lacked nothing; 6
Job 4:11 The strong lion perishes for lack of prey 4
31:19 if I have seen any one perish for lack of clothing 4
38:41 cry to God, and wander about for lack of food? 4
Ps 34:10 but those who seek the LORD lack no good thing. 6
Prv 5:23 He dies for lack of discipline 1
10:13 but a rod is for the back of him who lacks sense. 7
19 words are many, transgression is not lacking 5
21 but fools die for lack of sense. 6
11:12 He who belittles his neighbor lacks sense 7
12: 9 than one who plays the great man but lacks bread. 7
26:20 For lack of wood the fire goes out; 2
28:16 A ruler who lacks understanding is a cruel 7
31:11 he will have no lack of gain. 6
Ecc 1:15 and what is lacking cannot be numbered. 9
6: 2 that he lacks nothing of all that he desires 6
9: 8 let not oil be lacking on your head. 6
10: 3 when the fool walks on the road, he lacks sense 6
Sng 7: 2 navel is a . . bowl that never lacks mixed wine. 6
Isa 24:11 There is an outcry in the streets for lack of wine; •
50: 2 fish stink for lack of water, and die of thirst. 1
59:15 Truth is lacking, and he who departs from evil 12
Jer 33:17 David shall never lack a man to sit on the throne 10
18 and the Levitical priests shall never lack a man 10
35:19 shall never lack a man to stand before me. 10
44:18 we have lacked everything 6
Ezk 4:17 I will do this that they may lack bread and water 6

Hos 4: 6 My people are destroyed for lack of knowledge; 4
Ams 4: 6 and lack of bread in all your places 8
Mat 19:20 what do I still lack? 28
Mrk 10:21 You lack one thing 28
Lke 18:22 One thing you still lack 24
22:35 did you lack anything?" They said, "Nothing. 28
1Co 1: 7 you are not lacking in any spiritual gift 28
2Co 8:15 he who gathered little had no lack. 19
Col 1:24 what is lacking in Christ's afflictions 29
1Th 3:10 supply what is lacking in your faith? 29
Tit 3:13 see that they lack nothing. 24
Jas 1: 4 be perfect and complete, lacking in nothing. 24
5 If any of you lacks wisdom, let him ask God 24
2:15 If a brother or sister is . . in lack of daily food 24
2Pe 1: 9 For whoever lacks these things is blind 25
Jdt 8: 9 because they were faint for lack of water 26
Wis 14: 4 even if a man lacks skill, he may put to sea. 14
19: 4 which their torments still lacked 24
Sir 3:13 even if he is lacking in understanding 15
10:27 one who goes about boasting, but lacks bread. 16
11:12 who lacks strength and abounds in poverty 30
14:10 it is lacking at his table. 22
19:23 there is a fool who merely lacks wisdom. 20
24 God-fearing man who lacks intelligence 23
28 by lack of strength he is prevented from sinning 21
22:11 Weep for the dead, for he lacks the light 17
11 weep for the fool, for he lacks intelligence 17
23:10 will not lack bruises 20
25: 2 an adulterous old man who lacks good sense. 20
37:21 since he is lacking in all wisdom. 27
47:23 ample in folly and lacking in understanding 18
51:24 Why do you say you are lacking in these things 28

lack means 1. ἀπορέω
Wis 11:17 did not lack the means 1

lack of intelligence 1. ἄνοια
Wis 15:18 when judged by their lack of intelligence; 1

lack of self-control 1. ἀκρασία
1Co 7: 5 tempt you through lack of self-control. 1

lack strength 1. ἀσθενέω
1Mc 2:61 none . . will lack strength. 1

lackey 1. διάκονος
4Mc 9:17 he replied, "You abominable lackeys 1

lacking 1. עדר 2. שׁבת
Lev 2:13 you shall not let the salt . . be lacking 2
1Kg 4:27 each . . in his month; they let nothing be lacking. 1

lad 1. יֶלֶד 2. נַעַר 3. παιδάριον 4. παιδίον 5. παῖς
Gen 21:12 Be not displeased because of the lad 2
17 God heard the voice of the lad; 2
17 Fear not; for God has heard the voice of the lad 2
18 Arise, lift up the lad, and hold him fast 2
19 filled the skin . . and gave the lad a drink. 2
20 God was with the lad, and he grew up; 2
22: 5 I and the lad will go yonder and worship 2
12 He said, "Do not lay your hand on the lad 2
37: 2 he was a lad with the sons of Bilhah and Zilpah 2
30 The lad is gone; and I, where shall I go? 1
42:22 Did I not tell you not to sin against the lad? 1
43: 8 Send the lad with me, and we will arise and go 2
44:22 said to my lord, 'The lad cannot leave his father 2
30 when I come . . and the lad is not with us 2
30 then, as his life is bound up in the lad's life •
31 when he sees that the lad is not with us, he will die 2
32 For your servant became surety for the lad 2
33 let your servant . . remain instead of the lad 2
33 let the lad go back with his brothers. 2
34 go back to my father if the lad is not with me? 2
48:16 the angel . . bless the lads; and in them let my 2
Jdg 16:26 Samson said to the lad who held him by the hand 2
1Sm 20:21 I will send the lad, saying, 'Go, find the arrows.' 2
21 If I say to the lad, 'Look, the arrows are 2
35 Jonathan went out . . and with him a little lad. 2
36 And he said to his lad, "Run and find the arrows 2
36 As the lad ran, he shot an arrow beyond him. 2
37 And when the lad came to the place of the arrow 2
37 Jonathan called after the lad and said 2
38 Jonathan called after the lad, "Hurry, make haste 2
38 Jonathan's lad gathered up the arrows 2
39 But the lad knew nothing; 2
40 And Jonathan gave his weapons to his lad, and said 2
41 as soon as the lad had gone, David rose from beside 2
2Sm 17:18 But a lad saw them, and told Ab'salom; 2
Joh 6: 9 a lad here who has five barley loaves and two fish; 3
Act 20:12 they took the lad away alive 5
Tob 10: 4 his wife said to him, "The lad has perished 4
Sus 1:45 the holy spirit of a young lad named Daniel; 3

ladder 1. סֻלָּם 2. κλίμαξ
Gen 28:12 he dreamed that there was a ladder set up 1
1Mc 5:30 carrying ladders and engines of war 2
11:59 from the Ladder of Tyre to the borders of Egypt. 2

lade 1. עמס
Neh 4:17 carried burdens were laden in such a way 1

laden 1. כָּבֵד
1Sm 16:20 Jesse took an ass laden with bread •
Isa 1: 4 Ah, sinful nation, a people laden with iniquity 1

heavily laden 1. כבד
Ezk 27:25 and heavily laden in the heart of the seas. 1

heavy laden 1. φορτίζω
Mat 11:28 Come to me, all who labor and are heavy laden 1

lady 1. שָׂרָה 2. κυρία
Jdg 5:29 Her wisest ladies make answer, nay, she gives 1
Est 1:18 the ladies of Persia and Media who have heard 1
2Jn 1: 1 The elder to the elect lady and her children 2
5 And now I beg you, lady, not as though I were writing 2

lady of honor 1. יָקָר
Ps 45: 9 of kings are among your ladies of honor; 1

lag behind 1. חשׁל
Deu 25:18 cut off at your rear all who lagged behind you; 1

laggard 1. ἐσχατίζω
1Mc 5:53 Judas kept rallying the laggards 1

lair 1. אֶרֶב 2. מָעוֹן 3. מַרְבֵּץ
Job 37: 8 Then the beasts go into their lairs, 1
Jer 9:11 make Jerusalem a heap of ruins, a lair of jackals; 2
10:22 to make . . Judah a desolation, a lair of jackals. 2
Zep 2:15 desolation she has become, a lair for wild beasts 3

lake 1. יָם 2. λίμνη
Deu 33:23 O Naph'tali . . possess the lake and the south. 1
Job 14:11 As waters fail from a lake, and a river wastes away 1
Lke 5: 1 he was standing by the lake of Gennes'aret. 2
2 he saw two boats by the lake 2
8:22 Let us go across to the other side of the lake. 2
23 a storm of wind came down on the lake 2
33 the herd rushed down the steep bank into the lake 2
Rev 19:20 These two were thrown alive into the lake of fire 2
20:10 thrown into the lake of fire and sulphur 2
14 Death and Hades were thrown into the lake of fire 2
14 This is the second death, the lake of fire; 2
15 he was thrown into the lake of fire. 2
21: 8 in the lake that burns with fire and sulphur 2
2Mc 12:16 the adjoining lake, a quarter of a mile wide 2

lama 1. λαμά
Mat 27:46 Eli, Eli, la'ma sabach-tha'ni? 1
Mrk 15:34 E'lo-i, E'lo-i, la'ma sabach-tha'ni? 1

lamb 1. בֶּן צֹאן 2. טָלֶה 3. כֶּבֶשׂ 4. כִּבְשָׂה 5. כַּר 6. כֶּשֶׂב 7. כִּשְׂבָּה 8. צֹאן 9. שֶׂה 10. אִמַּר (A) 11. ἀμνός 12. ἀρνήν 13. ἀρνίον
Gen 22: 7 but where is the lamb for a burnt offering? 9
8 Abraham said, "God will provide himself the lamb 9
30:32 spotted sheep and every black lamb 9
33 among the goats and black among the lambs 6
35 every lamb that was black, and put them in charge 6
40 Jacob separated the lambs, and set the faces 6
Exd 12: 3 a lamb according to their fathers' houses 9
3 take . . a lamb for a household; 9
4 if the household is too small for a lamb, then a man 9
4 you shall make your count for the lamb. 9
5 Your lamb shall be without blemish, a male 9
6 Israel shall kill their lambs in the evening. •
21 said to them, "Select lambs for yourselves 8
13:13 firstling of an ass you shall redeem with a lamb 9
29:38 two lambs a year old day by day continually. 3
39 One lamb you shall offer in the morning 3
39 the other lamb you shall offer in the evening; 3
40 with the first lamb a tenth measure of fine flour 3
41 the other lamb you shall offer in the evening 3
34:20 an ass you shall redeem with a lamb 9
Lev 3: 7 If he offers a lamb for his offering 6
4:32 If he brings a lamb as his offering 3
35 he shall remove as the fat of the lamb is removed 6
5: 6 a female from the flock, a lamb or a goat 7
7 if he cannot afford a lamb, then he shall bring 9
9: 3 Take . . a calf and a lamb, both a year old 3
12: 6 bring . . a lamb a year old for a burnt offering 3
8 if she cannot afford a lamb, then she shall take 9
14:13 he shall kill the lamb in the place where 3
24 priest shall take the lamb of the guilt offering 3
25 he shall kill the lamb of the guilt offering 3
17: 3 If any man . . kills an ox or a lamb or a goat 6
22:23 A bull or a lamb which has a part too long 9
23:18 you shall present with the bread seven lambs 3
20 wave offering before the LORD, with the two lambs 3
Num15: 5 offering, or for the sacrifice, for each lamb. 3
28: 4 The one lamb you shall offer in the morning 3
4 the other lamb you shall offer in the evening; 3
7 offering shall be a fourth of a hin for each lamb; 3
8 The other lamb you shall offer in the evening; 3
13 cereal offering for every lamb; 3
14 drink offerings . . a fourth of a hin for a lamb; 3
21 tenth shall you offer for each of the seven lambs; 3
29 a tenth for each of the seven lambs; 3
29: 4 one tenth for each of the seven lambs; 3
10 a tenth for each of the seven lambs 3
15 a tenth for each of the fourteen lambs; 3
18 cereal offering . . for the rams, and for the lambs 3
21 cereal offering . . and for the lambs 3
24 cereal offering . . and for the lambs 3
27 cereal offering . . for the lambs 3
30 cereal offering . . for the lambs 3
33 cereal offering . . for the lambs 3
37 cereal offering . . and for the lambs 3
Deu 32:14 fat of lambs and rams, herds of Bashan and goats 5
1Sm 7: 9 Samuel took a sucking lamb and offered it 2
15: 9 and of the oxen and of the fatlings, and the lambs 5
17:34 when there came a lion, or a bear, and took a lamb 9
2Sm 12: 4 but he took the poor man's lamb, and prepared it 4
6 and he shall restore the lamb fourfold 4
2Kg 3: 4 Moab . . had to deliver . . 100,000 lambs 5
1Ch 29:21 and 1,000 lambs, with their drink offerings 3
2Ch 29:21 they brought . . seven lambs, and seven he-goats 3
22 killed the lambs and their blood was thrown 3
32 number of the burnt offerings . . 200 lambs; 3
35: 7 contributed . . lambs and kids from the flock 3
8 for the passover offerings 2,600 lambs and kids •
9 for the passover offerings 5,000 lambs and kids •
Ezr 6:17 offered . . 200 rams, 400 lambs 10
7:17 with all diligence buy bulls, rams, and lambs 10
8:35 96 rams, 77 lambs 3
Ps 114: 4 skipped like rams, the hills like lambs. 1
6 skip like rams? O hills, like lambs? 1
Prv 27:26 the lambs will provide your clothing 3
Isa 1:11 in the blood of bulls, or of lambs, or of he-goats. 3
5:17 Then shall the lambs graze as in their pasture 3
11: 6 The wolf shall dwell with the lamb 3
16: 1 They have sent lambs to the ruler of the land 5
34: 6 gorged with fat, with the blood of lambs and goats 5
40:11 he will gather the lambs in his arms 2
53: 7 like a lamb that is led to the slaughter 9
65:25 The wolf and the lamb shall feed together 2
66: 3 he who sacrifices a lamb, 9
Jer 11:19 But I was like a gentle lamb led to the slaughter. 3
51:40 will bring them down like lambs to the slaughter 5
Ezk 27:21 your favored dealers in lambs, rams, and goats; 5
39:18 of rams, of lambs, and of goats, of bulls, 5
46: 4 shall be six lambs without blemish and a ram 3
5 with the lambs shall be as much as he is able 3
6 bull without blemish, and six lambs and a ram 3
7 and with the lambs as much as he is able 3
11 with the lambs as much as one is able to give 3
13 He shall provide a lamb a year old 3
15 Thus the lamb and the meal offering and the oil 3
Hos 4:16 LORD now feed them like a lamb in a broad pasture? 3
Ams 6: 4 and eat lambs from the flock, and calves 5
Lke 10: 3 I send you out as lambs in the midst of wolves. 12
Joh 1:29 Behold, the Lamb of God, who takes away the sin 11
36 and said, "Behold, the Lamb of God! 11
21:15 He said to him, "Feed my lambs. 13
Act 8:32 As . . a lamb before its shearer is dumb 11
1Pe 1:19 like that of a lamb without blemish or spot. 11
Rev 5: 6 I saw a Lamb standing, as though it had been slain 13
8 the 24 elders fell down before the Lamb 13
12 Worthy is the Lamb who was slain, to receive power 13
13 To him who sits upon the throne and to the Lamb 13
6: 1 I saw when the Lamb opened one of the seven seals 13
16 hide us . . from the wrath of the Lamb; 13
7: 9 standing before the throne and before the Lamb 13
10 Salvation belongs . . to the Lamb! 13
14 made them white in the blood of the Lamb. 13
17 For the Lamb in the midst of the throne will be 13
8: 1 When the Lamb opened the seventh seal •
12:11 they have conquered him by the blood of the Lamb 13
13: 8 the book of life of the Lamb that was slain. 13
11 it had two horns like a lamb 13
14: 1 Then I looked, and lo, on Mount Zion stood the Lamb 13
4 it is these who follow the Lamb wherever he goes; 13
4 redeemed . . as first fruits for God and the Lamb 13
10 and in the presence of the Lamb. 13
15: 3 and the song of the Lamb, saying 13
17:14 they will make war on the Lamb 13
14 and the Lamb will conquer them 13
19: 7 for the marriage of the Lamb has come 13
9 invited to the marriage supper of the Lamb. 13
21: 9 Come, I will show you the Bride, the wife of the Lamb. 13
14 twelve names of the twelve apostles of the Lamb. 13
22 its temple is the Lord God . . and the Lamb. 13
23 God is its light, and its lamp is the Lamb. 13
27 only those . . written in the Lamb's book of life 13
22: 1 flowing from the throne of God and of the Lamb 13
3 but the throne of God and of the Lamb shall be in it 13
1Es 1: 7 gave to the people . . 30,000 lambs and kids 12
6:29 for bulls and rams and lambs 12
7: 7 They offered . . 100 bulls, 200 rams, 400 lambs 12
8:14 both gold and silver for bulls and rams and lambs 12
66 72 lambs, and as a thank offering twelve he-goats 12
Wis 19: 9 ranged like horses, and leaped like lambs 11
Sir 13:17 What fellowship has a wolf with a lamb? 11
46:16 he offered in sacrifice a sucking lamb. 12

47: 3 with bears as with lambs of the flock. 12
Aza 1:16 with tens of thousands of fat lambs; 12

male lamb 1. כֶּבֶשׂ
Lev 14:10 on the eighth day he shall take two male lambs 1
12 the priest shall take one of the male lambs 1
21 shall take one male lamb for a guilt offering 1
23:12 you shall offer a male lamb a year old 1
19 offer . . two male lambs a year old as a sacrifice 1
Num 6:12 bring a male lamb a year old for a guilt offering; 1
14 one male lamb a year old . . for a burnt offering 1
7:15 ram, one male lamb a year old, for a burnt offering; 1
17 peace offerings . . five male lambs a year old. 1
21 ram, one male lamb a year old, for a burnt offering; 1
23 peace offerings . . five male lambs a year old. 1
27 ram, one male lamb a year old, for a burnt offering; 1
29 peace offerings . . five male lambs a year old. 1
33 ram, one male lamb a year old, for a burnt offering; 1
35 peace offerings . . five male lambs a year old. 1
39 ram, one male lamb a year old, for a burnt offering; 1
41 peace offerings . . five male lambs a year old. 1
45 ram, one male lamb a year old, for a burnt offering; 1
47 peace offerings . . five male lambs a year old. 1
51 ram, one male lamb a year old, for a burnt offering; 1
53 peace offerings . . five male lambs a year old. 1
57 ram, one male lamb a year old, for a burnt offering; 1
59 peace offerings . . five male lambs a year old. 1
63 ram, one male lamb a year old, for a burnt offering; 1
65 peace offerings . . five male lambs a year old. 1
69 ram, one male lamb a year old, for a burnt offering; 1
71 peace offerings . . five male lambs a year old. 1
75 ram, one male lamb a year old, for a burnt offering; 1
77 peace offerings . . five male lambs a year old. 1
81 ram, one male lamb a year old, for a burnt offering; 1
83 peace offerings . . five male lambs a year old. 1
87 burnt offering . . twelve male lambs a year old 1
88 peace offerings . . male lambs a year old 60 1
15:11 or for each of the male lambs or the kids. 1
28: 3 two male lambs a year old without blemish 1
9 two male lambs a year old without blemish 1
11 seven male lambs a year old without blemish; 1
19 a burnt offering . . seven male lambs a year old; 1
27 a burnt offering . . seven male lambs a year old; 1
29: 2 seven male lambs a year old without blemish; 1
8 a burnt offering . . seven male lambs a year old; 1
13 burnt offering . . fourteen male lambs a year old 1
17 fourteen male lambs a year old without blemish 1
20 fourteen male lambs a year old without blemish 1
23 fourteen male lambs a year old without blemish 1
26 fourteen male lambs a year old without blemish 1
29 fourteen male lambs a year old without blemish 1
32 fourteen male lambs a year old without blemish 1
36 seven male lambs a year old without blemish 1

paschal lamb 1. πάσχα
1Co 5: 7 Christ, our paschal lamb, has been sacrificed. 1

passover lamb 1. פֶּסַח 2. πάσχα
Exd 12:21 Select lambs . . kill the passover lamb. 1
2Ch 30:15 killed the passover lamb on the fourteenth day 1
17 Levites had to kill the passover lamb 1
35: 1 killed the passover lamb on the fourteenth day 1
6 kill the passover lamb, and sanctify yourselves 1
11 killed the passover lamb 1
13 they roasted the passover lamb with fire 1
Ezr 6:20 killed the passover lamb for all the returned 1
Mrk 14:12 when they sacrificed the passover lamb 2
Lke 22: 7 on which the passover lamb had to be sacrificed. 2
1Es 1: 1 he killed the passover lamb 2
6 kill the passover lamb 2
12 roasted the passover lamb with fire, as required; 2
7:12 they sacrificed the passover lamb 2

lame 1. פִּסֵּחַ 2. צלה 3. χωλός
Lev 21:18 a man blind or lame, or one who has a mutilated face 1
Deu 15:21 if it has any blemish, if it is lame or blind 1
2Sm 5: 6 but the blind and the lame will ward you off 1
8 up the water shaft to attack the lame and . . blind 1
8 The blind and the lame shall not come 1
9:13 Now he was lame in both his feet. 1
19:26 For your servant is lame. 1
Job 29:15 I was eyes to the blind, and feet to the lame. 1
Isa 33:23 even the lame will take the prey. 1
Jer 31: 8 the blind and the lame, the woman with child 1
Mic 4: 6 In that day, says the LORD, I will assemble the lame 2
7 and the lame I will make the remnant; 2
Zep 3:19 And I will save the lame and gather the outcast 2
Mal 1: 8 when you offer those that are lame or sick 1
13 what has been taken by violence or is lame or sick 1
Mat 11: 5 the blind receive their sight and the lame walk 3
15:30 crowds came to him, bringing with them the lame 3
31 the maimed whole, the lame walking 3
18: 8 it is better for you to enter life maimed or lame 3
21:14 the blind and the lame came to him in the temple 3
Mrk 9:45 it is better for you to enter life lame 3
Lke 7:22 the blind receive their sight, the lame walk 3
14:13 invite the poor, the maimed, the lame, the blind 3
21 bring in the poor and maimed and blind and lame.' 3
Joh 5: 3 a multitude of invalids, blind, lame, paralyzed. 3
Act 3: 2 a man lame from birth was being carried 3
8: 7 many who were paralyzed or lame were healed. 3
Heb 12:13 so that what is lame may not be put out of joint 3

become lame 1. פסח
2Sm 4: 4 as she fled in her haste, he fell, and became lame. 1

lame man 1. פִּסֵּחַ 2. claudus
Prv 26: 7 Like a lame man's legs, which hang useless 1
Isa 35: 6 then shall the lame man leap like a hart 1
2Es 2:21 do not ridicule a lame man, protect the maimed 2

lament 1. אבל 2. אָבֵל 3. אלה 4. אנה 5. וְעָקָה 6. מִסְפֵּד 7. נהג 8. נהה 9. נְהִי 10. ספד 11. קדר 12. קִין 13. קִינָה 14. קנן 15. תנה 16. θρηνέω 17. θρῆνος 18. πενθέω 19. προσοδύρομαι 20. φωνὴ θρηνέω 21. doleo 22. lugeo
Gen 50:10 they lamented there with a very great 10
Jdg 11:40 went . . to lament the daughter of Jephthah 15
1Sm 7: 2 all the house of Israel lamented after the LORD. 8
2Sm 1:17 David lamented with this lamentation over Saul 12
3:33 And the king lamented for Abner, saying 12
2Ch 35:25 spoken of Josi'ah in their laments to this day. 13
25 behold, they are written in the Laments. 13
Est 4: 3 with fasting and weeping and lamenting 6
9:31 with regard to their fasts and their lamenting. 5
Ps 35:14 I went about as one who laments his mother 2
Isa 3:26 her gates shall lament and mourn; 4
19: 8 The fishermen will mourn and lament 1
Jer 4: 8 For this gird you with sackcloth, lament and wail; 10
9:20 teach to your daughters a lament 9
14: 2 her people lament on the ground 11
16: 4 They shall not be lamented 10
5 Do not enter the house of mourning, or go to lament 10
6 they shall not be buried, and no one shall lament 10
22:18 They shall not lament for him, saying, 'Ah lord!' 10
18 They shall not lament for him, saying, 'Ah lord!' 10
25:33 They shall not be lamented, or gathered, or buried; 10
34: 5 and lament for you, saying, "Alas, lord! 10
49: 3 Gird yourselves with sackcloth, lament, and run 10
Ezk 27:32 raise a lamentation for you, and lament over you 14
Jol 1: 8 Lament like a virgin girded with sackcloth 3
13 Gird on sackcloth and lament, O priests 10
Mic 1: 8 For this I will lament and wail; 10
Nah 2: 7 her maidens lamenting, moaning like doves 7
Lke 23:27 women who bewailed and lamented him. 16
Joh 16:20 you will weep and lament 16
1Es 1:32 Jeremiah the prophet lamented for Josiah 16
2Es 7:65 Let the human race lament 22
65 all who have been born lament 22
8:16 about thy inheritance, for whom I lament 22
16: 2 and wail for your children, and lament for them 21
Wis 18:10 their piteous lament for their children 20
19: 3 were lamenting at the graves of their dead 19
Sir 38:16 begin the lament 17
51:19 lamented my ignorance of her. 18
1Mc 1:27 Every bridegroom took up the lament 17
3Mc 4: 6 raising a lament instead of a wedding song 17
4Mc 16:12 did not wail with such a lament for any of them 17
lament *See also* utter.

lament bitterly 1. ἀποδύρομαι
3Mc 4:12 to lament bitterly the ignoble misfortune 1

cause to lament 1. אבל
Lam 2: 8 he caused rampart and wall to lament 1

lamentable 1. δυσαίακτος
3Mc 6:31 instead of a bitter and lamentable death 1

lamentation 1. אֲנִיָּה 2. מִסְפֵּד 3. נְהִי 4. קִינָה 5. γόος 6. θρῆνος 7. κλαυθμός 8. κοπετός 9. ὀδυρμός 10. οἶκτος 11. πανόδυρτος 12. planctus 13. suspiro
Gen 50:10 with a very great and sorrowful lamentation; 2
2Sm 1:17 David lamented with this lamentation over Saul 4
Isa 29: 2 and there shall be moaning and lamentation 1
43:14 the shouting . . will be turned to lamentations. 1
Jer 6:26 make mourning . . most bitter lamentation; 2
7:29 raise a lamentation on the bare heights 4
9:10 lamentation for the pastures of the wilderness 4
31:15 heard in Ramah, lamentation and bitter weeping. 3
48:38 in the squares there is nothing but lamentation; 2
Lam 2: 5 he has multiplied . . mourning and lamentation. 1
Ezk 2:10 there were written on it words of lamentation 4
19: 1 take up a lamentation for the princes of Israel 4
14 This is a lamentation 4
14 a lamentation, and has become a lamentation. 4
26:17 they will raise a lamentation over you 4
27: 2 Now you, son of man, raise a lamentation over Tyre 4
32 they raise a lamentation for you 4
28:12 raise a lamentation over the king of Tyre, and say 4
32: 2 raise a lamentation over Pharaoh king of Egypt 4
16 This is a lamentation which shall be chanted; 4
Ams 5: 1 take up over you in lamentation, O house of Israel 4
16 to wailing those who are skilled in lamentation 3
8:10 turn . . all your songs into lamentation; 4
Mic 1: 8 I will make lamentation like the jackals 2
Mat 2:18 wailing and loud lamentation, Rachel weeping 9
Act 8: 2 made great lamentation over him. 8
2Es 10:12 My lamentation is not like the earth's 12
16:18 when there shall be much lamentation 13
Tob 2: 6 all your festivities into lamentation 6
Jdt 7:29 Then great and general lamentation arose 7
1Mc 2:70 Israel mourned for him with great lamentation. 8
4:39 mourned with great lamentation 8
9:20 all Israel made great lamentation for him 8
13:26 All Israel bewailed him with great lamentation 8
2Mc 11: 6 with lamentations and tears, besought the Lord 9
3Mc 1:18 filled . . with groans and lamentations. 5
4: 2 mourning, lamentation, and tearful cries 11
8 lamentations instead of good cheer 6
5:49 and giving way to lamentation and groans 10

bitter lamentation 1. נהה
Mic 2: 4 and wail with bitter lamentation, and say 1

lamp 1. מָאוֹר 2. מְנוֹרָה 3. נִיר 4. נֵר 5. λαμπάς 6. λύχνος 7. lucerna 8. lumen
Exd 25: 6 oil for the lamps, spices for the anointing oil 1
37 you shall make the seven lamps for it; 4
37 the lamps shall be set up so as to give light 4
27:20 that a lamp may be set up to burn continually. 4
30: 7 when he dresses the lamps he shall burn it 4
8 when Aaron sets up the lamps in the evening 4
35:14 with its utensils and its lamps, and the oil 4
37:23 he made its seven lamps and its snuffers 4
39:37 the lampstand of pure gold and its lamps 4
37 its lamps with the lamps set and all its utensils 4
40: 4 bring in the lampstand, and set up its lamps. 4
25 set up the lamps before the LORD; 4
Lev 24: 2 bring you . . oil . . for the lamp, that a light 1
4 He shall keep the lamps in order 2
Num 4: 9 with its lamps, its snuffers, its trays 4
8: 2 When you set up the lamps, the seven lamps 4
2 seven lamps shall give light in front 4
3 Aaron . . set up its lamps to give light in front 4
1Sm 3: 3 the lamp of God had not yet gone out 4
2Sm 21:17 no more . . lest you quench the lamp of Israel. 4
22:29 Yea, thou art my lamp, O LORD 4
1Kg 7:49 the flowers, the lamps, and the tongs, of gold; 4
11:36 that David . . have a lamp before me in Jerusalem 3
15: 4 the LORD his God gave him a lamp in Jerusalem 3
2Kg 4:10 put there for him a bed, a table, a chair, and a lamp 2
8:19 he promised to give a lamp to him and to his sons 3
1Ch 28:15 weight of the golden lampstands and their lamps 4
15 weight of gold for each lampstand and its lamps 4
15 weight of silver for a lampstand and its lamps 4
2Ch 4:20 the lampstands and their lamps of pure gold 4
21 flowers, the lamps, and the tongs, of purest gold; 4
13:11 that its lamps may burn every evening; 4
21: 7 promised to give a lamp to him and to his sons 3
29: 7 They also shut the doors . . and put out the lamps 4
Job 18: 6 dark in his tent, and his lamp above him is put out. 4
21:17 often is it that the lamp of the wicked is put out? 4
29: 3 when his lamp shone upon my head 4
Ps 18:28 Yea, thou dost light my lamp; 4
119:105 Thy word is a lamp to my feet and a light to my path. 4
132:17 I have prepared a lamp for my anointed. 4
Prv 6:23 commandment is a lamp and the teaching a light 4
13: 9 but the lamp of the wicked will be put out. 4
20:20 his lamp will be put out in utter darkness. 4
27 The spirit of man is the lamp of the LORD 4
21: 4 eyes and a proud heart, the lamp of the wicked 4
24:20 lamp of the wicked will be put out. 4
31:18 Her lamp does not go out at night. 4
Jer 25:10 of the millstones and the light of the lamp. 4
Zep 1:12 At that time I will search Jerusalem with lamps 4
Zec 4: 2 with a bowl on the top of it, and seven lamps on it 4
2 on each of the lamps which are on the top of it. 4
Mat 5:15 Nor do men light a lamp and put it under a bushel 6
6:22 The eye is the lamp of the body. So, if your eye 6
25: 1 ten maidens who took their lamps 5
3 For when the foolish took their lamps 5
4 the wise took flasks of oil with their lamps. 5
7 trimmed their lamps. 5
8 for our lamps are going out.' 5
Mrk 4:21 Is a lamp brought in to be put under a bushel 6
Lke 8:16 No one after lighting a lamp covers it 6
11:33 No one after lighting a lamp puts it in a cellar 6
34 Your eye is the lamp of your body 6
36 as when a lamp with its rays gives you light. 6
12:35 Let your loins be girded and your lamps burning 6
15: 8 does not light a lamp and sweep the house and seek 6
Joh 5:35 He was a burning and shining lamp 6
2Pe 1:19 as to a lamp shining in a dark place 6
Rev 18:23 and the light of a lamp shall shine in thee no more; 6
21:23 God is its light, and its lamp is the Lamb. 6
22: 5 they need no light of lamp or sun 6
2Es 10: 2 Then we all put out the lamps 8
12:42 and like a lamp in a dark place 7
14:25 light in your heart the lamp of understanding 7
Jdt 10:22 with silver lamps carried before him. 5
Sir 26:17 Like the shining lamp on the holy lampstand 6
LJr 1:19 They light lamps 6
1Mc 4:50 lighted the lamps on the lampstand 6

2Mc 1: 8 we lighted the lamps and we set out the loaves. 6
10: 3 they burned incense and lighted lamps 6

lampstand 1. מְנוֹרָה 2. נֶבְרְשָׁה (A) 3. λυχνία 4. candelabrum

Exd 25:31 you shall make a lampstand of pure gold. 1
31 The base and the shaft of the lampstand shall be 1
32 three branches of the lampstand out of one side 1
32 three branches of the lampstand out of the other 1
33 –so for the six branches going out of the lampstand; 1
34 on the lampstand itself four cups made like 1
35 the six branches going out from the lampstand. 1
26:35 the lampstand on the south side 1
30:27 its utensils, and the lampstand and its utensils 1
31: 8 pure lampstand with all its utensils 1
35:14 the lampstand also for the light 1
37:17 He also made the lampstand of pure gold. 1
17 The base and the shaft of the lampstand were made 1
18 three branches of the lampstand out of one side 1
18 three branches of the lampstand out of the other 1
19 for the six branches going out of the lampstand. 1
20 on the lampstand itself were four cups made like 1
39:37 the lampstand of pure gold and its lamps 1
40: 4 you shall bring in the lampstand, and set up 1
24 he put the lampstand in the tent of meeting 1
Lev 24: 4 the lamps in order upon the lampstand of pure gold 1
Num 3:31 their charge was . . the lampstand, the altars 1
4: 9 cover the lampstand for the light, with its lamps 1
8: 2 shall give light in front of the lampstand. 1
3 its lamps to give light in front of the lampstand 1
4 workmanship of the lampstand, hammered work 1
4 so he made the lampstand. 1
1Kg 7:49 the lampstands of pure gold, five on the south 1
1Ch 28:15 weight of the golden lampstands and their lamps 1
15 weight of gold for each lampstand and its lamps 1
15 weight of silver for a lampstand and its lamps 1
15 the use of each lampstand in the service 1
2Ch 4: 7 he made ten golden lampstands as prescribed 1
20 the lampstands and their lamps of pure gold 1
13:11 care for the golden lampstand 1
Jer 52:19 and the lampstands, and the dishes for incense 1
Dan 5: 5 wrote on the plaster . . opposite the lampstand; 2
Zec 4: 2 I said, "I see, and behold, a lampstand all of gold 1
11 trees on the right and the left of the lampstand? 1
Heb 9: 2 in which were the lampstand and the table 3
Rev 1:12 and on turning I saw seven golden lampstands 3
13 the midst of the lampstands one like a son of man 3
20 seven stars . . and the seven golden lampstands 3
20 the seven lampstands are the seven churches. 3
2: 1 who walks among the seven golden lampstands. 3
5 and remove your lampstand from its place 3
11: 4 two lampstands which stand before the Lord 3
2Es 10:22 the light of our lampstand has been put out 4
Sir 26:17 Like the shining lamp on the holy lampstand 3
1Mc 1:21 the golden altar, the lampstand for the light 3
4:49 and brought the lampstand . . into the temple. 3
50 lighted the lamps on the lampstand 3

lance 1. רֹמַח 2. λόγχη

1Kg 18:28 cut themselves . . with swords and lances 1
2Mc 5: 2 fully armed with lances and drawn swords– 2

land 1. אֲדָמָה 2. אִי 3. אֶרֶץ 4. גְּבוּל 5. חֵלֶק 6. יַבָּשָׁה 7. שָׂדֶה 8. ἀγρός 9. γῆ 10. κλῆρος 11. ξηρός 12. πεδίον 13. τόπος 14. χερσαῖος 15. χώρα 16. χωρίον 17. regio 18. terra 19. territorium

Gen 2:11 which flows around the whole land of Havilah 3
12 the gold of that land is good; 3
13 which flows around the whole land of Cush. 3
4:16 Cain . . dwelt in the land of Nod, east of Eden. 3
10: 5 These are the sons of Japheth in their lands 3
10 Accad, all of them in the land of Shinar. 3
11 From that land he went into Assyria 3
20 languages, their lands, and their nations. 3
31 by their families, their languages, their lands 3
11: 2 they found a plain in the land of Shinar 3
28 before his father Terah in the land of his birth 3
31 of the Chalde'ans to go into the land of Canaan; 3
12: 1 house to the land that I will show you. 3
5 and they set forth to go to the land of Canaan. 3
5 When they had come to the land of Canaan 3
6 Abram passed through the land to the place 3
6 At that time the Canaanites were in the land. 3
7 To your descendants I will give this land. 3
10 Now there was a famine in the land. 3
10 for the famine was severe in the land. 3
13: 6 that the land could not support both of them 3
7 the Per'izzites dwelt in the land. 3
9 Is not the whole land before you? 3
10 like the land of Egypt, in the direction of Zo'ar; 3
12 Abram dwelt in the land of Canaan 3
15 for all the land which you see I will give to you 3
17 the breadth of the land, for I will give it to you. 3
15: 7 to give you this land to possess. 3
13 your descendants will be sojourners in a land 3
18 To your descendants I give this land 3
19 the land of the Ken'ites, the Ken'izzites •
16: 3 had dwelt ten years in the land of Canaan 3
17: 8 give . . the land of your sojournings 3
8 land of your sojournings, all the land of Canaan 3
19:28 looked down . . toward all the land of the valley 3
28 and beheld, and lo, the smoke of the land went up 3
20:15 Abim'elech said, "Behold, my land is before you; 3
21:21 took a wife for him from the land of Egypt. 3
23 and with the land where you have sojourned. 3
32 returned to the land of the Philistines. 3
34 many days in the land of the Philistines. 3
22: 2 and go to the land of Mori'ah 3
23: 2 Sarah died . . in the land of Canaan; 3
7 bowed to the Hittites, the people of the land. 3
12 bowed down before the people of the land. 3
13 in the hearing of the people of the land 3
19 of Mamre (that is, Hebron) in the land of Canaan. 3
24: 5 willing to follow me to this land; must I then take 3
5 must I then take your son back to the land 3
7 house and from the land of my birth 3
7 To your descendants I will give this land,' 3
37 of the Canaanites, in whose land I dwell; 3
26: 1 Now there was a famine in the land 3
2 dwell in the land of which I shall tell you. 3
3 Sojourn in this land, and I will be with you 3
3 to your descendants I will give all these lands 3
4 will give to your descendants all these lands; 3
12 Isaac sowed in that land, and reaped 3
22 and we shall be fruitful in the land. 3
27:46 marries . . one of the women of the land 3
28: 4 take possession of the land of your sojournings 3
13 the land on which you lie I will give to you 3
15 and will bring you back to this land; 1
29: 1 and came to the land of the people of the east. 3
31: 3 Return to the land of your fathers 3
13 go forth from this land, and return to the land 3
13 return to the land of your birth.' 3
18 to go to the land of Canaan to his father Isaac. 3
32: 3 before him to Esau his brother in the land of Se'ir 3
33:18 the city of Shechem, which is in the land of Canaan 3
19 bought . . the piece of land on which he had 7
34: 1 Dinah . . went out to visit the women of the land; 3
2 son of Hamor the Hivite, the prince of the land 3
10 You shall dwell with us; and the land shall be open 3
21 let them dwell in the land and trade in it 3
21 for behold, the land is large enough for them; 3
30 odious to the inhabitants of the land 3
35: 6 Luz . . which is in the land of Canaan 3
12 The land which I gave to Abraham and Isaac I will 3
12 I will give the land to your descendants after 3
22 While Israel dwelt in that land Reuben went 3
36: 5 who were born to him in the land of Canaan. 3
6 which he had acquired in the land of Canaan; 3
6 he went into a land away from his brother Jacob. 3
7 the land of their sojournings could not support 3
16 the chiefs of El'iphaz in the land of Edom; 3
17 these are the chiefs of Reu'el in the land of Edom; 3
20 Se'ir the Horite, the inhabitants of the land 3
21 the Horites, the sons of Se'ir in the land of Edom. 3
30 according to their clans in the land of Se'ir. 3
31 the kings who reigned in the land of Edom, before 3
34 Husham of the land of the Te'manites reigned 3
43 in the land of their possession. 3
37: 1 dwelt in the land of his father's sojournings 3
1 his father's sojournings, in the land of Canaan. 3
40:15 I was indeed stolen out of the land of the Hebrews; 3
41:19 such as I had never seen in all the land of Egypt. 3
29 plenty throughout all the land of Egypt 3
30 plenty will be forgotten in the land of Egypt; 3
30 land of Egypt; the famine will consume the land 3
31 the plenty will be unknown in the land by reason 3
33 let Pharaoh . . set him over the land of Egypt. 3
34 proceed to appoint overseers over the land 3
34 the produce of the land of Egypt during the seven 3
36 a reserve for the land against the seven years 3
36 famine which are to befall the land of Egypt 3
36 that the land may not perish through the famine. 3
41 Behold, I have set you over all the land of Egypt. 3
43 Thus he set him over all the land of Egypt. 3
44 lift up hand or foot in all the land of Egypt. 3
45 Joseph went out over the land of Egypt. 3
46 Joseph . . went through all the land of Egypt. 3
48 years when there was plenty in the land of Egypt 3
52 made me fruitful in the land of my affliction. 3
53 plenty that prevailed in the land of Egypt came 3
54 There was famine in all lands; but in all the land 3
54 but in all the land of Egypt there was bread. 3
55 When all the land of Egypt was famished 3
56 when the famine had spread over all the land 3
56 for the famine was severe in the land of Egypt. 3
42: 5 for the famine was in the land of Canaan. 3
6 Now Joseph was governor over the land; 3
6 he it was who sold to all the people of the land. 3
7 They said, "From the land of Canaan, to buy food. 3
9 you have come to see the weakness of the land. 3
12 the weakness of the land that you have come 3
13 twelve brothers, the sons of one man in the land 3
29 came to Jacob their father in the land of Canaan 3
30 The man, the lord of the land, spoke roughly to us 3
30 The man . . took us to be spies of the land. 3
32 this day with our father in the land of Canaan.' 3
33 Then the man, the lord of the land, said to us 3
34 and you shall trade in the land.' 3
43: 1 Now the famine was severe in the land. 3
11 do this: take some of the choice fruits of the land 3
44: 8 the money . . we brought back to you from the land 3
45: 6 the famine has been in the land these two years; 3
8 made me . . ruler over all the land of Egypt. 3
10 you shall dwell in the land of Goshen 3
17 load your beasts and go back to the land of Canaan; 3
18 and I will give you the best of the land of Egypt 3
18 and you shall eat the fat of the land.' 3
19 from the land of Egypt for your little ones 3
20 for the best of all the land of Egypt is yours.' 3
25 and came to the land of Canaan to their father 3
26 Joseph is . . ruler over all the land of Egypt. 3
46: 6 goods, which they had gained in the land of Canaan 3
12 but Er and Onan died in the land of Canaan 3
20 to Joseph in the land of Egypt were born Manas'seh 3
28 and they came into the land of Goshen. 3
31 My brothers . . who were in the land of Canaan 3
34 in order that you may dwell in the land of Goshen; 3
47: 1 my brothers . . have come from the land of Canaan; 3
1 they are now in the land of Goshen. 3
4 We have come to sojourn in the land; for there is no 3
4 for the famine is severe in the land of Canaan; 3
4 let your servants dwell in the land of Goshen. 3
6 The land of Egypt is before you; 3
6 settle . . in the best of the land; 3
6 let them dwell in the land of Goshen; 3
11 and gave them a possession in the land of Egypt 3
11 the best of the land, in the land of Ram'eses 3
11 the best of the land, in the land of Ram'eses 3
13 Now there was no food in all the land; 3
13 famine was very severe, so that the land of Egypt 3
13 land of Egypt and the land of Canaan languished 3
14 all the money that was found in the land of Egypt 3
14 money . . in the land of Canaan, for the grain 3
15 was all spent in the land of Egypt and in the land 3
15 in the land of Egypt and in the land of Canaan 3
18 nothing left . . but our bodies and our lands. 1
19 Why should we die . . both we and our land? 1
19 Buy us and our land for food, and we with our land 1
19 we with our land will be slaves to Pharaoh; 1
19 and that the land may not be desolate. 1
20 Joseph bought all the land of Egypt for Pharaoh; 1
20 The land became Pharaoh's; 3
22 Only the land of the priests he did not buy; 1
22 therefore they did not sell their land. 1
23 Behold, I have this day bought you and your land 1
23 seed for you, and you shall sow the land. 1
26 made it a statute concerning the land of Egypt 1
26 the land of the priests alone did not become 1
27 Thus Israel dwelt in the land of Egypt 3
27 Thus Israel dwelt . . in the land of Goshen; 3
28 Jacob lived in the land of Egypt seventeen years; 3
48: 3 God . . appeared to me . . in the land of Canaan 3
4 and will give this land to your descendants 3
5 were born to you in the land of Egypt before I came 3
7 Rachel to my sorrow died in the land of Canaan 3
21 but God . . will bring you again to the land 3
49:15 he saw . . that the land was pleasant; 3
30 to the east of Mamre, in the land of Canaan 3
50: 5 in my tomb . . in the land of Canaan, 3
7 went up . . all the elders of the land of Egypt 3
8 their herds were left in the land of Goshen. 3
11 When the inhabitants of the land, the Canaanites 3
13 for his sons carried him to the land of Canaan 3
24 God will . . bring you up out of this land 3
24 to the land which he swore to Abraham, 3
Exd 1: 7 so that the land was filled with them. 3
10 lest they . . escape from the land. 3
2:15 Moses fled . . and stayed in the land of Mid'ian; 3
22 he said, "I have been a sojourner in a foreign land. 3
3: 8 and to bring them up out of that land 3
8 bring them up . . to a good and broad land 3
8 to . . a land flowing with milk and honey 3
17 bring you . . to the land of the Canaanites 3
17 to . . a land flowing with milk and honey. 3
4:20 Moses . . went back to the land of Egypt; 3
5: 5 Behold, the people of the land are now many and you 3
12 scattered . . throughout all the land of Egypt 3
6: 1 he will drive them out of his land. 3
4 covenant . . to give them the land of Canaan 3
4 the land in which they dwelt as sojourners. 3
8 I will bring you into the land which I swore 3
11 let the people of Israel go out of his land. 3
13 the people of Israel out of the land of Egypt. 3
26 Bring out . . Israel from the land of Egypt 3
28 when the LORD spoke to Moses in the land of Egypt 3
7: 2 let the people of Israel go out of his land. 3
3 multiply my . . wonders in the land of Egypt 3
4 bring forth my hosts . . out of the land of Egypt 3
19 shall be blood throughout all the land of Egypt 3
21 was blood throughout all the land of Egypt. 3
8: 5 cause frogs to come upon the land of Egypt!' 3
6 the frogs came up and covered the land of Egypt. 3
7 brought frogs upon the land of Egypt. 3
14 and the land stank. 3
16 gnats throughout all the land of Egypt.' 3

17 gnats throughout all the land of Egypt. 3
22 on that day I will set apart the land of Goshen 3
24 and in all the land of Egypt the land was ruined 3
24 and in all the land of Egypt the land was ruined 3
25 Go, sacrifice to your God within the land. 3
9: 5 the LORD will do this thing in the land. 3
9 become fine dust over all the land of Egypt 3
9 throughout all the land of Egypt. 3
22 that there may be hail in all the land of Egypt 3
22 hail . . throughout the land of Egypt. 3
23 the LORD rained hail upon the land of Egypt; 3
24 heavy hail, such as had never been in all the land 3
25 in the field throughout all the land of Egypt 3
26 Only in the land of Goshen, where the people 3
10: 5 they shall cover the face of the land 3
5 cover . . the land, so that no one can see the land; 3
12 Stretch out your hand over the land of Egypt 3
12 that they may come upon the land of Egypt 3
12 that they may . . eat every plant in the land 3
13 stretched forth his rod over the land of Egypt 3
13 brought an east wind upon the land all that day 3
14 the locusts came up over all the land of Egypt 3
15 For they covered the face of the whole land 3
15 covered . . so that the land was darkened 3
15 they ate all the plants in the land and all 3
15 through all the land of Egypt. 3
21 there may be darkness over the land of Egypt 3
22 there was thick darkness in all the land of Egypt 3
11: 3 Moreover, the man Moses was very great in the land 3
5 all the first-born in the land of Egypt shall die 3
6 be a great cry throughout all the land of Egypt 3
9 that my wonders may be multiplied in the land 3
10 let the people of Israel go out of his land. 3
12: 1 The LORD said to Moses and Aaron in the land 3
12 For I will pass through the land of Egypt 3
12 I will smite all the first-born in the land 3
13 pass over you . . when I smite the land of Egypt. 3
17 I brought your hosts out of the land of Egypt 3
19 he is a sojourner or a native of the land. 3
25 when you come to the land which the LORD will give 3
29 smote all the first-born in the land of Egypt 3
33 urgent . . to send them out of the land in haste; 3
41 hosts of the LORD went out from the land of Egypt. 3
42 by the LORD, to bring them out of the land of Egypt; 3
48 he shall be as a native of the land. 3
51 Israel out of the land of Egypt by their hosts. 3
13: 5 brings you into the land of the Canaanites 3
5 to give you, a land flowing with milk and honey 3
11 brings you into the land of the Canaanites 3
15 slew all the first-born in the land of Egypt 3
17 lead them by way of the land of the Philistines 3
18 Israel went up out of the land of Egypt equipped 3
14: 3 They are entangled in the land; 3
16: 1 after they had departed from the land of Egypt. 3
3 that we had died by the hand of the LORD in the land 3
6 who brought you out of the land of Egypt 3
32 when I brought you out of the land of Egypt.' 3
35 forty years, till they came to a habitable land; 3
35 they came to the border of the land of Canaan. 3
18: 3 he said, "I have been a sojourner in a foreign land") 3
19: 1 Israel had gone forth out of the land of Egypt 3
20: 2 God, who brought you out of the land of Egypt 3
12 be long in the land which the LORD your God gives 1
22:21 for you were strangers in the land of Egypt. 3
23: 9 for you were strangers in the land of Egypt. 3
10 For six years you shall sow your land 3
26 None shall . . be barren in your land; 3
29 in one year, lest the land become desolate 3
30 until you are increased and possess the land. 3
31 for I will deliver the inhabitants of the land 3
33 They shall not dwell in your land, lest they make 3
29:46 who brought them forth out of the land of Egypt 3
32: 1 who brought us up out of the land of Egypt 3
4 who brought you up out of the land of Egypt! 3
7 whom you brought up out of the land of Egypt 3
8 who brought you up out of the land of Egypt!' 3
11 thou has brought forth out of the land of Egypt 3
13 all this land that I have promised I will give 3
23 who brought us up out of the land of Egypt 3
33: 1 whom you have brought up out of the land of Egypt 3
1 go up . . to the land of which I swore to Abraham 3
3 Go up to a land flowing with milk and honey; 3
34:12 a covenant with the inhabitants of the land 3
15 make a covenant with the inhabitants of the land 3
24 neither shall any man desire your land, when you 3
Lev 11:45 who brought you up out of the land of Egypt 3
14:34 When you come into the land of Canaan, which I give 3
34 in a house in the land of your possession 3
16:22 bear all their iniquities . . to a solitary land 3
18: 3 not . . as they do in the land of Egypt 3
3 not . . as they do in the land of Canaan 3
25 the land became defiled, so that I punished 3
25 the land vomited out its inhabitants 3
27 all of these abominations the men of the land did 3
27 so that the land became defiled) 3
28 lest the land vomit you out, when you defile it 3
19: 9 When you reap the harvest of your land 3
23 When you come into the land and plant 3
29 lest the land fall into harlotry 3

29 and the land become full of wickedness 3
33 When a stranger sojourns with you in your land 3
34 for you were strangers in the land of Egypt 3
36 your God, who brought you out of the land of Egypt 3
20: 2 the people of the land shall stone him 3
4 if the people of the land do at all hide their eyes 3
22 that the land where I am bringing you to dwell 3
24 I have said to you, 'You shall inherit their land 1
24 a land flowing with milk and honey.' I am the LORD 3
22:24 you shall not . . sacrifice within your land 3
33 who brought you out of the land of Egypt 3
23:10 When you come into the land which I give you 3
22 when you reap the harvest of your land 3
39 when you have gathered in the produce of the land 3
43 when I brought them out of the land of Egypt 3
25: 2 When you come into the land which I give to you 3
2 the land shall keep a sabbath to the LORD 3
4 shall be a sabbath of solemn rest for the land 3
5 it shall be a year of solemn rest for the land 3
6 The sabbath of the land shall provide food 3
7 and for the beasts that are in your land 3
9 the trumpet throughout all your land 3
10 proclaim liberty throughout the land to all 3
18 so you will dwell in the land securely 3
19 The land will yield its fruit, and you will eat 3
23 The land shall not be sold in perpetuity 3
23 for the land is mine; for you are strangers 3
24 you shall grant a redemption of the land 3
38 God, who brought you forth out of the land of Egypt 3
38 to give you the land of Canaan, and to be your God 3
42 whom I brought forth out of the land of Egypt 3
45 who have been born in your land 3
55 whom I brought forth out of the land of Egypt 3
26: 1 you shall not set up a figured stone in your land 3
4 the land shall yield its increase 3
5 you shall . . dwell in your land securely 3
6 I will give peace in the land 3
6 I will remove evil beasts from the land 3
6 the sword shall not go through your land 3
13 God, who brought you forth out of the land of Egypt 3
20 your land shall not yield its increase 3
20 the trees of the land shall not yield their fruit 3
32 I will devastate the land 3
33 your land shall be a desolation 3
34 Then the land shall enjoy its sabbaths 3
34 while you are in your enemies' land 3
34 then the land shall rest, and enjoy its sabbaths 3
36 into their hearts in the lands of their enemies 3
38 the land of your enemies shall eat you up 3
39 are left shall pine away in your enemies' lands 3
41 I . . brought them into the land of their enemies 3
42 and I will remember the land 3
43 the land shall be left by them 3
44 when they are in the land of their enemies 3
45 whom I brought forth out of the land of Egypt 3
27:16 If a man dedicates to the LORD part of the land 7
24 field shall return . . to whom the land belongs 3
30 All the tithe of the land . . is the LORD'S 3
30 tithe of the land, whether of the seed of the land 3
Num 1: 1 after they had come out of the land of Egypt 3
3:13 I slew all the first-born in the land of Egypt 3
8:17 slew all the first-born in the land of Egypt 3
9: 1 after they had come out of the land of Egypt, saying 3
10: 9 go to war in your land against the adversary 3
30 I will depart to my own land and to my kindred. 3
11:12 to the land which thou didst swear to give 1
13: 2 Send men to spy out the land of Canaan 3
16 men whom Moses sent to spy out the land. 3
17 Moses sent them to spy out the land of Canaan 3
18 see what the land is, and whether the people 3
19 whether the land that they dwell in is good or bad 3
20 whether the land is rich or poor 3
20 bring some of the fruit of the land. 3
21 spied out the land from the wilderness of Zin 3
25 they returned from spying out the land. 3
26 showed them the fruit of the land. 3
27 told him, "We came to the land to which you sent us; 3
28 Yet the people who dwell in the land are strong 3
29 Amal'ekites dwell in the land of the Negeb; 3
32 an evil report of the land which they had spied out 3
32 land . . is a land that devours its inhabitants; 3
32 land . . is a land that devours its inhabitants; 3
14: 2 Would that we had died in the land of Egypt! 3
3 Why does the LORD bring us into this land, to fall 3
6 who were among those who had spied out the land 3
7 The land . . is an exceedingly good land. 3
7 The land . . is an exceedingly good land. 3
8 he will bring us into this land and give it to us 3
8 land which flows with milk and honey. 3
9 do not fear the people of the land 3
14 they will tell the inhabitants of this land. 3
16 was not able to bring this people into the land 3
23 shall see the land which I swore to give 3
24 my servant Caleb . . I will bring into the land 3
30 not one shall come into the land where I swore 3
31 shall know the land which you have despised. 3
34 number of the days in which you spied out the land 3
36 men whom Moses sent to spy out the land 3
36 by bringing up an evil report against the land 3

37 the men who brought up an evil report of the land 3
38 of those men who went to spy out the land. 3
15: 2 When you come into the land you are to inhabit 3
18 When you come into the land to which I bring you 3
19 when you eat of the food of the land 3
41 LORD . . who brought you out of the land of Egypt 3
16:13 brought us up out of a land flowing with milk 3
14 not brought us into a land flowing with milk 3
18:13 first ripe fruits of all that is in their land 3
20 You shall have no inheritance in their land 3
20:12 not bring this assembly into the land which I 3
17 Now let us pass through your land. 3
23 Mount Hor, on the border of the land of Edom 3
24 Aaron . . shall not enter the land which I have 3
21: 4 set out . . to go around the land of Edom; 3
22 Let me pass through your land; 3
24 Israel . . took possession of his land 3
26 taken all his land out of his hand 3
31 Thus Israel dwelt in the land of the Amorites. 3
34 him into your hand, and all his people, and his land; 3
35 they slew him . . and they possessed his land. 3
22: 5 near the River, in the land of Amaw to call him 3
6 to defeat them and drive them from the land; 3
13 Go to your own land; for the LORD has refused 3
26: 4 who came forth out of the land of Egypt, were 3
19 Er and Onan died in the land of Canaan. 3
53 To these the land shall be divided 3
55 the land shall be divided by lot; 3
27:12 see the land which I have given to . . Israel. 3
32: 1 they saw the land of Jazer and the land of Gilead 3
1 they saw the land of Jazer and the land of Gilead 3
4 land which the LORD smote before . . Israel 3
4 land which the LORD smote . . is a land for cattle; 3
5 let this land be given to your servants 3
7 discourage . . Israel from going over into the land 3
8 sent them from Ka'desh-bar'nea to see the land. 3
9 went up to the Valley of Eshcol, and saw the land 3
9 discouraged . . Israel from going into the land 3
11 shall see the land which I swore to give 1
17 cities because of the inhabitants of the land. 3
22 and the land is subdued before the LORD 3
22 and this land shall be your possession 3
29 the land shall be subdued before you 3
29 give them the land of Gilead for a possession; 3
30 possessions among you in the land of Canaan. 3
32 pass over armed . . into the land of Canaan 3
33 the land and its cities with their territories 3
33 the cities of the land throughout the country. 3
33: 1 when they went forth out of the land of Egypt 3
37 at Mount Hor, on the edge of the land of Edom. 3
38 after . . Israel had come out of the land of Egypt 3
40 king . . dwelt in the Negeb in the land of Canaan 3
51 pass over the Jordan into the land of Canaan 3
52 drive out all the inhabitants of the land 3
53 take possession of the land and settle in it 3
53 for I have given the land to you to possess it. 3
54 You shall inherit the land by lot according 3
55 if you do not drive out the inhabitants of the land 3
55 shall trouble you in the land where you dwell. 3
34: 2 When you enter the land of Canaan (this is the land 3
2 Canaan (this is the land that shall fall to you 3
2 inheritance, the land of Canaan in its full extent) 3
12 your land with its boundaries all round. 3
13 This is the land which you shall inherit by lot 3
17 who shall divide the land to you for inheritance 3
18 leader . . to divide the land for inheritance. 3
29 divide the inheritance . . in the land of Canaan. 3
35:10 When you cross the Jordan into the land of Canaan 3
14 shall give . . three cities in the land of Canaan 3
28 may return to the land of his possession. 3
32 no ransom . . that he may return to dwell in the land 3
33 shall not thus pollute the land in which you live; 3
33 for blood pollutes the land 3
33 no expiation can be made for the land 3
34 You shall not defile the land in which you live 3
36: 2 my lord to give the land for inheritance by lot 3
Deu 1: 5 Beyond the Jordan, in the land of Moab 3
7 by the seacoast, the land of the Canaanites 3
8 Behold, I have set the land before you; go 3
8 take possession of the land which the LORD swore 3
21 LORD your God has set the land before you; go up 3
22 that they may explore the land for us, and bring us 3
25 took in their hands some of the fruit of the land 3
25 'It is a good land which the LORD our God gives us.' 3
27 he has brought us forth out of the land of Egypt 3
35 Not one . . shall see the good land which I swore 3
36 to him and to his children I will give the land 3
2: 5 for I will not give you any of their land 3
9 not give you any of their land for a possession 3
12 as Israel did to the land of their possession 3
19 not give you any of the land of the sons of Ammon 3
20 That also is known as a land of Reph'aim; 3
24 Sihon the Amorite, king of Heshbon, and his land; 3
27 'Let me pass through your land; I will go only 3
29 into the land which the LORD our God gives to us.' 3
31 I have begun to give Sihon and his land over to you; 3
31 take possession, that you may occupy his land.' 3
37 land of the sons of Ammon you did not draw near 3
3: 2 I have given him and all his people and his land 3

8 took the land at that time out of the hand 3
12 When we took possession of this land at that time 3
13 whole of that Bashan is called the land of Reph'aim. 3
18 LORD your God has given you this land to possess; 3
20 occupy the land which the LORD your God gives 3
25 Let me . . see the good land beyond the Jordan 3
28 he shall put them in possession of the land 3
4: 1 live, and go in and take possession of the land 3
5 should do them in the land which you are entering 3
14 teach you . . that you might do them in the land 3
21 swore . . that I should not enter the good land 3
22 must die in this land, I must not go over the Jordan; 3
22 go over and take possession of that good land. 3
25 When you . . have grown old in the land 3
26 that you will soon utterly perish from the land 3
38 to give you their land for an inheritance 3
40 that you may prolong your days in the land 1
46 in the land of Sihon the king of the Amorites, who 3
47 took possession of his land and the land of Og 3
47 possession of . . the land of Og the king of Bashan 3
5: 6 LORD . . who brought you out of the land of Egypt 3
15 servant in the land of Egypt, and the LORD your God 3
16 in the land which the LORD your God gives you. 1
31 do them in the land which I give them to possess.' 3
33 live long in the land which you shall possess. 3
6: 1 to teach you, that you may do them in the land 3
3 in a land flowing with milk and honey. 3
10 when the LORD your God brings you into the land 3
12 LORD, who brought you out of the land of Egypt 3
18 that you may . . take possession of the good land 3
23 that he might bring us in and give us the land 3
7: 1 brings you into the land which you are entering 3
13 in the land which he swore to your fathers to give 1
8: 1 possess the land which the LORD swore to give 3
7 LORD your God is bringing you into a good land 3
7 good land, a land of brooks of water 3
8 a land of wheat and barley, of vines and fig trees 3
8 a land of olive trees and honey 3
9 land in which you will eat bread 3
9 a land whose stones are iron, and out of whose hills 3
10 bless the LORD . . for the good land he has given 3
14 LORD . . who brought you out of the land of Egypt 3
9: 4 LORD has brought me in to possess this land'; 3
5 are you going in to possess their land; 3
6 LORD . . not giving you this good land to possess 3
7 from the day you came out of the land of Egypt 3
23 take possession of the land which I have given you 3
28 lest the land from which thou didst bring us say 3
28 LORD was not able to bring them into the land 3
10: 7 Jot'bathah, a land with brooks of water. 3
11 that they may go in and possess the land 3
19 for you were sojourners in the land of Egypt. 3
11: 3 to Pharaoh the king of Egypt and to all his land; 3
8 and go in and take possession of the land 3
9 in the land which the LORD swore to your fathers 1
9 land flowing with milk and honey. 3
10 land which you are entering to take possession 3
10 land . . is not like the land of Egypt 3
11 land which you are going over to possess is a land 3
11 land of hills and valleys, which drinks water 3
12 land which the LORD your God cares for; 3
14 he will give the rain for your land in its season 3
17 no rain, and the land yield no fruit, and you perish 1
17 perish quickly off the good land which the LORD 3
21 that your days . . may be multiplied in the land 1
25 upon all the land that you shall tread 3
29 when the LORD your God brings you into the land 3
30 land of the Canaanites who live in the Arabah 3
31 pass over . . to go in to take possession of the land 3
12: 1 which you shall be careful to do in the land 3
10 when you go over the Jordan, and live in the land 3
19 as long as you live in your land. 1
29 dispossess them and dwell in their land 3
13: 5 LORD . . who brought you out of the land of Egypt 3
10 LORD . . who brought you out of the land of Egypt 3
15: 4 (for the LORD will bless you in the land 3
7 towns within your land which the LORD . . gives 3
11 For the poor will never cease out of the land; 3
11 brother, to the needy and to the poor, in the land. 3
15 remember . . you were a slave in the land of Egypt 3
16: 3 came out of the land of Egypt in hurried flight 3
3 remember the day . . came out of the land of Egypt. 3
20 live and inherit the land which the LORD . . gives 3
17:14 When you come to the land which the LORD . . gives 3
18: 9 come into the land which the LORD your God gives 3
19: 1 whose land the LORD your God gives you 3
2 set apart three cities for you in the land 3
3 divide into three parts the area of the land 3
8 gives you all the land which he promised to give 3
10 blood be shed in your land which the LORD . . gives 3
14 inheritance which you will hold in the land 3
20: 1 LORD . . brought you up out of the land of Egypt. 3
21: 1 If in the land which the LORD your God gives you 1
23 not defile your land which the LORD your God 1
23: 7 Egyptian . . you were a sojourner in his land. 3
20 bless you in all that you undertake in the land 3
24: 4 not bring guilt upon the land which the LORD 3
14 or one of the sojourners who are in your land 3
22 remember that you were a slave in the land of Egypt; 3

25:15 that your days may be prolonged in the land 1
19 in the land which the LORD your God gives you 3
26: 1 come into the land which the LORD your God gives 3
2 fruit . . which you harvest from your land 3
3 declare . . that I have come into the land 3
9 brought us into this place and gave us this land 3
9 gave us . . land flowing with milk and honey. 3
15 a land flowing with milk and honey.' 3
27: 2 Jordan to the land which the LORD your God gives 3
3 pass over to enter the land which the LORD 3
3 land flowing with milk and honey, as the LORD 3
28: 8 bless you in the land which the LORD your God 3
11 abound . within the land which the LORD swore 1
12 to give the rain of your land in its season 3
21 until he has consumed you off the land which you 1
24 will make the rain of your land powder and dust; 3
52 walls . . come down throughout all your land; 3
52 all your towns throughout all your land 3
63 you shall be plucked off the land 1
29: 1 make with . . Israel in the land of Moab 3
2 LORD did before your eyes in the land of Egypt 3
2 LORD did . . to Pharaoh . . and to all his land 3
8 took their land, and gave it for an inheritance 3
16 You know how we dwelt in the land of Egypt 3
22 foreigner who comes from a far land, would say 3
22 when they see the afflictions of that land 3
23 whole land brimstone and salt, and a burnt-out 3
24 'Why has the LORD done thus to this land? 3
25 when he brought them out of the land of Egypt 3
27 anger of the LORD was kindled against this land 3
28 LORD uprooted them from their land in anger 1
28 cast them into another land, as at this day.' 3
30: 5 LORD your God will bring you into the land 3
16 LORD your God will bless you in the land 3
18 not live long in the land which you . . possess. 1
20 you may dwell in the land which the LORD swore 1
31: 4 as he did to Sihon and Og . . and to their land 3
7 for you shall go with this people into the land 3
13 as long as you live in the land which you are going 1
16 harlot after the strange gods of the land 3
20 into the land flowing with milk and honey 1
21 brought them into the land that I swore to give. 3
23 shall bring the children of Israel into the land 3
32:10 He found him in a desert land, and in the howling 3
43 makes expiation for the land of his people. 1
47 thereby you shall live long in the land 1
49 Nebo . . in the land of Moab, opposite Jericho; 3
49 view the land of Canaan, which I give to . . Israel 3
52 For you shall see the land before you; 3
52 not go . . into the land which I give to the people 3
33:13 of Joseph he said, "Blessed by the LORD be his land •
21 He chose the best of the land for himself •
28 Israel dwelt . . in a land of grain and wine; 3
34: 1 LORD showed him all the land. Gilead as far as Dan 3
2 all Naph'tali, the land of E'phraim and Manas'seh 3
2 all the land of Judah as far as the Western Sea 3
4 This is the land of which I swore to Abraham 3
5 Moses . . died there in the land of Moab 3
6 buried him in the valley in the land of Moab 3
11 LORD sent him to do in the land of Egypt, to Pharaoh 3
11 to do in the land of Egypt, to . . all his land 3
Jos 1: 2 go over . . into the land which I am giving to them 3
4 all the land of the Hittites . . shall be 3
6 you shall cause this people to inherit the land 3
11 take . . the land which the LORD your God gives you 3
13 LORD your God is . . and will give you this land. 3
14 shall remain in the land which Moses gave you 3
15 and they also take possession of the land 3
15 you shall return to the land of your possession 3
15 and shall possess it, the land which Moses . . gave •
2: 1 saying, "Go, view the land, especially Jericho. 3
2 have come here tonight to search out the land. 3
3 they have come to search out all the land. 3
9 I know that the LORD has given you the land 3
9 the inhabitants of the land melt away before you. 3
14 we will deal . . when the LORD gives us the land. 3
18 when we come into the land, you shall bind this 3
24 the LORD has given all the land into our hands; 3
24 moreover all the inhabitants of the land are 3
5: 6 LORD swore that he would not let them see the land 3
6 a land flowing with milk and honey. 3
11 they ate of the produce of the land 3
12 when they ate of the produce of the land; 3
12 Israel . . ate of the fruit of the land of Canaan 3
6:22 said to the two men who had spied out the land 3
27 was with Joshua; and his fame was in all the land. 3
7: 2 Joshua . . said to them, "Go up and spy out the land 3
9 Canaanites and all the inhabitants of the land 3
8: 1 the king of Ai, and his people, his city, and his land; 3
9:24 had commanded . . Moses to give you all the land 3
24 and to destroy all the inhabitants of the land 3
10:40 Joshua defeated the whole land 3
42 took all these kings and their land at one time 3
11: 3 the Hivites under Hermon in the land of Mizpah. 3
16 Joshua took all that land 3
16 all the Negeb and all the land of Goshen 3
22 none . . left in the land of the people of Israel; 3
23 Joshua took the whole land 3
23 And the land had rest from war. 3

12: 1 Now these are the kings of the land 3
1 took possession of their land beyond the Jordan 3
6 and Moses . . gave their land for a possession •
7 the kings of the land whom Joshua . . defeated 3
7 and Joshua gave their land to the tribes •
8 the land of the Hittites, the Amorites •
13: 1 there remains yet very much land to be possessed. 3
2 This is the land that yet remains: all the regions 3
4 in the south, all the land of the Canaanites 3
5 the land of the Geb'alites, and all Lebanon 3
6 only allot the land to Israel for an inheritance •
7 Now . . divide this land for an inheritance 3
21 the princes of Sihon, who dwelt in the land. 3
25 and half the land of the Ammonites, to Aro'er 3
14: 1 which . . Israel received in the land of Canaan 3
4 no portion was given to the Levites in the land 3
5 as the LORD commanded . . they allotted the land. 3
7 sent me from Ka'desh-bar'nea to spy out the land; 3
9 the land . . shall be an inheritance for you 3
15 And the land had rest from war. 3
15:19 since you have set me in the land of the Negeb 3
17: 5 ten . . besides the land of Gilead and Bashan 3
6 The land of Gilead was allotted to the rest 3
8 The land of Tap'puah belonged to Manas'seh 3
10 the land to the south being E'phraim's •
12 Canaanites persisted in dwelling in that land. 3
15 clear ground for yourselves in the land 3
18: 1 the land lay subdued before them. 3
3 be slack to go in and take possession of the land 3
4 that they may set out and go up and down the land 3
6 you shall describe the land in seven divisions 3
8 who went to write the description of the land 3
8 Go up and down and write a description of the land 3
9 So the men went and passed up and down in the land 3
10 there Joshua apportioned the land to the people 3
19:49 territories of the land as inheritances 3
51 they finished dividing the land. 3
21: 2 they said to them at Shiloh in the land of Canaan 3
43 LORD gave . . all the land which he swore to give 3
22: 4 your home in the land where your possession lies 3
7 a possession . . in the land west of the Jordan. •
9 at Shiloh, which is in the land of Canaan 3
9 parting . . to go to the land of Gilead 3
9 their own land of which they had possessed 3
10 to the region . . that lies in the land of Canaan 3
11 an altar at the frontier of the land of Canaan 3
13 the Gadites and . . Manas'seh, in the land of Gilead 3
15 the Gadites, and . . Manas'seh, in the land of Gilead 3
19 if your land is unclean, pass over into the LORD's 3
19 the LORD's land where the . . tabernacle stands 3
32 Reubenites and the Gadites in the land of Gilead 3
32 returned from . . Gilead to the land of Canaan 3
33 to destroy the land where the Reubenites 3
23: 5 and you shall possess their land, as . . promised 3
13 till you perish from off this good land 1
15 destroyed you from off this good land 1
16 you shall perish quickly from off the good land 3
24: 3 and led him through all the land of Canaan 3
8 Then I brought you to the land of the Amorites 3
8 and you took possession of their land 3
13 I gave you a land on which you had not labored 3
15 the gods of the Amorites in whose land you dwell; 3
17 our God who brought us . . up from the land of Egypt 3
18 the peoples, the Amorites who lived in the land; 3
Jdg 1: 2 behold, I have given the land into his hand. 3
15 since you have set me in the land of the Negeb, give 3
26 the man went to the land of the Hittites and built 3
27 Canaanites persisted in dwelling in that land. 3
32 the Canaanites, the inhabitants of the land; 3
33 the Canaanites, the inhabitants of the land; 3
2: 1 you up from Egypt, and brought you into the land 3
2 no covenant with the inhabitants of this land; 3
6 his inheritance to take possession of the land. 3
12 who had brought them out of the land of Egypt; 3
3:11 So the land had rest 40 years. Then Oth'niel the son 3
30 And the land had rest for 80 years. 3
5:31 And the land had rest for 40 years. 3
6: 4 they would . . destroy the produce of the land 3
5 so that they wasted the land as they came in. 3
9 drove them out before you, and gave you their land; 3
10 the gods of the Amorites, in whose land you dwell 3
8:28 the land had rest 40 years in the days of Gideon 3
9:37 men are coming down from the center of the land 3
10: 4 30 cities . . which are in the land of Gilead. 3
8 beyond the Jordan in the land of the Amorites 3
11: 3 Jephthah fled . . and dwelt in the land of Tob; 3
5 went to bring Jephthah from the land of Tob; 3
12 that you have come to me to fight against my land? 3
13 Israel . . took away my land, from the Arnon 3
15 Israel did not take away the land of Moab 3
15 Israel did not take . . the land of the Ammonites 3
17 Let us pass, we pray, through your land'; but the king 3
18 went around the land of Edom and the land of Moab 3
18 went around the land of Edom and the land of Moab 3
18 and arrived on the east side of the land of Moab 3
19 Let us pass . . through your land to our country.' 3
21 took possession of all the land of the Amorites 3
12:12 and was buried at Ai'jalon in the land of Zeb'ulun. 3
15 and was buried at Pira'thon in the land of E'phraim 3

18: 2 sent . . to spy out the land and to explore it; 3
2 they said to them, "Go and explore the land. 3
9 we have seen the land, and behold, it is very 3
9 be slow to go, and enter in and possess the land. 3
10 The land is broad; yea, God has given it 3
17 five men who had gone to spy out the land went up 3
30 until the day of the captivity of the land. 3
19:30 people of Israel came up out of the land of Egypt 3
20: 1 people of Israel . . including the land of Gilead 3
21:12 the camp at Shiloh, which is in the land of Canaan. 3
21 and go to the land of Benjamin. 3
Rut 1: 1 In the days when . . there was a famine in the land 3
7 went on the way to return to the land of Judah. 3
2:11 left your father and mother and your native land 3
4: 3 Na'omi . . is selling the parcel of land 7
1Sm 6: 5 and images of your mice that ravage the land 3
5 his hand from off you and your gods and your land. 3
9 if it goes up on the way to its own land 4
9: 4 and passed through the land of Shal'ishah 3
4 they passed through the land of Sha'alim 3
4 Then they passed through the land of Benjamin 3
5 When they came to the land of Zuph, Saul said to his 3
16 I will send to you a man from the land of Benjamin 3
12: 6 brought your fathers up out of the land of Egypt. 3
13: 3 Saul blew the trumpet throughout all the land 3
7 crossed . . Jordan to the land of Gad and Gilead. 3
17 one . . turned toward Ophrah, to the land of Shu'al 3
19 no smith . . throughout all the land of Israel; 3
14:14 half a furrow's length in an acre of land. 7
29 Jonathan said, "My father has troubled the land; 3
21:11 Is not this David the king of the land? 3
22: 5 depart, and go into the land of Judah. 3
23:23 if he is in the land, I will search him out 3
27 the Philistines have made a raid upon the land. 3
27: 1 I should escape to the land of the Philistines; 3
8 were the inhabitants of the land from of old 3
8 of the land . . as far as Shur, to the land of Egypt. 3
9 David smote the land 3
28: 3 put the mediums and the wizards out of the land. 3
9 cut off the mediums and . . wizards from the land. 3
29:11 to return to the land of the Philistines. 3
30:16 behold, they were spread abroad over all the land 3
16 taken from the land of the Philistines 3
16 spoil they had taken . . from the land of Judah. 3
31: 9 sent . . throughout the land of the Philistines 3
2Sm 3:12 To whom does the land belong? Make your covenant 3
5: 6 the Jeb'usites, the inhabitants of the land 3
9: 7 I will restore to you all the land of Saul 7
10 you and your sons . . shall till the land for him 1
10: 2 servants came into the land of the Ammonites. 3
15: 4 Oh that I were judge in the land! 3
17:26 and Ab'salom encamped in the land of Gilead. 3
19: 9 and now he has fled out of the land from Ab'salom. 3
29 I have decided: you and Ziba shall divide the land. 7
21:14 they buried the bones . . in the land of Benjamin 3
14 And . . God heeded supplications for the land. 3
24: 6 came . . and to Kadesh in the land of the Hittites; 3
8 when they had gone through all the land, they came 3
13 Shall three years of famine come . . in your land? 3
13 there be three days' pestilence in your land? 3
25 So the LORD heeded supplications for the land 3
1Kg 4:10 (to him belonged Socoh and all the land of Hepher); 3
19 Geber . . in the land of Gilead, the country 3
19 And there was one officer in the land of Judah. 3
21 the Euphra'tes to the land of the Philistines 3
6: 1 after . . Israel came out of the land of Egypt 3
8: 9 of Israel, when they came out of the land of Egypt. 3
21 when he brought them out of the land of Egypt. 3
34 bring them again to the land which thou gavest 1
36 grant rain upon thy land, which thou hast given 3
37 famine in the land . . pestilence or blight 3
40 live in the land which thou gavest 1
46 carried away captive to the land of the enemy 3
47 the land to which they have been carried captive 3
47 supplication . . in the land of their captors 3
48 repent . . in the land of their enemies 3
48 repent . . and pray to thee toward their land 3
9: 7 cut off Israel from the land which I have given 1
8 the LORD done thus to this land and to this house?' 3
9 brought their fathers out of the land of Egypt 3
11 gave to Hiram . . cities in the land of Galilee. 3
13 So they are called the land of Cabul to this day. 3
18 and Tamar in the wilderness, in the land of Judah 3
19 in Lebanon, and in all the land of his dominion. 3
21 descendants who were left after them in the land 3
26 E'zion-ge'ber . . in the land of Edom. 3
10: 6 The report was true which I heard in my own land 3
13 she turned and went back to her own land 3
15 which came . . from the governors of the land. 3
11:18 and assigned him . . food, and gave him land. 3
12:28 who brought you up out of the land of Egypt. 3
14:15 root up Israel out of this good land which he gave 1
24 were also male cult prostitutes in the land. 3
15:12 put . . the male cult prostitutes out of the land 3
20 all Chin'neroth, with all the land of Naph'tali. 3
17: 7 dried up, because there was no rain in the land. 3
18: 5 Go through the land to all the springs of water 3
6 they divided the land between them 3
20: 7 the king . . called all the elders of the land 3
22:46 he exterminated from the land. 3
2Kg 2:19 but the water is bad, and the land is unfruitful. 3
3:27 they withdrew . . and returned to their own land. 3
4:38 when there was a famine in the land. 3
5: 2 carried off a little maid from the land of Israel 3
4 so spoke the maiden from the land of Israel. 3
6:23 Syrians came no more . . into the land of Israel. 3
8: 1 called for a famine, and it will come upon the land 3
2 and sojourned in the land of the Philistines 3
3 woman returned from the land of the Philistines 3
3 to appeal to the king for her house and her land. 7
5 appealed to the king for her house and her land. 7
6 from the day that she left the land until now. 3
10:33 from the Jordan eastward, all the land of Gilead 3
11: 3 while Athali'ah reigned over the land. 3
14 and all the people of the land rejoicing 3
18 the people of the land went to the house of Ba'al 3
19 he took . . and all the people of the land; 3
20 So all the people of the land rejoiced; 3
13:20 Moabites used to invade the land in the spring 3
15: 5 king's son . . governing the people of the land. 3
19 Pul the king of Assyria came against the land; 3
20 turned back, and did not stay there in the land. 3
29 Gilead, and Galilee, all the land of Naph'tali; 3
16:15 burnt offering of all the people of the land, and their 3
17: 5 Then the king of Assyria invaded all the land 3
7 who had brought them up out of the land of Egypt 3
23 Israel was exiled from their own land to Assyria 1
26 do not know the law of the god of the land; 3
26 they do not know the law of the god of the land. 3
27 and teach them the law of the god of the land. 3
36 the LORD, who brought you out of the land of Egypt 3
18:25 Go up against this land, and destroy it.' 3
32 come and take you away to a land like your own land 3
32 come and take you away to a land like your own land 3
32 a land like your own land, a land of grain and wine 3
32 of grain and wine, a land of bread and vineyards 3
32 and vineyards, a land of olive trees and honey 3
33 Has any of the gods . . ever delivered his land 3
19: 7 he shall hear a rumor and return to his own land; 3
7 cause him to fall by the sword in his own land.' 3
11 what the kings of Assyria have done to all lands 3
17 have laid waste the nations and their lands 3
37 slew him . . and escaped into the land of Ar'arat. 3
21: 8 out of the land which I gave to their fathers 1
24 the people of the land slew all those who had 3
24 the people of the land made Josi'ah his son king 3
23:24 abominations that were seen in the land of Judah 3
30 the people of the land took Jeho'ahaz 3
33 put him in bonds at Riblah in the land of Hamath 3
33 Pharaoh Neco . . laid upon the land a tribute 3
35 he taxed the land to give the money 3
35 He exacted the . . of the people of the land 3
24: 7 king of Egypt did not come again out of his land 3
14 none . . except the poorest people of the land. 3
15 wives, his officials, and the chief men of the land 3
25: 3 there was no food for the people of the land. 3
12 captain . . left some of the poorest of the land 3
19 commander . . who mustered the people of the land; 3
19 and sixty men of the people of the land 3
21 put them to death at Riblah in the land of Hamath. 3
21 So Judah was taken into exile out of its land. 1
22 over the people who remained in the land of Judah 3
24 dwell in the land, and serve the king of Babylon 3
1Ch 1:43 These are the kings who reigned in the land of Edom 3
45 Husham of the land of the Te'manites reigned 3
2:22 Ja'ir, who had 23 cities in the land of Gilead 3
4:40 the land was very broad, quiet, and peaceful; 3
5: 9 cattle had multiplied in the land of Gilead. 3
11 in the land of Bashan as far as Sal'ecah 3
23 the half-tribe of Manas'seh dwelt in the land 3
25 the peoples of the land, whom God had destroyed 3
6:55 to them they gave Hebron in the land of Judah 3
7:21 the men of Gath who were born in the land slew 3
10: 9 throughout the land of the Philistines 3
11: 4 the Jeb'usites were, the inhabitants of the land. 3
13: 2 our brethren who remain in all the land of Israel 3
14:17 the fame of David went out into all lands 3
16:18 saying, "To you I will give the land of Canaan 3
19: 2 came to Hanun in the land of the Ammonites 3
3 to search and to overthrow and to spy out the land? 3
21:12 sword of the LORD, pestilence upon the land 3
22: 2 the aliens who were in the land of Israel 3
5 of fame and glory throughout all lands; 3
18 the inhabitants of the land into my hand; 3
18 land is subdued before the LORD and his people. 3
28: 8 that you may possess this good land 3
2Ch 2:17 census of all the aliens who were in the land 3
6: 5 I brought my people out of the land of Egypt 3
25 bring them again to the land which thou gavest 1
27 forgive the sin . . and grant rain upon thy land 3
28 If there is famine in the land, if there is 3
31 days that they live in the land which thou gavest 1
36 carried away captive to a land far or near; 3
37 land to which they have been carried captive 3
37 supplication . . in the land of their captivity 3
38 if they repent . . in the land of their captivity 3
38 if they repent . . and pray toward their land 3
7:13 When I . . command the locust to devour the land 3
14 will forgive their sin and heal their land. 3
20 will pluck you up from the land which I have given 1
21 'Why has the LORD done thus to this land and to this 3
22 LORD . . who brought them out of the land of Egypt 3
8: 6 to build . . in all the land of his dominion. 3
8 descendants who were left after them in the land 3
17 to E'zion-Ge'ber and Eloth . . in the land of Edom. 3
9: 5 The report was true which I heard in my own land 3
11 never was seen the like of them before in the land 3
12 So she turned and went back to her own land 3
14 kings of Arabia and the governors of the land 3
26 he ruled . . to the land of the Philistines 3
28 horses were imported . . from all lands. 3
13: 9 made priests . . like the people of other lands? 3
14: 1 In his days the land had rest for ten years. 3
6 fortified cities in Judah, for the land had rest. 3
7 the land is still ours 3
15: 5 afflicted all the inhabitants of the lands. 3
8 from all the land of Judah and Benjamin 3
17: 2 set garrisons in the land of Judah 3
10 fell upon all the kingdoms of the lands 3
19: 3 for you destroyed the Ashe'rahs out of the land 3
5 He appointed judges in the land 3
20: 7 O our God, drive out the inhabitants of this land 3
10 when they came from the land of Egypt 3
22:12 while Athali'ah reigned over the land. 3
23:13 all the people of the land rejoicing 3
20 he took . . all the people of the land; 3
21 all the people of the land rejoiced; 3
26:21 Jotham . . governing the people of the land. 3
30: 9 find compassion . . and return to this land. 3
25 sojourners who came out of the land of Israel 3
32: 4 the brook that flowed through the land 3
13 have done to all the peoples of other lands? 3
13 gods of the nations of those lands at all able 3
13 at all able to deliver their lands out of my hand? 3
17 Like the gods of the nations of the lands 3
21 returned with shame of face to his own land. 3
31 about the sign that had been done in the land 3
33: 8 no more remove the foot of Israel from the land 1
25 people of the land slew all . . who had conspired 3
25 people of the land made Josi'ah his son king 3
34: 7 throughout all the land of Israel. 3
8 when he had purged the land and the house 3
36: 1 people of the land took Jeho'ahaz 3
3 king of Egypt . . laid upon the land a tribute 3
21 until the land had enjoyed its sabbaths. 3
Ezr 3: 3 fear . . because of the peoples of the lands 3
4: 4 people of the land discouraged the people 3
6:21 from the pollutions of the peoples of the land 3
9: 1 not separated . . from the peoples of the lands 3
2 mixed itself with the peoples of the lands. 3
7 been given into the hand of the kings of the lands 3
11 land which you are entering, to take possession 3
11 land unclean with the pollutions of the peoples 3
11 pollutions of the peoples of the lands 3
12 that you may be strong, and eat the good of the land 3
10: 2 foreign women from the peoples of the land 3
11 separate yourselves from the peoples of the land 3
Neh 4: 4 plundered in a land where they are captives. 3
5:14 appointed . . governor in the land of Judah 3
16 held to the work . . and acquired no land; 7
9: 8 to his descendants the land of the Canaanite 3
10 servants and all the people of his land 3
15 thou didst tell them to go in to possess the land 3
22 took possession of the land of Sihon king 3
22 took possession of . . the land of Og king 3
23 bring them into the land which thou hadst told 3
24 descendants went in and possessed the land 3
24 subdue . . inhabitants of the land 3
24 with their kings and the peoples of the land 3
25 captured fortified cities and a rich land 1
30 into the hand of the peoples of the lands. 3
35 did not serve thee . . in the large and rich land 3
36 land that thou gavest to our fathers to enjoy 3
10:28 separated . . from the peoples of the lands 3
30 not give our daughters to the peoples of the land 3
31 if the peoples of the land bring in wares 3
Est 10: 1 King Ahasu-e'rus laid tribute on the land 3
Job 1: 1 a man in the land of Uz, whose name was Job 3
10 his possessions have increased in the land. 3
10:21 not return, to the land of gloom and deep darkness 3
22 the land of gloom and chaos 3
12:15 if he sends them out, they overwhelm the land. 3
15:19 to whom alone the land was given 3
22: 8 The man with power possessed the land 3
24:18 their portion is cursed in the land; 3
28:13 it is not found in the land of the living. 3
30: 8 they have been whipped out of the land. 3
31:38 If my land has cried out against me 1
37:13 for correction, or for his land, or for love 3
38:26 to bring rain on a land where no man is 3
42:15 in all the land there were no women so fair as Job's 3
Ps 10:16 the nations shall perish from his land. 3
16: 3 As for the saints in the land, they are the noble 3
25:13 his children shall possess the land. 3
27:13 the goodness of the LORD in the land of the living! 3
35:20 but against those who are quiet in the land they 3
37: 3 you will dwell in the land, and enjoy security. 3

9 who wait for the LORD shall possess the land. 3
11 the meek shall possess the land 3
22 those blessed by the LORD shall possess the land 3
29 The righteous shall possess the land 3
34 he will exalt you to possess the land; 3
41: 2 he is called blessed in the land; 3
42: 6 I remember thee from the land of Jordan 3
44: 3 for not by their own sword did they win the land 3
49:11 though they named lands their own. 1
52: 5 he will uproot you from the land of the living. 3
60: 2 Thou hast made the land to quake 3
63: 1 my flesh faints for thee, as in a dry and weary land 3
72:16 May there be abundance of grain in the land; 3
74: 8 burned all the meeting places of God in the land. 3
20 the dark places of the land are full 3
78:12 he wrought marvels in the land of Egypt 3
54 he brought them to his holy land, to the mountain 4
80: 9 it took deep root and filled the land. 3
81: 5 when he went out over the land of Egypt. 3
10 who brought you up out of the land of Egypt. 3
85: 1 LORD, thou wast favorable to thy land; 3
9 that glory may dwell in our land. 3
12 our land will yield its increase. 3
88:12 or thy saving help in the land of forgetfulness? 3
100: 1 Make a joyful noise to the LORD, all the lands! 3
101: 6 I will look with favor on the faithful in the land 3
8 morning I will destroy all the wicked in the land 3
105:11 saying, "To you I will give the land of Canaan 3
16 When he summoned a famine on the land 3
23 Jacob sojourned in the land of Ham. 3
27 wrought his signs . . miracles in the land of Ham. 3
28 He sent darkness, and made the land dark; •
30 Their land swarmed with frogs 3
32 lightning that flashed through their land. 3
35 which devoured all the vegetation in their land 3
36 He smote all the first-born in their land 3
44 he gave them the lands of the nations; 3
106:22 wondrous works in the land of Ham 3
24 Then they despised the pleasant land 3
27 scattering them over the lands. 3
38 land was polluted with blood. 3
107: 3 gathered in from the lands, from the east 3
34 a fruitful land into a salty waste 3
35 turns . . a parched land into springs of water. 3
112: 2 His descendants will be mighty in the land; 3
116: 9 I walk before the LORD in the land of the living. 3
135:12 gave their land as a heritage 3
136:21 gave their land as a heritage 3
137: 4 How shall we sing the LORD'S song in a foreign land? 1
140:11 Let not the slanderer be established in the land; 3
141: 7 rock which one cleaves and shatters on the land 3
142: 5 my refuge, my portion in the land of the living. 3
143: 6 my soul thirsts for thee like a parched land. 3
Prv 2:21 For the upright will inhabit the land 3
22 but the wicked will be cut off from the land 3
10:30 but the wicked will not dwell in the land. 3
12:11 He who tills his land will have plenty of bread 1
21:19 It is better to live in a desert land 3
28: 2 When a land transgresses it has many rulers; 3
19 He who tills his land will have plenty of bread 1
29: 4 By justice a king gives stability to the land 3
31:23 when he sits among the elders of the land. 3
Ecc 5: 9 an advantage to a land with cultivated fields. 3
10:16 Woe to you, O land, when your king is a child 3
17 Happy are you, O land, when your king is the son 3
Sng 2:12 the voice of the turtledove is heard in our land. 3
Isa 1: 7 in your very presence aliens devour your land; 1
19 If . . obedient, you shall eat the good of the land; 3
2: 7 Their land is filled with silver and gold 3
7 their land is filled with horses 3
8 Their land is filled with idols; 3
4: 2 the fruit of the land shall be the pride and glory 3
5: 8 you are made to dwell alone in . . the land. 3
30 if one look to the land, behold, darkness 3
6:11 without men, and the land is utterly desolate 1
12 forsaken places are many in the midst of the land. 3
7:16 the land before whose two kings you are in dread 1
18 for the bee which is in the land of Assyria. 3
22 every one that is left in the land will eat curds 3
24 for all the land will be briers and thorns; 3
8: 8 wings will fill the breadth of your land 3
21 They will pass through the land •
9: 1 he brought into contempt the land of Zeb'ulun 3
1 he brought into contempt . . the land of Naph'tali 3
2 those who dwelt in a land of deep darkness 3
19 wrath of the LORD of hosts the land is burned 3
11:16 Israel when they came up from the land of Egypt. 3
13: 5 come from a distant land . . the end of the heavens 3
14 and every man will flee to his own land. 3
14: 1 choose Israel, and will set them in their own land 1
2 Israel will possess them in the LORD'S land 1
20 because you have destroyed your land 3
25 that I will break the Assyrian in my land 3
15: 8 For a cry has gone round the land of Moab; 4
9 a lion . . for the remnant of the land. 1
16: 1 They have sent lambs to the ruler of the land 3
4 he who tramples . . has vanished from the land 3
18: 1 Ah, land of whirring wings . . beyond the rivers 3
2 a nation . . whose land the rivers divide. 3
7 a nation . . whose land the rivers divide 3
19:10 the pillars of the land will be crushed •
17 the land of Judah will become a terror 1
18 five cities in the land of Egypt which speak 3
19 altar to the LORD in the midst of the land of Egypt 3
20 a sign . . in the land of Egypt; 3
21: 1 it comes from the desert, from a terrible land. 3
14 with bread, O inhabitants of the land of Tema. 3
22:18 and throw you like a ball into a wide land; 3
23: 1 From the land of Cyprus it is revealed to them. 3
10 Overflow your land like the Nile 3
13 Behold the land of the Chalde'ans! 3
26: 1 this song will be sung in the land of Judah 3
10 in the land of uprightness he deals perversely 3
15 thou hast enlarged all the borders of the land. 3
19 on the land of the shades thou wilt let it fall. 3
27:13 those who were lost in the land of Assyria 3
13 those who were driven out to the land of Egypt 3
28:22 decree of destruction . . upon the whole land. 3
30: 6 Through a land of trouble and anguish 3
32: 2 like the shade of a great rock in a weary land. 3
33: 9 The land mourns and languishes; 3
17 they will behold a land that stretches afar. 3
34: 6 LORD has . . a great slaughter in the land of Edom. 3
7 Their land shall be soaked with blood 3
9 her land shall become burning pitch. 3
36:10 I have come up against this land to destroy it? 3
10 said to me, Go up against this land, and destroy it.' 3
17 and take you away to a land like your own land 3
17 and take you away to a land like your own land 3
17 like your own land, a land of grain and wine 3
17 of grain and wine, a land of bread and vineyards. 3
18 delivered his land out of the hand of . . Assyria? 3
37: 7 he shall hear a rumor, and return to his own land; 3
7 I will make him fall by the sword in his own land.' 3
11 what the kings of Assyria have done to all lands 3
18 laid waste all the nations and their lands 3
38 slew him . . and escaped into the land of Ar'arat. 3
38:11 I shall not see the LORD in the land of the living; 3
41:18 a pool of water, and the dry land springs of water. 3
44: 3 For I will pour water on the thirsty land •
45:19 I did not speak in secret, in a land of darkness; 3
49: 8 to establish the land, to apportion the desolate 3
12 from the west, and these from the land of Syene. 3
19 desolate places and your devastated land– 3
53: 8 that he was cut off out of the land of the living 3
57:13 he who takes refuge in me shall possess the land 3
60:18 Violence shall no more be heard in your land 3
21 they shall possess the land for ever 3
61: 7 in your land you shall possess a double portion; 3
62: 4 and your land shall no more be termed Desolate; 3
4 called My delight is in her, and your land Married; 3
4 delights in you, and your land shall be married. 3
65:16 blesses himself in the land shall bless himself 3
16 takes an oath in the land shall swear by the God 3
66: 8 Shall a land be born in one day? 3
Jer 1: 1 who were in An'athoth in the land of Benjamin 3
14 upon all the inhabitants of the land. 3
18 against the whole land, against the kings 3
18 Judah . . its priests, and the people of the land. 3
2: 2 followed me in the wilderness, in a land not sown. 3
6 the LORD who brought us up from the land of Egypt 3
6 in the wilderness, in a land of deserts and pits 3
6 in a land of drought and deep darkness 3
6 in a land that none passes through 3
7 I brought you into a plentiful land 3
7 But when you came in you defiled my land 3
15 They have made his land a waste; 3
31 wilderness to Israel, or a land of thick darkness? 3
3: 1 Would not that land be greatly polluted? 3
2 have polluted the land with your vile harlotry. 3
9 she polluted the land, committing adultery 3
16 you have multiplied and increased in the land 3
18 they shall come from the land of the north 3
18 the land that I gave your fathers for a heritage. 3
19 and give you a pleasant land, a heritage 3
4: 5 and say, "Blow the trumpet through the land; 3
7 forth from his place to make your land a waste; 3
16 Besiegers come from a distant land; 3
20 the whole land is laid waste. 3
27 The whole land shall be a desolation; 3
5:19 forsaken me and served foreign gods in your land 3
19 serve strangers in a land that is not yours.' 3
30 An . . and horrible thing has happened in the land 3
6: 8 lest I make you a desolation, an uninhabited land. 3
12 my hand against the inhabitants of the land 3
20 or sweet cane from a distant land? 3
7: 7 in the land that I gave of old to your fathers 3
22 day that I brought them out of the land of Egypt 3
25 that your fathers came out of the land of Egypt 3
34 for the land shall become a waste. 3
8:16 at . . their stallions the whole land quakes. 3
16 They come and devour the land 3
19 my people from the length and breadth of the land 3
9: 3 not truth has grown strong in the land; 3
12 Why is the land ruined and laid waste 3
19 utterly shamed, because we have left the land 3
10:18 I am slinging out the inhabitants of the land 3
11: 4 when I brought them out of the land of Egypt 3
5 to give them a land flowing with milk and honey 3
7 when I brought them up out of the land of Egypt 3
19 let us cut him off from the land of the living 3
12: 4 How long will the land mourn 3
5 And if in a safe land you fall down 3
11 The whole land is made desolate 3
12 sword of the LORD devours from one end of the land 3
14 Behold, I will pluck them up from their land 1
15 each to his heritage and each to his land. 3
13:13 all the inhabitants of this land 3
14: 4 since there is no rain on the land 3
8 why shouldst thou be like a stranger in the land 3
15 Sword and famine shall not come on this land 3
18 and priest ply their trade through the land 3
15: 7 I have winnowed them . . in the gates of the land; 3
10 a man of strife and contention to the whole land! 3
14 serve your enemies in a land which you do not know 3
16: 3 and the fathers who begot them in this land 3
6 Both great and small shall die in this land; 3
13 therefore I will hurl you out of this land 3
13 hurl you out of this land into a land 3
14 the people of Israel out of the land of Egypt 3
15 For I will bring them back to their own land 1
18 because they have polluted my land 3
17: 4 serve your enemies in a land which you do not know 3
26 from the land of Benjamin, from the Shephe'lah 3
18:16 making their land a horror, a thing to be hissed 3
22:10 he shall return no more to see his native land. 3
12 and he shall never see this land again. 3
27 to the land to which they will long to return 3
28 and cast into a land which they do not know? 3
29 O land, land, land, hear the word of the LORD! 3
29 O land, land, land, hear the word of the LORD! 3
29 O land, land, land, hear the word of the LORD! 3
23: 5 execute justice and righteousness in the land. 3
7 the people of Israel out of the land of Egypt 3
8 Then they shall dwell in their own land. 1
10 For the land is full of adulterers; 3
10 because of the curse the land mourns 3
15 ungodliness has gone forth into all the land. 3
24: 5 from this place to the land of the Chalde'ans. 3
6 and I will bring them back to this land. 3
8 the remnant of Jerusalem who remain in this land 3
8 and those who dwell in the land of Egypt. 3
10 destroyed from the land which I gave to them 1
25: 5 and dwell upon the land which the LORD has given 1
9 and I will bring them against this land 3
11 This whole land shall become a ruin and a waste 3
12 and that nation, the land of the Chalde'ans 3
12 making the land an everlasting waste. 3
13 I will bring upon that land all the words 3
20 all the kings of the land of Uz 3
20 all the kings of the land of the Philistines 3
38 for their land has become a waste 3
26:17 certain of the elders of the land arose and spoke 3
20 against this city and against this land 3
27: 6 all these lands into the hand of Nebuchadnez'zar 3
7 until the time of his own land comes; 3
10 that you will be removed far from your land 1
11 I will leave on its own land, to till it and dwell 1
30: 3 I will bring them back to the land which I gave 3
10 offspring from the land of their captivity. 3
31:16 they shall come back from the land of the enemy. 3
23 they shall use these words in the land of Judah 3
32 to bring them out of the land of Egypt 3
32: 8 which is at An'athoth in the land of Benjamin 3
15 vineyards shall again be bought in this land. 3
20 hast shown signs and wonders in the land of Egypt 3
21 bring thy people Israel out of the land of Egypt 3
22 thou gavest them this land 3
22 to give them, a land flowing with milk and honey; 3
41 I will plant them in this land in faithfulness 3
43 Fields shall be bought in this land 3
44 and sealed and witnessed, in the land of Benjamin 3
33:11 will restore the fortunes of the land as at first 3
13 the cities of the Negeb, in the land of Benjamin 3
15 execute justice and righteousness in the land. 3
34:13 when I brought them out of the land of Egypt 3
19 people of the land who passed between the parts 3
35: 7 may live many days in the land where you sojourn. 1
11 king of Babylon came up against the land, we said 3
15 you shall dwell in the land which I gave to you 1
36:29 will certainly come and destroy this land 3
37: 1 king of Babylon made king in the land of Judah 3
2 nor the people of the land listened to the words 3
7 is about to return to Egypt, to its own land. 3
12 from Jerusalem to go to the land of Benjamin 3
19 will not come against you and against this land'? 3
39: 5 king of Babylon, at Riblah, in the land of Hamath; 3
10 left in the land of Judah some of the poor people 3
40: 4 See, the whole land is before you; 3
6 among the people who were left in the land. 3
7 Gedali'ah the son of Ahi'kam governor in the land 3
7 of the poorest of the land who had not been taken 3
9 Dwell in the land, and serve the king of Babylon 3
11 and in Edom and in other lands heard that the king 3
12 they had been driven and came to the land of Judah 3
41: 2 Babylon had appointed governor in the land. 3
18 king of Babylon had made governor over the land. 3

42:10 If you will remain in this land 3
12 mercy on you and let you remain in your own land. 1
13 if you say, 'We will not remain in this land,' 3
14 saying, 'No, we will go to the land of Egypt 3
16 shall overtake you there in the land of Egypt; 3
43: 4 to remain in the land of Judah. 3
5 who had returned to live in the land of Judah 3
7 And they came into the land of Egypt 3
11 He shall come and smite the land of Egypt 3
12 he shall clean the land of Egypt, as a shepherd 3
13 Heliop'olis which is in the land of Egypt; 3
44: 1 all the Jews that dwelt in the land of Egypt 3
1 at Memphis, and in the land of Pathros 3
8 in the land of Egypt where you have come to live 3
9 which they committed in the land of Judah 3
12 have set their faces to come to the land of Egypt 3
12 in the land of Egypt they shall fall; 3
13 I will punish those who dwell in the land of Egypt 3
14 who have come to live in the land of Egypt 3
14 or survive or return to the land of Judah 3
15 people who dwelt in Pathros in the land of Egypt 3
21 kings and your princes, and the people of the land 3
22 therefore your land has become a desolation 3
24 all you of Judah who are in the land of Egypt 3
26 all you of Judah who dwell in the land of Egypt 3
26 of any man of Judah in all the land of Egypt, saying 3
27 all the men of Judah who are in the land of Egypt 3
28 return from the land of Egypt to the land of Judah 3
28 return from the land of Egypt to the land of Judah 3
28 the remnant of Judah, who came to the land of Egypt 3
45: 4 I am plucking up-that is, the whole land. 3
46:13 king of Babylon to smite the land of Egypt 3
16 to our own people and to the land of our birth 3
27 your offspring from the land of . . captivity. 3
47: 2 they shall overflow the land 3
2 and every inhabitant of the land shall wail. 3
48:24 all the cities of the land of Moab, far and near. 3
33 been taken away from the fruitful land of Moab; 3
50: 1 concerning the land of the Chalde'ans 3
3 which shall make her a land a desolation 3
8 and go out of the land of the Chalde'ans 3
16 and every one shall flee to his own land. 3
18 punishment on the king of Babylon and his land 3
21 Go up against the land of Meratha'im 3
22 The noise of battle is in the land 3
25 has a work to do in the land of the Chalde'ans. 3
28 they flee and escape from the land of Babylon 3
38 it is a land of images, and they are mad over idols. 3
45 purposes . . against the land of the Chalde'ans 3
51: 2 they shall empty her land 3
4 fall down slain in the land of the Chalde'ans 3
5 the land of the Chalde'ans is full of guilt 3
28 deputies, and every land under their dominion. 3
29 The land trembles and writhes in pain 3
29 to make the land of Babylon a desolation 3
43 become a horror, a land of drought and a desert 3
43 drought and a desert, a land in which no one dwells 3
46 be not fearful at the report heard in the land 3
46 violence is in the land 3
47 her whole land shall be put to shame 3
52 through all her land the wounded shall groan. 3
54 destruction from the land of the Chalde'ans! 3
52: 6 there was no food for the people of the land. 3
9 king of Babylon at Riblah in the land of Hamath 3
16 the guard left some of the poorest of the land 3
25 of the army who mustered the people of the land; 3
25 60 men of the people of the land, who were found 3
27 put them to death at Riblah in the land of Hamath. 3
27 So Judah was carried captive out of its land. 1
Lam 4:21 O daughter of Edom, dweller in the land of Uz; 3
Ezk 1: 3 in the land of the Chalde'ans by the river Chebar; 3
6:14 and make the land desolate and waste 3
7: 2 thus says the Lord GOD to the land of Israel: An end! 1
2 end has come upon the four corners of the land. 3
7 Your doom has come to you, O inhabitant of the land; 3
23 Because the land is full of bloody crimes 3
27 the people of the land are palsied by terror. 3
8:12 For they say . . the LORD has forsaken the land. 3
17 that they should fill the land with violence 3
9: 9 the land is full of blood 3
9 for they say, 'The LORD has forsaken the land 3
11:15 to us this land is given for a possession. 3
17 I will give you the land of Israel. 1
12: 6 cover your face, that you may not see the land; 3
12 that he may not see the land with his eyes. 3
13 bring him to Babylon in the land of the Chalde'ans 3
19 say of the people of the land, Thus says the Lord 3
19 inhabitants of Jerusalem in the land of Israel 1
19 their land will be stripped of all it contains 3
20 and the land shall become a desolation; 3
22 proverb that you have about the land of Israel 1
13: 9 nor shall they enter the land of Israel; 1
14:13 a land sins against me by acting faithlessly 3
15 If I cause wild beasts to pass through the land 3
16 but the land would be desolate. 3
17 Or if I bring a sword upon that land, and say 3
17 and say, Let a sword go through the land; 3
19 Or if I send a pestilence into that land 3
15: 8 I will make the land desolate 3

16: 3 and your birth are of the land of the Canaanites; 3
29 harlotry also with the trading land of Chalde'a; 3
17: 4 its young twigs and carried it to a land of trade 3
5 Then he took of the seed of the land and planted it 3
13 The chief men of the land he had taken away 3
18: 2 this proverb concerning the land of Israel 1
19: 4 they brought him with hooks to the land of Egypt. 3
7 the land was appalled and all who were in it 3
13 in the wilderness, in a dry and thirsty land. 3
20: 5 making myself known to them in the land of Egypt 3
6 that I would bring them out of the land of Egypt 3
6 into a land that I had searched out for them 3
6 a land flowing with milk and honey •
6 milk and honey, the most glorious of all lands. 3
8 against them in the midst of the land of Egypt. 3
9 in bringing them out of the land of Egypt. 3
10 So I led them out of the land of Egypt 3
15 that I would not bring them into the land 3
15 had given them, a land flowing with milk and honey •
15 milk and honey, the most glorious of all lands 3
28 For when I had brought them into the land 3
36 in the wilderness of the land of Egypt 3
38 bring them out of the land where they sojourn 3
38 but they shall not enter the land of Israel. 1
40 Israel, all of them, shall serve me in the land; 3
42 when I bring you into the land of Israel 1
46 and prophesy against the forest land in the Negeb 7
21: 2 prophesy against the land of Israel 1
3 say to the land of Israel, Thus says the LORD 1
19 both of them shall come forth from the same land. 3
30 in the land of your origin, I will judge you. 3
32 your blood shall be in the midst of the land; 3
22:24 say to her, You are a land that is not cleansed 3
29 The people of the land have practiced extortion 3
30 and stand in the breach before me for the land 3
23:15 of Babylonians whose native land was Chalde'a. 3
19 when she played the harlot in the land of Egypt 3
27 your harlotry brought from the land of Egypt; 3
48 Thus will I put an end to lewdness in the land 3
25: 3 over the land of Israel when it was made desolate 1
6 the malice within you against the land of Israel 1
26:20 or have a place in the land of the living. 3
27:17 Judah and the land of Israel traded with you; 3
28:25 then they shall dwell in their own land 1
29: 9 the land of Egypt shall be a desolation 3
10 I will make the land of Egypt an utter waste 3
12 I will make the land of Egypt a desolation 3
14 and bring them back to the land of Pathros 3
14 to the land of Pathros, the land of their origin; 3
19 I will give the land of Egypt to Nebuchadrez'zar 3
20 I have given him the land of Egypt 3
30: 5 Libya, and the people of the land that is in league 3
11 nations, shall be brought in to destroy the land; 3
11 against Egypt, and fill the land with the slain. 3
12 and will sell the land into the hand of evil men; 3
12 I will bring desolation upon the land 3
13 shall no longer be a prince in the land of Egypt; 3
13 I will put fear in the land of Egypt. 3
23 and disperse them throughout the lands. 3
25 he shall stretch it out against the land of Egypt; 3
31:12 lie broken in all the watercourses of the land; 3
32: 6 I will drench the land even to the mountains 3
8 put darkness upon your land, says the Lord GOD. 3
15 I make the land of Egypt desolate and when the land 3
15 when the land is stripped of all that fills it 3
23 who spread terror in the land of the living. 3
24 who spread terror in the land of the living 3
25 terror . . was spread in the land of the living 3
26 they spread terror in the land of the living. 3
27 of the mighty men was in the land of the living. 3
32 For he spread terror in the land of the living; 3
33: 2 and say to them, If I bring the sword upon a land 3
2 the people of the land take a man from among them 3
3 if he sees the sword coming upon the land 3
24 waste places in the land of Israel keep saying 1
24 was only one man, yet he got possession of the land; 3
24 the land is surely given us to possess. 3
25 and shed blood; shall you then possess the land? 3
26 shall you then possess the land? 3
28 I will make the land a desolation and a waste; 3
29 when I have made the land a desolation and a waste 3
34:13 and will bring them into their own land; 1
25 and banish wild beasts from the land 3
27 they shall be secure in their land; 1
28 nor shall the beasts of the land devour them; 3
29 shall no more be consumed with hunger in the land 3
36: 5 against all Edom, who gave my land to themselves 3
6 prophesy concerning the land of Israel, 1
17 when the house of Israel dwelt in their own land 1
18 for the blood which they had shed in the land 3
20 yet they had to go out of his land. 3
24 and bring you into your own land. 1
28 dwell in the land which I gave to your fathers; 3
34 the land that was desolate shall be tilled 3
35 This land that was desolate has become 3
37:12 I will bring you home into the land of Israel. 1
14 I will place you in your own land; 1
21 from all sides, and bring them to their own land; 1
22 I will make them one nation in the land 3

25 shall dwell in the land where your fathers dwelt 3
38: 2 set your face toward Gog, of the land of Magog 3
8 in the latter years you will go against the land 3
8 the land where people were gathered •
9 you will be like a cloud covering the land 3
11 go up against the land of unwalled villages; 3
16 my people Israel, like a cloud covering the land. 3
16 I will bring you against my land 3
18 when Gog shall come against the land of Israel 1
19 shall be a great shaking in the land of Israel; 1
39:12 burying them, in order to cleanse the land. 3
13 All the people of the land will bury them; 3
14 They will set apart men to pass through the land 3
14 bury those remaining upon the face of the land 3
15 when these pass through the land and any one sees 3
16 Thus shall they cleanse the land. 3
26 when they dwell securely in their land 1
27 and gathered them from their enemies' lands 3
28 and then gathered them into their own land. 1
40: 2 in the visions of God into the land of Israel, 3
45: 1 When you allot the land as a possession 3
1 a portion of the land as a holy district 3
4 It shall be the holy portion of the land; 3
7 to the prince shall belong the land on both sides •
7 the western to the eastern boundary of the land. •
8 they shall let the house of Israel have the land 3
16 the people of the land shall give this offering 3
22 for himself and all the people of the land 3
46: 3 The people of the land shall worship 3
9 When the people of the land come before the LORD 3
47:13 boundaries by which you shall divide the land 3
14 this land shall fall to you as your inheritance. 3
15 This shall be the boundary of the land 3
18 the Jordan between Gilead and the land of Israel; 3
21 you shall divide this land among you 3
48:12 portion from the holy portion of the land 3
14 not alienate this choice portion of the land 3
29 the land which you shall allot as an inheritance 3
Dan 8: 9 exceedingly great . . toward the glorious land. •
9: 6 spoke . . to all the people of the land. 3
7 all the lands to which thou hast driven them 3
15 didst bring thy people out of the land of Egypt 3
11: 9 latter . . shall return into his own land. 1
16 stand in the glorious land, and all of it 3
19 face . . toward the fortresses of his own land; 3
28 he shall return to his land with great substance 3
28 shall work his will, and return to his own land. 3
39 shall divide the land for a price. 1
41 He shall come into the glorious land. 3
42 land of Egypt shall not escape. 3
Hos 1: 2 for the land commits great harlotry 3
11 and they shall go up from the land 3
2: 3 like a wilderness, and set her like a parched land 3
15 at the time when she came out of the land of Egypt. 3
18 abolish the bow, the sword, and war from the land; 3
23 and I will sow him for myself in the land. 3
4: 1 a controversy with the inhabitants of the land. 3
1 There is . . no knowledge of God in the land; 3
3 the land mourns, and all who dwell in it languish 3
7:16 shall be their derision in the land of Egypt. 3
9: 3 They shall not remain in the land of the LORD; 3
11: 5 They shall return to the land of Egypt 3
11 trembling . . like doves from the land of Assyria; 3
12: 9 I am the LORD your God from the land of Egypt; 3
12 (Jacob fled to the land of Aram 7
13: 4 I am the LORD your God from the land of Egypt; 3
5 knew you in the wilderness, in the land of drought; 3
Jol 1: 2 give ear, all inhabitants of the land! 3
6 For a nation has come up against my land 3
14 the elders and all the inhabitants of the land 3
2: 1 Let all the inhabitants of the land tremble 3
3 The land is like the garden of Eden before them 3
18 Then the LORD became jealous for his land 3
20 and drive him into a parched and desolate land 3
21 Fear not, O land; be glad and rejoice 1
3: 2 scattered them . . and have divided up my land 3
19 they have shed innocent blood in their land. 3
Ams 2:10 Also I brought you up out of the land of Egypt 3
10 and led you . . to possess the land of the Amorite. 3
3: 1 family which I brought up out of the land of Egypt 3
9 to the strongholds in the land of Egypt, and say 3
11 An adversary shall surround the land 3
5: 2 forsaken on her land, with none to raise her up. 1
7: 2 they had finished eating the grass of the land 3
4 devoured the . . deep and was eating up the land. 5
10 the land is not able to bear all his words. 3
11 and Israel must go into exile away from his land 1
12 flee away to the land of Judah, and eat bread there 3
17 and your land shall be parceled out by line; 1
17 you yourself shall die in an unclean land 1
17 shall surely go into exile away from its land.' 1
8: 4 and bring the poor of the land to an end 3
8 Shall not the land tremble on this account 3
11 when I will send a famine on the land; 3
9: 7 Did I not bring up Israel from the land of Egypt 3
15 I will plant them upon their land 1
15 plucked up out of the land which I have given them 1
Obd 1:19 of the Shephe'lah the land of the Philistines; •
19 they shall possess the land of E'phraim 7

19 the land of E'phraim and the land of Sama'ria 7
Jon 1:13 the men rowed hard to bring the ship back to land 6
2: 6 I went down to the land whose bars closed upon me 3
Mic 5: 5 when the Assyrian comes into our land 3
6 shall rule the land of Assyria with the sword 3
6 rule . . the land of Nimrod with the drawn sword; 3
6 the Assyrian when he comes into our land 3
11 I will cut off the cities of your land 3
6: 4 For I brought you up from the land of Egypt 3
7:15 in the days when you came out of the land of Egypt 3
Nah 3:13 The gates of your land are wide open to your foes; 3
Hab 3: 7 the curtains of the land of Mid'ian did tremble. 3
Zep 2: 3 Seek the LORD, all you humble of the land 3
5 is against you, O Canaan, land of the Philistines; 3
9 like Gomor'rah, a land possessed by nettles •
11 each in its place, all the lands of the nations. 2
Hag 1:11 called for a drought upon the land and the hills 3
2: 4 take courage, all you people of the land 3
Zec 1:21 against the land of Judah to scatter it. 3
2: 6 ho! Flee from the land of the north, says the LORD; 3
12 inherit Judah as his portion in the holy land 1
3: 9 remove the guilt of this land in a single day. 3
5: 3 that goes out over the face of the whole land; 3
6 he said, "This is their iniquity in all the land. 3
11 To the land of Shinar, to build a house for it; 3
7: 5 Say to all the people of the land and the priests 3
14 Thus the land they left was desolate 3
14 the pleasant land was made desolate. 3
9: 1 word of the LORD is against the land of Hadrach 3
16 jewels of a crown they shall shine on his land. 1
10:10 I will bring them home from the land of Egypt 3
10 I will bring them to the land of Gilead 3
11: 6 on the inhabitants of this land, says the LORD. 3
16 For lo, I am raising up in the land a shepherd 3
12:12 The land shall mourn, each family by itself; 3
13: 2 I will cut off the names of the idols from the land 3
2 also I will remove from the land the prophets 3
5 the land has been my possession since my youth. 1
8 In the whole land, says the LORD 3
14:10 The whole land shall be turned into a plain 3
Mal 3:12 for you will be a land of delight, says the LORD 3
4: 6 lest I come and smite the land with a curse. 3
Mat 2: 6 you, O Bethlehem, in the land of Judah, are by no 9
20 his mother, and go to the land of Israel, for those 9
21 his mother, and went to the land of Israel. 9
4:15 The land of Zeb'ulun and the land of Naph'tali 9
15 The land of Zeb'ulun and the land of Naph'tali 9
10:15 for the land of Sodom and Gomor'rah 9
11:24 day of judgment for the land of Sodom 9
14:24 many furlongs distant from the land 9
34 they came to land at Gennesaret. 9
19:29 sisters or father or mother or children or lands 8
23:15 you traverse sea and land 11
27:45 there was darkness over all the land 9
Mrk 4: 1 the whole crowd was beside the sea on the land. 9
6:47 he was alone on the land. 9
53 they came to land at Gennes'aret 9
10:29 mother or father or children or lands 8
30 mothers and children and lands 8
15:33 there was darkness over the whole land 9
Lke 4:25 when there came a great famine over all the land; 9
26 in the land of Sidon •
5: 3 he asked him to put out a little from the land. 9
11 when they had brought their boats to land 9
8:27 And as he stepped out on land 9
12:16 The land of a rich man brought forth plentifully; 15
14:35 is fit neither for the land nor for the dunghill; 9
23:44 darkness over the whole land until the ninth hour 9
Joh 3:22 After this Jesus . . went into the land of Judea; 9
6:21 immediately the boat was at the land 9
21: 8 they were not far from the land 9
9 When they got out on land, they saw a charcoal fire 9
Act 4:34 as many as were possessors of lands or houses 16
5: 3 to keep back part of the proceeds of the land? 16
8 Tell me whether you sold the land for so much. 16
7: 3 Depart from your land and from your kindred 9
3 go into the land which I will show you.' 9
4 Then he departed from the land of the Chalde'ans 9
4 God removed him from there into this land 9
6 aliens in a land belonging to others 9
29 and became an exile in the land of Mid'ian 9
40 this Moses who led us out from the land of Egypt 9
13:17 during their stay in the land of Egypt 9
19 destroyed seven nations in the land of Canaan 9
19 he gave them their land as an inheritance 9
27:14 a tempestuous wind . . struck down from the land; •
27 sailors suspected that they were nearing land. 15
39 when it was day, they did not recognize the land 9
43 make for the land 9
44 so it was that all escaped to land. 9
28: 7 lands belonging to the chief man of the island 16
Heb 6: 7 land which has drunk the rain that . . falls 9
8: 9 to lead them out of the land of Egypt 9
11: 9 By faith he sojourned in the land of promise 9
9 as in a foreign land •
15 If they had been thinking of that land •
29 the people crossed the Red Sea as if on dry land 9
Jde 1: 5 he who saved a people out of the land of Egypt 9
Rev 10: 2 right foot on the sea, and his left foot on the land 9

5 the angel whom I saw standing on sea and land 9
8 angel who is standing on the sea and on the land. 9
1Es 1:58 Until the land has enjoyed its sabbaths 9
4: 2 who rule over land and sea and all that is in them? 9
15 to every people that rules over sea and land. 9
28 Do not all lands fear to touch him? 15
56 He wrote that land and wages should be provided 10
5:50 joined them from the other peoples of the land. 9
50 all the peoples of the land were hostile to them 9
72 the peoples of the land 9
7:13 the abominations of the peoples of the land 9
8:69 the alien peoples of the land 9
70 mixed with the alien peoples of the land 9
83 'The land which you are entering 9
83 a land polluted with the pollution of the aliens 9
83 the pollution of the aliens of the land 9
85 may be strong and eat the good things of the land 9
87 the uncleanness of the peoples of the land. 9
92 foreign women from the peoples of the land 9
9: 9 separate . . from the peoples of the land 9
2Es 1: 7 not I who brought them out of the land of Egypt 18
21 I divided fertile lands among you 18
2: 9 whose land lies in lumps of pitch 18
4:19 for the land is assigned to the forest 18
21 For as the land is assigned to the forest 18
5: 1 and the land shall be barren of faith. 17
3 the land which you now see ruling 17
17 entrusted to you in the land of their exile? 17
24 from all the lands of the world thou hast chosen 18
7:26 the land which now is hidden shall be disclosed. 18
8:17 I see the failings of us who dwell in the land 18
9: 8 and will see my salvation in my land 18
13:33 every man shall leave his own land 17
40 led away from their own land into captivity 18
40 and they were taken into another land. 18
42 which they had not kept in their own land. 17
14:31 Then land was given to you for a possession 18
31 to you for a possession in the land of Zion 18
15: 6 For iniquity has spread throughout every land 18
10 to live any longer in the land of Egypt 18
11 as before, and will destroy all its land. 18
30 a portion of the land of the Assyrians 18
33 from the land of the Assyrians an enemy in ambush 19
60 and shall destroy a part of your land 19
62 your land and your mountains 19
Tob 1: 3 who went with me into the land of the Assyrians 15
4 in the land of Israel, while I was still a young man 9
3:15 in the land of my captivity 9
4:12 their posterity will inherit the land. 9
6: 3 seized the fish and threw it up on the land. 9
13: 6 I give him thanks in the land of my captivity 9
14: 4 will be scattered . . from the good land 9
5 bring them back into their land 9
Jdt 1: 9 Raamses and the whole land of Goshen 9
12 also all the inhabitants of the land of Moab 9
2:27 sacked their cities and ravaged their lands 12
3: 3 Behold, our buildings, and all our land 13
8 given to him to destroy all the gods of the land 9
5: 9 go to the land of Canaan 9
12 he afflicted the whole land of Egypt 9
15 they lived in the land of the Amorites 9
7: 4 These men will now lick up the face of the whole land 9
18 covered the whole face of the land 9
8:22 the captivity of the land 9
AEs 13:16 redeem for thyself out of the land of Egypt. 9
Wis 12: 3 Those who dwelt of old in thy holy land 9
7 the land most precious of all to thee 9
16:19 to destroy the crops of the unrighteous land. 9
18:15 into the midst of the land that was doomed 9
19: 7 and dry land emerging where water had stood before 9
19 land animals were transformed 14
19 and creatures that swim moved over to the land. 9
Sir 10:16 The Lord has overthrown the lands of the nations 15
37: 3 why were you formed to cover the land with deceit? 11
39: 4 travel through the lands of foreign nations 9
43: 3 At noon it parches the land 15
45:22 in the land of the people he has no inheritance 9
46: 8 into a land flowing with milk and honey. 9
47:24 so as to remove them from their land. 9
48:15 carried away captive from their land 9
Bar 1: 8 to return them to the land of Judah–the silver 9
9 had carried away . . the people of the land 9
19 Lord brought our fathers out of the land of Egypt 9
20 he brought our fathers out of the land of Egypt 9
20 to give to us a land flowing with milk and honey. 9
2:11 didst bring thy people out of the land of Egypt 9
21 remain in the land which I gave to your fathers. 9
23 the whole land will be a desolation without 9
30 in the land of their exile they will come 9
32 they will praise me in the land of their exile 9
34 land which I swore to give to their fathers 9
35 remove . . from the land which I have given them. 9
3:10 why is it that you are in the land of your enemies 9
LJr 1:61 the wind likewise blows in every land. 15
72 a reproach in the land. 15
1Mc 1: 1 who came from the land of Kittim 9
16 he determined to become king of the land of Egypt 9
19 the fortified cities in the land of Egypt 9
19 he plundered the land of Egypt. 9

24 Taking them all, he departed to his own land 9
28 Even the land shook for its inhabitants 9
44 to follow customs strange to the land 9
52 they did evil in the land; 9
2:56 Caleb . . received an inheritance in the land. 9
3: 8 he destroyed the ungodly out of the land; •
24 the rest fled into the land of the Philistines. 9
29 caused in the land by abolishing the laws 9
36 distribute their land. 9
39 to go into the land of Judah and destroy it 9
41 from Syria and the land of the Philistines 9
4:22 they all fled into the land of the Philistines. 9
5:13 all our brethren who were in the land of Tob •
45 to go to the land of Judah. 9
48 Let us pass through your land to get to our land 9
48 Let us pass through your land to get to our land 9
53 till he came to the land of Judah. 9
65 fought the sons of Esau in the land to the south 9
66 to go into the land of the Philistines 9
68 Azotus in the land of the Philistines 9
68 returned to the land of Judah. 9
6: 5 the armies which had gone into the land of Judah 9
13 I am perishing of deep grief in a strange land. 9
49 since it was a sabbatical year for the land. 9
7: 6 and have driven us out of our land. 9
7 brought upon us and upon the land of the king 15
10 came with a large force into the land of Judah 9
22 They gained control of the land of Judah 9
50 the land of Judah had rest for a few days. 9
8: 3 what they had done in the land of Spain 15
10 they plundered them, conquered the land 9
16 to control all their land 9
23 May all go well . . at sea and on land for ever 11
32 fight you on sea and on land.' 11
9: 1 sent . . into the land of Judah a second time 9
53 he took the sons of the leading men of the land 15
57 the land of Judah had rest for two years. 9
69 Then he decided to depart to his own land. 9
72 formerly taken from the land of Judah 9
72 then he turned and departed to his own land 9
10:13 each left his place and departed to his own land. 9
30 I will not collect them from the land of Judah 9
33 taken as a captive from the land of Judah 9
37 in the land of Judah. 9
39 Ptolemais and the land adjoining it •
55 you returned to the land of your fathers 9
67 came from Crete to the land of his fathers. 9
72 fathers were twice put to flight in their own land. 9
11:34 from the crops of the land 9
38 the land was quiet before him 9
52 the land was quiet before him. 9
12: 4 safe conduct to the land of Judah. 9
46 they returned to the land of Judah. 9
52 So they all reached the land of Judah safely 9
13: 1 invade the land of Judah and destroy it 9
12 with a large army to invade the land of Judah 9
22 He marched off and went into the land of Gilead. †
24 Trypho turned back and departed to his own land. 9
32 he brought great calamity upon the land. 9
14: 4 The land had rest all the days of Simon 9
8 They tilled their land in peace 9
11 He established peace in the land 9
13 No one was left in the land to fight them 9
15:10 Antiochus set out and invaded the land of his fathers 9
14 he pressed the city hard from land and sea 9
29 you have done great damage in the land 9
33 neither taken foreign land nor seized foreign property 9
35 great damage among the people and to our land 15
2Mc 1: 1 those in the land of Judea 15
7 the holy land and the kingdom 9
2:21 they seized the whole land 15
4:26 was driven as a fugitive into the land of Ammon. 15
5:21 he could sail on the land and walk on the sea 9
3Mc 6: 3 perishing as foreigners in a foreign land. 9
15 when they were in the land of their enemies 9
7:20 they had been brought safely by land and sea 9

land (2) 1. ἀναβαίνω 2. κατάγω 3. κατέρχομαι
Act 18:22 When he had landed at Caesare'a, he went up 3
21: 3 sailed to Syria, and landed at Tyre 3
1Mc 10: 1 landed and occupied Ptolemais 1
3Mc 7:19 when they had landed in peace 2

allotted land 1. גּוֹרָל
Ps 125: 3 not rest upon the land allotted to the righteous 1

land beyond 1. עֵבֶר 2. ὑπερέκεινα
Isa 9: 1 will make glorious . . the land beyond the Jordan 1
2Co 10:16 that we may preach the gospel in lands beyond you 2

common land 1. מִגְרָשׁ
Lev 25:34 fields of common land belonging to their cities 1
2Ch 11:14 left their common lands and their holdings 1
31:19 sons of Aaron . . in the fields of common land 1

desolate land 1. מְשׁוֹאָה
Job 38:27 to satisfy the waste and desolate land 1

dry land 1. חֲרָבָה 2. יַבָּשָׁה 3. יַבֶּשֶׁת 4. צִיָּה 5. *ξηρά*
Gen 1: 9 and let the dry land appear. 2
10 God called the dry land Earth 2
7:22 everything on the dry land in whose nostrils 1
Exd 14:21 and made the sea dry land, and the waters . . divided. 1
Neh 9:11 went through the midst of the sea on dry land; 2
Ps 66: 6 He turned the sea into dry land; 2
95: 5 for his hands formed the dry land. 3
Isa 35: 1 The wilderness and the dry land shall be glad 4
Jon 1: 9 God of heaven, who made the sea and the dry land. 2
2:10 it vomited out Jonah upon the dry land. 2
Hag 2: 6 heavens and the earth and the sea and the dry land; 1
Sir 39:22 His blessing covers the dry land like a river 5

fertile land 1. כַּרְמֶל
2Ch 26:10 in the hills and in the fertile lands 1

fruitful land 1. כַּרְמֶל
Isa 10:18 The glory of his forest and of his fruitful land 1
Jer 4:26 I looked, and lo, the fruitful land was a desert 1

garden land 1. כַּרְמֶל
Mic 7:14 alone in a forest in the midst of a garden land; 1

grazing land 1. נָוֶה
Ezk 34:14 there they shall lie down in good grazing land 1

native land 1. *πατρίς*
4Mc 1:11 their native land was purified through them. 1
4:20 at the very citadel of our native land 1

land of silence 1. דּוּמָה
Ps 94:17 soul . . soon have dwelt in the land of silence. 1

land on a border 1. *ὅριον*
1Mc 6:25 but also against all the lands on their borders. 1

open land 1. מִגְרָשׁ
Ezk 48:17 the city shall have open land 1

parched land 1. צְחִיחָה
Ps 68: 6 but the rebellious dwell in a parched land. 1

pasture land 1. מִגְרָשׁ
Num35: 2 the Levites pasture lands round about the cities 1
3 their pasture lands shall be for their cattle 1
4 pasture lands of the cities, which you shall give 1
5 belong to them as pasture land for their cities. 1
7 All the cities . . with their pasture lands. 1
Jos 14: 4 with their pasture lands for their cattle 1
21: 2 along with their pasture lands for our cattle. 1
3 Israel gave . . cities and pasture lands 1
8 cities and their pasture lands . . Israel gave 1
11 They gave . . along with the pasture lands 1
13 they gave Hebron . . with its pasture lands 1
13 they gave . . Libnah with its pasture lands 1
14 Jattir with its pasture lands, Eshtemo'a with its 1
14 Jattir with . . Eshtemo'a with its pasture lands 1
15 Holon with its pasture lands, Debir with its 1
15 Holon with its . . Debir with its pasture lands 1
16 A'in with its pasture lands, Juttah with its 1
16 A'in with its . . Juttah with its pasture lands 1
16 A'in with . . Beth-she'mesh with its pasture lands 1
17 Gibeon with its pasture lands, Geba with its 1
17 Gibeon with its . . Geba with its pasture lands 1
18 An'athoth with its pasture lands, and Almon 1
18 An'athoth . . and Almon with its pasture lands 1
19 thirteen cities with their pasture lands. 1
21 Shechem . . with its pasture lands in the hill 1
21 given Shechem . . Gezer with its pasture lands 1
22 Kib'za-im with its pasture lands, Beth-hor'on 1
22 Beth-hor'on with its pasture lands 1
23 El'teke with its pasture lands, Gib'bethon 1
23 El'teke . . Gib'bethon with its pasture lands 1
24 Ai'jalon with its pasture lands, Gath-rim'mon 1
24 Gath-rim'mon with its pasture lands 1
25 Ta'anach with its pasture lands, and Gath-rim'mon 1
25 and Gath-rim'mon with its pasture lands 1
26 cities . . ten in all with their pasture lands. 1
27 given . . Golan in Bashan with its pasture lands 1
27 and Beesh'terah with its pasture lands 1
28 of Is'sachar, Ki'shion with its pasture lands 1
28 Ki'shion with . . Dab'erath with its pasture lands 1
29 Jarmuth with its pasture lands, En-gan'nim 1
29 Jarmuth with . . En-gan'nim with its pasture lands 1
30 and out of . . Asher, Mishal with its pasture lands 1
30 Mishal with its . . Abdon with its pasture lands 1
31 Helkath with its pasture lands, and Rehob 1
31 Helkath with . . and Rehob with its pasture lands 1
32 Kedesh in Galilee with its pasture lands 1
32 Ham'moth-dor with its pasture lands 1
32 and Kartan with its pasture lands 1
33 in all thirteen cities with their pasture lands. 1
34 were given . . Jok'ne-am with its pasture lands 1
34 Jok'ne-am . . Kartah with its pasture lands 1
35 Dimnah with its pasture lands, Na'halal with its 1
35 Dimnah with . . Na'halal with its pasture lands 1
36 out of . . Reuben, Bezer with its pasture lands 1
36 Bezer with its . . Jahaz with its pasture lands 1
37 Ked'emoth with its pasture lands, and Meph'a-ath 1
37 and Meph'a-ath with its pasture lands 1
38 of Gad, Ramoth in Gilead with its pasture lands 1
38 Mehana'im with its pasture lands 1
39 Heshbon with its pasture lands, Jazer with its 1
39 Heshbon with its . . Jazer with its pasture lands 1
41 48 cities with their pasture lands. 1
42 cities had each its pasture lands round about it; 1
1Ch 5:16 in all the pasture lands of Sharon to their limits 1
6:55 Hebron . . and its surrounding pasture lands 1
57 Hebron, Libnah with its pasture lands, Jattir 1
57 Jattir, Eshtemo'a with its pasture lands 1
58 Hilen with its pasture lands 1
58 Debir with its pasture lands 1
59 Ashan with its pasture lands 1
59 Beth-she'mesh with its pasture lands; . 1
60 Geba with its pasture lands, Al'emeth 1
60 Geba . . Al'emeth with its pasture lands 1
60 Al'emeth . . An'athoth with its pasture lands. 1
64 gave . . the cities with their pasture lands. 1
67 cities of refuge: Shechem with its pasture lands 1
67 of refuge . . Gezer with its pasture lands 1
68 Jok'me-am with its pasture lands 1
68 Beth-hor'on with its pasture lands 1
69 Ai'jalon with its pasture lands 1
69 Gath-rim'mon with its pasture lands 1
70 Aner with its pasture lands, and Bil'e-am 1
70 Aner . . and Bil'e-am with its pasture lands 1
71 given . . Golan in Bashan with its pasture lands 1
71 were given . . Ash'taroth with its pasture lands; 1
72 tribe of Is'sachar: Kedesh with its pasture lands 1
72 of Is'sachar . . Dab'erath with its pasture lands 1
73 Ramoth with its pasture lands, and Anem 1
73 Ramoth . . and Anem with its pasture lands; 1
74 out of . . Asher: Mashal with its pasture lands 1
74 out of . . Asher . . Abdon with its pasture lands 1
75 Hukok with its pasture lands, and Rehob 1
75 Hukok . . and Rehob with its pasture lands; 1
76 Kedesh in Galilee with its pasture lands 1
76 Ham'mon with its pasture lands, and Kiria-tha'im 1
76 and Kiria-tha'im with its pasture lands. 1
77 of Zeb'ulun: Rim'mono with its pasture lands 1
77 of Zeb'ulun . . Tabor with its pasture lands 1
78 Bezer in the steppe with its pasture lands 1
78 Jahzah with its pasture lands 1
79 Ked'emoth with its pasture lands, and Meph'a-ath 1
79 and Meph'a-ath with its pasture lands; 1
80 Ramoth in Gilead with its pasture lands 1
80 Mahana'im with its pasture lands 1
81 Heshbon with its pasture lands, and Jazer 1
81 Heshbon . . and Jazer with its pasture lands. 1
13: 2 in the cities that have pasture lands 1

salt land 1. מְלֵחָה
Job 39: 6 and the salt land for his dwelling place? 1
Jer 17: 6 He shall dwell . . in an uninhabited salt land. 1

strange land 1. *ξένος*
2Mc 9:28 among the mountains in a strange land. 1

landing 1. מִפְרָץ
Jdg 5:17 Asher sat . . settling down by his landings. 1

landmark 1. גְּבוּל 2. גְּבוּלָה
Deu 19:14 shall not remove your neighbor's landmark 1
27:17 'Cursed . . who removes his neighbor's landmark.' 1
Job 24: 2 Men remove landmarks; they seize flocks 2
Prv 22:28 Remove not the ancient landmark 1
23:10 Do not remove an ancient landmark or enter 1
Hos 5:10 have become like those who remove the landmark; 1

lane 1. *ῥύμη*
Lke 14:21 Go out quickly to the streets and lanes of the city 1
Tob 13:18 all her lanes will cry 'Hallelujah!' 1

language 1. לָשׁוֹן 2. שָׂפָה 3. לְשָׁן (A) 4. *γλῶσσα* 5. *διάλεκτος* 6. *φωνή*
Gen 10: 5 each with his own language 1
20 by their families, their languages 1
31 by their families, their languages, their lands 1
11: 1 the whole earth had one language and few words. 2
6 and they have all one language; 2
7 there confuse their language 2
9 because there the LORD confused the language 2
Deu 28:49 nation whose language you do not understand 1
2Kg 18:26 speak to your servants in the Aramaic language *
Neh 13:24 half . . spoke the language of Ashdod *
24 they could not speak the language of Judah *
24 Judah, but the language of each people. 1
Est 1:22 sent . . to every people in its own language 1
22 speak according to the language of his people. 1
3:12 to . . every people in its own language; 1
8: 9 an edict . . to every people in its own language 1
9 to the Jews in their script and their language. 1
Isa 19:18 cities . . which speak the language of Canaan 2
Jer 5:15 a nation whose language you do not know 1
Ezk 3: 5 a people of foreign speech and a hard language 1
6 peoples of foreign speech and a hard language 1
Dan 3: 4 commanded, O peoples, nations, and languages 3
7 all the peoples, nations, and languages fell down 3
29 Any people, nation, or language that speaks 3
4: 1 King . . to all peoples, nations, and languages 3
5:19 all peoples, nations, and languages trembled 3
6:25 wrote to all the peoples, nations, and languages 3
7:14 all peoples, nations, and languages should serve 3
Act 1:19 the field was called in their language Akel'dama 5
2: 6 each one heard them speaking in his own language. 5
8 each of us in his own native language? 5
21:40 he spoke to them in the Hebrew language, saying 5
22: 2 he addressed them in the Hebrew language 5
26:14 heard a voice saying to me in the Hebrew language 5
1Co 14:10 There are doubtless many different languages 6
11 if I do not know the meaning of the language 6
Sir 0: 2 when translated into another language 4
2Mc 7: 8 He replied in the language of his fathers 6
21 the language of their fathers 6
12:37 In the language of their fathers 6
15:29 in the language of their fathers. 6
36 which is called Adar in the Syrian language 6
4Mc 12: 7 exhorted him in the Hebrew language 6
16:15 said to your sons in the Hebrew language 6

strange language 1. לעז 2. *ἀλλόγλωσσος*
Ps 114: 1 house of Jacob from a people of strange language 1
Bar 4:15 a shameless nation, of a strange language 2

languish 1. אמל 2. אֻמְלַל 3. דאב 4. דְּאָבוֹן 5. כלה 6. לאה 7. להה
Gen 47:13 Canaan languished by reason of the famine. 7
Deu 28:65 LORD will give you there . . a languishing soul; 4
Ps 6: 2 Be gracious to me, O LORD, for I am languishing; 2
68: 9 thou didst restore thy heritage as it languished; 6
119:81 My soul languishes for thy salvation; 5
Isa 16: 8 For the fields of Heshbon languish 1
19: 8 they . . languish who spread nets upon the water. 1
24: 4 the world languishes and withers; 1
4 the heavens languish together with the earth. 1
7 The wine mourns, the vine languishes 1
33: 9 The land mourns and languishes; 1
Jer 14: 2 Judah mourns and her gates languish; 1
15: 9 She who bore seven has languished; 1
31:12 and they shall languish no more. 3
25 and every languishing soul I will replenish. 3
Lam 2: 8 rampart and wall . . they languish together. 1
Hos 4: 3 the land mourns, and all who dwell in it languish 1
Jol 1:10 the wine fails, the oil languishes. 1
12 The vine withers, the fig tree languishes. 1

lantern 1. *φανός*
Joh 18: 3 went there with lanterns and torches 1

lap 1. בֶּגֶד 2. בֶּרֶךְ 3. חֵיק 4. חֹצֶן 5. *κόλπος*
2Kg 4:20 to his mother, the child sat on her lap till noon 2
39 and gathered from it his lap full of wild gourds 1
Neh 5:13 I also shook out my lap and said, "So may God shake 4
Prv 16:33 The lot is cast into the lap 3
Lke 6:38 good measure . . will be put into your lap 5

lap (2) 1. לקק
Jdg 7: 5 Every one that laps the water with his tongue 1
5 that laps the water with his tongue, as a dog laps 1
6 of those that lapped, putting their hands 1
7 With the 300 men that lapped I will deliver 1

lapse 1. *χρόνος*
2Mc 10: 3 they offered sacrifices, after a lapse of two years 1

large 1. גָּדוֹל 2. רַב 3. רבה 4. רחב 5. רָחָב 6. רַחֲבַת יָדַיִם 7. *βαρύς* 8. *δαψιλής* 9. *ἱκανός* 10. *μέγας* 11. *πηλίκος* 12. *πλῆθος* 13. *πολύς* 14. magnus
Gen 29: 2 The stone on the well's mouth was large 1
30:43 exceedingly rich, and had large flocks 2
34:21 for behold, the land is large enough for them; 6
Num13:28 cities are fortified and very large; and besides 1
26:54 a large tribe you shall give a large inheritance 2
56 divided . . between the larger and the smaller. 2
33:54 a large tribe you shall give a large inheritance 2
54 a large tribe you shall give a large inheritance 3
35: 8 from the larger tribes you shall take many 2
Deu 20: 1 see . . an army larger than your own 2
25:13 not . . two kinds of weights, a large and a small. 1
14 not . . two kinds of measures, a large and a small. 1
27: 2 set up large stones, and plaster them with plaster; 1
Jos 19: 9 the portion of . . Judah was too large for them 2
1Kg 10:16 King Solomon made 200 large shields of beaten gold; *
2Ch 26:10 he had large herds, both in the Shephe'lah 2
Neh 7: 4 city was wide and large, but the people within it 4
9:35 did not serve thee . . in the large and rich land 5
13: 5 prepared for Tobi'ah a large chamber 1
Isa 5: 9 houses shall be desolate, large and beautiful 1
8: 1 Take a large tablet and write upon it 1
30:23 your cattle will graze in large pastures; 4
Jer 41: 9 was the large cistern which King Asa had made 10
43: 9 Take in your hands large stones, and hide them 1

Ezk 17:15 that they might give him horses and a large army. 2
23:32 your sister's cup which is deep and large; 5
43:14 and from the smaller ledge to the larger ledge 1
Mat 19: 2 large crowds followed him, and he healed them 13
26: 9 this ointment might have been sold for a large sum 13
Mrk 4:32 and puts forth large branches 10
14:15 he will show you a large upper room 10
16: 4 the stone was rolled back; –it was very large. 10
Lke 5:29 was a large company of tax collectors and others 13
7:12 a large crowd from the city was with her. 9
8:32 Now a large herd of swine was feeding there 9
22:12 he will show you a large upper room furnished; 10
Joh 21:11 hauled the net ashore, full of large fish, 153 10
Act 11:24 a large company was added to the Lord. 9
26 and taught a large company of people 9
22:28 I bought this citizenship for a large sum. 13
Gal 6:11 See with what large letters I am writing to you 11
2Es 11: 4 the middle head was larger than the other heads 14
12:26 your seeing that the large head disappeared 14
Tob 7: 8 and set large servings of food before them. 13
Jdt 5: 3 How large is their army 12
Sir 51:28 Get instruction with a large sum of silver 13
1Mc 1:17 with a large fleet. 10
29 he came to Jerusalem with a large force. 7
3:10 a large force from Samaria 10
31 raise a large fund. 10
5:26 – all these cities were strong and large– 10
30 behold, a large company, that could not be counted 13
38 it is a very large force. 13
45 a very large company 10
46 This was a large and very strong city on the road 10
52 they crossed the Jordan into the large plain 10
6:41 the army was very large and strong. 10
7:10 came with a large force into the land of Judah 13
11 they saw that they had come with a large force. 13
27 So Nicanor came to Jerusalem with a large force 13
8: 6 with cavalry and chariots and a very large army. 13
9:37 from Nadabath with a large escort. 10
43 he came with a large force on the sabbath day 13
60 He started to come with a large force 13
10: 2 he assembled a very large army 13
48 Now Alexander the king assembled large forces 10
66 he assembled a large force 10
77 3,000 cavalry and a large army 10
11:63 had come to Kadesh in Galilee with a large army 13
12:24 with a larger force than before 13
42 Trypho saw that he had come with a large army 13
13: 1 Trypho had assembled a large army 13
12 with a large army to invade the land of Judah 13
14:24 sent Numenius to Rome with a large gold shield 10
16: 5 behold, a large force of infantry and horsemen 13
2Mc 1:31 the liquid . . be poured upon large stones. 10
3Mc 5: 2 large handfuls of frankincense 8

large *See also* grow.

large one 1. *μέγας*
Lke 12:18 I will pull down my barns, and build larger ones; 1

very large 1. *πολύς*
Mrk 4: 1 a very large crowd gathered about him 1

largeness 1. רֹחַב
1Kg 4:29 God gave Solomon . . and largeness of mind like 1

lash 1. *μαστίζω*
2Co 11:24 I have received . . the 40 lashes less one. *
Wis 5:11 lashed by the beat of its pinions 1

lashing 1. *μάστιξ*
Sir 26: 6 a tongue-lashing makes it known to all. 1

last 1. אַחַר 2. אַחֲרוֹן 3. אַחֲרִית 4. יֶתֶר 5. מֶרְחָק 6. נֶפֶשׁ 7. פַּעַם 8. תמם 9. עַד אָחֳרֵין (A) 10. *εἰς τέλος* 11. *ἔσχατος* 12. *λοιπός* 13. *οὐραγέω* 14. *ποτέ* 15. *τελευταῖος* 16. *τέλος* 17. *ὑπόλειμμα* 18. *ὕστερος* 19. novus
Gen 2:23 the man said, "This at last is bone of my bones 7
33: 2 children, and Rachel and Joseph last of all. 2
7 and last Joseph and Rachel drew near 1
Num 2:31 They shall set out last, standard by standard. 2
14:33 until the last of your dead bodies lies 8
Deu 28:54 grudge food . . to the last of the children 4
Rut 3:10 you have made this last kindness greater 2
2Sm 15:17 and they halted at the last house. 5
19:11 Why should you be the last to bring the king back 2
12 should you be the last to bring back the king?' 2
23: 1 Now these are the last words of David 2
1Ch 23:27 for by the last words of David these were 2
29:29 acts of King David, from first to last, are written 2
2Ch 9:29 the acts of Solomon, from the first to last 2
12:15 Now the acts of Rehobo'am, from first to last 2
16:11 The acts of Asa, from first to last, are written 2
20:34 rest of the acts . . from first to last 2
25:26 rest of the deeds of Amazi'ah, from first to last 2
26:22 the rest of the acts of Uzzi'ah, from first to last 2
28:26 his acts and all his ways, from first to last 2
35:27 his acts, first and last, behold, they are written 2
Neh 8:18 day by day, from the first day to the last day 2
Job 11:20 their hope is to breathe their last. 6
19:25 at last he will stand upon the earth; 2
Ps 68:25 the singers in front, the minstrels last 1
Prv 23:32 At the last it bites like a serpent 3
Isa 41: 4 I, the LORD, the first, and with the last; I am He. 2
44: 6 I am the first and I am the last; 2
48:12 I called! I am He, I am the first, and I am the last. 2
Jer 50:12 Lo, she shall be the last of the nations 3
17 now at last Nebuchadrez'zar king of Babylon 2
Dan 4: 8 At last Daniel came in before me 9
8: 3 higher one came up last. 2
Ams 4: 2 with hooks, even the last of you with fishhooks. 3
Mat 5:26 get out till you have paid the last penny. 11
19:30 many that are first will be last 11
30 first will be last, and the last first. 11
20: 8 beginning with the last, up to the first.' 11
12 saying, 'These last worked only one hour 11
14 I choose to give to this last as I give to you. 11
16 the last will be first, and the first last. 11
16 the last will be first, and the first last. 11
26:60 At last two came forward 18
27:64 the last fraud will be worse than the first. 11
Mrk 9:35 If any one would be first, he must be last of all 11
10:31 many that are first will be last 11
31 first will be last, and the last first. 11
12:22 Last of all the woman also died. 11
Lke 11:26 the last state of that man becomes worse 11
12:59 till you have paid the very last copper. 11
13:30 behold, some are last who will be first 11
30 some are first who will be last. 11
Joh 6:39 but raise it up at the last day. 11
40 I will raise him up at the last day. 11
44 I will raise him up at the last day. 11
54 I will raise him up at the last day. 11
7:37 On the last day of the feast, the great day 11
11:24 rise again in the resurrection at the last day. 11
12:48 will be his judge on the last day. 11
Act 2:17 in the last days it shall be, God declares 11
27:20 hope of our being saved was at last abandoned. 12
Rom 1:10 I may now at last succeed in coming to you. 14
1Co 4: 9 God has exhibited us apostles as last of all 11
15: 8 Last of all, as to one untimely born 11
26 The last enemy to be destroyed is death. 11
45 the last Adam became a life-giving spirit. 11
52 at the last trumpet. For the trumpet will sound 11
1Th 2:16 God's wrath has come upon them at last! 10
2Ti 3: 1 in the last days there will come times of stress. 11
Heb 1: 2 in these last days he has spoken to us by a Son 11
Jas 5: 3 You have laid up treasure for the last days. 11
1Pe 1: 5 salvation ready to be revealed in the last time. 11
2Pe 3: 3 scoffers will come in the last days 11
1Jn 2:18 Children, it is the last hour; 11
18 therefore we know that it is the last hour. 11
Jde 1:18 In the last time there will be scoffers 11
Rev 1:17 saying, "Fear not, I am the first and the last 11
2: 8 The words of the first and the last 11
15: 1 angels with seven plagues, which are the last 11
21: 9 the seven bowls full of the seven last plagues 11
22:13 I am the Alpha and the Omega, the first and the last 11
2Es 5:42 just as for those who are last 19
6:34 lest you be hasty concerning the last times.' 19
7:73 how will they answer in the last times? 19
77 it will not be shown to you until the last times. 19
84 torment laid up for themselves in the last days. 19
87 they are to be judged in the last times. 19
95 and the glory which awaits them in the last days. 19
116I answered and said, "This is my first and last word 19
8:50 those who inhabit the world in the last times 19
63 the signs which thou wilt do in the last times 19
10:59 to those who dwell on earth in the last days 19
11: 9 let the heads be reserved for the last. 19
12: 9 and the last events of the times. 19
23 In its last days the Most High will raise up 19
25 and perform his last actions. 19
28 he also shall fall by the sword in the last days. 19
13:18 what is reserved for the last days 19
20 and not to see what shall happen in the last days. 19
46 Then they dwelt there until the last times 19
14:22 those who wish to live in the last days may live. 19
46 but keep the 70 that were written last 19
Sir 6:28 For at last you will find the rest she gives 11
12:12 at last you will realize the truth of my words 11
32:11 Leave in good time and do not be the last 13
33:16 I was the last on watch 11
51:14 I will search for her to the last. 11
1Mc 6:53 had consumed the last of the stores. 17
2Mc 3:31 one who was lying quite at his last breath. 11
5: 5 at last the city was being taken 16
7: 9 when he was at his last breath, he said 11
41 Last of all, the mother died, after her sons. 11
3Mc 5:49 thought that this was their last moment of life 18
49 who were drawing their last milk. 15

last (2) 1. אמן 2. היה 3. נשג 4. עמד 5. *γίνομαι* 6. *διὰ παντός* 7. *εἰς τὸν αἰῶνα* 8. *ἐπὶ πολύ* 9. *μένω* 10. spatium habeo
Lev 26: 5 your threshing shall last to the time of vintage 3
5 the vintage shall last to the time for sowing 3
Deu 28:59 afflictions severe and lasting, and sicknesses 1
59 bring . . sicknesses grievous and lasting. 1
Jdg 14:17 wept . . the seven days that their feast lasted; 2
Est 1: 5 the king gave . . a banquet lasting for seven days *
Ps 81:15 their fate would last for ever. 2
Prv 27:24 for riches do not last for ever; *
Jer 32:14 in a . . vessel, that they may last for a long time. 4
Heb 13:14 For here we have no lasting city 9
2Es 7:43 For it will last for about a week of years. 10
Tob 8:19 a wedding feast . . which lasted fourteen days. *
Jdt 13: 1 because the banquet had lasted long. 5
AEs 13: 2 to settle . . in lasting tranquillity 6
Sir 11:17 what he approves will have lasting success. 7
33 lest he give you a lasting blemish. 7
22:12 Mourning for the dead lasts seven days *
12 for a fool or an ungodly man it lasts all his life. *
49:13 The memory of Nehemiah also is lasting 8

last man 1. קָצֶה
Gen 19: 4 all the people to the last man 1

last one 1. *ἔσχατος*
1Es 8:39 Of the sons of Adonikam, the last ones 1
Sir 24:28 the last one has not fathomed her; 1

last thing 1. *ἔσχατος*
Sir 48:24 By the spirit of might he saw the last things 1

very last 1. תמם
Jos 8:24 and all of them to the very last had fallen 1

latch 1. חֹר
Sng 5: 4 My beloved put his hand to the latch 1

late 1. אַחֲרוֹן 2. אָפִיל 3. יוֹם מָחָר 4. מִן 5. מִקְּרֹב 6. *ἀκόλουθος* 7. *ἐν* 8. *μετά* 9. *μετὰ ταῦτα* 10. *μετὰ ὕστερον* 11. *μετὰ χρόνον* 12. *μετέπειτα* 13. *ὄψιμος* 14. *ὄψιος* 15. *πολύς* 16. *ὕστερος* 17. *ὥρα πολλή*
Gen 30:33 my honesty will answer for me later, when you 3
38:24 About three months later Judah was told 4
Exd 9:32 for they are late in coming up.) 2
Deu 32:17 sacrificed to . . new gods that had come in of late 5
1Sm 25:38 And about ten days later the LORD smote Nabal; *
2Sm 11: 2 It happened, late one afternoon . . that he saw *
Ezr 8:13 Of the sons of Adoni'kam, those who came later 1
Mrk 6:35 when it grew late, his disciples came to him 17
35 This is a lonely place, and the hour is now late; 15
11:11 as it was already late 14
Lke 15:13 Not many days later, the younger son gathered all 8
22:58 a little later some one else saw him and said 8
Joh 20:26 Eight days later 8
1Ti 4: 1 in later times some will depart from the faith 16
Heb 4: 8 God would not speak later of another day. 9
12:11 later it yields the . . fruit of righteousness 16
Jas 5: 7 until it receives the early and the late rain 13
Sir 27:23 later he will twist his speech 16
1Mc 1:29 Two years later the king sent to the cities 8
11:18 But King Ptolemy died three days later 7
2Mc 4:17 a fact which later events will make clear. 6
8:25 obliged to return because the hour was late. *
14: 1 Three years later, word came to Judas and his men 11
3Mc 1: 3 a Jew by birth who later changed his religion 16
3:24 a sudden disorder should later arise against us 12
4Mc 12: 7 as we shall tell a little later 10

lately 1. *προσφάτως*
Act 18: 2 lately come from Italy with his wife Priscilla 1

later than 1. *μετά*
Heb 7:28 the word of the oath, which came later than the law 1

later thing 1. אַחֲרוֹן
Ecc 1:11 nor . . any remembrance of later things 1

latrine 1. מוֹצָאָה
2Kg 10:27 house of Ba'al, and made it a latrine to this day. 1

latter 1. אַחֲרוֹן 2. אַחֲרִית 3. אַחֲרִית (A) 4. *ἔσχατος* 5. *ἕτερος* 6. *μέν* 7. *ὁ δέ*
Exd 4: 8 the first sign, they may believe the latter sign. 1
Num24:14 people will do to your people in the latter days. 2
Deu 4:30 all these things come upon you in the latter days 2
24: 3 latter husband dislikes her and writes her 1
3 the latter husband dies, who took her to be his wife 1
Job 8: 7 your latter days will be very great. 2
Isa 2: 2 It shall come to pass in the latter days 2
9: 1 in the latter time he will make glorious the way 1
Jer 23:20 In the latter days you will understand it 2
30:24 In the latter days you will understand this. 2
48:47 restore the fortunes of Moab in the latter days 2
49:39 in the latter days I will restore the fortunes 2
Ezk 38: 8 in the latter years you will go against the land 2
16 In the latter days I will bring you 2
Dan 2:28 made known . . what will be in the latter days. 3
10:14 what is to befall your people in the latter days. 2
11: 9 latter shall come into the realm of the king *
Hos 3: 5 come . . to his goodness in the latter days. 2

Mic 4: 1 It shall come to pass in the latter days 2
Hag 2: 9 latter splendor of this house shall be greater 1
Php 1:16 The latter do it out of love 6
Rev 2:19 and that your latter works exceed the first. 4
Wis 19:16 the latter . . afflicted with . . sufferings 7
1Mc 11:34 the latter . . were added to Judea from Samaria. *
2Mc 14:31 When the latter became aware that . . 5

lattice 1. אֶשְׁנָב 2. חֲרַכִּים 3. שְׂבָכָה

Jdg 5:28 the mother of Sis'era gazed through the lattice 1
2Kg 1: 2 Ahazi'ah fell through the lattice 3
Prv 7: 6 I have looked out through my lattice 1
Sng 2: 9 gazing in . . looking through the lattice. 2

laud 1. שבח

Ps 145: 4 One generation shall laud thy works to another 1

laugh 1. לָבוּז 2. לעג 3. צחק 4. שחק 5. γελάω 6. γέλως 7. ἐπιγελάω 8. καταγελάω 9. συγγελάω

Gen 17:17 Then Abraham fell on his face and laughed 3
18:12 Sarah laughed to herself, saying 3
13 LORD said to Abraham, "Why did Sarah laugh, 3
15 I did not laugh"; for she was afraid. 3
15 she was afraid. He said, "No, but you did laugh. 3
21: 6 every one who hears will laugh over me. 3
38:23 keep the things as her own, lest we be laughed at; 1
Job 5:22 At destruction and famine you shall laugh 4
39:18 she laughs at the horse and his rider. 4
22 He laughs at fear, and is not dismayed; 4
41:29 he laughs at the rattle of javelins. 4
Ps 2: 4 He who sits in the heavens laughs; 4
37:13 the LORD laughs at the wicked 4
52: 6 see, and fear, and shall laugh at him, saying 4
59: 8 But thou, O LORD, dost laugh at them; 4
80: 6 our enemies laugh among themselves. 2
Prv 1:26 I also will laugh at your calamity; 4
29: 9 fool only rages and laughs, and there is no quiet. 4
31:25 she laughs at the time to come. 4
Ecc 3: 4 a time to weep, and a time to laugh; 4
Ezk 23:32 you shall be laughed at and held in derision 3
Hab 1:10 They laugh at every fortress 4
Mat 9:24 And they laughed at him. 8
Mrk 5:40 And they laughed at him. 8
Lke 6:21 Blessed are you that weep now, for you shall laugh. 5
25 Woe to you that laugh now, for you shall mourn 5
8:53 they laughed at him, knowing that she was dead. 8
1Es 4:31 If she smiles at him, he laughs 5
Tob 2: 8 my neighbors laughed at me and said 7
Jdt 12:12 if we do not embrace her she will laugh at us. 8
Sir 21:20 A fool raises his voice when he laughs 6
30:10 Do not laugh with him 9
Bel 1: 7 Then Daniel laughed, and said, "Do not be deceived 5
19 Then Daniel laughed 5
4Mc 5:28 you shall have no such occasion to laugh at me 5

laugh to scorn 1. לעג 2. שחק 3. ἐκγελάω

2Ch 30:10 but they laughed them to scorn, and mocked them. 2
Job 22:19 the innocent laugh them to scorn 1
Wis 4:18 the Lord will laugh them to scorn 3

laughing stock 1. καταγελάω

4Mc 6:20 and during that time be a laughing stock to all 1

laughingstock 1. שְׂחֹק 2. ἐπίχαρμα 3. κατάγελως

Job 12: 4 I am a laughingstock to my friends; 1
4 me, a just and blameless man, am a laughingstock. 1
Ps 44:14 made us . . a laughingstock among the peoples. †
Jer 20: 7 I have become a laughingstock all the day; 1
Lam 3:14 I have become the laughingstock of all peoples 1
Sir 6: 4 make him the laughingstock of his enemies. 2
18:31 make you the laughingstock of your enemies. 2
42:11 lest she make you a laughingstock 2
1Mc 10:70 I have become a laughingstock and reproach 3

laughter 1. צחק 2. שְׂחֹק 3. γέλως

Gen 21: 6 Sarah said, "God has made laughter for me; 1
Job 8:21 He will yet fill your mouth with laughter 2
Ps 126: 2 Then our mouth was filled with laughter 2
Prv 14:13 Even in laughter the heart is sad 2
Ecc 2: 2 I said of laughter, "It is mad 2
7: 3 Sorrow is better than laughter 2
6 as the crackling . . so is the laughter of the fools; 2
10:19 Bread is made for laughter, and wine gladdens 2
Jas 4: 9 Let your laughter be turned to mourning 3
Sir 19:30 A man's attire and open-mouthed laughter 3
27:13 their laughter is wantonly sinful. 3

launch 1. κατάρχω 2. mitto

2Es 9:34 what was sown or what was launched 2
2Mc 4:40 launched an unjust attack 1

laver 1. כִּיּוֹר

Exd 30:18 You shall also make a laver of bronze 1
28 all its utensils and the laver and its base; 1
31: 9 laver and its base 1
35:16 all its utensils, the laver and its base; 1
38: 8 he made the laver of bronze and its base of bronze 1
39:39 all its utensils; the laver and its base; 1
40: 7 place the laver between the tent of meeting 1
11 You shall also anoint the laver and its base 1
30 he set the laver between the tent of meeting 1
Lev 8:11 the laver and its base, to consecrate them 1
1Kg 7:30 at the four corners were supports for a laver. 1
38 he made ten lavers of bronze; each laver held 1
38 he made ten lavers . . each laver held 40 baths 1
38 each laver measured four cubits 1
38 and there was a laver for each of the ten stands. 1
43 the ten stands, and the ten lavers upon the stands; 1
2Kg 16:17 Ahaz cut off the frames . . and removed the laver 1
2Ch 4: 6 He also made ten lavers in which to wash 1
14 stands also, and the lavers upon the stands 1

lavish 1. זול 2. רב 3. רבה 4. שפך 5. ἄφθονος 6. περισσεύω

Est 1: 7 wine was lavished according to the bounty 2
Isa 46: 6 Those who lavish gold from the purse 1
Ezk 16:15 and lavished your harlotries on any passer-by. 4
Hos 2: 8 and who lavished upon her silver and gold 3
Eph 1: 8 which he lavished upon us. 6
3Mc 5: 2 maddened by the lavish abundance of liquor 5

lavishly 1. μεγαλομερῶς

3Mc 6:33 king . . gave thanks to heaven unceasingly and lavishly 1

law 1. דָּת 2. מִשְׁפָּט 3. תּוֹרָה 4. דָּת (A) 5. δικαίωμα 6. κρίσις 7. νομικός 8. νόμιμος 9. νομοθεσία 10. νόμος 11. πρόσταγμα 12. lex

Gen 26: 5 Abraham obeyed . . my statutes, and my laws. 3
Exd 12:49 There shall be one law for the native 3
13: 9 that the law of the LORD may be in your mouth; 3
16: 4 I may prove them, whether they will walk in my law 3
28 refuse to keep my commandments and my laws? 3
24:12 tables of stone, with the law and the commandment 3
Lev 6: 9 This is the law of the burnt offering 3
14 this is the law of the cereal offering 3
25 This is the law for the sin offering 3
7: 1 This is the law of the guilt offering 3
7 like the sin offering, there is one law for them 3
11 this is the law of the sacrifice of peace 3
37 This is the law of the burnt offering 3
11:46 This is the law pertaining to beast and bird 3
12: 7 This is the law for her who bears a child 3
13:59 This is the law for a leprous disease in a garment 3
14: 2 This shall be the law of the leper for the day 3
32 This is the law for him in whom is a leprous 3
54 This is the law for any leprous disease 3
57 This is the law for leprosy 3
15: 3 this is the law of his uncleanness *
32 This is the law for him who has a discharge 3
24:22 have one law for the sojourner and for the native 2
26:46 These are the statutes and ordinances and laws 3
Num 5:29 This is the law in cases of jealousy, when a wife 3
30 the priest shall execute upon her all this law. 3
6:13 this is the law for the Nazirite 3
21 This is the law for the Nazirite who takes a vow. 3
21 according to the law for his separation 3
15:16 One law and one ordinance shall be for you 3
29 one law for him who does anything unwittingly 3
19: 2 statute of the law which the LORD has commanded 3
14 This is the law when a man dies in a tent 3
31:21 This is the statute of the law which the LORD 3
Deu 1: 5 Moses undertook to explain this law, saying 3
4: 8 righteous as all this law which I set before you 3
44 This is the law which Moses set before . . Israel; 3
17:18 write for himself in a book a copy of this law 3
19 fear the LORD . . keeping all the words of this law 3
27: 3 shall write upon them all the words of this law 3
8 write upon the stones all the words of this law 3
26 not confirm the words of this law by doing them.' 3
28:58 If . . not careful to do all the words of this law 3
61 which is not recorded in the book of this law 3
29:21 curses of the covenant written in this . . law. 3
29 that we may do all the words of this law. 3
30:10 keep . . which are written in this book of the law 3
31: 9 Moses wrote this law, and gave it to the priests 3
11 read this law before all Israel in their hearing. 3
12 may . . be careful to do all the words of this law 3
24 finished writing the words of this law in a book 3
26 Take this book of the law, and put it by the side 3
32:46 may be careful to do all the words of this law. 3
33: 4 when Moses commanded us a law, as a possession 3
10 They shall teach . . Israel thy law; 3
Jos 1: 7 to all the law which Moses my servant commanded 3
8 book of the law shall not depart out of your mouth 3
8:31 as it is written in the book of the law of Moses 3
32 he wrote upon the stones a copy of the law of Moses 3
34 all the words of the law, the blessing and . . curse 3
34 to all that is written in the book of the law. 3
22: 5 observe the commandment and the law which Moses 3
23: 6 all that is written in the book of the law of Moses 3
24:26 Joshua wrote these . . in the book of the law of God; 3
1Kg 2: 3 the charge . . as it is written in the law of Moses 3
2Kg 10:31 Jehu was not careful to walk in the law of the LORD 3
14: 6 what is written in the book of the law of Moses 3
17:13 in accordance with all the law which I commanded 3
26 do not know the law of the god of the land; 2
26 they do not know the law of the god of the land. 2
27 and teach them the law of the god of the land. 2
34 follow the statutes or the ordinances or the law 3
37 and the law and the commandment which he wrote 3
21: 8 all the law that my servant Moses commanded 3
22: 8 I have found the book of the law in the house 3
11 the king heard the words of the book of the law 3
23:24 that he might establish the words of the law 3
25 who turned . . according to all the law of Moses; 3
1Ch 16:40 all that is written in the law of the LORD 3
22:12 over Israel you may keep the law of the LORD 3
2Ch 6:16 heed to their way, to walk in my law as you have 3
12: 1 he forsook the law of the LORD, and all Israel 3
14: 4 to keep the law and the commandment. 3
15: 3 For a long time Israel was . . without law; 3
17: 9 taught . . having the book of the law of the LORD 3
19:10 concerning bloodshed, law or commandment 3
23:18 as it is written in the law of Moses 3
25: 4 according to what is written in the law 3
30:16 accustomed posts according to the law of Moses 3
31: 3 as it is written in the law of the LORD. 3
4 might give themselves to the law of the LORD. 3
21 in accordance with the law and the commandments 3
33: 8 do all that I have commanded them, all the law 3
34:14 Hilki'ah . . found the book of the law of the LORD 3
15 found the book of the law in the house of the LORD"; 3
19 When the king heard the words of the law 3
35:26 what is written in the law of the LORD 3
Ezr 3: 2 as it is written in the law of Moses the man of God. 3
7: 6 Ezra . . was a scribe skilled in the law of Moses 3
10 Ezra had set his heart to study the law of the LORD 3
12 Ezra . . scribe of the law of the God of heaven. 4
14 according to the law of your God 4
21 Ezra . . scribe of the law of the God of heaven 4
25 all such as know the laws of your God; 4
26 not obey the law of your God and the law of the king 4
26 not obey the law of your God and the law of the king 4
10: 3 let it be done according to the law. 3
Neh 8: 1 Ezra . . to bring the book of the law of Moses 3
2 Ezra . . brought the law before the assembly 3
3 ears of all . . were attentive to the book of the law. 3
7 helped the people to understand the law 3
8 read from the book, from the law of God, clearly 3
9 people wept when they heard the words of the law. 3
13 came . . in order to study the words of the law. 3
14 found it written in the law that the LORD 3
18 by day . . he read from the book of the law of God. 3
9: 3 read from the book of the law of the LORD their God 3
13 give them right ordinances and true laws 3
14 commandments and statutes and a law by Moses 3
26 rebelled . . and cast thy law behind their back 3
29 warn them in order to turn them back to thy law. 3
34 not kept thy law or heeded thy commandments 3
10:28 separated themselves . . to the law of God 3
29 enter into a curse and an oath to walk in God's law 3
34 burn upon the altar . . as it is written in the law. 3
36 first-born . . as it is written in the law 3
12:44 gather . . portions required by the law 3
13: 3 When the people heard the law, they separated 3
Est 1: 8 And drinking was according to the law 1
13 toward all who were versed in law and judgment 1
15 According to the law, what is to be done 1
19 let it be written among the laws of the Persians 1
3: 8 their laws are different from . . other people 1
8 and they do not keep the king's laws 1
4:11 if any man or woman goes . . there is but one law; 1
16 I will go to the king, though it is against the law; 1
Ps 1: 2 his delight is in the law of the LORD 3
2 on his law he meditates day and night. 3
19: 7 The law of the LORD is perfect, reviving the soul; 3
37:31 The law of his God is in his heart; 3
40: 8 O my God; thy law is within my heart. 3
55:19 because they keep no law, and do not fear God. †
78: 5 testimony in Jacob, and appointed a law in Israel 3
10 but refused to walk according to his law. 3
89:30 If his children forsake my law 3
94:12 O LORD, and whom thou dost teach out of thy law 3
105:45 to the end that they should . . observe his laws. 3
119: 1 Blessed are those . . who walk in the law of the LORD! 3
18 that I may behold wondrous things out of thy law. 3
29 graciously teach me thy law! 3
34 Give me understanding, that I may keep thy law 3
44 I will keep thy law continually, for ever and ever; 3
51 I do not turn away from thy law. 3
53 because of the wicked, who forsake thy law. 3
55 I remember thy name . . O LORD, and keep thy law. 3
61 the wicked ensnare me, I do not forget thy law. 3
70 heart is gross like fat, but I delight in thy law. 3
72 The law of thy mouth is better to me 3
77 that I may live; for thy law is my delight. 3
85 men who do not conform to thy law. 3
92 If thy law had not been my delight 3
97 how I love thy law! It is my meditation all the day. 3
109 continually, but I do not forget thy law. 3
113 I hate double-minded men, but I love the law. 3
126 for the LORD to act, for thy law has been broken. 3
136 streams of tears, because men do not keep thy law. 3
142 righteous for ever, and thy law is true. 3

150 with evil purpose; they are far from thy law. 3
153 deliver me, for I do not forget thy law. 3
163 I hate and abhor falsehood, but I love thy law. 3
165 Great peace have those who love thy law; 3
174 O LORD, and thy law is my delight. 3
Prv 28: 4 Those who forsake the law praise the wicked 3
4 but those who keep the law strive against them. 3
7 He who keeps the law is a wise son 3
9 If one turns away his ear from hearing the law 3
29:18 but blessed is he who keeps the law. 3
Isa 2: 3 For out of Zion shall go forth the law 3
5:24 they have rejected the law of the LORD of hosts 3
24: 5 for they have transgressed the laws 3
42: 4 and the coastlands wait for his law. 3
21 to magnify his law and make it glorious. 3
24 and whose law they would not obey? 3
51: 4 for a law will go forth from me, and my justice 3
7 the people in whose heart is my law; 3
Jer 2: 8 Those who handle the law did not know me; 3
5: 4 not know the way of the LORD, the law of their God. 2
5 they know the way of the LORD, the law of their God. 2
6:19 as for my law, they have rejected it. 3
8: 8 say, 'We are wise, and the law of the LORD is with us 3
9:13 the LORD says: "Because they have forsaken my law 3
16:11 and have forsaken me and have not kept my law 3
18:18 for the law shall not perish from the priest 3
26: 4 to walk in my law which I have set before you 3
31:33 says the LORD: I will put my law within them 3
32:23 But they did not obey thy voice or walk in thy law; 3
44:10 nor have they feared, nor walked in my law 3
23 or walk in his law and in his statutes 3
Lam 2: 9 the law is no more, and . . no vision from the LORD. 3
Ezk 7:26 but the law perishes from the priest 3
22:26 Her priests have done violence to my law 3
43:11 known to them all its ordinances and all its laws; 3
11 and perform all its laws and all its ordinances. 5
12 This is the law of the temple 3
12 Behold, this is the law of the temple. 3
44: 5 of the temple of the LORD and all its laws; 3
24 They shall keep my laws and my statutes 3
Dan 6: 5 find it in connection with the law of his God. 4
8 according to the law of the Medes 4
12 according to the law of the Medes and Persians 4
15 law of the Medes and Persians that no interdict 4
7:25 shall think to change the times and the law; 4
9:10 not obeyed . . by following his laws, 3
11 All Israel has transgressed thy law and turned 3
11 which are written in the law of Moses the servant 3
13 As it is written in the law of Moses 3
Hos 4: 6 And since you have forgotten the law of your God 3
8: 1 broken my covenant, and transgressed my law. 3
12 Were I to write for him my laws by ten thousands 3
Ams 2: 4 because they have rejected the law of the LORD 3
Mic 4: 2 For out of Zion shall go forth the law 3
Hab 1: 4 the law is slacked and justice never goes forth. 3
Zep 3: 4 they do violence to the law. 3
Zec 7:12 lest they should hear the law and the words 3
Mal 4: 4 Remember the law of my servant Moses 3
Mat 5:17 come to abolish the law and the prophets 10
18 not a dot, will pass from the law until all is 10
7:12 do so to them; for this is the law and the prophets. 10
11:13 the prophets and the law prophesied until John; 10
12: 5 Or have you not read in the law 10
22:36 which is the great commandment in the law? 10
40 On these two commandments depend all the law 10
23:23 have neglected the weightier matters of the law 10
Lke 2:22 purification according to the law of Moses 10
23 as it is written in the law of the Lord 10
24 according to what is said in the law of the Lord 10
27 to do for him according to the custom of the law 10
39 according to the law of the Lord 10
10:26 What is written in the law? How do you read? 10
16:16 The law and the prophets were until John 10
17 than for one dot of the law to become void. 10
24:44 everything written about me in the law of Moses 10
Joh 1:17 For the law was given through Moses; 10
45 We have found him of whom Moses in the law . . wrote 10
7:19 Did not Moses give you the law? 10
19 Yet none of you keeps the law. 10
23 so that the law of Moses may not be broken 10
49 this crowd, who do not know the law, are accursed. 10
51 Does our law judge a man 10
8: 5 Now in the law Moses commanded us to stone such. 10
17 In your law it is written 10
10:34 Jesus answered them, "Is it not written in your law 10
12:34 crowd answered him, "We have heard from the law 10
15:25 to fulfil the word that is written in their law 10
18:31 judge him by your own law 10
19: 7 The Jews answered him, "We have a law 10
7 by that law he ought to die 10
Act 6:13 to speak words against this holy place and the law; 10
7:53 you who received the law as delivered by angels 10
13:15 After the reading of the law and the prophets 10
39 you could not be freed by the law of Moses. 10
15: 5 to charge them to keep the law of Moses. 10
18:13 worship God contrary to the law. 10
15 questions about words and names and your own law 10
21:20 they are all zealous for the law 10
24 you yourself live in observance of the law. 10
28 against the people and the law and this place; 10
22: 3 the strict manner of the law of our fathers 10
12 one Anani'as, a devout man according to the law 10
23: 3 Are you sitting to judge me according to the law 10
29 he was accused about questions of their law 10
24:14 believing everything laid down by the law 10
25: 8 Neither against the law . . nor . . the temple 10
28:23 both from the law of Moses and from the prophets. 10
Rom 2:12 and all who have sinned under the law 10
12 all who have sinned . . will be judged by the law. 10
13 it is not the hearers of the law who are righteous 10
13 but the doers of the law who will be justified. 10
14 When Gentiles who have not the law 10
14 Gentiles . . do by nature what the law requires 10
14 they are a law to themselves 10
14 even though they do not have the law. 10
15 what the law requires is written on their hearts 10
17 if you call yourself a Jew and rely upon the law 10
18 because you are instructed in the law 10
20 having in the law the embodiment of knowledge 10
23 You who boast in the law, do you dishonor God 10
23 do you dishonor God by breaking the law? 10
25 Circumcision . . is of value if you obey the law; 10
25 if you break the law, your circumcision becomes 10
26 uncircumcised keeps the precepts of the law 10
27 physically uncircumcised but keep the law 10
27 you who have . . circumcision but break the law. 10
3:19 Now we know that whatever the law says 10
19 the law . . speaks to those who are under the law 10
20 justified in his sight by works of the law 10
20 since through the law comes knowledge of sin. 10
21 righteousness . . manifested apart from law 10
21 the law and the prophets bear witness to it 10
28 man is justified by faith apart from works of law. 10
31 Do we then overthrow the law by this faith? 10
31 By no means! On the contrary, we uphold the law. 10
4:13 The promise . . did not come through the law 10
14 If it is the adherents of the law who are . . heirs 10
15 For the law brings wrath 10
15 but where there is no law there is no transgression 10
16 not only to the adherents of the law 10
5:13 sin indeed was in the world before the law 10
13 but sin is not counted where there is no law. 10
20 Law came in, to increase the trespass; 10
6:14 since you are not under law but under grace. 10
15 Are we to sin because we are not under law 10
7: 1 for I am speaking to those who know the law- 10
1 law is binding on a person only during his life? 10
2 a married woman is bound by law to her husband 10
2 she is discharged from the law concerning . . husband 10
3 But if her husband dies she is free from that law 10
4 have died to the law through the body of Christ 10
5 our sinful passions, aroused by the law 10
6 But now we are discharged from the law 10
7 What then shall we say? That the law is sin? 10
7 Yet, if it had not been for the law 10
7 if the law had not said, "You shall not covet. 10
8 Apart from the law sin lies dead. 10
9 I was once alive apart from the law 10
12 So the law is holy, and the commandment is holy 10
14 We know that the law is spiritual; but I am carnal 10
16 I agree that the law is good. 10
21 I find it to be a law that when I want to do right 10
22 For I delight in the law of God, in my inmost self. 10
23 another law at war with the law of my mind 10
23 another law at war with the law of my mind 10
23 to the law of sin which dwells in my members. 10
25 I of myself serve the law of God with my mind 10
25 but with my flesh I serve the law of sin. 10
8: 2 For the law of the Spirit of life in Christ Jesus 10
2 has set me free from the law of sin and death. 10
3 For God has done what the law . . could not do 10
4 the just requirement of the law might be fulfilled 10
7 it does not submit to God's law, indeed it cannot; 10
9:31 who pursued the righteousness which is based on law 10
31 Israel . . did not succeed in fulfilling that law 10
10: 4 For Christ is the end of the law 10
5 the righteousness which is based on the law 10
13: 8 he who loves his neighbor has fulfilled the law. 10
10 therefore love is the fulfilling of the law. 10
1Co 9: 8 Does not the law say the same? 10
9 For it is written in the law of Moses 10
20 to those under the law I became as one under the law 10
20 to those under the law I became as one under the law 10
20 though not being myself under the law 10
20 that I might win those under the law. 10
14:21 In the law it is written, "By men of strange tongues 10
34 be subordinate, as even the law says. 10
15:56 the power of sin is the law. 10
Gal 2:16 a man is not justified by works of the law 10
16 not by works of the law 10
16 by works of the law shall no one be justified. 10
19 For I through the law died to the law 10
19 For I through the law died to the law 10
21 if justification were through the law 10
3: 2 Did you receive the Spirit by works of the law 10
5 by works of the law, or by hearing with faith? 10
10 all who rely on works of the law are under a curse; 10
10 abide by all things written in the book of the law 10
11 no man is justified before God by the law 10
12 the law does not rest on faith 10
13 Christ redeemed us from the curse of the law 10
17 the law, which came 430 years afterward 10
18 For if the inheritance is by the law 10
19 Why then the law? 10
21 Is the law then against the promises of God? 10
21 if a law had been given which could make alive 10
21 then righteousness would indeed be by the law. 10
23 we were confined under the law 10
24 the law was our custodian until Christ came 10
4: 4 born of woman, born under the law 10
5 to redeem those who were under the law 10
21 Tell me, you who desire to be under law 10
21 do you not hear the law? 10
5: 3 he is bound to keep the whole law. 10
4 you who would be justified by the law 10
14 For the whole law is fulfilled in one word 10
18 led by the Spirit you are not under the law. 10
23 self-control; against such there is no law. 10
6: 2 and so fulfil the law of Christ. 10
13 do not themselves keep the law 10
Eph 2:15 the law of commandments and ordinances 10
Php 3: 5 a Hebrew born of Hebrews; as to the law a Pharisee 10
6 as to righteousness under the law blameless. 10
9 not having a righteousness of my own, based on law 10
1Ti 1: 8 Now we know that the law is good 10
9 the law is not laid down for the just 10
Tit 3: 9 dissensions, and quarrels over the law 7
Heb 7: 5 have a commandment in the law 10
12 necessarily a change in the law as well. 10
19 for the law made nothing perfect 10
28 Indeed, the law appoints men in their weakness 10
28 the word of the oath, which came later than the law 10
8: 4 priests who offer gifts according to the law. 10
10 I will put my laws into their minds 10
9:19 every commandment of the law had been declared 10
22 under the law 10
10: 1 since the law has but a shadow of the good things 10
8 these are offered according to the law) 10
16 I will put my laws on their hearts 10
28 A man who has violated the law of Moses dies 10
Jas 1:25 he who looks into the perfect law 10
25 the perfect law, the law of liberty 10
2: 8 If you really fulfill the royal law 10
9 are convicted by the law as transgressors. 10
10 For whoever keeps the whole law 10
11 you have become a transgressor of the law. 10
12 those . . to be judged under the law of liberty. 10
4:11 speaks evil against the law and judges the law. 10
11 speaks evil against the law and judges the law. 10
11 if you judge the law, you are not a doer of the law 10
11 if you judge the law, you are not a doer of the law 10
1Es 1:33 his understanding of the law of the Lord 10
48 transgressed the laws of the Lord 8
5:51 as it is commanded in the law 10
8: 3 a scribe skilled in the law of Moses 10
7 he omitted nothing from the law of the Lord 10
8 Ezra the priest and reader of the law of the Lord 10
9 Ezra the priest and reader of the law of the Lord 10
12 in accordance with what is in the law of the Lord 10
19 reader of the law of the Most High God 10
21 all things prescribed in the law of God 10
23 all those who know the law of your God 10
24 all who transgress the law of your God 10
24 all who transgress . . the law of the kingdom •
87 we turned back again to transgress thy law 10
94 to you and to all who obey the law of the Lord. 10
9:39 they told Ezra . . to bring the law of Moses 10
40 Ezra the chief priest brought the law 10
40 for . . all the priests to hear the law 10
41 all the multitude gave attention to the law. 10
42 Ezra the priest and reader of the law 10
45 Then Ezra took up the book of the law 10
46 when he opened the law, they all stood erect 10
48 the Levites, taught the law of the Lord 10
50 now they were all weeping as they heard the law- 10
2Es 1: 8 for they have not obeyed my law 12
2:40 who have fulfilled the law of the Lord. 12
3:19 to give the law to the descendants of Jacob 12
20 so that thy law might bring forth fruit in them. 12
22 the law was in the people's heart 12
4:23 the law of our fathers has been made of no effect 12
5:27 thou hast given the law which is approved by all. 12
7:17 thou hast ordained in thy law 12
20 the law of God which is set before them 12
24 They scorned his law, and denied his covenants; 12
72 and though they obtained the law 12
79 and who have despised his law 12
81 they have scorned the law of the Most High. 12
89 might keep the law of the Lawgiver perfectly. 12
94 they kept the law which was given them in trust. 12
133 who turn in repentance to his law; 12
8:12 and instructed him in thy law 12
29 regard those who have gloriously taught thy law. 12
56 and were contemptuous of his law 12
9:11 as many as scorned my law 12
31 For behold, I sow my law in you 12
32 though our fathers received the law 12

32 yet the fruit of the law did not perish 12
36 who have received the law and sinned will perish 12
37 the law, however, does not perish but remains 12
13:38 and will destroy them without effort by the law 12
54 and have searched out my law; 12
14:21 For thy law has been burned 12
22 the things which were written in thy law 12
30 received the law of life, which they did not keep 12
Tob 6:12 according to the law of Moses 10
7:12 Take her right now, in accordance with the law 6
13 Here she is; take her according to the law of Moses 10
14: 9 keep the law and the commandments 10
Jdt 11:12 all that God by his laws has forbidden them to eat. 10
AEs 13: 4 have laws contrary to those of every nation 10
5 a strange manner of life and laws 10
15:10 our law applies only to the people. Come near 11
16:15 are governed by most righteous laws 10
19 permit the Jews to live under their own laws. 8
Wis 2:11 let our might be our law of right 10
12 he reproaches us for sins against the law 10
6: 4 you did not rule rightly, nor keep the law 10
18 love of her is the keeping of her laws 10
18 giving heed to her laws 10
9: 5 with little understanding of judgment and laws; 10
14:16 Then the ungodly custom . . was kept as a law 10
16: 6 to remind them of thy law's command. 10
18: 4 the imperishable light of the law was to be given 10
9 and with one accord agreed to the divine law 10
Sir 0: 1 given to us through the law and the prophets 10
1 to the reading of the law and the prophets 10
2 Not only this work, but even the law itself, 10
2:16 who love him will be filled with the law. 10
9:15 your discussion be about the law of the Most High. 10
15: 1 he who holds to the law will obtain wisdom. 10
17:11 allotted to them the law of life. 10
19:17 let the law of the Most High take its course. 10
20 in all wisdom there is the fulfilment of the law. 10
24 highly prudent man who transgresses the law. 10
21:11 Whoever keeps the law controls his thoughts 10
23:23 first of all, she has disobeyed the law of the Most High 10
24:23 the law which Moses commanded us 10
32:15 He who seeks the law will be filled with it 10
24 He who believes the law 10
33: 2 A wise man will not hate the law 10
3 A man of understanding will trust in the law 10
3 the law is as dependable as . . Urim. 10
34: 8 the law will be fulfilled 10
35: 1 He who keeps the law makes many offerings 10
39: 1 the study of the law of the Most High 10
8 will glory in the law of the Lord's covenant. 10
41: 8 who have forsaken the law of the Most High God! 10
42: 2 of the law of the Most High and his covenant 10
44:20 he kept the law of the Most High 10
45: 5 the law of life and knowledge 10
17 to enlighten Israel with his law. 10
46:14 By the law of the Lord he judged the congregation 10
49: 4 they forsook the law of the Most High 10
Bar 2: 2 what is written in the law of Moses 10
28 thou didst command him to write thy law 10
4: 1 She is . . the law that endures for ever 10
12 because they turned away from the law of God. 10
Sus 1: 3 taught . . according to the law of Moses. 10
62 acting in accordance with the law of Moses 10
1Mc 1:49 so that they should forget the law 10
52 Many of the people, every one who forsook the law 10
56 The books of the law which they found 10
57 if any one adhered to the law 10
2:21 to desert the law and the ordinances. 10
26 Thus he burned with zeal for the law 10
27 Let every one who is zealous for the law 10
42 every one who offered himself willingly for the law. 10
48 rescued the law out of the hands of the Gentiles 10
50 Now, my children, show zeal for the law 10
58 Elijah because of great zeal for the law 10
64 be courageous and grow strong in the law 10
67 You shall rally about you all who observe the law 10
68 heed what the law commands. 10
3:21 we fight for our lives and our laws. 8
29 caused in the land by abolishing the laws 8
48 they opened the book of the law 10
56 return to his home, according to the law. 10
4:42 He chose blameless priests devoted to the law 10
47 Then they took unhewn stones, as the law directs 10
53 they rose and offered sacrifice, as the law directs 10
6:59 let them live by their laws as they did before 8
59 it was on account of their laws 8
10:14 who had forsaken the law and the commandments 10
37 let them live by their own laws 10
13: 3 done for the laws and the sanctuary 10
48 settled in it men who observed the law 10
14:14 he sought out the law 10
29 their sanctuary and the law might be preserved; 10
15:21 punish them according to their law. 10
2Mc 1: 4 open your heart to his law and his commandments 10
2: 2 after giving them the law 10
3 the law should not depart from their hearts. 10
18 as he promised through the law 10
22 the laws that were about to be abolished 10
3: 1 the laws were very well observed 10
4: 2 a zealot for the laws. 10
17 to show irreverence to the divine laws 10
5: 8 hated as a rebel against the laws 10
15 a traitor both to the laws and to his country. 10
6: 1 to forsake the laws of their fathers 10
1 and cease to live by the laws of God 10
5 which were forbidden by the laws. 10
23 moreover according to the holy God-given law 9
28 for the revered and holy laws 10
7: 2 rather than transgress the laws of our fathers. 10
9 because we have died for his laws. 10
11 because of his laws I disdain them 10
23 forget yourselves for the sake of his laws. 10
30 I obey the command of the law 10
37 give up body and life for the laws of our fathers 10
8:21 to die for their laws and their country 10
36 because they followed the laws ordained by him. 10
10:26 as the law declares. 10
11:31 for the Jews to enjoy their own food and laws 10
12:40 which the law forbids the Jews to wear 10
13:10 who were on the point of being deprived of the law 10
14 the laws, temple, city, country, and commonwealth 10
15: 9 Encouraging them from the law and the prophets 10
3Mc 1:12 Even after the law had been read to him 10
23 die courageously for the ancestral law 10
3: 4 and conducted themselves by his law 10
7:10 transgressed against . . the law of God 10
12 who had transgressed the law of God. 10
4Mc 1:17 This, in turn, is education in the law 10
34 forbidden to us by the law 10
2: 5 Thus the law says, "You shall not covet 10
6 In fact, since the law has told us not to covet 10
8 adopts a way of life in accordance with the law 10
9 he is ruled by the law through his reason 10
10 the law prevails even over affection for parents 10
14 when reason, through the law, can prevail 10
23 To the mind he gave the law 10
4:23 if any . . should be found observing the ancestral law 10
5: 4 He was a man of priestly family, learned in the law 7
16 persuaded to govern our lives by the divine law 10
16 more powerful than our obedience to the law. 10
18 Even if . . our law were not truly divine 10
21 for in either case the law is equally despised. 10
25 we believe that the law was established by God 10
29 concerning the keeping of the law 10
33 to break the ancestral law by my own act. 10
34 I will not play false to you, O law that trained me 10
35 honored priesthood and knowledge of the law. 9
6:21 and not protect our divine law even to death. 10
27 I am dying . . for the sake of the law. 10
30 he resisted . . for the sake of the law. 10
7: 7 O man in harmony with the law 10
8 those who are administrators of the law 10
8:25 Not even the law itself would arbitrarily slay 10
9: 2 we should practice ready obedience to the law 10
15 because I protect the divine law. 10
11: 5 and live according to his virtuous law? 10
12 to show our endurance for the law. 10
17 those of the divine law that are set over us; 10
13: 9 let us die . . for the sake of the law 10
13 let us use our bodies as a bulwark for the law. 10
22 our discipline in the law of God. 10
24 Since they had been educated by the same law 10
15: 9 their ready obedience to the law 10
29 O mother of the nation, vindicator of the law 10
16:16 Fight zealously for our ancestral law. 10
18: 1 obey this law and exercise piety in every way 10
10 he taught you the law and the prophets. 10

under the law 1. *ἔννομος*

1Co 9:21 but under the law of Christ 1

without law 1. *ἄνομος*

1Co 9:21 not being without law toward God 1

without the law 1. *ἀνόμως*

Rom 2:12 All who have sinned without the law 1
12 will also perish without the law 1

law-abiding 1. *νόμιμος*

4Mc 7:15 of venerable gray hair and of law-abiding life 1

lawbreaker 1. *παράνομος*

2Mc 13: 7 it came about that Menelaus the lawbreaker died 1

lawful 1. מִשְׁפָּט 2. שַׁלִּיט (A) 3. *ἔνθεσμος* 4. *ἔξεστι* 5. *καθίημι* 6. *νόμιμος*

Ezr 7:24 not be lawful to impose tribute, custom, or toll 2
Ezk 18: 5 is righteous and does what is lawful and right 1
19 When the son has done what is lawful and right 1
21 all my statutes and does what is lawful and right 1
27 and does what is lawful and right, he shall save 1
33:14 if he turns from his sin and does what is lawful 1
16 he has done what is lawful and right 1
19 does what is lawful and right, he shall live by it. 1
Mat 12: 2 your disciples are doing what is not lawful to do 4
4 which it was not lawful for him to eat 4
10 they asked him, "Is it lawful to heal on the sabbath? 4
12 So it is lawful to do good on the sabbath. 4
14: 4 It is not lawful for you to have her. 4
19: 3 Is it lawful to divorce one's wife for any cause? 4
22:17 Is it lawful to pay taxes to Caesar, or not? 4
27: 6 It is not lawful to put them into the treasury 4
Mrk 2:24 Look, why are they doing what is not lawful 4
26 which it is not lawful for any but the priests 4
3: 4 Is it lawful on the sabbath to do good or to do harm 4
6:18 is not lawful for you to have your brother's wife. 4
10: 2 Is it lawful for a man to divorce his wife? 4
12:14 Is it lawful to pay taxes to Caesar, or not? 4
Lke 6: 2 doing what is not lawful to do on the sabbath? 4
4 it is not lawful for any but the priests to eat 4
9 is it lawful on the sabbath to do good or to do harm 4
14: 3 Is it lawful to heal on the sabbath, or not? 4
20:22 Is it lawful for us to give tribute to Caesar 4
Joh 5:10 it is not lawful for you to carry your pallet. 4
18:31 It is not lawful for us to put any man to death. 4
Act 16:21 customs which it is not lawful . . to accept 4
22:25 lawful . . to scourge a man who is a Roman citizen 4
1Co 6:12 All things are lawful for me 4
12 All things are lawful for me 4
10:23 All things are lawful 4
23 All things are lawful 4
Jdt 11:13 although it is not lawful 5
2Mc 4:11 he destroyed the lawful ways of living 6
3Mc 2:21 having heard the lawful supplication 3

lawfully 1. *νόμιμος* 2. *νομίμως*

1Ti 1: 8 if any one uses it lawfully 2
4Mc 5:36 nor my long life lived lawfully. 1

lawgiver 1. *νομοθέτης* 2. legislator

Jas 4:12 There is one lawgiver and judge 1
2Es 7:89 might keep the law of the Lawgiver perfectly. 2

lawless 1. *ἀθέμιτος* 2. *ἄθεσμος* 3. *ἄνομος* 4. *ἀνόμως* 5. *παράνομος*

1Ti 1: 9 for the lawless and disobedient 3
1Pe 4: 3 living in . . carousing, and lawless idolatry. 1
2Pe 2: 8 he was vexed . . with their lawless deeds) 3
Wis 15:17 what he makes with lawless hands is dead 3
Sir 34:18 the gifts of the lawless are not acceptable. 3
Aza 1: 9 hast given us into the hands of lawless enemies 3
1Mc 1:11 In those days lawless men came forth from Israel 5
34 stationed there a sinful people, lawless men. 5
2:44 struck down . . lawless men in their wrath 3
3: 5 He searched out and pursued the lawless 3
7: 5 the lawless and ungodly men of Israel 3
9:23 the lawless emerged in all parts of Israel 3
58 Then all the lawless plotted and said, "See! 3
69 So he was greatly enraged at the lawless men 3
10:61 A group of pestilent men from Israel, lawless men 5
11:21 certain lawless men who hated their nation 5
14:14 and did away with every lawless and wicked man. 3
2Mc 8: 4 the lawless destruction of the innocent babies 5
17 keeping before their eyes the lawless outrage 4
3Mc 5:12 he quite failed in his lawless purpose 2
20 the destruction of the lawless Jews! 1
6: 4 exalted with lawless insolence 3
9 the abominable and lawless Gentiles. 3
12 the senseless insolence of the lawless 3

lawless deed 1. *ἀνόμημα*

Wis 1: 9 to convict him of his lawless deeds; 1
3:14 the eunuch whose hands have done no lawless deed 1
4:20 their lawless deeds will convict them 1

lawless man 1. *ἄθεσμος* 2. *ἄνομος*

Act 2:23 and killed by the hands of lawless men. 2
2Pe 3:17 carried away with the error of lawless men 1
Wis 17: 2 when lawless men supposed 2
Sir 16: 4 through a tribe of lawless men 2
1Mc 3: 6 Lawless men shrank back for fear of him 2
11:25 certain lawless men of his nation 2

lawless one 1. *ἄνομος*

2Th 2: 8 then the lawless one will be revealed 1
9 The coming of the lawless one •

lawlessly 1. *ἀθέσμως* 2. *ἀνομέω*

Aza 1: 6 have sinfully and lawlessly departed from thee 2
3Mc 6:26 Who . . so lawlessly encompassed..those 1

lawlessness 1. *ἀνομέω* 2. *ἀνομία* 3. *παρανομία*

Prv 11:30 but lawlessness takes away lives. •
2Th 2: 3 the man of lawlessness is revealed 2
7 the mystery of lawlessness is already at work; 2
Heb 1: 9 loved righteousness and hated lawlessness; 2
1Jn 3: 4 one who commits sin is guilty of lawlessness; 2
4 sin is lawlessness. 2
1Es 1:49 committed many acts of . . lawlessness 1
Wis 5: 7 We took our fill of the paths of lawlessness 2
23 Lawlessness will lay waste the whole earth 2
Sir 21: 3 All lawlessness is like a two-edged sword 2
1Mc 3:20 come against us in great pride and lawlessness 2
4Mc 9: 3 Tyrant and counselor of lawlessness 3

lawsuit 1. κρίμα 2. κρίσις
1Co 6: 7 To have lawsuits at all with one another 1
Sir 29:19 will fall into lawsuits. 2

lawyer 1. νομικός
Mat 22:35 one of them, a lawyer, asked him a question 1
Lke 7:30 the Pharisees and the lawyers rejected 1
10:25 a lawyer stood up to put him to the test, saying 1
11:45 One of the lawyers answered him, "Teacher 1
46 he said, "Woe to you lawyers also! 1
52 Woe to you lawyers! 1
14: 3 Jesus spoke to the lawyers and Pharisees, saying 1
Tit 3:13 speed Zenas the lawyer and Apol'los on their way 1

lay 1. היה 2. חול 3. טמן 4. יסד 5. יצג 6. יקש 7. ירה 8. מלט 9. נוח 10. נטל 11. נשא 12. נתן 13. סמך 14. עלל 15. עמד 16. עמס 17. ערך 18. פגע 19. שום 20. שוב 21. שית 22. שכב 23. שכן 24. שלח 25. שפת 26. יהב (A) 27. שום (A) 28. שוה (A) 29. ἀνακλίνω 30. βάλλω 31. γίνομαι 32. ἐκτείνω 33. ἐμβάλλω 34. ἐπιβάλλω 35. ἐπίθεσις 36. ἐπιτίθημι 37. καθίζω 38. καταβάλλω 39. κεῖμαι 40. κλίνω 41. προστίθημι 42. τίθημι 43. confirmo 44. depono 45. repono
Gen 9:23 garment, laid it upon both their shoulders 19
15:10 in two, and laid each half over against the other; 12
22: 6 wood of the burnt offering, and laid it on Isaac 19
9 Isaac his son, and laid him on the altar 19
12 He said, "Do not lay your hand on the lad 24
30:41 Jacob laid the rods in the runnels 19
42 the feebler of the flock he did not lay them there 19
37:22 here in the wilderness, but lay no hand upon 24
48:14 right hand and laid it upon the head of E'phraim 21
17 Joseph saw that his father laid his right hand 21
Exd 5: 8 number of bricks . . you shall lay upon them 19
7: 4 then I will lay my hand upon Egypt and bring forth 12
23 he did not lay even this to heart. 21
16:23 left over lay by to be kept till the morning.' 9
24 So they laid it by till the morning, as Moses bade 9
21:22 according as the woman's husband shall lay upon 21
30 If a ransom is laid on him, then he shall give 21
30 he shall give . . whatever is laid upon him. 21
24:11 he did not lay his hand on the chief men 24
29:10 Aaron and his sons shall lay their hands upon 13
15 Aaron and his sons shall lay their hands upon 13
19 Aaron and his sons shall lay their hands upon 13
40:18 Moses erected the tabernacle; he laid its bases 12
Lev 1: 4 he shall lay his hand upon the head of the burnt 13
2:15 oil upon it, and lay frankincense on it 19
3: 2 he shall lay his hand upon the head 13
8 laying his hand upon the head of his offering 13
13 lay his hand upon its head, and kill it 13
4: 4 lay his hand on the head of the bull 13
15 shall lay their hands upon the head of the bull 13
24 shall lay his hand upon the head of the goat 13
29 he shall lay his hand on the head 13
33 lay his hand upon the head of the sin offering 13
8:14 Aaron and his sons laid their hands upon the head 13
18 Aaron and his sons laid their hands on the head 13
22 Aaron and his sons laid their hands on the head 13
10: 1 put fire in it, and laid incense on it 19
16:21 Aaron shall lay both his hands upon the head 13
24:14 all who heard him lay their hands upon his head 13
26:31 I will lay your cities waste 12
Num 8:10 Israel shall lay their hands upon the Levites 13
12 Then the Levites shall lay their hands upon 13
11:11 dost lay the burden of all this people upon me? 19
16:18 took his censer, and . . laid incense upon them 19
46 Take your censer . . and lay incense on it 19
27:18 Take Joshua . . and lay your hand upon him; 13
23 he laid his hands upon him, and commissioned him 13
Deu 4:39 know therefore this day, and lay it to your heart 20
7:15 he will lay them upon all who hate you. 12
11:25 LORD . . will lay the fear of you and the dread 12
26: 6 Egyptians . . laid upon us hard bondage. 12
32:46 Lay to heart all the words which I enjoin upon you 19
34: 9 for Moses had laid his hands upon him; 13
Jos 2:19 but if a hand is laid upon any one who is with you 1
8: 2 lay an ambush against the city, behind it. 19
Jdg 6:26 build an altar . . with stones laid in due order; •
37 I am laying a fleece of wool on the threshing 5
9:24 come and their blood be laid upon Abim'elech 19
48 and took it up and laid it on his shoulder. 19
Rut 3:15 measured out six measures . . and laid it upon her; 21
4:16 Na'omi took the child and laid him in her bosom 21
1Sm 19:13 Michal took an image and laid it on the bed 19
25:18 and 200 cakes of figs, and laid them on asses. 19
2Sm 13:19 she laid her hand on her head, and went away, crying 19
1Kg 3:20 took my son . . and laid it in her bosom, and laid 22
20 in her bosom, and laid her dead son in my bosom. 22
8:47 if they lay it to heart . . and repent 20
12:11 my father laid upon you a heavy yoke, I will add 16
13:29 took up the body . . and laid it upon the ass 9
30 he laid the body in his own grave; 9
31 bury me . . lay my bones beside his bones. 9
17:19 carried him up . . and laid him upon his own bed. 22
18:23 cut it in pieces and lay it on the wood 19
23 prepare the other bull and lay it on the wood 12
33 and cut the bull in pieces and laid it on the wood. 19
20: 6 and lay hands on whatever pleases them 19
2Kg 4:21 she went up and laid him on the bed of the man of God 22
29 and lay my staff upon the face of the child. 19
31 Geha'zi went on . . and laid the staff upon the face 19
5:23 and laid them upon two of his servants; 12
10: 8 Lay them in two heaps at the entrance of the gate 19
11:16 So they laid hands on her; 19
13:16 And Eli'sha laid his hands upon the king's hands. 19
20: 7 take and lay it on the boil, that he may recover. 19
23:33 Pharaoh Neco . . laid upon the land a tribute 12
2Ch 6:37 yet if they lay it to heart in the land 20
10:11 now, whereas my father laid upon you a heavy yoke 16
16:14 They laid him on a bier which had been filled 22
23:15 laid hands on her; and she went into the entrance 19
24: 9 tax that Moses . . laid upon Israel •
29:23 they laid their hands upon them 13
31: 6 laid them in heaps. 12
Ezr 3: 6 foundation of the temple . . was not yet laid. 4
5: 8 huge stones, and timber is laid in the walls; 27
16 Shesh-baz'zar came and laid the foundations 26
Neh 10:32 We also lay upon ourselves the obligation 15
13:21 If you do so again I will lay hands on you. 24
Est 2:21 angry and sought to lay hands on King Ahasu-e'rus. 24
3: 6 But he disdained to lay hands on Mor'decai alone. 24
6: 2 who had sought to lay hands upon King Ahasu-e'rus. 24
8: 7 hanged . . because he would lay hands on the Jews. 24
9: 2 Jews gathered . . to lay hands on such as sought 24
10 but they laid no hand on the plunder. 24
15 but they laid no hands on the plunder. 24
16 but they laid no hands on the plunder. 24
10: 1 King Ahasu-e'rus laid tribute on the land 19
Job 6: 2 all my calamity laid in the balances! 11
9:33 no umpire . . who might lay his hand upon us both. 21
16:15 and have laid my strength in the dust. 14
21: 5 be appalled, and lay your hand upon your mouth. 19
22:24 if you lay gold in the dust 21
23: 4 I would lay my case before him 17
29: 9 from talking, and laid their hand on their mouth; 19
34:13 who laid on him the whole world? 19
37:15 Do you know how God lays his command upon them 19
38: 6 were its bases sunk, or who laid its cornerstone 7
40: 4 I answer thee? I lay my hand on my mouth. 19
41: 8 Lay hands on him; think of the battle; 19
Ps 7: 5 my life to the ground, and lay my soul in the dust. 23
22:15 thou dost lay me in the dust of death. 25
64: 5 they talk of laying snares secretly 3
66:11 thou didst lay affliction on our loins; 19
79: 1 heathen . . have laid Jerusalem in ruins. 19
84: 3 where she may lay her young, at thy altars 21
89:40 thou hast laid his strongholds in ruins. 19
119:110 The wicked have laid a snare for me 12
139: 5 layest thy hand upon me. 21
141: 9 Keep me from the trap which they have laid for me 6
Prv 29:25 The fear of man lays a snare 12
Ecc 7: 2 end of all men, and the living will lay it to heart. 12
9: 1 But all this I laid to heart, examining it all 12
Isa 30:32 punishment which the LORD lays upon them 9
34:15 There shall the owl nest and lay and hatch 8
47: 7 that you did not lay these things to heart 19
53: 6 the LORD has laid on him the iniquity of us all. 18
57: 1 righteous . . perishes, and no one lays it to heart; 19
Jer 6:21 I will lay before this people stumbling blocks 12
12:11 land is made desolate, but no man lays it to heart. 19
18:22 dug a pit to take me, and laid snares for my feet. 3
Lam 3:28 Let him sit . . in silence when he has laid it on him; 10
4: 6 overthrown in a moment, no hand being laid on it. 2
Ezk 3:20 I lay a stumbling block before him, he shall die; 12
4: 1 you, O son of man, take a brick and lay it before you 12
4 I will lay the punishment of the house of Israel 19
6: 5 I will lay the dead bodies of the people of Israel 12
11: 7 Your slain whom you have laid in the midst of it 19
21:29 to be laid on the necks of the unhallowed wicked 12
25:14 I will lay my vengeance upon Edom 12
17 I am the LORD, when I lay my vengeance upon them. 12
32:19 Go down, and be laid with the uncircumcised. 22
27 whose swords were laid under their heads 12
29 are laid with those who are slain by the sword; 12
32 he shall be laid among the uncircumcised 22
35: 4 I will lay your cities waste 19
36:29 and make it abundant and lay no famine upon you. 12
37: 6 I will lay sinews upon you 12
39:21 and my hand which I have laid on them. 19
40:42 on which the instruments were to be laid 9
43 the flesh of the offering was to be laid. •
42:14 outer court without laying there the garments 9
44:19 ministering, and lay them in the holy chambers; 9
Dan 2: 5 torn . . and your houses shall be laid in ruins. 27
3:29 limb from limb, and their houses laid in ruins; 28
6:17 stone was brought and laid upon the mouth 27
Jol 1: 7 It has laid waste my vines 19
Jon 1:14 this man's life, and lay not on us innocent blood; 12
Mic 1: 7 and all her idols I will lay waste; 19
5: 1 siege is laid against us; with a rod they strike 19
7:16 they shall lay their hands on their mouths; 19
Hag 2:18 that the foundation of the LORD'S temple was laid 4
Zec 4: 9 hands of Zerub'babel have laid the foundation 4
8: 9 was laid, that the temple might be built. 4
Mal 1: 3 I have laid waste his hill country 19
2: 2 if you will not lay it to heart to give glory 19
2 cursed them, because you do not lay it to heart. 19
Mat 3:10 Even now the axe is laid to the root of the trees; 39
8:20 but the Son of man has nowhere to lay his head. 40
9:18 but come and lay your hand on her 36
19:13 that he might lay his hands on them and pray 36
15 he laid his hands on them and went away. 36
23: 4 and lay them on men's shoulders 36
26:50 Then they came up and laid hands on Jesus 34
27:60 laid it in his own new tomb 42
Mrk 5:23 Come and lay your hands on her 36
6:29 they came and took his body, and laid it in a tomb. 42
56 they laid the sick in the market places 42
10:16 laying his hands upon them. 42
14:46 they laid hands on him and seized him. 34
15:46 laid him in a tomb 42
47 the mother of Joses saw where he was laid. 42
16: 6 he is not here; see the place where they laid him. 42
18 they will lay their hands on the sick 36
Lke 2: 7 laid him in a manger 29
3: 9 Even now the axe is laid to the root of the trees; 39
4:40 he laid his hands on every one of them 36
5:18 they sought to bring him in and lay him before Jesus; 42
6:48 who dug deep, and laid the foundation upon rock; 42
9:58 the Son of man has nowhere to lay his head. 40
14:29 Otherwise, when he has laid a foundation 42
15: 5 when he has found it, he lays it on his shoulders 36
20:19 the chief priests tried to lay hands on him 34
21:12 before all this they will lay their hands on you 34
22:53 you did not lay hands on me 32
23:26 and laid on him the cross, to carry it behind Jesus. 36
53 and laid him in a rock-hewn tomb 42
53 where no one had ever yet been laid. 39
55 saw the tomb, and how his body was laid; 42
Joh 7:30 no one laid hands on him 34
44 but no one laid hands on him. 34
11:34 he said, "Where have you laid him? 42
19:41 a new tomb where no one had ever been laid. 42
42 they laid Jesus there. 42
20: 2 we do not know where they have laid him. 42
13 I do not know where they have laid him. 42
15 tell me where you have laid him 42
Act 3: 2 whom they laid daily at that gate of the temple 42
4:35 laid it at the apostles' feet 42
37 laid it at the apostles' feet. 42
5: 2 laid it at the apostles' feet. 42
15 laid them on beds and pallets 42
7:16 laid in the tomb 42
8:17 Then they laid their hands on them 36
18 through the laying on of the apostles' hands 35
19 any one on whom I lay my hands 36
9:12 Anani'as come in and lay his hands on him 36
17 And laying his hands on him he said 36
37 they laid her in an upper room. 42
13: 3 they laid their hands on them and sent them off. 36
29 down from the tree, and laid him in a tomb. 42
36 David . . fell asleep, and was laid with his fathers 41
21:27 the Jews from Asia . . laid hands on him 34
Rom 9:33 Behold, I am laying in Zion a stone 42
1Co 3:10 I laid a foundation 42
11 For no other foundation can any one lay 42
11 than that which is laid, which is Jesus Christ. 39
6: 4 why do you lay them before those 37
7:35 not to lay any restraint upon you 34
1Ti 5:22 Do not be hasty in the laying on of hands 36
2Ti 1: 6 within you through the laying on of my hands; 35
Heb 6: 1 not laying again a foundation of repentance 38
2 the laying on of hands 35
1Pe 2: 6 Behold, I am laying in Zion a stone, 42
Rev 1:17 But he laid his right hand upon me, 42
2:24 to you I say, I do not lay upon you any other burden; 30
1Es 6: 9 with costly timber laid in the walls. 42
20 laid the foundations of the house of the Lord 33
8:22 to be laid on any of the priests or Levites 31
2Es 6: 2 and before the foundations of paradise were laid 43
7:105 neither shall any one lay a burden on another ‡
10:24 and lay aside your many sorrows 44
14:15 lay to one side the thoughts 45
Sir 50:28 he who lays them to heart will become wise. 42
Sus 1:34 two elders . . laid their hands upon her head. 42
Bel 1: 1 When King Astyages was laid with his fathers 41
1Mc 14:31 lay hands on their sanctuary 32

lay a beam 1. קרה
Neh 3: 3 laid its beams and set its doors 1
6 laid its beams and set its doors, its bolts 1
Ps 104: 3 hast laid the beams of thy chambers on the waters 1

lay a case 1. ἐμφανίζω
Act 24: 1 They laid before the governor their case 1

lay a charge 1. ערך
Ps 50:21 rebuke you, and lay the charge before you. 1

lay a charge against 1. ἔγκλημα
Act 25:16 concerning the charge laid against him. 1

lay a claim 1. ἀντιποιέω
1Mc 15: 3 I intend to lay claim to the kingdom 1

lay a commandment upon 1. mando
2Es 3: 7 thou didst lay upon him one commandment of thine; 1

lay a crafty plan 1. ערם סוד
Ps 83: 3 They lay crafty plans against thy people; 1

lay a foundation 1. יסד 2. מוּסָד 3. θεμελιόω 4. ὑποβάλλω
Jos 6:26 At the cost of his .. shall he lay its foundation 1
1Kg 5:17 in order to lay the foundation of the house 1
6:37 the foundation of the house of the LORD was laid 1
16:34 he laid its foundation at the cost of Abi'ram 1
2Ch 8:16 foundation of the house of the LORD was laid 2
Ezr 3:10 builders laid the foundation of the temple 1
11 foundation of the house of the LORD was laid. 1
12 saw the foundation of this house being laid 1
Job 38: 4 when I laid the foundation of the earth? 1
Ps 102:25 Of old thou didst lay the foundation of the earth 1
Isa 28:16 I am laying in Zion for a foundation a stone 1
44:28 and of the temple, 'Your foundation shall be laid.' 1
48:13 My hand laid the foundation of the earth 1
51:13 Maker, who .. laid the foundations of the earth 1
16 and laying the foundations of the earth 1
54:11 and lay your foundations with sapphires. 1
1Es 2:18 laying the foundations for a temple. 4
5:57 they laid the foundation of the temple of God 3
6:11 laying the foundations of this structure?' 3
Sir 50: 2 He laid the foundations 3

lay a heavy burden 1. כבד
Neh 5:15 former governors .. laid heavy burdens 1

lay a snare 1. נקשׁ 2. קושׁ
1Sm 28: 9 Why then are you laying a snare for my life 1
Ps 38:12 Those who seek my life lay their snares 1
Isa 29:21 lay a snare for him who reproves in the gate 2

lay a tribute 1. ענשׁ
2Ch 36: 3 king of Egypt .. laid upon the land a tribute 1

lay an oath 1. אלה
1Sm 14:24 Saul laid an oath on the people, saying, "Cursed be 1

lay an oath upon 1. שׁבע
Jos 6:26 Joshua laid an oath upon them at that time, saying 1
26 Joshua laid an oath upon them at that time, saying 1

lay aside 1. ἀποτίθημι 2. ἀφαιρέω 3. τίθημι
Joh 13: 4 rose from supper, laid aside his garments 3
Heb 12: 1 Therefore .. let us also lay aside every weight 1
2Mc 14: 7 Therefore I have laid aside my ancestral glory 2

lay away 1. ἀπόκειμαι
Lke 19:20 your pound, which I kept laid away in a napkin; 1

lay bare 1. גלה 2. ערה 3. τραχηλίζω
2Sm 22:16 the foundations of the world were laid bare 1
Ps 18:15 the foundations of the world were laid bare 1
Isa 3:17 the LORD will lay bare their secret parts. 2
Ezk 13:14 so that its foundation will be laid bare; 1
16:36 Because your shame was laid bare •
Hab 3:13 of the wicked, laying him bare from thigh to neck. 2
Zep 2:14 for her cedar work will be laid bare. 2
Heb 4:13 all are open and laid bare 3

lay before 1. ἀνατίθημι
Act 25:14 Festus laid Paul's case before the king, saying 1
Gal 2: 2 I laid before them .. the gospel 1

lay beside 1. παρανακλίνω
Sir 47:19 you laid your loins beside women 1

lay desolate 1. שׁמם
Ezk 35:12 They are laid desolate, they are given us 1

lay down 1. יצק 2. נוח 3. נטה 4. קום 5. שׂום 6. ἀποτίθημι 7. κατά 8. κεῖμαι 9. τίθημι
Jos 4: 3 lay them down in the place where you lodge 2
8 carried them over .. and laid them down there. 2
7:23 and they laid them down before the LORD. 1
Est 9:31 and as they had laid down for themselves 4
Job 17: 3 Lay down a pledge for me with thyself; 5
Ams 2: 8 they lay themselves down beside every altar 3
Lke 19:21 you take up what you did not lay down 9
22 a severe man, taking up what I did not lay down 9
Joh 10:11 The good shepherd lays down his life 9
15 I lay down my life for the sheep. 9
17 the Father loves me, because I lay down my life 9
18 I lay it down of my own accord 9
18 I have power to lay it down 9
13:37 I will lay down my life for you. 9
38 Jesus answered, "Will you lay down your life for me? 9
15:13 that a man lay down his life for his friends. 9
Act 7:58 the witnesses laid down their garments 6
24:14 believing everything laid down by the law 7
1Ti 1: 9 the law is not laid down for the just 8
1Jn 3:16 we know love, that he laid down his life for us; 9
16 we ought to lay down our lives for the brethren. 9

lay flat 1. נפל
Jdg 7:13 turned it upside down, so that the tent lay flat. 1

lay heavy 1. כבד
Exd 5: 9 Let heavier work be laid upon the men 1

lay hold 1. אחז 2. חזק 3. מצא 4. תפשׂ 5. ἀντιλαμβάνω 6. κρατέω
Jdg 19:29 and laying hold of his concubine he divided her 2
1Sm 15:27 Saul laid hold upon the skirt of his robe 2
1Kg 1:51 for, lo, he has laid hold of the horns of the altar 1
9: 9 forsook the LORD .. and laid hold on other gods 2
11:30 Ahi'jah laid hold of the new garment 4
13: 4 Lay hold of him. 4
2Ch 7:22 forsook the LORD .. and laid hold on other gods 2
Job 8:15 he lays hold of it, but it does not endure. 2
18: 9 seizes him by the heel, a snare lays hold of him. 2
Ps 116: 3 pangs of Sheol laid hold on me; 3
Prv 3:18 She is a tree of life to those who lay hold of her; 2
Ecc 2: 3 how to cheer my body .. and how to lay hold on folly 1
Sng 7: 8 climb the palm tree and lay hold of its branches. 1
Isa 27: 5 Or let them lay hold of my protection 2
Jer 6:23 They lay hold on bow and spear, they are cruel 2
26: 8 the people laid hold of him, saying, "You shall die! 4
50:42 They lay hold of bow and spear; they are cruel 2
Ezk 14: 5 I may lay hold of the hearts of the house of Israel 4
Zec 14:13 each will lay hold on the hand of his fellow 2
Mat 12:11 will not lay hold of it and lift it out? 6
Bar 3:20 way to knowledge .. nor laid hold of her. 5

lay in order 1. ערך
Gen 22: 9 Abraham .. laid the wood in order 1
Lev 1: 7 and lay wood in order upon the fire 1
8 the priests shall lay the pieces .. in order 1
12 the priest shall lay them in order upon the wood 1
6:12 he shall lay the burnt offering in order upon it 1
Jos 2: 6 the stalks of flax which she had laid in order 1

lay in ruins 1. נתץ 2. שׁחת
Jer 4:26 all its cities were laid in ruins before the LORD 1
Lam 2: 5 The Lord has .. laid in ruins its strongholds; 2
6 laid in ruins the place of his appointed feasts; 2
8 The LORD determined to lay in ruins the wall 2

lay low 1. חלשׁ 2. טול 3. ירד 4. כרע 5. נפל 6. שׁכב 7. שׁפל 8. καταστρώννυμι 9. humilio
Job 14:10 But man dies, and is laid low; man breathes his last 1
41: 9 he is laid low even at the sight of him. 2
Ps 78:31 and laid low the picked men of Israel. 4
Prv 7:26 for many a victim has she laid low; 5
Isa 13:11 and lay low the haughtiness of the ruthless. 7
14: 8 you were laid low, no hewer comes up against us.' 6
12 to the ground, you who laid the nations low! 1
25:11 the LORD will lay low his pride 7
12 will bring down, lay low, and cast to the ground 7
26: 5 He lays it low, lays it low to the ground 7
5 lays it low to the ground, casts it to the dust. 7
32:19 and the city will be utterly laid low. 7
Zec 10:11 The pride of Assyria shall be laid low 3
2Es 10:22 our harp has been laid low 9
11:42 and have laid low the walls of those 9
2Mc 15:27 they laid low no less than 35,000 men 8

lay open 1. פתח
Ezk 25: 9 therefore I will lay open the flank of Moab 1

lay out 1. ἐκτίθημι 2. περιστέλλω
Act 27:30 under pretense of laying out anchors 1
Tob 12:13 in order to go and lay out the dead 2
Sir 38:16 Lay out his body with the honor due him 2

lay people 1. בְּנֵי הָעָם
2Ch 35: 5 fathers' houses of your brethren the lay people 1
7 Then Josi'ah contributed to the lay people 1
12 fathers' houses of the lay people 1
13 carried them quickly to all the lay people. 1

lay secretly 1. מוֹקֵשׁ
Ps 64: 5 they talk of laying snares secretly 1

lay siege 1. חנה 2. סמך 3. צור
Jos 10:31 Joshua passed .. to Lachish, and laid siege to it 1
34 and they laid siege to it, and assaulted it; 1
1Kg 15:27 and all Israel were laying siege to Gib'bethon. 3
2Kg 25: 1 came .. against Jerusalem, and laid siege to it; 1
Isa 21: 2 Go up, O Elam, lay siege, O Media; 3
Jer 52: 4 they laid siege to it and built siegeworks 1
Ezk 24: 2 The king of Babylon has laid siege to Jerusalem 2

lay up 1. טמן 2. נוח 3. פְּקִדָּה 4. צבר 5. צפן 6. שׂום 7. ἀποθησαυρίζω 8. ἀπόκειμαι 9. θησαυρίζω 10. κεῖμαι 11. ταμιεύω 12. τηρέω 13. τίθημι 14. apud 15. repono
Gen 39:16 Then she laid up his garment by her 2
41:35 let them .. lay up grain under the authority 4
Deu 11:18 You shall therefore lay up these words of mine 6
14:28 all the tithe .. and lay it up within your towns; 2
1Sm 10:25 wrote .. in a book and laid it up before the LORD. 2
Job 15:20 all the years that are laid up for the ruthless. 5
20:26 Utter darkness is laid up for his treasures; 1
22:22 lay up his words in your heart. 6
Ps 31:19 abundant is thy goodness, which thou hast laid up 5
119:11 I have laid up thy word in my heart 5
Prv 10:14 Wise men lay up knowledge 5
13:22 sinner's wealth is laid up for the righteous. 5
Sng 7:13 all choice fruits .. which I have laid up for you 5
Isa 15: 7 and what they have laid up they carry away 3
Mat 6:19 Do not lay up for yourselves treasures on earth 9
20 lay up for yourselves treasures in heaven 9
Lke 1:66 all who heard them laid them up in their hearts 13
12:19 Soul, you have ample goods laid up for many years; 10
2Co 12:14 children ought not to lay up for their parents 9
Col 1: 5 because of the hope laid up for you in heaven 8
1Ti 6:19 thus laying up for themselves a good foundation 7
2Ti 4: 8 is laid up for me the crown of righteousness 8
2Es 7:77 a treasure of works laid up with the Most High 15
83 they shall see the reward laid up for those 15
84 torment laid up for themselves in the last days. 15
8:33 who have many works laid up with thee 15
13:56 for there is a reward laid up with the Most High. 14
14: 8 Lay up in your heart the signs 15
Sir 29:11 Lay up your treasure 13
Man 1:13 Do not be angry with me for ever or lay up evil for me 12
2Mc 12:45 that is laid up for those who fall asleep in godliness 8
4Mc 12:12 justice has laid up for you .. eternal fire 11

lay up in store 1. כמס
Deu 32:34 Is not this laid up in store with me, sealed up 1

lay up treasure 1. ἀποθησαυρίζω 2. θησαυρίζω
Lke 12:21 So is he who lays up treasure for himself 2
Jas 5: 3 You have laid up treasure for the last days. 2
Tob 4: 9 you will be laying up a good treasure 2
Sir 3: 4 like one who lays up treasure. 1

lay upon 1. ἐπιβάλλω 2. ἐπίθεσις 3. ἐπίκειμαι 4. ἐπιτίθημι
Mrk 6: 5 he laid his hands upon a few sick people 4
7:32 they besought him to lay his hand upon him. 4
8:23 and laid his hands upon him 4
25 Then again he laid his hands upon his eyes 4
Lke 13:13 he laid his hands upon her 4
Joh 11:38 it was a cave, and a stone lay upon it. 3
Act 6: 6 they prayed and laid their hands upon them. 4
12: 1 Herod the king laid violent hands upon some 1
15:28 to lay upon you no greater burden than these 4
19: 6 when Paul had laid his hands upon them 4
1Co 9:16 For necessity is laid upon me 3
1Ti 4:14 the council of elders laid their hands upon you 2
Tob 6:16 and lay upon them some of the heart .. of the fish 4
AEs 12: 2 preparing to lay hands upon Artaxerxes the king; 1
2Mc 1:21 the wood and what was laid upon it. 3

lay wait 1. ארב
Jdg 9:34 rose up by night, and laid wait against Shechem 1
43 took his men .. and laid wait in the fields; 1

lay waste 1. בקק 2. חרב 3. יצת 4. שׁדד 5. שׁמם 6. שְׁמָמָה 7. חרב (A) 8. ἐρημόω 9. desero 10. devasto
Num 21:30 we laid waste until fire spread to Med'eba. 5
2Kg 19:17 the kings of Assyria have laid waste the nations 2
Ezr 4:15 That was why this city was laid waste. 7
Ps 79: 7 devoured Jacob, and laid waste his habitation. 5
Isa 15: 1 Because Ar is laid waste in a night Moab is undone; 4
1 because Kir is laid waste in a night 4
23: 1 Wail, O ships of Tarshish, for Tyre is laid waste 4
14 Wail .. for your stronghold is laid waste. 4
24: 1 Behold, the LORD will lay waste the earth 1
3 The earth shall be utterly laid waste 1
37:18 kings of Assyria have laid waste all the nations 2
42:15 I will lay waste mountains and hills 2
49:17 and those who laid you waste go forth from you. 2
60:12 those nations shall be utterly laid waste. 2
Jer 4:20 the whole land is laid waste. 4
9:10 they are laid waste so that no one passes through 3
12 Why is the land ruined and laid waste 3
10:25 and have laid waste his habitation. 5
48: 1 Woe to Nebo, for it is laid waste! 4
20 Tell it by the Arnon, that Moab is laid waste. 4
49: 3 Wail, O Heshbon, for Ai is laid waste! 4
51:55 For the LORD is laying Babylon waste 4
Ezk 12:20 And the inhabited cities shall be laid waste 2
19: 7 their strongholds, and laid waste their cities; 2
26: 2 I shall be replenished, now that she is laid waste 2
19 When I make you a city laid waste, like the cities 2
29:12 40 years among cities that are laid waste. 2
30: 7 in the midst of cities that are laid waste. 2
Hos 2:12 And I will lay waste her vines and her fig trees 5
Jol 1:10 The fields are laid waste, the ground mourns; 4
Ams 7: 9 the sanctuaries of Israel shall be laid waste 2
Nah 1: 5 the earth is laid waste before him •
Zep 1:13 and their houses laid waste. 6
3: 6 I have laid waste their streets 2
Zec 11: 3 for the jungle of the Jordan is laid waste! 4
Mat 12:25 divided against itself is laid waste 8

Lke 11:17 Every kingdom divided against itself is laid waste 8
Rev 18:17 In one hour all this wealth has been laid waste. 8
19 In one hour she has been laid waste. 8
1Es 2:23 That is why this city was laid waste. 8
4: 8 if he tells them to lay waste, they lay waste 8
8 if he tells them to lay waste, they lay waste 8
45 when Judea was laid waste by the Chaldeans. 8
2Es 10:21 you see that our sanctuary has been laid waste 9
15:49 to lay waste your houses 10
Wis 5:23 Lawlessness will lay waste the whole earth 8
Sir 21: 4 Terror and violence will lay waste riches 8
4 thus the house of the proud will be laid waste. 8
1Mc 2:12 our beauty, and our glory have been laid waste 8

lazy 1. ἀργός
Tit 1:12 are always liars, evil beasts, lazy gluttons. 1
Sir 37:11 with a lazy servant about a big task 1

lead 1. אשר 2. בוא 3. דרך 4. הלך 5. יבל 6. ידע 7. משך 8. נהג 9. נהל 10. נחה 11. נסע 12. עבר 13. רדה 14. רעה 15. שׂר 16. ἄγω 17. ἀνάγω 18. ἀπάγω 19. ἀφηγέομαι 20. διάγω 21. ἐγγίζω 22. εἰς 23. εἰσάγω 24. εἰσφέρω 25. ἐκφέρω 26. ἐν 27. ἡγέομαι 28. κατάρχω 29. ὁδηγέω 30. παράγω 31. παρατάσσω 32. προάγω 33. προέρχομαι 34. προηγέομαι 35. προκόπτω 36. πρωτεύω 37. πρῶτος 38. φέρω 39. adduco 40. duco 41. induco
Gen 24:27 the LORD has led me in the way to the house 10
48 the LORD . . who had led me by the right way to take 10
33:14 I will lead on slowly, according to the pace 9
48:15 the God who has led me all my life long to this day 14
Exd 3: 1 and he led his flock to the west side 8
13:17 God did not lead them by way of the land 10
21 pillar of cloud to lead them along the way 10
15:13 Thou hast led in thy steadfast love the people 10
22 Then Moses led Israel onward from the Red Sea 11
32:34 now go, lead the people to the place of which I have 10
Deu 8: 2 the LORD your God has led you these 40 years 4
15 led you through the great and terrible wilderness 4
29: 5 I have led you 40 years in the wilderness; 4
19 lead to the sweeping away of moist and dry alike. •
32:12 LORD alone did lead him, and there was no foreign 10
Jos 24: 3 I took . . and led him through all the land 4
Jdg 4: 9 which you are going will not lead to your glory •
2Kg 6:19 And he led them to Sama'ria. 4
9: 2 bid him rise . . and lead him to an inner chamber. 2
1Ch 15:21 lead with lyres according to the Shem'inith. •
2Ch 23:13 singers . . leading in the celebration. 6
36:14 All the leading priests and the people likewise 15
Ezr 8:24 Then I set apart twelve of the leading priests 15
10: 5 made the leading priests . . take oath 15
Neh 9:12 pillar of cloud thou didst lead them in the day 10
19 pillar of cloud which led them in the way did not 10
Ps 5: 8 Lead me, O LORD, in thy righteousness 10
23: 2 He leads me beside still waters; 9
3 He leads me in paths of righteousness 10
25: 5 Lead me in thy truth, and teach me 3
9 He leads the humble in what is right, and teaches 3
27:11 lead me on a level path because of my enemies. 10
31: 3 for thy name's sake lead me and guide me 10
43: 3 let them lead me, let them bring me to thy holy hill 10
45:14 in many-colored robes she is led to the king 5
60: 9 to the fortified city? Who will lead me to Edom? 10
61: 2 Lead thou me to the rock that is higher than I; 10
68:27 There is Benjamin, the least of them, in the lead 13
77:20 Thou didst lead thy people like a flock 10
78:14 In the daytime he led them with a cloud 10
53 He led them in safety, so that they were not afraid; 10
80: 1 Shepherd . . who leadest Joseph like a flock! 8
106: 9 he led them through the deep as through a desert. 4
107: 7 he led them by a straight way, till they reached 3
108:10 Who will lead me to Edom? 10
110: 3 day you lead your host upon the holy mountains. •
119:35 Lead me in the path of thy commandments 3
136:16 to him who led his people through the wilderness 4
139:10 even there thy hand shall lead me 10
24 lead me in the way everlasting! 10
143:10 Let thy good spirit lead me on a level path! 10
Prv 4:11 I have led you in the paths of uprightness. 3
6:22 When you walk, they will lead you; 10
10:16 The wage of the righteous leads to life •
12:28 but the way of error leads to death. •
15:24 The wise man's path leads upward to life, that he •
16:29 leads him in a way that is not good. 4
19:23 The fear of the LORD leads to life; •
21: 5 plans of the diligent lead surely to abundance •
Sng 8: 2 I would lead you and bring you into the house 8
Isa 9:16 for those who lead this people lead them astray 1
16 and those who are led by them are swallowed up. 1
11: 6 together, and a little child shall lead them. 8
42:16 I will lead the blind in a way that they know not 4
48:17 your God . . who leads you in the way you should go. 3
21 thirsted not when he led them through . . deserts; 4
49:10 for he who has pity on them will lead them 8
53: 7 like a lamb that is led to the slaughter 5
57:18 I will lead him and requite him with comfort 10
60:11 the nations, with their kings led in procession. 8
63:13 who led them through the depths? 4
14 thou didst lead thy people 8
Jer 2: 6 who led us in the wilderness, in a land of deserts 4
17 the LORD your God, when he led you in the way? 4
11:19 But I was like a gentle lamb led to the slaughter. 5
23: 8 and led the descendants of the house of Israel 2
31: 9 and with consolations I will lead them back 5
Ezk 37: 2 he led me round among them; 12
39: 2 and lead you against the mountains of Israel; 2
40:24 he led me toward the south 4
41: 7 on the side of the temple a stairway led upward •
46:21 and led me to the four corners of the court; 12
47: 3 and then led me through the water; 12
4 measured 1,000, and led me through the water; 12
4 measured 1,000, and led me through the water; 12
6 Then he led me back along the bank of the river. 4
Hos 11: 4 I led them with cords of compassion 7
Ams 2:10 and led you 40 years in the wilderness 4
Mat 6:13 And lead us not into temptation, But deliver us 24
7:13 the way is easy, that leads to destruction 18
14 the way is hard, that leads to life 18
15:14 if a blind man leads a blind man, both will fall 29
26:57 led him to Ca'iaphas the high priest 18
Mrk 8:23 led him out of the village 25
14:53 they led Jesus to the high priest 18
Lke 4: 1 Jesus . . was led by the Spirit 16
29 led him to the brow of the hill 16
6:39 Can a blind man lead a blind man? 29
11: 4 lead us not into temptation. 24
22:47 the man called Judas, one of the twelve, was leading 33
Joh 18:13 First they led him to Annas 16
28 they led Jesus from the house of Ca'iaphas 16
Act 8:32 As a sheep led to the slaughter 16
12:10 they came to the iron gate leading into the city. 38
16:12 the leading city of the district of Macedo'nia 37
17: 4 not a few of the leading women. 37
Rom 2: 4 God's kindness is meant to lead you to repentance? 16
5:18 one man's trespass led to condemnation for all 22
18 one man's act . . leads to acquittal and life 22
6:16 slaves . . either of sin, which leads to death 22
16 or of obedience, which leads to righteousness? 22
8:14 all who are led by the Spirit of God are sons of God 16
2Co 7:10 that leads to salvation and brings no regret 22
Gal 5:18 if you are led by the Spirit 16
1Ti 2: 2 we may lead a quiet and peaceable life 20
2Ti 2:16 it will lead people into more and more ungodliness 35
Heb 3:12 leading you to fall away from the living God. 26
1Es 9:16 the leading men of their fathers' houses 27
2Es 1:18 saying, 'Why hast thou led us into this wilderness 39
3: 6 And thou didst lead him into the garden 41
13:40 whom Shalmaneser . . led captive 40
15:10 my people is led like a flock to the slaughter 40
Tob 12: 3 he has led me back to you safely, he cured my wife 16
Jdt 1:13 he led his forces against King Arphaxad 31
5: 3 Who rules over them as king, leading their army? 27
14 he led them by the way of Sinai and Kadesh-barnea 16
6:11 the slaves took him and led him out of the camp 16
10:20 all his servants came out and led her into the tent. 23
11:19 Then I will lead you through the middle of Judea 16
19 you will lead them like sheep 16
15:13 leading all the women 27
Wis 6:20 the desire for wisdom leads to a kingdom. 17
7:12 I rejoiced in them all, because wisdom leads them; 27
19:11 when desire led them to ask for luxurious food; 32
Sir 0: 1 was himself also led to write something 32
27:15 The strife of the proud leads to bloodshed •
37:30 gluttony leads to nausea. 21
42: 1 do not let partiality lead you to sin •
45: 5 led him into the thick darkness 23
Bar 5: 6 they went forth . . led away by their enemies 16
9 For God will lead Israel with joy 27
1Mc 5:11 Timothy is leading their forces. 27
23 led them to Judea with great rejoicing. 16
7: 5 were led by Alcimus, who wanted to be high priest. 27
9: 2 They went by the road which leads to Gilgal •
2Mc 1:19 when our fathers were . . led captive to Persia 16
23 Jonathan led, and the rest responded 28
8:23 then, leading the first division himself 34
10: 1 the Lord leading them on, recovered the temple 32
29 they were leading the Jews. 19
13:15 He stabbed the leading elephant and its rider. 36
4Mc 10: 1 the third was led 16
11:13 the sixth, a mere boy, was led 16
17 When he had said this, they led him to the wheel. 30

lead (2) 1. עֹפֶרֶת 2. μολιβός 3. plumbum
Exd 15:10 they sank as lead in the mighty waters. 1
Num31:22 only . . the bronze, the iron, the tin, and the lead 1
Job 19:24 Oh that with an iron pen and lead they were graven 1
Jer 6:29 the lead is consumed by the fire; 1
Ezk 22:18 bronze and tin and iron and lead in the furnace 1
20 As men gather silver and bronze and iron and lead 1
27:12 wealth of every kind; silver, iron, tin, and lead 1
2Es 7:52 will you add to them lead and clay? 3
55 and also iron and lead and clay; 3
56 and lead than iron, and clay than lead.' 3
56 and lead than iron, and clay than lead.' 3
Sir 22:14 What is heavier than lead? 2
47:18 amassed silver like lead. 2

lead a host of captives 1. αἰχμαλωτεύω
Eph 4: 8 When he ascended on high he led a host of captives 1

lead a life 1. περιπατέω 2. converso
Eph 4: 1 to lead a life worthy of the calling 1
Col 1:10 to lead a life worthy of the Lord 1
1Th 2:12 to lead a life worthy of God 1
2Es 7:122 those who have led a pure life 2

lead about 1. περιάγω
2Mc 4:38 and led him about the whole city 1

lead along 1. יבל
Ps 45:15 With joy and gladness they are led along 1

lead aright 1. κατευθύνω
Sir 49: 2 He was led aright in converting the people 1

lead astray 1. נטה 2. שגה 3. שוב 4. תעה 5. ἀπάγω 6. ἀποπλανάω 7. ἀφίστημι 8. πλανάω 9. φθείρω 10. seduco
Prv 12:26 but the way of the wicked leads them astray. 4
20: 1 whoever is led astray by it is not wise. 2
Isa 9:16 for those who lead this people lead them astray 4
19:13 cornerstones of her tribes . . led Egypt astray. 4
30:28 on the jaws . . a bridle that leads astray. 4
44:20 feeds on ashes; a deluded mind has led him astray 1
47:10 your wisdom and your knowledge led you astray 3
Jer 23:13 they prophesied . . and led my people Israel astray. 4
32 and lead my people astray by their lies 4
50: 6 lost sheep; their shepherds have led them astray 4
Hos 4:12 For a spirit of harlotry has led them astray 4
Ams 2: 4 but their lies have led them astray, 4
Mic 3: 5 the prophets who lead my people astray, who cry 4
Mat 24: 4 Take heed that no one leads you astray. 8
5 'I am the Christ,' and they will lead many astray. 8
11 false prophets will arise and lead many astray. 8
24 show great signs and wonders, so as to lead astray 8
Mrk 13: 5 Take heed that no one leads you astray. 8
6 and they will lead many astray. 8
22 to lead astray, if possible, the elect. 6
Lke 21: 8 he said, "Take heed that you are not led astray 8
Joh 7:12 others said, "No, he is leading the people astray. 8
47 The Pharisees answered them, "Are you led astray 8
1Co 12: 2 you were led astray to dumb idols 5
2Co 11: 3 your thoughts will be led astray 9
Tit 3: 3 once foolish, disobedient, led astray 8
1Es 3:18 It leads astray the minds of all who drink it. 8
2Es 7:92 might not lead them astray from life into death. 10
Wis 2:21 Thus they reasoned, but they were led astray 8
11:15 thoughts, which led them astray 8
Sir 3:24 For their hasty judgment has led many astray 8
13: 8 Take care not to be led astray 6
15:12 Do not say, "It was he who led me astray 8
19: 2 Wine and women lead intelligent men astray 7
31: 5 he who pursues money will be led astray by it. 2
2Mc 2: 2 nor to be led astray in their thoughts 6
6:25 they should be led astray because of me 8

lead away 1. הלך 2. נהג 3. נחה 4. שבה 5. ἄγω 6. ἀπάγω 7. ἀποφέρω 8. διάγω 9. παραφέρω 10. facio
Deu 28:37 among . . peoples where the LORD will lead you away. 2
Jdg 5:12 Arise, Barak, lead away your captives, 4
1Sm 30:22 each man may lead away his wife and children 2
Job 12:17 He leads counselors away stripped 1
19 He leads priests away stripped 1
23 he enlarges nations, and leads them away. 3
Ps 125: 5 the LORD will lead away with evildoers! 1
Isa 20: 4 so shall . . Assyria lead away the Egyptians 2
Mat 27: 2 and led him away and delivered him to Pilate 6
31 and led him away to crucify him. 6
Mrk 14:44 seize him and lead him away under guard. 6
15: 1 they bound Jesus and led him away 7
16 the soldiers led him away inside the palace 6
Lke 13:15 and lead it away to water it? 6
22:54 Then they seized him and led him away 5
66 they led him away to their council, and they said 6
23:26 as they led him away 6
32 Two others also, who were criminals, were led away 5
Heb 13: 9 led away by diverse and strange teachings 9
1Es 1:56 The survivors he led away to Babylon 6
2Es 13:40 tribes which were led away from their own land 10
Jdt 2: 9 I will lead them away captive 5
Bar 4:16 They led away the widow's beloved sons 6
Sus 1:45 And as she was being led away to be put to death 6
3Mc 1: 3 Dositheus . . had led the king away 8
4: 5 a multitude of . . old men . . was being led away 5

lead away captive 1. αἰχμαλωτεύω
Jdt 5:18 and were led away captive to a foreign country 1

lead by the hand 1. χειραγωγέω
Act 9: 8 so they led him by the hand 1
22:11 I was led by the hand by those who were with me 1

lead captive 1. שבה 2. αἰχμαλωτίζω
Ps 68:18 leading captives in thy train, and receiving 1
Lke 21:24 and be led captive among all nations 2

lead down 1. κατάγω
Tob 13: 2 he leads down to Hades, and brings up again 1
Wis 16:13 thou dost lead men down to the gates of Hades 1

lead forth 1. יבל 2. יצא 3. נסע 4. ריק 5. educo
Gen 14:14 he led forth his trained men, born in his house 4
Job 38:32 Can you lead forth the Maz'zaroth in their season 2
Ps 78:52 Then he led forth his people like sheep 3
105:37 Then he led forth Israel with silver and gold 2
43 he led forth his people with joy 2
Isa 55:12 you shall go out in joy, and be led forth in peace; 1
Hos 9:13 E'phraim must lead forth his sons to slaughter. 2
2Es 16:67 so God will lead you forth 5

lead gently 1. נהל
Isa 40:11 and gently lead those that are with young. 1

lead in procession 1. דדה
Ps 42: 4 went with the throng, and led them in procession 1

lead in triumph 1. θριαμβεύω
2Co 2:14 who in Christ always leads us in triumph 1

lead into sin 1. חטא
Ecc 5: 6 Let not your mouth lead you into sin 1

lead into unfaithfulness 1. זנה
2Ch 21:11 led the inhabitants . . into unfaithfulness 1
13 led Judah . . into unfaithfulness 1
13 house of Ahab led Israel into unfaithfulness 1

lead off 1. סור 2. ἐφέλκω
Lam 3:11 he led me off my way and tore me to pieces; 1
LJr 1:43 when one of them is led off by one of the passers-by 2

lead out 1. יצא 2. נהג 3. ἐξάγω 4. κατάγω 5. educo
Num27:17 who shall lead them out and bring them in; 1
2Sm 5: 2 it was you that led out and brought in Israel; 1
1Ch 11: 2 it was you that led out and brought in Israel; 1
20: 1 Jo'ab led out the army, and ravaged the country 2
2Ch 25:11 Amazi'ah took courage, and led out his people 2
Ps 68: 6 God . . leads out the prisoners to prosperity; 1
78:26 by his power he led out the south wind; 2
Jer 38:22 were being led out to the princes of the king 1
23 All your wives and your sons shall be led out 1
Ezk 14:22 any survivors to lead out sons and daughters 1
20:10 So I led them out of the land of Egypt 1
42: 1 Then he led me out into the inner court 1
15 he led me out by the gate which faced east 1
Mrk 15:20 they led him out to crucify him. 3
Lke 24:50 Then he led them out as far as Bethany 3
Joh 10: 3 he calls his own sheep by name and leads them out. 3
Act 7:36 He led them out 3
40 this Moses who led us out from the land of Egypt 3
13:17 with uplifted arm he led them out of it. 3
21:38 and led the 4,000 men of the Assassins out 3
Heb 8: 9 to lead them out of the land of Egypt 3
2Es 3:17 when thou didst lead his descendants out 5
14: 4 I sent him and led my people out of Egypt 5
Jdt 7: 6 Holofernes led out all his cavalry 3
3Mc 7: 5 They also led them out with harsh treatment 4

lead round 1. סבב
Exd 13:18 God led the people round by the way 1
Ezk 47: 2 and led me round on the outside to the outer gate 1

lead the life 1. περιπατέω
1Co 7:17 Only, let every one lead the life 1

lead through 1. διάγω
Wis 10:18 and led them through deep waters; 1

lead to execution 1. ἀπάγω
AEs 12: 3 when they confessed they were led to execution. 1

lead up 1. עלה 2. ἀνάγω 3. ἀναφέρω 4. adduco
Jdg 6: 8 I led you up from Egypt and brought you out 1
1Ch 17: 5 not dwelt in a house since the day I led up Israel 1
Ezk 40:22 seven steps led up to it; 1
26 there were seven steps leading up to it 1
49 breadth twelve cubits; and ten steps led up to it; 1
Mat 4: 1 Then Jesus was led up by the Spirit 2
17: 1 and led them up a high mountain apart. 3
Mrk 9: 2 led them up a high mountain apart by themselves; 3
2Es 14: 4 and I led him up on Mount Sinai 4

leaden 1. עֹפֶרֶת
Zec 5: 7 behold, the leaden cover was lifted 1
8 and thrust down the leaden weight upon its mouth. 1

leader 1. אַיִל 2. אשר 3. גָּדוֹל 4. נָגִיד 5. נָשִׂיא
6. עַתּוּד 7. פִּנָּה 8. פָּקִיד 9. פֶּרַע 10. קָצִין 11. ראשׁ
12. שַׂר 13. ἀρχηγός 14. ἄρχων 15. ἀφηγέομαι
16. ἡγεμών 17. ἡγέομαι 18. καθηγεμών
19. προηγέομαι 20. προοδηγός 21. προστατέω
22. πρῶτος 23. φύλαρχος 24. ducatus 25. dux
26. megestanes
Exd 15:15 the leaders of Moab, trembling seizes them; 1
16:22 and when all the leaders of the congregation 5
34:31 Aaron and all the leaders of the congregation 5
35:27 the leaders brought onyx stones and stones 5
Num 1:16 the leaders of their ancestral tribes 5
44 the help of the leaders of Israel, twelve men 5
2: 3 the leader of the people of Judah being Nahshon 5
5 the leader of the people of Is'sachar 5
7 leader of the people of Zeb'ulun being Eli'ab 5
10 the leader of the people of Reuben being Eli'zur 5
12 the leader of the people of Simeon 5
14 the leader of the people of Gad being Eli'asaph 5
18 leader of the people of E'phraim being Eli'shama 5
20 leader of the people of Manas'seh being Gama'liel 5
22 leader of the people of Benjamin being Abi'dan 5
25 leader of the people of Dan being Ahi-e'zer 5
27 leader of the people of Asher being Pa'giel 5
29 leader of the people of Naph'tali being Ahi'ra 5
3:32 chief over the leaders of the Levites 5
4:34 Moses and Aaron and the leaders 5
46 whom Moses and Aaron and the leaders of Israel 5
7: 2 leaders of Israel, heads of their fathers' houses 5
2 leaders of the tribes, who were over those 5
3 wagon for every two of the leaders 5
10 leaders offered offerings for the dedication 5
10 leaders offered their offering before 5
11 shall offer their offering, one leader each day 5
18 Nethan'el the son of Zu'ar, the leader of Is'sachar 5
24 Eli'ab the . . leader of the men of Zeb'ulun 5
30 Eli'zur the . . leader of the men of Reuben 5
36 Shelu'mi-el the . . leader of the men of Simeon 5
42 Eli'asaph the . . leader of the men of Gad 5
48 Eli'shama the . . leader of the men of E'phraim 5
54 he leader of the men of Manas'seh 5
60 Abi'dan the . . leader of the men of Benjamin 5
66 Ahie'zer the . . leader of the men of Dan 5
72 Pa'giel the . . leader of the men of Asher 5
78 Ahi'ra the . . leader cf the men of Naph'tali 5
84 offering . . from the leaders of Israel 5
10: 4 if they blow only one, then the leaders 5
13: 2 send a man, every one a leader among them. 5
16: 2 with . . 250 leaders of the congregation 5
17: 2 get from them rods . . from all their leaders 5
6 their leaders gave him rods, one for each leader 5
6 their leaders gave him rods, one for each leader 5
27: 2 stood . . before the leaders 5
31:13 Moses, and Elea'zar the priest, and all the leaders 5
32: 2 said to . . the leaders of the congregation 5
34:18 You shall take one leader of every tribe 5
22 Of the tribe of the sons of Dan a leader, Bukki 5
23 of the tribe of the sons of Manas'seh a leader, 5
24 of the tribe of the sons of E'phraim a leader, Kemu'el 5
25 Of the tribe of the sons of Zeb'ulun a leader 5
26 Of the tribe of the sons of Is'sachar a leader 5
27 of the tribe of the sons of Asher a leader 5
28 Of the tribe of the sons of Naph'tali a leader 5
36: 1 spoke before Moses and before the leaders 5
Jos 9:15 the leaders of the congregation swore to them. 5
18 the leaders of the congregation had sworn 5
18 the congregation murmured against the leaders. 5
19 But all the leaders said to all the congregation 5
21 And the leaders said to them, "Let them live. 5
21 they became . . as the leaders had said of them. 5
13:21 whom Moses defeated with the leaders of Mid'ian 5
17: 4 Elea'zar the priest and Joshua . . and the leaders 5
Jdg 5: 2 That the leaders took the lead in Israel 9
10:18 And the people, the leaders of Gilead, said 12
11: 6 Come and be our leader, that we may fight 10
11 and the people made him head and leader over them; 10
1Sm 14:38 Come hither, all you leaders of the people; 7
1Kg 8: 1 the leaders of the fathers' houses of . . Israel 5
11:24 and became leader of a marauding band 12
14: 7 exalted you . . and made you leader over my people 4
16: 2 and made you leader over my people Israel 4
1Ch 4:42 having as their leaders Pelati'ah, Ne-ari'ah 11
9:34 leaders, who lived in Jerusalem. 11
11:42 a leader of the Reubenites, and 30 with him 11
12: 4 Ishma'iah of Gibeon . . a leader over the 30; •
13: 1 with the commanders . . with every leader. 4
15:22 Chenani'ah, leader of the Levites in music 12
27 Chenani'ah the leader of the music of the singers 12
22:17 David also commanded all the leaders of Israel 12
23: 2 David assembled all the leaders of Israel 12
27:22 These were the leaders of the tribes of Israel. 12
28: 4 chose Judah as leader, and in the house of Judah 4
29: 6 as did also the leaders of the tribes 12
24 All the leaders and the mighty men, and also all 12
2Ch 1: 2 to the judges, and to all the leaders in all Israel 5
5: 2 the heads . . the leaders of the fathers' houses 5
Neh 4:16 leaders stood behind all the house of Judah 12
9:17 appointed a leader to return to their bondage 11
11: 1 Now the leaders of the people lived in Jerusalem; 12
17 Mattani'ah . . leader to begin the thanksgiving 11
12:42 singers sang with Jezrahi'ah as their leader. 8
Isa 3: 6 saying: "You have a mantle; you shall be our leader 10
7 you shall not make me leader of the people. 10
12 your leaders mislead you, and confuse the course 2
14: 9 the shades . . all who were leaders of the earth; 6
55: 4 a leader and commander for the peoples. 4
Jer 40:13 Now Joha'nan the son of Kare'ah and all the leaders 12
41:11 and all the leaders of the forces with him heard 12
13 saw Joha'nan the son of Kare'ah and all the leaders 12
16 leaders of the forces with him took all the rest 12
Zec 10: 3 I will punish the leaders; 6
Lke 22:26 the leader as one who serves. 17
Act 5:31 God exalted him . . as Leader and Savior 13
28:17 he called together the local leaders of the Jews 22
Heb 13: 7 Remember your leaders 17
17 Obey your leaders and submit to them 17
24 Greet all your leaders and all the saints 17
1Es 1:49 Even the leaders of the people and of the priests 17
5: 8 Mispar, Reeliah, Rehum, and Baanah, their leaders 19
9 the men of the nation and their leaders 19
6:12 who the leaders are 15
8:44 who were leaders and men of understanding; 17
49 David and the leaders 17
54 I set apart twelve of the leaders of the priests 23
59 the leaders of the priests and the Levites 23
69 The people of Israel and the leaders 14
70 the leaders and the nobles 19
96 leaders of the priests and Levites of all Israel 23
9:12 let the leaders of the multitude stay 19
2Es 1:13 I gave you Moses as leader and Aaron as priest; 25
39 to them I will give as leaders Abraham, Isaac 24
9: 3 wavering of leaders, confusion of princes 25
15:16 for their king or the chief of their leaders. 26
Jdt 5: 5 Then Achior, the leader of all the Ammonites, said 17
6:17 had said in the presence of the Assyrian leaders 14
7: 8 the leaders of the Moabites 17
13:18 to strike the head of the leader of our enemies. 14
14:19 When the leaders of the Assyrian army heard this 14
Sir 9:17 so a people's leader is proved wise by his words. 17
10:20 Among brothers their leader is worthy of honor 17
33:18 you leaders of the congregation, hearken. 17
44: 4 leaders of the people in their deliberations 17
45:24 leader of the sanctuary and of his people 21
46:18 he wiped out the leaders of the people of Tyre 17
50: 1 The leader of his brethren 3
Aza 1:15 no prince, or prophet, or leader, no burnt offering 17
1Mc 2:17 You are a leader, honored and great in this city 14
3:55 After this Judas appointed leaders of the people 17
5: 6 many people with Timothy as their leader. 17
18 Azariah, a leader of the people 17
9:30 to take his place as our ruler and leader 17
35 sent his brother as leader of the multitude 17
61 who were leaders in this treachery 13
10:37 Let their . . leaders be of their own number 14
12:53 they said, "They have no leader or helper 14
13: 8 You are our leader in place of Judas 17
42 commander and leader of the Jews. 17
14:35 they made him their leader and high priest 17
41 Simon should be their leader and high priest 17
2Mc 1:13 when the leader reached Persia 16
16 and struck down the leader and his men 16
10:21 he gathered the leaders of the people 17
28 the other made rage their leader in the fight. 18
12:36 their ally and leader in the battle. 20
14: 6 whose leader is Judas Maccabeus 15
16 At the command of the leader 17
20 the leader had informed the people 17
21 the leaders set a day •
4Mc 5: 4 one man, Eleazar by name, leader of the flock 22
12: 5 a leader in the government of the kingdom. 15

leader of the tribe 1. φύλαρχος
1Es 7: 8 the twelve leaders of the tribes of Israel; 1

leadership 1. ἥγησις
1Mc 9:31 Jonathan at that time accepted the leadership 1

excellent leadership 1. εὐκοσμία
Sir 32: 2 receive a wreath for your excellent leadership. 1

under the leadership 1. בְּיַד 2. διά 3. ἡγέομαι
4. προηγέομαι
Num33: 1 went . . under the leadership of Moses and Aaron. 1
Heb 3:16 left Egypt under the leadership of Moses. 2
1Es 5:36 under the leadership of Cherub, Addan, and Immer 3
2Mc 4:40 under the leadership of . . Auranus 4

leading man 1. ראשׁ 2. ἡγέομαι 3. πρῶτος
Ezr 7:28 gathered leading men from Israel to go up 1
8:16 Then I sent for Elie'zer . . leading men 1
17 Iddo, the leading man at the place Casiphi'a 1
Mrk 6:21 and the leading men of Galilee. 3
Act 13:50 the Jews incited . . the leading men of the city 3
15:22 leading men among the brethren 2
1Es 8:45 the leading man at the place of the treasury 2
1Mc 9:53 he took the sons of the leading men of the land 2

leaf 1. דֶּלֶת 2. עָלֶה 3. פַּח 4. צֵלָע 5. עֳפִי (A)
6. φύλλον 7. folium
Gen 3: 7 they sewed fig leaves together 2

Exd 39: 3 gold leaf was hammered and cut into threads 3
Lev 26:36 sound of a driven leaf shall put them to flight 2
1Kg 6:34 the two leaves of the one door were folding 4
34 the two leaves of the other door were folding. 4
Job 13:25 Wilt thou frighten a driven leaf 2
30: 4 They pick mallow and the leaves of bushes 2
Ps 1: 3 fruit in its season, and its leaf does not wither. 2
Isa 1:30 For you shall be like an oak whose leaf withers 2
33: 9 and Bashan and Carmel shake off their leaves. •
34: 4 host shall fall, as leaves fall from the vine 2
4 like leaves falling from the fig tree. •
64: 6 We all fade like a leaf, and our iniquities, 2
Jer 8:13 even the leaves are withered 2
17: 8 for its leaves remain green 2
Ezk 41:24 The doors had two leaves apiece 1
24 two swinging leaves for each door. 1
47:12 Their leaves will not wither nor their fruit 2
12 will be for food, and their leaves for healing. 2
Dan 4:12 Its leaves were fair and its fruit abundant 5
14 strip off its leaves and scatter its fruit; 5
21 whose leaves were fair and its fruit abundant 5
Mat 21:19 found nothing on it but leaves only 6
24:32 becomes tender and puts forth its leaves 6
Mrk 11:13 seeing in the distance a fig tree in leaf 6
13 When he came to it, he found nothing but leaves 6
13:28 becomes tender and puts forth its leaves 6
Rev 22: 2 the leaves . . were for the healing of the nations 6
2Es 1:20 I covered you with the leaves of trees. 7
Sir 6: 3 will devour your leaves and destroy your fruit 6
14:18 Like flourishing leaves on a spreading tree 6

fresh leaf 1. טֶרֶף
Ezk 17: 9 so that all its fresh sprouting leaves wither? 1

green leaf 1. עָלֶה
Prv 11:28 righteous will flourish like a green leaf. 1

olive leaf 1. זַיִת
Gen 8:11 and lo, in her mouth a freshly plucked olive leaf; 1

leafy 1. עָבוֹת 2. עָלֶה
Lev 23:40 take . . boughs of leafy trees, and willows 1
Neh 8:15 bring branches of . . palm, and other leafy trees 2
Ezk 6:13 under every leafy oak, wherever they offered 1
20:28 wherever they saw any high hill or any leafy tree 1

league 1. בְּרִית 2. מַסֵּכָה 3. נוח עַל 4. *στάδιον*
1Kg 15:19 Let there be a league between me and you 1
19 go, break your league with Ba'asha king of Israel 1
2Ch 16: 3 Let there be a league between me and you 1
3 go, break your league with Ba'asha king of Israel 1
Job 5:23 you shall be in league with the stones 1
Isa 7: 2 was told, "Syria is in league with E'phraim 3
30: 1 and who make a league, but not of my spirit 2
Ezk 30: 5 Libya, and the people of the land that is in league 1
2Mc 11: 5 about five leagues from Jerusalem 4

leak 1. דלף
Ecc 10:18 and through indolence the house leaks. 1

lean 1. נטה 2. סמך 3. רפק 4. שען 5. *ἐπερείδω* 6. *στηρίζω*
Num21:15 extends to the seat of Ar, and leans to the border 4
Jdg 16:26 the pillars . . that I may lean against them. 4
2Sm 1: 6 and there was Saul leaning upon his spear; 4
2Kg 5:18 my master goes into . . leaning on my arm, and I bow 4
7: 2 the captain on whose hand the king leaned said 4
17 appointed the captain on whose hand he leaned 4
18:21 will pierce the hand of any man who leans on it. 2
Job 8:15 He leans against his house, but it does not stand; 4
Ps 62: 3 all of you, like a leaning wall, a tottering fence? 1
71: 6 Upon thee I have leaned from my birth; 2
Sng 8: 5 Who is that coming up . . leaning upon her beloved 3
Isa 10:20 Jacob will no more lean upon him that smote them 4
20 but will lean upon the LORD, the Holy One of Israel 4
36: 6 will pierce the hand of any man who leans on it. 2
Ezk 29: 7 when they leaned upon you, you broke 4
Ams 5:19 and leaned with his hand against the wall 2
Mic 3:11 yet they lean upon the LORD and say 4
AEs 15: 3 leaning daintily on one 5
Sir 15: 4 He will lean on her and will not fall 6

lean (2) 1. רָזֶה 2. רַק
Gen 41:27 The seven lean and gaunt cows that came up after 2
Ezk 34:20 judge between the fat sheep and the lean sheep. 1

lean close 1. *προσκύπτω*
2Mc 7:27 leaning close to him 1

leanness 1. כַּחַשׁ
Job 16: 8 my leanness has risen up against me 1

leap 1. דלג 2. מַשָּׁק 3. נתר 4. עלה 5. פוש 6. פזז 7. רקד 8. שקק 9. *ἅλλομαι* 10. *διασκιρτάω* 11. *ἐμπηδάω* 12. *ἐφάλλομαι* 13. *σκιρτάω*
Gen 31:10 he-goats which leaped upon the flock were 4
12 the goats that leap upon the flock are striped 4
Lev 11:21 legs . . with which to leap on the earth 3
2Sm 6:16 saw . . David leaping and dancing before the LORD; 6
Job 37: 1 my heart trembles, and leaps out of its place. 3
Sng 2: 8 Behold, he comes, leaping upon the mountains 1
Isa 33: 4 as locusts leap, men leap upon it. 2
4 as locusts leap, men leap upon it. 8
35: 6 then shall the lame man leap like a hart 1
Jol 2: 5 they leap on the tops of the mountains 7
9 They leap upon the city, they run upon the walls; 8
Zep 1: 9 punish every one who leaps over the threshold 1
Mal 4: 2 go forth leaping like calves from the stall. 5
Lke 1:41 the babe leaped in her womb 13
44 the babe in my womb leaped for joy. 13
Act 3: 8 walking and leaping and praising God. 9
19:16 the man in whom the evil spirit was leaped on them 12
Wis 5:21 and will leap to the target as from a well-drawn bow 9
17:19 the unseen running of leaping animals 13
18:15 thy all-powerful word leaped from heaven 9
19: 9 ranged like horses, and leaped like lambs 10
1Mc 9:48 leaped into the Jordan 11

leap for joy 1. *σκιρτάω*
Lke 6:23 Rejoice in that day, and leap for joy 1

leap forth 1. זנק 2. מלט
Deu 33:22 Dan is a lion's whelp, that leaps forth from Bashan. 1
Job 41:19 Out of his mouth . . sparks of fire leap forth. 2

make leap 1. רעש
Job 39:20 Do you make him leap like the locust? 1

leap out 1. *ἐξάλλομαι*
1Mc 13:44 The men in the siege engine leaped out into the city 1

leap over 1. דלג
2Sm 22:30 Yea, by thee . . and by my God I can leap over a wall. 1
Ps 18:29 by my God I can leap over a wall. 1

leap up 1. *ἀναπηδάω* 2. *ἐξάλλομαι* 3. *παραπηδάω*
Act 3: 8 And leaping up he stood and walked 2
Tob 6: 2 A fish leaped up from the river 1
4Mc 11: 1 the fifth leaped up, saying 3

learn 1. אלף 2. בין 3. ידע 4. למד 5. לֶקַח 6. ספר 7. ראה 8. שמע 9. ידע (A) 10. *γινώσκω* 11. *γνῶσις* 12. *ἐπιγινώσκω* 13. *ἐπιστήμη* 14. *μανθάνω* 15. *μεταλαμβάνω* 16. *παιδεύω* 17. *παραλαμβάνω* 18. *πυνθάνομαι* 19. *συνοράω* 20. scio
Gen 24:21 gazed at her in silence to learn whether the LORD 3
42: 1 When Jacob learned that there was grain in Egypt 7
Deu 4:10 that they may learn to fear me all the days 4
5: 1 you shall learn them and be careful to do them. 4
14:23 may learn to fear the LORD your God always. 4
17:19 read in it . . that he may learn to fear the LORD 4
18: 9 not learn to follow the abominable practices 4
31:12 may hear and learn to fear the LORD your God 4
13 may hear and learn to fear the LORD your God 4
Rut 3:18 Wait . . until you learn how the matter turns out 3
1Sm 4: 6 they learned that the ark of the LORD had come 3
19: 3 and if I learn anything I will tell you. 7
26: 4 and learned of a certainty that Saul had come. 3
Ezr 4:15 learn that this city is a rebellious city 9
7:11 Ezra . . learned in matters of the commandments 6
Est 2:11 Mor'decai walked . . to learn how Esther was 3
4: 1 When Mor'decai learned all that had been done 3
5 to go to Mor'decai to learn what this was and why 3
Job 23: 5 I would learn what he would answer me 3
Ps 106:35 with the nations and learned to do as they did. 4
119: 7 when I learn thy righteous ordinances. 4
71 I was afflicted, that I might learn thy statutes. 4
73 that I may learn thy commandments. 4
141: 6 then . . learn that the word of the LORD is true. 8
Prv 1: 5 wise man also may hear and increase in learning 5
8: 5 O simple ones, learn prudence; 2
9: 9 teach a righteous man . . increase in learning. 5
22:25 lest you learn his ways and entangle yourself 1
30: 3 I have not learned wisdom, nor have I knowledge 4
Isa 1:17 learn to do good; seek justice 4
2: 4 neither shall they learn war any more. 4
26: 9 inhabitants of the world learn righteousness. 4
10 If favor . . he does not learn righteousness; 4
29:13 fear of me is a commandment of men learned by rote; 4
Jer 10: 2 Learn not the way of the nations, nor be dismayed 4
12:16 if they will diligently learn the ways of my 4
Ezk 19: 3 a young lion, and he learned to catch prey; 4
6 he learned to catch prey; he devoured men. 4
Dan 4:32 until you have learned that the Most High rules 9
Mic 4: 3 neither shall they learn war any more; 4
Mat 9:13 Go and learn what this means, 'I desire mercy 14
11:29 Take my yoke upon you, and learn from me 14
24:32 From the fig tree learn its lesson 14
Mrk 13:28 From the fig tree learn its lesson 14
15:45 he learned from the centurion that he was dead 10
Lke 7:37 when she learned that he was at table 12
9:11 When the crowds learned it, they followed him 10
23: 7 when he learned 12
Joh 6:45 who has heard and learned from the Father 14
7:51 giving him a hearing and learning what he does? 10
12: 9 great crowd of the Jews learned that he was there 10
Act 14: 6 they learned of it and fled to Lystra and Derbe 19
17:13 when the Jews of Thessaloni'ca learned 10
21:34 as he could not learn the facts 10
23:27 having learned that he was a Roman citizen. 14
34 When he learned that he was from Cili'cia 18
24: 8 will be able to learn from him about everything 12
28: 1 then learned that the island was called Malta. 12
1Co 4: 6 learn by us not to go beyond what is written 14
14:31 so that all may learn and all be encouraged; 14
Eph 4:20 You did not so learn Christ!- 14
Php 4: 9 What you have learned and received and heard 14
11 I have learned, in whatever state I am, to be content. 14
Col 1: 7 as you learned it from Ep'aphras 14
1Th 4: 1 as you learned from us how you ought to live 17
1Ti 1:20 that they may learn not to blaspheme. 16
2:11 Let a woman learn in silence 14
5: 4 let them first learn their religious duty 14
13 Besides that, they learn to be idlers 14
2Ti 3:14 as for you, continue in what you have learned 14
14 knowing from whom you learned it 14
Tit 3:14 learn to apply themselves to good deeds 14
Heb 5: 8 he learned obedience through what he suffered; 14
Rev 2:24 you in Thyati'ra . . who have not learned 10
3: 9 and learn that I have loved you. 11
14: 3 No one could learn that song except the 144,000 14
1Es 2:22 will learn that this city was rebellious 10
5:67 they learned that . . 12
2Es 12:36 you alone were worthy to learn this secret 20
Tob 1:19 When I learned that I was being searched 12
5: 8 I may learn to what tribe he belongs 12
13 because I tried to learn your tribe and family. 12
Jdt 11:16 Therefore, when I, your servant, learned all this 12
AEs 12: 2 learned that they were preparing to lay hands 14
Wis 6: 1 learn, O judges of the ends of the earth. 14
9 that you may learn wisdom and not transgress. 14
7:13 I learned without guile 14
21 I learned . . what is secret 10
9:10 that I may learn what is pleasing to thee. 10
13 For what man can learn the counsel of God? 10
17 Who has learned thy counsel 10
10:12 learn that godliness is more powerful 10
11: 9 they learned how the ungodly were tormented 10
16 that they might learn 10
16:26 thy sons . . might learn 14
Sir 8: 8 learn how to serve great men. •
9 they themselves learned from their fathers; 14
9 learn how to give an answer in time of need. •
18:19 Before you speak, learn 14
37: 8 learn first what is his interest 10
Bar 3: 9 life, O Israel; give ear, and learn wisdom! 10
14 Learn where there is wisdom, where there is 14
20 they have not learned the way to knowledge 10
23 have not learned the way to wisdom, nor given 10
Sus 1:48 condemned . . without learning the facts? 12
1Mc 2:39 When Mattathias and his friends learned of it 10
3:11 When Judas learned of it, he went out to meet him 10
42 also learned what the king had commanded to do 12
6:17 when Lysias learned that the king was dead 12
7:31 When Nicanor learned 10
42 let the rest learn 10
9:32 When Bacchides learned of this 10
63 When Bacchides learned of this 10
70 When Jonathan learned of this 12
10:72 Ask and learn who I am 14
80 Jonathan learned that there was an ambush 10
12:22 now that we have learned this 10
13:14 Trypho learned that Simon had risen up 12
2Mc 2: 7 When Jeremiah learned of it 10
4:21 Antiochus learned that . . 15
7: 2 What do you intend to ask and learn from us? 14
12: 8 But learning that the men in Jamnia 15
21 When Timothy learned of the approach of Judas 15
3Mc 1: 1 When Philopator learned 14
4Mc 1:17 by which we learn divine matters reverently 14
4: 4 When Apollonius learned the details 10
5: 4 He was a man of priestly family, learned in the law 13
9: 5 as though . . you learned nothing from Eleazar 14
10:16 you may learn from them 14

learn a better way 1. *μεταπαιδεύω*
4Mc 2: 7 even a drunkard can learn a better way 1

learn by divination 1. נחש
Gen 30:27 I have learned by divination that the LORD 1

learn prudence 1. ערם
Prv 19:25 Strike a scoffer . . simple will learn prudence; 1

learn the secret 1. *μυέω*
Php 4:12 I have learned the secret of facing plenty and hunger 1

learning 1. מַדָּע 2. *γράμμα* 3. *γράμματα οἶδα* 4. *γραμματεία*
Dan 1:17 God gave them learning and skill in all letters 1
Joh 7:15 this man has learning, when he has never studied? 3
Act 26:24 your great learning is turning you mad. 2
Sir 44: 4 in understanding of learning for the people 4

least 1. דָּבָר 2. צָעִיר 3. קָטָן 4. רַק 5. ἀλλά γε 6. ἐλάχιστος 7. ἐλαχύς 8. καὶ ἄν 9. μηδείς 10. μικρός 11. οὐ 12. πάντως 13. vel

Gen 24:55 remain with us a while, at least ten days; •
Exd 5:11 but your work will not be lessened in the least.' 1
Jdg 3: 2 war to such at least as had not known it before. 4
6:15 in Manas'seh, and I am the least in my family. 2
Ps 68:27 There is Benjamin, the least of them, in the lead 2
Jer 6:13 For from the least to the greatest of them 3
31:34 know me, from the least of them to the greatest 3
Jon 3: 5 from the greatest of them to the least of them. 3
Mat 2: 6 are by no means least among the rulers of Judah; 6
5:19 relaxes one of the least of these commandments 7
19 so, shall be called least in the kingdom of heaven; 6
11:11 yet he who is least in the kingdom of heaven 10
25:40 to one of the least of these my brethren 7
45 as you did it not to one of the least of these 7
Lke 7:28 yet he who is least in the kingdom of God 10
9:48 who is least among you all is the one who is great. 10
Act 5:15 at least his shadow might fall on some of them. 8
8:10 all gave heed . . from the least to the greatest 10
1Co 9: 2 If to others I am not an apostle, at least I am to you; 5
15: 9 For I am the least of the apostles 6
2Co 11: 5 I think that I am not in the least inferior 9
Heb 8:11 from the least of them to the greatest. 10
2Es 13:42 there at least they might keep their statutes 13
Sir 23:21 where he least suspects it, he will be seized. 11
2Mc 8:35 he regarded as of the least account 7
3Mc 1:15 why should not I at least enter 12

very least 1. ἐλάχιστος

Eph 3: 8 To me, though I am the very least of all the saints 1

leather 1. עוֹר 2. תַּחַשׁ 3. δερμάτινος

2Kg 1: 8 He wore . . with a girdle of leather 1
Ezk 16:10 and shod you with leather, I swathed you 2
Mat 3: 4 a garment of camel's hair, and a leather girdle 3
Mrk 1: 6 a leather girdle around his waist 3

leave 1. אַחֲרֵי 2. אַחֲרִית 3. גרם 4. הלך מִן 5. הלך מֵעִם 6. חדל 7. יצא 8. יצג 9. ישב 10. יתר 11. יֶתֶר 12. יֶתֶר הַפְּלֵיטָה 13. לון 14. מֵעִמָּד 15. מצא 16. מִתּוֹךְ 17. נוח 18. נטשׁ 19. נסע מִן 20. נתן 21. סור 22. עבר מִן 23. עדר 24. עוֹד 25. עזב 26. קום 27. רפה 28. שׂוּם 29. שָׂרִיד 30. שׁאר 31. שְׁאֵרִית 32. שׁלח 33. שׁבק (A) 34. ἀναζεύγνυμι 35. ἀνίημι 36. ἀνίστημι 37. ἀπαίρω 38. ἀπαλλάσσω 39. ἀπέρχομαι 40. ἀπό 41. ἀπολείπω 42. ἀπὸ προσώπου 43. ἀποχωρέω 44. ἀφίημι 45. ἀφίστημι 46. γίνομαι 47. δίδωμι 48. δίδωμι τόπον 49. ἐάω 50. ἐγκαταλείπω 51. εἰμί 52. ἐκβαίνω 53. ἐκπορεύομαι 54. ἐξεγείρω 55. ἐξέρχομαι 56. καταλείπω 57. μεταβαίνω 58. παραχωρέω 59. παρέχω 60. περιλείπομαι 61. περισσεύω 62. πορεύω 63. πορεύω ἀπό 64. ὑπολείπω 65. ὑπολιμπάνω 66. χωρίζω 67. derelinquo 68. proficiscor 69. recedo 70. relinquo 71. remaneo 72. subremaneo 73. supero

Gen 2:24 Therefore a man leaves his father and his mother 25
7:23 Only Noah was left, and those that were with him 30
28:10 Jacob left Beer-sheba, and went toward Haran. 7
15 for I will not leave you until I have done that 25
31:14 inheritance left to us in our father's house? 24
32: 8 then the company which is left will escape. 30
24 Jacob was left alone; and a man wrestled with him 10
33:15 Esau said, "Let me leave with you some of the men 8
39: 6 he left all that he had in Joseph's charge; 25
12 But he left his garment in her hand, and fled 25
13 when she saw that he had left his garment 25
15 he left his garment with me, and fled and got out 25
18 he left his garment with me, and fled out 25
42:33 leave one of your brothers with me 17
38 for his brother is dead, and he only is left. 30
44:20 and he alone is left of his mother's children; 10
22 said to my lord, 'The lad cannot leave his father 25
22 for if he should leave his father 25
28 one left me, and I said, Surely he has been torn 7
47:18 there is nothing left in the sight of my lord 30
50: 8 their herds were left in the land of Goshen. 25
Exd 2:20 where is he? Why have you left the man? 25
8: 9 the frogs . . be left only in the Nile. 30
11 they shall be left only in the Nile. 30
9:21 did not regard . . left his slaves and his cattle 25
10: 5 they shall eat what is left to you after the hail 12
12 that they may . . eat . . all that the hail has left. 30
15 they ate all . . which the hail had left; 10
19 not a single locust was left in all the country 30
16:19 Let no man leave any of it till the morning. 10
20 some left part of it till the morning 10
23: 5 you shall refrain from leaving him with it 25
11 what they leave the wild beasts may eat. 11
34:25 of the passover be left until the morning. 13
Lev 2: 3 what is left of the cereal offering 10
10 what is left of the cereal offering 10
7:15 he shall not leave any of it until the morning 17
10:12 Elea'zar and Ith'amar, his sons who were left 10
16 Ithamar, the sons of Aaron who were left 10
16:23 linen garments . . and shall leave them there 17
19:10 leave them for the poor and for the sojourner 25
22:30 you shall leave none of it until morning 10
23:22 you shall leave them for the poor 25
26:36 as for those of you that are left 30
39 those of you that are left shall pine away 30
43 the land shall be left by them 25
Num 9:12 They shall leave none of it until the morning 30
10:31 he said, "Do not leave us, I pray you, for you know 25
21:35 until there was not one survivor left to him; 30
25: 7 Phin'ehas . . rose and left the congregation 16
26:65 There was not left a man of them 10
Deu 2:14 the time from our leaving Ka'desh-bar'nea until 4
34 destroyed every city . . we left none remaining; 30
3: 3 smote him until no survivor was left to him. 30
11 only Og . . was left of the remnant of the Reph'aim; 30
4:27 you will be left few in number among the nations 30
7:20 until those who are left and hide themselves 30
28:51 who also shall not leave you grain, wine, or oil 30
55 because he has nothing left him, in the siege 30
62 multitude, you shall be left few in number; 30
Jos 2:11 and there was no courage left in any man 26
8:17 There was not a man left . . who did not go out 30
17 they left the city open, and pursued Israel. 25
22 there was left none that survived or escaped. 30
10:28 he utterly destroyed . . he left none remaining; 30
30 and he smote it . . he left none remaining in it; 30
33 Joshua smote . . until he left none remaining. 30
37 he left none remaining . . and utterly destroyed 30
39 and utterly destroyed . . he left none remaining; 30
40 he left none remaining, but utterly destroyed 30
11: 8 they smote them, until they left none remaining. 30
11 destroying . . there was none left that breathed 10
14 and they did not leave any that breathed. 10
22 There was none of the Anakim left in the land 10
13:12 he alone was left of the remnant of the Reph'aim 30
23: 7 be mixed with these nations left here among you 30
12 the remnant of these nations left here among you 30
Jdg 2:21 any of the nations that Joshua left when he died 25
23 the LORD left those nations, not driving them out 17
3: 1 the nations which the LORD left, to test Israel 17
4:16 the edge of the sword; not a man was left. 30
6: 4 they would . . leave no sustenance in Israel 30
8:10 all who were left of all the army of the people 10
9: 5 Jotham the youngest son of Jerubba'al was left 10
9 Shall I leave my fatness, by which gods and men are 6
11 Shall I leave my sweetness and my good fruit 6
13 Shall I leave my wine which cheers gods and men 6
16:17 If I be shaved, then my strength will leave me 21
19 began to torment him, and his strength left him. 21
20 And he did not know that the LORD had left him. 21
18:24 take my gods . . and go away, and what have I left? 24
21: 7 What shall we do for wives for those who are left 10
16 What shall we do for wives for those who are left 10
Rut 1: 3 and she was left with her two sons. 30
16 Ruth said, "Entreat me not to leave you or to return 25
2: 8 not . . glean in another field or leave this one 22
11 you left your father and mother and . . land 25
16 also pull out some . . and leave it for her to glean 25
1Sm 2:36 every one who is left in your house shall come 10
5: 4 only the trunk of Dagon was left to him. 30
10: 9 When he turned his back to leave Samuel 5
11:11 scattered, so that no two . . were left together. 30
14:36 let us not leave a man of them. 30
17:20 David rose . . and left the sheep with a keeper 18
22 And David left the things in charge of the keeper 18
28 with whom have you left those few sheep 18
20: 6 David . . asked leave of me to run to Bethlehem •
28 David . . asked leave of me to go to Bethlehem; 14
22: 4 he left them with the king of Moab, and they stayed 17
24: 7 Saul rose up and left the cave, and went . . his way. •
25:22 if by morning I leave so much as one male 30
34 there had not been left to Nabal 10
30:21 men . . who had been left at the brook Besor; 9
2Sm 5:21 And the Philistines left their idols there 25
8: 4 David . . left enough for 100 chariots. 10
9: 1 Is there still any one left of the house of Saul 10
13:30 slain all the king's . . and not one of them is left. 10
14: 7 Thus they would quench my coal which is left 30
7 and leave to my husband neither name nor remnant 28
15:16 the king left ten concubines to keep the house. 25
16:21 concubines, whom he has left to keep the house; 17
17:12 of him . . the men with him not one will be left. 10
22 by daybreak not one was left who had not crossed 23
19:19 on the day my lord the king left Jerusalem; 7
20: 3 concubines whom he had left to care for the house 17
1Kg 7:47 Solomon left all the vessels unweighed 17
8:57 God be with us . . may he not leave us or forsake us; 25
9:20 the people who were left of the Amorites 10
21 descendants who were left after them in the land 10
15:18 and the gold that were left in the treasures 10
29 he left to . . Jerobo'am not one that breathed 30
16:11 he did not leave him a single male of his kinsmen 30
17:17 so severe that there was no breath left in him. 10
18:22 I, even I only, am left a prophet of the LORD; 10
19: 3 came to Beer-sheba . . and left his servant there. 17
10 I, even I only, am left; and they seek my life 10
14 I, even I only, am left; and they seek my life 10
18 Yet I will leave 7,000 in Israel 30
20 he left the oxen, and ran after Eli'jah, and said 25
20:30 the wall fell upon . . men that were left. 10
2Kg 2: 2 As the LORD lives . . I will not leave you. 25
4 As the LORD lives . . I will not leave you. 25
6 As the LORD lives . . I will not leave you. 25
3:25 only its stones were left in Kir-har'eseth 30
4:30 As the LORD lives . . I will not leave you. 25
43 says the LORD, 'They shall eat and have some left.' 10
44 they ate, and had some left, according to the word 10
7: 7 and forsook . . leaving the camp as it was, and fled •
13 those who are left here will fare like the whole 30
8: 6 from the day that she left the land until now. 25
10:11 Jehu slew . . until he left him none remaining. 30
21 there was not a man left who did not come. 30
13: 7 there was not left to Jeho'ahaz an army 30
14:26 for there was none left, bond or free •
17:18 none was left but the tribe of Judah only. 30
19: 4 lift up your prayer for the remnant that is left. 15
8 for he heard that the king had left Lachish. 19
20:17 carried to Babylon; nothing shall be left, says 10
25:11 the rest of the people who were left in the city 30
12 captain . . left some of the poorest of the land 30
22 whom Nebuchadnez'zar king of Babylon had left 30
1Ch 14:12 left their gods there, and David gave command 25
16:37 David left Asaph and his brethren there 25
39 he left Zadok the priest and his brethren •
18: 4 but left enough for 100 chariots. 10
2Ch 8: 7 All the people who were left of the Hittites 10
8 from their descendants who were left after them 10
11:14 left their common lands and their holdings 25
21:17 so that no son was left to him except Jeho'ahaz 30
24:25 departed from him, leaving him severely wounded 25
28:14 the armed men left the captives and the spoil 25
31:10 we have eaten and had enough and have plenty left; 10
10 we have this great store left. 10
32:31 God left him to himself, in order to try him 25
34:21 for those who are left in Israel and in Judah 30
Ezr 9: 8 to leave us a remnant, and to give us a secure hold 30
12 leave it for an inheritance to your children •
15 left a remnant that has escaped, as at this day. 30
Neh 6: 1 reported . . that there was no breach left in it 10
3 work stop while I leave it and come down to you? 27
13: 6 after some time I asked leave of the king •
Est 7: 8 As the words left the mouth of the king 7
Job 16: 6 if I forbear, how much of it leaves me? 4
20:21 There was nothing left after he had eaten; 29
26 what is left in his tent will be consumed. 29
21:34 There is nothing left of your answers 30
22:20 what they left the fire has consumed.' 11
39:11 will you leave to him your labor? 25
14 For she leaves her eggs to the earth 25
41:32 Behind him he leaves a shining wake; •
Ps 17:14 may they leave something over to their babes. 17
19: 5 forth like a bridegroom leaving his chamber 7
49:10 must perish and leave their wealth to others. 25
106:11 their adversaries; not one of them was left. 10
119:121 do not leave me to my oppressors. 17
Prv 9: 6 Leave simpleness, and live 25
14: 7 Leave the presence of a fool, for there you do not 4
25:28 like a city broken into and left without walls. •
28: 3 beating rain that leaves no food. •
29:15 child left to himself brings shame 32
31: 8 for the rights of all who are left desolate. •
Ecc 2:18 I hated all my toil . . seeing that I must leave it 17
21 a man who has . . must leave all to be enjoyed 20
10: 4 do not leave your place 17
Isa 1: 8 And the daughter of Zion is left like a booth 10
9 If the LORD . . had not left us a few survivors 10
4: 3 he who is left in Zion and remains in Jerusalem 30
7:22 every one that is left in the land will eat curds 10
10: 3 and where will you leave your wealth? 25
11:11 recover the remnant which is left of his people 30
16 for the remnant which is left of his people 30
17: 6 Gleanings will be left in it, as when an olive tree 30
18: 6 They shall all of them be left to the birds of prey 25
24: 6 inhabitants . . scorched, and few men are left. 30
12 Desolation is left in the city 30
30:11 leave the way, turn aside from the path 21
17 you shall flee, till you are left like a flagstaff 10
37: 4 lift up your prayer for the remnant that is left.' 15
8 for he had heard that the king had left Lachish. 19
39: 6 be carried to Babylon; nothing shall be left 10
49:21 I was left alone; whence then have these come?' 30
65:15 You shall leave your name to my chosen for a curse 17
Jer 3:20 Surely, as a faithless wife leaves her husband •
9: 2 that I might leave my people and go away from them! 25
19 utterly shamed, because we have left the land 25
11:23 and none of them shall be left. 31
14: 9 and we are called by thy name; leave us not. 17
17:11 in the midst of his days they will leave him 25
18:14 Does the snow of Lebanon leave the crags 25
25:38 Like a lion he has left his covert 25
27:11 I will leave on its own land, to till it 17
18 vessels which are left in the house of the LORD 10
19 rest of the vessels which are left in this city. 10
21 vessels which are left in the house of the LORD 10
34: 7 against all the cities of Judah that were left 10
38: 4 hands of the soldiers who are left in this city 30

9 hunger, for there is no bread left in the city. 24
22 Behold, all the women left in the house of the king 30
39: 9 the rest of the people who were left in the city 30
10 left in the land of Judah some of the poor people 30
40: 6 among the people who were left in the land. 30
11 heard that the king of Babylon had left a remnant 20
41:10 and all the people who were left at Mizpah 30
42: 2 for we are left but a few of many, as your eyes see us 30
43: 6 Nebu'zarad'an the captain of the guard had left 17
44: 7 from the midst of Judah, leaving you no remnant? 10
48:28 Leave the cities, and dwell in the rock 25
49: 9 came to you, would they not leave gleanings? 30
11 Leave your fatherless children, I will keep them 25
50:20 for I will pardon those whom I leave as a remnant. 30
26 destroy her utterly; let nothing be left of her. 31
52:15 the rest of the people who were left in the city 30
16 the guard left some of the poorest of the land 30
Lam 1:13 he turned me back; he has left me stunned, faint 20
Ezk 6: 8 Yet I will leave some of you alive. 10
12 he that is left and is preserved shall die 30
9: 8 And while they were smiting, and I was left alone 30
14:22 Yet, if there should be left in it any survivors 10
16:39 shall strip you . . and leave you naked and bare. 17
23:29 and leave you naked and bare 25
31:12 Foreigners . . will cut it down and leave it. 18
12 peoples . . will go from its shadow and leave it. 18
36:36 Then the nations that are left round about you 30
47:11 not become fresh; they are to be left for salt. 20
Dan 2: 1 spirit was troubled, and his sleep left him. •
44 nor . . its sovereignty be left to another people. 33
4:15 leave the stump of its roots in the earth 33
23 but leave the stump of its roots in the earth 33
26 commanded to leave the stump of the roots 33
10: 8 I was left alone and saw this great vision 30
8 great vision, and no strength was left in me; 30
13 left him there with the prince of . . Persia 10
17 no strength remains . . no breath is left in me. 30
Hos 4:12 and they have left their God to play the harlot. •
9:12 I will bereave them till none is left. †
12:14 so his LORD will leave his bloodguilt upon him 18
Jol 1: 4 What the cutting locust left, the swarming locust 11
4 What the swarming locust left, the hopping locust 11
4 what the hopping locust left, the destroying locust 11
2:14 turn and repent, and leave a blessing behind him 30
16 Let the bridegroom leave his room 7
Ams 5: 3 went forth 1,000 shall have 100 left 30
3 which went forth 100 shall have ten left 30
9: 1 what are left of them I will slay with the sword 2
Obd 1: 5 gatherers . . would they not leave gleanings? 30
Zep 2: 5 and I will destroy you till no inhabitant is left. •
3: 3 wolves that leave nothing till the morning. 3
12 I will leave in the midst of you a people humble 30
13 those who are left in Israel; 31
Hag 2: 3 Who is left among you that saw this house 30
Zec 7:14 Thus the land they left was desolate 1
11: 9 let those that are left devour the flesh of one 30
12:14 all the families that are left, each by itself 30
13: 8 and perish, and one third shall be left alive. 10
Mal 1: 3 and left his heritage to jackals of the desert. •
4: 1 it will leave them neither root nor branch. 25
Mat 4:11 Then the devil left him, and behold, angels came 44
13 leaving Nazareth he went and dwelt in Caper'na-um 56
20 Immediately they left their nets and followed 44
22 Immediately they left the boat and their father 44
5:24 leave your gift there before the altar and go; 44
8:15 he touched her hand, and the fever left her 44
22 Jesus said to him, "Follow me, and leave the dead 44
34 they begged him to leave their neighborhood. 57
10:14 as you leave that house or town. 55
13:36 Then he left the crowds and went into the house. 44
16: 4 So he left them and departed. 56
18:12 does he not leave the 99 on the mountains 44
19: 5 said, 'For this reason a man shall leave his father 56
27 Lo, we have left everything and followed you 44
29 every one who has left houses or brothers 44
21:17 leaving them, he went out of the city to Bethany 56
22:22 they left him and went away. 44
25 having no children left his wife to his brother. 44
24: 1 Jesus left the temple and was going away 55
2 there will not be left here one stone 44
40 one is taken and one is left. 44
41 one is taken and one is left. 44
26:44 So, leaving them again, he went away 44
Mrk 1:18 immediately they left their nets and followed 44
20 they left their father Zeb'edee in the boat 44
29 immediately he left the synagogue 55
31 the fever left her; and she served them. 44
42 immediately the leprosy left him 39
4:36 leaving the crowd, they took him with them 44
6:10 stay there until you leave the place. 55
11 when you leave, shake off the dust 53
7: 8 You leave the commandment of God 44
17 when he had entered the house, and left the people 40
29 the demon has left your daughter. 55
8:13 he left them, and getting into the boat again 44
10: 1 he left there and went to the region of Judea 36
7 a man shall leave his father and mother 56
28 Lo, we have left everything and followed you. 44
29 there is no one who has left house or brothers 44

46 as he was leaving Jericho with his disciples 53
12:12 so they left him and went away. 44
19 if a man's brother dies and leaves a wife 56
19 leaves a wife, but leaves no child 44
20 when he died left no children; 44
21 the second took her, and died, leaving no children; 56
22 the seven left no children 44
13: 2 There will not be left here one stone upon another 44
34 when he leaves home 44
14:52 he left the linen cloth and ran away naked. 56
Lke 4:38 he arose and left the synagogue 40
39 rebuked the fever, and it left her 44
42 and would have kept him from leaving them; 62
5:11 they left everything and followed him. 44
13 immediately the leprosy left him. 39
28 he left everything, and rose and followed him. 56
9: 5 when you leave that town shake off the dust 55
39 shatters him, and will hardly leave him. 43
60 Leave the dead to bury their own dead 44
10:30 robbers . . departed, leaving him half dead. 44
40 Lord, do you not care that my sister has left me 56
12:39 he would not have left his house to be broken into. 44
15: 4 does not leave the 99 in the wilderness 56
17:34 one will be taken and the other left. 44
35 one will be taken and the other left. 44
18:28 Lo, we have left our homes and followed you. 44
29 there is no man who has left house or wife 44
19:44 they will not leave one stone upon another in you; 44
20:31 likewise all seven left no children and died. 56
21: 6 the days will come when there shall not be left 44
Joh 4: 3 he left Judea and departed again to Galilee. 44
28 the woman left her water jar, and went away 44
52 Yesterday at the seventh hour the fever left him. 44
6:13 fragments . . left by those who had eaten. 61
7: 3 Leave here and go to Judea 57
8: 9 Jesus was left alone with the woman 56
29 he who sent me is with me; he has not left me alone 44
10:12 leaves the sheep and flees 44
14:18 I will not leave you desolate; I will come to you. 44
27 Peace I leave with you; my peace I give to you 44
16:28 I am leaving the world and going to the Father. 44
32 will leave me alone 44
Act 5:41 Then they left the presence of the council 63
12:10 immediately the angel left him. 45
13:13 John left them and returned to Jerusalem; 43
14:17 yet he did not leave himself without witness 44
16:39 took them out and asked them to leave the city. 39
18: 1 After this he left Athens and went to Corinth. 66
2 had commanded all the Jews to leave Rome 66
7 he left there and went to the house of . . Titius 57
19 they came to Ephesus, and he left them there 56
19:12 diseases left them and the evil spirits came out 38
21: 3 leaving it on the left we sailed to Syria 56
23:32 leaving the horsemen to go on with him. 49
24:27 Felix left Paul in prison. 56
25:14 There is a man left prisoner by Felix; 56
27:40 they cast off the anchors and left them in the sea 49
Rom 9:29 If the Lord of hosts had not left us children 50
11: 3 and I alone am left, and they seek my life. 64
12:19 but leave it to the wrath of God; 48
2Co 12: 8 that it should leave me; 45
Eph 5:31 For this reason a man shall leave his father 56
Php 4:15 when I left Macedo'nia 55
1Th 4:15 who are left until the coming of the Lord 60
17 then we who are alive, who are left 60
2Ti 4:13 bring the cloak that I left with Carpus at Tro'as 41
20 Troph'imus I left ill at Mile'tus. 41
Tit 1: 5 This is why I left you in Crete 41
Heb 2: 8 he left nothing outside his control 44
3:16 left Egypt under the leadership of Moses. 55
6: 1 let us leave the elementary doctrine of Christ 44
11:27 By faith he left Egypt 56
12: 8 If you are left without discipline •
1Pe 2:21 Christ also suffered . . leaving you an example 65
Jde 1: 6 the angels that . . left their proper dwelling 41
1Es 4:20 A man leaves his own father, who brought him up 50
8: 6 left Babylon on the new moon of the first month 55
78 to leave to us a root and a name in thy holy place 56
88 to destroy us without leaving a root or seed 56
89 we are left as a root to this day. 56
2Es 3:11 thou didst leave one of them 67
5:18 like a shepherd who leaves his flock •
19 He heard what I said and left me. 69
7:30 so that no one shall be left. 67
78 as the spirit leaves the body to return again 69
140 there would probably be left only very few 67
12: 5 and not even a little strength is left in me •
39 Then he left me. 68
42 For of all the prophets you alone are left to us 73
13:16 alas for those who will be left in those days! 67
16 And still more, alas for those who are not left! 67
17 For those who are not left will be sad 67
19 alas for those also who are left 67
22 As for what you said about those who are left 67
24 those who are left are more blessed than those 67
26 and he will direct those who are left. 67
33 every man shall leave his own land 67
41 they would leave the multitude of the nations 67
48 those who are left of your people 67

16:23 for the earth shall be left desolate 67
24 No one shall be left to cultivate the earth 67
28 For out of a city, ten shall be left 70
29 three or four olives may be left on every tree 70
30 some clusters may be left by those who search 72
31 in those days three or four shall be left by those 71
32 the earth shall be left desolate 70
Tob 1: 8 I was left an orphan by my father. 56
20 nothing was left to me except my wife Anna 56
8:20 he should not leave 55
9: 3 For Raguel has sworn that I should not leave; 55
10: 7 every day to the road by which they had left 39
11: 2 Are you not aware . . of how you left your father? 44
12:13 did not hesitate to rise and leave your dinner 56
14: 8 now, my son, leave Nineveh 39
Jdt 2: 5 When you leave my presence 55
14 Holofernes left the presence of his master 55
5: 8 For they had left the ways of their ancestors 52
9 Then their God commanded them to leave 55
6:13 left him lying at the foot of the hill 44
7:22 there was no strength left in them any longer. •
8: 7 her husband Manasseh had left her gold 64
13: 2 Judith was left alone in the tent 64
4 no one . . was left in the bedchamber 56
14: 8 from the day she left 55
AEs 13: 7 leave our government completely secure 59
Wis 2: 9 everywhere let us leave signs of enjoyment 56
8:13 leave an everlasting remembrance 41
10: 8 also left for mankind a reminder of their folly 41
14 when he was in prison she did not leave him 44
12:11 didst leave them unpunished for their sins. 47
14: 6 left to the world the seed of a new generation. 41
Sir 6: 3 will be left like a withered tree. 44
8:11 Do not get up and leave an insolent fellow 42
11:19 until he leaves them to others and dies. 56
14:15 leave the fruit of your labors to another 56
15:14 he left him in the power of his own inclination. 44
23:11 the scourge will not leave his house 45
22 it is with a woman who leaves her husband 56
26 She will leave her memory for a curse 56
24:33 leave it to all future generations. 56
27:12 Among stupid people watch for a chance to leave •
32:11 Leave in good time and do not be the last 54
33:25 leave his hands idle, and he will seek liberty. 35
31 If you ill-treat him, and he leaves and runs away 37
38:12 let him not leave you, for there is need of him. 45
39:11 he will leave a name greater than 1,000 56
32 have thought this out and left it in writing 44
44: 8 There are some of them who have left a name 56
17 therefore a remnant was left to the earth 46
47:23 left behind him one of his sons, ample in folly 56
48:15 the people were left very few in number 56
Bar 2:13 we are left, few in number, among the nations 56
4:19 Go, my children, go; for I have been left desolate. 56
LJr 1:47 They have left only lies and reproach 56
1Mc 1:48 to leave their sons uncircumcised 44
2:18 as . . those . . left in Jerusalem have done. 56
28 left all that they had in the city. 50
3:32 He left Lysias . . in charge of the king's affairs 56
5:18 he left Joseph, the son of Zechariah 56
6: 2 weapons left there by Alexander 56
36 they never left it. 45
54 Few men were left in the sanctuary 64
7:20 left with him a force to help him 44
46 not even one of them was left. 56
9: 6 until no more than 800 of them were left. 56
8 He became faint, but he said to those who were left 56
10 and leave no cause to question our honor. 56
65 Jonathan left Simon his brother in the city 41
10:13 each left his place and departed to his own land. 56
79 Apollonius had secretly left 1,000 cavalry behind 41
11:64 left his brother Simon in the country. 56
70 not one of them was left except Mattathias 56
12:47 2,000 of whom he left in Galilee 44
13: 4 I alone am left. 56
15:14 and permitted no one to leave or enter it. 53
2Mc 1:31 the liquid that was left 60
2:28 leaving the responsibility for exact details 58
4:29 Menelaus left . . Lysimachus as deputy 41
29 while Sostratus left Crates •
31 leaving Andronicus . . to act as his deputy. 56
5:11 raging inwardly, he left Egypt 34
22 he left governors to afflict the people 56
6:28 leave to the young a noble example 56
31 leaving in his death an example of nobility 56
9:24 they would know to whom the government was left. 56
10:19 Maccabeus left Simon and Joseph 41
12:18 in one place he had left a very strong garrison. 56
19 whom Timothy had left in the stronghold 56
13:23 who had been left in charge of the government 41
24 left Hegemonides as governor 56
3Mc 5: 6 the Jews were left without any aid 51
4Mc 13:27 those who were left endured 64
18: 5 he left Jerusalem 37

leave alive 1. חיה 2. ὑπολείπω

1Sm 27: 9 David . . left neither man nor woman alive 1
Jdt 10:19 Surely not a man of them had better be left alive 2

leave all alone 1. μονόω
1Ti 5: 5 She who is a real widow, and is left all alone 1

leave an inheritance 1. נחל
Prv 13:22 A good man leaves an inheritance 1

leave behind 1. יתר 2. עזב 3. שאר 4. καταλείπω 5. περιλείπομαι
Exd 10:26 Our cattle . . not a hoof shall be left behind 3
1Sm 30: 9 Besor, where those stayed who were left behind. 1
13 my master left me behind because I fell sick 2
Ezk 24:21 your daughters whom you left behind shall fall 2
1Th 3: 1 we were willing to be left behind at Athens alone 4
Sir 30: 4 for he has left behind him one like himself; 4
6 left behind him an avenger against his enemies 4
4Mc 13:18 Those who were left behind said 5

leave defenseless 1. ערה
Ps 141: 8 in thee I seek refuge; leave me not defenseless! 1

leave desolate 1. ἐρημόω
Bar 4:12 I was left desolate because of the sins 1

leave dry and barren 1. χερσόω
Wis 4:19 they will be left utterly dry and barren 1

leave for an inheritance 1. נחל 2. κατακληρονομέω
1Ch 28: 8 leave it for an inheritance to your children 1
1Es 8:85 leave it for an inheritance 2

leave free 1. נוח
Ezk 41:11 on the part of the platform that was left free 1
11 the breadth of the part that was left free 1

leave hanging 1. κρεμάννυμι
2Sm 18: 9 and he was left hanging between heaven and earth 1

leave home 1. ἀναχωρέω
Tob 1:19 I left home in fear. 1

leave in trust 1. παρατίθημι
Tob 1:14 I left ten talents of silver in trust with Gabael 1
4: 1 the money which he had left in trust with Gabael 1
20 the ten talents . . which I left in trust with Gabael 1

make leave 1. נדח
Deu 13: 5 to make you leave the way in which the LORD 1

leave no one 1. ἐκλείπω
1Mc 14:13 No one was left in the land to fight them 1

leave off 1. חדל 2. עזב
Gen 11: 8 earth, and they left off building the city. 1
Neh 5:10 Let us leave off this interest. 2
Jer 44:18 since we left off burning incense to the queen 1

leave off speaking 1. חרש
Jer 38:27 So they left off speaking with him 1

leave open 1. פתח
Exd 21:33 When a man leaves a pit open, or when a man digs 1

leave out 1. נפל 2. ἐκβάλλω ἔξωθεν 3. omitto
Est 6:10 Leave out nothing that you have mentioned. 1
Rev 11: 2 court outside the temple; leave that out 2
2Es 2:14 for I left out evil and created good 3

leave over 1. יתר 2. עדף 3. περίσσευμα 4. περισσεύω
Exd 16:23 and all that is left over lay by to be kept 2
Lev 19: 6 anything left over until the third day 1
Rut 2:14 and she ate . . and she had some left over. 1
18 food she had left over after being satisfied. 1
Mat 14:20 baskets full of the broken pieces left over. 4
15:37 baskets full of the broken pieces left over. 4
Mrk 8: 8 they took up the broken pieces left over 3
Lke 9:17 they took up what was left over 4
Joh 6:12 Gather up the fragments left over 4

leave one's post 1. λειποτακτέω
4Mc 9:23 Do not leave your post in my struggle 1

leave remaining 1. יתר
Ezk 39:28 I will leave none of them remaining 1

leave the right way 1. ἀφίστημι
Sir 15:11 Do not say, "Because of the Lord I left the right way"; 1

leave to fate 1. παροράω
3Mc 3: 9 such . . ought not be left to its fate 1

leave undone 1. סור
Jos 11:15 Joshua did; he left nothing undone 1

leave unpunished 1. נקה
Jer 30:11 I will by no means leave you unpunished. 1
46:28 I will by no means leave you unpunished. 1

leave unsatisfied 1. ריק
Isa 32: 6 to leave the craving of the hungry unsatisfied 1

leave without 1. שבת
Rut 4:14 LORD, who has not left you . . without next of kin; 1

leaven 1. חמץ 2. חָמֵץ 3. מַחְמֶצֶת 4. שְׂאֹר 5. ζύμη 6. ζυμόω
Exd 12:15 you shall put away leaven out of your houses 4
15 if any one eats what is leavened . . that person 2
19 no leaven shall be found in your houses; 4
19 for if any one eats what is leavened 3
20 You shall eat nothing leavened; 3
34 people took their dough before it was leavened 1
39 for it was not leavened, because they were thrust 2
13: 7 and no leaven shall be seen with you in all 4
34:25 offer the blood of my sacrifice with leaven; 2
Lev 2:11 No cereal offering . . shall be made with leaven 2
11 you shall burn no leaven nor any honey 4
6:17 It shall not be baked with leaven 2
7:13 his offering with cakes of leavened bread 2
23:17 they shall be baked with leaven, as first fruits 2
Deu 16: 4 No leaven . . seen with you in all your territory 4
Hos 7: 4 the kneading of the dough until it is leavened. 1
Ams 4: 5 of thanksgiving of that which is leavened 2
Mat 13:33 The kingdom of heaven is like leaven 5
33 till it was all leavened. 6
16: 6 beware of the leaven of the Pharisees 5
11 Beware of the leaven of the Pharisees 5
12 to beware of the leaven of bread 5
Mrk 8:15 Take heed, beware of the leaven of the Pharisees 5
15 the leaven of Herod. 5
Lke 12: 1 the leaven of the Pharisees, which is hypocrisy. 5
13:21 It is like leaven which a woman took and hid 5
21 till it was all leavened. 6
1Co 5: 6 a little leaven leavens the whole lump? 5
6 a little leaven leavens the whole lump? 6
7 Cleanse out the old leaven 5
8 celebrate the festival, not with the old leaven 5
8 the old leaven, the leaven of malice and evil 5
Gal 5: 9 A little leaven leavens the whole lump. 5
9 A little leaven leavens the whole lump. 6

ledge 1. כַּרְכֹּב 2. עֲזָרָה
Exd 27: 5 you shall set it under the ledge of the altar 1
38: 4 network of bronze, under its ledge, extending 1
Ezk 43:14 from the base on the ground to the lower ledge 2
14 and from the smaller ledge to the larger ledge 2
14 and from the smaller ledge to the larger ledge 2
17 The ledge also shall be square 2
20 on the four corners of the ledge, and upon the rim 2
45:19 the four corners of the ledge of the altar 2

leech 1. עֲלוּקָה
Prv 30:15 The leech has two daughters; "Give, give," they cry. 1

leek 1. חָצִיר
Num11: 5 We remember the . . leeks, the onions 1

lees 1. שֶׁמֶר
Jer 48:11 Moab . . has settled on his lees; 1
Zep 1:12 the men who are thickening upon their lees 1

left 1. שמאל 2. שְׂמֹאל 3. שְׂמָאלִי 4. ἀριστερός 5. εὐώνυμος 6. levus 7. sinister
Gen 24:49 I may turn to the right hand or to the left. 2
Exd 14:22 on their right hand and on their left. 2
29 on their right hand and on their left. 2
Lev 14:15 pour it into the palm of his own left hand 3
16 the oil that is in his left hand, and sprinkle some 3
26 some of the oil into the palm of his own left hand 3
27 oil that is in his left hand seven times 3
Num20:17 not turn aside to the right hand or to the left 2
22:26 no way to turn either to the right or to the left. 2
Deu 2:27 turn aside neither to the right nor to the left. 2
5:32 not turn aside to the right hand or to the left. 2
17:11 not turn . . either to the right hand or to the left. 2
20 not turn . . either to the right hand or to the left; 2
28:14 do not turn . . to the right hand or to the left 2
Jos 1: 7 turn not from it to the right hand or to the left 2
23: 6 turning . . neither to the right hand nor to the left 2
Jdg 3:21 Ehud reached with his left hand, took the sword 2
7:20 the jars, holding in their left hands the torches 2
1Sm 6:12 they turned neither to the right nor to the left 2
2Sm 2:19 turned neither to the right hand nor to the left 2
21 Turn aside to your right hand or to your left 2
16: 6 mighty men were on his right hand and on his left. 2
1Kg 22:19 standing . . on his right hand and on his left; 2
2Kg 22: 2 did not turn aside to the right hand or to the left. 2
23: 8 which were on one's left at the gate of the city. 2
2Ch 18:18 all the host of heaven standing . . on his left; 2
34: 2 he did not turn aside to the right or to the left. 2
Neh 12:38 other company . . went to the left 1
Prv 4:27 Do not swerve to the right or to the left; 2
Ecc 10: 2 but a fool's heart toward the left. 2
Isa 9:20 and they devour on the left, but are not satisfied; 2
54: 3 will spread abroad to the right and to the left 2
Ezk 1:10 the four had the face of an ox on the left side 2
4: 4 Then lie upon your left side 2
21:16 Cut sharply to right and left 3
39: 3 then I will strike your bow from your left hand 2
Jon 4:11 who do not know their right hand from their left 2
Zec 4: 3 on the right of the bowl and the other on its left. 2
11 trees on the right and the left of the lampstand? 2
12: 6 they shall devour to the right and to the left 2
Mat 20:21 one at your right hand and one at your left 5
23 to sit at my right hand and at my left 5
25:33 the goats at the left. 5
27:38 one on the right and one on the left. 5
Mrk 10:37 one at your left, in your glory. 4
40 to sit at my right hand or at my left 5
15:27 one on his right and one on his left. 5
Lke 23:33 one on the right and one on the left. 4
Act 21: 3 leaving it on the left we sailed to Syria 5
2Co 6: 7 for the right hand and for the left; 4
Rev 10: 2 right foot on the sea, and his left foot on the land 5
1Es 9:44 on his left Pedaiah, Mishael, Malchijah 5
2Es 7: 7 and deep water on the left; 7
11:35 the head . . devoured the one on the left. 6
1Mc 2:22 to the right hand or to the left. 4
5:46 they could not go round it to the right or to the left; 4
6:45 he killed men right and left 5
9:16 When those on the left wing saw 4

go left 1. שמאל
Gen 13: 9 take the right hand, then I will go to the left. 1

left hand 1. שמאל 2. שְׂמֹאל 3. ἀριστερός
Gen 13: 9 If you take the left hand 2
48:13 E'phraim . . toward Israel's left hand 2
13 Manas'seh in his left hand toward Israel's right 2
14 and his left hand upon the head of Manas'seh 2
Jdg 16:29 right hand on the one and his left hand on the other 2
1Ch 6:44 On the left hand were their brethren the sons 2
12: 2 with either the right or the left hand; 1
Neh 8: 4 Zechari'ah, and Meshul'lam on his left hand. 2
Job 23: 9 on the left hand I seek him, but I cannot behold him; 2
Prv 3:16 in her left hand are riches and honor. 2
Sng 2: 6 O that his left hand were under my head 2
8: 3 O that his left hand were under my head 2
Dan 12: 7 his right hand and his left hand toward heaven; 2
Mat 6: 3 when you give alms, do not let your left hand know 3
25:41 Then he will say to those at his left hand •
1Es 4:30 slap the king with her left hand. 3

left-handed 1. אִטֵּר יַד־יְמִינוֹ
Jdg 3:15 Ehud . . the Benjaminite, a left-handed man. 1
20:16 were 700 picked men who were left-handed 1

leg 1. כֶּרַע 2. מַרְגְּלוֹת 3. רֶגֶל 4. שׁוֹק 5. שָׁק (A) 6. πούς 7. σκέλος
Exd 12: 9 its head with its legs and its inner parts. 1
25:26 the rings to the four corners at its four legs. 3
29:17 and wash its entrails and its legs, and put them 1
37:13 the rings to the four corners at its four legs. 3
Lev 1: 9 its entrails and its legs he shall wash with water 1
13 the entrails and the legs he shall wash with water 1
4:11 the bull . . with its head, its legs, its entrails 1
8:21 when the entrails and the legs were washed 1
9:14 he washed the entrails and the legs, and burned 1
11:21 may eat those which have legs above their feet 1
Deu 28:35 LORD will smite you on the knees and on the legs 4
1Sm 9:24 the cook took up the leg and the upper portion 4
17: 6 And he had greaves of bronze upon his legs 3
Ps 147:10 nor his pleasure in the legs of a man; 4
Prv 26: 7 Like a lame man's legs, which hang useless 4
Sng 5:15 His legs are alabaster columns, set upon bases 4
Isa 47: 2 uncover your legs, pass through the rivers. 4
Ezk 1: 7 Their legs were straight 3
Dan 2:33 its legs of iron, its feet partly of iron 5
10: 6 arms and legs like the gleam of burnished bronze 2
Ams 3:12 from the mouth of the lion two legs, or a piece 1
Joh 19:31 that their legs might be broken 7
32 the soldiers came and broke the legs of the first 7
33 they did not break his legs. 7
Rev 10: 1 and his legs like pillars of fire. 6
4Mc 10: 6 his fingers and arms and legs and elbows. 7

legal 1. νόμος
Heb 7:16 a legal requirement concerning bodily descent 1

legion 1. λεγιών
Mat 26:53 send me more than twelve legions of angels? 1
Mrk 5: 9 He replied, "My name is Legion; for we are many. 1
15 in his right mind, the man who had had the legion; 1
Lke 8:30 And he said, "Legion 1

legislation 1. νομοθεσία
4Mc 17:16 admire the athletes of the divine legislation? 1

leisure 1. ἀργία 2. εὐκαιρέω 3. ἡσυχία 4. σχολή
Mrk 6:31 they had no leisure even to eat. 2
AEs 14:16 I do not wear it on the days when I am at leisure. 3
Wis 13:13 he takes and carves with care in his leisure 1
Sir 38:24 depends on the opportunity of leisure 4

lend 1. לוה 2. נשה 3. נתן 4. עבט 5. שאל 6. γίνομαι 7. δανείζω 8. κίχρημι 9. χρέος

Exd 22:25 If you lend money to any of my people with you who 1
Lev 25:37 You shall not lend him your money at interest 3
Deu 15: 2 shall release what he has lent to his neighbor; 2
6 lend to many nations, but you shall not borrow; 4
8 lend him sufficient for his need, 4
28:12 lend to many nations, but you shall not borrow. 1
44 He shall lend to you, and you shall not lend to him; 1
44 He shall lend to you, and you shall not lend to him; 1
1Sm 1:28 Therefore I have lent him to the LORD; 5
28 as long as he lives, he is lent to the LORD. 5
2:20 for the loan which she lent to the LORD"; 5
Neh 5:10 Moreover I . . lending them money and grain. 2
Ps 37:26 He is ever giving liberally and lending 1
112: 5 well with the man who deals generously and lends 1
Prv 19:17 He who is kind to the poor lends to the LORD 1
Jer 15:10 I have not lent, nor have I borrowed 2
Ezk 18: 8 does not lend at interest or take any increase 3
13 lends at interest, and takes increase; 3
Lke 6:34 if you lend to those from whom you hope to receive 7
34 Even sinners lend to sinners 7
35 do good, and lend, expecting nothing in return 7
11: 5 Friend, lend me three loaves; 8
Jdt 11:22 to lend strength to our hands 6
Wis 15: 8 required to return the soul that was lent him. 9
Sir 8:12 Do not lend to a man who is stronger than you 7
12 if you do lend anything, be as one who has lost it. 7
20:15 today he lends and tomorrow he asks it back 7
29: 1 He that shows mercy will lend to his neighbor 7
2 Lend to your neighbor in the time of his need 7
7 many have refused to lend *
4Mc 2: 8 to lend without interest to the needy 7

lend for interest 1. נשך

Deu 23:19 interest on anything that is lent for interest. 1

lend upon interest 1. נשך

Deu 23:19 not lend upon interest to your brother 1
20 To a foreigner you may lend upon interest 1
20 to your brother you shall not lend upon interest; 1

lender 1. לוה

Prv 22: 7 borrower is the slave of the lender. 1
Isa 24: 2 as with the lender, so with the borrower; 1
Sir 29: 6 If the lender exert pressure *

length 1. אֹרֶךְ 2. קוֹמָה 3. רֹב 4. βῆμα 5. μακρότης 6. μῆκος 7. ποτέ

Gen 6:15 the length of the ark 300 cubits 1
13:17 Arise, walk through the length and the breadth 1
Exd 25:10 two cubits and a half shall be its length 1
17 two cubits and a half shall be its length 1
23 two cubits shall be its length 1
26: 2 The length of each curtain shall be 28 cubits 1
8 The length of each curtain shall be 30 cubits 1
13 what remains in the length of the curtains 1
16 Ten cubits shall be the length of a frame 1
27:11 likewise for its length on the north side 1
18 The length of the court shall be 100 cubits 1
28:16 a span its length and a span its breadth. 1
30: 2 A cubit shall be its length 1
36: 9 The length of each curtain was 28 cubits 1
15 The length of each curtain was 30 cubits 1
21 Ten cubits was the length of a frame 1
37: 1 two cubits and a half was its length 1
6 two cubits and a half was its length 1
10 two cubits was its length, a cubit its breadth 1
25 its length was a cubit, and its breadth was a cubit; 1
38: 1 five cubits was its length, and five cubits its 1
39: 9 a span its length and a span its breadth 1
Deu 3:11 Nine cubits was its length, and four cubits 1
30:20 for that means life to you and length of days 1
Jdg 3:16 himself a sword with two edges, a cubit in length; 1
1Sm 28:20 Saul fell at once full length upon the ground 2
1Kg 6:24 Five cubits was the length of one wing *
24 and five cubits the length of the other wing *
7: 2 its length was 100 cubits 1
6 he made the Hall of Pillars; its length was 50 cubits 1
2Ch 3: 3 the length . . was 60 cubits, and the breadth 1
8 most holy place; its length . . was twenty cubits; 1
Job 12:12 and understanding in length of days. 1
Ps 21: 4 gavest it to him, length of days for ever and ever. 1
Prv 3: 2 length of days and years of life 1
Isa 57:10 You were wearied with the length of your way 3
Ezk 31: 7 in its greatness, in the length of its branches; 1
40: 5 the length of the measuring reed in the man's hand *
5 each being a cubit and a handbreadth in length; *
18 corresponding to the length of the gates; 1
20 He measured its length and its breadth. 1
21 its length was 50 cubits 1
25 its length was 50 cubits 1
29 its length was 50 cubits 1
33 its length was 50 cubits 1
36 windows round about; its length was 50 cubits 1
49 The length of the vestibule was twenty cubits 1
41: 2 he measured the length of the nave 40 cubits 1
4 he measured the length of the room, twenty cubits 1
12 and its length 90 cubits. 1
15 Then he measured the length of the building 1
42: 2 The length of the building which was on the north 1
11 the same length and breadth, with the same exits 1
45: 7 corresponding in length to one of the tribal 1
48: 8 in length equal to one of the tribal portions 1
9 be 25,000 cubits in length, 1
10 and 25,000 in length on the southern side 1
13 25,000 cubits in length and 10,000 in breadth. 1
13 The whole length shall be 25,000 cubits 1
15 5,000 cubits in breadth and 25,000 in length *
18 The remainder of the length alongside the holy 1
Zec 2: 2 what is its breadth and what is its length. 1
5: 2 a flying scroll; its length is twenty cubits 1
Lke 23: 9 he questioned him at some length †
Act 7: 5 not even a foot's length 4
Eph 3:18 what is the breadth and length and height 6
Php 4:10 now at length you have revived your concern 7
Rev 21:16 its length the same as its breadth; 6
16 its length and breadth and height are equal. 6
Jdt 7: 3 spread out . . in length from Bethulia to Cyamon 6
4Mc 13:20 the brothers dwelt the same length of time *
18:19 this is your life and the length of your days.' 5

length and breadth 1. מֶרְחָק

Jer 8:19 the cry . . from the length and breadth of the land 1

furrow's length 1. מַעֲנָה

1Sm 14:14 within . . half a furrow's length in an acre 1

great length 1. πολύς

Wis 8:12 when I speak at greater length 1

length of days 1. μακροβίωσις 2. μακροημέρευσις

Sir 30:22 the rejoicing of a man is length of days. 2
Bar 3:14 discern where there is length of days, and life 1

length of time 1. πολυχρόνιος

Wis 4: 8 For old age is not honored for length of time 1

lengthen 1. ארך 2. נטה 3. אַרְכָּה (A) 4. πλεονάζω 5. προστίθημι

1Kg 3:14 if you will . . then I will lengthen your days. 1
2Kg 20:10 easy thing for the shadow to lengthen ten steps; 2
Isa 54: 2 lengthen your cords and strengthen your stakes. 1
Jer 6: 4 for the shadows of evening lengthen! 2
Dan 4:27 perhaps be a lengthening of your tranquillity. 3
Sir 48:23 he lengthened the life of the king. 5
2Mc 2:32 it is foolish to lengthen the preface 4

lentil 1. עֲדָשָׁה

Gen 25:34 Jacob gave Esau bread and pottage of lentils 1
2Sm 17:28 brought . . meal, parched grain, beans and lentils 1
23:11 where there was a plot of ground full of lentils; 1
Ezk 4: 9 you, take wheat and barley, beans and lentils 1

leopard 1. נָמֵר 2. נְמַר (A) 3. πάρδαλις

Sng 4: 8 dens of lions, from the mountains of leopards. 1
Isa 11: 6 and the leopard shall lie down with the kid 1
Jer 5: 6 A leopard is watching against their cities 1
13:23 change his skin or the leopard his spots? 1
Dan 7: 6 another, like a leopard, with four wings of a bird 2
Hos 13: 7 like a leopard I will lurk beside the way. 1
Hab 1: 8 Their horses are swifter than leopards 1
Rev 13: 2 And the beast that I saw was like a leopard 3
Sir 28:23 like a leopard it will mangle them. 3

leopard-like 1. παρδάλεος

4Mc 9:28 These leopard-like beasts tore out his sinews 1

leper 1. צרע 2. λεπρός

Lev 13:45 The leper who has the disease shall wear torn 1
14: 2 This shall be the law of the leper for the day 1
3 Then, if the leprous disease is healed in the leper 1
22: 4 None of the line of Aaron who is a leper or suffers 1
Num 5: 2 put out of the camp every leper 1
2Kg 5: 1 He was a mighty man of valor, but he was a leper. 1
11 wave his hand over the place, and cure the leper. 1
27 So he went out from his presence a leper 1
7: 3 Now there were four men who were lepers 1
8 when these lepers came . . they went into a tent 1
15: 5 he was a leper to the day of his death 1
2Ch 26:21 King Uzzi'ah was a leper to the day of his death 1
21 being a leper dwelt in a separate house 1
23 for they said, "He is a leper. 1
Mat 8: 2 behold, a leper came to him and knelt before him 2
10: 8 Heal the sick, raise the dead, cleanse lepers 2
11: 5 the lame walk, lepers are cleansed 2
26: 6 at Bethany in the house of Simon the leper 2
Mrk 1:40 a leper came to him beseeching him, and kneeling 2
14: 3 at Bethany in the house of Simon the leper 2
Lke 4:27 there were many lepers in Israel 2
7:22 lepers are cleansed, and the deaf hear 2
17:12 as he entered a village, he was met by ten lepers 2

leprosy 1. צָרַעַת 2. λέπρα

Lev 13: 8 shall pronounce him unclean; it is leprosy 1
9 When a man is afflicted with leprosy 1
11 it is a chronic leprosy in the skin of his body 1
12 if the leprosy breaks out in the skin 1
12 breaks out . . so that the leprosy covers all 1
13 if the leprosy has covered all his body 1
15 raw flesh is unclean, for it is leprosy 1
20 it is the disease of leprosy, it has broken out 1
25 if it appears deeper . . then it is leprosy 1
30 it is an itch, a leprosy of the head or the beard 1
42 it is leprosy breaking out on his bald head 1
43 the appearance of leprosy in the skin of the body 1
51 the disease is a malignant leprosy; it is unclean 1
52 for it is a malignant leprosy; it shall be burned 1
14: 7 upon him who is to be cleansed of leprosy 1
44 it is a malignant leprosy in the house 1
55 for leprosy in a garment or in a house 1
57 This is the law for leprosy 1
Deu 24: 8 Take heed, in an attack of leprosy, to be very 1
2Kg 5: 3 He would cure him of his leprosy. 1
6 my servant, that you may cure him of his leprosy. 1
7 this man sends . . to me to cure a man of his leprosy? 1
27 the leprosy of Na'aman shall cleave to you 1
2Ch 26:19 leprosy broke out on his forehead 1
Mat 8: 3 And immediately his leprosy was cleansed. 2
Mrk 1:42 immediately the leprosy left him 2
Lke 5:12 there came a man full of leprosy 2
13 immediately the leprosy left him. 2

leprous 1. צרע 2. צָרַעַת

Exd 4: 6 behold, his hand was leprous, as white as snow. 1
Lev 13: 2 a spot, and it turns into a leprous disease 2
3 than the skin of his body, it is a leprous disease 2
25 pronounce him unclean; it is a leprous disease 2
27 it is a leprous disease 2
47 When there is a leprous disease in a garment 2
49 it is a leprous disease and shall be shown 2
55 the leprous spot is on the back or on the front *
59 This is the law for a leprous disease in a garment 2
14: 3 Then, if the leprous disease is healed in the leper 2
32 law for him in whom is a leprous disease 2
34 and I put a leprous disease in a house 2
54 This is the law for any leprous disease 2
Num 12:10 behold, Miriam was leprous, as white as snow. 1
10 towards Miriam, and behold, she was leprous. 1
2Sm 3:29 without one who has a discharge, or who is leprous 1
2Ch 26:20 behold, he was leprous in his forehead! 1

leprous man 1. צרע

Lev 13:44 he is a leprous man, he is unclean 1

less 1. ἐλάσσων 2. ἥσσων 3. μᾶλλον 4. παρά

1Co 12:16 that would not make it any less a part of the body. †
2Co 11:24 I have received . . the 40 lashes less one. 4
12:15 If I love you the more, am I to be loved the less? 2
1Ti 5: 9 if she is not less than 60 years of age 1
Heb 12:25 much less shall we escape 3
2Mc 4:40 advanced in years and no less advanced in folly. 2
5: 5 Jason took no less than 1,000 men 1
10:18 When no less than 9,000 took refuge 1
12: 4 not less than 200. 1
10 not less than 5,000 Arabs with 500 horsemen 1
15:18 Their concern for wives . . lay upon them less heavily 2
27 they laid low no less than 35,000 men 2

any less 1. παρά

1Co 12:15 that would not make it any less a part of the body. 1

how much less 1. אַף כִּי

1Kg 8:27 how much less this house which I have built! 1
2Ch 6:18 how much less this house which I have built! 1
32:15 How much less will your God deliver you 1
Job 15:16 how much less one who is abominable and corrupt 1
25: 6 how much less man, who is a maggot 1
35:14 How much less when you say that you do not see him 1
Ezk 15: 5 how much less, when the fire has consumed it 1

less than 1. מִן

Job 11: 6 God exacts of you less than your guilt deserves. 1
Isa 40:17 they are accounted by him as less than nothing 1

lessen 1. גרע 2. ἐλαττονόω 3. ἐλαττόω 4. μικρύνω

Exd 5: 8 you shall by no means lessen it; for they are idle; 1
11 but your work will not be lessened in the least.' 1
19 by no means lessen your daily number of bricks. 1
Sir 17:25 pray in his presence and lessen your offenses. 4
19: 6 for one who hates gossip evil is lessened. 2
28: 8 Refrain from strife, and you will lessen sins 3

lesson 1. διδαχή 2. παιδεία 3. παραβολή

Mat 24:32 From the fig tree learn its lesson 3
Mrk 13:28 From the fig tree learn its lesson 3
1Co 14:26 a hymn, a lesson, a revelation, a tongue 1
Sir 9: 1 do not teach her an evil lesson to your own hurt. 2

lest 1. אֲשֶׁר לֹא 2. בַּל 3. בִּלְתִּי 4. וְ 5. וְאַל 6. וְלֹא 7. לֹא 8. לְבִלְתִּי לֹא 9. לְמַעַן לֹא 10. מִן 11. פֶּן 12. דִּי לְמָה (A) 13. ἵνα 14. ἵνα μή 15. μή 16. μήποτε 17. μήπως 18. ut non

Gen 3: 3 garden, neither shall you touch it, lest you die.' 11

22 good and evil; and now, lest he put forth his hand 11
4:15 a mark on Cain, lest any who came upon him should 8
11: 4 a name for ourselves, lest we be scattered abroad 11
14:23 lest you should say, 'I have made Abram rich.' 6
19:15 two daughters who are here, lest you be consumed 11
17 flee to the hills, lest you be consumed. 11
19 flee to the hills, lest the disaster overtake me 11
26: 7 lest the men of the place should kill me 11
9 I thought, 'Lest I die because of her.' 11
32:11 for I fear him, lest he come and slay us all 11
38: 9 semen on the ground, lest he should give 3
23 keep the things as her own, lest we be laughed at; 11
45:11 provide for you . . lest you and your household 11
Exd 1:10 deal shrewdly with them, lest they multiply 11
5: 3 the LORD our God, lest he fall upon us 11
13:17 Lest the people repent when they see war 11
19:21 warn the people, lest they break through 11
22 lest the LORD break out upon them. 11
24 the LORD, lest he break out against them. 11
20:19 but let not God speak to us, lest we die. 11
23:29 in one year, lest the land become desolate 11
33 They shall not dwell in your land, lest they make 11
28:35 shall be heard . . when he comes out, lest he die. 6
43 lest they bring guilt upon themselves and die. 6
30:20 they shall wash with water, lest they die. 6
21 wash their hands and their feet, lest they die 6
33: 3 go up among you, lest I consume you in the way 11
34:12 Take heed to yourself, lest you make a covenant 11
12 lest it become a snare in the midst of you. 11
15 lest you make a covenant with the inhabitants 11
Lev 8:35 lest you die; for so I am commanded 6
10: 6 do not rend your clothes, lest you die 6
6 lest wrath come upon all the congregation •
7 do not go out . . lest you die 11
9 Drink no wine . . lest you die 6
11:43 shall not defile . . lest you become unclean 6
14:36 lest all that is in the house be declared unclean 6
15:31 lest they die in their uncleanness by defiling 6
16: 2 the mercy seat which is upon the ark, lest he die 6
13 cover the mercy seat . . lest he die 6
18:28 lest the land vomit you out, when you defile it 6
19:17 reason with your neighbor, lest you bear sin 6
29 lest the land fall into harlotry 6
22: 9 keep my charge, lest they bear sin for it and die 6
Num 4:15 must not touch the holy things, lest they die. •
20 not go in to look . . lest they die. •
14:42 Do not go up lest you be struck down before 6
16:26 lest you be swept away with all their sins. 11
34 for they said, "Lest the earth swallow us up! 11
40 lest he become as Korah and as his company– 6
17:10 an end of their murmurings . . lest they die. 6
18: 3 lest they, and you, die. 6
22 lest they bear sin and die. •
32 not profane the holy things . . lest you die.' 6
20:18 not pass through, lest I come out with the sword 11
Deu 1:42 lest you be defeated before your enemies.' 6
4: 9 take heed . . lest you forget the things 11
9 take heed . . lest they depart from your heart 11
16 beware lest you act corruptly by making 11
19 beware lest you lift up your eyes to heaven 11
23 Take heed . . lest you forget the covenant 11
6:12 then take heed lest you forget the LORD 11
15 lest the anger of the LORD your God be kindled 11
7:22 lest the wild beasts grow too numerous for you. 11
25 not . . take it for yourselves, lest you be ensnared 11
8:11 Take heed lest you forget the LORD your God, by not 11
12 lest, when you have eaten and are full 11
17 Beware lest you say in your heart, 'My power 4
9:28 lest the land from which thou didst bring us say 11
11:16 Take heed lest your heart be deceived 11
15: 9 Take heed lest there be a base thought 11
17:17 not multiply wives . . lest his heart turn away; 6
18:16 me not . . see this great fire any more, lest I die.' 6
19: 6 lest the avenger of blood in hot anger pursue 11
10 lest innocent blood be shed in your land 6
20: 5 go back to his house, lest he die in the battle 11
6 go back to his house, lest he die in the battle 11
7 go back to his house, lest he die in the battle 11
8 go back . . lest the heart of his fellows melt 6
22: 9 lest the whole yield be forfeited 11
24:15 lest he cry against you to the LORD, and it be sin 6
25: 3 but not more; lest, if one should go on to beat him 11
29:18 Beware lest there be among you a man or woman 11
18 lest there be among you a root bearing poisonous 11
32:27 lest their adversaries should judge amiss, lest 11
27 lest they should say, "Our hand is triumphant 11
Jos 2:16 Go into the hills, lest the pursuers meet you; 11
6:18 keep yourselves from . . lest..you take any 11
9:20 This we will do to them . . lest wrath be upon us 6
22:27 to be a witness . . lest your children say to our 6
24:27 it shall be a witness . . lest you deal falsely 11
Jdg 7: 2 into their hand, lest Israel vaunt themselves 11
9:54 kill me, lest men say of me, 'A woman killed him.' 11
14:15 Entice your husband to tell . . lest we burn you 11
18:25 heard among us, lest angry fellows fall upon you 11
Rut 2:22 go out with his maidens, lest . . you be molested. 6
4: 6 I cannot . . lest I impair my own inheritance. 11
1Sm 4: 9 Take courage . . lest you become slaves 11
9: 5 Come, let us go back, lest my father cease to care 11

13:19 Lest the Hebrews make . . swords or spears"; 11
15: 6 go down from among . . lest I destroy you with them; 11
20: 3 'Let not Jonathan know this, lest he be grieved.' 11
27:11 Lest they should tell about us 11
29: 4 lest in the battle he become an adversary to us. 6
31: 4 thrust me . . lest these uncircumcised come 11
2Sm 1:20 Tell it not . . lest the daughters . . rejoice 11
20 Tell it not . . lest the daughters of..exult. 11
12:28 gather the rest . . and take it; lest I take the city 11
13:25 let us not all go, lest we be burdensome to you. 6
15:14 go in haste, lest he overtake us quickly 11
17:16 pass over; lest the king and all . . be swallowed 11
20: 6 pursue him, lest he get himself fortified cities 11
21:17 You shall no more . . lest you quench the lamp 6
1Kg 18:44 Prepare . . and go down, lest the rain stop you.' 7
1Ch 10: 4 lest these uncircumcised come and make sport 11
2Ch 35:21 Cease opposing God, who is with me, lest he destroy 5
Ezr 7:23 lest his wrath be against the realm of the king 12
Job 32:13 Beware lest you say, 'We have found wisdom; 11
36:18 Beware lest wrath entice you into scoffing; 11
Ps 2:12 kiss his feet, lest he be angry, and you perish 11
7: 2 lest like a lion they rend me, dragging me away 11
13: 3 lighten my eyes, lest I sleep the sleep of death; 11
4 lest my enemy say, "I have prevailed over him"; 11
4 lest my foes rejoice because I am shaken. •
28: 1 lest, if thou be silent to me, I become like those 11
50:22 lest I rend, and there be none to deliver! 11
59:11 Slay them not, lest my people forget; 11
91:12 lest you dash your foot against a stone. 11
125: 3 lest the righteous put forth their hands 9
143: 7 lest I be like those who go down to the Pit. 4
Prv 5: 9 lest you give your honor to others 11
10 lest strangers take their fill of your strength 11
20:13 Love not sleep, lest you come to poverty; 11
22:25 lest you learn his ways and entangle yourself 11
24:18 lest the LORD see it, and be displeased 11
25:10 lest he who hears you bring shame upon you 11
16 only enough . . lest you be sated with it and vomit 11
17 lest he become weary of you and hate you. 11
26: 4 lest you be like him yourself. 11
5 lest he be wise in his own eyes. 11
30: 6 Do not add to his words, lest he rebuke you 11
9 lest I be full, and deny thee, and say, 11
9 lest I be poor, and steal, and profane the name 11
10 lest he curse you, and you be held guilty. 11
31: 5 lest they drink and forget what has been decreed 11
Ecc 7:21 Do not give heed . . lest you hear your servant 1
Isa 6:10 shut their eyes; lest they see with their eyes 11
14:21 lest they rise and possess the earth 2
27: 3 Lest any one harm it, I guard it night and day; 11
28:22 do not scoff, lest your bonds be made strong; 11
33:15 who shakes his hands, lest they hold a bribe 10
36:18 Beware lest Hezeki'ah mislead you by saying 11
48: 5 lest you should say, 'My idol did them 11
7 lest you should say, 'Behold, I knew them.' 11
Jer 1:17 dismayed by them, lest I dismay you before them. 11
4: 4 lest my wrath go forth like fire, and burn 11
6: 8 warned, O Jerusalem, lest I be alienated from you; 11
8 lest I make you a desolation, an uninhabited land. 11
10:24 not in thy anger, lest thou bring me to nothing. 11
21:12 lest my wrath go forth like fire 11
37:20 to the house of Jonathan . . lest I die there. 6
38:19 lest I be handed over to them and they abuse me. 11
Ezk 18:30 Repent and turn . . lest iniquity be your ruin. •
44:19 lest they communicate holiness to the people 6
Dan 1:10 fear lest my lord the king, who appointed •
Hos 2: 3 lest I strip her naked 11
Ams 5: 6 Seek the LORD and live, lest he break out like fire 11
Zec 7:12 lest they should hear the law and the words 10
Mal 4: 6 lest I come and smite the land with a curse. 11
Mat 4: 6 will bear you up, lest you strike your foot 16
5:25 with him to court, lest your accuser hand you over 16
7: 6 lest they trample them under foot and turn 16
13:15 lest they should perceive with their eyes 16
29 lest in gathering the weeds you root up the wheat 16
15:32 lest they faint on the way. 16
26: 5 lest there be a tumult among the people. 14
27:64 lest his disciples go and steal him away 16
Mrk 3: 9 because of the crowd, lest they should crush him; 14
4:12 lest they should turn again, and be forgiven. 16
13:36 lest he come suddenly and find you asleep. 15
14: 2 lest there be a tumult of the people. 16
Lke 4:11 lest you strike your foot against a stone.' 16
11:35 be careful lest the light in you be darkness. 15
12:58 lest he drag you to the judge 16
14: 8 lest a more eminent man than you be invited by him; 16
12 lest they also invite you in return 16
16:28 lest they also come into this place of torment.' 14
21:34 lest your hearts be weighed down 16
Joh 3:20 lest his deeds should be exposed. 14
12:35 lest the darkness overtake you 14
40 lest they should see with their eyes 14
42 lest they should be put out of the synagogue 14
Act 13:40 lest there come upon you what is said 15
27:42 lest any should swim away and escape; 15
28:27 lest they should perceive with their eyes 16
Rom 11:25 Lest you be wise in your own conceits 14
15:20 lest I build on another man's foundation 14
1Co 1:15 lest any one should say that you were baptized 14

17 lest the cross of Christ be emptied of its power. 14
7: 5 then come together again, lest Satan tempt you 14
8: 9 Only take care lest this liberty of yours 15
13 lest I cause my brother to fall. 14
9:27 lest after preaching to others 15
10:12 thinks that he stands take heed lest he fall. 15
11:34 lest you come together to be condemned 14
2Co 9: 4 lest if some Macedo'nians come with me and find 15
Gal 2: 2 lest somehow I should be running 15
6: 1 Look to yourself, lest you too be tempted. 15
Eph 2: 9 not because of works, lest any man should boast. 14
Php 2:27 lest I should have sorrow upon sorrow. 14
Col 3:21 lest they become discouraged. 14
Heb 2: 1 lest we drift away from it. 16
3:12 lest there be in any of you an evil . . heart 16
4: 1 lest any of you be judged to have failed 16
2Pe 3:17 beware lest you be carried away with the error 14
Rev 18: 4 Come out of her . . lest you take part in her sins 14
4 Come out of her . . lest you share in her plagues; 14
2Es 6:34 lest you be hasty concerning the last times.' 18
10:34 do not forsake me, lest I die before my time. 18
Jdt 7: 9 lest his army be defeated. 14
12: 2 Judith said, "I cannot eat it, lest it be an offense; 14
Wis 4:11 lest evil change his understanding 15
16:11 lest they should fall into deep forgetfulness 14
Sir 1:30 Do not exalt yourself lest you fall 14
2: 7 turn not aside, lest you fall. 14
6: 2 lest your soul be torn in pieces like a bull. 14
7: 6 lest you be unable to remove iniquity 15
6 lest you be partial to a powerful man 16
8: 1 lest you fall into his hands. 16
2 lest his resources outweigh yours 16
4 lest your ancestors be disgraced. 14
10 lest you be burned in his flaming fire. 15
11 lest he lie in ambush against your words. 14
15 lest he be burdensome to you 14
19 lest you drive away your good luck. 15
9: 3 lest you fall into her snares. 16
4 lest you be caught in her intrigues. 16
5 lest you stumble and incur penalties for her. 16
6 lest you lose your inheritance. 14
9 lest your heart turn aside to her 16
13 lest he rob you of your life 14
11:33 lest he give you a lasting blemish. 16
12: 5 lest by means of it he subdue you 15
12 Do not put him next to you, lest he overthrow you 15
12 lest he try to take your seat of honor 16
13:10 Do not push forward, lest you be repulsed 15
10 not remain at a distance, lest you be forgotten. 14
18:32 lest you become impoverished by its expense. 15
23:14 lest you be forgetful in their presence 16
26:10 lest, when she finds liberty, she use it to her hurt. 14
28:26 Beware lest you err with your tongue 17
26 lest you fall before him who lies in wait. 15
29:20 take heed to yourself lest you fall. 15
30:10 lest you have sorrow with him 14
12 lest he become stubborn and disobey you 16
31:16 do not chew greedily, lest you be hated. 15
17 do not be insatiable, lest you give offense. 16
33:19 lest you change your mind and must ask for it. 14
37: 8 lest he cast the lot against you 16
42: 9 when she is young, lest she do not marry 16
9 if married, lest she be hated; 16
10 while a virgin, lest she be defiled 16
10 having a husband, lest she prove unfaithful 16
10 though married, lest she be barren. 16
11 lest she make you a laughingstock 16
LJr 1:27 lest they fall to the ground 16
1Mc 4:45 lest it bring reproach upon them 16
13:17 lest he arouse great hostility among the people 16
2Mc 6:24 he said, "lest many of the young should suppose 13
3Mc 2:17 lest the transgressors boast in their wrath 14
23 fearing lest he should lose his life 15
3:24 we have taken precautions lest . . 16
4Mc 4:13 lest King Seleucus suppose 16

let 1. ἐάω 2. εἰσδέχομαι

Act 19:30 the disciples would not let him; 1
2Mc 10:36 and let in the rest of the force 2

let alone 1. חדל מִן 2. מלט 3. נוח 4. רפה 5. שית מִן 6. שבק (A) 7. ἀφίημι 8. ἐάω 9. dimitto

Exd 4:26 So he let him alone. 4
14:12 Let us alone and let us serve the Egyptians'? 1
32:10 now therefore let me alone, that my wrath may burn 3
Deu 9:14 let me alone, that I may destroy them 4
Jdg 11:37 let me alone two months, that I may go and wander 4
2Sm 16:11 Let him alone, and let him curse; 3
2Kg 4:27 Let her alone, for she is in bitter distress; 4
23:18 Let him be . . " So they let his bones alone 2
Ezr 6: 7 Let the work on this house of God alone; 6
Job 7:16 Let me alone, for my days are a breath. 1
19 nor let me alone till I swallow my spittle? 4
10:20 Let me alone, that I may find a little comfort 5
Hos 4:17 E'phraim is joined to idols, let him alone. 3
Mat 15:14 Let them alone; they are blind guides 7
Mrk 14: 6 Jesus said, "Let her alone; why do you trouble her? 7
Lke 13: 8 he answered him, 'Let it alone, sir, this year also 7

Joh 12: 7 Jesus said, "Let her alone 7
Act 5:38 keep away from these men and let them alone 7
2Es 9:41 she said . . "Let me alone, my lord, that I may weep 9
2Mc 6:13 In fact, not to let the impious alone for long 8

let down 1. ירד 2. נטה 3. רפה 4. שלח 5. *καθίημι* 6. *χαλάω*
Gen 24:14 'Pray let down your jar that I may drink,' 2
18 and she quickly let down her jar upon her hand 1
46 She quickly let down her jar from her shoulder 1
Jos 2:15 she let them down by a rope through the window 1
18 in the window through which you let us down; 1
1Sm 19:12 So Michal let David down through the window; 1
Jer 38: 6 the guard, letting Jeremiah down by ropes. 4
11 he let down to Jeremiah in the cistern by ropes. 4
Ezk 1:24 when they stood still, they let down their wings. 3
25 when they stood still, they let down their wings. 3
Mrk 2: 4 let down the pallet on which the paralytic lay. 6
Lke 5: 4 and let down your nets for a catch. 6
5 But at your word I will let down the nets. 6
19 and let him down with his bed through the tiles 5
Act 9:25 and let him down over the wall 5
10:11 a great sheet, let down by four corners upon the earth 5
11: 5 a great sheet, let down from heaven by four corners 5
2Co 11:33 let down in a basket through a window in the wall 6

let loose 1. מְשַׁלַּח 2. נתר 3. שלח
Gen 49:21 Naph'tali is a hind let loose 3
Exd 22: 5 When a man . . lets his beast loose and it feeds 3
Lev 26:22 I will let loose the wild beasts among you 3
Job 6: 9 that he would let loose his hand and cut me off! 2
Ps 78:49 He let loose on them his fierce anger, wrath 3
Isa 7:25 will become a place where cattle are let loose 1
Ezk 7: 3 I will let loose my anger upon you 3

let out 1. נתן 2. פטר 3. *ἐκδίδωμι* 4. *ῥίπτω*
Prv 17:14 beginning of strife is like letting out water; 2
Sng 8:11 he let out the vineyard to keepers; 1
Mat 21:33 and let it out to tenants 3
41 and let out the vineyard to other tenants 3
Mrk 12: 1 built a tower, and let it out to tenants 3
Lke 20: 9 A man planted a vineyard, and let it out to tenants 3
Act 27:29 they let out four anchors from the stern 4

lethech 1. לֶתֶךְ
Hos 3: 2 bought her for . . a homer and a lethech of barley. 1

letter 1. אִגֶּרֶת 2. כְּתָב 3. מִכְתָּב 4. סֵפֶר 5. אִגְּרָה (A) 6. נִשְׁתְּוָן (A) 7. *βιβλίον* 8. *γράμμα* 9. *γραφή* 10. *γράφω* 11. *ἐπιστολή*
2Sm 11:14 David wrote a letter to Jo'ab, and sent it 4
15 In the letter he wrote, "Set Uri'ah in the forefront 4
1Kg 21: 8 she wrote letters in Ahab's name and sealed them 4
8 she sent the letters to the elders and the nobles 4
9 she wrote in the letters, "Proclaim a fast 4
11 As it was written in the letters 4
2Kg 5: 5 I will send a letter to the king of Israel. 4
6 he brought the letter to the king of Israel 4
6 When this letter reaches you, know that I have 4
7 when the king of Israel read the letter 4
10: 1 Jehu wrote letters, and sent them to Sama'ria 4
2 Now then, as soon as this letter comes to you 4
6 he wrote to them a second letter, saying, "If you are 4
7 when the letter came . . they took the king's sons 4
19:14 Hezeki'ah received the letter from the hand 4
20:12 sent envoys with letters and a present 4
2Ch 2:11 Huram . . answered in a letter which he sent 2
21:12 a letter came to him from Eli'jah . . saying 3
30: 1 Hezeki'ah . . wrote letters also to E'phraim 1
6 with letters from the king and his princes 1
32:17 he wrote letters to cast contempt on the LORD 4
Ezr 4: 7 letter was written in Aramaic and translated. 6
8 wrote a letter against Jerusalem to Ar-ta-xerx'es 1
11 copy of the letter that they sent–"To Ar-ta-xerx'es 1
18 letter which you sent to us has been plainly read 6
23 the copy of King Ar-ta-xerx'es' letter was read 6
5: 5 then answer be returned by letter concerning it. 6
6 copy of the letter which Tat'tenai . . sent 5
7:11 This is a copy of the letter which King 6
Neh 2: 7 let letters be given me to the governors 1
8 letter to Asaph, the keeper of the king's forest 1
9 governors . . and gave them the king's letter. 1
6: 5 sent his servant . . with an open letter in his hand. 1
17 nobles of Judah sent many letters to Tobi'ah 1
17 Tobi'ah's letters came to them. •
19 Tobi'ah sent letters to make me afraid. 1
Est 1:22 he sent letters to all the royal provinces 4
3:13 Letters were sent by couriers to . . provinces 4
8: 5 order . . to revoke the letters devised by Haman 4
10 and letters were sent by mounted couriers 4
9:20 and sent letters to all the Jews who were 4
26 because of all that was written in this letter 1
29 confirming this second letter about Purim. 1
30 Letters were sent to all the Jews . . in words 4
Isa 37:14 Hezeki'ah received the letter . . and read it; 4
39: 1 envoys with letters and a present to Hezeki'ah 4
Jer 29: 1 These are the words of the letter which Jeremiah 4
3 The letter was sent by the hand of Ela'sah •
25 You have sent letters in your name 4
29 Zephani'ah the priest read this letter 4
Dan 1:17 learning and skill in all letters and wisdom; 4
Act 9: 2 asked him for letters to the synagogues 11
15:23 with the following letter 10
30 they delivered the letter. 11
22: 5 From them I received letters to the brethren 11
23:25 he wrote a letter to this effect 11
33 delivered the letter to the governor 11
34 On reading the letter •
28:21 We have received no letters from Judea about you 8
Rom 16:22 I Tertius, the writer of this letter, greet you 11
1Co 5: 9 I wrote to you in my letter 11
16: 3 I will send those whom you accredit by letter 11
2Co 3: 1 do we need, as some do, letters of recommendation 11
2 our letter of recommendation 11
3 that you are a letter from Christ delivered by us 11
7 carved in letters on stone 8
7: 8 For even if I made you sorry with my letter 11
8 I see that that letter grieved you 11
10: 9 seem to be frightening you with letters. 11
10 For they say, "His letters are weighty and strong 11
11 what we say by letter when absent 11
Gal 6:11 See with what large letters I am writing to you 8
Col 4:16 when this letter has been read among you 11
16 see that you read also the letter from La-odice'a. •
1Th 5:27 I adjure you by the Lord that this letter be read 11
2Th 2: 2 by letter purporting to be from us 11
15 taught . . either by word of mouth or by letter. 11
3:14 any one refuses to obey what we say in this letter 11
17 This is the mark in every letter of mine 11
2Pe 3: 1 This is now the second letter that I have written 11
16 speaking of this as he does in all his letters. 11
1Es 2:16 wrote him the following letter 11
26 I have read the letter which you sent me 11
30 when the letter from King Artaxerxes was read 10
4:47 wrote letters for him to all the treasurers 11
48 he wrote letters to all the governors 11
61 he took the letters, and went to Babylon 11
6: 7 A copy of the letter which Sisinnes . . wrote 11
AEs 13: 1 This is a copy of the letter 11
6 those indicated to you in the letters of Haman 10
16: 1 The following is a copy of this letter 11
17 letters sent by Haman the son of Hammedatha 8
19 Therefore post a copy of this letter publicly 11
Sir 45:11 for a reminder, in engraved letters 9
LJr 1: 1 A copy of a letter which Jeremiah sent 11
1Mc 1:44 the king sent letters by messengers to Jerusalem 7
5:10 sent to Judas and his brothers a letter 8
14 While the letter was still being read 11
8:22 a copy of the letter which they wrote in reply 11
9:60 secretly sent letters to all his allies in Judea 11
10: 3 Demetrius sent Jonathan a letter 11
7 read the letter in the hearing of all the people 11
17 he wrote a letter and sent it to him 11
11:29 The king consented, and wrote a letter to Jonathan 11
31 the letter which we wrote concerning you 11
12: 2 He also sent letters to the same effect 11
4 the Romans gave them letters 11
5 This is a copy of the letter which Jonathan wrote 11
7 Already in time past a letter was sent to Onias 11
8 received the letter 11
10 since you sent your letter to us. •
17 greet you and deliver to you this letter from us 11
19 a copy of the letter which they sent to Onias 11
13:35 and wrote him a letter as follows 11
14:20 a copy of the letter which the Spartans sent 11
15: 1 sent a letter from the islands of the sea to Simon 11
15 with letters to the kings and countries 11
16:19 he sent letters to the captains 11
2Mc 2:13 letters of kings about votive offerings. 11
9:18 wrote to the Jews the following letter 11
11:16 The letter written to the Jews by Lysias 11
22 The king's letter ran thus 11
27 To the nation the king's letter was as follows 11
34 The Romans also sent them a letter 11
3Mc 3:11 wrote this letter against them 11
25 as soon as this letter shall arrive 11
30 The letter was written in the above form. 11
6:41 wrote the following letter for them 11
7:10 Upon receiving this letter 11

level 1. ישר 2. מִישׁוֹר 3. מֵישָׁר 4. סלל 5. ערר 6. שוה 7. *πεδινός* 8. *ποιέω*
Ps 27:11 lead me on a level path because of my enemies. 2
143:10 Let thy good spirit lead me on a level path! 2
Prv 15:19 but the path of the upright is a level highway. 4
Isa 26: 7 The way of the righteous is level; 3
28:25 When he has leveled its surface 6
40: 4 the uneven ground shall become level 2
45: 2 I will go before you and level the mountains 1
Jer 51:58 The broad wall of Babylon shall be leveled 5
Lke 6:17 he came down with them and stood on a level place 7
2Mc 14:33 I will level this precinct of God to the ground 8

level to the ground 1. *ἰσόπεδον ποιέω* 2. *ἰσόπεδον τίθημι* 3. *ἰσόπεδος*
2Mc 8: 3 and about to be leveled to the ground 3
9:14 which he was hastening to level to the ground 1
3Mc 5:43 and rapidly level it to the ground 2

levity 1. *εὐτραπελία*
Eph 5: 4 nor silly talk, nor levity, which are not fitting; 1

levy 1. מַס 2. עלה 3. רום
Num 31:28 levy for the LORD a tribute from the men of war 3
1Kg 5:13 King Solomon raised a levy of forced labor •
13 the levy numbered 30,000 men. 1
14 Adoni'ram was in charge of the levy. 1
9:15 forced labor which King Solomon levied to build 2
2Ch 24: 6 bring in . . the tax levied by Moses •

crown levy 1. *στέφανος*
1Mc 10:29 payment of tribute and salt tax and crown levies 1

forced levy 1. מַס
1Kg 9:21 Solomon made a forced levy of slaves 1
2Ch 8: 8 these Solomon made a forced levy and so they are 1

levy tribute 1. *ἀργυρολόγητος*
2Mc 11: 3 to levy tribute on the temple 1

lewd 1. זִמָּה 2. *ἀσυρής*
Jer 13:27 adulteries and neighings, your lewd harlotries 1
Ezk 16:27 who were ashamed of your lewd behavior. 1
Sir 23:13 Do not accustom your mouth to lewd vulgarity 2

lewdly 1. בְּזִמָּה
Ezk 22:11 another lewdly defiles his daughter-in-law; 1

lewdness 1. זִמָּה 2. נַבְלוּת
Ezk 16:43 Have you not committed lewdness in addition 1
58 You bear the penalty of your lewdness 1
22: 9 men commit lewdness in your midst. 1
23:21 Thus you longed for the lewdness of your youth 1
27 Thus I will put an end to your lewdness 1
29 Your lewdness and your harlotry 1
35 bear the consequences of your lewdness 1
44 to Oho'lah and to Ohol'ibah to commit lewdness. 1
48 Thus will I put an end to lewdness in the land 1
48 and not commit lewdness as you have done. 1
49 And your lewdness shall be requited upon you 1
24:13 Its rust is your filthy lewdness. 1
Hos 2:10 Now I will uncover her lewdness 2

liable 1. *ἔνοχος*
Mat 5:21 whoever kills shall be liable to judgment.' 1
22 his brother shall be liable to judgment 1
22 his brother shall be liable to the council 1
22 You fool!' shall be liable to the hell of fire. 1

liable to punishment 1. *ἔνοχος*
1Mc 14:45 shall be liable to punishment. 1

liar 1. אִישׁ כָּזָב 2. בַּד 3. דבר שֶׁקֶר 4. שֶׁקֶר 5. *ἀνὴρ ψεύστης* 6. *ἄνθρωπος ψευδής* 7. *ψευδής* 8. *ψευδολόγος* 9. *ψεύδω* 10. *ψεύστης* 11. mendax
Ps 63:11 for the mouths of liars will be stopped. 3
Prv 17: 4 liar gives heed to a mischievous tongue. 4
19:22 poor man is better than a liar. 1
Isa 44:25 who frustrates the omens of liars 2
Joh 8:44 for he is a liar and the father of lies. 10
55 I should be a liar like you 10
1Ti 1:10 immoral persons, sodomites, kidnapers, liars 10
4: 2 through the pretensions of liars 8
Tit 1:12 Cretans are always liars, evil beasts 10
1Jn 1:10 If we say we have not sinned, we make him a liar 10
2: 4 but disobeys his commandments is a liar 10
22 Who is the liar but he who denies 10
4:20 says, "I love God," and hates his brother, he is a liar; 10
5:10 He who does not believe God has made him a liar 10
Rev 21: 8 as for . . sorcerers, idolaters, and all liars 7
2Es 11:42 and have loved liars 11
Sir 15: 8 liars will never think of her. 5
20:25 A thief is preferable to a habitual liar 9
26 The disposition of a liar brings disgrace 6
25: 2 a beggar who is proud, a rich man who is a liar 10

libation 1. נֶסֶךְ 2. *σπονδή*
Exd 29:40 a fourth of a hin of wine for a libation. 1
41 with it a cereal offering and its libation 1
30: 9 and you shall pour no libation thereon. 1
2Ch 29:35 the libations for the burnt offerings. 1
Ps 16: 4 their libations of blood I will not pour out 1
Jer 44:17 the queen of heaven and pour out libations to her 1
18 queen of heaven and pouring out libations to her 1
19 queen of heaven and poured out libations to her 1
19 and poured out libations to her? 1
25 queen of heaven and to pour out libations to her. 1
Hos 9: 4 They shall not pour libations of wine to the LORD; •
1Es 6:31 libations may be made to the Most High God 2
AEs 14:17 I have not . . drunk the wine of the libations. 2

liberal 1. *εὐμετάδοτος* 2. *λαμπρός*
1Ti 6:18 be rich in good deeds, liberal and generous 1
Sir 31:23 Men will praise the one who is liberal with food 2

liberal man 1. נֶפֶשׁ בְּרָכָה
Prv 11:25 A liberal man will be enriched 1

liberality 1. יָד 2. ἁπλότης
Est 2:18 He also . . and gave gifts with royal liberality. 1
Rom 12: 8 he who contributes, in liberality; 2
2Co 8: 2 in a wealth of liberality on their part. 2

liberally 1. μετὰ ἁπλότητος 2. πολύς
Deu 15:14 furnish him liberally out of your flock †
Act 10: 2 gave alms liberally to the people 2
3Mc 3:21 the myriad affairs liberally entrusted to them 1

liberty 1. דְּרוֹר 2. רָחָב 3. ἄνεσις 4. ἄφεσις 5. ἐλευθερία 6. ἐξουσία
Lev 25:10 proclaim liberty throughout the land to all 1
Ps 119:45 I shall walk at liberty 2
Isa 61: 1 to proclaim liberty to the captives 1
Jer 34: 8 to make a proclamation of liberty to them 1
15 by proclaiming liberty, each to his neighbor 1
17 You have not obeyed me by proclaiming liberty 1
17 behold, I proclaim to you liberty to the sword 1
Ezk 46:17 it shall be his to the year of liberty; 1
Lke 4:18 to set at liberty those who are oppressed 4
Act 24:23 but should have some liberty 3
Rom 8:21 the glorious liberty of the children of God. 5
1Co 8: 9 Only take care lest this liberty of yours 6
10:29 why should my liberty be determined by another 5
Jas 1:25 the perfect law, the law of liberty 5
2:12 those . . to be judged under the law of liberty. 5
2Es 7:96 the spacious liberty which they are to receive •
Sir 26:10 lest, when she finds liberty, she use it to her hurt. 3
33:25 leave his hands idle, and he will seek liberty. 5

set at liberty 1. ἀπολύω
Act 28:18 they wished to set me at liberty 1

library 1. βιβλιοθήκη
2Mc 2:13 he founded a library 1

license 1. ἄδεια
3Mc 7:12 The king then . . granted them a general license 1

licentious 1. ἀσέλγεια
2Pe 2:18 entice with licentious passions of the flesh 1

licentious deed 1. ἀσέλγεια
3Mc 2:26 his uncounted licentious deeds 1

licentiousness 1. ἀσέλγεια
Mrk 7:22 coveting, wickedness, deceit, licentiousness 1
Rom 13:13 not in debauchery and licentiousness 1
2Co 12:21 impurity, immorality, and licentiousness 1
Gal 5:19 fornication, impurity, licentiousness 1
Eph 4:19 have given themselves up to licentiousness 1
1Pe 4: 3 living in licentiousness, passions 1
2Pe 2: 2 And many will follow their licentiousness 1
7 distressed by the licentiousness of the wicked 1
Jde 1: 4 pervert the grace of our God into licentiousness 1

lick 1. לחך 2. לקק 3. ἐπιλείχω
1Kg 21:19 In the place . . shall dogs lick your own blood.'" 2
Ps 72: 9 his enemies lick the dust! 1
Isa 49:23 bow down to you, and lick the dust of your feet. 1
Mic 7:17 they shall lick the dust like a serpent 1
Lke 16:21 moreover the dogs came and licked his sores. 3

lick up 1. לחך 2. לקק 3. ἐκλείχω
Num 22: 4 horde will now lick up all that is round about us 1
4 as the ox licks up the grass of the field. 1
1Kg 18:38 and licked up the water that was in the trench. 1
21:19 where dogs licked up the blood of Naboth 2
22:38 the dogs licked up his blood 2
Jdt 7: 4 These men will now lick up the face of the whole land 3

lid 1. דֶּלֶת
2Kg 12: 9 took a chest, and bored a hole in the lid of it 1

lie 1. הוה 2. היה 3. חבק 4. ידע 5. ידע מִשְׁכָּב 6. יצע 7. ישב 8. לון 9. מִשְׁכָּב 10. נפל 11. נתן שְׁכָבָה 12. רבע 13. רבץ 14. שׁכב 15. ἀνάκειμαι 16. ἀναπίπτω 17. ἀποκαθίστημι 18. βάλλω 19. γίνομαι 20. ἐγκαθίζω 21. εἰμί 22. ἐπίκειμαι 23. κατάκειμαι 24. κεῖμαι 25. κοιμάω 26. παράκειμαι 27. ῥίπτω 28. discumbo 29. iaceo 30. pono 31. recumbo
Gen 16:14 Beer-la'hai-roi; it lies between Kadesh and Bered. •
19:32 we will lie with him 14
33 the first-born went in, and lay with her father; 14
34 Behold, I lay last night with my father; 14
34 then you go in and lie with him 14
35 and the younger arose, and lay with him; 14
26:10 the people might easily have lain with your wife 14
28:13 the land on which you lie I will give to you 14
29: 2 lo, three flocks of sheep lying beside it; 13
30:15 Rachel said, "Then he may lie with you tonight 14
16 my son's mandrakes." So he lay with her that night 14
34: 2 he seized her and lay with her and humbled her. 14
7 wrought folly in Israel by lying with Jacob's 14
35:22 Reuben went and lay with Bilhah 14
38:26 And he did not lie with her again. 4
39: 7 cast her eyes upon Joseph, and said, "Lie with me. 14
10 he would not listen to her, to lie with her 14
12 caught him by his garment, saying, "Lie with me 14
14 he came in to me to lie with me, and I cried out 14
47:30 let me lie with my fathers; carry me out of Egypt 14
Exd 16:13 in the morning dew lay round about the camp. 14
22:16 and lies with her, he shall give 14
19 Whoever lies with a beast shall be put to death. 14
23: 5 see the ass . . lying under its burden 13
25:27 Close to the frame the rings shall lie, as holders 2
28:28 that it may lie upon the skilfully woven band 2
39:21 that it should lie upon the skilfully woven band 2
Lev 15: 4 Every bed on which he who has the discharge lies 14
18 If a man lies with a woman and has an emission 14
20 everything upon which she lies 14
24 if any man lies with her, and her impurity is on him 14
24 every bed on which he lies shall be unclean 14
26 Every bed on which she lies 14
33 the man who lies with a woman who is unclean 14
18:22 You shall not lie with a male as with a woman 14
23 you shall not lie with any beast and defile 11
23 woman give herself to a beast to lie with it 12
19:20 If a man lies carnally with a woman who is a slave 14
20:11 The man who lies with his father's wife 14
12 If a man lies with his daughter-in-law, both of them 14
13 If a man lies with a male as with a woman 14
15 If a man lies with a beast, he shall be put to death 14
16 If a woman . . lies with it, you shall kill 12
18 If a man lies with a woman having her sickness 14
20 If a man lies with his uncle's wife 14
26:34 enjoy its sabbaths as long as it lies desolate •
Num 5:13 if a man lies with her carnally, and it is hidden 14
19 If no man has lain with you, and if you have not 14
20 some man other than your husband has lain with you 11
14:33 last of your dead bodies lies in the wilderness. •
21:20 Bamoth to the valley lying in the region of Moab •
31:17 kill every woman who has known man by lying 9
18 young girls who have not known man by lying 9
35 women who had not known man by lying with him. 9
Deu 21: 1 any one is found slain, lying in the open country 10
22:22 man is found lying with the wife of another man 14
22 both . . shall die, the man who lay with the woman 14
23 man meets her in the city and lies with her 14
25 open country . . man seizes her and lies with her 14
25 then only the man who lay with her shall die. 14
28 not betrothed, and seizes her and lies with her 14
29 man who lay with her shall give to the father 14
27:20 'Cursed be he who lies with his father's wife 14
21 'Cursed be he who lies with any kind of beast.' 14
22 'Cursed be he who lies with his sister, whether 14
23 'Cursed be he who lies with his mother-in-law.' 14
28:30 betroth a wife, and another man shall lie with her; 14
Jos 8: 9 went to the place . . and lay between Bethel and Ai 7
15: 8 the mountain that lies over against the valley •
18:13 mountain that lies south of Lower Beth-hor'on. •
14 from the mountain that lies to the south •
22: 4 your home in the land where your possession lies •
10 to the region . . that lies in the land of Canaan •
Jdg 1:16 wilderness of Judah, which lies in the Negeb near •
3:25 and there lay their lord dead on the floor. 10
4:22 So he went in to her tent; and there lay Sis'era dead 10
7:12 Mid'ianites . . lay along the valley 10
16: 3 Samson lay till midnight, and at midnight he 14
5 see wherein his great strength lies •
6 Please tell me wherein your great strength lies •
15 not told me wherein your great strength lies. •
19:27 there was his concubine lying at the door 10
21:11 male and every woman that has lain with a male 5
12 virgins who had not known man by lying with him; 9
Rut 3: 4 when he lies down, observe the place where he lies; 14
8 and turned over, and behold, a woman lay at his feet! 14
14 she lay at his feet until the morning 14
1Sm 2:22 he heard . . how they lay with the women who served 14
3:15 Samuel lay until morning; 14
5: 4 his hands were lying cut off upon the threshold; •
19:24 he too prophesied . . and lay naked all that day 10
26: 5 and David saw the place where Saul lay, with Abner 14
5 Saul was lying within the encampment 14
7 there lay Saul sleeping within the encampment 14
7 lay Saul . . and Abner and the army lay around him. 14
2Sm 2:24 came to the hill of Ammah, which lies before Gi'ah •
4: 7 they came . . as he lay on his bed in his bedchamber 14
11: 4 she came to him, and he lay with her. 14
11 go . . to eat and to drink, and to lie with my wife? 14
13 in the evening he went out to lie on his couch 14
12: 3 and drink from his cup, and lie in his bosom 14
11 and he shall lie with your wives in the sight 14
16 and went in and lay all night upon the ground. 14
24 David . . went in to her, and lay with her; 14
13:11 and said to her, "Come, lie with me, my sister. 14
14 being stronger . . he forced her, and lay with her. 14
31 arose, and rent his garments, and lay on the earth; 14
1Kg 1: 2 let her lie in your bosom, that . . the king may be 14
3:19 this woman's son died . . because she lay on it. 14
21:27 rent his clothes . . fasted and lay in sackcloth 14
2Kg 4:32 Eli'sha . . saw the child lying dead on his bed. 14
34 Then he went up and lay upon the child 14
9:16 Jehu . . and went to Jezreel, for Joram lay there. 14
1Ch 9:27 for upon them lay the duty of watching •
2Ch 20:24 behold, they were dead bodies lying on the ground; 10
Est 4: 3 and most of them lay in sackcloth and ashes. 6
Job 7:21 For now I shall lie in the earth; thou wilt seek me 14
38:40 in their dens, or lie in wait in their covert? 7
40:21 Under the lotus plants he lies 14
Ps 41: 8 he will not rise again from where he lies. 14
57: 4 I lie in the midst of lions that greedily devour 14
88: 5 like the slain that lie in the grave 14
Prv 6: 9 How long will you lie there, O sluggard? 14
15:11 Sheol and Abaddon lie open before the LORD •
23:34 like one who lies on the top of a mast. 14
Ecc 4:11 Again, if two lie together, they are warm; 14
11: 3 the place where the tree falls, there it will lie. 1
Sng 1:13 to me a bag of myrrh, that lies between my breasts. 8
Isa 1: 7 Your country lies desolate . . cities are burned •
14:18 All the kings of the nations lie in glory 14
51:20 they lie at the head of every street 14
Jer 3: 2 Where have you not been lain with? 14
Lam 2:21 In the dust of . . streets lie the young and the old; 14
4: 5 those . . brought up in purple lie on ash heaps. 3
Ezk 4: 4 Then lie upon your left side 14
4 for the number of the days that you lie upon it 14
9 the number of days that you lie upon your side 14
6:13 when their slain lie among their idols 2
23: 8 in her youth men had lain with her and handled her 14
29: 3 dragon that lies in the midst of his streams 13
31:18 you shall lie among the uncircumcised 14
32:20 with her shall lie all her multitudes. 25
27 they do not lie with the fallen mighty men of old 14
28 shall be broken and lie among the uncircumcised 14
29 they lie with the uncircumcised 14
30 they lie uncircumcised with those who are slain 14
47:16 Bero'thah, Sib'raim (which lies on the border •
48:22 The portion of the prince shall lie between 2
Dan 2:28 Your dream . . as you lay in bed are these •
29 O king, as you lay in bed came thoughts •
4: 5 as I lay in bed the fancies and the visions •
10 visions of my head as I lay in bed were these •
13 I saw in the visions of my head as I lay in bed •
7: 1 dream and visions of his head as he lay in his bed. •
Ams 6: 4 Woe to those who lie upon beds of ivory 14
Mic 7: 5 your mouth from her who lies in your bosom; 14
Hag 1: 4 while this house lies in ruins? •
9 Because of my house that lies in ruins •
Zec 14: 4 the Mount of Olives which lies before Jerusalem •
Mat 8: 6 saying, "Lord, my servant is lying paralyzed 18
14 he saw his mother-in-law lying sick with a fever; 18
9: 2 a paralytic, lying on his bed 18
28: 6 Come, see the place where he lay. 24
Mrk 1:30 Now Simon's mother-in-law lay sick with a fever 23
2: 4 let down the pallet on which the paralytic lay. 23
7:30 she went home, and found the child lying in bed 18
Lke 2:12 lying in a manger. 24
16 the babe lying in a manger. 24
5:25 and took up that on which he lay, and went home 23
16:20 at his gate lay a poor man named Laz'arus 18
Joh 5: 3 In these lay a multitude of invalids, blind, lame 23
6 and knew that he had been lying there a long time 23
13:23 was lying close to the breast of Jesus; 15
25 lying thus, close to the breast of Jesus, he said 16
20: 5 he saw the linen cloths lying there 24
6 went into the tomb; he saw the linen cloths lying 24
7 and the napkin . . not lying with the linen cloths 24
12 sitting where the body of Jesus had lain 24
21: 9 a charcoal fire . . with fish lying on it, and bread. 22
Act 27:20 no small tempest lay on us 22
28: 8 It happened that the father of Publius lay sick 23
Rom 7: 8 Apart from the law sin lies dead. •
2Co 3:15 a veil lies over their minds; 24
Rev 9:10 power of hurting men . . lies in their tails. •
11: 8 their dead bodies will lie in the street •
21:16 The city lies foursquare 24
2Es 2: 9 whose land lies in lumps of pitch 29
3: 1 I was troubled as I lay on my bed 31
7: 8 there is only one path lying between them 30
9:27 after seven days, as I lay on the grass 28
10:30 behold, I lay there like a corpse 30
14:20 For the world lies in darkness 30
Jdt 3: 3 our sheepfolds with their tents, lie before you 26
6:13 left him lying at the foot of the hill 27
13:15 he lay in his drunken stupor 23
14:18 For look, here is Holofernes lying on the ground •
Wis 17: 2 they themselves lay as captives of darkness 24
Sir 8:11 lest he lie in ambush against your words. 20
38:13 when success lies in the hands of physicians •
43:32 Many things greater than these lie hidden 21
46:12 May their bones revive from where they lie •
49:10 revive from where they lie •
LJr 1:43 when one of them is led off . . and is lain with 25
Sus 1:20 so give your consent, and lie with us. 19
37 Then a young man . . came to her and lay with her. 16
1Mc 6: 9 He lay there for many days 21
16: 5 a stream lay between them. 21
2Mc 3:31 one who was lying quite at his last breath. 24
5:10 He who had cast out many to lie unburied •

12:39 to bring them back to lie with their kinsmen 17
15:18 Their concern for wives . . lay upon them less heavily 24
3Mc 2:22 he lay helpless on the ground *
4Mc 13:15 danger of eternal torment lying before those 24

lie (2) 1. דִּבַּר כָּזָב 2. כזב 3. כָּזָב 4. כחש 5. כַּחַשׁ 6. כֶּחָשׁ 7. שָׁוְא 8. שקר 9. שֶׁקֶר 10. שֶׁקֶר כִּזֵּב 11. כְּדַב (A) 12. καταψεύδω 13. ψευδής 14. ψεύδομαι 15. ψεῦδος

Exd 5: 9 that they may . . pay no regard to lying words. 9
Lev 6: 3 or has found what was lost and lied about it 4
19:11 nor deal falsely, nor lie to one another 8
Num23:19 God is not man, that he should lie 2
Jos 7:11 they have stolen, and lied, and put them among 4
Jdg 16:10 you have mocked me, and told me lies; please tell me 3
13 Until now you have mocked me, and told me lies; 3
1Sm 15:29 the Glory of Israel will not lie or repent; 8
1Kg 13:18 But he lied to him. 4
22:22 he said, 'I will go forth, and will be a lying spirit 9
23 the LORD has put a lying spirit in the mouth 9
2Kg 4:16 No, my lord . . do not lie to your maidservant. 2
2Ch 18:21 a lying spirit in the mouth of all his prophets.' 9
22 LORD has put a lying spirit in the mouth of these 9
Job 6:28 look at me; for I will not lie to your face. 2
13: 4 As for you, you whitewash with lies; 9
Ps 4: 2 will you love vain words, and seek after lies? 3
5: 6 Thou destroyest those who speak lies; 3
7:14 pregnant with mischief, and brings forth lies. 9
12: 2 Every one utters lies to his neighbor; 7
31:18 Let the lying lips be dumb 9
52: 3 lying more than speaking the truth. Selah 9
58: 3 they err from their birth, speaking lies. 3
59:12 For the cursing and lies which they utter 5
69: 4 would destroy me, those who attack me with lies. 9
78:36 they lied to him with their tongues. 2
89:35 I will not lie to David. 2
101: 7 no man who utters lies shall continue in my 9
109: 2 speaking against me with lying tongues. 9
119:69 The godless besmear me with lies 9
120: 2 Deliver me, O LORD, from lying lips 9
144: 8 whose mouths speak lies, and whose right hand 7
11 aliens, whose mouths speak lies, and whose right 7
Prv 6:17 haughty eyes, a lying tongue 9
19 a false witness who breathes out lies 3
10:18 He who conceals hatred has lying lips 9
12:19 but a lying tongue is but for a moment. 9
22 Lying lips are an abomination to the LORD 9
14: 5 A faithful witness does not lie 2
5 but a false witness breathes out lies. 3
25 but one who utters lies is a betrayer. 3
19: 5 he who utters lies will not escape. 3
9 he who utters lies will perish. 3
21: 6 The getting of treasures by a lying tongue 9
26:28 A lying tongue hates its victims 9
30: 8 Remove far from me falsehood and lying; 1
Isa 9:15 and the prophet who teaches lies is the tail; 9
28:15 for we have made lies our refuge 3
17 hail will sweep away the refuge of lies 3
30: 9 For they are a rebellious people, lying sons 6
32: 7 wicked devices to ruin the poor with lying words 9
44:20 or say, "Is there not a lie in my right hand? 9
57:11 fear, so that you lied, and did not remember me 2
59: 3 your lips have spoken lies, 9
4 they rely on empty pleas, they speak lies 7
13 and uttering from the heart lying words. 9
Jer 8: 8 the false pen of the scribes has made it into a lie. 9
9: 5 they have taught their tongue to speak lies; 9
13:25 you have forgotten me and trusted in lies. 9
14:14 The prophets are prophesying lies in my name; 9
14 They are prophesying to you a lying vision 9
16:19 Our fathers have inherited nought but lies 9
23:14 they commit adultery and walk in lies; 9
25 prophets have said who prophesy lies in my name 9
26 shall there be lies in the heart of the prophets *
26 in the heart of the prophets who prophesy lies 9
32 I am against those who prophesy lying dreams 9
32 and lead my people astray by their lies 9
27:10 For it is a lie which they are prophesying to you 9
14 for it is a lie which they are prophesying to you. 9
16 for it is a lie which they are prophesying to you. 9
28:15 and you have made this people trust in a lie. 9
29: 9 for it is a lie which they are prophesying to you 9
21 who are prophesying a lie to you in my name 9
23 and they have spoken in my name lying words 9
31 I did not send him, and has made you trust in a lie 9
43: 2 men said to Jeremiah, "You are telling a lie. 9
Ezk 13: 6 They have spoken falsehood and divined a lie; 3
7 and uttered a lying divination 3
8 you have uttered delusions and seen lies 3
9 the prophets . . who give lying divinations; 3
19 by your lies to my people, who listen to lies. 2
19 by your lies to my people, who listen to lies. 3
21:29 while they divine lies for you 3
22:28 seeing false visions and divining lies for them 3
Dan 2: 9 agreed to speak lying and corrupt words 11
11:27 shall speak lies at the same table, but to no avail; 3
Hos 4: 2 there is swearing, lying, killing, stealing 4
7:13 but they speak lies against me. 3
10:13 you have eaten the fruit of lies. 5
11:12 E'phraim has encompassed me with lies 5
Ams 2: 4 but their lies have led them astray, 3
Mic 2:11 If a man should go about and utter wind and lies 10
6:12 your inhabitants speak lies 9
Nah 3: 1 Woe to the bloody city, all full of lies and booty 5
Hab 2: 3 it hastens to the end–it will not lie. 2
18 has shaped it, a metal image, a teacher of lies? 9
Zep 3:13 they shall do no wrong and utter no lies 3
Zec 10: 2 utter nonsense, and the diviners see lies; 3
13: 3 not live, for you speak lies in the name of the LORD 9
Joh 8:44 for he is a liar and the father of lies. *
Act 5: 3 filled your heart to lie to the Holy Spirit 14
4 You have not lied to men but to God. 14
Rom 1:25 they exchanged the truth about God for a lie 15
9: 1 I am speaking the truth in Christ, I am not lying; 14
2Co 11:31 knows that I do not lie. 14
Gal 1:20 In what I am writing to you, before God, I do not lie!) 14
Col 3: 9 Do not lie to one another 14
1Ti 2: 7 (I am telling the truth, I am not lying) 14
1Jn 1: 6 we lie and do not live according to the truth; 14
2:21 and know that no lie is of the truth. 15
27 anointing teaches . . and is true, and is no lie 15
Rev 3: 9 who say that they are Jews and are not, but lie 14
14: 5 in their mouth no lie was found 15
Wis 1:11 a lying mouth destroys the soul. 12
14:28 prophesy lies, or live unrighteously 13
Sir 7:12 Do not devise a lie against your brother 15
13 Refuse to utter any lie 15
13 the habit of lying serves no good. *
20:24 A lie is an ugly blot on a man 15
41:17 Be ashamed . . of a lie, before a prince or a ruler; 13
51: 2 lips that utter lies 15
5 from an unclean tongue and lying words– 13
LJr 1:47 They have left only lies and reproach 13
Sus 1:55 Very well! You have lied against your own head 14
59 You also have lied against your own head 14

lie about 1. παράκειμαι 2. ῥίπτω

1Mc 11: 4 and the corpses lying about 2
2Mc 4:41 took handfuls of the ashes that were lying about 1

lie ahead 1. ἔμπροσθεν

Php 3:13 straining forward to what lies ahead 1

lie all night 1. לון

Job 24: 7 They lie all night naked, without clothing 1

lie awake 1. שקד

Ps 102: 7 I lie awake, I am like a lonely bird 1

lie behind 1. ὀπίσω

Php 3:13 one thing I do, forgetting what lies behind 1

lie broken 1. שבר

Ezk 31:12 its boughs will lie broken 1

lie buried 1. ἐγκηδεύομαι

4Mc 17: 9 Here lie buried an aged priest and an aged woman 1

lie carnally 1. נתן שְׁכָבָה לְזֶרַע

Lev 18:20 shall not lie carnally with your neighbor's wife 1

cause to lie down 1. נפל

Deu 25: 2 judge shall cause him to lie down and be beaten 1

lie close 1. ἀναπίπτω

Joh 21:20 the disciple . . who had lain close to his breast 1

lie close at hand 1. παράκειμαι

Rom 7:21 when I want to do right, evil lies close at hand. 1

lie dead 1. προπίπτω

2Mc 15:28 Nicanor, lying dead, in full armor. 1

lie desolate 1. שמם

Lev 26:35 As long as it lies desolate it shall have rest 1
43 enjoy its sabbaths while it lies desolate 1
2Ch 36:21 All the days that it lay desolate it kept sabbath 1
Lam 5:18 for Mount Zion which lies desolate; 1

lie down 1. רבע 2. רבץ 3. שכב 4. ἀναπίπτω

Gen 19: 4 before they lay down, the men of the city 3
33 he did not know when she lay down 3
35 not know when she lay down or when she arose. 3
28:11 his head and lay down in that place to sleep. 3
Lev 14:47 he who lies down in the house shall wash 3
26: 6 you shall lie down, and none shall make you afraid 3
Num22:27 the ass saw the angel . . she lay down under Balaam 2
23:24 it does not lie down till it devours the prey 3
24: 9 couched, he lay down like a lion, and like a lioness; 3
Deu 6: 7 when you lie down, and when you rise 3
11:19 by the way, and when you lie down, and when you rise 3
Jos 2: 8 Before they lay down, she came up to them 3
Rut 3: 4 when he lies down, observe the place where he lies; 3
4 then, go and uncover his feet and lie down; 3
7 he went to lie down at the end of the heap of grain. 3
7 she came . . and uncovered his feet, and lay down. 3
13 Lie down until the morning. 3
1Sm 3: 2 At that time Eli . . was lying down in his own place; 3
3 Samuel was lying down within the temple 3
5 But he said, "I did not call; lie down again. 3
5 So he went and lay down. 3
6 But he said, "I did not call, my son; lie down again. 3
9 Eli said to Samuel, "Go, lie down; and if he calls you 3
9 So Samuel went and lay down in his place. 3
9:25 a bed was spread . . and he lay down to sleep. *
2Sm 7:12 you lie down with your fathers 3
13: 5 Lie down on your bed, and pretend to be ill; 3
6 Amnon lay down, and pretended to be ill; 3
8 went to . . Amnon's house, where he was lying down. 3
1Kg 19: 5 he lay down and slept under a broom tree; 3
6 And he ate and drank, and lay down again. 3
21: 4 he lay down on his bed, and turned away his face 3
Job 3:13 For then I should have lain down and been quiet; 3
7: 4 When I lie down I say, 'When shall I arise?' 3
11:19 You will lie down, and none will make you afraid; 2
14:12 man lies down and rises not again; 3
20:11 vigor, but it will lie down with him in the dust. 3
21:26 They lie down alike in the dust 3
Ps 3: 5 I lie down and sleep; I wake again 3
4: 8 In peace I will both lie down and sleep; 3
104:22 get them away and lie down in their dens. 2
139: 3 Thou searchest out my path and my lying down 1
Prv 3:24 when you lie down, your sleep will be sweet. 3
6:22 when you lie down, they will watch over you; 3
23:34 like one who lies down in the midst of the sea 3
Isa 11: 6 and the leopard shall lie down with the kid 2
7 shall feed; their young shall lie down together; 2
13:21 But wild beasts will lie down there 2
14:30 the poor . . and the needy lie down in safety; 2
17: 2 they will be for flocks, which will lie down 2
27:10 there the calf grazes, there he lies down 2
43:17 they lie down, they cannot rise 3
50:11 have from my hand: you shall lie down in torment. 3
56:10 dogs, they cannot bark; dreaming, lying down 3
Jer 3:25 Let us lie down in our shame 3
Ezk 4: 6 you shall lie down a second time 3
34:14 there they shall lie down in good grazing land 2
Jon 1: 5 Jonah . . had lain down, and was fast asleep. 3
Zep 2: 7 and in the houses of Ash'kelon they shall lie down 2
14 Herds shall lie down in the midst of her 2
3:13 For they shall pasture and lie down 2
Jdt 12:16 Then Judith came in and lay down 4

lie fallow 1. נטש

Exd 23:11 let it rest and lie fallow 1

lie fast asleep 1. רדם

Jdg 4:21 he was lying fast asleep from weariness. 1

lie heavy 1. כבד 2. סמך 3. רַב

Ps 88: 7 Thy wrath lies heavy upon me 2
Ecc 6: 1 There is an evil . . and it lies heavy upon men 3
8: 6 although man's trouble lies heavy upon him. 3
Isa 24:20 earth . . its transgression lies heavy upon it 1

lie humbled 1. κατάκειμαι

Wis 17: 7 The delusions of their magic art lay humbled 1

lie in ambush 1. ארב 2. ἐνεδρεύω

Jos 8: 4 you shall lie in ambush against the city 1
Act 23:21 more than 40 of their men lie in ambush for him 2
Sir 5:14 do not lie in ambush with your tongue 2

lie in ruins 1. חָרֵב

Neh 2:17 Jerusalem lies in ruins with its gates burned. 1

lie in wait 1. ארב 2. חכה 3. צְדִיָּה 4. צוד 5. קוה 6. שׁוּר 7. ἐνεδρεύω 8. περικάθημαι

Exd 21:13 if he did not lie in wait for him, but God let him 4
Num35:20 hurled at him, lying in wait, so that he died 3
22 if he . . hurled anything on him without lying in wait 3
Deu 19:11 hates his neighbor, and lies in wait for him 1
Jdg 9:32 go by night . . and lie in wait in the fields. 1
16: 2 they surrounded the place and lay in wait for him 1
9 Now she had men lying in wait in an inner chamber. 1
12 the men lying in wait were in an inner chamber. 1
21:20 Go and lie in wait in the vineyards 1
1Sm 15: 5 Saul came . . and lay in wait in the valley. 7
22: 8 stirred up . . to lie in wait, as at this day. 1
13 he has risen against me, to lie in wait 1
Job 31: 9 I have lain in wait at my neighbor's door; 1
Ps 59: 3 For, lo, they lie in wait for my life; 1
119:95 The wicked lie in wait to destroy me; 5
Prv 1:11 Come with us, let us lie in wait for blood 1
18 these men lie in wait for their own blood 1
7:12 at every corner she lies in wait. 1
12: 6 The words of the wicked lie in wait for blood 1
23:28 She lies in wait like a robber 1
24:15 Lie not in wait as a wicked man against 1
Jer 5:26 they lurk like fowlers lying in wait. 6
Lam 3:10 He is to me like a bear lying in wait 1
4:19 they lay in wait for us in the wilderness. 1
Hos 6: 9 As robbers lie in wait for a man 2
Mic 7: 2 they all lie in wait for blood 1
Lke 11:54 lying in wait for him 7

Wis 2:12 Let us lie in wait for the righteous man 7
10:12 kept him safe from those who lay in wait for him 7
Sir 11:31 for he lies in wait, turning good into evil 7
32 a sinner lies in wait to shed blood. 7
14:22 lie in wait on her paths. 7
27:10 A lion lies in wait for prey 7
28 vengeance lies in wait for him like a lion. 7
28:26 lest you fall before him who lies in wait. 7
1Mc 5: 3 because they kept lying in wait for Israel 8

make lie down 1. רבץ 2. שׁכב
2Sm 8: 2 measured . . making them lie down on the ground; 2
Ps 23: 2 he makes me lie down in green pastures. 1
Sng 1: 7 Tell me . . where you make it lie down at noon; 1
Isa 13:20 will make their flocks lie down there. 1
Ezk 34:15 I will make them lie down, says the Lord GOD. 1
Hos 2:18 and I will make you lie down in safety. 2

never lie 1. ἀψευδής
Tit 1: 2 eternal life which God, who never lies, promised 1

lie polluted 1. חנף
Isa 24: 5 The earth lies polluted under its inhabitants; 1

lie prostrate 1. נפל 2. παράκειμαι 3. πρόπτωσις 4. πτῶσις 5. ῥίπτω
Deu 9:18 Then I lay prostrate before the LORD as before 1
25 I lay prostrate before the LORD for these 40 days 1
Ps 36:12 the evildoers lie prostrate, they are thrust down 1
Jdt 3: 2 Behold, we . . lie prostrate before you 2
10: 2 she rose from where she lay prostrate 4
2Mc 3:29 While he lay prostrate 5
13:12 with weeping and . . lying prostrate for three days 3

lie scattered 1. שׁפך
Lam 4: 1 holy stones lie scattered at . . every street. 1

lie sick 1. חלה
2Kg 1: 2 Ahazi'ah fell . . and lay sick; 1
Dan 8:27 I, Daniel, was overcome and lay sick for some days; 1

lie slain 1. חָלָל
2Sm 1:25 Jonathan lies slain upon thy high places. 1

lie still 1. שׁכב
Jdg 5:27 He sank, he fell, he lay still at her feet; 1
Ezk 32:21 they lie still, the uncircumcised, slain 1

lie stunned 1. רדם
Ps 76: 6 O God of Jacob, both rider and horse lay stunned. 1

lie subdued 1. כבשׁ
Jos 18: 1 the land lay subdued before them. 1

lie uncovered 1. גלה
Gen 9:21 became drunk, and lay uncovered in his tent. 1

lie upon the ground 1. χαμαιπετής
1Es 8:91 lying upon the ground before the temple 1

lie wallowing 1. גלל
2Sm 20:12 Ama'sa lay wallowing in his blood in the highway. 1

lie waste 1. חרב 2. חָרֵב 3. שׁאה 4. שׁמם
Neh 2: 3 when the city . . lies waste, and its gates 2
Isa 6:11 said: "Until cities lie waste without inhabitant 3
33: 8 highways lie waste, the wayfaring man ceases. 4
34:10 generation to generation it shall lie waste; 1

life 1. דָּם 2. דֶּרֶךְ 3. הַיִּים 4. חַי 5. חיה 6. חַיָּה 7. חַיִּים 8. חֶלֶד 9. יוֹם 10. יָחִיד 11. כֹּל הַיָּמִים 12. נֶפֶשׁ 13. עוֹלָם 14. חַיִּין (A) 15. ἀναστροφή 16. ἄνθρωπος 17. βίος 18. βιωτικός 19. ἑαυτοῦ 20. εἰμί 21. ζάω 22. ζωή 23. ἡμέρα 24. πνεῦμα 25. συμβίωσις 26. τρόπος 27. ψυχή 28. vita 29. vivifico 30. vivo
Gen 1:30 to . . everything that has the breath of life 6
2: 7 breathed into his nostrils the breath of life; 7
9 the tree of life also in the midst of the garden 7
3:14 dust you shall eat all the days of your life. 7
17 shall eat of it all the days of your life; 7
22 of the tree of life, and eat, and live for ever"- 7
24 sword . . to guard the way to the tree of life. 7
6:17 to destroy all flesh in which is the breath of life 7
7:11 In the 600th year of Noah's life 7
15 flesh in which there was the breath of life. 7
22 dry land in whose nostrils was the breath of life 7
9: 4 eat flesh with its life, that is, its blood. 12
5 brother I will require the life of man. 12
12:13 that my life may be spared on your account. 12
19:17 they said, "Flee for your life; 12
19 shown me great kindness in saving my life; 12
20 a little one?-and my life will be saved! 12
23: 1 these were the years of the life of Sarah. 7
25: 7 These are the days of the years of Abraham's life 7
17 These are the years of the life of Ish'mael 7
26:35 they made life bitter for Isaac and Rebekah. •
27:46 Rebekah said to Isaac, "I am weary of my life 7
46 of the land, what good will my life be to me?". 7
32:30 God face to face, and yet my life is preserved. 12
37:21 hands, saying, "Let us not take his life. 12
42:15 be tested: by the life of Pharaoh 4
16 or else, by the life of Pharaoh 4
44:30 then, as his life is bound up in the lad's life 12
30 then, as his life is bound up in the lad's life 12
32 in the sight of my father all my life.' 9
47: 8 How many are the days of the years of your life? 7
9 evil have been the days of the years of my life 7
9 to the days of the years of the life of my fathers 7
28 Jacob, the years of his life, were 147 years. 7
48:15 the God who has led me all my life long to this day •
Exd 1:14 made their lives bitter with hard service 7
4:19 all the men who were seeking your life are dead. 12
6:16 the years of the life of Levi being 137 years. 7
18 the years of the life of Kohath being 133 years. 7
20 the years of the life of Amram being 137 years. 7
21: 6 and he shall serve him for life. 13
23 harm follows, then you shall give life for life 12
23 harm follows, then you shall give life for life 12
30 for the redemption of his life whatever is laid 12
Lev 17:11 For the life of the flesh is in the blood 12
11 blood . . makes atonement, by reason of the life 12
14 For the life of every creature is the blood of it 12
14 for the life of every creature is its blood 12
19:16 not stand forth against the life of your neighbor 1
24:18 shall make it good, life for life 12
18 shall make it good, life for life 12
26:16 that waste the eyes and cause life to pine away. 12
Num16:38 men who have sinned at the cost of their lives; 12
35:31 shall accept no ransom for the life of a murderer 12
Deu 4: 9 depart from your heart all the days of your life; 7
6: 2 all his statutes . . all the days of your life; 7
12:23 do not eat the blood; for the blood is the life 12
23 you shall not eat the life with the flesh. 12
16: 3 all the days of your life you may remember the day 7
17:19 he shall read in it all the days of his life 7
19:21 You eye shall not pity; it shall be life for life 12
21 You eye shall not pity; it shall be life for life 12
24: 6 for he would be taking a life in pledge. 12
28:66 your life shall hang in doubt before you; 7
66 be in dread, and have no assurance of your life. 7
30:15 set before you . . life and good, death and evil. 7
19 set before you life and death, blessing and curse; 7
19 choose life, that you and your descendants 7
20 for that means life to you and length of days 7
32:47 For it is no trifle for you, but it is your life 7
Jos 1: 5 able to stand before you all the days of your life; 7
2:13 save alive . . and deliver our lives from death. 12
14 And the men said to her, "Our life for yours! 12
4:14 had stood in awe of Moses, all the days of his life. 7
9:24 we feared greatly for our lives because of you 12
Jdg 5:18 Zeb'ulun . . jeoparded their lives to the death; 12
9:17 for my father fought for you, and risked his life 12
12: 3 you would not deliver me, I took my life in my hand 12
16:30 more than those whom he had slain during his life. 7
18:25 fall upon you, and you lose your life 12
25 lose your life with the lives of your household. 12
Rut 4:15 He shall be to you a restorer of life 12
1Sm 1:11 I will give him to the LORD all the days of his life 7
7:15 Samuel judged Israel all the days of his life. 7
19: 5 for he took his life in his hand and he slew 12
11 If you do not save your life tonight, tomorrow you 12
20: 1 is my sin before your father, that he seeks my life? 12
22:23 he that seeks my life seeks your life; 12
23 he that seeks my life seeks your life; 12
23:15 Saul had come out to seek his life. 12
24:11 though you hunt my life to take it. 12
25:29 If men rise up to pursue you and to seek your life 12
29 the life of my lord shall be bound in the bundle 12
29 and the lives of your enemies he shall sling out 12
26:20 the king of Israel has come out to seek my life 27
21 my life was precious in your eyes this day; 12
24 as your life was precious this day in my sight 12
24 so may my life be precious in the sight of the LORD 12
28: 2 Very well, I will make you my bodyguard for life. 11
9 Why then are you laying a snare for my life 12
21 I have taken my life in my hand, and have hearkened 12
2Sm 1: 9 anguish has seized me, and yet my life . . lingers.' 12
23 In life and in death they were not divided; 7
4: 8 Ish-bo'sheth . . your enemy, who sought your life; 12
9 who has redeemed my life out of every adversity 12
14: 7 kill him for the life of his brother whom he slew'; 12
14 but God will not take away the life of him 12
15:21 wherever my lord . . whether for death or for life 7
16:11 my own son seeks my life; how much more now 12
17: 3 You seek the life of only one man 27
18:13 if I had dealt treacherously against his life 12
19: 5 your servants, who have this day saved your life 12
5 saved your life, and the lives of your sons 12
5 and the lives of your wives and your concubines 12
23:17 of the men who went at the risk of their lives? 12
1Kg 1:12 save your own life and the life of your son 12
12 your own life and the life of your son Solomon. 12
2:23 if this word does not cost Adoni'jah his life! 12
3:11 have not asked for yourself long life or riches 9
11 long life or riches or the life of your enemies 12
4:21 and served Solomon all the days of his life. 7
11:34 I will make him ruler all the days of his life 7
15: 5 that he commanded him all the days of his life 7
6 there was war . . all the days of his life. 7
19: 2 if I do not make your life as the life of one of them 12
2 if I do not make your life as the life of one of them 12
3 he was afraid, and he arose and went for his life 12
4 It is enough; now, O LORD, take away my life; 12
10 I . . am left; and they seek my life, to take it away. 12
14 I . . am left; and they seek my life, to take it away. 12
20:31 perhaps he will spare your life. 12
39 if . . he be missing, your life shall be for his life 12
39 if . . he be missing, your life shall be for his life 12
42 your life shall go for his life, and your people 12
42 your life shall go for his life, and your people 12
2Kg 1:13 let my life, and the life of these . . be precious 12
13 let my life, and the life of these . . be precious 12
14 but now let my life be precious in your sight. 12
7: 7 leaving the camp . . and fled for their lives. 12
10:24 who allows any . . escape shall forfeit his life. 12
20: 6 And I will add fifteen years to your life. 9
25:29 every day of his life he dined regularly 4
2Ch 1:11 not asked . . or the life of those who hate you 12
11 and have not even asked long life, but have asked 9
Ezr 6:10 may . . pray for the life of the king and his sons. 14
Est 7: 3 let my life be given me at my petition 12
7 Haman stayed to beg his life from Queen Esther 12
8:11 the Jews . . to gather and defend their lives 12
9:16 Jews who . . also gathered to defend their lives 12
Job 2: 4 All that a man has he will give for his life. 12
6 he is in your power; only spare his life. 12
3:20 that is in misery, and life to the bitter in soul 7
7: 7 Remember that my life is a breath; 7
16 I loathe my life; I would not live for ever. •
9:21 I regard not myself; I loathe my life. 7
10: 1 I loathe my life; 12
12 Thou has granted me life and steadfast love; 7
20 Are not the days of my life few? •
11:17 your life will be brighter than the noonday; 8
12:10 In his hand is the life of every living thing 12
13:14 and put my life in my hand. 12
24:22 God prolongs the life of the mighty by his power; •
22 they rise up when they despair of life. 7
27: 8 when God cuts him off, when God takes away his life? 12
31:30 I have not let my mouth sin by asking for his life 12
33:18 his life from perishing by the sword. 6
20 that his life loathes bread 6
22 his life to those who bring death. 6
28 my life shall see the light. 6
30 from the Pit, that he may see the light of life. 7
36:14 They die in youth, and their life ends in shame. 6
Ps 6: 4 Turn, O LORD, save my life; deliver me 12
7: 5 let him trample my life to the ground 7
16:11 Thou dost show me the path of life; 7
17:13 Deliver my life from the wicked by thy sword 12
14 from men whose portion in life is of the world. 7
21: 4 He asked life of thee; thou gavest it to him 7
22:20 Deliver . . my life from the power of the dog! 10
23: 6 and mercy shall follow me all the days of my life; 7
25:20 Oh guard my life, and deliver me; 12
26: 9 with sinners, nor my life with bloodthirsty men 7
27: 1 The LORD is the stronghold of my life; 7
4 in the house of the LORD all the days of my life 7
31:10 my life is spent with sorrow 7
13 together against me, as they plot to take my life. 12
34:12 What man is there who desires life 7
22 The LORD redeems the life of his servants; 12
35: 4 put to shame and dishonor who seek after my life! 12
7 without cause they dug a pit for my life. 12
17 from their ravages, my life from the lions! 10
36: 9 with thee is the fountain of life; 7
38:12 Those who seek my life lay their snares 12
39: 4 let me know how fleeting my life is! •
40:14 be put to shame . . who seek to snatch away my life; 12
42: 8 his song is with me, a prayer to the God of my life. 7
49: 8 for the ransom of his life is costly 12
54: 3 ruthless men seek my life; 12
4 the Lord is the upholder of my life. 12
56: 6 As they have waited for my life 12
13 that I may walk before God in the light of life. 7
59: 3 For, lo, they lie in wait for my life; 12
61: 6 Prolong the life of the king; may his years endure †
63: 3 Because thy steadfast love is better than life 7
9 those who seek to destroy my life shall go down 12
64: 1 preserve my life from dread of the enemy 7
70: 2 be put to shame and confusion who seek my life! 12
71:10 those who watch for my life consult together 12
72:13 He has pity . . and saves the lives of the needy. 12
14 From oppression . . he redeems their life; 12
74:19 do not forget the life of thy poor for ever. 6
78:50 but gave their lives over to the plague. 6
86: 2 Preserve my life, for I am godly; 12
14 band of ruthless men seek my life 12
88: 3 my life draws near to Sheol. 7
91:16 With long life I will satisfy him 9
94:21 band together against the life of the righteous 12
97:10 LORD . . preserves the lives of his saints; 12
103: 4 who redeems your life from the Pit 7

109:20 of those who speak evil against my life! 12
116: 4 O LORD, I beseech thee, save my life! 12
119:109 I hold my life in my hand continually 12
121: 7 LORD . . will keep your life. 12
128: 5 prosperity of Jerusalem all the days of you life! 7
133: 3 commanded the blessing, life for evermore. 7
143: 3 enemy . . has crushed my life to the ground; 6
Prv 1:18 they set an ambush for their own lives. 12
19 it takes away the life of its possessors. 12
2:19 nor do they regain the paths of life. 7
3: 2 length of days and years of life 7
16 Long life is in her right hand; 9
18 She is a tree of life to those who lay hold of her; 7
22 life for your soul and adornment for your neck. 7
4:10 Hear . . that the years of your life may be many. 7
13 guard her, for she is your life. 7
22 For they are life to him who finds them 7
23 for from it flow the springs of life. 7
5: 6 she does not take heed to the path of life; 7
6:23 reproofs of discipline are the way of life 7
26 but an adulteress stalks a man's very life. 12
7:23 he does not know that it will cost him his life. 12
8:35 For he who finds me finds life 7
9:11 For by me . . years will be added to your life. 7
10:11 The mouth of the righteous is a fountain of life 7
16 The wage of the righteous leads to life 7
17 He who heeds instruction is on the path to life 7
27 The fear of the LORD prolongs life 9
11:30 The fruit of the righteous is a tree of life 7
30 but lawlessness takes away lives. 12
12:10 righteous . . regard for the life of his beast 12
28 In the path of righteousness is life 7
13: 3 He who guards his mouth preserves his life; 12
8 The ransom of a man's life is his wealth 12
12 but a desire fulfilled is a tree of life. 7
14 The teaching of the wise is a fountain of life 7
14:25 A truthful witness saves lives 12
27 The fear of the LORD is a fountain of life 7
30 A tranquil mind gives life to the flesh 7
15: 4 A gentle tongue is a tree of life 7
24 The wise man's path leads upward to life, 7
16:15 In the light of a king's face there is life 7
17 he who guards his way preserves his life. 12
22 Wisdom is a fountain of life to him who has it 7
31 A hoary head . . is gained in a righteous life. 2
18:21 Death and life are in the power of the tongue 7
19:16 He who keeps the commandment keeps his life; 12
23 The fear of the LORD leads to life; 7
20: 2 he who provokes him to anger forfeits his life. 12
21:21 who pursues . . kindness will find life and honor. 7
22: 4 reward . . is riches and honor and life. 7
23 LORD . . despoil of life those who despoil them. 12
23:14 beat him with the rod . . save his life from Sheol. 12
29:10 who is blameless, and the wicked seek his life. 12
24 The partner of a thief hates his own life; 12
31:12 She does him good . . all the days of her life. 7
Ecc 2: 3 to do . . during the few days of their life. 7
17 I hated life, because . . was grievous to me; 7
5:18 the few days of his life which God has given him 7
20 For he will not much remember the days of his life 7
6: 3 but he does not enjoy life's good things •
12 while he lives the few days of his vain life 7
7:15 In my vain life I have seen everything; 9
15 a . . man who prolongs his life in his evil-doing. •
8:12 a sinner does evil . . and prolongs his life •
15 this will go with him . . through the days of life 7
9: 9 Enjoy life with the wife whom you love 7
9 all the days of your vain life which he has given 7
9 that is your portion in life and in your toil 7
10:19 Bread is . . for laughter, and wine gladdens life 7
Isa 4: 3 one who has been recorded for life in Jerusalem 7
38: 5 behold, I will add fifteen years to your life. 9
12 like a weaver I have rolled up my life; 7
16 and in all these is the life of my spirit. 7
17 thou hast held back my life from the pit 12
20 to stringed instruments all the days of our life 7
43: 4 I give . . peoples in exchange for your life. 12
57:10 you found new life for your strength 6
Jer 4:10 whereas the sword has reached their very life. 12
30 Your lovers despise you; they seek your life. 12
8: 3 Death shall be preferred to life 7
11:21 the men of An'athoth, who seek your life, and say 12
17:21 says the LORD: Take heed for the sake of your lives 12
18:20 Yet they have dug a pit for my life. 12
19: 7 and by the hand of those who seek their life. 12
9 and those who seek their life afflict them. 12
20:13 For he has delivered the life of the needy 12
21: 7 into the hand of those who seek their lives. 12
8 Behold, I set before you the way of life 7
9 and shall have his life as a prize of war. 12
22:25 give you into the hand of those who seek your life 12
31:12 their life shall be like a watered garden 12
34:20 and into the hand of those who seek their lives. 12
21 and into the hand of those who seek their lives 12
38: 2 he shall have his life as a prize of war, and live. 12
16 the hand of these men who seek your life. 12
17 then your life shall be spared 12
20 be well with you, and your life shall be spared. 12
39:18 you shall have your life as a prize of war 12
40:14 has sent Ish'mael . . to take your life? 12
15 Why should he take your life 12
42:20 you have gone astray at the cost of your lives. 12
44:30 and into the hand of those who seek his life 12
30 Babylon, who was his enemy and sought his life. 12
45: 5 but I will give you your life as a prize of war 12
46:26 into the hand of those who seek their life 12
49:37 and before those who seek their life; 12
51: 6 the midst of Babylon, let every man save his life! 12
13 your end has come, the thread of your life is cut. †
45 Let every man save his life from the fierce anger 12
52:33 every day of his life he dined . . at the king's 4
Lam 2:12 their life is poured out on their mothers' bosom. 12
19 Lift your hands . . for the lives of your children 12
3:58 taken up my cause . . thou has redeemed my life. 7
Ezk 3:19 but you will have saved your life. 12
21 you will have saved your life. 12
7:13 none can maintain his life. 6
14:14 they would deliver but their own lives 12
20 they would deliver but their own lives 12
17:17 cast up and siege walls built to cut off many lives 12
18:27 and does what is . . right, he shall save his life. 12
20:25 and ordinances by which they could not have life; 5
22:27 destroying lives to get dishonest gain. 12
32:10 tremble every moment, every one for his own life 12
33: 5 had taken warning, he would have saved his life. 12
9 but you will have saved your life. 12
15 and walks in the statutes of life 7
Dan 7:12 lives were prolonged for a season and a time. 14
12: 2 some to everlasting life, and some to shame 7
Ams 2:14 nor shall the mighty save his life; 12
15 nor shall he who rides the horse save his life; 12
Jon 1:14 O LORD, let us not perish for this man's life 12
2: 6 yet thou didst bring up my life from the Pit, O LORD 7
4: 3 now, O LORD, take my life from me, I beseech thee 12
Hab 2:10 you have forfeited your life. 12
Mal 2: 5 covenant of life and peace, and I gave them to him 7
15 God made and sustained for us the spirit of life? •
Mat 2:20 those who sought the child's life are dead. 27
6:25 I tell you, do not be anxious about your life 27
25 put on. Is not life more than food, and the body 27
7:14 the way is hard, that leads to life 22
10:39 He who finds his life will lose it 27
39 he who loses his life for my sake will find it. 27
16:25 For whoever would save his life will lose it 27
25 whoever loses his life for my sake will find it. 27
26 if he gains the whole world and forfeits his life? 27
26 Or what shall a man give in return for his life? 27
18: 8 it is better for you to enter life maimed or lame 22
9 it is better for you to enter life with one eye 22
19:16 to have eternal life? 22
17 If you would enter life, keep the commandments. 22
29 and inherit eternal life. 22
20:28 to give his life as a ransom for many. 27
25:46 but the righteous into eternal life. 22
Mrk 3: 4 to save life or to kill 27
8:35 For whoever would save his life will lose it; 27
35 whoever loses his life for my sake 27
36 to gain the whole world and forfeit his life? 27
37 For what can a man give in return for his life? 27
9:43 it is better for you to enter life maimed 22
45 it is better for you to enter life lame 22
10:17 what must I do to inherit eternal life? 22
30 in the age to come eternal life. 22
45 to give his life as a ransom for many. 27
Lke 1:75 before him all the days of our life. •
6: 9 to save life or to destroy it? 27
8:14 the cares and riches and pleasures of life 17
9:24 For whoever would save his life will lose it; 27
24 whoever loses his life for my sake, he will save it. 27
10:25 Teacher, what shall I do to inherit eternal life? 22
12:15 a man's life does not consist in the abundance 22
22 do not be anxious about your life 27
23 life is more than food 27
14:26 yes, and even his own life 27
17:33 Whoever seeks to gain his life will lose it 27
33 whoever loses his life will preserve it. •
18:18 what shall I do to inherit eternal life? 22
30 in the age to come eternal life. 22
21:34 drunkenness and cares of this life 18
Joh 1: 4 In him was life, and the life was the light of men. 22
4 In him was life, and the life was the light of men. 22
3:15 whoever believes in him may have eternal life. 22
16 should not perish but have eternal life. 22
36 He who believes in the Son has eternal life; 22
36 he who does not obey the Son shall not see life 22
4:14 a spring of water welling up to eternal life. 22
36 and gathers fruit for eternal life 22
5:24 he who hears . . has eternal life 22
24 has passed from death to life. 22
26 For as the Father has life in himself 22
26 he has granted the Son also to have life in himself 22
29 who have done good, to the resurrection of life 22
39 in them you have eternal life 22
40 you refuse to come to me that you may have life. 22
6:27 the food which endures to eternal life 22
33 gives life to the world. 22
35 Jesus said to them, "I am the bread of life 22
40 every one . . should have eternal life 22
47 he who believes has eternal life. 22
48 I am the bread of life. 22
51 bread which I shall give for the life of the world 22
53 you have no life in you; 22
54 he who . . drinks my blood has eternal life 22
63 the words . . are spirit and life. 22
68 You have the words of eternal life; 22
8:12 will have the light of life. 22
10:10 I came that they may have life 22
11 The good shepherd lays down his life 27
15 I lay down my life for the sheep. 27
17 the Father loves me, because I lay down my life 27
28 I give them eternal life 22
11:25 I am the resurrection and the life 22
12:25 He who loves his life loses it 27
25 he who hates his life in this world will keep it 27
25 will keep it for eternal life. 22
50 I know that his commandment is eternal life. 22
13:37 I will lay down my life for you. 27
38 Jesus answered, "Will you lay down your life for me? 27
14: 6 I am the way, and the truth, and the life 22
15:13 that a man lay down his life for his friends. 27
17: 2 to give eternal life to all 22
3 this is eternal life, that they know thee 22
20:31 believing you may have life in his name. 22
Act 2:28 Thou hast made known to me the ways of life 22
3:15 killed the Author of life 22
5:20 speak to the people all the words of this Life. 22
8:33 his life is taken up from the earth. 22
11:18 God has granted repentance unto life. 22
13:46 judge yourselves unworthy of eternal life 22
48 as many as were ordained to eternal life 22
17:25 gives to all men life and breath and everything. 22
20:10 Do not be alarmed, for his life is in him. 27
24 I do not account my life of any value 27
27:22 no loss of life among you, but only of the ship. 27
Rom 2: 7 he will give eternal life; 22
5:10 much more . . shall we be saved by his life. 22
17 reign in life through the one man Jesus Christ. 22
18 leads to acquittal and life for all men. 22
21 to eternal life through Jesus Christ our Lord. 22
6: 4 we too might walk in newness of life. 22
10 but the life he lives he lives to God. •
22 and its end, eternal life. 22
23 but the free gift of God is eternal life in Christ 22
7: 1 law is binding on a person only during his life 21
6 so that we serve . . in the new life of the Spirit. •
10 the very commandment which promised life 22
8: 2 For the law of the Spirit of life in Christ Jesus 22
6 to set the mind on the Spirit is life and peace. 22
38 neither death, nor life, nor angels 22
11: 3 and I alone am left, and they seek my life. 27
15 their acceptance mean but life from the dead? 22
16: 4 who risked their necks for my life 27
1Co 1:30 He is the source of your life in Christ Jesus 20
3:22 the world or life or death or the present 22
15:19 If for this life only we have hoped in Christ 22
2Co 1: 8 we despaired of life itself. 21
2:16 to the other a fragrance from life to life 22
16 to the other a fragrance from life to life 22
4:10 so that the life of Jesus may also be manifested 22
11 so that the life of Jesus may be manifested 22
12 death is at work in us, but life in you. 22
5: 4 what is mortal may be swallowed up by life. 22
Gal 1:13 For you have heard of my former life in Judaism 15
2:20 the life I now live in the flesh I live by faith •
6: 8 will from the Spirit reap eternal life. 22
Eph 4:18 alienated from the life of God 22
Php 1:20 whether by life or by death. 22
22 If it is to be life in the flesh 21
2:16 holding fast the word of life 22
30 risking his life to complete your service to me. 27
4: 3 whose names are in the book of life. 22
Col 2:10 you have come to fulness of life in him •
3: 3 your life is hid with Christ in God. 22
4 When Christ who is our life appears 22
1Ti 1:16 who were to believe in him for eternal life. 22
2: 2 we may lead a quiet and peaceable life 17
4: 8 as it holds promise for the present life 22
8 the present life and also for the life to come. •
6:12 the eternal life to which you were called 22
19 take hold of the life which is life indeed. 22
19 take hold of the life which is life indeed. •
2Ti 1: 1 the promise of the life which is in Christ Jesus. 22
10 brought life and immortality to light 22
Tit 1: 2 eternal life which God, who never lies, promised 22
3: 7 become heirs in hope of eternal life. 22
Heb 7: 3 has neither beginning of days nor end of life 22
16 by the power of an indestructible life. 22
11:35 that they might rise again to a better life. •
13: 5 Keep your life free from love of money 26
7 consider the outcome of their life 15
Jas 1:12 he will receive the crown of life 22
3:13 By his good life let him show his works 15
4:14 What is your life? 22
1Pe 3: 7 since you are joint heirs of the grace of life 22
10 He that would love life and see good days 22
2Pe 1: 3 all things that pertain to life and godliness 22
1Jn 1: 1 concerning the word of life- 22

2 the life was made manifest, and we saw it 22
2 and proclaim to you the eternal life 22
2:16 the lust of the eyes and the pride of life 17
25 this is what he has promised us, eternal life. 22
3:14 We know that we have passed out of death into life 22
15 no murderer has eternal life abiding in him. 22
16 we know love, that he laid down his life for us; 27
5:11 the testimony, that God gave us eternal life 22
11 eternal life, and this life is in his Son. 22
12 He who has the Son has life; 22
12 he who has not the Son of God has not life. 22
13 that you may know that you have eternal life. 22
16 he will ask, and God will give him life 22
20 This is the true God and eternal life. 22
3Jn 1: 3 and testified to the truth of your life •
Jde 1:21 the mercy of our Lord . . unto eternal life. 22
Rev 2: 7 I will grant to eat of the tree of life 22
10 and I will give you the crown of life. 22
3: 5 I will not blot his name out of the book of life; 22
11:11 a breath of life from God entered them 22
13: 8 name has not been written . . in the book of life 22
17: 8 names have not been written in the book of life 22
20:12 another book was opened, which is the book of life 22
15 name was not found written in the book of life 22
21: 6 I will give from the fountain of the water of life 22
27 only those . . written in the Lamb's book of life 22
22: 1 Then he showed me the river of the water of life 22
2 the tree of life with its twelve kinds of fruit 22
14 they may have the right to the tree of life 22
17 let him who desires take the water of life 22
19 God will take away his share in the tree of life 22
1Es 6:31 prayers be offered for their life. 22
2Es 2:12 The tree of life shall give them . . perfume 28
3: 5 thou didst breathe into him the breath of life 28
4:24 and our life is like a mist 28
52 I was not sent to tell you concerning your life 28
7:48 and removed us far from life 28
92 might not lead them astray from life into death. 28
98 whom they served in life 30
129 Choose for yourself life, that you may live!' 27
137 those who inhabit it would not have life; 29
138 one 10,000th of mankind could have life; 29
8:52 paradise is opened, the tree of life is planted 28
60 ungrateful to him who prepared life for them. 28
13:55 for you have devoted your life to wisdom 28
14:13 And now renounce the life that is corruptible 28
30 received the law of life, which they did not keep 28
16:61 and gave him breath and life and understanding 28
Tob 1: 3 all the days of my life 22
4: 3 Honor her all the days of your life 22
5 Live uprightly all the days of your life 22
5:19 the life that is given to us by the Lord is enough 21
12: 9 will have fulness of life; 22
14: 3 I have grown old and am about to depart this life. 21
Jdt 8:29 from the beginning of your life 23
10:15 You have saved your life 27
12:18 because my life means more to me today 21
13:20 because you did not spare your own life 27
16:22 she remained a widow all the days of her life 22
AEs 16:12 to deprive us of our kingdom and our life 24
Wis 1:12 Do not invite death by the error of your life 22
2: 1 Short and sorrowful is our life 17
4 our life will pass away 17
4: 9 a blameless life is ripe old age. 17
5: 4 We thought that his life was madness 17
7: 6 there is for all mankind one entrance into life 17
8: 5 If riches are a desirable possession in life 17
7 nothing in life is more profitable for men 17
16 and life with her has no pain 25
12:23 those who in folly of life lived unrighteously 22
13:11 a useful vessel that serves life's needs 22
18 for life he prays to a thing that is dead 22
14:12 the invention of them was the corruption of life 22
15: 9 his life is brief 17
10 his life is of less worth than clay 17
12 considered . . life a festival held for profit 17
17 since he has life, but they never have. 21
16:13 For thou hast power over life and death 22
Sir 4:12 Whoever loves her loves life 22
6:16 A faithful friend is an elixir of life 22
7:36 In all you do, remember the end of your life •
9:13 lest he rob you of your life 22
10: 9 for even in life his bowels decay. 3
29 who will honor the man that dishonors his own life? 22
11:14 Good things and bad, life and death 22
27 at the close of a man's life 16
15:17 Before a man are life and death 22
17:11 allotted to them the law of life. 22
20:22 A man may lose his life through shame 27
22:11 the life of the fool is worse than death. 22
12 for a fool or an ungodly man it lasts all his life. 22
23: 1 O Lord, Father and Ruler of my life 22
4 O Lord, Father and God of my life 27
25: 2 I am greatly offended at their life 27
28: 6 Remember the end of your life •
29:15 he has given his life for you. 27
21 The essentials for life are water and bread 22
22 Better is the life of a poor man 17
24 It is a miserable life to go from house to house 22
30:17 Death is better than a miserable life 22
22 Gladness of heart is the life of man 22
24 Jealousy and anger shorten life 23
31:27 Wine is like life to men 22
27 What is life to a man who is without wine? 22
33:14 life the opposite of death 22
23 At the time when you end the days of your life 22
34:17 he grants healing, life, and blessing. 22
21 The bread of the needy is the life of the poor; 22
37:18 good and evil, life and death 22
25 The life of a man is numbered by days 22
31 he who is careful to avoid it prolongs his life. 22
38:19 the life of the poor man weighs down his heart. 17
20 drive it away, remembering the end of life. •
39:26 Basic to all the needs of man's life 22
40:18 Life is sweet for the self-reliant and the worker 22
28 My son, do not lead the life of a beggar 22
29 his existence cannot be considered as life 22
41: 3 remember your former days and the end of life •
4 Whether life is for ten or 100 . . years 22
13 The days of a good life are numbered 22
45: 5 the law of life and knowledge 22
48:14 As in his life he did wonders 22
23 he lengthened the life of the king. 22
50: 1 who in his life repaired the house 22
51: 3 from the hand of those who sought my life 27
6 my life was very near to Hades beneath. 27
Bar 1:11 pray for the life of Nebuchadnezzar king 22
11 pray . . for the life of Belshazzar his son 22
3: 9 Hear the commandments of life, O Israel; give ear 22
14 discern where there is length of days, and life 22
Man 1:15 all the days of my life 22
1Mc 3:12 and used it in battle the rest of his life. 23
6:44 So he gave his life to save his people 19
13: 5 to spare my life in any time of distress 27
2Mc 3:31 to grant life 21
33 for his sake the Lord has granted you your life. 21
35 and made very great vows to the Savior of his life 21
6:19 rather than life with pollution 17
20 even for the natural love of life. 21
23 and his excellent life even from childhood 15
27 Therefore, by manfully giving up my life now 17
7: 9 you dismiss us from this present life 21
9 an everlasting renewal of life 22
14 there will be no resurrection to life! 22
22 It was not I who gave you life and breath 22
23 will in his mercy give life and breath back to you 22
36 our brothers . . have drunk of everflowing life 22
37 give up body and life for the laws of our fathers 27
9:28 the murderer . . came to the end of his life 17
10:13 he took poison and ended his life. 17
14:38 he had with all zeal risked body and life. 27
46 calling upon the Lord of life and spirit 22
3Mc 2:23 fearing lest he should lose his life 21
32 by paying money in exchange for life 21
4: 4 some . . reflected upon the uncertainty of life 17
6 to share married life 17
5:32 have been deprived of life instead of these 21
49 thought that this was their last moment of life 17
6: 1 throughout his life 17
12 deprived of life in the manner of traitors. 21
24 attempting to deprive of dominion and life 24
4Mc 1:15 with sound logic prefers the life of wisdom. 17
4: 1 who then held the high priesthood for life 17
6:18 maintained . . the reputation of such a life 17
29 take my life in exchange for theirs. 27
7: 4 his sacred life was consumed by tortures 27
7 philosopher of divine life! 17
15 of venerable gray hair and of law-abiding life 17
8:23 Why do we banish . . from this most pleasant life 17
9:25 the saintly youth broke the thread of life. 27
10:15 by the everlasting life of the pious 17
12:18 he will take vengeance both in this present life 17
19 so ended his life. •
13:20 growing . . through the same life 27
15: 3 religion that preserves them for eternal life 22
16:18 have had a share in the world and have enjoyed life 17
17:12 The prize was immortality in endless life. 22
18: 9 who lived out his life with good children 17
16 'There is a tree of life for those who do his will.' 22
19 this is your life and the length of your days.' 22

life *See also* give, span.

all life long 1. עוֹד
Num22:30 you have ridden all your life long to this day? 1

common life 1. *βίος*
2Mc 14:25 he . . settled down, and shared the common life. 1

godly life
2Ti 3:12 all who desire to live a godly life in Christ •

human life 1. נֶפֶשׁ
Ezk 22:25 they have devoured human lives; 1

long life 1. *ἡλικία* 2. *μακροημέρευσις*
Sir 1:12 gives gladness and joy and long life. 2
20 her branches are long life. 2
3: 6 will have long life 2
4Mc 5:36 nor my long life lived lawfully. 1

national life 1. *πολιτεία*
4Mc 8: 7 the ancestral tradition of your national life. 1

lifeblood 1. דָּם 2. דָּם לְנַפְשׁוֹת 3. דַּם נַפְשׁוֹת 4. נֵצַח
Gen 9: 5 For your lifeblood I will surely require 2
1Ch 11:19 Shall I drink the lifeblood of these men? 1
Isa 63: 3 their lifeblood is sprinkled upon my garments 4
6 and I poured out their lifeblood on the earth. 4
Jer 2:34 is found the lifeblood of guiltless poor; 3

lifeless 1. *ἄπνοος* 2. *ἄψυχος* 3. mortuus 4. sine anima
1Co 14: 7 If even lifeless instruments 2
2Es 3: 5 it gave thee Adam, a lifeless body 3
6:48 The dumb and lifeless water 4
Wis 14:29 for because they trust in lifeless idols 2
15: 5 they desire the lifeless form of a dead image. 1

lifeless thing 1. *ἄψυχος*
Wis 13:17 he is not ashamed to address a lifeless thing. 1

lifelong 1. *ζάω*
Heb 2:15 those who . . were subject to lifelong bondage. 1

lifetime 1. חַיִּים 2. חֶלֶד 3. עַל פְּנֵי 4. *ζωή* 5. vivo
Num 3: 4 served as priests in the lifetime of Aaron 3
2Sm 18:18 Ab'salom in his lifetime had . . set up for himself 1
Ps 30: 5 for a moment, and his favor is for a lifetime. 1
39: 5 my lifetime is as nothing in thy sight. 2
Lke 16:25 you in your lifetime received your good things 4
2Es 9:10 did not acknowledge me in their lifetime 5

lift 1. גדל 2. נוף 3. נשא 4. עלה 5. עמס 6. רום 7. שגב 8. נטל (A) 9. *αἴρω* 10. *ἀνορθόω* 11. *βαστάζω* 12. *ἐπαίρω* 13. levo
Gen 37:28 drew Joseph up and lifted him out of the pit 4
Exd 10:19 very strong west wind, which lifted the locusts 3
Num23:24 As a lioness . . as a lion it lifts itself; 3
Jos 8:31 stones, upon which no man has lifted an iron tool 2
1Sm 2: 8 he lifts the needy from the ash heap, to make them 6
2Kg 4:20 when he had lifted him, and brought him 3
19:22 Against whom . . and haughtily lifted your eyes? 3
1Ch 21:16 David lifted his eyes and saw the angel 3
Ezr 9: 6 O my God, I am ashamed and blush to lift my face 6
Job 5:11 those who mourn are lifted to safety. 7
Ps 3: 3 my glory, and the lifter of my head. 6
41: 9 bosom friend . . has lifted his heel against me. 1
113: 7 lifts the needy from the ash heap 6
Prv 30:13 There are those–how . . high their eyelids lift! 3
Isa 10:15 As if a rod should wield him who lifts it 6
15 or as if a staff should lift him who is not wood! 6
26 his rod . . and he will lift it as he did in Egypt. 3
37:23 your voice and haughtily lifted your eyes? 3
46: 7 They lift it upon their shoulders, they carry it 3
Jer 38:10 and lift Jeremiah the prophet out of the cistern 4
13 with ropes and lifted him out of the cistern. 4
Lam 2:19 Lift your hands to him for . . your children 3
Ezk 12: 6 you shall lift the baggage upon your shoulder 3
12 prince who is among them shall lift his baggage 3
Dan 4:34 Nebuchadnez'zar, lifted my eyes to heaven 8
Hab 3:10 gave forth its voice, it lifted its hands on high. 3
Zec 1:18 I lifted my eyes and saw, and behold, four horns! 3
2: 1 I lifted my eyes and saw, and behold, a man 3
5: 1 Again I lifted my eyes and saw 3
5 Lift your eyes, and see what this is that goes 3
7 behold, the leaden cover was lifted 3
9 I lifted my eyes and saw, and behold, two women 3
6: 1 again I lifted my eyes and saw 3
12: 3 all who lift it shall grievously hurt 5
Act 4:24 lifted their voices together to God and said 9
1Ti 2: 8 lifting holy hands without anger or quarreling; 12
Heb 12:12 Therefore lift your drooping hands 10
1Es 9:47 they lifted up their hands, and fell to the ground 9
2Es 13: 9 he neither lifted his hand nor held a spear 13
Jdt 11: 2 I would never have lifted my spear against them; 9
AEs 15: 7 Lifting his face, flushed with splendor 9
Sir 11:12 he lifts him out of his low estate 10
13: 2 Do not lift a weight beyond your strength 9
46: 2 How glorious he was when he lifted his hands 12
47: 4 when he lifted his hand with a stone in the sling 12
Bel 1:36 lifted him by his hair and set him down in Babylon 11

lift against 1. *ἐπαίρω*
Joh 13:18 He . . has lifted his heel against me.' 1

lift out 1. *ἐγείρω*
Mat 12:11 will not lay hold of it and lift it out? 1

lift the burden 1. *κουφίζω*
1Es 8:86 thou, O Lord, didst lift the burden of our sins 1

lift up 1. גאה 2. גבה 3. גלה 4. זקף 5. חשף 6. מַעַל 7. מַשְׂאֵת 8. נוף 9. נטל 10. נשא 11. נתן 12. נתק 13. סלל 14. עוד 15. קום 16. רום 17. רוֹמֵמוֹת 18. נטל (A) 19. רום (A) 20. *αἴρω* 21. *ἀνατείνω*

22. ἀνίστημι 23. ἀνυψόω 24. ἐγείρω 25. ἐπαίρω
26. μετεωρίζω 27. συνεγείρω 28. ὑψόω 29. extollo

Gen 13:10 Lot lifted up his eyes, and saw that the Jordan 10
14 Lift up your eyes, and look from the place 10
18: 2 He lifted up his eyes and looked, and behold 10
21:16 the child lifted up his voice and wept. 10
18 Arise, lift up the lad, and hold him fast 10
22: 4 On the third day Abraham lifted up his eyes 10
13 Abraham lifted up his eyes and looked 10
24:63 and he lifted up his eyes and looked 10
64 Rebekah lifted up her eyes, and when she saw Isaac 10
27:38 And Esau lifted up his voice and wept. 10
31:10 the flock I lifted up my eyes, and saw in a dream 10
12 he said, 'Lift up your eyes and see, all the goats 10
33: 1 Jacob lifted up his eyes and looked 10
39:15 when he heard that I lifted up my voice and cried 16
18 as soon as I lifted up my voice and cried, he left 16
40:13 within three days Pharaoh will lift up your head 10
19 Pharaoh will lift up your head-from you! 10
20 and lifted up the head of the chief butler 10
41:44 no man shall lift up hand or foot in all the land 16
43:29 he lifted up his eyes, and saw his brother 10
Exd 7:20 he lifted up the rod and struck the water that was 16
14:10 the people of Israel lifted up their eyes 10
16 Lift up your rod, and stretch out your hand over 16
23: 5 you shall help him to lift it up. 27
Lev 9:22 Then Aaron lifted up his hands toward the people 10
Num 6:26 The LORD lift up his countenance upon you 10
20:11 Moses lifted up his hand and struck the rock 16
24: 2 Balaam lifted up his eyes, and saw Israel 10
Deu 3:27 lift up your eyes westward and northward 10
4:19 beware lest you lift up your eyes to heaven 10
8:14 then your heart be lifted up, and you forget 16
17:20 his heart may not be lifted up above his brethren 16
22: 4 you shall help him to lift them up again. 15
27: 5 you shall lift up no iron tool upon them. 8
32:40 For I lift up my hand to heaven, and swear, As I live 10
Jos 4:18 soles of the . . feet were lifted up on dry ground 12
5:13 When Joshua . . he lifted up his eyes and looked 10
Jdg 2: 4 the people lifted up their voices and wept. 10
8:28 and they lifted up their heads no more. 10
19:17 he lifted up his eyes, and saw the wayfarer 10
21: 2 and they lifted up their voices and wept 10
Rut 1: 9 and they lifted up their voices and wept. 10
14 Then they lifted up their voices and wept again; 10
1Sm 6:13 when they lifted up their eyes and saw the ark 10
24:16 And Saul lifted up his voice and wept. 10
2Sm 2:22 How . . could I lift up my face to your brother Jo'ab? 10
3:32 the king lifted up his voice and wept at the grave 10
13:34 young man who kept the watch lifted up his eyes 10
36 sons came, and lifted up their voice and wept; 10
18:24 when he lifted up his eyes and looked, he saw a man 10
20:21 a man . . has lifted up his hand against King David; 10
1Kg 11:26 Jerobo'am . . lifted up his hand against the king. 16
27 why he lifted up his hand against the king. 16
2Kg 9:32 he lifted up his face to the window, and said 10
14:10 and your heart has lifted you up. 10
19: 4 lift up your prayer for the remnant that is left. 10
2Ch 25:19 your heart has lifted you up in boastfulness. 10
Neh 8: 6 answered, "Amen, Amen," lifting up their hands; 6
Job 10:15 If I am righteous, I cannot lift up my head 10
16 if I lift myself up, thou dost hunt me like a lion 1
11:15 then you will lift up your face without blemish; 10
22:26 in the Almighty, and lift up your face to God. 10
27:21 The east wind lifts him up and he is gone; 10
30:22 Thou liftest me up on the wind, 10
38:34 Can you lift up your voice to the clouds 16
Ps 4: 6 Lift up the light of thy countenance upon us 10
7: 6 lift thyself up against the fury of my enemies; 10
9:13 O thou who liftest me up from the gates of death 16
10:12 Arise, O LORD; O God, lift up thy hand; 10
24: 4 who does not lift up his soul to what is false 10
7 Lift up your heads, O gates! 10
7 be lifted up, O ancient doors! 10
9 Lift up your heads, O gates! 10
9 be lifted up, O ancient doors! 25
25: 1 To thee, O LORD, I lift up my soul. 10
27: 6 now my head shall be lifted up above my enemies 16
28: 2 I lift up my hands toward thy most holy 10
63: 4 I will lift up my hands and call on thy name. 10
68: 4 lift up a song to him who rides upon the clouds; 13
75: 4 and to the wicked, "Do not lift up your horn; 16
5 do not lift up your horn on high 16
6 not from the wilderness comes lifting up; 16
7 putting down one and lifting up another. 16
86: 4 for to thee, O Lord, do I lift up my soul. 10
93: 3 floods have lifted up, O LORD 10
3 O LORD, the floods have lifted up their voice 10
3 floods lift up their roaring. 10
107:25 stormy wind, which lifted up the waves of the sea. 16
110: 7 therefore he will lift up his head. 16
116:13 I will lift up the cup of salvation 10
121: 1 I lift up my eyes to the hills. 10
123: 1 To thee I lift up my eyes, O thou who art enthroned 10
131: 1 O LORD, my heart is not lifted up, my eyes are not 2
134: 2 Lift up your hands to the holy place, and bless 10
139:20 who lift themselves up against thee for evil! *
140: 9 Those who surround me lift up their head *
141: 2 lifting up of my hands as an evening sacrifice! 7
143: 8 way I should go, for to thee I lift up my soul. 10
146: 8 The LORD lifts up those who are bowed down; 4
147: 6 LORD lifts up the downtrodden 14
Ecc 4:10 For if they fall, one will lift up his fellow; 15
10 who is alone . . and has not another to lift him up. 15
Isa 2: 4 nation shall not lift up sword against nation 10
12 has a day . . against all that is lifted up and high; 10
13 all the cedars of Lebanon, lofty and lifted up; 10
6: 1 the Lord sitting upon a throne, high and lifted up; 10
10:24 lift up their staff against you as the Egyptians 10
24:14 They lift up their voices, they sing for joy; 10
26:11 O LORD, thy hand is lifted up, but they see it not 16
33: 3 at the lifting up of thyself nations are 17
10 now I will lift myself up; now I will be exalted. 16
37: 4 therefore lift up your prayer for the remnant 10
40: 4 Every valley shall be lifted up 10
9 lift up your voice with strength, O Jerusalem 16
9 herald of good tidings, lift it up, fear not; 16
26 Lift up your eyes on high and see 10
42: 2 He will not cry or lift up his voice 10
11 Let the desert and its cities lift up their voice 10
49:18 Lift up your eyes round about and see; 10
22 Behold, I will lift up my hand to the nations 10
51: 6 Lift up your eyes to the heavens 10
52: 8 Hark, your watchmen lift up their voice 10
13 prosper, he shall be exalted and lifted up 10
58: 1 spare not, lift up your voice like a trumpet; 16
60: 4 Lift up your eyes round about, and see; 10
62:10 lift up an ensign over the peoples. 16
63: 9 he lifted them up and carried them all the days 9
Jer 3: 2 Lift up your eyes to the bare heights, and see! 10
7:16 do not pray . . or lift up cry or prayer for them 10
11:14 or lift up a cry or prayer on their behalf 10
12: 8 she has lifted up her voice against me; 11
13:20 Lift up your eyes and see those who come 10
22 your skirts are lifted up, and you suffer 3
26 I myself will lift up your skirts over your face 5
22:20 cry out, and lift up your voice in Bashan; 11
23:39 therefore, behold, I will surely lift you up 10
51: 9 and has been lifted up even to the skies. 10
52:31 lifted up the head of Jehoi'achin king of Judah 10
Lam 3:41 Let us lift up our hearts and hands to God 10
Ezk 3:12 Then the Spirit lifted me up 10
14 The Spirit lifted me up and took me away 10
8: 3 the Spirit lifted me up between earth and heaven 10
5 Then he said to me, "Son of man, lift up your eyes now 10
5 So I lifted up my eyes toward the north, and behold 10
10:16 the cherubim lifted up their wings to mount up 10
19 cherubim lifted up their wings and mounted up 10
11: 1 The Spirit lifted me up, and brought me 10
22 Then the cherubim lifted up their wings 10
24 Spirit lifted me up and brought me in the vision 10
17:14 kingdom might be humble and not lift itself up 10
18: 6 or lift up his eyes to the idols of . . Israel 10
12 lifts up his eyes to the idols 10
15 or lift up his eyes to the idols . . of Israel 10
21:22 with a cry, to lift up the voice with shouting 16
23:27 you shall not lift up your eyes to the Egyptians 10
33:25 and lift up your eyes to your idols, and shed blood; 10
43: 5 the Spirit lifted me up, and brought me 10
Dan 5:20 heart was lifted up and his spirit was hardened 19
23 lifted up yourself against the Lord of heaven; 19
7: 4 lifted up from the ground and made to stand 18
10: 5 I lifted up my eyes and looked, and behold, a man 10
11:14 men of violence . . shall lift themselves up 10
Hos 13: 6 and their heart was lifted up; 16
Mic 4: 3 nation shall not lift up sword against nation 10
5: 9 hand shall be lifted up over your adversaries 16
Nah 3: 5 and will lift up your skirts over your face; 3
Zec 1:21 the nations who lifted up their horns 10
5: 9 lifted up the ephah between earth and heaven. 10
Mat 17: 8 when they lifted up their eyes, they saw no one 25
Mrk 1:31 he came and took her by the hand and lifted her up 24
9:27 Jesus took him by the hand and lifted him up 24
Lke 6:20 he lifted up his eyes on his disciples 25
16:23 in Hades, being in torment, he lifted up his eyes 25
17:13 and lifted up their voices and said 20
18:13 would not even lift up his eyes to heaven 25
24:50 and lifting up his hands he blessed them. 25
Joh 3:14 as Moses lifted up the serpent in the wilderness 28
14 so must the Son of man be lifted up 28
4:35 I tell you, lift up your eyes, and see how the fields 25
6: 5 Lifting up his eyes . . Jesus said 25
8:28 Jesus said, "When you have lifted up the Son of man 28
11:41 Jesus lifted up his eyes and said, "Father 20
12:32 when I am lifted up from the earth 28
34 How can you say . . the Son of man must be lifted up? 28
17: 1 he lifted up his eyes to heaven and said 25
Act 1: 9 he was lifted up 25
2:14 Peter . . lifted up his voice and addressed them 25
9:41 he gave her his hand and lifted her up 22
10:26 Peter lifted him up, saying, "Stand up; I too am a man. 24
14:11 they lifted up their voices, saying in Lycao'nian 25
22:22 then they lifted up their voices and said 25
Rev 10: 5 the angel . . lifted up his right hand to heaven 20
1Es 4:58 he lifted up his face to heaven toward Jerusalem 20
2Es 6: 4 before the heights of the air were lifted up 29
9:38 I lifted up my eyes and saw a woman on my right ‡
Jdt 16:11 they lifted up their voices 28
Sir 11: 1 The wisdom of a humble man will lift up his head 23
34:17 He lifts up the soul and gives light to the eyes 23
36: 3 Lift up thy hand against foreign nations 25
38: 3 The skill of the physician lifts up his head 23
40:26 Riches and strength lift up the heart 23
46:20 lifted up his voice out of the earth in prophecy 23
50:20 lifted up his hands over the whole congregation 25
1Mc 1: 3 he was exalted, and his heart was lifted up. 25
16:13 His heart was lifted up 28
3Mc 6: 5 Sennacherib . . was lifted up against your holy city 26
4Mc 6:26 he lifted up his eyes to God and said 21

lift up against 1. ἐπαίρω

Sir 48:18 he lifted up his hand against Zion 1

ligament 1. σύνδεσμος

Col 2:19 knit together through its joints and ligaments 1
4Mc 9:21 the ligaments joining his bones *

light 1. אור 2. אוֹר 3. אוֹרָה 4. יפע 5. מָאוֹר 6. נֹגַהּ
7. נְהָרָה 8. נֵר 9. נְהִיר (A) 10. נַהִירוּ (A) 11. ἅπτω
12. ἐξάπτω 13. καίω 14. λαμπάς 15. φαιδρός
16. φαῦσις 17. φέγγος 18. φῶς 19. φωστήρ
20. φωτεινός 21. φωτίζω 22. φωτισμός 23. ascendo
24. lumen 25. lux

Gen 1: 3 God said, "Let there be light"; and there was light 2
3 God said, "Let there be light"; and there was light 2
4 God saw that the light was good 2
4 and God separated the light from the darkness 2
5 God called the light Day 2
14 God said, "Let there be lights in the firmament 5
15 let them be lights in the firmament 5
16 God made the two great lights 5
16 two great lights, the greater light to rule 5
16 the lesser light to rule the night; 5
18 to separate the light from the darkness. 2
44: 3 As soon as the morning was light 2
Exd 10:23 people of Israel had light where they dwelt. 2
27:20 bring . . pure beaten olive oil for the light 5
35: 8 oil for the light, spices for the anointing oil 5
14 the lampstand also for the light 5
14 its lamps, and the oil for the light; 5
28 oil for the light, and for the anointing oil 5
39:37 all its utensils, and the oil for the light; 5
Lev 24: 2 that a light may be kept burning continually 8
Num 4: 9 cover the lampstand for the light, with its lamps 5
16 charge of the oil for the light 5
Jdg 16: 2 Let us wait till the light of the morning; 2
19:26 woman came and fell down . . till it was light. 2
1Sm 14:36 and despoil them until the morning light; 2
25:36 she told him nothing . . until the morning light. 2
29:10 and depart as soon as you have light. 2
2Sm 23: 4 he dawns on them like the morning light 2
2Kg 7: 9 if we are silent and wait until the morning light 2
Neh 9:12 pillar of fire . . to light for them the way 1
19 pillar of fire . . which lighted for them the way 1
Est 8:16 Jews had light and gladness and joy and honor. 3
Job 3: 4 May God above not seek it, nor light shine upon it. 7
9 let it hope for light, but have none 2
16 as infants that never see the light? 2
20 Why is light given to him that is in misery 2
23 Why is light given to a man whose way is hid *
10:22 gloom and chaos, where light is as darkness. 4
12:22 and brings deep darkness to light. 2
25 They grope in the dark without light; 2
17:12 The light,' they say, 'is near to the darkness.' 2
18: 5 Yea, the light of the wicked is put out 2
6 The light is dark in his tent 2
18 He is thrust from light into darkness 2
22:11 your light is darkened, so that you cannot see *
28 light will shine on your ways. 2
24:13 There are those who rebel against the light 2
16 shut themselves up; they do not know the light. 2
25: 3 Upon whom does his light not arise? 2
26:10 at the boundary between light and darkness. 2
28:11 the thing that is hid he brings forth to light. 2
29: 3 by his light I walked through darkness; 2
24 light of my countenance they did not cast down. 2
30:26 when I waited for light, darkness came. 2
33:28 my life shall see the light. 2
30 from the Pit, that he may see the light of life. 2
37:21 look on the light when it is bright in the skies 2
38:15 From the wicked their light is withheld 2
19 Where is the way to the dwelling of light 2
24 way to the place where the light is distributed 2
41:18 His sneezings flash forth light 2
Ps 4: 6 Lift up the light of thy countenance upon us 2
18:28 Yea, thou dost light my lamp; 1
27: 1 The LORD is my light and my salvation; 2
36: 9 in thy light do we see light. 2
9 in thy light do we see light. 2
37: 6 will bring forth your vindication as the light 2
38:10 the light of my eyes-it also has gone from me. 2
43: 3 Oh send out thy light and thy truth; 2
44: 3 hand, and thy arm, and the light of thy countenance; 2
49:19 his fathers, who will never more see the light. 2
56:13 that I may walk before God in the light of life. 2

78:14 with a cloud, and all the night with a fiery light. 2
89:15 who walk, O LORD, in the light of thy countenance 2
90: 8 our secret sins in the light of thy countenance. 5
97:11 Light dawns for the righteous 2
104: 2 coverest thyself with light as with a garment 2
112: 4 Light rises in the darkness for the upright; 2
119:105 Thy word is a lamp to my feet and a light to my path. 2
136: 7 to him who made the great lights 2
139:11 darkness cover me, and the light about me be night 2
12 for darkness is as light with thee. 3
Prv 4:18 path of the righteous is like the light of dawn 2
6:23 commandment is a lamp and the teaching a light 2
13: 9 The light of the righteous rejoices 2
15:30 The light of the eyes rejoices the heart 5
16:15 In the light of a king's face there is life 2
Ecc 2:13 wisdom excels folly as light excels darkness. 2
11: 7 Light is sweet, and it is pleasant . . to behold 2
12: 2 the light and the moon and the stars are darkened 2
Isa 2: 5 come, let us walk in the light of the LORD. 2
5:20 put darkness for light and light for darkness 2
20 put darkness for light and light for darkness 2
30 and the light is darkened by its clouds. 2
9: 2 who walked in darkness have seen a great light; 2
2 of deep darkness, on them has light shined. 2
10:17 The light of Israel will become a fire 2
13:10 their constellations will not give their light; 2
10 and the moon will not shed its light. 2
26:19 For thy dew is a dew of light 3
30:26 light of the moon will be as the light of the sun 2
26 light of the moon will be as the light of the sun 2
26 and the light of the sun will be sevenfold 2
26 sun will be sevenfold, as the light of seven days 2
42: 6 a covenant to the people, a light to the nations 2
16 I will turn the darkness before them into light 2
45: 7 I form light and create darkness 2
49: 6 I will give you as a light to the nations 2
50:10 servant, who walks in darkness and has no light 6
11 Walk by the light of your fire 2
51: 4 from me, and my justice for a light to the peoples. 2
58: 8 Then shall your light break forth like the dawn 2
10 then shall your light rise in the darkness 2
59: 9 we look for light, and behold darkness 2
60: 1 Arise, shine; for your light has come 2
3 And nations shall come to your light 2
19 The sun shall be no more your light by day 2
19 but the LORD will be your everlasting light 2
20 for the LORD will be your everlasting light 2
Jer 4:23 and to the heavens, and they had no light. 2
13:16 while you look for light he turns it into gloom 2
25:10 of the millstones and the light of the lamp. 2
31:35 says the LORD, who gives the sun for light by day 2
35 order of the moon and the stars for light by night 2
Lam 3: 2 and brought me into darkness without any light; 2
Ezk 32: 7 the moon shall not give its light. 2
8 All the bright lights of heaven will I make dark 5
Dan 2:22 light dwells with him. 9
5:11 light and understanding and wisdom 10
14 light and understanding and excellent wisdom 10
Hos 6: 5 and my judgment goes forth as the light. 2
Ams 5:18 day of the LORD? It is darkness, and not light; 2
20 Is not the day of the LORD darkness, and not light 2
Mic 7: 8 I sit in darkness, the LORD will be a light to me. 2
9 He will bring me forth to the light; 2
Hab 3: 4 His brightness was like the light 2
11 at the light of thine arrows as they sped 2
Zec 14: 7 for at evening time there shall be light. 2
Mat 4:16 people who sat in darkness have seen a great light 18
16 region and shadow of death light has dawned. 18
5:14 You are the light of the world. A city set on a hill 18
15 Nor do men light a lamp and put it under a bushel 13
16 Let your light so shine before men, that they may 18
6:22 eye is sound, your whole body will be full of light; 20
23 darkness. If then the light in you is darkness 18
10:27 What I tell you in the dark, utter in the light 18
17: 2 and his garments became white as light. 18
24:29 the moon will not give its light 17
Mrk 4:22 nor is anything secret, except to come to light. 15
13:24 the moon will not give its light 17
Lke 2:32 a light for revelation to the Gentiles 18
8:16 No one after lighting a lamp covers it 11
16 that those who enter may see the light. 18
17 that shall not be known and come to light. 15
11:33 No one after lighting a lamp puts it in a cellar 11
33 those who enter may see the light. 18
35 be careful lest the light in you be darkness. 18
12: 3 have said in the dark shall be heard in the light 18
15: 8 does not light a lamp and sweep the house and seek 11
16: 8 more shrewd . . than the sons of light. 18
22:56 seeing him as he sat in the light and gazing at him 18
23:45 while the sun's light failed *
Joh 1: 4 In him was life, and the life was the light of men. 18
5 The light shines in the darkness 18
7 He came . . to bear witness to the light 18
8 He was not the light, but came to bear witness 18
8 but came to bear witness to the light. 18
9 The true light that enlightens every man 18
3:19 that the light has come into the world 18
19 and men loved darkness rather than light 18
20 For every one who does evil hates the light 18
20 hates the light, and does not come to the light 18
21 But he who does what is true comes to the light 18
5:35 willing to rejoice for a while in his light. 18
8:12 I am the light of the world 18
12 will have the light of life. 18
9: 5 I am the light of the world. 18
11: 9 because he sees the light of this world. 18
10 he stumbles, because the light is not in him. 18
12:35 The light is with you for a little longer 18
35 Walk while you have the light 18
36 While you have the light, believe in the light 18
36 While you have the light, believe in the light 18
36 that you may become sons of light 18
46 I have come as light into the world 18
Act 9: 3 suddenly a light from heaven flashed about him. 18
12: 7 a light shone in the cell 18
13:47 I have set you to be a light for the Gentiles 18
16:29 And he called for lights and rushed in 18
20: 8 There were many lights in the upper chamber 14
22: 6 a great light from heaven suddenly shone about me 18
9 Now those who were with me saw the light 18
11 I could not see because of the brightness of that light 18
26:13 I saw on the way a light from heaven 18
18 they may turn from darkness to light 18
23 he would proclaim light . . to the people 18
Rom 2:19 a light to those who are in darkness 18
13:12 Let us . . put on the armor of light; 18
2Co 4: 4 to keep them from seeing the light of the gospel 22
6 the God who said, "Let light shine out of darkness 18
6 to give the light of the knowledge of the glory 22
6:14 what fellowship has light with darkness? 18
11:14 Satan disguises himself as an angel of light. 18
Eph 5: 8 now you are light in the Lord 18
8 walk as children of light 18
9 for the fruit of light is found in all that is good 18
13 when anything is exposed by the light 18
13 for anything that becomes visible is light. 18
Php 2:15 among whom you shine as lights in the world 19
Col 1:12 the inheritance of the saints in light. 18
1Th 5: 5 For you are all sons of light 18
1Ti 6:16 dwells in unapproachable light 18
Jas 1:17 coming down from the Father of lights 18
1Pe 2: 9 called you out of darkness into . . light. 18
1Jn 1: 5 God is light and in him is no darkness at all. 18
7 if we walk in the light, as he is in the light 18
7 if we walk in the light, as he is in the light 18
2: 8 and the true light is already shining. 18
9 He who says he is in the light 18
10 He who loves his brother abides in the light 18
Rev 8:12 so that a third of their light was darkened; *
18:23 and the light of a lamp shall shine in thee no more; 18
21:23 for the glory of God is its light 21
24 By its light shall the nations walk; 18
22: 5 they need no light of lamp or sun 18
5 for the Lord God will be their light 21
1Es 8:79 to uncover a light for us in the house of the Lord 19
2Es 1:14 I provided light for you from a pillar of fire 25
2:35 because the eternal light will shine upon you 25
6:40 that a ray of light be brought forth 24
45 the light of the moon 24
7:42 night, or dawn or shining or brightness or light 25
97 how they are to be made like the light of the stars 24
10:22 the light of our lampstand has been put out 24
14:20 and its inhabitants are without light. 24
25 I will light in your heart the lamp 23
Tob 10: 5 you who are the light of my eyes? 18
14:10 how he brought him from light into darkness 18
Jdt 13:13 they kindled a fire for light 16
AEs 10: 6 there was light and the sun and abundant water 18
11:11 light came, and the sun rose 18
Wis 5: 6 the light of righteousness did not shine on us 18
7:10 I chose to have her rather than light 18
26 For she is a reflection of eternal light 18
29 Compared with the light 18
16:28 and must pray to thee at the dawning of the light; 18
17:20 was illumined with brilliant light 18
18: 1 for thy holy ones there was very great light. 18
4 their enemies deserved to be deprived of light 18
4 the imperishable light of the law was to be given 18
Sir 17:31 Yet its light fails *
22:11 Weep for the dead, for he lacks the light 18
24:27 It makes instruction shine forth like light 18
32:16 like a light they will kindle righteous deeds. 18
42:16 The sun looks down on everything with its light 21
43: 7 a light that wanes when it has reached the full. 19
50:29 the light of the Lord is his path. 18
Bar 1:12 he will give light to our eyes, and we shall live 21
3:14 where there is light for the eyes, and peace. 18
20 Young men have seen the light of day, and have 18
33 he who sends forth the light, and it goes, called it 18
4: 2 take her; walk toward the shining of her light. 18
5: 9 lead Israel with joy, in the light of his glory 18
LJr 1:19 They light lamps 13
19 even more than they light for themselves *
Aza 1:48 Bless the Lord, light and darkness 18
1Mc 1:21 the golden altar, the lampstand for the light 18
4:50 lighted the lamps on the lampstand 12
2Mc 1: 8 we lighted the lamps and we set out the loaves. 12
32 when the light from the altar shone back 18
10: 3 they burned incense and lighted lamps *
12: 9 the glow of the light was seen in Jerusalem 17
3Mc 6: 4 manifesting the light of your mercy 17
7 Daniel . . you brought up to the light unharmed. 18

light (2) 1. קַל 2. *ἐλαφρός* 3. *κοῦφος* 4. *λεπτός* 5. *ὀλίγος* 6. *παίγνιον*

Ps 62: 9 they are together lighter than a breath. *
Jer 3: 9 Because harlotry was so light to her 1
Mat 11:30 For my yoke is easy, and my burden is light. 2
Lke 12:48 he . . shall receive a light beating 5
Wis 5:11 the light air . . is traversed by . . its wings 3
14 like a light hoarfrost driven away by a storm 4
12:26 who have not heeded the warning of light rebukes 6

light (3) 1. נפל 2. עוּף 3. *ἐφίπταμαι*

2Sm 17:12 we shall light upon him as the dew falls *
Prv 23: 5 When your eyes light upon it, it is gone; 2
Isa 9: 8 a word . . and it will light upon Israel; 1
LJr 1:22 Bats, swallows, and birds light on their bodies 3

light *See* give.

light the way 1. *φωταγωγέω*

4Mc 17: 5 after lighting the way of your star-like . . sons 1

light thing 1. קלל

1Kg 16:31 had been a light thing for him to walk in the sins 1
2Kg 3:18 This is a light thing in the sight of the LORD; 1
Isa 49: 6 is too light a thing that you should be my servant 1

light up 1. אור 2. *λάμπω*

Ps 77:18 thy lightnings lighted up the world; 1
Lke 17:24 For as lightning flashes and lights up the sky 2

lighten 1. קלל 2. *ἐπικουφίζω* 3. *κουφίζω*

1Sm 6: 5 he will lighten his hand from off you 1
1Kg 12: 4 lighten the hard service of your father 1
9 'Lighten the yoke that your father put upon us'? 1
10 made our yoke heavy, but do you lighten it for us'; 1
2Ch 10: 4 lighten the hard service of your father 1
9 'Lighten the yoke that your father put upon us'? 1
10 made our yoke heavy, but do you lighten it for us'; 1
Jon 1: 5 into the sea, to lighten it for them. 1
Act 27:38 they lightened the ship 3
4Mc 9:31 I lighten my pain 2

lighten (2) 1. אור 2. נגה

2Sm 22:29 Yea, thou art . . and my God lightens my darkness. 2
Ps 13: 3 lighten my eyes, lest I sleep the sleep of death; 1
18:28 the LORD my God lightens my darkness. 2
97: 4 His lightnings lighten the world; 1

lightly 1. מְאֹד 2. עַל נְקַלָּה

Jer 2:36 How lightly you gad about, changing your way! 1
6:14 They have healed the wound of my people lightly 2
8:11 They have healed the wound of my people lightly 2

lightning 1. אוֹר 2. אֵשׁ 3. בָּרָק 4. חֲזִיז 5. לַפִּיד 6. *ἀστραπή* 7. coruscatio 8. coruscus

Exd 19:16 third day there were thunders and lightnings 3
20:18 the thunderings and the lightnings 5
2Sm 22:15 And he sent out . . lightning, and routed them. 3
Job 28:26 a way for the lightning of the thunder; 4
36:30 Behold, he scatters his lightning about him 1
32 He covers his hands with the lightning 1
37: 3 his lightning to the corners of the earth. 1
4 he does not restrain the lightnings *
11 the clouds scatter his lightning. 1
15 causes the lightning of his cloud to shine? 1
38:35 Can you send forth lightnings, that they may go 3
Ps 18:14 he flashed forth lightnings, and routed them. 3
77:18 thy lightnings lighted up the world; 3
97: 4 His lightnings lighten the world; 3
105:32 lightning that flashed through their land. 2
135: 7 who makes lightnings for the rain 3
144: 6 Flash forth the lightning and scatter them 3
Jer 10:13 He makes lightnings for the rain 3
51:16 He makes lightnings for the rain 3
Ezk 1:13 and out of the fire went forth lightning. 3
21:10 for slaughter, polished to flash like lightning! 3
15 glittering sword; ah! it is made like lightning 3
28 polished to glitter and to flash like lightning 3
Dan 10: 6 his face like the appearance of lightning 3
Nah 2: 4 gleam like torches, they dart like lightning. 3
Zec 9:14 and his arrow go forth like lightning; 3
Mat 24:27 For as the lightning comes from the east 6
28: 3 His appearance was like lightning 6
Lke 10:18 I saw Satan fall like lightning from heaven. 6
17:24 For as lightning flashes and lights up the sky 6
2Es 6: 2 and before the flashes of lightning shone 8
7:40 or cloud or thunder or lightning or wind or water 7
10:25 and her countenance flashed like lightning 8
Wis 5:21 Shafts of lightning will fly with true aim 6
Sir 32:10 Lightning speeds before the thunder 6
43:13 speeds the lightnings of his judgment. 6
LJr 1:61 the lightning, when it flashes, is widely seen 6
Aza 1:51 Bless the Lord, lightnings and clouds 6

like 1. כְּ 2. דמה 3. כְּ 4. כַּאֲשֶׁר 5. כִּדְמוּת 6. כְּמוֹ
7. כֵּן 8. לְ 9. מַעֲשֶׂה 10. מֹשֶׁל 11. מֹשֶׁל כְּ 12. מֹשֶׁל עִם
13. עַד 14. עִם 15. שׁוה 16. דמה (A) 17. כְּ (A)
18. לְ (A) 19. ἀφομοιόω 20. εἰμί 21. εἰς 22. ἔοικα
23. ἔπισος 24. ἴσος 25. ἰσόψυχος 26. καθά
27. καθάπερ 28. καθόσπερ 29. καθώς 30. κατά
31. οἷος 32. ὅμοιος 33. ὁμοιόω 34. ὁμοίωμα
35. ὁποῖος 36. οὗτος 37. οὕτως 38. παρομοιάζω
39. σύμμορφος 40. τοιοῦτος 41. τοιοῦτος οἷος
42. τρόπος 43. ὡς 44. ὡσαύτως 45. ὡς ἐάν 46. ὡσεί
47. ὥσπερ 48. adsimilo 49. in 50. quasi 51. sicut
52. similis 53. similo 54. species 55. ut

Gen 3: 5 your eyes will be opened, and you will be like God 3
22 Behold, the man has become like one of us 3
10: 9 Like Nimrod a mighty hunter before the LORD. 3
13:10 watered everywhere like the garden of the LORD 3
10 like the land of Egypt, in the direction of Zo'ar; 3
19:28 land went up like the smoke of a furnace. 3
25:25 came forth red, all his body like a hairy mantle; 3
27:23 his hands were hairy like his brother Esau's 3
28:14 descendants shall be like the dust of the earth 3
31:26 carried away my daughters like captives 3
33:10 to see your face is like seeing the face of God 3
38:11 feared that he would die, like his brothers. 3
41:49 stored up grain in great abundance, like the sand 3
44:18 for you are like Pharaoh himself. 3
Exd 1:19 the Hebrew women are not like the Egyptian women; 3
4: 7 it was restored like the rest of his flesh. 3
8:10 know that there is no one like the LORD our God. 3
9:14 that there is none like me in all the earth. 3
15: 5 they went down into the depths like a stone. 6
7 thy fury, it consumes them like stubble. 3
11 Who is like thee, O LORD, among the gods? 3
11 Who is like thee, majestic in holiness, terrible 3
16:31 it was like coriander seed, white, and the taste 3
31 taste of it was like wafers made with honey. 3
19:18 the smoke of it went up like the smoke of a kiln 3
24:10 pavement of sapphire stone, like the very heaven 3
17 glory of the LORD was like a devouring fire 3
28:14 two chains of pure gold, twisted like cords; •
15 like the work of the ephod you shall make it; 3
21 they shall be like signets, each engraved •
22 make . . twisted chains like cords, of pure gold; •
32 an opening . . like the opening in a garment 3
36 engrave on it, like the engraving of a signet •
30:32 you shall make no other like it in composition; 3
33 Whoever compounds any like it or whoever puts 3
38 Whoever makes any like it to use as perfume 3
34: 1 Cut two tables of stone like the first; 3
4 Moses cut two tables of stone like the first; 3
39: 6 engraved like the engravings of a signet •
8 breastpiece . . like the work of the ephod 3
14 they were like signets, each engraved •
15 on the breastpiece twisted chains like cords 9
23 the opening of the robe in it was like the opening 3
30 wrote upon it an inscription, like the engraving •
Lev 4:26 like the fat of sacrifice of peace offerings 3
6:17 like the sin offering and the guilt offering 3
21 in baked pieces like a cereal offering •
7: 7 The guilt offering is like the sin offering 3
9:15 offered it for sin, like the first sin offering 3
13:43 swelling . . like the appearance of leprosy 3
14:13 for the guilt offering, like the sin offering 3
26:19 I will make your heavens like iron 3
19 I will make . . your earth like brass 3
39 they shall pine away like them •
Num 9:15 over the tabernacle like the appearance of fire 3
11: 7 Now the manna was like coriander seed 3
7 manna . . its appearance like that of bdellium. 3
8 taste of it was like the taste of cakes baked 3
13:33 we seemed to ourselves like grasshoppers 3
23:10 let my end be like his! 3
24: 6 Like valleys that stretch afar 3
6 like gardens beside a river 3
6 like aloes that the LORD has planted 3
6 like cedar trees beside the waters. 3
9 couched, he lay down like a lion, and like a lioness; 3
9 couched, he lay down like a lion, and like a lioness; 3
28: 8 like the cereal offering of the morning 3
8 like its drink offering, you shall offer it 3
Deu 2:11 like the Anakim they were also known as Reph'idim 3
7:26 bring an abominable thing . . become accursed like it 3
8:20 Like the nations that the LORD makes to perish 3
10: 1 Hew two tables of stone like the first, and come up 3
3 hewed two tables of stone like the first 3
11:10 land . . is not like the land of Egypt 3
10 like a garden of vegetables; 3
12:16 blood . . pour it out upon the earth like water. 3
24 you shall pour it out upon the earth like water. 3
15:23 blood . . pour it out on the ground like water. 3
17:14 king over me, like all the nations . . round about 3
18: 7 he may minister . . like all his fellow-Levites 3
15 LORD . . will raise up for you a prophet like me 6
18 I will raise up for them a prophet like you 6
22:26 case is like that of a man attacking 3
29:23 an overthrow like that of Sodom and Gomor'rah 3
32:11 Like an eagle that stirs up its nest 3
33:20 Gad couches like a lion, he tears the arm 3
26 There is none like God, O Jesh'urun, who rides 3
29 O Israel! Who is like you, a people saved by the LORD 6
34:10 not arisen a prophet since in Israel like Moses 3
11 none like him for all the signs and the wonders •
Jos 10: 2 Gibeon was a . . city, like one of the royal cities 3
14 There has been no day like it before or since 3
11: 4 in number like the sand that is upon the seashore 3
Jdg 5:31 O LORD! But thy friends be like the sun as he rises 3
6: 5 would come up . . coming like locusts for number; 3
7:12 lay along the valley like locusts for multitude; 3
13: 6 and his countenance was like the countenance 3
16: 7 I shall become weak, and be like any other man. 3
11 I shall become weak, and be like any other man. 3
12 he snapped the ropes off his arms like a thread. 3
13 I shall become weak, and be like any other man. •
17 and I shall become weak, and be like any other man. 3
17:11 the young man became to him like one of his sons. 3
Rut 4:11 the LORD make the woman . . like Rachel and Leah 3
12 and may your house be like the house of Perez 3
1Sm 2: 2 There is none holy like the LORD 3
2 none besides thee; there is no rock like our God. 3
4: 7 nothing like this has happened before. 3
9 Take courage, and acquit yourselves like men 8
9 to you; acquit yourselves like men and fight. 8
8: 5 a king to govern us like all the nations. 3
20 that we also may be like all the nations 3
10:24 There is none like him among all the people. 6
13: 5 and troops like the sand on the seashore 3
17: 7 And the shaft of his spear was like a weaver's beam 3
36 this . . Philistine shall be like one of them 3
21: 9 David said, "There is none like that; give it to me. 6
25:36 he was holding a feast . . like the feast of a king. 3
26:15 Are you not a man? Who is like you in Israel? 6
20 to seek my life, like one who hunts a partridge 4
2Sm 5:20 The LORD has broken . . like a bursting flood. 3
7: 9 a great name, like the name of the great ones 3
22 there is none like thee, and there is no God 6
23 What . . nation on earth is like thy people Israel 3
9:11 Mephib'osheth ate . . like one of the king's sons. 3
12: 3 lie in his bosom, and it was like a daughter to him. 3
14: 2 behave like a woman who has been mourning 3
14 we are like water spilt on the ground 3
17 the king is like the angel of God to discern good 3
20 lord has wisdom like the wisdom of the angel of God 3
17: 8 they are enraged, like a bear robbed of her cubs 3
10 valiant . . whose heart is like the heart of a lion 3
18:14 I will not waste time like this with you. 7
27 of the foremost is like the running of Ahi'ma-az 3
32 May the enemies of . . be like that young man. 3
19:27 But my lord the king is like the angel of God; 3
21:19 the shaft of whose spear was like a weaver's beam. 3
22:34 He made my feet like hinds' feet, and set me secure 3
43 stamped them down like the mire of the streets. 3
23: 4 he dawns on them like the morning light 3
4 he dawns on them . . like the sun shining forth •
4 he dawns . . like rain that makes grass to sprout •
6 godless men are all like thorns . . thrown away; 3
1Kg 3:12 none like you has been before you and none like 3
12 and none like you shall arise after you. 3
4:29 largeness of mind like the sand on the seashore 3
5: 6 who knows how to cut timber like the Sido'nians. 3
7: 8 His own house . . was of like workmanship. 3
8 Solomon also made a house like this hall 3
26 made like the brim of a cup, like the flower 3
26 made like the brim . . like the flower of a lily; 3
33 The wheels were made like a chariot wheel; 3
8:23 LORD . . there is no God like thee, in heaven above 6
10:20 The like of it was never made in any kingdom. 7
12:32 a feast . . like the feast that was in Judah 3
14: 8 and yet you have not been like my servant David 3
16: 3 I will make your house like the house of Jerobo'am 3
7 in being like the house of Jerobo'am 3
18:44 a little cloud like a man's hand is rising 3
20:25 muster an army like the army that you have lost 3
27 encamped before them like two little flocks 3
21:22 I will make your house like the house of Jerobo'am 3
22 I will make your house . . like the house of Ba'asha 3
25 There was none who sold himself . . like Ahab 3
22:13 let your word be like the word of one of them 3
2Kg 3: 2 the LORD, though not like his father and mother 3
5:14 flesh was restored like the flesh of a . . child 3
7:13 will fare like the whole multitude of Israel 3
9: 9 make the house of Ahab like the house of Jerobo'am 3
9 and like the house of Ba'asha the son of Ahi'jah. 3
20 And the driving is like the driving of Jehu 3
13: 7 and made them like the dust at threshing. 3
14: 3 And he did . . yet not like David his father; 3
17:15 commanded . . that they should not do like them. 3
18: 5 was none like him among all the kings of Judah 6
32 come and take you away to a land like your own land 3
19:26 and have become like plants of the field •
26 have become like plants . . and like tender grass •
26 like tender grass, like grass on the housetops; •
23:25 there was no king like him, who turned to the LORD 6
25 Before . . nor did any like him arise after him. 6
25:17 And the second pillar had the like 3
1Ch 4:27 their family multiply like the men of Judah. 13
11:23 a spear like a weaver's beam; 3
12: 8 whose faces were like the faces of lions •
22 until there was a great army, like an army of God. 3
14:11 my enemies by my hand, like a bursting flood. 3
17: 8 like the name of the great ones of the earth. 3
20 There is none like thee, O LORD 3
21 What other nation . . is like thy people Israel 3
20: 5 the shaft of whose spear was like a weaver's beam. 3
29:15 our days on the earth are like a shadow 3
2Ch 1:12 such as . . none after you shall have the like. 3
3:16 He made chains like a necklace and put them •
4: 5 its brim was made like the brim of a cup 3
5 brim was made . . like the flower of a lily; •
6:14 said, "O LORD, God of Israel, there is no God like thee 3
9:11 there never was seen the like of them before 3
19 The like of it was never made in any kingdom. 7
13: 9 made priests . . like the people of other lands? 3
14:11 O LORD, there is none like thee to help 14
18:12 let your word be like the word of one of them 3
21:19 like the fires made for his fathers. 3
28: 1 not do what was right . . like his father David. 3
30: 7 Do not be like your fathers and your brethren 3
26 there had been nothing like this in Jerusalem. 3
32:17 Like the gods . . who have not delivered 3
35:18 No passover like it had been kept in Israel since 3
Neh 13:26 Among the many nations there was no king like him 3
Job 1: 8 Job, that there is none like him on the earth 3
2: 3 Job, that there is none like him on the earth 3
3:24 my groanings are poured out like water. 3
7: 1 are not his days like the days of a hireling? 3
2 Like a slave who longs for the shadow 3
2 like a hireling who looks for his wages 3
9:26 They go by like skiffs of reed, like an eagle 14
26 They go by . . like an eagle swooping on the prey. 3
10:10 Didst thou not pour me out like milk and curdle me 3
10 pour me out like milk and curdle me like cheese? 3
16 if I lift myself up, thou dost hunt me like a lion 3
11:17 its darkness will be like the morning. 3
12:25 he makes them stagger like a drunken man. 3
13:28 Man wastes away like a rotten thing 3
28 rotten thing, like a garment that is moth-eaten. 3
14: 2 He comes forth like a flower, and withers; 3
2 he flees like a shadow, and continues not. 3
6 that he may enjoy, like a hireling, his day. 3
9 bud and put forth branches like a young plant. 6
15:16 corrupt, a man who drinks iniquity like water! 3
24 against him, like a king prepared for battle. 3
33 He will shake off his unripe grape, like the vine 3
33 and cast off his blossom, like the olive tree. 3
16:14 he runs upon me like a warrior. 3
21 like that of a man with his neighbor. ‡
17: 7 all my members are like a shadow. 3
19:10 I am gone, and my hope has he pulled up like a tree. 3
22 Why do you, like God, pursue me? 6
20: 7 he will perish for ever like his own dung; 3
8 He will fly away like a dream, and not be found; 3
8 he will be chased away like a vision of the night. 3
21:11 They send forth their little ones like a flock 3
18 That they are like straw before the wind 3
18 like chaff that the storm carries away? 3
24: 5 like wild asses in the desert they go forth •
20 wickedness is broken like a tree.' 3
24 they wither and fade like the mallow; 3
24 they are cut off like the heads of grain. 3
27:16 Though he heap up silver like dust 3
16 silver like dust, and pile up clothing like clay; 3
18 The house which he builds is like a spider's web 3
18 like a booth which a watchman makes. 3
20 Terrors overtake him like a flood; 3
29:14 my justice was like a robe and a turban. 3
25 as chief, and I dwelt like a king among his troops 3
25 like one who comforts mourners. 4
30:15 my prosperity has passed away like a cloud. 3
18 it binds me about like the collar of my tunic. 3
31:37 like a prince I would approach him. 6
32:19 Behold, my heart is like wine that has no vent; 3
19 like new wineskins, it is ready to burst. 3
34: 7 What man is like Job, who drinks up scoffing 3
7 man is like Job, who drinks up scoffing like water 3
36 because he answers like wicked men. 3
35: 8 Your wickedness concerns a man like yourself 3
36:22 exalted in his power; who is a teacher like him? 3
37:18 Can you, like him, spread out the skies 14
38: 3 Gird up your loins like a man, I will question you 3
14 It is changed like clay under the seal 3
14 it is dyed like a garment. 6
30 The waters become hard like stone 3
39:20 Do you make him leap like the locust? 3
40: 7 Gird up your loins like a man; I will question you 3
9 Have you an arm like God, and can you thunder 3
9 like God, and can you thunder with a voice like his? 3
15 Behold, Be'hemoth . . he eats grass like an ox. 3
17 He makes his tail stiff like a cedar; 6
18 his limbs like bars of iron. 3
41:18 his eyes are like the eyelids of the dawn. 3
30 His underparts are like sharp potsherds; •
30 he spreads himself like a threshing sledge •
31 He makes the deep boil like a pot; 3
31 he makes the sea like a pot of ointment. 3
33 there is not his like, a creature without fear. 10

Ps 1: 3 He is like a tree planted by streams of water 3
4 but are like chaff which the wind drives away. 3
2: 9 dash them in pieces like a potter's vessel. 3
7: 2 lest like a lion they rend me, dragging me away 3
10: 9 he lurks in secret like a lion in his covert; 3
11: 1 can you say to me, "Flee like a bird to the mountains; •
17:12 They are like a lion eager to tear, as a young lion 3
18:33 He made my feet like hinds' feet 3
42 I cast them out like the mire of the streets. 3
19: 5 forth like a bridegroom leaving his chamber 3
5 like a strong man runs its course with joy. 3
22:13 like a ravening and roaring lion. •
14 I am poured out like water 3
14 all my bones are out of joint; my heart is like wax 3
15 my strength is dried up like a potsherd 3
29: 6 He makes Lebanon to skip like a calf 6
6 skip like a calf, and Si'rion like a young wild ox. 6
31:12 I have passed out of mind like one who is dead; 3
12 I have become like a broken vessel. 3
32: 9 Be not like a horse or a mule 3
35: 5 Let them be like chaff before the wind 3
10 All my bones shall say, "O LORD, who is like thee 3
36: 6 Thy righteousness is like the mountains of God 3
6 thy judgments are like the great deep; •
37: 2 For they will soon fade like the grass, and wither 3
2 like the grass, and wither like the green herb. 3
20 of the LORD are like the glory of the pastures 3
20 they vanish-like smoke they vanish away. 3
35 towering like a cedar of Lebanon. 3
38: 4 they weigh like a burden too heavy for me. 3
13 I am like a deaf man, I do not hear 3
13 like a dumb man who does not open his mouth. 3
14 Yea, I am like a man who does not hear 3
39:11 thou dost consume like a moth what is dear to him; 3
12 passing guest, a sojourner, like all my fathers. 3
44:11 Thou hast made us like sheep for slaughter 3
45: 1 my tongue is like the pen of a ready scribe. •
49:12 he is like the beasts that perish. 11
14 Like sheep they are appointed for Sheol; 3
20 he is like the beasts that perish. 11
50:21 you thought that I was one like yourself. 3
52: 2 Your tongue is like a sharp razor 3
8 I am like a green olive tree in the house of God. 3
55: 6 I say, "O that I had wings like a dove! I would fly away 3
58: 4 They have venom like the venom of a serpent 5
4 a serpent, like the deaf adder that stops its ear 6
7 Let them vanish like water that runs away; 6
7 like grass let them be trodden down and wither. 6
8 be like the snail which dissolves into slime 6
8 like the untimely birth that never sees the sun. •
59: 6 Each evening they come back, howling like dogs 3
14 Each evening they come back, howling like dogs 3
62: 3 all of you, like a leaning wall, a tottering fence? 3
64: 3 who whet their tongues like swords 3
3 who aim bitter words like arrows •
71:19 O God, who is like thee? 3
72: 6 May he be like rain that falls on the mown grass 3
6 like rain . . like showers that water the earth! 3
16 may its fruit be like Lebanon; and may men blossom 3
16 from the cities like the grass of the field! 3
73: 5 they are not stricken like other men. 14
20 They are like a dream when one awakes 3
22 I was like a beast toward thee. •
77:13 What god is great like our God? 3
20 Thou didst lead thy people like a flock 3
78: 8 that they should not be like their fathers 3
13 and made the waters stand like a heap. 6
16 caused waters to flow down like rivers. 3
27 he rained flesh upon them like dust 3
27 like dust, winged birds like the sand of the seas; 3
33 he made their days vanish like a breath 1
52 Then he led forth his people like sheep 3
52 guided them in the wilderness like a flock. 3
57 acted treacherously like their fathers; 3
57 they twisted like a deceitful bow. 3
65 like a strong man shouting because of wine. 3
69 He built his sanctuary like the high heavens 3
69 like the earth, which he has founded for ever. 3
79: 3 blood like water round about Jerusalem 3
5 Will thy jealous wrath burn like fire? 6
80: 1 Shepherd . . who leadest Joseph like a flock! 3
82: 7 nevertheless, you shall die like men 3
7 die like men, and fall like any prince. 3
83:11 Make their nobles like Oreb and Zeeb 3
11 all their princes like Zebah and Zalmun'na 3
13 O my God, make them like whirling dust 3
13 like whirling dust, like chaff before the wind. 3
86: 8 There is none like thee among the gods, O Lord 3
8 nor are there any works like thine. 3
88: 5 like one forsaken among the dead •
5 like the slain that lie in the grave 6
5 like those whom thou dost remember no more •
17 They surround me like a flood all day long; 3
89: 6 Who among the heavenly beings is like the LORD 2
10 Thou didst crush Rahab like a carcass 3
37 Like the moon it shall be established for ever; 3
46 How long will thy wrath burn like fire? 6
90: 5 dream, like grass which is renewed in the morning 3
9 our years come to an end like a sigh. 6
92: 7 though the wicked sprout like grass 6
10 thou hast exalted my horn like that of the wild ox; 3
12 The righteous flourish like the palm tree 3
12 The righteous . . grow like a cedar in Lebanon. 3
97: 5 The mountains melt like wax before the LORD 3
102: 3 For my days pass away like smoke 3
3 my bones burn like a furnace. 3
4 My heart is smitten like grass, and withered; 3
6 I am like a vulture of the wilderness, like an owl 2
6 like a vulture . . like an owl of the waste places; 3
7 lie awake, I am like a lonely bird on the housetop. 3
9 For I eat ashes like bread 3
11 My days are like an evening shadow; 3
11 I wither away like grass. 3
26 they will all wear out like a garment. 3
26 changest them like a raiment, and they pass away; 3
103: 5 so that your youth is renewed like the eagle's. 3
15 As for man, his days are like grass; 3
15 man . . flourishes like a flower of the field; 3
104: 2 who hast stretched out the heavens like a tent 3
105:41 flowed through the desert like a river. •
107:27 they reeled and staggered like drunken men 3
41 makes their families like flocks. 3
109:18 may it soak into his body like water 3
18 may it soak . . like oil into his bones! 3
19 May it be like a garment which he wraps round him 3
19 like a belt with which he daily girds himself! 3
23 I am gone, like a shadow at evening; 3
23 I am shaken off like a locust. 3
110: 3 From the womb of the morning like dew your youth •
113: 5 Who is like the LORD our God, who is seated on high 3
114: 4 mountains skipped like rams 3
4 skipped like rams, the hills like lambs. 3
6 O mountains, that you skip like rams? 3
6 skip like rams? O hills, like lambs? 3
115: 8 who make them are like them; so are all who trust 6
118:12 surrounded me like bees, they blazed like a fire 3
12 they blazed like a fire of thorns; 3
119:70 their heart is gross like fat 3
83 For I have become like a wineskin in the smoke 3
162I rejoice at thy word like one who finds 3
176I have gone astray like a lost sheep; 3
125: 1 Those who trust in the LORD are like Mount Zion 3
126: 1 fortunes of Zion, we were like those who dream. 3
4 fortunes . . like the watercourses in the Negeb! 3
127: 4 Like arrows in the hand of a warrior are the sons 3
128: 3 wife . . like a fruitful vine within your house; 3
3 your children will be like olive shoots 3
129: 6 Let them be like the grass on the housetops 3
131: 2 like a child quieted at its mother's breast; 3
2 like a child that is quieted is my soul. 3
133: 2 It is like the precious oil upon the head 3
3 It is like the dew of Hermon 3
135:18 Like them be those who make them!- 6
143: 3 has made me sit in darkness like those long dead. 3
6 my soul thirsts for thee like a parched land. 3
7 lest I be like those who go down to the Pit. 12
144: 4 Man is like a breath, his days . . passing shadow. 2
4 like a breath, his days are like a passing shadow. 3
12 our sons in their youth be like plants full grown 3
12 our daughters like corner pillars cut 3
147:16 He gives snow like wool; he scatters hoarfrost 3
16 he scatters hoarfrost like ashes. 3
17 He casts forth his ice like morsels; 3
Prv 1:12 like Sheol let us swallow them alive and whole 3
12 like those who go down to the Pit; 3
27 when panic strikes you like a storm 3
27 when . . your calamity comes like a whirlwind 3
2: 4 if you seek it like silver 3
4:18 path of the righteous is like the light of dawn 3
19 The way of the wicked is like deep darkness; 3
6: 5 save yourself like a gazelle from the hunter 3
5 like a bird from the hand of the fowler. 3
11 poverty will come upon you like a vagabond 3
11 want like an armed man. 3
8:30 then I was beside him, like a master workman; •
10:23 It is like sport to a fool to do wrong 3
26 Like vinegar to the teeth, and smoke to the eyes 3
11:22 Like a gold ring in a swine's snout is a beautiful •
28 righteous will flourish like a green leaf. 3
12: 4 brings shame is like rottenness in his bones. 3
18 one whose rash words are like sword thrusts 3
16:15 favor is like the clouds that bring the . . rain. 3
24 Pleasant words are like a honeycomb •
27 his speech is like a scorching fire. 3
17: 8 A bribe is like a magic stone in the eyes of him •
14 beginning of strife is like letting out water; •
18: 8 words of a whisperer are like delicious morsels; 3
11 like a high wall protecting him. 3
19 A brother helped is like a strong city 43
19 but quarreling is like the bars of a castle. 3
19:12 A king's wrath is like the growling of a lion 3
12 but his favor is like dew upon the grass. 3
20: 2 dread wrath of a king is like the growling of a lion; 3
5 The purpose in a man's mind is like deep water •
23: 5 flying like an eagle toward heaven. 3
7 for he is like one who is inwardly reckoning. 6
28 She lies in wait like a robber 3
32 At the last it bites like a serpent 3
32 At the last it . . stings like an adder. 3
34 like one who lies down in the midst of the sea 3
34 like one who lies on the top of a mast. 3
24:34 poverty will come upon you like a robber •
34 want like an armed man. 3
25:11 fitly spoken is like apples of gold in a setting •
12 Like a gold ring or an ornament of gold •
13 Like the cold of snow in the time of harvest 3
14 Like clouds and wind without rain is a man •
18 Like a war club, or a sword, or sharp arrow. •
19 like a bad tooth or a foot that slips. •
20 like one who takes off a garment on a cold day •
20 like vinegar on a wound. •
25 Like cold water to a thirsty soul, so is good news •
26 Like a muddied spring or a polluted fountain •
28 like a city broken into and left without walls. •
26: 1 Like snow in summer or rain in harvest 3
2 Like a sparrow in its flitting, like a swallow 3
2 in its flitting, like a swallow in its flying 3
4 lest you be like him yourself. 3
7 Like a lame man's legs, which hang useless •
8 Like one who binds the stone in the sling 3
9 Like a thorn that goes up into the hand •
10 Like an archer who wounds everybody is he who •
11 Like a dog that returns to his vomit is a fool 3
17 like one who takes a passing dog by the ears. •
18 Like a madman who throws firebrands, arrows 3
22 words of a whisperer are like delicious morsels; 3
23 Like the glaze covering an earthen vessel •
27: 8 Like a bird that strays from its nest 3
28:15 Like a roaring lion or a charging bear •
31:14 She is like the ships of the merchant 3
Ecc 6:12 few days of . . life, which he passes like a shadow? 3
7:12 For the protection of wisdom is like . . of money; •
8: 1 Who is like the wise man? 3
13 neither will he prolong his days like a shadow 3
9:12 Like fish which are taken . . so the sons of men are 3
12 like birds which are caught . . so the sons of men 3
10: 7 and princes walking on foot like slaves. 3
12:11 The sayings of the wise are like goads 3
11 like nails firmly fixed are the . . sayings 3
Sng 1: 5 I am very dark . . like the tents of Kedar 3
5 I am very dark . . like the curtains of Solomon. 3
7 why should I be like one who wanders beside 3
2: 9 My beloved is like a gazelle, or a young stag. 2
17 turn, my beloved, be like a gazelle 2
3: 6 What is that coming . . like a column of smoke 3
4: 1 Your hair is like a flock of goats 3
2 Your teeth are like a flock of shorn ewes 3
3 Your lips are like a scarlet thread 3
3 Your cheeks are like halves of a pomegranate 3
4 Your neck is like the tower of David 3
5 Your two breasts are like two fawns 3
11 the scent of your garments is like . . Lebanon. 3
5:12 His eyes are like doves beside springs of water 3
13 His cheeks are like beds of spices 3
15 His appearance is like Lebanon 3
6: 5 Your hair is like a flock of goats 3
6 Your teeth are like a flock of ewes 3
7 Your cheeks are like halves of a pomegranate 3
10 Who is this that looks forth like the dawn 6
7: 1 Your rounded thighs are like jewels 6
3 breasts are like two fawns, twins of a gazelle. 3
4 Your neck is like an ivory tower. 3
4 Your nose is like a tower of Lebanon 3
5 Your head crowns you like Carmel 3
5 and your flowing locks are like purple; 3
7 and your breasts are like its clusters. 2
8 Oh, may your breasts be like clusters of the vine 3
8 and the scent of your breath like apples 3
9 and your kisses like the best wine that goes down 3
8: 1 O that you were like a brother to me 3
10 I was a wall, and my breasts were like towers; 3
14 Make haste . . and be like a gazelle or a young stag 2
Isa 1: 8 Zion is left like a booth in a vineyard 3
8 Zion is left . . like a lodge in a cucumber field 3
8 like a lodge in a . . field, like a besieged city. 3
9 we should have been like Sodom, and . . Gomor'rah. 3
9 been like Sodom, and become like Gomor'rah. 8
18 sins are like scarlet, they shall be white as snow; 3
18 though they are red like crimson 3
18 red like crimson, they shall become like wool. 3
30 For you shall be like an oak whose leaf withers 3
30 like an oak . . and like a garden without water. 3
2: 6 full . . of soothsayers like the Philistines 3
3: 9 they proclaim their sin like Sodom 3
5:24 as rottenness, and their blossom go up like dust; 3
28 their horses' hoofs seem like flint 3
28 like flint, and their wheels like the whirlwind. 3
29 Their roaring is like a lion, like young lions 3
29 like a lion, like young lions they roar; 3
30 growl . . like the roaring of the sea. 3
6:13 it will be burned again, like a terebinth or an oak 3
9:18 For wickedness burns like a fire, it consumes 3
19 burned, and the people are like fuel for the fire; 3
10: 6 to tread them down like the mire of the streets. 3
9 Is not Calno like Car'chemish? 3
9 Is not Hamath like Arpad? 3
9 Is not Sama'ria like Damascus? 3

13 like a bull I have brought down those who sat 3
14 found like a nest the wealth of the peoples; 3
16 burning . . kindled, like the burning of fire. 3
11: 7 and the lion shall eat straw like the ox. 3
13: 8 they will be in anguish like a woman in travail. 3
14 like a hunted gazelle, or like sheep 3
14 or like sheep with none to gather them 3
19 Babylon . . will be like Sodom and Gomor'rah 3
14:17 who made the world like a desert 3
19 cast out . . like a loathed untimely birth 3
19 to . . the Pit, like a dead body trodden under foot 3
16: 2 Like fluttering birds 3
2 fluttering birds, like scattered nestlings •
3 make your shade like night at the height of noon; 3
11 Therefore my soul moans like a lyre for Moab 3
14 In three years, like the years of a hireling 3
17: 3 the remnant of Syria will be like the glory 3
9 cities will be like the deserted places 3
12 they thunder like the thundering of the sea! 3
12 they roar like the roaring of mighty waters! 3
13 The nations roar like the roaring of many waters 3
13 like chaff on the mountains before the wind 3
18: 4 from my dwelling like clear heat in sunshine 3
4 like a cloud of dew in the heat of harvest. 3
19:16 In that day the Egyptians will be like women 3
21: 3 pangs . . like the pangs of a woman in travail; 3
22:18 and throw you like a ball into a wide land; 3
23 I will fasten him like a peg in a sure place •
23:10 Overflow your land like the Nile 3
15 for 70 years, like the days of one king. 3
24:20 The earth staggers like a drunken man, it sways 3
20 The earth staggers . . it sways like a hut; 3
25: 4 for the blast of the ruthless is like a storm 3
5 like heat in a dry place. 3
26:17 Like a woman with child, who writhes and cries out 6
27: 9 stones of the altars like chalkstones crushed 3
10 forsaken, like the wilderness; 3
28: 2 like a storm of hail, a destroying tempest 3
2 like a storm of mighty, overflowing waters 3
4 will be like a first-ripe fig before the summer 3
29: 2 she shall be to me like an Ariel. 3
4 come from the ground like the voice of a ghost 3
5 your foes shall be like small dust 3
5 multitude of the ruthless like passing chaff. 3
7 shall be like a dream, a vision of the night. 3
11 this has become to you like the words of a book 3
30:13 iniquity . . like a break in a high wall 3
14 its breaking is like that of a potter's vessel 3
17 you shall flee, till you are left like a flagstaff 3
17 like a flagstaff . . like a signal on a hill. 3
27 and his tongue is like a devouring fire; 3
28 his breath is like an overflowing stream 3
33 the breath of the LORD, like a stream of brimstone 3
31: 5 Like birds hovering, so the LORD . . will protect 3
32: 2 Each will be like a hiding place from the wind 3
2 like streams of water in a dry place 3
2 like the shade of a great rock in a weary land. 3
33: 9 Sharon is like a desert; 3
12 like thorns cut down, that are burned in the fire. •
34: 4 and the skies roll up like a scroll. 3
4 like leaves falling from the fig tree. 3
35: 1 shall rejoice and blossom; like the crocus 3
6 then shall the lame man leap like a hart 3
36:17 and take you away to a land like your own land 3
37:27 and have become like plants of the field •
27 like plants of the field and like tender grass •
27 like tender grass, like grass on the housetops •
38:12 removed from me like a shepherd's tent; 3
12 like a weaver I have rolled up my life; 3
13 like a lion he breaks all my bones; 3
14 Like a swallow or a crane I clamor 3
14 Like . . a crane I clamor, I moan like a dove. 3
40: 6 all its beauty is like the flower of the field. 3
11 He will feed his flock like a shepherd 3
15 Behold, the nations are like a drop from a bucket 3
15 behold, he takes up the isles like fine dust. 3
22 and its inhabitants are like grasshoppers; 3
22 who stretches out the heavens like a curtain 3
22 and spreads them like a tent to dwell in; 3
24 and the tempest carries them off like stubble. 3
25 that I should be like him? says the Holy One. 15
31 they shall mount up with wings like eagles 3
41: 2 he makes them like dust with his sword 3
2 like dust . . like driven stubble with his bow. 3
15 and you shall make the hills like chaff; 3
42:13 The LORD goes forth like a mighty man 3
13 like a man of war he stirs up his fury; 3
14 now I will cry out like a woman in travail 3
43:17 they are extinguished, quenched like a wick 3
44: 4 They shall spring up like grass amid waters 3
4 like grass . . like willows by flowing streams. 3
7 Who is like me? Let him proclaim it 3
22 swept away your transgressions like a cloud 3
22 like a cloud, and your sins like mist; 3
46: 9 there is no other; I am God, and there is none like me 3
47:14 they are like stubble, the fire consumes them; 3
48:10 Behold, I have refined you, but not like silver; 1
18 Then your peace would have been like a river 3
18 and your righteousness like the waves of the sea; 3
19 your offspring would have been like the sand 3
19 the sand, and your descendants like its grains; 3
49: 2 He made my mouth like a sharp sword 3
50: 7 therefore I have set my face like a flint 3
9 Behold, all of them will wear out like a garment; 3
51: 3 and will make her wilderness like Eden 3
3 like Eden, her desert like the garden of the LORD; 3
6 for the heavens will vanish like smoke 3
6 like smoke, the earth will wear out like a garment 3
6 and they who dwell in it will die like gnats; 6
8 For the moth will eat them up like a garment 3
8 and the worm will eat them like wool; 3
12 who dies, of the son of man who is made like grass •
20 the head of every street like an antelope in a net; 3
23 and you have made your back like the ground 3
23 and like the street for them to pass over. 3
53: 2 For he grew up before him like a young plant 3
2 a young plant, and like a root out of dry ground; 3
6 All we like sheep have gone astray; 3
7 like a lamb that is led to the slaughter 3
7 and like a sheep that before its shearers is dumb 3
54: 6 For the LORD has called you like a wife forsaken 3
6 like a wife of youth when she is cast off 3
9 this is like the days of Noah to me: as I swore that •
56:12 will be like this day, great beyond measure. 3
57:20 But the wicked are like the tossing sea; 3
58: 1 spare not, lift up your voice like a trumpet; 3
4 Fasting like yours this day will not make 3
5 Is it to bow down his head like a rush 3
8 Then shall your light break forth like the dawn 3
11 you shall be like a watered garden, like a spring 3
11 like a watered garden, like a spring of water 3
59:10 We grope for the wall like the blind 3
10 we grope like those who have no eyes; 3
10 among those in full vigor we are like dead men. 3
11 We all growl like bears, 3
11 growl like bears, we moan and moan like doves; 3
19 for he will come like a rushing stream 3
60: 8 Who are these that fly like a cloud, 3
8 like a cloud, and like doves to their windows? 3
63: 2 garments like his that treads in the wine press? 3
13 Like a horse in the desert, they did not stumble. 3
14 Like cattle that go down into the valley 3
19 like those over whom thou hast never ruled •
19 like those who are not called by thy name. •
64: 6 We have all become like one who is unclean 3
6 all our righteous deeds are like a polluted garment. 3
6 We all fade like a leaf, and our iniquities, 3
6 and our iniquities, like the wind, take us away. 3
65:22 like the days of a tree shall the days of my people 3
25 the lion shall eat straw like the ox; 3
66: 3 He who slaughters an ox is like him who kills a man; •
3 sacrifices a lamb, like him who breaks a dog's neck •
3 a cereal . . like him who offers swine's blood; •
3 frankincense, like him who blesses an idol. •
12 I will extend prosperity to her like a river 3
12 of the nations like an overflowing stream; 3
14 your bones shall flourish like the grass; 3
15 come in fire, and his chariots like the stormwind 3
Jer 2:30 devoured your prophets like a ravening lion. 3
3: 2 awaiting lovers like an Arab in the wilderness. 3
4: 4 lest my wrath go forth like fire, and burn 3
13 Behold, he comes up like clouds 3
13 his chariots like the whirlwind; 3
17 Like keepers of a field are they against her 3
5:16 Their quiver is like an open tomb 3
26 they lurk like fowlers lying in wait. 3
27 Like a basket full of birds, their houses are full 3
6: 9 like a grape-gatherer pass your hand again over 3
23 the sound of them is like the roaring sea; 3
8: 6 like a horse plunging headlong into battle. 3
9: 3 They bend their tongue like a bow; •
12 land ruined and laid waste like a wilderness 3
22 men shall fall like dung upon the open field 3
22 men shall fall . . like sheaves after the reaper 3
10: 5 idols are like scarecrows in a cucumber field 3
6 There is none like thee, O LORD; thou art great 3
7 in all their kingdoms there is none like thee. 3
16 Not like these is he who is the portion of Jacob 3
11:19 But I was like a gentle lamb led to the slaughter. 3
12: 3 Pull them out like sheep for the slaughter 3
8 has become to me like a lion in the forest 3
9 Is my heritage to me like a speckled bird of prey? •
13:10 shall be like this waistcloth 3
21 pangs . . like those of a woman in travail? 6
24 I will scatter you like chaff driven by the wind 3
14: 6 they pant for air like jackals; 3
8 why shouldst thou be like a stranger in the land 3
8 like a wayfarer who turns aside to tarry 3
9 Why shouldst thou be like a man confused 3
9 a man confused, like a mighty man who cannot save? 3
15:18 Wilt thou be to me like a deceitful brook 6
18 like a deceitful brook, like waters that fail? 3
17: 6 He is like a shrub in the desert 3
8 He is like a tree planted by water 3
11 Like the partridge that gathers a brood •
18: 6 Behold, like the clay in the potter's hand 3
13 among the nations, who has heard the like of this? 3
17 Like the east wind I will scatter them 3
19:12 making this city like Topheth. 3
13 shall be defiled like the place of Topheth. 3
20:16 like the cities which the LORD overthrew 3
21:12 lest my wrath go forth like fire 3
23: 9 I am like a drunken man, like a man overcome 3
9 I am like a drunken man, like a man overcome 3
12 their way shall be to them like slippery paths 3
14 all of them have become like Sodom to me 3
14 Sodom to me, and its inhabitants like Gomor'rah. 3
29 Is not my word like fire, says the LORD 3
29 and like a hammer which breaks the rock in pieces? 3
24: 2 had very good figs, like first-ripe figs 3
5 Like these good figs, so I will regard as good 3
8 Like the bad figs which are so bad 3
25:30 and shout, like those who tread grapes 3
34 and you shall fall like choice rams. 3
38 Like a lion he has left his covert 3
26: 6 then I will make this house like Shiloh 3
9 the LORD, saying, 'This house shall be like Shiloh 3
20 prophesied . . in words like those of Jeremiah. 3
29:17 I will make them like vile figs which are so bad 3
22 The LORD make you like Zedeki'ah and Ahab 3
30: 6 with his hands on his loins like a woman in labor? 3
7 Alas! that day is so great there is none like it; 3
31:12 their life shall be like a watered garden 3
18 I was chastened, like an untrained calf; 3
32 not like the covenant which I made 3
34:18 I will make like the calf which they cut in two •
46: 7 Who is this, rising like the Nile 3
7 like the Nile, like rivers whose waters surge? 3
8 Egypt rises like the Nile 3
8 like the Nile, like rivers whose waters surge. 3
18 the LORD of hosts, like Tabor among the mountains 3
18 and like Carmel by the sea, shall one come. 3
21 soldiers in her midst are like fatted calves; 3
22 She makes a sound like a serpent gliding away; 3
22 against her with axes, like those who fell trees. 3
48: 6 Save yourselves! Be like a wild ass in the desert! 3
28 Be like the dove that nests 3
36 Therefore my heart moans for Moab like a flute 3
36 my heart moans like a flute for the men 3
38 for I have broken Moab like a vessel 3
40 Behold, one shall fly swiftly like an eagle 3
41 shall be in that day like the heart of a woman 3
49:19 Behold, like a lion coming up from the jungle 3
19 For who is like me? Who will summon me? 3
22 one shall mount up and fly swiftly like an eagle 3
22 like the heart of a woman in her pangs. 3
23 they melt in fear, they are troubled like the sea •
50: 9 Their arrows are like a skilled warrior 3
11 as a heifer at grass, and neigh like stallions 3
26 pile her up like heaps of grain, and destroy her 6
42 The sound of them is like the roaring of the sea; 3
44 Behold, like a lion coming up from the jungle 3
44 For who is like me? Who will summon me? 3
51:19 Not like these is he who is the portion of Jacob 3
27 bring up horses like bristling locusts. 3
33 daughter of Babylon is like a threshing floor 3
34 he has swallowed me like a monster; 3
38 They shall roar together like lions; 3
38 they shall growl like lions' whelps. 3
40 will bring them down like lambs to the slaughter 3
40 lambs to the slaughter, like rams and he-goats. 3
55 Their waves roar like many waters 3
52:22 And the second pillar had the like 3
Lam 1: 1 How like a widow has she become, she that was great 3
6 Her princes have become like harts 3
12 Look and see if there is any sorrow like my sorrow 3
20 in the house it is like death. 3
2: 3 he has burned like a flaming fire in Jacob 3
4 He has bent his bow like an enemy 3
4 bent his bow . . with his right hand set like a foe; 3
4 he has poured out his fury like fire. 3
5 The Lord has become like an enemy 3
6 He has broken down his booth like that of a garden 3
12 faint like wounded men in the streets of the city 3
18 tears stream down like a torrent day and night! 3
19 Pour out your heart like water before 3
3: 6 dwell in darkness like the dead of long ago. 3
10 He is to me like a bear lying in wait •
10 He is . . a bear lying in wait, like a lion in hiding; •
52 I have been hunted like a bird by . . my enemies 3
4: 3 cruel, like the ostriches in the wilderness. 3
7 the beauty of their form was like sapphire. •
5: 3 our mothers are like widows. 3
Ezk 1: 7 of their feet were like the sole of a calf's foot 3
7 and they sparkled like burnished bronze. 3
13 something that looked like burning coals 3
13 like torches moving to and fro among the living 3
14 darted to and fro, like a flash of lightning. 3
16 was like the gleaming of a chrysolite; 3
22 likeness of a firmament, shining like crystal 3
24 their wings like the sound of many waters 3
24 many waters, like the thunder of the Almighty 3
24 a sound of tumult like the sound of a host; 3
26 of a throne, in appearance like sapphire; 3
27 gleaming bronze, like the appearance of fire 3
28 Like the appearance of the bow 3
2: 8 be not rebellious like that rebellious house; 3

3: 9 Like adamant harder than flint have I made 3
13 wheels . . that sounded like a great earthquake. •
23 like the glory which I had seen by the river 3
5: 9 and the like of which I will never do again. 6
7:16 like doves of the valleys, all of them moaning 3
19 and their gold is like an unclean thing; •
8: 2 it was like the appearance of brightness 3
2 of brightness, like gleaming bronze. 3
4 like the vision that I saw in the plain. 3
10: 1 appeared above them something like a sapphire 3
5 like the voice of God Almighty when he speaks. 3
9 of the wheels was like sparkling chrysolite. 3
13: 4 Your prophets have been like foxes among ruins 3
20 let the souls that you hunt go free like birds. 8
15: 6 Like the wood of the vine among the trees 4
16: 7 and grow up like a plant of the field. 3
16 the like has never been, nor ever shall be. •
31 Yet you were not like a harlot 3
44 proverb about you, 'Like mother, like daughter. 3
44 proverb about you, 'Like mother, like daughter. •
57 you have become like her an object of reproach 3
17: 5 He set it like a willow twig •
19:10 Your mother was like a vine in a vineyard 3
20:32 Let us be like the nations, like the tribes 3
32 like the tribes of the countries, and worship 3
21:10 for slaughter, polished to flash like lightning! •
15 glittering sword; ah! it is made like lightning 8
23 But to them it will seem like a false divination; 3
28 polished to glitter and to flash like lightning •
22:25 are like a roaring lion tearing the prey; 3
27 Her princes in the midst of her are like wolves 3
23:15 all of them looking like officers •
20 whose members were like those of asses •
20 and whose issue was like that of horses. •
25: 8 the house of Judah is like all the other nations 3
26:19 waste, like the cities that are not inhabited 3
27:32 destroyed like Tyre in the midst of the sea? 3
30:24 groan before him like a man mortally wounded. •
31: 2 Whom are you like in your greatness? 2
8 no tree in the garden of God was like it in beauty. 2
18 Whom are you thus like in glory and in greatness 2
32: 2 but you are like a dragon in the seas; 3
14 and cause their rivers to run like oil 3
33:32 lo, you are to them like one who sings love songs 3
36:17 like the uncleanness of a woman in her impurity. 3
35 desolate has become like the garden of Eden 3
37 to do for them: to increase their men like a flock. 3
38 Like the flock for sacrifices 3
38 for sacrifices, like the flock at Jerusalem 3
38: 9 You will advance, coming on like a storm 3
9 you will be like a cloud covering the land 3
16 my people Israel, like a cloud covering the land. 3
40: 2 mountain, on which was a structure like a city 3
3 there was a man, whose appearance was like bronze 3
25 in its vestibule, like the windows of the others; 3
42: 6 they had no pillars like the pillars of the outer 3
43: 2 his coming was like the sound of many waters; 3
3 vision I saw was like the vision which I had seen 3
3 like the vision which I had seen by the river 3
45:14 the cor, like the homer, contains ten baths •
47:10 of very many kinds, like the fish of the Great Sea. 3
Dan 1:19 among them all none was found like Daniel 3
2:35 became like the chaff of the summer threshing 17
40 like iron which crushes, it shall break and crush 17
3:25 appearance of the fourth is like a son of the gods. 18
4:25 made to eat grass like an ox, and you shall be wet 17
32 shall be made to eat grass like an ox; 17
33 driven from among men, and ate grass like an ox 17
33 till . . his nails were like birds' claws. 17
5:11 light . . and wisdom, like the wisdom of the gods 17
21 fed grass like an ox, and his body was wet 17
7: 4 The first was like a lion and had eagles' wings. 17
4 made to stand upon two feet like a man; 17
5 behold, another beast, a second one, like a bear. 16
6 another, like a leopard, with four wings of a bird 17
8 horn were eyes like the eyes of a man, and a mouth 17
9 as snow, and the hair of his head like pure wool; 17
13 clouds of heaven there came one like a son of man 17
9:12 not been done the like of what has been done 3
10: 6 His body was like beryl, 3
6 his face like the appearance of lightning 3
6 his eyes like flaming torches, his arms and legs 3
6 arms and legs like the gleam of burnished bronze 3
6 sound of his words like the noise of a multitude. 3
11:40 king . . shall rush upon him like a whirlwind •
12: 3 shine like the brightness of the firmament; 3
3 shine . . like the stars for ever and ever. 3
Hos 1:10 people of Israel shall be like the sand of the sea 3
2: 3 and make her like a wilderness 3
3 like a wilderness, and set her like a parched land 3
4: 9 And it shall be like people, like priest; 3
9 And it shall be like people, like priest; 3
16 Like a stubborn heifer, Israel is stubborn; 3
16 LORD now feed them like a lamb in a broad pasture? 3
5:10 have become like those who remove the landmark; 3
10 upon them I will pour out my wrath like water. 3
12 Therefore I am like a moth to E'phraim 3
12 I am . . like dry rot to the house of Judah. 3
14 For I will be like a lion to E'phraim 3
14 and like a young lion to the house of Judah. 3
6: 4 Your love is like a morning cloud, like the dew 3
4 Your love is . . like the dew that goes early away. 3
7: 4 they are like a heated oven 6
6 For like an oven their hearts burn with intrigue; 3
6 in the morning it blazes like a flaming fire. 3
11 E'phraim is like a dove, silly and without sense 3
12 I will bring them down like birds of the air; 3
16 They turn to Ba'al; they are like a treacherous bow 3
9: 1 Rejoice not, O Israel! Exult not like the peoples; 3
4 Their bread shall be like mourners' bread; 3
10 Like grapes in the wilderness, I found Israel. 3
10 Like the first fruit on the fig tree 3
10 became detestable like the thing they loved. 3
11 E'phraim's glory shall fly away like a bird- 3
10: 4 so judgment springs up like poisonous weeds 3
7 perish, like a chip on the face of the waters. 3
11: 8 How can I make you like Admah! 3
8 How can I treat you like Zeboi'im! 3
10 the LORD, he will roar like a lion; 3
11 they shall come trembling like birds from Egypt 3
11 trembling . . like doves from the land of Assyria; 3
12:11 their altars also shall be like stone heaps 3
13: 3 Therefore they shall be like the morning mist 3
3 they shall be . . like the dew that goes early away 3
3 like the chaff that swirls from the threshing 3
3 they shall be . . like smoke from a window. 3
7 So I will be to them like a lion 6
7 like a leopard I will lurk beside the way. 3
8 will fall upon them like a bear robbed of her cubs 3
8 and there I will devour them like a lion 3
14: 6 his beauty shall be like the olive 3
6 and his fragrance like Lebanon. 3
7 fragrance shall be like the wine of Lebanon. 3
8 I am like an evergreen cypress 3
Jol 1: 8 Lament like a virgin girded with sackcloth 3
2: 2 Like blackness there is spread 3
2 their like has never been from of old 3
3 The land is like the garden of Eden before them 3
4 appearance is like the appearance of horses 3
4 and like war horses they run. 3
5 like the crackling of a flame of fire devouring 3
5 like a powerful army drawn up for battle. 3
7 Like warriors they charge 3
7 they charge, like soldiers they scale the wall. 3
9 they enter through the windows like a thief. 3
Ams 2: 9 whose height was like the height of the cedars 3
5: 6 lest he break out like fire in the house of Joseph 3
24 But let justice roll down like waters 3
24 and righteousness like an ever-flowing stream. 3
6: 5 and like David invent . . instruments of music; 3
8: 8 and all of it rise like the Nile, and be tossed 3
8 and sink again, like the Nile of Egypt? 3
10 I will make it like the mourning for an only son 3
10 mourning . . and the end of it like a bitter day. 3
9: 5 and all of it rises like the Nile, and sinks again 3
5 and sinks again, like the Nile of Egypt; 3
7 Are you not like the Ethiopians to me 3
Obd 1: 4 Though you soar aloft like the eagle 3
11 you were like one of them. 3
Mic 1: 4 valleys will be cleft, like wax before the fire 3
4 like waters poured down a steep place. 3
8 I will make lamentation like the jackals 3
8 the jackals, and mourning like the ostriches. 3
2:12 I will set them together like sheep in a fold 3
12 like sheep in a fold, like a flock in its pasture 3
3: 3 and chop them up like meat in a kettle 3
3 like meat in a kettle, like flesh in a caldron. 3
4: 9 that pangs have seized you like a woman in travail? 3
10 groan, O daughter of Zion, like a woman in travail; 3
5: 7 the midst of many peoples like dew from the LORD 3
7 dew from the LORD, like showers upon the grass 3
8 like a lion among the beasts of the forest 3
8 like a young lion among the flocks of sheep 3
7: 4 The best of them is like a brier 3
10 be trodden down like the mire of the streets. 3
17 they shall lick the dust like a serpent 3
17 lick . . like the crawling things of the earth; 3
18 Who is a God like thee, pardoning iniquity 3
Nah 1: 6 His wrath is poured out like fire 3
10 Like entangled thorns they are consumed 3
10 they are consumed, like dry stubble. 3
2: 3 The chariots flash like flame when mustered 3
4 they gleam like torches 3
4 gleam like torches, they dart like lightning. 3
7 her maidens lamenting, moaning like doves 3
8 Nin'eveh is like a pool whose waters run away. 3
3:12 All your fortresses are like fig trees •
15 It will devour you like the locust. 3
15 Multiply yourselves like the locust 3
15 multiply like the grasshopper! 3
17 Your princes are like grasshoppers 3
17 your scribes like clouds of locusts 3
Hab 1: 8 they fly like an eagle swift to devour. 3
9 They gather captives like sand. 3
11 they sweep by like the wind and go on, guilty men •
14 For thou makest men like the fish of the sea 3
14 like crawling things that have no ruler. 3
2: 5 as wide as Sheol; like death he has never enough. 3
3: 4 His brightness was like the light 3
19 he makes my feet like hinds' feet, he makes me tread 3
Zep 1:17 that they shall walk like the blind 3
17 their blood shall be poured out like dust 3
17 poured out like dust, and their flesh like dung. 3
2: 2 you are driven away like the drifting chaff 3
9 Moab shall become like Sodom 3
9 and the Ammonites like Gomor'rah 3
13 a desolation, a dry waste like the desert. 3
Hag 2:23 says the LORD, and make you like a signet ring; 3
Zec 1: 4 Be not like your fathers 3
4: 1 like a man that is wakened out of his sleep. 3
5: 9 they had wings like the wings of a stork 3
7:12 They made their hearts like adamant •
9: 3 heaped up silver like dust, and gold like the dirt 3
3 like dust, and gold like the dirt of the streets. 3
7 it shall be like a clan in Judah 3
7 Ekron shall be like the Jeb'usites. 3
13 O Greece, and wield you like a warrior's sword. 3
14 and his arrow go forth like lightning; 3
15 they shall drink their blood like wine 6
15 their blood like wine, and be full like a bowl 3
15 drenched like the corners of the altar. 3
16 like the jewels of a crown they shall shine 3
10: 2 Therefore the people wander like sheep; 6
3 will make them like his proud steed in battle. 3
5 Together they shall be like mighty men in battle 3
7 Then E'phraim shall become like a mighty warrior 3
12: 6 I will make the clans of Judah like a blazing pot 3
6 Judah . . like a flaming torch among sheaves; 3
8 the feeblest . . on that day shall be like David 3
8 the house of David shall be like God 3
8 like God, like the angel of the LORD, at their head. 3
14:15 plague like this plague shall fall on the horses 3
Mal 3: 2 he is like a refiner's fire and like fullers' soap 3
2 he is like a refiner's fire and like fullers' soap 3
3 sons of Levi and refine them like gold and silver 3
4: 1 For behold, the day comes, burning like an oven 3
2 go forth leaping like calves from the stall. 3
Mat 3:16 saw the Spirit of God descending like a dove 46
6: 5 you must not be like the hypocrites; for they love 43
8 Do not be like them, for your Father knows 33
9 Pray then like this: Our Father who art in heaven 36
16 you fast, do not look dismal, like the hypocrites 43
29 his glory was not arrayed like one of these. 43
7:24 will be like a wise man who built his house 33
26 and does not do them will be like a foolish man 33
9:33 Never was anything like this seen in Israel. 36
36 like sheep without a shepherd. 46
10:25 the disciple to be like his teacher 43
25 and the servant like his master 43
11:16 It is like children sitting in the market places 32
12:13 and it was restored, whole like the other. 43
13:31 The kingdom of heaven is like a grain of mustard 32
33 The kingdom of heaven is like leaven 32
43 Then the righteous will shine like the sun 43
44 The kingdom of heaven is like treasure 32
45 Again, the kingdom of heaven is like a merchant 32
47 Again, the kingdom of heaven is like a net 32
52 like a householder who brings out of his treasure 32
17: 2 and his face shone like the sun 43
18: 3 unless you turn and become like children 43
4 Whoever humbles himself like this child 43
20: 1 For the kingdom of heaven is like a householder 32
22:30 but are like angels in heaven. 43
39 a second is like it, You shall love your neighbor 32
23:27 you are like whitewashed tombs 38
28: 3 His appearance was like lightning 43
4 the guards trembled and became like dead men. 43
Mrk 1:10 the Spirit descending upon him like a dove; 43
2:12 saying, "We never saw anything like this! 36
4:31 It is like a grain of mustard seed 43
6:15 It is a prophet, like one of the prophets of old. 43
34 because they were like sheep without a shepherd; 43
8:24 I see men; but they look like trees, walking. 43
9:26 it came out, and the boy was like a corpse 46
10:15 receive the kingdom of God like a child 43
12:25 are like angels in heaven. 43
13:34 It is like a man going on a journey 43
Lke 6:40 every one . . will be like his teacher. 43
47 I will show you what he is like 32
48 he is like a man building a house, who dug deep 32
49 like a man who built a house on the ground 32
7:31 what are they like? 32
32 They are like children sitting in the market place 32
10:18 I saw Satan fall like lightning from heaven. 43
11:44 you are like graves which are not seen 43
12:27 was not arrayed like one of these. 43
36 be like men who are waiting for their master 32
13:18 What is the kingdom of God like? 20
19 It is like a grain of mustard seed which a man took 32
21 It is like leaven which a woman took and hid 32
18:11 I thank thee that I am not like other men 47
11 or even like this tax collector. 43
17 receive the kingdom of God like a child 43
21:34 and that day come upon you suddenly like a snare; •
22:31 he might sift you like wheat 43
Joh 7:46 No man ever spoke like this man! 36
8:55 I should be a liar like you 32

9: 9 others said, "No, but he is like him. 32
Act 2: 2 a sound . . like the rush of a mighty wind 47
6:15 his face was like the face of an angel. 46
9:18 something like scales fell from his eyes 43
10:11 something descending, like a great sheet 43
11: 5 like a great sheet 43
17:29 we ought not to think that the Deity is like gold 32
19:25 with the workmen of like occupation 40
Rom 5:14 sins . . not like the transgression of Adam 34
15 But the free gift is not like the trespass. 43
16 the free gift is not like . . that one man's sin. 43
6: 5 if we have been united with him in a death like his 34
5 be united with him in a resurrection like his. •
9:29 we would have fared like Sodom 43
29 fared like Sodom and been made like Gomor'rah. 43
1Co 3: 3 of the flesh, and behaving like ordinary men? 30
10 like a skilled master builder 43
4: 9 like men sentenced to death 43
13:11 When I was a child, I spoke like a child 43
11 I thought like a child, I reasoned like a child; 43
11 I thought like a child, I reasoned like a child; 43
2Co 1:17 Do I make my plans like a worldly man 30
2:17 For we are not, like so many, peddlers of God's word; 43
3:13 not like Moses, who put a veil over his face 27
11:23 I am talking like a madman •
Gal 4:28 we, brethren, like Isaac, are children of promise. 30
5:21 envy, drunkenness, carousing, and the like 32
Eph 2: 3 like the rest of mankind. 43
Php 2:20 I have no one like him 25
3:21 to be like his glorious body 39
1Th 2: 7 like a nurse taking care of her children. 45
11 for you know how, like a father with his children 43
4: 5 like heathen who do not know God; 27
5: 2 the day of the Lord will come like a thief 43
4 for that day to surprise you like a thief. 43
1Ti 5: 1 treat younger men like brothers 43
2 older women like mothers 43
2 younger women like sisters, in all purity. 43
2Ti 2: 9 suffering and wearing fetters like a criminal. 43
17 their talk will eat its way like gangrene 43
Heb 1:11 they will all grow old like a garment 43
12 like a mantle thou wilt roll them up 46
7:27 He has no need, like those high priests 47
8: 9 like the covenant that I made with their fathers 30
12:16 that no one be immoral or irreligious like Esau 43
Jas 1: 6 he who doubts is like a wave of the sea 22
10 like the flower of the grass he will pass away. 43
23 he is like a man who observes his natural face 22
24 and at once forgets what he was like. 35
5: 3 their rust . . will eat your flesh like fire 43
1Pe 1:19 like that of a lamb without blemish or spot. 43
24 All flesh is like grass 43
24 and all its glory like the flower of grass. 43
2: 2 Like newborn babes, long for . . spiritual milk 43
5 like living stones be yourselves built 43
25 For you were straying like sheep 43
4: 6 that though judged in the flesh like men 30
6 they might live in the spirit like God. 30
5: 8 the devil prowls around like a roaring lion 43
2Pe 2:12 like irrational animals, creatures of instinct 43
3:10 But the day of the Lord will come like a thief 43
1Jn 3: 2 we know that when he appears we shall be like him 32
12 and not be like Cain who was of the evil one 29
Rev 1:10 and I heard behind me a loud voice like a trumpet 43
13 the midst of the lampstands one like a son of man 32
14 his eyes were like a flame of fire 43
15 his feet were like burnished bronze 32
15 and his voice was like the sound of many waters; 43
16 face was like the sun shining in full strength 43
2:18 the Son of God, who has eyes like a flame of fire 43
18 and whose feet are like burnished bronze. 32
3: 3 If you will not awake, I will come like a thief 43
4: 1 which I had heard speaking to me like a trumpet 43
3 he . . appeared like jasper and carnelian 32
3 a rainbow that looked like an emerald. 32
6 there is as it were a sea of glass, like crystal. 32
7 the first living creature like a lion 32
7 the second living creature like an ox 32
7 the fourth living creature like a flying eagle. 32
6:12 the full moon became like blood 43
14 the sky vanished like a scroll that is rolled up 43
8: 8 something like a great mountain, burning 43
10 great star fell from heaven, blazing like a torch 43
9: 2 rose smoke like the smoke of a great furnace 43
3 were given power like the power of scorpions 43
5 their torture was like the torture of a scorpion 43
7 the locusts were like horses arrayed for battle; 32
7 their faces were like human faces 43
8 their hair like women's hair, and their teeth like 43
8 and their teeth like lions' teeth; 43
9 they had scales like iron breastplates 43
9 the noise of their wings was like the noise 43
10 They have tails like scorpions, and stings 32
17 and the heads of the horses were like lions' heads 43
19 their tails are like serpents, with heads 32
10: 1 his face was like the sun, and his legs like 43
1 and his legs like pillars of fire. 43
3 called out with a loud voice, like a lion roaring; 47
11: 1 Then I was given a measuring rod like a staff 32
12:15 The serpent poured water like a river 43
13: 2 And the beast that I saw was like a leopard 32
2 the beast that I saw . . its feet were like a bear's 43
2 the beast . . its mouth was like a lion's mouth. 43
4 Who is like the beast, and who can fight against it? 32
11 it had two horns like a lamb 32
11 and it spoke like a dragon. 43
14: 2 a voice from heaven like the sound of many waters 43
2 a voice . . like the sound of loud thunder; 43
2 like the sound of harpers playing on their harps 43
14 and seated on the cloud one like a son of man 32
16: 3 the sea, and it became like the blood of a dead man 43
13 I saw . . three foul spirits like frogs; 43
15 ("Lo, I am coming like a thief! 43
18:18 What city was like the great city? 32
21 angel took up a stone like a great millstone 43
19: 6 like the sound of many waters 43
6 like the sound of mighty thunderpeals, crying 43
12 His eyes are like a flame of fire 43
20: 8 their number is like the sand of the sea. 43
21:11 its radiance like a most rare jewel, like a jasper 32
11 its radiance like a most rare jewel, like a jasper 43
1Es 1:20 No passover like it had been kept in Israel 40
2Es 4:24 why we pass from the world like locusts 55
24 and our life is like a mist 55
36 When the number of those like yourselves ‡
41 the chambers of the souls are like the womb. 48
5:18 like a shepherd who leaves his flock 51
52 not like those whom you bore before 52
6:17 its sound was like the sound of many waters. 51
24 friends shall make war on friends like enemies 55
56 that they are like spittle 48
7: 4 so that it is like a river. 52
61 they who are now like a mist 48
62 out of the dust like the other created things! 51
97 how their face is to shine like the sun 51
8:51 the glory of those who are like yourself 52
62 but only to you and a few like you. 52
10:12 My lamentation is not like the earth's 52
25 and her countenance flashed like lightning 54
30 behold, I lay there like a corpse 55
33 to me, "Stand up like a man, and I will instruct you. 55
11:14 so that it disappeared like the first. 51
18 and held the rule like the former ones 51
37 I looked, and behold, a creature like a lion 51
12:42 like a cluster of grapes from the vintage 51
42 and like a lamp in a dark place 51
42 and like a haven for a ship saved from a storm. 51
13: 3 this wind made something like the figure of a man ‡
20 to pass from the world like a cloud 51
14: 9 with those who are like you 52
39 it was full of something like water 51
39 but its color was like fire. 52
15:10 my people is led like a flock to the slaughter 50
23 and the sinners, like straw that is kindled. 50
30 shall go forth like wild boars of the forest 55
50 the glory . . shall wither like a flower 51
51 You shall be weakened like a wretched woman 55
61 you shall be broken down by them like stubble 49
61 and they shall be like fire to you. •
16:23 the dead shall be cast out like dung 50
40 be like strangers on the earth. 50
41 Let him that sells be like one who will flee 50
41 let him that buys be like one who will lose; 50
42 be like one who will not make a profit 50
42 be like one who will not live in it; 50
43 let him that sows be like one who will not reap 50
43 like one who will not gather the grapes; 50
44 like those who will have no children 50
44 that do not marry, like those who are widowed. 50
51 Therefore do not be like her or her works. 53
59 who has spread out the heaven like an arch 50
71 They shall be like mad men, sparing no one 50
Tob 8: 6 let us make a helper for him like himself.' 32
14: 5 though it will not be like the former one 31
Jdt 2:20 a mixed crowd like a swarm of locusts 43
20 like the dust of the earth 43
8:16 God is not like man, to be threatened 43
16 nor like a human being, to be won over by pleading. 43
10:19 who have women like this among them 40
11:19 will lead them like sheep that have no shepherd 43
12: 3 where can we get more like it for you? 32
13 become today like one of the . . Assyrians 43
16:12 were wounded like the children of fugitives 43
15 at thy presence the rocks shall melt like wax 43
AEs 14:16 I abhor it like a menstruous rag 43
15:13 I saw you, my lord, like an angel of God 43
Wis 2: 3 the spirit will dissolve like empty air. 43
4 like the traces of a cloud 43
4 be scattered like mist 43
3: 6 like gold in the furnace he tried them 43
6 like a sacrificial burnt offering 43
7 will run like sparks through the stubble. 43
5: 9 All those things have vanished like a shadow 43
9 like a rumor that passes by; 43
10 like a ship that sails through the billowy water 43
14 like chaff carried by the wind 43
14 like a light hoarfrost driven away by a storm 43
14 it is dispersed like smoke before the wind 43
14 it passes like the remembrance of a guest 43
23 like a tempest it will winnow them away. 43
7: 1 I also am mortal, like all men 24
3 my first sound was a cry, like that of all. 32
11:14 their thirst was not like that of the righteous. 32
22 like a speck that tips the scales 43
22 like a drop of morning dew 43
12:24 they were deceived like foolish babes. •
15:16 no man can form a god which is like himself. 32
16:29 will melt like wintry frost 43
29 and flow away like waste water. 43
19: 9 they ranged like horses 43
9 ranged like horses, and leaped like lambs 43
Sir 3: 4 like one who lays up treasure. 43
16 Whoever forsakes his father is like a blasphemer 43
4:10 Be like a father to orphans 43
10 you will then be like a son of the Most High 43
30 Do not be like a lion in your home 43
6: 2 lest your soul be torn in pieces like a bull. 43
3 will be left like a withered tree. 43
19 Come to her like one who plows and sows 43
21 will weigh him down like a heavy testing stone 43
22 wisdom is like her name 30
31 You will wear her like a glorious robe •
31 put her on like a crown of gladness. •
7:12 nor do the like to a friend. 32
9: 8 by it passion is kindled like a fire. 43
10 A new friend is like new wine •
10: 2 Like the magistrate of the people 30
2 like the ruler of the city 30
11:30 Like a decoy partridge in a cage •
30 like a spy he observes your weakness; 43
12:10 like the rusting of copper, so is his wickedness. 43
11 will be to him like one who has polished a mirror 43
13:15 Every creature loves its like 32
16 a man clings to one like himself. 32
14:17 All living beings become old like a garment 43
18 Like flourishing leaves on a spreading tree 43
22 Pursue wisdom like a hunter 43
15: 2 She will come to meet him like a mother 43
2 like the wife of his youth she will welcome him. 43
16:21 Like a tempest which no man can see •
17: 3 He endowed them with strength like his own 30
22 A man's almsgiving is like a signet with the Lord 43
22 like the apple of his eye. 43
18:10 Like a drop of water from the sea 43
23 do not be like a man who tempts the Lord. 43
19:11 suffer pangs like a woman in labor with a child. 43
12 Like an arrow stuck in the flesh of the thigh •
20: 4 Like a eunuch's desire to violate a maiden 37
15 he opens his mouth like a herald 43
19 like a story told at the wrong time •
29 like a muzzle on the mouth they avert reproofs. 43
21: 3 All lawlessness is like a two-edged sword 43
8 like one who gathers stones for his burial mound. 43
9 like tow gathered together •
13 will increase like a flood 43
13 and his counsel like a flowing spring. 43
14 The mind of a fool is like a broken jar 43
16 A fool's narration is like a burden on a journey 43
18 Like a house that has vanished 43
19 like manacles on his right hand. 43
21 education is like a golden ornament 43
21 like a bracelet on the right arm. 43
22: 6 Like music in mourning •
7 like one who glues potsherds together •
17 like the stucco decoration 43
23:16 The soul heated like a burning fire 43
24: 3 covered the earth like a mist. 43
13 I grew tall like a cedar in Lebanon 43
13 like a cypress on the heights of Hermon. 43
14 I grew tall like a palm tree in En-ge'di 43
14 like rose plants in Jericho 43
14 like a beautiful olive tree in the field 43
14 like a plane tree I grew tall. 43
15 Like cassia and camel's thorn 43
15 like choice myrrh I spread a pleasant odor 43
15 like galbanum, onycha, and stacte 43
15 like the fragrance of frankincense 43
16 Like a terebinth I spread out my branches 43
17 Like a vine I caused loveliness to bud 43
25 It fills men with wisdom, like the Pishon 43
25 like the Tigris at the time of the first fruits. 43
26 full of understanding, like the Euphrates 43
26 like the Jordan at harvest time. 43
27 It makes instruction shine forth like light 43
27 like the Gihon at the time of vintage. 43
30 I went forth like a canal from a river 43
30 like a water channel into a garden. 43
32 again make instruction shine forth like the dawn 43
33 I will again pour out teaching like prophecy 43
25:17 darkens her face like that of a bear. 43
26: 7 taking hold of her is like grasping a scorpion. 43
16 Like the sun rising in the heights of the Lord •
17 Like the shining lamp on the holy lampstand •
18 Like pillars of gold on a base of silver •
27:11 the fool changes like the moon. 43
20 has escaped like a gazelle from a snare. 43
28 vengeance lies in wait for him like a lion. 43

28: 4 Does he have no mercy toward a man like himself 32
23 will be sent out against them like a lion 43
23 like a leopard it will mangle them. 43
29:18 has shaken them like a wave of the sea 43
30: 4 for he has left behind him one like himself; 32
18 like offerings of food placed upon a grave. *
20 like a eunuch who embraces a maiden and groans. 47
31:16 Eat like a human being what is set before you 43
27 Wine is like life to men 23
32:16 like a light they will kindle righteous deeds. 43
33: 2 like a boat in a storm. 43
5 The heart of a fool is like a cart wheel *
5 and his thoughts like a turning axle. 43
6 A stallion is like a mocking friend 43
16 like one who gleans after the grape-gatherers 43
16 like a grape-gatherer I filled my wine press. 43
34: 5 like a woman in travail the mind has fancies. 43
20 Like one who kills a son before his father's eyes *
36:23 her husband is not like other men. 30
38:22 Remember my doom, for yours is like it 37
39:12 I am filled, like the moon at the full. 43
13 bud like a rose growing by a stream of water; 43
14 send forth fragrance like frankincense 43
14 put forth blossoms like a lily 43
22 His blessing covers the dry land like a river 43
22 drenches it like a flood. 43
40: 6 like one who has escaped from the battle-front; 43
13 wealth of the unjust will dry up like a torrent 43
13 crash like a loud clap of thunder in a rain. 43
17 Kindness is like a garden of blessings 43
27 The fear of the Lord is like a garden of blessing 43
43:14 the clouds fly forth like birds. 43
17 He scatters the snow like birds flying down 43
17 its descent is like locusts alighting. 43
19 He pours the hoarfrost upon the earth like salt 43
20 the water puts it on like a breastplate. 43
21 withers the tender grass like fire. 43
44:19 no one has been found like him in glory; 32
21 he would multiply him like the dust of the earth 43
21 exalt his posterity like the stars 43
45: 6 a holy man like him, of the tribe of Levi. 32
11 with precious stones engraved like signets *
12 inscribed like a signet with "Holiness *
47:14 You overflowed like a river with understanding. 43
18 you gathered gold like tin 43
18 amassed silver like lead. 43
48: 1 Then the prophet Elijah arose like a fire 43
1 his word burned like a torch. 43
19 they were in anguish, like women in travail. 43
49: 1 like a blending of incense 21
1 like music at a banquet of wine. 43
11 He was like a signet on the right hand 43
14 No one like Enoch has been created on earth 41
15 no man like Joseph has been born, and his bones are 43
50: 3 a reservoir like the sea in circumference. 46
6 Like the morning star among the clouds 43
6 like the moon when it is full; 43
7 like the sun shining upon the temple 43
7 like the rainbow gleaming in glorious clouds; 43
8 like roses in the days of the first fruits 43
8 like lilies by a spring of water 43
8 like a green shoot on Lebanon on a summer day; 43
9 like fire and incense in the censer 43
9 like a vessel of hammered gold 43
10 like an olive tree putting forth its fruit 43
10 like a cypress towering in the clouds. 43
12 like a young cedar on Lebanon 43
12 they surrounded him like the trunks of palm trees 43
Bar 1:11 days on earth may be like the days of heaven. 43
2: 2 done the like of what he has done in Jerusalem 26
4:26 taken away like a flock carried off by the enemy. 43
LJr 1:11 They deck their gods out with garments like men 43
14 Like a local ruler the god holds a scepter 43
39 like stones from the mountain 33
54 they are like crows between heaven and earth. 47
55 the gods will be burnt in two like beams. 47
67 shine like the sun or give light like the moon. 43
67 shine like the sun or give light like the moon. 43
70 Like a scarecrow in a cucumber bed 47
71 like a thorn bush in a garden 19
71 like a dead body cast out in the darkness. 44
Aza 1:27 like a moist whistling wind 43
Sus 1:27 nothing like this had ever been said about Susanna. 40
1Mc 2: 8 Her temple has become like a man without honor; 43
3: 3 Like a giant he put on his breastplate 43
4 He was like a lion in his deeds 33
4 like a lion's cub roaring for prey. 43
45 Jerusalem was uninhabited like a wilderness; 43
4:47 and built a new altar like the former one. 30
6:39 the hills . . gleamed like flaming torches. 43
9:29 no one like him to go against our enemies 32
11: 1 great forces, like the sand by the seashore 43
2Mc 7:37 I, like my brothers, give up body and life 27
8:35 and made his way alone like a runaway slave 42
10: 6 wandering in the . . caves like wild animals. 42
3Mc 4: 9 They were brought on board like wild animals 42
4Mc 6:10 like a noble athlete the old man 28
7: 1 like a most skilful pilot 47
5 in setting his mind firm like a jutting cliff 47
14 by reason like that of Isaac †
19 like our patriarchs Abraham and Isaac and Jacob 47
11:10 he was completely curled back like a scorpion 42
14:14 Even unreasoning animals, like mankind 32
15:15 the flesh of the head . . exposed like masks. 47
17: 3 Nobly set like a roof on the pillars of your sons 28

like (2) 1. אהב 2. חפץ 3. *βούλημα* 4. *βούλομαι* 5. *θέλω*
Ps 109:17 He did not like blessing; may it be far from him! 2
Prv 15:12 A scoffer does not like to be reproved; 1
Mrk 12:38 who like to go about in long robes 5
Lke 20:46 the scribes, who like to go about in long robes 5
Act 25:22 I should like to hear the man myself. 4
2Co 11:12 who would like to claim 5
1Pe 4: 3 for doing what the Gentiles like to do 3
Tob 5:11 Tobit said to him, "I should like to know, my brother 4

like *See* make.

become like 1. דמה 2. משל 3. *ὁμοιόω* 4. *συμμορφίζω*
Job 30:19 I have become like dust and ashes. 2
Ps 28: 1 I become like those who go down to the Pit. 2
Isa 1: 9 been like Sodom, and become like Gomor'rah. 1
14:10 as weak as we! You have become like us!' 2
Php 3:10 becoming like him in his death 4
Sir 13: 1 will become like him. 3

become at all like 1. *ἀφομοιόω*
LJr 1: 5 take care not to become at all like the foreigners 1

just like 1. עִם 2. *ὥσπερ*
Ecc 2:16 How the wise man dies just like the fool! 1
LJr 1:20 They are just like a beam of the temple 2

like to put first 1. *φιλοπρωτεύω*
3Jn 1: 9 Diot'rephes, who likes to put himself first 1

likely to fail 1. *ἐπισφάλλω*
Wis 9:14 our designs are likely to fail 1

liken 1. דמה 2. שוה 3. *ὁμοιόω* 4. adsimilo
Isa 40:18 To whom then will you liken God 1
46: 5 To whom will you liken me and make me equal 1
Lam 2:13 What can I liken to you, that I may comfort you 2
Ezk 31: 3 Behold, I will liken you to a cedar in Lebanon *
2Es 5:42 He said to me, "I shall liken my judgment to a circle; 4
Wis 7: 9 Neither did I liken to her any priceless gem 3
Sir 25:11 to whom shall be likened the one who holds it fast? 3
36:12 whom thou hast likened to a first-born son. 3

likeness 1. דְּמוּת 2. תַּבְנִית 3. תְּמוּנָה 4. *ἀπείκασμα* 5. *εἰκών* 6. *ὁμοιότης* 7. *ὁμοιόω* 8. *ὁμοίωμα* 9. *ὁμοίωσις* 10. similitudo
Gen 1:26 Let us make man in our image, after our likeness 1
5: 1 man, he made him in the likeness of God. 1
3 son in his own likeness, after his image 1
Exd 20: 4 not make . . any likeness of anything 3
Deu 4:16 form of any figure, the likeness of male or female 2
17 likeness of any beast that is on the earth 2
17 likeness of any winged bird that flies in the air 2
18 likeness of anything that creeps on the ground 2
18 likeness of any fish that is in the water 2
5: 8 'You shall not make . . any likeness of anything 3
Isa 40:18 you liken God, or what likeness compare with him? 1
Ezk 1: 5 came the likeness of four living creatures. 1
10 As for the likeness of their faces 1
16 and the four had the same likeness 1
22 there was the likeness of a firmament, shining 1
26 there was the likeness of a throne 1
26 and seated above the likeness of a throne 1
26 was a likeness as it were of a human form. 1
28 Such was the appearance of the likeness 1
10:10 the four had the same likeness 1
22 as for the likeness of their faces 1
41:17 the nave were carved likenesses *
Dan 10:16 one in the likeness of the sons of men touched 1
Mat 22:20 Whose likeness and inscription is this? 5
Mrk 12:16 Whose likeness and inscription is this? 5
Lke 20:24 Whose likeness and inscription has it? 5
Act 14:11 The gods have come down to us in the likeness of men! 7
Rom 8: 3 his own Son in the likeness of sinful flesh 8
2Co 3:18 changed into his likeness 5
4: 4 the glory of Christ, who is the likeness of God. 5
Php 2: 7 being born in the likeness of men. 8
Heb 7:15 in the likeness of Melchiz'edek 6
Jas 3: 9 we curse men, who are made in the likeness of God. 9
2Es 8: 6 mortal who bears the likeness of a human being ‡
10:49 behold, you saw her likeness, how she mourned 10
Wis 13:10 likenesses of animals, or a useless stone 4
14:19 forced the likeness to take more beautiful form 6
Sir 34: 3 the likeness of a face confronting a face. 8
4Mc 15: 4 a wondrous likeness both of mind and of form. 6

after the likeness 1. *κατά*
Eph 4:24 created after the likeness of God 1

likewise 1. גַּם 2. וְ 3. כָּהֵן 4. כֵּן 5. *ὅμοιος* 6. *ὅμοιος τρόπος* 7. *ὁμοίως* 8. *οὗτος* 9. *οὕτως* 10. *πάλιν* 11. *παραπλησίως* 12. *τὸ αὐτό* 13. *ὡσαύτως* 14. *ὥστε καί* 15. similiter
Gen 32:19 He likewise instructed the second and the third 1
23 across the stream, and likewise everything *
33: 7 Leah likewise and her children drew near 1
Exd 22:30 You shall do likewise with your oxen 4
23:11 You shall do likewise with your vineyard 4
26: 4 and likewise you shall make loops on the edge 4
27:11 likewise for its length on the north side 4
36:11 likewise he made them on the edge of the outmost 4
Deu 12:30 serve their gods?-that I also may do likewise.' 4
15:17 And to your bondwoman you shall do likewise. 4
Jdg 1: 3 and I likewise will go with you 1
7: 5 likewise every one that kneels down to drink. 2
17 And he said to them, "Look at me, and do likewise; 4
1Sm 14:22 Likewise, when all the men . . they too followed 2
2Sm 10:14 when the Ammonites saw . . they likewise fled 2
1Kg 7:18 Likewise he made pomegranates; in two rows 2
8:41 Likewise when a foreigner . . comes from a far 1
2Kg 17:41 So these nations . . their children likewise 1
1Ch 12:38 likewise all the rest of Israel 1
19:15 the Ammonites . . likewise fled before Abi'shai 1
23:30 and praising the LORD, and likewise at evening. 4
2Ch 1:17 likewise through them these were exported 4
6:32 Likewise when a foreigner . . comes from a far 1
32:29 likewise provided cities for himself 2
36:14 likewise were exceedingly unfaithful 1
Neh 5:18 fowls likewise were prepared for me *
10:34 likewise cast lots, the priests, the Levites *
Jer 40:11 Likewise, when all the Jews who were in Moab 1
Ezk 18:14 and fears, and does not do likewise 3
40:16 likewise the vestibule had windows round about 4
Mrk 12:21 the third likewise; 13
Lke 3:11 he who has food, let him do likewise. 7
10:32 So likewise a Levite, when he came to the place 7
37 Jesus said to him "Go and do likewise." 7
13: 3 unless you repent you will all likewise perish. 7
5 unless you repent you will all likewise perish. 13
17:28 Likewise as it was in the days of Lot 7
31 likewise let him who is in the field not turn back. 7
20:31 likewise all seven left no children and died. 13
22:20 likewise the cup after supper, saying, "This cup 13
36 let him who has a purse take it, and likewise a bag. 7
Joh 5:19 whatever he does, that the Son does likewise. 7
Rom 1:27 the men likewise gave up natural relations 7
4:12 likewise the father of the circumcised *
7: 4 Likewise, my brethren, you have died to the law 14
8:26 Likewise the Spirit helps us in our weakness; 13
1Co 7: 3 likewise the wife to her husband. 7
4 likewise the husband does not rule 7
22 Likewise he who was free when called 7
Php 2:18 Likewise you also should be glad and rejoice 12
1Ti 3: 8 Deacons likewise must be serious 13
11 The women likewise must be serious 13
Tit 2: 3 Bid the older women likewise to be reverent 13
6 Likewise urge the younger men 13
Heb 2:14 he himself likewise partook of the same nature 11
1Pe 3: 1 Likewise you wives, be submissive 7
7 Likewise you husbands, live considerately 7
5: 5 Likewise you that are younger be subject 7
Jde 1: 7 cities, which likewise acted immorally 6
Rev 8:12 from shining, and likewise a third of the night. 7
1Es 4: 6 Likewise those who do not serve in the army 10
6:30 likewise wheat and salt and wine and oil 7
8:20 likewise up to 100 cors of wheat 7
2Es 4:17 likewise also the plan of the waves of the sea 15
Tob 12:12 I was likewise present with you. 13
Sir 13:19 likewise the poor are pastures for the rich. 8
20 likewise a poor man is an abomination 9
24:11 In the beloved city likewise 5
33:15 they likewise are in pairs 9
40:14 likewise transgressors will utterly fail. 8
49: 7 likewise to build and to plant. 13
LJr 1:28 likewise their wives preserve some with salt 13
35 Likewise they are not able to give either wealth 13
61 the wind likewise blows in every land. 12
2Mc 2:12 Likewise Solomon also kept the eight days. 13
15:13 Then likewise a man appeared 9
3Mc 6:33 Likewise also the king 13
4Mc 11:15 we ought likewise to die for the same principles. 5

liking 1. *βούλομαι* 2. *ἐπιθυμία* 3. *θέλημα*
2Ti 4: 3 teachers to suit their own likings 2
Wis 16:21 was changed to suit every one's liking. 1
Sir 32:17 will find a decision according to his liking. 3

lily 1. שׁוּשַׁן 2. *κρίνον* 3. lilium
1Kg 7:19 the capitals . . were of lily-work, four cubits. 1
22 upon the tops of the pillars was lily-work. 1
26 made like the brim . . like the flower of a lily; 1
2Ch 4: 5 brim was made . . like the flower of a lily; 1
Ps 69: 0 To the choirmaster: according to Lilies. 1
Sng 2: 1 I am a rose of Sharon, a lily of the valleys. 1
2 As a lily among brambles, so is my love 1
16 he pastures his flock among the lilies. 1
4: 5 like two fawns . . that feed among the lilies. 1

5:13 His lips are lilies, distilling liquid myrrh. 1
6: 2 to pasture his flock . . and to gather lilies. 1
3 he pastures his flock among the lilies. 1
7: 2 belly is a heap of wheat, encircled with lilies. 1
Hos 14: 5 he shall blossom as the lily 1
Mat 6:28 about clothing? Consider the lilies of the field 2
Lke 12:27 Consider the lilies, how they grow 2
2Es 2:19 mighty mountains on which roses and lilies grow; 3
5:24 thou hast chosen for thyself one lily 3
Sir 39:14 put forth blossoms like a lily 2
50: 8 like lilies by a spring of water 2

limb 1. בַּד 2. גֶּרֶם 3. הַדָּם (A) 4. קְטַר חֲרַץ (A) 5. *μέλος*
Job 18:13 the first-born of death consumes his limbs. 1
40:18 his limbs like bars of iron. 2
41:12 I will not keep silence concerning his limbs 1
Dan 2: 5 torn limb from limb, and your houses . . laid 3
5: 6 limbs gave way, and his knees knocked together. 4
2Mc 9: 7 to torture every limb of his body. 5
3Mc 2:22 besides being paralyzed in his limbs 5
4Mc 9:13 his limbs were dislocated *
17 Cut my limbs, burn my flesh, and twist my joints. 5

limb by limb 1. לַעֲצָמִים 2. *κατὰ μέλος*
Jdg 19:29 hold of his concubine he divided her, limb by limb 1
2Mc 7: 7 rather than have your body punished limb by limb? 2

limb too long 1. שׂרע
Lev 21:18 who has a mutilated face or a limb too long 1

lime 1. שִׂיד
Isa 33:12 the peoples will be as if burned to lime 1
Ams 2: 1 he burned to lime the bones of the king of Edom. 1

limit 1. גרע 2. חֹק 3. קֵץ 4. קָצֶה 5. תּוֹצָאָה 6. תַּכְלִית 7. *ἀριθμός* 8. *ἐλαττόω* 9. *μέτρον*
1Ch 5:16 the pasture lands of Sharon to their limits. 5
Job 11: 7 Can you find out the limit of the Almighty? 6
15: 8 do you limit wisdom to yourself? 1
Ps 119:96 I have seen a limit to all perfection 3
Prv 8:29 when he assigned to the sea its limit 2
Nah 3: 9 was her strength . . and that without limit; 4
2Co 10:13 keep to the limits God has apportioned us 9
Sir 17: 2 He gave to men few days, a limited time 7
39:18 none can limit his saving power. 8

beyond limit 1. *ἄμετρος*
2Co 10:13 we will not boast beyond limit 1
15 We do not boast beyond limit, in other men's labors; 1

limitation 1. *ἀσθένεια*
Rom 6:19 because of your natural limitations. 1

limp 1. פסח 2. צלע
Gen 32:31 he passed Penu'el, limping because of his thigh. 2
1Kg 18:26 they limped about the altar which they had made. 1

line 1. חֶבֶל 2. חוּט 3. פְּתִיל 4. קָו
Num34: 7 from the Great Sea you shall mark out your line *
2Sm 8: 2 he defeated Moab, and measured them with a line 1
2 two lines he measured to be put to death 1
2 two . . put to death, and one full line to be spared. 1
1Kg 7:15 a line of twelve cubits measured its 2
23 a line of 30 cubits measured its circumference. 4
2Ch 4: 2 round . . and a line of 30 cubits measured 4
Job 38: 5 Or who stretched the line upon it? 4
Ps 16: 6 The lines have fallen for me in pleasant places; 1
Isa 28:10 precept upon precept, line upon line 4
10 precept upon precept, line upon line 4
10 line upon line, line upon line, here a little 4
10 line upon line, line upon line, here a little 4
13 precept upon precept, line upon line 4
13 precept upon precept, line upon line 4
13 line upon line, line upon line 4
13 line upon line, line upon line 4
17 I will make justice the line 4
34:11 He shall stretch the line of confusion over it 4
17 his hand . . portioned it out to them with the line; 4
44:13 The carpenter stretches a line, he marks it out 4
Jer 31:39 the measuring line shall go out farther 4
Lam 2: 8 he marked it off by the line; 4
Ezk 40: 3 a line of flax and a measuring reed in his hand; 3
47: 3 Going on eastward with a line in his hand 4
Ams 7:17 and your land shall be parceled out by line; 1
Mic 2: 5 you will have none to cast the line by lot 1
Zec 2: 1 behold, a man with a measuring line in his hand! 1

line (2) 1. זֶרַע 2. *σπέρμα*
Lev 22: 4 None of the line of Aaron who is a leper 1
Ps 89:29 I will establish his line for ever 1
36 His line shall endure for ever 1
1Mc 7:14 A priest of the line of Aaron has come with the army 2

line (3) 1. בנה 2. חפה
1Kg 6:15 He lined the walls of the house on the inside 1
2Ch 3: 5 nave he lined with cypress, and covered it 2
7 he lined the house with gold-its beams 2

battle line 1. מִלְחָמָה 2. מַעֲרָכָה
Jdg 20:20 Israel drew up the battle line against them 1
22 again formed the battle line in the same place 1
1Sm 4:12 A man of Benjamin ran from the battle line 2
17:20 the host was going forth to the battle line 2
48 David ran quickly toward the battle line to meet 2

measuring line 1. קָו
2Kg 21:13 stretch over Jerusalem the measuring line 1
Zec 1:16 the measuring line shall be stretched out 1

line of battle 1. *παράταξις*
1Es 1:30 his servants took him out of the line of battle. 1

line up 1. *παρεμβάλλω*
1Mc 16: 6 Then he and his army lined up against them 1

lineage 1. *γενεά* 2. *γένος* 3. *πατριά*
Lke 2: 4 because he was of the house and lineage of David 3
1Es 5: 5 of the house of David, of the lineage of Phares 1
37 not prove by their fathers' houses or lineage 1
Tob 5:13 of a good and noble lineage. 1
1Mc 3:32 Lysias, a distinguished man of royal lineage 2

linen 1. אֵטוּן 2. בַּד 3. בּוּץ 4. פֵּשֶׁת 5. *λίνον*
Exd 28:42 you shall make for them linen breeches to cover 2
39:28 and the linen breeches of fine twined linen 2
Lev 6:10 the priest shall put on his linen garment 2
10 and put his linen breeches upon his body 2
13:47 disease . . whether a woolen or a linen garment 4
48 disease . . whether a woolen or a linen garment 4
52 woolen or linen, or anything of skin 4
59 leprous disease in a garment of wool or linen 4
16: 4 He shall put on the holy linen coat 2
4 and shall have the linen breeches on his body 2
4 He shall . . be girded with the linen girdle 2
4 and wear the linen turban 2
23 Aaron . . shall put off the linen garments 2
32 make atonement, wearing the holy linen garments 2
Deu 22:11 not wear a mingled stuff, wool and linen together. 4
1Sm 2:18 Samuel was . . a boy girdled with a linen ephod. 2
22:18 he killed . . persons who wore the linen ephod. 2
2Sm 6:14 and David was girded with a linen ephod. 2
1Ch 4:21 the house of linen workers at Beth-ashbe'a; 3
15:27 and David wore a linen ephod. 2
Prv 7:16 colored spreads of Egyptian linen; 1
Jer 13: 1 Go and buy a linen waistcloth 4
Ezk 9: 2 with them was a man clothed in linen 2
3 he called to the man clothed in linen 2
11 lo, the man clothed in linen, with the writing case 2
10: 2 And he said to the man clothed in linen 2
6 And when he commanded the man clothed in linen 2
7 put it into the hands of the man clothed in linen 2
44:17 they shall wear linen garments; 4
18 They shall have linen turbans upon their heads 4
18 and linen breeches upon their loins; 4
Dan 10: 5 behold, a man clothed in linen, 2
12: 6 I said to the man clothed in linen, who was above 2
7 The man clothed in linen, who was above the waters 2
Rev 15: 6 seven angels . . robed in pure bright linen 5
Jdt 16: 8 and put on a linen gown to deceive him. 5
LJr 1:72 By the purple and linen that rot upon them *

fine linen 1. בּוּץ 2. שֵׁשׁ 3. *βύσσινος* 4. *βύσσος*
Gen 41:42 and arrayed him in garments of fine linen 2
Exd 26: 1 with ten curtains of fine twined linen and blue 2
31 scarlet stuff and fine twined linen; 2
36 scarlet stuff and fine twined linen 2
27: 9 court shall have hangings of fine twined linen 2
16 a screen . . of . . fine twined linen 2
18 with hangings of fine twined linen and bases 2
28: 5 purple and scarlet stuff, and fine twined linen. 2
6 and scarlet stuff, and of fine twined linen 2
8 purple and scarlet stuff, and fine twined linen. 2
15 purple and scarlet stuff, and fine twined linen 2
39 weave the coat in checker work of fine linen 2
39 you shall make a turban of fine linen 2
35:23 scarlet stuff or fine linen or goats' hair 2
36: 8 they were made of fine twined linen and blue 2
35 purple and scarlet stuff and fine twined linen; 2
38: 9 hangings of the court were of fine twined linen 2
16 hangings . . were of fine twined linen. 2
18 purple and scarlet stuff and fine twined linen; 2
39: 2 purple and scarlet stuff, and fine twined linen. 2
5 purple and scarlet stuff, and fine twined linen; 2
24 scarlet stuff and fine twined linen. *
27 coats, woven of fine linen, for Aaron and his sons 2
28 the turban of fine linen, and the caps 2
28 the caps of fine linen, and the linen breeches 2
29 and the linen breeches of fine twined linen 2
29 and the girdle of fine twined linen 2
1Ch 15:27 David was clothed with a robe of fine linen 1
2Ch 2:14 trained to work in . . fabrics and fine linen 1
3:14 veil of . . and crimson fabrics and fine linen 1
5:12 arrayed in fine linen, with cymbals, harps 1
Est 1: 6 caught up with cords of fine linen and purple 1
8:15 crown and a mantle of fine linen and purple 1
Prv 31:22 her clothing is fine linen and purple. 2
Ezk 16:13 and your raiment was of fine linen, and silk 2
27:16 embroidered work, fine linen, coral, and agate. 1
Lke 16:19 who was clothed in purple and fine linen 4
Rev 18:12 cargo of . . fine linen, purple, silk and scarlet 3
16 the great city that was clothed in fine linen 3
19: 8 it was granted her to be clothed with fine linen 3
8 fine linen is the righteous deeds of the saints. 3
14 arrayed in fine linen, white and pure 3
1Es 3: 6 a turban of fine linen 3

fine twined linen 1. שֵׁשׁ
Exd 25: 4 scarlet stuff and fine twined linen, goats' hair 1
35: 6 scarlet stuff and fine twined linen; goats' hair 1
25 purple and scarlet stuff and fine twined linen; 1
35 purple and scarlet stuff and fine twined linen 1
36:37 scarlet stuff and fine twined linen 1
38:23 purple and scarlet stuff and fine twined linen. 1
39: 3 into the fine twined linen, in skilled design. 1
8 purple and scarlet stuff, and fine twined linen. 1

linger 1. מהה
Gen 19:16 he lingered; so the men seized him and his wife 1
2Sm 1: 9 anguish has seized me, and yet my life . . lingers.' †

lintel 1. אַיִל 2. מַשְׁקוֹף
Exd 12: 7 two doorposts and the lintel of the houses 2
22 and touch the lintel and the two doorposts 2
23 the blood on the lintel and on the two doorposts 2
1Kg 6:31 the lintel and the doorposts formed a pentagon. 1

lion 1. אֲרִי 2. אַרְיֵה 3. כְּפִיר 4. לְבִי 5. לָבִיא 6. לַיִשׁ 7. שַׁחַל 8. אַרְיֵה (A) 9. *λέων* 10. leo
Gen 49: 9 Judah is a lion's whelp; 2
9 he couched as a lion, and as a lioness; 2
Num23:24 As a lioness . . as a lion it lifts itself; 1
24: 9 couched, he lay down like a lion, and like a lioness; 1
Deu 33:20 Gad couches like a lion, he tears the arm 5
22 Dan is a lion's whelp, that leaps forth from Bashan. 2
Jdg 14: 6 him, and he tore the lion asunder as one tears a kid; *
8 he turned aside to see the carcass of the lion 2
8 a swarm of bees in the body of the lion, and honey. 2
9 had taken the honey from the carcass of the lion. 2
18 sweeter than honey? What is stronger than a lion? 1
1Sm 17:34 when there came a lion, or a bear, and took a lamb 1
36 Your servant has killed both lions and bears; 1
37 The LORD who delivered me from the paw of the lion 1
2Sm 1:23 they were stronger than lions. 1
17:10 valiant . . whose heart is like the heart of a lion 2
23:20 He also went down and slew a lion in a pit 1
1Kg 7:29 on the panels . . were lions, oxen, and cherubim. 1
29 both above and below the lions and oxen 1
36 and on its panels, he carved cherubim, lions 1
10:19 and two lions standing beside the arm rests 1
20 twelve lions stood there, one on each end of a step 1
13:24 a lion met him on the road and killed him. 2
24 the lion also stood beside the body. 2
25 the body . . in the road, and the lion standing 2
26 the LORD has given him to the lion, which has torn 2
28 found his body . . and the ass and the lion 2
28 The lion had not eaten the body or torn the ass. 2
20:36 as soon as you have gone . . a lion shall kill you. 2
36 as soon as he . . a lion met him and killed him. 2
2Kg 17:25 the LORD sent lions among them, which killed some 1
26 therefore he has sent lions among them 1
1Ch 11:22 slew a lion in a pit on a day when snow had fallen. 1
12: 8 whose faces were like the faces of lions 2
2Ch 9:18 two lions standing beside the arm rests 2
19 while twelve lions stood there, one on each end 2
Job 4:10 The roar of the lion, the voice of the fierce lion 2
10 The roar of the lion, the voice of the fierce lion 7
11 The strong lion perishes for lack of prey 6
10:16 if I lift myself up, thou dost hunt me like a lion 7
28: 8 the lion has not passed over it. 7
38:39 Can you hunt the prey for the lion 5
Ps 7: 2 lest like a lion they rend me, dragging me away 2
10: 9 he lurks in secret like a lion in his covert; 2
17:12 They are like a lion eager to tear, as a young lion 2
22:13 like a ravening and roaring lion. 2
21 Save me from the mouth of the lion 2
35:17 from their ravages, my life from the lions! 3
57: 4 I lie in the midst of lions that greedily devour 4
91:13 You will tread on the lion and the adder 7
Prv 19:12 A king's wrath is like the growling of a lion 3
20: 2 dread wrath of a king is like the growling of a lion; 3
22:13 The sluggard says, "There is a lion outside! 1
26:13 The sluggard says, "There is a lion in the road! 7
13 sluggard says, " . . There is a lion in the streets! 1
28: 1 but the righteous are bold as a lion. 3
15 roaring lion or a charging bear is a wicked ruler 1
30:30 the lion, which is mightiest among beasts 6
Ecc 9: 4 for a living dog is better than a dead lion. 2
Sng 4: 8 Depart . . from the dens of lions 2
Isa 5:29 Their roaring is like a lion, like young lions 5
11: 6 the calf and the lion and the fatling together 3
7 and the lion shall eat straw like the ox. 2
15: 9 a lion for those of Moab who escape 2
30: 6 from where come the lioness and the lion 6
31: 4 As a lion or a young lion growls over his prey 2

35: 9 No lion shall be there, nor shall any ravenous 2
38:13 like a lion he breaks all my bones; 1
65:25 the lion shall eat straw like the ox; 2
Jer 2:15 The lions have roared against him 3
30 devoured your prophets like a ravening lion. 2
4: 7 A lion has gone up from his thicket 2
5: 6 Therefore a lion from the forest shall slay them 2
12: 8 has become to me like a lion in the forest 2
25:38 Like a lion he has left his covert 3
49:19 Behold, like a lion coming up from the jungle 2
50:17 Israel is a hunted sheep driven away by lions. 2
44 Behold, like a lion coming up from the jungle 2
51:38 They shall roar together like lions; 3
38 they shall growl like lions' whelps. 2
Lam 3:10 He is . . a bear lying in wait, like a lion in hiding; 1
Ezk 1:10 the four had the face of a lion on the right side 2
10:14 and the third the face of a lion 2
19: 2 say: What a lioness was your mother among lions! 2
6 He prowled among the lions; he became a young lion 2
22:25 are like a roaring lion tearing the prey; 1
32: 2 You consider yourself a lion among the nations 3
Dan 6: 7 to you, O king, shall be cast into the den of lions. 8
12 shall be cast into the den of lions? 8
16 brought and cast into the den of lions. 8
19 king arose and went in haste to the den of lions. 8
20 has your God . . able to deliver you from the lions 8
22 My God sent his angel and shut the lions' mouths 8
24 den of lions-they, their children, and their wives; 8
24 lions overpowered them and broke all 8
27 who has saved Daniel from the power of the lions 8
7: 4 The first was like a lion and had eagles' wings. 8
Hos 5:14 For I will be like a lion to E'phraim 7
11:10 the LORD, he will roar like a lion; 2
13: 7 So I will be to them like a lion 7
8 and there I will devour them like a lion 5
Jol 1: 6 its teeth are lions' teeth 2
Ams 3: 4 Does a lion roar in the forest, when he has no prey? 2
8 The lion has roared; who will not fear? 2
12 the shepherd rescues from the mouth of the lion 1
5:19 as if a man fled from a lion, and a bear met him; 1
Mic 5: 8 like a lion among the beasts of the forest 2
Nah 2:11 Where is the lions' den, the cave of the young lions 2
11 where the lion brought his prey 2
12 The lion tore enough for his whelps 2
Zep 3: 3 Her officials within her are roaring lions; 2
Zec 11: 3 Hark, the roar of the lions, for the jungle 3
2Ti 4:17 So I was rescued from the lion's mouth. 9
Heb 11:33 received promises, stopped the mouths of lions 9
1Pe 5: 8 the devil prowls around like a roaring lion 9
Rev 4: 7 the first living creature like a lion 9
5: 5 lo, the Lion of the tribe of Judah . . has conquered 9
9: 8 and their teeth like lions' teeth; 9
17 and the heads of the horses were like lions' heads 9
10: 3 called out with a loud voice, like a lion roaring; 9
13: 2 the beast . . its mouth was like a lion's mouth. 9
1Es 4:24 he faces lions, and he walks in darkness 9
2Es 11:37 I looked, and behold, a creature like a lion 10
12: 1 While the lion was saying these words 10
31 as for the lion whom you saw rousing up 10
16: 6 Can one drive off a hungry lion in the forest 10
AEs 14:13 Put eloquent speech in my mouth before the lion 9
Wis 11:17 a multitude of bears, or bold lions 9
Sir 4:30 Do not be like a lion in your home 9
13:19 Wild asses . . are the prey of lions 9
21: 2 Its teeth are lion's teeth 9
25:16 I would rather dwell with a lion and a dragon 9
27:10 A lion lies in wait for prey 9
28 vengeance lies in wait for him like a lion. 9
28:23 will be sent out against them like a lion 9
47: 3 He played with lions as with young goats 9
Bel 1:31 They threw Daniel into the lions' den 9
32 There were seven lions in the den 9
34 to Babylon, to Daniel, in the lions' den. 9
1Mc 2:60 was delivered from the mouth of the lions. 9
3: 4 He was like a lion in his deeds 9
3Mc 6: 7 cast down . . to lions as food for wild beasts 9
4Mc 16: 3 The lions surrounding Daniel were not so savage 9
21 Daniel the righteous was thrown to the lions 9
18:13 He praised Daniel in the den of the lions 9

lion cub 1. σκύμνος
1Mc 3: 4 like a lion's cub roaring for prey. 1

like a lion 1. λεοντηδόν
2Mc 11:11 They hurled themselves like lions against the enemy 1

young lion 1. כְּפִיר 2. כְּפִיר אֲרָיוֹת
Jdg 14: 5 And behold, a young lion roared against him; 2
Job 4:10 the teeth of the young lions, are broken. 1
38:39 or satisfy the appetite of the young lions 1
Ps 17:12 eager to tear, as a young lion lurking in ambush. 1
34:10 The young lions suffer want and hunger; 1
58: 6 tear out the fangs of the young lions, O LORD! 1
91:13 young lion and the serpent you will trample 1
104:21 The young lions roar for their prey 1
Isa 5:29 like a lion, like young lions they roar; 1
31: 4 As a lion or a young lion growls over his prey 1
Ezk 19: 2 She couched in the midst of young lions 1
3 he became a young lion, and he learned to catch 1
5 another of her whelps and made him a young lion. 1
6 He prowled among the lions; he became a young lion 1
41:19 the face of a young lion toward the palm tree 1
Hos 5:14 and like a young lion to the house of Judah. 1
Ams 3: 4 Does a young lion cry out from his den, 1
Mic 5: 8 like a young lion among the flocks of sheep 1
Nah 2:11 Where is the lions' den, the cave of the young lions 1
13 and the sword shall devour your young lions; 1

lioness 1. לָבִי 2. לְבִיָּא 3. לָבִיא
Gen 49: 9 he couched as a lion, and as a lioness; 3
Num23:24 As a lioness it rises up and as a lion 3
24: 9 couched, he lay down like a lion, and like a lioness; 3
Job 4:11 the whelps of the lioness are scattered. 3
Isa 30: 6 from where come the lioness and the lion 3
Ezk 19: 2 say: What a lioness was your mother among lions! 2
Jol 1: 6 it has the fangs of a lioness. 3
Nah 2:12 and strangled prey for his lionesses; 1

lip 1. חֵךְ 2. מוּצֶקֶת 3. פֶּה 4. שָׂפָה 5. שָׂפָם 6. στόμα 7. χεῖλος 8. labia
Exd 6:12 to me, who am a man of uncircumcised lips? 4
30 Moses said . . "Behold, I am of uncircumcised lips; 4
Lev 5: 4 Or if any one utters with his lips a rash oath 4
Num30: 6 under . . any thoughtless utterance of her lips 4
8 void . . the thoughtless utterance of her lips 4
12 then whatever proceeds out of her lips 4
Deu 23:23 be careful to perform what has passed your lips 4
1Sm 1:13 only her lips moved, and her voice was not heard; 4
Job 2:10 In all this Job did not sin with his lips. 4
8:21 with laughter, and your lips with shouting. 4
11: 5 oh, that God would speak, and open his lips to you 4
13: 6 listen to the pleadings of my lips. 4
15: 6 your own lips testify against you. 4
16: 5 the solace of my lips would assuage your pain. 4
23:12 not departed from the commandment of his lips; 4
27: 4 my lips will not speak falsehood 4
32:20 I must open my lips and answer. 4
33: 3 what my lips know they speak sincerely. 4
Ps 12: 2 with flattering lips . . they speak. 4
3 May the LORD cut off all flattering lips 4
4 our lips are with us; who is our master? 4
16: 4 not pour out or take their names upon my lips. 4
17: 1 Give ear to my prayer from lips free of deceit! 4
4 by the word of thy lips I have avoided the ways 4
21: 2 and hast not withheld the request of his lips. 4
31:18 Let the lying lips be dumb 4
34:13 from evil, and your lips from speaking deceit. 4
40: 9 lo, I have not restrained my lips, as thou knowest 4
45: 2 grace is poured upon your lips; 4
50:16 or take my covenant on your lips? 3
51:15 O Lord, open thou my lips 4
59: 7 with their mouths, and snarling with their lips- 4
12 the sin of their mouths, the words of their lips 4
63: 3 my lips will praise thee. 4
5 my mouth praises thee with joyful lips 4
66:14 that which my lips uttered and my mouth promised 4
71:23 My lips will shout for joy, when I sing praises 4
89:34 alter the word that went forth from my lips. 4
119:13 With my lips I declare all the ordinances 4
171 My lips will pour forth praise 4
120: 2 Deliver me, O LORD, from lying lips 4
140: 3 under their lips is the poison of vipers. Selah 4
9 let the mischief of their lips overwhelm them! 4
141: 3 O LORD, keep watch over the door of my lips! 4
Prv 5: 2 that . . your lips may guard knowledge. 4
3 For the lips of a loose woman drip honey 4
6: 2 if you are snared in the utterance of your lips •
8: 6 from my lips will come what is right; 4
7 wickedness is an abomination to my lips. 4
10:13 lips of him who has understanding wisdom is found 4
18 He who conceals hatred has lying lips 4
19 but he who restrains his lips is prudent. 4
21 The lips of the righteous feed many 4
32 lips of the righteous know what is acceptable 4
12:13 man is ensnared by the transgression of his lips 4
19 Truthful lips endure for ever 4
22 Lying lips are an abomination to the LORD 4
13: 3 he who opens wide his lips comes to ruin. 4
14: 3 but the lips of the wise will preserve them. 4
15: 7 The lips of the wise spread knowledge; 4
16:10 Inspired decisions are on the lips of a king; 4
13 Righteous lips are the delight of a king 4
23 adds persuasiveness to his lips. 4
30 he who compresses his lips brings evil to pass. 4
17: 4 An evildoer listens to wicked lips; 4
28 when he closes his lips, he is deemed intelligent. 4
18: 6 A fool's lips bring strife 4
7 A fool's . . lips are a snare to himself. 4
20 man . . is satisfied by the yield of his lips. 4
20:15 but the lips of knowledge are a precious jewel. 4
22:18 pleasant . . if all of them are ready on your lips. 4
23:16 soul . . rejoice when your lips speak what is right. 4
24: 2 for . . their lips talk of mischief. 4
26 He who gives a right answer kisses the lips. 4
28 do not deceive with your lips. 4
26:23 smooth lips with an evil heart. 4
24 He who hates, dissembles with his lips 4
27: 2 stranger, and not your own lips. 4
Ecc 10:12 but the lips of a fool consume him. 4
Sng 4: 3 Your lips are like a scarlet thread 4
11 Your lips distil nectar, my bride; 4
5:13 His lips are lilies, distilling liquid myrrh. 4
7: 9 goes down smoothly, gliding over lips and teeth. 4
Isa 6: 5 For I am lost; for I am a man of unclean lips 4
5 I dwell in the midst of a people of unclean lips; 4
7 Behold, this has touched your lips; 4
11: 4 with the breath of his lips . . slay the wicked. 4
28:11 by men of strange lips and with an alien tongue 4
29:13 honor me with their lips, while their hearts are 4
30:27 his lips are full of indignation 4
57:18 creating for his mourners the fruit of the lips. 4
59: 3 your lips have spoken lies, 4
Jer 7:28 truth has perished; it is cut off from their lips. 3
17:16 that which came out of my lips was before thy face. 4
Lam 3:62 The lips and . . of my assailants are against me 4
Ezk 24:17 do not cover your lips 5
22 you shall not cover your lips 5
29:21 I will open your lips among them. 3
33:31 for with their lips they show much love 3
Dan 10:16 likeness of the sons of men touched my lips; 4
Hos 8: 1 Set the trumpet to your lips 1
14: 2 and we will render the fruit of our lips. 4
Mic 3: 7 they shall all cover their lips 5
Hab 3:16 my body trembles, my lips quiver at the sound; 4
Zec 4: 2 with seven lips on each of the lamps 2
Mal 2: 6 no wrong was found on his lips. 4
7 For the lips of a priest should guard knowledge 4
Mat 15: 8 'This people honors me with their lips 7
Mrk 7: 6 This people honors me with their lips 7
Lke 22:71 We have heard it ourselves from his own lips. 6
Rom 3:13 The venom of asps is under their lips. 7
10: 8 The word is near you, on your lips and in your heart 6
9 if you confess with your lips that Jesus is Lord 6
10 and he confesses with his lips and so is saved. 6
1Co 14:21 by the lips of foreigners 7
Heb 13:15 the fruit of lips that acknowledge his name. 7
1Pe 2:22 no guile was found on his lips. 6
3:10 let him keep . . his lips from speaking guile; 7
1Es 4:46 vowed to the King of heaven with your own lips. 6
2Es 13:10 and from his lips a flaming breath 8
Jdt 2: 2 and recounted fully, with his own lips 6
9:10 By the deceit of my lips strike down the slave 7
15:13 wearing garlands and with songs on their lips. 6
Sir 1:24 the lips of many will tell of his good sense. 7
29 keep watch over your lips. 7
12:16 An enemy will speak sweetly with his lips 7
14: 1 does not blunder with his lips 6
15: 9 is not fitting on the lips of a sinner 6
20:19 continually on the lips of the ignorant. 6
20 A proverb from a fool's lips will be rejected 6
24 it is continually on the lips of the ignorant. 6
21: 5 The prayer of a poor man goes from his lips 6
25 The lips of strangers will speak of these things 7
22:27 a seal of prudence upon my lips 7
23: 8 The sinner is overtaken through his lips 7
34: 8 wisdom is made perfect in truthful lips. 6
37:22 may be trustworthy on his lips. 6
39:15 with songs on your lips, and with lyres 7
50:20 pronounce the blessing of the Lord with his lips 7
51: 2 lips that utter lies 7

upper lip 1. שָׂפָם
Lev 13:45 he shall cover his upper lip and cry, 'Unclean 1

liquid 1. דְּרוֹר 2. עבר 3. ὕδωρ 4. χυλός
Exd 30:23 Take . . of liquid myrrh 500 shekels 1
Sng 5: 5 my hands dripped . . my fingers with liquid myrrh 2
13 His lips are lilies, distilling liquid myrrh. 2
2Mc 1:20 they had not found fire but thick liquid 3
21 to sprinkle the liquid on the wood 3
31 the liquid that was left 3
33 the liquid had appeared 3
4Mc 6:25 poured stinking liquids into his nostrils. 4

liquor 1. πόματος
3Mc 5: 2 maddened by the lavish abundance of liquor 1

list 1. מִסְפָּר
1Ch 25: 1 list of those who did the work and of their duties 1
27: 1 This is the list of the people of Israel 1
2Es 2:40 conclude the list of your people •

list of names 1. ὀνοματογραφία
1Es 6:12 list of the names of those who are at their head 1
8:49 the list of all their names was reported. 1

listen 1. אזן 2. קשב 3. שמע 4. שמע בקול 5. ἀκοή 6. ἀκούω 7. ἀκροάομαι 8. εἰσακούω 9. ἐπακούω 10. ἐπακροάομαι 11. μανθάνω 12. πειθαρχέω 13. προσέχω 14. audio 15. exaudio
Gen 3:17 you have listened to the voice of your wife 3
18:10 Sarah was listening at the tent door behind him 3
23:15 My lord, listen to me; a piece of land 3
27: 5 Now Rebekah was listening when Isaac spoke 3
34:17 if you will not listen to us and be circumcised 3

39:10 he would not listen to her, to lie with her 3
42:21 when he besought us and we would not listen; 3
22 But you would not listen. So now there comes 3
Exd 4: 1 they will not believe me or listen to my voice 3
6: 9 Israel; but they did not listen to Moses 3
12 the people of Israel have not listened to me; 3
12 how then shall Pharaoh listen to me, who am a man 3
30 how then shall Pharaoh listen to me? 3
7: 4 Pharaoh will not listen to you; 3
13 and he would not listen to them; as the LORD had 3
22 Pharaoh . . would not listen to them; 3
8:15 hardened his heart, and would not listen to them; 3
19 was hardened, and he would not listen to them; 3
9:12 he did not listen to them; as the LORD had spoken 3
11: 9 Pharaoh will not listen to you; 3
16:20 they did not listen to Moses; some left part of it 3
18:19 Listen now to my voice; I will give you counsel 3
Deu 13: 3 you shall not listen to the words of that prophet 3
8 you shall not yield to him or listen to him 3
Jos 24:10 but I would not listen to Balaam; 3
Jdg 2:17 yet they did not listen to their judges; 3
9: 7 Listen to me, you men of Shechem, that God may 3
7 Listen to me . . that God may listen to you. 3
11:17 your land'; but the king of Edom would not listen. 3
13: 9 God listened to the voice of Mano'ah, and the angel 3
19:25 the men would not listen to him. So the man seized 3
20:13 the Benjaminites would not listen to the voice 3
Rut 2: 8 Now, listen, my daughter, do not go to glean 3
1Sm 2:25 would not listen to the voice of their father; 3
8:19 people refused to listen to the voice of Samuel; 3
24: 9 Why do you listen to the words of men 3
30:24 Who would listen to you in this matter? 3
2Sm 12:18 we spoke to him, and he did not listen to us; 4
13:14 But he would not listen to her; and . . he forced her 4
16 But he would not listen to her. 3
19:35 Can I still listen to the voice of singing men 3
20:17 Listen to the words of your maidservant. 3
17 Listen to . . " And he answered, "I am listening. 3
2Kg 14:11 Amazi'ah would not listen. 3
17:14 they would not listen, but were stubborn 3
40 However they would not listen 3
18:12 not obey . . they neither listened nor obeyed. 3
31 Do not listen to Hezeki'ah; for thus says the king 3
32 do not listen to Hezeki'ah when he misleads you 3
21: 9 they did not listen, and Manas'seh seduced them 3
2Ch 25:16 done this and have not listened to my counsel. 3
20 Amazi'ah would not listen; for it was of God 3
35:22 did not listen to the words of Neco from . . God 3
Ezr 8:23 listened to our entreaty. *
Neh 13:27 then listen to you and do all this great evil 3
Est 3: 4 spoke to him . . and he would not listen to them 3
Job 9:16 not believe that he was listening to my voice. 1
13: 6 listen to the pleadings of my lips. 2
17 Listen carefully to my words 3
15: 8 Have you listened in the council of God? 3
21: 2 Listen carefully to my words 3
29:21 Men listened to me, and waited, and kept silence 3
32:10 say, 'Listen to me; let me also declare my opinion 3
11 I listened for your wise sayings 1
33: 1 hear my speech, O Job, and listen to all my words. 1
31 Give heed, O Job, listen to me; 3
33 If not, listen to me; be silent, 3
34:16 hear this; listen to what I say. 1
Ps 34:11 Come, O sons, listen to me, I will teach you 3
61: 1 Hear my cry, O God, listen to my prayer; 2
66:18 the Lord would not have listened. 3
19 But truly God has listened; he has given heed 3
81: 8 O Israel, if you would but listen to me! 3
11 my people did not listen to my voice; 3
13 O that my people would listen to me 3
Prv 1:24 Because I have called and you refused to listen *
33 he who listens to me will dwell secure 3
5: 7 now, O sons, listen to me 3
13 I did not listen to the voice of my teachers 3
7:24 now, O sons, listen to me 3
8:32 now, my sons, listen to me 3
34 Happy is the man who listens to me 3
12:15 but a wise man listens to advice. 3
13: 1 but a scoffer does not listen to rebuke. 3
17: 4 An evildoer listens to wicked lips; 2
19:20 Listen to advice and accept instruction 3
25:12 wise reprover to a listening ear. 3
29:12 ruler listens to falsehood, all his officials 2
Ecc 5: 1 to draw near to listen is better than to offer 3
Sng 8:13 my companions are listening for your voice; 2
Isa 1:15 though you make many prayers, I will not listen; 3
34: 1 Let the earth listen, and all that fills it; 3
36:16 Do not listen to Hezeki'ah; 3
42:23 Who . . will attend and listen for the time to come? 3
49: 1 Listen to me, O coastlands, and hearken 3
51: 4 Listen to me, my people, and give ear to me, my nation 2
65:12 you did not answer, when I spoke, you did not listen 3
66: 4 when I spoke they did not listen; 3
Jer 6:10 Behold, their ears are closed, they cannot listen; 2
7:13 I spoke to you persistently you did not listen 3
26 yet they did not listen to me, or incline their ear 3
27 but they will not listen to you. 3
8: 6 I have given heed and listened 3
11: 4 Listen to my voice, and do all that I command you. 3
11 though they cry to me, I will not listen to them. 3
14 for I will not listen when they call to me 3
12:17 But if any nation will not listen 3
13:11 but they would not listen. 3
17 if you will not listen, my soul will weep in secret 3
16:12 his stubborn evil will, refusing to listen to me; 3
17:23 Yet they did not listen or incline their ear 3
24 But if you listen to me, says the LORD 3
27 if you do not listen to me, to keep the sabbath day 3
18:10 does evil in my sight, not listening to my voice 3
22:21 but you said, 'I will not listen.' 3
23:16 Do not listen to the words of the prophets 3
18 or who has given heed to his word and listened? 3
25: 3 but you have not listened. 3
4 You have neither listened nor inclined 3
7 Yet you have not listened to me, says the LORD 3
26: 3 It may be they will listen, and every one turn 3
4 Thus says the LORD: If you will not listen to me 3
27: 9 do not listen to your prophets, your diviners 3
14 Do not listen to the words of the prophets 3
16 Do not listen to the words of your prophets 3
17 Do not listen to them; serve the king of Babylon 3
28:15 Listen, Hanani'ah, the LORD has not sent you 3
29: 8 and do not listen to the dreams which they dream 3
19 but you would not listen, says the LORD. 3
32:33 they have not listened to receive instruction. 3
34:14 But your fathers did not listen to me 3
35:13 Will you not receive instruction and listen 3
14 but you have not listened to me. 3
15 But you did not incline your ear or listen to me. 3
17 I have spoken to them and they have not listened 3
36:25 he would not listen to them. 3
37: 2 nor the people of the land listened to the words 3
14 But Iri'jah would not listen to him 3
38:15 if I give you counsel, you will not listen to me. 3
44: 5 But they did not listen or incline their ear 3
16 we will not listen to you. 3
Ezk 3: 6 if I sent you to such, they would listen to you. 3
7 But the house of Israel will not listen to you; 3
7 for they are not willing to listen to me; 3
13:19 by your lies to my people, who listen to lies. 3
20: 8 they rebelled against me and would not listen 3
39 now and hereafter, if you will not listen to me; 3
Dan 9: 6 have not listened to thy servants the prophets 3
Ams 5:23 to the melody of your harps I will not listen. 3
Zep 3: 2 She listens to no voice 3
Mal 2: 2 If you will not listen 3
Mat 10:14 if any one will not receive you or listen 6
17: 5 listen to him. 6
18:15 If he listens to you, you have gained your brother. 6
16 if he does not listen, take one or two others along 6
Mrk 4: 3 Listen! A sower went out to sow. 6
9: 7 This is my beloved Son; listen to him. 6
Lke 2:46 listening to them and asking them questions; 6
9:35 This is my Son, my Chosen; listen to him! 6
10:39 listened to his teaching. 6
Joh 6:60 This is a hard saying; who can listen to it? 6
9:27 you would not listen 6
31 We know that God does not listen to sinners 6
31 God listens to him 6
10:20 he is mad; why listen to him? 6
Act 3:22 You shall listen to him in whatever he tells you. 6
23 every soul that does not listen to that prophet 6
4:19 to listen to you rather than to God 6
13:16 Men of Israel, and you that fear God, listen. 6
14: 9 He listened to Paul speaking 6
15:12 they listened to Barnabas and Paul 6
13 Brethren, listen to me. 6
16:25 the prisoners were listening to them 10
22:22 Up to this word they listened to him 6
26: 3 therefore I beg you to listen to me patiently. 6
27:21 you should have listened to me 12
28:28 they will listen. 6
1Co 14:21 they will not listen to me, says the Lord. 8
2Co 6: 2 At the acceptable time I have listened to you 9
2Ti 3: 7 who will listen to anybody 11
4: 4 will turn away from listening to the truth 5
Jas 2: 5 Listen, my beloved brethren. 6
1Jn 4: 5 and the world listens to them. 6
6 We are of God. Whoever knows God listens to us 6
6 and he who is not of God does not listen to us. 6
2Es 1:26 When you call upon me, I will not listen to you 15
2: 1 but they would not listen to them 14
9 So will I do to those who have not listened to me 14
5:32 he said to me,"Listen to me 14
6:17 When I heard this, I rose to my feet and listened 14
7: 2 he said to me, "Rise, Ezra, and listen to the words 14
49 He answered me and said, "Listen to me, Ezra 14
10:38 He answered me and said, "Listen to me 14
11:38 Listen and I will speak to you 14
16:35 Listen now to these things, and understand them 14
Tob 6:12 Now listen to my plan 6
15 Now listen to me, brother 6
Jdt 8:11 Listen to me, rulers of the people of Bethulia! 6
32 Judith said to them, "Listen to me 6
14: 1 Then Judith said to them, "Listen to me, my brethren 6
Wis 6: 1 Listen therefore, O kings, and understand 6
Sir 3: 1 Listen to me your father, O children 6
6:23 Listen, my son, and accept my judgment 6
33 If you love to listen you will gain knowledge 6
35 Be ready to listen to every narrative 7
14:23 will also listen at her doors; 7
16:24 Listen to me, my son, and acquire knowledge 6
21:24 It is ill-mannered for a man to listen at a door 7
23: 7 Listen, my children 6
31:22 Listen to me, my son, and do not disregard me 6
34:24 to whose voice will the Lord listen? 8
26 who will listen to his prayer? 8
35:13 will listen to the prayer of one who is wronged. 8
39:13 Listen to me, O you holy sons 8
1Mc 2:65 always listen to him; he shall be your father. 6
5:61 they did not listen to Judas and his brothers. 6
2Mc 7:25 Since the young man would not listen to him at all 13
3Mc 2:10 you would listen to our petition 8

listen diligently 1. קשב
Isa 21: 7 let him listen diligently, very diligently. 1

listen in silence 1. חרשׁ
Isa 41: 1 Listen to me in silence, O coastlands; 1

attentive listener 1. εἰς ὦτα ἀκούω
Sir 25: 9 he who speaks to attentive listeners. 1

literal 1. γράμμα
Rom 2:29 a matter of the heart, spiritual and not literal. 1

litter 1. מִטָּה 2. צָב 3. φορεῖον
Sng 3: 7 Behold, it is the litter of Solomon! 1
Isa 66:20 in chariots, and in litters, and upon mules 2
2Mc 9: 8 carried in a litter 3

litter (2) 1. מָלֵא
2Kg 7:15 way was littered with garments and equipment 1

little 1. וְעֵיר 2. לְמַטָּה 3. מעט 4. מְעַט 5. צָעִיר 6. קָטָן 7. קָטֹן 8. βραχύς 9. βραχύς τι 10. ἐλασσόω 11. ἐλαχύς 12. μέρος 13. μετρίως 14. μικρός 15. ὀλίγος 16. πάρεργος 17. τις 18. minutus 19. modicus 20. parvus
Gen 1:16 the lesser light to rule the night; 7
18: 4 Let a little water be brought, and wash your feet 4
24:17 and said, "Pray give me a little water 4
43 Pray give me a little water from your jar to drink 4
30:30 For you had little before I came 4
43: 2 Go again, buy us a little food. 4
11 and carry down to the man a present, a little balm 4
11 a present, a little balm and a little honey 4
44:25 when our father said, 'Go again, buy us a little food 4
Exd 16:17 Israel did so; they gathered, some more, some less. 3
23:30 Little by little I will drive them out 4
30 Little by little I will drive them out 4
Num 22:18 not go beyond the command . . to do less or more. 6
Deu 7:22 clear away these nations . . little by little; 4
22 clear away these nations . . little by little; 4
28:38 carry much seed . . and shall gather little in; 4
Jdg 4:19 give me a little water to drink; for I am thirsty. 4
1Sm 2:19 his mother used to make for him a little robe 7
9:21 Am I not . . from the least of the tribes of Israel? 6
14:29 because I tasted a little of this honey. 4
43 I tasted a little honey with the tip of the staff 4
15:17 Though you are little in your own eyes, are you not 7
20:35 Jonathan went out . . and with him a little lad. 7
22:15 servant has known nothing . . much or little. 7
2Sm 12: 3 the poor man had nothing but one little ewe lamb 6
8 if this were too little, I would add to you as much 4
16: 1 When David had passed a little beyond the summit 4
19:36 Your servant will go a little way over the Jordan 4
1Kg 3: 7 I am but a little child; I do not know how to go out 7
11:17 Hadad fled . . Hadad being yet a little child. 6
17:10 Bring me a little water . . that I may drink. 4
12 handful of meal in a jar, and a little oil in a cruse; 4
13 first make me a little cake of it and bring it to me 6
18:44 a little cloud like a man's hand is rising 6
2Kg 5: 2 the Syrians . . had carried off a little maid 6
14 was restored like the flesh of a little child 7
10:18 Ahab served Ba'al a little; 4
18:24 captain among the least of my master's servants 6
1Ch 12:14 the lesser over 100 and the greater over 1,000. 6
Ezr 9: 8 grant us a little reviving in our bondage. 4
13 punished us less than our iniquities deserved 2
Job 10:20 Let me alone, that I may find a little comfort 4
36: 2 Bear with me a little, and I will show you 1
Ps 8: 5 Yet thou hast made him little less than God 4
37:16 Better is a little that the righteous has 4
Prv 6:10 A little sleep, a little slumber 4
10 A little sleep, a little slumber 4
10 a little folding of the hands to rest 4
10:20 the mind of the wicked is of little worth. 4
15:16 Better is a little with the fear of the LORD 4
16: 8 Better is a little with righteousness 4
24:33 A little sleep, a little slumber, a little folding 4
33 A little sleep, a little slumber, a little folding 4
33 slumber, a little folding of the hands to rest 4
Ecc 5:12 sleep of a laborer, whether he eats little or much 4
9:14 There was a little city with few men in it; 6
10: 1 so a little folly outweighs wisdom and honor. 4

Sng 2:15 foxes, the little foxes, that spoil the vineyards 6
8: 8 We have a little sister, and she has no breasts. 6
Isa 7:13 O house of David! Is it too little for you to weary men 4
10:25 in a very little while my indignation will come 4
11: 6 together, and a little child shall lead them. 7
26:20 hide yourselves for a little while 4
28:10 line upon line, here a little, there a little. 1
10 line upon line, here a little, there a little. 1
13 line upon line, here a little, there a little; 1
13 line upon line, here a little, there a little; 1
32:10 In little more than a year you will shudder •
36: 9 captain among the least of my master's servants 6
Jer 8:10 the least to the greatest every one is greedy 7
42: 1 all the people from the least to the greatest 7
8 and all the people from the least to the greatest 7
44:12 from the least to the greatest, they shall die 7
Ezk 16:47 within a very little time you were more corrupt 4
Dan 8: 9 Out of one of them came forth a little horn 7
11:34 When they fall, they shall receive a little help. 4
Ams 6:11 into fragments, and the little house into bits. 7
Mic 5: 2 who are little to be among the clans of Judah 5
Hag 1: 6 You have sown much, and harvested little; 4
9 You have looked for much, and, lo, it came to little; 4
Zec 1:15 while I was angry but a little 4
Mat 10:42 whoever gives to one of these little ones 14
25:21 you have been faithful over a little 15
23 you have been faithful over a little 15
26:39 going a little farther he fell on his face 14
73 After a little while the bystanders came up 14
Mrk 1:19 And going on a little farther 15
14:35 going a little farther, he fell on the ground 14
Lke 5: 3 he asked him to put out a little from the land. 15
7:47 he who is forgiven little, loves little. 15
47 he who is forgiven little, loves little. 15
12:32 Fear not, little flock 14
22:58 a little later some one else saw him and said 8
Joh 6: 7 buy enough bread for each of them to get a little 9
7:33 I shall be with you a little longer 14
12:35 The light is with you for a little longer 14
13:33 Little children, yet a little while I am with you. 14
14:19 Yet a little while 14
16:16 A little while, and you will see me no more 14
16 again a little while, and you will see me. 14
17 A little while, and you will not see me 14
17 again a little while, and you will see me 14
18 They said, "What does he mean by 'a little while'? 14
19 what I meant by saying, 'A little while . . 14
19 again a little while, and you will see me'? 14
Act 14:28 remained no little time with the disciples. 15
19:23 there arose no little stir concerning the Way. 15
24 brought no little business to the craftsmen. 15
20:12 were not a little comforted. 13
27:28 a little farther on they sounded again 8
Rom 15:24 once I have enjoyed your company for a little. 12
1Co 5: 6 a little leaven leavens the whole lump? 14
2Co 8:15 he who gathered little had no lack. 14
10: 8 even if I boast a little too much of our authority 17
11: 1 bear with me in a little foolishness 14
16 so that I too may boast a little. 14
Gal 5: 9 A little leaven leavens the whole lump. 14
1Ti 5:23 No longer drink only water, but use a little wine 15
Heb 10:37 yet a little while, and the coming one shall come 14
Jas 3: 5 So the tongue is a little member and boasts 14
Rev 3: 8 I know that you have but little power 14
6:11 they were each . . told to rest a little longer 14
17:10 when he comes he must remain only a little while. 15
20: 3 After that he must be loosed for a little while. 14
2Es 8: 2 but only a little dust from which gold comes 20
11: 3 wings; but they became little, puny wings. 18
25 I looked, and behold, these little wings planned ‡
12: 5 and not even a little strength is left in me 19
40 from the least to the greatest 20
Tob 4: 8 afraid to give according to the little you have. 15
12: 8 A little with righteousness is better 15
Wis 3: 5 Having been disciplined a little 15
7: 9 because all gold is but a little sand in her sight 15
9: 5 with little understanding of judgment and laws; 11
13: 6 Yet these men are little to be blamed 15
15: 8 after a little while goes to the earth 15
16: 6 they were troubled for a little while as a warning 15
Sir 0: 2 differ not a little as originally expressed. 14
3 I found opportunity for no little instruction. 14
20:12 There is a man who buys much for a little 15
15 He gives little and upbraids much 15
29:23 Be content with little or much. 14
31:19 How ample a little is for a well-disciplined man! 15
38:24 he who has little business may become wise. 10
40: 6 He gets little or no rest 15
42: 4 of acquiring much or little; 15
51:16 I inclined my ear a little and received her 15
27 See with your eyes that I have labored little 15
2Mc 3:14 no little distress throughout the whole city. 14
30 which a little while before was full of fear 14
6:29 a little before had acted . . with good will 14
9:10 the man who a little while before had thought 14
15:19 were in no little distress 16
4Mc 6:20 if we should survive for a little while 15
12: 7 as we shall tell a little later 14

little by little 1. עַל יָד 2. *κατὰ βραχύ* 3. *κατὰ μικρόν* 4. *κατ' ὀλίγον* 5. paulatim

Prv 13:11 he who gathers little by little will increase 1
2Es 6:29 While he spoke to me, behold, little by little 5
Wis 12: 2 Therefore thou dost correct little by little 4
8 to destroy them little by little 2
10 judging them little by little 2
Sir 19: 1 will fail little by little. 3
2Mc 8: 8 gaining ground little by little 3

little one 1. טַף 2. מִצְעָר 3. עֲוִיל 4. עוֹלֵל 5. צָעִיר 6. צער 7. קָטֹן 8. זְעֵיר (A) 9. *μικρός* 10. parvulus

Gen 19:20 city . . is a little one. 2
20 city . . is it not a little one? 2
34:29 all their wealth, all their little ones 1
43: 8 both we and you and also our little ones. 1
45:19 wagons . . for your little ones and for your wives 1
46: 5 carried . . their little ones, and their wives 1
47:24 and as food for your little ones. 1
50:21 I will provide for you and your little ones. 1
Exd 10:10 if ever I let you and your little ones go! 1
Num 14: 3 Our wives and our little ones will become a prey; 1
31 your little ones, who you said would become a prey 1
16:27 wives, their sons, and their little ones. 1
31: 9 took captive the women . . and their little ones; 1
17 therefore, kill every male among the little ones 1
32:16 We will build . . cities for our little ones 1
17 our little ones shall live in the . . cities 1
24 Build cities for your little ones 1
26 Our little ones, our wives, our flocks, and all our 1
Deu 1:39 your little ones, who you said would become a prey 1
3:19 your wives, your little ones, and your cattle 1
20:14 women and the little ones the cattle 1
29:11 your little ones, your wives, and the sojourner 1
31:12 Assemble the people, men, women, and little ones 1
Jos 1:14 Your wives, your little ones, and your cattle 1
8:35 all . . Israel, and the women, and the little ones 1
Jdg 18:21 departed, putting the little ones and the cattle 1
21:10 Go and smite . . also the women and the little ones. 1
2Sm 15:22 his men and all the little ones who were with him. 1
2Kg 8:12 and dash in pieces their little ones 4
2Ch 20:13 with their little ones, their wives 1
Job 21:11 They send forth their little ones like a flock 3
Ps 137: 9 Happy shall he be who takes your little ones 4
Isa 60:22 The least one shall become a clan 7
Jer 49:20 little ones of the flock shall be dragged away; 5
50:45 little ones of their flock shall be dragged away; 5
Dan 7: 8 came up among them another horn, a little one 8
Hos 13:16 their little ones shall be dashed in pieces 4
Nah 3:10 her little ones were dashed in pieces 4
Zec 13: 7 I will turn my hand against the little ones. 6
Mat 18: 6 one of these little ones who believe in me 9
10 that you do not despise one of these little ones; 9
14 that one of these little ones should perish. 9
Mrk 9:42 one of these little ones who believe in me 9
Lke 17: 2 that he should cause one of these little ones to sin. 9
2Es 10:22 our little ones have been cast out 10

seem little 1. מעט

Neh 9:32 let not all the hardship seem little to thee 1

seem a little thing 1. קלל

1Sm 18:23 Does it seem . . a little thing to become the king's 1

very little 1. מִזְעָר 2. מְעַט מִזְעָר 3. *ἐλάχιστος*

Isa 10:25 in a very little while my indignation will come 1
29:17 Is it not yet a very little while until Lebanon 2
Lke 16:10 He who is faithful in a very little 3
10 he who is dishonest in a very little 3
19:17 Because you have been faithful in a very little 3

very little thing 1. *ἐλαχύς*

Jdt 16:16 all fat for burnt offerings . . is a very little thing 1

live 1. אכל 2. גור 3. הלך 4. חַי 5. חיה 6. חַיָּה 7. חַיּוֹת 8. חַיִּים 9. יוֹם 10. ישב 11. מָגוֹר 12. מוֹשָׁב 13. מִחְיָה 14. עמד 15. שכן 16. חַי (A) 17. חיה (A) 18. יתב (A) 19. *αἴδης* 20. *ἀληθινός* 21. *ἀναστρέφω* 22. *ἀναστροφή* 23. *ἄρτος* 24. *αὐλίζομαι* 25. *βίος* 26. *βιοτεύω* 27. *βιόω* 28. *βίωσις* 29. *γίνομαι* 30. *διάθεσις* 31. *διατρίβω* 32. *ἐγκατοικέω* 33. *εἰμί* 34. *ἐμβιόω* 35. *ἐμμένω* 36. *ἐνοικέω* 37. *ἐπιδημέω* 38. *ἔχω* 39. *ἔχω ψυχήν* 40. *ζάω* 41. *ζωή* 42. *ζῷον* 43. *ζωτικός* 44. *κάθημαι* 45. *κατά* 46. *κατοικέω* 47. *κατοίκησιν ἔχω* 48. *μένω* 49. *μετέχω* 50. *οἰκέω* 51. *οἰκία* 52. *παροικέω* 53. *περίειμι* 54. *περιπατέω* 55. *ποιέω* 56. *πολιτεύομαι* 57. *πορεύω* 58. *στοιχέω* 59. *συζάω* 60. *συμβιόω* 61. *συμβίωσις* 62. *συμπαραμένω* 63. *συναναστρέφω* 64. *συνοικέω* 65. *ὑπάρχω* 66. *φρονέω* 67. *χράομαι* 68. *ψυχή* 69. converso 70. converto 71. habeo 72. habito 73. inhabito 74. praesens 75. sum 76. vivo 77. vivus

Gen 1:20 waters bring forth swarms of living creatures 4
21 God created . . every living creature that moves 4
24 Let the earth bring forth living creatures 4
2: 7 breath of life; and man became a living being. 4
19 whatever the man called every living creature 4
3:20 Eve, because she was the mother of all living. 4
22 of the tree of life, and eat, and live for ever"- 4
5: 3 When Adam had lived 130 years 5
5 Thus all the days that Adam lived were 930 years 5
6 When Seth had lived 105 years 5
7 Seth lived after the birth of Enosh 807 years 5
9 When Enosh had lived 90 years 5
10 Enosh lived after the birth of Kenan 815 years 5
12 When Kenan had lived 70 years 5
13 Kenan lived after the birth of Ma-hal'alel 5
15 When Ma-hal'alel had lived 65 years 5
16 Ma-hal'alel lived after the birth of Jared 5
18 When Jared had lived 162 years 5
19 Jared lived after the birth of Enoch 800 years 5
21 When Enoch had lived 65 years 5
25 When Methu'selah had lived 187 years 5
26 Methu'selah lived after the birth of Lamech 5
28 When Lamech had lived 182 years 5
30 Lamech lived after the birth of Noah 595 years 5
6:19 of every living thing of all flesh 4
8:21 destroy every living creature as I have done. 4
9: 3 Every moving thing that lives shall be food 4
10 with every living creature that is with you 4
12 me and you and every living creature that is 4
15 you and every living creature of all flesh; 4
16 covenant between God and every living creature 4
28 After the flood Noah lived 350 years; 5
10:30 The territory in which they lived extended 12
11:11 Shem lived after the birth of Arpach'shad 5
12 When Arpach'shad had lived 35 years 5
13 Arpach'shad lived after the birth of Shelah 5
14 When Shelah had lived 30 years 5
15 Shelah lived after the birth of Eber 403 years 5
16 When Eber had lived 34 years 5
17 Eber lived after the birth of Peleg 430 years 5
18 When Peleg had lived 30 years 5
19 Peleg lived after the birth of Re'u 209 years 5
20 When Re'u had lived 32 years 5
21 Re'u lived after the birth of Serug 207 years 5
22 When Serug had lived 30 years 5
23 Serug lived after the birth of Nahor 200 years 5
24 When Nahor had lived 29 years 5
25 Nahor lived after the birth of Terah 119 years 5
26 When Terah had lived 70 years 5
12:12 they will kill me, but they will let you live. 5
14:13 the Hebrew, who was living by the oaks of Mamre 15
17:18 O that Ish'mael might live in thy sight! 5
20: 7 and you shall live. But if you do not 5
21:20 the lad . . lived in the wilderness 10
21 He lived in the wilderness of Paran; 10
23: 1 Sarah lived 127 years; 8
25: 6 and while he was still living he sent them away 4
22 and she said, "If it is thus, why do I live? •
27:40 By your sword you shall live, and you shall serve 5
31:32 one with whom you find your gods shall not live. 5
42: 2 buy grain . . that we may live, and not die. 5
18 Joseph said to them, "Do this and you will live 5
43: 8 that we may live and not die, both we and you 5
47:19 give us seed, that we may live, and not die 5
22 priests . . lived on the allowance 1
28 Jacob lived in the land of Egypt seventeen years; 5
50:22 and Joseph lived 110 years. 5
Exd 1:16 but if it is a daughter, she shall live. 5
17 midwives . . let the male children live. 5
18 Why have you . . let the male children live? 5
22 but you shall let every daughter live. 5
9:16 for this purpose have I let you live, to show you 14
19:13 whether beast or man, he shall not live.' 5
21:35 then they shall sell the live ox and divide 4
33:20 for man shall not see me and live. 5
Lev 11:10 of the living creatures that are in the waters 4
46 law pertaining to . . every living creature 4
14: 4 take . . two living birds and cedarwood 4
6 He shall take the living bird with the cedarwood 4
6 dip them and the living bird in the blood 4
7 shall let the living bird go into the open field 4
51 the scarlet stuff, along with the living bird 4
52 cleanse the house . . with the living bird 4
53 he shall let the living bird go out of the city 4
16:20 he shall present the live goat 4
21 both his hands upon the head of the live goat 4
18: 5 my ordinances, by doing which a man shall live 5
25: 6 servant and the sojourner who lives with you 2
35 a sojourner he shall live with you 4
36 that your brother may live beside you 4
Num 4:19 deal thus with them, that they may live and not die 5
14:21 truly, as I live, and as all the earth shall be 4
28 Say to them, 'As I live,' says the LORD 4
16:48 he stood between the dead and the living; 4
21: 8 every one who is bitten when he sees it, shall live. 5
9 man, he would look at the bronze serpent and live. 5
22:33 just now I would have slain you and let her live. 5
24:23 Alas, who shall live when God does this? 5
31:15 Moses said to them, "Have you let all the women live? 5
32:17 little ones shall live in the fortified cities 10
35:25 live in it until the death of the high priest 10
33 shall not thus pollute the land in which you live; •

34 You shall not defile the land in which you live 10
Deu 1: 4 king of the Amorites, who lived in Heshbon 10
4 king of Bashan, who lived in Ash'taroth 10
44 Amorites who lived in that hill country came out 10
2: 4 your brethren the sons of Esau, who live in Se'ir; 10
8 our brethren the sons of Esau who live in Se'ir 10
10 Emim formerly lived there, a people great and many 10
12 The Horites also lived in Se'ir formerly 10
20 Reph'aim formerly lived there, but the Ammonites 10
22 he did for the sons of Esau, who live in Se'ir 10
23 for the Avvim, who lived in villages as far as Gaza 10
29 as the sons of Esau who live in Se'ir . . did for me 10
29 as . . the Moabites who live in Ar did for me 10
4: 1 which I teach you, and do them; that you may live 5
10 fear me all the days that they live upon the earth 4
33 hear the voice of a god speaking . . and still live? 5
46 king of the Amorites, who lived at Heshbon 10
47 who lived to the east beyond the Jordan; •
5:24 day seen God speak with man and man still live. 5
26 heard the voice of the living God speaking 4
26 heard the voice . . as we have, and has still lived? 5
33 that you may live, and that it may go well with you 5
8: 1 that you may live and multiply 5
3 man does not live by bread alone 5
3 alone, but that man lives by everything that 5
12 when you . . have built goodly houses and live 10
11:30 land of the Canaanites who live in the Arabah 10
31 when you possess it and live in it 10
12: 1 all the days that you live upon the earth. 4
10 when you go over the Jordan, and live in the land 10
10 gives you rest . . so that you live in safety 10
19 as long as you live in your land. •
16:20 justice, you shall follow, that you may live 5
18: 6 comes from any of your towns . . where he lives– 2
21:19 city at the gate of the place where he lives •
26: 1 taken possession of it, and live in it 10
30: 6 heart and with all your soul, that you may live. 5
16 If you obey . . then you shall live and multiply 5
19 life, that you and your descendants may live 5
31:13 as long as you live in the land which you are going 4
21 (for it will live unforgotten in the mouths •
32:40 I lift up my hand . . and swear, As I live for ever 4
33: 6 Let Reuben live, and not die, nor let his men be few. 5
Jos 3:10 you shall know that the living God is among you 4
6:17 only Rahab the harlot and all who . . shall live 5
8:35 and the sojourners who lived among them. 3
9: 7 men of Israel said . . "Perhaps you live among us; 10
15 and made a covenant with them, to let them live; 5
20 This we will do to them, and let them live 5
21 And the leaders said to them, "Let them live. 5
24: 2 Your fathers lived of old beyond the Euphra'tes 10
7 and you lived in the wilderness a long time. 10
8 who lived on the other side of the Jordan; 10
18 the peoples, the Amorites who lived in the land; 10
Jdg 8:19 as the LORD lives, if you had saved them alive 4
9:41 so that they could not live on at Shechem. 10
10: 1 and he lived at Shamir in the hill country 10
17: 8 departed . . to live where he could find a place; 2
10 a year, and a suit of apparel, and your living. 13
Rut 1: 4 They lived there about ten years; 10
2:20 kindness has not forsaken the living or the dead! 4
23 and she lived with her mother-in-law. 10
3:13 as the LORD lives, I will do the part . . for you. 4
1Sm 1:26 As you live, my lord, I am the woman 4
28 as long as he lives, he is lent to the LORD. 5
10:24 And all the people shouted, "Long live the king! 5
14:39 For as the LORD lives . . he shall surely die. 4
45 As the LORD lives, there shall not one hair . . fall 4
17:26 who . . should defy the armies of the living God? 4
36 he has defied the armies of the living God. 4
55 As your soul lives, O king, I cannot tell. 4
19: 6 As the LORD lives, he shall not be put to death. 4
20: 3 But truly, as the LORD lives . . there is but a step 4
3 as the LORD lives and as your soul lives 4
21 for, as the LORD lives, it is safe for you 4
31 as long as the son of Jesse lives upon the earth 4
25:26 as the LORD lives, and as your soul lives 4
26 as the LORD lives, and as your soul lives 4
28 evil shall not be found in you so long as you live. 9
29 my lord shall be bound in the bundle of the living 4
34 For as surely as the LORD the God of Israel lives 4
26:10 As the LORD lives, the LORD will smite him; 4
16 As the LORD lives, you deserve to die 4
28:10 Saul swore to her by the LORD, "As the LORD lives 4
29: 6 As the LORD lives, you have been honest 4
2Sm 1:10 I was sure . . he could not live after he had fallen; 5
2:27 As God lives, if you had not spoken, surely the men 4
4: 9 As the LORD lives, who has redeemed my life 4
11:11 As you live, and as your soul lives, I will not do 4
11 As you live, and as your soul lives, I will not do 4
12: 5 As the LORD lives, the man . . deserves to die; 4
22 LORD . . be gracious to me, that the child may live?' 4
14:11 As the LORD lives, not one hair . . shall fall 4
19 As surely as you live, my lord the king, one cannot 4
15:21 As the LORD lives, and as my lord the king lives 4
21 As the LORD lives, and as my lord the king lives 4
19:34 How many years have I still to live 8
20: 3 they were shut up . . living as if in widowhood. 7
22:47 The LORD lives; and blessed be my rock, and exalted 4

1Kg 1:25 before him, and saying, 'Long live King Adoni'jah!' 5
29 As the LORD lives, who has redeemed my soul 4
31 and said, "May my lord King David live for ever. 5
34 the trumpet, and say, 'Long live King Solomon! 5
39 and all the people said, "Long live King Solomon! 5
2:24 as the LORD lives, who has established me 4
3:22 No, the living child is mine, and the dead child is 4
22 dead child is yours, and the living child is mine. 4
23 your son is dead, and my son is the living one.' 4
25 Divide the living child in two, and give half 4
26 give her the living child, and by no means slay it. 4
27 Give the living child to the first woman, and by no 4
8:40 fear thee all the days that they live in the land 4
17: 1 As the LORD the God of Israel lives 4
12 As the LORD your God lives, I have nothing baked 4
23 and Eli'jah said, "See, your son lives. 4
18:10 As the LORD your God lives, there is no nation 4
15 As the LORD of hosts lives . . I will surely show 4
20:32 Your servant Ben-ha'dad says, 'Pray, let me live.' 5
32 And he said, "Does he still live? He is my brother. 4
22:14 Micai'ah said, "As the LORD lives . . that I will 4
2Kg 2: 2 As the LORD lives, and as you yourself live, I will 4
2 As the LORD lives, and as you yourself live, I will 4
4 As the LORD lives, and as you yourself live, I will 4
4 As the LORD lives, and as you yourself live, I will 4
6 As the LORD lives, and as you yourself live, I will 4
6 As the LORD lives, and as you yourself live, I will 4
3:14 As the LORD of hosts lives, whom I serve, were it not 4
4: 7 pay your debts, and you . . can live on the rest. 5
8 went on to Shunem, where a wealthy woman lived •
30 As the LORD lives, and as you yourself live, I will 4
30 As the LORD lives, and as you yourself live, I will 4
5:16 As the LORD lives, whom I serve, I will receive 4
20 As the LORD lives, I will run after him 4
7: 4 if they spare our lives we shall live 5
10:19 whoever is missing shall not live. 5
14:17 Amazi'ah . . lived fifteen years after the death 5
18:32 and take you away . . that you may live, and not die. 5
19: 4 whom his master . . has sent to mock the living God 4
16 words . . which he has sent to mock the living God. 4
25:30 every day a portion, as long as he lived. 4
1Ch 9:34 leaders, who lived in Jerusalem. 10
2Ch 6:31 walk in thy ways all the days that they live 4
8:11 My wife shall not live in the house of David 10
18:13 Micai'ah said, "As the LORD lives, what my God says 4
19:10 from your brethren who live in their cities 10
23:11 anointed him, and they said, "Long live the king. 5
25:25 Amazi'ah . . lived fifteen years after the death 5
31: 4 commanded the people who lived in Jerusalem 10
6 people . . who lived in the cities of Judah 10
Ezr 2:70 some . . lived in Jerusalem and its vicinity; 10
70 temple servants lived in their towns 10
4:17 rest of their associates who live in Sama'ria 18
Neh 2: 3 Let the king live for ever! Why should not my face 5
3:26 temple servants living on Ophel repaired 10
4:12 When the Jews who lived by them came they said 10
12 From all the places where they live •
6:11 man such as I could go into the temple and live? 5
7:73 priests . . and all Israel, lived in their towns. 10
9:29 by the observance of which a man shall live 5
11: 1 Now the leaders of the people lived in Jerusalem; 10
1 one out of ten to live in Jerusalem the holy city 10
2 men who willingly offered to live in Jerusalem. 10
3 chiefs of the province who lived in Jerusalem; 10
3 every one lived on his property in their towns 10
4 Jerusalem lived certain of the sons of Judah 10
6 sons of Perez who lived in Jerusalem were 468 10
21 temple servants lived on Ophel; 10
25 some . . lived in Kir'iath-ar'ba and its villages 10
31 people of Benjamin also lived from Geba onward •
13:16 Men of Tyre also, who lived in the city, 10
Est 4:11 king holds out the . . scepter that he may live. 5
9:19 Jews of the villages, who live in the open towns 10
Job 7:16 I loathe my life; I would not live for ever. 5
8:17 about the stoneheap; he lives among the rocks. 40
14:14 If a man die, shall he live again? 5
15:28 and has lived in desolate cities 15
18:19 no survivor where he used to live. 11
19:25 For I know that my Redeemer lives 4
21: 7 Why do the wicked live, reach old age 5
27: 2 As God lives, who has taken away my right 4
28: 4 open shafts in a valley away from where men live; 2
13 it is not found in the land of the living. 4
21 It is hid from the eyes of all living 4
30:23 death, and to the house appointed for all living. 4
42:16 after this Job lived 140 years 5
Ps 18:46 The LORD lives; and blessed be my rock 4
22:26 praise the LORD! May your hearts live for ever! 5
27:13 the goodness of the LORD in the land of the living! 4
42: 2 My soul thirsts for God, for the living God. 4
49: 9 that he should continue to live on for ever 5
18 Though, while he lives, he counts himself happy 8
52: 5 he will uproot you from the land of the living. 4
63: 4 I will bless thee as long as I live; 8
66: 9 who has kept us among the living 4
69:28 Let them be blotted out of the book of the living; 4
72: 5 May he live while the sun endures 62
15 Long may he live, may gold of Sheba be given to him! 5
84: 2 my heart and flesh sing for joy to the living God. 4

89:48 What man can live and never see death? 5
103: 5 who satisfies you with good as long as you live •
104:33 I will sing to the LORD as long as I live; 8
107:36 hungry dwell, and they establish a city to live in; 12
116: 2 therefore I will call on him as long as I live. 9
9 I walk before the LORD in the land of the living. 4
118:17 I shall not die, but I shall live, and recount 5
119:17 that I may live and observe thy word. 5
77 Let thy mercy come to me, that I may live; 5
116 according to thy promise, that I may live 5
144 give me understanding that I may live. 5
175 Let me live, that I may praise thee 5
142: 5 my refuge, my portion in the land of the living. 4
146: 2 I will praise the LORD as long as I live; 8
Prv 4: 4 keep my commandments, and live; 5
7: 2 keep my commandments and live 5
9: 6 Leave simpleness, and live 5
11:19 He who is steadfast in righteousness will live 5
15:27 but he who hates bribes will live. 5
19:10 It is not fitting for a fool to live in luxury •
21: 9 It is better to live in a corner of the housetop 10
19 It is better to live in a desert land 10
25:24 better to live in a corner of the housetop 10
Ecc 3:12 and enjoy themselves as long as they live; 8
4: 2 more fortunate than the living who are . . alive; 4
15 I saw all the living who move about under the sun 4
6: 3 and lives many years, so that the days . . are many 5
6 Even though he should live 1,000 years 5
8 knows how to conduct himself before the living? 4
12 good for man while he lives the few days of his 4
7: 2 end of all men, and the living will lay it to heart. 4
9: 3 and madness is in their hearts while they live 4
4 But he who is joined with all the living has hope 4
4 for a living dog is better than a dead lion. 4
5 For the living know that they will die 4
11: 8 if a man lives many years, let him rejoice in them 5
Sng 4:15 a garden fountain, a well of living water 4
Isa 8:19 they consult the dead on behalf of the living? 4
26:14 They are dead, they will not live; 5
19 Thy dead shall live, their bodies shall rise. 5
37: 4 king of Assyria has sent to mock the living God 4
17 words . . which he has sent to mock the living God. 4
38:11 I shall not see the LORD in the land of the living; 4
16 O Lord, by these things men live 5
19 The living, the living, he thanks thee, as I do 4
19 the living, he thanks thee, as I do this day; 4
49:18 As I live, says the LORD, you shall put them 4
53: 8 that he was cut off out of the land of the living 4
55: 3 come to me; hear, that your soul may live; 5
65:20 there be in it an infant that lives but a few days •
Jer 2:13 have forsaken me, the fountain of living waters 4
4: 2 if you swear, 'As the LORD lives,' in truth, in justice 4
5: 2 Though they say, "As the LORD lives 4
10:10 the LORD is the true God; he is the living God 4
11:19 let us cut him off from the land of the living 4
12:16 my people, to swear by my name, 'As the LORD lives 4
16:14 As the LORD lives who brought up the people 4
15 but 'As the LORD lives who brought up the people 4
17:13 forsaken the LORD, the fountain of living water. 4
21: 9 shall live and shall have his life as a prize 5
22:24 As I live, says the LORD 4
23: 7 when men shall no longer say, 'As the LORD lives 4
8 'As the LORD lives who brought up and led 4
36 and you pervert the words of the living God 4
27:12 and serve him and his people, and live. 5
17 serve the king of Babylon and live. 5
29: 5 Build houses and live in them; 10
28 exile will be long; build houses and live in them 10
32 shall not have any one living among this people 10
35: 7 but you shall live in tents all your days 10
7 that you may live many days in the land 5
10 but we have lived in tents 10
11 So we are living in Jerusalem. 10
38: 2 but he who goes out to the Chalde'ans shall live; 5
2 he shall have his life as a prize of war, and live. 5
16 to Jeremiah, "As the LORD lives, who made our souls 4
17 and you and your house shall live. 5
42:15 set your faces to enter Egypt and go to live there 2
17 to go to Egypt to live there shall die by the sword 2
22 in the place where you desire to go to live. 2
43: 2 not send you to say, 'Do not go to Egypt to live there'; 2
5 all the remnant of Judah who had returned to live 2
44: 8 in the land of Egypt where you have come to live 2
12 to come to the land of Egypt to live 2
14 who have come to live in the land of Egypt 2
26 saying, 'As the Lord GOD lives.' 4
28 who came to the land of Egypt to live 2
46:18 As I live, says the King, whose name is the LORD 4
49:16 you who live in the clefts of the rock 15
52:34 until the day of his death as long as he lived. 4
Lam 3:39 Why should a living man complain 4
4:20 Under his shadow we shall live among . . nations. 5
Ezk 3:21 he shall surely live, because he took warning; 5
5:11 Wherefore, as I live, says the Lord GOD 4
7:13 not return to what he has sold, while they live. 6
13:19 and keeping alive persons who should not live 5
14:16 as I live, says the Lord GOD, they would deliver 4
18 though these three men were in it, as I live 4
20 as I live, says the Lord GOD, they would deliver 4

Book	Ref	Context	No.
	16: 6	I said to you in your blood, 'Live	5
	46	who lived with her daughters to the north of you;	10
	46	your younger sister, who lived to the south of you	10
	48	As I live, says the Lord GOD	4
	17:16	As I live, says the Lord GOD	4
	19	Therefore thus says the Lord GOD: As I live, surely	4
	18: 3	As I live, says the Lord GOD	4
	9	he shall surely live, says the Lord GOD.	5
	13	shall he then live? He shall not live.	5
	13	shall he then live? He shall not live.	5
	17	he shall not die . . he shall surely live.	5
	19	to observe all my statutes, he shall surely live.	5
	21	he shall surely live; he shall not die.	5
	22	righteousness which he has done he shall live.	5
	23	rather that he should turn from his way and live?	5
	24	things that the wicked man does, shall he live?	5
	28	he shall surely live, he shall not die.	5
	32	says the Lord GOD; so turn, and live.	5
	20: 3	As I live, says the Lord GOD	4
	11	ordinances, by whose observance man shall live.	5
	13	ordinances, by whose observance man shall live;	5
	21	ordinances, by whose observance man shall live;	5
	31	As I live, says the Lord GOD	4
	33	As I live, says the Lord GOD	4
	26:20	or have a place in the land of the living.	4
	32:23	who spread terror in the land of the living.	4
	24	who spread terror in the land of the living	4
	25	terror . . was spread in the land of the living	4
	26	they spread terror in the land of the living.	4
	27	of the mighty men was in the land of the living.	4
	32	For he spread terror in the land of the living;	4
	33:10	waste away because of them; how then can we live?	5
	11	Say to them, As I live, says the Lord GOD	4
	11	but that the wicked turn from his way and live;	5
	12	the righteous shall not be able to live	5
	13	I say to the righteous that he shall surely live	5
	15	he shall surely live, he shall not die.	5
	16	what is lawful and right, he shall surely live.	5
	19	does what is lawful and right, he shall live by it.	5
	27	Say this to them, Thus says the Lord GOD: As I live	4
	34: 8	As I live, says the Lord GOD	4
	35: 6	therefore, as I live, says the Lord GOD	4
	11	as I live, says the Lord GOD, I will deal with you	4
	37: 3	he said to me, "Son of man, can these bones live?	5
	5	cause breath to enter you, and you shall live.	5
	6	and put breath in you, and you shall live;	5
	9	breathe upon these slain, that they may live.	5
	10	the breath came into them, and they lived	5
	14	I will put my Spirit within you, and you shall live	5
	45: 5	as their possession for cities to live in.	46
	47: 9	every living creature which swarms will live	4
	9	every living creature which swarms will live	5
	9	everything will live where the river goes.	4
Dan	2: 4	O king, live for ever! Tell your servants the dream	17
	30	any wisdom . . more than all the living	16
	3: 9	O king, live for ever!	17
	4:17	that the living may know that the Most High rules	16
	34	praised and honored him who lives for ever;	16
	5:10	queen said, "O king, live for ever!	17
	6: 6	said to him, "O King Darius, live for ever!	17
	20	O Daniel, servant of the living God,	16
	21	Then Daniel said to the king, "O king, live for ever	17
	26	before the God of Daniel, for he is the living God	16
	12: 7	heard him swear by him who lives for ever	4
Hos	1:10	it shall be said to them, "Sons of the living God.	4
	4:15	and swear not, "As the LORD lives.	4
	6: 2	he will raise us up, that we may live before him.	5
Ams	5: 4	to the house of Israel: "Seek me and live;	5
	6	Seek the LORD and live, lest he break out like fire	5
	14	Seek good, and not evil, that you may live;	5
	8:14	who swear . . and say, 'As thy god lives, O Dan,'	4
	14	O Dan,' and, 'As the way of Beer-sheba lives,'	4
Obd	1: 3	you who live in the clefts of the rock	15
Jon	4: 3	for it is better for me to die than to live.	8
	8	It is better for me to die than to live.	8
Hab	2: 4	but the righteous shall live by his faith.	5
Zep	2: 9	Therefore, as I live," says the LORD of hosts	4
Zec	1: 5	And the prophets, do they live for ever?	5
	10: 9	with their children they shall live and return.	5
	13: 3	You shall not live, for you speak lies	5
	14: 8	living waters shall flow out from Jerusalem	4
Mat	4: 4	written, 'Man shall not live by bread alone	40
	9:18	lay your hand on her, and she will live.	40
	16:16	You are the Christ, the Son of the living God.	40
	22:32	He is not God of the dead, but of the living.	40
	23:30	saying, 'If we had lived in the days of our fathers	33
	26:63	I adjure you by the living God	40
Mrk	5: 3	who lived among the tombs	47
	23	so that she may be made well, and live.	40
	7: 5	Why do your disciples not live	54
	12:27	He is not God of the dead, but of the living;	40
	44	put in everything she had, her whole living.	25
Lke	2:36	lived with her husband seven years	40
	4: 4	It is written, 'Man shall not live by bread alone.'	40
	7:25	those who . . live in luxury are in kings' courts.	65
	8:27	he lived not in a house but among the tombs.	48
	10:28	You have answered right; do this, and you will live.	40
	15:12	he divided his living between them.	25
	13	he squandered his property in loose living.	40
	30	who has devoured your living with harlots	25
	20:38	Now he is not God of the dead, but of the living	40
	38	all live to him.	40
	21: 4	put in all the living that she had.	25
	19	By your endurance you will gain your lives.	68
	24: 5	Why do you seek the living among the dead?	40
Joh	4:10	and he would have given you living water.	40
	11	where do you get that living water?	40
	50	Jesus said to him, "Go; your son will live.	40
	51	his servants . . told him that his son was living	40
	53	Jesus had said to him, "Your son will live";	40
	5:25	those who hear will live.	40
	6:51	I am the living bread which came down from heaven;	40
	51	if any one eats of this bread, he will live for ever;	40
	57	As the living Father sent me	40
	57	I live because of the Father	40
	57	he who eats me will live because of me.	40
	58	he who eats this bread will live for ever.	40
	7:38	shall flow rivers of living water.'	40
	11:25	who believes in me, though he die, yet shall he live	40
	26	whoever lives and believes in me	40
	14:19	because I live, you will live also.	40
	19	because I live, you will live also.	40
Act	1:20	let there be no one to live in it	46
	7: 2	in Mesopota'mia, before he lived in Haran	46
	4	lived in Haran	46
	4	this land in which you are now living;	46
	38	he received living oracles to give to us.	40
	9:22	confounded the Jews who lived in Damascus	46
	32	he came down also to the saints that lived at Lydda.	46
	10:42	judge of the living and the dead.	40
	11:29	send relief to the brethren who lived in Judea;	46
	13:27	For those who live in Jerusalem and their rulers	46
	14:15	turn from these vain things to a living God	40
	15:26	men who have risked their lives	68
	17:21	the foreigners who lived there	37
	24	God . . does not live in shrines made by man	46
	26	to live on all the face of the earth	46
	28	'In him we live and move and have our being'	40
	20:18	You yourselves know how I lived among you	29
	21:24	you yourself live in observance of the law.	58
	22:12	well spoken of by all the Jews who lived there	46
	22	he ought not to live.	40
	23: 1	I have lived before God in all good conscience	56
	25:24	shouting that he ought not to live any longer.	40
	26: 5	I have lived as a Pharisee.	40
	27:10	not only of . . the ship, but also of our lives.	68
	28: 4	justice has not allowed him to live.	40
	30	he lived there two whole years at his own expense	35
Rom	1:17	He who through faith is righteous shall live.	40
	6: 2	How can we who died to sin still live in it?	40
	8	we believe that we shall also live with him.	59
	10	but the life he lives he lives to God.	40
	10	but the life he lives he lives to God.	40
	7: 2	woman is bound . . to her husband as long as he lives;	40
	3	an adulteress if she lives with another man	29
	5	While we were living in the flesh	•
	8: 5	For those who live according to the flesh	33
	5	but those who live according to the Spirit	•
	12	not to the flesh, to live according to the flesh–	40
	13	if you live according to the flesh you will die	40
	13	put to death the deeds of the body you will live.	40
	9:26	they will be called 'sons of the living God.'	40
	10: 5	which is based on the law shall live by it.	40
	12: 1	to present your bodies as a living sacrifice	40
	16	Live in harmony with one another;	66
	14: 7	None of us lives to himself	40
	8	If we live, we live to the Lord	40
	8	If we live, we live to the Lord	40
	8	whether we live or whether we die, we are the Lord's.	40
	9	For to this end Christ died and lived again	40
	9	be Lord both of the dead and of the living.	40
	11	As I live, says the Lord, every knee shall bow to me	40
	15: 5	to live in such harmony with one another	66
1Co	5: 1	a man is living with his father's wife.	38
	7:12	she consents to live with him	50
	13	he consents to live with her	50
	29	who have wives live as though they had none	33
	39	A wife is bound to her husband as long as he lives.	40
	9: 6	have no right to refrain from working for a living?	•
	15:45	The first man Adam became a living being	40
2Co	3: 3	not with ink but with the Spirit of the living God	40
	4:11	while we live we are always being given up	40
	5: 1	if the earthly tent we live in is destroyed	51
	15	that those who live might live no longer	40
	15	that those who live might live no longer	40
	6: 9	as dying, and behold we live	40
	16	For we are the temple of the living God; as God said	40
	16	I will live in them and move among them	36
	10: 3	For though we live in the world	54
	13: 4	lives by the power of God	40
	4	in dealing with you we shall live with him	40
Gal	2:14	If you, though a Jew, live like a Gentile	40
	19	that I might live to God.	40
	20	it is no longer I who live	40
	20	Christ who lives in me	40
	20	the life I now live in the flesh I live by faith	40
	20	the life I now live in the flesh I live by faith	40
	3:11	He who through faith is righteous shall live";	40
	12	He who does them shall live by them.	40
	5:25	If we live by the Spirit	40
Eph	1:12	to live for the praise of his glory.	33
	2: 3	Among these we all once lived	21
	4:17	you must no longer live as the Gentiles do	54
Php	1:21	For to me to live is Christ, and to die is gain.	40
	3:17	mark those who so live as you have an example in us	54
	18	live as enemies of the cross of Christ.	54
Col	2: 6	so live in him	54
	20	you live as if you still belonged to the world	40
	3: 7	In these you once walked, when you lived in them.	40
1Th	1: 9	to serve a living and true God	20
	3: 8	for now we live, if you stand fast in the Lord.	40
	4: 1	how you ought to live and to please God	54
	5:10	whether we wake or sleep we might live with him.	40
2Th	3: 6	any brother who is living in idleness	54
	11	we hear that some of you are living in idleness	54
	12	to earn their own living.	23
1Ti	3:15	which is the church of the living God	40
	4:10	because we have our hope set on the living God	40
	5: 6	she . . is dead even while she lives.	40
2Ti	2:11	If we have died with him, we shall also live with him;	59
	3:12	all who desire to live a godly life in Christ	40
	4: 1	who is to judge the living and the dead	40
Tit	2:12	to live sober, upright, and godly lives in this world	40
	12	to live sober, upright, and godly lives in this world	•
Heb	3:12	leading you to fall away from the living God.	40
	4:12	For the word of God is living and active	40
	5:13	every one who lives on milk	49
	7: 8	one of whom it is testified that he lives.	40
	25	since he always lives to make intercession	40
	9:14	to serve the living God.	40
	10:20	by the new and living way which he opened for us	40
	31	to fall into the hands of the living God.	40
	38	my righteous one shall live by faith	40
	11: 9	living in tents with Isaac and Jacob	46
	12: 9	be subject to the Father of spirits and live?	40
	22	the city of the living God	40
Jas	4:15	If the Lord wills, we shall live	40
1Pe	1: 3	we have been born anew to a living hope	40
	23	through the living and abiding word of God;	40
	2: 4	Come to him, to the living stone, rejected by men	40
	5	like living stones be yourselves built	40
	16	Live as free men, yet without using your freedom	•
	16	but live as servants of God.	•
	24	we might die to sin and live to righteousness.	40
	3: 7	husbands, live considerately with your wives	64
	4: 2	so as to live for the rest of the time in the flesh	27
	3	living in licentiousness, passions	57
	5	who is ready to judge the living and the dead.	40
	6	they might live in the spirit like God.	40
2Pe	2: 8	saw and heard as he lived among them	32
	18	escaped from those who live in error.	21
	3:11	in lives of holiness and godliness	22
1Jn	1: 6	we lie and do not live according to the truth;	55
	3:16	we ought to lay down our lives for the brethren.	68
	4: 9	so that we might live through him.	40
Rev	4: 9	thanks to him . . who lives for ever and ever	40
	10	worship him who lives for ever and ever;	40
	7: 2	another angel . . with the seal of the living God	40
	17	and he will guide them to springs of living water;	41
	8: 9	a third of the living creatures in the sea died	39
	10: 6	swore by him who lives for ever and ever	40
	12:11	they loved not their lives even unto death.	68
	13:14	which was wounded by the sword and yet lived;	40
	15: 7	the wrath of God who lives for ever and ever;	40
1Es	2: 6	let each man, wherever he may live, be helped	50
	16	living in Samaria and other places	50
	16	against those who were living in Judea	46
	25	living in Samaria and Syria and Phoenicia	50
	4:38	lives and prevails for ever and ever.	40
	5:73	as long as King Cyrus lived	41
2Es	2:14	because I live, says the Lord.	76
	3: 2	and the wealth of those who lived in Babylon.	72
	4:12	to come here and live in ungodliness	76
	26	and if you live long, you will often marvel	76
	51	Do you think that I shall live until those days?	76
	5: 4	if the Most High grants that you live	76
	45	If therefore all creatures will live at one time	•
	6:21	and these shall live and dance.	76
	51	to live in it, where there are 1,000 mountains;	73
	7:14	the living pass through the difficult and vain	76
	21	what they should do to live	76
	46	who among the living is there	74
	82	make a good repentance that they may live.	76
	89	During the time that they lived in it	‡
	109	for the one who was dead, that he might live	76
	117	For what good is it to all that they live in sorrow	76
	121	but we have lived wickedly?	69
	124	because we have lived in unseemly places?	69
	126	For while we lived and committed iniquity	76
	129	Choose for yourself life, that you may live!'	76
	136	abound more and more to those now living	75
	8: 5	for you have been given only a short time to live.	76
	6	by which every mortal . . may be able to live.	76
	25	For as long as I live I will speak	76
	28	those who have lived wickedly in thy sight	69
	9:43	though I lived with my husband 30 years.	71
	12:33	he will set them living before his judgment seat	77

13:41 where mankind had never lived 73
14: 9 and henceforth you shall live with my Son 70
22 those who wish to live in the last days may live. 76
22 those who wish to live in the last days may live. 76
15:10 I will not allow them to live any longer 72
14 Alas for the world and for those who live in it! 72
16:22 many of those who live on the earth shall perish 73
42 be like one who will not live in it; 72
Tob 3: 6 it is better for me to die than to live 40
15 Why should I live? 40
4: 5 Live uprightly all the days of your life 55
7 Give alms . . to all who live uprightly 55
5: 3 I will pay him wages as long as I live 40
6:14 the lives of my father and mother 41
8:17 and bring their lives to fulfilment in health 41
12: 6 exalt him . . in the presence of all the living 40
10 who commit sin are the enemies of their own lives. 41
13: 1 Blessed is God who lives for ever 40
4 exalt him in the presence of all the living; 40
14:10 do not live in Nineveh any longer 24
Jdt 1: 6 all those who lived along the Euphrates 46
7 sent to all who lived in Persia 46
7 all who lived in the west 46
7 those who lived in Cilicia and Damascus 46
7 all who lived along the seacoast 46
10 all who lived in Egypt 46
11 all who lived in the whole region 46
2:12 as I live, and by the power of my kingdom 40
23 the Ishmaelites who lived along the desert *
28 the people who lived along the seacoast 46
28 those who lived in Sur and Ocina 46
28 all who lived in Jamnia 46
28 Those who lived in Azotus and Ascalon 46
4: 1 the people of Israel living in Judea 46
11 their children, living at Jerusalem 46
5: 3 what people . . lives in the hill country 44
4 they alone, of all who live in the west 46
7 At one time they lived in Mesopotamia 52
8 lived there for a long time. 52
10 and lived there as long as they had food 52
15 they lived in the land of the Amorites 50
16 lived there a long time. 46
7:10 the height of the mountains where they live 36
27 for we will be slaves, but our lives will be spared 68
8: 4 Judith had lived at home as a widow 33
24 their lives depend upon us 68
10: 2 the house where she lived on sabbaths 31
3 while her husband Manasseh was living. 41
11: 2 your people who live in the hill country 46
4 Have courage; you will live 40
7 Nebuchadnezzar . . lives 40
7 will live by your power under Nebuchadnezzar 40
14 the people living there have been doing this 46
23 shall live in the house of King Nebuchadnezzar 44
12: 4 Judith replied, "As your soul lives, my lord 40
13:16 As the Lord lives, who has protected me 40
14: 4 you and all who live within the borders of Israel 46
15: 8 who lived at Jerusalem 46
AEs 13: 2 to settle the lives of my subjects 25
17 that we may live and sing praise to thy name, O Lord; 40
16:16 sons of the Most High, the most mighty living God 40
19 permit the Jews to live under their own laws. 67
Wis 1:13 he does not delight in the death of the living. 40
4:10 while living among sinners he was taken up. 40
16 will condemn the ungodly who are living 40
5:15 the righteous live for ever 40
7:28 nothing so much as the man who lives with wisdom. 64
8: 3 She glorifies her noble birth by living with God 61
9 I determined to take her to live with me 60
12: 6 these parents who murder helpless lives 68
23 those who in folly of life lived unrighteously 27
13: 7 as they live among his works they keep searching 21
14: 5 therefore men trust their lives 68
17 since they lived at a distance 50
22 they live in great strife due to ignorance 40
24 keep either their lives or their marriages pure 25
28 prophesy lies, or live unrighteously 40
15:11 and breathed into him a living spirit. 43
18:12 the living were not sufficient even to bury them 40
23 and cut off its way to the living. 40
Sir 0: 1 make . . progress in living according to the law 28
3 prepared . . to live according to the law. 26
3:12 do not grieve him as long as he lives; 41
4: 1 My son, deprive not the poor of his living 41
7:33 Give graciously to all the living 40
9:12 not be held guiltless as long as they live. 19
13: 5 If you own something, he will live with you 60
16:30 with all kinds of living beings 42
18: 1 He who lives for ever created the whole universe; 40
25: 7 a man who lives to see the downfall of his foes; 40
8 happy is he who lives with an intelligent wife 64
33:19 as long as you live 41
34:13 The spirit of those who fear the Lord will live 40
22 To take away a neighbor's living is to murder him; 34
37:26 his name will live for ever. 40
27 My son, test your soul while you live 41
38:32 men can neither sojourn nor live there. 54
39: 9 his name will live through all generations. 40
41:19 of theft, in the place where you live 52
42:23 All these things live and remain for ever 40
44: 9 who have perished as though they had not lived; 65
14 their name lives to all generations. 40
45:16 He chose him out of all the living 40
50:26 Those who live on Mount Seir, and the Philistines 44
Bar 1:12 we shall live under the protection 40
3:37 she appeared upon earth and lived among men. 63
4: 1 All who hold her fast will live 41
LJr 1: 7 and he is watching your lives. 68
46 The men . . will certainly not live very long themselves 29
Sus 1: 1 a man living in Babylon whose name was Joakim. 50
Bel 1: 5 the living God, who created heaven and earth 40
6 Do you not think that Bel is a living God? 40
24 You cannot deny that this is a living god 40
25 he is the living God. 40
1Mc 2:13 Why should we live any longer? 41
20 will live by the covenant of our fathers. 57
33 do what the king commands, and you will live. 40
40 refuse to fight with the Gentiles for our lives 68
50 give your lives for the covenant of our fathers. 68
3:21 we fight for our lives and our laws. 68
4:35 how ready they were either to live or to die nobly 40
5: 2 the descendants of Jacob who lived among them. 33
9 the Israelites who lived in their territory 33
6:23 to live by what he said and to follow his commands. 57
55 King Antiochus while still living 40
59 let them live by their laws as they did before 57
9: 9 Let us rather save our own lives now 68
44 Let us rise up now and fight for our lives 68
58 his men are living in quiet and confidence 46
71 he would not try to harm him as long as he lived. 41
10:37 let them live by their own laws 57
12:51 they would fight for their lives 68
2Mc 6: 1 and cease to live by the laws of God 56
25 for the sake of living a brief moment longer 40
26 yet whether I live or die 40
7:33 if our living Lord is angry for a little while 40
9: 9 while he was still living in anguish and pain 40
11:25 live according to the customs of . . 56
12: 3 the Jews who lived among them 50
14:10 For as long as Judas lives 53
15: 4 the living Lord himself, the Sovereign in heaven 40
3Mc 3: 1 those Jews who lived in Alexandria 45
8 they lived under tyranny 30
6: 6 had voluntarily surrendered their lives to the flames 68
10 our lives have become entangled in impieties 25
28 the sons of the almighty and living God of heaven 40
7: 6 we barely spared their lives 40
4Mc 5:22 as though living by it were irrational 27
26 to eat what will be most suitable for our lives 68
36 nor my long life lived lawfully. 25
6:18 who have lived in accordance with truth to old age 40
7:19 do not die to God, but live in God. 40
8:26 when we can live in peace if we obey the king? 40
9: 7 if you take our lives because of our religion 68
11: 5 and live according to his virtuous law? 40
13:13 who gave us our lives 68
24 and brought up in right living 25
16:25 those who die for the sake of God live in God 40
17:18 and live through blessed eternity. 27
18:17 'Shall these dry bones live?' 40

live abroad 1. *παροικία*
Sir 0: 3 publish the book for those living abroad 1

live according 1. *ποιέω*
Sir 51:18 For I resolved to live according to wisdom 1

live again 1. *ἀντικαταλλάσσω* 2. revivesco
2Es 14:35 the judgment will come, when we shall live again; 2
Sir 46:12 live again in their sons! 1

live among 1. *ἐννέμω* 2. *παροικέω*
2Mc 12: 8 to wipe out the Jews who were living among them 2
3Mc 3:25 you are to send to us those who live among you 1

live as a philosopher 1. *φιλόσοφος*
4Mc 7:21 What person who lives as a philosopher 1

live at peace 1. *εἰρηνεύω*
Sir 41: 1 one who lives at peace among his possessions 1

live hereafter 1. sum
2Es 8:46 are for those who will live hereafter. 1

live in harmony 1. *συμπεριφέρω*
Sir 25: 1 a wife and a husband who live in harmony. 1

live in luxury 1. שְׁמַן חֵלֶק 2. *τρυφάω*
Hab 1:16 by them he lives in luxury, and his food is rich. 1
Jas 5: 5 You have lived on the earth in luxury 2
Sir 14: 4 others will live in luxury on his goods. 2

live in peace 1. *εἰρηνεύω*
2Co 13:11 agree with one another, live in peace 1

live in pleasure 1. *σπαταλάω*
Jas 5: 5 You have lived on the earth . . in pleasure; 1

live long 1. ארך 2. ארך יָמִים 3. חיה 4. *ἐμμένω* 5. *μακρόβιος* 6. *μακροχρόνιος* 7. *μόνος*
Deu 4:26 you will not live long upon it 2
5:33 and that you may live long in the land 1
11: 9 that you may live long in the land 2
22: 7 may go well with you, and that you may live long. 2
30:18 not live long in the land which you . . possess. 2
32:47 thereby you shall live long in the land 2
2Sm 16:16 Long live the king! Long live the king! 3
16 Long live the king! Long live the king! 3
2Kg 11:12 they clapped . . and said, "Long live the king! 3
Eph 6: 3 that you may live long on the earth. 6
Wis 3:17 Even if they live long 5
Sir 39:11 if he lives long 4
1Mc 7:38 and let them live no longer. 7

make live 1. חיה 2. vivifico
Isa 38:16 Oh, restore me to health and make me live! 1
2Es 8:13 for he is thy creation; and thou wilt make him live 2

live now 1. praesens
2Es 8:46 Things that are present are for those who live now 1

live on 1. *σιτέομαι*
2Mc 5:27 they continued to live on what grew wild 1

live out 1. *ἐπιζάω*
4Mc 18: 9 who lived out his life with good children 1

live out half 1. חצה
Ps 55:23 treachery shall not live out half their days. 1

live peaceably 1. *εἰρηνεύω*
Rom 12:18 If possible . . live peaceably with all. 1
Sir 44: 6 living peaceably in their habitations 1
2Mc 12: 4 because they wished to live peaceably 1

live piously 1. *εὐσεβέω*
4Mc 9: 6 the aged men . . lived piously while enduring torture 1

live quietly 1. *εὐσταθέω* 2. *ἡσυχάζω*
1Th 4:11 to aspire to live quietly 2
2Mc 12: 2 Nicanor . . would not let them live quietly and in peace. 1

live subject 1. *πολιτεύομαι*
4Mc 2:23 one who lives subject to this will rule a kingdom 1

live together 1. *συζάω*
2Co 7: 3 to die together and to live together. 1

livelihood 1. *βίος*
Sir 31: 4 The poor man toils as his livelihood diminishes 1

liver 1. כָּבֵד 2. *ἧπαρ*
Exd 29:13 take . . the appendage of the liver 1
22 take . . the appendage of the liver 1
Lev 3: 4 the appendage of the liver which he shall take 1
10 the appendage of the liver which he shall take 1
15 appendage of the liver which he shall take away 1
4: 9 the appendage of the liver which he shall take 1
7: 4 the appendage of the liver which he shall take 1
8:16 he took . . the appendage of the liver 1
25 he took . . the appendage of the liver 1
9:10 the kidneys and the appendage of the liver 1
19 the kidneys, and the appendage of the liver 1
Ezk 21:21 he consults the teraphim, he looks at the liver. 1
Tob 6: 4 take the heart and liver and gall 2
6 of what use is the liver and heart and gall 2
7 He replied, "As for the heart and liver 2
16 some of the heart and liver of the fish 2
8: 2 and put the heart and liver of the fish upon them 2

where one lives 1. *οἴκησις*
Jdt 7:14 strewn about in the streets where they live. 1

livestock 1. מִקְנֶה 2. רְכוּשׁ
Gen 31:18 he drove away all his cattle, all his livestock 2
Num 35: 3 pasture lands shall be . . for their livestock 2
1Ch 5:21 They carried off their livestock 1

living man 1. חַי
Ps 143: 2 for no man living is righteous before thee. 1

now living 1. praesens
2Es 7:20 Let many perish who are now living 1
14:20 I will reprove the people who are now living 1

living one 1. *ζάω*
Rev 1:18 and the living one; I died, and behold I am alive 1

living thing 1. חַי 2. חַיָּה 3. יְקוּם 4. *ψυχὴ ζωή*
Gen 1:28 dominion . . over every living thing that moves 2
6:19 of every living thing of all flesh 1
7: 4 every living thing that I have made 3
23 He blotted out every living thing 3

8:17 Bring . . every living thing that is with you 2
Lev 11: 2 These are the living things which you may eat 2
Deu 11: 6 tents, and every living thing that followed them 3
Job 12:10 In his hand is the life of every living thing 1
Ps 104:25 living things both small and great. 2
145:16 satisfiest the desire of every living thing. 1
Rev 16: 3 and every living thing died that was in the sea. 4

lizard 1. לְטָאָה 2. שְׂמָמִית

Lev 11:30 the gecko, the land crocodile, the lizard 1
Prv 30:28 lizards you can take in your hands 2

lo 1. הֵן 2. הִנֵּה 3. אֲרוּ (A) 4. *ἰδού*

Gen 8:11 and lo, in her mouth a freshly plucked olive leaf; 2
15:12 and lo, a dread and great darkness fell upon him. 2
19:28 and beheld, and lo, the smoke of the land went up 2
29: 2 lo, three flocks of sheep lying beside it; 2
37: 7 and lo, my sheaf arose and stood upright; 2
39: 8 his master's wife, "Lo, having me my master has no 1
48:11 and lo, God has let me see your children also. 2
Exd 2: 6 saw the child; and lo, the babe was crying. 2
3: 2 a bush; and he looked, and lo, the bush was burning 2
18: 6 when one told Moses, "Lo, your father-in-law Jethro 4
19: 9 the LORD said to Moses, "Lo, I am coming to you 2
Num22:38 Balaam said to Balak, "Lo, I have come to you! 2
23: 6 lo, he and all the princes of Moab were standing 2
9 lo, a people dwelling alone 1
17 lo, he was standing beside his burnt offering 2
Deu 22:17 lo, he has made shameful charges against her 2
Jos 14:10 and now, lo, I am this day 85 years old. 2
Jdg 7:13 Behold, I dreamed a dream; and lo, a cake of barley 2
13: 5 for lo, you shall conceive and bear a son. No razor 2
1Sm 21:14 Lo, you see the man is mad; why then have you 2
24:10 Lo, this day your eyes have seen how the LORD gave 2
25:36 lo, he was holding a feast in his house 2
2Sm 1: 6 and lo, the chariots and the horsemen were close 2
15:24 And Abi'athar came up, and lo, Zadok came also 2
24:17 David spoke . . and said, "Lo, I have sinned 2
1Kg 1:51 for, lo, he has laid hold of the horns of the altar 2
2Kg 1:14 Lo, fire came down . . and consumed the two 2
6:20 they saw; and lo, they were in the midst of Sama'ria. 2
7:15 and, lo, all the way was littered with garments 2
13:21 as a man was being buried, lo, a . . band was seen 2
2Ch 29: 9 For lo, our fathers have fallen by the sword 2
Job 5:27 Lo, this we have searched out; it is true. 2
9:11 Lo, he passes by me, and I see him not; 1
13: 1 Lo, my eye has seen all this 1
26:14 Lo, these are but the outskirts of his ways; 1
Ps 11: 2 for lo, the wicked bend the bow 2
37:36 Again I passed by, and, lo, he was no more; 2
40: 7 Lo, I come; in the roll of the book it is written of me; 2
9 lo, I have not restrained my lips, as thou knowest 2
48: 4 lo, the kings assembled, they came on together. 2
59: 3 For, lo, they lie in wait for my life; 2
68:33 lo, he sends forth his voice, his mighty voice. 1
73:27 For lo, those who are far from thee shall perish; 2
83: 2 For lo, thy enemies are in tumult; 2
92: 9 For, lo, thy enemies, O LORD, for, lo, thy enemies 2
9 O LORD, for, lo, thy enemies shall perish; 2
127: 3 Lo, sons are a heritage from the LORD 2
128: 4 Lo, thus shall the man be blessed who fears 2
132: 6 Lo, we heard of it in Eph'rathah, we found it 2
139: 4 lo, O LORD, thou knowest it altogether. 1
Prv 7:10 lo, a woman meets him, dressed as a harlot 2
24:31 lo, it was all overgrown with thorns; 2
Sng 2:11 lo, the winter is past, the rain is over and gone. 2
Isa 5:26 and lo, swiftly, speedily it comes! 2
25: 9 It will be said on that day, "Lo, this is our God; 2
38:17 Lo, it was for my welfare 2
49:12 Lo, these shall come from afar 2
12 and lo, these from the north and from the west 2
Jer 1:15 For, lo, I am calling all the tribes of the kingdoms 2
4:23 I looked on the earth, and lo, it was waste and void; 2
24 looked on the mountains, and lo, they were quaking 2
25 I looked, and lo, there was no man 2
26 I looked, and lo, the fruitful land was a desert 2
8: 9 lo, they have rejected the word of the LORD 2
30:10 O Israel; for lo, I will save you from afar 2
46:27 for lo, I will save you from afar 2
50:12 Lo, she shall be the last of the nations 2
Ezk 2: 9 a hand . . and, lo, a written scroll was in it; 2
3:23 and, lo, the glory of the LORD stood there 2
8: 2 Then I beheld, and, lo, a form 2
8 and when I dug in the wall, lo, there was a door. 2
17 Lo, they put the branch to their nose. 2
9: 2 lo, six men came from the direction of the upper 2
11 lo, the man clothed in linen, with the writing case 2
15: 4 Lo, it is given to the fire for fuel; 2
23:39 And lo, this is what they did in my house. 2
40 far, to whom a messenger was sent, and lo, they came. 2
30: 9 the day of Egypt's doom; for, lo, it comes! 2
21 and lo, it has not been bound up, to heal it 2
33:32 lo, you are to them like one who sings love songs 2
37: 2 and lo, they were very dry. 2
Dan 7: 6 After this I looked, and lo, another, like a leopard 3
10:20 lo, the prince of Greece will come. 2
Ams 4:13 For lo, he who forms the mountains 2
7: 1 and lo, it was the latter growth after the king's 2

9: 9 For lo, I will command, and shake the house 2
Hab 1: 6 For lo, I am rousing the Chalde'ans 2
Hag 1: 9 You have looked for much, and, lo, it came to little; 2
Zec 2:10 lo, I come and I will dwell in the midst of you 2
9: 4 But lo, the Lord will strip her of her possessions 2
9 O daughter of Jerusalem! Lo, your king comes to you; 2
11: 6 Lo, I will cause men to fall 2
16 For lo, I am raising up in the land a shepherd 2
12: 2 Lo, I am about to make Jerusalem a cup of reeling 2
Mat 2: 9 and lo, the star which they had seen in the East 4
3:17 lo, a voice from heaven, saying, "This is my beloved 4
17: 5 He was still speaking, when lo, a bright cloud 4
19:27 Lo, we have left everything and followed you 4
24:23 Then if any one says to you, 'Lo, here is the Christ!' 4
25 Lo, I have told you beforehand. 4
26 So, if they say to you, 'Lo, he is in the wilderness,' 4
26 if they say, 'Lo, he is in the inner rooms' 4
28: 7 Lo, I have told you. 4
20 lo, I am with you always, to the close of the age. 4
Mrk 10:28 Lo, we have left everything and followed you. 4
Lke 13: 7 Lo, these three years I have come seeking fruit 4
15:29 Lo, these many years I have served you 4
17:21 nor will they say, 'Lo, here it is!' or 'There!' 4
23 they will say to you, 'Lo, there!' or 'Lo, here!' 4
23 they will say to you, 'Lo, there!' or 'Lo, here!' 4
18:28 Lo, we have left our homes and followed you. 4
Act 27:24 lo, God has granted you all those who sail with you.' 4
1Co 15:51 Lo! I tell you a mystery 4
Heb 10: 7 I said, 'Lo, I have come to do thy will, O God,' 4
9 he added, "Lo, I have come to do thy will. 4
Rev 4: 1 After this I looked, and lo, in heaven an open door! 4
2 I was in the Spirit, and lo, a throne stood in heaven 4
5: 5 lo, the Lion of the tribe of Judah . . has conquered 4
14: 1 Then I looked, and lo, on Mount Zion stood the Lamb 4
14 Then I looked, and lo, a white cloud 4
16:15 ("Lo, I am coming like a thief! 4
Jdt 9: 6 'Lo, we are here' 4
Sir 24:31 lo, my canal became a river 4

load 1. טען 2. טרח 3. כבד 4. מַשָּׂא 5. נשא 6. עמס 7. *ἐπιτίθημι* 8. *φορτίζω* 9. *φορτίον* 10. gravo

Gen 42:26 Then they loaded their asses with their grain 5
44:13 rent their clothes, and every man loaded his ass 6
45:17 Say to your brothers, 'Do this: load your beasts 1
23 he sent as follows: ten asses loaded with the good 5
23 sent . . ten she-asses loaded with grain, bread 5
2Kg 8: 9 all kinds of goods of Damascus, 40 camel loads. 4
Neh 13:15 heaps of grain and loading them on asses; 6
Job 37:11 He loads the thick cloud with moisture; 2
Isa 46: 1 are loaded as burdens on weary beasts. 6
Lam 5:13 and boys stagger under loads of wood. *
Hab 2: 6 and loads himself with pledges! 3
Lke 11:46 you load men with burdens hard to bear 8
Gal 6: 5 For each man will have to bear his own load. 9
2Es 2:18 twelve trees loaded with various fruits 10
Jdt 15:11 she took them and loaded her mule 7

loaf 1. כִּכָּר 2. לֶחֶם 3. *ἄρτος*

Exd 29:23 one loaf of bread, and one cake of bread with oil 1
Lev 23:17 bring . . two loaves of bread to be waved *
Jdg 8: 5 Pray, give loaves of bread to the people who 1
1Sm 2:36 implore . . for a piece of silver or a loaf of bread 1
10: 3 another carrying three loaves of bread 1
4 will greet you and give you two loaves of bread *
17:17 an ephah of . . parched grain, and these ten loaves 2
21: 3 Give me five loaves of bread, or whatever is here. *
25:18 Ab'igail made haste, and took 200 loaves 2
2Sm 16: 1 a couple of asses . . bearing 200 loaves of bread *
1Kg 14: 3 Take with you ten loaves, some cakes, and a jar 2
2Kg 4:42 bringing . . twenty loaves of barley 2
1Ch 16: 3 loaf of bread, a portion of meat, and a cake 1
Prv 6:26 for a harlot may be hired for a loaf of bread 1
Jer 37:21 and a loaf of bread was given him daily 1
Mat 14:17 We have only five loaves here and two fish. 3
19 and taking the five loaves and the two fish 3
19 broke and gave the loaves to the disciples 3
15:34 Jesus said to them, "How many loaves have you? 3
36 he took the seven loaves and the fish 3
16: 9 Do you not remember the five loaves 3
10 Or the seven loaves of the 4,000 3
Mrk 6:38 How many loaves have you? Go and see. 3
41 taking the five loaves and the two fish 3
41 blessed, and broke the loaves 3
44 those who ate the loaves were 5,000 men. 3
52 for they did not understand about the loaves 3
8: 5 he asked them, "How many loaves have you? 3
6 he took the seven loaves 3
14 they had only one loaf with them in the boat. 3
19 I broke the five loaves for the 5,000 3
Lke 9:13 We have no more than five loaves and two fish 3
16 taking the five loaves and the two fish 3
11: 5 Friend, lend me three loaves; 3
Joh 6: 9 a lad here who has five barley loaves and two fish; 3
11 Jesus then took the loaves 3
13 fragments from the five barley loaves 3
26 because you ate your fill of the loaves. 3
2Mc 1: 8 we lighted the lamps and we set out the loaves. 3

loaf of bread 1. *ἄρτος*

Mat 4: 3 command these stones to become loaves of bread. 1

loan 1. שְׁאֵלָה 2. *δάνος*

1Sm 2:20 give you children . . for the loan which she lent 1
Sir 29: 4 Many persons regard a loan as a windfall 2
5 will kiss another's hands until he gets a loan *

loath

Job 20:13 he is loath to let it go, and holds it in his mouth †

loathe 1. בוס 2. געל 3. זהם 4. לאה 5. מאס 6. קוט 7. קוץ 8. שנא 9. תעב 10. *βδελύσσομαι*

Exd 7:18 will loathe to drink water from the Nile. 4
Num21: 5 no food and . . we loathe this worthless food. 7
Job 7:16 I loathe my life; I would not live for ever. 5
9:21 I regard not myself; I loathe my life. 5
10: 1 I loathe my life; 6
33:20 that his life loathes bread 3
Ps 95:10 40 years I loathed that generation and said 6
107:18 they loathed any kind of food 9
139:21 do I not loathe them that rise up against thee? 6
Prv 27: 7 He who is sated loathes honey 1
Isa 14:19 cast out . . like a loathed untimely birth 9
Jer 14:19 Does thy soul loathe Zion? 2
Ezk 16:37 all those you loved and all those you loathed; 8
45 mother, who loathed her husband and her children; 2
45 your sisters, who loathed their husbands 2
20:43 you shall loathe yourselves for all the evils 6
36:31 you will loathe yourselves for your iniquities 6
Sir 11: 2 nor loathe a man because of his appearance. 10
16: 8 whom he loathed on account of their insolence. 10
20: 8 Whoever uses too many words will be loathed 10

loathing 1. *βδελύσσομαι*

Wis 11:24 hast loathing for none of the things 1

loathsome 1. דְּוַי 2. זָרָא 3. חנן 4. קוט 5. רַע 6. שֶׁקֶץ

Num11:20 month, until it . . becomes loathsome to you 2
Job 2: 7 Satan . . afflicted Job with loathsome sores 5
6: 7 they are as food that is loathsome to me. 1
19:17 loathsome to the sons of my own mother. 3
Ezk 6: 9 they will be loathsome in their own sight 4
8:10 kinds of creeping things, and loathsome beasts 6

local 1. *χώρα*

Act 28:17 he called together the local leaders of the Jews *
LJr 1:14 Like a local ruler the god holds a scepter 1

locality 1. *τόπος*

3Mc 2:26 he framed evil reports in the various localities; 1

lock 1. נעל 2. *κλεῖθρον* 3. *κλείω*

Jdg 3:23 of the roof chamber upon him, and locked them. 1
24 saw that the doors of the roof chamber were locked 1
Sng 4:12 A garden locked is my sister, my bride 1
12 my bride, a garden locked, a fountain sealed. 1
Act 5:23 We found the prison securely locked 3
LJr 1:18 make . . secure with doors and locks and bars 2

lock (2) 1. מַחְלָפָה 2. פֶּרַע 3. צִיצִת 4. קְוֻצּוֹת 5. *πλόκαμος*

Num 6: 5 shall let the locks of hair of his head grow long. 2
Jdg 16:13 If you weave the seven locks of my head 1
14 Deli'lah took the seven locks of his head and wove *
19 and had him shave off the seven locks of his head. 1
Sng 5: 2 wet with dew, my locks with the drops of the night. 4
11 his locks are wavy, black as a raven. 4
Ezk 8: 3 the form of a hand, and took me by a lock of my head; 3
44:20 shave their heads or let their locks grow long; 2
3Mc 1: 4 wailing and tears, her locks all disheveled 5

lock up 1. *καταδέω* 2. *κλείω*

Sir 28:24 lock up your silver and gold 1
42: 6 where there are many hands, lock things up. 2

flowing locks 1. דַּלַּת רֹאשׁ

Sng 7: 5 and your flowing locks are like purple; 1

locust 1. אַרְבֶּה 2. גֵּב 3. גֹּבַי 4. גוֹב 5. גָּזָם 6. חָגָב 7. יֶלֶק 8. צְלָצַל 9. *ἀκρίς* 10. locusta

Exd 10: 4 tomorrow I will bring locusts into your country 1
12 Stretch out your hand . . for the locusts 1
13 the east wind had brought the locusts. 1
14 the locusts came up over all the land of Egypt 1
14 such a dense swarm of locusts as had never been 1
19 wind, which lifted the locusts and drove them 1
19 not a single locust was left in all the country 1
Lev 11:22 you may eat: the locust according to its kind 1
Deu 28:38 gather little in; for the locust shall consume 1
42 trees and the fruit . . locust shall possess. 8
Jdg 6: 5 would come up . . coming like locusts for number; 1
7:12 lay along the valley like locusts for multitude; 1
1Kg 8:37 pestilence or blight or mildew or locust 1
2Ch 6:28 if there is . . mildew or locust or caterpillar; 1
7:13 When I . . command the locust to devour the land 6
Job 39:20 Do you make him leap like the locust? 1
Ps 78:46 the fruit of their labor to the locust. 1

105:34 He spoke, and the locusts came, and young locusts 1
109:23 I am shaken off like a locust. 1
Prv 30:27 locusts have no king, yet all of them march in rank; 1
Isa 33: 4 as locusts leap, men leap upon it. 2
Jer 46:23 because they are more numerous than locusts; 1
51:14 Surely I will fill you with men, as many as locusts 7
27 bring up horses like bristling locusts. 7
Ams 4: 9 and your olive trees the locust devoured; 5
7: 1 behold, he was forming locusts 3
Nah 3:15 It will devour you like the locust. 7
15 Multiply yourselves like the locust 7
16 The locust spreads its wings and flies away. 7
17 your scribes like clouds of locusts 4
Mat 3: 4 waist; and his food was locusts and wild honey. 9
Mrk 1: 6 ate locusts and wild honey. 9
Rev 9: 3 Then from the smoke came locusts on the earth 9
7 the locusts were like horses arrayed for battle; 9
2Es 4:24 why we pass from the world like locusts 10
Jdt 2:20 a mixed crowd like a swarm of locusts 9
Wis 16: 9 were killed by the bites of locusts and flies 9
Sir 43:17 its descent is like locusts alighting. 9

bald locust 1. סָלְעָם
Lev 11:22 may eat . . the bald locust according to its kind 1

cutting locust 1. גָּזָם
Jol 1: 4 What the cutting locust left, the swarming locust 1

destroying locust 1. חָסִיל
Jol 1: 4 hopping locust left, the destroying locust has eaten. 1

hopping locust 1. יֶלֶק
Jol 1: 4 swarming locust left, the hopping locust has eaten 1
4 what the hopping locust left, the destroying locust 1

swarming locust 1. אַרְבֶּה
Jol 1: 4 cutting locust left, the swarming locust has eaten 1
4 What the swarming locust left, the hopping locust 1
2:25 the years which the swarming locust has eaten 1

young locust 1. יֶלֶק
Ps 105:34 locusts came, and young locusts without number; 1

lodge 1. ישׁב 2. לון 3. מְלוּנָה 4. נוח 5. שׁכב
6. αὐλίζομαι 7. ἐνίστημι 8. καταλύω 9. ξενίζω
Gen 24:23 room in your father's house for us to lodge in? 2
25 We have . . room to lodge in. 2
32:13 he lodged there that night, and took 2
21 and he himself lodged that night in the camp. 2
Num22: 8 Lodge here this night, and I will bring back word 2
Jos 2: 1 into the house of a harlot . . and lodged there. 5
3: 1 and they came to the Jordan, and lodged there 2
4: 3 lay them . . in the place where you lodge tonight. 2
Jdg 18: 2 came . . to the house of Micah, and lodged there. 2
19: 4 days; so they ate and drank, and lodged there. 2
7 urged him, till he lodged there again. 2
9 lodge here and let your heart be merry; 2
Rut 1:16 and where you lodge I will lodge; 2
16 and where you lodge I will lodge; 2
1Sm 7: 2 the day that the ark was lodged at Kir'iath-je'arim 1
2Sm 17:16 Do not lodge tonight at the fords 2
1Kg 17:19 into the upper chamber, where he lodged 1
19: 9 he came to a cave, and lodged there; 2
1Ch 9:27 they lodged round about the house of God; 2
Neh 13:20 lodged outside Jerusalem once or twice. 2
21 Why do you lodge before the wall? If you do so again •
Job 31:32 the sojourner has not lodged in the street; 2
Ps 55: 7 I would lodge in the wilderness, Selah 2
Ecc 7: 9 for anger lodges in the bosom of fools. 4
Sng 7:11 go . . into the fields, and lodge in the villages; 2
Isa 1: 8 Zion is left . . like a lodge in a cucumber field 3
21 Righteousness lodged in her, but now murderers. 2
21:13 In the thickets in Arabia you will lodge 2
Jer 4:14 How long shall your evil thoughts lodge within 2
Zep 2:14 the hedgehog shall lodge in her capitals; 2
Mat 21:17 went out of the city to Bethany and lodged there. 6
Lke 9:12 to lodge and get provisions 8
21:37 went out and lodged on the mount called Olivet. 6
Act 10: 6 he is lodging with Simon, a tanner 9
18 Simon who was called Peter was lodging there. 9
32 he is lodging in the house of Simon 9
21:16 Mnason of Cyprus . . with whom we should lodge. 9
Sir 14:25 will lodge in an excellent lodging place; 8
24: 7 I sought in whose territory I might lodge. 6
36:26 has no home, and lodges wherever night finds him? 8
51:23 lodge in my school. 6
2Mc 3:17 the pain lodged in his heart. 7

lodge for the night 1. לוּן
Isa 10:29 at Geba they lodge for the night; Ramah trembles 1

lodging 1. ξενία 2. οἰκία
Act 28:23 they came to him at his lodging in great numbers. 1
Sir 29:28 scolding about lodging 2

lodging place 1. מָלוֹן 2. κατάλυμα
Gen 42:27 to give his ass provender at the lodging place 1
43:21 when we came to the lodging place we opened 1
Exd 4:24 At a lodging place on the way the LORD met him 1
Jer 9: 2 I had in the desert a wayfarers' lodging place 1
Sir 14:25 will lodge in an excellent lodging place; 2
1Mc 3:45 it was a lodging place for the Gentiles 2

loftily 1. מָרוֹם
Ps 73: 8 with malice; loftily they threaten oppression. 1

loftiness 1. גֹּבַהּ
Jer 48:29 of his loftiness, his pride, and his arrogance 1

lofty 1. גָּבֹהַּ 2. נשׂא 3. רום 4. שׂגב 5. תָּלוּל
6. ὑπεροχή 7. eminens
Job 22:12 See the highest stars, how lofty they are! 3
Prv 30:13 There are those–how lofty are their eyes 3
Isa 2:12 has a day against all that is proud and lofty 3
13 all the cedars of Lebanon, lofty and lifted up; 3
14 high mountains, and against all the lofty hills; 2
10:33 the great . . and the lofty will be brought low. 1
26: 5 the inhabitants of the height, the lofty city. 4
30:25 upon every lofty mountain and every high hill 1
57: 7 Upon a . . lofty mountain you have set your bed 2
15 the high and lofty One who inhabits eternity 2
Ezk 17:22 I myself will take a sprig from the lofty top 3
22 will plant it upon a high and lofty mountain; 5
31:14 no trees by the waters may grow to lofty height •
Zep 1:16 and against the lofty battlements. 1
1Co 2: 1 the testimony of God in lofty words or wisdom. 6
2Es 15:40 shall pour out upon every high and lofty place 7

lofty place 1. רָמָה
Ezk 16:24 and made yourself a lofty place in every square; 1
25 you built your lofty place and prostituted 1
31 and making your lofty place in every square. 1
39 and break down your lofty places; 1

log 1. עֵץ 2. קוֹרָה 3. δοκός 4. ξύλον
2Kg 6: 2 go to the Jordan and each of us get there a log 2
5 as one was felling a log, his axe head fell 2
Ecc 10: 9 and he who splits logs is endangered by them. 1
Ezk 24: 5 pile the logs under it; boil its pieces •
10 Heap on the logs, kindle the fire, boil well 1
Mat 7: 3 but do not notice the log that is in your own eye? 3
4 when there is the log in your own eye? 3
5 hypocrite, first take the log out of your own eye 3
Lke 6:41 do not notice the log that is in your own eye? 3
42 you . . do not see the log that is in your own eye 3
42 hypocrite, first take the log out of your own eye 3
1Es 5:55 to bring cedar logs from Lebanon 4

log (2) 1. לֹג
Lev 14:10 mixed with oil, and one log of oil 1
12 offer it . . along with the log of oil 1
15 Then the priest shall take some of the log of oil 1
21 oil for a cereal offering, and a log of oil 1
24 the lamb of the guilt offering, and the log of oil 1

logic 1. λόγος
4Mc 1:15 with sound logic prefers the life of wisdom. 1

loin 1. חָלָץ 2. כֶּסֶל 3. מָתְנַיִם 4. λαγών 5. ὀσφῦς
Gen 37:34 put sackcloth upon his loins, and mourned for his 3
Exd 12:11 your loins girded, your sandals on your feet 3
28:42 from the loins to the thighs they shall reach; 3
Lev 3: 4 kidneys with the fat that is on them at the loins 2
10 with the fat that is on them at the loins 2
15 with the fat that is on them at the loins 2
4: 9 with the fat that is on them at the loins 2
7: 4 with the fat that is on them at the loins 2
Deu 33:11 crush the loins of his adversaries 3
2Sm 20: 8 a girdle with a sword . . fastened upon his loins 3
1Kg 2: 5 innocent blood upon the girdle about my loins 3
12:10 little finger is thicker than my father's loins. 3
18:46 Eli'jah . . girded up his loins and ran before Ahab 3
20:31 sackcloth on our loins and ropes upon our heads 3
32 they girded sackcloth on their loins 3
2Kg 1: 8 with a girdle of leather about his loins. 3
4:29 Gird up your loins, and take my staff . . and go. 3
9: 1 Gird up your loins, and take this flask of oil 3
2Ch 10:10 little finger is thicker than my father's loins. 3
Job 12:18 binds a waistcloth on their loins. 3
15:27 with his fat, and gathered fat upon his loins 2
31:20 if his loins have not blessed me 1
38: 3 Gird up your loins like a man, I will question you 1
40: 7 Gird up your loins like a man; I will question you 1
16 Behold, his strength in his loins, and his power 3
Ps 38: 7 For my loins are filled with burning 2
66:11 thou didst lay affliction on our loins; 3
69:23 make their loins tremble continually. 3
Prv 31:17 She girds her loins with strength 3
Isa 11: 5 and faithfulness the girdle of his loins. 1
20: 2 Go, and loose the sackcloth from your loins 3
21: 3 Therefore my loins are filled with anguish; 3
32:11 make . . bare, and gird sackcloth upon your loins. 1
45: 1 ungird the loins of kings, to open doors 3
48: 1 and who came forth from the loins of Judah; •
Jer 1:17 But you, gird up your loins; 3
13: 1 buy a linen waistcloth, and put it on your loins 3
2 and put it on my loins. 3
4 which you have bought, which is upon your loins 3
11 For as the waistcloth clings to the loins of a man 3
30: 6 then do I see every man with his hands on his loins 1
48:37 and on the loins is sackcloth. 3
Ezk 1:27 upward from what had the appearance of his loins 3
27 from what had the appearance of his loins I saw 3
8: 2 below what appeared to be his loins it was fire 3
2 above his loins it was like the appearance 3
23:15 girded with belts on their loins 3
29: 7 you broke, and made all their loins to shake; 3
44:18 and linen breeches upon their loins; 3
47: 4 through the water; and it was up to the loins. 3
Dan 10: 5 whose loins were girded with gold of Uphaz. 3
Ams 8:10 I will bring sackcloth upon all loins 3
Nah 2: 1 Man the ramparts; watch the road; gird your loins; 3
10 anguish is on all loins, all faces grow pale! 3
Lke 12:35 Let your loins be girded and your lamps burning 5
Eph 6:14 having girded your loins with truth 5
Heb 7:10 for he was still in the loins of his ancestor 5
Jdt 4:14 with their loins girded with sackcloth 5
8: 5 girded sackcloth about her loins 5
Sir 35:18 till he crushes the loins of the unmerciful 5
47:19 you laid your loins beside women 4
2Mc 10:25 girded their loins with sackcloth 5

lonely 1. בדד 2. בָּדָד 3. יָחִיד 4. ἔρημος 5. μόνος
Ps 25:16 be gracious to me; for I am lonely and afflicted. 3
102: 7 lie awake, I am like a lonely bird on the housetop. 1
Lam 1: 1 How lonely sits the city that was full of people! 2
Mat 14:15 This is a lonely place, and the day is now over 4
Mrk 1:35 he rose and went out to a lonely place 4
6:31 Come away by yourselves to a lonely place 4
32 in the boat to a lonely place by themselves. 4
35 This is a lonely place, and the hour is now late; 4
Lke 4:42 he departed and went into a lonely place 4
9:12 we are here in a lonely place. 4
Bar 4:16 bereaved the lonely woman of her daughters. 5

lonely place 1. ἔρημος
Mat 14:13 he withdrew from there in a boat to a lonely place 1

lonely woman 1. μόνος
Bar 4:16 bereaved the lonely woman of her daughters. 1

long 1. אֲצִיל 2. ארך 3. אָרֵךְ 4. אֹרֶךְ 5. אֶרֶךְ
6. אֹרֶךְ יָמִים 7. בְּ 8. בושׁ 9. בְּיָמִים 10. בְּכָל עֵת
11. בְּעוֹד 12. יסף 13. יסף עוֹד 14. כְּבָר 15. כְּיָמִים
16. כָּל יָמִים 17. כָּל עוֹד 18. לִפְנֵי 19. מדד - 20. מִן
21. מָתַי 22. עַד 23. עוֹד 24. עוֹלָם 25. קֶדֶם 26. רַב
27. רֹב 28. רבה 29. רָחֹק 30. תְּמוֹל 31. αἰώνιος
32. ἄχρι 33. ἄχρις 34. διά 35. ἐκ παλαιῶν χρόνων
36. ἐν 37. ἐξ ἱκανῶν χρόνων 38. ἐπὶ πολύ 39. ἔτι
40. ἔτι χρόνον 41. ἐφ' ὅσον 42. ἕως 43. ἤδη
44. ἱκανός 45. μακρός 46. μεγαλύνω 47. μέγας
48. μέχρις 49. μῆκος 50. μικρός 51. ὅσος 52. ὅταν
53. ὅτε 54. πάλαι 55. πάσας τὰς ἡμέρας 56. ποδήρης
57. πολύς 58. πολὺς χρόνος 59. πρός 60. τοσοῦτο
61. τοσοῦτος 62. χρόνος 63. amplius 64. amplus
65. dum 66. iam 67. multus 68. tempus 69. tot tempus
Gen 4:12 When you till the ground, it shall no longer yield 12
17: 5 No longer shall your name be Abram 23
26: 8 When he had been there a long time 5
35:10 no longer shall your name be called Jacob 23
48:15 the God who has led me all my life long to this day •
Exd 2: 3 when she could hide him no longer she took for him 23
5: 7 You shall no longer give the people straw to make 12
9:28 I will let you go, and you shall stay no longer. 12
33 the rain no longer poured upon the earth. •
19:13 When the trumpet sounds a long blast •
20:12 that your days may be long in the land 2
27: 1 altar . . five cubits long and five cubits broad; 5
9 hangings . . 100 cubits long for one side; 5
11 there shall be hangings 100 cubits long 5
16 there shall be a screen twenty cubits long •
38:18 it was twenty cubits long and five cubits high 5
Lev 13:46 He shall remain unclean as long as he has 16
26:34 enjoy its sabbaths as long as it lies desolate 16
35 As long as it lies desolate it shall have rest 16
Num 9:18 as long as the cloud rested over the tabernacle 16
20:15 we dwelt in Egypt a long time; 26
Deu 1: 6 'You have stayed long enough at this mountain; 26
2: 3 going about this mountain country long enough; 26
10:16 be no longer stubborn. 23
11:21 as long as the heavens are above the earth. 15
12:19 as long as you live in your land. 16
14:24 if the way is too long for you, so that you 28
19: 6 overtake him, because the way is long 28
20:19 When you besiege a city for a long time, making war 26
31: 2 I am no longer able to go out and come in. 23
13 as long as you live in the land which you are going 16
32: 5 dealt corruptly . . they are no longer his children •
33:12 encompasses him all the day long •
Jos 5: 1 and there was no longer any spirit in them •
9:13 shoes . . are worn out from the very long journey. 27
11:18 Joshua made war a long time with all those kings. 26
23: 1 A long time afterward, when the LORD had given 26

Jdg 2:14 they could no longer withstand their enemies. *
5:28 Why is his chariot so long in coming? 8
18:31 set up . . as long as the house of God was at Shiloh. 16
1Sm 1:18 and ate, and her countenance was no longer sad. *
28 as long as he lives, he is lent to the LORD. 16
10:24 And all the people shouted, "Long live the king! *
20:31 as long as the son of Jesse lives upon the earth 16
25:15 we did not miss . . as long as we went with them; 16
28 evil shall not be found in you so long as you live. 20
2Sm 3: 1 There was a long war between the house of Saul 4
1Kg 1:25 before him, and saying, 'Long live King Adoni'jah!' *
34 the trumpet, and say, 'Long live King Solomon! *
39 and all the people said, "Long live King Solomon! *
3:11 have not asked for yourself long life or riches 26
6: 2 The house . . for the LORD was 60 cubits long 5
3 The vestibule . . was twenty cubits long 5
17 The house . . the nave . . , was 40 cubits long. *
20 The inner sanctuary was twenty cubits long 5
7:27 each stand was four cubits long, four cubits wide 5
8: 8 the poles were so long that the ends . . were seen 2
12:28 You have gone up to Jerusalem long enough. 26
2Kg 9:22 so long as the harlotries and . . are so many? 22
25:30 every day a portion, as long as he lived 16
1Ch 23:26 Levites no longer need to carry the tabernacle *
2Ch 1:11 and have not even asked long life, but have asked 26
3: 4 The vestibule . . was twenty cubits long 5
4: 1 He made an altar of bronze, twenty cubits long 5
5: 9 the poles were so long that the ends of the poles 2
6:13 bronze platform five cubits long, five . . wide 5
15: 3 For a long time Israel was without the true God 26
23:11 anointed him, and they said, "Long live the king. *
26: 5 as long as he sought the LORD, God made him prosper 9
35: 3 you need no longer carry it upon your shoulders. *
Neh 2:17 that we may no longer suffer disgrace. 23
Est 5:13 all this does me no good, so long as I see Mor'decai 10
Job 7: 4 But the night is long, and I am full of tossing 19
11: 9 Its measure is longer than the earth 4
24:20 their name is no longer remembered; 23
27: 3 as long as my breath is in me 17
Ps 25: 5 for thee I wait all the day long. *
32: 3 wasted away through my groaning all day long. *
35:28 and of thy praise all the day long. *
38:12 meditate treachery all the day long. *
39: 1 so long as the wicked are in my presence. 11
44:15 All day long my disgrace is before me *
22 Nay, for thy sake we are slain all the day long *
56: 1 all day long foemen oppress me; *
2 my enemies trample upon me all day long *
5 All day long they seek to injure my cause; *
63: 4 I will bless thee as long as I live; 7
71:24 will talk of thy righteous help all the day long *
72: 5 as long as the moon, throughout all generations! *
15 Long may he live, may gold of Sheba be given to him! *
17 for ever, his fame continue as long as the sun! 18
73:14 For all the day long I have been stricken *
74: 9 there is no longer any prophet 23
88:17 They surround me like a flood all day long; *
89:36 his throne as long as the sun before me. *
91:16 With long life I will satisfy him 5
103: 5 who satisfies you with good as long as you live *
104:33 I will sing to the LORD as long as I live; 7
116: 2 therefore I will call on him as long as I live. 7
119:152Long have I known from thy testimonies 25
120: 6 Too long have I had my dwelling among those 26
123: 4 Too long our soul has been sated with the scorn 26
143: 3 has made me sit in darkness like those long dead. 24
146: 2 I will praise the LORD as long as I live; 7
Prv 1:22 How long, O simple ones, will you love being simple? 21
3:16 Long life is in her right hand; 5
6: 9 How long will you lie there, O sluggard? 21
7:19 husband . . has gone on a long journey; 29
21:26 All day long the wicked covets *
Ecc 2:16 seeing . . all will have been long forgotten. 14
3:12 and enjoy themselves as long as they live; 7
4:13 and foolish king, who will no longer take advice *
Isa 7: 8 that it will no longer be a people.) *
30:33 For a burning place has long been prepared; 30
Jer 16:14 says the LORD, when it shall no longer be said 23
20: 8 has become for me a . . derision all day long. *
23: 7 when men shall no longer say, 'As the LORD lives 23
29:28 Your exile will be long; 4
31:29 In those days they shall no longer say 23
34 And no longer shall each man teach his neighbor 23
33:24 they are no longer a nation in their sight. 23
44:22 The LORD could no longer bear your evil doings 23
48:42 Moab shall be destroyed and be no longer a people *
51:44 The nations shall no longer flow to him; 23
52:34 until the day of his death as long as he lived 16
Lam 1:13 he has left me stunned, faint all the day long. *
3: 3 surely against me he turns . . the whole day long. *
14 the burden of their songs all day long. *
62 my assailants are against me all the day long. *
5:20 why dost thou so long forsake us? 6
Ezk 4: 5 so long shall you bear the punishment *
12:25 It will no longer be delayed, but in your days 23
28 None of my words will be delayed any longer 23
17: 3 A great eagle with great wings and long pinions 3
24:27 you shall speak and be no longer dumb. 23
30:13 shall no longer be a prince in the land of Egypt; 23
33:22 my mouth was opened, and I was no longer dumb. 23
34:10 no longer shall the shepherds feed themselves. 23
22 I will save my flock, they shall no longer be a prey; 23
29 no longer suffer the reproach of the nations. 23
36:12 you shall no longer bereave them of children. 13
14 therefore you shall no longer devour men 23
14 and no longer bereave your nation of children 23
15 you shall no longer bear the disgrace 23
15 and no longer cause your nation to stumble 23
37:22 they shall be no longer two nations 23
22 and no longer divided into two kingdoms. 23
40: 5 reed in the man's hand was six long cubits *
7 the side rooms, one reed long, and one reed broad; 5
30 vestibules round about, 25 cubits long 5
42 a cubit and a half long, and a cubit and a half broad 5
43 And hooks, a handbreadth long, were fastened *
47 he measured the court, 100 cubits long 5
41: 8 measured a full reed of six long cubits. 1
13 he measured the temple, 100 cubits long; 5
13 building with its walls, 100 cubits long; 5
22 cubits high, two cubits long, and two cubits broad; 5
42: 4 ten cubits wide and 100 cubits long 49
7 opposite the chambers, 50 cubits long. 5
8 on the outer court were 50 cubits long 5
8 opposite the temple were 100 cubits long. *
20 It had a wall around it, 500 cubits long 5
43:16 be square, twelve cubits long by twelve broad. 5
17 square, fourteen cubits long by fourteen broad 5
45: 1 holy district, 25,000 cubits long 5
3 a section 25,000 cubits long 5
5 section, 25,000 cubits long 5
6 25,000 cubits long; 5
46:22 small courts, 40 cubits long and 30 broad; 5
Hos 2:16 and no longer will you call me, 'My Ba'al.' 23
12: 1 and pursues the east wind all day long; *
Zep 3:11 shall no longer be haughty in my holy mountain. 23
Zec 11: 6 For I will no longer have pity on the inhabitants 23
14:21 no longer be a trader in the house of the LORD 23
Mal 2:13 because he no longer regards the offering 23
Mat 5:13 It is no longer good for anything except to be 39
9:15 guests mourn as long as the bridegroom 51
23: 5 and their fringes long 46
25:19 Now after a long time 57
Mrk 2:19 As long as they have the bridegroom with them 62
12:40 for a pretense make long prayers 45
Lke 8:27 for a long time he had worn no clothes 44
20: 9 went into another country for a long while. 44
47 and for a pretense make long prayers 45
23: 8 he had long desired to see him 37
Joh 5: 6 and knew that he had been lying there a long time 57
7:33 I shall be with you a little longer 40
9: 5 As long as I am in the world 52
11: 6 he stayed two days longer in the place where he was. *
12:35 The light is with you for a little longer 40
14: 9 Jesus said to him, "Have I been with you so long 62
Act 8:11 for a long time he had amazed them with his magic. 44
14: 3 So they remained for a long time 44
18:18 After this Paul stayed many days longer 39
20 When they asked him to stay for a longer period 57
20: 9 as Paul talked still longer 57
11 he conversed with them a long while 44
27:21 As they had been long without food 57
Rom 7: 2 woman is bound . . to her husband as long as he lives; *
8:36 we are being killed all the day long; *
10:21 All day long I have held out my hands *
16:25 the mystery which was kept secret for long ages 31
1Co 7:39 A wife is bound to her husband as long as he lives. 51
Gal 4: 1 I mean that the heir, as long as he is a child 51
1Th 3: 6 and long to see us, as we long to see you- *
Heb 3:13 as long as it is called "today 33
4: 7 saying through David so long afterward 60
9: 8 as long as the outer tent is still standing *
17 as long as the one who made it is alive. 53
10: 2 would no longer have any consciousness of sin. 39
2Pe 1:13 I think it right, as long as I am in this body 41
Rev 1:13 clothed with a long robe and with a golden girdle †
6:11 they were each . . told to rest a little longer 40
1Es 3:22 before long they draw their swords. 57
5:73 as long as King Cyrus lived 62
8:90 we can no longer stand in thy presence 39
2Es 4:26 and if you live long, you will often marvel ‡
6:28 the truth, which has been so long without fruit 68
8:25 For as long as I live I will speak 65
25 as long as I have understanding I will answer. 65
10:27 behold, the woman was no longer visible to me 63
11:13 and it continued to reign a long time. 67
17 After you no one shall rule as long as you 68
40 for so long you have dwelt on the earth 69
12:15 the second . . shall hold sway for a longer time 64
13:45 Through that region there was a long way to go 67
14:41 my mouth was opened, and was no longer closed. 63
15: 8 I will be silent no longer 66
Tob 5: 3 I will pay him wages as long as I live 42
9: 4 if I delay long he will be greatly distressed. 47
Jdt 1: 2 three cubits thick and six cubits long 49
5: 8 lived there for a long time. 57
10 and lived there as long as they had food 48
16 lived there a long time. 57
17 As long as they did not sin against their God 42
8:31 we will no longer be faint. 39
13: 1 because the banquet had lasted long. 38
16:25 for a long time after her death. 57
AEs 13: 7 those who have long been and are now hostile 54
Wis 4:13 he fulfilled long years; 45
14:24 they no longer keep . . their marriages pure 39
17: 2 prisoners of long night 45
18:20 the wrath did not long continue. 38
24 upon his long robe the whole world was depicted 56
Sir 3:12 do not grieve him as long as he lives; 36
9:12 not be held guiltless as long as they live. 42
10:10 A long illness baffles the physician 45
33:19 as long as you live 36
41:12 longer than 1,000 great stores of gold. *
46: 4 did not one day become as long as two? 59
Bar 4:35 for a long time she will be inhabited by demons. 57
LJr 1: 3 for a long time, up to seven generations 45
1Mc 8:19 They went to Rome, a very long journey 57
9:55 so that he could no longer say a word 39
71 he would not try to harm him as long as he lived. 55
2Mc 6: 1 Not long after this 58
13 In fact, not to let the impious alone for long 58
21 because of their long acquaintance with him 35
10: 6 not long before, during the feast of booths 50
12:36 men had been fighting for a long time and were weary 57
14:10 For as long as Judas lives 32
4Mc 3: 7 had been attacking the Philistines all day long 34
5: 7 Although you have had them for so long a time 61
7:13 his body no longer tense and firm 43

long (2) 1. חכה 2. חשק 3. חֵשֶׁק 4. יאב 5. כלה 6. כסף 7. נשא נֶפֶשׁ 8. ערג 9. פוח 10. פקד 11. קוה 12. שאף 13. תאב 14. תַּאֲבָה 15. תַּאֲוָה 16. *ἐπιθυμέω* 17. *ἐπιθυμία* 18. *ἐπιποθέω* 19. *ἐπιπόθησις* 20. *ἐπιπόθητος* 21. *ἐπιποθίαν ἔχω* 22. *ποθέω* 23. concupisco

Gen 31:30 you longed greatly for your father's house 6
34: 8 my son Shechem longs for your daughter; 2
Deu 28:32 eyes . . fail with longing for them all the day; *
2Sm 13:39 spirit of the king longed to go forth to Ab'salom; 5
Job 3:21 who long for death, but it comes not 1
7: 2 Like a slave who longs for the shadow 12
14:15 thou wouldest long for the work of thy hands. 6
36:20 Do not long for the night, when peoples are cut off 12
Ps 12: 5 I will place him in the safety for which he longs. 9
38: 9 Lord, all my longing is known to thee 15
42: 1 As a hart longs for flowing streams 8
1 so longs my soul for thee, O God. 8
84: 2 soul longs, yea, faints for the courts of the LORD; 6
119:20 My soul is consumed with longing 14
40 Behold, I long for thy precepts; 13
131I pant, because I long for thy commandments. 4
174I long for thy salvation, O LORD 13
Isa 21: 4 the twilight I longed for has been turned 3
Jer 22:27 to the land to which they will long to return 7
Lam 2:16 Ah, this is the day we longed for; now we have it; 11
Ezk 23:21 Thus you longed for the lewdness of your youth 10
Mat 13:17 prophets and righteous men longed to see 16
Rom 1:11 For I long to see you 18
15:23 since I have longed for many years to come to you 21
2Co 5: 2 long to put on our heavenly dwelling 18
7: 7 as he told us of your longing, your mourning 19
11 what indignation, what alarm, what longing 19
9:14 while they long for you and pray for you 18
Php 2:26 for he has been longing for you all 18
4: 1 my brethren, whom I love and long for 20
1Th 3: 6 and long to see us, as we long to see you- 18
2Ti 1: 4 I long night and day to see you 18
1Pe 1:12 things into which angels long to look. 16
2: 2 long for the pure spiritual milk 18
Rev 9: 6 they will long to die, and death will fly from them. 16
18:14 The fruit for which thy soul longed has gone 17
2Es 16:27 one man will long to see another 23
Wis 4: 2 they long for it when it has gone 22
6:11 long for them, and you will be instructed. 22
8: 8 if any one longs for wide experience 22

long *See* grow.

how long 1. אַחֲרֵי מָתַי 2. כַּמָּה 3. כַּמָּה יְמֵי 4. עַד 5. עַד אָן 6. עַד אָנָה 7. עַד מָה 8. עַד מָתַי 9. *ἕως πότε* 10. *μέχρι τίνος* 11. *πόσος χρόνος* 12. quantum 13. usquequo

Exd 10: 3 'How long will you refuse to humble yourself 8
7 How long shall this man be a snare to us? 8
16:28 the LORD said to Moses, "How long do you refuse 6
Num14:11 How long will this people despise me? 6
11 how long will they not believe in me 6
27 How long shall this wicked congregation murmur 8
24:22 How long shall Asshur take you away captive? 7
Jos 18: 3 How long will you be slack to go in and take 6
1Sm 1:14 How long will you be drunken? Put away your wine 8
16: 1 How long will you grieve over Saul 8
2Sm 2:26 How long will it be before you bid your people 8
1Kg 18:21 How long will you go limping with two . . opinions? 8
Neh 2: 6 How long will you be gone, and when will you return 8
Job 7:19 How long wilt thou not look away from me 2
8: 2 How long will you say these things 5

18: 2 How long will you hunt for words? 6
19: 2 How long will you torment me 6
Ps 4: 2 O men, how long shall my honor suffer shame? 7
2 How long will you love vain words •
6: 3 sorely troubled. But thou, O LORD–how long? 8
13: 1 How long, O LORD? Wilt thou forget me for ever? 6
1 How long wilt thou hide thy face from me? 6
2 How long must I bear pain in my soul 6
2 How long shall my enemy be exalted over me? 6
35:17 How long, O LORD, wilt thou look on? Rescue me 2
62: 3 How long will you set upon a man to shatter him 6
74: 9 there is none among us who knows how long. 7
10 How long, O God, is the foe to scoff? 8
79: 5 How long, O LORD? Wilt thou be angry for ever? 7
80: 4 how long . . be angry with thy people's prayers? 8
82: 2 How long will you judge unjustly 8
89:46 How long, O LORD? Wilt thou hide thyself for ever? 4
46 How long will thy wrath burn like fire? •
90:13 Return, O LORD! How long? Have pity on thy servants! 8
94: 3 O LORD, how long shall the wicked 8
3 O LORD . . how long shall the wicked exult? 8
119:84 How long must thy servant endure? 3
Prv 1:22 How long will scoffers delight in their scoffing •
Isa 6:11 Then I said, "How long, O Lord? 8
Jer 4:14 How long shall your evil thoughts lodge within 8
21 How long must I see the standard 8
12: 4 How long will the land mourn 8
13:27 How long will it be before you are made clean? 1
23:26 How long shall there be lies in the heart 8
31:22 How long will you waver, O faithless daughter? 8
47: 5 Anakim, how long will you gash yourselves? 8
Dan 8:13 For how long is the vision concerning 8
12: 6 How long shall it be till the end of these wonders? 8
Hos 8: 5 How long will it be till they are pure 8
Hab 1: 2 O LORD, how long shall I cry for help 6
2: 6 who heaps up what is not his own–for how long? 8
Zec 1:12 how long wilt thou have no mercy on Jerusalem 8
Mat 17:17 how long am I to be with you 9
17 How long am I to bear with you? 9
Mrk 9:19 how long am I to be with you? 9
19 How long am I to bear with you? Bring him to me. 9
21 Jesus asked his father, "How long has he had this? 11
Lke 9:41 how long am I to be with you and bear with you? 9
Joh 10:24 How long will you keep us in suspense? 9
Rev 6:10 how long before thou wilt judge and avenge 9
2Es 1: 9 How long shall I endure them 13
4:33 How long and when will these things be? ‡
35 'How long are we to remain here? 13
6:59 How long will this be so? 13
7:74 For how long the time is 12
1Mc 6:22 How long will you fail to do justice 9
3Mc 5:40 O king, how long will you try us 10

how long till 1. עַד אָנָה
Jer 47: 6 Ah, sword of the LORD! How long till you are quiet? 1

too long 1. שרע
Lev 22:23 A bull or a lamb which has a part too long 1

very long 1. *πολυχρόνιος*
LJr 1:46 The men . . will certainly not live very long themselves 1

long with sleeves 1. פַּס
Gen 37: 3 old age; and he made him a long robe with sleeves. 1
23 the long robe with sleeves that he wore; 1
32 they sent the long robe with sleeves 1
2Sm 13:18 Now she was wearing a long robe with sleeves; 1

long-suffering 1. *μακρόθυμος*
Man 1: 7 of great compassion, long-suffering 1

any longer 1. עוֹד 2. *ἔτι* 3. *μηκέτι* 4. adhuc 5. iam
1Sm 27: 1 Saul will despair of seeking me any longer 1
2Kg 6:33 Why should I wait for the LORD any longer? 1
Act 25:24 shouting that he ought not to live any longer. 3
2Es 4:40 her womb can keep the child within her any longer. 4
5:49 a woman . . does not bring forth any longer 4
15:10 to live any longer in the land of Egypt 5
Tob 14:10 do not live in Nineveh any longer 3
Jdt 7:22 there was no strength left in them any longer. 2
1Mc 2:13 Why should we live any longer? 2

no longer 1. גמר 2. לֹא יסף 3. *ἀντί* 4. *μηκέτι* 5. *οὐ* 6. *οὐκ ἔτι* 7. *οὐκέτι* 8. nusquam
Ps 12: 1 Help, LORD; for there is no longer any that is godly; 1
Lam 4:15 men said . . "They shall stay with us no longer. 2
22 he will keep you in exile no longer; 2
Mat 19: 6 So they are no longer two but one flesh 7
Mrk 1:45 so that Jesus could no longer openly enter a town 4
2: 2 so that there was no longer room for them 4
7:12 then you no longer permit him to do anything 7
9: 8 they no longer saw any one with them but Jesus 7
10: 8 So they are no longer two but one flesh. 7
Lke 15:19 I am no longer worthy to be called your son 7
21 I am no longer worthy to be called your son.' 7
16: 2 you can no longer be steward.' 6
20:40 For they no longer dared to ask him any question. 7
Joh 4:42 It is no longer because of your words 7
6:66 and no longer went about with him. 7
11:54 Jesus therefore no longer went about openly 7
14:30 I will no longer talk much with you 7
15:15 No longer do I call you servants 7
16:21 she no longer remembers the anguish 7
25 when I shall no longer speak to you in figures 7
Rom 6: 6 and we might no longer be enslaved to sin. 4
9 death no longer has dominion over him. 7
7:17 So then it is no longer I that do it, but sin 7
20 it is no longer I that do it, but sin 7
11: 6 it is no longer on the basis of works; 7
6 otherwise grace would no longer be grace. 7
14:15 you are no longer walking in love. 7
15:23 But now, since I no longer have any room for work 4
2Co 5:15 that those who live might live no longer 4
16 we regard him thus no longer. 7
Gal 2:20 it is no longer I who live 7
3:18 it is no longer by promise 7
25 we are no longer under a custodian; 7
4: 7 So through God you are no longer a slave but a son 7
Eph 2:19 you are no longer strangers and sojourners 7
4:14 so that we may no longer be children 4
17 you must no longer live as the Gentiles do 4
28 Let the thief no longer steal 4
1Th 3: 1 Therefore when we could bear it no longer 4
5 For this reason, when I could bear it no longer 4
1Ti 5:23 No longer drink only water, but use a little wine 4
Phm 1:16 no longer as a slave but more than a slave 7
Heb 10:18 there is no longer any offering for sin. 7
26 there no longer remains a sacrifice for sins 7
1Pe 4: 2 no longer by human passions but by the will of God 4
1Es 1: 4 You need no longer carry it upon your shoulders 5
2:24 no longer have access to Coelesyria 7
2Es 4:23 and the written covenants no longer exist; 8
Tob 1:15 I could no longer go into Media. 7
2: 8 He is no longer afraid that he will be put to death 7
Jdt 10:10 and they could no longer see her. 7
1Mc 2:11 no longer free, she has become a slave. 3
5:44 they could stand before Judas no longer. 5
13:39 whatever other tax . . shall be collected no longer. 4
2Mc 4:14 the priests were no longer intent upon their service 4
9:13 who would no longer have mercy on him 7
3Mc 4:17 they were no longer able to take the census of the Jews 4

no longer any 1. *οὐδὲ ἔτι*
Rev 12: 8 there was no longer any place for them in heaven. 1

eager longing 1. *ἀποκαραδοκία*
Rom 8:19 For the creation waits with eager longing 1

longingly 1. אוה
2Sm 23:15 And David said longingly, "O that some one would 1
1Ch 11:17 David said longingly, "O that some one 1

look 1. אחז 2. בין 3. בְּעֵינַיִם 4. בקשׁ 5. הִנֵּה 6. חזה 7. מַרְאֶה 8. נבט 9. עַיִן 10. פנה 11. פָּנִים 12. צוץ 13. צפה 14. קוה 15. קרא 16. ראה 17. שׂבר 18. שׂוּם עַיִן 19. שׁעה 20. שׁקף 21. חזה (A) 22. *ἀναβλέπω* 23. *ἀναζητέω* 24. *ἀποβλέπω* 25. *ἀτενίζω* 26. *ἀφοράω* 27. *βλέπω* 28. *γίνομαι* 29. *εἶδον* 30. *ἐμβλέπω* 31. *ἐνατενίζω* 32. *ἐπεῖδον* 33. *ἐπέχω* 34. *ἐπιβλέπω* 35. *ἐπισκέπτομαι* 36. *ἐφοράω* 37. *ζητέω* 38. *ἡγέομαι* 39. *θεάομαι* 40. *θεωρέω* 41. *ἰδού* 42. *κατανοέω* 43. *ὅρασις* 44. *ὁράω* 45. *παρακύπτω* 46. *περιβλέπω* 47. *προσδέχομαι* 48. *προσδοκάω* 49. *προσοράω* 50. *πρόσωπον* 51. *σκοπέω* 52. *σκοπός* 53. *συνοράω* 54. aspectus 55. aspicio 56. considero 57. conspicio 58. respicio 59. spero 60. video
Gen 8:13 Noah removed the covering of the ark, and looked 16
9:16 When the bow is in the clouds, I will look upon it 16
13:14 Lift up your eyes, and look from the place 16
15: 5 Look toward heaven, and number the stars 8
16: 4 she looked with contempt on her mistress. 3
5 she looked on me with contempt. 3
18: 2 He lifted up his eyes and looked, and behold 16
16 from there, and they looked toward Sodom; 20
19:17 Flee for your life; do not look back or stop 8
26 Lot's wife behind him looked back 8
21:16 for she said, "Let me not look upon the death 16
22:13 Abraham lifted up his eyes and looked 16
24:63 and he lifted up his eyes and looked 16
29: 2 As he looked, he saw a well in the field 16
30:33 when you come to look into my wages with you. •
31:10 Jacob lifted up his eyes and looked 16
39: 6 Now Joseph was handsome and good-looking. 7
Exd 2:11 Moses . . looked on their burdens; 16
12 He looked this way and that, and seeing no one 10
3: 2 a bush; and he looked, and lo, the bush was burning 16
6 hid his face, for he was afraid to look at God. 8
5:21 they said . . "The LORD look upon you and judge 16
10:10 Look, you have some evil purpose in mind. 16
16:10 they looked toward the wilderness, and behold 10
33: 8 stood . . and looked after Moses, until he had 8
Lev 14:39 shall come again on the seventh day, and look 16
44 then the priest shall go and look 16
Num 11: 6 there is nothing at all but this manna to look at. 9
17: 9 they looked, and each man took his rod. 16
21: 9 man, he would look at the bronze serpent and live. 8
24: 1 he did not go, as at other times, to look for omens 15
20 he looked on Am'alek, and took up his discourse 16
21 he looked on the Ken'ite, and took up his discourse 16
Deu 9:16 I looked, and behold, you had sinned 16
28:32 while your eyes look on and fail with longing 16
Jos 5:13 When Joshua . . he lifted up his eyes and looked 16
8:20 when the men of Ai looked back, behold, the smoke 10
Jdg 7:17 And he said to them, "Look at me, and do likewise; 16
9:36 Look, men are coming down from the mountain tops! 5
37 Look, men are coming down from the center 5
43 he looked and saw the men coming out of the city 16
13:20 ascended . . while Mano'ah and his wife looked on; 16
16:27 3,000 . . who looked on while Samson made sport. 16
20:40 the Benjaminites looked behind them; and behold 10
1Sm 1:11 look on the affliction of thy maidservant 16
2:32 Then . . you will look with envious eye on all 8
6:19 because they looked into the ark of the LORD; 16
9: 3 Take . . and arise, go and look for the asses. 4
14:11 Look, Hebrews are coming out of the holes 5
16 watchmen of Saul in Gib'e-ah of Benjamin looked; 16
16: 6 When they came, he looked on Eli'ab and thought 16
7 Do not look on his appearance or on the height 8
7 man looks on the outward appearance, but the LORD 16
7 man looks on . . but the LORD looks on the heart. 16
17:42 And when the Philistine looked, and saw David 8
20:21 'Look, the arrows are on this side of you, take them,' 5
22 if I say . . 'Look, the arrows are beyond you,' then go; 5
24: 8 And when Saul looked behind him, David bowed 8
2Sm 1: 7 And when he looked behind him, he saw me 10
2:20 Abner looked behind him and said, "Is it you, As'ahel? 10
6:16 Michal . . looked out of the window, and saw 20
9: 8 What . . that you should look upon a dead dog 10
13:34 lifted up his eyes, and looked 16
15:27 Look, go back to the city in peace, 29
16:12 may be that the LORD will look upon my affliction 16
18:24 when he lifted up his eyes and looked, he saw a man 16
22:42 They looked, but there was none to save; 19
1Kg 12:16 Look now to your own house, David. 16
18:43 he said . . "Go up now, look toward the sea. 8
43 he went up and looked, and said, "There is nothing. 8
19: 6 he looked, and . . there was at his head a cake 8
2Kg 3:14 I would neither look at you, nor see you. 8
4:25 he said . . "Look, yonder is the Shu'nammite; 5
6:30 the people looked, and behold, he had sackcloth 16
32 Look, when the messenger comes, shut the door 16
9: 2 look there for Jehu the son of Jehosh'aphat 16
30 adorned her head, and looked out of the window. 20
11:14 when she looked, there was the king standing 16
1Ch 15:29 Michal . . looked out of the window 20
21:21 Ornan looked and saw David and went forth 8
2Ch 10:16 Look now to your own house, David. 16
13:14 when Judah looked, behold, the battle was 10
20:24 they looked toward the multitude; 10
23:13 when she looked, there was the king 16
26:20 Azari'ah . . and all the priests, looked at him 10
Neh 4:14 I looked, and arose, and said to the nobles 16
Est 1:17 causing them to look with contempt upon their †
Job 6:19 The caravans of Tema look, the travelers of Sheba 8
28 now, be pleased to look at me; 10
7: 2 like a hireling who looks for his wages 14
19 How long wilt thou not look away from me 19
14: 6 look away from him, and desist, that he may enjoy 19
17:13 If I look for Sheol as my house 14
20:17 He will not look upon the rivers 16
21: 5 Look at me, and be appalled 10
28:24 For he looks to the ends of the earth, 8
30:26 when I looked for good, evil came; 14
31: 1 how then could I look upon a virgin? 2
26 if I have looked at the sun when it shone 16
35: 5 Look at the heavens, and see; and behold the clouds 8
36:25 men have looked on it; man beholds it from afar. 6
37:21 now men cannot look on the light when it is bright 16
40:11 look on every one that is proud, and abase him. 16
12 Look on every one that is proud, and bring him low; 16
Ps 8: 3 When I look at thy heavens, the work of thy fingers 16
33:13 The LORD looks down from heaven, he sees all 8
34: 5 Look to him, and be radiant; 8
35:17 How long, O LORD, wilt thou look on? Rescue me 16
37:34 you will look on the destruction of the wicked. 16
54: 7 my eye has looked in triumph on my enemies. 16
59:10 my God will let me look in triumph on my enemies. 16
69:20 I looked for pity, but there was none; 14
91: 8 only look with your eyes and see the recompense 8
101: 5 man of haughty looks and arrogant heart 9
102:19 from heaven the LORD looked at the earth 8
104:27 These all look to thee, to give them their food 17
32 who looks on the earth and it trembles 8
113: 6 who looks far down upon the heavens and the earth? 16
114: 3 The sea looked and fled, Jordan turned back. 16
118: 7 I shall look in triumph on those who hate me. 16
119:37 Turn my eyes from looking at vanities; 16
153 Look on my affliction and deliver me 16
158 I look at the faithless with disgust 16
123: 2 eyes of servants look to the hand of their master •
2 so our eyes look to the LORD our God •

142: 4 I look to the right and watch, but there is none 8
145:15 The eyes of all look to thee, and thou gives them 17
Prv 4:25 Let your eyes look directly forward 8
14:15 but the prudent looks where he is going. 2
23:31 Do not look at wine when it is red 16
24:32 I looked and received instruction. 16
25:23 backbiting tongue, angry looks. 11
29:16 but the righteous will look upon their downfall. 16
Ecc 12: 3 those that look through the windows are dimmed 16
Sng 2: 9 gazing in . . looking through the lattice. 12
6:11 went down . . to look at the blossoms of the valley 16
13 return, return, that we may look upon you. 6
13 Why should you look upon the Shu'lammite 1
Isa 2:11 The haughty looks of man shall be brought low 9
5: 2 he looked for it to yield grapes 14
4 When I looked for it to yield grapes 14
7 he looked for justice, but behold, bloodshed; 14
30 if one look to the land, behold, darkness 8
8:22 they will look to the earth, but behold, distress 8
17: 7 and their eyes will look to the Holy One of Israel; 16
8 will not look to what their own fingers have made 16
18: 3 when a signal is raised on the mountains, look! 16
22: 4 Therefore I said: "Look away from me, let me weep 19
8 In that day you looked to the weapons of the House 8
11 you did not look to him who did it 8
31: 1 but do not look to the Holy One of Israel 19
33:15 who . . shuts his eyes from looking upon evil 16
38:14 My eyes are weary with looking upward. •
41:28 when I look there is no one; 16
42:18 Hear, you deaf; and look, you blind, that you may see! 8
51: 1 look to the rock from which you were hewn 8
2 Look to Abraham your father and to Sarah 8
6 eyes to the heavens, and look at the earth beneath; 8
53: 2 no form or comeliness that we should look at him 16
57: 8 loved their bed, you have looked on nakedness. 6
59: 9 we look for light, and behold darkness 14
11 we look for justice, but there is none; 14
63: 5 I looked, but there was no one to help; 8
64: 3 didst terrible things which we looked not for 14
66: 2 But this is the man to whom I will look 8
24 go forth and look on the dead bodies of the men 16
Jer 2:23 Look at your way in the valley; 16
4:23 I looked on the earth, and lo, it was waste and void; 16
24 I looked on the mountains 16
25 I looked, and lo, there was no man 16
26 I looked, and lo, the fruitful land was a desert 16
5: 1 Run to and fro . . look and take note! 16
3 O LORD, do not thy eyes look for truth? •
6:16 Thus says the LORD: "Stand by the roads, and look 16
8:15 We looked for peace, but no good came 14
13:16 while you look for light he turns it into gloom 14
14:19 We looked for peace, but no good came; 14
20: 4 They shall fall by the sword . . while you look on. 16
31:26 I awoke and looked, and my sleep was pleasant to me 16
39:12 Take him, look after him well and do him no harm 18
40: 4 to Babylon, come, and I will look after you well; 18
Lam 1:11 Look, O LORD, and behold, for I am despised. 16
12 Look and see if there is any sorrow like my sorrow 8
2:20 Look, O LORD, and see! With whom hast thou dealt 16
Ezk 1: 4 As I looked, behold, a stormy wind 16
13 something that looked like burning coals 7
15 Now as I looked at the living creatures 16
2: 6 nor be dismayed at their looks 11
9 I looked, behold, a hand was stretched out to me 16
3: 9 fear them not, nor be dismayed at their looks 11
8: 7 when I looked, behold, there was a hole in the wall. 16
10: 1 Then I looked, and behold, on the firmament 16
9 I looked, and behold, there were four wheels 16
21:21 he consults the teraphim, he looks at the liver. 16
23:15 all of them looking like officers 7
37: 8 as I looked, there were sinews on them, and flesh 16
40: 4 the man said to me, "Son of man, look with your eyes 16
44: 4 I looked, and behold, the glory of the LORD filled 16
Dan 2:34 As you looked, a stone was cut out by no human hand 21
7: 4 Then as I looked its wings were plucked off 21
6 After this I looked, and lo, another, like a leopard 21
9 As I looked, thrones were placed 21
11 looked then because of the sound 21
11 looked, the beast was slain, and its body 21
21 As I looked, this horn made war with the saints 21
10: 5 I lifted up my eyes and looked, and behold, a man 16
12: 5 Then I Daniel looked, and behold, two others stood 16
Jon 2: 4 how shall I again look upon thy holy temple? 8
Mic 7: 7 But as for me, I will look to the LORD 13
Nah 3: 5 and I will let nations look on your nakedness 16
7 all who look on you will shrink from you and say 16
Hab 1: 5 Look among the nations, and see; 16
13 than to behold evil and canst not look on wrong 8
13 why dost thou look on faithless men 8
3: 6 he looked and shook the nations; 16
Hag 1: 9 You have looked for much, and, lo, it came to little; 10
Zec 12:10 when they look on him whom they have pierced 8
Mat 5:28 I say to you that every one who looks at a woman 27
6:16 you fast, do not look dismal, like the hypocrites 28
26 Look at the birds of the air: they neither sow 30
11: 3 or shall we look for another? 48
12: 2 when the Pharisees saw it, they said to him, "Look 41
19:26 Jesus looked at them and said to them 30
22:11 But when the king came in to look at the guests 39

27:55 also many women there, looking on from afar 40
Mrk 2:24 Look, why are they doing what is not lawful 44
8:24 I see men; but they look like trees, walking. 44
10:27 Jesus looked at them and said 30
11:21 Peter remembered and said to him, "Master, look! 44
12:15 Bring me a coin, and let me look at it. 44
13: 1 one of his disciples said to him, "Look, Teacher 44
21 then if any one says to you, 'Look, here is the Christ!' 44
21 'Look, there he is!' do not believe it. 44
14:67 seeing Peter warming himself, she looked at him 30
15:40 There were also women looking on from afar 40
43 who was also himself looking for the kingdom of God 47
Lke 1:25 done to me in the days when he looked on me 32
2:25 looking for the consolation of Israel 47
38 all who were looking for the redemption of Jerusalem 47
48 your father and I have been looking for you anxiously. 37
7:19 Are you he . . or shall we look for another? 48
20 'Are you he . . or shall we look for another?' 48
9:62 puts his hand to the plow and looks back is fit 27
18:24 Jesus looking at him said, "How hard it is for those 44
20:17 he looked at them and said, "What then is this 30
21:29 Look at the fig tree, and all the trees; 29
22:38 they said, "Look, Lord, here are two swords. 41
61 the Lord turned and looked at Peter 30
23:51 he was looking for the kingdom of God. 47
Joh 1:36 and he looked at Jesus as he walked, and said 30
42 Jesus looked at him, and said, "So you are Simon 30
7:11 The Jews were looking for him at the feast 37
11:56 They were looking for Jesus 37
12:19 look, the world has gone after him. 44
13:22 The disciples looked at one another 27
19:37 They shall look on him whom they have pierced. 44
Act 1: 9 when he had said this, as they were looking 27
11 why do you stand looking into heaven? 27
3: 4 Look at us. 27
7:31 as he drew near to look, the voice of the Lord came 42
32 Moses trembled and did not dare to look. 42
10:19 3 men are looking for you. 37
21 I am the one you are looking for 37
11: 6 Looking at it closely I observed animals 42
25 Barnabas went to Tarsus to look for Saul; 23
27:12 looking northeast and southeast 27
2Co 3: 7 the Israelites could not look 25
4:18 because we look not to the things that are seen 51
10: 7 Look at what is before your eyes 27
Gal 6: 1 Look to yourself, lest you too be tempted. 52
Eph 5:15 Look carefully then how you walk 27
Php 2: 4 Let each of you look not only to his own interests 51
2Th 3:15 Do not look on him as an enemy 38
Heb 11:26 he looked to the reward. 24
12: 2 looking to Jesus the pioneer . . of our faith 26
Jas 1:25 he who looks into the perfect law 45
3: 4 Look at the ships also; though they are so great 41
1Pe 1:12 things into which angels long to look. 45
2Jn 1: 8 Look to yourselves, that you may not lose 27
Rev 4: 1 After this I looked, and lo, in heaven an open door! 44
3 a rainbow that looked like an emerald. 43
5: 3 able to open the scroll or to look upon it 27
4 no one was found worthy . . to look upon it. 27
11 Then I looked, and I heard around the throne 44
6:12 When he opened the sixth seal, I looked, and behold 44
7: 9 After this I looked, and behold, a great multitude 44
8:13 Then I looked and I heard an eagle crying 44
14: 1 Then I looked, and lo, on Mount Zion stood the Lamb 44
14 Then I looked, and lo, a white cloud 44
15: 5 After this I looked, and the temple . . was opened 44
1Es 4:33 the king and the nobles looked at one another 30
2Es 1:38 now, father, look with pride and see the people 55
4:48 I stood and looked, and behold, a flaming furnace 60
48 and when the flame had gone by I looked, and behold 60
7: 5 to reach the sea, to look at it or to navigate it 60
37 Look now, and understand whom you have denied 60
38 Look on this side and on that 60
66 they do not look for a judgment 59
8:23 whose look dries up the depths 54
10:27 I looked, and behold, the woman 60
11: 2 I looked, and behold, he spread his wings 60
3 I looked, and out of his wings 60
5 I looked, and behold, the eagle flew with his wings 60
7 I looked, and behold, the eagle rose 60
10 I looked, and behold, the voice did not come 60
12 I looked, and behold, on the right side one wing 60
20 I looked, and behold, in due course the wings 60
22 after this I looked, and behold, the twelve wings 60
24 I looked, and behold, two little wings separated 60
25 I looked, and behold, these little wings planned 60
26 I looked, and behold, one was set up 60
28 I looked, and behold, the two that remained 60
33 after this I looked, and behold, the middle head 60
35 I looked, and behold, the head on the right side 60
36 Then I heard a voice saying to me, "Look before you 57
37 I looked, and behold, a creature like a lion 60
44 the Most High has looked upon his times 58
12: 1 saying these words to the eagle, I looked 60
3 I looked, and behold, they also disappeared 60
13: 3 I looked, and behold, this wind made something 60
3 I looked, and behold, that man flew with the clouds ‡
3 wherever he turned his face to look 56
5 After this I looked, and behold, an . . multitude 60

6 I looked, and behold, he carved out for himself 60
8 After this I looked, and behold, all 60
Tob 5: 4 he went to look for a man 37
11 Are you looking for a tribe and a family 37
Jdt 4:15 to look with favor upon the whole house of Israel. 35
14:18 For look, here is Holofernes lying on the ground 41
AEs 15: 5 she looked happy, as if beloved 50
7 he looked at her in fierce anger 27
Wis 17:10 refusing to look even at the air 49
Sir 14:16 because in Hades one cannot look for luxury. 37
20:22 lose it because of his foolish look. 50
33:21 you should look to the hand of you sons. 30
34:15 To whom does he look? And who is his support? 33
40:29 When a man looks to the table of another 27
41:20 looking at a woman who is a harlot 43
42:16 The sun looks down on everything with its light 34
43:11 Look upon the rainbow, and praise him who made it 44
51: 7 I looked for the assistance of men 30
Bar 4:36 Look toward the east, O Jerusalem 46
5: 5 stand upon the height and look toward the east 46
Sus 1: 9 and turned away their eyes from looking to Heaven 27
20 Look, the garden doors are shut, no one sees us 41
Bel 1:18 the king looked at the table 34
19 Look at the floor, and notice whose footsteps 29
40 When he came to the den he looked in 30
1Mc 4: 5 so he looked for them in the hills 37
9:39 They raised their eyes and looked 44
45 For look! the battle is in front of us and behind us; 41
2Mc 3:17 which plainly showed to those who looked at him 40
7: 4 the brothers and the mother looked on. 53
16 he looked at the king, and said 44
28 to look at the heaven and the earth 22
12:45 if he was looking to the splendid reward 30
15: 8 now to look for the victory 48
34 they all, looking to heaven, blessed the Lord •
3Mc 5:30 with a threatening look he said 31
4Mc 13:13 all of them together looking at one another 36
15:18 the second in torments looked at you piteously 27
19 when you looked at the eyes of each one 40
17:10 looking to God and enduring torture 26

look after 1. שׁוּר 2. γίνομαι πρός 3. ἐπισκέπτομαι 4. ζητέω 5. ποιμαίνω

Hos 14: 8 It is I who answer and look after you. 1
Php 2:21 They all look after their own interests 4
Jde 1:12 carouse together, looking after themselves; 5
Sir 7:22 Do you have cattle? Look after them 3
2Mc 11:29 and look after your own affairs. 2

look aghast 1. תמה

Isa 13: 8 They will look aghast at one another; 1

look around 1. περιβλέπω

Mrk 3: 5 he looked around at them with anger 1
34 looking around on those who sat about him 1
5:32 he looked around to see who had done it. 1
9: 8 suddenly looking around they no longer saw 1
10:23 Jesus looked around and said to his disciples 1
Lke 6:10 he looked around on them all 1
Sir 9: 7 Do not look around in the streets of a city 1

look at one another 1. ראה

Gen 42: 1 he said to his sons, "Why do you look at one another 1

look at suspiciously 1. ὑποβλέπω

Sir 37:10 the one who looks at you suspiciously 1

look away 1. שׁעה

Ps 39:13 Look away from me, that I may know gladness 1

look back 1. פנה

Jer 46: 5 they look not back–terror on every side! 1
47: 3 the fathers look not back to the children 1

look closely 1. בין

1Kg 3:21 when I looked at it closely in the morning, behold 1

look down 1. נבט 2. שׁקף 3. καθοράω

Gen 19:28 he looked down toward Sodom and Gomor'rah 2
Exd 14:24 LORD . . looked down upon the host 2
Num 21:20 top of Pisgah which looks down upon the desert. 2
Deu 26:15 Look down from thy holy habitation, from heaven 2
1Sm 13:18 border that looks down upon the valley of Zebo'im 2
2Sm 24:20 when Arau'nah looked down, he saw the king 2
Ps 14: 2 The LORD looks down from heaven 2
53: 2 God looks down from heaven upon the sons of men 2
80:14 Look down from heaven, and see; 1
85:11 righteousness will look down from the sky. 2
102:19 that he looked down from his holy height 2
Isa 63:15 Look down from heaven and see 1
Lam 3:50 until the LORD from heaven looks down and sees; 2
Bar 2:16 O Lord, look down from thy holy habitation 3

look downcast 1. συμπίπτω τὸ πρόσωπον

Jdt 6: 9 do not look downcast 1

look favorably upon 1. ἐπιβλέπω

Tob 3: 3 Remember me and look favorably upon me 1

look forth 1.צפה 2.שגח 3.שקף

Ps 33:14 from where he sits enthroned he looks forth 2
Sng 6:10 Who is this that looks forth like the dawn 3
Hab 2: 1 and look forth to see what he will say to me 1

look forward 1.ἐκδέχομαι 2.προσδοκάω

Heb 11:10 he looked forward to the city 1
2Mc 15:20 all were now looking forward to the coming decision 2

look in amazement 1.תמה

Gen 43:33 and the men looked at one another in amazement. 1

look in anger 1.נפל פנים

Jer 3:12 I will not look on you in anger, for I am merciful 1

look in dismay 1.שמם

Ezk 4:17 and look at one another in dismay, and waste away 1

look intently 1.ἀτενίζω 2.διαβλέπω 3.καταμανθάνω 4.περιβλέπω

Mrk 8:25 he looked intently and was restored 2
Act 13: 9 Saul . . looked intently at him 1
14: 9 Paul, looking intently at him 1
23: 1 Paul, looking intently at the council, said 1
Tob 11: 5 Now Anna sat looking intently down the road 4
Sir 9: 5 Do not look intently at a virgin 3
8 look intently at beauty belonging to another; 3

look into 1.ἐμβλέπω 2.ἐπισκέπτομαι

1Es 8:12 in order to look into matters in Judea 2
Sir 42:18 he looks into the signs of the age. 1

look like 1.ὅμοιος

Rev 9: 7 on their heads were what looked like crowns 1

look one another 1.ראה

2Kg 14: 8 saying, "Come let us look one another in the face. 1
2Ch 25:17 Come, let us look one another in the face. 1

look out 1.שקף 2.βλέπω

Gen 26: 8 looked out of a window and saw Isaac 1
2Kg 9:32 Two or three eunuchs looked out at him. 1
Prv 7: 6 I have looked out through my lattice 1
Php 3: 2 Look out for the dogs 2
2 look out for the evil-workers 2
2 look out for those who mutilate the flesh. 2

look round 1.περιβλέπω

Mrk 11:11 when he had looked round at everything 1

look sad 1.σκυθρωπός

Lke 24:17 they stood still, looking sad. 1

look up 1.נשא עינים 2.αἴρω τοὺς ὀφθαλμούς 3.ἀναβλέπω 4.ἀνακύπτω 5.ἀτενίζω

Gen 37:25 Then they sat down to eat; and looking up they saw 1
Mat 14:19 he looked up to heaven, and blessed, and broke 3
Mrk 6:41 he looked up to heaven 3
7:34 looking up to heaven, he sighed, and said 3
8:24 he looked up and said, "I see men 3
16: 4 And looking up, they saw that the stone 3
Lke 9:16 he looked up to heaven, and blessed and broke them 3
19: 5 he looked up and said to him 3
21: 1 He looked up and saw the rich 3
28 look up and raise your heads 4
Joh 8:10 Jesus looked up and said to her, "Woman 4
Sus 1:35 she, weeping, looked up toward heaven 3
Man 1: 9 I am unworthy to look up and see the height 5
1Mc 4:12 When the foreigners looked up 2
5:30 At dawn they looked up 2

look upon 1.חזה 2.מַרְאֶה 3.נבט 4.ראה 5.εἰσοράω 6.ἐμβλέπω 7.ἐναντίον 8.ἐπεῖδον 9.ἐπιβλέπω 10.θεάομαι 11.aspicio 12.pervideo 13.video

Gen 24:16 The maiden was very fair to look upon 2
26: 7 of Rebekah"; because she was fair to look upon. 2
29:32 Because the LORD has looked upon my affliction; 4
Num 4:20 they shall not go in to look upon the holy things 4
15:39 shall be to you a tassel to look upon and remember 4
Job 10:15 with disgrace and look upon my affliction. 4
Ps 63: 2 I have looked upon thee in the sanctuary 1
84: 9 look upon the face of thine anointed! 3
Isa 33:20 Look upon Zion, the city of our appointed feasts! 1
38:11 I shall look upon man no more 3
Ezk 16: 8 When I passed by you again and looked upon you 4
Ams 5:22 your fatted beasts I will not look upon. 3
Hab 1: 3 make me see wrongs and look upon trouble? 3
Mrk 10:21 Jesus looking upon him loved him, and said to him 6
Lke 9:38 I beg you to look upon my son, for he is my only child; 9
Act 4:29 now, Lord, look upon their threats 8
1Jn 1: 1 That . . which we have looked upon and touched 10
2Es 8:26 O look not upon the sins of thy people 11
9:45 and looked upon my low estate 12
10:29 and he looked upon me; 13
Jdt 1:11 but looked upon him as only one man 7
4:13 the Lord . . looked upon their affliction 5
6:19 look this day upon the faces of those . . consecrated 9
13: 4 look in this hour upon the work of my hands 9
Sir 11:12 the eyes of the Lord look upon him for his good 9
16:19 shake with trembling when he looks upon them. 9
29 After this the Lord looked upon the earth 9
23:19 they look upon all the ways of men 9
33:15 Look upon all the works of the Most High 6
36: 1 look upon us 9
42:12 Do not look upon any one for beauty 6
Aza 1:32 and lookest upon the deeps 9
2Mc 1:27 look upon those who are rejected and despised 8
8: 2 They besought the Lord to look upon the people 8
3Mc 6: 3 look upon the descendants of Abraham, O Father 8

look well 1.בין

Ps 37:10 though you look well at his place, he will not be 1

look with envy 1.רצד

Ps 68:16 Why look you with envy, O many-peaked mountain 1

look with favor 1.עַיִן

Ps 101: 6 I will look with favor on the faithful in the land 1

look with greedy eye 1.ἐπιβλέπω

1Sm 2:29 Why then look with greedy eye at my sacrifices 1

without a backward look 1.ἀνεπιστρέπτως

3Mc 1:20 and without a backward look 1

good looks 1.κάλλος

Sir 11: 2 Do not praise a man for his good looks 1

loom 1.אֶרֶג 2.דַּלָּה

Jdg 16:14 and pulled away the pin, the loom, and the web. 1
Isa 38:12 he cuts me off from the loom; 2

loom (2) 1.שקף

Jer 6: 1 for evil looms out of the north 1

loop 1.לוּלִי

Exd 26: 4 you shall make loops of blue on the edge 1
4 and likewise you shall make loops on the edge •
5 50 loops you shall make on the one curtain 1
5 50 loops you shall make on the edge 1
5 the loops shall be opposite one another. 1
10 you shall make 50 loops on the edge 1
10 shall make 50 loops on the edge of the curtain 1
11 and put the clasps into the loops 1
36:11 he made loops of blue on the edge of the outmost 1
12 he made 50 loops on the one curtain 1
12 he made 50 loops on the edge of the curtain 1
12 the loops were opposite one another. 1
17 he made 50 loops on the edge of the outmost 1
17 made . . 50 loops on the edge of the other 1

loose 1.זור 2.פתח 3.רפה 4.שלח 5.שרא (A) 6.ἀσώτως 7.ἑταιρίζω 8.λύω

Job 12:18 He looses the bonds of kings 2
21 and looses the belt of the strong. 3
30:11 Because God has loosed my cord and humbled me 2
38:31 the Plei'ades, or loose the cords of Orion? 2
39: 5 Who has loosed the bonds of the swift ass 2
Ps 30:11 thou hast loosed my sackcloth 2
116:16 Thou hast loosed my bonds. 2
Prv 2:16 You will be saved from the loose woman 1
7: 5 to preserve you from the loose woman 1
Isa 5:27 not a waistcloth is loose, not a sandal-thong 2
20: 2 Go, and loose the sackcloth from your loins 2
52: 2 loose the bonds from your neck, O captive 2
58: 6 that I choose: to loose the bonds of wickedness 2
Ezk 5:16 I loose against you my deadly arrows of famine 4
16 destruction, which I will loose to destroy you 4
Dan 3:25 But I see four men loose, walking in the midst 5
Mat 16:19 whatever you loose on earth 8
19 shall be loosed in heaven. 8
18:18 whatever you loose on earth 8
18 loose on earth shall be loosed in heaven. 8
Lke 1:64 his mouth was opened and his tongue loosed •
13:16 be loosed from this bond on the sabbath day? 8
15:13 he squandered his property in loose living. 6
Act 2:24 having loosed the pangs of death 8
Rev 20: 3 After that he must be loosed for a little while. 8
7 Satan will be loosed from his prison 8
Jdt 9: 2 had loosed the girdle of a virgin to defile her 8
Sir 9: 3 Do not go to meet a loose woman 7
3Mc 6:27 Loose and untie their unjust bonds! 8
4Mc 12: 8 he said, "Let me loose, let me speak to the king 8

loose woman 1.זור

Prv 5: 3 For the lips of a loose woman drip honey 1
20 Why . . be infatuated, my son, with a loose woman 1
22:14 The mouth of a loose woman is a deep pit; 1

loosen 1.שמט 2.ἀνίημι

Jer 17: 4 You shall loosen your hand from your heritage 1
Act 27:40 loosening the ropes that tied the rudders 2

loot 1.שלח יד

Obd 1:13 you should not have looted his goods 1

lop the bough 1.סעף

Isa 10:33 Behold . . the LORD of hosts will lop the boughs 1

lord 1.אָדוֹן 2.אַדִּיר 3.בַּעַל 4.גְּבִיר 5.סֶרֶן 6.שַׂר 7.שׂרר 8.שלט 9.מָרֵא (A) 10.רַבְרְבָן (A) 11.δεσπότης 12.κυριεύω 13.κύριος 14.dominus

Gen 18: 3 said, "My lord, if I have found favor 1
19: 2 said, "My lords, turn aside, I pray you 1
18 Lot said to them, "Oh, no, my lords; 1
23: 6 Hear us, my lord; you are a mighty prince among us. 1
11 No, my lord, hear me; I give you the field 1
15 My lord, listen to me; a piece of land 1
24:18 She said, "Drink, my lord"; 1
27:29 Be lord over your brothers 4
37 Behold, I have made him your lord 4
31:35 she said to her father, "Let not my lord be angry 1
32: 4 you shall say to my lord Esau: Thus says 1
5 I have sent to tell my lord, in order that I may find 1
18 they are a present sent to my lord Esau; 1
33: 8 To find favor in the sight of my lord. 1
13 Jacob said to him, "My lord knows that the children 1
14 Let my lord pass on before his servant 1
14 lead on slowly . . until I come to my lord in Se'ir. 1
15 Let me find favor in the sight of my lord. 1
40: 1 his baker offended their lord the king of Egypt. 1
42:10 They said to him, "No, my lord, but to buy food 1
30 The man, the lord of the land, spoke roughly to us 1
33 Then the man, the lord of the land, said to us 1
43:20 said, "Oh, my lord, we came down the first time 1
44: 5 Is it not from this that my lord drinks 1
7 said to him, "Why does my lord speak such words 1
8 steal silver or gold from your lord's house? 1
9 let him die, and we also will be my lord's slaves. 1
16 Judah said, "What shall we say to my lord? 1
16 behold, we are my lord's slaves 1
18 Then Judah went up to him and said, "O my lord 1
18 I pray you, speak a word in my lord's ears 1
19 My lord asked his servants, saying 1
20 we said to my lord, 'We have a father, an old man 1
22 said to my lord, 'The lad cannot leave his father 1
24 we told him the words of my lord. 1
33 remain instead of the lad as a slave to my lord; 1
45: 8 has made me . . lord of all his house 1
9 God has made me lord of all Egypt; come down to me 1
47:18 We will not hide from my lord that our money 1
18 and the herds of cattle are my lord's; 1
18 there is nothing left in the sight of my lord 1
25 may it please my lord, we will be slaves 1
Exd 32:22 Aaron said, "Let not the anger of my lord burn hot; 1
Num11:28 Joshua . . said, "My lord Moses, forbid them. 1
12:11 Aaron said to Moses, "Oh, my lord, do not punish us 1
21:28 Ar of Moab, the lords of the heights of the Arnon. 3
32:25 Your servants will do as my lord commands. 1
27 before the LORD to battle, as my lord orders. 1
36: 2 LORD commanded my lord to give the land 1
2 my lord was commanded by the LORD to give 1
Deu 10:17 LORD your God is God of gods and Lord of lords 1
Jos 5:14 What does my lord bid his servant? 1
Jdg 3: 3 nations: the five lords of the Philistines 5
25 and there lay their lord dead on the floor. 1
4:18 said to him, "Turn aside, my lord, turn aside to me; 1
16: 5 the lords of the Philistines came to her and said 5
8 the lords of the Philistines brought her seven 5
18 she sent and called the lords of the Philistines 5
18 the lords of the Philistines came up to her 5
23 the lords of the Philistines gathered to offer 5
27 all the lords of the Philistines were there 5
30 house fell upon the lords and upon all the people 5
Rut 2:13 Then she said, "You are most gracious to me, my lord 1
1Sm 1:15 No, my lord, I am a woman sorely troubled; 1
26 Oh, my lord! As you live, my lord, I am the woman 1
26 As you live, my lord, I am the woman 1
5: 8 gathered . . all the lords of the Philistines 5
11 and gathered . . all the lords of the Philistines 5
6: 4 the number of the lords of the Philistines; 5
4 same plague was upon . . you and upon your lords. 5
12 the lords of the Philistines went after them 5
16 when the five lords of the Philistines saw it 5
18 all the cities . . belonging to the five lords 5
7: 7 the lords of the Philistines went up against 5
16:16 Let our lord now command your servants . . to seek 1
22:12 Hear now . . " And he answered, "Here I am, my lord. 1
24: 6 LORD forbid that I should do this thing to my lord 1
8 David . . called after Saul, "My lord the king! 1
10 I said, 'I will not put forth my hand against my lord; 1
25:24 Upon me alone, my lord, be the guilt; 1
25 Let not my lord regard this ill-natured fellow 1
25 your handmaid did not see the young men of my lord 1
26 Now then, my lord, as the LORD lives 1
26 enemies and those who seek to do evil to my lord 1
27 which your servant has brought to my lord 1
27 be given to the young men who follow my lord. 1
28 the LORD will certainly make my lord a sure house 1
28 my lord is fighting the battles of the LORD; 1
29 the life of my lord shall be bound in the bundle 1

30 LORD has done to my lord according to all the good 1
31 my lord shall have no cause of grief, or pangs 1
31 or for my lord taking vengeance himself. 1
31 And when the LORD has dealt well with my lord 1
41 to wash the feet of the servants of my lord. 1
26:15 have you not kept watch over your lord the king? 1
15 For one . . came in to destroy the king your lord. 1
16 kept watch over your lord, the LORD's anointed. 1
17 And David said, "It is my voice, my lord, O king. 1
18 he said, "Why does my lord pursue after his servant? 1
19 let my lord the king hear . . his servant. 1
29: 2 As the lords of the Philistines were passing 5
4 could this fellow reconcile himself to his lord? 1
6 Nevertheless the lords do not approve of you. 5
7 not displease the lords of the Philistines. 5
8 and fight against the enemies of my lord the king? 1
10 rise early . . with the servants of your lord 1
2Sm 1:10 I took . . and I have brought them here to my lord. 1
2: 5 you showed this loyalty to Saul your lord 1
7 and be valiant; for Saul your lord is dead 1
3:21 I . . will gather all Israel to my lord the king 1
4: 8 the LORD has avenged my lord the king . . on Saul 1
9:11 According to all that my lord the king commands 1
10: 3 princes . . said to Hanun their lord 1
11: 9 Uri'ah slept . . with all the servants of his lord 1
11 my lord Jo'ab . . are camping in the open field; 1
11 Jo'ab and the servants of my lord are camping 1
13 to lie on his couch with the servants of his lord 1
13:32 Let not my lord suppose that they have killed 1
33 let not my lord the king so take it to heart 1
14: 9 On me be the guilt, my lord the king 1
12 Pray let your handmaid speak a word to my lord 1
15 Now I have come to say this to my lord the king 1
17 The word of my lord the king will set me at rest'; 1
17 for my lord the king is like the angel of God 1
18 And the woman said, "Let my lord the king speak. 1
19 As surely as you live, my lord the king, one cannot 1
19 from anything that my lord the king has said. 1
20 But my lord has wisdom like . . the angel of God 1
22 I have found favor in your sight, my lord the king 1
15:15 ready to do whatever my lord the king decides. 1
21 As the LORD lives, and as my lord the king lives 1
21 wherever my lord the king shall be . . there also 1
16: 4 let me . . find favor in your sight, my lord the king. 1
9 Why should this dead dog curse my lord the king? 1
18:28 who raised their hand against my lord the king. 1
31 Cushite said, "Good tidings for my lord the king! 1
32 the enemies of my lord the king, and all who rise up 1
19:19 Let not my lord hold me guilty or remember how 1
19 on the day my lord the king left Jerusalem; 1
20 the first . . to come down to meet my lord the king. 1
26 "My lord, O king, my servant deceived me; 1
27 He . . slandered your servant to my lord the king. 1
27 But my lord the king is like the angel of God; 1
28 but men doomed to death before my lord the king; 1
30 since my lord the king has come safely home. 1
35 Why then . . be an added burden to my lord the king? 1
37 let him go over with my lord the king; 1
20: 6 take your lord's servants and pursue him 1
24: 3 while the eyes of my lord the king still see it; 1
3 why does my lord the king delight in this thing? 1
21 Why has my lord the king come to his servant? 1
22 Let my lord the king take and offer up what seems 1
1Kg 1: 2 Let a young maiden be sought for my lord the king 1
2 in your bosom, that my lord the king may be warm. 1
11 has become king and David our lord does not know 1
13 Did you not, my lord the king, swear 1
17 My lord, you swore to your maidservant by the LORD 1
18 is king, although you, my lord the king, do not know 1
20 now, my lord the king, the eyes of all Israel are 1
20 who shall sit on the throne of my lord the king 1
21 when my lord the king sleeps with his fathers 1
24 My lord the king, have you said, 'Adoni'jah shall 1
27 this thing been brought about by my lord the king 1
27 who should sit on the throne of my lord the king 1
31 and said, "May my lord King David live for ever. 1
33 Take with you the servants of your lord, and cause 1
36 May the LORD, the God of my lord the king, say so. 1
37 As the LORD has been with my lord the king, even 1
37 greater than the throne of my lord King David. 1
43 No, for our lord King David has made Solomon king; 1
47 came to congratulate our lord King David, saying 1
2:38 as my lord the king has said, so will your servant 1
3:17 my lord, this woman and I dwell in the same house; 1
26 my lord, give her the living child, and by no means 1
12:27 this people will turn again to their lord 1
18: 7 and said, "Is it you, my lord Eli'jah? 1
8 Go, tell your lord, 'Behold, Eli'jah is here.' 1
10 no nation or kingdom whither my lord has not sent 1
11 'Go, tell your lord, "Behold, Eli'jah is here."' 1
13 Has it not been told my lord what I did 1
14 'Go, tell your lord, "Behold, Eli'jah is here"'; 1
20: 4 As you say, my lord, O king, I am yours 1
9 Tell my lord the king, 'All that you first demanded 1
2Kg 2:19 the situation . . is pleasant, as my lord sees; 1
4:16 she said, "No, my lord, O man of God; do not lie 1
28 Then she said, "Did I ask my lord for a son? 1
5: 3 Would that my lord were with the prophet 1
4 Na'aman . . told his lord, "Thus and so spoke 1
6:12 None, my lord, O king; but Eli'sha . . tells the king 1
26 woman cried out to him, saying, "Help, my lord, 1
8: 5 And Geha'zi said, "My lord, O king, here is the woman 1
12 Haz'ael said, "Why does my lord weep? 1
1Ch 21: 3 my lord the king, all of them my lord's servants? 1
3 my lord the king, all of them my lord's servants? 1
3 Why then should my lord require this? 1
23 Take it; and let my lord the king do what seems good 1
2Ch 2:14 with your craftsmen, the craftsmen of my lord 1
15 of which my lord has spoken 1
13: 6 rose up and rebelled against his lord; 1
Ezr 8:25 king and his counselors and his lords 6
10: 3 according to the counsel of my lord 1
Neh 5:15 Even their servants lorded it over the people. 8
Est 1:22 that every man be lord in his own house 7
Ps 45:11 Since he is your lord, bow to him; 1
97: 5 before the LORD, before the Lord of all the earth. 1
105:21 he made him lord of his house, and ruler of all 1
110: 1 LORD says to my lord: "Sit at my right hand 1
136: 3 O give thanks to the Lord of lords 1
Ecc 8: 9 while man lords it over man to his hurt. 8
Isa 16: 8 lords of the nations . . struck down its branches 3
26:13 other lords besides thee have ruled over us 1
Jer 22:18 They shall not lament for him, saying, 'Ah lord!' 1
25:34 and roll in ashes, you lords of the flock 2
35 nor escape for the lords of the flock. 2
36 the cry of the shepherds, and the wail of the lords 2
34: 5 and lament for you, saying, "Alas, lord! 1
37:20 Now hear, I pray you, O my lord the king 1
38: 9 My lord the king, these men have done evil 1
Dan 1:10 fear lest my lord the king, who appointed 1
4:19 My lord, may the dream be for those who hate you 9
24 decree . . which has come upon my lord the king 9
36 counselors and my lords sought me 10
5: 1 made a great feast for 1,000 of his lords 10
2 king and his lords, his wives, and his concubines 10
3 king and his lords, his wives, and his concubines 10
9 his lords were perplexed. 10
10 because of the words of the king and his lords 10
23 lords, your wives, and your concubines have drunk 10
6:17 king sealed it . . with the signet of his lords 10
10:16 O my lord, by reason of the vision pains have come 1
17 How can my lord's servant talk with my lord? 1
17 How can my lord's servant talk with my lord? 1
19 Let my lord speak, for you have strengthened me. 1
12: 8 O my lord, what shall be the issue of these things? 1
Zec 1: 9 Then I said, 'What are these, my lord?' 1
4: 4 And I said . . "What are these, my lord? 1
5 Do you not know what these are?" I said, "No, my lord. 1
13 Do you not know what these are?" I said, "No, my lord. 1
6: 4 Then I said to the angel . . "What are these, my lord? 1
Mat 12: 8 For the Son of man is lord of the sabbath. 13
18:25 as he could not pay, his lord ordered him to be sold 13
27 the lord of that servant released him 13
31 they went and reported to their lord 13
32 Then his lord summoned him and said to him 13
34 in anger his lord delivered him to the jailers 13
25:11 'Lord, lord, open to us.' 13
Mrk 2:28 the Son of man is lord even of the sabbath. 13
Lke 6: 5 The Son of man is lord of the sabbath. 13
Act 25:26 nothing definite to write to my lord about him 13
1Co 8: 5 as indeed there are many "gods" and many "lords"- 13
1Ti 6:15 the King of kings and Lord of lords 12
1Pe 3: 6 as Sarah obeyed Abraham, calling him lord. 13
Rev 17:14 Lamb . . for he is Lord of lords and King of kings 13
19:16 a name inscribed, King of kings and Lord of lords. 13
1Es 2:17 To King Artaxerxes our lord 13
18 Now be it known to our lord the king 13
21 to speak to our lord the king 13
24 we now make known to you, O lord and king 13
4: 3 the king is stronger; he is their lord and master 12
14 Who then is their master, or who is their lord? 12
46 now, O lord the king, this is what I ask and request 13
6: 8 Let it be fully known to our lord the king 13
21 in the royal archives of our lord the king 13
22 if it is approved by our lord the king 13
2Es 2:44 Then I asked an angel, "Who are these, my lord? 14
4: 3 Then I said, "Yes, my lord. 14
5 I said, "Speak on, my lord. 14
22 Then I answered and said, "I beseech you, my lord 14
41 I said, "No, lord, it cannot. 14
5:33 I said, "Speak, my lord." And he said to me 14
34 I said, "No, my lord 14
35 he said . . "You cannot." And I said, "Why not, my lord? 14
7: 3 I said, "Speak, my lord." And he said to me 14
10 I said, "He cannot, lord." And he said to me 14
9:41 she said . . "Let me alone, my lord, that I may weep 14
10:34 I said, "Speak, my lord; only do not forsake me 14
Jdt 2: 5 the Great King, the lord of the whole earth 13
15 as his lord had ordered him to do 13
5: 5 Let my lord now hear a word 13
20 Now therefore, my master and lord 13
21 then let my lord pass them by; 13
6: 4 Nebuchadnezzar, the lord of the whole earth 13
7: 9 Let our lord hear a word 11
11 Therefore, my lord, do not fight against them 11
10:15 hurrying down to the presence of our lord 13
11: 4 the servants of my lord King Nebuchadnezzar. 13
5 I will tell nothing false to my lord this night. 13
6 my lord will not fail to achieve his purposes. 13
10 my lord and master, do not disregard what he said 13
11 now, in order that my lord may not be defeated 13
17 therefore, my lord, I will remain with you 13
22 those who have slighted my lord. 13
12: 4 Judith replied, "As your soul lives, my lord 13
6 Let my lord now command 13
13 come to my lord and be honored in his presence 13
14 Judith said, "Who am I, to refuse my lord? 13
18 Judith said, "I will drink now, my lord 13
14:13 Wake up our lord 13
AEs 15:13 I saw you, my lord, like an angel of God 13
14 For you are wonderful, my lord 13
Sir 51:10 I appealed to the Lord, the Father of my lord 13
1Mc 2:53 kept the commandment, and became lord of Egypt. 13
4Mc 2: 7 unless reason is clearly lord of the emotions? 13
7:23 courageous man is lord of his emotions. 13

lord it over 1. κατακυριεύω

Mat 20:25 the rulers of the Gentiles lord it over them 1
Mrk 10:42 lord it over them 1

lord over 1. κυριεύω 2. ὑπεραίρω

2Co 1:24 Not that we lord it over your faith 1
2Mc 5:23 who lorded it over his fellow citizens 2

sovereign Lord 1. δεσπότης

Act 4:24 Sovereign Lord, who didst make the heaven 1
Rev 6:10 O Sovereign Lord, holy and true, how long before 1

lordly 1. אַדִּיר 2. אֶדֶר

Jdg 5:25 she brought him curds in a lordly bowl. 1
Zec 11:13 the lordly price at which I was paid off by them. 2

lose 1. אבד 2. אֲבֵדָה 3. אסף 4. יצא 5. כרת 6. נפל 7. שׁכח 8. ἀπόλλυμι 9. ἀποστρέφω 10. ἀπώλεια 11. διαγίνομαι 12. διαπίπτω 13. διαφωνέω 14. ἐκλείπω 15. ἐκπίπτω 16. ἐλαττονόω 17. λήγω 18. amitto 19. perdo

Lev 6: 3 or has found what was lost and lied about it 2
Deu 22: 3 any lost thing . . which he loses and you find; 1
Jos 19:47 the territory of the Danites was lost to them 4
Jdg 18:25 fall upon you, and you lose your life 3
1Sm 9: 3 Now the asses of Kish, Saul's father, were lost. 1
20 As for your asses that were lost three days ago 1
1Kg 18: 5 save . . alive, and not lose some of the animals. 5
20:25 muster an army like the army that you have lost 6
Job 11:20 all way of escape will be lost to them 1
Ps 119:176 I have gone astray like a lost sheep; 1
Ecc 3: 6 a time to seek, and a time to lose; 1
5:14 and those riches were lost in a bad venture; 1
9: 5 but the memory of them is lost. 7
Isa 27:13 those who were lost in the land of Assyria 1
Jer 50: 6 My people have been lost sheep; 1
Ezk 19: 5 saw that she was baffled, that her hope was lost 1
34: 4 the lost you have not sought 1
16 I will seek the lost, and I will bring back 1
37:11 our hope is lost; we are clean cut off 1
Zep 3: 7 will not lose sight of all that I have enjoined 5
Mat 5:29 is better that you lose one of your members 8
30 is better that you lose one of your members 8
10: 6 go rather to the lost sheep 8
39 He who finds his life will lose it 8
39 he who loses his life for my sake will find it. 8
42 truly, I say to you, he shall not lose his reward. 8
15:24 I was sent only to the lost sheep 8
16:25 For whoever would save his life will lose it 8
25 whoever loses his life for my sake will find it. 8
Mrk 2:22 the wine is lost, and so are the skins 8
8:35 For whoever would save his life will lose it; 8
35 whoever loses his life for my sake 8
9:41 will by no means lose his reward. 8
Lke 9:24 For whoever would save his life will lose it; 8
24 whoever loses his life for my sake, he will save it. 8
25 loses or forfeits himself? 8
15: 4 if he has lost one of them 8
4 go after the one which is lost, until he finds it? 8
6 I have found my sheep which was lost.' 8
8 having ten silver coins, if she loses one coin 8
9 I have found the coin which I had lost.' 8
24 he was lost, and is found 8
32 he was lost, and is found.' 8
17:33 Whoever seeks to gain his life will lose it 8
33 whoever loses his life will preserve it. 8
19:10 the Son of man came to seek and to save the lost. 8
Joh 6:12 that nothing may be lost. 8
39 I should lose nothing of all that he has given me 8
12:25 He who loves his life loses it 8
17:12 none of them is lost but the son of perdition 8
18: 9 Of those whom thou gavest me I lost not one. 8
Act 27: 9 As much time had been lost 11
2Pe 3:17 lest you . . lose your own stability. 15
2Jn 1: 8 that you may not lose what you have worked for 8
Rev 18:14 thy dainties and thy splendor are lost to thee 8
2Es 2: 3 but with mourning and sorrow I have lost you 18
9:20 I considered my world, and behold, it was lost 19
10:11 she who lost so great a multitude 19
12 for I have lost the fruit of my womb 19

14:10 For the age has lost its youth 19
16:41 let him that buys be like one who will lose; 19
Tob 7: 7 When he heard that Tobit had lost his sight 8
14: 2 He was 58 years old when he lost his sight 8
Jdt 10:13 without losing one of his men, captured or slain. 13
Wis 16: 3 might lose the least remnant of appetite 9
Sir 2:14 Woe to you who have lost your endurance! 8
8:12 if you do lend anything, be as one who has lost it. 8
9: 6 lest you lose your inheritance. 8
19: 7 you will lose nothing at all. 16
20:22 A man may lose his life through shame 8
22 lose it because of his foolish look. 8
29:10 Lose your silver for the sake of a brother 8
10 do not let it rust under a stone and be lost. 10
14 a man who has lost his sense of shame 8
41: 2 one who is contrary, and has lost his patience! 8
2Mc 2:14 the books that had been lost on account of the war 12
9:11 he began to lose much of his arrogance 17
3Mc 2:23 fearing lest he should lose his life 14

lose courage 1. ἐκλύω
Heb 12: 5 nor lose courage when you are punished by him. 1

lose heart 1. נבל 2. ἀθυμέω 3. ἐγκακέω 4. ἐκλύω
2Sm 22:46 Foreigners lost heart, and came trembling out 1
Ps 18:45 Foreigners lost heart, and came trembling 1
Lke 18: 1 they ought always to pray and not lose heart. 3
2Co 4: 1 by the mercy of God, we do not lose heart. 3
16 So we do not lose heart 3
Gal 6: 9 if we do not lose heart. 4
Eph 3:13 I ask you not to lose heart 3
Jdt 7:22 Their children lost heart 2

lose one's mind 1. ἀπονοέω
1Es 4:26 Many men have lost their minds because of women 1

lose one's temper 1. πικραίνω
1Es 4:31 if she loses her temper with him, he flatters her 1

lose saltness 1. ἄναλος
Mrk 9:49 if the salt has lost its saltness 1

lose taste 1. μωραίνω
Mat 5:13 if salt has lost its taste, how shall its saltness 1
Lke 14:34 if salt has lost its taste 1

lose the seal 1. resigno
2Es 10:23 for she has now lost the seal of her glory 1

loss 1. נֶזֶק 2. ἀποβάλλω 3. ἀπορέω 4. ἐλάττωσις 5. ἐπ' ἐλαττώσει 6. ζημία
Est 7: 4 is not to be compared with the loss to the king. 1
Act 25:20 Being at a loss how to investigate these questions 3
27:10 the voyage will be with injury and much loss 6
21 incurred this injury and loss. 6
22 no loss of life among you, but only of the ship. 2
Php 3: 7 I counted as loss for the sake of Christ. 6
8 Indeed I count everything as loss 6
Tob 4:13 in shiftlessness there is loss and great want 4
Wis 18:11 the common man suffered the same loss as the king; *
Sir 18: 7 when he stops, he will be at a loss. 3
20: 2 will be kept from loss. 4
9 a windfall may result in a loss. 4
11 There are losses because of glory 4
22: 3 the birth of a daughter is a loss. 5
40:26 There is no loss in the fear of the Lord 4

loss of a child 1. שְׁכוֹל
Isa 47: 8 sit as a widow or know the loss of children 1
9 the loss of children and widowhood shall come 1

loss of sight 1. ἀορασία
Wis 19:17 They were stricken also with loss of sight 1

loss of sleep 1. ἀγρυπνία
2Mc 2:26 but calls for sweat and loss of sleep 1

loss of time 1. ישב
Exd 21:19 only he shall pay for the loss of his time 1

utterly at a loss 1. בושׁ
Jdg 3:25 they waited till they were utterly at a loss; 1

lost 1. גזר 2. דמה 3. שׁגה
Prv 5:23 because of his great folly he is lost. 3
Isa 6: 5 For I am lost; for I am a man of unclean lips 2
Lam 3:54 water closed over my head; I said, 'I am lost.' 1

lost thing 1. אֲבֵדָה
Exd 22: 9 lost thing, of which one says, 'This is it,' 1
Lev 6: 4 the lost thing which he found 1
Deu 22: 3 so . . do with any lost thing of your brother's 1

lot 1. גּוֹרָל 2. חֵלֶק 3. קֶסֶם 4. חֵלֶק (A) 5. κεῖμαι 6. κληρονομέω 7. κλῆρος 8. μερίζω 9. μέρος
Lev 16: 8 Aaron shall cast lots upon the two goats 1
8 one lot for the LORD and the other lot for Aza'zel 1
8 one lot for the LORD and the other lot for Aza'zel 1
9 the goat on which the lot fell for the LORD 1
10 the goat on which the lot fell for Aza'zel 1
Num26:55 the land shall be divided by lot; 1
56 inheritance shall be divided according to lot 1
33:54 inherit . . by lot according to your families; 1
54 wherever the lot falls to any man, that shall be his 1
34:13 This is the land which you shall inherit by lot 1
36: 2 my lord to give the land for inheritance by lot 1
3 be taken away from the lot of our inheritance. 1
Jos 14: 2 Their inheritance was by lot 1
15: 1 The lot for . . Judah according to their families 1
17:14 Why have you given me but one lot and one portion 1
17 you shall not have one lot only 1
18: 6 and I will cast lots for you here before the LORD 1
8 and I will cast lots for you here before the LORD 1
10 Joshua cast lots . . in Shiloh before the LORD; 1
11 The lot of the tribe of Benjamin . . came up 1
19: 1 The second lot came out for Simeon 1
10 The third lot came up for the tribe of Zeb'ulun 1
17 The fourth lot came out for Is'sachar 1
24 The fifth lot came out for the tribe of Asher 1
32 The sixth lot came out for the tribe of Naph'tali 1
40 The seventh lot came out for the tribe of Dan 1
51 inheritances . . distributed by lot at Shiloh 1
21: 4 The lot came out for the . . Ko'hathites. 1
4 those Levites . . received by lot from the tribes 1
5 Ko'hathites received by lot from the families 1
6 Gersonites received by lot . . thirteen cities. 1
8 These . . the people of Israel gave by lot 1
10 which went . . since the lot fell to them first. 1
Jdg 20: 9 we will do to Gib'e-ah: we will go up against it by lot 1
1Ch 6:54 families of Ko'hathites, for theirs was the lot 1
61 the Ko'hathites were given by lot . . ten cities. 1
65 They also gave them by lot . . these cities 1
24: 5 They organized them by lot, all alike 1
7 The first lot fell to Jehoi'arib 1
31 head . . and his younger brother alike, cast lots 1
25: 8 they cast lots for their duties, small and great 1
9 The first lot fell for Asaph to Joseph; 1
26:13 cast lots by fathers' houses, small and great 1
14 The lot for the east fell to Shelemi'ah. 1
14 They cast lots also for his son Zechari'ah 1
14 Zechari'ah . . and his lot came out for the north. 1
Neh 10:34 likewise cast lots, the priests, the Levites 1
11: 1 rest . . cast lots to bring one out of ten to live 1
Est 3: 7 they cast Pur, that is the lot, before Haman 1
9:24 and had cast Pur, that is the lot, 1
Ps 16: 5 my chosen portion and my cup; thou holdest my lot. 1
22:18 for my raiment they cast lots. 1
Prv 1:14 throw in your lot among us 1
16:33 The lot is cast into the lap 1
18:18 The lot puts an end to disputes 1
Ecc 3:22 a man should enjoy his work, for that is his lot; 2
5:18 for this is his lot. 2
19 to accept his lot and find enjoyment in his toil– 2
Isa 17:14 portion . . and the lot of those who plunder us. 1
34:17 He has cast the lot for them 1
57: 6 the smooth stones . . they, are your lot; 1
61: 7 of dishonor you shall rejoice in your lot; 2
Jer 13:25 This is your lot, the portion I have measured out 1
Ezk 21:22 Into his right hand comes the lot for Jerusalem 3
Dan 4:15 let his lot be with the beasts in the grass 4
23 let his lot be with the beasts of the field 4
Jol 3: 3 and have cast lots for my people 1
Obd 1:11 and foreigners . . cast lots for Jerusalem 1
Jon 1: 7 they said to one another, "Come, let us cast lots 1
7 So they cast lots, and the lot fell upon Jonah. 1
7 So they cast lots, and the lot fell upon Jonah. 1
Mic 2: 5 you will have none to cast the line by lot 1
Nah 3:10 for her honored men lots were cast 1
Zep 2:10 This shall be their lot in return for their pride *
Mat 27:35 they divided his garments among them by casting lots 7
Mrk 15:24 casting lots for them 7
Lke 23:34 they cast lots to divide his garments. 7
Joh 19:24 for my clothing they cast lots. 7
Act 1:26 they cast lots for them 7
26 the lot fell on Matthi'as 7
8:21 You have neither part nor lot in this matter 7
1Th 3: 3 You yourselves know that this is to be our lot. 5
Rev 21: 8 their lot shall be in the lake that burns 9
AEs 10:10 For this purpose he made two lots 7
11 these two lots came to the hour and moment and day 7
Wis 2: 9 because this is our portion, and this our lot. 7
5: 5 why is his lot among the saints? 7
Sir 14:15 what you acquired by toil to be divided by lot? 7
20:25 the lot of both is ruin. 6
25:19 may a sinner's lot befall her! 7
37: 8 lest he cast the lot against you 7
41: 9 when you die, a curse is your lot. 8

lot *See also* fall.

lotus plant 1. צֶאֱלִים
Job 40:21 Under the lotus plants he lies 1

lotus tree 1. צֶאֱלִים
Job 40:22 For his shade the lotus trees cover him; 1

loud 1. גָּדוֹל 2. המה 3. חזק 4. חָזָק 5. קוֹל 6. רום 7. תְּרוּעָה 8. βαρυηχής 9. ἰσχυρός 10. μέγας 11. πολύς 12. magnus
Gen 39:14 with me, and I cried out with a loud voice; 1
Exd 19:16 a very loud trumpet blast, so that all 4
19 sound of the trumpet grew louder, Moses spoke 3
Lev 25: 9 Then you shall send abroad the loud trumpet 7
Num14: 1 Then all the congregation raised a loud cry; *
Deu 5:22 spoke to all your assembly . . with a loud voice; 1
27:14 Levites shall declare . . with a loud voice 6
1Sm 28:12 When the woman . . she cried out with a loud voice; 1
2Sm 19: 4 the king cried with a loud voice, "O my son Ab'salom 1
1Kg 8:55 and blessed all the assembly . . with a loud voice 1
2Kg 18:28 Rab'shakeh stood and called out in a loud voice 1
2Ch 15:14 They took oath to the LORD with a loud voice 1
20:19 to praise the LORD . . with a very loud voice. 1
32:18 they shouted it with a loud voice in the language 1
Ezr 3:12 wept with a loud voice when they saw 1
10:12 Then all the assembly answered with a loud voice 1
Neh 9: 4 cried with a loud voice to the LORD their God. 1
Est 4: 1 went out . . wailing with a loud and bitter cry; 1
Ps 47: 1 all peoples! Shout to God with loud songs of joy! 5
102: 5 Because of my loud groaning my bones cleave 5
Prv 7:11 She is loud and wayward 2
27:14 He who blesses his neighbor with a loud voice 1
Isa 36:13 in a loud voice in the language of Judah 1
Ezk 8:18 though they cry in my ears with a loud voice 1
9: 1 Then he cried in my ears with a loud voice, saying 1
11:13 fell down upon my face, and cried with a loud voice 1
Zep 1:10 Second Quarter, a loud crash from the hills. 1
Mat 2:18 wailing and loud lamentation, Rachel weeping 11
24:31 will send out his angels with a loud trumpet call 10
27:46 Jesus cried with a loud voice 10
50 Jesus cried again with a loud voice 10
Mrk 1:26 convulsing him and crying with a loud voice 10
5: 7 crying out with a loud voice, he said 10
15:34 at the ninth hour Jesus cried with a loud voice 10
37 Jesus uttered a loud cry, and breathed his last. 10
Lke 1:42 she exclaimed with a loud cry, "Blessed are you 10
4:33 and he cried out with a loud voice 10
8:28 fell down before him, and said with a loud voice 10
17:15 turned back, praising God with a loud voice; 10
19:37 began to rejoice and praise God with a loud voice 10
23:23 demanding with loud cries 10
46 Then Jesus, crying with a loud voice, said, "Father 10
Joh 11:43 When he had said this, he cried with a loud voice 10
Act 7:57 they cried out with a loud voice 10
60 he knelt down and cried with a loud voice 10
8: 7 unclean spirits . . crying with a loud voice 10
14:10 said in a loud voice, "Stand upright on your feet. 10
16:28 Paul cried with a loud voice, "Do not harm yourself 10
26:24 Festus said with a loud voice, "Paul, you are mad 10
Heb 5: 7 with loud cries and tears 9
Rev 1:10 and I heard behind me a loud voice like a trumpet 10
5: 2 a strong angel proclaiming with a loud voice 10
12 saying with a loud voice, "Worthy is the Lamb 10
6:10 they cried out with a loud voice, "O Sovereign Lord 10
7: 2 he called with a loud voice to the four angels 10
10 crying out with a loud voice, "Salvation 10
8:13 I heard an eagle crying with a loud voice 10
10: 3 called out with a loud voice, like a lion roaring; 10
11:12 Then they heard a loud voice from heaven saying 10
15 and there were loud voices in heaven, saying 10
12:10 And I heard a loud voice in heaven, saying 10
14: 2 a voice . . like the sound of loud thunder; 10
7 and he said with a loud voice, "Fear God 10
9 another angel . . saying with a loud voice 10
15 another angel . . calling with a loud voice 10
18 another angel . . called with a loud voice 10
16: 1 Then I heard a loud voice from the temple 10
17 and a loud voice came out of the temple 10
19: 1 After this I heard what seemed to be a loud voice 10
17 and with a loud voice he called to all the birds 10
21: 3 I heard a loud voice from the throne saying 10
1Es 5:63 came . . with outcries and loud weeping 10
9:10 the multitude shouted and said with a loud voice 10
2Es 9:38 she was mourning and weeping with a loud voice 12
10:26 she suddenly uttered a loud and fearful cry 12
27 I was afraid, and cried with a loud voice and said 12
12:45 And they wept with a loud voice 12
Jdt 7:23 and cried out with a loud voice 10
29 they cried out to the Lord God with a loud voice. 10
9: 1 Judith cried out to the Lord with a loud voice 10
13:14 Then she said to them with a loud voice, "Praise God 10
14:16 he cried out with a loud voice and wept 10
Sir 40:13 crash like a loud clap of thunder in a rain. 10
Sus 1:24 Then Susanna cried out with a loud voice 10
42 Then Susanna cried out with a loud voice, and said 10
46 he cried with a loud voice, "I am innocent 10
Bel 1:18 looked at the table, and shouted in a loud voice 10
41 the king shouted with a loud voice 10
1Mc 2:19 Mattathias answered and said in a loud voice 10
27 cried out in the city with a loud voice, saying 10
3:54 they sounded the trumpets and gave a loud shout. 10
5:31 with trumpets and loud shouts 10
13: 8 they answered in a loud voice, "You are our leader 10
45 they cried out with a loud voice 10

3Mc 5:48 and heard the loud and tumultuous noise 8
51 and cried out in a very loud voice 10

loud-mouthed 1. *στόμα λαλέω*

Jde 1:16 loud-mouthed boasters, flattering people 1

loudly 1. *μεγαλωστί* 2. *μετὰ βοῆς* 3. *πολύς* 4. *φωνὴ μεγάλη*

1Ch 15:16 who should play loudly on musical instruments *
Mrk 5:38 people weeping and wailing loudly. 3
1Es 5:65 the multitude sounded the trumpets loudly 1
Sus 1:60 all the assembly shouted loudly and blessed God 4
3Mc 7:16 joyfully and loudly giving thanks to the one God 2

love 1. אהב 2. אֹהַב 3. אַהֲבָה 4. דּוֹד 5. חבב 6. חֶסֶד 7. חָסִיד 8. יְדִיד 9. עֲגָב 10. רחם 11. רַעְיָה 12. *ἀγαλλίαμα* 13. *ἀγαπάω* 14. *ἀγάπη* 15. *ἀγάπησις* 16. *ἀγαπητός* 17. *ἐπιθυμία* 18. *ἐράω* 19. *στέργω* 20. *στοργή* 21. *φιλέω* 22. *φιλία* 23. *φίλος* 24. *φιλόστοργος* 25. *φιλοτιμέομαι* 26. caritas 27. desidero 28. diligo

Gen 22: 2 your only son Isaac, whom you love 1
24:67 Rebekah, and she became his wife; and he loved her. 1
25:28 Isaac loved Esau, because he ate of his game; 1
28 ate of his game; but Rebekah loved Jacob. 1
27: 4 prepare for me savory food, such as I love 1
9 savory food for your father, such as he loves; 1
14 prepared savory food, such as his father loved. 1
29:18 Jacob loved Rachel; and he said 1
20 a few days because of the love he had for her. 3
30 Jacob went in to Rachel also, and he loved Rachel 1
32 surely now my husband will love me. 1
34: 3 he loved the maiden and spoke tenderly to her. 1
37: 3 Now Israel loved Joseph more than any other 1
4 brothers saw that their father loved him more 1
44:20 We have a . . brother . . and his father loves him. 1
Exd 20: 6 to thousands of those who love me 1
21: 5 I love my master, my wife, and my children; 1
Lev 19:18 you shall love your neighbor as yourself 1
34 and you shall love him as yourself 1
Deu 4:37 loved your fathers and chose their descendants 1
5:10 to thousands of those who love me 1
6: 5 shall love the LORD your God with all your heart 1
7: 8 because the LORD loves you, and is keeping 3
9 those who love him and keep his commandments 1
13 he will love you, bless you, and multiply you; 1
10:12 require . . but . . , to love him, to serve the LORD 3
15 LORD set his heart in love upon your fathers 3
18 loves the sojourner, giving him food 1
19 Love the sojourner therefore; 1
11: 1 You shall therefore love the LORD your God 1
13 my commandments . . to love the LORD your God 3
22 commandment . . loving the LORD your God 3
13: 3 to know whether you love the LORD your God 1
15:16 because he loves you and your household 1
19: 9 by loving the LORD your God and by walking 3
21:15 two wives, the one loved and the other disliked 1
15 borne him children, both the loved and the disliked 1
16 not treat the son of the loved as the first-born 1
23: 5 because the LORD your God loved you. 1
30: 6 love the LORD your God with all your heart 3
16 obey . . by loving the LORD your God 3
20 loving the LORD your God, obeying his voice 3
33: 3 Yea, he loved his people; all those consecrated 5
Jos 22: 5 the commandment and the law . . to love the LORD 3
23:11 Take good heed . . to love the LORD your God. 3
Jdg 14:16 You only hate me, you do not love me; you have put 1
16: 4 After this he loved a woman in the valley of Sorek 1
15 How can you say, 'I love you,' when your heart is not 1
Rut 4:15 your daughter-in-law who loves you . . has borne 1
1Sm 1: 5 although he loved Hannah, he would give . . only 1
16:21 Saul loved him greatly, and he became his 1
18: 1 and Jonathan loved him as his own soul. 1
3 because he loved him as his own soul. 3
16 But all Israel and Judah loved David; 1
20 Michal loved David; and they told Saul 1
22 king has delight . . and all his servants love you; 1
28 LORD was with David, and that all Israel loved him 1
20:17 Jonathan made David swear . . by his love for him; 3
17 for he loved him as he loved his own soul. 1
17 for he loved him as he loved his own soul. 3
2Sm 1:26 your love to me was wonderful, passing the love 3
26 your love to me was . . passing the love of women. 3
12:24 called his name Solomon. And the LORD loved him 1
13: 1 after a time Amnon, David's son, loved her. 1
4 I love Tamar, my brother Ab'salom's sister. 1
15 than the love with which he had loved her. 3
15 than the love with which he had loved her. 1
19: 6 you love those who hate you and hate those who 3
6 love . . who hate you and hate those who love you. 1
1Kg 3: 3 Solomon loved the LORD, walking in the statutes 1
5: 1 for Hiram always loved David. 1
10: 9 Because the LORD loved Israel for ever 3
11: 1 Now King Solomon loved many foreign women 1
2 Solomon clung to these in love. 3
2Ch 2:11 Because the LORD loves his people he has made you 3
9: 8 Because your God loved Israel 3
11:21 Rehobo'am loved Ma'acah . . above all his wives 1
19: 2 Should you . . love those who hate the LORD? 1
26:10 for he loved the soil. 1
Neh 1: 5 keeps . . with those who love him 1
Est 2:17 the king loved Esther more than all the women 1
Job 19:19 those whom I loved have turned against me. 1
37:13 for correction, or for his land, or for love 6
39:13 but are they the pinions and plumage of love? 7
Ps 4: 2 How long will you love vain words 1
5:11 that those who love thy name may exult in thee. 1
11: 5 his soul hates him that loves violence. 1
7 the LORD is righteous, he loves righteous deeds; 1
18: 1 I love thee, O LORD, my strength. 10
26: 8 O LORD, I love the habitation of thy house 1
31:23 Love the LORD, all you his saints! 1
33: 5 He loves righteousness and justice; 1
37:28 For the LORD loves justice; 1
40:16 those who love thy salvation say continually 1
45: 0 A Maskil of the Sons of Korah; a love song. 8
7 you love righteousness and hate wickedness. 1
47: 4 heritage for us, the pride of Jacob whom he loves. 1
52: 3 You love evil more than good 1
4 You love all words that devour 1
69:36 those who love his name shall dwell in it. 1
70: 4 May those who love thy salvation say evermore 1
78:68 the tribe of Judah, Mount Zion, which he loves. 1
87: 2 LORD loves the gates of Zion more than all 1
97:10 The LORD loves those who hate evil; *
109: 4 In return for my love they accuse me 3
5 reward me evil for good, and hatred for my love. 3
17 He loved to curse; let curses come on him! 1
116: 1 I love the LORD, because he has heard my voice 1
119:47 my delight in thy commandments, which I love. 1
48 I revere thy commandments, which I love 1
97 how I love thy law! It is my meditation all the day. 1
113 I hate double-minded men, but I love the law. 1
119 therefore I love thy testimonies. 1
127 Therefore I love thy commandments above gold 1
132 as is thy wont toward those who love thy name. 1
140 promise is well tried, and thy servant loves it. 1
159 Consider how I love thy precepts! 1
163 I hate and abhor falsehood, but I love thy law. 1
165 Great peace have those who love thy law; 1
167 thy testimonies; I love them exceedingly. 1
122: 6 May they prosper who love you! 1
145:20 LORD preserves all who love him; 1
146: 8 the LORD loves the righteous. 1
Prv 1:22 How long, O simple ones, will you love being simple? 1
3:12 for the LORD reproves him whom he loves 1
4: 6 love her, and she will guard you. 1
5:19 be infatuated always with her love. 3
7:18 Come, let us take our fill of love till morning; 4
18 Come, let us . . delight ourselves with love. 2
8:17 I love those who love me 1
17 I love those who love me 1
21 endowing with wealth those who love me 1
36 all who hate me love death. 1
9: 8 reprove a wise man, and he will love you. 1
10:12 but love covers all offenses. 3
12: 1 Whoever loves discipline loves knowledge 1
1 Whoever loves discipline loves knowledge 1
13:24 but he who loves him is diligent to discipline 1
15: 9 but he loves him who pursues righteousness. 1
17 Better is a dinner of herbs where love is 3
16:13 king, and he loves him who speaks what is right. 1
17: 9 He who forgives an offense seeks love 3
17 A friend loves at all times 1
19 He who loves transgression loves strife; 1
19 He who loves transgression loves strife; 1
18:21 those who love it will eat its fruits. 1
19: 8 He who gets wisdom loves himself; 1
20:13 Love not sleep, lest you come to poverty; 1
21:17 He who loves pleasure will be a poor man; 1
17 he who loves wine and oil will not be rich. 1
22:11 He who loves purity of heart, and whose speech 1
27: 5 Better is open rebuke than hidden love. 3
29: 3 He who loves wisdom makes his father glad 1
Ecc 3: 8 a time to love, and a time to hate; 1
5:10 He who loves money will not be satisfied 1
10 nor he who loves wealth, with gain 1
9: 1 whether it is love or hate man does not know. 3
6 Their love and their hate and their envy 3
9 Enjoy life with the wife whom you love 1
Sng 1: 2 For your love is better than wine 4
3 your name is . . therefore the maidens love you. 1
4 we will extol your love more than wine; 4
4 we will extol your . . rightly do they love you. 1
7 Tell me, you whom my soul loves, where you pasture 1
9 I compare you, my love, to a mare of . . chariots. 11
15 Behold, you are beautiful, my love; 11
2: 2 As a lily among . . so is my love among maidens. 11
4 He brought me . . and his banner over me was love. 3
5 refresh me with apples; for I am sick with love. 3
7 you stir not up nor awaken love until it please. 3
10 Arise, my love, my fair one, and come away; 11
13 Arise, my love, my fair one, and come away. 11
3: 1 by night I sought him whom my soul loves 1
2 I will rise . . I will seek him whom my soul loves. 1
3 Have you seen him whom my soul loves? 1
4 I found him whom my soul loves. 1
5 stir not up nor awaken love until it please. 3
4: 1 Behold, you are beautiful, my love 11
7 You are all fair, my love; there is no flaw in you. 11
10 How sweet is your love, my sister, my bride! 4
10 how much better is your love than wine 4
5: 2 Open to me, my sister, my love, my dove, 11
8 my beloved, that you tell him I am sick with love. 3
6: 4 You are beautiful as Tirzah, my love 11
7:12 There I will give you my love. 4
8: 4 I adjure . . that you stir not up nor awaken love 3
6 love is strong as death, jealousy is cruel 3
7 Many waters cannot quench love 3
7 a man offered for love all the wealth of his house 3
Isa 1:23 Every one loves a bribe and runs after gifts. 1
5: 1 my beloved a love song concerning his vineyard 4
43: 4 precious in my eyes, and honored, and I love you 1
48:14 LORD loves him; he shall perform his purpose 1
54: 8 with everlasting love I will have compassion 6
56: 6 to minister to him, to love the name of the LORD 3
10 dreaming, lying down, loving to slumber. 1
57: 8 you have loved their bed, you have looked 1
61: 8 I the LORD love justice, I hate robbery and wrong; 1
63: 9 in his love and in his pity he redeemed them; 3
66:10 Rejoice with Jerusalem . . all you who love her; 1
Jer 2: 2 the devotion of your youth, your love as a bride 3
25 It is hopeless, for I have loved strangers 1
5:31 my people love to have it 1
8: 2 and all the host of heaven, which they have loved 1
14:10 They have loved to wander thus 1
31: 3 I have loved you with an everlasting love; 1
3 I have loved you with an everlasting love; 3
Ezk 16: 8 behold, you were at the age for love; 4
37 all those you loved and all those you loathed; 1
23:17 the Babylonians came to her into the bed of love 4
33:32 lo, you are to them like one who sings love songs 9
Dan 9: 4 those who love him and keep his commandments 1
Hos 3: 1 Go again, love a woman who is beloved of a paramour 1
1 even as the LORD loves the people of Israel 3
1 they turn to other gods and love cakes of raisins. 1
4:18 they love shame more than their glory. 1
6: 4 Your love is like a morning cloud, like the dew 6
8:13 They love sacrifice; *
9: 1 You have loved a harlot's hire 1
15 I will love them no more; 3
10:11 a trained heifer that loved to thresh 1
11: 1 When Israel was a child, I loved him 1
4 with cords of compassion, with the bands of love 3
12: 6 return, hold fast to love and justice 6
7 he loves to oppress. 1
14: 4 I will love them freely, for my anger has turned 1
Ams 4: 5 publish . . for so you love to do, O people of Israel! 1
5:15 Hate evil, and love good, and establish justice 1
Mic 3: 2 you who hate the good and love the evil 1
6: 8 but to do justice, and to love kindness 3
Zep 3:17 he will renew you in his love; 3
Zec 8:17 love no false oath, for all these things I hate 1
19 therefore love truth and peace. 1
Mal 1: 2 I have loved you," says the LORD. 1
2 But you say, "How hast thou loved us? 1
2 Yet I have loved Jacob 1
2:11 the sanctuary of the LORD, which he loves 1
Mat 5:43 was said, 'You shall love your neighbor and hate 13
44 I say to you, Love your enemies and pray for those 13
46 For if you love those who love you, what reward 13
46 you love those who love you, what reward have you? 13
6: 5 not be like the hypocrites; for they love to stand 21
24 for either he will hate the one and love the other 13
10:37 He who loves father or mother more than me 21
37 and he who loves son or daughter more than me 21
19:19 You shall love your neighbor as yourself. 13
22:37 love the Lord your God with all your heart 13
39 a second is like it, You shall love your neighbor 13
23: 6 they love the place of honor at feasts 21
24:12 most men's love will grow cold. 14
Mrk 10:21 Jesus looking upon him loved him, and said to him 13
12:30 shall love the Lord your God with all your heart 13
31 You shall love your neighbor as yourself 13
33 to love him with all the heart 13
33 to love one's neighbor as oneself 13
Lke 6:27 Love your enemies, do good to those who hate you 13
32 If you love those who love you, what credit is that 13
32 If you love those who love you, what credit is that 13
32 even sinners love those who love them. 13
32 even sinners love those who love them. 13
35 love your enemies, and do good, and lend 13
7: 5 he loves our nation, and he built us our synagogue 13
42 Now which of them will love him more? 13
47 for she loved much 13
47 he who is forgiven little, loves little. 13
10:27 shall love the Lord your God with all your heart 13
11:42 neglect justice and the love of God 14
43 you love the best seat in the synagogues 13
16:13 either he will hate the one and love the other 13
20:46 and love salutations in the market places 25
Joh 3:16 God so loved the world that he gave his only Son 13
19 and men loved darkness rather than light 13
35 the Father loves the Son, and has given all things 13
5:20 For the Father loves the Son 21
42 I know that you have not the love of God 14

8:42 If God were your Father, you would love me 13
10:17 For this reason the Father loves me 13
11: 3 Lord, he whom you love is ill. 21
5 Jesus loved Martha and her sister and Laz'arus. 13
36 the Jews said, "See how he loved him! 21
12:25 He who loves his life loses it 21
43 for they loved the praise of men 13
13: 1 having loved his own who were in the world 13
1 he loved them to the end. 13
23 One of his disciples, whom Jesus loved 13
34 that you love one another 13
34 even as I have loved you 13
34 that you also love one another. 13
35 if you have love for one another. 14
14:15 If you love me, you will keep my commandments. 13
21 he it is who loves me 13
21 he who loves me will be loved by my Father 13
21 he who loves me will be loved by my Father 13
21 I will love him and manifest myself to him. 13
23 If a man loves me, he will keep my word 13
23 my Father will love him 13
24 He who does not love me does not keep my words 13
28 If you loved me, you would have rejoiced 13
31 so that the world may know that I love the Father. 13
15: 9 As the Father has loved me, so have I loved you; 13
9 so have I loved you; abide in my love. 13
9 so have I loved you; abide in my love. 14
10 you will abide in my love 14
10 just as I . . abide in his love. 14
12 This is my commandment, that you love one another 13
12 you love one another as I have loved you. 13
13 Greater love has no man than this 14
17 This I command you, to love one another. 13
19 the world would love its own 21
16:27 for the Father himself loves you 21
27 because you have loved me 21
17:23 and hast loved them even as thou hast loved me. 13
23 and hast loved them even as thou hast loved me. 13
24 given me in thy love for me 13
26 the love with which thou hast loved me 14
26 the love with which thou hast loved me 13
19:26 and the disciple whom he loved standing near 13
20: 2 the other disciple, the one whom Jesus loved 21
21: 7 That disciple whom Jesus loved said to Peter 13
15 Simon, son of John, do you love me more than these? 13
15 He said to him, "Yes, Lord; you know that I love you. 23
16 Simon, son of John, do you love me? 13
16 He said to him, "Yes, Lord; you know that I love you. 23
17 Simon, son of John, do you love me? 21
17 he said to him the third time, "Do you love me? 21
17 you know everything; you know that I love you 23
20 following them the disciple whom Jesus loved 13
Rom 5: 5 God's love has been poured into our hearts 14
8 But God shows his love for us 14
8:28 God works for good with those who love him 13
35 Who shall separate us from the love of Christ? 14
37 more than conquerors through him who loved us. 13
39 will be able to separate us from the love of God 14
9:13 As it is written, "Jacob I loved, but Esau I hated. 13
12: 9 Let love be genuine; hate what is evil 14
10 love one another with brotherly affection; 24
13: 8 Owe no one anything, except to love one another; 13
8 he who loves his neighbor has fulfilled the law. 13
9 You shall love your neighbor as yourself. 13
10 Love does no wrong to a neighbor; 14
10 therefore love is the fulfilling of the law. 14
14:15 you are no longer walking in love. 14
15:30 I appeal to you . . by the love of the Spirit 14
1Co 2: 9 what God has prepared for those who love him 13
4:21 with love in a spirit of gentleness? 14
8: 1 Knowledge" puffs up, but love builds up. 14
3 if one loves God, one is known by him. 13
13: 1 but have not love 14
2 but have not love, I am nothing. 14
3 if I deliver my body to be burned, but have not love 14
4 Love is patient and kind 14
4 love is not jealous or boastful; 14
5 Love does not insist on its own way •
7 Love bears all things, believes all things •
8 Love never ends 14
13 So faith, hope, love abide, these three 14
13 but the greatest of these is love. 14
14: 1 Make love your aim 14
16:14 Let all that you do be done in love. 14
22 If any one has no love for the Lord 21
24 My love be with you all in Christ Jesus. Amen. 14
2Co 2: 4 to let you know the abundant love that I have 14
8 I beg you to reaffirm your love for him. 14
5:14 For the love of Christ controls us 14
6: 6 kindness, the Holy Spirit, genuine love 14
8: 7 in all earnestness, and in your love for us 14
8 your love also is genuine. 14
24 So give proof, before the churches, of your love 14
9: 7 God loves a cheerful giver. 13
11:11 why? Because I do not love you? God knows I do! 13
12:15 If I love you the more, am I to be loved the less? 13
15 If I love you the more, am I to be loved the less? 13
13:11 the God of love and peace will be with you. 14
14 the love of God 14
Gal 2:20 the Son of God, who loved me and gave himself for me 13
5: 6 faith working through love. 14
13 through love be servants of one another. 14
14 You shall love your neighbor as yourself. 13
22 love, joy, peace, patience, kindness, goodness 14
Eph 1: 5 He destined us in love to be his sons 14
15 your love toward all the saints 14
2: 4 out of the great love with which he loved us 14
4 out of the great love with which he loved us 13
3:17 being rooted and grounded in love 14
19 to know the love of Christ 14
4: 2 forbearing one another in love 14
15 Rather, speaking the truth in love 14
16 makes bodily growth and upbuilds itself in love. 14
5: 2 walk in love, as Christ loved us 14
2 walk in love, as Christ loved us 13
25 Husbands, love your wives 13
25 Christ loved the church 13
28 Even so husbands should love their wives 13
28 He who loves his wife loves himself 13
28 He who loves his wife loves himself 13
33 let each one of you love his wife as himself 13
6:23 Peace be to the brethren, and love with faith 14
24 Grace be with all who love our Lord Jesus Christ 13
24 love our Lord Jesus Christ with love undying. •
Php 1: 9 my prayer that your love may abound more and more 14
16 The latter do it out of love 14
2: 1 any incentive of love 14
2 having the same love, being in full accord 14
4: 1 Therefore, my brethren, whom I love and long 16
Col 1: 4 the love which you have for all the saints 14
8 has made known to us your love in the Spirit. 14
2: 2 as they are knit together in love 14
3:14 above all these put on love 14
19 Husbands, love your wives 13
1Th 1: 3 work of faith and labor of love 14
3: 6 good news of your faith and love 14
12 may the Lord make you increase and abound in love 14
4: 9 taught by God to love one another; 13
10 indeed you do love all the brethren •
5: 8 put on the breastplate of faith and love 14
13 to esteem them very highly in love 14
2Th 1: 3 the love of every one of you for one another 14
2:10 because they refused to love the truth 14
16 who loved us and gave us eternal comfort 13
3: 5 May the Lord direct your hearts to the love of God 14
1Ti 1: 5 whereas the aim of our charge is love 14
14 the faith and love that are in Christ Jesus. 14
2:15 if she continues in faith and love and holiness 14
4:12 an example in speech and conduct, in love, in faith 14
6:11 aim at righteousness, godliness, faith, love 14
2Ti 1: 7 a spirit of power and love and self-control. 14
13 in the faith and love which are in Christ Jesus; 14
2:22 aim at righteousness, faith, love, and peace 14
3:10 my patience, my love, my steadfastness 14
4: 8 also to all who have loved his appearing. 13
10 Demas, in love with this present world 13
Tit 2: 2 sound in faith, in love, and in steadfastness. 14
3:15 Greet those who love us in the faith 25
Phm 1: 5 because I hear of your love 14
7 I have derived much joy and comfort from your love 14
9 yet for love's sake I prefer to appeal to you–I, Paul 14
Heb 1: 9 loved righteousness and hated lawlessness; 13
6:10 the love which you showed for his sake 14
10:24 to stir up one another to love and good works 14
12: 6 For the Lord disciplines him whom he loves 13
Jas 1:12 crown . . God has promised to those who love him. 13
2: 5 which he has promised to those who love him? 13
8 You shall love your neighbor as yourself 13
1Pe 1: 8 Without having seen him you love him; 13
22 love one another earnestly from the heart. 13
2:17 Honor all men. Love the brotherhood. Fear God. 13
3:10 He that would love life and see good days 13
4: 8 hold unfailing your love for one another 14
8 since love covers a multitude of sins. 14
5:14 Greet one another with the kiss of love. 14
2Pe 1: 7 and brotherly affection with love. 14
2:15 Balaam . . who loved gain from wrongdoing 13
1Jn 2: 5 in him truly love for God is perfected. 14
10 He who loves his brother abides in the light 13
15 Do not love the world or the things in the world. 13
15 If any one loves the world 13
15 love for the Father is not in him. 14
3: 1 See what love the Father has given us 14
10 nor he who does not love his brother. 13
11 that we should love one another 13
14 because we love the brethren. 13
14 He who does not love abides in death. 13
16 By this we know love, that he laid down his life 14
17 how does God's love abide in him? 14
18 let us not love in word or speech but in deed 13
23 we should believe . . and love one another 13
4: 7 Beloved, let us love one another; 13
7 let us love one another; for love is of God 14
7 and he who loves is born of God and knows God. 13
8 He who does not love does not know God; 13
8 for God is love. 14
9 In this the love of God was made manifest among us 14
10 In this is love, not that we loved God 14
10 not that we loved God but that he loved us 13
10 not that we loved God but that he loved us 13
11 Beloved, if God so loved us, we also ought to love 13
11 we also ought to love one another. 13
12 if we love one another, God abides in us 13
12 God abides in us and his love is perfected in us 14
16 So we know and believe the love God has for us. 14
16 God is love, and he who abides in love abides in God 14
16 God is love, and he who abides in love abides in God 14
17 In this is love perfected with us 14
18 There is no fear in love 14
18 but perfect love casts out fear. 14
18 and he who fears is not perfected in love. 14
19 We love, because he first loved us. 13
19 We love, because he first loved us. 13
20 If any one says, "I love God," and hates his brother 13
20 he who does not love his brother whom he has seen 13
20 cannot love God whom he has not seen. 13
21 he who loves God should love his brother also. 13
21 he who loves God should love his brother also. 13
5: 1 every one who loves the parent loves the child. 13
1 every one who loves the parent loves the child. 13
2 By this we know that we love the children of God 13
2 when we love God and obey his commandments. 13
3 the love of God, that we keep his commandments. 14
2Jn 1: 1 lady and her children, whom I love in the truth 13
3 from Jesus Christ . . in truth and love. 14
5 commandment . . that we love one another. 13
6 this is love, that we follow his commandments; 14
6 this is the commandment . . that you follow love •
3Jn 1: 1 to the beloved Ga'ius, whom I love in truth. 13
6 testified to your love before the church. 14
Jde 1: 2 May mercy, peace, and love be multiplied to you. 14
21 keep yourselves in the love of God; 14
Rev 1: 5 To him who loves us and has freed us from our sins 13
2: 4 you have abandoned the love you had at first. 14
19 'I know your works, your love and faith and service 14
3: 9 and learn that I have loved you. 13
19 Those whom I love, I reprove and chasten; 23
12:11 they loved not their lives even unto death. 13
22:15 every one who loves and practices falsehood. 21
1Es 4:24 he brings it back to the woman he loves. 18
25 A man loves his wife more than his father 13
2Es 3:14 thou didst love him 28
4:23 why the people whom you loved has been given over 28
5:27 to this people, whom thou hast loved 27
33 Or do you love him more than his Maker does? 28
40 the goal of the love 26
8:30 love those who have always put their trust 28
47 being able to love my creation more than I 28
47 able to love my creation more than I love it •
11:42 and have loved liars 28
Tob 4:13 now, my son, love your brethren 13
6:14 a demon is in love with her 21
13:10 love those within you who are distressed 13
12 blessed for ever will be all who love you. 13
14 How blessed are those who love you! 13
14: 7 all who love the Lord God in truth 13
AEs 14: 2 every part that she loved to adorn 12
Wis 1: 1 Love righteousness, you rulers of the earth 13
3: 9 the faithful will abide with him in love 14
4:10 There was one who pleased God and was loved by him 13
6:12 she is easily discerned by those who love her 13
17 concern for instruction is love of her 14
18 love of her is the keeping of her laws 14
7:10 I loved her more than health and beauty 13
28 for God loves nothing 13
8: 2 I loved her and sought her from my youth 21
3 the Lord of all loves her. 13
7 if any one loves righteousness 13
11:24 For thou lovest all things that exist 13
16:26 thy sons, whom thou didst love, O Lord 13
Sir 1:10 he supplied her to those who love him. 13
2:15 those who love him will keep his ways 13
16 who love him will be filled with the law. 13
3:17 then you will be loved by those whom God accepts. 13
26 whoever loves danger will perish by it. 14
4:10 he will love you more than does your mother. 13
12 Whoever loves her loves life 14
12 Whoever loves her loves life 13
14 the Lord loves those who love her. 13
14 the Lord loves those who love her. 13
6:33 If you love to listen you will gain knowledge 13
7:21 Let your soul love an intelligent servant 13
30 With all your might love your Maker 13
35 because for such deeds you will be loved. 13
13:15 Every creature loves its like 13
15:13 they are not loved by those who fear him. 16
27:17 Love your friend and keep faith with him 19
30: 1 He who loves his son will whip him often 14
31: 5 He who loves gold will not be justified 13
34:16 The eyes of the Lord are upon those who love him 13
40:20 the love of wisdom is better than both. 15
47: 8 he loved his Maker. 13
16 you were loved for your peace. 13
22 nor destroy the posterity of him who loved him 13
48:11 those who have been adorned in love 15
Bar 3:36 Jacob his servant and to Israel whom he loved. 13
Sus 1:20 we are in love with you; so give your consent 17

Bel 1:38 hast not forsaken those who love thee. 13
1Mc 4:33 the sword of those who love thee 13
3Mc 2:10 because you love the house of Israel 14
4Mc 2:11 It is superior to love for one's wife 22
12 It takes precedence over love for children 22
13:24 they loved one another all the more. 13
14:13 how complex is a mother's love for her children 20
14 have a sympathy and parental love 20
17 in the anguish of love 20
15: 3 She loved religion more 13

love a brother 1. φιλάδελφος
2Mc 15:14 This is a man who loves the brethren 1
4Mc 15:10 and loved their brothers and their mother 1

love a child 1. φιλότεκνος
Tit 2: 4 to love their husbands and children 1
4Mc 15: 4 the emotions of parents who love their children 1

love a child more 1. φιλότεκνος
4Mc 15: 6 mother . . more than any other . . loved her children. 1

love a fellow citizen 1. φιλοπολίτης
2Mc 14:37 a man who loved his fellow citizens 1

love a husband 1. φίλανδρος
Tit 2: 4 so train the young women to love their husbands 1

love a mother 1. φιλομήτωρ
4Mc 15:10 and loved their brothers and their mother 1

love an ornament 1. φιλόκοσμος
LJr 1: 9 as they would for a girl who loves ornaments; 1

brotherly love 1. φιλαδελφία
Heb 13: 1 Let brotherly love continue. 1
4Mc 13:26 they rendered their brotherly love more fervent. 1
14: 1 mastered the emotions of brotherly love. 1

love for a child 1. φιλοτεκνία
4Mc 14:13 how complex is a mother's love for her children 1
15:11 to suffer with them out of love for her children 1
23 to disregard her temporal love for her children. 1

love learning 1. φιλομαθέω
Sir 0: 1 those who love learning should be able to help 1
1 those who love learning should make . . progress 1

loyal love 1. חֶסֶד
1Sm 20:14 show me the loyal love of the LORD 1

natural love 1. φιλοστοργία
2Mc 6:20 even for the natural love of life. 1

love of glory 1. φιλοδοξία
AEs 13:12 not in insolence or pride or for any love of glory 1

love of money 1. φιλαργυρία
1Ti 6:10 For the love of money is the root of all evils 1

love of the brother 1. φιλαδελφία 2. φιλάδελφος
1Th 4: 9 But concerning love of the brethren 1
1Pe 1:22 for a sincere love of the brethren 1
3: 8 all of you, have . . love of the brethren 2

parental love 1. φιλοτεκνία
4Mc 15:25 nature, family, parental love 1
16: 3 her innate parental love 1

show much love 1. עָגַב
Ezk 33:31 for with their lips they show much love 1

steadfast love 1. חֶסֶד
Gen 24:12 I pray thee, and show steadfast love to my master 1
14 thou hast shown steadfast love to my master. 1
27 who has not forsaken his steadfast love 1
32:10 worthy of the least of all the steadfast love 1
39:21 LORD was with Joseph . . showed him steadfast love 1
Exd 15:13 Thou hast led in thy steadfast love the people 1
20: 6 showing steadfast love to thousands of those 1
34: 6 slow to anger, and abounding in steadfast love 1
7 keeping steadfast love for thousands 1
Num14:18 The LORD is . . abounding in steadfast love 1
19 according to the greatness of thy steadfast love 1
Deu 5:10 showing steadfast love to thousands 1
7: 9 God who keeps covenant and steadfast love 1
12 keep with you the covenant and the steadfast love 1
2Sm 2: 6 the LORD show steadfast love and faithfulness 1
7:15 but I will not take my steadfast love from him 1
15:20 the LORD show steadfast love and faithfulness 1
22:51 shows steadfast love to his anointed, to David 1
1Kg 3: 6 Thou hast shown great and steadfast love 1
6 hast kept for him this great and steadfast love 1
8:23 showing steadfast love to thy servants 1
1Ch 16:34 for his steadfast love endures for ever! 1
41 for his steadfast love endures for ever. 1
17:13 I will not take my steadfast love from him 1
2Ch 1: 8 Thou hast shown great and steadfast love 1
5:13 is good, for his steadfast love endures for ever 1
6:14 keeping covenant and showing steadfast love 1
42 Remember thy steadfast love for David 1
7: 3 is good, for his steadfast love endures for ever. 1
6 -for his steadfast love endures for ever- 1
20:21 for his steadfast love endures for ever. 1
Ezr 3:11 steadfast love endures for ever toward Israel. 1
7:28 extended . . his steadfast love before the king 1
9: 9 but has extended to us his steadfast love 1
Neh 1: 5 God who keeps covenant and steadfast love 1
9:17 thou art a God . . abounding in steadfast love 1
32 God, who keepest covenant and steadfast love 1
13:22 according to the greatness of thy steadfast love. 1
Job 10:12 Thou has granted me life and steadfast love; 1
Ps 5: 7 I through the abundance of thy steadfast love 1
6: 4 deliver me for the sake of thy steadfast love. 1
13: 5 I have trusted in thy steadfast love; 1
17: 7 Wondrously show thy steadfast love, O savior 1
18:50 and shows steadfast love to his anointed 1
21: 7 through the steadfast love of the Most High 1
25: 6 of thy mercy, O LORD, and of thy steadfast love 1
7 according to thy steadfast love remember me 1
10 All the paths of the LORD are steadfast love 1
26: 3 For thy steadfast love is before my eyes 1
31: 7 I will rejoice and be glad for thy steadfast love 1
16 save me in thy steadfast love! 1
21 for he has wondrously shown his steadfast love 1
32:10 steadfast love surrounds him who trusts 1
33: 5 earth is full of the steadfast love of the LORD. 1
18 on those who hope in his steadfast love 1
22 Let thy steadfast love, O LORD, be upon us 1
36: 5 Thy steadfast love, O LORD, extends to the heavens 1
7 How precious is thy steadfast love, O God! 1
10 O continue thy steadfast love to those who know 1
40:10 I have not concealed thy steadfast love 1
11 let thy steadfast love and thy faithfulness 1
42: 8 By day the LORD commands his steadfast love; 1
44:26 Deliver us for the sake of thy steadfast love! 1
48: 9 We have thought on thy steadfast love, O God 1
51: 1 O God, according to thy steadfast love; 1
52: 8 I trust in the steadfast love of God for ever 1
57: 3 God will send forth his steadfast love 1
10 For thy steadfast love is great to the heavens 1
59:10 My God in his steadfast love will meet me; 1
16 I will sing aloud of thy steadfast love 1
17 my fortress, the God who shows me steadfast love. 1
61: 7 steadfast love and faithfulness watch over him! 1
62:12 that to thee, O Lord, belongs steadfast love. 1
63: 3 Because thy steadfast love is better than life 1
66:20 or removed his steadfast love from me! 1
69:13 in the abundance of thy steadfast love answer me. 1
16 Answer me, O LORD, for thy steadfast love is good; 1
77: 8 Has his steadfast love for ever ceased? 1
85: 7 Show us thy steadfast love, O LORD 1
10 Steadfast love and faithfulness will meet; 1
86: 5 abounding in steadfast love to all who call 1
13 For great is thy steadfast love toward me; 1
15 abounding in steadfast love and faithfulness. 1
88:11 Is thy steadfast love declared in the grave 1
89: 1 I will sing of thy steadfast love, O LORD, for ever; 1
2 For thy steadfast love was established for ever 1
14 steadfast love and faithfulness go before thee. 1
24 faithfulness and my steadfast love . . be 1
28 My steadfast love I will keep for him for ever 1
33 I will not remove from him my steadfast love 1
49 Lord, where is thy steadfast love of old 1
90:14 Satisfy us . . with thy steadfast love 1
92: 2 to declare thy steadfast love in the morning 1
94:18 foot slips," thy steadfast love, O LORD, held me up. 1
98: 3 remembered his steadfast love 1
100: 5 LORD is good; his steadfast love endures for ever 1
103: 4 who crowns you with steadfast love and mercy 1
8 slow to anger and abounding in steadfast love. 1
11 so great is his steadfast love toward those who 1
17 steadfast love of the LORD is from everlasting 1
106: 1 for his steadfast love endures for ever! 1
7 not remember the abundance of thy steadfast love 1
45 to the abundance of his steadfast love. 1
107: 1 for his steadfast love endures for ever! 1
8 Let them thank the LORD for his steadfast love 1
15 Let them thank the LORD for his steadfast love 1
21 Let them thank the LORD for his steadfast love 1
31 Let them thank the LORD for his steadfast love 1
43 let men consider the steadfast love of the LORD. 1
108: 4 thy steadfast love is great above the heavens 1
109:21 because thy steadfast love is good, deliver me! 1
26 Save me according to thy steadfast love! 1
115: 1 for the sake of thy steadfast love and thy faithfulness! 1
117: 2 For great is his steadfast love toward us; 1
118: 1 he is good; his steadfast love endures for ever! 1
2 Israel say, "His steadfast love endures for ever. 1
3 Aaron say, "His steadfast love endures for ever. 1
4 His steadfast love endures for ever. 1
29 for his steadfast love endures for ever! 1
119:41 Let thy steadfast love come to me, O LORD 1
64 The earth, O LORD, is full of thy steadfast love; 1
76 Let thy steadfast love be ready to comfort me 1
88 In thy steadfast love spare my life 1
124 Deal . . according to thy steadfast love 1
149 Hear my voice in thy steadfast love; 1
159 Preserve . . according to thy steadfast love. 1
130: 7 For with the LORD there is steadfast love 1
136: 1 for his steadfast love endures for ever. 1
2 for his steadfast love endures for ever. 1
3 for his steadfast love endures for ever; 1
4 for his steadfast love endures for ever; 1
5 for his steadfast love endures for ever; 1
6 for his steadfast love endures for ever; 1
7 for his steadfast love endures for ever; 1
8 for his steadfast love endures for ever; 1
9 for his steadfast love endures for ever; 1
10 for his steadfast love endures for ever; 1
11 for his steadfast love endures for ever; 1
12 for his steadfast love endures for ever; 1
13 for his steadfast love endures for ever; 1
14 for his steadfast love endures for ever; 1
15 for his steadfast love endures for ever; 1
16 for his steadfast love endures for ever; 1
17 for his steadfast love endures for ever; 1
18 for his steadfast love endures for ever; 1
19 for his steadfast love endures for ever; 1
20 for his steadfast love endures for ever; 1
21 for his steadfast love endures for ever; 1
22 for his steadfast love endures for ever. 1
23 for his steadfast love endures for ever; 1
24 for his steadfast love endures for ever; 1
25 for his steadfast love endures for ever. 1
26 for his steadfast love endures for ever. 1
138: 2 for thy steadfast love and thy faithfulness; 1
8 thy steadfast love, O LORD, endures for ever. 1
143: 8 Let me hear in the morning of thy steadfast love 1
12 in thy steadfast love cut off my enemies 1
145: 8 slow to anger and abounding in steadfast love. 1
147:11 pleasure . . who hope in his steadfast love. 1
Isa 16: 5 a throne will be established in steadfast love 1
54:10 but my steadfast love shall not depart from you 1
55: 3 covenant, my steadfast, sure love for David. 1
63: 7 I will recount the steadfast love of the LORD 1
7 the abundance of his steadfast love. 1
Jer 9:24 that I am the LORD who practice steadfast love 1
16: 5 says the LORD, my steadfast love and mercy. 1
32:18 who showest steadfast love to thousands 1
33:11 for his steadfast love endures for ever! 1
Lam 3:22 The steadfast love of the LORD never ceases 1
32 to the abundance of his steadfast love; 1
Dan 9: 4 God, who keepest covenant and steadfast love 1
Hos 2:19 betroth you to me . . in justice, in steadfast love 1
6: 6 For I desire steadfast love and not sacrifice 1
10:12 reap the fruit of steadfast love; 1
Jol 2:13 slow to anger, and abounding in steadfast love 1
Jon 4: 2 slow to anger, and abounding in steadfast love 1
Mic 7:18 for ever because he delights in steadfast love. 1
20 Thou wilt show . . steadfast love to Abraham 1

tender love 1. φιλοστοργία
4Mc 15: 6 she had implanted in herself tender love toward them 1

love the good 1. φιλάγαθος
Wis 7:22 distinct, invulnerable, loving the good, keen 1

love the living 1. φιλόψυχος
Wis 11:26 O Lord who lovest the living. 1

loved one 1. אַהֲבָה
Sng 7: 6 How fair and pleasant you are, O loved one 1

loved thing 1. אָהַב
Hos 9:10 became detestable like the thing they loved. 1

loveliness 1. χάρις 2. pulchritudo
2Es 10:50 and the loveliness of her beauty. 2
Sir 24:17 Like a vine I caused loveliness to bud 1

lovely 1. אָהַב 2. טוֹב מַרְאֶה 3. יָדִיד 4. יְפַת מַרְאֶה 5. נָאוֶה 6. נָעִים 7. καλός 8. προσφιλής 9. ὡραῖος
Gen 29:17 but Rachel was beautiful and lovely. 4
2Sm 1:23 Saul and Jonathan, beloved and lovely! 6
Est 2: 7 the maiden was beautiful and lovely 2
Ps 84: 1 How lovely is thy dwelling place, O LORD of hosts! 3
Prv 5:19 a lovely hind, a graceful doe. 1
Sng 1:16 you are beautiful, my beloved, truly lovely. 6
4: 3 your mouth is lovely. 5
Php 4: 8 whatever is pure, whatever is lovely 8
1Es 4:18 then see a woman lovely in appearance and beauty 7
Jdt 8: 7 had a very lovely face 9

lover 1. אהב 2. אָהַב 3. אַהֲבָה 4. דּוֹד 5. עגב 6. רֵעַ 7. ἐραστής 8. amator
Ps 88:18 Thou hast caused lover and friend to shun me; 1
99: 4 Mighty King, lover of justice, thou hast 1
Sng 5: 1 Eat, O friends, and drink: drink deeply, O lovers! 4
Jer 2:33 How well you direct your course to seek lovers! 3
3: 1 You have played the harlot with many lovers; 6
2 By the waysides you have sat awaiting lovers •
4:30 Your lovers despise you; they seek your life. 5
22:20 cry . . for all your lovers are destroyed. 1
22 and your lovers shall go into captivity; 1

30:14 All your lovers have forgotten you; 1
Lam 1: 2 among all her lovers she has none to comfort her; 1
19 I called to my lovers but they deceived me; 1
Ezk 16:33 but you gave your gifts to all your lovers 1
36 uncovered in your harlotries with your lovers 1
37 therefore, behold, I will gather all your lovers 1
39 And I will give you into the hand of your lovers •
23: 5 and she doted on her lovers the Assyrians 1
9 I delivered her into the hands of her lovers 1
22 Behold, I will rouse against you your lovers 1
Hos 2: 5 For she said, 'I will go after my lovers 1
7 She shall pursue her lovers, but not overtake 1
10 uncover her lewdness in the sight of her lovers 1
12 These are my hire, which my lovers have given me.' 1
13 and went after her lovers, and forgot me 1
8: 9 E'phraim has hired lovers. 2
2Es 15:47 to please and glory in your lovers 8
51 so that you cannot receive your mighty lovers. 8
Wis 15: 6 Lovers of evil things 7

no lover of money 1. ἀφιλάργυρος
1Ti 3: 3 not quarrelsome, and no lover of money. 1

lover of God 1. φιλόθεος
2Ti 3: 4 lovers of pleasure rather than lovers of God 1

lover of goodness 1. φιλάγαθος
Tit 1: 8 but hospitable, a lover of goodness 1

lover of money 1. φιλάργυρος
Lke 16:14 The Pharisees, who were lovers of money, heard all 1
2Ti 3: 2 For men will be lovers of self, lovers of money 1
4Mc 2: 8 even though he is a lover of money 1

lover of pleasure 1. עָדִין 2. φιλήδονος
Isa 47: 8 Now therefore hear this, you lover of pleasures 1
2Ti 3: 4 lovers of pleasure rather than lovers of God 2

lover of self 1. φίλαυτος
2Ti 3: 2 For men will be lovers of self, lovers of money 1

lovesick 1. אמל
Ezk 16:30 How lovesick is your heart, says the Lord GOD 1

lovingly 1. אַהֲבָה
Sng 3:10 it was lovingly wrought within by the daughters 1

low 1. בֶּן אָדָם 2. מַטָּה 3. מִלְמַטָּה 4. קָטֹן 5. שחח 6. שָׁפָל 7. תַּחְתּוֹן 8. תַּחְתִּי 9. ἀγενής 10. ἔσχατος 11. κατώτερος 12. ὑποκάτω 13. ὑποκάτωθεν
Gen 6:16 make it with lower, second, and third decks. 8
Exd 28:27 attach them in front to the lower part of the two 3
39:20 to the lower part of the two shoulder-pieces 3
Deu 28:43 you shall come down lower and lower. 2
43 you shall come down lower and lower. 2
Jos 13:27 to the lower end of the Sea of Chin'nereth •
15:19 gave . . the upper springs and the lower springs. 8
16: 3 as far as the territory of Lower Beth-hor'on 7
18:13 mountain that lies south of Lower Beth-hor'on. 7
Jdg 1:15 gave her the upper . . and the lower springs. 8
1Kg 6: 6 The lowest story was five cubits broad 7
8 The entrance for the lowest story was 13
9:17 rebuilt Gezer) and Lower Beth-hor'on 7
1Ch 7:24 who built both Lower and Upper Beth-hor'on 7
2Ch 8: 5 He also built Upper . . and Lower Beth-Ho'ron 7
Est 1:20 will give honor to their husbands, high and low. 4
Ps 49: 2 both low and high, rich and poor together! 1
Ecc 12: 4 when the sound of the grinding is low 6
Isa 22: 9 you collected the waters of the lower pool 7
29: 4 from low in the dust your words shall come; 5
Ezk 17: 6 it sprouted and became a low spreading vine 6
24 the high tree, and make high the low tree 6
21:26 exalt that which is low, and abase that which is 6
40:18 this was the lower pavement. 7
19 distance from the inner front of the lower gate 7
41: 7 thus one went up from the lowest story to the top 7
42: 5 took more away from them than from the lower 7
6 set back from the ground more than the lower 7
43:14 from the base on the ground to the lower ledge 7
Lke 14: 9 will begin with shame to take the lowest place. 10
10 go and sit in the lowest place 10
1Co 1:28 God chose what is low and despised in the world 9
Eph 4: 9 descended into the lower parts of the earth? 11
Bar 2: 5 They were brought low and not raised up 12

low (2) 1. געה 2. קוֹל
1Sm 6:12 the cows went straight . . lowing as they went; 1
15:14 What then is . . the lowing of oxen which I hear? 2
Job 6: 5 when he has grass, or the ox low over his fodder? 1
Jer 9:10 and the lowing of cattle is not heard; 2
low *See* bring.

low part 1. תַּחְתִּי
Neh 4:13 in the lowest parts of the space behind the wall 1

low place 1. שֵׁפֶל
Ecc 10: 6 and the rich sit in a low place. 1

lower 1. ירד 2. נוח 3. ταπεινόω 4. χαλάω
Gen 44:11 every man quickly lowered his sack to the ground 1
Exd 17:11 whenever he lowered his hand, Am'alek prevailed. 2
Act 9:25 lowering him in a basket. 4
27:17 they lowered the gear, and so were driven. 4
30 had lowered the boat into the sea 4
Sir 29: 5 will lower his voice 3

lowland 1. שְׁפֵלָה
Deu 1: 7 Arabah, in the hill country and in the lowland 1
Jos 9: 1 the lowland all along the coast of the Great Sea 1
10:40 and the Negeb and the lowland and the slopes 1
11: 2 to the kings who were in . . the lowland 1
16 land of Goshen and the lowland and the Arabah 1
16 and the hill country of Israel and its lowland 1
12: 8 in the hill country, in the lowland, in the Arabah 1
15:33 And in the lowland, Eshta'ol, Zorah, Ashnah 1
Jdg 1: 9 the hill country, in the Negeb, and in the lowland. 1
Zec 7: 7 the South and the lowland were inhabited 1

lowliness 1. ταπεινοφροσύνη
Eph 4: 2 with all lowliness and meekness 1
Col 3:12 compassion, kindness, lowliness, meekness 1

lowly 1. דַּל 2. שַׁח עֵינַיִם 3. שפל 4. שָׁפָל 5. שְׁפַל (A) 6. πραΰς 7. ταπεινός 8. ταπείνωσις 9. humilis
Job 5:11 he sets on high those who are lowly 4
22:29 For God abases the proud, but he saves the lowly. 2
Ps 138: 6 For though the LORD is high, he regards the lowly; 4
Prv 16:19 better to be of a lowly spirit with the poor 4
29:23 but he who is lowly in spirit will obtain honor. 4
Jer 13:18 to the king and the queen mother: "Take a lowly seat 3
Ezk 29:14 there they shall be a lowly kingdom. 4
15 It shall be the most lowly of the kingdoms 4
Dan 4:17 sets over it the lowliest of men.' 5
Zep 3:12 in the midst of you a people humble and lowly. 4
Mat 11:29 for I am gentle and lowly in heart 7
Rom 12:16 do not be haughty, but associate with the lowly; 7
Php 3:21 who will change our lowly body 8
Jas 1: 9 Let the lowly brother boast in his exaltation 7
2Es 14:13 comfort the lowly among them 9
Jdt 9:11 thou art God of the lowly, helper of the oppressed 7
AEs 11:11 the lowly were exalted 7
Sir 10:14 has seated the lowly in their place. 6

lowly man 1. ἐλαχύς
Wis 6: 6 For the lowliest man may be pardoned in mercy 1

loyal 1. חָסִיד 2. ἀνδρεῖος 3. εὐνοέω 4. εὔνους 5. ὁμόσπονδος
2Sm 22:26 With the loyal thou dost show thyself loyal; 1
Ps 18:25 With the loyal thou dost show thyself loyal; 1
AEs 16:23 may mean salvation for us and the loyal Persians 3
Sir 26: 2 A loyal wife rejoices her husband 2
3Mc 3: 7 these people were loyal neither to the king 5
4Mc 4: 3 because I am loyal to the king's government 4

loyal deed 1. ἔλεος
Sir 46: 7 in the days of Moses he did a loyal deed 1

show oneself loyal 1. חסד
2Sm 22:26 With the loyal thou dost show thyself loyal; 1
Ps 18:25 With the loyal thou dost show thyself loyal; 1

loyal thing 1. πιστός
3Jn 1: 5 Beloved, it is a loyal thing you do 1

loyal to the government 1. ἡμέτερα φρονέω
AEs 16: 1 to those who are loyal to our government 1

loyally 1. חֶסֶד
Gen 21:23 but as I have dealt loyally with you 1
24:49 if you will deal loyally and truly with my master 1
47:29 and promise to deal loyally and truly with me. 1
2Sm 10: 2 I will deal loyally with Hanun the son of Nahash 1
2 I will . . as his father dealt loyally with me. 1
1Kg 2: 7 deal loyally with the sons of Barzil'lai 1
1Ch 19: 2 David said, "I will deal loyally with Hanun 1
2 for his father dealt loyally with me. 1

loyalty 1. חֶסֶד 2. πίστις
1Sm 20:15 and do not cut off your loyalty from my house 1
2Sm 2: 5 you showed this loyalty to Saul . . and buried him! 1
3: 8 I keep showing loyalty to the house of Saul 1
16:17 And Ab'salom said to Hushai, "Is this your loyalty 1
1Kg 2: 7 with such loyalty they met me when I fled •
Ps 101: 1 sing of loyalty and of justice; to thee, O LORD 1
Prv 3: 3 Let not loyalty and faithfulness forsake you; 1
14:22 who devise good meet loyalty and faithfulness. 1
16: 6 By loyalty and faithfulness iniquity is atoned 1
19:22 What is desired in a man is loyalty 1
20: 6 Many a man proclaims his own loyalty 1
28 Loyalty and faithfulness preserve the king 1
1Mc 14:35 loyalty which he had maintained 2
3Mc 3: 3 to maintain good will and unswerving loyalty 2
5:31 a full and firm loyalty to my ancestors. 2

loyalty to the law 1. εὐνομία
4Mc 7: 9 You, father, strengthened our loyalty to the law 1

true loyalty 1. חֶסֶד
Jon 2: 8 to vain idols forsake their true loyalty. 1

good luck 1. טוֹבָה
Sir 8:19 lest you drive away your good luck. 1

lukewarm 1. χλιαρός
Rev 3:16 you are lukewarm, and neither cold nor hot 1

luminary 1. מָאוֹר 2. φωστήρ
Ps 74:16 hast established the luminaries and the sun. 1
Wis 13: 2 the luminaries of heaven 2

lump 1. φύραμα 2. gleba
Rom 9:21 to make out of the same lump one vessel for beauty 1
11:16 If the dough . . is holy, so is the whole lump; 1
1Co 5: 6 a little leaven leavens the whole lump? 1
7 you may be a new lump 1
Gal 5: 9 A little leaven leavens the whole lump. 1
2Es 2: 9 whose land lies in lumps of pitch 2

lure 1. ἐξέλκω
Jas 1:14 when he is lured and enticed by his own desire. 1

lurk 1. ארב 2. ישב 3. צפן 4. שׁוּר
Ps 10: 9 he lurks in secret like a lion in his covert; 1
9 he lurks that he may seize the poor 1
17:12 eager to tear, as a young lion lurking in ambush. 2
56: 6 They band themselves together, they lurk 3
Jer 5:26 they lurk like fowlers lying in wait. •
Hos 13: 7 like a leopard I will lurk beside the way. 4

lurking place 1. מַחֲבֹא
1Sm 23:23 note . . all the lurking places where he hides 1

lust 1. הַוָּה 2. תַּאֲוָה 3. תַּזְנוּת 4. ἐπιθυμία 5. πορνεία 6. σάρξ 7. συνουσιασμός 8. cupio fornicari
Prv 11: 6 treacherous are taken captive by their lust. 1
Jer 2:24 Who can restrain her lust? 2
Ezk 23: 8 and poured out their lust upon her. 3
17 they defiled her with their lust; 3
Rom 1:24 God gave them up in the lusts of their hearts 4
Eph 4:22 is corrupt through deceitful lusts 4
1Th 4: 5 not in the passion of lust 4
2Pe 2:10 indulge in the lust of defiling passion 6
1Jn 2:16 the lust of the flesh and the lust of the eyes 4
16 the lust of the flesh and the lust of the eyes 4
17 the world passes away, and the lust of it; 4
Jde 1: 7 acted immorally and indulged in unnatural lust 6
2Es 15:47 who have always lusted after you. 8
Tob 8: 7 I am not taking this sister of mine because of lust 5
Sir 23: 6 Let neither gluttony nor lust overcome me 7
Sus 1:14 they confessed their lust. 4
56 and lust has perverted your heart. 4
4Mc 1: 3 namely, gluttony and lust 4

lust after 1. רוץ
Ps 68:30 Trample under foot those who lust after tribute; 1

lust for power 1. φιλαρχία
4Mc 2:15 lust for power, vainglory, boasting, arrogance 1

lustful 1. גְּדֵל בָּשָׂר 2. ἐπιθυμία 3. μετεωρισμός
Ezk 16:26 with the Egyptians, your lustful neighbors 1
Sir 26: 9 A wife's harlotry shows in her lustful eyes 3
Sus 1:11 their lustful desire to possess her. 2

lustfully 1. ἐπιθυμέω
Mat 5:28 who looks at a woman lustfully has already 1

lusty 1. שכה
Jer 5: 8 They were well-fed lusty stallions 1

lute 1. נֵבֶל 2. עָשׂוֹר 3. κινύρα
Ps 92: 3 to the music of the lute and the harp 2
150: 3 praise him with lute and harp! 1
1Mc 4:54 it was dedicated with songs and harps and lutes 3

luxuriant 1. בקק
Hos 10: 1 a luxuriant vine that yields its fruit. 1

luxurious 1. ἔδεσμα
Wis 19:11 when desire led them to ask for luxurious food; 1

luxury 1. תַּעֲנוּג 2. τρυφή
Prv 19:10 It is not fitting for a fool to live in luxury 1
Lke 7:25 those who . . live in luxury are in kings' courts. 2
Sir 11:27 The misery of an hour makes one forget luxury 2
14:16 because in Hades one cannot look for luxury. 2
18:32 Do not revel in great luxury 2
37:29 have an insatiable appetite for any luxury 2

lye 1. בֹּר 2. נֶתֶר
Job 9:30 If I wash myself . . and cleanse my hands with lye 1

Isa 1:25 I . . will smelt away your dross as with lye 1
Jer 2:22 Though you wash yourself with lye 2

lyre 1. כִּנּוֹר 2. קַתְרֹס (A) 3. *κινύρα* 4. *ψαλτήριον*

Gen 4:21 was the father of all those who play the lyre 1
31:27 with mirth and songs, with tambourine and lyre? 1
1Sm 10: 5 with harp, tambourine, flute, and lyre before them 1
16:16 seek out a man who is skilful in playing the lyre; 1
23 David took the lyre and played it with his hand; 1
18:10 and he raved . . while David was playing the lyre •
19: 9 as he sat in . . and David was playing the lyre. •
2Sm 6: 5 making merry . . with songs and lyres and harps 1
1Kg 10:12 king made . . lyres also and harps for the singers; 1
1Ch 13: 8 making merry . . with song and lyres and harps 1
15:16 on harps and lyres and cymbals, to raise sounds 1
21 lead with lyres according to the Shem'inith. 1
28 and made loud music on harps and lyres. 1
16: 5 and Je-i'el, who were to play harps and lyres; 1
25: 1 prophesy with lyres, with harps 1
3 Jedu'thun, who prophesied with the lyre 1
6 with cymbals, harps, and lyres for the service 1
2Ch 5:12 arrayed in fine linen, with . . harps, and lyres 1
9:11 algum wood steps . . lyres also and harps 1
20:28 to Jerusalem with harps and lyres and trumpets 1
29:25 Levites . . with cymbals, harps, and lyres 1
Neh 12:27 celebrate . . with cymbals, harps, and lyres. 1
Job 21:12 They sing to the tambourine and the lyre 1
30:31 My lyre is turned to mourning 1
Ps 33: 2 Praise the LORD with the lyre, make melody to him 1
43: 4 I will praise thee with the lyre, O God, my God. 1
49: 4 I will solve my riddle to the music of the lyre. 1
57: 8 Awake, my soul! Awake, O harp and lyre! 1
71:22 I will sing praises to thee with the lyre, O Holy One 1
81: 2 sound the timbrel, the sweet lyre with the harp. 1
92: 3 to the melody of the lyre. 1
98: 5 Sing praises to the LORD with the lyre 1
5 praises . . with the lyre and the sound of melody! 1
108: 2 Awake, O harp and lyre! I will awake the dawn! 1
137: 2 On the willows there we hung up our lyres 1
147: 7 make melody to our God upon the lyre! 1
149: 3 making melody to him with timbrel and lyre! 1
Isa 5:12 They have lyre and harp, timbrel and flute 1
16:11 Therefore my soul moans like a lyre for Moab 1
24: 8 has ceased, the mirth of the lyre is stilled. 1
30:32 will be to the sound of timbrels and lyres; 1
Ezk 26:13 the sound of your lyres shall be heard no more. 1
Dan 3: 5 hear the sound of the horn, pipe, lyre, trigon 2
7 heard the sound of the horn, pipe, lyre, trigon 2
10 hears the sound of the horn, pipe, lyre, trigon 2
15 hear the sound of the horn, pipe, lyre, trigon 2
Sir 39:15 with songs on your lips, and with lyres 3
151 1: 2 My hands made a harp, my fingers fashioned a lyre. 4

M

machine 1. μηχανή 2. ὄργανον
1Mc 9:67 and set fire to the machines of war. 1
4Mc 9:20 were falling off the axles of the machine. 2
26 they bound him to the torture machine and catapult. 2

machine of war 1. μηχανή
1Mc 9:64 and made machines of war. 1

machine to shoot arrows 1. σκορπίδιον
1Mc 6:51 machines to shoot arrows, and catapults. 1

war machine 1. μηχάνημα
4Mc 7: 4 besieged with many ingenious war machines 1

mad 1. הלל 2. שׁגע 3. ἄνοια 4. μαίνομαι 5. μανία
1Sm 21:14 you see the man is mad; why . . have you brought him 2
Ecc 2: 2 I said of laughter, "It is mad 1
Jer 50:38 it is a land of images, and they are mad over idols. 1
Hos 9: 7 The prophet is a fool, the man of the spirit is mad 2
Joh 10:20 Many of them said, "He has a demon, and he is mad 4
Act 12:15 They said to her, "You are mad. 4
26:24 Festus said with a loud voice, "Paul, you are mad 4
24 your great learning is turning you mad. 5
25 Paul said, "I am not mad, most excellent Festus 4
1Co 14:23 will they not say that you are mad? 4
2Mc 14: 5 an opportunity that furthered his mad purpose 3

mad *See also* drive, feign.

mad fellow 1. שׁגע
2Kg 9:11 Is all well? Why did this mad fellow come to you? 1

go mad 1. הלל
Jer 51: 7 nations drank . . therefore the nations went mad. 1

mad man 1. insanus
2Es 16:71 They shall be like mad men, sparing no one 1

madden 1. ἀγριόω 2. ἐπιμαίνομαι
3Mc 5: 2 maddened by the lavish abundance of liquor 1
4Mc 7: 5 broke the maddening waves of the emotion. 2

made by man 1. χειροποίητος
Act 17:24 God . . does not live in shrines made by man 1

thing made 1. מַעֲשֶׂה
Isa 29:16 that the thing made should say of its maker 1

madman 1. להלה 2. מְשׁוּגָּע 3. שׁגע 4. παραφρονέω 5. παράφρων
1Sm 21:15 Do I lack madmen, that you have brought this 2
Prv 26:18 Like a madman who throws firebrands, arrows 1
Jer 29:26 charge in the house of the LORD over every madman 3
2Co 11:23 I am talking like a madman 4
Wis 5:20 join with him to fight against the madmen. 5

madman *See also* play.

madness 1. הוֹלֵלָה 2. הוֹלֵלוֹת 3. שִׁגָּעוֹן 4. ἀλογιστία 5. ἀπόνοια 6. μανία 7. μανιώδης 8. παραφρονία
Deu 28:28 LORD will smite you with madness and blindness 3
Ecc 1:17 to know wisdom and to know madness and folly. 1
2:12 turned to consider wisdom and madness and folly; 1
7:25 to know . . and the foolishness which is madness. 1
9: 3 and madness is in their hearts while they live 1
10:13 and the end of his talk is wicked madness. 2
Zec 12: 4 horse with panic, and its rider with madness. 3
2Pe 2:16 a dumb ass . . restrained the prophet's madness. 8
Wis 5: 4 We thought that his life was madness 6
Sir 22:13 you will never be wearied by his madness. 5
3Mc 5:42 Phalaris in everything and filled with madness 4
45 had been brought virtually to a state of madness 7
4Mc 8: 5 not to display the same madness 6

madness *See also* display, feign.

sheer madness 1. ἀπόνοια
2Mc 6:29 the words . . were in their opinion sheer madness. 1

maggot 1. רִמָּה
Job 25: 6 how much less man, who is a maggot 1
Isa 14:11 maggots are the bed beneath you 1

magic 1. חֵן 2. μαγεία 3. μαγικός
Prv 17: 8 A bribe is like a magic stone in the eyes of him 1
Ezk 13:20 Behold, I am against your magic bands *
Act 8:11 for a long time he had amazed them with his magic. 2
Wis 17: 7 The delusions of their magic art lay humbled 3

magic *See also* art, band, practice.

magician 1. חַרְטֹם 2. חָרָשׁ 3. חַרְטֹם (A) 4. μάγος
Gen 41: 8 sent and called for all the magicians of Egypt 1
24 And I told it to the magicians, but there was no one 1
Exd 7:11 they also, the magicians of Egypt, did the same 1
22 the magicians of Egypt did the same 1
8: 7 the magicians did the same by their secret arts 1
18 The magicians tried by their secret arts 1
19 the magicians said to Pharaoh, "This is the finger 1
9:11 the magicians could not stand before Moses 1
11 boils were upon the magicians and upon all 1
Isa 3: 3 the skilful magician and the expert in charms. 2
Dan 1:20 better than all the magicians and enchanters 1
2: 2 commanded that the magicians, the enchanters 1
10 such a thing of any magician or enchanter 3
27 No wise men . . magicians, or astrologers 3
4: 7 magicians, the enchanters, the Chalde'ans 3
9 O Belteshaz'zar, chief of the magicians 3
5:11 chief of the magicians, enchanters, Chalde'ans 3
Act 13: 6 they came upon a certain magician 4
8 El'ymas the magician . . withstood them 4

magistrate 1. שׁפט (A) 2. תִּפְתָּיֵא (A) 3. ἄρχων 4. κριτής 5. στρατηγός
Ezr 7:25 appoint magistrates and judges who may judge 1
Dan 3: 2 assemble the . . magistrates, and all 2
3 magistrates, and all the officials 2
Lke 12:58 you go with your accuser before the magistrate 3
Act 16:20 when they had brought them to the magistrates 5
22 the magistrates tore the garments off them 5
35 when it was day, the magistrates sent the police 5
36 The magistrates have sent to let you go 5
38 police reported these words to the magistrates 5
Jdt 6:14 placed him before the magistrates of their city 3
Sir 10: 1 A wise magistrate will educate his people 4
2 Like the magistrate of the people 4
41:18 of a transgression, before a judge or magistrate; 3

magnanimous 1. μεγαλόψυχος
4Mc 15:10 self-controlled and brave and magnanimous 1

magnanimously 1. μεγαλοψύχως
3Mc 6:41 magnanimously expressing his concern 1

magnificence 1. μεγαλειότης 2. παράστασις
Act 19:27 she may even be deposed from her magnificence 1
1Es 1: 5 the magnificence of Solomon his son 1
1Mc 15:32 when he saw . . his great magnificence 2

magnificent 1. גדל 2. ἐκπρεπής 3. ἐνδόξως 4. μεγαλοπρεπής
1Ch 22: 5 for the LORD must be exceedingly magnificent 1
Tob 14:11 Tobias gave him a magnificent funeral. 3
13 he gave . . magnificent funerals 3
3Mc 2: 9 your magnificent manifestation 4
3:17 with magnificent and most beautiful offerings 2

magnificently 1. καλός 2. μεγαλομερῶς 3. μεγαλοπρεπῶς
2Mc 3:25 a magnificently caparisoned horse 1
4:22 welcomed magnificently by Jason and the city 2
49 provided magnificently for their funeral. 3

magnify 1. גדל 2. רבה 3. δοξάζω 4. θαυμάζω 5. μεγαλύνω
2Sm 7:26 and thy name will be magnified for ever, saying 1
1Ch 17:24 name will be established and magnified for ever 1
Job 19: 5 If indeed you magnify yourselves against me 1
Ps 34: 3 O magnify the LORD with me, and let us exalt 1
35:26 dishonor who magnify themselves against me! 1
69:30 I will magnify him with thanksgiving. 1
Isa 10:15 the saw magnify itself against him who wields it? 1
42:21 to magnify his law and make it glorious. 1
Jer 48:26 because he magnified himself against the LORD; 1
42 because he magnified himself against the LORD. 1
Ezk 35:13 And you magnified yourselves against me 1
Dan 8: 4 did as he pleased and magnified himself. 1
8 Then the he-goat magnified himself exceedingly; 1
11 magnified itself, even up to the Prince 1
25 in his mind he shall magnify himself. 1
11:36 exalt himself and magnify himself 1
37 for he shall magnify himself above all. 1
39 acknowledge him he shall magnify with honor. 2
Lke 1:46 Mary said, "My soul magnifies the Lord 5
Rom 11:13 an apostle to the Gentiles, I magnify my ministry 3
AEs 14:10 to magnify for ever a mortal king. 4
Sir 36: 4 so in them be thou magnified before us; 5
49:11 How shall we magnify Zerubbabel? 5

maid 1. אָמָה 2. נַעֲרָה 3. שִׁפְחָה 4. ἅβρα 5. δούλη 6. κοράσιον 7. παιδίσκη
Gen 16: 1 Sar'ai . . had an Egyptian maid whose name was 3
2 me from bearing children; go in to my maid; 3
3 Sar'ai . . took Hagar the Egyptian, her maid 3
5 I gave my maid to your embrace 3
6 Behold, your maid is in your power; 3
24:61 Then Rebekah and her maids arose 2
25:12 whom Hagar the Egyptian, Sarah's maid, bore 3
29:24 Laban gave his maid Zilpah to his daughter Leah 3
24 Zilpah to his daughter Leah to be her maid. 3
29 Laban gave his maid Bilhah to his daughter 3
29 Bilhah to his daughter Rachel to be her maid. 3
30: 3 Then she said, "Here is my maid Bilhah; go in to her 1
4 she gave him her maid Bilhah as a wife; 3
7 Rachel's maid Bilhah conceived again 3
9 she took her maid Zilpah and gave her to Jacob 3
10 Then Leah's maid Zilpah bore Jacob a son. 3
12 Leah's maid Zilpah bore Jacob a second son. 3
18 my hire because I gave my maid to my husband"; 3
32:22 took . . his two maids, and his eleven children 3
33: 1 among Leah and Rachel and the two maids. 3
2 he put the maids with their children in front 3
6 Then the maids drew near, they and their children 3
35:25 The sons of Bilhah, Rachel's maid: Dan 3
26 The sons of Zilpah, Leah's maid: Gad and Asher. 3
Exd 2: 5 saw the basket . . and sent her maid to fetch it. 1
2Sm 6:20 today before the eyes of his servants' maids 1
22 by the maids of whom you have spoken . . I shall be 1
2Kg 5: 2 the Syrians . . had carried off a little maid 2
Est 2: 9 and with seven chosen maids from the king's 2
9 and advanced her and her maids to the best place 2
4: 4 Esther's maids and her eunuchs came and told her 2
16 I and my maids will also fast as you do. 2
Ps 123: 2 as the eyes of a maid to the hand of her mistress 3
Prv 9: 3 She has sent out her maids to call 2
30:23 maid when she succeeds her mistress. 3
Isa 24: 2 as with the maid, so with her mistress; 3
Mat 26:69 a maid came up to him, and said 7
71 when he went out to the porch, another maid saw him *
Mrk 14:66 one of the maids of the high priest came; 7
69 the maid saw him 7
Lke 22:56 Then a maid, seeing him as he sat in the light 7
Joh 18:17 The maid who kept the door said to Peter 7
Act 12:13 a maid named Rhoda came to answer. 7
Tob 3: 7 was reproached by her father's maids 7
8 the maids said to her *

8:12 Send one of the maids to see whether he is alive 7
13 the maid opened the door and went 7
Jdt 8:10 she sent her maid 4
33 I will go out with my maid 4
10: 2 called her maid and went down into the house 4
5 gave her maid a bottle of wine and a flask of oil 4
10 Judith went out, she and her maid with her 7
17 100 men to accompany her and her maid 4
12:15 her maid went 5
19 drank before him what her maid had prepared. 5
13: 3 told her maid to stand outside the bedchamber 5
9 gave Holofernes' head to her maid 4
16:23 She set her maid free 4
AEs 15: 2 Then . . she took her two maids with her 4
7 the maid who went before her. 4
Sus 1:15 she went in as before with only two maids 6
17 She said to her maids, "Bring me oil and ointments 6
19 When the maids had gone out, the two elders rose 6
21 and this was why you sent your maids away. 6
36 this woman came in with two maids 7
36 shut the garden doors, and dismissed the maids. 7

maid who keeps the door 1. *θυρωρός*
Joh 18:16 went out and spoke to the maid who kept the door 1

maiden 1. אָמָה 2. בַּת 3. בְּתוּלָה 4. יַלְדָּה 5. נַעֲרָה 6. עַלְמָה 7. רֶחֶם 8. *νεᾶνις* 9. *παρθένος*
Gen 24:14 Let the maiden to whom I shall say 5
16 The maiden was very fair to look upon 5
28 the maiden ran and told her mother's household 5
55 her mother said, "Let the maiden remain with us 5
57 They said, "We will call the maiden, and ask her. 5
34: 3 he loved the maiden and spoke tenderly to her. 5
4 Get me this maiden for my wife. 4
12 only give me the maiden to be my wife. 5
Exd 2: 5 and her maidens walked beside the river; 5
Jdg 5:30 dividing the spoil?–A maiden or two for every man; 7
Rut 2: 5 Bo'az said to his servant . . "Whose maiden is this? 5
6 It is the Moabite maiden, who came back with Na'omi 5
8 do not go to . . but keep close to my maidens. 5
22 It is well . . that you go out with his maidens 5
23 she kept close to the maidens of Bo'az 5
3: 2 Bo'az our kinsman, with whose maidens you were? 5
1Sm 25:42 Ab'igail . . and her five maidens attended her; 5
1Kg 1: 2 Let a young maiden be sought for my lord the king 3
3 they sought for a beautiful maiden throughout 5
4 The maiden was very beautiful; and she became 5
2Kg 5: 4 Thus and so spoke the maiden from . . Israel. 5
Est 2: 4 let the maiden who pleases the king be queen 5
7 the maiden was beautiful and lovely 5
8 many maidens were gathered in Susa the capital 5
9 And the maiden pleased him and won his favor; 5
12 came for each maiden to go in to King Ahasu-e'rus 5
13 when the maiden went in to the king in this way 5
Job 41: 5 or will you put him on leash for your maidens? 5
Ps 68:25 between them maidens playing timbrels 6
78:63 their maidens had no marriage song. 3
148:12 Young men and maidens together 3
Prv 27:27 enough . . maintenance for your maidens. 5
30:19 way of a man with a maiden. 6
31:15 provides food . . and tasks for her maidens. 5
Sng 1: 3 your name is . . therefore the maidens love you. 6
2: 2 As a lily among . . so is my love among maidens. 2
6: 8 80 concubines, and maidens without number. 6
9 The maidens saw her and called her happy; 2
7: 1 How graceful are your feet . . O queenly maiden! 2
6 How fair . . you are . . delectable maiden! ‡
Jer 2:32 Can a maiden forget her ornaments 3
31:13 Then shall the maidens rejoice in the dance 3
51:22 I break in pieces the young man and the maiden; 3
Lam 1: 4 her maidens have been dragged away 3
18 my maidens and . . men have gone into captivity. 3
2:10 the maidens of Jerusalem have bowed their heads 3
21 my maidens and my young men have fallen 3
3:51 grief at the fate of all the maidens of my city. 2
Ezk 9: 6 slay old men outright, young men and maidens 3
Nah 2: 7 her maidens lamenting, moaning like doves 1
Zec 9:17 young men flourish, and new wine the maidens. 3
Mat 25: 1 ten maidens who took their lamps 9
7 Then all those maidens rose 9
11 Afterward the other maidens came also, saying 9
Sir 20: 4 Like a eunuch's desire to violate a maiden 8
30:20 like a eunuch who embraces a maiden and groans. 8
1Mc 1:26 maidens and young men became faint 9
2Mc 3:19 Some of the maidens who were kept indoors 9

young maiden 1. נַעֲרָה
1Sm 9:11 they met young maidens coming out to draw water 1

maidenhood
Ezk 16: 7 and became tall and arrived at full maidenhood; •

maidservant 1. אָמָה 2. שִׁפְחָה 3. *δούλη* 4. *κοράσιον* 5. *παιδίσκη*
Gen 12:16 maidservants, she-asses, and camels. 2
24:35 gold, menservants and maidservants, camels 2
30:43 had large flocks, maidservants and menservants 2
31:33 into the tent of the two maidservants 1
32: 5 I have . . menservants, and maidservants; 2
Exd 11: 5 even to the first-born of the maidservant who is 2
20:10 or your maidservant, or your cattle 1
17 covet . . his manservant, or his maidservant 1
Deu 5:14 your manservant, or your maidservant, or your ox 1
14 that your manservant and your maidservant 1
21 not desire . . his manservant, or his maidservant 1
12:12 rejoice . . you . . and your maidservants 1
18 eat . . you . . and your maidservant, and the Levite 1
16:11 rejoice . . you and . . your maidservant 1
14 rejoice . . you and . . your maidservant 1
Jdg 9:18 made Abim'elech, the son of his maidservant 1
19:19 with bread and wine for me and your maidservant 1
Rut 2:13 you have . . spoken kindly to your maidservant 2
13 though I am not one of your maidservants. 2
3: 9 And she answered, "I am Ruth, your maidservant 1
9 spread your skirt over your maidservant 1
1Sm 1:11 look on the affliction of thy maidservant 1
11 and remember me, and not forget thy maidservant 1
11 but wilt give to thy maidservant a son 1
16 Do not regard your maidservant as a base woman 1
18 Let your maidservant find favor in your eyes. 2
8:16 He will take your menservants and maidservants 2
2Sm 17:17 a maidservant used to go and tell them 2
20:17 Listen to the words of your maidservant. 1
1Kg 1:13 Did you not . . swear to your maidservant, saying 1
17 My lord, you swore to your maidservant by the LORD 1
3:20 took my son . . while your maidservant slept 1
2Kg 4: 2 Your maidservant has nothing in the house 2
16 No, my lord . . do not lie to your maidservant. 2
5:26 sheep and oxen, menservants and maidservants? 2
Ezr 2:65 besides their menservants and maidservants 1
Neh 7:67 besides their menservants and maidservants 1
Job 19:15 my maidservants count me as a stranger; 1
31:13 the cause of my manservant or my maidservant 1
Jol 2:29 Even upon the menservants and maidservants 2
Lke 12:45 to beat the menservants and the maidservants 5
Act 2:18 yea, and on my menservants and my maidservants 3
1Es 5: 1 menservants and maidservants, and their cattle. 5
41 besides menservants and maidservants 5
42 their menservants and maidservants were 7,337; 5
Jdt 11: 5 let your maidservant speak in your presence 5
6 if you follow out the words of your maidservant 5
12:13 This beautiful ma idservant will please come 5
16:12 The sons of maidservants have pierced them through; 4
Wis 9: 5 For I am thy slave and the son of thy maidservant 5
Sir 41:22 of meddling with his maidservant 5

mail 1. קַשְׂקֶשֶׂת
1Sm 17: 5 and he was armed with a coat of mail 1
mail *See also* coat.

maim 1. שׁבר 2. *ἀνάπηρος* 3. *κυλλός* 4. mancus
Zec 11:16 or seek the wandering, or heal the maimed 1
Mat 15:30 the lame, the maimed, the blind, the dumb 3
31 the dumb speaking, the maimed whole 3
18: 8 it is better for you to enter life maimed or lame 3
Mrk 9:43 it is better for you to enter life maimed 3
Lke 14:13 invite the poor, the maimed, the lame, the blind 2
21 bring in the poor and maimed and blind and lame.' 2
2Es 2:21 do not ridicule a lame man, protect the maimed 4

main 1. כֹּל
Jos 8:13 the main encampment which was north of the city 1
main *See also* principle, street, strength.

main part 1. רֵאשִׁית
Dan 11:41 Edom and Moab and the main part of the Ammonites. 1

mainland 1. שָׂדֶה
Ezk 26: 6 her daughters on the mainland shall be slain 1
8 He will slay . . your daughters on the mainland; 1
17 who imposed your terror on all the mainland! •

mainstay 1. רֵאשִׁית
Jer 49:35 break the bow of Elam, the mainstay of their might; 1

maintain 1. חזק 2. מוט יָד 3. נצב 4. עשה 5. *διατηρέω* 6. *διαφυλάσσω* 7. *διεξάγω* 8. *ἔχω* 9. *καθίστημι* 10. *κατέχω* 11. *μένω* 12. *προφέρω* 13. *συντηρέω* 14. *τηρέω* 15. *φυλάσσω* 16. habeo
Lev 25:35 brother . . cannot maintain himself with you 2
35 brother . . cannot maintain himself with you 1
1Kg 8:45 then hear . . and maintain their cause. 4
49 hear . . and maintain their cause 4
59 and may he maintain the cause of his servant 4
2Ch 6:35 then hear . . and maintain their cause. 4
39 hear thou . . and maintain their cause 4
Ps 9: 4 For thou hast maintained my just cause; 4
140:12 LORD maintains the cause of the afflicted 4
Prv 15:25 but maintains the widow's boundaries. 3
31: 9 maintain the rights of the poor and needy. •
Ezk 7:13 none can maintain his life. 1
1Co 11: 2 maintain the traditions 10
Eph 4: 3 eager to maintain the unity of the Spirit 14
1Pe 2:12 Maintain good conduct among the Gentiles 8
2Es 6:32 which you have maintained from your youth. 16
Jdt 8: 7 she maintained this estate. 11
Sir 28: 5 If he himself, being flesh, maintains wrath 5
1Mc 14:35 loyalty which he had maintained 13
2Mc 9:26 to maintain your present good will, each of you 13
10:12 attempted to maintain peaceful relations 7
11:19 If you will maintain your good will toward 13
15:30 the man who maintained his youthful good will 6
3Mc 1:12 did not cease to maintain that he ought to enter 12
3: 3 The Jews . . continued to maintain good will 15
19 By maintaining their manifest ill-will toward us 9
4Mc 6:18 have maintained in accordance with law 15
17: 4 maintaining firm an enduring hope in God. 8

maintain a force of mercenaries 1. *ξενοτροφέω*
2Mc 10:14 he maintained a force of mercenaries 1

maintain right 1. יכח 2. צדק
Job 16:21 he would maintain the right of a man with God 1
Ps 82: 3 maintain the right of the afflicted 2

maintain rights 1. דִּין
Prv 31: 9 maintain the rights of the poor and needy. 1
maintaining *See* exact.

maintenance 1. חזק 2. חַיִּים 3. *ξενία*
1Ch 26:27 for the maintenance of the house of the LORD. 1
Prv 27:27 enough . . maintenance for your maidens. 2
1Mc 10:36 let the maintenance be given them 3

majestic 1. אַדִּיר 2. אדר 3. גָּאוֹן 4. הוֹד 5. *μεγαλεῖος* 6. *μεγαλοπρεπής* 7. *μεγαλωσύνη*
Exd 15:11 Who is like thee, majestic in holiness, terrible 2
Job 37: 4 he thunders with his majestic voice 3
39:20 His majestic snorting is terrible. 4
Ps 8: 1 our Lord, how majestic is thy name in all the earth! 1
9 our Lord, how majestic is thy name in all the earth! 1
76: 4 more majestic than the everlasting mountains. 1
Isa 10:34 and Lebanon with its majestic trees will fall. 1
30:30 the LORD will cause his majestic voice to be heard 4
60:15 I will make you majestic for ever 3
Ezk 32:18 her and the daughters of majestic nations 1
2Pe 1:17 the voice was borne to him by the Majestic Glory 6
Sir 18: 5 Who can measure his majestic power? 7
2Mc 3:34 report to all men the majestic power of God. 5
majestically *See* adorn.

majesty 1. אַדִּיר 2. גַּאֲוָה 3. גָּאוֹן 4. גֵּאוּת 5. גְּדוּלָּה 6. הָדָר 7. הוֹד 8. שְׂאֵת 9. הֲדַר (A) 10. *ἐπιφάνεια* 11. *μεγαλεῖος* 12. *μεγαλειότης* 13. *μεγαλοπρεπής* 14. *μεγαλωσύνη*
Exd 15: 7 In the greatness of thy majesty 3
Deu 33:17 His firstling bull has majesty 6
26 who rides . . in his majesty through the skies. 2
1Ch 16:27 Honor and majesty are before him; 6
29:11 Thine, O LORD, is . . the victory, and the majesty; 7
25 and bestowed upon him such royal majesty 7
Est 1: 4 he showed . . the splendor and pomp of his majesty 5
Job 13:11 Will not his majesty terrify you 8
31:23 I could not have faced his majesty. 8
37:22 God is clothed with terrible majesty. 7
40:10 Deck yourself with majesty and dignity; 3
Ps 21: 5 splendor and majesty thou dost bestow upon him. 6
29: 4 voice of the LORD is full of majesty. 6
45: 3 O mighty one, in your glory and majesty! 6
4 In your majesty ride forth victoriously 6
68:34 God, whose majesty is over Israel 2
93: 1 The LORD reigns; he is robed in majesty; 4
96: 6 Honor and majesty are before him; 6
104: 1 Thou art clothed with honor and majesty 6
111: 3 Full of honor and majesty is his work 6
145: 5 On the glorious splendor of thy majesty 7
Isa 2:10 and hide . . and from the glory of his majesty. 3
19 the glory of his majesty, when he rises to terrify 3
21 the glory of his majesty, when he rises to terrify 3
24:14 over the majesty of the LORD they shout 3
26:10 and does not see the majesty of the LORD. 4
33:21 there the LORD in majesty will be for us 1
35: 2 the majesty of Carmel and Sharon. 6
2 the glory of the LORD, the majesty of our God. 6
Jer 22:18 lament for him, saying, 'Ah lord!' or 'Ah his majesty!' 7
Lam 1: 6 From . . Zion has departed all her majesty. 6
Dan 4:30 by my mighty power . . for the glory of my majesty? 9
36 my majesty and splendor returned to me. 9
5:18 kingship and greatness and glory and majesty; 9
11:21 contemptible person to whom royal majesty 7
Mic 5: 4 in the majesty of the name of the LORD his God. 3
Nah 2: 2 For the LORD is restoring the majesty of Jacob 3
2 the majesty of Jacob as the majesty of Israel 3
Lke 9:43 all were astonished at the majesty of God 12
Heb 1: 3 he sat down at the right hand of the Majesty on high 14
8: 1 right hand of the throne of the Majesty in heaven 14
2Pe 1:16 but we were eyewitnesses of his majesty. 12
Jde 1:25 to the only God . . be glory, majesty, dominion 14
1Es 4:40 the power and the majesty of all the ages. 12
Tob 13: 6 I show his power and majesty 14
7 my soul . . will rejoice in his majesty. 14
AEs 15: 6 clothed in the full array of his majesty 10
Wis 18:24 thy majesty on the diadem upon his head. 14
Sir 2:18 as his majesty is, so also is his mercy. 14

17: 8 to show them the majesty of his works. 11
13 Their eyes saw his glorious majesty 11
39:15 ascribe majesty to his name 14
43:15 In his majesty he amasses the clouds 11
44: 2 apportioned . . his majesty from the beginning. 14
2Mc 15:13 marvelous majesty and authority. 13

majority 1. מַרְבִּית 2. πολύς
1Ch 12:29 the majority had hitherto kept their allegiance 1
Act 27:12 the majority advised to put to sea from there 2
2Co 2: 6 this punishment by the majority is enough; 2
3Mc 2:32 the majority acted firmly 2

make 1. בנה 2. בער 3. ברא 4. דבר 5. היה 6. הרג
7. יסף 8. יצק 9. יצג 10. יצר 11. כרת 12. לבב
13. לקח לְ 14. מלא 15. מְלָאכָה 16. מַעֲשֶׂה 17. נדר
18. נכה 19. נסך 20. נפל 21. נתן 22. עבד 23. עבר
24. עלה 25. עשה 26. פלם 27. פעל 28. פקד 29. קום
30. שום 31. שוה 32. שית 33. עבד (A) 34. קום (A)
35. שום (A) 36. ἄγω 37. αἰτέω 38. ἀναγκάζω
39. ἀναδείκνυμι 40. ἀναλαμβάνω 41. ἀποδίδωμι
42. γίνομαι 43. γίνομαι περί 44. δημιουργέω
45. διατίθημι 46. δίδωμι 47. δίδωμι γίνομαι 48. δράω
49. ἐγείρω 50. εἰμί 51. εἶπον 52. εἰς 53. ἐμβάλλω
54. ἔξειμι 55. ἐπί 56. ἐργάζομαι 57. εὔχομαι 58. ἔχω
59. ἵνα 60. ἵστημι 61. καθίστημι 62. καταρτίζω
63. κατασκευάζω 64. κατατίθημι 65. κατεφίσταμαι
66. κατέχω 67. κερδαίνω 68. κτάομαι 69. κτίζω
70. λαλέω 71. λαμβάνω 72. νοσσεύω 73. οἰκοδομέω
74. ὅπως 75. παρεισφέρω 76. παρέχω 77. ποιέω
78. ποίησις 79. πολεμέω 80. πόνος 81. πρός
82. προσφέρω 83. στέλλω 84. συντελέω
85. συντίθημι 86. τάσσω 87. τίθημι 88. ὑπάρχω
89. ὥστε 90. capio 91. cogito 92. deduco 93. dispono
94. exhibeo 95. facio 96. fio 97. plasmo 98. pono

Gen 1: 7 God made the firmament and separated the waters 25
16 God made the two great lights 25
16 he made the stars also. *
25 God made the beasts of the earth 25
26 Let us make man in our image, after our likeness 25
31 God saw everything that he had made 25
2: 4 In the day that the LORD God made the earth 25
18 be alone; I will make him a helper fit for him. 25
22 the rib . . he made into a woman 1
3: 1 other wild creature that the LORD God had made. 25
7 leaves together and made themselves aprons. 25
21 made for Adam and for his wife garments of skins 25
5: 1 When God created man, he made him in the likeness 25
6: 6 the LORD was sorry that he had made man 25
7 air, for I am sorry that I have made them. 25
13 I have determined to make an end of all flesh; *
14 Make yourself an ark of gopher wood; 25
14 ark of gopher wood; make rooms in the ark 25
15 This is how you are to make it 25
16 Make a roof for the ark, and finish it to a cubit 25
16 make it with lower, second, and third decks. 25
7: 4 living thing that I have made I will blot out 25
8: 6 the window of the ark which he had made 25
9: 6 for God made man in his own image. 25
12 covenant which I make between me and you 21
11: 4 let us make a name for ourselves 25
12: 2 I will make of you a great nation 25
13: 4 to the place where he had made an altar 25
16 I will make your descendants as the dust 30
14: 2 these kings made war with Bera king of Sodom 25
15:18 On that day the LORD made a covenant with Abram 11
17: 2 I will make my covenant between me and you 21
5 Abraham; for I have made you the father 21
6 I will make nations of you, and kings shall come 21
20 princes, and I will make him a great nation. 21
18: 6 Make ready quickly three measures of fine meal *
6 measures of fine meal, knead it, and make cakes. 25
19: 3 and he made them a feast 25
21: 6 Sarah said, "God has made laughter for me; 25
8 and Abraham made a great feast 25
13 I will make a nation of the son of the slave woman 30
18 for I will make him a great nation. 30
27 to Abim'elech, and the two men made a covenant. 11
32 they made a covenant at Beer-sheba. 11
26:28 and let us make a covenant with you 11
30 he made them a feast, and they ate and drank. 25
35 they made life bitter for Isaac and Rebekah. 5
27:37 Isaac answered Esau, "Behold, I have made him 30
29:22 all the men of the place, and made a feast. 25
31:46 and they took stones, and made a heap; 25
32:12 I will do you good, and make your descendants 30
33:17 built . . a house, and made booths for his cattle; 25
35: 1 dwell there; and make there an altar to the God who 25
3 to Bethel, that I may make there an altar to the God 25
37: 3 old age; and he made him a long robe with sleeves. 25
40:20 Pharaoh's birthday, he made a feast for all his 25
43:18 to make slaves of us and seize our asses. 13
45: 8 and he has made me a father to Pharaoh 30
9 God has made me lord of all Egypt; come down to me 30
46: 3 for I will there make of you a great nation. 30
47:26 Joseph made it a statute concerning the land 30
48: 4 and I will make of you a company of peoples 21
20 God make you as E'phraim and as Manas'seh 30
50:10 and he made a mourning for his father seven days. 25
Exd 2: 3 she took for him a basket made of bulrushes *
14 He answered, "Who made you a prince and a judge 30
4:11 the LORD said to him, "Who has made man's mouth? 30
11 man's mouth? Who makes him dumb, or deaf 30
5: 8 the number of bricks which they made heretofore 25
16 No straw . . yet they say to us, 'Make bricks!' 25
7: 1 to Moses, "See, I make you as God to Pharaoh; 21
12: 4 you shall make your count for the lamb. *
14:21 and made the sea dry land, and the waters were 30
15:17 place, O LORD, which thou has made for thy abode 27
25 There the LORD made for them a statute 30
16:31 taste of it was like wafers made with honey. *
18:25 Moses . . made them heads over the people 21
20: 4 You shall not make for yourself a graven image 25
11 for in six days the LORD made heaven and earth 25
23 You shall not make gods of silver to be with me 25
23 nor shall you make for yourselves gods of gold. 25
24 An altar of earth you shall make for me 25
25 if you make me an altar of stone, you shall not 25
22:16 he shall . . make her his wife. *
23:32 You shall make no covenant with them 11
24: 8 the covenant which the LORD has made with you 11
25: 8 let them make me a sanctuary, that I may dwell 25
9 so you shall make it. 25
10 They shall make an ark of acacia wood; 25
11 you shall make upon it a molding of gold round 25
13 You shall make poles of acacia wood, and overlay 25
17 Then you shall make a mercy seat of pure gold; 25
18 you shall make two cherubim of gold; 25
18 of hammered work shall you make them 25
19 Make one cherub on the one end 25
19 with the mercy seat shall you make the cherubim 25
23 you shall make a table of acacia wood; 25
24 You shall . . make a molding of gold around 25
25 shall make around it a frame a handbreadth wide 25
26 you shall make for it four rings of gold 25
28 You shall make the poles of acacia wood 25
29 you shall make its plates and dishes for incense 25
29 of pure gold you shall make them. 25
31 you shall make a lampstand of pure gold. 25
31 the lampstand shall be made of hammered work; 25
37 you shall make the seven lamps for it; 25
39 Of a talent of pure gold shall it be made, with all 25
40 see that you make them after the pattern for them 25
26: 1 you shall make the tabernacle with ten curtains 25
1 cherubim skilfully worked shall you make them. 25
4 you shall make loops of blue on the edge 25
4 and likewise you shall make loops on the edge 25
5 50 loops you shall make on the one curtain 25
5 50 loops you shall make on the edge 25
6 you shall make 50 clasps of gold 25
7 You shall also make curtains of goats' hair 25
7 eleven curtains shall you make. 25
10 you shall make 50 loops on the edge 25
11 you shall make 50 clasps of bronze 25
14 you shall make for the tent a covering of tanned 25
15 you shall make upright frames 25
18 You shall make the frames for the tabernacle 25
19 40 bases of silver you shall make 25
22 tabernacle westward you shall make six frames. 25
23 you shall make two frames for corners 25
26 you shall make bars of acacia wood 25
29 shall make their rings of gold for holders 25
31 you shall make a veil of blue and purple 25
31 in skilled work shall it be made, with cherubim. 25
36 you shall make a screen for the door of the tent 25
37 you shall make for the screen five pillars 25
27: 1 You shall make the altar of acacia wood 25
2 you shall make horns for it on its four corners; 25
3 You shall make pots for it to receive its ashes 25
3 all its utensils you shall make of bronze. 25
4 You shall also make for it a grating 25
4 upon the net you shall make four bronze rings 25
6 you shall make poles for the altar 25
8 You shall make it hollow, with boards; 25
8 as it has been shown . . so shall it be made. 25
9 You shall make the court of the tabernacle. 25
28: 2 you shall make holy garments for Aaron 25
3 that they make Aaron's garments to consecrate 25
4 These are the garments which they shall make 25
4 they shall make holy garments for Aaron 25
6 they shall make the ephod of gold, of blue 25
13 you shall make settings of gold filigree 25
15 you shall make a breastpiece of judgment 25
15 like the work of the ephod you shall make it; 25
15 of . . fine twined linen shall you make it. 25
22 you shall make for the breastpiece twisted 25
23 you shall make for the breastpiece two rings 25
26 you shall make two rings of gold, and put them 25
27 you shall make two rings of gold, and attach them 25
31 you shall make the robe of the ephod all of blue. 25
33 On its skirts you shall make pomegranates 25
36 you shall make a plate of pure gold, and engrave 25
39 shall make a turban of fine linen, and you shall 25
39 shall make a girdle embroidered 25
40 for Aaron's sons you shall make coats and girdles 25
40 you shall make them for glory and beauty. 25
42 you shall make for them linen breeches to cover 25
29: 2 You shall make them of fine wheat flour. 25
30: 1 You shall make an altar to burn incense upon; 25
1 of acacia wood shall you make it. 25
3 make for it a molding of gold round about. 25
4 two golden rings shall you make for it; 25
4 on two opposite sides of it shall you make them 25
5 You shall make the poles of acacia wood 25
18 You shall also make a laver of bronze 25
25 you shall make of these a sacred anointing oil 25
32 you shall make no other like it in composition; 25
35 make an incense blended as by the perfumer 25
37 the incense which you shall make 25
37 incense . . you shall not make for yourselves; 25
38 Whoever makes any like it to use as perfume 25
31: 6 that they may make all that I have commanded you 25
17 in six days the LORD made heaven and earth 25
32: 1 said to him, "Up, make us gods, who shall go before us; 25
4 fashioned it . . and made a molten calf; 25
8 they have made for themselves a molten calf 25
10 but of you I will make a great nation. 25
20 he took the calf which they had made, and burnt it 25
23 For they said to me, 'Make us gods, who shall go 25
31 they have made for themselves gods of gold. 25
35 a plague . . because they made the calf 25
35 because they made the calf which Aaron made. 25
34:10 he said, "Behold, I make a covenant. 11
12 Take heed to yourself, lest you make a covenant 11
15 lest you make a covenant with the inhabitants 11
17 You shall make for yourself no molten gods. 25
27 I have made a covenant with you and with Israel. 11
35:10 come and make all that the LORD has commanded 25
36: 8 able men among the workmen made the tabernacle 25
8 they were made of fine twined linen and blue 25
11 he made loops of blue on the edge of the outmost 25
11 he made them on the edge of the outmost curtain 25
12 he made 50 loops on the one curtain 25
12 he made 50 loops on the edge of the curtain 25
13 he made 50 clasps of gold 25
14 He also made curtains of goats' hair for a tent 25
14 over the tabernacle; he made eleven curtains. 25
17 he made 50 loops on the edge of the outmost 25
18 he made 50 clasps of bronze to couple the tent 25
19 he made for the tent a covering of tanned rams' 25
20 he made the upright frames for the tabernacle 25
23 The frames for the tabernacle he made thus 25
24 he made 40 bases of silver under the twenty frames 25
25 on the north side, he made twenty frames 25
27 for . . the tabernacle westward he made six frames. 25
28 he made two frames for corners 25
29 he made two of them thus, for the two corners. 25
31 he made bars of acacia wood, five for the frames 25
33 he made the middle bar to pass through 25
34 and made their rings of gold for holders 25
35 he made the veil of blue and purple and scarlet 25
35 with cherubim skilfully worked he made it. 25
36 for it he made four pillars of acacia 25
37 He also made a screen for the door of the tent 25
37: 1 Bez'alel made the ark of acacia wood; 25
2 and made a molding of gold around it. 25
4 And he made poles of acacia wood 25
6 he made a mercy seat of pure gold; 25
7 he made two cherubim of hammered gold; 25
7 on the two ends of the mercy seat he made them 25
8 mercy seat he made the cherubim on its two ends. 25
10 He also made the table of acacia wood; 25
11 he overlaid it with pure gold, and made a molding 25
12 he made around it a frame a handbreadth wide 25
12 made a molding of gold around the frame. 25
15 He made the poles of acacia wood to carry 25
16 he made the vessels of pure gold which were to be 25
17 He also made the lampstand of pure gold. 25
17 The base and the shaft of the lampstand were made 25
23 he made its seven lamps and its snuffers 25
24 He made it and all its utensils of a talent 25
25 He made the altar of incense of acacia wood; 25
26 and he made a molding of gold round about it 25
27 made two rings of gold on it under its molding 25
28 he made the poles of acacia wood, and overlaid 25
29 He made the holy anointing oil also, and the pure 25
38: 1 He made the altar of burnt offering also 25
2 He made horns for it on its four corners; 25
3 he made all the utensils of the altar, the pots 25
3 all its utensils he made of bronze. 25
4 he made for the altar a grating, a network 25
6 he made the poles of acacia wood, and overlaid 25
7 he made it hollow, with boards. 25
8 he made the laver of bronze and its base of bronze 25
9 he made the court; for the south side the hangings 25
22 Bez'alel . . made all that the LORD commanded 25
28 he made hooks for the pillars 25
30 with it he made the bases for the door of the tent 25
39: 1 they made finely wrought garments 25
1 they made the holy garments for Aaron; 25
2 he made the ephod of gold, blue and purple 25
4 They made for the ephod shoulder-pieces 25
8 He made the breastpiece, in skilled work 25
9 It was square; the breastpiece was made double 25

15 they made on the breastpiece twisted chains 25
16 they made two settings of gold filigree 25
19 Then they made two rings of gold 25
20 they made two rings of gold, and attached them 25
22 He also made the robe of the ephod 25
24 On the skirts of the robe they made pomegranates 25
25 They also made bells of pure gold 25
27 They also made the coats, woven of fine linen 25
30 they made the plate of the holy crown of pure gold 25
Lev 2: 7 it shall be made of fine flour with oil 25
8 you shall bring the cereal offering that is made 25
11 No cereal offering . . shall be made with leaven 25
6:21 It shall be made with oil on a griddle 25
7:35 portion . . from the offerings made by fire *
13:48 in a skin or in anything made of skin 15
49 in anything made of skin, it is a leprous disease *
19: 4 Do not . . make for yourselves molten gods 25
19 a garment of cloth made of two kinds of stuff *
28 You shall not make any cuttings in your flesh 21
22:22 you shall not . . make of them an offering by fire 21
23:17 bread . . made of two tenths of an ephah *
26: 1 You shall make for yourselves no idols 25
11 I will make my abode among you 21
19 I will make your heavens like iron 21
46 which the LORD made between him and the people 21
27:25 twenty gerahs shall make a shekel 5
Num 5:21 then . . LORD make you an execration and an oath 21
21 when the LORD makes your thigh fall away 21
6: 3 he shall drink no vinegar made from wine *
8: 4 so he made the lampstand. 25
10: 2 Make two silver trumpets; of hammered work 25
2 trumpets; of hammered work you shall make them; 25
11: 8 people . . boiled it in pots, and made cakes of it; 25
14:12 I will make of you a nation greater and mightier 25
15: 3 to make a pleasing odor to the LORD 25
38 bid them to make tassels on the corners 25
16:38 let them be made into hammered plates 25
18: 8 whatever is kept of the offerings made to me *
21: 8 Make a fiery serpent, and set it on a pole; 25
9 Moses made a bronze serpent, and set it on a pole; 25
29 He has made his sons fugitives, and his daughters 21
Deu 1:11 LORD . . make you a 1,000 times as many as you are 7
4:16 lest you act corruptly by making a graven image 25
23 covenant of the LORD . . which he made with you 11
23 make a graven image in the form of anything 25
25 if you act corruptly by making a graven image 25
5: 2 The LORD our God made a covenant with us in Horeb. 11
3 Not with . . did the LORD make this covenant 11
8 You shall not make for yourself a graven image 25
7: 2 utterly destroy them; you shall make no covenant 11
9: 9 tables of the covenant which the LORD made 11
12 they have made themselves a molten image.' 25
14 I will make of you a nation mightier and greater 25
16 you had made yourselves a molten calf; 25
21 sinful thing, the calf which you had made 25
10: 1 come up to me . . and make an ark of wood. 25
3 I made an ark of acacia wood, and hewed two tables 25
5 put the tables in the ark which I had made; 25
22 made you as the stars of heaven for multitude. 30
14: 1 not . . make any baldness on your foreheads 30
16:21 beside the altar of the LORD . . you shall make. 25
20:12 if it makes no peace . . but makes war against you 25
20 siegeworks against the city that makes war 25
22: 8 new house, you shall make a parapet for your roof 25
12 make yourself tassels on the four corners 25
17 he has made shameful charges against her, saying 30
23:21 When you make a vow to the LORD your God 17
26:19 set you high above all nations that he has made 25
27:15 'Cursed . . man who makes a graven or molten image 25
15 image . . a thing made by the hands of a craftsman *
28:13 LORD will make you the head, and not the tail; 21
24 LORD will make the rain of your land powder 21
68 promised that you should never make again; *
29: 1 LORD commanded Moses to make with . . Israel 11
1 covenant which he had made with them at Horeb. 11
12 sworn covenant . . LORD your God makes with you 11
14 Nor . . with you only that I make this sworn covenant 11
25 forsook the covenant . . which he made with them 11
31:16 break my covenant which I have made with them. 11
32: 6 father, who . . made you and established you? 25
15 then he forsook God who made him 25
Jos 5: 2 Make flint knives and circumcise the people 25
3 Joshua made flint knives, and circumcised 25
6:18 make the camp of Israel a thing for destruction 30
8:28 burned Ai, and made it for ever a heap of ruins 30
9: 6 from a far country; so now make a covenant with us. 11
7 then how can we make a covenant with you? 11
11 We are your servants . . make a covenant with us. 11
15 Joshua made peace with them, and made a covenant 25
15 and made a covenant with them, to let them live; 11
16 after they had made a covenant with them 11
27 But Joshua made them that day hewers of wood 21
11:18 Joshua made war a long time with all those kings. 25
17: 1 Then allotment was made to the tribe of Manas'seh 5
2 allotments were made to the rest of . . Manas'seh *
21:45 promises which the LORD had made to . . Israel 4
22:25 For the LORD has made the Jordan a boundary 21
28 the copy of the altar . . which our fathers made 25
33 Israel . . spoke no more of making war against 24

24:25 Joshua made a covenant with the people that day 11
25 Joshua . . made statutes and ordinances 30
Jdg 2: 2 you shall make no covenant with the inhabitants 11
3:16 And Ehud made for himself a sword with two edges 25
6: 2 people of Israel made for themselves the dens 25
8:27 Gideon made an ephod of it and put it in his city 25
33 turned again . . and made Ba'al-be'rith their god. 30
11:11 and the people made him head and leader over them; 30
39 did . . according to his vow which he had made. 17
14:10 down to the woman, and Samson made a feast there; 25
17: 3 I consecrate the silver . . to make a graven image 25
4 the silversmith, who made it into a graven image 25
5 the man Micah had a shrine, and he made an ephod 25
18:24 You take my gods which I made, and the priest, and go 25
27 taking what Micah had made, and the priest who 25
31 they set up Micah's graven image which he made 25
21:15 the LORD had made a breach in the tribes 25
Rut 4:11 May the LORD make the woman . . like Rachel 21
1Sm 2:19 his mother used to make for him a little robe 25
6: 5 make images of your tumors and . . of your mice 25
8: 1 Samuel . . made his sons judges over Israel. 30
12 appoint . . and to make his implements of war 25
11: 1 Make a treaty with us, and we will serve you. 11
12:22 it has pleased the LORD to make you a people 25
13:19 Lest the Hebrews make . . swords or spears"; 25
14:14 the first slaughter, which Jonathan . . made 18
17:25 the king will . . make his father's house free 25
18: 3 Then Jonathan made a covenant with David 11
13 Saul removed him . . and made him a commander 30
22: 7 will he make you all commanders of thousands 30
23:18 the two of them made a covenant before the LORD; 11
25:28 the LORD will certainly make my lord a sure house 25
39 Then David . . wooed Ab'igail, to make her his wife. 13
28: 2 Very well, I will make you my bodyguard for life. 30
30:25 he made it a statute and an ordinance for Israel 30
2Sm 3:12 Make your covenant with me, and . . my hand shall be 11
13 And he said, "Good; I will make a covenant with you; 11
20 David made a feast for Abner and the men 25
21 that they may make a covenant with you 11
5: 3 King David made a covenant with them at Hebron 11
7: 9 and I will make for you a great name 25
11 declares . . that the LORD will make you a house. 25
23 God went to redeem . . making himself a name 30
13: 6 Tamar come and make a couple of cakes in my sight 12
10 And Tamar took the cakes she had made 25
22:12 He made darkness around him his canopy 32
34 He made my feet like hinds' feet, and set me secure 31
23: 5 For he has made with me an everlasting covenant 30
1Kg 2:24 of David my father, and who has made me a house 25
3:15 offerings, and made a feast for all his servants. 25
5: 9 I will make it into rafts to go by sea to the place 30
12 and the two of them made a treaty. 11
6: 4 he made for the house windows with recessed 25
5 and he made side chambers all around. 25
6 outside of the house he made offsets on the wall 21
20 He also made an altar of cedar. 77
23 he made two cherubim of olivewood 25
31 For the entrance . . he made doors of olivewood; 25
33 he made for the entrance to the nave doorposts 25
7: 6 he made the Hall of Pillars; its length was 50 cubits 25
7 he made the Hall of the Throne 25
8 Solomon also made a house like this hall 25
9 All these were made of costly stones *
14 full of wisdom . . for making any work in bronze. 25
16 He also made two capitals of molten bronze 25
17 he made two nets of checker work with wreaths 77
18 he made pomegranates; in two rows round about 25
23 he made the molten sea; it was round, ten cubits 25
26 its brim was made like the brim of a cup 16
27 He also made the ten stands of bronze; 25
31 its opening was round, as a pedestal is made 16
33 The wheels were made like a chariot wheel; 16
37 After this manner he made the ten stands; 25
38 he made ten lavers of bronze; each laver held 25
40 Hiram also made the pots, the shovels 25
45 vessels . . which Hiram made for King Solomon 25
48 So Solomon made all the vessels that were 25
8:20 the LORD has fulfilled his promise which he made; 4
21 covenant . . which he made with our fathers 11
38 whatever supplication is made by any man 5
9:21 Solomon made a forced levy of slaves 24
22 of the people of Israel Solomon made no slaves; 21
10: 9 he has made you king, that you may execute justice 30
12 the king made of the almug wood supports 25
16 King Solomon made 200 large shields of beaten gold; 25
17 he made 300 shields of beaten gold; *
18 The king also made a great ivory throne 25
20 The like of it was never made in any kingdom. 25
11:34 I will make him ruler all the days of his life 32
12:28 king took counsel, and made two calves of gold. 25
31 He also made houses on high places 25
32 sacrificing to the calves that he had made. 25
32 he placed in Bethel the priests . . he had made. 25
33 He went up to the altar which he had made in Bethel 25
13:33 Jerobo'am . . made priests for the high places 25
14: 7 exalted you . . and made you leader over my people 21
9 and have gone and made for yourself other gods 25
15 they have made their Ashe'rim, provoking the LORD 25
26 all the shields of gold which Solomon had made; 25

27 Rehobo'am made in their stead shields of bronze 25
15:12 removed all the idols that his fathers had made. 25
13 she had an abominable image made for Ashe'rah; 25
16: 2 I exalted you out of the dust and made you leader 21
3 I will make your house like the house of Jerobo'am 21
33 Ahab made an Ashe'rah. 25
17:13 first make me a little cake of it and bring it to me 25
13 and afterward make for yourself and your son. 25
18:26 they limped about the altar which they had made. 25
32 And he made a trench about the altar 25
19: 2 if I do not make your life as the life of one of them 30
20:34 So he made a covenant with him and let him go. 11
21:22 I will make your house like the house of Jerobo'am 21
22:11 Zedeki'ah . . made for himself horns of iron 25
48 Jehosh'aphat made ships . . to go to Ophir for gold; 25
2Kg 3: 2 the pillar of Ba'al which his father had made. 25
16 'I will make this dry stream-bed full of pools.' 25
4:10 Let us make a small roof chamber with walls 25
6: 2 and let us make a place for us to dwell there. 25
7: 2 If the LORD . . should make windows in heaven 25
19 If the LORD . . should make windows in heaven 25
8:28 He went with Joram . . to make war against Haz'ael *
9: 9 I will make the house of Ahab like . . of Jerobo'am 21
10:27 house of Ba'al, and made it a latrine to this day. 30
11: 4 he made a covenant with them . . and he showed them 11
17 Jehoi'ada made a covenant between the LORD 11
12:13 there were not made . . basins of silver, snuffers 25
13: 7 king . . destroyed them and made them like the dust 30
16:11 in accordance with . . so Uri'ah the priest made it 25
17:15 and his covenant that he made with their fathers 11
16 made for themselves molten images of two calves; 25
16 they made an Ashe'rah, and worshiped all the host 25
29 But every nation still made gods of its own 25
29 the high places which the Samaritans had made 25
30 the men of Babylon made Suc'coth-be'noth 25
30 the men of Cuth made Nergal, the men of Hamath 25
30 Cuth made Nergal, the men of Hamath made Ashi'ma 25
31 and the Av'vites made Nibhaz and Tartak; 25
35 The LORD made a covenant with them 11
38 forget the covenant that I have made with you. 11
18: 4 broke . . the bronze serpent that Moses had made 25
31 Make your peace with me and come out to me; 25
19:15 O LORD . . thou hast made heaven and earth. 25
20:20 how he made the pool and the conduit and brought 25
21: 3 he erected altars for Ba'al, and made an Ashe'rah 25
7 the graven image of Ashe'rah that he had made 25
23: 3 king stood . . and made a covenant before the LORD 11
4 to bring out . . all the vessels made for Ba'al 25
12 altars . . which the kings of Judah had made 25
12 altars which Manas'seh had made in the two courts 25
19 the shrines . . which kings of Israel had made 25
24:13 vessels . . which Solomon king of Israel had made 25
25:16 As for the . . which Solomon had made for the house 25
1Ch 5:10 in the days of Saul they made war on the Hagrites 25
19 made war upon the Hagrites, Jetur, Naphish 25
9:31 was in charge of making the flat cakes. 16
11: 3 David made a covenant with them at Hebron 11
12:18 David . . made them officers of his troops. 21
16:16 the covenant which he made with Abraham 11
26 are idols; but the LORD made the heavens. 25
17: 8 I will make for you a name 25
21 making for thyself a name 30
22 didst make thy people Israel to be thy people 21
18: 8 with it Solomon made the bronze sea 25
21:29 which Moses had made in the wilderness 25
23: 5 the instruments which I have made for praise. 25
26:10 not the first-born, his father made him chief 30
28:18 for the altar of incense made of refined gold *
19 All this he made clear by the writing *
2Ch 1: 3 which Moses the servant of the LORD had made 25
5 that Bez'alel the son of Uri, son of Hur, had made 25
15 king made silver and gold as common . . as stone 21
15 king . . made cedar as plentiful as the sycamore 21
2:11 LORD loves his people he has made you king 21
12 LORD . . who made heaven and earth 25
3: 5 nave he lined . . and made palms and chains on it. 24
8 And he made the most holy place; 25
10 most holy place he made two cherubim of wood 25
14 he made the veil of blue and purple and crimson 25
15 he made two pillars 35 cubits high 25
16 He made chains like a necklace and put them 25
16 made 100 pomegranates, and put them 25
4: 1 He made an altar of bronze, twenty cubits long 25
2 Then he made the molten sea; it was round 25
5 its brim was made like the brim of a cup 16
6 He also made ten lavers in which to wash 25
7 he made ten golden lampstands as prescribed 25
8 made ten tables, and placed them in the temple 25
8 And he made 100 basins of gold. 25
9 made the court of the priests, and the great court 25
11 Huram also made the pots, the shovels 25
14 He made the stands also, and the lavers upon 25
16 for these Huram-abi made of burnished bronze 25
18 made all these things in great quantities 25
19 Solomon made all the things that were 25
5: 8 cherubim made a covering above the ark and its *
10 LORD made a covenant with the people of Israel 11
6:10 the LORD has fulfilled his promise which he made; 4
11 the covenant of the LORD he made with . . Israel. 11

13 Solomon had made a bronze platform . . and set it 25
29 whatever prayer . . is made by any man or by all 5
7: 6 instruments . . David made for giving thanks 25
7 bronze altar Solomon had made could not hold 25
15 to the prayer that is made in this place. •
20 make it a proverb and a byword among all peoples. 21
8: 8 these Solomon made a forced levy and so they are 24
9 of the people of Israel Solomon made no slaves 21
9: 8 he has made you king over them, that you may 21
11 king made of the algum wood steps for the house 25
15 King Solomon made 200 large shields of . . gold; 25
16 he made 300 shields of beaten gold; •
17 The king also made a great ivory throne 25
19 The like of it was never made in any kingdom. 25
27 king made silver as common in Jerusalem as stone 21
11:15 for the calves which he had made. 25
12: 9 the shields of gold which Solomon had made; 25
10 Rehobo'am made in their stead shields of bronze 25
13: 8 golden calves which Jerobo'am made you for gods. 25
9 made priests for yourselves 25
15:16 she had made an abominable image for Ashe'rah. 25
18:10 Zedeki'ah . . made for himself horns of iron 25
20:37 LORD will destroy what you have made. 16
21: 7 the covenant which he had made with David 11
11 he made high places in the hill country of Judah 25
19 His people made no fire in his honor 25
19 like the fires made for his fathers. •
22: 5 went with Jeho'ram . . to make war against Haz'ael •
23: 3 all the assembly made a covenant with the king 11
16 Jehoi'ada made a covenant between himself 11
24: 8 the king commanded, and they made a chest 25
9 proclamation was made throughout Judah 21
14 made utensils for the house of the LORD 25
25:16 Have we made you a royal counselor? 21
26:11 in the muster made by Je-i'el the secretary •
13 307,500, who could make war with mighty power 25
15 In Jerusalem he made engines 25
28: 2 He even made molten images for the Ba'als; 25
24 Ahaz . . made himself altars in . . Jerusalem. 25
25 he made high places to burn incense to other gods 25
29: 8 he has made them an object of horror 21
10 it is in my heart to make a covenant with the LORD 11
24 sin offering should be made for all Israel. •
30: 5 decreed to make a proclamation throughout all 23
7 so that he made them a desolation, as you see. 21
32: 5 He also made weapons and shields in abundance. 25
27 made for himself treasuries for silver, for gold 25
33: 3 erected altars to the Ba'als, and made Ashe'rahs 25
7 image of the idol which he had made he set 25
22 all the images that Manas'seh his father had made 25
34:31 king . . made a covenant before the LORD 11
35:25 They made these an ordinance in Israel; 21
Ezr 4:15 that search may be made in the book of the records •
19 made a decree, and search has been made 30
19 made a decree, and search has been made •
19 rebellion and sedition have been made in it. 33
21 make a decree that these men be made to cease 30
21 city be not rebuilt, until a decree is made by me. 35
5:13 Cyrus . . made a decree that this house of God 35
14 Shesh-baz'zar, whom he had made governor; 35
6: 1 Darius the king made a decree, and search was made 35
1 make a decree, and search was made in Babylonia •
8 I make a decree regarding what you shall do 35
11 I make a decree that if any one alters this edict 35
11 his house shall be made a dunghill. 33
12 I Darius make a decree; let it be done 35
7:13 I make a decree that any one of the people 35
21 make a decree to all the treasurers 35
10: 3 Therefore let us make a covenant with our God 11
7 proclamation was made throughout Judah 23
Neh 8: 4 pulpit which they had made for the purpose; 25
12 send portions and to make great rejoicing 25
15 branches . . to make booths, as it is written. 25
16 people . . made booths for themselves 25
17 assembly . . made booths and dwelt in the booths; 25
9: 6 thou hast made heaven, the heaven of heavens 25
8 thou . . didst make with him the covenant to give 11
18 Even when they had made . . a molten calf and said 25
38 make a firm covenant and write it 11
13:26 God made him king over all Israel; 21
Est 1:20 when the decree made by the king is proclaimed 25
5:14 Let a gallows 50 cubits high be made 25
14 pleased Haman, and he had the gallows made. 25
9:17 they . . made that a day of feasting and gladness. 25
18 and rested . . making that a day of feasting 25
22 should make them days of feasting and gladness 25
Job 7:20 watcher of men? Why hast thou made me thy mark? 30
9: 9 who made the Bear and Orion, the Plei'ades 25
10: 8 Thy hands fashioned and made me; 25
9 Remember that thou hast made me of clay; 25
17: 6 He has made me a byword of the peoples 9
12 They make night into day; 30
25: 2 with God; he makes peace in his high heaven. 25
26:13 By his wind the heavens were made fair; •
27:18 like a booth which a watchman makes. 25
28:26 when he made a decree for the rain 25
31: 1 I have made a covenant with my eyes; 11
15 Did not he who made me in the womb make him? 25
15 Did not he who made me in the womb make him? 25

24 If I have made gold my trust 30
33: 4 The spirit of God has made me 25
38: 9 when I made clouds its garment 30
40:15 Behold, Be'hemoth, which I made as I made you; 25
15 Behold, Be'hemoth, which I made as I made you; •
19 let him who made him bring near his sword! 25
41: 4 Will he make a covenant with you to take him 11
15 His back is made of rows of shields •
31 he makes the sea like a pot of ointment. 30
Ps 2: 8 I will make the nations your heritage 21
7:13 deadly weapons, making his arrows fiery shafts. 27
15 He makes a pit, digging it out, and falls 11
15 falls into the hole which he has made. 27
9:15 The nations have sunk in the pit which they made; 25
18:11 He made darkness his covering around him 32
32 girded me with strength, and made my way safe. 21
33 He made my feet like hinds' feet 31
43 thou didst make me the head of the nations; 30
21: 6 Yea, thou dost make him most blessed for ever; 32
9 make them as a blazing oven when you appear. 32
33: 6 By the word of the LORD the heavens were made 25
39: 5 Behold, thou hast made my days a few handbreadths 21
8 Make me not the scorn of the fool! 30
40: 4 Blessed is the man who makes the LORD his trust 30
44:11 Thou hast made us like sheep for slaughter 21
13 Thou hast made us the taunt of our neighbors 30
14 Thou hast made us a byword among the nations 30
45:16 you will make them princes in all the earth. 32
50: 5 my faithful ones, who made a covenant with me 11
52: 7 See the man who would not make God his refuge 30
69:11 When I made sackcloth my clothing 21
12 the drunkards make songs about me. •
73:28 I have made the Lord GOD my refuge 32
74:17 thou hast made summer and winter. 10
78:50 He made a path for his anger; he did not spare them 26
80: 6 Thou dost make us the scorn of our neighbors; 30
81: 5 He made it a decree in Joseph, when he went out 30
83: 5 against thee they make a covenant- 11
11 Make their nobles like Oreb and Zeeb 32
13 O my God, make them like whirling dust 32
84: 6 valley of Baca they make it a place of springs; 32
85:13 make his footsteps a way. 30
86: 9 nations thou hast made shall come and bow down 25
88: 8 thou hast made me a thing of horror to them. 32
89: 3 I have made a covenant with my chosen one 11
27 I will make him the first-born 21
91: 9 Because you have made the LORD your refuge 30
95: 5 The sea is his, for he made it; 25
96: 5 but the LORD made the heavens. 25
100: 3 LORD . . is he that made us, and we are his; 25
104: 3 who makest the clouds thy chariot 30
4 who makest the winds thy messengers 25
19 Thou hast made the moon to mark the seasons; 25
20 Thou makest darkness, and it is night 32
24 In wisdom hast thou made them all; 25
105: 9 covenant which he made with Abraham 11
21 he made him lord of his house, and ruler of all 30
106:19 made a calf in Horeb and worshiped 25
107:29 he made the storm be still 29
41 makes their families like flocks. 30
109: 4 accuse me, even as I make prayer for them. •
110: 1 till I make your enemies your footstool. 32
113: 9 making her the joyous mother of children. •
115: 8 who make them are like them; so are all who trust 25
15 blessed by the LORD, who made heaven and earth! 25
118:24 This is the day which the LORD has made; 25
119:73 Thy hands have made and fashioned me; 25
121: 2 help . . from the LORD, who made heaven and earth. 25
124: 8 LORD, who made heaven and earth. 25
134: 3 LORD bless . . he who made heaven and earth! 25
135: 7 who makes lightnings for the rain 25
18 Like them be those who make them!- 25
136: 5 to him who by understanding made the heavens 25
7 to him who made the great lights 25
139:15 not hidden . . when I was being made in secret 25
145: 9 his compassion is over all that he has made. 16
146: 6 who made heaven and earth, the sea, and all that 25
147:14 He makes peace in your borders; he fills you 30
Prv 6:34 For jealousy makes a man furious •
8:26 before he had made the earth with its fields 25
13:10 By insolence the heedless make strife 21
14:30 but passion makes the bones rot. •
16: 4 The LORD has made everything for its purpose 27
20:12 ear and the . . eye, the LORD has made them both. 25
25 snare . . to reflect only after making his vows. •
30:26 yet they make their homes in the rocks; 30
31:22 She makes herself coverings; 25
24 She makes linen garments and sells them; 25
Ecc 2: 5 I made myself gardens and parks 25
6 I made myself pools . . to water the forest 25
3:11 He has made everything beautiful in its time; 25
14 God has made it so, in order that men should fear 25
7:14 God has made the one as well as the other 25
29 God made man upright, but they have sought out 25
10:19 Bread is made for laughter, and wine gladdens 25
11: 5 do not know the work of God who makes everything. 25
12:12 Of making many books there is no end 25
Sng 1: 6 they made me keeper of the vineyards; 30
11 We will make you ornaments of gold 25

3: 9 Solomon made himself a palanquin from the wood 25
10 He made its posts of silver, its back of gold 25
Isa 2: 8 hands, to what their own fingers have made. 25
20 of silver and their idols of gold, which they made 25
3: 4 I will make boys their princes 21
7 you shall not make me leader of the people. 30
5: 6 I will make it a waste; it shall not be pruned 32
10:23 For the Lord, the LORD of hosts, will make a full end 25
13: 9 the LORD comes . . to make the earth a desolation 30
14:17 who made the world like a desert 30
23 I will make it a possession of the hedgehog 30
16: 3 make your shade like night at the height of noon; 32
17: 8 will not look to what their own fingers have made 25
22:11 You made a reservoir between the two walls 25
23:13 they razed her palaces, they made her a ruin. 30
25: 2 For thou hast made the city a heap 30
6 will make for all peoples a feast of fat things 25
27: 5 let them make peace with me. 25
5 let them make peace with me. 25
9 when he makes all the stones of the altars 30
11 he who made them will not have compassion on them 25
28:15 you have said, "We have made a covenant with death 11
15 for we have made lies our refuge 30
17 I will make justice the line 30
29:16 should say of its maker, "He did not make me"; 25
30: 1 and who make a league, but not of my spirit 19
31: 7 idols . . your hands have sinfully made for you. 25
36:16 Make your peace with me and come out to me; 25
37:16 thou hast made heaven and earth. 25
40:23 and makes the rulers of the earth as nothing. 25
41: 2 he makes them like dust with his sword 21
15 Behold, I will make of you a threshing sledge 30
15 and you shall make the hills like chaff; 30
18 I will make the wilderness a pool of water 30
43: 7 I created for my glory, whom I formed and made 25
16 Thus says the LORD, who makes a way in the sea 21
19 I will make a way in the wilderness 30
44: 2 Thus says the LORD who made you, who formed you 25
9 All who make idols are nothing 10
15 also he makes a god and worships it 27
15 makes it a graven image and falls down before it. 25
17 the rest of it he makes into a god, his idol; 25
19 and shall I make the residue of it an abomination? 25
24 I am the LORD, who made all things 25
45: 7 I make weal and create woe 25
9 say to him who fashions it, 'What are you making'? 25
12 I made the earth, and created man upon it; 25
18 (he is God!), who formed the earth and made it 25
46: 4 I have made, and I will bear; 25
6 hire a goldsmith, and he makes it into a god; 25
49: 2 He made my mouth like a sharp sword 30
2 he made me a polished arrow 30
11 And I will make all my mountains a way 30
50: 2 I dry up the sea, I make the rivers a desert; 30
3 and make sackcloth their covering. 30
51: 3 and will make her wilderness like Eden 30
10 that didst make the depths of the sea a way 30
12 who dies, of the son of man who is made like grass 21
23 and you have made your back like the ground 30
53: 5 upon him was the chastisement that made us whole •
9 they made his grave with the wicked 21
10 when he makes himself an offering for sin 30
54:12 I will make your pinnacles of agate 30
55: 3 I will make with you an everlasting covenant 11
4 Behold, I made him a witness to the peoples 21
57: 8 you have made a bargain for yourself with them 11
16 the spirit, and I have made the breath of life. 25
59: 2 but your iniquities have made a separation 5
6 will not cover themselves with what they make. 16
60:15 I will make you majestic for ever 30
17 I will make your overseers peace 30
61: 8 I will make an everlasting covenant with them. 11
62: 7 Jerusalem and makes it a praise in the earth. 30
63:12 to make for himself an everlasting name 25
14 to make for thyself a glorious name. 25
66: 2 All these things my hand has made 25
22 earth which I will make shall remain before me 25
Jer 1:18 And I, behold, I make you this day a fortified city 21
2: 7 and made my heritage an abomination. 30
15 They have made his land a waste; 32
28 where are your gods that you made for yourself? 25
3:16 it shall not be made again. 25
4: 7 forth from his place to make your land a waste; 30
27 yet I will not make a full end. 25
5:10 and destroy, but make not a full end; 25
14 behold, I am making my words in your mouth a fire 21
18 says the LORD, I will not make a full end of you. 25
6: 8 lest I make you a desolation, an uninhabited land. 30
26 make mourning as for an only son 25
27 made you an assayer and tester among my people 21
7:18 knead dough, to make cakes for the queen of heaven; 25
8: 8 the false pen of the scribes has made it into a lie. 25
9:11 I will make Jerusalem a heap of ruins 21
11 and I will make the cities of Judah a desolation 21
10:11 gods who did not make the heavens and the earth 22
12 It is he who made the earth by his power 25
13 He makes lightnings for the rain 25
22 to make the cities of Judah a desolation 30
11:10 my covenant which I made with their fathers. 11

12:10 they have made my pleasant portion a desolate 21
11 They have made it a desolation; 30
13:16 turns it into gloom and makes it deep darkness. 32
15: 4 I will make them a horror to all the kingdoms 21
20 I will make you to this people a fortified wall 21
16:20 Can man make for himself gods? Such are no gods! 25
17: 5 man who trusts in man and makes flesh his arm 30
18: 4 And the vessel he was making of clay was spoiled 25
16 making their land a horror, a thing to be hissed 30
19: 8 And I will make this city a horror 30
12 making this city like Topheth. 21
20: 4 Behold, I will make you a terror to yourself 21
22: 6 yet surely I will make you a desert 32
24: 9 I will make them a horror to all the kingdoms 21
25: 9 and make them a horror, a hissing 30
12 making the land an everlasting waste. 30
18 its kings and princes, to make them a desolation 21
26: 6 then I will make this house like Shiloh 21
6 I will make this city a curse for all the nations 21
27: 2 Make yourself thongs and yoke-bars 25
5 and my outstretched arm have made the earth 25
28:13 but I will make in their place bars of iron. 25
29:17 I will make them like vile figs which are so bad 21
18 will make them a horror to all the kingdoms 21
22 The LORD make you like Zedeki'ah and Ahab 30
26 The LORD has made you priest instead of Jehoi'ada 21
30:11 I will make a full end of all the nations 25
11 but of you I will not make a full end. 25
16 all who prey on you I will make a prey. 21
31:21 make yourself guideposts; 30
31 says the LORD, when I will make a new covenant 11
32 the covenant which I made with their fathers 11
33 But this is the covenant which I will make 11
32:17 'Ah Lord GOD! It is thou who hast made the heavens 25
20 and hast made thee a name, as at this day. 25
40 I will make with them an everlasting covenant 11
33: 2 Thus says the LORD who made the earth 25
14 fulfil the promise I made to the house of Israel 4
18 and to make sacrifices for ever. 25
34: 8 after King Zedeki'ah had made a covenant 11
13 I made a covenant with your fathers 11
15 and you made a covenant before me 11
17 I will make you a horror to all the kingdoms 21
18 terms of the covenant which they made before me 11
18 I will make like the calf which they cut in two 21
22 I will make the cities of Judah a desolation 21
37:15 for it had been made a prison. 25
38:16 to Jeremiah, "As the LORD lives, who made our souls 25
26 I made a humble plea to the king 20
41: 9 cistern which King Asa had made for defense 25
18 whom the king of Babylon had made governor 28
44:19 we made cakes for her bearing her image 25
25 will surely perform our vows that we have made 17
46:28 I will make a full end of all the nations 25
28 but of you I will not make a full end. 25
49:15 behold, I will make you small among the nations 21
20 Therefore hear the plan which the LORD has made 8
30 Nebuchadrez'zar king of Babylon has made a plan 8
50: 3 which shall make her a land a desolation 32
45 Therefore hear the plan which the LORD has made 8
51:15 It is he who made the earth by his power 25
16 He makes lightnings for the rain 25
25 and make you a burnt mountain. 21
29 to make the land of Babylon a desolation 30
34 he has made me an empty vessel, he has swallowed 9
52:20 and the stands, which Solomon the king had made 25
Lam 3:11 he led me off my way and . . he has made me desolate; 30
45 Thou hast made us offscouring and refuse 30
Ezk 3: 8 I have made your face hard against their faces 21
9 harder than flint have I made your forehead; 21
17 I have made you a watchman for the house of Israel; 21
4: 9 and put them into a single vessel, and make bread 25
5:14 Moreover I will make you a desolation 21
6:14 and make the land desolate and waste 21
7:20 they made their abominable images 25
20 therefore I will make it an unclean thing to them. 21
23 and make a desolation. 25
11:13 wilt thou make a full end of the remnant of Israel? 25
12: 6 I have made you a sign for the house of Israel. 21
13:18 and make veils for the heads of persons 25
14: 8 I will make him a sign and a byword and cut him off 30
15 and they ravage it, and it be made desolate 5
15: 3 Is wood taken from it to make anything? 25
8 I will make the land desolate 21
16:16 and made for yourself gaily decked shrines 25
17 and made for yourself images of men 25
24 and made yourself a lofty place in every square; 25
31 and making your lofty place in every square. 25
17:13 and made a covenant with him 11
19: 5 another of her whelps and made him a young lion. 30
20:17 or make a full end of them in the wilderness. 25
21:15 glittering sword; ah! it is made like lightning 25
19 And make a signpost, make it at the head of the way 3
19 a signpost, make it at the head of the way to a city; 3
27 A ruin, ruin, ruin I will make it; 30
22: 3 and that makes idols to defile herself! 25
4 and defiled by the idols which you have made; 25
4 I have made you a reproach to the nations 21
13 at the dishonest gain which you have made 25
23:46 and make them an object of terror and a spoil. 21
24: 6 piece after piece, without making any choice. †
17 Sigh, but not aloud; make no mourning for the dead. 25
25: 4 among you and make their dwellings in your midst; 21
5 I will make Rabbah a pasture for camels 21
13 I will make it desolate; from Teman even to Dedan 21
26: 4 scrape her soil from her, and make her a bare rock. 21
14 I will make you a bare rock; 21
15 when slaughter is made in the midst of you? 6
19 When I make you a city laid waste, like the cities 21
27: 5 They made all your planks of fir trees from Senir; 1
5 took a cedar from Lebanon to make a mast for you. 25
6 Of oaks of Bashan they made your oars; 25
6 they made your deck of pines from the coasts 25
29: 3 dragon . . that says, 'My Nile is my own; I made it 25
9 Because you said, 'The Nile is mine, and I made it 25
10 I will make the land of Egypt an utter waste 21
12 I will make the land of Egypt a desolation 21
31: 9 I made it beautiful in the mass of its branches 25
32:15 I make the land of Egypt desolate and when the land 21
25 They have made her a bed among the slain 21
33: 2 from among them, and make him their watchman; 21
7 I have made a watchman for the house of Israel; 21
28 I will make the land a desolation and a waste; 21
29 when I have made the land a desolation and a waste 21
34:25 I will make with them a covenant of peace 11
26 I will make them and the places round about 21
35: 3 I will make you a desolation and a waste. 21
7 I will make Mount Se'ir a waste and a desolation; 21
9 I will make you a perpetual desolation 21
14 of the whole earth I will make you desolate. 25
36:30 I will make the fruit of the tree and the increase •
37:19 with it the stick of Judah, and make them one stick 25
22 I will make them one nation in the land 25
26 I will make a covenant of peace with them; 11
39:10 for they will make their fires of the weapons; 2
14 they will make their search. •
45:25 he shall make the same provision for sin 25
46:16 If the prince makes a gift to any of his sons 21
17 if he makes a gift out of his inheritance 21
23 with hearths made at the bottom of the rows 25
Dan 3: 1 King Nebuchadnez'zar made an image of gold 33
10 You, O king, have made a decree 35
15 fall down and worship the image which I have made 33
29 make a decree: Any people, nation, or language 35
4: 6 I made a decree that all the wise men of Babylon 35
5: 1 King Belshaz'zar made a great feast 33
11 made him chief of the magicians, enchanters 34
6:11 found Daniel making petition and supplication •
26 I make a decree, that in all my royal dominion 35
7:21 horn made war with the saints, and prevailed over 33
9:15 hast made thee a name, as at this day 25
11: 6 shall come to the king of the north to make peace; 25
Hos 2: 3 and make her as in the day she was born 9
3 and make her like a wilderness 30
12 I will make them a forest 30
15 and make the Valley of Achor a door of hope. •
18 And I will make for you a covenant on that day 11
8: 4 With their silver and gold they made idols 25
6 in Israel? A workman made it; it is not God. 25
10: 4 with empty oaths they make covenants; 11
11: 8 How can I make you like Admah! 21
12: 1 they make a bargain with Assyria 11
13: 2 and make for themselves molten images, idols 25
2 idols skilfully made of their silver •
Jol 2:17 and make not thy heritage a reproach, 21
19 and I will no more make you a reproach 21
Ams 4:13 who makes the morning darkness, and treads 25
5: 8 He who made the Plei'ades and Orion 25
26 your images, which you made for yourselves; 25
8:10 I will make it like the mourning for an only son 30
9:14 and they shall make gardens and eat their fruit. 25
Obd 1: 2 Behold, I will make you small among the nations 21
Jon 1: 9 God of heaven, who made the sea and the dry land. 25
16 offered a sacrifice to the LORD and made vows. 17
4: 5 east of the city, and made a booth for himself 25
Mic 1: 6 I will make Sama'ria a heap in the open country 30
8 I will make lamentation like the jackals 25
16 make yourselves as bald as the eagle †
4: 7 and the lame I will make the remnant; 30
13 I will make your horn iron and your hoofs bronze; 30
6:16 that I may make you a desolation 21
Nah 1: 8 he will make a full end of his adversaries 25
9 He will make a full end; 25
14 I will make your grave, for you are vile. 30
3: 6 and make you a gazingstock. 30
Hab 1:14 For thou makest men like the fish of the sea 25
2:18 in his own creation when he makes dumb idols! 25
3:19 he makes my feet like hinds' feet, he makes me tread 30
Zep 1:18 sudden end he will make of all the inhabitants 25
2:13 and he will make Nin'eveh a desolation, a dry waste 30
3:20 yea, I will make you renowned and praised 21
Hag 2: 5 according to the promise that I made you 11
23 says the LORD, and make you like a signet ring; 30
Zec 6:11 Take from them silver and gold, and make a crown 25
7:12 They made their hearts like adamant 30
14 the pleasant land was made desolate. 30
8:16 judgments that are true and make for peace •
9:13 Judah as my bow; I have made E'phraim its arrow. 14
10: 1 from the LORD who makes the storm clouds 25
3 will make them like his proud steed in battle. 30
11:10 covenant which I had made with all the peoples. 11
12: 2 Lo, I am about to make Jerusalem a cup of reeling 30
3 On that day I will make Jerusalem a heavy stone 30
6 I will make the clans of Judah like a blazing pot 30
Mal 2: 9 and so I make you despised and abased before all 21
15 Has not the one God made and sustained for us 25
Mat 3: 3 way of the Lord, make his paths straight. 77
4:19 me, and I will make you fishers of men. 77
5:25 Make friends quickly with your accuser 50
32 unchastity, makes her an adultress; and whoever 77
36 head, for you cannot make one hair white or black. 77
9:16 and a worse tear is made. 42
12:16 ordered them not to make him known. 77
33 Either make the tree good, and its fruit good 77
33 or make the tree bad, and its fruit bad 77
14:22 Then he made the disciples get into the boat 38
17: 4 if you wish, I will make three booths here 77
19: 4 he who made them from the beginning 69
4 made them male and female 77
20:12 you have made them equal to us 77
21:13 but you make it a den of robbers. 77
23:15 to make a single proselyte 77
15 you make him twice as much a child of hell 77
25:16 he made five talents more. 67
17 he who had the two talents made two talents more. 67
20 here I have made five talents more.' 67
22 here I have made two talents more.' 67
Mrk 1: 3 make his paths straight- 77
17 Follow me and I will make you become fishers of men. 77
2:21 the new from the old, and a worse tear is made. 42
23 as they made their way 77
27 sabbath was made for man, not man for the sabbath; 42
3:12 he strictly ordered them not to make him known. 77
6:45 he made his disciples get into the boat 38
7:37 he even makes the deaf hear and the dumb speak. 77
9: 5 let us make three booths 77
10: 6 'God made them male and female.' 77
11:17 you have made it a den of robbers. 77
12:42 put in two copper coins, which make a penny. 50
14:60 Have you no answer to make? •
61 he was silent and made no answer •
15: 4 Pilate again asked . . "Have you no answer to make? •
5 Jesus made no further answer •
Lke 3: 4 make his paths straight. 77
5 the crooked shall be made straight 52
5 the rough ways shall be made smooth; 52
5:29 Levi made him a great feast in his house 77
34 Can you make wedding guests fast 77
8:17 nothing is hid that shall not be made manifest 42
9:33 let us make three booths 77
11:40 Did not he who made the outside make the inside 77
40 he who made the outside make the inside also? 77
12:14 Man, who made me a judge or divider over you? 61
58 make an effort to settle with him on the way 46
16: 9 make friends . . by means of unrighteous mammon 77
19:18 Lord, your pound has made five pounds.' 77
42 that . . you knew the things that make for peace 81
46 you have made it a den of robbers. 77
20:43 till I make thy enemies a stool for thy feet.' 87
Joh 1: 3 all things were made through him 42
3 without him was not anything made that was made. 42
3 without him was not anything made that was made. 42
10 and the world was made through him 42
2:15 And making a whip of cords, he drove them all 77
16 not make my Father's house a house of trade. 77
4: 1 Jesus was making and baptizing more disciples 77
46 Cana in Galilee, where he had made the water wine. 77
5:18 making himself equal with God. 77
6:10 Jesus said, "Make the people sit down. 77
15 and take him by force to make him king 77
7:23 on the sabbath I made a man's whole body well? 77
8:33 How is it that you say, 'You will be made free'? 42
9: 6 made clay of the spittle 77
11 He answered, "The man called Jesus made clay 77
14 Now it was a sabbath day when Jesus made the clay 77
10:33 because you, being a man, make yourself God. 77
12: 2 There they made him a supper; Martha served 77
14:23 we will come to him and make our home with him. 77
15: 3 You are already made clean by the word •
17: 5 glory which I had . . before the world was made. 50
18:18 officers had made a charcoal fire 77
19: 7 because he has made himself the Son of God. 77
12 every one who makes himself a king 77
23 they took his garments and made four parts 77
Act 2:35 till I make thy enemies a stool for thy feet.' 87
36 God has made him both Lord and Christ 77
3:12 as though . . we have made him walk? 77
4:24 Sovereign Lord, who didst make the heaven 77
7:10 who made him governor over Egypt 61
27 Who made you a ruler and a judge over us? 61
35 Who made you a ruler and a judge? 61
40 saying to Aaron, 'Make for us gods to go before us 77
43 the figures which you made to worship 77
44 he who spoke to Moses directed him to make it 77
50 Did not my hand make all these things?' 77
8: 2 made great lamentation over him. 77
9:39 tunics and other garments which Dorcas made 77

10:40 made him manifest; 47
12: 5 prayer for him was made to God by the church. 42
14: 5 an attempt was made by both Gentiles and Jews 42
15 a living God who made the heaven and the earth 77
15:18 who has made these things known from of old.' 77
17:24 The God who made the world and everything in it 77
26 he made from one every nation of men 77
18:12 the Jews made a united attack upon Paul 65
19:24 a silversmith, who made silver shrines of Ar'temis 77
26 saying that gods made with hands are not gods. 42
20: 3 when a plot was made against him by the Jews 42
28 in which the Holy Spirit has made you overseers 87
22: 1 hear the defense which I now make before you. •
23:12 When it was day, the Jews made a plot 77
13 There were more than 40 who made this conspiracy. 77
25:17 I made no delay, but on the next day took my seat 77
26: 6 hope in the promise made by God to our fathers 42
11 and tried to make them blaspheme 38
28 In a short time you think to make me a Christian! 77
27:40 they made for the beach. 66
43 themselves overboard . . and make for the land 54
28:25 they departed, after Paul had made one statement 51
Rom 4:11 to make him the father of all who believe 50
17 I have made you the father of many nations 87
5:19 by one man's disobedience many were made sinners 61
19 by one man's . . many will be made righteous. 61
6:12 to make you obey their passions. 52
9:20 say to its molder, "Why have you made me thus? 77
21 to make out of the same lump one vessel for beauty 77
22 the vessels of wrath made for destruction 62
13:14 and make no provision for the flesh 77
14:19 Let us then pursue what makes for peace •
20 but it is wrong for any one to make others fall †
15:26 pleased to make some contribution for the poor 77
1Co 1:30 whom God made our wisdom, our righteousness 42
6:15 make them members of a prostitute? Never! 77
9:18 I may make the gospel free of charge 87
11: 8 man was not made from woman, 50
12 as woman was made from man •
12:15 that would not make it any less a part of the body. 50
16 that would not make it any less a part of the body. 50
16: 2 so that contributions need not be made when I come. 42
2Co 1: 9 that was to make us rely not on ourselves 50
2: 3 from those who should have made me rejoice •
5:21 For our sake he made him to be sin who knew no sin 77
Gal 3:16 Now the promises were made to Abraham 51
Eph 1:22 has made him the head over all things 46
2:14 For he is our peace, who has made us both one 77
15 one new man in place of the two, so making peace 77
3: 7 Of this gospel I was made a minister 42
4:16 makes bodily growth and upbuilds itself in love. 77
6:18 making supplication for all the saints •
Php 1: 4 making my prayer with joy 77
1Th 2: 3 nor is it made with guile; •
6 though we might have made demands 50
3:12 may the Lord make you increase and abound in love •
2Th 2:11 to make them believe what is false 52
1Ti 2: 1 thanksgivings be made for all men 77
6:13 who . . before Pontius Pilate made the good confession •
Heb 1: 3 When he had made purification for sins 77
7 Of the angels he says, "Who makes his angels winds 77
13 till I make thy enemies a stool for thy feet"? 87
5: 5 did not exalt himself to be made a high priest 42
7:22 makes Jesus the surety of a better covenant. 42
8: 5 See that you make everything 77
9 like the covenant that I made with their fathers 77
9:17 as long as the one who made it is alive. 45
10:13 his enemies should be made a stool for his feet. 87
11: 3 was made out of things which do not appear. 42
12:13 make straight paths for your feet 77
19 a voice whose words made the hearers entreat •
27 as of what has been made 77
Jas 3: 9 we curse men, who are made in the likeness of God. 42
18 sown in peace by those who make peace. 77
4: 4 makes himself an enemy of God. 61
1Pe 3:15 Always be prepared to make a defense to any one 81
2Pe 1: 5 make every effort to supplement your faith 75
2: 6 he condemned them . . and made them an example 87
1Jn 1:10 If we say we have not sinned, we make him a liar 77
5:10 He who does not believe God has made him a liar 77
15 we have obtained the requests made of him. 37
Rev 1: 6 made us a kingdom, priests to his God and Father 77
3: 9 I will make those in the synagogue of Satan 46
9 make them come and bow down before your feet 77
12 I will make him a pillar in the temple of my God; 77
5:10 hast made them a kingdom and priests to our God 77
11: 7 the beast . . will make war upon them and conquer 77
12:17 went off to make war on the rest of her offspring 77
13: 7 Also it was allowed to make war on the saints 77
12 and makes the earth and its inhabitants worship 77
13 even making fire come down from heaven to earth 77
14 bidding them to make an image for the beast 77
14: 7 and worship him who made heaven and earth 77
17:16 they will make her desolate and naked 77
19:11 and in righteousness he judges and makes war. 79
19 kings . . with their armies gathered to make war 77
21: 5 Behold, I make all things new. 77
21 each of the gates made of a single pearl 50
1Es 1:25 went to make war at Carchemish on the Euphrates 49
34 made him king in succession to Josiah his father. 39
37 made Jehoiakim his brother king of Judea 39
46 made Zedekiah king of Judea and Jerusalem. 39
2: 3 the Lord Most High, has made me king of the world 39
3:19 It makes equal the mind of the king and the orphan 77
21 makes every one talk in millions. 77
21 It makes all hearts feel rich 77
4: 4 If he tells them to make war on one another 77
17 Women make men's clothes; they bring men glory 77
43 the vow which you made to build Jerusalem 57
5: 3 he made them go up with them. 77
6:31 libations may be made to the Most High God 82
9: 3 a proclamation was made throughout Judea 42
8 Now then make confession and give glory 46
2Es 1:13 and made safe highways for you 94
23 and made the stream sweet. 95
2: 1 and made my counsels void. 95
3: 5 and he was made alive in thy presence. 95
15 didst make with him an everlasting covenant 93
18 move the world, and make the depths to tremble 95
4:13 and they made a plan 91
14 Come, let us go and make war against the sea 95
14 that we may make for ourselves more forests.' 95
15 the waves of the sea also made a plan and said, 'Come 91
19 I answered and said, "Each has made a foolish plan 91
23 the law of our fathers has been made of no effect 92
5:26 from all the flocks that have been made 97
6: 6 they were made through me 95
38 'Let heaven and earth be made,' 96
44 These were made on the third day. 95
54 as ruler over all the works which thou hadst made; 95
7:11 For I made the world for their sake 95
11 what had been made was judged. 95
12 so the entrances of this world were made narrow 95
50 the Most High has made not one world but two. 95
60 they who have made my glory to prevail now 95
62 if the mind is made out of the dust 95
63 so that the mind might not have been made from it. 96
70 When the Most High made the world 95
82 because they cannot now make a good repentance 95
8: 1 The Most High made this world for the sake of many 95
2 very much clay from which earthenware is made 96
14 to what purpose was he made? 96
23 whose indignation makes the mountains melt 95
60 the name of him who made them 95
9: 2 to visit the world which he has made. 95
13 and for whose sake the age was made. ‡
18 before the world was made for them to dwell 96
10:14 the earth . . has . . given . . to him who made her.' 95
22 and our strong men made powerless. 95
11:39 which I had made to reign in my world 95
46 for the judgment and mercy of him who made it.' 95
13: 3 this wind made something like the figure of a man ‡
14:26 some things you shall make public 95
45 Make public the 24 books that you wrote first 98
15:19 but shall make an assault upon their houses 95
16:42 be like one who will not make a profit 90
55 He said, "Let the earth be made," and it was made 96
55 He said, "Let the earth be made," and it was made 95
55 Let the heaven be made," and it was made. 96
55 Let the heaven be made," and it was made. 95
62 Almighty God; who made all things and searches 95
Tob 3: 4 thou madest us a byword of reproach •
4: 7 begrudge the gift when you make it 77
8 make your gift from them in proportion 77
16 let your eye begrudge the gift when you made it. 77
19 ask him that your ways may be made straight 42
8: 6 Thou madest Adam and gavest him Eve his wife 77
6 let us make a helper for him like himself.' 77
Jdt 1: 2 he made the walls 70 cubits high 77
4 he made its gates, which were 70 cubits high 77
5 Nebuchadnezzar made war against King Arphaxad 77
5:11 and set them to making bricks 80
11 humbled them and made slaves of them. 87
6: 1 the disturbance made by the men outside the council •
7: 1 make war on the Israelites. 77
24 not making peace with the Assyrians. 70
8:14 God, who made all these things 77
9:13 Make my deceitful words to be their wound 46
14: 9 made a joyful noise in their city. 46
16:14 thou didst speak, and they were made 42
AEs 10: 6 Esther, whom the king married and made queen. 77
10 For this purpose he made two lots 77
13: 2 in order to make my kingdom peaceable •
10 For thou hast made heaven and earth 77
16: 5 have been made in part responsible 61
21 God . . has made this day to be a joy to his chosen 77
24 It shall be made not only impassable for men 61
Wis 1: 9 inquiry will be made 50
13 because God did not make death 77
16 they made a covenant with him 87
2:23 made him in the image of his own eternity 77
5: 4 held in derision and made a byword of reproach •
6: 7 because he himself made both small and great 77
22 make knowledge of her clear 87
7:27 makes them friends of God, and prophets; 63
9: 1 who hast made all things by thy word 77
2 have dominion over the creatures thou hast made 42
9 was present when thou didst make the world 77
10:21 and made the tongues of babes speak clearly. 87
11:24 none of the things which thou hast made 77
24 thou wouldst not have made anything 63
12:12 destruction of nations which thou didst make 77
13:11 with pleasing workmanship make a useful vessel 63
15 then he makes for it a niche that befits it 77
14: 8 so is he who made it 77
12 the idea of making idols •
15 a father . . made an image of his child 77
17 made a visible image of the king 77
15: 6 who either make or desire or worship them. 48
7 making all in like manner •
8 this man who was made of earth a short time before 42
13 he makes from earthy matter fragile vessels 44
16 For a man made them 77
17 what he makes with lawless hands is dead 56
16:24 creation, serving thee who hast made it 77
28 to make it known that one must rise before the sun 50
19: 4 made them forget what had happened 53
Sir 1:15 She made among men an eternal foundation 72
4: 7 Make yourself beloved in the congregation 77
6: 4 make him the laughingstock of his enemies. 77
11 In prosperity he will make himself your equal 50
11:27 The misery of an hour makes one forget luxury 77
14:19 the man who made it will pass away with it. 56
16:14 He will make room for every act of mercy 77
26 when he made them, he determined their divisions. 78
17: 3 made them in his own image. 77
6 He made for them tongue and eyes •
18:31 make you the laughingstock of your enemies. 77
20:13 The wise man makes himself beloved 77
23 needlessly make him an enemy. 68
27:14 their quarrels make a man stop his ears. •
28:25 make balances and scales for your words 77
25 make a door and a bolt for your mouth. 77
29: 6 he has needlessly made him his enemy 68
31:27 It has been created to make men glad. 52
32: 1 If they make you master of the feast 61
13 bless him who made you 77
33: 9 some of them he made ordinary days. 87
13 so men are in the hand of him who made them 77
38: 8 the pharmacist makes of them a compound 77
39: 5 to rise early to seek the Lord who made him 77
42: 7 make a record of all that you give out or take in. •
11 lest she make you a laughingstock 77
24 he has made nothing incomplete. 77
43: 5 Great is the Lord who made it 77
6 He made the moon also •
11 Look upon the rainbow, and praise him who made it 77
33 For the Lord has made all things 77
44:18 Everlasting covenants were made with him 87
45: 7 He made an everlasting covenant with him 60
9 to make their ringing heard in the temple 77
46:17 made his voice heard with a mighty sound; 77
50:16 they made a great noise 77
51:17 I made progress therein 42
Bar 1: 8 silver vessels which Zedekiah . . had made 77
2:11 and hast made thee a name, as at this day 77
23 I will make to cease from the cities of Judah 77
26 house . . thou hast made as it is today 87
35 I will make an everlasting covenant with them 60
3:34 They shone with gladness for him who made them. 77
4: 7 For you provoked him who made you 77
LJr 1: 4 you will see gods made of silver and gold and wood •
9 make crowns for the heads of their gods 63
45 They are made by carpenters and goldsmiths 63
46 The men that make them will certainly not live 63
46 how then can . . things . . made by them be gods? 63
50 Since they are made of wood 88
Aza 1:27 made the midst of the furnace like a . . wind 77
Bel 1:13 they had made a hidden entrance 77
27 made cakes, which he fed to the dragon 77
Man 1: 2 thou who hast made heaven and earth 77
1Mc 1:11 Let us go and make a covenant with the Gentiles 45
2:15 king's officers . . came . . to make them offer sacrifice. 59
3:14 he said, "I will make a name for myself 77
4:49 They made new holy vessels 77
5:42 but make them all enter the battle. •
57 So they said, "Let us also make a name for ourselves; 77
6:41 All who heard the noise made by their multitude •
49 He made peace with the men of Beth-zur 77
52 The Jews also made engines of war to match theirs 77
58 make peace with them and with all their nation 77
7: 9 the ungodly Alcimus, whom he made high priest 60
8:30 any addition or deletion that they may make •
9:64 and made machines of war. 77
70 he sent ambassadors to him to make peace with him 85
10: 4 for he said, "Let us act first to make peace with him 87
4 before he makes peace with Alexander against us 87
16 Come now, we will make him our friend and ally. 77
54 will make gifts to you and to her 46
65 and made him general and governor of the province. 87
11: 9 Come, let us make a covenant with each other 85
27 made him to be regarded as one of his . . friends. 77
37 Now therefore take care to make a copy of this 77
51 they threw down their arms and made peace 77
57 and make you one of the friends of the king. •
59 Simon his brother he made governor 61

62 he made peace with them 46
13:37 we are ready to make a general peace with you 77
43 He made a siege engine 77
45 asking Simon to make peace with them; 46
50 Then they cried to Simon to make peace with them 71
53 so he made him commander of all the forces 87
14:35 they made him their leader and high priest 87
39 he made him one of the king's friends 77
15:25 continually . . making engines of war 77
27 the agreements he formerly had made with Simon 85
38 Then the king made Cendebeus commander-in-chief 61
2Mc 1:34 and enclosed the place and made it sacred. 77
3: 4 who had been made captain of the temple 61
9 he told about the disclosure that had been made 42
18 to make a general supplication 55
20 they all made entreaty. 77
33 high priest . . was making the offering of atonement 77
5: 1 Antiochus made his second invasion of Egypt. 83
3 attacks and counterattacks made on this side 42
5 suddenly made an assault upon the city 84
6:23 making a high resolve, worthy of his years 40
7:28 God did not make them out of things that existed. 77
8:15 the covenants made with their fathers •
21 and made them ready to die for their laws •
29 they made common supplication 77
35 and made his way alone like a runaway slave 77
9: 4 I will make Jerusalem a cemetery of Jews. 77
14 to level to the ground and to make a cemetery 73
15 make, all of them, equal to citizens of Athens; 77
10: 3 and made another altar of sacrifice 77
16 after making solemn supplication 77
28 the other made rage their leader in the fight. 86
11: 2 He intended to make the city a home for Greeks 77
12:12 agreed to make peace with them 36
45 Therefore he made atonement for the dead 77
14:26 he took the covenant that had been made 42
15: 9 he made them the more eager. 61
3Mc 1: 9 and made thank-offerings 41
2: 5 you made them an example 61
9 you made it a firm foundation 77
3:21 to make them participants in our regular . . rites. 61
29 to be made unapproachable and burned with fire 42
4:11 well suited to make them an obvious spectacle 36
5:17 make the present portion of the banquet joyful 64
6:40 they made the petition for their dismissal. 77
7:10 immediately hurry to make their departure 43
4Mc 6: 8 to make him get up again after he fell. 74
29 Make my blood their purification 77
10:14 a fire hot enough to make me play the coward. 89
12:13 are made of the same elements as you 42
13: 6 make it calm 76
17:24 this made them brave and courageous 58
18: 7 I guarded the rib from which woman was made. 73
19 'I kill and I make alive 77
151 1: 2 My hands made a harp, my fingers fashioned a lyre. 77

make a beam 1. קרה
Neh 2: 8 give me timber to make beams for the gates 1

make a bed 1. יצע 2. στρωννύω
Ps 139: 8 If I make my bed in Sheol, thou art there! 1
Act 9:34 Jesus Christ heals you; rise and make your bed. 2

make a beginning 1. חלל 2. ἄρχω
Ezr 3: 8 Zerub'babel . . and Jeshua . . made a beginning 1
1Es 5:56 Zerubbabel . . made a beginning 2

make a binding agreement 1. ἵστημι καὶ ἵστημι
Tob 7:11 until you make a binding agreement with me. 1

make a boast 1. גדל 2. דבר 3. הלל
Ps 12: 3 cut off . . the tongue that makes great boasts 2
34: 2 My soul makes its boast in the LORD; 3
97: 7 to shame, who make their boast in worthless idols; 3
Zep 2: 8 and made boasts against their territory. 1

make a breach 1. בקע
2Kg 25: 4 Then a breach was made in the city; 1

make a cake 1. לבב
2Sm 13: 8 And she took dough, and kneaded it, and made cakes 1

make a calf 1. μοσχοποιέω
Act 7:41 they made a calf in those days 1

make a change 1. ἐξαλλοιόω
3Mc 3:21 and we ventured to make a change 1

make a choice 1. ἐκλέγομαι
Act 15: 7 in the early days God made choice among you 1

make a circuit 1. περιέρχομαι
Act 28:13 we made a circuit and arrived at Rhe'gium 1

make a circuitous 1. סבב
2Kg 3: 9 when they had made a circuitous march of seven days 1

make a complaint 1. ἐντυγχάνω
1Mc 11:25 lawless men . . kept making complaints against him 1

make a confession 1. ὁμολογέω
1Ti 6:12 when you made the good confession in the presence 1

make a conspiracy 1. קשר
1Kg 16:20 acts of Zimri, and the conspiracy which he made 1
2Kg 12:20 His servants arose and made a conspiracy 1
14:19 they made a conspiracy against him in Jerusalem 1
15:15 the deeds of . . and the conspiracy which he made 1
30 Then Hoshe'a . . made a conspiracy against Pekah 1
2Ch 25:27 they made a conspiracy against him in Jerusalem 1

make a covenant 1. כרת 2. διατίθημι
Gen 31:44 Come now, let us make a covenant, you and I, 1
1Kg 8: 9 LORD made a covenant with the people of Israel 1
Heb 8:10 This is the covenant that I will make 2
10:16 This is the covenant that I will make with them 2

make a covering 1. סכך
1Kg 8: 7 cherubim made a covering above the ark and its 1

make a cutting 1. שרט
Lev 21: 5 nor make any cuttings in their flesh 1

make a decision 1. βουλεύω
1Mc 2:41 So they made this decision that day 1

make a deduction 1. גרע
Lev 27:18 a deduction shall be made from your valuation 1

make a defense 1. ἀπολογέομαι 2. ἀπολογία 3. ἀπομάχομαι
Act 19:33 wishing to make a defense to the people. 1
24:10 I cheerfully make my defense. 1
25:16 and had opportunity to make his defense 2
26: 1 Paul stretched out his hand and made his defense 1
2 I am to make my defense today 1
24 as he thus made his defense 1
2Mc 12:27 and made a vigorous defense 3
13:26 Lysias . . made the best possible defense 1

make a demand 1. ἀπαιτέω
Sir 31:31 do not afflict him by making demands of him. 1

make a desolation 1. שמם
Ezk 30:14 I will make Pathros a desolation 1

make a destruction 1. שחת
2Ch 12:12 so as not to make a complete destruction; 1

make a difference 1. διαφέρω
Gal 2: 6 what they were makes no difference to me 1

make a direct voyage 1. εὐθυδρομέω
Act 16:11 we made a direct voyage to Sam'o-thrace 1

make a display of wisdom 1. σοφίζω
Sir 10:26 Do not make a display of your wisdom 1

make a distinction 1. בדל 2. פלה 3. διακρίνω
Exd 9: 4 the LORD will make a distinction between 2
11: 7 you may know that the LORD makes a distinction 2
Lev 11:47 to make a distinction between the unclean 1
20:25 You shall therefore make a distinction 1
Act 11:12 to go with them, making no distinction 3
15: 9 he made no distinction between us and them 3
Jas 2: 4 made distinctions among yourselves 3

make a dwelling 1. שכן 2. κατασκηνόω
Deu 33:12 makes his dwelling between his shoulders. 1
Sir 24: 8 he said, 'Make your dwelling in Jacob 2

make a eunuch 1. εὐνουχίζω
Mat 19:12 who have been made eunuchs by men 1
12 who have made themselves eunuchs 1

make a fire 1. אור 2. בער 3. שרף
2Ch 16:14 they made a very great fire in his honor. 3
Isa 27:11 women come and make a fire of them. 1
Ezk 39: 9 they will make fires of them for seven years; 2

make a fool 1. הלל
Job 12:17 judges he makes fools. 1
Isa 44:25 the omens of liars, and makes fools of diviners; 1

make a freewill offering 1. נדב
1Ch 29: 6 the heads . . made their freewill offerings 1
Ezr 2:68 Some of the heads . . made freewill offerings 1
3: 5 every one who made a freewill offering to the LORD. 1

make a full effort 1. ἀτενίζω
1Es 6:28 full effort be made to help the men 1

make a full end 1. כלה
Ezk 20:13 in the wilderness, to make a full end of them. 1

make a gift 1. יהב 2. δίδωμι
Job 6:22 Have I said, 'Make me a gift'? 1
Sir 41:22 do not upbraid after making a gift; 2

make a good showing 1. εὐπροσωπέω
Gal 6:12 those who want to make a good showing in the flesh 1

make a grant 1. ἵστημι
1Mc 13:38 All the grants that we have made to you 1

make a great boast 1. μεγαλαυχέω
Sir 48:18 made great boasts in his arrogance. 1

make a habitation 1. שכן
Deu 12: 5 to put his name and make his habitation there; 1

make a harlot 1. זנה
Lev 19:29 not profane your daughter by making her a harlot 1

make a honeycomb 1. κηρογονία
4Mc 14:19 at the time for making honeycombs 1

make a journey 1. הלך 2. πορεύω
Gen 42:38 befall him on the journey that you are to make 1
Act 22: 6 As I made my journey and drew near to Damascus 2
Tob 9: 5 Raphael made the journey and stayed over night 2

make a joyful noise 1. רוע
Ps 66: 1 Make a joyful noise to God, all the earth; 1
95: 1 make a joyful noise to the rock of our salvation! 1
2 make a joyful noise to him with songs of praise! 1
98: 4 Make a joyful noise to the LORD, all the earth; 1
6 make a joyful noise before the King, the LORD! 1
100: 1 Make a joyful noise to the LORD, all the lands! 1

make a landing 1. ἐκβαίνω
1Mc 15: 4 and intend to make a landing in the country 1

make a league 1. כרת
1Sm 22: 8 when my son makes a league with the son of Jesse 1

make a loan 1. נשה 2. נשה מַשָּׁאָה
Deu 24:10 When you make your neighbor a loan of any sort 2
11 man to whom you make the loan shall bring 1

make a long blast 1. משך
Jos 6: 5 when they make a long blast with the ram's horn 1

make a mark 1. תוה
1Sm 21:13 and made marks on the doors of the gate 1

make a marriage alliance 1. חתן
1Kg 3: 1 Solomon made a marriage alliance with Pharaoh 1
2Ch 18: 1 he made a marriage alliance with Ahab. 1

make a memorial offering 1. זכר
Isa 66: 3 who makes a memorial offering of frankincense 1

make a misstep 1. πλημμελέω
Sir 9:13 if you approach him, make no misstep 1

make a mistake 1. πταίω
Jas 3: 2 For we all make many mistakes 1
2 if any one makes no mistakes in what he says 1

make a nest 1. κατασκηνόω
Mat 13:32 so that the birds of the air come and make nests 1
Mrk 4:32 the birds of the air can make nests in its shade. 1
Lke 13:19 the birds of the air made nests in its branches. 1

make a payment 1. ἀποδίδωμι
Mat 18:25 ordered him to be sold . . and payment to be made. 1

make a petition 1. שאל 2. בעא (A)
1Sm 1:17 God . . grant your petition which you have made 1
27 LORD has granted . . petition which I made to him. 1
Dan 6: 7 whoever makes petition to any god or man 2
11 found Daniel making petition and supplication 2
12 that any man who makes petition to any god or man 2
13 but makes his petition three times a day. 2

make a plan 1. βουλεύω
2Co 1:17 Do I make my plans like a worldly man 1
1Mc 16:13 made treacherous plans against Simon and his sons 1
2Mc 15: 1 he made plans to attack them 1

make a plot 1. חשב
Jer 18:18 Come, let us make plots against Jeremiah 1

make a prayer 1. עתר 2. פלל 3. προσεύχομαι
Job 22:27 You will make your prayer to him, and he will hear 1
Ps 72:15 May prayer be made for him continually 2
Mrk 12:40 for a pretense make long prayers 3
Lke 20:47 and for a pretense make long prayers 3

make a pretense
Jos 8:15 Joshua and all . . made a pretense of being beaten •

make a prey 1. בזז 2. שלל 3. συλαγωγέω
Gen 34:29 in the houses, they captured and made their prey. 1
Isa 59:15 he who departs from evil makes himself a prey. 2

Ezk 26:12 They will make . . a prey of your merchandise; 1
Col 2: 8 makes a prey of you by philosophy and empty deceit 3

make a prince 1. שׂרר
Num16:13 that you must also make yourself a prince over us? 1

make a proclamation 1. עבר קול 2. קרא 3. שׁמע 4. κηρύσσω
1Kg 15:22 King Asa made a proclamation to all Judah 3
2Ch 36:22 made a proclamation throughout all his kingdom 1
Ezr 1: 1 Cyrus . . made a proclamation throughout all 1
Jer 34: 8 to make a proclamation of liberty to them 2
1Es 2: 2 made a proclamation throughout all his kingdom 4
1Mc 5:49 Judas ordered proclamation to be made to the army 4

make a promise 1. ἐπαγγέλλομαι
Gal 3:19 to whom the promise had been made 1
Heb 6:13 For when God made a promise to Abraham 1
Sir 20:23 A man may for shame make promises to a friend 1

make a proposal 1. ἐκτίθημι
2Mc 11:36 that we may make proposals appropriate for you. 1

make a public spectacle 1. traduco
2Es 16:64 will make a public spectacle of all of you. 1

make a raid 1. נשׁט 2. פשׁט 3. ἐξοδεύω
Jdg 15: 9 Philistines came up . . and made a raid on Lehi. 1
1Sm 23:27 the Philistines have made a raid upon the land. 2
27: 8 went up, and made raids upon the Gesh'urites 2
10 Against whom have you made a raid today? 2
30: 1 the Amal'ekites had made a raid upon the Negeb 2
14 We had made a raid upon the Negeb 2
1Ch 14: 9 Now the Philistines had come and made a raid 2
13 Philistines yet again made a raid in the valley. 2
2Ch 28:18 the Philistines had made raids on the cities 2
Job 1:17 three companies, and made a raid upon the camels 2
1Mc 15:41 go out and make raids along the highways of Judea 3

make a reckoning 1. חשׁב
Lev 25:52 he shall make a reckoning with him 1

make a record 1. γράφω 2. καταγράφω
AEs 12: 4 The king made a permanent record of these things 1
1Mc 14:27 they made a record on bronze tablets 2

make a report 1. ἀπαγγέλλω 2. προσφωνέω
1Es 6: 6 until word could be sent . . and a report made. 2
1Mc 5:14 and made a similar report; 1

make a request 1. בקשׁ 2. שׁאל 3. בעא (A)
Jdg 8:24 Gideon said to them, "Let me make a request of you; 2
1Kg 2:16 I have one request to make of you; do not refuse me. 2
20 I have one small request to make of you; do not 2
20 Make your request, my mother; for I will not refuse 2
Neh 2: 4 king said to me, "For what do you make request? 1
Dan 2:49 Daniel made request of the king, and he appointed 3

make a revelation 1. גלה אֹזֶן 2. ἀποκαλύπτω
2Sm 7:27 thou, O LORD . . hast made this revelation 1
1Co 14:30 If a revelation is made to another sitting 2

make a sacrifice 1. זבח
1Ch 21:28 he made his sacrifices there. 1

make a search 1. ἐπισκέπτομαι
1Es 2:21 search may be made in the records of your fathers. 1
26 I ordered search to be made 1
6:21 let search be made in the royal archives 1
23 Darius commanded that search be made 1

make a separation 1. בדל
Ezk 42:20 to make a separation between the holy 1

make a servant 1. עבד
Jer 30: 8 strangers shall no more make servants of them. 1

make a sign 1. διανεύω 2. ἐννεύω
Lke 1:22 he made signs to them and remained dumb. 1
62 And they made signs to his father 2

make a sin offering 1. חטא
2Ch 29:24 priests . . made a sin offering with their blood 1

make a slaughter 1. נכה
1Sm 6:19 the LORD had made a great slaughter 1
23: 5 fought . . and made a great slaughter among them. 1

make a slave 1. עבד 2. δουλόω 3. καταδουλόω
Gen 47:21 as for the people, he made slaves of them 3
Lev 25:46 you may make slaves of them 1
Jer 25:14 great kings shall make slaves even of them; 1
27: 7 and great kings shall make him their slave. 1
1Co 9:19 I have made myself a slave to all 2
2Co 11:20 For you bear it if a man makes slaves of you 3
Wis 19:14 these made slaves of guests 2

make a slip 1. ὀλισθάνω
Sir 19:16 A person may make a slip without intending it. 1
25: 8 has not made a slip with his tongue 1

make a smoke 1. καπνίζω
Tob 6: 7 make a smoke from these before the man or woman 1
16 so as to make a smoke. 1
8: 2 the heart . . of the fish upon them and made a smoke. 1

make a sound 1. הגה 2. קול
Ps 115: 7 they do not make a sound in their throat. 1
Jer 46:22 She makes a sound like a serpent gliding away; 2

make a spoil 1. שׁלל
Ezk 26:12 They will make a spoil of your riches 1

make a stand 1. עמד
Est 9: 2 And no one could make a stand against them 1

make a success 1. εὐοδόω
Tob 11: 1 because he had made his journey a success 1

make a test 1. נסה
Ecc 2: 1 I will make a test of pleasure; enjoy yourself. 1

make a thing 1. ποίημα
Rom 1:20 the things that have been made. 1

make a tonsure 1. קרח
Lev 21: 5 They shall not make tonsures upon their heads 1

make a tour of inspection 1. ἐφοδεύω
2Mc 3: 8 ostensibly to make a tour of inspection 1

make a treaty 1. כרת 2. ἵστημι
1Sm 11: 2 On this condition I will make a treaty with you 1
1Mc 8:29 the Romans make a treaty with the Jewish people. 2

make a tumult 1. θορυβέω
Mat 9:23 flute players, and the crowd making a tumult 1
Mrk 5:39 Why do you make a tumult and weep? 1

make a variety 1. ἀλλοιόω
Sir 38:27 each is diligent in making a great variety 1

make a visit 1. ἔρχομαι
2Co 2: 1 not to make you another painful visit. 1

make a votive offering 1. ἀνατίθημι
2Mc 5:16 the votive offerings which other kings had made 1

make a vow 1. נדר 2. εὔχομαι
Gen 28:20 Jacob made a vow, saying, "If God will be with me 1
31:13 you anointed a pillar and made a vow to me. 1
Jdg 11:30 Jephthah made a vow to the LORD, and said, "If thou 1
Ps 76:11 Make your vows to the LORD your God 1
Isa 19:21 they will make vows to the LORD and perform them. 1
1Es 5:53 all who had made any vow to God 2
Sir 18:23 Before making a vow, prepare yourself 2
LJr 1:35 if one makes a vow to them and does not keep it 2
2Mc 3:35 and made very great vows to the Savior of his life 2
9:13 Then the abominable fellow made a vow to the Lord 2

make a wager 1. ערב
2Kg 18:23 make a wager with my master the king of Assyria 1
Isa 36: 8 make a wager with my master the king of Assyria 1

make a will 1. διατίθημι
Heb 9:16 a will is involved, the death of the one who made it 1

make abominable 1. שׁקץ 2. βδελύσσομαι
Lev 11:43 You shall not make yourselves abominable 1
20:25 not make yourselves abominable by beast 1
1Mc 1:48 They were to make themselves abominable 2

make abundant 1. רבה
Ezk 36:29 I will summon the grain and make it abundant 1
29 I will summon the grain and make it abundant 1
30 I will make . . the increase of the field abundant 1
30 I will make . . the increase of the field abundant 1

make afraid 1. בהל 2. חרד 3. ירא 4. דחל (A) 5. ἐκφοβέω
Lev 26: 6 you shall lie down, and none shall make you afraid 2
2Sm 14:15 I have . . because the people have made me afraid; 3
Ezr 4: 4 people of Judah, and made them afraid to build 1
Neh 6:14 prophets who wanted to make me afraid. 3
19 Tobi'ah sent letters to make me afraid. 3
Job 11:19 You will lie down, and none will make you afraid; 2
Isa 17: 2 for flocks . . and none will make them afraid. 2
Jer 30:10 quiet and ease, and none shall make him afraid. 2
46:27 quiet and ease, and none shall make him afraid. 2
Ezk 34:28 dwell securely, and none shall make them afraid. 2
39:26 in their land with none to make them afraid 2
Dan 4: 5 I had a dream which made me afraid; 4
Mic 4: 4 and none shall make them afraid; 2
Zep 3:13 and none shall make them afraid. 2
1Mc 14:12 there was none to make them afraid. 5

make agile 1. פזז
Gen 49:24 bow remained unmoved, his arms were made agile 1

make alive 1. חיה
Deu 32:39 I kill and I make alive; I wound and I heal; 1
2Kg 5: 7 Am I God, to kill and to make alive 1
Eph 2: 1 And you he made alive •

make alive together 1. συζωοποιέω
Eph 2: 5 made us alive together with Christ 1
Col 2:13 God made alive together with him 1

already make a beginning 1. προενάρχομαι
2Co 8: 6 as he had already made a beginning 1

make amends 1. נוח 2. רצה
Lev 26:41 if . . they make amends for their iniquity 2
43 they shall make amends for their iniquity 2
Ecc 10: 4 deference will make amends for great offenses. 1

make an accusation 1. κατηγορέω
Act 24:19 they ought . . to make an accusation 1

make an alliance 1. חבר 2. προστίθημι 3. συμμαχέω
Dan 11: 6 After some years they shall make an alliance 1
23 from the time that an alliance is made with him 1
1Mc 8: 1 all who made an alliance with them 2
15:19 or make alliance with those who war against them. 3

make an answer 1. מַעֲנֶה
Prv 15:23 To make an apt answer is a joy to a man 1

make an appeal 1. παρακαλέω
2Co 5:20 God making his appeal through us 1

make an appointment 1. יעד
1Sm 21: 2 I have made an appointment with the young men •
Job 2:11 They made an appointment together to come 1

make an argument 1. יכח
Job 19: 5 and make my humiliation an argument against me 1

make an assertion 1. διαβεβαιόομαι
1Ti 1: 7 the things about which they make assertions. 1

make an eloquent response 1. ἀντιρρητορεύω
4Mc 6: 1 When Eleazar . . had made eloquent response 1

make an end 1. כלה 2. כָּלָה 3. כרת 4. נלה
Exd 31:18 made an end of speaking with him upon Mount Sinai 1
Lev 16:20 when he has made an end of atoning 1
Num17:10 may make an end of their murmurings against me 1
Deu 7:22 you may not make an end of them at once, lest 1
20: 9 when the officers have made an end of speaking 1
2Kg 10:25 So as soon as he had made an end of offering 1
13:17 fight . . until you have made an end of them. 1
19 struck down Syria until you had made an end of it 1
2Ch 20:23 they had made an end of the inhabitants of Se'ir 1
Neh 9:31 in thy great mercies thou didst not make an end 2
Ps 119:87 They have almost made an end of me on earth; 1
Isa 33: 1 when you have made an end of dealing 4
Zec 9: 6 I will make an end of the pride of Philistia. 3

make an examination 1. ראה
Lev 13: 8 the priest shall make an examination 1
10 the priest shall make an examination 1
13 then the priest shall make an examination 1
20 the priest shall make an examination 1
39 the priest shall make an examination 1
14: 3 the priest shall make an examination 1
48 if the priest comes and makes an examination 1

make an example 1. δειγματίζω 2. παραδειγματίζω
Col 2:15 made a public example of them 1
AEs 14:11 make an example of the man who began this 2

make an exchange 1. מור
Lev 27:10 if he makes any exchange of beast for beast 1

make an excuse 1. παραιτέω
Lke 14:18 they all alike began to make excuses 1

make an expedition 1. στρατοπεδεύω
2Mc 9:23 on the occasions when he made expeditions 1

make an ingathering 1. אסף
Deu 16:13 seven days, when you make your ingathering 1

make an offering 1. עשׂה 2. קטר 3. קרב 4. רום 5. καρπόω 6. προσφέρω
Exd 35:24 Every one who could make an offering of silver 4
Lev 7:25 animal of which an offering by fire is made 3
Num 7:18 Nethan'el the son of Zu'ar . . made an offering; 3
1Ch 6:49 Aaron and his sons made offerings upon the altar 2
2Ch 25:14 worshiped them, making offerings to them. 2
Ps 66:15 I will make an offering of bulls and goats. Selah 1
Ezk 45:13 This is the offering which you shall make 4

Hos 4:13 and make offerings upon the hills 2
Lke 5:14 and make an offering for your cleansing 6
1Es 1:11 to make the offering to the Lord 6
4:52 the commandment to make seventeen offerings; 6
Sir 7: 9 when I make an offering to the Most High God 6
Aza 1:15 no place to make an offering before thee 5

make an opening 1. ἐξορύσσω
Mrk 2: 4 and when they had made an opening 1

make an oration 1. δημηγορέω
Act 12:21 Herod . . made an oration 1

make angry 1. παροργίζω
Rom 10:19 with a foolish nation I will make you angry. 1

make answer 1. ענה 2. ἀποκρίνομαι 3. ἀποκρίνω
Jdg 5:29 Her wisest ladies make answer, nay, she gives 1
1Sm 26:22 And David made answer, "Here is the spear, O king! 1
29: 9 And A'chish made answer to David, "I know 1
Mat 26:62 Have you no answer to make? 2
27:12 he made no answer. 2
Lke 23: 9 but he made no answer. 2
Sir 33: 4 make your answer. 3

make arrangement 1. τάσσω
1Es 1:15 according to the arrangement made by David 1

make as rebel 1. מרד
Jos 22:19 do not rebel against the LORD, or make us as rebels 1

make ashamed 1. ἐντρέπω
1Co 4:14 I do not write this to make you ashamed 1

make atonement 1. כפר 2. ἐξιλάσκομαι
Exd 29:33 those things with which atonement was made 1
36 when you make atonement for it, and shall anoint 1
37 Seven days you shall make atonement 1
30:10 Aaron shall make atonement upon its horns 1
10 he shall make atonement for it once in the year 1
15 offering to make atonement for yourselves. 1
16 so as to make atonement for yourselves. 1
32:30 perhaps I can make atonement for your sin. 1
Lev 1: 4 it shall be accepted for him to make atonement 1
4:20 the priest shall make atonement for them 1
26 so the priest shall make atonement for him 1
31 the priest shall make atonement for him 1
35 the priest shall make atonement for him 1
5: 6 and the priest shall make atonement for him 1
10 the priest shall make atonement for him 1
13 Thus the priest shall make atonement for him 1
16 the priest shall make atonement for him 1
18 the priest shall make atonement for him 1
6: 7 the priest shall make atonement for him 1
30 blood . . to make atonement in the holy place 1
7: 7 the priest who makes atonement with it 1
8:15 consecrated it, to make atonement for it 1
34 to be done to make atonement for you 1
9: 7 make atonement for yourself and for the people 1
7 the people, and make atonement for them 1
10:17 to make atonement for them before the LORD 1
12: 7 before the LORD, and make atonement for her 1
8 the priest shall make atonement for her 1
14:18 Then the priest shall make atonement for him 1
19 to make atonement for him who is to be cleansed 1
20 Thus the priest shall make atonement for him 1
21 offering to be waved, to make atonement for him 1
29 to make atonement for him before the LORD 1
31 the priest shall make atonement before the LORD 1
53 he shall make atonement for the house 1
15:15 the priest shall make atonement for him 1
30 the priest shall make atonement for her 1
16: 6 and shall make atonement for himself 1
10 alive before the LORD to make atonement over it 1
11 Aaron . . shall make atonement for himself 1
16 thus he shall make atonement for the holy place 1
17 he enters to make atonement in the holy place 1
17 has made atonement for himself and for his house 1
18 go out to the altar . . and make atonement for it 1
24 and make atonement for himself and for the people 1
27 whose blood was brought in to make atonement 1
30 for on this day shall atonement be made for you 1
32 priest . . shall make atonement 1
33 he shall make atonement for the sanctuary 1
33 he shall make atonement for the tent of meeting 1
33 he shall make atonement for the priests 1
34 that atonement may be made for the people 1
17:11 upon the altar to make atonement for your souls 1
11 for it is the blood that makes atonement 1
19:22 the priest shall make atonement for him 1
23:28 to make atonement for you before the LORD your God 1
Num 5: 8 ram . . with which atonement is made for him. 1
6:11 make atonement for him, because he sinned 1
8:12 to make atonement for the Levites. 1
19 to make atonement for the people of Israel 1
21 Aaron made atonement for them to cleanse them. 1
15:25 the priest shall make atonement for all 1
28 the priest shall make atonement before the LORD 1
28 when he sins unwittingly, to make atonement 1
16:46 Take your censer . . and make atonement for them; 1
47 the incense, and made atonement for the people 1
25:13 and made atonement for the people of Israel 1
28:22 for a sin offering, to make atonement for you 1
30 with one male goat, to make atonement for you. 1
29: 5 a sin offering, to make atonement for you; 1
31:50 to make atonement for ourselves before the LORD 1
1Ch 6:49 and to make atonement for Israel 1
2Ch 29:24 made a sin offering . . to make atonement 1
Neh 10:33 sin offerings to make atonement for Israel 1
Sir 45:16 to make atonement for the people. 2
23 made atonement for Israel. 2

make attentive 1. קשב
Prv 2: 2 making your ear attentive to wisdom 1

make away 1. ἐπαναιρέω
2Mc 14: 2 having made away with Antiochus 1

make bald 1. קרח
Ezk 27:31 they make themselves bald for you 1
Mic 1:16 Make yourselves bald and cut off your hair 1

make bare 1. ערר
Isa 32:11 strip, and make yourselves bare 1

make be at peace 1. שלם
Prv 16: 7 makes even his enemies to be at peace with him. 1

make beautiful 1. καλλωπίζω
Jdt 10: 4 and made herself very beautiful 1

make bitter 1. מרה 2. מרר 3. πικραίνω
Exd 1:14 made their lives bitter with hard service 2
Job 27: 2 the Almighty, who has made my soul bitter; 1
Ps 106:33 made his spirit bitter, and he spoke words that 1
Rev 8:11 men died of the water, because it was made bitter. 3
10:10 when I had eaten it my stomach was made bitter. 3

make blameless 1. תמם
Job 22: 3 is it gain to him if you make your ways blameless? 1

make bricks 1. לבן
Exd 5: 7 no longer give the people straw to make bricks 1
14 not done . . your task of making bricks today 1

make bright 1. φωτίζω
Rev 18: 1 and the earth was made bright with his splendor. 1

make broad 1. πλατύνω
Mat 23: 5 they make their phylacteries broad 1

make by hands 1. χειροποίητος
Eph 2:11 which is made in the flesh by hands- 1

make captive 1. αἰχμαλωτίζω
Rom 7:23 making me captive to the law of sin 1

cause to make war 1. πολεμέω
4Mc 4:21 and caused Antiochus himself to make war on them. 1

make cheerful 1. יטב
Prv 15:13 A glad heart makes a cheerful countenance 1

make childless 1. שכל
1Sm 15:33 As your sword has made women childless 1

make clean 1. זכה 2. καθαρίζω
Prv 20: 9 Who can say, "I have made my heart clean; 1
30 strokes make clean the innermost parts. *
Isa 1:16 Wash yourselves; make yourselves clean; 1
Mat 8: 2 saying, "Lord, if you will, you can make me clean. 2
Mrk 1:40 If you will, you can make me clean. 2
42 the leprosy left him, and he was made clean. 2
Lke 5:12 Lord, if you will, you can make me clean. 2
Sir 34: 4 From an unclean thing what will be made clean? 2

make clear 1. נגד 2. שקע 3. δηλόω 4. διασαφέω
5. ἐμφανίζω 6. φανερόω
2Sm 19: 6 For you have made it clear today 1
Ezk 32:14 Then I will make their waters clear 2
Col 4: 4 that I may make it clear, as I ought to speak. 6
Heb 11:14 For people who speak thus make it clear 5
2Mc 2: 9 It was also made clear that . . 4
4:17 a fact which later events will make clear. 3

make common 1. נתן לָרֹב
1Kg 10:27 the king made silver as common . . as stone 1

make competent 1. ἱκανόω
2Co 3: 6 who has made us competent to be ministers 1

make confession 1. ידא 2. ידה 3. נתן תּוֹדָה
4. ἀνθομολογέομαι 5. ἐξαγορεύω
Ezr 10: 1 While Ezra prayed and made confession 1
11 make confession to the LORD the God of your fathers 3
Neh 9: 3 for another fourth of it they made confession 2
Dan 9: 4 I prayed . . and made confession, saying, "O Lord 2
1Es 8:91 Ezra was praying and making his confession 4
Bar 1:14 make your confession in the house of the Lord 5

make confident 1. πείθω
Php 1:14 most of the brethren have been made confident 1

make contemptible 1. קלל
2Sm 6:22 I will make myself yet more contemptible 1

make corrupt 1. שחת
Zep 3: 7 they were eager to make all their deeds corrupt. 1

make credible 1. ἐπιστοποιέω
4Mc 7: 9 you made your words of divine philosophy credible. 1

make crooked 1. עוה 2. עות 3. עקש 4. διαστρέφω
Ecc 7:13 who can make straight what he has made crooked? 2
Isa 59: 8 they have made their roads crooked 3
Lam 3: 9 blocked my ways . . he has made my paths crooked. 1
Act 13:10 stop making crooked the straight paths of the Lord 4

make dark 1. חשך 2. קדר
Ps 105:28 He sent darkness, and made the land dark; 1
Ezk 32: 7 cover the heavens, and make their stars dark; 2
8 bright lights of heaven will I make dark over you 2

make deep 1. עמק
Isa 30:33 its pyre made deep and wide, with fire and wood 1
Hos 5: 2 And they have made deep the pit of Shittim; 1

make desolate 1. בלק 2. צדה 3. שָׁמָּה 4. שמם
5. ἐρημόω
Lev 26:31 I will . . make your sanctuaries desolate 4
Job 16: 7 worn me out; he has made desolate all my company. 4
Isa 24: 1 lay waste the earth and make it desolate 1
Jer 12:11 The whole land is made desolate 4
Ezk 25: 3 over the land of Israel when it was made desolate 4
36: 3 Because, yea, because they made you desolate, 3
Dan 8:13 transgression that makes desolate 4
9:27 upon the wing . . come one who makes desolate 4
11:31 set up the abomination that makes desolate. 4
12:11 time . . the abomination that makes desolate 4
Ams 7: 9 the high places of Isaac shall be made desolate 4
Mic 6:13 making you desolate because of your sins. 4
Zep 3: 6 their cities have been made desolate 2
Sir 16: 4 it will be made desolate. 5
49: 6 made her streets desolate 5

make dim 1. ἐκτήκω
Sir 18:18 the gift of a grudging man makes the eyes dim. 1

make disciples 1. μαθητεύω
Mat 28:19 Go therefore and make disciples of all nations 1
Act 14:21 When they . . had made many disciples 1

make distribution 1. διαδίδωμι
Act 4:35 distribution was made to each as any had need. 1

make drunk 1. שכר
Deu 32:42 I will make my arrows drunk with blood 1
2Sm 11:13 he ate . . and drank, so that he made him drunk; 1
Isa 63: 6 in my anger, I made them drunk in my wrath 1
Jer 48:26 Make him drunk, because he magnified himself 1
51:39 I will prepare them a feast and make them drunk 1
57 I will make drunk her princes and her wise men 1
Hab 2:15 and makes them drunk, to gaze on their shame! 1

make drunken 1. שכר
Jer 51: 7 a golden cup . . making all the earth drunken; 1

make dry 1. יבש
Nah 1: 4 He rebukes the sea and makes it dry 1

make dust 1. דקק
2Ch 34: 4 made dust of them and strewed it over the graves 1

make easy 1. εὐκοπία
2Mc 2:25 to make it easy for those . . inclined to memorize 1

make entreaty 1. עתר
Exd 8:28 Make entreaty for me. 1

make envious 1. παραζηλόω
Sir 30: 3 will make his enemies envious 1

make equal 1. שוה 2. ὁμοιόω
Isa 46: 5 To whom will you liken me and make me equal 1
Sir 45: 2 He made him equal in glory to the holy ones 2

make evident 1. ἐκφαίνω
3Mc 4: 1 enmity . . was now made evident and outspoken. 1

make evil 1. רעע
Mic 3: 4 because they have made their deeds evil. 1

make expiation 1. כפר 2. ἐξιλάσκομαι
3. ἱλάσκομαι
Num35:33 no expiation can be made for the land 1
Deu 32:43 makes expiation for the land of his people. 1
2Sm 21: 3 What shall I do . . ? And how shall I make expiation 1
Heb 2:17 to make expiation for the sins of the people. 3
Sir 28: 5 who will make expiation for his sins? 2

make faint 1. רכך

Job 23:16 God has made my heart faint; 1

make famous 1. יטב

1Kg 1:47 Your God make the name of Solomon more famous 1

make fat 1. שמן

Isa 6:10 Make the heart of this people fat 1

make few in number 1. מעט 2. ὀλιγοποιέω

Lev 26:22 I will . . make you few in number 1
Sir 48: 2 by his zeal he made them few in number. 2

make fillets 1. חשק

Exd 38:28 overlaid their capitals and made fillets 1

make firm 1. אמץ

Job 4: 4 you have made firm the feeble knees. 1
Prv 8:28 when he made firm the skies above 1
Isa 35: 3 weak hands, and make firm the feeble knees. 1

make foolish 1. הלל 2. סכל 3. μωραίνω

Ecc 7: 7 Surely oppression makes the wise man foolish 1
Isa 44:25 wise men back, and makes their knowledge foolish 2
1Co 1:20 Has not God made foolish the wisdom of the world? 3

make free 1. ἐλευθερόω

Joh 8:32 the truth will make you free. 1
36 if the Son makes you free, you will be free indeed. 1

make friendship 1. רעה

Prv 22:24 Make no friendship with a man given to anger 1

make fruitful 1. פרה

Lev 26: 9 I will have regard for you and make you fruitful 1
Ps 105:24 LORD made his people very fruitful 1

make full 1. ἀναπληρόω 2. πληρόω

Act 2:28 thou wilt make me full of gladness 2
Sir 24:26 It makes them full of understanding 1

make full use 1. καταχράομαι

1Co 9:18 not making full use of my right 1

make fully known 1. πληρόω

Col 1:25 to make the word of God fully known 1

make gain 1. בצע

Ezk 22:12 and make gain of your neighbors by extortion; 1

make glad 1. חדה 2. יטב 3. שמח 4. εὐφραίνω

Ps 21: 6 make him glad with the joy of thy presence. 1
45: 8 stringed instruments make you glad; 3
46: 4 a river whose streams make glad the city of God 3
90:15 Make us glad as many days as thou hast afflicted 3
92: 4 For thou, O LORD, hast made me glad by thy work; 3
Prv 10: 1 A wise son makes a glad father 3
12:25 but a good word makes him glad. 3
15:20 A wise son makes a glad father 3
27: 9 Oil and perfume make the heart glad 3
11 Be wise, my son, and make my heart glad 3
29: 3 He who loves wisdom makes his father glad 3
Ecc 7: 3 by sadness of countenance the heart is made glad. 2
Jer 20:15 A son is born to you," making him very glad. 3
Hos 7: 3 By their wickedness they make the king glad 3
2Co 2: 2 For if I cause you pain, who is there to make me glad 4
Tob 8:16 Blessed art thou, because thou hast made me glad. 4
13:14 they will be made glad for ever. 4
Sir 40:14 A generous man will be made glad 4
1Mc 3: 7 he made Jacob glad by his deeds 4

make glorious 1. אדר 2. כבד 3. δοξάζω

Isa 9: 1 he will make glorious the way of the sea 2
42:21 to magnify his law and make it glorious. 1
60:13 and I will make the place of my feet glorious. 2
Sir 36: 6 make thy hand and thy right arm glorious. 3
50:11 he made the court of the sanctuary glorious. 3
1Mc 14:15 He made the sanctuary glorious 3

make good 1. שלם

Exd 21:34 the owner of the pit shall make it good; 1
Lev 24:18 He who kills a beast shall make it good 1
21 He who kills a beast shall make it good 1

make great 1. גדל 2. יטב 3. רבה 4. שגא 5. μεγαλύνω 6. ὑψόω

Rut 3:10 you have made this last kindness greater 2
2Sm 22:36 Thou hast given . . and thy help made me great. 3
1Kg 1:37 and make his throne greater than the throne of my 1
47 and make his throne greater than your throne.' 1
1Ch 29:12 in thy hand it is to make great and to give strength 1
2Ch 1: 1 was with him and made him exceedingly great. 1
Job 12:23 He makes nations great, and he destroys them 4
Ps 18:35 hand supported me, and thy help made me great. 3
Ecc 2: 4 I made great works; I built houses and planted 1
Ams 8: 5 we may make the ephah small and the shekel great 1
Act 13:17 The God of this people . . made the people great 6
Sir 45: 2 made him great in the fears of his enemies. 5

make happy 1. μακαρίζω

Sir 25:23 the wife who does not make her husband happy. 1

make haste 1. אוץ 2. אמץ 3. בהל 4. ברח 5. חוש 6. חפז 7. מהר 8. קדם 9. רוץ 10. κατασπεύδω 11. σπεύδω 12. festino

Gen 19:22 Make haste, escape there; for I can do nothing 7
43:30 Then Joseph made haste, for his heart yearned 7
45: 9 Make haste and go up to my father and say to him 7
13 Make haste and bring my father down here. 7
Exd 34: 8 And Moses made haste to bow his head 7
Jos 8:14 he . . made haste and went out early 7
19 and they made haste to set the city on fire. 7
Jdg 9:48 What you have seen me do, make haste to do 7
20:37 men in ambush made haste and rushed upon Gib'e-ah 5
1Sm 9:12 Make haste; he has come just now to the city 7
20:38 Jonathan called after the lad, "Hurry, make haste 5
23:26 and David was making haste to get away from Saul 6
27 messenger came . . saying, "Make haste and come; 7
25:18 Ab'igail made haste, and took 200 loaves 7
23 Ab'igail . . made haste, and alighted from the ass 7
34 unless you had made haste and come to meet me 7
42 Ab'igail made haste and rose and mounted on an ass 7
2Sm 19:16 Shim'e-i . . made haste to come down with the men 7
1Kg 12:18 King Rehobo'am made haste to mount his chariot 2
20:41 he made haste to take the bandage away 7
2Ch 10:18 King Rehobo'am made haste to mount his chariot 2
35:21 God has commanded me to make haste. 3
Est 6:10 Make haste, take the robes and the horse 7
Ps 38:22 Make haste to help me, O Lord, my salvation! 5
40:13 deliver me! O LORD, make haste to help me! 5
69:17 for I am in distress, make haste to answer me. 7
70: 1 O LORD, make haste to help me! 5
71:12 be not far from me; O my God, make haste to help me! 5
141: 1 I call upon thee, O LORD; make haste to me! 5
143: 7 Make haste to answer me, O LORD! My spirit fails! 7
Prv 1:16 they make haste to shed blood. 7
6:18 feet that make haste to run to evil 7
19: 2 he who makes haste with his feet misses his way. 1
Sng 1: 4 Draw me after you, let us make haste. 9
8:14 Make haste, my beloved, and be like a gazelle 4
Isa 5:19 who say: "Let him make haste, let him speed his work 7
59: 7 and they make haste to shed innocent blood; 7
Jer 9:18 let them make haste and raise a wailing over us 7
Jon 4: 2 That is why I made haste to flee to Tarshish; 8
Lke 19: 5 Zacchae'us, make haste and come down 11
6 he made haste and came down 11
Act 22:18 Make haste and get quickly out of Jerusalem 11
2Es 4:42 For just as a woman who is in travail makes haste 12
5:44 The creation cannot make more haste 12
Sir 50:17 all the people together made haste 10
2Mc 11:37 Therefore make haste and send some men 11

make havoc 1. πορθέω

Act 9:21 Is not this the man who made havoc in Jerusalem 1

make headway 1. ἐλαύνω

Mrk 6:48 he saw that they were making headway painfully 1

make heavy 1. כבד 2. קשה 3. βαρύνω

1Kg 12: 4 Your father made our yoke heavy. 2
10 'Your father made our yoke heavy 1
14 My father made your yoke heavy 1
2Ch 10: 4 Your father made our yoke heavy. 2
10 'Your father made our yoke heavy 1
14 My father made your yoke heavy, but I will add to it; 1
Isa 6:10 Make the heart . . fat, and their ears heavy 1
47: 6 on the aged you made your yoke exceedingly heavy. 1
Sir 33:28 if he does not obey, make his fetters heavy. 3
1Mc 8:31 Why have you made your yoke heavy 3

make high 1. גבה 2. ὑψόω

Prv 17:19 he who makes his door high seeks destruction. 1
Jer 49:16 Though you make your nest as high as the eagle's 1
Ezk 17:24 bring low the high tree, and make high the low tree 1
1Mc 13:27 he made it high that it might be seen 2

make holy 1. קדש 2. ἁγιάζω 3. καθαγιάζω 4. ὁσιόω 5. sanctifico

2Ch 30:17 to make it holy to the LORD. 1
2Es 2:41 that your people . . may be made holy. 5
Wis 6:10 they will be made holy who observe holy things 4
Sir 33:12 some of them he made holy 2
2Mc 1:26 preserve thy portion and make it holy. 3

make ill 1. חלה

2Sm 13: 2 Amnon was so tormented that he made himself ill 1

make inquiry 1. פקד 2. בקר (A) 3. διερωτάω

Ezr 7:14 sent . . to make inquiries about Judah 2
Job 31:14 When he makes inquiry, what shall I answer him? 1
Act 10:17 having made inquiry for Simon's house 3

make intercession 1. פגע 2. ἐντυγχάνω

Isa 53:12 and made intercession for the transgressors. 1
Heb 7:25 since he always lives to make intercession 2

make jealous 1. παραζηλόω

Rom 10:19 make you jealous of those who are not a nation; 1
11:11 so as to make Israel jealous. 1
14 in order to make my fellow Jews jealous, and thus 1

make joyful 1. שמח 2. iucundo

Ezr 6:22 LORD had made them joyful, and had turned 1
Isa 56: 7 and make them joyful in my house of prayer; 1
2Es 12:34 he will make them joyful until the end comes 2

make judgment 1. פלל

Ezk 16:52 you have made judgment favorable 1

make judicious 1. שכל

Prv 16:23 The mind of the wise makes his speech judicious 1

make king 1. מלך 2. ἀναδείκνυμι 3. βασιλεύω

Jdg 9: 6 Beth-millo, and they went and made Abim'elech king 1
16 good faith and honor when you made Abim'elech king 1
18 and have made Abim'elech . . king over . . Shechem 1
1Sm 8:22 Hearken to their voice, and make them a king. 1
11:15 they made Saul king before the LORD in Gilgal. 1
12: 1 I have hearkened . . and have made a king over you. 1
15:11 I repent that I have made Saul king; 1
35 And the LORD repented that he had made Saul king 1
2Sm 2: 9 he made him king over Gilead and the Ash'urites 1
1Kg 1:43 No, for our lord King David has made Solomon king; 1
3: 7 thou hast made thy servant king in place of David 1
11:24 they went . . and made him king in Damascus. 1
12: 1 all Israel had come to Shechem to make him king. 1
20 and made him king over all Israel. 1
16:16 all Israel made Omri . . king over Israel 1
21 half . . followed Tibni . . to make him king 1
2Kg 10: 5 We will not make any one king; do whatever is good 1
14:21 people of Judah took Azari'ah . . and made him king 1
17:21 When . . they made Jerobo'am the son of Nebat king. 1
21:24 the people of the land made Josi'ah his son king 1
23:30 and made him king in his father's stead. 1
34 Pharaoh Neco made Eli'akim the son of Josi'ah king 1
24:17 the king of Babylon made Mattani'ah . . king 1
1Ch 11:10 to make him king, according to the word of the LORD 1
12:31 were expressly named to come and make David king. 1
38 intent to make David king over all Israel 1
38 were of a single mind to make David king. 1
23: 1 David . . made Solomon his son king over Israel. 1
28: 4 took pleasure in me to make me king over all Israel 1
29:22 And they made Solomon . . king the second time 1
2Ch 1: 8 Thou . . hast made me king in his stead. 1
9 for thou hast made me king over a people as many 1
11 may rule my people over whom I have made you king 1
10: 1 all Israel had come to Shechem to make him king. 1
11:22 for he intended to make him king. 1
22: 1 inhabitants of Jerusalem made Ahazi'ah . . king 1
26: 1 Judah took Uzzi'ah . . and made him king 1
33:25 people of the land made Josi'ah his son king 1
36: 1 made him king in his father's stead in Jerusalem. 1
4 the king of Egypt made Eli'akim his brother king 1
10 made . . Zedeki'ah king over Judah and Jerusalem. 1
Jer 37: 1 whom Nebuchadrez'zar king of Babylon made king 1
Ezk 17:16 the place where the king dwells who made him king 1
Hos 8: 4 They made kings, but not through me. 1
1Es 1:43 when he was made king he was eighteen years old 2
1Mc 8:13 Those whom they wish to help and to make kings 3
13 Those whom they wish to help . . they make kings 3

make known 1. ידע 2. יצא 3. נגד 4. נכר 5. שמע 6. ידע (A) 7. ἀναγνωρίζω 8. γινώσκω 9. γνωρίζω 10. δηλόω 11. ἐμφανίζω 12. ἐξηγέομαι 13. ἐπικοινωνέω 14. λέγω 15. προγινώσκω 16. σημαίνω 17. ὑποδείκνυμι

Gen 45: 1 when Joseph made himself known to his brothers. 1
Exd 6: 3 by my name the LORD I did not make myself known 1
Lev 4:23 if the sin which he has committed is made known 1
28 when the sin which he has committed is made known 1
Num12: 6 I the LORD make myself known to him in a vision 1
Deu 4: 9 make them known to your children 1
Rut 3: 3 do not make yourself known to the man until 1
1Sm 9:27 that I may make known to you the word of God. 5
1Ch 16: 8 make known his deeds among the peoples! 1
17:19 in making known all these great things. 1
Ezr 4:16 We make known to the king that, if this city 6
Neh 9:14 thou didst make known to them thy holy sabbath 1
Est 1:17 this deed . . will be made known to all women 2
2:10 Esther had not made known her people or kindred 3
10 Mor'decai had charged her not to make it known. 3
20 Now Esther had not made known her kindred 3
3: 6 they had made known to him the people of Mor'decai 3
Ps 9:16 The LORD has made himself known 1
25:14 he makes known to them his covenant. 1
98: 2 The LORD has made known his victory 1
103: 7 He made known his ways to Moses 1
105: 1 make known his deeds among the peoples! 1
106: 8 that he might make known his mighty power. 1
145:12 to make known to the sons of men thy mighty deeds 1
Prv 1:23 I will make my words known to you. 1
20:11 Even a child makes himself known by his acts 4
22:19 I have made them known to you today, even to you. 1
Isa 12: 4 make known his deeds among the nations 1
19:12 make known what the LORD of hosts has purposed 14
21 the LORD will make himself known 1
38:19 makes known to the children thy faithfulness. 1

48: 3 went forth from my mouth and I made them known; 5
64: 2 to make thy name known to thy adversaries 1
Jer 11:18 The LORD made it known to me and I knew; 1
Ezk 16: 2 make known to Jerusalem her abominations 1
20: 5 making myself known to them in the land of Egypt 1
9 I made myself known to them in bringing them out 1
35:11 I will make myself known among you, when I judge 1
38:23 and make myself known in the eyes of many 1
39: 7 I will make known in the midst of my people Israel; 1
43:11 make known to them all its ordinances 1
Dan 2: 5 if you do not make known to me the dream and its 6
9 if you do not make the dream known to me 6
15 Then Ar'ioch made the matter known to Daniel. 6
17 Daniel . . made the matter known to Hanani'ah 6
23 hast now made known to me what we asked of thee 6
23 for thou hast made known to us the king's matter. 6
25 found . . a man who can make known to the king 6
26 Are you able to make known to me the dream 6
28 made known to King Nebuchadnez'zar what will be 6
29 who reveals mysteries made known to you what is 6
30 in order that the interpretation may be made known 6
45 great God has made known to the king what shall be 6
4: 6 make known to me the interpretation 6
7 could not make known to me its interpretation. 6
18 not able to make known to me the interpretation 6
5: 8 make known to the king the interpretation. 6
15 writing and make known to me its interpretation; 6
16 writing and make known to me its interpretation 6
17 king and make known to him the interpretation. 6
7:16 told me, and made known to me the interpretation 6
8:19 make known to you what shall be at the latter end 1
Hab 3: 2 in the midst of the years make it known; 1
Lke 2:15 this thing . . which the Lord has made known to us. 9
17 they made known the saying which had been told 9
Joh 1:18 he has made him known. 12
15:15 all that I have heard . . I have made known to you. 9
17:26 I made known to them thy name 9
26 and I will make it known 9
Act 2:28 Thou hast made known to me the ways of life 9
7:13 Joseph made himself known to his brothers 7
Rom 9:22 What if God, desiring . . to make known his power 9
23 in order to make known the riches of his glory 9
16:26 is made known to all nations 9
Eph 1: 9 he has made known to us in all wisdom and insight 9
3: 3 the mystery was made known to me by revelation 9
5 not made known to the sons of men 9
10 might now be made known to the principalities 9
Php 4: 6 let your requests be made known to God. 9
Col 1: 8 has made known to us your love in the Spirit. 10
27 To them God chose to make known 9
2Pe 1:16 made known to you the power and coming of our Lord 9
Rev 1: 1 he made it known by sending his angel 16
1Es 2:24 Therefore we now make known to you, O lord 17
Tob 13: 4 Make his greatness known there 17
AEs 14:12 Remember, O Lord; make thyself known in this time 8
Wis 6:13 She hastens to make herself known 15
18:18 one here . . made known why they were dying; 11
Sir 26: 6 a tongue-lashing makes it known to all. 13
3Mc 2: 6 You made known your mighty power 9
3:21 we made known to all our amnesty 9

make known beforehand 1. προγινώσκω
Wis 18: 6 That night was made known beforehand 1

make lamentation 1. בכה 2. ספד 3. θρηνέω 4. κόπτω
2Sm 11:26 she made lamentation for her husband. 2
Job 27:15 buries, and their widows make no lamentation. 1
Ps 78:64 their widows made no lamentation. 1
1Es 1:32 have made lamentation for him to this day 3
1Mc 9:20 all Israel made great lamentation for him 4

make less 1. חסר
Ps 8: 5 Yet thou hast made him little less than God 1

make level 1. ὁμαλισμός
Bar 5: 7 the valleys filled up, to make level ground 1

make light 1. ἀθετέω 2. ἀμελέω
Mat 22: 5 But they made light of it and went off 2
Wis 5: 1 those who make light of his labors. 1

make like 1. דמה 2. שוה (A) 3. ὁμοιόω 4. adsimilo 5. similo
Isa 14:14 ascend . . I will make myself like the Most High.' 1
Dan 5:21 mind was made like that of a beast 2
Rom 9:29 fared like Sodom and been made like Gomor'rah. 3
Heb 2:17 had to be made like his brethren in every respect 3
2Es 7:97 how they are to be made like the light of the stars 4
8:44 called thy own image because he is made like thee 5
44 hast thou also made him like the farmer's seed? 5
15:47 For you have made yourself like her 4
Wis 13:14 or makes it like some worthless animal 3

make like almond 1. שקד
Exd 25:33 three cups made like almonds, each with capital 1
33 and three cups made like almonds 1
34 on the lampstand . . four cups made like almonds 1
37:19 three cups made like almonds, each with capital 1
19 three cups made like almonds, each with capital 1
20 four cups made like almonds, with their capitals 1

make long 1. ארך
Ps 129: 3 plowers . . made long their furrows. 1

make loud music 1. שמע
1Ch 15:28 and made loud music on harps and lyres. 1

make low 1. שפל 2. ἐλαττόω 3. ταπεινόω
Isa 40: 4 and every mountain and hill be made low; 1
Heb 2: 7 Thou didst make him . . lower than the angels 2
9 for a little while was made lower than the angels 2
Bar 5: 7 ordered that . . everlasting hills be made low 3

make manifest 1. δείκνυμι 2. ἐνδείκνυμι 3. φανερόω 4. ostendo
Mrk 4:22 there is nothing hid, except to be made manifest; 3
Joh 9: 3 that the works of God might be made manifest in him. 3
Col 1:26 now made manifest to his saints. 3
1Ti 6:15 this will be made manifest at the proper time 1
1Pe 1:20 He . . was made manifest at the end of the times 3
1Jn 1: 2 the life was made manifest, and we saw it 3
2 eternal life which . . was made manifest to us- 3
4: 9 In this the love of God was made manifest among us 3
2Es 8:54 the treasure of immortality is made manifest. 4
13:36 Zion will come and be made manifest to all people 4
2Mc 9: 8 making the power of God manifest to all. 2

make many 1. עצם 2. רבה 3. πλεονάζω 4. πληθύνω
Jos 24: 3 led him through . . and made his offspring many. 2
1Ch 27:23 to make Israel as many as the stars of heaven. 2
Job 41: 3 Will he make many supplications to you? 2
Isa 1:15 though you make many prayers, I will not listen; 2
51: 2 called him, and I blessed him and made him many. 2
Jer 15: 8 I have made their widows more in number 1
Ezk 22:25 they have made many widows in the midst of her. 2
Sir 35: 1 He who keeps the law makes many offerings 3
Aza 1:13 to make their descendants as many as the stars 4

make marriage 1. חתן
Gen 34: 9 Make marriages with us; give your daughters 1
Deu 7: 3 You shall not make marriages with them 1
Jos 23:12 join the remnant . . and make marriages with them 1

make melody 1. זמר 2. ψάλλω
Jdg 5: 3 I will sing, I will make melody to the LORD 1
Ps 27: 6 I will sing and make melody to the LORD. 1
33: 2 make melody to him with the harp of ten strings! 1
57: 7 my heart is steadfast! I will sing and make melody! 1
108: 1 I will sing and make melody! Awake, my soul! 1
147: 7 make melody to our God upon the lyre! 1
149: 3 making melody to him with timbrel and lyre! 1
Eph 5:19 singing and making melody to the Lord 2

make mention 1. זכר 2. μνημονεύω
Gen 40:14 to make mention of me to Pharaoh, and so get me out 1
Exd 23:13 make no mention of the names of other gods 1
Jos 23: 7 or make mention of the names of their gods 1
Job 28:18 No mention shall be made of coral or of crystal; 1
Heb 11:22 made mention of the exodus of the Israelites 2

make merry 1. יטב 2. שחק 3. εὐφραίνω 4. παίζω
Jdg 19:22 As they were making their hearts merry, behold 1
1Sm 18: 7 the women sang to one another as they made merry 2
2Sm 6: 5 David and all . . Israel were making merry 2
21 and I will make merry before the LORD. 2
1Ch 13: 8 making merry before God with all their might 2
15:29 saw King David dancing and making merry; 2
Jer 30:19 and the voices of those who make merry. 2
Lke 15:23 let us eat and make merry; 3
24 they began to make merry. 3
29 that I might make merry with my friends. 3
32 It was fitting to make merry and be glad 3
Rev 11:10 rejoice over them and make merry and exchange 3
1Es 5: 3 all their brethren were making merry 4

make mirth 1. שוש
Ezk 21:10 Or do we make mirth? You have despised the rod 1

make more 1. προσεργάζομαι
Lke 19:16 'Lord, your pound has made ten pounds more.' 1

make more sure 1. βέβαιος
2Pe 1:19 we have the prophetic word made more sure. 1

make mouths 1. פטר בְּשָׂפָה
Ps 22: 7 All who see me mock at me, they make mouths at me 1

make much 1. גדל 2. ζηλόω
Job 7:17 What is man, that thou dost make so much of him 1
Gal 4:17 They make much of you, but for no good purpose 2
17 to shut you out, that you may make much of them 2

make naked 1. ערה
Lev 20:18 he has made naked her fountain 1
19 for that is to make naked one's near kin 1

make null and void 1. פרר
Num30:12 if her husband makes them null and void on the day 1
15 if he makes them null and void after he has heard 1

make numerous 1. רבה
Deu 30: 5 make you more prosperous and numerous 1

make obedient 1. κάμπτω τὸν τράχηλον
Sir 7:23 make them obedient from their youth. 1

make obeisance 1. שחה 2. προσκυνέω
Gen 43:28 And they bowed their heads and made obeisance. 1
Jdt 10:23 she prostrated herself and made obeisance to him 2

make obstinate 1. אמץ
Deu 2:30 hardened his spirit and made his heart obstinate 1

make odious 1. באש
Gen 34:30 brought trouble on me by making me odious 1
2Sm 16:21 you have made yourself odious to your father 1
1Ch 19: 6 that they had made themselves odious to David 1

make of iron 1. ἀσίδηρος
Wis 17:16 thus was kept shut up in a prison not made of iron; 1

make of wood 1. ξύλινος
LJr 1:39 These things that are made of wood 1
57 Gods made of wood and overlaid with silver 1

make offensive 1. באש רֵיחַ
Exd 5:21 because you have made us offensive in the sight 1

make oil 1. צהר
Job 24:11 among the olive rows of the wicked they make oil; 1

make on high 1. רום
Job 39:27 the eagle mounts up and makes his nest on high? 1

make one's aim 1. διώκω 2. φιλοτιμέομαι
1Co 14: 1 Make love your aim 1
2Co 5: 9 we make it our aim to please him. 2

make one's ambition 1. φιλοτιμέομαι
Rom15:20 thus making it my ambition to preach the gospel 1

make one's home 1. לון
Job 39:28 makes his home in the fastness of the rocky crag. 1

make one's own 1. καταλαμβάνω
Php 3:12 I press on to make it my own 1
12 because Christ Jesus has made me his own. 1
13 I do not consider that I have made it my own 1

make one's way 1. ἐνδύνω
2Ti 3: 6 those who make their way into households 1

make out to be an offender 1. חטא
Isa 29:21 who by a word make a man out to be an offender 1

make over 1. קום
Gen 23:17 field, throughout its whole area, was made over 1
20 were made over to Abraham as a possession 1

make overseer 1. פקד
Gen 39: 4 and he made him overseer of his house and put him 1
5 he made him overseer in his house and over all 1

make overwise 1. חכם יוֹתֵר
Ecc 7:16 and do not make yourself overwise; 1

make peace 1. שלם 2. εἰρηνοποιέω
Deu 20:12 if it makes no peace with you, but makes war 1
Jos 10: 1 and how . . Gibeon had made peace with Israel 1
4 for it has made peace with Joshua and . . Israel. 1
11:19 was not a city that made peace with . . Israel 1
2Sm 10:19 when all the kings . . they made peace with Israel 1
1Kg 22:44 Jehosh'aphat also made peace with . . Israel. 1
1Ch 19:19 made peace with David, and became subject to him. 1
Prv 10:10 but he who boldly reproves makes peace. 2
Col 1:20 making peace by the blood of his cross. 2

make perfect 1. כלל 2. ἐπιτελέω 3. τελειόω 4. τελείωσις 5. τελέω
Ezk 27: 4 your builders made perfect your beauty. 1
11 they made perfect your beauty. 1
2Co 7: 1 make holiness perfect in the fear of God. 2
12: 9 for my power is made perfect in weakness 5
Heb 2:10 make the pioneer of their salvation perfect 3
5: 9 being made perfect he became the source . . 3
7:19 for the law made nothing perfect 3
28 the oath . . appoints a Son who has been made perfect 3
10: 1 it can never . . make perfect those who draw near. 3
11:40 apart from us they should not be made perfect. 3
12:23 to the spirits of just men made perfect 3
Sir 34: 8 wisdom is made perfect in truthful lips. 4

make plain 1. באר 2. פרש 3. φανερόω
Num15:34 not been made plain what should be done to him. 2

Hab 2: 2 Write the vision; make it plain upon tablets 1
2Co 11: 6 made this plain to you in all things. 3

make pleasant 1. ἡδύνω
Sir 40:21 The flute and the harp make pleasant melody 1

make plentiful 1. נתן לָרֹב
1Kg 10:27 he made cedar as plentiful as the sycamore 1

make pliable 1. κάμπτω
Sir 38:30 makes it pliable with his feet 1

make poor 1. ירשׁ
1Sm 2: 7 The LORD makes poor and makes rich; 1

make preparation 1. כון 2. ἑτοιμάζω 3. κατασκευάζω
1Ch 12:39 their brethren had made preparation for them. 1
22: 5 I will therefore make preparation for it. 1
28: 2 and I made preparations for building. 1
Heb 9: 6 These preparations having thus been made 3
Tob 5:16 his son made the preparations for the journey. 2

make prey 1. בזז
Isa 10: 2 that they may make the fatherless their prey! 1

make proclamation 1. זעק 2. קרא 3. כרז (A) 4. διαγγέλλω
Exd 32: 5 and Aaron made proclamation and said, "Tomorrow 2
Lev 23:21 you shall make proclamation on the same day 2
Dan 5:29 proclamation was made concerning him, 3
Jon 3: 7 he made proclamation and published 1
Sir 43: 2 The sun, when it appears, making proclamation 4

make progress 1. ἐπιπροσθέω
Sir 0: 1 those who love learning should make . . progress 1

make prosperous 1. יטב 2. יתר 3. צלח
Deu 30: 5 make you more prosperous and numerous 1
9 LORD . . will make you abundantly prosperous 2
Jos 1: 8 for then you shall make your way prosperous 3

make provision 1. כול 2. כון
1Kg 4: 7 each man had to make provision for one month 1
1Ch 29:19 the palace for which I have made provision. 2

make queen 1. מלך
Est 2:17 set the royal crown on her head and made her queen 1

make rare 1. יקר
Isa 13:12 I will make men more rare than fine gold 1

make ready 1. אסר 2. כון 3. עשׂה 4. διασκευάζω 5. ἐπισκευάζομαι 6. ἑτοιμάζω
Gen 43:16 and slaughter an animal and make ready 2
25 they made ready the present for Joseph's coming 2
46:29 Then Joseph made ready his chariot and went up 1
Exd 14: 6 So he made ready his chariot and took his army 1
Jdg 13:16 if you make ready a burnt offering, then offer it 3
2Kg 9:21 Joram said, "Make ready." And they made ready 1
21 Make ready." And they made ready his chariot. 1
2Ch 29:19 we have made ready and sanctified; 2
Ps 59: 4 for no fault of mine, they run and make ready. 2
Prv 21:31 The horse is made ready for the day of battle 2
Isa 30:33 yea, for the king it is made ready 2
Ezk 7:14 They have blown the trumpet and made all ready; 2
Mat 22: 4 Behold, I have made ready my dinner 6
Lke 1:17 to make ready for the Lord a people prepared. 6
9:52 he sent messengers . . to make ready for him; 6
12:47 but did not make ready or act according to his will 6
22:12 there make ready. 6
Act 21:15 we made ready and went up to Jerusalem. 5
Rev 8: 6 angels who had . . trumpets made ready to blow them. 6
19: 7 and his Bride has made herself ready; 6
Sir 39:31 be made ready on earth for their service 6
1Mc 6:33 his troops made ready for battle 4

make ready provision 1. ציד
Jos 9: 4 they . . went and made ready provisions 1

make rejoicing 1. εὐφραίνω
1Es 9:54 to make great rejoicing; 1

make repairs 1. חזק בֶּדֶק
2Kg 12: 6 the priests had made no repairs on the house. 1
12 to buy timber and . . stone for making repairs 1

make requital 1. שׁלם
Job 34:33 Will he then make requital to suit you 1

make response 1. ענה
Deu 26: 5 make response before the LORD your God 1

make restitution 1. שׁוב 2. שׁלם
Exd 22: 1 He shall make restitution; if he has nothing 2
5 he shall make restitution from the best 2
6 the fire shall make full restitution. 2
11 the oath, and he shall not make restitution. 2
12 he shall make restitution to its owner. 2
13 he shall not make restitution for what has been 2
14 he shall make full restitution. 2
15 he shall not make restitution; if it was hired 2
Lev 5:16 He shall also make restitution 2
Num 5: 7 he shall make full restitution for his wrong 1
8 restitution may be made for the wrong 1

make return 1. שׁוב
2Ch 32:25 Hezeki'ah did not make return 1

make rich 1. דשׁן 2. עשׁר 3. πλουτιέω 4. πλουτίζω
Gen 14:23 lest you should say, 'I have made Abram rich.' 2
1Sm 2: 7 The LORD makes poor and makes rich; 2
Prv 10: 4 but the hand of the diligent makes rich. 2
22 The blessing of the LORD makes rich 2
Isa 34: 7 and their soil made rich with fat. 1
2Co 6:10 as poor, yet making many rich 4
Wis 10:11 she stood by him and made him rich. 4
2Mc 7:24 he would make him rich and enviable 3

make room 1. נגשׁ 2. רחב
Gen 26:22 For now the LORD has made room for us 2
Prv 18:16 A man's gift makes room for him and brings him 2
Isa 49:20 too narrow for me; make room for me to dwell in.' 1

make ruler 1. משׁל 2. שׁלט (A) 3. καθίστημι
Dan 2:48 made him ruler over the whole province 2
11:39 shall make them rulers over many 1
1Mc 6:14 and made him ruler over all his kingdom. 3

make sacred 1. ἁγιάζω
Mat 23:17 or the temple that has made the gold sacred? 1
19 or the altar that makes the gift sacred? 1

make safe
2Sm 22:33 God is my strong refuge, and has made my way safe. •

make search 1. בקשׁ 2. דרשׁ 3. חקר 4. בקר (A)
Deu 13:14 shall inquire and make search and ask diligently 3
Jos 2:22 for the pursuers had made search all along the way 1
Jdg 6:29 after they had made search and inquired 2
1Ch 26:31 In the 40th year of David's reign search was made 2
Ezr 5:17 let search be made in the royal archives there 4

make secure 1. אמץ 2. חבשׁ 3. כון 4. ἀσφαλίζω 5. ὀχυρόω
2Ch 11:17 for three years they made Rehobo'am . . secure 1
Ps 40: 2 set my feet upon a rock, making my steps secure. 3
Ezk 27:24 colored stuff, bound with cords and made secure; 2
Mat 27:64 Therefore order the sepulchre to be made secure 4
65 go, make it as secure as you can. 4
66 So they went and made the sepulchre secure 4
LJr 1:18 so the priests make their temples secure 5

make sharp 1. שׁנן
Ps 140: 3 They make their tongue sharp as a serpent's 1

make shipwreck 1. ναυαγέω
1Ti 1:19 certain persons . . made shipwreck of . . faith 1

make sick 1. חלה
Deu 29:22 sicknesses with which the LORD has made it sick- 1
Prv 13:12 Hope deferred makes the heart sick 1

make slow 1. ארך
Prv 19:11 Good sense makes a man slow to anger 1

make small 1. מעט 2. קטן
Ezk 29:15 I will make them so small that they will never 1
Ams 8: 5 that we may make the ephah small 2

make smooth 1. פלס
Isa 26: 7 thou dost make smooth the path of the righteous. 1

make sorry 1. λυπέω
2Co 7: 8 For even if I made you sorry with my letter 1

make special 1. פלא
Lev 27: 2 When a man makes a special vow of persons 1
Num 6: 2 When either a man or a woman makes a special vow 1

make speechless 1. γλωσσοτομέω
4Mc 10:19 you will not make our reason speechless. 1

make sport 1. מִשְׂחָק 2. עלל 3. ענג 4. צחק 5. שׂחק 6. ἐμπαίζω
Exd 10: 2 tell . . how I have made sport of the Egyptians 2
Num22:29 Because you have made sport of me. 2
Jdg 16:25 Call Samson, that he may make sport for us. 5
25 called Samson . . and he made sport before them. 4
27 and women, who looked on while Samson made sport. 5
1Sm 6: 6 After he had made sport of them, did not they let 2
31: 4 come and thrust me through, and make sport of me. 2
1Ch 10: 4 these uncircumcised come and make sport of me. 2
Job 30: 1 they make sport of me, men who are younger than I 5
Isa 57: 4 Of whom are you making sport? Against whom do you 3
Hab 1:10 At kings they scoff, and of rulers they make sport. 1
1Mc 9:26 he took vengeance on them and made sport of them. 6

make stiff 1. חפץ
Job 40:17 He makes his tail stiff like a cedar; 1

make straight 1. ישׁר 2. תקן 3. ἀνορθόω 4. εὐθύνω
Ps 5: 8 make thy way straight before me. 1
Prv 3: 6 he will make straight your paths. 1
Ecc 1:15 What is crooked cannot be made straight 2
7:13 who can make straight what he has made crooked? 2
Isa 40: 3 make straight in the desert a highway for our God. 1
45:13 and I will make straight all his ways; 1
Lke 13:13 immediately she was made straight 3
Joh 1:23 'Make straight the way of the Lord,' 4
Sir 2: 6 make your ways straight, and hope in him. 4

make strong 1. אמץ 2. גבר 3. חזק 4. חלץ 5. עצם 6. στερεόω
2Sm 3: 6 Abner was making himself strong in the house 3
2Ch 11:11 He made the fortresses strong 3
12 in all the cities, and made them very strong. 3
Ps 80:17 son of man whom thou hast made strong for thyself! 1
105:24 LORD . . made them stronger than their foes. 5
Prv 31:17 She . . makes her arms strong. 1
Isa 28:22 do not scoff, lest your bonds be made strong; 3
58:11 with good things, and make your bones strong; 4
Jer 51:12 make the watch strong; set up watchmen; 3
Dan 9:27 make a strong covenant with many for one week; 2
Zec 10:12 I will make them strong in the LORD 2
Act 3: 7 his feet and ankles were made strong. 6
16 his name . . has made this man strong 6

make supplication 1. חנן 2. פלל 3. δέω
1Kg 8:33 pray and make supplication to thee in this house; 1
47 repent, and make supplication to thee in the land 1
59 I have made supplication before the LORD 1
9: 3 your supplication, which you have made before me; 1
2Ch 6:24 when they . . pray and make supplication to thee 1
37 lay it to heart . . repent, and make supplication 1
Est 4: 8 go to the king to make supplication to him 1
Job 8: 5 seek God and make supplication to the Almighty 1
Ps 30: 8 to the LORD I made supplication 1
142: 1 with my voice I make supplication to the LORD 1
Isa 45:14 They will make supplication to you, saying 2
Sir 39: 5 will make supplication before the Most High 3
5 make supplication for his sins. 3

make sure 1. אמן 2. כון 3. קום
Lev 25:30 the house . . shall be made sure in perpetuity 3
1Sm 23:22 Go, make yet more sure; know and see the place 2
2Sm 7:16 your house and your kingdom shall be made sure 1

make sweet 1. γλυκαίνω
Sir 38: 5 Was not water made sweet with a tree 1
47: 9 to make sweet melody with their voices. 1

make sweet melody 1. יטב נגן
Isa 23:16 Make sweet melody, sing many songs 1

make the ceiling 1. ספן
1Kg 6: 9 he made the ceiling . . of beams and planks 1

make the circuit 1. κυκλόω 2. στρέφω
1Es 4:34 it makes the circuit of the heavens 2
Sir 24: 5 I have made the circuit of the vault of heaven 1

make the most 1. ἐξαγοράζω
Eph 5:16 making the most of the time 1
Col 4: 5 making the most of the time. 1

make tight 1. תקע
Jdg 16:13 weave . . with the web and make it tight •
14 she made them tight with the pin, and said to him 1

make trial 1. נסה 2. δοκιμάζω 3. πειράζω
Jdg 6:39 pray, let me make trial only this once 1
Act 15:10 Now therefore why do you make trial of God 3
Wis 2:19 and make trial of his forbearance. 2

make trouble 1. עכר
Prv 15:27 unjust gain makes trouble for his household 1

make unclean 1. טמא
Lev 22: 5 a creeping thing by which he may be made unclean 1
Num 6: 7 if they die, shall he make himself unclean; 1

make up 1. ἀναπληρόω 2. ἐκπληρόω 3. ἑτοιμάζω 4. προαιρέω
1Co 16:17 because they have made up for your absence; 1
2Co 9: 7 Each one must do as he has made up his mind 4
Tob 7:16 Sister, make up the other room, and take her into it. 3
2Mc 8:10 Nicanor determined to make up . . the tribute 2

make up one's mind 1. κρίνω
2Co 2: 1 I made up my mind not to make you another . . visit 1

make use 1. χράομαι 2. χράω
1Co 9:12 Nevertheless, we have not made use of this right 1
15 I have made no use of any of these rights 1
Wis 2: 6 and make use of the creation to the full as in youth. 2

make void 1. בקק 2. פרר 3. ἀκυρόω 4. καταργέω
Num30: 8 then he shall make void her vow which was on her 2
12 her vows . . her husband has made them void 2
13 Any vow . . her husband may make void. 2
Jer 19: 7 in this place I will make void the plans of Judah 1
Mat 15: 6 you have made void the word of God. 3
Mrk 7:13 thus making void the word of God 3
Gal 3:17 so as to make the promise void. 4

make war 1. לחם 2. עלה לַצָּבָא 3. παράταξις ἰσχυρός 4. πολεμάω 5. bello 6. debello
Deu 20:19 making war against it in order to take it 1
Jos 10: 5 went . . against Gibeon, and made war against it. 1
22:12 Israel gathered . . to make war against them. 2
Jdg 11: 4 a time the Ammonites made war against Israel. 1
5 when the Ammonites made war against Israel 1
27 and you do me wrong by making war on me; 1
2Ch 17:10 they made no war against Jehosh'aphat. 1
26: 6 He went out and made war against the Philistines 1
Jer 21: 2 king of Babylon is making war against us; 1
Rev 17:14 they will make war on the Lamb 4
1Es 4: 6 who do not serve in the army or make war 4
2Es 6:24 At that time friends shall make war on friends 6
13:31 they shall plan to make war against one another 5
Jdt 5:23 a people with no strength or power for making war. 3
6: 2 not to make war against the people of Israel 4
1Mc 3:14 I will make war on Judas and his companions 4
5: 3 Judas made war on the sons of Esau in Idumea 4
57 let us go and make war on the Gentiles around us. 4
8:26 to the enemy who makes war 4
12:40 but might make war on him 4
53 Now therefore let us make war on them 4
14: 1 so that he could make war against Trypho. 4
15:19 should not seek their harm or make war against them 4
39 to make war on the people 4

make war against 1. debello
2Es 13: 5 to make war against the man who came up 1

make way
Lev 26:10 clear out the old to make way for the new •

make well 1. σῴζω
Mat 9:21 touch his garment, I shall be made well. 1
Mrk 5:23 so that she may be made well, and live. 1
28 If I touch even his garments, I shall be made well. 1

make white 1. לבן 2. λευκαίνω
Dan 11:35 refine and to cleanse them and to make them white 1
12:10 Many shall . . make themselves white 1
Jol 1: 7 their branches are made white. 1
Rev 7:14 they have washed their robes and made them white 2

make wholesome 1. רפא
2Kg 2:21 Thus says . . I have made this water wholesome; 1

make wide 1. רחב
Isa 30:33 its pyre made deep and wide, with fire and wood 1
57: 8 bed, you have gone up to it, you have made it wide; 1

make willing 1. נדב
Exd 25: 2 from every man whose heart makes him willing 1

make wise 1. חכם 2. שכל
Gen 3: 6 the tree was to be desired to make one wise 2
Job 35:11 makes us wiser than the birds of the air? 1
Ps 19: 7 the testimony . . is sure, making wise the simple; 1
119:98 Thy commandment makes me wiser than my enemies 1

make with hands 1. ἀχειροποίητος 2. χειροποίητος
Mrk 14:58 will destroy this temple that is made with hands 2
58 I will build another, not made with hands.' 1
Act 7:48 Most High does not dwell in houses made with hands 2
2Co 5: 1 a house not made with hands 1
Heb 9:11 more perfect tent (not made with hands 2
24 not into a sanctuary made with hands 2
Jdt 8:18 which worshiped gods made with hands 2
Wis 14: 8 the idol made with hands is accursed 2

make without hands 1. ἀχειροποίητος
Col 2:11 a circumcision made without hands 1

make worthy 1. ἀξιόω 2. καταξιόω
2Th 1: 5 you may be made worthy of the kingdom of God 2
11 that our God may make you worthy of his call 1

maker 1. חָרָשׁ 2. יצר 3. משל 4. עשה 5. פעל 6. קנה 7. δημιουργός 8. ποιέω 9. facio
Gen 14:19 by God Most High, maker of heaven and earth; 6
22 LORD God Most High, maker of heaven and earth 6
Job 4:17 Can a man be pure before his Maker? 4
32:22 else would my Maker soon put an end to me. 4
35:10 Where is God my Maker, who gives songs in the night 4
36: 3 ascribe righteousness to my Maker. 5
Ps 95: 6 bow down, let us kneel before the LORD, our Maker! 4
149: 2 Let Israel be glad in his Maker 4
Prv 14:31 He who oppresses a poor man insults his Maker 4
17: 5 He who mocks the poor insults his Maker; 4
22: 2 rich and the poor . . LORD is the maker of them all. 4
Isa 17: 7 In that day men will regard their Maker 4
29:16 that the thing made should say of its maker 4
45: 9 Woe to him who strives with his Maker 2
11 the LORD, the Holy One of Israel, and his Maker 2
16 the makers of idols go in confusion together. 1
51:13 and have forgotten the LORD, your Maker 4
54: 5 For your Maker is your husband, the LORD of hosts 4
Ezk 20:49 saying of me, 'Is he not a maker of allegories? 3
Hos 8:14 For Israel has forgotten his Maker 4
Hab 2:18 profit is an idol when its maker has shaped it 2
Heb 11:10 the city . . whose builder and maker is God. 7
2Es 5:33 Or do you love him more than his Maker does? 9
Sir 7:30 With all your might love your Maker 8
10:12 his heart has forsaken his Maker. 8
38:15 He who sins before his Maker 8
39:28 calm the anger of their Maker. 8
47: 8 he loved his Maker. 8

malcontent 1. μεμψίμοιρος
Jde 1:16 These are grumblers, malcontents 1

male 1. אִישׁ 2. זָכוּר 3. זָכָר 4. שתן בְּקִיר 5. ἀρσενικός 6. ἄρσην
Gen 1:27 in the image of God . . male and female he created 3
5: 2 Male and female he created them, and he blessed 3
6:19 they shall be male and female. 3
7: 2 all clean animals, the male and his mate; 1
2 that are not clean, the male and his mate; 1
3 birds of the air also, male and female 3
9 two and two, male and female, went into the ark 3
16 they that entered, male and female of all flesh 3
17:10 Every male among you shall be circumcised. 3
12 every male throughout your generations 3
14 Any uncircumcised male who is not circumcised 3
23 every male among the men of Abraham's house 3
34:15 as we are and every male of you be circumcised. 3
22 that every male among us be circumcised as they 3
24 and every male was circumcised 3
25 the city unawares, and killed all the males. 3
Exd 12: 5 lamb . . without blemish, a male a year old; 3
48 let all his males be circumcised, then he may come 3
13:12 your cattle that are males shall be the LORD'S. 3
15 sacrifice to the LORD all the males that first 3
23:17 shall all your males appear before the LORD God. 2
34:19 the womb is mine, all your male cattle 5
23 all your males appear before the LORD God 2
Lev 1: 3 he shall offer a male without blemish 3
10 he shall offer a male without blemish 3
3: 1 an animal from the herd, male or female 3
6 an animal from the flock, male or female 3
4:23 as his offering a goat, a male without blemish 3
6:18 Every male among the children of Aaron may eat 3
29 Every male among the priests may eat of it 3
7: 6 Every male among the priests may eat of it 3
12: 2 a woman conceives, and bears a male child 3
7 for her who bears a child, either male or female 3
15:33 for any one, male or female, who has a discharge 3
18:22 You shall not lie with a male as with a woman 3
20:13 If a man lies with a male as with a woman 3
22:19 you shall offer a male without blemish 3
27: 3 then your valuation of a male from twenty years 3
5 your valuation shall be for a male twenty shekels 3
6 your valuation shall be for a male five shekels 3
7 then your valuation for a male shall be fifteen 3
Num 1: 2 the number of . . every male, head by head; 3
20 every male from twenty years old and upward 3
22 every male from twenty years old and upward 3
3:15 every male from a month old and upward you shall 3
22 all the males from a month old and upward was 7,500 3
28 According to the number of all the males 3
34 number of all the males from a month old 3
39 all the males from a month old and upward 3
40 Number all the first-born males of the people 3
43 all the first-born males . . were 22,273. 3
5: 3 you shall put out both male and female 3
18:10 every male may eat of it; it is holy to you. 3
26:62 23,000, every male from a month old and upward; 3
31: 7 warred against Mid'ian . . and slew every male. 3
17 therefore, kill every male among the little ones 3
Deu 4:16 form of any figure, the likeness of male or female 3
15:19 firstling males that are born of your herd 3
16:16 all your males shall appear before the LORD 2
20:13 hand you shall put all its males to the sword 2
Jos 5: 4 all the males of the people . . had died on the way 3
17: 2 these were the male descendants of Manas'seh 3
Jdg 21:11 every male and every woman that has lain 3
11 male and every woman that has lain with a male 3
1Sm 25:22 I leave . . one male of all who belong to him. 4
34 had not been left to Nabal so much as one male. 4
1Kg 11:15 Jo'ab the commander . . slew every male in Edom 3
16 until he had cut off every male in Edom); 3
14:10 and will cut off from Jerobo'am every male 4
16:11 he did not leave him a single male of his kinsmen 4
21:21 I . . will cut off from Ahab every male, bond or free 4
2Kg 9: 8 I will cut off from Ahab every male . . in Israel. 4
2Ch 31:16 males from three years old and upwards 3
19 portions to every male among the priests 3
Mal 1:14 Cursed be the cheat who has a male in his flock 3
Mat 19: 4 made them male and female 6
Mrk 10: 6 'God made them male and female.' 6
Lke 2:23 Every male that opens the womb shall be called holy 6
Gal 3:28 there is neither male nor female 6
Rev 12: 5 she brought forth a male child, one who is to rule 6
13 he pursued the woman who had borne the male child. 6
1Mc 5:28 killed every male by the edge of the sword 5
35 he killed every male in it 5
51 He destroyed every male by the edge of the sword 5
4Mc 15:30 O more noble than males in steadfastness 6
male *See also* Levite, barren, child, goat, lamb, member, singer, slave.

malevolent 1. κακοήθης
4Mc 1:25 there exists even a malevolent tendency 1

malice 1. רַע 2. שְׁאָט 3. βασκανία 4. διάθεσις 5. κακία 6. κακοήθεια 7. πονηρία
Ps 41: 5 My enemies say of me in malice: "When will he die 1
73: 8 They scoff and speak with malice; 1
Ezk 25: 6 and rejoiced with all the malice within you 2
15 and took vengeance with malice of heart 2
Mat 22:18 Jesus, aware of their malice, said 7
Rom 1:29 all . . wickedness, evil, covetousness, malice. 5
1Co 5: 8 the old leaven, the leaven of malice and evil 5
Eph 4:31 with all malice 5
Col 3: 8 wrath, malice, slander, and foul talk 5
Tit 3: 3 passing our days in malice and envy 5
1Pe 2: 1 So put away all malice and all guile 5
2Mc 4: 4 was intensifying the malice of Simon. 5
5:23 In his malice toward the Jewish citizens 4
3Mc 2:25 he increased in his deeds of malice 5
3:22 in their innate malice 6
4Mc 1: 4 the emotions . . such as malice 6
26 thirst for honor, rivalry, and malice; 3
2:15 vainglory, boasting, arrogance, and malice. 3
3: 4 No one of us can eradicate malice 6
4 we are not overcome by malice. 6

malicious 1. חָמָס 2. κακοήθης 3. malignus
Exd 23: 1 with a wicked man, to be a malicious witness. 1
Deu 19:16 If a malicious witness rises against any man 1
Ps 35:11 Malicious witnesses rise up; 1
2Es 11:45 and your malicious heads 3
4Mc 2:16 repels all these malicious emotions 2
malicious *See also* intent, joy.

maliciously 1. מְזִמָּה
Ps 139:20 men who maliciously defy thee 1
maliciously *See also* accuse, contrive.

malign
Mat 10:25 how much more will they malign •

malignant 1. מאר
Lev 13:51 the disease is a malignant leprosy; it is unclean 1
52 for it is a malignant leprosy; it shall be burned 1
14:44 it is a malignant leprosy in the house 1

malignity 1. κακοήθεια
Rom 1:29 Full of envy, murder, strife, deceit, malignity 1

mallet 1. הַלְמוּת
Jdg 5:26 She put . . her right hand to the workmen's mallet; 1

mallow 1. מַלּוּחַ 2. μολόχη
Job 24:24 they wither and fade like the mallow; 2
30: 4 They pick mallow and the leaves of bushes 1

maltreat 1. αἰκίζομαι 2. καταικίζω
2Mc 7:13 they maltreated and tortured the fourth 1
15 brought forward the fifth and maltreated him. 1
4Mc 12:13 to maltreat and torture them in this way? 2
13:27 watching their brothers being maltreated 2

mammon 1. μαμωνᾶς
Mat 6:24 the other. You cannot serve God and mammon. 1
Lke 16: 9 make friends . . by means of unrighteous mammon 1
11 not been faithful in the unrighteous mammon 1
13 You cannot serve God and mammon. 1

man 1. אָדָם 2. אֶחָד 3. אִישׁ 4. אֱנוֹשׁ 5. בֶּטֶן 6. בֵּן 7. בֶּן אָדָם 8. בֶּן אִישׁ 9. בַּעַל 10. גִּבּוֹר 11. גֶּבֶר 12. זָכָר 13. מַת 14. נַעַר 15. נֶפֶשׁ 16. נצר 17. עֶבֶד 18. עַם 19. אִישׁ (A) 20. אֱנָשׁ (A) 21. בַּר אֱנָשׁ (A) 22. גְּבַר (A) 23. גִּבָּר (A) 24. ἀδελφός 25. ἀνδρεῖος 26. ἀνήρ 27. ἄνθρωπος 28. ἄρσην 29. αὐτός 30. εἷς 31. ζάω 32. ἴδιος 33. κατὰ ἄνθρωπον 34. κύριος 35. λαός 36. ὁ 37. ὁ μετά 38. ὁ παρά 39. ὁ περί 40. ὁ σύν 41. ὁ ὑπό 42. πᾶς 43. τις 44. τίς 45. υἱός 46. χεῖλος 47. homo 48. humanus 49. natus 50. vir

Gen 1:26 Let us make man in our image, after our likeness 1
27 God created man in his own image 1
2: 5 and there was no man to till the ground; 1
7 the LORD God formed man of dust from the ground 1
7 breath of life; and man became a living being. 1
8 and there he put the man whom he had formed. 1
15 The LORD God took the man and put him 1
16 the LORD God commanded the man, saying 1
18 not good that the man should be alone; 1
19 every bird of the air, and brought them to the man 1
19 whatever the man called every living creature 1
20 The man gave names to all cattle 1
20 but for the man there was not found a helper fit 1
21 God caused a deep sleep to fall upon the man 1
22 rib which the LORD God had taken from the man 1
22 made into a woman and brought her to the man. 1
23 the man said, "This at last is bone of my bones 1
23 Woman, because she was taken out of Man. 3
24 Therefore a man leaves his father and his mother 3
25 the man and his wife were both naked 1
3: 8 and the man and his wife hid themselves 1
9 the LORD God called to the man 1
12 The man said, "The woman whom thou gavest 1
20 The man called his wife's name Eve 1
22 Behold, the man has become like one of us 1
24 He drove out the man; 1
4: 1 I have gotten a man with the help of the LORD. 3
23 I have slain a man for wounding me 3
26 time men began to call upon the name of the LORD. •
5: 1 When God created man, he made him in the likeness 1
2 them and named them Man when they were created. 1
6: 1 When men began to multiply on the face 1
2 that the daughters of men were fair; 1
3 the LORD said, "My spirit shall not abide in man 1
4 the sons of God came in to the daughters of men 1
4 that were of old, the men of renown. 3
5 the wickedness of man was great in the earth 1
6 that he had made man on the earth 1
7 I will blot out man whom I have created 1
7 man and beast and creeping things 1
9 Noah was a righteous man, blameless 3
7:21 that swarm upon the earth, and every man; 1
23 man and animals and creeping things and birds 1
8:21 never again curse the ground because of man 1
21 for the imagination of man's heart is evil 1
9: 5 of every beast I will require it and of man; 1
5 of man; of every man's brother I will require 3
5 brother I will require the life of man. 1
6 Whoever sheds the blood of man 1
6 by man shall his blood be shed; 1
6 for God made man in his own image. 1
11: 2 as men migrated from the east, they found a plain •
5 the tower, which the sons of men had built. 1
12:20 Pharaoh gave men orders concerning him; 3
13:13 Now the men of Sodom were wicked, great sinners 3
14:24 the share of the men who went with me; 3
15: 4 This man shall not be your heir; •
16:12 He shall be a wild ass of a man 1
17:17 Shall a child be born to a man who is 100 years old? 6
23 every male among the men of Abraham's house 3
27 all the men of his house, those born in the house 3
18: 2 behold, three men stood in front of him. 3
16 Then the men set out from there 3
22 the men turned from there, and went toward Sodom; 3
19: 4 before they lay down, the men of the city 3
4 the men of Sodom, both young and old 3
5 Where are the men who came to you tonight? 3
6 the door to the men, shut the door after him •
8 I have two daughters who have not known man; 3
8 only do nothing to these men 3
9 Then they pressed hard against the man Lot 3
10 the men put forth their hands 3
11 they struck with blindness the men 3
12 the men said to Lot, "Have you any one else here? 3
16 he lingered; so the men seized him and his wife 3
31 Our father is old, and there is not a man on earth 3
20: 3 woman whom you have taken; for she is a man's wife. 9
7 Now then restore the man's wife; 3
8 and the men were very much afraid. 3
24:13 the daughters of the men of the city are coming 3
16 fair to look upon, a virgin, whom no man had known. 3
21 The man gazed at her in silence to learn 3
22 the man took a gold ring weighing a half shekel 3
26 The man bowed his head and worshiped the LORD 3
29 and Laban ran out to the man, to the spring. 3
30 words of Rebekah his sister, "Thus the man spoke 3
30 Thus the man spoke to me," he went to the man; 3
32 the man came into the house; and Laban ungirded 3
32 his feet and the feet of the men who were with him. 3
54 he and the men who were with him ate and drank 3
58 Will you go with this man?" She said, "I will go. 3
59 sent away . . Abraham's servant and his men. 3
61 Rebekah . . followed the man; 3
65 said to the servant, "Who is the man yonder 3
25:27 Esau was a skilful hunter, a man of the field 3
27 Jacob was a quiet man, dwelling in tents. 3
26: 7 When the men of the place asked him about his wife 3
7 lest the men of the place should kill me 3
11 Whoever touches this man or his wife shall be put 3
13 the man became rich, and gained more and more 3
27:11 Esau is a hairy man, and I am a smooth man. 3
11 Esau is a hairy man, and I am a smooth man. 3
29:19 you than that I should give her to any other man; 3
22 Laban gathered together all the men of the place 3
30:43 Thus the man grew exceedingly rich 3
31:50 although no man is with us, remember 3
32: 6 he is coming to meet you, and 400 men with him. 3
24 Jacob was left alone; and a man wrestled with him 3
25 When the man saw that he did not prevail •
28 with God and with men, and have prevailed. 3
33: 1 Esau was coming, and 400 men with him. 3
15 leave with you some of the men who are with me. 18
34: 7 the men were indignant and very angry, because he 3
20 spoke to the men of their city, saying 3
21 These men are friendly with us; let them dwell 3
22 Only on this condition will the men agree 3
37:15 a man found him wandering in the fields; 3
15 in the fields; and the man asked him 3
17 the man said, "They have gone away 3
38:21 he asked the men of the place, "Where is the harlot 3
22 and also the men of the place say, 'No harlot has 3
25 By the man to whom these belong, I am with child. 3
39: 2 with Joseph, and he became a successful man; 3
11 none of the men of the house was there in the house 3
14 she called to the men of her household and said 3
41:33 let Pharaoh select a man discreet and wise 3
38 Can we find such a man as this 3
44 and without your consent no man shall lift up 3
42:11 We are all sons of one man, we are honest men 3
13 twelve brothers, the sons of one man in the land 3
25 to replace every man's money in his sack 3
30 The man, the lord of the land, spoke roughly to us 3
33 Then the man, the lord of the land, said to us 3
35 emptied their sacks, behold, every man's bundle 3
43: 3 Judah said to him, "The man solemnly warned us 3
5 we will not go down, for the man said to us 3
6 to tell the man that you had another brother? 3
7 They replied, "The man questioned us carefully 3
11 and carry down to the man a present, a little balm 3
13 also your brother, and arise, go again to the man; 3
14 may God Almighty grant you mercy before the man 3
15 the men took the present, and they took double 3
16 Bring the men into the house, and slaughter 3
16 for the men are to dine with me at noon. 3
17 The man did as Joseph bade him, 3
17 and brought the men to Joseph's house. 3
18 the men were afraid because they were brought 3
21 and there was every man's money in the mouth of his 3
24 when the man had brought the men into Joseph's 3
24 the man had brought the men into Joseph's house 3
33 and the men looked at one another in amazement. 3
44: 1 Fill the men's sacks with food, as much as they can 3
3 the men were sent away with their asses. 3
4 Up, follow after the men; and when you overtake 3
11 Then every man quickly lowered his sack 3
11 to the ground, and every man opened his sack. 3
13 rent their clothes, and every man loaded his ass 3
15 know that such a man as I can indeed divine? 3
17 Only the man in whose hand the cup was found 3
26 for we cannot see the man's face unless our 3
46:32 the men are shepherds, for they have been keepers 3
47: 2 he took five men and presented them to Pharaoh. 3
6 and if you know any able men among them, 3
49: 6 for in their anger they slay men 3
Exd 2: 1 Now a man from the house of Levi went and took 3
13 he said to the man that did the wrong, "Why do you •
20 where is he? Why have you left the man? 3
21 Moses was content to dwell with the man 3
4:11 the LORD said to him, "Who has made man's mouth? 1
19 for all the men who were seeking your life are 3
5: 9 Let heavier work be laid upon the men 3
6:12 to me, who am a man of uncircumcised lips? •
7:12 For every man cast down his rod, and they became 3
8:17 and there came gnats on man and beast; 1
18 So there were gnats on man and beast. 1
9: 9 breaking out in sores on man and beast 1
10 and it became boils breaking out in sores on man 1
19 hail shall come down upon every man and beast 1
22 hail . . upon man and beast and every plant 1
25 struck . . both man and beast; and the hail struck 1
10: 7 How long shall this man be a snare to us? •
7 Let the men go, that they may serve the LORD 3
11 No! Go, the men among you, and serve the LORD 11
11: 2 that they ask, every man of his neighbor and every 3
3 Moreover, the man Moses was very great in the land 3
7 of the people of Israel, either man or beast 3
12: 3 they shall take every man a lamb according 3
4 a man and his neighbor next to his house shall •
12 smite all . . both man and beast; 1
37 about 600,000 men on foot, besides women 11
13: 2 first to open the womb . . both of man and of beast 1
13 Every first-born of man among your sons you shall 1
15 first-born of man and the first-born of cattle. 1
15: 3 The LORD is a man of war; the LORD is his name. 3
16:16 Gather of it, every man of you, as much as he can eat; 3
19 Let no man leave any of it till the morning. 3
29 remain every man of you in his place, let no man go 3
29 let no man go out of his place on the seventh day. 3
17: 9 Moses said to Joshua, "Choose for us men, and go out 3
18:16 I decide between a man and his neighbor 3
21 Moreover choose able men from all the people 3
21 choose . . men who are trustworthy 3
21 and place such men over the people as rulers •
25 Moses chose able men out of all Israel 3
19:13 whether beast or man, he shall not live.' 3
21: 7 When a man sells his daughter as a slave 3
12 Whoever strikes a man so that he dies shall be put 3
14 if a man willfully attacks another to kill him 3
16 Whoever steals a man, whether he sells him or is 3
18 When men quarrel and one strikes the other 3
18 his fist and the man does not die but keeps his bed •
19 then if the man rises again and walks abroad •
20 When a man strikes his slave, male or female 3
22 When men strive together, and hurt a woman 3
26 When a man strikes the eye of his slave 3
28 When an ox gores a man or a woman to death 3
29 if . . it kills a man or a woman 3
31 If it gores a man's son or daughter, he shall be •
33 When a man leaves a pit open, or . . digs a pit 3
33 when a man digs a pit and does not cover it 3
35 When one man's ox hurts another's, so that it dies 3
22: 1 If a man steals an ox or a sheep, and kills it 3
5 When a man causes a field or vineyard to be grazed 3
7 If a man delivers to his neighbor money or goods 3
7 If . . it is stolen out of the man's house 3
10 If a man delivers to his neighbor an ass or an ox 3
14 If a man borrows anything of his neighbor, and it 3
16 If a man seduces a virgin who is not betrothed 3
31 You shall be men consecrated to me; therefore you 3
25: 2 from every man whose heart makes him willing 3
31: 6 I have given to all able men ability •
32: 1 as for this Moses, the man who brought us up out 3
23 as for this Moses, the man who brought us up 3
27 Put every man his sword on his side, and go 3
27 go . . and slay every man his brother 3
27 slay . . every man his companion, and every man 3
27 slay . . every man his neighbor.' 3
28 there fell of the people that day about 3,000 men. 3
33: 4 they mourned; and no man put on his ornaments. 3
8 all the people rose up, and every man stood 3
10 rise up and worship, every man at his tent door. 3
11 Moses face to face, as a man speaks to his friend. 3
20 for man shall not see me and live. 1
34: 3 No man shall come up with you, 3
3 let no man be seen throughout all the mountain; 3
35:22 So they came, both men and women; 3
22 every man dedicating an offering of gold 3
23 every man with whom was found blue or purple 3
29 All the men and women, the people of Israel 3
36: 1 Bez'alel and Oho'liab and every able man in whom 3
2 called . . every able man in whose mind the LORD 3
6 Let neither man nor woman do anything more 3
38:26 from twenty years old and upward, 603,550 men. •
Lev 1: 2 When any man of you brings an offering to the LORD 1
3: 1 If a man's offering is a sacrifice of peace •
5: 4 any sort of rash oath that men swear 1
5 When a man is guilty in any of these, he shall •
6: 3 in any of all the things which men do and sin 1
7:21 an unclean thing, whether the uncleanness of man 1
13: 2 When a man has on the skin of his body a swelling 1
9 When a man is afflicted with leprosy 1
29 When a man or woman has a disease on the head 3
38 When a man or a woman has spots on the skin 3
40 If a man's hair has fallen from his head, he is bald 3
41 if a man's hair has fallen from his forehead •
14:11 priest . . shall set the man who is to be cleansed 3
15: 2 When any man has a discharge from his body 3
16 if a man has an emission of semen, he shall bathe 3
18 If a man lies with a woman and has an emission 3
24 if any man lies with her, and her impurity is on him 3
33 the man who lies with a woman who is unclean 3
16:17 There shall be no man in the tent of meeting 1
21 by the hand of a man who is in readiness 3
17: 3 If any man of the house of Israel kills an ox 3
4 bloodguilt shall be imputed to that man 3
4 he has shed blood; and that man shall be cut off 3
8 Any man of the house of Israel 3
9 that man shall be cut off from his people 3
10 If any man of the house of Israel 3
13 Any man also of the people of Israel 3
18: 5 my ordinances, by doing which a man shall live 1
27 all of these abominations the men of the land did 3
19:20 If a man lies carnally with a woman who is a slave 3
20 betrothed to another man and not yet ransomed 3
20: 2 Any man of the people of Israel, or of the strangers 3
3 I myself will set my face against that man 3
4 do at all hide their eyes from that man 3
5 then I will set my face against that man 3
10 If a man commits adultery with the wife 3
11 The man who lies with his father's wife 3
12 If a man lies with his daughter-in-law, both of them 3
13 If a man lies with a male as with a woman 3
14 If a man takes a wife and her mother also 3
15 If a man lies with a beast, he shall be put to death 3
17 If a man takes his sister, a daughter of his father 3
18 If a man lies with a woman having her sickness 3
20 If a man lies with his uncle's wife 3

21 If a man takes his brother's wife, it is impurity 3
27 A man or a woman who is a medium or a wizard 3
21:18 a man blind or lame, or one who has a mutilated face 3
19 or a man who has an injured foot or an injured hand 3
20 a man with a defect in his sight or an itching •
21 no man of the descendants of Aaron the priest 3
22: 4 a man who has had an emission of semen 3
5 or a man from whom he may take uncleanness 1
14 if a man eats of a holy thing unwittingly 3
24:10 woman's son and a man of Israel quarreled 3
17 He who kills a man shall be put to death 3
19 When a man causes a disfigurement 3
20 as he has disfigured a man, he shall be disfigured 1
21 he who kills a man shall be put to death 1
25:26 If a man has no one to redeem it 3
27 let him . . pay back the overpayment to the man 3
29 If a man sells a dwelling house in a walled city 3
27: 2 When a man makes a special vow of persons 3
8 if a man is too poor to pay your valuation •
9 If it is an animal such as men offer as an offering •
9 all of such that any man gives to the LORD is holy •
11 then the man shall bring the animal •
14 When a man dedicates his house to be holy 3
16 If a man dedicates to the LORD part of the land 3
20 sold the field to another man, it shall not be 3
23 the man shall give the amount of the valuation 3
26 a firstling . . no man may dedicate; whether ox 3
28 no devoted thing that a man devotes to the LORD 3
28 no devoted thing . . whether of man or beast 1
29 who is to be utterly destroyed from among men 1
31 If a man wishes to redeem any of his tithe 3
33 A man shall not inquire whether it is good or bad •
Num 1: 4 there shall be with you a man from each tribe 3
5 these are the names of the men who shall attend 3
17 Moses . . took these men who have been named 3
44 twelve men, each representing his fathers' house. 3
3:13 first-born in Israel, both of man and of beast; 1
5: 6 When a man or woman commits any of the sins 3
6 any of the sins that men commit by breaking faith 1
8 if the man has no kinsman to whom restitution 3
10 every man's holy things shall be his; 3
10 whatever any man gives to the priest shall be his. 3
12 If any man's wife goes astray and acts 3
13 if a man lies with her carnally, and it is hidden 3
15 then the man shall bring his wife to the priest 3
19 If no man has lain with you, and if you have not 3
20 some man other than your husband has lain with you 3
30 or when the spirit of jealousy comes upon a man 3
31 The man shall be free from iniquity, but the woman 3
6: 2 When either a man or a woman makes a special vow 3
9 if any man dies very suddenly beside him •
7:24 Eli'ab the . . leader of the men of Zeb'ulun 6
30 Eli'zur the . . leader of the men of Reuben 6
36 Shelu'mi-el the . . leader of the men of Simeon 6
42 Eli'asaph the . . leader of the men of Gad 6
48 Eli'shama the . . leader of the men of E'phraim 6
54 Gama'liel the . . leader of the men of Manas'seh 6
60 Abi'dan the . . leader of the men of Benjamin 6
66 Ahie'zer the . . leader of the men of Dan 6
72 Pa'giel the . . leader of the men of Asher 6
78 Ahi'ra the . . leader of the men of Naph'tali 6
8:17 first-born . . are mine, both of man and of beast; 1
9: 6 there were certain men who were unclean 3
6 unclean through touching the dead body of a man 1
7 those men said to him, "We are unclean 3
7 unclean through touching the dead body of a man; 1
10 If any man of you or of your descendants 3
13 the man who is clean and is not on a journey, yet 3
13 shall be cut off . . that man shall bear his sin. 3
10:14 standard of the camp of the men of Judah set out 6
15 over the host of the tribe of the men of Is'sachar 6
16 over the host of the tribe of the men of Zeb'ulun 6
19 over the host of the tribe of the men of Simeon 6
20 over the host of the tribe of the men of Gad 6
22 standard of the camp of the men of E'phraim set out 6
23 over the host of the tribe of the men of Manas'seh 6
24 over the host of the tribe of the men of Benjamin 6
25 Then the standard of the camp of the men of Dan 6
26 over the host of the tribe of the men of Asher 6
27 over the host of the tribe of the men of Naph'tali 6
11:10 weeping . . every man at the door of his tent; 3
16 Gather for me 70 men of the elders of Israel 3
24 he gathered 70 men of the elders of the people 3
26 Now two men remained in the camp, one named Eldad 3
12: 3 Now the man Moses was very meek, 3
3 very meek, more than all men that were on the face 1
13: 2 Send men to spy out the land of Canaan 3
2 each tribe of their fathers shall you send a man 3
3 all of them men who were heads of the people 3
16 names of the men whom Moses sent to spy out 3
24 which the men of Israel cut down from there. 6
31 Then the men who had gone up with him said 3
32 people that we saw in it are men of great stature. 3
14:15 Now if thou dost kill this people as one man 3
22 none of the men who have seen my glory and my signs 3
36 men whom Moses sent to spy out the land 3
37 the men who brought up an evil report of the land 3
38 of those men who went to spy out the land. 3
15:32 found a man gathering sticks on the sabbath day. 3
35 LORD said to Moses, "The man shall be put to death; 3
16: 2 took men; and they rose up before Moses •
2 250 . . chosen from the assembly, well-known men; 3
7 man whom the LORD chooses shall be the holy one. 3
14 Will you put out the eyes of these men? 3
18 every man took his censer, and they put fire 3
22 shall one man sin, and wilt thou be angry with all 3
26 Depart . . from the tents of these wicked men 3
29 If these men die the common death of all men •
29 If these men die the common death of all men 1
29 or if they are visited by the fate of all men 1
30 know that these men have despised the LORD. 3
32 men that belonged to Korah and all their goods. 1
35 consumed the 250 men offering the incense. 3
17: 5 the rod of the man whom I choose shall sprout; 3
18:15 opens the womb of all flesh, whether man or beast 1
15 the first-born of man you shall redeem 1
19: 9 man who is clean shall gather up the ashes 3
13 Whoever touches . . body of any man who has died 1
14 This is the law when a man dies in a tent 1
16 Whoever . . touches . . a bone of a man, or a grave 1
20 man who is unclean and does not cleanse himself 3
20:20 Edom came out against them with many men 18
21: 9 if a serpent bit any man, he would look 3
23 He gathered all his men together, and went out 18
22: 9 God came . . and said, "Who are these men with you? 3
20 If the men have come to call you, rise, go with them; 3
35 angel of the LORD said to Balaam, "Go with the men; 3
23:19 God is not man, that he should lie 3
19 God is not . . a son of man, that he should repent. 1
24: 3 oracle of the man whose eye is opened 11
15 the oracle of the man whose eye is opened 11
25: 5 Every one of you slay his men who have yoked 3
8 went after the man of Israel into the inner room 3
8 both of them, the man of Israel and the woman 3
14 The name of the slain man of Israel . . was Zimri 3
26:10 when the fire devoured 250 men; 3
64 not a man of those numbered by Moses and Aaron 3
65 There was not left a man of them 3
27: 8 If a man dies, and has no son 3
16 LORD . . appoint a man over the congregation 3
18 Joshua the son of Nun, a man in whom is the spirit 3
30: 2 When a man vows a vow to the LORD, or swears 3
16 statutes . . as between a man and his wife 3
31: 3 Arm men from among you for the war, 3
11 spoil and all the booty, both of man and of beast. 1
17 kill every woman who has known man by lying 3
18 young girls who have not known man by lying 12
21 Elea'zar the priest said to the men of war 3
26 count of the booty . . both of man and of beast 1
28 levy for the LORD a tribute from the men of war 3
32 remaining of the spoil that the men of war took 18
35 women who had not known man by lying with him. 12
42 separated from that of the men who had gone to war- 3
49 Your servants have counted the men of war 3
49 men of war . . there is not a man missing from us. 3
53 men of war had taken booty, every man for himself.) 3
53 men of war had taken booty, every man for himself.) 3
32:11 Surely none of the men who came up out of Egypt 3
14 risen in your fathers' stead, a brood of sinful men 3
34:17 names of the men who shall divide the land to you 3
19 These are the names of the men 3
29 These are the men whom the LORD commanded •
35:17 with a stone in the hand, by which a man may die •
18 with a weapon of wood . . by which a man may die •
23 or used a stone, by which a man may die •
28 For the man must remain in his city of refuge •
Deu 1:13 Choose wise, understanding, and experienced men 3
15 heads of your tribes, wise and experienced men 3
16 judge righteously between a man and his brother 3
17 you shall not be afraid of the face of man 3
22 'Let us send men before us, that they may explore 3
23 I took twelve men of you, one man for each tribe; 3
23 I took twelve men of you, one man for each tribe; 3
31 how the LORD . . bore you, as a man bears his son 3
35 Not one of these men of this evil generation 3
41 And every man of you girded on his weapons of war 3
2:14 entire generation, that is, the men of war 3
16 when all the men of war had perished and were dead 3
34 destroyed every city, men, women, and children; 13
3: 6 destroying every city, men, women, and children. 13
18 all your men of valor shall pass over armed 6
20 then you shall return every man to his possession 3
4: 3 destroyed . . all the men who followed the Ba'al 3
28 gods of wood and stone, the work of men's hands 1
32 since the day that God created man upon the earth 1
5:24 day seen God speak with man and man still live. 1
24 day seen God speak with man and man still live. •
7:24 not a man shall be able to stand against you 3
8: 3 man does not live by bread alone 1
3 but that man lives by everything that proceeds 1
5 as a man disciplines his son, the LORD your God 3
11:25 No man shall be able to stand against you; 3
12: 8 every man doing whatever is right in his own eyes; 3
16:17 every man shall give as he is able, according 3
17: 2 a man or woman who does what is evil 3
5 bring . . man or woman who has done this evil thing 3
5 stone that man or woman to death with stones. 3
12 The man who acts presumptuously, by not obeying 3
12 who acts presumptuously . . that man shall die; 3
19: 6 mortally, though the man did not deserve to die •
11 if any man hates his neighbor, and lies in wait 3
11 man flees into one of these cities •
15 A single witness shall not prevail against a man 3
16 If a malicious witness rises against any man 3
20: 5 What man is there that has built a new house 3
5 die in the battle and another man dedicate it. 3
6 what man is there that has planted a vineyard 3
6 lest he die . . and another man enjoy its fruit. 3
7 what man is there that has betrothed a wife 3
7 die in the battle and another man take her.' 3
8 What man is there that is fearful 3
19 Are the trees in the field men that they should be 1
21:15 If a man has two wives, the one loved and the other 3
18 If a man has a stubborn and rebellious son 3
21 all the men of the city shall stone him to death 3
22 if a man has committed a crime punishable 3
22: 5 woman . . not wear anything that pertains to a man 11
5 nor shall a man put on a woman's garment; 11
13 If a man takes a wife, and goes in to her 3
16 I gave my daughter to this man to wife 3
18 elders of that city shall take the man and whip 3
21 men of her city shall stone her to death 3
22 man is found lying with the wife of another man 3
22 man is found lying with the wife of another man 9
22 both . . shall die, the man who lay with the woman 3
23 man meets her in the city and lies with her 3
24 man because he violated his neighbor's wife; 3
25 if . . a man meets a young woman who is betrothed 3
25 open country . . man seizes her and lies with her 3
25 then only the man who lay with her shall die. 3
26 like that of a man attacking and murdering 3
28 If a man meets a virgin who is not betrothed 3
29 then the man who lay with her shall give 3
30 A man shall not take his father's wife 3
23:10 among you any man who is not clean by reason 3
24: 1 When a man takes a wife and marries her 3
2 if she goes and becomes another man's wife 3
5 When a man is newly married, he shall not go out 3
6 No man . . take a mill or an upper millstone in pledge; •
7 If a man is found stealing one of his brethren 3
11 man to whom you make the loan shall bring 3
12 if . . poor man, you shall not sleep in his pledge; 3
16 every man shall be put to death for his own sin. 3
25: 1 If there is a dispute between men, and they come 3
7 if the man does not wish to take his brother's wife 3
9 So shall it be done to the man who does not build up 3
11 When men fight with one another, and the wife 3
27:14 Levites shall declare to all the men of Israel 3
15 'Cursed be the man who makes a graven or molten 3
28:30 betroth a wife, and another man shall lie with her; 3
54 man who is the most tender and delicately bred 3
68 male and female slaves, but no man will buy you. •
29:10 stand this day all of you . . all the men of Israel 3
18 lest there be . . a man or woman or family or tribe 3
20 anger of the LORD . . smoke against that man 3
25 Then men would say, 'It is because they forsook •
31:12 Assemble the people, men, women, and little ones 3
32: 8 when he separated the sons of men, he fixed 1
25 the sucking child with the man of gray hairs. 3
26 make the remembrance . . cease from among men 4
33: 1 blessing with which Moses the man of God blessed 3
6 Let Reuben live, and not die, nor let his men be few. 13
34: 6 no man knows the place of his burial to this day. 3
Jos 1: 5 No man shall be able to stand before you 3
14 but all the men of valor among you shall pass over 10
2: 1 And Joshua . . sent two men secretly from Shittim 3
2 certain men of Israel have come here tonight 3
3 Bring forth the men that have come to you 3
4 the woman had taken the two men and hidden them; 3
4 True, men came to me, but I did not know where 3
5 the men went out; where the men went I do not know; 3
5 the men went out; where the men went I do not know; 3
7 the men pursued . . them on the way to the Jordan 3
9 and said to the men, "I know that the LORD has given 3
14 And the men said to her, "Our life for yours! 3
17 The men said to her, "We will be guiltless 3
23 Then the two men came down again from the hills 3
3:12 Now . . take twelve men from the tribes of Israel 3
12 take twelve men . . from each tribe a man. 3
4: 2 Take twelve men from the people, from each . . a man 3
2 Take twelve men . . from each tribe a man 3
4 Joshua called the twelve men from the people 3
4 whom he had appointed, a man from each tribe; 3
8 And the men of Israel did as Joshua commanded 6
5: 4 all the males of . . all the men of war, had died 3
6 all the nation, the men of war that came forth 3
13 a man stood before him with his drawn sword 3
6: 3 march . . all the men of war going around the city 3
21 all in the city, both men and women, young and old 3
22 said to the two men who had spied out the land 3
26 Cursed . . be the man that rises up and rebuilds 3
7: 2 Joshua sent men from Jericho to Ai . . and said 3
2 And the men went up and spied out Ai. 3
3 let . . 2,000 or 3,000 men go up and attack 3
4 and they fled before the men of Ai 3
5 the men of Ai killed about 36 men of them 3
5 the men of Ai killed about 36 men of them 3

8: 1 take all the fighting men with you, and arise 18
3 Joshua arose, and all the fighting men, to go up 18
11 And all the fighting men who were with him went up 18
12 he took about 5,000 men, and set them in ambush 3
14 his people, the men of the city, made haste 3
17 There was not a man left . . who did not go out 3
20 when the men of Ai looked back, behold, the smoke 3
21 then they turned back and smote the men of Ai. 3
25 both men and women, were 12,000 3
31 stones, upon which no man has lifted an iron tool •
9: 6 and said to him and to the men of Israel 3
7 But the men of Israel said to the Hivites 3
14 the men partook of their provisions 3
10: 2 it was greater than Ai, and all its men were mighty. 3
6 And the men of Gibeon sent to Joshua . . in Gilgal 3
8 there shall not a man of them stand before you. 3
11 the men of Israel killed with the sword. 6
12 LORD gave the Amorites over to the men of Israel; 6
14 when the LORD hearkened to the voice of a man; 3
18 the cave, and set men by it to guard them; 3
20 When Joshua and the men of Israel had finished 6
21 not a man moved his tongue against . . Israel. 3
24 Joshua summoned all the men of Israel, and said 3
24 Joshua . . and said to the chiefs of the men of war 3
11:14 every man they smote with the edge of the sword 1
14: 6 what the LORD said to Moses the man of God 3
15 this Arba was the greatest man among the Anakim. 1
17: 1 were allotted . . because he was a man of war. 3
18: 4 Provide three men from each tribe, and I will send 3
8 So the men started on their way; 3
9 So the men went and passed up and down in the land 3
23: 9 no man has been able to withstand you to this day. 3
10 One man of you puts to flight 1,000 3
24:11 and the men of Jericho fought against you 9
Jdg 1: 8 the men of Judah fought against Jerusalem 6
9 the men of Judah went down to fight against 6
24 the spies saw a man coming out of the city 3
25 sword, but they let the man and all his family go. 3
26 the man went to the land of the Hittites and built 3
3:15 Ehud . . the Benjaminite, a left-handed man. 3
17 Eglon king of Moab. Now Eglon was a very fat man. 3
28 Moabites, and allowed not a man to pass over. 3
29 Moabites, all strong, able-bodied men; not a man 3
29 strong, able-bodied men; not a man escaped. 3
4: 6 commands you, 'Go, gather your men at Mount Tabor •
10 10,000 men went up at his heels; and Deb'orah 3
13 and all the men who were with him 18
14 from Mount Tabor with 10,000 men following him 3
16 the edge of the sword; not a man was left. 2
20 and if any man comes and asks you, 'Is any one here?' 3
22 and I will show you the man whom you are seeking. 3
5:30 dividing the spoil?–A maiden or two for every man; 11
6:12 him, "The LORD is with you, you mighty man of valor. 10
16 and you shall smite the Mid'ianites as one man. 3
27 Gideon took ten men of his servants, and did 3
27 too afraid of his family and the men of the town 3
28 When the men of the town rose early in the morning 3
30 the men of the town said to Jo'ash, "Bring out 3
7: 4 he of whom I say to you, 'This man shall go with you,' •
4 of whom I say to you, 'This man shall not go with you,' •
6 of those that lapped . . was 300 men; 3
7 With the 300 men . . I will deliver you 3
8 every man to his tent, but retained the 300 men; 3
13 behold, a man was telling a dream to his comrade; 3
14 sword of Gideon the son of Jo'ash, a man of Israel; 3
16 he divided the 300 men into three companies 3
19 Gideon and the 100 men who were with him came 3
23 the men of Israel were called out from Naph'tali 3
24 So all the men of E'phraim were called out 3
8: 1 the men of E'phraim said to him, "What is this 3
4 he and the 300 men who were with him 3
5 he said to the men of Succoth, "Pray, give loaves 3
8 and the men of Penu'el answered him as the men 3
8 Penu'el answered him as the men of Succoth had 3
9 he said to the men of Penu'el, "When I come again 3
10 about 15,000 men, all who were left of all the army •
10 there had fallen 120,000 men who drew the sword. 3
14 the officials and elders of Succoth, 77 men. 3
15 he came to the men of Succoth, and said, "Behold 3
15 we should give bread to your men who are faint?' 3
16 briers and with them taught the men of Succoth. 3
17 the tower of Penu'el, and slew the men of the city. 3
18 Where are the men whom you slew at Tabor? 3
21 for as the man is, so is his strength. 3
22 Then the men of Israel said to Gideon, "Rule over us 3
9: 3 words . . in the ears of all the men of Shechem; 9
5 slew his brothers the sons of Jerubba'al, 70 men 3
7 Listen to me, you men of Shechem, that God may 9
9 my fatness, by which gods and men are honored 3
13 Shall I leave my wine which cheers gods and men 3
18 and have slain his sons, 70 men on one stone 3
23 spirit between Abim'elech and the men of Shechem; 9
23 and the men of Shechem dealt treacherously 9
24 blood be laid . . upon the men of Shechem 9
25 the men of Shechem put men in ambush against him 9
26 and the men of Shechem put confidence in him. 9
28 Zebul his officer serve the men of Hamor 3
32 go . . you and the men that are with you, and lie 18
33 when he and the men that are with him come out 18
34 Abim'elech and all the men . . with him rose up 18
35 and Abim'elech and the men that were with him rose 18
36 when Ga'al saw the men, he said to Zebul, "Look, 18
36 Look, men are coming down from the mountain tops! 18
36 You see the shadow . . as if they were men. 3
37 men are coming down from the center of the land 18
38 Are not these the men whom you despised? 18
39 Ga'al went out at the head of the men of Shechem 9
42 following day the men went out into the fields. 18
43 He took his men and divided them into three 18
43 he looked and saw the men coming out of the city 18
48 he and all the men that were with him; 18
48 he said to the men that were with him 18
49 of Shechem also died, about 1,000 men and women. 3
51 people of the city fled to it, all the men and women 3
55 the men of Israel saw that Abim'elech was dead 3
57 all the wickedness of the men of Shechem 3
10: 1 Tola the son of Pu'ah, son of Dodo, a man of Is'sachar 3
18 Who is the man that will begin to fight 3
11:39 She had never known a man. 3
12: 1 The men of E'phraim were called to arms 3
4 Then Jephthah gathered all the men of Gilead 3
4 and the men of Gilead smote E'phraim 3
5 the men of Gilead said to him, "Are you 3
13: 2 there was a certain man of Zorah, of the tribe 3
6 A man of God came to me, and his countenance was 3
8 let the man of God whom thou didst send come again 3
10 Behold, the man who came to me the other day 3
11 Mano'ah arose . . and came to the man and said 3
11 Are you the man who spoke to this woman? 3
14:18 the men of the city said to him on the seventh day 3
19 to Ash'kelon and killed 30 men of the town 3
15:10 the men of Judah said, "Why have you come up 3
11 Then 3,000 men of Judah went down to the cleft 3
15 jawbone of an ass . . and with it he slew 1,000 men. 3
16 with the jawbone of an ass have I slain 1,000 men 3
16: 7 I shall become weak, and be like any other man. 1
9 Now she had men lying in wait in an inner chamber. •
11 I shall become weak, and be like any other man. 1
13 I shall become weak, and be like any other man. •
17 and I shall become weak, and be like any other man. 1
19 she called a man, and had him shave off the seven 3
27 the house was full of men and women; all the lords 3
27 on the roof there were about 3,000 men and women 3
17: 1 There was a man of the hill country of E'phraim 3
5 the man Micah had a shrine, and he made an ephod 3
8 the man departed from . . Bethlehem . . to live 3
11 And the Levite was content to dwell with the man; 3
18: 2 the Danites sent five able men from the whole 3
7 the five men departed, and came to La'ish 3
11 600 men of the tribe of Dan, armed . . set forth 3
14 the five men who had gone to spy out the country 3
16 600 men of the Danites, armed with their weapons 3
17 the five men who had gone to spy out the land went 3
17 with the 600 men armed with weapons of war 3
19 be priest to the house of one man, or to be priest 3
22 the men who were in the houses . . were called out 3
19: 6 the two men sat and ate and drank together; •
6 the girl's father said to the man, "Be pleased 3
7 when the man rose up to go, his father-in-law urged 3
9 the man and his concubine and his servant rose up 3
10 the man would not spend the night; he rose up 3
15 no man took them into his house to spend 3
16 an old man was coming from his work in the field 3
16 the man was from the hill country of E'phraim 3
16 Gib'e-ah; the men of the place were Benjaminites 3
17 the old man said, "Where are you going? 3
20 the old man said, "Peace be to you; I will care for all 3
22 the men of the city, base fellows, beset the house 3
22 they said to the old man, the master of the house 3
22 Bring out the man who came into your house, that we 3
23 the man, the master of the house, went out to them 3
23 seeing that this man has come into my house 3
24 but against this man do not do so vile a thing. 3
25 the men would not listen to him. So the man seized 3
25 the man seized his concubine, and put her out 3
26 woman . . fell down at the door of the man's house 3
28 and the man rose up and went away to his home. 3
20: 1 congregation assembled as one man to the LORD 3
2 of God, 400,000 men on foot that drew the sword. 3
5 the men of Gib'e-ah rose against me, and beset 9
8 all the people arose as one man, saying, "We will not 3
10 take ten men of a 100 throughout all the tribes 3
11 all the men of Israel gathered against the city 3
11 gathered against the city, united as one man. 3
12 tribes of Israel sent men through all the tribe 3
13 give up the men, the base fellows in Gib'e-ah 3
15 mustered . . 26,000 men that drew the sword 3
15 Gib'e-ah, who mustered 700 picked men. 3
16 were 700 picked men who were left-handed 3
17 the men of Israel, apart from Benjamin, mustered 3
17 Israel . . mustered 400,000 men that drew sword 3
17 men that drew sword; all these were men of war. 3
20 the men of Israel went out to battle against 3
20 the men of Israel drew up the battle line against 3
21 felled . . 22,000 men of the Israelites. 3
22 But the people, the men of Israel, took courage 3
25 felled . . 18,000 men of the people of Israel 3
25 of Israel; all these were men who drew the sword. •
31 and kill some . . about 30 men of Israel. 3
32 the men of Israel said, "Let us flee, and draw them 6
33 all the men of Israel rose up out of their place 3
34 came . . 10,000 picked men out of all Israel 3
35 men of Israel destroyed 25,100 men of Benjamin 6
35 men of Israel destroyed 25,100 men of Benjamin 3
35 25,100 . . all these were men who drew the sword. •
36 The men of Israel gave ground to Benjamin 3
38 signal between the men of Israel and the men 3
39 the men of Israel should turn in battle. 3
39 to smite and kill about 30 men of Israel; 3
41 the men of Israel turned, and the men of Benjamin 3
41 the men of Benjamin were dismayed, for they saw 3
42 they turned their backs before the men of Israel 3
44 18,000 men of Benjamin fell, all of them men 3
44 men of Benjamin fell, all of them men of valor. 3
45 5,000 men of them were cut down in the highways 3
45 to Gidom, and 2,000 men of them were slain. 3
46 fell . . 25,000 men that drew the sword 3
46 men that drew the sword, all of them men of valor. 3
47 600 men turned and fled toward the wilderness 3
48 the men of Israel turned back against 3
48 smote . . men and beasts and all that they found. 50
21: 1 the men of Israel had sworn at Mizpah, "No one of us 3
10 sent thither 12,000 of their bravest men 3
12 virgins who had not known man by lying with him; 3
Rut 1: 1 a certain man of Bethlehem in Judah went 3
2 The name of the man was Elim'elech 3
2: 1 a kinsman of her husband's, a man of wealth 3
19 Blessed be the man who took notice of you. •
19 The man's name with whom I worked today is Bo'az. 3
20 The man is a relative of ours, one of our nearest 3
3: 3 do not make yourself known to the man until 3
8 At midnight the man was startled, and turned over 3
16 Then she told her all that the man had done for her 3
18 Wait . . for the man will not rest, but will settle 3
4: 2 he took ten men of the elders of the city, and said 3
1Sm 1: 1 There was a certain man of Ramatha'im-zo'phim 3
3 Now this man used to go up year by year 3
21 the man Elka'nah and all his house went up to offer 3
2: 9 for not by might shall a man prevail. 3
13 The custom . . when any man offered sacrifice 3
15 and say to the man who was sacrificing, "Give meat 3
16 if the man said to him, "Let them burn the fat first 3
17 the men treated the offering . . with contempt. 3
25 If a man sins against a man, God will mediate 3
25 If a man sins against a man, God will mediate 3
25 if a man sins against the LORD, who can intercede 3
26 to grow . . in favor with the LORD and with men. 3
27 And there came a man of God to Eli, and said to him 3
33 The man of you whom I shall not cut off 3
33 all the increase . . shall die by the sword of men. 3
4: 2 slew about 4,000 men on the field of battle. 3
9 Take courage, and acquit yourselves like men 3
9 to you; acquit yourselves like men and fight. 3
12 A man of Benjamin ran from the battle line 3
13 when the man came into the city and told the news 3
14 Then the man hastened and came and told Eli. 3
16 the man said to Eli, "I . . come from the battle; 3
18 neck was broken . . for he was an old man, and heavy. 3
5: 7 the men of Ashdod saw how things were, they said 3
9 and he afflicted the men of the city 3
12 the men who did not die were stricken with tumors 3
6:10 The men did so, and took two milch cows 3
15 the men of Beth-she'mesh offered burnt offerings 3
19 And he slew some of the men of Beth-she'mesh 3
19 he slew 70 men of them, and the people mourned 3
20 the men of Beth-she'mesh said, "Who is able to stand 3
7: 1 the men of Kir'iath-je'arim came and took up the ark 3
11 the men of Israel went out of Mizpah and pursued 3
8:22 Samuel then said to the men of Israel 3
9: 1 There was a man of Benjamin whose name was Kish 3
1 name was Kish . . a Benjaminite, a man of wealth; 3
2 There was not a man . . more handsome than he; 3
6 there is a man of God in this city 3
6 a man of God . . and he is a man that is held in honor; 3
7 But if we go, what can we bring the man? 3
7 and there is no present to bring to the man of God. 3
8 I have . . silver, and I will give it to the man of God 3
9 when a man went to inquire of God, he said, "Come 3
10 they went to the city where the man of God was. 3
16 I will send to you a man from the land of Benjamin 3
17 Here is the man of whom I spoke to you! 3
10: 2 you will meet two men by Rachel's tomb 3
3 three men going up to God at Bethel will meet you 3
6 prophesy . . and be turned into another man. 3
12 And a man of the place answered, "And who is 3
22 they inquired again . . "Did the man come hither? 3
26 Saul also went . . and with him went men of valor 45
27 But some . . said, "How can this man save us? •
11: 1 all the men of Jabesh said to Nahash, "Make a treaty 3
5 they told him the tidings of the men of Jabesh. 3
7 and they came out as one man. 3
8 the men of Israel were 300,000 6
8 and the men of Judah 30,000. 3
9 Thus shall you say to the men of Ja'besh-gil'ead 3
9 the messengers came and told the men of Jabesh 3
10 Therefore the men of Jabesh said 3
12 Bring the men, that we may put them to death. 3

13 Saul said, "Not a man shall be put to death this day 3
15 Saul and all the men of Israel rejoiced greatly. 3
13: 2 Saul chose 3,000 men of Israel; •
6 the men of Israel saw that they were in straits 3
14 the LORD has sought out a man after his own heart; 3
15 people who were present with him, about 600 men. 3
14: 2 the people who were with him were about 600 men 3
8 we will cross over to the men, and we will show 3
12 And the men of the garrison hailed Jonathan 3
14 that first slaughter . . was of about twenty men 3
22 when all the men of Israel who had hid themselves 3
24 And the men of Israel were distressed that day; 3
24 Cursed be the man who eats food until . . evening 3
28 'Cursed be the man who eats food this day.' 3
36 let us not leave a man of them. 3
39 was not a man among all the people that answered •
52 when Saul saw any strong man, or any valiant man 3
52 when Saul saw any strong man, or any valiant man 3
15: 3 do not spare them, but kill both man and woman 3
4 200,000 men on foot, and 10,000 men of Judah. 3
29 for he is not a man, that he should repent. 1
16: 7 for the LORD sees not as man sees; 1
7 man looks on the outward appearance, but the LORD 1
16 seek out a man who is skilful in playing the lyre; 3
17 Provide for me a man who can play well, and bring 3
18 who is skilful in playing, a man of valor 3
18 skilful in playing, a man of valor, a man of war 3
18 prudent in speech, and a man of good presence; 3
17: 2 And Saul and the men of Israel were gathered 3
8 Choose a man for yourselves, and let him come down 3
10 give me a man, that we may fight together. 3
12 the man was already old and advanced in years. 3
19 all the men of Israel, were in the valley of Elah 3
24 All the men of Israel, when they saw the man, fled 3
24 All . . Israel, when they saw the man, fled from him 3
25 And the men of Israel said, "Have you seen this man 3
25 Have you seen this man who has come up? 3
25 the man who kills him, the king will enrich 3
26 And David said to the men who stood by him 3
26 What . . for the man who kills this Philistine 3
27 So shall it be done to the man who kills him. 3
28 Now Eli'ab . . heard when he spoke to the men; 3
32 Let no man's heart fail because of him; 1
33 and he has been a man of war from his youth. 3
52 And the men of Israel and Judah rose with a shout 3
18: 5 David . . so that Saul set him over the men of war. 3
23 seeing that I am a poor man and of no repute? 3
27 David arose and went, along with his men 3
21: 7 a certain man of the servants of Saul was there 3
14 you see the man is mad; why . . have you brought him 3
22: 2 And there were with him about 400 men. 3
6 was discovered, and the men who were with him. 3
19 both men and women, children and sucklings, oxen 3
23: 3 David's men said to him, "Behold, we are afraid here 3
5 And David and his men went to Kei'lah, and fought 3
8 go down to Kei'lah, to besiege David and his men. 3
11 Will the men of Kei'lah surrender me into his hand? 9
12 Will the men of Kei'lah surrender me and my men 9
12 surrender me and my men into the hand of Saul? 3
13 Then David and his men . . arose and departed 3
24 David and his men were in the wilderness of Ma'on 3
25 And Saul and his men went to seek him. 3
26 Saul went . . David and his men on the other side 3
26 Saul and his men were closing in 3
26 Saul and . . were closing in upon David and his men 3
24: 2 Then Saul took 3,000 chosen men out of all Israel 3
2 Saul took . . and went to seek David and his men 3
3 David and his men were sitting in the . . cave. 3
4 And the men of David said to him, "Here is the day 3
6 He said to his men, "The LORD forbid that I . . do this 3
7 David persuaded his men with these words 3
9 Why do you listen to the words of men 1
19 if a man finds his enemy, will he let him go away 3
22 but David and his men went up to the stronghold. 3
25: 2 a man in Ma'on, whose business was in Carmel. 3
2 The man was very rich; he had 3,000 sheep 3
3 Now the name of the man was Nabal 3
3 but the man was churlish and ill-behaved; 3
11 give it to men who come from I do not know where? 3
13 David said to his men, "Every man gird on his sword! 3
13 and about 400 men went up after David 3
15 men were very good to us, and we suffered no harm 3
20 David and his men came down . . and she met them. 3
29 If men rise up to pursue you and to seek your life 1
26: 2 Saul arose and . . with 3,000 chosen men of Israel 3
15 Are you not a man? Who is like you in Israel? 3
19 but if it is men, may they be cursed before the LORD 7
27: 2 David . . and the 600 men who were with him 3
3 David dwelt with A'chish at Gath, he and his men 3
8 Now David and his men went up, and made raids 3
9 David . . left neither man nor woman alive 3
11 And David saved neither man nor woman alive 3
28: 1 you and your men are to go out with me in the army. 3
8 Saul . . went, he and two men with him; 3
14 An old man is coming up; and he is wrapped in a robe. 3
29: 2 and David and his men were passing on in the rear 3
4 Send the man back, that he may return to the place 3
4 Would it not be with the heads of the men here? 3
11 David set out with his men early in the morning 3
30: 1 David and his men came to Ziklag on the third day 3
3 when David and his men came to the city, they found 3
9 David set out, and the 600 men who were with him 3
10 David went on with the pursuit, he and 400 men; 3
17 not a man of them escaped, except 400 young men 3
17 not a man of them escaped, except 400 young men 3
21 Then David came to the 200 men 3
22 fellows among the men who had gone with David 3
31 the places where David and his men had roamed. 3
31: 1 the men of Israel fled before the Philistines 3
6 Saul died, and his three sons . . and all his men 3
7 men of Israel . . on the other side of the valley 3
7 saw that the men of Israel had fled and that Saul 3
12 valiant men arose, and went all night 3
2Sm 1: 2 a man came from Saul's camp, with his clothes rent 3
11 and so did all the men who were with him; 3
2: 3 And David brought up his men who were with him 3
4 the men of Judah came, and . . anointed David king 3
4 It was the men of Ja'besh-gil'ead who buried Saul 3
5 sent messengers to the men of Ja'besh-gil'ead 3
17 Abner and the men of Israel were beaten before 3
27 surely the men would have given up the pursuit 18
28 all the men stopped, and pursued Israel no more 18
29 Abner and his men went . . through the Arabah; 3
30 were missing . . nineteen men besides As'ahel. 3
31 servants . . had slain of Benjamin 360 of Abner's men. 3
32 And Jo'ab and his men marched all night 3
3:20 Abner came with twenty men to David at Hebron 3
20 feast for Abner and the men who were with him. 3
39 these men the sons of Zeru'iah are too hard for me. 3
4: 2 Now Saul's son had two men who were captains 3
2 sons of Rimmon a man of Benjamin from Be-er'oth 6
11 when wicked men have slain a righteous man 3
11 when wicked men have slain a righteous man 3
5: 6 And the king and his men went to Jerusalem 3
21 and David and his men carried them away. 3
6:19 the whole multitude of Israel, both men and women 3
7:14 I will chasten him with the rod of men 3
14 chasten him . . with the stripes of the sons of men; 1
8: 5 David slew 22,000 men of the Syrians. 3
10: 5 meet them, for the men were greatly ashamed. 3
6 hired . . the king of Ma'acah with 1,000 men 3
6 hired . . the men of Tob, 12,000 men. 3
6 hired . . the men of Tob, 12,000 men. 3
8 Zobah and of Rehob, and the men of Tob and Ma'acah 3
10 the rest of his men he put in the charge of Abi'shai 18
18 David slew of the Syrians the men of 700 chariots •
11:16 Uri'ah to . . where he knew there were valiant men. 3
17 the men of the city came out and fought with Jo'ab; 3
23 The men gained an advantage over us, and came out 3
12: 1 There were two men in a certain city 3
4 Now there came a traveler to the rich man 3
4 but he took the poor man's lamb, and prepared it 3
4 and prepared it for the man who had come to him. 3
5 anger was greatly kindled against the man; 3
5 the man who has done this deserves to die; 3
7 Nathan said to David, "You are the man. 3
13: 3 and Jon'adab was a very crafty man. 3
14: 7 Give up the man who struck his brother •
16 from . . the hand of the man who would destroy me 3
15: 1 a chariot and horses, and 50 men to run before him. 3
2 when any man had a suit to come before the king 3
3 there is no man deputed by the king to hear you. •
4 every man with a suit or cause might come to me 3
5 whenever a man came near to do obeisance to him 3
6 so Ab'salom stole the hearts of the men of Israel. 3
11 200 men from Jerusalem who were invited guests 3
13 the men of Israel have gone after Ab'salom. 3
22 It'tai . . passed on, with all his men 3
16: 5 came out a man of the family of the house of Saul 3
7 Begone . . you man of blood, you worthless fellow! 3
8 See, your ruin is on you; for you are a man of blood. 3
13 So David and his men went on the road 3
15 Ab'salom and all the people, the men of Israel, came 3
18 the LORD and this people and all the men of Israel 3
17: 1 Let me choose 12,000 men 3
3 You seek the life of only one man 26
8 You know . . your father and his men are mighty men 3
12 of . . all the men with him not one will be left. 3
14 And Ab'salom and all the men of Israel said 3
18 to the house of a man at Bahu'rim, who had a well 3
24 Ab'salom crossed . . with all the men of Israel. 3
25 Ama'sa was the son of a man named Ithra 3
18: 1 Then David mustered the men who were with him 18
2 And the king said to the men, "I myself will also go 18
3 But the men said, "You shall not go out. 18
7 And the men of Israel were defeated there 18
7 the slaughter there was great . . 20,000 men. •
10 And a certain man saw it, and told Jo'ab 3
11 Jo'ab said to the man who told him, "What, 3
12 But the man said to Jo'ab, "Even if I felt in my hand 3
24 when he . . looked, he saw a man running alone. 3
26 And the watchman saw another man running; 3
26 watchman . . said, "See, another man running alone! 3
27 He is a good man, and comes with good tidings. 3
28 has delivered up the men who raised their hand 3
19: 7 not a man will stay with you this night; 3
14 he swayed the heart of all the men of Judah as one 3
14 swayed the heart of all the men of Judah as one man; 3
16 come down with the men of Judah to meet King David 3
17 and with him were 1,000 men from Benjamin. 3
28 all my father's house were but men doomed to death 3
32 he had provided . . for he was a very wealthy man. 3
41 all the men of Israel came to the king, and said 3
41 Why have our brethren the men of Judah stolen you 3
41 brought the king . . and all David's men with him? 3
42 All the men of Judah answered the men of Israel 3
42 All the men of Judah answered the men of Israel 3
43 And the men of Israel answered the men of Judah 3
43 And the men of Israel answered the men of Judah 3
43 But the words of the men of Judah were fiercer 3
43 were fiercer than the words of the men of Israel. 3
20: 2 the men of Israel withdrew from David 3
2 but the men of Judah followed their king 3
4 Call the men of Judah together to me 3
11 And one of Jo'ab's men took his stand by Ama'sa 14
12 and when the man saw that all the people stopped 3
15 all the men . . with Jo'ab came and besieged him 18
21 a man of the hill country . . has lifted up his hand 3
21: 5 The man who consumed us and planned to destroy us 3
12 took the bones . . from the men of Ja'besh-gil'ead 9
17 Then David's men adjured him, "You shall no more go 3
20 war at Gath, where there was a man of great stature 3
22:26 with the blameless man thou dost show thyself 10
49 thou didst deliver me from men of violence. 3
23: 1 the oracle of the man who was raised on high 11
3 When one rules justly over men 1
6 godless men are all like thorns . . thrown away; •
7 the man who touches them arms himself with iron 3
9 and the men of Israel withdrew. 3
10 the men returned after him . . to strip the slain. 18
11 and the men fled from the Philistines. 18
17 Shall I drink the blood of the men who went 3
18 he wielded his spear against 300 men •
20 Benai'ah . . was a valiant man of Kabzeel, a doer 3
21 And he slew an Egyptian, a handsome man. 3
24: 9 in Israel there were 800,000 valiant men 3
9 and the men of Judah were 500,000. 3
14 but let me not fall into the hand of man. 1
15 died . . from Dan to Beer-sheba 70,000 men. 3
1Kg 1: 5 prepared . . and 50 men to run before him. 3
6 He was also a very handsome man; and he was born •
42 for you are a worthy man and bring good news. 3
52 If he prove to be a worthy man, not one of his hairs 6
2: 2 Be strong, and show yourself a man 3
4 shall not fail you a man on the throne of Israel.' 3
9 hold him not guiltless, for you are a wise man; you 3
32 slew with the sword two men more righteous 3
4: 7 twelve officers . . each man had to make •
31 he was wiser than all other men, wiser than Ethan 1
34 men came from all peoples to hear the wisdom •
5:13 the levy numbered 30,000 men. 3
7:14 his father was a man of Tyre, a worker in bronze; 3
8: 2 all the men of Israel assembled to King Solomon 3
25 a man before me to sit upon the throne of Israel 3
31 If a man sins . . and is made to take an oath 3
38 supplication is made by any man or by all 1
39 knowest the hearts of all the children of men); 1
46 for there is no man who does not sin 1
9: 5 There shall not fail you a man upon the throne 3
11:18 took men with them from Paran and came to Egypt 3
24 he gathered men about him and became leader 3
28 The man Jerobo'am was very able 3
12:22 the word of God came to Shemai'ah the man of God 3
13: 1 behold, a man of God came out of Judah 3
2 the man cried against the altar . . and said •
2 and men's bones shall be burned upon you.' 1
4 when the king heard the saying of the man of God 3
5 the sign which the man of God had given 3
6 the king said to the man of God, "Entreat now 3
6 the man of God entreated the LORD; 3
7 the king said to the man of God, "Come home with me 3
8 the man of God said to the king 3
11 came and told him all that the man of God had done 3
12 the way which the man of God . . had gone. 3
14 he went after the man of God, and found him 3
14 Are you the man of God who came from Judah? 3
21 he cried to the man of God who came from Judah 3
25 men passed by, and saw the body thrown in the road 3
26 It is the man of God, who disobeyed the word 3
29 the prophet took up the body of the man of God 3
31 the grave in which the man of God is buried; 3
14:10 as a man burns up dung until it is all gone. •
17:18 What have you against me, O man of God? 3
24 Now I know that you are a man of God 3
18:13 how I hid 100 men of the LORD's prophets 3
22 Ba'al's prophets are 450 men. 3
44 a little cloud like a man's hand is rising 3
20: 7 Mark now, and see how this man is seeking trouble; •
12 When Ben-ha'dad heard . . he said to his men 17
17 Men are coming out from Sama'ria. 3
20 each killed his man; the Syrians fled 3
28 a man of God came near and said to the king 3
30 the wall fell upon . . men that were left. 3
33 the men were watching for an omen 3
35 a certain man of the sons of the prophets said 3
35 Strike me, I pray." But the man refused 3
37 he found another man, and said, "Strike me, I pray. 3

37 Strike me, I pray." And the man struck him, smiting 3
39 a soldier turned and brought a man to me, and said 3
39 said, 'Keep this man; if by any means he be missing 3
42 you have let go . . the man whom I had devoted 3
21:11 the men of his city . . did as Jez'ebel had sent word 3
22: 6 king . . gathered the prophets . . , about 400 men 3
8 There is yet one man by whom we may inquire 3
34 a certain man drew his bow at a venture 3
2Kg 1: 6 There came a man to meet us, and said to us, 'Go back 3
7 What kind of man was he who came to meet you 3
9 the king sent to him a captain of 50 men *
9 O man of God, the king says, 'Come down.' 3
10 If I am a man of God, let fire come down from heaven 3
11 the king sent to him another captain of 50 men *
11 O man of God, this is the king's order, 'Come down 3
12 If I am a man of God, let fire come down from heaven 3
13 O man of God, I pray you, let my life . . be precious 3
14 consumed the two former captains of 50 men *
2: 7 50 men of the sons of the prophets also went 3
16 there are with your servants 50 strong men; 3
17 he said, "Send." They sent therefore 50 men; 3
19 Now the men of the city said to Eli'sha, "Behold 3
4: 7 She came and told the man of God, and he said, "Go 3
9 I perceive that this is a holy man of God 3
16 she said, "No, my lord, O man of God; do not lie 3
21 she went up and laid him on the bed of the man of God 3
22 Send . . that I may quickly go to the man of God 3
25 So she . . came to the man of God at Mount Carmel. 3
25 When the man of God saw her coming, he said 3
27 when she came to the mountain to the man of God 3
27 But the man of God said, "Let her alone 3
40 And they poured out for the men to eat. 3
40 cried out, "O man of God, there is death in the pot! 3
41 and said, "Pour out for the men, that they may eat. 18
42 A man came from Ba'al-shal'ishah, bringing 3
42 A man came . . bringing the man of God bread 3
42 Eli'sha said, "Give to the men, that they may eat. 18
43 How am I to set this before 100 men? 3
43 Give them to the men, that they may eat 18
5: 1 Na'aman . . was a great man with his master 3
7 this man sends . . to me to cure a man of his leprosy? 3
8 when Eli'sha the man of God heard . . he sent 3
14 dipped . . according to the word of the man of God; 3
15 Then he returned to the man of God 3
20 Geha'zi, the servant of Eli'sha the man of God, said 3
24 and he sent the men away, and they departed. 3
26 when the man turned from his chariot to meet you? 3
6: 6 Then the man of God said, "Where did it fall? 3
9 the man of God sent word to the king of Israel 3
10 sent to the place of which the man of God told him. 3
15 When the servant of the man of God rose early 3
19 I will bring you to the man whom you seek. 3
20 LORD, open the eyes of these men, that they may see. *
32 the king had dispatched a man from his presence; 3
7: 2 the captain . . said to the man of God, "If the LORD 3
3 Now there were four men who were lepers 3
13 Let some men take five of the remaining horses *
17 so that he died, as the man of God had said 3
18 when the man of God had said to the king 3
19 the captain had answered the man of God 3
8: 2 and did according to the word of the man of God; 3
4 talking with Geha'zi the servant of the man of God 3
7 when it was told him, "The man of God has come here 3
8 Take a present . . and go to meet the man of God 3
11 And the man of God wept. 3
10:21 there was not a man left who did not come. 3
24 Now Jehu had stationed 80 men outside 3
24 man who allows any . . to escape shall forfeit 3
25 Go in and slay them; let not a man escape. 3
11: 9 each brought his men who were to go off duty 3
12: 4 the money which a man's heart prompts him to bring 3
15 the men into whose hand they delivered the money 3
13:19 Then the man of God was angry with him, and said 3
21 as a man was being buried, lo, a . . band was seen 3
21 and the man was cast into the grave of Eli'sha; 3
21 and as soon as the man touched the bones of Eli'sha 3
15:20 from Israel, that is, from all the wealthy men 10
20 50 shekels of silver from every man 3
25 conspired . . with 50 men of the Gileadites 3
17:30 the men of Babylon made Suc'coth-be'noth 3
30 the men of Cuth made Nergal, the men of Hamath 3
30 Cuth made Nergal, the men of Hamath made Ashi'ma 3
18:27 and to you, and not to the men sitting on the wall 3
19:18 no gods, but the work of men's hands, wood and stone; 1
20:14 What did these men say? And whence did they come 3
22:15 says the LORD . . 'Tell the man who sent you to me 3
23: 2 the king went . . and with him all the men of Judah 3
14 and filled their places with the bones of men. 1
16 word of the LORD which the man of God proclaimed 3
17 And the men of the city told him, "It is the tomb 3
17 It is the tomb of the man of God who came from Judah 3
18 And he said, "Let him be; let no man move his bones. 3
20 the altars, and burned the bones of men upon them. 1
24:15 wives, his officials, and the chief men of the land *
16 brought captive to Babylon all the men of valor 3
25: 4 the king with all the men of war fled by night 3
19 officer who had been in command of the men of war 3
19 took . . and five men of the king's council 3
19 and 60 men of the people of the land 3
23 when all the captains . . and their men heard 3
24 Gedali'ah swore to them and their men, saying 3
25 Ish'mael . . came with ten men, and attacked 3
1Ch 4:12 These are the men of Recah. 3
22 and the men of Co-ze'ba, and Jo'ash, and Saraph 3
27 their family multiply like the men of Judah. 6
42 some of them, 500 men of the Simeonites 3
5:21 They carried off . . 100,000 men alive. 1
24 mighty warriors, famous men 3
6:31 These are the men whom David put in charge *
7:21 the men of Gath who were born in the land slew 3
40 All of these were men of Asher 6
40 Their number . . for service in war, was 26,000 men. 3
8:40 sons of Ulam were men who were mighty warriors 3
9:13 very able men for . . the service of the house 10
10: 1 men of Israel fled before the Philistines 3
7 when all the men of Israel who were in the valley 3
12 all the valiant men arose 3
11:13 and the men fled from the Philistines. 18
19 Shall I drink the lifeblood of these men? 3
20 he wielded his spear against 300 men and slew them *
22 Benai'ah . . was a valiant man of Kabzeel 3
23 an Egyptian, a man of great stature, five cubits 3
12:15 These are the men who crossed the Jordan *
16 some of the men of Benjamin and Judah 6
19 Some of the men of Manas'seh deserted to David *
20 to Ziklag these men of Manas'seh deserted to him *
22 men kept coming to David to help him *
24 The men of Judah bearing shield and spear were 6
30 men of valor, famous men in their fathers' houses. 3
34 were 37,000 men armed with shield and spear. *
35 Of the Danites 28,600 men equipped for battle. *
37 120,000 men armed with all the weapons of war. *
38 All these, men of war, arrayed in battle order 3
16: 3 distributed to all Israel, both men and women 3
17: 9 violent men shall waste them no more, as formerly 6
18: 5 David slew 22,000 men of the Syrians. 3
19: 5 When David was told concerning the men 3
5 for the men were greatly ashamed. 3
11 the rest of his men he put in the charge of Abi'shai 18
18 David slew of the Syrians the men of 7,000 chariots *
20: 6 at Gath, where there was a man of great stature 3
21: 5 Israel there were 1,100,000 men who drew the sword 3
13 but let me not fall into the hand of man. 1
14 and there fell 70,000 men of Israel. 3
22: 9 son shall be born to you; he shall be a man of peace. 3
23: 3 numbered, and the total was 38,000 men. 11
14 sons of Moses the man of God were named among 3
24: 4 chief men were found among the sons of Elea'zar 11
26: 6 rulers . . for they were men of great ability. 10
7 brethren were able men, Eli'hu and Semachi'ah. 6
8 able men qualified for the service; 62 of O'bed-e'dom 3
9 Meshelemi'ah had sons and brethren, able men 6
12 corresponding to their chief men, had duties 11
30 Hashabi'ah and his brethren, 1,700 men of ability 6
31 men of great ability . . were found at Jazer 10
32 2,700 men of ability, heads of fathers' houses 6
27:32 being a man of understanding and a scribe; 3
29: 1 for the palace will not be for man but for the LORD 1
2Ch 2: 2 Solomon assigned 70,000 men 3
7 now send me a man skilled to work in gold, silver 3
13 Now I have sent a skilled man . . Huram-abi. 3
14 and his father was a man of Tyre. 3
5: 3 all the men of Israel assembled before the king 3
6: 5 I chose no man as prince over my people Israel; 3
16 'There shall never fail you a man before me to sit 3
18 will God dwell indeed with man on the earth? 1
22 If a man sins . . and is made to take an oath 3
29 whatever prayer . . is made by any man or by all 1
30 only, knowest the hearts of the children of men); 1
36 If they sin . . -for there is no man who does not sin- 1
7:18 'There shall not fail you a man to rule Israel.' 3
8:14 for so David the man of God had commanded. 3
11: 2 word of the LORD came to Shemai'ah the man of God 3
4 Return every man to his home 3
13: 3 having an army of valiant men of war 10
3 army of valiant men of war, 400,000 picked men; 3
15 Then the men of Judah raised the battle shout. 3
15 when the men of Judah shouted, God defeated 3
16 The men of Israel fled before Judah 6
17 there fell slain of Israel 500,000 picked men. 3
18 Thus the men of Israel were subdued at that time 6
18 the men of Judah prevailed 6
14: 8 280,000 men from Benjamin,that carried shields *
9 with an army of 1,000,000 men and 300 chariots 6
11 O LORD . . let not man prevail against thee. 4
13 The men of Judah carried away very much booty. *
15:13 put to death, whether young or old, man or woman. 3
17:17 with 200,000 men armed with bow and shield *
18: 5 gathered the prophets together, 400 men 3
7 yet one man by whom we may inquire of the LORD 3
33 a certain man drew his bow at a venture 3
19: 6 you judge not for man but for the LORD; 1
20: 2 Some men came and told Jehosh'aphat *
10 behold, the men of Ammon and Moab and Mount Se'ir 6
13 all the men of Judah stood before the LORD *
22 set an ambush against the men of Ammon, Moab 6
23 For the men of Ammon and Moab rose against 6
27 returned, every man of Judah and Jerusalem 3
23: 8 They each brought his men, who were to go off duty 3
10 every man with his weapon in his hand 3
24:24 the army of the Syrians had come with few men 3
25: 4 but every man shall die for his own sin. 3
7 a man of God came to him and said 3
9 Amazi'ah said to the man of God 3
9 man of God answered, "The LORD is able to give you 3
11 to the Valley of Salt and smote 10,000 men of Se'ir. 6
12 The men of Judah captured another 10,000 alive 6
13 the men of the army whom Amazi'ah sent back 6
14 he brought the gods of the men of Se'ir 6
22 every man fled to his home. 3
26:17 80 priests of the LORD who were men of valor; 6
28: 6 Pekah . . slew 120,000 . . , all of them men of valor 6
8 The men of Israel took captive 200,000 6
12 Certain chiefs also of the men of E'phraim 3
15 the men . . rose and took the captives 3
30:11 Only a few men of Asher, of Manas'seh, 3
16 according to the law of Moses the man of God; 3
31: 1 every man to his possession. 3
19 men in the several cities who were designated 3
32:19 gods . . which are the work of men's hands. 1
34:12 the men did the work faithfully. 3
23 Thus says the LORD . . 'Tell the man who sent you 3
30 king went up . . with all the men of Judah 3
Ezr 1: 4 survivor . . be assisted by the men of his place 3
2: 2 number of the men of the people of Israel 3
22 men of Neto'phah, 56. 3
23 men of An'athoth, 128. 3
27 men of Michmas, 122. 3
28 men of Bethel and Ai, 223. 3
3: 1 people gathered as one man to Jerusalem. 3
2 as it is written in the law of Moses the man of God. 3
4:11 Your servants, the men of the province . . send 20
21 make a decree that these men be made to cease 22
5: 4 names of the men who are building this building? 22
10 write down the names of the men at their head. 22
6: 8 cost is to be paid to these men in full 22
8: 3 Zechari'ah, with whom were registered 150 men. 12
4 son of Zerahi'ah, and with him 200 men. 12
5 son of Jaha'ziel, and with him 300 men. 12
6 Ebed the son of Jonathan, and with him 50 men. 12
7 Jeshai'ah the son of Athali'ah, and with him 70 men. 12
8 Zebadi'ah the son of Michael, and with him 80 men. 12
9 Obadi'ah the son of Jehi'el, and with him 218 men. 12
10 Shelo'mith . . of Josi-phi'ah, and with him 160 men. 12
11 son of Be'bai, and with him 28 men. 12
12 Joha'nan the son of Hak'katan, and with him 110 men 12
13 sons of Adoni'kam . . and with them 60 men. 12
14 Uthai and Zaccur, and with them 70 men. 12
18 brought us a man of discretion, 3
10: 1 very great assembly of men, women, and children 3
9 Then all the men of Judah and Benjamin assembled 3
16 Ezra . . selected men, heads of fathers' houses 3
17 end of all the men who had married foreign women. 3
Neh 1: 2 Hana'ni . . came with certain men out of Judah; 3
11 grant him mercy in the sight of this man. 3
2:12 Then I arose in the night, I and a few men with me; 3
3: 2 next to him the men of Jericho built. 3
7 repaired . . the men of Gibeon and of Mizpah 3
22 priests, the men of the Plain, repaired. 3
4:18 The man who sounded the trumpet was beside me. *
22 Let every man and his servant pass the night 3
23 neither I . . nor my servants nor the men of the guard 3
5:13 So may God shake out every man from his house 3
17 there were at my table 150 men, Jews and officials 3
6:11 I said, "Should such a man as I flee? 3
11 man such as I could go into the temple and live? *
7: 2 more faithful and God-fearing man than many. 3
7 number of the men of the people of Israel 3
26 men of Bethlehem and Neto'phah, 188. 3
27 men of An'athoth, 128. 3
28 men of Beth-az'maveth, 42. 3
29 men of Kir'iath-je'arim, Chephi'rah 3
30 men of Ramah and Geba, 621. 3
31 men of Michmas, 122. 3
32 men of Bethel and Ai, 123. 3
33 men of the other Nebo, 52. 3
8: 1 people gathered as one man into the square 3
2 assembly, both men and women and all who could 3
3 read . . in the presence of the men and the women 3
9:29 by the observance of which a man shall live 1
11: 2 blessed all the men who willingly offered 3
6 All the sons of Perez . . were 468 valiant men. 3
12:24 commandment of David the man of God 3
36 musical instruments of David the man of God; 3
44 that day men were appointed over the chambers 3
13:15 saw . . men treading wine presses on the sabbath *
Est 1:14 the men next to him being Carshe'na, Shethar *
22 that every man be lord in his own house 3
2:23 the men were both hanged on the gallows. *
4:11 if any man or woman goes . . there is but one law; 3
6: 6 What shall be done to the man whom the king 3
7 For the man whom the king delights to honor 3
9 array the man whom the king delights to honor 3
9 and let him conduct the man on horseback *
9 done to the man whom the king delights to honor.' 3
11 done to the man whom the king delights to honor. 3
9: 4 the man Mor'decai grew more and more powerful. 3

6 the Jews slew and destroyed 500 men 3
12 In Susa . . the Jews have slain 500 men 3
15 and they slew 300 men in Susa; 3
Job 1: 1 was a man in the land of Uz, whose name was Job 3
1 was Job; and that man was blameless and upright 3
3 this man was the greatest of all the people 3
8 a blameless and upright man, who fears God 3
2: 3 a blameless and upright man, who fears God 3
4 All that a man has he will give for his life. 3
3:23 Why is light given to a man whose way is hid 11
4:13 of the night, when deep sleep falls on men 3
17 Can mortal man be righteous before God? 4
17 Can a man be pure before his Maker? 11
5: 7 man is born to trouble as the sparks fly upward. 1
17 Behold, happy is the man whom God reproves; 4
6:26 when the speech of a despairing man is wind? •
7: 1 Has not man a hard service upon earth 4
17 What is man, that thou dost make so much of him 4
20 If I sin, what do I do to thee, thou watcher of men? 1
9: 2 it is so: but how can a man be just before God? 4
32 For he is not a man, as I am, that I might answer him 3
10: 4 Hast thou eyes of flesh? Dost thou see as man sees? 4
5 Are thy days as the days of man, or thy years 4
5 thy days as the days of man, or thy years as man's 11
11: 2 a man full of talk be vindicated? 3
3 Should your babble silence men, and when you mock 13
11 For he knows worthless men; when he sees iniquity 13
12 a stupid man will get understanding 3
12 when a wild ass's colt is born a man. 1
12:14 if he shuts a man in, none can open. 3
13: 9 Or can you deceive him, as one deceives a man? 4
28 Man wastes away like a rotten thing •
14: 1 Man that is born of a woman is of few days 1
10 But man dies, and is laid low; man breathes his last 11
10 man breathes his last, and where is he? 1
12 man lies down and rises not again; 3
14 If a man die, shall he live again? 11
19 so thou destroyest the hope of man. 4
15: 7 Are you the first man that was born? 1
14 What is man, that he can be clean? 4
16 corrupt, a man who drinks iniquity like water! 3
28 in houses which no man should inhabit •
16:10 Men have gaped at me with their mouth •
21 he would maintain the right of a man with God 11
21 like that of a man with his neighbor. 7
17: 6 I am one before whom men spit. •
20: 4 from of old, since man was placed upon earth 1
29 This is the wicked man's portion from God 1
21: 4 As for me, is my complaint against man? 1
33 all men follow after him, and those who go before 1
22: 2 Can a man be profitable to God? 11
8 The man with power possessed the land 3
15 you keep to the old way which wicked men have trod? 13
24: 2 Men remove landmarks; they seize flocks •
25: 4 How then can man be righteous before God? 4
6 how much less man, who is a maggot 4
6 and the son of man, who is a worm! 1
27:13 This is the portion of a wicked man with God 1
28: 3 Men put an end to darkness •
4 open shafts in a valley away from where men live; •
4 they hang afar from men, they swing to and fro. 4
9 Man puts his hand to the flinty rock •
13 Man does not know the way to it 4
28 he said to man, 'Behold, the fear of the Lord 1
29:21 Men listened to me, and waited, and kept silence •
30: 1 they make sport of me, men who are younger than I •
2 could I gain from . . men whose vigor is gone? •
5 They are driven out from among men; •
31:31 if the men of my tent have not said, 13
33 if I have concealed my transgressions from men 1
32: 1 these three men ceased to answer Job 3
5 was no answer in the mouth of these three men 3
8 the spirit in a man, the breath of the Almighty 4
13 have found wisdom; God may vanquish him, not man. 3
21 or use flattery toward any man. 1
33:12 I will answer you. God is greater than man. 4
14 though man does not perceive it. •
15 the night, when deep sleep falls upon men 3
16 then he opens the ears of men, and terrifies them 3
17 that he may turn man aside from his deed 1
17 man aside from his deed, and cut off pride from man; 11
19 Man is also chastened with pain upon his bed •
23 to declare to man what is right for him; 1
26 then man prays to God, and he accepts him •
26 He recounts to men his salvation 4
27 he sings before men, and says: 'I sinned 3
29 all these things, twice, three times, with a man 11
34: 7 What man is like Job, who drinks up scoffing 11
8 with evildoers and walks with wicked men? 3
9 For he has said, 'It profits a man nothing 11
10 Therefore, hear me, you men of understanding 3
11 according to the work of a man he will requite him 1
15 man would return to dust. 1
21 For his eyes are upon the ways of a man 3
23 For he has not appointed a time for any man to go 3
26 for their wickedness in the sight of men •
29 who can behold him, whether it be a nation or a man? 1
30 that a godless man should not reign 1
34 Men of understanding will say to me 3
34 the wise man who hears me will say 11
36 because he answers like wicked men. 3
35: 8 Your wickedness concerns a man like yourself 3
8 and your righteousness a son of man. 1
36:24 to extol his work, of which men have sung. 3
25 men have looked on it; man beholds it from afar. 1
25 men have looked on it; man beholds it from afar. 4
28 skies pour down, and drop upon man abundantly. 1
37: 7 He seals up the hand of every man 1
7 every man, that all men may know his work. 3
20 Did a man ever wish that he would be swallowed up? 3
21 now men cannot look on the light when it is bright •
24 men fear him; he does not regard any who are wise 3
38: 3 Gird up your loins like a man, I will question you 11
26 to bring rain on a land where no man is 3
26 on the desert in which there is no man; 1
40: 7 Gird up your loins like a man; I will question you 11
41: 9 Behold, the hope of a man is disappointed; •
Ps 1: 1 Blessed is the man who walks not in the counsel 3
4: 2 O men, how long shall my honor suffer shame? 8
5: 6 LORD abhors bloodthirsty and deceitful men. 3
8: 4 what is man that thou art mindful of him 4
4 and the son of man that thou dost care for him? 1
9:19 Arise, O LORD! Let not man prevail; 4
20 O LORD! Let the nations know that they are but men! 4
10:18 so that man who is of the earth may strike terror 4
11: 4 behold, his eyelids test, the children of men. 1
12: 1 have vanished from among the sons of men. 1
8 as vileness is exalted among the sons of men. 1
14: 2 looks down from heaven upon the children of men 1
17: 4 With regard to the works of men, by the word 1
14 from men by thy hand, O LORD . . whose portion 13
14 from men whose portion in life is of the world. 13
18:25 with the blameless man thou dost show thyself 11
48 thou didst deliver me from men of violence. 3
21:10 their children from among the sons of men. 1
22: 6 I am a worm, and no man; scorned by men, 3
6 scorned by men, and despised by the people. 1
25:12 Who is the man that fears the LORD? 3
26: 4 I do not sit with false men 13
9 with sinners, nor my life with bloodthirsty men 3
31:19 take refuge in thee, in the sight of the sons of men! 1
20 thou hidest them from the plots of men; 3
32: 2 the man to whom the LORD imputes no iniquity 1
33:13 looks down from heaven, he sees all the sons of men; 1
34: 8 Happy is the man who takes refuge in him! 11
12 What man is there who desires life 3
36: 6 man and beast thou savest, O LORD. 1
7 men take refuge in the shadow of thy wings. 1
37: 7 over the man who carries out evil devices! 3
23 The steps of a man are from the LORD 11
37 there is posterity for the man of peace. 3
38:14 Yea, I am like a man who does not hear 3
39: 5 Surely every man stands as a mere breath! Selah 1
6 Surely man goes about as a shadow! 3
11 When thou dost chasten man with rebukes for sin 3
11 surely every man is a mere breath! Selah 1
40: 4 Blessed is the man who makes the LORD his trust 11
43: 1 from deceitful and unjust men deliver me! 3
45: 2 You are the fairest of the sons of men; 1
49: 7 Truly no man can ransom himself 3
12 Man cannot abide in his pomp, he is like the beasts 1
20 Man cannot abide in his pomp, he is like the beasts 1
52: 7 See the man who would not make God his refuge 11
53: 2 God looks down from heaven upon the sons of men 1
55:23 men of blood and treachery shall not live 3
56: 1 Be gracious to me, O God, for men trample upon me; 4
11 in God I trust without fear. What can man do to me? 1
57: 4 of lions that greedily devour the sons of men; 1
58: 1 you gods? Do you judge the sons of men uprightly? 1
11 Men will say, "Surely there is a reward 1
59: 2 save me from bloodthirsty men. 3
60:11 help against the foe, for vain is the help of man! 1
62: 3 How long will you set upon a man to shatter him 3
12 For thou dost requite a man according to his work. 3
64: 6 For the inward mind and heart of a man are deep! 3
9 Then all men will fear; 1
66: 5 he is terrible in his deeds among men. 7
12 thou didst let men ride over our heads; 4
68:18 receiving gifts among men 1
73: 5 They are not in trouble as other men are; 4
5 they are not stricken like other men. 1
76: 5 all the men of war were unable to use their hands. 3
10 Surely the wrath of men shall praise thee; 1
78:25 Man ate of the bread of the angels; 3
60 at Shiloh, the tent where he dwelt among men 1
80:17 But let thy hand be upon the man of thy right hand 3
17 son of man whom thou hast made strong for thyself! 1
82: 7 nevertheless, you shall die like men 1
84: 5 Blessed are the men whose strength is in thee 1
12 O LORD of hosts, blessed is the man who trusts 1
88: 4 I am a man who has no strength 11
89:47 what vanity thou hast created all the sons of men! 1
48 What man can live and never see death? 11
90: 0 A Prayer of Moses, the man of God. 3
3 Thou turnest man back to the dust, and sayest 4
3 Thou . . sayest, "Turn back, O children of men! 1
5 Thou dost sweep men away; •
92: 6 The dull man cannot know 3
94:10 He who teaches men knowledge 1
11 the LORD, knows the thoughts of man 1
12 Blessed is the man whom thou dost chasten, O LORD 11
101: 5 man of haughty looks and arrogant heart •
102:21 that men may declare in Zion the name of the LORD •
103:15 As for man, his days are like grass; 4
104:14 plants for man to cultivate 1
15 wine to gladden the heart of man 4
15 bread to strengthen man's heart. 4
23 Man goes forth to his work and to his labor 1
105:17 he had sent a man ahead of them, Joseph 3
106:16 men in the camp were jealous of Moses and Aaron •
107: 8 for his wonderful works to the sons of men! 1
15 for his wonderful works to the sons of men! 1
21 for his wonderful works to the sons of men! 1
31 for his wonderful works to the sons of men! 1
43 let men consider the steadfast love of the LORD. •
108:12 grant us help . . for vain is the help of man! 1
112: 1 Blessed is the man who fears the LORD 3
5 well with the man who deals generously and lends 3
115: 4 idols are silver and gold, the work of men's hands. 1
16 but the earth he has given to the sons of men. 1
116:11 I said . . "Men are all a vain hope. 1
118: 6 the LORD . . I do not fear. What can man do to me? 1
8 It is better to . . than to put confidence in man. 1
119:85 men who do not conform to thy law. •
134 Redeem me from man's oppression 1
136 streams of tears, because men do not keep thy law. •
124: 2 when men rose up against us 1
127: 5 Happy is the man who has his quiver full of them! 11
128: 4 thus shall the man be blessed who fears the LORD. 11
135: 8 smote the first-born . . both of man and of beast; 1
15 idols . . silver and gold, the work of men's hands. 1
139:19 O that . . men of blood would depart from me 3
140: 1 Deliver me, O LORD, from evil men; 1
1 preserve me from violent men 3
4 preserve me from violent men, who have planned 3
11 let evil hunt down the violent man speedily! 3
141: 4 wicked . . in company with men who work iniquity; 3
144: 3 O LORD, what is man that thou dost regard him 1
3 LORD, what is . . son of man that thou dost think 4
4 Man is like a breath, his days . . passing shadow. 1
145:12 to make known to the sons of men thy mighty deeds 1
146: 3 Put not your trust in princes, in a son of man 1
147:10 nor his pleasure in the legs of a man; 3
Prv 1: 2 That men may know wisdom and instruction •
18 these men lie in wait for their own blood •
2:12 delivering you from . . men of perverted speech 3
15 men whose paths are crooked •
3: 4 favor and good repute in the sight of God and man. 1
13 Happy is the man who finds wisdom 1
13 Happy is . . the man who gets understanding 1
30 Do not contend with a man for no reason 1
31 Do not envy a man of violence 3
5:21 For a man's ways are before the eyes of the LORD 3
6:11 want like an armed man. 3
12 A worthless person, a wicked man 3
19 a man who sows discord among brothers. •
26 but an adulteress stalks a man's very life. 3
27 Can a man carry fire in his bosom 3
30 Do not men despise a thief if he steals to satisfy •
34 For jealousy makes a man furious 11
8: 4 To you, O men, I call, and my cry is to the sons of men. 3
4 To you, O men, I call, and my cry is to the sons of men. 1
31 delighting in the sons of men. 1
34 Happy is the man who listens to me 1
10:23 wise . . is pleasure to a man of understanding. 3
11:12 but a man of understanding remains silent. 3
17 A man who is kind benefits himself 3
20 Men of perverse mind are an abomination •
24 One man gives freely, yet grows all the richer; •
12: 2 but a man of evil devices he condemns. 3
3 A man is not established by wickedness 1
6 but the mouth of the upright delivers men. •
8 A man is commended according to his good sense 3
9 Better is a man of humble standing who works •
14 fruit of his words a man is satisfied with good 3
14 and the work of a man's hand comes back to him. 1
23 A prudent man conceals his knowledge 1
25 Anxiety in a man's heart weighs him down 3
27 but the diligent man will get precious wealth. 1
13: 2 From the fruit of his mouth a good man eats good 3
7 One man pretends to be rich, yet has nothing; •
8 The ransom of a man's life is his wealth 3
17 A bad messenger plunges men into trouble •
14:12 There is a way which seems right to a man 3
14 good man with the fruit of his deeds. 3
17 A man of quick temper acts foolishly •
17 but a man of discretion is patient. 3
15:11 how much more the hearts of men! 7
18 A hot-tempered man stirs up strife 3
20 but a foolish man despises his mother. 1
21 but a man of understanding walks aright. 3
23 To make an apt answer is a joy to a man 3
16: 1 The plans of the mind belong to man 1
2 All the ways of a man are pure in his own eyes 3
6 by the fear of the LORD a man avoids evil. •
7 When a man's ways please the LORD 3
9 A man's mind plans his way 1

14 wise man will appease it. 3
25 There is a way which seems right to a man 3
27 A worthless man plots evil 3
28 A perverse man spreads strife 3
29 A man of violence entices his neighbor 3
17:12 Let a man meet a she-bear robbed of her cubs 3
13 If a man returns evil for good *
18 A man without sense gives a pledge, and becomes 1
20 A man of crooked mind does not prosper *
27 who has a cool spirit is a man of understanding. 3
18: 4 The words of a man's mouth are deep waters; 3
12 Before destruction a man's heart is haughty 3
14 A man's spirit will endure sickness; 3
16 A man's gift makes room for him and brings him 1
20 From the fruit of his mouth a man is satisfied; 5
19: 1 than a man who is perverse in speech, and is a fool. *
2 It is not good for a man to be without knowledge 15
3 When a man's folly brings his way to ruin 1
6 every one is a friend to a man who gives gifts. 3
11 Good sense makes a man slow to anger 1
19 A man of great wrath will pay the penalty; *
21 Many are the plans in the mind of a man 3
22 What is desired in a man is loyalty 1
20: 3 It is an honor for a man to keep aloof from strife; 3
5 The purpose in a man's mind is like deep water 3
5 but a man of understanding will draw it out. 3
6 Many a man proclaims his own loyalty 1
6 but a faithful man who can find? 3
16 Take a man's garment when he has given surety *
17 Bread gained by deceit is sweet to a man 3
24 A man's steps are ordered by the LORD; 11
24 how then can man understand his way? 1
25 It is a snare for a man to say rashly, "It is holy 1
27 The spirit of man is the lamp of the LORD 1
21: 2 Every way of a man is right in his own eyes 3
16 A man who wanders from the way of understanding 1
17 He who loves pleasure will be a poor man; 3
20 but a foolish man devours it. 1
28 but the word of a man who hears will endure. 3
22:24 Make no friendship with a man given to anger 9
24 nor go with a wrathful man 3
29 Do you see a man skilful in his work? 3
23: 2 put a knife . . if you are a man given to appetite. 9
6 Do not eat the bread of a man who is stingy; *
21 drowsiness will clothe a man with rags. *
28 increases the faithless among men. 1
24: 1 not envious of evil men, nor desire to be with them; 3
5 A wise man is mightier than a strong man 11
5 man of knowledge than he who has strength; 3
9 scoffer is an abomination to men. 1
12 will he not requite man according to his work? 1
29 not say, "I . . pay the man back for what he has done. 3
30 I passed by . . the vineyard of a man without sense; 1
34 want like an armed man. 3
25: 1 proverbs of Solomon which the men of Hezeki'ah 3
14 man who boasts of a gift he does not give. 3
18 man who bears false witness against 3
28 A man without self-control is like a city broken 3
26:12 Do you see a man who is wise in his own eyes? 3
19 man who deceives his neighbor and says, "I am only 3
21 so is a quarrelsome man for kindling strife. 3
27: 8 from its nest, is a man who strays from his home. 3
13 Take a man's garment when he has given surety *
17 sharpens iron, and one man sharpens another. 3
19 so the mind of man reflects the man. 1
19 so the mind of man reflects the man. 1
20 never satisfied are the eyes of man. 1
21 man is judged by his praise. 3
28: 2 but with men of understanding and knowledge 1
3 A poor man who oppresses the poor is a . . rain 11
5 Evil men do not understand justice 3
11 A rich man is wise in his own eyes, but a poor man 3
12 but when the wicked rise, men hide themselves. 1
14 Blessed is the man who fears the LORD always; 1
17 If a man is burdened with the blood of another 1
20 A faithful man will abound with blessings 3
21 but for a piece of bread a man will do wrong. 11
22 A miserly man hastens after wealth 3
23 who rebukes a man will afterward find more favor 1
24 companion of a man who destroys. 3
28 When the wicked rise, men hide themselves 1
29: 5 A man who flatters his neighbor spreads a net 11
6 An evil man is ensnared in his transgression 3
9 If a wise man has an argument with a fool, the fool 3
10 Bloodthirsty men hate one who is blameless 3
20 Do you see a man who is hasty in his words? 3
22 A man of wrath stirs up strife 3
22 man given to anger causes much transgression. 9
23 A man's pride will bring him low 1
25 The fear of man lays a snare 1
26 but from the LORD a man gets justice. 3
27 An unjust man is an abomination to the righteous 3
30: 1 The man says to Ith'i-el, to Ith'i-el and Ucal 11
2 Surely I am too stupid to be a man. 3
2 I have not the understanding of a man. 1
14 to devour the . . needy from among men. 1
19 way of a man with a maiden. 11
Ecc 1: 3 What does man gain by all the toil 1
8 All . . are full of weariness; a man cannot utter it; 3
13 God has given to the sons of men to be busy with. 1
2: 3 I might see what was good for the sons of men to do 1
8 I got . . and many concubines, man's delight. 7
12 for what can the man do who comes after the king? 1
18 I must leave it to the man who will come after me; 1
21 a man who has toiled with wisdom and knowledge 1
21 leave all to be enjoyed by a man who did not toil 1
22 What has a man from all the toil and strain 1
24 There is nothing better for a man than that he 1
26 For to the man who pleases him God gives wisdom 1
3:10 the business that God has given to the sons of men 1
11 also he has put eternity into man's mind *
13 it is God's gift to man that every one should eat *
14 God . . in order that men should fear before him. *
18 I said . . with regard to the sons of men that God is 1
19 the fate of the sons of men and the fate of beasts 1
19 and man has no advantage over the beasts; 1
21 Who knows whether the spirit of man goes upward 7
22 nothing better than that a man . . enjoy his work 1
4: 4 come from a man's envy of his neighbor. 3
12 a man might prevail against one who is alone *
6: 1 There is an evil . . and it lies heavy upon men 1
2 a man to whom God gives wealth, possessions 3
3 If a man begets 100 children . . but he does 3
7 All the toil of man is for his mouth 1
10 it is known what man is, and that he is not able 1
11 the more vanity, and what is man the better? 1
12 good for man while he lives the few days of his 1
12 For who can tell man what will be after him 1
7: 2 this is the end of all men 1
5 better for a man to hear the rebuke of the wise 3
14 God has . . so that man may not find out anything 1
20 Surely there is not a righteous man on earth 1
21 Do not give heed to all the things that men say *
28 One man among 1,000 I found 1
29 God made man upright, but they have sought out 1
8: 1 A man's wisdom makes his face shine 1
6 although man's trouble lies heavy upon him. 1
8 No man has power to retain the spirit 1
9 while man lords it over man to his hurt. 1
9 while man lords it over man to his hurt. 1
11 the heart of the sons of men is fully set to do evil. 1
15 man has no good thing under the sun but to eat 1
17 man cannot find out the work that is done 1
17 However much man may toil . . he will not find it 1
9: 1 whether it is love or hate man does not know. 1
3 also the hearts of men are full of evil 7
12 For man does not know his time. 1
12 the sons of men are snared at an evil time 1
14 There was a little city with few men in it; 3
15 But there was found in it a poor wise man 3
15 Yet no one remembered that poor man. 3
10:14 no man knows what is to be, and who can tell him 1
11: 8 if a man lives many years, let him rejoice in them 1
12: 3 keepers . . tremble, and the strong men are bent 3
5 because man goes to his eternal home 1
13 Fear God . . for this is the whole duty of man. 1
Sng 8: 7 a man offered for love all the wealth of his house 3
Isa 2: 9 So man is humbled, and men are brought low– 1
9 So man is humbled, and men are brought low– 3
11 The haughty looks of man shall be brought low 1
11 brought low, and the pride of men shall be humbled; 3
17 the haughtiness of man shall be humbled 1
17 humbled, and the pride of men shall be brought low; 3
20 men will cast forth their idols of silver 1
22 Turn away from man in whose nostrils is breath 1
3: 6 When a man takes hold of his brother in the house 3
25 Your men shall fall by the sword . . in battle. 13
4: 1 seven women shall take hold of one man in that day 3
5: 3 inhabitants of Jerusalem and men of Judah, judge 3
7 the men of Judah are his pleasant planting; 3
13 their honored men are dying of hunger 13
15 Man is bowed down, and men are brought low 3
15 Man is bowed down, and men are brought low 3
22 valiant men in mixing strong drink 3
6: 5 Woe . . For I am lost; for I am a man of unclean lips 3
11 cities . . and houses without men 1
12 the LORD removes men far away 1
7:13 for you to weary men, that you weary my God also? 3
21 In that day a man will keep alive a young cow 3
24 With bow and arrows men will come there *
9:19 like fuel for the fire; no man spares his brother. 3
13: 7 hands . . be feeble, and every man's heart will melt 4
12 I will make men more rare than fine gold 4
14 every man will turn to his own people 3
14 and every man will flee to his own land. 3
14:16 Is this the man who made the earth tremble 3
17: 7 In that day men will regard their Maker 1
19: 2 they will fight, every man against his brother 3
2 and every man against his neighbor 3
24: 6 inhabitants . . scorched, and few men are left. 4
29:13 fear of me is a commandment of men learned by rote; 3
19 men shall exult in the Holy One of Israel. 1
21 who by a word make a man out to be an offender 1
31: 3 The Egyptians are men, and not God; 1
8 the Assyrian shall fall by a sword, not of man; 3
8 and a sword, not of man, shall devour him; 1
33: 8 are despised, there is no regard for man. 4
36: 6 will pierce the hand of any man who leans on it. 3
12 to you, and not to the men sitting on the wall 3
37:19 they were no gods, but the work of men's hands 1
38:11 I shall look upon man no more 1
39: 3 and said to him, "What did these men say? 3
41:14 Fear not, you worm Jacob, you men of Israel! 13
42:13 like a man of war he stirs up his fury; 3
43: 4 Because . . I love you, I give men in return for you 1
44:11 and the craftsmen are but men; 1
13 he shapes it into the figure of a man 3
13 the figure of a man, with the beauty of a man 1
15 Then it becomes fuel for a man; 1
45:12 I made the earth, and created man upon it; 1
14 the Sabe'ans, men of stature, shall come over to you 3
46:11 the man of my counsel from a far country. 3
47: 3 I will take vengeance, and I will spare no man. 1
50: 2 Why, when I came, was there no man? 3
51: 7 fear not the reproach of men, and be not dismayed 4
12 who are you that you are afraid of man who dies 4
12 who dies, of the son of man who is made like grass 1
52:14 and his form beyond that of the sons of men– 1
53: 3 He was despised and rejected by men; 3
3 a man of sorrows, and acquainted with grief; 3
55: 7 his way, and the unrighteous man his thoughts; 3
56: 2 Blessed is the man who does this 4
2 and the son of man who holds it fast 1
57: 1 devout men are taken away . . no one understands. 3
58: 5 the fast that I choose, a day for a man to humble 1
59:16 He saw that there was no man 3
66: 3 He who slaughters an ox is like him who kills a man; 3
24 go forth and look on the dead bodies of the men 3
Jer 2: 6 that none passes through, where no man dwells?' 3
16 the men of Memphis . . have broken the crown 6
3: 1 If a man divorces his wife and she goes from him 3
1 she goes from him and becomes another man's wife 3
4: 3 For thus says the LORD to the men of Judah 3
4 remove the foreskin of your hearts, O men of Judah 3
25 I looked, and lo, there was no man 1
29 cities are forsaken, and no man dwells in them. 3
5: 1 Search her squares to see if you can find a man 3
26 lying in wait. They set a trap; they catch men. 3
6:23 upon horses, set in array as a man for battle 3
7: 2 all you men of Judah who enter these gates *
20 on this place, upon man and beast 1
8: 4 says the LORD: When men fall, do they not rise again? *
6 no man repents of his wickedness 3
9:12 Who is the man so wise that he can understand this? 3
22 The dead bodies of men shall fall like dung 1
10: 4 Men deck it with silver and gold; *
14 Every man is stupid and without knowledge; 1
23 I know, O LORD, that the way of man is not in himself 1
23 it is not in man who walks to direct his steps. 3
11: 2 and speak to the men of Judah 3
3 Cursed be the man who does not heed the words 3
9 There is revolt among the men of Judah 3
21 says the LORD concerning the men of An'athoth 3
23 For I will bring evil upon the men of An'athoth 3
12: 4 because men said, "He will not see our latter end. *
5 If you have raced with men on foot *
11 land is made desolate, but no man lays it to heart. 3
13:11 For as the waistcloth clings to the loins of a man 3
14: 9 Why shouldst thou be like a man confused 3
15:10 Woe . . my mother, that you bore me, a man of strife 3
16:20 Can man make for himself gods? Such are no gods! 1
17: 5 says the LORD: "Cursed is the man who trusts in man 11
5 says the LORD: "Cursed is the man who trusts in man 1
7 Blessed is the man who trusts in the LORD 11
10 to give to every man according to his ways 3
25 men of Judah and the inhabitants of Jerusalem; 3
18:11 Now, therefore, say to the men of Judah 3
21 May their men meet death by pestilence 3
19:10 in the sight of the men who go with you 3
11 Men shall bury in Topheth *
20:15 Cursed be the man who brought the news 3
16 Let that man be like the cities 3
21: 6 the inhabitants of this city, both man and beast; 1
22: 8 and every man will say to his neighbor 3
28 Is this man Coni'ah a despised, broken pot 3
30 says the LORD: "Write this man down as childless 3
30 childless, a man who shall not succeed in his days; 11
23: 7 when men shall no longer say, 'As the LORD lives *
9 I am like a drunken man . . a man overcome by wine 3
9 I am like a drunken man . . a man overcome by wine 11
24 Can a man hide himself in secret places 3
34 I will punish that man and his household. 3
26:11 This man deserves the sentence of death 3
16 This man does not deserve the sentence of death 3
20 There was another man who prophesied 3
22 Then King Jehoi'akim sent to Egypt certain men 3
27: 5 with the men and animals that are on the earth 1
30: 6 Ask now, and see, can a man bear a child? 12
6 then do I see every man with his hands on his loins 11
31:22 a new thing on the earth: a woman protects a man. 11
27 with the seed of man and the seed of beast. 1
30 each man who eats sour grapes 1
32:19 whose eyes are open to all the ways of men 7
32 priests and their prophets, the men of Judah 3
43 It is a desolation, without man or beast; 1
33: 5 and to fill them with the dead bodies of men 1
10 which you say, 'It is a waste without man or beast 1

10 desolate, without man or inhabitant or beast 1
12 In this place which is waste, without man or beast 1
17 David shall never lack a man to sit on the throne 3
18 and the Levitical priests shall never lack a man 3
34: 5 so men shall burn spices for you and lament •
18 the men who transgressed my covenant 3
35: 4 sons of Hanan the son of Igdali'ah, the man of God 3
13 Go and say to the men of Judah 3
19 shall never lack a man to stand before me. 3
36: 6 shall read them also in the hearing of all the men •
29 and will cut off from it man and beast? 1
31 and upon the men of Judah, all the evil 3
38: 4 Let this man be put to death 3
4 this man is not seeking . . welfare of this people 3
9 My lord the king, these men have done evil 3
10 Take three men with you from here 3
11 E'bed-mel'ech took the men with him and went 3
16 or deliver you into the hand of these men 3
39:17 and you shall not be given into the hand of the men 3
40: 7 men heard that the king of Babylon had appointed 3
7 and had committed to him men, women, and children 3
8 went to Gedali'ah at Mizpah- . . they and their men. 3
9 Gedali'ah . . swore to them and their men, saying 3
41: 1 the chief officers of the king, came with ten men 3
2 Ish'mael the son of Nethani'ah and the ten men 3
5 80 men arrived from Shechem and Shiloh 3
7 Ish'mael the son of Nethani'ah and the men with him 3
8 there were ten men among them who said to Ish'mael 3
9 cast all the bodies of the men whom he had slain 3
12 they took all their men and went to fight 3
15 Ish'mael . . escaped from Joha'nan with eight men 3
42:17 All the men who set their faces to go to Egypt 3
43: 2 and all the insolent men said to Jeremiah 3
6 the men, the women, the children, the princesses 11
9 in the sight of the men of Judah 3
44: 7 to cut off from you man and woman, infant and child 3
15 all the men who knew that their wives had offered 3
20 Jeremiah said to all the people, men and women 11
26 no more be invoked by the mouth of any man of Judah 3
27 all the men of Judah who are in the land of Egypt 3
46: 9 Let the warriors go forth: men of Ethiopia and Put •
47: 2 Men shall cry out 1
48:14 do you say, 'We are heroes and mighty men of war'? 3
31 for all Moab; for the men of Kir-he'res I mourn. 3
36 moans like a flute for the men of Kir-he'res; 3
49:15 you small among the nations, despised among men. 1
18 no man shall dwell there, no man shall sojourn 3
18 no man shall sojourn in her. 1
29 men shall cry to them: 'Terror on every side!' •
33 no man shall dwell there, no man shall sojourn 3
33 no man shall sojourn in her. 7
50: 3 both man and beast shall flee away. 1
40 says the LORD, so no man shall dwell there 3
40 and no son of man shall sojourn in her. 1
42 arrayed as a man for battle against you 3
51: 6 the midst of Babylon, let every man save his life! 3
14 Surely I will fill you with men, as many as locusts 1
17 Every man is stupid and without knowledge; 1
22 with you I break in pieces man and woman; 3
43 and through which no son of man passes. 1
45 Let every man save his life from the fierce anger 3
62 nothing shall dwell in it, neither man nor beast 1
52: 7 the men of war fled and went out from the city 3
25 officer who had been in command of the men of war 3
25 the men of war, and seven men of the king's council 3
25 60 men of the people of the land, who were found 3
Lam 3: 1 I am the man who has seen affliction under the rod 11
27 It is good for a man that he bear the yoke 11
33 he does not . . afflict or grieve the sons of men. 3
35 to turn aside the right of a man 11
36 to subvert a man in his cause 1
39 Why should a living man complain 1
39 a living man complain, a man, about the punishment 11
4:15 Away! Unclean!" men cried at them; •
15 men said among the nations, "They shall stay •
18 Men dogged our steps so that we could not walk •
Ezk 1: 5 their appearance: they had the form of men 1
10 each had the face of a man in front; 1
2: 1 And he said to me, "Son of man, stand upon your feet 1
3 Son of man, I send you to the people of Israel 1
6 And you, son of man, be not afraid of them 1
8 But you, son of man, hear what I say to you; 1
3: 1 he said to me, "Son of man, eat what is offered to you; 1
3 Son of man, eat this scroll that I give you 1
4 Son of man, go, get you to the house of Israel 1
10 Son of man, all my words that I shall speak to you 1
17 Son of man, I have made you a watchman 1
25 O son of man, behold, cords will be placed upon you 1
4: 1 you, O son of man, take a brick and lay it before you 1
16 Son of man, behold, I will break the staff of bread 1
5: 1 And you, O son of man, take a sharp sword; 1
6: 2 Son of man, set your face toward the mountains 1
7: 2 And you, O son of man, thus says the Lord GOD 1
8: 2 lo, a form that had the appearance of a man; 26
5 Then he said to me, "Son of man, lift up your eyes now 1
6 Son of man, do you see what they are doing 1
8 Then said he to me, "Son of man, dig in the wall"; 1
11 And before them stood 70 men of the elders 3
12 Then he said to me, "Son of man, have you seen 1
12 in the dark, every man in his room of pictures? 3
15 he said to me, "Have you seen this, O son of man? 1
16 behold, at the door . . were about 25 men 3
17 he said to me, "Have you seen this, O son of man? 1
9: 2 six men came from the direction of the upper gate 3
2 with them was a man clothed in linen 3
3 he called to the man clothed in linen 3
4 and put a mark upon the foreheads of the men 3
11 lo, the man clothed in linen, with the writing case 3
10: 2 And he said to the man clothed in linen 3
3 the south side of the house, when the man went in; 3
6 And when he commanded the man clothed in linen 3
7 put it into the hands of the man clothed in linen •
14 and the second face was the face of a man 1
11: 1 at the door of the gateway there were 25 men; 3
2 And he said to me, "Son of man, these are the men 1
2 And he said to me, "Son of man, these are the men 3
4 prophesy against them, prophesy, O son of man. 1
15 Son of man, your brethren, even your brethren 1
12: 2 Son of man, you dwell in the midst of a rebellious 1
3 son of man, prepare for yourself an exile's 1
4 in their sight, as men do who must go into exile. •
9 Son of man, has not the house of Israel 1
18 Son of man, eat your bread with quaking 1
22 Son of man, what is this proverb that you have 1
27 Son of man, behold, they of the house of Israel say 1
13: 2 Son of man, prophesy against the prophets 1
17 son of man, set your face against the daughters 1
14: 3 Son of man, these men have taken their idols 1
3 men have taken their idols into their hearts 3
4 Any man of the house of Israel 3
8 I will set my face against that man 3
13 Son of man, when a land sins against me by acting 1
13 famine upon it, and cut off from it man and beast 1
14 even if these three men, Noah, Daniel, and Job 3
15 no man may pass through because of the beasts; •
16 even if these three men were in it 3
17 and I cut off from it man and beast; 1
18 though these three men were in it, as I live 3
19 with blood, to cut off from it man and beast; 1
21 and pestilence, to cut off from it man and beast! 1
15: 2 Son of man, how does the wood of the vine surpass 1
3 Do men take a peg from it to hang any vessel on? •
16: 2 Son of man, make known to Jerusalem her 1
17 and made for yourself images of men 12
33 Men give gifts to all harlots; •
17: 2 Son of man, propound a riddle 1
15 Can a man escape who does such things? •
18: 5 If a man is righteous and does what is lawful 3
8 executes true justice between man and man 3
8 executes true justice between man and man 3
14 if this man begets a son who sees all the sins •
24 man turns away from his righteousness •
26 man turns away from his righteousness •
19: 3 he learned to catch prey; he devoured men. 1
6 he learned to catch prey; he devoured men. 1
20: 3 Son of man, speak to the elders of Israel 1
4 Will you judge them, son of man, will you judge them? 1
8 they did not every man cast away the detestable 3
11 ordinances, by whose observance man shall live. 1
13 ordinances, by whose observance man shall live; 1
21 ordinances, by whose observance man shall live; 1
27 Therefore, son of man, speak to the house of Israel 1
46 Son of man, set your face toward the south 1
21: 2 Son of man, set your face toward Jerusalem 1
6 Sigh therefore, son of man; 1
9 Son of man, prophesy and say, Thus says the Lord 1
12 Cry and wail, son of man, for it is against my people; 1
14 Prophesy therefore, son of man; clap your hands 1
19 Son of man, mark two ways for the sword of the king 1
28 son of man, prophesy, and say, Thus says the Lord 1
31 I will deliver you into the hands of brutal men 3
22: 2 And you, son of man, will you judge 1
9 There are men in you who slander to shed blood 3
9 and men in you who eat upon the mountains; •
9 men commit lewdness in your midst. •
10 In you men uncover their fathers' nakedness; •
12 In you men take bribes to shed blood; •
18 Son of man, the house of Israel has become dross 1
20 As men gather silver and bronze and iron and lead •
24 Son of man, say to her, You are a land that is not 1
30 I sought for a man among them who should build up 3
23: 2 Son of man, there were two women, the daughters 1
7 upon them, the choicest men of Assyria all of them; 6
8 in her youth men had lain with her and handled her •
14 she saw men portrayed upon the wall, the images 3
36 Son of man, will you judge Oho'lah and Ohol'ibah? 1
40 They even sent for men to come from far 3
42 with men of the common sort drunkards were 3
43 Then I said, Do not men now commit adultery •
44 they have gone in to her, as men go in to a harlot. •
45 But righteous men shall pass judgment on them 3
24: 2 Son of man, write down the name of this day 1
16 Son of man, behold, I am about to take the delight 1
25 you, son of man, on the day when I take from them 1
25: 2 Son of man, set your face toward the Ammonites 1
13 against Edom, and cut off from it man and beast; 1
26: 2 Son of man, because Tyre said concerning 1
27: 2 Now you, son of man, raise a lamentation over Tyre 1
10 Lud and Put were in your army as your men of war; 3
11 The men of Arvad and Helech were upon your walls 6
13 they exchanged the persons of men 1
15 The men of Rhodes traded with you; 6
27 men of war who are in you, with all your company 3
28: 2 Son of man, say to the prince of Tyre 1
2 yet you are but a man, and no god 1
9 though you are but a man, and no god 1
12 Son of man, raise a lamentation over the king 1
21 Son of man, set your face toward Sidon 1
29: 2 Son of man, set your face against Pharaoh 1
8 and will cut off from you man and beast; 1
11 No foot of man shall pass through it 1
18 Son of man, Nebuchadrez'zar king of Babylon made 1
30: 2 Son of man, prophesy, and say, Thus says the Lord 1
21 Son of man, I have broken the arm of Pharaoh king 1
24 groan before him like a man mortally wounded. •
31: 2 Son of man, say to Pharaoh king of Egypt and to his 1
14 to death, to the nether world among mortal men 7
32: 2 Son of man, raise a lamentation over Pharaoh king 1
13 no foot of man shall trouble them any more 1
18 Son of man, wail over the multitude of Egypt 1
33: 2 Son of man, speak to your people and say to them 1
2 the people of the land take a man from among them 3
6 that man is taken away in his iniquity •
7 you, son of man, I have made a watchman 1
10 And you, son of man, say to the house of Israel 1
12 And you, son of man, say to your people 1
21 a man who had escaped from Jerusalem came to me •
22 by the time the man came to me in the morning; •
24 Son of man, the inhabitants of these waste places 1
30 son of man, your people who talk together 1
34: 2 Son of man, prophesy against the shepherds 1
35: 2 Son of man, set your face against Mount Se'ir 1
36: 1 son of man, prophesy to the mountains of Israel 1
10 I will multiply men upon you 1
11 I will multiply upon you man and beast; 1
12 Yea, I will let men walk upon you, even my people 1
13 Because men say to you, 'You devour men •
13 You devour men, and you bereave your nation 1
14 therefore you shall no longer devour men 1
17 Son of man, when the house of Israel dwelt 1
20 men said of them, 'These are the people of the LORD •
37 to do for them: to increase their men like a flock. 1
38 the waste cities be filled with flocks of men. 1
37: 3 he said to me, "Son of man, can these bones live? 1
9 Prophesy to the breath, prophesy, son of man, 1
11 Then he said to me, "Son of man 1
16 Son of man, take a stick and write on it, 'For Judah 1
38: 2 Son of man, set your face toward Gog 1
14 Therefore, son of man, prophesy, and say to Gog 1
20 all the men that are upon the face of the earth 1
21 every man's sword will be against his brother. 3
39: 1 And you, son of man, prophesy against Gog, 1
14 They will set apart men to pass through the land 3
15 pass through the land and any one sees a man's bone 1
17 As for you, son of man, thus says the Lord GOD 1
40: 3 When he brought me there, behold, there was a man 3
4 the man said to me, "Son of man, look with your eyes 3
4 the man said to me, "Son of man, look with your eyes 1
5 the length of the measuring reed in the man's hand 3
41:19 face of a man toward the palm tree on the one side 1
43: 6 While the man was standing beside me, I heard one 3
7 Son of man, this is the place of my throne 1
10 And you, son of man, describe to the house of Israel 1
18 he said to me, "Son of man, thus says the Lord GOD 1
44: 5 And the LORD said to me, "Son of man, mark well 1
47: 3 the man measured 1,000 cubits 3
6 And he said to me, "Son of man, have you seen this? 1
Dan 2:10 not a man on earth who can meet the king's demand; 20
25 found . . a man who can make known to the king 22
38 given . . the sons of men, the beasts of the field 20
3:10 made a decree, that every man who hears the sound 20
12 men, O king, pay no heed to you; they do not serve 22
13 Then they brought these men before the king. 22
20 ordered certain mighty men of his army to bind 23
21 men were bound in their mantles, their tunics 22
22 slew those men who took up Shadrach, Meshach 22
23 these three men, Shadrach, Meshach, and Abed'nego 22
24 Did we not cast three men bound into the fire? 22
25 But I see four men loose, walking in the midst 22
27 not had any power over the bodies of those men; •
4:16 let his mind be changed from a man's 20
17 know that the Most High rules the kingdom of men 20
17 sets over it the lowliest of men.' 19
25 that you shall be driven from among men 20
25 know that the Most High rules the kingdom of men 20
32 you shall be driven from among men 20
32 Most High rules the kingdom of men 20
33 driven from among men, and ate grass like an ox 20
5: 5 fingers of a man's hand appeared and wrote 20
11 man in whom is the spirit of the holy gods. 22
21 driven from among men, and his mind was made 21
21 knew . . Most High God rules the kingdom of men 20
6: 5 Then these men said, "We shall not find any ground 22
7 makes petition to any god or man for 30 days 20
11 men came by agreement and found Daniel making 22
12 that any man who makes petition to any god or man 20
12 petition to any god or man within 30 days 20

15 men came by agreement to the king, and said 22
24 men who had accused Daniel were brought and cast 22
26 all my royal dominion men tremble and fear *
7: 4 made to stand upon two feet like a man; 20
4 mind of a man was given to it. 20
8 horn were eyes like the eyes of a man, and a mouth 20
13 clouds of heaven there came one like a son of man 20
8:15 before me one having the appearance of a man. 11
16 I heard a man's voice between the banks of the U'lai 1
16 Gabriel, make this man understand the vision. *
17 said to me, "Understand, O son of man, 1
9: 7 men of Judah, to the inhabitants of Jerusalem 3
21 man Gabriel, whom I had seen in the vision 3
10: 5 behold, a man clothed in linen, 3
7 men who were with me did not see the vision 3
11 said to me, "O Daniel, man greatly beloved, give heed 3
16 likeness of the sons of men touched my lips; 1
18 one having the appearance of a man touched me 1
19 said, "O man greatly beloved, fear not, 3
11:14 men of violence among your own people 6
12: 6 I said to the man clothed in linen, who was above 3
7 The man clothed in linen, who was above the waters 3
Hos 3: 3 not play the harlot, or belong to another man; 3
4:14 for the men themselves go aside with harlots *
6: 9 As robbers lie in wait for a man 3
9: 7 The prophet is a fool, the man of the spirit is mad 3
11: 9 for I am God and not man, the Holy One in your midst 3
13: 1 When E'phraim spoke, men trembled; *
2 Sacrifice to these, they say. Men kiss calves! 1
Jol 1:12 and gladness fails from the sons of men. 1
3: 9 Let all the men of war draw near, let them come up. 3
Ams 4:13 and declares to man what is his thought; 1
5:19 as if a man fled from a lion, and a bear met him; 3
6: 9 if ten men remain in one house, they shall die. 3
Obd 1: 9 every man from Mount Esau will be cut off 3
Jon 1:10 Then the men were exceedingly afraid 3
10 the men knew that he was fleeing 3
13 the men rowed hard to bring the ship back to land 3
14 O LORD, let us not perish for this man's life 3
16 Then the men feared the LORD exceedingly 3
3: 7 Let neither man nor beast, herd nor flock 1
8 but let man and beast be covered with sackcloth 1
Mic 2: 2 they oppress a man and his house 11
2 they oppress . . a man and his inheritance. 3
11 If a man should go about and utter wind and lies 3
12 a flock in its pasture, a noisy multitude of men. 1
4: 4 but they shall sit every man under his vine 3
5: 5 we will raise against him . . eight princes of men; 1
7 showers . . which tarry not for men nor wait 3
7 which tarry not . . nor wait for the sons of men. 1
6: 8 He has showed you, O man, what is good; 1
11 Shall I acquit the man with wicked scales *
7: 2 and there is none upright among men; 1
6 a man's enemies are the men of his own house. 3
6 a man's enemies are the men of his own house. 3
Nah 2: 1 Man the ramparts; watch the road; gird your loins; 16
Hab 1:13 the wicked swallows up the man more righteous *
14 For thou makest men like the fish of the sea 1
2: 5 the arrogant man shall not abide. 11
8 for the blood of men and violence to the earth 1
17 for the blood of men and violence to the earth 1
Zep 1: 3 I will sweep away man and beast; 1
12 the men who are thickening upon their lees 3
17 I will bring distress on men 1
3: 4 Her prophets are wanton, faithless men; 3
6 cities have been made desolate, without a man 3
Hag 1:11 upon men and cattle, and upon all their labors. 1
Zec 1: 8 behold, a man riding upon a red horse! 3
10 the man who was standing among the myrtle trees 3
21 scattered Judah, so that no man raised his head; 3
2: 1 behold, a man with a measuring line in his hand! 3
4 because of the multitude of men and cattle in it. 1
3: 8 who sit before you, for they are men of good omen 3
4: 1 like a man that is wakened out of his sleep. 3
6:12 Behold, the man whose name is the Branch 3
7: 2 sent Share'zer and Reg'em-mel'ech and their men 3
8:10 For before those days there was no wage for man 1
10 for I set every man against his fellow. 3
23 In those days ten men from the nations 3
10: 1 who gives men showers of rain, to every one *
11: 6 Lo, I will cause men to fall 1
12: 1 and formed the spirit of man within him 1
13: 7 against the man who stands next to me 11
Mal 2: 7 men should seek instruction from his mouth *
12 for the man who does this, any to witness or answer 3
3: 8 Will man rob God? Yet you are robbing me. 1
17 I will spare them as a man spares his son 3
Mat 1:19 Joseph, being a just man and unwilling to put her 26
4: 4 But he answered, "It is written, 'Man shall not live 27
19 me, and I will make you fishers of men. 27
5:11 Blessed are you when men revile you *
12 for so men persecuted the prophets who were *
13 thrown out and trodden under foot by men. 27
15 Nor do men light a lamp and put it under a bushel *
16 your light so shine before men, that they may see 27
19 and teaches men so, shall be called least 27
6: 1 Beware of practicing your piety before men 27
2 that they may be praised by men. Truly, I say to you 27
5 that they may be seen by men. Truly, I say to you 27
14 For if you forgive men their trespasses 27
15 if you do not forgive men their trespasses 27
16 may be seen by men. Truly, I say to you, they have 27
18 fasting may not be seen by men but by your Father 27
30 will he not . . more clothe you, O men of little faith? *
7: 9 Or what man of you, if his son asks him for bread 27
12 So whatever you wish that men would do to you, do 27
24 will be like a wise man who built his house 26
26 will be like a foolish man who built his house 26
8: 9 For I am a man under authority, with soldiers 27
12 there men will weep and gnash their teeth. *
20 but the Son of man has nowhere to lay his head. 27
26 Why are you afraid, O men of little faith? *
27 the men marveled, saying, "What sort of man is this 27
27 the men marveled, saying, "What sort of man is this 27
9: 6 you may know that the Son of man has authority 27
8 God, who had given such authority to men. 27
9 he saw a man called Matthew 27
10:17 Beware of men; for they will deliver you up 27
23 before the Son of man comes. 27
32 So every one who acknowledges me before men 27
33 whoever denies me before men, I also will deny 27
35 For I have come to set a man against his father 27
36 a man's foes will be those of his own household. 27
11: 8 To see a man clothed in soft raiment? 27
19 the Son of man came eating and drinking 27
12: 8 For the Son of man is lord of the sabbath. 27
10 behold, there was a man with a withered hand 27
11 said to them, "What man of you, if he has one sheep 27
12 Of how much more value is a man than a sheep! 27
13 Then he said to the man, "Stretch out your hand. 27
31 every sin and blasphemy will be forgiven men 27
32 whoever says a word against the Son of man 27
35 The good man out of his good treasure 27
35 and the evil man out of his evil treasure 27
36 on the day of judgment men will render account 27
40 so will the Son of man be three days 27
41 The men of Nin'eveh will arise at the judgment 26
43 When the unclean spirit has gone out of a man 27
45 the last state of that man becomes worse 27
13:24 The kingdom of heaven may be compared to a man 27
25 while men were sleeping, his enemy came and sowed 27
31 which a man took and sowed in his field; 27
37 He who sows the good seed is the Son of man; 27
41 The Son of man will send his angels 27
44 which a man found and covered up 27
14:21 those who ate were about 5,000 men 26
35 when the men of that place recognized him 26
15: 9 teaching as doctrines the precepts of men.' 27
11 not what goes into the mouth defiles a man 27
11 what comes out of the mouth, this defiles a man. 27
18 and this defiles a man. 27
20 These are what defile a man 27
20 to eat with unwashed hands does not defile a man. 27
38 Those who ate were 4,000 men 26
16:13 Who do men say that the Son of man is? 27
13 Who do men say that the Son of man is? 27
23 are not on the side of God, but of men. 27
26 For what will it profit a man 27
26 Or what shall a man give in return for his life? 27
27 For the Son of man is to come with his angels 27
28 before they see the Son of man coming 27
17: 9 until the Son of man is raised from the dead. 27
12 So also the Son of man will suffer at their hands. 27
14 a man came up to him and kneeling before him said 27
22 Son of man is to be delivered into the hands of men 27
22 Son of man is to be delivered into the hands of men 27
18: 7 woe to the man by whom the temptation comes! 27
12 If a man has a 100 sheep 27
19: 5 said, 'For this reason a man shall leave his father 27
6 let not man put asunder. 27
10 If such is the case of a man with his wife 27
12 who have been made eunuchs by men 27
26 With men this is impossible 27
28 the Son of man shall sit on his glorious throne 27
20:18 the Son of man will be delivered 27
28 the Son of man came not to be served but to serve 27
21:25 From heaven or from men? 27
26 if we say, 'From men,' we are afraid of the multitude; 27
28 What do you think? A man had two sons 27
22:11 he saw there a man who had no wedding garment; 27
13 there men will weep and gnash their teeth.' *
16 for you do not regard the position of men. 27
24 If a man dies, having no children 44
23: 4 and lay them on men's shoulders 27
5 They do all their deeds to be seen by men 27
7 being called rabbi by men. 27
13 you shut the kingdom of heaven against men 27
28 So you also outwardly appear righteous to men 27
24:27 so will be the coming of the Son of man. 27
30 the sign of the Son of man in heaven 27
30 see the Son of man coming on the clouds of heaven 27
37 so will be the coming of the Son of man. 27
39 so will be the coming of the Son of man. 27
40 Then two men will be in the field *
44 the Son of man is coming at an hour 27
51 there men will weep and gnash their teeth. *
25:14 For it will be as when a man going on a journey 27
24 Master, I knew you to be a hard man 27
30 there men will weep and gnash their teeth.' *
31 When the Son of man comes in his glory 27
26: 2 the Son of man will be delivered up 27
24 The Son of man goes as it is written of him 27
24 woe to that man by whom the Son of man is betrayed! 27
24 woe to that man by whom the Son of man is betrayed! 27
24 It would have been better for that man 27
45 Son of man is betrayed into the hands of sinners. 27
48 The one I shall kiss is the man; seize him. *
64 hereafter you will see the Son of man 27
72 I do not know the man. 27
74 I do not know the man. 27
27:32 they came upon a man of Cyre'ne, Simon by name 27
32 this man they compelled to carry his cross. 27
57 there came a rich man from Arimathe'a 27
Mrk 1:17 Follow me and I will make you become fishers of men. 27
23 in their synagogue a man with an unclean spirit; 27
2: 3 bringing to him a paralytic carried by four men. *
10 Son of man has authority on earth to forgive sins"- 27
27 sabbath was made for man, not man for the sabbath; 27
27 sabbath was made for man, not man for the sabbath; 27
28 the Son of man is lord even of the sabbath. 27
3: 1 a man was there who had a withered hand. 27
3 he said to the man who had the withered hand 27
5 said to the man, "Stretch out your hand. 27
28 all sins will be forgiven the sons of men 27
4:26 as if a man should scatter seed upon the ground 27
5: 2 a man with an unclean spirit 27
8 Come out of the man, you unclean spirit! 27
15 in his right mind, the man who had had the legion; *
18 the man who had been possessed with demons *
6:12 and preached that men should repent. *
20 knowing that he was a righteous and holy man 26
44 those who ate the loaves were 5,000 men. 26
7: 7 teaching as doctrines the precepts of men.' 27
8 and hold fast the tradition of men. 27
11 you say, 'If a man tells his father or his mother 27
15 there is nothing outside a man 27
15 the things which come out of a man are what defile 27
18 whatever goes into a man from outside 27
20 What comes out of a man is what defiles a man. 27
20 What comes out of a man is what defiles a man. 27
21 out of the heart of man, come evil thoughts 27
23 they defile a man. 27
32 they brought to him a man who was deaf *
8:24 I see men; but they look like trees, walking. 27
27 he asked his disciples, "Who do men say that I am? 27
31 the Son of man must suffer many things 27
33 you are not on the side of God, but of men. 27
36 what does it profit a man, to gain the whole world 27
37 For what can a man give in return for his life? 27
38 of him will the Son of man also be ashamed 27
9: 9 until the Son of man should have risen 27
12 how is it written of the Son of man 27
31 The Son of man will be delivered 27
31 delivered into the hands of men 27
38 we saw a man casting out demons in your name 44
10: 2 Is it lawful for a man to divorce his wife? 26
4 Moses allowed a man to write a certificate *
7 'For this reason a man shall leave his father 27
9 let not man put asunder. 27
17 a man ran up and knelt before him, and asked him 30
27 With men it is impossible, but not with God 27
33 Son of man will be delivered to the chief priests 27
45 Son of man also came not to be served but to serve 27
11:30 Was the baptism of John from heaven or from men? 27
32 But shall we say, 'From men'? 27
12: 1 A man planted a vineyard 27
14 for you do not regard the position of men 27
19 if a man's brother dies and leaves a wife 44
19 the man must take the wife, and raise up children 24
13:26 then they will see the Son of man coming in clouds 27
34 It is like a man going on a journey 27
14:13 a man carrying a jar of water will meet you 27
21 For the Son of man goes as it is written of him 27
21 woe to that man by whom the Son of man is betrayed! 27
21 woe to that man by whom the Son of man is betrayed! 27
21 better for that man if he had not been born. 27
41 Son of man is betrayed into the hands of sinners. 27
44 The one I shall kiss is the man *
62 the Son of man seated at the right hand of Power 27
71 I do not know this man of whom you speak. 27
15: 7 there was a man called Barab'bas. *
12 Then what shall I do with the man *
39 he said, "Truly this man was the Son of God! 27
Lke 1:25 to take away my reproach among men. 27
27 a virgin betrothed to a man whose name was Joseph 26
2:14 on earth peace among men with whom he is pleased! 27
25 Now there was a man in Jerusalem 27
25 this man was righteous and devout 27
52 increased . . in favor with God and man. 27
4: 4 It is written, 'Man shall not live by bread alone.' 27
33 a man who had the spirit of an unclean demon 27
5: 8 Depart from me, for I am a sinful man, O Lord. 26
10 henceforth you will be catching men. 27
12 there came a man full of leprosy 26
18 men were bringing on a bed a man who was paralyzed 26
18 men were bringing on a bed a man who was paralyzed 27
20 Man, your sins are forgiven you. 27

24 Son of man has authority on earth to forgive 27
24 he said to the man who was paralyzed–"I say to you •
6: 5 The Son of man is lord of the sabbath. 27
6 a man was there whose right hand was withered. 27
8 he said to the man who had the withered hand 26
22 Blessed are you when men hate you 27
22 revile you . . on account of the Son of man! 27
26 Woe to you, when all men speak well of you 27
31 as you wish that men would do to you, do so to them. 27
45 The good man out of the good treasure of his heart 27
45 the evil man out of his evil treasure produces evil; •
48 he is like a man building a house, who dug deep 27
49 like a man who built a house on the ground 27
7: 8 I am a man set under authority 27
12 behold, a man who had died was being carried out •
20 when the men had come to him, they said 26
25 A man clothed in soft clothing? 27
31 shall I compare the men of this generation 27
34 The Son of man has come eating and drinking; 27
8:27 there met him a man from the city who had demons 26
29 commanded the unclean spirit to come out of the man 27
33 Then the demons came out of the man 27
35 found the man from whom the demons had gone 27
38 The man from whom the demons had gone begged 26
41 there came a man named Ja'irus 26
49 a man from the ruler's house came and said 44
9:14 For there were about 5,000 men. 26
22 saying, "The Son of man must suffer many things 27
25 what does it profit a man if he gains the whole world 27
26 of him will the Son of man be ashamed 27
30 behold, two men talked with him, Moses and Eli'jah 26
32 his glory and the two men who stood with him. 26
33 as the men were parting from him •
38 behold, a man from the crowd cried, "Teacher 26
44 the Son of man is to be delivered 27
44 to be delivered into the hands of men. 27
49 we saw a man casting out demons in your name 44
57 As they were going along the road, a man said to him 44
58 the Son of man has nowhere to lay his head. 27
10:30 A man was going down from Jerusalem to Jericho 27
36 the man who fell among the robbers? •
11:24 When the unclean spirit has gone out of a man 27
26 the last state of that man becomes worse 27
30 For as Jonah became a sign to the men of Nin'eveh †
30 so will the Son of man be to this generation. 27
31 arise . . with the men of this generation 26
32 The men of Nin'eveh will arise at the judgment 26
44 men walk over them without knowing it. 27
46 you load men with burdens hard to bear 27
12: 8 every one who acknowledges me before men 27
8 the Son of man also will acknowledge 27
9 he who denies me before men 27
10 every one who speaks a word against the Son of man 27
14 Man, who made me a judge or divider over you? 27
15 a man's life does not consist in . . possessions •
16 The land of a rich man brought forth plentifully; 27
36 be like men who are waiting for their master 27
40 the Son of man is coming at an unexpected hour. 27
48 to whom men commit much •
13: 6 A man had a fig tree planted in his vineyard 44
19 It is like a grain of mustard seed which a man took 27
29 men will come from east and west •
14: 2 behold, there was a man before him who had dropsy. 27
12 He said also to the man who had invited him •
16 A man once gave a great banquet, and invited many; 27
24 none of those men who were invited shall taste 26
30 saying, 'This man began to build 27
35 men throw it away •
15: 4 What man of you, having 100 sheep 27
11 he said, "There was a man who had two sons; 27
16: 1 There was a rich man who had a steward 27
15 You are those who justify yourselves before men 27
15 what is exalted among men 27
19 There was a rich man 27
17:22 will desire to see one of the days of the Son of man 27
24 so will the Son of man be in his day. 27
26 so will it be in the days of the Son of man. 27
30 on the day when the Son of man is revealed. 27
18: 2 a judge who neither feared God nor regarded man; 27
4 Though I neither fear God nor regard man 27
8 Nevertheless, when the Son of man comes 27
10 Two men went up into the temple to pray 27
11 I thank thee that I am not like other men 27
27 impossible with men is possible with God. 27
31 everything that is written of the Son of man 27
19: 2 there was a man named Zacchae'us; 26
7 to be the guest of a man who is a sinner. 26
10 the Son of man came to seek and to save the lost. 27
21 I was afraid of you, because you are a severe man; 27
22 You knew that I was a severe man 27
20: 4 Was the baptism of John from heaven or from men? 27
6 if we say, 'From men,' all the people will stone us 27
9 A man planted a vineyard, and let it out to tenants 27
28 Moses wrote for us that if a man's brother dies 44
28 the man must take the wife and raise up children 24
21:26 men fainting with fear and with foreboding 27
27 then they will see the Son of man coming in a cloud 27
36 to stand before the Son of man. 27
22:10 a man carrying a jar of water will meet you 27
22 For the Son of man goes as it has been determined; 27
22 woe to that man by whom he is betrayed! 27
47 the man called Judas, one of the twelve, was leading •
48 would you betray the Son of man with a kiss? 27
58 Peter said, "Man, I am not. 27
60 Peter said, "Man, I do not know what you are saying. 27
63 Now the men who were holding Jesus mocked him 26
69 from now on the Son of man shall be seated 27
23: 4 I find no crime in this man. 27
6 he asked whether the man was a Galilean. 27
14 said to them, "You brought me this man 27
14 behold, I did not find this man guilty 27
19 a man who had been thrown into prison •
25 the man who had been thrown into prison •
47 Certainly this man was innocent! 27
50 Now there was a man named Joseph 26
50 member of the council, a good and righteous man 26
24: 4 behold, two men stood by them in dazzling apparel; 26
5 the men said to them, "Why do you seek the living •
7 the Son of man must be delivered 27
7 must be delivered into the hands of sinful men 27
Joh 1: 4 In him was life, and the life was the light of men. 27
6 was a man sent from God, whose name was John. 27
9 The true light that enlightens every man 27
13 born, not of blood nor of the will of man, but of God. 26
30 'After me comes a man who ranks before me 26
51 ascending and descending upon the Son of man. 27
2:10 said to him, "Every man serves the good wine first; 27
10 and when men have drunk freely, then the poor wine; •
25 and needed no one to bear witness of man; 27
25 for he himself knew what was in man. 27
3: 1 there was a man of the Pharisees, named Nicode'mus 27
4 How can a man be born when he is old? 27
13 but he who descended from heaven, the Son of man. 27
14 so must the Son of man be lifted up 27
19 and men loved darkness rather than light 27
4:20 Jerusalem is . . where men ought to worship. •
29 Come, see a man who told me all that I ever did. 27
50 The man believed the word that Jesus spoke to him 27
5: 5 One man was there, who had been ill for 38 years. 27
7 I have no man to put me into the pool 27
9 at once the man was healed 27
10 the Jews said to the man who was cured •
11 answered them, "The man who healed me said to me •
12 They asked him, "Who is the man who said to you 27
13 the man who had been healed did not know who •
15 The man went away and told the Jews 27
27 because he is the Son of man. 27
34 the testimony which I receive is from man 27
41 I do not receive glory from men. 27
6:10 the men sat down, in number about 5,000. 26
27 which the Son of man will give to you 27
50 a man may eat of it and not die. 27
53 eat the flesh of the Son of man and drink his blood 27
62 what if you were to see the Son of man ascending 27
7:22 you circumcise a man upon the sabbath. 27
23 If on the sabbath a man receives circumcision 27
23 on the sabbath I made a man's whole body well? 27
46 No man ever spoke like this man! 27
51 Does our law judge a man 27
8:17 the testimony of two men is true; 27
28 Jesus said, "When you have lifted up the Son of man 27
40 a man who has told you the truth 27
9: 1 As he passed by, he saw a man blind from his birth. 27
6 and anointed the man's eyes with the clay •
8 Is not this the man who used to sit and beg? •
9 He said, "I am the man. •
11 He answered, "The man called Jesus made clay 27
16 This man is not from God 27
16 How can a man who is a sinner do such signs? 27
18 the parents of the man who had received his sight •
24 they called the man who had been blind 27
24 we know that this man is a sinner. 27
30 The man answered, "Why, this is a marvel! 27
35 Do you believe in the Son of Man? 27
10:33 because you, being a man, make yourself God. 27
11:47 What are we to do? For this man performs many signs 27
50 one man should die for the people 27
12:23 The hour . . for the Son of man to be glorified. 27
34 How can you say . . the Son of man must be lifted up? 27
34 Who is this Son of man? 27
43 for they loved the praise of men 27
13:31 Now is the Son of man glorified 27
14:23 If a man loves me, he will keep my word 44
15: 6 If a man does not abide in me 44
13 that a man lay down his life for his friends. 44
17: 6 the men whom thou gavest me out of the world 27
18:14 expedient that one man should die for the people. 27
17 Are not you also one of this man's disciples? 27
26 a kinsman of the man whose ear Peter had cut off •
29 What accusation do you bring against this man? 27
19: 5 Pilate said to them, "Behold the man! 27
Act 1:10 behold, two men stood by them in white robes 26
11 said, "Men of Galilee, why do you stand looking 26
21 one of the men who have accompanied us 26
2: 5 devout men from every nation under heaven. 26
14 Men of Judea and all who dwell in Jerusalem 26
22 Men of Israel, hear these words 26
22 Jesus of Nazareth, a man attested to you by God 26
3: 2 a man lame from birth was being carried 26
12 Men of Israel, why do you wonder at this 26
16 the faith . . has given the man this perfect health •
4: 4 the number of the men came to about 5,000 26
9 by what means this man has been healed 27
12 no other name under heaven given among men 27
14 seeing the man that had been healed 27
16 saying, "What shall we do with these men? 27
22 man on whom this sign of healing was performed 27
5: 1 a man named Anani'as with his wife Sapphi'ra 26
4 You have not lied to men but to God. 27
14 multitudes both of men and women 26
25 The men whom you put in prison 26
28 you intend to bring this man's blood upon us. 27
29 We must obey God rather than men. 27
34 ordered the men to be put outside for a while. 27
35 he said to them, "Men of Israel 26
35 take care what you do with these men. 27
36 a number of men, about 400, joined him 26
38 keep away from these men and let them alone 27
38 if this plan or this undertaking is of men 27
6: 3 pick out from among you seven men of good repute 26
5 Stephen, a man full of faith and of the Holy Spirit 26
11 Then they secretly instigated men, who said 26
13 This man never ceases to speak words 27
7:26 Men, you are brethren, why do you wrong each other? 26
27 the man who was wronging his neighbor •
56 the Son of man standing at the right hand of God. 27
8: 2 Devout men buried Stephen 26
3 he dragged off men and women 26
9 there was a man named Simon 26
12 they were baptized, both men and women. 26
9: 2 if he found any belonging to the Way, men or women 26
7 The men who were traveling with him 26
11 a man of Tarsus named Saul †
12 he has seen a man named Anani'as come 26
13 I have heard from many about this man 26
21 Is not this the man who made havoc in Jerusalem •
33 There he found a man named Aene'as 27
38 the disciples . . sent two men to him entreating 26
10: 1 At Caesare'a there was a man named Cornelius 26
5 now send men to Joppa 26
17 behold, the men that were sent by Cornelius 26
19 three men are looking for you. 26
21 Peter went down to the men and said, "I am the one 26
22 a centurion, an upright and God-fearing man 26
26 Peter lifted him up, saying, "Stand up; I too am a man. 27
28 I should not call any man common or unclean. 27
30 behold, a man stood before me in bright apparel 26
11: 3 saying, "Why did you go to uncircumcised men 26
11 three men arrived at the house in which we were 26
12 we entered the man's house. 26
20 there were some of them, men of Cyprus and Cyre'ne 26
24 a good man, full of the Holy Spirit and of faith. 26
12:22 people shouted, "The voice of a god, and not of man! 27
13: 7 Proconsul, Sergius Paulus, a man of intelligence 26
16 Men of Israel, and you that fear God, listen. 26
21 Saul the son of Kish, a man of the tribe of Benjamin 26
22 a man after my heart, who will do all my will.' 26
14: 8 Now at Lystra there was a man sitting 26
11 The gods have come down to us in the likeness of men! 27
15 Men, why are you doing this? 26
15 We also are men, of like nature with you 27
15:17 the rest of men may seek the Lord 27
22 to choose men from among them 26
22 leading men among the brethren 26
25 to choose men and send them to you 26
26 men who have risked their lives 27
16: 9 a man of Macedo'nia was standing beseeching him 26
17 These men are servants of the Most High God 27
20 they said, "These men are Jews 27
30 Men, what must I do to be saved? 34
35 sent the police, saying, "Let those men go. 27
37 uncondemned, men who are Roman citizens 27
17:12 Greek women of high standing as well as men. 26
22 Paul . . said: "Men of Athens 26
26 he made from one every nation of men 27
29 by the art and imagination of man. 27
30 now he commands all men everywhere to repent 27
31 judge the world . . by a man whom he has appointed 26
34 some men joined him and believed 26
18: 7 went to the house of a man named Titius Justus 44
13 saying, "This man is persuading men to worship God 27
24 an eloquent man, well versed in the scriptures. 26
19:16 the man in whom the evil spirit was leaped on them 27
24 a man named Deme'trius, a silversmith 44
25 Men . . from this business we have our wealth. 26
35 Men of Ephesus, what man is there who does not 26
35 Men of Ephesus, what man is there who does not 27
37 you have brought these men here 26
20:30 will arise men speaking perverse things 26
21:11 bind the man who owns this girdle 26
23 We have four men who are under a vow; 26
26 Then Paul took the men 26
28 crying out, "Men of Israel, help! 26
28 This is the man who is teaching men everywhere 27
28 This is the man who is teaching men everywhere 42
38 and led the 4,000 men of the Assassins out 26
22: 4 delivering to prison both men and women 26

12 one Anani'as, a devout man according to the law 26
15 you will be a witness for him to all men 27
25 lawful . . to scourge a man who is a Roman citizen 27
26 this man is a Roman citizen. 27
23: 9 We find nothing wrong in this man. 27
21 more than 40 of their men lie in ambush for him 26
27 This man was seized by the Jews 26
30 there would be a plot against the man 26
24: 5 we have found this man a pestilent fellow 26
16 a clear conscience toward God and toward men. 27
25: 3 to have the man sent to Jerusalem •
5 if there is anything wrong about the man 26
14 There is a man left prisoner by Felix; 26
17 and ordered the man to be brought in. 26
22 I should like to hear the man myself. 27
23 the prominent men of the city 26
26:31 This man is doing nothing to deserve death 27
32 This man could have been set free 27
27:21 Paul then came forward among them and said, "Men 26
25 So take heart, men 26
28: 4 No doubt this man is a murderer 27
Rom 1:18 against all ungodliness and wickedness of men 27
23 for images resembling mortal man or birds 27
27 the men . . gave up natural relations with women 28
27 men committing shameless acts with men 28
27 men committing shameless acts with men 28
2: 1 you have no excuse, O man, whoever you are 27
3 Do you suppose, O man, that when you judge 27
16 God judges the secrets of men by Christ Jesus. 27
26 if a man who is uncircumcised keeps the . . law •
29 His praise is not from men but from God. 27
3: 4 Let God be true though every man be false 27
28 man is justified by faith apart from works of law. 27
4: 6 So also David pronounces a blessing upon the man 27
8 blessed is the man again 26
5:12 as sin came into the world through one man 27
12 death spread to all men because all men sinned- 27
15 the free gift in the grace of that one man Jesus 27
18 trespass led to condemnation for all men 27
18 leads to acquittal and life for all men. 27
19 by one man's disobedience many were made sinners 27
6:13 as men who have been brought from death to life •
7: 3 an adulteress if she lives with another man 26
3 and if she marries another man 26
24 Wretched man that I am! Who will deliver me 27
8:27 he who searches the hearts of men knows •
9:16 So it depends not upon man's will or exertion •
20 But who are you, a man, to answer back to God? 27
33 laying in Zion a stone that will make men stumble •
10: 5 the man who practices the righteousness 27
10 man believes with his heart and so is justified •
14 how are men to call upon him •
15 And how can men preach unless they are sent? •
11: 4 I have kept for myself 7,000 men who have not bowed 26
14: 1 As for the man who is weak in faith, welcome him •
2 while the weak man eats only vegetables. •
18 is acceptable to God and approved by men. 27
15:20 lest I build on another man's foundation •
1Co 1:25 For the foolishness of God is wiser than men 27
25 the weakness of God is stronger than men. 27
2: 5 your faith might not rest in the wisdom of men 27
9 nor the heart of man conceived 27
11 what person knows a man's thoughts 27
11 except the spirit of the man which is in him 27
14 The unspiritual man does not receive the gifts 27
3: 3 of the flesh, and behaving like ordinary men? 27
4 are you not merely men? 27
21 So let no one boast of men. 27
4: 9 a spectacle to the world, to angels and to men. 27
5: 1 a man is living with his father's wife. 44
5 you are to deliver this man to Satan •
6:18 Every other sin which a man commits 27
7: 1 It is well for a man not to touch a woman. 27
23 do not become slaves of men. 27
8:10 For if any one sees you, a man of knowledge, at table •
10:28 out of consideration for the man who informed •
11: 3 the head of every man is Christ 26
4 Any man who prays or prophesies with his head 26
7 For a man ought not to cover his head 26
7 woman is the glory of man. 26
8 man was not made from woman 26
8 was not made from woman, but woman from man. 26
9 Neither was man created for woman 26
9 was man created for woman, but woman for man.) 26
11 woman is not independent of man nor man of woman; 26
11 woman is not independent of man nor man of woman; 26
12 as woman was made from man 26
12 so man is now born of woman 26
14 for a man to wear long hair is degrading to him 26
28 Let a man examine himself, and so eat of the bread 27
13: 1 If I speak in the tongues of men and of angels 27
11 when I became a man, I gave up childish ways. 26
14: 2 who speaks in a tongue speaks not to men but to God; 27
3 On the other hand, he who prophesies speaks to men 27
15:19 we are of all men most to be pitied. 27
21 For as by a man came death 27
21 by a man has come also the resurrection 27
39 there is one kind for men, another for animals 27
45 The first man Adam became a living being 27
47 The first man was from the earth, a man of dust 27
47 The first man was from the earth, a man of dust 27
47 the second man is from heaven. 27
48 As was the man of dust •
48 as is the man of heaven •
49 Just as we have borne the image of the man of dust •
49 we shall also bear the image of the man of heaven. •
2Co 2:17 as men of sincerity, as commissioned by God •
3: 2 to be known and read by all men; 27
16 when a man turns to the Lord the veil is removed. •
4: 2 commend ourselves to every man's conscience 27
5:11 we persuade men 27
8:12 it is acceptable according to what a man has •
21 also in the sight of men. 27
24 our boasting about you to these men. •
10:18 not the man who commends himself that is accepted •
18 the man whom the Lord commends. •
11:20 For you bear it if a man makes slaves of you 44
12: 2 I know a man in Christ 27
3 I know that this man was caught up 27
4 which man may not utter. 27
5 On behalf of this man I will boast •
Gal 1: 1 Paul an apostle-not from men nor through man 27
1 from men nor through man, but through Jesus 27
10 Am I now seeking the favor of men, or of God? 27
10 Or am I trying to please men? 27
10 If I were still pleasing men 27
11 the gospel . . is not man's gospel. 33
12 I did not receive it from man, nor was I taught it 27
2:16 a man is not justified by works of the law 27
3: 7 So you see that it is men of faith who are the sons •
9 who are men of faith are blessed with Abraham •
15 no one annuls even a man's will, or adds to it 27
5: 3 to every man who receives circumcision 27
6: 1 Brethren, if a man is overtaken in any trespass 27
7 whatever a man sows, that he will also reap. 27
Eph 2:15 create in himself one new man in place of the two 27
3: 5 the sons of men in other generations 27
16 through his Spirit in the inner man 27
4: 8 he gave gifts to men. 27
14 by the cunning of men 27
5:31 For this reason a man shall leave his father 27
6: 7 as to the Lord and not to men 27
Php 2: 7 being born in the likeness of men. 27
4: 5 Let all men know your forbearance 27
Col 1:28 warning every man and teaching every man 27
28 teaching every man in all wisdom 27
28 that we may present every man mature in Christ. 27
3:23 work heartily, as serving the Lord and not men 27
1Th 1: 5 You know what kind of men we proved to be •
2: 4 not to please men, but to please God 27
6 nor did we seek glory from men 27
13 you accepted it not as the word of men 27
15 drove us out, and displease God and oppose all men 27
4: 8 disregards not man but God 27
2Th 2: 3 the man of lawlessness is revealed 27
3: 2 that we may be delivered from wicked and evil men; 27
1Ti 2: 1 thanksgivings be made for all men 27
4 who desires all men to be saved 27
5 there is one mediator between God and men 27
5 the man Christ Jesus 27
8 in every place the men should pray 26
12 to have authority over men 26
3: 5 if a man does not know how to manage his own 44
4:10 the living God, who is the Savior of all men 27
5:24 The sins of some men are conspicuous 27
6: 5 wrangling among men who are depraved in mind 27
9 plunge men into ruin and destruction. 27
11 as for you, man of God, shun all this 27
16 whom no man has ever seen or can see 27
2Ti 2: 2 entrust to faithful men 27
3: 2 For men will be lovers of self, lovers of money 27
8 men of corrupt mind and counterfeit faith; 27
13 while evil men . . will go on from bad to worse 27
17 that the man of God may be complete 27
Tit 1:14 commands of men who reject the truth. 27
2:11 has appeared for the salvation of all men 27
3: 2 to show perfect courtesy toward all men. 27
8 these are excellent and profitable to men. 27
10 As for a man who is factious 27
Heb 2: 6 What is man that thou art mindful of him 27
6 What is . . the son of man, that thou carest for him? 27
5: 1 every high priest chosen from among men 27
1 every high priest . . appointed to act on behalf of men 27
6:16 Men indeed swear by a greater than themselves 27
7: 6 this man who has not their genealogy •
8 Here tithes are received by mortal men 27
28 Indeed, the law appoints men in their weakness 27
8: 2 which is set up not by man but by the Lord. 27
9:27 just as it is appointed for men to die once 27
10:28 A man who has violated the law of Moses dies 44
29 the man who has spurned the Son of God •
11:19 God was able to raise men even from the dead •
12:14 Strive for peace with all men •
13: 6 I will not be afraid; what can man do to me? 27
17 as men who will have to give account •
Jas 1: 7 a double-minded man, unstable in all his ways 26
12 Blessed is the man who endures trial 26
19 Let every man be quick to hear, slow to speak 27
20 anger of man does not work the righteousness of God. 26
23 a man who observes his natural face in a mirror; 26
2: 2 For if a man with gold rings and in fine clothing 26
14 if a man says he has faith but has not works? 44
20 Do you want to be shown, you shallow man 27
24 You see that a man is justified by works 27
3: 2 he is a perfect man, able to bridle the whole body 26
9 and with it we curse men 27
5:17 Eli'jah was a man of like nature with ourselves 27
1Pe 2: 4 Come to him, to the living stone, rejected by men 27
8 A stone that will make men stumble •
15 put to silence the ignorance of foolish men. 27
4: 6 that though judged in the flesh like men 27
2Pe 1:21 no prophecy ever came by the impulse of man 27
21 men moved by the Holy Spirit spoke from God. 27
2:18 they entice . . men who have barely escaped •
19 whatever overcomes a man, to that he is enslaved. 44
3: 7 judgment and destruction of ungodly men. 27
1Jn 5: 9 If we receive the testimony of men 27
2Jn 1: 7 men who will not acknowledge the coming of Jesus •
Jde 1: 8 these men in their dreamings defile the flesh •
10 these men revile . . they do not understand •
Rev 1:13 the midst of the lampstands one like a son of man 27
4: 7 the third living creature with the face of a man 27
5: 9 and by thy blood didst ransom men for God •
6: 4 so that men should slay one another; •
8:11 men died of the water, because it was made bitter. 27
9: 5 the torture of a scorpion, when it stings a man. 27
6 in those days men will seek death and will not find it; 27
10 power of hurting men . . lies in their tails. 27
11: 9 men from the peoples and tribes and tongues •
13: 4 Men worshiped the dragon •
13 making fire come down . . in the sight of men; 27
14:14 and seated on the cloud one like a son of man 27
16: 2 and foul and evil sores came upon the men 27
6 men have shed the blood of saints and prophets •
8 and it was allowed to scorch men with fire; 27
9 men were scorched by the fierce heat 27
18 such as had never been since men were on the earth 27
21 great hailstones . . dropped on men from heaven 27
21 till men cursed God for the plague of the hail 27
21: 3 Behold, the dwelling of God is with men. 27
17 144 cubits by a man's measure, that is, an angel's. 27
1Es 1:12 the priests and Levites and the men of Judah †
34 the men of the nation took Jeconiah 36
2: 6 be helped by the men of his place with gold 36
27 that the men in it were given to rebellion and war 27
28 to prevent these men from building the city 27
3:22 When men drink •
24 since it forces men to do these things •
4: 2 Gentlemen, are not men strongest 27
14 is not the king great, and are not men many 27
16 brought up the very men who plant the vineyards •
17 Women make men's clothes; they bring men glory 27
17 Women make men's clothes; they bring men glory 27
17 men cannot exist without women. 27
18 If men gather gold and silver •
20 A man leaves his own father, who brought him up 27
23 A man takes his sword, and goes out to travel 27
25 A man loves his wife more than his father 27
37 all the sons of men are unrighteous 27
39 All men approve her deeds •
5: 4 These are the names of the men who went up 26
7 the men of Judea who came up out of . . captivity •
9 The number of the men of the nation •
18 The men of Netophah, 55. The men of Anathoth, 158. •
18 The men of Netophah, 55. The men of Anathoth, 158. •
18 The men of Bethasmoth, 42. •
19 The men of Kiriatharim, 25. •
19 The men of Chephirah and Beeroth, 743 •
20 The men of Ramah and Geba, 621. •
21 The men of Michmas, 122. The men of Bethel, 52. •
21 The men of Michmas, 122. The men of Bethel, 52. •
49 the directions in the book of Moses the man of God. 27
6:29 a portion be scrupulously given to these men 27
8:27 I gathered men from Israel to go up with me. 26
30 Zechariah, and with him 150 men enrolled. 26
31 the son of Zerahiah, and with him 200 men. 26
32 Shecaniah . . and with him 300 men 26
32 Obed the son of Jonathan, and with him 250 men. 26
33 the son of Gotholiah, and with him 70 men. 26
34 the son of Michael, and with him 70 men. 26
35 the son of Jehiel, and with him 212 men. 26
36 the son of Josiphiah, and with him 160 men. 26
37 the son of Bebai, and with him 28 men. 26
38 the son of Hakkatan, and with him 110 men. 26
39 Jeuel, and Shemaiah, and with them 70 men. 26
40 the son of Istalcurus, and with him 70 men. 26
46 to send us men to serve as priests •
47 brought us competent men of the sons of Mahli 26
48 and their sons, twenty men; 26
91 a very great throng . . , men and women and youths 26
92 the son of Jehiel, one of the men of Israel 45
9: 4 the men themselves expelled from the multitude •
5 Then the men of the tribe of Judah . . assembled •
16 the leading men of their fathers' houses 26
17 the cases of the men who had foreign wives 26
37 The priests and the Levites and the men of Israel •
40 all the multitude, men and women 27

41 in the presence of both men and women 26
2Es 3:36 Thou mayest indeed find individual men 47
5: 3 and men shall see it desolate. •
12 at that time men shall hope but not obtain 47
38 except he whose dwelling is not with men? 47
6:10 For the beginning of a man is his hand 47
10 and the end of a man is his heel ‡
26 they shall see the men who were taken up 47
39 the sound of man's voice was not yet there. 47
46 thou didst command them to serve man 47
7: 8 so that only one man can walk upon that path. 47
9 is given to a man for an inheritance 47
46 who among men that has not transgressed 49
78 that a man shall die 47
127 the contest which every man . . shall wage 47
8:34 what is man, that thou art angry with him 47
44 man, who has been formed by thy hands 47
59 did not intend that men should be destroyed; 47
10:14 the earth . . has . . given her fruit, that is, man 47
33 to me, "Stand up like a man, and I will instruct you. 50
54 for no work of man's building could endure 47
11:37 I heard how he uttered a man's voice to the eagle 47
13: 3 this wind made something like the figure of a man ‡
3 behold, that man flew with the clouds of heaven; 47
5 and behold, an innumerable multitude of men 47
5 the man who came up out of the sea. 47
12 I saw the same man come down from the mountain 47
25 As for your seeing a man come up from . . the sea 50
32 whom you saw as a man coming up from the sea. 50
51 Why did I see the man coming up from . . the sea? 50
14: 9 you shall be taken up from among men 47
14 cast away from you the burdens of man 48
22 that men may be able to find the path 47
37 I took the five men, as he commanded me 50
42 the Most High gave understanding to the five men 50
15:16 For there shall be unrest among men 47
17 For a man will desire to go into a city 47
19 A man shall have no pity upon his neighbors 47
36 a man's thigh and a camel's hock. 47
16:19 as scourges for the correction of men. •
21 men will imagine that peace is assured for them •
27 one man will long to see another 47
54 Behold, the Lord knows all the works of men 47
61 who formed man 47
65 when your sins come out before men 47
Tob 1: 9 When I became a man I married Anna 26
19 Then one of the men of Nineveh went and informed •
3:14 I am innocent of any sin with man 26
4:14 the wages of any man who works for you 27
5: 2 when I do not know the man? 29
3 Find a man to go with you 27
4 he went to look for a man 27
16 Go with this man 27
6: 7 make a smoke from these before the man or woman 27
8 anoint . . a man who has white films in his eyes 27
12 cannot give her to another man 26
12 you rather than any other man 27
7: 7 Son of that good and noble man! 27
8: 6 It is not good that the man should be alone 27
11: 6 so is the man who went with him! 27
12: 1 son, see to the wages of the man who went with you; 27
Jdt 1:11 but looked upon him as only one man 26
2: 5 take with you men confident in their strength 26
18 also plenty of food for every man 26
3: 5 The men came to Holofernes and told him all this. 26
6 took picked men from them as his allies. 26
4: 7 only wide enough for two men at the most. 26
9 every man of Israel cried out to God 26
11 the men and women of Israel, and their children 26
5:22 all the men standing around the tent 35
6: 1 the disturbance made by the men outside the council 26
3 the king's servants will destroy them as one man. 27
10 and hand him over to the men of Israel. 45
12 When the men of the city saw them 26
14 Then the men of Israel came down from their city 45
7: 2 their force of men of war was 170,000 infantry 26
11 not a man of your army will fall. 26
12 keep all the men in your forces with you 26
13 to keep watch that not a man gets out of the city. 26
18 they sent some of their men toward the south •
8:12 in the place of God among the sons of men? 27
14 nor find out what a man is thinking •
16 God is not like man, to be threatened 27
10: 4 to entice the eyes of all men who might see her. 26
10 the men of the city watched her 26
13 without losing one of his men, captured or slain. 26
14 When the men heard her words 26
17 They chose from their number 100 men 26
19 Surely not a man of them had better be left alive 26
11: 7 not only do men serve him because of you 27
9 the men of Bethulia spared him 26
14 They have sent men to Jerusalem •
13:12 When the men of her city heard her voice 26
19 will never depart from the hearts of men 27
14: 5 the man who despised the house of Israel •
6 in the hand of one of the men 26
11 every man took his weapons 26
15: 1 When the men in the tents heard it •
3 the men of Israel, every one that was a soldier 45
4 Uzziah sent men to Betomasthaim and Bebai •
13 while all the men of Israel followed 26
AEs 11: 3 a great man, serving in the court of the king. 27
13: 2 to re-establish the peace which all men desire. 27
5 stands constantly in opposition to all men 27
14 not set the glory of man above the glory of God 27
14:11 the man who began this against us. •
13 to hate the man who is fighting against us •
16: 4 not only take away thankfulness from among men 27
8 quiet and peaceable for all men 27
18 the man himself who did these things •
24 It shall be made not only impassable for men 27
Wis 1: 3 For perverse thoughts separate men from God •
2: 1 there is no remedy when a man comes to his end 27
23 for God created man for incorruption 27
3: 4 For though in the sight of men they were punished 27
4: 1 because it is known both by God and by men. 27
2 When it is present, men imitate it •
9 understanding is gray hair for men 27
5: 4 This is the man whom we once held in derision •
7: 2 the seed of a man and the pleasure of marriage. 26
14 for it is an unfailing treasure for men 27
20 the powers of spirits and the reasonings of men 27
28 nothing so much as the man who lives with wisdom. •
8: 7 nothing in life is more profitable for men 25
9: 2 by thy wisdom hast formed man, to have dominion 27
5 a man who is weak and short-lived 27
6 for even if one is perfect among the sons of men 27
13 For what man can learn the counsel of God? 27
18 men were taught what pleases thee 27
11:19 not only could their damage exterminate men •
20 men could fall at a single breath •
23 thou dost overlook men's sins 27
12: 8 since they were but men 27
12 to plead as an advocate for unrighteous men? 27
17 when men doubt the completeness of thy power •
13: 1 all men who were ignorant of God 27
3 If . . men assumed them to be gods •
4 if men were amazed at their power and working •
10 who give the name "gods" to the works of men's hands 27
13 he forms it like the image of a man 27
14: 4 even if a man lacks skill, he may put to sea. •
5 therefore men trust their lives 27
11 and became traps for the souls of men 27
14 through the vanity of men they entered the world 27
17 men could not honor monarchs in their presence 27
20 shortly before they had honored as a man. 27
21 men, in bondage to misfortune 27
31 not the power of the things by which men swear •
15: 8 this man who was made of earth a short time before •
16 For a man made them 27
16 no man can form a god which is like himself. 27
16: 1 Therefore those men were deservedly punished •
13 thou dost lead men down to the gates of Hades •
14 A man in his wickedness kills another 27
26 it is not the production of crops that feeds man 27
18:21 a blameless man was quick to act as their champion; 26
Sir 1:15 She made among men an eternal foundation 27
16 she satisfies men with her fruits; •
22 a man's anger tips the scale to his ruin. •
29 Be not a hypocrite in men's sight 27
2: 5 acceptable men in the furnace of humiliation. 27
18 not into the hands of men 27
3:11 For a man's glory comes from honoring his father 27
4: 2 nor anger a man in want. 26
5 nor give a man occasion to curse you; 27
5:13 a man's tongue is his downfall. 27
7:11 Do not ridicule a man who is bitter in soul 27
25 give her to a man of understanding. 26
35 Do not shrink from visiting a sick man 27
8: 1 Do not contend with a powerful man 27
2 Do not quarrel with a rich man 27
5 Do not reproach a man who is turning away from sin; 27
6 Do not disdain a man when he is old 27
12 Do not lend to a man who is stronger than you 27
9:13 Keep far from a man who has the power to kill 27
16 Let righteous men be your dinner companions 26
18 the man who is reckless in speech will be hated. 26
10: 5 The success of a man is in the hands of the Lord 26
7 hateful before the Lord and before men 27
11 when a man is dead 27
12 The beginning of man's pride 27
13 the man who clings to it pours out abominations. •
18 Pride was not created for men 27
23 nor is it proper to honor a sinful man. 26
24 greater than the man who fears the Lord. •
25 a man of understanding will not grumble. 26
27 Better is a man who works •
29 will justify the man that sins against himself? •
29 who will honor the man that dishonors his own life? •
31 A man honored in poverty, how much more in wealth! •
31 a man dishonored in wealth •
11: 2 Do not praise a man for his good looks 26
2 nor loathe a man because of his appearance. 27
4 his works are concealed from men. 27
11 There is a man who works, and toils, and presses on •
18 There is a man who is rich through his diligence •
26 to reward a man on the day of death 27
27 at the close of a man's life 27
28 a man will be known through his children. 26
29 Do not bring every man into your home 27
12: 3 No good will come to the man who persists in evil •
9 A man's enemies are grieved when he prospers 26
14 will pity a man who associates with a sinner •
13:16 a man clings to one like himself. 26
25 A man's heart changes his countenance 27
14: 1 Blessed is the man who does not blunder 26
3 Riches are not seemly for a stingy man 26
3 man; and of what use is property to an envious man? 27
5 If a man is mean to himself •
6 meaner than the man who is grudging to himself •
8 Evil is the man with a grudging eye •
19 the man who made it will pass away with it. •
20 Blessed is the man who meditates on wisdom 26
15: 1 The man who fears the Lord will do this •
7 Foolish men will not obtain her 27
7 sinful men will not see her. 26
12 for he had no need of a sinful man. 26
14 It was he who created man in the beginning 27
17 Before a man are life and death 27
19 he knows every deed of man. 27
16:12 he judges a man according to his deeds. 26
21 Like a tempest which no man can see 27
23 a senseless and misguided man thinks foolishly. 26
17: 1 The Lord created man out of earth 27
2 He gave to men few days, a limited time •
22 A man's almsgiving is like a signet with the Lord 26
30 For all things cannot be in men 27
30 since a son of man is not immortal. 27
32 all men are dust and ashes. 27
18: 7 When a man has finished, he is just beginning 27
8 What is man, and of what use is he? 27
9 The number of a man's days is great 27
13 The compassion of man is for his neighbor 27
17 Both are to be found in a gracious man. 26
23 do not be like a man who tempts the Lord. 27
27 A wise man is cautious in everything 27
19: 2 the man who consorts with harlots •
29 A man is known by his appearance 26
30 A man's attire and open-mouthed laughter 26
30 a man's manner of walking, show what he is. 27
20: 1 there is a man who keeps silent but is wise. •
4 a man who executes judgments by violence. •
7 A wise man will be silent until the right moment 27
9 There may be good fortune for a man in adversity 26
11 men who have raised their heads •
12 There is a man who buys much for a little •
15 such a one is a hateful man. 27
19 An ungracious man is like a story 27
21 A man may be prevented from sinning •
22 A man may lose his life through shame •
23 A man may for shame make promises to a friend •
24 A lie is an ugly blot on a man 27
27 a sensible man will please great men. 27
31 Better is the man who hides his folly 27
31 Better . . than the man who hides his wisdom. 27
21: 2 destroy the souls of men. 27
8 A man who builds his house •
15 When a man of understanding hears a wise saying •
20 a clever man smiles quietly. 26
22 a man of experience 27
23 a cultivated man remains outside. 26
24 It is ill-mannered for a man to listen at a door 27
22:15 of iron are easier to bear than a stupid man. 27
19 A man who pricks an eye will make tears fall •
23:10 the man who always swears and utters the Name •
11 A man who swears many oaths 26
15 A man accustomed to use insulting words 27
16 Two sorts of men multiply sins •
16 man who commits fornication with his near of kin 27
18 A man who breaks his marriage vows says 27
19 His fear is confined to the eyes of men 27
19 they look upon all the ways of men 27
23 brought forth children by another man. 26
24:25 It fills men with wisdom, like the Pishon •
25: 1 are beautiful in the sight of the Lord and of men; 27
2 My soul hates three kinds of men •
7 a man rejoicing in his children 27
7 a man who lives to see the downfall of his foes; •
26: 3 the blessings of the man who fears the Lord. •
28 intelligent men 26
28 a man who turns back from righteousness to sin •
27: 3 If a man is not steadfast and zealous •
4 so a man's filth remains in his thoughts. 27
5 the test of a man is in his reasoning. 27
6 discloses the cultivation of a man's mind. 27
7 Do not praise a man before you hear him reason 26
7 this is the test of men. 27
14 The talk of men given to swearing •
14 their quarrels make a man stop his ears. •
18 as a man destroys his enemy 27
27 If a man does evil, it will roll back upon him •
30 the sinful man will possess them. 26
28: 3 Does a man harbor anger against another 27
4 Does he have no mercy toward a man like himself 27
8 a man given to anger will kindle strife 27
9 a sinful man will disturb friends 26
10 in proportion to the strength of the man 27

19 Happy is the man who is protected from it *
29: 5 A man will kiss another's hands *
14 A good man will be surety for his neighbor 26
14 a man who has lost his sense of shame *
18 it has driven men of power into exile 26
22 sumptuous food in another man's house. *
28 things are hard to bear for a man who has feeling 27
30:22 Gladness of heart is the life of man 27
22 the rejoicing of a man is length of days. 26
25 A man of cheerful and good heart *
31:12 Are you seated at the table of a great man? 3
19 How ample a little is for a well-disciplined man! 27
23 Men will praise the one who is liberal with food 46
27 Wine is like life to men 27
27 What is life to a man who is without wine? *
27 It has been created to make men glad. 27
32:17 A sinful man will shun reproof 27
18 A man of judgment will not overlook an idea 26
33: 1 No evil will befall the man who fears the Lord *
2 A wise man will not hate the law 26
3 A man of understanding will trust in the law 27
10 All men are from the ground 27
13 so men are in the hand of him who made them 27
34: 1 A man of no understanding has vain and false hopes 26
9 An educated man knows many things 26
15 Blessed is the soul of the man who fears the Lord! *
20 the man who offers a sacrifice *
21 whoever deprives them of it is a man of blood. 27
25 If a man washes after touching a dead body *
26 if a man fasts for his sins 27
35: 7 The sacrifice of a righteous man is acceptable 26
19 till he repays the man according to his deeds 27
19 repays . . works of men 27
36:20 a man of experience will pay him back. 27
21 A woman will accept any man 28
23 her husband is not like other men. 27
25 a man will wander about and sigh. *
26 So who will trust a man that has no home 27
37:12 stay constantly with a godly man 26
14 a man's soul sometimes keeps him better informed 26
19 A man may be shrewd and the teacher of many 26
22 A man may be wise to his own advantage *
23 A wise man will instruct his own people 26
24 A wise man will have praise heaped upon him 26
25 The life of a man is numbered by days 26
38: 4 a sensible man will not despise them. 26
6 he gave skill to men 27
32 men can neither sojourn nor live there. *
39: 2 he will preserve the discourse of notable men 26
4 he tests the good and the evil among men. 27
26 Basic to all the needs of man's life 27
40: 1 Much labor was created for every man 27
3 the man who sits on a splendid throne *
4 the man who wears purple and a crown *
8 With all flesh, both man and beast 27
14 A generous man will be made glad 29
19 establish a man's name *
27 covers a man better than any glory. *
29 When a man looks to the table of another 26
29 He pollutes himself with another man's food 26
29 a man who is intelligent and well instructed 26
41: 1 a man without distractions 26
8 Woe to you, ungodly men, who have forsaken the law 26
11 The mourning of men is about their bodies 27
15 Better is the man who hides his folly 27
15 Better . . than the man who hides his wisdom. 27
23 will find favor with every man. 27
42: 8 will be approved before all men. 31
14 Better is the wickedness of a man 26
18 He searches out the abyss, and the hearts of men *
43: 4 A man tending a furnace works in burning heat *
44: 1 Let us now praise famous men 26
3 men renowned for their power 26
6 rich men furnished with resources 26
8 so that men declare their praise. *
10 these were men of mercy 26
23 The blessing of all men and the covenant 27
45: 1 the Lord brought forth a man of mercy 26
1 was beloved by God and man 27
18 Dathan and Abiram and their men 26
46:19 Samuel called men to witness before the Lord *
19 no man accused him. 27
47: 5 to slay a man mighty in war 27
49:15 no man like Joseph has been born, and his bones are 26
16 Shem and Seth were honored among men 27
51: 7 I looked for the assistance of men 27
Bar 1:15 to the men of Judah, to the inhabitants 27
2: 1 princes and against the men of Israel and Judah. 27
3:17 who hoard up silver and gold, in which men trust 27
37 she appeared upon earth and lived among men. 27
LJr 1: 4 which are carried on men's shoulders *
11 They deck their gods out with garments like men 27
18 a man who has offended a king 44
20 men say their hearts have melted *
26 they are carried on men's shoulders *
36 They cannot save a man from death 27
37 They cannot restore sight to a blind man 27
37 they cannot rescue a man who is in distress. 27
41 they bring him and pray Bel that the man may speak *
46 The men that make them will certainly not live *
51 they are not gods but the work of men's hands 27
53 they cannot . . give rain to men. 27
64 either to decide a case or to do good to men. 27
73 Better therefore is a just man who has no idols 27
Aza 1:60 Bless the Lord, you sons of men 27
Sus 1: 1 a man living in Babylon whose name was Joakim. 26
39 but we could not hold the man, for he was too strong *
Bel 1:20 the footsteps of men and women and children. 26
42 the men who had attempted his destruction *
Man 1: 7 repentest over the evils of men. 27
1Mc 1:11 In those days lawless men came forth from Israel 45
34 stationed there a sinful people, lawless men. 26
2: 8 Her temple has become like a man without honor; 26
18 as all the Gentiles and the men of Judah 26
31 men who had rejected the king's command 26
41 fight against every man who comes to attack us 27
44 struck down . . lawless men in their wrath 26
47 They hunted down the arrogant men 45
3:32 Lysias, a distinguished man of royal lineage 27
38 mighty men among the friends of the king 26
4: 2 Men from the citadel were his guides. 45
6 Judas appeared in the plain with 3,000 men 26
8 Judas said to the men who were with him 26
13 Then the men with Judas blew their trumpets *
29 Judas met them with 10,000 men. 26
30 the man who carried his armor. *
34 there fell of the army of Lysias 5,000 men 26
41 Then Judas detailed men to fight 26
5:13 and have destroyed about 1,000 men there. 26
15 men of Ptolemais and Tyre and Sidon *
17 Choose your men and go and rescue your brethren 26
20 Then 3,000 men were assigned to Simon 26
32 he said to the men of his forces 26
38 Judas sent men to spy out the camp *
42 Permit no man to encamp 27
47 the men of the city shut them out *
50 So the men of the forces encamped 26
58 they issued orders to the men of the forces *
59 Gorgias and his men came out of the city 26
62 they did not belong to the family of those men 26
63 The man Judas and his brothers 26
64 Men gathered to them and praised them. *
6: 3 his plan became known to the men of the city *
18 Now the men in the citadel kept hemming Israel *
35 with each elephant they stationed 1,000 men 26
37 upon each were four armed men 26
42 600 men of the king's army fell. 26
45 he killed men right and left *
49 He made peace with the men of Beth-zur *
54 Few men were left in the sanctuary 26
57 said . . to the men 26
58 Now then let us come to terms with these men 27
7: 1 sailed with a few men to a city by the sea 26
5 the lawless and ungodly men of Israel 26
7 Now then send a man whom you trust 26
19 seized many of the men who had deserted to him 26
24 took vengeance on the men who had deserted 26
28 I shall come with a few men to see you 26
32 About 500 men of the army of Nicanor fell 26
38 Take vengeance on this man and on his army 27
40 Judas encamped in Adasa with 3,000 men 26
46 men came out of all the villages of Judea round about *
8: 2 Men told him of their wars and of the brave deeds *
16 They trust one man each year to rule over them 27
9: 5 with him were 3,000 picked men. 26
12 the men with Judas also blew their trumpets. *
16 they . . followed close behind Judas and his men. *
48 Then Jonathan and the men with him leaped *
49 about 1,000 of Bacchides' men fell that day. 26
58 Jonathan and his men are living in quiet 38
60 telling them to seize Jonathan and his men 37
61 Jonathan's men seized about 50 of the men *
61 Jonathan's men seized about 50 of the men 26
62 Then Jonathan with his men, and Simon 37
63 and sent orders to the men of Judea. *
67 Simon and his men sallied out from the city 37
69 So he was greatly enraged at the lawless men 26
10: 7 the men in the citadel. *
9 the men in the citadel released the hostages *
15 men told him of the battles *
16 So he said, "Shall we find another such man? 26
32 station in it men of his own choice to guard it. 26
36 to the number of 30,000 men 26
61 A group of pestilent men from Israel, lawless men 26
61 A group of pestilent men from Israel, lawless men 26
72 Men will tell you that you cannot stand before us *
74 He chose 10,000 men 26
75 the men of the city closed its gates *
76 the men of the city became afraid *
80 shot arrows at his men 35
81 his men stood fast, as Jonathan commanded 35
85 The number . . came to 8,000 men. 26
86 the men of the city came out to meet him *
11:20 In those days Jonathan assembled the men of Judea *
21 certain lawless men who hated their nation 26
43 you will do well to send me men who will help me 26
44 So Jonathan sent 3,000 stalwart men 26
45 the men of the city assembled within the city *
46 Then the men of the city seized the main streets *
47 they killed . . as many as 100,000 men. *
49 When the men of the city saw 36
61 the men of Gaza shut him out 36
70 All the men with Jonathan fled 36
73 When his men who were fleeing saw this 38
12: 1 he chose men and sent them to Rome 26
27 Jonathan commanded his men to be alert 38
28 Jonathan and his men were prepared for battle 38
29 Jonathan and his men did not know it 38
34 the men whom Demetrius had sent *
41 with 40,000 picked fighting men 26
45 choose for yourself a few men to stay with you 26
47 He kept with himself 3,000 men 26
48 the men of Ptolemais closed the gates and seized him †
50 been seized and had perished along with his men 37
53 and blot out the memory of them from among men. 27
13:21 Now the men in the citadel kept sending envoys 36
34 Simon also chose men and sent them to Demetrius 26
44 The men in the siege engine leaped out into the city 36
45 The men in the city, with their wives and children 36
48 settled in it men who observed the law 26
49 The men in the citadel at Jerusalem 36
52 he and his men dwelt there. 38
14:23 to receive these men with honor 26
32 he armed the men of his nation's forces 26
36 as were also the men in the city of David 36
42 and appoint men over its tasks and over the country *
15:26 Simon sent to Antiochus 2,000 picked men 26
16: 6 when his men saw him, they crossed over after him. 26
15 he gave them a great banquet, and hid men there. 26
16 Ptolemy and his men rose up, took their weapons *
21 he has sent men to kill you also. *
22 he seized the men who came to destroy him 26
2Mc 1:16 and struck down the leader and his men *
3: 4 a man named Simon, of the tribe of Benjamin *
11 a man of very prominent position 26
17 bodily trembling had come over the man 26
27 his men took him up and put him on a stretcher *
28 this man who had just entered the . . treasury *
32 offered sacrifice for the man's recovery. 26
34 report to all men the majestic power of God. *
4: 2 the man who was the benefactor of the city *
9 to enrol the men of Jerusalem *
31 Andronicus, a man of high rank *
35 displeased at the unjust murder of the man. 26
40 a man advanced in years *
41 threw them . . at Lysimachus and his men. 39
44 three men sent by the senate presented the case 26
5: 5 Jason took no less than 1,000 men *
22 more barbarous than the man who appointed him; *
25 he ordered his men to parade under arms. 41
6: 6 A man could neither keep the sabbath *
18 a man now advanced in age and of noble presence 26
20 as men ought to go *
21 Those . . took the man aside 26
26 I should avoid the punishment of men 27
7:14 One cannot but choose to die at the hands of men 27
16 Because you have authority among men 27
21 she fired her woman's reasoning with a man's courage 28
23 who shaped the beginning of man 27
34 you, unholy wretch, you most defiled of all men 27
8: 2 which had been profaned by ungodly men 27
8 When Philip saw that the man was gaining ground 26
9 a man of experience in military service. 26
16 Maccabeus gathered his men together 39
22 to command a division, putting 1,500 men under each. *
32 a most unholy man 26
9: 2 Antiochus and his men were defeated *
10 no one was able to carry the man *
10:16 Maccabeus and his men 39
19 left . . also Zacchaeus and his men 40
20 the men with Simon, who were money-hungry *
21 and accused these men of having sold their brethren *
25 Maccabeus and his men 39
29 five resplendent men on horses 26
33 Then Maccabeus and his men were glad 39
34 The men within . . blasphemed terribly *
11: 2 gathered about 80,000 men and all his cavalry *
6 When Maccabeus and his men got word 39
9 ready to assail not only men 27
12: 3 some men of Joppa did so ungodly a deed as this †
5 he gave orders to his men 26
8 the men in Jamnia meant . . to wipe out the Jews *
11 Judas and his men won the victory 39
14 Judas and his men 39
15 Judas and his men 39
19 more than 10,000 men. 26
20 Maccabeus . . set men in command of the divisions *
22 often they were injured by their own men 32
23 and destroyed as many as 30,000 men. 26
24 Dositheus and Sosipater and their men 39
35 a certain Dositheus, one of Bacenor's men *
35 who was on horseback and was a strong man 26
36 Esdris and his men 39
37 then he charged against Gorgias' men 39
39 Judas and his men went to take up the bodies 39
13: 1 word came to Judas and his men 39
14 exhorting his men to fight nobly to the death 40

15 He gave his men the watchword, "God's victory 39
15 slew as many as 2,000 men in the camp 26
21 Rhodocus, a man from the ranks of the Jews •
22 attacked Judas and his men, was defeated; 39
14: 1 Three years later, word came to Judas and his men 39
13 with orders to kill Judas and scatter his men 40
18 hearing of the valor of Judas and his men 39
24 he was warmly attached to the man. 26
28 when the man had done no wrong. 26
30 he gathered not a few of his men 39
31 he had been cleverly outwitted by the man 26
31 and commanded them to hand the man over. 26
32 did not know where the man was whom he sought •
37 a man who loved his fellow citizens 26
15: 1 Judas and his men were in the region of Samaria 39
6 a public monument of victory over Judas and his men 39
8 he exhorted his men not to fear the attack 40
12 a noble and good man 26
13 Then likewise a man appeared 26
14 This is a man who loves the brethren •
25 Nicanor and his men advanced with trumpets 39
26 Judas and his men met the enemy in battle 39
27 they laid low no less than 35,000 men •
30 the man who was ever . . the defender •
30 the man who maintained his youthful good will •
3Mc 1: 3 so it turned out that this man incurred the vengeance •
29 not only the men but also the walls 27
2: 5 consumed with fire and sulphur the men of Sodom †
15 your dwelling . . is unapproachable by man. 27
3: 2 by men who conspired to do them ill 27
5 they were established in good repute among all men. 27
7: 6 the clemency which we have toward all men 27
9 not man but the Ruler over every power 27
15 In that day they put to death more than 300 men 26
4Mc 1:24 a man will see if he reflects on this experience 43
2:21 Now when God fashioned man 27
4: 1 the noble and good man, Onias 26
15 an arrogant and terrible man 26
5: 4 He was a man of priestly family, learned in the law •
6: 5 the courageous and noble man, as a true Eleazar •
30 the holy man died nobly in his tortures 26
7:16 because of piety an aged man despised tortures 26
23 only the wise and courageous man •
8:19 O men and brothers, should we not fear 26
10: 5 Enraged by the man's boldness 26
12:13 a man, were you not ashamed, you most savage beast 27
14:11 reason had full command over these men 26
15:23 devout reason, giving her heart a man's courage •
30 more manly than men in endurance! 26
16: 2 not only that men have ruled over the emotions 26
14 you have proved more powerful than a man. 26
18: 3 were not only admired by men 27

man *See also* able, accursed, aged, another, any, armed, arrogant, band, best, blameless, blind, certain, chief, chosen, collection, common, cruel, dead, deaf, depraved, devout, discerning, discreet, drowsy, drunken, dumb, each, eminent, every, evil, faithful, faithless, famous, favored, few, fierce, first, foolish, free, generous, godless, godly, good, great, greedy, grudging, guilty, haired, hanged, happy, hated, haughty, highly, hired, holy, honest, honorable, honored, humble, hungry, illustrious, immoral, impure, inferior, innocent, insolent, insubordinate, intelligent, just, lame, last, lawless, leading, leprous, liberal, living, lowly, mad, made, many, married, merciless, mighty, minded, miserable, modest, most, mounted, no, noble, obscure, old, one, only, oppressed, ordinary, other, patient, perverse, pestilent, picked, play, poor, position, powerful, principal, profane, proud, prudent, reliable, rich, right, righteous, ruthless, seafaring, senseless, sensible, seven, sick, singer, singing, skilful, skilled, slain, slave, slothful, some, spiritual, stingy, stouthearted, strong, such, thirsty, thrice, trained, treacherous, two, understanding, unfortunate, ungodly, ungrateful, unintelligent, unmarried, unrighteous, unwise, upright, valiant, violent, wayfaring, weak, wicked, willing, wise, worldly, worthless, wounded, wrathful, young.

all men 1. ἅπας 2. πᾶς 3. omnis

Mat 19:11 Not all men can receive this saying 2
Mrk 5:20 and all men marveled. 2
Lke 3:15 all men questioned in their hearts concerning John 2
Joh 2:25 because he knew all men 2
12:32 I . . will draw all men to myself. 2
13:35 all men will know that you are my disciples 2
Act 1:24 Lord, who knowest the hearts of all men 2
4:21 all men praised God for what had happened. 2
17:25 since he himself gives to all men life and breath 2
31 of this he has given assurance to all men 2
Rom 3: 9 all men, both Jews and Greeks, are under . . sin 2
5:12 death spread to all men because all men sinned– 2
11:32 For God has consigned all men to disobedience 2
1Co 9:19 For though I am free from all men 2
22 I have become all things to all men 2
10:33 just as I try to please all men in everything I do 2
Gal 6:10 as we have opportunity, let us do good to all men 2
Eph 3: 9 to make all men see what is the plan of the mystery 2
1Th 3:12 abound in love to one another and to all men 2
Jas 1: 5 let him ask God, who gives to all men generously 2
1Pe 2:17 Honor all men. Love the brotherhood. Fear God. 2
Rev 19:18 and the flesh of all men, both free and slave 2
2Es 8:62 I have not shown this to all men 3
Tob 13: 8 Let all men speak 2
Jdt 5:22 all the men from the seacoast and from Moab 2
Wis 7: 1 I also am mortal, like all men 1
12:13 whose care is for all men 2
16:12 it was thy word, O Lord, which heals all men. 2
2Mc 3:36 he bore testimony to all men 2
5: 4 Therefore all men prayed 2
8 pursued by all men 2
24 and commanded him to slay all the grown men 2

man binding 1. δεσμεύω

Jdt 8: 3 overseeing the men who were binding sheaves 1

man by man 1. לַגְּבָרִים 2. εἰς ἄνδρας

Jos 7:14 the household . . shall come near man by man. 1
17 and he brought near the . . Zer'ahites man by man 1
18 and he brought near his household man by man 1
1Sm 10:21 he brought the . . Matrites near man by man 2

man greedy for gain 1. בצע

Ps 10: 3 man greedy for gain curses and renounces the LORD. 1

man in ambush 1. ארב 2. ἔνεδρον

Jdg 9:25 the men of Shechem put men in ambush against him 1
20:29 Israel set men in ambush round about Gib'e-ah. 1
33 the men of Israel who were in ambush rushed out 1
36 because they trusted to the men in ambush 1
37 the men in ambush made haste and rushed 1
37 the men in ambush moved out and smote all the city 1
38 between the men of Israel and the men in ambush 1
1Mc 11:69 Then the men in ambush emerged from their places 2

man in harmony 1. σύμφωνος

4Mc 7: 7 O man in harmony with the law 1

man in humble circumstances 1. ταπεινός

Sir 29: 8 be patient with a man in humble circumstances 1

man of a strange tongue 1. ἑτερόγλωσσος

1Co 14:21 In the law it is written, "By men of strange tongues 1

man of age 1. γῆρας

4Mc 7:15 O man of blessed age and of venerable gray hair 1

man of authority 1. δυνατός

Act 25: 5 let the men of authority among you go down with me 1

man of discernment 1. בין

Prv 16:21 The wise of heart is called a man of discernment 1

man of double mind 1. δίψυχος

Jas 4: 8 purify your hearts, you men of double mind. 1

man of high estate 1. בֶּן אִישׁ

Ps 62: 9 men of high estate are a delusion; 1

man of insight 1. בין

Ezr 8:16 Joi'arib and Elna'than, who were men of insight 1

man of integrity 1. תָּמִים

Prv 2:21 men of integrity will remain in it; 1

man of little faith 1. ὀλιγόπιστος

Mat 16: 8 O men of little faith 1
Lke 12:28 how much more . . you, O men of little faith! 1

man of low estate 1. בֶּן אָדָם

Ps 62: 9 Men of low estate are but a breath 1

man of note 1. ἐπίσημος

Rom 16: 7 they are men of note among the apostles 1

man of old 1. רִאשׁוֹן 2. ἀρχαῖος 3. πρεσβύτερος

Deu 19:14 neighbor's landmark, which the men of old have set. 1
Mat 5:21 You have heard that it was said to the men of old 2
33 to the men of old, 'You shall not swear falsely 2
Heb 11: 2 the men of old received divine approval. 3

man of pride 1. ὑπερηφανία

Sir 15: 8 She is far from men of pride 1

man of rank 1. נשׂא פָּנִים

Isa 3: 3 the captain of 50 and the man of rank 1

man of skill 1. ידע

Ecc 9:11 bread to the wise . . nor favor to the men of skill; 1

man of strength 1. ἰσχύω

Jdt 9:11 nor thy might upon men of strength 1

man of the flesh 1. σάρκινος

1Co 3: 1 as men of the flesh, as babes in Christ. 1

man of understanding 1. בין 2. ἐπιστήμων 3. συνετός

Prv 1: 5 man of understanding acquire skill 1
14: 6 but knowledge is easy for a man of understanding. 1
33 Wisdom . . in the mind of a man of understanding 1
17:10 A rebuke goes deeper into a man of understanding 1
24 man of understanding sets his face toward 1
19:25 reprove a man of understanding, and he will gain 1
1Es 8:44 who were leaders and men of understanding; 2
Sir 9:15 your conversation be with men of understanding 3

man of violence 1. βιαστής

Mat 11:12 men of violence take it by force. 1

man on foot 1. רַגְלִי 2. πεζός

1Sm 15: 4 numbered them . . 200,000 men on foot 1
Sir 16:10 nor for the 600,000 men on foot 2

man on horseback 1. רכב סוס

2Kg 9:18 So a man on horseback went to meet him, and said 1

man sentenced to death 1. ἐπιθανάτιος

1Co 4: 9 like men sentenced to death 1

man who dies 1. νεκρός

LJr 1:32 as some do at a funeral feast for a man who has died. 1

man who has feelings like 1. ὁμοιοπαθέω

4Mc 12:13 men who have feelings like yours 1

man who has understanding 1. ידע בִּינָה

1Ch 12:32 Is'sachar men who had understanding of the times 1

man who practices 1. עשׂה

Ps 101: 7 No man who practices deceit shall dwell in my 1

man who serves 1. עמד

1Ch 6:33 These are the men who served and their sons. 1

man who sins 1. חָטָא

Num 16:38 the censers of these men who have sinned 1

man who utters 1. דבר

Ps 101: 7 no man who utters lies shall continue in my 1

man whom one pays 1. μίσθιος

Tob 5:11 a man whom you will pay to go with your son 1

man-child 1. גֶּבֶר

Job 3: 3 the night which said, 'A man-child is conceived.' 1

man-made 1. χειροποίητος

Bel 1: 5 Because I do not revere man-made idols 1

man-pleaser 1. ἀνθρωπάρεσκος

Eph 6: 6 not in the way of eye-service, as men-pleasers 1
Col 3:22 not with eyeservice, as men-pleasers 1

manacle 1. χειροπέδη

Sir 21:19 like manacles on his right hand. 1

manage 1. ἰσχύω 2. προΐστημι

Act 27:16 we managed with difficulty to secure the boat; 1
1Ti 3: 4 He must manage his own household well 2
5 man does not know how to manage his own household 2
12 let them manage their children . . well 2

mandrake 1. דּוּדַי

Gen 30:14 Reuben went and found mandrakes in the field 1
14 Give me, I pray, some of your son's mandrakes. 1
15 Would you take away my son's mandrakes also? 1
15 lie with you tonight for your son's mandrakes. 1
16 have hired you with my son's mandrakes." So he lay 1
Sng 7:13 The mandrakes give forth fragrance 1

manfully 1. ἀνδρείως 2. ἀνδρωδῶς

1Mc 6:31 burned these with fire, and fought manfully. 2
2Mc 6:27 Therefore, by manfully giving up my life now 1
14:43 and manfully threw himself down into the crowd. 2

manger 1. φάτνη

Lke 2: 7 laid him in a manger 1
12 lying in a manger. 1
16 the babe lying in a manger. 1
13:15 untie his ox or his ass from the manger 1

mangle 1. αἰκίζω 2. καταικίζω 3. λυμαίνω

Sir 28:23 like a leopard it will mangle them. 3
3Mc 5:42 mangled by the knees and feet of the beasts 1
4Mc 9:15 you are mangling me in this manner 2

manhood 1. אוֹן 2. ἀνήρ

Hos 12: 3 and in his manhood he strove with God. 1
Eph 4:13 to mature manhood 2
1Mc 13:53 Simon saw that John his son had reached manhood 2

manifest 1. ידע 2. ראה 3. δείκνυμι 4. ἔκδηλος 5. ἐμφανής 6. ἐμφανίζω 7. ἐπιφαίνω 8. ἐπιφάνεια 9. ἐπιφανής 10. φαιδρός 11. φανερός 12. φανερόω 13. manifestus 14. ostendo 15. pareo

Ps 77:14 who hast manifested thy might among the peoples. 1
90:16 Let thy work be manifest to thy servants 2
Isa 24:23 before his elders he will manifest his glory. •
Lke 8:17 nothing is hid that shall not be made manifest 10

Joh 2:11 Jesus did at Cana . . and manifested his glory; 12
14:21 I will love him and manifest myself to him. 6
22 manifest yourself to us, and not to the world? 6
17: 6 I have manifested thy name to the men 12
Act 2:20 the great and manifest day. 9
4:16 is manifest to all the inhabitants of Jerusalem 10
10:40 made him manifest; 5
Rom 3:21 righteousness . . manifested apart from law 12
1Co 3:13 each man's work will become manifest 10
2Co 4:10 Jesus may also be manifested in our bodies. 12
11 so that the life of Jesus may be manifested 12
1Ti 3:16 He was manifested in the flesh 12
2Ti 1:10 manifested through the appearing of our Savior 12
Tit 1: 3 at the proper time manifested in his word 12
1Pe 5: 4 when the chief Shepherd is manifested 12
2Es 7:35 and the reward shall be manifested 14
9: 5 the beginning is evident, and the end manifest; 13
6 the beginnings are manifest in wonders 13
16:73 the tested quality of my elect shall be manifest 15
Wis 1: 2 manifests himself to those who do not distrust 6
7:21 both what is secret and what is manifest 5
16:21 For thy sustenance manifested thy sweetness 6
Sir 6:22 is not manifest to many. 10
LJr 1:51 It will be manifest to all the nations and kings 11
Man 1:14 in me thou wilt manifest thy goodness 3
1Mc 15: 9 so that your glory will become manifest 10
2Mc 9: 8 making the power of God manifest to all. 10
14:15 upholds . . by manifesting himself. 8
15:34 the Lord who had manifested himself 9
3Mc 3:19 By maintaining their manifest ill-will toward us 4
5:35 praised the manifest Lord God, King of kings 9
51 manifest himself and be merciful to them 8
6: 4 manifesting the light of your mercy 7

manifest *See also* make.

become manifest 1. *φαίνω* 2. pareo
2Es 14:35 the names of the righteous will become manifest 2
1Mc 11:12 their enmity became manifest. 1

manifest one's glory 1. כבד
Ezk 28:22 I will manifest my glory in the midst of you. 1

manifest one's holiness 1. קדשׁ
Ezk 20:41 I will manifest my holiness among you 1
28:22 judgments in her, and manifest my holiness in her; 1
25 and manifest my holiness in them 1

manifestation 1. *ἀνάδειξις* 2. *ἐπιφάνεια* 3. *φανέρωσις*
Lke 1:80 till the day of his manifestation to Israel. 1
1Co 12: 7 To each is given the manifestation of the Spirit 3
2Mc 3:24 caused so great a manifestation 2
12:22 the manifestation to them of him who sees all 2
15:27 were greatly gladdened by God's manifestation. 2
3Mc 5: 8 in a glorious manifestation rescue them 2

manifestation of the Spirit 1. *πνεῦμα*
1Co 14:12 you are eager for manifestations of the Spirit 1

manifold 1. כָּפֶל 2. רבב 3. *πολυμερής* 4. *πολυποίκιλος*
Job 11: 6 For he is manifold in understanding. 1
Ps 104:24 O LORD, how manifold are thy works! 2
Eph 3:10 the manifold wisdom of God 4
Wis 7:22 is intelligent, holy, unique, manifold, subtle 3

manifold more 1. *πολλαπλασίων*
Lke 18:30 who will not receive manifold more in this time 1

mankind 1. אָדָם 2. בְּשַׂר אִישׁ 3. *ἄνθρωπος* 4. *ἀνθρώπων γένος* 5. *βίος* 6. *σάρξ* 7. genus humanum 8. homo
Job 12:10 living thing and the breath of all mankind. 2
Isa 13:12 rare than . . and mankind than the gold of Ophir. 1
Jer 32:20 and to this day in Israel and among all mankind 1
Zep 1: 3 I will cut off mankind from the face of the earth 1
Eph 2: 3 like the rest of mankind. •
Rev 9: 4 but only those of mankind who have not the seal 3
15 angels . . ready . . to kill a third of mankind. 3
18 By . . three plagues a third of mankind was killed 3
20 rest of mankind, who were not killed by . . plagues 3
14: 4 redeemed from mankind as first fruits for God 3
2Es 7:138 not one 10,000th of mankind 8
8:15 About all mankind thou knowest best 8
13:41 where mankind had never lived 7
Tob 8: 6 From them the race of mankind has sprung 3
Wis 7: 6 there is for all mankind one entrance into life •
10: 8 also left for mankind a reminder of their folly 5
14:21 this became a hidden trap for mankind 6
Sir 45: 4 he chose him out of all mankind. 5
LJr 1:26 revealing to mankind their worthlessness. 3
2Mc 7:28 Thus also mankind comes into being. 4
4Mc 14:14 Even unreasoning animals, like mankind 3

mankind *See also* hater.

manliness *See* awake.

more manly 1. *ἀνδρεῖος*
4Mc 15:30 more manly than men in endurance! 1

manna 1. מָן 2. *μάννα* 3. manna
Exd 16:31 Now the house of Israel called its name manna; 1
33 Take a jar, and put an omer of manna in it, and place 1
35 the people of Israel ate the manna forty years 1
35 they ate the manna, till they came to the border 1
Num 11: 6 there is nothing at all but this manna to look at. 1
7 Now the manna was like coriander seed 1
9 When the dew fell . . the manna fell with it. 1
Deu 8: 3 let you hunger and fed you with manna 1
16 who fed you in the wilderness with manna 1
Jos 5:12 And the manna ceased on the morrow, when they ate 1
12 and the people of Israel had manna no more 1
Neh 9:20 didst not withhold thy manna from their mouth 1
Ps 78:24 he rained down upon them manna to eat 1
Joh 6:31 Our fathers ate the manna in the wilderness 2
49 Your fathers ate the manna in the wilderness 2
Heb 9: 4 which contained a golden urn holding the manna 2
Rev 2:17 To him who conquers I will give some . . manna 2
2Es 1:19 and gave you manna for food 3

manner 1. אֹרַח 2. דָּבָר 3. דֶּרֶךְ 4. כָּכָה 5. מִשְׁפָּט 6. *νόμος* 7. *τρόπος*
Gen 18:11 to be with Sarah after the manner of women. 1
19:31 to come in to us after the manner of all the earth. 3
Exd 12:11 In this manner you shall eat it: your loins girded 4
Deu 15: 2 this is the manner of the release: every creditor 2
Jos 6:15 and marched around the city in the same manner 5
Jdg 18: 7 in security, after the manner of the Sido'nians 5
Rut 4: 7 this was the manner of attesting in Israel. •
1Kg 7:37 After this manner he made the ten stands; •
2Kg 17:33 So they . . after the manner of the nation 5
34 they do according to the former manner. 5
40 but they did according to their former manner. 5
Neh 6: 4 I answered them in the same manner. •
Ezk 20:30 after the manner of your fathers and go astray 3
Ams 4:10 among you a pestilence after the manner of Egypt; 3
Rom 1:29 They were filled with all manner of wickedness •
2Mc 10: 6 in the manner of the feast of booths 7
14:46 This was the manner of his death. 7
15:12 of modest bearing and gentle manner 7
3Mc 5:36 reconvened the party in the same manner 6
6:12 deprived of life in the manner of traitors. 7
7:13 When they had applauded him in fitting manner •
4Mc 4: 1 despite all manner of slander 7
6: 1 in this manner had made eloquent response 7
9:15 you are mangling me in this manner 7
15: 4 In what manner might I express 7

manner *See also* shameful.

all manner
Ps 144:13 garners be full, providing all manner of store; †

kindly manner 1. *φιλοφρόνως*
4Mc 8: 5 I admire . . every one of you in a kindly manner 1

like manner 1. כְּכֹל הַדְּבָרִים הָאֵלֶּה 2. *ὁμοίως* 3. *ὡσαύτως* 4. similiter
Jer 27:12 To Zedeki'ah king of Judah I spoke in like manner 1
Mrk 4:16 these in like manner are the ones •
Lke 16:25 Laz'arus in like manner evil things 2
Jde 1: 8 Yet in like manner these men . . defile the flesh 2
2Es 4:15 in like manner the waves of the sea also 4
Wis 15: 7 making all in like manner 2
3Mc 7:19 there too in like manner they decided to observe 3

manner of life 1. מִשְׁפָּט 2. *ἀναστροφή* 3. *βίος* 4. *βίωσις* 5. *πολιτεύομαι*
Jdg 13:12 what is to be the boy's manner of life 1
Act 26: 4 My manner of life from my youth . . is known 4
Eph 4:22 which belongs to your former manner of life 2
Php 1:27 Only let your manner of life be worthy 5
Wis 2:15 his manner of life is unlike that of others 3

manner of walking 1. *βῆμα*
Sir 19:30 a man's manner of walking, show what he is. 1

strange manner of life 1. *ξενίζω*
AEs 13: 5 a strange manner of life and laws 1

strict manner 1. *ἀκρίβεια*
Act 22: 3 educated according to the strict manner of the law 1

unworthy manner 1. *ἀναξίως*
1Co 11:27 drinks the cup of the Lord in an unworthy manner 1

manner worthy of a brother 1. *ἀδελφοπρεπῶς*
4Mc 10:12 in a manner worthy of his brothers 1

good manners 1. *παιδεία*
Sir 31:17 first to stop eating, for the sake of good manners 1

manservant 1. עֶבֶד 2. *δοῦλος* 3. *παῖς*
Gen 12:16 and he had sheep, oxen, he-asses, menservants 1
24:35 herds, silver and gold, menservants 1
30:43 had large flocks, maidservants and menservants 1
32: 5 I have oxen, asses, flocks, menservants 1
Exd 20:10 you, or your son, or your daughter, your manservant 1
17 covet . . his manservant, or his maidservant 1
Deu 5:14 your manservant, or your maidservant, or your ox 1
14 that your manservant and your maidservant 1
21 not desire . . his manservant, or his maidservant 1
12:12 rejoice . . you and . . your menservants 1
18 eat . . you and your . . manservant 1
16:11 rejoice . . you and . . your manservant 1
14 rejoice . . you and . . your manservant 1
1Sm 8:16 He will take your menservants and maidservants 1
2Kg 5:26 sheep and oxen, menservants and maidservants? 1
Ezr 2:65 besides their menservants and maidservants 1
Neh 7:67 besides their menservants and maidservants 1
Job 31:13 If I have rejected the cause of my manservant 1
Jol 2:29 Even upon the menservants and maidservants 1
Lke 12:45 to beat the menservants and the maidservants 3
Act 2:18 yea, and on my menservants and my maidservants 2
1Es 5: 1 menservants and maidservants, and their cattle. 3
41 besides their menservants and maidservants 3
42 their menservants and maidservants were 7,337; 3

manslayer 1. נכה 2. רצח 3. *ἀνδροφόνος*
Num 35: 6 where you shall permit the manslayer to flee 2
11 manslayer who kills any person without intent 2
12 that the manslayer may not die until he stands 2
24 between the manslayer and the avenger of blood 1
25 congregation shall rescue the manslayer 2
26 if the manslayer shall at any time go beyond 2
27 avenger of blood slays the manslayer 2
28 manslayer may return to . . his possession. 2
Deu 4:42 that the manslayer might flee there 2
19: 3 so that any manslayer can flee to them. 2
4 This is the provision for the manslayer 2
6 avenger of blood . . pursue the manslayer 2
Jos 20: 3 that the manslayer . . may flee there; 2
1Ti 1: 9 for . . murderers of mothers, for manslayers 3

mantelet 1. סֹכֵךְ
Nah 2: 5 they hasten to the wall, the mantelet is set up. 1

mantle 1. אַדֶּרֶת 2. מִטְפַּחַת 3. מַעֲטֶה 4. מַעֲטָפָה 5. מְעִיל 6. רְדִיד 7. שִׂמְלָה 8. תַּכְרִיךְ 9. סַרְבָּל (A) 10. *ἐσθής* 11. *ἱμάτιον* 12. *περιβόλαιον*
Gen 25:25 came forth red, all his body like a hairy mantle; 1
Exd 12:34 kneading bowls being bound up in their mantles 7
22:27 covering, it is his mantle for his body; 7
Jos 7:21 among the spoil a beautiful mantle from Shinar 1
24 and the silver and the mantle and the bar of gold 1
Rut 3:15 Bring the mantle you are wearing and hold it out. 2
1Kg 19:13 Eli'jah . . wrapped his face in his mantle 1
19 Eli'jah passed . . and cast his mantle upon him. 1
2Kg 2: 8 Eli'jah took his mantle, and rolled it up 1
13 he took up the mantle of Eli'jah that had fallen 1
14 Then he took the mantle of Eli'jah that had fallen 1
Ezr 9: 3 When I heard this, I rent my garments and my mantle 5
5 I rose . . with my garments and my mantle rent 5
Est 8:15 #crown and a mantle of fine linen and purple 8
Ps 109:29 they be wrapped in their own shame as in a mantle! 5
Sng 5: 7 beat me, they wounded me, they took away my mantle 6
Isa 3: 6 saying: "You have a mantle; you shall be our leader 7
7 n my house there is neither bread nor mantle 7
22 the festal robes, the mantles, the cloaks 4
59:17 and wrapped himself in fury as a mantle. 5
61: 3 the mantle of praise instead of a faint spirit; 3
Dan 3:21 bound in their mantles, their tunics, their hats 9
27 mantles were not harmed, and no smell of fire 9
Zec 13: 4 not put on a hairy mantle in order to deceive 1
Mat 24:18 to take his mantle. 11
Mrk 10:50 throwing off his mantle he sprang up 11
13:16 not turn back to take his mantle. 11
Lke 22:36 who has no sword sell his mantle and buy one. 11
Act 12: 8 Wrap your mantle around you and follow me. 11
Heb 1:12 like a mantle thou wilt roll them up 12
1Es 8:71 I rent my garments and my holy mantle 10
73 with my garments and my holy mantle rent 10

manure 1. *κόπριον*
Lke 13: 8 till I dig about it and put on manure. 1

many 1. גָּדוֹל 2. הַרְבֵּה 3. כָּבֵד 4. מְאֹד 5. מִכֹּל 6. מִסְפָּר 7. מֵרֹב 8. עצם 9. רַב 10. רֹב 11. רבב 12. רבה 13. רֹב מְאֹד מְאֹד 14. שִׁפְעָה 15. שַׂגִּיא (A) 16. *εἷς* 17. *ἕως* 18. *ἱκανός* 19. *καθώς* 20. *μακρός* 21. *ὅσος* 22. *οὐχ ἧττον* 23. *ὄχλος* 24. *πλῆθος* 25. *πληθύνω* 26. *πολλάκις* 27. *πολλαχόθεν* 28. *πολύπαις* 29. *πολύς* 30. *συχνός* 31. *τοσοῦτος* 32. *ὑπέρ* 33. multitudo 34. multus 35. quotquot 36. tantus
Gen 9:10 the earth with you, as many as came out of the ark. 5
21:34 Abraham sojourned many days in the land 9
37:34 Jacob . . mourned for his son many days. 9
45: 7 sent me . . to keep alive for you many survivors. 1
50: 3 for so many are required for embalming. •
20 to bring it about that many people should be kept 9
Exd 1: 9 people of Israel are too many and too mighty 9
2:23 In the course of those many days 9

5: 5 Behold, the people of the land are now many and you 9
12:38 and very many cattle, both flocks and herds. 3
19:21 to the LORD to gaze and many of them perish. 9
Lev 11:42 whatever has many feet, all the swarming things 12
15:25 If a woman has a discharge of blood for many days 9
25:16 If the years are many you shall increase the price 10
51 If there are still many years, according to them 9
26:21 more plagues . . sevenfold as many as your sins •
Num 9:19 cloud continued over the tabernacle many days 9
13:18 whether they are few or many 9
20:20 Edom came out against them with many men 3
21: 6 so that many people of Israel died. 9
22: 3 great dread of the people, because they were many; 9
15 princes, more in number and more honorable 9
24: 7 his seed shall be in many waters 9
35: 8 from the larger tribes you shall take many 12
Deu 1:11 LORD . . make you a 1,000 times as many as you are •
46 you remained at Kadesh many days 9
2: 1 for many days we went about Mount Se'ir. 9
10 Emim . . a people great and many, and tall 9
21 a people great and many, and tall as the Anakim; 9
3: 5 besides very many unwalled villages. 12
19 your cattle (I know that you have many cattle) 9
7: 1 the LORD . . clears away many nations before you 9
15: 6 lend to many nations, but you shall not borrow; 9
6 rule over many nations, but they shall not rule 9
23:24 eat your fill of grapes, as many as you wish •
25: 3 go on to beat him with more stripes than these 9
28:12 lend to many nations, but you shall not borrow. 9
31:17 many evils and troubles will come upon them 9
21 when many evils and troubles have come upon them 9
32: 7 of old, consider the years of many generations; •
Jos 11: 4 they came . . with very many horses and chariots. 9
22: 3 not forsaken your brethren these many days 9
8 Go . . with much wealth, and with very many cattle 9
Jdg 7: 2 The people with you are too many for me to give 9
4 LORD said to Gideon, "The people are still too many; 9
8:30 Gideon had 70 sons . . for he had many wives. 9
9:40 many fell wounded, up to the entrance of the gate. 9
16:24 ravager of our country, who has slain many of us. 12
30 whom he slew at his death were more than those 9
1Sm 2: 5 but she who has many children is forlorn. 9
14: 6 hinder the LORD from saving by many or by few. 9
25:10 There are many servants . . breaking away 11
26:25 You will do many things and will succeed in them. •
2Sm 1: 4 many of the people also have fallen and are dead; 12
12: 2 The rich man had very many flocks and herds; 12
13:34 many people were coming from the Horona'im road 9
14: 2 who has been mourning many days for the dead; 9
18: 8 forest devoured more people . . than the sword. 2
22:17 he took me, he drew me out of many waters. 9
24: 3 God add . . 100 times as many as they are •
1Kg 2:38 So Shim'e-i dwelt in Jerusalem many days. 9
4:20 Judah and Israel were as many as the sand 9
7:47 unweighed, because there were so many of them; 13
8: 5 so many sheep . . that they could not be counted 7
11: 1 Now King Solomon loved many foreign women 9
17:15 she, and he, and her household ate for many days. •
18: 1 After many days the word of the LORD came 9
25 and prepare it first, for you are many; 9
2Kg 9:22 so long as the harlotries and . . are so many? 9
19:23 With my many chariots I have gone up the heights 10
1Ch 4:27 but his brothers had not many children 9
5:22 For many fell slain, because the war was of God. 9
7: 4 36,000, for they had many wives and sons. 12
22 E'phraim their father mourned many days 9
8:40 warriors, bowmen, having many sons and grandsons 12
21: 3 add to his people 100 times as many as they are! •
23:11 but Je'ush and Beri'ah had not many sons 12
17 but the sons of Rehabi'ah were very many. 12
24: 4 Since more chief men were found among the sons 9
28: 5 of all my sons (for the LORD has given me many sons 9
2Ch 1: 9 over a people as many as the dust of the earth. 9
5: 6 the ark, sacrificing so many sheep and oxen 10
16: 8 a huge army with exceedingly many chariots 4
24:27 Accounts . . of the many oracles against him 10
26:10 he built towers . . and hewed out many cisterns 9
30:13 many people came together in Jerusalem to keep 9
17 For there were many in the assembly who had not 9
18 many of them from E'phraim, Manas'seh, Is'sachar 9
32: 4 A great many people were gathered 9
23 many brought gifts to the LORD to Jerusalem 9
Ezr 3:12 many of the priests and Levites and heads 9
12 wept . . though many shouted aloud for joy; 9
5:11 rebuilding the house . . built many years ago 15
10:13 people are many, and it is a time of heavy rain; 9
Neh 5: 2 With our sons and our daughters, we are many; 9
6:17 nobles of Judah sent many letters to Tobi'ah 12
18 For many in Judah were bound by oath to him 9
7: 2 more faithful and God-fearing man than many. 9
9:28 many times thou didst deliver them 9
30 Many years thou didst bear with them 9
13:26 Among the many nations there was no king like him 9
Est 1: 4 he showed . . for many days, 180 days 9
2: 8 many maidens were gathered in Susa the capital 9
4: 3 and most of them lay in sackcloth and ashes. 9
8:17 many from . . the country declared themselves Jews 9
Job 1: 3 500 she-asses, and very many servants; 9
4: 3 Behold, you have instructed many 9
5:25 know also that your descendants shall be many 9
11:19 many will entreat your favor. 9
16: 2 I have heard many such things; 9
23:14 many such things are in his mind. 9
32: 7 Let days speak, and many years teach wisdom. 10
Ps 3: 1 O LORD, how many are my foes! 11
1 how many are my foes! Many are rising against me; 9
2 many are saying of me, there is no help for him 9
4: 6 many who say, "O that we might see some good! 9
5:10 because of their many transgressions cast them out 10
18:16 he took me, he drew me out of many waters. 9
22:12 Many bulls encompass me, strong bulls of Bashan 9
25:19 Consider how many are my foes 12
29: 3 God of glory thunders, the LORD, upon many waters. 9
31:13 Yea, I hear the whispering of many- 9
32:10 Many are the pangs of the wicked; 9
34:12 who desires life, and covets many days •
19 Many are the afflictions of the righteous; 9
37:16 Better . . than the abundance of many wicked. 9
38:19 many are those who hate me wrongfully. 11
40: 3 a song of praise to our God. Many will see and fear 9
5 they would be more than can be numbered. 8
12 they are more than the hairs of my head; 8
55:18 many are arrayed against me. 9
56: 2 for many fight against me proudly. 9
69: 4 More in number than the hairs of my head 11
71: 7 I have been as a portent to many; 9
20 Thou who hast made me see many sore troubles 9
90:15 Make us glad as many days as thou hast afflicted •
15 as many years as we have seen evil. •
93: 4 Mightier than the thunders of many waters 9
94:19 cares of my heart are many, thy consolations 10
97: 1 LORD reigns; let . . the many coastlands be glad! 9
106:43 Many times he delivered them 9
119:157 Many are my persecutors and my adversaries 9
135:10 who smote many nations and slew mighty kings 9
139:18 If I would count them, they are more than the sand. 12
144: 7 rescue me and deliver me from the many waters 9
Prv 4:10 Hear . . that the years of your life may be many. 12
7:26 for many a victim has she laid low; 9
10:19 words are many, transgression is not lacking 10
21 The lips of the righteous feed many 9
14:20 but the rich has many friends. 9
15:22 but with many advisers they succeed. 10
19: 4 Wealth brings many new friends 9
6 Many seek the favor of a generous man 9
21 Many are the plans in the mind of a man 9
20: 6 Many a man proclaims his own loyalty 9
28: 2 When a land transgresses it has many rulers; 9
27 but he who hides his eyes will get many a curse. 9
29:26 Many seek the favor of a ruler 9
31:29 Many women have done excellently 9
Ecc 2: 8 I got . . and many concubines, man's delight. •
5: 3 dream comes . . and a fool's voice with many words. 10
6: 3 and lives many years, so that the days . . are many 9
3 many years, so that the days of his years are many 9
11 The more words, the more vanity 12
11 The more words, the more vanity 12
7:22 many times you have yourself cursed others. 9
29 but they have sought out many devices. 9
10: 6 folly is set in many high places 9
11: 1 for you will find it after many days. 10
8 if a man lives many years, let him rejoice in them 12
8 remember that the days of darkness will be many. 12
12:12 Of making many books there is no end 12
Sng 8: 7 Many waters cannot quench love 9
Isa 2: 3 many peoples shall come, and say: "Come, let us go up 9
4 shall judge . . and shall decide for many peoples; 9
5: 9 many houses shall be desolate, large . . houses 9
6:12 forsaken places are many in the midst of the land. 11
8: 7 the waters of the River, mighty and many 9
15 many shall stumble thereon; they shall fall 9
17:12 Ah, the thunder of many peoples 9
13 The nations roar like the roaring of many waters 9
22: 9 the breaches of the city of David were many 12
23: 3 were on many waters; your revenue was the grain 9
16 Make sweet melody, sing many songs 2
24:22 and after many days they will be punished. 10
31: 1 who trust in chariots because they are many 9
37:24 With my many chariots I have gone up the heights 10
47: 9 in spite of your many sorceries 10
12 in your enchantments and your many sorceries 10
13 You are wearied with your many counsels; 10
52:14 As many were astonished at him-his appearance 9
15 shall he startle many nations; 9
53:11 my servant, make many to be accounted righteous; 9
12 yet he bore the sin of many, and made intercession 9
58:12 raise up the foundations of many generations; †
61: 4 the devastations of many generations. †
66:16 and those slain by the LORD shall be many. 11
Jer 2:28 for as many as your cities are your gods, O Judah. 6
3: 1 You have played the harlot with many lovers; 9
5: 6 because their transgressions are many 11
11:13 For your gods have become as many as your cities 6
13 as many as the streets of Jerusalem 6
12:10 Many shepherds have destroyed my vineyard 9
13: 6 And after many days the LORD said to me 9
14: 7 for our backslidings are many, we have sinned 11
16:16 I am sending for many fishers, says the LORD 9
16 and afterwards I will send for many hunters 9
20:10 I hear many whispering. Terror is on every side! 9
22: 8 And many nations will pass by this city 9
25:14 many nations and great kings shall make slaves 9
27: 7 then many nations . . shall make him their slave. 9
28: 8 and pestilence against many countries 9
35: 7 that you may live many days in the land 9
36:32 and many similar words were added to them. 9
37:16 and remained there many days 9
42: 2 for we are left but a few of many, as your eyes see us 12
46:11 In vain you have used many medicines; 12
50:41 many kings are stirring from the farthest parts 9
51:13 O you who dwell by many waters, rich in treasures 9
14 Surely I will fill you with men, as many as locusts •
55 Their waves roar like many waters 9
Lam 1:22 for my groans are many and my heart is faint. 9
Ezk 1:24 their wings like the sound of many waters 9
3: 6 not to many peoples of foreign speech 9
12:27 The vision that he sees is for many days hence 9
16:41 judgments upon you in the sight of many women; 9
51 you have committed more abominations than they 12
17: 9 not take . . many people to pull it from its roots. 9
17 cast up and siege walls built to cut off many lives 9
21:15 hearts may melt, and many fall at all their gates. 12
26: 3 and will bring up many nations against you 9
7 with horsemen and a host of many soldiers. 9
10 His horses will be so many that their dust will 14
27: 3 merchant of the peoples on many coastlands 9
15 many coastlands were your own special markets 9
33 came from the seas, you satisfied many peoples; 9
31:15 many waters shall be stopped; 9
32: 3 throw my net over you with a host of many peoples; 9
9 I will trouble the hearts of many peoples 9
10 I will make many peoples appalled at you 9
13 all its beasts from beside many waters; 9
33:24 but we are many; the land is surely given us 9
37: 2 behold, there were very many upon the valley; 9
38: 6 with all his hordes-many peoples are with you. 9
8 After many days you will be mustered; 9
8 gathered from many nations upon the mountains 9
9 and all your hordes, and many peoples with you. 9
15 you and many peoples with you, all of them riding 9
22 rain upon him and his hordes and the many peoples 9
23 make myself known in the eyes of many nations. 9
39:27 my holiness in the sight of many nations. 9
43: 2 his coming was like the sound of many waters; 9
47: 7 I saw upon the bank of the river very many trees 9
9 there will be very many fish; 9
10 its fish will be of very many kinds 9
Dan 2:48 gave Daniel high honors and many great gifts 15
8:25 Without warning he shall destroy many; 9
26 vision, for it pertains to many days hence. 9
9:27 make a strong covenant with many for one week; 9
11:14 many shall rise against the king of the south; 9
18 face to the coastlands, and shall take many 9
26 army . . swept away, and many shall fall down slain 9
33 people who are wise shall make many understand 9
34 many shall join themselves to them with flattery; 9
39 shall make them rulers over many 9
40 with chariots and horsemen, and with many ships; 9
44 to exterminate and utterly destroy many. 9
12: 2 many of those who sleep in the dust of the earth 9
3 who turn many to righteousness, like the stars 9
4 Many shall run to and fro 9
10 Many shall purify themselves 9
Hos 3: 3 I said to her, "You must dwell as mine for many days; 9
4 For the children of Israel shall dwell many days 9
Ams 5:12 For I know how many are your transgressions 9
8: 3 the dead bodies shall be many; 9
Jon 4:11 city, in which there are more than 120,000 persons 12
Mic 4: 2 many nations shall come, and say: "Come, let us go up 9
3 He shall judge between many peoples 9
11 Now many nations are assembled against you 9
13 you shall beat in pieces many peoples 9
5: 7 in the midst of many peoples like dew 9
8 among the nations, in the midst of many peoples 9
Nah 1:12 says the LORD, "Though they be strong and many 9
Hab 2: 8 Because you have plundered many nations 9
10 shame to your house by cutting off many peoples; 9
Zec 2:11 many nations shall join themselves to the LORD 9
7: 3 in the fifth month, as I have done for so many years? •
8:20 yet come, even the inhabitants of many cities; 9
22 Many peoples and strong nations shall come 9
10: 8 they shall be as many as of old. 12
Mal 2: 6 he turned many from iniquity. 9
8 you have caused many to stumble 9
Mat 3: 7 when he saw many of the Pharisees and Sad'ducees 29
7:13 and those who enter by it are many. 29
22 On that day many will say to me, 'Lord, Lord 29
22 and do many mighty works in your name?' 29
8:11 I tell you, many will come from east and west 29
16 That evening they brought to him many 29
9:10 behold, many tax collectors and sinners came 29
10:31 you are of more value than many sparrows. 29
12:15 And many followed him, and he healed them all 29
13:17 I say to you, many prophets and righteous men 29
58 he did not do many mighty works there 29
14:24 the boat by this time was many furlongs distant 29

36 and as many as touched it were made well. 21
15:30 the blind, the dumb, and many others 29
18:21 As many as seven times? 17
19:30 many that are first will be last 29
20:28 to give his life as a ransom for many. 29
22: 9 invite to the marriage feast as many as you find.' 21
14 For many are called, but few are chosen. 29
24: 5 For many will come in my name, saying 29
5 'I am the Christ,' and they will lead many astray. 29
10 then many will fall away, and betray one another 29
11 many false prophets will arise 29
11 false prophets will arise and lead many astray. 29
26:28 my blood . . which is poured out for many 29
60 though many false witnesses came forward 29
27:52 many bodies of the saints who had fallen asleep 29
53 went into the holy city and appeared to many. 29
55 There were also many women there 29
Mrk 1:34 healed many who were sick with various diseases 29
34 and cast out many demons 29
2: 2 And many were gathered together 29
15 many tax collectors and sinners were sitting 29
15 there were many who followed him. 29
3:10 he had healed many 29
4:33 With many such parables he spoke the word to them 29
5: 9 He replied, "My name is Legion; for we are many. 29
26 who had suffered much under many physicians 29
6: 2 many who heard him were astonished, saying 29
13 they cast out many demons, and anointed with oil 29
13 anointed with oil many that were sick 29
31 many were coming and going 29
33 Now many saw them going, and knew them 29
56 as many as touched it were made well. 21
7: 4 many other traditions which they observe 29
10:31 many that are first will be last 29
45 to give his life as a ransom for many. 29
48 many rebuked him, telling him to be silent 29
11: 8 many spread their garments on the road 29
12: 5 so with many others 29
41 Many rich people put in large sums. 29
13: 6 Many will come in my name, saying, 'I am he!' 29
6 and they will lead many astray. 29
14:24 my blood . . which is poured out for many. 29
56 For many bore false witness against him 29
15:41 also many other women who came up with him 29
Lke 1: 1 many have undertaken to compile a narrative 29
14 many will rejoice at his birth; 29
16 he will turn many of the sons of Israel to the Lord 29
2:34 the fall and rising of many in Israel 29
35 thoughts out of many hearts may be revealed. 29
3:18 So, with many other exhortations, he preached 29
4:25 were many widows in Israel in the days of Eli'jah 29
27 there were many lepers in Israel 29
41 demons also came out of many, crying 29
7:21 he cured many of diseases and plagues 29
21 on many that were blind he bestowed sight. 29
47 I tell you, her sins, which are many, are forgiven 29
8: 3 Joan'na . . and Susanna, and many others 29
29 For many a time it had seized him 29
30 he said, "Legion"; for many demons had entered him. 29
10:24 many prophets and kings desired to see 29
12: 7 Fear not; you are of more value than many sparrows. 29
19 Soul, you have ample goods laid up for many years; 29
13:24 many, I tell you, will seek to enter 29
14:16 A man once gave a great banquet, and invited many; 29
15:13 Not many days later, the younger son gathered all 29
29 Lo, these many years I have served you 31
21: 8 many will come in my name, saying, 'I am he!' 29
22:65 they spoke many other words against him 29
Joh 2:23 many believed in his name when they saw the signs 29
4:39 Many Samaritans from that city believed in him 29
41 And many more believed because of his word. 29
6: 9 but what are they among so many? 31
60 Many of his disciples, when they heard it, said 29
66 After this many of his disciples drew back 29
7:31 Yet many of the people believed in him; they said 29
8:30 As he spoke thus, many believed in him. 29
10:20 Many of them said, "He has a demon, and he is mad 29
32 I have shown you many good works from the Father; 29
41 many came to him; and they said, "John did no sign 29
42 many believed in him there. 29
11:19 many of the Jews had come to Martha and Mary 29
45 Many of the Jews therefore, who had come with Mary 29
47 What are we to do? For this man performs many signs 29
55 many went up from the country to Jerusalem 29
12:11 on account of him many of the Jews were going away 29
37 Though he had done so many signs before them 31
42 many even of the authorities believed in him 29
14: 2 In my Father's house are many rooms 29
19:20 Many of the Jews read this title 29
20:30 Now Jesus did many other signs 29
21:11 although there were so many, the net was not torn. 31
25 there are also many other things which Jesus did; 29
Act 1: 3 presented himself alive . . by many proofs 29
5 before many days you shall be baptized 29
2:40 he testified with many other words and exhorted 29
43 many wonders and signs were done 29
4: 4 many of those who heard the word believed 29
34 as many as were possessors of lands or houses 21
5:12 Now many signs and wonders were done 29
6: 7 a great many of the priests 29
8: 7 spirits came out of many who were possessed 29
7 many who were paralyzed or lame were healed. 29
25 many villages of the Samaritans. 29
9:13 I have heard from many about this man 29
23 When many days had passed 18
42 many believed in the Lord. 29
43 in Joppa for many days with one Simon, a tanner. 18
12:12 many were gathered together and were praying. 18
13:31 for many days he appeared 29
43 many Jews and devout converts to Judaism 29
48 as many as were ordained to eternal life 21
14:21 When they . . had made many disciples 18
22 through many tribulations 29
15:32 exhorted the brethren with many words 29
35 with many others also. 29
16:18 this she did for many days 29
23 when they had inflicted many blows upon them 29
17: 4 as did a great many of the devout Greeks 29
12 Many of them therefore believed 29
18: 8 many of the Corinthians hearing Paul believed 29
10 I have many people in this city. 29
18 After this Paul stayed many days longer 18
19:18 Many also of those who were now believers came 29
20: 8 There were many lights in the upper chamber 18
24:10 many years you have been judge over this nation 29
25: 7 bringing against him many serious charges 29
14 as they stayed there many days 29
26:10 I not only shut up many of the saints in prison 29
27:20 when neither sun nor stars appeared for many a day 29
28:10 They presented many gifts to us 29
Rom 4:17 I have made you the father of many nations 29
18 that he should become the father of many nations; 29
5:15 For if many died through one man's trespass 29
15 the grace of God . . abounded for many. 29
16 the free gift following many trespasses brings 29
19 by one man's disobedience many were made sinners 29
19 by one man's . . many will be made righteous. 29
8:29 he might be the first-born among many brethren. 29
12: 4 For as in one body we have many members 29
5 so we, though many, are one body in Christ 29
15:23 since I have longed for many years to come to you 29
16: 2 a helper of many and of myself as well. 29
1Co 1:26 not many of you were wise 29
26 not many were powerful 29
26 not many were of noble birth; 29
4:15 you do not have many fathers 29
8: 5 as indeed there are many "gods" and many "lords"- 29
5 as indeed there are many "gods" and many "lords"- 29
10:17 we who are many are one body 29
33 not seeking my own advantage, but that of many 29
11:30 That is why many of you are weak and ill, 29
12:12 For just as the body is one and has many members 29
12 all the members of the body, though many, are one 29
14 body does not consist of one member but of many. 29
20 As it is, there are many parts, yet one body. 29
14:10 There are doubtless many different languages 31
16: 9 there are many adversaries. 29
2Co 1:11 so that many will give thanks on our behalf 29
11 granted us in answer to many prayers. 29
2: 4 anguish of heart and with many tears 29
17 For we are not, like so many, peddlers of God's word; 29
6:10 as poor, yet making many rich 29
8:22 and found earnest in many matters 29
9:12 also overflows in many thanksgivings to God. 29
11:18 since many boast of worldly things 29
27 in toil . . through many a sleepless night 26
12:21 I may have to mourn over many of those who sinned 29
Gal 1:14 I advanced in Judaism beyond many of my own age 29
3:16 referring to many; but, referring to one 29
27 For as many of you as were baptized into Christ 21
4:27 the children of the desolate one are many more 29
Php 3:18 many, of whom I have often told you and now tell you 29
1Ti 6: 9 into a snare, into many senseless . . desires 29
10 pierced their hearts with many pangs. 29
12 in the presence of many witnesses. 29
2Ti 2: 2 have heard from me before many witnesses 29
Tit 1:10 For there are many insubordinate men 29
Heb 2:10 in bringing many sons to glory 29
9:28 Christ . . offered once to bear the sins of many 29
11:12 as many as the stars of heaven 19
12:15 by it the many become defiled; 29
Jas 3: 1 Let not many of you become teachers, my brethren 29
2 For we all make many mistakes 29
2Pe 2: 2 And many will follow their licentiousness 29
1Jn 2:18 so now many antichrists have come; 29
4: 1 many false prophets have gone out into the world 29
2Jn 1: 7 For many deceivers have gone out into the world 29
Rev 1:15 and his voice was like the sound of many waters; 29
5:11 I heard . . the voice of many angels 29
8:11 the waters became wormwood, and many men died 29
9: 9 like the noise of many chariots with horses 29
10:11 prophesy about many peoples and nations 29
14: 2 a voice from heaven like the sound of many waters 29
17: 1 the great harlot who is seated upon many waters 29
19: 6 like the sound of many waters 29
12 and on his head are many diadems; 29
1Es 1:49 committed many acts of sacrilege 29
2: 9 from many whose hearts were stirred. 29
4:14 is not the king great, and are not men many 29
27 Many have perished, or stumbled, or sinned 29
5:64 while many came with trumpets and a joyful noise 29
6:14 the house was built many years ago 29
8:11 Let as many as are so disposed, therefore, depart 21
2Es 1:10 For their sake I have overthrown many kings 34
3:12 children and peoples and many nations 34
25 This was done for many years 34
29 my soul has seen many sinners 34
4:34 but the Highest hastens on behalf of many. 34
5: 7 one whom the many do not know 34
8 There shall be chaos also in many places 34
10 it shall be sought by many but shall not be found 34
28 why hast thou given over the one to the many 34
28 and scattered thine only one among the many? 34
6:17 its sound was like the sound of many waters. 34
7:20 Let many perish who are now living 34
47 bring delight to few, but torments to many. 34
51 that the righteous are not many but few 34
110and many others prayed for many? 34
110and many others prayed for many? 34
8: 1 The Most High made this world for the sake of many 34
3 Many have been created, but few shall be saved. 34
33 who have many works laid up with thee 34
41 just as the farmer sows many seeds 34
50 For many miseries will affect those 34
9:10 as many as did not acknowledge me 35
11 as many as scorned my law 35
15 are more who perish than those who will be saved 34
10: 9 to mourn over so many who have come into being 36
24 and lay aside your many sorrows 33
38 the Most High has revealed many secrets to you. 34
57 For you are more blessed than many 34
12: 7 righteous before thee beyond many others 34
13:13 many people came to him, some of whom were joyful 34
26 whom the Most High has been keeping for many ages 34
14: 4 Mount Sinai, where I kept him with me many days; 34
5 I told him many wondrous things 34
24 prepare for yourself many writing tablets 34
15:29 nations . . shall come out with many chariots 34
16:18 the beginning of famine, when many shall perish; 34
22 many of those who live on the earth shall perish 34
70 For in many places and in neighboring cities •
Tob 1: 3 I performed many acts of charity to my brethren 29
16 I performed many acts of charity to my brethren. 29
18 in his anger he put many to death 29
3: 5 now thy many judgments are true 29
4: 4 she faced many dangers for you 29
8 If you have many possessions 24
13:11 Many nations will come from afar 29
Jdt 1: 6 Many nations joined the forces of the Chaldeans. 29
4:13 the people fasted many days throughout Judea 29
5: 9 much gold and silver and very many cattle. 29
18 they were utterly defeated in many battles 29
8:11 the Lord turns and helps us within so many days. •
11:16 as many as shall hear about them. 21
16:22 Many desired to marry her 29
AEs 13: 2 Having become ruler of many nations 29
16: 5 many of those who are set in places of authority 29
Wis 6: 2 you that . . boast of many nations. 23
Sir 0: 1 many great teachings have been given to us 29
1:24 the lips of many will tell of his good sense. 29
3:24 For their hasty judgment has led many astray 29
6: 6 Let those that are at peace with you be many 29
22 is not manifest to many. 29
8: 2 gold has ruined many 29
9: 8 many have been misled by a woman's beauty 29
11: 5 Many kings have had to sit on the ground 29
6 Many rulers have been greatly disgraced 29
10 My son, do not busy yourself with many matters 29
13 raises up his head, so that many are amazed at him. 29
29 many are the wiles of the crafty. 29
32 From a spark of fire come many burning coals 25
13:22 If a rich man slips, his helpers are many 29
16: 5 Many such things my eye has seen 29
17 Among so many people I shall not be known 29
20:14 he has many eyes instead of one. 29
27: 1 Many have committed sin for a trifle 29
28:13 he has destroyed many who were at peace. 29
14 Slander has shaken many 29
18 Many have fallen by the edge of the sword 29
18 not so many as have fallen because of the tongue. •
29: 4 Many persons regard a loan as a windfall 29
7 many have refused to lend 29
30:23 sorrow has destroyed many 29
31: 6 Many have come to ruin because of gold 29
25 wine has destroyed many. 29
34: 7 For dreams have deceived many 29
37:19 A man may be shrewd and the teacher of many 29
31 Many have died of gluttony 29
39: 9 Many will praise his understanding 29
42: 6 where there are many hands, lock things up. 29
51: 3 from the many afflictions that I endured 29
Bar 1:12 we shall serve them many days and find favor 29
4:12 a widow and bereaved of many; I was left desolate 29
35 fire will come upon her . . for many days 20
LJr 1: 3 you will remain there for many years 29
Man 1: 9 more in number than the sand of the sea 32
10 I am weighted down with many an iron fetter 29

1Mc 1: 2 He fought many battles, conquered strongholds 29
3 plundered many nations 24
9 so did their sons after them for many years; 29
11 lawless men . . misled many, saying 29
11 many evils have come upon us. 29
18 many were wounded and fell. 29
30 destroyed many people of Israel. 29
43 Many even from Israel 29
52 Many of the people, every one who forsook the law 29
62 many in Israel stood firm 29
2:16 Many from Israel came to them 29
18 honored with silver and gold and many gifts. 29
29 Then many who were seeking righteousness 29
32 Many pursued them, and overtook them 29
3: 7 He embittered many kings 29
11 Many were wounded and fell, and the rest fled. 29
18 It is easy for many to be hemmed in by few 29
18 no difference between saving by many or by few. 29
5: 6 many people with Timothy as their leader. 29
7 He engaged in many battles with them 29
12 many of us have fallen 24
21 fought many battles against the Gentiles 29
22 as many as 3,000 of the Gentiles fell 16
26 Many of them have been shut up in Bozrah and Bosor 29
34 As many as 8,000 of them fell that day. 16
60 as many as 2,000 of the people of Israel 16
6: 9 He lay there for many days 29
24 have put to death as many of us as they have caught 21
31 many days they fought and built engines of war; 29
51 he encamped before the sanctuary for many days. 29
52 fought for many days. 29
7:19 seized many of the men who had deserted to him 29
8:10 Many of them were wounded and fell 29
11 as many as ever opposed them, they destroyed 21
12 as many as have heard of their fame 21
9: 2 they took it and killed many people. 29
6 many slipped away from the camp 29
17 many on both sides were wounded and fell. 29
20 they mourned many days and said 29
22 have not been recorded, for they were very many. 29
39 tambourines and musicians and many weapons. 29
40 Many were wounded and fell 29
64 he fought against it for many days 29
69 he killed many of them 29
10:28 grant you many immunities and give you gifts. 29
60 silver and gold and many gifts 29
11: 1 gathered great forces . . and many ships 29
20 he built many engines of war to use against it. 29
27 in as many other honors as he had formerly had 21
40 he stayed there many days. 29
47 killed on that day as many as 100,000 men 16
65 and fought against it for many days and hemmed it in. 29
74 As many as 3,000 of the foreigners fell 16
12:13 many afflictions . . have encircled us 29
13 many wars have encircled us 29
13:26 mourned for him many days. 29
49 many of them perished from famine. 18
15: 4 those who have devastated many cities 29
29 you have taken possession of many places 29
16: 8 many of them were wounded and fell 29
2Mc 1:20 after many years had passed 18
35 he exchanged many excellent gifts. 29
2:27 However, to secure the gratitude of many 29
3:26 inflicting many blows on him. 29
4:35 not only Jews, but many also of other nations 29
39 When many acts of sacrilege had been committed 29
39 many of the gold vessels had already been stolen. 29
42 As a result, they wounded many of them 29
5: 9 who had driven many from their own country 30
10 He who had cast out many to lie unburied 24
14 as many were sold into slavery as were slain 22
18 they were involved in many sins 29
6:24 he said, "lest many of the young should suppose 29
9: 6 with many and strange infliction. 29
12:12 they might really be useful in many ways 29
23 and destroyed as many as 30,000 men. 16
25 with many words he had confirmed his . . promise 29
28 killed as many as 25,000 of those who were within 16
13: 8 he had committed many sins against the altar 29
15 slew as many as 2,000 men in the camp 16
3Mc 1: 5 many captives also were taken. 29
2: 6 inflicting many and varied punishments 29
13 because of our many and great sins 29
26 many of his friends . . followed his will. 29
6: 5 showing your power to many nations. 29
4Mc 1: 7 prove to you from many and various examples 27
21 pleasure and pain have many consequences. 29
28 there are many offshoots of these plants 29
3: 7 had slain many of them. 29
5: 4 when many persons had been rounded up 29
4 and known to many in the tyrant's court 29
7: 4 besieged with many ingenious war machines 29
18 as many as attend to religion with a whole heart 21
10: 1 many repeatedly urged him to save himself 29
11:20 so many of us brothers have been summoned 31
12: 6 who had been bereaved of so many sons 31
15: 7 because of the many pains she suffered with each 29
11 though so many factors influenced the mother 31
16: 4 so many and such great emotions 31
8 In vain, my sons, I endured many birth-pangs for you 29
10 I who had so many and beautiful children 28
18:15 'Many are the afflictions of the righteous.' 29

many *See also* bring, color, give, grow, make, put, sorrow, thousand, time, use, way, word.

many and various 1. πολυτρόπος
4Mc 3:21 and caused many and various disasters. 1

become many 1. πληθύνω
Sir 47:24 Their sins became exceedingly many 1

cause many 1. πληθύνω
1Mc 1: 9 they caused many evils on the earth. 1

how many 1. כַּמָּה 2. עַד כַּמָּה 3. ὅσος 4. πόσος 5. quantus
Gen 47: 8 How many are the days of the years of your life? 1
2Sm 19:34 How many years have I still to live 1
1Kg 22:16 How many times shall I adjure you that you speak 1
2Ch 18:15 king said to him, "How many times shall I adjure you 2
Job 13:23 How many are my iniquities and my sins? 1
Mat 15:34 Jesus said to them, "How many loaves have you? 4
16: 9 and how many baskets you gathered? 4
10 and how many baskets you gathered? 4
Mrk 6:38 How many loaves have you? Go and see. 4
8: 5 he asked them, "How many loaves have you? 4
19 how many baskets full of broken pieces 4
20 how many baskets full of broken pieces 4
15: 4 See how many charges they bring against you. 4
Lke 15:17 How many of my father's hired servants have bread 4
Act 21:20 how many thousands there are among the Jews 4
2Es 2:48 how great and many are the wonders of the Lord God 5
4: 7 How many dwellings are in the heart of the sea 5
7 or how many streams are at the source of the deep 5
7 or how many streams are above the firmament 5
Sir 20:17 How many will ridicule him, and how often! 3
4Mc 1:14 how many kinds of emotions there are 4
15:22 How great and how many torments 4

how many things 1. πόσος
Mat 27:13 hear how many things they testify against you? 1

many in number 1. πολύς
Heb 7:23 The former priests were many in number 1

many men 1. πολύς
1Es 4:26 Many men have lost their minds because of women 1
AEs 16: 2 the more proud do many men become. 1
Sir 29:18 Being surety has ruined many men 1

many persons 1. πολύς
Act 10:27 he went in and found many persons gathered; 1
Sir 31:18 If you are seated among many persons 1

many things 1. רַב 2. πολύς 3. τοσοῦτος 4. multus
Isa 42:20 He sees many things, but does not observe them; 1
Mat 13: 3 he told them many things in parables, saying 2
16:21 he must go to Jerusalem and suffer many things 2
Mrk 4: 2 he taught them many things in parables 2
6:34 he began to teach them many things. 2
7:13 many such things you do. 2
8:31 the Son of man must suffer many things 2
9:12 suffer many things and be treated with contempt? 2
15: 3 the chief priests accused him of many things. 2
Lke 9:22 saying, "The Son of man must suffer many things 2
10:41 you are anxious and troubled about many things; 2
11:53 and to provoke him to speak of many things 2
17:25 first he must suffer many things and be rejected 2
Joh 16:12 I have yet many things to say to you 2
Act 26: 9 I . . was convinced that I ought to do many things 2
Gal 3: 4 Did you experience so many things in vain? 3
2Es 12:23 and they shall renew many things in it 4
Sir 27:24 I have hated many things 2
34: 9 An educated man knows many things 2
11 I have seen many things in my travels 2
43:32 Many things greater than these lie hidden 2

too many to count 1. ἀναρίθμητος
Wis 18:12 they . . had corpses too many to count 1

very many 1. πολύς 2. multus plurimus
2Es 13:50 then he will show them very many wonders. 2
Sir 45: 9 with very many golden bells round about 1

many-colored *See* robe.

many-headed 1. πολυκέφαλος
4Mc 7:14 he rendered the many-headed rack ineffective. 1

many-peaked 1. גַּבְנֹן
Ps 68:15 O many-peaked mountain, mountain of Bashan! 1
16 Why look you with envy, O many-peaked mountain 1

mar 1. מִשְׁחָת 2. שחת
Lev 19:27 You shall not . . mar the edges of your beard 2
Isa 52:14 astonished at him–his appearance was so marred 1

marauder 1. גְּדוּד
Jer 18:22 thou bringest the marauder suddenly upon them! 1

marauding *See* band.

marble 1. אֶבֶן שַׁיִשׁ 2. שֵׁשׁ 3. μάρμαρος
1Ch 29: 2 quantities of . . precious stones, and marble. 1
Est 1: 6 caught up . . to silver rings and marble pillars 2
6 a mosaic pavement of porphyry, marble 2
Rev 18:12 articles of costly wood, bronze, iron and marble 3

march 1. בוא 2. דרך 3. דֶּרֶךְ 4. הלך 5. יצא 6. נסע 7. עבר 8. סלה 9. צָבָא 10. צעד 11. צְעָדָה 12. ἀναζεύγνυμι 13. ἀπαίρω 14. ἀπέρχομαι ὁδόν 15. ἐξέρχομαι 16. ἐπιστρατεύω 17. καταστρατοπεδεύω 18. ὁδοιπορία 19. ὀξεῖα πορεία 20. ὀρθρίζω 21. πορεία 22. πορεύω 23. στρατεύω
Exd 14:10 behold, the Egyptians were marching after them; 6
Num 2: 9 They shall set out first on the march. 9
24 They shall set out third on the march. •
12:15 people did not set out on the march till Miriam •
Jdg 5: 4 when thou didst march from the region of Edom 10
21 March on, my soul, with might! 2
1Sm 29: 6 right that you should march out and in with me 1
2Sm 2:29 and marching the whole forenoon they came 4
32 And Jo'ab and his men marched all night 4
5:24 hear the sound of marching in the . . balsam trees 11
2Kg 3: 8 Then he said, "By which way shall we march? 8
9 when they had made a circuitous march of seven days 3
11:19 brought the king . . marching through the gate 1
1Ch 14:15 sound of marching in the tops of the balsam trees 11
2Ch 23:20 marching through the upper gate 1
Ps 68: 7 when thou didst march through the wilderness 10
Prv 30:27 locusts have no king, yet all of them march in rank; 5
Isa 63: 1 marching in the greatness of his strength? •
Jer 46:22 for her enemies march in force 4
Jol 2: 7 They march each on his way, they do not swerve 4
8 not jostle one another, each marches in his path; 4
Hab 1: 6 who march through the breadth of the earth 4
Zec 9: 8 as a guard, so that none shall march to and fro; 7
Jdt 2:21 They marched for three days from Nineveh 14
1Mc 5:36 From there he marched on and took Chaspho 13
58 they marched against Jamnia. 22
6:41 noise made . . by the marching of the multitude 18
11:67 they marched to the plain of Hazor 20
12:50 and kept marching in close formation 22
14: 1 marched into Media to secure help 22
16: 4 they marched against Cendebeus 22
5 they arose and marched into the plain 22
2Mc 4:22 Then he marched into Phoenicia. 17
12:10 on their march against Timothy 21
26 Then Judas marched against Carnaim 15
27 he marched also against Ephron 16
3Mc 4: 5 forced to march at a swift pace 19
4Mc 4:22 He speedily marched against them 12
18: 5 marched against the Persians. 23

march *See also* order.

march against 1. ἐπιστρατεύω
3Mc 5:43 and would also march against Judea 1

march along opposite 1. ἀντιπαράγω
1Mc 13:20 Simon . . kept marching along opposite him 1

march around 1. סבב
Jos 6: 3 You shall march around the city, all the men of war 1
4 you shall march around the city seven times 1
7 Go forward; march around the city 1
14 they marched around the city once, and returned 1
15 and marched around the city in the same manner 1
15 they marched around the city seven times. 1

march away 1. ἀπαίρω
1Mc 6:32 Then Judas marched away from the citadel 1
7:10 they marched away and came with a large force 1
12:25 So he marched away from Jerusalem 1

march down 1. ירד
Jdg 5:11 down to the gates marched the people of the LORD. 1
13 Then down marched the remnant of the noble; 1
13 the people of the LORD marched down for him 1
14 from Machir marched down the commanders 1

forced march 1. ὅρμημα
1Mc 6:33 and took his army by a forced march along the road 1

march forth 1. הלך 2. ἀπαίρω
Zec 9:14 and march forth in the whirlwinds of the south. 1
1Mc 12:40 he marched forth and came to Beth-shan. 2

march in triumph 1. πομπεύω
Wis 4: 2 it marches crowned in triumph 1

march off 1. ἀπαίρω
1Mc 5:66 Then he marched off 1
9: 4 then they marched off and went to Berea 1
13:22 He marched off and went into the land of Gilead. 1

march off with forces 1. ἀναστρατοπεδεύω
2Mc 3:35 he marched off with his forces to the king. 1

march out 1. יצא 2. ἀπαίρω 3. ἐξάγω 4. ἐξέρχομαι 5. ἐξοδεύω 6. ἔξοδος 7. ἐξορμάω
Jdg 2:15 Whenever they marched out . . the LORD was against 1
1Sm 29: 6 right that you should march out and in with me 1
2Sm 18: 4 army marched out by hundreds and by thousands. 1
2Kg 3: 6 King Jeho'ram marched out of Sama'ria at that time 1
Jdt 1: 4 so that his armies could march out in force 6
1Mc 3:57 Then the army marched out 2
9:11 the army of Bacchides marched out from the camp 2
10: 2 and marched out to meet him in battle. 4
11:15 Ptolemy marched out 3
2Mc 12:19 Sosipater . . marched out and destroyed those 5
13:13 he determined to march out 4
3Mc 1: 1 and marched out to the region near Raphia 7

march through 1. διοδεύω
1Mc 12:32 and marched through all that region. 1
33 and marched through the country as far as Askalon 1

march up 1. עלה 2. ἀναβαίνω
Jos 10: 9 having marched up all night from Gilgal. 1
2Kg 16: 9 the king of Assyria marched up against Damascus 1
Rev 20: 9 And they marched up over the broad earth 2

mare 1. סוּסָה
Sng 1: 9 I compare you . . to a mare of Pharoah's chariots. 1

mariner 1. מַלָּח
Ezk 27: 9 ships of the sea with their mariners were in you 1
27 your mariners and your pilots, your caulkers 1
29 The mariners and all the pilots of the sea stand 1
Jon 1: 5 Then the mariners were afraid, and each cried 1

marital *See* right.

mark 1. אוֹת 2. בין 3. ידע 4. כְּתֹבֶת 5. מַטָּרָה 6. מִפְגָּע 7. נכר 8. ראה 9. שׂוּם 10. שׁמר 11. תאר 12. תָּו 13. ἀνάδειξις 14. δίδωμι χάραγμα 15. εἰμὶ ἐπί 16. ἐπέχω 17. ἐπισημαίνω 18. ἴχνος 19. σημεῖον 20. σκοπέω 21. στίγμα 22. τύπος 23. χάραγμα 24. signo
Gen 4:15 And the LORD put a mark on Cain 1
38:25 And she said, "Mark, I pray you, whose these are 7
Exd 13:16 It shall be as a mark on your hand or frontlets 1
Lev 19:28 or tattoo any marks upon you: I am the LORD 4
1Sm 20:20 shoot three arrows . . as though I shot at a mark. 5
2Sm 13:28 Mark when Amnon's heart is merry with wine 8
1Kg 20: 7 Mark now, and see how this man is seeking trouble; 3
Job 7:20 watcher of men? Why hast thou made me thy mark? 6
10:14 If I sin, thou dost mark me 10
36:32 lightning, and commands it to strike the mark. •
Ps 37:37 Mark the blameless man, and behold the upright 10
50:22 Mark this, then, you who forget God 2
130: 3 LORD . . mark iniquities, Lord, who could stand? 10
Isa 44:13 with planes, and marks it with a compass; 11
Lam 3:12 he bent his bow and set me as a mark for his arrow. 5
Ezk 9: 4 and put a mark upon the foreheads of the men 12
6 but touch no one upon whom is the mark. 12
21:19 Son of man, mark two ways for the sword of the king 9
20 mark a way for the sword to come to Rabbah 9
44: 5 And the LORD said to me, "Son of man, mark well †
5 mark well those who may be admitted to the temple †
Lke 14: 7 when he marked how they chose the places of honor 16
Joh 20:25 place my finger in the mark of the nails 22
Gal 6:17 I bear on my body the marks of Jesus. 21
Php 3:17 mark those who so live as you have an example in us 20
2Th 3:17 This is the mark in every letter of mine 19
Rev 13:16 to be marked on the right hand or the forehead 14
17 that no one can buy or sell unless he has the mark 23
14: 9 receives a mark on his forehead or on his hand 23
11 and whoever receives the mark of its name. 23
16: 2 the men who bore the mark of the beast 23
19:20 those who had received the mark of the beast 23
20: 4 and had not received its mark on their foreheads 23
2Es 2:23 commit them to the grave and mark it 24
Wis 8:21 it was a mark of insight to know whose gift she was •
Sir 13:26 The mark of a happy heart is a cheerful face 18
36:23 If kindness and humility mark her speech 15
43: 6 to mark the times and to be an everlasting sign. 13
2Mc 2: 6 Some . . came up to mark the way 17

mark *See also* make, miss, put.

mark of pride 1. ἁδρύνω
1Mc 8:14 or worn purple as a mark of pride 1

mark off 1. כון 2. נטה
Isa 40:12 Who has . . marked off the heavens with a span 1
Lam 2: 8 he marked it off by the line; 2

mark out 1. חקק 2. תאה 3. תאר
Num34: 7 from the Great Sea you shall mark out your line 2
8 from Mount Hor you shall mark it out 2
10 You shall mark out your eastern boundary •
Prv 8:29 when he marked out the foundations of the earth 1
Isa 44:13 stretches a line, he marks it out with a pencil; 3

mark the season 1. מוֹעֵד
Ps 104:19 Thou hast made the moon to mark the seasons; 1

market 1. סחר 2. רְחוֹב 3. πλατεία
Prv 1:20 in the markets she raises her voice; 2
7:12 now in the street, now in the market 2
Ezk 27:15 many coastlands were your own special markets 1
Jdt 1:14 plundered its markets 3

market *See also* administration.

meat market 1. μάκελλον
1Co 10:25 Eat whatever is sold in the meat market 1

market place 1. רְחוֹב 2. ἀγορά
Ps 55:11 and fraud do not depart from its market place. 1
Mat 11:16 It is like children sitting in the market places 2
20: 3 he saw others standing idle in the market place; 2
23: 7 salutations in the market places 2
Mrk 6:56 they laid the sick in the market places 2
7: 4 when they come from the market place 2
12:38 to have salutations in the market places 2
Lke 7:32 They are like children sitting in the market place 2
11:43 and salutations in the market places. 2
20:46 and love salutations in the market places 2
Act 16:19 and dragged them into the market place 2
17:17 he argued . . in the market place every day 2
1Es 2:18 repairing its market places and walls 2
Tob 2: 3 strangled and thrown into the market place. 2

marriage 1. לְאִשָּׁה 2. γαμέω 3. γάμος 4. γυνή
Gen 34: 8 I pray you, give her to him in marriage. 1
21 let us take their daughters in marriage 1
38:14 she had not been given to him in marriage. 1
41:45 and he gave him in marriage As'enath 1
Jdg 12: 9 30 daughters he gave in marriage outside his clan •
21: 1 give his daughter in marriage to Benjamin. 1
1Kg 7: 8 daughter whom he had taken in marriage. •
11: 2 You shall not enter into marriage with them •
19 he gave him in marriage the sister of his own wife •
1Ch 2:35 Sheshan gave his daughter in marriage to Jarha •
Ps 78:63 their maidens had no marriage song. †
Dan 2:43 they will mix with one another in marriage •
Joh 2: 1 there was a marriage at Cana in Galilee 3
2 Jesus also was invited to the marriage 3
1Co 7:27 Are you free from a wife? Do not seek marriage. 4
1Ti 4: 3 who forbid marriage 2
Heb 13: 4 Let marriage be held in honor among all 3
Rev 19: 7 for the marriage of the Lamb has come 3
9 those who are invited to the marriage supper 3
Tob 3:17 give . . in marriage to Tobias the son of Tobit 4
6:10 I will suggest that she be given to you in marriage 4
12 we will celebrate the marriage. 3
15 she will be given to you in marriage. 4
11:19 Tobias' marriage was celebrated for seven days 3
Wis 13:17 possessions and his marriage and children 3
14:24 keep either their lives or their marriages pure 3
26 sex perversion, disorder in marriage, adultery 3
1Mc 11: 9 I will give you in marriage my daughter •
3Mc 1:19 who had recently been arrayed for marriage •

marriage *See also* bed, feast, festival, give, make, present, refrain, vow.

married man 1. γαμέω
1Co 7:33 the married man is anxious about worldly affairs 1

married woman 1. γαμέω
1Co 7:34 the married woman is anxious about worldly affairs 1

marrow 1. חֵלֶב 2. מֹחַ 3. μυελός
Job 21:24 full of fat and the marrow of his bones moist. 2
Ps 63: 5 My soul is feasted as with marrow and fat 1
Heb 4:12 the division . . of joints and marrow 3

marrow *See also* full.

marry 1. בוא אֶל 2. בוא בְּ 3. בעל 4. בַּעַל אִשָּׁה 5. היה 6. היה לְאִישׁ 7. היה לְאִשָּׁה 8. ישב 9. לקח 10. לקח אִשָּׁה 11. לקח לְאִשָּׁה 12. נשא 13. γαμέω 14. γαμίζω 15. γαμικός 16. γίνομαι 17. ἐπιγαμβρεύω 18. ἔχω ἄνδρα 19. λαμβάνω 20. λαμβάνω γυναῖκα 21. παρακμάζω 22. συνοικέω 23. συνοικίζω 24. ὕπανδρος 25. nubo
Gen 19:14 his sons-in-law, who were to marry his daughters 9
27:46 If Jacob marries one of the Hittite women 9
28: 1 and charged him, "You shall not marry 9
6 You shall not marry one of the Canaanite women 10
38: 2 he married her and went in to her 9
Exd 21: 3 if he comes in married, then his wife shall go out 4
Lev 21: 7 They shall not marry a harlot or a woman who has 9
7 neither shall they marry a woman divorced 9
14 or a harlot, these he shall not marry 9
22:12 If a priest's daughter is married to an outsider 5
Num12: 1 because of the Cushite woman whom he had married 9
1 for he had married a Cushite woman; 9
30: 6 if she is married to a husband 5
36: 3 married to any of the sons of the other tribes 7
6 Let them marry whom they think best; 7
6 only, they shall marry within the family 7
11 daughters of Zeloph'ehad, were married to sons 7
12 married into the families of . . Manas'seh 7
Deu 24: 1 When a man takes a wife and marries her 3
5 When a man is newly married, he shall not go out 10
25: 5 wife . . shall not be married outside the family •
Jos 23:12 so that you marry their women and they yours 2
Rut 1:13 Would you therefore refrain from marrying? 6
2Sm 17:25 a man named Ithra . . who had married Ab'igal 1
1Ch 2:19 Caleb married Ephrath, who bore him Hur. 9
21 the daughter of Machir . . whom he married 9
4:17 Bith'i-ah . . whom Mered married; 9
23:22 their kinsmen, the sons of Kish, married them. 12
Ezr 10: 2 married foreign women from the peoples 8
10 You have trespassed and married foreign women 8
17 end of all the men who had married foreign women. 8
18 sons . . who had married foreign women 8
44 All these had married foreign women 12
Neh 13:23 Jews . . married women of Ashdod, Ammon, 8
27 against our God by marrying foreign women? 8
Isa 54: 1 be more than the children of her that is married 3
62: 4 called My delight is in her, and your land Married; 3
4 delights in you, and your land shall be married. 3
5 as a young man marries a virgin, so shall your sons 3
5 man marries a virgin, so shall your sons marry you 3
Ezk 44:22 They shall not marry a widow, or a divorced woman 11
Mal 2:11 and has married the daughter of a foreign god. 3
Mat 5:32 adultress; and whoever marries a divorced woman 13
19: 9 and marries another, commits adultery. 13
10 it is not expedient to marry. 13
22:24 his brother must marry the widow 17
25 the first married, and died 13
30 they neither marry nor are given in marriage 13
24:38 marrying and giving in marriage 13
Mrk 6:17 because he had married her. 13
10:11 Whoever divorces his wife and marries another 13
12 if she divorces her husband and marries another 13
12:25 they neither marry nor are given in marriage 13
Lke 14:20 I have married a wife, and therefore I cannot come.' 13
16:18 divorces his wife and marries another 13
18 he who marries a woman divorced from her husband 13
17:27 They ate, they drank, they married 14
20:34 Jesus said to them, "The sons of this age marry 13
35 neither marry nor are given in marriage 13
Rom 7: 2 a married woman is bound by law to her husband 24
3 and if she marries another man 16
1Co 7: 9 they should marry 13
9 it is better to marry than to be aflame with passion. 13
10 To the married I give charge, not I but the Lord 13
28 if you marry, you do not sin 13
28 if a girl marries she does not sin 13
28 Yet those who marry will have worldly troubles •
36 let him do as he wishes: let them marry–it is no sin. 13
38 So that he who marries his betrothed does well; 14
39 she is free to be married to whom she wishes 13
Gal 4:27 more than the children of her that is married. 18
1Ti 5:11 they desire to marry 13
14 I would have younger widows marry, bear children 13
1Es 5:38 the sons of Jaddus who had married Agia 20
8:70 sons have married the daughters of these people 22
92 have married foreign women 23
9: 7 broken the law and married foreign women 23
36 All these had married foreign women 23
2Es 16:44 them that marry, like those 25
44 them that do not marry, like those 25
Tob 1: 9 When I became a man I married Anna 20
4:12 do not marry a foreign woman 19
Jdt 16:22 Many desired to marry her •
AEs 10: 6 Esther, whom the king married and made queen. 13
Sir 42: 9 when she is young, lest she do not marry 21
9 if married, lest she be hated; 22
10 though married, lest she be barren. 22
2Mc 1:14 For under pretext of intending to marry her 22
14:25 he urged him to marry and have children; 13
25 he married, settled down 13
3Mc 4: 6 to share married life 15
4Mc 16: 9 others married and without offspring 13

marsh 1. בִּצָּה 2. גֶּבֶא 3. ἕλος
Job 8:11 Can papyrus grow where there is no marsh? 1
40:21 in the covert of the reeds and in the marsh. 1
Ezk 47:11 its swamps and marshes will not become fresh; 2
1Mc 9:42 they returned to the marshes of the Jordan. 3
45 on this side and on that, with marsh and thicket; 3

marshal 1. טִפְסָר 2. ספר 3. ἐπισκέπτομαι 4. συντάσσω
Jdg 5:14 from Zeb'ulun those who bear the marshal's staff; 2
Jer 51:27 appoint a marshal against her, bring up horses 1
Jdt 2:16 as a great army is marshaled for a campaign. 4
Sir 17:32 He marshals the host of the height of heaven 3

martyr 1. μάρτυς
Rev 17: 6 drunk with . . the blood of the martyrs of Jesus. 1

marvel 1. פלא 2. פֶּלֶא 3. ἀποθαυμάζω 4. ἐκθαυμάζω 5. θαυμάζω 6. θαυμαστός 7. miror
Exd 34:10 Before all your people I will do marvels 1
Ps 78:12 In the sight of their fathers he wrought marvels 2

Mat 8:10 When Jesus heard him, he marveled 5
27 the men marveled, saying, "What sort of man is this 5
9:33 the dumb man spoke; and the crowds marveled 5
21:20 When the disciples saw it they marveled, saying 5
22:22 When they heard it, they marveled 5
Mrk 5:20 and all men marveled. 5
6: 6 he marveled because of their unbelief 5
Lke 1:63 they all marveled. 5
2:33 marveled at what was said about him; 5
7: 9 When Jesus heard this he marveled at him 5
8:25 they were afraid, and they marveled 5
9:43 they were all marveling at everything he did 5
11:14 the dumb man spoke, and the people marveled. 5
20:26 marveling at his answer they were silent. 5
Joh 3: 7 Do not marvel that I said to you 5
4:27 They marveled that he was talking with a woman 5
5:20 that you may marvel. 5
28 Do not marvel at this 5
7:15 The Jews marveled at it, saying, "How is it 5
21 I did one deed, and you all marvel at it. 5
9:30 The man answered, "Why, this is a marvel! 6
2Th 1:10 to be marveled at in all who have believed 5
Rev 17: 6 When I saw her I marveled greatly. 5
7 But the angel said to me, "Why marvel? I will tell you 5
8 the dwellers . . will marvel to behold the beast 5
2Es 4:26 and if you live long, you will often marvel 7
Jdt 10:19 they marveled at her beauty 5
23 they all marveled at the beauty of her face 5
11:20 they marveled at her wisdom and said 5
Wis 11:14 at the end of the events they marveled at him 5
Sir 43:18 The eye marvels at the beauty of its whiteness 4
24 we marvel at what we hear. 5
47:17 the countries marveled at you. 3
2Mc 1:22 a great fire blazed up, so that all marveled. 5
3Mc 1:10 he marveled at the good order of the temple 5
4Mc 1:11 marveled at their courage and endurance 5
9:26 all were marveling at his courageous spirit 5
17:17 The tyrant himself and all his council marveled 5

marvelous 1.פלא 2.פֶּלֶא 3.θαυμάσιος 4.θαυμαστός
Ps 118:23 This . . LORD's doing; it is marvelous in our eyes. 1
131: 1 things too great and too marvelous for me. 1
Isa 29:14 with this people, wonderful and marvelous; 2
Zec 8: 6 If it is marvelous in the sight of the remnant 1
6 should it also be marvelous in my sight 1
Mat 21:42 it is marvelous in our eyes'? 4
Mrk 12:11 it is marvelous in our eyes'? 4
1Pe 2: 9 out of darkness into his marvelous light. 4
Jdt 11: 8 you are . . marvelous in military strategy. 4
Wis 10:17 she guided them along a marvelous way 4
19: 8 after gazing on marvelous wonders. 4
Sir 38: 6 he might be glorified in his marvelous works. 3
39:20 nothing is marvelous to him. 3
43: 2 a marvelous instrument, the work of the Most High. 4
25 for in it are strange and marvelous works 3
29 marvelous is his power. 4
48:14 so in death his deeds were marvelous. 3
Aza 1:20 Deliver us in accordance with thy marvelous works 3
2Mc 15:13 marvelous majesty and authority. 4
marvelous *See also* work.

do a marvelous thing 1.פלא
Isa 29:14 again do marvelous things with this people 1

marvelous thing 1.פלא
Job 5: 9 marvelous things without number 1
9:10 and marvelous things without number. 1
Ps 98: 1 O sing . . for he has done marvelous things! 1
Mic 7:15 I will show them marvelous things. 1

marvelously 1.פלא 2.θαυμάσιος σφόδρα 3.θαυμαστός
2Ch 26:15 fame spread far, for he was marvelously helped 1
Jdt 10:14 she was in their eyes marvelously beautiful 2
Sir 43: 8 increasing marvelously in its phases 3

act marvelously 1.παραδοξάζω
2Mc 3:30 they praised the Lord who had acted marvelously 1

mask 1.προσωπεῖον
4Mc 15:15 the flesh of the head . . exposed like masks. 1

mason 1.גדר 2.חצב 3.חָרָשׁ אֶבֶן 4.חָרָשׁ אֶבֶן קִיר 5.חָרָשׁ קִיר 6.λατόμος
2Sm 5:11 sent . . cedar trees, also carpenters and masons 4
2Kg 12:12 and to the masons 1
22: 6 carpenters, and to the builders, and to the masons 1
1Ch 14: 1 king of Tyre sent . . also masons and carpenters 5
22:15 stonecutters, masons, carpenters 3
2Ch 24:12 hired masons and carpenters to restore 2
Ezr 3: 7 gave money to the masons and the carpenters 2
1Es 5:54 they gave money to the masons and the carpenters 6

masonry
Ezk 46:23 a row of masonry, with hearths made at the bottom •

mass 1.מֻצָּק 2.מלא 3.רב 4.πλῆθος
Job 16:10 they mass themselves together against me. 2
38:38 when the dust runs into a mass 1
Ezk 19:11 seen in its height with the mass of its branches. 3
31: 9 I made it beautiful in the mass of its branches 3
2Mc 2:24 because of the mass of material 4
5: 3 brandishing of shields, massing of spears 4
3Mc 2: 7 pursued them with chariots and a mass of troops 4

mass of people 1.πλῆθος 2.συστροφή
3Mc 5:41 it is crowded with masses of people 2
46 city now being filled with countless masses of people 1

massacre 1.ἐκκεντέω
2Mc 12: 6 massacred those who had taken refuge there. 1

mast 1.חִבֵּל 2.תֹּרֶן
Prv 23:34 like one who lies on the top of a mast. 1
Isa 33:23 it cannot hold the mast firm in its place 2
Ezk 27: 5 took a cedar from Lebanon to make a mast for you. 2

master 1.אָדוֹן 2.אָמָן 3.בעל 4.בַּעַל 5.משל 6.שלט 7.δεσπόζω 8.δεσπότης 9.ἐπικρατέω 10.ἐπιστάτης 11.ἡγέομαι 12.καθηγητής 13.κατακυριεύω 14.κρατέω 15.κυριεύω 16.κύριος 17.ῥαββί 18.ῥαββουνί 19.σώφρων 20.τυραννέω 21.dominus
Gen 4: 7 its desire is for you, but you must master it. 5
24: 9 thigh of Abraham his master, and swore to him 1
10 Then the servant took ten of his master's camels 1
10 taking all sorts of choice gifts from his master; 1
12 he said, "O LORD, God of my master Abraham 1
12 I pray thee, and show steadfast love to my master 1
14 thou hast shown steadfast love to my master. 1
27 Blessed be the LORD, the God of my master Abraham 1
27 love and his faithfulness toward my master. 1
27 the way to the house of my master's kinsmen. 1
35 The LORD has greatly blessed my master 1
36 Sarah my master's wife bore a son to my master 1
36 Sarah my master's wife bore a son to my master 1
37 My master made me swear, saying 1
39 I said to my master, 'Perhaps the woman will not 1
42 and said, 'O LORD, the God of my master Abraham 1
44 whom the LORD has appointed for my master's son.' 1
48 blessed the LORD, the God of my master Abraham 1
48 the daughter of my master's kinsman for his son. 1
49 if you will deal loyally and truly with my master 1
51 let her be the wife of your master's son 1
54 Send me back to my master. 1
56 let me go that I may go to my master. 1
65 The servant said, "It is my master. 1
39: 2 he was in the house of his master the Egyptian 1
3 his master saw that the LORD was with him 1
7 after a time his master's wife cast her eyes upon 1
8 he refused and said to his master's wife 1
8 his master's wife, "Lo, having me my master has no 1
16 his garment by her until his master came home 1
19 When his master heard the words which his wife 1
20 Joseph's master took him and put him 1
40: 7 with him in custody in his master's house 1
Exd 21: 4 If his master gives him a wife and she bears him 1
4 children shall be her master's and he shall go out 1
5 I love my master, my wife, and my children; 1
6 then his master shall bring him to God 1
6 his master shall bore his ear through with an awl; 1
8 If she does not please her master 1
32 the owner shall give to the master 30 shekels 1
Deu 23:15 not give up to his master a slave who has escaped 1
15 slave who has escaped from his master to you; 1
Jdg 19:11 and the servant said to his master, "Come now, let us 1
12 his master said to him, "We will not turn aside 1
22 they said to the old man, the master of the house 4
23 the man, the master of the house, went out to them 4
26 at the door of the man's house where her master was 1
27 her master rose up in the morning 1
1Sm 20:38 gathered up the arrows, and came to his master. 1
25:10 servants . . breaking away from their masters. 1
14 David sent messengers . . to salute our master; 1
17 for evil is determined against our master 1
30:13 my master left me behind because I fell sick 1
15 kill me, or deliver me into the hands of my master 1
2Sm 9: 9 I have given to your master's son. 1
10 that your master's son may have bread to eat; 1
10 Mephib'osheth your master's son shall always eat 1
12: 8 I gave you your master's house, and . . wives 1
8 I gave . . and your master's wives into your bosom 1
16: 3 And the king said, "And where is your master's son? 1
1Kg 11:23 Rezon . . who had fled from his master Hadade'zer 1
22:17 These have no master; let each return to his home 1
2Kg 2: 3 the LORD will take away your master from over you? 1
5 the LORD will take away your master from over you? 1
16 strong men; pray, let them go, and seek your master; 1
5: 1 Na'aman . . was a great man with his master 1
18 when my master goes into the house of Rimmon 1
20 See, my master has spared this Na'aman the Syrian 1
22 he said, "All is well. My master has sent me to say 1
25 He went in, and stood before his master 1
6: 5 he cried out, "Alas, my master! It was borrowed. 1
15 the servant said, "Alas, my master! What shall we do? 1
22 they may eat and drink and go to their master. 1
23 he sent them away, and they went to their master. 1
32 Is not the sound of his master's feet behind him? 1
8:14 he departed from Eli'sha, and came to his master 1
9: 7 strike down the house of Ahab your master 1
11 When Jehu came out to the servants of his master 1
31 Is it peace, you Zimri, murderer of your master? 1
10: 2 your master's sons are with you, and there are 1
3 select the best and fittest of your master's sons 1
3 and fight for your master's house. 1
6 take the heads of your master's sons, and come to me 1
9 It was I who conspired against my master 1
18:23 make a wager with my master the king of Assyria 1
24 captain among the least of my master's servants 1
27 Has my master sent me to speak these words 1
27 to speak these words to your master and to you 1
19: 4 his master the king of Assyria has sent to mock 1
6 Say to your master, 'Thus says the LORD: Do not be 1
1Ch 12:19 he will desert to his master Saul. 1
2Ch 18:16 LORD said, 'These have no master; 1
Job 3:19 the slave is free from his master. 1
Ps 12: 4 our lips are with us; who is our master? 1
123: 2 eyes of servants look to the hand of their master 1
Prv 25:13 refreshes the spirit of his masters. 1
27:18 he who guards his master will be honored. 1
30:10 Do not slander a servant to his master 1
Ecc 2:19 Yet he will be master of all for which I toiled 6
Sng 7: 1 thighs are like jewels, the work of a master hand. 2
Isa 1: 3 ox knows its owner, and the ass its master's crib; 4
19: 4 the Egyptians into the hand of a hard master; 1
22:18 you shall die . . you shame of your master's house. 1
24: 2 as with the slave, so with his master; 1
36: 8 make a wager with my master the king of Assyria 1
9 captain among the least of my master's servants 1
12 Has my master sent me to speak these words 1
12 speak these words to your master and to you 1
37: 4 Rab'shakeh, whom his master the king of Assyria 1
6 Isaiah said to them, "Say to your master 1
Jer 3:14 for I am your master; I will take you, one from a city 3
27: 4 Give them this charge for their masters 1
4 This is what you shall say to your masters 1
Zep 1: 9 who fill their master's house with violence 1
Mal 1: 6 A son honors his father, and a servant his master. 1
6 if I am a master, where is my fear? says the LORD 1
Mat 6:24 No one can serve two masters; for either he will 16
10:24 nor a servant above his master; 16
25 and the servant like his master 16
15:27 crumbs that fall from their master's table. 16
23:10 Neither be called masters 12
10 you have one master, the Christ. 12
24:45 whom his master has set over his household 16
46 whom his master when he comes will find so doing. 16
48 'My master is delayed,' 16
50 the master of that servant will come on a day 16
25:18 dug in the ground and hid his master's money. 16
19 the master of those servants came 16
20 Master, you delivered to me five talents 16
21 His master said to him 16
21 enter into the joy of your master.' 16
22 Master, you delivered to me two talents 16
23 His master said to him 16
23 enter into the joy of your master.' 16
24 Master, I knew you to be a hard man 16
26 his master answered him 16
26:25 Judas, who betrayed him, said, "Is it I, Master? 17
49 he came up to Jesus at once and said, "Hail, Master! 17
Mrk 9: 5 Master, it is well that we are here 17
10:51 Master, let me receive my sight. 18
11:21 Peter remembered and said to him, "Master, look! 17
13:35 when the master of the house will come 16
14:45 he went up to him at once, and said, "Master! 17
Lke 5: 5 Master, we toiled all night and took nothing! 10
8:24 they went and woke him, saying, "Master, Master 10
24 they went and woke him, saying, "Master, Master 10
45 When all denied it, Peter said, "Master 10
9:33 Master, it is well that we are here 10
49 John answered, "Master, we saw a man 10
12:36 be like men who are waiting for their master 16
37 those servants whom the master finds awake 16
42 whom his master will set over his household 16
43 his master when he comes will find so doing. 16
45 'My master is delayed in coming,' 16
46 the master of that servant will come 16
47 that servant who knew his master's will 16
14:21 came and reported this to his master 16
23 the master said to the servant, 'Go out 16
16: 3 since my master is taking the stewardship away 16
5 summoning his master's debtors one by one 16
5 he said to the first, 'How much . . owe my master?' 16
8 The master commended the dishonest steward 16
13 No servant can serve two masters 16
17:13 lifted up their voices and said, "Jesus, Master 10
Joh 13:16 a servant is not greater than his master 16
15:15 servant does not know what his master is doing; 16
20 'A servant is not greater than his master.' 16
Act 19:16 mastered all of them, and overpowered them 13
Rom 14: 4 It is before his own master that he stands 16
4 for the Master is able to make him stand. 16

Eph 6: 5 those who are your earthly masters 16
9 Masters, do the same to them 16
9 he who is both their Master and yours is in heaven 16
Col 3:22 those who are your earthly masters 16
4: 1 Masters, treat your slaves justly and fairly 16
1 knowing that you also have a Master in heaven. 16
1Ti 6: 1 regard their masters as worthy of all honor 8
2 Those who have believing masters 8
2Ti 2:21 consecrated and useful to the master of the house 8
Tit 1: 8 lover of goodness, master of himself, upright 19
2: 9 Bid slaves to be submissive to their masters 8
1Pe 2:18 Servants, be submissive to your masters 8
2Pe 2: 1 even denying the Master who bought them 8
Jde 1: 4 and deny our only Master and Lord, Jesus Christ. 8
1Es 4: 3 the king is stronger; he is their lord and master 7
14 Who then is their master, or who is their lord? 7
2Es 7:104 or a son his father, or a master his servant 21
Jdt 2:14 Holofernes left the presence of his master 16
5:20 Now therefore, my master and lord 8
6:13 returned to their master. 16
11:10 my lord and master, do not disregard what he said 16
13: 1 shut out the attendants from his master's presence 16
AEs 13: 2 master of the whole world 9
14:12 King of the gods and Master of all dominion! 9
Wis 10:14 and authority over his masters 20
18:11 was punished with the same penalty as the master 8
Sir 3: 7 he will serve his parents as his masters. 8
28:22 It will not be master over the godly 14
32: 1 If they make you master of the feast 11
4Mc 1: 4 it masters the emotions 15
2:24 if reason is master of the emotions 8
5:23 we master all pleasures and desires 14
6:34 when it masters even external agonies 9
35 not only that reason has mastered agonies 14
35 also that it masters pleasures 14
13: 4 the brothers mastered both emotions and pains. 9
14: 1 mastered the emotions of brotherly love. 14
18: 2 devout reason is master of all emotions 8

master *See also* builder, cultivator, workman.

master of the house 1. *οἰκοδεσπότης*
Mat 10:25 called the master of the house Be-el'zebul 1

mastery *See* gain, get.

mastic tree 1. *σχῖνος*
Sus 1:54 He answered, "Under a mastic tree. 1

match 1. *οὗτος* 2. *πρός* 3. *συμφωνέω*
Lke 5:36 the piece from the new will not match the old. 3
2Co 8:11 matched by your completing it 1
1Mc 6:52 The Jews also made engines of war to match theirs 2

match strength 1. *συγκρίνω*
1Mc 10:71 let us match strength with each other there 1

mate 1. אִשָּׁה 2. יחם 3. רְעוּת
Gen 7: 2 all clean animals, the male and his mate; 1
2 that are not clean, the male and his mate; 1
31:10 In the mating season of the flock I lifted up 2
Isa 34:15 the kites be gathered, each one with her mate. 3
16 none shall be without her mate. 3

material 1. *σαρκικός* 2. *ὕλη*
Exd 28: 8 shall be of the same workmanship and materials *
1Ch 22: 5 David provided materials in great quantity *
Prv 25: 4 dross . . and the smith has material for a vessel; *
Rom 15:27 to be of service to them in material blessings. 1
2Mc 1:21 materials for the sacrifices were presented *
31 the materials of the sacrifice were consumed *
33 Nehemiah . . had burned the materials of the sacrifice *
2:24 because of the mass of material 2

material *See also* benefit.

same material 1. מִן
Exd 39: 5 was of the same materials and workmanship 1

matter 1. אֹמֶר 2. דָּבָר 3. חֵפֶץ 4. מַעֲשֶׂה 5. מִלָּה (A) 6. *ἐκ* 7. *λόγος* 8. *οὗτος* 9. *πρᾶγμα* 10. *πρᾶξις* 11. *τίς*
Gen 24: 9 swore to him concerning this matter. 2
Exd 18:22 every great matter they shall bring to you 2
22 any small matter they shall decide themselves; 2
26 any small matter they decided themselves. 2
Lev 5: 1 whether he has seen or come to know the matter *
6: 2 by deceiving his neighbor in a matter of deposit *
Num 25:18 they beguiled you in the matter of Pe'or 2
18 they beguiled you in . . the matter of Cozbi 2
31:16 to act . . against the LORD in the matter of Pe'or 2
Deu 3:26 suffice you; speak no more to me of this matter. 2
Jos 22:20 break faith in the matter of the devoted things *
Rut 3:18 Wait . . until you learn how the matter turns out 2
18 the man will not rest, but will settle the matter 2
1Sm 10:16 about the matter of the kingdom . . he did not tell 2
11: 4 reported the matter in the ears of the people; 2
20:19 where you hid . . when the matter was in hand 4
23 as for the matter of which you and I have spoken 2
39 only Jonathan and David knew the matter. 2
21: 2 The king has charged me with a matter, and said 2
2 Let no one know anything of the matter 2
30:24 Who would listen to you in this matter? 2
2Sm 11:25 Do not let this matter trouble you 2
19:42 Why then are you angry over this matter? 2
20:18 ask counsel at Abel'; and so they settled a matter. *
21: 4 It is not a matter of silver or gold between us *
1Kg 5: 8 all you desire in the matter of cedar and cypress *
15: 5 what was right . . except in the matter of Uri'ah 2
2Kg 5:18 In this matter may the LORD pardon your servant 2
18 the LORD pardon your servant in this matter. 2
1Ch 2: 7 transgressed in the matter of the devoted thing *
27: 1 in all matters concerning the divisions that 2
2Ch 8:15 king had commanded . . concerning any matter 2
19:11 Amari'ah . . is over you in all matters of the LORD; 2
11 Zebedi'ah . . in all the king's matters; 2
24: 5 see that you hasten the matter. 2
32:31 matter of the envoys of the princes of Babylon *
Ezr 4:22 take care not to be slack in this matter; *
5:17 let the king send us his pleasure in this matter. *
7:11 Ezra . . learned in matters of the commandments 2
10: 9 trembling because of this matter 2
13 we have greatly transgressed in this matter. 2
14 till the fierce wrath of our God over this matter 2
16 tenth month they sat down to examine the matter; 2
Neh 11:24 at the king's hand in all matters concerning 2
Est 9:26 and of what they had faced in this matter *
Job 9:19 If it is a matter of justice, who can summon him? *
19:28 The root of the matter is found in him'; 2
22:28 You will decide on a matter 1
Prv 17: 9 but he who repeats a matter alienates a friend. 2
Ecc 3: 1 and a time for every matter under heaven 3
17 for he has appointed a time for every matter 3
5: 8 If you see . . do not be amazed at the matter; 3
8: 3 go . . do not delay when the matter is unpleasant 2
6 For every matter has its time and way 3
10:20 or some winged creature tell the matter. 2
12:13 The end of the matter; all has been heard. 2
Ezk 16:20 Were your harlotries so small a matter *
Dan 1:14 hearkened to them in this matter, and tested them 2
20 every matter of wisdom and understanding 2
2:15 Then Ar'ioch made the matter known to Daniel. 5
17 Daniel . . made the matter known to Hanani'ah 5
23 for thou hast made known to us the king's matter. 5
3:16 have no need to answer you in this matter. *
5:15 could not show the interpretation of the matter. 5
26 This is the interpretation of the matter: 5
7: 1 down the dream, and told the sum of the matter. 5
28 Here is the end of the matter. 5
28 but I kept the matter in my mind. 5
Mrk 9:10 So they kept the matter to themselves 7
10:10 the disciples asked him again about this matter. *
Act 8:21 You have neither part nor lot in this matter 7
15: 6 gathered together to consider this matter. 7
18:14 a matter of wrongdoing or vicious crime 11
15 a matter of questions about words and names *
28:23 he expounded the matter to them *
Rom 2:29 and real circumcision is a matter of the heart *
1Co 7: 1 concerning the matters about which you wrote. *
2Co 7:11 proved yourselves guiltless in the matter. 9
8:10 in this matter I give my advice *
14 but that as a matter of equality 6
22 and found earnest in many matters *
1Th 4: 6 wrong his brother in this matter 9
2Pe 1:20 a matter of one's own interpretation *
2:12 reviling in matters of which they are ignorant *
1Es 2:20 we think it best not to neglect such a matter *
8:12 in order to look into matters in Judea *
70 from the beginning of this matter 9
9:13 the wrath of the Lord over this matter. 9
14 undertook the matter on these terms *
16 to investigate the matter. 9
2Es 4:35 in their chambers ask about these matters *
10:31 What is the matter with you? *
13:56 and explain weighty and wondrous matters to you. *
Tob 7: 8 let the matter be settled. 9
AEs 10: 5 the dream that I had concerning these matters 7
16: 7 investigation of matters close at hand. *
Sir 3:23 matters too great for human understanding *
5:15 In great and small matters do not act amiss *
11: 9 argue about a matter which does not concern you 9
10 My son, do not busy yourself with many matters 10
15:15 to act faithfully is a matter of your own choice. *
31:15 in every matter be thoughtful. 9
1Mc 3:48 to inquire into those matters *
10:35 annoy any of them about any matter. 9
63 bring charges against him about any matter 9
2Mc 1:33 When this matter became known 9
34 the king investigated the matter 9
2:26 it is no light matter 9
30 to discuss matters from every side 7
11:17 and have asked about the matters indicated therein. *
20 concerning these matters and their details *
36 as to the matters which . . are to be referred *
13:13 march out and decide the matter by the help of God 9
14: 9 the details of this matter *
15:17 to decide the matter 9
37 This . . is how matters turned out with Nicanor. *
3Mc 1: 4 matters were . . in favor of Antiochus 9
3: 2 While these matters were being arranged *
8 expected that matters would change; 8
4:19 he was clearly convinced about the matter *
5:27 inquired what the matter was 9
30 in regard to these matters *
40 again revoking your decree in the matter? 9
46 and urged the king on to the matter at hand. *
4Mc 1:16 the knowledge of divine and human matters 9
17 by which we learn divine matters reverently *
2: 9 In all other matters *
4: 5 On receiving authority to deal with this matter *
5:20 in matters either small or great *

matter (2) 1. *ὕλη*
Wis 11:17 which created the world out of formless matter 1
15:13 he makes from earthy matter fragile vessels 1

matter of counsel 1. *συμβουλία*
Sir 37:11 in any matter of counsel. 1

matter pertaining to this life 1. *βιωτικός*
1Co 6: 3 How much more, matters pertaining to this life! 1

small matter 1. מְעַט
Gen 30:15 a small matter that you have taken away my husband 1

weighty matter 1. *βαρύς*
Mat 23:23 have neglected the weightier matters of the law 1

mattock 1. אֵת
1Sm 13:20 to sharpen his plowshare, his mattock, his axe 1
21 was a pim for the plowshares and for the mattocks 1

mature 1. *ἱκανός* 2. *τέλειος* 3. *τελεσφορέω*
Lke 8:14 their fruit does not mature. 3
1Co 2: 6 Yet among the mature we do impart wisdom 2
14:20 be babes in evil, but in thinking be mature. 2
Eph 4:13 to mature manhood 2
Php 3:15 Let those of us who are mature be thus minded; 2
Col 1:28 that we may present every man mature in Christ. 2
4:12 may stand mature and fully assured 2
Heb 5:14 solid food is for the mature 2
1Mc 16: 3 you by His mercy are mature in years 1

maturity 1. *ἀκμή* 2. *τελειότης*
Heb 6: 1 let us . . go on to maturity 2
4Mc 18: 9 In the time of my maturity 1

maturity *See also* come, comes.

maxim 1. זִכָּרוֹן 2. *παροιμία*
Job 13:12 Your maxims are proverbs of ashes 1
Sir 8: 8 busy yourself with their maxims 2

meadow 1. כַּר 2. כָּרָה 3. pratum
Ps 65:13 the meadows clothe themselves with flocks 1
Zep 2: 6 shall be pastures, meadows for shepherds 2
2Es 15:42 and grass of the meadows, and their grain. 3

meal 1. לֶחֶם 2. *ἄρτος* 3. *βρῶσις* 4. *δεῖπνον*
1Sm 20:27 Why has not the son of Jesse come to the meal 1
1Co 11:21 in eating, each one goes ahead with his own meal 4
Heb 12:16 who sold his birthright for a single meal. 3
Sir 31:21 get up in the middle of the meal *
41:19 Be ashamed of selfish behavior at meals 2

meal (2) 1. קֶמַח
Gen 18: 6 Make ready quickly three measures of fine meal 1
Num 5:15 offering . . a tenth of an ephah of barley meal; 1
2Sm 17:28 brought . . wheat, barley, meal, parched grain 1
1Kg 4:22 provision for one day was . . and 60 cors of meal 1
17:12 nothing baked, only a handful of meal in a jar 1
14 The jar of meal shall not be spent, and the cruse 1
16 The jar of meal was not spent 1
2Kg 4:41 Then bring meal." And he threw it into the pot 1
1Ch 12:40 abundant provisions of meal, cakes of figs 1
Isa 47: 2 Take the millstones and grind meal 1
Hos 8: 7 grain has no heads, it shall yield no meal; 1

meal *See* offering, serve, take.

coarse meal 1. עֲרִיסָה
Num 15:20 first of your coarse meal you shall present 1
21 Of the first of your coarse meal you shall give 1
Neh 10:37 bring the first of our coarse meal 1
Ezk 44:30 give to the priests the first of your coarse meal 1

fine meal 1. סֹלֶת
2Kg 7: 1 a measure of fine meal shall be sold for a shekel 1
16 So a measure of fine meal was sold for a shekel 1
18 and a measure of fine meal for a shekel 1

sacrificial meal 1. *θυσία*
2Mc 6:21 he was eating the flesh of the sacrificial meal 1

mealtime 1. עֵת הָאֹכֶל 2. *ἀρίστου ὥρα*
Rut 2:14 And at mealtime Bo'az said to her, "Come here 1
Sus 1:13 Let us go home, for it is mealtime. 2

mean 1. *διερμηνεύω* 2. *εἰμί* 3. *ἑρμηνεύω* 4. *θέλω εἰμί* 5. *λαλέω* 6. *λέγω* 7. *λέγω μεθερμηνεύω* 8. *λόγος* 9. *μεθερμηνεύω* 10. *ὅτι* 11. *ποιέω* 12. *φημί* 13. sum

Gen 33: 8 Esau said, "What do you mean by all his company •
41:32 the doubling of Pharaoh's dream means that •
Exd 12:26 'What do you mean by this service?' •
13:14 when . . your son asks you, 'What does this mean?' •
Deu 29:24 What means the heat of this great anger?' •
30:20 for that means life to you and length of days •
Jos 4: 6 'What do those stones mean to you?' •
21 your children ask . . 'What do these stones mean?' •
1Sm 4: 6 What does this great shouting . . mean? •
1Kg 1:41 he said, "What does this uproar in the city mean? •
22:22 the LORD said to him, 'By what means?' •
Ezk 17:12 Do you not know what these things mean? •
24:19 Will you not tell us what these things mean for us •
37:18 Will you not show us what you mean by these? •
Mat 1:23 Emman'u-el" (which means, God with us). 9
9:13 Go and learn what this means, 'I desire mercy 2
12: 7 if you had known what this means, 'I desire mercy 2
13:38 and the good seed means the sons of the kingdom 2
26:70 I do not know what you mean. 6
27:33 (which means the place of a skull) 2
Mrk 5:41 which means, "Little girl, I say to you, arise. 2
9:10 what the rising from the dead meant. 2
14:68 I neither know nor understand what you mean. 6
15:22 Gol'gotha (which means the place of a skull). 9
34 which means, "My God, my God, why hast thou 9
Lke 8: 9 his disciples asked him what this parable meant 2
15:26 asked what this meant. 2
18:36 he inquired what this meant. 2
Joh 1:38 And they said to him, "Rabbi" (which means Teacher) 7
41 We have found the Messiah" (which means Christ). 9
42 You shall be called Cephas" (which means Peter). 3
7:36 What does he mean by saying, 'You will seek me 8
9: 7 Go, wash in the pool of Silo'am" (which means Sent) 3
11:13 they thought that he meant taking rest in sleep. 6
16:18 They said, "What does he mean by 'a little while'? 2
18 We do not know what he means. 5
19 what I meant by saying, 'A little while . . 10
20:16 Rab-bo'ni!" (which means Teacher) 6
Act 2:12 What does this mean? 4
4:36 Barnabas (which means, Son of encouragement) 2
9:36 a disciple named Tabitha, which means Dorcas. 1
10:17 as to what the vision which he had seen might mean 2
17:20 wish to know therefore what these things mean 4
Rom 9: 8 This means that it is not the children 2
1Co 1:12 What I mean is that each one of you says 6
7:29 I mean, brethren, the appointed time has grown 12
10:29 I mean his conscience, not yours–do not eat it 6
15:29 Otherwise, what do people mean by being baptized 11
Gal 3:17 This is what I mean 6
4: 1 I mean that the heir, as long as he is a child 6
Eph 4: 9 In saying, "He ascended," what does it mean 2
2Es 10:25 While I was wondering what this meant 13
AEs 16:23 may mean salvation for us and the loyal Persians 2
2Mc 1:36 called this "nephthar," which means purification 1
14: 7 I mean the high priesthood 6
14 would mean prosperity for themselves. 2
4Mc 1: 2 virtue–I mean, of course, rational judgment. 6

mean (2) 1. אמר 2. דמה 3. זמם 4. חפץ 5. חשב 6. עשה 7. *βούλομαι* 8. *θέλω*

Gen 50:20 As for you, you meant evil against me; 5
20 but God meant it for good, to bring it about 5
Exd 2:14 Do you mean to kill me as you killed the Egyptian? 1
Deu 19:19 do to him as he had meant to do to his brother; 3
Jdg 13:23 If the LORD had meant to kill us, he would not have 4
20: 5 they meant to kill me, and they ravished my 2
Isa 3:15 What do you mean by crushing my people •
22: 1 What do you mean that you have gone up, all of you •
Jer 4:30 what do you mean that you dress in scarlet 6
Ezk 18: 2 What do you mean by repeating this proverb •
Jon 1: 6 and said to him, "What do you mean, you sleeper? •
Mrk 6:48 He meant to pass by them 8
Rom 2: 4 God's kindness is meant to lead you to repentance? •
11:12 Now if their trespass means riches for the world •
12 if their failure means riches for the Gentiles •
12 how much more will their full inclusion mean! •
15 if their rejection means the reconciliation •
15 what will their acceptance mean but life •
1Co 5:10 not at all meaning the immoral of this world •
6:13 Food is meant for the stomach •
13 The body is not meant for immorality •
2Co 8:13 I do not mean that others should be eased •
Php 1:22 that means fruitful labor for me •
1Es 5:66 find out what the sound of the trumpets meant. •
Wis 18: 8 by the same means by which thou didst punish •
Sir 39: 3 he will seek out the hidden meanings of proverbs •
2Mc 12: 8 meant in the same way to wipe out the Jews 7
3Mc 1: 3 incurred the vengeance meant for the king. •

mean (3) 1. *ἄσημος*

Act 21:39 from Tarsus in Cili'cia, a citizen of no mean city 1

mean (4) 1. *πονηρός*

Sir 14: 5 If a man is mean to himself 1
6 meaner than the man who is grudging to himself 1
9 mean injustice withers the soul. 1

mean *See* take.

mean more 1. *μεγαλύνω*

Jdt 12:18 because my life means more to me today 1

meaning 1. פִּתְרוֹן 2. *δύναμις* 3. *μεθερμηνεύω* 4. cogitamentum 5. distinctio 6. intellectus

Gen 21:29 What is the meaning of these seven ewe lambs •
40: 5 dream, and each dream with its own meaning. 1
41:11 he and I, each having a dream with its own meaning. 1
Deu 6:20 What is the meaning of the testimonies •
Act 13: 8 that is the meaning of his name 3
1Co 14:11 if I do not know the meaning of the language 2
2Es 7:127 This is the meaning of the contest 4
10:40 This therefore is the meaning of the vision. 6
12: 8 and meaning of this terrifying vision 5

without meaning 1. *τοσοῦτος*

1Co 14:10 and none is without meaning; 1

means 1. *διά* 2. *ἐκ* 3. *ἐν* 4. *μηχανή* 5. *μόρος* 6. *σκεῦος*

Lev 25:54 if he is not redeemed by these means •
Jdg 16: 5 and by what means we may overpower him •
2Ch 18:20 And the LORD said to him, 'By what means?' •
Prv 13: 8 but a poor man has no means of redemption. •
Jer 30:11 I will by no means leave you unpunished. †
46:28 I will by no means leave you unpunished. †
Nah 1: 3 and the LORD will by no means clear the guilty. •
Lke 16: 9 make friends . . by means of unrighteous mammon 2
Joh 11: 4 the Son of God may be glorified by means of it. 1
Act 4: 9 by what means this man has been healed •
2Pe 3: 5 an earth formed out of water and by means of water 1
Rev 9:19 their tails . . and by means of them they wound. 3
Wis 12:27 being punished by means of them 3
Sir 12: 5 lest by means of it he subdue you 3
33: 3 as dependable as an inquiry by means of Urim. •
1Mc 14:10 furnished them with the means of defense 6
3Mc 3: 1 and put to death by the most cruel means. 5
4:19 had been bribed to contrive a means of escape 4
4Mc 1:19 since by means of it reason rules 2
4:24 by means of his decrees 1

means (2) 1. מַחֲשָׁבָה 2. *δύναμις* 3. *ἐὰν ἔχω* 4. *ὑπάρχω*

2Sm 14:14 who devises means not to keep his banished one 1
Lke 8: 3 others, who provided for them out of their means. 4
2Co 8: 3 they gave according to their means, as I can testify 2
3 beyond their means, of their own free will 2
Sir 8:13 Do not give surety beyond your means 2
14:11 treat yourself well, according to your means 3

means *See* lack.

base means 1. *κακός*

Wis 15:12 must get money however one can, even by base means. 1

by all means 1. *πάντως*

1Sm 6: 3 but by all means return him a guilt offering. †
2Sm 17:16 Do not lodge tonight . . but by all means pass over; †
1Co 9:22 that I might by all means save some. 1

by any means

1Kg 20:39 said, 'Keep this man; if by any means he be missing †

by no means 1. אַל 2. לֹא 3. *μὴ γίνομαι* 4. *οὐδαμῶς* 5. *οὐ μή*

Exd 5: 8 you shall by no means lessen it; for they are idle; 2
19 You shall by no means lessen your daily number 2
34: 7 who will by no means clear the guilty †
Num 14:18 but he will by no means clear the guilty †
1Kg 3:26 give her the living child, and by no means slay it. 1
27 Give the living child . . and by no means slay it; 2
Mat 2: 6 are by no means least among the rulers of Judah; 4
Mrk 9:41 will by no means lose his reward. 5
Rom 3: 4 By no means! Let God be true 3
6 By no means! For then how could God judge the world? 3
31 By no means! On the contrary, we uphold the law. 3
6: 2 By no means! How can we who died to sin still live 3
15 Are we to sin . . ? By no means! 3
7: 7 That the law is sin? By no means! 3
13 Did . . bring death to me? By no means! 3
9:14 Is there injustice on God's part? By no means! 3
11: 1 I ask, then, has God rejected his people? By no means! 3
11 I ask, have they stumbled so as to fall? By no means! 3
3Mc 1:11 the king was by no means persuaded. 4
2:24 he by no means repented 4

means of gain 1. *πορισμός*

1Ti 6: 5 imagining that godliness is a means of gain. 1

sufficient means 1. דַּי

Lev 25:26 and finds sufficient means to redeem it 1
28 if he has not sufficient means to get it back 1

meantime

Lke 12: 1 In the meantime •

meanwhile 1. וְ 2. *ἐν τούτοις*

Gen 37:36 Meanwhile the Mid'ianites had sold him in Egypt 1
2Ch 20:13 Meanwhile all the men of Judah stood 1
3Mc 1:24 Meanwhile the crowd . . was engaged in prayer 2

measure 1. אֵיפָה 2. חֹק 3. יֶתֶר 4. מדד 5. מדה 6. מִדָּה 7. מִסְפָּר 8. מְשׂוּרָה 9. מַתְכֹּנֶת 10. סְאָה 11. סְאָה 12. סבב 13. ספר 14. פּוּרָה 15. שָׁלִשׁ 16. תֹּכֶן 17. *βάτος* 18. *βοήθεια* 19. *ἐξαριθμέω* 20. *ἐξεύρεσις* 21. *κόρος* 22. *μέρος* 23. *μετρέω* 24. *μέτρον* 25. *πόσος* 26. *σάτον* 27. mensura 28. mensuro 29. meto

Gen 18: 6 Make ready quickly three measures of fine meal 10
41:49 stored up grain . . until he ceased to measure it 13
49 measure it, for it could not be measured. 7
Exd 16:18 when they measured it with an omer 4
26: 2 all the curtains shall have one measure. 6
8 the eleven curtains shall have the same measure. 6
36: 9 all the curtains had the same measure. 6
15 the eleven curtains had the same measure. 6
Num 35: 5 you shall measure, outside the city 4
Deu 21: 2 they shall measure the distance to the cities 4
25:14 not . . two kinds of measures, a large and a small. 1
15 full and just weight . . a full and just measure 1
Rut 3:15 and he measured out six measures of barley •
17 saying, "These six measures of barley he gave to me •
1Sm 25:18 five measures of parched grain, and 100 clusters 10
2Sm 8: 2 he defeated Moab, and measured them with a line 4
2 two lines he measured to be put to death 4
1Kg 6:25 The other cherub also measured ten cubits; •
25 both cherubim had the same measure and . . form. 6
7: 9 costly stones, hewn according to measure, sawed 6
37 cast alike, of the same measure and the same form. 6
38 each laver measured four cubits •
18:32 as great as would contain two measures of seed. 11
2Kg 7: 1 a measure of fine meal shall be sold for a shekel 11
1 and two measures of barley for a shekel 11
16 So a measure of fine meal was sold for a shekel 11
16 and two measures of barley for a shekel 11
18 Two measures of barley shall be sold for a shekel 11
18 and a measure of fine meal for a shekel 11
1Ch 23:29 and all measures of quantity or size. •
2Ch 4: 2 30 cubits measured its circumference. 12
Job 11: 9 Its measure is longer than the earth 6
28:25 and meted out the waters by measure; 6
Ps 39: 4 my end, and what is the measure of my days; 6
147: 5 his understanding is beyond measure. 7
Prv 20:10 Diverse weights and diverse measures are both 1
Isa 5:14 Sheol has . . opened its mouth beyond measure 2
40:12 has measured the waters in the hollow of his hand 4
12 enclosed the dust of the earth in a measure 15
56:12 will be like this day, great beyond measure. 3
65: 7 I will measure into their bosom payment 4
Jer 31:37 If the heavens above can be measured 5
39 the measuring line shall go out farther 6
33:22 and the sands of the sea cannot be measured 4
Ezk 4:11 And water you shall drink by measure 8
16 they shall drink water by measure and in dismay. 8
40: 3 a line of flax and a measuring reed in his hand; 6
5 the length of the measuring reed in the man's hand 6
5 so he measured the thickness of the wall, one reed; 5
6 and measured the threshold of the gate 5
8 Then he measured the vestibule of the gateway 5
11 Then he measured the breadth of the opening 5
13 Then he measured the gate from the back of the one 5
14 He measured also the vestibule, twenty cubits; •
19 He measured the distance from the inner front 5
20 He measured its length and its breadth. 4
23 he measured from gate to gate, 100 cubits. 5
24 he measured its jambs and its vestibule; 4
27 he measured from gate to gate toward the south 5
28 he measured the south gate; it was of the same size 5
32 he measured the gate; it was of the same size 5
35 north gate, and he measured it; it had the same size 4
47 he measured the court, 100 cubits long 5
48 and measured the jambs of the vestibule 5
41: 1 he brought me to the nave, and measured the jambs; 5
2 he measured the length of the nave 40 cubits 5
3 and measured the jambs of the entrance 5
4 he measured the length of the room, twenty cubits 5
5 Then he measured the wall of the temple 5
8 of the side chambers measured a full reed •
13 he measured the temple, 100 cubits long; 4
15 Then he measured the length of the building 4
42:15 Now when he had finished measuring the interior 6
15 and measured the temple area round about. 4
16 He measured the east side with the measuring 4
16 measured the east side with the measuring reed 6
16 500 cubits by the measuring reed. 6
17 Then he turned and measured the north side 4
17 500 cubits by the measuring reed. 6
18 Then he turned and measured the south side 4
18 500 cubits by the measuring reed. 6
19 Then he turned to the west side and measured 4
19 500 cubits by the measuring reed. 6
20 He measured it on the four sides. It had a wall 4
45: 3 in the holy district you shall measure 4
11 ephah and the bath shall be of the same measure 16
11 the homer shall be the standard measure. 9
47: 3 the man measured 1,000 cubits 5
4 Again he measured 1,000, and led me through 5

4 Again he measured 1,000, and led me through 5
5 Again he measured 1,000, and it was a river 5
48:10 shall have an allotment measuring 25,000 cubits *
30 north side, which is to be 4,500 cubits by measure 6
33 south side, which is to be 4,500 cubits by measure 6
Dan 8:23 transgressors have reached their full measure *
Hos 1:10 sea, which can be neither measured nor numbered; 4
Mic 6:10 and the scant measure that is accursed? 1
Hab 3: 6 He stood and measured the earth; 4
Hag 2:16 When one came to a heap of twenty measures *
16 when one came to the winevat to draw 50 measures 14
Zec 1:16 the measuring line shall be stretched out *
2: 1 behold, a man with a measuring line in his hand! 6
2 To measure Jerusalem, to see what is its breadth 4
Mat 7: 2 you will be judged, and the measure you give 24
2 you give will be the measure you get. 23
13:33 in three measures of flour 26
23:32 Fill up, then, the measure of your fathers. 24
Mrk 4:24 the measure you give will be the measure you get 24
Lke 6:38 good measure, pressed down, shaken together 24
38 the measure you give will be the measure you get 24
13:21 took and hid in three measures of flour 26
16: 6 He said, 'A 100 measures of oil.' 17
7 He said, 'A 100 measures of wheat.' 21
Joh 3:34 for it is not by measure that he gives the Spirit; 24
Act 27:17 they took measures to undergird the ship 18
Rom 12: 3 the measure of faith which God has assigned him. 24
2Co 2: 5 in some measure–not to put it too severely 22
10:12 But when they measure themselves by one another 23
Eph 4: 7 us according to the measure of Christ's gift. 24
13 measure of the stature of the fulness of Christ; 24
1Th 2:16 so as always to fill up the measure of their sins. *
Rev 11: 1 Rise and measure the temple of God and the altar 23
2 do not measure the court outside the temple; 23
21:15 And he who talked to me had a measuring rod of gold 24
15 to measure the city and its gates and walls. 23
16 and he measured the city with his rod 23
17 He also measured its wall 23
17 144 cubits by a man's measure, that is, an angel's. 24
1Es 8:78 now in some measure mercy has come to us from thee 25
2Es 4: 5 or measure for me a measure of wind 27
5 or measure for me a measure of wind ‡
37 measured the times by measure 28
37 measured the times by measure 27
37 or arouse them until that measure is fulfilled.' 27
6: 4 the measures of the firmaments were named 27
16:57 who has measured the sea and its contents; 29
Wis 4: 8 nor measured by number of years; 23
11:20 thou hast arranged all things by measure 24
Sir 6:15 no scales can measure his excellence. *
18: 5 Who can measure his majestic power? 19
Bar 3:18 are anxious, whose labors are beyond measure? 20

measure *See also* 1/10, get, give, line.

beyond measure 1. רבה מְאֹד 2. καθ' ὑπερβολήν 3. ὑπερπερισσῶς 4. inaestimabilis
1Kg 4:29 wisdom and understanding beyond measure 1
Mrk 7:37 they were astonished beyond measure, saying 3
Rom 7:13 might become sinful beyond measure. 2
2Es 8:21 whose throne is beyond measure 4

measure by measure 1. בְּסַאסְּאָה
Isa 27: 8 Measure by measure, by exile thou didst contend 1

measure carefully 1. metior
2Es 9: 1 Measure carefully in your mind 1

measure circumference 1. סבב
1Kg 7:15 twelve cubits measured its circumference; 1
23 a line of 30 cubits measured its circumference. 1

full measure 1. שָׁלִישׁ 2. תֹּם 3. ἐκπλήρωσις 4. πλησμονή
Ps 80: 5 given them tears to drink in full measure. 1
Isa 47: 9 widowhood shall come upon you in full measure 2
Sir 1:16 To fear the Lord is wisdom's full measure 4
2Mc 6:14 they have reached the full measure of their sins; 3

just measure 1. מִשְׁפָּט
Jer 10:24 Correct me, O LORD, but in just measure; 1
30:11 I will chasten you in just measure 1
46:28 I will chasten you in just measure 1

like measure 1. τοσοῦτο
Rev 18: 7 give her a like measure of torment and mourning. 1

measure of length 1. מִדָּה
Lev 19:35 in measures of length or weight or quantity 1

measure of life 1. חֶלֶד
Ps 89:47 Remember, O Lord, what the measure of life is 1

measure out 1. מַד 2. מדה
Rut 3:15 and he measured out six measures of barley 2
Jer 13:25 is your lot, the portion I have measured out to you 1

strong measure 1. ἰσχύς
1Es 8:95 we are with you to take strong measures. 1

measurement 1. מִדָּה 2. מֵמַד
1Kg 7:11 costly stones, hewn according to measurement 1
2Ch 3: 3 Solomon's measurements for building the house ‡
Job 38: 5 Who determined its measurements 2

measuring *See* rod.

meat 1. בָּשָׂר 2. טִבְחָה 3. צָלִי 4. שְׁאֵר 5. βρῶμα 6. κρέας 7. σάρξ 8. caro
Num 11: 4 Israel . . said, "O that we had meat to eat!. 1
13 Where am I to get meat to give to all this people? 1
13 they weep . . and say, 'Give us meat, that we may eat.' 1
18 you shall eat meat; for you have wept 1
18 Who will give us meat to eat? For it was well with us 1
18 LORD will give you meat, and you shall eat. 1
21 thou hast said, 'I will give them meat 1
33 While the meat was yet between their teeth 1
Jdg 6:19 the meat he put in a basket, and the broth he put 1
20 to him, "Take the meat and the unleavened cakes 1
21 angel . . touched the meat and the unleavened 1
1Sm 2:13 servant would come, while the meat was boiling 1
15 Give meat for the priest to roast; 1
15 he will not accept boiled meat from you, but raw. 1
25:11 my meat that I have killed for my shearers 2
2Sm 6:19 to each a cake of bread, a portion of meat, and a cake 8
1Kg 17: 6 ravens brought him bread and meat in the morning 1
6 ravens brought . . bread and meat in the evening; 1
1Ch 16: 3 loaf of bread, a portion of meat, and a cake *
Job 31:31 that has not been filled with his meat?' 1
Ps 78:20 also give bread, or provide meat for his people? 4
Prv 23:20 Be not . . among gluttonous eaters of meat; 1
Isa 44:16 he eats flesh, he roasts meat and is satisfied; 3
Dan 10: 3 no delicacies, no meat or wine entered my mouth 1
Mic 3: 3 and chop them up like meat in a kettle 7
Rom 14:21 it is right not to eat meat or drink wine 6
1Co 8:13 I will never eat meat 6
2Es 9:24 and taste no meat and drink no wine 8
2Mc 6:21 urged him to bring meat of his own providing 6
4Mc 6:15 We will set before you some cooked meat 5
10: 1 to save himself by tasting the meat. *

meat *See also* eat, market.

meddle 1. עבר 2. περιεργάζομαι 3. περιεργία
Prv 26:17 He who meddles in a quarrel not his own is like one 1
Sir 3:23 Do not meddle in what is beyond your tasks 2
41:22 of meddling with his maidservant 3

mediate 1. פלל 2. μεσίτης
1Sm 2:25 If a man sins against a man, God will mediate 1
Heb 8: 6 the covenant he mediates is better 2

mediator 1. ליץ 2. μεσίτης
Job 33:23 If there be for him an angel, a mediator 1
Isa 43:27 and your mediators transgressed against me. 1
1Ti 2: 5 there is one mediator between God and men 2
Heb 9:15 Therefore he is the mediator of a new covenant 2
12:24 to Jesus, the mediator of a new covenant 2

medicine 1. גֵּהָה 2. רְפָאָה 3. φάρμακον
Prv 17:22 A cheerful heart is a good medicine 1
Jer 30:13 no medicine for your wound, no healing for you. 2
46:11 In vain you have used many medicines; 2
Sir 38: 4 The Lord created medicines from the earth 3

mediocre 1. μετρίως
2Mc 15:38 if it is poorly done and mediocre 1

meditate 1. הגה 2. שׂיח 3. διανοέω 4. μελετάω 5. μεριμνάω
Gen 24:63 Isaac went out to meditate in the field 2
Jos 1: 8 but you shall meditate on it day and night 1
Ps 1: 2 on his law he meditates day and night. 1
38:12 meditate treachery all the day long. 1
63: 6 meditate on thee in the watches of the night; 1
77: 3 I moan; I meditate, and my spirit faints. 2
6 in the night; I meditate and search my spirit 2
12 I will meditate on all thy work 1
119:15 I will meditate on thy precepts 2
23 thy servant will meditate on thy statutes. 2
27 I will meditate on thy wondrous works. 2
48 I will meditate on thy statutes. 2
78 as for me, I will meditate on thy precepts. 2
148 awake . . that I may meditate upon thy promise. 2
143: 5 I meditate on all that thou hast done; 1
145: 5 on thy wondrous works, I will meditate. 2
Wis 12:22 we may meditate upon thy goodness when we judge 5
Sir 6:37 meditate at all times on his commandments 4
14:20 Blessed is the man who meditates on wisdom 4
39: 7 He will . . meditate on his secrets. 3

meditate beforehand 1. προμελετάω
Lke 21:14 not to meditate beforehand how to answer 1

meditation 1. הָגוּת 2. הִגָּיוֹן 3. שִׂיחַ 4. שִׂיחָה
Job 15: 4 and hindering meditation before God. 4
Ps 19:14 Let . . the meditation of my heart be acceptable 2
49: 3 meditation of my heart shall be understanding. 1
104:34 May my meditation be pleasing to him 3
119:97 how I love thy law! It is my meditation all the day. 4
99 for thy testimonies are my meditation. 4

medium 1. אוֹב 2. בַּעֲלַת אוֹב 3. שׁאל אוֹב
Lev 19:31 Do not turn to mediums or wizards; do not seek them 1
20: 6 If a person turns to mediums and wizards 1
27 A man or a woman who is a medium or a wizard 1
Deu 18:11 charmer, or a medium, or a wizard, or a necromancer. 3
1Sm 28: 3 And Saul had put the mediums and the wizards out 1
7 Seek out for me a woman who is a medium, 2
7 Behold, there is a medium at Endor. 2
9 what Saul has done, how he has cut off the mediums 1
2Kg 21: 6 and dealt with mediums and with wizards. 1
23:24 Josi'ah put away the mediums and the wizards 1
1Ch 10:13 Saul . . also consulted a medium 1
2Ch 33: 6 dealt with mediums and with wizards. 1
Isa 8:19 when they say to you, "Consult the mediums 1
19: 3 the sorcerers, and the mediums and the wizards; 1

meek 1. עָנָו 2. πραΰς 3. mansuetus
Num 12: 3 Now the man Moses was very meek, 1
Ps 10:17 O LORD, thou wilt hear the desire of the meek; 1
37:11 the meek shall possess the land 1
Isa 11: 4 and decide with equity for the meek of the earth; 1
29:19 The meek shall obtain fresh joy in the LORD 1
Mat 5: 5 Blessed are the meek, for they shall inherit 2
2Es 11:42 for you have afflicted the meek 3

meekness 1. πραότης 2. πραΰτης
2Co 10: 1 by the meekness and gentleness of Christ 2
Eph 4: 2 with all lowliness and meekness 2
Col 3:12 compassion, kindness, lowliness, meekness 2
Jas 1:21 receive with meekness the implanted word 2
3:13 let him show his works in the meekness of wisdom. 2
Sir 1:27 he delights in fidelity and meekness. 1
3:17 My son, perform your tasks in meekness 2
45: 4 faithfulness and meekness 2

meet 1. בוא 2. היה 3. ידע 4. יעד 5. לִפְנֵי 6. מוֹעֵד 7. מצא 8. עשה 9. פגע 10. פגשׁ 11. פָּנִים 12. קדם 13. קרא 14. קרב 15. קרה 16. חוה (A) 17. ἀναλαμβάνω 18. ἀπαντάω 19. ἀπάντησις 20. γίνομαι 21. εἰς 22. εἰσέρχομαι 23. ἐμπίπτω 24. ἐπί 25. ἐπισυναγωγή 26. εὑρίσκω 27. ἔχω 28. ἥκω εἰς τὸ αὐτό 29. κομίζω 30. ὁράω τὸ πρόσωπον 31. περιπίπτω 32. πρός 33. συγκεράννυμι 34. συμβάλλω 35. συμμείγνυμι 36. συνάγω 37. συναντάω 38. συνάντησις 39. συνάπτω 40. συνέρχομαι 41. συντυγχάνω 42. τυγχάνω 43. ὑπαντάω 44. ὑπάντησις
Gen 14:17 king of Sodom went out to meet him at the Valley 13
18: 2 ran from the tent door to meet them 13
19: 1 When Lot saw them, he rose to meet them 13
24:17 Then the servant ran to meet her, and said 13
65 Who is . . walking in the field to meet us? 13
29:13 Laban . . ran to meet him, and embraced him 13
30:16 Leah went out to meet him, and said 13
32: 1 Jacob went on his way and the angels of God met him; 9
6 We came to . . Esau, and he is coming to meet you 13
17 When Esau my brother meets you, and asks you 10
19 shall say the same thing to Esau when you meet him 7
33: 4 Esau ran to meet him, and embraced him 13
8 What do you mean by all his company which I met? 10
46:29 Joseph . . went up to meet Israel his father 13
Exd 3:18 The LORD, the God of the Hebrews, has met with us; 15
4:14 and behold, he is coming out to meet you 13
24 on the way the LORD met him and sought to kill him. 10
27 Aaron, "Go into the wilderness to meet Moses. 13
27 So he went, and met him at the mountain of God 10
5: 3 they said, "The God of the Hebrews has met with us; 13
20 They met Moses and Aaron, who were waiting 9
18: 7 Moses went out to meet his father-in-law 13
19:17 brought the people out . . to meet God; 13
23: 4 If you meet your enemy's ox or his ass going astray 9
25:22 There I will meet you 4
27:21 In the tent of meeting, outside the veil 6
28:43 when they go into the tent of meeting 6
29: 4 to the door of the tent of meeting, and wash them 6
10 shall bring the bull before the tent of meeting. 6
11 at the door of the tent of meeting 6
30 when he comes into the tent of meeting 6
32 shall eat . . at the door of the tent of meeting. 6
42 offering . . at the door of the tent of meeting 6
42 tent of meeting . . where I will meet with you 4
43 There I will meet with the people of Israel 4
44 I will consecrate the tent of meeting 6
30: 6 over the testimony, where I will meet with you. 4
16 appoint it for the service of the tent of meeting; 6
18 put it between the tent of meeting and the altar 6
20 When they go into the tent of meeting, or when they 6
26 you shall anoint with it the tent of meeting 6
36 before the testimony in the tent of meeting 6
36 the tent of meeting where I shall meet with you; 4
31: 7 tent of meeting, and the ark of the testimony 6
33: 7 and he called it the tent of meeting. 6
7 every one . . would go out to the tent of meeting 6
35:21 offering to be used for the tent of meeting 6

38: 8 ministered at the door of the tent of meeting. 6
30 bases for the door of the tent of meeting 6
39:32 tabernacle of the tent of meeting was finished; 6
40 of the tabernacle, for the tent of meeting; 6
40: 2 erect the tabernacle of the tent of meeting. 6
6 door of the tabernacle of the tent of meeting 6
7 laver between the tent of meeting and the altar 6
12 to the door of the tent of meeting 6
22 he put the table in the tent of meeting 6
24 he put the lampstand in the tent of meeting 6
26 he put the golden altar in the tent of meeting 6
29 door of the tabernacle of the tent of meeting 6
30 between the tent of meeting and the altar 6
32 when they went into the tent of meeting 6
34 Then the cloud covered the tent of meeting 6
35 Moses was not able to enter the tent of meeting 6
Lev 1: 1 and spoke to him from the tent of meeting 6
3 offer it at the door of the tent of meeting 6
5 that is at the door of the tent of meeting 6
3: 2 kill it at the door of the tent of meeting 6
8 killing it before the tent of meeting 6
13 and kill it before the tent of meeting 6
4: 4 to the door of the tent of meeting before the LORD 6
5 blood . . and bring it to the tent of meeting 6
7 which is in the tent of meeting 6
7 which is at the door of the tent of meeting 6
14 and bring it before the tent of meeting 6
16 the blood of the bull to the tent of meeting 6
18 the altar which is in the tent of meeting 6
18 which is at the door of the tent of meeting 6
6:16 in the court of the tent of meeting they shall eat 6
26 in the court of the tent of meeting 6
30 any blood is brought into the tent of meeting 6
8: 3 congregation at the door of the tent of meeting 6
4 assembled at the door of the tent of meeting 6
31 Boil the flesh at the door of the tent of meeting 6
33 the door of the tent of meeting for seven days 6
35 At the door of the tent of meeting 6
9: 5 brought . . before the tent of meeting 6
23 Moses and Aaron went into the tent of meeting 6
10: 7 do not go out from the door of the tent of meeting 6
9 no wine . . when you go into the tent of meeting 6
12: 6 the priest at the door of the tent of meeting 6
14:11 the LORD, at the door of the tent of meeting 6
23 bring them . . to the door of the tent of meeting 6
15:14 before the LORD to the door of the tent of meeting 6
29 to the priest, to the door of the tent of meeting 6
16: 7 before the LORD at the door of the tent of meeting 6
16 so he shall do for the tent of meeting 6
17 There shall be no man in the tent of meeting 6
20 holy place and the tent of meeting and the altar 6
23 Then Aaron shall come into the tent of meeting 6
33 he shall make atonement for the tent of meeting 6
17: 4 bring it to the door of the tent of meeting 6
5 to the priest at the door of the tent of meeting 6
6 altar of the LORD at the door of the tent of meeting 6
9 does not bring it to the door of the tent of meeting 6
19:21 to the LORD, to the door of the tent of meeting 6
24: 3 in the tent of meeting, Aaron shall keep it 6
Num 1: 1 in the wilderness of Sinai, in the tent of meeting 6
2: 2 they shall encamp facing the tent of meeting 6
17 Then the tent of meeting shall set out 6
3: 7 perform . . before the tent of meeting 6
8 all the furnishings of the tent of meeting 6
25 the charge . . in the tent of meeting was to be 6
25 the screen for the door of the tent of meeting 6
38 before the tent of meeting toward the sunrise 6
4: 3 to do the work in the tent of meeting. 6
4 service of . . Kohath in the tent of meeting 6
15 things of the tent of meeting which the sons 6
23 for service, to do the work in the tent of meeting. 6
25 carry . . the tent of meeting with its covering 6
25 screen for the door of the tent of meeting 6
28 This is the service . . in the tent of meeting 6
30 service, to do the work of the tent of meeting. 6
31 whole of their service in the tent of meeting 6
33 whole of their service in the tent of meeting 6
35 enter the service, for work in the tent of meeting; 6
37 all who served in the tent of meeting 6
39 enter the service for work in the tent of meeting– 6
41 Gershon, all who served in the tent of meeting 6
43 enter the service, for work in the tent of meeting– 6
47 enter to do the work . . in the tent of meeting 6
6:10 to the priest to the door of the tent of meeting 6
13 be brought to the door of the tent of meeting 6
18 shave . . at the door of the tent of meeting 6
7: 5 used in doing the service of the tent of meeting 6
89 when Moses went into the tent of meeting to speak 6
8: 9 present the Levites before the tent of meeting 6
15 shall go in to do service at the tent of meeting 6
19 to do the service . . at the tent of meeting 6
22 to do their service in the tent of meeting 6
24 work in the service of the tent of meeting; 6
26 minister . . in the tent of meeting 6
10: 3 at the entrance of the tent of meeting. 6
11:16 bring them to the tent of meeting 6
12: 4 Come out, you three, to the tent of meeting. 6
14:10 glory . . appeared at the tent of meeting to all 6
16:18 they stood at the entrance of the tent of meeting 6
19 at the entrance of the tent of meeting. 6
42 they turned toward the tent of meeting; 6
43 came to the front of the tent of meeting 6
50 to Moses at the entrance of the tent of meeting 6
17: 4 deposit them in the tent of meeting 6
4 before the testimony, where I meet with you. 4
18: 4 shall join you, and attend to the tent of meeting 6
6 to do the service of the tent of meeting. 6
21 their service in the tent of meeting. 6
22 Israel shall not come near the tent of meeting 6
23 shall do the service of the tent of meeting 6
31 return for your service in the tent of meeting. 6
19: 4 toward the front of the tent of meeting 6
20: 6 went . . to the door of the tent of meeting 6
22:36 Balak . . went out to meet him at the city of Moab 13
23: 3 perhaps the LORD will come to meet me; 13
4 God met Balaam; and Balaam said to him 15
15 Stand here . . while I meet the LORD yonder. 15
16 LORD met Balaam, and put a word in his mouth 15
25: 6 weeping at the door of the tent of meeting. 6
27: 2 stood . . at the door of the tent of meeting 6
31:13 went forth to meet them outside the camp. 13
54 gold . . and brought it into the tent of meeting 6
35:19 when he meets him, he shall put him to death. 9
21 put the murderer to death, when he meets him. 9
Deu 22:23 man meets her in the city and lies with her 7
25 if . . a man meets a young woman who is betrothed 7
28 If a man meets a virgin who is not betrothed 7
23: 4 not meet you with bread and with water on the way 12
31:14 present yourselves in the tent of meeting 6
14 presented themselves in the tent of meeting. 6
Jos 2:16 Go into the hills, lest the pursuers meet you; 9
8:14 made haste and went . . to meet Israel in battle; 13
9:11 Take provisions . . and go to meet them 13
18: 1 at Shiloh, and set up the tent of meeting there; 6
19:51 before . . LORD, at the door of the tent of meeting. 6
Jdg 4: 7 Jabin's army, to meet you by the river Kishon •
18 Ja'el came out to meet Sis'era, and said to him 13
22 Ja'el went out to meet him, and said to him 13
6:35 and Naph'tali; and they went up to meet them. 13
11:31 comes forth from the doors of my house to meet me 13
34 his daughter came out to meet him with timbrels 13
15:14 the Philistines came shouting to meet him; 13
19: 3 girl's father saw him, he came with joy to meet him. 13
1Sm 2:22 served at the entrance to the tent of meeting. 6
9:11 they met young maidens coming out to draw water 7
13 Now go up, for you will meet him immediately. 7
10: 2 you will meet two men by Rachel's tomb 7
3 three men going up to God at Bethel will meet you 7
5 you will meet a band of prophets coming down 9
7 when these signs meet you, do whatever your hand 1
10 When they came . . a band of prophets met him; 13
13:10 and Saul went out to meet him and salute him. 13
15:12 And Samuel rose early to meet Saul in the morning; 13
16: 4 The elders of the city came to meet him trembling 13
17:48 Philistine . . came and drew near to meet David 13
48 David ran quickly . . to meet the Philistine. 13
18: 6 the women came . . to meet King Saul, with timbrels 13
21: 1 Ahim'elech came to meet David trembling, and said 13
25:20 David and his men came down . . and she met them. 10
32 the LORD . . who sent you this day to meet me! 13
34 unless you had made haste and come to meet me 13
30:21 they went out to meet David and to meet the people 13
21 they went out to meet David and to meet the people 13
2Sm 2:13 went out and met them at the pool of Gibeon; 10
6:20 But Michal . . came out to meet David, and said 13
10: 5 When it was told David, he sent to meet them 13
15:32 Hushai . . came to meet him with his coat rent 13
16: 1 Ziba the servant of Mephib'osheth met him 13
19:15 came . . to meet the king and to bring the king over 13
16 come down with the men of Judah to meet King David 13
20 the first . . to come down to meet my lord the king. 13
24 And Mephib'osheth . . came down to meet the king; 13
25 And when he came from Jerusalem to meet the king 13
20: 8 When they were at . . Ama'sa came to meet them. 5
1Kg 2: 7 with such loyalty they met me when I fled 14
8 when he came down to meet me at the Jordan, I swore 13
19 the king rose to meet her, and bowed down to her; 13
5: 9 you shall meet my wishes by providing food 8
8: 4 brought up the ark . . the tent of meeting, and all 6
13:24 a lion met him on the road and killed him. 7
18: 7 as Obadi'ah was on the way, behold, Eli'jah met him; 13
16 Obadi'ah went to meet Ahab, and told him; 13
16 Obadi'ah . . told him; and Ahab went to meet Eli'jah. 13
20:36 as soon as he . . a lion met him and killed him. 7
21:18 Arise, go down to meet Ahab . . who is in Sama'ria; 13
2Kg 1: 3 Arise, go up to meet the messengers of the king 13
6 There came a man to meet us, and said to us, 'Go back 13
7 who came to meet you and told you these things? 13
2:15 they came to meet him, and bowed to the ground 13
4:26 run at once to meet her, and say to her, Is it well 13
29 If you meet any one, do not salute him; 7
31 he returned to meet him, and told him 13
5:21 he alighted from the chariot to meet him, and said 13
26 when the man turned from his chariot to meet you? 13
8: 8 Take a present . . and go to meet the man of God 13
9 So Haz'ael went to meet him, and took a present 13
9:17 and send to meet them, and let him say, 'Is it peace?' 13
18 So a man on horseback went to meet him, and said 13
21 set out, each in his chariot, and went to meet Jehu 13
21 to meet Jehu, and met him at the property of Naboth 7
10:13 Jehu met the kinsmen of Ahazi'ah . . and he said 7
15 he met Jehon'adab the son of Rechab 7
15 he met Jehon'adab . . coming to meet him; 13
16:10 When King Ahaz went . . to meet Tig'lath-pile'ser 13
23:29 Josi'ah went to meet him; and Pharaoh Neco slew him 13
1Ch 6:32 before the tabernacle of the tent of meeting 6
9:21 at the entrance of the tent of meeting. 6
12:17 David went out to meet them and said to them 5
19: 5 When David was told . . he sent to meet them 13
23:32 they shall keep charge of the tent of meeting 6
2Ch 1: 3 at Gibeon; for the tent of meeting of God 6
6 which was at the tent of meeting 6
13 from before the tent of meeting 6
5: 5 they brought up the ark, the tent of meeting 6
14:10 Asa went out to meet him 5
15: 2 he went out to meet Asa, and said to him, "Hear me, 5
19: 2 the son of Hana'ni the seer went out to meet him 11
22: 7 came there he went out with Jeho'ram to meet Jehu •
8 Jehu . . met the princes of Judah 7
28: 9 he went out to meet the army that came to Sama'ria 5
Neh 6: 2 Come and let us meet together in one 4
13: 2 not meet the children of Israel with bread 12
Job 5:14 They meet with darkness in the daytime 10
39:21 in his strength; he goes out to meet the weapons. 13
Ps 10: 6 I shall not meet adversity. •
21: 3 For thou dost meet him with goodly blessings; 12
59:10 My God in his steadfast love will meet me; 12
85:10 Steadfast love and faithfulness will meet; 10
Prv 7:10 lo, a woman meets him, dressed as a harlot 13
15 now I have come out to meet you, to seek you eagerly 13
14: 7 for there you do not meet words of knowledge. 3
22 who devise good meet loyalty and faithfulness. •
17:12 Let a man meet a she-bear robbed of her cubs 10
Ecc 8: 5 He who obeys a command will meet no harm 3
Sng 8: 1 If I met you outside, I would kiss you 7
Isa 7: 3 the LORD said to Isaiah, "Go forth to meet Ahaz 13
14: 9 Sheol . . is stirred up to meet you when you come 13
21:14 bring water, meet the fugitive with bread 12
34:14 wild beasts shall meet with hyenas 10
41: 2 from the east whom victory meets at every step? 13
64: 5 Thou meetest him that joyfully works 9
Jer 18:21 May their men meet death by pestilence 2
41: 6 Ish'mael . . came out from Mizpah to meet them 13
6 he met them, he said to them, "Come in to Gedali'ah 10
51:31 One runner runs to meet another 13
31 one messenger to meet another, to tell the king 13
Dan 2:10 not a man on earth who can meet the king's demand; 16
Hos 12: 4 He met God at Bethel, and there God spoke with him– 7
Ams 4:12 do this to you, prepare to meet your God, O Israel! 13
5:19 as if a man fled from a lion, and a bear met him; 9
9:10 who say, 'Evil shall not overtake or meet us.' 12
Zec 2: 3 and another angel came forward to meet him 13
Mat 8:28 country of the Gadarenes, two demoniacs met him 43
34 behold, all the city came out to meet Jesus 44
25: 1 went to meet the bridegroom. 44
6 'Behold, the bridegroom! Come out to meet him.' 19
28: 9 behold, Jesus met them and said, "Hail! 43
Mrk 5: 2 there met him out of the tombs a man 43
14:13 a man carrying a jar of water will meet you 18
Lke 8:27 there met him a man from the city who had demons 43
9:37 a great crowd met him. 37
14:31 whether he is able with 10,000 to meet him 43
17:12 as he entered a village, he was met by ten lepers 18
22:10 a man carrying a jar of water will meet you 37
Joh 4:51 As he was going down, his servants met him 43
11:30 still in the place where Martha had met him. 43
12:13 went out to meet him, crying, "Hosanna! 44
18: 2 Jesus often met there with his disciples. 36
Act 10:25 When Peter entered, Cornelius met him 37
11:26 For a whole year they met with the church 36
13:43 when the meeting of the synagogue broke up •
16:16 met by a slave girl who had a spirit of divination 43
17:18 Epicurean and Stoic philosophers met him 34
20:14 when he met us at Assos, we took him on board 34
22:30 the chief priests and all the council to meet 40
25:16 before the accused met the accusers face to face 27
28:15 came as far as the Forum of Ap'pius . . to meet us 19
1Co 11:20 When you meet together, it is not the Lord's supper 40
1Th 4:17 in the clouds to meet the Lord in the air 19
2Th 2: 1 our assembling to meet him 24
Heb 4: 2 because it did not meet with faith in the hearers. 33
7: 1 met Abraham returning from the slaughter 37
10 when Melchiz'edek met him. 37
10:25 not neglecting to meet together 25
Jas 1: 2 Count it all joy . . when you meet various trials 31
1Es 9: 4 if any did not meet there within two or three days 18
Tob 7: 1 Sarah met them and greeted them 43
11:16 Then Tobit went out to meet his daughter-in-law 38
Jdt 5: 4 why have they . . refused to come out and meet me? 19
10:11 an Assyrian patrol met her 37
15: 9 when they met her they all blessed her 22
Wis 6:16 meets them in every thought. 43
19: 5 they themselves might meet a strange death. 26
Sir 19:29 is known by his face, when you meet him. 19
31: 6 their destruction has met them face to face. 20
36: 9 may those who harm thy people meet destruction. 26
40:23 A friend or a companion never meets one amiss 18

1Mc 3:11 When Judas learned of it, he went out to meet him 38
16 Judas went out to meet him with a small company. 38
17 when they saw the army coming to meet them 38
4:29 Judas met them with 10,000 men. 37
5:25 who met them peaceably 18
39 Judas went to meet them. 38
59 came out of the city to meet them in battle. 38
7:30 he was afraid of him and would not meet him again. 30
31 he went out to meet Judas in battle 38
43 So the armies met in battle 39
9:39 came out . . to meet them with tambourines 38
10: 2 and marched out to meet him in battle. 38
39 to meet the necessary expenses of the sanctuary. 21
49 The two kings met in battle, and the army 39
53 I met him in battle 39
56 meet me at Ptolemais 18
58 Alexander the king met him 18
59 the king wrote to Jonathan to come to meet him. 38
60 went with pomp to Ptolemais and met the two kings; 18
71 come down to the plain to meet us 32
74 Simon his brother met him to help him. 37
86 came out to meet him with great pomp. 38
11: 2 and went to meet him 37
2 Alexander . . had commanded them to meet him 37
6 Jonathan met the king at Joppa with pomp 37
15 marched out and met him with a strong force 18
22 to meet him for a conference at Ptolemais 18
60 the people of the city met him and paid him honor. 18
68 the army of the foreigners met him in the plain; 18
68 they themselves met him face to face. 18
12:25 met them in the region of Hamath 18
41 Jonathan went out to meet him 19
16: 5 a large force . . was coming to meet them 38
2Mc 3: 7 When Apollonius met the king 35
5: 8 Finally he met a miserable end 42
12 to cut down relentlessly every one they met 23
8:14 before he ever met them 41
10:35 and with savage fury cut down every one they met. 23
13: 8 he met his death in ashes. 29
14:21 set a day on which to meet by themselves 28
30 was meeting him more rudely than . . his custom 19
3Mc 5: 2 so that the Jews might meet their doom. 38
6:30 they had expected to meet their destruction. 17
7:14 any whom they met of their fellow-countrymen 23
151 1: 6 I went out to meet the Philistine 38

meet *See also* chance, go, run.

meet again 1. ἔρχομαι ἐπὶ τὸ αὐτό
Sus 1:14 But turning back, they met again; 1

come to meet 1. קדם 2. ὑπαντάω
Job 30:27 days of affliction come to meet me. 1
Ps 79: 8 let thy compassion come speedily to meet us 1
Sir 15: 2 She will come to meet him like a mother 2

meet in battle 1. συμμείγνυμι
2Mc 15:26 Judas and his men met the enemy in battle 1

meet the test 1. δόκιμος
2Co 13: 7 not that we may appear to have met the test 1

meet together 1. יעד 2. פגשׁ
Neh 6:10 Let us meet together in the house of God 1
Prv 22: 2 The rich and the poor meet together; 2
29:13 The poor man and the oppressor meet together; 2

meeting of the council 1. συνέδριον
2Mc 14: 5 was invited by Demetrius to a meeting of the council 1

meeting place 1. מוֹעֵד
Ps 74: 8 they burned all the meeting places of God 1

melodious 1. εὐμελής
Wis 17:18 a melodious sound of birds 1
3Mc 7:16 praise and all kinds of melodious songs. †

melody 1. הִגָּיוֹן 2. זִמְרָה 3. μέλος
Ps 92: 3 to the melody of the lyre. 1
98: 5 praises . . with the lyre and the sound of melody! 2
Ams 5:23 to the melody of your harps I will not listen. 2
Sir 32: 6 the melody of music with good wine. 3
40:21 The flute and the harp make pleasant melody 3
47: 9 to make sweet melody with their voices. 3
50:18 in sweet and full-toned melody. 3

melody *See also* make.

melon 1. אֲבַטִּחִים
Num11: 5 We remember the . . cucumbers, the melons 1

melt 1. הִתּוּךְ 2. ירד 3. מוג 4. מסה 5. מסס 6. נתך 7. ἐκλείχω 8. τηκτός 9. τήκω 10. ardesco 11. liquesco
Exd 16:21 but when the sun grew hot, it melted. 5
Deu 20: 8 lest the heart of his fellows melt as his heart.' 5
Jos 2:11 And as soon as we heard it, our hearts melted 5
5: 1 their heart melted, and there was no . . spirit 5
7: 5 hearts of the people melted, and became as water. 5
Jdg 15:14 caught fire, and his bonds melted off his hands. 5
2Sm 17:10 the valiant man . . will utterly melt with fear; 5
Ps 22:14 my heart is like wax, it is melted within my breast; 5
46: 6 he utters his voice, the earth melts. 3
68: 2 as wax melts before fire, let the wicked perish 5
97: 5 The mountains melt like wax before the LORD 5
147:18 He sends forth his word, and melts them; 4
Isa 13: 7 hands . . be feeble, and every man's heart will melt 5
15: 3 in . . squares every one wails and melts in tears. 2
19: 1 heart of the Egyptians will melt within them. 5
Ezk 21: 7 When it comes, every heart will melt 5
15 that their hearts may melt, and many fall 3
22:20 to blow the fire upon it in order to melt it; 6
20 and I will put you in and melt you. 6
21 you shall be melted in the midst of it. 6
22 As silver is melted in a furnace, so you shall be 1
22 you shall be melted in the midst of it; 6
24:11 may burn, that its filthiness may be melted in it 6
Ams 9: 5 GOD of hosts, he who touches the earth and it melts 3
Mic 1: 4 And the mountains will melt under him 5
Nah 1: 5 The mountains quake before him, the hills melt; 3
2Pe 3:12 and the elements will melt with fire! 9
2Es 13: 4 all who heard his voice melted as wax melts 10
4 as wax melts when it feels the fire. 11
Jdt 16:15 at thy presence the rocks shall melt like wax 9
Wis 16:22 Snow and ice withstood fire without melting 9
27 For what was not destroyed by fire was melted 9
29 will melt like wintry frost 9
19:21 nor did they melt the . . heavenly food. 8
Sir 38:28 the breath of the fire melts his flesh 9
LJr 1:20 men say their hearts have melted 7
1Mc 4:32 melt the boldness of their strength 9

melt away 1. דלף 2. מוג 3. מסס 4. ἀναλύω 5. tabesco
Exd 15:15 all the inhabitants of Canaan have melted away. 2
Jos 2: 9 the inhabitants of the land melt away before you. 2
Ps 107:26 their courage melted away in their evil plight; 2
112:10 wicked man . . gnashes his teeth and melts away; 3
119:28 My soul melts away for sorrow; 1
2Es 8:23 indignation makes the mountains melt away 5
Sir 3:15 as frost in fair weather, your sins will melt away. 4

melt easily 1. εὔτηκτος
Wis 19:21 the crystalline, easily melted kind of heavenly food. 1

melt in fear 1. מוג
Isa 8: 6 melt in fear before Rezin and the son of Remali'ah; •
14:31 O city; melt in fear, O Philistia, all of you! 1
Jer 49:23 they melt in fear, they are troubled like the sea 1

make melt 1. מסה 2. מסס
Deu 1:28 Our brethren have made our hearts melt, saying 2
Jos 14: 8 my brethren . . made the heart of the people melt; 1

member 1. בֵּן 2. בָּשָׂר 3. יֵצֶר 4. נֶפֶשׁ 5. עֵקֶר 6. ἐκ σπέρματος 7. μέλος 8. ὁ ἐκ 9. membrum
Gen 36: 6 Esau took . . all the members of his household 4
Lev 25:47 sells . . to a member of the stranger's family 5
1Ch 5:23 members of the half-tribe of Manas'seh dwelt 1
Job 17: 7 all my members are like a shadow. 3
Ezk 23:20 whose members were like those of asses 2
Mat 5:29 is better that you lose one of your members 7
30 is better that you lose one of your members 7
Rom 6:13 Do not yield your members to sin 7
13 yield . . your members to God as instruments 7
19 as you once yielded your members to impurity 7
19 so now yield your members to righteousness 7
7: 5 sinful passions . . were at work in our members 7
23 but I see in my members another law 7
23 to the law of sin which dwells in my members. 7
11: 1 I myself am . . a member of the tribe of Benjamin. •
12: 4 For as in one body we have many members 7
4 and all the members do not have the same function 7
5 and individually members one of another. 7
1Co 6: 5 to decide between members of the brotherhood •
15 know that your bodies are members of Christ 7
15 Shall I therefore take the members of Christ 7
15 make them members of a prostitute? Never! 7
12:12 For just as the body is one and has many members 7
12 all the members of the body, though many, are one 7
14 body does not consist of one member but of many. 7
25 members may have the same care for one another. 7
26 If one member suffers, all suffer together 7
26 if one member is honored, all rejoice together. 7
27 individually members of it. 7
Eph 4:25 we are members one of another. 7
5:30 because we are members of his body. 7
Jas 3: 5 So the tongue is a little member and boasts 7
6 an unrighteous world among our members 7
4: 1 Is it not your passions . . at war in your members? 7
2Es 8: 8 and dost furnish it with members 9
10 from the members . . (that is, from the breasts) 9
Tob 1: 9 I married Anna, a member of our family 6
3Mc 1:11 not even members of their own nation were allowed 8
4Mc 9:14 though broken in every member 7
10:20 we let our bodily members be mutilated. 7

male member 1. שָׁפְכָה
Deu 23: 1 He . . whose male member is cut off 1

member of the council 1. βουλευτής
Mrk 15:43 Joseph of Arimathe'a, a . . member of the council 1
Lke 23:50 He was a member of the council 1

member of the court 1. σύντροφος
Act 13: 1 Man'a-en a member of the court of Herod 1

member of the household 1. οἰκεῖος
Eph 2:19 you are . . members of the household of God 1

member of the same body 1. σύσσωμος
Eph 3: 6 Gentiles are . . members of the same body 1

members *See* disjoint.

memoir 1. ὑπομνηματισμός
2Mc 2:13 in the memoirs of Nehemiah 1

memorable deed 1. זִכָּרוֹן
Est 6: 1 gave orders to bring the book of memorable deeds 1

memorial 1. זָכַר 2. זִכָּרוֹן 3. שֵׁם 4. μνημόσυνον 5. ὄνομα
Exd 12:14 This day shall be for you a memorial day 2
13: 9 as a memorial between your eyes, that the law 2
17:14 Write this as a memorial in a book and recite it 2
Lev 23:24 a memorial proclaimed with blast of trumpets 2
Num31:54 as a memorial for the people of Israel 2
Jos 4: 7 stones shall be to . . Israel a memorial for ever. 2
Neh 2:20 no portion or right or memorial in Jerusalem. 2
Isa 26: 8 thy memorial name is the desire of our soul. 1
55:13 and it shall be to the LORD for a memorial 3
Act 10: 4 have ascended as a memorial before God. 4
Sir 44: 9 there are some who have no memorial 4
Bar 4: 5 Take courage, my people, O memorial of Israel! 4
1Mc 8:22 as a memorial of peace and alliance 4
13:29 suits of armor for a permanent memorial 5
2Mc 6:31 example of nobility and a memorial of courage 4

memorial *See also* offering, portion.

memorize 1. διὰ μνήμης ἀναλαμβάνω
2Mc 2:25 to make it easy for those . . inclined to memorize 1

memory 1. זֵכֶר 2. μνήμη 3. μνημόσυνον 4. memoria
Job 18:17 His memory perishes from the earth 1
Ps 9: 6 the very memory of them has perished. 1
109:15 may his memory be cut off from the earth! 1
Prv 10: 7 The memory of the righteous is a blessing 1
Ecc 9: 5 but the memory of them is lost. 1
Mat 26:13 what she has done will be told in memory of her. 3
Mrk 14: 9 what she has done will be told in memory of her. 3
2Es 14:40 for my spirit retained its memory; 4
Wis 4: 1 in the memory of virtue is immortality 2
19 the memory of them will perish. 2
11:12 groaning at the memory of what had occurred. 2
Sir 10:17 extinguished the memory of them from the earth. 3
23:26 She will leave her memory for a curse 3
35: 7 the memory of it will not be forgotten. 3
39: 9 his memory will not disappear 3
45: 1 Moses, whose memory is blessed. 3
46:11 may their memory be blessed! 3
49: 1 The memory of Josiah 3
13 The memory of Nehemiah also is lasting 3
1Mc 3: 7 his memory is blessed for ever. 3
35 banish the memory of them from the place 3
12:53 and blot out the memory of them from among men. 3
2Mc 7:20 admirable and worthy of honorable memory 2

mend 1. צרר 2. רפא 3. καταρτίζω
Jos 9: 4 took . . wineskins, worn-out and torn and mended 1
Jer 19:11 potter's vessel, so that it can never be mended. 2
Mat 4:21 with Zeb'edee their father, mending their nets 3
Mrk 1:19 who were in their boat mending the nets. 3

begin to mend 1. κομψότερον ἔχω
Joh 4:52 So he asked them the hour when he began to mend 1

mend one's ways 1. καταρτίζω
2Co 13:11 Mend your ways, heed my appeal 1

menial *See* use.

menstrual 1. נִדָּה
Lev 18:19 while she is in her menstrual uncleanness 1

menstruation 1. נִדָּה
Lev 12: 2 time of her menstruation, she shall be unclean 1
5 she shall be unclean . . as in her menstruation 1

woman in menstruation 1. ἀποκαθῆμαι
LJr 1:29 Sacrifices . . may be touched by women in menstruation 1

menstruous 1. καταμήνιος 2. menstruo
2Es 5: 8 menstruous women shall bring forth monsters. 2
AEs 14:16 I abhor it like a menstruous rag 1

mental 1. ψυχικός
4Mc 1:32 Some desires are mental, others are physical 1
mental *See also* effort.

mention 1. בוא 2. דבר 3. זכר 4. נקב 5. קרא 6. μνείαν ποιέω 7. προεῖπον 8. dico 9. loquor 10. supradico
Jos 21: 9 gave the following cities mentioned by name 5
1Sm 4:18 When he mentioned the ark of God, Eli fell over 3
1Ch 4:38 these mentioned by name were princes 1
6:65 these cities which are mentioned by name. 5
2Ch 28:15 men who have been mentioned by name rose and took 4
Ezr 8:20 These were all mentioned by name. 4
Est 6:10 Leave out nothing that you have mentioned. 2
Ps 87: 4 know me I mention Rahab and Babylon; 3
Isa 19:17 every one to whom it is mentioned will fear 3
Jer 20: 9 If I say, "I will not mention him 3
23:36 'the burden of the LORD' you shall mention no more 3
Hos 2:17 and they shall be mentioned by name no more. 3
Ams 6:10 Hush! We must not mention the name of the LORD. 3
Rom 1: 9 I mention you always in my prayers 6
1Th 1: 2 constantly mentioning you in our prayers 6
2Es 5:40 the things that were mentioned 8
7:87 worse than all the ways that have been mentioned 10
98 all that have been mentioned 10
13:21 the things which you have mentioned. 9
2Mc 14: 8 through the folly of those whom I have mentioned 7
mention *See also* make.

mention before 1. προδηλόω
3Mc 4:14 the hard labor . . briefly mentioned before 1

mention previously 1. προαποδείκνυμι 2. προεῖπον 3. προσημαίνω
2Mc 4: 1 The previously mentioned Simon 2
23 the brother of the previously mentioned Simon 3
3Mc 2:25 by the previously mentioned drinking companions 1
4:17 the previously mentioned interval of time 2

mercenary 1. μισθωτός 2. ξένος
1Mc 6:29 mercenary forces came to him 1
15: 3 and have recruited a host of mercenary troops *
2Mc 10:24 gathered a tremendous force of mercenaries 2
mercenary *See also* enlist, maintain.

merchandise 1. מַעֲרָב 2. סַחַר 3. רְכֻלָּה
Prv 31:18 perceives that her merchandise is profitable. 2
Isa 23:18 Her merchandise . . will be dedicated to the LORD; 2
18 her merchandise will supply abundant food 2
45:14 wealth of Egypt and the merchandise of Ethiopia 2
Ezk 26:12 They will make . . a prey of your merchandise; 3
27:13 and vessels of bronze for your merchandise. 1
17 they exchanged for your merchandise wheat 1
19 calamus were bartered for your merchandise. 1
25 traveled for you with your merchandise. 1
27 Your riches, your wares, your merchandise 1
27 your caulkers, your dealers in merchandise 1
33 with your abundant wealth and merchandise 1
34 your merchandise and all your crew have sunk 1

merchant 1. כְּנַעַן 2. כְּנַעֲנִי 3. סחר 4. רכל 5. ἔμπορος
Gen 23:16 the weights current among the merchants. 3
1Kg 10:15 which came . . from the traffic of the merchants 4
2Ch 9:14 that which the traders and merchants brought; 3
Neh 3:31 repaired as far as the house . . of the merchants 4
32 goldsmiths and the merchants repaired. 4
13:20 merchants and sellers of all kinds of wares 4
Job 41: 6 Will they divide him up among the merchants? 1
Prv 31:14 She is like the ships of the merchant 3
24 she delivers girdles to the merchant. 2
Sng 3: 6 with all the fragrant powders of the merchant? 4
Isa 23: 2 Be still . . O merchants of Sidon; 3
3 you were the merchant of the nations. 3
8 Tyre . . whose merchants were princes 3
Ezk 17: 4 and set it in a city of merchants. 4
27: 3 merchant of the peoples on many coastlands 4
36 The merchants among the peoples hiss at you; 3
38:13 Sheba and Dedan and the merchants of Tarshish 3
Nah 3:16 increased your merchants more than the stars 4
Mat 13:45 like a merchant in search of fine pearls 5
Rev 18: 3 the merchants of the earth have grown rich 5
11 the merchants of the earth weep and mourn for her 5
15 The merchants of these wares, who gained wealth 5
23 thy merchants were the great men of the earth 5
Sir 26:29 A merchant can hardly keep from wrongdoing 5
37:11 with a merchant about barter 5
42: 5 of profit from dealing with merchants 5
Bar 3:23 merchants of Merran and Teman, the story-tellers 5
2Mc 8:34 who had brought the 1,000 merchants to buy the Jews 5

merciful 1. חֶמְלָה 2. חנן 3. חֶסֶד 4. חָסִיד 5. רַחוּם 6. רחם 7. ἐλεέω 8. ἐλεήμων 9. ἔλεος 10. ἱλάσκομαι 11. ἵλεως 12. οἰκτίρμων 13. οἰκτίρω 14. φιλελεήμων 15. misereo 16. misericors
Gen 19:16 by the hand, the LORD being merciful to him 1
Exd 34: 6 a God merciful and gracious, slow to anger 5
Deu 4:31 for the LORD your God is a merciful God; 5
1Kg 20:31 kings of the house of Israel are merciful kings; 3
2Ch 30: 9 For the LORD your God is gracious and merciful 5
Neh 9:17 God ready to forgive, gracious and merciful 5
31 for thou art a gracious and merciful God. 5
Ps 57: 1 Be merciful to me, O God, be merciful to me 2
1 Be merciful to me, O God, be merciful to me 2
86:15 O Lord, art a God merciful and gracious 5
103: 8 The LORD is merciful and gracious 5
111: 4 LORD is gracious and merciful. 5
112: 4 LORD is gracious, merciful, and righteous. 5
116: 5 Gracious . . and righteous; our God is merciful. 6
145: 8 The LORD is gracious and merciful 5
Jer 3:12 I will not look on you in anger, for I am merciful 4
Jol 2:13 for he is gracious and merciful, slow to anger 5
Jon 4: 2 thou art a gracious God and merciful 5
Mat 5: 7 Blessed are the merciful, for they shall obtain 8
Lke 6:36 Be merciful, even as your Father is merciful. 12
36 Be merciful, even as your Father is merciful. 12
18:13 'God, be merciful to me a sinner!' 10
Heb 2:17 become a merciful and faithful high priest 8
8:12 For I will be merciful toward their iniquities 11
Jas 5:11 how the Lord is compassionate and merciful. 12
2Es 2:31 for I am merciful, says the Lord Almighty. 16
7:132 that the Most High is now called merciful 16
8:31 thou, because of us sinners, are called merciful. 16
32 then thou wilt be called merciful. 16
36 when thou art merciful to those who have no store 15
Tob 6:17 and cry out to the merciful God, and he will save you 8
7:12 The merciful God will guide you both for the best. 8
11:17 God had been merciful to him 7
14: 9 be merciful and just 14
Wis 11:23 thou art merciful to all 7
Sir 2:11 For the Lord is compassionate and merciful 8
48:20 they called upon the Lord who is merciful 8
50:19 in prayer before him who is merciful 8
1Mc 2:57 David, because he was merciful 9
2Mc 1:24 awe-inspiring and strong and just and merciful 8
8:29 besought the merciful Lord 8
11: 9 they all together praised the merciful God 8
13:12 besought the merciful Lord with weeping 8
3Mc 5: 7 their merciful God and Father 8
51 manifest himself and be merciful to them 13
4Mc 6:28 Be merciful to your people 11
8:14 whatever justice you revere will be merciful 11
9:24 may become merciful to our nation 11
12:17 to be merciful to our nation; 11

merciful again 1. repropitio
2Es 10:24 that the Mighty One may be merciful to you again 1

all merciful 1. πολυέλεος
3Mc 6: 9 all-merciful and protector of all 1

very merciful 1. εὐΐλατος 2. πολυέλεος
1Es 8:53 we found him very merciful 1
Man 1: 7 long-suffering, and very merciful 2

merciless 1. אַכְזָרִי 2. ἀνελεήμων
Prv 5: 9 lest you give . . your years to the merciless; 1
Wis 12: 5 their merciless slaughter of children 2
merciless *See also* foe.

merciless man 1. ἀνελεήμων
Sir 37:11 with a merciless man about kindness 1

mercilessly 1. לֹא חמל
Hab 1:17 and mercilessly slaying nations for ever? 1

mercy 1. חמל 2. חנן 3. חֶסֶד 4. רחם 5. רַחֲמִים 6. תְּחִנָּה 7. רַחֲמִין (A) 8. ἐλεάω 9. ἐλεέω 10. ἐλεημοσύνη 11. ἔλεος 12. ἱλάσκομαι 13. ἵλεως 14. οἰκτιρμός 15. φειδώ 16. misereo 17. misereor 18. misericordia
Gen 43:14 may God Almighty grant you mercy before the man 5
Deu 13:17 show you mercy, and have compassion on you 5
Jos 11:20 and should receive no mercy but be exterminated 6
2Sm 24:14 into the hand of the LORD, for his mercy is great; 5
1Ch 21:13 the hand of the LORD, for his mercy is very great; 5
Neh 1:11 grant him mercy in the sight of this man. 5
9:19 thou in thy great mercies didst not forsake them 5
27 according to thy great mercies thou didst give 5
28 deliver them according to thy mercies. 5
31 in thy great mercies thou didst not make an end 5
Ps 23: 6 Surely goodness and mercy shall follow me 3
25: 6 Be mindful of thy mercy, O LORD 5
40:11 Do not thou, O LORD, withhold thy mercy from me 5
51: 1 Have mercy on me, O God, according to thy steadfast 2
1 according to thy abundant mercy blot out my 5
69:16 according to thy abundant mercy, turn to me. 5
103: 4 who crowns you with steadfast love and mercy 5
119:77 Let thy mercy come to me, that I may live; 5
156 Great is thy mercy, O LORD; 5
123: 3 Have mercy upon us, O LORD, have mercy upon us 2
Prv 12:10 but the mercy of the wicked is cruel. 5
Isa 13:18 they will have no mercy on the fruit of the womb; 4
47: 6 gave them into your hand, you showed them no mercy 5
55: 7 return to the LORD, that he may have mercy on him 4
60:10 I smote you, but in my favor I have had mercy on you. 4
63: 7 which he has granted them according to his mercy 5
Jer 6:23 they are cruel and have no mercy 4
16: 5 says the LORD, my steadfast love and mercy. 3
31:20 I will surely have mercy on him, says the LORD. 4
42:12 I will grant you mercy 5
12 that he may have mercy on you and let you remain 4
50:42 they are cruel, and have no mercy. 4
Lam 2: 2 Lord has destroyed without mercy all . . Jacob; 1
21 hast slain them, slaughtering without mercy. 1
3:22 his mercies never come to an end; 5
Dan 2:18 told them to seek mercy of the God of heaven 7
9: 9 To the Lord our God belong mercy and forgiveness; 5
18 but on the ground of thy great mercy. 5
Hos 2:19 betroth you . . in steadfast love, and in mercy. 3
Hab 3: 2 in wrath remember mercy. 4
Zec 1:12 how long wilt thou have no mercy on Jerusalem 4
7: 9 Render true judgments, show kindness and mercy 3
Mat 9:13 Go and learn what this means, 'I desire mercy 11
27 Have mercy on us, Son of David. 9
12: 7 'I desire mercy, and not sacrifice,' 11
15:22 Have mercy on me, O Lord, Son of David 9
17:15 Lord, have mercy on my son, for he is an epileptic 9
18:33 you have had mercy on your fellow servant 9
33 as I had mercy on you?' 9
20:30 Have mercy on us, Son of David! 9
31 Lord, have mercy on us, Son of David! 9
23:23 justice and mercy and faith 11
Mrk 5:19 how he has had mercy on you. 9
10:47 Jesus, Son of David, have mercy on me! 9
48 Son of David, have mercy on me! 9
Lke 1:50 his mercy is on those who fear him 11
54 in remembrance of his mercy 11
58 the Lord had shown great mercy to her 11
72 to perform the mercy promised to our fathers 11
78 through the tender mercy of our God 11
10:37 He said, "The one who showed mercy on him. 11
16:24 he called out, 'Father Abraham, have mercy 9
17:13 Jesus, Master, have mercy on us. 9
18:38 he cried, "Jesus, Son of David, have mercy on me! 9
39 Son of David, have mercy on me! 9
Rom 9:15 I will have mercy on whom I have mercy 9
15 I will have mercy on whom I have mercy 9
16 upon man's will or exertion, but upon God's mercy. 8
23 the riches of his glory for the vessels of mercy 11
11:31 by the mercy shown to you they . . receive mercy. 11
32 that he may have mercy upon all. 9
12: 1 I appeal to you . . by the mercies of God 14
15: 9 the Gentiles might glorify God for his mercy. 11
1Co 7:25 one who by the Lord's mercy is trustworthy. 9
2Co 1: 3 Father of mercies and God of all comfort 14
4: 1 having this ministry by the mercy of God 9
Gal 6:16 Peace and mercy be upon all who walk by this rule 11
Eph 2: 4 God, who is rich in mercy 11
Php 2:27 God had mercy on him, and not only on him but on me 9
1Ti 1: 2 Grace, mercy, and peace from God the Father 11
2Ti 1: 2 Grace, mercy, and peace from God the Father 11
16 May the Lord grant mercy 11
18 may the Lord grant him to find mercy from the Lord 11
Tit 3: 5 in virtue of his own mercy 11
Heb 4:16 we may receive mercy and find grace 11
10:28 dies without mercy 14
Jas 2:13 without mercy to one who has shown no mercy 11
13 yet mercy triumphs over judgment. 11
3:17 wisdom . . is . . full of mercy and good fruits 11
1Pe 1: 3 By his great mercy we have been born anew 11
2Jn 1: 3 Grace, mercy, and peace will be with us, from God 11
Jde 1: 2 May mercy, peace, and love be multiplied to you. 11
21 wait for the mercy of our Lord Jesus Christ 11
23 on some have mercy with fear 8
1Es 8:78 now in some measure mercy has come to us from thee 11
2Es 1:25 When you beg mercy of me, I will show you no mercy. 18
2: 4 Go, my children, and ask for mercy from the Lord.' 18
31 and will show mercy to them 18
32 and proclaim mercy to them 18
4:24 and we are not worthy to obtain mercy. 18
7:115 no one will then be able to have mercy on him 17
132 because he has mercy on those 17
8:11 and afterwards thou wilt guide him in thy mercy. 18
45 and have mercy on thy inheritance 16
45 for thou hast mercy on thy own creation. 16
11:46 for the judgment and mercy of him who made it.' 18
12:34 he will deliver in mercy the remnant of my people 18
48 and to seek mercy on account of the humiliation 18
14:34 and after death you shall obtain mercy. 18
Tob 3: 2 all thy deeds and all thy ways are mercy and truth 10
6:17 he will save you and have mercy on you 9
8:16 thou hast treated us according to thy great mercy. 11
17 Show them mercy, O Lord 11
17 in health and happiness and mercy. 11
13: 6 if he will accept you and have mercy on you? 10
14: 5 God will again have mercy on them 9
7 showing mercy to our brethren. 11
Jdt 7:30 the Lord our God will restore to us his mercy 11
13:14 has not withdrawn his mercy 11
AEs 13: 6 destroyed . . without pity or mercy 15
17 have mercy upon thy inheritance 12
Wis 3: 9 because grace and mercy are upon his elect 11
4:15 God's grace and mercy are with his elect 11
6: 6 For the lowliest man may be pardoned in mercy 11

9: 1 O God of my fathers and Lord of mercy 11
11: 9 though they were being disciplined in mercy 11
12:22 when we are judged we may expect mercy. 11
15: 1 patient, and ruling all things in mercy. 11
16:10 thy mercy came to their help and healed them. 11
Sir 2: 7 You who fear the Lord, wait for his mercy 11
9 for good things, for everlasting joy and mercy. 11
18 as his majesty is, so also is his mercy. 11
5: 6 Do not say, "His mercy is great 14
6 both mercy and wrath are with him 11
16:11 mercy and wrath are with the Lord 11
12 As great as his mercy, so great is also his reproof; 11
17:29 How great is the mercy of the Lord 10
18: 5 who can fully recount his mercies? 11
11 pours out his mercy upon them. 11
28: 4 Does he have no mercy toward a man like himself 11
29: 1 He that shows mercy will lend to his neighbor 11
35:19 makes them rejoice in his mercy. 11
20 Mercy is as welcome when he afflicts them 11
36: 1 Have mercy upon us, O Lord, the God of all 9
12 Have mercy, O Lord, upon the people 9
44:10 these were men of mercy 11
45: 1 the Lord brought forth a man of mercy 11
47:22 the Lord will never give up his mercy 11
50:22 deals with us according to his mercy. 11
24 May he entrust to us his mercy! 11
51: 3 in the greatness of thy mercy and of thy name 11
8 Then I remembered thy mercy, O Lord 11
29 May your soul rejoice in his mercy 11
Bar 2:19 we bring before thee our prayer for mercy 11
3: 2 have mercy, for we have sinned before thee. 9
4:22 because of the mercy which soon will come to you 10
5: 9 mercy and righteousness that come from him. 10
Aza 1:12 do not withdraw thy mercy from us 11
15 to make an offering before thee or to find mercy. 11
19 in thy forbearance and in thy abundant mercy. 11
67 his mercy endures for ever. 11
68 his mercy endures for ever. 11
Man 1: 6 yet . . unsearchable is thy promised mercy 11
7 in the multitude of thy mercies 14
14 thou wilt save me in thy great mercy 11
1Mc 3:44 to pray and ask for mercy and compassion. 11
4:24 he is good, for his mercy endures for ever. 11
13:46 according to your mercy. 11
16: 3 you by His mercy are mature in years 11
2Mc 2: 7 shows his mercy. 13
6:16 Therefore he never withdraws his mercy from us. 11
7:23 will in his mercy give life and breath back to you 11
29 in God's mercy I may get you back again 11
37 appealing to God to show mercy soon to our nation 13
8: 3 to have mercy on the city 9
5 the wrath of the Lord had turned to mercy. 11
27 allotted it to them as the beginning of mercy. 11
9:13 who would no longer have mercy on him 9
11:10 the Lord had mercy on them. 9
3Mc 2:19 reveal your mercy at this hour. 11
20 Speedily let your mercies overtake us 14
6: 2 governing all creation with mercy 14
4 manifesting the light of your mercy 11
39 the Lord of all most gloriously revealed his mercy 11

mercy *See also* act, appeal, find, obtain, receive.

do an act of mercy 1. *ἐλεέω*

Rom12: 8 he who does acts of mercy, with cheerfulness. 1

mercy seat 1. כַּפֹּרֶת 2. *ἱλαστήριον*

Exd 25:17 Then you shall make a mercy seat of pure gold; 1
18 cherubim . . on the two ends of the mercy seat. 1
19 of one piece with the mercy seat shall you make 1
20 overshadowing the mercy seat with their wings 1
20 toward the mercy seat shall the faces . . be. 1
21 you shall put the mercy seat on the top of the ark; 1
22 from above the mercy seat . . I will speak 1
26:34 You shall put the mercy seat upon the ark 1
30: 6 before the mercy seat that is over the testimony 1
31: 7 the ark . . and the mercy seat that is thereon 1
35:12 the ark with its poles, the mercy seat, and the veil 1
37: 6 he made a mercy seat of pure gold; 1
7 on the two ends of the mercy seat he made them 1
8 of one piece with the mercy seat 1
9 overshadowing the mercy seat with their wings 1
9 toward the mercy seat were the faces 1
39:35 the ark . . with its poles and the mercy seat; 1
40:20 and set the mercy seat above on the ark; 1
Lev 16: 2 before the mercy seat which is upon the ark 1
2 I will appear in the cloud upon the mercy seat 1
13 the cloud of the incense may cover the mercy seat 1
14 sprinkle it . . on the front of the mercy seat 1
14 and before the mercy seat he shall sprinkle 1
15 sprinkling it upon the mercy seat and before 1
15 sprinkling it . . before the mercy seat 1
Num 7:89 voice speaking to him from above the mercy seat 1
1Ch 28:11 plan of . . the room for the mercy seat; 1
Heb 9: 5 cherubim of glory overshadowing the mercy seat. 2

show mercy 1. חנן 2. רחם 3. חנן (A) 4. *ἐλεάω*
5. *ἐλεέω* 6. *εὐιλατεύω* 7. misereo

Exd 33:19 will show mercy on whom I will show mercy. 2
19 will show mercy on whom I will show mercy. 2
Deu 7: 2 make no covenant with them, and show no mercy 1
Isa 30:18 he exalts himself to show mercy to you. 2
Dan 4:27 iniquities by showing mercy to the oppressed 3
2Es 1:25 When you beg mercy of me, I will show you no mercy. 7
Tob 13: 2 For he afflicts, and he shows mercy 4
5 again he will show mercy 5
9 he will show mercy to the sons of the righteous. 5
Jdt 16:15 thou wilt continue to show mercy. 6

mercy upon 1. חנן 2. רחם 3. *ἐλεέω*

Ps 123: 2 look to the LORD our God, till he have mercy upon 1
3 Have mercy upon us, O LORD, have mercy upon us 1
3 Have mercy upon us, O LORD, have mercy upon us 1
Jer 33:26 and will have mercy upon them. 2
Ezk 39:25 and have mercy upon the whole house of Israel; 2
Rom 9:18 So then he has mercy upon whomever he wills 3
Tob 8: 4 let us pray that the Lord may have mercy upon us. 3
11:15 thou hast had mercy upon me 3
2Mc 2:18 he will soon have mercy upon us 3
3Mc 6:12 watch over us now and have mercy upon us 3

without mercy 1. *ἀνέλεος*

Jas 2:13 For judgment is without mercy 1

mere 1. אַךְ 2. *ἀλλά* 3. *καί*

2Kg 18:20 Do you think that mere words are strategy 1
Ps 39: 5 Surely every man stands as a mere breath! Selah *
11 surely every man is a mere breath! Selah *
Prv 14:23 but mere talk tends only to want. *
29:19 By mere words a servant is not disciplined *
Isa 36: 5 you think . . mere words are strategy and power 1
Hos 10: 4 They utter mere words; *
2Th 3:11 mere busybodies, not doing any work. 2
Wis 11:19 the mere sight of them could kill by fright. 3

mere *See also* boy, chance.

merely 1. *μόνος*

Est 7: 4 If we had been sold merely as slaves, men and women *
Rom 4:12 circumcised who are not merely circumcised 1
1Co 3: 4 are you not merely men? *
Tob 12:19 All these days I merely appeared to you *
Wis 16: 4 while to these it was merely shown 1
18:25 merely to test the wrath was enough. 1
Sir 19:23 there is a fool who merely lacks wisdom. *

merit 1. *ἀξία*

Sir 38:17 observe the mourning according to his merit 1

merrily 1. שָׂמֵחַ

Est 5:14 then go merrily with the king to the dinner. 1

merry 1. טוֹב 2. יטב 3. שכר 4. *εὐφραίνω*
5. *εὐφροσύνη* 6. *ἡδέως*

Gen 43:34 they drank and were merry with him. 3
Jdg 16:25 when their hearts were merry, they said, "Call 1
19: 6 spend the night, and let your heart be merry. 2
9 lodge here and let your heart be merry; 2
Rut 3: 7 Bo'az had eaten and drunk, and his heart was merry 2
1Sm 25:36 And Nabal's heart was merry within him 1
2Sm 13:28 Mark when Amnon's heart is merry with wine 1
Est 1:10 when the heart of the king was merry with wine 1
Ecc 9: 7 Go, eat . . and drink your wine with a merry heart; *
Jer 31:13 and the young men and the old shall be merry. *
Lke 12:19 take your ease, eat, drink, be merry.' 4
Tob 7: 9 Raguel said to Tobias, "Eat, drink, and be merry; 6
11 But for the present be merry 6
Jdt 12:13 drink wine and be merry with us 5
17 Drink now, and be merry with us! 5
Sir 32: 2 that you may be merry on their account 4

merry *See also* make.

merry-hearted 1. שִׂמְחֵי לֵב

Isa 24: 7 vine languishes, all the merry-hearted sigh. 1

merrymaker 1. שחק

Jer 15:17 I did not sit in the company of merrymakers 1
31: 4 shall go forth in the dance of the merrymakers. 1

merrymaking 1. *εὐφροσύνη*

Sir 31:31 do not despise him in his merrymaking 1

message 1. דָּבָר 2. מַלְאָכוּת 3. קְרִיאָה 4. שְׁמוּעָה
5. *ἀγγελία* 6. *κήρυγμα* 7. *λέγω* 8. *λόγος* 9. *ῥῆμα*

Num22: 7 came to Balaam, and gave him Balak's message. 1
Jdg 3:19 and said, "I have a secret message for you, O king. 1
20 And Ehud said, "I have a message from God for you. 1
11:28 the king . . did not heed the message of Jephthah 1
2Sm 12:25 LORD . . sent a message by Nathan the prophet; *
19:11 David sent this message to Zadok and Abi'athar 1
1Kg 5: 8 I have heard the message which you have sent to me; *
20:12 When Ben-ha'dad heard this message . . he said 1
Prv 26: 6 He who sends a message by the hand of a fool 1
Isa 28: 9 and to whom will he explain the message? 4
19 be sheer terror to understand the message. 4
Jon 3: 2 proclaim to it the message that I tell you. 3
Hag 1:13 spoke to the people with the LORD's message 2
Mrk 16:20 confirmed the message 8
Act 11:14 he will declare to you a message 9
13:26 sent the message of this salvation. 8
1Co 2: 4 my speech and my message 6
2Co 5:19 the message of reconciliation. 8
2Ti 4:15 he strongly opposed our message. 8
17 gave me strength to proclaim the message fully 6
Heb 2: 2 For if the message declared by angels was valid 8
4: 2 the message which they heard did not benefit 8
12:19 that no further messages be spoken to them 8
1Jn 1: 5 the message we have heard from him and proclaim 5
3:11 message which you have heard from the beginning 5
1Mc 5:16 When Judas and the people heard these messages 8
48 Judas sent them this friendly message 8
7:27 treacherously sent . . this peaceable message 8
10:25 he sent a message to them in the following words *
51 with the following message 8
69 Then he sent the following message to Jonathan 7
11:42 Demetrius sent this message to Jonathan 7

message *See also* give, send.

message come 1. *προσπίπτω*

2Mc 14:28 When this message came to Nicanor 1

messenger 1. מַלְאָךְ 2. נגד 3. צִיר 4. *ἄγγελος*
5. *ἀπόστολος* 6. angelus

Gen 32: 3 Jacob sent messengers before him to Esau 1
6 the messengers returned to Jacob, saying 1
Num20:14 Moses sent messengers from Kadesh to the king 1
21:21 Then Israel sent messengers to Sihon king 1
22: 5 sent messengers to Balaam the son of Be'or 1
24:12 Did I not tell your messengers whom you sent to me 1
Deu 2:26 I sent messengers from the wilderness 1
Jos 6:17 because she hid the messengers that we sent. 1
25 she hid the messengers whom Joshua sent to spy 1
7:22 Joshua sent messengers, and they ran to the tent; 1
Jdg 6:35 And he sent messengers throughout all Manas'seh; 1
35 And he sent messengers to Asher, Zeb'ulun 1
7:24 Gideon sent messengers throughout all the hill 1
9:31 he sent messengers to Abim'elech at Aru'mah 1
11:12 Then Jephthah sent messengers to the king 1
13 king . . answered the messengers of Jephthah 1
14 Jephthah sent messengers again to the king 1
17 Israel then sent messengers to the king of Edom 1
19 Israel then sent messengers to Sihon king 1
1Sm 6:21 So they sent messengers to the inhabitants 1
11: 3 send messengers through all the territory 1
4 When the messengers came to Gib'e-ah of Saul 1
7 sent them . . by the hand of the messengers 1
9 they said to the messengers . . "Thus shall you say 1
9 the messengers came and told the men of Jabesh 1
16:19 Saul sent messengers to Jesse, and said, "Send me 1
19:11 Saul sent messengers to David's house to watch 1
14 when Saul sent messengers to take David, she said 1
15 Saul sent the messengers to see David, saying 1
16 when the messengers came in . . the image was 1
20 Then Saul sent messengers to take David; 1
20 Spirit of God came upon the messengers of Saul 1
21 When it was told Saul, he sent other messengers 1
21 And Saul sent messengers again the third time 1
23:27 a messenger came to Saul, saying, "Make haste 1
25:14 David sent messengers . . to salute our master; 1
42 she went after the messengers of David 1
31: 9 and sent messengers throughout the land *
2Sm 2: 5 David sent messengers to . . Ja'besh-gil'ead 1
3:12 Abner sent messengers to David at Hebron, saying 1
14 David sent messengers to Ish-bo'sheth Saul's son 1
26 When Jo'ab came . . he sent messengers after Abner 1
5:11 And Hiram king of Tyre sent messengers to David 1
11: 4 David sent messengers, and took her; 1
19 and he instructed the messenger, "When you have 1
22 the messenger went, and came and told David all 1
23 The messenger said to David, "The men gained 1
25 David said to the messenger, "Thus shall you say 1
12:27 Jo'ab sent messengers to David, and said 1
15:13 And a messenger came to David, saying 2
1Kg 19: 2 Then Jez'ebel sent a messenger to Eli'jah saying 1
20: 2 he sent messengers into the city to Ahab 1
5 The messengers came again, and said, "Thus says 1
9 So he said to the messengers of Ben-ha'dad 1
9 the messengers departed and brought him word 1
22:13 the messenger who went to summon Micai'ah said 1
2Kg 1: 2 he sent messengers, telling them, "Go, inquire 1
3 to meet the messengers of the king of Sama'ria 1
5 The messengers returned to the king 1
16 Because you have sent messengers to inquire 1
5:10 Eli'sha sent a messenger to him, saying, "Go and wash 1
6:32 before the messenger arrived Eli'sha said 1
32 Look, when the messenger comes, shut the door 1
7:15 And the messengers returned, and told the king. 1
9:18 The messenger reached them, but he is not coming 1
10: 8 the messenger came and told him, "They have 1
14: 8 Then Amazi'ah sent messengers to Jeho'ash 1
16: 7 So Ahaz sent messengers to Tig'lath-pile'ser 1
17: 4 he had sent messengers to So, king of Egypt 1
19: 9 he sent messengers again to Hezeki'ah, saying 1
14 received . . from the hand of the messengers 1
23 By your messengers you have mocked the Lord 1
1Ch 10: 9 sent messengers throughout the land *

14: 1 Hiram king of Tyre sent messengers to David 1
19: 2 David sent messengers to console him 1
16 sent messengers and brought out the Syrians 1
2Ch 18:12 messenger who went to summon Micai'ah said to him 1
36:15 sent persistently to them by his messengers 1
16 they kept mocking the messengers of God 1
Neh 6: 3 I sent messengers to them, saying, "I am doing 1
Job 1:14 there came a messenger to Job, and said 1
Ps 104: 4 who makest the winds thy messengers 1
Prv 13:17 A bad messenger plunges men into trouble 1
16:14 A king's wrath is a messenger of death 1
17:11 cruel messenger will be sent against him. 1
25:13 Like the cold of snow . . is a faithful messenger 3
Ecc 5: 6 do not say before the messenger that it was 1
Isa 14:32 will one answer the messengers of the nation? 1
18: 2 Go, you swift messengers, to a nation 1
23: 2 your messengers passed over the sea 1
37: 9 when he heard it, he sent messengers to Hezeki'ah 1
14 the letter from the hand of the messengers 1
42:19 or deaf as my messenger whom I send? 1
44:26 and performs the counsel of his messengers; 1
Jer 49:14 and a messenger has been sent among the nations 3
51:31 one messenger to meet another, to tell the king 2
Ezk 23:16 and sent messengers to them in Chalde'a. 1
40 far, to whom a messenger was sent, and lo, they came. 1
30: 9 that day swift messengers shall go forth from me 1
Obd 1: 1 and a messenger has been sent among the nations 3
Nah 2:13 voice of your messengers shall no more be heard. 1
Hag 1:13 Then Haggai, the messenger of the LORD, spoke 1
Mal 2: 7 for he is the messenger of the LORD of hosts. 1
3: 1 messenger of the covenant in whom you delight 1
1 messenger of the covenant in whom you delight 1
Mat 11:10 'Behold, I send my messenger before thy face 4
Mrk 1: 2 Behold, I send my messenger before thy face 4
Lke 7:24 When the messengers of John had gone 4
27 Behold, I send my messenger before thy face 4
9:52 he sent messengers ahead of him 4
2Co 8:23 messengers of the churches, the glory of Christ. 5
12: 7 a messenger of Satan, to harass me 4
Php 2:25 your messenger and minister to my need 5
Jas 2:25 when she received the messengers 4
1Es 1:50 sent by his messenger to call them back 4
51 they mocked his messengers 4
2Es 1:40 who is also called the messenger of the Lord. 6
Jdt 1:11 they sent back his messengers empty-handed 4
3: 1 they sent messengers to sue for peace, and said 4
Sir 43:26 Because of him his messenger finds the way 4
1Mc 1:44 the king sent letters by messengers to Jerusalem 4
5:14 behold, other messengers . . came from Galilee 4
7:10 he sent messengers to Judas and his brothers 4
41 When the messengers from the king spoke •
151 1: 4 It was he who sent his messenger and took me 4

messenger *See also* send.

secret messenger 1. רגל

2Sm 15:10 Ab'salom sent secret messengers throughout all 1

metal *See* image.

mete out 1. כון

Job 28:25 and meted out the waters by measure; 1

method 1. *χράομαι*

AEs 16: 9 by changing our methods 1
2Mc 13: 4 by the method which is the custom in that place. •

mid-course 1. דֶּרֶךְ

Ps 102:23 He has broken my strength in mid-course; 1

midday 1. מַחֲצִית הַיּוֹם 2. צָהֳרַיִם 3. *ἡμέρα μέση* 4. *μεσημβρινός*

1Kg 18:29 as midday passed, they raved 2
Neh 8: 3 read . . from early morning until midday 1
Act 26:13 At midday, O king, I saw on the way a light 3
1Es 9:41 from early morning until midday 4

middle 1. חֲצִי 2. תָּוֶךְ 3. תִּיכוֹן 4. *μέσος* 5. *μεσότης* 6. *μεσόω* 7. medium

Exd 26:28 The middle bar, halfway up the frames, shall pass 3
36:33 he made the middle bar to pass through 3
Num35: 5 the city being in the middle; 2
Deu 3:16 with the middle of the valley as a boundary 2
Jos 12: 2 from the middle of the valley as far as the river 2
13: 9 and the city that is in the middle of the valley 2
16 and the city that is in the middle of the valley 2
Jdg 7:19 came . . at the beginning of the middle watch 2
16:29 Samson grasped the two middle pillars 2
2Sm 10: 4 and cut off their garments in the middle 1
24: 5 from the city that is in the middle of the valley 2
1Kg 6: 6 the middle one was six cubits broad 3
8 one went up by stairs to the middle story 3
8 by stairs . . from the middle story to the third. 3
27 wings touched . . in the middle of the house. 2
8:64 the king consecrated the middle of the court 2
2Kg 20: 4 before Isaiah had gone out of the middle court 3
1Ch 19: 4 cut off their garments in the middle 1
2Ch 7: 7 Solomon consecrated the middle of the court 2
Jer 39: 3 king of Babylon came and sat in the middle gate 2
Ezk 15: 4 and the middle of it is charred, is it useful 2
41: 7 to the top story through the middle story. 2
42: 5 the lower and middle chambers in the building. 3
6 more than the lower and the middle ones. 3
Lke 22:55 had kindled a fire in the middle of the courtyard 4
Joh 7:14 About the middle of the feast 6
Act 1:18 falling headlong he burst open in the middle 4
17:22 Paul, standing in the middle of the Are-op'agus 4
Rev 22: 2 through the middle of the street of the city; 4
2Es 11: 4 the middle head was larger than the other heads 7
29 (the one which was in the middle) awoke 7
33 the middle head also suddenly disappeared 7
12:21 when the middle of its time draws near 7
Jdt 11:19 Then I will lead you through the middle of Judea 4
Wis 7:18 the beginning and end and middle of times 5
Sir 31:21 get up in the middle of the meal 4
1Mc 10:63 Go forth with him into the middle of the city 4
2Mc 14:44 he fell in the middle of the empty space. 4
3Mc 5:14 since it was nearly the middle of the tenth hour 6

midheaven 1. *μεσουράνημα*

Rev 8:13 heard an eagle crying . . as it flew in midheaven 1
14: 6 Then I saw another angel flying in midheaven 1
19:17 he called to all the birds that fly in midheaven 1

midnight 1. חֲצוֹת הַלַּיְלָה 2. חֲצוֹת לַיְלָה 3. חֲצִי הַלַּיְלָה 4. תּוֹךְ הַלַּיְלָה 5. *μέση νύξ* 6. *μεσονύκτιον* 7. *μέσος τῆς νυκτός* 8. *μεσόω τῆς νυκτός*

Exd 11: 4 says the LORD: About midnight I will go forth 1
12:29 At midnight the LORD smote all the first-born 3
Jdg 16: 3 Samson lay till midnight, and at midnight he 3
3 till midnight, and at midnight he arose and took 3
Rut 3: 8 At midnight the man was startled, and turned over 3
1Kg 3:20 she arose at midnight, and took my son from beside 4
Job 34:20 at midnight the people are shaken and pass away 2
Ps 119:62 At midnight I rise to praise thee 2
Mat 25: 6 at midnight there was a cry 5
Mrk 13:35 in the evening, or at midnight, or at cockcrow 6
Lke 11: 5 go to him at midnight and say to him, 'Friend 6
Act 16:25 about midnight Paul and Silas were praying 6
20: 7 he prolonged his speech until midnight. 6
27:27 about midnight the sailors suspected 7
Jdt 12: 5 she slept until midnight 8

midst 1. בֵּין 2. חֲצִי 3. לֵב 4. קֶרֶב 5. תָּוֶךְ 6. גַּו (A) 7. *ἀνὰ μέσον* 8. *ἐντός* 9. *μέσος* 10. *μεταξύ* 11. in 12. medietas 13. medium 14. penes

Gen 1: 6 a firmament in the midst of the waters 5
2: 9 the tree of life also in the midst of the garden 5
3: 3 the tree which is in the midst of the garden 5
19:29 God . . sent Lot out of the midst of the overthrow 5
48:16 grow into a multitude in the midst of the earth. 4
Exd 3: 2 in a flame of fire out of the midst of a bush; 5
8:22 that I am the LORD in the midst of the earth. 4
9:24 flashing continually in the midst of the hail 5
11: 4 midnight I will go forth in the midst of Egypt; 5
14:22 people of Israel went into the midst of the sea 5
23 went in after them into the midst of the sea 5
27 the Egyptians in the midst of the sea. 5
15:19 on dry ground in the midst of the sea. 5
23:25 I will take sickness away from the midst of you. 4
24:16 he called to Moses out of the midst of the cloud. 5
25: 8 sanctuary, that I may dwell in their midst. 5
34: 9 let the Lord, I pray thee, go in the midst of us 4
12 lest it become a snare in the midst of you. 4
Lev 15:31 by defiling my tabernacle that is in their midst 5
16:16 with them in the midst of their uncleannesses 5
Num 2:17 with the camp of the Levites in the midst 5
5: 3 their camp, in the midst of which I dwell. 5
14:14 thou, O LORD, art in the midst of this people; 4
16:33 they perished from the midst of the assembly. 5
45 Get away from the midst of this congregation 5
47 ran into the midst of the assembly and behold 5
19: 6 cast them into the midst of the burning 5
20 shall be cut off from the midst of the assembly 5
33: 8 passed through the midst of the sea 5
35:34 land . . in the midst of which I dwell; 5
34 LORD dwell in the midst of the people of Israel. 5
Deu 1:42 Do not go up or fight, for I am not in the midst of you; 4
4:12 LORD spoke to you out of the midst of the fire; 5
15 spoke to you at Horeb out of the midst of the fire 5
33 voice of a god speaking out of the midst of the fire 5
34 take a nation . . from the midst of another nation 4
36 you heard his words out of the midst of the fire. 5
5: 4 LORD spoke . . out of the midst of the fire 5
22 mountain out of the midst of the fire, the cloud 5
23 heard the voice out of the midst of the darkness 5
24 heard his voice out of the midst of the fire; 5
26 living God speaking out of the midst of fire 5
6:15 LORD your God in the midst of you is a jealous God; 4
7:21 LORD your God is in the midst of you 4
9:10 spoken with you . . out of the midst of the fire 5
10: 4 LORD had spoken to you . . out of the midst of the fire 5
11: 6 swallowed them up . . in the midst of all Israel; 4
13: 5 So you shall purge the evil from the midst of you. 4
16 spoil into the midst of its open square, and burn 5
17: 7 So you shall purge the evil from the midst of you. 4
19:19 you shall purge the evil from the midst of you. 4
21: 8 not the guilt . . in the midst of thy people Israel; 4
9 guilt of innocent blood from your midst 4
21 so you shall purge the evil from your midst; 4
22:21 you shall purge the evil from the midst of you. 4
24 so you shall purge the evil from the midst of you. 4
23:14 LORD your God walks in the midst of your camp 4
16 he shall dwell with you, in your midst, in the place 4
24: 7 so you shall purge the evil from the midst of you. 4
29:16 how we came through the midst of the nations 4
32:51 broke faith . . in the midst of the people of Israel 5
51 holy in the midst of the people of Israel. 5
Jos 3:17 stood on dry ground in the midst of the Jordan 5
4: 3 Take . . from here out of the midst of the Jordan 5
5 Pass on . . into the midst of the Jordan, and take up 5
8 twelve stones out of the midst of the Jordan 5
9 set up twelve stones in the midst of the Jordan 5
10 the priests . . stood in the midst of the Jordan 5
18 priests . . came up from the midst of the Jordan 5
7:13 There are devoted things in the midst of you 4
8:22 they were in the midst of Israel, some on this side 5
10:13 The sun stayed in the midst of heaven 2
13:13 Geshur and Ma'acath dwell in the midst of Israel 4
16:10 the Canaanites have dwelt in the midst 4
19: 1 its inheritance was in the midst of . . Judah. 5
9 inheritance in the midst of their inheritance. 5
21:41 The cities . . in the midst of the possession 5
22:31 Today we know that the LORD is in the midst of us 5
24: 5 I plagued Egypt with what I did in the midst of it; 4
Jdg 12: 4 Gileadites, in the midst of E'phraim and Manas'seh 5
18:20 graven image, and went in the midst of the people. 4
20:42 cities destroyed them in the midst of them. 5
1Sm 11:11 they came into the midst of the camp 5
16:13 and anointed him in the midst of his brothers; 4
2Sm 1:25 the mighty fallen in the midst of the battle! 5
3:27 Jo'ab took him aside into the midst of the gate 5
23:12 But he took his stand in the midst of the plot 5
1Kg 3: 8 thy servant is in the midst of thy people whom 5
8:51 out of Egypt, from the midst of the iron furnace). 5
20:39 servant went out into the midst of the battle; 4
2Kg 6:20 they saw; and lo, they were in the midst of Sama'ria. 5
1Ch 11:14 he took his stand in the midst of the plot 5
2Ch 20:14 in the midst of the assembly. 5
Neh 4:11 not know or see till we come into the midst of them 5
9:11 went through the midst of the sea on dry land; 5
Est 4: 1 and went out into the midst of the city 5
Ps 22:22 in the midst of the congregation I will praise 5
46: 5 God is in the midst of her, she shall not be moved; 4
48: 9 steadfast love, O God, in the midst of thy temple. 4
55:11 ruin is in its midst; 4
57: 4 I lie in the midst of lions that greedily devour 5
74: 4 Thy foes have roared in the midst of thy holy place; 4
12 working salvation in the midst of the earth. 4
78:28 he let them fall in the midst of their camp 4
82: 1 in the midst of the gods he holds judgment 4
102:24 God . . take me not hence in the midst of my days 2
109:30 I will praise him in the midst of the throng. 5
110: 2 Rule in the midst of your foes! 4
116:19 house of the LORD, in your midst, O Jerusalem. 5
135: 9 who in thy midst, O Egypt, sent signs and wonders 5
136:14 made Israel pass through the midst of it 5
138: 7 Though I walk in the midst of trouble 4
Prv 23:34 like one who lies down in the midst of the sea 3
Isa 4: 4 cleansed . . from its midst by a spirit 4
5: 2 he built a watchtower in the midst of it 5
8 made to dwell alone in the midst of the land. 4
25 corpses were as refuse in the midst of the streets. 4
6: 5 I dwell in the midst of a people of unclean lips; 5
12 forsaken places are many in the midst of the land. 4
7: 6 set up the son of Ta'be-el as king in the midst of it 5
10:23 full end, as decreed, in the midst of all the earth. 4
12: 6 for great in your midst is the Holy One of Israel. 4
19:19 altar to the LORD in the midst of the land of Egypt 5
24 Israel . . a blessing in the midst of the earth 4
24:13 thus it shall be in the midst of the earth among 4
25:11 he will spread out his hands in the midst of it 4
29:23 his children, the work of my hands, in his midst 4
41:18 and fountains in the midst of the valleys; 5
52:11 go out from the midst of her, purify yourselves 5
58: 9 If you take away from the midst of you the yoke 5
61: 9 and their offspring in the midst of the peoples; 5
63:11 he who put in the midst of them his holy Spirit 4
66:17 go into the gardens, following one in the midst 5
Jer 6: 1 Flee for safety . . from the midst of Jerusalem! 4
12:16 they shall be built up in the midst of my people. 5
14: 9 Yet thou, O LORD, art in the midst of us 4
17:11 in the midst of his days they will leave him 2
21: 4 bring them together into the midst of this city. 5
30:21 their ruler shall come forth from their midst; 4
44: 7 from the midst of Judah, leaving you no remnant? 5
46:21 soldiers in her midst are like fatted calves; 4
50: 8 Flee from the midst of Babylon 5
37 and upon all the foreign troops in her midst 5
51: 6 Flee from the midst of Babylon 5
45 Go out of the midst of her, my people! 5
47 and all her slain shall fall in the midst of her. 5
63 and cast it into the midst of the Euphra'tes 5
52:25 men . . who were found in the midst of the city. 5
Lam 1: 3 overtaken her in the midst of her distress. 1
15 Lord flouted all my mighty men in the midst of me; 4
4:13 her priests, who shed in the midst of her the blood 4

Ezk 1: 4 in the midst of the fire, as it were gleaming 5
5 And from the midst of it came the likeness 5
13 In the midst of the living creatures 9
5: 2 shall burn in the fire in the midst of the city 5
8 I will execute judgments in the midst of you 5
10 fathers shall eat their sons in the midst of you 5
12 and be consumed with famine in the midst of you; 5
6: 7 And the slain shall fall in the midst of you 5
7: 4 while your abominations are in your midst. 5
9 while your abominations are in your midst. 5
11: 7 Your slain whom you have laid in the midst of it 5
7 you shall be brought forth out of the midst of it. 5
9 And I will bring you forth out of the midst of it 5
11 nor shall you be the flesh in the midst of it; 5
23 the LORD went up from the midst of the city 5
12: 2 you dwell in the midst of a rebellious house 5
13:14 when it falls, you shall perish in the midst of it; 5
14: 8 and cut him off from the midst of my people; 5
9 and will destroy him from the midst of my people 5
16:53 restore your own fortunes in the midst of them 5
19: 2 She couched in the midst of young lions 5
20: 8 against them in the midst of the land of Egypt. 5
21:32 your blood shall be in the midst of the land; 5
22: 3 A city that sheds blood in the midst of her 5
7 the sojourner suffers extortion in your midst; 5
9 men commit lewdness in your midst. 5
13 at the blood which has been in the midst of you. 5
19 I will gather you into the midst of Jerusalem. 5
21 you shall be melted in the midst of it. 5
22 you shall be melted in the midst of it; 5
25 Her princes in the midst of her are like a roaring 5
25 they have made many widows in the midst of her. 5
27 Her princes in the midst of her are like wolves 4
24: 7 the blood she has shed is still in the midst of her; 5
25: 4 among you and make their dwellings in your midst; •
26: 5 She shall be in the midst of the sea 5
12 soil they will cast into the midst of the waters. 5
15 when slaughter is made in the midst of you? 5
27:27 you, with all your company that is in your midst 5
32 destroyed like Tyre in the midst of the sea? 5
28:14 in the midst of the stones of fire you walked. 5
16 the guardian cherub drove you out from the midst 5
18 I brought forth fire from the midst of you; 5
22 I will manifest my glory in the midst of you. 5
23 the slain shall fall in the midst of her 5
29: 3 dragon that lies in the midst of his streams 5
4 I will draw you up out of the midst of your streams 5
12 desolation in the midst of desolated countries; 5
30: 7 desolated in the midst of desolated countries 5
7 in the midst of cities that are laid waste. 5
32:21 with their helpers, out of the midst of Sheol 5
37: 1 and set me down in the midst of the valley; 5
26 and will set my sanctuary in the midst of them 5
28 when my sanctuary is in the midst of them 5
39: 7 I will make known in the midst of my people Israel; 5
43: 7 I will dwell in the midst of the people of Israel 5
9 I will dwell in their midst for ever. 5
48: 8 to the west, with the sanctuary in the midst of it. 5
10 with the sanctuary of the LORD in the midst of it. 5
15 In the midst of it shall be the city; 5
21 with the sanctuary of the temple in its midst 5
22 in the midst of that which belongs to the prince. 5
Dan 3:25 four men loose, walking in the midst of the fire 6
4:10 saw, and behold, a tree in the midst of the earth; 6
Hos 11: 9 for I am God and not man, the Holy One in your midst 4
Jol 2:27 You shall know that I am in the midst of Israel 4
Ams 2: 3 I will cut off the ruler from its midst 4
3: 9 and see . . the oppressions in her midst. 4
5:17 wailing, for I will pass through the midst of you 4
6: 4 eat . . and calves from the midst of the stall; 5
7: 8 a plumb line in the midst of my people Israel; 4
10 against you in the midst of the house of Israel; 4
Mic 3:11 Is not the LORD in the midst of us? 4
5: 7 Jacob shall be in the midst of many peoples 4
8 among the nations, in the midst of many peoples 4
7:14 alone in a forest in the midst of a garden land; 5
Nah 3:13 Behold, your troops are women in your midst. 4
Hab 3: 2 In the midst of the years renew it; 4
2 in the midst of the years make it known; 4
Zep 2:14 Herds shall lie down in the midst of her 5
3:11 from your midst your proudly exultant ones 4
12 I will leave in the midst of you a people humble 4
15 The King of Israel, the LORD, is in your midst; 4
17 The LORD, your God, is in your midst, 4
Zec 2:10 I will dwell in the midst of you, says the LORD. 5
11 I will dwell in the midst of you, and you shall know 5
8: 3 to Zion, and will dwell in the midst of Jerusalem 5
8 bring them to dwell in the midst of Jerusalem; 5
12: 6 Judah like a blazing pot in the midst of wood •
14: 1 the spoil . . will be divided in the midst of you. 4
Mat 10:16 I send you out as sheep in the midst of wolves 9
18: 2 he put him in the midst of them 9
20 there am I in the midst of them. 9
Mrk 9:36 he took a child, and put him in the midst of them; 9
14:60 stood up in the midst, and asked Jesus 9
Lke 4:30 passing through the midst of them he went away. 9
35 when the demon had thrown him down in the midst 9
5:19 through the tiles into the midst before Jesus. 9
10: 3 I send you out as lambs in the midst of wolves. 9
17:21 behold, the kingdom of God is in the midst of you. 8
Joh 8: 3 placing her in the midst 9
Act 2:22 signs which God did through him in your midst 9
4: 7 when they had set them in the midst, they inquired 9
Php 2:15 in the midst of a . . perverse generation 9
Heb 2:12 in the midst of the congregation 9
Jas 1:11 rich man fade away in the midst of his pursuits. •
Rev 1:13 in the midst of the lampstands one like a son 9
6: 6 a voice in the midst of the four living creatures 9
7:17 For the Lamb in the midst of the throne will be 7
2Es 2: 8 who conceal the unrighteous in your midst 14
43 In their midst was a young man of great stature 13
11:10 but from the midst of his body. 12
12:17 but from the midst of his body 13
18 In the midst of the time of that kingdom ‡
16:40 in the midst of the calamities be like strangers 11
58 has enclosed the sea in the midst of the waters 13
61 and put a heart in the midst of his body 13
Jdt 6:16 they set Achior in the midst of all their people 9
11:19 I will set your throne in the midst of it 9
14:19 shouts arose in the midst of the camp. 9
16: 3 brought me to his camp, in the midst of the people. 9
Wis 4:14 took him quickly from the midst of wickedness. 9
12: 5 initiates from the midst of a heathen cult 9
16:19 even in the midst of water 10
18:15 into the midst of the land that was doomed 9
Sir 1:30 cast you down in the midst of the congregation 9
9:13 Know that you are walking in the midst of snares 9
11: 8 nor interrupt a speaker in the midst of his words. 9
14:27 will dwell in the midst of her glory. •
15: 5 will open his mouth in the midst of the assembly. 9
24: 1 will glory in the midst of her people. 9
42:12 do not sit in the midst of women; 9
48:17 brought water into the midst of it 9
51: 4 from the midst of fire which I did not kindle 9
Aza 1: 1 they walked about in the midst of the flames 9
2 in the midst of the fire he opened his mouth 9
27 made the midst of the furnace like a . . wind 9
66 delivered us from the midst of the . . furnace 9
66 from the midst of the fire he has delivered us. 9
Sus 1:34 the two elders stood up in the midst of the people 9
48 Taking his stand in the midst of them, he said 9
1Mc 6:45 He . . ran into the midst of the phalanx to reach it 9
16: 7 and placed the horsemen in the midst of the infantry 9

very midst 1. *αὐτός*

4Mc 15:23 in the very midst of her emotions 1

midwife 1. ילד

Gen 35:17 midwife said to her, "Fear not; for now you will 1
38:28 a hand; and the midwife took and bound on his hand 1
Exd 1:15 the king of Egypt said to the Hebrew midwives 1
17 the midwives feared God 1
18 the king of Egypt called the midwives, and said 1
19 The midwives said to Pharaoh, "Because the Hebrew 1
19 are delivered before the midwife comes to them. 1
20 So God dealt well with the midwives; 1
21 because the midwives feared God 1

midwife *See also* serve.

frightening mien 1. *φοβερός*

2Mc 3:25 a rider of frightening mien 1

might 1. אוֹן 2. גְּבוּרָה 3. זְרוֹעַ 4. חֹזֶק 5. חַיִל 6. כֹּחַ 7. מְאֹד 8. עַז 9. עֹז 10. עֱזוּז 11. עָצוּם 12. עֹצֶם 13. קֶרֶן 14. גְּבוּרָה (A) 15. תְּקֹף (A) 16. *ἀλκή* 17. *δύναμις* 18. *δυναστεία* 19. *ἰσχύς* 20. *κράτος* 21. *μέγας* 22. *μέγεθος* 23. potentia

Gen 49: 3 Reuben, you are my first-born, my might 6
Num14:13 for thou didst bring up this people in thy might 6
Deu 6: 5 love the LORD your God with . . all your might. 7
8:17 My power and the might of my hand have gotten me 12
Jdg 5:21 March on, my soul, with might! 9
31 friends be like the sun as he rises in his might. 2
6:14 said, "Go in this might of yours and deliver Israel 6
16:30 Then he bowed with all his might; and the house 6
1Sm 2: 9 for not by might shall a man prevail. 6
2Sm 6: 5 Israel were making merry . . with all their might •
14 David danced before the LORD with all his might; 9
1Kg 15:23 the acts of Asa, all his might, and all that he did 2
16: 5 the acts of Ba'asha, and what he did, and his might 2
27 acts of Omri . . and the might that he showed 2
22:45 acts of Jehosh'aphat, and his might that he showed 2
2Kg 10:34 acts of Jehu, and all that he did, and all his might 2
13: 8 acts of Jeho'ahaz and all that he did, and his might 2
12 the might with which he fought against Amazi'ah 2
14:15 acts of Jeho'ash . . and his might, and how he fought 2
28 acts of Jerobo'am . . and his might, how he fought 2
20:20 deeds of Hezeki'ah, and all his might, and how he 2
23:25 heart and . . all his soul and with all his might 7
1Ch 13: 8 making merry before God with all their might 9
29:12 In thy hand are power and might; 2
30 with accounts of all his rule and his might 2
2Ch 6:41 thy resting place, thou and the ark of thy might. 9
20: 6 In thy hand are power and might 2
30:21 singing with all their might to the LORD. 9
Est 10: 2 the acts of his power and might, and . . account 2
Job 12:13 With God are wisdom and might; 2
30:21 with the might of thy hand thou dost persecute 12
39:19 Do you give the horse his might? 2
Ps 10:10 is crushed, sinks down, and falls by his might. 11
33:17 by its great might it cannot save. 5
54: 1 O God, by thy name, and vindicate me by thy might. 2
59:16 I will sing of thy might; 9
65: 6 the mountains, being girded with might; 2
66: 7 who rules by his might for ever 2
68:28 Summon thy might, O God; show thy strength, O God 9
71:18 till I proclaim thy might to all the generations 3
74:13 Thou didst divide the sea by thy might; 9
77:14 who hast manifested thy might among the peoples. 9
78: 4 his might, and the wonders which he has wrought. 10
80: 2 Stir up thy might, and come to save us! 2
132: 8 resting place, thou and the ark of thy might. 9
145: 6 Men . . proclaim the might of thy terrible acts 10
Ecc 9:10 Whatever your hand finds . . do it with your might; 6
16 But I say that wisdom is better than might 2
Isa 11: 2 understanding, the spirit of counsel and might 2
33:13 and you who are near, acknowledge my might. 2
40:10 Behold, the Lord GOD comes with might 4
26 by the greatness of his might 1
29 to him who has no might he increases strength. 1
42:25 the heat of his anger and the might of battle; 10
63:15 Where are thy zeal and thy might? 2
Jer 9:23 let not the mighty man glory in his might 2
10: 6 thou art great, and thy name is great in might. 2
16:21 I will make them know my power and my might 2
23:10 Their course is evil, and their might is not right. 2
49:35 break the bow of Elam, the mainstay of their might; 2
Lam 2: 3 He has cut down in . . anger all the might of Israel; 13
17 he has made . . and exalted the might of your foes. 13
Ezk 7:24 I will put an end to their proud might 8
30: 6 her proud might shall come down; 9
18 of Egypt, and her proud might shall come to an end; 9
32:29 all her princes, who for all their might are laid 2
30 all the terror which they caused by their might; 2
33:28 her proud might shall come to an end; 9
Dan 2:20 name of God . . to whom belong wisdom and might. 14
37 given the . . power, and the might, and the glory. 15
Mic 3: 8 and with justice and might, to declare to Jacob 2
7:16 nations shall . . be ashamed of all their might; 2
Nah 1: 3 The LORD is slow to anger and of great might 6
Hab 1:11 guilty men, whose own might is their god! 6
Zec 4: 6 Not by might, nor by power, but by my Spirit 5
Eph 1:19 according to the working of his great might 19
3:16 he may grant you to be strengthened with might 17
6:10 in the strength of his might. 19
Col 1:11 with all power, according to his glorious might 20
2Th 1: 9 exclusion . . from the glory of his might 19
2Pe 2:11 angels, though greater in might and power 19
Rev 5:12 to receive . . might and honor and glory 19
13 honor and glory and might for ever and ever! 20
7:12 honor and power and might be to our God for ever 19
2Es 15:16 in their might have no respect for their king 23
Jdt 4:15 they cried out to the Lord with all their might 17
5:15 by their might destroyed . . the inhabitants of Heshbon 19
6: 3 They cannot resist the might of our cavalry. 20
9: 7 the Assyrians are increased in their might 17
8 Break their strength by thy might 17
11 nor thy might upon men of strength 18
14 thou art God, the God of all power and might 17
13: 4 O Lord God of all might 17
8 she struck his neck twice with all her might 19
AEs 14:19 O God, whose might is over all 19
Wis 2:11 let our might be our law of right 19
11:21 who can withstand the might of thy arm? 20
Sir 3:20 For great is the might of the Lord 18
6:26 keep her ways with all your might. 17
7:30 With all your might love your Maker 17
16: 7 the ancient giants who revolted in their might. 19
36: 3 let them see thy might. 18
48:24 By the spirit of might he saw the last things 21
1Mc 6:47 when the Jews saw the royal might 19
2Mc 12:28 with power shatters the might of his enemies 16
15:24 By the might of thy arm 22
3Mc 3:11 not considering the might of the supreme God 20
5:13 to show the might of his all-powerful hand 20
6:12 you, O Eternal One, who have all might and all power 16
13 cower today in fear of your invincible might 17

show might 1. חזק

2Ch 16: 9 show his might in behalf of those whose heart is 1

mightily 1. בְּחָזְקָה 2. מְאֹד 3. *δυνατῶς* 4. *ἐν δυνάμει* 5. *ἐξ ἰσχύος* 6. *εὐρώστως* 7. *κατὰ κράτος*

Gen 7:19 the waters prevailed so mightily upon the earth 2
Jer 25:30 he will roar mightily against his fold, and shout †
Jon 3: 8 with sackcloth, and let them cry mightily to God; 1
Act 19:20 the word . . grew and prevailed mightily. 7
Col 1:29 the energy which he mightily inspires within me. 4
AEs 13:18 all Israel cried out mightily 5
Wis 6: 6 mighty men will be mightily tested. 3
8: 1 She reaches mightily from one end of the earth 6

mightily *See also* come.

mighty 1. אַבִּיר 2. אַדִּיר 3. אַיִל 4. אֵיתָן 5. אֵל
6. אֱלֹהִים 7. אַמִּיץ 8. אמץ 9. גִּבּוֹר 10. גְּבוּרָה 11. גבר
12. גָּדוֹל 13. חָזָק 14. חַיִל 15. חֲסִין 16. כַּבִּיר 17. כֹּחַ
18. מְאֹד 19. עַז 20. עֹז 21. עָצוּם 22. עצם 23. קַו קָו
24. רַב 25. חַיִל (A) 26. רַב (A) 27. תַּקִּיף (A)
28. תְּקֵף (A) 29. *βίαιος* 30. *δεινός* 31. *δύναμαι*
32. *δύναμις* 33. *δυναστεία* 34. *δυνάστης* 35. *δυνατός*
36. *ἰσχυρός* 37. *ἰσχύς* 38. *κραταιός* 39. *κράτος*
40. *κρείσσων* 41. *μεγαλεῖος* 42. *μέγας* 43. *σφοδρός*
44. immensus 45. possum 46. validus

Gen 10: 9 He was a mighty hunter before the LORD; 9
9 Like Nimrod a mighty hunter before the LORD. 9
18:18 Abraham shall become a great and mighty nation 21
23: 6 Hear us, my lord; you are a mighty prince among us. 6
26:16 for you are much mightier than we. 22
30: 8 With mighty wrestlings I have wrestled with my 6
49:26 The blessings of your father are mighty 11
Exd 1: 9 Israel are too many and too mighty for us. 21
3:19 not let you go unless compelled by a mighty hand. 13
15:10 they sank as lead in the mighty waters. 2
32:11 with great power and with a mighty hand? 13
Num14:12 you a nation greater and mightier than they. 21
22: 6 curse this people . . since they are too mighty 21
Deu 3:24 show . . thy greatness and thy mighty hand; 13
4:34 by a mighty hand and an outstretched arm 13
38 driving out . . nations greater and mightier 21
5:15 with a mighty hand and an outstretched arm; 13
6:21 LORD brought us out of Egypt with a mighty hand; 13
7: 1 Jeb'usites, seven nations greater and mightier 21
8 the LORD has brought you out with a mighty hand 13
19 saw, the . . mighty hand, and the outstretched arm 13
9: 1 nations greater and mightier than yourselves 21
14 nation mightier and greater than they.' 21
26 brought out of Egypt with a mighty hand. 13
10:17 great, the mighty, and the terrible God 9
11: 2 consider . . mighty hand and his outstretched arm 13
23 nations greater and mightier than yourselves. 21
26: 5 became a nation, great, mighty, and populous. 21
8 LORD brought us out of Egypt with a mighty hand 13
34:11 for all the mighty power and all the great 13
Jos 4:24 all . . may know that the hand of the LORD is mighty; 13
10: 2 it was greater than Ai, and all its men were mighty. 9
Jdg 5:13 LORD marched down for him against the mighty. 9
23 to the help of the LORD against the mighty. 9
6:12 him, "The LORD is with you, you mighty man of valor. 14
11: 1 Now Jephthah the Gileadite was a mighty warrior 14
1Sm 2: 4 The bows of the mighty are broken 9
4: 5 Israel gave a mighty shout, so that the earth 12
8 deliver us from the power of these mighty gods? 2
7:10 the LORD thundered with a mighty voice that day 12
2Sm 1:19 How are the mighty fallen! 9
21 For there the shield of the mighty was defiled 9
22 from the fat of the mighty, the bow . . turned not 9
25 How are the mighty fallen in the midst 9
27 How are the mighty fallen, and the weapons of war 9
22:18 delivered me . . for they were too mighty for me. 8
1Kg 8:42 hear of thy great name, and thy mighty hand 13
1Ch 5:24 mighty warriors, famous men 14
7: 2 mighty warriors of their generations 14
5 of Is'sachar were in all 87,000 mighty warriors 14
7 heads of fathers' houses, mighty warriors; 14
9 heads of their fathers' houses, mighty warriors 14
11 sons of Jedi'a-el . . mighty warriors 14
40 men of Asher . . approved, mighty warriors 14
8:40 sons of Ulam were men who were mighty warriors 14
12: 8 mighty and experienced warriors 14
28 Zadok, a young man mighty in valor 9
2Ch 6:32 comes . . for the sake of . . thy mighty hand 13
13: 3 with 800,000 picked mighty warriors. 14
14:11 between the mighty and the weak. 24
26:13 307,500, who could make war with mighty power 14
32:21 cut off all the mighty warriors and commanders 14
Ezr 4:20 mighty kings have been over Jerusalem, who ruled 27
7:28 before all the king's mighty officers. 9
Neh 9:11 into the depths, as a stone into mighty waters. 19
32 our God, the great and mighty and terrible God 9
Job 5:15 the needy from the hand of the mighty. 13
9: 4 He is wise in heart, and mighty in strength 7
12:19 and overthrows the mighty. 4
24:22 God prolongs the life of the mighty by his power; 1
34:17 Will you condemn him who is righteous and mighty 16
20 the mighty are taken away by no human hand. 1
24 He shatters the mighty without investigation 16
35: 9 call for help because of the arm of the mighty. 24
36: 5 Behold, God is mighty, and does not despise any; 16
5 he is mighty in strength of understanding. 16
41:25 When he raises himself up the mighty are afraid; 5
Ps 18:17 for they were too mighty for me. 8
20: 6 with mighty victories by his right hand. 10
24: 8 the King of glory? The LORD, strong and mighty 9
8 LORD, strong and mighty, the LORD, mighty in battle! 9
35:18 in the mighty throng I will praise thee. 21
38:19 Those who are my foes without cause are mighty 22
50: 3 round about him a mighty tempest. 18
62: 7 my mighty rock, my refuge is God. 20
68:15 O mighty mountain, mountain of Bashan; 6
17 With mighty chariotry, twice 10,000 6
33 lo, he sends forth his voice, his mighty voice. 20
69: 4 mighty are those who would destroy me 22
77:12 I will meditate . . and muse on thy mighty deeds. •
80:10 the mighty cedars with its branches; 5
89: 8 O LORD God of hosts, who is mighty as thou art 15
10 didst scatter thy enemies with thy mighty arm. 20
13 Thou hast a mighty arm; strong is thy hand 10
19 I have set the crown upon one who is mighty 9
93: 4 Mightier than the thunders of many waters 2
4 mightier than the waves of the sea 2
4 LORD on high is mighty! 2
99: 4 Mighty King, lover of justice, thou hast 20
103:20 O you his angels, you mighty ones who do his word 17
110: 2 LORD sends forth from Zion your mighty scepter. 20
112: 2 His descendants will be mighty in the land; 9
135:10 who smote many nations and slew mighty kings 21
150: 1 praise him in his mighty firmament! 20
Prv 16:32 He who is slow to anger is better than the mighty 9
21:22 A wise man scales the city of the mighty 9
24: 5 A wise man is mightier than a strong man 40
30:26 badgers are a people not mighty, yet they make 21
30 the lion, which is mightiest among beasts 9
Isa 8: 7 the waters of the River, mighty and many 21
9: 6 be called "Wonderful Counselor, Mighty God 9
10:21 return, the remnant of Jacob, to the mighty God. 9
17:12 they roar like the roaring of mighty waters! 16
18: 2 a nation mighty and conquering 23
7 a nation mighty and conquering 23
28: 2 Behold, the Lord has one who is mighty and strong; 13
2 like a storm of mighty, overflowing waters 16
43:16 a way in the sea, a path in the mighty waters 19
49:24 Can the prey be taken from the mighty 9
25 Even the captives of the mighty shall be taken 9
56:11 The dogs have a mighty appetite; 19
60:22 a clan, and the smallest one a mighty nation; 21
62: 8 has sworn by his right hand and by his mighty arm 20
63: 1 It is I, announcing vindication, mighty to save. 24
Jer 32:18 O great and mighty God whose name is the LORD 9
19 great in counsel and mighty in deed; 24
48:14 do you say, 'We are heroes and mighty men of war'? 14
17 say, 'How the mighty scepter is broken 20
50:41 a mighty nation and many kings are stirring 12
51:55 laying . . waste, and stilling her mighty voice. 12
Ezk 17:17 Pharaoh with his mighty army and great company 12
20:33 says the Lord GOD, surely with a mighty hand 13
34 with a mighty hand and an outstretched arm 13
26:11 your mighty pillars will fall to the ground. 20
17 O city renowned, that was mighty on the sea 13
31:11 I will give it into the hand of a mighty one 3
32:21 The mighty chiefs shall speak of them 9
38:15 riding on horses, a great host, a mighty army; 24
39:18 You shall eat the flesh of the mighty 9
Dan 2:31 This image, mighty and of exceeding brightness 26
3:20 ordered certain mighty men of his army to bind 25
4: 3 How great are his signs, how mighty his wonders! 27
30 Babylon, which I have built by my mighty power 28
8: 6 ran at him in his mighty wrath. 17
9:15 out of the land of Egypt with a mighty hand 13
11: 3 Then a mighty king shall arise, who shall rule 9
25 war with an exceedingly great and mighty army; 21
Ams 2:14 nor shall the mighty save his life; 9
16 who is stout of heart among the mighty shall flee 9
Jon 1: 4 there was a mighty tempest on the sea 12
Hab 3:15 trample the sea . . the surging of mighty waters. 24
Mat 3:11 he who is coming after me is mightier than I 36
Mrk 1: 7 After me comes he who is mightier than I 36
Lke 1:49 for he who is mighty has done great things for me 35
52 he has put down the mighty from their thrones 34
3:16 he who is mightier than I is coming 36
24:19 a prophet mighty in deed and word before God 35
Act 2: 2 a sound . . like the rush of a mighty wind 29
11 the mighty works of God 41
7:22 he was mighty in his words and deeds. 35
2Th 1: 7 with his mighty angels in flaming fire 32
Heb 11:34 became mighty in war 36
1Pe 5: 6 under the mighty hand of God 38
Rev 10: 1 another mighty angel coming down from heaven 36
18: 2 And he called out with a mighty voice 36
8 for mighty is the Lord God who judges her. 36
10 alas! thou great city, thou mighty city, Babylon! 36
21 Then a mighty angel took up a stone 36
19: 6 like the sound of mighty thunderpeals, crying 36
1Es 2:27 mighty and cruel kings ruled in Jerusalem 36
8:47 by the mighty hand of our Lord 38
61 by the mighty hand of our Lord 38
2Es 2:19 seven mighty mountains on which roses . . grow 44
15:11 I will bring them out with a mighty hand 45
40 great and mighty clouds 46
51 so that you cannot receive your mighty lovers. 45
16:16 an arrow shot by a mighty archer does not return 46
Wis 5:23 a mighty wind will rise against them 32
6: 8 a strict inquiry is in store for the mighty. 38
18: 5 didst destroy them all together by a mighty flood. 43
Sir 15:18 he is mighty in power and sees everything; 36
16:11 he is mighty to forgive, and he pours out wrath. 34
21: 7 He who is mighty in speech is known from afar 35
29:13 more than a mighty shield 39
34:16 a mighty protection and strong support 33
36: 8 let people recount thy mighty deeds. 41
46: 1 Joshua the son of Nun was mighty in war 38
6 hailstones of mighty power 38
17 made his voice heard with a mighty sound; 42
47: 5 to slay a man mighty in war 35
Bar 2:11 out of the land of Egypt with a mighty hand 38
1Mc 2:42 Hasideans, mighty warriors of Israel 32
66 has been a mighty warrior from his youth 32
3:38 mighty men among the friends of the king 35
9:21 How is the mighty fallen, the savior of Israel! 35
10:19 a mighty warrior and worthy to be our friend. 37
2Mc 7:17 see how his mighty power will torture you 41
11:13 because the mighty God fought on their side 31
3Mc 2: 6 You made known your mighty power •
4Mc 15:25 she saw mighty advocates 30

mighty *See also* bull, doing, grow, host, power, strength, warrior, wave, work.

mighty act 1. גְּבוּרָה

Deu 3:24 what god . . do such works and mighty acts as thine? 1
Ps 145: 4 to another, and shall declare thy mighty acts. 1

become mighty 1. חזק

2Ch 27: 6 Jotham became mighty 1

mighty deed 1. גְּבוּרָה 2. *μεγαλεῖος*

Ps 71:16 With the mighty deeds of the Lord GOD I will come 1
145:12 to make known to the sons of men thy mighty deeds 1
150: 2 Praise him for his mighty deeds; praise him 1
Sir 18: 4 who can search out his mighty deeds? 2

mighty man 1. אַבִּיר 2. גִּבּוֹר 3. גְּבוּרָה 4. עָצוּם
5. *δυνατός* 6. *ἰσχυρός*

Gen 6: 4 These were the mighty men that were of old 2
10: 8 he was the first on earth to be a mighty man. 2
Jos 6: 2 Jericho, with its king and mighty men of valor. 2
8: 3 and Joshua chose 30,000 mighty men of valor 2
10: 7 Joshua went up . . and all the mighty men of valor. 2
2Sm 10: 7 he sent Jo'ab and all the host of the mighty men. 2
16: 6 people and all the mighty men were on his right 2
17: 8 You know . . your father and his men are mighty men 2
10 all Israel knows that your father is a mighty man 2
20: 7 and the Pel'ethites, and all the mighty men; 2
23: 8 the names of the mighty men whom David had 2
9 next . . among the three mighty men was Elea'zar 2
16 Then the three mighty men broke through the camp 2
17 These things did the three mighty men. 2
22 and won a name beside the three mighty men. 2
1Kg 1: 8 and David's mighty men were not with Adoni'jah. 2
10 he did not invite . . Benai'ah or the mighty men 2
2Kg 5: 1 He was a mighty man of valor, but he was a leper. 2
24:14 all the princes, and all the mighty men of valor 2
1Ch 11:10 Now these are the chiefs of David's mighty men 2
11 This is an account of David's mighty men 2
12 next . . among the three mighty men was Elea'zar 2
18 the three mighty men broke through the camp •
19 These things did the three mighty men. 2
24 won a name beside the three mighty men. 2
26 The mighty men of the armies were As'ahel 2
12: 1 were among the mighty men who helped him in war. 2
4 Ishma'iah of Gibeon, a mighty man among the 30 2
21 for they were all mighty men of valor 2
25 the Simeonites, mighty men of valor for war, 7,100 2
30 Of the E'phraimites 20,800, mighty men of valor 2
19: 8 he sent Jo'ab and all the army of the mighty men. 2
27: 6 Benai'ah who was a mighty man of the 30 2
28: 1 with the palace officials, the mighty men 2
29:24 All the leaders and the mighty men, and also all 2
2Ch 14: 8 all these were mighty men of valor. 2
17:13 He had . . mighty men of valor, in Jerusalem. 2
14 Adnah . . with 300,000 mighty men of valor 2
16 Amasi'ah . . with 200,000 mighty men of valor. 2
17 Of Benjamin: Eli'ada, a mighty man of valor 2
25: 6 hired . . 100,000 mighty men of valor from Israel 2
26:12 heads of fathers' houses of mighty men of valor 2
28: 7 Zichri, a mighty man of E'phraim, slew Ma-asei'ah 2
32: 3 he planned with his officers and his mighty men 2
Neh 3:16 repaired to . . the house of the mighty men. 2
11:14 their brethren, mighty men of valor, 128; 2
Ps 52: 1 Why do you boast, O mighty man, of mischief done 2
Sng 3: 7 litter of Solomon! About it are 60 mighty men 2
7 About it are 60 . . of the mighty men of Israel 2
Isa 3: 2 the mighty man and the soldier 2
25 fall by the sword and your mighty men in battle. 3
13: 3 have summoned my mighty men to execute my anger 2
21:17 archers of the mighty men of the sons of Kedar 2
42:13 The LORD goes forth like a mighty man 2
Jer 5:16 they are all mighty men. 2
9:23 let not the mighty man glory in his might 2
14: 9 a man confused, like a mighty man who cannot save? 2
Lam 1:15 Lord flouted all my mighty men in the midst of me; 1
Ezk 32:27 they do not lie with the fallen mighty men of old 2
27 for the terror of the mighty men was in the land 2
39:20 horses and riders, with mighty men 2
Dan 8:24 destroy mighty men and the people of the saints. 4
Jol 3: 9 Prepare war, stir up the mighty men. 2
Obd 1: 9 And your mighty men shall be dismayed, O Teman 2
Nah 2: 3 The shield of his mighty men is red 2
Zep 1:14 the mighty man cries aloud there. 2

Zec 10: 5 Together they shall be like mighty men in battle 2
Rev 19:18 to eat . . the flesh of mighty men 6
Wis 6: 6 mighty men will be mightily tested. 5
Sir 13: 2 a man mightier and richer than you 6
Bar 1: 4 in the hearing of the mighty men and the princes 5
9 carried away . . the mighty men and the people 5
1Mc 4: 3 he and his mighty men moved out 5

most mighty 1. *μέγας*
AEs 16:16 sons of the Most High, the most mighty living God 1

mighty one 1. אָבִיר 2. אַיִל 3. אֵל 4. גִּבּוֹר 5. *δυνάστης* 6. *δυνατός* 7. fortis
Gen 49:24 by the hands of the Mighty One of Jacob 1
Jos 22:22 The Mighty One, God, the LORD! The Mighty One, God 3
22 God, the LORD! The Mighty One, God, the LORD! 3
1Ch 1:10 he began to be a mighty one in the earth. 4
Ps 45: 3 Gird your sword upon your thigh, O mighty one 4
50: 1 The Mighty One, God the LORD, speaks and summons 3
132: 2 to the LORD and vowed to the Mighty One of Jacob 1
5 dwelling place for the Mighty One of Jacob. 1
Isa 1:24 the LORD of hosts, the Mighty One of Israel 1
49:26 and your Redeemer, the Mighty One of Jacob. 1
60:16 and your Redeemer, the Mighty One of Jacob. 1
Ezk 31:11 I will give it into the hand of a mighty one 2
32:12 to fall by the swords of mighty ones, all of them 4
2Es 6:32 for the Mighty One has seen your uprightness 7
9:45 and we gave great glory to the Mighty One. 7
10:24 that the Mighty One may be merciful to you again 7
11:43 and your pride to the Mighty One. 7
12:47 the Mighty One has not forgotten you 7
Jdt 16: 7 For their mighty one did not fall 6
Sir 46: 5 He called upon the Most High, the Mighty One 5
6 he wholly followed the Mighty One. 5
16 He called upon the Lord, the Mighty One 5

show oneself mighty 1. גבר
Isa 42:13 he shows himself mighty against his foes. 1

migrate 1. נסע
Gen 11: 2 as men migrated from the east, they found a plain 1

milch 1. ינק 2. עול
Gen 32:15 30 milch camels and their colts, 40 cows 1
1Sm 6: 7 take and prepare a new cart and two milch cows 2
10 and took two milch cows and yoked them to the cart 2

mildew 1. יֵרָקוֹן
Deu 28:22 smite you . . with blasting, and with mildew; 1
1Kg 8:37 pestilence or blight or mildew or locust 1
2Ch 6:28 if there is pestilence or blight or mildew 1
Ams 4: 9 I smote you with blight and mildew; 1
Hag 2:17 I smote you . . with blight and mildew and hail; 1

mildness 1. *ἐπιείκεια*
Wis 12:18 sovereign in strength dost judge with mildness 1

mile 1. *μίλιον*
Mat 5:41 forces you to go one mile, go with him two miles. 1
41 forces you to go one mile, go with him two miles. •
mile *See also* more, quarter.
miles *See* seven, two.

military 1. *πολεμικός* 2. *πόλεμος*
Jdt 11: 8 you are . . marvelous in military strategy. 2
2Mc 8: 9 a man of experience in military service. 1
military *See also* equipment, force, tribune.

milk 1. חָלָב 2. חֶמְאָה 3. *γάλα* 4. lac
Gen 18: 8 Then he took curds, and milk, and the calf 1
49:12 and his teeth white with milk. 1
Exd 3: 8 to . . a land flowing with milk and honey 1
17 to . . a land flowing with milk and honey. 1
13: 5 to give you, a land flowing with milk and honey 1
23:19 You shall not boil a kid in its mother's milk. 1
33: 3 Go up to a land flowing with milk and honey; 1
34:26 You shall not boil a kid in its mother's milk. 1
Lev 20:24 a land flowing with milk and honey.' I am the LORD 1
Num13:27 flows with milk and honey, and this is its fruit. 1
14: 8 land which flows with milk and honey. 1
16:13 out of a land flowing with milk and honey 1
14 into a land flowing with milk and honey 1
Deu 6: 3 in a land flowing with milk and honey. 1
11: 9 land flowing with milk and honey. 1
14:21 You shall not boil a kid in its mother's milk. 1
26: 9 gave us . . land flowing with milk and honey. 1
15 a land flowing with milk and honey.' 1
27: 3 land flowing with milk and honey, as the LORD 1
31:20 into the land flowing with milk and honey 1
32:14 Curds from the herd, and milk from the flock 1
Jos 5: 6 a land flowing with milk and honey. 1
Jdg 4:19 she opened a skin of milk and gave him a drink 1
5:25 He asked water and she gave him milk 1
Job 10:10 Didst thou not pour me out like milk and curdle me 1
29: 6 when my steps were washed with milk 2
Prv 27:27 there will be enough goats' milk for your food 1
30:33 For pressing milk produces curds 1
Sng 4:11 honey and milk are under your tongue; 1
5: 1 I drink my wine with my milk. 1
12 His eyes are like doves . . bathed in milk 1
Isa 7:22 because of the abundance of milk which they give 1
28: 9 Those who are weaned from the milk 1
55: 1 Come, buy wine and milk without money 1
60:16 You shall suck the milk of nations 1
Jer 11: 5 to give them a land flowing with milk and honey 1
32:22 to give them, a land flowing with milk and honey; 1
Lam 4: 7 princes were purer than snow, whiter than milk; 1
Ezk 20: 6 a land flowing with milk and honey 1
15 had given them, a land flowing with milk and honey 1
25: 4 they shall drink your milk. 1
Jol 3:18 and the hills shall flow with milk 1
1Co 3: 2 I fed you with milk, not solid food 3
9: 7 without getting some of the milk? 3
Heb 5:12 You need milk, not solid food 3
13 every one who lives on milk 3
1Pe 2: 2 long for the pure spiritual milk 3
2Es 2:19 number of springs flowing with milk and honey 4
8:10 milk should be supplied 4
Sir 39:26 iron and salt and wheat flour and milk and honey 3
46: 8 into a land flowing with milk and honey. 3
Bar 1:20 to give to us a land flowing with milk and honey. 3
3Mc 5:49 who were drawing their last milk. 3
milk *See also* drink.

mill 1. טְחוֹן 2. רֵחַיִם 3. *μύλος*
Exd 11: 5 the maidservant who is behind the mill; 2
Num11: 8 ground it in mills or beat it in mortars 2
Deu 24: 6 No man . . take a mill or an upper millstone in pledge; 2
Jdg 16:21 fetters; and he ground at the mill in the prison. •
Lam 5:13 Young men are compelled to grind at the mill; 1
Mat 24:41 Two women will be grinding at the mill 3

millet 1. דֹּחַן
Ezk 4: 9 and barley, beans and lentils, millet and spelt 1

millions 1. *τάλαντον*
1Es 3:21 makes every one talk in millions. 1

millstone 1. פֶּלַח 2. רֵחַיִם 3. *λίθος μυλικός* 4. *μύλινος* 5. *μύλος*
Jdg 9:53 woman threw an upper millstone upon Abim'elech's 1
2Sm 11:21 Did not a woman cast an upper millstone upon him 1
Job 41:24 hard as a stone, hard as the nether millstone. 1
Isa 47: 2 Take the millstones and grind meal 2
Jer 25:10 the grinding of the millstones and the light 2
Mat 18: 6 have a great millstone fastened round his neck 5
Lke 17: 2 if a millstone were hung round his neck 3
Rev 18:21 angel took up a stone like a great millstone 4
22 the millstone shall be heard in thee no more; 5
millstone *See also* upper.

great millstone 1. *μύλος ὀνικός*
Mrk 9:42 if a great millstone were hung round his neck 1

upper millstone 1. רֶכֶב
Deu 24: 6 No man . . take a mill or an upper millstone in pledge; 1

mina 1. מָנֶה 2. *μνᾶ*
1Kg 10:17 three minas of gold went into each shield; 1
Ezr 2:69 gave to . . the work . . gold, 5,000 minas of silver 1
Neh 7:71 gave into the treasury . . 2,200 minas of silver. 1
72 rest of the people gave . . 2,000 minas of silver 1
Ezk 45:12 your mina shall be 50 shekels. 1
1Es 5:45 1,000 minas of gold, 5,000 minas of silver 2
45 1,000 minas of gold, 5,000 minas of silver 2
1Mc 14:24 a large gold shield weighing 1,000 minas 2
15:18 have brought a gold shield weighing 1,000 minas. 2
3Mc 1: 4 promising to give them each two minas of gold 2

mince 1. טפף
Isa 3:16 mincing along as they go, tinkling with . . feet; 1

mind 1. יֵצֶר 2. לֵב 3. לֵבָב 4. נֶגֶד פָּנִים 5. נֶפֶשׁ 6. רוּחַ 7. בָּל (A) 8. לֵב (A) 9. לְבַב (A) 10. *γνώμη* 11. *γνῶσις* 12. *διάνοια* 13. *ἐγκατά* 14. *ἐνθύμημα* 15. *καρδία* 16. *λογισμός* 17. *νεφρός* 18. *νόημα* 19. *νοῦς* 20. *πνεῦμα* 21. *φρήν* 22. *φρονέω* 23. *φρόνημα* 24. *ψυχή* 25. animus 26. cor 27. mens 28. sensus 29. vas
Exd 10:10 Look, you have some evil purpose in mind. 4
14: 5 the mind of Pharaoh and his servants was changed 3
28: 3 whom I have endowed with an able mind 6
36: 2 called . . every able man in whose mind the LORD 2
Deu 5:29 Oh that they had such a mind as this always 3
28:28 LORD will smite you with . . confusion of mind; 3
29: 4 LORD has not given you a mind to understand 2
30: 1 call them to mind among all the nations 2
Jdg 16:17 he told her all his mind, and said to her, "A razor has 2
18 When Deli'lah saw that he had told her all his mind 2
18 Come up this once, for he has told me all his mind. 2
1Sm 2:35 do according to what is in my heart and in my mind; 5
9:19 go and will tell you all that is on your mind. 3
20 As for your asses . . do not set your mind on them 2
14: 7 Do all that your mind inclines to . . I am with you 3
7 I am with you, as is your mind so is mine. 3
2Sm 19:19 let not the king bear it in mind. 2
1Kg 3: 9 Give . . an understanding mind to govern thy 2
12 I give you a wise and discerning mind, so that none 2
4:29 God gave Solomon . . and largeness of mind like 2
8:48 repent with all their mind and . . all their heart 3
10: 2 she told him all that was on her mind. 3
24 hear his wisdom, which God had put into his mind. 2
11:11 this has been your mind and you have not kept •
2Kg 6:11 the mind of the king of Syria was . . troubled 2
9:15 If this is your mind, then let no one slip out 5
1Ch 12:38 all the rest of Israel were of a single mind 2
22:19 set your mind and heart to seek the LORD your God. 5
28: 9 serve him with . . and with a willing mind; 5
12 the plan of all that he had in mind for the courts 6
2Ch 6:38 if they repent with all their mind and . . heart 5
9: 1 to Solomon, she told him all that was on her mind. 3
23 his wisdom, which God had put into his mind. 2
Neh 4: 6 For the people had a mind to work. 2
6: 8 for you are inventing them out of your own mind. 2
7: 5 Then God put it into my mind to assemble 2
Job 7:17 that thou dost set thy mind upon him 2
17: 4 thou hast closed their minds to understanding 2
23:14 many such things are in his mind. •
Ps 7: 9 thou who triest the minds and hearts 2
26: 2 O LORD, and try me; test my heart and my mind. 2
31:12 I have passed out of mind like one who is dead; 2
Prv 10:20 the mind of the wicked is of little worth. 2
11:20 Men of perverse mind are an abomination 2
12: 8 but one of perverse mind is despised. 2
14:30 A tranquil mind gives life to the flesh 2
33 Wisdom . . in the mind of a man of understanding 2
15: 7 spread knowledge; not so the minds of fools. 2
14 mind . . who has understanding seeks knowledge 2
28 The mind of the righteous ponders how to answer 2
16: 1 The plans of the mind belong to man 2
9 A man's mind plans his way 2
23 The mind of the wise makes his speech judicious 2
17:16 should a fool . . buy wisdom, when he has no mind? 2
20 A man of crooked mind does not prosper 2
18:15 An intelligent mind acquires knowledge 2
19:21 Many are the plans in the mind of a man 2
20: 5 The purpose in a man's mind is like deep water 2
22:17 apply your mind to my knowledge; 2
23:12 Apply your mind to instruction and your ear 2
19 my son, and be wise, and direct your mind in the way. 2
33 your mind utter perverse things. 2
24: 2 for their minds devise violence 2
25: 3 so the mind of kings is unsearchable. 2
27:19 so the mind of man reflects the man. 2
28:26 He who trusts in his own mind is a fool; 2
Ecc 1:13 I applied my mind to seek and to search out 2
16 and my mind has had great experience of wisdom 2
17 I applied my mind to know wisdom and . . madness 2
2: 3 I searched with my mind how to cheer my body 2
3 my mind still guiding me with wisdom 2
23 even in the night his mind does not rest. 2
3:11 also he has put eternity into man's mind 2
7: 7 and a bribe corrupts the mind. 2
25 I turned my mind to know and to search out 2
28 my mind has sought . . but I have not found. 5
8: 5 the mind of a wise man will know the time and way. 2
9 while applying my mind to all that is done 2
16 When I applied my mind to know wisdom 2
11:10 Remove vexation from your mind, and put away pain 2
Isa 10: 7 does not so intend, and his mind does not so think; 3
7 does not so think; but it is in his mind to destroy 3
21: 4 My mind reels, horror has appalled me; 3
26: 3 in perfect peace, whose mind is stayed on thee 1
32: 4 The mind of the rash will have good judgment 3
6 speaks folly, and his mind plots iniquity 2
33:18 Your mind will muse on the terror 2
44:18 and their minds, so that they cannot understand. 2
20 feeds on ashes; a deluded mind has led him astray 2
46: 8 Remember this and consider, recall it to mind 2
65:17 the former things shall not . . come into mind. 2
Jer 3:16 It shall not come to mind, or be remembered 2
7:31 I did not command, nor did it come into my mind. 2
11:20 who triest the heart and the mind 2
12: 3 thou seest me, and triest my mind toward thee. 2
14:14 divination, and the deceit of their own minds. 2
17:10 I the LORD search the mind and try the heart 2
19: 5 not command or decree, nor did it come into my mind; 2
20:12 O LORD . . who seest the heart and the mind 2
23:16 they speak visions of their own minds 2
20 and accomplished the intents of his mind. 2
30:24 and accomplished the intents of his mind. 2
32:35 did not command them, nor did it enter into my mind 2
44:21 Did it not come into his mind? 2
51:50 let Jerusalem come into your mind 3
Lam 3:21 But this I call to mind, and therefore I have hope 2
Ezk 11: 5 I know the things that come into your mind. 6
13: 2 say to those who prophesy out of their own minds 2
17 your people, who prophesy out of their own minds; 2
20:32 What is in your mind shall never happen 6
38:10 On that day thoughts will come into your mind 3
40: 4 and set your mind upon all that I shall show you 2
Dan 2:30 that you may know the thoughts of your mind. 8
4:16 let his mind be changed from a man's 8
16 let a beast's mind be given to him; 9

5:21 mind was made like that of a beast 8
6:14 distressed, and set his mind to deliver Daniel; 7
7: 4 mind of a man was given to it. 9
28 but I kept the matter in my mind. 8
8:25 in his mind he shall magnify himself. 3
10:12 first day that you set your mind to understand 2
11:27 two kings, their minds shall be bent on mischief; 3
Mat 22:37 with all your soul, and with all your mind. 12
Mrk 12:30 with all your soul, and with all your mind 12
Lke 10:27 with all your strength, and with all your mind; 12
21:14 Settle it therefore in your minds 15
24:45 Then he opened their minds 19
Act 14: 2 poisoned their minds against the brethren. 24
15:24 unsettling your minds 24
Rom 1:21 and their senseless minds were darkened. 15
28 God gave them up to a base mind 19
7:23 another law at war with the law of my mind 19
25 I of myself serve the law of God with my mind 19
8: 6 To set the mind on the flesh is death 23
6 to set the mind on the Spirit is life and peace. 23
7 the mind that is set on the flesh is hostile to God; 23
27 knows what is the mind of the Spirit 23
11:34 For who has known the mind of the Lord 19
12: 2 but be transformed by the renewal of your mind 19
14: 5 Let every one be fully convinced in his own mind. 19
1Co 1:10 be united in the same mind and the same judgment. 19
2:16 For who has known the mind of the Lord 19
16 we have the mind of Christ. 19
14:14 my spirit prays but my mind is unfruitful. 19
15 I will pray with the mind also 19
15 I will sing with the mind also. 19
19 I would rather speak five words with my mind . . than 19
2Co 2:13 my mind could not rest 20
3:14 their minds were hardened 18
15 a veil lies over their minds; 15
4: 4 blinded the minds of the unbelievers 18
7:13 because his mind has been set at rest by you all. 20
9: 7 Each one must do as he has made up his mind 15
Eph 2: 3 following the desires of body and mind 12
4:17 in the futility of their minds; 19
23 be renewed in the spirit of your minds 19
Php 1:27 with one mind striving side by side for the faith 24
2: 2 complete my joy by being of the same mind 22
2 being in full accord and of one mind. 22
5 Have this mind among yourselves 22
4: 7 keep your hearts and your minds in Christ Jesus. 18
Col 1:21 you, who once were estranged and hostile in mind 12
2:18 puffed up without reason by his sensuous mind 19
2Th 2: 2 not to be quickly shaken in mind or excited 19
1Ti 6: 5 who are depraved in mind and bereft of the truth 19
2Ti 3: 8 men of corrupt mind and counterfeit faith; 19
Tit 1:15 their very minds and consciences are corrupted. 19
Heb 8:10 I will put my laws into their minds 12
10:16 and write them on their minds 12
1Pe 1:13 Therefore gird up your minds, be sober 12
2Pe 3: 1 aroused your sincere mind by way of reminder; 12
Rev 2:23 that I am he who searches mind and heart 17
17: 9 This calls for a mind with wisdom 19
13 These are of one mind and give over their power 10
17 to carry out his purpose by being of one mind 10
1Es 3:18 It leads astray the minds of all who drink it. 12
19 It makes equal the mind of the king and the orphan 12
4:26 Many men have lost their minds because of women 12
2Es 4:11 how then can your mind comprehend the way 29
5:33 Are you greatly disturbed in mind over Israel? 27
7:16 why have you not considered in your mind 26
62 if the mind is made out of the dust 28
63 so that the mind might not have been made from it. 28
64 now the mind grows with us 28
71 for you have said that the mind grows with us. 28
9: 1 Measure carefully in your mind •
10:31 your understanding and the thoughts of your mind 26
36 Or is my mind deceived, and my soul dreaming? 28
12: 3 in great perplexity of mind and great fear 27
5 am still weary in mind and very weak in my spirit 25
13:16 For as I consider it in my mind, alas for those 28
30 bewilderment of mind shall come over those 27
14:34 If you, then, will rule over your minds 28
Tob 4:19 do not let them be blotted out of your mind. 15
Jdt 8:14 and find out his mind or comprehend his thought 19
11:10 keep it in your mind, for it is true 15
16: 9 her beauty captivated his mind 24
AEs 11:12 after he awoke he had it on his mind 15
Wis 4:12 roving desire perverts the innocent mind. 19
8:17 and thought upon them in my mind 15
9:15 this earthy tent burdens the thoughtful mind. 19
Sir 1:28 do not approach him with a divided mind. 15
3:26 A stubborn mind will be afflicted at the end 15
27 A stubborn mind will be burdened by troubles 15
29 The mind of the intelligent man 15
4: 3 Do not add to the troubles of an angry mind 15
6:37 It is he who will give insight to your mind 15
8: 2 gold . . has perverted the minds of kings. 15
11:30 so is the mind of a proud man 15
12:16 in his mind he will plan to throw you into a pit 15
14:21 He who reflects in his mind on her ways 15
16:20 no mind will reflect on this 15
17: 6 he gave them ears and a mind for thinking. 15
21:14 The mind of a fool is like a broken jar 13
17 they will ponder his words in their minds. 15
26 The mind of fools is in their mouth 15
26 the mouth of wise men is in their mind. 15
22:16 so the mind firmly fixed on a reasonable counsel 15
17 A mind settled on an intelligent thought 15
23: 2 the discipline of wisdom over my mind! 15
25:23 A dejected mind, a gloomy face, and a wounded heart 15
27: 6 discloses the cultivation of a man's mind. 15
32:12 Amuse yourself there, and do what you have in mind 14
34: 5 like a woman in travail the mind has fancies. 15
6 do not give your mind to them. 15
36:19 so an intelligent mind detects false words. 15
20 A perverse mind will cause grief 15
40: 5 his sleep at night confuses his mind. 11
6 he is troubled by the visions of his mind 15
43:18 the mind is amazed at its falling. 15
Sus 1: 9 And they perverted their minds 19
1Mc 3:31 He was greatly perplexed in mind 24
2Mc 5:21 because his mind was elated. 15
14:20 it had appeared that they were of one mind 10
15: 8 to keep in mind the former times 19
3Mc 1:25 to change his arrogant mind 19
4: 1 which had long ago been in their minds 12
16 with a mind alienated from truth 21
5:28 he had implanted in the king's mind a forgetfulness 12
30 because . . his whole mind had been deranged 18
39 wondering at his instability of mind 12
42 the changes of mind which had come about within 24
47 he had filled his impious mind with a deep rage 21
4Mc 1:15 Now reason is the mind 19
35 checked by the temperate mind 19
2: 1 the desires of the mind 24
16 the temperate mind repels all these 19
18 the temperate mind is able to get the better 19
22 he enthroned the mind among the senses 19
23 To the mind he gave the law •
3: 3 No one of us can eradicate anger from the mind 24
17 the temperate mind can conquer the drives 19
5:11 adopt a mind appropriate to your years 19
7: 5 in setting his mind firm like a jutting cliff 12
8:29 all with one voice together, as from one mind, said 24
11:14 I am their equal in mind. 12
25 not been able to persuade us to change our mind 16
13: 4 The supremacy of the mind over these 12
14: 6 moved in harmony with the guidance of the mind 24
11 since the mind of woman despised . . agonies 19
15: 4 a wondrous likeness both of mind and of form. 24
16:13 as though having a mind like adamant 19

mind (2) 1. μέλει 2. πράσσω

1Co 7:21 Were you a slave when called? Never mind. 1
1Th 4:11 to mind your own affairs 2

mind *See* call, change, come, consider, induce, keep, lose, make, man, savage, set.

anxious mind 1. μετεωρίζομαι

Lke 12:29 nor be of anxious mind. 1

humble mind 1. ταπεινόφρων

1Pe 3: 8 have . . a tender heart and a humble mind. 1

inward mind 1. קֶרֶב

Ps 64: 6 For the inward mind and heart of a man are deep! 1

right mind 1. σωφρονέω

Mrk 5:15 sitting there, clothed and in his right mind 1
Lke 8:35 and found the man . . clothed and in his right mind 1
2Co 5:13 if we are in our right mind, it is for you. 1

same mind 1. ὁμόψυχος

4Mc 14:20 she was of the same mind as Abraham. 1

minded 1. βούλομαι 2. φρονέω

Php 3:15 Let those of us who are mature be thus minded; 2
15 if in anything you are otherwise minded 2
1Es 8:16 whatever you and your brethren are minded to do 1

double minded 1. δίψυχος

Jas 1: 7 a double-minded man, unstable in all his ways 1

double minded man 1. סֵעֵף

Ps 119:113I hate double-minded men, but I love the law. 1

mindful 1. זכר 2. פקד 3. ἐντρέπω 4. μιμνήσκω 5. συνείδησις 6. memor

1Ch 16:15 He is mindful of his covenant for ever 1
Neh 9:17 not mindful of the wonders which thou didst 1
Ps 8: 4 what is man that thou art mindful of him 1
9:12 For he who avenges blood is mindful of them; 1
25: 6 Be mindful of thy mercy, O LORD 1
105: 8 He is mindful of his covenant for ever 1
111: 5 he is ever mindful of his covenant. 1
115:12 The LORD has been mindful of us; he will bless us; 1
Zep 2: 7 For the LORD their God will be mindful of them 2
1Pe 2:19 one is approved if, mindful of God, he endures pain 5
2Es 16:20 nor be always mindful of the scourges. 6
Tob 2: 2 who is mindful of the Lord 4
Sir 4:25 be mindful of your ignorance. 3

mine 1. μέταλλον

1Mc 8: 3 to get control of the silver and gold mines there 1

mingle 1. בלל 2. מסך 3. ערב 4. δίδωμι 5. μείγνυμι 6. commisceo

Exd 29:40 a tenth measure of fine flour mingled 1
Ps 102: 9 mingle tears with my drink 2
106:35 mingled with the nations and learned to do 3
Isa 19:14 LORD . . mingled within her a spirit of confusion; 2
Mat 27:34 they offered him wine to drink, mingled with gall; 5
Lke 13: 1 the Galileans whose blood Pilate had mingled 5
Rev 8: 3 given much incense to mingle with the prayers 4
15: 2 appeared to be a sea of glass mingled with fire 5
2Es 13:11 All these were mingled together 6

mingle with myrrh 1. σμυρνίζω

Mrk 15:23 they offered him wine mingled with myrrh 1

mingled stuff 1. שַׁעַטְנֵז

Deu 22:11 not wear a mingled stuff, wool and linen together. 1

no mingling 1. ἀμειξία

2Mc 14:38 when there was no mingling with the Gentiles 1

minister 1. היה שרת 2. עבד 3. עמד 4. צבא 5. שרת 6. διακονέω 7. διάκονος 8. δυνάστης 9. θεραπεύω 10. λατρεύω 11. λειτουργέω 12. λειτουργικός 13. λειτουργός 14. παρίστημι 15. ὑπηρετέω 16. ὑπηρέτης

Exd 28:35 it shall be upon Aaron when he ministers 5
43 come near the altar to minister in the holy place; 5
29:30 when he comes . . to minister in the holy place. 5
30:20 when they come near the altar to minister 5
35:19 the finely wrought garments for ministering 5
38: 8 the . . women who ministered at the door 4
39: 1 garments, for ministering in the holy place; 5
26 upon the skirts of the robe for ministering; 5
41 the finely worked garments for ministering 5
Num 3: 6 set them . . that they may minister to him. 5
7 as they minister at the tabernacle 2
8 attend . . as they minister at the tabernacle. 2
31 vessels . . with which the priests minister 5
8:26 minister to their brethren in the tent 5
11:28 Joshua the son of Nun, the minister of Moses 5
16: 9 to stand before the congregation to minister 5
18: 2 that they may join you and minister to you 5
Deu 10: 8 to stand before the LORD to minister to him 5
17:12 by not obeying the priest who stands to minister 5
18: 5 chosen him . . to stand and minister in the name 5
7 then he may minister in the name of the LORD 5
7 who stand to minister there before the LORD. •
21: 5 LORD your God has chosen them to minister to him 5
Jos 1: 1 LORD said to Joshua the son of Nun, Moses' minister 5
Jdg 20:28 Phin'ehas . . ministered before it in those days) 3
1Sm 2:11 And the boy ministered to the LORD 1
18 Samuel was ministering before the LORD 5
3: 1 Samuel was ministering to the LORD under Eli. 5
1Kg 1: 4 she became the king's nurse and ministered to him; 5
15 old, and Ab'ishag . . was ministering to the king). 5
8:11 priests could not stand to minister 5
19:21 he . . went after Eli'jah, and ministered to him. 5
1Ch 6:32 They ministered with song 5
15: 2 and to minister to him for ever. 5
16: 4 Levites as ministers before the ark of the LORD 5
37 to minister continually before the ark 5
23:13 minister to him and pronounce blessings 5
26:12 ministering in the house of the LORD; 5
2Ch 5:14 priests could not stand to minister 5
13:10 We have priests ministering to the LORD 5
23: 6 priests and ministering Levites; they may enter 5
29:11 LORD has chosen you . . to minister to him 5
11 LORD has chosen you . . to be his ministers 5
31: 2 minister in the gates of the camp of the LORD 5
Ezr 8:17 to send us ministers for the house of our God. 5
Neh 10:36 priests who minister in the house of our God 5
39 priests that minister, and the gatekeepers 5
12:44 priests and the Levites who ministered. 3
Ps 101: 6 way that is blameless shall minister to me. 5
103:21 all his hosts, his ministers that do his will! 5
104: 4 who makest . . fire and flame thy ministers. 5
Isa 56: 6 join themselves to the LORD, to minister to him 5
60: 7 the rams of Nebai'oth shall minister to you; 5
10 and their kings shall minister to you; 5
61: 6 men shall speak of you as the ministers of our God; 5
Jer 33:21 with the Levitical priests my ministers. 5
22 and the Levitical priests who minister to me. 5
Ezk 40:46 may come near to the LORD to minister to him. 5
42:14 the garments in which they minister 5
43:19 of Zadok, who draw near to me to minister to me 5
44:11 They shall be ministers in my sanctuary 5
12 they ministered to them before their idols 5
15 shall come near to me to minister to me; 5
16 they shall approach my table, to minister to me 5
17 they minister at the gates of the inner court, 5
19 garments in which they have been ministering 5
27 the inner court, to minister in the holy place 5
45: 4 for the priests, who minister in the sanctuary 5
4 and approach the LORD to minister to him; 5

5 shall be for the Levites who minister 5
46:24 These are the kitchens where those who minister 5
Jol 1: 9 The priests mourn, the ministers of the LORD. 5
13 lament, O priests, wail, O ministers of the altar. 5
13 pass the night in sackcloth, O ministers of my God! 5
2:17 let the priests, the ministers of the LORD, weep 5
Mat 4:11 behold, angels came and ministered to him. 6
25:44 and did not minister to thee?' 6
27:55 followed Jesus from Galilee, ministering to him; 6
Mrk 1:13 the angels ministered to him. 6
15:41 followed him, and ministered to him 6
Lke 1: 2 eyewitnesses and ministers of the word 16
Act 8:27 an Ethiopian, a eunuch, a minister of the Can'dace 8
20:34 these hands ministered to my necessities 15
Rom 13: 6 for the authorities are ministers of God 13
15:16 to be a minister of Christ Jesus to the Gentiles 13
2Co 3: 6 competent to be ministers of a new covenant 7
Eph 3: 7 Of this gospel I was made a minister 7
6:21 faithful minister in the Lord 7
Php 2:25 your messenger and minister to my need 13
Col 1: 7 He is a faithful minister of Christ on our behalf 7
23 of which I, Paul, became a minister. 7
25 of which I became a minister 7
4: 7 he is a beloved brother and faithful minister 7
1Ti 4: 6 you will be a good minister of Christ Jesus 7
Heb 1:14 all ministering spirits sent forth to serve 12
8: 2 a minister in the sanctuary and the true tent 13
1Es 1: 5 minister before your brethren *
4:54 in which they were to minister. 10
Tob 1: 7 sons of Levi who ministered at Jerusalem 9
Jdt 4:14 the priests who . . ministered to the Lord 11
11:13 priests who minister in the presence of our God 14
Wis 16:21 ministering to the desire of the one who took it 15
Sir 4:14 Those who serve her will minister to the Holy One; 11
7:30 do not forsake his ministers. 13
24:10 In the holy tabernacle I ministered before him 11
45:15 to minister to the Lord 11
1Mc 10:42 it belongs to the priests who minister there. 11

minister as priest 1. כהן
Deu 10: 6 his son Elea'zar ministered as priest in his stead 1

minister in the priest's office 1. כהן
Num 3: 3 ordained to minister in the priest's office. 1

ministering woman 1. צבא
Exd 38: 8 the mirrors of the ministering women 1

ministry 1. יָד 2. שרת 3. διακονία 4. λειτουργία
2Ch 7: 6 David offered praises by their ministry; 1
8:14 for their offices of praise and ministry 2
Lke 3:23 Jesus, when he began his ministry *
Act 1:17 allotted his share in this ministry. 3
25 this ministry and apostleship 3
6: 4 to prayer and to the ministry of the word. 3
20:24 the ministry which I received from the Lord 3
21:19 done among the Gentiles through his ministry. 3
Rom 11:13 an apostle to the Gentiles, I magnify my ministry 3
2Co 4: 1 having this ministry by the mercy of God 3
5:18 gave us the ministry of reconciliation; 3
6: 3 so that no fault may be found with our ministry 3
Eph 4:12 to equip the saints for the work of ministry 3
Col 4:17 the ministry which you have received in the Lord. 3
2Ti 4: 5 fulfil your ministry. 3
Heb 8: 6 Christ has obtained a ministry 4
Wis 18:21 he brought forward the shield of his ministry 4

minstrel 1. נגן 2. μουσικός
2Kg 3:15 But now bring me a minstrel. 1
15 when the minstrel played, the power of the LORD 1
Ps 68:25 the singers in front, the minstrels last 1
Rev 18:22 and the sound of harpers and minstrels 2

mint 1. ἡδύοσμον
Mat 23:23 you tithe the mint and dill and cummin 1
Lke 11:42 you tithe the mint and rue and every herb 1

mint (2) 1. ποιέω
1Mc 15: 6 I permit you to mint your own coinage 1

miracle 1. מוֹפֵת 2. פלא 3. δύναμις
Exd 4:21 do . . before Pharaoh all the miracles which I 1
7: 9 'Prove yourselves by working a miracle,' 1
Ps 78:11 the miracles that he had shown them. 2
43 in Egypt, and his miracles in the fields of Zo'an. 1
105: 5 Remember the wonderful works . . his miracles 1
27 wrought his signs . . miracles in the land of Ham. 1
Act 8:13 seeing signs and great miracles performed 3
19:11 did extraordinary miracles by the hands of Paul 3
1Co 12:10 to another the working of miracles 3
29 Are all teachers? Do all work miracles? 3
Gal 3: 5 works miracles among you 3
Heb 2: 4 signs and wonders and various miracles 3
miracle *See also* worker.

mire 1. בֹּץ 2. חֹמֶר 3. טִיט 4. יָוֵן 5. רֶפֶשׁ 6. βόρβορος
2Sm 22:43 stamped them down like the mire of the streets. 3
Job 30:19 God has cast me into the mire 2
41:30 himself like a threshing sledge on the mire. 3
Ps 18:42 I cast them out like the mire of the streets. 3
69: 2 I sink in deep mire, where there is no foothold; 4
14 rescue me from sinking in the mire; 3
Isa 10: 6 to tread them down like the mire of the streets. 2
57:20 cannot rest, and its waters toss up mire and dirt. 5
Jer 38: 6 there was no water in the cistern, but only mire 3
6 and Jeremiah sank in the mire. 3
22 now that your feet are sunk in the mire 1
Mic 7:10 be trodden down like the mire of the streets. 3
2Pe 2:22 and the sow is washed only to wallow in the mire. 6

mirror 1. מַרְאָה 2. רְאִי 3. ἔσοπτρον
Exd 38: 8 made the laver . . from the mirrors 1
Job 37:18 spread out the skies, hard as a molten mirror? 2
1Co 13:12 now we see in a mirror dimly, but then face to face. 3
Jas 1:23 a man who observes his natural face in a mirror; 3
Wis 7:26 a spotless mirror of the working of God 3
Sir 12:11 will be to him like one who has polished a mirror 3

mirth 1. מָשׂוֹשׂ 2. שִׂמְחָה 3. שָׂשׂוֹן 4. εὐφροσύνη
Gen 31:27 I might have sent you away with mirth and songs 2
Ps 137: 3 required of us songs, and our tormentors, mirth 2
Ecc 7: 4 but the heart of fools is in the house of mirth. 2
Isa 24: 8 The mirth of the timbrels is stilled 1
8 has ceased, the mirth of the lyre is stilled. 1
Jer 7:34 from the streets of Jerusalem the voice of mirth 3
16: 9 the voice of mirth and the voice of gladness 3
25:10 I will banish from them the voice of mirth 3
33:11 the voice of mirth and the voice of gladness 3
Hos 2:11 And I will put an end to all her mirth, her feasts 1
1Es 3:20 It turns every thought to feasting and mirth 4
Bar 2:23 the voice of mirth and the voice of gladness 4

miry 1. יָוֵן 2. טִין (A)
Ps 40: 2 out of the miry bog, and set my feet upon a rock 1
Dan 2:41 just as you saw iron mixed with the miry clay. 2
43 As you saw the iron mixed with miry clay 2

miscarriage 1. יצא יֶלֶד 2. שכל
Exd 21:22 a woman with child, so that there is a miscarriage 1
2Kg 2:21 death nor miscarriage shall come from it. 2

miscarry 1. שכל
Gen 31:38 your ewes and your she-goats have not miscarried 1
Hos 9:14 Give them a miscarrying womb and dry breasts. 1

mischance 1. פֶּרֶץ
Ps 144:14 suffering no mischance or failure in bearing; 1

mischief 1. אָוֶן 2. מְזִמָּה 3. עָמָל 4. רָעָה 5. רעע
Jdg 15: 3 to the Philistines, when I do them mischief. 4
1Kg 11:25 an adversary . . doing mischief as Hadad did; 4
Job 15:35 They conceive mischief and bring forth evil 3
Ps 7:14 conceives evil, and is pregnant with mischief 3
16 His mischief returns upon his own head 3
10: 7 under his tongue are mischief and iniquity. 3
21:11 if they devise mischief, they will not succeed. 2
28: 3 while mischief is in their hearts. 4
36: 3 The words of his mouth are mischief and deceit; 1
4 He plots mischief while on his bed; 1
41: 6 empty words, while his heart gathers mischief; 1
52: 1 Why do you boast, O mighty man, of mischief done 4
55:10 mischief and trouble are within it 1
94:20 wicked rulers . . who frame mischief by statute? 3
140: 9 let the mischief of their lips overwhelm them! 3
Prv 24: 2 for . . their lips talk of mischief. 3
Isa 59: 4 they conceive mischief and bring forth 3
Dan 11:27 two kings, their minds shall be bent on mischief; 5

mischief-maker 1. בַּעַל מְזִמּוֹת 2. ἀλλοτριεπίσκοπος
Prv 24: 8 plans to do evil will be called a mischief-maker. 1
1Pe 4:15 let none of you suffer as . . a mischief-maker; 2

mischievous 1. הַוָּה
Prv 17: 4 liar gives heed to a mischievous tongue. 1

misdeed 1. ἀνομία 2. κακία
Heb 10:17 remember their sins and their misdeeds no more. 1
4Mc 2:12 one punishes them for misdeeds. 2

miserable 1. עָמֵל 2. κακός 3. κακῶς 4. πικρός 5. πονηρός 6. ταλαίπωρος 7. τάλας 8. miser
Job 16: 2 miserable comforters are you all. 1
Mat 21:41 put those wretches to a miserable death 3
2Es 15:47 woe to you, miserable wretch! 8
Wis 3:11 whoever despises wisdom . . is miserable 6
13:10 miserable, with their hopes set on dead things 6
15:14 most foolish, and more miserable than an infant 7
Sir 29:24 It is a miserable life to go from house to house 5
30:17 Death is better than a miserable life 4
2Mc 5: 8 Finally he met a miserable end 2

miserable man 1. ταλαίπωρος
Wis 13:10 miserable . . are the men 1

most miserable 1. ἄθλιος 2. δυσάθλιος
3Mc 4: 4 and shed tears at the most miserable expulsion 2
5:49 the end of their most miserable suspense 1

miserably 1. τάλας 2. pessime
2Es 7:120 but we have miserably failed? 2
4Mc 12: 4 be miserably tortured and die before your time 1

miserly 1. רַע
Prv 28:22 A miserly man hastens after wealth 1

misery 1. עֹמֶל 2. עָמָל 3. κάκωσις 4. πτωχεία 5. ταλαιπωρία 6. extritio 7. miseria
Jdg 10:16 he became indignant over the misery of Israel. 2
Job 3:20 Why is light given to him that is in misery 1
7: 3 nights of misery are apportioned to me. 2
11:16 You will forget your misery; 2
20:22 all the force of misery will come upon him. 1
Ps 31:10 my strength fails because of my misery 4
Prv 31: 7 drink and . . remember their misery no more. 2
Rom 3:16 in their paths are ruin and misery 5
Jas 5: 1 howl for the miseries that are coming upon you. 5
2Es 8:50 For many miseries will affect those 7
15:15 For the sword and misery draw near them 6
Sir 11:27 The misery of an hour makes one forget luxury 3
2Mc 6: 9 One could see, therefore, the misery 5

great misery 1. πόνος πονηρός
Bar 2:25 They perished in great misery, by famine 1

misfortune 1. אָוֶן 2. נֵכֶר 3. פֶּגַע רַע 4. פִּיד 5. רַע 6. רָעָה 7. ἀκληρέω 8. ἄτοπος 9. ἀτυχία 10. δυσημερία 11. δυσπέτημα 12. κακός 13. συμφορά 14. ταλαιπωρία 15. casus
Num 11: 1 people complained . . about their misfortunes; 5
23:21 He has not beheld misfortune in Jacob; 1
1Kg 5: 4 there is neither adversary nor misfortune. 3
Job 12: 5 there is contempt for misfortune; 4
Prv 13:21 Misfortune pursues sinners 6
Obd 1:12 your brother in the day of his misfortune; 2
Act 28: 6 saw no misfortune come to him 8
2Es 10:43 her telling you about the misfortune of her son 15
48 and that misfortune had overtaken her 15
Wis 14:21 in bondage to misfortune or to royal authority 13
1Mc 3:42 Judas . . saw that misfortunes had increased 12
59 to see the misfortunes of our nation 12
2Mc 4: 1 had been the real cause of the misfortune. 12
5: 6 success . . is the greatest misfortune 10
20 the place itself shared in the misfortunes 11
10: 4 they might never again fall into such misfortunes 12
12:30 kind treatment of them in times of misfortune 9
14: 8 our whole nation is now in no small misfortune. 7
14 the misfortunes and calamities of the Jews 9
3Mc 4:12 the ignoble misfortune of their brothers 14

misguide 1. πλανάω
Sir 16:23 a senseless and misguided man thinks foolishly. 1

mislead 1. מַדּוּחַ 2. נשא 3. סות 4. שגה 5. תעה 6. ἀναπείθω 7. πλανάω
Deu 27:18 'Cursed be he who misleads a blind man on the road.' 4
2Kg 18:32 do not listen . . when he misleads you by saying 3
2Ch 32:11 Is not Hezeki'ah misleading you . . when he tells 3
15 do not let Hezeki'ah deceive you or mislead you 3
Prv 28:10 misleads the upright into an evil way will fall 4
Isa 3:12 your leaders mislead you, and confuse the course 5
36:18 Beware lest Hezeki'ah mislead you by saying 3
Lam 2:14 have seen for you oracles false and misleading. 1
Ezk 13:10 Because, yea, because they have misled my people 2
Wis 15: 4 the evil intent of human art misled us 7
Sir 9: 8 many have been misled by a woman's beauty 7
1Mc 1:11 lawless men . . misled many, saying 6

mismate 1. ἑτεροζυγέω
2Co 6:14 Do not be mismated with unbelievers 1

misrepresent 1. ψευδόμαρτυς
1Co 15:15 We are even found to be misrepresenting God 1

misrepresent a fact 1. διαβάλλω
2Mc 3:11 the impious Simon had misrepresented the facts. 1

miss 1. חטא 2. לא פקד 3. עדר 4. פקד 5. ἐπισκέπτω 6. deficio
Num 31:49 men of war . . there is not a man missing from us. 4
Jdg 20:16 could sling a stone at a hair, and not miss. 1
1Sm 20: 6 If your father misses me at all, then say 4
18 Tomorrow is the new moon; and you will be missed 4
19 And on the third day you will be greatly missed; 5
25: 7 and we did them no harm, and they missed nothing 4
15 we did not miss anything when . . in the fields 4
21 nothing was missed of all that belonged to him; 4
30:19 Nothing was missing, whether small or great 3
2Sm 2:30 there were missing of David's servants nineteen 4
1Kg 20:39 if . . he be missing, your life shall be for his life 4
2Kg 10:19 call to me all . . let none be missing 4
19 whoever is missing shall not live. 4
Job 5:24 you shall inspect your fold and miss nothing. 1
Prv 8:36 he who misses me injures himself; 1
Isa 34:16 Not one of these shall be missing; 3

40:26 because he is strong in power not one is missing. 3
Jer 3:16 not come to mind, or be remembered, or missed; 2
23: 4 neither shall any be missing, says the LORD. 4
2Es 16:13 and will not miss when they begin to be shot 6
Jdt 14:15 with his head cut off and missing. •

miss the mark 1. ἀστοχέω
1Ti 6:21 some have missed the mark as regards the faith. 1

miss the way 1. חטא
Prv 19: 2 he who makes haste with his feet misses his way. 1

missile 1. βέλος
2Mc 5: 3 hurling of missiles 1
12:27 great stores of war engines and missiles 1

mission 1. דֶּרֶךְ 2. ἀποστολή 3. διακονία 4. πρεσβεία
1Sm 15:18 And the LORD sent you on a mission, and said 1
20 I have gone on the mission on which the LORD sent 1
Act 12:25 when they had fulfilled their mission 3
2Co 11:12 in their boasted mission •
Gal 2: 8 the mission to the circumcised 2
2Mc 4:11 who went on the mission to establish friendship 4

mission *See also* send.
misspent *See* toil.
misstep *See* make.

mist 1. אֵד 2. נָשִׂיא 3. עָנָן 4. שֶׂכְוִי 5. ἀτμίς 6. ἀχλύς 7. ὁμίχλη 8. vapor
Gen 2: 6 a mist went up from the earth 1
Job 36:27 the drops of water, he distils his mist in rain 1
38:36 or given understanding to the mists? 4
Isa 44:22 like a cloud, and your sins like mist; 3
Jer 10:13 he makes the mist rise from the ends of the earth. 2
51:16 he makes the mist rise from the ends of the earth. 2
Hos 13: 3 Therefore they shall be like the morning mist 3
Act 13:11 Immediately mist and darkness fell upon him 6
Jas 4:14 For you are a mist that appears for a little time 5
2Pe 2:17 waterless springs and mists driven by a storm; 7
2Es 4:24 and our life is like a mist ‡
7:61 they who are now like a mist 8
Wis 2: 4 be scattered like mist 7
Sir 24: 3 covered the earth like a mist. 7
43:22 A mist quickly heals all things 7

mistake 1. שְׁגָגָה 2. ἄγνοια
Ecc 5: 6 and do not say . . that it was a mistake; 1
1Es 8:75 our mistakes have mounted up to heaven 2
Sir 23: 3 in order that my mistakes may not be multiplied 2

mistake *See also* make.

mistress 1. בַּעֲלָה 2. גְּבֶרֶת
Gen 16: 4 she looked with contempt on her mistress. 2
8 She said, "I am fleeing from my mistress Sar'ai. 2
9 Return to your mistress, and submit to her. 2
1Kg 17:17 the son of the woman, the mistress of the house 1
2Kg 5: 3 She said to her mistress, "Would that my lord 2
Ps 123: 2 as the eyes of a maid to the hand of her mistress 2
Prv 30:23 maid when she succeeds her mistress. 2
Isa 24: 2 as with the maid, so with her mistress; 2
47: 5 no more be called the mistress of kingdoms. 2
7 You said, "I shall be mistress for ever 2
Nah 2: 7 its mistress is stripped, she is carried off •

mix 1. בּוא בְּ 2. בלל 3. מהל 4. מסך 5. מֶסֶךְ 6. מִרְקַחַת 7. ערב 8. עֵרֶב 9. ערב (A) 10. δίδωμι 11. ἐπιμίγνυμι 12. ἐπίμικτος 13. κεράννυμι 14. μείγνυμι 15. συγκεράννυμι
Exd 12:38 A mixed multitude also went up with them 8
29: 2 unleavened cakes mixed with oil, and unleavened 2
Lev 2: 4 cakes of fine flour mixed with oil 2
5 shall be of fine flour unleavened, mixed with oil 2
7:10 every cereal offering, mixed with oil or dry 2
12 offer . . unleavened cakes mixed with oil 2
9: 4 and a cereal offering mixed with oil 2
14:10 an ephah of fine flour mixed with oil, and one log 2
21 a tenth of an ephah of fine flour mixed with oil 2
23:13 two tenths of an ephah of fine flour mixed with oil 2
Num 6:15 cakes of fine flour mixed with oil 2
7:13 fine flour mixed with oil for a cereal offering; 2
19 fine flour mixed with oil for a cereal offering; 2
25 fine flour mixed with oil for a cereal offering; 2
31 fine flour mixed with oil for a cereal offering; 2
37 fine flour mixed with oil for a cereal offering; 2
43 fine flour mixed with oil for a cereal offering; 2
49 fine flour mixed with oil for a cereal offering; 2
55 fine flour mixed with oil for a cereal offering; 2
61 fine flour mixed with oil for a cereal offering; 2
67 fine flour mixed with oil for a cereal offering; 2
73 fine flour mixed with oil for a cereal offering; 2
79 fine flour mixed with oil for a cereal offering; 2
8: 8 cereal offering of fine flour mixed with oil 2
15: 4 fine flour, mixed with a fourth of a hin of oil; 2
6 fine flour, mixed with a third of a hin of oil; 2
9 fine flour, mixed with half a hin of oil 2
28: 5 cereal offering, mixed with a fourth of a hin 2
9 fine flour for a cereal offering, mixed with oil 2
12 fine flour for a cereal offering, mixed with oil 2
12 fine flour for a cereal offering, mixed with oil 2
13 fine flour mixed with oil as a cereal offering 2
20 cereal offering of fine flour mixed with oil; 2
28 cereal offering of fine flour mixed with oil 2
29: 3 cereal offering of fine flour mixed with oil 2
9 cereal offerings of fine flour mixed with oil 2
14 cereal offering of fine flour mixed with oil 2
Jos 23: 7 you may not be mixed with these nations left here 1
1Ch 9:30 Others . . prepared the mixing of the spices. 6
Ezr 9: 2 holy race has mixed itself with the peoples 7
Ps 75: 8 there is a cup, with foaming wine, well mixed; 5
Prv 9: 2 slaughtered her beasts, she has mixed her wine 4
5 eat of my bread and drink of the wine I have mixed. 4
Isa 1:22 Your silver . . dross, your wine mixed with water. 3
5:22 valiant men in mixing strong drink 4
Dan 2:41 just as you saw iron mixed with the miry clay. 9
43 As you saw the iron mixed with miry clay 9
43 they will mix with one another in marriage 9
43 not hold . . just as iron does not mix with clay. 9
Hos 7: 8 E'phraim mixes himself with the peoples; 2
Rev 8: 7 there followed hail and fire, mixed with blood 14
18: 6 mix a double draught for her in the cup she mixed. 13
6 mix a double draught for her in the cup she mixed. 13
1Es 8:70 mixed with the alien peoples of the land 11
87 mixing with the uncleanness of the peoples 11
Jdt 2:20 Along with them went a mixed crowd 12
Sir 18:15 My son, do not mix reproach with your good deeds 10
Bel 1:11 set forth the food and mix and place the wine 13
2Mc 15:39 wine mixed with water is sweet and delicious 15

mix with frankincense 1. λιβανόομαι
3Mc 5:45 wine mixed with frankincense 1

mixed *See* offering, tribes, wine.

well mixed 1. רבך 2. בלל רבך
Lev 6:21 you shall bring it well mixed, in baked pieces 1
7:12 cakes of fine flour well mixed with oil 2

mixture 1. μίγμα
Joh 19:39 came bringing a mixture of myrrh and aloes 1

moan 1. אֲנָחָה 2. הגה 3. המה 4. קוֹל 5. תַּאֲנִיָּה
Ps 6: 6 I am weary with my moaning; 1
55:17 at noon I utter my complaint and moan 3
77: 3 I think of God, and I moan; I meditate 3
Isa 16:11 Therefore my soul moans like a lyre for Moab 3
29: 2 and there shall be moaning and lamentation 5
38:14 Like . . a crane I clamor, I moan like a dove. 2
59:11 growl like bears, we moan and moan like doves; 2
11 growl like bears, we moan and moan like doves; 2
Jer 48:36 Therefore my heart moans for Moab like a flute 3
36 my heart moans like a flute for the men 3
Ezk 7:16 like doves of the valleys, all of them moaning 3
Nah 2: 7 her maidens lamenting, moaning like doves 4

moat 1. חָרוּץ
Dan 9:25 built again with squares and moat 1

mob 1. ὄχλος 2. πλῆθος
Act 21:36 the mob of the people followed, crying 2
Sir 26: 5 The slander of a city, the gathering of a mob 1

mobile 1. εὐκίνητος
Wis 7:22 holy, unique, manifold, subtle, mobile, clear 1

more mobile 1. κινητικός
Wis 7:24 For wisdom is more mobile than any motion; 1

mock 1. התל 2. חרף 3. ליץ 4. לעב 5. לעג 6. לַעַג 7. קלס 8. קַלָּסָה 9. שחק 10. תלל 11. תעע 12. διαχλευάζω 13. ἐκμυκτηρίζω 14. ἐμπαιγμός 15. ἐμπαίζω 16. καταγελάω 17. μυκτηρίζω 18. μωκός 19. χλευάζω
Gen 27:12 I shall seem to be mocking him, and bring a curse 11
Jdg 16:10 you have mocked me, and told me lies; please tell me 10
13 Until now you have mocked me, and told me lies; 10
15 You have mocked me these three times, and you have 10
1Kg 18:27 at noon Eli'jah mocked them, saying, "Cry aloud 1
2Kg 19: 4 whom his master . . has sent to mock the living God 2
16 words . . which he has sent to mock the living God. 2
22 Whom have you mocked and reviled? 2
23 you have mocked the Lord, and you have said 2
2Ch 30:10 but they laughed them to scorn, and mocked them. 5
36:16 they kept mocking the messengers of God 4
Job 9:23 he mocks at the calamity of the innocent. 5
11: 3 when you mock, shall no one shame you? 5
21: 3 I will speak, and after I have spoken, mock on. 5
Ps 22: 7 All who see me mock at me, they make mouths at me 5
35:16 they impiously mocked more and more •
79: 4 mocked and derided by those round about us. 6
89:51 which they mock the footsteps of thy anointed. 2
Prv 1:26 I will mock when panic strikes you 5
17: 5 He who mocks the poor insults his Maker; 5
19:28 A worthless witness mocks at justice 3
30:17 eye that mocks a father and scorns to obey 5
Isa 37: 4 king of Assyria has sent to mock the living God 2
17 words . . which he has sent to mock the living God. 2
23 'Whom have you mocked and reviled? 2
24 By your servants you have mocked the Lord 2
Jer 20: 7 laughingstock all the day; every one mocks me. 5
Lam 1: 7 foe gloated over her, mocking at her downfall. 9
Ezk 22: 4 and a mocking to all the countries. 8
5 will mock you, you infamous one, full of tumult. 7
Mat 20:19 to be mocked and scourged and crucified 15
27:29 kneeling before him they mocked him, saying 15
31 when they had mocked him 15
41 with the scribes and elders, mocked him, saying 15
Mrk 10:34 they will mock him, and spit upon him, and scourge 15
15:20 when they had mocked him 15
31 also the chief priests mocked him to one another 15
Lke 14:29 all who see it begin to mock him 15
18:32 will be mocked and shamefully treated and spit upon; 15
22:63 who were holding Jesus mocked him and beat him; 15
23:11 Herod . . mocked him 15
36 The soldiers also mocked him 15
Act 2:13 others mocking said 12
17:32 some mocked; but others said, "We will hear you 19
Gal 6: 7 Do not be deceived; God is not mocked 17
Heb 11:36 Others suffered mocking and scourging 14
1Es 1:51 they mocked his messengers 13
AEs 14:11 do not let them mock at our downfall 16
Wis 12:25 thou didst send thy judgment to mock them. 14
Sir 33: 6 A stallion is like a mocking friend 18
1Mc 7:34 he mocked them and derided them and defiled them 17

mocker 1. הֲתֻלִּים 2. ליץ
Job 17: 2 Surely there are mockers about me 1
Prv 20: 1 Wine is a mocker, strong drink a brawler; 2
Hos 7: 5 he stretched out his hand with mockers. 2

mockery 1. ἐμπαιγμός
Sir 27:28 Mockery and abuse issue from the proud man 1

mockingly 1. χλευάζω
Wis 11:14 though they had mockingly rejected him 1

model 1. דְּמוּת 2. τύπος
2Kg 16:10 Ahaz sent to Uri'ah the priest a model of the altar 1
Tit 2: 7 in all respects a model of good deeds 2

moderate 1. μέτριος
Sir 31:20 Healthy sleep depends on moderate eating 1

moderation 1. ἐπιεικῶς 2. μέτρον 3. σωφροσύνη
Sir 31:27 if you drink it in moderation 2
2Mc 4:37 wept because of the moderation and good conduct 3
9:27 treat you with moderation and kindness. 1

modest 1. αἰδήμων 2. αἰσχυντηρός
Sir 26:15 A modest wife adds charm to charm 2
2Mc 15:12 of modest bearing and gentle manner 1
4Mc 8: 3 seven brothers–handsome, modest, noble 1

modest man 1. αἰσχυντηρός
Sir 32:10 approval precedes a modest man. 1

modestly 1. μετά αἰδοῦς
1Ti 2: 9 women should adorn themselves modestly 1

modesty 1. αἰδώς 2. εὐσχημοσύνη 3. σωφροσύνη
1Co 12:23 treated with greater modesty 2
1Ti 2:15 in faith and love and holiness, with modesty. 3
3Mc 1:19 neglecting proper modesty 1

moist 1. רָוֶה 2. שקה 3. δρόσος
Deu 29:19 lead to the sweeping away of moist and dry alike. 1
Job 21:24 full of fat and the marrow of his bones moist. 2
Aza 1:27 like a moist whistling wind 3

moisten 1. רסס
Ezk 46:14 one third of a hin of oil to moisten the flour 1

moisten with dew 1. δροσίζω
3Mc 6: 6 moistening the fiery furnace with dew 1

moisture 1. רִי 2. ἰκμάς
Job 37:11 He loads the thick cloud with moisture; 1
Lke 8: 6 it withered away, because it had no moisture. 2

mold 1. γλυφή 2. πλάσμα 3. πλάσσω
Rom 9:20 Will what is molded say to its molder 2
Wis 7: 1 in the womb of a mother I was molded into flesh 1
15: 7 and laboriously molds each vessel for our service 3
9 he molds counterfeit gods. 3

mold *See also* brick.

molder 1. πλάσσω
Rom 9:20 Will what is molded say to its molder 1

molding 1. זֵר
Exd 25:11 make upon it a molding of gold round about. 1
24 and make a molding of gold around it. 1
25 make . . a molding of gold around the frame. 1

30: 3 make for it a molding of gold round about. 1
4 under its molding on two opposite sides of it 1
37: 2 and made a molding of gold around it. 1
11 and made a molding of gold around it. 1
12 made a molding of gold around the frame. 1
26 and he made a molding of gold round about it 1
27 under its molding, on two opposite sides of it 1

moldy 1. נִקֻּד
Jos 9: 5 and all their provisions were dry and moldy. 1
12 it was still warm . . but now..it is dry and moldy; 1

mole 1. חֲפַרְפֶּרֶת
Isa 2:20 cast forth their idols . . to the moles 1

molest 1. נגע 2. פגע 3. *ἐμπαροχλέω* 4. *ὑβρίζω*
Rut 2: 9 Have I not charged the young men not to molest you? 1
22 lest in another field you be molested. 2
Act 14: 5 to molest them and to stone them 4
2Mc 11:31 none of them shall be molested in any way 3

molten 1. יצק 2. מַסֵּכָה
Exd 32: 4 fashioned it . . and made a molten calf; 2
8 they have made for themselves a molten calf 2
34:17 You shall make for yourself no molten gods. 2
Lev 19: 4 Do not . . make for yourselves molten gods 2
Num33:52 destroy all their molten images 2
Deu 9:16 you had made yourselves a molten calf; 2
1Kg 7:16 made two capitals of molten bronze, to set upon 1
23 he made the molten sea; it was round, ten cubits 1
2Ch 4: 2 Then he made the molten sea; it was round 1
Neh 9:18 Even when they had made . . a molten calf and said 2
Job 37:18 spread out the skies, hard as a molten mirror? 1

molten *See also* image.

moment 1. בלע 2. מעט 3. פַּעַם 4. פֶּתַע 5. רגע
6. רֶגַע 7. שָׁעָה (A) 8. *ἄτομος* 9. *καιρός* 10. *ὀλίγος*
11. *ὅς* 12. *πάρειμι* 13. *ῥοπή* 14. *στιγμή* 15. *τότε*
16. *ὥρα* 17. pungo
Exd 33: 5 if for a single moment I should go up among you 6
Num 4:20 look upon the holy things even for a moment 1
16:21 that I may consume them in a moment. 6
45 Get away . . that I may consume them in a moment. 6
Rut 2: 7 she has . . without resting even for a moment. 2
Ezr 9: 8 now for a brief moment favor has been shown 6
Job 20: 5 the joy of the godless but for a moment? 6
34:20 In a moment they die; 6
Ps 6:10 shall turn back, and be put to shame in a moment. 6
30: 5 For his anger is but for a moment 6
73:19 How they are destroyed in a moment 6
Prv 6:15 in a moment he will be broken beyond healing. 4
12:19 but a lying tongue is but for a moment. 5
Isa 47: 9 These two things shall come to you in a moment 6
54: 7 For a brief moment I forsook you 6
8 In overflowing wrath for a moment I hid my face 6
66: 8 Shall a nation be brought forth in one moment? 3
Jer 4:20 my tents are destroyed, my curtains in a moment. 6
Lam 4: 6 of Sodom, which was overthrown in a moment 6
Dan 4:19 Then Daniel . . was dismayed for a moment 7
Mat 8:13 And the servant was healed at that very moment. 16
26:16 from that moment he sought an opportunity 15
Lke 4: 5 the kingdoms of the world in a moment of time 14
1Co 15:52 in a moment, in the twinkling of an eye 8
Gal 2: 5 we did not yield submission even for a moment 16
Heb 12:11 For the moment all discipline seems painful 12
2Es 16:38 there will not be a moment's delay 17
Tob 3:17 At that very moment Tobit returned 9
Jdt 13: 9 after a moment she went out 10
14: 8 until the moment of her speaking to them. 11
AEs 10:11 came to the hour and moment and day of decision 9
Sir 3:31 at the moment of his falling he will find support. 9
18:24 moment of vengeance when he turns away his face. 9
40: 7 at the moment of his rescue he wakes up 9
2Mc 9:11 he was tortured with pain every moment. 14
3Mc 5:49 thought that this was their last moment of life 13

every moment 1. לִרְגָעִים
Job 7:18 every morning, and test him every moment? 1
Isa 27: 3 I, the LORD, am its keeper; every moment I water it 1
Ezk 26:16 sit upon the ground and tremble every moment 1
32:10 they shall tremble every moment 1

moment longer 1. *ἀκαριαῖος*
2Mc 6:25 for the sake of living a brief moment longer 1

right moment 1. *καιρός*
Sir 1:23 A patient man will endure until the right moment 1
24 He will hide his words until the right moment 1
20: 7 A wise man will be silent until the right moment 1
7 a braggart and fool goes beyond the right moment. 1

very moment 1. *ἐξαυτῆς*
Act 11:11 At that very moment three men arrived 1

momentary 1. *παραυτίκα*
2Co 4:17 this slight momentary affliction 1

monarch 1. *τύραννος*
Wis 6: 9 To you then, O monarchs, my words are directed 1
21 O monarchs over the peoples, honor wisdom 1
8:15 dread monarchs will be afraid of me 1
12:14 nor can any king or monarch confront thee 1
14:16 at the command of monarchs 1
17 men could not honor monarchs in their presence *

money 1. כֶּסֶף 2. כְּסַף (A) 3. *ἀργύριον* 4. *διάφορος*
5. *νόμισμα* 6. *τιμή* 7. *χαλκός* 8. *χρῆμα*
Gen 17:12 in your house, or bought with your money 1
13 he that is bought with your money 1
23 born in his house or bought with his money 1
27 those bought with money from a foreigner 1
31:15 he has been using up the money given for us. 1
42:25 to replace every man's money in his sack 1
27 he saw his money in the mouth of his sack; 1
28 said to his brothers, "My money has been put back; 1
35 every man's bundle of money was in his sack; 1
35 every man's bundle of money was in his sack; 1
43:12 Take double the money with you; 1
12 carry back with you the money that was returned 1
15 took double the money with them, and Benjamin; 1
18 and they said, "It is because of the money 1
21 and there was every man's money in the mouth of his 1
21 in the mouth of his sack, our money in full weight; 1
22 we have brought other money down in our hand 1
22 We do not know who put our money in our sacks. 1
23 I received your money. 1
44: 1 and put each man's money in the mouth of his sack 1
2 put my cup . . with his money for the grain. 1
8 Behold, the money which we found in the mouth 1
47:14 Joseph gathered up all the money that was found 1
14 Joseph brought the money into Pharaoh's house. 1
15 when the money was all spent in the land of Egypt 1
15 Give us food . . For our money is gone. 1
16 exchange for your cattle, if your money is gone. 1
18 We will not hide . . that our money is all spent; 1
Exd 12:44 every slave that is bought for money may eat of it 1
21:11 go out for nothing, without payment of money. 1
21 to be punished; for the slave is his money. 1
34 he shall give money to its owner 1
22: 7 If a man delivers to his neighbor money or goods 1
17 he shall pay money equivalent to the marriage 1
25 If you lend money to any of my people with you who 1
30:16 you shall take the atonement money 1
Lev 22:11 if a priest buys a slave as his property for money 1
25:37 You shall not lend him your money at interest 1
27:15 he shall add a fifth of the valuation in money 1
19 he shall add a fifth of the valuation in money 1
Num 3:48 give the money by which the excess number of them 1
49 Moses took the redemption money from those 1
50 he took the money, 1,365 shekels 1
51 gave the redemption money to Aaron and his sons 1
Deu 2: 6 purchase food from them for money, that you may eat 1
6 buy water of them for money, that you may drink. 1
28 You shall sell me food for money, that I may eat 1
28 You . . give me water for money, that I may drink; 1
14:25 then you shall turn it into money, and bind up 1
25 money, and bind up the money in your hand, and go 1
26 spend the money for whatever you desire, oxen 1
21:14 not sell her for money, you shall not treat her 1
23:19 interest on money, interest on victuals 1
Jdg 16:18 came up . . and brought the money in their hands. 1
17: 4 when he restored the money to his mother 1
1Kg 21: 2 I will give you its value in money. 1
6 Give me your vineyard for money; 1
15 which he refused to give you for money; 1
2Kg 5:26 to accept money and garments, olive orchards 1
12: 4 All the money of the holy things which is brought 1
4 the money for which each man is assessed 1
4 -the money from the assessment of persons- 1
4 the money which a man's heart prompts him to bring 1
7 take no more money from your acquaintances 1
8 they should take no more money from the people 1
9 put in it all the money . . brought into the house 1
10 they saw that there was much money in the chest 1
10 counted and tied up . . the money that was found 1
11 they would give the money that was weighed out 1
13 from the money that was brought into the house 1
15 the men into whose hand they delivered the money 1
16 The money from the guilt offerings and . . the sin 1
16 the money from the sin offerings was not brought 1
15:20 Men'ahem exacted the money from Israel 1
22: 4 the money which has been brought into the house 1
7 no accounting shall be asked . . for the money 1
9 Your servants have emptied out the money 1
23:35 he taxed the land to give the money 1
2Ch 24: 5 gather from all Israel money to repair 1
11 when they saw that there was much money in it 1
11 and collected money in abundance. 1
14 brought the rest of the money before the king 1
34: 9 delivered the money that had been brought 1
14 bringing out the money that had been brought 1
17 emptied out the money that was found in the house 1
Ezr 3: 7 gave money to the masons and the carpenters 1
7:17 With this money, then, you shall . . buy bulls 2
Neh 5: 4 We have borrowed money for the king's tax 1
10 Moreover I . . lending them money and grain. 1
11 Return . . 100th of money, grain, wine, and oil 1
Est 3:11 The money is given to you, the people also, 1
4: 7 and the exact sum of money that Haman had 1
Ps 15: 5 who does not put out his money at interest 1
Prv 7:20 he took a bag of money with him; 1
Ecc 5:10 He who loves money will not be satisfied 1
10 who loves money will not be satisfied with money; 1
7:12 For . . wisdom is like the protection of money; 1
10:19 wine gladdens . . and money answers everything. 1
Isa 43:24 You have not bought me sweet cane with money 1
52: 3 and you shall be redeemed without money. 1
55: 1 and he who has no money, come, buy and eat! 1
1 Come, buy wine and milk without money 1
2 Why do you spend your money for that which is not 1
Jer 32: 9 weighed out the money to him, seventeen shekels 1
10 got witnesses, and weighed the money on scales. 1
25 Buy the field for money and get witnesses 1
44 Fields shall be bought for money 1
Mic 3:11 its prophets divine for money; 1
Mat 22:19 Show me the money for the tax. 5
25:18 dug in the ground and hid his master's money. 3
27 to have invested my money with the bankers 3
27: 6 since they are blood money. 6
28:12 counsel, they gave a sum of money to the soldiers 3
15 they took the money and did as they were directed; 3
Mrk 6: 8 a staff; no bread, no bag, no money in their belts; 7
12:41 the multitude putting money into the treasury. 7
14:11 they were glad, and promised to give him money. 3
Lke 9: 3 no staff, nor bag, nor bread, nor money 3
19:15 these servants, to whom he had given the money 3
23 Why then did you not put my money into the bank 3
22: 5 they were glad, and engaged to give him money. 3
Act 4:37 brought the money 8
8:18 he offered them money 8
20 you could obtain the gift of God with money! 8
24:26 he hoped that money would be given him by Paul 8
1Es 5:54 they gave money to the masons and the carpenters 3
Tob 4: 1 the money which he had left in trust with Gabael 3
2 explain to him about the money before I die? *
5: 2 how can I obtain the money 3
3 go and get the money. 3
18 Do not add money to money 3
18 Do not add money to money 3
9: 2 go to Gabael at Rages in Media and get the money 3
10: 2 there is no one to give him the money? 3
10 half of his property in slaves, cattle, and money. 3
12: 3 he obtained the money for me 3
Sir 7:18 Do not exchange a friend for money 4
21: 8 who builds his house with other people's money 8
29: 5 in speaking of his neighbor's money 8
6 the borrower has robbed him of his money 8
31: 5 he who pursues money will be led astray by it. 4
51:25 Get these things for yourselves without money. 3
Bar 1: 6 they collected money, each giving what he could; 3
10 Herewith we send you money; so buy with the money 3
10 buy with the money burnt offerings 3
LJr 1:28 The priests . . use the money *
35 they are not able to give either wealth or money; 7
1Mc 3:29 saw that the money in the treasury was exhausted 3
8:26 not give or supply grain, arms, money, or ships 3
28 shall be given no grain, arms, money, or ships 3
13:15 the money that Jonathan your brother owed 3
17 he sent to get the money and the sons 3
18 Because Simon did not send him the money 3
15: 6 mint your own coinage as money for your country 5
2Mc 3: 7 he told him of the money 8
7 to effect the removal of the aforesaid money. 8
11 also some money of Hyrcanus, son of Tobias *
13 this money must in any case be confiscated *
4: 1 who had informed about the money 8
19 Those who carried the money *
20 this money was intended . . for . . Hercules *
23 to carry the money to the king 8
27 any of the money promised to the king. 8
8:25 the money of those who had come to buy them 8
10:21 having sold their brethren for money 3
3Mc 2:32 by paying money in exchange for life 8
4Mc 3:20 had both appropriated money to them 8
4:10 going up with his armed forces to seize the money 8

money *See also* bag, borrow, box, earn, free, get, love, lover, piece, sum.

money for redemption 1. גְּאֻלָּה
Lev 25:52 he shall refund the money for his redemption 1

money to the king 1. *βασιλικός*
1Mc 10:43 because he owes money to the king or has any debt 1

tribute money 1. *φόρος*
1Mc 15:30 tribute money of the places which you have conquered 1
31 the tribute money of the cities 1

money-changer 1. *κερματιστής* 2. *κολλυβιστής*
Mat 21:12 and he overturned the tables of the money-changers 2
Mrk 11:15 he overturned the tables of the money-changers 2
Joh 2:14 and the money-changers at their business. 1
15 and he poured out the coins of the money-changers 2

money-hungry 1. *φιλαργυρέω*

2Mc 10:20 the men with Simon, who were money-hungry 1

money-making 1. *πορισμός*

Wis 13:19 money-making and work and success with his hands 1

money-value 1. כֶּסֶף

Lev 27:18 then the priest shall compute the money-value 1

moneylender 1. *δανειστής*

Sir 29:28 the reproach of the moneylender. 1

mongrel 1. מַמְזֵר

Zec 9: 6 a mongrel people shall dwell in Ashdod; 1

monster 1. תַּנִּין 2. monstrum

Jer 51:34 he has swallowed me like a monster; 1
2Es 5: 8 menstruous women shall bring forth monsters. 2

monster *See also* sea.

huge sea monster 1. *κῆτος*

3Mc 6: 8 in the belly of a huge, sea-born monster 1

monstrous 1. *ἄπλατος* 2. *τέρας*

Wis 17:15 now were driven by monstrous specters 2
3Mc 4:11 had been built with a monstrous perimeter wall 1

month 1. חֹדֶשׁ 2. יֶרַח 3. יֶרַח יָמִים 4. יְרַח (A) 5. *μήν* 6. mensis

Gen 7:11 in the second month, on the seventeenth day 1
11 on the seventeenth day of the month 1
8: 4 in the seventh month, on the seventeenth day 1
4 on the seventeenth day of the month 1
5 to abate until the tenth month; 1
5 in the tenth month, on the first day of the month 1
5 in the tenth month, on the first day of the month 1
13 In the 601st year, in the first month 1
13 the first day of the month, the waters were dried 1
14 In the second month, on the 27th day of the month 1
14 In the second month, on the 27th day of the month 1
29:14 And he stayed with him a month. 1
38:24 About three months later Judah was told 1
Exd 2: 2 he was a goodly child, she hid him three months. 2
12: 2 This month shall be for you the beginning 1
2 month shall be for you the beginning of months; 1
2 it shall be the first month of the year for you. 1
3 on the tenth day of this month they shall take 1
6 keep it until the fourteenth day of this month 1
18 on the fourteenth day of the month at evening 1
18 so until the twenty-first day of the month 1
13: 4 This day you are to go forth, in the month of Abib. 1
5 you shall keep this service in this month. 1
16: 1 on the fifteenth day of the second month 1
23:15 at the appointed time in the month of Abib 1
34:18 at the time appointed in the month Abib; 1
18 for in the month Abib you came out from Egypt. 1
40: 2 On the first day of the first month you shall 1
17 And in the first month in the second year 1
17 second year, on the first day of the month 1
Lev 16:29 in the seventh month, on the tenth day of the month 1
29 in the seventh month, on the tenth day of the month 1
23: 5 the first month, on the fourteenth day of the month 1
5 on the fourteenth day of the month in the evening 1
6 fifteenth day of the same month is the feast 1
24 In the seventh month, on the first day of the month 1
24 In the seventh month, on the first day of the month 1
27 On the tenth day of this seventh month is the day 1
32 on the ninth day of the month beginning at evening 1
34 On the fifteenth day of this seventh month 1
39 On the fifteenth day of the seventh month 1
41 you shall keep it in the seventh month 1
25: 9 on the tenth day of the seventh month 1
27: 6 If the person is from a month old up to five years 1
Num 1: 1 on the first day of the second month 1
18 on the first day of the second month 1
3:15 every male from a month old and upward you shall 1
22 all the males from a month old and upward was 7,500 1
28 males, from a month old and upward . . were 8,600 1
34 males from a month old and upward was 6,200. 1
39 all the males from a month old and upward 1
40 all the first-born males . . from a month old 1
43 first-born males . . from a month old and upward 1
9: 1 in the first month of the second year after 1
3 fourteenth day of this month, in the evening 1
5 they kept the passover in the first month •
5 first month, on the fourteenth day of the month 1
11 In the second month on the fourteenth day 1
22 Whether it was two days, or a month, or a longer time 1
10:10 feasts, and at the beginnings of your months 1
11 In the second year, in the second month 1
11 second month, on the twentieth day of the month 1
11:20 a whole month, until it comes out at your nostrils 1
21 give them meat, that they may eat a whole month!' 1
18:16 (at a month old you shall redeem them) 1
20: 1 into the wilderness of Zin in the first month 1
26:62 23,000, every male from a month old and upward; 1
28:11 At the beginnings of your months you shall offer 1
14 this is the burnt offering of each month 1
14 offering . . throughout the months of the year. 1
16 fourteenth day of the first month is the LORD'S 1
17 on the fifteenth day of this month is a feast; 1
29: 1 On the first day of the seventh month 1
7 On the tenth day of this seventh month 1
12 On the fifteenth day of the seventh month 1
33: 3 They set out from Ram'eses in the first month 1
3 set out . . the fifteenth day of the first month; 1
38 died . . on the first day of the fifth month. 1
Deu 1: 3 year, on the first day of the eleventh month 1
16: 1 Observe the month of Abib, and keep the passover 1
1 in the month of Abib the LORD your God brought you 1
21:13 shall remain in your house and bewail . . a full month; 2
33:14 with the . . rich yield of the months 2
Jos 4:19 people came . . on the tenth day of the first month 1
5:10 passover on the fourteenth day of the month 1
Jdg 11:37 let me alone two months, that I may go and wander 1
38 And he sent her away for two months; 1
39 at the end of two months, she returned to her 1
19: 2 at Bethlehem . . and was there some four months. 1
20:47 and abode at the rock of Rimmon four months. 1
1Sm 6: 1 in the country of the Philistines seven months. 1
20:34 and ate no food the second day of the month 1
27: 7 number of the days . . was a year and four months. 1
2Sm 2:11 the time that . . was seven years and six months. 1
5: 5 he reigned over Judah seven years and six months 1
6:11 the ark of the LORD remained . . three months; 1
24: 8 at the end of nine months and twenty days. 1
13 Or will you flee three months before your foes 1
1Kg 4: 7 each . . had to make provision for one month 1
27 officers supplied . . each one in his month; they 1
5:14 he sent them to Lebanon, 10,000 a month in relays; 1
14 be a month in Lebanon and two months at home; 1
14 be a month in Lebanon and two months at home; 1
6: 1 in the fourth year . . in the month of Ziv 1
1 in the month of Ziv, which is the second month 1
37 the foundation . . was laid, in the month of Ziv. 2
38 in the month of Bul, which is the eighth month 1
38 in the month of Bul, which is the eighth month 1
8: 2 feast in the month Eth'anim, which is the seventh 2
2 the month Eth'anim, which is the seventh month. 1
11:16 Jo'ab and all Israel remained there six months 1
12:32 a feast on the fifteenth day of the eighth month 1
33 on the fifteenth day in the eighth month 1
33 eighth month, in the month which he had devised 1
2Kg 15: 8 reigned over Israel in Sama'ria six months. 1
13 Shallum . . and he reigned one month in Sama'ria. 3
23:31 and he reigned three months in Jerusalem. 1
24: 8 Jehoi'achin . . and he reigned three months 1
25: 1 in the ninth year of his reign, in the tenth month 1
1 in the tenth month, on the tenth day of the month 1
3 On the ninth day of the fourth month the famine 1
8 In the fifth month, on the seventh day of the month 1
8 In the fifth month, on the seventh day of the month 1
25 in the seventh month, Ish'mael . . came with ten men 1
27 in the 37th year . . in the twelfth month 1
27 in the twelfth month, on the 27th day of the month 1
1Ch 3: 4 where he reigned for seven years and six months. 1
12:15 the men who crossed the Jordan in the first month 1
13:14 in his house three months 1
21:12 or three months of devastation by your foes 1
27: 1 and went, month after month throughout the year 1
1 and went, month after month throughout the year 1
2 charge of the first division in the first month; 1
3 of all the commanders . . for the first month. 1
4 in charge of the division of the second month; 1
5 third commander, for the third month, was Benai'ah 1
7 As'ahel . . was fourth, for the fourth month 1
8 commander, for the fifth month, was Shamhuth 1
9 Sixth, for the sixth month, was Ira, the son 1
10 Seventh, for the seventh month, was Helez 1
11 Eighth, for the eighth month, was Sib'becai 1
12 Ninth, for the ninth month, was Abi-e'zer 1
13 Tenth, for the tenth month, was Ma'harai 1
14 Eleventh, for the eleventh month, was Benai'ah 1
15 Twelfth, for the twelfth month, was Heldai 1
2Ch 3: 2 He began to build in the second month 1
5: 3 at the feast which is in the seventh month. 1
7:10 On the 23rd day of the seventh month he 1
15:10 in the third month of the fifteenth year 1
29: 3 In the first year of his reign, in the first month 1
17 to sanctify on the first day of the first month 1
17 and on the eighth day of the month they came 1
17 on the sixteenth day of the first month 1
30: 2 to keep the passover in the second month 1
13 feast of unleavened bread in the second month 1
15 on the fourteenth day of the second month. 1
31: 7 In the third month they began to pile up the heaps 1
7 finished them in the seventh month. 1
35: 1 lamb on the fourteenth day of the first month. 1
36: 2 he reigned three months in Jerusalem. 1
9 reigned three months and ten days in Jerusalem. 1
Ezr 3: 1 When the seventh month came 1
6 From the first day of the seventh month 1
8 in the second year . . in the second month 1
6:15 finished on the third day of the month of Adar 4
19 On the fourteenth day of the first month 1
7: 8 came to Jerusalem in the fifth month 1
9 first day of the first month he began to go up 1
9 first day of the fifth month he came to Jerusalem 1
8:31 twelfth day of the first month, to go to Jerusalem; 1
10: 9 ninth month, on the twentieth day of the month. 1
9 ninth month, on the twentieth day of the month. 1
16 On the first day of the tenth month they sat down 1
17 by the first day of the first month they had come 1
Neh 1: 1 Now it happened in the month of Chislev 1
2: 1 month of Nisan, in the twentieth year of King 1
6:15 finished . . 25th day of the month Elul •
7:73 seventh month had come, the children of Israel 1
8: 2 on the first day of the seventh month. 1
14 booths during the feast of the seventh month 1
9: 1 Now on the 24th day of this month 1
Est 2:12 being twelve months under the regulations 1
12 six months with oil of myrrh and six . . with spices 1
12 six months with spices and ointments for women- 1
16 taken . . into his royal palace in the tenth month 1
16 in the tenth month, which is the month of Tebeth 1
3: 7 In the first month, which is the month of Nisan 1
7 In the first month, which is the month of Nisan 1
7 cast it month after month till the twelfth month 1
7 cast it month after month till the twelfth month 1
7 cast it month after month till the twelfth month 1
7 the twelfth month, which is the month of Adar. •
12 summoned on the thirteenth day of the first month 1
13 in one day, the thirteenth day of the twelfth month 1
13 of the twelfth month, which is the month of Adar 1
8: 9 summoned at that time, in the third month, 1
9 in the third month, which is the month of Sivan 1
12 on the thirteenth day of the twelfth month 1
12 of the twelfth month, which is the month of Adar. 1
9: 1 in the twelfth month, which is the month of Adar 1
1 in the twelfth month, which is the month of Adar 1
15 also on the fourteenth day of the month of Adar 1
17 was on the thirteenth day of the month of Adar 1
19 hold the fourteenth day of the month of Adar 1
21 keep the fourteenth day of the month Adar 1
22 and as the month that had been turned for them 1
Job 3: 6 let it not come into the number of the months. 2
7: 3 I am allotted months of emptiness 2
14: 5 the number of his months is with thee 1
21:21 when the number of their months is cut off? 1
29: 2 Oh, that I were as in the months of old 2
39: 2 Can you number the months that they fulfil 2
Jer 1: 3 the captivity of Jerusalem in the fifth month. 1
2:24 in her month they will find her. 1
28: 1 in the fifth month of the fourth year, Hanani'ah 1
17 In that same year, in the seventh month 1
36: 9 the fifth year of Jehoi'akim . . in the ninth month 1
22 It was the ninth month, and the king was sitting 1
39: 1 Zedeki'ah king of Judah, in the tenth month 1
2 in the fourth month, on the ninth day of the month 1
2 in the fourth month, on the ninth day of the month 1
41: 1 In the seventh month, Ish'mael . . came 1
52: 4 in the ninth year of his reign, in the tenth month 1
4 tenth month, on the tenth day of the month 1
6 On the ninth day of the fourth month the famine 1
12 In the fifth month, on the tenth day 1
12 the fifth month, on the tenth day of the month 1
31 in the twelfth month, on the 25th day 1
31 on the 25th day of the month 1
Ezk 1: 1 In the 30th year, in the fourth month 1
1 in the fourth month, on the fifth day of the month 1
2 On the fifth day of the month (it was the fifth year 1
8: 1 In the sixth year, in the sixth month 1
1 in the sixth month, on the fifth day of the month 1
20: 1 In the seventh year, in the fifth month 1
1 the fifth month, on the tenth day of the month 1
24: 1 In the ninth year, in the tenth month, on the tenth 1
1 in the tenth month, on the tenth day of the month 1
26: 1 In the eleventh year, on the first day of the month 1
29: 1 In the tenth year, in the tenth month 1
1 the tenth month, on the twelfth day of the month 1
17 in the first month, on the first day of the month 1
17 in the first month, on the first day of the month 1
30:20 In the eleventh year, in the first month 1
20 the first month, on the seventh day of the month 1
31: 1 In the eleventh year, in the third month 1
1 in the third month, on the first day of the month 1
32: 1 In the twelfth year, in the twelfth month 1
1 in the twelfth month, on the first day of the month 1
17 In the twelfth year, in the first month 1
17 on the fifteenth day of the month 1
33:21 in the tenth month, on the fifth day of the month 1
21 in the tenth month, on the fifth day of the month 1
39:12 For seven months the house of Israel will be 1
14 at the end of seven months they will make their 1
40: 1 on the tenth day of the month 1
45:18 In the first month, on the first day of the month •
18 In the first month, on the first day of the month 1
20 shall do the same on the seventh day of the month 1
21 first month, on the fourteenth day of the month •
21 first month, on the fourteenth day of the month 1
25 seventh month, on the fifteenth day of the month •
25 seventh month, on the fifteenth day of the month 1
47:12 they will bear fresh fruit every month 1
Dan 4:29 end of twelve months he was walking on the roof 4
10: 4 On the 24th day of the first month 1
Ams 4: 7 when there were yet three months to the harvest; 1

Hag 1: 1 in the sixth month, on the first day of the month 1
1 in the sixth month, on the first day of the month 1
15 on the 24th day of the month, in the sixth month 1
15 day of the month, in the sixth month. *
2: 1 in the seventh month, on the 21st day of the month *
1 in the seventh month, on the 21st day of the month 1
10 On the 24th day of the ninth month *
18 from the 24th day of the ninth month. *
20 on the 24th day of the month 1
Zec 1: 1 In the eighth month, in the second year of Darius 1
7 On the 24th day of the eleventh month 1
7 the eleventh month which is the month of Shebat 1
7: 1 fourth day of the ninth month, which is Chislev. 1
3 Should I mourn and fast in the fifth month 1
5 and mourned in the fifth month and in the seventh *
8:19 fast of the fourth month, and the fast of the fifth 1
11: 8 In one month I destroyed the three shepherds. 2
Lke 1:24 for five months she hid herself, saying 5
26 In the sixth month the angel Gabriel was sent 5
36 the sixth month with her who was called barren. 5
56 Mary remained with her about three months 5
4:25 the heaven was shut up three years and six months 5
Act 7:20 brought up for three months in his father's house; 5
18:11 he stayed a year and six months 5
19: 8 and for three months spoke boldly 5
20: 3 There he spent three months 5
28:11 After three months we set sail 5
Gal 4:10 You observe days, and months, and seasons 5
Jas 5:17 for three years and six months it did not rain 5
Rev 9: 5 were allowed to torture them for five months 5
10 their power of hurting men for five months lies 5
15 ready for the hour, the day, the month, and the year 5
11: 2 they will trample over the holy city for 42 months. 5
13: 5 it was allowed to exercise authority for 42 months; 5
22: 2 tree of life . . yielding its fruit each month; 5
1Es 1: 1 the fourteenth day of the first month 5
35 he reigned three months in Judah and Jerusalem. 5
44 reigned three months and ten days in Jerusalem. 5
5: 6 in the month of Nisan, the first month. 5
6 in the month of Nisan, the first month. 5
47 When the seventh month came 5
53 from the new moon of the seventh month 5
56 in the second month 5
57 new moon of the second month in the second year 5
7: 5 the 23rd day of the month of Adar 5
10 the fourteenth day of the first month 5
8: 6 the fifth month (this was the king's seventh year); 5
6 left Babylon on the new moon of the first month 5
6 arrived . . on the new moon of the fifth month 5
61 on the twelfth day of the first month 5
9: 5 this was the ninth month 5
5 on the twentieth day of the month. 5
16 on the new moon of the tenth month 5
17 the new moon of the first month. 5
37 On the new moon of the seventh month 5
40 on the new moon of the seventh month. 5
2Es 4:40 when her nine months have been completed 6
6:21 premature children at three and four months 6
8: 8 and for nine months the womb 6
16:38 Just as a woman with child, in the ninth month 6
Jdt 2: 1 on the 22nd day of the first month 5
8: 4 three years and four months. 5
16:20 before the sanctuary for three months 5
AEs 10:13 observe these days in the month of Adar 5
13 on the fourteenth and fifteenth of that month 5
13: 6 on the fourteenth day of the twelfth month 5
16:20 the thirteenth day of the twelfth month, Adar 5
Sir 43: 8 The month is named for the moon 5
Bar 1: 2 in the fifth year, on the seventh day of the month 5
1Mc 1:58 those found month after month in the cities. 5
58 those found month after month in the cities. 5
59 And on the 25th day of the month 5
4:52 on the 25th day of the ninth month 5
52 the ninth month, which is the month of Chislev 5
59 the 25th day of the month of Chislev. 5
7:43 on the thirteenth day of the month of Adar 5
9: 3 In the first month of the 152nd year 5
54 In the 153rd year, in the second month 5
10:21 in the seventh month 5
13:51 the 23rd day of the second month, in the 171st year 5
16:14 his sons, in the 177th year, in the eleventh month 5
14 the eleventh month, which is the month of Shebat. 5
2Mc 1: 9 in the month of Chislev, in the 188 year. 5
7:27 I carried you nine months in my womb 5
10: 5 on the 25th day of the same month 5
15:36 the thirteenth day of the twelfth month 5

first month 1. רִאשׁוֹן
Exd 12:18 In the first month, on the fourteenth day 1

whole month 1. *μὴν ἡμερῶν*
Jdt 3:10 and remained for a whole month 1

monthly 1. *κατὰ μῆνα*
2Mc 6: 7 the monthly celebration of the king's birthday 1

months *See* three.

monument 1. יָד 2. צִיּוּן 3. *μνημεῖον*
1Sm 15:12 he set up a monument for himself and turned 1
2Sm 18:18 and it is called Ab'salom's monument to this day. 1
2Kg 23:17 Then he said, "What is yonder monument that I see? 2
1Ch 18: 3 to set up his monument at the river Euphra'tes. 1
Isa 56: 5 within my walls a monument and a name better 1
Mat 23:29 adorn the monuments of the righteous 3
Wis 10: 7 standing as a monument to an unbelieving soul. 3
1Mc 13:27 Simon built a monument over the tomb of his father *

monument of victory 1. *τρόπαιον*
2Mc 15: 6 a public monument of victory over Judas and his men 1

moon 1. יָרֵחַ 2. יֶרַע 3. לְבָנָה 4. *σελήνη* 5. luna
Gen 37: 9 behold, the sun, the moon, and eleven stars were 2
Deu 4:19 when you see the sun and the moon and the stars 1
17: 3 worshipped . . sun or the moon or any of the host 2
Jos 10:12 Sun, stand . . and thou Moon in the valley 2
13 And the sun stood still, and the moon stayed 2
2Kg 23: 5 burned incense to Ba'al, to the sun, and the moon 2
Job 25: 5 Behold, even the moon is not bright 2
26: 9 He covers the face of the moon *
31:26 sun when it shone, or the moon moving in splendor 2
Ps 8: 3 moon and the stars which thou hast established; 2
72: 5 as long as the moon, throughout all generations! 1
7 and peace abound, till the moon be no more! 2
89:37 Like the moon it shall be established for ever; 2
104:19 Thou hast made the moon to mark the seasons; 1
121: 6 not smite you by day, nor the moon by night. 1
136: 9 the moon and stars to rule over the night 2
148: 3 Praise him, sun and moon 2
Ecc 12: 2 the light and the moon and the stars are darkened 2
Sng 6:10 that looks forth like the dawn, fair as the moon 3
Isa 13:10 and the moon will not shed its light. 2
24:23 moon will be confounded, and the sun ashamed; 3
30:26 light of the moon will be as the light of the sun 3
60:19 nor for brightness shall the moon give light 2
20 no more go down, nor your moon withdraw itself; 1
Jer 8: 2 they shall be spread before the sun and the moon 2
31:35 fixed order of the moon and the stars for light 2
Ezk 32: 7 the moon shall not give its light. 1
Jol 2:10 The sun and the moon are darkened 2
31 The sun . . to darkness, and the moon to blood 2
3:15 The sun and the moon are darkened 2
Hab 3:11 The sun and moon stood still in their habitation 2
Mat 24:29 the moon will not give its light 4
Mrk 13:24 the moon will not give its light 4
Lke 21:25 there will be signs in sun and moon and stars 4
Act 2:20 the moon into blood 4
1Co 15:41 one glory of the sun, and another glory of the moon 4
Rev 6:12 the full moon became like blood 4
8:12 third of the sun was struck, and a third of the moon 4
12: 1 clothed with the sun, with the moon under her feet 4
21:23 the city has no need of sun or moon to shine upon it 4
2Es 5: 4 and the moon during the day. 5
6:45 the light of the moon 5
7:39 a day that has no sun or moon or stars 5
Sir 27:11 the fool changes like the moon. 4
43: 6 He made the moon also 4
7 From the moon comes the sign for feast days 4
8 The month is named for the moon *
50: 6 like the moon when it is full; 4
LJr 1:60 sun and moon and stars . . are obedient. 4
67 shine like the sun or give light like the moon. 4
Aza 1:40 Bless the Lord, sun and moon 4
4Mc 17: 5 The moon in heaven, with the stars 4

moon *See also* day.

moon at the full 1. *διχομηνία*
Sir 39:12 I am filled, like the moon at the full. 1

full moon 1. כֶּסֶא
Ps 81: 3 Blow the trumpet at the new moon, at the full moon 1
Prv 7:20 at full moon he will come home. 1

new moon 1. חדשׁ 2. חֹדֶשׁ 3. *νεομηνία* 4. neomenia
Exd 19: 1 On the third new moon after the people of Israel 2
Num29: 6 besides the burnt offering of the new moon 2
1Sm 20: 5 tomorrow is the new moon, and I should not fail 2
18 Tomorrow is the new moon; and you will be missed 2
24 when the new moon came, the king sat down to eat 2
27 on the second day, the morrow after the new moon 2
2Kg 4:23 Why . . today? It is neither new moon nor sabbath. 2
1Ch 23:31 to the LORD on sabbaths, new moons, and feast days 2
2Ch 2: 4 offerings . . on the sabbaths and the new moons 2
8:13 commandment . . for the sabbaths, the new moons 2
31: 3 burnt offerings for the sabbaths, the new moons 2
Ezr 3: 5 offerings at the new moon and . . appointed feasts 2
Neh 10:33 sabbaths, the new moons, the appointed feasts 2
Ps 81: 3 Blow the trumpet at the new moon, at the full moon 2
Isa 1:13 New moon and sabbath and . . assemblies 2
14 Your new moons and your . . feasts my soul hates; 2
47:13 who at the new moons predict what shall befall 2
66:23 From new moon to new moon, and from sabbath 2
23 new moon to new moon, and from sabbath to sabbath 1
23 new moon to new moon, and from sabbath to sabbath 2
Ezk 45:17 and drink offerings, at the feasts, the new moons 2
46: 1 on the day of the new moon it shall be opened. 2
3 the LORD on the sabbaths and on the new moons. 2
6 day of the new moon he shall offer a young bull 2
Hos 2:11 her mirth, her feasts, her new moons, her sabbaths 2
5: 7 the new moon shall devour them with their fields. 2
Ams 8: 5 When will the new moon be over, that we may sell 2
Col 2:16 a festival or a new moon or a sabbath. 3
1Es 5:52 on sabbaths and at new moons 3
53 from the new moon of the seventh month 3
57 on the new moon of the second month 3
8: 6 left Babylon on the new moon of the first month 3
6 arrived . . on the new moon of the fifth month 3
9:16 on the new moon of the tenth month 3
17 the new moon of the first month. 3
37 On the new moon of the seventh month 3
40 on the new moon of the seventh month. 3
2Es 1:31 for I have rejected your feast days, and new moons 4
1Mc 10:34 sabbaths and new moons and appointed days 3

moor to the shore 1. *προσορμίζω*
Mrk 6:53 they came to land . . and moored to the shore. 1

moral 1. *ἦθος*
1Co 15:33 Bad company ruins good morals. 1

morale 1. *εὐθαρσής*
3Mc 1: 7 he strengthened the morale of his subjects. 1

morbid *See* craving.

more 1. גָּדוֹל 2. דָּבָר 3. הַרְבֵּה 4. טוֹב 5. יסף
6. יסף עוד 7. יתר 8. כֹּה 9. כֵּן 10. עַד 11. עוֹד 12. עַתָּה
13. רַב 14. רבה 15. רַבִּים 16. שֵׁנִי 17. עַל (A)
18. *ἄλλος* 19. *ἀπό* 20. *ἐν* 21. *ἕτερος* 22. *ἔτι*
23. *μᾶλλον* 24. *μέγας* 25. *ὅσος* 26. *παρά*
27. *περισσεύω* 28. *περισσός* 29. *περισσοτέρως*
30. *πικρός* 31. *πολύς* 32. *πρὸς ταῦτα* 33. *προστίθημι*
34. *τοσοῦτο* 35. adhuc 36. adhuc alius 37. alius
38. amplus 39. magis 40. magnus 41. multus
42. quamdiu 43. tanto magis 44. tantum
Gen 32:28 he said, "Your name shall no more be called Jacob 11
37: 5 to his brothers they only hated him the more. 11
8 yet more for his dreams and for his words. 5
38:26 She is more righteous than I, inasmuch as I did not †
44:23 you shall see my face no more.' 5
Exd 1:12 the more they were oppressed †
12 the more they multiplied 9
12 they multiplied and the more they spread abroad. 9
9:29 there will be no more hail, that you may know that 11
11: 1 Yet one plague more I will bring upon Pharaoh 11
16:17 Israel did so; they gathered, some more, some less. 14
30:15 The rich shall not give more, and the poor shall 14
36: 6 man nor woman do anything more for the offering 11
7 was sufficient to do all the work, and more. 7
Lev 13: 5 then the priest shall shut him up seven days more 16
33 shut up the person . . for seven days more 16
54 and he shall shut it up seven days more 16
17: 7 So they shall no more slay their sacrifices 11
Num 8:25 withdraw from the work . . and serve no more 11
11:25 they prophesied. But they did so no more. 5
18: 5 there be wrath no more upon the people of Israel. 11
20:19 let me only pass through on foot, nothing more. 2
22:15 princes, more in number and more honorable †
18 not go beyond the command . . to do less or more. 1
19 that I may know what more the LORD will say to me. 5
Deu 3:26 suffice you; speak no more to me of this matter. 5
5:22 words the LORD spoke . . and he added no more. *
25 if we hear the voice of the LORD our God any more 11
25: 3 Forty stripes may be given him, but not more; 5
Jos 5:12 and the people of Israel had manna no more 11
7:12 I will be with you no more, unless you destroy 5
10:11 were more who died because of the hailstones 15
22:33 Israel . . spoke no more of making war against *
Jdg 8:28 and they lifted up their heads no more. 5
10:13 other gods; therefore I will deliver you no more. 5
13:21 angel . . appeared no more to Mano'ah 6
Rut 1:17 May the LORD do so to me and more also if even death 5
4:15 who loves you, who is more to you than seven sons 4
1Sm 1: 8 why do you . . ? Am I not more to you than ten sons? 4
2: 3 Talk no more so very proudly 14
14:44 God do so to me and more also; you shall surely die 5
18: 8 and what more can he have but the kingdom? 11
29 Saul was still more afraid of David. 5
20:13 the LORD do so to Jonathan, and more also 5
25:22 God do so to David and more also 8
26:21 return, my son David, for I will no more do you harm 11
27: 4 it was told Saul . . he sought for him no more. 6
28:15 God . . turned away from me and answers me no more *
2Sm 2:28 all the men stopped, and pursued Israel no more 11
3: 9 God do so to Abner, and more also, if I do not 5
35 God do so to me and more also, if I taste bread 5
5:13 David took more concubines and wives 11
13 and more sons and daughters were born to David. 11
7:10 dwell in their own place, and be disturbed no more; 11
10 and violent men shall afflict them no more 5
20 And what more can David say to thee? 6
10:19 Syrians feared to help the Ammonites any more. 11
19:13 God do so to me, and more also, if you are not 5
29 Why speak any more of your affairs? I have decided 11

21:17 You shall no more go out with us to battle 11
1Kg 2:23 God do so to me and more also if this word does not 5
10: 5 there was no more spirit in her. 11
19: 2 So may the gods do to me, and more also, if I do not 5
20:10 The gods do so to me, and more also, if the dust 5
2Kg 2:12 And he saw him no more. 11
6:16 those . . with us are more than those..with them. 15
23 the Syrians came no more on raids into the land 6
31 May God do so to me, and more also, if the head 5
12: 7 take no more money from your acquaintances •
8 they should take no more money from the people •
1Ch 14: 3 David took more wives in Jerusalem 11
3 and David begot more sons and daughters. 11
17: 9 dwell in their own place, and be disturbed no more; 11
9 violent men shall waste them no more, as formerly 5
18 And what more can David say to thee 6
2Ch 9: 4 there was no more spirit in her. 11
15:19 there was no more war until the 35th year 10
33: 8 no more remove the foot of Israel from the land 5
23 but this Amon incurred guilt more and more. 14
23 but this Amon incurred guilt more and more. 14
Est 1:19 Vashti is to come no more before King Ahasu-e'rus •
6: 6 Whom would the king delight to honor more than me? 7
Job 7: 8 The eye of him who sees me will behold me no more; •
10 he returns no more to his house 11
20: 9 The eye which saw him will see him no more 5
27:19 He goes to bed rich, but will do so no more; 33
32:15 They are discomfited, they answer no more; 11
16 because they stand there, and answer no more? 11
34:31 borne chastisement; I will not offend any more; •
Ps 10:18 man who is of the earth may strike terror no more. 6
28: 5 he will break them down and build them up no more. •
69:26 whom thou hast wounded, they afflict still more. †
71:14 and will praise thee yet more and more. †
14 and will praise thee yet more and more. †
78:17 Yet they sinned still more against him 5
83: 4 let the name of Israel be remembered no more! 11
88: 5 like those whom thou dost remember no more 11
103:16 it is gone, and its place knows it no more. 11
104:35 let the wicked be no more! 11
123: 3 for we have had more than enough of contempt. 13
130: 6 more than watchmen for the morning. •
Prv 31: 7 drink and . . remember their misery no more. 11
Ecc 2: 7 and flocks, more than any who had been before me 3
9: 5 the dead know nothing, and . . have no more reward; 11
6 they have no more for ever any share in all that is 11
Isa 1:13 Bring no more vain offerings; 5
5: 4 What more was there to do for my vineyard 11
10:20 Jacob will no more lean upon him that smote them 6
15: 6 the new growth fails, the verdure is no more. •
23:12 You will no more exult, O . . daughter of Sidon; 11
24: 9 No more do they drink wine with singing; •
25: 2 the palace of aliens is a city no more •
26:21 disclose . . and will no more cover her slain. 11
29:22 Jacob shall no more be ashamed 12
22 no more shall his face grow pale. 12
30:19 who dwell at Jerusalem; you shall weep no more. •
32: 5 The fool will no more be called noble 11
33:19 You will see no more the insolent people •
38:11 I shall look upon man no more 11
47: 1 you shall no more be called tender and delicate. 5
5 for you shall no more be called the mistress 5
51:22 the bowl of my wrath you shall drink no more; 5
52: 1 shall no more come into you the uncircumcised 6
54: 4 of your widowhood you will remember no more. 11
9 waters of Noah should no more go over the earth 11
60:18 Violence shall no more be heard in your land 11
19 The sun shall be no more your light by day 11
20 Your sun shall no more go down 11
62: 4 You shall no more be termed Forsaken 11
4 and your land shall no more be termed Desolate; 11
65:19 no more shall be heard in it the sound of weeping 11
20 No more shall . . be in it an infant that lives 11
Jer 2:31 We are free, we will come no more to thee'? 11
3:16 in those days, says the LORD, they shall no more say 11
17 no more stubbornly follow their own evil heart. 11
7:32 when it will no more be called Topheth 11
11:19 that his name be remembered no more. 11
19: 6 when this place shall no more be called Topheth 11
22:10 he shall return no more to see his native land. 11
11 away from this place: "He shall return here no more 11
23: 4 and they shall fear no more, nor be dismayed 11
36 'the burden of the LORD' you shall mention no more 11
25:27 Drink, be drunk and vomit, fall and rise no more •
30: 8 strangers shall no more make servants of them. 11
31:12 and they shall languish no more. 6
34 and I will remember their sin no more. 11
42:18 You shall see this place no more. 11
44:26 that my name shall no more be invoked by the mouth 11
48: 2 the renown of Moab is no more. 11
49: 7 Is wisdom no more in Teman? Has counsel perished 11
10 his brothers, and his neighbors; and he is no more. •
50:39 she shall be peopled no more for ever 11
51:64 say, 'Thus shall Babylon sink, to rise no more •
Lam 4: 7 their bodies were more ruddy than coral †
Ezk 5:16 when I bring more and more famine upon you •
16 when I bring more and more famine upon you •
12:23 they shall no more use it as a proverb in Israel. 11
24 For there shall be no more any false vision 11
13:15 The wall is no more, nor those who daubed it •
21 they shall be no more in your hand as prey; 11
23 you shall no more see delusive visions •
14:11 that the house of Israel may go no more astray 11
11 nor defile themselves any more 11
16:41 you shall also give hire no more. 11
42 I will be calm, and will no more be angry. 11
18: 3 this proverb shall no more be used by you 11
19: 9 that his voice should no more be heard 11
20:39 but my holy name you shall no more profane 11
21:32 you shall be no more remembered; •
25:10 may be remembered no more among the nations •
26:13 the sound of your lyres shall be heard no more. 11
21 you shall be no more; though you be sought •
27:36 to a dreadful end and shall be no more for ever. •
28:19 to a dreadful end and shall be no more for ever. •
24 for . . Israel there shall be no more a brier 11
32:13 no foot of man shall trouble them any more •
34:28 They shall no more be a prey to the nations 11
29 shall no more be consumed with hunger in the land 11
43: 7 house of Israel shall no more defile my holy name 11
45: 8 my princes shall no more oppress my people; 11
Dan 3:19 seven times more than it was wont to be heated. 17
11: 2 Behold, three more kings shall arise in Persia; 11
Hos 1: 6 for I will no more have pity on the house of Israel 6
2:17 and they shall be mentioned by name no more. 11
4: 7 The more they increased, the more they sinned •
7 The more they increased, the more they sinned •
9:15 I will love them no more; 5
10: 1 The more his fruit increased †
11: 2 The more I called them, the more they went from me; •
2 The more I called them, the more they went from me; 9
14: 3 will say no more, 'Our God,' to the work of our hands. 11
Jol 2:19 and I will no more make you a reproach 11
Ams 5: 2 Fallen, no more to rise, is the virgin Israel; 5
Jon 1:11 For the sea grew more and more tempestuous. •
11 For the sea grew more and more tempestuous. •
13 for the sea grew more and more tempestuous •
13 for the sea grew more and more tempestuous •
Mic 5:12 and you shall have no more soothsayers; •
13 shall bow down no more to the work of your hands; 11
Nah 1:12 I have afflicted you, I will afflict you no more. 11
14 No more shall your name be perpetuated; 11
2:13 voice of your messengers shall no more be heard. 11
Zep 3:15 you shall fear evil no more. 11
Zec 13: 2 so that they shall be remembered no more; 11
14:11 inhabited, for there shall be no more curse; 11
Mat 5:37 simply 'Yes' or 'No'; anything more than this comes 28
47 what more are you doing than others? Do not even 28
6:25 put on. Is not life more than food, and the body 31
25 than food, and the body more than clothing? •
26 them. Are you not of more value than they? 23
30 will he not much more clothe you, O men 23
7:11 how much more will your Father who is in heaven 23
10:25 how much more will they malign 23
11: 9 Yes, I tell you, and more than a prophet. 28
13:12 For to him who has will more be given •
18:13 rejoices over it more than over the 99 23
20:10 they thought they would receive more 31
31 but they cried out the more 24
21:36 Again he sent other servants, more than the first; 31
25:16 he made five talents more. 18
17 he who had the two talents made two talents more. 18
20 bringing five talents more, saying 18
20 here I have made five talents more.' 18
22 here I have made two talents more.' 18
29 For to every one who has will more be given •
26:53 he will at once send me more than twelve legions 31
Mrk 4:25 For to him who has will more be given •
7:36 the more he charged them 25
36 the more zealously they proclaimed it. 23
10:48 he cried out all the more, "Son of David, have mercy 23
12:43 this poor widow has put in more than all 31
Lke 3:13 Collect no more than is appointed you. 31
7:26 Yes, I tell you, and more than a prophet. 28
42 Now which of them will love him more? 31
43 The one, I suppose, to whom he forgave more. 31
8:18 to him who has will more be given •
9:13 We have no more than five loaves and two fish 31
11:13 how much more will the heavenly Father give 23
12: 4 after that have no more that they can do. 28
23 life is more than food 31
23 the body more than clothing. •
24 Of how much more value are you than the birds! 23
28 how much more will he clothe you 23
48 of him . . they will demand the more. 28
15: 7 more joy in heaven over one sinner who repents •
18:39 he cried out all the more 23
19:26 to every one who has will more be given •
21: 3 this poor widow has put in more than all of them; 31
Joh 4: 1 making and baptizing more disciples than John 31
41 And many more believed because of his word. 31
7:31 will he do more signs than this man has done? 31
12:43 more than the praise of God. 23
15: 2 he prunes, that it may bear more fruit. 31
19: 8 he was the more afraid; 23
21:15 Simon, son of John, do you love me more than these? 31
Act 4:22 the man . . was more than 40 years old. 31
20:35 'It is more blessed to give than to receive.' 23
22: 2 they were the more quiet. And he said 23
23:13 There were more than 40 who made this conspiracy. 31
21 more than 40 of their men lie in ambush for him 31
24:11 it is not more than twelve days since I went up 31
25: 6 stayed among them not more than eight or ten days 31
27:11 centurion paid more attention to the captain 23
Rom 5: 9 much more shall we be saved by him from the wrath 23
10 much more . . shall we be saved by his life. 23
15 much more have the grace of God and the free gift 23
17 much more will those . . reign in life 23
11:12 how much more will their full inclusion mean! 23
24 how much more will these natural branches 23
1Co 9:12 do not we still more 23
19 a slave to all, that I might win the more. 31
14:18 I speak in tongues more than you all; 23
2Co 3:11 what is permanent must have much more splendor. 20
7: 7 so that I rejoiced still more. 23
12:15 If I love you the more, am I to be loved the less? 29
Gal 4:27 the children of the desolate one are many more 23
Php 1: 9 my prayer that your love may abound more and more 23
9 my prayer that your love may abound more and more 23
2:12 as in my presence but much more in my absence 23
3: 4 I have more: 23
4:18 I have received full payment, and more; I am filled 27
1Th 2:17 we endeavored the more eagerly 29
2Ti 2:16 it will lead people into more and more ungodliness 31
16 it will lead people into more and more ungodliness 31
Phm 1:16 especially to me but how much more to you 23
Heb 3: 3 the builder of a house has more honor than the house. 31
7:15 This becomes even more evident 28
8:12 I will remember their sins no more. 22
9:14 how much more shall the blood of Christ 23
10:17 remember their sins and their misdeeds no more. 22
25 all the more as you see the Day drawing near. 23
11:32 what more shall I say? 22
12: 9 Shall we not much more be subject to the Father 23
26 Yet once more I will shake not only the earth •
27 This phrase, "Yet once more," indicates . . •
Jas 4: 6 But he gives more grace; therefore it says 24
2Pe 1:10 more zealous to confirm your call and election 23
Rev 7:16 They shall hunger no more, neither thirst 22
1Es 2:28 to take care that nothing more be done 26
4:25 A man loves his wife more than his father 23
5:41 All those of Israel, twelve or more years of age 19
58 the Levites who were twenty or more years of age 19
2Es 1:21 What more can I do for you? says the Lord. 35
2:43 but he was more exalted than they 39
3:12 to be more ungodly than were their ancestors. 41
4:14 that we may make for ourselves more forests.' 37
15 there also we may gain more territory 37
45 whether more time is to come than has passed 41
50 for as the rain is more than the drops 38
5:33 Or do you love him more than his Maker does? 41
7:136 abound more and more to those now living 39
9:23 if you will let seven days more pass 36
10:11 Who then ought to mourn the more 39
23 And, what is more than all, the seal of Zion 40
12:39 wait here seven days more, so that you may be shown 36
13:16 And still more, alas for those who are not left! 41
24 those who are left are more blessed than those 39
56 after three more days I will tell you 37
14:17 the more shall evils be multiplied 44
16:47 the more they adorn their cities, their houses 42
48 the more angry I will be with them for their sins 43
Jdt 7:30 Let us hold out for five more days 22
12: 3 where can we get more like it for you? •
AEs 16: 2 the more proud do many men become. 24
Wis 8: 6 who more than she is fashioner of what exists? 23
12:22 thou scourgest our enemies 10,000 times more •
Sir 3:18 The greater you are, the more you must humble 34
4:10 he will love you more than does your mother. 23
11:11 is so much the more in want. 23
24:21 Those who eat me will hunger for more 22
21 those who drink me will thirst for more. 22
29:11 it will profit you more than gold. 23
34:11 I understand more than I can express. 31
40: 8 upon sinners seven times more 32
LJr 1:19 even more than they light for themselves 31
1Mc 3:30 give more lavishly than preceding kings. 27
9:72 came no more into their territory. 22
10:88 he honored Jonathan still more; 33
15:31 500 talents more 18
2Mc 4: 9 he promised to pay 150 more 21
10:23 he destroyed more than 20,000 31
12:19 more than 10,000 men. 31
4Mc 9:30 you are being tortured more than I 31
15: 3 She loved religion more 23
5 they are more devoted to their children. 23
18:20 to the catapult and back again to more tortures 30

more *See also* abound, acceptable, accurately, all, ancient, any, austere, barbarous, beautiful, bitter, bitterly, build, clearly, closely, convincingly, cruelly, desirable, distant, diverse, eager, earnest, earnestly, equitable, even, evil, exactly, excellent, faithful, far, fervent, fitting, fragile, frequent, give, graciously, greedy, grievous, grow, hear, inflame, intense, love, make, manifold, manly, mean, mobile, much, necessary, never, no, noble, numerous, often, once, painful, perfect, powerful, precious, profitable, put, quickly, rare, richly, royal, rudely, savage, senseless, shrewd, spend, still, striking, sympathetic, tell, terrifying, tolerable, value, vehemently, violent.

more also 1. יָסַף

1Sm 3:17 May God do so to you and more also, if you hide 1

more and more 1. הָלַךְ 2. יָסַף 3. προβαίνω

Gen 26:13 the man became rich, and gained more and more 1
1Sm 14:19 the tumult in the camp . . increased more and more; 1
Ps 35:16 they impiously mocked more and more •
Hos 13: 2 And now they sin more and more 2
Jdt 16:23 She became more and more famous 3

more and more people 1. πολύς

2Co 4:15 so that as grace extends to more and more people 1

any more 1. יָסַף 2. יָסַף עוֹד 3. עוֹד 4. ἔτι 5. adicio

Gen 8:12 she did not return to him any more. 2
Lev 27:20 it shall not be redeemed any more 3
Deu 18:16 me not . . see this great fire any more, lest I die.' 3
2Sm 2:28 pursued . . no more, nor did they fight any more. 1
2Kg 21: 8 I will not cause . . Israel to wander any more 1
1Ch 19:19 not willing to help the Ammonites any more. 3
Job 7:10 nor does his place know him any more. 3
20: 9 nor will his place any more behold him. 3
Isa 2: 4 neither shall they learn war any more. 3
23:10 Overflow . . there is no restraint any more. 3
30:20 yet your Teacher will not hide himself any more 3
Mic 4: 3 neither shall they learn war any more; 3
Mat 22:46 did any one dare to ask him any more questions. 4
Mrk 5: 3 no one could bind him any more 4
Lke 20:36 for they cannot die any more 4
Rev 7:16 shall hunger no more, neither thirst any more; 4
18:11 since no one buys their cargo any more 4
21: 4 neither . . mourning nor crying nor pain any more 4
2Es 8:55 Therefore do not ask any more questions 5

how much more 1. אַף 2. אַף כִּי 3. μήτιγε 4. ποσαχῶς

Deu 31:27 how much more after my death! 2
1Sm 21: 5 how much more today will their vessels be holy? 2
23: 3 how much more then if we go to Kei'lah 1
2Sm 4:11 How much more . . shall I not now require 1
16:11 how much more now may this Benjaminite! 2
Job 4:19 how much more those who dwell in houses of clay 1
Prv 11:31 how much more the wicked and the sinner! 1
15:11 how much more the hearts of men! 2
19: 7 how much more do his friends go far from him! 2
21:27 how much more when he brings it with evil intent. 2
Ezk 14:21 How much more when I send upon Jerusalem 2
1Co 6: 3 How much more, matters pertaining to this life! 3
Sir 10:31 A man honored in poverty, how much more in wealth! 4
31 how much more in poverty! 4

more than 1. כִּי אִם 2. לֹא 3. לִפְנֵי 4. מִן 5. עַל 6. מִן (A) 7. ἀπό 8. ἐπάνω 9. οὐ 10. παρά 11. ὑπέρ 12. prae 13. super

Gen 3: 1 more subtle than any other wild creature 4
29:30 he loved Rachel more than Leah, and served Laban 4
37: 3 loved Joseph more than any other of his children 4
4 father loved him more than all his brothers 4
Num12: 3 very meek, more than all men that were on the face 4
Deu 7: 7 not . . more in number than any other people 4
30: 5 more prosperous and numerous than their fathers 4
1Sm 9: 2 There was not a man . . more handsome than he; 4
18:30 David had more success than all the servants 4
24:17 He said to David, "You are more righteous than I; 4
2Sm 19:43 We have . . and in David also we have more than you. 4
20: 6 Now Sheba . . will do us more harm than Ab'salom; 4
1Kg 1:47 make the name of Solomon more famous than yours 4
2:32 two men more righteous and better than himself 4
14:22 sins . . more than all that their fathers 4
16:25 and did more evil than all who were before him. 4
30 did evil . . more than all that were before him. 4
2Kg 6:10 he saved himself there more than once or twice. 2
13: 7 was not . . an army of more than 50 horsemen 1
21: 9 to do more evil than the nations had done 4
11 more wicked than all that the Amorites did 4
1Ch 4: 9 Jabez was more honorable than his brothers; 4
2Ch 29:34 were more upright in heart than the priests 4
33: 9 did more evil than the nations whom the LORD 4
Neh 7: 2 more faithful and God-fearing man than many. 4
Est 2:17 the king loved Esther more than all the women 4
17 found grace and . . more than all the virgins 4
4:13 that . . you will escape any more than all 4
Job 3:21 and dig for it more than for hid treasures; 4
34:19 nor regards the rich more than the poor 3
35:11 who teaches us more than the beasts of the earth 4
42:12 the latter days of Job more than his beginning; 4
Ps 4: 7 Thou hast put more joy in my heart than they have 4
19:10 More to be desired are they than gold 4
52: 3 You love evil more than good 4
3 lying more than speaking the truth. Selah 4
69:31 This will please the LORD more than an ox or a bull 4
76: 4 more majestic than the everlasting mountains. 4
87: 2 gates of Zion more than all the dwelling places 4
119:99 I have more understanding than all my teachers 4
100I understand more than the aged 4
130: 6 more than watchmen for the morning, 4
Prv 3:15 She is more precious than jewels 4
21: 3 more acceptable to the LORD than sacrifice 4
26:12 There is more hope for a fool than for him. 4
28:23 more favor than he who flatters with his tongue. 4
29:20 There is more hope for a fool than for him. 4
31:10 good wife . . is far more precious than jewels. 4
Ecc 7:19 Wisdom gives strength . . more than ten rulers 4
26 I found more bitter than death the woman whose 4
Sng 1: 4 we will extol your love more than wine; 4
5: 9 What is your beloved more than another beloved 4
9 What is your beloved more than another beloved 4
Isa 13:12 I will make men more rare than fine gold 4
32:10 In little more than a year you will shudder 5
54: 1 be more than the children of her that is married 4
Jer 48:32 More than for Jazer I weep for you, O vine of Sibmah! 4
Ezk 5: 6 wickedly rebelled . . more than the nations 4
6 and against my statutes more than the countries 4
7 Because you are more turbulent than the nations 4
16:47 you were more corrupt than they in all your ways. 4
52 in which you acted more abominably than they 4
52 they are more in the right than you. 4
23:11 yet she was more corrupt than she in her doting 4
36:11 and will do more good to you than ever before. 4
42: 5 took more away from them than from the lower 4
6 set back from the ground more than the lower 4
Dan 2:30 any wisdom . . more than all the living 6
Hos 4:18 they love shame more than their glory. •
Nah 3:16 increased your merchants more than the stars 4
Hab 1: 8 horses . . more fierce than the evening wolves; 4
13 swallows up the man more righteous than he? 4
Mat 10:37 He who loves father or mother more than me 11
37 and he who loves son or daughter more than me 11
Mrk 14: 5 ointment . . sold for more than 300 denarii 8
Rom 12: 3 not to think of himself more highly than he ought 10
1Co 15: 6 Then he appeared to more than 500 brethren 8
2Co 12: 6 no one may think more of me than he sees in me 11
Gal 3:20 Now an intermediary implies more than one 9
Phm 1:16 no longer as a slave but more than a slave 11
21 knowing that you will do even more than I say. 11
2Es 5:44 cannot make more haste than the Creator 13
7:56 silver is more abundant than gold 13
59 rejoices more than he who has what is plentiful. 13
125the faces . . shall shine more than the stars 13
8:47 able to love my creation more than I love it 13
10:57 For you are more blessed than many 12
12:24 its inhabitants more oppressively than all 13
Wis 7:10 I loved her more than health and beauty 11
15:13 this man, more than all others, knows 10
14 most foolish, and more miserable than an infant 11
16:19 at another time . . it burned more intensely than fire 11
Sir 24:29 for her thought is more abundant than the sea 7
29:13 more than a mighty shield 11
13 more than a heavy spear 11
40:22 the green shoots of grain more than both. 11
25 good counsel is esteemed more than both. 11
1Mc 7:23 it was more than the Gentiles had done. 11
2Mc 8:24 they slew more than 9,000 of the enemy 11
30 they killed more than 20,000 of them 11
14:39 Nicanor . . sent more than 500 soldiers to arrest him; 11
3Mc 7:15 In that day they put to death more than 300 men 11
4Mc 9: 3 do not pity us more than we pity ourselves. 11

more than a mile 1. στάδιοι ἐννέα

2Mc 12:10 When they had gone more than a mile from there 1

more than conqueror 1. ὑπερνικάω

Rom 8:37 in all these things we are more than conquerors 1

more than enough 1. שָׂבָע

Ps 17:14 may their children have more than enough; 1

more than ever 1. μᾶλλον

Act 5:14 more than ever believers were added to the Lord 1

more than that 1. οὐ μόνον δέ

Rom 5: 3 More than that, we rejoice in our sufferings 1

yet more 1. יָסַף 2. עוֹד 3. ἔτι

1Sm 23:22 Go, make yet more sure; know and see the place 2
2Sm 6:22 will make myself yet more contemptible than this 2
2Ch 28:22 distress he became yet more faithless 1
Sir 39:12 I have yet more to say, which I have thought upon 3

moreover 1. אַף 2. אַף כִּי 3. גַּם 4. וְ 5. וְגַם 6. וְעוֹד 7. וְעַתָּה 8. עוֹד 9. עַתָּה 10. וְ (A) 11. ἀλλά 12. ἀλλὰ καί 13. δέ 14. ἐπὶ τούτοις 15. ἔτι 16. ἔτι τε 17. λοιπός 18. μᾶλλον 19. πλήν 20. πρὸς τούτοις 21. adhuc 22. autem 23. et

Gen 17:16 I will bless her, and moreover I will give you a son 3
22:24 Moreover, his concubine, whose name was Reumah 3
32:18 my lord Esau; and moreover he is behind us.' 3
20 you shall say, 'Moreover your servant Jacob is 3
38:24 played the harlot; and moreover she is with child 3
41:44 Moreover Pharaoh said to Joseph, "I am Pharaoh 4
57 Moreover, all the earth came to Egypt to Joseph 4
48:22 Moreover I have given to you rather 4
Exd 5: 2 and moreover I will not let Israel go. 3
6: 5 Moreover I have heard the groaning of the people 3
11: 3 Moreover, the man Moses was very great in the land 3
18:21 Moreover choose able men from all the people 4
26: 1 Moreover you shall make the tabernacle 4
30:22 Moreover, the LORD said to Moses 4
Lev 7:26 Moreover you shall eat no blood whatever 4
14:46 Moreover he who enters the house while it is shut 4
Num16:14 Moreover you have not brought us into a land 1
18:26 Moreover you shall say to the Levites, 'When you 4
35:31 Moreover you shall accept no ransom 4
Deu 1:28 moreover we have seen the sons of the Anakim 3
39 Moreover your little ones . . shall go in there 4
7:20 Moreover the LORD your God will send hornets 3
26:13 moreover I have given it to the Levite 3
Jos 2:24 moreover all the inhabitants of the land are 3
1Sm 2:15 Moreover, before the fat was burned 3
12:23 Moreover as for me, far be it . . that I should sin 3
28:19 Moreover the LORD will give . . into the hand 3
2Sm 7:11 Moreover the LORD declares to you 4
12:27 fought against Rabbah; moreover, I have taken 3
15: 4 Ab'salom said moreover, "Oh that I were judge 4
17: 1 Moreover Ahith'ophel said to Ab'salom 4
8 Hushai said moreover, "You know that 4
1Kg 1:47 Moreover the king's servants came 5
2: 5 Moreover you know also what Jo'ab the son 5
7:30 Moreover each stand had four bronze wheels 4
10:11 Moreover the fleet of Hiram, which brought gold 5
14:14 Moreover the LORD will raise up . . a king 4
16: 7 Moreover the word of the LORD came by the prophet 5
2Kg 18:25 Moreover, is it without the LORD that I have come 9
21:16 Moreover Manas'seh shed . . much innocent blood 5
23:15 Moreover the altar at Bethel . . he pulled down 5
24 Moreover Josi'ah put away the mediums 5
1Ch 16: 4 Moreover he appointed certain of the Levites 4
17:10 Moreover I declare to you that the LORD 4
29: 3 Moreover, in addition to all that I have provided 8
2Ch 1: 5 Moreover the bronze altar . . was there before 4
9:10 Moreover the servants of Huram and the servants 3
12:12 moreover, conditions were good in Judah. 3
19: 8 Moreover in Jerusalem Jehosh'aphat appointed 3
21:11 Moreover he made high places in the hill country 3
26: 9 Moreover Uzzi'ah built towers in Jerusalem 4
11 Moreover Uzzi'ah had an army of soldiers 4
27: 4 Moreover he built cities in the hill country 4
Ezr 6: 8 Moreover I make a decree regarding what you 10
Neh 5:10 Moreover I and my brethren and my servants 3
14 Moreover from the time that I was appointed 3
17 Moreover there were at my table 150 men •
6:17 Moreover in those days the nobles of Judah sent 3
Est 7: 9 Moreover, the gallows . . is standing in Haman's 3
Ps 19:11 Moreover by them is thy servant warned; 3
Ecc 3:16 Moreover I saw . . that in the place of justice 6
6: 5 moreover it has not seen the sun or known 3
Isa 30:26 Moreover the light of the moon will be 4
36:10 Moreover, is it without the LORD that I have come 7
Jer 2:16 Moreover, the men of Memphis and Tah'panhes have 3
20: 5 Moreover, I will give all the wealth of the city 4
25:10 Moreover, I will banish from them the voice 4
Ezk 3:10 Moreover he said to me, "Son of man 4
4:16 Moreover he said to me, "Son of man, behold 4
5:14 Moreover I will make you a desolation 4
12:17 Moreover the word of the LORD came to me 4
20:12 Moreover I gave them my sabbaths, as a sign 3
15 Moreover I swore to them in the wilderness 3
23 Moreover I swore to them in the wilderness 3
25 Moreover I gave them statutes that were not good 3
22: 1 Moreover the word of the LORD came to me, saying 4
23:38 Moreover this they have done to me 8
28:11 Moreover the word of the LORD came to me 4
Hab 2: 5 Moreover, wine is treacherous; 2
Zec 4: 8 Moreover the word of the LORD came to me, saying 4
Lke 16:21 moreover the dogs came and licked his sores. 12
24:22 Moreover, some women of our company amazed us. 11
Act 2:26 moreover my flesh will dwell in hope. 15
21:28 moreover he also brought Greeks into the temple 16
1Co 4: 2 Moreover it is required of stewards 17
1Ti 3: 7 moreover he must be well thought of by outsiders 13
1Es 4:10 Moreover, he reclines, he eats and drinks 20
2Es 2:11 Moreover, I will take back to myself their glory 23
8:57 Moreover they have even trampled upon . . 21
11:32 Moreover this head gained control 22
1Mc 6:24 moreover, they have put to death 19
10:42 Moreover, the 5,000 shekels of silver 14
2Mc 6:23 moreover according to the holy God-given law 18
8:19 Moreover, he told them of the times when . . 13

morning 1. אוֹר הַבֹּקֶר 2. בֹּקֶר 3. מִשְׁחָר 4. שַׁחַר 5. שָׁכַם 6. ἑωθινός 7. ὀρθρινός 8. ὄρθρος 9. πρωΐ 10. πρωΐα 11. πρωΐθεν 12. πρωϊνός 13. mane

Gen 1: 5 there was evening and there was morning, one day 2
8 And there was evening and there was morning 2
13 there was evening and there was morning 2
19 was evening and there was morning, a fourth day 2
23 evening and there was morning, a fifth day 2
31 evening and there was morning, a sixth day. 2
19:15 When morning dawned, the angels urged Lot 4
27 Abraham went early in the morning to the place 2
20: 8 Abim'elech rose early in the morning 2

21:14 Abraham rose early in the morning 2
22: 3 Abraham rose early in the morning 2
24:54 When they arose in the morning, he said, "Send me 2
26:31 In the morning they rose early and took oath 2
28:18 Jacob rose early in the morning 2
29:25 in the morning, behold, it was Leah; 2
31:55 Early in the morning Laban arose 2
40: 6 When Joseph came to them in the morning 2
41: 8 in the morning his spirit was troubled; 2
44: 3 As soon as the morning was light 2
49:27 wolf, in the morning devouring the prey 2
Exd 7:15 Go to Pharaoh in the morning, as he is going out 2
8:20 Rise up early in the morning and wait for Pharaoh 2
9:13 Rise up early in the morning and stand before 2
10:13 and when it was morning the east wind had brought 2
12:10 you shall let none of it remain until the morning 2
10 anything that remains until the morning 2
22 go out of the door of his house until the morning. 2
14:24 And in the morning watch the LORD 2
27 sea returned . . when the morning appeared; 2
16: 7 in the morning you shall see the glory of the LORD 2
8 LORD gives . . in the morning bread to the full 2
12 in the morning you shall be filled with bread; 2
13 in the morning dew lay round about the camp. 2
19 Let no man leave any of it till the morning. 2
20 some left part of it till the morning 2
21 Morning by morning they gathered it, each as much 2
21 Morning by morning they gathered it, each as much 2
23 left over lay by to be kept till the morning.' 2
24 So they laid it by till the morning, as Moses bade 2
18:13 stood about Moses from morning till evening. 2
14 stand about you from morning till evening? 2
19:16 On the morning of the third day there were 2
23:18 fat of my feast remain until the morning. 2
24: 4 he rose early in the morning, and built an altar 2
27:21 tend it from evening to morning before the LORD. 2
29:34 if any . . of the bread, remain until the morning 2
39 One lamb you shall offer in the morning 2
41 offer in the evening . . as in the morning 2
30: 7 every morning when he dresses the lamps he shall 2
34: 2 Be ready in the morning, and come up in the morning 2
2 Be ready in the morning, and come up in the morning 2
4 he rose early in the morning and went up 2
25 of the passover be left until the morning. 2
36: 3 bringing him freewill offerings every morning 2
Lev 6: 9 upon the altar all night until the morning 2
12 the priest shall burn wood on it every morning 2
20 fine flour . . half of it in the morning 2
7:15 he shall not leave any of it until the morning 2
9:17 besides the burnt offering of the morning 2
19:13 not remain with you all night until the morning 2
22:30 you shall leave none of it until morning 2
24: 3 keep it in order from evening to morning 2
Num 9:12 They shall leave none of it until the morning 2
15 like the appearance of fire until morning. 2
21 cloud remained from evening until morning; 2
21 cloud was taken up in the morning, they set out 2
14:40 rose early in the morning, and went up 2
16: 5 In the morning the LORD will show who is his 2
22:13 Balaam rose in the morning, and said 2
21 Balaam rose in the morning, and saddled his ass 2
28: 4 The one lamb you shall offer in the morning 2
8 like the cereal offering of the morning 2
23 these besides the burnt offering of the morning 2
Deu 16: 4 nor shall any . . remain all night until morning. 2
7 morning you shall turn and go to your tents. 2
28:67 morning you shall say, 'Would it were evening!' 2
67 at evening you shall say, 'Would it were morning!' 2
Jos 3: 1 Early in the morning Joshua rose and set out 2
6:12 Then Joshua rose early in the morning 2
7:14 In the morning . . you shall be brought near 2
16 Joshua rose early in the morning 2
8:10 And Joshua arose early in the morning 2
Jdg 6:28 When the men of the town rose early in the morning 2
31 for him shall be put to death by morning. 2
9:33 in the morning, as soon as the sun is up, rise early 2
16: 2 Let us wait till the light of the morning; 2
19: 5 arose early in the morning, and he prepared to go; 2
8 he arose early in the morning to depart; 2
9 arise early in the morning for your journey •
25 and abused her all night until the morning. 2
26 as morning appeared, the woman came and fell down 2
27 her master rose up in the morning 2
20:19 Israel rose in the morning, and encamped against 2
Rut 2: 7 she has continued from early morning until now 2
3:13 in the morning, if he will do . . well; let him do it; 2
13 Lie down until the morning. 2
14 she lay at his feet until the morning 2
1Sm 1:19 They rose early in the morning and worshiped 2
3:15 Samuel lay until morning; 2
5: 4 But when they rose early on the next morning 2
9:19 today you . . and in the morning I will let you go 2
11:11 they came into . . the camp in the morning watch 2
14:36 and despoil them until the morning light; 2
15:12 And Samuel rose early to meet Saul in the morning; 2
17:16 came . . and took his stand, morning and evening. 5
20 David rose early in the morning 2
19: 2 take heed . . in the morning, stay in a secret place 2
11 watch him, that he might kill him in the morning. 2
20:35 In the morning Jonathan went out into the field 2
25:22 if by morning I leave so much as one male 2
34 by morning there had not been left . . one male. 1
36 she told him nothing . . until the morning light. 2
37 in the morning, when the wind had gone out of Nabal 2
29:10 rise early in the morning with the servants 2
10 start early in the morning, and depart as soon 2
11 David set out with his men early in the morning 2
2Sm 2:27 have given up the pursuit . . in the morning. 2
11:14 In the morning David wrote a letter to Jo'ab 2
13: 4 why are you so haggard morning after morning? 2
4 why are you so haggard morning after morning? 2
23: 4 he dawns on them like the morning light 2
4 the sun shining forth upon a cloudless morning 2
24:11 when David arose in the morning, the word . . came 2
15 from the morning until the appointed time; 2
1Kg 3:21 When I rose in the morning to nurse my child 2
21 when I looked at it closely in the morning, behold 2
17: 6 ravens brought him bread and meat in the morning 2
18:26 called on . . Ba'al from morning until noon, saying 2
2Kg 3:20 The next morning, about the time of offering 2
22 they rose early in the morning, and the sun shone 2
7: 9 if we are silent and wait until the morning light 2
10: 8 Lay them in two heaps . . until the morning. 2
9 in the morning, when he went out, he stood, and said 2
16:15 burn the morning burnt offering, and the evening 2
19:35 when men arose early in the morning, behold 2
1Ch 9:27 and they had charge of opening it every morning. 2
16:40 continually morning and evening 2
23:30 stand every morning, thanking and praising 2
2Ch 2: 4 and for burnt offerings morning and evening 2
13:11 They offer . . every morning and every evening 2
20:20 they rose early in the morning and went out 2
31: 3 burnt offerings of morning and evening 2
Ezr 3: 3 offered . . burnt offerings morning and evening. 2
Est 2:14 in the morning she came back to the second harem 2
5:14 and in the morning . . have Mor'decai hanged 2
Job 1: 5 he would rise early in the morning 2
3: 9 nor see the eyelids of the morning; 4
4:20 Between morning and evening they are destroyed; 2
11:17 its darkness will be like the morning. 2
24:17 For deep darkness is morning to all of them; 2
38: 7 when the morning stars sang together 2
12 Have you commanded the morning since your days 2
Ps 5: 3 O LORD, in the morning thou dost hear my voice; 2
3 in the morning I prepare a sacrifice for thee 2
30: 5 for the night, but joy comes with the morning. 2
55:17 Evening and morning and at noon I utter 2
59:16 sing aloud of thy steadfast love in the morning. 2
65: 8 thou makest the outgoings of the morning 2
73:14 been stricken, and chastened every morning. 2
88:13 in the morning my prayer comes before thee. 2
90: 5 dream, like grass which is renewed in the morning 2
6 in the morning it flourishes and is renewed; 2
14 Satisfy us in the morning with thy . . love 2
92: 2 to declare thy steadfast love in the morning 2
110: 3 From the womb of the morning like dew your youth 3
130: 6 more than watchmen for the morning, 2
6 more than watchmen for the morning. 2
139: 9 If I take the wings of the morning and dwell 4
143: 8 Let me hear in the morning of thy steadfast love 2
Prv 7:18 Come, let us take our fill of love till morning; 2
27:14 loud voice, rising early in the morning 2
Ecc 10:16 and your princes feast in the morning! 2
11: 6 In the morning sow your seed 2
Isa 5:11 Woe to those who rise early in the morning 2
17:11 and make them blossom in the morning that you sow; 2
14 Before morning, they are no more! 2
21:12 Morning comes, and also the night. 2
28:19 for morning by morning it will pass through 2
19 for morning by morning it will pass through 2
37:36 and when men arose early in the morning 2
38:13 I cry for help until morning; 2
50: 4 Morning by morning he wakens, he wakens my ear 2
4 Morning by morning he wakens, he wakens my ear 2
Jer 20:16 let him hear a cry in the morning 2
21:12 says the LORD: "'Execute justice in the morning 2
Lam 3:23 they are new every morning; 2
Ezk 12: 8 In the morning the word of the LORD came to me 2
24:18 I spoke to the people in the morning 2
18 on the next morning I did as I was commanded. 2
33:22 by the time the man came to me in the morning; 2
46:13 morning by morning he shall provide it. 2
13 morning by morning he shall provide it. 2
14 a cereal offering with it morning by morning 2
14 a cereal offering with it morning by morning 2
15 the oil shall be provided, morning by morning 2
15 the oil shall be provided, morning by morning 2
Dan 8:14 said to him, "For 2,300 evenings and mornings; 2
26 vision of the evenings and the mornings 2
Hos 6: 4 Your love is like a morning cloud, like the dew 2
7: 6 in the morning it blazes like a flaming fire. 2
13: 3 Therefore they shall be like the morning mist 2
Ams 4: 4 bring your sacrifices every morning 2
13 who makes the morning darkness, and treads 4
5: 8 and turns deep darkness into the morning 2
Mic 2: 1 When the morning dawns, they perform it 2
Zep 3: 3 wolves that leave nothing till the morning. 2
5 every morning he shows forth his justice 2
Mat 16: 3 in the morning 9
20: 1 a householder who went out early in the morning 9
21:18 In the morning, as he was returning to the city 9
27: 1 When morning came 10
Mrk 1:35 in the morning, a great while before day, he rose 9
11:20 As they passed by in the morning 9
13:35 at midnight, or at cockcrow, or in the morning- 9
15: 1 And as soon as it was morning 9
Act 28:23 from morning till evening 9
Rev 2:28 I will give him the morning star. 12
22:16 the offspring of David, the bright morning star. 12
1Es 1:11 this they did in the morning. 12
5:50 burnt offerings . . morning and evening. 12
2Es 7:40 water or air, or darkness or evening or morning 13
Jdt 12: 5 Along toward the morning watch she arose 6
14: 2 as soon as morning comes and the sun rises 8
Wis 11:22 like a drop of morning dew 7
Sir 18:26 From morning to evening conditions change 11
50: 6 Like the morning star among the clouds 6
Bel 1:12 when you return in the morning 9
16 Early in the morning the king rose and came 9
1Mc 9:13 the battle raged from morning till evening. 11
12:29 his men did not know it until morning 9

morning *See also* early, get, star.

morning by morning 1. לִבְקָרִים
Ps 101: 8 Morning by morning I will destroy all the wicked 1

early morning 1. אוֹר 2. ὄρθριος 3. ὄρθρος 4. πρωΐα 5. πρωΐθεν
Neh 8: 3 read . . from early morning until midday 1
1Es 9:41 from early morning until midday 3
Sir 47:10 the sanctuary resounded from early morning. 4
1Mc 10:80 men from early morning till late afternoon. 5
3Mc 5:23 as soon as the cock had crowed in the early morning 2

every morning 1. לִבְקָרִים
Job 7:18 dost visit him every morning 1
Isa 33: 2 Be our arm every morning, our salvation 1

next morning 1. מָחֳרָת
Jdg 6:38 rose early next morning and squeezed the fleece 1

morrow 1. בֹּקֶר 2. מָחֳרָת 3. αὔριον 4. ἐπαύριον
Exd 9: 6 on the morrow the LORD did this thing; 2
18:13 On the morrow Moses sat to judge the people 2
32: 6 they rose up early on the morrow, and offered 2
30 On the morrow Moses said to the people, "You have 2
Lev 7:16 on the morrow what remains of it shall be eaten 2
19: 6 the same day . . or on the morrow 2
23:11 on the morrow after the sabbath the priest shall 2
15 you shall count from the morrow 2
16 50 days to the morrow after the seventh sabbath 2
Num16:41 on the morrow all . . Israel murmured against 2
17: 8 on the morrow Moses went into the tent 2
22:41 on the morrow Balak took Balaam and brought him 1
Jos 5:11 on the morrow after the passover, on that very day 2
12 And the manna ceased on the morrow, when they ate 2
Jdg 21: 4 on the morrow the people rose early, and built 2
1Sm 11:11 on the morrow Saul put the people in . . companies; 2
18:10 on the morrow an evil spirit . . rushed upon Saul 2
20:27 on the second day, the morrow after the new moon 2
31: 8 On the morrow . . came to strip the slain 2
2Kg 8:15 on the morrow he took the coverlet and dipped it 2
1Ch 10: 8 On the morrow, when the Philistines came 2
Jer 20: 3 On the morrow, when Pashhur released Jeremiah 2
Act 4: 3 put them in custody until the morrow 3
5 On the morrow 3
20: 7 intending to depart on the morrow 4
21: 8 On the morrow we departed and came to Caesare'a; 4
22:30 on the morrow, desiring to know the real reason 4
23:32 on the morrow they returned to the barracks 4
25:23 So on the morrow Agrippa and Berni'ce came 4

morsel 1. פַּת 2. ψωμίον
Gen 18: 5 while I fetch a morsel of bread 1
Jdg 19: 5 Strengthen your heart with a morsel of bread 1
Rut 2:14 eat some bread, and dip your morsel in the wine. 1
1Sm 2:36 Put me . . that I may eat a morsel of bread."' 1
28:22 let me set a morsel of bread before you; and eat 1
2Sm 12: 3 it used to eat of his morsel, and drink from his cup 1
1Kg 17:11 Bring me a morsel of bread in your hand. 1
Job 31:17 or have eaten my morsel alone 1
Ps 147:17 He casts forth his ice like morsels; 1
Prv 17: 1 Better is a dry morsel with quiet 1
23: 8 will vomit up the morsels which you have eaten 1
Joh 13:26 I shall give this morsel when I have dipped it 2
26 when he had dipped the morsel, he gave it to Judas 2
27 after the morsel, Satan entered into him 2
30 after receiving the morsel 2

morsel *See also* delicious.

mortal 1. εἰς θάνατον 2. θάνατος 3. θνητός 4. πρὸς θάνατον 5. σάρκινος 6. φθαρτός 7. corruptibilis 8. corruptus 9. mortalis
Job 4:17 Can mortal man be righteous before God? •
Ezk 31:14 to death, to the nether world among mortal men •
Rom 1:23 for images resembling mortal man or birds 6

6:12 Let not sin . . reign in your mortal bodies 3
8:11 will give life to your mortal bodies also 3
1Co 15:54 the mortal puts on immortality 3
2Co 4:11 Jesus may be manifested in our mortal flesh. 3
5: 4 what is mortal may be swallowed up by life. 3
1Jn 5:16 his brother committing what is not a mortal sin 4
16 give him life for those whose sin is not mortal. 4
16 There is sin which is mortal; 4
17 but there is sin which is not mortal. 4
Rev 13: 3 One of its heads seemed to have a mortal wound 1
3 but its mortal wound was healed 2
12 the first beast, whose mortal wound was healed. 2
2Es 2:45 they who have put off mortal clothing 9
7:15 why are you moved, seeing that you are mortal? 9
88 they shall be separated from their mortal body. 7
8: 6 every mortal who bears the likeness of a human 8
14:14 put away from you mortal thoughts 9
AEs 14:10 to magnify for ever a mortal king. 5
Wis 7: 1 I also am mortal, like all men 3
9:14 For the reasoning of mortals is worthless 3
15:17 He is mortal 3
2Mc 7:16 mortal though you are 6
9:12 no mortal should think that he is equal to God. 3
3Mc 3:29 useless for all time to any mortal creature. 3

mortal *See also* nature.

mortally 1. נֶפֶשׁ

Deu 19: 6 overtake him . . and wound him mortally 1
11 attacks . . wounds him mortally so that he dies 1
Ezk 30:24 groan before him like a man mortally wounded. •

mortar 1. חֵמָר 2. מְדֹכָה 3. מַכְתֵּשׁ 4. מֶלֶט

Gen 11: 3 had brick for stone, and bitumen for mortar. 1
Exd 1:14 hard service, in mortar and brick 1
Num11: 8 ground it in mills or beat it in mortars 2
Prv 27:22 Crush a fool in a mortar with a pestle along 3
Isa 41:25 he shall trample on rulers as on mortar 1
Jer 43: 9 and hide them in the mortar in the pavement 4
Nah 3:14 go into the clay, tread the mortar 1
Zep 1:11 Wail, O inhabitants of the Mortar! 3

mortgage 1. ערב

Neh 5: 3 We are mortgaging our fields, our vineyards 1

mosaic *See* pavement.

most 1. מְאֹד 2. מִן 3. μάλιστα 4. πᾶς 5. πλεῖον μέρος 6. πολύς 7. σφόδρα 8. ὑπὲρ πάντας 9. super omnes

Gen 34:19 Now he was the most honored of all his family. 2
Exd 26:33 separate . . the holy place from the most holy. †
34 the ark . . in the most holy place. †
29:37 consecrate it, and the altar shall be most holy; †
30:10 it is most holy to the LORD. †
29 consecrate them, that they may be most holy; †
36 it shall be for you most holy. †
40:10 and the altar shall be most holy. †
Lev 2: 3 it is a most holy part of the offerings by fire †
10 it is a most holy part of the offering by fire †
6:17 it is a thing most holy, like the sin offering †
25 be killed before the LORD; it is most holy †
29 the priests may eat of it; it is most holy †
7: 1 law of the guilt offering. It is most holy †
6 it shall be eaten in a holy place; it is most holy †
10:12 unleavened beside the altar, for it is most holy †
17 since it is a thing most holy and has been given †
14:13 belongs to the priest; it is most holy †
21:22 He may eat the bread . . both of the most holy †
24: 9 since it is for him a most holy portion †
27:28 every devoted thing is most holy to the LORD †
Num 4: 4 in the tent of meeting: the most holy things. †
19 when they come near to the most holy things †
18: 9 This shall be yours of the most holy things †
9 shall be most holy to you and to your sons. †
10 In a most holy place shall you eat of it; †
Deu 28:54 man who is the most tender and delicately bred 1
56 most tender and delicately bred woman among you •
Jdg 5:24 Most blessed of women be Ja'el, the wife of Heber •
24 be Ja'el . . of tent-dwelling women most blessed. •
Rut 2:13 Then she said, "You are most gracious to me, my lord •
2Sm 23:19 He was the most renowned of the 30
1Kg 6:16 as an inner sanctuary, as the most holy place. †
7:50 innermost part . . the most holy place †
8: 6 the inner sanctuary . . in the most holy place †
1Ch 6:49 for all the work of the most holy place †
11:21 He was the most renowned of the 30 •
23:13 was set apart to consecrate the most holy things †
2Ch 3: 8 And he made the most holy place; †
10 In the most holy place he made two cherubim †
4:22 for the inner doors to the most holy place †
5: 7 inner sanctuary . . in the most holy place †
31:14 to apportion . . the most holy offerings. †
Ezr 2:63 not to partake of the most holy food †
Neh 7:65 not to partake of the most holy food, until †
Est 6: 9 handed . . to one of the king's most noble princes; •
Ps 21: 6 Yea, thou dost make him most blessed for ever; •
28: 2 lift up my hands toward thy most holy sanctuary. •
Jer 3:19 a heritage most beauteous of all nations. †
6:26 make mourning . . most bitter lamentation; •
Ezk 20: 6 milk and honey, the most glorious of all lands. •
15 milk and honey, the most glorious of all lands •
28: 7 upon you, the most terrible of the nations; •
29:15 It shall be the most lowly of the kingdoms •
30:11 people with him, the most terrible of the nations •
31:12 Foreigners, the most terrible of the nations •
32:12 all of them most terrible among the nations. †
41: 4 And he said to me, This is the most holy place. †
42:13 the priests . . shall eat the most holy offerings; †
13 there they shall put the most holy offerings †
43:12 upon the top of the mountain shall be most holy. †
44:13 nor come near . . the things that are most sacred; †
45: 3 shall be the sanctuary, the most holy place. †
48:12 a most holy place, adjoining the territory †
Dan 9:24 to anoint a most holy place. †
Mic 7: 4 the most upright of them a thorn hedge. •
Mat 11:20 where most of his mighty works had been done 6
21: 8 Most of the crowd spread their garments 6
Mrk 9:26 so that most of them said, "He is dead. 6
Act 19:32 most of them did not know why they had come 6
1Co 10: 5 with most of them God was not pleased 6
14:27 let there be only two or at most three 6
15: 6 most of whom are still alive 6
2Co 9: 2 your zeal has stirred up most of them. 6
Php 1:14 most of the brethren have been made confident 6
2Es 10: 6 You most foolish of women 9
Jdt 4: 7 only wide enough for two men at the most. 4
AEs 15: 6 he was most terrifying. 7
Sir 16:21 so most of his works are concealed. 6
Bel 1: 2 was the most honored of his friends. 8
2Mc 1:14 to secure most of its treasures as a dowry. 6
36 by most people it is called naphtha. 6
8: 7 the nights most advantageous for such attacks. 3
24 wounded and disabled most of Nicanor's army 5
9:25 often entrusted and commended to most of you 6
11:12 Most of them got away stripped and wounded 6
12:24 because he held the parents of most of them 6
3Mc 4:18 although most of them were still in the country 6

most *See also* abominable, amazing, appropriate, beautiful, certainly, complex, comprehensive, cruel, dear, defiled, evil, excellent, favorable, foolish, gladly, glorious, gloriously, grievous, hateful, high, holy, impious, incredible, insolently, make, mighty, miserable, painful, philosophical, pitiable, pitiful, pity, pleasant, precious, rare, righteous, savage, sincere, skilful, subtle, suitable, sweet, tearful, unholy, valued, wicked, wise.

most men 1. πολύς

Mat 24:12 most men's love will grow cold. 1

most of all 1. μάλιστα

Act 20:38 sorrowing most of all because of the word . . spoken 1

moth 1. עָשׁ 2. σής

Job 4:19 in the dust, who are crushed before the moth. 1
Ps 39:11 thou dost consume like a moth what is dear to him; 1
Isa 50: 9 like a garment; the moth will eat them up. 1
51: 8 For the moth will eat them up like a garment 1
Hos 5:12 Therefore I am like a moth to E'phraim 1
Mat 6:19 treasures on earth, where moth and rust consume 2
20 in heaven, where neither moth nor rust consumes 2
Lke 12:33 where no thief approaches and no moth destroys. 2
Sir 42:13 for from garments comes the moth 2

moth-eaten 1. עָשׁ אכל 2. σητόβρωτος

Job 13:28 rotten thing, like a garment that is moth-eaten. 1
Jas 5: 2 and your garments are moth-eaten. 2

mother 1. אֵם 2. בֶּטֶן 3. γενέτις 4. μήτηρ 5. ὁ 6. τίκτω 7. mater

Gen 2:24 Therefore a man leaves his father and his mother 1
3:20 Eve, because she was the mother of all living. 1
17:16 she shall be a mother of nations; kings of peoples •
20:12 my father but not the daughter of my mother; 1
21:21 and his mother took a wife for him from the land 1
24:28 the maiden ran and told her mother's household 1
53 he also gave to her brother and to her mother 1
55 Her brother and her mother said, "Let the maiden 1
60 be the mother of thousands of ten thousands; •
67 Isaac was comforted after his mother's death. 1
27:11 Jacob said to Rebekah his mother 1
13 mother said to him, "Upon me be your curse, my son; 1
14 took them and brought them to his mother; 1
14 and his mother prepared savory food 1
29 may your mother's sons bow down to you. 1
28: 2 to the house of Bethu'el your mother's father 1
2 daughters of Laban your mother's brother. 1
5 the brother of Rebekah, Jacob's and Esau's mother. 1
7 that Jacob had obeyed his father and his mother 1
29:10 the daughter of Laban his mother's brother 1
10 saw . . the sheep of Laban his mother's brother 1
10 watered the flock of Laban his mother's brother. 1
30:14 in the field, and brought them to his mother Leah. 1
32:11 slay us all, the mothers with the children. 1
37:10 Shall I and your mother and your brothers indeed 1
43:29 and saw his brother Benjamin, his mother's son 1
44:20 and he alone is left of his mother's children; 1
Exd 2: 8 So the girl went and called the child's mother. 1
20:12 Honor your father and your mother, that your days 1
21:15 Whoever strikes his father or his mother shall 1
17 Whoever curses his father or his mother shall be 1
23:19 You shall not boil a kid in its mother's milk. 1
34:26 You shall not boil a kid in its mother's milk. 1
Lev 18: 7 which is the nakedness of your mother 1
7 she is your mother, you shall not uncover her 1
9 of your father or the daughter of your mother 1
13 not uncover the nakedness of your mother's sister 1
13 for she is your mother's near kinswoman 1
19: 3 one of you shall revere his mother and father 1
20: 9 For every one who curses his father or his mother 1
9 he has cursed his father or his mother, his blood 1
14 If a man takes a wife and her mother also 1
17 takes . . a daughter of his mother, and sees her 1
19 uncover the nakedness of your mother's sister 1
21: 2 his nearest of kin, his mother, his father, his son 1
11 even for his father or for his mother 1
22:27 it shall remain seven days with its mother 1
28 whether the mother is a cow or a ewe •
24:11 His mother's name was Shelo'mith, 1
Num 6: 7 Neither for his father nor for his mother 1
12:12 consumed when he comes out of his mother's womb. 1
Deu 5:16 'Honor your father and your mother 1
13: 6 If your brother, the son of your mother . . entices 1
14:21 You shall not boil a kid in its mother's milk. 1
21:13 remain in your house and bewail . . her mother 1
18 son, who will not obey . . the voice of his mother 1
19 his father and his mother shall take hold of him 1
22: 6 mother sitting upon the young or upon the eggs 1
6 you shall not take the mother with the young; 1
7 let the mother go, but the young you may take 1
15 then the father of the young woman and her mother 1
27:16 'Cursed . . who dishonors his father or his mother.' 1
22 sister, whether the . . daughter of his mother.' 1
33: 9 who said of his father and mother, 'I regard . . not'; 1
Jos 2:13 and save alive my father and mother, my brothers 1
18 gather into your house your father and mother 1
6:23 and brought out Rahab, and her father and mother 1
Jdg 5: 7 you arose, Deb'orah, arose as a mother in Israel. 1
28 the mother of Sis'era gazed through the lattice 1
8:19 said, "They were my brothers, the sons of my mother; 1
9: 1 went to Shechem to his mother's kinsmen and said 1
1 them and to the whole clan of his mother's family 1
3 his mother's kinsmen spoke all these words on his 1
14: 2 he came up, and told his father and mother 1
3 his father and mother said to him, "Is there not 1
4 His father and mother did not know that it was 1
5 Samson went down with his father and mother 1
6 he did not tell his father or his mother what he 1
9 he came to his father and mother, and gave some 1
16 Behold, I have not told my father nor my mother 1
16:17 have been a Nazirite to God from my mother's womb. 1
17: 2 he said to his mother, "The 1,100 pieces of silver 1
2 And his mother said, "Blessed be my son 1
3 he restored the . . silver to his mother; 1
3 restored the . . silver . . ; and his mother said 1
4 when he restored the money to his mother 1
4 his mother took 200 pieces of silver 1
Rut 1: 8 Go, return each of you to her mother's house. 1
2:11 you left your father and mother and . . land 1
1Sm 2:19 his mother used to make for him a little robe 1
15:33 so shall your mother be childless among women. 1
20:30 and to the shame of your mother's nakedness? 1
22: 3 Pray let my father and my mother stay with you 1
2Sm 17:25 of Nahash, sister of Zeru'iah, Jo'ab's mother. 1
19:37 die . . near the grave of my father and my mother. 1
20:19 to destroy a city which is a mother in Israel; 1
1Kg 1:11 Nathan said to Bathshe'ba the mother of Solomon 1
2:13 came to Bathshe'ba the mother of Solomon. 1
19 and had a seat brought for the king's mother; 1
20 Make your request, my mother; for I will not refuse 1
22 King Solomon answered his mother, "And why do you 1
3:27 by no means slay it; she is its mother. 1
11:26 Jerobo'am . . whose mother's name was Zeru'ah 1
14:21 His mother's name was Na'amah the Ammonitess. 1
31 His mother's name was Na'amah the Ammonitess. 1
15: 2 His mother's name was Ma'acah the daughter 1
10 His mother's name was Ma'acah the daughter 1
13 He also removed Ma'acah his mother 1
17:23 took the child . . and delivered him to his mother; 1
19:20 Let me kiss my father and my mother 1
22:42 His mother's name was Azu'bah the daughter 1
52 walked in . . and in the way of his mother 1
2Kg 3: 2 the LORD, though not like his father and mother 1
13 Go to . . and the prophets of your mother. 1
4:19 The father said . . "Carry him to his mother. 1
20 he had lifted him, and brought him to his mother 1
30 the mother of the child said, "As the LORD lives 1
8:26 His mother's name was Athali'ah; 1
9:22 the harlotries and the sorceries of your mother 1
11: 1 Athali'ah the mother of Ahazi'ah saw that her son 1
12: 1 His mother's name was Zib'iah of Beer-sheba. 1
14: 2 His mother's name was Jeho-ad'din of Jerusalem. 1
15: 2 His mother's name was Jecoli'ah of Jerusalem. 1
33 His mother's name was Jeru'sha the daughter 1
18: 2 His mother's name was Abi the daughter 1
21: 1 His mother's name was Heph'zibah. 1
19 His mother's name was Meshul'lemeth 1
22: 1 His mother's name was Jedi'dah the daughter 1
23:31 His mother's name was Hamu'tal the daughter 1

36 His mother's name was Zebi'dah 1
24: 8 His mother's name was Nehush'ta the daughter 1
12 gave himself up . . himself, and his mother, and his 1
15 he carried away . . the king's mother 1
18 His mother's name was Hamu'tal the daughter 1
1Ch 2:26 wife . . At'arah; she was the mother of Onam. 1
3: 2 the third Ab'salom, whose mother was Ma'acah •
2 the fourth Adoni'jah, whose mother was Haggith; •
4: 9 and his mother called his name Jabez, saying 1
2Ch 12:13 His mother's name was Na'amah the Ammonitess. 1
13: 2 mother's name was Micai'ah the daughter of U'riel 1
15:16 Even Ma'acah, his mother, King Asa removed 1
20:31 His mother's name was Azu'bah 1
22: 2 His mother's name was Athali'ah 1
3 his mother was his counselor in doing wickedly. 1
10 Athali'ah the mother of Ahazi'ah saw that her son 1
24: 1 his mother's name was Zib'iah of Beer-sheba. 1
25: 1 His mother's name was Jeho-ad'dan of Jerusalem. 1
26: 3 His mother's name was Jecoli'ah of Jerusalem. 1
27: 1 His mother's name was Jeru'shah 1
29: 1 His mother's name was Abi'jah 1
Est 2: 7 Esther . . for she had neither father nor mother; 1
7 and when her father and her mother died 1
Job 1:21 he said, "Naked I came from my mother's womb 1
3:10 it did not shut the doors of my mother's womb 4
17:14 if I say . . to the worm, 'My mother,' or 'My sister,' 1
19:17 loathsome to the sons of my own mother. 2
31:18 from his mother's womb I guided him 1
Ps 22: 9 thou didst keep me safe upon my mother's breasts. 1
10 since my mother bore me thou hast been my God. 1
27:10 For my father and my mother have forsaken me 1
35:14 I went about as one who laments his mother 1
50:20 you slander your own mother's son. 1
51: 5 in iniquity, and in sin did my mother conceive me. 1
69: 8 I have become . . an alien to my mother's sons. 1
71: 6 thou art he who took me from my mother's womb. 1
109:14 let not the sin of his mother be blotted out! 1
113: 9 making her the joyous mother of children. 1
131: 2 like a child quieted at its mother's breast; 1
139:13 thou didst knit me together in my mother's womb. 1
Prv 1: 8 reject not your mother's teaching; 1
4: 3 son . . the only one in the sight of my mother 1
6:20 My son . . forsake not your mother's teaching. 1
10: 1 but a foolish son is a sorrow to his mother. 1
15:20 but a foolish man despises his mother. 1
19:26 who does violence . . and chases away his mother 1
20:20 If one curses his father or his mother 1
23:22 do not despise your mother when she is old. 1
25 Let your father and mother be glad 1
28:24 He who robs his father or his mother and says, "That 1
29:15 left to himself brings shame to his mother. 1
30:11 those who . . do not bless their mothers. 1
17 eye . . mocks a father and scorns to obey a mother 1
31: 1 words of Lemuel . . which his mother taught him 1
Ecc 5:15 As he came from his mother's womb he shall go again 1
Sng 1: 6 My mother's sons were angry with me 1
3: 4 until I had brought him into my mother's house 1
11 with the crown with which his mother crowned him 1
6: 9 My dove . . is only one, the darling of her mother 1
8: 1 a brother to me, that nursed at my mother's breast! 1
2 lead you and bring you into the house of my mother 1
5 There your mother was in travail with you 1
Isa 8: 4 the child knows how to cry 'My father' or 'My mother 1
49: 1 from the body of my mother he named my name. 1
50: 1 Where is your mother's bill of divorce 1
1 for . . transgressions your mother was put away. 1
66:13 As one whom his mother comforts, so I will comfort 1
Jer 15: 8 I have brought against the mothers of young men 1
10 Woe is me, my mother, that you bore me 1
16: 3 and concerning the mothers who bore them 1
7 to drink for his father or his mother. 1
20:14 The day when my mother bore me 1
17 so my mother would have been my grave 1
22:26 I will hurl you and the mother who bore you 1
50:12 your mother shall be utterly shamed 1
52: 1 His mother's name was Hamu'tal 1
Lam 2:12 They cry to their mothers, "Where is bread and wine? 1
12 their life is poured out on their mothers' bosom. 1
5: 3 our mothers are like widows. 1
Ezk 16: 3 father was an Amorite, and your mother a Hittite. 1
44 proverb about you, 'Like mother, like daughter. 1
45 You are the daughter of your mother 1
45 mother was a Hittite and your father an Amorite. 1
19: 2 say: What a lioness was your mother among lions! 1
10 Your mother was like a vine in a vineyard 1
22: 7 Father and mother are treated with contempt 1
23: 2 there were two women, the daughters of one mother; 1
44:25 however, for father or mother, for son or daughter 1
Hos 2: 2 Plead with your mother, plead–
5 For their mother has played the harlot; 1
4: 5 and I will destroy your mother. 1
10:14 mothers were dashed in pieces with . . children. 1
Mic 7: 6 the daughter rises up against her mother 1
Zec 13: 3 his father and mother who bore him will say to him 1
3 mother who bore him shall pierce him through 1
Mat 1:18 When his mother Mary had been betrothed 4
2:11 saw the child with Mary his mother, and they fell 4
13 Rise, take the child and his mother, and flee 4
14 he rose and took the child and his mother by night 4
20 Rise, take the child and his mother, and go 4
21 he rose and took the child and his mother, and went 4
10:35 and a daughter against her mother 4
37 He who loves father or mother more than me 4
12:46 behold, his mother and his brothers stood 4
48 Who is my mother, and who are my brothers? 4
49 he said, "Here are my mother and my brothers! 4
50 is my brother, and sister, and mother. 4
13:55 Is not his mother called Mary? 4
14: 8 Prompted by her mother, she said 4
11 and she brought it to her mother. 4
15: 4 'Honor your father and your mother,' 4
4 'He who speaks evil of father or mother 4
5 you say, 'If any one tells his father or his mother 4
19: 5 leave his father and mother 4
19 Honor your father and mother 4
29 sisters or father or mother or children or lands 4
20:20 the mother of the sons of Zeb'edee came up to him 4
27:56 Mary the mother of James and Joseph 5
56 the mother of the sons of Zeb'edee. 4
Mrk 3:31 his mother and his brothers came 4
32 Your mother and your brothers are outside 4
33 he replied, "Who are my mother and my brothers? 4
34 he said, "Here are my mother and my brothers! 4
35 my brother, and sister, and mother. 4
5:40 and took the child's father and mother 4
6:24 she went out, and said to her mother 4
28 the girl gave it to her mother. 4
7:10 For Moses said, 'Honor your father and your mother'; 4
10 'He who speaks evil of father or mother 4
11 you say, 'If a man tells his father or his mother 4
12 to do anything for his father or mother 4
10: 7 a man shall leave his father and mother 4
19 Do not defraud, Honor your father and mother.' 4
29 house or brothers or sisters or mother or father 4
30 brothers and sisters and mothers and children 4
15:40 Mary the mother of James the younger and of Joses •
47 Mary Mag'dalene and Mary the mother of Joses saw •
16: 1 Mary Mag'dalene, and Mary the mother of James •
Lke 1:15 with the Holy Spirit, even from his mother's womb. 4
43 that the mother of my Lord should come to me? 4
60 his mother said, "Not so, he shall be called John. 4
2:33 his father and his mother marveled 4
34 Simeon blessed them and said to Mary his mother 4
48 his mother said to him, "Son, why have you treated us 4
51 his mother kept all these things in her heart. 4
7:12 the only son of his mother, and she was a widow 4
15 he gave him to his mother. 4
8:19 Then his mother and his brothers came to him 4
20 he was told, "Your mother and your brothers 4
21 My mother and my brothers are those who hear 4
51 the father and mother of the child. 4
12:53 mother against daughter 4
53 daughter against her mother 4
14:26 his own father and mother and wife and children 4
18:20 Honor your father and mother.' 4
24:10 Mary the mother of James and the other women •
Joh 2: 1 at Cana . . and the mother of Jesus was there; 4
3 When the wine failed, the mother of Jesus said 4
5 His mother said to the servants 4
12 with his mother and his brothers 4
3: 4 Can he enter a second time into his mother's womb 4
6:42 Jesus . . whose father and mother we know? 4
19:25 standing by the cross of Jesus were his mother 4
25 standing by the cross of Jesus were his mother 4
26 When Jesus saw his mother 4
26 he said to his mother, "Woman, behold, your son! 4
27 Then he said to the disciple, "Behold, your mother! 4
Act 1:14 with the women and Mary the mother of Jesus 4
12:12 Mary . . mother of John whose other name was Mark 4
Rom 16:13 Greet Rufus . . also his mother and mine. 4
Gal 4:26 Jerusalem above is free, and she is our mother. 4
Eph 5:31 shall leave his father and mother 4
6: 2 Honor your father and mother 4
1Ti 5: 2 older women like mothers 4
2Ti 1: 5 your grandmother Lo'is and your mother Eunice 4
Rev 17: 5 Babylon the great, mother of harlots 4
1Es 4:21 with no thought of his father or his mother 4
25 loves . . more than his father or his mother. 4
2Es 1:28 a mother her daughters or a nurse her children 7
2: 2 The mother who bore them says to them, 'Go 7
5 in addition to the mother of the children 7
6 and bring their mother to ruin 7
15 Mother, embrace your sons 7
17 Do not fear, mother of sons, for I have chosen you 7
30 Rejoice, O mother, with your sons 7
5:35 Or why did not my mother's womb become my grave 7
50 Is our mother . . still young? 7
10: 7 For Zion, the mother of us all, is in deep grief 7
8 but we, the whole world, for our mother. ‡
13:55 and called understanding your mother. 7
Tob 1: 8 as Deborah my father's mother had commanded me 4
4: 3 do not neglect your mother 4
13 because shiftlessness is the mother of famine. 4
5:17 Anna, his mother, began to weep, and said to Tobit 4
6:14 the lives of my father and mother 4
7:17 the mother comforted her daughter in her tears •
10: 7 my father and mother have given up hope 4
11:17 blessed are your father and your mother. 4
14:10 Bury me properly, and your mother with me 4
Jdt 8:26 the sheep of Laban, his mother's brother. 4
Wis 7: 1 in the womb of a mother I was molded into flesh 4
12 I did not know that she was their mother. 3
Sir 3: 2 confirmed the right of the mother over her sons. 4
4 whoever glorifies his mother 4
6 whoever obeys the Lord will refresh his mother; 4
9 a mother's curse uproots their foundations. 4
11 a disgrace . . not to respect their mother. 4
16 whoever angers his mother is cursed by the Lord. 4
4:10 Be . . instead of a husband to their mother 4
10 he will love you more than does your mother. 4
7:27 do not forget the birth pangs of your mother. 4
15: 2 She will come to meet him like a mother 4
23:14 Remember your father and mother 4
40: 1 the day they come forth from their mother's womb 4
1 till the day they return to the mother of all. 4
41:17 before your father or mother 4
1Mc 1:61 they hung the infants from their mothers' necks. •
13:28 for his father and mother and four brothers. 4
2Mc 7: 1 seven brothers and their mother 4
4 the rest of the brothers and the mother 4
5 the brothers and their mother 4
20 The mother was especially admirable 4
25 the king called the mother to him 4
41 Last of all, the mother died, after her sons. 4
3Mc 1:18 virgins . . rushed out with their mothers 6
20 Mothers and nurses 4
5:49 parents and children, mothers and daughters 4
4Mc 1: 8 Eleazar and the seven brothers and their mother. 4
10 with their mother, died for the sake of nobility 4
8: 3 seven brothers . . along with their aged mother 4
4 grouped about their mother as if in a chorus 4
20 have compassion on our mother's age; 4
10: 2 the same mother bore me 4
12: 6 he sent for the boy's mother 4
7 when his mother had exhorted him 4
14:12 the mother of the seven young men 4
13 how complex is a mother's love for her children •
20 did not sway the mother of the young men 4
15: 1 more desirable to the mother than her children! 4
2 Two courses were open to this mother 4
4 Especially is this true of mothers 4
5 Considering that mothers are the weaker sex 4
6 The mother of the seven boys 4
6 more than any other mother, loved her children. 4
11 though so many factors influenced the mother 4
12 Instead, the mother urged them on 4
13 nurture and indomitable suffering by mothers! 4
14 This mother . . did not change her attitude. 4
16 O mother, tried now by more bitter pains 4
21 children in torture calling to their mother. 4
22 how many torments the mother then suffered 4
24 this noble mother disregarded all these 4
26 this mother held two ballots 4
29 O mother of the nation, vindicator of the law 4
16: 1 advanced in years and mother of seven sons 4
4 the mother quenched so many . . emotions 4
5 though a mother 4
6 I am now the mother of none! 4
12 the sacred and God-fearing mother did not wail 4
14 O mother, soldier of God in the cause of religion 4
17: 2 O mother, who . . nullified . . the tyrant 4
4 Take courage, therefore, O holy-minded mother 4
7 they saw the mother of the seven children 4
13 the mother of the seven sons 4
18: 6 The mother of seven sons 4
23 the sons of Abraham with their . . mother 4

mother *See also* love, queen.

nursing mother 1. ינק
Isa 49:23 and their queens your nursing mothers. 1

mother of seven 1. ἑπταμήτωρ
4Mc 16:24 the mother of the seven encouraged 1

without mother 1. ἀμήτωρ
Heb 7: 3 He is without father or mother or genealogy 1

mother-in-law 1. חָמוֹת 2. חֹתֵן 3. πενθερά
Deu 27:23 'Cursed be he who lies with his mother-in-law.' 2
Rut 1:14 kissed her mother-in-law, but Ruth clung to her. 1
2:11 All that you have done for your mother-in-law 1
18 she showed her mother-in-law what she had gleaned 1
19 her mother-in-law said to her, "Where did you glean 1
19 she told her mother-in-law with whom she had 1
23 and she lived with her mother-in-law. 1
3: 1 Then Na'omi her mother-in-law said to her 1
6 and did just as her mother-in-law had told her. 1
16 And when she came to her mother-in-law, she said 1
17 not go back empty-handed to your mother-in-law. 1
Mic 7: 6 the daughter-in-law against her mother-in-law; 1
Mat 8:14 he saw his mother-in-law lying sick with a fever; 3
10:35 a daughter-in-law against her mother-in-law; 3
Mrk 1:30 Now Simon's mother-in-law lay sick with a fever 3
Lke 4:38 Now Simon's mother-in-law was ill with a high fever 3
12:53 mother-in-law against her daughter-in-law 3

53 daughter-in-law against her mother-in-law. 3
mother-in-law *See also* father-in-law.

mother-of-pearl 1. דַּר
Est 1: 6 mosaic . . of porphyry, marble, mother-of-pearl 1

motion 1. κατασείω 2. κίνησις 3. νεύω
Act 12:17 motioning to them with his hand to be silent 1
13:16 So Paul stood up, and motioning with his hand said 1
19:33 Alexander motioned with his hand 1
21:40 motioned with his hand to the people 1
24:10 when the governor had motioned to him to speak 3
Wis 7:24 For wisdom is more mobile than any motion; 2

motive
2Mc 14:30 this austerity did not spring from the best motives •

mottle 1. בָּרֹד
Gen 31:10 the flock were striped, spotted, and mottled. 1
12 upon the flock are striped, spotted, and mottled; 1

mould 1. τυπόω
Sir 38:30 He moulds the clay with his arm 1

mound 1. סֹלְלָה 2. תֵּל
Jos 11:13 none of the cities that stood on mounds 2
2Sm 20:15 they cast up a mound against the city, and it stood 1
Jer 30:18 the city shall be rebuilt upon its mound 2
49: 2 Rabbah . . it shall become a desolate mound 2
Ezk 4: 2 and cast up a mound against it; 1
17:17 will not help him in war, when mounds are cast up 1
21:22 to cast up mounds, to build siege towers. 1
26: 8 and throw up a mound against you 1

burial mound 1. χειμών
Sir 21: 8 like one who gathers stones for his burial mound. 1

siege mound 1. סֹלְלָה
2Kg 19:32 or cast up a siege mound against it. 1
Isa 37:33 or cast up a siege mound against it. 1
Jer 6: 6 cast up a siege mound against Jerusalem. 1
32:24 siege mounds have come up to the city to take it 1
33: 4 to make a defense against the siege mounds 1

mount 1. הַר 2. ὄρος
Gen 22:14 On the mount of the LORD it shall be provided. 1
Num10:33 set out from the mount of the LORD three days' 1
1Kg 19: 8 ate and drank, and went . . to Horeb the mount of God. 1
11 stand upon the mount before the LORD. 1
2Kg 23:13 to the south of the mount of corruption 1
16 as Josi'ah turned, he saw the tombs . . on the mount; 1
Ps 68:16 at the mount which God desired for his abode 1
87: 1 On the holy mount stands the city he founded; 1
Isa 10:32 shake . . fist at the mount of the daughter of Zion 1
14:13 sit on the mount of assembly in the far north; 1
16: 1 lambs . . to the mount of the daughter of Zion. 1
Ezk 35: 3 Behold, I am against you, mount Se'ir 1
Lke 19:29 at the mount that is called Olivet 2
21:37 went out and lodged on the mount called Olivet. 2
Act 1:12 Then they returned to Jerusalem from the mount 2

mount (2) 1. הַר 2. ἐπιβαίνω 3. κτῆνος 4. mons
Gen 14: 6 the Horites in their Mount Se'ir 1
Exd 19:11 the LORD will come down upon Mount Sinai 1
18 Mount Sinai was wrapped in smoke 1
20 the LORD came down upon Mount Sinai, to the top 1
23 The people cannot come up to Mount Sinai; 1
24:16 The glory of the LORD settled on Mount Sinai 1
31:18 made an end of speaking with him upon Mount Sinai 1
33: 6 stripped themselves . . from Mount Horeb onward. 1
34: 2 come up in the morning to Mount Sinai 1
4 went up on Mount Sinai, as the LORD had commanded 1
29 When Moses came down from Mount Sinai 1
32 the LORD had spoken with him in Mount Sinai. 1
Lev 7:38 which the LORD commanded Moses on Mount Sinai 1
25: 1 The LORD said to Moses on Mount Sinai 1
26:46 statutes . . on Mount Sinai by Moses 1
27:34 for the people of Israel on Mount Sinai. 1
Num 3: 1 when the LORD spoke with Moses on Mount Sinai. 1
20:22 people of Israel . . came to Mount Hor. 1
23 the LORD said to Moses and Aaron at Mount Hor 1
25 Aaron and Elea'zar . . bring them up to Mount Hor; 1
27 they went up Mount Hor in the sight of all 1
21: 4 From Mount Hor they set out by the way to the Red Sea 1
28: 6 offering, which was ordained at Mount Sinai 1
33:23 from Kehela'thah, and encamped at Mount Shepher. 1
24 out from Mount Shepher, and encamped at Hara'dah. 1
37 set out from Kadesh, and encamped at Mount Hor 1
38 went up Mount Hor at the command of the LORD 1
39 Aaron was 123 years old when he died on Mount Hor. 1
41 set out from Mount Hor, and encamped at Zalmo'nah. 1
34: 7 you shall mark out your line to Mount Hor 1
8 from Mount Hor you shall mark it out 1
Deu 1: 2 from Horeb by the way of Mount Se'ir 1
2: 1 for many days we went about Mount Se'ir. 1
5 I have given Mount Se'ir to Esau as a possession. 1
3: 8 from the valley of the Arnon to Mount Hermon 1
4:48 from Aro'er . . as far as Mount Si'rion 1
11:29 set the blessing on Mount Ger'izim and the curse 1
29 set the blessing . . and the curse on Mount Ebal. 1
27: 4 set up these stones . . on Mount Ebal 1
12 these shall stand upon Mount Ger'izim to bless 1
13 stand upon Mount Ebal for the curse: Reuben, Gad 1
32:49 "Ascend this mountain of the Ab'arim, Mount Nebo 1
50 as Aaron your brother died in Mount Hor 1
33: 2 he shone forth from Mount Paran 1
34: 1 Moses went up from the plains of Moab to Mount Nebo. 1
Jos 8:30 Joshua built an altar in Mount Ebal to the LORD 1
33 Israel . . half of them in front of Mount Ger'izim 1
33 half . . and half of them in front of Mount Ebal 1
11:17 lowland from Mount Halak, that rises toward Se'ir 1
17 in the valley of Lebanon below Mount Hermon. 1
12: 1 from the valley of the Arnon to Mount Hermon 1
5 and ruled over Mount Hermon and Sal'ecah 1
7 from Ba'al-gad in the valley . . to Mount Halak 1
13: 5 from Ba'al-gad below Mount Hermon to the entrance 1
11 and all Mount Hermon, and all Bashan to Sal'ecah; 1
15: 9 and from there to the cities of Mount Ephron; 1
10 boundary circles west of Ba'alah to Mount Se'ir 1
10 along to the northern shoulder of Mount Je'arim 1
11 to Shik'keron, and passes along to Mount Ba'alah 1
Jdg 3: 3 Hivites who dwelt on Mount Lebanon, from Mount 1
3 Lebanon, from Mount Ba'al-her'mon as far 1
4: 6 Go, gather your men at Mount Tabor, taking 10,000 1
12 the son of Abin'o-am had gone up to Mount Tabor 1
14 Barak went down from Mount Tabor with 10,000 men 1
9: 7 he went and stood on the top of Mount Ger'izim 1
48 Abim'elech went up to Mount Zalmon 1
1Sm 31: 1 Israel fled . . and fell slain on Mount Gilbo'a. 1
8 Saul and his three sons fallen on Mount Gilbo'a. 1
2Sm 1: 6 By chance I happened to be on Mount Gilbo'a; 1
15:30 David went up the ascent of the Mount of Olives •
1Kg 18:19 send and gather all Israel to me at Mount Carmel 1
20 and gathered the prophets . . at Mount Carmel. 1
2Kg 2:25 From there he went on to Mount Carmel 1
4:25 So she . . came to the man of God at Mount Carmel. 1
19:31 and out of Mount Zion a band of survivors. 1
1Ch 4:42 some of them . . went to Mount Se'ir 1
5:23 very numerous from Bashan to . . Mount Hermon. 1
10: 1 men of Israel . . fell slain on Mount Gilbo'a. 1
8 found Saul and his sons fallen on Mount Gilbo'a. 1
2Ch 3: 1 house of the LORD in Jerusalem on Mount Mori'ah 1
13: 4 Then Abi'jah stood up on Mount Zemara'im 1
20:10 behold, the men of Ammon and Moab and Mount Se'ir 1
22 an ambush against the men of . . Mount Se'ir 1
23 rose against the inhabitants of Mount Se'ir 1
Ps 42: 6 land of Jordan and of Hermon, from Mount Mizar. 1
48: 2 joy of all the earth, Mount Zion, in the far north 1
11 let Mount Zion be glad! 1
74: 2 Remember Mount Zion, where thou hast dwelt. 1
78:68 the tribe of Judah, Mount Zion, which he loves. 1
125: 1 Those who trust in the LORD are like Mount Zion 1
Isa 4: 5 create over the whole site of Mount Zion 1
8:18 the LORD of hosts, who dwells on Mount Zion. 1
10:12 the Lord has finished all his work on Mount Zion 1
18: 7 to Mount Zion, the place of the name of the LORD 1
24:23 for the LORD of hosts will reign on Mount Zion 1
28:21 For the LORD will rise up as on Mount Pera'zim 1
29: 8 the nations be that fight against Mount Zion. 1
31: 4 LORD . . will come down to fight upon Mount Zion 1
37:32 and out of Mount Zion a band of survivors. 1
Jer 4:15 from Dan and proclaims evil from Mount E'phraim. 1
Lam 5:18 for Mount Zion which lies desolate; 1
Ezk 35: 2 "Son of man, set your face against Mount Se'ir 1
7 I will make Mount Se'ir a waste and a desolation; 1
15 you shall be desolate, Mount Se'ir, and all Edom 1
Jol 2:32 for in Mount Zion and in Jerusalem there shall be 1
Obd 1: 8 out of Edom, and understanding out of Mount Esau? 1
9 every man from Mount Esau will be cut off 1
17 in Mount Zion there shall be those that escape 1
19 Those of the Negeb shall possess Mount Esau 1
21 Saviors shall go up to Mount Zion to rule 1
21 shall go up to Mount Zion to rule Mount Esau; 1
Mic 4: 7 the LORD will reign over them in Mount Zion 1
Hab 3: 3 came from Teman . . the Holy One from Mount Paran. 1
Zec 14: 4 his feet shall stand on the Mount of Olives 1
4 the Mount of Olives shall be split in two 1
4 one half of the Mount shall withdraw northward 1
Mat 21: 5 humble, and mounted on an ass 2
Act 23:24 Also provide mounts for Paul to ride 3
2Es 2:33 from the Lord on Mount Horeb to go to Israel 4
42 I, Ezra, saw on Mount Zion a great multitude 4
3:17 thou didst bring them to Mount Sinai. 4
13:35 he shall stand on the top of Mount Zion. 4
14: 4 and I led him up on Mount Sinai 4
Sir 50:26 those who live on Mount Seir •

mount (3) 1. כָּבַשׁ 2. גדל 3. עלה 4. רכב
Deu 28:43 sojourner . . mount above you higher and higher; 3
1Sm 25:42 Ab'igail made haste and rose and mounted on an ass 4
30:17 400 young men, who mounted camels and fled. 4
2Sm 13:29 all . . arose, and each mounted his mule and fled. 4
1Kg 12:18 King Rehobo'am made haste to mount his chariot 3
13:13 they saddled the ass for him and he mounted it. 4
2Ch 10:18 King Rehobo'am made haste to mount his chariot 3
Ezr 9: 6 our guilt has mounted up to the heavens. 2
Est 8:10 and letters were sent by mounted couriers 1
14 the couriers, mounted on their swift horses 4
Ps 78:21 against Jacob, his anger mounted against Israel; 3
Jer 46: 4 Harness the horses; mount, O horsemen! 3

mount a chariot 1. רכב
2Kg 9:16 Jehu mounted his chariot, and went to Jezreel 1

high mount 1. מָרוֹם
Ps 68:18 Thou didst ascend the high mount 1

mount up 1. גבה 2. עלה 3. רום 4. רמם 5. ὑπερφέρω
Job 20: 6 Though his height mount up to the heavens 2
39:27 Is it at your command that the eagle mounts up 1
Ps 107:26 mounted up to heaven, they went down to the depths; 2
Isa 40:31 they shall mount up with wings like eagles 2
Jer 49:22 one shall mount up and fly swiftly like an eagle 2
51:53 Though Babylon should mount up to heaven 2
Ezk 10:15 And the cherubim mounted up. 4
16 the cherubim lifted up their wings to mount up 3
17 when they mounted up, these mounted up with them; 3
17 when they mounted up, these mounted up with them; 4
19 cherubim lifted up their wings and mounted up 4
1Es 8:75 our mistakes have mounted up to heaven 5

mountain 1. הַר 2. סֶלַע 3. צוּר 4. טוּר (A) 5. ὄρος 6. mons
Gen 7:19 all the high mountains under the whole heaven 1
20 the waters prevailed above the mountains 1
8: 4 ark came to rest upon the mountains of Ar'arat. 1
5 of the month, the tops of the mountains were seen. 1
12: 8 Thence he removed to the mountain on the east 1
14:10 into them, and the rest fled to the mountain. 1
22: 2 one of the mountains of which I shall tell you. 1
31:54 Jacob offered a sacrifice on the mountain 1
54 ate bread and tarried all night on the mountain. 1
49:26 beyond the blessings of the eternal mountains 5
Exd 3: 1 and came to Horeb, the mountain of God. 1
12 you shall serve God upon this mountain. 1
4:27 met him at the mountain of God and kissed him. 1
15:17 bring them in, and plant them on thy own mountain 1
18: 5 he was encamped at the mountain of God. 1
19: 2 there Israel encamped before the mountain. 1
3 LORD called to him out of the mountain, saying 1
12 Take heed that you do not go up into the mountain 1
12 touches the mountain shall be put to death; 1
13 they shall come up to the mountain. 1
14 Moses went down from the mountain to the people 1
16 a thick cloud upon the mountain 1
17 took their stand at the foot of the mountain. 1
18 and the whole mountain quaked greatly. 1
20 LORD came down . . to the top of the mountain; 1
20 the LORD called Moses to the top of the mountain 1
23 bounds about the mountain, and consecrate it.' 1
20:18 sound of the trumpet and the mountain smoking 1
24: 4 built an altar at the foot of the mountain 1
12 Come up to me on the mountain, and wait there; 1
13 Moses went up into the mountain of God. 1
15 Then Moses went up on the mountain, and the cloud 1
15 and the cloud covered the mountain. 1
17 like a devouring fire on the top of the mountain 1
18 And Moses . . went up on the mountain. 1
18 And Moses was on the mountain 40 days 1
25:40 which is being shown you on the mountain. 1
26:30 which has been shown you on the mountain. 1
27: 8 as it has been shown you on the mountain, so shall 1
32: 1 Moses delayed to come down from the mountain 1
12 to slay them in the mountains, and to consume 1
15 Moses turned, and went down from the mountain 1
19 broke them at the foot of the mountain. 1
34: 2 present yourself . . on the top of the mountain. 1
3 let no man be seen throughout all the mountain; 1
3 let no flocks or herds feed before that mountain. 1
29 in his hand as he came down from the mountain 1
Num20:28 Aaron died there on the top of the mountain. 1
28 Moses and Elea'zar came down from the mountain. 1
23: 7 king of Moab from the eastern mountains 1
9 For from the top of the mountains I see him 3
27:12 Go up into this mountain to Ab'arim, and see 1
33:47 encamped in the mountains of Ab'arim, before Nebo. 1
48 set out from the mountains of Ab'arim 1
Deu 1: 6 'You have stayed long enough at this mountain; 1
4:11 came near and stood at the foot of the mountain 1
11 mountain burned with fire to the heart of heaven 1
5: 4 LORD spoke with you face to face at the mountain 1
5 you did not go up into the mountain. He said 1
22 LORD spoke to all your assembly at the mountain 1
23 while the mountain was burning with fire 1
9: 9 up the mountain to receive the tables of stone 1
9 I remained on the mountain 40 days and 40 nights 1
10 spoken with you on the mountain out of the midst 1
15 I turned and came down from the mountain 1
15 mountain was burning with fire; 1
21 brook that descended out of the mountain. 1
10: 1 come up to me on the mountain, and make an ark 1
3 went up the mountain with the two tables 1
4 the LORD had spoken to you on the mountain 1
5 Then I turned and came down from the mountain 1

10 I stayed on the mountain, as at the first time 1
12: 2 served their gods, upon the high mountains 1
32:22 sets on fire the foundations of the mountains. 1
49 Ascend this mountain of the Ab'arim, Mount Nebo 1
50 die on the mountain which you ascend 1
33:15 with the finest produce of the ancient mountains 1
19 They shall call peoples to their mountain; 1
Jos 15: 8 the boundary goes up to the top of the mountain 1
9 boundary extends from the top of the mountain 1
18:13 upon the mountain that lies south 1
14 southward from the mountain that lies . . south 1
16 boundary goes down to the border of the mountain 1
24:30 Tim'nath-se'rah . . north of the mountain of Ga'ash. 1
Jdg 2: 9 of E'phraim, north of the mountain of Ga'ash. 1
5: 5 The mountains quaked before the LORD, yon Sinai 1
6: 2 made . . the dens which are in the mountains 1
9:25 men in ambush against him on the mountain tops 1
36 Look, men are coming down from the mountain tops! 1
36 You see the shadow of the mountains as if they 1
11:37 that I may go and wander on the mountains 1
38 and bewailed her virginity upon the mountains. 1
1Sm 17: 3 Philistines stood on the mountain on . . one side 1
3 Israel stood on the mountain on the other side 1
23:26 Saul went on one side of the mountain 1
26 David . . on the other side of the mountain; 1
25:20 and came down under cover of the mountain 1
26:13 and stood afar off on the top of the mountain 1
20 like one who hunts a partridge in the mountains. 1
2Sm 1:21 Ye mountains of Gilbo'a, let there be no dew or rain 1
13:34 the Horona'im road by the side of the mountain. 1
21: 6 hang . . at Gibeon on the mountain of the LORD. •
9 they hanged them on the mountain before the LORD 1
1Kg 11: 7 high place . . on the mountain east of Jerusalem. 1
19:11 a great and strong wind rent the mountains 1
22:17 I saw all Israel scattered upon the mountains 1
2Kg 2:16 cast him upon some mountain or into some valley. 1
4:27 when she came to the mountain to the man of God 1
6:17 the mountain was full of horses and chariots 1
19:23 I have gone up the heights of the mountains 1
1Ch 12: 8 who were swift as gazelles upon the mountains 1
2Ch 18:16 I saw all Israel scattered upon the mountains 1
33:15 built on the mountain of the house of the LORD 1
Job 9: 5 he who removes mountains, and they know it not 1
14:18 the mountain falls and crumbles away 1
24: 8 They are wet with the rain of the mountains 1
28: 9 and overturns mountains by the roots. 1
39: 1 Do you know when the mountain goats bring forth? 2
8 He ranges the mountains as his pasture 1
40:20 For the mountains yield food for him 1
Ps 11: 1 can you say to me, "Flee like a bird to the mountains; 1
18: 7 the foundations also of the mountains trembled 1
30: 7 thou hadst established me as a strong mountain; 1
36: 6 Thy righteousness is like the mountains of God 1
46: 2 though the mountains shake in the heart of the sea; 1
3 though the mountains tremble with its tumult. 1
48: 1 His holy mountain 1
65: 6 by thy strength hast established the mountains 1
68:15 O mighty mountain, mountain of Bashan; 1
15 O mighty mountain, mountain of Bashan; 1
15 O many-peaked mountain, mountain of Bashan! 1
15 O many-peaked mountain, mountain of Bashan! 1
16 Why look you with envy, O many-peaked mountain 1
72: 3 the mountains bear prosperity for the people 1
16 on the tops of the mountains may it wave; 1
76: 4 more majestic than the everlasting mountains. 1
78:54 the mountain which his right hand had won. 1
80:10 The mountains were covered with its shade 1
83:14 as the flame sets the mountains ablaze 1
90: 2 Before the mountains were brought forth 1
95: 4 heights of the mountains are his also. 1
97: 5 The mountains melt like wax before the LORD 1
99: 9 LORD our God, and worship at his holy mountain; 1
104: 6 waters stood above the mountains. 1
8 The mountains rose, the valleys sank down 1
13 From thy lofty abode . . waterest the mountains; 1
18 The high mountains are for the wild goats; 1
32 who touches the mountains and they smoke! 1
110: 3 day you lead your host upon the holy mountains. 1
114: 4 mountains skipped like rams 1
6 O mountains, that you skip like rams? 1
125: 2 As the mountains are round about Jerusalem 1
133: 3 dew . . which falls on the mountains of Zion! 1
144: 5 Touch the mountains that they smoke! 1
148: 9 Mountains and all hills 1
Prv 8:25 Before the mountains had been shaped 1
27:25 herbage of the mountains is gathered 1
Sng 2: 8 Behold, he comes, leaping upon the mountains 1
17 or a young stag upon rugged mountains. 1
4: 6 I will hie me to the mountain of myrrh 1
8 dens of lions, from the mountains of leopards. 1
8:14 or a young stag upon the mountains of spices. 1
Isa 2: 2 the mountain of the house of the LORD shall be 1
2 house of the LORD . . the highest of the mountains 1
3 mountain of the LORD . . house of the God of Jacob; 1
14 against all the high mountains, and . . hills; 1
5:25 smote them, and the mountains quaked; 1
11: 9 shall not hurt or destroy in all my holy mountain; 1
13: 4 a tumult on the mountains as of a great multitude! 1
14:25 and upon my mountains trample him under foot; 1
17:13 like chaff on the mountains before the wind 1
18: 3 when a signal is raised on the mountains, look! 1
6 be left to the birds of prey of the mountains 1
22: 5 a day of . . a shouting to the mountains. 1
25: 6 On this mountain the LORD of hosts will make 1
7 he will destroy on this mountain the covering 1
10 the hand of the LORD will rest on this mountain 1
27:13 worship . . on the holy mountain at Jerusalem. 1
30:17 left like a flagstaff on the top of a mountain 1
25 upon every lofty mountain and every high hill 1
29 to the mountain of the LORD, to the Rock of Israel. 1
34: 3 the mountains shall flow with their blood. 1
37:24 I have gone up the heights of the mountains 1
40: 4 and every mountain and hill be made low; 1
9 Get you up to a high mountain, O Zion 1
12 weighed the mountains in scales 1
41:15 you shall thresh the mountains and crush them 1
42:11 let them shout from the top of the mountains. 1
15 I will lay waste mountains and hills 1
44:23 break forth into singing, O mountains 1
45: 2 I will go before you and level the mountains 1
49:11 And I will make all my mountains a way 1
13 break forth, O mountains, into singing! 1
52: 7 beautiful upon the mountains are the feet of him 1
54:10 For the mountains may depart and the hills be 1
55:12 the mountains and the hills before you shall 1
56: 7 these I will bring to my holy mountain 1
57: 7 Upon a . . lofty mountain you have set your bed 1
13 the land, and shall inherit my holy mountain. 1
64: 1 that the mountains might quake at they presence- 1
3 the mountains quaked at thy presence. 1
65: 7 because they burned incense upon the mountains 1
9 and from Judah inheritors of my mountains; 1
11 forsake the LORD, who forget my holy mountain 1
25 shall not hurt or destroy in all my holy mountain 1
66:20 upon dromedaries, to my holy mountain Jerusalem 1
Jer 3:23 are a delusion, the orgies on the mountains. 1
4:24 I looked on the mountains 1
9:10 Take up weeping and wailing for the mountains 1
13:16 your feet stumble on the twilight mountains 1
16:16 hunt them from every mountain and every hill 1
17: 3 on the mountains in the open country. 1
18:14 Do the mountain waters run dry •
26:18 and the mountain of the house a wooded height. 1
31: 5 plant vineyards upon the mountains of Sama'ria; 1
46:18 the LORD of hosts, like Tabor among the mountains 1
50: 6 astray, turning them away on the mountains; 1
6 from mountain to hill they have gone 1
51:25 Behold, I am against you, O destroying mountain 1
25 and make you a burnt mountain. 1
Lam 4:19 they chased us on the mountains, they lay in wait 1
Ezk 6: 2 set your face toward the mountains of Israel 1
3 You mountains of Israel, hear the word of the Lord 1
3 Thus says the Lord GOD to the mountains 1
13 on all the mountain tops, under every green tree 1
7: 7 and not of joyful shouting upon the mountains. 1
16 they will be on the mountains, like doves 1
11:23 and stood upon the mountain which is on the east 1
17:22 will plant it upon a high and lofty mountain; 1
23 on the mountain height of Israel will I plant it 1
18: 6 if he does not eat upon the mountains 1
11 but eats upon the mountains 1
15 who does not eat upon the mountains 1
19: 9 no more be heard upon the mountains of Israel. 1
20:40 my holy mountain, the mountain height of Israel 1
40 my holy mountain, the mountain height of Israel 1
22: 9 and men in you who eat upon the mountains; 1
28:14 you were on the holy mountain of God; 1
16 as a profane thing from the mountain of God 1
31:12 On the mountains and in all the valleys 1
32: 5 I will strew your flesh upon the mountains 1
6 I will drench the land even to the mountains 1
33:28 the mountains of Israel shall be so desolate 1
34: 6 scattered, they wandered over all the mountains 1
13 I will feed them on the mountains of Israel 1
14 upon the mountain heights of Israel 1
14 on fat pasture they shall feed on the mountains 1
35: 8 I will fill your mountains with the slain; 1
12 you uttered against the mountains of Israel 1
36: 1 son of man, prophesy to the mountains of Israel 1
1 O mountains of Israel, hear the word of the LORD. 1
4 O mountains of Israel, hear the word of the Lord 1
4 says the Lord GOD to the mountains and the hills 1
6 and say to the mountains and hills, to the ravines 1
8 you, O mountains of Israel, shall shoot forth 1
37:22 nation in the land, upon the mountains of Israel; 1
38: 8 gathered from many nations upon the mountains 1
20 the mountains shall be thrown down 1
39: 2 and lead you against the mountains of Israel; 1
4 You shall fall upon the mountains of Israel 1
17 sacrificial feast upon the mountains of Israel 1
40: 2 and set me down upon a very high mountain 1
43:12 upon the top of the mountain shall be most holy. 1
Dan 2:35 stone . . became a great mountain and filled 4
45 stone was cut from a mountain by no human hand 4
11:45 between the sea and the glorious holy mountain; 1
Hos 4:13 They sacrifice on the tops of the mountains 1
10: 8 and they shall say to the mountains, Cover us 1
Jol 2: 1 sound the alarm on my holy mountain! 1
2 blackness there is spread upon the mountains 1
5 they leap on the tops of the mountains 1
3:17 LORD your God, who dwell in Zion, my holy mountain. 1
18 in that day the mountains shall drip sweet wine 1
Ams 3: 9 Assemble . . upon the mountains of Sama'ria 1
4: 1 cows of Bashan, who are in the mountains of Sama'ria 1
13 he who forms the mountains, and creates the wind 1
6: 1 those who feel secure on the mountain of Sama'ria 1
9:13 the mountains shall drip sweet wine 1
Obd 1:16 For as you have drunk upon my holy mountain 1
Jon 2: 6 at the roots of the mountains. 1
Mic 1: 4 And the mountains will melt under him 1
3:12 and the mountain of the house a wooded height. 1
4: 1 the mountain . . of the LORD shall be established 1
1 be established as the highest of the mountains 1
2 Come, let us go up to the mountain of the LORD 1
6: 1 Arise, plead your case before the mountains 1
2 Hear, you mountains, the controversy of the LORD 1
7:12 from sea to sea and from mountain to mountain. 1
12 from sea to sea and from mountain to mountain. 1
Nah 1: 5 The mountains quake before him, the hills melt; 1
15 on the mountains the feet of him who brings good 1
3:18 Your people are scattered on the mountains 1
Hab 3: 6 then the eternal mountains were scattered 1
10 The mountains saw thee, and writhed; 1
Zep 3:11 shall no longer be haughty in my holy mountain. 1
Zec 4: 7 What are you, O great mountain? 1
6: 1 chariots came out from between two mountains; 1
1 and the mountains were mountains of bronze. 1
1 and the mountains were mountains of bronze. 1
8: 3 the mountain of the LORD of hosts, the holy 1
3 of the LORD of hosts, the holy mountain. 1
14: 5 the valley of my mountains shall be stopped up 1
5 the valley of the mountains shall touch the side 1
Mat 4: 8 Again, the devil took him to a very high mountain 5
5: 1 Seeing the crowds, he went up on the mountain 5
8: 1 When he came down from the mountain 5
14:23 he went up on the mountain by himself to pray 5
15:29 he went up on the mountain, and sat down there. 5
17: 1 and led them up a high mountain apart. 5
9 as they were coming down the mountain 5
20 you will say to this mountain 5
18:12 does he not leave the 99 on the mountains 5
21:21 but even if you say to this mountain 5
24:16 let those who are in Judea flee to the mountains; 5
28:16 to the mountain to which Jesus had directed 5
Mrk 3:13 And he went up on the mountain 5
5: 5 on the mountains he was always crying out 5
6:46 he went up on the mountain to pray. 5
9: 2 led them up a high mountain apart by themselves; 5
9 as they were coming down the mountain 5
11:23 Truly, I say to you, whoever says to this mountain 5
13:14 let those who are in Judea flee to the mountains; 5
Lke 3: 5 every mountain and hill shall be brought low 5
6:12 In these days he went out to the mountain to pray; 5
9:28 and went up on the mountain to pray. 5
37 when they had come down from the mountain 5
21:21 let those who are in Judea flee to the mountains 5
23:30 they will begin to say to the mountains, 'Fall on us'; 5
Joh 4:20 Our fathers worshiped on this mountain; 5
21 neither on this mountain nor in Jerusalem 5
6: 3 Jesus went up on the mountain 5
15 Jesus withdrew again to the mountain by himself. 5
1Co 13: 2 if I have all faith, so as to remove mountains 5
Heb 8: 5 the pattern which was shown you on the mountain. 5
11:38 wandering over deserts and mountains 5
12:20 If even a beast touches the mountain 5
2Pe 1:18 for we were with him on the holy mountain. 5
Rev 6:14 every mountain and island was removed 5
15 hid . . among the rocks of the mountains 5
16 calling to the mountains and the rocks, "Fall on us 5
8: 8 something like a great mountain, burning 5
16:20 and no mountains were to be found; 5
17: 9 the seven heads are seven mountains 5
21:10 he carried me away to a great, high mountain 5
1Es 4: 4 they go, and conquer mountains, walls, and towers. 5
2Es 2:19 seven mighty mountains on which roses . . grow 6
6:51 to live in it, where there are 1,000 mountains; 6
8:23 whose indignation makes the mountains melt 6
13: 6 he carved out for himself a great mountain 6
7 or place from which the mountain was carved 6
12 I saw the same man come down from the mountain 6
36 the mountain carved out without hands. 6
15:42 destroy cities and walls, mountains and hills 6
58 who are in the mountains and highlands 6
62 your land and your mountains 6
16:60 and pools on the tops of the mountains 6
Tob 1:21 they fled to the mountains of Ararat 5
Jdt 1:15 He captured Arphaxad in the mountains of Ragae 5
2:21 mountain which is to the north of Upper Cilicia. 5
6: 4 their mountains will be drunk with their blood 5
7: 4 neither the high mountains nor the valleys 5
10 the height of the mountains where they live 5
10 not easy to reach the tops of their mountains. 5
12 flows from the foot of the mountain- 5
13 We . . will go up to the tops of the nearby mountains 5
10:10 watched her until she had gone down the mountain 5
13:10 and went up the mountain to Bethulia 5
14:11 they went out . . to the passes in the mountains. 5

16: 4 came down from the mountains of the north 5
15 mountains shall be shaken to their foundations 5
Wis 9: 8 a temple on thy holy mountain 5
17:19 an echo thrown back from a hollow of the mountains 5
Sir 16:19 mountains . . and the foundations of the earth 5
43: 4 the sun burns the mountains three times as much 5
16 At his appearing the mountains are shaken 5
21 He consumes the mountains 5
Bar 5: 7 every high mountain and the everlasting hills 5
LJr 1:39 like stones from the mountain 5
63 sent from above to consume mountains and woods 5
Aza 1:53 Bless the Lord, mountains and hills 5
1Mc 4:38 bushes sprung up . . as on one of the mountains 5
9:38 and went up and hid under cover of the mountain. 5
40 the rest fled to the mountain 5
11:37 a conspicuous place on the holy mountain.' 5
68 set an ambush against him in the mountains 5
2Mc 2: 4 he went out to the mountain 5
5:27 kept himself . . alive in the mountains 5
9: 8 he could weigh the high mountains in a balance 5
28 among the mountains in a strange land. 5
10: 6 wandering in the mountains and caves 5

mountain *See also* country, district, slope.

mountain-sheep 1. זֶמֶר
Deu 14: 5 the ibex, the antelope, and the mountain-sheep 1

mounted man 1. רֶכֶב סוּסִים
2Kg 7:14 they took two mounted men, and the king sent them 1

mourn 1. אבל 2. אֵבֶל 3. אָבֵל 4. אָוֶן 5. אנה 6. בכה 7. הגה 8. הֶגֶה 9. מִסְפֵּד 10. מַרְזֵחַ 11. ספד 12. קדר 13. קְדֹרַנִּית 14. תַּאֲנִיָּה 15. *ἐν πένθει* 16. *θρηνέω* 17. *κλαίω* 18. *κοπετός* 19. *κόπτω* 20. *μελανία* 21. *ὀδυρμός* 22. *οἰμωγή* 23. *ὀλοφύρομαι* 24. *πενθέω* 25. *πένθος* 26. *στολή* 27. dolor 28. lugeo 29. ululo
Gen 23: 2 and Abraham went in to mourn for Sarah and to weep 11
27:41 The days of mourning for my father 2
37:34 Jacob . . mourned for his son many days. 1
35 No, I shall go down to Sheol to my son, mourning. 3
50:10 and he made a mourning for his father seven days. 2
11 saw the mourning on the threshing floor of Atad 2
11 This is a grievous mourning to the Egyptians. 2
Exd 33: 4 people heard these evil tidings, they mourned; 1
Num14:39 people mourned greatly. 1
Deu 26:14 I have not eaten of the tithe while I was mourning 4
34: 8 then the days of weeping and mourning for Moses 2
1Sm 6:19 he slew 70 men of them, and the people mourned 1
25: 1 all Israel assembled and mourned for him 11
28: 3 Samuel . . died, and all Israel had mourned for him 11
2Sm 1:12 they mourned and wept and fasted until evening 11
3:31 and gird on sackcloth, and mourn before Abner. 11
11:27 And when the mourning was over, David sent 2
13:37 And David mourned for his son day after day. 1
14: 2 be a mourner, and put on mourning garments; 2
2 who has been mourning many days for the dead; 1
19: 1 the king is weeping and mourning for Ab'salom. 1
2 So the victory that day was turned into mourning 2
1Kg 13:29 and brought it back . . to mourn and to bury him. 11
30 they mourned over him, saying, "Alas, my brother! 11
14:13 all Israel shall mourn for him, and bury him; 11
18 all Israel buried him and mourned for him 11
1Ch 7:22 E'phraim their father mourned many days 1
2Ch 35:24 All Judah and Jerusalem mourned for Josi'ah. 1
Ezr 10: 6 mourning over the faithlessness of the exiles. 1
Neh 1: 4 I sat down and wept, and mourned for days; 1
8: 9 This day is holy . . do not mourn or weep. 1
Est 4: 3 there was great mourning among the Jews 2
6:12 Haman . . mourning and with his head covered. 3
9:22 and from mourning into a holiday; 2
Job 5:11 those who mourn are lifted to safety. 12
14:22 he mourns only for himself. 1
30:31 My lyre is turned to mourning 2
Ps 30:11 Thou hast turned for me my mourning into dancing; 9
35:14 laments his mother, bowed down and in mourning. 12
38: 6 all the day I go about mourning. 12
42: 9 Why hast thou forgotten me? Why go I mourning 12
43: 2 why hast thou cast me off? Why go I mourning 12
Ecc 3: 4 a time to mourn, and a time to dance; 11
7: 2 It is better to go to the house of mourning 2
4 The heart of the wise is in the house of mourning; 2
Isa 3:26 her gates shall lament and mourn; 1
16: 7 Mourn, utterly stricken, for the raisin-cakes 7
19: 8 The fishermen will mourn and lament 5
22:12 Lord GOD of hosts called to weeping and mourning 9
24: 4 The earth mourns and withers 1
7 The wine mourns, the vine languishes 1
33: 9 The land mourns and languishes; 1
60:20 and your days of mourning shall be ended. 2
61: 2 vengeance of our God; to comfort all who mourn; 3
3 to grant to those who mourn in Zion– 3
3 the oil of gladness instead of mourning 2
66:10 rejoice with her in joy, all you who mourn over her; 1
Jer 4:28 For this the earth shall mourn 1
6:26 make mourning as for an only son 2
8:21 I mourn, and dismay has taken hold on me. 12
12: 4 How long will the land mourn 1
11 made it a desolation; desolate, it mourns to me. 1
14: 2 Judah mourns and her gates languish; 1
16: 5 says the LORD: Do not enter the house of mourning 10
23:10 because of the curse the land mourns 1
31:13 I will turn their mourning into joy 2
48:31 for all Moab; for the men of Kir-he'res I mourn. 7
Lam 1: 4 The roads to Zion mourn, for none come to . . feasts; 3
2: 5 he has multiplied . . mourning and lamentation. 14
5:15 our dancing has been turned to mourning. 2
Ezk 2:10 on it words of lamentation and mourning and woe. 8
7:12 Let not the buyer rejoice, nor the seller mourn 1
27 The king mourns, the prince is wrapped in despair 1
24:16 yet you shall not mourn or weep 11
17 Sigh, but not aloud; make no mourning for the dead. 2
23 you shall not mourn or weep, but you shall pine 11
27:31 in bitterness of soul, with bitter mourning. 9
Dan 10: 2 days I, Daniel, was mourning for three weeks. 1
Hos 4: 3 the land mourns, and all who dwell in it languish 1
10: 5 Its people shall mourn for it 1
Jol 1: 9 The priests mourn, the ministers of the LORD. 1
10 The fields are laid waste, the ground mourns; 1
2:12 with fasting, with weeping, and with mourning; 9
Ams 1: 2 the pastures of the shepherds mourn 1
5:16 They shall call the farmers to mourning 2
8: 8 and every one mourn who dwells in it 1
10 I will turn your feasts into mourning 2
10 I will make it like the mourning for an only son 2
9: 5 earth and it melts, and all who dwell in it mourn 1
Mic 1: 8 the jackals, and mourning like the ostriches. 2
Zec 7: 3 Should I mourn and fast in the fifth month 6
5 When you fasted and mourned in the fifth month 11
12:10 whom they have pierced, they shall mourn for him 11
10 mourn for him, as one mourns for an only child 9
11 the mourning in Jerusalem will be as great 9
11 as great as the mourning for Hadadrim'mon 9
12 The land shall mourn, each family by itself; 11
Mal 3:14 walking as in mourning before the LORD of hosts? 13
Mat 5: 4 Blessed are those who mourn, for they shall be 24
9:15 Jesus said to them, "Can the wedding guests mourn 24
11:17 we wailed, and you did not mourn.' 19
24:30 then all the tribes of the earth will mourn 19
Mrk 16:10 as they mourned and wept. 24
Lke 6:25 you shall mourn and weep. 24
1Co 5: 2 you are arrogant! Ought you not rather to mourn? 24
7:30 those who mourn as though they were not mourning 17
30 those who mourn as though they were not mourning 17
2Co 7: 7 as he told us of your longing, your mourning 21
12:21 I may have to mourn over many of those who sinned 24
Jas 4: 9 Be wretched and mourn and weep. 24
9 Let your laughter be turned to mourning 25
Rev 18: 7 give her a like measure of torment and mourning. 25
7 I am no widow, mourning I shall never see,' 25
8 plagues . . pestilence and mourning and famine 25
11 the merchants of the earth weep and mourn for her 24
15 fear of her torment, weeping and mourning aloud 24
19 as they wept and mourned, crying out, "Alas, alas 24
21: 4 neither shall there be mourning nor crying 25
1Es 1:32 in all Judea they mourned for Josiah 24
8:72 as I mourned over this iniquity 24
9: 2 he was mourning over the great iniquities 24
2Es 5:20 I fasted seven days, mourning and weeping 29
9:38 and behold, she was mourning and weeping 28
41 that I may weep for myself and continue to mourn 27
10: 4 but without ceasing mourn and fast until I die. 28
8 It is most appropriate to mourn now 28
8 because we are all mourning, and to be sorrowful 28
9 to mourn over so many who have come into being 28
11 Who then ought to mourn the more 28
39 and mourned greatly over Zion. 28
41 whom you saw mourning and began to console- 28
44 you saw her likeness, how she mourned for her son 28
15:12 Let Egypt mourn, and its foundations 28
13 Let the farmers that till the ground mourn 28
16:33 Virgins shall mourn 28
33 women shall mourn 28
33 their daughters shall mourn 28
Tob 2: 6 Your feasts shall be turned into mourning 25
10: 4 Then she began to mourn for him, and said 16
7 she never stopped mourning for her son Tobias 16
Jdt 16: 8 For she took off her widow's mourning 26
24 the house of Israel mourned for her seven days. 24
AEs 13:17 turn our mourning into feasting 25
14: 2 put on the garments of distress and mourning 25
Wis 19: 3 while they were still busy at mourning 25
Sir 7:34 mourn with those who mourn. 24
34 mourn with those who mourn. 24
19:26 There is a rascal bowed down in mourning 20
22: 6 Like music in mourning 25
12 Mourning for the dead lasts seven days 25
38:17 observe the mourning according to his merit 25
41:11 The mourning of men is about their bodies 25
48:24 comforted those who mourned in Zion. 24
Bel 1:40 the king came to mourn for Daniel 24
1Mc 1:25 Israel mourned deeply in every community 25
27 she who sat in the bridal chamber was mourning. 24
39 her feasts were turned into mourning 25
40 her exaltation was turned into mourning. 25
2:14 Mattathias . . put on sackcloth, and mourned greatly. 24
39 they mourned for them deeply. 24
70 Israel mourned for him with great lamentation. 19
3:51 thy priests mourn in humiliation. 15
4:39 mourned with great lamentation 19
9:20 they mourned many days and said 24
41 Thus the wedding was turned into mourning 25
12:52 they mourned for Jonathan and his companions 24
52 all Israel mourned deeply. 24
13:26 mourned for him many days. 24
3Mc 4: 2 among the Jews there was incessant mourning 25
3 what streets were not filled with mourning 18
6:32 Putting an end to all mourning and wailing 22
4Mc 16: 5 she would have mourned over them 23

make mourn 1. אבל
Ezk 31:15 I will make the deep mourn for it 1

no one to mourn 1. *ἀπένθητος*
2Mc 5:10 He . . had no one to mourn for him 1

mourner 1. אבל 2. אָבֵל 3. אָוֶן 4. ספד 5. lugeo
Job 29:25 like one who comforts mourners. 2
Ecc 12: 5 and the mourners go about the streets; 4
Isa 57:18 creating for his mourners the fruit of the lips. 2
Jer 16: 7 No one shall break bread for the mourner 1
Ezk 24:17 nor eat the bread of mourners. 5
22 nor eat the bread of mourners. 5
Hos 9: 4 Their bread shall be like mourners' bread; 3

mourner *See also* pretend.

mournful 1. *γοερός*
3Mc 5:25 with most tearful supplication and mournful dirges 1

mourning 1. luctus
2Es 2: 3 but with mourning and sorrow I have lost you 1
10: 6 do you not see our mourning, and what has happened 1

mourning woman 1. קִין
Jer 9:17 Consider, and call for the mourning women to come; 1

mouse 1. עַכְבָּר
Lev 11:29 the weasel, the mouse, the great lizard 1
1Sm 6: 4 Five golden tumors and five golden mice 1
5 make . . and images of your mice that ravage 1
11 the box with the golden mice and the . . tumors. 1
18 the golden mice, according to the number of all 1
Isa 66:17 swine's flesh and the abomination and mice 1

mouth 1. חֵךְ 2. מִדְבָּר 3. פֶּה 4. פָּנִים 5. קָצֶה 6. שָׂפָה 7. פֻּם (A) 8. *γλῶσσα* 9. *στόμα* 10. os
Gen 4:11 from the ground, which has opened its mouth 3
8:11 and lo, in her mouth a freshly plucked olive leaf; 3
29: 2 The stone on the well's mouth was large 3
3 would roll the stone from the mouth of the well 3
3 back in its place upon the mouth of the well. 3
8 the stone is rolled from the mouth of the well; 3
10 Jacob . . rolled the stone from the well's mouth 3
42:27 he saw his money in the mouth of his sack; 3
28 has been put back; here it is in the mouth of my sack •
43:12 that was returned to the mouth of your sacks; 3
21 and there was every man's money in the mouth of his 3
44: 1 and put each man's money in the mouth of his sack 3
2 put my cup . . in the mouth of the sack 3
8 money which we found in the mouth of our sacks 3
45:12 see, that it is my mouth that speaks to you. 3
Exd 4:11 the LORD said to him, "Who has made man's mouth? 3
12 I will be with your mouth and teach you what you 3
15 speak to him and put the words in his mouth; 3
15 I will be with your mouth and with his mouth 3
15 I will be with your mouth and with his mouth 3
16 and he shall be a mouth for you 3
13: 9 that the law of the LORD may be in your mouth; 3
23:13 nor let such be heard out of your mouth. 3
Num12: 8 With him I speak mouth to mouth, clearly 3
8 With him I speak mouth to mouth, clearly 3
16:30 ground opens its mouth, and swallows them up 3
32 earth opened its mouth and swallowed them up 3
22:28 LORD opened the mouth of the ass, and she said 3
38 word that God puts in my mouth, that must I speak. 3
23: 5 the LORD put a word in Balaam's mouth, and said 3
12 take heed to speak what the LORD puts in my mouth? 3
16 LORD met Balaam, and put a word in his mouth 3
26:10 the earth opened its mouth and swallowed them up 3
30: 2 according to all that proceeds out of his mouth. 3
Deu 8: 3 that proceeds out of the mouth of the LORD. 3
11: 6 how the earth opened its mouth and swallowed 3
18:18 I will put my words in his mouth, and he shall speak 3
23:23 vowed . . what you have promised with your mouth. 3
30:14 very near you . . in your mouth and in your heart 3
31:19 this song, and teach it . . put it in their mouths 3
21 unforgotten in the mouths of their descendants); 3
32: 1 let the earth hear the words of my mouth. 3
Jos 1: 8 book of the law shall not depart out of your mouth 3
6:10 neither shall any word go out of your mouth 3
10:18 Roll great stones against the mouth of the cave 3
22 Open the mouth of the cave, and bring . . out to me 3
27 set great stones against the mouth of the cave 3
15: 5 east boundary is . . to the mouth of the Jordan. 5
5 from the bay of the sea at the mouth of the Jordan; 5
Jdg 7: 6 that lapped, putting their hands to their mouths 3

9:38 Where is your mouth now, you who said, 'Who is 3
11:35 I have opened my mouth to the LORD, and I cannot 3
36 father, if you have opened your mouth to the LORD 3
36 according to what has gone forth from your mouth 3
18:19 Keep quiet, put your hand upon your mouth, and come 3
1Sm 1:12 As she continued . . Eli observed her mouth. 3
2: 1 My mouth derides my enemies, because I rejoice 3
3 let not arrogance come from your mouth; 3
14:26 honey was . . but no man put his hand to his mouth; 3
27 and dipped it in . . and put his hand to his mouth; 3
17:35 I went . . and delivered it out of his mouth; 3
2Sm 1:16 your own mouth has testified against you, saying 3
14: 3 speak thus . . " So Jo'ab put the words in her mouth. 3
19 put . . these words in the mouth of your handmaid. 3
17:19 took and spread a covering over the well's mouth 4
18:25 If he is alone, there are tidings in his mouth. 3
22: 9 Smoke went . . devouring fire from his mouth; 3
1Kg 8:15 fulfilled what he promised with his mouth 3
24 thou didst speak with thy mouth, and with thy hand 3
17:24 the word of the LORD in your mouth is truth. 3
19:18 leave . . every mouth that has not kissed him. 3
22:22 a lying spirit in the mouth of all his prophets.' 3
23 lying spirit in the mouth of all . . your prophets; 3
2Kg 4:34 putting his mouth upon his mouth 3
34 putting his mouth upon his mouth 3
19:28 put my hook in your nose and my bit in your mouth 6
2Ch 6: 4 promised with his mouth to David . . saying 3
15 yea, thou didst speak with thy mouth 3
18:21 a lying spirit in the mouth of all his prophets.' 3
22 LORD has put a lying spirit in the mouth of these 3
35:22 not listen to the words . . from the mouth of God 3
36:12 Jeremiah . . spoke from the mouth of the LORD. 3
21 word of the LORD by the mouth of Jeremiah 3
22 that the word of the LORD by the mouth of Jeremiah 3
Ezr 1: 1 that the word of the LORD by the mouth of Jeremiah 3
Neh 9:20 didst not withhold thy manna from their mouth 3
Est 7: 8 As the words left the mouth of the king 3
Job 3: 1 Job opened his mouth and cursed the day of his 3
5:15 he saves the fatherless from their mouth 3
16 poor have hope, and injustice shuts her mouth. 3
7:11 Therefore I will not restrain my mouth; 3
8: 2 and the words of your mouth be a great wind? 3
21 He will yet fill your mouth with laughter 3
9:20 I am innocent, my own mouth would condemn me; 3
15: 5 For your iniquity teaches your mouth 3
6 Your own mouth condemns you, and not I; 3
13 and let such words go out of your mouth? 3
16: 5 I could strengthen you with my mouth 3
10 Men have gaped at me with their mouth 3
19:16 I must beseech him with my mouth. 3
20:12 Though wickedness is sweet in his mouth 3
13 he is loath to let it go, and holds it in his mouth 1
21: 5 be appalled, and lay your hand upon your mouth. 3
22:22 Receive instruction from his mouth 3
23: 4 and fill my mouth with arguments. 3
12 treasured in my bosom the words of his mouth. 3
29: 9 from talking, and laid their hand on their mouth; 3
23 they opened their mouths as for the spring rain. 3
31:27 enticed, and my mouth has kissed my hand; 3
30 I have not let my mouth sin by asking for his life 1
32: 5 was no answer in the mouth of these three men 3
33: 2 Behold, I open my mouth; 3
2 I open my mouth; the tongue in my mouth speaks. 1
35:16 Job opens his mouth in empty talk 3
37: 2 the rumbling that comes from his mouth. 3
40: 4 what shall I answer thee? I lay my hand on my mouth 3
23 though Jordan rushes against his mouth. 3
41:19 Out of his mouth go flaming torches; 3
21 a flame comes forth from his mouth. 3
Ps 5: 9 For there is no truth in their mouth; 3
8: 2 by the mouth of babes and infants 3
10: 7 His mouth is filled with cursing and deceit 3
17: 3 my mouth does not transgress. 3
10 with their mouths they speak arrogantly. 3
18: 8 devouring fire from his mouth; glowing coals 3
19:14 Let the words of my mouth . . be acceptable 3
22:13 they open wide their mouths at me 3
21 Save me from the mouth of the lion 3
33: 6 all their host by the breath of his mouth. 3
34: 1 his praise shall continually be in my mouth. 3
35:21 They open wide their mouths against me; 3
36: 3 The words of his mouth are mischief and deceit; 3
37:30 The mouth of the righteous utters wisdom 3
38:13 like a dumb man who does not open his mouth. 3
14 does not hear, and in whose mouth are no rebukes. 3
39: 1 I will bridle my mouth 3
9 I am dumb, I do not open my mouth; 3
40: 3 He put a new song in my mouth, a song of praise 3
49: 3 My mouth shall speak wisdom; 3
50:19 You give your mouth free rein for evil 3
51:15 my mouth shall show forth thy praise. 3
54: 2 O God; give ear to the words of my mouth. 3
58: 6 O God, break the teeth in their mouths; 3
59: 7 There they are, bellowing with their mouths 3
12 the sin of their mouths, the words of their lips 3
62: 4 They bless with their mouths 3
63: 5 my mouth praises thee with joyful lips 3
11 for the mouths of liars will be stopped. 3
66:14 that which my lips uttered and my mouth promised 3
69:15 or the pit close its mouth over me. 3
71: 8 My mouth is filled with thy praise 3
15 My mouth will tell of thy righteous acts 3
73: 9 They set their mouths against the heavens 3
78: 1 incline your ears to the words of my mouth! 3
2 I will open my mouth in a parable; 3
30 while the food was still in their mouths 3
36 they flattered him with their mouths; 3
81:10 Open your mouth wide, and I will fill it. 3
89: 1 with my mouth I will proclaim thy faithfulness 3
107:42 all wickedness stops its mouth. 3
109: 2 wicked and deceitful mouths are opened against •
30 With my mouth I will give great thanks to the LORD; 3
115: 5 They have mouths, but do not speak; 3
119:13 I declare all the ordinances of thy mouth. 3
43 take not the word of truth utterly out of my mouth 3
72 The law of thy mouth is better to me 3
88 that I may keep the testimonies of thy mouth. 3
103 words to my taste, sweeter than honey to my mouth! 3
131 With open mouth I pant 3
126: 2 Then our mouth was filled with laughter 3
135:16 They have mouths, but they speak not 3
17 nor is there any breath in their mouths. 3
138: 4 for they have heard the words of thy mouth; 3
141: 3 Set a guard over my mouth, O LORD 3
7 their bones be strewn at the mouth of Sheol. 3
144: 8 whose mouths speak lies, and whose right hand 3
11 aliens, whose mouths speak lies, and whose right 3
145:21 My mouth will speak the praise of the LORD 3
Prv 2: 6 from his mouth come knowledge and understanding; 3
4: 5 do not turn away from the words of my mouth. 3
5: 7 do not depart from the words of my mouth. 3
6: 2 if you are . . caught in the words of your mouth; 3
7:24 O sons . . be attentive to the words of my mouth. 3
8: 7 for my mouth will utter truth; 1
8 All the words of my mouth are righteous; 3
10: 6 but the mouth of the wicked conceals violence. 3
11 The mouth of the righteous is a fountain of life 3
11 but the mouth of the wicked conceals violence. 3
31 The mouth of the righteous brings forth wisdom 3
32 but the mouth of the wicked, what is perverse. 3
11: 9 With his mouth the godless man would destroy 3
11 but it is overthrown by the mouth of the wicked. 3
12: 6 but the mouth of the upright delivers men. 3
13: 2 From the fruit of his mouth a good man eats good 3
3 He who guards his mouth preserves his life; 3
15: 2 but the mouths of fools pour out folly. 3
14 but the mouths of fools feed on folly. 3
28 mouth of the wicked pours out evil things. 3
16:10 his mouth does not sin in judgment. 3
26 worker's . . mouth urges him on. 3
18: 4 The words of a man's mouth are deep waters; 3
6 A fool's . . mouth invites a flogging. 3
7 A fool's mouth is his ruin 3
20 From the fruit of his mouth a man is satisfied; 3
19:24 will not even bring it back to his mouth. 3
28 mouth of the wicked devours iniquity. 3
20:17 but afterward his mouth will be full of gravel. 3
21:23 He who keeps his mouth and his tongue keeps 3
22:14 The mouth of a loose woman is a deep pit; 3
24: 7 in the gate he does not open his mouth. 3
26: 7 proverb in the mouth of fools. 3
9 Like a thorn . . proverb in the mouth of fools. 3
15 wears him out to bring it back to his mouth. 3
28 flattering mouth works ruin. 3
27: 2 Let another praise you, and not your own mouth; 3
30:20 adulteress: she eats, and wipes her mouth, and says 3
32 put your hand on your mouth. 3
31: 8 Open your mouth for the dumb 3
9 Open your mouth, judge righteously 3
26 She opens her mouth with wisdom 3
Ecc 5: 2 Be not rash with your mouth, nor . . hasty to utter 3
6 Let not your mouth lead you into sin 3
6: 7 All the toil of man is for his mouth 3
10:12 The words of a wise man's mouth win him favor 3
13 The beginning of the words of his mouth is 3
Sng 1: 2 you would kiss me with the kisses of your mouth! 3
4: 3 your mouth is lovely. 2
Isa 1:20 for the mouth of the LORD has spoken. 3
5:14 Sheol has . . opened its mouth beyond measure 3
6: 7 he touched my mouth, and said: "Behold 3
9:12 Philistines . . devour Israel with open mouth. 3
17 and an evildoer, and every mouth speaks folly. 3
10:14 that moved a wing, or opened the mouth, or chirped. 3
11: 4 he shall smite the earth with the rod of his mouth 3
29:13 Because this people draw near with their mouth 3
34:16 For the mouth of the LORD has commanded 3
37:29 put my hook in your nose and my bit in your mouth 6
40: 5 together, for the mouth of the LORD has spoken. 3
45:23 from my mouth has gone forth in righteousness 3
48: 3 they went forth from my mouth 3
49: 2 He made my mouth like a sharp sword 3
51:16 I have put my words in your mouth, and hid you 3
52:15 kings shall shut their mouths because of him; 3
53: 7 and he was afflicted, yet he opened not his mouth; 3
7 is dumb, so he opened not his mouth. 3
9 no violence, and there was no deceit in his mouth. 3
55:11 shall my word be that goes forth from my mouth; 3
57: 4 Against whom do you open your mouth wide 3
58:14 your father, for the mouth of the LORD has spoken. 3
59:21 and my words which I have put in your mouth 3
21 my words . . shall not depart out of your mouth 3
21 of your mouth, or out of the mouth of your children 3
21 or out of the mouth of your children's children 3
62: 2 a new name which the mouth of the LORD will give. 3
Jer 1: 9 the LORD put forth his hand and touched my mouth; 3
9 Behold, I have put my words in your mouth. 3
5:14 behold, I am making my words in your mouth a fire 3
9: 8 with his mouth each speaks peaceably 3
12 To whom has the mouth of the LORD spoken 3
20 and let your ear receive the word of his mouth; 3
12: 2 art near in their mouth and far from their heart. 3
15:19 you shall be as my mouth. They shall turn to you 3
23:16 of their own minds, not from the mouth of the LORD. 3
44:25 and your wives have declared with your mouths 3
26 no more be invoked by the mouth of any man of Judah 3
48:28 that nests in the sides of the mouth of a gorge. 3
51:44 and take out of his mouth what he has swallowed. 3
Lam 3:29 let him put his mouth in the dust 3
38 from the mouth of the Most High that good and evil 3
Ezk 2: 8 open your mouth, and eat what I give you. 3
3: 2 I opened my mouth, and he gave me the scroll to eat. 3
3 I ate it; and it was in my mouth as sweet as honey. 3
17 whenever you hear a word from my mouth 3
27 But when I speak with you, I will open your mouth 3
4:14 nor has foul flesh come into my mouth. 3
16:56 a byword in your mouth in the day of your pride 3
63 confounded, and never open your mouth again 3
21:22 to open the mouth with a cry, to lift up the voice 3
24:27 your mouth will be opened to the fugitive 3
33: 7 whenever you hear a word from my mouth 3
22 he had opened my mouth by the time the man came 3
22 my mouth was opened, and I was no longer dumb. 3
34:10 I will rescue my sheep from their mouths 3
35:13 yourselves against me with your mouth 3
Dan 4:31 While the words were still in the king's mouth 7
6:17 stone was . . laid upon the mouth of the den 7
22 My God sent his angel and shut the lions' mouths 7
7: 5 had three ribs in its mouth between its teeth; 7
8 eyes of a man, and a mouth speaking great things. 7
20 had eyes and a mouth that spoke great things 7
10: 3 no delicacies, no meat or wine entered my mouth 3
16 touched my lips; then I opened my mouth and spoke. 3
Hos 2:17 will remove the names of the Ba'als from her mouth 3
6: 5 I have slain them by the words of my mouth 3
Jol 1: 5 for it is cut off from your mouth. 3
Ams 3:12 the shepherd rescues from the mouth of the lion 3
Mic 3: 5 against him who puts nothing into their mouths. 3
4: 4 for the mouth of the LORD of hosts has spoken. 3
6:12 and their tongue is deceitful in their mouth. 3
7: 5 guard . . your mouth from her who lies 3
16 they shall lay their hands on their mouths; 3
Nah 3:12 if shaken they fall into the mouth of the eater. 3
Zep 3:13 be found in their mouth a deceitful tongue. 3
Zec 5: 8 and thrust down the leaden weight upon its mouth. 3
8: 9 these words from the mouth of the prophets 3
9: 7 I will take away its blood from its mouth 3
14:12 their tongues shall rot in their mouths. 3
Mal 2: 6 True instruction was in his mouth 3
7 men should seek instruction from his mouth 3
Mat 4: 4 word that proceeds from the mouth of God.' 9
5: 2 he opened his mouth and taught them, saying 9
12:34 the abundance of the heart the mouth speaks. 9
13:35 I will open my mouth in parables 9
15:11 not what goes into the mouth defiles a man 9
11 what comes out of the mouth, this defiles a man. 9
17 Do you not see that whatever goes into the mouth 9
18 what comes out of the mouth 9
17:27 when you open its mouth you will find a shekel; 9
21:16 Out of the mouth of babes and sucklings 9
Lke 1:64 immediately his mouth was opened 9
70 as he spoke by the mouth of his holy prophets 9
4:22 the gracious words which proceeded out of his mouth; 9
6:45 his mouth speaks. 9
19:22 I will condemn you out of your own mouth 9
21:15 for I will give you a mouth and wisdom 9
Joh 19:29 held it to his mouth. 9
Act 1:16 spoke beforehand by the mouth of David 9
3:18 foretold by the mouth of all the prophets 9
21 God spoke by the mouth of his holy prophets 9
4:25 by the mouth of our father David, thy servant 9
8:32 so he opens not his mouth. 9
35 Then Philip opened his mouth 9
10:34 Peter opened his mouth and said: "Truly I perceive 9
11: 8 nothing . . unclean has ever entered my mouth.' 9
15: 7 by my mouth the Gentiles should hear the word 9
27 who . . will tell you the same things by word of mouth. •
18:14 when Paul was about to open his mouth 9
22:14 to see the Just One and to hear a voice from his mouth 9
23: 2 to strike him on the mouth. 9
Rom 3:14 Their mouth is full of curses and bitterness. 9
19 so that every mouth may be stopped 9
2Co 6:11 Our mouth is open to you, Corinthians 9
Eph 4:29 Let no evil talk come out of your mouths 9
6:19 opening my mouth boldly to proclaim the mystery 9
Col 3: 8 malice, slander, and foul talk from your mouth. 9
2Th 2: 8 slay him with the breath of his mouth 9
15 taught . . either by word of mouth or by letter. •

2Ti 4:17 So I was rescued from the lion's mouth. 9
Heb 11:33 received promises, stopped the mouths of lions 9
Jas 3: 3 If we put bits into the mouths of horses 9
10 From the same mouth come blessing and cursing. 9
Rev 1:16 from his mouth issued a sharp two-edged sword 9
2:16 and war against them with the sword of my mouth. 9
3:16 I will spew you out of my mouth. 9
9:17 and smoke and sulphur issued from their mouths. 9
18 smoke and sulphur issuing from their mouths. 9
19 For the power of the horses is in their mouths 9
10: 9 bitter . . but sweet as honey in your mouth. 9
10 it was sweet as honey in my mouth 9
11: 5 fire pours out from their mouth and consumes 9
12:15 The serpent poured water . . out of his mouth 9
16 earth opened its mouth and swallowed the river 9
16 river which the dragon had poured from his mouth 9
13: 2 the beast . . its mouth was like a lion's mouth. 9
2 the beast . . its mouth was like a lion's mouth. 9
5 a mouth uttering haughty and blasphemous words 9
6 it opened its mouth to utter blasphemies 9
14: 5 in their mouth no lie was found 9
16:13 I saw, issuing from the mouth of the dragon 9
13 I saw, issuing . . from the mouth of the beast 9
13 issuing . . from the mouth of the false prophet 9
19:15 From his mouth issues a sharp sword 9
21 the sword that issues from his mouth; 9
1Es 1:28 words . . from the mouth of the Lord. 9
47 words . . from the mouth of the Lord. 9
57 the word of the Lord by the mouth of Jeremiah 9
2: 1 the word of the Lord by the mouth of Jeremiah 9
4:19 with open mouths stare at her 9
31 the king would gaze at her with mouth agape 9
2Es 9:28 my mouth was opened, and I began to speak 10
13: 4 whenever his voice issued from his mouth 10
10 from his mouth as it were a stream of fire 10
27 fire and a storm coming out of his mouth 10
14:38 Ezra, open your mouth and drink what I give you 10
39 Then I opened my mouth, and behold, a full cup 10
41 my mouth was opened, and was no longer closed. 10
15: 1 the prophecy which I will put in your mouth 10
Jdt 5: 5 a word from the mouth of your servant 9
5 No falsehood shall come from your servant's mouth. 9
11:19 not a dog will so much as open its mouth to growl 8
AEs 13:17 not destroy the mouth of those who praise thee. 9
14: 9 to abolish what thy mouth has ordained 9
9 to stop the mouths of those who praise thee 9
10 to open the mouths of the nations 9
13 Put eloquent speech in my mouth before the lion 9
Wis 1:11 a lying mouth destroys the soul. 9
8:12 they will put their hands on their mouths. 9
10:21 because wisdom opened the mouth of the dumb 9
Sir 5:12 if not, put your hand on your mouth. 9
15: 5 will open his mouth in the midst of the assembly. 9
20:15 he opens his mouth like a herald 9
29 like a muzzle on the mouth they avert reproofs. 9
21:26 The mind of fools is in their mouth 9
26 the mouth of wise men is in their mind. 9
22:22 If you have opened your mouth 9
27 O that a guard were set over my mouth 9
23: 9 Do not accustom your mouth to oaths 9
13 Do not accustom your mouth to lewd vulgarity 9
24: 2 she will open her mouth 9
3 I came forth from the mouth of the Most High 9
26:12 As a thirsty wayfarer opens his mouth 9
27:23 In your presence his mouth is all sweetness 9
28:12 both come out of your mouth. 9
25 make a door and a bolt for your mouth. 9
29:24 you may not open your mouth; 9
30:18 poured out upon a mouth that is closed 9
39: 5 he will open his mouth in prayer 9
17 at the word of his mouth. 9
40:30 In the mouth of the shameless begging is sweet 9
49: 1 it is sweet as honey to every mouth 9
51:25 I opened my mouth and said 9
Aza 1: 2 he opened his mouth and said 9
10 now we cannot open our mouths 9
28 the three, as with one mouth, praised 9
Sus 1:61 out of their own mouths Daniel had convicted 9
1Mc 2:60 was delivered from the mouth of the lions. 9
9:55 his mouth was stopped and he was paralyzed 9
3Mc 2:20 put praises in the mouth of those . . downcast 9
4:16 with a profane mouth 9
4Mc 5:36 You . . not stain the honorable mouth of my old age 9

mouth *See also* foam, open, roof.

mouth of the womb 1. מַשְׁבֵּר
Hos 13:13 does not present himself at the mouth of the womb. 1

mouths *See* make.

move 1. הלך 2. חלף 3. חרץ 4. מוט 5. מוש 6. נדב
7. נדד 8. נוע 9. נסע 10. נשא 11. סות 12. עבר
13. עתק 14. פוק 15. רחף 16. רמש 17. ἄγω
18. ἀνίστημι 19. εἰμί 20. ἐπικινέω 21. κινέω
22. μεταβαίνω 23. σαίνω 24. σαλεύω 25. ὑπάγω
26. φέρω 27. commoveo 28. moveo 29. recedo
Gen 1: 2 and the Spirit of God was moving over the face 15
21 God created . . every living creature that moves 16
28 every living thing that moves upon the earth. 16
7:21 all flesh died that moved upon the earth 16
8:19 everything that moves upon the earth, went forth 16
26:22 he moved from there and dug another well 13
Exd 13:20 they moved on from Succoth, and encamped at Etham 9
14:19 the angel . . moved and went behind them; 9
19 and the pillar of cloud moved from before them 9
17: 1 Israel moved on from the wilderness of Sin 9
35:21 and every one whose spirit moved him 6
26 women whose hearts were moved with ability spun 10
29 the people . . whose heart moved them to bring 6
Lev 11:46 living creature that moves through the waters 16
Jos 10:21 not a man moved his tongue against . . Israel. 3
Jdg 9:26 Ga'al . . moved into Shechem with his kinsmen; 12
1Sm 1:13 only her lips moved, and her voice was not heard; 8
2Sm 7: 7 In all places where I have moved with . . Israel 1
2Kg 23:18 And he said, "Let him be; let no man move his bones. 8
1Ch 16:30 yea, the world stands firm, never to be moved. 4
17: 6 In all places where I have moved with Israel 1
Job 2: 3 although you moved me against him 11
9:11 he moves on, but I do not perceive him. 2
31:26 sun when it shone, or the moon moving in splendor 1
Ps 10: 6 He thinks in his heart, "I shall not be moved; 4
15: 5 He who does these things shall never be moved. 4
16: 8 he is at my right hand, I shall not be moved. 4
21: 7 love of the Most High he shall not be moved. 4
30: 6 I said in my prosperity, "I shall never be moved. 4
46: 5 God is in the midst of her, she shall not be moved; 4
55:22 he will never permit the righteous to be moved. 4
62: 2 I shall not be greatly moved. 4
69:34 the seas and everything that moves therein. 16
93: 1 world is established; it shall never be moved; 4
96:10 world is established, it shall never be moved; 4
112: 6 For the righteous will never be moved; 4
121: 3 He will not let your foot be moved 4
125: 1 Mount Zion, which cannot be moved, but abides 4
Prv 12: 3 root of the righteous will never be moved. 4
Isa 10:14 and there was none that moved a wing 7
40:20 to set up an image that will not move. 4
41: 7 fasten it with nails so that it cannot be moved. 4
46: 7 it stands there; it cannot move from its place. 5
Jer 10: 4 with hammer and nails so that it cannot move. 14
Mat 17:20 say to this mountain, 'Move from here to there,' 22
20 and it will move 22
23: 4 will not move them with their finger. 21
Act 17:28 'In him we live and move and have our being' 21
1Co 12: 2 however you may have been moved. 17
1Th 3: 3 that no one be moved by these afflictions 23
2Pe 1:21 men moved by the Holy Spirit spoke from God. 26
1Es 8:72 all who were ever moved at the word of the Lord 20
2Es 3:18 shake the earth, and move the world 27
4:37 he will not move or arouse them 27
6:41 that one part might move upward 29
7:15 why are you moved, seeing that you are mortal? 28
Jdt 7: 1 to break camp and move against Bethulia *
12:16 he was moved with great desire to possess her 24
Sir 18:26 all things move swiftly before the Lord. 19
LJr 1:27 it cannot move itself 21
Aza 1:57 whales and all creatures that move in the waters 21
1Mc 2: 1 moved from Jerusalem and settled in Modein. 18
4Mc 4:13 Moved by these words 25
14: 6 moved in harmony with the guidance of the mind 21
6 as though moved by an immortal spirit of devotion *

move about 1. הלך
2Sm 7: 6 have been moving about in a tent for my dwelling. 1
Ecc 4:15 I saw all the living who move about under the sun 1

move about freely 1. עצר
1Ch 12: 1 he could not move about freely because of Saul 1

all that move 1. זיז
Ps 50:11 all that moves in the field is mine. 1
80:13 all that move in the field feed on it. 1

move along 1. διακινέω
3Mc 5:23 Hermon . . began to move them along in
the . . colonnade 1

move among 1. ἐμπεριπατέω
2Co 6:16 I will live in them and move among them 1

move camp 1. ἀναζεύγνυμι
Jdt 7: 2 all their warriors moved their camp that day; 1

move deeply 1. ἐμβριμάομαι
Joh 11:33 he was deeply moved in spirit and troubled; 1
38 Then Jesus, deeply moved again, came to the tomb 1

move down 1. גלש
Sng 4: 1 flock of goats, moving down the slopes of Gilead. 1
6: 5 flock of goats, moving down the slopes of Gilead. 1

move forward 1. ἀπαίρω
Jdt 7:17 the army of the Ammonites moved forward 1

move in choral dance 1. χορεύω
4Mc 14: 7 the seven days of creation move in choral dance 1

move out 1. משך 2. ἀπαίρω
Jdg 20:37 the men in ambush moved out and smote all the city 1
1Mc 4: 1 this division moved out by night 2
3 he and his mighty men moved out 2

move over 1. μεταβαίνω
Wis 19:19 and creatures that swim moved over to the land. 1

move tent 1. אהל
Gen 13:12 Lot dwelt . . and moved his tent as far as Sodom. 1
18 Abram moved his tent, and came and dwelt 1

move to and fro 1. הלך 2. קלל
Jer 4:24 and all the hills moved to and fro. 2
Ezk 1:13 like torches moving to and fro among the living 1

move to jealousy 1. קנא
Ps 78:58 moved him to jealousy with their graven images. 1

move to pity 1. נחם
Jdg 2:18 for the LORD was moved to pity by their groaning 1

move with anger 1. מרר
Dan 11:11 king of the south, moved with anger, shall come out 1

move with pity 1. σπλαγχνίζομαι
Mrk 1:41 Moved with pity, he stretched out his hand 1

deeply moved 1. רגז
2Sm 18:33 And the king was deeply moved, and went . . and wept; 1

movement 1. κινέω 2. motus
2Es 6: 3 before the powers of movement were established 2
Wis 5:11 is traversed by the movement of its wings 1

moving thing 1. רֶמֶשׂ
Gen 9: 3 Every moving thing that lives shall be food 1

mow 1. גֵּז 2. ἀμάω
Ams 7: 1 was the latter growth after the king's mowings. 1
Jas 5: 4 the wages of the laborers who mowed your fields 2

mow down 1. חלש
Exd 17:13 Joshua mowed down Am'alek and his people 1

mown *See* grass.

much 1. גָּדוֹל 2. דָּבָר 3. כַּאֲשֶׁר 4. כַּבִּיר 5. כֹּל 6. כָּנָף
7. כְּפֶה 8. לְכֹל 9. לְפִי 10. לָרֹב 11. מְאֹד 12. מִרְבָּה
13. עַד 14. עַל אֲשֶׁר 15. רַב 16. רֹב 17. רבה
18. שַׂגִּיא (A) 19. ἁπλῶς 20. εἰ μή 21. ἕως 22. ἱκανός
23. ἴσος 24. καθ' ὅσον ἄν 25. κατά 26. μέγας 27. ὅσος
28. οὗτος 29. πληθύνω 30. πολύς 31. τοσοῦτος
32. copiosus 33. multus 34. quantum 35. sicut
36. valde
Gen 20: 8 and the men were very much afraid. 11
26:16 for you are much mightier than we. 11
43:34 portion was five times as much as any of theirs. *
44: 1 sacks with food, as much as they can carry 3
Exd 14:28 into the sea; not so much as one of them remained. 13
16: 5 it will be twice as much as they gather daily. 14
16 Gather of it, every man of you, as much as he can eat; 9
21 they gathered it, each as much as he could eat; 7
22 the sixth day they gathered twice as much bread *
Lev 14:21 But if he is poor and cannot afford so much *
Deu 2: 5 not so much as for the sole of the foot to tread *
12:15 slaughter and eat . . as much as you desire 5
20 you may eat as much flesh as you desire. 5
21 may eat within your towns as much as you desire. 5
28:38 carry much seed into the field, and shall gather 15
Jos 13: 1 there remains yet very much land to be possessed. 17
22: 8 Go back to your homes with much wealth 15
8 gold, bronze, and iron, and with much clothing; 17
1Sm 2:16 burn the fat . . and then take as much as you wish 3
17:24 Israel . . fled from him, and were much afraid. 11
19: 1 But Jonathan, Saul's son, delighted much in David. 11
21:12 and was much afraid of A'chish the king of Gath. 11
22:15 servant has known nothing . . much or little. 1
25:22 if by morning I leave so much as one male *
34 had not been left to Nabal so much as one male. 13
2Sm 3:22 arrived . . from a raid, bringing much spoil 15
8: 8 And from . . King David took very much bronze. 17
14:25 there was no one so much to be praised 11
1Kg 9:11 timber and gold, as much as he desired 8
10: 2 with camels bearing spices, and very much gold 15
25 Every one of them brought . . so much year by year. 2
2Kg 10:18 served Ba'al . . but Jehu will serve him much. 17
12:10 they saw that there was much money in the chest 15
21: 6 He did much evil in the sight of the LORD 17
16 Manas'seh shed very much innocent blood 17
1Ch 18: 8 and from Cun . . David took very much bronze; 15
22: 8 have shed much blood and have waged great wars; 16
8 because you have shed so much blood before me 15
14 beyond weighing, for there is so much of it; 16
2Ch 9: 1 camels bearing spices and very much gold 16

24 brought his present . . so much year by year. 2
14:13 The men of Judah carried away very much booty. 17
14 for there was much plunder in them. 15
20:25 three days in taking the spoil, it was so much. 15
24:11 when they saw that there was much money in it 15
25:13 killed 3,000 people in them, and took much spoil. 15
27: 3 did much building on the wall of Ophel. 10
28: 8 they also took much spoil from them 15
32: 4 kings of Assyria come and find much water? 15
33: 6 He did much evil in the sight of the LORD 17
Ezr 7:22 oil, and salt without prescribing how much. •
Neh 2: 2 Then I was very much afraid. 17
4:10 strength . . is failing, and there is much rubbish; 17
Job 31:25 because my hand had gotten much; 4
42:10 the LORD gave Job twice as much as he had before. •
Ps 19:10 desired are they than gold, even much fine gold; 15
119:14 I delight as much as in all riches. •
Prv 7:21 With much seductive speech she persuades him; 16
13:23 The fallow ground of the poor yields much food 15
15: 6 house of the righteous there is much treasure 15
25:27 It is not good to eat much honey 17
29:22 man given to anger causes much transgression. 15
Ecc 1:18 For in much wisdom is much vexation 16
18 For in much wisdom is much vexation 15
5: 3 For a dream comes with much business 16
12 sleep of a laborer, whether he eats little or much 17
17 all his days . . in much vexation and sickness 17
20 For he will not much remember the days of his life 17
9:18 but one sinner destroys much good. 17
12:12 and much study is a weariness of the flesh. 17
Jer 2:22 you wash yourself with lye and use much soap 17
Ezk 17: 7 great eagle with great wings and much plumage; 15
23:32 and held in derision, for it contains much; 12
46: 7 and with the lambs as much as he is able •
11 with the lambs as much as one is able to give •
Dan 6:14 when he heard these words, was much distressed 18
7: 5 it was told, 'Arise, devour much flesh.' 18
Jon 4:11 more than 120,000 persons . . and also much cattle? 15
Hag 1: 6 You have sown much, and harvested little; 17
9 You have looked for much, and, lo, it came to little; 17
Mat 6:30 oven, will he not much more clothe you, O men 30
13: 5 where they had not much soil 30
25:21 I will set you over much 30
23 I will set you over much 30
27:19 for I have suffered much over him today 30
Mrk 4: 5 where it had not much soil 30
5:26 who had suffered much under many physicians 30
6:20 When he heard him, he was much perplexed 30
Lke 6:34 to receive as much again. 23
7:47 for she loved much 30
10:40 Martha was distracted with much serving 30
12:48 Every one to whom much is given 30
48 of him will much be required 30
48 to whom men commit much 30
16:10 is faithful also in much 30
10 is dishonest also in much. 30
Joh 3:23 near Salim, because there was much water there; 30
6:10 Now there was much grass in the place 30
11 so also the fish, as much as they wanted. 27
7:12 much muttering about him among the people 30
8:26 I have much to say about you and much to judge 30
26 I have much to say about you and much to judge •
12:24 if it dies, it bears much fruit. 30
14:30 I will no longer talk much with you 30
15: 5 he it is that bears much fruit 30
8 that you bear much fruit 30
Act 5: 8 Tell me whether you sold the land for so much. 31
8 she said, "Yes, for so much. 31
8: 8 there was much joy in that city. 30
15: 7 after there had been much debate, Peter rose 30
16:16 brought her owners much gain by soothsaying. 30
20: 2 and had given them much encouragement 30
24: 2 Since through you we enjoy much peace 30
27: 9 As much time had been lost 22
10 the voyage will be with injury and much loss 30
Rom 3: 2 Much in every way. 30
5: 9 much more shall we be saved by him from the wrath 30
10 much more . . shall we be saved by his life. 30
15 much more have the grace of God and the free gift 30
17 much more will those . . reign in life 30
9:22 endured with much patience the vessels of wrath 30
1Co 2: 3 in weakness and in much fear and trembling; 30
9:11 is it too much if we reap your material benefits? 26
2Co 2: 4 I wrote you out of much affliction and anguish 30
3:11 what is permanent must have much more splendor. 30
8:15 He who gathered much had nothing over 30
Php 2:12 as in my presence but much more in my absence 30
1Th 1: 6 received the word in much affliction 30
1Ti 3: 8 not double-tongued, not addicted to much wine 30
Phm 1: 7 I have derived much joy and comfort from your love 30
Heb 1: 4 having become as much superior to angels as . . 31
5:11 About this we have much to say 30
12: 9 Shall we not much more be subject to the Father 30
25 much less shall we escape 30
2Jn 1:12 Though I have much to write to you 30
3Jn 1:13 I had much to write to you 30
Rev 5: 4 I wept much that no one was found worthy to open 30
8: 3 given much incense to mingle with the prayers 30
1Es 9:11 we have sinned too much in these things. 30
2Es 7:66 For it is much better with them than with us 33
131 so much as joy over those 35
9:22 because with much labor I have perfected them. 33
46 I brought him up with much care. 33
10:56 you will hear as much as your ears can hear. 34
11:32 and with much oppression dominated 33
40 have held sway over the world with much terror 33
13: 8 all . . were much afraid, yet dared to fight. 36
19 they shall see great dangers and much distress 33
16:18 when there shall be much lamentation 32
Tob 12: 8 is better than much with wrongdoing 30
Jdt 4: 9 they humbled themselves with much fasting. 26
5: 9 settled, and prospered, with much gold and silver •
11:13 it is not lawful . . so much as to touch these things •
19 not a dog will so much as open its mouth to growl •
AEs 16: 7 be seen not so much from the more ancient records 31
Wis 7:28 nothing so much as the man who lives with wisdom. 20
13: 9 for if they had the power to know so much 31
Sir 9:14 As much as you can, aim to know your neighbors 25
11:11 is so much the more in want. 31
12:18 whisper much, and change his expression. 30
13:11 he will test you through much talk 30
14:13 reach out and give to him as much as you can. 25
20:12 There is a man who buys much for a little 30
15 He gives little and upbraids much 30
22:13 Do not talk much with a foolish man 29
29:23 Be content with little or much. 26
31:12 do not say, "There is certainly much upon it! 30
32: 8 Speak concisely, say much in few words 30
33:27 idleness teaches much evil. 30
38:11 as much as you can afford. 6
40: 1 Much labor was created for every man 26
42: 4 of acquiring much or little; 30
5 of much discipline of children 30
43:27 Though we speak much we cannot reach the end 30
30 exalt him as much as you can 24
46:19 not so much as a pair of shoes 21
51:16 I found for myself much instruction. 30
27 have labored little and found myself much rest. 30
28 you will gain by it much gold. 30
1Mc 4:23 they seized much gold and silver 30
9:39 and saw a tumultuous procession with much baggage; 30
10:87 returned to Jerusalem with much booty. 30
11:48 seized much spoil on that day 30
51 they returned to Jerusalem with much spoil. 30
15:26 silver and gold and much military equipment. 22
16:11 he had much silver and gold 30
2Mc 2:32 adding only so much to what has already been said; 31
6: 6 nor so much as confess himself to be a Jew. 19
7:26 After much urging on his part 30
8:20 destroyed 120,000 and took much booty. 30
9:11 he began to lose much of his arrogance 30
15:11 not so much with confidence in shields •
14 loves the brethren and prays much for the people 30
3Mc 5:22 they did not so much employ the duration of the night 28

much *See also* acquire, ask, better, bring, care, gather, half, less, love, make, more, perplex, rather, three, twice, value.

much as able 1. מַתַּת יָד
Ezk 46: 5 with the lambs shall be as much as he is able 1

do much 1. יסף 2. περισσεύω 3. προσθέω
1Kg 16:33 Ahab did more to provoke the LORD . . to anger 1
Job 34:32 if I have done iniquity, I will do it no more 1
Ps 120: 3 what more . . be done to you, you deceitful tongue? 1
1Th 4: 1 just as you are doing, you do so more and more. 2
10 we exhort you, brethren, to do so more and more 2
Sir 21: 1 Have you sinned, my son? Do so no more 3

much experience 1. πολύπειρος
Sir 34: 9 things, and one with much experience will speak 1

how much 1. מָה 2. ὅσος 3. πόσος 4. τις 5. ὡς 6. quanto 7. quantum
Job 16: 6 if I forbear, how much of it leaves me? 1
Sng 4:10 how much better is your love than wine 1
Mat 7:11 how much more will your Father who is in heaven 3
10:25 how much more will they malign 3
12:12 Of how much more value is a man than a sheep! 3
Mrk 5:19 tell them how much the Lord has done for you 2
20 how much Jesus had done for him 2
Lke 8:39 and declare how much God has done for you 2
39 proclaiming . . how much Jesus had done for him. 2
11:13 how much more will the . . Father give the Holy Spirit 3
12:24 Of how much more value are you than the birds! 3
28 how much more will he clothe you 3
16: 5 he said to the first, 'How much . . owe my master?' 3
7 Then he said to another, 'And how much do you owe?' 3
Act 9:13 how much evil he has done 2
16 how much he must suffer for the sake of my name. 2
Rom 11:12 how much more will their full inclusion mean! 3
24 how much more will these natural branches 3
Phm 1:16 especially to me but how much more to you 3
Heb 9:14 how much more shall the blood of Christ 3
10:29 How much worse punishment . . will be deserved 3
2Es 4:30 how much ungodliness it has produced until now 7
31 how much fruit of ungodliness 7
12:44 how much better it would have been for us 6
Tob 7: 2 How much the young man resembles my cousin Tobit! 5
Wis 13: 3 know how much better than these is their Lord 3
4 how much more powerful is he who formed them. 3
Sir 11:19 he does not know how much time will pass 4
20: 2 How much better it is to reprove 5
Bel 1: 6 see how much he eats and drinks every day? 2

however much 1. בְּשֶׁל אֲשֶׁר
Ecc 8:17 However much man may toil . . he will not find it 1

much less 1. אַף כִּי
Prv 19:10 much less for a slave to rule over princes. 1

much more 1. הֵנָּה הֵנָּה 2. רבה 3. ὅσος 4. περισσότερος 5. περισσοτέρως 6. πολύς
Exd 36: 5 The people bring much more than enough for doing 2
2Sm 12: 8 I would add to you as much more. 1
2Ch 25: 9 The LORD is able to give you much more than this. 2
Mrk 12:33 much more than all whole burnt offerings 4
Php 1:14 much more bold to speak the word of God 5
Heb 3: 3 counted worthy of . . much more glory than Moses 6
8: 6 which is as much more excellent than the old as . . 3

much more than 1. ὅσον οὐ
Jdt 12:20 much more than he had ever drunk in any one day 1

much the more 1. μᾶλλον
Lke 5:15 so much the more the report went abroad 1

too much 1. περισσότερος 2. multitudo
2Co 10: 8 even if I boast a little too much of our authority 1
2Es 8:43 or if it has been ruined by too much rain 2

very much 1. πολύς 2. multus magis
2Es 8: 2 it provides very much clay 2
2Mc 8:30 they divided very much plunder 1

mud 1. טִיט
Zec 10: 5 mighty men in battle, trampling the foe in the mud 1

muddy 1. רפס
Prv 25:26 Like a muddied spring or a polluted fountain 1

mulberry 1. μόρα
1Mc 6:34 the juice of grapes and mulberries 1

mule 1. פֶּרֶד 2. פִּרְדָּה 3. ἡμίονος
2Sm 13:29 all . . arose, and each mounted his mule and fled. 1
18: 9 Ab'salom was riding upon his mule 1
9 the mule went under the . . branches of a great oak 1
9 while the mule that was under him went on. 1
1Kg 1:33 cause Solomon my son to ride on my own mule 2
38 and caused Solomon to ride on King David's mule 2
44 they have caused him to ride on the king's mule; 2
10:25 garments, myrrh, spices, horses, and mules 1
18: 5 find grass and save the horses and mules alive 1
2Kg 5:17 let there be given . . two mules' burden of earth; 1
1Ch 12:40 bringing food . . camels and on mules and on oxen 1
2Ch 9:24 his present . . myrrh, spices, horses, and mules 1
Ezr 2:66 Their horses were 736, their mules were 245 1
Neh 7:68 Their horses were 736, their mules 245 3
Ps 32: 9 Be not like a horse or a mule 1
Isa 66:20 in litters, and upon mules, and upon dromedaries 1
Ezk 27:14 for your wares horses, war horses, and mules. 1
Zec 14:15 on the horses, the mules, the camels, the asses 1
1Es 5:43 245 mules, and 5,525 asses. 3
Jdt 2:17 camels and asses and mules for transport 3
15:11 she took them and loaded her mule 3

multiply 1. כבד 2. כבר 3. עתר 4. פרץ 5. רבב 6. רבה 7. רַב עשה 8. שגא (A) 9. πληθύνω 10. multiplico
Gen 1:22 Be fruitful and multiply and fill the waters 6
22 and let birds multiply on the earth 6
28 Be fruitful and multiply, and fill the earth 6
3:16 I will greatly multiply your pain 6
6: 1 When men began to multiply on the face 5
8:17 and be fruitful and multiply upon the earth. 6
9: 1 Be fruitful and multiply, and fill the earth. 6
7 be fruitful and multiply 6
7 on the earth and multiply in it. 6
16:10 I will so greatly multiply your descendants 6
17: 2 you, and will multiply you exceedingly. 6
20 make him fruitful and multiply him exceedingly; 6
22:17 I will multiply your descendants as the stars 6
26: 4 I will multiply your descendants as the stars 6
24 will bless you and multiply your descendants 6
28: 3 make you fruitful and multiply you 6
35:11 I am God Almighty: be fruitful and multiply; 6
47:27 were fruitful and multiplied exceedingly. 6
48: 4 I will make you fruitful, and multiply you 6
Exd 1: 7 they multiplied and grew exceedingly strong; 6
10 deal shrewdly with them, lest they multiply 6
12 the more they multiplied 6
20 the people multiplied and grew very strong. 6
7: 3 and though I multiply my signs and wonders 6
11: 9 that my wonders may be multiplied in the land 6
23:29 lest . . the wild beasts multiply against you. 5

32:13 I will multiply your descendants as the stars 6
Lev 26: 9 and make you fruitful and multiply you 6
Deu 1:10 the LORD your God has multiplied you, and behold 6
6: 3 that you may multiply greatly, as the LORD 6
7:13 he will love you, bless you, and multiply you; 6
8: 1 that you may live and multiply 6
13 when your herds and flocks multiply 6
13 when . . your silver and gold is multiplied 6
13 when . . all that you have is multiplied 6
11:21 that your days . . may be multiplied in the land 6
13:17 multiply you, as he swore to your fathers 6
17:16 Only he must not multiply horses for himself 6
16 in order to multiply horses 6
17 not multiply wives for himself, lest his heart 6
17 nor . . greatly multiply for himself silver and gold. 6
28:63 as the LORD took delight in . . multiplying you 6
30:16 If you obey . . then you shall live and multiply 6
1Ch 4:27 their family multiply like the men of Judah. 6
5: 9 cattle had multiplied in the land of Gilead. 6
Neh 9:23 multiply their descendants as the stars 6
Job 9:17 and multiplies my wounds without cause; 6
27:14 If his children are multiplied 6
29:18 I shall multiply my days as the sand 6
34:37 among us, and multiplies his words against God. 6
35: 6 if your transgressions are multiplied 5
16 he multiplies words without knowledge. 2
Ps 16: 4 who choose another god multiply their sorrows; 6
40: 5 Thou hast multiplied, O LORD my God, thy wondrous 7
107:38 By his blessing they multiply greatly; 6
Prv 6:35 nor be appeased though you multiply gifts. 6
9:11 For by me your days will be multiplied 6
Ecc 10:14 A fool multiplies words, though no man knows 6
Isa 9: 3 Thou hast multiplied the nation 6
57: 9 Molech with oil and multiplied your perfumes; 6
59:12 our transgressions are multiplied before thee 5
Jer 3:16 And when you have multiplied and increased 6
23: 3 and they shall be fruitful and multiply. 6
29: 6 multiply there, and do not decrease. 6
30:19 I will multiply them, and they shall not be few; 6
33:22 I will multiply the descendants of David 6
Lam 2: 5 he has multiplied . . mourning and lamentation. 6
Ezk 11: 6 You have multiplied your slain in this city 6
16:25 to any passer-by, and multiplying your harlotry. 6
26 multiplying your harlotry, to provoke me 6
29 You multiplied your harlotry 6
35:13 and multiplied your words against me; I heard it. 3
36:10 I will multiply men upon you 6
11 I will multiply upon you man and beast; 6
37:26 I will bless them and multiply them 6
Dan 4: 1 to all peoples . . Peace be multiplied to you! 8
6:25 Darius wrote . . "Peace be multiplied to you. 8
Hos 4:10 they shall play the harlot, but not multiply; 4
8:11 E'phraim has multiplied altars for sinning 6
14 and Judah has multiplied fortified cities; 6
12: 1 they multiply falsehood and violence; 6
10 it was I who multiplied visions 6
Ams 4: 4 to Gilgal, and multiply transgression; 6
Nah 3:15 Multiply yourselves like the locust 1
15 multiply like the grasshopper! 1
Mat 24:12 because wickedness is multiplied 9
Act 6: 7 the number of the disciples multiplied greatly 9
7:17 the people grew and multiplied in Egypt 9
9:31 it was multiplied. 9
12:24 the word of God grew and multiplied. 9
2Co 9:10 supply and multiply your resources 9
Heb 6:14 saying, "Surely I will bless you and multiply you. 9
1Pe 1: 2 May grace and peace be multiplied to you. 9
2Pe 1: 2 May grace and peace be multiplied to you 9
Jde 1: 2 May mercy, peace, and love be multiplied to you. 9
2Es 3:12 When those who dwelt on earth began to multiply 10
7:111and unrighteousness has multiplied 10
14:17 the more shall evils be multiplied 10
Sir 6: 5 A pleasant voice multiplies friends 9
5 a gracious tongue multiplies courtesies. 9
11:10 if you multiply activities 9
16: 2 If they multiply , do not rejoice in them 9
23: 3 in order that my mistakes may not be multiplied 9
16 Two sorts of men multiply sins 9
44:21 he would multiply him like the dust of the earth 9
48:16 others multiplied sins. 9
Man 1: 9 my transgressions are multiplied, O Lord 9
9 O Lord, they are multiplied! 9
10 multiplying offenses. 9

multitude 1. הָמוֹן 2. מְלֹא 3. מַרְבִּית 4. עַם 5. קָהָל 6. רַב 7. רֹב 8. שִׁפְעָה 9. *βόμβησις* 10. *ὄχλος* 11. *ὄχλος πολύς* 12. *πλῆθος* 13. *πληθύς* 14. multiplico 15. multitudo 16. turba

Gen 16:10 that they cannot be numbered for multitude. 7
17: 4 be the father of a multitude of nations. 1
5 you the father of a multitude of nations. 1
32:12 which cannot be numbered for multitude.' 7
48:16 grow into a multitude in the midst of the earth. 7
19 shall become a multitude of nations. 2
Exd 12:38 A mixed multitude also went up with them 6
23: 2 You shall not follow a multitude to do evil; 6
2 in a suit, turning aside after a multitude 6
Num32: 1 sons of Gad had a very great multitude of cattle; 6
Deu 1:10 you are . . as the stars of heaven for multitude. 7
10:22 made you as the stars of heaven for multitude. 7
28:62 you were as the stars of heaven for multitude 7
Jdg 7:12 lay along the valley like locusts for multitude; 7
12 sand which is upon the seashore for multitude. 7
1Sm 13: 5 like the sand on the seashore in multitude; 7
14:16 the multitude was surging hither and thither. 1
2Sm 6:19 all the people, the whole multitude of Israel 1
17:11 all Israel . . as the sand by the sea for multitude 7
1Kg 3: 8 cannot be numbered or counted for multitude. 7
20:13 Have you seen all this great multitude? 1
28 give all this great multitude into your hand 1
2Kg 7:13 will fare like the whole multitude of Israel 1
25:11 together with the rest of the multitude 1
2Ch 14:11 in thy name we have come against this multitude. 1
20: 2 great multitude is coming against you from Edom 1
12 we are powerless against this great multitude 1
15 be not dismayed at this great multitude; 1
24 they looked toward the multitude; 1
30:18 multitude of the people . . had not cleansed 3
31:18 enrolled with . . the whole multitude; 5
Est 10: 3 and popular with the multitude of his brethren 7
Job 11: 2 Should a multitude of words go unanswered 7
31:34 because I stood in great fear of the multitude 1
35: 9 Because of the multitude of oppressions 7
Ps 42: 4 of thanksgiving, a multitude keeping festival. 1
Prv 14:28 In a multitude of people is the glory of a king 7
Isa 1:11 What to me is the multitude of your sacrifices? 7
5:13 their multitude is parched with thirst. 1
14 nobility of Jerusalem and her multitude go down 1
13: 4 tumult on the mountains as of a great multitude! 4
16:14 contempt, in spite of all his great multitude 1
29: 5 the multitude of your foes shall be like . . dust 1
5 the multitude of the ruthless like . . chaff. 1
7 the multitude of all the nations that fight 1
8 shall the multitude of all the nations be 1
60: 6 A multitude of camels shall cover you 8
Jer 46:16 Your multitude stumbled and fell, and they said 12
Lam 1: 5 suffer for the multitude of her transgressions; 7
Ezk 7:12 for wrath is upon all their multitude. 1
13 For wrath is upon all their multitude; 1
14 for my wrath is upon all their multitude. 1
14: 4 because of the multitude of his idols 7
23:42 The sound of a carefree multitude was with her; 1
28:18 By the multitude of your iniquities 7
30:15 and cut off the multitude of Thebes. 1
31: 2 say to Pharaoh king of Egypt and to his multitude 1
18 Pharaoh and all his multitude, says the Lord GOD. 1
32:12 I will cause your multitude to fall by the swords 1
12 Egypt, and all its multitude shall perish. 1
16 chant it; over Egypt, and over all her multitude 1
18 Son of man, wail over the multitude of Egypt 1
20 with her shall lie all her multitudes. 1
24 Elam . . and all her multitude about her grave; 1
25 among the slain with all her multitude 1
26 their multitude, their graves round about them 1
31 he will comfort himself for all his multitude 1
32 slain by the sword, Pharaoh and all his multitude 1
39:11 there Gog and all his multitude will be buried; 1
Dan 10: 6 sound of his words like the noise of a multitude. 1
11:10 war and assemble a multitude of great forces 1
11 raise a great multitude, but it shall be given 1
12 when the multitude is taken, his heart shall be 1
13 king of the north shall again raise a multitude 1
Hos 10:13 trusted . . in the multitude of your warriors 7
Jol 3:14 Multitudes, multitudes, in the valley 1
14 multitudes, in the valley of decision! 1
Zec 2: 4 because of the multitude of men and cattle in it. 7
Mat 21:26 if we say, 'From men,' we are afraid of the multitude; 10
46 they feared the multitudes 10
Mrk 3: 7 a great multitude from Galilee followed 12
8 from about Tyre and Sidon a great multitude 12
7:33 taking him aside from the multitude privately 10
8:34 he called to him the multitude 10
10:46 his disciples and a great multitude 10
11:18 because all the multitude was astonished 10
12:12 feared the multitude 10
41 watched the multitude 10
Lke 1:10 the whole multitude of the people were praying 12
2:13 with the angel a multitude of the heavenly host 12
3: 7 the multitudes that came out to be baptized by him 10
10 the multitudes asked him, "What then shall we do? 10
5:15 great multitudes gathered to hear 10
6:17 a great multitude of people from all Judea 12
7: 9 turned and said to the multitude that followed 10
8:45 the multitudes surround you and press upon you! 10
12: 1 so many thousands of the multitude 10
13 One of the multitude said to him, "Teacher 10
54 He also said to the multitudes 10
14:25 Now great multitudes accompanied him 10
18:36 hearing a multitude going by 10
19:37 the whole multitude of the disciples 12
39 some of the Pharisees in the multitude said 10
22: 6 an opportunity . . in the absence of the multitude. 10
23: 4 the chief priests and the multitudes 10
27 followed him a great multitude of the people 12
48 the multitudes who assembled to see the sight 10
Joh 5: 3 In these lay a multitude of invalids, blind, lame 12
6: 2 a multitude followed him 11
5 seeing that a multitude was coming to him 10
Act 2: 6 at this sound the multitude came together 12
5:14 multitudes both of men and women 12
6: 5 what they said pleased the whole multitude 12
8: 6 the multitudes with one accord gave heed 10
13:45 when the Jews saw the multitudes 10
14:14 and rushed out among the multitude, crying 10
Jas 5:20 and will cover a multitude of sins. 12
1Pe 4: 8 since love covers a multitude of sins. 12
Rev 7: 9 a great multitude which no man could number 10
17:15 peoples and multitudes and nations and tongues 10
19: 1 a loud voice of a great multitude in heaven 10
6 what seemed to be the voice of a great multitude 10
1Es 2:30 with horsemen and a multitude in battle array 10
5:65 the multitude sounded the trumpets loudly 10
8:91 there was great weeping among the multitude. 12
9: 2 the great iniquities of the multitude. 12
4 the multitude of those who had returned 12
6 all the multitude sat in the open square 12
10 Then all the multitude shouted 12
11 the multitude is great and it is winter 12
12 let the leaders of the multitude stay 12
38 the whole multitude gathered with one accord 12
40 all the multitude, men and women 12
41 all the multitude gave attention to the law. 12
45 in the sight of the multitude 12
47 all the multitude answered, "Amen. 12
49 the Levites who were teaching the multitude 12
2Es 2:42 I, Ezra, saw on Mount Zion a great multitude 16
3:16 and Jacob became a great multitude. 15
5:27 from all the multitude of peoples 14
7:61 I will not grieve over the multitude of those 15
139and blot out the multitude of their sins 15
140only very few of the innumerable multitude. 15
8:41 and plants a multitude of seedlings 15
55 questions about the multitude . . who perish. 15
63 thou hast now shown me a multitude of the signs 15
9:22 let the multitude perish 15
10:10 a multitude . . are destined for destruction. 15
11 she who lost so great a multitude 15
13 the multitude that is now in it goes as it came'; 15
13: 5 and behold, an innumerable multitude of men 15
9 he saw the onrush of the approaching multitude 15
11 and fell on the onrushing multitude 15
11 nothing was seen of the innumerable multitude 15
12 another multitude which was peaceable. 15
28 yet destroying the onrushing multitude 15
34 an innumerable multitude shall be gathered 15
39 another multitude that was peaceable 15
41 they would leave the multitude of the nations 15
47 the multitude gathered together in peace. 15
49 when he destroys the multitude of the nations 15
16:68 behold, the burning wrath of a great multitude 16
Jdt 2:20 a multitude that could not be counted. 12
5:10 there they became a great multitude 12
7: 2 a very great multitude. 12
18 they formed a vast multitude. 12
16: 4 their multitude blocked up the valleys 12
Wis 6: 2 Give ear, you that rule over multitudes 12
24 A multitude of wise men 12
8:10 I shall have glory among the multitudes 10
11:15 a multitude of irrational creatures 12
17 to send upon them a multitude of bears 12
14:20 the multitude, attracted by the charm of his work 12
16: 1 tormented by a multitude of animals. 12
18: 5 thou didst . . take away a multitude of their children 12
20 a plague came upon the multitude in the desert 12
Sir 5: 6 he will forgive the multitude of my sins 12
7: 9 He will consider the multitude of my gifts 12
16: 1 Do not desire a multitude of useless children 12
3 do not rely on their multitude 12
34:19 a multitude of sacrifices. 12
35:18 till he takes away the multitude of the insolent 12
42:11 put you to shame before the great multitude. 12
44:19 the great father of a multitude of nations 12
Bar 2:29 this very great multitude will surely turn 9
LJr 1: 5 you see the multitude before and behind them 10
Man 1: 7 in the multitude of thy mercies 12
9 because of the multitude of my iniquities. 12
1Mc 3:17 fight against so great and strong a multitude 12
6:41 All who heard the noise made by their multitude 12
41 noise made . . by the marching of the multitude 12
9:35 sent his brother as leader of the multitude 10
2Mc 12:27 with multitudes of people of all nationalities. 12
3Mc 4: 5 a multitude of gray-headed old men 12
17 because of their innumerable multitude 13
7:13 their priests and the whole multitude 12

great multitude 1. רַב 2. *πολυπληθία*

2Ch 13: 8 because you are a great multitude 1
2Mc 8:16 not to fear the great multitude of Gentiles 2

noisy multitude 1. הוּם

Mic 2:12 a flock in its pasture, a noisy multitude of men. 1

multitude of the people 1. *ἐθνοπλήθης*

4Mc 7:11 Aaron . . ran through the multitude of the people 1

murder 1. דָּם 2. הרג 3. מות 4. רצח 5. ἀποκτείνω 6. αὐθέντης 7. κατακτείνω 8. σφάζω 9. φονεὺς γίνομαι 10. φονεύω 11. φόνος 12. homicidium
Deu 22:26 man attacking and murdering his neighbor; 4
Jdg 20: 4 the husband of the woman who was murdered 4
1Kg 2: 5 Abner . . and Ama'sa . . , whom he murdered 2
Ps 10: 8 in hiding places he murders the innocent. 2
94: 6 widow . . sojourner, and murder the fatherless; 4
Jer 7: 9 Will you steal, murder, commit adultery 4
41: 4 On the day after the murder of Gedali'ah 3
Hos 4: 2 they break all bounds and murder follows murder. 1
2 they break all bounds and murder follows murder. 1
6: 9 they murder on the way to Shechem 4
Mat 15:19 evil thoughts, murder, adultery, fornication 11
23:31 you are sons of those who murdered the prophets. 10
35 murdered between the sanctuary and the altar. 10
Mrk 7:21 fornication, theft, murder, adultery 11
15: 7 who had committed murder in the insurrection 11
Lke 23:19 thrown into prison . . for murder. 11
25 for insurrection and murder . . they asked for 11
Act 7:52 whom you have now betrayed and murdered 9
9: 1 Saul, still breathing threats and murder 11
Rom 1:29 Full of envy, murder, strife, deceit, malignity 11
1Jn 3:12 not be like Cain who . . murdered his brother. 8
12 And why did he murder him? 8
Rev 9:21 nor did they repent of their murders 11
2Es 1:26 and your feet are swift to commit murder. 12
Wis 12: 6 these parents who murder helpless lives 6
14:25 all is a raging riot of blood and murder 11
Sir 34:22 To take away a neighbor's living is to murder him; 10
2Mc 4: 3 even murders were committed 11
35 displeased at the unjust murder of the man. 11
36 with regard to the unreasonable murder of Onias 5
4Mc 11: 3 by murdering me you will incur punishment 7
12:11 were you not ashamed to murder his servants 7
murder *See also* deed.

murderer 1. בֶּן רצח 2. הרג 3. נכה 4. רצח 5. ἀνδροφονέω 6. ἀνδρόφονος 7. ἀνθρωποκτόνος 8. μιαιφόνος 9. φονεύς
Num35:16 iron, so that he died, he is a murderer; 4
16 the murderer shall be put to death. 4
17 with a stone . . and he died, he is a murderer; 4
17 the murderer shall be put to death. 4
18 weapon of wood . . and he died, he is a murderer; 4
18 the murderer shall be put to death. 4
19 avenger of blood . . put the murderer to death; 4
21 shall be put to death; he is a murderer; 4
21 avenger of blood shall put the murderer to death 4
30 the murderer shall be put to death on the evidence 4
31 shall accept no ransom for the life of a murderer 4
2Kg 6:32 see how this murderer has sent to take off my head? 1
9:31 Is it peace, you Zimri, murderer of your master? 2
14: 6 not put to death the children of the murderers; 3
Job 24:14 The murderer rises in the dark 4
Isa 1:21 Righteousness lodged in her, but now murderers. 4
Jer 4:31 Woe is me! I am fainting before murderers. 2
Mat 22: 7 sent his troops and destroyed those murderers 9
Joh 8:44 He was a murderer from the beginning 7
Act 3:14 asked for a murderer to be granted to you 9
28: 4 No doubt this man is a murderer 9
1Pe 4:15 let none of you suffer as a murderer, or a thief 9
1Jn 3:15 Any one who hates his brother is a murderer 7
15 no murderer has eternal life abiding in him. 7
Rev 21: 8 as for murderers, fornicators, sorcerers 9
22:15 Outside are the . . fornicators and murderers 9
2Mc 9:28 the murderer and blasphemer 6
12: 6 attacked the murderers of his brethren 8
4Mc 9:15 not because I am a murderer 5

murderous 1. φονώδης
4Mc 10:17 the bloodthirsty, murderous . . Antiochus 1

murmur 1. לון 2. רגן 3. תְּלֻנָּה 4. γογγύζω 5. γογγυσμός 6. διαγογγύζω
Exd 15:24 the people murmured against Moses, saying, "What 1
16: 2 Israel murmured against Moses and Aaron 1
7 he has heard your murmurings against the LORD. 3
7 what are we, that you murmur against us? 1
8 LORD has heard your murmurings which you murmur 3
8 your murmurings which you murmur against 1
8 Your murmurings are not against us but against 3
9 LORD, for he has heard your murmurings.' 3
12 I have heard the murmurings of the people 3
17: 3 and the people murmured against Moses 1
Num14: 2 people . . murmured against Moses and Aaron; 1
27 this wicked congregation murmur against me? 1
27 heard the murmurings of the people of Israel 3
27 murmurings . . which they murmur against me. 1
29 all your number . . who have murmured against me 1
16:11 what is Aaron that you murmur against him? 1
41 all . . murmured against Moses 1
17: 5 thus I will make to cease from me the murmurings 3
5 murmurings . . which they murmur against you. 1
10 may make an end of their murmurings against me 3
Deu 1:27 murmured in your tents, and said, 'Because the LORD 2
Jos 9:18 the congregation murmured against the leaders. 1
Ps 106:25 murmured in their tents, and did not obey 2
Isa 29:24 those who murmur will accept instruction. 2
Lke 5:30 the Pharisees and their scribes murmured 4
15: 2 the Pharisees and the scribes murmured, saying 6
19: 7 when they saw it they all murmured 6
Joh 6:41 The Jews then murmured at him, because he said 4
43 Do not murmur among yourselves. 4
61 knowing in himself that his disciples murmured 4
Act 6: 1 the Hellenists murmured against the Hebrews 5
Wis 1:10 the sound of murmurings does not go unheard. 5
11 Beware then of useless murmuring 5
Sir 46: 7 stilled their wicked murmuring. 5

murmur against 1. καταγογγύζω
1Mc 11:39 the troops were murmuring against Demetrius. 1

make murmur 1. לון
Num14:36 made all the congregation to murmur against him 1

muscle 1. שָׁרִיר 2. σάρξ
Job 40:16 his power in the muscles of his belly. 1
4Mc 7:13 his muscles flabby, his sinews feeble 2

muse 1. הגה 2. הָגִיג 3. שׂיח 4. שִׂיחַ
1Kg 18:27 he is a god; either he is musing, or he has gone aside 4
Ps 39: 3 As I mused, the fire burned; 2
77:12 I will meditate . . and muse on thy mighty deeds. 3
143: 5 I muse on what thy hands have wrought. 3
Isa 33:18 Your mind will muse on the terror 1

music 1. הָמוֹן 2. מַשָּׂא 3. נְגִינָה 4. שִׁיר 5. שׁמע 6. זְמָר(A) 7. μουσικός 8. συμφωνία
1Ch 15:22 Chenani'ah, leader of the Levites in music 2
22 should direct the music, for he understood it. 2
27 Chenani'ah the leader of the music of the singers 2
16:42 had trumpets and cymbals for the music 5
25: 6 in the music in the house of the LORD 4
2Ch 7: 6 Levites . . with the instruments for music 4
34:12 Levites . . skilful with instruments of music 4
Ps 49: 4 I will solve my riddle to the music of the lyre. •
92: 3 to the music of the lute and the harp •
Lam 5:14 old men have quit . . the young men their music. 3
Ezk 26:13 I will stop the music of your songs 1
Dan 3: 5 hear the sound of . . every kind of music 6
7 heard the sound of . . every kind of music 6
10 hears the sound of . . every kind of music 6
15 hear the sound of . . every kind of music 6
Ams 6: 5 invent for themselves instruments of music; 4
Lke 15:25 he heard music and dancing. 8
1Es 4:63 they feasted, with music and rejoicing 7
5: 2 with the music of drums and flutes; 7
Sir 22: 6 Like music in mourning 7
32: 3 do not interrupt the music. 7
5 a concert of music at a banquet of wine. 7
6 the melody of music with good wine. 7
40:20 Wine and music gladden the heart 7
49: 1 like music at a banquet of wine. 7
music *See also* instrument, make.

musical 1. שִׁיר 2. μουσικός
1Ch 15:16 who should play loudly on musical instruments 1
2Ch 5:13 raised, with . . and other musical instruments 1
23:13 singers with their musical instruments 1
Neh 12:36 musical instruments of David the man of God; 1
Sir 44: 5 those who composed musical tunes 2
musical *See also* instrument.

musician 1. חצץ 2. μουσικός 3. ψάλτης
Jdg 5:11 To the sound of musicians at the watering places 1
1Es 5:42 245 musicians and singers. 3
1Mc 9:39 tambourines and musicians and many weapons. 2
41 the voice of their musicians into a funeral dirge. 2

must 1. ἀνάγκη 2. δεῖ 3. ἔχω ἀνάγκην 4. ἵνα 5. μᾶλλον 6. ὁράω 7. οὖν 8. oportet
Gen 20:13 I said to her, 'This is the kindness you must do me •
43:23 your God and the God of your father must have put •
45:13 You must tell my father of all my splendor •
47:29 when the time drew near that Israel must die •
Exd 8:27 We must go three days' journey •
10: 9 for we must hold a feast to the LORD. •
25 Moses said, "You must also let us have sacrifices •
26 Our cattle also must go with us; •
26 cattle . . we must take of them to serve the LORD •
26 we do not know with what we must serve the LORD •
12:16 what every one must eat, that only may be prepared •
Lev 13:44 the priest must pronounce him unclean •
19:23 be forbidden to you, it must not be eaten •
22:21 to be accepted it must be perfect •
Num23:12 Must I not take heed to speak what the LORD •
35:28 For the man must remain in his city of refuge •
Deu 31:14 Behold, the days approach when you must die; •
Jos 22:18 that you must turn away this day from . . the LORD? •
Jdg 14: 3 all our people, that you must go to take a wife •
21:17 There must be an inheritance for the survivors •
Rut 3:17 for he said, 'You must not go back empty-handed •
1Sm 2:16 No, you must give it now; and if not, I will take it •
6: 5 So you must make images of your tumors and . . mice •
9:13 till he comes, since he must bless the sacrifice; •
2Sm 14:14 We must all die, we are like water spilt •
1Kg 18:27 or perhaps he is asleep and must be awakened. •
1Ch 22: 5 for the LORD must be exceedingly magnificent •
14 timber and stone . . To these you must add. •
Ezr 10:12 It is so; we must do as you have said. •
Ecc 2:18 I hated all my toil . . seeing that I must leave it •
21 a man who has . . must leave all to be enjoyed •
10:10 he must put forth more strength; •
Jer 25:28 Thus says the LORD of hosts: You must drink! †
36:16 We must report all these words to the king. †
49:12 did not deserve to drink the cup must drink it †
12 You shall not go unpunished, but you must drink. †
Lam 5: 4 We must pay for the water we drink •
4 We must pay for . . the wood we get must be bought. •
Mat 5:48 You, therefore, must be perfect, as your heavenly •
6: 5 when you pray, you must not be like the hypocrites; •
16:21 he must go to Jerusalem and suffer many things 2
17:10 the scribes say that first Eli'jah must come? 2
19:16 Teacher, what good deed must I do •
20:26 whoever would be great . . must be your servant •
27 whoever would be first . . must be your slave; •
22:24 his brother must marry the widow •
24: 6 this must take place, but the end is not yet. 2
44 Therefore you also must be ready •
26:35 Even if I must die with you, I will not deny you. 2
54 that it must be so? 2
Mrk 8:31 the Son of man must suffer many things 2
9:11 the scribes say that first Eli'jah must come 2
35 If any one would be first, he must be last of all •
10:17 what must I do to inherit eternal life? •
43 whoever would be great . . must be your servant •
44 whoever would be first . . must be slave of all. •
12:19 the man must take the wife, and raise up children 4
13: 7 do not be alarmed; this must take place 2
10 gospel must first be preached to all nations. 2
14:31 If I must die with you, I will not deny you. 2
Lke 2:49 you not know that I must be in my Father's house? 2
4:43 he said to them, "I must preach the good news 2
5:38 new wine must be put into fresh wineskins. •
9:22 saying, "The Son of man must suffer many things 2
12:40 You also must be ready; for the Son of man is coming •
13:33 I must go on my way today and tomorrow 2
14:18 I must go out and see it 3
17: 4 you must forgive him. •
25 first he must suffer many things and be rejected 2
19: 5 I must stay at your house today. 2
20:28 the man must take the wife and raise up children 4
21: 9 this must first take place 2
22:37 this scripture must be fulfilled in me 2
24: 7 the Son of man must be delivered 2
44 everything . . must be fulfilled. 2
Joh 3: 7 that I said to you, 'You must be born anew.' 2
14 so must the Son of man be lifted up 2
30 He must increase, but I must decrease. 2
30 He must increase, but I must decrease. •
4:24 must worship in spirit and truth. 2
6:28 What must we do, to be doing the works of God? •
9: 4 We must work the works of him who sent me 2
10:16 I must bring them also 2
12:26 If any one serves me, he must follow me •
34 How can you say . . the Son of man must be lifted up? 2
20: 9 the scripture, that he must rise from the dead. 2
Act 1:22 one of these men must become with us a witness 2
3:21 whom heaven must receive 2
4:12 no other name . . by which we must be saved. 2
19 you must judge; •
5:29 We must obey God rather than men. 2
9:16 I will show him how much he must suffer 2
10:15 What God has cleansed, you must not call common. •
11: 9 'What God has cleansed you must not call common.' •
14:22 saying that . . we must enter the kingdom of God. 2
16:30 Men, what must I do to be saved? 2
19:21 After I have been there, I must also see Rome. 2
20:35 by so toiling one must help the weak 2
23:11 so you must bear witness also at Rome. 2
26:23 that the Christ must suffer •
27:24 you must stand before Caesar 2
Rom 2:22 You who say that one must not commit adultery •
6:11 you also must consider yourselves dead to sin •
13: 5 Therefore one must be subject 1
1Co 10: 8 We must not indulge in immorality as some of them •
9 We must not put the Lord to the test, as some of them •
11:19 for there must be factions among you 2
15:25 For he must reign 2
53 perishable nature must put on the imperishable 2
53 this mortal nature must put on immortality. 2
2Co 1:11 You also must help us by prayer •
3: 9 the dispensation . . must far exceed it in splendor. 5
5:10 For we must all appear before the judgment seat 2
9: 7 Each one must do as he has made up his mind •
11:21 To my shame, I must say, we were too weak for that! •
30 If I must boast 2
12: 1 I must boast; there is nothing to be gained by it 2
13: 1 Any charge must be sustained •
Eph 4:17 you must no longer live as the Gentiles do •
5: 3 covetousness must not even be named among you •
Col 3:13 so you also must forgive. •

1Ti 3: 2 Now a bishop must be above reproach 2
4 He must manage his own household well •
6 He must not be a recent convert •
7 moreover he must be well thought of by outsiders 2
8 Deacons likewise must be serious •
9 they must hold the mystery of the faith •
11 The women likewise must be serious •
5:10 she must be well attested for her good deeds •
6: 2 Those . . must not be disrespectful •
2 rather they must serve all the better •
2Ti 2:24 the Lord's servant must not be quarrelsome 2
Tit 1: 7 For a bishop, as God's steward, must be blameless 2
7 he must not be arrogant or quick-tempered •
9 he must hold firm to the sure word as taught •
11 they must be silenced 2
Heb 2: 1 Therefore we must pay the closer attention 2
9:16 the death . . must be established. 1
11: 6 must believe that he exists 2
Jas 1: 7 For that person must not suppose •
2Pe 1:20 First of all you must understand this •
3: 3 First of all you must understand this •
Jde 1:17 you must remember, beloved, the predictions •
Rev 1: 1 show to his servants what must soon take place; 2
4: 1 I will show you what must take place after this. 2
10:11 You must again prophesy about many peoples 2
13:10 if any one slays . . with the sword must he be slain 2
17:10 when he comes he must remain only a little while. 2
19:10 but he said to me, "You must not do that! 6
20: 3 After that he must be loosed for a little while. 2
22: 6 to show his servants what must soon take place. 2
1Es 4:22 Hence you must realize that women rule over you! 2
2Es 6:16 for they know that their end must be changed. 8
9:12 these must in torment acknowledge it 8
Tob 11: 8 You therefore must anoint his eyes with the gall; •
12: 1 he must also be given more. 2
Jdt 5:22 insisted that he must be put to death. •
Wis 12:19 the righteous man must be kind 2
16:28 to make it known that one must rise before the sun 2
28 and must pray to thee at the dawning of the light; •
Sir 3:18 the more you must humble yourself •
8: 7 remember that we all must die. •
13 be concerned as one who must pay. •
13: 3 he must add apologies. •
14:17 the decree from of old is, "You must surely die! •
33:19 lest you change your mind and must ask for it. •
LJr 1: 6 It is thou, O Lord, whom we must worship. 2
2Mc 2:29 the master builder . . must be concerned •
3Mc 5:37 How many times . . must I give you orders 2
4Mc 13: 1 everyone must concede •
16: 1 it must be admitted †
22 You too must have the same faith in God 7

mustard seed 1. σίναπι

Mat 13:31 like a grain of mustard seed 1
17:20 if you have faith as a grain of mustard seed 1
Mrk 4:31 It is like a grain of mustard seed 1
Lke 13:19 It is like a grain of mustard seed which a man took 1
17: 6 If you had faith as a grain of mustard seed 1

muster 1. אסף 2. מנה 3. פקד 4. פְּקֻדָּה 5. צבא 6. קבץ 7. ἀριθμέω 8. παρεμβάλλω 9. συλλοχάω

Jos 8:10 Joshua arose early . . and mustered the people 3
Jdg 20:15 the Benjaminites mustered out of their cities 3
15 Gib'e-ah, who mustered 700 picked men. 3
17 Israel . . mustered 400,000 men that drew sword 3
21: 9 For when the people were mustered, behold, not one 3
1Sm 11: 8 When he mustered them at Bezek, the men of Israel 3
13: 5 the Philistines mustered to fight with Israel 1
11 the Philistines had mustered at Michmash 1
2Sm 18: 1 Then David mustered the men who were with him 3
1Kg 20:15 he mustered the servants of the governors 3
15 after them he mustered all the people of Israel 3
25 muster an army like the army that you have lost 2
26 Ben-ha'dad mustered the Syrians, and went up 3
27 the people of Israel were mustered 3
2Kg 3: 6 Jeho'ram marched out . . and mustered all Israel. 3
6:24 Ben-ha'dad king of Syria mustered his entire army 6
25:19 commander . . who mustered the people of the land; 5
1Ch 19: 7 Ammonites were mustered from their cities 1
2Ch 17:14 This was the muster of them by fathers' houses 4
25: 5 He mustered those twenty years old and upward 3
26:11 according to the numbers in the muster 4
Isa 13: 4 The LORD of hosts is mustering a host for battle. 3
Jer 52:25 of the army who mustered the people of the land; 5
Ezk 38: 8 After many days you will be mustered; 3
Jdt 2:15 mustered the picked troops by divisions 7
1Mc 4:28 he mustered 60,000 picked infantrymen 9
10:77 he mustered 3,000 cavalry 8

muster in array 1. כון

Nah 2: 3 chariots flash like flame when mustered in array 1

mute 1. σιωπάω

4Mc 10:18 God hears also those who are mute. 1

mutilate 1. חרם 2. חרץ 3. ἀκρωτηριάζω 4. ἀποκόπτω

Lev 21:18 a man blind or lame, or one who has a mutilated face 1
22:22 Animals blind or disabled or mutilated 2
Gal 5:12 who unsettle you would mutilate themselves! 4
4Mc 10:20 we let our bodily members be mutilated. 3

mutilate the flesh 1. κατατομή

Php 3: 2 look out for those who mutilate the flesh. 1

mutilation 1. מָשְׁחָת

Lev 22:25 a blemish in them, because of their mutilation 1

mutter 1. הגה 2. γογγύζω 3. γογγυσμός

Isa 8:19 the mediums and the wizards who chirp and mutter 1
59: 3 spoken lies, your tongue mutters wickedness. 1
Joh 7:12 much muttering about him among the people 3
32 heard the crowd thus muttering about him 2

mutual 1. εἰς ἀλλήλους

Rom 14:19 makes for peace and for mutual upbuilding. 1

mutual *See also* help.

mutually *See* encourage.

muzzle 1. חסם 2. κημόω 3. φιμός 4. φιμόω

Deu 25: 4 not muzzle an ox when it treads out the grain. 1
1Co 9: 9 not muzzle an ox when it is treading out the grain. 2
1Ti 5:18 not muzzle an ox when it is treading out the grain 4
Sir 20:29 like a muzzle on the mouth they avert reproofs. 3

myriad 1. μυριάς 2. μύριος

Jde 1:14 Behold, the Lord came with his holy myriads 1
Rev 5:11 angels, numbering myriads of myriads 1
11 angels, numbering myriads of myriads 1
Jdt 16: 4 he came with myriads of his warriors 1
3Mc 3:21 the myriad affairs liberally entrusted to them 2

myrrh 1. לֹט 2. מֹר 3. נֵשֶׁק 4. μύρον 5. σμύρνα

Gen 37:25 with their camels bearing gum, balm, and myrrh 1
43:11 a little honey, gum, myrrh, pistachio nuts 1
Exd 30:23 Take . . of liquid myrrh 500 shekels 2
1Kg 10:25 garments, myrrh, spices, horses, and mules 3
2Ch 9:24 his present . . garments, myrrh, spices, horses 3
Est 2:12 six months with oil of myrrh and six . . with spices 2
Ps 45: 8 your robes are all fragrant with myrrh and aloes 2
Prv 7:17 perfumed my bed with myrrh, aloes, and cinnamon. 2
Sng 1:13 My beloved is to me a bag of myrrh 2
3: 6 of smoke, perfumed with myrrh and frankincense 2
4: 6 I will hie me to the mountain of myrrh 2
14 with all trees of frankincense, myrrh and aloes 2
5: 1 I gather my myrrh with my spice, I eat my honeycomb 2
5 I arose to open . . and my hands dripped with myrrh 2
5 my hands dripped . . my fingers with liquid myrrh 2
13 His lips are lilies, distilling liquid myrrh. 2
Mat 2:11 gifts, gold and frankincense and myrrh. 5
Joh 19:39 came bringing a mixture of myrrh and aloes 5
Rev 18:13 cinnamon, spice, incense, myrrh, frankincense 4
Sir 24:15 like choice myrrh I spread a pleasant odor 5

myrrh *See also* mingle.

myrrh-perfumed 1. μυροβρεχής

3Mc 4: 6 their myrrh-perfumed hair sprinkled with ashes 1

myrtle 1. הֲדַס

Neh 8:15 bring branches of olive, wild olive, myrtle, palm 1
Isa 41:19 the cedar, the acacia, the myrtle, and the olive; 1
55:13 instead of the brier shall come up the myrtle; 1

myrtle tree 1. הֲדַס

Zec 1: 8 standing among the myrtle trees in the glen; 1
10 the man who was standing among the myrtle trees 1
11 angel . . who was standing among the myrtle trees 1

something mysterious 1. ἄδηλος

3Mc 1:17 something mysterious was occurring. 1

mysterious thing 1. סתר (A)

Dan 2:22 he reveals deep and mysterious things; 1

mystery 1. רָז (A) 2. μυέω 3. μυστήριον

Dan 2:18 mercy of the God . . concerning this mystery 1
19 mystery was revealed to Daniel in a vision 1
27 can show . . the mystery which the king has asked 1
28 there is a God in heaven who reveals mysteries 1
29 who reveals mysteries made known to you what is 1
30 mystery been revealed to me, but in order that 1
47 Truly, your God is . . a revealer of mysteries 1
47 for you have been able to reveal this mystery. 1
4: 9 know . . that no mystery is difficult for you 1
Rom 11:25 I want you to understand this mystery, brethren 3
16:25 revelation of the mystery which was kept secret 3
1Co 4: 1 stewards of the mysteries of God. 3
13: 2 and understand all mysteries and all knowledge 3
14: 2 he utters mysteries in the Spirit. 3
15:51 Lo! I tell you a mystery 3
Eph 1: 9 has made known . . the mystery of his will 3
3: 3 how the mystery was made known to me 3
4 perceive my insight into the mystery of Christ 3
9 to make all men see what is the plan of the mystery 3
5:32 This mystery is a profound one 3
6:19 to proclaim the mystery of the gospel 3
Col 1:26 the mystery hidden for ages and generations 3
27 the riches of the glory of this mystery 3
2: 2 the knowledge of God's mystery, of Christ 3
4: 3 to declare the mystery of Christ 3
2Th 2: 7 the mystery of lawlessness is already at work; 3
1Ti 3: 9 they must hold the mystery of the faith 3
16 Great indeed . . is the mystery of our religion 3
Rev 1:20 As for the mystery of the seven stars 3
10: 7 the mystery of God, as he announced to his 3
17: 5 on her forehead was written a name of mystery 3
7 I will tell you the mystery of the woman 3
Wis 14:23 or celebrate secret mysteries 3
3Mc 2:30 who have been initiated into the mysteries 2

myth 1. μῦθος

1Ti 1: 4 nor to occupy themselves with myths 1
4: 7 godless and silly myths 1
2Ti 4: 4 will turn away . . and wander into myths. 1
Tit 1:14 instead of giving heed to Jewish myths 1
2Pe 1:16 For we did not follow cleverly devised myths 1

N

nail 1. מַסְמֵר 2. ἧλος 3. προσηλόω
1Ch 22: 3 iron for nails for the doors of the gates 1
2Ch 3: 9 The weight of the nails was one shekel to 50 1
Ecc 12:11 like nails firmly fixed are the . . sayings 1
Isa 41: 7 fasten it with nails so that it cannot be moved. 1
Jer 10: 4 they fasten it with hammer and nails 1
Joh 20:25 Unless I see in his hands the print of the nails 2
25 place my finger in the mark of the nails 2
Col 2:14 this he set aside, nailing it to the cross. 3

nail (2) 1. צִפֹּרֶן 2. טְפַר (A)
Deu 21:12 she shall shave her head and pare her nails. 1
Dan 4:33 till . . his nails were like birds' claws. 2

naked 1. מַעֲרֹם 2. עֵירֹם 3. עֶרְוָה 4. עָרוֹם 5. γυμνός
6. nudus
Gen 2:25 the man and his wife were both naked 4
3: 7 they knew that they were naked; 2
10 afraid, because I was naked; and I hid myself. 2
11 He said, "Who told you that you were naked? 2
Exd 28:42 linen breeches to cover their naked flesh; 3
1Sm 19:24 he too prophesied . . and lay naked all that day 4
2Ch 28:15 with the spoil they clothed all that were naked 1
Job 1:21 he said, "Naked I came from my mother's womb 4
21 from my mother's womb, and naked shall I return; 4
22: 6 and stripped the naked of their clothing. 4
24: 7 They lie all night naked, without clothing 4
10 They go about naked, without clothing; hungry 4
26: 6 Sheol is naked before God 4
Ecc 5:15 As he came . . he shall go again, naked as he came 4
Isa 20: 2 and he had done so, walking naked and barefoot- 4
3 my servant Isaiah has walked naked and barefoot 4
4 both the young and the old, naked and barefoot 4
58: 7 when you see the naked, to cover him 4
Ezk 16: 7 your hair had grown; yet you were naked and bare. 2
22 your youth, when you were naked and bare 2
39 shall strip you . . and leave you naked and bare. 2
18: 7 and covers the naked with a garment 2
16 and covers the naked with a garment 2
23:29 and leave you naked and bare 2
Hos 2: 3 lest I strip her naked 4
Ams 2:16 the mighty shall flee away naked in that day 4
Mic 1: 8 will lament and wail; I will go stripped and naked; 4
Mat 25:36 I was naked and you clothed me 5
38 naked and clothe thee? 5
43 naked and you did not clothe me 5
44 thirsty or a stranger or naked or sick 5
Mrk 14:52 he left the linen cloth and ran away naked. 5
Act 19:16 they fled out of that house naked and wounded. 5
2Co 5: 3 so that by putting it on we may not be found naked. 5
Rev 3:17 you are wretched, pitiable, poor, blind, and naked. 5
16:15 that he may not go naked and be seen exposed!") 5
17:16 they will make her desolate and naked 5
2Es 2:20 defend the orphan, clothe the naked 6
Tob 1:17 I would give . . my clothing to the naked 5
4:16 Give . . of your clothing to the naked 5

naked *See also* make.

nakedness 1. יַד 2. מַעֲרֶה 3. עֵירֹם 4. עֶרְוָה 5. עֶרְיָה
6. ἀσχημοσύνη 7. γυμνότης
Gen 9:22 Ham . . saw the nakedness of his father 4
23 covered the nakedness of their father; 4
23 they did not see their father's nakedness. 4
Exd 20:26 that your nakedness be not exposed on it.' 4
Lev 18: 6 approach any one . . to uncover nakedness 4
7 shall not uncover the nakedness of your father 4
7 which is the nakedness of your mother 4
7 your mother, you shall not uncover her nakedness 4
8 not uncover the nakedness of your father's wife 4
8 your father's wife; it is your father's nakedness 4
9 shall not uncover the nakedness of your sister 4
10 not uncover the nakedness of your son's daughter 4
10 their nakedness is your own nakedness 4
10 their nakedness is your own nakedness 4
11 the nakedness of your father's wife's daughter 4
12 not uncover the nakedness of your father's sister 4
13 not uncover the nakedness of your mother's sister 4
14 uncover the nakedness of your father's brother 4
15 uncover the nakedness of your daughter-in-law 4
15 son's wife, you shall not uncover her nakedness 4
16 not uncover the nakedness of your brother's wife 4
16 brother's wife; she is your brother's nakedness 4
17 You shall not uncover the nakedness of a woman 4
17 her daughter's daughter to uncover her nakedness 4
18 uncovering her nakedness while her sister is 4
19 not approach a woman to uncover her nakedness 4
20:11 The man . . has uncovered his father's nakedness 4
17 If a man . . sees her nakedness, and she sees his 4
17 If . . she sees his nakedness, it is a shameful 4
17 he has uncovered his sister's nakedness 4
18 If a man . . uncovers her nakedness 4
19 You shall not uncover the nakedness 4
20 he has uncovered his uncle's nakedness 4
21 he has uncovered his brother's nakedness 4
Deu 28:48 serve your enemies . . in nakedness, and in want 3
1Sm 20:30 and to the shame of your mother's nakedness? 4
Isa 47: 3 Your nakedness shall be uncovered 4
57: 8 loved their bed, you have looked on nakedness. 1
Lam 1: 8 despise her, for they have seen her nakedness; 4
Ezk 16: 8 my skirt over you, and covered your nakedness; 4
36 your nakedness uncovered in your harlotries 4
37 and will uncover your nakedness to them 4
37 to them, that they may see all your nakedness. 4
22:10 In you men uncover their fathers' nakedness; 4
23:10 These uncovered her nakedness; they seized her 4
18 harlotry so openly and flaunted her nakedness 4
29 nakedness of your harlotry shall be uncovered. 4
Hos 2: 9 and my flax, which were to cover her nakedness. 4
Mic 1:11 inhabitants of Shaphir, in nakedness and shame; 5
Nah 3: 5 and I will let nations look on your nakedness 2
Rom 8:35 or famine, or nakedness, or peril, or sword? 7
Rev 3:18 keep the shame of your nakedness from being seen 7
Sir 29:21 clothing and a house to cover one's nakedness. 6

name 1. אמר 2. דבר 3. זכר 4. זֵכֶר 5. נקב 6. נקב שֵׁם
7. קרא 8. קרא בְּשֵׁם 9. קרא לְ 10. קרא שֵׁם
11. שׂום שֵׁם 12. שֵׁם 13. שׂום שְׁם (A) 14. שְׁם (A)
15. ἀνώνυμος 16. καλέω 17. καλέω τὸ ὄνομα 18. λέγω
19. ὄνομα 20. ὀνομάζω 21. nomen 22. nomino
Gen 2:11 The name of the first is Pishon; 12
13 The name of the second river is Gihon; 12
14 the name of the third river is Tigris 12
19 every living creature, that was its name. 12
20 The man gave names to all cattle 12
3:20 The man called his wife's name Eve 12
4:17 built a city, and called the name of the city 12
17 name of the city after the name of his son, Enoch. 12
19 took two wives; the name of the one was Adah 12
19 one was Adah, and the name of the other Zillah. 12
21 His brother's name was Jubal; 12
25 she bore a son and called his name Seth 12
26 was born, and he called his name Enosh. 12
26 time men began to call upon the name of the LORD. 12
5: 2 created them, and he blessed them and named them 10
3 a son . . after his image, and named him Seth. 10
29 called his name Noah, saying, "Out of the ground 12
10:25 born two sons: the name of the one was Peleg 12
25 was divided, and his brother's name was Joktan. 12
11: 4 let us make a name for ourselves 12
9 Therefore its name was called Ba'bel 12
29 the name of Abram's wife was Sar'ai 12
29 and the name of Nahor's wife, Milcah 12
12: 2 I will bless you, and make your name great 12
8 to the LORD and called on the name of the LORD. 12
13: 4 there Abram called on the name of the LORD. 12
16: 1 had an Egyptian maid whose name was Hagar; 12
11 you shall call his name Ish'mael; 12
13 she called the name of the LORD who spoke to her 12
15 the name of his son, whom Hagar bore, Ish'mael. 12
17: 5 No longer shall your name be Abram 12
5 be Abram, but your name shall be Abraham; 12
15 you shall not call her name Sar'ai, but Sarah 12
15 her name Sar'ai, but Sarah shall be her name. 12
19 and you shall call his name Isaac. 12
19:22 Therefore the name of the city was called Zo'ar. 12
37 first-born bore a son, and called his name Moab; 12
38 bore a son, and called his name Ben-ammi; 12
21: 3 Abraham called the name of his son who was born 12
12 through Isaac shall your descendants be named. 7
33 and called there on the name of the LORD 12
22:14 Abraham called the name of that place 12
24 Moreover, his concubine, whose name was Reumah 12
23:16 the silver which he had named in the hearing 2
24:29 Rebekah had a brother whose name was Laban; 12
25: 1 took another wife, whose name was Ketu'rah. 12
13 These are the names of the sons of Ish'mael 12
13 sons . . named in the order of their birth 12
16 these are their names, by their villages 12
25 like a hairy mantle; so they called his name Esau. 12
26 hold of Esau's heel; so his name was called Jacob. 12
30 Therefore his name was called Edom. 12
26:18 he gave them the names which his father had given 12
20 he called the name of the well Esek 12
21 he called its name Sitnah. 12
22 did not quarrel; so he called its name Reho'both 12
25 and called upon the name of the LORD 12
33 therefore the name of the city is Beer-sheba 12
27:36 Esau said, "Is he not rightly named Jacob? 10
28:19 He called the name of that place Bethel; 12
19 but the name of the city was Luz at the first. 12
29:16 had two daughters; the name of the older was Leah 12
16 was Leah, and the name of the younger was Rachel. 12
32 she called his name Reuben; for she said 12
33 this son also"; and she called his name Simeon. 12
34 therefore his name was called Levi. 12
35 therefore she called his name Judah; 12
30: 6 given me a son"; therefore she called his name Dan 12
8 have prevailed"; so she called his name Naph'tali. 12
11 Good fortune!" so she called his name Gad. 12
13 will call me happy"; so she called his name Asher. 12
18 she called his name Is'sachar. 12
20 she called his name Zeb'ulun. 12
21 bore a daughter, and called her name Dinah. 12
24 she called his name Joseph 12
28 name your wages, and I will give it. 5
31:48 Therefore he named it Galeed 10
32: 2 he called the name of that place Mahana'im. 12
27 he said to him, "What is your name? 12
28 he said, "Your name shall no more be called Jacob 12
29 Then Jacob asked him, "Tell me, I pray, your name. 12
29 But he said, "Why is it that you ask my name? 12
30 Jacob called the name of the place Peni'el 12
33:17 therefore the name of the place is called 12
35: 8 so the name of it was called Al'lon-bacuth. 12
10 God said to him, "Your name is Jacob; 12
10 no longer shall your name be called Jacob 12
10 be called Jacob, but Israel shall be your name. 12
10 his name was called Israel. 12
15 Jacob called the name of the place where God 12
18 she called his name Ben-o'ni; 12
18 Ben-o'ni; but his father called his name Benjamin *
36:10 These are the names of Esau's sons 12
32 Edom, the name of his city being Din'habah. 12
35 in his stead, the name of his city being Avith. 12
39 the name of his city being Pau; 12
39 his wife's name was Mehet'abel 12
40 These are the names of the chiefs of Esau 12
40 by their names: the chiefs Timna, Alvah, Jetheth 12
38: 1 to a certain Adullamite, whose name was Hirah. 12
2 a certain Canaanite whose name was Shua; 12
3 bore a son, and he called his name Er. 12
4 bore a son, and she called his name Onan. 12
5 bore a son, and she called his name Shelah. 12

6 took a wife . . and her name was Tamar. 12
29 Therefore his name was called Perez. 12
30 his hand; and his name was called Zerah. 12
41:45 Pharaoh called Joseph's name Zaph'enath-pane'ah 12
51 Joseph called the name of the first-born 12
52 The name of the second he called E'phraim 12
46: 8 Now these are the names of the descendants 12
48: 6 shall be called by the name of their brothers 12
16 in them let my name be perpetuated, 12
16 be perpetuated, and the name of my fathers 12
49:24 by the name of the Shepherd, the Rock of Israel 12
50:11 Therefore the place was named A'bel-mizraim; 10
Exd 1: 1 These are the names of the sons of Israel 12
15 Hebrew midwives, one of whom was named Shiph'rah 12
2:10 her son; and she named him Moses, for she said 10
22 She bore a son, and he called his name Gershom; 12
3:13 'What is his name?' what shall I say to them? 12
15 this is my name for ever, and thus I am to be 12
5:23 For since I came to Pharaoh to speak in thy name 12
6: 3 by my name the LORD I did not make myself known 12
16 These are the names of the sons of Levi according 12
9:16 so that my name may be declared throughout all 12
15: 3 The LORD is a man of war; the LORD is his name. 12
23 it was bitter; therefore it was named Marah. 10
16:31 Now the house of Israel called its name manna; 12
17: 7 he called the name of the place Massah 12
15 Moses built an altar and called the name of it 12
18: 3 two sons, of whom the name of the one was Gershom 12
4 the name of the other was Elie'zer 12
20: 7 You shall not take the name of the LORD your God 12
7 hold him guiltless who takes his name in vain. 12
24 place where I cause my name to be remembered 12
23:13 make no mention of the names of other gods 12
21 for my name is in him. 12
28: 9 engrave on them the names of the sons of Israel 12
10 six of their names on the one stone, and the names 12
10 the names of the remaining six on the other stone 12
11 engrave the two stones with the names of the sons 12
12 Aaron shall bear their names before the LORD 12
21 There shall be twelve stones with their names 12
21 stones with their names according to the names 12
21 like signets, each engraved with its name 12
29 Aaron shall bear all the names of the sons of Israel 12
31: 2 See, I have called by name Bez'alel and son of Uri 12
33:12 I know you by name, and you have also found favor 12
17 found favor in my sight, and I know you by name. 12
19 will proclaim before you my name 'The LORD'; 12
34: 5 the LORD . . proclaimed the name of the LORD. 12
14 the LORD, whose name is Jealous, is a jealous God) 12
35:30 See, the LORD has called by name Bez'alel 12
39: 6 engraved . . according to the names of the sons 12
14 There were twelve stones with their names 12
14 stones with their names according to the names 12
14 like signets, each engraved with its name 12
Lev 18:21 fire to Molech, and so profane the name of your God 12
19:12 you shall not swear by my name falsely 12
12 and so profane the name of your God: I am the LORD 12
20: 3 defiling my sanctuary and profaning my holy name 12
21: 6 shall . . not profane the name of their God 12
22: 2 may not profane my holy name: I am the LORD 12
32 you shall not profane my holy name 12
24:11 the Israelite woman's son blasphemed the Name 12
11 His mother's name was Shelo'mith, 12
16 He who blasphemes the name of the LORD 12
16 when he blasphemes the Name, shall be put to death 12
Num 1: 2 census . . according to the number of names 12
5 these are the names of the men who shall attend 12
17 Moses . . took these men who have been named 6
18 registered . . according to the number of names 12
20 according to the number of names, head by head 12
22 according to the number of names, head by head 12
24 according to the number of the names 12
26 according to the number of names 12
28 according to the number of names 12
30 according to the number of names 12
32 according to the number of names 12
34 to the number of names, from twenty years old 12
36 according to the number of names 12
38 according to the number of names, from twenty 12
40 according to the number of names, from twenty 12
42 according to the number of names, from twenty 12
3: 2 These are the names of the sons of Aaron 12
3 these are the names of the sons of Aaron 12
17 these were the sons of Levi by their names 12
18 these are the names of the sons of Gershon 12
40 taking their number by names. 12
43 first-born . . according to the number of names 12
4:32 shall assign by name the objects which they 12
6:27 shall they put my name upon the people of Israel 12
11: 3 name of that place was called Tab'erah 12
26 Now two men remained in the camp, one named Eldad 12
26 two men remained . . the other named Medad 12
34 name of that place was called Kib'roth-hatta'avah 12
13: 4 these were their names: From the tribe of Reuben 12
16 names of the men whom Moses sent to spy out 12
17: 2 Write each man's name upon his rod 12
3 write Aaron's name upon the rod of Levi. 12
21: 3 so the name of the place was called Hormah. 12
25:14 The name of the slain man of Israel . . was Zimri 12
15 name of the Mid'ianite woman who was slain 12
26:33 names of the daughters of Zeloph'ehad were 12
46 the name of the daughter of Asher was Serah. 12
53 inheritance according to the number of names. 12
55 according to the names of the tribes 12
59 name of Amram's wife was Joch'ebed the daughter 12
27: 1 names of his daughters were: Mahlah, Noah, Hoglah 12
4 Why should the name of our father be taken away 12
32:38 Nebo, and Ba'al-me'on (their names to be changed) 12
38 gave other names to the cities which they built. 12
42 Kenath . . and called it Nobah, after his own name. 12
34:17 names of the men who shall divide the land to you 12
19 These are the names of the men 12
Deu 3:14 Ja'ir . . called the villages after his own name 12
5:11 not take the name of the LORD your God in vain 12
11 not hold him guiltless who takes his name in vain. 12
6:13 you shall serve him, and swear by his name. 12
7:24 shall make their name perish from under heaven; 12
9:14 I may . . blot out their name from under heaven; 12
10: 8 stand before the LORD . . to bless in his name 12
20 fear the LORD . . by his name you shall swear. 12
12: 3 destroy their name out of that place. 12
5 to put his name and make his habitation there; 12
11 LORD . . will choose, to make his name dwell there 12
21 place . . LORD . . will choose to put his name there 12
14:23 LORD . . will choose, to make his name dwell there 12
24 which the LORD . . chooses, to set his name there 12
16: 2 place . . LORD will choose, to make his name dwell 12
6 LORD . . will choose, to make his name dwell in it 12
11 LORD . . choose, to make his name dwell there. 12
18: 5 stand and minister in the name of the LORD 12
7 may minister in the name of the LORD his God 12
19 my words which he shall speak in my name 12
20 prophet who presumes to speak a word in my name 12
20 prophet . . who speaks in the name of other gods 12
22 when a prophet speaks in the name of the LORD 12
21: 5 chosen them . . to bless in the name of the LORD 12
22:14 brings an evil name upon her, saying, 'I took 12
19 brought an evil name upon a virgin of Israel; 12
25: 6 first son . . succeed to the name of his brother 12
6 that his name may not be blotted out of Israel. 12
7 refuses to perpetuate his brother's name 12
10 the name of his house shall be called in Israel 12
26: 2 LORD . . choose, to make his name dwell there. 12
28:10 see that you are called by the name of the LORD; 12
58 that you may fear this glorious and awful name 12
29:20 LORD would blot out his name from under heaven. 12
32: 3 For I will proclaim the name of the LORD. 12
Jos 2: 1 into the house of a harlot whose name was Rahab 12
5: 9 And so the name of this place is called Gilgal 12
7: 9 surround us, and cut off our name from the earth; 12
9 what wilt thou do for thy great name? 12
26 the name of that place is called the Valley 12
9: 9 because of the name of the LORD your God; 12
14:15 Now the name of Hebron formerly was Kir'iath-ar'ba; 12
15:15 the name of Debir formerly was Kir'iath-se'pher. 12
17: 3 these are the names of his daughters: Mahlah, Noah 12
19:47 after the name of Dan their ancestor. 12
21: 9 gave the following cities mentioned by name 12
23: 7 or make mention of the names of their gods 12
Jdg 1:10 now the name of Hebron was formerly Kir'iath-ar'ba 12
11 The name of Debir was formerly Kir'iath-se'pher. 12
17 So the name of the city was called Hormah. 12
23 (Now the name of the city was formerly Luz.) 12
26 Hittites and built a city, and called its name Luz; 12
26 called its name Luz; that is its name to this day. 12
2: 5 And they called the name of that place Bochim; 12
8:31 bore him a son, and he called his name Abim'elech. 12
13: 2 a certain man of Zorah . . whose name was Mano'ah; 12
6 him whence he was, and he did not tell me his name; 12
17 What is your name, so that, when your words come 12
18 Why do you ask my name, seeing it is wonderful? 12
24 the woman bore a son, and called his name Samson; 12
15:19 Therefore the name of it was called En-hakkor'e; 12
16: 4 he loved a woman . . whose name was Deli'lah. 12
17: 1 was a man of . . E'phraim, whose name was Micah. 12
18:29 they named the city Dan, after the name of Dan 10
29 the city Dan, after the name of Dan their ancestor 12
29 but the name of the city was La'ish at the first. 12
Rut 1: 2 The name of the man was Elim'elech 12
2 man was Elim'elech and the name of his wife Na'omi 12
2 the names of his two sons were Mahlon and Chil'ion; 12
4 the name of the one was Orpah 12
4 the one was Orpah and the name of the other Ruth. 12
2: 1 Now Na'omi had a kinsman . . whose name was Bo'az. 12
19 The man's name with whom I worked today is Bo'az. 12
4: 5 restore the name of the dead to his inheritance. 12
10 to be my wife, to perpetuate the name of the dead 12
10 to be my wife . . that the name of the dead may not be 12
14 and may his name be renowned in Israel! 12
17 the women of the neighborhood gave him a name 12
17 They named him Obed; he was the father of Jesse 10
1Sm 1: 1 whose name was Elka'nah the son of Jero'ham 12
2 He had two wives; the name of the one was Hannah 12
2 was Hannah, and the name of the other Penin'nah. 12
20 and bore a son, and she called his name Samuel 12
4:21 And she named the child Ich'abod, saying 9
7:12 took a stone . . and called its name Ebene'zer; 12
8: 2 The name of his first-born son was Jo'el 12
2 first-born . . and the name of his second, Abi'jah; 12
9: 1 There was a man of Benjamin whose name was Kish 12
2 he had a son whose name was Saul 12
12:22 not cast away his people, for his great name's sake 12
14: 4 name of the one was Bozez, and the . . other Seneh. 12
4 the one was Bozez, and the name of the other Seneh. 12
49 and the names of his two daughters were these 12
49 the name of the first-born was Merab 12
49 and the name of the younger Michal; 12
50 and the name of Saul's wife was Ahin'o-am 12
50 the name of the commander of his army was Abner 12
16: 3 and you shall anoint for me him whom I name to you. 1
17: 4 there came out . . a champion named Goliath 12
12 an Eph'rathite of Bethlehem in Judah, named Jesse 12
13 the names of his three sons who went to the battle 12
23 the Philistine of Gath, Goliath by name, came up 12
45 but I come to you in the name of the LORD of hosts 12
18:30 so that his name was highly esteemed. 12
20:16 let not the name of Jonathan be cut off 19
42 we have sworn both of us in the name of the LORD 12
21: 7 his name was Do'eg the E'domite 12
22:20 one of the sons . . named Abi'athar, escaped 12
24:21 not destroy my name out of my father's house. 12
25: 3 Now the name of the man was Nabal 12
3 man was Nabal, and the name of his wife Ab'igail. 12
5 go to Nabal, and greet him in my name. 12
9 they said all this to Nabal in the name of David; 12
25 as his name is, so is he; 12
25 Nabal is his name, and folly is with him; 12
28: 8 and bring up for me whomever I shall name to you. 1
2Sm 3: 7 Now Saul had a concubine, whose name was Rizpah 12
4: 2 the name of the one was Ba'anah 12
2 one was Ba'anah, and the name of the other Rechab 12
4 and became lame. And his name was Mephib'osheth. 12
5:14 these are the names of those who were born to him 12
20 the name of that place is called Ba'al-pera'zim. 12
6: 2 which is called by the name of the LORD of hosts 12
18 he blessed the people in the name of the LORD 12
7: 9 and I will make for you a great name 12
9 a great name, like the name of the great ones 12
13 He shall build a house for my name 12
23 God went to redeem . . making himself a name 12
26 and thy name will be magnified for ever, saying 12
8:13 And David won a name for himself. 12
9: 2 a servant of the house of Saul whose name was Ziba 12
12 Mephib'osheth had a . . son, whose name was Mica. 12
12:24 and she bore a son, and he called his name Solomon. 12
25 he called his name Jedidi'ah, because of the LORD. 12
28 lest I take the city, and it be called by my name. 12
13: 1 had a beautiful sister, whose name was Tamar; 12
3 But Amnon had a friend, whose name was Jon'adab 12
14: 7 and leave to my husband neither name nor remnant 12
27 three sons, and one daughter whose name was Tamar; 12
16: 5 man of the . . house of Saul, whose name was Shim'e-i 12
17:25 was the son of a man named Ithra the Ish'maelite 12
18:18 I have no son to keep my name in remembrance"; 12
18 he called the pillar after his own name 12
20: 1 a worthless fellow, whose name was Sheba 12
22:50 I will extol thee . . and sing praises to thy name. 12
23: 8 These are the names of the mighty men whom David 12
18 and slew them, and won a name beside the three. 12
22 and won a name beside the three mighty men. 12
1Kg 1:47 Your God make the name of Solomon more famous 12
3: 2 house had yet been built for the name of the LORD. 12
4: 8 These were their names: Ben-hur, in the hill 12
5: 3 not build a house for the name of the LORD his God 12
5 to build a house for the name of the LORD my God 12
5 'Your son . . shall build the house for my name.' 12
7:21 pillar on the south and called its name Jachin; 12
21 the pillar on the north and called its name Bo'az. 12
8:16 to build a house, that my name might be there; 12
17 to build a house for the name of the LORD 12
18 it was in your heart to build a house for my name 12
19 your son . . shall build the house for my name.' 12
20 house for the name of the LORD, the God of Israel. 12
29 place of which thou . . said, 'My name shall be there,' 12
33 turn again to thee, and acknowledge thy name 12
35 if they pray . . and acknowledge thy name 12
41 comes from a far country for thy name's sake 12
42 hear of thy great name, and thy mighty hand 12
43 that all . . may know thy name and fear thee 12
43 house which I have built is called by thy name. 12
44 and the house which I have built for thy name 12
48 and the house which I have built for thy name; 12
9: 3 consecrated this house . . and put my name there 12
7 the house which I have consecrated for my name 12
10: 1 fame of Solomon concerning the name of the LORD 12
11:26 Jerobo'am . . whose mother's name was Zeru'ah 12
36 the city where I have chosen to put my name. 12
13: 2 a son shall be born to . . David, Josi'ah by name; 12
14:21 the LORD had chosen . . to put his name there. 12
21 His mother's name was Na'amah the Ammonitess. 12
31 His mother's name was Na'amah the Ammonitess. 12
15: 2 His mother's name was Ma'acah the daughter 12
10 His mother's name was Ma'acah the daughter 12
16:24 and called the name of the city . . Sama'ria 12
24 Sama'ria, after the name of Shemer, the owner 12
18:24 you call on the name of your god 12
24 I will call on the name of the LORD; 12

25 call on the name of your god, but put no fire to it. 12
26 they prepared it, and called on the name of Ba'al 12
31 word of the LORD came . . "Israel shall be your name"; 12
32 he built an altar in the name of the LORD. 12
21: 8 she wrote letters in Ahab's name and sealed them 12
22:16 that you speak . . the truth in the name of the LORD? 12
42 His mother's name was Azu'bah the daughter 12
2Kg 2:24 he cursed them in the name of the LORD. 12
5:11 come . . and stand, and call on the name of the LORD 12
8:26 His mother's name was Athali'ah; 12
12: 1 His mother's name was Zib'iah of Beer-sheba. 12
14: 2 His mother's name was Jeho-ad'din of Jerusalem. 12
7 called it Jok'the-el, which is its name to this day. 12
27 that he would blot out the name of Israel 12
15: 2 His mother's name was Jecoli'ah of Jerusalem. 12
33 mother's name was Jeru'sha the daughter of Zadok. 12
17:34 the children of Jacob, whom he named Israel. 11
18: 2 His mother's name was Abi the daughter 12
21: 1 His mother's name was Heph'zibah. 12
4 the LORD had said, "In Jerusalem will I put my name. 12
7 In this house . . I will put my name for ever; 12
19 His mother's name was Meshul'lemeth 12
22: 1 His mother's name was Jedi'dah the daughter 12
23:27 the house of which I said, My name shall be there. 12
31 His mother's name was Hamu'tal the daughter 12
34 and changed his name to Jehoi'akim. 12
36 His mother's name was Zebi'dah 12
24: 8 His mother's name was Nehush'ta the daughter 12
17 and changed his name to Zedeki'ah. 12
18 His mother's name was Hamu'tal the daughter 12
1Ch 1:19 To Eber were born two sons: the name of the one was 12
19 two sons . . the name of his brother Joktan. 12
43 son of Be'or, the name of whose city was Din'habah 12
46 and the name of his city was Avith. 12
50 Hadad . . and the name of his city was Pa'i 12
50 his wife's name Mehet'abel the daughter of Matred 12
2:26 also had another wife, whose name was At'arah; 12
29 The name of Abi'shur's wife was Ab'ihail 12
34 had an Egyptian slave, whose name was Jarha. 12
4: 3 and the name of their sister was Hazzelelpo'ni. 12
9 and his mother called his name Jabez, saying 12
38 these mentioned by name were princes 12
41 These, registered by name 12
6:17 names of the sons of Gershom: Libni and Shim'e-i. 12
65 these cities which are mentioned by name. 12
7:15 The name of his sister was Ma'acah. 12
15 And the name of the second was Zeloph'ehad; 12
16 Ma'acah . . she called his name Peresh; 12
16 Peresh; and the name of his brother was Sheresh; 12
23 E'phraim . . called his name Beri'ah 12
8:29 Je-i'el . . the name of his wife was Ma'acah. 12
38 Azel had six sons, and these are their names 12
9:35 Je-i'el, and the name of his wife was Ma'acah 12
44 Azel had six sons and these are their names 12
11:20 slew them, and won a name beside the three. 12
24 won a name beside the three mighty men. 12
12:31 were expressly named to come and make David king. 12
13: 6 which is called by the name of the LORD 12
14: 4 names of the children whom he had in Jerusalem 12
11 the name of that place is called Ba'al-pera'zim. 12
16: 2 he blessed the people in the name of the LORD 12
8 O give thanks to the LORD, call on his name 12
10 Glory in his holy name; 12
29 Ascribe to the LORD the glory due his name; 12
35 that we may give thanks to thy holy name 12
41 the rest of those chosen and expressly named 5
17: 8 I will make for you a name 12
8 like the name of the great ones of the earth. 12
21 making . . a name for great and terrible things 12
24 thy name will be established and magnified 12
21:19 word, which he had spoken in the name of the LORD. 12
22: 7 in my heart to build a house to the name of the LORD 12
8 you shall not build a house to my name 12
9 for his name shall be Solomon 12
10 He shall build a house for my name. 12
19 into a house built for the name of the LORD. 12
23:13 and pronounce blessings in his name for ever. 12
14 sons of Moses . . named among the tribe of Levi. 7
24 number of the names of the individuals 12
28: 3 God said . . 'You may not build a house for my name 12
29:13 thank thee, our God, and praise thy glorious name 12
16 for building thee a house for thy holy name 12
2Ch 2: 1 to build a temple for the name of the LORD 12
4 to build a house for the name of the LORD my God 12
6: 5 I chose no city . . that my name might be there 12
6 I have chosen Jerusalem that my name may be there 12
7 David . . to build a house for the name of the LORD 12
8 it was in your heart to build a house for my name 12
9 your son . . shall build the house for my name.' 12
10 I have built the house for the name of the LORD 12
20 place where thou hast promised to set thy name 12
24 when they turn again and acknowledge thy name 12
26 pray toward this place, and acknowledge thy name 12
32 from a far country for the sake of thy great name 12
33 that all . . may know thy name and fear thee, as do 12
33 house which I have built is called by thy name. 12
34 the house which I have built for thy name 12
38 the house which I have built for thy name 12
7:14 if my people who are called by my name humble 12
16 this house that my name may be there for ever; 12
20 this house, which I have consecrated for my name 12
12:13 the LORD had chosen . . to put his name there. 12
13 His mother's name was Na'amah the Ammonitess. 12
13: 2 mother's name was Micai'ah the daughter of U'riel 12
14:11 in thy name we have come against this multitude. 12
18:15 nothing but the truth in the name of the LORD? 12
20: 8 built thee in it a sanctuary for thy name, saying 12
9 for thy name is in this house 12
26 therefore the name of that place has been called 12
31 His mother's name was Azu'bah 12
22: 2 His mother's name was Athali'ah 12
24: 1 his mother's name was Zib'iah of Beer-sheba. 12
25: 1 His mother's name was Jeho-ad'dan of Jerusalem. 12
26: 3 His mother's name was Jecoli'ah of Jerusalem. 12
27: 1 His mother's name was Jeru'shah 12
28: 9 prophet . . was there, whose name was Oded; 12
15 men who have been mentioned by name rose and took 12
29: 1 His mother's name was Abi'jah 12
31:19 men . . designated by name to distribute 12
33: 4 In Jerusalem shall my name be for ever. 12
7 In this house . . I will put my name for ever; 12
18 seers who spoke to him in the name of the LORD 12
36: 4 changed his name to Jehoi'akim; 12
Ezr 2:61 Barzil'lai . . and was called by their name 12
5: 1 prophesied . . in the name of the God of Israel 14
4 What are the names of the men who are building 14
10 asked them their names, for your information 14
10 write down the names of the men at their head. 14
14 delivered to one whose name was Shesh-baz'zar 14
6:12 May the God who has caused his name to dwell there 14
8:13 names being Eliph'elet, Jeu'el, and Shemai'ah 12
20 These were all mentioned by name. 12
10:16 heads . . each of them designated by name. 12
Neh 1: 9 place . . I have chosen, to make my name dwell 12
11 thy servants who delight to fear thy name; 12
6:13 could give me an evil name, in order to taunt me. 12
7:63 Barzil'lai (who . . was called by their name). 12
9: 5 Blessed be thy glorious name which is exalted 12
7 the God who didst . . give him the name Abraham; 12
10 thou didst get thee a name, as it is to this day. 12
13:25 I made them take oath in the name of God, saying *
Est 2: 5 there was a Jew in Susa . . whose name was Mor'decai 12
14 unless the king . . and she was summoned by name. 12
22 and Esther told the king in the name of Mor'decai. 12
3:12 it was written in the name of King Ahasu-e'rus 12
8: 8 write as you please . . in the name of the king 12
8 an edict written in the name of the king 12
10 The writing was in the name of King Ahasu-e'rus 12
Job 1: 1 was a man in the land of Uz, whose name was Job 12
21 blessed be the name of the LORD. 12
18:17 he has no name in the street. 12
24:20 their name is no longer remembered; *
42:14 he called the name of the first Jemi'mah; 12
14 first Jemi'mah; and the name of the second Kezi'ah; 12
14 and the name of the third Ker'en-hap'puch. 12
Ps 5:11 that those who love thy name may exult in thee. 12
7:17 I will sing praise to the name of the LORD 12
8: 1 our Lord, how majestic is thy name in all the earth! 12
9 our Lord, how majestic is thy name in all the earth! 12
9: 2 I will sing praise to thy name, O Most High. 12
5 thou hast blotted out their name for ever 12
10 those who know thy name put their trust in thee 12
16: 4 not pour out or take their names upon my lips. 12
18:49 among the nations, and sing praises to thy name. 12
20: 1 The name of the God of Jacob protect you! 12
5 in the name of our God set up our banners! 12
7 we boast of the name of the LORD our God. 12
22:22 I will tell of thy name to my brethren; 12
23: 3 in paths of righteousness for his name's sake. 12
25:11 For thy name's sake, O LORD, pardon my guilt 12
29: 2 Ascribe to the LORD the glory of his name; 12
30: 4 O you his saints, and give thanks to his holy name. 4
31: 3 for thy name's sake lead me and guide me 12
33:21 glad in him, because we trust in his holy name. 12
34: 3 let us exalt his name together! 12
41: 5 When will he die, and his name perish? 12
44: 5 through thy name we tread down our assailants. 12
8 we will give thanks to thy name for ever. Selah 12
20 If we had forgotten the name of our God 12
45:17 I will cause your name to be celebrated 12
48:10 As thy name, O God, so thy praise reaches to the ends 12
49:11 though they named lands their own. 8
52: 9 I will proclaim thy name, for it is good 12
54: 1 Save me, O God, by thy name, and vindicate me 12
6 I will give thanks to thy name, O LORD, for it is good. 12
61: 5 given me the heritage of those who fear thy name. 12
8 So will I ever sing praises to thy name 12
63: 4 I will lift up my hands and call on thy name. 12
66: 2 sing the glory of his name; 12
4 sing praises to thee, sing praises to thy name. 12
68: 4 Sing to God, sing praises to his name; 12
4 his name is the LORD, exult before him! 12
69:30 I will praise the name of God with a song; 12
36 those who love his name shall dwell in it. 12
72:17 May his name endure for ever 12
19 Blessed be his glorious name for ever; 12
74: 7 they desecrated the dwelling place of thy name. 12
10 Is the enemy to revile thy name for ever? 12
18 an impious people reviles thy name. 12
21 let the poor and needy praise thy name. 12
75: 1 call on thy name and recount thy wondrous deeds. 12
76: 1 In Judah God is known, his name is great in Israel. 12
79: 6 on the kingdoms that do not call on thy name! 12
9 O God of our salvation, for the glory of thy name; 12
9 deliver us, and forgive our sins, for thy name's sake! 12
80:18 give us life, and we will call on thy name! 12
83: 4 let the name of Israel be remembered no more! 12
16 shame, that they may seek thy name, O LORD. 12
18 them know that thou alone, whose name is the LORD 12
86: 9 before thee, O Lord, and shall glorify thy name. 12
11 unite my heart to fear thy name. 12
12 I will glorify thy name for ever. 12
89:12 Tabor and Hermon joyously praise thy name. 12
16 who exult in thy name all the day 12
24 in my name shall his horn be exalted. 12
91:14 I will protect him, because he knows my name. 12
92: 1 good to . . sing praises to thy name, O Most High; 12
96: 2 Sing to the LORD, bless his name; 12
8 Acribe to the LORD the glory due his name; 12
97:12 O you righteous, and give thanks to his holy name! 4
99: 3 praise thy great and terrible name! Holy is he! 12
6 Samuel . . among those who called on his name. 12
100: 4 Give thanks to him, bless his name! 12
102:12 thy name endures to all generations. 4
15 The nations will fear the name of the LORD 12
21 that men may declare in Zion the name of the LORD 12
103: 1 all that is within me, bless his holy name! 12
105: 1 O give thanks to the LORD, call on his name 12
3 Glory in his holy name; 12
106: 8 Yet he saved them for his name's sake 12
47 that we may give thanks to thy holy name 12
109:13 his name be blotted out in the second generation! 12
21 my Lord, deal on my behalf for thy name's sake; 12
111: 9 Holy and terrible is his name! 12
113: 1 O servants of the LORD, praise the name of the LORD! 12
2 Blessed be the name of the LORD from this time 12
3 name of the LORD is to be praised! 12
115: 1 O LORD, not to us, but to thy name give glory 12
116: 4 Then I called on the name of the LORD: "O LORD 12
13 I will . . call on the name of the LORD 12
17 I will . . call on the name of the LORD. 12
118:10 in the name of the LORD I cut them off! 12
11 in the name of the LORD I cut them off! 12
12 in the name of the LORD I cut them off! 12
26 Blessed be he who enters in the name of the LORD! 12
119:55 I remember thy name in the night, O LORD 12
132as is thy wont toward those who love thy name. 12
122: 4 for Israel, to give thanks to the name of the LORD. 12
124: 8 Our help is in the name of the LORD, 12
129: 8 do not say . . We bless you in the name of the LORD! 12
135: 1 Praise the name of the LORD, give praise 12
3 sing to his name, for he is gracious! 12
13 Thy name, O LORD, endures for ever, 12
138: 2 give thanks to thy name for thy steadfast love 12
2 exalted above everything thy name and thy word. 12
140:13 Surely the righteous . . give thanks to thy name; 12
142: 7 out of prison, that I may give thanks to thy name! 12
143:11 For thy name's sake, O LORD, preserve my life! 12
145: 1 God and King, and bless thy name for ever and ever. 12
2 bless thee, and praise thy name for ever and ever. 12
21 all flesh bless his holy name for ever and ever. 12
147: 4 stars, he gives to all of them their names. 12
148: 5 Let them praise the name of the LORD! 12
13 Let them praise the name of the LORD 12
13 name of the LORD, for his name alone is exalted; 12
149: 3 Let them praise his name with dancing 12
Prv 10: 7 but the name of the wicked will rot. 12
18:10 The name of the LORD is a strong tower; 12
21:24 Scoffer" is the name of the proud, haughty man 12
22: 1 good name . . be chosen rather than great riches 12
30: 4 What is his name, and what is his son's name? 12
4 What is his name, and what is his son's name? 12
9 I be poor, and steal, and profane the name of my God. 12
Ecc 6: 4 and in darkness its name is covered; 12
10 Whatever has come to be has already been named 10
7: 1 A good name is better than precious ointment; 12
Sng 1: 3 oils are fragrant, your name is oil poured out; 12
Isa 4: 1 only let us be called by your name; 12
7:14 bear a son, and shall call his name Imman'u-el. 12
8: 3 Call his name Ma'her-shal'al-hash-baz; 12
9: 6 and his name will be called "Wonderful Counselor 12
12: 4 Give thanks to the LORD, call upon his name; 12
4 make known . . proclaim that his name is exalted. 12
14:20 May . . evildoers nevermore be named! 7
22 and will cut off from Babylon name and remnant 12
18: 7 Zion, the place of the name of the LORD of hosts. 12
24:15 glory . . to the name of the LORD, the God of Israel. 12
25: 1 my God; I will exalt thee, I will praise thy name; 12
26: 8 thy memorial name is the desire of our soul. 12
13 ruled over us, but thy name alone we acknowledge. 12
29:23 his children . . they will sanctify my name; 12
30:27 Behold, the name of the LORD comes from far 12
34:12 They shall name it No Kingdom There 7
40:26 their host by number, calling them all by name; 12
41:25 and he shall call on my name; 12
42: 8 I am the LORD, that is my name; 12
43: 1 I have redeemed you; I have called you by name 12

7 every one who is called by my name 12
44: 5 another will call himself by the name of Jacob 12
5 and surname himself by the name of Israel. 12
45: 3 I . . the God of Israel, who call you by your name. 12
4 I call you by your name, I surname you 12
47: 4 Our Redeemer-the LORD of hosts is his name 12
48: 1 of Jacob, who are called by the name of Israel 12
1 who swear by the name of the LORD, and confess 12
2 God of Israel; the LORD of hosts is his name. 12
9 For my name's sake I defer my anger 12
11 I do it, for how should my name be profaned? 19
19 their name would never be cut off or destroyed 12
49: 1 from the body of my mother he named my name. 3
1 from the body of my mother he named my name. 12
50:10 has no light, yet trusts in the name of the LORD 12
51:15 that its waves roar-the LORD of hosts is his name 12
52: 5 and continually all the day my name is despised. 12
6 Therefore my people shall know my name; 12
54: 5 is your husband, the LORD of hosts is his name; 12
56: 5 a monument and a name better than sons 12
5 an everlasting name which shall not be cut off. 12
6 to minister to him, to love the name of the LORD 12
57:15 One who inhabits eternity, whose name is Holy 12
59:19 they shall fear the name of the LORD from the west 12
60: 9 for the name of the LORD your God, and for the Holy 12
62: 2 called by a new name which the mouth of the LORD 12
63:12 to make for himself an everlasting name 12
14 to make for thyself a glorious name. 12
16 O LORD . . our Redeemer from of old is thy name. 12
19 like those who are not called by thy name. 12
64: 2 to make thy name known to thy adversaries 12
7 There is no one that calls upon thy name 12
65: 1 here am I," to a nation that did not call on my name. 12
15 You shall leave your name to my chosen for a curse 12
15 his servants he will call by a different name. 12
66: 5 who hate you and cast you out for my name's sake 12
22 shall your descendants and your name remain. 12
Jer 7:10 in this house, which is called by my name, and say 12
11 Has this house, which is called by my name 12
12 in Shiloh, where I made my name dwell at first 12
14 I will do to the house which is called by my name 12
30 in the house which is called by my name 12
10: 6 thou art great, and thy name is great in might. 12
16 the LORD of hosts is his name. 12
25 and upon the peoples that call not on thy name; 12
11:19 that his name be remembered no more. 12
21 and say, "Do not prophesy in the name of the LORD 12
12:16 my people, to swear by my name, 'As the LORD lives 12
13:11 might be for me a people, a name, a praise, and a glory 12
14: 7 act, O LORD, for thy name's sake; 12
9 and we are called by thy name; leave us not. 12
14 The prophets are prophesying lies in my name; 12
15 concerning the prophets who prophesy in my name 12
21 Do not spurn us, for thy name's sake; 12
15:16 for I am called by thy name, O LORD, God of hosts. 12
16:21 they shall know that my name is the LORD. 12
20: 3 The LORD does not call your name Pashhur 12
9 not mention him, or speak any more in his name 12
23: 6 And this is the name by which he will be called 12
25 prophets have said who prophesy lies in my name 12
27 who think to make my people forget my name 12
27 even as their fathers forgot my name for Ba'al? 12
25:29 work evil at the city which is called by my name 12
26: 9 Why have you prophesied in the name of the LORD 12
16 he has spoken to us in the name of the LORD our God. 12
20 another . . who prophesied in the name of the LORD 12
27:15 but they are prophesying falsely in my name 12
29: 9 a lie which they are prophesying to you in my name; 12
21 who are prophesying a lie to you in my name 12
23 and they have spoken in my name lying words 12
25 You have sent letters in your name 12
31:35 the LORD of hosts is his name 12
32:18 mighty God whose name is the LORD of hosts 12
20 and hast made thee a name, as at this day. 12
34 in the house which is called by my name 12
33: 2 formed it to establish it-the LORD is his name 12
9 And this city shall be to me a name of joy, a praise 12
16 And this is the name by which it will be called •
34:15 before me in the house which is called by my name; 12
16 but then you turned around and profaned my name 12
37:13 a sentry there named Iri'jah the son of Shelemi'ah 12
44:16 which you have spoken to us in the name of the LORD 12
26 I have sworn by my great name, says the LORD 12
26 that my name shall no more be invoked by the mouth 12
46:17 Call the name of Pharaoh, king of Egypt, 'Noisy one 12
18 As I live, says the King, whose name is the LORD 12
48:15 says the King, whose name is the LORD of hosts. 12
17 who are round about him, and all who know his name; 12
50:34 Redeemer is strong; the LORD of hosts is his name. 12
51:19 the LORD of hosts is his name. 12
57 says the King, whose name is the LORD of hosts. 12
52: 1 His mother's name was Hamu'tal 12
Lam 3:55 I called on thy name, O LORD, from the depths 12
Ezk 20: 9 I acted for the sake of my name 12
14 But I acted for the sake of my name 12
22 withheld my hand, and acted for the sake of my name 12
29 its name is called Bamah to this day 12
39 but my holy name you shall no more profane 12
44 the LORD, when I deal with you for my name's sake 12
23: 4 Oho'lah was the name of the elder 12
4 and Ohol'ibah the name of her sister. •
4 As for their names, Oho'lah is Sama'ria 12
24: 2 write down the name of this day, this very day. 12
36:20 whereever they came, they profaned my holy name 12
21 I had concern for my holy name 12
22 I am about to act, but for the sake of my holy name 12
23 I will vindicate the holiness of my great name 12
39: 7 my holy name I will make known in the midst of my 12
7 I will not let my holy name be profaned any more; 12
25 I will be jealous for my holy name. 12
43: 7 house of Israel shall no more defile my holy name 12
8 They have defiled my holy name 12
48: 1 These are the names of the tribes 12
31 gates . . being named after the tribes of Israel. 12
35 the name of the city henceforth shall be 12
Dan 1: 7 chief of the eunuchs gave them names: Daniel 12
2:20 Blessed be the name of God for ever and ever. 14
26 king said to Daniel, whose name was Belteshaz'zar 14
4: 8 Daniel . . named Belteshaz'zar after the name 14
8 named Belteshaz'zar after the name of my god 14
19 Daniel, whose name was Belteshaz'zar 14
5:12 this Daniel, whom the king named Belteshaz'zar. 13
9: 6 spoke in thy name to our kings, our princes 12
15 hast made thee a name, as at this day 12
18 behold . . the city which is called by thy name; 12
19 thy city and thy people are called by thy name. 12
10: 1 revealed to Daniel, who was named Belteshaz'zar. 10
12: 1 every one whose name . . found written in the book. •
Hos 1: 4 And the LORD said to him, "Call his name Jezreel; 12
6 the LORD said to him, "Call her name Not pitied 12
9 And the LORD said, "Call his name Not my people 12
2:17 will remove the names of the Ba'als from her mouth 12
17 and they shall be mentioned by name no more. 12
12: 5 the LORD the God of hosts, the LORD is his name 4
Jol 2:26 and praise the name of the LORD your God 12
32 that all who call upon the name of the LORD 12
Ams 2: 7 the same maiden, so that my holy name is profaned; 12
4:13 of the earth- the LORD, the God of hosts, is his name! 12
5: 8 surface of the earth, the LORD is his name 12
27 says the LORD, whose name is the God of hosts. 12
6:10 "Hush! We must not mention the name of the LORD. 12
9: 6 who calls . . the LORD is his name. 12
12 Edom and all the nations who are called by my name 12
Mic 4: 5 all the peoples walk each in the name of its god 12
5 but we will walk in the name of the LORD our God 12
5: 4 in the majesty of the name of the LORD his God. 12
6: 9 and it is sound wisdom to fear thy name 12
Nah 1:14 No more shall your name be perpetuated; 12
Zep 1: 4 cut off . . the name of the idolatrous priests; 12
3: 9 that all of them may call on the name of the LORD 12
12 They shall seek refuge in the name of the LORD 12
Zec 5: 4 the house of him who swears falsely by my name; 12
6:12 Behold, the man whose name is the Branch 12
10:12 they shall glory in his name," says the LORD. 12
11: 7 staffs; one I named Grace, the other I named Union. 9
7 staffs; one I named Grace, the other I named Union. 9
13: 2 I will cut off the names of the idols from the land 12
3 not live, for you speak lies in the name of the LORD 12
9 They will call on my name, and I will answer them. 12
14: 9 on that day the LORD will be one and his name one. 12
Mal 1: 6 to you, O priests, who despise my name. 12
6 You say, 'How have we despised thy name? 12
11 my name is great among the nations, says the LORD 12
11 in every place incense is offered to my name 12
11 my name is great among the nations, says the LORD 12
14 my name is feared among the nations. 12
2: 2 will not lay it to heart to give glory to my name 12
5 he feared me, he stood in awe of my name. 12
3:16 who feared the LORD and thought on his name. 12
4: 2 for you who fear my name the sun of righteousness 12
Mat 1:21 you shall call his name Jesus, for he will save his 19
23 a son, and his name shall be called Emman'u-el 19
25 she had borne a son; and he called his name Jesus. 19
6: 9 Father who art in heaven, Hallowed be thy name. 19
7:22 Lord, Lord, did we not prophesy in your name 19
22 and cast out demons in your name 19
22 and do many mighty works in your name?' 19
10: 2 The names of the twelve apostles are these 19
22 you will be hated by all for my name's sake 19
12:21 in his name will the Gentiles hope. 19
18: 5 one such child in my name receives me; 19
20 For where two or three are gathered in my name 19
19:29 for my name's sake, will receive a hundredfold 19
21: 9 Blessed is he who comes in the name of the Lord! 19
23:39 'Blessed is he who comes in the name of the Lord.' 19
24: 5 For many will come in my name, saying 19
9 hated by all nations for my name's sake. 19
27:32 they came upon a man of Cyre'ne, Simon by name 19
57 a rich man from Arimathe'a, named Joseph 19
28:19 baptizing them in the name of the Father 19
Mrk 5: 9 Jesus asked him, "What is your name? 19
9 He replied, "My name is Legion; for we are many. 19
22 Ja'irus by name 19
6:14 Jesus' name had become known 19
9:37 receives one such child in my name receives me; 19
38 we saw a man casting out demons in your name 19
39 no one who does a mighty work in my name 19
41 because you bear the name of Christ 19
11: 9 Blessed is he who comes in the name of the Lord! 19
13: 6 Many will come in my name, saying, 'I am he!' 19
13 you will be hated by all for my name's sake 19
16:17 in my name they will cast out demons 19
Lke 1: 5 there was a priest named Zechari'ah 19
5 her name was Elizabeth. 19
13 you shall call his name John. 19
26 to a city of Galilee named Nazareth 19
27 a virgin betrothed to a man whose name was Joseph 19
27 and the virgin's name was Mary. 19
31 you shall call his name Jesus. 19
49 holy is his name. 19
59 would have named him Zechari'ah after his father 16
61 None of your kindred is called by this name. 19
63 for a writing tablet, and wrote, "His name is John. 19
2:21 he was called Jesus, the name given by the angel 19
25 was a man in Jerusalem, whose name was Simeon 19
5:27 he went out, and saw a tax collector, named Levi 19
6:13 chose from them twelve, whom he named apostles; 20
14 Simon, whom he named Peter, and Andrew 20
22 and cast out your name as evil 19
8:30 Jesus then asked him, "What is your name? 19
41 there came a man named Ja'irus 19
9:48 Whoever receives this child in my name 19
49 we saw a man casting out demons in your name 19
10:17 even the demons are subject to us in your name! 19
20 rejoice that your names are written in heaven. 19
38 a woman named Martha received him 19
11: 2 hallowed be thy name. Thy kingdom come. 19
13:35 'Blessed is he who comes in the name of the Lord!' 19
16:20 at his gate lay a poor man named Laz'arus 19
19: 2 there was a man named Zacchae'us; 19
38 the King who comes in the name of the Lord 19
21: 8 many will come in my name, saying, 'I am he!' 19
12 before kings and governors for my name's sake. 19
17 you will be hated by all for my name's sake. 19
23:50 Now there was a man named Joseph 19
24:13 two of them were going to a village named Emma'us 19
18 Then one of them, named Cle'opas, answered him 19
47 preached in his name to all nations 19
Joh 1: 6 was a man sent from God, whose name was John. 19
12 to all who received him, who believed in his name 19
2:23 many believed in his name when they saw the signs 19
3: 1 there was a man of the Pharisees, named Nicode'mus 19
18 not believed in the name of the only Son of God. 19
5:43 I have come in my Father's name 19
43 if another comes in his own name 19
10: 3 he calls his own sheep by name and leads them out. 19
25 The works that I do in my Father's name 19
12:13 Blessed is he who comes in the name of the Lord 19
28 Father, glorify thy name. 19
14:13 Whatever you ask in my name, I will do it 19
14 if you ask anything in my name, I will do it. 19
26 Holy Spirit, whom the Father will send in my name 19
15:16 whatever you ask the Father in my name 19
16:23 he will give it to you in my name 19
24 Hitherto you have asked nothing in my name 19
26 In that day you will ask in my name 19
17: 6 I have manifested thy name to the men 19
11 keep them in thy name, which thou hast given me 19
12 While I was with them, I kept them in thy name 19
26 I made known to them thy name 19
18:10 The slave's name was Malchus. 19
20:31 believing you may have life in his name. 19
Act 2:21 whoever calls on the name of the Lord 19
38 in the name of Jesus Christ 19
3: 6 in the name of Jesus Christ of Nazareth, walk. 19
16 his name, by faith . . has made this man strong 19
16 by faith in his name 19
4: 7 By what power or by what name did you do this? 19
10 by the name of Jesus Christ of Nazareth 19
12 no other name under heaven given among men 19
17 to speak no more to any one in this name. 19
18 not to speak or teach at all in the name of Jesus. 19
30 through the name of thy holy servant Jesus. 19
5: 1 a man named Anani'as with his wife Sapphi'ra 19
28 We strictly charged you not to teach in this name 19
34 a Pharisee in the council named Gama'li-el 19
40 charged them not to speak in the name of Jesus 19
41 were counted worthy to suffer dishonor for the name. 19
7:58 at the feet of a young man named Saul. 16
8: 9 there was a man named Simon 19
12 the name of Jesus Christ 19
16 baptized in the name of the Lord Jesus. 19
9:10 there was a disciple at Damascus named Anani'as. 19
11 a man of Tarsus named Saul 19
12 he has seen a man named Anani'as come 19
14 to bind all who call upon thy name. 19
15 he is a chosen instrument of mine to carry my name 19
16 how much he must suffer for the sake of my name. 19
21 those who called on this name 19
27 he had preached boldly in the name of Jesus. 19
29 preaching boldly in the name of the Lord. 19
33 There he found a man named Aene'as 19
36 Now there was at Joppa a disciple named Tabitha 19
10: 1 At Caesare'a there was a man named Cornelius 19
43 receives forgiveness of sins through his name. 19
48 baptized in the name of Jesus Christ 19
11:28 one of them named Ag'abus stood up 19

12:13 a maid named Rhoda came to answer. 19
13: 6 a Jewish false prophet, named Bar-Jesus. 19
8 that is the meaning of his name 19
15:14 to take out of them a people for his name. 19
17 all the Gentiles who are called by my name 19
16: 1 A disciple was there, named Timothy 19
14 One who heard us was a woman named Lydia 19
18 I charge you in the name of Jesus Christ 19
17:34 a woman named Dam'aris and others with them. 19
18: 2 he found a Jew named Aq'uila, a native of Pontus 19
7 went to the house of a man named Titius Justus 19
15 questions about words and names and your own law 19
24 Now a Jew named Apol'los, a native of Alexandria 19
19: 5 baptized in the name of the Lord Jesus. 19
13 undertook to pronounce the name of the Lord 20
14 Seven sons of a Jewish high priest named Sceva •
17 the name of the Lord Jesus was extolled. 19
24 a man named Deme'trius, a silversmith 19
20: 9 a young man named Eu'tychus 19
21:10 a prophet named Ag'abus came down from Judea. 19
13 die at Jerusalem for the name of the Lord Jesus. 19
22:16 and wash away your sins, calling on his name.' 19
26: 9 in opposing the name of Jesus of Nazareth. 19
27: 1 a centurion of the Augustan Cohort, named Julius. 19
28: 7 the chief man of the island, named Publius 19
Rom 1: 5 for the sake of his name among all the nations 19
2:24 The name of God is blasphemed among the Gentiles 19
9: 7 Through Isaac shall your descendants be named. 16
17 so that my name may be proclaimed in all the earth 19
10:13 For, "every one who calls upon the name of the Lord 19
15: 9 thee among the Gentiles, and sing to thy name"; 19
20 not where Christ has already been named 20
1Co 1: 2 call on the name of our Lord Jesus Christ 19
10 by the name of our Lord Jesus Christ 19
13 were you baptized in the name of Paul? 19
15 say that you were baptized in my name. 19
5: 4 in the name of the Lord Jesus 19
6:11 justified in the name of the Lord Jesus Christ 19
Eph 1:21 and above every name that is named 19
21 and above every name that is named 20
3:15 every family in heaven and on earth is named 20
5: 3 covetousness must not even be named among you 20
20 in the name of our Lord Jesus Christ 19
Php 2: 9 the name which is above every name 19
9 the name which is above every name 19
10 at the name of Jesus every knee should bow 19
4: 3 whose names are in the book of life. 19
Col 3:17 do everything in the name of the Lord Jesus 19
2Th 1:12 that the name of our Lord Jesus may be glorified 19
3: 6 in the name of our Lord Jesus Christ 19
1Ti 6: 1 name of God and the teaching may not be defamed. 19
2Ti 2:19 every one who names the name of the Lord depart 20
19 every one who names the name of the Lord depart 19
Heb 1: 4 the name he has obtained 19
2:12 saying, "I will proclaim thy name to my brethren 19
7: 2 by translation of his name •
11 rather than one named after the order of Aaron? 18
11:18 Through Isaac shall your descendants be named. 16
13:15 the fruit of lips that acknowledge his name. 19
Jas 2: 7 Is it not they who blaspheme that honorable name 19
5:10 the prophets who spoke in the name of the Lord. 19
14 anointing him with oil in the name of the Lord; 19
1Pe 4:14 If you are reproached for the name of Christ 19
16 but under that name let him glorify God. 19
1Jn 3:23 believe in the name of his Son Jesus Christ 19
5:13 to you who believe in the name of the Son of God 19
Rev 2: 3 and bearing up for my name's sake 19
13 you hold fast my name and you did not deny my faith 19
17 with a new name written on the stone 19
3: 1 you have the name of being alive, and you are dead. 19
4 Yet you have still a few names in Sardis 19
5 I will not blot his name out of the book of life; 19
5 I will confess his name before my Father 19
8 you have kept my word and have not denied my name 19
12 and I will write on him the name of my God 19
12 the name of my God, and the name of the city 19
12 the name of my God . . and my own new name. 19
6: 8 a pale horse, and its rider's name was Death 19
8:11 The name of the star is Wormwood. 19
9:11 his name in Hebrew is Abad'don 19
11:18 those who fear thy name, both small and great 19
13: 1 and a blasphemous name upon its heads. 19
6 God, blaspheming his name and his dwelling 19
8 name has not been written . . in the book of life 19
17 the name of the beast or the number of its name. 19
17 the name of the beast or the number of its name. 19
14: 1 144,000 who had his name and his Father's name 19
1 144,000 who had his name and his Father's name 19
11 and whoever receives the mark of its name. 19
15: 2 the beast and its image and the number of its name 19
4 Who shall not fear and glorify thy name, O Lord? 19
16: 9 and they cursed the name of God 19
17: 3 beast which was full of blasphemous names 19
5 on her forehead was written a name of mystery 19
8 names have not been written in the book of life 19
19:12 he has a name inscribed which no one knows 19
13 the name by which he is called is The Word of God. 19
16 and on his thigh he has a name inscribed 19
20:15 name was not found written in the book of life •
21:12 and on the gates the names of the twelve tribes 19
14 twelve names of the twelve apostles of the Lamb. 19
22: 4 and his name shall be on their foreheads. 19
1Es 1:48 made him swear by the name of the Lord 19
4:63 the temple which is called by his name 19
5: 4 These are the names of the men who went up 19
38 was called by his name. 19
6: 1 they prophesied to them in the name of the Lord 19
33 the Lord, whose name is there called upon 19
8:39 their names being Eliphelet, Jeuel, and Shemaiah 19
78 to leave to us a root and a name in thy holy place 19
88 without leaving a root or seed or name? 19
9:16 all of them by name 19
2Es 1:16 You have not exulted in my name 21
22 thirsty and blaspheming my name 21
24 and will give them my name 21
2: 7 let their names be blotted out from the earth 21
16 because I recognize my name in them. 21
45 and they have confessed the name of God 21
47 who had stood valiantly for the name of the Lord. 21
3:13 one of them, whose name was Abraham; 21
23 raise up for thyself a servant, named David. 21
24 didst command him to build a city for thy name 21
4: 1 the angel . . whose name was Uriel, answered 21
25 what will he do for his name, by which we are called? 21
5:26 thou hast named for thyself one dove 22
6: 4 the measures of the firmaments were named 22
49 the name of one thou didst call Behemoth 21
49 and the name of the other Leviathan. 21
7:60 and through them my name has now been honored. 21
8:60 who were created have defiled the name of him 21
10:22 the name by which we are called has been profaned; 21
14:35 the names of the righteous will become manifest 21
Tob 3:11 blessed is thy holy and honored name for ever. 19
15 I did not stain my name or the name of my father 19
15 I did not stain my name or the name of my father 19
5:11 like to know . . your people and your name. 19
6:10 he has an only daughter named Sarah 19
8: 5 and blessed by thy holy and glorious name for ever. 19
11:14 blessed is thy name for ever 19
12: 6 It is good to praise God and to exalt his name 19
13:11 will come from afar to the name of the Lord God 19
Jdt 9: 7 the Lord is thy name. 19
8 the tabernacle where thy glorious name rests 19
14: 7 those who hear your name will be alarmed. 19
16: 2 exalt him, and call upon his name. 19
AEs 10: 8 gathered to destroy the name of the Jews. 19
13:17 that we may live and sing praise to thy name, O Lord; 19
Wis 2: 4 Our name will be forgotten in time 19
10:20 they sang hymns, O Lord, to thy holy name 19
14: 8 the perishable thing was named a god. 20
21 the name that ought not to be shared. 19
27 the worship of idols not to be named 15
Sir 6: 1 a bad name incurs shame and reproach 19
22 wisdom is like her name 19
15: 6 will acquire an everlasting name. 19
17:10 they will praise his holy name 19
22:14 what is its name except "Fool"? 19
36:12 the people called by thy name 19
15 fulfil the prophecies spoken in thy name. 19
37: 1 some friends are friends only in name. 19
26 his name will live for ever. 19
39: 9 his name will live through all generations. 19
11 he will leave a name greater than 1,000 19
15 ascribe majesty to his name 19
35 bless the name of the Lord. 19
40:19 establish a man's name 19
41:11 the evil name of sinners will be blotted out. 19
12 Have regard for your name 19
13 a good name endures for ever. 19
43: 8 The month is named for the moon 19
44: 8 There are some of them who have left a name 19
14 their name lives to all generations. 19
45:15 serve as priest and bless his people in his name. 19
46: 1 in accordance with his name 19
11 The judges also, with their respective names 19
12 the name of those who have been honored 19
47:10 while they praised God's holy name 19
13 that he might build a house for his name 19
16 Your name reached to far-off islands, and you were 19
18 In the name of the Lord God 19
50:20 to glory in his name; 19
51: 1 I give thanks to thy name 19
3 in the greatness of thy mercy and of thy name 19
11 I will praise thy name continually 19
12 I will bless the name of the Lord. 19
Bar 2:11 and hast made thee a name, as at this day 19
15 his descendants are called by thy name. 19
26 house which is called by thy name thou hast made 19
32 land of their exile, and will remember my name 19
3: 5 in this crisis remember thy power and thy name. 19
7 in order that we should call upon thy name 19
4:30 for he who named you will comfort you. 20
5: 4 For your name will for ever be called by God 19
Aza 1: 3 thy name is glorified for ever. 19
11 For thy name's sake do not give us up utterly 19
20 give glory to thy name, O Lord! 19
30 blessed is thy glorious, holy name 19
Sus 1: 1 a man living in Babylon whose name was Joakim. 19
2 a wife named Susanna, the daughter of Hilkiah 19
45 the holy spirit of a young lad named Daniel; 19
Man 1: 3 sealed it with thy terrible and glorious name; 19
1Mc 2:51 receive great honor and an everlasting name. 19
3:14 he said, "I will make a name for myself 19
4:33 let all who know thy name praise thee with hymns. 19
5:57 So they said, "Let us also make a name for ourselves; 19
63 wherever their name was heard. 19
6:17 he named him Eupator. 17
44 to win for himself an everlasting name. 19
7:37 didst choose this house to be called by thy name 19
14:43 contracts . . should be written in his name 19
2Mc 3: 4 a man named Simon, of the tribe of Benjamin •
8: 4 the blasphemies committed against his name 19
15 called them by his holy and glorious name. 19
12:13 Its name was Caspin. 19
3Mc 2: 9 sanctified this place for your name 19
9 the glory of your great and honored name. 19
14 holy place . . dedicated to your glorious name. 19
4Mc 5: 4 one man, Eleazar by name, leader of the flock 19

name *See also* bear, give, use, utter.

other name 1. ἐπικαλέω

Act 12:12 the mother of John whose other name was Mark 1
12 Mary, the mother of John whose other name was Mark 1
25 John whose other name was Mark. 1

namely 1. וְ 2. לְ 3. ὅς τε

Num 1:32 Joseph, namely, of the people of E'phraim •
2Kg 25:23 they came . . namely, Ish'mael the son of Nethani'ah •
1Ch 5:26 carried them away, namely, the Reubenites •
6:39 namely, Asaph the son of Berechi'ah, son of Shim'e-a •
7: 2 heads of their fathers' houses, namely of Tola •
Ezr 2: 6 Pa'hath-moab, namely the sons of Jeshua and Jo'ab 2
16 sons of Ater, namely of Hezeki'ah, 98. 2
8:17 namely, to send us ministers for the house •
18 namely Sherebi'ah with his sons and kinsmen 1
Neh 7:11 Pa'hath-mo'ab, namely the sons of Jeshua and Jo'ab 2
21 sons of Ater, namely of Hezeki'ah, 98. 2
39 sons of Jedai'ah, namely the house of Jeshua, 973. 2
43 Jeshua, namely of Kad'mi-el of the sons of Ho'devah 2
Dan 9: 2 number of years . . namely, 70 years. •
Rom 1:20 namely, his eternal power and deity 3
1Es 5:15 The sons of Ater, namely of Hezekiah, 92. •
8:47 the son of Levi, son of Israel, namely Sherebiah •
4Mc 1: 3 namely, gluttony and lust •
4 namely anger, fear, and pain. •

names *See* list.

naphtha 1. νάφθα 2. νεφθαί

Aza 1:23 naphtha, pitch, tow, and brush. 1
2Mc 1:36 by most people it is called naphtha. 2

napkin 1. σουδάριον

Lke 19:20 your pound, which I kept laid away in a napkin; 1
Joh 20: 7 the napkin, which had been on his head 1

nard 1. נֵרְדְּ 2. νάρδος

Sng 1:12 the king was . . my nard gave forth its fragrance. 1
4:13 with all choicest fruits, henna with nard 1
14 nard and saffron, calamus and cinnamon 1
Mrk 14: 3 ointment of pure nard, very costly 2
Joh 12: 3 Mary took a pound of costly ointment of pure nard 2

narration 1. ἐξήγησις

Sir 21:16 A fool's narration is like a burden on a journey 1

narrative 1. διήγημα 2. διήγησις 3. ἱστορία

Lke 1: 1 many have undertaken to compile a narrative 2
Sir 6:35 Be ready to listen to every narrative 2
2Mc 2:24 who wish to enter upon the narratives of history 1
32 let us begin our narrative 2
4Mc 3:19 a narrative demonstration of temperate reason. 3

narrative *See also* recast.

narrow 1. אוּץ 2. אטם 3. צַר 4. צרר 5. קצר 6. στενός 7. angustus

Num22:26 angel of the LORD . . stood in a narrow place 3
Jos 17:15 the hill country of E'phraim is too narrow for you. 1
Prv 23:27 an adventuress is a narrow well. 3
Isa 28:20 the covering too narrow to wrap oneself in it. 3
49:19 you will be too narrow for your inhabitants 4
20 say in your ears: 'The place is too narrow for me; 3
Ezk 40:16 windows . . narrowing inwards into their jambs 2
42: 5 Now the upper chambers were narrower 5
Mat 7:13 Enter by the narrow gate; for the gate is wide 6
14 For the gate is narrow and the way is hard 6
Lke 13:24 Strive to enter by the narrow door 6
2Es 7: 4 it has an entrance set in a narrow place 7
5 unless he passes through the narrow part? 7
7 the entrance to it is narrow 7
12 so the entrances of this world were made narrow 7
13:43 the narrow passages of the Euphrates river. 7
Jdt 4: 7 the approach was narrow 6

narrow *See also* path.

narrowness 1. στενότης

2Mc 12:21 because of the narrowness of all the approaches. 1

nation 1. אֶרֶץ 2. גּוֹי 3. לְאֹם 4. עַם 5. אֻמָּה (A)
6. *γένος* 7. *ἔθνος* 8. *φυλή* 9. *φῦλον* 10. gens
11. natio

Gen 10: 5 language, by their families, in their nations. 2
20 languages, their lands, and their nations. 2
31 their languages, their lands, and their nations. 2
32 from these the nations spread abroad 2
32 from these the nations spread abroad 2
12: 2 make of you a great nation, and I will bless you 2
15:14 I will bring judgment on the nation 2
17: 4 be the father of a multitude of nations. 2
5 you the father of a multitude of nations. 2
6 I will make nations of you, and kings shall come 2
16 she shall be a mother of nations; kings of peoples 2
20 princes, and I will make him a great nation. 2
18:18 Abraham shall become a great and mighty nation 2
18 mighty nation, and all the nations of the earth 2
21:13 I will make a nation of the son of the slave woman 2
18 for I will make him a great nation. 2
22:18 all the nations of the earth bless themselves 2
25:23 the LORD said to her, "Two nations are in your womb 2
26: 4 all the nations of the earth shall bless 2
27:29 Let peoples serve you, and nations bow down to you. 3
35:11 a nation and a company of nations shall come 2
11 a company of nations shall come from you 2
46: 3 for I will there make of you a great nation. 2
48:19 shall become a multitude of nations. 2
Exd 9:24 never been in . . Egypt since it became a nation. 2
19: 6 be to me a kingdom of priests and a holy nation. 2
32:10 but of you I will make a great nation. 2
33:13 Consider too that this nation is thy people. 2
34:10 in all the earth or in any nation 2
24 For I will cast out nations before you 2
Lev 18:24 the nations I am casting out before you defiled 2
28 as it vomited out the nation that was before you 2
20:23 you shall not walk in the customs of the nation 2
25:44 from among the nations that are round about you 2
26:33 I will scatter you among the nations 2
38 you shall perish among the nations 2
45 I brought forth . . in the sight of the nations 2
Num14:12 I will make of you a nation greater and mightier 2
15 then the nations who have heard thy fame will say 2
23: 9 not reckoning itself among the nations! 2
24: 8 he shall eat up the nations his adversaries 2
20 Am'alek was the first of the nations, but in the end 2
Deu 4: 6 great nation is a wise and understanding people.' 2
7 what great nation is there that has a god so near 2
8 what great nation is there, that has statutes 2
27 you will be left few in number among the nations 2
34 has any god ever attempted to go and take a nation 2
34 take a nation . . from the midst of another nation 2
38 driving out before you nations greater 2
7: 1 the LORD . . clears away many nations before you 2
1 Jeb'usites, seven nations greater and mightier 2
17 These nations are greater than I; how can I 2
22 LORD . . will clear away these nations before you 2
8:20 Like the nations that the LORD makes to perish 2
9: 1 nations greater and mightier than yourselves 2
4 it is because of the wickedness of these nations 2
5 because of the wickedness of these nations 2
14 I will make of you a nation mightier and greater 2
11:23 LORD will drive out all these nations before you 2
23 dispossess nations greater and mightier 2
12: 2 places where the nations . . served their gods 2
29 When the LORD . . cuts off before you the nations 2
30 How did these nations serve their gods?-that I 2
15: 6 lend to many nations, but you shall not borrow; 2
6 rule over many nations, but they shall not rule 2
17:14 king over me, like all the nations . . round about 2
18: 9 abominable practices of those nations. 2
14 For these nations . . give heed to soothsayers 2
19: 1 LORD . . cuts off the nations whose land the LORD 2
20:15 which are not cities of the nations here. 2
26: 5 few in number; and there he became a nation, great 2
19 set you high above all nations that he has made 2
28: 1 set you high above all the nations of the earth. 2
12 lend to many nations, but you shall not borrow. 2
33 A nation which you have not known shall eat up 4
36 nation that neither you nor your fathers 2
49 LORD will bring a nation against you from afar 2
49 nation whose language you do not understand 2
50 nation of stern countenance, who shall not 2
65 among these nations you shall find no ease 2
29:16 how we came through the midst of the nations 2
18 turns . . to go and serve the gods of those nations; 2
24 yea, all the nations would say, 'Why has the LORD 2
30: 1 call them to mind among all the nations 2
31: 3 LORD . . will destroy these nations before you 2
32: 8 Most High gave to the nations their inheritance 2
21 I will provoke them with a foolish nation. 2
28 For they are a nation void of counsel 2
43 Praise his people, O you nations; for he avenges 2
Jos 3:17 stood . . until all the nation finished passing 2
4: 1 When all the nation had finished passing over 2
5: 6 till all the nation, the men of war . . perished 2
8 When the circumcising of all the nation was done 2
10:13 the nation took vengeance on their enemies. 2
23: 3 all that the LORD . . has done to all these nations 2
4 I have allotted . . those nations that remain 2
4 with all the nations that I have already cut off 2
7 be mixed with these nations left here among you 2
9 driven out before you great and strong nations; 2
12 the remnant of these nations left here among you 2
13 continue to drive out these nations before you; 2
Jdg 2:21 any of the nations that Joshua left when he died 2
23 the LORD left those nations, not driving them out 2
3: 1 these are the nations which the LORD left, to test 2
3 These are the nations: the five lords •
1Sm 8: 5 a king to govern us like all the nations. 2
20 be like all the nations, and that our king may 2
2Sm 7:23 What other nation on earth is like thy people 2
23 by driving out . . a nation and its gods? 2
8:11 the silver and . . from all the nations he subdued 2
22:44 thou didst keep me as the head of the nations; 2
50 I will extol thee, O LORD, among the nations 2
1Kg 4:31 his fame was in all the nations round about. 2
11: 2 the nations concerning which the LORD had said 2
14:24 all the abominations of the nations 2
18:10 no nation or kingdom whither my lord has not sent 2
10 he would take an oath of the kingdom or nation 2
2Kg 16: 3 practices of the nations whom the LORD drove out 2
17: 8 customs of the nations whom the LORD drove out 2
11 as the nations did whom the LORD carried away 2
15 they followed the nations that were round about 2
26 The nations which you have carried away 2
29 But every nation still made gods of its own 2
29 every nation in the cities in which they dwelt; 2
33 after the manner of the nation from among whom 2
41 these nations feared the LORD and also served 2
18:33 Has any of the gods of the nations ever delivered 2
19:12 Have the gods of the nations delivered them 2
12 the nations which my fathers destroyed, Gozan •
17 have laid waste the nations and their lands 2
21: 2 practices of the nations whom the LORD drove out 2
9 to do more evil than the nations had done 2
1Ch 14:17 LORD brought the fear of him upon all nations. 2
16:20 wandering from nation to nation 2
20 wandering from nation to nation 2
24 Declare his glory among the nations 2
31 let them say among the nations, "The LORD reigns! 2
35 gather and save us from among the nations 2
17:21 What other nation on earth is like thy people 2
21 in driving out nations before thy people 2
18:11 which he had carried off from all the nations 2
2Ch 15: 6 nation against nation and city against city 2
6 nation against nation and city against city 2
20: 6 not rule over all the kingdoms of the nations? 2
28: 3 abominable practices of the nations 2
32:13 gods of the nations of those lands at all able 2
14 nations which my fathers utterly destroyed 2
15 for no god of any nation or kingdom has been able 2
17 Like the gods of the nations of the lands 2
23 he was exalted in the sight of all nations 2
33: 2 abominable practices of the nations 2
9 did more evil than the nations whom the LORD 2
36:14 following all the abominations of the nations; 2
Ezr 4:10 rest of the nations whom the great and noble 5
Neh 5: 8 brethren who have been sold to the nations; 2
9 prevent the taunts of the nations our enemies? 2
17 came to us from the nations which were about us. 2
6: 6 It is reported among the nations, and Geshem also 2
16 all the nations round about us were afraid 2
13:26 Among the many nations there was no king like him 2
Job 12:23 He makes nations great, and he destroys them 2
23 he enlarges nations, and leads them away. 2
34:29 who can behold him, whether it be a nation or a man? 2
Ps 2: 1 Why do the nations conspire, and the peoples plot 2
8 I will make the nations your heritage 2
9: 5 Thou hast rebuked the nations 2
15 The nations have sunk in the pit which they made; 2
17 depart to Sheol, all the nations that forget God. 2
19 let the nations be judged before thee! 2
20 O LORD! Let the nations know that they are but men! 2
10:16 the nations shall perish from his land. 2
18:43 thou didst make me the head of the nations; 2
49 I will extol thee, O LORD, among the nations 2
22:27 all the families of the nations shall worship 2
28 to the LORD, and he rules over the nations. 2
33:10 LORD brings the counsel of the nations to nought; 2
12 Blessed is the nation whose God is the LORD 2
44: 2 with thy own hand didst drive out the nations 2
11 hast scattered us among the nations. 2
14 Thou hast made us a byword among the nations 2
46: 6 The nations rage, the kingdoms totter; 2
10 I am God. I am exalted among the nations 2
47: 3 peoples under us, and nations under our feet. 3
8 God reigns over the nations; 2
57: 9 I will sing praises to thee among the nations. 3
59: 5 Awake to punish all the nations; 2
8 thou dost hold all the nations in derision. 2
66: 7 for ever, whose eyes keep watch on the nations- 2
67: 2 upon earth, thy saving power among all nations. 2
4 Let the nations be glad and sing for joy 3
4 with equity and guide the nations upon earth. 3
72:11 kings fall down before him, all nations serve him! 2
17 all nations call him blessed! 2
78:55 He drove out nations before them; 2
79: 6 out thy anger on the nations that do not know thee 2
10 Why should the nations say, "Where is their God? 2
10 be known among the nations before our eyes! 2
80: 8 thou didst drive out the nations and plant it. 2
82: 8 for to thee belong all the nations! 2
83: 4 They say, "Come, let us wipe them out as a nation; 2
86: 9 nations thou hast made shall come and bow down 2
94:10 He who chastens the nations, does he not chastise? 2
96: 3 Declare his glory among the nations 2
10 Say among the nations, "The LORD reigns! 2
98: 2 his vindication in the sight of the nations. 2
102:15 The nations will fear the name of the LORD 2
105:13 wandering from nation to nation 2
13 wandering from nation to nation 2
44 he gave them the lands of the nations; 2
106: 5 that I may rejoice in the gladness of thy nation 2
27 disperse their descendants among the nations 2
35 mingled with the nations and learned to do 2
41 he gave them into the hand of the nations 2
47 O LORD . . and gather us from among the nations 2
108: 3 I will sing praises to thee among the nations. 3
110: 6 He will execute judgment among the nations 2
111: 6 in giving them the heritage of the nations. 2
113: 4 The LORD is high above all nations 2
115: 2 Why should the nations say, "Where is their God? 2
117: 1 Praise the LORD, all nations! 2
118:10 All nations surrounded me; in the name of the LORD 2
126: 2 then they said among the nations, "The LORD 2
135:10 who smote many nations and slew mighty kings 2
15 The idols of the nations are silver and gold 2
147:20 He has not dealt thus with any other nation; 2
149: 7 to wreak vengeance on the nations 2
Prv 14:34 Righteousness exalts a nation 2
24:24 will be cursed by peoples, abhorred by nations; 3
Isa 1: 4 Ah, sinful nation, a people laden with iniquity 2
2: 2 and all the nations shall flow to it 2
4 He shall judge between the nations 2
4 nation shall not lift up sword against nation 2
4 nation shall not lift up sword against nation 2
5:26 He will raise a signal for a nation afar off 2
9: 1 land beyond the Jordan, Galilee of the nations. 2
3 Thou hast multiplied the nation 2
10: 6 Against a godless nation I send him 2
7 to destroy, and to cut off nations not a few; 2
11:10 ensign to the peoples; him shall the nations seek 2
12 He will raise an ensign for the nations 2
12: 4 make known his deeds among the nations 4
13: 4 Hark, an uproar of kingdoms, of nations gathering 2
14: 6 that ruled the nations in anger 2
9 their thrones all who were kings of the nations. 2
12 to the ground, you who laid the nations low! 2
18 All the kings of the nations lie in glory 2
26 the hand . . stretched out over all the nations. 2
32 will one answer the messengers of the nation? 2
16: 8 lords of the nations . . struck down its branches 2
17:12 Ah, the roar of nations, they roar like the roaring 3
13 The nations roar like the roaring of many waters 3
18: 2 swift messengers, to a nation, tall and smooth 2
2 a nation mighty and conquering 2
7 a nation mighty and conquering 2
23: 3 you were the merchant of the nations. 2
24:13 in the midst of the earth among the nations 4
25: 3 cities of ruthless nations will fear thee. 2
7 the veil that is spread over all nations. 2
26: 2 that the righteous nation which keeps faith 2
15 thou hast increased the nation, O LORD 2
15 O LORD, thou hast increased the nation; 2
29: 7 the multitude of all the nations that fight 2
8 multitude of all the nations be that fight 2
30:28 to sift the nations with the sieve 2
33: 3 lifting up of thyself nations are scattered; 2
34: 1 Draw near, O nations, to hear, and hearken, O peoples 2
2 For the LORD is enraged against all the nations 2
36:18 Has any of the gods of the nations delivered 2
37:12 Have the gods of the nations delivered them 2
12 the nations which my fathers destroyed •
18 kings of Assyria have laid waste all the nations 1
40:15 Behold, the nations are like a drop from a bucket 2
17 All the nations are as nothing before him 2
41: 2 He gives up nations before him 2
42: 1 he will bring forth justice to the nations. 2
6 a covenant to the people, a light to the nations 2
43: 9 Let all the nations gather together 2
45: 1 to subdue nations before him and ungird 2
20 draw near together, you survivors of the nations! 2
49: 6 I will give you as a light to the nations 2
7 to one deeply despised, abhorred by the nations 2
22 Behold, I will lift up my hand to the nations 2
51: 4 Listen to me, my people, and give ear to me, my nation 3
52:10 his holy arm before the eyes of all the nations; 2
15 shall he startle many nations; 2
54: 3 and your descendants will possess the nations 2
55: 5 Behold, you shall call nations that you know not 2
5 and nations that knew you not shall run to you 2
58: 2 as if they were a nation that did righteousness 2
60: 3 And nations shall come to your light 2
5 the wealth of the nations shall come to you. 2
11 men may bring to you the wealth of the nations 2
12 the nation and kingdom that will not serve you 2

12 those nations shall be utterly laid waste. 2
16 You shall suck the milk of nations 2
22 a clan, and the smallest one a mighty nation; 2
61: 6 you shall eat the wealth of the nations 2
9 descendants shall be known among the nations 2
11 praise to spring forth before all the nations. 2
62: 2 The nations shall see your vindication 2
64: 2 that the nations might tremble at thy presence! 2
65: 1 here am I," to a nation that did not call on my name. 2
66: 8 Shall a nation be brought forth in one moment? 2
12 the wealth of the nations like an overflowing 2
18 and I am coming to gather all nations and tongues; 2
19 from them I will send survivors to the nations 2
19 they shall declare my glory among the nations. 2
20 brethren from all the nations as an offering 2
Jer 1: 5 I appointed you a prophet to the nations. 2
10 set you this day over nations and over kingdoms 2
2:11 Has a nation changed its gods 2
3:17 and all nations shall gather to it 2
19 a heritage most beauteous of all nations. 2
4: 2 then nations shall bless themselves in him 2
7 a destroyer of nations has set out 2
16 Warn the nations that he is coming; 2
5: 9 shall I not avenge myself on a nation such as this? 2
15 Behold, I am bringing upon you a nation from afar 2
15 It is an enduring nation, it is an ancient nation 2
15 It is an enduring nation, it is an ancient nation 2
15 a nation whose language you do not know 2
29 shall I not avenge myself on a nation such as this? 2
6:18 hear, O nations, and know, O congregation 2
22 a great nation is stirring 2
7:28 the nation that did not obey the voice of the LORD 2
9: 9 shall I not avenge myself on a nation such as this? 2
16 I will scatter them among the nations 2
26 for all these nations are uncircumcised 2
10: 2 Learn not the way of the nations, nor be dismayed 2
2 because the nations are dismayed at them 2
7 Who would not fear thee, O King of the nations? 2
7 for among all the wise ones of the nations 2
10 the nations cannot endure his indignation. 2
25 Pour out thy wrath upon the nations 2
12:17 But if any nation will not listen 2
14:22 the false gods of the nations that can bring rain? 2
16:19 to thee shall the nations come 2
18: 7 If at any time I declare concerning a nation 2
8 if that nation, concerning which I have spoken 2
9 And if at any time I declare concerning a nation 2
13 thus says the LORD: Ask among the nations 2
22: 8 And many nations will pass by this city 2
25: 9 and against all these nations round about; 2
11 these nations shall serve the king of Babylon 2
12 I will punish the king of Babylon and that nation 2
13 Jeremiah prophesied against all the nations. 2
14 many nations and great kings shall make slaves 2
15 make all the nations to whom I send you drink it. 2
17 all the nations to whom the Lord sent me 2
31 the LORD has an indictment against the nations; 2
32 Behold, evil is going forth from nation to nation 2
32 Behold, evil is going forth from nation to nation 2
26: 6 I will make this city a curse for all the nations 2
27: 7 All the nations shall serve him and his son 2
7 then many nations . . shall make him their slave. 2
8 But if any nation or kingdom will not serve 2
8 I will punish that nation with the sword 2
11 nation which will bring its neck under the yoke 2
13 as the LORD has spoken concerning any nation 2
28:11 king of Babylon from the neck of all the nations 2
14 upon the neck of all these nations an iron yoke 2
29:14 and gather you from all the nations 2
18 a hissing, and a reproach among all the nations 2
30:11 I will make a full end of all the nations 2
31: 7 and raise shouts for the chief of the nations; 2
10 Hear the word of the LORD, O nations, and declare it 2
36 cease from being a nation before me for ever. 2
33: 9 and a glory before all the nations of the earth 2
24 they are no longer a nation in their sight. 2
36: 2 against Israel and Judah and all the nations 2
43: 5 all the nations to which they had been driven 2
44: 8 and a taunt among all the nations of the earth? 2
46: 1 Jeremiah the prophet concerning the nations. 2
12 The nations have heard of your shame 2
28 I will make a full end of all the nations 2
48: 2 Come, let us cut her off from being a nation! 2
49:14 and a messenger has been sent among the nations 2
15 behold, I will make you small among the nations 2
31 Rise up, advance against a nation at ease 2
36 shall be no nation to which those driven out 2
50: 2 Declare among the nations and proclaim 2
3 out of the north a nation has come up against her 2
9 against Babylon a company of great nations 2
12 Lo, she shall be the last of the nations 2
23 How Babylon has become a horror among the nations! 2
41 a mighty nation and many kings are stirring 2
46 and her cry shall be heard among the nations. 2
51: 7 the nations drank of her wine 2
7 of her wine, therefore the nations went mad. 2
20 weapon of war: with you I break nations in pieces; 2
27 on the earth, blow the trumpet among the nations; 2
27 prepare the nations for war against her 2
28 Prepare the nations for war against her 2
41 How Babylon has become a horror among the nations! 2
44 The nations shall no longer flow to him; 2
58 the nations weary themselves only for fire. 3
Lam 1: 1 a widow . . she that was great among the nations! 2
3 she dwells now among the nations 2
10 yea, she has seen the nations invade her 2
2: 9 her king and princes are among the nations; 2
4:15 men said among the nations, "They shall stay 2
17 we watched for a nation which could not save. 2
20 Under his shadow we shall live among . . nations. 2
Ezk 2: 3 a nation of rebels, who have rebelled against me; 2
4:13 among the nations whither I will drive them. 2
5: 5 I have set her in the center of the nations 2
6 wickedly rebelled . . more than the nations 2
7 Because you are more turbulent than the nations 2
7 according to the ordinances of the nations 2
8 in the midst of you in the sight of the nations. 2
14 of reproach among the nations round about you 2
15 a warning and a horror, to the nations round about 2
6: 8 When you have among the nations some who escape 2
9 will remember me among the nations 2
7:24 I will bring the worst of the nations to take 2
11:12 ordinances of the nations that are round about 2
16 Though I removed them far off among the nations 2
12:15 when I disperse them among the nations 2
16 abominations among the nations where they go 2
16:14 your renown went forth among the nations 2
19: 4 The nations sounded an alarm against him; 2
8 the nations set against him snares on every side; 2
20: 9 in the sight of the nations among whom they dwelt 2
14 not be profaned in the sight of the nations 2
22 not be profaned in the sight of the nations 2
23 that I would scatter them among the nations 2
32 Let us be like the nations, like the tribes 2
41 holiness among you in the sight of the nations. 2
22: 4 I have made you a reproach to the nations 2
15 I will scatter you among the nations 2
16 profaned through you in the sight of the nations; 2
23:30 because you played the harlot with the nations 2
25: 7 and will hand you over as spoil to the nations; 2
8 the house of Judah is like all the other nations 2
10 may be remembered no more among the nations 2
26: 3 and will bring up many nations against you 2
5 she shall become a spoil to the nations; 2
28: 7 upon you, the most terrible of the nations; 2
25 my holiness in them in the sight of the nations 2
29:12 I will scatter the Egyptians among the nations 2
15 and never again exalt itself above the nations; 2
15 they will never again rule over the nations. 2
30: 3 a day of clouds, a time of doom for the nations. 2
11 people with him, the most terrible of the nations 2
23 I will scatter the Egyptians among the nations 2
26 I will scatter the Egyptians among the nations 2
31: 6 under its shadow dwelt all great nations. 2
11 into the hand of a mighty one of the nations; 2
12 Foreigners, the most terrible of the nations 2
16 I will make the nations quake at the sound 2
17 who dwelt under its shadow among the nations 2
32: 2 You consider yourself a lion among the nations 2
9 when I carry you captive among the nations 2
12 all of them most terrible among the nations. 2
16 the daughters of the nations shall chant it; 2
18 her and the daughters of majestic nations 2
34:28 They shall no more be a prey to the nations 2
29 no longer suffer the reproach of the nations. 2
35:10 These two nations and these two countries shall 2
36: 3 became the possession of the rest of the nations 2
4 derision to the rest of the nations round about; 2
5 my hot jealousy against the rest of the nations 2
6 you have suffered the reproach of the nations; 2
7 I swear that the nations that are round about you 2
13 you bereave your nation of children, 2
14 and no longer bereave your nation of children 2
15 let you hear any more the reproach of the nations 2
15 and no longer cause your nation to stumble 2
19 I scattered them among the nations 2
20 when they came to the nations 2
21 Israel caused to be profaned among the nations 2
22 name, which you have profaned among the nations 2
23 name, which has been profaned among the nations 2
23 the nations will know that I am the LORD 2
24 For I will take you from the nations 2
30 the disgrace of famine among the nations. 2
36 Then the nations that are left round about you 2
37:21 I will take the people of Israel from the nations 2
22 I will make them one nation in the land 2
22 they shall be no longer two nations 2
28 the nations will know that I the LORD sanctify 2
38: 8 gathered from many nations upon the mountains 4
8 its people were brought out from the nations 4
12 the people who were gathered from the nations 2
16 against my land, that the nations may know me 2
23 make myself known in the eyes of many nations. 2
39: 7 the nations shall know that I am the LORD 2
21 I will set my glory among the nations; 2
21 all the nations shall see my judgment 2
23 the nations shall know that the house of Israel 2
27 my holiness in the sight of many nations. 2
28 because I sent them into exile among the nations 2
28 of them remaining among the nations any more; •
Dan 3: 4 commanded, O peoples, nations, and languages 5
7 all the peoples, nations, and languages fell down 5
29 Any people, nation, or language that speaks 5
4: 1 King . . to all peoples, nations, and languages 5
5:19 all peoples, nations, and languages trembled 5
6:25 wrote to all the peoples, nations, and languages 5
7:14 all peoples, nations, and languages should serve 5
8:22 four kingdoms shall arise from his nation 2
12: 1 since there was a nation till that time; 2
Hos 8: 8 they are among the nations as a useless vessel. 2
10 Though they hire allies among the nations 2
9:17 they shall be wanderers among the nations. 2
10:10 and nations shall be gathered against them 4
Jol 1: 6 For a nation has come up against my land 2
2:17 heritage a reproach, a byword among the nations. 2
19 no more make you a reproach among the nations. 2
3: 2 I will gather all the nations 2
2 they have scattered them among the nations 2
8 will sell them to the Sabe'ans, to a nation far off; 2
9 Proclaim this among the nations: Prepare war 2
11 Hasten and come, all you nations round about 2
12 Let the nations bestir themselves, and come up 2
12 I will sit to judge all the nations round about. 2
Ams 6: 1 the notable men of the first of the nations 2
14 For behold, I will raise up against you a nation 2
9: 9 shake the house of Israel among all the nations 2
12 Edom and all the nations who are called by my name 2
Obd 1: 1 and a messenger has been sent among the nations 2
2 Behold, I will make you small among the nations 2
15 the day of the LORD is near upon all the nations. 2
16 all the nations round about shall drink; 2
Mic 4: 2 many nations shall come, and say: "Come, let us go up 2
3 and shall decide for strong nations afar off; 2
3 nation shall not lift up sword against nation 2
3 nation shall not lift up sword against nation 2
7 and those who were cast off, a strong nation; 2
11 Now many nations are assembled against you 2
5: 8 the remnant of Jacob shall be among the nations 2
15 vengeance upon the nations that did not obey. 2
7:16 The nations shall see and be ashamed 2
Nah 3: 4 who betrays nations with her harlotries 2
5 and I will let nations look on your nakedness 2
Hab 1: 5 Look among the nations, and see; 2
6 the Chalde'ans, that bitter and hasty nation 2
17 and mercilessly slaying nations for ever? 2
2: 5 He gathers for himself all nations 2
8 Because you have plundered many nations 2
13 and nations weary themselves for nought? 3
3: 6 he looked and shook the nations; 2
12 thou didst trample the nations in anger. 2
Zep 2: 1 and hold assembly, O shameless nation 2
5 Woe to you . . you nation of the Cher'ethites! 2
9 the survivors of my nation shall possess them. 2
11 each in its place, all the lands of the nations. 2
3: 6 I have cut off nations; 2
8 For my decision is to gather nations 2
Hag 2: 7 I will shake all nations, so that the treasures 2
7 that the treasures of all nations shall come 2
14 and with this nation before me, says the LORD; 2
22 the strength of the kingdoms of the nations 2
Zec 1:15 I am very angry with the nations that are at ease; 2
21 to cast down the horns of the nations who lifted 2
2: 8 after his glory sent me to the nations 2
11 many nations shall join themselves to the LORD 2
7:14 among all the nations which they had not known. 2
8:13 been a byword of cursing among the nations 2
22 Many peoples and strong nations shall come 2
23 In those days ten men from the nations 2
9:10 he shall command peace to the nations; 2
10: 9 Though I scattered them among the nations 4
12: 3 the nations of the earth will come together 2
9 all the nations that come against Jerusalem. 2
14: 2 For I will gather all the nations 2
3 will go forth and fight against those nations 2
14 the wealth of all the nations round about 2
16 Then every one that survives of all the nations 2
18 plague with which the LORD afflicts the nations 2
19 punishment to all the nations that do not go up 2
Mal 1:11 my name is great among the nations, says the LORD 2
11 my name is great among the nations, says the LORD 2
14 my name is feared among the nations. 2
3: 9 you are robbing me; the whole nation of you. 2
12 Then all nations will call you blessed 2
Mat 21:43 given to a nation producing the fruits of it. 7
24: 7 For nation will rise against nation 7
7 For nation will rise against nation 7
9 hated by all nations for my name's sake. 7
14 as a testimony to all nations 7
25:32 Before him will be gathered all the nations 7
28:19 Go therefore and make disciples of all nations 7
Mrk 11:17 a house of prayer for all the nations 7
13: 8 For nation will rise against nation 7
8 For nation will rise against nation 7
10 gospel must first be preached to all nations. 7
Lke 7: 5 he loves our nation, and he built us our synagogue 7
12:30 all the nations of the world seek these things; 7
21:10 he said to them, "Nation will rise against nation 7

10 he said to them, "Nation will rise against nation 7
24 and be led captive among all nations 7
25 upon the earth distress of nations 7
23: 2 We found this man perverting our nation 7
24:47 preached in his name to all nations 7
Joh 11:48 and destroy both our holy place and our nation. 7
50 the whole nation should not perish. 7
51 Jesus should die for the nation 7
52 not for the nation only 7
18:35 Your own nation and the chief priests 7
Act 2: 5 devout men from every nation under heaven. 7
7: 7 I will judge the nation which they serve,' said God 7
45 when they dispossessed the nations 7
8: 9 and amazed the nation of Sama'ria 7
10:22 who is well spoken of by the whole Jewish nation 7
35 in every nation any one who fears him 7
13:19 when he had destroyed seven nations in the land 7
14:16 allowed all the nations to walk in their own ways; 7
17:26 he made from one every nation of men 7
24: 2 reforms are introduced on behalf of this nation 7
10 many years you have been judge over this nation 7
17 I came to bring to my nation alms and offerings. 7
26: 4 spent from the beginning among my own nation 7
28:19 though I had no charge to bring against my nation. 7
Rom 1: 5 for the sake of his name among all the nations 7
4:17 I have made you the father of many nations 7
18 that he should become the father of many nations; 7
10:19 make you jealous of those who are not a nation; 7
19 with a foolish nation I will make you angry. 7
16:26 is made known to all nations 7
Gal 3: 8 saying, "In you shall all the nations be blessed. 7
1Ti 3:16 preached among the nations 7
1Pe 2: 9 you are . . a holy nation, God's own people 7
Rev 2:26 I will give him power over the nations 7
5: 9 every tribe and tongue and people and nation 7
7: 9 multitude . . from every nation, from all tribes 7
10:11 prophesy about many peoples and nations 7
11: 2 for it is given over to the nations 7
9 the peoples and tribes and tongues and nations 7
18 The nations raged, but thy wrath came 7
12: 5 one who is to rule all nations with a rod of iron 7
13: 7 every tribe and people and tongue and nation 7
14: 6 to every nation and tribe and tongue and people; 7
8 she who made all nations drink the wine 7
15: 4 All nations shall come and worship thee 7
16:19 and the cities of the nations fell 7
17:15 peoples and multitudes and nations and tongues 7
18: 3 all nations have drunk the wine of her . . passion 7
23 and all nations were deceived by thy sorcery. 7
19:15 a sharp sword with which to smite the nations 7
20: 3 that he should deceive the nations no more 7
8 and will come out to deceive the nations 7
21:24 By its light shall the nations walk; 7
26 the glory and the honor of the nations. 7
22: 2 leaves . . were for the healing of the nations. 7
1Es 1:32 throughout the whole nation of Israel. 6
34 the men of the nation took Jeconiah 7
36 fined the nation 100 talents of silver 7
49 beyond all the unclean deeds of all the nations 7
5: 9 The number of the men of the nation 7
6:33 may the Lord . . destroy every king and nation 7
8:10 of the Jewish nation and of the priests 7
14 together with what is given by the nation 7
2Es 1:11 I have destroyed all nations before them 10
24 I will turn to other nations 10
2: 7 Let them be scattered among the nations 10
8 O wicked nation, remember what I did to Sodom 10
28 The nations shall envy you 10
34 I say to you, O nations that hear and understand 10
3: 7 From him there sprang nations and tribes 10
8 every nation walked after its own will 10
12 children and peoples and many nations 10
32 Or has another nation known thee besides Israel? 10
33 I have traveled widely among the nations 10
35 what nation has kept thy commandments so well? 10
36 but nations thou wilt not find. 10
6:48 the nations might declare thy wondrous works. 11
56 other nations which have descended from Adam 10
57 now, O Lord, behold, these nations 10
7:37 the nations that have been raised from the dead 10
9: 3 tumult of peoples, intrigues of nations 10
13:33 when all the nations hear his voice 10
37 he, my Son, will reprove the assembled nations 10
41 they would leave the multitude of the nations 10
49 when he destroys the multitude of the nations 10
15:15 and nation shall rise up to fight against nation 10
15 and nation shall rise up to fight against nation 10
29 The nations of the dragons of Arabia 11
Tob 3: 4 the nations among which we have been dispersed. 7
4:19 none of the nations has understanding 7
13: 3 Acknowledge him before the nations 7
5 will gather us from all the nations 7
6 I show his power . . to a nation of sinners 7
11 Many nations will come from afar 7
Jdt 1: 6 Many nations joined the forces of the Chaldeans. 7
8 those among the nations of Carmel and Gilead 7
3: 8 all nations should worship Nebuchadnezzar 7
4: 1 had done to the nations 7
5:21 if there is no transgression in their nation 7
8:20 he will not disdain us or any of our nation. 6
9:14 cause thy whole nation and every tribe to know 7
11:10 our nation cannot be punished 6
13:20 when our nation was brought low 6
14: 7 In every nation 7
15: 9 you are the great pride of our nation! 6
16:17 Woe to the nations that rise up against my people! 7
AEs 10: 8 The nations are those that gathered 7
9 my nation, this is Israel, who cried out to God 7
9 wonders, which have not occurred among the nations 7
10 one for all the nations. 7
11 before God and among all the nations. 7
11: 7 at their roaring every nation prepared for war 7
7 to fight against the nation of the righteous 7
9 the whole righteous nation was troubled 7
13: 2 Having become ruler of many nations 7
4 among all the nations in the world 8
4 have laws contrary to those of every nation 7
14: 5 didst take Israel out of all the nations 7
10 to open the mouths of the nations 7
16:11 the good will that we have for every nation 7
13 together with their whole nation. 7
Wis 3: 8 They will govern nations and rule over peoples 7
6: 2 you that . . boast of many nations. 7
8:14 nations will be subject to me; 7
10: 5 when the nations . . had been confounded 7
15 wisdom delivered from a nation of oppressors. 7
12:12 accuse thee for the destruction of nations 7
17: 2 they held the holy nation in their power 7
Sir 4:15 He who obeys her will judge the nations 7
10: 8 Sovereignty passes from nation to nation 7
8 Sovereignty passes from nation to nation 7
15 The Lord has plucked up the roots of the nations 7
16 The Lord has overthrown the lands of the nations 7
16: 6 in a disobedient nation wrath was kindled. 7
9 a nation devoted to destruction 7
17:17 He appointed a ruler for every nation 7
24: 6 in the whole earth, and in every people and nation 7
28:14 scattered them from nation to nation 7
14 scattered them from nation to nation 7
29:18 they have wandered among foreign nations. 7
35:18 repays vengeance on the nations 7
36: 2 the fear of thee to fall upon all the nations. 7
3 Lift up thy hand against foreign nations 7
39: 4 travel through the lands of foreign nations 7
10 Nations will declare his wisdom 7
23 The nations will incur his wrath 7
44:19 the great father of a multitude of nations 7
21 nations would be blessed through his posterity; 7
46: 6 He hurled down war upon that nation 7
6 so that the nations might know his armament 7
49: 5 they gave . . their glory to a foreign nation 7
50:25 With two nations my soul is vexed 7
25 the third is no nation: 7
Bar 2:13 among the nations where thou hast scattered us. 7
29 turn into a small number among the nations 7
3:16 Where are the princes of the nations, and those 7
4: 6 you were sold to the nations 7
15 For he brought against them a nation from afar 7
15 a shameless nation, of a strange language 7
LJr 1:51 It will be manifest to all the nations and kings 7
67 show signs in the heavens and among the nations 7
Aza 1:14 For we, O Lord, have become fewer than any nation 7
1Mc 1: 3 plundered many nations 7
4 and ruled over countries, nations, and princes 7
2:10 What nation has not inherited her palaces 7
19 the nations that live under the rule of the king 7
3:59 to see the misfortunes of our nation 7
6:58 make peace with them and with all their nation 7
8:23 with the Romans and with the nation of the Jews 7
25 the nation of the Jews shall act as their allies 7
27 if war comes first to the nation of the Jews 7
9:29 to deal with those of our nation who hate us. 7
10: 5 to him and to his brothers and his nation. 7
20 to be the high priest of your nation 7
25 King Demetrius to the nation of the Jews, greeting 7
11:21 certain lawless men who hated their nation 7
25 certain lawless men of his nation 7
30 to the nation of the Jews, greeting. 7
33 To the nation of the Jews, who are our friends 7
38 recruited from the islands of the nations 7
42 do these things for you and your nation 7
42 I will confer great honor on you and your nation 7
12: 3 Jonathan the high priest and the Jewish nation 7
6 the senate of the nation, the priests 7
53 all the nations round about them 7
13: 6 I will avenge my nation and the sanctuary 7
6 the nations have gathered together out of hatred 7
36 to the elders and nation of the Jews, greeting. 7
14: 4 He sought the good of his nation 7
6 He extended the borders of his nation 7
28 the people and the rulers of the nation 7
29 resisted the enemies of their nation 7
29 they brought great glory to their nation. 7
30 Jonathan rallied the nation 7
32 then Simon rose up and fought for his nation 7
32 he armed the men of his nation's forces 7
35 glory which he had resolved to win for his nation 7
35 which he had maintained toward his nation 7
15: 1 to all the nation; 7
2 to the nation of the Jews, greeting. 7
9 upon you and your nation and the temple 7
16: 3 go out and fight for our nation 7
2Mc 4:35 not only Jews, but many also of other nations 7
5:19 the nation for the sake of the holy place 7
19 the place for the sake of the nation. 7
20 the misfortunes that befell the nation 7
6:14 in the case of the other nations 7
31 but to the great body of his nation. 7
7:37 appealing to God to show mercy soon to our nation 7
38 which has justly fallen on our whole nation. 6
10: 4 blasphemous and barbarous nations. 7
8 the whole nation of the Jews 7
11: 3 as he did on the sacred places of the other nations 7
25 that this nation also be free from disturbance 7
27 To the nation the king's letter was as follows 7
14: 8 our whole nation is now in no small misfortune. 6
9 to take thought for . . our hard-pressed nation 6
34 and called upon the constant Defender of our nation 7
3Mc 1:11 not even members of their own nation were allowed 7
2:33 to be enemies of the Jewish nation 7
3: 2 a hostile rumor . . against the Jewish nation 6
6 their good service to their nation 6
15 not rule the nations inhabiting Coele-Syria 7
19 they become the only people among all nations 7
20 since we treat all nations with benevolence. 7
5: 5 the whole nation would experience 9
6: 4 light of your mercy upon the nation of Israel. 6
5 showing your power to many nations. 7
9 those of the nation of Israel 6
13 who have power to save the nation of Jacob. 6
26 from the beginning differed from all nations 7
7: 4 ill-will . . toward all nations. 7
10 those of the Jewish nation 6
4Mc 1:11 the downfall of tyranny over their nation 7
3: 7 together with the soldiers of his nation 7
4: 1 unable to injure Onias in the eyes of the nation 7
18 high priest and ruler of the nation. 7
19 Jason changed the nation's way of life 7
26 tried to compel everyone in the nation 7
9:24 may become merciful to our nation 7
12:17 to be merciful to our nation; 7
15:29 O mother of the nation, vindicator of the law 7
16:16 you are called to bear witness for the nation. 7
17: 8 a reminder to the people of our nation 7
10 They vindicated their nation 6
20 our enemies did not rule over our nation 7
21 a ransom for the sin of our nation. 7
18: 4 Because of them the nation gained peace 7

nation *See also* ancestor.

another nation 1. ἀλλόφυλος

Act 10:28 to visit any one of another nation 1

one nation 1. πανεθνί

Wis 19: 8 those . . passed through as one nation 1

national *See* life.

nationalities *See* people.

all nations 1. πάμφυλος

2Mc 8: 9 no fewer than 20,000 Gentiles of all nations 1

native 1. אֶזְרָח 2. מוֹלֶדֶת 3. βάρβαρος 4. γένος 5. ἐγχώριος 6. ἴδιος 7. πάτριος

Exd 12:19 cut off . . whether he is a sojourner or a native 1
48 he shall be as a native of the land. 1
49 There shall be one law for the native 1
Lev 16:29 do no work, either the native or the stranger 1
17:15 whether he is a native or a sojourner 1
18:26 the native or the stranger who sojourns among you 1
19:34 stanger . . shall be to you as the native 1
23:42 all that are native in Israel shall dwell 1
24:16 the sojourner as well as the native 1
22 have one law for the sojourner and for the native 1
Num 9:14 both for the sojourner and for the native. 1
15:13 who are native shall do these things in this way 1
29 for him who is native among the people of Israel 1
30 high hand, whether he is native or a sojourner 1
Rut 2:11 left your father and mother and your native land 2
4:10 not be cut off . . from the gate of his native place; •
Jer 22:10 he shall return no more to see his native land. 2
Ezk 23:15 of Babylonians whose native land was Chalde'a. 2
Act 4:36 a Levite, a native of Cyprus 4
18: 2 he found a Jew named Aq'uila, a native of Pontus 4
24 Now a Jew named Apol'los, a native of Alexandria 4
28: 2 the natives showed us unusual kindness 3
4 When the natives saw the creature 3
1Es 6:25 one course of new native timber 5
Wis 16:23 the fire . . even forgot its native power. 6
2Mc 7:27 she spoke in their native tongue as follows 7

native *See also* land.

native-born 1. אֶזְרָח

Ezk 47:22 They shall be to you as native-born sons of Israel; 1

natural 1. *γένεσις* 2. *ἑαυτοῦ* 3. *κατὰ φύσιν* 4. *σάρξ* 5. *φυσικός*

Rom 1:26 exchanged natural relations for unnatural 5
27 the men . . gave up natural relations with women 5
6:19 because of your natural limitations. 4
11:21 For if God did not spare the natural branches 3
24 will . . natural branches be grafted back 3
Jas 1:23 a man who observes his natural face in a mirror; 1
4Mc 2: 8 he is forced to act contrary to his natural ways 2

natural *See also* force, love.

nature 1. *ἄνθρωπος* 2. *γένεσις* 3. *γένος* 4. *ὄνομα* 5. *σπέρμα* 6. *ὑπόστασις* 7. *φύσις* 8. natura

Joh 8:44 When he lies, he speaks according to his own nature •
Rom 2:14 Gentiles . . do by nature what the law requires 7
11:24 cut from what is by nature a wild olive tree 7
24 grafted, contrary to nature, into a cultivated 7
1Co 11:14 Does not nature itself teach you 7
2Co 4:16 Though our outer nature is wasting away 1
16 our inner nature is being renewed every day. •
Gal 4: 8 in bondage to beings that by nature are no gods; 7
Eph 2: 3 we were by nature children of wrath 7
4:22 Put off your old nature 1
24 put on the new nature 1
Col 3: 9 seeing that you have put off the old nature 1
10 and have put on the new nature •
Heb 1: 3 and bears the very stamp of his nature 6
2:14 he himself likewise partook of the same nature •
Jas 3: 6 setting on fire the cycle of nature 2
2Pe 1: 4 and become partakers of the divine nature. 7
1Jn 3: 9 for God's nature abides in him, and he cannot sin 5
2Es 14:14 and divest yourself now of your weak nature 8
Wis 7:20 the natures of animals 7
13: 1 were foolish by nature 7
19: 6 whole creation in its nature was fashioned anew 3
18 on a harp the notes vary the nature of the rhythm 4
20 water forgot its fire-quenching nature. 7
4Mc 5: 8 Why, when nature has granted it to us 7
9 wrong to spurn the gifts of nature. 7
25 we know that in the nature of things 7
13:27 nature and companionship and virtuous habits 7
15:13 O sacred nature and affection of parental love 7
25 nature, family, parental love 7

nature *See also* concerned, endowed.

evil nature 1. *κακοήθεια*

AEs 16: 6 the false trickery of their evil natures 1

invisible nature 1. *ἀόρατος*

Rom 1:20 his invisible nature, namely, his eternal power 1

like nature 1. *ὁμοιοπαθής*

Act 14:15 We also are men, of like nature with you 1
Jas 5:17 Eli'jah was a man of like nature with ourselves 1

mortal nature 1. *θνητός*

1Co 15:53 this mortal nature must put on immortality. 1

perishable nature 1. *φθαρτός*

1Co 15:53 perishable nature must put on the imperishable 1

nausea 1. *χολέρα*

Sir 31:20 distress of sleeplessness . . nausea and colic 1
37:30 gluttony leads to nausea. 1

nave 1. בַּיִת 2. בַּיִת גָּדוֹל 3. הֵיכָל

1Kg 6: 3 The vestibule in front of the nave of the house 3
5 the house, both the nave and the inner sanctuary; 3
17 the nave in front of the inner sanctuary 3
33 he made for the entrance to the nave doorposts 3
7:50 and for the doors of the nave of the temple. 3
2Ch 3: 4 The vestibule in front of the nave of the house •
5 nave he lined with cypress, and covered it 2
13 cherubim stood on their feet, facing the nave. 1
4:22 and for the doors of the nave of the temple 3
Ezk 41: 1 Then he brought me to the nave 3
2 he measured the length of the nave 40 cubits •
4 and its breadth, twenty cubits, beyond the nave. 3
15 The nave of the temple and the inner room 3
17 the nave were carved likenesses •
21 The doorposts of the nave were squared; 3
23 nave and the holy place had each a double door. 3
25 And on the doors of the nave were carved cherubim 3

navel 1. שֹׁר

Sng 7: 2 Your navel is a rounded bowl that never lacks 1

navel *See also* string.

navigate 1. dominor

2Es 7: 5 to reach the sea, to look at it or to navigate it 1

nay 1. אַף 2. וְאִם לֹא 3. כִּי 4. לֹא

Jos 22:24 Nay, but we did it from fear that in time to come 2
24:21 the people said . . "Nay; but we will serve the LORD. 4
Jdg 5:29 make answer, nay, she gives answer to herself 1
Ps 44:22 Nay, for thy sake we are slain all the day long 3
58: 2 Nay, in your hearts you devise wrongs; 1
Isa 28:11 Nay, but by men of strange lips *

near 1. אֶל 2. אֵצֶל 3. אֵת 4. בְּ 5. לְ 6. מִן הוּא 7. נגשׁ 8. עַל 9. עַל יַד 10. עִם 11. קָצֶה 12. קרב 13. קָרֹב 14. קִרְבָה 15. *ἐγγύς* 16. *ἐν* 17. *κατά* 18. *κατὰ χεῖρας* 19. *μετά* 20. *παραπλήσιος* 21. *περί* 22. *πλησίον* 23. *πρός* 24. *προσάγω* 25. *πρὸς κεῖμαι* 26. *σύνεγγυς* 27. ad

Gen 19:20 Behold, yonder city is near enough to flee to 13
35: 4 hid them under the oak which was near Shechem. 10
37:12 to pasture their father's flock near Shechem. 4
45:10 you shall be near me, you and your children 12
Exd 13:17 land of the Philistines, although that was near; 12
Lev 10: 3 I will show myself holy among those who are near me 12
18:17 they are your near kinswomen; it is wickedness •
21: 2 his nearest of kin, his mother, his father, his son 13
3 (who is near to him because she has had no husband 13
Num 13:21 Zin to Rehob, near the entrance of Hamath. 5
22: 5 at Pethor, which is near the River, in the land 8
41 from there he saw the nearest of the people. 11
23:13 you shall see only the nearest of them 11
Deu 4: 7 has a god so near to it as the LORD our God is to us 13
13: 7 whether near you or far off from you 13
15: 9 The seventh year, the year of release is near,' 12
21: 3 elders of the city . . nearest to the slain man 13
6 elders of that city nearest to the slain man 13
22: 2 if he is not near you, or if you do not know him 12
30:14 word is very near you; it is in your mouth 12
Jos 3: 4 Yet there shall be a space . . do not come near it. 1
7: 2 from Jericho to Ai, which is near Beth-a'ven 10
Jdg 1:16 of Judah, which lies in the Negeb near Arad; •
3:19 back at the sculptured stones near Gilgal 3
4:11 the oak in Za-anan'nim, which is near Kedesh. 3
18:22 the men who were in the houses near Micah's house 10
19:11 When they were near Jebus, the day was far spent 10
14 the sun went down on them near Gib'e-ah 2
Rut 3:12 yet there is a kinsman nearer than I. 13
2Sm 13:23 at Ba'al-ha'zor, which is near E'phraim 10
19:37 die . . near the grave of my father and my mother. 10
42 Because the king is near of kin to us. 12
1Kg 8:46 captive to the land of the enemy, far off or near; 13
59 Let these words of mine . . be near to the LORD 13
9:26 E'zion-ge'ber, which is near Eloth on the shore 3
21: 2 Give me . . because it is near my house; 2
2Ch 6:36 carried away captive to a land far or near; 13
21:16 of the Arabs who are near the Ethiopians; 9
Est 9:20 all the provinces of . . both near and far 13
Job 17:12 The light,' they say, 'is near to the darkness.' 12
41:16 One is so near to another that no air can come 7
Ps 22:11 Be not far from me, for trouble is near 13
34:18 The LORD is near to the brokenhearted, and saves 13
73:28 for me it is good to be near God; 14
119:151 thou art near, O LORD 12
145:18 The LORD is near to all who call upon him 12
148:14 his saints, for the people of Israel who are near 12
Prv 7: 8 passing along the street near her corner 2
10:14 but the babbling of a fool brings ruin near. 13
27:10 Better is a neighbor who is near than a brother 12
Isa 13: 6 Wail, for the day of the LORD is near; 12
18: 2 to a people feared near and far 6
7 from a people feared near and far 6
26:17 cries out in her pangs, when she is near her time 12
33:13 and you who are near, acknowledge my might. 13
50: 8 he who vindicates me is near. 12
55: 6 the LORD . . call upon him while he is near; 12
57:19 peace, to the far and to the near, says the LORD; 12
Jer 12: 2 art near in their mouth and far from their heart. 13
25:26 all the kings of the north, far and near 13
35: 4 which was near the chamber of the princes 2
41:17 and stayed at Geruth Chimham near Bethlehem 2
48:16 The calamity of Moab is near at hand 12
24 all the cities of the land of Moab, far and near. 13
Ezk 6:12 he that is near shall fall by the sword; 12
7: 7 the time has come, the day is near, a day of tumult 12
11: 3 who say, 'The time is not near to build houses; 12
22: 5 Those who are near and those who are far from you 13
30: 3 For the day is near, the day of the LORD is near; 12
3 For the day is near, the day of the LORD is near; 12
44:25 defile themselves by going near to a dead person; •
Dan 8:17 came near where I stood; and when he came 2
9: 7 all Israel . . near and those that are far away 13
Jol 1:15 Alas for the day! For the day of the LORD is near 12
2: 1 for the day of the LORD is coming, it is near 12
3:14 day of the LORD is near in the valley of decision. 12
Obd 1:15 the day of the LORD is near upon all the nations. 12
Zep 1:14 The great day of the LORD is near 12
14 day of the LORD is near, near and hastening fast; 12
Mat 24:32 you know that summer is near. 15
33 you know that he is near, at the very gates. 15
Mrk 13:28 you know that summer is near. 15
29 you know that he is near, at the very gates. 15
Lke 19:11 because he was near to Jerusalem 15
21:30 know that the summer is already near. 15
31 you know that the kingdom of God is near. 15
Joh 3:23 John also was baptizing at Ae'non near Salim 15
4: 5 near the field that Jacob gave to his son Joseph. 22
6:19 walking on the sea and drawing near to the boat 15
23 However, boats from Tiber'i-as came near the place 15
9:40 Some of the Pharisees near him heard this 19
11:18 Bethany was near Jerusalem, about two miles off 15
54 from there to the country near the wilderness 15
19:20 the place . . was near the city 15
Act 1:12 the mount called Olivet, which is near Jerusalem 15
9:38 Since Lydda was near Joppa 15
27: 8 Fair Havens, near which was the city of Lase'a. 15
27 sailors suspected that they were nearing land. 24
Rom 10: 8 The word is near you, on your lips and in your heart 15
13:11 For salvation is nearer to us now 15
2Co 11:23 with countless beatings, and often near death. 16
Eph 2:13 have been brought near in the blood of Christ. 15
17 preached . . peace to those who were near; 15
Php 2:27 Indeed he was ill, near to death 20
Heb 6: 8 it is worthless and near to being cursed 15
Rev 1: 3 for the time is near. 15
22:10 for the time is near. 15
2Es 5:19 and do not come near me for seven days 27
Tob 3:15 he has . . no near kinsman or kinsman's son 15
Jdt 2:21 near the mountain 22
3: 9 Then he came to the edge of Esdraelon, near Dothan 22
4: 6 opposite the plain near Dothan 22
7: 3 They encamped in the valley near Bethulia 22
18 which is near Chusi beside the brook Mochmur. 22
16:24 her own nearest kindred. 15
Wis 6:19 immortality brings one near to God; 15
Sir 14:24 he who encamps near her house 26
25 he will pitch his tent near her 18
26:12 drinks from any water near him 26
1Mc 3:40 they encamped near Emmaus in the plain. 22
4:18 Gorgias and his force are near us in the hills. 15
7:31 to meet Judas in battle near Caphar-salama. 17
8:12 They have subdued kings far and near 15
2Mc 4:33 a place of sanctuary at Daphne near Antioch. 25
6:11 Others who had assembled in the caves near by 22
7:14 when he was near death, he said 23
11: 8 while they were still near Jerusalem 23
13:14 he pitched his camp near Modein. 21
3Mc 1: 1 and marched out to the region near Raphia 17
25 the elders near the king 21
6:31 those disgracefully treated and near to death 22
4Mc 8: 4 summoned them nearer and said 22
12: 2 He summoned him to come nearer 22
10 Running to the nearest of the braziers 22

near *See also* bring, come, draw, get, go, kin, kinsman, kinswoman, stand.

near of kin 1. שְׁאֵר בָּשָׂר 2. *σῶμα σαρκός*

Lev 18: 6 None of you shall approach any one near of kin 1
Sir 23:16 man who commits fornication with his near of kin 2

very near 1. *σύνεγγυς*

Sir 51: 6 my life was very near to Hades beneath. 1

nearby 1. *παράκειμαι* 2. *πλησίον*

Jdt 5: 5 that dwells in the nearby mountain district 2
7:13 We . . will go up to the tops of the nearby mountains 2
3Mc 6:17 even the nearby valleys resounded with them 1

nearly 1. *μέχρι* 2. *σχεδόν*

Php 2:30 for he nearly died for the work of Christ 1
3Mc 5:14 since it was nearly the middle of the tenth hour 2

necessarily 1. *ἐξ ἀνάγκης*

Heb 7:12 necessarily a change in the law as well. 1

necessary 1. *ἀναγκαῖος* 2. *ἀνάγκη* 3. *δεῖ* 4. *δέον* 5. *ἐπιτήδειος* 6. *καθήκω* 7. *χρεία*

Mat 18: 7 For it is necessary that temptations come 2
Lke 24:26 necessary that the Christ should suffer 3
Act 13:46 necessary that the word of God should be spoken 1
15: 5 It is necessary to circumcise them 3
17: 3 explaining and proving that it was necessary 3
2Co 9: 5 So I thought it necessary to urge the brethren 1
Php 2:25 I have thought it necessary to send to you 1
Heb 8: 3 hence it is necessary for this priest also . . 1
9:23 Thus it was necessary . . 2
Jde 1: 3 I found it necessary to write appealing to you 2
1Es 8:18 whatever else occurs to you as necessary 7
Wis 16: 4 it was necessary 3
Sir 0: 1 it is necessary not only that the readers 3
1Mc 10:39 to meet the necessary expenses of the sanctuary. 6
14:34 whatever was necessary for their restoration. 5
2Mc 1:18 we thought it necessary to notify you 4
9:21 I have deemed it necessary 1
12:39 by that time it had become necessary 7
13:20 Judas sent in to the garrison whatever was necessary. 3
4Mc 14:18 why is it necessary to demonstrate sympathy 3

highly necessary 1. *ἀναγκαῖος*

Sir 0: 3 It seemed highly necessary that I should 1

more necessary 1. *ἀναγκαῖος*

Php 1:24 is more necessary on your account. 1

necessary thing 1. *ἐπάναγκες*

Act 15:28 no greater burden than these necessary things 1

necessity 1. ἀνάγκη 2. χρεία
Act 20:34 these hands ministered to my necessities 2
1Co 7:37 under no necessity 1
9:16 For necessity is laid upon me 1
Tob 4: 9 against the day of necessity. 1
AEs 14:16 Thou knowest my necessity 1

neck 1. גַּרְגְּרוֹת 2. גָּרוֹן 3. מַפְרֶקֶת 4. נֶפֶשׁ 5. עֹרֶף 6. צַוָּאר 7. צַוָּאר (A) 8. αὐχήν 9. τράχηλος
Gen 27:16 his hands and upon the smooth part of his neck; 6
40 you shall break his yoke from your neck. 6
33: 4 embraced him, and fell on his neck and kissed him 6
41:42 of fine linen, and put a gold chain about his neck; 6
45:14 he fell upon his brother Benjamin's neck and wept 6
14 and Benjamin wept upon his neck. 6
46:29 and fell on his neck, and wept on his neck 6
29 and wept on his neck a good while. 6
49: 8 your hand shall be on the neck of your enemies; 5
Lev 5: 8 he shall wring its head from its neck 5
Deu 28:48 he will put a yoke of iron upon your neck, until 6
Jos 10:24 put your feet upon the necks of these kings. 6
24 they came near, and put their feet on their necks. 6
Jdg 5:30 dyed work embroidered for my neck as spoil? 6
8:21 crescents . . on the necks of their camels. 6
26 collars that were about the necks of their camels. 6
1Sm 4:18 Eli fell over backward . . and his neck was broken 3
2Ch 36:13 stiffened his neck and hardened his heart 5
Neh 3: 5 nobles did not put their necks to the work 6
9:16 stiffened their neck and did not obey 5
17 stiffened their neck and appointed a leader 5
29 stubborn shoulder and stiffened their neck 5
Job 16:12 he seized me by the neck and dashed me to pieces; 5
39:19 Do you clothe his neck with strength? 6
41:22 In his neck abides strength 6
Ps 69: 1 O God! For the waters have come up to my neck. 4
75: 5 or speak with insolent neck. 6
105:18 his neck was put in a collar of iron; 4
Prv 1: 9 for they are . . pendants for your neck. 1
3: 3 bind them about your neck 1
22 life for your soul and adornment for your neck. 1
6:21 tie them about your neck. 1
29: 1 He who is often reproved, yet stiffens his neck 5
Sng 1:10 your neck with strings of jewels. 6
4: 4 Your neck is like the tower of David 6
7: 4 Your neck is like an ivory tower. 6
Isa 3:16 haughty and walk with outstretched necks 2
8: 8 overflow and pass on, reaching even to the neck; 6
10:27 his yoke will be destroyed from your neck. 6
30:28 overflowing stream that reaches up to the neck; 6
48: 4 are obstinate, and your neck is an iron sinew 5
52: 2 loose the bonds from your neck, O captive 6
Jer 7:26 or incline their ear, but stiffened their neck. 5
17:23 or incline their ear, but stiffened their neck 5
19:15 because they have stiffened their neck 5
27: 2 thongs and yoke-bars, and put them on your neck. 6
8 and put its neck under the yoke of the king 6
11 nation which will bring its neck under the yoke 6
12 Bring your necks under the yoke of the king 6
28:10 took the yoke-bars from the neck of Jeremiah 6
11 king of Babylon from the neck of all the nations 6
12 yoke-bars from off the neck of Jeremiah 6
14 I have put upon the neck of all these nations 6
30: 8 that I will break the yoke from off their neck 6
Lam 1:14 My transgressions . . they were set upon my neck; 6
5: 5 With a yoke on our necks we are hard driven; 6
Ezk 16:11 bracelets on your arms, and a chain on your neck. 2
21:29 to be laid on the necks of the unhallowed wicked 6
Dan 5: 7 purple, and have a chain of gold about his neck 7
16 purple, and have a chain of gold about your neck 7
29 purple, a chain of gold was put about his neck 7
Hos 10:11 and I spared her fair neck; 6
Mic 2: 3 evil, from which you cannot remove your necks; 6
Hab 3:13 of the wicked, laying him bare from thigh to neck. 6
Mat 18: 6 have a great millstone fastened round his neck 9
Mrk 9:42 if a great millstone were hung round his neck 9
Lke 17: 2 if a millstone were hung round his neck 9
Act 15:10 by putting a yoke upon the neck of the disciples 9
Rom 16: 4 who risked their necks for my life 9
1Es 1:48 he stiffened his neck and hardened his heart 9
3: 6 a necklace about his neck; 9
Jdt 13: 8 she struck his neck twice with all her might 9
16: 9 the sword severed his neck. 9
AEs 15:11 and touched it to her neck; 9
Sir 6:24 Put . . your neck into her collar. 9
30:12 Bow down his neck in his youth *
33:26 Yoke and thong will bow the neck 9
51:26 Put your neck under the yoke 9
Bar 4:25 you . . will tread upon their necks. 9
1Mc 1:61 they hung the infants from their mothers' necks. 9
3Mc 4: 8 their necks encircled with ropes instead of garlands 8
9 some were fastened by the neck to the benches 9

neck *See also* break.

necked 1. עֹרֶף
Exd 32: 9 and behold, it is a stiff-necked people; 1
33: 3 for you are a stiff-necked people. 1
5 You are a stiff-necked people; if for a single 1
34: 9 although it is a stiff-necked people; 1

necklace 1. עֲנָק 2. צַוְּרוֹן 3. μανιάκης
2Ch 3:16 He made chains like a necklace and put them *
Ps 73: 6 Therefore pride is their necklace; 1
Sng 4: 9 with a glance . . with one jewel of your necklace. 2
1Es 3: 6 a necklace about his neck; 3

necromancer 1. דרשׁ אֶל הַמֵּתִים
Deu 18:11 charmer, or a medium, or a wizard, or a necromancer. 1

nectar 1. נֹפֶת
Sng 4:11 Your lips distil nectar, my bride; 1

need 1. דָּבָר 2. מַחְסוֹר 3. צֹרֶךְ 4. חשׁח (A) 5. חַשְׁחָה (A) 6. ἀνάγκη 7. ἀπορέω 8. δεῖ 9. εἰμί 10. ἔνδεια 11. ἐπιδέομαι 12. ἐπιμέλεια 13. ἐπιτήδειος 14. ὀφείλω 15. προσδέομαι 16. πρὸς τὰς χρείας 17. ὑστερέω 18. ὑστέρημα 19. χράομαι 20. χρεία 21. χρείαν ἔχω
Gen 33:15 What need is there? Let me find favor in the sight *
Lev 13:36 the priest need not seek for the yellow hair *
Num 4:26 do all that needs to be done with regard to them. *
Deu 15: 8 lend him sufficient for his need, whatever it may be. 2
18:22 you need not be afraid of him. *
1Ch 23:26 Levites no longer need to carry the tabernacle *
2Ch 2:16 will cut whatever timber you need from Lebanon 3
20:17 You will not need to fight in this battle; *
35: 3 you need no longer carry it upon your shoulders. *
15 did not need to depart from their service *
Ezr 6: 9 whatever is needed . . let that be given to them 5
Job 33: 7 Behold, no fear of me need terrify you; *
Jer 2:24 None who seek her need weary themselves; *
52:34 given him by the king according to his daily need 1
Ezk 39:10 they will not need to take wood out of the field *
Dan 3:16 have no need to answer you in this matter. 4
Mat 3:14 I need to be baptized by you, and do you come to me? 21
6: 8 Father knows what you need before you ask him. 21
9:12 Those who are well have no need of a physician 20
14:16 Jesus said, "They need not go away 20
15: 5 he need not honor his father.' *
21: 3 'The Lord has need of them,' 20
26:65 Why do we still need witnesses? 21
Mrk 2:17 Those who are well have no need of a physician 20
25 when he was in need and was hungry 21
11: 3 say, 'The Lord has need of it 20
14:63 Why do we still need witnesses? 21
Lke 5:31 Those who are well have no need of a physician 20
9:11 cured those who had need of healing. 20
15: 7 who need no repentance. 21
19:31 you shall say this, 'The Lord has need of it. 20
34 they said, "The Lord has need of it. 20
22:71 they said, "What further testimony do we need? 20
Joh 2:25 and needed no one to bear witness of man; 21
13:10 He who has bathed does not need to wash 20
29 Buy what we need for the feast 20
16:30 need none to question you 20
Act 2:45 distributed them to all, as any had need. 20
4:35 distribution was made to each as any had need. 20
17:25 as though he needed anything 15
28:10 they put on board whatever we needed. 16
Rom 12:13 Contribute to the needs of the saints 20
1Co 5:10 since then you would need to go out of the world. 14
12:21 eye cannot say to the hand, "I have no need of you 20
21 the head to the feet, "I have no need of you. 20
16: 2 so that contributions need not be made when I come. *
2Co 11: 9 my needs were supplied by the brethren 18
Eph 4:28 that he may be able to give to those in need. 20
Php 2:25 your messenger and minister to my need 20
4:19 my God will supply every need of yours 20
1Th 1: 8 so that we need not say anything. 20
4: 9 you have no need to have any one write to you 20
5: 1 you have no need to have anything written to you. 20
Tit 3:14 so as to help cases of urgent need 20
Heb 5:12 you need some one to teach you again 21
12 You need milk, not solid food 21
7:11 what further need would there have been 20
27 He has no need . . to offer sacrifices daily 6
10:36 you have need of endurance 20
1Jn 2:27 and you have no need that any one should teach you; 20
3:17 has the world's goods and sees his brother in need 20
Rev 3:17 For you say, I am rich . . and I need nothing; 20
21:23 the city has no need of sun or moon to shine upon it 20
22: 5 they need no light of lamp or sun 20
1Es 1: 4 You need no longer carry it upon your shoulders 9
16 no one needed to depart from his duties 9
Wis 11: 5 they themselves received benefit in their need. 7
13:11 a useful vessel that serves life's needs *
16 it is only an image and has need of help. 20
16:25 according to the desire of those who had need 8
Sir 3:22 you do not need what is hidden. 20
8: 9 learn how to give an answer in time of need. 20
11:12 There is another who is slow and needs help 15
23 Do not say, "What do I need 20
13: 4 if you are in need he will forsake you. 17
6 When he needs you he will deceive you 21
6 will speak to you kindly and say, "What do you need? 20
14: 1 and need not suffer grief for sin. *
15:12 for he had no need of a sinful man. 20
18:25 in the days of wealth think of poverty and need. 10
29: 2 Lend to your neighbor in the time of his need 20
3 on every occasion you will find what you need. 20
9 because of his need do not send him away empty. 10
27 brother has come to stay with me; I need my house. 20
32: 7 Speak, young man, if there is need of you 20
33:31 as your own soul you will need him 11
38: 1 according to your need of him 20
12 let him not leave you, for there is need of him. 20
39:26 Basic to all the needs of man's life 20
33 he will supply every need in its hour. 20
40:26 with it there is no need to seek for help. *
41: 2 one who is in need and is failing in strength 11
42:21 he needs no one to be his counselor. 15
23 remain for ever for every need 20
LJr 1:59 a household utensil that serves its owner's need 19
1Mc 3:28 ordered them to be ready for any need. 20
16:14 and attending to their needs 12
2Mc 2:15 if you have need of them 20
11:18 everything that needed to be brought before him 8
3Mc 6:30 and everything else needed for a festival 13

need *See also* time.

need more urgently 1. ἐπείγω
2Mc 10:19 where he was more urgently needed. 1

no need 1. ἀπροσδεής
1Mc 12: 9 Therefore, though we have no need of these things 1
3Mc 2: 9 though you have no need of anything 1

no need to be ashamed 1. ἀνεπαίσχυντος
2Ti 2:15 a workman who has no need to be ashamed 1

need of nothing 1. ἀπροσδεής
2Mc 14:35 O Lord of all, who hast need of nothing 1

need of repair 1. בֶּדֶק
2Kg 12: 5 wherever any need of repairs is discovered. 1

thing needed 1. ἐπιτήδειος
Jas 2:16 the things needed for the body 1

needful 1. חֹק 2. χρεία
Prv 30: 8 feed me with the food that is needful for me 1
Lke 10:42 one thing is needful 2

needle 1. βελόνη 2. ῥαφίς
Mat 19:24 for a camel to go through the eye of a needle 2
Mrk 10:25 a camel to go through the eye of a needle 2
Lke 18:25 to go through the eye of a needle 1

needlessly 1. διὰ κενῆς 2. δωρεάν
Sir 20:23 needlessly make him an enemy. 2
23:11 if he has sworn needlessly 1
29: 6 he has needlessly made him his enemy 2
7 afraid of being defrauded needlessly. 2

needlework 1. מַעֲשֶׂה
Exd 26:36 a screen . . embroidered with needlework. 1
27:16 fine twined linen, embroidered with needlework; 1
28:39 make a girdle embroidered with needlework. 1
36:37 fine twined linen, embroidered with needlework; 1
38:18 screen . . was embroidered with needlework 1
39:29 scarlet stuff, embroidered with needlework; 1

needs *See* attend.

needy 1. אֶבְיוֹן 2. אִישׁ אֶבְיוֹן 3. בֶּן אֶבְיוֹן 4. דַּל 5. עָנִי 6. δέω 7. ἐνδεής 8. ἐπιδεής 9. ἐπιδέομαι 10. egens
Deu 15:11 wide your hand to . . the needy and to the poor 5
24:14 not oppress a hired servant who is poor and needy 1
1Sm 2: 8 he lifts the needy from the ash heap, to make them 1
Job 5:15 the needy from the hand of the mighty. 1
24:14 that he may kill the poor and needy; 1
Ps 9:18 For the needy shall not always be forgotten 1
12: 5 because the needy groan, I will now arise 1
35:10 the weak and needy from him who despoils him? 1
37:14 bend their bows, to bring down the poor and needy 1
40:17 As for me, I am poor and needy; 1
68:10 goodness, O God, thou didst provide for the needy. 5
69:33 For the LORD hears the needy, and does not despise 1
70: 5 I am poor and needy; hasten to me, O God! 1
72: 4 give deliverance to the needy 3
12 For he delivers the needy when he calls 1
13 He has pity on the weak and the needy 1
13 He has pity . . and saves the lives of the needy. 1
74:21 let the poor and needy praise thy name. 1
82: 4 Rescue the weak and the needy; 1
86: 1 answer me, for I am poor and needy. 1
107:41 he raises up the needy out of affliction 1
109:16 pursued the poor and needy . . to their death. 2
22 poor and needy, and my heart is stricken within 1
31 For he stands at the right hand of the needy 1
113: 7 lifts the needy from the ash heap 1
140:12 LORD . . executes justice for the needy. 1
Prv 14:31 but he who is kind to the needy honors him. 1
30:14 to devour the . . needy from among men. 1
31: 9 maintain the rights of the poor and needy. 1
20 She . . reaches out her hands to the needy. 1
Isa 10: 2 to turn aside the needy from justice and to rob 4

14:30 the poor . . and the needy lie down in safety; 1
25: 4 a stronghold to the needy in his distress 1
26: 6 the feet of the poor, the steps of the needy. 4
32: 7 even when the plea of the needy is right. 1
41:17 the poor and needy seek water, and there is none 1
Jer 5:28 they do not defend the rights of the needy. 1
20:13 For he has delivered the life of the needy 1
22:16 He judged the cause of the poor and needy; 1
Ezk 16:49 but did not aid the poor and needy. 1
18:12 oppresses the poor and needy, commits robbery 1
22:29 they have oppressed the poor and needy 1
Ams 2: 6 for silver, and the needy for a pair of shoes 1
4: 1 Sama'ria, who oppress the poor, who crush the needy 1
5:12 take a bribe, and turn aside the needy in the gate. 1
8: 4 Hear this, you who trample upon the needy 1
6 that we may buy . . the needy for a pair of sandals 1
Act 4:34 There was not a needy person among them 7
2Es 2:20 give to the needy, defend the orphan 10
Sir 4: 1 do not keep needy eyes waiting. 9
5 Do not avert your eye from the needy 6
31: 4 when he rests he becomes needy. 8
34:21 The bread of the needy is the life of the poor; 9
4Mc 2: 8 to lend without interest to the needy 6

neglect 1. לֹא דרשׁ 2. עזב 3. פרע 4. ἀμελέω 5. ἀφίημι 6. ἐγκαταλείπω 7. ἐπιλανθάνομαι 8. παραθεωρέω 9. πάρειμι 10. παρέρχομαι 11. παροράω 12. ὑπεροράω 13. neglego

1Ch 13: 3 for we neglected it in the days of Saul. 1
Neh 10:39 We will not neglect the house of our God. 2
Prv 8:33 Hear instruction and be wise, and do not neglect 3
Mat 23:23 have neglected the weightier matters of the law 5
23 without neglecting the others. 5
Lke 11:42 neglect justice and the love of God 10
42 without neglecting the others. 9
Act 6: 1 neglected in the daily distribution. 8
1Ti 4:14 Do not neglect the gift you have 4
Heb 2: 3 if we neglect such a great salvation 4
10:25 not neglecting to meet together 6
13: 2 Do not neglect to show hospitality to strangers 7
16 Do not neglect to do good 7
1Es 2:20 we think it best not to neglect such a matter 12
2Es 1:34 because . . they have neglected my commandment 13
Tob 4: 3 do not neglect your mother 12
AEs 13:16 Do not neglect thy portion 12
Wis 19:22 thou hast not neglected to help them at all times 12
Sir 7:10 nor neglect to give alms. 11
38:16 do not neglect his burial. 12
2Mc 4:14 neglecting the sacrifices 4
3Mc 1:19 neglecting proper modesty •
6:15 did I neglect them 12

negligent 1. שלה 2. παραβλέπω 3. σχεδιάζω

2Ch 29:11 not now be negligent, for the LORD has chosen you 1
Sir 38: 9 My son, when you are sick do not be negligent 2
Bar 1:19 we have been negligent, in not heeding his voice. 3

negotiate a second time 1. δευτερολογέω

2Mc 13:22 The king negotiated a second time 1

neigh 1. מִצְהָלָה 2. צהל 3. χρεμετίζω

Jer 5: 8 each neighing for his neighbor's wife. 2
8:16 at the sound of the neighing of their stallions 1
13:27 abominations, your adulteries and neighings 1
50:11 as a heifer at grass, and neigh like stallions 2
Sir 33: 6 he neighs under every one who sits on him. 3

neighbor 1. סָבִיב 2. עָמִית 3. קָרֹב 4. רֵעַ 5. רְעוּת 6. שָׁכֵן 7. קָרֵב (A) 8. ἀστυγείτων 9. γειτνιάω 10. γείτων 11. ἕτερος 12. κύκλος 13. παροικία 14. πάροικος 15. περιοικέω 16. περίοικος 17. πλησίον 18. civis 19. proximus 20. vicinus

Exd 3:22 each woman shall ask of her neighbor . . jewelry 6
11: 2 that they ask, every man of his neighbor and every 4
2 that they ask . . every woman of her neighbor 5
12: 4 a man and his neighbor next to his house shall 6
18:16 I decide between a man and his neighbor 4
20:16 not bear false witness against your neighbor. 4
17 You shall not covet your neighbor's house; 4
17 you shall not covet your neighbor's wife 4
17 covet . . anything that is your neighbor's. 4
22: 7 If a man delivers to his neighbor money or goods 4
8 he has put his hand to his neighbor's goods. 4
9 he . . shall pay double to his neighbor. 4
10 If a man delivers to his neighbor an ass or an ox 4
11 has not put his hand to his neighbor's property; 4
14 If a man borrows anything of his neighbor, and it 4
26 ever you take your neighbor's garment in pledge 4
32:27 slay . . every man his neighbor.' 3
Lev 6: 2 by deceiving his neighbor in a matter of deposit 2
2 robbery, or if he has oppressed his neighbor 2
18:20 shall not lie carnally with your neighbor's wife 2
19:13 You shall not oppress your neighbor or rob him 4
15 in righteousness shall you judge your neighbor 2
16 not stand forth against the life of your neighbor 4
17 but you shall reason with your neighbor 2
18 you shall love your neighbor as yourself 4
20:10 commits adultery with the wife of his neighbor 4
24:19 a man causes a disfigurement in his neighbor 2
25:14 if you sell to your neighbor or buy 2
14 If you . . buy from your neighbor 2
15 the jubilee, you shall buy from your neighbor 2
Deu 1: 7 go to . . all their neighbors in the Arabah 6
4:42 who kills his neighbor unintentionally 4
5:20 'Neither . . bear false witness against your neighbor. 4
21 'Neither shall you covet your neighbor's wife; 4
21 not desire your neighbor's house, his field 4
21 not desire . . anything that is your neighbor's.' 4
15: 2 shall release what he has lent to his neighbor; 4
2 he shall not exact it of his neighbor, his brother 4
19: 4 If any one kills his neighbor unintentionally 4
5 into the forest with his neighbor to cut wood 4
5 head slips . . and strikes his neighbor 4
6 not at enmity with his neighbor in time past. •
11 if any man hates his neighbor, and lies in wait 4
14 shall not remove your neighbor's landmark 4
22:24 man because he violated his neighbor's wife; 4
26 man attacking and murdering his neighbor; 4
23:24 When you go into your neighbor's vineyard 4
25 When you go into your neighbor's standing grain 4
25 not put a sickle to your neighbor's standing grain. 4
24:10 When you make your neighbor a loan of any sort 4
27:17 'Cursed . . who removes his neighbor's landmark.' 4
24 'Cursed be he who slays his neighbor in secret.' 4
Jos 9:16 they heard that they were their neighbors 3
20: 5 he killed his neighbor unwittingly 4
1Sm 15:28 and has given it to a neighbor of yours 4
28:17 and given it to your neighbor, David. 4
2Sm 12:11 take your wives . . and give them to your neighbor 4
1Kg 8:31 If a man sins against his neighbor and is 4
2Kg 4: 3 Go outside, borrow vessels of all your neighbors 6
1Ch 12:40 also their neighbors, from as far as Is'sachar 3
2Ch 6:22 If a man sins against his neighbor and is made 4
Job 16:21 like that of a man with his neighbor. 4
31: 9 I have lain in wait at my neighbor's door; 4
Ps 12: 2 Every one utters lies to his neighbor; 4
15: 3 nor takes up a reproach against his neighbor; 3
28: 3 who speak peace with their neighbors 4
31:11 a horror to my neighbors, an object of dread 6
44:13 Thou hast made us the taunt of our neighbors 6
79: 4 We have become a taunt to our neighbors 6
12 sevenfold into the bosom of our neighbors 6
80: 6 Thou dost make us the scorn of our neighbors; 6
89:41 he has become the scorn of his neighbors. 6
101: 5 Him who slanders his neighbors secretly 4
Prv 3:28 Do not say to your neighbor, "Go, and come again 4
29 Do not plan evil against your neighbor 4
6: 1 if you have become surety for your neighbor 4
3 for you have come into your neighbor's power 4
3 go, hasten, and importune your neighbor. 4
29 So is he who goes in to his neighbor's wife; 4
11: 9 mouth the godless man would destroy his neighbor 4
12 He who belittles his neighbor lacks sense 4
14:20 The poor is disliked even by his neighbor 4
21 He who despises his neighbor is a sinner 4
16:29 A man of violence entices his neighbor 4
17:18 becomes surety in the presence of his neighbor. 4
21:10 his neighbor finds no mercy in his eyes. 4
24:28 not a witness against your neighbor without cause 4
25: 8 do in the end, when your neighbor puts you to shame? 4
9 Argue your case with your neighbor himself 4
17 Let your foot be seldom in your neighbor's house 4
18 who bears false witness against his neighbor 4
26:19 man who deceives his neighbor and says, "I am only 4
27:10 Better is a neighbor who is near than a brother 6
14 He who blesses his neighbor with a loud voice 4
29: 5 A man who flatters his neighbor spreads a net 4
Ecc 4: 4 come from a man's envy of his neighbor. 4
Isa 3: 5 oppress . . his fellow and every man his neighbor; 4
9:20 not satisfied; each devours his neighbor's flesh 7
19: 2 and every man against his neighbor 4
41: 6 Every one helps his neighbor 4
Jer 5: 8 each neighing for his neighbor's wife. 4
6:21 together, neighbor and friend shall perish. 6
9: 4 Let every one beware of his neighbor 4
4 and every neighbor goes about as a slanderer. 4
5 Every one deceives his neighbor 4
8 each speaks peaceably to his neighbor 4
20 a lament, and each to her neighbor a dirge. 5
12:14 says the LORD concerning all my evil neighbors 6
19: 9 and every one shall eat the flesh of his neighbor 4
22: 8 and every man will say to his neighbor 4
13 who makes his neighbor serve him for nothing 4
23:35 Thus shall you say, every one to his neighbor 4
29:23 committed adultery with their neighbors' wives 4
31:34 And no longer shall each man teach his neighbor 4
34:15 by proclaiming liberty, each to his neighbor 4
17 every one to his brother and to his neighbor; 4
49:10 destroyed, and his brothers, and his neighbors; 6
18 Sodom and Gomor'rah and their neighbor cities 6
50:40 Sodom and Gomor'rah and their neighbor cities 6
Lam 1:17 Jacob that his neighbors should be his foes; 1
Ezk 16:26 with the Egyptians, your lustful neighbors 6
57 for the daughters of Edom and all her neighbors 1
18: 6 does not defile his neighbor's wife 4
11 upon the mountains, defiles his neighbor's wife 4
15 does not defile his neighbor's wife 4
22:11 commits abomination with his neighbor's wife; 4
12 and make gain of your neighbors by extortion; 4
28:24 thorn to hurt them among all their neighbors 1
26 execute judgments upon all their neighbors 1
33:26 each of you defiles his neighbor's wife; 4
Mic 7: 5 Put no trust in a neighbor 4
Hab 2:15 Woe to him who makes his neighbors drink 4
Zec 3:10 every one of you will invite his neighbor 4
Mat 5:43 was said, 'You shall love your neighbor and hate 17
19:19 You shall love your neighbor as yourself. 17
22:39 You shall love your neighbor as yourself. 17
Mrk 12:31 You shall love your neighbor as yourself 17
33 to love one's neighbor as oneself 17
Lke 1:58 her neighbors and kinsfolk heard 16
65 fear came on all their neighbors 15
10:27 and your neighbor as yourself. 17
29 And who is my neighbor? 17
36 proved neighbor to the man 17
14:12 your brothers or your kinsmen or rich neighbors 10
15: 6 he calls together his friends and his neighbors 10
9 she calls together her friends and neighbors 10
Joh 9: 8 The neighbors and those who had seen him before 10
Act 7:27 the man who was wronging his neighbor 17
Rom 13: 8 he who loves his neighbor has fulfilled the law. 11
9 You shall love your neighbor as yourself. 17
10 Love does no wrong to a neighbor; 17
15: 2 let each of us please his neighbor for his good 17
1Co 10:24 the good of his neighbor. 11
Gal 5:14 You shall love your neighbor as yourself. 17
6: 4 in himself alone and not in his neighbor. 11
Eph 4:25 let every one speak the truth with his neighbor 17
Jas 2: 8 You shall love your neighbor as yourself 17
4:12 But who are you that you judge your neighbor? 17
2Es 5:11 one country shall ask its neighbor 19
9:45 I and my husband and all my neighbors 18
10: 2 and all my neighbors attempted to console me 18
16:19 A man shall have no pity upon his neighbors 19
16:70 For in many places and in neighboring cities 20
Tob 2: 8 my neighbors laughed at me and said 17
Jdt 7: 4 and every one said to his neighbor 17
10:19 and every one said to his neighbor 17
Sir 5:12 If you have understanding, answer your neighbor; 17
6:17 as he is, so is his neighbor also. 17
9:14 As much as you can, aim to know your neighbors 17
10: 6 Do not be angry with your neighbor for any injury 17
13:15 every person his neighbor; 17
15: 5 She will exalt him above his neighbors 17
16: 8 He did not spare the neighbors of Lot 13
17:14 gave commandment . . concerning his neighbor. 17
18:13 The compassion of man is for his neighbor 17
19:14 Question a neighbor, perhaps he did not say it 17
17 Question your neighbor before you threaten him; 17
22:23 Gain the trust of your neighbor in his poverty 17
25: 1 friendship between neighbors 17
18 Her husband takes his meals among the neighbors 17
27:18 destroyed the friendship of your neighbor. 17
19 you have let your neighbor go 17
28: 2 Forgive your neighbor the wrong he has done 17
7 do not be angry with your neighbor 17
29: 1 He that shows mercy will lend to his neighbor 17
2 Lend to your neighbor in the time of his need 17
2 in turn, repay your neighbor promptly. 17
5 in speaking of his neighbor's money 17
14 A good man will be surety for his neighbor 17
20 Assist your neighbor according to your ability 17
31:14 do not crowd your neighbor at the dish. •
15 Judge your neighbor's feelings by your own 17
31 Do not reprove your neighbor at a banquet of wine 17
34:22 To take away a neighbor's living is to murder him; 17
Bar 4: 9 and she said: "Hearken, you neighbors of Zion 14
14 Let the neighbors of Zion come 14
24 the neighbors of Zion have now seen your capture 14
Sus 1:62 had wickedly planned to do to their neighbor; 17
1Mc 2:40 each said to his neighbor 17
12:33 Askalon and the neighboring strongholds 17
2Mc 4:32 he had sold to Tyre and the neighboring cities. 12
6: 8 was issued to the neighboring Greek cities 8
9:25 the neighbors to my kingdom 9
3Mc 1: 6 decided to visit the neighboring cities 17
3:10 some of their neighbors and friends 10
4Mc 2: 5 You shall not covet your neighbor's wife 17
5 or anything that is your neighbor's 17

neighborhood 1. בּוֹאֲךָ 2. ὁ περί 3. ὅριον 4. παροίκησις 5. χώρα

Jdg 6: 4 of the land, as far as the neighborhood of Gaza 1
11:33 from Aro'er to the neighborhood of Minnith 1
Mat 8:34 they begged him to leave their neighborhood. 3
Mrk 5:17 to beg Jesus to depart from their neighborhood. 3
6:55 and ran about the whole neighborhood 5
Act 28: 7 Now in the neighborhood of that place were lands 2
Sir 21:28 is hated in his neighborhood. 4

woman of the neighborhood 1. שָׁכֵן

Rut 4:17 the women of the neighborhood gave him a name 1

neither 1. אַיִן 2. אַל 3. אִם 4. בַּל 5. בִּלְתִּי 6. גַּם אַיִן 7. גַּם לֹא 8. וְ 9. וְאַיִן 10. וְאַל 11. וְלֹא 12. כִּי לֹא 13. לֹא

14. לֹא וְ 15. לֹא מִן 16. מִן 17. καὶ γὰρ οὐ 18. μή
19. μηδέ 20. μήτε 21. οὐ 22. οὐδέ 23. οὐδείς 24. οὔτε
25. οὕτως οὐδέ 26. nec 27. neque 28. non

Gen 3: 3 garden, neither shall you touch it, lest you die.' 11
8:21 neither will I ever again destroy every living 11
31:29 you speak to Jacob neither good nor bad.' 16
45: 6 there will be neither plowing nor harvest. 1
Exd 10: 6 as neither your fathers nor your grandfathers *
15 neither tree nor plant of the field, through all *
12:39 could not tarry, neither had they prepared 7
34:24 neither shall any man desire your land, when you 13
25 neither shall the sacrifice of the feast 13
28 he neither ate bread nor drank water. 13
36: 6 proclaimed throughout the camp, "Let neither man 2
Lev 3:17 a statute . . that you eat neither fat nor blood *
7:18 neither shall it be credited to him 13
17:12 neither shall any stranger who sojourns among *
18:23 neither shall any woman give herself to a beast *
19: 9 neither shall you gather the gleanings after *
10 neither shall you gather the fallen grapes *
21: 7 neither shall they marry a woman divorced *
12 neither shall he go out of the sanctuary *
22:25 neither shall you offer as the bread of your God *
23:14 you shall eat neither bread nor grain parched *
25:11 A jubilee . . in it you shall neither sow 13
26:44 I will not spurn them, neither will I abhor them 8
27:33 neither shall he exhange it; and if he exchanges 8
Num 6: 7 Neither for his father nor for his mother *
14:44 neither the ark of the covenant of the LORD *
18:20 neither shall you have any portion among them; 13
20:17 neither will we drink water from a well; 11
23:25 Neither curse them at all, nor bless them at all. 7
Deu 2:27 turn aside neither to the right nor to the left. 13
4:28 gods . . that neither see, nor hear, nor eat, nor smell. 13
5:18 'Neither shall you commit adultery. 11
19 'Neither shall you steal. 11
20 'Neither shall you bear false witness 11
21 'Neither shall you covet your neighbor's wife; 11
7:16 your eye shall not pity them; neither shall you 11
9: 9 I neither ate bread nor drank water. 13
18 I neither ate bread nor drank water 13
13: 6 other gods,' which neither you nor your fathers 13
21: 4 valley . . which is neither plowed nor sown 13
7 neither did our eyes see it shed. 13
23:17 neither shall there be a cult prostitute 11
26:13 not transgressed . . neither have I forgotten 11
28:36 nation that neither you nor your fathers 13
39 but you shall neither drink of the wine nor 13
64 gods . . neither you nor your fathers have known. 13
30:11 commandment . . not too hard for you, neither 11
13 Neither is it beyond the sea, that you should say 11
Jos 1: 9 be not frightened, neither be dismayed; 10
6:10 You shall not shout . . neither shall any word go 11
23: 6 turning aside from it neither to the right hand 5
Jdg 11:34 beside her he had neither son nor daughter. 1
13:14 from the vine, neither let her drink wine 10
21:22 we did not take . . neither did you give them 12
1Sm 1:15 I have drunk neither wine nor strong drink 14
6:12 they turned neither to the right nor to the left 13
13:22 there was neither sword nor spear found 13
16: 8 And he said, "Neither has the LORD chosen this one. 7
9 And he said, "Neither has the LORD chosen this one. 7
20:31 neither you nor your kingdom shall be 13
21: 8 I have brought neither my sword nor my weapons 7
27: 9 David . . left neither man nor woman alive 11
11 And David saved neither man nor woman alive 11
2Sm 2:19 he turned neither to the right . . nor to the left 13
13:22 But Ab'salom spoke to Amnon neither good nor bad; 15
14: 7 and leave to my husband neither name nor remnant *
19:24 he had neither dressed his feet, nor . . his beard 13
21: 4 neither is it for us to put any man to death 9
1Kg 3:26 It shall be neither mine nor yours; divide it. 7
5: 4 there is neither adversary nor misfortune. 1
6: 7 neither hammer nor axe nor any tool of iron 13
11: 2 You shall not . . neither shall they with you 13
13: 9 You shall neither eat bread, nor drink water 13
16 neither will I eat bread nor drink water with you 13
17 You shall neither eat bread nor drink water 13
17: 1 there shall be neither dew nor rain these years *
16 neither did the cruse of oil fail 11
22:31 Fight with neither small nor great, but only 13
2Kg 2:21 neither death nor miscarriage shall come 13
3:14 I would neither look at you, nor see you. 3
4:23 Why . . today? It is neither new moon nor sabbath. 13
18:12 not obey . . they neither listened nor obeyed. 11
2Ch 18:30 Fight with neither small nor great 13
Ezr 9:12 neither take their daughters for your sons *
10: 6 neither eating bread nor drinking water; *
Neh 4:23 neither I nor my brethren nor my servants *
5:14 neither I nor my brethren ate the food allowance *
Est 2: 7 Esther . . for she had neither father nor mother; 1
4:16 a fast . . and neither eat nor drink for three days 2
5: 9 Haman saw . . that he neither rose nor trembled 13
Ps 82: 5 They have neither knowledge nor understanding 13
121: 4 keeps Israel will neither slumber nor sleep. 13
Prv 30: 8 give me neither poverty nor riches; *
Ecc 7:17 Be not wicked overmuch, neither be a fool; 10
8:13 the wicked, neither will he prolong his days 11

16 how neither day nor night one's eyes see sleep; 6
Sng 8: 7 cannot quench love, neither can floods drown it. 11
Isa 2: 4 neither shall they learn war any more. 11
3: 7 in my house there is neither bread nor mantle 1
23: 4 I have neither travailed nor given birth 13
4 I have neither reared young men nor brought up 13
30: 5 that brings neither help nor profit 13
44: 9 their witnesses neither see nor know 4
49:10 neither scorching wind nor sun shall smite them 11
51:14 go down to the Pit, neither shall his bread fail. 11
55: 8 neither are your ways my ways, says the LORD. 11
Jer 9:16 whom neither they nor their fathers have known; 13
10: 5 cannot do evil, neither is it in them to do good. 6
16:13 which neither you nor your fathers have known 13
19: 4 neither they nor their fathers nor the kings 13
23: 4 neither shall any be missing, says the LORD. 11
25: 4 You have neither listened nor inclined 11
35: 6 shall not drink wine, neither you nor your sons *
36:24 Yet neither the king, nor any of his servants 13
37: 2 But neither he nor his servants nor the people 13
44: 3 knew not, neither they, nor you, nor your fathers. *
51:62 nothing shall dwell in it, neither man nor beast 16
Ezk 7:11 neither shall there be preeminence among them. 11
14:16 they would deliver neither sons nor daughters; 3
18 they would deliver neither sons nor daughters 13
20 they would deliver neither son nor daughter; 3
22:26 neither have they taught the difference 11
29:18 yet neither he nor his army got anything 11
43: 7 neither they, nor their kings, by their harlotry *
Dan 11:20 shall be broken, neither in anger nor in battle. 11
24 neither his fathers nor his fathers' fathers 13
Hos 1:10 sea, which can be neither measured nor numbered; 13
Jon 3: 7 Let neither man nor beast, herd nor flock 2
Mic 4: 3 neither shall they learn war any more; 11
Zep 1:18 Neither their silver nor their gold shall be 7
Zec 8:10 neither was there any safety from the foe 1
14: 6 that day there shall be neither cold nor frost. 13
Mal 4: 1 it will leave them neither root nor branch. 13
Mat 6:15 neither will your Father forgive 22
20 in heaven, where neither moth nor rust consumes 24
26 of the air: they neither sow nor reap nor gather 21
28 how they grow; they neither toil nor spin; 21
9:17 Neither is new wine put into old wineskins 22
11:18 For John came neither eating nor drinking 20
21:27 he said to them, "Neither will I tell you 22
22:29 neither the scriptures nor the power of God. 18
30 they neither marry nor are given in marriage 24
23:10 Neither be called masters 19
13 you neither enter yourselves 21
25:13 you know neither the day nor the hour. 21
Mrk 11:33 Neither will I tell you by what authority 22
12:24 you know neither the scriptures nor the power of God 18
25 they neither marry nor are given in marriage 24
14:68 I neither know nor understand what you mean. 24
Lke 12:24 Consider the ravens: they neither sow nor reap 21
24 they have neither storehouse nor barn 21
27 they neither toil nor spin 21
14:35 is fit neither for the land nor for the dunghill; 24
16:31 neither will they be convinced 22
18: 2 a judge who neither feared God nor regarded man; 21
4 Though I neither fear God nor regard man 21
20: 8 Jesus said to them, "Neither will I tell you 22
35 neither marry nor are given in marriage 24
23:15 neither did Herod, for he sent him back to us. 22
Joh 1:25 if you are neither the Christ, nor Elijah 21
4:21 neither on this mountain nor in Jerusalem 24
8:11 Jesus said, "Neither do I condemn you 22
19 Jesus answered, "You know neither me nor my Father 24
14:17 because it neither sees him nor knows him 21
27 neither let them be afraid. 19
15: 4 neither can you, unless you abide in me. 25
Act 8:21 You have neither part nor lot in this matter 24
9: 9 neither ate nor drank. 21
15:10 neither our fathers nor we have been able to bear? 24
19:37 neither sacrilegious nor blasphemers 24
23:12 an oath neither to eat nor drink 20
21 an oath neither to eat nor drink 20
24:13 Neither can they prove to you 22
25: 8 Neither against the law . . nor . . the temple 24
27:20 when neither sun nor stars appeared for many a day 20
Rom 8:38 For I am sure that neither death, nor life 24
11:21 neither will he spare you. 22
1Co 3: 7 neither he who plants nor he who waters is 24
6: 9 neither the immoral, nor idolaters 24
7:19 For neither circumcision counts for anything *
11: 9 Neither was man created for woman 17
Gal 3:28 There is neither Jew nor Greek 21
28 there is neither slave nor free 21
28 there is neither male nor female 21
5: 6 neither circumcision nor uncircumcision 24
6:15 For neither circumcision counts for anything 24
Heb 7: 3 has neither beginning of days nor end of life 20
10: 8 Thou hast neither desired nor taken pleasure in 21
Rev 3:15 'I know your works: you are neither cold nor hot. 24
16 you are lukewarm, and neither cold nor hot 24
7:16 shall hunger no more, neither thirst any more; 22
21: 4 neither shall there be mourning nor crying 24
2Es 2:12 they shall neither toil nor become weary. 28
4: 8 neither did I ever ascend into heaven.' 27

5:44 neither can the world hold at one time those 26
7:105 neither shall any one lay a burden on another ‡
10: 4 and I will neither eat nor drink 27
12:48 neither forsaken you nor withdrawn from you 28
13: 9 he neither lifted his hand nor held a spear 28
15: 8 neither will I tolerate their . . practices. 26
Jdt 7: 4 neither the high mountains nor the valleys 24
Wis 6:23 neither will I travel in the company of . . envy 24
7: 9 Neither did I liken to her any priceless gem 22
12:13 For neither is there any god besides thee 24
14:13 neither have they existed from the beginning 24
15: 4 neither has the evil intent . . misled us 24
15 these have neither the use of their eyes to see 24
16:12 For neither herb nor poultice cured them 24
Sir 16:27 they neither hunger nor grow weary 24
23: 6 Let neither gluttony nor lust overcome me *
30:19 it can neither eat nor smell 24
35:18 neither will he be patient with them 22
38:32 men can neither sojourn nor live there. 21
LJr 1:66 For they can neither curse nor bless kings; 24
1Mc 12:36 so that its garrison could neither buy nor sell. 20
15:33 neither taken . . nor seized foreign property 24
2Mc 6: 6 A man could neither keep the sabbath 24
3Mc 3: 7 these people were loyal neither to the king 20
4:11 they could neither communicate 19
4Mc 2: 9 he neither gleans his harvest 20
7: 6 you neither defiled your sacred teeth 21
8:27 the youths . . neither said any of these things 23
15:21 Neither the melodies of sirens nor . . swans 21

nephew 1. ἐξάδελφος

Tob 1:22 He was my nephew. 1
11:18 Ahikar and his nephew Nadab came 1

nephthar 1. νεφθαρ

2Mc 1:36 his associates called this "nephthar" 1

nest 1. קֵן 2. קנן 3. שׁכן 4. κατασκήνωσις

Num24:21 your nest is set in the rock; 1
Deu 22: 6 come upon a bird's nest, in any tree or on the ground 1
32:11 Like an eagle that stirs up its nest 1
Job 29:18 Then I thought, ' shall die in my nest 1
39:27 the eagle mounts up and makes his nest on high? 1
Ps 84: 3 swallow a nest for herself 1
Prv 27: 8 Like a bird that strays from its nest 1
Isa 10:14 found like a nest the wealth of the peoples; 1
34:15 There shall the owl nest and lay and hatch 2
Jer 22:23 O inhabitant of Lebanon, nested among the cedars 2
48:28 Be like the dove that nests 2
49:16 Though you make your nest as high as the eagle's 1
Ezk 17:23 in . . its branches birds of every sort will nest. 3
Obd 1: 4 though your nest is set among the stars 1
Hab 2: 9 evil gain for his house, to set his nest on high 1
Mat 8:20 Foxes have holes, and birds of the air have nests; 4
Lke 9:58 Foxes have holes, and birds of the air have nests; 4

nest *See also* build, make.

make a nest 1. קנן

Ezk 31: 6 birds of the air made their nests in its boughs; 1

nestling 1. קֵן 2. ἐννοσσοποιέομαι

Isa 16: 2 fluttering birds, like scattered nestlings 1
4Mc 14:16 hatch the nestlings and ward off the intruder. 2

net 1. חֵרֶם 2. מַכְמֹר 3. מִכְמָר 4. מִכְמֶרֶת 5. מָצוֹד
6. מְצוֹדָה 7. מְצוּדָה 8. רֶשֶׁת 9. שְׂבָכָה
10. ἀμφίβληστρον 11. δίκτυον 12. σαγήνη

Exd 27: 4 upon the net you shall make four bronze rings 8
5 the net shall extend halfway down the altar. 8
1Kg 7:17 nets of checker work with wreaths of chain work 9
17 a net for the one capital, and a net for the other 11
17 the one capital, and a net for the other capital. 11
Job 18: 8 For he is cast into a net by his own feet 8
19: 6 put me in the wrong, and closed his net about me. 5
Ps 9:15 in the net . . has their own foot been caught. 8
10: 9 he seizes the poor when he draws him into his net. 8
25:15 for he will pluck my feet out of the net. 8
31: 4 take me out of the net which is hidden for me 8
35: 7 For without cause they hid their net for me; 8
8 let the net which they hid ensnare them; 8
57: 6 They set a net for my steps; my soul was bowed down. 8
66:11 Thou didst bring us into the net; 7
140: 5 trap for me, and with cords they have spread a net 8
141:10 Let the wicked together fall into their own nets 2
Prv 1:17 For in vain is a net spread in the sight of any bird; 8
29: 5 flatters his neighbor spreads a net for his feet. 8
Ecc 7:26 the woman whose heart is snares and nets 1
9:12 Like fish which are taken in an evil net 6
Isa 19: 8 they . . languish who spread nets upon the water. 4
51:20 the head of every street like an antelope in a net; 3
Lam 1:13 he spread a net for my feet; he turned me back; 8
Ezk 12:13 I will spread my net over him, and he shall be taken 8
17:20 I will spread my net over him, and he shall be taken 8
19: 8 they spread their net over him; he was taken 8
26: 5 midst of the sea a place for the spreading of nets; 1
14 you shall be a place for the spreading of nets; 1
32: 3 Thus says the Lord GOD: I will throw my net over you 8
47:10 it will be a place for the spreading of nets; 1

Hos 5: 1 a snare at Mizpah, and a net spread upon Tabor. 8
7:12 As they go, I will spread over them my net; 8
Mic 7: 2 and each hunts his brother with a net. 1
Hab 1:15 he drags them out with his net 1
16 Therefore he sacrifices to his net 1
17 Is he then to keep on emptying his net 1
Mat 4:18 Andrew his brother, casting a net into the sea; 10
20 Immediately they left their nets and followed 11
21 with Zeb'edee their father, mending their nets 11
13:47 like a net which was thrown into the sea 12
Mrk 1:18 immediately they left their nets and followed 11
19 who were in their boat mending the nets. 11
Lke 5: 2 were washing their nets. 11
4 and let down your nets for a catch. 11
5 But at your word I will let down the nets. 11
6 as their nets were breaking 11
Joh 21: 6 Cast the net on the right side of the boat 11
8 dragging the net full of fish 11
11 hauled the net ashore, full of large fish, 153 11
11 although there were so many, the net was not torn. 11

net *See also* cast.

nether 1. תַּחְתִּי

Job 41:24 hard as a stone, hard as the nether millstone. 1
Ezk 26:20 I will make you to dwell in the nether world 1
31:14 to death, to the nether world among mortal men 1
16 will be comforted in the nether world. 1
18 down with the trees of Eden to the nether world; 1
32:18 to the nether world, to those who have gone down 1
24 went down uncircumcised into the nether world 1
2Pe 2: 4 God . . committed them to pits of nether gloom •
17 the nether gloom of darkness has been reserved. •

nether *See also* gloom.

nettle 1. חָרוּל 2. קִמּוֹשׁ

Job 30: 7 under the nettles they huddle together. 1
Prv 24:31 ground was covered with nettles 1
Isa 34:13 nettles and thistles in its fortresses. 2
Hos 9: 6 Nettles shall possess their precious things 2
Zep 2: 9 like Gomor'rah, a land possessed by nettles 1

network 1. רֶשֶׁת 2. שְׂבָכָה

Exd 27: 4 also make for it a grating, a network of bronze; 1
38: 4 made . . a network of bronze, under its ledge 1
1Kg 7:18 in two rows round about upon the one network 2
20 projection which was beside the network; 2
41 the two networks to cover the two bowls 2
42 400 pomegranates for the two networks 2
42 two rows of pomegranates for each network 2
2Kg 25:17 a network and pomegranates, all of bronze 2
17 the second pillar had the like, with the network. 2
2Ch 4:12 the two networks to cover the two bowls 2
13 400 pomegranates for the two networks 2
13 two rows of pomegranates for each network 2
Jer 52:22 a network and pomegranates, all of bronze 2
23 pomegranates . . upon the network round about. 2

never 1. אַיִן 2. אַל 3. אַל לְעוֹלָם 4. בַּל 5. בַּל לָנֶצַח 6. בַּל לְעוֹלָם 7. וְלֹא 8. לֹא 9. לֹא יֹסֵף 10. לֹא כָּל הַיָּמִים 11. לֹא לָנֶצַח 12. לֹא לְעוֹלָם 13. לֹא מֵעוֹלָם 14. לֹא עַד עוֹלָם 15. לֹא עוֹד 16. לֹא עוֹלָם 17. לְבִלְתִּי 18. נֵצַח 19. תָּמִיד לֹא 20. לָא (A) 21. לָא לְעָלְמִין (A) 22. εἰ 23. μή 24. μὴ γίνομαι 25. μηδαμῶς 26. μηδέ 27. μηδέποτε 28. μή εἰς τὸν αἰῶνα 29. μὴ τὸ σύνολον 30. οὐ 31. οὐδέ 32. οὐδὲ μή 33. οὐδέποτε 34. οὐθὲν ἕως τοῦ αἰῶνος 35. οὐκ εἰς τὸν αἰῶνα 36. οὐ μή 37. οὐ μή εἰς τὸν αἰῶνα 38. οὐ μὴ ἔτι 39. οὐ μήποτε 40. οὔτε 41. οὔτε πώποτε 42. οὐχ ἕως αἰῶνος 43. ποτέ 44. πώποτε 45. in sempiterno 46. non 47. non umquam 48. numquam 49. nusquam

Gen 8:21 I will never again curse the ground 9
41:19 gaunt and thin, such as I had never seen in all 8
44:28 torn to pieces; and I have never seen him since. 8
Exd 9:18 heavy hail . . such as never has been in Egypt 8
24 very heavy hail, such as had never been in all 8
10:14 swarm of locusts as had never been before 8
11: 6 a great cry . . such as there has never been 8
14:13 Egyptians . . you shall never see again. 9
Lev 18:30 keep my charge never to practice any of these 17
30 and never to defile yourselves by them 8
Num19: 2 red heifer . . upon which a yoke has never come. 8
Deu 13:11 shall . . never again do any such wickedness 7
15:11 For the poor will never cease out of the land; 8
17:16 You shall never return that way again.' 9
19:20 rest . . shall never again commit any such evil 9
21: 3 heifer which has never been worked 8
28:68 promised that you should never make again; 9
32:17 They sacrificed to . . gods they had never known 8
17 new gods . . your fathers had never dreaded. 8
Jdg 2: 1 I said, 'I will never break my covenant with you 16
11:39 She had never known a man. 8
16:17 A razor has never come upon my head; for I have been •
19:30 Such a thing has never happened or been seen 8
1Sm 6: 7 two . . cows upon which there has never come a yoke 8
2Sm 3:29 may the house of Jo'ab never be without one who has 2
12:10 the sword shall never depart from your house 14
14:10 bring him . . and he shall never touch you again. 15
1Kg 1: 6 His father had never at any time displeased him 8
8:25 There shall never fail you a man before me to sit 8
10:20 The like of it was never made in any kingdom. 8
22: 8 I hate him, for he never prophesies good 8
1Ch 16:30 yea, the world stands firm, never to be moved. 4
2Ch 6:16 'There shall never fail you a man before me to sit 8
9:11 there never was seen the like of them before 8
19 The like of it was never made in any kingdom. 8
18: 7 never prophesies good concerning me, but always 1
Ezr 9:12 never seek their peace or prosperity 14
Est 9:28 Purim . . never fall into disuse among the Jews 8
Job 3:16 as infants that never see the light? 8
7: 7 my eye will never again see good. 8
8:18 it will deny him, saying, 'I have never seen you.' 8
21:25 bitterness of soul, never having tasted of good. 8
24: 1 why do those who know him never see his days? 8
30:27 My heart is in turmoil, and is never still; 8
Ps 10:11 he has hidden his face, he will never see it. 5
15: 5 He who does these things shall never be moved. 12
30: 6 I said in my prosperity, "I shall never be moved. 6
31: 1 let me never be put to shame; 3
34: 5 be radiant; so your faces shall never be ashamed. 2
49: 9 to live on for ever, and never see the Pit. 8
55:22 he will never permit the righteous to be moved. 12
58: 8 like the untimely birth that never sees the sun. 4
71: 1 I take refuge; let me never be put to shame! 3
77: 7 spurn for ever, and never again be favorable? 9
80:18 Then we will never turn back from thee; 8
89:48 What man can live and never see death? 8
93: 1 world is established; it shall never be moved; 4
96:10 world is established, it shall never be moved; 4
104: 5 so that it should never be shaken. 4
112: 6 For the righteous will never be moved; 12
119:93 I will never forget thy precepts; 12
141: 5 but let the oil of the wicked never anoint my head; 2
Prv 10:30 The righteous will never be removed 6
12: 3 root of the righteous will never be moved. 4
27:20 Sheol and Abaddon are never satisfied 8
20 never satisfied are the eyes of man. 8
30:15 Three things are never satisfied; 8
15 never satisfied; four never say, "Enough 8
16 fire which never says, "Enough. 8
Ecc 4: 8 and his eyes are never satisfied with riches 8
8 no end to all his toil . . so that he never asks •
7:20 not a . . man on earth who does good and never sins. 8
Sng 7: 2 navel is a . . bowl that never lacks mixed wine. 2
Isa 13:20 It will never be inhabited or dwelt 11
25: 2 is a city no more, it will never be rebuilt. 12
33:20 tent, whose stakes will never be plucked up 5
48: 7 before today you have never heard of them 8
8 You have never heard, you have never known 8
8 You have never heard, you have never known 8
19 their name would never be cut off or destroyed 8
51: 6 for ever, and my deliverance will never be ended. 8
56:11 a mighty appetite; they never have enough. 8
62: 6 day and all the night they shall never be silent. 19
63:19 like those over whom thou hast never ruled 13
Jer 19:11 potter's vessel, so that it can never be mended. 15
20:11 Their eternal dishonor will never be forgotten. 8
33:17 David shall never lack a man to sit on the throne 8
18 and the Levitical priests shall never lack a man 8
35:19 shall never lack a man to stand before me. 10
50: 5 covenant which will never be forgotten. 8
Lam 3:22 The steadfast love of the LORD never ceases 8
22 his mercies never come to an end; 8
Ezk 4:14 Ah Lord GOD! behold, I have never defiled myself; 8
14 up till now I have never eaten what died of itself 8
5: 9 I will do with you what I have never yet done 8
16:16 the like has never been, nor ever shall be. 8
20:32 What is in your mind shall never happen 8
26:14 you shall never be rebuilt; 15
21 you will never be found again, says the Lord GOD. 12
Dan 2:44 set up a kingdom which shall never be destroyed 21
6:26 his kingdom shall never be destroyed 20
12: 1 such as never has been since there was a nation 8
Hos 12: 8 but all his riches can never offset the guilt 8
Jol 2: 2 their like has never been from of old 8
Ams 7: 8 my people Israel; I will never again pass by them; 9
13 but never again prophesy at Bethel 9
8: 2 my people Israel; I will never again pass by them. 9
7 Surely I will never forget any of their deeds. 18
Nah 1:15 never again shall the wicked come against you 9
Hab 1: 4 the law is slacked and justice never goes forth. 11
2: 5 as wide as Sheol; like death he has never enough. 8
Hag 1: 6 you eat, but you never have enough; 1
6 you drink, but you never have your fill; 1
Mat 5:20 Pharisees, you will never enter the kingdom 36
26 you will never get out till you have paid the last 36
7:23 And then will I declare to them, 'I never knew you; 33
9:33 Never was anything like this seen in Israel. 33
13:14 You shall indeed hear but never understand 36
14 and you shall indeed see but never perceive. 36
16:22 God forbid, Lord! This shall never happen to you. 36
18: 3 you will never enter the kingdom of heaven. 36
13 more than over the 99 that never went astray. 23
21:16 Yes, have you never read 33
21 if you have faith and never doubt 23
42 Have you never read in the scriptures 33
24:21 until now, no, and never will be. 36
26:33 I will never fall away. 33
Mrk 2:12 saying, "We never saw anything like this! 33
25 he said to them, "Have you never read what David did 33
3:29 never has forgiveness 35
13:19 never will be. 36
Lke 12:59 I tell you, you will never get out 36
15:29 I never disobeyed your command 33
29 yet you never gave me a kid, that I might make merry 33
23:29 the wombs that never bore 30
29 and the breasts that never gave suck!' 30
Joh 4:14 water that I shall give him will never thirst 37
5:37 His voice you have never heard 41
37 his form you have never seen; 40
6:35 he who believes in me shall never thirst. 36
7:15 this man has learning, when he has never studied? 23
8:33 and have never been in bondage to any one 44
51 if any one keeps my word, he will never see death. 37
52 he will never taste death.' 37
9:32 Never since the world began has it been heard 30
10:28 they shall never perish 37
11:26 shall never die 37
13: 8 Peter said to him, "You shall never wash my feet. 37
Act 6:13 This man never ceases to speak words 30
10:14 never eaten anything that is common or unclean. 33
13:41 a deed you will never believe 36
14: 8 he was a cripple from birth, who had never walked. 33
19: 2 never even heard that there is a Holy Spirit. 31
28:26 You shall indeed hear but never understand 36
26 you shall indeed see but never perceive. 36
Rom 10:14 to believe in him of whom they have never heard? 30
12:11 Never flag in zeal, be aglow with the Spirit 23
16 associate with the lowly; never be conceited. 23
19 Beloved, never avenge yourselves 23
14:13 but rather decide never to put a stumbling block 23
15:21 They shall see who have never been told of him 30
21 shall understand who have never heard of him. 30
1Co 6:15 make them members of a prostitute? Never! 24
7:21 a slave when called? Never mind. But if you can 23
8:13 I will never eat meat 37
13: 8 Love never ends 33
1Th 2: 5 never used either words of flattery, as you know 43
1Ti 5:19 Never admit any charge against an elder 23
2Ti 3: 7 can never arrive at a knowledge of the truth. 27
Heb 1:12 thou art the same, and thy years will never end. 30
3:11 'They shall never enter my rest.' 22
18 swear that they should never enter his rest 22
4: 3 They shall never enter my rest 22
5 They shall never enter my rest. 22
10: 1 it can never . . make perfect those who draw near. 33
11 which can never take away sins. 33
13: 5 he has said, "I will never fail you nor forsake you. 36
2Pe 1:10 for if you do this you will never fall; 39
2:21 better for them never to have known the way 23
Rev 3:12 the temple of my God; never shall he go out of it 38
4: 8 and day and night they never cease to sing 30
16:18 such as had never been since men were on the earth 30
18: 7 I am no widow, mourning I shall never see,' 36
14 lost to thee, never to be found again! 36
21:25 and its gates shall never be shut by day- 36
2Es 3:15 thou wouldst never forsake his descendants 47
4: 8 I never went down into the deep 46
7:14 they can never receive those things 46
8:47 Never do so! 48
11:19 and then were never seen again. 49
13:41 where mankind had never lived 48
16:67 your iniquities, never to commit them again 45
Tob 3: 9 May we never see a son or daughter of yours! 28
6: 7 that person will never be troubled again. 36
10: 7 she never stopped mourning for her son Tobias 30
Jdt 8:13 but you will never know anything! 34
18 never in our generation 30
11: 1 I have never hurt any one 30
2 I would never have lifted my spear against them; 30
13:19 will never depart from the hearts of men 42
Wis 2: 2 hereafter we shall be as though we had never been; 30
10: 8 their failures could never go unnoticed. 26
12:10 their way of thinking would never change. 37
15:17 since he has life, but they never have. 33
Sir 4:25 Never speak against the truth 23
7: 1 Do no evil, and evil will never befall you. 36
36 then you will never sin. 35
9: 9 Never dine with another man's wife 29
12:10 Never trust your enemy 28
15: 8 liars will never think of her. 36
16:28 they will never disobey his word. 42
19: 7 Never repeat a conversation 27
16 Who has never sinned with his tongue? 30
22:13 you will never be wearied by his madness. 36
23: 7 the one who observes it will never be caught. 36
12 may it never be found in the inheritance of Jacob! 23
14 then you will wish that you had never been born 23
15 will never become disciplined all his days. 36
16 will never cease until the fire burns him up. 36
17 he will never cease until he dies. 36
27:16 he will never find a congenial friend. 36
38: 8 His works will never be finished 36
39: 9 it will never be blotted out 42

43:10 they never relax in their watches. 36
45:13 there never were such beautiful things 30
47:22 the Lord will never give up his mercy 36
22 never blot out the descendants of his chosen one 32
51:18 I shall never be put to shame. 36
Bar 2:35 I will never again remove my people Israel 30
Bel 1: 7 it never ate or drank anything. 30
35 Habakkuk said, "Sir, I have never seen Babylon 30
1Mc 2:48 they never let the sinner gain the upper hand. 30
6:36 they never left it. 30
2Mc 6:16 Therefore he never withdraws his mercy from us. 33
15:36 never to let this day go unobserved 25
3Mc 3:16 who never cease from their folly. 27
7: 4 our government would never be firmly established 27
11 never be favorably disposed toward . . government. 27
4Mc 6:17 May we . . never think so basely 23
12:12 these throughout all time will never let you go. 30
never *See also* cease, lie, suffice, think.

never again 1. אַל יֹסֵף 2. בִּלְתִּי 3. לֹא לְעוֹלָם 4. לֹא עוֹד 5. μηκέτι 6. οὐκ αἰῶνα αἰῶνος 7. οὐκέτι
Gen 9:11 never again shall all flesh be cut off 4
11 never again shall there be a flood to destroy 4
15 the waters shall never again become a flood 4
Exd 10:28 take heed to yourself; never see my face again; 1
1Kg 10:10 never again came such an abundance of spices 4
Jer 22:12 and he shall never see this land again. 4
Ezk 5: 9 and the like of which I will never do again. 4
16:63 confounded, and never open your mouth again 4
29:15 and never again exalt itself above the nations; 4
15 they will never again rule over the nations. 2
16 it shall never again be the reliance of the house 4
36:30 may never again suffer the disgrace of famine 4
Jol 2:26 And my people shall never again be put to shame. 3
27 And my people shall never again be put to shame. 3
3:17 and strangers shall never again pass through it. 4
Ams 8:14 they shall fall, and never rise again. 4
9:15 they shall never again be plucked up 4
Mrk 9:25 come out of him, and never enter him again. 5
Rom 6: 9 For we know that Christ . . will never die again; 7
Tob 6: 7 that person will never be troubled again. 7
17 and will never again return 6
2Mc 10: 4 they might never again fall into such misfortunes 5

never amiss 1. εἰς καιρόν
Sir 40:23 A friend or a companion never meets one amiss 1

never more 1. עַד נֵצַח לֹא
Ps 49:19 his fathers, who will never more see the light. 1

never-ending 1. עוֹלָם
Ezk 25:15 to destroy in never-ending enmity; 1

nevermore 1. לֹא
Isa 14:20 May . . evildoers nevermore be named! 1

nevertheless 1. אֲבָל 2. אוּלָם 3. אַךְ 4. אָכֵן 5. אֶפֶס 6. אֶפֶס כִּי 7. וְ 8. כִּי 9. כִּי אִם 10. רַק 11. בְּרַם (A) 12. ἀλλά 13. μέν 14. ὅμως 15. πλήν 16. autem 17. et
Gen 48:19 also shall be great; nevertheless his younger 2
Exd 32:34 Nevertheless, in the day when I visit, I will visit 7
Lev 11: 4 Nevertheless among those that chew the cud 3
36 Nevertheless a spring or a cistern 3
25:32 Nevertheless the cities of the Levites 7
Num18:15 nevertheless the first-born of man 3
24:22 nevertheless Kain shall be wasted. 9
25: 9 Nevertheless those that died by the plague 7
31:23 Nevertheless it shall also be purified 3
Deu 23: 5 Nevertheless the LORD . . would not hearken 7
Jdg 1:33 nevertheless the inhabitants of Beth-she'mesh 7
4: 9 surely go with you; nevertheless, the road 6
1Sm 29: 6 Nevertheless the lords do not approve of you. 7
9 nevertheless the commanders . . have said 3
2Sm 5: 7 Nevertheless David took the stronghold of Zion 7
12:14 Nevertheless, because by this deed you have 5
1Kg 8:19 nevertheless you shall not build 10
11:34 Nevertheless I will not take the whole kingdom 7
15: 4 Nevertheless for David's sake the LORD . . gave 8
14 Nevertheless the heart of Asa was wholly true 10
20: 6 nevertheless I will send my servants to you 9
2Kg 3: 3 Nevertheless he clung to the sin of Jerobo'am 10
12: 3 Nevertheless the high places were not taken 10
13: 6 Nevertheless they did not depart from the sins 3
15: 4 Nevertheless the high places were not taken 10
35 Nevertheless the high places were not removed; 10
1Ch 11: 5 Nevertheless David took the stronghold of Zion 7
2Ch 6: 9 nevertheless you shall not build the house 10
12: 8 Nevertheless they shall be servants to him 8
15:17 Nevertheless the heart of Asa was blameless 10
19: 3 Nevertheless some good is found in you 1
33:17 Nevertheless the people still sacrificed 1
35:22 Nevertheless Josi'ah would not turn away 7
Neh 9:26 Nevertheless they were disobedient 7
31 Nevertheless in thy great mercies 7
13:26 nevertheless foreign women made even him to sin. *
Est 5:10 Nevertheless Haman restrained himself 7
Ps 73:23 Nevertheless I am continually with thee; 7
82: 7 nevertheless, you shall die like men 4
106:44 Nevertheless he regarded their distress 7
Ezk 3:21 Nevertheless if you warn the righteous man 7
20:17 Nevertheless my eye spared them 7
Dan 5:17 nevertheless I will read the writing to the king 11
Jon 1:13 Nevertheless the men rowed hard to bring 7
Mat 26:39 nevertheless, not as I will, but as thou wilt. 15
Lke 10:11 nevertheless know this 15
20 Nevertheless do not rejoice in this 15
13:33 Nevertheless I must go on my way today 15
18: 8 Nevertheless, when the Son of man comes 15
22:42 nevertheless not my will, but thine, be done. 15
Joh 12:42 Nevertheless . . the authorities believed 14
16: 7 Nevertheless I tell you the truth 12
1Co 9:12 Nevertheless, we have not made use of this right 12
10: 5 Nevertheless with most of them 12
11:11 (Nevertheless, in the Lord 15
14:19 nevertheless, in church I would rather speak 12
2Es 7:22 Nevertheless they were not obedient 16
12:18 nevertheless it shall not fall then 17
Sir 29: 8 Nevertheless, be patient 15
2Mc 14:18 Nevertheless Nicanor . . shrank from deciding 14
15: 5 Nevertheless, he did not succeed 14
3Mc 3: 6 Nevertheless those of other races paid no heed 13
4Mc 15:11 Nevertheless, though so many factors 14

new 1. חָדָשׁ 2. καινός 3. καινότης 4. νέος 5. πρόσφατος
Exd 1: 8 Now there arose a new king over Egypt 1
Lev 26:10 clear out the old to make way for the new 1
Deu 20: 5 What man is there that has built a new house 1
22: 8 When you build a new house, you shall make 1
Jos 9:13 these wineskins were new when we filled them 1
Jdg 5: 8 When new gods were chosen, then war was 1
15:13 they bound him with two new ropes, and brought him 1
16:11 If they bind me with new ropes that have not been 1
12 Deli'lah took new ropes and bound him with them 1
1Sm 6: 7 take and prepare a new cart and two milch cows 1
2Sm 6: 3 And they carried the ark of God upon a new cart 1
3 and Uzzah and Ahi'o . . were driving the new cart 1
21:16 Ish'bi-be'nob . . who was girded with a new sword 1
1Kg 11:29 Now Ahi'jah had clad himself with a new garment; 1
30 Ahi'jah laid hold of the new garment 1
2Kg 2:20 He said, "Bring me a new bowl, and put salt in it. 1
1Ch 13: 7 they carried the ark of God upon a new cart 1
2Ch 20: 5 in the house of the LORD, before the new court 1
Job 32:19 like new wineskins, it is ready to burst. 1
Ps 33: 3 Sing to him a new song, play skillfully 1
40: 3 He put a new song in my mouth, a song of praise 1
96: 1 O sing to the LORD a new song; 1
98: 1 O sing to the LORD a new song, 1
144: 9 I will sing a new song to thee, O God; 1
149: 1 Sing to the LORD a new song, his praise 1
Prv 19: 4 Wealth brings many new friends *
Ecc 1: 9 and there is nothing new under the sun. 1
10 Is there a thing of which it is said, "See, this is new"? 1
Sng 7:13 over . . are all choice fruits, new as well as old 1
Isa 41:15 a threshing sledge, new, sharp, and having teeth; 1
42:10 Sing to the LORD a new song 1
57:10 you found new life for your strength *
62: 2 and you shall be called by a new name 1
65:17 For behold, I create new heavens and a new earth; 1
17 For behold, I create new heavens and a new earth; 1
66:22 the new heavens and the new earth 1
22 new heavens and the new earth which I will make 1
Jer 26:10 took their seat in the entry of the New Gate 1
31:31 says the LORD, when I will make a new covenant 1
36:10 at the entry of the New Gate of the LORD'S house. 1
Lam 3:23 they are new every morning; 1
Ezk 11:19 and put a new spirit within them; 1
18:31 and get yourselves a new heart and a new spirit! 1
31 and get yourselves a new heart and a new spirit! 1
36:26 A new heart I will give you, and a new spirit 1
26 and a new spirit I will put within you; 1
Mat 9:17 Neither is new wine put into old wineskins 4
17 but new wine is put into fresh wineskins 4
13:52 what is new and what is old. 2
26:29 until that day when I drink it new with you 2
27:60 laid it in his own new tomb 2
Mrk 1:27 What is this? A new teaching! 2
2:21 the new from the old, and a worse tear is made. 2
22 no one puts new wine into old wineskins 4
22 new wine is for fresh skins. 4
14:25 when I drink it new in the kingdom of God. 2
16:17 they will speak in new tongues; 2
Lke 5:36 No one tears a piece from a new garment 2
36 if he does, he will tear the new 2
36 the piece from the new will not match the old. 2
37 no one puts new wine into old wineskins 4
37 if he does, the new wine will burst the skins 4
38 new wine must be put into fresh wineskins. 4
39 no one after drinking old wine desires new 4
22:20 the new covenant in my blood. 2
Joh 13:34 A new commandment I give to you 2
19:41 there was a garden, and in the garden a new tomb 2
Act 17:19 May we know what this new teaching is 2
21 telling or hearing something new. 2
Rom 7: 6 so that we serve . . in the new life of the Spirit. 3
1Co 5: 7 you may be a new lump 4
11:25 This cup is the new covenant in my blood 2
2Co 3: 6 competent to be ministers of a new covenant 2
5:17 if any one is in Christ, he is a new creation 2
17 the old has passed away, behold, the new has come. 2
Gal 6:15 nor uncircumcision, but a new creation. 2
Eph 2:15 create in himself one new man in place of the two 2
4:24 put on the new nature 2
Col 3:10 and have put on the new nature 4
Heb 8: 8 when I will establish a new covenant 2
13 In speaking of a new covenant 2
9:15 Therefore he is the mediator of a new covenant 2
10:20 by the new and living way which he opened for us 5
12:24 to Jesus, the mediator of a new covenant 4
2Pe 3:13 we wait for new heavens and a new earth 2
13 we wait for new heavens and a new earth 2
1Jn 2: 7 Beloved, I am writing you no new commandment 2
8 Yet I am writing you a new commandment 2
2Jn 1: 5 as though I were writing you a new commandment 2
Rev 2:17 with a new name written on the stone 2
3:12 the new Jerusalem which comes down from my God 2
12 the name of my God . . and my own new name. 2
5: 9 they sang a new song, saying, "Worthy art thou 2
14: 3 and they sing a new song before the throne 2
21: 1 Then I saw a new heaven and a new earth; 2
1 Then I saw a new heaven and a new earth; 2
2 new Jerusalem, coming down out of heaven from God 2
5 Behold, I make all things new. 2
1Es 6: 9 building . . a great new house for the Lord 2
25 one course of new native timber 2
Jdt 16: 2 Raise to him a new psalm 2
13 I will sing to my God a new song 2
Wis 14: 6 left to the world the seed of a new generation. *
19:11 Afterward they saw also a new kind of birds 4
Sir 9:10 A new friend is like new wine 4
10 A new friend is like new wine 4
1Mc 4:47 and built a new altar like the former one. 2
49 They made new holy vessels 2
53 on the new altar of burnt offering 2
2Mc 2:29 the master builder of a new house 2
4:11 and introduced new customs contrary to the law. *
new *See also* god, grain, growth, moon, put, wine, world.

ever new 1. חלף
Job 29:20 glory fresh with me, and my bow ever new in my hand 1

new one 1. πρόσφατος
Sir 9:10 a new one does not compare with him 1

something new 1. בְּרִיאָה
Num16:30 if the LORD creates something new 1

new thing 1. חָדָשׁ
Isa 42: 9 have come to pass, and new things I now declare; 1
43:19 Behold, I am doing a new thing; now it springs forth 1
48: 6 From this time forth I make you hear new things 1
Jer 31:22 For the LORD has created a new thing on the earth 1

newborn 1. ילד 2. ἀρτιγέννητος 3. νεογνός
Jer 14: 5 hind in the field forsakes her newborn calf 1
1Pe 2: 2 Like newborn babes, long for . . spiritual milk 2
3Mc 1:20 nurses abandoned even newborn children 3

newly 1. חָדָשׁ 2. νεωστί
Deu 24: 5 When a man is newly married, he shall not go out 1
Jdt 4: 3 all the people of Judea were newly gathered together 2
newly *See also* created.

newness 1. καινότης
Rom 6: 4 we too might walk in newness of life. 1

news 1. בְּשֹׂרָה 2. דָּבָר 3. שְׁמוּעָה 4. שֵׁמַע 5. γινώσκω 6. λόγος 7. περί
1Sm 4:13 when the man came into the city and told the news *
2Sm 4: 4 news about Saul and Jonathan came from Jezreel; 3
10 which was the reward I gave him for his news. 1
11:18 and told David all the news about the fighting; 2
19 When you have finished telling all the news 2
1Kg 2:28 When the news came to Jo'ab . . Jo'ab fled 3
2Kg 9:15 out of the city to go and tell the news in Jezreel. *
Prv 15:30 good news refreshes the bones. 3
25:25 Like cold water . . good news from a far country. 3
Jer 37: 5 who were besieging Jerusalem heard news of them 4
Ezk 24:26 will come to you to report to you the news. *
Nah 3:19 All who hear the news of you clap their hands 4
Mrk 1:45 to spread the news 6
Act 11:22 News of this came to the ears of the church 6
Php 2:19 so that I may be cheered by news of you. 5
1Mc 6: 8 When the king heard this news, he was astounded 6
2Mc 5:11 When news of what had happened reached the king 7
9: 3 news came to him of what had happened to Nicanor *
news *See also* bring, carry, preach, receive, tell.

news come 1. προσαγγέλλω
2Mc 9:24 if . . any unwelcome news came 1

good news 1. בְּשֹׂרָה
2Kg 7: 9 This day is a day of good news; if we are silent 1

good news come 1.εὐαγγελίζω
Heb 4: 2 For good news came to us just as to them 1

next 1.אַחַר 2.אַחֲרוֹן 3.אַחֲרֵי 4.אֶל יַד 5.אֶל עֵבֶר 6.מָחֳרָת 7.מִשְׁנֶה 8.עַל 9.עַל יַד 10.קָרֹב 11.שֵׁנִי 12.δεύτερος 13.δὴ τοίνυν 14.ἐγγύς 15.ἑξῆς 16.ἐπαύριον 17.ἔρχομαι 18.ἕτερος 19.ἐχομένως 20.ἔχω 21.καί 22.μεταξύ 23.παρά 24.sequor
Gen 17:21 bear to you at this season next year. 1
Exd 2:13 When he went out the next day, behold, two Hebrews 11
12: 4 a man and his neighbor next to his house shall 10
28:26 put them . . on its inside edge next to the ephod. 5
39:19 on its inside edge next to the ephod. 5
Num 2: 5 Those to encamp next to him shall be the tribe 8
12 those to encamp next to him shall be the tribe 8
20 next to him shall be the tribe of Manas'seh 8
27 those to encamp next to him shall be the tribe 8
11:32 people rose . . all night, and all the next day 6
27:11 his kinsman that is next to him of his family 10
1Sm 5: 4 But when they rose early on the next morning 6
17:13 Eli'ab the first-born, and next to him Abin'adab 7
23:17 you shall be king . . and I shall be next to you; 7
2Sm 11:12 Uri'ah remained . . that day, and the next. 6
14:30 See, Jo'ab's field is next to mine, and he has barley 4
23: 9 And next to him among the three . . men was Elea'zar 3
11 And next to him was Shammah, the son of Agee 3
1Kg 1: 6 handsome man; and he was born next after Ab'salom. *
2Kg 3:20 The next morning, about the time of offering *
6:29 And on the next day I said to her, 'Give your son 1
1Ch 11:12 next to him . . was Elea'zar the son of Dodo 3
29:21 and on the next day offered burnt offerings 6
2Ch 17:15 next to him Jehoha'nan the commander, with 280,000 9
16 next to him Amasi'ah the son of Zichri 9
18 next to him Jeho'zabad with a 180,000 armed 9
Neh 3: 2 next to him the men of Jericho built. 9
2 next to them Zaccur the son of Imri built. 9
4 next to them Mer'emoth the son of Uri'ah 9
4 next to them Meshul'lam the son of Berechi'ah 9
4 next to them Zadok the son of Ba'ana repaired. 9
5 next to them the Teko'ites repaired; 9
7 next to them repaired Melati'ah the Gib'eonite 9
8 Next to them Uz'ziel the son of Harhai'ah 9
8 Next to him Hanani'ah, one of the perfumers 9
9 Next to them Rephai'ah the son of Hur, ruler of half 9
10 Next to them Jedai'ah the son of Haru'maph 9
10 next to him Hattush the son of Hashabnei'ah 9
12 Next to him Shallum the son of Hallo'hesh 9
17 next to him Hashabi'ah, ruler of half the district 9
19 next to him Ezer the son of Jeshua, ruler of Mizpah 9
Est 1:14 the men next to him being Carshe'na, Shethar 10
Ps 48:13 that you may tell the next generation 2
78: 6 that the next generation might know them 2
Ezk 24:18 on the next morning I did as I was commanded. *
Mat 10:23 flee to the next 18
27:62 Next day, that is, after the day of Preparation 16
Mrk 1:38 he said to them, "Let us go on to the next towns 20
Lke 9:37 On the next day 15
Act 13:42 might be told them the next sabbath. 22
44 The next sabbath almost the whole city gathered 17
20:15 the next day we touched at Samos 18
21: 1 the next day to Rhodes . . from there to Pat'ara 15
26 the next day he purified himself with them 20
1Es 3: 7 because of his wisdom he shall sit next to Darius 12
4:42 you shall sit next to me, and be called my kinsman. 20
2Es 11:13 Then the next wing arose and reigned 24
Tob 7:14 Next he called his wife Edna 21
Jdt 16:24 all those who were next of kin to her husband 14
Sir 12:12 Do not put him next to you, lest he overthrow you 23
1Mc 4:28 the next year 17
5:35 Next he turned aside to Alema 21
2Mc 7:15 Next they brought forward the fifth 19
12:39 On the next day 20
4Mc 1:16 Wisdom, next, is the knowledge of . . 13
next *See also* day, door, eldest, morning, stand, woman, year.

next in authority 1.מִשְׁנֶה
2Ch 28: 7 Elka'nah the next in authority to the king. 1

next in rank 1.מִשְׁנֶה
Est 10: 3 Mor'decai the Jew was next in rank to . . Ahasu-e'rus 1

next of kin 1.גאל 2.קָרֹב
Lev 25:25 his next of kin shall come and redeem 2
Rut 3: 9 spread your skirt over . . for you are next of kin. 1
4: 1 the next of kin, of whom Bo'az had spoken, came by. 1
3 Then he said to the next of kin 1
6 the next of kin said, "I cannot redeem it for myself 1
8 when the next of kin said to Bo'az, "Buy it 1
14 who has not left you this day without next of kin; 1

niche 1.οἴκημα
Wis 13:15 then he makes for it a niche that befits it 1

niggardliness 1.πονηρία
Sir 31:24 their testimony to his niggardliness 1

niggardly 1.πονηρός
Sir 31:24 complain of the one who is niggardly with food 1

nigh 1.קָרֹב
Num24:17 I see him, but not now; I behold him, but not nigh 1
nigh *See also* draw.

well nigh 1.כְּאַיִן
Ps 73: 2 my steps had well nigh slipped. 1

night 1.לַיְלָה 2.עֶרֶב 3.לֵילְיָא(A) 4.ἀωρία 5.νύκτωρ 6.νύξ 7.nox
Gen 1: 5 the light Day, and the darkness he called Night 1
14 to separate the day from the night; 1
16 the lesser light to rule the night; 1
18 to rule over the day and over the night 1
7: 4 send rain upon the earth 40 days and 40 nights; 1
12 rain fell upon the earth 40 days and 40 nights. 1
8:22 and winter, day and night, shall not cease. 1
14:15 he divided his forces against them by night 1
19:33 they made their father drink wine that night; 1
35 they made their father drink wine that night 1
20: 3 Abim'elech in a dream by night, and said to him 1
26:24 the LORD appeared to him the same night and said 1
30:16 my son's mandrakes." So he lay with her that night 1
31:24 God came to Laban the Aramean in a dream by night 1
39 whether stolen by day or stolen by night. 1
40 by day the heat consumed me, and the cold by night 1
32:13 he lodged there that night, and took 1
21 and he himself lodged that night in the camp. 1
22 The same night he arose and took his two wives 1
40: 5 one night they both dreamed 1
41:11 we dreamed on the same night, he and I 1
46: 2 God spoke to Israel in visions of the night 1
Exd 10:13 upon the land all that day and all that night; 1
12: 8 They shall eat the flesh that night, roasted; 1
12 pass through . . that night, and I will smite 1
30 Pharaoh rose up in the night, he, and all his 1
31 he summoned Moses and Aaron by night, and said 1
42 It was a night of watching by the LORD, to bring 1
42 so this same night is a night of watching kept 1
42 so this same night is a night of watching kept *
13:21 and by night in a pillar of fire to give them light 1
21 that they might travel by day and by night; 1
22 the pillar of fire by night did not depart 1
14:20 and the night passed without one coming near 6
20 without one coming near the other all night. 1
21 the sea back by a strong east wind all night 1
24:18 Moses was on the mountain 40 days and 40 nights. 1
34:28 he was there with the LORD 40 days and 40 nights; 1
40:38 and fire was in it by night, in the sight of all 1
Lev 6: 9 upon the altar all night until the morning 1
8:35 you shall remain day and night for seven days 1
Num 9:16 continually . . appearance of fire by night. 1
21 if it continued for a day and a night 1
11: 9 When the dew fell upon the camp in the night 1
32 the people rose all that day, and all night 1
14: 1 raised a loud cry; and the people wept that night. 1
14 goest before . . in a pillar of fire by night. 1
22: 8 Lodge here this night, and I will bring back word 1
19 Pray, now, tarry here this night also 1
20 God came to Balaam at night and said to him 1
Deu 1:33 who went before you . . in fire by night 1
9: 9 I remained on the mountain 40 days and 40 nights 1
11 at the end of 40 days and 40 nights the LORD gave me 1
18 I lay prostrate . . 40 days and 40 nights; 1
25 before the LORD for these 40 days and 40 nights 1
10:10 I stayed on the mountain . . 40 days and 40 nights 1
16: 1 LORD your God brought you out of Egypt by night. 1
23:10 by reason of what chances to him by night 1
28:66 night and day you shall be in dread 1
Jos 1: 8 but you shall meditate on it day and night 1
8: 3 Joshua . . and sent them forth by night. 1
9 but Joshua spent that night among the people. 1
13 But Joshua spent that night in the valley. 1
10: 9 having marched up all night from Gilgal. 1
Jdg 6:25 That night the LORD said to him, "Take your father's 1
27 too afraid . . to do it by day, he did it by night. 1
40 God did so that night; for it was dry on the fleece 1
7: 9 That same night the LORD said to him, "Arise, 1
9:32 go by night . . and lie in wait in the fields. 1
34 Abim'elech and all . . with him rose up by night 1
16: 2 and lay in wait for him all night at the gate 1
2 They kept quiet all night, saying, "Let us wait till 1
19:25 and abused her all night until the morning. 1
20: 5 and beset the house round about me by night; 1
Rut 1:12 even if I should have a husband this night 1
3:13 Remain this night, and in the morning 1
1Sm 14:34 So every one . . brought his ox with him that night 1
36 Let us go down after the Philistines by night 1
15:11 was angry; and he cried to the LORD all night. 1
16 tell you what the LORD said to me on this night. 1
19:11 That night Saul sent messengers to David's house 1
24 and lay naked all that day and all that night. 1
25:16 they were a wall to us both by night and by day 1
26: 7 David and Abi'shai went to the army by night; 1
28: 8 and they came to the woman by night. 1
20 he had eaten nothing all day and all night. 1
25 Then they rose and went away that night. 1
30:12 or drunk water for three days and three nights. 1
31:12 valiant men arose, and went all night 1
2Sm 2:29 Abner . . went all that night through the Arabah; 1
32 And Jo'ab and his men marched all night 1
4: 7 and went by the way of the Arabah all night 1
7: 4 But that same night the word of the LORD came 1
19: 7 not a man will stay with you this night; 1
21:10 or the beasts of the field by night. 1
1Kg 3: 5 the LORD appeared to Solomon in a dream by night; 1
19 this woman's son died in the night, because she lay 1
8:29 eyes may be open night and day toward this house 1
59 words . . be near to the LORD our God day and night 1
19: 8 and went . . 40 days and 40 nights to Horeb 1
2Kg 6:14 and they came by night, and surrounded the city. 1
7:12 the king rose in the night, and said 1
8:21 Joram passed over to Za'ir . . and rose by night 1
19:35 And that night the angel of the LORD went forth 1
25: 4 the king with all the men of war fled by night 1
1Ch 9:33 for they were on duty day and night. 1
17: 3 same night the word of the LORD came to Nathan 1
2Ch 1: 7 In that night God appeared to Solomon 1
6:20 eyes may be open day and night toward this house 1
7:12 Then the LORD appeared to Solomon in the night 1
21: 9 Jeho'ram . . rose by night and smote the E'domites 1
35:14 busied in offering . . the fat parts until night; 1
Neh 1: 6 prayer . . I now pray before thee day and night 1
2:12 Then I arose in the night, I and a few men with me; 1
13 I went out by night by the Valley Gate 1
15 Then I went up in the night by the valley 1
4: 9 set a guard as a protection . . day and night. 1
22 may be a guard for us by night and may labor by day. 1
6:10 at night they are coming to kill you. 1
9:12 by a pillar of fire in the night to light for them 1
19 nor the pillar of fire by night which lighted 1
Est 4:16 neither eat nor drink . . three days, night or day. 1
6: 1 On that night the king could not sleep; 1
Job 2:13 on the ground seven days and seven nights 1
3: 3 the night which said, 'A man-child is conceived.' 1
6 That night–let thick darkness seize it! 1
7 Yea, let that night be barren; 1
4:13 Amid thoughts from visions of the night 1
5:14 and grope at noonday as in the night. 1
7: 3 nights of misery are apportioned to me. 1
4 But the night is long, and I am full of tossing 2
17:12 They make night into day; 1
20: 8 he will be chased away like a vision of the night. 1
24:14 in the night he is as a thief. 1
27:20 in the night a whirlwind carries him off. 1
30:17 The night racks my bones, and the pain 1
33:15 In a dream, in a vision of the night, 1
34:25 he overturns them in the night 1
35:10 Where is God my Maker, who gives songs in the night 1
36:20 Do not long for the night, when peoples are cut off 1
Ps 1: 2 on his law he meditates day and night. 1
6: 6 every night I flood my bed with tears; 1
16: 7 in the night also my heart instructs me. 1
17: 3 if thou visitest me by night, if thou testest me 1
19: 2 night to night declares knowledge. 1
2 night to night declares knowledge. 1
22: 2 I cry by day . . and by night, but find no rest. 1
30: 5 Weeping may tarry for the night 2
32: 4 For day and night thy hand was heavy upon me; 1
42: 3 My tears have been my food day and night 1
8 at night his song is with me 1
55:10 Day and night they go around it on its walls; 1
74:16 Thine is the day, thine also the night; 1
77: 2 in the night my hand is stretched out 1
6 I commune with my heart in the night; 1
78:14 with a cloud, and all the night with a fiery light. 1
88: 1 I cry out in the night before thee. 1
90: 4 yesterday . . is past, or as a watch in the night. 1
91: 5 You will not fear the terror of the night 1
92: 2 to declare . . thy faithfulness by night 1
104:20 Thou makest darkness, and it is night 1
105:39 fire to give light by night. 1
119:55 I remember thy name in the night, O LORD 1
148 My eyes are awake before the watches of the night *
121: 6 not smite you by day, nor the moon by night. 1
134: 1 who stand by night in the house of the LORD! 1
136: 9 the moon and stars to rule over the night 1
139:11 darkness cover me, and the light about me be night 1
12 not dark to thee, the night is bright as the day; 1
Prv 7: 9 at the time of night and darkness. 1
31:15 She rises while it is yet night and provides food 1
18 Her lamp does not go out at night. 1
Ecc 2:23 even in the night his mind does not rest. 1
8:16 how neither day nor night one's eyes see sleep; 1
Sng 3: 1 bed by night I sought him whom my soul loves 1
8 each with his sword . . against alarms by night. 1
5: 2 wet with dew, my locks with the drops of the night. 1
Isa 4: 5 smoke and the shining of a flaming fire by night; 1
15: 1 Because Ar is laid waste in a night Moab is undone; 1
1 Kir is laid waste in a night Moab is undone. 1
16: 3 make your shade like night at the height of noon; 1
21: 8 by day, and at my post I am stationed whole nights. 1
11 calling . . Watchman, what of the night? 1
11 what of the night? Watchman, what of the night? 1
12 Morning comes, and also the night. 1
26: 9 My soul yearns for thee in the night 1
27: 3 Lest any one harm it, I guard it night and day; 1
28:19 it will pass through, by day and by night; 1

29: 7 shall be like a dream, a vision of the night. 1
30:29 a song as in the night when a holy feast is kept; 1
34:10 Night and day it shall not be quenched; 1
38:12 from day to night thou dost bring me to an end; 1
13 from day to night thou dost bring me to an end. 1
60:11 day and night they shall not be shut; 1
19 shall the moon give light to you by night; 1
62: 6 day and all the night they shall never be silent. 1
Jer 6: 5 let us attack by night, and destroy her palaces! 1
9: 1 that I might weep day and night for the slain 1
14:17 Let my eyes run down with tears night and day 1
16:13 there you shall serve other gods day and night 1
31:35 order of the moon and the stars for light by night 1
33:20 If you can break . . my covenant with the night 1
20 and night will not come at their appointed time 1
25 not established my covenant with day and night 1
36:30 to the heat by day and the frost by night. 1
39: 4 they fled, going out of the city at night 1
49: 9 If thieves came by night, would they not destroy 1
52: 7 went out from the city by night by the way of a gate 1
Lam 1: 2 She weeps bitterly in the night 1
2:18 tears stream down like a torrent day and night! 1
19 Arise, cry out in the night, at the . . watches! 1
Dan 2:19 mystery was revealed . . in a vision of the night. 3
5:30 night Belshaz'zar the Chalde'an king was slain. 3
7: 2 Daniel said, "I saw in my vision by night, 3
7 After this I saw in the night visions, 3
13 I saw in the night visions, and behold 3
Hos 4: 5 the prophet also shall stumble with you by night; 1
7: 6 all night their anger smolders; 1
Ams 5: 8 into the morning, and darkens the day into night 1
Obd 1: 5 If thieves came to you, if plunderers by night 1
Jon 1:17 belly of the fish three days and three nights. 1
4:10 into being in a night, and perished in a night. 1
10 into being in a night, and perished in a night. 1
Mic 3: 6 it shall be night to you, without vision 1
Zec 1: 8 I saw in the night, and behold, a man 1
14: 7 day (it is known to the LORD), not day and not night 1
Mat 2:14 he rose and took the child and his mother by night 6
4: 2 And he fasted 40 days and 40 nights 6
12:40 For as Jonah was three days and three nights 6
40 three nights in the heart of the earth. 6
14:25 in the fourth watch of the night he came to them 6
26:31 You will all fall away because of me this night 6
34 this very night, before the cock crows 6
28:13 said, "Tell people, 'His disciples came by night 6
Mrk 4:27 sleep and rise night and day 6
5: 5 Night and day among the tombs 6
6:48 about the fourth watch of the night he came 6
14:30 this very night, before the cock crows twice 6
Lke 2: 8 keeping watch over their flock by night. 6
37 with fasting and prayer night and day. 6
5: 5 Master, we toiled all night and took nothing! 6
12:20 This night your soul is required of you 6
17:34 in that night there will be two in one bed 6
18: 7 who cry to him day and night 6
21:37 at night he went out and lodged on the mount 6
Joh 3: 2 This man came to Jesus by night and said to him 6
9: 4 night comes, when no one can work. 6
11:10 if any one walks in the night, he stumbles 6
13:30 he immediately went out; and it was night. 6
19:39 who had at first come to him by night 6
21: 3 that night they caught nothing. 6
Act 5:19 at night an angel of the Lord opened the . . doors 6
9:24 were watching the gates day and night, to kill him; 6
25 his disciples took him by night 6
12: 6 The very night 6
16: 9 a vision appeared to Paul in the night 6
33 he took them the same hour of the night 6
17:10 sent . . Silas away by night to Beroe'a 6
18: 9 the Lord said to Paul one night in a vision 6
20:31 I did not cease night or day to admonish every one 6
23:11 The following night the Lord stood by him 6
23 At the third hour of the night get ready 6
31 took Paul and brought him by night to Antip'atris. 6
26: 7 as they earnestly worship night and day 6
27:23 this very night there stood by me an angel 6
27 When the fourteenth night had come 6
Rom 13:12 the night is far gone, the day is at hand. 6
1Co 11:23 the Lord Jesus on the night when he was betrayed 6
1Th 2: 9 worked night and day, that we might not burden any 6
3:10 praying earnestly night and day that we may see 6
5: 2 day of the Lord will come like a thief in the night 6
5 we are not of the night or of darkness. 6
7 For those who sleep sleep at night 6
7 those who get drunk are drunk at night. 6
2Th 3: 8 with toil and labor we worked night and day 6
1Ti 5: 5 in supplications and prayers night and day; 6
2Ti 1: 3 I long night and day to see you 6
Rev 4: 8 and day and night they never cease to sing 6
7:15 and serve him day and night within his temple; 6
8:12 from shining, and likewise a third of the night. 6
12:10 who accuses them day and night before our God. 6
14:11 and they have no rest, day or night 6
20:10 they will be tormented day and night for ever 6
21:25 and there shall be no night there; 6
22: 5 And night shall be no more; 6
1Es 1:14 the priests were offering the fat until night 4
2Es 3:14 the end of the times, secretly by night. 7
5: 4 and the sun shall suddenly shine forth at night 7
7 one . . shall make his voice heard by night 7
16 Now on the second night Phaltiel . . came to me 7
31 the angel who had come to me on a previous night 7
6:12 thou didst show me in part on a previous night. 7
30 I have come to show you these things this night. ‡
36 on the eighth night my heart was troubled 7
7: 1 who had been sent to me on the former nights 7
42 or noon or night, or dawn or shining or brightness 7
9:44 I besought the Most High, night and day. 7
10: 3 that I might be quiet, I got up in the night and fled 7
58 tomorrow night you shall remain here. 7
59 So I slept that night and the following one 7
11: 1 On the second night I had a dream 7
12: 5 with which I have been terrified this night. 7
13: 1 After seven days I dreamed a dream in the night; 7
14:42 and ate their bread at night. 7
43 and was not silent at night. 7
Tob 2: 9 On the same night I returned from burying him 6
6:15 this very night she will be given to you 6
7:11 when each came to her he died in the night 6
8: 9 Then they both went to sleep for the night. 6
10: 7 throughout the nights she never stopped 6
Jdt 6:21 all that night they called on the God of Israel 6
7: 5 they remained on guard all that night. 6
11: 5 I will tell nothing false to my lord this night. 6
17 serves the God of heaven day and night 6
17 every night your servant will go out 6
12: 7 and went out each night to the valley of Bethulia 6
13:14 but has destroyed our enemies . . this very night! 6
Wis 7:30 for it is succeeded by the night 6
10:17 a starry flame through the night. 6
17: 2 prisoners of long night 6
5 avail to illumine that hateful night. 6
14 throughout the night 6
21 over those men alone heavy night was spread 6
18: 6 night was made known beforehand to our fathers 6
14 and night in its swift course was now half gone 6
Sir 38:27 labors by night as well as by day 5
40: 5 his sleep at night confuses his mind. 6
Bar 2:25 cast out to the heat of day and the frost of night. 6
Aza 1:47 Bless the Lord, nights and days 6
Bel 1:15 In the night the priests came with their wives 6
1Mc 4: 1 this division moved out by night 6
5 When Gorgias entered the camp of Judas by night 6
5:29 He departed from there at night 6
50 all that day and all the night 6
9:58 he will capture them all in one night. 6
12:26 to fall upon the Jews by night. 6
27 so as to be ready all night for battle 6
13:22 that night a very heavy snow fell 6
2Mc 8: 7 He found the nights most advantageous 6
12: 6 He set fire to the harbor by night 5
9 he attacked the people of Jamnia by night 6
13:10 to call upon the Lord day and night 6
15 he attacked the king's pavilion at night 5
3Mc 1: 2 and crossed over by night to the tent of Ptolemy 5
5:11 from the beginning, night and day 6
19 while it was still night 6
22 employ the duration of the night in sleep 6

night *See also* camp, continue, hag, lie, lodge, part, pass, spend, stay, tarry, through, watch.

all night 1. לון
2Sm 12:16 and went in and lay all night upon the ground. 1
Job 29:19 with the dew all night on my branches 1

night and a day 1. *νυχθήμερον*
2Co 11:25 a night and a day I have been adrift at sea; 1

night finds 1. *ὀψίζω*
Sir 36:26 and lodges wherever night finds him? 1

last night 1. אֶמֶשׁ
Gen 19:34 Behold, I lay last night with my father; 1
31:29 but the God of your father spoke to me last night 1
42 God saw . . and rebuked you last night. 1

remain all night 1. לון
Lev 19:13 wages . . shall not remain with you all night 1
Deu 16: 4 nor shall any . . remain all night until morning. 1
21:23 his body shall not remain all night upon the tree 1

sleepless night 1. *ἀγρυπνία*
2Co 11:27 in toil . . through many a sleepless night 1

through the night 1. *ἔννυχον*
3Mc 5: 5 arranged for . . continued custody through the night 1

nighthawk 1. תַּחְמָס
Lev 11:16 the ostrich, the nighthawk, the sea gull, the hawk 1
Deu 14:15 the ostrich, the nighthawk, the sea gull, the hawk 1

nimble 1. *εὔζωνος*
Sir 36:26 who will trust a nimble robber 1

nine 1. תֵּשַׁע 2. *ἐννέα* 3. novem
Num 29:26 On the fifth day nine bulls, two rams, fourteen 1
34:13 LORD has commanded to give to the nine tribes 1
Deu 3:11 Nine cubits was its length, and four cubits 1
Jos 13: 7 divide this land . . to the nine tribes 1
14: 2 commanded . . for the nine and one-half tribes. 1
15:44 nine cities with their villages. 1
54 nine cities with their villages. 1
21:16 nine cities out of these two tribes; 1
2Sm 24: 8 at the end of nine months and twenty days. 1
2Kg 17: 1 Hoshe'a . . and he reigned nine years. 1
1Ch 3: 8 Eli'shama, Eli'ada, and Eliph'elet, nine. 1
Lke 17:17 Were not ten cleansed? Where are the nine? 2
2Es 4:40 when her nine months have been completed 3
8: 8 and for nine months the womb 3
14:11 and nine of its parts have already passed *
Sir 25: 7 With nine thoughts I have gladdened my heart 2
2Mc 7:27 I carried you nine months in my womb 2

nine others 1. *δέκατος γίνομαι*
2Mc 5:27 Judas Maccabeus, with about nine others, got away 1

nineteen 1. תְּשַׁע עֶשְׂרֵה
Jos 19:38 nineteen cities with their villages. 1
2Sm 2:30 were missing . . nineteen men besides As'ahel. 1

nineteenth 1. תְּשַׁע עֶשְׂרֵה
2Kg 25: 8 was the nineteenth year of King Nebuchadnez'zar 1
1Ch 24:16 the nineteenth to Pethahi'ah, the twentieth 1
25:26 nineteenth, to Mallo'thi, 1
Jer 52:12 which was the nineteenth year of King 1

ninth 1. תְּשִׁיעִי 2. תֵּשַׁע 3. *ἔνατος* 4. nonus
Lev 23:32 on the ninth day of the month beginning at evening 2
25:22 until the ninth year, when its produce comes 1
Num 7:60 On the ninth day Abi'dan . . of the men of Benjamin 1
2Kg 17: 6 In the ninth year of Hoshe'a 1
18:10 which was the ninth year of Hoshe'a king of Israel 2
25: 1 in the ninth year of his reign, in the tenth month 1
3 On the ninth day of the fourth month the famine 2
1Ch 12:12 Joha'nan eighth, Elza'bad ninth 1
24:11 the ninth to Jeshua, the tenth to Shecani'ah 1
25:16 ninth to Mattani'ah, his sons and his brethren 1
27:12 Ninth . . was Abi-e'zer of An'athoth, a Benjaminite; 1
12 Ninth, for the ninth month, was Abi-e'zer 1
Ezr 10: 9 ninth month, on the twentieth day of the month. 1
Jer 36: 9 the fifth year of Jehoi'akim . . in the ninth month 1
22 It was the ninth month, and the king was sitting 1
39: 1 In the ninth year of Zedeki'ah king of Judah 1
2 in the fourth month, on the ninth day of the month 2
52: 4 in the ninth year of his reign, in the tenth month 1
6 On the ninth day of the fourth month the famine 2
Ezk 24: 1 In the ninth year, in the tenth month, on the tenth 1
Hag 2:10 On the 24th day of the ninth month 1
18 from the 24th day of the ninth month. 1
Zec 7: 1 fourth day of the ninth month, which is Chislev. 1
Mat 20: 5 the sixth hour and the ninth hour 3
27:45 over all the land until the ninth hour. 3
46 about the ninth hour Jesus cried 3
Mrk 15:33 over the whole land until the ninth hour. 3
34 at the ninth hour Jesus cried with a loud voice 3
Lke 23:44 darkness over the whole land until the ninth hour 3
Act 3: 1 going up . . at the hour of prayer, the ninth hour. 3
10: 3 About the ninth hour of the day 3
30 I was keeping the ninth hour of prayer in my house; 3
Rev 21:20 the eighth beryl, the ninth topaz 3
1Es 9: 5 this was the ninth month 3
2Es 16:38 Just as a woman with child, in the ninth month 4
1Mc 4:52 on the 25th day of the ninth month 3

no 1. אֲבָל 2. אַיִן 3. אַל 4. אִם 5. אֶפֶס 6. בַּל 7. בְּלִי 8. בִּלְתִּי 9. חָלִילָה 10. חָסֵר 11. כִּי 12. לֹא 13. לֹא כֹּל 14. לֹא עוֹד 15. לְבִלְתִּי 16. מִן 17. פֶּן 18. לָא (A) 19. *ἀλλά* 20. *ἀλλ' ἰδού* 21. *ἄνευ* 22. *ἄτερ* 23. *εἰ* 24. *ἐν μηδενί* 25. *μά* 26. *μή* 27. *μηδαμῶς* 28. *μηδέ* 29. *μηδείς* 30. *μὴ πᾶς* 31. *μήτε* 32. *μή τις* 33. *οὐ* 34. *οὐδαμός* 35. *οὐδέ* 36. *οὐδείς* 37. *οὐκ ἔνι* 38. *οὐ μή* 39. *οὐ πᾶς* 40. *οὔπω* 41. *οὔτε* 42. *οὐ τις* 43. *οὐχί* 44. *παρ' οὐδέν* 45. ne 46. nec 47. neque 48. non
Gen 2: 5 and there was no man to till the ground; 2
4: 5 for Cain and his offering he had no regard. 12
12 When you till the ground, it shall no longer yield 12
8: 9 the dove found no place to set her foot 12
11:30 Now Sar'ai was barren; she had no child. 2
13: 8 Let there be no strife between you and me 3
15: 3 Behold, thou hast given me no offspring; 12
16: 1 Now Sar'ai, Abram's wife, bore him no children. 12
17: 5 No longer shall your name be Abram 12
19 God said, "No, but Sarah your wife shall bear 1
18:15 she was afraid. He said, "No, but you did laugh. 12
19 No, for I have chosen him *
19: 2 They said, "No; we will spend the night 12
18 Lot said to them, "Oh, no, my lords; 3
20:11 There is no fear of God at all in this place 2
23:11 No, my lord, hear me; I give you the field 12
24:16 fair to look upon, a virgin, whom no man had known. 12
26:29 that you will do us no harm, just as we have not *
30: 1 When Rachel saw that she bore Jacob no children 12
31:50 although no man is with us, remember 2

32:28 he said, "Your name shall no more be called Jacob 12
33:10 Jacob said, "No, I pray you, if I have found favor 3
35:10 no longer shall your name be called Jacob 12
37:22 Reuben said to them, "Shed no blood; 3
22 in the wilderness, but lay no hand upon him 3
24 The pit was empty, there was no water in it. 2
35 refused to be comforted, and said, "No, I shall go •
38:21 And they said, "No harlot has been here. 12
22 men of the place say, 'No harlot has been here.' 12
39: 6 and having him he had no concern for anything 12
8 my master has no concern about anything 12
23 the keeper of the prison paid no heed to anything 2
41:21 had eaten them no one would have known that they 12
44 and without your consent no man shall lift up 12
42:10 They said to him, "No, my lord, but to buy food 12
12 He said to them, "No, it is the weakness of the land 12
44:23 you shall see my face no more.' 12
45: 1 no one stayed with him when Joseph made 12
20 Give no thought to your goods 3
47: 4 for there is no pasture for your servants' flocks 2
13 Now there was no food in all the land; 2
Exd 2: 3 when she could hide him no longer she took for him 12
12 and seeing no one he killed the Egyptian and hid 2
5: 7 You shall no longer give the people straw to make 12
9 that they may . . pay no regard to lying words. 3
16 No straw is given to your servants, yet they say 2
18 Go now, and work; for no straw shall be given you 12
8:22 so that no swarms of flies shall be there; 15
9:26 in the land of Goshen . . there was no hail. 12
28 I will let you go, and you shall stay no longer. 12
29 there will be no more hail, that you may know that 12
33 the rain no longer poured upon the earth. 12
10: 5 cover . . the land, so that no one can see the land; 12
11 No! Go, the men among you, and serve the LORD 12
12:13 I will pass over you, and no plague 12
16 no work shall be done on those days; 12
19 no leaven shall be found in your houses; 12
43 passover: no foreigner shall eat of it; 12
45 No sojourner or hired servant may eat of it. 12
48 But no uncircumcised person shall eat of it. 12
13: 3 no leavened bread shall be eaten. 12
7 no leavened bread shall be seen with you 12
7 and no leaven shall be seen with you in all 12
14:11 Is it because there are no graves in Egypt 2
15:22 went . . in the wilderness and found no water. 12
16:18 and he that gathered little had no lack; 12
19 Let no man leave any of it till the morning. 3
24 become foul, and there were no worms in it. 12
29 let no man go out of his place on the seventh day. 3
17: 1 there was no water for the people to drink. 2
19:13 no hand shall touch him, but he shall be stoned 12
20: 3 You shall have no other gods before me. 12
21: 8 he shall have no right to sell her to a foreign 12
22 a miscarriage, and yet no harm follows 12
22: 2 there shall be no bloodguilt for him; 2
23: 8 you shall take no bribe, for a bribe blinds 12
13 make no mention of the names of other gods 12
32 You shall make no covenant with them 12
30: 9 You shall offer no unholy incense thereon 12
9 and you shall pour no libation thereon. 12
12 that there be no plague among them 12
32 you shall make no other like it in composition; 12
33: 4 they mourned; and no man put on his ornaments. 12
34: 3 No man shall come up with you, 12
3 let no man be seen throughout all the mountain; 3
3 let no flocks or herds feed before that mountain. 3
14 for you shall worship no other god, for the LORD 12
17 You shall make for yourself no molten gods. 12
35: 3 you shall kindle no fire in all your habitations 12
Lev 2:11 No cereal offering which you bring to the LORD 12
11 you shall burn no leaven nor any honey 12
5:11 he shall put no oil upon it 12
11 and shall put no frankincense on it 12
6:30 no sin offering shall be eaten from which any 12
7:23 You shall eat no fat, of ox, or sheep, or goat 12
24 any other use, but on no account shall you eat it 12
26 Moreover you shall eat no blood whatever 12
10: 9 Drink no wine nor strong drink, you nor your sons 3
13: 4 if the spot . . appears no deeper than the skin 2
26 if . . it is no deeper than the skin, but is dim 2
31 if . . it appears no deeper than the skin 2
31 if . . there is no black hair in it 2
32 if . . there is in it no yellow hair 2
32 the itch appears to be no deeper than the skin 2
34 if . . it appears to be no deeper than the skin 2
16:17 There shall be no man in the tent of meeting 12
29 shall afflict yourselves, and shall do no work 12
17: 7 So they shall no more slay their sacrifices 12
12 No person among you shall eat blood 12
19:15 You shall do no injustice in judgment 12
35 You shall do no wrong in judgment 12
20:14 that there may be no wickedness among you 12
21: 3 (who is near to him because she has had no husband 12
18 For no one who has a blemish shall draw near 12
21 no man of the descendants of Aaron the priest 12
22:13 daughter . . has no child, and returns to her 2
13 yet no outsider shall eat of it 12
21 must be perfect; there shall be no blemish in it 12
23: 3 you shall do no work; it is a sabbath to the LORD 12
7 convocation; you shall do no laborious work 12
8 convocation; you shall do no laborious work 12
21 you shall do no laborious work: it is a statute 12
25 You shall do no laborious work 12
28 you shall do no work on this same day; for it is a day 12
31 You shall do no work: it is a statute for ever 12
35 convocation; you shall do no laborious work 12
36 solemn assembly; you shall do no laborious work 12
25:26 If a man has no one to redeem it 12
31 the villages which have no wall around them 2
36 Take no interest from him or increase 3
26: 1 You shall make for yourselves no idols 12
1 and erect no graven image or pillar 12
37 have no power to stand before your enemies 12
27:26 a firstling . . no man may dedicate; whether ox 12
28 no devoted thing that a man devotes to the LORD 12
29 No one devoted, who is to be utterly destroyed 12
Num 1:53 that there may be no wrath upon the congregation 12
3: 4 they had no children. So Elea'zar and Ith'amar 12
5: 8 if the man has no kinsman to whom restitution 2
13 there is no witness against her 2
15 shall pour no oil upon it and put no frankincense 12
15 no oil upon it and put no frankincense on it 12
19 If no man has lain with you, and if you have not 12
6: 3 he shall drink no vinegar made from wine 12
5 no razor shall come upon his head; 12
8:19 there may be no plague among the people of Israel 12
25 withdraw from the work . . and serve no more 12
26 minister . . and they shall do no service. 12
11:25 they prophesied. But they did so no more. 12
14:18 but he will by no means clear the guilty 12
18: 4 no one else shall come near you. 12
5 there be wrath no more upon the people of Israel. 12
20 You shall have no inheritance in their land 12
23 they shall have no inheritance. 12
24 have no inheritance among the people of Israel. 12
32 you shall bear no sin by reason of it 12
19: 2 red heifer . . in which there is no blemish 2
15 open vessel, which has no cover fastened upon it 2
20: 2 Now there was no water for the congregation; 12
5 It is no place for grain, or figs, or vines 12
5 evil place . . and there is no water to drink. 2
21: 5 For there is no food and no water, and we loathe 2
5 For there is no food and no water, and we loathe 2
22:26 in a narrow place, where there was no way to turn 2
30 I ever accustomed to do so to you?" And he said, "No. 12
23:23 For there is no enchantment against Jacob 12
23 For there is . . no divination against Israel; 12
26:33 Now Zeloph'ehad the son of Hepher had no sons 12
62 because there was no inheritance given to them 12
27: 3 died for his own sin; and he had no sons. 12
4 taken away from his family, because he had no son? 2
8 If a man dies, and has no son 2
9 if he has no daughter, then you shall give 2
10 if he has no brothers, then you shall give 2
11 if his father has no brothers, then you shall give 2
17 may not be as sheep which have no shepherd. 2
28:18 the first day . . you shall do no laborious work 12
25 you shall do no laborious work. 12
26 holy convocation; you shall do no laborious work 12
29: 1 convocation; you shall do no laborious work. 12
7 afflict yourselves; you shall do no work 12
12 holy convocation; you shall do no laborious work 12
35 solemn assembly: you shall do no laborious work. 12
30: 5 no vow of hers, no pledge . . shall stand; 12
5 no vow of hers, no pledge . . shall stand; •
33:14 Reph'idim, where there was no water for the people 12
35:30 no person shall be put to death on the testimony 12
31 shall accept no ransom for the life of a murderer 12
32 you shall accept no ransom for him who has fled 12
33 no expiation can be made for the land 12
36: 9 no inheritance shall be transferred from one 12
Deu 1:39 children . . have no knowledge of good or evil 12
2: 5 no, not so much as for the sole of the foot to tread •
3: 3 smote him until no survivor was left to him. 8
26 suffice you; speak no more to me of this matter. 3
4:12 you heard the sound of words, but saw no form; 2
15 Since you saw no form on the day that the LORD 12
35 the LORD is God; there is no other besides him. 2
39 know . . the LORD is God . . ; there is no other. 2
5: 7 You shall have no other gods before me. 12
22 words the LORD spoke . . and he added no more. 12
7: 2 utterly destroy them; you shall make no covenant 12
2 make no covenant with them, and show no mercy 12
8:15 thirsty ground where there was no water 2
10: 9 no portion or inheritance with his brothers; 12
16 be no longer stubborn. 12
17 God, who is not partial and takes no bribe. 12
11:17 he shut up the heavens, so that there be no rain 12
17 no rain, and the land yield no fruit, and you perish 12
25 No man shall be able to stand against you; 12
12:12 since he has no portion or inheritance with you. 2
14:27 Levite . . has no portion or inheritance with you. 2
29 Levite, because he has no portion or inheritance 2
15: 4 there will be no poor among you (for the LORD 12
19 shall do no work with the firstling of your herd 12
16: 3 You shall eat no leavened bread with it; 12
4 No leaven . . seen with you in all your territory 12
8 seventh day . . you shall do no work on it. 12
18: 1 Levi . . no portion or inheritance with Israel; 12
2 no inheritance among their brethren; the LORD 12
20:12 if it makes no peace with you, but makes war 12
21:14 Then, if you have no delight in her, you shall let 12
22:26 woman there is no offense punishable by death 2
23: 2 No bastard shall enter the assembly of the LORD; 12
3 No Ammonite or Moabite shall enter the assembly 12
17 no cult prostitute of the daughters of Israel 12
22 if you refrain from vowing, it . . no sin in you. 12
24: 1 if then she finds no favor in his eyes 12
6 No man . . take a mill or an upper millstone in pledge; 12
25: 5 dwell together, and one of them dies and has no son 2
12 cut off her hand; your eye shall have no pity. 12
27: 5 you shall lift up no iron tool upon them. 12
28:65 among these nations you shall find no ease 12
65 there shall be no rest for the sole of your foot; 12
66 be in dread, and have no assurance of your life. 12
68 male and female slaves, but no man will buy you. 2
29:23 growing nothing, where no grass can sprout 12
31: 2 I am no longer able to go out and come in. 12
32: 5 dealt corruptly . . they are no longer his children 12
12 LORD alone . . there was no foreign god with him. 2
17 They sacrificed to demons which were no gods 12
20 children in whom is no faithfulness. 12
21 have stirred me to jealousy with what is no god; 12
21 So I will stir them to jealousy with . . no people; 12
28 there is no understanding in them. 2
39 I, even I, am he, and there is no god beside me; 2
47 For it is no trifle for you, but it is your life 12
34: 6 no man knows the place of his burial to this day. 12
Jos 1: 5 No man shall be able to stand before you 12
2:11 and there was no courage left in any man 14
5: 1 and there was no longer any spirit in them 12
12 and the people of Israel had manna no more 12
14 No; but as commander of the army . . I have now come. 12
7:12 I will be with you no more, unless you destroy 12
8:20 and they had no power to flee this way or that 12
31 stones, upon which no man has lifted an iron tool 12
10:14 There has been no day like it before or since 12
11:20 and should receive no mercy but be exterminated 8
13:14 To the tribe of Levi . . Moses gave no inheritance; 12
33 to the tribe of Levi Moses gave no inheritance; 12
14: 3 but to the Levites he gave no inheritance 12
4 no portion was given to the Levites in the land 12
17: 3 Now Zeloph'ehad . . had no sons, but only daughters; 12
18: 7 The Levites have no portion among you 2
20: 5 he killed . . unwittingly, having had no enmity 12
22:25 you have no portion in the LORD. 2
27 You have no portion in the LORD. 2
33 Israel . . spoke no more of making war against 12
23: 9 no man has been able to withstand you to this day. 12
Jdg 2: 2 you shall make no covenant with the inhabitants 12
14 they could no longer withstand their enemies. 12
3: 1 all in Israel who had no experience of any war 12
4:18 turn aside to me; have no fear." So he turned aside 3
20 man comes and asks you, 'Is any one here?' say, No. 2
5:19 they got no spoils of silver. 12
6: 4 they would . . leave no sustenance in Israel 12
4 leave no sustenance . . and no sheep or ox or ass. 12
8:28 and they lifted up their heads no more. 12
10:13 other gods; therefore I will deliver you no more. 12
12: 5 E'phraimite?" When he said, "No," they said to him 12
13: 2 his wife was barren and had no children. 12
3 Behold, you are barren and have no children; 12
4 beware, and drink no wine or strong drink, and eat 3
5 bear a son. No razor shall come upon his head 12
7 bear a son; so then drink no wine or strong drink 3
21 angel . . appeared no more to Mano'ah and to his wife. 12
15:13 No; we will only bind you and give you into their 12
17: 6 there was no king in Israel; every man did what was 2
18: 1 In those days there was no king in Israel. 2
1 until then no inheritance . . had fallen to them. 12
7 the Sido'nians and had no dealings with any one. 2
10 where there is no lack of anything that is 2
28 there was no deliverer because it was far 2
28 from Sidon, and they had no dealings with any one. 2
19: 1 In those days, when there was no king in Israel 2
15 no man took them into his house to spend 2
19 with your servants; there is no lack of anything. 2
23 No, my brethren, do not act so wickedly; 3
28 Get up, let us be going." But there was no answer. 2
21: 1 No one of us shall give his daughter in marriage 12
8 no one had come . . from Ja'besh-gil'ead 12
25 In those days there was no king in Israel; 2
Rut 1:10 No, we will return with you to your people. 11
13 No, my daughters, for it is exceedingly bitter 3
4: 4 there is no one besides you to redeem it 2
1Sm 1: 2 but Hannah had no children. 2
11 to the LORD . . and no razor shall touch his head. 12
15 No, my lord, I am a woman sorely troubled; 12
18 and ate, and her countenance was no longer sad. 12
2: 2 none besides thee; there is no rock like our God. 2
3 Talk no more so very proudly 3
12 they had no regard for the LORD. 12
16 No, you must give it now; and if not, I will take it 12
24 No, my sons; it is no good report that I hear 3
24 No, my sons; it is no good report that I hear 12
3: 1 was rare . . there was no frequent vision. 2
8:19 No! but we will have a king over us 12

9: 7 and there is no present to bring to the man of God. 2
10:19 and you have said, 'No! but set a king over us.' 12
27 they despised him, and brought him no present. 12
11:11 scattered, so that no two . . were left together. 12
12:12 you said to me, 'No, but a king shall reign over us,' 12
13:19 Now there was no smith . . throughout all the land 12
14:26 honey was . . but no man put his hand to his mouth; 2
17:32 Let no man's heart fail because of him; 3
50 there was no sword in the hand of David. 2
18:25 The king desires no marriage present except 2
20:21 it is safe for you and there is no danger. 2
34 Jonathan rose . . and ate no food the second day 12
21: 4 I have no common bread at hand, but . . holy bread; 2
6 there was no bread there but . . of the Presence 12
22:15 time that I have inquired of God for him? No! 9
24:11 see that there is no wrong or treason in my hands. 2
25: 7 and we did them no harm, and they missed nothing 12
15 men were very good to us, and we suffered no harm 12
31 my lord shall have no cause of grief, or pangs 12
26:12 No man saw it, or knew it, nor did any awake; 2
19 driven me out this day that I should have no share *
21 return, my son David, for I will no more do you harm 12
27: 4 when it was told Saul . . he sought for him no more. 12
28:10 no punishment shall come upon you for this 4
13 The king said to her, "Have no fear; what do you see? 3
15 God has turned away . . and answers me no more 12
20 and there was no strength in him 12
29: 3 I have found no fault in him to this day. 12
30: 2 they killed no one, but carried them off 12
2Sm 1:21 Gilbo'a, let there be no dew or rain upon you 3
2:28 all the men stopped, and pursued Israel no more 12
6:23 And Michal . . had no child to the day of her death. 12
7:10 dwell in their own place, and be disturbed no more; 12
10 and violent men shall afflict them no more 12
22 is none like thee, and there is no God besides thee 2
12: 6 because he did this . . and because he had no pity. 12
13:12 She answered him, "No, my brother, do not force me; 3
16 But she said to him, "No, my brother; 3
25 No, my son, let us not all go 3
14: 6 they quarreled . . there was no one to part them 2
25 there was no one so much to be praised 12
25 to . . his head there was no blemish in him. 12
15: 3 there is no man deputed by the king to hear you. 2
14 else there will be no escape for us from Ab'salom; 12
26 'I have no pleasure in you,' behold, here I am 12
16:18 No; for whom the LORD . . have chosen, his I will be 12
18:18 I have no son to keep my name in remembrance"; 2
20 but today you shall carry no tidings 12
22 you will have no reward for the tidings? 2
20: 1 We have no portion in David, and . . no inheritance 2
1 and we have no inheritance in the son of Jesse; 12
21: 5 so that we should have no place in all . . Israel 16
17 You shall no more go out with us to battle 12
24:24 king said . . "No, but I will buy it of you for a price; 12
1Kg 1:43 No, for our lord King David has made Solomon king; 1
2:30 he said, "No, I will die here." Then Benai'ah brought 12
3: 2 because no house had yet been built for the name 12
13 I give you . . so that no other king shall compare 12
18 there was no one else with us in the house, only we 2
22 No, the living child is mine, and the dead child is 12
22 No, the dead child is yours, and the living child is 12
23 No; but your son is dead, and my son is the living 12
5: 6 there is no one . . who knows how to cut timber 2
6:18 all was cedar, no stone was seen. 2
8:16 I chose no city . . in which to build a house 12
23 LORD . . there is no God like thee, in heaven above 2
35 and there is no rain because they have sinned 12
46 for there is no man who does not sin 2
60 may know that the LORD is God; there is no other. 2
9:22 of the people of Israel Solomon made no slaves; 12
10: 5 there was no more spirit in her. 12
12 no such almug wood has come or been seen, 12
12:16 We have no inheritance in the son of Jesse. 12
13:22 he said to you, "Eat no bread, and drink no water"; 3
22 he said to you, "Eat no bread, and drink no water"; 3
17: 7 the brook dried up, because there was no rain 12
17 so severe that there was no breath left in him. 12
18:10 there is no nation . . whither my lord has not sent 4
23 and lay it on the wood, but put no fire to it; 12
23 and lay it on the wood, and put no fire to it. 12
25 call on the name of your god, but put no fire to it. 12
26 O Ba'al, answer us!" But there was no voice 2
29 they raved on . . but there was no voice; 2
19: 4 take . . my life; for I am no better than my fathers. 12
21: 4 turned away his face, and would eat no food. 12
5 Why is your spirit so vexed that you eat no food? 2
22:17 scattered . . as sheep that have no shepherd; 2
17 These have no master; let each return to his home 12
47 There was no king in Edom; a deputy was king. 2
2Kg 1: 3 Is it because there is no God in Israel that you 2
6 Is it because there is no God in Israel that you 2
16 is it because there is no God in Israel 2
17 became king . . because Ahazi'ah had no son. 12
2:12 And he saw him no more. 12
3: 9 there was no water for the army or for the beasts 12
11 Is there no prophet of the LORD here 2
13 No; it is the LORD who has called these three kings 3
4:14 Well, she has no son, and her husband is old. 2
16 No, my lord . . do not lie to your maidservant. 3
31 but there was no sound or sign of life. 2
41 And there was no harm in the pot. 12
5:15 there is no God in all the earth but in Israel; 2
6:23 the Syrians came no more on raids into the land 12
7: 5 when they came . . behold, there was no one there. 2
10 there was no one to be seen or heard there, nothing 2
9:37 Jez'ebel shall be as dung . . so that no one can say 12
10:23 see that there is no servant of the LORD here 17
12: 6 the priests had made no repairs on the house. 12
7 take no more money from your acquaintances 3
8 priests agreed . . they should take no more money 8
17: 4 and offered no tribute to the king of Assyria 12
19: 3 and there is no strength to bring them forth. 2
18 they were no gods, but the work of men's hands, wood 12
22: 7 But no accounting shall be asked from them 12
23:18 And he said, "Let him be; let no man move his bones. 3
22 no such passover had been kept since the days 12
25 there was no king like him, who turned to the LORD 12
25: 3 there was no food for the people of the land. 12
1Ch 2:34 Now Sheshan had no sons, only daughters; 12
12:17 although there is no wrong in my hands 12
15: 2 'No one but the Levites may carry the ark of God 12
16:22 Touch not my anointed ones, do my prophets no harm! 3
17: 9 dwell in their own place, and be disturbed no more; 12
9 violent men shall waste them no more, as formerly 12
20 O LORD, and there is no God besides thee 2
21:24 to Ornan, "No, but I will buy it for the full price; 12
23:17 Elie'zer had no other sons 12
22 Elea'zar died having no sons, but only daughters; 12
26 Levites no longer need to carry the tabernacle 2
24: 2 Nadab and Abi'hu died . . and had no children 12
28 Of Mahli: Elea'zar, who had no sons. 12
29:15 are like a shadow, and there is no abiding. 2
2Ch 6: 5 I chose no city in all the tribes of Israel 12
5 I chose no man as prince over my people Israel; 12
14 said, "O LORD, God of Israel, there is no God like thee 2
26 When heaven is shut up and there is no rain 12
36 If they sin . . -for there is no man who does not sin- 2
7:13 When I shut up the heavens so that there is no rain 12
8: 9 of . . Israel Solomon made no slaves for his work; 12
9: 4 there was no more spirit in her. 12
9 there were no spices such as those 12
10:16 We have no inheritance in the son of Jesse. 12
13: 9 becomes a priest of what are no gods. 12
14: 6 no war in those years, for the LORD gave him peace. 2
15: 5 there was no peace to him who went out 2
19 there was no more war until the 35th year 12
17:10 they made no war against Jehosh'aphat. 12
18:16 as sheep that have no shepherd; 2
16 LORD said, 'These have no master; 12
19: 7 is no perversion of justice with the LORD our God 2
21:17 so that no son was left to him except Jeho'ahaz 12
19 His people made no fire in his honor 12
20 he departed with no one's regret. 12
23:19 no one should enter who was in any way unclean. 18
26:18 it will bring you no honor from the LORD God. 12
32:15 for no god of any nation or kingdom has been able 12
33: 8 no more remove the foot of Israel from the land 12
10 The LORD spoke . . but they gave no heed. 12
35: 3 you need no longer carry it upon your shoulders. 2
18 No passover like it had been kept in Israel since 12
36:16 till there was no remedy. 2
17 had no compassion on young man or virgin 12
Ezr 4:16 you will then have no possession in the province 18
9:14 that there should be no remnant, nor any to escape? 2
Neh 2:12 told no one what my God had put into my heart to do 12
12 no beast with me but the beast on which I rode. 2
14 there was no place for the beast that was under me 2
17 that we may no longer suffer disgrace. 12
20 no portion or right or memorial in Jerusalem. 2
5:16 held to the work . . and acquired no land; 12
6: 1 reported . . that there was no breach left in it 12
8 No such things as you say have been done 12
7: 4 people . . were few and no houses had been built. 2
13: 1 no Ammonite or Moabite should ever enter 12
19 no burden might be brought in on the sabbath day. 12
26 Among the many nations there was no king like him 12
Est 1:19 Vashti is to come no more before King Ahasu-e'rus 12
5:12 Even Queen Esther let no one come . . but myself. 12
13 all this does me no good, so long as I see Mor'decai 2
9: 2 And no one could make a stand against them 12
10 but they laid no hand on the plunder. 12
15 but they laid no hands on the plunder. 12
16 but they laid no hands on the plunder. 12
Job 2:13 no one spoke a word to him 2
3: 7 let no joyful cry be heard in it. 3
26 I have no rest; but trouble comes. 12
4:18 Even in his servants he puts no trust 12
5: 4 there is no one to deliver them. 2
12 that their hands achieve no success. 12
19 in seven there shall no evil touch you. 12
6:13 In truth I have no help in me 2
29 Turn, I pray, let no wrong be done. 3
7: 8 The eye of him who sees me will behold me no more; 12
10 he returns no more to his house 12
8:11 Can papyrus grow where there is no marsh? 12
11 Can reeds flourish where there is no water? 7
9:25 they flee away, they see no good. 12
33 There is no umpire between us 12
11: 3 when you mock, shall no one shame you? 2
13:15 Behold, he will slay me; I have no hope; 12
15: 3 or in words with which he can do no good? 12
15 Behold, God puts no trust in his holy ones 12
19 no stranger passed among them). 12
28 in houses which no man should inhabit 12
16:17 although there is no violence in my hands 12
18 let my cry find no resting place. 3
18:17 he has no name in the street. 12
19 He has no offspring or descendant 12
19 no survivor where he used to live. 2
19: 7 I call aloud, but there is no justice. 2
16 I call to my servant, but he gives me no answer; 12
20: 9 The eye which saw him will see him no more 12
18 of his trading he will get no enjoyment. 12
20 Because his greed knew no rest 12
21: 9 safe from fear, and no rod of God is upon them. 12
22: 5 There is no end to your iniquities. 2
7 You have given no water to the weary to drink 12
23: 6 No; he would give heed to me. 12
24: 7 naked, without clothing, and have no covering 2
12 yet God pays no attention to their prayer. 12
15 waits for the twilight, saying, 'No eye will see 12
18 no treader turns toward their vineyards. 12
20 their name is no longer remembered; 12
21 and do no good to the widow. 12
26: 2 How you have helped him who has no power! 12
2 How you have saved the arm that has no strength! 12
3 How you have counseled him who has no wisdom 12
6 naked before God, and Abaddon has no covering. 2
27:15 buries, and their widows make no lamentation. 12
19 He goes to bed rich, but will do so no more; 12
28: 7 That path no bird of prey knows 12
18 No mention shall be made of coral or of crystal; 12
29:24 I smiled on them when they had no confidence; 12
30:13 they promote my calamity; no one restrains them. 12
17 the pain that gnaws me takes no rest. 12
32: 3 he was angry . . because they had found no answer 12
5 was no answer in the mouth of these three men 2
15 They are discomfited, they answer no more; 12
16 because they stand there, and answer no more? 12
19 Behold, my heart is like wine that has no vent; 12
33: 7 Behold, no fear of me need terrify you; 12
9 I am pure, and there is no iniquity in me. 12
34:19 who shows no partiality to princes 12
20 the mighty are taken away by no human hand. 12
22 There is no gloom or deep darkness 2
27 had no regard for any of his ways 12
32 if I have done iniquity, I will do it no more 12
36:16 into a broad place where there was no cramping 12
38:11 and said, 'Thus far shall you come, and no farther 12
26 to bring rain on a land where no man is 12
26 on the desert in which there is no man; 12
39:16 though her labor be in vain, yet she has no fear; 7
17 and given her no share in understanding. 12
40: 5 twice, but I will proceed no further. 12
41:10 No one is so fierce that he dares to stir him up. 12
16 near to another that no air can come between 12
42: 2 no purpose of thine can be thwarted. 12
15 there were no women so fair as Job's daughters; 12
Ps 3: 2 are saying of me, there is no help for him in God. 2
5: 9 For there is no truth in their mouth; 2
6: 5 For in death there is no remembrance of thee; 2
10: 4 all his thoughts are, "There is no God. 2
18 man who is of the earth may strike terror no more. 6
14: 1 The fool says in his heart, "There is no God. 2
3 there is none that does good, no, not one. 2
4 Have they no knowledge, all the evildoers 12
15: 3 does no evil to his friend, nor takes up a reproach 12
16: 2 Thou art my Lord; I have no good apart from thee. 6
17: 3 testest me, thou wilt find no wickedness in me; 6
19: 3 There is no speech, nor are there words; 2
22: 2 I cry by day . . and by night, but find no rest. 12
6 I am a worm, and no man; scorned by men, 12
23: 4 I fear no evil; for thou art with me; 12
28: 5 he will break them down and build them up no more. 12
32: 2 the man to whom the LORD imputes no iniquity 12
2 in whose spirit there is no deceit. 2
34: 9 for those who fear him have no want! 2
10 but those who seek the LORD lack no good thing. 12
36: 1 there is no fear of God before his eyes. 2
38: 3 There is no soundness in my flesh 2
3 there is no health in my bones because of my sin. 2
7 there is no soundness in my flesh. 2
14 does not hear, and in whose mouth are no rebukes. 2
44:12 for a trifle, demanding no high price for them. 12
49: 7 Truly no man can ransom himself 12
50: 9 I will accept no bull from your house 12
51:16 For thou hast no delight in sacrifice; 12
53: 1 The fool says in his heart, "There is no God. 2
3 there is none that does good, no, not one. 2
4 Have those who work evil no understanding 12
55:19 because they keep no law, and do not fear God. 2
59: 3 For no transgression or sin of mine, O LORD 12
4 for no fault of mine, they run and make ready. 7
62:10 Put no confidence in extortion 3
10 in extortion, set no vain hopes on robbery; 3
63: 1 as in a dry and weary land where no water is. 7
69: 2 I sink in deep mire, where there is no foothold; 2

25 let no one dwell in their tents. 3
27 may they have no acquittal from thee. 3
72:12 he delivers . . the poor and him who has no helper. 2
73: 4 For they have no pangs; their bodies are sound 2
10 turn and praise them; and find no fault in them. •
74: 9 there is no longer any prophet 2
78:22 because they had no faith in God 12
63 their maidens had no marriage song. 12
64 their widows made no lamentation. 12
81: 9 There shall be no strange god among you; 12
83: 4 let the name of Israel be remembered no more! 12
84:11 No good thing does the LORD withhold 12
88: 4 I am a man who has no strength 2
5 like those whom thou dost remember no more 12
91:10 no evil shall befall you 12
10 no scourge come near your tent. 12
92:15 my rock, and there is no unrighteousness in him. 12
101: 7 No man who practices deceit shall dwell in my 12
7 no man who utters lies shall continue in my 12
102:27 thou art the same, and thy years have no end. 12
103:16 it is gone, and its place knows it no more. 12
104:35 let the wicked be no more! 2
105:14 he allowed no one to oppress them; 12
15 Touch not my anointed ones, do my prophets no harm! 3
106:24 land, having no faith in his promise. 12
107: 4 finding no way to a city to dwell in; 12
119: 3 who also do no wrong, but walk in his ways! 12
133let no iniquity get dominion over me. 3
142: 4 no refuge remains to me, no man cares for me. †
4 no refuge remains to me, no man cares for me. 2
143: 2 for no man living is righteous before thee. 12
144:14 suffering no mischance or failure in bearing; 2
14 there be no cry of distress in our streets! 2
146: 3 Put not your trust in . . whom there is no help. 2
Prv 3:30 Do not contend . . when he has done you no harm. 12
6: 4 Give your eyes no sleep 3
4 Give . . your eyelids no slumber; •
32 He who commits adultery has no sense; 10
35 He will accept no compensation 12
8:24 When there were no depths I was brought forth 2
24 when . . no springs abounding with water. 2
9:13 A foolish woman . . is wanton and knows no shame. 6
10:22 makes rich, and he adds no sorrow with it. 12
11:14 Where there is no guidance, a people falls; 2
12:11 follows worthless pursuits has no sense. 10
21 No ill befalls the righteous 12
13: 8 but a poor man has no means of redemption. 12
14: 4 Where there are no oxen, there is no grain; 2
4 Where there are no oxen, there is no grain; •
10 no stranger shares its joy. 12
15:21 Folly is a joy to him who has no sense 10
17:16 should a fool . . buy wisdom, when he has no mind? 2
21 father of a fool has no joy. 12
18: 2 A fool takes no pleasure in understanding 12
21:10 his neighbor finds no mercy in his eyes. 12
30 No wisdom, no understanding, no counsel, can avail 2
30 No wisdom, no understanding, no counsel, can avail 2
30 No wisdom, no understanding, no counsel, can avail 2
22:24 Make no friendship with a man given to anger 3
24:20 for the evil man has no future; 12
25:10 shame upon you, and your ill repute have no end. 12
26:20 where there is no whisperer, quarreling ceases. 2
28: 3 beating rain that leaves no food. 2
17 let him be a fugitive until death; let no one help 3
24 robs . . and says, "That is no transgression 2
29: 9 fool only rages and laughs, and there is no quiet. 2
18 Where there is no prophecy the people cast off 2
30:20 adulteress . . says, "I have done no wrong. 12
27 locusts have no king, yet all of them march in rank; 2
31: 7 drink and . . remember their misery no more. 12
11 he will have no lack of gain. 12
Ecc 1:11 There is no remembrance of former things 2
2:10 I kept my heart from no pleasure 13
16 of the fool there is no enduring remembrance 2
3:19 and man has no advantage over the beasts; 2
4: 8 a person who has no one, either son or brother 2
8 there is no end to all his toil . . so that he never asks 2
13 and foolish king, who will no longer take advice 12
16 there was no end of all the people; he was over all 2
5: 4 do not delay . . for he has no pleasure in fools. 2
6: 3 but he does not enjoy . . and also has no burial 12
6 Even though he should live . . yet enjoy no good 12
8: 5 He who obeys a command will meet no harm 12
8 No man has power to retain the spirit 2
8 there is no discharge from war 2
15 man has no good thing under the sun but to eat 2
9: 5 the dead know nothing, and . . have no more reward; 2
6 they have no more for ever any share in all that is 2
10 there is no work or thought or knowledge 2
15 Yet no one remembered that poor man. 12
10:11 there is no advantage in a charmer. 2
14 no man knows what is to be, and who can tell him 12
12: 1 when you will say, "I have no pleasure in them"; 2
12 Of making many books there is no end 2
Sng 3: 1 I called him, but he gave no answer. 33
4: 7 You are all fair, my love; there is no flaw in you. 2
5: 6 I sought him . . I called him, but he gave no answer 12
8: 8 We have a little sister, and she has no breasts. 2
Isa 1: 6 there is no soundness in it, but bruises and sores 2

13 Bring no more vain offerings; 12
2: 7 filled . . and there is no end to their treasures; 2
7 and there is no end to their chariots. 2
5: 6 command the clouds that they rain no rain upon it. 16
7: 8 that it will no longer be a people.) •
8:20 for this word which they speak there is no dawn. 2
9: 1 there will be no gloom for her . . in anguish. 12
7 his government and of peace there will be no end 2
17 and has no compassion on their fatherless 12
19 like fuel for the fire; no man spares his brother. 12
10:20 Jacob will no more lean upon him that smote them 12
13:17 Medes . . who have no regard for silver 12
18 they will have no mercy on the fruit of the womb; 12
20 no Arab will pitch his tent there 12
20 no shepherds will make their flocks lie down 12
14: 8 you were laid low, no hewer comes up against us.' 12
31 the north, and there is no straggler in his ranks. 2
15: 6 the new growth fails, the verdure is no more. 12
16:10 and in the vineyards no songs are sung 12
10 no songs are sung, no shouts are raised; 12
10 no treader treads out wine in the presses; 12
23:10 Overflow . . there is no restraint any more. 2
12 You will no more exult, O . . daughter of Sidon; 12
12 over to Cyprus, even there you will have no rest. 12
24: 9 No more do they drink wine with singing; 12
25: 2 the palace of aliens is a city no more •
26:18 We have wrought no deliverance in the earth 6
21 disclose . . and will no more cover her slain. 12
27: 4 I have no wrath. 2
9 no Ashe'rim or incense altars will remain 12
11 he that formed them will show them no favor. 12
28: 8 full of vomit, no place is without filthiness. 7
28 No, he does not thresh it for ever; 12
29:16 say of him who formed it, "He has no understanding"? 12
22 Jacob shall no more be ashamed 12
22 no more shall his face grow pale. 12
30:16 you said, "No! We will speed upon horses 12
19 who dwell at Jerusalem; you shall weep no more. 12
32: 5 The fool will no more be called noble 12
33: 8 are despised, there is no regard for man. 12
19 You will see no more the insolent people 12
21 a place . . where no galley with oars can go 6
24 no inhabitant will say, "I am sick"; 6
34:12 They shall name it No Kingdom There 2
35: 9 No lion shall be there, nor shall any ravenous 12
37: 3 and there is no strength to bring them forth. 2
19 they were no gods, but the work of men's hands 12
38:11 I shall look upon man no more 12
40:29 to him who has no might he increases strength. 2
41:28 when I look there is no one; 2
28 among these there is no counselor who 2
42: 8 my glory I give to no other 12
43:10 Before me no god was formed 12
11 I, I am the LORD, and besides me there is no savior. 2
12 when there was no strange god among you; 2
44: 6 first and I am the last; besides me there is no god. 2
8 a God besides me? There is no Rock; I know not any. 2
12 strength fails, he drinks no water and is faint. 12
19 No one considers, nor is there knowledge 12
45: 5 I am the LORD, and there is no other 2
5 there is no other, besides me there is no God; 2
6 I am the LORD, and there is no other. 2
9 Does the clay say . . 'Your work has no handles'? 2
14 God is with you only, and there is no other 2
14 there is no other, no god besides him.' 5
18 I am the LORD, and there is no other. 2
20 have no knowledge who carry about . . idols 12
21 there is no other god besides me 2
22 Turn to me . . For I am God, and there is no other. 2
46: 9 for I am God, and there is no other; 2
47: 1 you shall no more be called tender and delicate. 12
3 I will take vengeance, and I will spare no man. 12
5 for you shall no more be called the mistress 12
6 gave them into your hand, you showed them no mercy 12
14 No coal for warming oneself is this 2
14 No coal for warming . . no fire to sit before! •
15 they wander about . . there is no one to save you. 2
48:22 There is no peace," says the LORD, "for the wicked. 2
49:15 have no compassion on the son of her womb? 16
50: 2 Why, when I came, was there no man? 2
2 Why . . When I called, was there no one to answer? 2
2 cannot redeem? Or have I no power to deliver? 2
10 servant, who walks in darkness and has no light 2
51:22 the bowl of my wrath you shall drink no more; 12
52: 1 shall no more come into you the uncircumcised 12
11 depart, go out thence, touch no unclean thing; 3
53: 2 he had no form or comeliness that we should look 12
2 and no beauty that we should desire him. 12
9 in his death, although he had done no violence 12
9 no violence, and there was no deceit in his mouth. 12
54: 4 of your widowhood you will remember no more. 12
9 waters of Noah should no more go over the earth 16
17 no weapon that is fashioned against you shall 12
55: 1 and he who has no money, come, buy and eat! 2
56:11 The shepherds also have no understanding; 12
57: 1 righteous . . perishes, and no one lays it to heart; 2
21 There is no peace, says my God, for the wicked. 2
58: 3 humbled ourselves, and thou takest no knowledge 12
59: 8 and there is no justice in their paths; 2

8 no one who goes in them knows peace. 12
10 we grope like those who have no eyes; 2
15 it displeased him that there was no justice. 2
16 He saw that there was no man 2
16 wondered that there was no one to intervene; 2
60:18 Violence shall no more be heard in your land 12
19 The sun shall be no more your light by day 12
20 Your sun shall no more go down 12
62: 4 You shall no more be termed Forsaken 12
4 and your land shall no more be termed Desolate; 12
6 You who put the LORD in remembrance, take no rest 3
7 give him no rest until he establishes Jerusalem 3
63: 3 alone, and from the peoples no one was with me; 2
5 I looked, but there was no one to help; 2
5 I was appalled, but there was no one to uphold; 2
64: 4 of old no one has heard or perceived by the ear 12
4 no eye has seen a God besides thee 12
7 There is no one that calls upon thy name 2
65:19 no more shall be heard in it the sound of weeping 12
20 No more shall . . be in it an infant that lives 12
Jer 2: 6 that none passes through, where no man dwells?' 12
11 changed its gods, even though they are no gods? 12
13 broken cisterns, that can hold no water. 12
30 smitten your children, they took no correction; 12
31 We are free, we will come no more to thee'? 12
3:16 in those days, says the LORD, they shall no more say 12
17 no more stubbornly follow their own evil heart. 12
4:22 stupid children, they have no understanding. 12
23 and to the heavens, and they had no light. 2
25 I looked, and lo, there was no man 2
29 cities are forsaken, and no man dwells in them. 2
5: 3 Thou hast smitten them, but they felt no anguish; 12
7 and have sworn by those who are no gods. 12
12 He will do nothing; no evil will come upon us 12
6:10 an object of scorn, they take no pleasure in it. 12
14 saying, 'Peace, peace,' when there is no peace. 2
15 No, they were not at all ashamed; 12
23 they are cruel and have no mercy 12
7: 8 Behold, you trust in deceptive words to no avail. 8
32 when it will no more be called Topheth 12
32 bury in Topheth, because there is no room 2
8: 6 no man repents of his wickedness 2
11 saying, 'Peace, peace,' when there is no peace. 2
12 No, they were not at all ashamed; 12
13 there are no grapes on the vine 2
15 We looked for peace, but no good came 2
22 Is there no balm in Gilead? Is there no physician 2
22 no balm in Gilead? Is there no physician there? 2
9: 4 and put no trust in any brother; 3
5 and no one speaks the truth; 12
10 they are laid waste so that no one passes through 7
12 like a wilderness, so that no one passes through? 7
10:14 images are false, and there is no breath in them. 12
20 there is no one to spread my tent again 2
11:19 that his name be remembered no more. 12
12:11 land is made desolate, but no man lays it to heart. 2
12 no flesh has peace. 2
14: 3 they come to the cisterns, they find no water 12
4 since there is no rain on the land 12
5 forsakes her . . calf because there is no grass. 12
6 their eyes fail because there is no herbage. 2
18 trade through the land, and have no knowledge. 12
19 Why hast thou smitten us so . . there is no healing 2
19 We looked for peace, but no good came; 2
16: 6 they shall not be buried, and no one shall lament 12
7 No one shall break bread for the mourner 12
13 for I will show you no favor. 12
14 says the LORD, when it shall no longer be said 12
19 worthless things in which there is no profit. 2
20 Can man make for himself gods? Such are no gods! 12
17:24 and bring in no burden by the gates of this city 8
24 but keep the sabbath day holy and do no work on it 8
19: 6 when this place shall no more be called Topheth 12
11 because there will be no place else to bury. 2
22: 3 And do no wrong or violence to the alien 3
10 he shall return no more to see his native land. 12
11 away from this place: "He shall return here no more 12
28 a despised, broken pot, a vessel no one cares for? 2
23: 4 and they shall fear no more, nor be dismayed 12
7 when men shall no longer say, 'As the LORD lives 12
14 so that no one turns from his wickedness; 8
17 they say, 'No evil shall come upon you. 12
36 'the burden of the LORD' you shall mention no more 12
25: 6 Then I will do you no harm. 12
27 Drink, be drunk and vomit, fall and rise no more 12
30: 5 heard a cry of panic, of terror, and no peace. 2
8 strangers shall no more make servants of them. 12
11 I will by no means leave you unpunished. 12
13 no medicine for your wound, no healing for you. •
13 no medicine for your wound, no healing for you. 2
31:12 and they shall languish no more. 12
29 In those days they shall no longer say 12
34 And no longer shall each man teach his neighbor 12
34 and I will remember their sin no more. 12
33:24 they are no longer a nation in their sight. •
34: 9 so that no one should enslave a Jew, his brother. 8
35: 6 But they answered, "We will drink no wine 12
8 that he commanded us, to drink no wine all our days 8
9 We have no vineyard or field or seed; 12

14 gave to his sons, to drink no wine, has been kept; 8
36:19 and let no one know where you are. 3
38: 6 there was no water in the cistern, but only mire 2
9 hunger, for there is no bread left in the city. 2
24 said to Jeremiah, "Let no one know of these words 3
39:12 Take him, look after him well and do him no harm 3
40:15 Let me go and slay Ish'mael . . and no one will know 12
42:14 saying, 'No, we will go to the land of Egypt 12
17 they shall have no remnant or survivor 12
18 You shall see this place no more. 12
44: 2 they are a desolation, and no one dwells in them 2
5 to turn . . and burn no incense to other gods. 8
7 from the midst of Judah, leaving you no remnant? 8
17 had plenty of food, and prospered, and saw no evil. 12
22 The LORD could no longer bear your evil doings 12
26 that my name shall no more be invoked by the mouth †
45: 3 I am weary with my groaning, and I find no rest. 12
46:11 there is no healing for you. 2
28 I will by no means leave you unpunished. 12
48: 2 the renown of Moab is no more. 2
8 come upon every city, and no city shall escape; 12
9 become a desolation, with no inhabitant in them. 2
33 no one treads them with shouts of joy; 12
38 a vessel for which no one cares, says the LORD. 2
42 Moab shall be destroyed and be no longer a people •
49: 1 says the LORD: "Has Israel no sons? Has he no heir? 2
1 says the LORD: "Has Israel no sons? Has he no heir? 2
7 Is wisdom no more in Teman? Has counsel perished 2
10 his brothers, and his neighbors; and he is no more. 2
18 no man shall dwell there, no man shall sojourn 12
18 no man shall sojourn in her. 12
31 that has no gates or bars, that dwells alone. 12
33 no man shall dwell there, no man shall sojourn 12
33 no man shall dwell there, no man shall sojourn 12
36 shall be no nation to which those driven out 12
50:14 you that bend the bow; shoot at her, spare no arrows 3
29 Encamp round about her; let no one escape. 3
39 she shall be peopled no more for ever 12
40 says the LORD, so no man shall dwell there 12
40 and no son of man shall sojourn in her. 12
42 they are cruel, and have no mercy. 12
51:17 images are false, and there is no breath in them. 12
26 No stone shall be taken from you for a corner 12
26 for a corner and no stone for a foundation •
43 drought and a desert, a land in which no one dwells 12
43 and through which no son of man passes. 12
44 The nations shall no longer flow to him; 12
64 say, 'Thus shall Babylon sink, to rise no more 12
52: 6 there was no food for the people of the land. 12
Lam 1: 3 now among the nations, but finds no resting place; 12
6 Her princes . . like harts that find no pasture; 12
9 she took no thought of her doom; 12
9 her fall is terrible, she has no comforter. 2
2: 9 and her prophets obtain no vision from the LORD. 12
18 Give yourself no rest, your eyes no respite! 3
18 Give yourself no rest, your eyes no respite! 3
3:44 wrapped thyself . . so that no prayer can pass 16
4: 6 overthrown in a moment, no hand being laid on it. 12
16 no honor was shown to the priests 12
16 no honor was shown . . no favor to the elders. 12
5: 5 we are . . driven; we are weary, we are given no rest. 12
12 no respect is shown to the elders. 12
Ezk 3:18 and you give him no warning, nor speak to warn 12
5:11 my eye will not spare, and I will have no pity. 12
9: 5 shall not spare, and you shall show no pity; 3
6 but touch no one upon whom is the mark. 3
12:23 they shall no more use it as a proverb in Israel. 12
24 For there shall be no more any false vision 12
25 It will no longer be delayed, but in your days 12
13:10 saying, 'Peace,' when there is no peace; 2
15 The wall is no more, nor those who daubed it 2
16 visions of peace for her, when there was no peace 2
21 they shall be no more in your hand as prey; 12
23 you shall no more see delusive visions 12
14:11 that the house of Israel may go no more astray 12
15 no man may pass through because of the beasts; 7
16: 5 No eye pitied you, to do any of these things to you 12
34 you gave hire, while no hire was given to you; 12
41 you shall also give hire no more. 12
42 I will be calm, and will no more be angry. 12
18: 3 this proverb shall no more be used by you 4
7 commits no robbery, gives his bread to the hungry 12
16 exacts no pledge, commits no robbery 12
16 exacts no pledge, commits no robbery 12
17 takes no interest or increase 12
32 For I have no pleasure in the death of any one 12
19: 9 that his voice should no more be heard 12
14 so that there remains in it no strong stem 12
14 in it no strong stem, no scepter for a ruler. •
20:39 but my holy name you shall no more profane 12
21:32 you shall be no more remembered; 12
22:26 they have made no distinction between the holy 12
24:17 Sigh, but not aloud; make no mourning for the dead. 12
27 you shall speak and be no longer dumb. 12
25:10 may be remembered no more among the nations 12
26:13 the sound of your lyres shall be heard no more. 12
21 you shall be no more; though you be sought 2
27:36 to a dreadful end and shall be no more for ever. 2
28: 2 yet you are but a man, and no god 12
3 wiser than Daniel; no secret is hidden from you; 12
9 and no god, in the hands of those who wound you 12
19 to a dreadful end and shall be no more for ever. 2
24 for . . Israel there shall be no more a brier 12
29:11 No foot of man shall pass through it 12
11 no foot of beast shall pass through it; 12
30:13 shall no longer be a prince in the land of Egypt; 12
31: 8 no tree in the garden of God was like it in beauty. 13
14 in order that no trees by the waters may grow 13
14 no trees that drink water may reach up to them 13
32:13 no foot of man shall trouble them any more 12
33:11 I have no pleasure in the death of the wicked •
15 in the statutes of life, committing no iniquity; 8
22 my mouth was opened, and I was no longer dumb. 12
34: 5 were scattered, because there was no shepherd; 7
8 since there was no shepherd; 2
10 no longer shall the shepherds feed themselves. 12
22 I will save my flock, they shall no longer be a prey; 12
28 They shall no more be a prey to the nations 12
29 shall no more be consumed with hunger in the land 12
29 no longer suffer the reproach of the nations. 12
36:12 you shall no longer bereave them of children. 12
14 therefore you shall no longer devour men 12
14 and no longer bereave your nation of children 12
15 you shall no longer bear the disgrace 12
15 and no longer cause your nation to stumble 12
29 and make it abundant and lay no famine upon you. 12
37: 8 but there was no breath in them. 2
22 they shall be no longer two nations 12
22 and no longer divided into two kingdoms. 12
38:11 without walls, and having no bars or gates 2
42: 6 they had no pillars like the pillars of the outer 2
43: 7 house of Israel shall no more defile my holy name 12
44: 2 it shall not be opened, and no one shall enter by it; 12
9 No foreigner, uncircumcised in heart and flesh 12
21 No priest shall drink wine, when he enters 13
28 They shall have no inheritance; 12
28 you shall give them no possession in Israel; 12
45: 8 my princes shall no more oppress my people; 12
46: 9 no one shall return by way of the gate by which he 12
Dan 2:10 no great and powerful king has asked such a thing 18
27 No wise men, enchanters, magicians 18
34 As you looked, a stone was cut out by no human hand 18
45 stone was cut from a mountain by no human hand 18
3:12 men, O king, pay no heed to you; they do not serve 18
16 have no need to answer you in this matter. 18
27 no smell of fire had come upon them. 18
29 no other god who is able to deliver in this way. 18
4: 9 know . . that no mystery is difficult for you 18
6: 2 account, so that the king might suffer no loss. 18
4 could find no ground for complaint or any fault 18
4 faithful, and no error or fault was found in him. 18
13 pays no heed to you, O king, or the interdict 18
15 no interdict or ordinance which the king 18
18 no diversions were brought to him, and sleep fled 18
22 also before you, O king, I have done no wrong. 18
23 no kind of hurt was found upon him 18
8: 4 no beast could stand before him, 12
7 ram had no power to stand before him 12
7 no one who could rescue the ram from his power. 12
25 but, by no human hand, he shall be broken. 5
10: 3 ate no delicacies, no meat or wine entered 12
3 no delicacies, no meat or wine entered my mouth 12
8 great vision, and no strength was left in me; 12
8 I retained no strength. 12
16 pains have come upon me, and I retain no strength. 12
17 For now no strength remains in me, and no breath 12
17 no strength remains . . no breath is left in me. 12
11:15 for there shall be no strength to stand. 2
27 shall speak lies at the same table, but to no avail; 12
37 He shall give no heed to the gods of his fathers 12
Hos 1: 6 for I will no more have pity on the house of Israel 12
2: 4 Upon her children also I will have no pity 12
10 and no one shall rescue her out of my hand. 12
16 and no longer will you call me, 'My Ba'al.' 12
17 and they shall be mentioned by name no more. 12
4: 1 There is no faithfulness or kindness 2
1 There is . . no knowledge of God in the land; 2
4 Yet let no one contend, and let none accuse 3
8: 7 The standing grain has no heads 2
7 grain has no heads, it shall yield no meal; 7
13 but the LORD has no delight in them. 12
9:11 no birth, no pregnancy, no conception! 16
11 no birth, no pregnancy, no conception! 16
11 no birth, no pregnancy, no conception! 16
15 I will love them no more; 12
16 their root is dried up, they shall bear no fruit. 6
10: 3 We have no king, for we fear not the LORD 2
13: 4 you know no God but me 12
4 and besides me there is no savior. 2
14: 3 will say no more, 'Our God,' to the work of our hands. 12
Jol 1:18 perplexed because there is no pasture for them; 2
2:19 and I will no more make you a reproach 12
Ams 3: 4 Does a lion roar in the forest, when he has no prey? 2
5 Does a bird fall . . when there is no trap for it? 2
4: 7 upon one city, and send no rain upon another city; 12
5: 2 Fallen, no more to rise, is the virgin Israel; 12
20 and not light, and gloom with no brightness in it? 12
21 and I take no delight in your solemn assemblies. 12
6:10 Is there still any one with you?" he shall say, "No"; 5
7:14 answered . . "I am no prophet, nor a prophet's son 12
9: 9 a sieve, but no pebble shall fall upon the earth. 12
Obd 1: 7 trap under you–there is no understanding of it. 2
18 there shall be no survivor to the house of Esau; 12
Mic 2: 8 who pass by trustingly with no thought of war. •
10 Arise and go, for this is no place to rest; 12
3: 7 cover their lips, for there is no answer from God. 2
11 No evil shall come upon us. 12
4: 9 Now why do you cry aloud? Is there no king in you? 2
5:12 and you shall have no more soothsayers; 12
13 shall bow down no more to the work of your hands; 12
7: 1 there is no cluster to eat 2
1 no first-ripe fig which my soul desires. •
5 Put no trust in a neighbor 3
5 have no confidence in a friend; 3
Nah 1: 3 and the LORD will by no means clear the guilty. 12
12 I have afflicted you, I will afflict you no more. 12
14 No more shall your name be perpetuated; 12
2: 9 There is no end of treasure, or wealth 2
13 voice of your messengers shall no more be heard. 12
3: 1 full of lies and booty–no end to the plunder! 12
17 they fly away; no one knows where they are. 12
19 There is no assuaging your hurt 2
Hab 1:14 like crawling things that have no ruler. 12
2:19 there is no breath at all in it. 2
3:17 the olive fail and the fields yield no food 12
17 Though . . there be no herd in the stalls 2
Zep 2: 5 and I will destroy you till no inhabitant is left. 2
3: 2 She listens to no voice 12
2 listens to no voice, she accepts no correction. 12
5 The LORD within her is righteous, he does no wrong; 12
5 but the unjust knows no shame. 12
11 you shall no longer be haughty 12
13 they shall do no wrong and utter no lies 12
13 they shall do no wrong and utter no lies 12
15 you shall fear evil no more. 12
Hag 1: 6 you clothe yourselves, but no one is warm; 2
2:12 does it become holy?'" The priests answered, "No 12
Zec 1:12 how long wilt thou have no mercy on Jerusalem 12
21 scattered Judah, so that no man raised his head; 12
4: 5 Do you not know what these are?" I said, "No, my lord. 12
13 Do you not know what these are?" I said, "No, my lord. 12
7:14 was desolate, so that no one went to and fro •
8:10 For before those days there was no wage for man 12
17 love no false oath, for all these things I hate 3
9: 8 no oppressor shall again overrun them 12
10:10 and to Lebanon, till there is no room for them. 12
11: 5 their own shepherds have no pity on them. 12
6 For I will no longer have pity on the inhabitants 12
13: 2 so that they shall be remembered no more; 12
5 he will say, 'I am no prophet, I am a tiller of the soil; 12
14:11 inhabited, for there shall be no more curse; 12
17 there will be no rain upon them. 12
21 no longer be a trader in the house of the LORD 12
Mal 1: 8 offer blind animals in sacrifice, is that no evil? 2
8 offer those that are lame or sick, is that no evil? 2
10 I have no pleasure in you, says the LORD of hosts 2
2: 6 no wrong was found on his lips. 12
13 because he no longer regards the offering 2
Mat 5:37 Let what you say be simply 'Yes' or 'No'; 33
6: 1 you will have no reward from your Father who is 33
2 when you give alms, sound no trumpet before you 26
8:28 so fierce that no one could pass that way. 26
9:12 Those who are well have no need of a physician 33
10: 5 and enter no town of the Samaritans 26
9 Take no gold, nor silver, nor copper in your belts 26
10 no bag for your journey, nor two tunics 26
26 So have no fear of them; for nothing is covered 26
11: 6 blessed is he who takes no offense at me. 26
11 has risen no one greater than John the Baptist 33
27 and no one knows the Father except the Son 35
12:25 no city or house divided against itself 33
39 but no sign shall be given to it 33
13: 5 since they had no depth of soil 26
6 since they had no root they withered away. 26
21 yet he has no root in himself 33
29 he said, 'No, lest in gathering the weeds you root up 33
14:27 Take heart, it is I; have no fear. 26
16: 4 but no sign shall be given to it 33
7 We brought no bread. 33
8 the fact that you have no bread? 33
17: 7 Rise, and have no fear. 26
20:13 Friend, I am doing you no wrong 33
22:11 he saw there a man who had no wedding garment; 33
23 who say that there is no resurrection 26
24 If a man dies, having no children 26
25 having no children left his wife to his brother. 26
24: 4 Take heed that no one leads you astray. 26
21 until now, no, and never will be. 35
22 no human being would be saved 33
25: 3 they took no oil with them; 33
42 for I was hungry and you gave me no food 33
42 I was thirsty and you gave me no drink 33
26:62 Have you no answer to make? 36
27:12 he made no answer. 36
14 he gave him no answer, not even to a single charge; 33
Mrk 2:17 Those who are well have no need of a physician 33
4: 5 since it had no depth of soil; 26

6 since it had no root it withered away. 26
7 it yielded no grain. 33
17 they have no root in themselves 33
40 Why are you afraid? Have you no faith? 40
5:26 no better but rather grew worse. 29
6: 5 he could do no mighty work there 36
8 a staff; no bread, no bag, no money in their belts; 26
8 a staff; no bread, no bag, no money in their belts; 26
8 a staff; no bread, no bag, no money in their belts; 26
50 Take heart, it is I; have no fear. 26
8:12 Truly, I say to you, no sign shall be given 23
16 We have no bread. 33
17 Why do you discuss the fact that you have no bread? 33
9: 3 as no fuller on earth could bleach them. 33
12:18 who say that there is no resurrection 26
19 leaves a wife, but leaves no child 26
20 when he died left no children; 33
21 the second took her, and died, leaving no children; 26
22 the seven left no children 33
31 no other commandment greater than these. 33
32 there is no other but he; 33
13:20 no human being would be saved 39
14:60 Have you no answer to make? 36
61 he was silent and made no answer 36
15: 4 Pilate again asked him, "Have you no answer to make 36
5 Jesus made no further answer 36
Lke 1: 7 they had no child, because Elizabeth was barren 33
15 he shall drink no wine nor strong drink 38
33 of his kingdom there will be no end. 33
34 How shall this be, since I have no husband? 33
2: 7 because there was no place for them in the inn. 33
3:13 Collect no more than is appointed you. 29
4:24 no prophet is acceptable in his own country. 36
35 he came out of him, having done him no harm. 29
5:19 no way to bring him in, because of the crowd 26
31 Those who are well have no need of a physician 33
6:43 For no good tree bears bad fruit 33
7:23 blessed is he who takes no offense at me. 26
33 For John the Baptist has come eating no bread 33
33 has come eating no bread and drinking no wine 31
44 you gave me no water for my feet 33
45 You gave me no kiss 33
8: 6 it withered away, because it had no moisture. 26
13 but these have no root 33
27 for a long time he had worn no clothes 33
51 he permitted no one to enter with him 33
9: 3 no staff, nor bag, nor bread, nor money 31
13 We have no more than five loaves and two fish 33
10: 4 Carry no purse, no bag, no sandals 26
4 Carry no purse, no bag, no sandals 26
4 Carry no purse, no bag, no sandals 26
11:29 it seeks a sign, but no sign shall be given to it 33
36 whole body is full of light, having no part dark 26
12: 4 after that have no more that they can do. 26
33 where no thief approaches and no moth destroys. 33
33 where no thief approaches and no moth destroys. 35
51 No, I tell you, but rather division; 33
13: 3 I tell you, No 33
5 I tell you, No 33
15: 7 who need no repentance. 33
16:13 No servant can serve two masters 36
30 he said, 'No, father Abraham 33
17:18 Was no one found to return and give praise to God 33
20:21 and show no partiality 33
27 those who say that there is no resurrection 26
31 likewise all seven left no children and died. 33
22:35 When I sent you out with no purse or bag or sandals 22
36 let him who has no sword sell his mantle 26
23: 4 I find no crime in this man. 36
9 but he made no answer. 36
22 I have found in him no crime deserving death 36
Joh 1:21 Are you the prophet?" And he answered, "No. 33
47 Behold, an Israelite indeed, in whom is no guile! 33
2: 3 the mother of Jesus said to him, "They have no wine. 33
3:27 John answered, "No one can receive anything 33
4: 9 For Jews have no dealings with Samaritans. 33
17 The woman answered him, "I have no husband. 33
17 You are right in saying, 'I have no husband'; 33
44 that a prophet has no honor in his own country. 33
5: 7 I have no man to put me into the pool 33
6:53 you have no life in you; 33
63 the flesh is of no avail 36
7:12 others said, "No, he is leading the people astray. 33
18 in him there is no falsehood. 33
52 no prophet is to rise from Galilee. 33
8:37 because my word finds no place in you. 33
44 because there is no truth in him 33
9: 9 others said, "No, but he is like him. 33
41 If you were blind, you would have no guilt 33
10:28 no one shall snatch them out of my hand. 33
41 many came to him; and they said, "John did no sign 36
12:27 No, for this purpose I have come to this hour. 19
13: 8 If I do not wash you, you have no part in me. 33
14:30 He has no power over me; 33
15: 2 Every branch of mine that bears no fruit 26
22 now they have no excuse for their sin. 33
18:38 I find no crime in him. 36
19: 4 that you may know that I find no crime in him. 36
6 for I find no crime in him. 33

9 But Jesus gave no answer. 33
11 You would have no power over me 36
15 We have no king but Caesar. 33
21: 5 They answered him, "No. 33
Act 3: 6 I have no silver and gold, but I give you what I have; 33
4:12 no other name under heaven given among men 35
17 it may spread no further among the people 26
32 no one said that any of the things . . was his own 35
7: 5 yet he gave him no inheritance in it 33
5 though he had no child. 33
11 our fathers could find no food. 33
10:14 Peter said, "No, Lord 27
34 Truly I perceive that God shows no partiality 33
11: 8 I said, 'No, Lord 27
12 to go with them, making no distinction 29
12:18 there was no small stir among the soldiers 33
13:25 No, but after me one is coming 20
37 he whom God raised up saw no corruption. 33
14:28 remained no little time with the disciples. 33
15: 2 when Paul and Barnabas had no small dissension 33
9 he made no distinction between us and them 36
24 although we gave them no instructions 33
28 no greater burden than these necessary things 29
16:37 No! let them come themselves and take us out. 33
18:17 But Gallio paid no attention to this. 36
19: 2 they said, "No 19
23 there arose no little stir concerning the Way. 33
24 brought no little business to the craftsmen. 33
40 no cause that we can give to justify this 29
21:39 from Tarsus in Cili'cia, a citizen of no mean city 33
23: 8 the Sad'ducees say that there is no resurrection 26
14 an oath to taste no food till we have killed Paul. 29
24: 4 to detain you no further 26
25:10 to the Jews I have done no wrong 36
17 I made no delay, but on the next day took my seat 29
18 they brought no charge in his case 36
27:20 no small tempest lay on us 33
22 no loss of life among you, but only of the ship. 36
28: 5 shook off the creature . . and suffered no harm. 36
6 saw no misfortune come to him 29
18 no reason for the death penalty in my case. 29
19 though I had no charge to bring against my nation. 33
21 We have received no letters from Judea about you 41
Rom 2:11 For God shows no partiality. 33
3: 9 What then? Are we Jews any better off? No, not at all; 33
10 as it is written: "None is righteous, no, not one; *
11 no one understands, no one seeks for God. 33
11 no one understands, no one seeks for God. 33
12 no one does good, not even one. 33
18 There is no fear of God before their eyes. 33
20 For no human being will be justified in his sight 39
22 all who believe. For there is no distinction; 33
27 No, but on the principle of faith. 33
4:15 but where there is no law there is no transgression 33
15 but where there is no law there is no transgression 35
20 No distrust made him waver 33
5:13 but sin is not counted where there is no law. 26
6:14 For sin will have no dominion over you 33
8: 1 no condemnation for those who are in Christ 33
37 No, in all these things we are more 19
9:21 Has the potter no right over the clay 33
10:12 there is no distinction between Jew and Greek; 33
12:20 No, "if your enemy is hungry, feed him; 19
13: 1 For there is no authority except from God 33
3 Would you have no fear of him who is in authority? 26
10 Love does no wrong to a neighbor; 33
14 and make no provision for the flesh 26
14:22 happy is he who has no reason to judge himself 26
1Co 1:10 that there be no dissensions among you 26
29 so that no human being might boast 26
2: 9 What no eye has seen, nor ear heard 33
6: 5 Can it be that there is no man among you 33
7:25 I have no command of the Lord 33
30 those who buy as though they had no goods 26
31 as though they had no dealings with it 26
36 let him do as he wishes: let them marry–it is no sin. 33
37 under no necessity 26
8: 4 there is no God but one. 33
8 We are no worse off if we do not eat 41
8 and no better off if we do. 41
9: 6 Or is it only Barnabas and I who have no right 33
15 I have made no use of any of these rights 33
16 that gives me no ground for boasting 33
10:13 No temptation has overtaken you 33
20 No, I imply that what pagans sacrifice 19
11:16 we recognize no other practice 33
22 Shall I commend you in this? No, I will not. *
12:21 eye cannot say to the hand, "I have no need of you 33
21 the head to the feet, "I have no need of you. 33
25 that there may be no discord in the body 26
15:12 there is no resurrection of the dead? 33
13 if there is no resurrection of the dead 33
16:11 So let no one despise him 26
22 If any one has no love for the Lord 33
2Co 1:17 like a worldly man, ready to say Yes and No at once? 33
18 our word to you has not been Yes and No. 33
19 was not Yes and No; but in him it is always Yes. 33
3:10 has come to have no splendor at all 33
5:21 For our sake he made him to be sin who knew no sin 26

6: 3 We put no obstacle in any one's way 29
3 so that no fault may be found with our ministry 26
7: 5 our bodies had no rest 36
9 so that you suffered no loss through us. 24
8:15 he who gathered little had no lack. 33
11:14 no wonder, for even Satan disguises himself 33
12: 6 so that no one may think more of me than he sees 26
Gal 2: 6 what they were makes no difference to me 36
6 God shows no partiality 33
16 by works of the law shall no one be justified. 33
4: 1 the heir . . is no better than a slave 36
8 in bondage to beings that by nature are no gods; 26
12 You did me no wrong; 36
5: 2 Christ will be of no advantage to you. 36
10 you will take no other view than mine 36
23 self-control; against such there is no law. 33
26 Let us have no self-conceit 26
26 have no self-conceit, no provoking of one another *
26 no envy of one another. *
Eph 2:12 having no hope and without God in the world. 26
4:27 give no opportunity to the devil. 28
29 Let no evil talk come out of your mouths 30
5: 4 Let there be no filthiness, nor silly talk *
5 no fornicator or impure man 39
11 Take no part in the unfruitful works of darkness 26
6: 9 there is no partiality with him. 33
Php 3: 3 put no confidence in the flesh. 33
4:15 no church entered into partnership with me 36
Col 2: 8 See to it that no one makes a prey of you 26
16 Therefore let no one pass judgment on you 26
23 they are of no value 42
3:25 there is no partiality. 33
1Th 4: 9 you have no need to have any one write to you 33
13 you may not grieve as others do who have no hope. 26
5: 1 you have no need to have anything written to you. 33
3 there will be no escape. 38
2Th 2: 3 Let no one deceive you in any way 26
1Ti 2:12 I permit no woman to teach 33
3: 3 no drunkard, . . not violent but gentle 26
11 no slanderers, but temperate 26
5:14 give the enemy no occasion to revile us. 29
6:16 whom no man has ever seen or can see 36
2Ti 2: 4 No soldier on service gets entangled 36
14 avoid disputing about words, which does no good 36
Tit 1:11 by teaching . . what they have no right to teach. 26
Heb 4:11 no one fall by the same sort of disobedience. 26
13 before him no creature is hidden 33
7:27 He has no need . . to offer sacrifices daily 33
8: 7 there would have been no occasion for a second. 33
12 I will remember their sins no more. 38
9:22 there is no forgiveness of sins. 33
10: 2 would no longer have any consciousness of sin. 29
6 thou hast taken no pleasure. 33
17 remember their sins and their misdeeds no more. 26
38 if he shrinks back, my soul has no pleasure in him. 33
12:15 no "root of bitterness" spring up 32
17 he was rejected for he found no chance to repent 33
19 no further messages be spoken to them. 26
13:10 those who serve the tent have no right to eat. 33
14 For here we have no lasting city 33
Jas 1: 6 let him ask in faith, with no doubting 29
17 Father of lights with whom there is no variation 37
25 being no hearer that forgets but a doer that acts 33
2: 1 show no partiality as you hold the faith 26
13 without mercy to one who has shown no mercy 26
17 So faith by itself, if it has no works, is dead. 26
3: 2 if any one makes no mistakes in what he says 33
8 no human being can tame the tongue 36
5:12 let your yes be yes and your no be no 33
12 let your yes be yes and your no be no 33
1Pe 2:10 Once you were no people but now you are God's 33
22 He committed no sin; 33
22 no guile was found on his lips. 35
3:14 Have no fear of them, nor be troubled 26
2Pe 1:20 no prophecy of scripture is a matter of one's own 39
21 no prophecy ever came by the impulse of man 33
1Jn 1: 8 If we say we have no sin, we deceive ourselves 33
2: 7 Beloved, I am writing you no new commandment 33
10 and in it there is no cause for stumbling. 33
21 and know that no lie is of the truth. 39
27 and you have no need that any one should teach you; 33
27 anointing teaches . . and is true, and is no lie 33
3: 5 and in him there is no sin. 33
15 no murderer has eternal life abiding in him. 39
4:18 There is no fear in love 33
3Jn 1: 4 No greater joy can I have than this 33
Rev 7: 1 that no wind might blow on earth or sea 26
16 They shall hunger no more, neither thirst 33
11: 6 shut the sky, that no rain may fall during the days 26
14: 5 in their mouth no lie was found 33
11 and they have no rest, day or night 33
16:20 and no mountains were to be found; 33
18: 7 I am no widow, mourning I shall never see,' 33
20: 6 Over such the second death has no power 33
11 and no place was found for them. 33
21:22 And I saw no temple in the city 33
23 the city has no need of sun or moon to shine upon it 33
25 and there shall be no night there; 33
22: 5 they need no light of lamp or sun 33

1Es 1:16 no one needed to depart from his duties 33
20 No passover like it had been kept in Israel 33
2:29 that such wicked proceedings go no further 26
4:11 no one may go away to attend to his own affairs 33
21 with no thought of his father or his mother 41
37 There is no truth in them 33
39 With her there is no partiality or preference 33
49 that no officer or satrap . . forcibly enter 30
8:22 no tribute or any other tax 29
90 we can no longer stand in thy presence 33
2Es 1:25 When you beg mercy of me, I will show you no mercy. 48
34 your sons will have no children 48
35 to whom I have shown no signs 48
36 They have seen no prophets 48
2: 6 so that they may have no offspring. 45
3:33 and their labor has borne no fruit 47
4: 9 and you have given me no answer about them! 48
41 I said, "No, lord, it cannot. 48
5:34 I said, "No, my lord 48
42 there is no slowness 48
42 for those who are first there is no haste. 46
7:39 a day that has no sun or moon or stars 47
8:32 who have no works of righteousness 48
36 to those who have no store of good works. 48
45 No, O Lord who art over us! 48
9:24 a field of flowers where no house has been built 48
24 and taste no meat and drink no wine 48
24 and taste no meat and drink no wine 48
43 Your servant was barren and had no child 48
10:27 behold, the woman was no longer visible to me 48
51 remain in the field where no house had been built 48
53 where there was no foundation of any building 48
54 for no work of man's building could endure 46
11:42 the walls of those who did you no harm. 48
12:45 For we are no better than those who died there. 46
13:52 Just as no one can explore or know 48
52 so no one on earth can see my Son 48
14:41 my mouth was opened, and was no longer closed. 48
15: 8 I will be silent no longer 48
16 in their might have no respect for their king 48
19 A man shall have no pity upon his neighbors 48
16:23 there shall be no one to console them 48
24 No one shall be left to cultivate the earth 48
32 because no sheep will go along them. 48
33 shall mourn because they have no bridegrooms; 48
33 because they have no husbands 48
33 because they have no helpers. 48
44 like those who will have no children 48
53 Let no sinner say that he has not sinned 48
77 so that no one can pass through! 48
Tob 3: 8 have had no benefit from any of them. 33
15 he has no child to be his heir 33
15 he has . . no near kinsman or kinsman's son 35
6:14 they have no other son to bury them. 33
10: 9 Tobias replied, "No, send me back to my father. 43
12: 2 it would do me no harm to give him half 33
13: 2 there is no one who can escape his hand. 33
Jdt 5: 5 No falsehood shall come from your servant's mouth. 33
21 if there is no transgression in their nation 33
23 a people with no strength or power for making war. 33
7:19 there was no way of escape from them. 33
22 there was no strength left in them any longer. 33
25 For now we have no one to help us 33
31 if these days pass by, and no help comes for us 26
8: 8 No one spoke ill of her 33
14 No, my brethren, do not provoke the Lord our God 27
20 we know no other god but him 33
28 there is no one who can deny your words. 33
31 we will no longer be faint. 33
9:14 no other who protects the people of Israel 33
11: 4 No one will hurt you, but all will treat you well 33
19 will lead them like sheep that have no shepherd 33
13:16 yet he committed no act of sin with me 33
16:25 no one ever again spread terror among the people 33
AEs 13: 9 there is no one who can oppose thee 33
11 is no one who can resist thee, who art the Lord. 33
14: 3 help me, who am alone and have no helper but thee 26
11 do not surrender thy scepter to what has no being; 26
14 am alone and have no helper but thee, O Lord. 26
18 no joy since the day that I was brought here 33
Wis 1:11 because no secret word is without result 33
14 there is no destructive poison in them 33
2: 1 there is no remedy when a man comes to his end 33
1 no one has been known to return from Hades. 33
5 there is no return from our death 33
7 let no flower of spring pass by us. 26
3:14 the eunuch whose hands have done no lawless deed 26
17 they will be held of no account 36
18 If they die young, they will have no hope 33
18 no consolation in the day of decision. 35
4: 3 will be of no use 33
5:10 when it has passed no trace can be found 33
11 no evidence of its passage is found 36
11 afterward no sign of its coming is found there; 33
13 we had no sign of virtue to show 36
6:14 He . . will have no difficulty 33
22 I will hide no secrets from you 33
7: 5 no king has had a different beginning 36
8:16 companionship with her has no bitterness 33
16 and life with her has no pain 35
14:24 they no longer keep . . their marriages pure 41
29 swear wicked oaths and expect to suffer no harm. 33
16: 9 no healing was found for them 33
17: 5 no power of fire was able to give light 36
18: 2 thy holy ones . . were doing them no injury 33
Sir 0: 3 I found opportunity for no little instruction. 33
2:13 Woe to the faint heart, for it has no trust! 33
3:10 your father's dishonor is no glory to you. 33
28 The affliction of the proud has no healing 33
6:15 no scales can measure his excellence. 33
7: 1 Do no evil, and evil will never befall you. 26
13 the habit of lying serves no good. 33
8:16 where no help is at hand, he will strike you down. 33
9:13 if you approach him, make no misstep 26
12: 3 No good will come to the man who persists in evil 33
13:22 he speaks sensibly, and receives no attention. 33
15:12 for he had no need of a sinful man. 33
16: 9 showed no pity for a nation 33
20 no mind will reflect on this 33
21 Like a tempest which no man can see 33
20: 6 is one who keeps silent because he has no answer 33
16 A fool will say, "I have no friend 33
16 there is no gratitude for my good deeds 33
21 when he rests he feels no remorse. 33
21: 1 Have you sinned, my son? Do so no more 26
3 there is no healing for its wound. 33
14 it will hold no knowledge. 39
25:15 There is no venom worse than a snake's venom 33
15 no wrath worse than an enemy's wrath. 33
25 Allow no outlet to water 26
25 Allow . . no boldness of speech in an evil wife. 28
26:15 no balance can weigh the value of a chaste soul. 39
28: 4 Does he have no mercy toward a man like himself 33
30:11 Give him no authority in his youth 26
16 There is no wealth better than health of body 33
16 there is no gladness above joy of heart. 33
23 there is no profit in it. 33
31:22 no sickness will overtake you. 39
31 speak no word of reproach to him 26
33: 1 No evil will befall the man who fears the Lord 33
22 bring no stain upon your honor. 26
35:12 with him is no partiality. 33
36:25 Where there is no fence 33
25 where there is no wife 33
26 So who will trust a man that has no home 26
37:11 pay no attention to these 26
13 no one is more faithful to you than it is. 33
38:21 Do not forget, there is no coming back 33
21 you do the dead no good, and you injure yourself. 33
39:17 No one can say, "What is this?" "Why is that? 33
21 No one can say, "What is this?" "Why is that? 33
34 no one can say, "This is worse than that 33
40: 6 He gets little or no rest 36
26 There is no loss in the fear of the Lord 33
26 with it there is no need to seek for help. 33
41: 4 there is no inquiry about it in Hades. 33
42:20 No thought escapes him 39
44: 9 there are some who have no memorial 33
19 no one has been found like him in glory; 33
45:13 No outsider ever put them on 33
22 in the land of the people he has no inheritance 36
22 he has no portion among the people 33
46:19 no man accused him. 33
49:15 no man like Joseph has been born, and his bones are 35
50:25 the third is no nation: 33
51: 7 there was no one to help me 33
Bar 3:17 men trust, and there is no end to their getting; 33
25 It is great and has no bounds; it is high 33
28 so they perished because they had no wisdom 26
31 No one knows the way to her, or is concerned about 33
35 This is our God; no other can be compared to him! 33
4:13 They had no regard for his statutes 33
15 nation . . who had no respect for an old man 33
15 nation . . who . . had no pity for a child. 35
LJr 1:24 when they were being cast, they had no feeling. 35
25 there is no breath in them. 33
26 Having no feet, they are carried 21
42 they have no sense. 33
51 there is no work of God in them. 36
56 they can offer no resistance to a king or any enemies. 38
56 they can offer no resistance to a king or any enemies. 26
69 we have no evidence whatever that they are gods; 36
73 Better therefore is a just man who has no idols 33
Aza 1:15 at this time there is no prince, or prophet 33
15 no prince, or prophet, or leader, no burnt offering 35
15 no place to make an offering before thee 33
17 will be no shame for those who trust in thee. 33
Bel 1:18 and with you there is no deceit, none at all. 33
41 there is no other besides thee. 33
Man 1:10 I have no relief 33
1Mc 3:18 no difference between saving by many or by few. 33
5:42 Permit no man to encamp 30
6:49 because they had no provisions there 33
53 they had no food in storage 33
7:11 they paid no attention to their words 33
18 they said, "There is no truth or justice in them 33
28 Let there be no fighting between me and you 26
38 and let them live no longer. 26
8:16 there is no envy or jealousy among them. 33
28 to the enemy allies shall be given no grain, arms 33
9: 7 he had no time to assemble them. 33
10 and leave no cause to question our honor. 26
29 no one like him to go against our enemies 33
45 there is no place to turn. 33
55 so that he could no longer say a word 33
72 came no more into their territory. 33
10:38 obey no other authority but the high priest. 26
61 the king paid no attention to them. 33
73 where there is no stone or pebble, or place to flee. 33
11:38 there was no opposition to him 36
12:25 no opportunity to invade his own country. 33
53 they said, "They have no leader or helper 33
2Mc 2:26 it is no light matter 33
3:14 no little distress throughout the whole city. 33
4:13 who was ungodly and no high priest 33
17 it is no light thing to show irreverence 33
25 possessing no qualification for the high priesthood 36
34 with no regard for justice 33
40 advanced in years and no less advanced in folly. 36
5: 5 Jason took no less than 1,000 men 33
10 he had no funeral of any sort 35
10 he had . . no place in the tomb of his fathers. 41
7: 8 and said to them, "No. 43
14 there will be no resurrection to life! 33
8: 9 in command of no fewer than 20,000 Gentiles 33
9:12 no mortal should think that he is equal to God. 26
10:17 killing no fewer than 20,000. 33
18 When no less than 9,000 took refuge 33
24 and collected the cavalry . . in no small number 33
12: 3 as though there were no ill will to the Jews; 29
14: 3 realized that there was no way for him to be safe 33
8 our whole nation is now in no small misfortune. 33
28 when the man had done no wrong. 29
15:19 were in no little distress 33
27 they laid low no less than 35,000 men 36
3Mc 3: 6 Nevertheless those of other races paid no heed 34
7 they attached no ordinary reproach to them. 33
9 when it had committed no offense. 29
5:42 the king . . took no account of the changes of mind 44
6:24 secretly devising acts of no advantage to the kingdom. 26
4Mc 3: 2 No one of us can eradicate that kind of desire 33
3 No one of us can eradicate anger from the mind 33
4 No one of us can eradicate malice 33
5:16 there is no compulsion more powerful 36
28 you shall have no such occasion to laugh at me 33
6:35 and in no respect yields to them. 29
7: 3 in no way did he turn the rudder of religion 36
4 No city besieged 33
20 No contradiction therefore arises 36
10:15 No, by the blessed death of my brothers 25
17: 1 so that no one might touch her body. 26
18: 8 No seducer corrupted me on a desert plain 35

no *See also* account, advantage, answer, avail, because, child, consideration, doubt, effect, excuse, existence, help, knowledge, long, longer, means, mingling, need, offense, opportunity, power, purpose, reason, relief, remain, repute, road, sense, strength, thought, understanding, use, way.

no again 1. μηκέτι
Mat 21:19 May no fruit ever come from you again! 1

no any one 1. οὐδείς
1Co 3:11 For no other foundation can any one lay 1

no anything 1. μηδείς 2. οὐδείς
Mat 5:13 no longer good for anything except to be thrown out 2
Php 4: 6 Have no anxiety about anything 1

no at all 1. οὐδείς
1Jn 1: 5 God is light and in him is no darkness at all. 1

no even 1. οὐδέ
Mrk 6:31 they had no leisure even to eat. 1

no ever 1. οὐδέποτε 2. οὐ μή 3. numquam
Joh 7:46 No man ever spoke like this man! 1
2Es 7:105 no one shall ever pray for another on that day 3
Wis 3: 1 no torment will ever touch them. 2

no man 1. μηδείς 2. οὐδείς
Mat 22:16 teach the way of God . . and care for no man; 2
23: 9 call no man your father on earth •
Mrk 12:14 we know that you are true, and care for no man 2
Lke 18:29 there is no man who has left house or wife 2
Joh 7: 4 For no man works in secret 2
15:13 Greater love has no man than this 2
Act 18:10 no man shall attack you to harm you 2
Gal 3:11 no man is justified before God by the law 2
6:17 Henceforth let no man trouble me 1
Eph 5:29 For no man ever hates his own flesh 2
1Th 4: 6 that no man transgress, and wrong his brother •
1Jn 4:12 No man has ever seen God; 2
Rev 7: 9 a great multitude which no man could number 2
Wis 15:16 no man can form a god which is like himself. 2

no more 1. אַיִן 2. אפס 3. אֶפֶס 4. בַּל 5. בְּלִי 6. בִּלְתִּי 7. דמה 8. חדל 9. לֹא יֹסִף 10. מִן הַרְבֵּה 11. ἐάω ἕως 12. μή 13. μὴ ἔτι 14. μηκέτι 15. μήποτε 16. οὐ 17. οὐκέτι 18. οὐ μὴ ἔτι 19. οὔτε 20. οὗτος

Gen 42:13 this day with our father, and one is no more. 1
32 one is no more, and the youngest is this day 1
36 my children: Joseph is no more, and Simeon is no 1
36 and Simeon is no more, and now you would take 1
Rut 1:18 when Na'omi saw that she was . . she said no more. 8
1Sm 30: 4 and wept, until they had no more strength to weep. 1
2Sm 14:11 that the avenger of blood slay no more 10
2Ch 20:25 they took . . until they could carry no more. 1
Job 8:22 the tent of the wicked will be no more. 1
14:12 till the heavens are no more he will not awake 6
Ps 37:10 Yet a little while, and the wicked will be no more; 1
36 Again I passed by, and, lo, he was no more; 1
39:13 I may know gladness, before I depart and be no more! 1
59:13 in wrath, consume them till they are no more 1
72: 7 and peace abound, till the moon be no more! 5
140:10 Let them be cast into pits, no more to rise! 4
Prv 10:25 When the tempest passes, the wicked is no more 1
12: 7 The wicked are overthrown and are no more 1
Isa 5: 8 who add field to field, until there is no more room 3
16: 4 When the oppressor is no more 2
17:14 Before morning, they are no more! 1
19: 7 will dry up, be driven away, and be no more. 1
Lam 2: 9 the law is no more, and . . no vision from the LORD. 1
4:16 has scattered them, he will regard them no more; 9
5: 7 Our fathers sinned, and are no more; 1
Zep 1:11 For all the traders are no more; 7
Mat 2:18 to be consoled, because they were no more. 16
Lke 22:51 Jesus said, "No more of this! 11
Joh 5:14 Sin no more, that nothing worse befall you. 14
14:19 the world will see me no more 17
16:10 you will see me no more; 17
16 A little while, and you will see me no more 17
17:11 now I am no more in the world 17
Act 4:17 let us warn them to speak no more to any one 14
8:39 the eunuch saw him no more 17
13:34 no more to return to corruption 14
20:25 all you . . will see my face no more. 17
38 that they should see his face no more 17
Rom 14:13 Then let us no more pass judgment on one another 14
1Co 15:34 Come to your right mind, and sin no more 12
Jas 3:12 No more can salt water yield fresh. 19
Rev 10: 6 that there should be no more delay 17
18:21 Babylon . . shall be found no more; 18
22 sound of harpers . . shall be heard in thee no more 18
22 a craftsman . . shall be found in thee no more; 18
22 the millstone shall be heard in thee no more; 18
23 and the light of a lamp shall shine in thee no more; 18
23 the voice . . shall be heard in thee no more; 18
20: 3 that he should deceive the nations no more 13
21: 1 earth had passed away, and the sea was no more. 17
4 and death shall be no more 17
22: 3 There shall no more be anything accursed 17
5 And night shall be no more; 17
Tob 3:13 Command . . that I hear reproach no more. 14
15 command . . that I hear reproach no more. 14
12:21 Then they stood up; but they saw him no more. 17
Sir 13:17 No more has a sinner with a godly man. 20
19:13 if he did anything, so that he may do it no more. 15
21: 1 Do so no more, but pray about your former sins. 14

no more than 1. לֹא כִּי אִם 2. ἀλλ' ἤ 3. μόλις

2Kg 9:35 they found no more of her than the skull 1
Sir 32: 7 no more than twice, and only if asked. 3
1Mc 9: 6 until no more than 800 of them were left. 2

no one 1. אַיִן 2. אִישׁ אַיִן 3. אַל 4. אַל אִישׁ 5. אַל פְּלִיט 6. אֶפֶס 7. בְּלִי 8. בִּלְתִּי אִישׁ 9. לֹא אִישׁ 10. לְבִלְתִּי 11. μηδείς 12. μή τις 13. οὐ 14. οὐδείς 15. οὐ τις 16. πᾶς οὐ 17. πᾶς οὐδέ 18. τίς 19. nec quisquam 20. nemo

Gen 40: 8 dreams, and there is no one to interpret them. 1
41:15 and there is no one who can interpret it; 1
24 there was no one who could explain it to me. 1
Exd 8:10 know that there is no one like the LORD our God. 1
Num 16:40 so that no one who is not a priest 9
Deu 22:27 woman cried for help there was no one to rescue 1
28:26 there shall be no one to frighten them away. 1
29 there shall be no one to help you. 1
31 there shall be no one to help you. 1
1Sm 11: 3 if there is no one to save us, we will give . . up 1
21: 1 Why are you alone, and no one with you? 2
2 Let no one know anything of the matter 4
22: 8 No one discloses to me when my son makes a league 1
1Kg 15:17 permit no one to go out or come in to Asa 7
18:26 there was no voice, and no one answered. 1
29 there was no voice; no one answered, no one heeded. 1
29 there was no voice; no one answered, no one heeded. 1
2Kg 9:15 let no one slip out of the city to go and tell 5
23:10 that no one might burn his son or his daughter 8
1Ch 16:21 he allowed no one to oppress them; 9
2Ch 16: 1 that he might permit no one to go out or come 10
22: 9 had no one able to rule the kingdom. 1
23: 6 Let no one enter the house of the LORD 3
Est 1: 8 drinking . . no one was compelled; 1
4: 2 no one might enter the king's gate clothed 1
Prv 1:24 stretched out my hand and no one has heeded 1
28: 1 The wicked flee when no one pursues 1
Ecc 4: 1 and they had no one to comfort them! 1
1 and there was no one to comfort them. 1
Isa 47: 8 in your heart, "I am, and there is no one besides me 6
10 in your wickedness, you said, "No one sees me"; 1
10 in your heart, "I am, and there is no one besides me 6
57: 1 men are taken away, while no one understands. 1
59: 4 No one enters suit justly, 1
4 no one goes to law honestly 1
60:15 forsaken and hated, with no one passing through 1
66: 4 because, when I called, no one answered 1
Jer 30:17 an outcast: 'It is Zion, for whom no one cares!' 1
Lam 4: 4 the children beg for food, but no one gives to them. 1
Dan 8: 4 there was no one who could rescue from his power; 1
Mat 6:24 No one can serve two masters; for either he will 14
9:16 no one puts a piece of unshrunk cloth 14
30 See that no one knows it. 11
11:27 and no one knows the Son except the Father 14
16:20 strictly charged the disciples to tell no one 11
17: 8 when they lifted up their eyes, they saw no one 14
9 Tell no one the vision 11
20: 7 They said to him, 'Because no one has hired us.' 14
22:46 no one was able to answer him a word 14
24:36 of that day and hour no one knows 14
Mrk 2:21 No one sews a piece of unshrunk cloth 14
22 no one puts new wine into old wineskins 14
3:27 no one can enter a strong man's house 14
5: 3 no one could bind him any more 14
4 no one had the strength to subdue him. 14
37 he allowed no one to follow him except Peter 14
43 he strictly charged them that no one should know 11
7:36 he charged them to tell no one 11
8:30 he charged them to tell no one about him. 11
9: 9 he charged them to tell no one what they had seen 11
39 no one who does a mighty work in my name 14
10:18 Why do you call me good? No one is good but God 14
29 there is no one who has left house or brothers 14
11: 2 a colt . . on which no one has ever sat 14
14 May no one ever eat fruit from you again. 11
12:34 after that no one dared to ask him any question. 14
13: 5 Take heed that no one leads you astray. 18
32 of that day or that hour no one knows 14
Lke 3:14 Rob no one by violence or by false accusation 11
5:14 he charged him to tell no one 11
36 No one tears a piece from a new garment 14
37 no one puts new wine into old wineskins 14
39 no one after drinking old wine desires new 14
8:16 No one after lighting a lamp covers it 14
56 he charged them to tell no one what had happened. 11
9:21 he . . commanded them to tell this to no one 11
36 they kept silence and told no one in those days 11
62 No one who puts his hand to the plow 14
10: 4 salute no one on the road. 11
22 no one knows who the Son is except the Father 14
11:33 No one after lighting a lamp puts it in a cellar 14
15:16 no one gave him anything. 14
18:19 Why do you call me good? No one is good but God 14
19:30 a colt . . on which no one has ever yet sat 11
23:53 where no one had ever yet been laid. 14
Joh 1:18 No one has ever seen God; 14
2:25 and needed no one to bear witness of man; 15
3: 2 for no one can do these signs that you do 14
13 No one has ascended into heaven but he who 14
32 yet no one receives his testimony; 14
5:22 The Father judges no one 14
6:44 No one can come to me 14
65 This is why I told you that no one can come to me 14
7:13 Yet for fear of the Jews no one spoke openly 14
27 no one will know where he comes from. 14
30 no one laid hands on him 14
44 but no one laid hands on him. 14
8:10 Woman, where are they? Has no one condemned you? 14
11 She said, "No one, Lord. 14
15 You judge according to the flesh, I judge no one. 14
20 but no one arrested him 14
9: 4 night comes, when no one can work. 14
10:18 No one takes it from me 14
29 no one is able to snatch them out of the Father's hand 14
13:28 no one at the table knew why he said this to him. 14
14: 6 no one comes to the Father, but by me. 14
15:24 done among them the works which no one else did 14
16:22 no one will take your joy from you. 14
19:41 a new tomb where no one had ever been laid. 14
Act 1:20 let there be no one to live in it •
4:12 there is salvation in no one else 14
5:23 when we opened it we found no one inside. 14
9: 7 hearing the voice but seeing no one. 11
20:33 I coveted no one's silver or gold or apparel. 14
23:22 Tell no one that you have informed me of this. 11
25:11 no one can give me up to them 14
Rom 10:11 No one who believes in him will be put to shame 16
12:17 Repay no one evil for evil 11
13: 8 Owe no one anything, except to love one another; 11
1Co 2:11 So also no one comprehends the thoughts of God 14
15 is himself to be judged by no one. 14
3:18 Let no one deceive himself 11
21 So let no one boast of men. 11
10:24 Let no one seek his own good 11
12: 3 no one speaking by the Spirit of God ever says 14
3 no one can say "Jesus is Lord 14
14: 2 no one understands him, but he utters mysteries 14
28 if there is no one to interpret •
2Co 5:16 we regard no one from a human point of view 14
7: 2 we have wronged no one, we have corrupted no one 14
2 we have wronged no one, we have corrupted no one 14
2 we have taken advantage of no one. 14
8:20 We intend that no one should blame us 18
11:16 I repeat, let no one think me foolish 18
Gal 3:15 no one annuls even a man's will, or adds to it 14
Eph 5: 6 Let no one deceive you with empty words 11
Php 2:20 I have no one like him 14
Col 2: 4 I say this in order that no one may delude you 11
18 Let no one disqualify you 11
1Th 3: 3 that no one be moved by these afflictions 11
1Ti 4:12 Let no one despise your youth 11
2Ti 4:16 At my first defense no one took my part 14
Tit 2:15 Let no one disregard you. 11
3: 2 to speak evil of no one, to avoid quarreling 11
Heb 6:13 since he had no one greater by whom to swear 14
7:13 from which no one has ever served at the altar. 14
12:14 holiness without which no one will see the Lord. 14
15 no one fail to obtain the grace of God 18
16 that no one be immoral or irreligious like Esau 18
Jas 1:13 Let no one say . . "I am tempted by God 11
13 God cannot be tempted . . and . . tempts no one; 14
1Jn 2:23 No one who denies the Son has the Father. 17
3: 6 No one who abides in him sins; 16
6 no one who sins has either seen him or known him. 16
7 Little children, let no one deceive you. 11
9 No one born of God commits sin; 16
Rev 2:17 a new name . . which no one knows except him 14
3: 7 the true one . . who opens and no one shall shut 14
7 the true one . . who shuts and no one opens. 14
8 an open door, which no one is able to shut; 14
11 hold fast . . so that no one may seize your crown. 11
5: 3 no one in heaven or on earth or under the earth 14
4 that no one was found worthy to open the scroll 14
13:17 that no one can buy or sell unless he has the mark 12
14: 3 No one could learn that song except the 144,000 14
15: 8 and no one could enter the temple 14
18:11 since no one buys their cargo any more 14
19:12 he has a name inscribed which no one knows 14
1Es 8:22 no one has authority to impose any tax upon them. 11
2Es 7:30 so that no one shall be left. 20
105 no one shall ever pray for another on that day 20
115 no one will then be able to have mercy on him 20
8:35 there is no one among those who have been born 20
35 there is no one who has not transgressed. •
9:18 and no one opposed me then, for no one existed; 20
18 and no one opposed me then, for no one existed; 19
11: 6 and no one spoke against him 20
17 After you no one shall rule as long as you 20
14:21 so no one knows the things which have been done 20
36 let no one come to me now 20
36 and let no one seek me for 40 days. •
16:71 They shall be like mad men, sparing no one 20
Tob 6:14 he harms no one except those who approach her. 14
10: 2 there is no one to give him the money? 14
Jdt 13: 4 no one, either small or great, was left 14
14:15 when no one answered 14
Wis 1: 8 therefore no one who utters unrighteous things 14
2: 4 no one will remember our works 14
5 because it is sealed up and no one turns back. 14
Sir 11:28 Call no one happy before his death 11
12:14 So no one will pity a man •
14: 6 No one is meaner than the man who is grudging •
19:27 where no one notices, he will forestall you. 13
23:18 no one sees me. Why should I fear? 14
25:10 no one superior to him who fears the Lord. 13
27:22 no one can keep him from them. 14
36:10 There is no one but ourselves. 13
42:21 he needs no one to be his counselor. 14
48:12 no one brought him into subjection. 14
49:14 No one like Enoch has been created on earth 14
Bar 4:12 Let no one rejoice over me, a widow 11
Sus 1:16 And no one was there except the two elders 14
20 Look, the garden doors are shut, no one sees us 14
1Mc 4: 5 he found no one there 14
5:48 No one will do you harm 14
10:35 No one shall have authority to exact anything 14
63 no one is to bring charges against him 11
63 let no one annoy him for any reason. 11
15:14 and permitted no one to leave or enter it. 14
2Mc 9:10 no one was able to carry the man 14
3Mc 1:13 no one there had stopped him. 14
7: 8 with no one in any place doing them harm at all 11

no whatever 1. οὐδαμῶς

2Mc 11: 4 He took no account whatever of the power of God 1

yet no 1. טֶרֶם

Gen 2: 5 when no plant of the field was yet in the earth 1
5 and no herb of the field had yet sprung up- 1

nobility 1. הָדָר 2. γενναιότης 3. εὐγένεια 4. καλοκἀγαθία

Isa 5:14 nobility of Jerusalem and her multitude go down 1
2Mc 6:31 leaving in his death an example of nobility 2
4Mc 3:18 by nobility of reason spurn all domination 4
8: 4 struck by their appearance and nobility 3
11:22 equipped with nobility, will die with my brothers 4
13:25 A common zeal for nobility 4
15: 9 because of the nobility of her sons 4

nobility and goodness 1. καλοκἀγαθία

4Mc 1:10 for the sake of nobility and goodness 1

noble 1. אַדִּיר 2. גָּדוֹל 3. חֹר 4. כבד 5. נָגִיד 6. נָדִיב 7. פַּרְתְּמִים 8. יַקִּיר(A) 9. ἀγαθός 10. γενναῖος 11. εὐγενής 12. καλός 13. μεγιστάν 14. τιμή

Num21:18 well . . which the nobles of the people delved 6
Jdg 5:13 down marched the remnant of the noble; the people 1
1Kg 21: 8 she sent the letters to the elders and the nobles 3
11 the men of his city, the elders and the nobles 3
2Ch 23:20 he took the captains, the nobles, the governors 1
Ezr 4:10 nations whom the great and noble Osnap'par 8
Neh 2:16 I had not yet told the Jews, the priests, the nobles 3
3: 5 Teko'ites repaired; but their nobles did not put 1
4:14 said to the nobles and to the officials 3
19 I said to the nobles and to the officials 3
5: 7 charges against the nobles and the officials. 3
6:17 nobles of Judah sent many letters to Tobi'ah 3
7: 5 assemble the nobles and the officials 3
10:29 join with their brethren, their nobles, and enter 1
13:17 I remonstrated with the nobles of Judah and said 3
Est 1: 3 and the nobles and governors of the provinces 7
6: 9 handed . . to one of the king's most noble princes; 7
Job 29:10 the voice of the nobles was hushed 5
34:18 'Worthless one,' and to nobles, 'Wicked man'; 6
Ps 16: 3 As for the saints in the land, they are the noble 1
83:11 Make their nobles like Oreb and Zeeb 6
149: 8 to bind . . their nobles with fetters of iron 4
Prv 8:16 by me princes rule, and nobles govern the earth. 6
Isa 13: 2 wave . . for them to enter the gates of the nobles. 6
32: 5 The fool will no more be called noble 6
8 he who is noble devises noble things 6
34:11 and the plummet of chaos over its nobles. 3
Jer 14: 3 Her nobles send their servants for water; 1
27:20 and all the nobles of Judah and Jerusalem– 3
39: 6 the king of Babylon slew all the nobles of Judah. 3
Ezk 17: 8 and bear fruit, and become a noble vine. 1
23 and bear fruit, and become a noble cedar; 1
Jon 3: 7 By the decree of the king and his nobles 2
Nah 3:18 O king of Assyria; your nobles slumber. 1
Lke 21: 5 it was adorned with noble stones and offerings 12
Rom12:17 take thought for what is noble in the sight of all 12
1Ti 3: 1 he desires a noble task. 12
2Ti 2:20 some for noble use, some for ignoble. 14
21 he will be a vessel for noble use 14
1Es 1:38 Jehoiakim put the nobles in prison 13
3: 1 all the nobles of Media and Persia 13
9 the king and the three nobles of Persia 13
14 summoned all the nobles of Persia and Media 13
4:33 the king and the nobles looked at one another 13
8:26 his counselors and all his friends and nobles. 13
55 king himself and his counselors and the nobles 13
70 the leaders and the nobles 13
Tob 5:13 of a good and noble lineage. 12
7: 7 Son of that good and noble man! 12
Jdt 2: 2 all his officers and all his nobles 13
1Mc 9:37 a daughter of one of the great nobles of Canaan 13
2Mc 4:12 the noblest of the young men 9
6:18 a man now advanced in age and of noble presence 12
28 leave to the young a noble example 10
7:21 Filled with a noble spirit 10
12:42 the noble Judas exhorted the people 10
15:12 a noble and good man 12
17 so noble and so effective in arousing valor 12
4Mc 4: 1 the noble and good man, Onias 12
6: 5 the courageous and noble man, as a true Eleazar 11
10 like a noble athlete the old man 10
7: 8 their own blood and noble sweat 10
8: 3 seven brothers-handsome, modest, noble 12
9:13 the noble youth was stretched out around this 11
24 Fight the sacred and noble battle for religion. 11
27 they heard this noble decision. 11
10: 3 I do not renounce the noble kinship 11
15 I will not renounce our noble brotherhood. 11
11:12 through these noble sufferings 10
15:24 this noble mother disregarded all these 10
16:16 noble is the contest to which you are called 10

noble *See also* birth, bravery.

noble man 1. נָדִיב

Prv 17:26 to flog noble men is wrong. 1

more noble 1. γενναῖος 2. εὐγενής

Act 17:11 Now these Jews were more noble 2
4Mc 15:30 O more noble than males in steadfastness 1

noble thing 1. נָגִיד 2. נְדִיבָה

Prv 8: 6 Hear, for I will speak noble things 1
Isa 32: 8 he who is noble devises noble things 2
8 and by noble things he stands. 2

nobleman 1. ἄνθρωπος εὐγενής 2. μεγιστάν

Lke 19:12 A nobleman went into a far country 1
Sir 10:24 The nobleman, and the judge, and the ruler 2

nobly 1. γενναῖος 2. γενναίως 3. εὐγενής 4. εὐγενῶς

1Mc 4:35 how ready they were either to live or to die nobly 2
2Mc 6:28 die a good death willingly and nobly 2
7: 5 the brothers . . encouraged one another to die nobly, 2
11 said nobly, "I got these from Heaven 2
8:16 exhorted them . . to fight nobly 2
13:14 exhorting his men to fight nobly to the death 2
14:42 preferring to die nobly 4
4Mc 6:22 die nobly for your religion! 3
30 the holy man died nobly in his tortures 3
9:22 he nobly endured the rackings. 3
12:14 by dying nobly fulfilled their service to God 3
13:11 another said, "Bear up nobly 3
15:32 endured nobly and withstood the wintry storms 1
17: 3 Nobly set like a roof on the pillars of your sons 1

nobody 1. אֵין אִישׁ 2. μηδείς

Jdg 19:18 to my home; and nobody takes me into his house. 1
1Th 4:12 be dependent on nobody. 2

nod 1. νεῦμα

2Mc 8:18 is able with a single nod to strike down 1

noise 1. הָמוֹן 2. קוֹל 3. שָׁאוֹן 4. μεγάλη φωνή 5. φωνή

Exd 32:17 heard the noise of the people as they shouted 2
17 There is a noise of war in the camp. 2
1Sm 4: 6 the Philistines heard the noise of the shouting 2
1Kg 1:40 joy, so that the earth was split by their noise. 2
45 an uproar. This is the noise that you have heard. 2
2Kg 11:13 Athali'ah heard the noise of the guard 2
2Ch 23:12 When Athali'ah heard the noise of the people 2
Ps 55: 3 by the noise of the enemy 2
Isa 24: 8 the noise of the jubilant has ceased 3
25: 5 Thou dost subdue the noise of the aliens; 3
29: 6 with earthquake and great noise, with whirlwind 2
31: 4 by their shouting or daunted at their noise 1
33: 3 At the thunderous noise peoples flee 2
Jer 4:29 At the noise of horseman and archer 2
47: 3 At the noise of the stamping of the hoofs 2
50:22 The noise of battle is in the land 2
51:54 The noise of great destruction from the land *
55 the noise of their voice is raised; 3
Ezk 26:10 your walls will shake at the noise 2
37: 7 and as I prophesied, there was a noise 2
Dan 10: 6 sound of his words like the noise of a multitude. 2
Ams 5:23 Take away from me the noise of your songs; 1
Rev 9: 9 the noise of their wings was like the noise 5
9 like the noise of many chariots with horses 5
1Es 5:64 while many came with trumpets and a joyful noise 4
Jdt 14: 9 made a joyful noise in their city. 5
AEs 11: 5 Behold, noise and confusion 5
Sir 50:16 they made a great noise 5
1Mc 6:41 All who heard the noise made by their multitude 5
9:13 The earth was shaken by the noise of the armies 5

noise *See also* make.

loud noise 1. ῥοιζηδόν

2Pe 3:10 then the heavens will pass away with a loud noise 1

tumultuous noise 1. θόρυβος

3Mc 5:48 and heard the loud and tumultuous noise 1

noisy 1. המה 2. ἠχέω

Prv 9:13 A foolish woman is noisy; 1
1Co 13: 1 I am a noisy gong or a clanging cymbal. 2

noisy *See also* multitude.

noisy one 1. שָׁאוֹן

Jer 46:17 king of Egypt, 'Noisy one who lets the hour go by.' 1

nomad 1. νομάς

2Mc 12:11 The defeated nomads besought Judas 1

none 1. אַיִן 2. אֵין אֶחָד 3. אַל 4. אַל אִישׁ 5. אַל כֹּל 6. אִם 7. אֶפֶס 8. בַּל 9. בְּלִי 10. בִּלְתִּי 11. כֹּל לֹא 12. לֹא 13. לֹא אֶחָד 14. לֹא אִישׁ 15. לֹא אִשָּׁה 16. לֹא כֹל 17. לֹא מִכֹּל 18. רַק לֹא 19. אָחֳרָן לָא (A) 20. לָא (A) 21. μή 22. μηδέ 23. μηδείς 24. μὴ εἷς 25. μή τις 26. οὐ 27. οὐ ἅπαντες 28. οὐδέ 29. οὐδείς 30. οὐδὲ λόγος 31. οὐ πᾶς 32. οὔτε 33. οὔτε τις 34. οὔ τις 35. οὐ τίς 36. πᾶς

Gen 23: 6 none of us will withhold from you his sepulchre 14
28:17 This is none other than the house of God 1
39:11 none of the men of the house was there in the house 1
41:39 there is none so discreet and wise as you are; 1
Exd 9:14 that you may know that there is none like me in all 1
12:10 you shall let none of it remain until the morning 12
22 and none of you shall go out of the door 12
15:26 I will put none of the diseases upon you which I 11
16:26 on the seventh day . . there will be none. 12
27 went out to gather, and they found none. 12
23:15 None shall appear before me empty-handed. 12
26 None shall cast her young or be barren 12
34:20 And none shall appear before me empty. 12
Lev 18: 6 None of you shall approach any one near of kin 12
26 and do none of these abominations 16
21: 1 say to them that none of them shall defile 12
17 Say to Aaron, None of your descendants 12
22: 4 None of the line of Aaron who is a leper or suffers 12
30 you shall leave none of it until morning 12
26: 6 you shall lie down, and none shall make you afraid 1
17 you shall flee when none pursues you 1
36 sword, and they shall fall when none pursues 1
37 they shall stumble . . though none pursues 1
Num 7: 9 to the sons of Kohath he gave none 12
9:12 They shall leave none of it until the morning 12
14:22 none of the men who have seen my glory and my signs †
23 none of those who despised me shall see it. 11
32:11 Surely none of the men who came up out of Egypt *
12 none except Caleb . . and Joshua the son of Nun *
Deu 2:34 destroyed every city . . we left none remaining; 12
7:15 none of the evil diseases of Egypt . . will he inflict 12
13:17 None of the devoted things shall cleave 12
23: 2 none of his descendants shall enter 12
3 none belonging to them shall enter the assembly 12
32:39 there is none that can deliver out of my hand. 1
33:26 There is none like God, O Jesh'urun, who rides 1
34:11 none like him for all the signs and the wonders *
Jos 6: 1 was shut up . . none went out, and none came in. 1
1 was shut up . . none went out, and none came in. 1
8:22 there was left none that survived or escaped. 10
10:28 he utterly destroyed . . he left none remaining; 12
30 and he smote it . . he left none remaining in it; 12
33 Joshua smote . . until he left none remaining. 10
37 he left none remaining . . and utterly destroyed 12
39 and utterly destroyed . . he left none remaining; 12
40 he left none remaining, but utterly destroyed 12
11: 8 they smote them, until they left none remaining. 10
11 destroying . . there was none left that breathed 16
13 none of the cities . . on mounds did Israel burn 16
22 There was none of the Anakim left in the land 12
Jdg 20: 8 his tent, and none of us will return to his house. 14
1Sm 2: 2 There is none holy like the LORD 1
2 There is none holy . . there is none besides thee; 1
3:19 LORD was with him and let none of his words fall 17
10:24 There is none like him among all the people. 1
14:24 So none of the people tasted food. 16
21: 9 take it, for there is none but that here. 1
9 David said, "There is none like that; give it to me. 1
22: 8 none of you is sorry for me or discloses to me that 1
2Sm 7:22 there is none like thee, and there is no God 1
22:42 They looked, but there was none to save; 1
1Kg 3:12 none like you has been before you and none like 12
12 and none like you shall arise after you. 12
10:21 all . . were of pure gold; none were of silver 1
12:20 There was none that followed the house of David 12
15:22 Asa made a proclamation . . none was exempt 1
21:25 There was none who sold himself . . like Ahab 18
2Kg 5:16 he said, "As the LORD lives . . I will receive none. 6
6:12 None, my lord, O king; but Eli'sha . . tells the king 12
9:10 eat Jez'ebel . . and none shall bury her. 1
10:11 Jehu slew . . until he left him none remaining. 10
14 and slew them . . and he spared none of them. 14
19 call to me all . . let none be missing 4
14:26 none left . . and there was none to help Israel. 1
26 for there was none left, bond or free 7
17:18 none was left but the tribe of Judah only. 12
18: 5 there was none like him among all the kings 12
24:14 none remained, except the poorest people 12
1Ch 17:20 There is none like thee, O LORD 1
2Ch 1:12 such as none of the kings had who were before you 12
12 such as . . none after you shall have the like. 12
14:11 O LORD, there is none like thee to help 1
13 the Ethiopians fell until none remained alive; 1
20: 6 so that none is able to withstand thee. 1
24 bodies lying on the ground; none had escaped. 1
35:18 none of the kings of Israel had kept such 12
Ezr 8:15 I found there none of the sons of Levi. 12
9:15 none can stand before thee because of this. 1
Neh 4:23 none of us took off our clothes; 1
Job 1: 8 Job, that there is none like him on the earth 1
2: 3 Job, that there is none like him on the earth 1
3: 9 let it hope for light, but have none 1
10: 7 there is none to deliver out of thy hand? 1
11:19 You will lie down, and none will make you afraid; 1
12:14 If he tears down, none can rebuild; 12
14 if he shuts a man in, none can open. 12
18:15 In his tent dwells that which is none of his; 9
29:12 the fatherless who had none to help him. 12
32:12 behold, there was none that confuted Job 1
33:13 He will answer none of my words'? 16
35:10 But none says, 'Where is God my Maker 12
Ps 7: 2 rend me, dragging me away, with none to rescue. 1
10:15 seek out his wickedness till thou find none. 8
14: 1 there is none that does good. 1
3 there is none that does good, no, not one. 1
18:41 They cried for help, but there was none to save 1
22:11 trouble is near and there is none to help. 1

25: 3 Yea, let none that wait for thee be put to shame; 16
34:22 none . . who take refuge in him will be condemned. 16
40: 5 none can compare with thee! 1
50:22 lest I rend, and there be none to deliver! 1
53: 1 there is none that does good. 1
3 there is none that does good, no, not one. 1
59: 5 spare none of those who treacherously plot 5
69:20 I looked for pity, but there was none; 1
20 for comforters, but I found none. 12
71:11 seize him, for there is none to deliver him. 1
74: 9 there is none among us who knows how long. 12
79: 3 there was none to bury them. 1
81:11 Israel would have none of me. 12
86: 8 There is none like thee among the gods, O Lord 1
105:37 there was none among his tribes who stumbled. 1
107:12 they fell down, with none to help. 1
109:12 Let there be none to extend kindness to him 3
139:16 when as yet there was none of them. 13
142: 4 watch, but there is none who takes notice of me; 1
Prv 1:25 would have none of my reproof 12
30 would have none of my counsel 12
2:19 none who go to her come back 11
6:29 none who touches her will go unpunished. 16
Sng 8: 1 I would kiss you, and none would despise me. 12
Isa 1:31 shall burn together, with none to quench them. 1
5:27 None is weary, none stumbles, none slumbers 1
27 None is weary, none stumbles, none slumbers 1
27 None is weary, none stumbles, none slumbers 12
29 they carry it off, and none can rescue. 1
10:14 and there was none that moved a wing 12
13:14 or like sheep with none to gather them 1
17: 2 for flocks . . and none will make them afraid. 1
22:22 he shall open, and none shall shut; 1
22 and he shall shut, and none shall open. 1
24:10 every house is shut up so that none can enter. *
33: 1 with whom none has dealt treacherously! 12
34:10 none shall pass through it for ever and ever. 1
16 none shall be without her mate. 15
41:17 the poor and needy seek water, and there is none 1
26 There was none who declared it 1
26 none who proclaimed, none who heard your words. 1
26 none who proclaimed, none who heard your words. 1
42:22 they have become a prey with none to rescue 1
22 a spoil with none to say, "Restore! 1
43:13 there is none who can deliver from my hand; 1
45: 6 from the west, that there is none besides me; 7
21 a . . God and a Savior; there is none besides me. 1
46: 9 there is no other; I am God, and there is none like me 7
51:18 There is none to guide her among all the sons 1
18 there is none to take her by the hand among 1
59:11 we look for justice, but there is none; 1
Jer 2: 6 in a land that none passes through 14
24 None who seek her need weary themselves; 16
4: 4 go forth like fire, and burn with none to quench it 1
7:33 and none will frighten them away. 1
9:22 sheaves after the reaper, and none shall gather 1
10: 6 There is none like thee, O LORD; thou art great 1
7 in all their kingdoms there is none like thee. 1
11:23 and none of them shall be left. 12
13:19 The cities of Negeb are shut up, with none to open 1
14:16 victims of famine and sword, with none to bury 1
21:12 go forth like fire, and burn with none to quench it 1
22:30 for none of his offspring shall succeed 14
30: 7 Alas! that day is so great there is none like it; 1
10 quiet and ease, and none shall make him afraid. 1
13 There is none to uphold your cause 1
35:14 and they drink none to this day 12
36:30 He shall have none to sit upon the throne of David 12
44:14 so that none of the remnant of Judah who have come 12
46:27 quiet and ease, and none shall make him afraid. 1
49: 5 with none to gather the fugitives. 1
50: 3 her land a desolation, and none shall dwell in it; 12
20 shall be sought in Israel, and there shall be none; 1
20 and sin in Judah, and none shall be found; 12
32 shall stumble and fall, with none to raise him up 1
Lam 1: 2 among all her lovers she has none to comfort her; 1
4 Zion mourn, for none come to the appointed feasts; 9
7 her people fell . . and there was none to help her 1
17 Zion stretches . . but there is none to comfort 1
21 Hear how I groan; there is none to comfort me. 1
2:22 and on the day of . . none escaped or survived; 12
4:14 defiled . . none could touch their garments. 12
5: 8 Slaves rule over us; there is none to deliver us 1
Ezk 7:11 none of them shall remain, nor their abundance 12
13 none can maintain his life. 14
14 but none goes to battle, for my wrath is upon all 1
25 they will seek peace, but there shall be none. 1
12:28 None of my words will be delayed any longer 16
16:34 none solicited you to play the harlot; 12
18:11 who does none of these duties 16
22 None of the transgressions which he has 16
24 None of the righteous deeds which he has done 16
22:30 that I should not destroy it; but I found none. 12
33:13 none of his righteous deeds shall be remembered; 16
16 None of the sins that he has committed 16
28 be so desolate that none will pass through. 1
34: 6 with none to search or seek for them. 1
28 dwell securely, and none shall make them afraid. 1
39:26 in their land with none to make them afraid 1

28 I will leave none of them remaining 12
46:18 so that none of my people shall be dispossessed 12
Dan 1:19 among them all none was found like Daniel 12
2:11 none can show it to the king except the gods 19
4:35 none can stay his hand or say to him, "What doest 20
10:21 none who contends by my side 2
11:16 none shall stand before him; 1
45 yet he shall come to his end, with none to help him. 1
12:10 none of the wicked shall understand; 16
Hos 4: 4 Yet let no one contend, and let none accuse 4
5:14 I will carry off, and none shall rescue. 1
7: 7 and none of them calls upon me. 1
9:12 I will bereave them till none is left. †
11: 7 appointed to the yoke, and none shall remove it. 12
Jol 2:27 that I, the LORD, am your God and there is none else. 1
Ams 5: 2 forsaken on her land, with none to raise her up. 1
6 and it devour, with none to quench it for Bethel 1
Mic 2: 5 you will have none to cast the line by lot 12
4: 4 and none shall make them afraid; 1
5: 8 and tears in pieces, and there is none to deliver. 1
7: 2 and there is none upright among men; 1
Nah 2: 8 Halt! Halt!" they cry; but none turns back. 1
11 where his cubs were, with none to disturb? 1
3:18 scattered on the mountains with none to gather 1
Zep 2:15 that said to herself, "I am and there is none else 7
3: 6 waste their streets so that none walks in them; 9
13 and none shall make them afraid. 1
Zec 7:10 none of you devise evil against his brother 4
9: 8 as a guard, so that none shall march to and fro; *
11: 6 I will deliver none from their hand. 12
Mal 2:15 let none be faithless to the wife of his youth. 3
Mat 12:43 but he finds none. 26
26:60 they found none 26
Mrk 14:55 they found none. 26
Lke 1:61 None of your kindred is called by this name. 29
3:11 let him share with him who has none 21
4:26 Eli'jah was sent to none of them 29
27 none of them was cleansed 29
7:28 none is greater than John 29
11:24 finding none he says, 'I will return to my house 21
13: 6 he came seeking fruit on it and found none. 26
7 I find none 26
14:24 For I tell you, none of those men who were invited 29
16:26 none may cross from there to us.' 22
18:34 they understood none of these things 29
21:15 none of your adversaries will be able 27
Joh 4:27 but none said, "What do you wish? 29
7:19 Yet none of you keeps the law. 29
16: 5 yet none of you asks me, 'Where are you going?' 29
30 need none to question you 35
17:12 I have guarded them, and none of them is lost 29
21:12 none of the disciples dared ask him, "Who are you? 29
Act 5:13 None of the rest dared join them 29
11:19 speaking the word to none except Jews. 29
24:23 none of his friends should be prevented 23
26:26 none of these things has escaped his notice 29
28:21 none of the brethren coming here has reported 33
Rom 3:10 as it is written: "None is righteous, no, not one; 26
14: 7 None of us lives to himself 29
7 and none of us dies to himself. 29
1Co 1:14 I am thankful that I baptized none of you 29
2: 8 None of the rulers of this age understood this; 29
4: 6 that none of you may be puffed up in favor of one 24
7:29 who have wives live as though they had none 21
14:10 and none is without meaning; 29
Gal 1:19 I saw none of the other apostles 26
1Th 5:15 See that none of you repays evil for evil 25
Heb 3:13 that none of you may be hardened 25
1Pe 4:15 let none of you suffer as a murderer, or a thief 25
1Es 1:21 none of the kings of Israel 31
8:42 When I found there none of the sons of the priests 26
9:51 send portions to those who have none; 21
54 to give portions to those who had none 21
Tob 4:17 give none to sinners. 21
19 none of the nations has understanding 31
Jdt 6: 4 he has spoken; none of his words shall be in vain. 26
9 I have spoken and none of my words shall fail. 29
12: 3 none of your people is here with us. 26
16:14 there is none that can resist thy voice. 26
AEs 10: 5 none of them has failed to be fulfilled. 30
Wis 2: 9 Let none of us fail to share in our revelry 23
4: 3 none of their illegitimate seedlings 26
11:24 hast loathing for none of the things 29
Sir 10:24 none of them is greater 34
18: 4 To none has he given power to proclaim his works; 29
27:24 hated many things, but none to be compared to him; 26
39:18 none can limit his saving power. 26
51: 7 there was none. 26
LJr 1:19 though their gods can see none of them. 29
28 give none to the poor or helpless. 32
Sus 1:43 Yet I have done none of the things 23
Bel 1:18 and with you there is no deceit, none at all. 28
1Mc 2:61 none who put their trust in him will lack strength 36
7:17 there was none to bury them. 26
14: 7 there was none to oppose him. 26
12 there was none to make them afraid. 26
44 none of the people or priests shall be permitted 29
2Mc 11:31 none of them shall be molested in any way 29
3Mc 2:28 None of those who do not sacrifice 23

4Mc 14: 4 None of the seven youths proved coward 29
15:11 in the case of none of them 29
16: 6 I am now the mother of none! 29

none *See also* remaining.

nonsense 1. אָוֶן
Zec 10: 2 For the teraphim utter nonsense 1

noon 1. עֵת צָהֳרַיִם 2. צָהֳרַיִם 3. *μεσημβρία* 4. *μέσον ἡμέρας* 5. meridies
Gen 43:16 for the men are to dine with me at noon. 2
25 the present for Joseph's coming at noon 2
1Kg 18:26 called on . . Ba'al from morning until noon, saying 2
27 at noon Eli'jah mocked them, saying, "Cry aloud 2
20:16 And they went out at noon 2
2Kg 4:20 to his mother, the child sat on her lap till noon 2
Ps 55:17 Evening and morning and at noon I utter 2
Sng 1: 7 Tell me . . where you make it lie down at noon; 2
Isa 16: 3 make your shade like night at the height of noon; 2
59:10 we stumble at noon as in the twilight 2
Jer 6: 4 war against her; up, and let us attack at noon! 2
20:16 a cry in the morning and an alarm at noon 1
Ams 8: 9 I will make the sun go down at noon 2
Zep 2: 4 Ashdod's people shall be driven out at noon 2
Act 22: 6 about noon a great light from heaven 3
2Es 7:42 or noon or night, or dawn or shining or brightness 5
Sir 43: 3 At noon it parches the land 3
Sus 1: 7 When the people departed at noon 4

noonday 1. צָהֳרַיִם
Deu 28:29 grope at noonday, as the blind grope in darkness 1
2Sm 4: 5 Ish-bo'sheth, as he was taking his noonday rest. 1
Job 5:14 and grope at noonday as in the night. 1
11:17 your life will be brighter than the noonday; 1
Ps 37: 6 as the light, and your right as the noonday. 1
91: 6 nor the destruction that wastes at noonday. 1
Isa 58:10 in the darkness and your gloom be as the noonday. 1
Jer 15: 8 against the mothers . . a destroyer at noonday; 1

noonday *See also* sun.

noontide 1. דֳּמִי
Isa 38:10 I said, In the noontide of my days I must depart; 1

nor 1. אוֹ 2. אַיִן 3. אִם 4. אַף אַיִן 5. גַּם לֹא 6. וְ 7. וְאֵין 8. וְאַל 9. וְאִם 10. וּבַל 11. וְגַם 12. וְגַם לֹא 13. וְלֹא 14. וּמָה 15. לֹא 16. לֹא וְ 17. עַד 18. וְ(A) 19. *ἤ* 20. *ἵνα μή* 21. *καί* 22. *καὶ μή* 23. *καί οὐ* 24. *καί οὐ μή* 25. *καὶ οὕτως* 26. *μή* 27. *μηδέ* 28. *μήτε* 29. *οὐ* 30. *οὐδέ* 31. *οὐ μή* 32. *οὔτε* 33. nec 34. neque
Gen 31:29 you speak to Jacob neither good nor bad.' 17
39: 9 nor has he kept back anything from me except 13
45: 6 there will be neither plowing nor harvest. 6
49:10 nor the ruler's staff from between his feet 6
Exd 10: 6 as neither your fathers nor your grandfathers 6
14 as had never been before, nor ever shall be again. 13
15 neither tree nor plant of the field, through all 6
23 they did not see one another, nor did any rise 13
11: 6 there has never been, nor ever shall be again. 13
20:23 nor shall you make for yourselves gods of gold. 13
22:28 You shall not revile God, nor curse a ruler 13
23: 2 multitude to do evil; nor shall you bear witness 13
3 nor shall you be partial to a poor man in his suit. 13
13 nor let such be heard out of your mouth. 15
24 bow down to their gods, nor serve them 15
24 nor serve them, nor do according to their works 15
30: 9 no unholy incense thereon, nor burnt offering 6
9 nor burnt offering, nor cereal offering; 6
34:28 he neither ate bread nor drank water. 15
36: 6 Let neither man nor woman do anything more 6
Lev 2:11 you shall burn no leaven nor any honey 6
3:17 a statute . . that you eat neither fat nor blood 6
10: 9 Drink no wine nor strong drink, you nor your sons 6
9 Drink no wine nor strong drink, you nor your sons 6
12: 4 she shall not . . nor come into the sanctuary 6
19:11 You shall not steal, nor deal falsely 13
11 nor deal falsely, nor lie to one another 13
19 nor shall there come upon you a garment of cloth 15
21: 5 nor shave off the edges of their beards 13
5 nor make any cuttings in their flesh 13
10 The priest . . shall not . . nor rend his clothes 13
11 shall not . . nor defile himself, even for his 15
12 nor profane the sanctuary of his God 13
23:14 eat neither bread nor grain parched or fresh 6
22 nor shall you gather the gleanings 13
25:11 neither sow, nor reap what grows of itself 13
11 nor gather the grapes from the undressed vines 13
37 nor give him your food for profit 13
Num 6: 7 Neither for his father nor for his mother 6
7 Neither for . . nor for brother or sister 6
9:12 none of it until the morning, nor break a bone of it; 15
14:44 neither the ark . . nor Moses, departed out 6
16:14 nor given us inheritance of fields 6
23:21 nor has he seen trouble in Israel. 13
25 Neither curse them at all, nor bless them at all. 5
Deu 2:27 turn aside neither to the right nor to the left. 6
4: 2 You shall not add to the word . . nor take from it; 13
28 gods . . that neither see, nor hear, nor eat, nor smell. 13

28 gods . . that neither see, nor hear, nor eat, nor smell. 13
28 gods . . that neither see, nor hear, nor eat, nor smell. 13
8: 3 you did not know, nor did your fathers know; 15
9: 9 I neither ate bread nor drank water. 15
18 I neither ate bread nor drank water 15
13: 6 other gods,' which neither you nor your fathers 6
8 nor shall your eye pity him, nor shall you spare 13
8 nor shall your eye pity him, nor shall you spare 13
8 nor shall you spare him, nor shall you conceal him; 13
15:19 nor shear the firstling of your flock. 15
16: 4 nor shall any of the flesh . . remain all night 13
17:17 nor . . greatly multiply for himself silver and gold. 15
21: 4 valley . . which is neither plowed nor sown 15
22: 5 nor shall a man put on a woman's garment; 13
30 nor shall he uncover her who is his father's. 13
24:16 nor . . children be put to death for the fathers; 15
28:36 nation that neither you nor your fathers 6
39 but you shall neither . . nor gather the grapes; 13
64 gods . . neither you nor your fathers have known. 6
29:14 Nor is it with you only that I make this . . covenant 13
33: 6 Let Reuben live, and not die, nor let his men be few. 6
34: 7 his eye was not dim, nor his natural force abated. 13
Jos 22:26 altar, not for burnt offering, nor for sacrifice 13
28 made, not for burnt offerings, nor for sacrifice 13
23: 6 turning . . neither to the right hand nor to the left 6
Jdg 11:34 beside her he had neither son nor daughter. 1
14:16 Behold, I have not told my father nor my mother 6
1Sm 1:15 I have drunk neither wine nor strong drink 6
6:12 they turned neither to the right nor to the left 6
13:22 there was neither sword nor spear found 6
20:31 neither you nor your kingdom shall be 6
21: 8 I have brought neither my sword nor my weapons 11
26:12 No man saw it, or knew it, nor did any awake; 6
27: 9 David . . left neither man nor woman alive 6
11 And David saved neither man nor woman alive 6
2Sm 1:21 be no dew or rain . . nor upsurging of the deep! 6
2:19 turned neither to the right hand nor to the left 6
28 pursued . . no more, nor did they fight any more. 13
12:17 he would not, nor did he eat food with them. 13
13:22 But Ab'salom spoke to Amnon neither good nor bad; 17
14: 7 leave . . neither name nor remnant upon the face 6
19:24 neither dressed his feet, nor trimmed his beard 13
24 nor trimmed his beard, nor washed his clothes 13
1Kg 3:26 It shall be neither mine nor yours; divide it. 5
5: 4 there is neither adversary nor misfortune. 2
6: 7 so that neither hammer nor axe nor . . was heard 6
7 so that neither hammer nor axe nor . . was heard •
13: 9 neither eat bread, nor drink water, nor return 13
9 eat bread, nor drink water, nor return by the way 13
16 neither will I eat bread nor drink water with you 13
17 You shall neither eat bread nor drink water 13
17 nor return by the way that you came.' 15
17: 1 there shall be neither dew nor rain these years 6
22:31 Fight with neither small nor great, but only 6
2Kg 2:21 death nor miscarriage shall come from it. 6
3:14 I would neither look at you, nor see you. 9
4:23 Why . . today? It is neither new moon nor sabbath. 13
13:23 and would not destroy them; nor has he cast them 6
18: 5 none like him among . . nor among those who were 6
12 not obey . . they neither listened nor obeyed. 13
23:25 Before . . nor did any like him arise after him. 6
1Ch 4:27 nor did all their family multiply like the men 13
21:24 nor offer burnt offerings which cost me 6
2Ch 18:30 Fight with neither small nor great •
30: 3 nor had the people assembled in Jerusalem 15
Ezr 9:14 that there should be no remnant, nor any to escape? 6
10: 6 neither eating bread nor drinking water; 13
13 Nor is this a work for one day or for two; 13
Neh 4:23 neither I nor my brethren nor my servants 6
23 neither I . . nor my servants nor the men of the guard 6
23 neither I . . nor my servants nor the men of the guard 6
5:14 neither I nor my brethren ate the food allowance 6
7:61 but they could not prove . . nor their descent 6
9:19 nor the pillar of fire by night which lighted 6
Est 2: 7 Esther . . for she had neither father nor mother; 6
4:16 a fast . . and neither eat nor drink for three days 8
5: 9 Haman saw . . that he neither rose nor trembled 13
9:28 nor should the commemoration of these days 13
Job 3: 4 May God above not seek it, nor light shine upon it. 8
9 nor see the eyelids of the morning; 8
10 nor hide trouble from my eyes. 6
26 I am not at ease, nor am I quiet; I have no rest; 13
5: 6 nor does trouble sprout from the ground; 13
7:10 nor does his place know him any more. 13
19 nor let me alone till I swallow my spittle? 15
8:20 nor take the hand of evildoers. 13
15:29 nor will he strike root in the earth; 13
20: 9 nor will his place any more behold him. 13
28:17 nor can it be exchanged for jewels of fine gold. 6
19 nor can it be valued in pure gold. 15
32: 9 nor the aged that understand what is right. 6
34:19 nor regards the rich more than the poor 13
35:13 an empty cry, nor does the Almighty regard it. 13
41:26 not avail; nor the spear, the dart, or the javelin. •
Ps 1: 1 nor stands in the way of sinners 13
1 nor sits in the seat of scoffers; 13
5 nor sinners in the congregation of the righteous; 6
6: 1 not in thy anger, nor chasten me in thy wrath. 8
15: 3 nor takes up a reproach against his neighbor; 13
19: 3 There is no speech, nor are there words; 7
26: 4 with false men, nor do I consort with dissemblers; 13
9 with sinners, nor my life with bloodthirsty men 6
36:11 nor the hand of the wicked drive me away. 8
38: 1 not in thy anger, nor chasten me in thy wrath! 6
44: 3 nor did their own arm give them victory; 13
6 not in my bow do I trust, nor can my sword save me. 13
18 nor have our steps departed from thy way 6
50: 9 bull from your house, nor he-goat from your folds. •
82: 5 They have neither knowledge nor understanding 13
86: 8 nor are there any works like thine. 2
91: 5 of the night, nor the arrow that flies by day •
6 nor the pestilence that stalks in darkness •
6 nor the destruction that wastes at noonday. •
103: 9 nor will he keep his anger for ever. 13
10 nor requite us according to our iniquities. 13
109:12 nor any to pity his fatherless children! 8
115:17 nor do any that go down into silence. 13
121: 4 keeps Israel will neither slumber nor sleep. 13
6 not smite you by day, nor the moon by night. •
135:17 nor is there any breath in their mouths. 4
147:10 nor his pleasure in the legs of a man; 15
Prv 2:19 nor do they regain the paths of life. 13
6:35 nor be appeased though you multiply gifts. 15
22:24 nor go with a wrathful man 6
24: 1 not envious of evil men, nor desire to be with them; 8
30: 3 not learned . . nor have I knowledge of the Holy One. 6
8 give me neither poverty nor riches; 6
Ecc 1: 8 the eye is not . . nor the ear filled with hearing. 13
11 nor will there be any remembrance of later 12
3:14 nothing . . added to it, nor anything taken from it; 6
5: 2 Be not rash . . nor let your heart be hasty to utter 8
10 nor he who loves wealth, with gain 13
8: 8 no discharge . . nor will wickedness deliver 13
16 how neither day nor night one's eyes see sleep; 6
9:11 nor the battle to the strong, nor bread to the wise 13
11 nor the battle to the wise, nor bread to the wise 12
11 bread to the wise, nor riches to the intelligent 12
11 bread to the wise . . nor favor to the men of skill; 12
10:20 nor in your bedchamber curse the rich; 8
Sng 2: 7 you stir not up nor awaken love until it please. †
3: 5 stir not up nor awaken love until it please. †
8: 4 I adjure . . that you stir not up nor awaken love 14
Isa 3: 7 n my house there is neither bread nor mantle 7
8:12 do not fear what they fear, nor be in dread. 13
9:13 did not turn . . nor seek the LORD of hosts. 6
23: 4 I have neither travailed nor given birth 13
4 reared young men nor brought up virgins. •
28:27 nor is a cart wheel rolled over cummin; 6
30: 5 that brings neither help nor profit 13
32: 5 nor the knave said to be honorable. 13
33:20 nor will any of its cords be broken. 10
21 with oars can go, nor stately ship can pass. 13
35: 9 nor shall any ravenous beast come up on it; 10
40:16 nor are its beasts enough for a burnt offering. 7
42: 8 give to no other, nor my praise to graven images. 6
43:10 no god was formed, nor shall there be any after me. 13
18 Remember not . . nor consider the things of old. 8
44: 8 Fear not, nor be afraid; 8
9 their witnesses neither see nor know 10
18 They know not, nor do they discern; 13
19 nor is there knowledge or discernment to say 13
49:10 neither scorching wind nor sun shall smite them 16
57:16 not contend for ever, nor will I always be angry; 13
60:19 nor for brightness shall the moon give light 13
20 no more go down, nor your moon withdraw itself; 13
Jer 4:28 I have not relented nor will I turn back. 13
5:12 nor shall we see sword or famine. 13
15 nor can you understand what they say. 13
6:20 nor your sacrifices pleasing to me. 13
25 Go not forth into the field, nor walk on the road; 8
7:31 I did not command, nor did it come into my mind. 13
8:13 are no grapes on the vine, nor figs on the fig tree; 7
9:16 whom neither they nor their fathers have known; 6
10: 2 nor be dismayed at the signs of the heavens 8
14:13 shall not see the sword, nor shall you have famine 13
14 I did not send them, nor did I command them 13
15:10 I have not lent, nor have I borrowed 13
17 in the company of merrymakers, nor did I rejoice; 6
16: 2 nor shall you have sons or daughters 13
4 shall not be lamented, nor shall they be buried; 13
7 nor shall any one give him the cup of consolation 13
13 which neither you nor your fathers have known 6
17 nor is their iniquity concealed from my eyes. 13
17:16 nor have I desired the day of disaster 13
18:18 perish from the priest, nor counsel from the wise 6
18 from the wise, nor the word from the prophet. 6
23 nor blot out their sin from thy sight. 6
19: 4 neither they nor their fathers nor the kings 6
4 their fathers nor the kings of Judah have known; 6
5 not command or decree, nor did it come into my mind; 13
22: 3 nor shed innocent blood in this place. 8
10 Weep not for him who is dead, nor bemoan him; 8
23: 4 and they shall fear no more, nor be dismayed 13
25: 4 neither listened nor inclined your ears to hear 13
35 nor escape for the lords of the flock. 6
30:10 says the LORD, nor be dismayed, O Israel; 8
32:35 did not command them, nor did it enter into my mind 13
35: 6 shall not drink wine, neither you nor your sons 6
36:24 nor any of his servants who heard all these words 6
24 was afraid, nor did they rend their garments. 13
37: 2 But neither he nor his servants nor the people 6
2 But neither he nor his servants nor the people 6
44: 3 knew not, neither they, nor you, nor your fathers. •
3 knew not, neither they, nor you, nor your fathers. 6
10 nor have they feared, nor walked in my law 13
10 nor have they feared, nor walked in my law 13
46: 6 The swift cannot flee . . nor the warrior escape; 8
27 nor be dismayed, O Israel; 8
48:11 nor has he gone into exile; so his taste remains 13
50:39 nor inhabited for all generations. 13
51:62 nothing shall dwell in it, neither man nor beast 17
Ezk 2: 6 not afraid of them, nor be afraid of their words 8
6 nor be dismayed at their looks 8
3: 9 fear them not, nor be dismayed at their looks 13
18 nor speak to warn the wicked from his wicked way 13
4:14 nor has foul flesh come into my mouth. 13
7: 4 And my eye will not spare you, nor will I have pity; 13
9 And my eye will not spare, nor will I have pity; 13
11 none of them shall remain, nor their abundance 13
11 remain, nor their abundance, nor their wealth; 13
12 Let not the buyer rejoice, nor the seller mourn 8
8:18 my eye will not spare, nor will I have pity; 13
9:10 As for me, my eye will not spare, nor will I have pity 13
11:11 nor shall you be the flesh in the midst of it; 6
12 nor executed my ordinances, but have acted 13
13: 9 nor be enrolled in the register of the house 13
9 nor shall they enter the land of Israel; 13
15 The wall is no more, nor those who daubed it 7
23 see delusive visions nor practice divination; 13
14:11 nor defile themselves any more 13
16 they would deliver neither sons nor daughters; 3
18 they would deliver neither sons nor daughters 6
20 they would deliver neither son nor daughter; 3
16: 4 nor were you washed with water to cleanse you 13
4 nor rubbed with salt, nor swathed with bands. 13
4 nor rubbed with salt, nor swathed with bands. 13
16 the like has never been, nor ever shall be. 13
18:20 nor the father suffer for the iniquity of the son; 13
20: 8 nor did they forsake the idols of Egypt. 13
18 nor observe their ordinances, nor defile 8
18 nor defile yourselves with their idols. 8
44 nor according to your corrupt doings 6
24:16 not mourn or weep nor shall your tears run down. 13
17 nor eat the bread of mourners. 13
22 nor eat the bread of mourners. 13
29:18 neither he nor his army got anything from Tyre 6
31: 8 not rival it, nor the fir trees equal its boughs; 15
32:13 nor shall the hoofs of beasts trouble them. 13
34:28 nor shall the beasts of the land devour them; 13
43: 7 neither they, nor their kings, by their harlotry 6
44:13 nor come near any of my sacred things 6
47:12 leaves will not wither nor their fruit fail 13
Dan 2:44 nor . . its sovereignty be left to another people. 18
10: 3 nor did I anoint myself at all, 13
11: 4 nor according to the dominion with which he ruled 13
20 shall be broken, neither in anger nor in battle. 13
24 neither his fathers nor his fathers' fathers 6
Hos 1: 7 I will not deliver them by bow, nor by sword 6
7 nor by war, nor by horses, nor by horsemen. 6
7 nor by war, nor by horses, nor by horsemen. •
7 nor by war, nor by horses, nor by horsemen. 6
10 sea, which can be neither measured nor numbered; 13
4:14 nor your brides when they commit adultery; •
15 Enter not into Gilgal, nor go up to Beth-a'ven 8
7:10 nor seek him, for all this. 13
Jol 2: 2 never been from of old, nor will be again after 13
Ams 2:14 nor shall the mighty save his life; 13
15 nor shall he who rides the horse save his life; 13
7:14 answered . . "I am no prophet, nor a prophet's son 13
8:11 not a famine of bread, nor a thirst for water 13
Jon 3: 7 Let neither man nor beast, herd nor flock 6
7 Let neither man nor beast, herd nor flock 6
4:10 which you did not labor, nor did you make it grow 13
Mic 5: 7 which tarry not . . nor wait for the sons of men. 13
Hab 3:17 fig tree do not blossom, nor fruit be on the vines 7
Zep 1:12 The LORD will not do good, nor will he do ill.' 13
18 Neither their silver nor their gold shall be 5
3:13 nor shall there be found in their mouth 13
Zec 4: 6 Not by might, nor by power, but by my Spirit 13
14: 6 that day there shall be neither cold nor frost. •
Mal 4: 1 it will leave them neither root nor branch. 6
Mat 5:15 Nor do men light a lamp and put it under a bushel 30
6:20 in heaven, where neither moth nor rust consumes 32
25 what you shall drink, nor about your body 27
26 of the air: they neither sow nor reap nor gather 30
26 they neither sow nor reap nor gather into barns 30
28 how they grow; they neither toil nor spin; 30
7:18 nor can a bad tree bear good fruit. 30
10: 9 Take no gold, nor silver, nor copper in your belts 27
9 Take no gold, nor silver, nor copper in your belts 27
10 no bag for your journey, nor two tunics 27
10 nor two tunics, nor sandals, nor a staff 27
10 nor two tunics, nor sandals, nor a staff 27
24 nor a servant above his master; 30
11:18 For John came neither eating nor drinking 28
12: 4 nor for those who were with him 30
19 nor will any one hear his voice in the streets; 30

13:13 hearing they do not hear, nor do they understand. 30
22:29 neither the scriptures nor the power of God. 27
30 they neither marry nor are given in marriage 32
46 nor from that day did any one dare to ask him 30
23:13 nor allow those who would enter to go in. 30
24:36 not even the angels of heaven, nor the Son 30
25:13 you know neither the day nor the hour. 30
Mrk 4:22 nor is anything secret, except to come to light. 30
12:24 you know neither the scriptures nor the power of God 27
25 they neither marry nor are given in marriage 32
13:15 let him . . not go down, nor enter his house 27
32 nor the Son, but only the Father. 30
14:68 I neither know nor understand what you mean. 32
Lke 1:15 he shall drink no wine nor strong drink 21
6:43 nor again does a bad tree bear good fruit; 30
44 nor are grapes picked from a bramble bush. 30
8:17 nor anything secret that shall not be known 30
9: 3 no staff, nor bag, nor bread, nor money 28
3 no staff, nor bag, nor bread, nor money 28
3 no staff, nor bag, nor bread, nor money 28
12:22 nor about your body, what you shall put on. 27
24 Consider the ravens: they neither sow nor reap 30
24 they have neither storehouse nor barn 30
27 they neither toil nor spin 30
29 nor be of anxious mind. 22
14:35 is fit neither for the land nor for the dunghill; 32
17:21 nor will they say, 'Lo, here it is!' or 'There!' 30
18: 2 a judge who neither feared God nor regarded man; 22
4 Though I neither fear God nor regard man 30
20:35 neither marry nor are given in marriage 32
Joh 1:13 born, not of blood nor of the will of the flesh 30
13 born, not of blood . . nor of the will of man 30
25 if you are neither the Christ, nor Elijah 30
25 neither the Christ, nor Elijah, nor the prophet? 30
4:15 that I may not thirst, nor come here to draw. 27
21 neither on this mountain nor in Jerusalem 32
6:24 Jesus was not there, nor his disciples 30
8:19 Jesus answered, "You know neither me nor my Father 32
9:21 nor do we know who opened his eyes 19
13:16 nor is he who is sent greater than he who sent him. 30
14:17 because it neither sees him nor knows him 30
16: 3 because they have not known the Father, nor me. 30
Act 2:27 nor let thy Holy One see corruption. 30
31 nor did his flesh see corruption. 32
8:21 You have neither part nor lot in this matter 30
9: 9 neither ate nor drank. 30
13:27 nor understand the utterances of the prophets 21
15:10 neither our fathers nor we have been able to bear? 32
17:25 nor is he served by human hands 30
19:37 neither sacrilegious nor blasphemers 32
20:24 not . . of any value nor as precious to myself *
23: 8 there is no resurrection, nor angel, nor spirit; 28
8 there is no resurrection, nor angel, nor spirit; 28
12 an oath neither to eat nor drink 28
21 an oath neither to eat nor drink 28
25: 8 Neither against the law . . nor . . the temple 32
8 nor against the temple, nor against Caesar 32
27:20 when neither sun nor stars appeared for many a day 28
Rom 2:28 nor is true circumcision something external 30
8:38 neither death, nor life, nor angels 32
38 neither death, nor life, nor angels 32
38 nor principalities, nor things present 32
38 nor things present, nor things to come, nor powers 32
38 nor things present, nor things to come, nor powers 32
38 nor things present, nor things to come, nor powers 32
39 nor height, nor depth, nor anything else 32
39 nor height, nor depth, nor anything else 32
39 nor depth, nor anything else in all creation 32
1Co 2: 9 What no eye has seen, nor ear heard 29
9 nor the heart of man conceived 29
3: 7 neither he who plants nor he who waters is 32
6: 9 neither the immoral, nor idolaters 32
9 nor adulterers, nor sexual perverts 32
9 nor adulterers, nor sexual perverts 32
10 nor thieves, nor the greedy, nor drunkards 32
10 nor thieves, nor the greedy, nor drunkards 32
10 nor thieves, nor the greedy, nor drunkards 29
10 nor revilers, nor robbers 29
10 nor revilers, nor robbers 29
7:19 nor uncircumcision 21
9:15 nor am I writing this 29
10:10 nor grumble, as some of them did 27
11:11 woman is not independent of man nor man of woman; 32
16 nor do the churches of God. 30
12:21 nor again the head to the feet 19
15:50 nor does the perishable inherit 30
2Co 7:12 nor on account of the one who suffered the wrong 30
Gal 1: 1 Paul an apostle–not from men nor through man 30
12 I did not receive it from man, nor was I taught it 32
17 nor did I go up to Jerusalem 30
3:28 There is neither Jew nor Greek 30
28 there is neither slave nor free 30
28 there is neither male nor female 21
5: 6 neither circumcision nor uncircumcision 32
6:15 nor uncircumcision, but a new creation. 32
Eph 5: 4 nor silly talk, nor levity, which are not fitting; 21
4 nor silly talk, nor levity, which are not fitting; 19
1Th 2: 3 nor is it made with guile; 30
6 nor did we seek glory from men 32
1Ti 1: 4 nor to occupy themselves with myths 27
5:22 nor participate in another man's sins 27
6:17 nor to set their hopes on uncertain riches 27
2Ti 1: 8 nor of me his prisoner 27
Tit 2:10 nor to pilfer, but to show entire and true fidelity 26
Heb 7: 3 has neither beginning of days nor end of life 28
9:25 Nor was it to offer himself repeatedly 30
10: 8 Thou hast neither desired nor taken pleasure in 30
12: 5 nor lose courage when you are punished by him. 27
13: 5 he has said, "I will never fail you nor forsake you. 30
1Pe 3:14 Have no fear of them, nor be troubled 27
1Jn 3:10 nor he who does not love his brother. 21
Rev 3:15 'I know your works: you are neither cold nor hot. 32
16 you are lukewarm, and neither cold nor hot 32
7:16 sun shall not strike them, nor any scorching heat 30
9:20 nor give up worshiping demons and idols of gold 20
21 nor did they repent of their murders 23
21: 4 neither shall there be mourning nor crying 32
4 neither . . mourning nor crying nor pain any more 32
27 nor any one who practices abomination 21
1Es 4:11 nor do they disobey him. 30
2Es 2:12 they shall neither toil nor become weary. 34
4: 8 nor as yet into hell 34
7:66 nor do they know of any torment or salvation 33
76 nor number yourself among those 34
10: 4 and I will neither eat nor drink 34
12:48 neither forsaken you nor withdrawn from you 34
13: 9 he neither lifted his hand nor held a spear 34
16:20 nor be always mindful of the scourges. 33
Jdt 7: 4 neither the high mountains nor the valleys 32
4 neither the high mountains . . nor the hills 32
8:14 nor find out what a man is thinking 23
16 nor like a human being, to be won over by pleading. 30
18 nor in these present days 30
27 nor has he taken revenge upon us 23
9:11 nor thy might upon men of strength 30
11:10 nor can the sword prevail against them 29
16: 7 nor did the sons of the Titans smite him 30
7 nor did tall giants set upon him 30
Wis 1: 4 nor dwell in a body enslaved to sin. 30
12 nor bring on destruction by the works of your hands; 27
2:10 nor regard the gray hairs of the aged. 27
22 nor hope for the wages of holiness 30
22 nor discern the prize for blameless souls; 30
4: 8 nor measured by number of years; 30
15 nor take such a thing to heart 27
5:10 nor track of its keel in the waves; 30
6: 4 you did not rule rightly, nor keep the law 30
4 nor walk according to the purpose of God 30
7 nor show deference to greatness 30
12:14 nor can any king or monarch confront thee 30
13: 1 nor did they recognize the craftsman 32
14:13 nor will they exist for ever. 32
15: 4 nor the fruitless toil of painters 30
15 nor nostrils with which to draw breath 32
15 nor ears with which to hear 32
15 nor fingers to feel 32
16:12 For neither herb nor poultice cured them 30
14 nor set free the imprisoned soul. 30
17: 5 nor did the brilliant flames of the stars avail 32
19:21 nor did they melt the . . heavenly food. 30
Sir 3:21 nor investigate what is beyond your power. 22
4: 2 nor anger a man in want. 22
3 nor delay your gift to a beggar. 22
4 nor turn your face away from the poor. 22
5 nor give a man occasion to curse you; 22
27 nor show partiality to a ruler. 22
30 nor be a faultfinder with your servants. 21
5: 1 nor say, "I have enough. 22
7 nor postpone it from day to day 22
9 nor follow every path 22
7: 4 nor the seat of honor from the king. 27
5 nor display your wisdom before the king. 21
10 nor neglect to give alms. 22
12 nor do the like to a friend. 27
14 nor repeat yourself in your prayer. 22
8: 3 nor heap wood on his fire. 22
9: 7 nor wander about in its deserted sections. 22
9 nor revel with her at wine 22
10:18 nor fierce anger for those born of women. 30
23 nor is it proper to honor a sinful man. 23
26 nor glorify yourself 22
11: 2 nor loathe a man because of his appearance. 22
4 nor exalt yourself 22
8 nor interrupt a speaker in the midst of his words. 22
9 nor sit with sinners when they judge a case. 22
12: 8 nor will an enemy be hidden in adversity. 23
13: 2 nor associate with a man 22
11 nor trust his abundance of words 22
16: 1 nor rejoice in ungodly sons. 27
10 nor for the 600,000 men on foot 25
27 they neither hunger nor grow weary 32
18: 6 nor is it possible to trace the wonders 23
15 nor cause grief by your words 21
19:22 nor is there prudence 23
23: 6 Let neither gluttony nor lust overcome me 21
28:16 nor will he settle down in peace. 30
30:19 it can neither eat nor smell 32
34:14 nor play the coward, for he is his hope. 31
35:14 nor the widow when she pours out her story. 21
38:32 men can neither sojourn nor live there. 30
33 nor do they attain eminence 23
33 nor do they understand the sentence of judgment; 29
47:22 nor cause any of his works to perish 24
22 nor destroy the posterity of him who loved him 24
Bar 3:20 the way to knowledge, nor understood her paths 30
20 way to knowledge . . nor laid hold of her. 30
22 She has not been heard of . . nor seen in Teman; 30
23 the way to wisdom, nor given thought to her paths. 30
27 God did not choose them, nor give them the way 30
4:13 nor tread the paths of discipline 30
LJr 1:64 one must not think . . nor call them gods 32
66 For they can neither curse nor bless kings; 32
1Mc 2:34 nor will we do what the king commands 30
4:27 nor had they turned out as the king had commanded 23
12:36 so that its garrison could neither buy nor sell. 28
15:33 neither taken foreign land nor seized foreign property 32
2Mc 2: 2 nor to be led astray in their thoughts 22
6: 6 nor observe the feasts of his fathers 32
6 nor so much as confess himself to be a Jew. 32
7:22 nor I who set in order the elements 23
3Mc 3: 7 loyal neither to the king nor to his authorities 28
4:11 nor in any way claim 27
4Mc 2: 9 nor gathers the last grapes from the vineyard 28
5:29 nor will I transgress the sacred oaths 32
34 nor will I renounce you, beloved self-control. 30
35 nor will I reject you, honored priesthood 30
36 nor my long life lived lawfully. 30
7: 6 nor profaned your stomach 30
8:24 nor take hollow pride in being put to the rack. 27
15:18 nor when the second in torments looked at you 30
18 nor when the third expired; 29
19 nor did you weep 30
21 the melodies of sirens nor the songs of swans 30
16: 3 nor was the . . furnace . . so intensely hot 30
11 Nor when I die 30
12 nor did she dissuade any of them from dying 30
12 nor did she grieve as they were dying 30
18: 8 nor did the destroyer, the deceitful serpent 30

nor even 1. *μηδέ* 2. *οὐδέ*

3Mc 1:11 nor even all of the priests 1
4Mc 8:27 nor even seriously considered them. 2

normal 1. *ἴδιος*

Wis 19:20 Fire even in water retained its normal power 1

north 1. מִשְּׂמֹאל 2. צָפוֹן 3. שְׂמֹאל 4. שְׂמָאלִי 5. *ἀριστερός* 6. *βορέας* 7. *βορρᾶς* 8. septentriones

Gen 14:15 pursued them to Hobah, north of Damascus. 3
28:14 to the west and to the east and to the north 2
Exd 26:20 the tabernacle, on the north side twenty frames 2
35 you shall put the table on the north side. 2
27:11 likewise for its length on the north side 2
36:25 side of the tabernacle, on the north side 2
38:11 for the north side 100 cubits, their pillars 20 2
40:22 on the north side of the tabernacle 2
Lev 1:11 he shall kill it on the north side of the altar 2
Num 3:35 to encamp on the north side of the tabernacle. 2
35: 5 shall measure . . for the north side 2,000 cubits 2
Jos 8:13 the main encampment which was north of the city 2
15: 5 the boundary on the north side runs from the bay 2
6 boundary . . passes along north of Beth-arabah; 2
11 boundary goes out to . . the hill north of Ekron 2
16: 6 the boundary . . on the north is Mich-me'thath; 2
17:10 and that to the north being Manas'seh's 2
10 on the north Asher is reached, and on the east 2
18: 5 house of Joseph in their territory on the north. 2
12 On the north side their boundary began 2
12 boundary goes up the shoulder north of Jericho 2
18 passing on to the north of the shoulder 2
19 passes . . north of the shoulder of Beth-hoglah; 2
19:14 on the north the boundary turns . . to Han'nathon 2
27 then it continues in the north to Cabul 3
24:30 Tim'nath-se'rah . . north of the mountain of Ga'ash 2
Jdg 2: 9 of E'phraim, north of the mountain of Ga'ash. 2
7: 1 the camp of Mid'ian was north of them, by the hill 2
21:19 Shiloh, which is north of Bethel, on the east 2
1Sm 14: 5 one crag rose on the north in front of Michmash 2
1Kg 7:21 he set up the pillar on the north and called its 4
25 twelve oxen, three facing north, three facing 2
39 stands . . and five on the north side of the house; 1
49 lampstands . . south side and five on the north 3
2Kg 11:11 from the south . . to the north side of the house 4
16:14 he removed . . and put it on the north side of his altar. 2
1Ch 9:24 on the four sides, east, west, north and south; 2
26:14 Zechari'ah . . and his lot came out for the north. 2
17 on the north four each day, on the south four 2
2Ch 3:17 one on the south, the other on the north; 3
17 pillars . . Jachin, and that on the north Bo'az. 4
4: 4 It stood upon twelve oxen, three facing north 2
7 set them in the temple . . and five on the north. 3
8 placed them in the temple . . five on the north. 3
23:10 from the south . . to the north side of the house 4
Job 26: 7 He stretches out the north over the void 2
37:22 Out of the north comes golden splendor; 2
Ps 48: 2 joy of all the earth, Mount Zion, in the far north 2

89:12 The north and the south, thou hast created them; 2
107: 3 gathered in from . . north and from the south. 2
Prv 25:23 The north wind brings forth rain; 2
Ecc 1: 6 wind blows . . south, and goes round to the north; 2
11: 3 and if a tree falls to the south or to the north 2
Isa 14:13 sit on the mount of assembly in the far north; 2
31 For smoke comes out of the north 2
41:25 I stirred up one from the north, and he has come 2
43: 6 I will say to the north, Give up 2
49:12 and lo, these from the north and from the west 2
Jer 1:13 I see a boiling pot, facing away from the north. 2
14 Out of the north evil shall break forth 2
15 all the tribes of the kingdoms of the north 2
3:18 they shall come from the land of the north 2
4: 6 stay not, for I bring evil from the north 2
6: 1 for evil looms out of the north 2
22 Behold, a people is coming from the north country 2
10:22 a great commotion out of the north country 2
13:20 and see those who come from the north. 2
15:12 Can one break iron, iron from the north, and bronze? 2
16:15 the people of Israel out of the north country 2
23: 8 the house of Israel out of the north country 2
25: 9 behold, I will send for all the tribes of the north 2
26 all the kings of the north, far and near 2
31: 8 Behold, I will bring them from the north country 2
46: 6 in the north by the river Euphra'tes 2
10 in the north country by the river Euphra'tes. 2
20 but a gadfly from the north has come upon her. 2
24 into the hand of a people from the north. 2
47: 2 Behold, waters are rising out of the north 2
50: 3 out of the north a nation has come up against her 2
9 company of great nations, from the north country; 2
41 Behold, a people comes from the north; 2
51:48 come against them out of the north, says the LORD. 2
Ezk 1: 4 behold, a stormy wind came out of the north 2
8: 3 gateway of the inner court that faces north 2
5 your eyes now in the direction of the north. 2
5 So I lifted up my eyes toward the north, and behold 2
5 behold, north of the altar gate, in the entrance 2
14 he brought me to the entrance of the north gate 2
9: 2 direction of the upper gate, which faces north 2
16:46 who lived with her daughters to the north of you; 3
20:47 all faces from south to north shall be scorched 2
21: 4 against all flesh from south to north; 2
23:24 And they shall come against you from the north 7
26: 7 bring upon Tyre from the north Nebuchadrez'zar 2
32:30 The princes of the north are there, all of them 2
38: 6 from the uttermost parts of the north 2
15 place out of the uttermost parts of the north 2
39: 2 from the uttermost parts of the north, and lead you 2
40:19 Then he went before me to the north 2
20 there was a gate which faced toward the north 2
23 And opposite the gate on the north, as on the east 2
35 Then he brought me to the north gate 2
40 the entrance of the north gate were two tables; 2
44 one at the side of the north gate facing south 2
44 at the side of the south gate facing north. 2
46 the chamber which faces north is for the priests 2
41:11 one door toward the north, and another door 2
42: 1 led me out into the inner court, toward the north 2
1 and opposite the building on the north. 2
2 The length of the building which was on the north 2
4 their doors were on the north. 2
11 they were similar to the chambers on the north 2
13 The north chambers and the south chambers 2
17 Then he turned and measured the north side 2
44: 4 he brought me by way of the north gate to the front 2
46: 9 he who enters by the north gate to worship 2
9 by the south gate shall go out by the north gate 2
19 north row of the holy chambers for the priests; 2
47: 2 Then he brought me out by way of the north gate 2
15 On the north side, from the Great Sea 2
17 Damascus, with the border of Hamath to the north. 2
17 This shall be the north side. 2
48:16 its dimensions: the north side 4,500 cubits 2
17 open land: on the north 250 cubits, on the south 250 2
30 north side, which is to be 4,500 cubits by measure 2
Dan 11: 6 shall come to the king of the north to make peace; 2
7 enter the fortress of the king of the north 2
8 refrain from attacking the king of the north. 2
11 come out and fight with the king of the north; 2
13 king of the north shall again raise a multitude 2
15 Then the king of the north shall come and throw up 2
40 king of the north shall rush upon him like 2
44 tidings from the east and the north shall alarm 2
Ams 8:12 wander from sea to sea, and from north to east; 2
Zep 2:13 he will stretch out his hand against the north 2
Zec 2: 6 ho! Flee from the land of the north, says the LORD; 2
6: 6 the black horses goes toward the north country 2
8 Behold, those who go toward the north country 2
8 have set my Spirit at rest in the north country. 2
Lke 13:29 come from east and west, and from north and south 7
Rev 21:13 on the east three gates, on the north three gates 7
2Es 15:34 from the east, and from the north to the south 8
38 from the north, and another part from the west. 8
Jdt 2:21 mountain which is to the north of Upper Cilicia. 5
16: 4 came down from the mountains of the north 7
Sir 43:17 the tempest from the north and the whirlwind 6
20 The cold north wind blows 6

north *See also* end, side, toward, wind.

northeast 1. κατὰ λίβα
Act 27:12 looking northeast and southeast 1

northeaster 1. εὐρακύλων
Act 27:14 soon a tempestuous wind, called the northeaster 1

northerly *See* direction.

northern 1. מִצָּפוֹן 2. צָפוֹן
Num34: 7 your northern boundary: from the Great Sea 2
9 this shall be your northern boundary. 2
Jos 11: 2 the kings who were in the northern hill country 1
15: 8 at the northern end of the valley of Reph'aim; 2
10 along to the northern shoulder of Mount Je'arim 1
18:19 boundary ends at the northern bay of the Salt Sea 2
Ezk 47:17 which is on the northern border of Damascus 2
48: 1 Beginning at the northern border, from the sea 2
1 Hazar-e'non (which is on the northern border 2
10 measuring 25,000 cubits on the northern side 2

northerner 1. צְפוֹנִי
Jol 2:20 I will remove the northerner far from you 1

northward 1. צָפוֹנָה
Gen 13:14 place where you are, northward and southward 1
Deu 2: 3 going about . . long enough; turn northward. 1
3:27 lift up your eyes westward and northward 1
Jos 13: 3 from . . northward to the boundary of Ekron 1
15: 7 boundary goes up to Debir . . and so northward 1
19:27 and touches . . Iph'tahel northward to Beth-emek 1
Dan 8: 4 charging westward and northward and southward; 1
Zec 14: 4 one half of the Mount shall withdraw northward 1

nose 1. אַף
Gen 24:47 I put the ring in her nose, and the bracelets 1
2Kg 19:28 put my hook in your nose and my bit in your mouth 1
Job 40:24 with hooks, or pierce his nose with a snare? 1
41: 2 Can you put a rope in his nose, or pierce his jaw 1
Ps 115: 6 have ears, but do not hear; noses, but do not smell. 1
Prv 30:33 pressing the nose produces blood 1
Sng 7: 4 Your nose is like a tower of Lebanon 1
Isa 3:21 the signet rings and nose rings; 1
37:29 I will put my hook in your nose 1
Ezk 8:17 Lo, they put the branch to their nose. 1
16:12 I put a ring on your nose, and earrings in your ears 1
23:25 They shall cut off your nose and your ears 1

nostril 1. אַף 2. נְחִיר 3. μυκτήρ 4. ῥίς
Gen 2: 7 breathed into his nostrils the breath of life; 1
7:22 dry land in whose nostrils was the breath of life 1
Exd 15: 8 At the blast of thy nostrils the waters piled up 1
Num11:20 a whole month, until it comes out at your nostrils 1
2Sm 22: 9 Smoke went up from his nostrils, and . . fire 1
16 at the blast of the breath of his nostrils. 1
Job 27: 3 the spirit of God is in my nostrils; 1
41:20 Out of his nostrils comes forth smoke 2
Ps 18: 8 Smoke went up from his nostrils 1
15 O LORD, at the blast of the breath of thy nostrils. 1
Isa 2:22 Turn away from man in whose nostrils is breath 1
65: 5 These are a smoke in my nostrils, 1
Lam 4:20 The breath of our nostrils, the LORD'S anointed 1
Ams 4:10 the stench of your camp go up into your nostrils; 1
Wis 2: 2 because the breath in our nostrils is smoke 4
15:15 nor nostrils with which to draw breath 4
4Mc 6:25 poured stinking liquids into his nostrils. 3
15:19 and saw in their nostrils the signs 3

notable 1. γνωστός 2. ἐπίσημος 3. μετὰ δόξης 4. ὀνομαστός
Act 4:16 a notable sign has been performed through them 1
AEs 16:22 you shall observe this . . as a notable day 2
Sir 39: 2 he will preserve the discourse of notable men 4
3Mc 6:28 has granted an unimpeded and notable stability 3

note 1. נבט 2. ὁράω 3. σημειόω
Ps 10:14 yea, thou dost note trouble and vexation 1
Rom11:22 Note then the kindness and the severity of God 2
2Th 3:14 note that man, and have nothing to do with him 3
Jdt 10: 7 and noted how her face was altered •

note (2) 1. ἦχος 2. φθόγγος
1Co 14: 7 flute or the harp, do not give distinct notes 2
Wis 19:18 on a harp the notes vary the nature of the rhythm 2
18 on a harp . . while each note remains the same 1

note *See* man, take.

nothing 1. אַיִן 2. אֵין דָּבָר 3. אֵין כֹּל 4. אֵין מְאוּמָה 5. אַךְ 6. אַל 7. אַל דָּבָר 8. אַל כֹּל 9. אֶפֶס 10. בְּלִי 11. בְּלִי מָה 12. בִּלְתִּי 13. חִנָּם 14. כִּי אִם 15. כֹּל דָּבָר לֹא 16. כֹּל לֹא 17. לֹא 18. לֹא דָּבָר 19. לֹא לֶחֶם 20. לֹא מְאוּמָה 21. לֹא מְלָאכָה 22. לֹא רַק 23. מְאוּמָה 24. רַק 25. תֹּהוּ 26. לָא (A) 27. לָא צְבוּ (A) 28. μή 29. μηδείς 30. μηδέ τις 31. μή τις 32. μὴ τίς 33. οὐ 34. οὐδείς 35. οὐθείς 36. οὐ μὴ πᾶς 37. οὐ πᾶν ῥῆμα 38. οὐ πᾶς λόγος 39. οὔτε 40. οὔ τις 41. οὐ τίς 42. nihil 43. nolo
Gen 11: 6 nothing that they propose . . will now be impossible 16
14:24 I will take nothing but what the young men have •
19: 8 only do nothing to these men 7
22 for I can do nothing till you arrive 18
26:29 we . . have done to you nothing but good 24
29:15 should you therefore serve me for nothing? 13
40:15 and here also I have done nothing that they 23
47:18 there is nothing left in the sight of my lord 17
Exd 9: 4 a distinction . . so that nothing shall die 18
12:20 You shall eat nothing leavened; 16
16:18 he that gathered much had nothing over 17
21: 2 in the seventh he shall go out free, for nothing. 13
11 she shall go out for nothing, without payment 13
22: 1 if he has nothing, then he shall be sold 1
Num 6: 4 eat nothing that is produced by the grapevine 17
11: 5 We remember the fish we ate in Egypt for nothing 13
6 there is nothing at all but this manna to look at. 1
16:26 Depart . . and touch nothing of theirs 8
20:19 let me only pass through on foot, nothing more. 1
22:16 Let nothing hinder you from coming to me; 6
23:11 behold, you have done nothing but bless them. •
Deu 2: 7 LORD . . been with you; you have lacked nothing.' 18
8: 9 a land . . in which you will lack nothing 16
15: 9 your eye be hostile . . and you give him nothing 17
20:16 you shall save alive nothing that breathes 17
22:26 But to the young woman you shall do nothing; 17
28:55 because he has nothing left him, in the siege 10
29:23 burnt-out waste, unsown, and growing nothing 17
Jos 2:22 pursuers had made search . . and found nothing. 17
11:15 left nothing undone of all that the LORD had 18
Jdg 13: 4 drink no wine . . and eat nothing unclean 8
7 drink no wine . . and eat nothing unclean 8
14: 6 as one tears a kid; and he had nothing in his hand. 23
18: 7 dwelt in security . . lacking nothing that is 2
1Sm 3:18 Samuel told him . . and hid nothing from him. •
4: 7 nothing like this has happened before. 17
14: 6 nothing can hinder the LORD from saving 1
20: 2 my father does nothing . . without disclosing it 18
39 But the lad knew nothing; 20
22:15 your servant has known nothing of all this 18
25: 7 and we did them no harm, and they missed nothing 20
21 nothing was missed of all that belonged to him; 20
36 she told him nothing at all until the morning 18
27: 1 there is nothing better for me than . . escape 1
28:20 he had eaten nothing all day and all night. 19
29: 6 I have found nothing wrong in you 17
30:19 Nothing was missing, whether small or great 17
2Sm 12: 3 the poor man had nothing but one little ewe lamb 3
15:11 they went in their simplicity, and knew nothing. 18
17:19 spread a covering . . and nothing was known of it. 18
18:13 (and there is nothing hidden from the king) 15
19: 6 commanders and servants are nothing to you; 1
1Kg 4:27 each . . in his month; they let nothing be lacking. 18
8: 9 There was nothing in the ark except the two 1
10: 3 there was nothing hidden from the king 18
17:12 I have nothing baked, only a handful of meal †
18:43 he went up and looked, and said, "There is nothing. 1
43 he went up and looked, and said, "There is nothing. 23
22:16 that you speak to me nothing but the truth 22
2Kg 4: 2 Your maidservant has nothing in the house 3
7:10 there was no one . . nothing but the horses tied 14
10:10 there shall fall to the earth nothing of the word 17
20:13 there was nothing . . that Hezeki'ah did not show 18
15 there is nothing . . that I did not show them. 18
17 carried to Babylon; nothing shall be left, says 18
2Ch 5:10 was nothing in the ark except the two tables 1
9: 2 there was nothing hidden from Solomon 17
18:15 speak to me nothing but the truth 17
30:26 there had been nothing like this in Jerusalem. 17
Ezr 4: 3 You have nothing to do with us in building a house 17
Neh 2: 2 This is nothing else but sadness of the heart. 1
5:12 We will restore these and require nothing 17
8:10 portions to him for whom nothing is prepared; 1
9:21 sustain them . . and they lacked nothing; 17
Est 2:15 asked for nothing except what Hegai . . advised. 18
6: 3 servants . . said, "Nothing has been done for him. 18
10 Leave out nothing that you have mentioned. 7
Job 5:24 you shall inspect your fold and miss nothing. 17
8: 9 for we are but of yesterday, and know nothing 17
20:21 There was nothing left after he had eaten; 1
21:34 There is nothing left of your answers •
22: 6 exacted pledges of your brothers for nothing 13
24:25 and show that there is nothing in what I say? 6
26: 7 over the void, and hangs the earth upon nothing. 11
34: 9 For he has said, 'It profits a man nothing 17
Ps 19: 6 there is nothing hid from its heat. 1
39: 5 my lifetime is as nothing in thy sight. 1
49:17 For when he dies he will carry nothing away; 16
73:25 there is nothing upon earth that I desire 17
101: 4 far from me; I will know nothing of evil. 17
119:165who love thy law; nothing can make them stumble. 1
Prv 3:15 nothing you desire can compare with her. 16
8: 8 there is nothing twisted or crooked in them. 1
13: 4 The soul of the sluggard craves, and gets nothing 1
7 One man pretends to be rich, yet has nothing; 3

20: 4 he will seek at harvest and have nothing. 1
22:27 If you have nothing with which to pay, why 1
29:24 hears the curse, but discloses nothing. 17
Ecc 1: 9 and there is nothing new under the sun. 3
2:11 and there was nothing to be gained under the sun. 1
24 There is nothing better for a man than that he 1
3:12 there is nothing better for them than to be happy 1
14 nothing can be added to it, nor anything taken 1
22 there is nothing better than that a man should 1
5:14 he is father . . but he has nothing in his hand. 4
15 he shall go . . and shall take nothing for his toil 20
6: 2 that he lacks nothing of all that he desires 1
9: 5 For the living know . . but the dead know nothing 4
Isa 10: 4 Nothing remains but to crouch 12
19:15 nothing for Egypt which head or tail . . may do. 17
34:12 and all its princes shall be nothing. 9
39: 2 There was nothing in his house or in all his realm 18
4 nothing in my storehouses that I did not show 18
6 be carried to Babylon; nothing shall be left 18
40:17 All the nations are as nothing before him 1
17 they are accounted by him as less than nothing 9
23 and makes the rulers of the earth as nothing. 25
41:11 those who strive against you shall be as nothing 1
24 Behold, you are nothing, and your work is nought; 1
29 they are all a delusion; their works are nothing; 9
44: 9 All who make idols are nothing 25
10 casts an image, that is profitable for nothing? 12
47:11 come on you suddenly, of which you know nothing. 17
49: 4 I have spent my strength for nothing and vanity; 25
52: 3 For thus says the LORD: "You were sold for nothing 13
4 and the Assyrian oppressed them for nothing. 9
5 seeing that my people are taken away for nothing? 13
Jer 5:12 and have said, 'He will do nothing; no evil will come 17
6: 6 there is nothing but oppression within her. •
12:13 have tired themselves out but profit nothing. 17
13: 7 waistcloth was spoiled; it was good for nothing. 16
10 like this waistcloth, which is good for nothing. 16
22:13 who makes his neighbor serve him for nothing 13
30:14 have forgotten you; they care nothing for you; 17
32:17 Nothing is too hard for thee 15
23 they did nothing of all thou didst command them 17
30 and the sons of Judah have done nothing but evil 5
30 sons of Israel have done nothing but provoke me 5
38: 5 for the king can do nothing against you. 2
14 I will ask you a question; hide nothing from me. 7
25 what the king said to you; hide nothing from us 6
39:10 some of the poor people who owned nothing 4
42: 4 I will tell you; I will keep nothing back from you. 18
48:38 in the squares there is nothing but lamentation; 1
50:26 destroy her utterly; let nothing be left of her. 6
51:62 cut it off, so that nothing shall dwell in it 12
Lam 1:12 Is it nothing to you, all you who pass by? 17
Ezk 13: 3 follow their own spirit, and have seen nothing! 12
15: 5 Behold, when it was whole, it was used for nothing; 21
31: 8 were as nothing compared with its branches; 17
44:17 they shall have nothing of wool on them 17
Dan 4:35 inhabitants . . are accounted as nothing; 26
6:17 nothing might be changed concerning Daniel. 27
9:26 anointed one . . cut off, and shall have nothing; 1
Jol 2: 3 desolate wilderness, and nothing escapes them. 17
Ams 3: 4 cry out from his den, if he has taken nothing? 12
5 a snare spring up . . when it has taken nothing? 17
7 the Lord GOD does nothing, without revealing his 18
Mic 3: 5 against him who puts nothing into their mouths. 17
Zep 3: 3 wolves that leave nothing till the morning. 17
Hag 2: 3 do you see it now? Is it not in your sight as nothing? 1
19 and the olive tree still yield nothing? 17
Mat 8: 4 See that you say nothing to any one; but go •
10:26 So have no fear of them; for nothing is covered 34
13:34 he said nothing to them without a parable. 34
15:32 and have nothing to eat 41
17:20 and nothing will be impossible to you. 34
21:19 found nothing on it but leaves only 34
23:16 If any one swears by the temple, it is nothing 34
18 If any one swears by the altar, it is nothing 34
27:19 Have nothing to do with that righteous man 29
24 So when Pilate saw that he was gaining nothing 34
Mrk 1:44 said to him, "See that you say nothing to any one 29
4:22 there is nothing hid, except to be made manifest; 33
6: 8 charged them to take nothing for their journey 29
7:15 there is nothing outside a man 34
8: 1 they had nothing to eat 32
2 have nothing to eat; 41
11:13 When he came to it, he found nothing but leaves 34
14:51 with nothing but a linen cloth about his body †
16: 8 they said nothing to any one, for they were afraid. 34
Lke 1:37 For with God nothing will be impossible. 37
4: 2 he ate nothing in those days 34
5: 5 Master, we toiled all night and took nothing! 34
6:35 do good, and lend, expecting nothing in return 29
8:17 nothing is hid that shall not be made manifest 33
9: 3 he said to them, "Take nothing for your journey 29
10:19 nothing shall hurt you. 34
11: 6 I have nothing to set before him'; 33
12: 2 Nothing is covered up that will not be revealed 34
22:35 did you lack anything?" They said, "Nothing. 34
23:15 nothing deserving death has been done by him; 34
41 this man has done nothing wrong. 34
Joh 4:11 you have nothing to draw with, and the well is deep; 39
5:14 Sin no more, that nothing worse befall you. 31
19 the Son can do nothing of his own accord 34
30 I can do nothing on my own authority 34
6:12 that nothing may be lost. 31
39 I should lose nothing of all that he has given me 28
7:26 here he is, speaking openly, and they say nothing 34
8:28 I do nothing on my own authority 34
44 and has nothing to do with the truth 33
54 If I glorify myself, my glory is nothing 34
9:33 If this man were not from God, he could do nothing. 34
10:13 is a hireling and cares nothing for the sheep. 33
11:49 You know nothing at all; 34
12:19 You see that you can do nothing 34
15: 5 for apart from me you can do nothing. 34
16:23 In that day you will ask nothing of me 34
24 Hitherto you have asked nothing in my name 34
18:20 I have said nothing secretly. 34
21: 3 that night they caught nothing. 34
Act 4:14 they had nothing to say in opposition. 34
5:36 were dispersed and came to nothing. 34
8:24 nothing of what you have said may come upon me. 29
9: 8 when his eyes were opened, he could see nothing 34
13:28 could charge him with nothing deserving death 29
17:21 nothing except telling or hearing something 34
19:27 the temple . . may count for nothing 34
36 you ought to be quiet and do nothing rash. 29
21:24 is nothing in what they have been told about you 34
23: 9 We find nothing wrong in this man. 34
29 charged with nothing deserving death 29
25:11 if there is nothing in their charges against me 34
25 I found that he had done nothing deserving death; 29
26 nothing definite to write to my lord about him 40
26:22 saying nothing but what the prophets . . said 34
31 This man is doing nothing to deserve death 34
27:33 without food, having taken nothing. 29
28:17 though I had done nothing against the people 34
Rom 7:18 For I know that nothing good dwells within me 33
9:11 and had done nothing either good or bad 30
14:14 persuaded . . that nothing is unclean in itself; 34
1Co 2: 2 For I decided to know nothing among you 40
11:22 humiliate those who have nothing 28
13: 2 but have not love, I am nothing. 34
3 but have not love, I gain nothing. 34
2Co 1:13 For we write you nothing but what you can read 33
6:10 as having nothing, and yet possessing 29
17 touch nothing unclean; then I will welcome you 28
8:15 He who gathered much had nothing over 33
9: 4 to say nothing of you 28
12: 1 I must boast; there is nothing to be gained by it 33
11 even though I am nothing. 34
Gal 2: 6 those, I say, who were of repute added nothing to me; 34
6: 3 when he is nothing 29
Php 2: 3 Do nothing from selfishness or conceit 29
2Th 3:14 note that man, and have nothing to do with him 28
1Ti 4: 4 nothing is to be rejected 34
5:21 doing nothing from partiality. 29
6: 4 is puffed up with conceit, he knows nothing 29
7 for we brought nothing into the world 34
Tit 1:15 to the corrupt and unbelieving nothing is pure; 34
2: 8 having nothing evil to say of us. 29
3:13 see that they lack nothing. 29
Phm 1:14 I preferred to do nothing without your consent 34
19 to say nothing of your owing me 28
Heb 2: 8 he left nothing outside his control 34
7:14 Moses said nothing about priests. 34
19 for the law made nothing perfect 34
Jas 1: 4 be perfect and complete, lacking in nothing. 29
1Pe 3: 6 if you do right and let nothing terrify you. 29
3Jn 1: 7 they . . have accepted nothing from the heathen 29
Rev 3:17 For you say, I am rich . . and I need nothing; 34
21:27 But nothing unclean shall enter it 36
1Es 2:28 to take care that nothing more be done 29
4:36 with him there is nothing unrighteous. 34
40 there is nothing unrighteous in her judgment. 34
5:70 You have nothing to do with us 33
8: 7 he omitted nothing from the law of the Lord 29
2Es 6:10 seek for nothing else, Ezra! 43
56 thou hast said that they are nothing 42
57 these nations, which are reputed as nothing 42
11:23 nothing remained on the eagle's body 42
13:11 suddenly nothing was seen of the . . multitude 42
Tob 1:20 nothing was left to me except my wife Anna 34
7:11 Tobias said, "I will eat nothing here 34
10: 7 she ate nothing in the daytime 33
12 do nothing to grieve her. 28
Jdt 11: 5 I will tell nothing false to my lord this night. 33
Wis 4: 5 not ripe enough to eat, and good for nothing. 34
7: 8 I accounted wealth as nothing 34
25 nothing defiled gains entrance into her. 34
28 for God loves nothing 34
8: 7 nothing in life is more profitable for men 34
9: 6 he will be regarded as nothing. 34
13:13 useful for nothing 34
17: 9 For even if nothing disturbing frightened them 29
12 fear is nothing but surrender of the helps 34
Sir 6:15 nothing so precious as a faithful friend 33
8:16 because blood is as nothing in his sight 34
18 do nothing that is to be kept secret 28
18:22 Let nothing hinder you from paying a vow 28
33 when you have nothing in your purse. 34
19: 7 you will lose nothing at all. 35
20:10 There is a gift that profits you nothing 33
14 A fool's gift will profit you nothing 33
23:27 nothing is better than the fear of the Lord 34
27 nothing sweeter than to heed the commandments 34
25: 3 You have gathered nothing in your youth 33
26:14 nothing so precious as a disciplined soul. 33
32:19 Do nothing without deliberation 29
33:29 do nothing without discretion. 29
39:19 nothing can be hid from his eyes. 33
20 nothing is marvelous to him. 34
40: 7 wonders that his fear came to nothing. 34
42:21 Nothing can be added or taken away 39
24 he has made nothing incomplete. 34
48:13 Nothing was too hard for him 38
LJr 1:45 they can be nothing but what the craftsmen wish 34
70 a scarecrow . . that guards nothing 34
Sus 1:63 because nothing shameful was found in her. 33
Bel 1:35 I know nothing about the den. 33
2Mc 7:12 for he regarded his sufferings as nothing. 34
12: 4 because they . . suspected nothing 29
14:23 and did nothing out of the way 34
4Mc 2:17 he did nothing against them in anger 33
8:11 if you disobey, nothing remains for you but to die 34
9: 5 as though . . you learned nothing from Eleazar 33

nothing *See also* bring, cost, eat, need, profit, say, take.

nothing at all 1. אַיִן אֶפֶס
Isa 41:12 who war against you shall be as nothing at all. 1

do nothing 1. חשה
Jdg 18: 9 And will you do nothing? Do not be slow to go 1

empty nothing 1. הֶבֶל
Job 21:34 How then will you comfort me with empty nothings? 1

nothing ever 1. *οὐδέποτε* 2. *πώποτε οὐκ*
Act 11: 8 nothing common or unclean has ever entered 1
Sus 1:27 nothing like this had ever been said about Susanna. 2

nothing except 1. *μόνον*
Wis 17: 6 Nothing was shining through to them except . . 1

nothing more to do 1. *παραιτέομαι*
Tit 3:10 have nothing more to do with him 1

nothing to do 1. *παραιτέομαι*
1Ti 4: 7 Have nothing to do with godless . . myths 1
2Ti 2:23 Have nothing to do with . . controversies 1

notice 1. *αἰσθάνομαι* 2. *γινώσκω* 3. *ἐπιγινώσκω* 4. *κατανοέω* 5. *συνοράω*
Mat 7: 3 but do not notice the log that is in your own eye? 4
Lke 6:41 do not notice the log that is in your own eye? 4
Act 27:39 they noticed a bay with a beach 4
Sir 19:27 where no one notices, he will forestall you. 3
LJr 1:20 They do not notice 1
Bel 1:19 notice whose footsteps these are. 2
2Mc 14:26 Alcimus noticed their good will for one another 5
30 noticing that Nicanor was more austere 5

notice *See also* escape, give, take.

notify 1. ידע (A) 2. *διασαφέω*
Ezr 7:24 notify you that it shall not be lawful to impose 1
2Mc 1:18 we thought it necessary to notify you 2

notion 1. *διάλημψις* 2. *λόγος*
2Mc 3:32 fearing that the king might get the notion 1
4Mc 3: 1 This notion is entirely ridiculous 2

notorious 1. *διάδηλος* 2. *ἔκκλητος* 3. *ἐπίσημος* 4. *ὑπεροχὴν ποιέω*
Mat 27:16 they had then a notorious prisoner 3
Sir 42:11 notorious among the people 2
2Mc 13: 6 notorious for other crimes. 4
3Mc 2: 5 who were notorious for their vices 1

notwithstanding 1. וְ
Num26:11 Notwithstanding, the sons of Korah did not die. 1

nought 1. אָוֶן 2. אַיִן 3. אַךְ 4. הֶבֶל 5. חִנָּם 6. רֵיק 7. שָׁוְא
Job 1: 9 answered the LORD, "Does Job fear God for nought? 5
Ps 39: 6 Surely for nought are they in turmoil; 4
Isa 40:23 who brings princes to nought 2
41:24 Behold, you are nothing, and your work is nought; •
Jer 16:19 Our fathers have inherited nought but lies 3
51:58 The peoples labor for nought 6
Hos 12:11 they shall surely come to nought; 7
Ams 5: 5 go into exile, and Bethel shall come to nought. 1
Hab 2:13 and nations weary themselves for nought? 6

nought *See also* bring, come, set.

nourish 1. גדל 2. כול 3. *ἐκτρέφω* 4. *ἐντρέφω* 5. *ἐπιχορηγέω* 6. *συντρέφω* 7. *τρέφω* 8. nutrio
Isa 44:14 he plants a cedar and the rain nourishes it. 1

Ezk 31: 4 The waters nourished it, the deep made it grow 1
Zec 11:16 or heal the maimed, or nourish the sound 2
Eph 5:29 nourishes and cherishes it 3
Col 2:19 nourished and knit together through its joints 5
1Ti 4: 6 nourished on the words of the faith 4
Rev 12: 6 place prepared by God, in which to be nourished 7
14 to the place where she is to be nourished 7
2Es 2:25 Good nurse, nourish your sons 8
8:11 may be nourished for a time 8
4Mc 13:21 brotherly-loving souls are nourished; 6

nourisher 1. כּוּל

Rut 4:15 a restorer of life and a nourisher of your old age; 1

all nourishing 1. *παντοτρόφος*

Wis 16:25 it served thy all-nourishing bounty 1

nourishment 1. esca

2Es 9:26 the nourishment they afforded satisfied me. 1

now 1. אוּלָם 2. אָז 3. אַחֲרֵי 4. אַךְ 5. אָנָּא 6. אַף 7. אֵפוֹא 8. גַּם 9. הֵא 10. הַיּוֹם 11. הַיּוֹם הַזֶּה 12. הֵנָּה 13. הִנֵּה 14. זֶה 15. כָּ 16. כָּעֵת 17. נָא 18. עַל כֵּן 19. עֵת 20. עַתָּה 21. פַּעַם 22. כְּעַן (A) 23. כְּעֶנֶת (A) 24. *ἀλλά* 25. *ἀπ' ἄρτι* 26. *ἄρτι* 27. *γάρ* 28. *γίνομαι* 29. *γοῦν* 30. *δέ* 31. *δή* 32. *ἤδη* 33. *καί* 34. *καὶ ἰδού* 35. *λοιπός* 36. *μέν* 37. *μὲν γάρ* 38. *μὲν οὖν* 39. *νῦν* 40. *νυνί* 41. *ὁράω* 42. *οὐκέτι* 43. *οὖν* 44. *πάλιν* 45. *παρὰ πόδας* 46. *τοίνυν* 47. *τότε* 48. autem 49. enim 50. et 51. iam 52. modo 53. nam 54. nunc 55. praesens 56. vero

Gen 3:22 good and evil; and now, lest he put forth his hand 20
4:11 now you are cursed from the ground 20
12:19 Now then, here is your wife, take her, and be gone. 20
16: 2 Sar'ai said to Abram, "Behold now, the LORD has 17
19: 9 Now we will deal worse with you than with them. 20
20: 7 Now then restore the man's wife; 20
21:23 now therefore swear to me here by God 20
22:12 for now I know that you fear God 20
24:42 O LORD . . if now thou wilt prosper the way 17
49 Now then, if you will deal loyally and truly 20
26:22 For now the LORD has made room for us 20
29 You are now the blessed of the LORD. 20
27: 3 Now then, take your weapons, your quiver 20
8 Now therefore, my son, obey my word as I command 20
19 now sit up and eat of my game 17
36 behold, now he has taken away my blessing. 20
43 Now therefore, my son, obey my voice; 20
29:32 surely now my husband will love me. 20
34 Now this time my husband will be joined to me 20
30:20 now my husband will honor me 21
30 But now when shall I provide for my own household 20
31:13 Now arise, go forth from this land, and return 20
16 now then, whatever God has said to you, do. 20
28 Now you have done foolishly. 20
30 now you have gone away because you longed 20
42 surely now you would have sent me away 20
44 Come now, let us make a covenant, you and I; 20
32: 4 I have sojourned with Laban, and stayed until now 20
10 and now I have become two companies. 20
37:14 he said to him, "Go now, see if it is well 17
20 Come now, let us kill him and throw him into one 20
32 This we have found; see now whether it is your son's 17
41:33 Now therefore let Pharaoh select a man discreet 20
43:10 not delayed, we would now have returned twice. 20
44:30 Now therefore, when I come to your servant 20
33 Now therefore, let your servant, I pray you 20
45: 5 now do not be distressed, or angry 20
12 now your eyes see, and the eyes of my brother 13
46:30 Israel said to Joseph, "Now let me die 21
34 keepers of cattle from our youth even until now 20
47: 1 they are now in the land of Goshen. 13
4 and now, we pray you, let your servants dwell 20
23 Now here is seed for you, and you shall sow 9
29 If now I have found favor in your sight, 17
48: 5 now your two sons, who were born to you in the land 20
50: 4 Joseph spoke . . saying, "If now I have found favor 17
5 Now therefore let me go up, I pray you, and bury my 20
17 And now, we pray you, forgive the transgression 20
Exd 3: 9 now, behold, the cry of the people of Israel 20
18 and now, we pray you, let us go a three days' journey 20
4:12 Now therefore go, and I will be with your mouth 20
5: 5 Behold, the people of the land are now many and you 20
18 Go now, and work; for no straw shall be given you 20
6: 1 the LORD said to Moses, "Now you shall see what I 20
9:18 in Egypt from the day it was founded until now. 20
19 Now therefore send, get your cattle and all that 20
10:17 Now therefore, forgive my sin, I pray you 20
11: 2 Speak now in the hearing of the people 17
15:15 Now are the chiefs of Edom dismayed; 2
18:11 Now I know that the LORD is greater than all gods 20
19 Listen now to my voice; I will give you counsel 20
19: 5 Now therefore, if you will obey my voice and keep 20
32:10 now therefore let me alone, that my wrath may burn 20
30 You have sinned a great sin. And now I will go up 20
32 now, if thou wilt forgive their sin–and if not, blot 20
34 now go, lead the people to the place of which I have 20
33: 5 So now put off your ornaments from you 20
13 Now therefore, I pray thee, if I have found favor 20
13 show me now thy ways, that I may know thee 17
34: 9 he said, "If now I have found favor in thy sight 17
Num11: 6 now our strength is dried up, and there is nothing 20
23 Now you shall see whether my word will come true 20
14:17 now, I pray thee, let the power of the LORD be 20
19 forgiven this people, from Egypt even until now. 12
41 Why now are you trangressing the command 14
16: 8 Moses said to Korah, "Hear now, you sons of Levi 17
20:10 Hear now, you rebels; shall we bring forth water 17
17 Now let us pass through your land. 17
22: 4 horde will now lick up all that is round about us 20
6 Come now, curse this people for me 20
11 now come, curse them for me; 20
19 Pray, now, tarry here this night also 20
33 just now I would have slain you and let her live. 20
34 Now therefore, if it is evil in thy sight, I will go 20
38 Have I now any power at all to speak anything? 20
23:23 now it shall be said of Jacob and Israel 16
27 Come now, I will take you to another place; 17
24:11 Therefore now flee to your place; 20
14 now, behold, I am going to my people; 20
17 I see him, but not now; I behold him, but not nigh 20
31:17 Now . . kill every male among the little ones 20
Deu 2:13 'Now rise up, and go over the brook Zered.' 20
4: 1 now, O Israel, give heed to the statutes 20
32 For ask now of the days that are past 17
5:25 Now therefore why should we die? 20
10:12 now, Israel, what does the LORD your God require 20
22 now the LORD your God has made you as the stars 20
26:10 now I bring the first of the fruit of the ground 20
31:19 Now therefore write this song, and teach it 20
32:39 'See now that I, even I, am he, and there is no god 20
Jos 1: 2 Moses my servant is dead; now therefore arise 20
2:12 Now then, swear to me by the LORD that as I have 20
3:12 Now therefore take twelve men from the tribes 20
5:14 as commander of the army of the LORD I . . now come. 20
7:19 give glory to . . and tell me now what you have done; 17
9: 6 We have come from a far . . so now make a covenant 20
11 We are your servants; come now, make a covenant 20
12 was still . . but now, behold, it is dry and moldy 20
19 We have sworn . . and now we may not touch them. 20
23 Now therefore you are cursed 20
25 And now, behold, we are in your hand 20
13: 7 Now therefore divide this land 20
14:10 And now . . the LORD has kept me alive, as he said 20
11 my strength now is as my strength was then, for war 20
12 now give me this . . of which the LORD spoke 20
22: 4 now the LORD . . has given rest to your brethren 20
19 But now, if your land is unclean, pass over 4
26 Let us now build an altar, not for burnt offering 17
31 now you have saved the people . . from the hand 2
23:14 And now I am about to go the way of all the earth 13
24:14 Now therefore fear the LORD, and serve him 20
Jdg 2: 3 So now I say, I will not drive them out before you; 8
6:13 us up from Egypt?' But now the LORD has cast us off 20
17 If now I have found favor with thee, then show me 17
22 Lord GOD! For now I have seen the angel of the LORD 18
7: 3 Now therefore proclaim in the ears of the people 20
8: 2 What have I done now in comparison with you? 20
9:16 Now therefore, if you acted in good faith 20
32 Now therefore, go by night, you and the men 20
38 whom you despised? Go out now and fight with them. 20
11: 7 Why have you come to me now . . in trouble 20
8 That is why we have turned to you now, that you may 20
13 took away my land . . now therefore restore it 20
25 Now are you any better than Balak the son 20
36 now that the LORD has avenged you on your enemies 3
13:12 Now when your words come true, what is to be 20
23 shown us all these things, or now announced to us 16
14: 2 at Timnah; now get her for me as my wife. 20
15:18 shall I now die of thirst, and fall into the hands 20
16:13 Until now you have mocked me, and told me lies; 12
17: 3 now therefore I will restore it to you. 20
13 Now I know that the LORD will prosper me, because I 20
18:14 Now therefore consider what you will do. 20
19: 9 now the day has waned toward evening; pray tarry 17
11 Come now, let us turn aside . . and spend the night 17
20: 9 now this is what we will do to Gib'e-ah: we will go up 20
13 Now therefore give up the men . . that we may put 20
21:22 did you give . . else you would now be guilty. 16
Rut 2: 7 she has continued from early morning until now 20
3: 2 Now is not Bo'az our kinsman 20
11 And now, my daughter, do not fear 20
12 And now it is true that I am a near kinsman 20
1Sm 2:16 No, you must give it now; and if not, I will take it 20
30 I promised . . '; but now the LORD declares: 'Far be it 20
6: 7 Now then, take and prepare a new cart and two 20
8: 5 you are old . . now appoint for us a king to govern 20
9 Now then, hearken to their voice; 20
9: 9 he who is now called a prophet was formerly 10
13 Now go up, for you will meet him immediately. 20
10: 2 are found, and now your father has ceased to care 13
19 Now therefore present yourselves before 20
11: 5 Now Saul was coming from the field 13
12: 2 And now, behold, the king walks before you; 20
7 Now therefore stand still, that I may plead 20
10 We have sinned . . but now deliver us out 20
13 And now behold the king whom you have chosen 20
16 Now therefore stand . . and see this great thing 20
13:13 now the LORD would have established 20
14 But now your kingdom shall not continue; 20
14:30 now the slaughter . . has not been great. 20
15: 1 now therefore hearken to the words of the LORD. 20
3 Now go and smite Am'alek, and utterly destroy all 20
25 Now therefore, I pray, pardon my sin, and return 20
30 yet honor me now before the elders of my people 20
16:15 Behold now, an evil spirit from God is tormenting 17
16 Let our lord now command your servants . . to seek 17
17:29 What have I done now? Was it not but a word? 20
18:21 Saul said . . "You shall now be my son-in-law. 10
22 now then become the king's son-in-law. 20
20:29 now, if I have found favor . . let me get away 20
21: 3 Now then, what have you at hand? Give me five 20
22: 7 Saul said . . "Hear now, you Benjaminites; 17
12 Saul said, "Hear now, son of Ahi'tub." 17
23:20 Now come down, O king 20
24:20 now, behold, I know that you shall surely be king 20
25: 7 now your shepherds have been with us 20
17 Now therefore know this and consider 20
26 Now then, my lord, as the LORD lives 20
26 now then let your enemies . . be as Nabal. 20
27 now let this present . . be given to the young men 20
26: 8 now therefore let me pin him to the earth 20
11 but take now the spear that is at his head 20
16 And now see where the king's spear is, and the jar 20
19 Now therefore let my lord the king hear the words 20
20 Now therefore, let not my blood fall to the earth 20
27: 1 I shall now perish one day by the hand of Saul; 20
28:22 Now therefore, you also hearken to your handmaid; 20
29: 7 go back now; and go peaceably 20
8 from the day I entered your service until now 11
10 Now then rise early . . and depart as soon as you 20
2Sm 2: 6 Now may the LORD show steadfast love . . to you! 20
7 Now therefore let your hands be strong 20
3:18 Now then bring it about; for the LORD has promised 20
4:11 shall I not now require his blood at your hand 20
7: 2 See now, I dwell in a house of cedar 17
8 Now therefore thus you shall say to my servant 20
25 And now, O LORD God, confirm for ever the word 20
28 now, O Lord GOD, thou art God, and thy words 20
29 now therefore may it please thee to bless 20
11:25 for the sword devours now one and now another; 15
25 for the sword devours now one and now another; 15
12:10 Now therefore the sword shall never depart 20
23 But now he is dead; why should I fast? 20
28 Now, then, gather the rest of the people together 20
13:13 Now therefore, I pray you, speak to the king; 20
20 Has Amnon . . been with you? Now hold your peace 20
33 Now therefore let not my lord . . take it to heart 20
14: 7 And now the whole family has risen against 13
15 Now I have come to say this to my lord the king 20
21 Then the king said to Jo'ab, "Behold now, I grant this; 17
32 Now therefore let me go into the presence 20
15:34 as I have been . . so now I will be your servant,' 20
16:11 how much more now may this Benjaminite! 20
17: 9 even now he has hidden himself in one of the pits 20
16 Now therefore send quickly and tell David, 'Do not 20
19: 7 Now therefore arise, go out and speak kindly 20
7 evil . . come upon you from your youth until now. 20
9 and now he has fled out of the land from Ab'salom. 20
10 Now therefore why do you say nothing about 20
20: 6 Now Sheba . . will do us more harm than Ab'salom; 20
24:10 But now, O LORD, I pray thee, take away the iniquity 20
13 Now consider, and decide what answer 20
16 and said . . "It is enough; now stay your hand. 20
1Kg 1:12 Now therefore come, let me give you counsel 20
18 And now, behold, Adoni'jah is king, although you, my 20
20 now, my lord the king, the eyes of all Israel are 20
2: 9 Now therefore hold him not guiltless, for you are 20
16 now I have one request to make of you; do not refuse 20
24 Now therefore as the LORD lives, who has 20
3: 7 now, O LORD my God, thou hast made thy servant 20
5: 4 now the LORD my God has given me rest 20
6 Now therefore command that cedars . . be cut 20
8:25 Now therefore, O LORD . . keep with thy servant 20
26 Now therefore, O God . . let thy word be confirmed 20
11:22 you are now seeking to go to your own country 13
12: 4 Now therefore lighten the hard service 20
11 now, whereas my father laid upon you a heavy yoke 20
16 Look now to your own house, David. 20
26 Now the kingdom will turn back 20
13: 6 Entreat now the favor of the LORD your God 17
17:12 and now, I am gathering a couple of sticks 13
24 Now I know that you are a man of God 20
18:11 now you say, 'Go, tell your lord 20
14 now you say, 'Go, tell your lord 20
19 Now therefore send and gather all Israel to me 20
43 he said . . "Go up now, look toward the sea. 17
19: 4 It is enough; now, O LORD, take away my life; 20
20: 7 Mark now, and see how this man is seeking trouble; 17
31 Behold now, we have heard that the kings 17
21: 7 Do you now govern Israel? Arise, and eat bread 20
22:23 Now therefore behold, the LORD has put 20
2Kg 1:14 but now let my life be precious in your sight. 20
2:16 Behold now, there are . . 50 strong men; 17
3:15 But now bring me a minstrel. 20

23 Now then, Moab, to the spoil! 20
4: 9 she said to her husband, "Behold now, I perceive 17
13 Say now to her, See, you have taken all this trouble 17
5: 8 Let him come now to me, that he may know 17
15 accept now a present from your servant. 20
7: 4 So now come, let us go over to the . . Syrians; 20
9 now therefore come, let us go and tell 20
8: 6 from the day that she left the land until now. 20
9:12 they said, "That is not true; tell us now. 17
26 Now therefore take him up and cast him on the plot 20
34 See now to this cursed woman, and bury her; 17
10: 2 Now then, as soon as this letter comes to you 20
19 Now therefore call to me all the prophets of Ba'al 20
12: 7 Now therefore take no more money 20
13:19 now you will strike down Syria only three times. 20
23 nor has he cast them from his presence until now. 20
18:20 On whom do you now rely, that you have rebelled 20
21 Behold, you are relying now on Egypt 20
23 Come now, make a wager with my master the king 20
19:19 So now, O LORD our God, save us, I beseech thee 20
25 I planned from days of old what now I bring to pass 20
20: 3 Remember now, O LORD . . how I have walked before 5
1Ch 8:32 Now these also dwelt opposite their kinsmen. 6
17: 7 Now therefore thus shall you say to my servant 20
23 now, O LORD, let the word which thou hast spoken 20
26 now, O LORD, thou art God, and thou hast promised 20
27 now therefore may it please thee to bless 20
21: 8 But now, I pray thee, take away the iniquity 20
12 Now decide what answer I shall return to him 20
15 It is enough; now stay your hand. 20
22:11 Now, my son, the LORD be with you 20
19 Now set your mind and heart to seek the LORD 20
28: 8 Now therefore in the sight of all Israel 20
10 Take heed now, for the LORD has chosen you to build 20
29:13 now we thank thee, our God, and praise 20
17 now I have seen thy people . . offering freely 20
2Ch 1: 9 thy promise to David my father be now fulfilled 20
10 Give me now wisdom and knowledge to go out 20
2: 7 now send me a man skilled to work in gold, silver 20
13 Now I have sent a skilled man . . Huram-abi. 20
15 Now therefore the wheat and barley, oil and wine 20
6:16 Now therefore, O LORD . . keep with . . David 20
17 Now therefore, O LORD, God of Israel, let thy word be 20
40 Now, O my God, let thy eyes be open and thy ears 20
41 now arise, O LORD God, and go to thy resting place 20
7:15 Now my eyes will be open and my ears attentive 20
16 For now I have chosen and consecrated this house 20
10: 4 Now therefore lighten the hard service 20
11 now, whereas my father laid upon you a heavy yoke 20
16 Look now to your own house, David. 20
13: 8 now you think to withstand the kingdom 20
16: 9 for from now on you will have wars. 20
18:22 Now therefore behold, the LORD has put 20
19: 7 Now then, let the fear of the LORD be upon you; 20
20:10 now behold, the men of Ammon and Moab 20
25:19 now stay at home; why should you provoke trouble 20
28:10 now you intend to subjugate the people of Judah 20
11 Now hear me, and send back the captives 20
29: 5 Hear me, Levites! Now sanctify yourselves 20
10 Now it is in my heart to make a covenant 20
11 not now be negligent, for the LORD has chosen you 20
31 You have now consecrated yourselves to the LORD; 20
30: 8 Do not now be stiff-necked as your fathers were 20
32:15 Now therefore do not let Hezeki'ah deceive you 20
35: 3 Now serve the LORD your God and his people Israel. 20
Ezr 4:10 rest of the province Beyond the River, and now 23
11 Your servants . . send greeting. And now 23
13 Now be it known to the king that, if this city 22
14 Now because we eat the salt of the palace 22
17 To Rehum . . and Shim'shai . . , greeting. And now 16
5:16 from that time until now it has been in building 22
6: 6 Now therefore, Tat'tenai, governor 22
7:12 And now I make a decree that any one of the people 23
9: 8 now for a brief moment favor has been shown 20
10 now, O our God, what shall we say after this? 20
10: 2 even now there is hope for Israel in spite 20
11 Now then make confession to the LORD the God 20
Neh 5: 5 Now our flesh is as the flesh of our brethren 20
6: 7 now it will be reported to the king 20
7 now come, and let us take counsel together. 20
9 But now, O God, strengthen thou my hands. 20
9:32 Now therefore, our God, the great and mighty 20
Job 4: 5 now it has come to you, and you are impatient; 20
7 Think now, who that was innocent ever perished? 17
5: 1 Call now; is there any one who will answer you? 17
6:21 Such you have now become to me; you see 20
28 now, be pleased to look at me; 20
7:21 For now I shall lie in the earth; thou wilt seek me 20
13: 6 Hear now my reasoning 17
16: 7 Surely now God has worn me out; 20
19 Even now, behold, my witness is in heaven 20
30: 1 now they make sport of me, men who are younger 20
9 now I have become their song, I am a byword to them. 20
16 now my soul is poured out within me; 20
33: 1 now, hear my speech, O Job, and listen 1
35:15 now, because his anger does not punish 20
37:21 now men cannot look on the light when it is bright 20
42: 5 by the hearing of the ear, but now my eye sees thee; 20
8 Now therefore take seven bulls and seven rams 20
Ps 2:10 Now therefore, O kings, be wise; be warned, O rulers 20
12: 5 because the needy groan, I will now arise 20
17:11 They track me down; now they surround me; 20
20: 6 Now I know that the LORD will help his anointed; 20
27: 6 now my head shall be lifted up above my enemies 20
37:25 I have been young, and now am old; 8
39: 7 now, Lord, for what do I wait? My hope is in thee. 20
69: 4 What I did not steal must I now restore? 2
119:67 I went astray; but now I keep thy word. 20
124: 1 If . . the LORD who was on our side, let Israel now say– 17
129: 1 let Israel now say– 17
Prv 5: 7 now, O sons, listen to me 20
7:12 now in the street, now in the market 21
12 now in the street, now in the market 21
24 now, O sons, listen to me 20
8:32 now, my sons, listen to me 20
Ecc 2: 1 Come now, I will make a test of pleasure; 17
Sng 3: 2 I will rise now and go about the city 17
Isa 1:18 Come now, let us reason together, says the LORD 17
21 Righteousness lodged in her, but now murderers. 20
5: 3 now, O inhabitants of Jerusalem and men of Judah 20
5 now I will tell you what I will do to my vineyard. 20
16:14 now the LORD says, "In three years 20
28:22 Now therefore do not scoff 20
30: 8 now, go, write it before them on a tablet 20
33:10 Now I will arise," says the LORD 20
10 now I will lift myself up; now I will be exalted. 20
10 now I will lift myself up; now I will be exalted. 20
36: 5 On whom do you now rely, that you have rebelled 20
8 Come now, make a wager with my master the king 20
37:20 now, O LORD our God, save us from his hand 20
26 I planned from days of old what now I bring to pass 20
38: 3 said, "Remember now, O LORD, I beseech thee 5
43: 1 now thus says the LORD, he who created you 20
19 Behold, I am doing a new thing; now it springs forth 20
44: 1 But now hear, O Jacob my servant 20
47: 8 Now therefore hear this, you lover of pleasures 20
48: 7 They are created now, not long ago; 20
16 And now the Lord GOD has sent me and his Spirit. 20
49: 5 now the LORD says, who formed me from the womb 20
19 surely now you will be too narrow 20
52: 5 Now therefore what have I here, says the LORD 20
Jer 2:18 And now what do you gain by going to Egypt 20
3: 4 Have you not just now called to me, 'My father 20
4:12 Now it is I who speak in judgment upon them. 20
7:12 Go now to my place that was in Shiloh 17
13 And now, because you have done all these things 20
14:10 now he will remember their iniquity and punish 20
18:11 Now, therefore, say to the men of Judah 20
25: 5 saying, 'Turn now, every one of you, 17
26:13 Now therefore amend your ways and your doings 20
27: 6 Now I have given all these lands into the hand 20
16 will now shortly be brought back from Babylon, 20
28: 7 Yet hear now this word which I speak 17
29:27 Now why have you not rebuked Jeremiah 20
30: 6 Ask now, and see, can a man bear a child? 17
32:36 Now therefore thus says the LORD 20
35:15 Turn now every one of you from his evil way 17
37:20 Now hear, I pray you, O my lord the king 20
38:20 Obey now the voice of the LORD in what I say to you 17
40: 4 Now, behold, I release you today from the chains 20
42:22 Now therefore know for a certainty 20
44: 7 now thus says the LORD God of hosts 20
50:17 now at last Nebuchadrez'zar king of Babylon 14
Ezk 4:14 up till now I have never eaten what died of itself 20
7: 3 Now the end is upon you 20
8 Now I will soon pour out my wrath upon you 20
17:12 Say now to the rebellious house, Do you not know 17
18:25 Hear now, O house of Israel: Is my way not just? 17
19:13 Now it is transplanted in the wilderness 20
23:43 Then I said, Do not men now commit adultery 20
26:18 Now the isles tremble on the day of your fall; 20
27:34 Now you are wrecked by the seas, in the depths 19
39:25 Now I will restore the fortunes of Jacob 20
43: 9 Now let them put away their idolatry 20
Dan 2:23 hast now made known to me what we asked of thee 22
3:15 Now if you are ready when you hear the sound 22
4:37 Now I, Nebuchadnez'zar, praise and extol and honor 22
5:12 Now let Daniel be called, 22
15 Now the wise men, the enchanters 22
16 Now if you can read the writing and make known 22
6: 8 Now, O king, establish the interdict 22
9:15 now, O Lord our God, who didst bring thy people out 20
17 Now therefore, O our God, hearken to the prayer 20
22 O Daniel, I have now come out to give you wisdom 20
10:11 stand upright, for now I have been sent to you. 20
17 For now no strength remains in me, and no breath 20
20 But now I will return to fight against the prince 20
11: 2 now I will show you the truth. 20
Hos 2: 7 for it was better with me then than now.' 20
10 Now I will uncover her lewdness 20
4:16 can the LORD now feed them like a lamb in a broad 20
5: 3 for now, O E'phraim, you have played the harlot 20
7 Now the new moon shall devour them 20
7: 2 Now their deeds encompass them 20
8:13 Now he will remember their iniquity 20
10: 2 now they must bear their guilt. 20
3 For now they will say: "We have no king 20
13: 2 And now they sin more and more 20
10 Where now is your king, to save you; 7
13 for now he does not present himself at the mouth 19
Jol 2:12 Yet even now," says the LORD, "return to me 20
3: 7 But now I will stir them up from the place 13
Ams 6: 7 shall now be the first of those to go into exile 20
7:16 Now therefore hear the word of the LORD. 20
Jon 4: 3 Therefore now, O LORD, take my life from me 20
Mic 4: 9 Now why do you cry aloud? Is there no king in you? 20
10 for now you shall go forth from the city 20
11 Now many nations are assembled against you 20
5: 1 Now you are walled about with a wall; 20
4 for now he shall be great to the ends of the earth. 20
7: 4 now their confusion is at hand. 20
10 now she will be trodden down like the mire 20
Nah 1:13 And now I will break his yoke from off you 20
Hag 1: 5 Now therefore thus says the LORD of hosts 20
2: 2 Speak now to Zerub'babel the son of She-al'ti-el 17
3 do you see it now? Is it not in your sight as nothing? 20
4 Yet now take courage, O Zerub'babel, says the LORD; 20
15 Pray now, consider what will come to pass 20
Zec 3: 8 Hear now, O Joshua the high priest 17
8:11 now I will not deal with the remnant of this 20
9: 8 for now I see with my own eyes. 20
Mal 1: 9 now entreat the favor of God 20
2: 1 now, O priests, this command is for you. 20
Mat 1:18 Now the birth of Jesus Christ took place in this 30
2: 1 Now when Jesus was born in Bethlehem of Judea 30
13 Now when they had departed, behold, an angel 30
3: 4 Now John wore a garment of camel's hair 30
15 But Jesus answered him, "Let it be so now; 26
4:12 Now when he heard that John had been arrested 30
8:18 Now when Jesus saw great crowds around him 30
11:12 From the days of John the Baptist until now 26
14:15 This is a lonely place, and the day is now over 32
15:32 because they have been with me now three days 32
16:13 Now when Jesus came into the district 30
19: 1 Now when Jesus had finished these sayings 28
20:10 Now when the first came 33
22:25 Now there were seven brothers among us 30
41 Now while the Pharisees were gathered together 30
24:21 from the beginning of the world until now 39
25:19 Now after a long time 30
26: 6 Now when Jesus was at Bethany 30
17 Now on the first day of Unleavened Bread 30
26 Now as they were eating, Jesus took bread 30
48 Now the betrayer had given them a sign, saying 30
59 Now the chief priests and the whole council 30
65 You have now heard his blasphemy. 39
69 Now Peter was sitting outside in the courtyard. 30
27:11 Now Jesus stood before the governor 30
15 Now at the feast the governor was accustomed 30
20 Now the chief priests and the elders persuaded 30
42 let him come down now from the cross 39
43 let God deliver him now, if he desires him 39
45 Now from the sixth hour there was darkness 30
28: 1 Now after the sabbath 30
16 Now the eleven disciples went to Galilee 30
Mrk 1: 6 Now John was clothed in camel's hair 33
14 Now after John was arrested 30
30 Now Simon's mother-in-law lay sick with a fever 30
2: 6 Now some of the scribes were sitting there 30
18 Now John's disciples and the Pharisees 33
5:11 Now a great herd of swine was feeding there 30
6:33 Now many saw them going, and knew them 33
35 This is a lonely place, and the hour is now late; 32
7:26 Now the woman was a Greek 30
8: 2 because they have been with me now three days 32
14 Now they had forgotten to bring bread 33
10:30 receive a hundredfold now in this time 39
13:19 the creation which God created until now 39
14:44 Now the betrayer had given them a sign, saying 30
55 Now the chief priests and the whole council 30
15: 6 Now at the feast he used to release for them one 30
32 Let the Christ, the King of Israel, come down now 39
16: 9 Now when he rose early on the first day of the week 30
Lke 1: 8 Now while he was serving as priest before God 30
57 Now the time came for Elizabeth to be delivered 30
2:25 Now there was a man in Jerusalem 34
29 now lettest thou thy servant depart in peace 39
41 Now his parents went to Jerusalem every year 33
3: 9 Even now the axe is laid to the root of the trees; 32
21 Now when all the people were baptized 30
4:38 Now Simon's mother-in-law was ill with a high fever 30
40 Now when the sun was setting 30
6:21 Blessed are you that hunger now 39
21 Blessed are you that weep now, for you shall laugh. 39
25 Woe to you that are full now, for you shall hunger. 39
25 Woe to you that laugh now, for you shall mourn 39
7: 2 Now a centurion had a slave who was dear to him 30
39 Now when the Pharisee who had invited him saw it 30
42 Now which of them will love him more? 43
8:11 Now the parable is this 30
32 Now a large herd of swine was feeding there 30
40 Now when Jesus returned, the crowd welcomed him 30
9: 7 Now Herod the tetrarch heard of all that was done 30
12 Now the day began to wear away 30
18 Now it happened that as he was praying alone 33
28 Now about eight days after these sayings 30
32 Now Peter and those who were with him were heavy 30

10:31 Now by chance a priest was going down that road; 30
38 Now as they went on their way, he entered a village; 30
11: 7 door is now shut, and my children are with me in bed; 32
14 Now he was casting out a demon that was dumb 33
39 Now you Pharisees cleanse the outside of the cup 39
13:10 Now he was teaching in one of the synagogues 30
14: 7 Now he told a parable to those who were invited 30
17 'Come; for all is now ready.' 32
25 Now great multitudes accompanied him 30
15: 1 Now the tax collectors and sinners 30
25 Now his elder son was in the field 30
16:25 now he is comforted here, and you are in anguish. 39
17:16 Now he was a Samaritan. 33
18:15 Now they were bringing even infants to him 30
19:37 As he was now drawing near 32
42 now they are hid from your eyes. 39
20: 3 I also will ask you a question; now tell me 33
29 Now there were seven brothers 43
38 Now he is not God of the dead, but of the living 30
21:28 Now when these things begin to take place, look up 30
22: 1 Now the feast of Unleavened Bread drew near 30
18 from now on I shall not drink of the fruit 39
36 But now, let him who has a purse take it 39
63 Now the men who were holding Jesus mocked him 33
69 from now on the Son of man shall be seated 39
23:44 It was now about the sixth hour 32
47 Now when the centurion saw what had taken place 30
50 Now there was a man named Joseph 34
24:10 Now it was Mary Mag'dalene and Joan'na 30
29 it is toward evening and the day is now far spent 32
Joh 1:24 Now they had been sent from the Pharisees. 33
44 Now Philip was from Beth-sa'ida, the city of Andrew 30
2: 6 Now six stone jars were standing there 30
8 Now draw some out, and take it to the steward 39
10 but you have kept the good wine until now. 26
23 Now when he was in Jerusalem at the Passover 30
3: 1 Now there was a man of the Pharisees 30
25 Now a discussion arose between John's disciples 43
4: 1 Now when the Lord knew that the Pharisees 43
18 and he whom you now have is not your husband; 39
23 But the hour is coming, and now is 39
54 This was now the second sign that Jesus did 44
5: 2 Now there is in Jerusalem by the Sheep Gate a pool 30
9 Now that day was the sabbath. 30
13 Now the man who had been healed did not know 30
25 the hour is coming, and now is 39
6: 4 Now the Passover . . was at hand. 30
10 Now there was much grass in the place 30
17 It was now dark 32
42 does he now say, 'I have come down from heaven' 39
7: 2 Now the Jews' feast of Tabernacles was at hand. 30
39 Now this he said about the Spirit 30
8: 5 Now in the law Moses commanded us to stone such. 30
40 now you seek to kill me 39
52 Now we know that you have a demon 39
9:14 Now it was a sabbath day when Jesus made the clay 30
19 How then does he now see? 26
21 how he now sees we do not know 39
25 one thing I know, that though I was blind, now I see. 26
41 now that you say, 'We see,' your guilt remains. 39
11: 1 Now a certain man was ill, Laz'arus of Bethany 30
5 Now Jesus loved Martha and her sister 30
8 the Jews were but now seeking to stone you 39
13 Now Jesus had spoken of his death 30
17 Now when Jesus came 43
22 even now I know that whatever you ask from God 39
30 Now Jesus had not yet come to the village 30
55 Now the Passover of the Jews was at hand 30
57 Now the chief priests . . had given orders 30
12:20 Now among those who went up to worship 30
27 Now is my soul troubled. And what shall I say? 39
31 Now is the judgment of this world 39
31 now shall the ruler of this world be cast out; 39
13: 1 Now before the feast of the Passover 30
7 What I am doing you do not know now 26
19 I tell you this now, before it takes place 25
28 Now no one at the table knew why he said this 30
31 Now is the Son of man glorified 39
33 as I said to the Jews so now I say to you 26
36 Where I am going you cannot follow me now 39
37 Peter said . . "Lord, why cannot I follow you now? 26
14:29 now I have told you before it takes place 39
15:22 now they have no excuse for their sin. 39
24 now they have seen and hated 39
16: 5 now I am going to him who sent me 39
12 you cannot bear them now. 26
22 you have sorrow now, but I will see you again 39
29 Ah, now you are speaking plainly, not in any figure! 39
30 Now we know that you know all things 39
31 Jesus answered them, "Do you now believe? 26
17: 5 now, Father, glorify thou me in thy own presence 39
7 Now they know that everything . . is from thee; 39
13 now I am coming to thee 39
18: 2 Now Judas, who betrayed him, also knew the place; 30
18 Now the servants and officers 30
25 Now Simon Peter was . . warming himself 30
40 Now Barab'bas was a robber. 30
19:14 Now it was the day of Preparation of the Passover; 30
28 knowing that all was now finished 32

41 Now in the place where he was crucified 30
20: 1 Now on the first day of the week 30
24 Now Thomas, one of the twelve, called the Twin 30
30 Now Jesus did many other signs 36
21: 6 now they were not able to haul it 42
12 Now none of the disciples dared ask him 30
14 This was now the third time 32
Act 1:18 (Now this man bought a field 43
2: 5 Now there were dwelling in Jerusalem Jews 30
37 Now when they heard this 30
3: 1 Now Peter and John were going up to the temple 30
17 now, brethren, I know that you acted in ignorance 39
4:13 Now when they saw the boldness of Peter and John 30
29 now, Lord, look upon their threats 39
32 Now the company of those who believed 30
5:12 Now many signs and wonders were done 30
21 Now the high priest came 30
24 Now when the captain of the temple 30
6: 1 Now in these days 30
7: 4 this land in which you are now living; 39
11 Now there came a famine throughout all Egypt 30
30 Now when 40 years had passed 33
34 now come, I will send you to Egypt.' 39
52 whom you have now betrayed and murdered 39
54 Now when they heard these things 30
8: 4 Now those who were scattered went about 43
14 Now when the apostles at Jerusalem heard 30
18 Now when Simon saw 30
25 Now when they had testified and spoken the word 43
32 Now the passage of the scripture 30
9: 3 Now as he journeyed he approached Damascus 30
10 Now there was a disciple at Damascus 30
32 Now as Peter went here and there among them all 30
36 Now there was at Joppa a disciple named Tabitha 30
10: 5 now send men to Joppa 39
17 Now while Peter was inwardly perplexed 30
33 Now therefore we are all here present 39
11: 1 Now the apostles and the brethren 30
19 Now those who were scattered 43
27 Now in these days prophets came down 30
12:11 Now I am sure that the Lord has sent his angel 39
18 Now when day came, there was no small stir 30
20 Now Herod was angry with the people of Tyre 30
13: 1 Now in the church at Antioch there were prophets 30
11 now, behold, the hand of the Lord is upon you 39
13 Now Paul and his company set sail from Paphos 30
31 who are now his witnesses to the people. 39
14: 1 Now at Ico'nium they entered together 30
8 Now at Lystra there was a man sitting 33
15:10 Now therefore why do you make trial of God 39
16:36 now therefore come out and go in peace. 39
37 do they now cast us out secretly 39
17: 1 Now when they had passed through Amphip'olis 30
11 Now these Jews were more noble 30
16 Now while Paul was waiting for them at Athens 30
21 Now all the Athenians and the foreigners 30
30 now he commands all men everywhere to repent 39
32 Now when they heard of the resurrection 30
18: 6 From now on I will go to the Gentiles. 39
24 Now a Jew named Apol'los, a native of Alexandria 30
19:21 Now after these events 30
32 Now some cried one thing, some another 43
20:22 now, behold, I am going to Jerusalem 39
25 now, behold, I know 39
32 now I commend you to God 39
22: 1 hear the defense which I now make before you. 40
9 Now those who were with me saw the light 30
16 now why do you wait? Rise and be baptized 39
23:15 give notice now to the tribune to bring him down 39
16 Now the son of Paul's sister heard of their ambush; 30
21 now they are ready 39
24:13 prove to you what they now bring up against me. 40
17 Now after some years I came to bring to my nation 30
25: 1 Now when Festus had come into his province 43
13 Now when some days had passed 30
26: 6 now I stand here on trial for hope in the promise 39
27:22 I now bid you take heart 39
39 Now when it was day 30
28: 7 Now in the neighborhood of that place were lands 30
Rom 1:10 I may now at last succeed in coming to you. 32
3:19 Now we know that whatever the law says 30
21 But now the righteousness of God 40
4: 4 Now to one who works, his wages are not reckoned 30
5: 9 Since . . we are now justified by his blood 39
11 we have now received our reconciliation. 39
6:19 so now yield your members to righteousness 39
21 get from the things of which you are now ashamed? 39
22 But now that you have been set free from sin 40
7: 6 But now we are discharged from the law 40
16 Now if I do what I do not want, I agree that the law is 30
20 Now if I do what I do not want, it is no longer I 30
8: 1 There is therefore now no condemnation 39
22 whole creation has been groaning . . until now; 39
24 Now hope that is seen is not hope. 30
11:12 Now if their trespass means riches for the world 30
13 Now I am speaking to you Gentiles. 30
30 but now have received mercy 39
31 so they have now been disobedient in order that 39
13:11 how it is full time now for you to wake from sleep. 32

11 For salvation is nearer to us now 39
15:23 But now, since I no longer have any room for work 40
16:25 Now to him who is able to strengthen you 30
26 but is now disclosed 39
1Co 2:12 Now we have received not the spirit of the world 30
3:12 Now if any one builds on the foundation with gold 30
4:13 we have become, and are now, as the refuse 26
7: 1 Now concerning the matters 30
25 Now concerning the unmarried, I have no command 30
29 from now on, let those who have wives live 35
8: 1 Now concerning food offered to idols 30
10: 6 Now these things are warnings for us 30
11 Now these things happened to them as a warning 30
12: 1 Now concerning spiritual gifts, brethren 30
4 Now there are varieties of gifts 30
13:12 now we see in a mirror dimly, but then face to face. 26
12 Now I know in part; then I shall understand fully 26
14: 5 Now I want you all to speak in tongues 30
6 Now, brethren, if I come to you speaking in tongues 39
15: 1 Now I would remind you, brethren 30
12 Now if Christ is preached as raised from the dead 30
16: 1 Now concerning the contribution for the saints 30
7 For I do not want to see you now just in passing 26
12 it was not at all his will to come now 39
15 Now, brethren, you know that the household 30
2Co 3: 7 Now if the dispensation of death 30
17 Now the Lord is the Spirit 30
5:16 From now on, therefore, we regard 39
6: 2 Behold, now is the acceptable time 39
2 behold, now is the day of salvation. 39
8: 7 Now as you excel in everything 24
22 who is now more earnest than ever 40
9: 1 Now it is superfluous for me to write to you 37
13: 2 I warn them now while absent 39
Gal 1: 9 As we have said before, so now I say again 26
10 Am I now seeking the favor of men, or of God? 26
23 now preaching the faith he once tried to destroy 39
2:20 the life I now live in the flesh I live by faith 39
3: 3 are you now ending with the flesh? 39
11 Now it is evident that no man is justified 30
16 Now the promises were made to Abraham 30
20 Now an intermediary implies more than one 30
23 Now before faith came 30
4: 9 now that you have come to know God 39
20 to be present with you now and to change my tone 26
25 Now Hagar is Mount Sinai in Arabia 30
28 Now we, brethren, like Isaac, are children 30
29 so it is now. 39
5: 2 Now I, Paul, say to you 41
19 Now the works of the flesh are plain 30
Eph 2: 2 the spirit that is now at work 39
13 now in Christ Jesus you . . have been brought 40
3: 5 has now been revealed to his holy apostles 39
10 might now be made known to the principalities 39
20 Now to him who . . is able to do 30
4:17 Now this I affirm and testify in the Lord 43
5: 8 now you are light in the Lord 39
6:21 Now that you also may know how I am 30
Php 1: 5 from the first day until now. 39
20 with full courage now as always 39
30 which you saw and now hear to be mine. 39
2:12 so now, not only as in my presence 39
3:18 many, of whom I have often told you and now tell you 39
4:10 now at length you have revived your concern 32
Col 1:22 now reconciled in his body of flesh by his death 40
24 Now I rejoice in my sufferings for your sake 39
26 now made manifest to his saints. 39
3: 8 now put them all away: anger, wrath, malice, slander 40
1Th 3: 6 now that Timothy has come to us from you 26
8 for now we live, if you stand fast in the Lord. 39
11 Now may our God and Father himself 30
2Th 2: 1 Now concerning the coming of our Lord Jesus 30
6 you know what is restraining him now 39
7 only he who now restrains it will do 26
16 Now may our Lord Jesus Christ himself 30
3: 6 Now we command you, brethren 30
12 Now such persons we command and exhort 30
16 Now may the Lord of peace himself give you peace 30
1Ti 1: 8 Now we know that the law is good 30
3: 2 Now a bishop must be above reproach 43
4: 1 Now the Spirit expressly says 30
2Ti 1:10 now has manifested through the appearing of . . 39
3:10 Now you have observed my teaching, my conduct 30
Phm 1: 9 I, Paul, an ambassador and now a prisoner also 40
11 now he is indeed useful to you and to me.) 40
Heb 2: 8 Now in putting everything in subjection to him 27
3: 5 Now Moses was faithful in all God's house 33
7:11 Now if perfection had been attainable 43
8: 1 Now the point in what we are saying is this 30
4 Now if he were on earth, he would not be a priest 43
9: 1 Now even the first covenant had regulations 43
5 Of these things we cannot now speak in detail. 39
24 now to appear in the presence of God on our behalf. 39
11: 1 Now faith is the assurance of things hoped for 30
5 Now before he was taken 27
12:26 now he has promised 39
13:20 Now may the God of peace 30
Jas 4:13 Come now, you who say, "Today or tomorrow we . . go 39
5: 1 Come now, you rich, weep and howl for the miseries 39

1Pe 1: 6 now for a little while you may have to suffer 26
8 though you do not now see him you believe in him 26
12 the things which have now been announced to you 39
2:10 but now you are God's people; 39
10 but now you have received mercy. 39
25 you . . have now returned to the Shepherd 39
3:13 Now who is there to harm you if you are zealous 33
21 Baptism, which corresponds to this, now saves you 39
2Pe 3: 1 This is now the second letter that I have written 32
7 the heavens and earth that now exist 39
18 glory both now and to the day of eternity. Amen. 39
1Jn 2:18 so now many antichrists have come; 39
28 now, little children, abide in him 39
3: 2 Beloved, we are God's children now; 39
4: 3 antichrist . . and now it is in the world 39
2Jn 1: 5 And now I beg you, lady, not as though I were writing 39
Jde 1: 5 Now I desire to remind you 30
24 Now to him who is able to keep you from falling 30
25 before all time and now and for ever. Amen. 39
Rev 1:19 Now write what you see 43
6: 1 Now I saw when the Lamb opened one of the . . seals 33
8: 6 Now the seven angels who had the seven trumpets 33
12: 7 Now war arose in heaven, Michael and his angels 33
10 Now the salvation and the power . . have come 26
1Es 1: 4 Now worship the Lord your God 39
27 now the Lord is with me! 39
33 these that are now told 39
2:18 Now be it known to our lord the king 39
19 Now if this city is built and the walls finished 43
24 Therefore we now make known to you, O lord 39
28 Therefore I have now issued orders 39
3: 1 Now King Darius gave a great banquet 33
4:28 now do you not believe me? 39
46 now, O lord the king, this is what I ask and request 39
6: 1 Now in the second year of the reign of Darius 30
20 in . . construction from that time until now 39
21 Now therefore, if it seems wise, O king 39
8:78 now in some measure mercy has come to us from thee 39
82 now, O Lord, what shall we say 39
90 Behold, we are now before thee in our iniquities; 39
92 even now there is hope for Israel. 39
9: 8 Now then make confession and give glory 39
50 now they were all weeping as they heard the law- 33
2Es 1:30 But now, what shall I do to you? 52
38 now, father, look with pride and see the people 54
2: 4 now what can I do for you? 52
45 now they are being crowned, and receive palms. 52
3:34 Now therefore weigh in a balance our iniquities 54
4: 9 now I have asked you only about fire and wind 54
18 If now you were a judge between them 49
30 how much ungodliness it has produced until now 54
31 Consider now for yourself how much fruit 48
5: 1 Now concerning the signs 48
3 the land which you now see ruling 54
13 and if you pray again, and weep as you do now 54
16 Now on the second night Phaltiel . . came to me 50
28 now, O Lord, why hast thou given over the one 54
45 it might even now be able to support all of them 54
50 Since thou hast now given me the opportunity 51
50 Or is she now approaching old age? 51
6: 5 before the imaginations of those who now sin 54
35 Now after this I wept again and fasted seven days 50
57 now, O Lord, behold, these nations 54
7: 9 If now that city is given to a man 48
15 now why are you disturbed 54
26 that the city which now is not seen shall appear ‡
26 the land which now is hidden shall be disclosed. 54
45 O sovereign Lord, I said then and I say now 54
47 now I see that the world to come 54
60 they who have made my glory to prevail now 54
60 and through them my name has now been honored. 54
61 they who are now like a mist 54
64 now the mind grows with us 54
71 now understand from your own words 54
78 Now, concerning death, the teaching is 53
82 because they cannot now make a good repentance 51
88 Now this is the order of those 53
96 they rejoice that they have now escaped 54
104 Just as now a father does not send his son 54
111 the righteous have prayed for the ungodly now 52
117 they live in sorrow now 55
132 that the Most High is now called merciful 54
136 abound more and more to those now living 55
8: 8 the body which is now fashioned in the womb 54
15 now I will speak out 54
61 Therefore my judgment is now drawing near; 52
63 thou hast now shown me a multitude of the signs 54
9: 9 those who have now abused my ways shall be amazed 54
15 I said before, and I say now, and will say it again 54
18 when I was preparing for those who now exist 54
19 now those who have been created in this world 54
10: 4 now I intend not to return to the city 51
8 It is most appropriate to mourn now 54
9 Now ask the earth, and she will tell you 49
13 the multitude that is now in it goes as it came'; 55
15 Now, therefore, keep your sorrow to yourself 54
23 for she has now lost the seal of her glory 54
37 Now therefore I entreat you to give your servant 54
42 you do not now see the form of a woman 54
44 whom you now behold as an established city 54
50 now the Most High, seeing that you are . . grieved 54
12: 6 Therefore I will now beseech the Most High 54
12 it was not explained to him as I now explain 54
49 Now go, every one of you to his house 54
13:15 now show me also the interpretation 54
46 and now, when they are about to come again 54
14: 7 now I say to you; 54
13 Now therefore, set your house in order 54
13 And now renounce the life that is corruptible 51
14 and divest yourself now of your weak nature 51
16 evils worse than those which you have now seen 54
33 now you are here 54
36 let no one come to me now 54
15:27 now calamities have come upon the whole earth 51
16:35 Listen now to these things, and understand them 56
Tob 1: 4 Now when I was in my own country 33
10 Now when I was carried away captive to Nineveh 33
22 Now Ahikar was cupbearer, keeper of the signet 30
3: 5 now thy many judgments are true 39
6 now deal with me according to thy pleasure; 39
6 Command that I now be released from my distress 32
12 now, O Lord, I have turned my eyes . . toward thee. 39
4:13 now, my son, love your brethren 39
20 now let me explain to you about the ten talents 39
6: 1 Now as they proceeded on their way 30
12 Now listen to my plan 39
14 Now I am the only son my father has 39
14 now I fear that I may die 39
15 Now listen to me, brother 39
8: 7 now, O Lord, I am not taking this sister of mine 39
10: 1 Now his father Tobit was counting each day 33
12 they are now your parents 39
11: 5 Now Anna sat looking intently down the road 33
9 I have seen you, my child; now I am ready to die. 39
12:14 now God sent me to heal you 39
20 now give thanks to God 39
14: 8 now, my son, leave Nineveh 39
11 now, my children, consider 39
Jdt 5: 5 Let my lord now hear a word 31
19 now they have returned to their God 39
20 Now therefore, my master and lord 39
6: 7 Now my slaves are going to take you back 33
7: 4 These men will now lick up the face of the whole land 39
25 For now we have no one to help us 39
26 Now call them in and surrender the whole city 39
8:24 Now therefore, brethren, let us set an example 39
9: 5 thou hast designed the things that are now 39
7 Behold now, the Assyrians 27
11: 2 even now, if your people . . had not slighted me 39
3 now tell me why you have fled from them 39
9 Now as for the things Achior said in your council 39
11 now, in order that my lord may not be defeated 39
12: 6 Let my lord now command 31
11 Go now and persuade the Hebrew woman 31
17 Drink now, and be merry with us! 31
18 Judith said, "I will drink now, my lord 31
13: 3 Now Judith had told her maid . . 33
5 For now is the time to help thy inheritance 39
14: 8 Now tell me what you have done during these days. 39
AEs 12: 1 Now Mordecai took his rest in the courtyard 33
13: 7 those who have long been and are now hostile 39
15 now, O Lord God and King, God of Abraham 39
14: 6 now we have sinned before thee 39
8 now they are not satisfied 39
18 since the day that I was brought here until now 39
16:23 both now and hereafter it may mean salvation 39
Wis 14:15 he now honored as a god 39
20 the multitude . . now regarded as an object of worship 39
17:15 now were driven by monstrous specters 36
15 now were paralyzed by their souls' surrender 30
Sir 11:19 I have found rest, and now I shall enjoy my goods! 39
39:35 now sing praise with all your heart and voice 39
42:15 I will now call to mind the works of the Lord 31
44: 1 Let us now praise famous men 31
50:22 now bless the God of all 39
Bar 2:11 And now, O Lord God of Israel, who didst bring 39
3: 4 O Lord Almighty, God of Israel, hear now the prayer 31
4:24 the neighbors of Zion have now seen your capture 39
LJr 1: 4 Now in Babylon you will see gods made of silver 40
Aza 1:10 now we cannot open our mouths 39
18 now with all our heart we follow thee 39
23 Now the king's servants . . did not cease 33
Sus 1:31 Now Susanna was a woman of great refinement 30
43 And now I am to die! 41
52 your sins have now come home 39
54 Now then, if you really saw her, tell me this 39
58 Now then, tell me 39
Bel 1: 3 Now the Babylonians had an idol called Bel 33
10 Now there were 70 priests of Bel 33
32 these were not given to them now 47
33 Now the prophet Habakkuk was in Judea 33
Man 1:11 now I bend the knee of my heart 39
1Mc 1:54 Now on the fifteenth day of Chislev 33
2:18 Now be the first to come 39
49 Now the days drew near for Mattathias to die 33
49 Arrogance and reproach have now become strong 39
50 Now, my children, show zeal for the law 39
65 Now behold . . Simeon . . is wise in counsel; 33
3:42 Now Judas and his brothers saw 33
4: 1 Now Gorgias took 5,000 infantry 33
10 now let us cry to Heaven 39
18 stand now against our enemies and fight them 39
5: 9 Now the Gentiles in Gilead gathered together 33
12 Now then come and rescue us from their hands 39
55 Now while Judas and Jonathan were in Gilead 33
6:11 into what a great flood I now am plunged! 39
12 now I remember the evils I did in Jerusalem 39
18 Now the men in the citadel kept hemming Israel 33
40 Now a part of the king's army was spread out 33
58 Now then let us come to terms with these men 39
7: 7 Now then send a man whom you trust 39
39 Now Nicanor went out from Jerusalem 33
8: 1 Now Judas heard of the fame of the Romans 33
32 If now they appeal again for help against you 43
9: 5 Now Judas was encamped in Elasa 33
9 Let us rather save our own lives now 39
22 Now the rest of the acts of Judas 33
30 So now we have chosen you today to take his place 39
44 Let us rise up now and fight for our lives 31
46 Cry out now to Heaven that you may be delivered 39
58 So now let us bring Bacchides back 39
10:15 Now Alexander the king heard of all the promises 33
16 Come now, we will make him our friend and ally. 39
27 now continue still to keep faith with us 39
29 now I free you 39
41 they shall give from now 39
48 Now Alexander the king assembled large forces 33
54 now therefore let us establish friendship 39
54 give me now your daughter as my wife 39
56 now I will do for you as you wrote 39
71 If you now have confidence in your forces 39
73 now you will not be able to withstand my cavalry 39
79 Now Apollonius had . . left 1,000 cavalry 33
11:14 Now Alexander the king was in Cilicia 30
37 Now therefore take care to make a copy of this 39
38 Now when Demetrius the king saw 33
39 Now Trypho had formerly been one 30
41 Now Jonathan sent to Demetrius . . the request 33
43 Now then you will do well to send me men 39
12:18 now please send us a reply to this. 39
22 now that we have learned this 39
24 Now Jonathan heard 33
45 Dismiss them now to their homes 39
53 Now therefore let us make war on them 39
13: 5 now, far be it from me to spare my life 39
16 Send now 100 talents of silver 39
21 Now the men in the citadel kept sending envoys 30
15: 5 now . . I confirm to you all the tax remissions 39
30 Now then, hand over the cities 39
34 Now that we have the opportunity 30
37 Now Trypho embarked on a ship 30
16: 3 now I have grown old 40
11 Now Ptolemy . . had been appointed governor 33
14 Now Simon was visiting the cities of the country 30
2Mc 1: 6 We are now praying for you here. 39
9 now see that you keep the feast of booths 39
3:28 but was now unable to help himself 26
6:12 Now I urge those who read this book 43
18 a man now advanced in age and of noble presence 32
27 Therefore, by manfully giving up my life now 39
7:23 since you now forget yourselves 39
10: 1 Now Maccabeus . . recovered the temple 30
10 Now we will tell what took place under Antiochus 40
24 Now Timothy . . gathered a tremendous force 30
13:10 now if ever to help those who . . 39
14: 3 Now a certain Alcimus . . realized that . . 30
36 now, O holy One, Lord of all holiness 39
46 with his blood now completely drained from him 32
15: 8 now to look for the victory 39
20 When all were now looking forward 32
23 now, O Sovereign of the heavens, send a good angel 39
3Mc 1: 6 Now that he had foiled the plot 30
26 and began now to approach 32
2:13 see now, O holy King 39
31 Now some, however . . readily gave themselves up 43
4: 1 was now made evident and outspoken. 39
5: 8 rescue them from the fate now prepared for them. 45
14 now, since it was . . the middle of the tenth hour 32
38 Equip the elephants now once more 39
40 ordering now for a third time 32
45 Now when the beasts had been brought 30
46 the city now being filled with countless masses 32
51 they stood now at the gates of death. 32
6: 9 now, you who hate insolence . . reveal yourself 39
12 watch over us now and have mercy upon us 39
24 you are now attempting to deprive of dominion 32
28 from the time of our ancestors until now 39
29 since they now had escaped death. 26
4Mc 1:15 Now reason is the mind 46
18 Now the kinds of wisdom are rational judgment 30
30 Observe now first of all 46
2:21 Now when God fashioned man 27
3: 6 Now this can be explained more clearly 29
9 Now all the rest were at supper 38
19 The present occasion now invites us 32
4: 1 Now there was a certain Simon 27
6:18 if we . . should now change our course 39

26 When he was now burned to his very bones 32
33 now that reason has conquered the emotions 40
14: 9 Even now, we ourselves shudder as we hear 39
15:16 O mother, tried now by more bitter pains 39
17:18 they now stand before the divine throne 39

just now 1. הַיּוֹם 2. עַתָּה זֶה 3. עַתָּה זֶה

1Sm 9:12 Make haste; he has come just now to the city 1
2Kg 5:22 There have just now come to me . . two young men 3
22 There have just now come to me . . two young men 2

now on 1. *εἰς τὸ λοιπόν*

Jdt 11: 4 you will live, tonight and from now 1

right now 1. *ἀπὸ τοῦ νῦν*

Tob 7:12 Take her right now, in accordance with the law 1

now then 1. עַתָּה

Gen 12:19 Now then, here is your wife, take her, and be gone. 1

nowadays 1. הַיּוֹם

1Sm 25:10 many servants nowadays . . breaking away 1

nowhere 1. אָנֶה וָאָנָה 2. *μή* 3. *μηδαμόθεν* 4. *οὐ ποῦ*

2Kg 5:25 And he said, "Your servant went nowhere. 1
Mat 8:20 but the Son of man has nowhere to lay his head. 4
10: 5 Go nowhere among the Gentiles 2
Lke 9:58 the Son of man has nowhere to lay his head. 4
12:17 I have nowhere to store my crops?' 4
Wis 17:10 though it nowhere could be avoided. 3

nudge 1. *νύσσω*

3Mc 5:14 approached the king and nudged him. 1

null 1. *κενόω*

Rom 4:14 If . . faith is null and the promise is void. 1

nullify 1. *ἀθετέω* 2. *ἀκυρόω* 3. *καταλύω* 4. *καταργέω*

Rom 3: 3 faithlessness nullify the faithfulness of God? 4
Gal 2:21 I do not nullify the grace of God 1
1Es 6:32 nullify any of the things herein written 2
1Mc 14:44 permitted to nullify any of these decisions 1
45 Whoever . . nullifies any of them 1
4Mc 2: 3 he nullified the frenzy of the passions. 2
8:15 their right reasoning nullified his tyranny. 3
17: 2 nullified the violence of the tyrant 3

number 1. אִישׁ 2. דָּבָר 3. היה 4. מִכְסָה 5. מלא 6. מנה 7. מִסְפָּר 8. מִפְקָד 9. מַתְכֹּנֶת 10. נשׂא מִסְפָּר 11. ספר 12. סְפֹרָה 13. עבר 14. פקד 15. רֹב 16. רבב 17. מְנֵה (A) 18. מִנְיָן (A) 19. *ἀριθμέω* 20. *ἀριθμός* 21. *ἐναρίθμιος* 22. *ἱκανός* 23. *καταλογίζομαι* 24. *καταριθμέω* 25. *ὁ αὐτός* 26. *ὄχλος* 27. *πλῆθος* 28. numero 29. numerus

Gen 15: 5 Look toward heaven, and number the stars 11
5 number the stars, if you are able to number them. 11
16:10 that they cannot be numbered for multitude. 11
32:12 which cannot be numbered for multitude.' 11
34:30 my numbers are few, and if they gather themselves 7
46:15 his sons and his daughters numbered 33 •
47:12 according to the number of their dependents. •
Exd 5: 8 the number of bricks which they made heretofore 9
19 by no means lessen your daily number of bricks. 2
12: 4 shall take according to the number of persons; 4
16:16 according to the number of the persons whom each 7
23:26 I will fulfil the number of your days. 7
30:12 when you number them, that there be no plague 14
12 no plague among them when you number them. 14
13 Each who is numbered in the census shall give 13
14 Every one who is numbered in the census 13
38:25 those of the congregation who were numbered 14
26 for every one who was numbered in the census 13
Lev 25:15 According to the number of years after 7
15 and according to the number of years for crops 7
16 the number of the crops that he is selling to you 7
50 according to the number of his release of years 7
Num 1: 2 census . . according to the number of names 7
3 you and Aaron shall number them 14
18 registered . . according to the number of names 7
19 So he numbered them in the wilderness of Sinai. 14
20 according to the number of names, head by head 7
21 the number of the tribe of Reuben was 46,500 14
22 those of them that were numbered, according 14
22 according to the number of names, head by head 7
23 the number of the tribe of Simeon was 59,300 14
24 according to the number of the names 7
25 the number of the tribe of Gad was 45,650 14
26 according to the number of names 7
27 the number of the tribe of Judah was 74,600 14
28 according to the number of names 7
29 the number of the tribe of Is'sachar was 54,400 14
30 according to the number of names 7
31 the number of the tribe of Zeb'ulun was 57,400 14
32 according to the number of names 7
33 the number of the tribe of E'phraim was 40,500 14
34 according to the number of names 7
35 the number of the tribe of Manas'seh was 32,200 14
36 according to the number of names 7
37 the number of the tribe of Benjamin was 35,400 14
38 according to the number of names, from twenty 7
39 the number of the tribe of Dan was 62,700 14
40 according to the number of names, from twenty 7
41 the number of the tribe of Asher was 41,500 14
42 according to the number of names, from twenty 7
43 the number of the tribe of Naph'tali was 53,400 14
44 These are those who were numbered 14
44 whom Moses and Aaron numbered with the help 14
45 So the whole number of the people of Israel 14
46 their whole number was 603,550. 14
47 the Levites were not numbered by their 14
49 Only the tribe of Levi you shall not number 14
2: 4 his host as numbered being 74,600 14
6 his host as numbered being 54,400. 14
8 his host as numbered being 57,400. 14
9 The whole number of the camp of Judah 14
11 his host as numbered being 46,500. 14
13 his host as numbered being 59,300 14
15 his host as numbered being 45,650 14
16 The whole number of the camp of Reuben 14
19 his host as numbered being 40,500 14
21 his host as numbered being 32,200 14
23 his host as numbered being 35,400 14
24 The whole number of the camp of E'phraim 14
26 his host as numbered being 62,700 14
28 his host as numbered being 41,500 14
30 his host as numbered being 53,400 14
31 The whole number of the camp of Dan is 157,600 14
32 Israel as numbered by their fathers' houses; 14
32 all . . who were numbered by their companies 14
33 the Levites were not numbered among the people 14
3:15 Number the sons of Levi, by fathers' houses 14
15 every male . . you shall number. 14
16 So Moses numbered them according to the word 14
22 Their number according to the number of all 14
22 Their number according to the number of all 7
28 According to the number of all the males 7
34 number according to the number of all the males 14
34 number of all the males from a month old 7
39 All who were numbered of the Levites 14
39 Moses and Aaron numbered at the commandment 14
40 Number all the first-born males of the people 14
40 taking their number by names. 7
42 Moses numbered all the first-born 14
43 first-born . . according to the number of names 7
43 first-born males . . as numbered were 22,273. 14
46 over and above the number of the male Levites •
4:23 you shall number them, all who can enter 14
29 number them by their . . fathers' houses; 14
30 number them, every one that can enter the service 14
34 Moses . . numbered the sons of the Ko'hathites 14
36 their number by families was 2,750. 14
37 number of the families of the Ko'hathites 14
37 Ko'hathites . . Moses and Aaron numbered 14
38 number of the sons of Gershon, by their families 14
40 number by their families and their fathers' 14
41 number of the families of the sons of Gershon 14
41 whom Moses and Aaron numbered according 14
42 The number of the families of the sons of Merar'i 14
44 their number by families was 3,200. 14
45 numbered of the families of the sons of Merar'i 14
45 whom Moses and Aaron numbered according 14
46 All those who were numbered of the Levites 14
46 Moses and Aaron and the leaders . . numbered 14
48 those who were numbered of them were 8,580. 14
49 thus they were numbered by him 14
7: 2 leaders . . were over those who were numbered 14
11:21 The people among whom I am number 600,000 on foot; •
14:29 all your number, numbered from twenty years old 14
29 all your number, numbered from twenty years old 7
34 According to the number of the days in which you 7
15:12 According to the number that you prepare 7
12 do with every one according to their number. 7
16: 2 rose up . . with a number of the people of Israel 1
22:15 princes, more in number and more honorable •
23:10 dust of Jacob, or number the fourth part of Israel? 7
26: 7 Reubenites; and their number was 43,730. 14
18 sons of Gad according to their number, 40,500. 14
22 families of Judah according to their number 14
25 families of Is'sachar according to their number 14
27 Zeb'ulunites according to their number, 60,500. 14
34 Manas'seh; and their number was 52,700. 14
37 E'phraim according to their number, 32,500. 14
41 sons of Benjamin . . and their number was 45,600. 14
43 Shu'hamites, according to their number 14
47 sons of Asher according to their number, 53,400. 14
50 Naph'tali . . their number was 45,400. 14
51 number of the people of Israel, 601,730. 14
53 inheritance according to the number of names. 7
54 inheritance according to its numbers. 14
57 These are the Levites as numbered according 14
62 those numbered of them were 23,000 14
62 not numbered among the people of Israel 14
63 These were those numbered by Moses and Elea'zar 14
63 numbered the people of Israel in the plains 14
64 not a man of those numbered by Moses and Aaron 14
64 numbered the people of Israel in the wilderness 14
29:18 cereal offering . . by number, according 7
21 cereal offering . . by number 7
24 cereal offering . . by number 7
27 cereal offering . . by number 7
30 cereal offering . . by number 7
33 cereal offering . . by number 7
37 cereal offering . . by number 7
31:36 the half . . was in number 337,500 sheep 7
Deu 4:27 you will be left few in number among the nations 7
7: 7 not . . more in number than any other people 16
25: 2 beaten in his presence with a number of stripes 7
26: 5 Egypt and sojourned there, few in number; •
32: 8 according to the number of the sons of God. 7
Jos 4: 5 to the number of the tribes of the people of Israel 7
8 twelve . . according to the number of the tribes 7
11: 4 a great host, in number like the sand that is upon 15
Jdg 6: 5 would come up . . coming like locusts for number; 15
7: 6 And the number of those that lapped, putting 7
12 and their camels were without number, as the sand 7
21:23 and took their wives, according to their number 7
1Sm 6: 4 the number of the lords of the Philistines; 7
18 mice, according to the number of all the cities 7
13:15 Saul numbered the people . . present with him 14
14:17 Saul said . . "Number and see who has gone from us. 14
17 when they had numbered, behold, Jonathan and his 14
15: 4 summoned the people, and numbered them in Tela'im 14
27: 7 the number of the days . . was a year 7
2Sm 2:15 Then they arose and passed over by number 7
21:20 and six toes on each foot, 24 in number; 7
24: 1 he incited David . . "Go, number Israel and Judah. 6
2 Go through all . . Israel . . and number the people 14
2 that I may know the number of the people. 7
4 went out . . to number the people of Israel. 14
9 Jo'ab gave the sum of the numbering of the people 8
10 smote him after he had numbered the people. 11
1Kg 3: 8 cannot be numbered or counted for multitude. 6
5:13 the levy numbered 30,000 men. 3
8: 5 that they could not be counted or numbered. 6
18:31 according to the number of the tribes of the sons 7
1Ch 7: 2 their number in the days of David being 22,600 7
40 Their number enrolled by genealogies 7
12:23 the numbers of the divisions of the armed troops 7
16:19 they were few in number, and of little account 7
20: 6 on each hand, and six toes on each foot, 24 in number •
21: 1 Satan . . incited David to number Israel. 6
2 Go, number Israel, from Beer-sheba to Dan 11
2 bring me a report, that I may know their number. 7
5 Jo'ab gave the sum of the numbering of the people 8
6 not include Levi and Benjamin in the numbering 14
17 Was it not I who gave command to number the people 6
22: 4 cedar timbers without number; 7
15 and all kinds of craftsmen without number 7
23: 3 The Levites, 30 years old and upward, were numbered 11
24 registered according to the number of the names 7
27 number of the Levites from twenty years old 7
31 according to the number required of them 7
25: 7 The number of them along with their brethren 7
27: 1 each division numbering 24,000 •
23 David did not number those below twenty years 10
24 Jo'ab . . began to number, but did not finish; 6
24 the number was not entered in the chronicles 7
2Ch 5: 6 that they could not be counted or numbered. 6
12: 3 people were without number who came with him 7
26:11 army . . in divisions according to the numbers 7
12 The whole number of the heads of fathers' houses 7
29:32 The number of the burnt offerings 7
35: 7 lambs and kids . . to the number of 30,000 7
Ezr 1: 9 this was the number of them: 1,000 basins 7
2: 2 number of the men of the people of Israel 7
3: 4 offered the daily burnt offerings by number 7
6:17 according to the number of the tribes of Israel. 18
Neh 7: 7 number of the men of the people of Israel 7
Est 5:11 riches, the number of his sons, all the promotions 15
9:11 the number of those slain in Susa . . was reported 7
Job 1: 5 burnt offerings according to the number of them 7
3: 6 let it not come into the number of the months. 7
5: 9 marvelous things without number 7
9:10 and marvelous things without number. 7
14: 5 the number of his months is with thee 7
16 For then thou wouldest number my steps 11
21:21 when the number of their months is cut off? 7
25: 3 Is there any number to his armies? 7
31: 4 Does not he see my ways, and number all my steps? 11
36:26 the number of his years is unsearchable. 7
38:21 the number of your days is great! 7
37 Who can number the clouds by wisdom? 11
39: 2 Can you number the months that they fulfil 11
Ps 40: 5 they would be more than can be numbered. 11
12 For evils have encompassed me without number; 7
48:12 about Zion, go round about her, number her towers 11
69: 4 More in number than the hairs of my head •
71:15 for their number is past my knowledge. 12
90:12 teach us to number our days that we may get 6
105:12 When they were few in number, of little account 7
34 locusts came, and young locusts without number; 7
147: 4 He determines the number of the stars 7
Ecc 1:15 and what is lacking cannot be numbered. 6
Sng 6: 8 80 concubines, and maidens without number. 7
Isa 40:26 He who brings out their host by number 7

53:12 and was numbered with the transgressors; 6
Jer 2:32 people have forgotten me days without number. 7
15: 8 I have made their widows more in number •
33:22 As the host of heaven cannot be numbered 11
46:23 numerous than locusts; they are without number. 7
52:28 This is the number of the people whom •
Lam 4:18 our days were numbered; for our end had come. 5
Ezk 4: 4 for the number of the days that you lie upon it 7
5 For I assign to you a number of days, 390 days 7
5 390 days, equal to the number of the years •
9 the number of days that you lie upon your side 7
5: 3 And you shall take from these a small number 7
20:37 and I will let you go in by number. 20
Dan 5:26 MENE, God has numbered the days of your kingdom 17
9: 2 perceived in the books the number of years 7
Hos 1:10 the number of the people . . shall be like the sand 7
10 sea, which can be neither measured nor numbered; 11
Jol 1: 6 against my land, powerful and without number; 7
Mat 10:30 even the hairs of your head are all numbered. 19
Mrk 5:13 and the herd, numbering about 2,000 •
Lke 12: 7 Why, even the hairs of your head are all numbered. 19
22: 3 who was of the number of the twelve; 20
Joh 6:10 the men sat down, in number about 5,000. 20
Act 1:17 he was numbered among us 24
2:47 the Lord added to their number day by day 25
4: 4 the number of the men came to about 5,000 20
5:36 a number of men, about 4,000, joined him 20
6: 7 the number of the disciples multiplied greatly 20
11:21 a great number that believed turned to the Lord. 20
16: 5 they increased in numbers daily. 20
19:19 a number of those who practiced magic arts 22
27: 7 We sailed slowly for a number of days 22
Rom 9:27 Though the number of the sons of Israel be 20
Rev 5:11 angels, numbering myriads of myriads 20
6:11 until the number of their fellow servants •
7: 4 I heard the number of the sealed 20
9 a great multitude which no man could number 19
9:16 The number of the troops of cavalry was twice 20
16 number of the troops . . I heard their number. 20
13:17 the name of the beast or the number of its name. 20
18 let him . . reckon the number of the beast 20
18 number of the beast, for it is a human number 20
18 the number of the beast . . its number is 666. 20
15: 2 the beast and its image and the number of its name 20
20: 8 their number is like the sand of the sea. 20
1Es 2:13 The number of these was 20
5: 9 The number of the men of the nation 20
7: 8 the number of the twelve leaders of the tribes 20
2Es 2:26 for I will require them from among your number. 29
38 the number of those who have been sealed. 29
40 Take again your full number, O Zion 29
41 The number of your children . . is full 29
42 a great multitude, which I could not number 28
3: 7 peoples and clans without number. 29
29 I saw ungodly deeds without number 29
4:32 When heads of grain without number are sown 29
36 When the number of those like yourselves 29
37 and numbered the times by number 28
37 and numbered the times by number 29
16:56 and he knows the number of the stars. 29
Jdt 2: 5 the number of 120,000 foot soldiers •
17 He collected a vast number of camels and asses 27
7:18 supply trains spread out in great number 26
9:11 For thy power depends not upon numbers 27
10:17 They chose from their number 100 men •
Wis 4: 8 nor measured by number of years; 20
5: 5 Why has he been numbered among the sons of God? 23
11:20 measure and number and weight. 20
Sir 18: 9 The number of a man's days is great 20
26: 1 the number of his days will be doubled. 20
37:25 The life of a man is numbered by days 20
38:29 all his output is by number. 21
41:13 The days of a good life are numbered 20
42: 7 let it be by number and weight 20
45:11 according to the number of the tribes of Israel; 20
Bar 2:13 we are left, few in number, among the nations •
Man 1: 9 more in number than the sand of the sea 20
1Mc 2:18 you . . will be numbered among the friends of the king •
38 to the number of 1,000 persons. •
4: 8 Do not fear their numbers 27
6:30 The number of his forces 20
9: 6 When they saw the huge number of the enemy forces 27
10:36 to the number of 30,000 men •
37 Let their . . leaders be of their own number •
85 The number of those who fell by the sword •
11:45 to the number of 120,000 •
2Mc 2:24 considering the flood of numbers involved 20
8:16 to the number 6,000 20
3Mc 5: 2 all the elephants–500 in number 20
4Mc 8: 5 the beauty and the number of such brothers 27
16:13 the whole number of her sons 20

number *See also* few, give, increase, make, many.

number among 1. connumero
2Es 7:76 nor number yourself among those 1

excess number 1. עדף
Num 3:48 by which the excess number of them is redeemed 1

full number 1. πλήρωμα
Rom 11:25 until the full number of the Gentiles come in 1

great number 1. גָּדוֹל 2. לָרֹב 3. רֹב 4. πολύς
2Ch 15: 9 great numbers had deserted to him from Israel 3
20:25 found cattle in great numbers, goods, clothing 2
28: 5 took captive a great number of his people 1
29:35 Besides the great number of burnt offerings 2
30: 5 had not kept it in great numbers as prescribed. 2
24 sanctified themselves in great numbers. 2
Act 28:23 they came to him at his lodging in great numbers. 4

number of people 1. πλῆθος
2Mc 5:26 and killed great numbers of people. 1

same number 1. תֹּכֶן 2. totidem
Exd 5:18 you shall deliver the same number of bricks. 1
2Es 2:19 the same number of springs 2

small number 1. μικρός 2. ὀλίγος
Bar 2:29 multitude will surely turn into a small number 1
2Mc 10:24 and collected the cavalry . . in no small number 2

sufficient number 1. מַדַּי
2Ch 30: 3 sanctified themselves in sufficient number 1

untold number 1. ἀμύθητος
2Mc 12:16 and slaughtered untold numbers 1

vast number 1. πλῆθος
Jdt 7: 4 When the Israelites saw their vast numbers 1
Wis 19:10 the river spewed out vast numbers of frogs. 1

very great number 1. πολύς
1Es 2: 9 a very great number of votive offerings 1

whole number 1. קְצָה
Jdg 18: 2 sent . . men from the whole number of their tribe 1

without number 1. ἀναρίθμητος
Sir 37:25 the days of Israel are without number. 1

numerous 1. רַב 2. πολύς
Jos 17:14 but one lot . . although I am a numerous people 1
15 If you are a numerous people, go up to the forest 1
17 You are a numerous people, and have great power; 1
1Mc 11:24 gold and clothing and numerous other gifts 2
16: 7 the cavalry of the enemy were very numerous. 2

numerous *See also* grow, make.

more numerous 1. רבב
Jer 46:23 because they are more numerous than locusts; 1

very numerous 1. רבה
1Ch 5:23 were very numerous from Bashan to Ba′al-her′mon 1

nurse 1. אמן 2. אִשָּׁה ינק 3. ינק 4. סכן 5. ἀνατρέφω 6. γαλακτοτροφία 7. θηλάζω 8. τιθηνός 9. τροφός 10. nutrix
Gen 24:59 sent away Rebekah their sister and her nurse 3
35: 8 Deb′orah, Rebekah's nurse, died 3
Exd 2: 7 Shall I go and call you a nurse from the Hebrew 2
7 call . . a nurse . . to nurse the child for you? 3
9 Take this child away, and nurse him for me 3
9 So the woman took the child and nursed him. 3
Num 11:12 Carry . . as a nurse carries the sucking child 1
Rut 4:16 Na′omi took the child . . and became his nurse. 1
1Sm 1:23 the woman remained and nursed her son 3
2Sm 4: 4 and his nurse took him up, and fled; 1
1Kg 1: 2 and let her wait upon the king, and be his nurse; 4
4 she became the king's nurse and ministered to him; 4
3:21 When I rose in the morning to nurse my child 3
2Kg 11: 2 and she put him and his nurse in a bedchamber. 3
2Ch 22:11 she put him and his nurse in a bedchamber. 3
Sng 8: 1 a brother to me, that nursed at my mother's breast! 3
1Th 2: 7 like a nurse taking care of her children. 9
2Es 1:28 a mother her daughters or a nurse her children 10
2:25 Good nurse, nourish your sons 10
Wis 7: 4 I was nursed with care in swaddling cloths. 5
2Mc 7:27 nursed you for three years 7
3Mc 1:20 Mothers and nurses 8
4Mc 16: 7 fruitless nurturings and wretched nursings! 6

nursing *See* infant, mother.

nursling 1. ינק
Lam 4: 4 The tongue of the nursling cleaves . . for thirst; 1

nurture 1. τιθηνία 2. τρέφω 3. τροφεία
Bar 4:11 With joy I nurtured them 2
4Mc 15:13 nurture and indomitable suffering by mothers! 3
16: 7 fruitless nurturings and wretched nursings! 1

common nurture 1. συντροφία
4Mc 13:22 they grow stronger from this common nurture 1

nurture in common 1. συντροφία
3Mc 5:32 an affection arising from our nurture in common 1

nut 1. אֱגוֹז
Sng 6:11 I went down to the nut orchard 1

nut *See also* pistachio.

O

O that 1. אַחֲלַי 2. מִי נתן
Job 6: 8 O that I might have my request 2
Ps 14: 7 O that deliverance for Israel would come 2
53: 6 O that deliverance for Israel would come 2
55: 6 I say, "O that I had wings like a dove! I would fly away 2
119: 5 O that my ways may be steadfast 1

oak 1. אַיִל 2. אֵלָה 3. אַלָּה 4. אֵלוֹן 5. אַלּוֹן 6. quercus
Gen 12: 6 to the place at Shechem, to the oak of Moreh. 4
13:18 and came and dwelt by the oaks of Mamre 4
14:13 the Hebrew, who was living by the oaks of Mamre 4
18: 1 the LORD appeared to him by the oaks of Mamre 4
35: 4 hid them under the oak which was near Shechem. 2
8 died, and she was buried under an oak below Bethel; 5
Deu 11:30 over against Gilgal, beside the oak of Moreh? 4
Jos 19:33 its boundary ran . . from the oak in Za-anan'nim 4
24:26 and set it up there under the oak in the sanctuary 3
Jdg 4:11 his tent as far away as the oak in Za-anan'nim 4
6:11 the angel . . came and sat under the oak at Ophrah 2
19 brought them to him under the oak and presented 2
9: 6 made . . king, by the oak of the pillar at Shechem. 4
37 coming from the direction of the Diviners' Oak. 4
1Sm 10: 3 go on . . further and come to the oak of Tabor; 4
2Sm 18: 9 mule went under the thick branches of a great oak 2
9 Ab'salom was . . and his head caught fast in the oak 2
10 Behold, I saw Ab'salom hanging in an oak. 2
14 of Ab'salom, while he was still alive in the oak. 2
1Kg 13:14 and found him sitting under an oak; 2
1Ch 10:12 they buried their bones under the oak in Jabesh 2
Ps 29: 9 voice of the LORD makes the oaks to whirl 2
Isa 1:29 be ashamed of the oaks in which you delighted; 1
30 For you shall be like an oak whose leaf withers 2
2:13 cedars . . and against all the oaks of Bashan; 5
6:13 it will be burned again, like a terebinth or an oak 5
44:14 he chooses a holm tree or an oak and lets it grow 5
57: 5 you who burn with lust among the oaks 1
61: 3 that they may be called oaks of righteousness 1
Ezk 6:13 under every leafy oak, wherever they offered 2
27: 6 Of oaks of Bashan they made your oars; 5
Hos 4:13 make offerings upon the hills, under oak, poplar 5
Ams 2: 9 and who was as strong as the oaks; 5
Zec 11: 2 Wail, oaks of Bashan 5
2Es 14: 1 On the third day, while I was sitting under an oak 6
oak *See also* evergreen.

oar 1. מָשׁוֹט 2. שַׁיִט
Isa 33:21 a place . . where no galley with oars can go 2
Ezk 27: 6 Of oaks of Bashan they made your oars; 1
29 from their ships come all that handle the oar. 1

oath 1. אָלָה 2. שְׁבוּעָה 3. ἐνόρκως 4. ὁρκισμός 5. ὅρκος 6. ὁρκωμοσία
Gen 24: 8 then you will be free from this oath of mine; 2
41 then you will be free from my oath 1
41 give her to you, you will be free from my oath.' 1
26: 3 I will fulfil the oath which I swore 2
28 LORD is with you; so we say, let there be an oath 1
Exd 22:11 an oath by the LORD shall be between them both 2
11 the owner shall accept the oath, and he shall not •
Lev 5: 4 any sort of rash oath that men swear 2
Num 5:21 then . . LORD make you an execration and an oath 2
30: 2 When a man . . swears an oath to bind himself 2
10 if she . . bound herself by a pledge with an oath 2
13 Any vow and any binding oath to afflict herself 2
Deu 7: 8 LORD loves you, and is keeping the oath 2
Jos 2:17 We will be guiltless with respect to this oath 2
20 we shall be guiltless with respect to your oath 2
9:20 because of the oath which we swore to them. 2
Jdg 21: 5 they had taken a great oath concerning him who 2
1Sm 14:26 no man put . . for the people feared the oath. 2
2Sm 21: 7 the oath of the LORD which was between them 2
1Kg 2:43 Why then have you not kept your oath to the LORD 2
8:31 If a man sins . . and is made to take an oath 1
31 comes and swears his oath before thine altar 1
2Ch 6:22 If a man sins . . and is made to take an oath 1
15:15 all Judah rejoiced over the oath; 2
Neh 6:18 For many in Judah were bound by oath to him 2
10:29 enter into a curse and an oath to walk in God's law 2
Ps 119:106 I have sworn an oath and confirmed it •
132:11 The LORD swore to David a sure oath •
Ecc 8: 2 and because of your sacred oath be not dismayed; 2
9: 2 and he who swears is as he who shuns an oath. 2
Jer 11: 5 that I may perform the oath which I swore 2
Ezk 16:59 who have despised the oath 1
17:13 made a covenant with him, putting him under oath. 1
16 who made him king, whose oath he despised 1
18 he despised the oath and broke the covenant 1
19 surely my oath which he despised, and my covenant 1
21:23 false divination; they have sworn solemn oaths; 2
Dan 9:11 curse and oath which are written in the law 2
Hos 10: 4 with empty oaths they make covenants; 1
Zec 8:17 love no false oath, for all these things I hate 2
Mat 14: 7 so that he promised with an oath to give her 5
9 because of his oaths and his guests 5
26:72 again he denied it with an oath 5
Mrk 6:26 because of his oaths and his guests 5
Lke 1:73 the oath which he swore to our father Abraham 5
Act 2:30 knowing that God had sworn with an oath to him 5
Heb 6:16 disputes an oath is final for confirmation. 5
17 he interposed with an oath 5
7:20 it was not without an oath. 6
21 took their office without an oath 6
21 this one was addressed with an oath 6
28 the word of the oath, which came later than the law 6
Jas 5:12 do not swear . . with any other oath 5
1Es 8:93 Let us take an oath to the Lord about this 6
Tob 8:20 Raguel declared by oath to Tobias 3
Jdt 8:11 you have even sworn and pronounced this oath 5
30 and made us take an oath which we cannot break. 5
Wis 12:21 to whose fathers thou gavest oaths 5
18: 6 the oaths in which they trusted. 5
22 the oaths and covenants given to our fathers. 5
Sir 23: 9 Do not accustom your mouth to oaths 5
44:21 Therefore the Lord assured him by an oath 5
1Mc 6:62 he broke the oath he had sworn 4
7:18 violated . . the oath which they swore. 5
2Mc 7:24 promised with oaths 5
14:32 when they declared on oath that they did not know 5
33 and swore this oath •
15:10 pointing out . . their violation of oaths. 5
3Mc 5:42 he firmly swore an irrevocable oath 5
4Mc 5:29 the sacred oaths of my ancestors 5
oath *See also* bind, break, charge, give, lay, promise, swear, take, utter.

obedience 1. יְקָהָה 2. εὐπείθεια 3. ὑπακοή 4. ὑποταγή
Gen 49:10 to him shall be the obedience of the peoples. 1
Rom 1: 5 to bring about the obedience of faith 3
5:19 by one man's obedience many will be made righteous. 3
6:16 or of obedience, which leads to righteousness? 3
15:18 to win obedience from the Gentiles 3
16:19 For while your obedience is known to all 3
26 to bring about the obedience of faith– 3
2Co 7:15 as he remembers the obedience of you all 3
9:13 glorify God by your obedience 4
10: 6 when your obedience is complete. 3
Phm 1:21 Confident of your obedience, I write to you 3
Heb 5: 8 he learned obedience through what he suffered; 3
1Pe 1: 2 sanctified . . for obedience to Jesus Christ 3
22 Having purified your souls by your obedience 3
4Mc 5:16 more powerful than our obedience to the law. 2

ready obedience 1. εὐπείθεια
4Mc 9: 2 we should practice ready obedience to the law 1
15: 9 their ready obedience to the law 1

obedient 1. שׁמע 2. εὐήκοος 3. πειθαρχέω 4. ὑπακοή 5. ὑπακούω 6. ὑπήκοος 7. ὑποτάσσω 8. persuasum
Exd 24: 7 we will do, and we will be obedient. 1
Isa 1:19 If you are willing and obedient, you shall eat 1
Lke 2:51 was obedient to them 7
Act 6: 7 the priests were obedient to the faith. 5
Rom 6:16 if you yield . . to any one as obedient slaves 4
2Co 2: 9 know whether you are obedient in everything. 6
Eph 6: 5 Slaves, be obedient 5
Php 2: 8 became obedient unto death, even death on a cross 6
Tit 3: 1 to be obedient, to be ready for any honest work 3
1Pe 1:14 As obedient children, do not be conformed 4
2Es 7:22 they were not obedient, and spoke against him 8
Sir 42:23 are all obedient. 5
LJr 1:60 sun and moon and stars . . are obedient. 2
obedient *See also* make.

become obedient 1. ὑπακούω
Rom 6:17 you . . have become obedient from the heart 1
obeisance *See* make.

do obeisance 1. שׁחה
Exd 18: 7 Moses . . did obeisance and kissed him; 1
1Sm 24: 8 David bowed . . to the earth, and did obeisance. 1
28:14 he bowed . . face to the ground, and did obeisance. 1
2Sm 1: 2 he fell to the ground and did obeisance. 1
9: 6 came . . and fell on his face and did obeisance. 1
8 And he did obeisance, and said 1
14: 4 fell on her face to the ground, and did obeisance 1
22 Jo'ab fell . . to the ground, and did obeisance 1
15: 5 whenever a man came near to do obeisance to him 1
16: 4 And Ziba said, "I do obeisance; let me ever find 1
24:20 Arau'nah went forth, and did obeisance to the king 1
1Kg 1:16 Bathshe'ba bowed and did obeisance to the king 1
31 bowed . . and did obeisance to the king, and said 1
53 And he came and did obeisance to King Solomon; 1
1Ch 21:21 did obeisance to David with his face to the ground 1
29:20 the LORD, and did obeisance to the king. 1
2Ch 24:17 princes of Judah . . did obeisance to the king; 1
Est 3: 2 And all . . bowed down and did obeisance to Haman; 1
2 But Mor'decai did not bow down or do obeisance. 1
5 Mor'decai did not bow down or do obeisance to him 1

obelisk 1. מַצֵּבָה
Jer 43:13 He shall break the obelisks of Heliop'olis 1

obey 1. יְקָהָה 2. מִשְׁמַעַת 3. עשׂה 4. עשׂה מַאֲמַר 5. שׁמע 6. שׁמע לְקֹל 7. שׁמר 8. עבד (A) 9. שׁמע (A) 10. ἀκολουθέω 11. ἀκούω 12. ἀπειθέω 13. εἰσακούω 14. ἐνακούω 15. ἐπακουστός 16. εὐπείθεια 17. εὐπειθω 18. πειθαρχέω 19. πείθω 20. ποιέω 21. ποιέω κατά 22. πράσσω 23. ὑπακοή 24. ὑπακούω 25. ὑπήκοος 26. obaudio 27. oboedio
Gen 22:18 because you have obeyed my voice. 5
26: 5 Abraham obeyed my voice and kept my charge 5
27: 8 Now therefore, my son, obey my word as I command 5
13 only obey my word, and go, fetch them to me. 5
43 Now therefore, my son, obey my voice; 5
28: 7 that Jacob had obeyed his father and his mother 5
Exd 7:16 and behold, you have not yet obeyed. 5
19: 5 if you will obey my voice and keep my covenant 5
Num 27:20 congregation of the LORD the people of Israel may obey. 5
Deu 4:30 return to the LORD your God and obey his voice 5
8:20 because you would not obey the voice of the LORD 5
9:23 did not believe him or obey his voice. 5
11:13 if you will obey my commandments which I command 5
27 blessing, if you obey the commandments 5
28 curse, if you do not obey the commandments 5
13: 4 keep his commandments and obey his voice 5
18 if you obey the voice of the LORD your God, keeping 5
15: 5 if only you will obey the voice of the LORD 5
17:12 by not obeying the priest who stands to minister 5
21:18 son, who will not obey the voice of his father 5

20 This our son . . will not obey our voice; 5
26:14 I have obeyed the voice of the LORD my God 5
17 walk in his ways . . and will obey his voice; 5
27:10 therefore obey the voice of the LORD your God 5
28: 1 if you obey the voice of the LORD your God 5
2 if you obey the voice of the LORD your God. 5
13 if you obey the commandments of the LORD your God 5
15 if you will not obey the voice of the LORD your God 5
45 you did not obey the voice of the LORD your God 5
62 you did not obey the voice of the LORD your God. 5
30: 2 obey his voice in all that I command you this day 5
8 again obey the voice of the LORD, and keep all 5
10 if you obey the voice of the LORD your God, to keep 5
16 If you obey the commandments of the LORD your God 13
20 loving . . obeying his voice, and cleaving to him; 5
34: 9 Israel obeyed him, and did as the LORD 5
Jos 1:17 we obeyed Moses in all things, so we will obey you; 5
17 Just as we obeyed Moses . . so we will obey you; 5
22: 2 have obeyed my voice in all that I have commanded 5
24:24 LORD . . we will serve, and his voice we will obey. 5
Jdg 2: 2 But you have not obeyed my command. What is this 5
17 who had obeyed the commandments of the LORD 5
20 and have not obeyed my voice 5
3: 4 whether Israel would obey the commandments 5
1Sm 15:19 Why then did you not obey the voice of the LORD? 5
20 I have obeyed the voice of the LORD, I have gone 5
22 as in obeying the voice of the LORD? 5
22 to obey is better than sacrifice, and to hearken 5
24 I feared the people and obeyed their voice. 5
28:18 Because you did not obey the voice of the LORD 5
2Sm 22:45 as soon as they heard of me, they obeyed me. 5
1Kg 2:42 And you said to me, 'What you say is good; I obey.' 5
6:12 walk in my statutes and obey my ordinances 3
20:36 Because you have not obeyed the voice of the LORD 5
2Kg 10: 6 If you are on my side, and if you are ready to obey me 6
18:12 they did not obey the voice of the LORD their God 5
12 not obey . . they neither listened nor obeyed. 3
22:13 fathers have not obeyed the words of this book 5
1Ch 29:23 and he prospered, and all Israel obeyed him. 5
Ezr 7:26 Whoever will not obey the law of your God 8
Neh 9:16 did not obey thy commandments; 5
17 refused to obey, and were not mindful 5
29 did not obey thy commandments, but sinned 5
29 stiffened their neck and would not obey. 5
Est 2:20 Esther obeyed Mor'decai just as when she was 4
Ps 18:44 As soon as they heard of me they obeyed me; 5
106:25 murmured . . did not obey the voice of the LORD. 5
Prv 30:17 eye . . mocks a father and scorns to obey a mother 1
Ecc 8: 5 He who obeys a command will meet no harm 7
Isa 11:14 Edom and Moab, and the Ammonites shall obey them. 2
42:24 and whose law they would not obey? 5
50:10 fears the LORD and obeys the voice of his servant 5
Jer 3:13 that you have not obeyed my voice, says the LORD. 5
25 we have not obeyed the voice of the LORD our God.". 5
7:23 But this command I gave them, 'Obey my voice 5
24 But they did not obey or incline their ear 5
28 the nation that did not obey the voice of the LORD 5
9:13 have not obeyed my voice, or walked in accord 5
11: 7 even to this day, saying, Obey my voice. 5
8 Yet they did not obey or incline their ear 5
22: 4 For if you will indeed obey this word 3
21 that you have not obeyed my voice. 5
25: 8 Because you have not obeyed my words 5
26:13 and obey the voice of the LORD your God 5
32:23 But they did not obey thy voice or walk in thy law; 5
34:10 they obeyed, all the princes and all the people 5
10 they obeyed and set them free. 5
17 You have not obeyed me by proclaiming liberty 5
35: 8 We have obeyed the voice of Jon'adab 5
10 and have obeyed and done all that Jon'adab 5
14 for they have obeyed their father's command. 5
16 but this people has not obeyed me. 5
18 Because you have obeyed the command of Jon'adab 5
38:20 Obey now the voice of the LORD in what I say to you 5
40: 3 Because you sinned . . and did not obey his voice 5
42: 6 we will obey the voice of the LORD our God 5
6 when we obey the voice of the LORD our God. 5
21 you have not obeyed the voice of the LORD your God 5
43: 4 the people did not obey the voice of the LORD 5
7 for they did not obey the voice of the LORD. 5
44:23 and did not obey the voice of the LORD 5
Ezk 11:20 and keep my ordinances and obey them; 3
Dan 7:27 all dominions shall serve and obey them.' 9
9:10 not obeyed the voice of the LORD our God 5
11 turned aside, refusing to obey thy voice. 5
14 we have not obeyed his voice. 5
Mic 5:15 vengeance upon the nations that did not obey. 5
Hag 1:12 the people, obeyed the voice of the LORD their God 5
Zec 6:15 if you will diligently obey the voice of the LORD 5
Mat 8:27 that even winds and sea obey him? 24
Mrk 1:27 they obey him. 24
4:41 Who then is this, that even wind and sea obey him? 24
Lke 8:25 commands even wind and water, and they obey him? 24
17: 6 it would obey you. 24
Joh 3:36 he who does not obey the Son shall not see life 12
Act 5:29 We must obey God rather than men. 18
32 whom God has given to those who obey him. 18
7:39 Our fathers refused to obey him 25
Rom 2: 8 those who are factious and do not obey the truth 12
8 and do not obey the truth, but obey wickedness 19
25 Circumcision . . is of value if you obey the law; 22
6:12 to make you obey their passions. 24
16 you are slaves of the one whom you obey 24
10:16 But they have not all obeyed the gospel; 24
2Co 10: 5 take every thought captive to obey Christ 23
Gal 5: 7 who hindered you from obeying the truth? 19
Eph 6: 1 Children, obey your parents in the Lord 24
Php 2:12 Therefore, my beloved, as you have always obeyed 24
Col 3:20 Children, obey your parents in everything 24
22 Slaves, obey in everything 24
2Th 1: 8 who do not obey the gospel of our Lord Jesus. 24
3:14 any one refuses to obey what we say in this letter 24
Heb 5: 9 the source of . . salvation to all who obey him 24
11: 8 By faith Abraham obeyed 24
13:17 Obey your leaders and submit to them 19
Jas 3: 3 that they may obey us 19
1Pe 3: 1 though they do not obey the word 12
6 as Sarah obeyed Abraham, calling him lord. 24
20 who formerly did not obey 12
4:17 the end of those who do not obey the gospel of God? 12
1Jn 5: 2 when we love God and obey his commandments. 20
1Es 4: 3 whatever he says to them they obey. 14
10 All his people and his armies obey him 14
12 since he is to be obeyed in this fashion? 15
5:69 For we obey your Lord just as you do 11
8:94 to you and to all who obey the law of the Lord. 18
2Es 1: 8 for they have not obeyed my law 27
24 You would not obey me, O Judah. 26
Jdt 2: 3 every one who had not obeyed his command 10
Sir 3: 6 whoever obeys the Lord will refresh his mother; 13
4:15 He who obeys her will judge the nations 24
24:22 Whoever obeys me will not be put to shame 24
33:28 if he does not obey, make his fetters heavy. 18
Bar 2:10 Yet we have not obeyed his voice, to walk 11
22 But if you will not obey the voice of the Lord 11
24 we did not obey thy voice, to serve the king 11
29 If you will not obey my voice, this very great 11
30 For I know that they will not obey me, for they are 11
31 give them a heart that obeys and ears that hear; 11
3:33 he . . called it, and it obeyed him in fear; 24
Aza 1: 6 have not obeyed thy commandments; 11
1Mc 1:50 whoever does not obey the command of the king 21
2:19 Even if all the nations . . obey him 11
22 We will not obey the king's words 11
10:38 obey no other authority but the high priest. 24
12:43 commanded his friends and his troops to obey him 24
14:43 that he should be obeyed by all 11
2Mc 7:30 I will not obey the king's command 24
30 I obey the command of the law 11
4Mc 6: 4 Obey the king's commands! 19
8: 6 so I can be a benefactor to those who obey me. 17
17 to accept kind treatment if we obey him 19
26 when we can live in peace if we obey the king? 19
10:13 obey the king and save yourself. 19
12: 4 You too, if you do not obey, will be . . tortured 19
6 to obey and save himself. 16
15:10 they obeyed her even to death 19
18: 1 obey this law and exercise piety in every way 19

object 1. כְּלִי 2. σκεῦος

Exd 35:22 rings and armlets, all sorts of gold objects 1
Num 4:32 shall assign by name the objects which they 1
Ps 31:11 an object of dread to my acquaintances; •
Ezk 5:14 make you a desolation and an object of reproach •
16:57 you have become like her an object of reproach •
23:46 and make them an object of terror and a spoil. •
Wis 14:21 men . . bestowed on objects of stone or wood the name •
15: 6 and fit for such objects of hope •
Sir 38:28 his eyes are on the pattern of the object 2

object (2) 1. ἀντιλέγω

Act 28:19 when the Jews objected 1
3Mc 2:28 Those who object to this are to be taken by force 1

object of astonishment 1. שַׁמָּה

2Ch 29: 8 made them an object of . . astonishment 1

object of hissing 1. שְׁרֵקָה

2Ch 29: 8 he has made them an object of . . hissing 1

object of horror 1. זַעֲוָה

2Ch 29: 8 he has made them an object of horror 1

object of pity 1. ἔλεον

3Mc 4: 4 the common object of pity before their eyes 1

object of scorn 1. חֶרְפָּה

Ps 109:25 I am an object of scorn to my accusers; 1
Jer 6:10 the word of the LORD is to them an object of scorn 1

object of worship 1. σέβασμα

Act 17:23 and observed the objects of your worship 1
2Th 2: 4 every so-called god or object of worship 1
Wis 14:20 the multitude . . now regarded as an object of worship 1

object one worships 1. σέβασμα

Wis 15:17 he is better than the objects he worships 1

without objection 1. ἀναντιρρήτως

Act 10:29 So when I was sent for, I came without objection 1

oblation 1. מִנְחָה 2. προσφορά 3. oblatio

1Kg 18:29 until the time of the offering of the oblation 1
36 at the time of the offering of the oblation 1
2Es 1:31 When you offer oblations to me, I will turn my face 3
3:24 in it to offer thee oblations from what is thine. 3
Aza 1:15 no burnt offering, or sacrifice, or oblation 2

obligate

Neh 10:35 obligate ourselves to bring the first fruits •

obligation 1. מִצְוָה 2. δίκαιος 3. φύλαγμα

Neh 10:32 lay upon ourselves the obligation to charge 1
1Mc 8:26 they shall keep their obligations 3
28 they shall keep these obligations 3
11:33 who . . fulfil their obligations to us 2

obligation *See also* free.

under obligation 1. ὀφειλέτης

Rom 1:14 I am under obligation both to Greeks 1

oblige 1. συγκλείω

1Ch 9:25 were obliged to come in every seven days •
2Mc 8:25 obliged to return because the hour was late. 1

obscure 1. עָמֵק 2. ἀμαυρός

Isa 33:19 the people of an obscure speech which you cannot 1
Wis 4:12 obscures what is good 2

obscure man 1. חָשֹׁךְ

Prv 22:29 he will not stand before obscure men. 1

obscurity 1. αἴνιγμα

Sir 39: 3 be at home with the obscurities of parables 1

observance 1. עשה 2. ἄγω 3. φυλάσσω

Neh 9:29 ordinances, by the observance of which a man 1
Ezk 20:11 ordinances, by whose observance man shall live. 1
13 ordinances, by whose observance man shall live; 1
21 ordinances, by whose observance man shall live; 1
Act 16: 4 delivered to them for observance the decisions 3
21:24 you yourself live in observance of the law. 3
3Mc 3: 2 the observance of their customs. •
6:36 instituted the observance of the . . days 2

observance of the law 1. εὐνομία

4Mc 3:20 because of their observance of the law 1
4:24 to put an end to the people's observance of the law 1
18: 4 by reviving observance of the law in the homeland 1

observe 1. בין 2. ידע 3. נצר 4. פקד 5. ראה 6. שכל 7. שמר 8. ἀναθεωρέω 9. ἐπιβλέπω 10. ἐπιθεωρέω 11. θεωρέω 12. κατανοέω 13. ὁράω 14. παρακολουθέω 15. provideo

Exd 3:16 I have observed you and what has been done to you 4
1Sm 1:12 As she continued . . Eli observed her mouth. 7
2Sm 20:10 But Ama'sa did not observe the sword which was 7
Rut 3: 4 when he lies down, observe the place where he lies; 2
Job 39: 1 Do you observe the calving of the hinds? 7
Ps 33:15 of them all, and observes all their deeds. 1
Prv 21:12 The righteous observes the house of the wicked; 6
23: 1 observe carefully what is before you; 1
26 My son . . let your eyes observe my ways. 3
Ecc 8: 9 All this I observed while applying my mind to all 5
11: 4 He who observes the wind will not sow; 7
Isa 42:20 He sees many things, but does not observe them; 7
Jer 33:24 you not observed what these people are saying 5
Dan 1:13 let our appearance . . be observed by you 5
Act 11: 6 I observed animals and beasts of prey 13
17:23 and observed the objects of your worship 8
2Ti 3:10 Now you have observed my teaching, my conduct 14
Jas 1:23 a man who observes his natural face in a mirror; 12
24 he observes himself and goes away 12
2Es 6:32 and has also observed the purity 15
Jdt 10:14 heard her words, and observed her face 12
Sir 11:30 like a spy he observes your weakness; 9
24:34 Observe that I have not labored for myself alone 13
1Mc 4:35 and observed the boldness •
2Mc 9:23 I observed that . . 11
3Mc 1:27 When those who were around him observed this 11
6:17 when the Jews observed this 11
4Mc 1:30 Observe now first of all 10
14:13 Observe how complex is a mother's love 11

observe (2) 1. חגג 2. נצר 3. עשׂה 4. קום 5. שׁמר 6. ἄγω 7. ἀσκέω 8. διαφυλάσσω 9. ἐννοέω 10. ἐπί 11. κρατέω 12. παρατηρέω 13. περιπατέω 14. ποιέω 15. ποιητής 16. συντηρέω 17. τηρέω 18. φρονέω 19. φυλάσσω 20. χράομαι 21. custodio 22. observo

Exd 12:14 you shall observe it as an ordinance for ever. 1
17 you shall observe the feast of unleavened bread 5
17 therefore you shall observe this day 5
24 You shall observe this rite as an ordinance 5
27:21 It shall be a statute for ever to be observed •
31:16 observing the sabbath throughout 3
34:11 Observe what I command you this day. 5
22 you shall observe the feast of weeks 3
Lev 19:37 And you shall observe all my statutes 5
23:24 you shall observe a day of solemn rest •
26: 3 walk in my statutes and observe my commandments 5
Num15:22 err, and do not observe all these commandments 3
Deu 5:12 'Observe the sabbath day, to keep it holy 5
16: 1 Observe the month of Abib, and keep the passover 5
12 you shall be careful to observe these statutes. 3
33: 9 they observed thy word, and kept they covenant. 5
Jos 22: 5 Take good care to observe the commandment 3
Jdg 13:14 thing; all that I commanded her let her observe. 5
1Ch 22:13 to observe the statutes and the ordinances 3
28: 8 observe and seek out all the commandments 5
Neh 10:29 observe and do all the commandments of the LORD 5
Est 9:31 that these days of Purim should be observed 4
Ps 78:56 did not observe his testimonies 5
105:45 to the end that they should . . observe his laws. 2
106: 3 Blessed are they who observe justice 5
119: 8 I will observe thy statutes; O forsake me not 5
17 that I may live and observe thy word. 5
34 keep thy law and observe it with my whole heart. 5
106an oath . . to observe thy righteous ordinances. 5
146save me, that I may observe thy testimonies. 5
Ezk 18: 9 and is careful to observe my ordinances 3
17 observes my ordinances, and walks in my statutes; 3
19 and has been careful to observe all my statutes 5
20:18 nor observe their ordinances, nor defile 5
19 and be careful to observe my ordinances 3
21 and were not careful to observe my ordinances 5
36:27 and be careful to observe my ordinances. 5
37:24 and be careful to observe my statutes. 5
43:11 that they may observe and perform all its laws 5
Mat 19:20 All these I have observed 19
23: 3 so practice and observe whatever they tell you 17
28:20 teaching them to observe all 17
Mrk 7: 3 observing the tradition of the elders; 11
4 many other traditions which they observe 11
10:20 Teacher, all these I have observed from my youth. 19
Lke 18:21 he said, "All these I have observed from my youth. 19
Act 21:21 not to circumcise . . or observe the customs. 13
Rom14: 6 He who observes the day, observes it in honor 18
6 the day, observes it in honor of the Lord. 18
Gal 4:10 You observe days, and months, and seasons 12
2Es 7:21 what they should observe to avoid punishment. 22
9:32 did not keep it, and did not observe the statutes; 21
15:24 do not observe my commandments," says the Lord; 22
AEs 10:13 observe these days in the month of Adar •
16:22 you shall observe this with all good cheer 6
Wis 6:10 they will be made holy who observe holy things 19
Sir 4:20 Observe the right time, and beware of evil 16
23: 7 the one who observes it will never be caught. 19
38:17 observe the mourning according to his merit 14
41:14 My children, observe instruction and be at peace; 16
Aza 1: 7 we have not observed them or done them 16
1Mc 1:13 observe the ordinances of the Gentiles. 14
2:61 so observe, from generation to generation 9
67 You shall rally about you all who observe the law 15
4:59 observed with gladness and joy for eight days 6
13:48 settled in it men who observed the law 14
2Mc 3: 1 the laws were very well observed 16
6: 6 nor observe the feasts of his fathers 8
11 to observe the seventh day secretly 6
10: 8 should observe these days every year. 6
13:23 yielded and swore to observe all their rights 10
15: 4 who ordered us to observe the seventh day 7
3Mc 7:19 they decided to observe these days 6
4Mc 5: 7 when you observe the religion of the Jews. 20

observe a sign 1. παρατήρησις

Lke 17:20 is not coming with signs to be observed; 1

observe intently 1. ἀτενίζω

3Mc 2:26 intently observing the king's purpose 1

observe the law 1. πολιτεύω

4Mc 4:23 if any . . should be found observing the ancestral law 1

observer 1. ἐπισκοπός

Wis 1: 6 a true observer of his heart 1

obsolete *See* treat.

become obsolete 1. παλαιόω

Heb 8:13 what is becoming obsolete and growing old 1

obstacle 1. ἐγκοπή 2. ἐπαίρω 3. πρόσκομμα

1Co 9:12 we endure anything rather than put an obstacle 1
2Co 10: 5 every proud obstacle to the knowledge of God 2
Sir 39:24 just as they are obstacles to the wicked. 3

obstacle in the way 1. προσκοπή

2Co 6: 3 We put no obstacle in any one's way 1

obstinacy 1. στερέωσις

Sir 28:10 in proportion to the obstinacy of strife 1

obstinate 1. קָשֶׁה

Isa 48: 4 Because I know that you are obstinate 1

obstinate *See also* make.

obstruction 1. מִכְשׁוֹל

Isa 57:14 remove every obstruction from my people's way. 1

obtain 1. חזק 2. מצא 3. נשׂג 4. פוק 5. תמך 6. εἰς 7. ἐπιτυγχάνω 8. ἔχω 9. ἵστημι 10. κατακληρονομέω 11. καταλαμβάνω 12. κατέχω 13. κληρονομέω 14. κομίζω 15. κρατέω 16. κτάομαι 17. λαγχάνω 18. λαμβάνω 19. περιποιέω 20. περιποίησις 21. στέλλω 22. τυγχάνω 23. φέρω 24. consequor 25. inpetro

Prv 8:35 he who finds me . . obtains favor from the LORD; 4
12: 2 A good man obtains favor from the LORD 4
18:22 finds a wife . . obtains favor from the LORD. 4
29:23 but he who is lowly in spirit will obtain honor. 5
Isa 35:10 they shall obtain joy and gladness 3
51:11 they shall obtain joy and gladness 3
Lam 2: 9 and her prophets obtain no vision from the LORD. 2
Dan 11:21 obtain the kingdom by flatteries. 1
Act 8:20 you could obtain the gift of God with money! 16
20:28 which he obtained with the blood of his own Son. 19
27:13 supposing that they had obtained their purpose 15
Rom 5: 2 we have obtained access to this grace 9
8:21 and obtain the glorious liberty 6
11: 7 Israel failed to obtain what it sought. 7
7 The elect obtained it, but the rest were hardened 7
1Co 9:24 So run that you may obtain it. 11
Php 3:12 Not that I have already obtained this 18
1Th 5: 9 to obtain salvation through our Lord Jesus 20
2Th 2:14 may obtain the glory of our Lord Jesus Christ. 20
2Ti 2:10 they also may obtain salvation in Christ Jesus 22
Heb 1: 4 the name he has obtained 13
14 for the sake of those who are to obtain salvation? 13
6:15 thus Abraham . . obtained the promise. 7
8: 6 Christ has obtained a ministry 22
Jas 4: 2 you covet and cannot obtain; so you fight 7
1Pe 1: 9 you obtain the salvation of your souls. 14
3: 9 that you may obtain a blessing. 13
5: 4 you will obtain the unfading crown of glory. 14
2Pe 1: 1 obtained a faith of equal standing with ours 17
1Jn 5:15 we have obtained the requests made of him. 8
2Es 4:24 and we are not worthy to obtain mercy. 24
5:12 at that time men shall hope but not obtain 25
7:72 and though they obtained the law 24
14:34 and after death you shall obtain mercy. 24
Tob 5: 2 how can I obtain the money 18
12: 3 he obtained the money for me 23
Wis 7:14 those who get it obtain friendship with God 21
Sir 4:13 Whoever holds her fast will obtain glory 13
16 If he has faith in her he will obtain her 10
15: 1 he who holds to the law will obtain wisdom. 11
7 Foolish men will not obtain her 11
22: 4 A sensible daughter obtains her husband 13
46: 9 his children obtained it for an inheritance; 12
2Mc 4:32 he had obtained a suitable opportunity 18
3Mc 2:33 They remained resolutely hopeful of obtaining help 22

obtain *See also* fail.

obtain a child 1. בנה

Gen 16: 2 may be . . I shall obtain children by her. 1

obtain an inheritance 1. נחל

Jos 19: 9 Simeon obtained an inheritance in the midst 1

obtain by corruption 1. ὑπονοθεύω

2Mc 4: 7 Jason . . obtained the high priesthood by corruption 1

obtain fresh 1. יסף

Isa 29:19 The meek shall obtain fresh joy in the LORD 1

obtain mercy 1. רחם 2. ἐλεέω

Prv 28:13 confesses and forsakes them will obtain mercy. 1
Mat 5: 7 the merciful, for they shall obtain mercy. 2

obtain pity 1. רחם

Hos 2: 1 and to your sister, "She has obtained pity. 1

obtain release 1. ἀποδίδωμι

1Mc 9:70 and obtain release of the captives. 1

wrongfully obtain 1. ἄδικος

Sir 34:18 what has been wrongfully obtained 1

obvious 1. ἐπιπόλαιος

3Mc 2:31 an obvious abhorrence of the price to be exacted 1

obvious *See also* spectacle.

obviously 1. εἰκότως 2. φαίνω

4Mc 1:32 reason obviously rules over both. 2
9: 2 we are obviously putting our forefathers to shame 1

occasion 1. תֹּאֲנָה 2. תְּנוּאָה 3. ἀφορμή 4. καιρός 5. τόπος

Jdg 14: 4 seeking an occasion against the Philistines. 1
1Sm 22:22 I have occasioned the death of all the persons •
Ezr 7:20 which you have occasion to provide •
Job 33:10 Behold, he finds occasions against me 2
1Ti 5:14 give the enemy no occasion to revile us. 3
Heb 8: 7 there would have been no occasion for a second. 5
Tob 4:19 Bless the Lord God on every occasion 4
Sir 4: 5 nor give a man occasion to curse you; 5
29: 3 on every occasion you will find what you need. 4
1Mc 8:25 as the occasion may indicate to them. 4
27 as the occasion may indicate to them. 4
12:11 remember you constantly on every occasion 4
2Mc 9:23 on the occasions when he made expeditions 4
4Mc 3:19 The present occasion now invites us 4

occasion *See also* fit, seek.

occasion offers 1. מצא יָד

Jdg 9:33 you, you may do to them as occasion offers. 1

occasion to laugh 1. γέλως

4Mc 5:28 you shall have no such occasion to laugh at me 1

occupant 1. εἰμί ἐν

1Mc 13:11 he drove out its occupants and remained there. 1

occupation 1. מְלָאכָה 2. מַעֲשֶׂה 3. ἀσχολία 4. περί

Gen 46:33 When Pharaoh . . says, 'What is your occupation? 2
47: 3 is your occupation?" And they said to Pharaoh 2
Jon 1: 8 What is your occupation? And whence do you come? 1
Act 19:25 with the workmen of like occupation 4
3Mc 5:34 each to his own occupation. 3

occupied *See* keep.

occupy 1. הלך 2. ἀναστρέφω 3. προσέχω 4. συνέχω

Ps 131: 1 I do not occupy myself with things too great 1
Act 18: 5 Paul was occupied with preaching 4
1Ti 1: 4 nor to occupy themselves with myths 3
Sir 38:25 who drives oxen and is occupied with their work 2

occupy (2) 1. בוא 2. ירשׁ 3. καταλαμβάνω 4. κατέχω 5. κρατέω 6. προκαταλαμβάνω

Num13:30 Caleb . . said, "Let us go up at once, and occupy it; 2
Deu 2:31 take possession, that you may occupy his land.' 2
3:20 occupy the land which the LORD your God gives 2
Neh 2: 8 make beams . . for the house which I shall occupy. 1
1Es 4:50 all the country which they would occupy 5
Jdt 5:19 have occupied Jerusalem 4
1Mc 10: 1 landed and occupied Ptolemais 3
2Mc 10:36 they occupied the city. 6

occupy ground 1. ἐμβατεύω

2Mc 2:30 the duty . . to occupy the ground 1

occur 1. γίνομαι 2. εἰμί 3. ἥκω 4. παρέρχομαι 5. ὑποπίπτω 6. contingo 7. facio

Act 13:12 when he saw what had occurred 1
Heb 9:15 since a death has occurred which redeems them 1
1Es 8:18 whatever else occurs to you as necessary 5
2Es 9: 5 everything that has occurred in the world 7
13:32 and the signs occur which I showed you before 6
AEs 10: 9 wonders, which have not occurred among the nations 1
Wis 11:12 groaning at the memory of what had occurred. 4
Sir 20:18 the downfall of the wicked will occur speedily. 3
48:25 He revealed what was to occur to the end of time 2
1Mc 9:24 In those days a very great famine occurred 1
14:29 Since wars often occurred in the country 1
3Mc 1:17 something mysterious was occurring. 1

odious 1. εἰδέχθεια

Wis 16: 3 because of the odious creatures sent to them 1

odious *See also* make.

become odious 1. באשׁ

1Sm 13: 4 Israel had become odious to the Philistines. 1
2Sm 10: 6 Ammonites saw . . they had become odious to David 1

odor 1. רֵיחַ 2. ὄζω 3. ὀσμή 4. odor

Gen 8:21 when the LORD smelled the pleasing odor 1
Exd 29:18 it is a pleasing odor, an offering by fire 1
25 burn them . . as a pleasing odor before the LORD; 1
41 for a pleasing odor, an offering by fire 1
Lev 1: 9 an offering by fire, a pleasing odor to the LORD 1
13 offering by fire, a pleasing odor to the LORD 1
17 offering by fire, a pleasing odor to the LORD 1
2: 2 an offering by fire, a pleasing odor to the LORD 1
9 an offering by fire, a pleasing odor to the LORD 1

12 be offered on the altar for a pleasing odor 1
3: 5 offering by fire, a pleasing odor to the LORD 1
16 as food offered by fire for a pleasing odor 1
4:31 upon the altar for a pleasing odor to the LORD 1
6:15 on the altar, a pleasing odor to the LORD 1
21 offer it for a pleasing odor to the LORD 1
8:21 burned . . as a burnt offering, a pleasing odor 1
28 a pleasing odor, an offering by fire to the LORD 1
17: 6 and burn the fat for a pleasing odor to the LORD 1
23:13 to be offered by fire to the LORD, a pleasing odor 1
18 an offering by fire, a pleasing odor to the LORD 1
26:31 I will not smell your pleasing odors 1
Num15: 3 to make a pleasing odor to the LORD 1
7 a pleasing odor to the LORD. 1
10 offering by fire, a pleasing odor to the LORD. 1
13 offering by fire, a pleasing odor to the LORD. 1
14 offering by fire, a pleasing odor to the LORD 1
24 a burnt offering, a pleasing odor to the LORD 1
18:17 offering by fire, a pleasing odor to the LORD; 1
28: 2 food for my offerings by fire, my pleasing odor 1
6 ordained at Mount Sinai for a pleasing odor 1
8 offering by fire, a pleasing odor to the LORD. 1
13 for a burnt offering of pleasing odor 1
24 offering by fire, a pleasing odor to the LORD; 1
27 burnt offering, a pleasing odor to the LORD; 1
29: 2 a burnt offering, a pleasing odor to the LORD 1
6 a pleasing odor, an offering by fire to the LORD. 1
8 burnt offering to the LORD, a pleasing odor 1
13 offering by fire, a pleasing odor to the LORD 1
36 offering by fire, a pleasing odor to the LORD 1
Ezk 6:13 they offered pleasing odor to all their idols. 1
16:19 and honey–you set before them for a pleasing odor 1
20:28 there they sent up their soothing odors 1
41 As a pleasing odor I will accept you 1
Joh 11:39 by this time there will be an odor 2
2Es 6:44 and odors of inexpressible fragrance 4
Tob 8: 3 when the demon smelled the odor 3
odor *See also* make.

evil odor 1. באשׁ
Ecc 10: 1 Dead flies make . . ointment give off an evil odor; 1

pleasant odor 1. εὐωδία
Sir 24:15 like choice myrrh I spread a pleasant odor 1

pleasing odor 1. εὐωδία
1Es 1:12 in brass pots and caldrons, with a pleasing odor 1
Sir 35: 6 its pleasing odor rises before the Most High. 1
45:16 incense and a pleasing odor 1
50:15 a pleasing odor to the Most High, the King of all. 1

off 1. מִן 2. מֵעַל 3. מִשָּׁם 4. עַל 5. ἀπό 6. ἐκ 7. κατά
Gen 8:13 the waters were dried from off the earth; 4
Lev 14: 9 he shall shave all his hair off his head •
Num16:46 censer, and put fire therein from off the altar 4
Deu 6:15 destroy you from off the face of the earth. 4
11:17 perish quickly off the good land which the LORD 2
28:21 until he has consumed you off the land which you 2
63 you shall be plucked off the land 2
Jos 23:13 till you perish from off this good land 4
15 destroyed you from off this good land 4
16 you shall perish quickly from off the good land 4
Jdg 15:14 caught fire, and his bonds melted off his hands. 1
16:12 he snapped the ropes off his arms like a thread. 2
1Sm 6: 5 lighten his hand from off you and your gods 4
2Sm 17:23 saddled his ass, and went off home to his own city. •
2Kg 16:17 and he took down the sea from off the bronze oxen 4
24:13 and carried off all the treasures 3
Job 24: 4 They thrust the poor off the road; 1
Prv 30:14 to devour the poor from off the earth, the needy 1
Ecc 7:24 That which is, is far off, and deep, very deep; •
Jer 22:24 ring on my right hand, yet I would tear you off 3
28:12 had broken the yoke-bars from off the neck 2
30: 8 that I will break the yoke from off their neck 2
Ezk 45: 3 you shall measure off a section 1
Mic 3: 2 who tear the skin from off my people 4
2 who tear . . their flesh from off their bones; 4
3 of my people, and flay their skin from off them 4
Nah 1:13 And now I will break his yoke from off you 4
Joh 11:18 Bethany was near Jerusalem, about two miles off 5
21: 8 about 100 yards off. 5
Act 12: 7 the chains fell off his hands. 6
27: 5 the sea which is off Cili'cia and Pamphyl'ia 7
7 arrived with difficulty off Cni'dus 7
7 sailed under the lee of Crete off Salmo'ne. 7
Jdt 13: 9 Then she tumbled his body off the bed 5
off *See also* afar, bad, beat, better, break, carry, cast, cut, drag, draw, drive, drop, fall, far, fight, get, give, go, hasten, lead, leave, march, mark, pay, pluck, pull, put, remove, rinse, round, run, rush, scale, scrape, send, set, shake, shave, shut, strip, take, tear, throw, ward, wash, way, wear, well, wipe, wring.

off duty
2Kg 11: 5 those who come off duty on the sabbath •
9 his men who were to go off duty on the sabbath •
2Ch 23: 4 of you priests and Levites who come off duty •
8 men, who were to go off duty on the sabbath •

off guard 1. בֶּטַח
Jdg 8:11 attacked the army; for the army was off its guard. 1

offend 1. אשׁם 2. חבל 3. חטא 4. לאה 5. ἀδικέω 6. ἁμαρτάνω 7. πλημμελέω 8. προσκόπτω 9. προσοχθίζω 10. σκανδαλίζω 11. pecco
Gen 40: 1 and his baker offended their lord the king 3
Job 4: 2 one ventures a word with you, will you be offended? 4
34:31 borne chastisement; I will not offend any more; 2
Ezk 25:12 has grievously offended in taking vengeance 1
Mat 15:12 Do you know that the Pharisees were offended 10
Act 25: 8 nor against Caesar have I offended at all. 6
2Es 12:41 How have we offended you 11
Sir 7: 7 Do not offend against the public 6
23:11 if he offends, his sin remains on him 7
25: 2 I am greatly offended at their life 9
30:13 you may not be offended by his shamelessness. 8
LJr 1:14 though unable to destroy any one who offends it. 6
18 a man who has offended a king 5

offender 1. חַטָּא 2. ὀφειλέτης
1Kg 1:21 I and my son Solomon will be counted offenders. 1
Lke 13: 4 worse offenders than all the others 2
offender *See also* make.

offense 1. חֵטְא 2. נֶגֶף 3. פֶּשַׁע 4. רִשְׁעָה 5. ἁμάρτημα 6. πρόσκομμα 7. προσόχθισμα 8. σκάνδαλον
Gen 31:36 Jacob said to Laban, "What is my offense? 3
Deu 19:15 for any wrong in connection with any offense 1
22:26 woman there is no offense punishable by death 1
25: 2 number of stripes in proportion to his offense. 4
Prv 10:12 but love covers all offenses. 3
17: 9 He who forgives an offense seeks love 3
19:11 it is his glory to overlook an offense. 3
Ecc 10: 4 deference will make amends for great offenses. 1
Isa 8:14 he will become a sanctuary, and a stone of offense 2
Jdt 5:20 and we find out their offense 8
8:22 we shall be an offense and a reproach 6
12: 2 Judith said, "I cannot eat it, lest it be an offense; 8
Sir 17:25 pray in his presence and lessen your offenses. 6
27:23 with your own words he will give offense. 8
Man 1:10 multiplying offenses. 7
1Mc 13:39 We pardon any errors and offenses committed 5
offense *See also* commit, give, take.

no offense 1. ἀπρόσκοπος
1Co 10:32 Give no offense to Jews or to Greeks 1

unwitting offense 1. ἀγνόημα
Tob 3: 3 do not punish me . . for my unwitting offenses 1

offensive 1. προσόχθισμα
Sir 27:13 The talk of fools is offensive 1
3Mc 2:18 as offensive houses are trampled down.' 1
offensive *See also* make.

offer 1. זבח 2. זֶבַח 3. מצא 4. נגשׁ 5. נוף 6. נטה 7. נטל 8. נשׂא 9. נתן 10. עלה 11. עשׂה 12. פלל 13. פשׂק 14. פתח 15. קטר 16. קרא 17. קרב 18. רום 19. שׁחט 20. תְּרוּמָה 21. דבח (A) 22. קרב (A) 23. ἀνάγω 24. ἀναφέρω 25. δίδωμι 26. θύω 27. καρπόω 28. παρέχω 29. ποιέω 30. προσάγω 31. προσφερής 32. προσφέρω 33. συντελέω 34. offero 35. porrigo
Gen 8:20 Noah . . offered burnt offerings on the altar. 10
22: 2 and offer him there as a burnt offering 10
Exd 18:12 Jethro . . offered a burnt offering •
22:29 You shall not delay to offer from the fulness •
23:18 You shall not offer the blood of my sacrifice 1
24: 5 young men . . who offered burnt offerings 10
29:27 which is offered from the ram of ordination 18
28 portion to be offered by the people of Israel 20
36 every day you shall offer a bull as a sin offering 11
38 Now this is what you shall offer upon the altar 11
39 One lamb you shall offer in the morning 11
39 the other lamb you shall offer in the evening; 11
41 the other lamb you shall offer in the evening 11
41 shall offer with it a cereal offering 11
30: 9 You shall offer no unholy incense thereon 10
32: 6 offered burnt offerings and brought peace 10
34:25 You shall not offer the blood of my sacrifice 19
40:29 offered upon it the burnt offering 10
Lev 1: 3 he shall offer a male without blemish 17
3 he shall offer it at the door of the tent 17
10 he shall offer a male without blemish 17
13 the priest shall offer the whole, and burn it 17
2:12 they shall not be offered on the altar 10
13 with all your offerings you shall offer salt 17
14 If you offer a cereal offering of first fruits 17
14 you shall offer for the cereal offering 17
3: 1 if he offers an animal from the herd 17
1 shall offer it without blemish before the LORD 17
3 he shall offer the fat covering the entrails 17
6 animal . . he shall offer it without blemish 17
7 If he offers a lamb for his offering 17
7 then he shall offer it before the LORD 17
9 he shall offer its fat, the fat tail entire 17
12 then he shall offer it before the LORD 17
14 Then he shall offer from it, as his offering 17
4: 3 let him offer for the sin which he has committed 17
14 shall offer a young bull for a sin offering 17
5: 8 who shall offer first the one for the sin offering 17
10 he shall offer the second for a burnt offering 11
6:14 The sons of Aaron shall offer it before the LORD 17
20 which Aaron and his sons shall offer to the LORD 17
21 offer it for a pleasing odor to the LORD 17
22 priest . . shall offer it to the LORD as decreed 11
7: 3 all its fat shall be offered, the fat tail 17
8 the priest who offers any man's burnt offering 17
8 skin of the burnt offering which he has offered 17
9 all . . shall belong to the priest who offers it 17
11 peace offerings which one may offer to the LORD 17
12 If he offers it for a thanksgiving 17
12 then he shall offer with the thank offering 17
14 of such he shall offer one cake from each offering 17
16 on the day that he offers his sacrifice 17
18 he who offers it shall not be accepted 17
29 He that offers the sacrifice of his peace 17
33 he among the sons of Aaron who offers the blood 17
34 the thigh that is offered I have taken 20
9: 2 without blemish, and offer them before the LORD 17
7 offer your sin offering and your burnt offering 11
16 he presented the burnt offering, and offered it 11
22 he came down from offering the sin offering 11
10: 1 and offered unholy fire before the LORD 17
14 the thigh that is offered you shall eat 20
15 The thigh that is offered and the breast 20
19 today they have offered their sin offering 17
12: 7 he shall offer it before the LORD 17
14:12 male lambs, and offer it for a guilt offering 17
19 The priest shall offer the sin offering 11
20 the priest shall offer the burnt offering 10
30 he shall offer, of the turtledoves 11
15:15 and the priest shall offer them 11
30 the priest shall offer one for a sin offering 11
16: 6 Aaron shall offer the bull as a sin offering 17
9 the goat . . and offer it as a sin offering 11
24 and come forth, and offer his burnt offering 11
17: 4 to offer it as a gift to the LORD 17
8 who offers a burnt offering or sacrifice 10
19: 5 you shall offer it so that you may be accepted 1
6 It shall be eaten the same day you offer it 2
21: 6 for they offer the offerings by fire to the LORD 17
8 You shall consecrate him, for he offers the bread 17
17 None . . may approach to offer the bread 17
21 shall come near to offer the LORD'S offerings 17
21 not come near to offer the bread of his God 17
22:15 holy things . . which they offer to the LORD 18
18 freewill offering which is offered to the LORD 17
19 to be accepted you shall offer a male •
20 You shall not offer anything that has a blemish 17
21 when any one offers a sacrifice of peace 17
22 Animals . . you shall not offer to the LORD 17
24 you shall not offer to the LORD or sacrifice 17
25 neither shall you offer as the bread of your God 17
23:12 you shall offer a male lamb a year old 11
19 you shall offer one male goat for a sin offering 11
27: 9 If it is an animal such as men offer as an offering 17
11 if it is an unclean animal such as is not offered 17
Num 3: 4 died . . when they offered unholy fire 17
6:11 the priest shall offer one for a sin offering 11
14 he shall offer his gift to the LORD 17
16 offer his sin offering and his burnt offering 11
17 offer the ram as a sacrifice of peace offering 11
17 priest shall offer also its cereal offering 11
20 together with . . the thigh that is offered; 20
7: 3 offered and brought their offerings before •
3 offered them before the tabernacle. 17
10 leaders offered offerings for the dedication 17
10 leaders offered their offering before 17
11 shall offer their offering, one leader each day 17
12 offered his offering the first day was Nahshon 17
19 he offered for his offering one silver plate 17
8:11 Aaron shall offer the Levites before the LORD 5
12 shall offer the one for a sin offering 11
13 shall offer them as a wave offering to the LORD. 5
15 when you . . offered them as a wave offering. 5
21 Aaron offered them as a wave offering 5
9: 7 why are we kept from offering the LORD'S offering 17
13 because he did not offer the LORD'S offering 17
15: 3 offer to the LORD from the herd or from the flock 11
4 who brings his offering shall offer to the LORD 17
7 drink . . you shall offer a third of a hin of wine 17
9 one shall offer with the bull a cereal offering 17
10 offer for the drink offering half a hin of wine 17
13 in offering an offering by fire, a pleasing odor 17
14 wishes to offer an offering by fire, a pleasing 11
24 all the congregation shall offer one young bull 11
27 sins unwittingly, he shall offer a female goat 17
16:35 consumed the 250 men offering the incense. 17
38 for they offered them before the LORD 17
39 censers, which those who were burned had offered; 17
18:15 which they offer to the LORD, shall be yours; 17
30 When you have offered from it the best of it 18
32 bear no sin . . when you have offered the best 18

23: 2 Balak and Balaam offered . . a bull and a ram. 10
4 I have offered upon each altar a bull and a ram. 10
14 offered a bull and a ram on each altar. 10
30 Balak . . offered a bull and a ram on each altar. 10
26:61 when they offered unholy fire before the LORD. 17
28: 2 take heed to offer to me in its due season.' 17
3 offering by fire . . you shall offer to the LORD 17
4 The one lamb you shall offer in the morning 11
4 the other lamb you shall offer in the evening; 11
8 The other lamb you shall offer in the evening; 11
8 you shall offer it as an offering by fire 11
11 you shall offer a burnt offering to the LORD 17
15 offered besides the continual burnt offering 11
19 offer an offering by fire, a burnt offering 17
20 three tenths . . shall you offer for a bull 11
21 tenth shall you offer for each of the seven lambs; 11
23 offer these besides the burnt offering 11
24 same way you shall offer daily, for seven days 11
24 offered besides the continual burnt offering 11
26 when you offer a cereal offering of new grain 17
27 offer a burnt offering, a pleasing odor 17
31 you shall offer them and their drink offering. 11
29: 2 you shall offer a burnt offering, a pleasing odor 11
8 you shall offer a burnt offering to the LORD 17
13 you shall offer a burnt offering 17
36 you shall offer a burnt offering 17
39 These you shall offer to the LORD 11
31:52 all the gold of the offering that they offered 18
Deu 12:13 Take heed that you do not offer 10
14 there you shall offer your burnt offerings 10
27 offer . . burnt offerings, the flesh and the blood 11
16: 2 offer the passover sacrifice to the LORD 1
6 there you shall offer the passover sacrifice 1
18: 3 priests' due . . from those offering a sacrifice 1
20:10 city to fight against it, offer terms of peace 16
26:14 I have not . . offered any of it to the dead; 9
27: 6 offer burnt offerings on it to the LORD your God; 10
33:19 mountain; there they offer right sacrifices; 1
Jos 8:31 they offered on it burnt offerings to the LORD 10
22:23 to offer burnt offerings or cereal offerings 10
Jdg 6:26 take the . . bull, and offer it as a burnt offering 10
28 and the second bull was offered upon the altar 10
13:16 ready a burnt offering, then offer it to the LORD 10
19 took the kid . . and offered it upon the rock 10
20:26 evening, and offered burnt offerings and peace 10
21: 4 and offered burnt offerings and peace 10
1Sm 1:21 went up to offer to the LORD the yearly sacrifice 1
2:13 The custom . . when any man offered sacrifice 1
19 she went up . . to offer the yearly sacrifice. 1
6:14 offered the cows as a burnt offering to the LORD. 10
15 the men of Beth-she'mesh offered burnt offerings 10
7: 9 lamb and offered it as a whole burnt offering 10
10: 8 I am coming to you to offer burnt offerings 10
13: 9 And he offered the burnt offering. 10
10 as he had finished offering the burnt offering 10
12 forced myself, and offered the burnt offering. 10
2Sm 6:17 and David offered burnt . . and peace offerings 10
18 finished offering the burnt offerings 10
15:12 And while Ab'salom was offering the sacrifices 1
24:12 Three things I offer you; choose one of them 7
24 I will not offer burnt offerings to the LORD my God 10
25 offered burnt offerings and peace offerings. 10
1Kg 3: 4 Solomon used to offer . . burnt offerings 10
8:29 prayer which thy servant offers toward this 12
54 as Solomon finished offering all this prayer 12
62 Israel . . offered sacrifice before the LORD. 1
63 Solomon offered . . to the LORD 22,000 oxen 1
64 he offered the burnt offering and the cereal 11
10: 5 burnt offerings which he offered at the house 10
12:27 go up to offer sacrifices in the house of the LORD 11
32 and he offered sacrifices upon the altar; 10
18:29 until the time of the offering of the oblation 10
36 at the time of the offering of the oblation 10
2Kg 3:20 about the time of offering the sacrifice, behold 10
27 offered him for a burnt offering upon the wall. 10
5:17 your servant will not offer burnt offering 11
10:19 I have a great sacrifice to offer to Ba'al; *
24 Then he went in to offer sacrifices 11
25 So as soon as he had made an end of offering 11
17: 4 and offered no tribute to the king of Assyria 10
1Ch 16: 1 offered burnt offerings and peace offerings 17
2 finished offering the burnt offerings 10
40 to offer burnt offerings to the LORD 10
21:10 'Thus says the LORD, Three things I offer you; 6
24 nor offer burnt offerings which cost me 10
23:31 burnt offerings are offered to the LORD 10
29:21 the next day offered burnt offerings to the LORD 10
2Ch 1: 6 offered 1,000 burnt offerings upon it. 10
6:20 hearken to the prayer which thy servant offers 12
7: 4 the king and all the people offered sacrifice 1
5 King Solomon offered as a sacrifice 1
7 for there he offered the burnt offering 11
8:13 offering according to the commandment of Moses 10
9: 4 burnt offerings which he offered at the house 10
13:11 They offer to the LORD . . burnt offerings 15
23:18 to offer burnt offerings to the LORD 10
24:14 offered burnt offerings in the house of the LORD 10
29: 7 not burned incense or offered burnt offerings 10
21 to offer them on the altar of the LORD. 10

27 commanded that the burnt offering be offered 10
29 When the offering was finished, the king 10
33:16 offered upon it sacrifices of peace offerings 1
35:12 burnt offerings . . to offer to the LORD 17
14 busied in offering the burnt offerings 10
16 to offer burnt offerings on the altar of the LORD 10
Ezr 3: 2 altar . . to offer burnt offerings upon it 10
3 offered burnt offerings upon it to the LORD 10
4 offered the daily burnt offerings by number 11
6 began to offer burnt offerings to the LORD. 10
6: 3 place where sacrifices are offered 21
17 offered at the dedication of this house of God 22
7:17 offer them upon the altar of the house of your God 22
8:25 all Israel there present had offered; 18
35 returned exiles, offered burnt offerings 17
Neh 12:43 offered great sacrifices that day and rejoiced 1
Job 1: 5 offer burnt offerings according to the number 10
Ps 4: 5 Offer right sacrifices, and put your trust 1
27: 6 I will offer in his tent sacrifices with shouts 1
51:19 then bulls will be offered on thy altar. 10
66:15 I will offer to thee burnt offerings of fatlings 10
106:28 ate sacrifices offered to the dead; *
107:22 let them offer sacrifices of thanksgiving 1
116:17 offer to thee the sacrifice of thanksgiving 1
Prv 7:14 I had to offer sacrifices *
Ecc 5: 1 is better than to offer the sacrifice of fools; 9
Sng 8: 7 a man offered for love all the wealth of his house 9
Isa 57: 7 and thither you went up to offer sacrifice. 1
66: 3 a cereal . . like him who offers swine's blood; *
Jer 14:12 they offer burnt offering and cereal offering 10
33:18 a man in my presence to offer burnt offerings 10
48:35 him who offers sacrifice in the high place 10
Ezk 3: 1 he said to me, "Son of man, eat what is offered to you; 3
6:13 they offered pleasing odor to all their idols. 9
16:25 offering yourself to any passer-by 13
20:28 there they offered their sacrifices 1
31 you offer your gifts and sacrifice your sons 8
43:18 when it is erected for offering burnt offerings 10
22 on the second day you shall offer a he-goat 17
23 you shall offer a bull without blemish 17
27 the priests shall offer upon the altar 11
44: 7 when you offer to me my food, the fat and the blood. 17
15 attend on me to offer me the fat and the blood 17
27 he shall offer his sin offering, says the Lord GOD 17
46: 2 The priests shall offer his burnt offering 11
4 offering that the prince offers to the LORD 17
6 day of the new moon he shall offer a young bull *
12 he shall offer his burnt offering 11
Ams 5:22 Even though you offer me your burnt offerings 10
8: 5 And the sabbath, that we may offer wheat for sale 14
Jon 1:16 they offered a sacrifice to the LORD 1
Hag 2:14 what they offer there is unclean. 17
Mal 1: 7 By offering polluted food upon my altar. 4
8 When you offer blind animals in sacrifice 4
8 when you offer those that are lame or sick 4
11 in every place incense is offered to my name 4
Mat 2:11 opening their treasures, they offered him gifts 32
5:24 your brother, and then come and offer your gift. 32
8: 4 and offer the gift that Moses commanded 32
27:34 they offered him wine to drink, mingled with gall; 25
Mrk 1:44 and offer for your cleansing what Moses commanded 32
15:23 they offered him wine mingled with myrrh 25
Lke 2:24 to offer a sacrifice 25
5:33 disciples of John fast often and offer prayers 29
6:29 offer the other also 28
Act 7:41 offered a sacrifice to the idol 23
42 Did you offer to me slain beasts and sacrifices 32
8:18 he offered them money 32
Rom 11:16 If the dough offered as first fruits is holy *
1Co 10:20 they offer to demons and not to God 26
Heb 5: 1 to offer gifts and sacrifices for sins. 32
7:27 He has no need . . to offer sacrifices daily 24
8: 3 every high priest is appointed to offer gifts 32
3 also to have something to offer. 32
4 since there are priests who offer gifts 32
9: 7 taking blood which he offers for himself 32
9 gifts and sacrifices are offered 32
14 who through the eternal Spirit offered himself 32
25 Nor was it to offer himself repeatedly 32
28 Christ . . offered once to bear the sins of many 32
10: 1 are continually offered year after year 32
2 would they not have ceased to be offered 32
8 these are offered according to the law) 32
12 when Christ had offered . . a single sacrifice 32
11: 4 Abel offered to God a more acceptable sacrifice 32
Jas 2:21 when he offered his son Isaac upon the altar? 24
1Pe 2: 5 offer spiritual sacrifices acceptable to God 24
1Es 1:18 sacrifices were offered on the altar of the Lord 32
4:52 to be offered on the altar every day 27
5:49 to offer burnt offerings upon it 32
50 they offered sacrifices at the proper times 24
51 offered the proper sacrifices every day *
53 began to offer sacrifices to God 32
7: 7 They offered . . 100 bulls, 200 rams, 400 lambs 32
8:15 to offer sacrifices upon the altar of their Lord 32
65 offered sacrifices to the Lord, the God of Israel 32
2Es 1:31 When you offer oblations to me, I will turn my face 34
3:24 in it to offer thee oblations from what is thine. 34
10:45 before any offering was offered in it. 34

46 built the city, and offered offerings 34
14:39 and behold, a full cup was offered to me 35
Tob 5:13 offered the first-born of our flocks 24
Jdt 4:14 Joakim . . offered the continual burnt offerings 32
9: 1 when that evening's incense was being offered 32
16:18 they offered their burnt offerings 24
Sir 34:20 the man who offers a sacrifice 30
35: 2 He who returns a kindness offers fine flour 31
38:11 Offer a sweet-smelling sacrifice 25
45:16 to offer sacrifice to the Lord 30
Bar 1:10 offer them upon the altar of the Lord our God; 24
LJr 1:28 the sacrifices that are offered to these gods *
1Mc 4:53 they rose and offered sacrifice, as the law directs 24
56 and offered burnt offerings with gladness 32
56 offered a sacrifice of deliverance and praise. 26
5:54 and offered burnt offerings 30
7:33 burnt offering . . being offered for the king. 32
12:11 at the sacrifices which we offer 32
2Mc 1: 8 we offered sacrifice and cereal offering 32
18 when Nehemiah . . offered sacrifices. 24
23 the priests offered prayer 29
2: 9 Solomon offered sacrifice 24
3:32 offered sacrifice for the man's recovery. 30
35 Then Heliodorus offered sacrifice to the Lord 24
10: 3 they offered sacrifices, after a lapse of two years 24
7 they offered hymns of thanksgiving to him 24
13:23 settled with them and offered sacrifice 30
3Mc 5:43 empty of those who offered sacrifices there. 33

offer *See also* occasion.

offer a bribe 1. שׁחד 2. *δωροκοπέω*

Job 6:22 Or, 'From your wealth offer a bribe for me'? 1
Sir 35:12 Do not offer him a bribe 2

offer a pledge 1. *δεξιάζω*

2Mc 4:34 and . . offered him sworn pledges 1

offer a prayer 1. פלל 2. *προσεύχομαι*

Ps 32: 6 let every one who is godly offer prayer to thee; 1
1Es 6:31 prayers be offered for their life. 2
Aza 1: 2 Then Azariah stood and offered this prayer 2

offer a sacrifice 1. זבח 2. קטר 3. קרב (A) 4. *θυσιάζω* 5. *θύω* 6. *προσφέρω* 7. sacrifico

Gen 31:54 Jacob offered a sacrifice on the mountain 1
46: 1 came to Beer-sheba, and offered sacrifices 1
Exd 5: 8 Let us go and offer sacrifice to our God.' 1
Lev 19: 5 When you offer a sacrifice of peace offerings 1
Deu 16: 5 You may not offer the passover sacrifice 1
Jdg 16:23 Philistines gathered to offer a . . sacrifice 1
Ezr 6:10 may offer pleasing sacrifices to the God 3
Ps 50:14 Offer to God a sacrifice of thanksgiving 1
Ams 4: 5 offer a sacrifice of thanksgiving of that 2
Act 14:13 and wanted to offer sacrifice with the people. 5
18 they . . restrained the people from offering sacrifice 5
Heb 5: 3 he is bound to offer sacrifice for his own sins 6
2Es 1: 6 have offered sacrifices to strange gods. 7
Wis 18: 9 the holy children of good men offered sacrifices 4
1Mc 1:51 to offer sacrifice, city by city. 4
59 they offered sacrifice on the altar 4
2:15 king's officers . . came . . to make them offer sacrifice. 4
23 to offer sacrifice upon the altar in Modein 4
11:34 To all those who offer sacrifice in Jerusalem 4
3Mc 1: 9 he offered sacrifice to the supreme God 5

offer a sin offering 1. חטא

Exd 29:36 shall offer a sin offering for the altar 1

offer as a burnt offering 1. *ὁλοκαρπόομαι*

4Mc 18:11 Isaac who was offered as a burnt offering 1

offer by fire 1. אִשֶּׁה

Lev 3:11 on he altar as food offered by fire to the LORD 1
16 as food offered by fire for a pleasing odor 1
23:13 to be offered by fire to the LORD, a pleasing odor 1
24: 7 memorial portion to be offered by fire to the LORD 1

offer for sale 1. מכר

Deu 28:68 offer yourselves for sale to your enemies 1

offer for sin 1. חטא

Lev 6:26 The priest who offers it for sin shall eat it 1
9:15 the goat . . and killed it, and offered it for sin 1

offer freely 1. נדב 2. נְדָבָה 3. נדב (A)

1Ch 29: 9 they had offered freely to the LORD; 1
17 I have freely offered all these things 1
17 seen thy people . . offering freely . . to thee 1
Ezr 1; 6 besides all that was freely offered. 1
7:13 who freely offers to go to Jerusalem, may go 3
15 king and his counselors have freely offered 3
Ps 110: 3 Your people will offer themselves freely 2

offer in sacrifice 1. *ἱερόθυτος* 2. *προσφορά*

1Co 10:28 This has been offered in sacrifice 1
Sir 46:16 he offered in sacrifice a sucking lamb. 2

offer incense 1. קטר
Jer 32:29 houses on whose roofs incense has been offered 1
44:15 their wives had offered incense to other gods 1

make offer 1. עבר
Ezk 20:26 in making them offer by fire all their first-born 1

offer of peace 1. εἰρηνεύω
1Mc 6:60 he sent to the Jews an offer of peace 1

offer praise 1. הלל
1Ch 23: 5 4,000 shall offer praises to the LORD 1
2Ch 7: 6 David offered praises by their ministry; 1

offer resistance 1. ἀνθίστημι
LJr 1:56 they can offer no resistance to a king or any enemies. 1

offer to drink 1. שקה
Jer 35: 2 then offer them wine to drink. 1

offer up 1. עבר 2. עלה 3. נסך (A) 4. ἀναφέρω 5. προσφέρω
Gen 22:13 took the ram, and offered it up as a burnt offering 2
Jdg 11:31 and I will offer him up for a burnt offering. 2
1Sm 7:10 As Samuel was offering up the burnt offering 2
2Sm 24:22 Let my lord . . take and offer up what seems good 2
1Kg 3:15 offered up burnt offerings and peace offerings 2
9:25 Solomon used to offer up burnt offerings 2
2Ch 8:12 Solomon offered up burnt offerings to the LORD 2
Job 42: 8 offer up for yourselves a burnt offering; 2
Jer 32:35 to offer up their sons and daughters to Molech 1
Ezk 23:37 have even offered up to them for food the sons 1
43:24 and offer them up as a burnt offering to the LORD. 2
Dan 2:46 offering and incense be offered up to him. 3
Heb 5: 7 In the days of his flesh, Jesus offered up prayers 5
7:27 did this once for all when he offered up himself. 4
11:17 Abraham, when he was tested, offered up Isaac 5
17 he . . was ready to offer up his only son 5
13:15 let us continually offer up a sacrifice 4

offer willingly 1. נדב 2. ἑκουσιάζομαι
Jdg 5: 2 that the people offered themselves willingly 1
9 commanders . . who offered themselves willingly 1
1Ch 29: 5 Who then will offer willingly, consecrating 1
14 that we should be able thus to offer willingly? 1
Neh 11: 2 blessed all the men who willingly offered 1
1Mc 2:42 every one who offered himself willingly for the law. 2

offer worship 1. עבר 2. λατρεύω
2Sm 15: 8 then I will offer worship to the LORD.' 1
Heb 12:28 thus let us offer to God acceptable worship 2

offering 1. זֶבַח 2. חַג 3. מִנְחָה 4. נְדָבָה 5. עבר 6. עֹלָה 7. קָרְבָּן 8. תְּנוּפָה 9. תְּרוּמָה 10. מִנְחָה (A) 11. ἀνάθημα 12. ἀναφέρω 13. διακονία 14. δόμα 15. δῶρον 16. θέμα 17. θυσία 18. λειτουργία 19. ὁ περί 20. ὀσμή 21. περί 22. προσάγω 23. προσφέρω 24. προσφορά 25. oblatio 26. offero
Gen 4: 3 Cain brought to the LORD an offering of the fruit 3
4 And the LORD had regard for Abel and his offering 3
5 for Cain and his offering he had no regard. 3
Exd 24: 5 who . . sacrificed peace offerings of oxen 1
25: 2 that they take for me an offering; 9
2 you shall receive the offering for me. 9
3 this is the offering which you shall receive 9
29:28 offered . . from their peace offerings; 1
28 it is their offering to the LORD. 9
30:13 half a shekel as an offering to the LORD. 9
14 Every one . . shall give the LORD'S offering. 9
15 give the LORD'S offering to make atonement 9
35: 5 Take from among you an offering to the LORD; 9
5 bring the LORD'S offering: gold, silver, and bronze 9
21 brought the LORD'S offering to be used 9
22 dedicating an offering of gold to the LORD. 8
24 who could make an offering of silver or bronze 9
24 brought it as the LORD'S offering; 9
36: 6 man nor woman do anything more for the offering 9
38:24 the gold from the offering, was 29 talents 8
Lev 1: 2 When any man of you brings an offering to the LORD 7
2 you shall bring your offering of cattle 7
3 If his offering is a burnt offering from the herd 7
14 If his offering to the LORD is a burnt offering 6
14 then he shall bring his offering of turtledoves 7
2: 1 any one brings a cereal offering as an offering 7
1 cereal offering as an offering to the LORD •
1 his offering shall be of fine flour 7
4 When you bring a cereal offering baked 7
4 baked in the oven as an offering •
5 if your offering is a cereal offering baked 7
7 if your offering is a cereal offering cooked 7
12 As an offering of first fruits you may bring them 7
13 with all your offerings you shall offer salt 7
3: 1 If a man's offering is a sacrifice of peace 7
2 shall lay his hand upon the head of his offering 7
6 If his offering for a sacrifice of peace 7
7 If he offers a lamb for his offering 7
8 laying his hand upon the head of his offering 7
12 If his offering is a goat 7
14 as his offering for an offering by fire 7
4:23 he shall bring as his offering a goat, a male 7
28 he shall bring for his offering a goat, a female 7
32 brings a lamb as his offering for a sin offering 7
5:11 then he shall bring, as his offering for the sin 7
6:20 This is the offering which Aaron and his sons 7
7:13 his offering with cakes of leavened bread 7
14 of such he shall offer one cake from each offering 7
14 as an offering to the LORD; it shall belong 9
15 shall be eaten on the day of his offering 7
16 his offering is a votive offering or a freewill 7
29 He shall bring his offering to the LORD 7
32 give to the priest as an offering 9
38 commanded . . bring their offerings to the LORD 7
9: 7 bring the offering of the people 7
15 Then he presented the people's offering 7
14:32 cannot afford the offerings for his cleansing •
22:12 she shall not eat of the offering of the holy 9
18 WHen any one . . presents his offering, whether 7
27 it shall be acceptable as an offering by fire 7
23:14 until you have brought the offering of your God 7
27: 9 If it is an animal such as men offer as an offering 7
11 such as is not offered as an offering to the LORD 7
Num 5: 9 every offering, all the holy things of the people 9
15 man shall . . bring the offering required of her 7
6:21 offering to the LORD shall be according 7
7: 3 brought their offerings before the LORD 7
10 leaders offered offerings for the dedication •
10 leaders offered their offering before 7
11 shall offer their offering, one leader each day 7
12 offered his offering the first day was Nahshon 7
13 his offering was one silver plate whose weight 7
17 was the offering of Nahshon the son of Ammin'adab 7
19 he offered for his offering one silver plate 7
23 was the offering of Nethan'el the son of Zu'ar. 7
25 his offering was one silver plate 7
29 This was the offering of Eli'ab the son of Helon. 7
31 his offering was one silver plate whose weight 7
35 was the offering of Eli'zur the son of Shed'eur. 7
37 his offering was one silver plate 7
41 offering of Shelu'mi-el the son of Zurishad'dai. 7
43 his offering was one silver plate, whose weight 7
47 was the offering of Eli'asaph the son of Deu'el. 7
49 his offering was one silver plate 7
53 was the offering of Eli'shama the son of Ammi'hud. 7
55 his offering was one silver plate 7
59 offering of Gama'liel the son of Pedah'zur. 7
61 his offering was one silver plate, whose weight 7
65 was the offering of Abi'dan the son of Gideo'ni. 7
67 his offering was one silver plate, whose weight 7
71 offering of Ahie'zer the son of Ammishad'dai. 7
73 his offering was one silver plate 7
77 was the offering of Pa'giel the son of Ochran. 7
79 his offering was one silver plate 7
83 This was the offering of Ahi'ra the son of Enan. 7
9: 7 why are we kept from offering the LORD'S offering 7
13 offer the LORD'S offering at its appointed time; 7
15: 4 who brings his offering shall offer to the LORD 7
19 when you eat . . you shall present an offering 9
20 meal you shall present a cake as an offering; 9
20 as an offering from the threshing floor 9
21 offering throughout your generations. 9
25 because . . they have brought their offering 7
16:15 Do not respect their offering. 3
18: 8 whatever is kept of the offerings made to me 9
9 This shall be yours . . every offering of theirs 7
11 This also is yours, the offering of their gift 9
19 All the holy offerings which the people 9
24 tithe . . they present as an offering to the LORD 9
26 you shall present an offering from it to the LORD 9
27 your offering shall be reckoned to you as though 9
28 shall you also present an offering to the LORD 9
28 give the LORD'S offering to Aaron the priest. 9
29 you shall present every offering due to the LORD 9
28: 2 My offering . . you shall take heed to offer to me 7
3 two male lambs . . as a continual offering. 6
31:29 give it to Elea'zar . . as an offering to the LORD. 9
41 tribute, which was the offering for the LORD 9
50 we have brought the LORD'S offering 7
52 all the gold of the offering that they offered 9
Deu 12: 6 thither you shall bring . . the offering 9
11 bring . . the offering that you present 9
17 not eat . . the offering that you present; 9
18:10 any one who burns his son . . as an offering •
Jos 22:23 or cereal offerings or peace offerings on it 1
1Sm 2:17 treated the offering of the LORD with contempt. 3
29 look with . . at my sacrifices and my offerings 3
29 choicest parts of every offering of my people 3
3:14 shall not be expiated by sacrifice or offering 3
10: 8 to offer . . and to sacrifice peace offerings. 1
11:15 sacrificed peace offerings before the LORD 1
26:19 If it is the LORD . . may he accept an offering; 3
2Kg 16: 3 He even burned his son as an offering 5
17:17 burned their sons and . . daughters as offerings 5
21: 6 And he burned his son as an offering •
23:10 burn his son or his daughter as an offering •
1Ch 16:29 bring an offering, and come before him! 3
2Ch 2: 4 and for the continual offering of the showbread •
28: 3 burned his sons as an offering •
30:24 1,000 bulls and 7,000 sheep for offerings •
33: 6 he burned his sons as an offering in the valley •
Ezr 3: 5 offerings at the new moon and . . appointed feasts •
5 offerings of every one who made a freewill •
8:25 offering for the house of our God which the king 9
Neh 10:34 cast lots . . for the wood offering, to bring it 7
13:31 provided for the wood offering, at appointed 7
Ps 20: 3 May he remember all your offerings 3
40: 6 Sacrifice and offering thou dost not desire; 3
96: 8 bring an offering, and come into his courts! 3
119:108 Accept my offerings of praise, O LORD, and teach me 4
Isa 1:13 Bring no more vain offerings; 3
40:20 chooses for an offering wood that will not rot; 9
43:23 I have not burdened you with offerings 3
66:20 from all the nations as an offering to the LORD 3
Ezk 16:21 delivered them up as an offering by fire to them? 5
20:28 presented the provocation of their offering; 7
40 your gifts, with all your sacred offerings. •
40:43 the flesh of the offering was to be laid. 7
42:13 the priests . . shall eat the most holy offerings; •
13 there they shall put the most holy offerings •
44:30 offering of all kinds from all your offerings 9
30 offering of all kinds from all your offerings 9
45:13 This is the offering which you shall make 9
15 This is the offering for cereal offerings •
16 the people of the land shall give this offering 9
Dan 2:46 King . . commanded that an offering and incense 10
9:27 shall cause sacrifice and offering to cease; 3
Ams 5:25 Did you bring to me sacrifices and offerings 3
Zep 3:10 my dispersed ones, shall bring my offering. 3
Mal 1:10 I will not accept an offering from your hand. 3
11 incense is offered to my name, and a pure offering; 3
13 lame or sick, and this you bring as your offering! 3
2: 3 dung upon your faces, the dung of your offerings 2
12 or to bring an offering to the LORD of hosts! 3
13 because he no longer regards the offering 3
3: 3 till they present right offerings to the LORD. 3
4 Then the offering of Judah and Jerusalem will be 3
8 we robbing thee?' In your tithes and offerings. 9
Mat 5:23 So if you are offering your gift at the altar 23
Lke 21: 5 it was adorned with noble stones and offerings 11
23:36 coming up and offering him vinegar 23
Joh 16: 2 will think he is offering service to God. 23
Act 21:26 the offering presented for every one of them. 24
24:17 I came to bring to my nation alms and offerings. 24
Rom 15:16 the offering of the Gentiles may be acceptable 24
2Co 9: 1 to write to you about the offering for the saints 13
Eph 5: 2 a fragrant offering and sacrifice to God. 24
Php 2:17 upon the sacrificial offering of your faith 18
4:18 a fragrant offering, a sacrifice acceptable 20
Heb 10: 5 Sacrifices and offerings thou hast not desired 24
6 in burnt offerings and sin offerings 21
8 in sacrifices and offerings and burnt offerings 24
8 burnt offerings and sin offerings 21
10 the offering of the body of Jesus Christ 24
11 offering repeatedly the same sacrifices 23
14 by a single offering he has perfected 24
18 there is no longer any offering for sin. 24
1Es 1:14 the priests were offering the fat until night 12
5:52 thereafter the continual offerings 24
2Es 10:45 before any offering was offered in it. 25
46 built the city, and offered offerings 25
13:13 and some were bringing others as offerings. 26
Tob 4:11 charity is an excellent offering 15
Jdt 4:14 the vows and freewill offerings of the people. 14
16:16 every sacrifice as a fragrant offering 20
Sir 14:11 present worthy offerings to the Lord. 24
30:18 like offerings of food placed upon a grave. 16
34:18 the offering is blemished 24
19 not pleased with the offerings of the ungodly; 24
35: 1 He who keeps the law makes many offerings 24
6 The offering of a righteous man 24
38:11 pour oil on your offering 24
50:13 with the Lord's offering in their hands 24
14 arranging the offering to the Most High 24
1Mc 1:54 sacrilege upon the altar of burnt offering. •
59 which was upon the altar of burnt offering. •
2Mc 2:11 because the sin offering had not been eaten. 19
9:16 he would adorn with the finest offerings 11
12:43 to provide for a sin offering 17
14:31 were offering the customary sacrifices 22
3Mc 3:17 honor it with magnificent and . . beautiful offerings 11
offering *See also* cup, make, offer, pour, sacrifice.

abominable offering 1. ἀποδιαστέλλω
2Mc 6: 5 The altar was covered with abominable offerings 1

baked offering 1. מַחֲבַת
1Ch 23:29 unleavened bread, the baked offering 1

burnt offering 1. מִנְחָה 2. עלה 3. עֹלָה 4. אשׁ (A) 5. עֲלָת (A) 6. ὁλοκάρπωμα 7. ὁλοκαύτωμα 8. ὁλοκαύτωσις
Gen 8:20 Noah . . offered burnt offerings on the altar. 3
22: 2 and offer him there as a burnt offering 3
3 and he cut the wood for the burnt offering 3
6 Abraham took the wood of the burnt offering 3

7 but where is the lamb for a burnt offering? 3
8 provide himself the lamb for a burnt offering 3
13 took the ram, and offered it up as a burnt offering 3
Exd 10:25 let us have sacrifices and burnt offerings 3
18:12 Jethro . . offered a burnt offering 3
20:24 your burnt offerings and your peace offerings 3
24: 5 offered burnt offerings and sacrificed peace 3
29:18 it is a burnt offering to the LORD; 3
25 on the altar in addition to the burnt offering 3
42 It shall be a continual burnt offering 3
30: 9 no unholy incense thereon, nor burnt offering 3
28 altar of burnt offering with all its utensils 3
31: 9 altar of burnt offering with all its utensils 3
32: 6 they rose up . . and offered burnt offerings 3
35:16 the altar of burnt offering, with its grating 3
38: 1 He made the altar of burnt offering also 3
40: 6 You shall set the altar of burnt offering before 3
10 shall also anoint the altar of burnt offering 3
29 he set the altar of burnt offering at the door 3
29 offered upon it the burnt offering 3
Lev 1: 3 If his offering is a burnt offering from the herd 3
4 lay his hand upon the head of the burnt offering 3
6 he shall flay the burnt offering and cut it 3
9 burn the whole on the altar, as a burnt offering 3
10 If his gift for a burnt offering is from the flock 3
13 it is a burnt offering, an offering by fire 3
14 If his offering to the LORD is a burnt offering 3
17 it is a burnt offering, an offering by fire 3
3: 5 burn it on the altar upon the burnt offering 3
4: 7 at the base of the altar of burnt offering 3
10 burn them upon the altar of burnt offering 3
18 at the base of the altar of burnt offering 3
24 in the place where they kill the burnt offering 3
25 put it on the horns of the altar of burnt offering 3
25 blood at the base of the altar of burnt offering 3
29 the sin offering in the place of burnt offering 3
30 put it on the horns of the altar of burnt offering 3
33 the place where they kill the burnt offering 3
34 put it on the horns of the altar of burnt offering 3
5: 7 sin offering and the other for a burnt offering 3
10 he shall offer the second for a burnt offering 3
6: 9 This is the law of the burnt offering 3
9 The burnt offering shall be on the hearth 3
10 which the fire has consumed the burnt offering 3
12 he shall lay the burnt offering in order upon it 3
25 In the place where the burnt offering is killed 3
7: 2 in the place where they kill the burnt offering 3
8 the priest who offers any man's burnt offering 3
8 skin of the burnt offering which he has offered 3
37 This is the law of the burnt offering 3
8:18 Then he presented the ram of the burnt offering 3
21 burned . . as a burnt offering, a pleasing odor 3
28 burned them on the altar with the burnt offering 3
9: 2 ram for a burnt offering, both without blemish 3
3 a calf and a lamb . . for a burnt offering 3
7 offer your sin offering and your burnt offering 3
12 he killed the burnt offering 3
13 they delivered the burnt offering to him 3
14 burned them with the burnt offering on the altar 3
16 he presented the burnt offering, and offered it 3
17 besides the burnt offering of the morning 3
22 the burnt offering and the peace offerings 3
24 the burnt offering and the fat upon the altar 3
10:19 their sin offering and their burnt offering 3
12: 6 bring . . a lamb a year old for a burnt offering 3
8 one for a burnt offering and the other for a sin 3
14:13 kill the sin offering and the burnt offering 3
19 And afterward he shall kill the burnt offering 3
20 the priest shall offer the burnt offering 3
22 a sin offering and the other a burnt offering 3
31 sin offering and the other for a burnt offering 3
15:15 sin offering and the other for a burnt offering 3
30 shall offer . . the other for a burnt offering 3
16: 3 a sin offering and a ram for a burnt offering 3
5 a sin offering, and one ram for a burnt offering 3
24 and come forth, and offer his burnt offering 3
24 offer . . the burnt offering of the people 3
17: 8 who offers a burnt offering or sacrifice 3
22:18 is offered to the LORD as a burnt offering 3
23:12 a male lamb . . as a burnt offering to the LORD 3
18 they shall be a burnt offering to the LORD 3
37 burnt offerings and cereal offerings 3
Num 6:11 shall offer . . the other for a burnt offering 3
14 one male lamb a year old . . for a burnt offering 3
16 offer his sin offering and his burnt offering 3
7:15 ram, one male lamb a year old, for a burnt offering; 3
21 ram, one male lamb a year old, for a burnt offering; 3
27 ram, one male lamb a year old, for a burnt offering; 3
33 ram, one male lamb a year old, for a burnt offering; 3
39 ram, one male lamb a year old, for a burnt offering; 3
45 ram, one male lamb a year old, for a burnt offering; 3
51 ram, one male lamb a year old, for a burnt offering; 3
57 ram, one male lamb a year old, for a burnt offering; 3
63 ram, one male lamb a year old, for a burnt offering; 3
69 ram, one male lamb a year old, for a burnt offering; 3
75 ram, one male lamb a year old, for a burnt offering; 3
81 ram, one male lamb a year old, for a burnt offering; 3
87 cattle for the burnt offering twelve bulls 3
8:12 shall offer . . the other for a burnt offering 3
10:10 blow the trumpets over your burnt offerings 3
15: 3 offer . . an offering by fire or a burnt offering 3
5 you shall prepare with the burnt offering 3
8 when you prepare a bull for a burnt offering 3
24 offer one young bull for a burnt offering 3
23: 3 Stand beside your burnt offering, and I will go; 3
6 Moab were standing beside his burnt offering. 3
15 Stand here beside your burnt offering 3
17 lo, he was standing beside his burnt offering 3
28: 6 It is a continual burnt offering 3
10 this is the burnt offering of every sabbath 3
10 the continual burnt offering and its drink 3
11 you shall offer a burnt offering to the LORD 3
13 for a burnt offering of pleasing odor 3
14 this is the burnt offering of each month 3
15 offered besides the continual burnt offering 3
19 an offering by fire, a burnt offering to the LORD 3
23 these besides the burnt offering of the morning 3
23 which is for a continual burnt offering. 3
24 offered besides the continual burnt offering 3
27 a burnt offering, a pleasing odor to the LORD 3
31 Besides the continual burnt offering 3
29: 2 you shall offer a burnt offering, a pleasing odor 3
6 besides the burnt offering of the new moon 3
6 besides . . the continual burnt offering 3
8 you shall offer a burnt offering to the LORD 3
11 besides . . the continual burnt offering 3
13 shall offer a burnt offering, an offering by fire 3
16 besides the continual burnt offering 3
19 besides the continual burnt offering 3
22 besides the continual burnt offering 3
25 besides the continual burnt offering 3
28 besides the continual burnt offering 3
31 besides the continual burnt offering 3
34 besides the continual burnt offering 3
36 shall offer a burnt offering, an offering by fire 3
38 besides the continual burnt offering 3
39 offer . . for your burnt offerings 3
Deu 12: 6 thither you shall bring your burnt offerings 3
11 bring . . your burnt offerings 3
13 do not offer your burnt offerings at every place 3
14 there you shall offer your burnt offerings 3
27 offer . . burnt offerings, the flesh and the blood 3
27: 6 offer burnt offerings on it to the LORD your God; 3
Jos 8:31 they offered on it burnt offerings to the LORD 3
22:23 to offer burnt offerings or cereal offerings 3
26 altar, not for burnt offering, nor for sacrifice 3
27 perform the service . . with our burnt offerings 3
28 made, not for burnt offerings, nor for sacrifice 3
29 an altar for burnt offering, cereal offering 3
Jdg 6:26 take the . . bull, and offer it as a burnt offering 3
11:31 and I will offer him up for a burnt offering. 3
13:16 if you make ready a burnt offering, then offer it 3
23 accepted a burnt offering and a cereal offering 3
20:26 offered burnt offerings and peace offerings 3
21: 4 offered burnt offerings and peace offerings. 3
1Sm 6:14 offered the cows as a burnt offering to the LORD. 3
15 the men of Beth-she'mesh offered burnt offerings 3
7: 9 took . . and offered it as a whole burnt offering 3
10 As Samuel was offering up the burnt offering 3
10: 8 to offer burnt offerings and to sacrifice 3
13: 9 Saul said, "Bring the burnt offering here to me 3
9 And he offered the burnt offering. 3
10 as he had finished offering the burnt offering 3
12 forced myself, and offered the burnt offering. 3
15:22 delight in burnt offerings and sacrifices 3
2Sm 6:17 and David offered burnt offerings 3
18 offering the burnt offerings and the peace 3
24:22 here are the oxen for the burnt offering 3
24 I will not offer burnt offerings to the LORD my God 3
25 offered burnt offerings and peace offerings. 3
1Kg 3: 4 Solomon used to offer . . burnt offerings 3
15 offered up burnt offerings and peace offerings 3
8:64 he offered the burnt offering and the cereal 3
64 receive the burnt offering and the cereal 3
9:25 offer up burnt offerings and peace offerings 3
10: 5 and his burnt offerings which he offered 3
18:33 pour it on the burnt offering, and on the wood. 3
38 fire . . fell, and consumed the burnt offering 3
2Kg 3:27 offered him for a burnt offering upon the wall. 3
5:17 will not offer burnt offering or sacrifice 3
10:24 he went in to offer . . burnt offerings. 3
25 he had made an end of offering the burnt offering 3
16:13 and burned his burnt offering 3
15 burn the morning burnt offering, and the evening 3
15 king's burnt offering, and his cereal offering 3
15 with the burnt offering of all the people 3
15 throw upon it all the blood of the burnt offering 3
1Ch 6:49 made offerings upon the altar of burnt offering 3
16: 1 offered burnt offerings and peace offerings 3
2 finished offering the burnt offerings 3
40 to offer burnt offerings to the LORD 3
40 to the LORD upon the altar of burnt offering 3
21:23 see, I give the oxen for burnt offerings 3
24 nor offer burnt offerings which cost me 3
26 presented burnt offerings and peace offerings 3
26 with fire . . upon the altar of burnt offering. 3
29 tabernacle . . and the altar of burnt offering 3
22: 1 and here the altar of burnt offering for Israel. 3
23:31 burnt offerings are offered to the LORD 3
29:21 the next day offered burnt offerings to the LORD 3
2Ch 1: 6 offered 1,000 burnt offerings upon it. 3
2: 4 and for burnt offerings morning and evening 3
4: 6 to rinse off what was used for the burnt offering 3
7: 1 fire . . consumed the burnt offering 3
7 for there he offered the burnt offering 3
7 could not hold the burnt offering 3
8:12 Solomon offered up burnt offerings to the LORD 3
13:11 They offer to the LORD . . burnt offerings 3
23:18 to offer burnt offerings to the LORD 3
24:14 both for the service and for the burnt offerings 2
14 offered burnt offerings in the house of the LORD 3
29: 7 not burned incense or offered burnt offerings 3
18 the altar of burnt offering and all its utensils 3
24 king commanded that the burnt offering 3
27 commanded that the burnt offering be offered 3
27 burnt offering began, the song to the LORD began 3
28 until the burnt offering was finished. 3
31 of a willing heart brought burnt offerings. 3
32 The number of the burnt offerings 3
32 all these were for a burnt offering to the LORD. 3
34 could not flay all the burnt offerings 3
35 Besides the great number of burnt offerings 3
35 the libations for the burnt offerings. 3
30:15 brought burnt offerings into the house 3
31: 2 priests and the Levites, for burnt offerings 3
3 contribution . . was for the burnt offerings 3
3 burnt offerings of morning and evening 3
3 burnt offerings for the sabbaths, the new moons 3
35:12 they set aside the burnt offerings 3
14 busied in offering the burnt offerings 3
16 to offer burnt offerings on the altar of the LORD 3
Ezr 3: 2 altar . . to offer burnt offerings upon it 3
3 offered burnt offerings upon it to the LORD 3
3 offered . . burnt offerings morning and evening. 3
4 offered the daily burnt offerings by number 3
5 after that the continual burnt offerings 3
6 began to offer burnt offerings to the LORD. 3
6: 3 place where . . burnt offerings are brought; 4
9 young bulls, rams, or sheep for burnt offerings 5
8:35 returned exiles, offered burnt offerings 3
35 all this was a burnt offering to the LORD 3
Neh 10:33 continual burnt offering, the sabbaths 3
Job 1: 5 offer burnt offerings according to the number 3
42: 8 offer up for yourselves a burnt offering; 3
Ps 40: 6 Burnt offering . . thou hast not required. 3
50: 8 your burnt offerings are continually before me. 3
51:16 were I to give a burnt offering, thou wouldst not 3
19 delight in right sacrifices, in burnt offerings 3
66:13 I will come into thy house with burnt offerings; 3
15 I will offer to thee burnt offerings of fatlings 3
Isa 1:11 I have had enough of burnt offerings of rams 3
19:21 worship with sacrifice and burnt offering 1
40:16 nor are its beasts enough for a burnt offering. 3
43:23 not brought me your sheep for burnt offerings 3
56: 7 their burnt offerings and their sacrifices 3
Jer 6:20 Your burnt offerings are not acceptable 3
7:21 Add your burnt offerings to your sacrifices 3
22 command them concerning burnt offerings 3
14:12 they offer burnt offering and cereal offering 3
17:26 bringing burnt offerings and sacrifices 3
19: 5 to burn their sons in the fire as burnt offerings 3
33:18 a man in my presence to offer burnt offerings 3
Ezk 40:38 gate, where the burnt offering was to be washed. 3
39 on which the burnt offering and the sin offering 3
42 tables of hewn stone for the burnt offering 3
42 instruments . . with which the burnt offerings 3
43:18 when it is erected for offering burnt offerings 3
24 and offer them up as a burnt offering to the LORD. 3
27 shall offer upon the altar your burnt offerings 3
44:11 they shall slay the burnt offering 3
45:15 offering for cereal offerings, burnt offerings 3
17 the prince's duty to furnish the burnt offerings 3
17 burnt offerings, and peace offerings 3
23 he shall provide as a burnt offering to the LORD 3
25 provision for sin offerings, burnt offerings 3
46: 2 The priests shall offer his burnt offering 3
4 The burnt offering that the prince offers 3
12 either a burnt offering or peace offerings 3
12 he shall offer his burnt offering 3
13 for a burnt offering to the LORD daily; 3
14 ordinance for the continual burnt offering. •
15 by morning, for a continual burnt offering. 3
Hos 6: 6 knowledge of God, rather than burnt offerings. 3
Ams 5:22 Even though you offer me your burnt offerings 3
Mic 6: 6 Shall I come before him with burnt offerings 3
Heb 10: 6 in burnt offerings and sin offerings 7
8 in sacrifices and offerings and burnt offerings 7
1Es 4:52 additional ten talents . . for burnt offerings 7
5:49 to offer burnt offerings upon it 8
50 they offered . . burnt offerings to the Lord 7
Jdt 4:14 Joakim . . offered the continual burnt offerings 8
16:16 all fat for burnt offerings . . is a very little thing 7
18 they offered their burnt offerings 7
Wis 3: 6 like a sacrificial burnt offering 6
Bar 1:10 buy with the money burnt offerings 7
Aza 1:15 no prince, or prophet, or leader, no burnt offering 8
16 as though it were with burnt offerings of rams 7

1Mc 1:45 to forbid burnt offerings and sacrifices 7
4:44 what to do about the altar of burnt offering 8
53 on the new altar of burnt offering 7
56 and offered burnt offerings with gladness 7
5:54 and offered burnt offerings 7
7:33 and to show him the burnt offering 8

offering by fire 1. אִשֶּׁה

Exd 29:18 it is . . an offering by fire to the LORD. 1
25 it is an offering by fire to the LORD. 1
41 an offering by fire to the LORD. 1
30:20 to burn an offering by fire to the LORD 1
Lev 1: 9 an offering by fire, a pleasing odor to the LORD 1
13 it is a burnt offering, an offering by fire 1
17 it is a burnt offering, an offering by fire 1
2: 2 an offering by fire, a pleasing odor to the LORD 1
3 part of the offerings by fire to the LORD 1
9 an offering by fire, a pleasing odor to the LORD 1
10 part of the offerings by fire to the LORD 1
11 no leaven nor any honey as an offering by fire 1
16 it is an offering by fire to the LORD 1
3: 3 as an offering by fire to the LORD 1
5 it is an offering by fire, a pleasing odor 1
9 peace offering as an offering by fire to the LORD 1
14 as his offering for an offering by fire 1
4:35 upon the offerings by fire to the LORD 1
5:12 the altar, upon the offerings by fire to the LORD 1
6:17 their portion of my offerings by fire 1
18 from the LORD'S offerings by fire 1
7: 5 burn them on the altar as an offering by fire 1
25 animal of which an offering by fire is made 1
30 shall bring . . offerings by fire to the LORD 1
35 portion . . from the offerings made by fire 1
8:21 a pleasing odor, an offering by fire to the LORD 1
28 a pleasing odor, an offering by fire to the LORD 1
10:12 remains of the offerings by fire to the LORD 1
13 due, from the offerings by fire to the LORD 1
15 bring with the offerings by fire of the fat 1
21: 6 for they offer the offerings by fire to the LORD 1
21 come near to offer the LORD'S offerings by fire 1
22:22 an offering by fire upon the altar to the LORD 1
23: 8 you shall present an offering by fire to the LORD 1
18 an offering by fire, a pleasing odor to the LORD 1
25 you shall present an offering by fire to the LORD 1
27 present an offering by fire to the LORD 1
36 Seven days you shall present offerings by fire 1
36 and present an offering by fire to the LORD 1
37 for presenting to the LORD offerings by fire 1
24: 9 a most holy portion out of the offerings by fire 1
Num15: 3 offer . . an offering by fire or a burnt offering 1
10 half a hin of wine, as an offering by fire 1
13 in offering an offering by fire, a pleasing odor 1
14 to offer an offering by fire, a pleasing odor 1
25 their offering, an offering by fire to the LORD 1
18:17 shall burn their fat as an offering by fire 1
28: 2 My offering, my food for my offerings by fire 1
3 This is the offering by fire which you shall offer 1
6 for a pleasing odor, an offering by fire to the LORD 1
8 you shall offer it as an offering by fire 1
13 of pleasing odor, an offering by fire to the LORD 1
19 an offering by fire, a burnt offering to the LORD 1
24 offer daily . . the food of an offering by fire 1
29: 6 a pleasing odor, an offering by fire to the LORD. 1
13 shall offer a burnt offering, an offering by fire 1
36 shall offer a burnt offering, an offering by fire 1
Deu 18: 1 eat the offerings by fire to the LORD 1
Jos 13:14 the offerings by fire . . are their inheritance 1
1Sm 2:28 I gave to . . your father all my offerings by fire 1

cereal offering 1. מִנְחָה 2. מִנְחָה (A) 3. μάννα 4. σεμίδαλις

Exd 29:41 with it a cereal offering and its libation 1
30: 9 nor burnt offering, nor cereal offering; 1
40:29 the burnt offering and the cereal offering; 1
Lev 2: 1 any one brings a cereal offering as an offering 1
3 what is left of the cereal offering 1
4 When you bring a cereal offering baked 1
5 if your offering is a cereal offering baked 1
6 pour oil on it; it is a cereal offering 1
7 offering is a cereal offering cooked in a pan 1
8 you shall bring the cereal offering that is made 1
9 the priest shall take from the cereal offering 1
10 what is left of the cereal offering 1
11 No cereal offering which you bring to the LORD 1
13 not season all your cereal offerings with salt 1
13 salt . . be lacking from your cereal offering 1
14 If you offer a cereal offering of first fruits 1
14 you shall offer for the cereal offering 1
15 lay frankincense on it; it is a cereal offering 1
5:13 be for the priest, as in the cereal offering 1
6:14 this is the law of the cereal offering 1
15 fine flour of the cereal offering with its oil 1
15 frankincense which is on the cereal offering 1
20 fine flour as a regular cereal offering 1
21 in baked pieces like a cereal offering 1
23 Every cereal offering of a priest 1
7: 9 every cereal offering baked in the oven 1
10 every cereal offering, mixed with oil or dry 1
37 of the burnt offering, of the cereal offering 1
9: 4 sacrifice before the LORD, and a cereal offering 1
17 he presented the cereal offering 1
10:12 cereal offering that remains of the offerings 1
14:10 a cereal offering of three tenths of an ephah 1
20 offer . . the cereal offering on the altar 1
21 fine flour mixed with oil for a cereal offering 1
31 a burnt offering, along with a cereal offering 1
23:13 the cereal offering with it shall be two tenths 1
16 then you shall present a cereal offering 1
18 a burnt offering . . with their cereal offering 1
37 burnt offerings and cereal offerings 1
Num 4:16 charge of . . the continual cereal offering 1
5:15 it is a cereal offering of jealousy 1
15 cereal offering of remembrance 1
18 in her hands the cereal offering of remembrance 1
18 which is the cereal offering of jealousy. 1
25 shall take the cereal offering of jealousy 1
25 shall wave the cereal offering before the LORD 1
26 take a handful of the cereal offering 1
6:15 cereal offering and their drink offerings. 1
17 priest shall offer also its cereal offering 1
7:13 fine flour mixed with oil for a cereal offering; 1
19 fine flour mixed with oil for a cereal offering; 1
25 fine flour mixed with oil for a cereal offering; 1
31 fine flour mixed with oil for a cereal offering; 1
37 fine flour mixed with oil for a cereal offering; 1
43 fine flour mixed with oil for a cereal offering; 1
49 fine flour mixed with oil for a cereal offering; 1
55 fine flour mixed with oil for a cereal offering; 1
61 fine flour mixed with oil for a cereal offering; 1
67 fine flour mixed with oil for a cereal offering; 1
73 fine flour mixed with oil for a cereal offering; 1
79 fine flour mixed with oil for a cereal offering; 1
87 all the cattle . . with their cereal offering; 1
8: 8 young bull and its cereal offering of fine flour 1
15: 4 shall offer to the LORD a cereal offering 1
6 for a ram, you shall prepare for a cereal offering 1
9 one shall offer with the bull a cereal offering 1
24 a burnt offering . . with its cereal offering 1
18: 9 This shall be yours . . every cereal offering 1
28: 5 of fine flour for a cereal offering 1
8 like the cereal offering of the morning 1
9 fine flour for a cereal offering, mixed with oil 1
12 fine flour for a cereal offering, mixed with oil 1
12 fine flour for a cereal offering, mixed with oil 1
13 fine flour mixed with oil as a cereal offering 1
20 also their cereal offering of fine flour 1
26 when you offer a cereal offering of new grain 1
28 also their cereal offering of fine flour 1
31 burnt offering and its cereal offering 1
29: 3 cereal offering of fine flour mixed with oil 1
6 the burnt offering . . and its cereal offering 1
6 burnt offering and its cereal offering 1
9 cereal offerings of fine flour mixed with oil 1
11 burnt offering and its cereal offering 1
14 and their cereal offering of fine flour 1
16 its cereal offering and its drink offering. 1
18 with the cereal offering and the drink offerings 1
19 burnt offering and its cereal offering 1
21 with the cereal offering and the drink offerings 1
22 burnt offering and its cereal offering 1
24 with the cereal offering and the drink offerings 1
25 its cereal offering and its drink offering. 1
27 with the cereal offering and the drink offerings 1
28 its cereal offering and its drink offering. 1
30 with the cereal offering and the drink offerings 1
31 its cereal offering, and its drink offerings. 1
33 with the cereal offering and the drink offerings 1
34 its cereal offering, and its drink offering. 1
37 and the cereal offering and the drink offerings 1
38 its cereal offering and its drink offering. 1
39 offer . . for your cereal offerings 1
Jos 22:23 to offer burnt offerings or cereal offerings 1
29 an altar for burnt offering, cereal offering 1
Jdg 13:19 So Mano'ah took the kid with the cereal offering 1
23 accepted a burnt offering and a cereal offering 1
1Kg 8:64 offered the . . and the cereal offering 1
64 receive the . . and the cereal offering 1
2Kg 16:13 burned his burnt . . and his cereal offering 1
15 burnt offering, and the evening cereal offering 1
15 king's burnt offering, and his cereal offering 1
15 burnt offering of . . and their cereal offering 1
1Ch 21:23 I give . . the wheat for a cereal offering. 1
23:29 the showbread, the flour for the cereal offering 1
2Ch 7: 7 could not hold . . the cereal offering 1
Ezr 7:17 cereal offerings and their drink offerings 2
Neh 10:33 showbread, the continual cereal offering 1
13: 5 previously put the cereal offering 1
9 with the cereal offering and the frankincense. 1
Isa 57: 6 to them . . you have brought a cereal offering. 1
66: 3 he who presents a cereal offering, 1
20 as the Israelites bring their cereal offering 1
Jer 14:12 they offer burnt offering and cereal offering 1
17:26 sacrifices, cereal offerings and frankincense 1
33:18 offer burnt offerings, to burn cereal offerings 1
41: 5 bringing cereal offerings and incense 1
Ezk 42:13 the cereal offering, the sin offering 1
44:29 They shall eat the cereal offering 1
45:15 This is the offering for cereal offerings 1
17 furnish the burnt offerings, cereal offerings 1
17 provide the sin offerings, cereal offerings 1
24 he shall provide as a cereal offering an ephah 1
25 and cereal offerings, and for the oil. 1
46: 5 cereal offering with the ram shall be an ephah 1
5 cereal offering with the lambs shall be as much 1
7 as a cereal offering he shall provide an ephah 1
11 cereal offering with a . . bull shall be an ephah 1
14 he shall provide a cereal offering with it 1
14 the flour, as a cereal offering to the LORD; 1
20 where they shall bake the cereal offering 1
Jol 1: 9 The cereal offering and the drink offering 1
13 cereal offering and drink offering are withheld 1
2:14 a cereal offering and a drink offering for the LORD 1
Ams 5:22 your burnt offerings and cereal offerings 1
Bar 1:10 prepare a cereal offering, and offer them 3
2Mc 1: 8 we offered sacrifice and cereal offering 4

consecrated offering 1. קֹדֶשׁ

2Ch 29:33 the consecrated offerings were 600 bulls 1

continual burnt offering 1. תָּמִיד

Dan 8:11 continual burnt offering was taken away 1
12 together with the continual burnt offering 1
13 concerning the continual burnt offering 1
11:31 shall take away the continual burnt offering. 1
12:11 from the time that the continual burnt offering 1

dedication offering 1. חֲנֻכָּה

Num 7:84 This was the dedication offering for the altar 1
88 This was the dedication offering for the altar 1

drink offering 1. נָסִיךְ 2. נֶסֶךְ 3. נָסַךְ (A) 4. σπονδή

Gen 35:14 and he poured out a drink offering on it 2
Lev 23:13 the drink offering with it shall be of wine 2
18 their cereal offering and their drink offerings 2
37 sacrifices and drink offerings 2
Num 4: 7 flagons for the drink offering; 2
6:15 cereal offering and their drink offerings. 2
17 priest shall offer also . . its drink offering. 2
15: 5 wine for the drink offering, a fourth of a hin 2
7 for the drink offering you shall offer a third 2
10 offer for the drink offering half a hin of wine 2
24 a burnt offering . . and its drink offering 2
28: 7 Its drink offering shall be a fourth of a hin 2
7 pour out a drink offering of strong drink 2
8 and like its drink offering, you shall offer it 2
9 a cereal offering . . and its drink offering 2
10 continual burnt offering and its drink offering 2
14 Their drink offerings shall be half a hin of wine 2
15 continual burnt offering and its drink offering 2
24 continual burnt offering and its drink offering 2
31 you shall offer them and their drink offering. 2
29: 6 its cereal offering, and their drink offering 2
11 its cereal offering, and their drink offerings 2
16 its cereal offering and its drink offering. 2
18 with the cereal offering and the drink offerings 2
19 its cereal offering, and their drink offerings 2
21 with the cereal offering and the drink offerings 2
22 its cereal offering and its drink offering. 2
24 with the cereal offering and the drink offerings 2
25 its cereal offering and its drink offering. 2
27 with the cereal offering and the drink offerings 2
28 its cereal offering and its drink offering. 2
30 with the cereal offering and the drink offerings 2
31 its cereal offering, and its drink offerings. 2
33 with the cereal offering and the drink offerings 2
34 its cereal offering, and its drink offering. 2
37 and the cereal offering and the drink offerings 2
38 its cereal offering and its drink offering. 2
39 offer . . for your drink offerings 2
Deu 32:38 who . . drank the wine of their drink offering? 1
2Kg 16:13 and poured his drink offering 2
15 cereal offering, and their drink offering; 2
1Ch 29:21 and 1,000 lambs, with their drink offerings 2
Ezr 7:17 cereal offerings and their drink offerings 3
Isa 57: 6 to them you have poured out a drink offering 2
Jer 7:18 they pour out drink offerings to other gods 2
19:13 and drink offerings have been poured out 2
32:29 and drink offerings have been poured out 2
Ezk 20:28 there they poured out their drink offerings. 2
45:17 and drink offerings, at the feasts, the new moons 2
Jol 1: 9 and the drink offering are cut off from the house 2
13 cereal offering and drink offering are withheld 2
2:14 a cereal offering and a drink offering for the LORD 2
1Mc 1:45 to forbid . . sacrifices and drink offerings 4

offering for sin 1. אָשָׁם

Isa 53:10 when he makes himself an offering for sin 1

freewill offering 1. נְדָבָה 2. תְּרוּמָה 3. נדב (A) 4. ἑκούσιος

Exd 35:29 as their freewill offering to the LORD. 1
36: 3 they received . . all the freewill offering 2
3 still kept bringing him freewill offerings 1
Lev 7:16 is a votive offering or a freewill offering 1
22:18 in payment of a vow or as a freewill offering 1

21 to fulfil a vow or as a freewill offering 1
23 too short you may present for a freewill offering 1
23:38 and besides all your freewill offerings 1
Num15: 3 to fulfil a vow or as a freewill offering 1
29:39 votive offerings and your freewill offerings 1
Deu 12: 6 bring . . your freewill offerings 1
17 You may not eat . . your freewill offerings 1
16:10 keep . . with the tribute of a freewill offering 1
2Ch 31:14 Ko're . . was over the freewill offerings to God 1
Ezr 1: 4 besides freewill offerings for the house of God 1
3: 5 every one who made a freewill offering to the LORD. 1
7:16 freewill offerings of the people 3
8:28 freewill offering to the LORD, 1
Ps 54: 6 a freewill offering I will sacrifice to thee; 1
Ezk 46:12 When the prince provides a freewill offering 1
12 offerings as a freewill offering to the LORD 1
Ams 4: 5 and proclaim freewill offerings, publish them; 1
Jdt 16:18 freewill offerings, and their gifts. 4

guilt offering 1. אָשָׁם 2. אַשְׁמָה 3. *περὶ πλημμελείας*

Lev 5: 6 he shall bring his guilt offering to the LORD 1
7 he shall bring, as his guilt offering to the LORD 1
15 he shall bring, as his guilt offering to the LORD 1
15 it is a guilt offering 1
16 for him with the ram of the guilt offering 1
18 valued by you at the price for a guilt offering 1
19 It is a guilt offering; he is guilty 1
6: 5 give it . . on the day of his guilt offering 2
6 he shall bring to the priest his guilt offering 1
6 valued by you at the price for a guilt offering 1
17 like the sin offering and the guilt offering 1
7: 1 This is the law of the guilt offering 1
2 they shall kill the guilt offering 1
5 to the LORD; it is a guilt offering 1
7 The guilt offering is like the sin offering 1
37 of the guilt offering, of the consecration 1
14:12 male lambs, and offer it for a guilt offering 1
13 for the guilt offering, like the sin offering 1
14 some of the blood of the guilt offering 1
17 upon the blood of the guilt offering 1
21 shall take one male lamb for a guilt offering 1
24 priest shall take the lamb of the guilt offering 1
25 he shall kill the lamb of the guilt offering 1
25 take some of the blood of the guilt offering 1
28 where the blood of the guilt offering was put 1
19:21 he shall bring a guilt offering for himself 1
21 shall bring . . a ram for a guilt offering 1
22 with the ram of the guilt offering 1
Num 6:12 bring a male lamb a year old for a guilt offering; 1
18: 9 This shall be yours . . every guilt offering 1
1Sm 6: 3 but by all means return him a guilt offering. 1
4 What is the guilt offering that we shall return 1
8 which you are returning . . as a guilt offering. 1
17 returned as a guilt offering to the LORD 1
2Kg 12:16 The money from the guilt offerings and . . the sin 1
Ezr 10:19 their guilt offering was a ram of the flock 1
Ezk 40:39 and the guilt offering were to be slaughtered. 1
42:13 and the guilt offering, for the place is holy. 1
44:29 the sin offering, and the guilt offering; 1
46:20 where the priests shall boil the guilt offering 1
Sir 7:31 the first fruits, the guilt offering 3

holy offering 1. קֹדֶשׁ

Exd 28:38 any guilt incurred in the holy offering 1
2Ch 31:14 to apportion . . the most holy offerings. 1
35:13 boiled the holy offerings in pots, in caldrons 1

meal offering 1. מִנְחָה

Ezk 46:15 Thus the lamb and the meal offering and the oil 1

memorial offering 1. זכר

Ps 38: 0 A Psalm of David, for the memorial offering. 1
70: 0 A Psalm of David, for the memorial offering. 1

mixed offering 1. רבך

1Ch 23:29 the baked offering, the offering mixed with oil 1

offering of atonement 1. *ἱλασμός*

2Mc 3:33 high priest . . was making the offering of atonement 1

offering of fruit 1. *κάρπωσις*

Sir 30:19 Of what use to an idol is an offering of fruit? 1

offering of praise 1. הִלּוּל

Lev 19:24 holy, an offering of praise to the LORD 1

ordination offering 1. מִלּוּא

Lev 8:28 as an ordination offering, a pleasing odor 1
31 in the basket of ordination offerings 1

passover offering 1. פֶּסַח

2Ch 35: 7 as passover offerings for all that were present 1
8 for the passover offerings 2,600 lambs and kids 1
9 gave to the Levites for the passover offerings 1

peace offering 1. שֶׁלֶם 2. *σωτήριος*

Exd 20:24 your burnt offerings and your peace offerings 1
32: 6 offerings and brought peace offerings; 1
Lev 3: 1 offering is a sacrifice of peace offering 1
3 from the sacrifice of the peace offering 1
6 a sacrifice of peace offering to the LORD 1
9 Then from the sacrifice of the peace offering 1
4:10 the ox of the sacrifice of the peace offerings) 1
26 like the fat of sacrifice of peace offerings 1
31 as the fat is removed from the peace offerings 1
35 from the sacrifice of peace offerings 1
6:12 shall burn on it the fat of the peace offerings 1
7:11 the law of the sacrifice of peace offerings 1
13 With the sacrifice of his peace offerings 1
14 who throws the blood of the peace offerings 1
15 the sacrifice of his peace offerings 1
18 sacrifice of his peace offering is eaten 1
20 sacrifice of the LORD'S peace offerings 1
21 the sacrifice of the LORD'S peace offerings 1
29 the sacrifice of his peace offerings to the LORD 1
29 from the sacrifice of his peace offerings 1
32 from the sacrifice of your peace offerings 1
33 offers the blood of the peace offerings 1
34 out of the sacrifices of their peace offerings 1
37 of the consecration, and of the peace offerings 1
9: 4 an ox and a ram for peace offerings, to sacrifice 1
18 the sacrifice of peace offerings for the people 1
22 the burnt offering and the peace offerings 1
10:14 sacrifices of the peace offerings of the people 1
17: 5 as sacrifices of peace offerings to the LORD 1
19: 5 offer a sacrifice of peace offerings to the LORD 1
22:21 any one offers a sacrifice of peace offerings 1
23:19 lambs a year old as a sacrifice of peace offerings 1
Num 6:14 one ram without blemish as a peace offering 1
17 ram as a sacrifice of peace offering to the LORD 1
18 under the sacrifice of the peace offering. 1
7:17 for the sacrifice of peace offerings, two oxen 1
23 for the sacrifice of peace offerings, two oxen 1
29 for the sacrifice of peace offerings, two oxen 1
35 for the sacrifice of peace offerings, two oxen 1
41 for the sacrifice of peace offerings, two oxen 1
47 for the sacrifice of peace offerings, two oxen 1
53 for the sacrifice of peace offerings, two oxen 1
59 for the sacrifice of peace offerings, two oxen 1
65 for the sacrifice of peace offerings, two oxen 1
71 for the sacrifice of peace offerings, two oxen 1
77 for the sacrifice of peace offerings, two oxen 1
83 for the sacrifice of peace offerings, two oxen 1
88 cattle for the sacrifice of peace offerings 1
10:10 over the sacrifices of your peace offerings; 1
15: 8 a bull for . . peace offerings to the LORD 1
29:39 offer . . for your peace offerings. 1
Deu 27: 7 sacrifice peace offerings, and shall eat there; 1
Jos 8:31 and sacrificed peace offerings. 1
22:27 offerings and sacrifices and peace offerings; 1
Jdg 20:26 offered burnt offerings and peace offerings 1
21: 4 offered burnt offerings and peace offerings. 1
1Sm 13: 9 Bring the . . here to me, and the peace offerings. 1
2Sm 6:17 offered burnt offerings and peace offerings 1
18 offering the burnt . . and the peace offerings 1
24:25 offered burnt offerings and peace offerings. 1
1Kg 3:15 offered up burnt offerings and peace offerings 1
8:63 Solomon offered as peace offerings to the LORD 1
64 and the fat pieces of the peace offerings. 1
64 and the fat pieces of the peace offerings. 1
9:25 offer up burnt offerings and peace offerings 1
2Kg 16:13 and threw the blood of his peace offerings upon 1
1Ch 16: 1 offered burnt offerings and peace offerings 1
2 finished offering . . the peace offerings 1
21:26 presented burnt offerings and peace offerings 1
2Ch 7: 7 offered . . the fat of the peace offerings 1
29:35 there was the fat of the peace offerings 1
30:22 sacrificing peace offerings and giving thanks 1
31: 2 priests and the Levites, for . . peace offerings 1
33:16 offered upon it sacrifices of peace offerings 1
Ezk 43:27 your burnt offerings and your peace offerings; 1
45:15 and peace offerings, to make atonement for them 1
17 and peace offerings, to make atonement 1
46: 2 his burnt offering and his peace offerings 1
12 either a burnt offering or peace offerings 1
12 offer his burnt offering or his peace offerings 1
Ams 5:22 and the peace offerings of your fatted beasts 1
Sir 35: 1 sacrifices a peace offering. 2
47: 2 As the fat is selected from the peace offering 2

sacrificial offering 1. *θυσιαστήριον*

1Co 9:13 share in the sacrificial offerings? 1

sin offering 1. חַטָּאָה 2. חַטָּאת 3. חַטָּיא (A) 4. *περὶ ἁμαρτίας*

Exd 29:14 it is a sin offering. 2
36 every day you shall offer a bull as a sin offering 2
30:10 with the blood of the sin offering of atonement 2
Lev 4: 3 a young bull . . to the LORD for a sin offering 2
8 all the fat of the bull of the sin offering 2
14 shall offer a young bull for a sin offering 2
20 as he did with the bull of the sin offering 2
21 it is the sin offering for the assembly 2
24 before the LORD; it is a sin offering 2
25 take some of the blood of the sin offering 2
29 lay his hand on the head of the sin offering 2
29 and kill the sin offering in the place 2
32 brings a lamb as his offering for a sin offering 2
33 lay his hand upon the head of the sin offering 2
33 kill it for a sin offering in the place 2
34 take some of the blood of the sin offering 2
5: 6 a lamb or a goat, for a sin offering 2
7 two young pigeons, one for a sin offering 2
8 who shall offer first the one for the sin offering 2
9 sprinkle some of the blood of the sin offering 2
9 at the base of the altar; it is a sin offering 2
11 tenth of an ephah of fine flour for a sin offering 2
11 no frankincense on it, for it is a sin offering 2
12 to the LORD; it is a sin offering 2
6:17 like the sin offering and the guilt offering 2
25 This is the law for the sin offering 2
25 shall the sin offering be killed before the LORD 2
30 no sin offering shall be eaten from which any 2
7: 7 The guilt offering is like the sin offering 2
37 of the cereal offering, of the sin offering 2
8: 2 the bull of the sin offering, and the two rams 2
14 Then he brought the bull of the sin offering 2
14 the head of the bull of the sin offering 2
9: 2 Take a bull calf for a sin offering, and a ram 2
3 Take a male goat for a sin offering, and a calf 2
7 offer your sin offering and your burnt offering 2
8 Aaron . . killed the calf of the sin offering 2
10 the appendage of the liver from the sin offering 2
15 took the goat of the sin offering 2
15 offered it for sin, like the first sin offering •
22 he came down from offering the sin offering 2
10:16 inquired about the goat of the sin offering 2
17 Why have you not eaten the sin offering 2
19 today they have offered their sin offering 2
19 If I had eaten the sin offering today 2
12: 6 a young pigeon or a turtledove for a sin offering 2
8 a burnt offering and the other for a sin offering 2
14:13 in the place where they kill the sin offering 2
13 for the guilt offering, like the sin offering 2
19 The priest shall offer the sin offering 2
22 the one shall be a sin offering and the other 2
31 one for a sin offering and the other 2
15:15 priest shall offer them, one for a sin offering 2
30 the priest shall offer one for a sin offering 2
16: 3 with a young bull for a sin offering and a ram 2
5 two male goats for a sin offering 2
6 Aaron shall offer the bull as a sin offering 2
9 the goat . . and offer it as a sin offering 2
11 Aaron shall present the bull as a sin offering 2
11 kill the bull as a sin offering for himself 2
15 Then he shall kill the goat of the sin offering 2
25 the fat of the sin offering he shall burn 2
27 the bull for the sin offering and the goat 2
27 the bull . . and the goat for the sin offering 2
23:19 you shall offer one male goat for a sin offering 2
Num 6:11 the priest shall offer one for a sin offering 2
14 one ewe lamb a year old . . as a sin offering 2
16 offer his sin offering and his burnt offering 2
7:16 one male goat for a sin offering; 2
22 one male goat for a sin offering; 2
28 one male goat for a sin offering; 2
34 one male goat for a sin offering; 2
40 one male goat for a sin offering; 2
46 one male goat for a sin offering; 2
52 one male goat for a sin offering; 2
58 one male goat for a sin offering; 2
64 one male goat for a sin offering; 2
70 one male goat for a sin offering; 2
76 one male goat for a sin offering; 2
82 one male goat for a sin offering; 2
87 twelve male goats for a sin offering; 2
8: 8 take another young bull for a sin offering. 2
12 shall offer the one for a sin offering 2
15:24 and one male goat for a sin offering. 2
25 brought . . their sin offering before the LORD 2
27 offer a female goat a year old for a sin offering. 2
18: 9 This shall be yours . . every sin offering 2
19:17 shall take some ashes of the burnt sin offering 2
28:15 Also one male goat for a sin offering to the LORD; 2
22 also one male goat for a sin offering 2
29: 5 one male goat for a sin offering, to make atonement 2
11 also one male goat for a sin offering 2
11 besides the sin offering of atonement 2
16 also one male goat for a sin offering 2
19 also one male goat for a sin offering 2
22 also one male goat for a sin offering 2
25 also one male goat for a sin offering 2
28 also one male goat for a sin offering; 2
31 also one male goat for a sin offering; 2
34 also one male goat for a sin offering; 2
38 also one male goat for a sin offering; 2
2Kg 12:16 the money from the sin offerings was not brought 2
2Ch 29:21 for a sin offering for the kingdom 2
23 the he-goats for the sin offering were brought 2
24 king commanded that . . the sin offering 2
Ezr 6:17 sin offering for all Israel twelve he-goats 3
8:35 as a sin offering twelve he-goats; 2
Neh 10:33 holy things, and the sin offerings to make 2
Ps 40: 6 sin offering thou hast not required. 1
Ezk 40:39 on which the burnt offering and the sin offering 2
42:13 the sin offering, and the guilt offering 2

43:19 says the Lord GOD, a bull for a sin offering. 2
21 You shall also take the bull of the sin offering 2
22 a he-goat without blemish for a sin offering; 2
25 you shall provide daily a goat for a sin offering; 2
44:27 he shall offer his sin offering, says the Lord GOD 2
29 the sin offering, and the guilt offering; 2
45:17 he shall provide the sin offerings 2
19 shall take some of the blood of the sin offering 2
22 a young bull for a sin offering. 2
23 and a he-goat daily for a sin offering. 2
25 make the same provision for sin offerings 2
46:20 boil the guilt offering and the sin offering, 2
Bar 1:10 burnt offerings and sin offerings and incense 4

thank offering 1. תּוֹדָה 2. *αἴνεσις* 3. *ὑπὲρ σωτηρίου* 4. *χάρις*

Lev 7:12 offer with the thank offering unleavened cakes 1
2Ch 29:31 come near, bring sacrifices and thank offerings 1
31 assembly brought . . thank offerings; 1
Ps 56:12 O God; I will render thank offerings to thee. 1
100: 0 A Psalm for the thank offering. 1
Jer 17:26 thank offerings to the house of the LORD. 1
33:11 those who sing, as they bring thank offerings 1
1Es 8:66 72 lambs, and as a thank offering twelve he-goats 3
Sir 35: 2 he who gives alms sacrifices a thank offering. 2
3Mc 1: 9 and made thank-offerings 4

votive offering 1. נֶדֶר 2. *ἀνάθεμα* 3. *ἀνάθημα* 4. *εὐχή* 5. *κατ' εὐχάς*

Lev 7:16 his offering is a votive offering or a freewill 1
22:23 but for a votive offering it cannot be accepted 1
23:38 and besides all your votive offerings 1
Num29:39 offer . . in addition to your votive offerings 1
Deu 12: 6 bring . . your votive offerings 1
11 bring . . all your votive offerings 1
17 You may not eat . . any of your votive offerings 1
26 holy things . . and your votive offerings 1
1Es 2: 7 the other things added as votive offerings 5
9 a very great number of votive offerings 4
Jdt 16:19 the canopy . . she gave as a votive offering to the Lord. 3
2Mc 2:13 letters of kings about votive offerings. 2

wave offering 1. תְּנוּפָה

Exd 29:24 wave them for a wave offering before the LORD. 1
26 take the breast . . and wave it for a wave offering 1
27 consecrate the breast of the wave offering 1
Lev 7:30 that the breast may be waved as a wave offering 1
8:27 waved them as a wave offering before the LORD 1
29 waved it for a wave offering before the LORD 1
9:21 the right thigh Aaron waved for a wave offering 1
10:15 to wave for a wave offering before the LORD 1
14:12 wave them for a wave offering before the LORD 1
24 the priest shall wave them for a wave offering 1
23:15 you brought the sheaf of the wave offering 1
20 first fruits as a wave offering before the LORD 1
Num 6:20 the priest shall wave them for a wave offering 1
8:11 as a wave offering from the people of Israel 1
13 shall offer them as a wave offering to the LORD. 1
15 when you . . offered them as a wave offering. 1
21 Aaron offered them as a wave offering 1
18:11 all the wave offerings of the people of Israel; 1

whole burnt offering 1. כָּלִיל 2. *ὁλοκαύτωμα*

Deu 13:16 as a whole burnt offering to the LORD your God 1
33:10 put . . whole burnt offering upon thy altar. 1
Ps 51:19 in burnt offerings and whole burnt offerings; 1
Mrk 12:33 much more than all whole burnt offerings 2
2Mc 2:10 fire . . consumed the whole burnt offerings. 2

office 1. כֵּן 2. מַצָּב 3. מִשְׁמֶרֶת 4. *ἀρχή* 5. *ἐπισκοπή* 6. *οἰκονομία* 7. *χρεία*

Gen 40:13 restore you to your office; and you shall place 1
41:13 I was restored to my office, and the baker was 1
Deu 17: 9 to the judge who is in office in those days •
19:17 priests and the judges . . in office in those days; •
26: 3 go to the priest who is in office at that time •
2Ch 8:14 he appointed . . the Levites for their offices 3
31:16 for their service according to their offices 3
17 Levites . . was according to their offices 3
35: 2 He appointed the priests to their offices 3
Isa 22:19 I will thrust you from your office 2
Act 1:20 'His office let another take.' 5
Col 1:25 the divine office which was given to me 6
1Ti 3: 1 If any one aspires to the office of bishop •
Heb 7:23 were prevented by death from continuing in office; •
1Mc 11:63 intending to remove him from office. 7
13:15 in connection with the offices he held 7
2Mc 4:10 When the king assented and Jason came to office 4
27 Menelaus held the office 4
50 remained in office, growing in wickedness 4
13: 3 thought that he would be established in office. 4
4Mc 4:17 if the office were conferred upon him 4

office *See also* due, minister, take.

high office 1. *ἡγεμονία*

Sir 7: 4 not seek from the Lord the highest office 1

office of trust 1. אֱמוּנָה

1Ch 9:22 established them in their office of trust. 1

priestly office 1. *ἱερατεία*

Heb 7: 5 descendants of Levi who receive the priestly office 1

tax office 1. *τελώνιον*

Mat 9: 9 a man called Matthew sitting at the tax office; 1
Mrk 2:14 the son of Alphaeus sitting at the tax office 1
Lke 5:27 a tax collector . . sitting at the tax office; 1

officer 1. אַדִּיר 2. נצב 3. נְצִיב 4. סָרִיס 5. עֶבֶד 6. פקד 7. פְּקֻדָּה 8. פָּקִיד 9. ראשׁ 10. שַׂר 11. שֹׁטֵר 12. שָׁלִישׁ 13. *ἀνήρ* 14. *ἄρχων* 15. *δυνατός* 16. *ἐπιστάτης* 17. *θεράπων* 18. *μεγιστάν* 19. *ὁ ἐπί* 20. *ὁ παρά* 21. *παῖς* 22. *πράκτωρ* 23. *στρατηγός* 24. *συγγενής* 25. *ὑπηρέτης* 26. *χιλίαρχος* 27. *χρεία*

Gen 37:36 sold him . . to Pot'i-phar, an officer of Pharaoh 4
39: 1 Pot'i-phar, an officer of Pharaoh, bought him 4
40: 2 Pharaoh was angry with his two officers 4
7 he asked Pharaoh's officers who were with him 4
Exd 14: 7 chariots . . with officers over all of them. 12
15: 4 his picked officers are sunk in the Red Sea. 12
Num11:16 whom you know to be . . officers over them; 11
31:14 Moses was angry with the officers of the army 6
48 officers . . of the army, . . , came near to Moses 6
Deu 1:15 heads over you, commanders . . and officers 11
16:18 appoint judges and officers in all your towns 11
20: 5 Then the officers shall speak to the people 11
8 officers shall speak further to the people 11
9 when the officers have made an end of speaking 11
29:10 heads . . your elders, and your officers, all 11
31:28 Assemble . . the elders . . and your officers 11
Jos 1:10 Joshua commanded the officers of the people 11
3: 2 the officers went through the camp 11
8:33 with their elders and officers and their judges 11
23: 2 elders and heads, their judges and officers 11
24: 1 the heads, the judges, and the officers of Israel; 11
Jdg 9:28 the son of Jerubba'al and Zebul his officer 8
1Sm 8:15 and give it to his officers and to his servants. 4
1Kg 4: 5 Azari'ah the son of Nathan was over the officers; 2
7 Solomon had twelve officers over all Israel, who 2
19 And there was one officer in the land of Judah. 3
27 those officers supplied provisions for King 2
5:16 Solomon's . . officers who were over the work 2
9:23 the chief officers who were over Solomon's work 10
14:27 and committed them to the hands of the officers 10
22: 9 the king of Israel summoned an officer and said 4
2Kg 10:25 Jehu said to the guard and to the officers, "Go 12
25 the guard and the officers cast them out 12
25:19 an officer who had been in command of the men 4
1Ch 12:14 These Gadites were officers of the army 9
18 David . . made them officers of his troops. 9
23: 4 6,000 shall be officers and judges 11
24: 5 there were officers of the sanctuary 10
5 there were . . the sanctuary and officers of God 10
26:26 officers of the thousands and the hundreds 10
29 outside duties . . as officers and judges. 11
27: 1 officers who served the king in all matters 11
28: 1 officers of the divisions that served the king 10
21 also the officers . . wholly at your command. 10
29: 6 and the officers over the king's work. 10
2Ch 8: 9 they were soldiers, and his officers 10
10 these were the chief officers of King Solomon 2
12:10 committed them to the hands of the officers 10
18: 8 the king of Israel summoned an officer and said 4
19:11 the Levites will serve you as officers. 11
24:11 chest was brought to the king's officers 7
11 secretary and the officer of the chief priest 8
26:11 in the muster made by . . Ma-asei'ah the officer 11
32: 3 he planned with his officers and his mighty men 10
21 cut off all the . . commanders and officers 10
Ezr 7:28 before all the king's mighty officers. 10
Neh 2: 9 sent with me officers of the army and horsemen. 10
Est 2: 3 the king appoint officers in all the provinces 8
Prv 6: 7 Without having any chief, officer or ruler 11
Isa 31: 9 and his officers desert the standard in panic 10
Jer 39: 3 the rest of the officers of the king of Babylon. 10
46:26 the hand of Nebuchadrez'zar . . and his officers. 5
52:25 he took an officer who had been in command 4
Ezk 23:15 all of them looking like officers 12
23 commanders all of them, officers and warriors 12
Nah 2: 5 officers are summoned, they stumble as they go 1
Mrk 6:21 a banquet for his courtiers and officers 26
Lke 12:58 lest . . the judge hand you over to the officer 22
58 the officer put you in prison. 22
22: 4 and conferred with the chief priests and officers 23
52 the chief priests and officers of the temple 23
Joh 7:32 the chief priests and Pharisees sent officers 25
45 The officers then went back to the chief priests 25
46 The officers answered 25
18: 3 some officers from the chief priests 25
12 their captain and the officers of the Jews 25
18 officers had made a charcoal fire 25
22 one of the officers standing by struck Jesus 25
19: 6 When the chief priests and the officers saw him 25
Act 5:22 when the officers came 25
26 captain with the officers went and brought them 25
1Es 4:49 no officer or satrap or governor or treasurer 15
Jdt 2: 2 He called together all his officers 17
14 generals, and officers of the Assyrian army 16
5:22 Holofernes' officers 18
12:10 did not invite any of his officers. 27
14: 3 rouse the officers of the Assyrian army 23
12 they went . . to all their officers. 14
1Mc 1: 6 So he summoned his most honored officers 21
8 his officers began to rule, each in his own place. 21
2:15 the king's officers . . came to the city of Modein 20
17 Then the king's officers spoke to Mattathias 20
25 At the same time he killed the king's officer 13
31 it was reported to the king's officers 13
5:40 Timothy said to the officers of his forces 14
10:37 Let their officers . . be of their own number 19
63 he said to his officers 14
11:63 the officers of Demetrius had come to Kadesh 14
3Mc 5:44 the friends and officers departed with great joy 24

chief officer 1. נָגִיד 2. פָּקִיד נָגִיד 3. רַב 4. *ἐπιστάτης*

1Ch 9:11 Ahi'tub . . chief officer of the house of God; 1
26:24 chief officer in charge of the treasuries. 1
27:16 Elie'zer the son of Zichri was chief officer; 1
2Ch 31:12 chief officer in charge of them was Conani'ah 1
13 Azari'ah the chief officer of the house of God. 1
35: 8 the chief officers of the house of God 1
Jer 20: 1 who was chief officer in the house of the LORD 2
39:13 all the chief officers of the king of Babylon 3
41: 1 Ish'mael . . one of the chief officers of the king 3
1Es 1: 8 the chief officers of the temple 4

chief officer of the temple 1. *ἱεροστάτης*

1Es 7: 2 the chief officers of the temple. 1

official 1. סָגָן 2. סָרִיס 3. עֶבֶד 4. עשׂה מְלָאכָה 5. פְּקֻחַ 6. רַב 7. שַׂר 8. שֹׁטֵר 9. שׁרת 10. טַרְפְּלָיֵא (A) 11. שִׁלְטוֹן (A) 12. *βασιλικός* 13. *λειτουργός* 14. *ὁ ἐπὶ τῶν χρειῶν* 15. *συγγενής*

Exd 23: 8 no bribe, for a bribe blinds the officials 5
Jdg 8: 6 the officials of Succoth said, "Are Zebah 7
14 wrote down . . the officials and elders 7
1Kg 1: 9 he invited . . and all the royal officials of Judah 3
4: 2 these were his high officials: Azari'ah the son 7
9:22 they were his officials, his commanders 3
10: 5 food of his table, the seating of his officials 3
2Kg 8: 6 So the king appointed an official for her, saying 2
24:15 king's wives, his officials, and the chief men 2
25:24 not be afraid because of the Chalde'an officials; 3
1Ch 28: 1 David assembled . . all the officials of Israel 7
1 officials of Israel, the officials of the tribes 7
2Ch 9: 4 food of his table, the seating of his officials 3
29:20 Hezeki'ah . . gathered the officials of the city 7
34:13 Levites were . . officials, and gatekeepers. 8
Ezr 4: 9 judges, the governors, the officials 10
8:20 temple servants, whom David and his officials 7
9: 1 officials approached me and said, "The people 7
2 hand of the officials and chief men 7
10: 8 by order of the officials and the elders 7
14 Let our officials stand for the whole assembly; 7
Neh 2:16 officials did not know where I had gone 1
16 I had not yet told the . . officials, and the rest 1
4:14 said to the nobles and to the officials 1
19 I said to the nobles and to the officials 1
5: 7 charges against the nobles and the officials. 1
17 there were at my table 150 men, Jews and officials 1
7: 5 assemble the nobles and the officials 1
12:40 house of God, and I and half of the officials 1
13:11 I remonstrated with the officials and said, "Why 1
Est 1: 8 the king had given orders to all the officials 6
9: 3 governors and the royal officials also helped 4
Prv 29:12 falsehood, all his officials will be wicked. 9
Isa 30: 4 For though his officials are at Zo'an 7
Dan 3: 2 assemble . . all the officials of the provinces 11
3 all the officials of the provinces 11
Zep 1: 8 I will punish the officials and the king's sons 7
3: 3 Her officials within her are roaring lions; 7
Joh 4:46 there was an official whose son was ill. 12
49 The official said to him, "Sir, come down 12
1Es 8:67 these officials honored the people •
Sir 10: 2 so are his officials 13
1Mc 10:33 let all officials cancel also the taxes •
42 which my officials have received every year •
12:45 the remaining troops and all the officials 14
13:37 to write to our officials to grant you release 14
3Mc 5:39 the officials who were at table with him 15
6:30 summoned the official in charge of the revenues •

official *See also* government.

chief official 1. רִאשׁוֹן

1Ch 18:17 the chief officials in the service of the king. 1

high official 1. גָּבֹהַּ

Ecc 5: 8 for the high official is watched by a higher 1

palace official 1. סָרִיס

2Kg 24:12 and his princes, and his palace officials. 1
1Ch 28: 1 with the palace officials, the mighty men 1

offscouring 1. סְחִי 2. περίψημα

Lam 3:45 Thou hast made us offscouring and refuse 1
1Co 4:13 the offscouring of all things. 2

offset 1. מִגְרָעָה 2. διάστημα 3. τοῖχος

1Kg 6: 6 outside of the house he made offsets on the wall 1
Ezk 41: 6 There were offsets all around the wall 2
7 corresponding to the enlargement of the offset 3
Hos 12: 8 but all his riches can never offset the guilt *

offshoot 1. παραφυάς

4Mc 1:28 there are many offshoots of these plants 1

offspring 1. בֵּן 2. זֶרַע 3. יֶלֶד 4. יצא יָרֵךְ 5. מוֹלֶדֶת 6. נִין 7. פְּרִי 8. צֶאֱצָא 9. ἀπόγονος 10. γένεσις 11. γένημα 12. γεννάω 13. γένος 14. σπέρμα 15. generatio

Gen 15: 3 Behold, thou hast given me no offspring; 2
17:12 any foreigner who is not of your offspring 2
19:32 lie with him, that we may preserve offspring 2
34 lie with him, that we may preserve offspring 2
21:13 the son . . because he is your offspring. 2
23 deal falsely . . with my offspring 6
38: 8 to her, and raise up offspring for your brother. 2
9 Onan knew that the offspring would not be his; 2
9 lest he should give offspring to his brother. 2
46: 6 into Egypt, Jacob and all his offspring with him 2
7 all his offspring he brought with him 2
26 own offspring, not including Jacob's sons' wives 4
48: 6 the offspring born to you after them shall be 5
Exd 1: 5 All the offspring of Jacob were 70 persons; 4
Num18:19 for you and for your offspring with you. 2
Deu 28:51 eat the offspring of your cattle and the fruit 7
53 you shall eat the offspring of your own body 7
59 LORD will bring on you and your offspring 2
30: 6 God will circumcise . . the heart of your offspring 2
Jos 24: 3 led him through . . and made his offspring many. 2
Jdg 8:30 Gideon had 70 sons, his own offspring 4
2Sm 4: 8 avenged my lord . . on Saul and on his offspring. 2
7:12 I will raise up your offspring after you 2
1Kg 1:48 granted one of my offspring to sit on my throne 14
1Ch 7:13 Jah'zi-el, Guni . . the offspring of Bilhah. 1
16:13 O offspring of Abraham his servant 2
17:11 I will raise up your offspring after you 2
Job 5:25 your offspring as the grass of the earth. 8
18:19 He has no offspring or descendant 6
21: 8 and their offspring before their eyes. 8
27:14 his offspring have not enough to eat. 8
39: 3 when they crouch, bring forth their offspring 3
Ps 21:10 You will destroy their offspring from the earth 7
105: 6 O offspring of Abraham, his servant 2
Isa 1: 4 offspring of evildoers, sons who deal corruptly! 2
14:22 cut off from Babylon . . offspring and posterity 6
22:24 of his father's house, the offspring and issue 8
41: 8 Israel . . the offspring of Abraham, my friend; 2
43: 5 I will bring your offspring from the east 2
44: 3 I will pour . . my blessing on your offspring. 8
45:19 I did not say to the offspring of Jacob 2
25 the offspring of Israel shall triumph and glory. 2
48:19 your offspring would have been like the sand 2
53:10 an offering for sin, he shall see his offspring 2
57: 3 offspring of the adulterer and the harlot. 2
4 of transgression, the offspring of deceit 2
61: 9 and their offspring in the midst of the peoples; 8
65:23 shall be the offspring of the blessed of the LORD 2
Jer 7:15 all your kinsmen, all the offspring of E'phraim. 2
22:30 for none of his offspring shall succeed 2
30:10 offspring from the land of their captivity. 2
36:31 I will punish him and his offspring 2
46:27 your offspring from the land of . . captivity. 2
Lam 2:20 Should women eat their offspring 7
Dan 11: 6 he and his offspring shall not endure; 2
Mal 2: 3 Behold, I will rebuke your offspring 2
15 what does he desire? Godly offspring. 2
Act 17:28 For we are indeed his offspring.' 13
29 Being then God's offspring 13
Gal 3:16 to Abraham and to his offspring 14
16 It does not say, "And to offsprings 14
16 And to your offspring," which is Christ. 14
19 till the offspring should come 14
29 then you are Abraham's offspring 14
Rev 12:17 went off to make war on the rest of her offspring 14
22:16 I am the root and the offspring of David 13
2Es 2: 6 so that they may have no offspring. 15
Wis 3:13 their offspring are accursed 10
16 the offspring of an unlawful union will perish. 10
Sus 1:56 You offspring of Canaan and not of Judah 14
1Mc 1:38 she became strange to her offspring 11
4Mc 14:14 parental love for their offspring. 12
15: 4 have a deeper sympathy toward their offspring 12
13 yearning of parents toward offspring 13
18: 1 offspring of the seed of Abraham 9

without offspring 1. ἀνόνητος

4Mc 16: 9 others married and without offspring 1

often 1. מִדֵּי 2. רבה 3. ἐνδελεχέω 4. ἐν πολλοῖς 5. ὁσάκις 6. ὁσάκις ἐάν 7. πλεονάκις 8. πολλά 9. πολλάκις 10. πυκνός 11. frequenter

1Sm 1: 7 as often as she went up . . she used to provoke her. 1
18:30 as often as they came out David had more success 1
2Sm 8:10 Hadade'zer had often been at war with To'i. *
1Kg 14:28 as often as the king went into the house 1
1Ch 18:10 for Hadade'zer had often been at war with To'u. *
2Ch 12:11 as often as the king went into the house 1
Ps 78:38 he restrained his anger often 2
Prv 29: 1 He who is often reproved, yet stiffens his neck *
Isa 28:19 As often as it passes through it will take you; 1
Jer 31:20 For as often as I speak against him, I do remember 1
Mat 17:15 for often he falls into the fire 9
15 and often into the water. 9
Mrk 5: 4 he had often been bound with fetters and chains 9
9:22 often cast him into the fire and into the water 9
Lke 5:33 disciples of John fast often and offer prayers 10
Joh 18: 2 Jesus often met there with his disciples. 9
Act 24:26 So he sent for him often and conversed with him. 10
26:11 I punished them often in all the synagogues 9
Rom 1:13 that I have often intended to come to you 9
15:22 I have so often been hindered from coming to you. 8
1Co 11:25 Do this, as often as you drink it 6
26 For as often as you eat this bread 6
2Co 8:22 whom we have often tested 4
11:23 with countless beatings, and often near death. 9
27 in hunger and thirst, often without food 9
Php 3:18 many, of whom I have often told you and now tell you 9
2Ti 1:16 he often refreshed me 9
Heb 6: 7 drunk the rain that often falls upon it 9
Rev 11: 6 with every plague, as often as they desire. 5
2Es 4:26 and if you live long, you will often marvel 11
5: 8 and fire shall often break out 11
8:47 often compared yourself to the unrighteous 11
Tob 1: 6 I alone went often to Jerusalem for the feasts 7
AEs 16: 5 often many of those . . have been involved 9
Sir 19:15 Question a friend, for often it is slander 9
30: 1 He who loves his son will whip him often 3
34:12 I have often been in danger of death 7
1Mc 14:29 Since wars often occurred in the country 9
2Mc 9:25 often entrusted and commended to most of you 9
12:22 often they were injured by their own men 9
3Mc 6:26 and often have accepted willingly the worst 7

how often 1. כַּמָּה 2. ποσάκις

Job 21:17 How often is it that the lamp of the wicked 1
Ps 78:40 How often they rebelled against him 1
Mat 18:21 Lord, how often shall my brother sin against me 2
23:37 How often would I have gathered your children 2
Lke 13:34 How often would I have gathered your children 2
Sir 20:17 How many will ridicule him, and how often! 2

more often 1. πυκνός

AEs 16: 2 The more often they are honored 1

oftentimes 1. πλεονάκις

3Mc 2:12 because oftentimes . . you helped them 1

oh 1. בִּי 2. גַּם 3. נָא

Gen 18:30 Then he said, "Oh let not the Lord be angry 3
32 Then he said, "Oh let not the Lord be angry 3
19:18 Lot said to them, "Oh, no, my lords; 3
43:20 said, "Oh, my lord, we came down the first time 1
Exd 4:10 Moses said to the LORD, "Oh, my Lord, I am not 1
13 he said, "Oh, my Lord, send, I pray, some other person. 1
Num12:11 Aaron said to Moses, "Oh, my lord, do not punish us 1
Deu 5:29 Oh that they had such a mind as this always *
1Sm 1:26 Oh, my lord! As you live, my lord, I am the woman 1
2Sm 15: 4 Oh that I were judge in the land! *
19:30 Mephib'osheth said . . "Oh, let him take it all 2
1Kg 3:17 Oh, my lord, this woman and I dwell in the same 1
26 Oh, my lord, give her the living child, and by no 1
2Kg 4:19 he said to his father, "Oh, my head, my head! *
Job 19:24 Oh that with an iron pen and lead they were graven *
31:35 Oh, that I had the indictment *
Ps 25:20 Oh guard my life, and deliver me; *
43: 3 Oh send out thy light and thy truth; *
60: 1 thou hast been angry; oh, restore us. *
61: 4 Oh to be safe under the shelter of thy wings! Selah *
101: 2 Oh when wilt thou come to me? *
119:97 Oh, how I love thy law! It is my meditation *
Sng 7: 8 Oh, may your breasts be like clusters of the vine 3
Isa 38:16 Oh, restore me to health and make me live! *
Jer 4:19 I writhe in pain! Oh, the walls of my heart! *
44: 4 Oh, do not do this abominable thing that I hate! 3
Mal 1:10 Oh, that there were one among you who would shut *

oh that 1. אִם 2. מִי נתן

1Ch 4:10 Jabez . . saying, "Oh that thou wouldst bless me 1
Job 11: 5 oh, that God would speak, and open his lips to you 2
13: 5 Oh that you would keep silent 2
14:13 Oh that thou wouldest hide me in Sheol 2
19:23 Oh that my words were written! 2
23 Oh that they were inscribed in a book! 2
23: 3 Oh, that I knew where I might find him 2
29: 2 Oh, that I were as in the months of old 2
31:35 Oh, that I had one to hear me! 2

oil 1. יִצְהָר 2. משח 3. שֶׁמֶן 4. מְשַׁח (A) 5. ἔλαιον

Gen 28:18 for a pillar and poured oil on the top of it. 3
35:14 drink offering on it, and poured oil on it. 3
Exd 25: 6 oil for the lamps, spices for the anointing oil 3
6 oil for the lamps, spices for the anointing oil 3
27:20 bring . . pure beaten olive oil for the light 3
29: 2 unleavened cakes mixed with oil, and unleavened 3
2 and unleavened wafers spread with oil. 3
7 you shall take the anointing oil 3
21 take . . the anointing oil, and sprinkle it 3
23 one cake of bread with oil, and one wafer 3
40 a fourth of a hin of beaten oil, and a fourth of a hin 3
30:24 of olive oil a hin; 3
25 you shall make of these a sacred anointing oil 3
25 a holy anointing oil it shall be. 3
31 anointing oil throughout your generations. 3
31:11 anointing oil and the fragrant incense 3
35: 8 oil for the light, spices for the anointing oil 3
8 oil for the light, spices for the anointing oil 3
14 its lamps, and the oil for the light; 3
15 the anointing oil and the fragrant incense 3
28 spices and oil for the light 3
28 oil for the light, and for the anointing oil 3
37:29 He made the holy anointing oil also, and the pure 3
39:37 all its utensils, and the oil for the light; 3
38 the anointing oil and the fragrant incense 3
40: 9 Then you shall take the anointing oil, and anoint 3
Lev 2: 1 he shall pour oil upon it, and put frankincense 3
2 take . . a handful of the fine flour and oil 3
4 cakes of fine flour mixed with oil 3
4 unleavened wafers spread with oil 3
5 shall be of fine flour unleavened, mixed with oil 3
6 you shall break it in pieces, and pour oil on it 3
7 it shall be made of fine flour with oil 3
15 you shall put oil upon it, and lay frankincense 3
16 burn . . part of the crushed grain and of the oil 3
5:11 he shall put no oil upon it 3
6:15 fine flour of the cereal offering with its oil 3
21 It shall be made with oil on a griddle 3
7:10 every cereal offering, mixed with oil or dry 3
12 offer . . unleavened cakes mixed with oil 3
12 unleavened wafers spread with oil, and cakes 3
12 cakes of fine flour well mixed with oil 3
8: 2 Take . . the anointing oil, and the bull of the sin 3
10 The Moses took the anointing oil, and anointed 3
12 poured some of the anointing oil on Aaron's head 3
26 took . . one cake of bread with oil, and one wafer 3
30 took some of the anointing oil and of the blood 3
9: 4 and a cereal offering mixed with oil 3
10: 7 for the anointing oil of the LORD is upon you 3
14:10 an ephah of fine flour mixed with oil, and one log 3
10 mixed with oil, and one log of oil 3
12 offer it . . along with the log of oil 3
15 Then the priest shall take some of the log of oil 3
16 dip his right finger in the oil that is in his left 3
16 sprinkle some oil with his finger seven times 3
17 some of the oil that remains in his hand 3
18 the rest of the oil that is in the priest's hand 3
21 a tenth of an ephah of fine flour mixed with oil 3
21 oil for a cereal offering, and a log of oil 3
24 the lamb of the guilt offering, and the log of oil 3
26 the priest shall pour some of the oil 3
27 sprinkle with his right finger some of the oil 3
28 shall put some of the oil that is in his hand 3
29 the rest of the oil that is in the priest's hand 3
21:10 upon whose head the anointing oil is poured 3
12 for the consecration of the anointing oil 3
23:13 two tenths of an ephah of fine flour mixed with oil 3
24: 2 to bring you pure oil from beaten olives 3
Num 4: 9 with its lamps . . and all the vessels for oil 3
16 charge of the oil for the light 3
16 charge of . . and the anointing oil 3
5:15 shall pour no oil upon it and put no frankincense 3
6:15 cakes of fine flour mixed with oil 3
15 unleavened wafers spread with oil 3
7:13 fine flour mixed with oil for a cereal offering; 3
19 fine flour mixed with oil for a cereal offering; 3
25 fine flour mixed with oil for a cereal offering; 3
31 fine flour mixed with oil for a cereal offering; 3
37 fine flour mixed with oil for a cereal offering; 3
43 fine flour mixed with oil for a cereal offering; 3
49 fine flour mixed with oil for a cereal offering; 3
55 fine flour mixed with oil for a cereal offering; 3
61 fine flour mixed with oil for a cereal offering; 3
67 fine flour mixed with oil for a cereal offering; 3
73 fine flour mixed with oil for a cereal offering; 3
79 fine flour mixed with oil for a cereal offering; 3
8: 8 cereal offering of fine flour mixed with oil 3
11: 8 like the taste of cakes baked with oil. 3
15: 4 fine flour, mixed with a fourth of a hin of oil; 3
6 fine flour mixed with a third of a hin of oil; 3
9 fine flour, mixed with half a hin of oil 3
18:12 All the best of the oil, and all the best of the wine 1
28: 5 mixed with a fourth of a hin of beaten oil. 3
9 fine flour for a cereal offering, mixed with oil 3
12 fine flour for a cereal offering, mixed with oil 3
12 fine flour for a cereal offering, mixed with oil 3
13 fine flour mixed with oil as a cereal offering 3

20 cereal offering of fine flour mixed with oil; 3
28 cereal offering of fine flour mixed with oil 3
29: 3 cereal offering of fine flour mixed with oil 3
9 cereal offerings of fine flour mixed with oil 3
14 cereal offering of fine flour mixed with oil 3
35:25 high priest who was anointed with the holy oil. 3
Deu 7:13 also bless . . grain and your wine and your oil 1
11:14 gather in your grain and your wine and your oil. 1
12:17 not eat . . the tithe of your grain . . or of your oil 1
14:23 you shall eat the tithe . . of your oil 1
18: 4 first fruits of . . your wine and of your oil 1
28:40 but you shall not anoint yourself with the oil; 3
51 who also shall not leave you grain, wine, or oil 1
32:13 made him suck . . oil out of the flinty rock. 3
33:24 let him dip his foot in oil. 3
1Sm 10: 1 Samuel took a vial of oil and poured it on his head 3
16: 1 Fill your horn with oil, and go; I will send you 3
13 Then Samuel took the horn of oil, and anointed him 3
2Sm 1:21 the shield of Saul, not anointed with oil. 3
14: 2 do not anoint yourself with oil, but behave like 3
1Kg 1:39 took the horn of oil . . and anointed Solomon. 3
5:11 Solomon gave . . and 20,000 cors of beaten oil. 3
17:12 handful of meal in a jar, and a little oil in a cruse; 3
14 not be spent, and the cruse of oil shall not fail 3
16 neither did the cruse of oil fail 3
2Kg 4: 2 has nothing in the house, except a jar of oil. 3
6 Then the oil stopped flowing. 3
7 Go, sell the oil and pay your debts 3
9: 1 take this flask of oil in your hand, and go 3
3 Then take the flask of oil, and pour it on his head 3
6 and the young man poured the oil on his head 3
20:13 silver, the gold, the spices, the precious oil, his 3
1Ch 9:29 over . . the oil, the incense, and the spices. 3
12:40 and wine and oil, oxen and sheep 3
23:29 the baked offering, the offering mixed with oil *
27:28 and over the stores of oil was Jo'ash. 3
2Ch 2:10 baths of wine, and 20,000 baths of oil. 3
15 Now therefore the wheat and barley, oil and wine 3
11:11 and put . . in them, stores of food, oil, and wine. 3
31: 5 gave in abundance the first fruits of . . oil 1
32:28 storehouses also for the yield of . . oil; 1
Ezr 3: 7 gave . . food, drink, and oil to the Sido'nians 3
6: 9 wheat, salt, wine, or oil, as the priests at Jerusalem 4
7:22 up to . . 100 baths of oil, and salt 4
Neh 5:11 Return . . 100th of money, grain, wine, and oil 1
10:37 bring . . fruit of every tree, the wine and the oil 1
39 bring the contribution of grain, wine, and oil 1
13: 5 previously put the . . tithes of grain, wine, and oil 1
12 Judah brought the tithe of the grain, wine, and oil 1
Est 2:12 six months with oil of myrrh and six . . with spices 3
Job 29: 6 the rock poured out for me streams of oil! 3
Ps 23: 5 thou anointest my head with oil, my cup overflows. 3
45: 7 with the oil of gladness above your fellows; 3
55:21 his words were softer than oil 3
89:20 with my holy oil I have anointed him; 3
92:10 thou hast poured over me fresh oil. 3
104:15 oil to make his face shine 3
109:18 may it soak . . like oil into his bones! 3
133: 2 It is like the precious oil upon the head 3
141: 5 but let the oil of the wicked never anoint my head; 3
Prv 5: 3 her speech is smoother than oil; 3
21:17 he who loves wine and oil will not be rich. 3
27: 9 Oil and perfume make the heart glad 3
16 or to grasp oil in his right hand. 3
Ecc 9: 8 let not oil be lacking on your head. 3
Sng 1: 3 oils are fragrant, your name is oil poured out; 3
4:10 and the fragrance of your oils than any spice! 3
Isa 1: 6 they are not pressed out . . or softened with oil. 3
21: 5 eat, they drink. Arise, O princes, oil the shield! 2
39: 2 silver, the gold, the spices, the precious oil 3
57: 9 You journeyed to Molech with oil and multiplied 3
61: 3 the oil of gladness instead of mourning 3
Jer 31:12 over the grain, the wine, and the oil 1
40:10 as for you, gather wine and summer fruits and oil 3
41: 8 we have stores of wheat, barley, oil, and honey 3
Ezk 16: 9 and anointed you with oil. 3
13 you ate fine flour and honey and oil. 3
18 and set my oil and my incense before them. 3
19 I fed you with fine flour and oil and honey 3
23:41 on which you had placed my incense and my oil. 3
27:17 wheat, olives and early figs, honey, oil, and balm. 3
32:14 and cause their rivers to run like oil 3
45:14 as the fixed portion of oil, one tenth of a bath 3
24 an ephah for each ram, and a hin of oil to each ephah 3
25 and cereal offerings, and for the oil. 3
46: 5 together with a hin of oil to each ephah. 3
7 together with a hin of oil to each ephah. 3
11 together with a hin of oil to an ephah. 3
14 one third of a hin of oil to moisten the flour 3
15 Thus the lamb and the meal offering and the oil 3
Hos 2: 5 give me . . my wool and my flax, my oil and my drink 3
8 I who gave her the grain, the wine, and the oil 1
22 and the earth shall answer . . the oil 1
12: 1 and oil is carried to Egypt. 3
Jol 1:10 the wine fails, the oil languishes. 1
2:19 Behold, I am sending to you grain, wine, and oil 1
24 the vats shall overflow with wine and oil. 1
Ams 6: 6 and anoint themselves with the finest oils 3
Mic 6: 7 pleased . . with ten thousands of rivers of oil? 3
15 tread olives, but not anoint yourselves with oil; 3
Hag 1:11 upon the grain, the new wine, the oil 1
2:12 or pottage, or wine, or oil, or any kind of food 3
Zec 4:12 two golden pipes from which the oil is poured out? *
Mat 25: 3 they took no oil with them; 5
4 the wise took flasks of oil with their lamps. 5
8 'Give us some of your oil 5
Mrk 6:13 anointed with oil many that were sick 5
Lke 7:46 You did not anoint my head with oil 5
10:34 bound up his wounds, pouring on oil and wine 5
16: 6 He said, 'A 100 measures of oil.' 5
Heb 1: 9 has anointed thee with the oil of gladness 5
Jas 5:14 let them pray over him, anointing him with oil 5
Rev 6: 6 but do not harm oil and wine! 5
18:13 wine, oil, fine flour and wheat, cattle and sheep 5
1Es 6:30 likewise wheat and salt and wine and oil 5
Jdt 10: 5 gave her maid a bottle of wine and a flask of oil 5
11:13 the tithes of the wine and oil 5
Sir 39:26 the blood of the grape, and oil and clothing. 5
45:15 ordained him, and anointed him with holy oil 5
Sus 1:17 She said to her maids, "Bring me oil and ointments 5
151 1: 4 and anointed me with his anointing oil. 5

oil *See also* make, pour.

anointing oil 1. שֶׁמֶן

Sng 1: 3 your anointing oils are fragrant 1

ointment 1. שֶׁמֶן 2. תַּמְרוּק 3. *μυρισμός* 4. *μύρον* 5. *σμῆγμα*

Est 2: 3 let their ointments be given them. 2
9 and he quickly provided her with her ointments 2
12 six months with spices and ointments for women- 2
Ecc 7: 1 A good name is better than precious ointment; 1
10: 1 Dead flies make the perfumer's ointment . . evil 1
Mat 26: 7 alabaster flask of very expensive ointment 4
9 For this ointment might have been sold *
12 In pouring this ointment on my body 4
Mrk 14: 3 a woman came with an alabaster flask of ointment 4
4 Why was the ointment thus wasted? 4
5 For this ointment might have been sold 4
Lke 7:37 a woman . . brought an alabaster flask of ointment 4
38 anointed them with the ointment. 4
46 she has anointed my feet with ointment. 4
23:56 prepared spices and ointments 4
Joh 11: 2 It was Mary who anointed the Lord with ointment 4
12: 3 Mary took a pound of costly ointment of pure nard 4
3 was filled with the fragrance of the ointment. 4
5 Why was this ointment not sold for 300 denarii 4
Jdt 10: 3 anointed herself with precious ointment 4
16: 8 She anointed her face with ointment 3
Sus 1:17 She said to her maids, "Bring me oil and ointments 5

ointment *See also* pot.

old 1. בְּכוֹר 2. בְּלוֹא 3. בֵּן 4. בַּת 5. גָּדוֹל 6. זקן 7. זָקֵן 8. זְקֵנָה 9. זָקֵן לְיָמִים 10. כַּבִּיר יָמִים 11. בַּר (A) 12. *γέρων* 13. *γηράσκω* 14. *γηράω* 15. *πολιά* 16. *πολυχρόνιος* 17. *πρέσβυς* 18. *πρεσβύτερος* 19. *χρόνος* 20. senex

Gen 5:32 After Noah was 500 years old 3
7: 6 Noah was 600 years old when the flood . . came 3
10:21 the elder brother of Japheth, children were born 5
11:10 When Shem was 100 years old 3
12: 4 Abram was 75 years old when he departed 3
16:16 Abram was 86 years old when Hagar bore Ish'mael 3
17: 1 When Abram was 99 years old the LORD appeared 3
12 He that is eight days old among you 3
17 Shall a child be born to a man who is 100 years old? 3
17 Shall Sarah, who is 90 years old, bear a child? 4
24 Abraham was 99 years old 3
25 Ish'mael his son was thirteen years old 3
18:11 Now Abraham and Sarah were old, advanced in age; 7
12 After I have grown old, and my husband is old 7
13 'Shall I indeed bear a child, now that I am old?' 6
19: 4 the men of Sodom, both young and old 7
31 Our father is old, and there is not a man on earth 7
21: 4 he was eight days old, as God had commanded him. 3
5 Abraham was 100 years old when . . Isaac was born 3
24: 1 Abraham was old, well advanced in years; 7
2 to his servant, the oldest of his house 7
36 a son to my master when she was old; 8
25:20 Isaac was 40 years old when he took to wife Rebekah 3
26 Isaac was 60 years old when she bore them. 3
26:34 When Esau was 40 years old, he took to wife Judith 3
27: 1 When Isaac was old and his eyes were dim 7
1 called Esau his older son, and said to him 5
2 Behold, I am old; I do not know the day of my death. 6
15 the best garments of Esau her older son 5
42 words of Esau her older son were told to Rebekah; 5
29:16 had two daughters; the name of the older was Leah 5
35:29 gathered to his people, old and full of days; 7
37: 2 Joseph, being seventeen years old 3
41:46 Joseph was 30 years old when he entered 3
44:12 he searched, beginning with the eldest 5
50:25 Joseph died, being 110 years old; 3
Exd 7: 7 Now Moses was 80 years old 3
7 Moses was 80 . . and Aaron 83 years old 3
10: 9 Moses said, "We will go with our young and our old; 7
12: 5 lamb . . without blemish, a male a year old; 3
29:38 two lambs a year old day by day continually. 3
30:14 from twenty years old and upward, shall give 3
38:26 from twenty years old and upward, 603,550 men. 3
Lev 9: 3 calf and a lamb, both a year old without blemish 3
12: 6 bring . . a lamb a year old for a burnt offering 3
14:10 and one ewe lamb a year old without blemish 4
23:12 you shall offer a male lamb a year old 3
18 present . . seven lambs a year old 3
19 offer . . two male lambs a year old as a sacrifice 3
27: 3 a male from twenty years old up to 60 years old 3
3 a male from twenty years old up to 60 years old 3
5 is from five years old up to twenty years old 3
5 is from five years old up to twenty years old 3
6 If the person is from a month old up to five years 3
6 up to five years old, your valuation shall be 3
7 if the person is 60 years old and upward 3
Num 1: 3 from twenty years old and upward, all in Israel 3
18 names from twenty years old and upward 3
20 every male from twenty years old and upward 3
22 every male from twenty years old and upward 3
24 from twenty years old and upward 3
26 from twenty years old and upward, every man able 3
28 from twenty years old and upward, every man able †
30 from twenty years old and upward, every man able 3
32 number of names, from twenty years old and upward 3
34 from twenty years old and upward, every man able 3
36 from twenty years old and upward, every man able 3
38 from twenty years old and upward, every man able 3
40 from twenty years old and upward, every man able 3
42 from twenty years old and upward, every man able 3
45 from twenty years old and upward, every man able 3
3:15 every male from a month old and upward you shall 3
22 all the males from a month old and upward was 7,500 3
28 from a month old and upward, there were 8,600 3
34 males from a month old and upward was 6,200. 3
39 all the males from a month old and upward 3
40 all the first-born males . . from a month old 3
43 first-born males . . from a month old and upward 3
4: 3 from 30 years old up to 50 years old 3
3 from 30 years old up to 50 years old 3
23 from 30 years old up to 50 years old 3
23 from 30 years old up to 50 years old 3
30 from 30 years old up to 50 years old 3
30 from 30 years old up to 50 years old 3
35 from 30 years old up to 50 years old 3
35 from 30 years old up to 50 years old 3
39 from 30 years old up to 50 years old 3
39 from 30 years old up to 50 years old 3
43 from 30 years old up to 50 years old 3
43 from 30 years old up to 50 years old 3
47 from 30 years old up to 50 years old 3
47 from 30 years old up to 50 years old 3
6:12 bring a male lamb a year old for a guilt offering; 3
14 one male lamb a year old . . for a burnt offering 3
14 one ewe lamb a year old . . as a sin offering 4
7:15 ram, one male lamb a year old, for a burnt offering; 3
17 peace offerings . . five male lambs a year old. 3
21 ram, one male lamb a year old, for a burnt offering; 3
23 peace offerings . . five male lambs a year old. 3
27 ram, one male lamb a year old, for a burnt offering; 3
29 peace offerings . . five male lambs a year old. 3
33 ram, one male lamb a year old, for a burnt offering; 3
35 peace offerings . . five male lambs a year old. 3
39 ram, one male lamb a year old, for a burnt offering; 3
41 peace offerings . . five male lambs a year old. 3
45 ram, one male lamb a year old, for a burnt offering; 3
47 peace offerings . . five male lambs a year old. 3
51 ram, one male lamb a year old, for a burnt offering; 3
53 peace offerings . . five male lambs a year old. 3
57 ram, one male lamb a year old, for a burnt offering; 3
59 peace offerings . . five male lambs a year old. 3
63 ram, one male lamb a year old, for a burnt offering; 3
65 peace offerings . . five male lambs a year old. 3
69 ram, one male lamb a year old, for a burnt offering; 3
71 peace offerings . . five male lambs a year old. 3
75 ram, one male lamb a year old, for a burnt offering; 3
77 peace offerings . . five male lambs a year old. 3
81 ram, one male lamb a year old, for a burnt offering; 3
83 peace offerings . . five male lambs a year old. 3
87 burnt offering . . twelve male lambs a year old 3
88 peace offerings . . male lambs a year old 60 3
8:24 from 25 years old and upward they shall go 3
14:29 numbered from twenty years old and upward, who 3
15:27 offer a female goat a year old for a sin offering. 4
18:16 (at a month old you shall redeem them) 3
26: 2 from twenty years old and upward 3
4 people, from twenty years old and upward 3
62 23,000, every male from a month old and upward; 3
28: 3 two male lambs a year old without blemish 3
9 two male lambs a year old without blemish 3
11 seven male lambs a year old without blemish; 3
19 a burnt offering . . seven male lambs a year old; 3
27 a burnt offering . . seven male lambs a year old; 3
29: 2 seven male lambs a year old without blemish; 3
8 a burnt offering . . seven male lambs a year old; 3
13 bulls, two rams, fourteen male lambs a year old; 3
17 second day . . fourteen male lambs a year old 3
20 third day . . fourteen male lambs a year old 3

23 fourth day . . fourteen male lambs a year old 3
26 fifth day . . fourteen male lambs a year old 3
29 sixth day . . fourteen male lambs a year old 3
32 seventh day . . fourteen male lambs a year old 3
36 burnt offering . . seven male lambs a year old 3
32:11 none . . from twenty years old and upward 3
33:39 Aaron was 123 years old when he died on Mount Hor. 3
Deu 28:50 not regard the person of the old or show favor 7
31: 2 said to them, "I am 120 years old this day; 3
34: 7 Moses was 120 years old when he died; 3
Jos 6:21 all in the city, both men and women, young and old 7
13: 1 Now Joshua was old and advanced in years; 7
1 You are old and advanced in years 6
14: 7 I was 40 years old when Moses . . sent me 3
10 and now, lo, I am this day 85 years old. 3
23: 1 and Joshua was old and well advanced in years 7
2 I am now old and well advanced in years; 6
24:29 Joshua . . died, being 110 years old. 3
Jdg 6:25 father's bull, the second bull seven years old 3
19:16 an old man was coming from his work in the field 7
17 the old man said, "Where are you going? 7
20 the old man said, "Peace be to you; I will care for all 7
22 they said to the old man, the master of the house 7
Rut 1:12 go your way, for I am too old to have a husband. 6
1Sm 1:24 she took him up . . along with a three-year-old bull 3
2:22 Now Eli was very old, and he heard all that his sons 7
4:15 Now Eli was 98 years old and his eyes were set 3
18 neck was broken . . for he was an old man, and heavy. 7
5: 9 afflicted the men of the city, both young and old 5
8: 5 you are old and your sons do not walk in your ways; 6
12: 2 I am old and gray, and behold, my sons are with you; 6
13: 1 Saul was . . years old when he began to reign; 3
17:12 the man was already old and advanced in years. 7
13 The three eldest sons of Jesse had followed Saul 5
14 the three eldest followed Saul 5
28 Now Eli'ab his eldest brother heard when he spoke 5
18:17 Here is my elder daughter Merab; I will give her 5
28:14 An old man is coming up; and he is wrapped in a robe. 7
2Sm 2:10 Ish-bo'shet . . was 40 years old when he began to reign 3
4: 4 He was five years old when the news . . came 3
5: 4 David was 30 years old when he began to reign 3
19:32 Barzil'lai was a very aged man, 80 years old; 3
35 I am this day 80 years old; can I discern 3
1Kg 1: 1 King David was old and advanced in years; 7
15 now the king was very old, and Ab'ishag 7
2:22 he is my elder brother, and on his side are 5
11: 4 when Solomon was old his wives turned away 8
13:11 there dwelt an old prophet in Bethel. 7
25 told it in the city where the old prophet dwelt. 7
14:21 Rehobo'am was 41 years old when he began to reign 3
15:23 But in his old age he was diseased in his feet. 8
22:42 Jehosh'aphat was 35 years old when he began 3
2Kg 3:21 who were able . . from the youngest to the oldest †
27 took his eldest son who was to reign in his stead 1
4:14 Well, she has no son, and her husband is old. 7
8:17 He was 32 years old when became king 3
26 Ahazi'ah was 22 years old when he began to reign 3
11:21 Jeho'ash was seven years old when he began 3
14: 2 He was 25 years old when he began to reign 3
21 people . . took Azari'ah, who was sixteen years old 3
15: 2 He was sixteen years old when he began to reign 3
33 He was 25 years old when he began to reign 3
16: 2 Ahaz was twenty years old when he began to reign 3
18: 2 He was 25 years old when he began to reign 3
21: 1 Manas'seh was twelve years old when he began 3
19 Amon was 22 years old when he began to reign 3
22: 1 Josi'ah was eight years old when he began to reign 3
23:31 Jeho'ahaz was 23 years old when he began to reign 3
36 Jehoi'akim was 25 years old when he began to reign 3
24: 8 Jehoi'achin was eighteen years old 3
18 Zedeki'ah was 21 years old when he became king 3
1Ch 2:21 whom he married when he was 60 years old; 3
23: 1 When David was old and full of days 7
3 The Levites, 30 years old and upward, were numbered 3
24 from twenty years old and upward 3
27 of the Levites from twenty years old and upward 3
2Ch 12:13 41 years old when he began to reign 3
15:13 put to death, whether young or old, man or woman. 5
20:31 35 years old when he began to reign 3
21: 5 was 32 years old when he became king 3
20 He was 32 years old when he began to reign 3
22: 2 was 42 years old when he began to reign 3
24: 1 Jo'ash was seven years old when he began to reign 3
15 Jehoi'ada . . was 130 years old at his death. 3
25: 1 Amazi'ah was 25 years old when he began 3
5 He mustered those twenty years old and upward 3
26: 1 Judah took Uzzi'ah, who was sixteen years old 3
3 Uzzi'ah was sixteen years old when he began 3
27: 1 Jotham was 25 years old when he began 3
8 was 25 years old when he began to reign 3
28: 1 Ahaz was twenty years old when he began to reign 3
29: 1 began to reign when he was 25 years old 3
31:15 portions to their brethren, old and young alike 5
16 males from three years old and upwards 3
17 Levites from twenty years old and upwards 3
33: 1 Manas'seh was twelve years old when he began 3
21 Amon was 22 years old when he began to reign 3
34: 1 Josi'ah was eight years old when he began to reign 3
36: 2 Jeho'ahaz was 23 years old when he 3
5 25 years old when he began to reign 3
9 Jehoi'achin was eight years old when he began 3
11 21 years old when he began to reign 3
Ezr 3: 8 Levites, from twenty years old and upward 3
Est 3:13 annihilate all Jews, young and old, women 7
Job 1:13 drinking wine in their eldest brother's house; 1
18 drinking wine in their eldest brother's house; 1
15:10 aged are among us, older than your father. 10
32: 4 waited to speak to Job because they were older 9
9 It is not the old that are wise 16
Ps 37:25 I have been young, and now am old; 6
Prv 22: 6 when he is old he will not depart from it. 6
23:22 do not despise your mother when she is old. 6
Ecc 4:13 Better is a . . youth than an old and foolish king 7
Isa 20: 4 both the young and the old, naked and barefoot 7
65:20 for the child shall die 100 years old 3
20 sinner 100 years old shall be accursed. 3
Jer 31:13 and the young men and the old shall be merry. 7
38:11 and took from there old rags and worn-out clothes 2
52: 1 Zedeki'ah 21 years old when he became king; 3
Lam 2:21 In the dust of . . streets lie the young and the old; 7
Ezk 16:46 your elder sister is Sama'ria 5
23: 4 Oho'lah was the name of the elder 5
46:13 He shall provide a lamb a year old 3
Dan 5:31 Darius . . being about 62 years old. 11
Mic 6: 6 with burnt offerings, with calves a year old? 3
Mat 2:16 in all that region who were two years old or under *
Lke 2:42 when he was twelve years old *
Joh 3: 4 How can a man be born when he is old? 12
8: 9 went away, one by one, beginning with the eldest 18
57 You are not yet 50 years old *
21:18 when you are old, you will stretch out your hands 13
Act 4:22 the man . . was more than 40 years old. *
7:23 When he was 40 years old 19
Rom 4:19 because he was about a 100 years old *
Heb 8: 6 which is as much more excellent than the old as . . *
1Es 1:34 who was 23 years old *
39 Jehoiakim was 25 years old *
43 when he was made king he was eighteen years old *
46 Zedekiah was 21 years old *
2Es 2:22 Protect the old and the young within your walls; 20
Tob 14: 2 He was 58 years old when he lost his sight *
11 He was 158 years old *
Jdt 16:23 until she was 105 years old *
Sir 6:18 until you are old you will keep finding wisdom. 15
8: 6 Do not disdain a man when he is old 14
32: 3 Speak, you who are older 17
1Mc 16: 2 Simon called in his two older sons Judas and John 18
2Mc 5:13 Then there was killing of young and old 18
4Mc 5:31 I am not so old and cowardly 12
9:11 Then . . the guards brought forward the eldest 17

old (2) 1. אָז 2. לְמִן עוֹלָם 3. מֵאָז 4. מֵעוֹלָם 5. עַד 6. עוֹלָם 7. פָּנִים 8. קֶדֶם 9. רִאשׁוֹן 10. רחק 12. *αἰών* 13. *ἀρχαῖος* 14. *ἀρχή* 15. *ἔκπαλαι* 16. *πάλαι* 17. ante

Gen 6: 4 These were the mighty men that were of old 6
Deu 32: 7 Remember the days of old, consider the years 6
Jos 24: 2 Your fathers lived of old beyond the Euphra'tes 4
1Sm 27: 8 were the inhabitants of the land from of old 6
2Sm 13:18 thus were the virgin daughters . . clad of old. *
2Kg 19:25 I planned from days of old what now I bring to pass 8
2Ch 3: 3 length, in cubits of the old standard, was 60 9
Ezr 4:15 sedition was stirred up in it from of old. 11
19 found that this city from of old has risen 11
Neh 12:46 For in the days of David and Asaph of old there was 8
Job 20: 4 Do you not know this from of old 5
29: 2 Oh, that I were as in the months of old 8
Ps 25: 6 for they have been from of old. 6
44: 1 didst perform in their days, in the days of old 8
55:19 humble them, he who is enthroned from of old; 8
74: 2 thy congregation, which thou hast gotten of old 8
12 Yet God my King is from of old, working salvation 8
77: 5 I consider the days of old, I remember the years 8
11 yea, I will remember thy wonders of old. 8
78: 2 I will utter dark sayings from of old 8
89:19 Of old thou didst speak in a vision 1
49 Lord, where is thy steadfast love of old 9
93: 2 thy throne is established from of old; 1
102:25 Of old thou didst lay the foundation of the earth 7
119:52 When I think of thy ordinances from of old 6
143: 5 I remember the days of old, I meditate on all that 8
Prv 8:22 LORD created me . . the first of his acts of old. 1
Isa 23: 7 exultant city whose origin is from days of old 8
25: 1 hast done wonderful things, plans formed of old 10
37:26 I planned from days of old what now I bring to pass 8
44: 7 Who has announced from of old the things to come? 6
8 have I not told you from of old and declared it? 1
45:21 Who told this long ago? Who declared it of old? 3
46: 9 remember the former things of old; for I am God 6
48: 3 The former things I declared of old 1
5 I declared them to you from of old 1
8 from of old your ear has not been opened. 1
51: 9 as in days of old, the generations of long ago. 8
63: 9 lifted . . up and carried them all the days of old. 6
11 Then he remembered the days of old, 6
16 O LORD . . our Redeemer from of old is thy name. 6
64: 4 of old no one has heard or perceived by the ear 6
Jer 7: 7 in the land that I gave of old to your fathers 2
25: 5 to you and your fathers from of old and for ever; 6
30:20 Their children shall be as they were of old 8
46:26 Egypt shall be inhabited as in the days of old 8
Lam 1: 7 precious things that were hers from days of old. 8
5:21 Restore us . . Renew our days as of old! 8
Ezk 26:20 who descend into the Pit, to the people of old 6
32:27 they do not lie with the fallen mighty men of old 12
Jol 2: 2 their like has never been from of old 6
Ams 9:11 and rebuild it as in the days of old; 6
Mic 5: 2 ruler in Israel, whose origin is from of old 8
7:14 in Bashan and Gilead as in the days of old. 6
20 hast sworn to our fathers from the days of old. 8
Hab 3: 6 His ways were as of old. 6
Zec 10: 8 they shall be as many as of old. *
Mal 3: 4 as in the days of old and as in former years. 6
Mrk 6:15 It is a prophet, like one of the prophets of old. *
Lke 1:70 the mouth of his holy prophets from of old 12
9: 8 by others that one of the old prophets had risen. 13
19 others, that one of the old prophets has risen. 13
Act 3:21 the mouth of his holy prophets from of old. 12
15:18 who has made these things known from of old.' 12
Heb 1: 1 God spoke of old to our fathers by the prophets; 16
2Pe 2: 3 from of old their condemnation has not been idle 15
1Es 2:23 kept setting up blockades in it from of old 12
26 this city from of old has fought against kings 12
2Es 9: 4 from the days that were of old 17
Tob 4:12 Noah, Abraham, Isaac, and Jacob, our fathers of old 12
Wis 12: 3 Those who dwelt of old in thy holy land 16
Sir 14:17 the decree from of old is, "You must surely die! 12
50:23 in our days in Israel, as in the days of old. 12
51: 8 thy work from of old 12
Bar 3:26 The giants were born there, who were famous of old 14

old (3) 1. יָשָׁן 2. עוֹלָם 3. *ἀρχαῖος* 4. *πάλαι* 5. *παλαιός* 6. *παλαιότης*

Lev 25:22 you will be eating old produce; until the ninth 1
22 until the ninth year . . you shall eat the old 1
26:10 clear out the old to make way for the new 1
Job 22:15 you keep to the old way which wicked men have trod? 2
Sng 7:13 over . . are all choice fruits, new as well as old 1
Isa 22:11 reservoir . . for the water of the old pool. 1
2Co 5:17 the old has passed away, behold, the new has come. 3
2Pe 1: 9 forgotten that he was cleansed from his old sins 4
Sir 9:10 Forsake not an old friend 3
2Mc 6:22 on account of his old friendship with them. 3
Mat 9:16 a piece of unshrunk cloth on an old garment 5
17 Neither is new wine put into old wineskins 5
13:52 what is new and what is old. 5
Mrk 2:21 sews a piece of unshrunk cloth on an old garment; 5
21 the new from the old, and a worse tear is made. 5
22 no one puts new wine into old wineskins 5
Lke 5:36 and puts it upon an old garment 5
36 the piece from the new will not match the old. 5
37 no one puts new wine into old wineskins 5
39 no one after drinking old wine desires new 5
39 for he says, 'The old is good.' 5
Rom 6: 6 We know that our old self was crucified with him 5
7: 6 so that we serve not under the old written code 6
1Co 5: 7 Cleanse out the old leaven 5
8 celebrate the festival, not with the old leaven 5
2Co 3:14 for to this day, when they read the old covenant 5
Eph 4:22 Put off your old nature 5
Col 3: 9 seeing that you have put off the old nature 5
1Jn 2: 7 I am writing you . . an old commandment 5
7 old commandment is the word which you have heard 5

old *See* age, folks, grow, relic, son, store, three, time, year.

become old 1. זקן 2. *παλαιόω* 3. senesco

1Sm 8: 1 When Samuel became old, he made his sons judges 1
2Es 5:49 a woman who has become old does not bring forth 3
Sir 14:17 All living beings become old like a garment 2

old man 1. זָקֵן 2. *γεραιός* 3. *γέρων* 4. *πρεσβύτερος* 5. *πρεσβύτης*

Gen 25: 8 Abraham . . died in a good old age, an old man 1
43:27 Is your father well, the old man of whom you spoke? 1
44:20 We have a father, an old man, and a young brother 1
Lev 19:32 You shall . . honor the face of an old man 1
1Sm 2:31 there will not be an old man in your house. 1
32 shall not be an old man in your house for ever. 1
1Kg 12: 6 King Rehobo'am took counsel with the old men 1
8 he forsook the counsel which the old men gave him 1
13 the counsel which the old men had given him 1
2Ch 10: 6 Then King Rehobo'am took counsel with the old men 1
8 he forsook the counsel which the old men gave him 1
13 forsaking the counsel of the old men 1
36:17 had no compassion on . . old man or aged; 1
Ezr 3:12 heads of fathers' houses, old men who had seen 1
Job 42:17 Job died, an old man, and full of days. 1
Ps 148:12 together, old men and children! 1
Prv 20:29 beauty of old men is their gray hair. 1
Isa 65:20 or an old man who does not fill out his days 1
Jer 51:22 I break in pieces the old man and the youth; 1
Lam 5:14 The old men have quit the city gate 1
Ezk 9: 6 slay old men outright, young men and maidens 1
Jol 2:28 your old men shall dream dreams 1
Zec 8: 4 Old men and old women shall again sit 1

Lke 1:18 I am an old man, and my wife is advanced in years. 5
Act 2:17 your old men shall dream dreams; 4
1Ti 5: 1 Do not rebuke an older man 4
Tit 2: 2 Bid the older men be temperate, serious, sensible 5
1Es 1:53 young man or virgin, old man or child 5
5:63 old men who had seen the former house 4
Tob 12: 4 The old man said, "He deserves it. 5
Sir 25: 2 an adulterous old man who lacks good sense. 3
Bar 4:15 nation . . who had no respect for an old man 5
1Mc 14: 9 Old men sat in the streets 4
3Mc 1:23 being barely restrained by the old men and the elders 2
4: 5 a multitude of gray-headed old men 2
4Mc 5: 6 Before I begin to torture you, old man 5
6: 2 First they stripped the old man 2
6 yet while the old man's eyes were raised to heaven 3
10 the old man, while being beaten, was victorious 3
7:13 though he was an old man 3
8: 5 the old man who has just been tortured 3

old people 1. γεραιός
3Mc 3:27 old people or children or even infants 1

thing of old 1. קַדְמֹנִי 2. ἀρχαῖος
Isa 43:18 Remember not . . nor consider the things of old. 1
Wis 8: 8 she knows the things of old 2

very old 1. ἐσχατογήρος
Sir 41: 2 very old and distracted over everything 1

old woman 1. זָקֵן 2. πρεσβύτερος 3. πρεσβῦτις
Zec 8: 4 old women shall again sit in the streets 1
1Ti 5: 2 older women like mothers 2
Tit 2: 3 Bid the older women likewise to be reverent 3

olive 1. זַיִת 2. עֵץ שֶׁמֶן 3. ἐλαία 4. oliva
Exd 27:20 that they bring to you pure beaten olive oil 1
30:24 of olive oil a hin; 1
Lev 24: 2 to bring you pure oil from beaten olives 1
Deu 28:40 for your olives shall drop off. 1
Jdg 15: 5 standing grain, as well as the olive orchards. 1
2Sm 15:30 David went up the ascent of the Mount of Olives 1
Neh 8:15 Go out to the hills and bring branches of olive 1
Ps 128: 3 your children will be like olive shoots 1
Isa 41:19 the cedar, the acacia, the myrtle, and the olive; 2
Ezk 27:17 wheat, olives and early figs, honey, oil, and balm. *
Hos 14: 6 his beauty shall be like the olive 1
Mic 6:15 you shall tread olives, but not anoint 1
Hab 3:17 Though . . the produce of the olive fail 1
Hag 2:19 and the olive tree still yield nothing? 1
Mat 21: 1 and came to Beth'phage, to the Mount of Olives 3
24: 3 As he sat on the Mount of Olives 3
26:30 they went out to the Mount of Olives. 3
Mrk 11: 1 to Beth'phage and Bethany, at the Mount of Olives 3
13: 3 on the Mount of Olives opposite the temple 3
14:26 they went out to the Mount of Olives. 3
Lke 19:37 at the descent of the Mount of Olives 3
22:39 went, as was his custom, to the Mount of Olives; 3
Joh 8: 1 Jesus went to the Mount of Olives. 3
2Es 16:29 three or four olives may be left on every tree 4
olive *See also* branch, leaf, orchard, row, wreath.

cultivated olive tree 1. καλλιέλαιος
Rom 11:24 grafted . . into a cultivated olive tree 1

olive tree 1. זַיִת 2. זַיִת יִצְהָר 3. ἐλαία
Deu 6:11 vineyards and olive trees, which you did not plant 1
8: 8 a land of olive trees and honey 1
24:20 When you beat your olive trees, you shall not 1
28:40 have olive trees throughout all your territory 1
Jdg 9: 8 and they said to the olive tree, 'Reign over us.' 1
9 the olive tree said to them, 'Shall I leave 1
2Kg 18:32 a land of olive trees and honey, that you may live 2
1Ch 27:28 Over the olive . . trees in the Shephe'lah was 1
Job 15:33 and cast off his blossom, like the olive tree. 1
Ps 52: 8 I am like a green olive tree in the house of God. 1
Isa 17: 6 Gleanings . . as when an olive tree is beaten- 1
24:13 as when an olive tree is beaten 1
Jer 11:16 The LORD once called you, 'A green olive tree 1
Ams 4: 9 and your olive trees the locust devoured; 1
Zec 4: 3 there are two olive trees by it 1
11 What are these two olive trees on the right 1
12 What are these two branches of the olive trees 1
Sir 24:14 like a beautiful olive tree in the field 3
50:10 like an olive tree putting forth its fruit 3

wild olive 1. עֵץ שֶׁמֶן 2. ἀγριέλαιος
Neh 8:15 bring branches of olive, wild olive, myrtle, palm 1
Rom 11:17 and you, a wild olive shoot, were grafted 2

wild olive tree 1. ἀγριέλαιος
Rom 11:24 cut from what is by nature a wild olive tree 1

olivewood 1. עֵץ שֶׁמֶן
1Kg 6:23 he made two cherubim of olivewood 1
31 For the entrance . . he made doors of olivewood; 1
32 He covered the two doors of olivewood 1
33 made for the . . nave doorposts of olivewood 1

oliveyard 1. זַיִת
Jos 24:13 you eat the fruit of vineyards and oliveyards 1

omen 1. אוֹת 2. מוֹפֵת 3. נַחַשׁ 4. οἰωνισμός
Num 24: 1 he did not go, as at other times, to look for omens 3
Isa 44:25 who frustrates the omens of liars 1
Zec 3: 8 who sit before you, for they are men of good omen 2
Sir 34: 5 Divinations and omens and dreams are folly 4
2Mc 5: 4 the apparition might prove to have been a good omen. *
omen *See also* watch.

clear omen 1. ἔνδειξις
Php 1:28 This is a clear omen to them of their destruction 1

omer 1. עֹמֶר
Exd 16:16 you shall take an omer apiece, according 1
18 when they measured it with an omer 1
22 gathered twice as much bread, two omers apiece; 1
32 the LORD has commanded: 'Let an omer of it be kept 1
33 Take a jar, and put an omer of manna in it, and place 1
36 An omer is the tenth part of an ephah.) 1

omit 1. λείπω 2. παραλείπω
1Es 8: 7 he omitted nothing from the law of the Lord 2
3Mc 4:13 not omitting any detail of their punishment. 1

once 1. אֶחָד 2. עוֹד 3. פַּעַם 4. פַּעַם אַחַת 5. ἅπαξ 6. εἶς
Gen 18:32 be angry, and I will speak again but this once. 3
Exd 10:17 forgive . . only this once, and entreat the LORD 3
30:10 make atonement upon its horns once a year; 1
10 he shall make atonement for it once in the year 1
Lev 16:34 for the people of Israel once in the year 1
Num 22:15 Once again Balak sent princes, more in number 2
Jos 6: 3 all the men of war going around the city once. 4
11 the ark . . to compass the city, going about it once; 4
14 they marched around the city once, and returned 4
Jdg 6:39 Gideon said . . let me speak but this once; 3
39 let me make trial only this once with the fleece 3
16:18 Come up this once, for he has told me all his mind. 3
28 and strengthen me, I pray thee, only this once, O God 3
1Kg 10:22 Once every three years the fleet . . used to come 1
2Kg 4:35 he got up . . and walked once to and fro in the house 1
6:10 he saved himself there more than once or twice. 1
2Ch 9:21 once every three years the ships of Tarshish 1
Neh 13:20 lodged outside Jerusalem once or twice. 3
Job 9: 3 could not answer him once in 1,000 times. 1
40: 5 I have spoken once, and I will not answer; 1
Ps 62:11 Once God has spoken; twice have I heard this 1
Jer 16:21 this once I will make them know my power 3
Hag 2: 6 Once again, in a little while, I will shake 1
2Co 11:25 once I was stoned 5
Php 4:16 you sent me help once and again. 5
Tit 3:10 after admonishing him once or twice 6
Heb 6: 4 those who have once been enlightened 5
9: 7 and he but once a year 5
27 just as it is appointed for men to die once 5
28 Christ . . offered once to bear the sins of many 5
10: 2 If the worshipers had once been cleansed 5
12:26 Yet once more I will shake not only the earth 5
27 This phrase, "Yet once more," indicates . . 5
3Mc 1:11 he only once a year 5

once (2) 1. בַּיּוֹם 2. מַהֵר 3. עַתָּה 4. ἄρτι 5. ἐξαυτῆς 6. εὐθέως 7. εὐθύς 8. καί 9. νῦν 10. παραυτίκα 11. παραχρῆμα 12. σπεύδω 13. συντόμως 14. ταχύς 15. amodo 16. statim
Num 11:15 If thou wilt deal thus with me, kill me at once †
13:30 Caleb . . said, "Let us go up at once, and occupy it; †
Deu 7:22 you may not make an end of them at once, lest 2
Jdg 2:23 left those nations, not driving them out at once 2
1Sm 28:20 Saul fell at once full length upon the ground 2
1Kg 1:13 Go in at once to King David, †
2Kg 4:26 run at once to meet her, and say to her, Is it well 3
Prv 12:16 The vexation of a fool is known at once 1
Zec 8:21 Let us go at once to entreat the favor of the LORD †
Mat 21:19 And the fig tree withered at once. 11
20 How did the fig tree wither at once? 11
25:16 He who had received the five talents went at once 6
26:49 he came up to Jesus at once and said, "Hail, Master! 6
53 he will at once send me more than twelve legions 4
27:48 one of them at once ran and took a sponge 6
Mrk 1:28 And at once his fame spread everywhere 7
43 sternly charged him, and sent him away at once 7
4:29 at once he puts in the sickle 7
6:25 I want you to give me at once the head of John 5
14:45 came, he went up to him at once, and said, "Master! 7
Lke 8:55 her spirit returned, and she got up at once 11
12:36 so that they may open to him at once when he comes 6
54 you say at once, 'A shower is coming' 6
13:25 When once the householder has risen up †
17: 7 'Come at once and sit down at table'? 6
21: 9 the end will not be at once. 6
Joh 5: 9 at once the man was healed 6
13:32 and glorify him at once. 7
18:27 at once the cock crowed. 6
19:34 at once there came out blood and water. 7
Act 10:16 the thing was taken up at once to heaven. 7
33 So I sent to you at once 5
16:33 he was baptized at once, with all his family. 11
21:30 at once the gates were shut. 6
32 He at once took soldiers and centurions 5
23:30 I sent him to you at once 5
2Co 1:17 like a worldly man, ready to say Yes and No at once? *
Jas 1:24 and at once forgets what he was like. 6
Rev 4: 2 At once I was in the Spirit, and lo, a throne stood 6
2Es 6:43 and at once the work was done. 16
7:75 or whether we shall be tormented at once? 15
Tob 2:12 Once when they paid her wages 8
4:14 but pay him at once 10
Jdt 10:15 Go at once to his tent 9
12:14 Surely whatever pleases him I will do at once 12
Wis 5:12 the air, thus divided, comes together at once 6
18:17 at once apparitions . . greatly troubled them 11
2Mc 3: 8 Heliodorus at once set out on his journey 6
4:10 he at once shifted his countrymen over to . . 6
6:28 he went at once to the rack. 6
3Mc 5:25 implored . . God to help them again at once. 13
4Mc 12: 9 they freed him at once. 14

once (3) 1. ποτέ
Gen 25:29 Once when Jacob was boiling pottage, Esau came *
Jdg 9: 8 trees once went forth to anoint a king over them; *
2Kg 6: 8 Once when the King of Syria was warring *
Jer 11:16 The LORD once called you, 'A green olive tree *
Lke 14:16 A man once gave a great banquet, and invited many; *
Rom 6:17 that you who were once slaves of sin *
19 as you once yielded your members to impurity *
7: 9 I was once alive apart from the law 1
11:30 Just as you were once disobedient to God 1
2Co 3:10 Indeed, in this case, what once had splendor *
5:16 even though we once regarded Christ *
Gal 1:23 He who once persecuted us 1
23 now preaching the faith he once tried to destroy 1
Eph 2: 2 in which you once walked 1
3 Among these we all once lived 1
13 you who once were far off 1
5: 8 for once you were darkness, but now you are light 1
Col 1:21 you, who once were estranged and hostile in mind 1
3: 7 In these you once walked, when you lived in them. 1
Tit 3: 3 For we ourselves were once foolish, disobedient 1
1Pe 2:10 Once you were no people but now you are God's 1
10 once you had not received mercy *
3: 5 So once the holy women . . used to adorn 1
Tob 1:14 and once at Rages in Media I left ten talents *
2: 8 he once ran away, and here he is *
Wis 5: 4 This is the man whom we once held in derision 1
14:15 honored as a god what was once a dead human being 1
Sus 1:15 Once, while they were watching 1

once (4) 1. πρῶτος 2. mox
Rom 15:24 once I have enjoyed your company for a little. 1
Gal 3:15 or adds to it, once it has been ratified. *
2Es 16: 6 when once it has begun to burn? 2
once *See* all, grant, when.

once a day 1. מֵעֵת עַד עֵת
Ezk 4:10 once a day you shall eat it. 1
11 once a day you shall drink. 1

once for all 1. אֶחָד 2. ἅπαξ 3. ἐφάπαξ
Ps 89:35 Once for all I have sworn by my holiness; 1
Rom 6:10 The death he died he died to sin, once for all 3
Heb 7:27 did this once for all when he offered up himself. 3
9:12 he entered once for all into the Holy Place 3
26 he has appeared once for all at the end of the age 2
10:10 the offering of . . Jesus Christ once for all. 3
1Pe 3:18 For Christ also died for sins once for all 2
Jde 1: 3 faith . . once for all delivered to the saints. 2
5 though you were once for all fully informed 2

once more 1. עוֹד 2. שׁוּב 3. δεύτερος 4. ἔτι 5. πάλιν 6. πάλιν ἄνωθεν 7. iterum
Jer 31:23 Once more they shall use these words 1
Zec 11:15 Take once more the implements of a . . shepherd. 1
Mal 3:18 Then once more you shall distinguish 2
Lke 23:20 Pilate addressed them once more 5
Joh 8: 8 once more he bent down and wrote with his finger 5
Gal 4: 9 whose slaves you want to be once more? 6
Rev 19: 3 Once more they cried, "Hallelujah! 3
2Es 5:22 and I began once more to speak words 7
3Mc 5:38 Equip the elephants now once more 4

one 1. אֶחָד 2. אִישׁ 3. דָּבָר 4. יַחְדָּו 5. חַד (A) 6. αὐτός 7. εἷς 8. μέν 9. μέρος 10. μόνος 11. ὁμόψηφος 12. solummodo 13. unus
Gen 1: 5 there was evening and there was morning, one day 1
9 waters . . be gathered together into one place 1
2:11 Pishon; it is the one which flows around the whole 1
21 and while he slept took one of his ribs 1
24 cleaves to his wife, and they become one flesh. 1
3:22 Behold, the man has become like one of us 1
4:19 took two wives; the name of the one was Adah 1
10:25 born two sons: the name of the one was Peleg 1
11: 1 the whole earth had one language and few words. 1
6 the LORD said, "Behold, they are one people 1

6 and they have all one language; 1
21:15 she cast the child under one of the bushes. 1
22: 2 as a burnt offering upon one of the mountains 1
26:10 One of the people might easily have lain 1
27:38 Have you but one blessing, my father? Bless me 1
45 Why should I be bereft of you both in one day? 1
32: 8 If Esau comes to the one company and destroys it 1
33:13 if they are overdriven for one day, all the flocks 1
34:16 we will dwell with you and become one people. 1
22 agree to dwell with us, to become one people 1
37:20 let us kill him and throw him into one of the pits; 1
40: 5 one night they both dreamed 1
41: 5 plump and good, were growing on one stalk. 1
22 saw in my dream seven ears growing on one stalk 1
25 said to Pharaoh, "The dream of Pharaoh is one; 1
26 good ears are seven years; the dream is one. 1
42:11 We are all sons of one man, we are honest men 1
13 twelve brothers, the sons of one man in the land 1
13 this day with our father, and one is no more. 1
16 Send one of you, and let him bring your brother 1
19 if you are honest men, let one of your brothers 1
27 as one of them opened his sack 1
32 one is no more, and the youngest is this day 1
33 leave one of your brothers with me 1
44:28 one left me, and I said, Surely he has been torn 1
48:22 I have given . . one mountain slope which I took 1
49:16 judge his people as one of the tribes of Israel. 1
Exd 1:15 Hebrew midwives, one of whom was named Shiph'rah 1
8:31 removed the . . flies . . not one remained. 1
9: 6 of the cattle of . . Israel not one died. 1
7 not one of the cattle of the Israelites was dead. 1
11: 1 Yet one plague more I will bring upon Pharaoh 1
12:46 In one house shall it be eaten; 1
49 There shall be one law for the native 1
14:28 into the sea; not so much as one of them remained. 1
17:12 held up his hands, one on one side, and the other 1
18: 3 two sons, of whom the name of the one was Gershom 1
23:29 I will not drive them out from before you in one 1
24: 3 all the people answered with one voice, and said 1
25:19 Make one cherub on the one end 1
19 Make one cherub on the one end 1
19 Make . . one cherub on the other end; 1
32 the lampstand out of one side of it and three 1
33 three cups . . on one branch 1
36 one piece of hammered work of pure gold. 1
26: 2 all the curtains shall have one measure. 1
5 50 loops you shall make on the one curtain 1
6 that the tabernacle may be one whole. 1
10 the curtain that is outmost in one set 1
11 and couple the tent together that it may be one 1
19 two bases under one frame for its two tenons 1
21 forty bases of silver, two bases under one frame 1
25 two bases under one frame, and two bases 1
26 the frames of the one side of the tabernacle 1
27: 9 hangings . . 100 cubits long for one side; 1
28:10 six of their names on the one stone, and the names 1
29: 1 Take one young bull and two rams without blemish 1
3 you shall put them in one basket and bring them 1
15 Then you shall take one of the rams 1
23 one loaf of bread, and one cake of bread with oil 1
23 one loaf of bread, and one cake of bread with oil 1
23 one cake of bread with oil, and one wafer 1
39 One lamb you shall offer in the morning 1
36:10 he coupled five curtains to one another 1
10 other five curtains he coupled to one another. 1
12 he made 50 loops on the one curtain 1
12 the loops were opposite one another. 1
13 he . . coupled the curtains one to the other 1
13 so the tabernacle was one whole. 1
18 tent together that it might be one whole. 1
24 two bases under one frame for its two tenons 1
26 bases of silver, two bases under one frame 1
31 the frames of the one side of the tabernacle 1
37: 3 two rings on its one side and two rings on its 1
8 one cherub on the one end, and one cherub 1
8 on the one end, and one cherub on the other end; 1
18 three branches of the lampstand out of one side 1
19 cups . . with capital and flower on one branch 1
22 the whole of it was one piece of hammered work 1
Lev 4: 2 If anyone sins . . and does any one of them 1
27 If any one of the common people sins unwittingly 1
5: 7 two young pigeons, one for a sin offering 1
6: 7 which one may do and thereby become guilty 1
7: 7 like the sin offering, there is one law for them 1
14 of such he shall offer one cake from each offering 1
8:26 he took one unleavened cake, and one cake of bread 1
26 took . . one cake of bread with oil, and one wafer 1
26 took . . one cake of bread with oil, and one wafer 1
12: 8 one for a burnt offering and the other for a sin 1
13: 2 brought . . to one of his sons the priests 1
14: 5 command them to kill one of the birds 1
10 and one ewe lamb a year old without blemish 1
10 mixed with oil, and one log of oil 1
12 the priest shall take one of the male lambs 1
21 shall take one male lamb for a guilt offering 1
22 the one shall be a sin offering and the other 1
31 one for a sin offering and the other 1
50 shall kill one of the birds in an earthen vessel 1
15:15 priest shall offer them, one for a sin offering 1
30 the priest shall offer one for a sin offering 1
16: 5 a sin offering, and one ram for a burnt offering 1
8 one lot for the LORD and the other lot for Aza'zel 1
22:28 shall not kill both her and her young in one day 1
23:18 present . . one young bull, and two rams 1
19 you shall offer one male goat for a sin offering 1
24:22 have one law for the sojourner and for the native 1
25:48 one of his brothers may redeem him 1
26:26 ten women shall bake your bread in one oven 1
Num 6:11 the priest shall offer one for a sin offering 1
14 one male lamb a year old . . for a burnt offering 1
14 one ewe lamb a year old . . as a sin offering 1
14 one ram without blemish as a peace offering 1
19 take . . one unleavened cake out of the basket 1
19 priest shall take . . one unleavened wafer 1
7: 3 wagon for every two . . for each one an ox; 1
11 shall offer their offering, one leader each day 1
13 his offering was one silver plate whose weight 1
13 one silver basin of 70 shekels 1
14 one golden dish of ten shekels, full of incense; 1
15 one young bull, one ram . . for a burnt offering; 1
15 one young bull, one ram . . for a burnt offering; 1
15 ram, one male lamb a year old, for a burnt offering; 1
16 one male goat for a sin offering; 1
19 he offered for his offering one silver plate 1
19 one silver basin of 70 shekels 1
20 one golden dish of ten shekels, full of incense; 1
21 one young bull, one ram . . for a burnt offering; 1
21 one young bull, one ram . . for a burnt offering; 1
21 ram, one male lamb a year old, for a burnt offering; 1
22 one male goat for a sin offering; 1
25 his offering was one silver plate 1
25 one silver basin of 70 shekels 1
26 one golden dish of ten shekels, full of incense; 1
27 one young bull, one ram . . for a burnt offering; 1
27 one young bull, one ram . . for a burnt offering; 1
27 ram, one male lamb a year old, for a burnt offering; 1
28 one male goat for a sin offering; 1
31 his offering was one silver plate whose weight 1
31 one silver basin of 70 shekels 1
32 one golden dish of ten shekels, full of incense; 1
33 one young bull, one ram . . for a burnt offering; 1
33 one young bull, one ram . . for a burnt offering; 1
33 ram, one male lamb a year old, for a burnt offering; 1
34 one male goat for a sin offering; 1
37 his offering was one silver plate 1
37 one silver basin of 70 shekels 1
38 one golden dish of ten shekels, full of incense; 1
39 one young bull, one ram . . for a burnt offering; 1
39 one young bull, one ram . . for a burnt offering; 1
39 ram, one male lamb a year old, for a burnt offering; 1
40 one male goat for a sin offering; 1
43 his offering was one silver plate, whose weight 1
43 one silver basin of 70 shekels 1
44 one golden dish of ten shekels, full of incense; 1
45 one young bull, one ram . . for a burnt offering; 1
45 one young bull, one ram . . for a burnt offering; 1
45 ram, one male lamb a year old, for a burnt offering; 1
46 one male goat for a sin offering; 1
49 his offering was one silver plate 1
49 one silver basin of 70 shekels 1
50 one golden dish of ten shekels, full of incense; 1
51 one young bull, one ram . . for a burnt offering; 1
51 one young bull, one ram . . for a burnt offering; 1
51 ram, one male lamb a year old, for a burnt offering; 1
52 one male goat for a sin offering; 1
55 his offering was one silver plate 1
56 one golden dish of ten shekels, full of incense; 1
57 one young bull, one ram . . for a burnt offering; 1
57 one young bull, one ram . . for a burnt offering; 1
57 ram, one male lamb a year old, for a burnt offering; 1
58 one male goat for a sin offering; 1
61 his offering was one silver plate, whose weight 1
61 one silver basin of 70 shekels 1
62 one golden dish of ten shekels, full of incense; 1
63 one young bull, one ram . . for a burnt offering; 1
63 one young bull, one ram . . for a burnt offering; 1
63 ram, one male lamb a year old, for a burnt offering; 1
64 one male goat for a sin offering; 1
67 his offering was one silver plate, whose weight 1
67 one silver basin of 70 shekels 1
68 one golden dish of ten shekels, full of incense; 1
69 one young bull, one ram . . for a burnt offering; 1
69 one young bull, one ram . . for a burnt offering; 1
69 ram, one male lamb a year old, for a burnt offering; 1
70 one male goat for a sin offering; 1
73 his offering was one silver plate 1
73 one silver basin of 70 shekels 1
74 one golden dish of ten shekels, full of incense; 1
75 one young bull, one ram . . for a burnt offering; 1
75 one young bull, one ram . . for a burnt offering; 1
75 ram, one male lamb a year old, for a burnt offering; 1
76 one male goat for a sin offering; 1
79 his offering was one silver plate 1
79 one silver basin of 70 shekels 1
80 one golden dish of ten shekels, full of incense; 1
81 one young bull, one ram . . for a burnt offering; 1
81 one young bull, one ram . . for a burnt offering; 1
81 ram, one male lamb a year old, for a burnt offering; 1
82 one male goat for a sin offering; 1
8:12 shall offer the one for a sin offering 1
9:14 you shall have one statute 1
10: 4 if they blow only one, then the leaders 1
11:19 You shall not eat one day, or two days, or five days 1
26 Now two men remained in the camp, one named Eldad 1
14:15 Now if thou dost kill this people as one man 1
15:15 there shall be one statute for you 1
16 One law and one ordinance shall be for you 1
16 One law and one ordinance shall be for you 1
24 offer one young bull for a burnt offering 1
24 and one male goat for a sin offering. 1
27 If one person sins unwittingly, he shall offer 1
29 one law for him who does anything unwittingly 1
16:15 I have not taken one ass from them, and I have not 1
15 I have not harmed one of them. 1
22 shall one man sin, and wilt thou be angry with all 1
17: 2 get from them rods, one for each fathers' house †
3 For there shall be one rod for the head of each 1
6 their leaders gave him rods, one for each leader 1
28: 4 The one lamb you shall offer in the morning 1
11 burnt offering . . two young bulls, one ram 1
12 cereal offering . . for the one ram; 1
15 Also one male goat for a sin offering to the LORD; 1
19 burnt offering . . two young bulls, one ram 1
22 also one male goat for a sin offering 1
27 burnt offering . . two young bulls, one ram 1
28 ephah for each bull, two tenths for one ram 1
30 with one male goat, to make atonement for you. 1
29: 2 burnt offering . . one young bull, one ram 1
2 burnt offering . . one young bull, one ram 1
4 one tenth for each of the seven lambs; 1
5 one male goat for a sin offering, to make atonement 1
8 burnt offering . . one young bull, one ram 1
8 burnt offering . . one young bull, one ram 1
9 ephah for the bull, two tenths for the one ram 1
11 also one male goat for a sin offering 1
16 also one male goat for a sin offering 1
19 also one male goat for a sin offering 1
22 also one male goat for a sin offering 1
25 also one male goat for a sin offering 1
28 also one male goat for a sin offering; 1
31 also one male goat for a sin offering; 1
34 also one male goat for a sin offering; 1
36 burnt offering . . one bull, one ram, seven 1
36 burnt offering . . one bull, one ram, seven 1
38 also one male goat for a sin offering; 1
31:28 tribute . . one out of 500, of the persons 1
30 take one drawn out of every 50, of the persons 1
47 from . . Israel's half Moses took one of every fifty 1
34:18 You shall take one leader of every tribe 1
35:30 no . . put to death on the testimony of one witness. 1
36: 8 shall be wife to one of the family of the tribe 1
Deu 1:23 I took twelve men of you, one man for each tribe; 1
35 Not one of these men of this evil generation 2
4:42 fleeing to one of these cities he might save his life 1
6: 4 Hear, O Israel: The LORD our God is one LORD; 1
12:14 place . . LORD will choose in one of your tribes 1
13:12 If you hear in one of your cities, which the LORD 1
15: 7 there is among you a poor man, one of your brethren 1
17: 6 not be put to death on the evidence of one witness. 1
19: 5 may flee to one of these cities and save his life; 1
11 man flees into one of these cities 1
21:15 two wives, the one loved and the other disliked 1
23:16 place . . he shall choose within one of your towns 1
24: 5 newly married . . shall be free at home one year 1
25: 5 If brothers dwell together, and one of them dies 1
11 wife of the one draws near to rescue her husband 1
28: 7 come out against you one way, and flee before you 1
25 go out one way against them, and flee seven ways 1
32:30 How should one chase 1,000, and two 1
Jos 3:13 the waters . . from above shall stand in one heap. 1
9: 2 they gathered together with one accord to fight 1
10: 2 Gibeon was a . . city, like one of the royal cities 1
42 took all these kings and their land at one time 1
12: 9 the king of Jericho, one, the king of Ai 1
9 the king of Ai, which is beside Bethel, one; 1
10 king of Jerusalem, one; the king of Hebron, one; 1
10 king of Jerusalem, one; the king of Hebron, one; 1
11 the king of Jarmuth, one; the king of Lachish, one; 1
11 the king of Jarmuth, one; the king of Lachish, one; 1
12 the king of Eglon, one; the king of Gezer, one; 1
12 the king of Eglon, one; the king of Gezer, one; 1
13 the king of Debir, one; the king of Geder, one; 1
13 the king of Debir, one; the king of Geder, one; 1
14 the king of Hormah, one; the king of Arad, one; 1
14 the king of Hormah, one; the king of Arad, one; 1
15 the king of Libnah, one; the king of Adullam, one; 1
15 the king of Libnah, one; the king of Adullam, one; 1
16 the king of Makke'dah, one; the king of Bethel, one; 1
16 the king of Makke'dah, one; the king of Bethel, one; 1
17 the king of Tap'puah, one; the king of Hepher, one; 1
17 the king of Tap'puah, one; the king of Hepher, one; 1
18 the king of Aphek, one; the king of Lashar'on, one; 1
18 the king of Aphek, one; the king of Lashar'on, one; 1
19 the king of Madon, one; the king of Hazor, one; 1
19 the king of Madon, one; the king of Hazor, one; 1
20 the king of Shim'ron-me'ron, one; 1
20 the king of Ach'shaph, one; 1

21 the king of Ta'anach, one; the king of Megid'do, one; 1
21 the king of Ta'anach, one; the king of Megid'do, one; 1
22 the king of Kedesh, one; the king of Jok'ne-am . . one; 1
22 of Kedesh, one; the king of Jok'ne-am in Carmel, one; 1
23 the king of Dor in Naphath-dor, one; 1
23 king of Dor . . one; the king of Goi'im in Galilee, one; 1
24 the king of Tirzah, one: in all, 31 kings. 1
17:14 Why have you given me but one lot and one portion 1
14 Why have you given me but one lot and one portion 1
17 you shall not have one lot only 1
20: 4 He shall flee to one of these cities 1
21:44 not one of all their enemies had withstood them 2
45 Not one of all the good promises . . had failed; 3
22:14 ten chiefs, one from each of the tribal families 1
23:10 One man of you puts to flight 1,000 1
14 not one thing has failed of all the good things 1
14 all have come . . not one of them has failed. 1
Jdg 6:16 and you shall smite the Mid'ianites as one man. 1
9: 2 70 . . rule over you, or that one rule over you?' 1
5 slew his brothers . . 70 men, upon one stone; 1
18 and have slain his sons, 70 men on one stone 1
37 and one company is coming from the direction 1
16:28 that I may be avenged . . for one of my two eyes. 1
29 he leaned . . upon them, his right hand on the one 1
17: 5 and installed one of his sons, who became his 1
11 the young man became to him like one of his sons. 1
18:19 be priest to the house of one man, or to be priest 1
19:13 let us draw near to one of these places, and spend 1
20: 1 congregation assembled as one man to the LORD 1
8 all the people arose as one man, saying, "We will not 1
11 gathered against the city, united as one man. 1
31 in the highways, one of which goes up to Bethel 1
21: 3 there . . be today one tribe lacking in Israel? 1
6 One tribe is cut off from Israel this day. 1
8 What one is there of the tribes of Israel that did 1
9 not one of the inhabitants of Ja'besh-gil'ead 2
Rut 1: 4 the name of the one was Orpah 1
2:13 though I am not one of your maidservants. 1
1Sm 1: 2 He had two wives; the name of the one was Hannah 1
5 he would give Hannah only one portion 1
2:36 Put me, I pray you, in one of the priest's places 1
6:12 the cows went straight . . along one highway 1
17 the golden tumors . . one for Ashdod, one for Gaza 1
17 the golden tumors . . one for Ashdod, one for Gaza 1
17 Ashdod, one for Gaza, one for Ash'kelon, one for Gath 1
17 Ashdod, one for Gaza, one for Ash'kelon, one for Gath 1
17 Gaza, one for Ash'kelon, one for Gath, one for Ekron; 1
9: 3 Take one of the servants . . and arise, go and look 1
10: 3 three men . . one carrying three kids, another 1
11: 7 and they came out as one man. 1
13:17 one company turned toward Ophrah, to the land 1
14: 4 name of the one was Bozez, and the . . other Seneh. 1
5 one crag rose on the north in front of Michmash 1
40 You shall be on one side, and I and Jonathan my son 1
45 shall not one hair of his head fall to the ground; •
16:18 One of the young men answered, "Behold, I have seen 1
17:36 this . . Philistine shall be like one of them 1
22:20 one of the sons . . named Abi'athar, escaped 1
25:14 But one of the young men told Ab'igail, Nabal's wife 1
22 if by morning I leave so much as one male •
34 had not been left to Nabal so much as one male. •
26: 8 pin him to the earth with one stroke of the spear 1
15 For one of the people came in to destroy the king 1
20 like one who hunts a partridge in the mountains. 1
22 Let one of the young men come over and fetch it. 1
27: 1 I shall now perish one day by the hand of Saul; 1
5 let a place be given me in one of the country towns 1
2Sm 1:15 Then David called one of the young men and said, "Go 1
2:21 Turn aside . . and seize one of the young men 1
25 Benjaminites gathered . . and became one band 1
3:13 I will make a covenant . . but one thing I require 1
4: 2 the name of the one was Ba'anah 1
6:20 one of the vulgar fellows . . uncovers himself! 1
8: 2 two . . put to death, and one full line to be spared. •
9:11 Mephib'osheth ate . . like one of the king's sons. 1
12: 1 two men . . the one rich and the other poor. 1
3 the poor man had nothing but one little ewe lamb 1
13:13 you would be as one of the wanton fools in Israel. 1
30 slain all the king's . . and not one of them is left. 1
14: 6 and one struck the other and killed him. 1
11 not one hair of your son shall fall to the ground. •
27 three sons, and one daughter whose name was Tamar; 1
17: 3 You seek the life of only one man 7
9 even now he has hidden himself in one of the pits 1
12 of him . . the men with him not one will be left. 1
22 by daybreak not one was left who had not crossed 1
19:14 swayed the heart of all the men of Judah as one man; 1
23: 8 against 800 whom he slew at one time. 1
24:12 Three things I offer you; choose one of them 1
1Kg 1:52 If . . not one of his hairs shall fall to the earth; •
2:16 I have one request to make of you; do not refuse me. 1
20 I have one small request to make of you; do not 1
3:17 The one woman said, "Oh, my lord, this woman and I 1
25 child in two, and give half to the one, and half 1
4: 7 each . . had to make provision for one month 1
19 And there was one officer in the land of Judah. 1
22 Solomon's provision for one day was 30 cors 1
6:24 Five cubits was . . one wing of the cherub 1
26 The height of one cherub was ten cubits, and so was 1
27 a wing of one touched the one wall 1
34 the two leaves of the one door were folding 1
36 of hewn stone and one course of cedar beams. •
7:15 Eighteen cubits was the height of one pillar 1
16 the height of the one capital was five cubits 1
17 a net for the one capital, and a net for the other 1
18 in two rows round about upon the one network 1
31 within a crown which projected upward one cubit; •
44 one sea, and the twelve oxen underneath the sea. 1
8:56 not one word has failed of all his good promise 1
10:14 weight of gold that came to Solomon in one year 1
20 twelve lions stood there, one on each end of a step •
11:13 I will give one tribe to your son 1
32 he shall have one tribe, for the sake of my servant 1
36 Yet to his son I will give one tribe 1
12:29 he set one in Bethel, and the other he put in Dan. 1
30 the people went to the one at Bethel 1
15:29 he left to . . Jerobo'am not one that breathed •
18: 6 Ahab went in one direction by himself 1
23 let them choose one bull for themselves 1
25 Choose for yourselves one bull and prepare it 1
40 Seize the prophets . . let not one of them escape. 2
19: 2 if I do not make your life as the life of one of them 1
20:29 Israel smote . . 100,000 foot soldiers in one day. 1
22: 8 There is yet one man by whom we may inquire 1
13 the words of the prophets with one accord are 1
13 let your word be like the word of one of them 1
2Kg 3:11 one of the king of Israel's servants answered 1
4: 1 the wife of one of the sons of the prophets cried 1
22 Send me one of the servants and one of the asses 1
22 Send me one of the servants and one of the asses 1
39 One of them went out . . to gather herbs 1
6: 3 Then one of them said, " . . go with your servants. 1
5 as one was felling a log, his axe head fell 1
12 one of his servants said, "None, my lord, O king; 1
7:13 one of his servants said, "Let some men take five 1
8:26 and he reigned one year in Jerusalem. 1
9: 1 Eli'sha . . called one of the sons of the prophets 1
15:13 Shallum . . and he reigned one month in Sama'ria. •
17:27 Send there one of the priests . . you carried away 1
28 one of the priests whom they had carried away 1
25:16 As for the two pillars, the one sea, and the stands 1
17 The height of the one pillar was eighteen cubits 1
1Ch 1:19 To Eber were born two sons: the name of the one was 1
11:11 his spear against 300 whom he slew at one time. 1
21:10 Three things I offer you; choose one of them 1
23:11 they became a father's house in one reckoning 1
24: 6 one father's house being chosen for Elea'zar 1
6 for Elea'zar and one chosen for Ith'amar. 1
2Ch 3: 9 weight . . one shekel to 50 shekels of gold. •
11 one wing of the one, of five cubits, touched 1
11 one wing of the one, of five cubits, touched 1
12 one wing . . touched the wall of the house 1
17 one on the south, the other on the north; 1
4:15 the one sea, and the twelve oxen underneath it. 1
9:13 weight of gold that came to Solomon in one year 1
19 one on each end of a step on the six steps. •
18: 7 yet one man by whom we may inquire of the LORD 1
12 Behold, the words of the prophets with one accord 1
12 let your word be like the word of one of them 1
22: 2 Ahazi'ah . . reigned one year in Jerusalem. 1
28: 6 Pekah . . slew 120,000 in Judah in one day 1
30:12 to give them one heart to do what the king 1
32:12 Before one altar you shall worship 1
Ezr 3: 1 people gathered as one man to Jerusalem. 1
6: 4 courses of great stones and one course of timber; 5
10:13 Nor is this a work for one day or for two; 1
Neh 1: 2 Hana'ni, one of my brethren, came with certain men 1
4:17 each with one hand labored on the work 1
5:18 prepared for one day was one ox and six choice 1
18 one day was one ox and six choice sheep; 1
8: 1 people gathered as one man into the square 1
11: 1 lots to bring one out of ten to live in Jerusalem 1
Est 3:13 and to annihilate all Jews . . in one day 1
4:11 if any man or woman goes . . there is but one law; 1
7: 9 one of the eunuchs in attendance on the king 1
8:12 to destroy . . upon one day throughout all 1
Job 2:10 You speak as one of the foolish women would 1
9:22 It is all one; therefore I say, he destroys both 1
14: 4 clean thing out of an unclean? There is not one. 1
31:15 And did not one fashion us in the womb? 1
33:23 an angel, a mediator, one of the 1,000 1
41:16 One is so near to another that no air can come 1
Ps 14: 3 there is none that does good, no, not one. 1
34:20 He keeps all his bones; not one of them is broken. 1
53: 3 there is none that does good, no, not one. 1
83: 5 Yea, they conspire with one accord; 4
106:11 their adversaries; not one of them was left. 1
Prv 1:14 we will all have one purse"- 1
Ecc 2:14 yet I perceived that one fate comes to all of them. 1
3:20 All go to one place . . and all turn to dust again. 1
4: 9 Two are better than one . . they have a good reward 1
10 For if they fall, one will lift up his fellow; 1
11 they are warm; but how can one be warm alone? 1
12 a man might prevail against one who is alone 1
6: 6 though he should . . do not all go to the one place? 1
7:28 One man among 1,000 I found 1
9: 2 since one fate comes to all, to the righteous 1
3 This is an evil in all . . that one fate comes to all; 1
18 but one sinner destroys much good. 1
12:11 the . . sayings which are given by one Shepherd. 1
Sng 4: 9 with a glance . . with one jewel of your necklace. 1
6: 9 My dove, my perfect one, is only one 1
Isa 4: 1 seven women shall take hold of one man in that day 1
5:10 ten acres of vineyard shall yield but one bath 1
6: 6 flew one of the seraphim to me, having in his hand 1
9:14 head and tail, palm branch and reed in one day- 1
10:17 burn and devour his thorns and briers in one day. 1
19:18 One of these will be called the City of the Sun. 1
23:15 for 70 years, like the days of one king. 1
27:12 you will be gathered one by one 1
12 you will be gathered one by one 1
30:17 1,000 shall flee at the threat of one 1
34:16 Not one of these shall be missing; 1
40:26 because he is strong in power not one is missing. 2
47: 9 two things shall come to you . . in one day; 1
51: 2 when he was but one I called him, and I blessed him 1
66: 8 Shall a land be born in one day? 1
8 Shall a nation be brought forth in one moment? 1
17 go into the gardens, following one in the midst 1
Jer 3:14 for I am your master; I will take you, one from a city 1
24: 2 One basket had very good figs, like first-ripe 1
32:39 I will give them one heart and one way 1
39 I will give them one heart and one way 1
35: 2 to the house of the LORD, into one of the chambers; 1
52:20 As for the two pillars, the one sea 1
21 the height of the one pillar was eighteen cubits 1
22 the height of the one capital was five cubits; 1
Ezk 1:15 a wheel . . one for each of the four of them. 1
10: 9 there were four wheels . . one beside each cherub; 1
14 every one had four faces 1
11:19 I will give them one heart 1
19: 3 she brought up one of her whelps; 1
23: 2 there were two women, the daughters of one mother; 1
34:23 I will set up over them one shepherd 1
37:17 join them together into one stick 1
17 that they may become one in your hand. 1
19 with it the stick of Judah, and make them one stick 1
19 that they may be one in my hand. 1
22 I will make them one nation in the land 1
22 one king shall be king over them all; 1
24 they shall all have one shepherd. 1
40: 5 so he measured the thickness of the wall, one reed; 1
5 of the wall, one reed; and the height, one reed. 1
6 the threshold of the gate, one reed deep; 1
7 the side rooms, one reed long, and one reed broad; 1
7 the side rooms, one reed long, and one reed broad; 1
7 vestibule of the gate at the inner end, one reed. 1
12 before the side rooms, one cubit on either side; 1
26 it had palm trees on its jambs, one on either side. 1
34 it had palm trees on its jambs, one on either side; •
37 it had palm trees on its jambs, one on either side; •
42 a cubit and a half broad, and one cubit high 1
44 one at the side of the north gate facing south 7
41:11 one door toward the north, and another door 1
43:13 its base shall be one cubit high •
13 base shall be one cubit high, and one cubit broad •
13 broad, with a rim of one span around its edge. 1
14 ledge, two cubits, with a breadth of one cubit; 1
14 four cubits, with a breadth of one cubit; 1
15 projecting upward, four horns, one cubit high. 1
17 and its base one cubit round about. •
45: 7 corresponding . . to one of the tribal portions 1
11 the bath containing one tenth of a homer 1
15 one sheep from every flock of 200 1
46:17 out of his inheritance to one of his servants 1
48: 1 from the east side to the west, Dan, one portion. 1
2 from the east side to the west, Asher, one portion. 1
3 the east side to the west, Naph'tali, one portion. 1
4 the east side to the west, Manas'seh, one portion. 1
5 the east side to the west, E'phraim, one portion. 1
6 from the east side to the west, Reuben, one portion. 1
7 from the east side to the west, Judah, one portion. 1
8 in length equal to one of the tribal portions 1
23 the east side to the west, Benjamin, one portion. 1
24 from the east side to the west, Simeon, one portion 1
25 the east side to the west, Is'sachar, one portion. 1
26 the east side to the west, Zeb'ulun, one portion. 1
27 from the east side to the west, Gad, one portion. 1
Dan 2: 9 dream known to me, there is but one sentence 5
6: 2 three presidents, of whom Daniel was one 5
7: 5 raised up on one side; it had three ribs 5
8: 3 one was higher than the other, and the higher one 1
9 Out of one of them came forth a little horn 1
13 Then I heard a holy one speaking; 1
13 another holy one said to the one that spoke 1
9:27 make a strong covenant with many for one week; 1
10:13 but Michael, one of the chief princes, came to help 1
12: 5 one on this bank of the stream and one on that bank 1
5 one on this bank . . one on that bank of the stream. 1
Hos 1:11 and they shall appoint for themselves one head; 1
Ams 4: 7 I would send rain upon one city, and send no rain 1
7 one field would be rained upon 1
8 three cities wandered to one city to drink water 1
6: 9 if ten men remain in one house, they shall die. 1
Obd 1:11 you were like one of them. 1
Zep 3: 9 and serve him with one accord. 1
Zec 4: 3 olive trees by it, one on the right of the bowl 1

8:21 the inhabitants of one city shall go to another 1
11: 7 staffs; one I named Grace, the other I named Union. 1
8 In one month I destroyed the three shepherds. 1
14: 9 on that day the LORD will be one and his name one. 1
9 on that day the LORD will be one and his name one. 1
Mal 2:10 Have we not all one father? 1
10 Has not one God created us? 1
10 Why then are we faithless to one another 1
15 Has not the one God made and sustained for us 1
Mat 5:19 Whoever then relaxes one of the least of these 7
29 is better that you lose one of your members 7
30 is better that you lose one of your members 7
36 head, for you cannot make one hair white or black. 7
41 forces you to go one mile, go with him two miles. 7
6:24 for either he will hate the one and love the other 7
24 or he will be devoted to one and despise 7
27 by being anxious can add one cubit to his span 7
29 his glory was not arrayed like one of these. 7
10:29 And not one of them will fall to the ground 7
42 whoever gives to one of these little ones 7
12:11 said to them, "What man of you, if he has one sheep 7
13:46 on finding one pearl of great value 7
17: 4 one for you and one for Moses and one for Eli'jah. 7
4 one for you and one for Moses and one for Eli'jah. 7
4 one for you and one for Moses and one for Eli'jah. 7
18: 5 Whoever receives one such child in my name 7
6 whoever causes one of these little ones . . to sin 7
10 that you do not despise one of these little ones; 7
12 and one of them has gone astray 7
12 and go in search of the one that went astray? •
14 that one of these little ones should perish. 7
16 if he does not listen, take one or two others along 7
24 one was brought to him who owed him 10,000 talents; 7
28 came upon one of his fellow servants 7
19: 5 and the two shall become one flesh'? 7
6 So they are no longer two but one flesh 7
16 behold, one came up to him, saying 7
17 One there is who is good 7
20:12 saying, 'These last worked only one hour 7
13 he replied to one of them 7
21 one at your right hand and one at your left 7
21 one at your right hand and one at your left 7
22:35 one of them, a lawyer, asked him a question 7
23: 8 you have one teacher, and you are all brethren. 7
9 you have one Father, who is in heaven. 7
10 you have one master, the Christ. 7
24:40 one is taken and one is left. 7
40 one is taken and one is left. 7
41 one is taken and one is left. 7
41 one is taken and one is left. 7
25:15 to another two, to another one 7
18 he who had received the one talent went 7
24 who had received the one talent came forward 7
40 as you did it to one of the least of these 7
45 as you did it not to one of the least of these 7
26:14 one of the twelve, who was called Judas Iscariot 7
21 I say to you, one of you will betray me. 7
22 and began to say to him one after another 7
40 So, could you not watch with me one hour? 7
47 Judas came, one of the twelve 7
51 behold, one of those who were with Jesus 7
27:15 for the crowd any one prisoner whom they wanted. 7
38 one on the right and one on the left. 7
38 one on the right and one on the left. 7
48 one of them at once ran and took a sponge 7
Mrk 5:22 Then came one of the rulers of the synagogue 7
6:15 It is a prophet, like one of the prophets of old. 7
8:14 they had only one loaf with them in the boat. 7
28 others say, Eli'jah; and others one of the prophets 7
9: 5 one for you and one for Moses and one for Eli'jah. 7
5 one for you and one for Moses and one for Eli'jah. 7
5 one for you and one for Moses and one for Eli'jah. 7
17 one of the crowd answered him, "Teacher 7
37 Whoever receives one such child in my name 7
42 one of these little ones who believe in me 7
10: 8 the two shall become one flesh 7
8 So they are no longer two but one flesh. 7
37 one at your right hand and one at your left 7
37 one at your right hand and one at your left 7
12: 6 He had still one other, a beloved son 7
16 Bring me a coin . . they brought one •
28 one of the scribes came up and heard 7
29 The Lord our God, the Lord is one; 7
32 you have truly said that he is one 7
13: 1 one of his disciples said to him, "Look, Teacher 7
14:10 Then Judas Iscariot, who was one of the twelve 7
18 Truly, I say to you, one of you will betray me 7
19 to say to him one after another, "Is it I? 7
20 He said to them, "It is one of the twelve 7
20 one who is dipping bread into the dish with me. 7
37 Simon, are you asleep? Could you not watch one hour? 7
43 Judas came, one of the twelve 7
44 The one I shall kiss is the man •
47 one of those who stood by drew his sword 7
66 one of the maids of the high priest came; 7
15: 6 he used to release for them one prisoner 7
27 one on his right and one on his left. 7
27 one on his right and one on his left. 7
Lke 4:40 he laid his hands on every one of them 7
5: 3 Getting into one of the boats, which was Simon's 7
12 While he was in one of the cities 7
17 On one of those days, as he was teaching 7
7:41 one owed 500 denarii, and the other 50. 7
8:12 The ones along the path are those who have heard; •
13 the ones on the rock •
22 One day he got into a boat with his disciples 7
9:33 one for you and one for Moses and one for Eli'jah 7
33 one for you and one for Moses and one for Eli'jah 7
33 one for you and one for Moses and one for Eli'jah 7
11:46 not touch the burdens with one of your fingers. 7
12: 6 not one of them is forgotten before God. 7
27 was not arrayed like one of these. 7
52 in one house there will be five divided 7
13:10 Now he was teaching in one of the synagogues 7
14: 1 One sabbath when he went to dine •
15: 4 if he has lost one of them 7
7 more joy in heaven over one sinner who repents 7
8 having ten silver coins, if she loses one coin 7
10 there is joy . . over one sinner who repents. 7
15 joined himself to one of the citizens 7
19 treat me as one of your hired servants."' 7
26 he called one of the servants 7
16:13 either he will hate the one and love the other 7
13 will be devoted to the one and despise the other. 7
17 than for one dot of the law to become void. 7
17: 2 that he should cause one of these little ones to sin. 7
15 Then one of them, when he saw that he was healed 7
22 will desire to see one of the days of the Son of man 7
34 in that night there will be two in one bed 7
34 one will be taken and the other left. 7
35 one will be taken and the other left. 7
18:10 one a Pharisee and the other a tax collector. 7
19:44 they will not leave one stone upon another in you; •
20: 1 One day, as he was teaching the people 7
12 this one they wounded and cast out. •
21: 6 stone upon another •
22:36 let him . . sell his mantle and buy one. •
47 the man called Judas, one of the twelve, was leading 7
50 one of them struck the slave of the high priest 7
23:39 One of the criminals who were hanged 7
24:18 Then one of them, named Cle'opas, answered him 7
Joh 1:40 One of the two who heard John speak . . was Andrew 7
6: 8 One of his disciples, Andrew 7
22 saw that there had been only one boat there 7
70 one of you is a devil? 7
71 he, one of the twelve, was to betray him. 7
7:21 Jesus answered them, "I did one deed 7
50 Nicode'mus . . who was one of them, said to them 7
8: 9 when they heard it, they went away, one by one 7
9 went away, one by one, beginning with the eldest 7
41 we have one Father, even God. 7
10:16 there shall be one flock, one shepherd. 7
16 there shall be one flock, one shepherd. 7
30 I and the Father are one. 7
11:49 one of them, Ca'iaphas 7
50 one man should die for the people 7
52 to gather into one the children of God 7
12: 2 Laz'arus was one of those at table with him. 7
4 Judas Iscariot, one of his disciples 7
13:21 Truly, truly, I say to you, one of you will betray me. 7
23 One of his disciples, whom Jesus loved 7
17:11 that they may be one, even as we are one. 7
11 that they may be one, even as we are one. •
21 they may all be one; even as thou, Father, art in me 7
22 that they may be one even as we are one 7
22 that they may be one even as we are one 7
23 that they may become perfectly one 7
18:14 expedient that one man should die for the people. 7
22 one of the officers standing by struck Jesus 7
26 One of the servants of the high priest . . asked 7
19:23 made four parts, one for each soldier 9
34 one of the soldiers pierced his side with a spear 7
20:12 one at the head and one at the feet. 7
12 one at the head and one at the feet. 7
24 Now Thomas, one of the twelve, called the Twin 7
Act 1:21 one of the men who have accompanied us •
22 one of these men must become with us a witness 7
24 show which one of these two thou hast chosen 7
2: 3 distributed and resting on each one of them. 7
6 each one heard them speaking in his own language. 7
4:32 who believed were of one heart and soul 7
32 no one said that any of the things . . was his own 7
11:28 one of them named Ag'abus stood up 7
12:10 they went out and passed on through one street; 7
17:26 he made from one every nation of men 7
27 Yet he is not far from each one of us 7
19:34 they all with one voice cried out 7
20:31 not cease . . to admonish every one with tears. 7
21: 7 stayed with them for one day. 7
19 he related one by one the things that God had done 7
26 the offering presented for every one of them. 7
23: 6 one part were Sad'ducees and the other Pharisees 7
17 Paul called one of the centurions and said 7
24:21 except this one thing which I cried out 7
28:13 after one day a south wind sprang up 7
25 they departed, after Paul had made one statement 7
Rom 2:22 You who say that one must not commit adultery •
28 For he is not a real Jew who is one outwardly •
29 He is a Jew who is one inwardly •
3:10 as it is written: "None is righteous, no, not one; 7
12 no one does good, not even one. 7
30 since God is one; and he will justify 7
4: 4 Now to one who works, his wages are not reckoned •
5:12 as sin came into the world through one man 7
15 the free gift in the grace of that one man Jesus 7
16 judgment following one trespass brought condemnation 7
19 by one man's disobedience many were made sinners 7
12: 4 For as in one body we have many members 7
5 so we, though many, are one body in Christ 7
15: 6 together you may with one voice glorify the God 7
1Co 4: 6 puffed up in favor of one against another. 7
6:16 becomes one body with her 7
16 as it is written, "The two shall become one flesh. 7
17 united to the Lord becomes one spirit with him. 7
8: 4 there is no God but one. 7
6 yet for us there is one God, the Father 7
6 one Lord, Jesus Christ 7
9:24 only one receives the prize 7
10:17 Because there is one bread, we who are many are one 7
17 we who are many are one body 7
17 we all partake of the one bread. 7
12: 9 to another gifts of healing by the one Spirit 7
11 All these are inspired by one and the same Spirit 7
12 For just as the body is one and has many members 7
12 all the members of the body, though many, are one 7
13 by one Spirit we were all baptized 7
13 we were all baptized into one body 7
13 all were made to drink of one Spirit. 7
14 body does not consist of one member but of many. 7
18 organs in the body, each one of them, as he chose. 7
20 As it is, there are many parts, yet one body. 7
26 If one member suffers, all suffer together 7
26 if one member is honored, all rejoice together. 7
14:27 each in turn; and let one interpret. 7
2Co 5:14 we are convinced that one has died for all; 7
11: 2 to present you as a pure bride to her one husband. 7
24 I have received . . the 40 lashes less one. 7
Gal 3:16 referring to many; but, referring to one 7
20 Now an intermediary implies more than one 7
20 but God is one. 7
28 for you are all one in Christ Jesus. 7
4:22 one by a slave and one by a free woman. 7
22 one by a slave and one by a free woman. 7
24 One is from Mount Sinai 7
5:14 For the whole law is fulfilled in one word 7
Eph 2:14 For he is our peace, who has made us both one 7
15 create in himself one new man in place of the two 7
16 might reconcile us both to God in one body 7
18 both have access in one Spirit to the Father. 7
4: 4 There is one body and one Spirit 7
4 There is one body and one Spirit 7
4 just as you were called to the one hope 7
5 one Lord, one faith, one baptism 7
5 one Lord, one faith, one baptism 7
5 one Lord, one faith, one baptism 7
6 one God and Father of us all, who is above all 7
5:31 the two shall become one flesh. 7
33 however, let each one of you love his wife 7
Php 1:27 I may hear of you that you stand firm in one spirit 7
27 with one mind striving side by side for the faith 7
2: 2 being in full accord and of one mind. 7
Col 3:15 to which indeed you were called in the one body. 7
4: 6 you may know how you ought to answer every one. 7
1Th 2:11 we exhorted each one of you 7
5:11 encourage one another and build one another up 7
2Th 1: 3 the love of every one of you for one another 7
1Ti 2: 5 For there is one God 7
5 there is one mediator between God and men 7
3: 2 the husband of one wife, temperate, sensible 7
12 Let deacons be the husband of one wife 7
5: 9 having been the wife of one husband; 7
Tit 1: 6 if any man is blameless, the husband of one wife 7
Heb 2:11 those who are sanctified have all one origin. 7
7:13 the one of whom these things are spoken •
21 this one was addressed with an oath •
8: 1 one who is seated at the right hand of the throne •
9: 2 a tent was prepared, the outer one •
16 a will is involved, the death of the one who made it •
17 as long as the one who made it is alive. •
24 a copy of the true one •
10:34 a better possession and an abiding one. •
11:16 a better country, that is, a heavenly one •
Jas 2:10 whoever . . fails in one point has become guilty 7
19 You believe that God is one; you do well. 7
4:12 There is one lawgiver and judge 7
2Pe 3: 8 do not ignore this one fact, beloved 7
8 with the Lord one day is as a 1,000 years 7
8 and a 1,000 years as one day. 7
Rev 5: 5 Then one of the elders said to me, "Weep not; 7
6: 1 I saw when the Lamb opened one of the seven seals 7
1 and I heard one of the four living creatures say 7
7:13 Then one of the elders addressed me, saying 7
13: 3 One of its heads seemed to have a mortal wound 7
15: 7 And one of the four living creatures gave 7
17: 1 Then one of the seven angels . . said to me 7
10 seven kings . . one is, the other has not yet come 7

12 receive authority as kings for one hour 7
13 These are of one mind and give over their power 7
17 to carry out his purpose by being of one mind 7
18:10 Babylon! In one hour has thy judgment come. 7
17 In one hour all this wealth has been laid waste. 7
19 In one hour she has been laid waste. 7
21: 9 Then came one of the seven angels 7
1Es 3: 5 Let each of us state what one thing is strongest; 7
4:34 returns to its place in one day. 7
6:25 one course of new native timber 7
9:11 This is not a work we can do in one day or two 7
2Es 3: 7 thou didst lay upon him one commandment of thine; 13
11 thou didst leave one of them 13
13 thou didst choose for thyself one of them 13
4: 4 If you can solve one of them for me 13
5:11 one country shall ask its neighbor *
23 from all its trees thou hast chosen one vine 13
24 thou hast chosen for thyself one region 13
24 thou hast chosen for thyself one lily 13
25 thou hast filled for thyself one river 13
26 thou hast named for thyself one dove 13
26 thou hast provided for thyself one sheep 13
27 thou hast gotten for thyself one people 13
28 why hast thou given over the one to the many 13
28 and dishonored the one root beyond the others 13
40 Just as you cannot do one of the things 13
43 Couldst thou not have created at one time those 13
44 neither can the world hold at one time those 13
45 certainly give life at one time to thy creation? 13
45 If therefore all creatures will live at one time *
45 to support all of them present at one time. 13
46 Request it therefore to produce ten at one time. 13
6:41 that one part might move upward *
51 one of the parts which had been dried up 13
7: 8 there is only one path lying between them 13
8 so that only one man can walk upon that path. 12
50 the Most High has made not one world but two. 13
9:21 and saved for myself one grape out of a cluster *
21 and one plant out of a great forest. *
10: 8 you are sorrowing for one son 13
11 or you who are grieving for one? 13
11: 6 not even one creature that was on the earth. 13
12 behold, on the right side one wing arose 13
26 I looked, and behold, one was set up 13
29 behold, one of the heads that were at rest 13
12:26 one of the kings shall die in his bed 13
28 the sword of one shall devour him who was with him; 13
15:33 shall beset them and destroy one of them 13
Tob 1:19 Then one of the men of Nineveh went and informed 7
2: 3 Father, one of our people has been strangled 7
8:12 Send one of the maids to see whether he is alive 7
12:15 I am Raphael, one of the seven holy angels 7
Jdt 1:11 but looked upon him as only one man 7
6: 3 the king's servants will destroy them as one man. 7
10:13 without losing one of his men, captured or slain. 7
11: 8 you are the one good man in the whole kingdom 10
18 not one of them will withstand you. *
12:13 one of the daughters of the Assyrians 7
20 in any one day since he was born. 7
14: 6 in the hand of one of the men 7
18 One Hebrew woman has brought disgrace 7
AEs 10:10 one for the people of God 7
10 one for all the nations. 7
13: 7 may in one day go down in violence to Hades 7
15: 3 leaning daintily on one 7
Wis 4:10 There was one who pleased God and was loved by him *
7: 6 there is for all mankind one entrance into life 7
27 Though she is but one, she can do all things 7
12: 9 to destroy them at one blow by dread wild beasts 7
17:17 with one chain of darkness they all were bound. 7
18: 5 one child had been exposed and rescued 7
12 by the one form of death 7
12 in one instant 7
Sir 1: 8 There is One who is wise, greatly to be feared 7
6: 6 let your advisers be one in 1,000 7
7: 8 even for one you will not go unpunished. 7
16: 3 one is better than 1,000 7
11 Even if there is only one stiff-necked person 7
20:14 he has many eyes instead of one. 7
32: 1 be among them as one of them 7
33:15 in pairs, one the opposite of the other. 7
34:23 When one builds and another tears down 7
24 When one prays and another curses 7
38:17 for one day, or two, to avoid criticism 7
42:20 not one word is hidden from him. 7
24 All things are twofold, one opposite the other 7
25 One confirms the good things of the other 7
46: 4 did not one day become as long as two? 7
Aza 1:28 the three, as with one mouth, praised 7
Sus 1:25 And one of them ran and opened the garden doors. 7
52 he summoned one of them and said to him 7
1Mc 1:41 all should be one people 7
3:45 not one of her children went in or out *
4:11 there is one who redeems and saves Israel. *
5:27 take and destroy all these men in one day. 7
6:43 one of the beasts was equipped with royal armor. 7
7:16 he seized 60 of them and killed them in one day 7
26 the king sent Nicanor, one of his honored princes 7
46 not even one of them was left. 7
8:14 Yet for all this not one of them has put on a crown 7
16 They trust one man each year to rule over them 7
16 they all heed the one man 7
9:37 a daughter of one of the great nobles of Canaan 7
58 he will capture them all in one night. 7
10:38 they are considered to be under one ruler 7
11:36 not one of these grants shall be canceled 7
70 not one of them was left except Mattathias 7
13:28 erected seven pyramids, opposite one another 7
43 battered and captured one tower. 7
14: 2 he sent one of his commanders to take him alive. 7
15:28 He sent to him Athenobius, one of his friends 7
2Mc 7: 2 One of them, acting as their spokesman, said 7
8:33 who had fled into one little house 7
14:20 it had appeared that they were of one mind 11
3Mc 3: 1 all should promptly be gathered into one place 6
7:16 giving thanks to the one God of their fathers *
4Mc 1:33 I for one think so. 8
8:29 all with one voice together, as from one mind, said 7
29 all with one voice together, as from one mind, said 6
14:12 the rackings of each one of her children. 7
15:19 you looked at the eyes of each one in his tortures 7

one after another 1. per tempus 2. singillatim

2Es 5:46 If you bear ten children, why one after another?' 1
11:19 they wielded power one after another 2

one and all 1. מִקָּצֶה

Isa 56:11 to their own way, each to his own gain, one and all. 1

one another 1. אִישׁ אֶל אָח 2. אִישׁ אֶל רֵעַ 3. אִישׁ אֵת רֵעַ 4. אִישׁ לְרֵעַ 5. שְׁנֵיהֶם 6. ἀλλήλων 7. ἑαυτοῦ 8. ἕκαστος πρὸς τὸν πλησίον 9. ἕκαστος τὸν πλησίον 10. ἕτερος 11. ἕτερος ἕτερον 12. πλησίον 13. alius alio 14. alteruter 15. invicem 16. sui ipse

Jdg 6:29 they said to one another, "Who has done this thing? 2
1Sm 10:11 the people said to one another, "What has come over 2
20:41 they kissed one another, and wept with one 3
41 kissed one another, and wept with one another 3
2Sm 14: 6 had two sons, and they quarreled with one another 5
2Kg 3:23 kings . . fought together, and slain one another. 3
7: 3 they said to one another, "Why do we sit here 2
6 so that they said to one another, "Behold, the king 1
9 they said to one another, "We are not doing right. 2
Est 9:19 they send choice portions to one another. 4
22 days for sending choice portions to one another 4
Dan 2:43 they will mix with one another in marriage *
Mat 21:25 And they argued with one another 7
24:10 then many will fall away, and betray one another 6
10 betray one another, and hate one another. 6
25:32 he will separate them one from another 6
Mrk 4:41 and said to one another, "Who then is this 6
8:16 they discussed it with one another, saying 6
9:34 on the way they had discussed with one another 6
49 be at peace with one another. 6
11:31 they argued with one another 7
12: 7 those tenants said to one another 7
15:31 mocked him to one another with the scribes 6
16: 3 And they were saying to one another 7
Lke 2:15 the shepherds said to one another, "Let us go over 6
4:36 they were all amazed and said to one another 6
6:11 discussed with one another what they might do 6
7:32 like children . . calling to one another 6
8:25 they marveled, saying to one another 6
12: 1 they trod upon one another 6
20: 5 they discussed it with one another, saying 7
22:23 they began to question one another 7
Joh 4:33 So the disciples said to one another 6
5:44 who receive glory from one another 6
7:35 The Jews said to one another 7
11:56 They were . . saying to one another 6
12:19 The Pharisees then said to one another 7
13:14 you also ought to wash one another's feet. 6
22 The disciples looked at one another 6
34 that you love one another 6
34 that you also love one another. 6
35 if you have love for one another. 6
15:12 This is my commandment, that you love one another 6
17 This I command you, to love one another. 6
16:17 Some of his disciples said to one another 6
19:24 they said to one another, "Let us not tear it 6
Act 4:15 they conferred with one another 6
19:38 let them bring charges against one another. 6
21: 5 we prayed and bade one another farewell. 6
26:31 when they had withdrawn, they said to one another 6
28: 4 they said to one another 6
Rom 1:27 men . . consumed with passion for one another 6
12: 5 and individually members one of another. 6
10 love one another with brotherly affection; 6
10 outdo one another in showing honor. 6
16 Live in harmony with one another; 6
13: 8 Owe no one anything, except to love one another; 6
14:13 Then let us no more pass judgment on one another 6
15: 5 to live in such harmony with one another 6
7 Welcome one another, therefore 6
14 and able to instruct one another. 6
16:16 Greet one another with a holy kiss. 6
1Co 6: 7 To have lawsuits at all with one another 7
7: 5 Do not refuse one another 6
11:33 wait for one another- 6
12:25 members may have the same care for one another. 6
16:20 Greet one another with a holy kiss. 6
2Co 10:12 But when they measure themselves by one another 7
12 and compare themselves with one another 7
13:12 Greet one another with a holy kiss 6
Gal 5:13 through love be servants of one another. 6
15 if you bite and devour one another take heed 6
15 you are not consumed by one another. 6
26 have no self-conceit, no provoking of one another 6
26 no envy of one another. 6
6: 2 Bear one another's burdens 6
Eph 4: 2 forbearing one another in love 6
25 we are members one of another. 6
32 be kind to one another, tenderhearted 6
32 forgiving one another, as God in Christ forgave 7
5:19 addressing one another in psalms and hymns 7
21 Be subject to one another 6
Col 3: 9 Do not lie to one another 6
13 forbearing one another 6
16 teach and admonish one another in all wisdom 7
1Th 3:12 abound in love to one another and to all men 6
4: 9 taught by God to love one another; 6
18 comfort one another with these words. 6
5:11 encourage one another and build one another up 6
15 always seek to do good to one another and to all. 6
2Th 1: 3 love of every one . . for one another 6
Tit 3: 3 hated by men and hating one another; 6
Heb 3:13 exhort one another every day 7
10:24 to stir up one another to love and good works 6
25 but encouraging one another *
Jas 4:11 Do not speak evil against one another, brethren. 6
5: 9 Do not grumble, brethren, against one another 6
16 Therefore confess your sins to one another 6
16 and pray for one another, that you may be healed. 6
1Pe 1:22 love one another earnestly from the heart. 6
4: 8 hold unfailing your love for one another 7
9 Practice hospitality . . to one another. 6
10 employ it for one another, as good stewards 7
5: 5 yourselves . . with humility toward one another 6
14 Greet one another with the kiss of love. 6
1Jn 1: 7 we have fellowship with one another 6
3:11 that we should love one another 6
23 we should believe . . and love one another 6
4: 7 Beloved, let us love one another; 6
11 we also ought to love one another. 6
12 if we love one another, God abides in us 6
2Jn 1: 5 commandment . . that we love one another. 6
Rev 6: 4 so that men should slay one another; 6
1Es 3: 4 the three young men . . said to one another 10
4: 4 If he tells them to make war on one another 11
2Es 5: 9 and all friends shall conquer one another 16
13:31 they shall plan to make war against one another 13
33 the warfare that they have against one another; 14
15:16 growing strong against one another 13
35 They shall dash against one another 15
Jdt 15: 2 they did not wait for one another 12
Wis 5: 3 They will speak to one another in repentance 7
14:24 they either treacherously kill one another 11
24 or grieve one another by adultery *
18:23 the dead had already fallen on one another in heaps 6
19:18 the elements changed places with one another 7
Sir 16:28 They do not crowd one another aside 9
1Mc 3:43 they said to one another 8
7:29 they greeted one another peaceably 6
10:54 let us establish friendship with one another; 7
56 so that we may see one another 6
11: 6 they greeted one another 6
12:50 they encouraged one another 7
2Mc 7: 5 the brothers . . encouraged one another to die nobly, 6
14:26 Alcimus noticed their good will for one another 6
3Mc 5:49 falling into one another's arms *
4Mc 13: 8 and encouraged one another, saying 6
13 all of them together looking at one another 6
23 the more sympathetic to one another. 6
24 they loved one another all the more. 7
25 their goodwill and harmony toward one another 6

one by one 1. εἷς ἕκαστος 2. καθ' ἕνα 3. ὁ καθεῖς

Lke 16: 5 summoning his master's debtors one by one 1
1Co 14:31 For you can all prophesy one by one 2
3Mc 5:34 the . . friends one by one sullenly slipped away 3
4Mc 15:14 who saw them tortured and burned one by one 2

one man 1. אֶחָד 2. εἷς 3. ὁμοθυμαδόν 4. ὃς μέν

Ezk 33:24 Abraham was only one man, yet he got possession 1
Joh 18:39 I should release one man for you at the Passover; 2
Rom 5:15 For if many died through one man's trespass 2
16 the free gift is not like . . that one man's sin. 2
17 If, because of one man's trespass, death reigned 2
17 death reigned through that one man 2
17 reign in life through the one man Jesus Christ. 2
18 one man's trespass led to condemnation for all 2
18 one man's act of righteousness leads 2
19 by one man's obedience many will be made righteous. 2
9:10 when Rebecca had conceived children by one man 2
14: 5 One man esteems one day as better than another 4

Heb 11:12 Therefore from one man, and him as good as dead 2
1Es 4: 7 yet he is only one man! 2
5:47 they gathered as one man in the square 3
58 the Levites, as one man pressing forward the work 3
Sir 16: 4 through one man of understanding 2
1Mc 8:16 they all heed the one man 2
4Mc 5: 4 one man, Eleazar by name, leader of the flock 2

only one 1. יָחִיד 2. *μόνος*

Prv 4: 3 son . . the only one in the sight of my mother 1
1Mc 10:70 You are the only one to rise up against us 2

one piece 1. בְּ 2. מִן

Exd 37: 8 of one piece with the mercy seat 2
1Kg 7:32 the axles . . were of one piece with the stands; 1

one place 1. תַּחַת

Lev 13:23 the spot remains in one place and does not spread 1
28 the spot remains in one place and does not spread 1

one thing 1. אֶחָד 2. בְּכֹה 3. כָּכָה 4. *εἷς*

1Kg 22:20 And one said one thing, and another said another. 2
2Ch 18:19 And one said one thing and another said another. 3
Ps 27: 4 One thing have I asked of the LORD, that will I seek 1
Ecc 7:27 adding one thing to another to find the sum 1
Mrk 10:21 You lack one thing 4
Lke 10:42 one thing is needful 4
18:22 One thing you still lack 4
Joh 9:25 one thing I know, that though I was blind, now I see. 4
Php 3:13 one thing I do, forgetting what lies behind 4

one way 1. אֶחָד

Job 33:14 For God speaks in one way, and in two 1

onion 1. בָּצָל

Num11: 5 We remember the . . leeks, the onions 1

only 1. אַךְ 2. אֶפֶס 3. בְּדַי 4. וְ 5. זוּלַת 6. יָחִיד 7. כִּי אִם 8. לְבַד 9. לְמַעַן 10. פֶּן 11. רַק 12. רַק יָחִיד 13. *ἄλλος οὐκ εἰ μή* 14. *δέ* 15. *ἐὰν μή* 16. *εἰ* 17. *εἰ μή* 18. *εἰ μή οὐ* 19. *εἷς* 20. *καί* 21. *μέν* 22. *μετά* 23. *μήν* 24. *μονογενής* 25. *μόνος* 26. *ὅσος* 27. *οὐ μή* 28. *οὗτος* 29. *πλήν* 30. *τε* 31. *τίς* 32. autem 33. nisi 34. non nisi 35. solummodo 36. solus 37. tantum 38. unicus

Gen 6: 5 the thoughts of his heart was only evil 11
7:23 Only Noah was left, and those that were with him 1
9: 4 Only you shall not eat flesh with its life 1
11: 6 this is only the beginning of what they will do; *
19: 8 only do nothing to these men 11
22: 2 your only son Isaac, whom you love 6
24: 8 this oath of mine; only you must not take my son 11
27:13 only obey my word, and go, fetch them to me. 1
32:10 for with only my staff I crossed this Jordan; *
34:12 only give me the maiden to be my wife. 4
15 Only on this condition will we consent to you 1
22 Only on this condition will the men agree 1
23 Only let us agree with them 1
37: 5 to his brothers they only hated him the more. *
41:40 only as regards the throne will I be greater 11
42:38 for his brother is dead, and he only is left. 8
44:17 Only the man in whose hand the cup was found *
47:22 Only the land of the priests he did not buy; 11
50: 8 only their children, their flocks . . were left 11
Exd 8: 9 the frogs . . be left only in the Nile. 11
11 they shall be left only in the Nile. 11
28 only you shall not go very far away. 11
29 only let not Pharaoh deal falsely again by not 11
9:26 Only in the land of Goshen, where the people 11
10:17 forgive . . only this once, and entreat the LORD 1
17 entreat the LORD . . only to remove this death 11
24 Go . . only let your flocks and your herds remain 11
12:16 one must eat, that only may be prepared by you. 8
14:14 you have only to be still. *
21:19 only he shall pay for the loss of his time 11
22:20 sacrifices to any god, save to the LORD only 8
27 for that is his only covering, it is his mantle 8
Lev 13: 6 it is only an eruption; and he shall wash *
Num 1:49 Only the tribe of Levi you shall not number 1
10: 4 if they blow only one, then the leaders *
12: 2 Has the LORD indeed spoken only through Moses? 11
14: 9 Only do not rebel against the LORD; and do not fear 1
20:19 let me only pass through on foot, nothing more. 11
22:20 but only what I bid you, that shall you do. 1
35 only the word which I bid you, that shall you 2
23:13 you shall see only the nearest of them 2
31:22 only the gold, the silver, the bronze, the iron 1
36: 6 only, they shall marry within the family 1
Deu 2:27 pass through your land; I will go only by the road *
28 only let me pass through on foot 11
35 only the cattle we took as spoil for ourselves 11
37 Only to the land of the sons of Ammon you did not 11
3:11 only Og . . was left of the remnant of the Reph'aim; 11
24 only begun to show thy servant thy greatness *
4: 9 Only take heed, and keep your soul diligently 11
12 words, but saw no form; there was only a voice. 5
12:16 Only you shall not eat the blood . . pour it out 11
23 Only be sure that you do not eat the blood; 11
15: 5 if only you will obey the voice of the LORD 11
23 Only you shall not eat its blood; you shall pour 11
16:20 Justice, and only justice, you shall follow *
17:16 Only he must not multiply horses for himself 11
19:15 only on the evidence of two witnesses, or of three *
20:20 Only the trees which you know are not trees 11
22:25 then only the man who lay with her shall die. *
28:13 you shall tend upward only, and not downward; 11
29 only oppressed and robbed continually 1
33 be only oppressed and crushed continually; 11
29:14 Nor is it with you only that I make this . . covenant 8
Jos 1: 7 Only be strong and very courageous 11
17 we will obey you; only may the LORD . . be with you 11
18 Only be strong and of good courage. 11
6:15 it was only on that day . . seven times. 11
17 only Rahab the harlot and all who . . shall live 11
24 only the silver and . . they put into the treasury 11
8: 2 only its spoil and its cattle you shall take 11
27 Only the cattle and the spoil . . Israel took 11
11:13 none . . did Israel burn, except Hazor only; 8
22 only in Gaza, in Gath, and in Ashdod, did some remain 11
13: 6 only allot the land to Israel for an inheritance 11
14: 4 no portion was . . but only cities to dwell 7
17: 3 Now Zeloph'ehad . . had no sons, but only daughters; 7
17 you shall not have one lot only *
22:19 only do not rebel against the LORD 4
Jdg 3: 2 it was only that the generations of the people 11
24 they thought, "He is only relieving himself 1
6:39 let me make trial only this once with the fleece 11
39 let it be dry only on the fleece, and on all 8
40 it was dry on the fleece only, and on all the ground 8
10:15 to thee; only deliver us, we pray thee, this day. 1
11:34 she was his only child; beside her he had neither 12
14:16 You only hate me, you do not love me; you have put 11
15:13 No; we will only bind you and give you into their *
16:28 and strengthen me, I pray thee, only this once, O God 1
19:20 for all your wants; only, do not spend the night 11
1Sm 1: 5 he would give Hannah only one portion *
13 only her lips moved, and her voice was not heard; 11
23 wait . . only, may the LORD establish his word. 1
5: 4 only the trunk of Dagon was left to him. 11
7: 3 direct your heart to the LORD, and serve him only 8
4 Israel put away . . and they served the LORD only. 8
8: 9 hearken to their voice; only, you shall . . warn 1
12:24 Only fear the LORD, and serve him faithfully 1
18:17 only be valiant for me and fight . . battles. 1
20:39 only Jonathan and David knew the matter. 1
21: 4 if only the young men have kept . . from women. 1
2Sm 15:20 You came only yesterday, and shall I today *
17: 2 I will strike down the king only 8
3 You seek the life of only one man 29
23:10 men returned after him only to strip the slain. 1
1Kg 3: 3 Solomon loved the LORD . . only, he sacrificed 11
18 no one else . . only we two were in the house. 5
8:25 shall never fail . . if only your sons take heed 11
39 thou, thou only, knowest the hearts of all 8
11:22 And he said to him, "Only let me go. †
12:20 but the tribe of Judah only. 5
14: 8 followed me . . doing only that which was right 11
13 he only of Jerobo'am shall come to the grave 8
17:12 I have nothing baked, only a handful of meal 7
18:22 I, even I only, am left a prophet of the LORD; 8
19:10 I, even I only, am left; and they seek my life 8
14 I, even I only, am left; and they seek my life 8
22:31 Fight with neither . . but only with the king 7
2Kg 3:25 only its stones were left in Kir-har'eseth *
5: 7 Am I God . . ? Only consider, and see how he is seeking 1
10:23 no . . among you, but only the worshipers of Ba'al. 8
13:19 now you will strike down Syria only three times. *
17:18 none was left but the tribe of Judah only. 11
21: 8 I will not . . if only they will be careful to do 11
1Ch 2:34 Now Sheshan had no sons, only daughters; 7
22:12 Only, may the LORD grant you discretion 1
23:22 Elea'zar died having no sons, but only daughters; 7
2Ch 6:16 if only your sons take heed to their way, to walk 11
30 (for thou, thou only, knowest the hearts . . of men); 8
18:30 Fight . . only with the king of Israel. 8
27: 2 only he did not invade the temple of the LORD. 11
30:11 Only a few men of Asher, of Manas'seh, 1
33: 8 if only they will be careful to do all that 11
17 at the high places, but only to the LORD their God. 11
Ezr 10:15 Only Jonathan the son of As'ahel and Jahzei'ah 1
Est 1:16 Not only to the king has Queen Vashti done wrong 8
Job 1:12 only upon himself do not put forth your hand. 11
2: 6 he is in your power; only spare his life. 1
13:20 Only grant two things to me, then I will not hide 1
14:22 He feels only the pain of his own body 1
22 he mourns only for himself. *
Ps 37: 8 Fret not yourself, it tends only to evil. 1
38:16 For I pray, "Only let them not rejoice over me 10
51: 4 Against thee, thee only, have I sinned 8
62: 2 He only is my rock and my salvation, my fortress; 1
4 They only plan to thrust him down 1
6 He only is my rock and my salvation, my fortress; 1
91: 8 only look with your eyes and see the recompense 11
139:11 If I say, "Let only darkness cover me 1
Prv 11:23 desire of the righteous ends only in good; 1
24 another withholds . . and only suffers want. 1
14:23 but mere talk tends only to want. 1
17:11 An evil man seeks only rebellion 1
18: 2 but only in expressing his opinion. 7
19:19 deliver him, you will only have to do it again. *
27 only to stray from the words of knowledge. *
20:25 snare . . to reflect only after making his vows. *
21: 5 but every one who is hasty comes only to want. 1
22:16 who . . gives to the rich, will only come to want. 1
25:16 If you have found honey, eat only enough for you *
26:19 deceives his neighbor and says, "I am only joking! *
29: 9 fool only rages and laughs, and there is no quiet. *
Ecc 2:12 after the king? Only what he has already done. *
26 he gives . . only to give to one who pleases God. *
Sng 6: 9 My dove, my perfect one, is only one *
Isa 4: 1 only let us be called by your name; 11
10:22 only a remnant of them will return. *
45:14 God is with you only, and there is no other 1
24 Only in the LORD, it shall be said of me 1
58: 4 you fast only to quarrel and to fight and to hit *
Jer 1: 6 I do not know how to speak, for I am only a youth. *
7 the LORD said to me, "Do not say, 'I am only a youth' *
3:13 Only acknowledge your guilt, that you rebelled 1
5: 4 I said, "These are only the poor, they have no sense; 1
7:10 only to go on doing all these abominations? 9
22:17 have eyes and heart only for your dishonest gain 7
26:15 Only know for certain that if you put me to death 1
34: 7 these were the only fortified cities of Judah *
37:10 and there remained of them only wounded men *
38: 6 there was no water in the cistern, but only mire 7
49: 9 destroy only enough for themselves? *
51:58 the nations weary themselves only for fire. 3
Ezk 33:24 Abraham was only one man, yet he got possession *
43: 8 with only a wall between me and them. *
44: 3 Only the prince may sit in it to eat bread *
20 they shall only trim the hair of their heads. †
22 not marry a widow . . but only a virgin 7
46:17 only his sons may keep a gift from his 1
Dan 11:24 plans against strongholds, but only for a time. *
Hos 9: 4 for their bread shall be for their hunger only; *
Ams 3: 2 You only have I known of all the families 11
Obd 1: 5 would they not steal only enough for themselves? *
Hab 2:13 from the LORD . . that peoples labor only for fire 3
Mal 3:15 evildoers not only prosper *
Mat 4:10 your God and him only shall you serve.' 25
5:47 And if you salute only your brethren, what more 25
8: 8 but only say the word 25
9:21 she said to herself, "If I only touch his garment 25
12: 4 but only for the priests? 17
24 It is only by Be-el'zebul, the prince of demons 17
14:17 We have only five loaves here and two fish. 17
36 they might only touch the fringe of his garment 25
15:24 I was sent only to the lost sheep 17
17: 8 they saw no one but Jesus only. 25
19:11 but only those to whom it is given. *
20:12 saying, 'These last worked only one hour *
21:19 found nothing on it but leaves only 25
21 not only do what has been done to the fig tree 25
24:36 but the Father only. 25
Mrk 5:36 Do not fear, only believe. 25
8:14 they had only one loaf with them in the boat. 18
9: 8 saw any one with them but Jesus only. 25
13:32 nor the Son, but only the Father. *
Lke 4: 8 him only shall you serve.' 25
26 sent to none of them but only to Zar'ephath 17
27 but only Na'aman the Syrian. 17
5:21 Who can forgive sins but God only? 25
7:12 the only son of his mother, and she was a widow 24
8:42 he had an only daughter, about twelve years of age 24
50 Do not fear; only believe, and she shall be well. 25
17:10 we have only done what was our duty.' *
24:18 the only visitor to Jerusalem who does not know 25
Joh 3:16 God so loved the world that he gave his only Son 24
18 not believed in the name of the only Son of God. 24
4: 2 Jesus . . did not baptize, but only his disciples) *
5:18 because he not only broke the sabbath 25
19 only what he sees the Father doing 15
44 do not seek the glory that comes from the only God?. 25
6:22 saw that there had been only one boat there 13
10:10 The thief comes only to steal and kill 18
11:52 not for the nation only 25
12: 9 they came, not only on account of Jesus 25
13: 9 not my feet only but also my hands and my head! 25
17: 3 they know thee the only true God 25
20 I do not pray for these only 25
Act 2:15 since it is only the third hour of the day; *
5: 2 brought only a part 31
8:16 they had only been baptized 25
18:25 though he knew only the baptism of John. 25
19:26 not only at Ephesus but . . throughout all Asia 25
27 danger not only . . disrepute 25
20:24 if only I may accomplish my course *
21:13 am ready not only to be imprisoned but even to die 25
26:10 I not only shut up many of the saints in prison 30
29 not only you but also all who hear me this day 25
27:10 not only of the cargo and the ship 25
22 no loss of life among you, but only of the ship. 29
Rom 1:32 they not only do them but approve 25
3:29 Or is God the God of Jews only? 25
4: 9 Is this blessing pronounced only upon the circumcised *
16 not only to the adherents of the law 25
5:11 Not only so, but we also rejoice in God 25

7: 1 law is binding on a person only during his life? 26
8:23 not only the creation, but we ourselves 25
9:10 not only so, but also when Rebecca had conceived 25
24 not from the Jews only but also from the Gentiles? 25
27 only a remnant of them will be saved; •
11:20 but you stand fast only through faith. •
13: 5 one must be subject, not only to avoid God's wrath 25
14: 2 while the weak man eats only vegetables. •
16: 4 to whom not only I . . give thanks 25
27 to the only wise God be glory for evermore 25
1Co 3: 7 but only God who gives the growth. •
15 but only as through fire. 28
7:17 Only, let every one lead the life 17
39 married to whom she wishes, only in the Lord. 25
8: 9 Only take care lest this liberty of yours 14
9: 6 Or is it only Barnabas and I who have no right 25
24 only one receives the prize •
14:27 let there be only two or at most three •
36 or are you the only ones it has reached? 25
15:19 If for this life only we have hoped in Christ 25
2Co 3:14 because only through Christ is it taken away. •
4: 3 it is veiled only to those who are perishing. •
7: 7 not only by his coming but also by the comfort 25
8 that letter grieved you, though only for a while. 20
8:10 you began not only to do but to desire 25
17 For he not only accepted our appeal 21
19 not only that, but he has been appointed 25
21 not only in the Lord's sight 25
9:12 not only supplies the wants of the saints 25
13: 8 but only for the truth. •
Gal 1:23 they only heard it said 25
2:10 only they would have us remember the poor 25
3: 2 Let me ask you only this 25
4:18 not only when I am present with you. 25
5:13 only do not use your freedom as an opportunity 25
6:12 only in order that they may not be persecuted 25
Eph 1:21 not only in this age 25
4:29 only such as is good for edifying 16
Php 1:18 What then? Only that in every way 29
27 Only let your manner of life be worthy 25
29 you should not only believe in him 25
2: 4 Let each of you look not only to his own interests •
12 so now, not only as in my presence 25
27 God had mercy on him, and not only on him but on me 25
3:16 Only let us hold true to what we have attained. 29
4:15 in giving and receiving except you only; 25
Col 2:17 These are only a shadow of what is to come •
4:11 the only men of the circumcision among my fellow 25
1Th 1: 5 for our gospel came to you not only in word 25
8 not only has the word of the Lord sounded forth 25
2: 8 ready to share with you not only the gospel of God 25
2Th 2: 7 only he who now restrains it will do 25
1Ti 1:17 the King of ages, immortal, invisible, the only God 25
5:13 not only idlers but gossips and busybodies 25
6:15 the blessed and only Sovereign 25
2Ti 2:14 which does no good, but only ruins the hearers. •
20 there are not only vessels of gold and silver. 25
4: 8 and not only to me but also to all 25
Heb 9: 7 into the second only the high priest goes 25
10 deal only with food and drink 25
17 a will takes effect only at death •
12:26 Yet once more I will shake not only the earth 25
Jas 1:22 But be doers of the word, and not hearers only 25
1Pe 2:18 be submissive . . not only to the kind and gentle 25
2Pe 2:22 and the sow is washed only to wallow in the mire. •
1Jn 2: 2 the expiation for our sins, and not for ours only 25
4: 9 that God sent his only Son into the world 24
5: 6 he who came . . not with the water only 25
2Jn 1: 1 and not only I but also all who know the truth 25
Jde 1: 4 and deny our only Master and Lord, Jesus Christ. 25
25 to the only God, our Savior through Jesus Christ 25
Rev 2:25 only hold fast what you have, until I come. 29
9: 4 but only those of mankind who have not the seal 17
17:10 when he comes he must remain only a little while. •
21:27 only those . . written in the Lamb's book of life 17
1Es 2:19 they will not only refuse to pay tribute 27
4: 7 yet he is only one man! 25
2Es 3:14 to him only didst thou reveal the end of the times 36
4: 9 now I have asked you only about fire and wind 34
21 can understand only what is on the earth 35
5:28 and scattered thine only one among the many? 38
47 it cannot, but only each in its own time. •
7: 8 there is only one path lying between them 36
8 so that only one man can walk upon that path. 34
34 only judgment shall remain, truth shall stand 36
42 only the splendor of the glory of the Most High 35
54 he said to me, "Not only that, but ask the earth 35
140 there would probably be left only very few 34
8: 2 but only a little dust from which gold comes 32
5 for you have been given only a short time to live. 36
62 but only to you and a few like you. 33
9:24 and eat only of the flowers of the field 35
24 and drink no wine, but eat only flowers 35
10:34 I said, "Speak, my lord; only do not forsake me 37
12:51 and I ate only of the flowers of the field 35
13:10 I saw only how he sent forth from his mouth 35
11 but only the dust of ashes and the smell of smoke. 35
16:47 who conduct business, do it only to be plundered; •

Tob 3:10 But she said, "I am the only child of my father 19
6:10 he has an only daughter named Sarah 24
11 for you are her only eligible kinsman. 25
14 Now I am the only son my father has 25
Jdt 1:11 but looked upon him as only one man •
2: 4 chief general of his army, second only to himself 22
3: 8 nations should worship Nebuchadnezzar only 25
4: 3 they had only recently returned from the captivity •
7:12 only . . take possession of the spring of water 20
8:34 Only, do not try to find out what I plan 14
11: 7 not only do men serve him because of you 25
23 You are not only beautiful in appearance •
12:10 Holofernes held a banquet for his slave only 25
14: 2 only do not go down. 20
AEs 14: 3 O my Lord, thou only art our King 25
16: 3 They not only seek to injure our subjects 25
4 not only take away thankfulness from among men 25
24 It shall be made not only impassable for men 25
Wis 10: 8 not only . . hindered from recognizing the good 25
11:19 not only could their damage exterminate men 25
13:16 it is only an image and has need of help. •
19:15 And not only so, but punishment of some sort 25
Sir 0: 1 it is necessary not only that the readers 25
2 Not only this work, but even the law itself, 25
16:11 Even if there is only one stiff-necked person •
37: 1 some friends are friends only in name. 25
45:13 but only his sons and his descendants 29
25 the heritage of the king is from son to son only 25
LJr 1:47 They have left only lies and reproach •
Aza 1:22 Let them know that thou art the Lord, the only God 25
Sus 1:15 she went in as before with only two maids 25
1Mc 10:14 Only in Beth-zur did some remain 29
11:42 Not only will I do these things for you 25
15:33 but only the inheritance of our fathers •
2Mc 2:29 only what is suitable for its adornment •
32 adding only so much to what has already been said; •
4:35 For this reason not only Jews . . were grieved 25
5: 7 in the end got only disgrace from his conspiracy •
6:31 his death an example . . not only to the young 25
7:24 Antiochus not only appealed to him in words 25
10:28 not only . . valor but their reliance upon the Lord 22
11: 9 ready to assail not only men 25
3Mc 1:11 only the high priest who was pre-eminent over all 25
11 he only once a year •
29 not only the men but also the walls 25
3: 1 not only was he enraged against those Jews 25
19 they become the only people among all nations 25
23 they not only spurn the priceless citizenship 25
5:50 Not only this, but when they considered the help 23
4Mc 2: 4 Not only is reason proved to rule 25
4:20 not only was a gymnasium constructed 25
5:24 we worship the only real God. 25
27 to compel us not only to transgress the law 25
6:35 not only that reason has mastered agonies 25
7: 6 which had room only for reverence and purity •
23 only the wise and courageous man 25
8: 5 Not only do I advise you 25
15 not only were they not afraid 25
9:10 the tyrant not only was angry 25
14: 1 they not only despised their agonies 25
9 they not only saw what was happening 25
9 yes, not only heard the direct word of threat 25
15: 9 Not only so, but also because of the nobility 23
16: 2 not only that men have ruled over the emotions 25
17:20 These . . are honored, not only with this honor 25
18: 2 reason is master . . not only of sufferings from within 25
3 were not only admired by men 25

only *See also* begin, begotten, child, if, one, ruler, son.

only a few men 1. ἀριθμός
1Mc 9:65 he went with only a few men. 1

only if 1. ἐάν
Sir 32: 7 no more than twice, and only if asked. 1

onrush 1. impetus
2Es 13: 9 he saw the onrush of the approaching multitude 1

onrushing 1. קְדוּמִים 2. impetus
Jdg 5:21 Kishon swept them away, the onrushing torrent 1
2Es 13:11 and fell on the onrushing multitude 2
28 yet destroying the onrushing multitude 2

onslaught 1. ἐπίτασις
2Mc 6: 3 utterly grievous was the onslaught of evil. 1

onward 1. אַחֲרֵי 2. הָלְאָה 3. מַעְלָה 4. ἐπέκεινα
Exd 15:22 Then Moses led Israel onward from the Red Sea •
33: 6 stripped themselves . . from Mount Horeb onward. •
Num 15:23 from the day . . and onward throughout 2
2Ch 32:23 he was exalted . . from that time onward. 1
Neh 11:31 people of Benjamin also lived from Geba onward •
Ezk 43:27 from the eighth day onward the priests shall 2
Hag 2:15 what will come to pass from this day onward. 3
18 Consider from this day onward 3
Sus 1:64 And from that day onward Daniel had a great 4

onward *See also* go.

onycha 1. שְׁחֵלֶת 2. ὄνυξ
Exd 30:34 sweet spices, stacte, and onycha, and galbanum 1
Sir 24:15 like galbanum, onycha, and stacte 2

onyx 1. אֶבֶן שֹׁהַם 2. יָשְׁפֵה 3. שֹׁהַם 4. σαρδόνυξ
Gen 2:12 land is good; bdellium and onyx stone are there. 3
Exd 25: 7 onyx stones, and stones for setting, for the ephod 3
28: 9 you shall take two onyx stones, and engrave 3
20 the fourth row a beryl, an onyx, and a jasper; 3
35: 9 onyx stones and stones for setting, for the ephod 3
27 leaders brought onyx stones and stones to be set 3
39: 6 The onyx stones were prepared 3
13 the fourth row, a beryl, an onyx, and a jasper; 3
1Ch 29: 2 great quantities of onyx and stones for setting 1
Job 28:16 the gold of Ophir, in precious onyx or sapphire. 3
Ezk 28:13 jasper, chrysolite, beryl, and onyx, sapphire 2
Rev 21:20 the fifth onyx, the sixth carnelian 4

open 1. בַּר 2. גלה 3. חוּץ 4. כל 5. לִפְנֵי 6. מַפְתֵּחַ 7. נתן פִּתְחוֹן 8. עַל פְּנֵי 9. פטר 10. פֶּטֶר 11. פִּטְרָה 12. פָּנִים 13. פער 14. פצה 15. פקח 16. פְּרָזָה 17. פרק 18. פרש 19. פתח 20. פִּתְחוֹן 21. פתר 22. שָׂדֶה 23. שתם 24. פתח (A) 25. ἄγω 26. ἀναπτύσσω 27. ἀνοίγω 28. ἄνοιξις 29. γίνομαι 30. γυμνός 31. διανοίγω 32. διαστέλλω 33. ἐγκαινίζω 34. ἐκπετάζω 35. ἐν 36. λύω 37. παρέχω 38. ποιέω 39. πρόκειμαι 40. σχίζω 41. φανερόω 42. χάσκω 43. aperio 44. apertus
Gen 3: 5 your eyes will be opened, and you will be like God 15
7 the eyes of both were opened 15
4:11 from the ground, which has opened its mouth 14
7:11 and the windows of the heavens were opened. 19
8: 6 Noah opened the window of the ark 19
21:19 Then God opened her eyes, and she saw a well 15
29:31 LORD saw that Leah was hated, he opened her womb; 19
30:22 God hearkened to her and opened her womb. 19
34:10 the land shall be open to you; dwell and trade in it 5
41:56 Joseph opened all the storehouses 19
42:27 as one of them opened his sack 19
43:21 opened our sacks, and there was every man's money 19
44:11 to the ground, and every man opened his sack. 19
Exd 2: 6 When she opened it she saw the child; 19
13: 2 first to open the womb among the people of Israel 10
34:19 All that opens the womb is mine, all your male 10
Lev 14: 7 shall let the living bird go into the open field 12
53 go out of the city into the open field 12
17: 5 sacrifices which they slay in the open field 12
Num 3:12 instead of every first-born that opens the womb 10
8:16 instead of all that open the womb, the first-born 11
16:30 ground opens its mouth, and swallows them up 14
32 earth opened its mouth and swallowed them up 19
18:15 Everything that opens the womb of all flesh 10
19:15 every open vessel . . is unclean. 19
16 Whoever in the open field touches one who is 8
22:28 LORD opened the mouth of the ass, and she said 19
31 Then the LORD opened the eyes of Balaam, 2
24: 3 oracle of the man whose eye is opened 23
15 the oracle of the man whose eye is opened 23
26:10 the earth opened its mouth and swallowed them up 19
Deu 11: 6 how the earth opened its mouth and swallowed 14
15: 8 open your hand to him, and lend him sufficient 19
11 You shall open wide your hand to your brother 19
20:11 if its answer to you is peace and it opens to you 19
28:12 LORD will open to you his good treasury 19
32:25 In the open the sword shall bereave 3
Jos 8:17 they left the city open, and pursued Israel. 19
24 slaughtering all . . of Ai in the open wilderness 22
10:22 Open the mouth of the cave, and bring . . out to me 19
Jdg 3:25 still did not open the doors of the roof chamber 19
25 took the key and opened them; and there lay their 19
4:19 I am thirsty." So she opened a skin of milk and gave 19
11:35 I have opened my mouth to the LORD, and I cannot 14
36 father, if you have opened your mouth to the LORD 14
19:27 when he opened the doors of the house and went out 19
1Sm 3:15 then he opened the doors of the house of the LORD. 19
1Kg 6:18 was carved in the form of gourds and open flowers; 9
29 of cherubim and palm trees and open flowers 9
32 of cherubim, palm trees, and open flowers; 9
35 carved cherubim and palm trees and open flowers; 21
8:29 eyes may be open night and day toward this house 19
52 Let thy eyes be open to the supplication 19
2Kg 4:35 child sneezed . . and the child opened his eyes. 15
6:17 O LORD, I pray thee, open his eyes that he may see. 15
17 LORD opened the eyes of the young man, and he saw; 15
20 LORD, open the eyes of these men, that they may see. 15
20 So the LORD opened their eyes, and they saw; 15
9: 3 Then open the door and flee; do not tarry. 19
10 Then he opened the door, and fled. 19
13:17 said, "Open the window eastward": and he opened it. 19
17 said, "Open the window eastward": and he opened it. 19
15:16 they did not open it to him, therefore he sacked it 19
19:16 open thy eyes, O LORD, and see; and hear the words 15
1Ch 9:27 and they had charge of opening it every morning. 6
2Ch 6:20 eyes may be open day and night toward this house 19
40 Now, O my God, let thy eyes be open and thy ears 19
7:15 Now my eyes will be open and my ears attentive 19
29: 3 opened the doors of the house of the LORD 19

Ezr 10:13 we cannot stand in the open. 3
Neh 1: 6 let thy ear be attentive, and thy eyes open 19
6: 5 sent his servant . . with an open letter in his hand. 19
7: 3 not the gates . . be opened until the sun is hot; 19
8: 5 Ezra opened the book in the sight of all 19
5 when he opened it all the people stood. 19
13:19 gave orders that they should not be opened until 19
Est 9:19 Jews of the villages, who live in the open towns 16
Job 3: 1 Job opened his mouth and cursed the day of his 19
11: 5 oh, that God would speak, and open his lips to you 19
12:14 if he shuts a man in, none can open. 19
14: 3 dost thou open thy eyes upon such a one 15
27:19 he opens his eyes, and his wealth is gone. 15
29:23 they opened their mouths as for the spring rain. 13
31:32 I have opened my doors to the wayfarer 19
32:20 I must open my lips and answer. 19
33: 2 Behold, I open my mouth; 19
16 then he opens the ears of men, and terrifies them 2
35:16 Job opens his mouth in empty talk 14
36:10 He opens their ears to instruction, and commands 2
15 opens their ear by adversity. 2
39: 4 they grow up in the open; they go forth 1
41:14 Who can open the doors of his face? 19
Ps 5: 9 their throat is an open sepulchre 19
38:13 like a dumb man who does not open his mouth. 19
39: 9 I am dumb, I do not open my mouth; 19
40: 6 but thou hast given me an open ear. †
51:15 O Lord, open thou my lips 19
78: 2 I will open my mouth in a parable; 19
23 he commanded . . and opened the doors of heaven; 19
104:28 when thou openest thy hand, they are filled 19
105:41 He opened the rock, and water gushed forth; 19
106:17 earth opened and swallowed up Dathan 19
109: 2 wicked and deceitful mouths are opened against 19
118:19 Open to me the gates of righteousness 19
119:18 Open my eyes, that I may behold wondrous things 2
131 With open mouth I pant 13
145:16 Thou openest thy hand, thou satisfiest 19
146: 8 the LORD opens the eyes of the blind. 15
Prv 15:11 Sheol and Abaddon lie open before the LORD •
20:13 open your eyes, and you will have plenty of bread. 15
24: 7 in the gate he does not open his mouth. 19
27: 5 Better is open rebuke than hidden love. 2
31: 8 Open your mouth for the dumb 19
9 Open your mouth, judge righteously 19
20 She opens her hand to the poor 18
26 She opens her mouth with wisdom 19
Sng 5: 2 Open to me, my sister, my love, my dove, 19
5 I arose to open to my beloved, and my hands dripped 19
6 I opened to my beloved, but my beloved had turned 19
7:12 see . . whether the grape blossoms have opened 19
Isa 5:14 Sheol has . . opened its mouth beyond measure 13
9:12 Philistines . . devour Israel with open mouth. 4
10:14 that moved a wing, or opened the mouth, or chirped. 14
22:22 he shall open, and none shall shut; 19
22 and he shall shut, and none shall open. 19
24:18 For the windows of heaven are opened 19
26: 2 Open the gates, that the righteous nation 19
28:24 does he continually open and harrow his ground? 19
35: 5 Then the eyes of the blind shall be opened 15
37:17 open thy eyes, O LORD, and see; 15
41:18 I will open rivers on the bare heights 19
42: 7 to open the eyes that are blind 15
20 his ears are open, but he does not hear. 15
45: 1 to open doors before him that gates may not 19
8 the earth open, that salvation may sprout forth 19
48: 8 from of old your ear has not been opened. 19
50: 5 The Lord GOD has opened my ear 19
53: 7 and he was afflicted, yet he opened not his mouth; 19
7 like a lamb . . so he opened not his mouth. 19
60:11 Your gates shall be open continually; 19
61: 1 the opening of the prison to those who are bound; 15
Jer 5:16 Their quiver is like an open tomb 19
9:22 men shall fall like dung upon the open field •
13:19 The cities of Negeb are shut up, with none to open 19
32:11 the terms and conditions, and the open copy; 2
14 this sealed deed of purchase and this open deed 2
19 whose eyes are open to all the ways of men 15
50:25 The LORD has opened his armory 19
26 open her granaries; pile her up like heaps 19
Ezk 1: 1 the heavens were opened, and I saw visions of God. 19
2: 8 open your mouth, and eat what I give you. 14
3: 2 I opened my mouth, and he gave me the scroll to eat. 19
27 But when I speak with you, I will open your mouth 19
16: 5 but you were cast out on the open field 12
63 confounded, and never open your mouth again 20
21:22 to open the mouth with a cry, to lift up the voice 19
24:27 your mouth will be opened to the fugitive 19
26: 2 the gate . . is broken, it has swung open to me; •
29: 5 you shall fall upon the open field 12
21 I will open your lips among them. 7
32: 4 on the ground, on the open field I will fling you 12
33:22 he had opened my mouth by the time the man came 19
22 my mouth was opened, and I was no longer dumb. 19
27 him that is in the open field I will give 12
37:12 says the Lord GOD: Behold, I will open your graves 19
13 know that I am the LORD, when I open your graves 19
39: 5 You shall fall in the open field; for I have spoken 12
41:11 the doors of the side chambers opened on the part •
44: 2 it shall not be opened, and no one shall enter by it; 19
46: 1 but on the sabbath day it shall be opened 19
1 on the day of the new moon it shall be opened. 19
12 the gate facing east shall be opened for him 19
Dan 6:10 where he had windows . . open toward Jerusalem; 24
7:10 court sat in judgment, and the books were opened. 24
9:18 open thy eyes and behold our desolations 15
10:16 touched my lips; then I opened my mouth and spoke. 19
Mic 2:13 He who opens the breach will go up before them; 17
Nah 2: 6 The river gates are opened 19
Zec 11: 1 Open your doors, O Lebanon 19
12: 4 But upon the house of Judah I will open my eyes 15
13: 1 shall be a fountain opened for the house of David 19
Mal 3:10 if I will not open the windows of heaven for you 19
Mat 2:11 Then, opening their treasures, they offered him 27
3:16 heavens were opened and he saw the Spirit of God 27
5: 2 he opened his mouth and taught them, saying 27
7: 7 knock, and it will be opened to you. 27
8 and to him who knocks it will be opened. 27
9:30 their eyes were opened 27
13:35 I will open my mouth in parables 27
17:27 when you open its mouth you will find a shekel; 27
20:33 They said to him, "Lord, let our eyes be opened. 27
25:11 'Lord, lord, open to us.' 27
27:52 the tombs also were opened 27
Mrk 1:10 immediately he saw the heavens opened 40
7:34 Eph'phatha," that is, "Be opened. 31
35 his ears were opened, his tongue was released 27
Lke 1:64 immediately his mouth was opened 27
2:23 Every male that opens the womb shall be called holy 31
3:21 the heaven was opened 27
4:17 He opened the book 26
11: 9 seek, and you will find; knock, and it will be opened 27
10 to him who knocks it will be opened. 27
12:36 so that they may open to him at once when he comes 27
13:25 to knock at the door, saying, 'Lord, open to us.' 27
24:31 their eyes were opened and they recognized him; 31
32 while he opened to us the scriptures? 31
45 Then he opened their minds 31
Joh 1:51 truly, I say to you, you will see heaven opened 27
9:10 They said to him, "Then how were your eyes opened? 27
14 when Jesus made the clay and opened his eyes. 27
17 since he has opened your eyes 27
21 nor do we know who opened his eyes 27
26 How did he open your eyes? 27
30 and yet he opened my eyes. 27
32 that any one opened the eyes of a man born blind. 27
10: 3 To him the gatekeeper opens 27
21 Can a demon open the eyes of the blind? 27
11:37 he who opened the eyes of the blind man 27
Act 5:19 an angel of the Lord opened the prison doors 27
23 when we opened it we found no one inside. 27
7:56 he said, "Behold, I see the heavens opened 31
8:32 so he opens not his mouth. 27
35 Then Philip opened his mouth 27
9: 8 when his eyes were opened, he could see nothing 27
40 she opened her eyes 27
10:11 saw the heaven opened, and something descending 27
34 Peter opened his mouth and said: "Truly I perceive 27
12:10 It opened to them of its own accord 27
14 in her joy she did not open the gate but ran 27
16 when they opened, they saw him and were amazed. 27
14:27 how he had opened a door of faith to the Gentiles. 27
16:14 opened her heart to give heed to what was said 31
26 immediately all the doors were opened 27
27 woke and saw that the prison doors were open 27
18:14 when Paul was about to open his mouth 27
19:38 the courts are open 25
26:18 to open their eyes 27
Rom 3:13 Their throat is an open grave 27
1Co 16: 9 for a wide door for effective work has opened 27
2Co 2:12 a door was opened for me in the Lord; 27
6:11 Our mouth is open to you, Corinthians 27
Eph 6:19 opening my mouth boldly to proclaim the mystery 28
Col 4: 3 God may open to us a door for the word 27
Tit 1: 6 not open to the charge of being profligate 35
Heb 4:13 all are open and laid bare 30
9: 8 the way into the sanctuary is not yet opened 41
10:20 by the new and living way which he opened for us 33
1Pe 3:12 and his ears are open to their prayer. •
Rev 3: 7 the true one . . who opens and no one shall shut 27
7 the true one . . who shuts and no one opens. 27
8 Behold, I have set before you an open door 27
20 if any one hears my voice and opens the door 27
4: 1 After this I looked, and lo, in heaven an open door! 27
5: 2 Who is worthy to open the scroll and break 27
3 no one . . was able to open the scroll or to look 27
4 that no one was found worthy to open the scroll 27
5 so that he can open the scroll and its seven seals. 27
9 Worthy . . to take the scroll and to open its seals 27
6: 1 I saw when the Lamb opened one of the seven seals 27
3 When he opened the second seal, I heard 27
5 When he opened the third seal, I heard 27
7 When he opened the fourth seal, I heard the voice 27
9 When he opened the fifth seal, I saw 27
12 When he opened the sixth seal, I looked, and behold 27
8: 1 When the Lamb opened the seventh seal 27
9: 2 he opened the shaft of the bottomless pit 27
10: 2 He had a little scroll open in his hand. 27
8 the scroll which is open in the hand of the angel 27
11:19 Then God's temple in heaven was opened 27
12:16 earth opened its mouth and swallowed the river 27
13: 6 it opened its mouth to utter blasphemies 27
15: 5 temple of the tent of witness in heaven was opened 27
19:11 Then I saw heaven opened, and behold, a white horse! 27
20:12 I saw the dead . . and books were opened. 27
12 another book was opened, which is the book of life 27
1Es 4:19 with open mouths stare at her 42
9:46 when he opened the law, they all stood erect 36
2Es 5:37 open for me the closed chambers 43
6:20 the books shall be opened before the firmament 43
8:52 because it is for you that paradise is opened 43
9:11 an opportunity of repentance was still open 44
28 my mouth was opened, and I began to speak 43
14:38 Ezra, open your mouth and drink what I give you 43
39 Then I opened my mouth, and behold, a full cup 43
41 my mouth was opened, and was no longer closed. 43
Tob 2:10 their fresh droppings fell into my open eyes 27
8:13 the maid opened the door and went 27
11: 7 I know, Tobias, that your father will open his eyes. 27
Jdt 10: 9 Order the gate of the city to be opened for me 27
9 they ordered the young men to open the gate 27
11:19 not a dog will so much as open its mouth to growl •
13:11 Open, open the gate! God, our God, is still with us 27
11 Open, open the gate! God, our God, is still with us 27
13 they opened the gate and admitted them 27
14:15 he opened it and went into the bedchamber 32
AEs 13: 2 open to travel throughout all its extent 37
14:10 to open the mouths of the nations 27
Wis 10:21 because wisdom opened the mouth of the dumb 27
Sir 15: 5 will open his mouth in the midst of the assembly. 27
20:15 he opens his mouth like a herald 27
22:22 If you have opened your mouth 27
24: 2 she will open her mouth 27
26:12 As a thirsty wayfarer opens his mouth 27
12 open her quiver to the arrow. 27
29:24 you may not open your mouth; 27
39: 5 he will open his mouth in prayer 27
43:14 Therefore the storehouses are opened 27
51:25 I opened my mouth and said 27
Bar 2:17 open thy eyes, O Lord, and see; for the dead who are 27
Aza 1: 2 in the midst of the fire he opened his mouth 27
10 now we cannot open our mouths 27
Sus 1:25 And one of them ran and opened the garden doors. 27
39 and he opened the doors and dashed out. 27
Bel 1:18 As soon as the doors were opened 27
1Mc 3:28 he opened his coffers 27
48 they opened the book of the law 34
5:48 they refused to open to him. 27
10:76 the men . . became afraid and opened the gates 27
11: 2 the people of the cities opened their gates to him 27
14: 5 opened a way to the isles of the sea. 38
2Mc 1: 4 May he open your heart to his law 31
16 Opening the secret door in the ceiling 27
14:44 as they quickly drew back, a space opened 29
4Mc 15: 2 Two courses were open to this mother 39

open *See also* air, break, burst, cleave, country, cut, field, land, lay, leave, rend, rip, slash, space, split, square, statement, street, tear.

open a shaft 1. פרץ
Job 28: 4 open shafts in a valley away from where men live; 1

open first 1. פָּטַר
Exd 13:12 to the LORD all that first opens the womb. 1
15 all the males that first open the womb; 1

open one's heart 1. χωρέω
2Co 7: 2 Open your hearts to us 1

open one's mouth 1. ἀναχάσκω
2Mc 6:18 Eleazar . . was being forced to open his mouth 1

open place 1. צְחִיחַ
Neh 4:13 space behind the wall, in open places, I stationed 1

open to all 1. πάμφυλος
4Mc 4:11 half dead in the temple area that was open to all 1

open to reason 1. εὐπειθής
Jas 3:17 wisdom from above is . . gentle, open to reason 1

open up 1. διαιρέω
Sir 27:25 a treacherous blow opens up wounds. 1

open wide 1. פצה 2. פשק 3. רחב
Ps 22:13 they open wide their mouths at me 1
35:21 They open wide their mouths against me; 3
81:10 Open your mouth wide, and I will fill it. 3
Prv 13: 3 he who opens wide his lips comes to ruin. 2
Isa 57: 4 Against whom do you open your mouth wide 3

wide open 1. פתח
Nah 3:13 The gates of your land are wide open to your foes; 1

open-mouthed 1. ὀδούς
Sir 19:30 A man's attire and open-mouthed laughter 1

opening 1. פֶּה 2. פֶּתַח 3. ὀπή
Exd 28:32 It shall have in it an opening for the head 1
32 with a woven binding around the opening 1
32 an opening . . like the opening in a garment 1
39:23 the opening of the robe in it was like the opening 1
23 the opening of the robe in it was like the opening 1
23 a garment, with a binding around the opening 1
1Kg 7:31 Its opening was within a crown which projected 1
31 its opening was round, as a pedestal is made 1
31 At its opening there were carvings; 1
Ezk 40:11 breadth of the opening of the gateway, ten cubits; 2
Jas 3:11 Does a spring pour forth from the same opening 3
opening *See also* make.

openly 1. μετὰ παρρησίας 2. παρρησία 3. προφανής 4. φανερῶς 5. palam
Mrk 1:45 so that Jesus could no longer openly enter a town 4
Joh 7: 4 if he seeks to be known openly 2
13 Yet for fear of the Jews no one spoke openly 2
26 here he is, speaking openly, and they say nothing 2
11:54 no longer went about openly among the Jews 2
18:20 I have spoken openly to the world 2
Act 28:31 teaching . . quite openly and unhindered. 1
2Es 14: 6 'These words you shall publish openly 5
Sir 51:13 I sought wisdom openly in my prayer. 3
openly *See also* carry.

operation 1. ἔργον
1Es 6:10 These operations are going on rapidly 1

opinion 1. דֵּעַ 2. לֵב 3. γνώμη 4. διαλαμβάνω 5. διαλογισμός 6. στόμα 7. ὑπόνοια
Job 32: 6 timid and afraid to declare my opinion to you. 1
10 say, 'Listen to me; let me also declare my opinion 1
17 I also will declare my opinion. 1
Prv 18: 2 but only in expressing his opinion. 2
Rom 14: 1 welcome him, but not for disputes over opinions. 5
1Co 7:25 I give my opinion as one who by the Lord's mercy 3
Sir 3:24 wrong opinion has caused their thoughts to slip. 7
13:24 poverty is evil in the opinion of the ungodly. 6
2Mc 6:29 the words . . were in their opinion sheer madness. 4
opinion *See also* different, hold.

vain opinion 1. κενοδοξία
4Mc 8:19 and give up this vain opinion 1

opponent 1. רֵעַ 2. ἀντιδιατίθημι 3. ἀντίκειμαι 4. ἐναντίος 5. ὁ κατά
2Sm 2:16 And each caught his opponent by the head 1
16 and thrust his sword in his opponent's side; 1
Php 1:28 not frightened in anything by your opponents. 3
2Ti 2:25 correcting his opponents with gentleness 2
Tit 2: 8 so that an opponent may be put to shame 4
2Mc 8:35 having been humbled . . by opponents 5

political opponent 1. ἀντιπολιτεύω
4Mc 4: 1 a political opponent of . . Onias 1

opportune 1. εὔθετον
Sus 1:15 while they were watching for an opportune day 1
opportune *See also* time.

opportunity 1. ἀνοχή 2. ἀφορμή 3. ἔξειμι 4. εὐκαιρέω 5. εὐκαιρία 6. εὔκαιρος 7. εὐκαίρως 8. ἡμέρα εὔκαιρος 9. καιρός 10. τόπος 11. locus 12. via
Mat 26:16 he sought an opportunity to betray him. 5
Mrk 6:21 an opportunity came 8
14:11 he sought an opportunity to betray him. 7
Lke 22: 6 sought an opportunity to betray him to them 5
Act 24:25 when I have an opportunity I will summon you. 9
25:16 and had opportunity to make his defense 10
Rom 7: 8 But sin, finding opportunity in the commandment 2
11 For sin, finding opportunity in the commandment 2
1Co 16:12 He will come when he has opportunity. 4
Gal 5:13 your freedom as an opportunity for the flesh 2
6:10 So then, as we have opportunity 9
Eph 4:27 give no opportunity to the devil. 10
Heb 11:15 they would have had opportunity to return. 9
2Es 5:50 Since thou hast now given me the opportunity 12
9:11 while an opportunity of repentance was . . open 11
Jdt 12:16 he had been waiting for an opportunity to deceive her 9
Wis 12:20 granting them time and opportunity 10
Sir 0: 3 I found opportunity for no little instruction. 2
12:16 if he finds an opportunity 9
19:28 he will do evil when he finds an opportunity. 9
38:24 depends on the opportunity of leisure 5
1Mc 11:42 if I find an opportunity. 5
12:25 no opportunity to invade his own country. 1
15:34 Now that we have the opportunity 9
2Mc 4:32 he had obtained a suitable opportunity 9
9:25 how the princes . . keep watching for opportunities 9
14: 5 he found an opportunity 9
29 he watched for an opportunity 6
4Mc 1:12 shortly have an opportunity to speak of this 3
opportunity *See also* avail, give.

no opportunity 1. ἀκαιρέομαι
Php 4:10 but you had no opportunity. 1

oppose 1. נוא 2. עמד על 3. שׂוּם לְ 4. ἀνθίστημι 5. ἀντεῖπον 6. ἀντιδοκέω 7. ἀντίκειμαι 8. ἀντιπράσσω 9. ἀντιτάσσω 10. ἀντιτίθημι 11. ἐναντιόομαι 12. ἐναντίος 13. contradico 14. contrarius 15. dico
Num 30: 5 will forgive her, because her father opposed her. 1
11 said nothing to her, and did not oppose her; 1
1Sm 15: 2 what Am'alek did . . in opposing them on the way 3
2Ch 35:21 Cease opposing God, who is with me, lest he destroy •
Ezr 10:15 Only Jonathan . . and Jahzei'ah . . opposed this 2
Act 18: 6 when they opposed and reviled him 9
26: 9 in opposing the name of Jesus of Nazareth. 12
Gal 2:11 I opposed him to his face 4
5:17 these are opposed to each other 7
1Th 2:15 drove us out, and displease God and oppose all men 12
2Th 2: 4 opposes and exalts himself 7
2Ti 3: 8 As Jannes and Jambres opposed Moses 4
8 these men also oppose the truth 4
4:15 he strongly opposed our message. 4
Jas 4: 6 God opposes the proud, but gives grace 9
1Pe 5: 5 God opposes the proud, but gives grace 9
1Es 1:27 Stand aside, and do not oppose the Lord. 11
2Es 5:29 those who opposed thy promises 13
9:18 and no one opposed me then, for no one existed; 13
11: 3 out of his wings there grew opposing wings 14
11 I counted his opposing wings, and behold 14
15: 3 the unbelief of those who oppose you. 15
AEs 13: 9 there is no one who can oppose thee 6
Wis 2:12 he is inconvenient to us and opposes our actions; 11
1Mc 8:11 as many as ever opposed them, they destroyed 4
14: 7 there was none to oppose him. 7
44 to oppose what he says 5
2Mc 14:29 Since it was not possible to oppose the king 8
3Mc 3: 7 hostile and greatly opposed to his government. 11
6:19 They opposed the forces of the enemy 4
4Mc 1: 6 opposed to justice, courage, and self-control 12
3:16 opposing reason to desire 10

oppose God 1. θεομάχος
Act 5:39 You might even be found opposing God! 1

oppose with philosophy 1. ἀντιφιλοσοφέω
4Mc 8:15 they also opposed . . with their own philosophy 1

opposite 1. אֶל 2. אֶל פְּנֵי 3. לְנֶגֶד 4. לְעֻמַּת 5. מוּל 6. מִמּוּל 7. מִנֶּגֶד 8. נֶגֶד 9. נֹכַח 10. עַד נֹכַח 11. עַל פְּנֵי 12. קֹבֶל 13. לְקֳבֵל (A) 14. ἄντικρυς 15. ἀντιπέρα 16. ἀπέναντι 17. ἀπό 18. ἐξ ἐναντίας 19. ἐπί 20. ἑτέρωθεν 21. κατά 22. κατὰ πρόσωπον 23. κατέναντι 24. contra
Gen 25:18 from Hav'ilah to Shur, which is opposite Egypt 11
Exd 26: 5 the loops shall be opposite one another. 12
35 lampstand . . opposite the table; 9
30: 4 on two opposite sides of it shall you make them •
36:12 the loops were opposite one another. 12
37:27 under its molding, on two opposite sides of it •
40:24 opposite the table on the south side 9
Num 21:11 in the wilderness which is opposite Moab 11
22: 5 they are dwelling opposite me. 6
Deu 3:29 we remained in the valley opposite Beth-pe'or. 5
4:46 in the valley opposite Beth-pe'or, in the land 5
32:49 Nebo . . in the land of Moab, opposite Jericho; 11
34: 1 top of Pisgah, which is opposite Jericho. 11
6 buried . . in the land of Moab opposite Beth-pe'or; 5
Jos 3:16 and the people passed over opposite Jericho. 8
15: 7 Gilgal, which is opposite the ascent of Adum'mim 9
18:14 that lies to the south, opposite Beth-hor'on 11
17 Geli'loth, which is opposite the ascent of Adum'mim; 9
Jdg 19:10 rose up and departed, and arrived opposite Jebus 10
20:43 from Nohah as far as opposite Gib'e-ah on the east. 9
1Sm 20:25 The king sat . . Jonathan sat opposite, and Abner •
2Sm 5:23 and come upon them opposite the balsam trees. 6
16:13 Shim'e-i went along on the hillside opposite him 4
1Kg 7: 4 and window opposite window in three tiers. 1
5 and window was opposite window in three tiers. 1
20:29 they encamped opposite one another seven days. 9
21:10 set two base fellows opposite him 8
13 the two base fellows came in and sat opposite him; 8
2Kg 3:22 the Moabites saw the water opposite them 7
26 to break through, opposite the king of Edom; 1
1Ch 8:32 Now these also dwelt opposite their kinsmen. 8
9:38 dwelt opposite their kinsmen in Jerusalem 8
14:14 and come upon them opposite the balsam trees. 6
2Ch 7: 6 opposite them the priests sounded trumpets; 8
Neh 3:10 Jedai'ah . . repaired opposite his house; 8
16 point opposite the sepulchres of David 8
19 opposite the ascent to the armory at the Angle. 7
23 Benjamin . . repaired opposite their house. 8
25 Palal . . repaired opposite the Angle 7
26 repaired to a point opposite the Water Gate 8
27 section opposite the great projecting tower 7
28 repaired, each one opposite his own house. 3
29 Zadok . . repaired opposite his own house. 8
30 Meshul'lam . . repaired opposite his chamber. 8
31 opposite the Muster Gate, and to the upper 8
7: 3 Appoint guards . . each opposite his own house. 8
12: 9 Bakbuki'ah and Unno . . stood opposite them 3
Est 5: 1 in the inner court . . opposite the king's hall. 9
1 king was . . opposite the entrance to the palace; 9
Ezk 40: 2 on which was a structure like a city opposite me. 16
23 And opposite the gate on the north, as on the east 8
42: 1 chambers which were opposite the temple yard 8
1 and opposite the building on the north. 8
7 toward the outer court, opposite the chambers 2
8 those opposite the temple were 100 cubits 11
10 On the south also, opposite the yard 2
10 opposite the yard and opposite the building 2
12 and opposite them was a dividing wall. •
13 opposite the yard are the holy chambers 2
Dan 5: 5 wrote on the plaster . . opposite the lampstand; 13
Mat 21: 2 saying to them, "Go into the village opposite you 23
27:61 sitting opposite the sepulchre. 16
Mrk 11: 2 said to them, "Go into the village opposite you 23
12:41 he sat down opposite the treasury 23
13: 3 on the Mount of Olives opposite the temple 23
Lke 8:26 which is opposite Galilee. 15
19:30 saying, "Go into the village opposite 23
Act 16: 7 when they had come opposite My'sia 21
20:15 we came the following day opposite Chi'os 14
2Es 7:36 and opposite it shall be the place of rest 24
36 and opposite it the paradise of delight. 24
14: 1 behold, a voice came out of a bush opposite me 24
Jdt 2:21 camped opposite Bectileth 17
4: 6 opposite the plain near Dothan 22
7:18 and encamped in the hill country opposite Dothan 16
Sir 33:14 Good is the opposite of evil 16
14 life the opposite of death 16
14 so the sinner is the opposite of the godly. 16
15 in pairs, one the opposite of the other. 23
42:24 All things are twofold, one opposite the other 23
1Mc 2:32 they encamped opposite them 19
3:46 went to Mizpah, opposite Jerusalem 23
5:37 encamped opposite Raphon 22
6:32 Beth- zechariah, opposite the camp of the king. 16
10:48 encamped opposite Demetrius. 18
13:28 erected seven pyramids, opposite one another 23
2Mc 15:33 hang up . . opposite the sanctuary. 23
3Mc 5:16 to recline opposite him. 14
4Mc 6: 4 while a herald opposite him cried out 20
opposite *See also* march, point, sides.

opposition 1. ἀγών 2. ἀνθίστημι 3. ἀντιπαραγωγή 4. παρά
Rom 16:17 difficulties, in opposition to the doctrine 4
1Th 2: 2 in the face of great opposition. 1
AEs 13: 5 stands constantly in opposition to all men 3
1Mc 11:38 there was no opposition to him 2
opposition *See also* say.

oppress 1. דחק 2. דַּךְ 3. ינה 4. לחץ 5. נגשׂ 6. ענה 7. עָנִי 8. עשׁק 9. עֹשֶׁק 10. צרר 11. רצץ 12. עֲנֵי (A) 13. ἐλαττόω 14. θλίβω 15. θραύω 16. καταδυναστεύω 17. καταπατέω 18. πονέω 19. ταπεινός 20. ταπεινόω
Gen 15:13 they will be oppressed for 400 years; 6
Exd 1:12 the more they were oppressed 6
3: 9 with which the Egyptians oppress them. 4
22:21 You shall not wrong a stranger or oppress him 4
23: 9 You shall not oppress a stranger; 4
Lev 6: 2 robbery, or if he has oppressed his neighbor 8
19:13 You shall not oppress your neighbor or rob him 8
Num 10: 9 war . . against the adversary who oppresses you 10
Deu 23:16 where it pleases him best; you shall not oppress 3
24:14 not oppress a hired servant who is poor and needy 8
28:29 only oppressed and robbed continually 8
33 be only oppressed and crushed continually; 8
Jdg 2:18 those who afflicted and oppressed them. 1
4: 3 he . . oppressed the people of Israel cruelly 4
6: 9 from the hand of all who oppressed you 4
10: 8 they crushed and oppressed . . Israel that year 11
8 For eighteen years they oppressed . . Israel •
12 the Amal'ekites, and the Ma'onites, oppressed you; 4
1Sm 10:18 of all the kingdoms that were oppressing you.' 4
12: 3 Or whom have I defrauded? Whom have I oppressed? 11
4 You have not defrauded us or oppressed us 11
8 Jacob went . . and the Egyptians oppressed them 20
2Kg 13: 4 he saw . . how the king of Syria oppressed them. 4
22 Haz'ael . . oppressed Israel all the days 4
1Ch 16:21 he allowed no one to oppress them; 8
Job 10: 3 Does it seem good to thee to oppress 8
Ps 9: 9 The LORD is a stronghold for the oppressed 2
10:18 do justice to the fatherless and the oppressed 2
56: 1 all day long foemen oppress me; 4
69:32 Let the oppressed see it and be glad; 7
76: 9 to establish judgment to save all the oppressed 7
103: 6 vindication . . for all who are oppressed. 8
105:14 he allowed no one to oppress them; 8
106:42 Their enemies oppressed them 4
119:122 let not the godless oppress me. 8
146: 7 who executes justice for the oppressed; 8
Prv 14:31 He who oppresses a poor man insults his Maker 8

22:16 oppresses the poor to increase his own wealth 8
28: 3 A poor man who oppresses the poor is a . . rain 8
Ecc 4: 1 And behold, the tears of the oppressed 8
5: 8 If you see in a province the poor oppressed 9
Isa 3: 5 the people will oppress one another, every man 5
14: 2 captors, and rule over those who oppressed them. 5
23:12 O oppressed virgin daughter of Sidon; 8
38:14 O Lord, I am oppressed; be thou my security! 8
52: 4 and the Assyrian oppressed them for nothing. 8
53: 7 He was oppressed, and he was afflicted 5
58: 3 your own pleasure, and oppress all your workers. 5
6 to let the oppressed go free 11
60:14 those who oppressed you shall come bending low 6
Jer 7: 6 if you do not oppress the alien 8
30:20 and I will punish all who oppress them. 4
50:33 The people of Israel are oppressed 8
Ezk 18: 7 does not oppress any one 3
12 oppresses the poor and needy, commits robbery 3
22:29 they have oppressed the poor and needy 3
45: 8 my princes shall no more oppress my people; 3
Dan 4:27 iniquities by showing mercy to the oppressed 12
Hos 5:11 E'phraim is oppressed, crushed in judgment 8
12: 7 he loves to oppress. 8
Ams 4: 1 Sama'ria, who oppress the poor, who crush the needy 8
6:14 and they shall oppress you from the entrance 4
Mic 2: 2 they oppress a man and his house 8
Zep 3: 1 rebellious and defiled, the oppressing city! 3
Zec 7:10 do not oppress the widow, the fatherless 8
Mal 3: 5 those who oppress the hireling in his wages 8
Lke 4:18 to set at liberty those who are oppressed 15
Act 10:38 healing all that were oppressed by the devil 16
Jas 2: 6 Is it not the rich who oppress you 16
Jdt 9:11 thou art God of the lowly, helper of the oppressed 13
16: 8 to exalt the oppressed in Israel 18
11 my oppressed people shouted for joy 19
Wis 2:10 Let us oppress the righteous poor man 16
15:14 all the enemies who oppressed thy people. 16
1Mc 10:46 how he had greatly oppressed them. 14
11:53 but oppressed him greatly. 14
2Mc 1:28 Afflict those who oppress 16
8: 2 to look upon the people who were oppressed by all 17
3Mc 2:12 when our fathers were oppressed 14

oppressed man 1. *καταπονέω*

Act 7:24 he defended the oppressed man and avenged him 1

oppression 1. חָמוֹץ 2. לַחַץ 3. מַעֲשַׁקָּה 4. עָמָל 5. עֹצֶר 6. עָקָה 7. עֲשׁוּקִים 8. עֹשֶׁק 9. שֹׁד 10. תֹּךְ 11. labor

Exd 3: 9 seen the oppression with which the Egyptians 2
Lev 6: 4 he took by robbery, or what he got by oppression 8
Deu 26: 7 saw our affliction, our toil, and our oppression; 2
2Kg 13: 4 for he saw the oppression of Israel 2
Job 35: 9 Because of the multitude of oppressions 7
Ps 10: 7 filled with cursing and deceit and oppression; 10
42: 9 mourning because of the oppression of the enemy? 2
43: 2 mourning because of the oppression of the enemy? 2
44:24 dost thou forget our affliction and oppression? 2
55: 3 because of the oppression of the wicked. 6
11 oppression and fraud do not depart from its 10
72:14 From oppression and violence he redeems 10
73: 8 with malice; loftily they threaten oppression. 8
107:39 low through oppression, trouble, and sorrow 5
119:134 Redeem me from man's oppression 8
Ecc 4: 1 I saw all the oppressions that are practiced 7
7: 7 Surely oppression makes the wise man foolish 8
Isa 1:17 seek justice, correct oppression; 1
10: 1 the writers who keep writing oppression 4
30:12 trust in oppression and perverseness 8
33:15 who despises the gain of oppressions 3
53: 8 By oppression and judgment he was taken away; 5
54:14 you shall be far from oppression 8
59:13 speaking oppression and revolt, 8
Jer 6: 6 there is nothing but oppression within her. 8
9: 6 Heaping oppression upon oppression *
6 Heaping oppression upon oppression 10
22:17 for practicing oppression and violence. 8
Ezk 45: 9 Israel! Put away violence and oppression 9
Ams 3: 9 and see . . the oppressions in her midst. 7
2Es 11:32 and with much oppression dominated 11
40 and over all the earth with grievous oppression; 11

oppressive 1. *βαρύς*

3Mc 6: 5 oppressive king of the Assyrians 1

oppressively 1. labore multo

2Es 12:24 its inhabitants more oppressively than all 1

oppressor 1. אִישׁ תְּכָכִים 2. ינה 3. לחץ 4. מֵץ 5. נגשׂ 6. ענה 7. עָרִיץ 8. עָשׁוֹק 9. עשק 10. צוק 11. *θλίβω* 12. *κατισχύω* 13. *τυραννέω*

Job 6:23 Or, 'Ransom me from the hand of oppressors'? 7
27:13 which oppressors receive from the Almighty 7
Ps 72: 4 give deliverance . . and crush the oppressor! 9
119:121 do not leave me to my oppressors. 9
Prv 29:13 The poor man and the oppressor meet together; 1
Ecc 4: 1 On the side of their oppressors there was power 9
Isa 3:12 My people–children are their oppressors 5
9: 4 staff for his shoulder, the rod of his oppressor 5
14: 4 How the oppressor has ceased 5
16: 4 When the oppressor is no more 4
19:20 when they cry to the LORD because of oppressors 3
49:26 I will make your oppressors eat their own flesh 2
51:13 fear . . because of the fury of the oppressor 10
13 And where is the fury of the oppressor? 10
Jer 21:12 and deliver from the hand of the oppressor 9
22: 3 and deliver from the hand of the oppressor 8
25:38 a waste because of the sword of the oppressor 2
46:16 because of the sword of the oppressor. 2
50:16 because of the sword of the oppressor 2
Zep 3:19 I will deal with all your oppressors. 6
Zec 9: 8 no oppressor shall again overrun them 5
Wis 10:11 When his oppressors were covetous 12
15 wisdom delivered from a nation of oppressors. 11
16: 4 upon those oppressors . . want should come 13

cruel oppressor 1. מַעֲשַׁקָּה

Prv 28:16 who lacks understanding is a cruel oppressor; 1

oracle 1. דָּבָר 2. מַשָּׂא 3. מַשְׂאֵת 4. נְאֻם 5. *λόγιον* 6. *χρηματισμός*

Num 24: 3 oracle of Balaam the sons of Be'or 4
3 oracle of the man whose eye is opened 4
4 oracle of him who hears the words of God 4
15 The oracle of Balaam the son of Be'or 4
15 the oracle of the man whose eye is opened 4
16 the oracle of him who hears the words of God 4
2Sm 16:23 was as if one consulted the oracle of God; 1
23: 1 The oracle of David, the son of Jesse 4
1 the oracle of the man who was raised on high 4
2Kg 9:25 the LORD uttered this oracle against him 2
2Ch 24:27 Accounts . . of the many oracles against him 2
Isa 13: 1 The oracle concerning Babylon which Isaiah 2
14:28 In the year that King Ahaz died came this oracle 2
15: 1 An oracle concerning Moab. 2
17: 1 An oracle concerning Damascus. 2
19: 1 An oracle concerning Egypt. 2
21: 1 oracle concerning the wilderness of the sea. 2
11 The oracle concerning Dumah. 2
13 The oracle concerning Arabia. 2
22: 1 The oracle concerning the valley of vision. 2
23: 1 The oracle concerning Tyre. 2
30: 6 An oracle on the beasts of the Negeb. 2
Lam 2:14 have seen for you oracles false and misleading. 3
Ezk 12:10 This oracle concerns the prince in Jerusalem 2
Nah 1: 1 An oracle concerning Nin'eveh. 2
Hab 1: 1 oracle of God which Habak'kuk the prophet saw. 2
Zec 9: 1 An Oracle The word of the LORD is against the land 2
12: 1 An Oracle The word of the LORD concerning Israel 2
Mal 1: 1 The oracle of the word of the LORD to Israel 2
Act 7:38 he received living oracles to give to us. 5
Rom 3: 2 the Jews are entrusted with the oracles of God. 5
1Pe 4:11 whoever speaks, as one who utters oracles of God; 5
Wis 16:11 To remind them of thy oracles they were bitten 5
Sir 45:10 with the oracle of judgment, Urim and Thummim; 5
2Mc 2: 4 the prophet, having received an oracle 6

oracle *See also* give.

oration *See* make.

orchard 1. גַּנָּה 2. כֶּרֶם 3. פַּרְדֵּס 4. *κῆπος*

Jdg 15: 5 standing grain, as well as the olive orchards. 2
Sng 4:13 Your shoots are an orchard of pomegranates 3
6:11 I went down to the nut orchard 1
Sir 24:31 I will water my orchard and drench my garden plot 4

olive orchard 1. זַיִת 2. olivetum

Exd 23:11 do likewise . . with your olive orchard. 1
1Sm 8:14 the best of your fields . . and olive orchards 1
2Kg 5:26 Was it a time to accept money and . . olive orchards 1
Neh 5:11 Return . . olive orchards, and their houses 1
9:25 possession of . . olive orchards and fruit 1
2Es 16:29 As in an olive orchard three or four olives 2

ordain 1. מלא 2. מלא יָד 3. נתן 4. עשה 5. צוה 6. קום 7. שׂום 8. שׁפת 9. *γράφω* 10. *διατάσσω* 11. *ἐκδίδωμι* 12. *ἐντέλλομαι* 13. *κοσμέω* 14. *ὁρίζω* 15. *ὁρισμός* 16. *πληρόω τὰς χεῖρας* 17. *προτάσσω* 18. *τάσσω* 19. dispono

Exd 28:41 anoint them and ordain them and consecrate 2
29: 9 Thus you shall ordain Aaron and his sons. 2
29 to be anointed in them and ordained in them. 2
33 eat those things . . to ordain and consecrate 2
35 through seven days shall you ordain them 1
32:29 you have ordained yourselves for the service 16
Lev 8:33 for it will take seven days to ordain you 2
Num 3: 3 anointed priests, whom he ordained to minister 2
28: 6 offering, which was ordained at Mount Sinai 4
2Sm 17:14 the LORD had ordained to defeat the good counsel 5
1Kg 12:33 he ordained a feast for the people of Israel 4
2Kg 23: 5 whom the kings . . had ordained to burn incense 3
2Ch 2: 4 the LORD our God, as ordained for ever for Israel. *
22: 7 ordained by God that the downfall of Ahazi'ah *
Est 9:27 the Jews ordained and took it upon themselves 6
Ps 44: 4 my God, who ordainest victories for Jacob. 12
Isa 26:12 O LORD, thou wilt ordain peace for us 8
Lam 2:17 as he ordained . . he has demolished without pity; 5
3:37 Who has . . unless the Lord has ordained it? 5
Hab 1:12 O LORD, thou hast ordained them as a judgment; 7
Act 10:42 the one ordained by God to be judge of the living 14
13:48 as many as were ordained to eternal life 18
Gal 3:19 ordained by angels through an intermediary. 10
1Es 1:32 it was ordained that this should always be done 11
2Es 7:17 thou hast ordained in thy law 19
Tob 1: 6 as it is ordained for all Israel 9
AEs 14: 9 to abolish what thy mouth has ordained 15
Sir 42:21 He has ordained the splendors of his wisdom 13
45:15 Moses ordained him 16
2Mc 8:36 because they followed the laws ordained by him. 17
3Mc 6:36 when they had ordained a public rite 14

ordained *See* way.

fiery ordeal 1. *πύρωσις*

1Pe 4:12 fiery ordeal which comes upon you to prove you 1

same ordeal 1. *ἰσοπολίτιδης*

4Mc 13: 9 who despised the same ordeal of the furnace. 1

order 1. דִּבְרָה 2. בְּ 3. כון 4. נשׁק 5. ערך 6. עֵרֶךְ 7. *διάθεσις* 8. *διοικέω* 9. *καθεξῆς* 10. *κόσμος* 11. *τάγμα* 12. *τάξις* 13. *τάσσω* 14. ordo

Gen 25:13 sons . . named in the order of their birth *
41:40 and all my people shall order themselves as you 4
Exd 28:10 their names . . in the order of their birth. 2
40:23 set the bread in order on it before the LORD; 6
2Sm 23: 5 an everlasting covenant, ordered in all things 5
2Kg 23: 4 high priest, and the priests of the second order *
2Ch 27: 6 ordered his ways before the LORD his God. 3
Ps 110: 4 priest for ever after the order of Melchiz'edek. 1
Act 11: 4 Peter began and explained to them in order: 9
1Co 14:40 all things should be done decently and in order. 12
15:23 each in his own order: Christ the first fruits 11
Heb 5: 6 a priest for ever, after the order of Melchiz'edek. 12
10 a high priest after the order of Melchiz'edek. 12
6:20 after the order of Melchiz'edek. 12
7:11 after the order of Melchiz'edek 12
11 rather than one named after the order of Aaron? 12
17 a priest for ever, after the order of Melchiz'edek. 12
1Es 1: 5 Stand in order in the temple 12
2Es 7:88 this is the order of those who have kept the ways 14
91 for they shall have rest in seven orders. 14
92 The first order, because they have striven 14
93 The second order, because they see 14
94 The third order, they see the witness 14
95 The fourth order, they understand the rest 14
96 The fifth order, they rejoice 14
97 The sixth order, when it is shown to them 14
98 The seventh order, which is greater than all 14
99 This is the order of the souls of the righteous 14
AEs 16:16 directed . . in the most excellent order. 7
Wis 8: 1 she orders all things well. 8
Sir 10: 1 the rule . . will be well ordered. 13
50:19 till the order of worship of the Lord was ended 10
Man 1: 2 made heaven and earth with all their order; 10

order (2) 1. בַּעֲבוּר 2. לְ 3. לְבַעֲבוּר 4. לְמַעַן 5. שֶׁ 6. דִּי (A) 7. עַל דִּבְרַת דִּי (A) 8. *εἴπως* 9. *εἰς* 10. *ἕνεκα* 11. *ἵνα* 12. *ὅπως* 13. *πρός* 14. ut

Gen 32: 5 I have sent to tell my lord, in order that I may find 2
46:34 you shall say . . in order that you may dwell 1
Deu 17:16 in order to multiply horses 4
20:19 making war against it in order to take it 2
Jos 11:20 in order that they should be utterly destroyed 4
Rut 4: 5 also buying Ruth . . in order to restore the name 2
2Sm 14:20 In order to change the course of affairs 3
24:21 To buy the . . in order to build an altar to the LORD 2
1Kg 5:17 they quarried . . in order to lay the foundation 2
6: 6 in order that the supporting beams should not 2
8:43 do . . in order that all . . may know thy name 4
2Kg 10:19 in order to destroy the worshipers of Ba'al. 4
2Ch 6:33 in order that all the peoples of the earth may 4
25:20 it was of God, in order that he might give them 4
32:18 in order that they might take the city. 4
31 in order to try him and to know 2
35:22 disguised himself in order to fight with him. 2
Ezr 4:15 in order that search may be made in the book 6
Neh 6:13 could give me an evil name, in order to taunt me. 4
8:13 came . . in order to study the words of the law. 2
9:26 warned them in order to turn them back to thee 2
29 warn them in order to turn them back to thy law. 2
Est 1:11 bring Queen Vashti . . in order to show 2
3: 4 they told Haman, in order to see whether 2
Ps 59: 0 sent men to watch his house in order to kill him. 2
119:101 from every evil way, in order to keep thy word. 4
Ecc 3:14 God has made it so, in order that men should fear 5
Jer 44:29 in order that you may know 4
Ezk 3:18 from his wicked way, in order to save his life 2
22:20 to blow the fire upon it in order to melt it; 2
31:14 in order that no trees by the waters may grow 4
39:12 burying them, in order to cleanse the land. 4
40: 4 you were brought here in order that I might show 4
46:20 in order not to bring them out into the outer 2
Dan 2:30 in order that the interpretation may be made known 7
11:14 lift themselves up in order to fulfil the vision; 2

Zec 13: 4 not put on a hairy mantle in order to deceive 4
Mat 6: 1 before men in order to be seen by them; 13
26: 4 took counsel together in order to arrest Jesus 11
Mrk 7: 9 in order to keep your tradition! 11
10: 2 Pharisees came up and in order to test him asked •
14:10 went to the chief priests in order to betray him 11
Lke 16:26 in order that . . none may cross from there to us 12
Joh 19:31 in order to prevent the bodies from remaining 11
Act 4:17 in order that it may spread no further 11
Rom 1:13 in order that I may reap some harvest among you 11
4:16 in order that the promise may rest on grace 11
7: 4 in order that we may bear fruit for God. 11
13 in order that sin might be shown to be sin 11
8: 4 in order that the just requirement of the law 11
17 in order that we may also be glorified with him. 11
29 in order that he might be the first-born 9
9:11 in order that God's purpose of election might 11
23 in order to make known the riches of his glory 11
11:14 in order to make my fellow Jews jealous, and thus 8
31 in order that by the mercy shown to you 11
15: 8 in order to confirm the promises 9
9 in order that the Gentiles might glorify God •
1Co 9:20 To the Jews I became as a Jew, in order to win Jews 11
11:19 in order that those who are genuine among you 11
14:19 in order to instruct others 11
2Co 7:12 in order that your zeal for us might be revealed 10
11: 8 accepting support from them in order to serve you. 13
12 to do, in order to undermine the claim 11
32 governor . . guarded the city . . in order to seize me •
13:10 in order that when I come 11
Gal 1:16 in order that I might preach him 11
2:16 in order to be justified by faith in Christ 11
6:12 only in order that they may not be persecuted 11
Php 3: 8 in order that I may gain Christ 11
Col 1:22 in order to present you holy . . before him •
2: 4 I say this in order that no one may delude you 11
Phm 1:13 in order that he might serve me on your behalf 11
14 in order that your goodness might not be . . 11
Heb 10: 9 in order to establish the second. 11
12:27 in order that what cannot be shaken may remain. 11
13:12 in order to sanctify the people 11
19 in order that I may be restored to you the sooner. 11
1Pe 3: 7 in order that your prayers may not be hindered. 9
4:11 in order that in everything God may be glorified 11
1Es 2:21 in order that . . search may be made 12
6:12 in order that we might inform you in writing 10
31 in order that libations may be made 12
8:12 in order to look into matters in Judea 12
85 in order that you may be strong 11
2Es 6:35 in order to complete the three weeks 14
8:49 in order to receive the greatest glory. 14
11:20 also rose up . . in order to rule 14
14:46 in order to give them to the wise 14
Tob 12:13 in order to go and lay out the dead 12
Jdt 3:10 in order to assemble all the supplies 9
8:27 scourges . . in order to admonish them. 9
11:11 now, in order that my lord may not be defeated 11
14:13 in order to be destroyed completely. 11
AEs 13: 2 in order to make my kingdom peaceable •
Wis 16: 3 in order that those men . . might lose . . appetite 11
23 in order that the righteous might be fed 11
19: 4 in order that they might fill up the punishment 11
Sir 0: 1 in order that . . those who love learning 12
3 in order to complete and publish the book 13
23: 3 in order that my mistakes may not be multiplied 12
30: 1 in order that he may rejoice 11
38: 5 in order that his power might be known? 9
Bar 3: 7 in order that we should call upon thy name •
LJr 1:18 in order that they may not be plundered 12
1Mc 12:36 in order to isolate it 11
14:29 in order that their sanctuary . . be preserved; 12
2Mc 1:18 in order that you also may celebrate 11
6:15 in order that he may not take vengeance on us 11
3Mc 2:30 In order that he might not appear to be an enemy 11

order (3) 1. אמר 2. דבר 3. דָּבָר 4. יָד 5. עֵצָה 6. צוה 7. צוה עַל 8. אמר (A) 9. מִלָּה (A) 10. εἶπον 11. ἐντέλλω 12. ἐντολή 13. ἐπίταγμα 14. ἐπιτάσσω 15. ἐπιτιμάω 16. κελεύω 17. κρίμα 18. λέγω 19. παραγγέλλω 20. παρακελεύω 21. πρόσταγμα 22. προστάσσω 23. ῥῆμα 24. ῥῆμα τοῦ στόματος 25. συντάσσω

Num32:27 before the LORD to battle, as my lord orders. 2
2Sm 18: 5 And the king ordered Jo'ab and Abi'shai and It'tai 6
2Kg 1:11 this is the king's order, 'Come down quickly!' 1
10:20 Jehu ordered, "Sanctify a solemn assembly 1
1Ch 25: 6 and Heman were under the order of the king. 4
2Ch 23:18 according to the order of David. 4
Ezr 6:13 did . . what Darius the king had ordered. •
10: 8 by order of the officials and the elders 5
Est 1:19 let a royal order go forth from him 3
2: 8 when the king's order and his edict were proclaimed 3
3:15 The couriers went in haste by order of the king 3
4: 5 called for Hathach . . and ordered him to go 6
17 went . . and did everything as Esther had ordered 7
8: 5 let an order be written to revoke the letters •
Prv 20:24 A man's steps are ordered by the LORD; •
Jer 36: 5 And Jeremiah ordered Baruch, saying 6
8 did all that Jeremiah the prophet ordered him 6
Dan 3:19 ordered the furnace heated seven times more 8
20 ordered certain mighty men of his army to bind 8
22 king's order was strict and the furnace very hot 9
Mat 12:16 ordered them not to make him known. 15
14:19 he ordered the crowds to sit down on the grass 16
18:25 as he could not pay, his lord ordered him to be sold 16
27:58 Then Pilate ordered it to be given to him. 16
64 Therefore order the sepulchre to be made secure 16
Mrk 3:12 he strictly ordered them not to make him known. 15
Joh 11:57 the Pharisees had given orders 12
Act 5:34 ordered the men to be put outside for a while. 16
12:19 and ordered that they should be put to death 16
21:33 ordered him to be bound with two chains 16
34 he ordered him to be brought into the barracks. 16
22:24 ordered him to be examined by scourging 10
23: 3 yet contrary to the law you order me to be struck? 16
30 ordering his accusers also to state before you 19
25: 6 ordered Paul to be brought. 16
17 and ordered the man to be brought in. 16
27:43 He ordered those who could swim 16
1Es 2:26 I ordered search to be made 14
4:57 everything that Cyrus had ordered to be done 10
6: 4 By whose order are you building this house 25
24 King Cyrus ordered the building of the house 22
7: 1 following the orders of King Darius 22
8:46 ordered them to tell Iddo and his brethren 11
67 they delivered the king's orders 21
Tob 8:18 he ordered his servants to fill in the grave. 16
Jdt 1:11 disregarded the orders of Nebuchadnezzar 23
2: 6 because they disobeyed my orders. 24
13 sure to carry them out just as I have ordered you; 22
15 as his lord had ordered him to do 16
4: 7 ordering them to seize the passes up 18
6:10 Then Holofernes ordered his slaves 22
7: 1 The next day Holofernes ordered his whole army 19
10: 9 Order the gate of the city to be opened for me 14
9 they ordered the young men to open the gate 25
12: 1 and ordered them to set a table for her 25
AEs 12: 5 the king ordered Mordecai to serve in the court 14
Sir 43:10 command of the Holy One they stand as ordered 17
Bar 5: 7 For God has ordered that every high mountain 25
LJr 1:63 does what it is ordered 25
Sus 1:32 the wicked men ordered her to be unveiled 16
Bel 1:14 Then Daniel ordered his servants to bring ashes 16
1Mc 3:28 ordered them to be ready for any need. 11
5:49 Judas ordered proclamation to be made to the army 14
15:41 as the king had ordered him. 25
2Mc 1:20 he ordered them to dip it out and bring it. 16
21 Nehemiah ordered the priests to sprinkle 16
31 Nehemiah ordered that . . 16
2: 1 Jeremiah the prophet ordered . . 16
4 ordered that the tent and the ark should follow 16
4:25 After receiving the king's orders he returned 12
5:25 he ordered his men to parade under arms. 19
7: 5 the king ordered them to take him to the fire 16
9: 4 he ordered his charioteer to drive 25
11:20 ordered these men and my representatives 11
13: 4 he ordered them to take him to Beroea 22
10 he ordered the people to call upon the Lord 19
12 exhorted them and ordered them to stand ready. 16
14:13 with orders to kill Judas and scatter his men 12
41 they ordered that fire be brought 16
15: 4 who ordered us to observe the seventh day 16
30 ordered them to cut off Nicanor's head and arm 22
3Mc 3: 1 he ordered that all should promptly be gathered 22
4:13 ordered in his rage 22
14 tortured with the outrages that he had ordered 19
5: 2 ordered him . . to drug all the elephants 16
4 proceeded faithfully to carry out the orders. 22
16 ordered those present . . to recline opposite 16
19 he had carried out completely the order given him 22
40 ordering now for a third time 22
6:30 ordered him to provide to the Jews 16
7: 8 We also have ordered each and every one to return 22
4Mc 5: 2 ordered the guards to seize . . every Hebrew 20
8: 6 I am able to punish those who disobey my orders 13
12 he ordered the instruments of torture 16

order *See* arrange, due, give, issue, keep, lay, prescribed, put, send, set.

order aright 1. שׂוּם

Ps 50:23 to him who orders his way aright I will show 1

battle order 1. מַעֲרָכָה 2. διασκευή

1Ch 12:38 All these, men of war, arrayed in battle order 1
2Mc 11:10 They advanced in battle order 2

fixed order 1. חֹק 2. חֻקָּה

Jer 31:35 fixed order of the moon and the stars for light 2
36 If this fixed order departs from before me 1

given order 1. διαστέλλω

Heb 12:20 they could not endure the order that was given 1

good order 1. εὐστάθεια 2. εὐσχήμων 3. εὐταξία 4. τάξις 5. τεταγμένως

1Co 7:35 but to promote good order 2
Col 2: 5 rejoicing to see your good order 4
1Mc 6:40 they advanced steadily and in good order. 5
3Mc 1:10 he marveled at the good order of the temple 3
3:26 in good order and in the best state. 1

order of march 1. נסע

Num10:28 was the order of march of the people of Israel 1

second order 1. מִשְׁנֶה

1Ch 15:18 with them their brethren of the second order 1

well ordered 1. κόσμος

Sir 26:16 beauty of a good wife in her well-ordered home. 1

orderly 1. καθεξῆς

Lke 1: 3 to write an orderly account for you 1

ordinance 1. חֹק 2. חֻקָּה 3. מִשְׁפָּט 4. קְיָם (A) 5. διάταγμα 6. δικαίωμα 7. δόγμα 8. νόμιμος 9. πρόσταγμα 10. iussio

Exd 12:14 you shall observe it as an ordinance for ever. 2
17 observe this day . . as an ordinance for ever. 2
24 You shall observe this rite as an ordinance 1
43 This is the ordinance of the passover 2
13:10 You shall therefore keep this ordinance 2
15:25 a statute and an ordinance and there he proved 3
21: 1 Now these are the ordinances which you shall set 3
24: 3 told . . all the ordinances; 3
Lev 5:10 for a burnt offering according to the ordinance 3
9:16 and offered it according to the ordinance 3
18: 4 You shall do my ordinances and keep my statutes 3
5 therefore keep my statutes and my ordinances 3
26 you shall keep my statutes and my ordinances 3
19:37 observe all my statutes and all my ordinances 3
20:22 all my statutes and all my ordinances, and do them 3
25:18 and keep my ordinances and perform them 3
26:15 if your soul abhors my ordinances 3
43 amends . . because they spurned my ordinances 3
46 These are the statutes and ordinances and laws 3
Num 9: 3 according to all its . . ordinances 3
14 passover and according to its ordinance 3
15:16 One law and one ordinance shall be for you 3
24 its drink offering, according to the ordinance 3
27:11 shall be to . . Israel a statute and ordinance 3
29: 6 according to the ordinance for them 3
18 by number, according to the ordinance; 3
21 by number, according to the ordinance; 3
24 by number, according to the ordinance; 3
27 by number, according to the ordinance; 3
30 by number, according to the ordinance; 3
33 by number, according to the ordinance; 3
37 by number, according to the ordinance; 3
35:24 judge . . in accordance with these ordinances; 3
29 these things shall be for a statute and ordinance 3
36:13 These are the commandments and the ordinances 3
Deu 4: 1 give heed to the statutes and the ordinances 3
5 I have taught you statutes and ordinances 3
8 that has statutes and ordinances so righteous 3
14 to teach you statutes and ordinances 3
45 testimonies, the statutes, and the ordinances 3
5: 1 Hear, O Israel, the statutes and the ordinances 3
31 tell you all . . the statutes and the ordinances 3
6: 1 commandment, the statutes and the ordinances 3
20 What is the meaning of . . the ordinances 3
7:11 be careful to do . . the ordinances 3
12 because you hearken to these ordinances 3
8:11 by not keeping . . his ordinances 3
11: 1 keep his charge, his statutes, his ordinances 3
32 statutes and the ordinances which I set 3
12: 1 These are the statutes and ordinances which you 3
26:16 you to do these statutes and ordinances; 3
17 keep his statutes . . and his ordinances 3
30:16 by keeping . . his statutes and his ordinances 3
33:10 They shall teach Jacob thy ordinances 3
Jos 24:25 and made statutes and ordinances for them 3
1Sm 30:25 he made it a statute and an ordinance for Israel 3
2Sm 22:23 For all his ordinances were before me 3
1Kg 2: 3 his statutes, his commandments, his ordinances 3
6:12 walk in my statutes and obey my ordinances 3
8:58 statutes, and his ordinances, which he commanded 3
9: 4 and keeping my statutes and my ordinances 3
11:33 and keeping my statutes and my ordinances 3
2Kg 17:34 follow the statutes or the ordinances or the law 3
37 the statutes and the ordinances and the law 3
1Ch 22:13 to observe the statutes and the ordinances 3
28: 7 in keeping my commandments and my ordinance 3
2Ch 7:17 and keeping my statutes and my ordinances 3
8:14 According to the ordinance of David his father 3
19:10 concerning . . statutes or ordinance 3
33: 8 all the law, the statutes, and the ordinances 3
35:13 with fire according to the ordinance; 3
25 They made these an ordinance in Israel; 1
Ezr 3: 4 offerings by number according to the ordinance 3
7:10 to teach his statutes and ordinances in Israel. 3
Neh 1: 7 not kept the . . statutes, and the ordinances 3
8:18 solemn assembly, according to the ordinance. 3

9:13 give them right ordinances and true laws 3
29 not obey . . but sinned against thy ordinances 3
10:29 observe . . his ordinances and his statutes. 3
Job 38:33 Do you know the ordinances of the heavens? 2
Ps 18:22 For all his ordinances were before me 3
19: 9 the ordinances of the LORD are true, and righteous 3
81: 4 an ordinance of the God of Jacob. 3
89:30 If . . do not walk according to my ordinances 3
119: 7 when I learn thy righteous ordinances. 3
13 I declare all the ordinances of thy mouth. 3
20 with longing for thy ordinances at all times. 3
30 I set thy ordinances before me. 3
39 for thy ordinances are good. 3
43 my hope is in thy ordinances. 3
52 When I think of thy ordinances from of old 3
62 praise . . because of thy righteous ordinances. 3
102I do not turn aside from thy ordinances 3
106an oath . . to observe thy righteous ordinances. 3
108O LORD, and teach me thy ordinances. 3
160every one of thy righteous ordinances endures 3
164I praise thee for thy righteous ordinances. 3
175let thy ordinances help me. 3
147:19 his statutes and ordinances to Israel. 3
20 other nation; they do not know his ordinances. 3
Isa 58: 2 and did not forsake the ordinance of their God; 3
Jer 8: 7 but my people know not the ordinance of the LORD. 3
33:25 and night and the ordinances of heaven and earth 2
Ezk 5: 6 has wickedly rebelled against my ordinances 3
6 by rejecting my ordinances and not walking in my 3
7 not walked in my statutes or kept my ordinances 3
7 according to the ordinances of the nations 3
11:12 nor executed my ordinances, but have acted 3
12 ordinances of the nations that are round about 3
20 and keep my ordinances and obey them; 3
18: 9 and is careful to observe my ordinances 3
17 observes my ordinances, and walks in my statutes; 3
20:11 my statutes and showed them my ordinances 3
13 walk in my statutes but rejected my ordinances 3
16 because they rejected my ordinances 3
18 nor observe their ordinances, nor defile 3
19 and be careful to observe my ordinances 3
21 and were not careful to observe my ordinances 3
24 because they had not executed my ordinances 3
25 and ordinances by which they could not have life; 3
36:27 and be careful to observe my ordinances. 3
37:24 They shall follow my ordinances and be careful 3
43:11 make known to them all its ordinances 2
11 and perform all its laws and all its ordinances. 2
18 These are the ordinances for the altar 2
44: 5 all the ordinances of the temple of the LORD 2
46:14 ordinance for the continual burnt offering. 2
Dan 6: 7 king should establish an ordinance and enforce 4
15 no interdict or ordinance which the king 4
9: 5 aside from thy commandments and ordinances; 3
Mal 4: 4 the statutes and ordinances that I commanded 3
Lke 1: 6 commandments and ordinances of the Lord 6
Eph 2:15 the law of commandments and ordinances 7
1Es 8: 7 taught all Israel all the ordinances 6
2Es 8:22 whose ordinance is strong 10
AEs 13: 4 disregard the ordinances of the kings 5
Sir 4:17 she will test him with her ordinances. 6
Bar 2:12 O Lord our God, against all thy ordinances. 6
1Mc 1:13 observe the ordinances of the Gentiles. 6
49 forget the law and change all the ordinances. 6
2:21 to desert the law and the ordinances. 6
40 for our lives and for our ordinances 6
2Mc 10: 8 They decreed by public ordinance and vote 9
4Mc 15:10 obeyed her . . in keeping the ordinances. 8

ordinary 1. חֹל 2. εἰς ἀριθμόν 3. τυγχάνω
Ezk 48:15 in length, shall be for ordinary use for the city 1
1Co 3: 3 of the flesh, and behaving like ordinary men? •
Sir 33: 9 some of them he made ordinary days. 2
3Mc 3: 7 they attached no ordinary reproach to them. 3

ordinary man 1. אָדָם
Exd 30:32 poured upon the bodies of ordinary men 1

ordination 1. מִלּוּא
Exd 29:22 (for it is a ram of ordination) 1
26 the ram of Aaron's ordination and wave it 1
27 which is offered from the ram of ordination 1
31 You shall take the ram of ordination 1
34 if any of the flesh for the ordination 1
Lev 8:22 Then he presented . . the ram of ordination 1
29 it was Moses' portion of the ram of ordination 1
33 for seven days, until the days of your ordination 1
ordination *See also* offering.

ore 1. אֶבֶן
Job 28: 2 copper is smelted from the ore. 1
3 search out to the farthest bound the ore in gloom 1

organ 1. μέλος 2. ὄργανον
1Co 12:18 as it is, God arranged the organs in the body 1
19 If all were a single organ, where would the body be? 1
4Mc 10:18 he said, "Even if you remove my organ of speech 2

organize 1. חלק 2. διατάσσω 3. ἐν συστέματι 4. συνίστημι 5. dispono
1Ch 23: 6 David organized them in divisions 1
24: 3 David organized them according 1
4 organized them under sixteen heads 1
5 They organized them by lot, all alike 1
2Ch 23:18 whom David had organized to be in charge 1
2Es 5:49 so have I organized the world which I created. 5
Jdt 2:16 he organized them as a great army is marshaled 2
1Mc 2:44 They organized an army, and struck down sinners 4
2Mc 8: 5 As soon as Maccabeus got his army organized 3
3Mc 4:16 organizing feasts in honor of all his idols 4

orgy 1. הָמוֹן
Jer 3:23 are a delusion, the orgies on the mountains. 1

origin 1. מוֹצָאָה 2. מְכוּרָה 3. קַדְמָה 4. γένεσις 5. ἐκ 6. nativitas
Isa 23: 7 exultant city whose origin is from days of old 3
Ezk 16: 3 Your origin . . are of the land of the Canaanites; 2
21:30 in the land of your origin, I will judge you. 2
29:14 to the land of Pathros, the land of their origin; 2
Mic 5: 2 ruler in Israel, whose origin is from of old 1
Heb 2:11 those who are sanctified have all one origin. 5
2Es 15:31 then the dragons, remembering their origin 6
Wis 12:10 their origin was evil 4
2Mc 7:23 and devised the origin of all things 4
original *See* historian.

originally
Sir 0: 2 For what was originally expressed in Hebrew •

originate 1. ἐξέρχομαι
1Co 14:36 What! Did the word of God originate with you 1

ornament 1. חֲלִי 2. עֲדִי 3. תּוֹר 4. κόσμος
Exd 33: 4 they mourned; and no man put on his ornaments. 2
5 So now put off your ornaments from you 2
6 stripped themselves of their ornaments 2
2Sm 1:24 who put ornaments of gold upon your apparel. 2
Prv 25:12 Like a gold ring or an ornament of gold 1
Sng 1:10 Your cheeks are comely with ornaments 3
11 We will make you ornaments of gold 3
Isa 49:18 you shall put them all on as an ornament 2
Jer 2:32 Can a maiden forget her ornaments 2
4:30 that you deck yourself with ornaments of gold 2
Ezk 7:20 beautiful ornament they used for vainglory 2
16:11 I decked you with ornaments 2
23:40 and decked yourself with ornaments; 2
Jdt 10: 4 put on . . her earrings and all her ornaments 4
Sir 6:30 Her yoke is a golden ornament 4
21:21 education is like a golden ornament 4
ornament *See also* love.

costly ornament 1. מִגְדָּנָה
Gen 24:53 gave to her brother and . . mother costly ornaments. 1

orphan 1. יָתוֹם 2. ὀρφανός 3. orfanus
Exd 22:22 You shall not afflict any widow or orphan. 1
Lam 5: 3 We have become orphans, fatherless; 1
Hos 14: 3 In thee the orphan finds mercy. 1
Mal 3: 5 hireling in his wages, the widow and the orphan 1
Jas 1:27 to visit orphans and widows in their affliction 2
1Es 3:19 It makes equal the mind of the king and the orphan 2
2Es 2:20 give to the needy, defend the orphan 3
Tob 1: 8 I was left an orphan by my father. 2
Sir 4:10 Be like a father to orphans 2
LJr 1:38 take pity on a widow or do good to an orphan. 2
2Mc 3:10 some deposits belonging to widows and orphans 2
8:28 the widows and orphans 2
30 to the orphans and widows, and also to the aged 2

osprey 1. עָזְנִיָּה
Lev 11:13 an abomination: the eagle, the vulture, the osprey 1
Deu 14:12 shall not eat: the eagle, the vulture, the osprey 1

ostensibly 1. ἔμφασις
2Mc 3: 8 ostensibly to make a tour of inspection 1

ostrich 1. בַּת יַעֲנָה 2. יָעֵן 3. רְנָנִים
Lev 11:16 the ostrich, the nighthawk, the sea gull, the hawk 1
Deu 14:15 the ostrich, the nighthawk, the sea gull, the hawk 1
Job 30:29 of jackals, and a companion of ostriches. 1
39:13 The wings of the ostrich wave proudly; 3
Isa 13:21 its houses . . there ostriches will dwell 1
34:13 the haunt of jackals, an abode for ostriches. 1
43:20 will honor me, the jackals and the ostriches; 1
Jer 50:39 in Babylon, and ostriches shall dwell in her; 1
Lam 4: 3 cruel, like the ostriches in the wilderness. 2
Mic 1: 8 the jackals, and mourning like the ostriches. 1

other 1. אָח 2. אֶחָד 3. אָחוֹת 4. אַחֵר 5. אִישׁ 6. אֵלֶּה 7. בִּלְתִּי 8. הֵם 9. הֵנָּה 10. זֶה 11. כֹּל 12. מִזֶּה 13. מִן 14. עוֹד 15. עַם 16. רֵעַ 17. שְׁאָר 18. שֵׁנִי 19. אָחֳרָן (A) 20. ἀλλήλων 21. ἄλλος 22. ἄλλος δέ 23. ἀλλότριος 24. ἄνθρωπος 25. δέ 26. εἷς 27. ἐκεῖνος 28. ἐπίλοιπος 29. ἕτερος 30. ἔτι 31. κἀκεῖνος 32. λοιπός 33. ὁ δέ 34. ὁ μέν 35. οὗτος 36. τις 37. τίς 38. τις δέ 39. τὶς δέ 40. τοιοῦτος 41. υἱός 42. aliquis 43. alius 44. alteruter 45. ceterus 46. ex 47. ille 48. residuus 49. secundus
Gen 3: 1 more subtle than any other wild creature •
4:19 one was Adah, and the name of the other Zillah. 18
5: 4 and he had other sons and daughters. •
7 and had other sons and daughters. •
10 and had other sons and daughters. •
13 Kenan . . had other sons and daughters. •
16 Ma-hal'alel . . had other sons and daughters. •
19 and had other sons and daughters. •
22 Enoch . . had other sons and daughters. •
26 and had other sons and daughters. •
30 Lamech . . had other sons and daughters. •
11:11 Shem lived . . and had other sons and daughters. •
13 Arpach'shad . . had other sons and daughters. •
15 Shelah . . had other sons and daughters. •
17 Eber lived . . and had other sons and daughters. •
19 Peleg . . had other sons and daughters. •
21 Re'u lived . . and had other sons and daughters. •
23 years, and had other sons and daughters. •
25 and had other sons and daughters. •
13:11 thus they separated from each other. 1
15:10 in two, and laid each half over against the other; 16
25:23 the one shall be stronger than the other •
29:27 we will give you the other also in return 10
31:49 when we are absent one from the other. 16
41: 3 behold, seven other cows, gaunt and thin, came up 4
3 stood by the other cows on the bank of the Nile. •
19 seven other cows came up after them 4
42: 5 Israel came to buy among the others who came •
43:14 may send back your other brother and Benjamin. 4
22 we have brought other money down in our hand 4
47:21 from one end of Egypt to the other. †
Exd 1:15 one . . was named Shiphrah and the other Pu'ah 18
14: 7 took . . all the other chariots of Egypt •
20 without one coming near the other all night. 10
17:12 one side, and the other on the other side; 2
12 one side, and the other on the other side; •
18: 4 the name of the other was Elie'zer 2
7 and they asked each other of their welfare 16
20: 3 You shall have no other gods before me. 4
21:18 strikes the other with a stone or with his fist 16
23:13 make no mention of the names of other gods 4
24: 2 the others shall not come near, and the people 8
25:12 and two rings on the other side of it. 18
19 Make . . one cherub on the other end; 12
32 branches of the lampstand out of the other side 18
33 three cups . . on the other branch 2
26: 3 the other five curtains shall be coupled to one •
6 shall . . couple the curtains one to the other 3
13 and the cubit on the other side, of what remains 10
27 the frames of the other side of the tabernacle 18
27:15 On the other side the hangings shall be fifteen 18
28:10 the names of the remaining six on the other stone 18
29:19 You shall take the other ram; 18
39 the other lamb you shall offer in the evening; 18
41 the other lamb you shall offer in the evening 18
30:32 you shall make no other like it in composition; •
32:15 on the one side and on the other were they written. 10
33:16 distinct . . from all other people that are upon •
34:14 for you shall worship no other god, for the LORD 4
36:10 the other five curtains he coupled •
13 he . . coupled the curtains one to the other 2
17 on the edge of the other connecting curtain. 18
32 five bars for the frames of the other side 18
37: 3 its one side and two rings on its other side. 18
8 on the one end, and one cherub on the other end; 10
18 branches of the lampstand out of the other side 18
19 with capital and flower, on the other branch 2
38:15 so for the other side; on this hand and that hand 18
Lev 5: 7 sin offering and the other for a burnt offering 2
6:11 put on other garments, and carry forth the ashes 4
7:24 The fat . . may be put to any other use •
8:22 Then he presented the other ram 18
11:23 all other winged insects which have four feet •
12: 8 a burnt offering and the other for a sin offering 2
14:22 a sin offering and the other a burnt offering 2
31 sin offering and the other for a burnt offering 2
42 shall take other stones and put them in the place 4
42 shall take other plaster and plaster the house 4
15:15 sin offering and the other for a burnt offering 2
30 shall offer . . the other for a burnt offering 2
16: 8 one lot for the LORD and the other lot for Aza'zel 2
Num 6:11 shall offer . . the other for a burnt offering 2
8:12 shall offer . . the other for a burnt offering 2
11:26 two men remained . . the other named Medad 18
31 about . . a day's journey on the other side •
24: 1 he did not go, as at other times, to look for omens •
28: 4 the other lamb you shall offer in the evening; 18
8 The other lamb you shall offer in the evening; 18
32:38 gave other names to the cities which they built. •
36: 3 sons of the other tribes of the people of Israel •
Deu 4:32 ask from one end of heaven to the other •
35 the LORD is God; there is no other besides him. 14
39 know . . the LORD is God . . ; there is no other. 14
5: 7 You shall have no other gods before me. 4

6:14 You shall not go after other gods 4
7: 4 turn away your sons . . to serve other gods; 4
7 not . . more in number than any other people •
8:19 forget . . and go after other gods and serve them 4
11:16 turn aside and serve other gods and worship 4
28 to go after other gods which you have not known. 4
13: 2 go after other gods,' which you have not known 4
6 entices . . saying, 'Let us go and serve other gods,' 4
13 go and serve other gods,' which you have not known 4
17: 3 gone and served other gods and worshipped them 4
18:20 prophet . . who speaks in the name of other gods 4
19: 9 you shall add three other cities to these three 14
21:15 two wives, the one loved and the other disliked 2
28:14 do not turn . . to go after other gods to serve 4
36 shall serve other gods, of wood and stone. 4
64 scatter . . from one end of the earth to the other; •
64 there . . serve other gods, of wood and stone 4
29:26 went and served other gods and worshiped them 4
30:17 drawn away to worship other gods and serve them 4
31:18 evil . . because they have turned to other gods. 4
20 they will turn to other gods and serve them 4
Jos 8:22 the others came forth from the city against them; 6
13: 8 With the other half of the tribe of Manas'seh •
22: 7 but to the other half Joshua had given •
23:16 and go and serve other gods and bow down to them. 4
24: 2 and they served other gods. 4
16 that we . . forsake the LORD, to serve other gods; 4
Jdg 2:12 they went after other gods, from among the gods 4
17 played the harlot after other gods and bowed 4
19 worse than their fathers, going after other gods 4
7: 7 and let all the others go every man to his home. 15
14 This is no other than the sword of Gideon 7
10:13 Yet you have forsaken me and served other gods; 4
13:10 the man who came to me the other day has appeared 27
16:29 hand on the one and his left hand on the other. 2
20:31 one . . goes up to Bethel and the other to Gib'e-ah 2
Rut 1: 4 the one was Orpah and the name of the other Ruth. 18
4: 7 one drew off his sandal and gave it to the other 16
1Sm 1: 2 was Hannah, and the name of the other Penin'nah. 18
8: 8 done to me . . forsaking me and serving other gods 4
14: 4 on the one side and a rocky crag on the other side 12
4 the one was Bozez, and the name of the other Seneh. 2
5 and the other on the south in front of Geba. 2
40 I and Jonathan my son will be on the other side. 2
19:21 When it was told Saul, he sent other messengers 4
23:26 David . . on the other side of the mountain; 10
26:19 driven me out . . saying, 'Go, serve other gods.' 4
28: 8 disguised himself and put on other garments 4
2Sm 2:13 one . . and the other on the . . side of the pool. 6
4: 2 one was Ba'anah, and the name of the other Rechab 18
7:23 What other nation on earth is like thy people 2
12: 1 two men . . the one rich and the other poor. 2
13:16 is greater than the other which you did to me. 4
14: 6 and one struck the other and killed him. 2
1Kg 3:13 no other king shall compare with you, all 5
22 the other woman said, "No, the living child is mine 4
23 the other says, 'No; but your son is dead, and my son is 10
25 two, and give half to the one, and half to the other. 2
26 But the other said, "It shall be neither mine nor 10
4:31 he was wiser than all other men, wiser than Ethan •
6:24 and five cubits . . the other wing of the cherub; 18
24 from the tip of one wing to the tip of the other. †
25 The other cherub also measured ten cubits; 18
26 ten cubits, and so was that of the other cherub. 18
27 a wing of the other cherub touched the other wall; 18
27 a wing of the other cherub touched the other wall; 18
27 their other wings touched . . in the middle •
27 wings touched each other in the middle †
34 the two leaves of the other door were folding. 18
7: 8 own house . . in the other court back of the hall 4
16 the height of the other capital was five cubits. 18
17 the one capital, and a net for the other capital. 18
18 he did the same with the other capital. 18
20 there were . . and so with the other capital. 18
8:60 may know that the LORD is God; there is no other. 14
9: 6 if you . . go and serve other gods and worship them 4
9 forsook the LORD . . and laid hold on other gods 4
11: 4 his wives turned away his heart after other gods; 4
10 that he should not go after other gods; 4
12:29 he set one in Bethel, and the other he put in Dan. 2
30 people went . . and to the other as far as Dan. 2
14: 9 made for yourself other gods, and molten images 4
18:23 I will prepare the other bull 2
2Kg 2: 8 water was parted to the one side and to the other 9
14 water was parted to the one side and to the other; 9
10:21 the house . . was filled from one end to the other. †
12: 7 summoned Jehoi'ada . . and the other priests •
17: 7 Israel had sinned . . and had feared other gods 4
35 You shall not fear other gods or bow yourselves 4
37 You shall not fear other gods 4
38 You shall not fear other gods 4
22:17 forsaken me and . . burned incense to other gods 4
1Ch 2:52 Shobal . . had other sons: Haro'eh, half •
9:29 Others . . were appointed over the furniture 13
30 Others . . prepared the mixing of the spices. •
33 the singers . . free from other service •
17:21 What other nation on earth is like thy people 2
23:17 Elie'zer had no other sons 4
2Ch 3:11 its other wing, of five cubits, touched the wing 4
11 wing . . touched the wing of the other cherub; 4
12 the other wing . . was joined to the wing 4
17 one on the south, the other on the north; 2
5:13 raised, with . . and other musical instruments •
7:19 turn aside . . and go and serve other gods 4
22 forsook the LORD . . and laid hold on other gods 4
13: 9 made priests . . like the people of other lands? •
28:25 he made high places to burn incense to other gods 4
29:34 until other priests had sanctified themselves •
32:13 have done to all the peoples of other lands? •
34:25 forsaken me and . . burned incense to other gods 4
35:21 What have we to do with each other, king of Judah? †
Ezr 1:10 bowls of silver, and 1,000 other vessels; 4
2:31 sons of the other Elam, 1,254. 4
7:24 temple servants, or other servants of this house •
Neh 4:17 one hand . . and with the other held his weapon. 2
7:33 men of the other Nebo, 52. 4
34 sons of the other Elam, 1,254. 4
8:15 bring branches of . . palm, and other leafy trees •
11: 1 while nine tenths remained in the other towns. •
12:38 other company of those who gave thanks went 18
Est 3: 8 different from those of every other people •
4:13 you will escape any more than all the other Jews. •
9:16 Now the other Jews . . also gathered to defend 17
Job 8:19 out of the earth others will spring. 4
31:10 let others bow down upon her. 4
34:24 sets others in their place. 4
Ps 49:10 must perish and leave their wealth to others. 4
73: 5 They are not in trouble as other men are; •
5 they are not stricken like other men. •
147:20 He has not dealt thus with any other nation; •
Prv 5: 9 lest you give your honor to others 4
18:17 until the other comes and examines him. 16
Ecc 3:19 fate . . is the same; as one dies, so dies the other. 10
7:14 God has made the one as well as the other 10
22 many times you have yourself cursed others. 4
Isa 26:13 other lords besides thee have ruled over us •
42: 8 my glory I give to no other 4
45: 5 I am the LORD, and there is no other 14
6 I am the LORD, and there is no other. 14
14 God is with you only, and there is no other 14
18 I am the LORD, and there is no other. 14
21 there is no other god besides me 14
22 Turn to me . . For I am God, and there is no other. 14
46: 9 for I am God, and there is no other; 14
56: 8 I will gather yet others to him •
Jer 1:16 they have burned incense to other gods 4
6:12 Their houses shall be turned over to others 4
7: 6 if you do not go after other gods to your own hurt 4
9 and go after other gods that you have not known 4
18 they pour out drink offerings to other gods 4
8:10 Therefore I will give their wives to others 4
11:10 they have gone after other gods to serve them; 4
13:10 and have gone after other gods to serve them 4
16:11 and have gone after other gods and have served 4
13 there you shall serve other gods day and night 4
19: 4 by burning incense in it to other gods 4
13 have been poured out to other gods 4
22: 9 and worshiped other gods and served them. 4
24: 2 but the other basket had very bad figs 2
25: 6 do not go after other gods to serve and worship 4
26:22 Elna'than the son of Achbor and others with him 5
32:29 offerings have been poured out to other gods 4
35:15 amend your doings, and do not go after other gods 4
40:11 and in Edom and in other lands heard that the king 11
44: 3 they went to burn incense and serve other gods 4
5 to turn . . and burn no incense to other gods. 4
8 burning incense to other gods 4
15 their wives had offered incense to other gods 4
Ezk 4: 8 so that you cannot turn from one side to the other †
9: 5 to the others he said in my hearing, "Pass through 6
10:11 the others followed without turning •
13:18 and keep other souls alive for your profit? •
16:34 different from other women in your harlotries; •
25: 8 the house of Judah is like all the other nations •
40:13 back of the one side room to the back of the other •
24 they had the same size as the others. 6
25 in its vestibule, like the windows of the others; 6
28 it was of the same size as the others. 6
29 its vestibule were of the same size as the others; 6
32 it was of the same size as the others. 6
33 its vestibule were of the same size as the others; 6
35 he measured it; it had the same size as the others. 6
36 its vestibule were of the same size as the others; •
40 on the other side of the vestibule of the gate 4
44 the other at the side of the south gate facing 2
42:14 they shall put on other garments before they go 4
44:19 they shall put on other garments 4
47: 7 very many trees on the one side and on the other. 12
Dan 3:21 bound in their . . hats, and their other garments •
29 no other god who is able to deliver in this way. 19
6: 3 distinguished above all the other presidents •
7:20 other horn which came up and before which three 19
8: 3 one was higher than the other, and the higher one 18
22 in place of which four others arose •
11: 4 plucked up and go to others besides these. 4
37 he shall not give heed to any other god •
12: 5 Then I Daniel looked, and behold, two others stood 4
Hos 3: 1 they turn to other gods and love cakes of raisins. 4
Zec 4: 3 on the right of the bowl and the other on its left. 2
11: 7 staffs; one I named Grace, the other I named Union. 2
14: 4 northward, and the other half southward. •
13 will be raised against the hand of the other; 16
Mat 4:21 going on from there he saw two other brothers 21
5:39 on the right cheek, turn to him the other also; 21
47 than others? Do not even the Gentiles do the same? •
6:24 for either he will hate the one and love the other 29
24 one and despise the other. You cannot serve God 29
12:13 and it was restored, whole like the other. 21
45 he goes and brings with him seven other spirits 29
13: 5 Other seeds fell on rocky ground 22
7 Other seeds fell upon thorns 22
8 Other seeds fell on good soil 22
15:30 the blind, the dumb, and many others 29
16:14 Some say John the Baptist, others say Eli'jah 21
14 others say Eli'jah, and others Jeremiah 29
17:25 From their sons or from others? 23
26 when he said, "From others 23
18:16 if he does not listen, take one or two others along 30
20: 3 he saw others standing idle in the market place; 21
6 he went out and found others standing 21
21: 8 others cut branches from the trees 21
36 Again he sent other servants, more than the first; 21
41 and let out the vineyard to other tenants 21
22: 4 Again he sent other servants, saying 21
23:23 without neglecting the others. 31
24:31 from one end of heaven to the other. †
25:11 Afterward the other maidens came also, saying 32
27:42 He saved others; he cannot save himself 21
49 the others said, "Wait, let us see 32
61 Mary Mag'dalene and the other Mary were there 21
28: 1 Mary Mag'dalene and the other Mary 21
Mrk 4: 5 Other seed fell on rocky ground 21
7 Other seed fell among thorns 21
8 other seeds fell into good soil 21
18 others are the ones sown among thorns 21
36 other boats were with him. 21
6:15 others said, "It is Eli'jah. 21
15 others said, "It is a prophet 21
7: 4 many other traditions which they observe 21
8:28 others say, Eli'jah; and others one of the prophets 21
28 others say, Eli'jah; and others one of the prophets 21
11: 8 and others spread leafy branches 21
12: 5 so with many others 21
6 He had still one other, a beloved son •
9 give the vineyard to others. 21
31 no other commandment greater than these. 21
32 there is no other but he; 21
15:31 saying, "He saved others; he cannot save himself. 21
41 also many other women who came up with him 21
Lke 3:18 So, with many other exhortations, he preached 29
4:43 preach the good news . . to the other cities also 29
5: 7 beckoned to their partners in the other boat 29
29 was a large company of tax collectors and others 21
6:29 offer the other also 21
7:41 one owed 500 denarii, and the other 50. 29
8: 3 Joan'na . . and Susanna, and many others 29
10 for others they are in parables 32
9: 8 by others that one of the old prophets had risen. 21
19 others say, Eli'jah 21
19 others, that one of the old prophets has risen. 21
10: 1 After this the Lord appointed 70 others 29
11:16 while others, to test him, sought from him a sign 29
26 seven other spirits more evil than himself 29
42 without neglecting the others. 31
13: 2 worse sinners than all the other Galileans •
4 all the others who dwelt in Jerusalem? 24
14:32 while the other is yet a great way off •
16:13 either he will hate the one and love the other 29
13 will be devoted to the one and despise the other. 29
17:24 and lights up the sky from one side to the other •
34 one will be taken and the other left. 29
35 one will be taken and the other left. 29
18: 9 to some who . . despised others 32
10 one a Pharisee and the other a tax collector. 29
11 I thank thee that I am not like other men 32
14 this man . . rather than the other 27
20:16 give the vineyard to others 21
22:65 they spoke many other words against him 29
23:32 Two others also, who were criminals, were led away 29
35 He saved others; let him save himself 21
40 the other rebuked him, saying, "Do you not fear God 29
Joh 4:38 others have labored, and you have entered 21
7:12 others said, "No, he is leading the people astray. 21
41 Others said, "This is the Christ. 21
9: 9 others said, "No, but he is like him. 21
16 others said, "How can a man who is a sinner 21
10:16 I have other sheep, that are not of this fold 21
21 Others said, "These are not the sayings 21
12:29 Others said, "An angel has spoken to him. 21
18:16 the other disciple, who was known to the high priest 21
34 did others say it to you about me? 21
19:18 There they crucified him, and with him two others 21
32 the other who had been crucified with him; 21
20: 2 went to Simon Peter and the other disciple 21
3 Peter then came out with the other disciple 21
4 the other disciple outran Peter 21
8 the other disciple, who reached the tomb first 21

25 the other disciples told him 21
30 Now Jesus did many other signs 21
21: 2 two others of his disciples were together. 21
8 the other disciples came in the boat 21
Act 2: 4 began to speak in other tongues 29
13 others mocking said 29
40 he testified with many other words and exhorted 29
4:12 no other name under heaven given among men 29
9:39 showing tunics and other garments *
15: 2 Paul and Barnabas and some of the others 21
35 with many others also. 29
17:18 Others said, "He seems to be a preacher 33
32 some mocked; but others said, "We will hear you 33
34 a woman named Dam'aris and others with them. 29
23: 6 one part were Sad'ducees and the other Pharisees 29
27: 1 Paul and some other prisoners 29
28:24 while others disbelieved. 33
Rom 2:21 who teach others, will you not teach yourself? 29
11:23 And even the others, if they do not persist 31
13: 9 You shall not covet," and any other commandment 29
14:20 but it is wrong for any one to make others fall *
1Co 3:11 For no other foundation can any one lay 21
6:13 God will destroy both one and the other 35
18 Every other sin which a man commits *
9: 2 If to others I am not an apostle, at least I am to you; 21
5 as the other apostles 32
12 If others share this rightful claim upon you 21
27 lest after preaching to others 21
11:16 we recognize no other practice 40
14:19 in order to instruct others 21
29 let the others weigh what is said. 21
15:37 perhaps of wheat or of some other grain. 32
16:12 to visit you with the other brethren *
2Co 2:16 to the other a fragrance from life to life 25
8: 8 to prove by the earnestness of others 29
13 others should be eased and you burdened 21
9:13 your contribution for them and for all others; *
11: 8 I robbed other churches by accepting support 21
13: 2 who sinned before and all the others 32
Gal 1:19 I saw none of the other apostles 29
5:10 you will take no other view than mine 21
Eph 3: 5 the sons of men in other generations 29
Php 1:15 but others from good will. 39
2: 3 count others better than yourselves. 20
4 but also to the interests of others. 29
3: 4 If any other man thinks he has reason 21
1Th 2: 6 whether from you or from others 21
4:13 you may not grieve as others do who have no hope. 32
5: 6 So then let us not sleep, as others do 32
1Ti 5:24 the sins of others appear later. 37
2Ti 2: 2 who will be able to teach others also. 29
Heb 11:36 Others suffered mocking and scourging 29
Jas 5:12 do not swear . . with any other oath 21
2Pe 3:16 as they do the other scriptures. 32
Rev 8:13 woe . . at the blasts of the other trumpets 32
17:10 seven kings . . one is, the other has not yet come 21
1Es 1:24 beyond any other people or kingdom *
2:13 2,410 silver bowls, and 1,000 other vessels. 21
16 living in Samaria and other places 21
17 the other judges of their council in Coelesyria 28
22 troubling both kings and other cities *
25 the others associated with them 32
4:18 gold and silver or any other beautiful thing *
19 gold or silver or any other beautiful thing. *
5:22 The sons of the other Elam and Ono, 725. 21
50 joined them from the other peoples of the land. 21
8:10 the priests and Levites and others in our realm 33
22 no tribute or any other tax 21
2Es 1:24 I will turn to other nations 43
2:11 and will give to these others *
27 others shall weep and be sorrowful 43
43 of great stature, taller than any of the others 47
5:28 and dishonored the one root beyond the others 43
6:41 and the other part remain beneath. *
49 and the name of the other Leviathan. 49
50 thou didst separate one from the other 44
56 other nations which have descended from Adam 48
7:62 out of the dust like the other created things! 45
85 how the habitations of the others are guarded 43
110and many others prayed for many? *
10:10 and others will come; and behold, almost all go 43
11: 4 the middle head was larger than the other heads 43
21 others of them rose up, but did not hold the rule. 42
29 for it was greater than the other two heads. *
12: 7 righteous before thee beyond many others *
15 for a longer time than any other of the 12. *
13:13 and some were bringing others as offerings. 46
Tob 6:14 they have no other son to bury them. 29
7:16 Sister, make up the other room, and take her into it. 29
14:10 the other received repayment 27
Jdt 8:20 we know no other god but him 29
9:14 no other who protects the people of Israel 21
11:21 from one end of the earth to the other *
AEs 15: 4 while the other followed carrying her train. 29
Wis 2:15 his manner of life is unlike that of others 21
8: 1 from one end of the earth to the other *
15:13 this man, more than all others, knows *
18 which are worse than all others 21
19:14 Others had refused to receive strangers 34
Sir 0: 1 the prophets and the others that followed them, 21
1 the prophets and the other books of our fathers, 21
11: 6 illustrious men have been handed over to others. 29
19 until he leaves them to others and dies. 29
14: 4 accumulates for others 21
4 others will live in luxury on his goods. 29
18 which sheds some and puts forth others 21
19: 4 One who trusts others too quickly *
33:15 in pairs, one the opposite of the other. 26
36:23 her husband is not like other men. 41
42:24 All things are twofold, one opposite the other 26
25 One confirms the good things of the other 26
48:16 others multiplied sins. 36
49: 5 for they gave their power to others 29
Bar 1:21 by serving other gods and doing what is evil 29
3:19 to Hades, and others have arisen in their place. 21
35 This is our God; no other can be compared to him! 29
Sus 1:14 and when each pressed the other for the reason 20
56 and commanded them to bring the other. 29
Bel 1:41 there is no other besides thee. 21
1Mc 5:14 behold, other messengers . . came from Galilee 29
27 have been shut up in the other cities of Gilead; 32
36 Bosor, and the other cities of Gilead. 32
6:20 he built siege towers and other engines of war. *
29 came to him from other kingdoms 29
43 It was taller than all the others †
8: 5 the others who rose up against them *
10:38 obey no other authority but the high priest. 21
72 who the others are that are helping us 32
11:24 gold and clothing and numerous other gifts 29
27 in as many other honors as he had formerly had 21
35 the other payments henceforth due to us 21
12: 2 to the Spartans and to other places. 29
11 both in our feasts and on other appropriate days 32
14 annoy you and our other allies and friends 32
45 the other strongholds and the remaining troops 32
13:39 whatever other tax has been collected 21
15: 5 and release from all the other payments 21
2Mc 2: 3 with other similar words he exhorted them 29
27 seeks the benefit of others 29
3:19 while others peered out of the windows. 37
4:32 other vessels, as it happened, he had sold to Tyre 29
35 not only Jews, but many also of other nations 21
41 others took handfuls of the ashes that were lying 38
5:16 the votive offerings which other kings had made 21
23 worse than the others did 21
6:11 Others who had assembled in the caves near by 29
14 in the case of the other nations 21
7:39 handled him worse than the others 21
8:14 Others sold all their remaining property 33
33 Callisthenes and some others *
9: 6 he had tortured the bowels of others 29
28 such as he had inflicted on others 29
10:28 the other made rage their leader in the fight. 33
36 Others who came up in the same way 29
36 Others broke open the gates 33
11: 3 as he did on the sacred places of the other nations 32
7 he urged the others to risk their lives with him 21
27 King Antiochus . . to the other Jews, greeting. 21
13: 6 notorious for other crimes. 21
3Mc 1:13 when he entered every other temple *
23 the same posture of supplication as the others. *
3: 2 a report that they hindered others *
4: 9 others had their feet secured by . . fetters 33
13 in precisely the same fashion as the others 27
5:49 others with babies at their breasts 29
4Mc 1:32 Some desires are mental, others are physical 33
2: 9 In all other matters 29
18 to correct some, and to render others powerless. 33
8: 2 others of the Hebrew captives be brought 21
14:16 the others . . hatch the nestlings 33
15:20 the flesh . . burned upon the flesh of other children *
20 corpses fallen on other corpses *
26 one bearing death and the other deliverance *
16: 9 others married and without offspring 33

other *See also* belong, clasp, end, hand, honor, kiss, name, punishment, race, side, some, time, times.

all other 1. λοιπός
2Mc 12:11 to help his people in all other ways. 1

any other 1. אַחֵר 2. אַחֵר 3. כֹּל 4. ἄλλος 5. πᾶς
Gen 29:19 you than that I should give her to any other man; 2
37: 3 loved Joseph more than any other of his children 3
Jdg 16: 7 I shall become weak, and be like any other man. 1
11 I shall become weak, and be like any other man. 1
13 I shall become weak, and be like any other man. *
17 and I shall become weak, and be like any other man. 3
Job 8:12 not cut down, they wither before any other plant. 3
Rev 2:24 to you I say, I do not lay upon you any other burden; 4
Tob 6:12 you rather than any other man 5
4Mc 15: 6 The mother . . more than any other mother 5

each other 1. ἀλλήλων 2. αὐτός 3. ἑαυτοῦ 4. εἰς ἀπὸ τοῦ ἑνός 5. ἕτερος ἕτερος
Lke 23:12 Herod and Pilate became friends with each other 1
12 they had been at enmity with each other. 2
24:14 talking with each other about all these things 1
17 which you are holding with each other as you walk? 1
32 They said to each other, "Did not our hearts burn 1
Act 7:26 Men, you are brethren, why do you wrong each other?' 1
15:39 so that they separated from each other 1
Rom 1:12 mutually encouraged by each other's faith 1
Gal 5:17 these are opposed to each other 1
Col 3:13 forgiving each other 3
1Es 1:26 What have we to do with each other, king of Judea? †
Tob 5: 9 he entered and they greeted each other. 1
Sus 1:10 they did not tell each other of their distress 1
13 They said to each other, "Let us go home 5
14 when they went out, they parted from each other. 1
51 Separate them far from each other 1
52 When they were separated from each other 4
54 did you see them being intimate with each other? 1
58 did you catch them being intimate with each other? 1
1Mc 10:71 let us match strength with each other there 3
11: 9 Come, let us make a covenant with each other 3
3Mc 5:49 they kissed each other, embracing relatives 1

other man 1. אַחֵר 2. ἀλλότριος 3. ἕτερος
Neh 5: 5 for other men have our fields and our vineyards. 1
1Co 14:17 the other man is not edified. 3
2Co 10:15 We do not boast beyond limit, in other men's labors; 2
1Mc 16:19 He sent other men to Gazara to do away with John 3
20 he sent other men to take possession of Jerusalem 3

other people 1. ἀλλότριος
Sir 21: 8 who builds his house with other people's money 1

other person 1. ἄλλος
Exd 4:13 he said, "Oh, my Lord, send, I pray, some other person. 1

other than 1. בִּלְעָדֵי 2. כִּי אִם 3. מִבַּלְעֲדֵי 4. מִלְּבַד
Gen 28:17 This is none other than the house of God 2
Num 5:20 some man other than your husband has lain with you 1
Jos 22:19 an altar other than the altar of the LORD our God. 3
29 building an altar . . other than the altar 4

other thing 1. alius 2. ἄλλος 3. λοιπός 4. παρεκτός 5. alius
Mrk 4:19 and the desire for other things 3
Joh 21:25 there are also many other things which Jesus did; 2
1Co 11:34 About the other things I will give directions 3
2Co 11:28 And, apart from other things 4
1Es 2: 7 besides the other things 2
6: 4 finishing all the other things? 2
2Es 13:56 I will tell you other things 5
3Mc 3:21 Among other things 1

other woman 1. λοιπός
Lke 24:10 it was . . the other women with them who told this 1

others *See* nine.

all others 1. prior
2Es 15:59 Unhappy above all others 1

otherwise 1. וְ 2. ἄλλως 3. εἰ μή 4. ἐπεί 5. ἐπεὶ ἄρα 6. ἑτέρως 7. ἵνα μήποτε
1Kg 1:21 Otherwise it will come to pass, when my lord 1
Lke 14:29 Otherwise, when he has laid a foundation 7
Rom 11: 6 otherwise grace would no longer be grace. 4
22 otherwise you too will be cut off. 4
1Co 7:14 Otherwise, your children would be unclean 5
14:16 Otherwise, if you bless with the spirit 4
15:29 Otherwise, what do people mean by being baptized 4
Php 3:15 if in anything you are otherwise minded 6
Heb 10: 2 Otherwise, would they not have ceased 4
1Mc 15:31 Otherwise we will come and conquer you. 3
4Mc 1:33 Otherwise how is it that . . 4
2: 7 Otherwise how could it be 4
4:13 otherwise he had scruples about doing so 2

otherwise *See also* teach.

otherwise than 1. בְּלֹא
2Ch 30:18 ate the passover otherwise than as prescribed. 1

ought 1. δεῖ 2. καθήκω 3. ὀφείλω 4. χρή 5. debeo
Gen 20: 9 have done to me things that ought not to be done. *
Lev 10:18 You certainly ought to have eaten it *
1Kg 2: 9 wise man; you will know what you ought to do to him *
1Ch 12:32 to know what Israel ought to do *
2Ch 13: 5 Ought you not to know that the LORD *
Neh 5: 9 Ought you not to walk in the fear of our God *
Mat 23:23 these you ought to have done 1
25:27 Then you ought to have invested my money 1
Mrk 13:14 set up where it ought not to be 1
Lke 11:42 these you ought to have done 1
12:12 what you ought to say. 1
13:14 There are six days on which work ought to be done; 1
16 ought not this woman . . be loosed from this bond 1
18: 1 to the effect that they ought always to pray 1
Joh 4:20 Jerusalem is . . where men ought to worship. 1
13:14 you also ought to wash one another's feet. 3
19: 7 by that law he ought to die 3
Act 17:29 we ought not to think that the Deity is like gold 3
19:36 you ought to be quiet and do nothing rash. 1
22:22 he ought not to live. 2

24:19 they ought to be here before you 1
25:10 Caesar's tribunal, where I ought to be tried 1
24 shouting that he ought not to live any longer. 1
26: 9 I . . was convinced that I ought to do many things 1
Rom 8:26 for we do not know how to pray as we ought 1
12: 3 more highly than he ought to think 1
15: 1 ought to bear with the failings of the weak 3
27 they ought also to be of service to them 3
1Co 5: 2 you are arrogant! Ought you not rather to mourn? *
8: 2 he does not yet know as he ought to know. 1
11: 7 For a man ought not to cover his head 3
10 That is why a woman ought to have a veil on her head 3
2Co 12:11 I ought to have been commended by you 3
14 children ought not to lay up for their parents 3
Eph 6:20 I may declare it boldly, as I ought to speak. 1
Col 4: 4 that I may make it clear, as I ought to speak. 1
6 you may know how you ought to answer every one. 1
1Th 4: 1 how you ought to live and to please God 1
2Th 3: 7 you yourselves know how you ought to imitate us; 1
1Ti 3:15 you may know how one ought to behave 1
2Ti 2: 6 ought to have the first share of the crops. 1
Heb 5:12 For though by this time you ought to be teachers 3
Jas 3:10 My brethren, this ought not to be so. 4
4:15 Instead you ought to say, "If the Lord wills *
2Pe 3:11 what sort of persons ought you to be 1
1Jn 2: 6 ought to walk in the same way in which he walked. 3
3:16 we ought to lay down our lives for the brethren. 3
4:11 we also ought to love one another. 3
3Jn 1: 8 So we ought to support such men 3
2Es 10: 9 it is she who ought to mourn 5
11 Who then ought to mourn the more 5
2Mc 6:20 as men ought to go 1
3Mc 1:12 did not cease to maintain that he ought to enter 1
12 I ought not to be. 1
3: 9 such . . ought not be left to its fate *
4Mc 11:15 we ought likewise to die for the same principles. 3
16:19 therefore you ought to endure any suffering 3

ought not to share 1. *ἀκοινώνητος*

Wis 14:21 the name that ought not to be shared. 1

out 1. בַּעַד 2. חוּץ 3. לְ 4. מִבֵּין 5. מִחוּץ 6. מִן 7. מֵעַל 8. מִקֶּרֶב 9. מִשָּׁם 10. מִתּוֹךְ 11. עַל 12. מִן (A) 13. *ἀπό* 14. *διά* 15. *ἐκ* 16. *ἐκπορεύω* 17. *ἐκτός* 18. *ἐν* 19. *ἐξέρχομαι* 20. *ἔξω* 21. *περί* 22. *πρὸς ἐκδημίαν* 23. *χάριν* 24. *χωρίς* 25. de 26. ex

Gen 2: 9 out of the ground the LORD God made to grow 6
19 out of the ground the LORD God formed every beast 6
23 Woman, because she was taken out of Man. 6
3:19 return to the ground, for out of it you were taken; 6
5:29 called his name Noah, saying, "Out of the ground 6
6:14 in the ark, and cover it inside and out with pitch. 5
8:10 again he sent forth the dove out of the ark; 6
19 the earth, went forth by families out of the ark. 6
19:24 fire from the LORD out of heaven; 6
29 God . . sent Lot out of the midst of the overthrow 6
30 Lot went up out of Zo'ar, and dwelt in the hills 6
23: 4 that I may bury my dead out of my sight. 6
8 I should bury my dead out of my sight, hear me 6
24:29 and Laban ran out to the man, to the spring. 2
29: 2 for out of that well the flocks were watered. 6
34:26 took Dinah out of Shechem's house, and went away. 6
37:21 he delivered him out of their hands, saying 6
22 -that he might rescue him out of their hand 6
28 drew Joseph up and lifted him out of the pit 6
39:13 in her hand, and had fled out of the house 2
18 garment with me, and fled out of the house. 2
40:15 I was indeed stolen out of the land of the Hebrews; 6
17 but the birds were eating it out of the basket 6
41: 2 behold, there came up out of the Nile seven cows 6
3 cows . . came up out of the Nile after them 6
14 brought him hastily out of the dungeon; 6
18 seven cows, fat and sleek, came up out of the Nile 6
45:25 they went up out of Egypt, and came to the land 6
47:30 carry me out of Egypt and bury me in their burying 6
50:24 God will . . bring you up out of this land 6
Exd 2:10 she said, "Because I drew him out of the water. 6
19 delivered us out of the hand of the shepherds 6
3: 2 in a flame of fire out of the midst of a bush; 6
4 God called to him out of the bush, "Moses, Moses! 6
8 I have come down to deliver them out of the hand 6
8 and to bring them up out of that land 6
10 my people, the sons of Israel, out of Egypt. 6
11 bring the sons of Israel out of Egypt? 6
12 you have brought forth the people out of Egypt 6
17 I will bring you up out of the affliction of Egypt 6
6:11 let the people of Israel go out of his land. 6
13 the people of Israel out of the land of Egypt. 6
7: 2 let the people of Israel go out of his land. 6
4 bring forth my hosts . . out of the land of Egypt 6
8:13 the frogs died out of the houses and courtyards 6
13 the frogs died . . out of the fields. 6
11:10 let the people of Israel go out of his land. 6
12:15 you shall put away leaven out of your houses 6
33 urgent . . to send them out of the land in haste; 6
13: 3 came out from Egypt, out of the house of bondage 6
18 Israel went up out of the land of Egypt equipped 6
17: 3 Why did you bring us up out of Egypt 6
18: 9 delivered them out of the hand of the Egyptians. 6
10 delivered you out of the hand of the Egyptians 6
10 delivered you . . out of the hand of Pharaoh. 6
25 Moses chose able men out of all Israel 6
19: 1 Israel had gone forth out of the land of Egypt 6
3 LORD called to him out of the mountain, saying 6
20: 2 brought you . . out of the house of bondage. 6
22: 7 If . . it is stolen out of the man's house 6
23:13 nor let such be heard out of your mouth. 11
24:16 he called to Moses out of the midst of the cloud. 6
25:32 three branches of the lampstand out of one side 6
32 branches of the lampstand out of the other side 6
29:23 out of the basket of unleavened bread 6
46 who brought them forth out of the land of Egypt 6
32: 1 who brought us up out of the land of Egypt 6
4 who brought you up out of the land of Egypt! 6
7 whom you brought up out of the land of Egypt 6
8 they have turned aside quickly out of the way 6
8 who brought you up out of the land of Egypt!' 6
11 thou has brought forth out of the land of Egypt 6
19 he threw the tables out of his hands and broke 6
23 who brought us up out of the land of Egypt 6
33: 1 whom you have brought up out of the land of Egypt 6
37:18 three branches of the lampstand out of one side 6
18 branches of the lampstand out of the other side 6
Lev 5:15 bring . . a ram without blemish out of the flock 6
18 priest a ram without blemish out of the flock 6
6: 6 a ram without blemish out of the flock 6
7:34 out of the sacrifices of their peace offerings 6
8:26 out of the basket of unleavened bread 6
10: 4 carry your brethren . . out of the camp 5
5 carried them in their coats out of the camp 5
11:45 who brought you up out of the land of Egypt 6
13:56 shall tear the spot out of the garment or the skin 6
14:45 he shall carry them forth out of the city 5
53 he shall let the living bird go out of the city 5
24: 9 a most holy portion out of the offerings by fire 6
25:12 you shall eat what it yields out of the field 6
38 God, who brought you forth out of the land of Egypt 6
42 whom I brought forth out of the land of Egypt 6
51 according to them he shall refund out 6
55 whom I brought forth out of the land of Egypt 6
26:13 God, who brought you forth out of the land of Egypt 6
45 whom I brought forth out of the land of Egypt 6
Num 5:25 offering of jealousy out of the woman's hand 6
6:19 take . . one unleavened cake out of the basket 6
11:20 Why did we come forth out of Egypt?"' 6
14:44 nor Moses, departed out of the camp. 6
16:13 brought us up out of a land flowing with milk 6
37 to take up the censers out of the blaze; 4
18:29 Out of all the gifts due to you 6
20: 5 why have you made us come up out of Egypt 6
10 shall we bring forth water for you out of this rock? 6
16 sent an angel and brought us forth out of Egypt; 6
21: 5 Why have you brought us up out of Egypt to die 6
26 taken all his land out of his hand 6
22:23 the ass turned aside out of the road 6
24:17 star shall come forth out of Jacob, and a scepter 6
17 and a scepter shall rise out of Israel 6
26: 4 who came forth out of the land of Egypt, were 6
30: 2 according to all that proceeds out of his mouth. 6
31: 5 provided, out of the thousands of Israel 6
28 one out of 500, of the persons and of the oxen 6
30 take one drawn out of every 50, of the persons 6
32:11 Surely none of the men who came up out of Egypt 6
33: 1 when they went forth out of the land of Egypt 6
Deu 1:27 he has brought us forth out of the land of Egypt 6
3: 8 took the land . . out of the hand of the two kings 6
4:12 LORD spoke to you out of the midst of the fire; 6
15 spoke to you at Horeb out of the midst of the fire 6
20 LORD . . brought you forth out of the iron furnace 6
20 out of the iron furnace, out of Egypt, to be a people 6
33 voice of a god speaking out of the midst of the fire 6
36 Out of heaven he let you hear his voice 6
36 you heard his words out of the midst of the fire. 6
5: 4 LORD spoke . . out of the midst of the fire 6
6 LORD . . who brought you out of the land of Egypt 6
6 LORD . . who brought you out of . . the house of bondage. 6
22 at the mountain out of the midst of the fire 6
23 heard the voice out of the midst of the darkness 6
24 heard his voice out of the midst of the fire; 6
26 living God speaking out of the midst of fire 6
6:12 LORD, who brought you out of the land of Egypt 6
12 LORD, who brought you . . out of the house of bondage. 6
21 LORD brought us out of Egypt with a mighty hand; 6
7: 6 out of all the people . . on the face of the earth. 6
8: 9 a land . . out of whose hills you can dig copper. 6
14 LORD . . who brought you out of the land of Egypt 6
14 LORD . . brought you . . , out of the house of bondage 6
15 who brought you water out of the flinty rock 6
9: 7 from the day you came out of the land of Egypt 6
10 spoken with you . . out of the midst of the fire 6
12 they have turned aside quickly out of the way 6
17 two tables, and cast them out of my two hands 6
21 into the brook that descended out of the mountain 6
26 thou hast brought out of Egypt with a mighty hand 6
10: 4 LORD had spoken to you . . out of the midst of the fire 6
12: 3 destroy their name out of that place. 6
5 LORD your God will choose out of all your tribes 6
13: 5 LORD . . who brought you out of the land of Egypt 6
5 LORD . . redeemed you out of the house of bondage 6
10 LORD . . who brought you out of the land of Egypt 6
10 LORD . . brought you . . out of the house of bondage. 6
14: 2 the LORD has chosen you . . out of all the peoples 6
15:11 For the poor will never cease out of the land; 8
14 furnish him liberally out of your flock 6
14 liberally . . out of your threshing floor 6
14 furnish him liberally . . out of your wine press; 6
16: 1 LORD your God brought you out of Egypt by night. 6
3 came out of the land of Egypt in hurried flight 6
3 remember the day . . came out of the land of Egypt. 6
6 passover . . at the time you came out of Egypt. 6
18: 5 LORD . . has chosen him out of all your tribes 6
6 Levite comes from any of your towns out of all Israel 6
20: 1 LORD . . brought you up out of the land of Egypt. 6
23: 4 on the way, when you came forth out of Egypt 6
24: 1 sends her out of his house, and she departs 6
1 sends her out . . and she departs out of his house 6
3 dislikes her . . and sends her out of his house 6
9 Miriam on the way as you came forth out of Egypt. 6
11 man . . shall bring the pledge out to you. 2
25:17 Am'alek did to you . . as you came out of Egypt 6
26: 8 LORD brought us out of Egypt with a mighty hand 6
13 I have removed the sacred portion out of my house 6
32:13 he made him suck honey out of the rock, and oil 6
13 made him suck . . oil out of the flinty rock. 6
39 there is none that can deliver out of my hand. 6
Jos 1: 8 book of the law shall not depart out of your mouth 6
2:19 If any one goes out of the doors of your house 6
4: 3 Take . . from here out of the midst of the Jordan 6
8 twelve stones out of the midst of the Jordan 6
16 the priests . . to come up out of the Jordan. 6
17 commanded the priests, "Come up out of the Jordan. 6
19 The people came up out of the Jordan on the tenth 6
20 twelve stones, which they took out of the Jordan 6
5: 4 all the males of the people who came out of Egypt 6
4 on the way . . after they had come out of Egypt. 6
5 born on the way . . after they had come out of Egypt 6
6 the men of war that came forth out of Egypt 6
7:23 they took them out of the tent and brought them 10
8:19 And the ambush rose quickly out of their place 6
9:26 and delivered them out of the hand of the people 6
21: 3 Israel gave . . out of their inheritance. 6
9 Out of the tribe of Judah and . . Simeon they gave 6
16 nine cities out of these two tribes; 6
17 then out of the tribe of Benjamin, Gibeon 6
20 the cities . . were out of the tribe of E'phraim. 6
23 and out of the tribe of Dan, El'teke 6
25 and out of the half-tribe of Manas'seh, Ta'anach 6
27 Gershonites . . were given out . . of Manas'seh 6
28 and out of the tribe of Is'sachar, Ki'shion 6
30 and out of the tribe of Asher, Mishal with its 6
32 and out of the tribe of Naph'tali, Kedesh 6
34 the rest . . were given out of the tribe of Zeb'ulun 6
36 and out of the tribe of Reuben, Bezer with its 6
38 and out of the tribe of Gad, Ramoth in Gilead 6
24:10 he blessed you; so I delivered you out of his hand. 6
17 up from . . Egypt, out of the house of bondage 6
Jdg 2:16 out of the power of those who plundered them. 6
3:22 for he did not draw the sword out of his belly; 6
5:28 Out of the window she peered, the mother of Sis'era 1
8:22 you have delivered us out of the hand of Mid'ian. 6
9: 4 they gave him 70 pieces of silver out of the house 6
10:12 cried to me, and I delivered you out of their hand. 6
15:17 he threw away the jawbone out of his hand; 6
16:25 they called Samson out of the prison 6
19:25 man seized his concubine, and put her out to them; 2
30 people of Israel came up out of the land of Egypt 6
20:14 the Benjaminites came together out of the cities 6
15 mustered out of their cities on that day 6
25 Benjamin went against them out of Gib'e-ah 6
33 all the men of Israel rose up out of their place 6
33 in ambush rushed out of their place west of Geba. 6
34 came . . 10,000 picked men out of all Israel 6
38 made a great cloud of smoke rise up out of the city 6
40 signal began to rise out of the city in a column 6
42 those who came out of the cities destroyed them 6
21:16 since the women are destroyed out of Benjamin? 6
1Sm 2:28 I chose him out of all the tribes . . to be my priest 6
7: 3 deliver you out of the hand of the Philistines. 6
8: 8 from the day I brought them up out of Egypt even 6
10:18 I brought up Israel out of Egypt, and I delivered 6
12: 6 brought your fathers up out of the land of Egypt. 6
8 who brought forth your fathers out of Egypt 6
10 deliver us out of the hand of our enemies 6
11 and delivered you out of the hand of your enemies 6
14:48 Israel out of the hands of those who plundered 6
15: 2 opposing them . . when they came up out of Egypt. 6
6 to . . Israel when they came up out of Egypt. 6
17:23 came up out of the ranks of the Philistines 6
35 I went . . and delivered it out of his mouth; 6
49 David put his hand in his bag and took out a stone 9
51 and took his sword and drew it out of its sheath 6
24: 2 Then Saul took 3,000 chosen men out of all Israel 6
13 'Out of the wicked comes forth wickedness'; 6
21 not destroy my name out of my father's house. 6
25:14 David sent messengers out of the wilderness 6

26:24 and may he deliver me out of all tribulation. 6
27: 1 I shall escape out of his hand. 6
28:13 I see a god coming up out of the earth. 6
17 the LORD has torn the kingdom out of your hand 6
2Sm 4: 9 who has redeemed my life out of every adversity 6
6: 3 and brought it out of the house of Abin'adab 6
16 Michal . . looked out of the window, and saw 1
8: 1 David took . . out of the hand of the Philistines. 6
12: 7 and I delivered you out of the hand of Saul; 6
11 raise up evil against you out of your own house; 6
13:18 So his servant put her out, and bolted the door 2
15:24 until the people had all passed out of the city. 6
17:21 After they had gone, the men came up out of the well 6
19: 9 and now he has fled out of the land from Ab'salom. 6
20:12 he carried Ama'sa out of the highway 6
22:13 Out of the brightness . . coals of fire flamed 6
46 and came trembling out of their fastnesses. 6
23:21 and snatched the spear out of the Egyptian's hand 6
1Kg 1:29 who has redeemed my soul out of every adversity 6
5:13 raised a levy of forced labor out of all Israel; 6
8: 1 bring up the ark . . out of the city of David 6
16 day that I brought my people Israel out of Egypt 6
21 when he brought them out of the land of Egypt. 6
53 thou didst bring our fathers out of Egypt, O Lord 6
9: 9 brought their fathers out of the land of Egypt 6
11:12 I will tear it out of the hand of your son. 6
32 the city which I have chosen out of all the tribes 6
34 I will not take the whole kingdom out of his hand; 6
35 I will take the kingdom out of his son's hand 6
12:28 who brought you up out of the land of Egypt. 6
13: 1 man . . came out of Judah by the word of the LORD 6
14:15 root up Israel out of this good land which he gave 7
21 city . . the LORD had chosen out of all the tribes 6
15:12 put . . the male cult prostitutes out of the land 6
16: 2 I exalted you out of the dust and made you leader 6
18:44 a little cloud . . is rising out of the sea. 6
20:42 you have let go out of your hand the man whom I had 6
22: 3 do not take it out of the hand of the king of Syria? 6
34 Turn about, and carry me out of the battle 6
2Kg 9:30 adorned her head, and looked out of the window. 1
17: 7 who had brought them up out of the land of Egypt 6
18 and removed them out of his sight; 6
20 until he had cast them out of his sight. 6
23 the LORD removed Israel out of his sight 6
36 the LORD, who brought you out of the land of Egypt 6
39 deliver you out of the hand of all your enemies. 6
18:29 he will not be able to deliver you out of my hand. 6
33 his land out of the hand of the king of Assyria? 6
34 Have they delivered Sama'ria out of my hand? 6
35 have delivered their countries out of my hand 6
35 the LORD should deliver Jerusalem out of my hand?' 6
19:31 for out of Jerusalem shall go forth a remnant 6
31 and out of Mount Zion a band of survivors. 6
20: 6 deliver . . out of the hand of the king of Assyria 6
21: 7 I have chosen out of all the tribes of Israel 6
8 out of the land which I gave to their fathers 6
23: 8 brought . . the priests out of the cities of Judah 6
16 and he sent and took the bones out of the tombs 6
18 the bones of the prophet who came out of Sama'ria. 6
27 I will remove Judah also out of my sight 6
24: 3 to remove them out of his sight, for the sins 6
25:21 So Judah was taken into exile out of its land. 6
1Ch 6:61 given by lot out of the family of the tribe 6
61 out of the half-tribe, the half of Manas'seh 6
62 out of the tribes of Is'sachar, Asher, Naph'tali 6
63 out of the tribes of Reuben, Gad, and Zeb'ulun. 6
65 out of the tribes of Judah, Simeon, and Benjamin 6
66 of their territory out of the tribe of E'phraim. 6
70 out of the half-tribe of Manas'seh, Aner 6
71 were given out of the half-tribe of Manas'seh 6
72 out of the tribe of Is'sachar: Kedesh . . Dab'erath 6
74 out of the tribe of Asher: Mashal . . Abdon 6
76 out of the tribe of Naph'tali: Kedesh 6
77 were allotted out of the tribe of Zeb'ulun 6
78 out of the tribe of Reuben: Bezer . . Jahzah 6
80 out of the tribe of Gad: Ramoth in Gilead 6
11:18 drew water out of the well of Bethlehem 6
23 and snatched the spear out of the Egyptian's hand 6
15:29 Michal . . looked out of the window 1
18: 1 its villages out of the hand of the Philistines. 6
2Ch 5: 2 to bring up the ark . . out of the city of David 6
12:13 out of all the tribes of Israel to put his name 6
13:11 set out the showbread on the table of pure gold *
15:17 the high places were not taken out of Israel. 6
19: 2 Because of this, wrath has gone out against you *
3 for you destroyed the Ashe'rahs out of the land 6
30:25 whole assembly that came out of Israel 6
25 sojourners who came out of the land of Israel 6
32:13 at all able to deliver their lands out of my hand? 6
15 How . . will your God deliver you out of my hand!' 6
33: 7 I have chosen out of all the tribes of Israel 6
Ezr 2: 1 people . . who came up out of the captivity 6
5:14 Nebuchadnez'zar had taken out of the temple 12
14 Cyrus the king took out of the temple of Babylon 12
6: 5 took out of the temple that is in Jerusalem 12
11 beam shall be pulled out of his house 12
7:20 may provide it out of the king's treasury. 12
10: 1 great assembly . . gathered to him out of Israel; 6
Neh 1: 2 Hana'ni . . came with certain men out of Judah; 6

4: 2 revive the stones out of the heaps of rubbish 6
6: 8 for you are inventing them out of your own mind. 6
7: 6 came up out of the captivity of those exiles 6
9: 7 bring him forth out of Ur of the Chalde'ans 6
18 'This is your God who brought you up out of Egypt,' 6
11: 1 lots to bring one out of ten to live in Jerusalem 6
13: 8 furniture of Tobi'ah out of the chamber. 2
Job 5: 5 the hungry eat, and he takes it even out of thorns; 6
8:10 and utter words out of their understanding? 6
19 out of the earth others will spring. 6
9: 6 who shakes the earth out of its place 6
10: 7 there is none to deliver out of thy hand? 6
12:22 He uncovers the deeps out of darkness 6
14: 4 Who can bring a clean thing out of an unclean? 6
12 he will not awake, or be roused out of his sleep. 6
15:22 not believe that he will return out of darkness 6
18: 4 or the rock be removed out of its place? 6
20: 3 out of my understanding a spirit answers me. 6
15 God casts them out of his belly. 6
25 It is drawn forth and comes out of his body 6
25 the glittering point comes out of his gall; 6
24:12 From out of the city the dying groan 6
27:21 he is gone; it sweeps him out of his place. 6
28: 2 Iron is taken out of the earth 6
5 As for the earth, out of it comes bread; 6
30: 8 they have been whipped out of the land. 6
36:16 He also allured you out of distress 6
37: 1 my heart trembles, and leaps out of its place. 6
22 Out of the north comes golden splendor; 6
38: 1 Then the LORD answered Job out of the whirlwind 6
13 the wicked be shaken out of it? 6
40: 6 Then the LORD answered Job out of the whirlwind 6
41:19 Out of his mouth go flaming torches; 6
20 Out of his nostrils comes forth smoke 6
Ps 14: 7 deliverance for Israel would come out of Zion! 6
18:12 Out of the brightness before him there broke 6
45 came trembling out of their fastnesses. 6
25:22 Redeem Israel, O God, out of all his troubles. 6
31:12 I have passed out of mind like one who is dead; 6
34: 6 heard him, and saved him out of all his troubles. 6
17 and delivers them out of all their troubles. 6
19 but the LORD delivers him out of them all. 6
40: 2 out of the miry bog, and set my feet upon a rock 6
50: 2 Out of Zion, the perfection of beauty, God shines 6
78:16 He made streams come out of the rock 6
80: 8 Thou didst bring a vine out of Egypt; 6
81:10 who brought you up out of the land of Egypt. 6
94:12 O LORD, and whom thou dost teach out of thy law 6
107:41 he raises up the needy out of affliction 6
118: 5 Out of my distress I called on the LORD; 6
119:18 that I may behold wondrous things out of thy law. 6
43 take not the word of truth utterly out of my mouth 6
130: 1 Out of the depths I cry to thee, O LORD! 6
142: 7 Bring me out of prison, that I may give thanks 6
143:11 In thy righteousness bring me out of trouble! 6
Prv 2:22 treacherous will be rooted out of it. 6
21:23 keeps his mouth . . keeps himself out of trouble. 6
Ecc 8:10 they used to go in and out of the holy place 6
Isa 2: 3 For out of Zion shall go forth the law 6
11: 1 of Jesse, and a branch shall grow out of his roots. 6
13:13 and the earth will be shaken out of its place 6
14:31 For smoke comes out of the north 6
24:18 he who climbs out of the pit shall be caught 6
26:21 the LORD is coming forth out of his place 6
29: 4 and your speech shall whisper out of the dust. 6
18 out of their . . darkness the eyes of the blind 6
30:14 or to dip up water out of the cistern. 6
36:18 his land out of the hand of the king of Assyria? 6
19 Have they delivered Sama'ria out of my hand? 6
20 have delivered their countries out of my hand 6
20 the LORD should deliver Jerusalem out of my hand?' 6
37:32 for out of Jerusalem shall go forth a remnant 6
32 and out of Mount Zion a band of survivors. 6
38: 6 this city out of the hand of the king of Assyria 6
53: 2 a young plant, and like a root out of dry ground; 6
8 that he was cut off out of the land of the living 6
59:21 my words . . shall not depart out of your mouth 6
21 of your mouth, or out of the mouth of your children 6
21 or out of the mouth of your children's children 6
63:11 up out of the sea the shepherds of his flock? 6
Jer 1:14 Out of the north evil shall break forth 6
6: 1 for evil looms out of the north 6
10:22 a great commotion out of the north country 6
11: 7 when I brought them up out of the land of Egypt 6
15: 1 Send them out of my sight, and let them go! 7
21 I will deliver you out of the hand of the wicked 6
16:13 therefore I will hurl you out of this land 7
14 the people of Israel out of the land of Egypt 6
15 the people of Israel out of the north country 6
15 out of all the countries where he had driven them 6
16 and every hill, and out of the clefts of the rocks. 6
17:22 And do not carry a burden out of your houses 6
23: 3 out of all the countries where I have driven them 6
7 the people of Israel out of the land of Egypt 6
8 the house of Israel out of the north country 6
8 out of all the countries where he had driven them 6
30: 7 yet he shall be saved out of it. 6
32: 4 shall not escape out of the hand of the Chalde'ans 6
38:10 and lift Jeremiah the prophet out of the cistern 6

13 with ropes and lifted him out of the cistern. 6
47: 2 Behold, waters are rising out of the north 6
48:44 he who climbs out of the pit shall be caught 6
50: 3 out of the north a nation has come up against her 6
51:48 come against them out of the north, says the LORD. 6
52:27 So Judah was carried captive out of its land. 7
Ezk 1: 4 behold, a stormy wind came out of the north 6
13 and out of the fire went forth lightning. 6
11: 7 you shall be brought forth out of the midst of it. 6
9 And I will bring you forth out of the midst of it 6
17 and assemble you out of the countries 6
19 I will take the stony heart out of their flesh 6
13: 2 say to those who prophesy out of their own minds 6
17 your people, who prophesy out of their own minds; 6
21 and deliver my people out of your hand 6
23 I will deliver my people out of your hand. 6
16: 5 of these things to you out of compassion for you; 3
20:34 and gather you out of the countries 6
41 and gather you out of the countries 6
21: 3 and will draw forth my sword out of its sheath 6
22:15 I will consume your filthiness out of you. 6
23:34 and pluck out your hair, and tear your breasts; ‡
24:10 boil well the flesh, and empty out the broth *
25: 7 and will make you perish out of the countries; 6
29: 4 I will draw you up out of the midst of your streams 6
32:21 with their helpers, out of the midst of Sheol 6
38:15 place out of the uttermost parts of the north 6
39: 3 make your arrows drop out of your right hand. 6
10 they will not need to take wood out of the field 6
10 out of the field or cut down any out of the forests 6
43: 6 I heard one speaking to me out of the temple; 6
46:16 a gift to any of his sons out of his inheritance 15
17 out of his inheritance to one of his servants 6
18 the people, thrusting them out of their property; 6
18 sons their inheritance out of his own property 6
47: 2 the water was coming out on the south side. 6
Dan 3:15 god that will deliver you out of my hands? 12
17 God . . will deliver us out of your hand, O king. 12
5: 2 vessels . . taken out of the temple in Jerusalem 12
3 vessels which had been taken out of the temple 12
6:23 commanded that Daniel be taken up out of the den. 12
23 Daniel was taken up out of the den, 12
7: 3 four great beasts came up out of the sea 12
17 four kings who shall arise out of the earth. 12
24 horns, out of this kingdom ten kings shall arise 12
8: 9 Out of one of them came forth a little horn 6
11:41 these shall be delivered out of his hand: Edom 6
Hos 2:10 and no one shall rescue her out of my hand. 6
11: 1 and out of Egypt I called my son. 6
Ams 2:10 Also I brought you up out of the land of Egypt 6
3: 1 family which I brought up out of the land of Egypt 6
6:10 take him up to bring the bones out of the house 6
9:15 plucked up out of the land which I have given them 7
Obd 1: 8 destroy the wise men out of Edom 6
8 out of Edom, and understanding out of Mount Esau? 6
Jon 2: 2 saying, "I called to the LORD, out of my distress 6
2 he answered me; out of the belly of Sheol I cried 6
4: 5 Then Jonah went out of the city and sat to the east 6
Mic 1: 3 behold, the LORD is coming forth out of his place 6
4: 2 For out of Zion shall go forth the law 6
7:17 shall come trembling out of their strongholds 6
Zec 4: 1 like a man that is wakened out of his sleep. 6
10: 4 Out of them shall come the cornerstone 6
4 out of them the tent peg, out of them the battle bow 6
4 out of them the tent peg, out of them the battle bow 6
4 of them the battle bow, out of them every ruler. 6
Mal 2: 3 I will put you out of my presence. *
Mat 2:15 spoken by the prophet, "Out of Egypt have I called 15
5:13 except to be thrown out and trodden under foot 20
7: 4 'Let me take the speck out of your eye,' 15
5 hypocrite, first take the log out of your own eye 15
5 to take the speck out of your brother's eye. 15
12:34 For out of the abundance of the heart 15
35 The good man out of his good treasure 15
35 and the evil man out of his evil treasure 15
13:41 and they will gather out of his kingdom 15
15:19 For out of the heart come evil thoughts, murder 15
21:16 Out of the mouth of babes and sucklings 15
39 they took him and cast him out of the vineyard 20
26:75 he went out and wept bitterly. 20
27:18 For he knew that it was out of envy 14
53 coming out of the tombs after his resurrection 15
Mrk 1:10 when he came up out of the water 15
45 but was out in the country 20
5: 2 there met him out of the tombs a man 15
10 not to send them out of the country. 20
7:15 the things which come out of a man are what defile 15
20 What comes out of a man is what defiles a man. 15
21 out of the heart of man, come evil thoughts 15
26 begged him to cast the demon out of her daughter. 15
8:23 led him out of the village 20
9: 7 a voice came out of the cloud 15
25 come out of him, and never enter him again. 15
11: 4 at the door out in the open street; 20
19 when evening came they went out of the city. 20
12: 8 and cast him out of the vineyard. 20
44 For they all contributed out of their abundance; 15
44 out of her poverty has put in everything she had 15
14:68 he went out into the gateway 20

15:10 For he perceived that it was out of envy 14
46 a tomb which had been hewn out of the rock 15
Lke 2: 8 there were shepherds out in the field *
35 thoughts out of many hearts may be revealed. 15
4:22 the gracious words which proceeded out of his mouth; 15
29 they rose up and put him out of the city 20
6:42 hypocrite, first take the log out of your own eye 15
45 The good man out of the good treasure of his heart 15
45 the evil man out of his evil treasure produces evil; 15
45 out of the abundance of the heart 15
8: 3 others, who provided for them out of their means. 15
9:35 a voice came out of the cloud, saying, "This is my Son 15
13:28 and you yourselves thrust out. 20
16: 4 when I am put out of the stewardship.' 15
19:22 I will condemn you out of your own mouth 15
20:15 they cast him out of the vineyard and killed him. 20
21: 4 for they all contributed out of their abundance 15
4 she out of her poverty put in all the living 15
21 let not those who are out in the country enter it; *
24:50 Then he led them out as far as Bethany 20
Joh 1:46 Can anything good come out of Nazareth? 15
2:15 he drove them all . . out of the temple; 15
4:30 They went out of the city and were coming to him. 15
7:38 'Out of his heart shall flow rivers 15
8:59 Jesus hid himself, and went out of the temple. 15
9:34 And they cast him out. 20
35 Jesus heard that they had cast him out 20
10: 9 and will go in and out and find pasture. 19
28 no one shall snatch them out of my hand. 15
29 no one is able to snatch them out of the Father's hand 15
11:43 Laz'arus, come out. 20
12:17 when he called Laz'arus out of the tomb 15
31 now shall the ruler of this world be cast out; 20
13: 1 to depart out of this world to the Father 15
15:19 I chose you out of the world 15
17: 6 the men whom thou gavest me out of the world 15
15 that thou shouldst take them out of the world 15
18:29 Pilate went out to them and said 20
19: 4 Pilate went out again, and said to them 20
4 See, I am bringing him out to you, that you may know 20
5 Jesus came out, wearing the crown of thorns 20
13 he brought Jesus out 20
20: 2 They have taken the Lord out of the tomb 15
Act 1: 9 a cloud took him out of their sight. 13
21 the Lord Jesus went in and out among us 19
4:15 had commanded them to go aside out of the council 20
7:10 rescued him out of all his afflictions 15
58 Then they cast him out of the city and stoned him; 20
8:39 when they came up out of the water 15
12:17 how the Lord had brought him out of the prison 15
13:17 with uplifted arm he led them out of it. 15
50 and drove them out of their district. 13
14:19 they stoned Paul and dragged him out of the city 20
15:14 to take out of them a people for his name. 15
16:30 brought them out and said 20
19:16 they fled out of that house naked and wounded. 15
21:30 seized Paul and dragged him out of the temple 20
22:18 Make haste and get quickly out of Jerusalem 15
Rom 9:21 to make out of the same lump one vessel for beauty 15
1Co 5:10 since then you would need to go out of the world. 15
2Co 2: 4 For I wrote you out of much affliction 15
4: 6 the God who said, "Let light shine out of darkness 15
8:11 completing it out of what you have. 15
12: 2 whether in the body or out of the body 17
3 whether in the body or out of the body 24
Eph 2: 4 out of the great love with which he loved us 14
4:29 Let no evil talk come out of your mouths 15
5:21 out of reverence for Christ. 18
Php 1:16 The latter do it out of love 15
17 the former proclaim Christ out of partisanship 15
2Th 2: 7 only he . . will do so until he is out of the way. 15
Heb 8: 9 to lead them out of the land of Egypt 15
11: 3 was made out of things which do not appear. 15
34 won strength out of weakness 13
1Pe 2: 9 called you out of darkness into . . light. 15
2Pe 3: 5 an earth formed out of water and by means of water 15
1Jn 4:18 but perfect love casts out fear. 20
3Jn 1:10 stops those . . and puts them out of the church. 15
Jde 1: 5 he who saved a people out of the land of Egypt 15
23 save some, by snatching them out of the fire; 15
Rev 3: 5 I will not blot his name out of the book of life; 15
12 the temple of my God; never shall he go out of it 20
12 city . . which comes down from my God out of heaven 15
16 I will spew you out of my mouth. 15
7: 4 sealed, out of every tribe of the sons of Israel 15
5 12,000 sealed out of the tribe of Judah 15
8 12,000 sealed out of the tribe of Benjamin. 15
14 they who have come out of the great tribulation; 15
11: 5 fire pours out from their mouth and consumes 15
12:15 The serpent poured water . . out of his mouth 15
13: 1 I saw a beast rising out of the sea 15
11 I saw another beast which rose out of the earth; 15
14:15 another angel came out of the temple, calling 15
17 another angel came out of the temple in heaven 15
18 Then another angel came out from the altar 15
15: 6 out of the temple came the seven angels 15
16:17 and a loud voice came out of the temple 13
18: 4 Come out of her, my people 15
21: 2 new Jerusalem, coming down out of heaven from God 15
10 Jerusalem coming down out of heaven from God 15
1Es 1:30 his servants took him out of the line of battle. 13
38 brought him up out of Egypt. 15
5: 7 who came up out of their sojourn in captivity 15
6:18 taken out of the house in Jerusalem 15
26 which Nebuchadnezzar took out of the house 15
29 out of the tribute of Coelesyria and Phoenicia 13
32 a beam should be taken out of his house 15
8:18 you may provide out of the royal treasury. 15
2Es 1: 7 not I who brought them out of the land of Egypt 25
7 out of the house of bondage? 25
2: 1 I brought this people out of bondage 25
31 I will bring them out of the hiding places 25
3:17 thou didst lead his descendants out of Egypt 26
7:62 if the mind is made out of the dust 25
138 if he did not give out of his goodness 25
9:21 and saved for myself one grape out of a cluster 25
21 and one plant out of a great forest. 25
11: 3 out of his wings there grew opposing wings 25
37 a creature . . was aroused out of the forest 25
12:31 the lion whom you saw rousing up out of the forest 25
13: 3 a man come up out of the heart of the sea ‡
5 the man who came up out of the sea. 25
27 fire and a storm coming out of his mouth 25
14: 1 behold, a voice came out of a bush opposite me 25
4 I sent him and led my people out of Egypt 25
16:28 For out of a city, ten shall be left 25
28 out of the field, two who have hidden themselves 26
72 and drive them out of their houses. 25
Tob 5:17 as he goes in and out before us? 16
Jdt 5: 4 why have they . . refused to come out and meet me? *
6: 5 take revenge on this race that came out of Egypt. 15
11 the slaves took him and led him out of the camp 20
12 they caught up their weapons and ran out of the city 20
7:13 to keep watch that not a man gets out of the city. 15
8:28 has been spoken out of a true heart 18
13:15 Then she took the head out of the bag and showed it 15
14: 2 let every valiant man . . go out of the city 20
16: 3 he has delivered me out of the hands of my pursuers 15
AEs 13:16 didst redeem for thyself out of the land of Egypt 15
14: 5 didst take Israel out of all the nations 15
Wis 11: 4 water was given them out of flinty rock 15
17 which created the world out of formless matter 15
15: 7 he fashions out of the same clay 15
19: 7 an unhindered way out of the Red Sea 15
7 a grassy plain out of the raging waves 15
Sir 11:12 he lifts him out of his low estate 15
17: 1 The Lord created man out of earth 15
45: 4 he chose him out of all mankind. 15
16 He chose him out of all the living 13
46: 8 out of 600,000 people on foot 13
20 lifted up his voice out of the earth in prophecy 15
47:21 a disobedient kingdom arose out of Ephraim. 15
50:27 who out of his heart poured forth wisdom. 13
Bar 1:20 he brought our fathers out of the land of Egypt 15
2:11 didst bring thy people out of the land of Egypt 15
24 bones . . would be brought out of their graves; 15
Aza 1:26 and drove the fiery flame out of the furnace 15
Sus 1:61 out of their own mouths Daniel had convicted 15
1Mc 2:48 rescued the law out of the hands of the Gentiles 15
3: 8 he destroyed the ungodly out of the land; 15
45 not one of her children went in or out 16
4:19 a detachment appeared, coming out of the hills. 15
5:59 Gorgias and his men came out of the city 15
9:73 he destroyed the ungodly out of Israel. 15
10:40 15,000 shekels of silver . . out of the king's revenues 13
13: 6 the nations have gathered together out of hatred 23
48 He cast out of it all uncleanness 15
14:36 so that the Gentiles were put out of the country 15
16: 4 John chose out of the country 20,000 warriors 15
2Mc 1:11 Having been saved by God out of grave dangers 15
3:18 People also hurried out of their houses 15
19 while others peered out of the windows. 14
7:28 God did not make them out of things that existed. 15
9: 7 so it came about that he fell out of his chariot 13
10: 3 striking fire out of flint 15
3Mc 4:11 to those from the city going out into the country 22
4Mc 5:13 any transgression that arises out of compulsion. 14
6:12 At that point, partly out of pity for his old age *
13 partly out of sympathy 18
13 partly out of admiration for his endurance 18
17 out of cowardice we feign a role unbecoming to us! *
8:12 to persuade them out of fear 14
15:11 to suffer with them out of love for her children 21

out *See also* beat, blot, break, breathe, bring, bulge, call, carry, carve, cast, cleanse, clear, come, count, cry, cut, dash, deal, deck, dig, dip, drag, drain, draw, drive, empty, fall, fill, find, flee, flow, follow, get, give, go, gouge, grow, gush, hammer, hasten, hew, hire, hold, hurl, hurry, jut, knock, lay, lead, leap, leave, let, lift, live, look, march, mark, measure, mete, move, parcel, pass, pay, peer, pick, pluck, point, portion, pour, press, proceed, pull, purge, put, quarry, reach, ride, rinse, root, run, rush, sally, scrape, search, seek, send, set, shake, shine, shout, shut, single, sling, slip, speak, spew, spit, spread, spy, step, stick, strain, stream, stretch, strike, sure, swell, take, tear, think, thresh, throw, thrust, tire, trace, tread, trick, turn, vomit, wear, weep, weigh, wipe, work, write.

outbid 1. ὑπερβάλλω
2Mc 4:24 outbidding Jason by 300 talents of silver. 1

outcast 1. נדח
Deu 30: 4 If your outcasts are in the uttermost parts 1
Ps 147: 2 LORD . . gathers the outcasts of Israel. 1
Isa 11:12 and will assemble the outcasts of Israel 1
16: 3 hide the outcasts, betray not the fugitive; 1
4 let the outcasts of Moab sojourn among you; 1
56: 8 the Lord GOD, who gathers the outcasts of Israel 1
Jer 30:17 because they have called you an outcast 1
Zep 3:19 And I will save the lame and gather the outcast 1

outcast *See also* keep.

outcome 1. אַחֲרִית 2. ἔκβασις 3. τέλος 4. χωρέω
Isa 41:22 consider them, that we may know their outcome; 1
Heb 13: 7 consider the outcome of their life 2
1Pe 1: 9 As the outcome of your faith you obtain 3
Wis 8: 8 the outcome of seasons and times. 2
2Mc 3:40 This was the outcome of the episode 4

outcry 1. זְעָקָה 2. צְוָחָה 3. צְעָקָה 4. κραυγή
Gen 18:20 Because the outcry against Sodom and Gomor'rah 1
21 have done altogether according to the outcry 3
19:13 to destroy this place, because the outcry 3
1Sm 4:14 When Eli heard the sound of the outcry, he said 3
Neh 5: 1 Now there arose a great outcry of the people 3
6 I was very angry when I heard their outcry 1
Isa 24:11 There is an outcry in the streets for lack of wine; 2
1Es 5:63 came . . with outcries and loud weeping 4

outdo 1. προηγέομαι
Rom 12:10 outdo one another in showing honor. 1

outer 1. חוּץ 2. חִיצוֹן 3. מִחוּץ 4. פָּנִים 5. ἔξω 6. ἐξώτερος 7. πρῶτος
1Kg 6:29 all the walls . . in the inner and outer rooms. 2
30 The floor . . in the inner and outer rooms. 2
2Kg 16:18 and the outer entrance for the king he removed 2
2Ch 33:14 built an outer wall for the city of David 2
Est 6: 4 just entered the outer court of the king's palace 2
Job 41:13 Who can strip off his outer garment? 4
Ezk 10: 5 the cherubim was heard as far as the outer court 2
40:17 Then he brought me into the outer court; 2
19 lower gate to the outer front of the inner court 3
20 toward the north, belonging to the outer court. 2
31 Its vestibule faced the outer court 2
34 Its vestibule faced the outer court 2
37 Its vestibule faced the outer court 2
41: 9 The thickness of the outer wall of the side 1
15 and the inner room and the outer vestibule 6
42: 3 the pavement which belonged to the outer court 2
6 pillars like the pillars of the outer court; 6
7 parallel to the chambers, toward the outer court 2
8 chambers on the outer court were 50 cubits 2
9 as one enters them from the outer court 2
14 they shall not go out of it into the outer court 2
44: 1 me back to the outer gate of the sanctuary 2
19 they go out into the outer court to the people 2
46:20 not to bring them out into the outer court 2
21 Then he brought me forth to the outer court 2
47: 2 and led me round on the outside to the outer gate 1
Mat 8:12 kingdom will be thrown into the outer darkness; 6
22:13 and cast him into the outer darkness; 6
25:30 into the outer darkness 6
2Co 4:16 Though our outer nature is wasting away 5
Heb 9: 2 a tent was prepared, the outer one 7
6 the priests go continually into the outer tent 7
8 as long as the outer tent is still standing 7

outfit
Ezk 12: 7 in the dark, carrying my outfit upon my shoulder *

outflank 1. ὑπερκεράω
Jdt 15: 5 those in Gilead and in Galilee outflanked them 1
1Mc 7:46 they outflanked the enemy 1

outflow of press 1. דֶּמַע
Exd 22:29 offer . . from the outflow of your presses. 1

outgoing 1. מוֹצָא
Ps 65: 8 thou makest the outgoings of the morning 1

outlay 1. אֲשֶׁר יצא
2Kg 12:12 and for any outlay upon the repairs of the house. 1

outlet 1. מוֹצָא 2. διέξοδος
2Ch 32:30 closed the upper outlet of the waters of Gihon 1
Sir 25:25 Allow no outlet to water 2

outline 1. ὑπογραμμός
2Mc 2:28 arriving at the outlines of the condensation. 1

outlive 1. ארך יָמִים אַחֲרֵי
Jos 24:31 all the days of the elders who outlived Joshua 1
Jdg 2: 7 all the days of the elders who outlived Joshua, 1

outlying part 1.קָצָה
Num11: 1 consumed some outlying parts of the camp. 1

outmost 1.קִיצוֹן 2.קָצָה
Exd 26: 4 loops of blue on the edge of the outmost curtain 2
4 make loops on the edge of the outmost curtain 1
10 the curtain that is outmost in one set 1
10 the curtain which is outmost in the second set. •
36:11 of blue on the edge of the outmost curtain 2
11 he made them on the edge of the outmost curtain 1
17 50 loops on the edge of the outmost curtain 1

outpost 1.קָצָה 2.προφυλακή
Jdg 7:11 he went down . . to the outposts of the armed men 1
Jdt 14: 2 going down . . against the Assyrian outpost 2
1Mc 12:27 he stationed outposts around the camp. 2

outpoured 1.שפך
Ps 79:10 avenging of the outpoured blood of thy servants 1

outpouring 1.שפך
Ezk 9: 8 in the outpouring of thy wrath upon Jerusalem? 1

output 1.ἐργασία
Sir 38:29 all his output is by number. 1

outrage 1.αἰκία 2.ἐνυβρίζω 3.ὕβρις
Heb 10:29 outraged the Spirit of grace 2
Wis 4:18 and an outrage among the dead for ever 3
2Mc 8:17 keeping before their eyes the lawless outrage 3
3Mc 4:14 tortured with the outrages that he had ordered 1
outrage *See also* commit, suffer.

outrageous 1.πάνδεινος 2.πλημμελής
Sir 10: 7 injustice is outrageous to both. 2
4Mc 4: 7 considering it outrageous 1
outrageous *See also* treatment.
outrageously *See* treat.

outright
Ezk 9: 6 slay old men outright, young men and maidens •

outrun 1.עבר 2.προτρέχω τάχιον
2Sm 18:23 Then Ahi'ma-az ran . . and outran the Cushite. 1
Joh 20: 4 the other disciple outran Peter 2

outside 1.בַּחוּץ 2.חוּץ 3.חִיצוֹן 4.פֶּתַח מִחוּץ 5.לַחוּץ 6.מִחוּץ 7.מִהַחוּץ 8.מִפָּה 9.ἐκτός 10.ἔξω 11.ἔξωθεν 12.κύκλος
Gen 9:22 of his father, and told his two brothers outside. 1
15: 5 he brought him outside and said 2
19:16 brought him forth and set him outside the city. 7
24:11 he made the camels kneel down outside the city 7
31 blessed of the LORD; why do you stand outside? 1
Exd 12:46 carry forth any of the flesh outside the house; 2
26:35 you shall set the table outside the veil 7
27:21 In the tent of meeting, outside the veil 7
29:14 you shall burn with fire outside the camp; 7
33: 7 take the tent and pitch it outside the camp 7
7 the tent of meeting, which was outside the camp. 7
40:22 north side of the tabernacle, outside the veil 7
Lev 4:12 whole bull he shall carry forth outside the camp 7
21 he shall carry forth the bull outside the camp 7
6:11 carry forth the ashes outside the camp 7
8:17 the bull . . he burned with fire outside the camp 7
9:11 the skin he burned with fire outside the camp 7
13:46 dwell alone in a habitation outside the camp 7
14: 8 but shall dwell outside his tent seven days 7
40 throw them into an unclean place outside the city 7
41 shall pour into an unclean place outside the city 7
16:27 bull . . shall be carried forth outside the camp 7
17: 3 If any man . . kills it outside the camp 7
24: 3 Outside the veil of the testimony, in the tent 7
Num 5: 3 male and female, putting them outside the camp 7
4 Israel did so, and drove them outside the camp. 7
12:14 Let her be shut up outside the camp seven days 7
15 Miriam was shut up outside the camp seven days; 7
15:35 stone him with stones outside the camp. 7
36 congregation brought him outside the camp 7
19: 3 she shall be taken outside the camp 7
9 deposit them outside the camp in a clean place; 7
31:13 went forth to meet them outside the camp. 2
19 Encamp outside the camp seven days; 2
35: 5 you shall measure, outside the city 7
27 outside the bounds of his city of refuge 7
Deu 23:10 not clean . . then he shall go outside the camp 7
12 place outside the camp and you shall go out to it; 7
13 when you sit down outside, you shall dig a hole 2
24:11 stand outside, and the man to whom you make 2
25: 5 wife . . shall not be married outside the family 2
Jos 6:23 and set them outside the camp of Israel. 7
Jdg 12: 9 30 daughters he gave in marriage outside his clan 2
9 and 30 daughters he brought in from outside 2
1Kg 6: 6 around the outside of the house he made offsets 2
8: 8 but they could not be seen from outside; 2
21:13 So they took him outside the city, and stoned him 7
2Kg 4: 3 Go outside, borrow vessels of all your neighbors 2
10:24 Now Jehu had stationed 80 men outside 1
23: 4 he burned them outside Jerusalem in the fields 7
6 he brought out . . outside Jerusalem to the brook 7
1Ch 26:29 appointed to outside duties for Israel 3
2Ch 5: 9 but they could not be seen from outside; 2
24: 8 set it outside the gate of the house of the LORD. 2
32: 3 water of the springs that were outside the city; 7
5 outside it he built another wall; 5
33:15 he threw them outside of the city. 2
Neh 11:16 who were over the outside work of the house of God; 3
13:20 lodged outside Jerusalem once or twice. 7
Prv 22:13 The sluggard says, "There is a lion outside! 2
24:27 Prepare your work outside, get everything ready 2
Sng 8: 1 If I met you outside, I would kiss you 1
Jer 21: 4 Chalde'ans . . besieging you outside the walls; 7
Ezk 40: 5 a wall all around the outside of the temple area 7
40 on the outside of the vestibule at the entrance 4
41 four tables on the outside of the side of the gate 8
41:17 even to the inner room, and on the outside. 2
25 of wood in front of the vestibule outside. 6
42: 7 was a wall outside parallel to the chambers 5
10 where the outside wall begins. •
43:21 it shall be burnt . . outside the sacred area. 7
47: 2 and led me round on the outside to the outer gate 2
Mat 12:46 his mother and his brothers stood outside 10
23:25 you cleanse the outside of the cup 11
26 that the outside also may be clean. 9
26:69 Now Peter was sitting outside in the courtyard. 10
Mrk 3:31 standing outside they sent to him and called 10
32 Your mother and your brothers are outside 10
4:11 for those outside everything is in parables; 10
7:15 there is nothing outside a man 11
18 into a man from outside cannot defile him 11
Lke 1:10 praying outside at the hour of incense 10
8:20 your brothers are standing outside 10
11:39 Now you Pharisees cleanse the outside of the cup 11
40 Did not he who made the outside make the inside 11
13:25 begin to stand outside and to knock at the door 10
Joh 18:16 while Peter stood outside at the door 10
20:11 Mary stood weeping outside the tomb 10
Act 5:34 ordered the men to be put outside for a while. 10
9:40 Peter put them all outside and knelt down 10
16:13 we went outside the gate to the riverside 10
21: 5 till we were outside the city 10
1Co 5:13 God judges those outside 10
6:18 is outside the body 9
Heb 13:11 are burned outside the camp. 10
12 Jesus also suffered outside the gate 10
13 Therefore let us go forth to him outside the camp 10
Rev 11: 2 do not measure the court outside the temple; 11
14:20 the wine press was trodden outside the city 11
22:15 Outside are the dogs and sorcerers 10
Jdt 6: 1 the disturbance made by the men outside the council 12
10:18 she waited outside the tent of Holofernes 10
13: 1 Bagoas closed the tent from outside 11
3 told her maid to stand outside the bedchamber 10
Sir 21:23 a cultivated man remains outside. 10
Bel 1: 7 this is but clay inside and brass outside 11
11 Behold, we are going outside 10
1Mc 15:30 outside the borders of Judea; 9
2Mc 1:16 threw them to the people outside. 10
outside *See also* go, put.

just outside 1.παρά
1Mc 7:47 and displayed them just outside Jerusalem. 1

outside one's control 1.ἀνυπότακτος
Heb 2: 8 he left nothing outside his control 1

outside the law 1.ἄνομος
1Co 9:21 To those outside the law I became as one outside 1
21 those outside the law I became as one outside the law 1
21 that I might win those outside the law. 1

outsider 1.זוּר 2.ἀλλογενής 3.ἀλλότριος 4.ἐκτός 5.ἔξωθεν 6.ἰδιώτης 7.ὁ ἔξω
Exd 29:33 but an outsider shall not eat of them 1
30:33 whoever puts any of it on an outsider shall be cut 1
Lev 22:10 An outsider shall not eat of a holy thing 1
12 If a priest's daughter is married to an outsider 1
13 yet no outsider shall eat of it 1
1Co 5:12 For what have I to do with judging outsiders? 7
14:16 how can any one in the position of an outsider say 6
23 outsiders or unbelievers enter 6
24 an unbeliever or outsider enters 6
Col 4: 5 Conduct yourselves wisely toward outsiders 7
1Th 4:12 that you may command the respect of outsiders 7
1Ti 3: 7 moreover he must be well thought of by outsiders 5
Sir 0: 1 help the outsiders by both speaking and writing, 4
45:13 No outsider ever put them on 2
18 Outsiders conspired against him, and envied him 3

outskirts 1.קָצָה 2.קָצֶה
Jos 18:15 side begins at the outskirts of Kir'iath-je'arim; 2
Jdg 7:17 when I come to the outskirts of the camp, do as I do. 2
19 Gideon . . came to the outskirts of the camp 2
1Sm 9:27 they were going down to the outskirts of the city 2
14: 2 Saul was staying in the outskirts of Gib'e-ah 2
Job 26:14 Lo, these are but the outskirts of his ways; 1

outspoken 1.παρρησία
3Mc 4: 1 enmity . . was now made evident and outspoken. 1

outspread 1.מֻטָּה
Isa 8: 8 outspread wings . . fill the breadth of your land 1

outstretched 1.נטה 2.פרשׂ 3.προτείνω 4.ὑψηλός
Exd 6: 6 I will redeem you with an outstretched arm 1
Deu 4:34 by a mighty hand and an outstretched arm 1
5:15 with a mighty hand and an outstretched arm; 1
7:19 saw, the . . mighty hand, and the outstretched arm 1
9:29 bring out . . by thy outstretched arm.' 1
11: 2 consider . . mighty hand and his outstretched arm 1
26: 8 with a mighty hand and an outstretched arm 1
1Kg 8:42 and thy mighty hand, and of thy outstretched arm) 1
54 knelt with hands outstretched toward heaven; 2
2Kg 17:36 with great power and with an outstretched arm; 1
2Ch 6:32 for the sake of . . hand, and thy outstretched arm 1
Ps 136:12 with a strong hand and an outstretched arm 1
Isa 3:16 haughty and walk with outstretched necks 1
Jer 21: 5 will fight against you with outstretched hand 1
27: 5 I who by my great power and my outstretched arm 1
32:17 thy great power and by thy outstretched arm! 1
21 with a strong hand and outstretched arm 1
Ezk 20:33 with a mighty hand and an outstretched arm 1
34 with a mighty hand and an outstretched arm 1
Bar 2:11 with great power and outstretched arm 4
2Mc 15:12 was praying with outstretched hands 3

outstrip 1.מהר
Isa 49:17 Your builders outstrip your destroyers 1

outward 1.חוּץ 2.ἔξωθεν
Num35: 4 shall reach from the wall of the city outward 1
1Pe 3: 3 Let not yours be the outward adorning 2
outward *See also* appearance.

outwardly 1.ἔξωθεν
Mat 23:27 which outwardly appear beautiful 1
28 So you also outwardly appear righteous to men 1

outweigh 1.יָקָר מִן 2.ἀνθίστημι
Ecc 10: 1 so a little folly outweighs wisdom and honor. 1
Sir 8: 2 lest his resources outweigh yours 2

outwit 1.גנב לֵב 2.נשׁא 3.στρατηγέω
Gen 31:20 Jacob outwitted Laban the Aramean, in that he did 1
Ps 89:22 The enemy shall not outwit him 2
2Mc 14:31 he had been cleverly outwitted by the man 3

oven 1.תַּנּוּר 2.κλίβανος
Exd 8: 3 frogs which shall come up . . into your ovens 1
Lev 2: 4 bring a cereal offering baked in the oven 1
7: 9 every cereal offering baked in the oven 1
11:35 whether oven or stove, it shall be broken 1
26:26 ten women shall bake your bread in one oven 1
Ps 21: 9 make them as a blazing oven when you appear. 1
Lam 5:10 Our skin is hot as an oven with . . heat of famine. 1
Hos 7: 4 they are like a heated oven 1
6 For like an oven their hearts burn with intrigue; 1
7 All of them are hot as an oven 1
Mal 4: 1 For behold, the day comes, burning like an oven 1
Mat 6:30 alive and tomorrow is thrown into the oven 2
Lke 12:28 tomorrow is thrown into the oven 2

over 1.אֶל 2.בְּ 3.בְּעַד 4.כְּ 5.לְ 6.לְנֶגֶד 7.לִפְנֵי 8.מִן 9.מֵעַל לְ 10.עַד 11.עדף 12.עַל פְּנֵי 13.עַל רֹאשׁ 14.בְּ(A) 15.לְ(A) 16.עַל(A) 17.διά 18.εἰς 19.ἐν 20.ἐπάνω 21.ἐπί 22.κατά 23.πέραν 24.περί 25.πλεονάζω 26.πληρόω 27.προΐστημι 28.πρός 29.ὑπέρ 30.casus 31.in 32.propter 33.super
Gen 1:18 to rule over the day and over the night 2
18 to rule over the day and over the night 2
26 let them have dominion over the fish of the sea 2
26 have dominion . . over the birds of the air 2
26 have dominion . . over the cattle 2
26 have dominion . . over all the earth 2
26 dominion . . over every creeping thing 2
28 and have dominion over the fish of the sea 2
28 and have dominion . . over the birds of the air 2
28 dominion . . over every living thing that moves 2
21: 6 every one who hears will laugh over me. 5
27:29 Be lord over your brothers 5
36:31 before any king reigned over the Israelites. 5
37: 8 Or are you indeed to have dominion over us? 2
41:57 the famine was severe over all the earth. 2
45: 8 made me . . ruler over all the land of Egypt. 2
26 Joseph is . . ruler over all the land of Egypt. 2
Exd 14: 4 I will get glory over Pharaoh and all his host; 2
17 I will get glory over Pharaoh and all his host 2
18 I have gotten glory over Pharaoh, his chariots 2
16:18 he that gathered much had nothing over 11
Lev 25:43 You shall not rule over him with harshness 2
46 over your brethren the people of Israel 2
46 you shall not rule, one over another 2

26:17 those who hate you shall rule over you 2
37 They shall stumble over one another 2
Num 3:32 chief over the leaders of the Levites •
11:16 whom you know to be . . officers over them; •
31:48 officers who were over the thousands of the army 5
Deu 15: 6 rule over many nations, but they shall not rule 2
6 rule . . nations, but they shall not rule over you. 2
Jos 10:12 when the LORD gave the Amorites over to . . Israel; 7
12: 5 and ruled over Mount Hermon and Sal'ecah 2
5 ruled over . . and over half of Gilead •
Jdg 3:22 after the blade, and the fat closed over the blade 3
8:22 Then the men of Israel said to Gideon, "Rule over us 2
23 Gideon said to them, "I will not rule over you 2
23 not rule over you, and my son will not rule over you; 2
23 not rule over you; the LORD will rule over you. 2
9: 2 that all 70 of the sons of Jerubba'al rule over you 2
2 70 . . rule over you, or that one rule over you?' 2
10:16 he became indignant over the misery of Israel. 2
18 He shall be head over all the inhabitants 5
11: 8 be our head over all the inhabitants of Gilead. 5
9 the Ammonites, and the LORD gives them over to me 7
14: 4 time the Philistines had dominion over Israel. 2
15:11 not know that the Philistines are rulers over us? 2
1Sm 8: 1 Samuel . . made his sons judges over Israel. 5
9:17 He it is who shall rule over my people. 2
10: 1 anointed you to be prince over his people Israel? 21
1 And you shall reign over the people of the LORD 19
13:13 established your kingdom over Israel for ever. 1
15:35 did not see Saul . . but Samuel grieved over Saul. 1
16: 1 How long will you grieve over Saul 1
17:39 And David girded his sword over his armor 9
50 David prevailed over the Philistine 8
51 Then David ran and stood over the Philistine 1
22:14 king's son-in-law, and captain over your bodyguard •
26:15 have you not kept watch over your lord the king? 1
30:16 behold, they were spread abroad over all the land 12
2Sm 1:24 Ye daughters of Israel, weep over Saul 1
2: 9 he made him king over Gilead and the Ash'urites 1
3:21 you may reign over all that your heart desires. 2
8:18 Benai'ah . . was over the Cher'ethites ‡
18:33 and went up to the chamber over the gate, and wept; •
20:21 his head shall be thrown to you over the wall. 3
23: 3 When one rules justly over men 2
23 And David set him over his bodyguard. 1
1Kg 4:21 Solomon ruled over all the kingdoms 2
24 he had dominion over all the region west 2
24 had dominion . . over all the kings west 2
8: 7 spread out their wings over the place of the ark 1
11:28 he gave him charge over all the forced labor 5
37 you shall reign over all that your soul desires 2
15: 9 Asa began to reign over Judah •
2Kg 2: 3 the LORD will take away your master from over you? 13
5 the LORD will take away your master from over you? 13
5:11 wave his hand over the place, and cure the leper. 1
9: 3 'Thus says the LORD, I anoint you king over Israel.' 1
6 I anoint you king over the people of the LORD 1
6 king over the people of the LORD, over Israel. 1
12 Thus says the LORD, I anoint you king over Israel.' 1
13:17 LORD's arrow . . the arrow of victory over Syria! 2
1Ch 1:43 the land of Edom before any king reigned over 5
12:14 the lesser over 100 and the greater over 1,000. 5
14 the lesser over 100 and the greater over 1,000. 5
23 to turn the kingdom of Saul over to him 1
29: 6 and the officers over the king's work. 5
12 and thou rulest over all. 2
2Ch 4: 5 it held over 3,000 baths. •
8:10 who exercised authority over the people. 2
9:26 he ruled over all the kings from the Euphra'tes 2
20: 6 not rule over all the kingdoms of the nations? 2
27 LORD had made them rejoice over their enemies. 8
23:14 the captains who were set over the army •
32:11 may give you over to die by famine and by thirst •
Ezr 4:20 ruled over the whole province Beyond the River 2
5: 1 the God of Israel, who was over them. 16
10:14 till the fierce wrath of our God over this matter 10
Neh 9:28 enemies, so that they had dominion over them; 2
37 power also over our bodies and over our cattle 2
11:22 singers, over the work of the house of God. 6
13: 4 appointed over the chambers of the house 2
Est 9: 1 enemies of . . hoped to get the mastery over them 2
1 the Jews should get the mastery over their foes 2
Job 34:13 Who gave him charge over the earth •
Ps 8: 6 given him dominion over the works of thy hands; 2
19:13 sins; let them not have dominion over me! 2
20: 5 May we shout for joy over your victory 2
22:17 they stare and gloat over me; 2
28 to the LORD, and he rules over the nations. 2
25: 2 let not my enemies exult over me. 5
29:10 The LORD sits enthroned over the flood; 5
30: 1 and hast not let my foes rejoice over me. 5
35:19 those rejoice over me who are wrongfully my foes 5
24 let them not rejoice over me! 5
37: 7 fret not yourself over him who prospers 2
7 over the man who carries out evil devices! 2
38:16 For I pray, "Only let them not rejoice over me 5
59:13 that men may know that God rules over Jacob 2
65: 3 When our transgressions prevail over us 8
66:12 thou didst let men ride over our heads; 5
103:19 his kingdom rules over all. 2
106:27 scattering them over the lands. 2
41 so that those who hated them ruled over them. 2
119:133 let no iniquity get dominion over me. 2
136: 8 the sun to rule over the day 2
9 the moon and stars to rule over the night 2
141: 3 Set a guard over my mouth, O LORD 5
Prv 4:19 they do not know over what they stumble. 2
17: 2 wisely will rule over a son who acts shamefully 2
19:10 much less for a slave to rule over princes. 2
22: 7 The rich rules over the poor 2
Ecc 3:19 and man has no advantage over the beasts; 8
4:16 the people; he was over all of them. 7
6: 8 what advantage has the wise man over the fool? 8
8: 8 power . . or authority over the day of death; 2
9 while man lords it over man to his hurt. 2
Isa 3: 4 boys . . princes, and babes shall rule over them. 2
12 are their oppressors, and women rule over them. 2
14: 2 captors, and rule over those who oppressed them. 2
16 who see you will stare at you, and ponder over you 1
19: 4 a fierce king will rule over them 2
23: 5 Egypt . . in anguish over the report about Tyre. 4
24:14 over the majesty of the LORD they shout 2
28:28 he drives his cart wheel over it with his horses •
34:11 and the plummet of chaos over its nobles. •
44:12 fashions it and works it over the coals; 2
63:19 like those over whom thou hast never ruled 2
Jer 15:20 they shall not prevail over you, for I am with you 5
29:26 charge in the house of the LORD over every madman 5
33:26 to rule over the seed of Abraham, Isaac, and Jacob. 1
41:18 king of Babylon had made governor over the land. 2
49:19 and I will appoint over her whomever I choose. 1
50:38 it is a land of images, and they are mad over idols. 2
44 I will appoint over her whomever I choose. 1
Lam 1: 7 foe gloated over her, mocking at her downfall. •
5: 8 Slaves rule over us; there is none to deliver us 2
18 Zion . . lies desolate; jackals prowl over it. 2
Ezk 7:16 all of them moaning, every one over his iniquity. 2
25: 3 Because you said, 'Aha!' over my sanctuary 1
3 over the land of Israel when it was made desolate 1
3 over the house of Judah when it went into exile; 1
27:31 they weep over you in bitterness of soul 1
29:15 they will never again rule over the nations. 2
34: 6 scattered, they wandered over all the mountains 2
35:15 As you rejoiced over the inheritance 5
37:22 one king shall be king over them all; 5
41: 6 stories, one over another, 30 in each story. 1
48: 1 border of Damascus over against Hamath 1
Dan 2:38 making you rule over them all-you are the head 14
39 kingdom of bronze . . rule over all the earth. 14
48 made him ruler over the whole province 16
48 chief prefect over all the wise men of Babylon. 16
49 and Abed'nego over the affairs of the province 16
3:12 appointed over the affairs of the province 16
27 not had any power over the bodies of those men; 14
4:16 let seven times pass over him. 16
17 sets over it the lowliest of men.' 16
23 with the beasts . . till seven times pass over 16
25 and seven times shall pass over you, 16
32 and seven times shall pass over you, 16
5:21 kingdom of men, and sets over it whom he will. 16
6: 1 Darius to set over the kingdom 120 satraps 16
2 to set . . over them three presidents, 16
3 king planned to set him over the whole kingdom. 16
7:21 horn made war with the saints, and prevailed over 15
11:39 shall make them rulers over many 2
Obd 1:12 you should not have gloated over . . your brother 2
12 you should not have rejoiced over the people 5
13 you should not have gloated over his disaster 2
Jon 2: 5 The waters closed in over me 10
4: 6 a plant, and made it come up over Jonah 9
Mic 7: 8 Rejoice not over me, O my enemy; 5
10 My eyes will gloat over her; 2
Nah 3: 3 bodies without end-they stumble over the bodies 2
Mat 2: 9 it came to rest over the place where the child 20
22 when he heard that Archela'us reigned over Judea •
10: 1 and gave them authority over unclean spirits •
18:13 if he finds it . . he rejoices over it 21
13 he rejoices . . more than over the 99 21
24:47 he will set him over all his possessions. 21
25:21 you have been faithful over a little 21
21 I will set you over much 21
23 you have been faithful over a little 21
23 I will set you over much 21
27:19 I have suffered much over him today in a dream. 17
37 over his head they put the charge against him 20
45 there was darkness over all the land 21
Mrk 6: 7 and gave them authority over the unclean spirits. •
10:42 those who are supposed to rule over the Gentiles •
15:33 there was darkness over the whole land 21
Lke 1:33 he will reign over the house of Jacob for ever; 21
2: 8 keeping watch over their flock by night. 21
4:25 when there came a great famine over all the land; 21
39 he stood over her and rebuked the fever 20
9: 1 gave them power and authority over all demons 21
10:19 authority . . over all the power of the enemy 20
11:44 men walk over them without knowing it. 20
12:14 who made me a judge or divider over you? 21
42 whom his master will set over his household 21
44 he will set him over all his possessions. 21
15: 7 more joy in heaven over one sinner who repents 21
7 more joy . . over one . . than over 99 21
10 there is joy . . over one sinner who repents. 21
18: 7 Will he delay long over them? 21
19:14 'We do not want this man to reign over us.' 21
17 you shall have authority over ten cities.' 20
19 he said . . 'And you are to be over five cities.' 20
27 who did not want me to reign over them 21
41 he drew near and saw the city he wept over it, 21
23:38 There was also an inscription over him 21
44 there was darkness over the whole land 21
Joh 3:25 a discussion arose . . over purifying. 24
7:43 there was a division among the people over him. 17
14:30 He has no power over me; 19
17: 2 since thou hast given him power over all flesh •
19:11 You would have no power over me 22
Act 7:10 who made him governor over Egypt 21
10 made him governor . . over all his household. 21
18 till there arose over Egypt another king 21
27 Who made you a ruler and a judge over us? 21
8: 2 made great lamentation over him. 21
9:25 and let him down over the wall 17
11:19 the persecution that arose over Stephen 21
28 there would be a great famine over all the world 21
12:18 no small stir . . over what had become of Peter. •
19:13 pronounce . . over those who had evil spirits 21
24:10 many years you have been judge over this nation •
Rom 5:14 death reigned . . even over those whose sins 21
9: 5 God who is over all be blessed for ever. 21
21 Has the potter no right over the clay •
32 They have stumbled over the stumbling stone •
14: 1 welcome him, but not for disputes over opinions. •
16:19 is known to all, so that I rejoice over you 21
2Co 3:13 not like Moses, who put a veil over his face 21
15 a veil lies over their minds; 21
8:15 He who gathered much had nothing over 25
12:21 I may have to mourn over many of those who sinned •
Gal 4:11 I am afraid I have labored over you in vain. 18
Eph 1:22 has made him the head over all things 29
3:13 not to lose heart over what I am suffering for you 19
1Th 5:12 are over you in the Lord and admonish you 27
Tit 3: 9 dissensions, and quarrels over the law •
Heb 3: 6 Christ was faithful over God's house as a son 21
10:21 a great priest over the house of God 21
11:21 bowing in worship over the head of his staff. 21
38 wandering over deserts and mountains 21
13:17 for they are keeping watch over your souls 29
Jas 2: 7 that honorable name which was invoked over you? 21
5: 7 waits for the . . fruit . . being patient over it 21
14 and let them pray over him, anointing him 21
Rev 2:26 I will give him power over the nations 21
6: 8 they were given power over a fourth of the earth 21
9:11 They have as king over them the angel 21
10: 1 mighty angel . . with a rainbow over his head 21
11: 2 for it is given over to the nations •
2 they will trample over the holy city for 42 months. •
6 power over the waters to turn them into blood 21
10 rejoice over them and make merry and exchange 21
13: 7 authority was given it over every tribe 21
14:18 the angel who has power over fire 21
16: 9 God who had power over these plagues 21
17:13 give over their power and authority to the beast; •
17 and giving over their royal power to the beast •
18 the great city which has dominion over the kings 21
18: 9 the kings . . will weep and wail over her 21
20 Rejoice over her, O heaven, O saints 21
20: 3 into the pit, and shut it and sealed it over him 20
6 Over such the second death has no power 21
9 And they marched up over the broad earth 21
1Es 3:12 truth is victor over all things. 29
5: 4 in the tribes, over their groups: 21
6: 5 the providence of the Lord was over the captives; 21
17 Cyrus reigned over the country of Babylonia •
8:72 round me, as I mourned over this iniquity 21
9: 2 he was mourning over the great iniquities 29
13 the wrath of the Lord over this matter. •
2Es 5:33 Are you greatly disturbed in mind over Israel? 31
6:54 over these thou didst place Adam 33
54 as ruler over all the works which thou hadst made; 33
57 domineer over us and devour us. •
7:60 I will rejoice over the few who shall be saved 33
61 I will not grieve over the multitude of those 33
131 joy over those to whom salvation is assured. 33
8: 6 O Lord who are over us, grant to thy servant 33
39 will rejoice over the creation of the righteous 33
39 I will rejoice . . over their pilgrimage also •
45 No, O Lord who art over us! 33
9:45 And I rejoiced greatly over him 33
10: 9 to mourn over so many who have come into being 30
39 and mourned greatly over Zion. 32
11: 2 and behold, he spread his wings over all the earth 31
5 to reign over the earth 33
5 the earth and over those who dwell in it. 33
12 and it reigned over all the earth. 33
32 and it had greater power over the world than all •
34 also ruled over the earth and its inhabitants. 33
40 have held sway over the world with much terror •
40 and over all the earth with grievous oppression; •
13:30 bewilderment of mind shall come over those 33

15:29 their hissing shall spread over the earth 33
44 all who are about her shall wail over her. •
16:14 shall not return until they come over the earth. 33
52 and righteousness will reign over us. 31
58 has suspended the earth over the water; 33
68 the burning wrath . . is kindled over you 33
Tob 1:21 over all the accounts of his kingdom 21
21 he appointed Ahikar . . over all the accounts 21
3: 4 thou gavest us over to plunder, captivity, and death; 18
13:14 those who grieved over all your afflictions 21
14: 4 Our brethren will be scattered over the earth 19
15 Before his death he rejoiced over Nineveh. 21
Jdt 1: 1 who ruled over the Assyrians •
1 who ruled over the Medes in Ecbatana– •
5: 3 Who rules over them as king, leading their army? 21
7: 3 and they spread out in breadth over Dothan 21
7 seized them and set guards of soldiers over them •
11: 3 tell me why you . . have come over to us 28
14: 2 set a captain over them 18
3 Then fear will come over them 21
15: 2 Fear and trembling came over them 21
AEs 13: 9 O Lord, Lord, King who rulest over all things •
14:19 O God, whose might is over all 21
16:21 God, who rules over all things •
Wis 3: 8 the Lord will reign over them for ever. •
9 he watches over his holy ones. •
4:15 he watches over his holy ones. 19
6:21 O monarchs over the peoples, honor wisdom •
9: 7 to be judge over thy sons and daughters. •
10:14 and authority over his masters •
12:16 sovereignty over all causes thee to spare all. •
14:26 confusion over what is good •
16:13 For thou hast power over life and death •
Sir 1:29 keep watch over your lips. 19
3: 2 the right of the mother over her sons. 21
8: 7 Do not rejoice over any one's death 21
9: 2 so that she gains mastery over your strength. 21
10: 4 and over it he will raise up the right man 21
17: 2 authority over the things upon the earth. •
22:27 O that a guard were set over my mouth 21
23: 2 O that whips were set over my thoughts 21
2 and the discipline of wisdom over my mind! 21
26:10 Keep strict watch over a headstrong daughter 21
28:22 It will not be master over the godly •
30:21 Do not give yourself over to sorrow 18
31: 1 Wakefulness over wealth wastes away one's flesh •
25 Do not aim to be valiant over wine 19
32:20 do not stumble over stony ground. 19
33:19 do not give power over yourself 21
38:29 he is always deeply concerned over his work 21
41: 2 very old and distracted over everything 24
42: 9 worry over her robs him of sleep •
11 Keep strict watch over a headstrong daughter 21
43:20 wind blows, and ice freezes over the water 21
46:13 and anointed rulers over his people. 21
48:15 were scattered over all the earth 19
50:20 lifted up his hands over the whole congregation 21
Bar 2:34 they will rule over it; and I will increase them •
3:30 Who has gone over the sea, and found her, and will 23
LJr 1:53 they cannot set up a king over a country •
62 the clouds to go over the whole world 21
Aza 1:22 the only God, glorious over the whole world. 21
Bel 1: 5 and has dominion over all flesh. •
Man 1: 7 repentest over the evils of men. 21
1Mc 1: 4 and ruled over countries, nations, and princes •
16 that he might reign over both kingdoms. 21
51 he appointed inspectors over all the people 21
5:40 If he crosses over to us first 28
51 Then he passed through the city over the slain. 20
6: 2 the . . king who first reigned over the Greeks. 19
14 and made him ruler over all his kingdom. 21
8:16 They trust one man each year to rule over them •
11: 9 you shall reign over your father's kingdom. •
57 set you over the four districts 21
66 of the city, and set a garrison over it. 21
13:27 Simon built a monument over the tomb of his father 21
14:42 that he should be governor over them 21
42 the sanctuary and appoint men over its tasks 21
42 appoint men . . over the country and the weapons 21
16:11 appointed governor over the plain of Jericho 18
2Mc 3:17 bodily trembling had come over the man 24
4:10 he at once shifted . . over to the Greek way of life. 28
5: 2 over all the city, for almost 40 days 22
6 setting up trophies of victory over enemies •
6 over enemies and not over fellow countrymen. •
12:16 the . . lake . . appeared to be running over with blood. 26
22 terror and fear came over the enemy 21
13:25 were indignant over the treaty 24
15: 6 erect a . . monument of victory over Judas and his men •
19 being anxious over the encounter •
3Mc 1:11 only the high priest who was pre-eminent over all •
2: 7 the Ruler over the whole creation. •
5:17 he urged them to give themselves over to revelry 18
28 This was the act of God who rules over all things •
51 imploring the Ruler over every power •
7: 9 not man but the Ruler over every power •
4Mc 1: 1 devout reason is sovereign over the emotions •
5 is it not sovereign over forgetfulness and ignorance? •
7 that reason is dominant over the emotions •
11 the downfall of tyranny over their nation 22
13 whether reason is sovereign over the emotions. •
19 Rational judgment is supreme over all of these •
30 over the emotions it is sovereign •
30 rational judgment is sovereign over the emotions •
2: 4 to rule . . also over every desire. •
10 the law prevails even over affection for parents •
12 It takes precedence over love for children •
13 It is sovereign over the relationship of friends •
14 reason . . can prevail even over enmity •
16 for it is sovereign over even this. •
22 as a sacred governor over them all. 21
3: 1 reason rules . . over those of the body. •
6:10 the old man . . was victorious over his torturers; •
31 devout reason is sovereign over the emotions. •
32 if the emotions had prevailed over reason •
7: 1 steered . . over the sea of the emotions 19
10 O supreme king over the passions, Eleazar! •
8:28 they were . . sovereign over agonies •
13: 1 devout reason is sovereign over the emotions. •
3 they prevailed over their emotions. •
4 The supremacy of the mind over these •
6 just as towers jutting out over harbors •
14:11 reason had full command over these men •
15: 1 O reason of the children, tyrant over the emotions! •
16: 1 devout reason is sovereign over the emotions. •
5 she would have mourned over them 21

over עַל

Gen 1:2; 8:1; 9:14; 11:8, 9; 26:21, 22; 37:8; 39:5; 41:33, 34, 40, 41, 43, 45, 56; 42:6; 49:22; 50:1, Exd 1:8, 11; 2:14; 5:14; 7:19[2]; 8:5[3], 6; 9:9; 10:12, 13, 14, 21; 14:7, 16, 21, 26, 27; 18:21, 25; 26:7, 12, 13; 30:6; 36:14; 40:19[2], 36, Lev 14:5, 6, 50; 16:10, 21; 26:16, Num 1:50[3]; 4:7, 8, 11, 13; 7:2; 8:7; 9:15, 17, 18, 19, 20, 22; 10:10[2], 11, 14, 15, 16, 18, 19, 20, 22, 23, 24, 25, 26, 27, 34; 12:10; 14:14; 16:13, 33; 27:16, Deu 1:15; 17:14, 15[3]; 21:6; 28:23, 36; 32:11, Jos 7:26; 8:29, Jdg 3:10; 6:2; 9:8[2], 9, 10, 11, 12, 13, 14, 15, 18, 22, 49; 11:11; 12:1, Rut 3:9, 1Sm 8:7, 9, 11, 19; 9:16; 10:1, 19; 11:12; 12:1, 12, 13, 14; 13:1, 14; 14:47; 15:1, 17, 26, 35; 16:1; 18:5; 19:20; 22:2; 23:17; 25:30; 26:16, 2Sm 1:17; 2:4, 7, 10, 11; 3:8, 10[2], 17, 34; 5:2[2], 3, 5[2], 12, 17; 6:21; 7:8, 11, 26; 8:15, 16; 11:23; 12:7; 17:19, 25; 18:1, 8, 17; 19:10, 22, 42; 20:8, 12, 1Kg 1:34, 35[2]; 2:11, 35; 4:1, 5, 7; 5:7, 16; 6:1; 8:16; 9:5, 23; 11:25, 37, 42; 12:17, 18, 20; 13:30; 14:2, 7, 14; 15:1, 25[2], 33; 16:2, 8, 9, 16, 18, 23, 29[2]; 18:3; 19:15, 16; 20:38; 22:41, 51, 2Kg 3:1; 8:13, 15; 9:29; 10:5[2], 36; 11:3, 18; 13:1, 10; 15:5, 8, 17, 23, 27; 17:1; 18:18, 37; 19:2; 21:13; 25:22, 1Ch 9:20, 29[2]; 11:2, 3, 25; 12:4, 38; 14:2, 8; 17:7, 10; 18:14, 15, 17; 21:16; 22:12; 23:1; 27:16, 25[2], 26, 27[2], 28[2], 29[2], 30[2]; 28:4[2], 5; 29:26, 27, 2Ch 1:9, 11, 13; 2:11; 5:8; 6:5, 6; 9:8, 30; 10:17, 18; 13:1, 5; 15:15; 19:11; 20:31; 22:12; 26:21; 31:14; 32:6; 34:4, 12, 13; 36:4, 10, Ezr 4:20; 10:6, Neh 5:15; 7:2; 9:37[2]; 11:9, 16, 21; 12:44[2]; 13:13, 19, 26, Est 3:12; 8:2, Job 6:5, 27[2]; 7:12; 8:16; 14:16, 17; 21:32; 26:7, 9; 28:8; 41:6, 34, Ps 7:7; 3:2; 1:11; 2:7; 7:2, 8; 7:5, 11; 0:8; 8:34; 9:15; 1:5; 3:18; 8:16; 7:9; 9:2; 08:5, 9; 10:6; 24:5; 41:3; 45:9, Prv 2:11; 6:22; 20:26; 23:30; 28:15, Ecc 1:12, 16; 2:20; 5:8, Sng 2:4, 8; 7:13, Isa 4:5[2]; 5:30; 8:7[2]; 9:7, 17; 10:15, 26; 11:8, 15; 14:26; 15:2[2], 7; 19:16; 22:15; 23:11; 25:7[2]; 28:27; 31:4; 34:11; 36:3, 22; 37:2; 44:16; 45:14; 62:5[2], 10; 66:10, Jer 1:10[2], 12; 6:9, 17; 9:18; 13:21, 26; 15:3; 18:21; 23:4; 30:15; 31:12[3], 28[2]; 40:11; 43:10; 44:27; 51:14, 48, Lam 1:10; 2:17; 3:54, Ezk 1:22, 25, 26; 5:1; 9:4; 10:1, 2, 18, 19; 11:22; 12:13; 16:8; 17:20; 19:8; 20:33; 26:17, 19; 27:2, 30, 32; 28:12; 32:2, 3, 8, 16[2], 18; 34:6, 23; 37:24, Dan 1:11; 8:12; 9:1, Hos 7:12; 8:1; 10:5, Ams 5:1; 6:6, Jon 2:3; 4:6, Mic 3:6; 4:7; 5:9; 7:18, Nah 3:5, 19, Zep 1:9; 3:17, Zec 1:16; 2:9; 5:3; 9:13, 14; 12:7, 10[2]; 14:9

over (2) 1. חלף 2. עבר 3. תמם 4. ἀπό 5. παρέρχομαι 6. συντελέω

2Sm 11:27 And when the mourning was over, David sent 2
Sng 2:11 lo, the winter is past, the rain is over and gone. 1
Isa 18: 5 For before the harvest, when the blossom is over 3
Ams 8: 5 When will the new moon be over, that we may sell 2
Mat 14:15 This is a lonely place, and the day is now over 5
Tob 8:20 before the days of the feast were over 6
2Mc 15:28 When the action was over 4

over *See* advantage, all, authority, bend, boast, bring, carry, change, climb, cloud, come, cross, deliver, dominance, domineer, dominion, double, escort, exercise, fall, far, gain, give, glide, go, graze, grow, hand, keep, leap, leave, lord, make, move, pass, ponder, pour, power, prevail, reign, rejoice, rule, run, send, set, seven, spread, sweep, take, think, times, tip, triumph, turn, voyage, watch, win.

over against 1. אֶל יַד 2. לְנֶגֶד 3. לִקְרַאת 4. מוּל 5. מִנֶּגֶד 6. נֶגֶד 7. עַל 8. עַל פְּנֵים

Gen 15:10 in two, and laid each half over against the other; 3
16:12 he shall dwell over against all his kinsmen. 8
21:16 Then she went, and sat down over against him 5
16 as she sat over against him, the child lifted up 5
25:18 he settled over against all his people. 8
Exd 14: 2 you shall encamp over against it, by the sea. 7
Deu 1: 1 the wilderness, in the Arabah over against Suph 4
11:30 over against Gilgal, beside the oak of Moreh? 4
Jos 15: 8 the mountain that lies over against the valley 8
19:46 Rakkon with the territory over against Joppa. 4
2Kg 2:15 sons of the prophets . . saw him over against them 5
1Ch 5:11 sons of Gad dwelt over against them 6
Neh 12:24 Hashabi'ah . . with their brethren over against 2
Ezk 41:16 Over against the threshold the temple was 6
48: 1 border of Damascus over against Hamath) 1

over and above 1. עדף

Num 3:46 over and above the number of the male Levites 1
49 over and above those redeemed by the Levites; 1

right over 1. ἐπάνω

Bel 1:36 and set him down in Babylon, right over the den 1

something over 1. יֶתֶר

Ps 17:14 may they leave something over to their babes. 1

overbearing 1. עָרִיץ 2. σκολιός

Ps 37:35 I have seen a wicked man overbearing 1
1Pe 2:18 be submissive . . also to the overbearing. 2

overboard *See* throw.

overcome 1. היה 2. הלם 3. חזק 4. יכל 5. נכה 6. עבר 7. רוד 8. ἀναιρέω 9. βαρύνω 10. ἐξίστημι 11. ἔρχομαι ἐπὶ τὴν κεφαλήν 12. ἡττάομαι 13. κάμπτω 14. καταλαμβάνω 15. καταφέρω 16. κατέχω 17. κρατέω 18. νικάω 19. περιβάλλω 20. περικρατέω 21. περιχέω 22. vinco

Num13:30 occupy it; for we are well able to overcome it. •
1Sm 30: 1 They had overcome Ziklag, and burned it with fire 5
1Kg 16:22 people who followed Omri overcame the people 3
Ps 55: 2 I am overcome by my trouble. I am distraught 7
Isa 28: 1 the rich valley of those overcome with wine! 2
Jer 20:10 then we can overcome him, and take our revenge 4
11 my persecutors . . they will not overcome me. 4
23: 9 like a drunken man, like a man overcome by wine 6
Dan 8:27 I, Daniel, was overcome and lay sick for some days; 1
Mrk 5:42 immediately overcome with amazement. 10
Lke 11:22 one stronger than he assails him and overcomes 18
Joh 1: 5 and the darkness has not overcome it. 14
16:33 be of good cheer, I have overcome the world. 18
Act 20: 9 overcome by sleep, he fell down 15
Rom 12:21 Do not be overcome by evil 18
21 but overcome evil with good. 18
2Pe 2:19 whatever overcomes a man, to that he is enslaved. 12
1Jn 2:13 because you have overcome the evil one 18
14 and you have overcome the evil one. 18
4: 4 you are of God, and have overcome them; 18
5: 4 For whatever is born of God overcomes the world; 18
4 this is the victory that overcomes the world 18
5 Who is it that overcomes the world 18
2Es 3:21 Adam . . transgressed and was overcome 22
6:28 and corruption shall be overcome 22
7:92 to overcome the evil thought which was formed 22
Jdt 8: 3 he was overcome by the burning heat 11
13: 2 he was overcome with wine. 21
Wis 2: 4 mist that is..overcome by its heat. 9
Sir 23: 6 Let neither gluttony nor lust overcome me 14
3Mc 5:12 he was overcome by so pleasant and deep a sleep 16
27 completely overcome by incomprehension 17
6:34 groaned as they . . were overcome by disgrace 19
4Mc 2: 2 by mental effort he overcame sexual desire. 20
3: 4 we are not overcome by malice. 13
4:13 had been overcome by human treachery 8
7:22 would not be able to overcome the emotions 20
9: 6 which our aged instructor also overcame. 18

overcome with fear 1. קוץ

Num22: 3 Moab was overcome with fear of the people 1

overconfident 1. πιστεύω

Sir 32:21 Do not be overconfident on a smooth way 1

overdrive 1. דפק

Gen 33:13 if they are overdriven for one day, all the flocks 1

overeat 1. ἐν πολλοῖς βρώμασιν

Sir 37:30 for overeating brings sickness 1

overextend 1. ὑπερεκτείνω

2Co 10:14 For we are not overextending ourselves 1

overflow 1. הלך עַל 2. מלא 3. עבר 4. עֶבְרָה 5. עַד בְּלִי דָי 6. פוץ 7. רְוָיָה 8. רחשׁ 9. שׁוק 10. שׁטף 11. שֶׁצֶף 12. ἐμπίμπλημι 13. ἐπικλύζω 14. περισσεύω 15. ὑπερπλεονάζω

Jos 3:15 the Jordan overflows all its banks 2
4:18 (AL#Jordan returned . . and overflowed all its banks 1
1Ch 12:15 when it was overflowing all its banks 2
Job 40:11 Pour forth the overflowings of your anger 4
Ps 23: 5 thou anointest my head with oil, my cup overflows. 7
45: 1 My heart overflows with a goodly theme; 8
73: 7 their hearts overflow with follies. 3
78:20 that water gushed out and streams overflowed. 10
Isa 8: 8 overflow and pass on, reaching even to the neck; 10
10:22 is decreed, overflowing with righteousness. 10
23:10 Overflow your land like the Nile 3
28: 2 like a storm of mighty, overflowing waters 10
30:28 his breath is like an overflowing stream 10
54: 8 In overflowing wrath for a moment I hid my face 11
66:12 of the nations like an overflowing stream; 10
Jer 47: 2 and shall become an overflowing torrent; 10
2 they shall overflow the land 10
Dan 11:10 which . . come on and overflow and pass through 10
40 come into countries . . overflow and pass through. 10
Jol 2:24 the vats shall overflow with wine and oil. 9
3:13 The vats overflow, for their wickedness is great. 9

Nah 1: 8 with an overflowing flood he will make a full end 3
Zec 1:17 My cities shall again overflow with prosperity 6
Mal 3:10 and pour down for you an overflowing blessing. 5
2Co 8: 2 overflowed in a wealth of liberality 14
9:12 also overflows in many thanksgivings to God. 14
1Ti 1:14 the grace of our Lord overflowed for me 15
Jdt 2: 8 be filled . . and overflow; 13
Sir 47:14 You overflowed like a river with understanding. 12

make overflow 1. צוף
Deu 11: 4 how he made the water of the Red Sea overflow them 1

overgrown 1. עלה
Prv 15:19 The way of a sluggard is overgrown with thorns *
24:31 lo, it was all overgrown with thorns; 1

overhear 1. שמע 2. ἀκούω
Jer 38:27 for the conversation had not been overheard. 1
AEs 12: 2 He overheard their conversation 2

overjoyed 1. ὑπερπερισσεύω 2. ὑπερχαίρω
2Co 7: 4 With all our affliction, I am overjoyed. 1
3Mc 7:20 they departed unharmed, free, and overjoyed 2

overlay 1. חפה 2. טוח 3. צפה 4. צִפּוּי 5. רקע 6. חפש
Exd 25:11 you shall overlay it with pure gold 3
11 within and without shall you overlay it 3
13 make poles . . and overlay them with gold. 3
24 You shall overlay it with pure gold 3
28 make the poles . . and overlay them with gold 3
26:29 You shall overlay the frames with gold 3
29 and you shall overlay the bars with gold. 3
32 four pillars of acacia overlaid with gold 3
37 pillars of acacia, and overlay them with gold; 3
27: 2 and you shall overlay it with bronze. 3
6 make poles . . and overlay them with bronze; 3
30: 3 you shall overlay it with pure gold 3
5 make the poles . . overlay them with gold. 3
36:34 he overlaid the frames with gold 3
34 and overlaid the bars with gold. 3
36 pillars of acacia, and overlaid them with gold; 3
38 He overlaid their capitals, and their fillets 3
37: 2 he overlaid it with pure gold within and without 3
4 made poles . . and overlaid them with gold 3
11 he overlaid it with pure gold, and made a molding 3
15 made the poles . . and overlaid them with gold. 3
26 He overlaid it with pure gold, its top 3
28 the poles . . and overlaid them with gold. 3
38: 2 and he overlaid it with bronze. 3
6 the poles . . and overlaid them with bronze. 3
17 the overlaying of their capitals was also 4
19 the overlaying of their capitals and their 4
28 pillars, and overlaid their capitals 3
1Kg 6:20 sanctuary . . and he overlaid it with pure gold. 3
21 Solomon overlaid the inside . . with pure gold 3
21 the inner sanctuary, and overlaid it with gold. 3
22 he overlaid the whole house with gold 3
22 Also the whole altar . . he overlaid with gold. 3
28 And he overlaid the cherubim with gold. 3
30 The floor of the house he overlaid with gold 3
32 he overlaid them with gold, and spread gold 3
35 he overlaid them with gold evenly applied 3
10:18 throne, and overlaid it with the finest gold. 3
2Kg 18:16 the doorposts which Hezeki'ah . . had overlaid 3
1Ch 29: 4 for overlaying the walls of the house 2
2Ch 3: 4 He overlaid it on the inside with pure gold. 3
8 he overlaid it with 600 talents of fine 1
9 And he overlaid the upper chambers with gold. 1
10 cherubim of wood and overlaid them with gold. 3
4: 9 the court, and overlaid their doors with bronze; 3
9:17 ivory throne, and overlaid it with pure gold. 3
Isa 40:19 The idol! . . a goldsmith overlays it with gold 5
Hab 2:19 Behold, it is overlaid with gold and silver 6

overlay with gold 1. περίχρυσος
LJr 1: 8 they . . are overlaid with gold and silver 1
39 and overlaid with gold and silver 1
50 and overlaid with gold and silver 1
55 wooden gods overlaid with gold or silver 1
70 gods of wood, overlaid with gold and silver. 1
71 their gods of wood, overlaid with gold and silver 1

overlay with silver 1. περιάργυρος
LJr 1:57 Gods made of wood and overlaid with silver 1

overlook 1. עבר 2. עַל פְּנֵי 3. צוֹפֶה פְּנֵי 4. שקף 5. ἐπιλανθάνω 6. παροράω 7. ὑπεροράω
Num23:28 to the top of Pe'or, that overlooks the desert. 4
Jos 18:16 of the mountain that overlooks the valley 2
Prv 19:11 it is his glory to overlook an offense. 1
Sng 7: 4 a tower of Lebanon, overlooking Damascus. 3
Act 17:30 The times of ignorance God overlooked 7
Heb 6:10 For God is not so unjust as to overlook your work 5
Wis 11:23 thou dost overlook men's sins 6
Sir 2:10 who ever called upon him and was overlooked? 7
28: 7 overlook ignorance. 6
32:18 A man of judgment will not overlook an idea 6

3Mc 1:27 not to overlook this unlawful and haughty deed. 6
4Mc 13: 4 cannot be overlooked 6

overmuch 1. רבה
Ecc 7:16 Be not righteous overmuch 1
17 Be not wicked overmuch, neither be a fool; 1

overpayment 1. עדף
Lev 25:27 let him . . pay back the overpayment to the man 1

overpower 1. יכל 2. שלט (A) 3. βαρύς 4. ἡττάομαι 5. ἰσχύω 6. multitudo
Jdg 16: 5 and by what means we may overpower him 1
Dan 6:24 lions overpowered them and broke all 2
Act 19:16 mastered all of them, and overpowered them 5
2Pe 2:20 again entangled in them and overpowered 4
2Es 10:28 into this overpowering bewilderment 6
3Mc 5:30 he was filled with an overpowering wrath 3
overpowering *See* anger.

overrun 1. עבר
Zec 9: 8 no oppressor shall again overrun them 1

oversee 1. נצח 2. ἐπί 3. ἐπόπτης
2Ch 2: 2 assigned . . and 3,600 to oversee them. 1
Jdt 8: 3 overseeing the men who were binding sheaves 2
3Mc 2:21 God, who oversees all things 3

oversee all 1. πανεπίσκοπος
Wis 7:23 all-powerful, overseeing all 1
overseeing *See* stand.

overseer 1. נצח 2. פקד 3. פְּקֻדָּה 4. פָּקִיד 5. ἐπισκοπός
Gen 41:34 Let Pharaoh proceed to appoint overseers over 4
2Ch 2:18 as overseers to make the people work. 1
31:13 Ismachi'ah, Mahath, and Benai'ah were overseers 4
34:17 delivered it into the hand of the overseers 2
Neh 11: 9 Jo'el the son of Zichri was their overseer; 4
14 overseer was Zab'diel the son of Haggedo'lim. 4
22 overseer of the Levites in Jerusalem was Uzzi 4
Isa 60:17 I will make your overseers peace 3
Act 20:28 in which the Holy Spirit has made you overseers 5
overseer *See also* make.

overshadow 1. סכך 2. ἐπισκιάζω 3. κατασκιάζω 4. σκιάζω
Exd 25:20 overshadowing the mercy seat with their wings 1
37: 9 wings above, overshadowing the mercy seat 1
Mat 17: 5 when lo, a bright cloud overshadowed them 2
Mrk 9: 7 a cloud overshadowed them 2
Lke 1:35 the power of the Most High will overshadow you; 2
9:34 a cloud came and overshadowed them 2
Heb 9: 5 cherubim of glory overshadowing the mercy seat. 3
Wis 19: 7 The cloud was seen overshadowing the camp 4

oversight 1. יָד 2. מִשְׁגֶּה 3. נצח 4. עַל 5. פקד 6. פְּקֻדָּה
Gen 43:12 mouth of your sacks; perhaps it was an oversight. 2
Num 3:32 to have oversight of those who had charge 6
4:16 oversight of all the tabernacle and all that is 6
28 work is to be under the oversight of Ith'amar 1
2Kg 12:11 the workmen who had the oversight of the house 5
22: 5 the workmen who have the oversight of the house 5
9 the workmen who have the oversight of the house 5
1Ch 26:30 the oversight of Israel westward of the Jordan 6
32 to have the oversight of the Reubenites 4
2Ch 34:10 who had the oversight of the house of the LORD; 5
12 Jahath and . . Meshul'lam, . . to have oversight. 5
Ezr 3: 8 Levites . . to have the oversight of the work 3
9 together took the oversight of the workmen 3
Ezk 44:11 having oversight at the gates of the temple, 6

overstuff 1. βιάζω
Sir 31:21 If you are overstuffed with food 1

overtake 1. דבק 2. דבק אַחֲרֵי 3. מצא 4. נגש 5. נשג 6. סוג 7. ἀπαντάω 8. εὑρίσκω 9. καταδιώκω 10. καταλαμβάνω 11. λαμβάνω 12. μετέρχομαι 13. παρακολουθέω 14. παρίημι 15. περιέχω 16. προκαταλαμβάνω 17. προλαμβάνω 18. contingo
Gen 19:19 flee to the hills, lest the disaster overtake me 1
31:25 Laban overtook Jacob. Now Jacob had pitched 5
44: 4 and when you overtake them, say to them, 'Why have 5
6 When he overtook them, he spoke to them these 5
Exd 14: 9 his army, and overtook them encamped at the sea 5
15: 9 I will overtake, I will divide the spoil 5
Deu 19: 6 pursue the manslayer and overtake him 5
28: 2 blessings shall come upon you and overtake you 5
15 these curses shall come upon you and overtake 5
45 these curses shall . . pursue you and overtake 5
Jos 2: 5 pursue them quickly, for you will overtake them. 5
Jdg 18:22 were called out, and they overtook the Danites. 1
20:42 the battle overtook them, and those who came out 1
1Sm 30: 8 Shall I pursue . . this band? Shall I overtake them? 5
8 you shall surely overtake and shall . . rescue. 5
31: 2 And the Philistines overtook Saul and his sons; 1

2Sm 15:14 go in haste, lest he overtake us quickly 5
2Kg 7: 9 if we are silent . . punishment will overtake us; 3
25: 5 pursued the king, and overtook him in the plains 5
1Ch 10: 2 the Philistines overtook Saul and his sons; 2
21:12 while the sword of your enemies overtakes you; 5
Job 27:20 Terrors overtake him like a flood; 5
31:29 that hated me, or exulted when evil overtook him 3
Ps 7: 5 let the enemy pursue me and overtake me 5
18:37 I pursued my enemies and overtook them; 5
40:12 iniquities have overtaken me, till I cannot see; 5
69:24 let thy burning anger overtake them. 5
Isa 59: 9 and righteousness does not overtake us; 5
Jer 39: 5 Chalde'ans pursued them, and overtook Zedeki'ah 5
42:16 then the sword which you fear shall overtake you 5
52: 8 and overtook Zedeki'ah in the plains of Jericho; 5
Lam 1: 3 her pursuers have all overtaken her 5
Hos 2: 7 She shall pursue her lovers, but not overtake 5
10: 9 Shall not war overtake them in Gib'e-ah? 5
Ams 9:10 who say, 'Evil shall not overtake or meet us.' 4
13 when the plowman shall overtake the reaper 4
Mic 2: 6 disgrace will not overtake us. 6
Zec 1: 6 did they not overtake your fathers? 5
Joh 12:35 lest the darkness overtake you 10
1Co 10:13 No temptation has overtaken you 11
Gal 6: 1 Brethren, if a man is overtaken in any trespass 17
2Es 10:48 and that misfortune had overtaken her 18
Tob 12: 7 Do good, and evil will not overtake you. 8
Jdt 11:11 a sin has overtaken them 10
Wis 14:30 just penalties will overtake them on two counts 12
Sir 11:10 if you pursue you will not overtake 10
23: 8 The sinner is overtaken through his lips 10
31:22 no sickness will overtake you. 7
Bar 4:25 Your enemy has overtaken you 9
1Mc 2:32 Many pursued them, and overtook them 10
12:30 he did not overtake them 10
2Mc 4:16 For this reason heavy disaster overtook them 15
8:11 the judgment . . that was about to overtake him. 13
3Mc 2:10 if . . tribulation should overtake us 10
13 we are . . overtaken by helplessness. 14
20 Speedily let your mercies overtake us 16
23 the severe punishment that had overtaken him 10

overthrow 1. דחה 2. הפך 3. הֲפֵכָה 4. הרס 5. כרע 6. כשל 7. מַהְפֵּכָה 8. נער 9. סלף 10. שלך 11. מגר (A) 12. ἀναστρέφω 13. ἀνατρέπω 14. κατακρημνίζω 15. κατάλυσις 16. καταλύω 17. καταπαλαίω 18. καταργέω 19. καταστρέφω 20. καταστρώννυμι 21. everto 22. subverto
Gen 19:21 I will not overthrow the city of which you have 2
25 he overthrew those cities, and all the valley 2
29 God . . sent Lot out of the midst of the overthrow 3
29 when he overthrew the cities in which Lot dwelt. 2
Exd 15: 7 thou overthrowest thy adversaries; 4
23:24 but you shall utterly overthrow them and break 4
Deu 29:23 an overthrow like that of Sodom and Gomor'rah 7
23 which the LORD overthrew in his anger and wrath- 2
2Sm 10: 3 to search . . and to spy it out, and to overthrow it? 2
11:25 strengthen your attack . . and overthrow it. 4
2Kg 3:25 And they overthrew the cities 4
1Ch 19: 3 to search and to overthrow and to spy out the land? 2
20: 1 And Jo'ab smote Rabbah, and overthrew it. 4
Ezr 6:12 overthrow any king or people that shall put 11
Job 12:19 and overthrows the mighty. 9
Ps 17:13 Arise, O LORD! confront them, overthrow them! 5
136:15 overthrew Pharaoh and his host in the Red Sea 8
Prv 11:11 but it is overthrown by the mouth of the wicked. 4
12: 7 The wicked are overthrown and are no more 2
13: 6 but sin overthrows the wicked. 9
14:32 The wicked is overthrown through his evil-doing 1
22:12 but he overthrows the words of the faithless. 9
24:16 but the wicked are overthrown by calamity. 6
Isa 1: 7 it is desolate, as overthrown by aliens. 7
13:19 Sodom and Gomor'rah when God overthrew them. 7
14:17 made . . like a desert and overthrew its cities 4
Jer 1:10 to break down, to destroy and to overthrow 4
6:15 they shall be overthrown," says the LORD. 6
8:12 when I punish them, they shall be overthrown 6
18:23 Let them be overthrown before thee; 6
20:16 like the cities which the LORD overthrew 2
31:28 break down, to overthrow, destroy, and bring evil 4
40 It shall not be uprooted or overthrown any more 4
49:18 As when Sodom and Gomor'rah . . were overthrown 7
50:40 As when God overthrew Sodom and Gomor'rah 7
Lam 4: 6 of Sodom, which was overthrown in a moment 2
Dan 8:11 place of his sanctuary was overthrown. 10
Ams 4:11 I overthrew some of you, as when God overthrew 2
11 as when God overthrew Sodom and Gomor'rah 7
Jon 3: 4 Yet 40 days, and Nin'eveh shall be overthrown! 2
Zep 1: 3 I will overthrow the wicked; *
Hag 2:22 to overthrow the throne of kingdoms; 2
22 and overthrow the chariots and their riders; 2
Act 5:39 you will not be able to overthrow them 16
Rom 3:31 Do we then overthrow the law by this faith? 18
1Co 10: 5 for they were overthrown in the wilderness. 20
2Es 1:10 For their sake I have overthrown many kings 22
16:46 plunder their goods, and overthrow their houses 21
Tob 14: 4 it will be overthrown 19
Jdt 1:13 overthrew the whole army of Arphaxad 12

Sir 10:16 The Lord has overthrown the lands of the nations 19
12:12 Do not put him next to you, lest he overthrow you 13
27: 3 his house will be quickly overthrown. 19
29:16 will overthrow the prosperity of his surety 13
2Mc 8:17 the overthrow of their ancestral way of life. 15
12:15 overthrew Jericho in the days of Joshua 14
4Mc 3:18 it can overthrow bodily agonies 17

overturn 1. הפך 2. ἀνατρέφω 3. καταστρέφω 4. περιτρέπω

Job 9: 5 when he overturns them in his anger; 1
28: 9 and overturns mountains by the roots. 1
34:25 Thus, knowing their works, he overturns them 1
Mat 21:12 and he overturned the tables of the money-changers 3
Mrk 11:15 he overturned the tables of the money-changers 3
Joh 2:15 and overturned their tables 2
Wis 5:23 evil-doing will overturn the thrones of rulers. 4
Sir 28:14 overturned the houses of great men. 3

overwhelm 1. בהל 2. הפך 3. כסה 4. ענה 5. שטף 6. שֶׁטֶף 7. שמם 8. ἐπικλύζω 9. ἐπιχέω 10. καταντλέω 11. καταπίνω 12. περαντλέω 13. συγκλύζω 14. συντρίβω 15. obtego 16. tego

Job 12:15 if he sends them out, they overwhelm the land. 2
22:10 sudden terror overwhelms you; 1
Ps 55: 5 come upon me, and horror overwhelms me. 3
78:53 but the sea overwhelmed their enemies. 3
88: 7 thou dost overwhelm me with all thy waves. Selah 4
90: 7 by thy wrath we are overwhelmed. 1
140: 9 let the mischief of their lips overwhelm them! 3
Prv 27: 4 Wrath is cruel, anger is overwhelming; 6
Isa 28:15 when the overwhelming scourge passes through 5
17 and waters will overwhelm the shelter. 5
18 when the overwhelming scourge passes through 5
43: 2 through the rivers, they shall not overwhelm you; 5
Ezk 3:15 I sat there overwhelmed among them seven days. 7
Hab 2:17 The violence done to Lebanon will overwhelm you; 3
2Co 2: 7 or he may be overwhelmed by excessive sorrow. 11
2Es 16:77 and overwhelmed by their iniquities 15
77 and its path overwhelmed with thorns 16
Wis 5:22 rivers will relentlessly overwhelm them; 13
17:15 sudden and unexpected fear overwhelmed them. 9
1Mc 10:82 they were overwhelmed by him and fled 14
3Mc 2: 7 you overwhelmed him in the depths of the sea 8
4Mc 7: 2 and overwhelmed by the mighty waves of tortures 10
15:32 overwhelmed from every side 12

overwhelm with passion 1. καταννύσσω

Sus 1:10 Both were overwhelmed with passion for her 1

overwise *See* make.

owe 1. ὀφειλέτης 2. ὀφείλω 3. προσοφείλω

Mat 18:24 one was brought to him who owed him 10,000 talents; 1
28 fellow servants who owed him a 100 denarii 2
28 'Pay what you owe.' 2
Lke 7:41 one owed 500 denarii, and the other 50. 2
16: 5 he said to the first, 'How much . . owe my master?' 2
7 Then he said to another, 'And how much do you owe?' 2
Rom 13: 8 Owe no one anything, except to love one another; 2
Phm 1:18 If he has wronged you at all, or owes you anything 2
19 say nothing of your owing me even your own self 3
1Mc 10:43 because he owes money to the king or has any debt 2
13:15 the money that Jonathan your brother owed 2
39 and cancel the crown tax which you owe 2
15: 8 Every debt you owe to the royal treasury *

owl 1. יַנְשׁוּף 2. כּוֹס 3. קִפּוֹז

Lev 11:17 the owl, the cormorant, the ibis 2
Ps 102: 6 like a vulture . . like an owl of the waste places; 2
Isa 34:11 the owl and the raven shall dwell in it. 1
15 There shall the owl nest and lay and hatch 3
Zep 2:14 the owl shall hoot in the window *

owl *See also* great.

little owl 1. כּוֹס

Deu 14:16 the little owl and the great owl, the water hen 1

own 1. εἰμί 2. ἔχω

Gen 23: 9 give me the cave of Mach-pe'lah, which he owns; †
Lev 14:35 then he who owns the house shall come and tell *
Act 21:11 bind the man who owns this girdle 1
Sir 13: 5 If you own something, he will live with you 2

owner 1. אָדוֹן 2. בַּעַל 3. קנה 4. κτάομαι 5. κύριος

Exd 21:28 but the owner of the ox shall be clear. 2
29 its owner has been warned but has not kept it 2
29 and its owner also shall be put to death. 2
32 the owner shall give to the master 30 shekels *
34 the owner of the pit shall make it good; 2
34 he shall give money to its owner 2
36 if . . its owner has not kept it 2
22: 8 If the thief is not found, the owner of the house 2
11 the owner shall accept the oath, and he shall not 2
12 he shall make restitution to its owner. 2
14 If . . it is hurt or dies, the owner not being 2
15 If the owner was with it, he shall not make 2
Lev 25:50 the time he was with his owner shall be rated *
1Kg 16:24 Sama'ria, after . . Shemer, the owner of the hill. 1
Job 31:39 caused the death of its owners; 2
Ecc 5:11 and what gain has their owner but to see them 2
13 riches were kept by their owner to his hurt 2
Isa 1: 3 The ox knows its owner, and the ass its . . crib; 3
Mat 20: 8 when evening came, the owner of the vineyard said 5
21:40 When therefore the owner of the vineyard comes 5
Mrk 12: 9 What will the owner of the vineyard do? 5
Lke 19:33 as they were untying the colt, its owners said 5
20:13 the owner of the vineyard said, 'What shall I do? 5
15 What then will the owner of the vineyard do to them? 5
Act 16:16 brought her owners much gain by soothsaying. 5
19 her owners saw that their hope of gain was gone 5
Gal 4: 1 though he is the owner of all the estate; 5
Tob 2:12 She used to send the product to the owners 5
13 Return it to the owners 5
14 told her to return it to the owners 5
LJr 1:59 a household utensil that serves its owner's need 4

owner of the ship 1. ναύκληρος

Act 27:11 to the captain and to the owner of the ship 1

ox 1. אֶלֶף 2. בָּקָר 3. פַּר 4. שׁוֹר 5. תּוֹר (A) 6. βοῦς 7. μόσχος 8. ταῦρος

Gen 12:16 and he had sheep, oxen, he-asses, menservants 2
20:14 Then Abim'elech took sheep and oxen 2
21:27 Abraham took sheep and oxen and gave them 2
32: 5 I have oxen, asses, flocks, menservants 4
49: 6 and in their wantonness they hamstring oxen. 4
Exd 20:17 covet . . his ox, or his ass, or anything 4
24 sacrifice . . your sheep and your oxen; 2
21:28 When an ox gores a man or a woman to death 4
28 the ox shall be stoned, and its flesh shall 4
28 but the owner of the ox shall be clear. 4
29 if the ox has been accustomed to gore in the past 4
29 the ox shall be stoned, and its owner also shall 4
32 If the ox gores a slave, male or female, the owner 4
32 and the ox shall be stoned. 4
33 a pit . . and an ox or an ass falls into it 4
35 When one man's ox hurts another's, so that it dies 4
35 then they shall sell the live ox and divide 4
36 Or if it is known that the ox has been accustomed 4
36 he shall pay ox for ox, and the dead beast shall be 4
36 he shall pay ox for ox, and the dead beast shall be 4
22: 1 If a man steals an ox or a sheep, and kills it 4
1 he shall pay five oxen for an ox, and four sheep 2
1 he shall pay five oxen for an ox, and four sheep 4
4 whether it is an ox or an ass or a sheep 4
9 whether it is for ox, for ass, for sheep 4
10 an ass or an ox or a sheep or any beast to keep 4
30 You shall do likewise with your oxen 4
23: 4 If you meet your enemy's ox or his ass going astray 4
12 that your ox and your ass may have rest 4
24: 5 sacrificed peace offerings of oxen to the LORD. 3
Lev 4:10 just as these are taken from the ox 4
7:23 You shall eat no fat, of ox, or sheep, or goat 4
9: 4 an ox and a ram for peace offerings, to sacrifice 4
18 He killed the ox also and the ram 4
19 the fat of the ox and of the ram, the fat tail 4
17: 3 If any man . . kills an ox or a lamb or a goat 4
27:26 whether ox or sheep, it is the LORD'S 4
Num 7: 3 offering . . six covered wagons and twelve oxen 2
3 wagon for every two . . for each one an ox; 4
6 Moses took the wagons and the oxen, and gave them 2
7 Two wagons and four oxen he gave to . . Gershon 2
8 four wagons and eight oxen he gave 2
17 for the sacrifice of peace offerings, two oxen 2
23 for the sacrifice of peace offerings, two oxen 2
29 for the sacrifice of peace offerings, two oxen 2
35 for the sacrifice of peace offerings, two oxen 2
41 for the sacrifice of peace offerings, two oxen 2
47 for the sacrifice of peace offerings, two oxen 2
53 for the sacrifice of peace offerings, two oxen 2
59 for the sacrifice of peace offerings, two oxen 2
65 for the sacrifice of peace offerings, two oxen 2
71 for the sacrifice of peace offerings, two oxen 2
77 for the sacrifice of peace offerings, two oxen 2
83 for the sacrifice of peace offerings, two oxen 2
22: 4 as the ox licks up the grass of the field. 4
40 Balak sacrificed oxen and sheep, and sent 2
31:28 tribute . . of the persons and of the oxen 2
30 one drawn out of every 50, of the persons, of the oxen 2
Deu 5:14 your ox, or your ass, or any of your cattle 4
21 not desire . . his ox, or his ass, or anything 4
14: 4 animals you may eat: the ox, the sheep, the goat 4
26 whatever you desire, oxen, or sheep, or wine 2
17: 1 not sacrifice . . an ox or a sheep 4
18: 3 offering a sacrifice, whether it be ox or sheep 4
22: 1 not see your brother's ox or his sheep go astray 4
4 You shall not see your brother's ass or his ox 4
10 You shall not plow with an ox and an ass together. 4
25: 4 not muzzle an ox when it treads out the grain. 4
28:31 Your ox shall be slain before your eyes 4
Jos 6:21 and women, young and old, oxen, sheep, and asses 4
7:24 and daughters, and his oxen and asses and sheep 4
Jdg 6: 4 leave no sustenance . . and no sheep or ox or ass. 4
1Sm 11: 5 Saul was coming from the field behind the oxen; 2
7 He took a yoke of oxen, and cut them in pieces 2
7 Whoever does not . . so shall it be done to his oxen! 2
12: 3 Whose ox have I taken? Or whose ass have I taken? 4
14:32 and took sheep and oxen and calves, and slew them 2
34 Let every man bring his ox or his sheep 4
34 So every one . . brought his ox with him that night 4
15: 3 infant and suckling, ox and sheep, camel and ass. 4
9 the best of . . and of the oxen and of the fatlings 2
14 What then is . . the lowing of oxen which I hear? 2
15 people spared the best of the sheep and . . oxen 2
21 But the people took of the spoil, sheep and oxen 2
22:19 children and sucklings, oxen, asses and sheep 4
27: 9 took away the sheep, the oxen, the asses, the camels 2
2Sm 6: 6 and took hold of it, for the oxen stumbled. 2
13 he sacrificed an ox and a fatling. 4
24:22 here are the oxen for the burnt offering 2
22 sledges and the yokes of the oxen for the wood. 2
24 David bought the threshing floor and the oxen 2
1Kg 1: 9 Adoni'jah sacrificed sheep, oxen, and fatlings 2
19 He has sacrificed oxen, fatlings, and sheep 4
25 and has sacrificed oxen, fatlings, and sheep 4
4:23 ten fat oxen, and twenty . . cattle 2
7:25 It stood upon twelve oxen, three facing north 2
29 on the panels . . were lions, oxen, and cherubim. 2
29 both above and below the lions and oxen 2
44 one sea, and the twelve oxen underneath the sea. 2
8: 5 sacrificing so many sheep and oxen that 2
63 Solomon offered . . 22,000 oxen 2
19:20 he left the oxen, and ran after Eli'jah, and said 2
21 and took the yoke of oxen, and slew them, and boiled 2
21 and boiled their flesh with the yokes of the oxen 2
2Kg 5:26 olive orchards and vineyards, sheep and oxen 2
16:17 and he took down the sea from off the bronze oxen 2
1Ch 12:40 bringing food . . camels and on mules and on oxen 2
40 and wine and oil, oxen and sheep 2
13: 9 to hold the ark, for the oxen stumbled. 2
21:23 see, I give the oxen for burnt offerings 2
2Ch 4: 4 It stood upon twelve oxen, three facing north 2
15 the one sea, and the twelve oxen underneath it. 2
5: 6 sacrificing so many sheep and oxen that they 2
7: 5 offered as a sacrifice 22,000 oxen 2
15:11 They sacrificed . . 700 oxen and 7,000 sheep. 2
18: 2 Ahab killed an abundance of sheep and oxen 2
Neh 5:18 one day was one ox and six choice sheep; 4
Job 1: 3 3,000 camels, 500 yoke of oxen 2
14 The oxen were plowing and the asses feeding 2
6: 5 when he has grass, or the ox low over his fodder? 4
24: 3 they take the widow's ox for a pledge. 4
40:15 Behold, Be'hemoth . . he eats grass like an ox. 2
42:12 had 14,000 sheep, 6,000 camels, 1,000 yoke of oxen 2
Ps 8: 7 sheep and oxen, and also the beasts of the field 1
69:31 This will please the LORD more than an ox or a bull 4
106:20 God for the image of an ox that eats grass. 4
Prv 7:22 follows her, as an ox goes to the slaughter 4
14: 4 Where there are no oxen, there is no grain; 1
4 abundant crops come by the strength of the ox. 4
15:17 Better is . . than a fatted ox and hatred with it. 4
Isa 1: 3 The ox knows its owner, and the ass its . . crib; 4
11: 7 and the lion shall eat straw like the ox. 2
22:13 behold . . slaying oxen and killing sheep 2
30:24 the oxen and the asses that till the ground 1
32:20 who let the feet of the ox and the ass range free. 4
65:25 the lion shall eat straw like the ox; 2
66: 3 He who slaughters an ox is like him who kills a man; 4
Ezk 1:10 the four had the face of an ox on the left side 4
Dan 4:25 made to eat grass like an ox, and you shall be wet 5
32 shall be made to eat grass like an ox; 5
33 driven from among men, and ate grass like an ox 5
5:21 fed grass like an ox, and his body was wet 5
Ams 6:12 Does one plow the sea with oxen? 2
Mat 22: 4 my oxen and my fat calves are killed 8
Lke 13:15 Does not each of you on the sabbath untie his ox 6
14: 5 a son or an ox that has fallen into a well 6
19 another said, 'I have bought five yoke of oxen 6
Joh 2:14 he found those who were selling oxen and sheep 6
15 he drove them all, with the sheep and oxen, out 6
Act 14:13 brought oxen and garlands to the gates 8
1Co 9: 9 not muzzle an ox when it is treading out the grain. 6
9 Is it for oxen that God is concerned? 6
1Ti 5:18 not muzzle an ox when it is treading out the grain 6
Rev 4: 7 the second living creature like an ox 7
Jdt 2:17 innumerable sheep and oxen and goats 6
Sir 38:25 who drives oxen and is occupied with their work 6

ox *See also* wild, yoke.

oxgoad 1. מַלְמַד בָּקָר

Jdg 3:31 killed 600 of the Philistines with an oxgoad; 1

P

pace 1. צַעַד 2. רֶגֶל 3. רכב
Gen 33:14 slowly, according to the pace of the cattle 2
14 lead on . . according to the pace of the children 2
2Sm 6:13 when those who bore the ark . . had gone six paces 1
2Kg 4:24 do not slacken the pace for me unless I tell you. 3

swift pace 1. ὁρμή
3Mc 4: 5 forced to march at a swift pace 1

pagan 1. ἔθνος
1Co 5: 1 of a kind that is not found even among pagans 1
10:20 No, I imply that what pagans sacrifice 1

become a pagan 1. ἀλλοφυλέω
4Mc 18: 5 able to compel the Israelites to become pagans 1

pain 1. חֵבֶל 2. חִיל 3. חִילָה 4. כאב 5. כְּאֵב 6. מַכְאוֹב 7. עֶצֶב 8. עֹצֶב 9. עִצָּבוֹן 10. צִיר 11. רָעָה 12. αἴσθησις 13. ἀλγηδών 14. ἄλγος 15. βάσανος 16. λυπέω 17. λύπη 18. ὀδύνη 19. πόνος 20. σπουδή 21. ὠδίν 22. dolor 23. maeror
Gen 3:16 multiply your pain in childbearing; 9
16 in pain you shall bring forth children 7
1Sm 4:19 bowed and gave birth; for her pains came upon her. 10
1Ch 4: 9 his name Jabez, saying, "Because I bore him in pain. 8
Job 6:10 I would even exult in pain unsparing; 3
16: 5 the solace of my lips would assuage your pain. •
6 If I speak, my pain is not assuaged 5
21:17 That God distributes pains in his anger? 1
30:17 the pain that gnaws me takes no rest. •
33:19 Man is also chastened with pain upon his bed 6
Ps 13: 2 How long must I bear pain in my soul ‡
38:17 For I am ready to fall, and my pain is ever with me. 6
69:29 I am afflicted and in pain; 4
Ecc 11:10 Remove . . and put away pain from your body; 11
Isa 14: 3 When the LORD has given you rest from your pain 8
17:11 flee away in a day of grief and incurable pain. 5
65:14 but you shall cry out for pain of heart 5
66: 7 before her pain came upon her she was delivered 1
Jer 6:24 taken hold of us, pain as of a woman in travail. 2
15:18 Why is my pain unceasing, my wound incurable 5
22:23 pangs come upon you, pain as of a woman in travail! 2
30:15 Your pain is incurable. 6
45: 3 Woe is me! for the LORD has added sorrow to my pain; 6
50:43 anguish seized him, pain as of a woman in travail. 2
51: 8 wail for her! Take balm for her pain; 6
Dan 10:16 by reason of the vision pains have come upon me 10
Mat 4:24 with various diseases and pains, demoniacs 15
2Co 2: 2 but the one whom I have pained? 16
3 so that when I came I might not suffer pain 17
1Pe 2:19 one is approved if, mindful of God, he endures pain 17
Rev 16:11 cursed the God of heaven for their pain and sores 19
21: 4 neither . . mourning nor crying nor pain any more 19
2Es 10:12 which I brought forth in pain and bore in sorrow; 23
16:38 Just as a woman . . has great pains about her womb 22
39 and pains will seize it on every side. 22
Jdt 16:17 they shall weep in pain for ever. 12
Wis 8:16 and life with her has no pain 18
Sir 0: 3 I should myself devote some pains and labor 20
27:29 pain will consume them before their death. 18
38: 7 By them he heals and takes away pain; 19
2Mc 3:17 the pain lodged in his heart. 14
9: 5 he was seized with a pain in his bowels 13
9 while he was still living in anguish and pain 13
11 he was tortured with pain every moment. 13
4Mc 1: 4 namely anger, fear, and pain. 19
20 two . . types . . are pleasure and pain 19
21 The emotions of both pleasure and pain 19
23 Fear precedes pain and sorrow comes after. 19
24 an emotion embracing pleasure and pain. 19
28 Just as pleasure and pain are two plants 19
6: 9 he bore the pains and scorned the punishment 19
9:31 I lighten my pain 19
13: 4 the brothers mastered both emotions and pains. 19
15: 7 because of the many pains she suffered with each 21
16 more bitter pains than even the birth-pangs 19
16:23 It is unreasonable . . not to withstand pain. 19

pain *See also* feel, full, writhe.

cause pain 1. λυπέω
2Co 2: 2 For if I cause you pain, who is there to make me glad 1
4 not to cause you pain but to let you know 1
5 if any one has caused pain, he has caused it not 1

cause bitter pain 1. מַר
Num 5:24 water . . enter into her and cause bitter pain. 1
27 water . . enter into her and cause bitter pain 1

great pain 1. עֳנִי
1Ch 22:14 With great pains I have provided for the house 1

painful 1. λύπη 2. μετὰ κόπων
Heb 12:11 For the moment all discipline seems painful 1
Sir 13:26 to devise proverbs requires painful thinking. 2

more excruciatingly painful 1. ἐπαλγής
4Mc 14:10 What could be more excruciatingly painful than this 1

most painful 1. χαλεπός
4Mc 8: 1 the most painful instruments of torture. 1

painfully 1. βασανίζω
Mrk 6:48 he saw that they were making headway painfully 1

painless 1. ἄπονος
4Mc 11:26 and the catapults painless 1

pains *See* take.

paint 1. כחל 2. משח 3. פּוּךְ 4. שׂוּם בַּפּוּךְ 5. ἐγκαίω 6. ζωγραφέω 7. ὁμοιόω
2Kg 9:30 she painted her eyes, and adorned her head 4
Jer 4:30 that you enlarge your eyes with paint? 3
22:14 and painting it with vermilion. 2
Ezk 23:40 For them you bathed yourself, painted your eyes 1
Sir 38:27 he sets his heart on painting a lifelike image 7
2Mc 2:29 one who undertakes its painting and decoration 5
4Mc 17: 7 to paint the history of your piety as an artist 6

paint *See also* cover.

red paint 1. μίλτος
Wis 13:14 giving it a coat of red paint 1

painter 1. σκιαγράφος
Wis 15: 4 nor the fruitless toil of painters 1

pair 1. צֶמֶד 2. שְׁנַיִם 3. δύο δύο 4. ζεῦγος
Gen 7: 2 Take with you seven pairs of all clean animals †
2 and a pair of the animals that are not clean 2
3 seven pairs of the birds of the air also •
Exd 25:35 a capital . . under each pair of the six branches 2
37:21 a capital of one piece with it under each pair 2
Jdg 15: 4 and put a torch between each pair of tails. 2
Isa 21: 7 When he sees riders, horsemen in pairs 1
9 And, behold, here come riders, horsemen in pairs! 1
Lke 2:24 a pair of turtledoves, or two young pigeons. 4
Sir 33:15 they likewise are in pairs 3

pair of sandals 1. נַעַל
Ams 8: 6 that we may buy . . the needy for a pair of sandals 1

pair of shoes 1. נַעַל 2. ὑπόδημα
Ams 2: 6 they sell . . the needy for a pair of shoes 1
Sir 46:19 not so much as a pair of shoes 2

palace 1. אַרְמוֹן 2. בִּירָה 3. בַּיִת 4. בֵּית מַלְכוּת 5. בִּיתָן 6. הֵיכָל 7. הֵיכָל (A) 8. αὐλή 9. βασίλειος 10. οἶκος
1Kg 4: 6 Ahi'shar was in charge of the palace; and Adoni'ram 3
21: 1 a vineyard in Jezreel, beside the palace of Ahab 6
2Kg 10: 5 he who was over the palace, and he who was over 3
11: 6 a third . . shall guard the palace; 3
16:18 way . . which had been built inside the palace 3
20:18 be eunuchs in the palace of the king of Babylon. 6
1Ch 29: 1 for the palace will not be for man but for the LORD 2
19 may build the palace for which I have made 2
2Ch 2: 1 to build a temple . . and a royal palace 3
12 who will build . . a royal palace for himself. 3
28: 7 slew . . Azri'kam the commander of the palace 3
36: 7 to Babylon and put them in his palace in Babylon. 6
19 burned all its palaces with fire, and destroyed 1
Ezr 4:14 Now because we eat the salt of the palace 6
Est 1: 5 in the court of the garden of the king's palace. 5
8 given orders to all the officials of his palace 3
9 also gave a banquet for the women in the palace 3
2: 8 Esther also was taken into the king's palace 3
9 with . . chosen maids from the king's palace 3
13 take with her from the harem to the king's palace. 3
16 Esther was taken . . into his royal palace 3
4:13 Think not that in the king's palace you will 3
5: 1 and stood in the inner court of the king's palace 3
1 was sitting on his . . throne inside the palace 4
1 king was . . opposite the entrance to the palace; 3
6: 4 just entered the outer court of the king's palace 3
7: 7 rose . . in wrath and went into the palace garden; 5
8 And the king returned from the palace garden 5
Ps 45: 8 From ivory palaces stringed instruments make 6
15 led along as they enter the palace of the king. 6
144:12 corner pillars cut for the structure of a palace; 6
Prv 30:28 yet it is in kings' palaces. 6
Isa 13:22 Hyenas . . and jackals in the pleasant palaces; 6
23:13 they razed her palaces, they made her a ruin. 1
25: 2 the palace of aliens is a city no more 1
32:14 For the palace will be forsaken 1
39: 7 be eunuchs in the palace of the king of Babylon. 6
Jer 6: 5 let us attack by night, and destroy her palaces! 1
9:21 into our windows, it has entered our palaces 1
17:27 and it shall devour the palaces of Jerusalem 1
30:18 the palace shall stand where it used to be. 1
32: 2 which was in the palace of the king of Judah. 3
43: 9 which is at the entrance to Pharaoh's palace 3
Lam 2: 5 he has destroyed all its palaces 1
7 he has delivered . . the walls of her palaces; 1
Dan 4: 4 Nebuchadnez'zar . . prospering in my palace. 7
29 walking on the roof of the royal palace of Babylon 7
5: 5 plaster of the wall of the king's palace 7
6:18 king went to his palace, and spent the night 7
Hos 8:14 has forgotten his Maker, and built palaces; 6
Nah 2: 6 river gates are opened, the palace is in dismay; 6
Mat 26: 3 people gathered in the palace of the high priest 8
Mrk 15:16 the soldiers led him away inside the palace 8
Lke 11:21 a strong man, fully armed, guards his own palace 8
Jdt 2: 1 there was talk in the palace of Nebuchadnezzar 10
18 gold and silver from the royal palace. 10
LJr 1:59 better also a wooden pillar in a palace 9
1Mc 2:10 What nation has not inherited her palaces 9
7: 2 he was entering the royal palace of his fathers 10
11:46 But the king fled into the palace 8

palace *See also* official.

palanquin 1. אַפִּרְיוֹן
Sng 3: 9 Solomon made himself a palanquin from the wood 1

palate 1. חֵךְ 2. φάρυγξ
Job 12:11 the ear try words as the palate tastes food? 1
34: 3 the ear tests words as the palate tastes food. 1
Sir 36:19 As the palate tastes the kinds of game 2

palatial 1. אַפֶּדֶן
Dan 11:45 pitch his palatial tents between the sea 1

pale 1. יֵרָקוֹן 2. פָּארוּר 3. χλωρός
Jer 30: 6 Why has every face turned pale? 1
Jol 2: 6 peoples are in anguish, all faces grow pale. 2

Nah 2:10 anguish is on all loins, all faces grow pale! 2
Rev 6: 8 a pale horse, and its rider's name was Death 3

pale *See also* grow, turn.

thick pall 1. βρόμος
Wis 11:18 or belch forth a thick pall of smoke 1

pallet 1. κράβαττος
Mrk 2: 4 let down the pallet on which the paralytic lay. 1
9 or to say, 'Rise, take up your pallet and walk'? 1
11 I say to you, rise, take up your pallet and go home. 1
12 immediately took up the pallet and went out 1
6:55 began to bring sick people on their pallets 1
Joh 5: 8 Rise, take up your pallet, and walk. 1
9 he took up his pallet and walked. 1
10 it is not lawful for you to carry your pallet. 1
11 'Take up your pallet, and walk.' 1
12 'Take up your pallet, and walk'? •
Act 5:15 laid them on beds and pallets 1

palm 1. תָּמָר 2. תֹּמֶר 3. תִּמֹרָה 4. φοῖνιξ 5. palma
Jdg 1:16 went up . . from the city of palms 1
3:13 and they took possession of the city of palms. 1
4: 5 sit under the palm of Deb'orah between Ramah 2
2Ch 3: 5 nave he lined . . and made palms and chains on it. 3
Neh 8:15 bring branches of olive, wild olive, myrtle, palm 1
Jol 1:12 Pomegranate, palm, and apple, all the trees 1
2Es 2:45 now they are being crowned, and receive palms. 5
46 and puts palms in their hands? 5
2Mc 14: 4 presenting to him a crown of gold and a palm 4

palm (2) 1. כַּף
Lev 14:15 pour it into the palm of his own left hand 1
26 some of the oil into the palm of his own left hand 1
2Kg 9:35 the skull and the feet and the palms of her hands. 1
Isa 49:16 Behold, I have graven you on the palms of my hands; 1

palm *See* frond.

palm branch 1. כִּפָּה 2. βαΐνη 3. βαΐον 4. φοῖνιξ
Isa 9:14 cut off . . head and tail, palm branch and reed 1
19:15 nothing . . palm branch or reed, may do. 1
Rev 7: 9 in white robes, with palm branches in their hands 4
1Mc 13:37 received the gold crown and the palm branch 2
51 the Jews entered it with praise and palm branches 3

palm tree 1. תָּמָר 2. תִּמֹרָה 3. φοῖνιξ
Exd 15:27 12 springs of water and 70 palm trees; 1
Lev 23:40 branches of palm trees, and boughs of leafy trees 1
Num33: 9 there were twelve springs of water and 70 palm trees 1
Deu 34: 3 Jericho the city of palm trees, as far as Zo'ar. 1
1Kg 6:29 with carved figures of cherubim and palm trees 2
32 with carvings of cherubim, palm trees 2
32 spread gold upon . . and upon the palm trees. 2
35 On them he carved cherubim and palm trees 2
7:36 he carved cherubim, lions, and palm trees 2
2Ch 28:15 at Jericho, the city of palm trees. 1
Ps 92:12 The righteous flourish like the palm tree 1
Sng 7: 7 You are stately as a palm tree 1
8 I say I will climb the palm tree and lay hold of its 1
Ezk 40:16 and on the jambs were palm trees. 2
22 its windows, its vestibule, and its palm trees 2
26 it had palm trees on its jambs, one on either side. 2
31 palm trees were on its jambs 2
34 it had palm trees on its jambs, one on either side; 2
37 it had palm trees on its jambs, one on either side; 2
41:18 of cherubim and palm trees 2
18 a palm tree between cherub and cherub. 2
19 face of a man toward the palm tree on the one side 2
19 toward the palm tree on the other side. 2
20 cherubim and palm trees were carved on the wall. 2
25 were carved cherubim and palm trees 2
26 there were recessed windows and palm trees 2
Joh 12:13 they took branches of palm trees 3
Sir 24:14 I grew tall like a palm tree in En-ge'di 3
50:12 they surrounded him like the trunks of palm trees 3

palsy by terror 1. בהל
Ezk 7:27 the people of the land are palsied by terror. 1

paltry 1. εὐτελής
Wis 10: 4 steering . . by a paltry piece of wood. 1

pamper 1. פנק 2. τιθηνέω
Prv 29:21 He who pampers his servant from childhood 1
Sir 30: 9 Pamper a child, and he will frighten you 2

pan 1. כִּיּוֹר 2. מַרְחֶשֶׁת 3. מַשְׂרֵת 4. צַלַּחַת 5. τήγανον
Lev 2: 7 offering is a cereal offering cooked in a pan 2
7: 9 all that is prepared on a pan or a griddle 2
1Sm 2:14 thrust it into the pan, or kettle, or caldron, or pot; 1
2Sm 13: 9 she took the pan and emptied it out before him 3
2Ch 35:13 boiled the holy offerings in pots . . and in pans 4
2Mc 7: 3 and gave orders that pans and caldrons be heated. 5
5 The smoke from the pan spread widely 5

pan *See also* fry.

panel 1. מִסְגֶּרֶת 2. ספן 3. שְׂחִיף 4. φατνόω
1Kg 7:28 stands: they had panels, and the panels were set 1
28 and the panels were set in the frames 1
29 on the panels that were set in the frames were 1
31 and its panels were square, not round. 1
32 the four wheels were underneath the panels; 1
35 its stays and its panels were of one piece with it. 1
36 and on its panels, he carved cherubim, lions 1
Jer 22:14 and cuts out windows for it, paneling it with cedar 2
Ezk 41:16 were paneled and round about all three had 4
16 the temple was paneled with wood round about 3
Hag 1: 4 yourselves to dwell in your paneled houses 2

pang 1. חֶבֶל 2. חִיל 3. חַרְצֻבָּה 4. מַכְאוֹב 5. מִכְשׁוֹל 6. מֵצַר 7. צִיר 8. צרר 9. ὀδύνη 10. ὠδίν 11. necessitas
Exd 15:14 pangs have seized on the inhabitants 2
1Sm 25:31 have no cause of grief, or pangs of conscience 5
Ps 32:10 Many are the pangs of the wicked; 4
73: 4 For they have no pangs; their bodies are sound 3
116: 3 pangs of Sheol laid hold on me; 6
Isa 13: 8 Pangs and agony will seize them; 7
21: 3 pangs have seized me, like . . a woman in travail; 7
3 pangs . . like the pangs of a woman in travail; 7
26:17 who writhes and cries out in her pangs 1
Jer 13:21 Will not pangs take hold of you 1
22:23 how you will groan when pangs come upon you 1
48:41 like the heart of a woman in her pangs; 8
49:22 like the heart of a woman in her pangs. 8
Hos 13:13 The pangs of childbirth come for him 1
Mic 4: 9 that pangs have seized you like a woman in travail? 2
Act 2:24 having loosed the pangs of death 10
1Ti 6:10 pierced their hearts with many pangs. 9
2Es 4:42 makes haste to escape the pangs of birth 11

pang *See also* birth, suffer.

pang of birth 1. ὠδίνω
Rev 12: 2 she cried out in her pangs of birth 1

panic 1. בהל 2. חֲרָדָה 3. מְהוּמָה 4. פַּחַד 5. רֶטֶט 6. תִּמָּהוֹן
1Sm 5: 9 LORD was against . . causing a very great panic 3
11 was a deathly panic throughout the whole city. 3
14:15 there was a panic in the camp, in the field 2
15 earth quaked; and it became a very great panic. 2
Ps 48: 5 they were in panic, they took to flight; 1
Prv 1:26 I will mock when panic strikes you 4
27 when panic strikes you like a storm 4
3:25 Do not be afraid of sudden panic 4
Jer 30: 5 Thus says the LORD: We have heard a cry of panic 2
49:24 she turned to flee, and panic seized her; 5
51:32 burned with fire, and the soldiers are in panic. 1
Lam 3:47 panic and pitfall have come upon us 4
Zec 12: 4 I will strike every horse with panic 6
14:13 a great panic from the LORD shall fall on them 3

panic *See also* desert, throw.

panic-stricken 1. καταπλήσσω
3Mc 2:23 panic-stricken in their exceedingly great fear. 1

pant 1. שׁאף
Ps 119:131 With open mouth I pant 1
Isa 42:14 a woman in travail, I will gasp and pant. 1
Jer 14: 6 they pant for air like jackals; 1

pant after 1. שׁאף
Job 5: 5 the thirsty pant after his wealth. 1

paper 1. χαρτηρίαν 2. χάρτης 3. carta
2Jn 1:12 I would rather not use paper and ink 2
2Es 15: 2 cause them to be written on paper 3
3Mc 4:20 both the paper and the pens they used for writing 1

papyrus 1. גֹּמֶא
Job 8:11 Can papyrus grow where there is no marsh? 1
Isa 18: 2 by the Nile, in vessels of papyrus upon the waters 1

parable 1. מָשָׁל 2. παραβολή 3. similitudo
Ps 78: 2 I will open my mouth in a parable; 1
Mat 13: 3 he told them many things in parables, saying 2
10 Why do you speak to them in parables? 2
13 This is why I speak to them in parables 2
18 Hear then the parable of the sower. 2
24 Another parable he put before them, saying 2
31 Another parable he put before them, saying 2
33 He told them another parable 2
34 All this Jesus said to the crowds in parables; 2
34 he said nothing to them without a parable. 2
35 I will open my mouth in parables 2
36 Explain to us the parable of the weeds 2
53 when Jesus had finished these parables 2
15:15 Peter said to him, "Explain the parable to us. 2
21:33 Hear another parable 2
45 priests and the Pharisees heard his parables 2
22: 1 again Jesus spoke to them in parables, saying 2
Mrk 3:23 said to them in parables 2
4: 2 he taught them many things in parables 2
10 asked him concerning the parables. 2
11 for those outside everything is in parables; 2
13 Do you not understand this parable? 2
13 How then will you understand all the parables? 2
30 what parable shall we use for it? 2
33 With many such parables he spoke the word to them 2
34 he did not speak to them without a parable 2
7:17 his disciples asked him about the parable. 2
12: 1 he began to speak to them in parables 2
12 he had told the parable against them 2
Lke 5:36 He told them a parable also 2
6:39 He also told them a parable 2
8: 4 he said in a parable 2
9 his disciples asked him what this parable meant 2
10 for others they are in parables 2
11 the parable is this: The seed is the word of God. 2
12:16 he told them a parable, saying, "The land 2
41 are you telling this parable for us or for all? 2
13: 6 he told this parable: "A man had a fig tree planted 2
14: 7 Now he told a parable to those who were invited 2
15: 3 he told them this parable 2
18: 1 he told them a parable 2
9 He also told this parable to some 2
19:11 he proceeded to tell a parable 2
20: 9 he began to tell the people this parable 2
19 he had told this parable against them. 2
21:29 he told them a parable 2
2Es 4:47 I will show you the interpretation of a parable. 3
8: 2 I tell you a parable, Ezra 3
Sir 3:29 the intelligent man will ponder a parable 2
39: 2 penetrate the subtleties of parables; 2
3 be at home with the obscurities of parables 2
47:15 you filled it with parables and riddles. 2
17 your songs and proverbs and parables 2

parable *See also* give.

parade about 1. περιάγω
2Mc 6:10 These . . they publicly paraded about the city 1

parade under arms 1. ἐξοπλησία
2Mc 5:25 he ordered his men to parade under arms. 1

paradise 1. παράδεισος 2. paradisus
Lke 23:43 I say to you, today you will be with me in Paradise. 1
2Co 12: 3 this man was caught up into Paradise 1
Rev 2: 7 the tree of life, which is in the paradise of God.' 1
2Es 4: 7 or which are the entrances of paradise?' 2
6: 2 and before the foundations of paradise were laid 2
7:36 and opposite it the paradise of delight. 2
123Or that a paradise shall be revealed 2
8:52 because it is for you that paradise is opened 2

paradoxical 1. παραδοκέω
4Mc 2:14 Do not consider it paradoxical 1

parallel 1. לְעֻמַּת
Ezk 42: 7 was a wall outside parallel to the chambers 1
48:21 the west border, parallel to the tribal portions 1

paralytic 1. παραλυτικός
Mat 4:24 pains, demoniacs, epileptics, and paralytics 1
9: 2 behold, they brought to him a paralytic 1
2 he said to the paralytic, "Take heart, my son 1
6 he then said to the paralytic–"Rise 1
Mrk 2: 3 bringing to him a paralytic carried by four men. 1
4 let down the pallet on which the paralytic lay. 1
5 he said to the paralytic 1
9 Which is easier, to say to the paralytic 1
10 he said to the paralytic– 1

paralyze 1. καταλύω 2. ξηρός 3. παραλυτικός 4. παραλύω
Mat 8: 6 my servant is lying paralyzed at home 3
Lke 5:18 men were bringing on a bed a man who was paralyzed 4
24 he said to the man who was paralyzed–"I say to you 4
Joh 5: 3 a multitude of invalids, blind, lame, paralyzed. 2
Act 8: 7 many who were paralyzed or lame were healed. 4
9:33 bedridden for eight years and was paralyzed. 4
Wis 17:15 now were paralyzed by their souls' surrender 4
19 it paralyzed them with terror. 4
1Mc 9:55 his mouth was stopped and he was paralyzed 4
3Mc 2:22 besides being paralyzed in his limbs 4
4Mc 11:24 We six boys have paralyzed your tyranny! 1

paramour 1. פִּלֶגֶשׁ 2. רֵעַ
Ezk 23:20 and doted upon her paramours there 1
Hos 3: 1 Go again, love a woman who is beloved of a paramour 2

parapet 1. מַעֲקֶה 2. ἔπαλξις
Deu 22: 8 new house, you shall make a parapet for your roof 1
Jdt 14: 1 hang it upon the parapet of your wall. 2

parbar 1. פַּרְוָר
1Ch 26:18 for the parbar on the west there were four 1
18 were four at the road and two at the parbar. 1

parcel 1. חֶלְקָה
Rut 4: 3 Na'omi . . is selling the parcel of land 1

parcel out 1. חלק
Ams 7:17 and your land shall be parceled out by line; 1

parch 1.חרב 2.חרר 3.יבשׁ 4.נשׁת 5.עִיף 6.צִחֶה 7.צִיָּה 8.קלה 9.ἀναξηραίνω
Lev 2:14 new grain from fresh ears, parched with fire 8
Ps 69: 3 I am weary with my crying; my throat is parched. 2
107:35 turns . . a parched land into springs of water. 7
143: 6 my soul thirsts for thee like a parched land. 5
Isa 5:13 their multitude is parched with thirst. 6
19: 5 dried up, and the river will be parched and dry; 3
41:17 and their tongue is parched with thirst 4
Hos 2: 3 like a wilderness, and set her like a parched land 7
13:15 his spring shall be parched; 1
Jol 2:20 and drive him into a parched and desolate land 7
Sir 43: 3 At noon it parches the land 9
parched *See* grain, ground, land.

parched place 1.חָרֵר
Jer 17: 6 dwell in the parched places of the wilderness 1

parchment 1.μεμβράνα
2Ti 4:13 also the books, and above all the parchments. 1

pardon 1.כסה 2.כפר 3.נשׂא 4.סלח 5.רצה 6.ἀφίημι 7.λύω 8.συγγνωστός 9.χάρις 10.ignosco
Exd 23:21 for he will not pardon your transgression; 3
34: 9 and pardon our iniquity and our sin 4
Num14:19 Pardon the iniquity of this people, I pray thee 4
20 LORD said, "I have pardoned, according to your word; 4
Deu 29:20 LORD would not pardon him, but rather the anger 4
1Sm 15:25 Now therefore, I pray, pardon my sin, and return 3
2Kg 5:18 In this matter may the LORD pardon your servant 4
18 when I . . the LORD pardon your servant in this 4
24: 4 innocent blood, and the LORD would not pardon. 4
2Ch 30:18 The good LORD pardon every one 2
Job 7:21 Why dost thou not pardon my transgression 3
Ps 25:11 O LORD, pardon my guilt, for it is great. 4
85: 2 thou didst pardon all their sin. Selah 1
Isa 40: 2 warfare is ended, that her iniquity is pardoned 5
55: 7 and to our God, for he will abundantly pardon. 4
Jer 5: 1 that I may pardon her. 4
7 How can I pardon you? 4
50:20 for I will pardon those whom I leave as a remnant. 4
Mic 7:18 Who is a God like thee, pardoning iniquity 3
2Es 7:139if he did not pardon those who were created 10
Wis 6: 6 For the lowliest man may be pardoned in mercy 8
18: 2 they begged their pardon 9
Sir 28: 2 then your sins will be pardoned when you pray. 7
1Mc 13:39 We pardon any errors and offenses committed 6
pardon *See also* beg.

pare 1.עשׂה
Deu 21:12 she shall shave her head and pare her nails. 1

parent 1.γεννάω 2.γονεύς 3.πατήρ 4.πρόγονος 5.parens
Mat 10:21 children will rise against parents 2
Mrk 13:12 children will rise against parents 2
Lke 2:27 when the parents brought in the child Jesus 2
41 Now his parents went to Jerusalem every year 2
43 His parents did not know it 2
8:56 her parents were amazed 2
18:29 house or wife or brothers or parents or children 2
21:16 You will be delivered up even by parents 2
Joh 9: 2 who sinned, this man or his parents 2
3 It was not that this man sinned, or his parents 2
18 until they called the parents of the man 2
20 His parents answered, "We know that this is our son 2
22 His parents said this 2
23 Therefore his parents said, "He is of age, ask him. 2
Rom 1:30 inventors of evil, disobedient to parents 2
2Co 12:14 children ought not to lay up for their parents 2
14 parents for their children. 2
Eph 6: 1 Children, obey your parents in the Lord 2
Col 3:20 Children, obey your parents in everything 2
1Ti 5: 4 and make some return to their parents 4
2Ti 3: 2 disobedient to their parents, ungrateful, unholy 2
Heb 11:23 was hid for three months by his parents 3
1Jn 5: 1 every one who loves the parent loves the child. 1
2Es 1: 6 the sins of their parents have increased in them 5
7:103fathers for sons or sons for parents 5
Tob 10:12 they are now your parents 2
Wis 4: 6 witnesses of evil against their parents 2
12: 6 these parents who murder helpless lives 2
Sir 3: 7 he will serve his parents as his masters. 1
7:28 Remember . . through your parents you were born; •
Sus 1: 3 Her parents were righteous 2
30 And she came, with her parents, her children 2
1Mc 10: 9 he returned them to their parents. 2
2Mc 12:24 because he held the parents of most of them 2
3Mc 5:31 Were your parents or children present 2
49 parents and children, mothers and daughters 2
6:14 The whole throng of infants and their parents 2
4Mc 2:10 the law prevails even over affection for parents 2
15: 4 the emotions of parents who love their children 2
13 yearning of parents toward offspring •

parental 1.γεννάω 2.γονεύς
4Mc 14:14 have a sympathy and parental love 1
15:13 O sacred nature and affection of parental love 2
parental *See also* love.

park 1.פַּרְדֵּס
Ecc 2: 5 I made myself gardens and parks 1

part 1.בֶּטֶן 2.בֶּתֶר 3.דָּבָר 4.חֲלָקָה 5.חֶלְקָה 6.חצה 7.לְ 8.מִן 9.מָקוֹם 10.בַּיִן נצל 11.סָרַח 12.פרד 13.פרס 14.ἀπό 15.διαμερίζω 16.ἐκ 17.ἐν 18.μέλος 19.μερίς 20.μέρος 21.ὅριον 22.παρά 23.σχίζω 24.τόπος 25.pars 26.portio
Exd 16:20 some left part of it till the morning 8
26:12 the part that remains of the curtains of the tent 11
28:27 to the lower part of the two shoulder-pieces •
29:12 shall take part of the blood of the bull and put it 8
20 you shall kill the ram, and take part of its blood 8
21 Then you shall take part of the blood 8
30:36 put part of it before the testimony in the tent 8
39:20 to the lower part of the two shoulder-pieces •
Lev 2: 3 it is a most holy part of the offerings by fire •
10 it is a most holy part of the offering by fire •
16 as its memorial portion part of the crushed grain 8
4: 6 sprinkle part of the blood seven times 8
11: 3 Whatever parts the hoof and is cloven-footed 13
4 chew the cud or part the hoof, you shall not eat 13
4 chews the cud but does not part the hoof 13
5 it chews the cud but does not part the hoof 13
6 chews the cud but does not part the hoof 13
7 the swine, because it parts the hoof and is cloven- 13
26 Every animal which parts the hoof but is not 13
22:23 A bull or a lamb which has a part too long •
25:25 If your brother . . sells part of his property 8
27:16 If a man dedicates to the LORD part of the land 8
22 is not a part of his possession by inheritance 8
Deu 14: 6 Every animal that parts the hoof and has the hoof 13
7 because they chew the cud but do not part the hoof 13
8 parts the hoof but does not chew the cud 13
Jos 9: 4 they on their part acted with cunning •
19: 9 formed part of the territory of Judah; •
Rut 1:17 May the LORD . . if even death parts me from you. 12
2: 3 to come to the part of the field belonging to Bo'az 5
1Sm 23:20 come . . and our part shall be to surrender him •
30:26 David . . sent part of the spoil to his friends 8
2Sm 14: 6 they quarreled . . there was no one to part them 10
1Kg 6:38 the house was finished in all its parts 3
7:50 for the doors of the innermost part of the house •
2Kg 2: 8 water was parted to the one side and to the other 6
14 water was parted to the one side and to the other 6
10:32 the LORD began to cut off parts of Israel. •
18:23 you are able on your part to set riders upon them. 7
2Ch 35: 5 let there be for each a part of a father's house 4
36: 7 carried part of the vessels of the . . LORD 8
Prv 20:27 searching all his innermost parts. 1
30 strokes make clean the innermost parts. 1
Isa 36: 8 horses, if you are able on your part to set riders 7
44:15 fuel . . he takes a part of it and warms himself 8
Jer 34:18 they cut in two and passed between its parts 2
19 who passed between the parts of the calf; 2
Ezk 4:11 shall drink by measure, the sixth part of a hin; •
5: 2 A third part you shall burn in the fire •
2 a third part you shall take and strike •
2 and a third part you shall scatter to the wind •
12 A third part of you shall die of pestilence •
12 a third part shall fall by the sword round about •
12 and a third part I will scatter to all the winds •
41:11 the doors of the side chambers opened on the part •
11 the breadth of the part that was left free 9
Ams 3:12 the corner of a couch and part of a bed. •
Lke 11:36 whole body is full of light, having no part dark 20
Joh 13: 8 If I do not wash you, you have no part in me. 20
19:23 they took his garments and made four parts 20
24 They parted my garments among them 15
Act 2:10 Egypt and the parts of Libya belonging to Cyre'ne 20
5: 2 brought only a part 20
3 to keep back part of the proceeds of the land? 14
8:21 You have neither part nor lot in this matter 19
20: 2 When he had gone through these parts 20
23: 6 one part were Sad'ducees and the other Pharisees 20
Rom 9:14 Is there injustice on God's part? By no means! 22
11:25 a hardening has come upon part of Israel 20
1Co 12:15 that would not make it any less a part of the body. 16
16 that would not make it any less a part of the body. 16
20 As it is, there are many parts, yet one body. 18
22 the parts of the body which seem to be weaker 18
23 those parts of the body which we think less honorable •
13:12 Now I know in part; then I shall understand fully 20
2Co 1:14 as you have understood in part 20
8: 2 in a wealth of liberality on their part. •
Eph 4: 9 descended into the lower parts of the earth? 20
16 when each part is working properly 20
Rev 16:19 The great city was split into three parts 20
2Es 4:45 whether for us the greater part has gone by. •
52 I can tell you in part 25
5:34 and to search out part of his judgment. 25
6:12 thou didst show me in part on a previous night. 25
41 that one part might move upward 25
41 and the other part remain beneath. 25
42 in the seventh part of the earth 25
42 six parts thou didst dry up 25
47 thou didst command the seventh part 25
50 the seventh part where the water had been 25
51 one of the parts which had been dried up 25
52 didst give the seventh part, the watery part 25
52 didst give the seventh part, the watery part •
7: 5 unless he passes through the narrow part? •
9: 1 when you see that a certain part . . are past 25
14:11 For the age is divided into twelve parts 25
11 and nine of its parts have already passed •
12 as well as half of the tenth part 25
12 so two of its parts remain •
12 besides half of the tenth part. 25
15:38 from the north, and another part from the west. 26
60 and shall destroy a part of your land 26
Tob 8: 3 he fled to the remotest parts of Egypt •
12:18 For I did not come as a favor on my part •
AEs 14: 2 every part that she loved to adorn 24
Wis 14:11 though part of what God created 17
Sir 45: 3 showed him part of his glory. •
1Mc 6:40 Now a part of the king's army was spread out 20
45 they parted before him on both sides. 23
9:23 the lawless emerged in all parts of Israel 21
12:37 part of the wall on the valley to the east •
2Mc 7:26 After much urging on his part •
14:22 to prevent sudden treachery on the part of the enemy 16

part (2) 1.הלך 2.ἀποσπάω 3.διαχωρίζω 4.διΐστημι 5.χωρίζω
Jos 22: 9 returned home, parting from the people of Israel 1
Lke 24:51 While he blessed them, he parted from them 4
Act 21: 1 when we had parted from them and set sail 2
Phm 1:15 Perhaps this is why he was parted from you 5
Sus 1:14 when they went out, they parted from each other. 3
part *See* 1/4, any, broad, choice, demolished, far, fat, hallowed, hinder, inferior, inmost, inner, innermost, inward, low, main, outlying, presentable, private, remote, responsible, rich, secret, take, unpresentable, uttermost, write.

do part of next of kin 1.גאל
Rut 3:13 if he will do the part of the next of kin for you 1
13 the part of the next of kin for you . . let him do it 1
13 he is not willing to do the part of the next of kin 1
13 do the part of the next of kin for you. 1

equal part 1.בַּד
Exd 30:34 spices . . (of each shall there be an equal part) 1

part left free 1.נוח
Ezk 41: 9 the part of the platform which was left free was 1

part of the night 1.φυλακή
Mat 24:43 in what part of the night the thief was coming 1

partake 1.אכל 2.לקח 3.ἐφάπτω 4.μεταλαμβάνω 5.μετέχω
Jos 9:14 the men partook of their provisions 2
Ezr 2:63 not to partake of the most holy food 1
Neh 7:65 not to partake of the most holy food, until 1
Act 2:46 partook of food with glad and generous hearts 4
1Co 10:17 we all partake of the one bread. 5
21 You cannot partake of the table of the Lord 5
30 If I partake with thankfulness 5
Heb 2:14 he himself likewise partook of the same nature 5
Wis 16: 3 might partake of delicacies. 5
2Mc 7: 1 to partake of unlawful swine's flesh. 3

make partake of a sacrifice 1.σπλαγχνίζω
2Mc 6: 8 and make them partake of the sacrifices 1

partake of the sacrifice 1.σπλαγχνισμός
2Mc 6: 7 to partake of the sacrifices 1

partaker 1.κοινωνός 2.μέτοχος 3.συγκοινωνός 4.συμμέτοχος
Eph 3: 6 partakers of the promise in Christ Jesus 4
Php 1: 7 you are all partakers with me of grace 3
Heb 6: 4 have become partakers of the Holy Spirit 2
1Pe 5: 1 a partaker in the glory that is to be revealed. 1
2Pe 1: 4 and become partakers of the divine nature. 1

partial 1.הדר 2.נכר פָּנִים 3.נשׂא פָּנִים 4.εὐλαβέομαι ἀπὸ προσώπου
Exd 23: 3 nor shall you be partial to a poor man in his suit. 1
Lev 19:15 you shall not be partial to the poor 3
Deu 1:17 You shall not be partial in judgment; 2
10:17 God, who is not partial and takes no bribe. 3
Prv 18: 5 It is not good to be partial to a wicked man 3
Sir 7: 6 lest you be partial to a powerful man 4

partiality 1.הַכָּרַת פָּנִים 2.מַשֹּׂא פָּנִים 3.נכר פָּנִים 4.δόξα προσώπου 5.λαμβάνω πρόσωπον 6.πρόσκλισις 7.προσωπολήμπτης 8.προσωπολημψία 9.πρόσωπον

2Ch 19: 7 or partiality, or taking bribes. 2
Prv 24:23 Partiality in judging is not good. 3
Isa 3: 9 Their partiality witnesses against them; 1
Lke 20:21 and show no partiality 9
Act 10:34 Truly I perceive that God shows no partiality 7
Rom 2:11 For God shows no partiality. 8
Gal 2: 6 God shows no partiality 9
Eph 6: 9 there is no partiality with him. 8
Col 3:25 there is no partiality. 8
1Ti 5:21 doing nothing from partiality. 6
Jas 2: 1 show no partiality as you hold the faith 8
1Es 4:39 With her there is no partiality or preference 5
Sir 4:22 Do not show partiality, to your own harm 9
27 nor show partiality to a ruler. 9
35:12 with him is no partiality. 4
13 will not show partiality in the case of a poor man; 9
42: 1 do not let partiality lead you to sin 9

show partiality 1.נכר פָּנִים 2.נשׂא פָּנִים 3.προσωποληπτέω

Deu 16:19 not pervert justice . . not show partiality; 1
Job 13: 8 Will you show partiality toward him 2
10 rebuke you if in secret you show partiality. 2
32:21 I will not show partiality to any person 2
34:19 who shows no partiality to princes 2
Ps 82: 2 How long . . show partiality to the wicked? Selah 2
Prv 28:21 To show partiality is not good; 1
Mal 2: 9 not kept my ways but have shown partiality 2
Jas 2: 9 But if you show partiality, you commit sin 3

participant 1.μέτοχος

3Mc 3:21 participants in our regular religious rites. 1

participate 1.κοινωνέω 2.μέτοχος

1Ti 5:22 nor participate in another man's sins 1
Heb 12: 8 in which all have participated 2
2Mc 5:20 afterward participated in its benefits 1

participation 1.κοινωνία

1Co 10:16 is it not a participation in the blood of Christ? 1
16 is it not a participation in the body of Christ? 1
Php 2: 1 any participation in the Spirit 1

parting 1.אֵם 2.διαχωρίζομαι

Ezk 21:21 king of Babylon stands at the parting of the way 1
Lke 9:33 as the men were parting from him 2

parting *See also* gift.

parting of ways 1.פֶּרֶק

Obd 1:14 should not have stood at the parting of the ways 1

partisanship 1.ἐριθεία

Php 1:17 the former proclaim Christ out of partisanship 1

partly 1.מִן (A) 2.מִנְּהֵין (A) 3.מִן קְצָת (A) 4.μέρος τι 5.ὁ δέ 6.ὁ μέν

Dan 2:33 its feet partly of iron and partly of clay. 2
33 its feet partly of iron and partly of clay. 2
41 toes partly of potter's clay and partly of iron 2
41 toes partly of potter's clay and partly of iron 2
42 toes of the feet were partly iron and partly clay 2
42 toes of the feet were partly iron and partly clay 2
42 kingdom shall be partly strong and partly brittle. 3
42 kingdom shall be partly strong and partly brittle. 1
1Co 11:18 I partly believe it 4
4Mc 6:12 At that point, partly out of pity for his old age 6
13 partly out of sympathy 5
13 partly out of admiration for his endurance 5

partner 1.חלק 2.κοινωνός 3.μέτοχος

Prv 29:24 The partner of a thief hates his own life; 1
Lke 5: 7 they beckoned to their partners 3
10 sons of Zeb'edee, who were partners with Simon. 2
1Co 7:15 if the unbelieving partner desires to separate •
10:18 partners in the altar? 2
20 I do not want you to be partners with demons. 2
2Co 8:23 As for Titus, he is my partner and fellow worker 2
Phm 1:17 if you consider me your partner 2
Heb 10:33 sometimes being partners with those so treated. 2
AEs 16:13 of Esther, the blameless partner of our kingdom 2
Sir 41:18 of unjust dealing, before your partner or friend; 2
42: 3 of keeping accounts with a partner 2

partnership 1.κοινωνία 2.μετοχή

2Co 6:14 what partnership have righteousness 2
Php 1: 5 thankful for your partnership in the gospel 1

partnership *See also* enter.

partridge 1.קֹרֵא 2.πέρδιξ

1Sm 26:20 like one who hunts a partridge in the mountains. 1
Jer 17:11 Like the partridge that gathers a brood 1
Sir 11:30 Like a decoy partridge in a cage 2

parts *See* divide, two.

party 1.אִישׁ 2.αἵρεσις 3.μερίς 4.μέρος

Exd 22: 9 the case of both parties shall come before God; •
Deu 19:17 then both parties to the dispute shall appear 1
Act 5:17 the party of the Sad'ducees 2
15: 5 who belonged to the party of the Pharisees 2
23: 9 some of the scribes of the Pharisees' party 4
26: 5 the strictest party of our religion 2
Wis 1:16 because they are fit to belong to his party. 3
2:24 those who belong to his party experience it. 3

party (2) 1.ὁμιλία 2.συμπόσιον

3Mc 5:18 After the party had been going on for some time 1
36 reconvened the party in the same manner 2

party *See* spirit.

both parties 1.οὗτος καὶ οὗτος

1Mc 8:30 terms are in effect both parties shall determine 1

circumcision party 1.ἐκ περιτομῆς

Act 11: 2 the circumcision party criticized him 1
Gal 2:12 fearing the circumcision party. 1
Tit 1:10 especially the circumcision party; 1

paschal *See* lamb.

pass 1.בוא 2.הלך 3.יצא 4.מוֹצָא 5.מלא 6.מִן 7.עבר 8.עבר דֶּרֶךְ 9.עדה 10.צבט 11.רבה 12.שׁכח 13.חלף(A) 14.ἀπέρχομαι 15.διαβαίνω 16.διαγίνομαι 17.διαπορεύομαι 18.διέρχομαι 19.ἐκβάλλω 20.ἐκπορεύομαι 21.ἔρχομαι 22.μεταβαίνω 23.μετάγω 24.παράγω 25.παραπορεύομαι 26.παρατρέχω 27.πάρειμι 28.παρέρχομαι 29.παροδεύω 30.πάροδος 31.πληρόω 32.προέρχομαι 33.ὑπερέχω 34.χωρέω 35.intermitto 36.pertranseo 37.praetereo 38.transeo

Gen 15:17 a flaming torch passed between these pieces. 7
18: 3 favor in your sight, do not pass by your servant. 7
5 after that you may pass on– 7
32:16 Jacob . . said to his servants, "Pass on before me 7
21 the present passed on before him; 7
31 The sun rose upon him as he passed Penu'el 7
33:14 Let my lord pass on before his servant 7
37:28 Then Mid'ianite traders passed by; 7
Exd 7:25 Seven days passed after the LORD had struck 5
14:20 and the night passed without one coming near 18
15:16 still as a stone, till thy people, O LORD, pass 7
16 the people pass by whom thou hast purchased. 7
17: 5 the LORD said to Moses, "Pass on before the people 7
33:22 while my glory passes by I will put you in a cleft 7
22 I will cover you . . until I have passed by; 7
34: 6 The LORD passed before him, and proclaimed 7
Lev 27:32 every tenth animal of all that pass under 7
Num 5:22 that brings the curse pass into your bowels 1
14: 7 The land, which we passed through to spy it out 7
20:17 Now let us pass through your land. 7
17 We will not pass through field or vineyard 7
19 let me only pass through on foot, nothing more. 7
21:22 Let me pass through your land; 7
23 not allow Israel to pass through his territory. 7
31:23 everything . . you shall pass through the fire 7
23 whatever . . you shall pass through the water. 7
33: 8 passed through the midst of the sea 7
Deu 2: 4 You are about to pass through the territory 7
27 'Let me pass through your land; I will go only 7
30 Sihon the king of Heshbon would not let us pass 7
23:23 be careful to perform what has passed your lips 4
Jos 3: 4 for you have not passed this way before. 7
6 Take up the ark . . and pass on before the people. 7
4: 5 Pass on before the ark . . into the midst 7
6: 7 let the armed men pass on before the ark 7
13 priests . . passed on, blowing the trumpets 2
10:29 Then Joshua passed on from Makke'dah . . to Libnah 7
31 Joshua passed on from Libnah . . to Lachish 7
34 Joshua passed on with all Israel from Lachish 7
18:18 and passing on to the north . . it goes down 7
19 the boundary passes on to the north 7
24:17 and among all the peoples through whom we passed; 7
Jdg 9:25 they robbed all who passed by them along that way; 7
11:17 Let us pass, we pray, through your land'; but the king 7
19 Let us pass, we pray, through your land to our 7
20 Sihon did not trust Israel to pass through his 7
29 Manas'seh, and passed on to Mizpah of Gilead 7
29 from Mizpah . . he passed on to the Ammonites. 7
18:13 they passed on from there . . and came 7
19:12 not turn aside . . but we will pass on to Gib'e-ah. 7
14 So they passed on and went their way; and the sun 7
18 We are passing from Bethlehem in Judah 7
Rut 2:14 she sat . . and he passed to her parched grain; 10
1Sm 7: 2 From . . a long time passed, some twenty years 11
9: 4 they passed through the hill country of E'phraim 7
4 and passed through the land of Shal'ishah 7
4 they passed through the land of Sha'alim 7
4 Then they passed through the land of Benjamin 7
27 Tell the servant to pass on before us 7
27 when he has passed on stop here . . for a while 7
15:12 turned, and passed on, and went down to Gilgal. 7
29: 2 the lords . . were passing on by hundreds 7
2 and David and his men were passing on in the rear 7
2Sm 1:26 your love to me was . . passing the love of women. 6
15:18 And all his servants passed by him; 7
18 all the 600 . . passed on before the king. 7
22 And David said to It'tai, "Go then, pass on. 7
22 It'tai the Gittite passed on, with all his men 7
23 the country wept . . as all the people passed by 7
23 all the people passed on toward the wilderness. 7
24 until the people had all passed out of the city. 7
16: 1 When David had passed a little beyond the summit 7
20:14 Sheba passed through all the tribes of Israel 7
1Kg 9: 8 every one passing by it will be astonished 7
13:25 men passed by, and saw the body thrown in the road 7
18:29 as midday passed, they raved 7
19:11 And behold, the LORD passed by 7
19 Eli'jah passed by him and cast his mantle 7
20:39 as the king passed, he cried to the king and said 7
2Kg 4: 8 So whenever he passed that way, he would turn 7
9 man of God, who is continually passing our way. 7
6: 9 Beware that you do not pass this place 7
26 as the king of Israel was passing by upon the wall 7
30 clothes–now he was passing by upon the wall–and 7
14: 9 a wild beast of Lebanon passed by and trampled 7
2Ch 7:21 every one passing by will be astonished, and say 7
25:18 wild beast of Lebanon passed by and trampled 7
Neh 2:14 no place for the beast that was under me to pass. 7
Job 9:11 Lo, he passes by me, and I see him not; 7
14: 5 hast appointed his bounds that he cannot pass 7
20 prevailest for ever against him, and he passes; 2
15:19 no stranger passed among them). 7
19: 8 He has walled up my way, so that I cannot pass 7
28: 8 the lion has not passed over it. 9
37:21 skies, when the wind has passed and cleared them. 7
Ps 31:12 I have passed out of mind like one who is dead; 12
37:36 Again I passed by, and, lo, he was no more; 7
57: 1 refuge, till the storms of destruction pass by. 7
66: 6 men passed through the river on foot. 7
78:39 but flesh, a wind that passes and comes not again. 2
89:41 All that pass by despoil him; 7
104: 9 Thou didst set a bound which they should not pass 7
129: 8 while those who pass by do not say, "The blessing 7
144: 4 like a breath, his days are like a passing shadow. 7
148: 6 he fixed their bounds which cannot be passed. 7
Prv 4:15 turn away from it and pass on. 7
7: 8 passing along the street near her corner 7
9:15 calling to those who pass 7
10:25 When the tempest passes, the wicked is no more 7
24:30 I passed by the field of a sluggard 7
26:10 he who hires a passing fool or drunkard. 7
17 like one who takes a passing dog by the ears. 7
Sng 3: 4 Scarcely had I passed them, when I found him 7
Isa 8: 8 overflow and pass on, reaching even to the neck; 7
29: 5 multitude of the ruthless like passing chaff. 7
33:21 with oars can go, nor stately ship can pass. 7
34:10 none shall pass through it for ever and ever. 7
41: 3 He pursues them and passes on safely 7
43: 2 you pass through the waters I will be with you; 7
Jer 5:22 a perpetual barrier which it cannot pass; 7
18:16 Every one who passes by it is horrified 7
19: 8 every one who passes by it will be horrified 7
22: 8 And many nations will pass by this city 7
33:13 flocks shall again pass under the hands 7
34:18 they cut in two and passed between its parts 7
19 who passed between the parts of the calf; 7
49:17 every one who passes by it will be horrified 7
50:13 one who passes by Babylon shall be appalled 7
51:43 and through which no son of man passes. 7
Lam 1:12 Is it nothing to you, all you who pass by? 8
4:21 Rejoice . . but to you also the cup shall pass; 7
Ezk 5: 1 razor and pass it over your head and your beard; 7
14 and in the sight of all that pass by. 7
17 pestilence and blood shall pass through you; 7
16: 6 And when I passed by you, and saw you weltering 7
8 When I passed by you again and looked upon you 7
26:18 isles . . in the sea are dismayed at your passing. 3
36:34 it was in the sight of all who passed by. 7
39:14 They will set apart men to pass through the land 7
15 when these pass through the land and any one sees 7
Dan 4:16 let seven times pass over him. 13
23 with the beasts . . till seven times pass over 13
25 seven times shall pass over you, 13
32 seven times shall pass over you, 13
9: 2 must pass before the end of the desolations 5
Ams 7: 8 my people Israel; I will never again pass by them; 7
8: 2 my people Israel; I will never again pass by them. 7
Jon 2: 3 all thy waves and thy billows passed over me. 7
Mic 1:11 Pass on your way, inhabitants of Shaphir 7
2: 8 who pass by trustingly with no thought of war. 7
13 they will break through and pass the gate 7
13 Their king will pass on before them 7
7:18 and passing over transgression for the remnant 7
Zep 2:15 Every one who passes by her hisses 7
Zec 10:11 They shall pass through the sea of Egypt 7
Mat 5:18 not a dot, will pass from the law until all is 28
8:28 so fierce that no one could pass that way. 28
9: 9 As Jesus passed on from there, he saw a man 24
27 as Jesus passed on from there 24
15:17 goes into the mouth passes into the stomach 34
17 into the stomach, and so passes on? 19
29 and passed along the Sea of Galilee 21
20:30 when they heard that Jesus was passing by 24
26:39 My father, if it be possible, let this cup pass 28
42 My Father, if this cannot pass unless I drink it 28

27:39 those who passed by derided him, 25
Mrk 2:14 as he passed on, he saw Levi the son of Alphaeus 24
6:48 He meant to pass by them 28
7:19 since it enters . . his stomach, and so passes on? 20
11:20 As they passed by in the morning 25
14:35 if it were possible, the hour might pass from him. 28
15:29 those who passed by derided him 25
Lke 16:26 in order that those who would pass from here 15
18:37 They told him, "Jesus of Nazareth is passing by. 28
19: 4 he was to pass that way. 18
Joh 5:24 has passed from death to life. 22
9: 1 As he passed by, he saw a man blind from his birth. 24
Act 7:30 Now when 40 years had passed 31
8:40 Philip . . and passing on he preached the gospel 18
9:23 When many days had passed 31
12:10 they had passed the first and the second guard 18
10 they went out and passed on through one street; 32
13:14 they passed on from Perga 18
16: 8 so, passing by My'sia, they went down to Tro'as. 28
25:13 Now when some days had passed 16
Rom 15:24 I hope to see you in passing as I go to Spain 17
1Co 10: 1 all passed through the sea 18
16: 7 For I do not want to see you now just in passing 30
Php 4: 7 the peace of God, which passes all understanding 33
Rev 9:12 The first woe has passed; 14
11:14 The second woe has passed; behold, the third woe 14
2Es 3:23 the times passed and the years were completed 38
4: 9 things through which you have passed 38
24 why we pass from the world like locusts 36
45 whether more time is to come than has passed 37
48 and behold, a flaming furnace passed by before me 38
49 after this a cloud full of water passed before me 38
49 and when the rainstorm had passed 38
50 so the quantity that passed was far greater 38
5:55 is aging and passing the strength of youth. 37
9:23 if you will let seven days more pass 35
13:20 to pass from the world like a cloud 36
14:11 and nine of its parts have already passed 38
15:60 as they pass they shall wreck the hateful city 38
Tob 1:21 not 50 days passed before . . 18
Jdt 5:21 then let my lord pass them by; 28
7:31 if these days pass by, and no help comes for us 18
Wis 1: 8 justice, when it punishes, will not pass him by. 29
2: 5 For our allotted time is the passing of a shadow 30
7 let no flower of spring pass by us. 29
5: 9 like a rumor that passes by; 26
10 when it has passed no trace can be found 15
14 it passes like the remembrance of a guest 29
6:22 I will not pass by the truth; 29
7:27 in every generation she passes into holy souls 22
10: 8 For because they passed wisdom by 29
17: 9 yet, scared by the passing of beasts 15
Sir 10: 8 Sovereignty passes from nation to nation 23
11:19 he does not know how much time will pass 28
14:14 let not your share of desired good pass by you. 28
23: 2 that it may not pass by my sins; 27
1Mc 5:48 we will simply pass by on foot 28
12:10 considerable time has passed 18
2Mc 1:20 after many years had passed 18
22 When this was done and some time had passed 18

pass (2) 1. מַעֲבָר 2. מַעְבָּרָה 3. ἀνάβασις 4. δίοδος

1Sm 13:23 Philistines went out to the pass of Michmash. 1
14: 4 In the pass, by which Jonathan sought to go over 2
Isa 10:29 they have crossed over the pass 2
Jdt 5: 1 had closed the passes in the hills 4
6: 7 put you in one of the cities beside the passes 3
14:11 they went out . . to the passes in the mountains. 3

pass (3) 1. עשה

Ecc 6:12 few days . . which he passes like a shadow? 1

pass (4) 1. דבר

2Kg 25: 6 king of Babylon . . who passed sentence upon him. 1
Jer 39: 5 and he passed sentence upon him. 1
52: 9 and he passed sentence upon him. 1

pass *See* bring.

pass again 1. שוב

Jer 6: 9 pass your hand again over its branches. 1

pass along 1. עבר 2. διέρχομαι 3. παράγω

Num34: 4 go on to Ha'zar-ad'dar, and pass along to Azmon; 1
Jos 15: 3 it goes out southward . . passes along to Zin 1
4 passes along to Azmon, goes out by the Brook 1
6 boundary . . passes along north of Beth-arabah; 1
7 and the boundary passes along to . . En-she'mesh 1
10 passes along to the . . shoulder of Mount Je'arim 1
10 down to Beth-she'mesh, and passes along by Timnah; 1
11 the boundary . . passes along to Mount Ba'alah 1
16: 2 from Bethel to Luz, it passes along to At'aroth 1
6 boundary . . passes along beyond it on the east 1
18:13 From there the boundary passes along southward 1
19:13 it passes along on the east . . to Gath-hepher 1
Ps 8: 8 whatever passes along the paths of the sea. 1
80:12 so that all who pass along the way pluck its fruit? 1
Lam 2:15 All who pass along the way clap their hands at you; 1
Mrk 1:16 And passing along by the Sea of Galilee 3
Lke 17:11 passing along between Sama'ria and Galilee. 2
Act 17:23 as I passed along . . I found also an altar 2

pass away 1. חלף 2. כלה 3. סור 4. עבר 5. פנה 6. עדה (A) 7. ἀπέρχομαι 8. καταργέω 9. παράγω 10. παρέρχομαι 11. discedo 12. pertranseo 13. transeo

Job 6:15 as a torrent-bed, as freshets that pass away 4
11:16 remember it as waters that have passed away. 4
30:15 my prosperity has passed away like a cloud. 4
34:20 at midnight the people are shaken and pass away 4
Ps 90: 9 For all our days pass away under thy wrath 5
102: 3 For my days pass away like smoke 2
26 changest them like a raiment, and they pass away; 1
Isa 2:18 the idols shall utterly pass away. 1
31: 9 His rock shall pass away in terror 4
Jer 8:13 and what I gave them has passed away from them. 4
Dan 7:14 everlasting dominion, which shall not pass away 6
Ams 6: 7 those who stretch themselves shall pass away. 3
Nah 1:12 they will be cut off and pass away. 4
Mat 5:18 till heaven and earth pass away, not an iota 10
24:34 this generation will not pass away 10
35 Heaven and earth will pass away 10
35 but my words will not pass away. 10
Mrk 13:30 this generation will not pass away 10
31 Heaven and earth will pass away 10
31 my words will not pass away. 10
Lke 16:17 it is easier for heaven and earth to pass away 10
21:32 this generation will not pass away 10
33 Heaven and earth will pass away 10
33 my words will not pass away. 10
1Co 7:31 the form of this world is passing away. 9
13: 8 as for prophecies, they will pass away 8
8 as for knowledge, it will pass away. 8
10 the perfect comes, the imperfect will pass away. 8
2Co 5:17 the old has passed away, behold, the new has come. 10
Jas 1:10 like the flower of the grass he will pass away. 10
2Pe 3:10 then the heavens will pass away with a loud noise 10
1Jn 2: 8 because the darkness is passing away 9
17 the world passes away, and the lust of it; 9
Rev 21: 1 first heaven and the first earth had passed away 7
4 for the former things have passed away. 7
2Es 4:29 if the place . . does not pass away 11
6:20 the age which is about to pass away 12
7:33 and compassion shall pass away 12
113 in which corruption has passed away 12
8:54 sorrows have passed away 13
Wis 2: 4 our life will pass away 10
Sir 14:19 the man who made it will pass away with it. 7

pass beyond 1. עבר

Jdg 3:26 and passed beyond the sculptured stones 1
1Sm 14:23 and the battle passed beyond Beth-a'ven. 1

pass by on the other side 1. ἀντιπαρέρχομαι

Lke 10:31 when he saw him he passed by on the other side. 1
32 a Levite . . passed by on the other side 1

cause to pass 1. עבר

Num27: 7 cause the inheritance . . to pass to them. 1
8 you shall cause his inheritance to pass to his 1
Ezk 14:15 If I cause wild beasts to pass through the land 1

come to pass 1. בוא 2. היה 3. γίνομαι 4. παραγίνομαι 5. fio 6. infero 7. venio

Gen 41:13 as he interpreted to us, so it came to pass; 2
Deu 13: 2 sign or wonder which he tells you comes to pass 1
18:22 if the word does not come to pass or come true 2
Jos 21:45 Not one . . had failed; all came to pass. 1
23:14 all have come to pass for you 1
Jdg 21: 3 why has this come to pass in Israel 2
1Sm 10: 9 and all these signs came to pass that day. 1
1Kg 1:21 it will come to pass, when my lord the king sleeps 2
13:32 the saying . . shall surely come to pass. 2
2Kg 15:12 (This was the promise . . And so it came to pass.) 2
Ps 105:19 until what he had said came to pass 1
Isa 2: 2 It shall come to pass in the latter days 2
7: 7 not stand, and it shall not come to pass. 2
42: 9 Behold, the former things have come to pass 1
48: 3 then suddenly I did them and they came to pass. 1
5 before they came to pass I announced them to you 1
Jer 12:16 And it shall come to pass 2
28: 9 when the word of that prophet comes to pass 1
30: 8 it shall come to pass in that day, says the LORD 2
31:28 it shall come to pass that as I have watched over 2
32:24 What thou didst speak has come to pass 2
52: 3 things came to such a pass in Jerusalem and Judah 2
Lam 3:37 Who has commanded and it came to pass 2
Ezk 11:13 And it came to pass, while I was prophesying 2
24:14 I the LORD have spoken; it shall come to pass 1
Jol 2:28 And it shall come to pass afterward 2
32 And it shall come to pass that all who call 2
Mic 4: 1 It shall come to pass in the latter days 2
Hag 2:15 what will come to pass from this day onward. •
Zec 6:15 this shall come to pass, if you will . . obey 2
Mrk 11:23 believes that what he says will come to pass 3
Lke 1:20 until the day that these things come to pass 3
Act 26:22 what . . Moses said would come to pass 3
1Co 15:54 then shall come to pass the saying that is written 3
1Th 3: 4 just as it has come to pass, and as you know. 3
2Es 7:26 when the signs . . will come to pass 7
8:37 it will come to pass according to your words. 5
13:32 when these things come to pass 5
58 whatever things come to pass in their seasons. 6
Jdt 9: 5 Yea, the things thou didst intend came to pass 3
Sir 48:25 the hidden things before they came to pass. 4

pass days 1. διάγω

Tit 3: 3 passing our days in malice and envy 1

pass judgment 1. שפט 2. κρίνω

Ezk 23:45 But righteous men shall pass judgment on them 1
Rom 2: 1 in passing judgment upon him you condemn 2
14: 3 him who abstains pass judgment on him who eats; 2
4 to pass judgment on the servant of another? 2
10 Why do you pass judgment on your brother? 2
13 Then let us no more pass judgment on one another 2
Col 2:16 Therefore let no one pass judgment on you 2

pass life 1. ago

2Es 8:31 have passed our lives in ways that bring death 1

make pass 1. עבר

Exd 33:19 I will make all my goodness pass before you 1
1Sm 16: 8 Jesse called . . and made him pass before Samuel. 1
9 Then Jesse made Shammah pass by. 1
10 Jesse made seven of his sons pass before Samuel. 1
Ps 136:14 made Israel pass through the midst of it 1
Ezk 20:37 I will make you pass under the rod 1

pass out 1. μεταβαίνω

1Jn 3:14 We know that we have passed out of death into life 1

pass over 1. סבב 2. עבר 3. פסח 4. πάρεσις 5. traiicio 6. transeo

Gen 31:52 I will not pass over this heap to you 2
52 you will not pass over this heap and this pillar 2
Exd 12:13 and when I see the blood, I will pass over you 3
23 the LORD will pass over the door, and will not 3
27 for he passed over the houses of the people 3
Num32:21 every armed man of you will pass over the Jordan 2
27 your servants will pass over, every man who 2
29 every man . . will pass with you over the Jordan 2
30 if they will not pass over with you armed 2
32 We will pass over armed before the LORD 2
33:51 When you pass over the Jordan into . . Canaan 2
Deu 2:18 This day you are to pass over the boundary of Moab 2
3:18 all your men of valor shall pass over armed 2
9: 1 O Israel; you are to pass over the Jordan this day 2
11:31 pass over the Jordan to go in to take possession 2
27: 2 day you pass over the Jordan to the land 2
3 pass over to enter the land which the LORD 2
4 passed over the Jordan, you shall set up 2
12 When you have passed over the Jordan, these shall 2
Jos 1:11 you are to pass over this Jordan, to go 2
14 all the men of valor . . shall pass over armed 2
2:23 came down . . and passed over and came to Joshua 2
3: 1 they . . lodged there before they passed over. 2
11 ark . . is to pass over before you into the Jordan. 2
14 when the people set out . . to pass over the Jordan 2
16 and the people passed over opposite Jericho. 2
17 when all Israel were passing over on dry ground 2
17 the nation finished passing over the Jordan. 2
4: 1 When all . . had finished passing over the Jordan 2
7 when it passed over the Jordan, the waters 2
10 The people passed over in haste; 2
11 when all the people had finished passing over 2
11 the ark of the LORD and the priests passed over 2
12 Gad and . . Manas'seh passed over 2
13 40,000 . . passed over before the LORD 2
22 'Israel passed over this Jordan on dry ground.' 2
23 God dried up the waters . . until you passed over 2
23 Red Sea, which he dried up . . until we passed over 2
22:19 pass over into the LORD's land 2
Jdg 3:28 Moabites, and allowed not a man to pass over. 2
8: 4 Gideon came to the Jordan and passed over 2
2Sm 2:15 Then they arose and passed over by number 2
17:16 Do not lodge tonight . . but by all means pass over; 2
2Kg 8:21 Joram passed over to Za'ir with all his chariots 1
2Ch 21: 9 Then Jeho'ram passed over with his commanders 2
Ps 103:16 for the wind passes over it, and it is gone 2
Isa 16: 8 its shoots spread abroad and passed over the sea. 2
23: 2 your messengers passed over the sea 2
6 Pass over to Tarshish, wail, O inhabitants 2
12 daughter of Sidon; arise, pass over to Cyprus 2
35: 8 the Holy Way; the unclean shall not pass over it 2
51:10 of the sea a way for the redeemed to pass over? 2
23 said to you, 'Bow down, that we may pass over'; 2
23 and like the street for them to pass over. 2
Jer 5:22 though they roar, they cannot pass over it. 2
48:32 vine of Sibmah! Your branches passed over the sea 2
Ams 6: 2 Pass over to Calneh, and see; 2
Rom 3:25 because . . he had passed over former sins; 4
2Es 7:86 how some of them will pass over into torments. •
12:29 two little wings passing over to the head 5
13:44 until they had passed over. 6
47 that they may be able to pass over 6

pass the night 1. לון
Neh 4:22 every man . . pass the night within Jerusalem 1
Jol 1:13 pass the night in sackcloth, O ministers of my God! 1

pass the time 1. διάγω
3Mc 6:35 the Jews . . passed the time in feasting 1

pass through 1. ברח 2. חלף 3. עבר 4. διαπορεύομαι 5. διέρχομαι 6. διοδεύω 7. παραπορεύομαι διά 8. ingredior 9. pertranseo 10. transeo
Gen 12: 6 Abram passed through the land to the place 3
30:32 let me pass through all your flock today 3
Exd 12:12 For I will pass through the land of Egypt 3
23 the LORD will pass through to slay the Egyptians; 3
26:28 bar . . shall pass through from end to end. 1
36:33 he made the middle bar to pass through 1
Num20:17 until we have passed through your territory. 3
18 You shall not pass through, lest I come out 3
20 Edom said, "You shall not pass through. 3
21:22 until we have passed through your territory. 3
Deu 2:28 only let me pass through on foot 3
29:16 midst of the nations through which you passed 3
Jos 1:11 Pass through the camp, and command the people 3
Jdg 11:29 and he passed through Gilead and Manas'seh 3
1Kg 18: 6 they divided the land . . to pass through it; 3
Neh 2: 7 let me pass through until I come to Judah; 3
Job 11:10 If he passes through, and imprisons 2
Ps 78:13 He divided the sea and let them pass through it 3
Isa 8:21 They will pass through the land 3
10:28 he has come to Ai'ath; he has passed through Migron 3
28:15 when the overwhelming scourge passes through 3
18 when the overwhelming scourge passes through 3
19 As often as it passes through it will take you; 3
19 for morning by morning it will pass through 3
47: 2 uncover your legs, pass through the rivers. 3
60:15 forsaken and hated, with no one passing through 3
Jer 2: 6 in a land that none passes through 3
9:10 they are laid waste so that no one passes through 3
12 like a wilderness, so that no one passes through? 3
Lam 3:44 wrapped . . so that no prayer can pass through. 3
Ezk 9: 5 Pass through the city after him, and smite; 3
14:15 no man may pass through because of the beasts; 3
29:11 No foot of man shall pass through it 3
11 no foot of beast shall pass through it; 3
33:28 be so desolate that none will pass through. 3
47: 5 and it was a river that I could not pass through 3
5 a river that could not be passed through. 3
Dan 11:10 which . . come on and overflow and pass through 3
40 come into countries . . overflow and pass through. 3
Jol 3:17 and strangers shall never again pass through it. 3
Ams 5:17 wailing, for I will pass through the midst of you 3
Mat 12:43 he passes through waterless places 5
Mrk 9:30 They went on . . and passed through Galilee 7
Lke 4:30 passing through the midst of them he went away. 5
11:24 he passes through waterless places seeking rest; 5
19: 1 He entered Jericho and was passing through. 5
Joh 4: 4 He had to pass through Samar'ia. 5
Act 14:24 Then they passed through Pisid'ia 5
15: 3 they passed through both Phoeni'cia and Sama'ria 5
17: 1 Now when they had passed through Amphip'olis 6
19: 1 Paul passed through the upper country 5
21 Paul resolved . . to pass through Macedo'nia 5
1Co 16: 5 visit you after passing through Macedo'nia 5
5 for I intend to pass through Macedo'nia 5
Heb 4:14 high priest who has passed through the heavens 5
2Es 3:19 thy glory passed through the four gates 10
5:11 Has righteousness . . passed through you? 9
7: 5 unless he passes through the narrow part? 10
9 unless he passes through the danger 9
14 the living pass through the difficult and vain 8
16:77 so that no one can pass through! 10
Jdt 2:24 and passed through Mesopotamia 5
10:10 and passed through the valley 5
13:10 they passed through the camp 5
Wis 14: 5 and passing through the billows on a raft 5
19: 8 those . . passed through as one nation 5
1Mc 5:48 Let us pass through your land to get to our land 5
51 Then he passed through the city over the slain. 5
66 and passed through Marisa. 4
11:62 he passed through the country as far as Damascus. 5

pass up 1. ἀνάβασις
Jdt 4: 7 to seize the passes up into the hills 1
7: 1 to seize the passes up into the hill country 1

pass up and down 1. עבר
Jos 18: 9 So the men went and passed up and down in the land 1

passage 1. דֶּרֶךְ 2. מַהֲלָךְ 3. עבר 4. περιοχή 5. πορεία 6. introitus
Num20:21 Edom refused to give Israel passage through 3
Ezk 42: 4 And before the chambers was a passage inward 2
11 with a passage in front of them; 1
12 on the east side, where one enters the passage •
Mrk 12:26 in the passage about the bush •
Lke 20:37 even Moses showed, in the passage about the bush •
Act 8:32 passage of the scripture which he was reading 4
2Es 13:43 the narrow passages of the Euphrates river. 6
Wis 5:11 no evidence of its passage is found 5

passage through 1. δίοδος
Jdt 7:22 and in the passages through the gates 1

passageway 1. ὁδός
LJr 1:43 the women . . sit along the passageways 1

passer-by 1. עבר 2. παράγω 3. παραπορεύομαι
Ezk 16:15 and lavished your harlotries on any passer-by. 1
25 offering yourself to any passer-by 1
Mrk 15:21 they compelled a passer-by, Simon of Cyre'ne 2
LJr 1:43 when one of them is led off by one of the passers-by 3

passing *See* guest.

passion 1. קִנְאָה 2. ἐπιθυμία 3. ἡδονή 4. θυμός 5. ὄρεξις 6. πάθημα 7. πάθος 8. πάσχω 9. φιλία
Prv 14:30 but passion makes the bones rot. 1
Act 1: 3 he presented himself alive after his passion 8
Rom 1:26 God gave them up to dishonorable passions. 7
27 men . . consumed with passion for one another 5
6:12 to make you obey their passions. 2
7: 5 our sinful passions, aroused by the law 6
1Co 7: 9 it is better to marry than to be aflame with passion. •
Gal 5:24 the flesh with its passions and desires. 6
Eph 2: 3 once lived in the passions of our flesh 2
Col 3: 5 fornication, impurity, passion, evil desire 7
1Th 4: 5 not in the passion of lust 7
2Ti 2:22 shun youthful passions 2
Tit 2:12 to renounce irreligion and worldly passions 2
3: 3 slaves to various passions and pleasures 2
Jas 4: 1 Is it not your passions . . at war in your members? 3
3 you ask wrongly, to spend it on your passions. 3
1Pe 1:14 the passions of your former ignorance 2
2:11 to abstain from the passions of the flesh 2
4: 2 no longer by human passions but by the will of God 2
3 living in licentiousness, passions 2
2Pe 1: 4 the corruption . . in the world because of passion 2
2:10 indulge in the lust of defiling passion 2
18 entice with licentious passions of the flesh 2
3: 3 scoffers . . following their own passions 2
Jde 1:16 malcontents, following their own passions 2
18 scoffers, following their own ungodly passions 2
Rev 14: 8 drink the wine of her impure passion. 4
18: 3 drunk the wine of her impure passion 4
Sir 9: 8 by it passion is kindled like a fire. 9
4Mc 2: 3 he nullified the frenzy of the passions. 7
7:10 O supreme king over the passions, Eleazar! 7
18 are able to control the passions of the flesh 7

passion *See also* overwhelm.

passion be strong 1. ὑπέρακμος
1Co 7:36 if his passions are strong, and it has to be 1

passover 1. פֶּסַח 2. πάσχα
Exd 12:11 It is the LORD'S passover. 1
27 It is the sacrifice of the LORD'S passover 1
43 This is the ordinance of the passover 1
48 stranger . . would keep the passover to the LORD 1
34:25 the sacrifice of the feast of the passover 1
Lev 23: 5 In the first month . . is the LORD'S passover 1
Num 9: 2 Israel keep the passover at its appointed time. 1
4 Israel that they should keep the passover. 1
5 they kept the passover in the first month 1
6 that they could not keep the passover on that day; 1
10 he shall still keep the passover to the LORD. 1
12 according to all the statute for the passover 1
13 yet refrains from keeping the passover 1
14 stranger . . will keep the passover to the LORD 1
14 according to the statute of the passover 1
28:16 On the fourteenth day . . is the LORD'S passover. 1
33: 3 on the day after the passover the people 1
Deu 16: 1 keep the passover to the LORD your God; 1
Jos 5:10 they kept the passover on the fourteenth day 1
11 on the morrow after the passover, on that very day 1
2Kg 23:21 Keep the passover to the LORD your God 1
22 no such passover had been kept since the days 1
23 this passover was kept to the LORD in Jerusalem. 1
2Ch 30: 1 to keep the passover to the LORD the God of Israel. 1
2 had taken counsel to keep the passover 1
5 should come and keep the passover to the LORD 1
18 ate the passover otherwise than as prescribed. 1
35: 1 Josi'ah kept a passover to the LORD in Jerusalem; 1
16 to keep the passover and to offer burnt 1
17 people of Israel . . present kept the passover 1
18 No passover like it had been kept in Israel since 1
18 none . . kept such a passover as was kept 1
19 eighteenth year . . this passover was kept. 1
Ezr 6:19 returned exiles kept the passover. 1
Ezk 45:21 you shall celebrate the feast of the passover 1
Mat 26: 2 after two days the Passover is coming 2
17 prepare for you to eat the passover? 2
18 keep the passover at your house 2
19 they prepared the passover. 2
Mrk 14: 1 It was now two days before the Passover 2
12 prepare for you to eat the passover? 2
14 where I am to eat the passover with my disciples?' 2
16 they prepared the passover. 2
Lke 2:41 every year at the feast of the Passover. 2
22: 1 which is called the Passover. 2
8 prepare the passover for us, that we may eat it. 2
11 where I am to eat the passover with my disciples?' 2
13 they prepared the passover. 2
15 I have earnestly desired to eat this passover 2
Joh 2:13 The Passover of the Jews was at hand 2
23 when he was in Jerusalem at the Passover feast 2
6: 4 the Passover, the feast of the Jews, was at hand. 2
11:55 Now the Passover of the Jews was at hand 2
55 many went up . . before the Passover 2
12: 1 Six days before the Passover 2
13: 1 Now before the feast of the Passover 2
18:28 might not be defiled, but might eat the passover. 2
39 I should release one man for you at the Passover; 2
19:14 Now it was the day of Preparation of the Passover; 2
Act 12: 4 after the Passover to bring him out to the people. 2
Heb 11:28 By faith he kept the Passover 2
1Es 1: 1 Josiah kept the passover to his Lord 2
6 keep the passover according to the commandment 2
8 gave to the priests for the passover 2,600 sheep 2
9 gave the Levites for the passover 5,000 sheep 2
13 they prepared the passover for themselves •
16 the Levites prepared the passover for them. •
17 the passover was kept 2
19 the people of Israel . . kept the passover 2
20 No passover like it had been kept in Israel 2
21 such a passover as was kept by Josiah 2
22 this passover was kept. 2
7:10 kept the passover on the fourteenth day 2

passover *See also* lamb, offering, sacrifice.

past 1. אָז 2. סור 3. עבר 4. ראשון 5. שוב 6. תְּמוֹל שִׁלְשֹׁם 7. γίνομαι 8. διαγίνομαι 9. ἔμπροσθεν 10. ἔμπροσθεν χρόνος 11. παρέρχομαι 12. παροίχομαι 13. πρότερος 14. pertranseo 15. praetereo 16. transeo
Gen 50: 4 when the days of weeping for him were past 3
Exd 21:29 if the ox has been accustomed to gore in the past 6
36 the ox has been accustomed to gore in the past 6
Deu 4:32 For ask now of the days that are past 4
1Sm 15:32 Surely the bitterness of death is past. 2
Job 14:13 thou wouldest conceal me until thy wrath be past 5
17:11 My days are past, my plans are broken off 3
Ps 71:15 for their number is past my knowledge. †
90: 4 1,000 years . . as yesterday when it is past 3
Sng 2:11 lo, the winter is past, the rain is over and gone. 3
Isa 16:13 the LORD spoke concerning Moab in the past. 1
26:20 for a little while until the wrath is past. 3
Jer 8:20 The harvest is past, the summer is ended 3
Mrk 16: 1 when the sabbath was past 8
Act 14:16 In past generations he allowed all the nations 12
2Ti 2:18 holding that the resurrection is past already. 7
1Pe 4: 3 Let the time that is past suffice 11
1Es 1:24 The events . . have been recorded in the past 10
2Es 4: 5 or call back for me the day that is past. 15
9: 1 a certain part of the predicted signs are past 16
12:40 people heard that the seven days were past 14
Sus 1:52 sins . . which you have committed in the past 13
3Mc 2: 4 those who in the past committed injustice 9

past (2) 1. παρά
Heb 11:11 even when she was past the age 1

past *See* glide, sail, time.

pastor 1. ποιμήν
Eph 4:11 some evangelists, some pastors and teachers 1

pasture 1. דֹּבֶר 2. כַּר 3. מִרְעֶה 4. מַרְעִית 5. נַהֲלֹל 6. נָוֶה 7. נָוָה 8. רעה 9. νομή
Gen 29: 7 water the sheep, and go, pasture them. 8
36:24 as he pastured the asses of Zib'eon his father. 8
37:12 brothers went to pasture their father's flock 8
13 Are not your brothers pasturing the flock 8
16 tell me . . where they are pasturing the flock. 8
47: 4 for there is no pasture for your servants' flocks 3
2Sm 7: 8 I took you from the pasture, from following 7
1Ch 4:39 to seek pasture for their flocks 3
40 where they found rich, good pasture 3
41 there was pasture there for their flocks. 3
17: 7 I took you from the pasture 7
27:29 Over the herds that pastured in Sharon was 8
Job 24: 2 they seize flocks and pasture them. 8
39: 8 He ranges the mountains as his pasture 3
Ps 23: 2 he makes me lie down in green pastures. 6
37:20 of the LORD are like the glory of the pastures 2
65:12 The pastures of the wilderness drip 6
74: 1 thy anger smoke against the sheep of thy pasture? 4
79:13 Then we thy people, the flock of thy pasture 4
83:12 take . . for ourselves of the pastures of God. 6
95: 7 he is our God, and we are the people of his pasture 4
100: 3 we are his people, and the sheep of his pasture. 4
Sng 1: 7 Tell me . . where you pasture your flock 8
8 pasture your kids beside the shepherd's tents. 8
6: 2 to the beds of spices, to pasture his flock 8
3 he pastures his flock among the lilies. 8

Isa 5:17 Then shall the lambs graze as in their pasture 1
7:19 on all the thornbushes, and on all the pastures. 5
30:23 your cattle will graze in large pastures; 2
32:14 a joy of wild asses, a pasture of flocks; 3
49: 9 on all bare heights shall be their pasture; 4
65:10 Sharon shall become a pasture for flocks 7
Jer 6: 3 around her, they shall pasture, each in his place. 8
9:10 lamentation for the pastures of the wilderness 6
23: 1 who destroy and scatter the sheep of my pasture! 4
10 and the pastures of the wilderness are dried up. 6
25:36 For the LORD is despoiling their pasture 4
50:19 I will restore Israel to his pasture 7
Lam 1: 6 Her princes . . like harts that find no pasture; 3
Ezk 25: 5 I will make Rabbah a pasture for camels 7
34:14 I will feed them with good pasture 3
14 heights of Israel shall be their pasture; 7
14 on fat pasture they shall feed on the mountains 3
18 not enough for you to feed on the good pasture 3
18 you must tread down . . the rest of your pasture; 3
31 you are my sheep, the sheep of my pasture 4
Jol 1:18 perplexed because there is no pasture for them; 3
19 For fire has devoured the pastures 6
20 has devoured the pastures of the wilderness. 6
2:22 for the pastures of the wilderness are green; 6
Ams 1: 2 the pastures of the shepherds mourn 6
Mic 2:12 like sheep in a fold, like a flock in its pasture 1
Zep 2: 6 And you, O seacoast, shall be pastures 6
7 on which they shall pasture 8
3:13 For they shall pasture and lie down 8
Joh 10: 9 and will go in and out and find pasture. 9
2Es 9:19 unfailing table and an inexhaustible pasture ‡
Sir 13:19 likewise the poor are pastures for the rich. 9

pasture *See also* land.

pasture a flock 1. רעה
Sng 2:16 he pastures his flock among the lilies. 1

broad pasture 1. מֶרְחָב
Hos 4:16 LORD now feed them like a lamb in a broad pasture? 1

pasture-fed 1. רְעִי
1Kg 4:23 fat oxen, and twenty pasture-fed cattle 1

patch 1. טלא 2. πλήρωμα
Jos 9: 5 with worn-out, patched sandals on their feet 1
Mat 9:16 for the patch tears away from the garment 2
Mrk 2:21 if he does, the patch tears away from it 2

pate 1. קָדְקֹד
Ps 7:16 on his own pate his violence descends. 1

path 1. אֹרַח 2. אֶרֶץ 3. דֶּרֶךְ 4. מְסִלָּה 5. מַעְגָּל 6. מַעְגָּלָה 7. נָתִיב 8. נְתִיבָה 9. שָׁבִיל 10. ἀτραπός 11. ἴχνος 12. ὁδός 13. τρίβος 14. τρίβω 15. τροχιά 16. semita
Gen 49:17 Dan shall be . . a viper by the path 1
Job 8:13 Such are the paths of all who forget God; 1
13:27 my feet in the stocks, and watchest all my paths; 1
18:10 for him in the ground, a trap for him in the path. 7
19: 8 he has set darkness upon my paths. 8
24:13 with its ways, and do not stay in its paths. 8
28: 7 That path no bird of prey knows 7
30:13 They break up my path, they promote my calamity; 8
33:11 my feet in the stocks, and watches all my paths. 1
38:20 that you may discern the paths to its home? 8
Ps 8: 8 whatever passes along the paths of the sea. 1
16:11 Thou dost show me the path of life; 1
17: 5 My steps have held fast to thy paths 5
23: 3 He leads me in paths of righteousness 5
25: 4 to know thy ways, O LORD; teach me thy paths. 1
10 All the paths of the LORD are steadfast love 1
27:11 lead me on a level path because of my enemies. 1
77:19 thy path through the great waters; 9
78:50 He made a path for his anger; he did not spare them 7
119:35 Lead me in the path of thy commandments 7
105 Thy word is a lamp to my feet and a light to my path. 8
139: 3 Thou searchest out my path and my lying down 1
142: 3 path where I walk they have hidden a trap for me. 1
143:10 Let thy good spirit lead me on a level path! 2
Prv 1:15 my son . . hold back your foot from their paths; 8
2: 8 guarding the paths of justice 1
9 Then you will understand . . every good path; 5
13 who forsake the paths of uprightness 1
15 men whose paths are crooked 1
18 her paths to the shades; 5
19 nor do they regain the paths of life. 1
20 keep to the paths of the righteous. 1
3: 6 he will make straight your paths. 1
17 all her paths are peace. 8
4:11 I have led you in the paths of uprightness. 5
14 Do not enter the path of the wicked 1
18 path of the righteous is like the light of dawn 1
26 Take heed to the path of your feet 5
5: 6 she does not take heed to the path of life; 1
21 he watches all his paths. 6
7:25 do not stray into her paths; 8
8: 2 in the paths she takes her stand; 8
20 I walk in . . the paths of justice 8
10:17 He who heeds instruction is on the path to life 1
12:28 In the path of righteousness is life 1
15:19 but the path of the upright is a level highway. 1
24 The wise man's path leads upward to life, that he 1
Isa 2: 3 us his ways and that we may walk in his paths. 1
3:12 mislead . . and confuse the course of your paths. 1
26: 7 thou dost make smooth the path of the righteous. 5
8 In the path of thy judgments, O LORD, we wait 1
30:11 leave the way, turn aside from the path 1
40:14 and who taught him the path of justice 1
41: 3 passes on safely, by paths his feet have not trod. 1
42:16 in paths . . they have not known I will guide them. 8
43:16 a way in the sea, a path in the mighty waters 8
59: 8 and there is no justice in their paths; 6
Jer 6:16 and look, and ask for the ancient paths 8
31: 9 a straight path in which they shall not stumble; 3
Lam 3: 9 blocked my ways . . he has made my paths crooked. 8
Hos 2: 6 against her, so that she cannot find her paths. 8
Jol 2: 7 they do not swerve from their paths. 1
8 not jostle one another, each marches in his path; 4
Mic 4: 2 may teach us his ways and we may walk in his paths. 1
Mat 3: 3 way of the Lord, make his paths straight. 13
13: 4 as he sowed, some seeds fell along the path 12
19 this is what was sown along the path. 12
Mrk 1: 3 make his paths straight- 13
4: 4 as he sowed, some seed fell along the path 12
15 the ones along the path, where the word is sown; 12
Lke 3: 4 make his paths straight. 13
8: 5 as he sowed, some fell along the path 12
12 The ones along the path are those who have heard; 12
Act 13:10 making crooked the straight paths of the Lord? 12
Rom 3:16 in their paths are ruin and misery 12
Heb 12:13 make straight paths for your feet 15
2Es 7: 8 there is only one path lying between them 16
8 so that only one man can walk upon that path. 16
48 and has shown us the paths of perdition 16
14:22 that men may be able to find the path 16
16:32 and all its paths shall bring forth thorns 16
77 and its path overwhelmed with thorns 16
Tob 4:19 all your paths and plans may prosper 14
Jdt 13:20 walking in the straight path before our God •
15: 2 fled by every path across the plain 12
Wis 5: 7 We took our fill of the paths of lawlessness 13
6:16 she graciously appears to them in their paths 13
9:18 thus the paths of those on earth were set right 13
10:10 she guided him on straight paths 13
12:24 For they went far astray on the paths of error 12
14: 3 because thou hast given it a path in the sea 12
Sir 5: 9 nor follow every path 10
14:22 lie in wait on her paths. 13
32:20 Do not go on a path full of hazards 12
22 give good heed to your paths. ‡
50:29 the light of the Lord is his path. 11
51:15 my foot entered upon the straight path •
Bar 3:20 the way to knowledge, nor understood her paths 13
23 the way to wisdom, nor given thought to her paths. 13
31 No one . . is concerned about the path to her. 13
4:13 nor tread the paths of discipline 13

path *See also* follow.

narrow path 1. מִשְׁעוֹל
Num22:24 stood in a narrow path between the vineyards 1

slippery path 1. חֲלַקְלַקּוֹת
Jer 23:12 their way shall be to them like slippery paths 1

tortuous path 1. διαστρέφω
Sir 4:17 at first she will walk with him on tortuous paths 1

pathless 1. לֹא דֶרֶךְ
Job 12:24 and makes them wander in a pathless waste. 1

pathway 1. δίοδος
Wis 5:12 so that no one knows its pathway. 1

patience 1. אֶרֶךְ אַפַּיִם 2. μακροθυμέω 3. μακροθυμία 4. ὑπομονή 5. longanimitas
Prv 25:15 With patience a ruler may be persuaded 1
Mat 18:26 'Lord, have patience with me, and I will pay you 2
29 'Have patience with me, and I will pay you.' 2
Lke 8:15 and bring forth fruit with patience. 4
Rom 2: 4 presume upon . . his . . forbearance and patience? 3
7 who by patience in well-doing seek for glory 4
8:25 if we hope . . we wait for it with patience. 4
9:22 endured with much patience the vessels of wrath 3
2Co 12:12 in all patience, with signs and wonders 4
Gal 5:22 love, joy, peace, patience, kindness, goodness 3
Eph 4: 2 lowliness and meekness, with patience 3
Col 1:11 for all endurance and patience with joy 3
3:12 kindness, lowliness, meekness, and patience 3
1Ti 1:16 might display his perfect patience 3
2Ti 3:10 my aim in life, my faith, my patience, my love 3
4: 2 be unfailing in patience and in teaching. 3
Heb 6:12 through faith and patience 3
Jas 5:10 As an example of suffering and patience 3
1Pe 3:20 when God's patience waited in the days of Noah 3
2Es 7:33 and patience shall be withdrawn; 5
134 patient, because he shows patience toward those 5
Sir 16:13 the patience of the godly will not be frustrated. 4
41: 2 one who is contrary, and has lost his patience! 4
1Mc 8: 4 gained control . . by their . . patience 3

patience *See also* endure.

patient 1. אָרֵךְ 2. ארך נֶפֶשׁ 3. μακροθυμέω 4. μακρόθυμος 5. ὑπομένω 6. ὑποφέρω 7. habeo longanimitatem 8. longanimis
Job 6:11 <h> NEPE$#what is my end, that I should be patient? 2
Prv 14:17 but a man of discretion is patient. 6
Ecc 7: 8 and the patient in spirit is better 1
Rom 12:12 Rejoice in your hope, be patient in tribulation 5
1Co 13: 4 Love is patient and kind 3
1Th 5:14 help the weak, be patient with them all. 3
Jas 5: 7 Be patient . . until the coming of the Lord. 3
7 waits for the . . fruit . . being patient over it 4
8 You also be patient. Establish your hearts 3
2Es 7:74 the Most High has been patient with those 7
134 patient, because he shows patience toward those 8
Wis 15: 1 patient, and ruling all things in mercy. 4
Sir 2: 4 in changes that humble you be patient. 3
18:11 Therefore the Lord is patient with them 3
29: 8 be patient with a man in humble circumstances 3
35:18 neither will he be patient with them 3

patient *See also* endurance.

patient man 1. μακρόθυμος
Sir 1:23 A patient man will endure until the right moment 1

patiently 1. μακρόθυμος 2. μακροθύμως
Act 26: 3 therefore I beg you to listen to me patiently. 2
2Co 1: 6 when you patiently endure the same sufferings •
2Mc 6:14 the Lord waits patiently to punish them 1

patiently *See also* bear, endure, take, wait.

patriarch 1. πατήρ 2. πατριάρχης
Act 2:29 the patriarch David 2
7: 8 Jacob of the twelve patriarchs. 2
9 the patriarchs . . sold him into Egypt 2
Rom 9: 5 to them belong the patriarchs 1
15: 8 to confirm the promises given to the patriarchs 1
Heb 7: 4 Abraham the patriarch gave him a tithe 2
4Mc 7:19 like our patriarchs Abraham and Isaac and Jacob 2
16:25 Isaac and Jacob and all the patriarchs. 2

patrimony 1. אָב
Deu 18: 8 besides . . receives from the sale of his patrimony. 1

patrol 1. הלך 2. προφυλακή
Zec 1:10 whom the LORD has sent to patrol the earth.' 1
11 We have patrolled the earth 1
6: 7 were impatient to get off and patrol the earth. 1
7 he said, "Go, patrol the earth." So they patrolled 1
7 patrol the earth." So they patrolled the earth. 1
Jdt 10:11 an Assyrian patrol met her 2

pattern 1. מַרְאֶה 2. תַּבְנִית 3. ὁμοίωμα 4. τύπος 5. ὑποτύπωσις
Exd 25: 9 concerning the pattern of the tabernacle 2
40 see that you make them after the pattern for them 2
Num 8: 4 according to the pattern which the LORD had shown 1
2Kg 16:10 Ahaz sent . . a model of the altar, and its pattern 2
Act 7:44 according to the pattern that he had seen. 4
2Ti 1:13 Follow the pattern of the sound words 5
Heb 8: 5 make everything according to the pattern 4
Sir 38:28 his eyes are on the pattern of the object 3
4Mc 6:19 become a pattern of impiety to the young 4

pause 1. pausa
2Es 2:24 Pause and be quiet, my people 1

pave 1. ψηφολογέω
Tob 13:17 will be paved with beryl and ruby 1

pave smoothly 1. ὁμαλίζω
Sir 21:10 The way of sinners is smoothly paved with stones 1

pavement 1. מַלְבֵּן 2. מַעֲשֶׂה 3. רִצְפָּה 4. ἔδαφος 5. λιθόστρωτος
Exd 24:10 under his feet . . a pavement of sapphire stone 2
2Ch 7: 3 with their faces to the earth on the pavement 3
Jer 43: 9 and hide them in the mortar in the pavement 1
Ezk 40:17 behold, there were chambers and a pavement 3
17 30 chambers fronted on the pavement. 3
18 the pavement ran along the side of the gates 3
18 this was the lower pavement. 3
42: 3 the pavement which belonged to the outer court 3
Joh 19:13 a place called The Pavement 5
Sir 20:18 A slip on the pavement 4

mosaic pavement 1. רִצְפָּה
Est 1: 6 couches . . on a mosaic pavement of porphyry 1

pavilion 1. סֻכָּה 2. αὐλή
Job 36:29 of the clouds, the thunderings of his pavilion? 1
Isa 4: 5 over all . . there will be a canopy and a pavilion. 1
2Mc 13:15 he attacked the king's pavilion at night 2

paw 1. יָד 2. כַּף 3. ἀνορύσσω
Lev 11:27 all that go on their paws, among the animals 2
1Sm 17:37 The LORD who delivered me from the paw of the lion 1
37 me from . . the lion and from the paw of the bear 1
Job 39:21 He paws in the valley, and exults in his strength; 3

pay 1. מִקְנָה 2. נשא 3. נתן 4. נתן מֶכֶר 5. עשר 6. שָׂכָר 7. שוב 8. שלם 9. שקל 10. יהב (A) 11. שׂוּם (A) 12. ἀναφέρω 13. ἀντικαταλλάσσω 14. ἀποδίδωμι 15. ἀποτιννύω 16. ἀποτίνω 17. δαπανάω 18. διαγράφω 19. δίδωμι 20. ἵστημι 21. ὀψώνιον 22. τελέω
Exd 21:19 only he shall pay for the loss of his time 3
22 and he shall pay as the judges determine. 3
36 he shall pay ox for ox, and the dead beast shall be 8
22: 1 he shall pay five oxen for an ox, and four sheep 8
4 he shall pay double. 8
7 if the thief is found, he shall pay double. 8
9 he . . shall pay double to his neighbor. 8
17 he shall pay money equivalent to the marriage 9
Lev 25:51 refund out of the price paid for him 1
27: 8 if a man is too poor to pay your valuation •
Num 20:19 if we drink of your water . . then I will pay for it; 4
Deu 23:21 make a vow . . you shall not be slack to pay it; 8
26:12 finished paying all the tithe of your produce 5
1Sm 1:21 offer . . the yearly sacrifice, and to pay his vow. •
2Sm 15: 7 let me . . pay my vow, which I have vowed to the LORD 8
1Kg 5: 6 I will pay you for your servants such wages 3
20:39 his life, or else you shall pay a talent of silver.' 9
2Kg 4: 7 Go, sell the oil and pay your debts 8
17: 3 Hoshe'a became his vassal, and paid him tribute. 7
1Ch 21:25 David paid Ornan 600 shekels of gold by weight 3
2Ch 26: 8 The Ammonites paid tribute to Uzzi'ah 3
27: 5 Ammonites paid him the same amount 7
Ezr 4:13 not pay tribute, custom, or toll 3
20 to whom tribute, custom, and toll were paid. 10
6: 4 let the cost be paid from the royal treasury. 10
8 cost is to be paid to these men in full 10
Est 3: 9 I will pay 10,000 talents of silver 9
4: 7 Haman had promised to pay into the . . treasuries 9
Job 22:27 he will hear you; and you will pay your vows. 8
Ps 22:25 my vows I will pay before those who fear him. 8
50:14 pay your vows to the Most High; 8
61: 8 praises to thy name, as I pay my vows day after day. 8
66:13 with burnt offerings; I will pay thee my vows 8
116:14 I will pay my vows to the LORD in the presence 8
18 I will pay my vows to the LORD in the presence 8
Prv 6:31 if he is caught, he will pay sevenfold; 8
7:14 today I have paid my vows; 8
19:19 A man of great wrath will pay the penalty; 2
22:27 If you have nothing with which to pay, why 8
Ecc 5: 4 When you vow a vow to God, do not delay paying it; 8
4 Pay what you vow. 8
5 better . . than that you should vow and not pay. 8
Lam 5: 4 We must pay for the water we drink •
Ezk 29:18 army got anything from Tyre to pay for the labor 6
Dan 3:12 men, O king, pay no heed to you; they do not serve 11
6:13 Daniel . . pays no heed to you, O king 11
Jon 1: 3 he paid the fare, and went on board, 3
2: 9 sacrifice to thee; what I have vowed I will pay. 8
Mat 5:26 get out till you have paid the last penny. 14
17:24 Does not your teacher pay the tax? 22
18:25 as he could not pay, his lord ordered him to be sold 14
26 and I will pay you everything.' 14
28 'Pay what you owe.' 14
29 'Have patience with me, and I will pay you.' 14
30 put him in prison till he should pay the debt. 14
34 till he should pay all his debt. 14
20: 8 Call the laborers and pay them their wages 14
22:17 Is it lawful to pay taxes to Caesar, or not? 19
26:15 And they paid him thirty pieces of silver. 20
Mrk 12:14 Is it lawful to pay taxes to Caesar, or not? 19
15 Should we pay them, or should we not? 19
Lke 7:42 When they could not pay, he forgave them both. 14
12:59 till you have paid the very last copper. 14
Act 21:24 pay their expenses 17
Rom 13: 6 For the same reason you also pay taxes 22
7 Pay all of them their dues 14
1Es 2:19 they will not only refuse to pay tribute 19
4: 6 they compel one another to pay taxes to the king. 12
6:25 the cost to be paid from the treasury of Cyrus 19
Tob 2:12 Once when they paid her wages 14
4:14 but pay him at once 14
5: 3 I will pay him wages as long as I live 19
14 tell me, what wages am I to pay you–a drachma a day 19
Sir 8:13 be concerned as one who must pay. 16
18:22 nothing hinder you from paying a vow promptly 14
20:12 pays for it seven times over. 15
29: 5 will pay in words of unconcern 14
1Mc 3:28 and gave a year's pay to his forces 21
8: 4 the rest paid them tribute every year. 19
7 decreed that he . . should pay a heavy tribute 19
10:41 which the government officials have not paid 14
44 paid from the revenues of the king. 19
45 also be paid from the revenues of the king. 19
64 when his accusers saw the honor that was paid him •
14:32 paid them wages. 19
2Mc 4: 9 he promised to pay 150 more 18
3Mc 2:32 by paying money in exchange for life 13
4Mc 4:17 he would pay the king 3,660 talents annually. 19

pay *See also* man.

pay a tithe 1. δεκατόω
Heb 7: 9 Levi himself . . paid tithes through Abraham 1

pay attention 1. בין לֵב 2. שׂוּם 3. ἐπέχω 4. ἐπιβλέπω 5. μέλει 6. πείθω 7. προσέχω 8. intendo
Job 24:12 yet God pays no attention to their prayer. 2
Prv 8: 5 O foolish men, pay attention. 1
Act 18:17 But Gallio paid no attention to this. 5
27:11 centurion paid more attention to the captain 6
Heb 2: 1 Therefore we must pay the closer attention 7
Jas 2: 3 you pay attention to the one who wears 4
2Pe 1:19 You will do well to pay attention to this 7
2Es 5:32 pay attention to me, and I will tell you more. 8
Sir 16:24 pay close attention to my words. 7
37:11 pay no attention to these 3
1Mc 7:11 they paid no attention to their words 7
10:61 the king paid no attention to them. 7
4Mc 1: 1 to pay earnest attention to philosophy. 7

pay back 1. גמל 2. שוב 3. שלם 4. ἀνταποδίδωμι 5. κομίζω
Gen 50:15 Joseph will . . pay us back for all the evil 2
Lev 25:27 let him . . pay back the overpayment to the man 2
Ps 37:21 The wicked borrows, and cannot pay back 3
Prv 24:29 not say, "I . . pay the man back for what he has done. 2
Jol 3: 4 Are you paying me back for something? 3
4 If you are paying me back, I will requite your deed 1
Col 3:25 will be paid back for the wrong he has done 5
Jdt 7:15 you will pay them back with evil 4
Sir 36:20 a man of experience will pay him back. 4

pay back in full 1. ἀνταποδίδωμι ἀνταπόδομα
1Mc 2:68 Pay back the Gentiles in full 1

pay heed 1. ראה 2. διαριθμέω 3. προσέχω
Gen 39:23 the keeper of the prison paid no heed to anything 1
Wis 13: 1 while paying heed to his works 3
Sir 28:16 Whoever pays heed to slander will not find rest 3
3Mc 3: 6 Nevertheless those of other races paid no heed 2

pay honor 1. δοξάζω 2. ἐνδόξως
1Mc 11:60 the people of the city met him and paid him honor. 2
14:39 and paid him high honors. 1

pay in full 1. מלא
Job 15:32 It will be paid in full before his time 1

pay no heed 1. ἀμελέω
Heb 8: 9 so I paid no heed to them, says the Lord. 1

pay off 1. יקר
Zec 11:13 the lordly price at which I was paid off by them. 1

pay out 1. יצא 2. נתן
2Kg 12:11 and they paid it out to the carpenters 1
15 delivered the money to pay out to the workmen 2

pay regard 1. שמר 2. שעה
Exd 5: 9 that they may . . pay no regard to lying words. 2
Ps 31: 6 Thou hatest those who pay regard to vain idols; 1
Jon 2: 8 Those who pay regard to vain idols 1

pay regularly 1. εὐτακτέω
2Mc 4:27 he did not pay regularly any of the money 1

pay reverence 1. ירא
Jdg 6:10 you shall not pay reverence to the gods 1

pay tribute 1. ὑπὸ φόρον
1Mc 8: 2 how they had . . forced them to pay tribute 1

without pay 1. δωρεάν
Mat 10: 8 You received without paying, give without pay. 1

without paying 1. δωρεάν
Mat 10: 8 You received without paying, give without pay. 1
2Th 3: 8 we did not eat any one's bread without paying 1

payment 1. אֶשְׂכָּר 2. כֶּסֶף 3. פְּעֻלָּה 4. ἀπαίτησις 5. δόμα
Exd 21:11 go out for nothing, without payment of money. •
Deu 23:18 not bring . . in payment for any vow •
Job 31:39 if I have eaten its yield without payment 2
Isa 65: 7 into . . bosom payment for their former doings. 3
Ezk 27:15 they brought you in payment ivory tusks 1
1Mc 10:29 and exempt all the Jews from payment of tribute •
11:35 the other payments henceforth due to us •
15: 5 and release from all the other payments 5
2Mc 4:28 When Sostratus . . kept requesting payment 4

payment *See also* make, receive.

full payment 1. πᾶς
Php 4:18 I have received full payment, and more; I am filled 1

payment of vow 1. נֶדֶר
Lev 22:18 offering, whether in payment of a vow 1

without payment 1. δωρεάν
Rev 21: 6 To the thirsty I will give . . without payment. 1
1Mc 10:33 I set free without payment 1

peace 1. בְּרָכָה 2. מֵישָׁר 3. מְנוּחָה 4. רֶגַע 5. שַׁלְוָה 6. שָׁלוֹם 7. שׁלם 8. שֶׁלֶם 9. שְׁלָם (A) 10. ἀταραξία 11. δεξιά 12. εἰρηνεύω 13. εἰρήνη 14. εἰρηνικός 15. ἡσυχία 16. σιωπάω 17. pax
Gen 15:15 you shall go to your fathers in peace; 6
26:29 good and have sent you away in peace. 6
31 and they departed from him in peace. 6
28:21 that I come again to my father's house in peace 6
44:17 but as for you, go up in peace to your father. 6
Exd 4:18 And Jethro said to Moses, "Go in peace. 6
18:23 also will go to their place in peace. 6
24: 5 who . . sacrificed peace offerings of oxen 8
29:28 offered . . from their peace offerings; 8
Lev 26: 6 I will give peace in the land 6
Num 6:26 lift up his countenance . . and give you peace. 6
25:12 Behold, I give to him my covenant of peace; 6
Deu 2:26 sent . . to Sihon . . , with words of peace, saying 6
20:11 if its answer to you is peace and it opens to you 6
23: 6 shall not seek their peace or their prosperity 6
Jos 9:15 Joshua made peace with them, and made a covenant 6
22:23 or cereal offerings or peace offerings on it 8
Jdg 4:17 there was peace between Jabin the king of Hazor 6
6:23 Peace be to you; do not fear, you shall not die. 6
24 Gideon built . . and called it, The LORD is peace. 6
8: 9 When I come again in peace, I will break down this 6
18: 6 Go in peace. The journey on which you go is under 6
19:20 the old man said, "Peace be to you; I will care for all 6
21:13 sent word . . and proclaimed peace to them. 6
1Sm 1:17 Go in peace, and the God of Israel grant 6
7:14 was peace also between Israel and the Amorites. 6
10: 8 to offer . . and to sacrifice peace offerings. 8
11:15 sacrificed peace offerings before the LORD 8
20:42 Go in peace, forasmuch as we have sworn both of us 6
25: 6 Peace be to you, and peace be to your house 6
6 Peace be to you, and peace be to your house 6
6 be to your house, and peace be to all that you have. 6
35 Go up in peace to your house; see, I have hearkened 6
2Sm 3:21 David sent Abner away; and he went in peace. 6
22 he had sent him away, and he had gone in peace. 6
23 he has let him go, and he has gone in peace. 6
15: 9 The king said to him, "Go in peace." So he arose 6
27 Look, go back to the city in peace, you and Abi'athar 6
17: 3 only one man, and all the people will be at peace. 6
1Kg 2: 5 avenging in time of peace blood which had been 6
6 do not let his gray head go down to Sheol in peace. 6
33 to David . . there shall be peace from the LORD 6
4:24 and he had peace on all sides round about him. 6
5:12 there was peace between Hiram and Solomon; 6
20:18 If they have come out for peace, take them alive; 6
22:17 let each return to his home in peace.' 6
27 feed him with scant fare . . until I come in peace."' 6
28 If you return in peace, the LORD has not spoken 6
2Kg 5:19 He said to him, "Go in peace. 6
9:17 and send to meet them, and let him say, 'Is it peace?' 6
18 and said, "Thus says the king, 'Is it peace?' 6
18 And Jehu said, "What have you to do with peace? 6
19 and said, "Thus the king has said, 'Is it peace?' 6
19 Jehu answered, "What have you to do with peace? 6
22 when Joram saw Jehu, he said, "Is it peace, Jehu? 6
22 What peace can there be, so long as the harlotries 6
31 Is it peace, you Zimri, murderer of your master? 6
18:31 Make your peace with me and come out to me; 1
20:19 if there will be peace and security in my days? 6
22:20 and you shall be gathered to your grave in peace 6
1Ch 12:18 Peace, peace to you, and peace to your helpers! 6
18 Peace, peace to you, and peace to your helpers! 6
18 Peace, peace to you, and peace to your helpers! 6
22: 9 son shall be born to you; he shall be a man of peace. 3
9 I will give peace and quiet to Israel in his days. 6
2Ch 15: 5 there was no peace to him who went out 6
18:16 let each return to his home in peace.' 6
26 fellow in prison . . until I return in peace.' 6
27 If you return in peace, the LORD has not spoken 6
34:28 you shall be gathered to your grave in peace 6
Ezr 5: 7 written as follows: "To Darius the king, all peace. 9
9:12 never seek their peace or prosperity 6
Est 9:30 Letters were sent . . in words of peace and truth 6
10: 3 and spoke peace to all his people. 6
Job 5:23 the beasts of the field shall be at peace with you. 7
12: 6 The tents of robbers are at peace 5
21:13 and in peace they go down to Sheol. 4
22:21 Agree with God, and be at peace; 7
25: 2 with God; he makes peace in his high heaven. 6
Ps 4: 8 In peace I will both lie down and sleep; 6
28: 3 who speak peace with their neighbors 6
29:11 May the LORD bless his people with peace! 6
34:14 from evil, and do good; seek peace, and pursue it. 6
35:20 For they do not speak peace 6

37:37 there is posterity for the man of peace. 6
72: 7 may righteousness flourish, and peace abound 6
85: 8 will speak peace to his people, to his saints 6
10 righteousness and peace will kiss each other. 6
119:165 Great peace have those who love thy law; 6
120: 6 long . . my dwelling among those who hate peace. 6
7 I am for peace; but when I speak, they are for war! 6
122: 6 Pray for the peace of Jerusalem! 6
7 Peace be within your walls, and security within 6
8 I will say, "Peace be within you! 6
125: 5 Peace be in Israel! 6
128: 6 Peace be upon Israel! 6
147:14 He makes peace in your borders; he fills you 6
Prv 3:17 all her paths are peace. 6
Ecc 3: 8 a time for war, and a time for peace. 6
Sng 8:10 I was in his eyes as one who brings peace. 6
Isa 9: 6 Mighty God, Everlasting Father, Prince of Peace. 6
7 his government and of peace there will be no end 6
26: 3 Thou dost keep him in perfect peace 6
12 O LORD, thou wilt ordain peace for us 6
27: 5 let them make peace with me. 6
5 let them make peace with me. 6
32:17 the effect of righteousness will be peace 6
33: 7 the envoys of peace weep bitterly. 6
36:16 Make your peace with me and come out to me; 1
39: 8 There will be peace and security in my days. 6
48:18 Then your peace would have been like a river 6
22 There is no peace," says the LORD, "for the wicked. 6
52: 7 who publishes peace, who brings good tidings 6
54:10 and my covenant of peace shall not be removed 6
55:12 you shall go out in joy, and be led forth in peace; 6
57: 2 he enters into peace; they rest in their beds 6
19 Peace, peace, to the far and to the near 6
19 peace, to the far and to the near, says the LORD; 6
21 There is no peace, says my God, for the wicked. 6
59: 8 The way of peace they know not 6
8 no one who goes in them knows peace. 6
60:17 I will make your overseers peace 6
Jer 6:14 saying, 'Peace, peace,' when there is no peace. 6
14 saying, 'Peace, peace,' when there is no peace. 6
14 saying, 'Peace, peace,' when there is no peace. 6
8:11 saying, 'Peace, peace,' when there is no peace. 6
11 saying, 'Peace, peace,' when there is no peace. 6
11 saying, 'Peace, peace,' when there is no peace. 6
15 We looked for peace, but no good came 6
12:12 no flesh has peace. 6
14:13 but I will give you assured peace in this place. 6
19 We looked for peace, but no good came; 6
16: 5 for I have taken away my peace from this people 6
28: 9 As for the prophet who prophesies peace 6
30: 5 heard a cry of panic, of terror, and no peace. 6
34: 5 You shall die in peace. 6
43:12 he shall go away from there in peace. 6
Lam 3:17 my soul is bereft of peace 6
Ezk 7:25 When anguish comes, they will seek peace 6
13:10 they have misled my people, saying, 'Peace,' 6
10 saying, 'Peace,' when there is no peace; 6
16 and saw visions of peace for her 6
16 visions of peace for her, when there was no peace 6
34:25 I will make with them a covenant of peace 6
37:26 I will make a covenant of peace with them; 6
Dan 4: 1 to all peoples . . Peace be multiplied to you! 9
6:25 Darius wrote . . "Peace be multiplied to you. 9
10:19 O man greatly beloved, fear not, peace be with you; 6
11: 6 shall come to the king of the north to make peace; 2
17 shall bring terms of peace and perform them. *
Mic 3: 5 who cry "Peace" when they have something to eat 6
5: 5 And this shall be peace, when the Assyrian comes 6
Nah 1:15 who brings good tidings, who proclaims peace! 6
Zec 8:12 For there shall be a sowing of peace; 6
16 judgments that are true and make for peace 6
19 therefore love truth and peace. 6
9:10 he shall command peace to the nations; 6
Mal 2: 5 covenant of life and peace, and I gave them to him 6
6 He walked with me in peace and uprightness 6
Mat 10:13 if the house is worthy, let your peace come upon it; 13
13 if it is not worthy, let your peace return to you. 13
34 Do not think that I have come to bring peace 13
34 I have not come to bring peace, but a sword. 13
Mrk 4:39 said to the sea, "Peace! Be still!" And the wind ceased 16
5:34 go in peace, and be healed of your disease. 13
9:49 be at peace with one another. 12
Lke 1:79 to guide our feet into the way of peace. 13
2:14 on earth peace among men with whom he is pleased! 13
29 now lettest thou thy servant depart in peace 13
7:50 Your faith has saved you; go in peace. 13
8:48 your faith has made you well; go in peace. 13
10: 5 'Peace be to this house!' 13
6 if a son of peace is there 13
6 your peace shall rest upon him 13
11:21 his goods are in peace; 13
12:51 you think that I have come to give peace on earth? 13
14:32 he sends an embassy and asks terms of peace. 13
19:38 Peace in heaven and glory in the highest! 13
42 that . . you knew the things that make for peace 13
Joh 14:27 Peace I leave with you; my peace I give to you 13
27 Peace I leave with you; my peace I give to you 13
16:33 that in me you may have peace 13
20:19 Peace be with you. 13
21 Jesus said to them again, "Peace be with you 13
26 stood among them, and said, "Peace be with you. 13
Act 9:31 the church . . had peace and was built up 13
10:36 preaching good news of peace by Jesus Christ 13
12:20 they asked for peace 13
15:33 they were sent off in peace by the brethren 13
16:36 now therefore come out and go in peace. 13
24: 2 Since through you we enjoy much peace 13
Rom 1: 7 Grace to you and peace from God our Father 13
2:10 and honor and peace for every one who does good 13
3:17 the way of peace they do not know. 13
5: 1 peace with God through our Lord Jesus Christ. 13
8: 6 to set the mind on the Spirit is life and peace. 13
14:17 kingdom of God is . . righteousness and peace 13
19 Let us then pursue what makes for peace 13
15:13 May the God of hope fill you with all joy and peace 13
33 The God of peace be with you all. Amen. 13
16:20 then the God of peace will soon crush Satan 13
1Co 1: 3 Grace to you and peace from God our Father 13
7:15 God has called us to peace. 13
14:33 For God is not a God of confusion but of peace 13
16:11 Speed him on his way in peace 13
2Co 1: 2 Grace to you and peace from God our Father 13
13:11 the God of love and peace will be with you. 13
Gal 1: 3 Grace to you and peace from God the Father 13
5:22 love, joy, peace, patience, kindness, goodness 13
6:16 Peace and mercy be upon all who walk by this rule 13
Eph 1: 2 Grace to you and peace from God our Father 13
2:14 For he is our peace, who has made us both one 13
15 one new man in place of the two, so making peace 13
17 he came and preached peace to you who were far off 13
17 preached . . peace to those who were near; 13
4: 3 the unity of the Spirit in the bond of peace. 13
6:15 the equipment of the gospel of peace; 13
23 Peace be to the brethren, and love with faith 13
Php 1: 2 Grace to you and peace from God our Father 13
4: 7 the peace of God, which passes all understanding 13
9 the God of peace will be with you. 13
Col 1: 2 Grace to you and peace from God our Father. 13
3:15 let the peace of Christ rule in your hearts 13
1Th 1: 1 Grace to you and peace. 13
5: 3 When people say, "There is peace and security 13
13 Be at peace among yourselves. 12
23 May the God of peace himself sanctify you wholly; 13
2Th 1: 2 Grace to you and peace from God the Father 13
3:16 Now may the Lord of peace himself give you peace 13
16 Lord of peace himself give you peace at all times 13
1Ti 1: 2 Grace, mercy, and peace from God the Father 13
2Ti 1: 2 Grace, mercy, and peace from God the Father 13
2:22 aim at righteousness, faith, love, and peace 13
Tit 1: 4 Grace and peace from God the Father 13
Phm 1: 3 Grace to you and peace from God our Father 13
Heb 7: 2 then he is also king of Salem, that is, king of peace. 13
12:14 Strive for peace with all men 13
13:20 the God of peace who brought again from the dead 13
Jas 2:16 Go in peace, be warmed and filled 13
3:18 the harvest of righteousness is sown in peace 13
18 sown in peace by those who make peace. 13
1Pe 1: 2 May grace and peace be multiplied to you. 13
3:11 let him seek peace and pursue it. 13
5:14 Peace to all of you that are in Christ. 13
2Pe 1: 2 May grace and peace be multiplied to you 13
3:14 without spot or blemish, and at peace. 13
2Jn 1: 3 Grace, mercy, and peace will be with us, from God 13
3Jn 1:15 Peace be to you. The friends greet you. 13
Jde 1: 2 May mercy, peace, and love be multiplied to you. 13
Rev 1: 4 Grace to you and peace from him who is and who was 13
6: 4 rider was permitted to take peace from the earth 13
1Es 8:85 do not seek ever to have peace with them 12
2Es 13:47 the multitude gathered together in peace. 17
16:21 men will imagine that peace is assured for them 17
Tob 13:14 They will rejoice in your peace. 13
14: 4 in Media there will be peace for a time. 13
Jdt 3: 1 they sent messengers to sue for peace, and said 14
7:24 not making peace with the Assyrians. 14
8:35 Uzziah and the rulers said to her, "Go in peace 13
AEs 13: 2 to re-establish the peace which all men desire. 13
Wis 3: 3 they are at peace. 13
14:22 they call such great evils peace. 13
Sir 1:18 making peace and perfect health to flourish. 13
6: 6 Let those that are at peace with you be many 12
13:18 What peace is there between a hyena and a dog? 13
18 what peace between a rich man and a poor man? 13
26: 2 he will complete his years in peace. 13
28: 9 inject enmity among those who are at peace. 12
13 he has destroyed many who were at peace. 12
16 nor will he settle down in peace. 15
41:14 My children, observe instruction and be at peace; 13
44:14 Their bodies were buried in peace 13
45:24 a covenant of peace was established with him 13
47:13 Solomon reigned in days of peace 13
16 you were loved for your peace. 13
50:23 grant that peace may be in our days in Israel 13
Bar 3:13 God, you would be dwelling in peace for ever. 13
14 where there is light for the eyes, and peace. 13
4:20 I have taken off the robe of peace 13
5: 4 Peace of righteousness and glory of godliness. 13
LJr 1: 3 I will bring you away from there in peace. 13
1Mc 6:49 He made peace with the men of Beth-zur 13
58 make peace with them and with all their nation 13
7:13 first . . to seek peace from them 13
28 I shall come . . to see you face to face in peace. 13
8:20 sent us to you to establish alliance and peace 13
22 as a memorial of peace and alliance 13
9:70 he sent ambassadors to him to make peace with him 13
10: 4 for he said, "Let us act first to make peace with him 13
4 before he makes peace with Alexander against us *
66 returned to Jerusalem in peace and gladness. 13
11:50 Grant us peace 11
51 they threw down their arms and made peace 13
62 he made peace with them 11
13:37 we are ready to make a general peace with you 13
40 let there be peace between us. 13
45 asking Simon to make peace with them; 11
50 Then they cried to Simon to make peace with them 11
14: 8 They tilled their land in peace 13
11 He established peace in the land 13
2Mc 1: 1 brethren in Egypt, Greeting, and good peace. 13
4 may he bring peace. 13
3: 1 the holy city was inhabited in unbroken peace 13
12: 2 would not let them live quietly and in peace. 15
12 agreed to make peace with them 13
14:10 impossible for the government to find peace. 13
3Mc 2:20 give us peace. 13
6:27 Send them back to their homes in peace 13
7:19 when they had landed in peace 13
4Mc 3:20 our fathers were enjoying profound peace 13
8:26 when we can live in peace if we obey the king? 10

peace *See also* gain, give, hold, live, make, offer, offering, terms.

peaceable 1. שׁלם 2. *εἰρηνικός* 3. *ἥμερος* 4. *ἡσύχιος* 5. *μετ᾽ εἰρήνης* 6. pacificus 7. quiesco

2Sm 20:19 those who are peaceable and faithful in Israel; 1
1Ti 2: 2 we may lead a quiet and peaceable life 4
Jas 3:17 wisdom from above is first pure, then peaceable 2
2Es 11:42 afflicted the meek and injured the peaceable; 7
13:12 another multitude which was peaceable. 6
39 another multitude that was peaceable 6
AEs 13: 2 in order to make my kingdom peaceable 3
16: 8 quiet and peaceable for all men 5
1Mc 1:30 Deceitfully he spoke peaceable words to them 2
7:10 with peaceable but treacherous words. 2
15 he spoke peaceable words . . and swore this oath 2
27 treacherously sent . . this peaceable message 2
10: 3 sent Jonathan a letter in peaceable words 2
47 he had been the first to speak peaceable words 2
11: 2 He set out for Syria with peaceable words 2

peaceably 1. בְּשָׁלוֹם 2. שָׁלוֹם 3. *εἰρηνικός* 4. *εἰρηνικῶς*

Gen 37: 4 hated him, and could not speak peaceably to him. 2
Jdg 11:13 my land . . now therefore restore it peaceably. 1
1Sm 16: 4 The elders . . and said, "Do you come peaceably? 2
5 And he said, "Peaceably; I have come to sacrifice 2
29: 7 go peaceably, that you . . not displease the lords 1
1Kg 2:13 she said, "Do you come peaceably? 2
13 Do you come peaceably?" He said, "Peaceably. 2
Jer 9: 8 each speaks peaceably to his neighbor 2
Sir 4: 8 answer him peaceably and gently. 3
1Mc 5:25 who met them peaceably 4
7:29 they greeted one another peaceably 4
33 came out . . to greet him peaceably 4

peaceably *See also* disposed, live.

peaceful 1. שָׁלֵו 2. שָׁלוֹם 3. *εἰρηνικός* 4. *εἰρηνικῶς*

1Ch 4:40 the land was very broad, quiet, and peaceful; 1
Isa 32:18 My people will abide in a peaceful habitation 2
Jer 25:37 and the peaceful folds are devastated 2
Mic 2: 8 you strip the robe from the peaceful *
Zec 6:13 peaceful understanding shall be between them 2
Heb 12:11 it yields the peaceful fruit of righteousness 3
2Mc 10:12 attempted to maintain peaceful relations 4
3Mc 6:32 formed choruses as a sign of peaceful joy. 3

peaceful *See also* settlement.

peacemaker 1. *εἰρηνοποιός*

Mat 5: 9 Blessed are the peacemakers, for they shall be 1

peacock 1. תֻּכִּיִּים

1Kg 10:22 bringing gold, silver, ivory, apes, and peacocks. 1
2Ch 9:21 come bringing . . ivory, apes, and peacocks. 1

peak 1. ראשׁ

Sng 4: 8 Depart from the peak of Ama'na, from . . Senir 1
8 Depart from . . from the peak of Senir and Hermon 1

peal of thunder 1. *βροντή*

Rev 4: 5 issue . . voices and peals of thunder 1
8: 5 there were peals of thunder, voices, flashes 1
11:19 flashes of lightning, voices, peals of thunder 1
16:18 flashes of lightning, voices, peals of thunder 1

pearl 1. פְּנִינִים 2. *μαργαρίτης*

Job 28:18 the price of wisdom is above pearls. 1

Mat 7: 6 and do not throw your pearls before swine 2
13:45 like a merchant in search of fine pearls 2
46 on finding one pearl of great value 2
1Ti 2: 9 not with braided hair or gold or pearls 2
Rev 17: 4 and bedecked with gold and jewels and pearls 2
18:12 cargo of gold, silver, jewels and pearls 2
16 bedecked with gold, with jewels, and with pearls! 2
21:21 And the twelve gates were twelve pearls 2
21 each of the gates made of a single pearl 2

peasantry 1. פְּרָזוֹן
Jdg 5: 7 The peasantry ceased in Israel, they ceased 1
11 LORD, the triumphs of his peasantry in Israel. 1

pebble 1. צְרוֹר 2. κόχλαξ
2Sm 17:13 until not even a pebble is to be found there. 1
Ams 9: 9 a sieve, but no pebble shall fall upon the earth. 1
1Mc 10:73 where there is no stone or pebble, or place to flee. 2

peddler 1. καπηλεύω
2Co 2:17 For we are not, like so many, peddlers of God's word; 1

pedestal
1Kg 7:31 its opening was round, as a pedestal is made *

pediment 1. מַרְצֶפֶת
2Kg 16:17 and put it upon a pediment of stone. 1

peel 1. פצל
Gen 30:37 fresh rods . . and peeled white streaks in them 1
38 He set the rods which he had peeled in front 1

peer 1. שקף 2. παρακύπτω
Jdg 5:28 Out of the window she peered, the mother of Sis'era 1
Sir 14:23 He who peers through her windows 2
21:23 A boor peers into the house from the door 2

peer out 1. διεκκύπτω
2Mc 3:19 while others peered out of the windows. 1

peg 1. יָתֵד
Exd 27:19 and all its pegs and all the pegs of the court 1
19 and all its pegs and all the pegs of the court 1
35:18 the pegs of the tabernacle and the pegs 1
18 the pegs of the tabernacle and the pegs 1
38:20 all the pegs for the tabernacle and for the court 1
31 gate of the court, all the pegs of the tabernacle 1
31 and all the pegs round about the court. 1
39:40 gate of the court, its cords, and its pegs; 1
Num 3:37 pillars . . with their bases and pegs and cords. 1
4:32 pillars . . with their bases, pegs, and cords 1
Jdg 4:21 Ja'el the wife of Heber took a tent peg 1
21 softly to him and drove the peg into his temple 1
Isa 22:23 I will fasten him like a peg in a sure place 1
25 the peg that was fastened in a sure place 1
Ezk 15: 3 Do men take a peg from it to hang any vessel on? 1
Zec 10: 4 out of them the tent peg, out of them the battle bow 1

tent peg 1. יָתֵד 2. πάσσαλος
Jdg 4:22 lay Sis'era dead, with the tent peg in his temple. 1
5:26 She put her hand to the tent peg and her right hand 1
Sir 14:24 will also fasten his tent peg to her walls; 2

pelican 1. קָאָת
Lev 11:18 the water hen, the pelican, the carrion vulture 1
Deu 14:17 pelican, the carrion vulture and the cormorant 1

pen 1. עֵט 2. κάλαμος
Job 19:24 Oh that with an iron pen and lead they were graven 1
Ps 45: 1 my tongue is like the pen of a ready scribe. 1
Jer 8: 8 the false pen of the scribes has made it into a lie. 1
17: 1 The sin of Judah is written with a pen of iron; 1
3Jn 1:13 but I would rather not write with pen and ink; 2
3Mc 4:20 both the paper and the pens they used for writing 2

penalty 1. עֹנֶשׁ 2. ἀντιμισθία 3. δίκη 4. ἐπιτίμιον 5. ζημία 6. τιμωρία
Prv 19:19 A man of great wrath will pay the penalty; 1
Ezk 16:58 You bear the penalty of your lewdness *
23:49 shall bear the penalty for your sinful idolatry; *
Rom 1:27 receiving in their own persons the due penalty 2
2Es 6:19 when I require . . the penalty of their iniquity *
Tob 3: 5 are true in exacting penalty from me for my sins *
Wis 14:30 just penalties will overtake them on two counts *
18:11 was punished with the same penalty as the master 3
Sir 9: 5 lest you stumble and incur penalties for her. 4
2Mc 4:48 quickly suffered the unjust penalty. 5
3Mc 7: 3 to punish them with barbarous penalties 6

penalty *See also* incur.

death penalty 1. θάνατος
Act 28:18 no reason for the death penalty in my case. 1

penalty for desecration 1. βεβήλωσις
Jdt 8:21 he will exact of us the penalty for its desecration. 1

just penalty 1. δίκη
Wis 14:31 the just penalty for those who sin 1

pencil 1. שֶׂרֶד
Isa 44:13 stretches a line, he marks it out with a pencil; 1

pendant 1. נְטִיפָה 2. עֲנָק
Jdg 8:26 the crescents and the pendants and the purple 1
Prv 1: 9 for they are . . pendants for your neck. 2
Isa 3:19 the pendants, the bracelets, and the scarfs; 1

penetrate 1. בוא 2. συνεισέρχομαι 3. χωρέω
Job 41:13 Who can penetrate his double coat of mail? 1
Wis 7:23 penetrating through all spirits 3
24 she pervades and penetrates all things. 3
Sir 39: 2 penetrate the subtleties of parables; 2

penitent 1. רַךְ
2Kg 22:19 your heart was penitent, and you humbled 1
2Ch 34:27 because your heart was penitent and you humbled 1

penknife 1. תַּעַר
Jer 36:23 the king would cut them off with a penknife 1

penny 1. ἀσσάριον 2. κοδράντης
Mat 5:26 get out till you have paid the last penny. 2
10:29 Are not two sparrows sold for a penny? 1
Mrk 12:42 put in two copper coins, which make a penny. 2
Lke 12: 6 Are not five sparrows sold for two pennies? 1

pentagon 1. חֲמִשִׁי
1Kg 6:31 the lintel and the doorposts formed a pentagon. 1

people 1. אָח 2. אִישׁ 3. אֻמָּה 4. אֶרֶץ 5. בֵּן 6. בְּנֵי עַם 7. בַּעַל 8. בַּת 9. גּוֹי 10. זֶרַע 11. ישׁב 12. לְאֹם 13. מִשְׁפָּחָה 14. נפץ 15. עַם 16. עַם וְעָם 17. בֵּן (A) 18. עַם (A) 19. ἄνθρωπος 20. αὐτός 21. γένος 22. δῆμος 23. ἔθνος 24. κατὰ σάρκα 25. κατοικέω 26. λαός 27. ὁ 28. ὄχλος 29. πλῆθος 30. πρόσωπον 31. σῶμα 32. υἱός 33. ψυχή 34. ψυχὴ ἀνθρώπου 35. gens 36. homo 37. plebs 38. populus
Gen 9:19 from these the whole earth was peopled. 14
10: 5 From these the coastland peoples spread. 9
11: 6 the LORD said, "Behold, they are one people 15
14:16 his goods, and the women and the people. 15
17:14 who is not . . shall be cut off from his people; 15
16 of nations; kings of peoples shall come from her. 15
19: 4 all the people to the last man 15
13 the outcry against its people has become great *
20: 4 he said, "Lord, wilt thou slay an innocent people? 9
23: 7 bowed to the Hittites, the people of the land. 15
11 in the presence of the sons of my people I give it 15
12 bowed down before the people of the land. 15
13 he said to Ephron in the hearing of the people 15
25: 8 Abraham . . was gathered to his people. 15
18 he settled over against all his people. 1
23 and two peoples, born of you, shall be divided; 12
26:10 One of the people might easily have lain 15
11 Abim'elech warned all the people, saying 15
27:29 Let peoples serve you, and nations bow down to you. 15
28: 3 that you may become a company of peoples. 15
29: 1 and came to the land of the people of the east. 5
32: 7 Jacob . . divided the people that were with him 15
34:16 we will dwell with you and become one people. 15
22 agree to dwell with us, to become one people 15
35: 6 he and all the people who were with him 15
29 he died and was gathered to his people 15
41:40 and all my people shall order themselves as you 15
55 Egypt was famished, the people cried to Pharaoh 15
42: 6 he it was who sold to all the people of the land. 15
47:21 as for the people, he made slaves of them 15
23 Joseph said to the people, "Behold, I have 15
48: 4 make of you a company of peoples, and will give 15
19 he also shall become a people, and he also shall be 15
49:10 to him shall be the obedience of the peoples. 15
16 Dan shall judge his people as one of the tribes 15
29 I am to be gathered to my people; bury me with my 15
33 Jacob . . was gathered to his people. 15
50:20 that many people should be kept alive 15
Exd 1: 9 he said to his people, "Behold, the people of Israel 15
9 Behold, the people of Israel are too many 15
12 Egyptians were in dread of the people of Israel. 5
13 they made the people of Israel serve with rigor 5
20 the people multiplied and grew very strong. 15
22 Then Pharaoh commanded all his people 15
2:11 when Moses had grown up, he went out to his people 1
11 an Egyptian beating a Hebrew, one of his people. 1
23 the people of Israel groaned under their 5
25 God saw the people of Israel 5
3: 7 I have seen the affliction of my people 15
9 the cry of the people of Israel has come to me 5
10 bring forth my people, the sons of Israel 15
12 you have brought forth the people out of Egypt 15
13 I come to the people of Israel and say to them 5
14 Say this to the people of Israel, 'I AM has sent me 5
15 Say this to the people of Israel, 'The LORD 5
21 I will give this people favor in the sight 15
4:16 He shall speak for you to the people; 15
21 so that he will not let the people go. 15
29 all the elders of the people of Israel. 5
30 did the signs in the sight of the people. 15
31 the people believed; and when they heard 15
31 that the LORD had visited the people of Israel 5
5: 1 Thus says the LORD . . 'Let my people go 15
4 why do you take the people away from their work? 15
5 Behold, the people of the land are now many and you 15
6 the taskmasters of the people and their foremen 15
7 no longer give the people straw to make bricks 15
10 the taskmasters and the foremen of the people 15
10 said to the people, "Thus says Pharaoh, 'I will not 15
12 So the people were scattered abroad throughout 15
14 the foremen of the people of Israel 5
15 Then the foremen of the people of Israel came 5
16 are beaten; but the fault is in your own people. 15
19 The foremen of the people of Israel saw that they 5
22 O LORD, why hast thou done evil to this people? 15
23 he has done evil to this people, and thou hast not 15
23 and thou hast not delivered thy people at all. 15
6: 5 I have heard the groaning of the people of Israel 5
6 Say therefore to the people of Israel 5
7 I will take you for my people, and I will be your God; 15
9 Moses spoke thus to the people of Israel; 5
11 tell Pharaoh . . to let the people of Israel go 5
12 Behold, the people of Israel have not listened 5
13 a charge to the people of Israel and to Pharaoh 5
13 a charge . . to bring the people of Israel out 5
26 Bring out the people of Israel from the land 5
27 bringing out the people of Israel from Egypt 5
7: 2 shall tell Pharaoh to let the people of Israel go 5
4 then I will . . bring forth my hosts, my people 15
5 when I . . bring out the people of Israel 5
14 Pharaoh . . refuses to let the people go. 15
16 Let my people go, that they may serve me 15
8: 1 Let my people go, that they may serve me. 15
3 into the houses . . of your people 15
4 you and on your people and on all your servants. 15
8 take away the frogs from me and from my people; 15
8 I will let the people go to sacrifice to the LORD. 15
9 for you and your servants and for your people 15
11 depart from . . your servants and your people; 15
20 Thus says the LORD, "Let my people go, 15
21 Else, if you will not let my people go, behold, I will 15
21 flies . . on . . your people, and into your houses; 15
22 the land of Goshen, where my people dwell 15
23 a division between my people and your people. 15
23 a division between my people and your people. 15
29 from his servants, and from his people 15
29 by not letting the people go to sacrifice 15
31 removed the swarms . . from his people; 15
32 Pharaoh . . and did not let the people go. 15
9: 1 Thus says the LORD . . "Let my people go 15
4 of all that belongs to the people of Israel. 5
6 of the cattle of the people of Israel not one 5
7 and he did not let the people go. 15
13 Thus says the LORD . . "Let my people go 15
14 plagues . . upon your servants and your people 15
15 I could have . . struck you and your people 15
17 are still exalting yourself against my people 15
26 Goshen, where the people of Israel were, there was 5
27 I and my people are in the wrong. 15
35 he did not let the people of Israel go; 5
10: 3 Let my people go, that they may serve me. 15
4 For if you refuse to let my people go, behold 15
23 but all the people of Israel had light 5
11: 2 Speak now in the hearing of the people 15
3 the LORD gave the people favor in the sight 15
3 Moses was very great . . in the sight of the people. 15
7 against any of the people of Israel 5
8 saying, 'Get you out, and all the people who follow 15
10 did not let the people of Israel go out 5
12:27 the houses of the people of Israel in Egypt 5
27 the people bowed their heads and worshiped. 15
28 Then the people of Israel went and did so; 5
31 and said, "Rise up, go forth from among my people 15
31 go forth . . both you and the people of Israel; 5
33 the Egyptians were urgent with the people 15
34 So the people took their dough before it was 15
35 The people of Israel had also done as Moses told 5
36 the LORD had given the people favor in the sight 15
37 the people of Israel journeyed from Ram'eses 5
40 The time that the people of Israel dwelt in Egypt 5
42 kept to the LORD by all the people of Israel 5
50 Thus did all the people of Israel; 5
51 brought the people of Israel out of the land 5
13: 2 first to open the womb among the people of Israel 5
3 Moses said to the people, "Remember this day 15
17 When Pharaoh let the people go, God did not lead 15
17 Lest the people repent when they see war 15
18 God led the people round by the way 15
18 the people of Israel went up out of the land 5
19 Joseph had solemnly sworn the people of Israel 5
22 did not depart from before the people. 15
14: 2 Tell the people of Israel to turn back and encamp 5
3 For Pharaoh will say of the people of Israel 5
5 king . . was told that the people had fled 15
5 mind . . was changed toward the people 15
8 king of Egypt and he pursued the people of Israel 5
10 the people of Israel lifted up their eyes 5
10 the people of Israel cried out to the LORD; 5

13 Moses said to the people, "Fear not, stand firm 15
15 Tell the people of Israel to go forward. 5
16 the people of Israel may go on dry ground through 5
22 the people of Israel went into the midst 5
29 the people of Israel walked on dry ground 5
31 Israel saw . . and the people feared the LORD; 15
15: 1 Moses and the people of Israel sang this song 5
13 Thou hast led . . the people whom thou hast 15
14 The peoples have heard, they tremble; 15
16 still as a stone, till thy people, O LORD, pass 15
16 the people pass by whom thou hast purchased. 15
19 the people of Israel walked on dry ground 5
24 the people murmured against Moses, saying, "What 15
16: 1 all the congregation of the people of Israel 5
2 the whole congregation of the people of Israel 5
4 and the people shall go out and gather a day's 15
6 Moses and Aaron said to all the people of Israel 5
9 the whole congregation of the people of Israel 5
10 whole congregation of the people of Israel 5
12 the murmurings of the people of Israel; 5
15 When the people of Israel saw it, they said to one 5
17 the people of Israel did so; they gathered 5
27 On the seventh day some of the people went out 15
30 So the people rested on the seventh day. 15
35 the people of Israel ate the manna forty years 5
17: 1 All the congregation of the people of Israel 5
1 there was no water for the people to drink. 15
2 Therefore the people found fault with Moses 15
3 the people thirsted there for water 15
3 and the people murmured against Moses 15
4 What shall I do with this people? 15
5 Pass on before the people, taking with you some 15
6 shall come out of it, that the people may drink. 15
13 Joshua mowed down Am'alek and his people 15
18: 1 God had done for Moses and for Israel his people 15
11 because he delivered the people from under 15
13 On the morrow Moses sat to judge the people 15
13 the people stood about Moses from morning till 15
14 all that he was doing for the people 15
14 What is this that you are doing for the people? 15
14 you sit alone, and all the people stand about you 15
15 Because the people come to me to inquire of God; 15
18 You and the people with you will wear yourselves 15
19 You shall represent the people before God 15
21 Moreover choose able men from all the people 15
21 and place such men over the people as rulers *
22 let them judge the people at all times; 15
23 all this people also will go to their place 15
25 Moses . . made them heads over the people 15
26 they judged the people at all times; 15
19: 1 after the people of Israel had gone forth 5
3 Thus you shall . . tell the people of Israel 5
5 you shall be my own possession among all peoples; 15
7 So Moses came and called the elders of the people 15
8 all the people answered together and said 15
8 reported the words of the people to the LORD. 15
9 that the people may hear when I speak with you 15
9 Moses told the words of the people to the LORD. 15
10 Go to the people and consecrate them today 15
11 come down . . in the sight of all the people. 15
12 you shall set bounds for the people round about 15
14 Moses went down from the mountain to the people 15
14 So Moses . . consecrated the people; 15
15 he said to the people, "Be ready by the third day; 15
16 all the people who were in the camp trembled. 15
17 Then Moses brought the people out of the camp 15
21 LORD said to Moses, "Go down and warn the people 15
23 Moses said to the LORD, "The people cannot come up 15
24 but do not let the priests and the people break 15
25 So Moses went down to the people and told them. 15
20:18 when all the people perceived the thunderings 15
18 the people were afraid and trembled; 15
20 Moses said to the people, "Do not fear; for God has 15
21 the people stood afar off, while Moses drew near 15
22 Moses, "Thus you shall say to the people of Israel 5
21: 8 have no right to sell her to a foreign people 15
22:25 If you lend money to any of my people with you who 15
28 nor curse a ruler of your people. 15
23:11 lie fallow, that the poor of your people may eat; 15
27 throw into confusion all the people against 15
24: 2 and the people shall not come up with him. 15
3 Moses came and told the people all the words 15
3 all the people answered with one voice, and said 15
5 he sent young men of the people of Israel 5
7 and read it in the hearing of the people; 15
8 Moses took the blood and threw it upon the people 15
11 on the chief men of the people of Israel; 5
17 in the sight of the people of Israel. 5
25: 2 Speak to the people of Israel, that they take 5
22 in commandment for the people of Israel. 5
27:20 you shall command the people of Israel 5
21 observed . . by the people of Israel. 5
28: 1 from among the people of Israel, to serve me 5
30 bear the judgment of the people of Israel 5
38 holy offering which the people of Israel hallow 5
29:28 perpetual due from the people of Israel 5
28 portion to be offered by the people of Israel 5
43 There I will meet with the people of Israel 5
45 I will dwell among the people of Israel 5

30:12 When you take the census of the people of Israel 5
16 atonement money from the people of Israel 5
16 it may bring the people of Israel to remembrance 5
31 you shall say to the people of Israel, 'This shall 5
33 . . shall be cut off from his people.' 15
38 use as perfume shall be cut off from his people. 15
31:13 Say to the people of Israel 5
14 that soul shall be cut off from among his people. 15
16 people of Israel shall keep the sabbath 5
17 sign for ever between me and the people of Israel 5
32: 1 the people saw that Moses delayed to come down 15
1 the people gathered themselves together 15
3 So all the people took off the rings of gold 15
6 the people sat down to eat and drink, and rose up 15
7 Go down; for your people, whom you brought up 15
9 I have seen this people, and behold, it is 15
9 and behold, it is a stiff-necked people; 15
11 why does thy wrath burn hot against thy people 15
12 repent of this evil against thy people. 15
14 the evil which he thought to do to his people. 15
17 heard the noise of the people as they shouted 15
20 and made the people of Israel drink it. 5
21 Moses said to Aaron, "What did this people do to you 15
22 you know the people, that they are set on evil. 15
25 when Moses saw that the people had broken loose 15
28 there fell of the people that day about three 15
30 On the morrow Moses said to the people, "You have 15
31 said, "Alas, this people have sinned a great sin; 15
34 now go, lead the people to the place of which I have 15
35 the LORD sent a plague upon the people 15
33: 1 Depart, go up hence, you and the people whom you 15
3 for you are a stiff-necked people. 15
4 When the people heard these evil tidings 15
5 Say to the people of Israel, 'You are a stiff-necked 15
5 You are a stiff-necked people; if for a single 15
6 the people of Israel stripped themselves 5
8 went out to the tent, all the people rose up 15
10 when all the people saw the pillar of cloud 15
10 all the people would rise up and worship 15
12 sayest to me, 'Bring up this people'; 15
13 Consider too that this nation is thy people. 15
16 have found favor in thy sight, I and thy people? 15
16 we are distinct, I and thy people, from all other 15
16 distinct . . from all other people that are upon 15
34: 9 although it is a stiff-necked people; 15
10 Before all your people I will do marvels 15
10 and all the people among whom you are shall see 15
30 when Aaron and all the people of Israel saw Moses 5
32 afterward all the people of Israel came near 5
34 told the people of Israel what he was commanded 5
35 the people of Israel saw the face of Moses 5
35: 1 Moses assembled all the . . people of Israel 5
4 all the congregation of the people of Israel 5
20 all the congregation of the people of Israel 5
29 All the men and women, the people of Israel 5
30 Moses said to the people of Israel, "See, the LORD 5
36: 3 freewill offering which the people of Israel 5
5 said to Moses, "The people bring much more 15
6 So the people were restrained from bringing; 15
39:32 the people of Israel had done according to all 5
42 so the people of Israel had done all the work. 5
40:36 the people of Israel would go onward; 5
Lev 1: 2 Speak to the people of Israel, and say to them 5
4: 2 Say to the people of Israel, If any one sins 5
3 who sins, thus bringing guilt on the people 15
7:20 person shall be cut off from his people 15
21 that person shall be cut off from his people 15
23 Say to the people of Israel, You shall eat no fat 5
25 person . . shall be cut off from his people 15
27 that person shall be cut off from his people 15
29 Say to the people of Israel, He that offers 5
34 I have taken from the people of Israel 5
34 as a perpetual due from the people of Israel 5
36 to be given them by the people of Israel 5
38 on the day that he commanded the people of Israel 5
9: 3 say to the people of Israel, 'Take a male goat 5
7 make atonement for yourself and for the people 15
7 the people, and make atonement for them 15
15 Then he presented the people's offering 15
15 the sin offering which was for the people 15
18 the sacrifice of peace offerings for the people 15
22 Then Aaron lifted up his hands toward the people 15
23 when they came out they blessed the people 15
23 the glory of the LORD appeared to all the people 15
24 when all the people saw it, they shouted 15
10: 3 before all the people I will be glorified.' 15
11 you are to teach the people of Israel 5
14 sacrifices of the peace offerings of the people 5
11: 2 Say to the people of Israel 5
12: 2 Say to the people of Israel, If a woman conceives 5
15: 2 Say to the people of Israel 5
31 you shall keep the people of Israel separate 5
16: 5 from the congregation of the people of Israel 5
15 the sin offering which is for the people 15
16 the uncleannesses of the people of Israel 5
19 from the uncleannesses of the people of Israel 5
21 all the iniquities of the people of Israel 5
24 offer . . the burnt offering of the people 15
24 and make atonement for himself and for the people 15

33 the priests and for all the people of the assembly 15
34 atonement may be made for the people of Israel 5
17: 2 Say to Aaron . . and to all the people of Israel 5
4 that man shall be cut off from among his people 15
5 the people of Israel may bring their sacrifices 5
9 that man shall be cut off from his people 15
10 and will cut him off from among his people 15
12 Therefore I have said to the people of Israel 5
13 Any man also of the people of Israel 5
14 therefore I have said to the people of Israel 5
18: 2 Say to the people of Israel, I am the LORD your God 5
29 shall be cut off from among their people 15
19: 2 to all the congregation of the people of Israel 5
8 that person shall be cut off from his people 15
16 not go . . as a slanderer among your people 15
18 any grudge against the sons of your own people 15
20: 2 Say to the people of Israel, Any man of the people 5
2 Any man of the people of Israel, or of the strangers 5
2 the people of the land shall stone him 15
3 and will cut him off from among his people 15
4 if the people of the land do at all hide their eyes 15
5 and will cut off from among their people 15
6 I . . will cut him off from among his people 15
17 in the sight of the children of their people 15
18 both . . shall be cut off from among their people 15
24 your God, who have separated you from the peoples 15
26 I . . have separated you from the peoples 15
21: 1 defile himself for the dead among his people 15
4 defile himself . . among his people 15
14 he shall take to wife a virgin of his own people 15
15 not profane his children among his people 15
24 spoke . . to all the people of Israel 5
22: 2 the holy things of the people of Israel 5
3 holy things, which the people of Israel dedicate 5
15 profane the holy things of the people of Israel 5
18 Say to . . all the people of Israel, When any one 5
32 I will be hallowed among the people of Israel 5
23: 2 Say to the people of Israel, The appointed feasts 5
10 Say to the people of Israel, When you come 5
24 Say to the people of Israel, In the seventh month 5
29 on this same day shall be cut off from his people 15
30 that person I will destroy from among his people 15
34 Say to the people of Israel, On the fifteenth day 5
43 may know that I made the people of Israel dwell 5
44 Thus Moses declared to the people of Israel 5
24: 2 Command the people of Israel to bring you . . oil 5
8 on behalf of the people of Israel as a covenant 5
10 went out among the people of Israel 5
15 say to the people of Israel, Whoever curses 5
23 So Moses spoke to the people of Israel 5
23 Thus the people of Israel did as the LORD 5
25: 2 Say to the people of Israel, When you come 5
33 their possession among the people of Israel 5
46 over . . the people of Israel you shall not rule 5
55 For to me the people of Israel are servants 5
26:12 be your God, and you shall be my people 15
46 between him and the people of Israel on Mount 5
27: 2 Say to the people of Israel 5
34 commandments . . for the people of Israel 5
Num 1: 2 all the congregation of the people of Israel 5
20 The people of Reuben, Israel's first-born 5
22 Of the people of Simeon, their generations 5
24 Of the people of Gad, their generations 5
26 Of the people of Judah, their generations 5
28 Of the people of Is'sachar, their generations 5
30 Of the people of Zeb'ulun, their generations 5
32 Of the people of Joseph, namely . . E'phraim 5
32 Joseph, namely, of the people of E'phraim 5
34 Of the people of Manas'seh, their generations 5
36 Of the people of Benjamin, their generations 5
38 Of the people of Dan, their generations 5
40 Of the people of Asher, their generations 5
42 Of the people of Naph'tali, their generations 5
45 So the whole number of the people of Israel 5
49 take a census of them among the people of Israel; 5
52 The people of Israel shall pitch their tents 5
53 upon the congregation of the people of Israel; 5
54 Thus did the people of Israel; they did according 5
2: 2 The people of Israel shall encamp each by his own 5
3 the leader of the people of Judah being Nahshon 5
5 the leader of the people of Is'sachar 5
7 leader of the people of Zeb'ulun being Eli'ab 5
10 the leader of the people of Reuben being Eli'zur 5
12 the leader of the people of Simeon 5
14 leader of the people of Gad being Eli'asaph 5
18 leader of the people of E'phraim being Eli'shama 5
20 leader of the people of Manas'seh being Gama'liel 5
22 leader of the people of Benjamin being Abi'dan 5
25 leader of the people of Dan being Ahi-e'zer 5
27 leader of the people of Asher being Pa'giel 5
29 leader of the people of Naph'tali being Ahi'ra 5
32 These are the people of Israel as numbered 5
33 not numbered among the people of Israel 5
34 Thus did the people of Israel. 5
3: 8 shall . . attend to the duties for the people 5
9 given to him from among the people of Israel. 5
12 the Levites from among the people of Israel 5
12 that opens the womb among the people of Israel. 5
38 whatever had to be done for the people of Israel; 5

40 all the first-born males of the people of Israel 5
41 all the first-born among the people of Israel 5
41 among the cattle of the people of Israel. 5
42 all the first-born among the people of Israel 5
45 all the first-born among the people of Israel 5
46 273 of the first-born of the people of Israel 5
50 from the first-born of the people of Israel 5
5: 2 Command the people of Israel that they put out 5
4 people of Israel did so, and drove them outside 5
4 as the LORD said . . so the people of Israel did. 5
6 Say to the people of Israel, When a man or woman 5
9 all the holy things of the people of Israel 5
12 Say to the people of Israel, If any man's wife 5
21 execration and an oath among your people 15
27 shall become an execration among her people. 15
6: 2 Say to the people of Israel, When either a man 5
23 Thus you shall bless the people of Israel 5
27 shall they put my name upon the people of Israel 5
8: 6 Take the Levites from among the people of Israel 5
9 assemble the whole . . of the people of Israel. 5
10 people of Israel shall lay their hands upon 5
11 as a wave offering from the people of Israel 5
14 Levites from among the people of Israel 5
16 given to me from among the people of Israel; 5
16 first-born of all the people of Israel 5
17 first-born among the people of Israel are mine 5
18 all the first-born among the people of Israel. 5
19 as a gift . . from among the people of Israel 5
19 to do the service for the people of Israel 5
19 to make atonement for the people of Israel 5
19 there may be no plague among the people of Israel 5
19 in case the people of Israel should come near 5
20 all the congregation of the people of Israel 5
20 people of Israel did to them. 5
9: 2 Let the people of Israel keep the passover 5
4 Moses told the people of Israel that they should 5
5 so the people of Israel did. 5
7 among the people of Israel? 5
10 Say to the people of Israel, If any man of you 5
13 that person shall be cut off from his people 15
17 after that the people of Israel set out; 5
17 there the people of Israel encamped. 5
18 command of the LORD the people of Israel set out 5
19 people of Israel kept the charge of the LORD 5
22 the people of Israel remained in camp 5
10:12 people of Israel set out by stages 5
28 was the order of march of the people of Israel 5
11: 1 people complained in the hearing of the LORD 15
2 Then the people cried to Moses; and Moses prayed 15
4 people of Israel also wept again 5
8 people went about and gathered it, and ground it 15
10 Moses heard the people weeping throughout 15
11 dost lay the burden of all this people upon me? 15
12 Did I conceive all this people? Did I bring them 15
13 Where am I to get meat to give to all this people? 15
14 I am not able to carry all this people alone 15
16 whom you know to be the elders of the people 15
17 they shall bear the burden of the people with you 15
18 say to the people, 'Consecrate yourselves 15
21 The people among whom I am number 600,000 on foot; 15
24 Moses . . told the people the words of the LORD; 15
24 he gathered 70 men of the elders of the people 15
29 Would that all the LORD'S people were prophets 15
32 the people rose all that day, and all night 15
33 anger of the LORD was kindled against the people 15
33 LORD smote the people with a very great plague. 15
34 there they buried the people who had the craving. 15
35 From . . the people journeyed to Haze'roth; 15
12:15 people did not set out on the march till Miriam 15
16 After that the people set out from Haze'roth 15
13: 2 Canaan, which I give to the people of Israel; 5
3 men who were heads of the people of Israel. 5
18 whether the people who dwell in it are strong 15
26 all the congregation of the people of Israel 5
28 Yet the people who dwell in the land are strong 15
30 Caleb quieted the people before Moses, and said 15
31 We are not able to go up against the people; 15
32 brought to the people of Israel an evil report 5
32 people that we saw in it are men of great stature. 15
14: 1 raised a loud cry; and the people wept that night. 15
2 all the people of Israel murmured against Moses 5
5 all . . congregation of the people of Israel. 5
7 said to all . . of the people of Israel 5
9 do not fear the people of the land 15
10 appeared . . to all the people of Israel. 5
11 How long will this people despise me? 15
13 for thou didst bring up this people in thy might 15
14 thou, O LORD, art in the midst of this people; 15
15 Now if thou dost kill this people as one man 15
16 was not able to bring this people into the land 15
19 Pardon the iniquity of this people, I pray thee 15
19 according as thou hast forgiven this people 15
27 heard the murmurings of the people of Israel 5
39 told these words to all the people of Israel 5
39 people mourned greatly. 15
15: 2 Say to the people of Israel, When you come 5
18 Say to the people of Israel, When you come 5
25 for all the congregation of the people of Israel 5
26 all the congregation of the people of Israel 5
29 for him who is native among the people of Israel 5
30 shall be cut off from among his people. 15
32 people of Israel were in the wilderness 5
38 Speak to the people of Israel, and bid them to make 5
16: 2 rose up . . with a number of the people of Israel 5
38 Thus they shall be a sign to the people of Israel. 5
40 to be a reminder to the people of Israel 5
41 all . . the people of Israel murmured against 5
41 You have killed the people of the LORD. 15
47 plague had already begun among the people; 15
47 made atonement for the people. 15
17: 2 Speak to the people of Israel, and get from them 5
5 murmurings of the people of Israel 5
6 Moses spoke to the people of Israel; 5
9 all the rods . . to all the people of Israel; 5
12 people of Israel said to Moses, "Behold, we perish 5
18: 5 there be wrath no more upon the people of Israel. 5
6 Levites from among the people of Israel; 5
8 consecrated things of the people of Israel; 5
11 all the wave offerings of the people of Israel; 5
19 offerings which the people of Israel present 5
20 portion and your inheritance among the people 5
22 henceforth the people of Israel shall not come 5
23 among the people of Israel they shall have no 5
24 For the tithe of the people of Israel 5
24 have no inheritance among the people of Israel. 5
26 When you take from the people of Israel the tithe 5
28 tithes . . you receive from the people of Israel; 5
32 holy things of the people of Israel 5
19: 2 Tell the people of Israel to bring you 5
9 for the congregation of the people of Israel 5
10 be to the people of Israel, and to the stranger 5
20: 1 people of Israel . . came into the wilderness 5
1 people stayed in Kadesh; and Miriam died there 15
3 people contended with Moses, and said, "Would that 15
12 did not . . sanctify me in the eyes of the people 5
13 Mer'ibah, where the people of Israel contended 5
19 people of Israel said to him, "We will go up 5
22 people of Israel . . came to Mount Hor. 5
24 Aaron shall be gathered to his people; 15
24 land which I have given to the people of Israel 5
26 Aaron shall be gathered to his people •
21: 2 If thou wilt indeed give this people into my hand 15
4 the people became impatient on the way. 15
5 the people spoke against God and against Moses 15
6 LORD sent fiery serpents among the people 15
6 sent fiery serpents . . and they bit the people 15
6 so that many people of Israel died. 15
7 people came to Moses, and said, "We have sinned 15
7 So Moses prayed for the people. 15
10 people of Israel set out, and encamped in Oboth. 5
16 LORD said to Moses, "Gather the people together 15
18 well . . which the nobles of the people delved 15
29 O Moab! You are undone, O people of Chemosh! 15
33 Og . . came out against them, he and all his people 15
34 him into your hand, and all his people, and his land; 15
35 they slew him, and his sons, and all his people 15
22: 1 Then the people of Israel set out, and encamped 5
3 Moab was in great dread of the people 15
3 overcome with fear of the people of Israel. 5
5 Behold, a people has come out of Egypt; they cover 15
6 Come now, curse this people for me 15
11 'Behold, a people has come out of Egypt 15
12 shall not curse the people, for they are blessed. 15
17 come, curse this people for me.' 15
41 from there he saw the nearest of the people. 15
23: 9 lo, a people dwelling alone 15
24 Behold, a people! As a lioness it rises up 15
24:14 now, behold, I am going to my people; 15
14 people will do to your people in the latter days. 15
14 people will do to your people in the latter days. 15
25: 1 in Shittim the people began to play the harlot 15
2 These invited the people to the sacrifices 15
2 people ate, and bowed down to their gods. 15
4 Take all the chiefs of the people, and hang them 15
6 one of the people of Israel came and brought 5
6 whole congregation of the people of Israel 5
8 plague was stayed from the people of Israel. 5
11 turned back my wrath from the people of Israel 5
11 not consume the people of Israel in my jealousy. 5
13 made atonement for the people of Israel.' 5
15 Zur . . head of the people of a fathers' house 3
26: 2 all the congregation of the people of Israel 5
4 Take a census of the people, from twenty years old •
4 people of Israel, who came forth out of . . Egypt 5
51 number of the people of Israel, 601,730. 5
62 not numbered among the people of Israel 5
62 no inheritance . . among the people of Israel. 5
63 numbered the people of Israel in the plains 5
64 numbered the people of Israel in the wilderness 5
27: 8 you shall say to the people of Israel, 'If a man dies 5
11 to the people of Israel a statute and ordinance 5
12 land which I have given to the people of Israel. 5
13 you also shall be gathered to your people 15
20 congregation of the people of Israel may obey. 5
21 both he and all the people of Israel with him 5
28: 2 Command the people of Israel, and say to them 5
29:40 Moses told the people of Israel everything 5
30: 1 heads of the tribes of the people of Israel 5
31: 2 Avenge the people of Israel on the Mid'ianites; 5
2 afterward you shall be gathered to your people. 15
3 Moses said to the people, "Arm men from among you 15
9 people of Israel took captive the women 5
12 the congregation of the people of Israel 5
16 these caused the people of Israel . . to act 5
30 from the people of Israel's half you shall take 5
42 From the people of Israel's half, which Moses 5
47 from the people of Israel's half Moses took 5
54 memorial for the people of Israel before 5
32: 7 you discourage the heart of the people of Israel 5
9 discouraged the heart of the people of Israel 5
15 you will destroy all this people. 15
17 take up arms, ready to go before the people of Israel 5
18 until the people of Israel have inherited 5
28 tribes of the people of Israel. 5
33: 1 These are the stages of the people of Israel 5
3 people of Israel went out triumphantly 5
5 the people of Israel set out from Ram'eses 5
14 where there was no water for the people to drink. 15
38 after the people of Israel had come out 5
40 heard of the coming of the people of Israel. 5
51 Say to the people of Israel, When you pass over 5
34: 2 Command the people of Israel, and say to them 5
13 Moses commanded the people of Israel, saying 5
29 divide the inheritance for the people of Israel 5
35: 2 Command the people of Israel, that they give 5
8 give from the possession of the people of Israel 5
10 Say to the people of Israel, When you cross 5
15 cities . . for refuge for the people of Israel 5
34 LORD dwell in the midst of the people of Israel. 5
36: 1 leaders, the heads . . of the people of Israel; 5
2 give the land . . by lot to the people of Israel; 5
3 sons of the other tribes of the people of Israel 5
4 when the jubilee of the people of Israel comes 5
5 Moses commanded the people of Israel 5
7 inheritance of the people of Israel shall not 5
7 every one of the people of Israel shall cleave 5
8 inheritance in any tribe of the people of Israel 5
8 every one of the people of Israel may possess 5
9 for each of the tribes of the people of Israel 5
13 LORD commanded by Moses to the people of Israel 5
Deu 1: 3 Moses spoke to the people of Israel according 5
28 The people are greater and taller than we; 15
2: 4 command the people, You are about to pass through 15
10 Emim . . a people great and many, and tall 15
16 men of war . . were dead from among the people 15
21 a people great and many, and tall as the Anakim; 15
25 put the dread and fear of you upon the peoples 15
32 Sihon came out . . and all his people, to battle 15
33 we defeated him and his sons and all his people. 15
3: 1 Og . . came out against us, he and all his people 15
2 I have given him and all his people and his land 15
3 gave into our hand Og also . . and all his people; 15
18 before your brethren the people of Israel. 5
28 for he shall go over at the head of this people 15
4: 6 will be your wisdom . . in the sight of the peoples 15
6 great nation is a wise and understanding people.' 15
10 Gather the people to me, that I may let them hear 15
19 LORD your God has allotted to all the peoples 15
20 be a people of his own possession, as at this day. 15
27 LORD will scatter you among the peoples 15
33 Did any people ever hear the voice of a god 15
5:28 'I have heard the words of this people 15
6:14 other gods, of the gods of the peoples 15
7: 6 For you are a people holy to the LORD your God; 15
6 chosen you to be a people for his own possession 15
6 chosen you . . out of all the people 15
7 not . . more in number than any other people 15
7 for you were the fewest of all peoples; 15
14 You shall be blessed above all peoples; 15
16 you shall destroy all the peoples that the LORD 15
19 so will the LORD your God do to all the peoples 15
9: 2 people great and tall, the sons of the Anakim 15
6 righteousness; for you are a stubborn people 15
12 for your people whom you have brought from Egypt 15
13 LORD said to me, 'I have seen this people, and behold 15
13 seen . . and behold, it is a stubborn people; 15
26 O Lord GOD, destroy not thy people and thy heritage 15
27 do not regard the stubbornness of this people 15
29 For they are thy people and thy heritage 15
10: 6 people of Israel journeyed 5
11 Arise, go on your journey at the head of the people 15
15 LORD . . chose . . , you above all peoples 15
13: 7 gods of the people that are round about you 15
9 afterwards the hand of all the people. 15
14: 2 For you are a people holy to the LORD your God 15
2 chosen you to be a people for his own possession 15
2 the LORD has chosen you . . out of all the peoples 15
21 for you are a people holy to the LORD your God. 15
16:18 judge the people with righteous judgment. 15
17: 7 death, and afterward the hand of all the people. 15
13 all the people shall hear, and fear, and not act 15
16 must not . . cause the people to return to Egypt 15
18: 3 this shall be the priests' due from the people 15
20: 2 priest shall come forward and speak to the people 15
5 officers shall speak to the people, saying, 'What 15
8 officers shall speak further to the people 15
9 made an end of speaking to the people 15

9 commanders . . appointed at the head of the people. 15
11 then all the people . . shall do forced labor 15
16 cities of these peoples that the LORD your God 15
21: 8 Forgive, O LORD, thy people Israel, whom thou hast 15
8 not the guilt . . in the midst of thy people Israel; 15
24: 7 one of his brethren, the people of Israel 5
26:15 bless thy people Israel and the ground 15
18 you are a people for his own possession 15
19 you shall be a people holy to the LORD your God 15
27: 1 Moses and the elders . . commanded the people 15
9 you have become the people of the LORD your God. 15
11 Moses charged the people the same day, saying 15
12 stand upon Mount Ger'izim to bless the people 15
15 all the people shall answer and say, 'Amen.' 15
16 all the people shall say, 'Amen.' 15
17 all the people shall say, 'Amen.' 15
18 all the people shall say, 'Amen.' 15
19 all the people shall say, 'Amen.' 15
20 all the people shall say, 'Amen.' 15
21 all the people shall say, 'Amen.' 15
22 all the people shall say, 'Amen.' 15
23 all the people shall say, 'Amen.' 15
24 all the people shall say, 'Amen.' 15
25 all the people shall say, 'Amen.' 15
26 all the people shall say, 'Amen.' 15
28: 9 establish you as a people holy to himself 15
10 all the peoples of the earth shall see that 15
32 sons . . shall be given to another people 15
37 among . . peoples where the LORD will lead you away. 15
64 LORD will scatter you among all peoples 15
29: 1 Moses to make with the people of Israel in . . Moab 5
13 that he may establish you this day as his people 15
30: 3 gather you again from all the peoples 15
31: 7 for you shall go with this people into the land 15
12 Assemble the people, men, women, and little ones 15
16 then this people will rise and play the harlot 15
19 this song, and teach it to the people of Israel; 5
19 witness for me against the people of Israel. 5
22 song . . and taught it to the people of Israel. 5
32: 6 requite . . you foolish and senseless people? 15
8 he fixed the bounds of the peoples according 15
9 For the LORD'S portion is his people 15
21 So I will stir them to jealousy with . . no people; 15
36 For the LORD will vindicate his people 15
43 Praise his people, O you nations; for he avenges 15
43 makes expiation for the land of his people. 15
44 recited . . song in the hearing of the people 15
49 give to the people of Israel for a possession; 5
50 die . . and be gathered to your people, as Aaron 15
50 died . . and was gathered to his people; 15
51 broke faith . . in the midst of the people of Israel 5
51 holy in the midst of the people of Israel. 5
52 land which I give to the people of Israel. 5
33: 3 Yea, he loved his people; all those consecrated 15
5 when the heads of the people were gathered 15
7 voice of Judah, and bring him in to his people. 15
17 with them he shall push the peoples, all of them 15
19 They shall call peoples to their mountain; 15
21 he came to the heads of the people, with Israel 15
29 O Israel! Who is like you, a people saved by the LORD 15
34: 8 people of Israel wept for Moses in . . Moab 5
9 so the people of Israel obeyed him, and did 5
Jos 1: 2 arise, go over this Jordan you and all this people 15
2 which I am giving to them, to the people of Israel. 5
6 you shall cause this people to inherit the land 15
10 Joshua commanded the officers of the people 15
11 Pass through the camp, and command the people 15
3: 1 rose and set out . . with all the people of Israel; 5
3 and commanded the people, "When you see the ark 15
5 Joshua said to the people, "Sanctify yourselves; 15
6 Take up the ark . . and pass on before the people. 15
6 took up the ark . . and went before the people. 15
9 Joshua said to the people of Israel, "Come hither 5
14 the people set out from their tents, to pass over 15
14 the priests bearing the ark . . before the people 15
16 and the people passed over opposite Jericho. 15
4: 2 Take twelve men from the people, from each . . a man 15
4 called the twelve men from the people of Israel 5
5 to the number of the tribes of the people of Israel 5
7 these stones shall be to the people of Israel 5
8 the number of the tribes of the people of Israel 5
10 the LORD commanded Joshua to tell the people 15
10 The people passed over in haste; 15
11 when all the people had finished passing over 15
11 and the priests passed over before the people. 15
12 passed over armed before the people of Israel 5
19 The people came up out of the Jordan on the tenth 15
21 And he said to the people of Israel 5
24 so that all the peoples of the earth may know that 15
5: 1 dried up . . the Jordan for the people of Israel 5
1 heart melted . . because of the people of Israel. 5
2 and circumcise the people of Israel again 5
3 Joshua . . and circumcised the people of Israel 5
4 all the males of the people who came out of Egypt 15
5 all the people who came out had been circumcised 15
5 all the people that were born on the way . . had not 15
6 the people of Israel walked 40 years 5
10 the people of Israel were encamped in Gilgal 5
12 and the people of Israel had manna no more 5
6: 1 was shut up . . because of the people of Israel; 5
5 all the people shall shout with a great shout; 15
5 and the people shall go up . . straight before 15
7 And he said to the people, "Go forward; 15
8 And as Joshua had commanded the people 15
10 Joshua commanded the people, "You shall not shout 15
16 Joshua said to the people, "Shout; 15
20 the people shouted, and the trumpets were blown. 15
20 soon as the people heard the sound of the trumpet 15
20 As soon as the . . the people raised a great shout 15
20 the people went up into the city, every man 15
7: 1 But the people of Israel broke faith in regard 5
1 of the LORD burned against the people of Israel. 5
3 Let not all the people go up . . they are but few. 15
3 do not make the whole people toil up there 15
4 about 3,000 went up there from the people; 15
5 And the hearts of the people melted, and became 15
7 why hast thou brought this people over the Jordan 15
12 Therefore the people of Israel cannot stand 5
13 Up, sanctify the people, and say 15
23 brought . . to Joshua and all the people of Israel; 5
8: 1 given into your hand the king of Ai, and his people 15
5 I, and all the people who are with me, will approach 15
9 but Joshua spent that night among the people. 15
10 Joshua arose early . . and mustered the people 15
10 and went up . . before the people to Ai. 15
14 he and all his people, the men of the city 15
16 all the people who were in the city were called 15
20 the people that fled . . turned back upon 15
25 all who fell . . were 12,000, all the people of Ai. 2
31 as Moses . . had commanded the people of Israel 5
32 in the presence of the people of Israel, he wrote 5
33 that they should bless the people of Israel. 15
9:17 And the people of Israel set out 5
18 But the people of Israel did not kill them 5
26 out of the hand of the people of Israel; 5
10: 4 peace with Joshua and with the people of Israel. 5
7 Joshua . . he and all the people of war with him 15
21 all the people returned . . to Joshua in the camp 15
21 against any of the people of Israel. 5
33 and Joshua smote him and his people 15
11: 7 Joshua came . . with all his people of war 15
14 spoil . . and the cattle, the people of Israel took 5
19 a city that made peace with the people of Israel 5
22 none . . left in the land of the people of Israel; 5
12: 1 the kings . . whom the people of Israel defeated 5
6 Moses . . and the people of Israel defeated them; 5
7 whom Joshua and the people of Israel defeated 5
13: 6 drive them out from before the people of Israel; 5
13 the people of Israel did not drive out 5
22 Balaam also . . the people of Israel killed 5
23 the border of the people of Reuben was the Jordan 5
31 these were allotted to the people of Machir 5
14: 1 the inheritances which the people of Israel 5
1 houses of the tribes of the people of Israel 5
4 For the people of Joseph were two tribes 5
5 The people of Israel did as the LORD commanded 5
6 Then the people of Judah came to Joshua at Gilgal; 5
8 my brethren . . made the heart of the people melt; 15
15: 1 The lot for the tribe of the people of Judah 5
12 is the boundary round about the people of Judah 5
13 he gave . . a portion among the people of Judah 5
20 inheritance of the tribe of the people of Judah 5
21 belonging to the tribe of the people of Judah 5
63 Jeb'usites . . the people of Judah could not drive 5
63 so the Jeb'usites dwell with the people of Judah 5
16: 4 The people of Joseph, Manas'seh and E'phraim 5
17:13 when the people of Israel grew strong 5
14 but one lot . . although I am a numerous people 15
15 If you are a numerous people, go up to the forest 15
17 You are a numerous people, and have great power; 15
18: 1 the whole . . of the people of Israel assembled 5
2 There remained among the people of Israel seven 5
3 Joshua said to the people of Israel, "How long 5
10 apportioned the land to the people of Israel 5
19:49 people of Israel gave an inheritance among them 5
51 houses of the tribes of the people of Israel 5
20: 2 Say to the people of Israel, 'Appoint the cities 5
9 cities designated for all the people of Israel 5
21: 1 houses of the tribes of the people of Israel; 5
3 the people of Israel gave to the Levites 5
8 These . . the people of Israel gave by lot 5
41 midst of the possession of the people of Israel 5
22: 9 parting from the people of Israel at Shiloh 5
11 And the people of Israel heard say 5
11 on the side that belongs to the people of Israel. 5
12 when the people of Israel heard of it 5
12 whole assembly of the people of Israel gathered 5
13 Then the people of Israel sent . . Phin'ehas 5
31 you have saved the people of Israel from the hand 5
32 to the land of Canaan, to the people of Israel 5
33 And the report pleased the people of Israel; 5
33 and the people of Israel blessed God 5
24: 2 Joshua said to all the people, "Thus says the LORD 15
16 Then the people answered, "Far be it from us 15
17 in all the way . . and among all the peoples 15
18 and the LORD drove out before us all the peoples 15
19 But Joshua said to the people, "You cannot serve 15
21 the people said to Joshua, "Nay; but we will serve 15
22 Then Joshua said to the people, "You are witnesses 15
24 And the people said to Joshua, "The LORD our God 15
25 Joshua made a covenant with the people that day 15
27 Joshua said to all the people, "Behold, this stone 15
28 Joshua sent the people away, every man to his 15
32 bones . . which the people of Israel brought up 5
Jdg 1: 1 the people of Israel inquired of the LORD 5
16 went up with the people of Judah from the city 5
16 Arad; and they went and settled with the people. 15
21 the people of Benjamin did not drive out 5
21 have dwelt with the people of Benjamin 5
2: 4 spoke these words to all the people of Israel 5
4 the people lifted up their voices and wept. 15
6 When Joshua dismissed the people, the people 15
6 the people of Israel went each to his 5
7 the people served the LORD all the days of Joshua 15
11 the people of Israel did what was evil 5
12 the gods of the peoples who were round about them 15
20 this people have transgressed my covenant 9
3: 2 generations of the people of Israel might know 5
5 the people of Israel dwelt among the Canaanites 5
7 the people of Israel did what was evil 5
8 the people of Israel served Cu'shan-rishatha'im 5
9 But when the people of Israel cried to the LORD 5
9 raised up a deliverer for the people of Israel 5
12 the people of Israel again did what was evil 5
14 the people of Israel served Eglon the king 5
15 when the people of Israel cried to the LORD 5
15 The people of Israel sent tribute by him to Eglon 5
18 sent away the people that carried the tribute. 15
27 and the people of Israel went down with him 5
4: 1 the people of Israel again did what was evil 5
3 the people of Israel cried to the LORD for help; 5
3 he . . oppressed the people of Israel cruelly 5
5 the people of Israel came up to her for judgment. 5
23 the king of Canaan before the people of Israel. 5
24 the hand of the people of Israel bore harder 5
5: 2 that the people offered themselves willingly 15
9 who offered themselves . . among the people. 15
11 down to the gates marched the people of the LORD. 15
13 the people of the LORD marched down for him 15
18 Zeb'ulun is a people that jeoparded their lives 15
6: 1 people of Israel did what was evil in the sight 5
2 people of Israel made for themselves the dens 5
3 Mid'ianites and the Amal'ekites and the people 5
6 the people of Israel cried for help to the LORD. 5
7 When the people of Israel cried to the LORD 5
8 the LORD sent a prophet to the people of Israel; 5
33 and the Amal'ekites and the people of the East 5
7: 1 Then Jerubba'al (that is, Gideon) and all the people 15
2 The people with you are too many for me to give 15
3 proclaim in the ears of the people, saying 15
4 LORD said to Gideon, "The people are still too many; 15
5 he brought the people down to the water; 15
6 but all the rest of the people knelt down to drink 15
8 he took the jars of the people from their hands 15
12 the Amal'ekites and all the people of the East 5
8: 5 give loaves of bread to the people who follow me; 15
10 were left of all the army of the people of the East; 5
28 Mid'ian was subdued before the people of Israel 5
33 the people of Israel turned again and played 5
34 the people of Israel did not remember the LORD 5
9:29 Would that this people were under my hand! 15
45 he took the city, and killed the people . . in it; 15
46 When all the people of the Tower of Shechem heard 7
47 told that all the people of the Tower of Shechem 7
49 every one of the people cut down his bundle 15
49 all the people of the Tower of Shechem also died 2
51 tower . . and all the people of the city fled to it 7
10: 6 the people of Israel again did what was evil 5
8 they oppressed all the people of Israel 5
10 the people of Israel cried to the LORD 5
11 the LORD said to the people of Israel, "Did I not 5
15 the people of Israel said to the LORD, "We have 5
17 and the people of Israel came together 5
18 And the people, the leaders of Gilead, said 15
11:11 and the people made him head and leader over them; 15
20 so Sihon gathered all his people together 15
21 the LORD . . gave Sihon and all his people 15
23 the Amorites from before his people Israel; 15
27 decide this day between the people of Israel 5
27 the people of Israel and the people of Ammon. 5
33 were subdued before the people of Israel. 5
12: 2 I and my people had a great feud 15
13: 1 the people of Israel again did what was evil 5
14: 3 kinsmen, or among all our people, that you must go 15
11 And when the people saw him, they brought 30 •
16:24 when the people saw him, they praised their god; 15
30 the lords and upon all the people that were in it. 15
18: 7 came to La'ish, and saw the people who were there 15
10 you will come to an unsuspecting people. 15
20 graven image, and went in the midst of the people. 15
27 came to La'ish, to a people quiet and unsuspecting 15
19:12 who do not belong to the people of Israel; 5
30 from the day that the people of Israel came up out 5
20: 1 all the people of Israel came out, from Dan 5
2 the chiefs of all the people, of all the tribes 15
2 themselves in the assembly of the people of God 15
3 heard that the people of Israel had gone up 5

3 the people of Israel said, "Tell us, how was this 5
7 Behold, you people of Israel, all of you, give 5
8 all the people arose as one man, saying, "We will not 15
10 provisions for the people, that when they come 15
13 the voice of their brethren, the people of Israel 5
14 to go out to battle against the people of Israel 5
18 The people of Israel arose and went up to Bethel 5
19 the people of Israel rose in the morning 5
22 But the people, the men of Israel, took courage 15
23 the people of Israel went up and wept 5
24 the people of Israel came near against 5
25 felled . . 18,000 men of the people of Israel 5
26 all the people of Israel, the whole army, went up 5
27 the people of Israel inquired of the LORD 5
30 the people of Israel went up against 5
31 the Benjaminites went out against the people 15
31 they began to smite and kill some of the people 15
21: 2 the people came to Bethel, and sat there till 15
4 on the morrow the people rose early, and built 15
5 the people of Israel said, "Which of all the tribes 5
6 the people of Israel had compassion 5
9 For when the people were mustered, behold, not one 15
15 the people had compassion on Benjamin 15
18 the people of Israel had sworn, "Cursed be he who 5
24 the people of Israel departed from there 5
Rut 1: 6 LORD had visited his people and given them food. 15
10 No, we will return with you to your people. 15
15 See, your sister-in-law has gone back to her people 15
16 your people shall be my people, and your God my God; 15
16 your people shall be my people, and your God my God; 15
2:11 and came to a people that you did not know before. 15
4: 4 and in the presence of the elders of my people. 15
9 Then Bo'az said to the elders and all the people 15
11 all the people who were at the gate, and the elders 15
1Sm 2:13 The custom of the priests with the people was 15
23 I hear of your evil dealings from all the people. 15
24 that I hear the people of the LORD spreading 15
28 my offerings by fire from the people of Israel. 5
29 parts of every offering of my people Israel? 15
4: 4 the people sent to Shiloh, and brought . . the ark 15
17 has also been a great slaughter among the people; 15
5:10 They have brought . . to slay us and our people. 15
11 Send . . that it may not slay us and our people. 15
6: 6 did not they let the people go, and they departed? *
13 Now the people of Beth-she'mesh were reaping *
19 he slew 70 men of them, and the people mourned 15
19 LORD had made a . . slaughter among the people. 15
7: 6 Samuel judged the people of Israel at Mizpah. 5
7 that the people of Israel had gathered at Mizpah 5
7 when the people of Israel heard of it they were 5
8 the people of Israel said to Samuel, "Do not cease 5
8: 7 Hearken to the voice of the people in all 15
10 Samuel told all . . to the people who were asking 15
19 But the people refused to listen to . . Samuel; 15
21 when Samuel had heard all the words of the people 15
9: 2 a man among the people of Israel more handsome 5
2 he was taller than any of the people. 15
12 the people have a sacrifice . . on the high place. 15
13 the people will not eat till he comes 15
16 anoint him to be prince over my people Israel. 15
16 He shall save my people from . . the Philistines; 15
16 I have seen the affliction of my people 15
17 He it is who shall rule over my people. 15
10: 1 anointed you to be prince over his people Israel? 26
1 And you shall reign over the people of the LORD 26
11 the people said to one another, "What has come over 15
17 Samuel called the people together to the LORD 15
18 he said to the people of Israel, "Thus says the LORD 5
23 when he stood among the people, he was taller 15
23 he was taller than any of the people 15
24 Samuel said to all the people, "Do you see him 15
24 There is none like him among all the people. 15
24 And all the people shouted, "Long live the king! 15
25 Samuel told the people the rights and duties 15
25 Then Samuel sent all the people away 15
11: 4 reported the matter in the ears of the people; 15
4 they reported . . and all the people wept aloud. 15
5 What ails the people, that they are weeping? 15
7 Then the dread of the LORD fell upon the people 15
11 Saul put the people in three companies; 15
12 Then the people said to Samuel, "Who is it that said 15
14 Samuel said to the people, "Come, let us go to Gilgal 15
15 all the people went to Gilgal . . made Saul king 15
12: 6 Samuel said to the people, "The LORD is witness 15
18 all the people . . feared the LORD and Samuel. 15
19 the people said to Samuel, "Pray for your servants 15
20 And Samuel said to the people, "Fear not; 15
22 the LORD will not cast away his people 15
22 pleased . . to make you a people for himself. 15
13: 2 the rest of the people he sent home 15
4 the people were called out to join Saul 15
6 were in straits (for the people were hard pressed) 15
6 the people hid themselves in caves and in holes 15
7 and all the people followed him trembling. 15
8 and the people were scattering from him. 15
11 I saw that the people were scattering from me 15
14 LORD has appointed him . . prince over his people 15
15 Saul numbered the people . . present with him 15
16 the people . . present with them, stayed in Geba 15
22 of any of the people with Saul and Jonathan; 15
14: 2 Saul was . . the people who were with him were 15
3 the people did not know that Jonathan had gone. 15
15 panic in . . in the field, and among all the people; 15
17 Then Saul said to the people who were with him 15
18 the ark of God went . . with the people of Israel. 5
20 Saul and all the people who were with him rallied 15
24 Saul laid an oath on the people, saying, "Cursed be 15
24 So none of the people tasted food. 15
25 And all the people came into the forest; 4
26 And when the people entered the forest, behold 15
26 no man put . . for the people feared the oath. 15
27 heard his father charge the people with the oath; 15
28 Then one of the people said, "Your father 15
28 Your father . . charged the people with an oath 15
28 And the people were faint. 15
30 How much better if the people had eaten freely 15
31 And the people were very faint; 15
32 the people flew upon the spoil, and took sheep 15
32 slew . . and the people ate them with the blood. 15
33 the people are sinning against the LORD 15
34 Disperse yourselves among the people, and say 15
34 So every one of the people brought his ox with him 15
38 Come hither, all you leaders of the people; 15
39 was not a man among all the people that answered 15
40 the people said to Saul, "Do what seems good to you. 15
41 guilt is in thy people Israel, give Thummim 38
41 and Saul were taken, but the people escaped. 15
45 Then the people said to Saul, "Shall Jonathan die 15
45 the people ransomed Jonathan, that he . . not die. 15
15: 1 sent me to anoint you king over his people Israel; 15
4 Saul summoned the people, and numbered them 15
6 you showed kindness to all the people of Israel 5
8 and utterly destroyed all the people 15
9 But Saul and the people spared Agag, and the best 15
15 the people spared the best of the sheep 15
21 But the people took of the spoil, sheep and oxen 15
24 I feared the people and obeyed their voice. 15
30 yet honor me now before the elders of my people 15
17:27 And the people answered him in the same way 15
30 and the people answered him again as before. 15
18: 5 And this was good in the sight of all the people 15
13 and he went out and came in before the people. 15
23: 8 And Saul summoned all the people to war 15
26:15 For one of the people came in to destroy the king 15
27:12 made himself . . abhorred by his people Israel; 15
30: 4 David and the people . . raised their voices 15
6 distressed; for the people spoke of stoning him 15
6 all the people were bitter in soul 15
20 and the people drove those cattle before him *
21 to meet David and . . the people who were with him; 15
21 when David drew near to the people he saluted 15
31: 9 the good news to their idols and to the people. 15
2Sm 1: 4 The people have fled from the battle 15
4 many of the people also have fallen and are dead; 15
12 for the people of the LORD and for the house 15
18 he said it should be taught to the people of Judah; 5
2:26 before you bid your people turn from the pursuit 15
30 when he had gathered all the people together 15
3:18 I will save my people Israel from . . Philistines 15
31 said to Jo'ab and to all the people . . with him 15
32 They buried Abner . . and all the people wept. 15
34 And all the people wept again over him. 15
35 Then all the people came to persuade David to eat 15
36 all the people took notice . . and it pleased them; 15
36 that the king did pleased all the people. 15
37 the people and all Israel understood that day 15
5: 2 You shall be shepherd of my people Israel 15
12 LORD had . . for the sake of his people Israel. 15
6: 2 went with all the people who were with him 15
18 he blessed the people in the name of the LORD 15
19 among all the people, the whole multitude 15
19 Then all the people departed, each to his house. 15
21 as prince over Israel, the people of the LORD 15
7: 6 I brought up the people of Israel from Egypt 5
7 where I have moved with all the people of Israel 5
7 whom I commanded to shepherd my people Israel 15
8 that you should be prince over my people Israel; 15
10 And I will appoint a place for my people Israel 15
11 that I appointed judges over my people Israel; 15
23 What . . nation on earth is like thy people Israel 15
23 Israel, whom God went to redeem to be his people 15
23 by driving out before his people a nation 15
24 thou didst establish . . thy people Israel 15
24 establish . . Israel to be thy people for ever; 15
8:15 justice and equity to all his people. 15
10:12 play the man for our people, and for the cities 15
13 Jo'ab and the people who were with him drew near 15
11: 7 asked how Jo'ab was doing, and how the people fared 15
17 some . . servants of David among the people fell. 15
12:28 Now, then, gather the rest of the people together 15
29 David gathered all the people together and went 15
31 And he brought forth the people who were in it 15
31 David and all the people returned to Jerusalem. 15
13:34 many people were coming from the Horona'im road 15
14:13 planned such a thing against the people of God? 15
15 I have . . because the people have made me afraid; 15
15:12 and the people with Ab'salom kept increasing. 15
17 the king went forth, and all the people after him; 15
23 the country wept . . as all the people passed by 15
23 all the people passed on toward the wilderness. 15
24 until the people had all passed out of the city. 15
30 all the people . . with him covered their heads 15
16: 6 all the people and . . mighty men were on his right 15
14 the king, and all the people who were with him 15
15 Ab'salom and all the people, the men of Israel, came 15
18 the LORD and this people and all the men of Israel 15
17: 2 and all the people who are with him will flee. 15
3 and I will bring all the people back to you 15
3 only one man, and all the people will be at peace. 15
8 he will not spend the night with the people. 15
9 when some of the people fall at the first attack *
9 slaughter among the people who follow Ab'salom.' 15
16 the king and all the people who are with him 15
22 David arose, and all the people who were with him 15
29 for David and the people with him to eat; 15
29 The people are hungry and weary and thirsty 15
18: 5 all the people heard when the king gave orders 15
8 forest devoured more people . . than the sword. 15
19: 2 was turned into mourning for all the people; 15
2 the people heard that day, "The king is grieving 15
3 And the people stole into the city that day 15
3 as people steal in who are ashamed when they flee 15
8 And the people were all told, "Behold, the king is 15
8 and all the people came before the king. 15
9 the people were at strife throughout . . Israel 15
39 Then all the people went over the Jordan 15
40 the people of Judah, and also half . . of Israel 15
40 all . . of Judah, and also half the people of Israel 15
20:12 and when the man saw that all the people stopped 15
13 all the people went on after Jo'ab to pursue Sheba 2
22 the woman went to all the people in her wisdom. 15
21: 2 the Gib'eonites were not of the people of Israel 5
2 the people of Israel had sworn to spare them 5
2 in his zeal for the people of Israel and Judah. 5
22:28 Thou dost deliver a humble people 15
44 didst deliver me from strife with the peoples; 15
44 people whom I had not known served me. 15
48 God who . . brought down peoples under me 15
24: 2 Go through all . . Israel . . and number the people 15
2 that I may know the number of the people. 15
3 May the LORD . . add to the people 100 times 15
4 went out . . to number the people of Israel. 15
9 Jo'ab gave the sum of the numbering of the people 15
10 smote him after he had numbered the people. 15
15 and there died of the people . . 70,000 men. 15
16 who was working destruction among the people 15
17 when he saw the angel who was smiting the people 15
21 the plague may be averted from the people. 15
1Kg 1:39 blew the trumpet; and all the people said, "Long 15
40 all the people went up after him, playing on pipes 15
3: 2 The people were sacrificing at the high places 15
8 in the midst of thy people whom thou hast chosen 15
8 a great people, that cannot be numbered 15
9 an understanding mind to govern thy people 15
9 for who is able to govern this thy great people? 15
4:30 the wisdom of all the people of the east, and all 5
34 men came from all peoples to hear the wisdom 15
5: 7 given . . a wise son to be over this great people. 15
16 had charge of the people who carried on the work. 15
6: 1 after the people of Israel came out of . . Egypt 5
13 I will . . and will not forsake my people Israel. 15
8: 1 of the fathers' houses of the people of Israel 5
9 LORD made a covenant with the people of Israel 5
16 day that I brought my people Israel out of Egypt 15
16 but I chose David to be over my people Israel.' 15
30 of thy servant and of thy people Israel 15
33 When thy people Israel are defeated . . if they 15
34 hear . . and forgive the sin of thy people Israel 15
36 forgive . . thy servants, thy people Israel 15
36 thou hast given to thy people as an inheritance. 15
38 prayer . . by any man or by all thy people Israel 15
41 a foreigner, who is not of thy people Israel, comes 15
43 all the peoples of the earth may know thy name 15
43 thy name and fear thee, as do thy people Israel 15
44 If thy people go out . . against their enemy 15
50 forgive thy people who have sinned against thee 15
51 they are thy people, and thy heritage 15
52 open . . to the supplication of thy people Israel 15
53 from among all the peoples of the earth, to be 15
56 the LORD who has given rest to his people Israel 15
59 maintain . . and the cause of his people Israel 15
60 that all the peoples of the earth may know 15
63 the king and all the people of Israel dedicated 5
66 On the eighth day he sent the people away; 15
66 LORD had shown to . . and to Israel his people. 15
9: 7 become a proverb and a byword among all peoples. 15
20 All the people who were left 15
20 the people . . who were not of the people of Israel- 5
21 whom the people of Israel were unable to destroy 5
22 of the people of Israel Solomon made no slaves; 5
23 had charge of the people who carried on the work. 15
11: 2 the LORD had said to the people of Israel 5
12: 5 said to them, "Depart . . " So the people went away. 15
6 How do you advise me to answer this people? 15
7 be a servant to this people today and serve them 15
9 What do you advise that we answer this people 15
10 Thus shall you speak to this people 15

12 Jerobo'am and all the people came to Rehobo'am 15
13 the king answered the people harshly 15
15 So the king did not hearken to the people; 15
16 when all Israel saw . . the people answered 15
17 But Rehobo'am reigned over the people of Israel 5
23 Judah and Benjamin, and to the rest of the people 15
24 against your kinsmen the people of Israel. 5
27 if this people go up to offer sacrifices 15
27 the heart of this people will turn again 15
28 he said to the people, "You have gone up •
30 the people went to the one at Bethel 15
31 and appointed priests from among all the people 15
33 he ordained a feast for the people of Israel 5
13:33 made priests . . again from among all the people; 15
14: 2 said of me that I should be king over this people. 15
7 Because I exalted you from among the people 15
7 and made you leader over my people Israel 15
24 the LORD drove out before the people of Israel. 5
16: 2 and made you leader over my people Israel 15
2 and have made my people Israel to sin 15
21 the people of Israel were divided into two parts; 15
21 half of the people followed Tibni. 15
22 the people who followed Omri overcame 15
22 overcame the people who followed Tibni 15
18:20 So Ahab sent to all the people of Israel 5
21 Eli'jah came near to all the people, and said 15
21 And the people did not answer him a word. 15
22 Eli'jah said to the people, "I, even I only, am left 15
24 And all the people answered, "It is well spoken. 15
30 Then Eli'jah said to all the people, "Come near to me"; 15
30 Come near . . "; and all the people came near to him. 15
37 that this people may know that thou, O LORD, art God 15
39 when . . the people saw it, they fell on their faces; 15
19:10 the people of Israel have forsaken thy covenant 5
14 the people of Israel have forsaken thy covenant 5
21 boiled their flesh . . and gave it to the people 15
20: 8 all the elders and all the people said to him 15
10 suffice . . for all the people who follow me. 15
15 after them he mustered all the people of Israel 15
27 the people of Israel were mustered 5
27 the people of Israel encamped before them 5
29 the people of Israel smote . . 100,000 foot soldiers 5
42 go for his life, and your people for his people.' 15
42 go for his life, and your people for his people.' 15
21: 9 and set Naboth on high among the people; 15
12 and set Naboth on high among the people. 15
13 brought a charge . . in the presence of the people 15
26 the LORD cast out before the people of Israel.) 5
22: 4 I am as you are, my people as your people 15
4 I am as you are, my people as your people 15
28 And he said, "Hear, all you peoples! 15
43 the people still sacrificed and burned incense 15
2Kg 3: 7 I will go; I am as you are, my people as your people 15
7 I will go; I am as you are, my people as your people 15
4:13 She answered, "I dwell among my own people. 15
6:18 Strike this people, I pray thee, with blindness. 9
30 the people looked, and behold, he had sackcloth 15
7:16 Then the people went out, and plundered the camp 15
17 and the people trod upon him in the gate 15
20 so it happened to him, for the people trod upon him 15
8:12 the evil that you will do to the people of Israel; 5
9: 6 I anoint you king over the people of the LORD 15
10: 9 when he went . . he stood, and said to all the people 15
18 Jehu assembled all the people, and said to them 15
11:13 heard the noise of the guard and of the people 15
13 she went into the house of the LORD to the people; 15
14 and all the people of the land rejoicing 15
17 between the LORD and the king and people 15
17 covenant . . that they should be the LORD's people; 15
17 and also between the king and the people. 15
18 Then all the people . . went to the house of Ba'al 15
19 he took . . and all the people of the land; 15
20 So all the people of the land rejoiced; 15
12: 3 the people continued to sacrifice and burn 15
8 they should take no more money from the people 15
13: 5 and the people of Israel dwelt in their homes 5
14: 4 the people still sacrificed and burned incense 15
21 all the people of Judah took Azari'ah 15
15: 4 the people still sacrificed and burned incense 15
5 king's son . . governing the people of the land. 15
29 and he carried the people captive to Assyria. •
35 the people still sacrificed and burned incense 15
16: 3 the LORD drove out before the people of Israel. 5
9 and took it, carrying its people captive to Kir •
15 burnt offering of all the people of the land, and their 15
17: 7 the people of Israel had sinned against the LORD 5
8 the LORD drove out before the people of Israel 5
9 And the people of Israel did secretly 5
22 The people of Israel walked in all the sins 5
24 the king of Assyria brought people from Babylon •
24 placed them in . . instead of the people of Israel; 5
32 and appointed . . all sorts of people as priests •
18: 4 the people of Israel had burned incense to it; 5
26 the hearing of the people who are on the wall. 15
36 the people were silent and answered him not 15
19:12 Rezeph, and the people of Eden who were 5
20: 5 and say to Hezeki'ah the prince of my people 15
21: 2 the LORD drove out before the people of Israel. 5
9 the LORD destroyed before the people of Israel. 5

24 the people of the land slew all those who had 15
24 the people of the land made Josi'ah his son king 15
22: 4 the keepers . . have collected from the people; 15
13 Go, inquire of the LORD for me, and for the people 15
23: 2 and the priests and the prophets, all the people 15
3 and all the people joined in the covenant. 15
21 king commanded all the people, "Keep the passover 15
30 the people of the land took Jeho'ahaz 15
35 He exacted the . . of the people of the land 15
24:14 none . . except the poorest people of the land. 15
25: 3 there was no food for the people of the land. 15
11 the rest of the people who were left in the city 15
19 commander . . who mustered the people of the land; 15
19 and 60 men of the people of the land 15
22 over the people who remained in the land of Judah 15
26 all the people . . arose, and went to Egypt; 15
1Ch 5:25 the peoples of the land, whom God had destroyed 15
6:64 the people of Israel gave the Levites the cities 5
9: 3 some of the people of Judah, Benjamin, E'phraim 5
10: 9 the good news to their idols and to the people. 15
11: 2 You shall be shepherd of my people Israel 15
2 you shall be prince over my people Israel 15
13: 4 the thing was right in the eyes of all the people. 15
14: 2 exalted for the sake of his people Israel. 15
16: 2 he blessed the people in the name of the LORD 15
8 make known his deeds among the peoples! 15
20 from one kingdom to another people 15
24 his marvelous works among all the peoples! 15
26 For all the gods of the peoples are idols; 15
28 Ascribe to the LORD, O families of the peoples 15
36 all the people said "Amen!" and praised the LORD. 15
43 Then all the people departed each to his house 15
17: 6 whom I commanded to shepherd my people 15
7 that you should be prince over my people Israel; 15
9 I will appoint a place for my people Israel 15
10 I appointed judges over my people Israel; 15
21 What other nation . . is like thy people Israel 15
21 Israel, whom God went to redeem to be his people 15
21 in driving out nations before thy people 15
22 didst make thy people Israel to be thy people 15
22 make thy people Israel to be thy people for ever; 15
18:14 justice and equity to all his people. 15
19:13 let us play the man for our people 15
14 Jo'ab and the people who were with him drew near 15
20: 3 he brought forth the people who were in it 15
3 David and all the people returned to Jerusalem. 15
21: 3 May the LORD add to his people 100 times 15
5 Jo'ab gave the sum of the numbering of the people 15
17 Was it not I who gave command to number the people 15
17 but let not the plague be upon thy people. 15
22 that the plague may be averted from the people. 15
22:18 land is subdued before the LORD and his people. 15
23:25 the God of Israel, has given peace to his people; 15
27: 1 This is the list of the people of Israel 5
28: 2 and said: "Hear me, my brethren and my people. 15
21 all the people will be wholly at your command. 15
29: 9 Then the people rejoiced because these had 15
14 But who am I, and what is my people 15
17 now I have seen thy people . . offering freely 15
18 such purposes and . . in the hearts of thy people 15
2Ch 1: 9 for thou hast made me king over a people as many 15
10 to go out and come in before this people 15
10 who can rule this thy people, that is so great? 15
11 may rule my people over whom I have made you king 15
2:11 Because the LORD loves his people he has made you 15
18 as overseers to make the people work. 15
5: 2 of the fathers' houses of the people of Israel 5
10 LORD made a covenant with the people of Israel 5
6: 5 I brought my people out of the land of Egypt 15
5 I chose no man as prince over my people Israel; 15
6 I have chosen David to be over my people Israel.' 15
11 covenant of the LORD . . made with the people 5
21 supplications . . and of thy people Israel 15
24 If thy people . . are defeated before the enemy 15
25 hear . . and forgive the sin of thy people Israel 15
27 the sin of thy servants, thy people Israel 15
27 land . . given to thy people as an inheritance. 15
29 prayer . . made by . . or by all thy people Israel 15
32 when a foreigner, who is not of thy people Israel 15
33 that all the peoples of the earth may know thy 15
33 may know thy name and fear thee, as do thy people 15
34 If thy people go out to battle against their 15
39 hear thou . . and forgive thy people who have 15
7: 4 the king and all the people offered sacrifice 15
5 So the king and all the people dedicated 15
10 he sent the people away to their homes, joyful 15
10 goodness that the LORD had shown . . his people. 15
13 When I . . or send pestilence among my people 15
14 if my people . . humble themselves, and pray 15
20 make it a proverb and a byword among all peoples. 15
8: 2 and settled the people of Israel in them. 5
7 All the people who were left of the Hittites 15
8 whom the people of Israel had not destroyed- 5
9 of the people of Israel Solomon made no slaves 5
10 who exercised authority over the people. 15
10: 5 So the people went away. 15
6 How do you advise me to answer this people? 15
7 If you will be kind to this people and please them 15
9 What do you advise that we answer this people 15

10 Thus shall you speak to the people who said to you 15
12 Jerobo'am and all the people came to Rehobo'am 15
15 the king did not hearken to the people; 15
16 the people answered the king 15
17 Rehobo'am reigned over the people of Israel 5
18 people of Israel stoned him to death 5
12: 3 people were without number who came with him 15
13: 9 made priests . . like the people of other lands? 15
17 Abi'jah and his people slew them 15
14:13 Asa and the people . . pursued them as far 15
16:10 Asa inflicted cruelties upon some of the people 15
17: 9 they went about . . and taught among the people. 15
18: 2 for him and for the people who were with him 15
3 I am as you are, my people as your people. 15
3 I am as you are, my people as your people. 15
27 Micai'ah . . said, "Hear, all you peoples! 15
19: 4 Jehosh'aphat . . went out again among the people 15
20: 7 drive out . . before thy people Israel 15
21 when he had taken counsel with the people 15
25 When Jehosh'aphat and his people came to take 15
33 people had not yet set their hearts upon the God 15
21:14 LORD will bring a great plague on your people 15
19 His people made no fire in his honor 15
23: 5 all the people shall be in the courts 15
6 all the people shall keep the charge of the LORD. 15
10 he set all the people as a guard for the king 15
12 noise of the people running and praising 15
12 she went into the house of the LORD to the people; 15
13 all the people of the land rejoicing 15
16 covenant between himself and all the people 15
16 that they should be the LORD'S people. 15
17 Then all the people went to the house of Ba'al 15
20 he took . . the governors of the people 15
20 he took . . all the people of the land; 15
21 all the people of the land rejoiced; 15
24:10 all the princes and all the people rejoiced 15
20 Zechari'ah . . he stood above the people, and said 15
23 destroyed all the princes of the people 15
23 princes of the people from among the people 15
25:11 Amazi'ah took courage, and led out his people 15
13 killed 3,000 people in them, and took much spoil. •
15 Why have you resorted to the gods of a people 15
15 gods . . which did not deliver their own people 15
26: 1 all the people of Judah took Uzzi'ah 15
21 Jotham . . governing the people of the land. 15
27: 2 the people still followed corrupt practices. 15
28: 3 the LORD drove out before the people of Israel. 5
5 took captive a great number of his people •
10 now you intend to subjugate the people of Judah 5
29:36 Hezeki'ah and all the people rejoiced 15
36 because of what God had done for the people; 15
30: 3 nor had the people assembled in Jerusalem 15
5 the people should come and keep the passover •
6 O people of Israel, return to the LORD 5
13 many people came together in Jerusalem to keep 15
18 multitude of the people . . had not cleansed 15
20 the LORD heard Hezeki'ah, and healed the people. 15
21 people of Israel . . kept the feast 5
22 people ate the food of the festival for seven •
27 priests and the Levites . . blessed the people 15
31: 1 people of Israel returned to their cities 5
4 commanded the people . . to give the portion due 15
5 people of Israel gave in abundance 5
6 people of Israel and Judah 5
8 blessed the LORD and his people Israel. 15
10 for the LORD has blessed his people 15
32: 4 A great many people were gathered 15
6 he set combat commanders over the people 15
8 people took confidence from the words 15
13 have done to all the peoples of other lands? 15
14 was able to deliver his people from my hand 15
15 able to deliver his people from my hand 15
17 have not delivered their people from my hands 15
17 God . . will not deliver his people from my hand. 15
18 the people of Jerusalem who were upon the wall 15
19 the gods of the peoples of the earth 15
33: 2 LORD drove out before the people of Israel. 5
9 LORD destroyed before the people of Israel. 5
10 The LORD spoke to Manas'seh and to his people 15
17 people still sacrificed at the high places 15
25 people of the land slew all . . who had conspired 15
25 people of the land made Josi'ah his son king 15
34:30 all the people both great and small; 15
33 territory that belonged to the people of Israel 5
35: 3 Now serve the LORD your God and his people Israel. 15
8 princes contributed willingly to the people 15
17 people . . who were present kept the passover 5
36: 1 people . . took Jeho'ahaz the son of Josi'ah 15
14 All the leading priests and the people likewise 15
15 he had compassion on his people 15
16 till the wrath of the LORD rose against his people 15
23 Whoever is among you of all his people 15
Ezr 1: 3 Whoever is among you of all his people, may his God 15
2: 1 Now these were the people of the province 5
2 number of the men of the people of Israel 15
70 priests, the Levites, and some of the people lived 15
3: 1 people gathered as one man to Jerusalem. 15
3 fear . . because of the peoples of the lands 15
11 all the people shouted with a great shout 15

13 people could not distinguish the sound 15
13 from the sound of the people's weeping 15
13 for the people shouted with a great shout 15
4: 4 people of the land discouraged the people 15
4 land discouraged the people of Judah 15
5:12 carried away the people to Babylonia. 18
6:12 overthrow any king or people that shall put 18
16 people of Israel, the priests and the Levites 17
21 eaten by the people of Israel who had returned 5
21 from the pollutions of the peoples of the land 9
7: 7 some of the people of Israel 5
13 any one of the people of Israel or their priests 18
16 freewill offerings of the people 18
25 judges who may judge all the people 18
8:15 As I reviewed the people and the priests, I found 15
36 aided the people and the house of God. 15
9: 1 people of Israel and the priests and the Levites 15
1 not separated . . from the peoples of the lands 15
2 mixed itself with the peoples of the lands. 15
11 land unclean with the pollutions of the peoples 15
14 intermarry with the peoples who practice 15
10: 1 for the people wept bitterly. 15
2 foreign women from the peoples of the land 15
9 all the people sat in the open square 15
11 separate yourselves from the peoples of the land 15
13 people are many, and it is a time of heavy rain; 15
Neh 1: 6 prayer . . for the people of Israel thy servants 5
6 confessing the sins of the people of Israel 5
8 unfaithful, I will scatter you among the peoples; 15
10 servants and thy people, whom thou hast redeemed 15
4: 6 For the people had a mind to work. 15
13 I stationed the people according 15
14 said to . . officials and to the rest of the people 15
19 said to . . officials and to the rest of the people 15
22 I also said to the people at that time, "Let every 15
5: 1 great outcry of the people and of their wives 15
13 And the people did as they had promised. 15
15 laid heavy burdens upon the people, and took 15
15 Even their servants lorded it over the people. 15
18 servitude was heavy upon this people. 15
19 all that I have done for this people. 15
7: 4 city . . large, but the people within it were few 15
5 assemble . . officials and the people 15
6 These were the people of the province who came up 5
7 number of the men of the people of Israel 15
72 rest of the people gave was 20,000 darics of gold 15
73 gatekeepers, the singers, some of the people 15
8: 1 people gathered as one man into the square 15
3 ears of all the people were attentive to the book 15
5 opened the book in the sight of all the people 15
5 for he was above all the people; and when he opened 15
5 when he opened it all the people stood. 15
6 all the people answered, "Amen, Amen," lifting up 15
7 helped the people to understand the law 15
7 while the people remained in their places. 15
8 so that the people understood the reading. *
9 Levites who taught the people said to all 15
9 taught the people said to all the people, "This day 15
9 For all the people wept when they heard the words 15
11 Levites stilled all the people, saying, "Be quiet 15
12 all the people went their way to eat and drink 15
13 day the heads of fathers' houses of all the people 15
14 people of Israel should dwell in booths during 5
16 people went out and brought them and made booths 15
17 from . . Jeshua . . people of Israel had not done 5
9: 1 people of Israel were assembled with fasting 5
10 servants and all the people of his land 15
22 thou didst give them kingdoms and peoples 15
24 with their kings and the peoples of the land 15
30 into the hand of the peoples of the lands. 15
32 come upon . . our fathers, and all thy people 15
10:14 chiefs of the people: Parosh, Pa'hath-mo'ab, Elam 15
28 The rest of the people, the priests, the Levites 15
28 separated . . from the peoples of the lands 15
30 not give our daughters to the peoples of the land 15
31 if the peoples of the land bring in wares 15
34 cast lots, the priests, the Levites, and the people 15
39 For the people of Israel and the sons of Levi 5
11: 1 Now the leaders of the people lived in Jerusalem; 15
1 rest of the people cast lots to bring one out 15
2 people blessed all the men who willingly 15
24 all matters concerning the people. 15
25 some of the people of Judah lived in Kir'iath-ar'ba 5
31 people of Benjamin also lived from Geba onward 5
12:30 purified the people and the gates and the wall. 15
38 I followed them with half of the people 15
13: 1 book of Moses in the hearing of the people; 15
3 When the people heard the law, they separated *
16 sold them on the sabbath to the people of Judah 5
24 Judah, but the language of each people. 15
Est 1: 5 for all the people present in Susa the capital 15
11 to show the peoples and the princes her beauty; 15
16 but also to all the princes and all the peoples 15
22 sent . . to every people in its own language 15
22 speak according to the language of his people. 15
2:10 Esther had not made known her people or kindred 15
20 had not made known her kindred or her people 15
3: 6 they had made known to him the people of Mor'decai 15
6 to destroy all the Jews, the people of Mor'decai 15
8 There is a certain people scattered abroad 15
8 scattered . . and dispersed among the peoples 15
8 different from those of every other people 15
11 The money is given to you, the people also, 15
12 and to the princes of all the peoples 16
12 to . . every people in its own language; 15
14 by proclamation to all the peoples to be ready 15
4: 8 go to the king . . and entreat him for her people. 15
11 and the people of the king's provinces know 15
7: 3 let my life be . . and my people at my request. 15
4 For we are sold, I and my people, to be destroyed 15
8: 6 to see the calamity that is coming to my people? 15
11 any armed force of any people or province 15
13 issued . . and by proclamation to all peoples 15
17 many from the peoples of the country declared 15
9: 2 for the fear of them had fallen upon all peoples. 15
10: 3 he sought the welfare of his people 15
3 and spoke peace to all his people. 10
Job 1: 3 the greatest of all the people of the east. 5
12: 2 No doubt you are the people 15
24 from the chiefs of the people of the earth 15
17: 6 He has made me a byword of the peoples 15
18:19 has no offspring or descendant among his people 15
34:20 at midnight the people are shaken and pass away 15
30 that he should not ensnare the people. 15
35: 9 the multitude of oppressions people cry out; *
36:20 night, when peoples are cut off in their place. 15
31 For by these he judges peoples; 15
Ps 2: 1 nations conspire, and the peoples plot in vain? 12
3: 6 I am not afraid of ten thousands of people 15
8 thy blessing be upon thy people! Selah 15
7: 7 Let the assembly of the peoples be gathered 12
8 The LORD judges the peoples; 15
9: 8 he judges the peoples with equity. 12
11 Tell among the peoples his deeds! 15
14: 4 all the evildoers who eat up my people 15
7 the LORD restores the fortunes of his people 15
18:27 For thou dost deliver a humble people; 15
43 didst deliver me from strife with the peoples; 26
43 people whom I had not known served me. 15
47 gave me vengeance and subdued peoples under me; 15
22: 6 scorned by men, and despised by the people. 15
31 proclaim his deliverance to a people yet unborn 15
28: 8 The LORD is the strength of his people 15
9 O save thy people, and bless thy heritage; 15
29:11 May the LORD give strength to his people! 15
11 May the LORD bless his people with peace! 15
33:10 LORD . . he frustrates the plans of the peoples. 15
12 the people whom he has chosen as his heritage! 15
43: 1 defend my cause against an ungodly people; 9
44: 2 thou didst afflict the peoples 12
12 Thou hast sold thy people for a trifle 15
14 made us . . a laughingstock among the peoples. 12
45: 5 the peoples fall under you. 15
10 forget your people and your father's house; 15
12 the people of Tyre will sue your favor with gifts 8
12 your favor with gifts, the richest of the people 15
17 therefore the peoples will praise you for ever 15
47: 1 Clap your hands, all peoples! Shout to God 15
3 He subdued peoples under us, and nations 15
9 The princes of the peoples gather 15
9 gather as the people of the God of Abraham. 15
49: 1 Hear this, all peoples! Give ear, all inhabitants 15
50: 4 to the earth, that he may judge his people 15
7 Hear, O my people, and I will speak 15
53: 4 who eat up my people as they eat bread 15
6 When God restores the fortunes of his people 15
56: 7 in wrath cast down the peoples, O God! 15
57: 9 give thanks to thee, O Lord, among the peoples; 15
59:11 Slay them not, lest my people forget; 15
60: 3 Thou hast made thy people suffer hard things; 15
62: 8 Trust in him at all times, O people; 15
65: 7 roaring of their waves, the tumult of the peoples; 12
66: 8 Bless our God, O peoples 15
67: 3 Let the peoples praise thee, O God; 15
3 O God; let all the peoples praise thee! 15
4 for thou dost judge the peoples with equity 15
5 Let the peoples praise thee, O God; 15
5 O God; let all the peoples praise thee! 15
68: 7 O God, when thou didst go forth before thy people 15
30 herd of bulls with the calves of the peoples. 15
30 scatter the peoples who delight in war. 15
35 God . . gives power and strength to his people. 15
72: 2 May he judge thy people with righteousness 15
3 the mountains bear prosperity for the people 15
4 May he defend the cause of the poor of the people 15
73:10 Therefore the people turn and praise them; 15
74:18 an impious people reviles thy name. 15
77:14 who hast manifested thy might among the peoples. 15
15 Thou didst with thy arm redeem thy people 15
20 Thou didst lead thy people like a flock 15
78: 1 Give ear, O my people, to my teaching; 15
20 also give bread, or provide meat for his people? 15
52 Then he led forth his people like sheep 15
62 He gave his people over to the sword 15
71 to be the shepherd of Jacob his people, of Israel 15
79:13 Then we thy people, the flock of thy pasture 15
80: 4 how long . . be angry with thy people's prayers? 15
81: 8 Hear, O my people, while I admonish you! 15
11 my people did not listen to my voice; 15
13 O that my people would listen to me 15
83: 3 They lay crafty plans against thy people; 15
85: 2 Thou didst forgive the iniquity of thy people; 15
6 that thy people may rejoice in thee? 15
8 will speak peace to his people, to his saints 15
87: 6 LORD records as he registers the peoples 15
89:15 Blessed are the people who know the festal shout 15
19 I have exalted one chosen from the people. 15
50 how I bear in my bosom the insults of the peoples 15
94: 5 They crush thy people, O LORD 15
8 Understand, O dullest of the people! 15
14 For the LORD will not forsake his people; 15
95: 7 he is our God, and we are the people of his pasture 15
10 They are a people who err in heart 15
96: 3 his marvelous works among all the peoples! 15
5 For all the gods of the peoples are idols; 15
7 Ascribe to the LORD, O families of the peoples 15
10 he will judge the peoples with equity. 15
13 He will judge . . the peoples with his truth. 15
97: 6 all the peoples behold his glory. 15
98: 9 will judge . . the peoples with equity. 15
99: 1 The LORD reigns; let the peoples tremble! 15
2 in Zion; he is exalted over all the peoples. 15
100: 3 we are his people, and the sheep of his pasture. 15
102:18 so that a people yet unborn may praise the LORD 15
22 when peoples gather together, and kingdoms 15
103: 7 made known his . . acts to the people of Israel. 5
105: 1 make known his deeds among the peoples! 15
13 from one kingdom to another people 15
20 the ruler of the peoples set him free; 15
24 LORD made his people very fruitful 15
25 He turned their hearts to hate his people 15
43 he led forth his people with joy 15
44 took possession of the fruit of the peoples' toil 12
106: 4 me, O LORD, when thou showest favor to thy people; 15
34 not destroy the peoples, as the LORD commanded 15
40 anger of the LORD was kindled against his people 15
48 let all the people say, "Amen!" Praise the LORD! 15
107:32 them extol him in the congregation of the people 15
108: 3 give thanks to thee, O LORD, among the peoples 15
110: 3 Your people will offer themselves freely 15
111: 6 He has shown his people the power of his works 15
9 He sent redemption to his people; 15
113: 8 make them sit with . . the princes of his people. 15
114: 1 house of Jacob from a people of strange language 15
116:14 pay my vows . . in the presence of all his people. 15
18 pay my vows . . in the presence of all his people 15
117: 1 Extol him, all peoples! 3
125: 2 so the LORD is round about his people 15
135:12 as a heritage, a heritage to his people Israel. 15
14 For the LORD will vindicate his people 15
136:16 to him who led his people through the wilderness 15
144: 2 who subdues the peoples under him. 15
15 Happy the people to whom such blessings fall! 15
15 Happy the people whose God is the LORD! 15
148:11 Kings of the earth and all peoples 12
14 He has raised up a horn for his people 15
14 his saints, for the people of Israel who are near 15
149: 4 For the LORD takes pleasure in his people; 15
7 to wreak . . chastisement on the peoples 12
Prv 11:14 Where there is no guidance, a people falls; 15
26 The people curse him who holds back grain 12
14:28 In a multitude of people is the glory of a king 15
28 but without people a prince is ruined. 12
34 but sin is a reproach to any people. 12
24:24 will be cursed by peoples, abhorred by nations; 15
28:15 bear is a wicked ruler over a poor people. 15
29: 2 righteous are in authority, the people rejoice; 15
2 but when the wicked rule, the people groan. 15
18 no prophecy the people cast off restraint 15
30:25 ants are a people not strong, yet they provide 15
26 badgers are a people not mighty, yet they make 15
31 he-goat, and a king striding before his people. *
Ecc 4:16 there was no end of all the people; he was over all 15
12: 9 the Preacher also taught the people knowledge 15
Isa 1: 3 but Israel . . my people does not understand. 15
4 Ah, sinful nation, a people laden with iniquity 15
10 Give ear . . you people of Gomor'rah! 15
2: 3 many peoples shall come, and say: "Come, let us go up 15
4 shall judge . . and shall decide for many peoples; 15
6 thou hast rejected thy people, the house of Jacob 15
3: 5 the people will oppress one another, every man 15
7 you shall not make me leader of the people. 15
12 My people–children are their oppressors 15
12 O my people, your leaders mislead you 15
13 to contend, he stands to judge his people. 26
14 judgment with the . . princes of his people 15
15 What do you mean by crushing my people 15
5:13 my people go into exile for want of knowledge; 15
25 anger of the LORD was kindled against his people 15
6: 5 I dwell in the midst of a people of unclean lips; 15
9 he said, "Go, and say to this people: 'Hear and hear 15
10 Make the heart of this people fat 15
7: 2 the heart of his people shook as the trees 15
8 that it will no longer be a people.) 15
17 The LORD will bring upon you and upon your people 15
8: 6 this people have refused the waters of Shilo'ah 15
9 Be broken, you peoples, and be dismayed; give ear 15

11 warned me not to walk in the way of this people 15
12 all that this people call conspiracy 15
19 should not a people consult their God? 15
9: 2 The people who walked in darkness have seen 15
9 all the people will know, E'phraim 15
13 The people did not turn to him who smote them 15
16 for those who lead this people lead them astray 15
19 burned, and the people are like fuel for the fire; 15
10: 2 and to rob the poor of my people of their right 15
6 and against the people of my wrath I command him 15
13 I have removed the boundaries of peoples 15
14 found like a nest the wealth of the peoples; 15
22 For though your people Israel be as the sand 15
24 O my people, who dwell in Zion, be not afraid 15
11:10 root of Jesse . . stand as an ensign to the peoples; 15
11 recover the remnant which is left of his people 15
14 they shall plunder the people of the east. 5
16 for the remnant which is left of his people 15
13:14 every man will turn to his own people 15
14: 2 the peoples will take them . . to their place 15
6 that smote the peoples in wrath 15
20 destroyed your land, you have slain your people. 15
32 in her the afflicted of his people find refuge. 15
17:12 Ah, the thunder of many peoples 15
18: 2 to a people feared near and far 15
7 to the LORD of hosts from a people tall and smooth 15
7 from a people feared near and far 15
19:25 Blessed be Egypt my people 15
22: 4 the destruction of the daughter of my people. 15
23:13 Chalde'ans! This is the people; it was not Assyria. 15
24: 2 it shall be, as with the people, so with the priest; 15
25: 3 Therefore strong peoples will glorify thee; 15
6 will make for all peoples a feast of fat things 15
7 the covering that is cast over all peoples 15
8 the reproach of his people he will take away 15
26:11 them see thy zeal for thy people, and be ashamed. 15
20 Come, my people, enter your chambers 15
27:11 For this is a people without discernment; 15
12 be gathered one by one, O people of Israel. 5
28: 5 a diadem of beauty, to the remnant of his people; 15
11 alien tongue the LORD will speak to this people 15
14 you scoffers, who rule this people in Jerusalem! 15
29:13 Because this people draw near with their mouth 15
14 again do marvelous things with this people 15
30: 5 shame through a people that cannot profit them 15
6 to a people that cannot profit them. 15
9 For they are a rebellious people, lying sons 15
19 Yea, O people in Zion who dwell at Jerusalem; 15
26 when the LORD binds up the hurt of his people 15
28 and to place on the jaws of the peoples a bridle 15
31: 6 you have deeply revolted, O people of Israel. 5
32:13 for the soil of my people growing up in thorns 15
18 My people will abide in a peaceful habitation 15
33: 3 At the thunderous noise peoples flee 15
12 the peoples will be as if burned to lime 15
19 You will see no more the insolent people 15
19 the people of an obscure speech which you cannot 15
24 the people who dwell there will be forgiven 15
34: 1 Draw near, O nations, to hear, and hearken, O peoples 12
5 for judgment . . upon the people I have doomed. 15
36:11 within the hearing of the people . . on the wall. 15
37:12 and the people of Eden who were in Tel-assar? 5
40: 1 Comfort, comfort my people, says your God. 15
7 The grass withers . . surely the people is grass. 15
41: 1 let the peoples renew their strength; 12
42: 5 who gives breath to the people upon it 15
6 I have given you as a covenant to the people 15
22 this is a people robbed and plundered 15
43: 4 I give . . peoples in exchange for your life. 12
8 Bring forth the people who are blind 15
9 and let the peoples assemble. 12
20 in the desert, to give drink to my chosen people 15
21 the people whom I formed for myself 15
47: 6 was angry with my people, I profaned my heritage; 15
49: 1 O coastlands, and hearken, you peoples from afar. 12
8 kept you and given you as a covenant to the people 15
13 For the LORD has comforted his people 15
22 to the nations, and raise my signal to the peoples; 15
51: 4 Listen to me, my people, and give ear to me, my nation 15
4 from me, and my justice for a light to the peoples. 15
5 has gone forth, and my arms will rule the peoples; 15
7 the people in whose heart is my law; 15
16 and saying to Zion, 'You are my people.' 15
22 your God who pleads the cause of his people 15
52: 4 My people went down at the first into Egypt 15
5 seeing that my people are taken away for nothing? 15
6 Therefore my people shall know my name; 15
9 Jerusalem; for the LORD has comforted his people 15
53: 8 stricken for the transgression of my people? 15
54: 3 possess . . and will people the desolate cities. 11
55: 4 Behold, I made him a witness to the peoples 12
4 a leader and commander for the peoples. 12
56: 3 LORD will surely separate me from his people"; 15
7 be called a house of prayer for all peoples. 15
57:14 remove every obstruction from my people's way. 15
58: 1 declare to my people their transgression 15
60: 2 cover the earth, and thick darkness the peoples; 12
21 Your people shall all be righteous; 15
61: 9 and their offspring in the midst of the peoples; 15
9 that they are a people whom the LORD has blessed. 10
62:10 through the gates, prepare the way for the people; 15
10 lift up an ensign over the peoples. 15
12 And they shall be called The holy people 15
63: 3 alone, and from the peoples no one was with me; 15
6 I trod down the peoples in my anger 15
8 For he said, Surely they are my people 15
14 thou didst lead thy people 15
18 Thy holy people possessed thy sanctuary 15
64: 9 Behold, consider, we are all thy people. 15
65: 2 my hands all the day to a rebellious people 15
3 a people who provoke me to my face continually 15
10 to lie down, for my people who have sought me. 15
18 Jerusalem a rejoicing, and her people a joy. 15
19 rejoice in Jerusalem, and be glad in my people; 15
22 the days of a tree shall the days of my people be 15
Jer 1:18 Judah . . its priests, and the people of the land. 15
2:11 But my people have changed their glory 15
13 for my people have committed two evils 15
31 Why then do my people say, 'We are free 15
32 Yet my people have forgotten me 15
4:10 utterly deceived this people and Jerusalem 15
11 At that time it will be said to this people 15
11 A hot wind . . toward the daughter of my people 15
22 For my people are foolish, they know me not; 15
5:14 this people wood, and the fire shall devour them. 15
19 when your people say, 'Why has the LORD our God •
21 Hear this, O foolish and senseless people 15
23 this people has a stubborn and rebellious heart; 15
26 For wicked men are found among my people; 15
31 my people love to have it 15
6: 1 Flee for safety, O people of Benjamin 5
14 They have healed the wound of my people lightly 15
19 behold, I am bringing evil upon this people 15
21 I will lay before this people stumbling blocks 15
22 Behold, a people is coming from the north country 15
26 O daughter of my people, gird on sackcloth 15
27 made you an assayer and tester among my people 15
7:12 did to it for the wickedness of my people Israel. 15
16 As for you, do not pray for this people 15
23 I will be your God, and you shall be my people; 15
33 And the dead bodies of this people will be food 15
8: 5 Why then has this people turned away 15
7 but my people know not the ordinance of the LORD. 15
11 They have healed the wound of my people lightly 15
19 Hark, the cry of the daughter of my people 15
21 For the wound of the daughter of my people 15
22 the daughter of my people not been restored? 15
9: 1 weep . . for the slain of the daughter of my people! 15
2 that I might leave my people and go away from them! 15
7 for what else can I do, because of my people? 15
15 Behold, I will feed this people with wormwood 15
10: 3 for the customs of the peoples are false. 15
25 and upon the peoples that call not on thy name; 13
11: 4 shall you be my people, and I will be your God 15
14 Therefore do not pray for this people 15
12:14 which I have given my people Israel to inherit 15
16 will diligently learn the ways of my people 15
16 even as they taught my people to swear by Ba'al 15
16 they shall be built up in the midst of my people. 15
13:10 This evil people, who refuse to hear my words 15
11 might be for me a people, a name, a praise, and a glory 15
14: 2 her people lament on the ground •
10 Thus says the LORD concerning this people 15
11 Do not pray for the welfare of this people. 15
16 people to whom they prophesy shall be cast out 15
17 for the virgin daughter of my people is smitten 15
15: 1 yet my heart would not turn toward this people. 15
7 I have bereaved them, I have destroyed my people; 15
20 I will make you to this people a fortified wall 15
16: 5 for I have taken away my peace from this people 15
10 And when you tell this people all these words 15
14 LORD lives who brought up the people of Israel 5
15 LORD lives who brought up the people of Israel 5
17:26 And people shall come from the cities of Judah •
18:15 But my people have forgotten me 15
19: 1 and take some of the elders of the people 15
4 Because the people have forsaken me •
7 and will cause their people to fall by the sword •
11 will I break this people and this city 15
14 Then Jeremiah . . said to all the people 15
21: 7 and the people in this city who survive 15
8 to this people you shall say: 'Thus says the LORD 15
22: 2 and your people who enter these gates. 15
4 they, and their servants, and their people. 15
23: 2 concerning the shepherds who care for my people 15
7 LORD lives who brought up the people of Israel 5
13 by Ba'al and led my people Israel astray. 15
22 they would have proclaimed my words to my people 15
27 who think to make my people forget my name 15
32 and lead my people astray by their lies 15
32 so they do not profit this people at all 15
33 When one of this people, or a prophet, or a priest 15
34 the prophet, priest, or one of the people who says 15
24: 7 and they shall be my people and I will be their God 15
25: 1 to Jeremiah concerning all the people of Judah 15
2 the prophet spoke to all the people of Judah 15
19 Egypt, his servants, his princes, all his people 15
26: 7 The priests and the prophets and all the people 15
8 LORD had commanded him to speak to all the people 15
8 the priests and the prophets and all the people 15
9 the people gathered about Jeremiah in the house 15
11 said to the princes and to all the people 15
12 spoke to all the princes and all the people 15
16 Then the princes and all the people said 15
17 and spoke to all the assembled people, saying 15
18 and said to all the people of Judah 15
24 so that he was not given over to the people 15
27:12 and serve him and his people, and live. 15
13 Why will you and your people die by the sword 15
16 Then I spoke to the priests and to all this people 15
28: 1 in the presence of the priests and all the people 15
5 in the presence of the priests and all the people 15
7 and in the hearing of all the people. 15
11 Hanani'ah spoke in the presence of all the people 15
15 and you have made this people trust in a lie. 15
29: 1 to the priests, the prophets, and all the people 15
16 concerning all the people who dwell in this city 15
25 to all the people who are in Jerusalem 15
32 shall not have any one living among this people 15
32 to see the good that I will do to my people 15
30: 3 when I will restore the fortunes of my people 15
22 And you shall be my people, and I will be your God. 15
31: 1 and they shall be my people. 15
2 The people who survived the sword found grace 15
7 give praise, and say, 'The LORD has saved his people 15
14 my people shall be satisfied with my goodness 15
33 I will be their God, and they shall be my people. 15
32:21 bring thy people Israel out of the land of Egypt 15
38 they shall be my people, and I will be their God. 15
42 brought all this great evil upon this people 15
33:24 you not observed what these people are saying 15
24 Thus they have despised my people 15
34: 1 the peoples were fighting against Jerusalem 15
8 made a covenant with all the people in Jerusalem 15
10 they obeyed, all the princes and all the people 15
19 people of the land who passed between the parts 15
35:16 but this people has not obeyed me. 15
36: 6 and on a fast day in the hearing of all the people 15
7 the LORD has pronounced against this people. 15
9 in the ninth month, all the people in Jerusalem 15
9 the people who came from the cities of Judah 15
10 Then, in the hearing of all the people, Baruch read 15
13 read the scroll in the hearing of the people. 15
14 scroll that you read in the hearing of the people 15
37: 2 But neither he nor his servants nor the people 15
4 was still going in and out among the people 15
12 to receive his portion there among the people. 15
18 have I done to you or your servants or this people 15
38: 1 words that Jeremiah was saying to all the people 15
4 weakening . . the hands of all the people 15
4 this man is not seeking . . welfare of this people 15
39: 8 The Chalde'ans burned . . the house of the people 15
9 the rest of the people who were left in the city 15
9 had deserted to him, and the people who remained. 15
10 left in the land of Judah some of the poor people 15
14 So he dwelt among the people. 15
40: 5 and dwell with him among the people; 15
6 among the people who were left in the land. 15
41:10 Ish'mael took captive all the rest of the people 15
10 king's daughters and all the people who were left 15
13 when all the people who were with Ish'mael saw 15
14 all the people whom Ish'mael had carried away 15
16 forces with him took all the rest of the people 15
42: 1 all the people from the least to the greatest 15
8 and all the people from the least to the greatest 15
43: 1 Jeremiah finished speaking to all the people 15
4 the people did not obey the voice of the LORD 15
44:15 people who dwelt in Pathros in the land of Egypt 15
20 Then Jeremiah said to all the people 15
20 all the people who had given him this answer 15
21 kings and your princes, and the people of the land 15
24 Jeremiah said to all the people and all the women 15
46:16 Arise, and let us go back to our own people 15
24 she shall be delivered into the hand of a people 15
48:42 Moab shall be destroyed and be no longer a people 15
46 Woe to you, O Moab! The people of Chemosh is undone 15
49: 1 and his people settled in its cities? 15
28 against Kedar! Destroy the people of the east! 5
50: 4 the people of Israel and the people of Judah 5
4 the people of Israel and the people of Judah 5
6 My people have been lost sheep; 15
16 every one shall turn to his own people 15
33 The people of Israel are oppressed 5
33 are oppressed, and the people of Judah with them; 5
39 she shall be peopled no more for ever 11
41 Behold, a people comes from the north; 15
51:45 Go out of the midst of her, my people! 15
58 The peoples labor for nought 15
52: 6 there was no food for the people of the land. 15
15 carried away . . some of the poorest of the people 15
15 the rest of the people who were left in the city 15
25 of the army who mustered the people of the land; 15
25 60 men of the people of the land, who were found 15
28 the people whom Nebuchadrez'zar carried away 15
Lam 1: 1 How lonely sits the city that was full of people! 15
7 When her people fell into the hand of the foe 15
11 All her people groan as they search for bread; 15

18 but hear, all you peoples, and behold my suffering; 15
2:11 the destruction of the daughter of my people 15
3:14 I have become the laughingstock of all peoples 15
45 made us offscouring and . . among the peoples. 15
48 the destruction of the daughter of my people. 15
4: 3 but the daughter of my people has become cruel 15
6 the chastisement of the daughter of my people 15
10 the destruction of the daughter of my people. 15
Ezk 2: 3 Son of man, I send you to the people of Israel 5
4 The people also are impudent and stubborn 5
3: 5 For you are not sent to a people of foreign speech 15
6 not to many peoples of foreign speech 15
11 go, get you to the exiles, to your people 15
25 so that you cannot go out among the people; •
4:13 Thus shall the people of Israel eat their bread 5
6: 5 I will lay the dead bodies of the people of Israel 5
7:27 the people of the land are palsied by terror. 15
11: 1 I saw among them . . princes of the people. 15
17 I will gather you from the peoples 15
20 they shall be my people, and I will be their God. 15
12:19 say of the people of the land, Thus says the Lord 15
13: 9 they shall not be in the council of my people 15
10 Because, yea, because they have misled my people 15
10 when the people build a wall, these prophets daub •
17 your face against the daughters of your people 15
18 Will you hunt down souls belonging to my people 15
19 You have profaned me among my people 15
19 by your lies to my people, who listen to lies. 15
21 and deliver my people out of your hand 15
23 I will deliver my people out of your hand. 15
14: 8 and cut him off from the midst of my people; 15
9 destroy him from the midst of my people Israel. 15
11 that they may be my people and I may be their God 15
17: 9 not take . . many people to pull it from its roots. 15
18:18 and did what is not good among his people 15
20:34 I will bring you out from the peoples 15
35 bring you into the wilderness of the peoples 15
41 when I bring you out from the peoples 15
21:12 Cry and wail, son of man, for it is against my people; 15
12 delivered over to the sword with my people. 15
22:29 The people of the land have practiced extortion 15
23:24 with chariots and wagons and a host of peoples; 15
24:18 I spoke to the people in the morning 15
19 the people said to me, "Will you not tell us 15
25: 4 I am handing you over to the people of the East 5
7 I will cut you off from the peoples 15
10 to the people of the East as a possession 5
14 vengeance upon Edom by the hand of my people 15
26: 2 Aha, the gate of the peoples is broken 15
11 he will slay your people with the sword; 15
20 who descend into the Pit, to the people of old 15
27: 3 merchant of the peoples on many coastlands 15
33 came from the seas, you satisfied many peoples; 15
36 The merchants among the peoples hiss at you; 15
28:19 All who know you among the peoples are appalled 15
25 from the peoples among whom they are scattered 15
29:13 I will gather the Egyptians from the peoples 15
30: 5 Libya, and the people of the land that is in league 5
11 people with him, the most terrible of the nations 15
31:12 the peoples of the earth will go from its shadow 15
32: 3 throw my net over you with a host of many peoples; 15
9 I will trouble the hearts of many peoples 15
10 I will make many peoples appalled at you 15
33: 2 Son of man, speak to your people and say to them 15
2 the people of the land take a man from among them 15
3 and blows the trumpet and warns the people; 15
6 so that the people are not warned 15
12 And you, son of man, say to your people 15
17 Yet your people say, 'The way of the Lord is not just 6
30 son of man, your people who talk together 15
31 they come to you as people come, and they sit 15
31 people come, and they sit before you as my people 15
34:13 I will bring them out from the peoples 15
30 the house of Israel, are my people, says the Lord 15
35: 5 and gave over the people of Israel 5
36: 3 you became the talk and evil gossip of the people; 15
8 and yield your fruit to my people Israel; 15
12 I will let men walk upon you, even my people Israel; 15
15 shall no longer bear the disgrace of the peoples 15
20 men said of them, 'These are the people of the LORD 15
28 you shall be my people, and I will be your God. 15
37:12 and raise you from your graves, O my people; 15
13 and raise you from your graves, O my people. 15
18 when your people say to you, 'Will you not show us 6
21 I will take the people of Israel from the nations 5
23 they shall be my people, and I will be their God. 15
27 I will be their God, and they shall be my people. 15
38: 6 with all his hordes–many peoples are with you. 15
8 the land where people were gathered •
8 its people were brought out from the nations •
9 and all your hordes, and many peoples with you. 15
11 fall upon the quiet people who dwell securely •
12 the people who were gathered from the nations 15
14 when my people Israel are dwelling securely 15
15 you and many peoples with you, all of them riding 15
16 you will come up against my people Israel 15
22 rain upon him and his hordes and the many peoples 15
39: 4 all your hordes and the peoples that are with you; 15
7 I will make known in the midst of my people Israel; 15

13 All the people of the land will bury them; 15
27 when I have brought them back from the peoples 15
42:14 they go near to that which is for the people. 15
43: 7 I will dwell in the midst of the people of Israel 5
44: 9 foreigners who are among the people of Israel 5
11 burnt offering and the sacrifice for the people 15
11 they shall attend on the people, to serve them. •
15 when the people of Israel went astray from me 5
19 they go out into the outer court to the people 15
19 lest they communicate holiness to the people 15
23 They shall teach my people the difference 15
45: 8 my princes shall no more oppress my people; 15
9 cease your evictions of my people, says the Lord 15
16 the people of the land shall give this offering 15
22 shall provide for himself and all the people 15
46: 3 The people of the land shall worship 15
9 When the people of the land come before the LORD 15
18 take any of the inheritance of the people 15
18 so that none of my people shall be dispossessed 15
20 and so communicate holiness to the people. 15
24 shall boil the sacrifices of the people. 15
48:11 go astray when the people of Israel went astray 5
Dan 2:44 nor . . its sovereignty be left to another people. 18
3: 4 commanded, O peoples, nations, and languages 18
7 Therefore, as soon as all the peoples heard 18
7 all the peoples, nations, and languages fell down 18
29 Any people, nation, or language that speaks 18
4: 1 King . . to all peoples, nations, and languages 18
5:19 all peoples, nations, and languages trembled 18
6:25 wrote to all the peoples, nations, and languages 18
7:14 all peoples, nations, and languages should serve 18
27 given to the people of the saints of the Most High; 18
8:24 destroy mighty men and the people of the saints. 15
9: 6 spoke . . to all the people of the land. 15
15 didst bring thy people out of the land of Egypt 15
16 Jerusalem and thy people have become a byword 15
19 thy city and thy people are called by thy name. 15
20 confessing my sin and the sin of my people Israel 15
24 concerning your people and your holy city 15
26 people of the prince who is to come shall destroy 15
10:14 understand what is to befall your people 15
11:14 men of violence among your own people 15
23 he shall become strong with a small people. 9
32 people who know their God shall stand firm 15
33 among the people who are wise shall make many 15
12: 1 great prince who has charge of your people. 6
1 but at that time your people shall be delivered 15
7 shattering of the power of the holy people 15
Hos 1: 9 for you are not my people and I am not your God. 15
10 the number of the people . . shall be like the sand 5
10 where it was said to them, "You are not my people 15
11 And the people of Judah . . shall be gathered 5
11 and the people of Israel shall be gathered 5
2: 1 Say to your brother, "My people," and to your sister 15
23 and I will say to Not my people, 'You are my people'; 15
3: 1 even as the LORD loves the people of Israel 5
4: 1 Hear the word of the LORD, O people of Israel; 5
6 My people are destroyed for lack of knowledge; 15
8 They feed on the sin of my people; 15
9 And it shall be like people, like priest; 15
12 My people inquire of a thing of wood 15
14 people without understanding . . come to ruin. 15
6:11 When I would restore the fortunes of my people 15
7: 8 E'phraim mixes himself with the peoples; 15
9: 1 Rejoice not, O Israel! Exult not like the peoples; 15
8 the watchman of E'phraim, the people of my God 15
10: 5 Its people shall mourn for it 15
10 I will come against the wayward people 5
14 the tumult of war shall arise among your people 15
11: 7 My people are bent on turning away from me; 15
Jol 2: 2 upon the mountains a great and powerful people; 15
6 Before them peoples are in anguish 15
16 gather the people. Sanctify the congregation; 15
17 weep and say, "Spare thy people, O LORD 15
17 Why should they say among the peoples 15
18 jealous for his land, and had pity on his people. 15
19 The LORD answered and said to his people 15
26 And my people shall never again be put to shame. 15
27 And my people shall never again be put to shame. 15
3: 2 on account of my people and my heritage Israel 15
3 and have cast lots for my people 15
6 You have sold the people of Judah and Jerusalem 5
16 But the LORD is a refuge to his people 15
16 a stronghold to the people of Israel. 5
19 for the violence done to the people of Judah 5
Ams 1: 5 and the people of Syria shall go into exile to Kir 15
2:11 it not indeed so, O people of Israel?" says the LORD. 5
3: 1 has spoken against you, O people of Israel 5
6 a trumpet blown . . and the people are not afraid? 15
12 shall the people of Israel who dwell in Sama'ria 5
4: 5 publish . . for so you love to do, O people of Israel! 5
7: 8 a plumb line in the midst of my people Israel; 15
15 LORD said to me, 'Go, prophesy to my people Israel.' 15
8: 2 The end has come upon my people Israel; 15
9: 7 O people of Israel?" says the LORD. 5
10 the sinners of my people shall die by the sword 15
14 I will restore the fortunes of my people Israel 15
Obd 1:12 not have rejoiced over the people of Judah 5
13 You should not have entered the gate of my people 15

20 exiles in Halah who are of the people of Israel 5
Jon 1: 8 What is your country? And of what people are you? 15
3: 5 the people of Nin'eveh believed God; 2
Mic 1: 2 Hear, you peoples, all of you; 15
9 it has reached to the gate of my people 15
2: 4 ruined; he changes the portion of my people; 15
8 But you rise against my people as an enemy; 15
9 The women of my people you drive out 15
11 he would be the preacher for this people! 15
3: 2 who tear the skin from off my people •
3 who eat the flesh of my people, and flay their skin 15
5 the prophets who lead my people astray, who cry 15
4: 1 and peoples shall flow to it 15
3 He shall judge between many peoples 15
5 all the peoples walk each in the name of its god 15
13 you shall beat in pieces many peoples 15
5: 3 brethren shall return to the people of Israel. 5
7 the midst of many peoples like dew from the LORD 15
8 among the nations, in the midst of many peoples 15
6: 2 for the LORD has a controversy with his people 15
3 O my people, what have I done to you? 15
5 O my people, remember what Balak king of Moab 15
16 so you shall bear the scorn of the peoples. 26
7:14 Shepherd thy people with thy staff 15
Nah 3: 4 betrays nations . . and peoples with her charms. 13
18 Your people are scattered on the mountains 15
Hab 2: 5 and collects as his own all peoples. 15
8 all the remnant of the peoples shall plunder you 15
10 shame to your house by cutting off many peoples; 15
13 from the LORD . . that peoples labor only for fire 15
3:13 wentest forth for the salvation of thy people 15
16 day of trouble to come upon people who invade us. 15
Zep 2: 4 Ashdod's people shall be driven out at noon •
8 how they have taunted my people 15
9 The remnant of my people shall plunder them 15
10 boasted against the people of the LORD of hosts. 15
3: 9 I will change the speech of the peoples 15
12 I will leave in the midst of you a people humble 15
20 and praised among all the peoples of the earth 15
Hag 1: 2 This people say the time has not yet come 15
12 high priest, with all the remnant of the people 15
12 the people feared before the LORD. 15
13 spoke to the people with the LORD's message 15
14 the spirit of all the remnant of the people; 15
2: 2 and to all the remnant of the people, and say 15
4 take courage, all you people of the land 15
14 Then Haggai said, "So is it with this people 15
Zec 2:11 to the LORD in that day, and shall be my people; 15
7: 2 Now the people of Bethel had sent Share'zer •
5 Say to all the people of the land and the priests 15
8: 6 of the remnant of this people in these days 15
7 I will save my people from the east country 15
8 they shall be my people and I will be their God 15
11 the remnant of this people as in the former days 15
12 this people to possess all these things. 15
20 says the LORD of hosts: Peoples shall yet come 15
22 Many peoples and strong nations shall come 15
9: 6 a mongrel people shall dwell in Ashdod; •
16 save them for they are the flock of his people; 15
10: 2 Therefore the people wander like sheep; •
11:10 covenant which I had made with all the peoples. 15
12: 2 a cup of reeling to all the peoples round about; 15
3 make Jerusalem a heavy stone for all the peoples; 15
4 every horse of the peoples with blindness. 15
6 right and to the left all the peoples round about 15
13: 9 I will say, 'They are my people'; 15
14: 2 the rest of the people shall not be cut off 15
12 LORD will smite all the peoples that wage war 15
Mal 1: 4 the people with whom the LORD is angry for ever. 15
2: 9 you despised and abased before all the people 15
Mat 1:21 he will save his people from their sins. 26
2: 4 scribes of the people, he inquired of them where 26
6 a ruler who will govern my people Israel.' 26
4:16 the people who sat in darkness have seen a great 26
23 disease and every infirmity among the people. 26
8: 4 for a proof to the people. •
12:23 all the people were amazed, and said 28
46 While he was still speaking to the people 28
13:15 For this people's heart has grown dull 26
14: 5 he feared the people 28
15: 8 'This people honors me with their lips 26
10 he called the people to him and said to them 28
19:13 The disciples rebuked the people; 20
21:23 the chief priests and the elders of the people 26
26: 3 the elders of the people gathered in the palace 26
5 lest there be a tumult among the people. 26
47 from the chief priests and the elders of the people. 26
27: 1 all the chief priests and the elders of the people 26
20 elders persuaded the people to ask for Barab'bas 28
25 all the people answered, "His blood be on us 26
64 steal him away, and tell the people 26
28:13 said, "Tell people, 'His disciples came by night •
Mrk 1: 5 and all the people of Jerusalem †
44 for a proof to the people. •
45 people came to him from every quarter. •
2:18 people came and said to him •
3:21 for people were saying, "He is beside himself. •
5:14 people came to see what it was that had happened. •
38 people weeping and wailing loudly. •

6:41 loaves . . to set before the people •
54 immediately the people recognized him •
7: 6 This people honors me with their lips 26
14 he called the people to him again, and said 28
17 when he had entered the house, and left the people 28
8: 6 to his disciples to set before the people •
9 there were about 4,000 people •
22 some people brought to him a blind man •
11:32 they were afraid of the people 28
14: 2 lest there be a tumult of the people. 26
Lke 1:10 the whole multitude of the people were praying 26
17 to make ready for the Lord a people prepared. 26
21 the people were waiting for Zechari'ah 26
68 he has visited and redeemed his people 26
77 to give knowledge of salvation to his people 26
2:10 a great joy which will come to all the people; 26
31 hast prepared in the presence of all peoples 26
32 for glory to thy people Israel. 26
3:15 As the people were in expectation 26
18 he preached good news to the people. 26
21 Now when all the people were baptized 26
4:42 the people sought him and came to him 28
5: 1 While the people pressed upon him 28
3 he sat down and taught the people from the boat. 28
14 as Moses commanded, for a proof to the people. •
6:17 a great multitude of people from all Judea 26
7: 1 all his sayings in the hearing of the people 26
16 God has visited his people! 26
29 the people and the tax collectors justified God 26
8: 4 people from town after town came to him •
35 Then people went out to see what had happened •
37 Then all the people of the surrounding country 29
42 As he went, the people pressed round him. 28
47 declared in the presence of all the people 26
9:13 go and buy food for all these people. 26
18 he asked them, "Who do the people say that I am? 28
53 the people would not receive him •
11:14 the dumb man spoke, and the people marveled. 28
13:14 ruler of the synagogue . . said to the people 28
17 the people rejoiced at all the glorious things 28
14:23 compel people to come in •
16: 4 so that people may receive me into their houses •
18:43 all the people, when they saw it, gave praise to God. 26
19:47 scribes and the principal men of the people 26
48 all the people hung upon his words. 26
20: 1 as he was teaching the people in the temple 26
6 if we say, 'From men,' all the people will stone us 26
9 he began to tell the people this parable 26
19 they feared the people 26
26 they were not able in the presence of the people 26
45 in the hearing of all the people 26
21:23 and wrath upon this people; 26
38 early in the morning all the people came to him 26
22: 2 they feared the people. 26
66 the assembly of the elders of the people 26
23: 5 they were urgent, saying, "He stirs up the people 26
13 chief priests and the rulers and the people 26
14 as one who was perverting the people 26
27 followed him a great multitude of the people 26
35 the people stood by, watching 26
24:19 before God and all the people 26
Joh 1:11 and his own people received him not. •
3:23 and people came and were baptized. •
4:28 went away into the city, and said to the people 19
6: 5 are we to buy bread, so that these people may eat? •
10 Jesus said, "Make the people sit down. 19
14 When the people saw the sign which he had done 19
22 the people who remained on the other side of the sea 28
24 when the people saw that Jesus was not there 28
7:12 much muttering about him among the people 28
12 others said, "No, he is leading the people astray. 28
20 The people answered, "You have a demon! 28
31 Yet many of the people believed in him; they said 28
40 some of the people said 28
43 there was a division among the people over him. 28
8: 2 all the people came to him 26
11:42 said this on account of the people standing by 28
50 one man should die for the people 26
18:14 expedient that one man should die for the people. 26
Act 2:47 having favor with all the people 26
3: 9 all the people saw him walking and praising God 26
11 all the people ran together to them 26
12 when Peter saw it he addressed the people 26
23 shall be destroyed from the people.' 26
4: 1 as they were speaking to the people 26
2 annoyed because they were teaching the people 26
8 Rulers of the people and elders 26
10 to all the people of Israel 26
17 it may spread no further among the people 26
21 no way to punish them, because of the people 26
25 the peoples imagine vain things? 26
27 with the Gentiles and the peoples of Israel 26
5:12 wonders were done among the people 26
13 the people held them in high honor. 26
16 people also gathered from the towns 29
20 speak to the people all the words of this Life. 26
25 standing in the temple and teaching the people. 26
26 they were afraid of being stoned by the people. 26
34 Gama'li-el . . held in honor by all the people 26
37 and drew away some of the people after him 26
6: 8 did great wonders and signs among the people. 26
12 they stirred up the people and the elders 26
7:17 the people grew and multiplied in Egypt 26
34 ill-treatment of my people that are in Egypt 26
51 You stiff-necked people •
10: 2 gave alms liberally to the people 26
41 not to all the people 26
42 he commanded us to preach to the people 26
11:26 and taught a large company of people •
12: 4 intending . . to bring him out to the people. 26
11 from all that the Jewish people were expecting. 26
20 Herod was angry with the people of Tyre and Sidon; •
22 people shouted, "The voice of a god, and not of man! 22
13:15 word of exhortation for the people, say it. 26
17 The God of this people Israel chose our fathers 26
17 chose our fathers and made the people great 26
24 preached . . to all the people of Israel. 26
31 who are now his witnesses to the people. 26
42 As they went out, the people begged •
14: 4 the people of the city were divided 29
13 and wanted to offer sacrifice with the people. 28
18 they scarcely restrained the people 28
19 having persuaded the people 28
15:14 to take out of them a people for his name. 26
17: 5 seeking to bring them out to the people. 22
8 the people and the city authorities 28
18:10 I have many people in this city. 26
19: 4 telling the people to believe 26
26 and turned away a considerable company of people •
33 wishing to make a defense to the people. 22
21:28 against the people and the law and this place; 26
30 and the people ran together 26
36 the mob of the people followed, crying 26
39 I beg you, let me speak to the people. 26
40 motioned with his hand to the people 26
23: 5 shall not speak evil of a ruler of your people.' 26
25:24 about whom the whole Jewish people petitioned 29
26:17 delivering you from the people 26
23 both to the people and to the Gentiles 26
28: 9 the rest of the people on the island who had diseases •
17 though I had done nothing against the people 26
26 'Go to this people, and say, You shall indeed hear 26
27 this people's heart has grown dull 26
Rom 9:25 Those who were not my people I will call 'my people,' 26
25 Those who were not my people I will call 'my people,' 26
26 where it was said to them, 'You are not my people,' 26
10:21 my hands to a disobedient and contrary people. 26
11: 1 I ask, then, has God rejected his people? By no means! 26
2 God has not rejected his people 26
15:10 Rejoice, O Gentiles, with his people"; 26
11 and let all the peoples praise him"; 26
1Co 1:11 For it has been reported to me by Chlo'e's people 27
10: 7 The people sat down to eat and drink 26
18 Consider the people of Israel 24
14:21 will I speak to this people 26
15:29 Otherwise, what do people mean by being baptized •
29 why are people baptized on their behalf? •
2Co 6:16 I will be their God, and they shall be my people. 26
9: 2 I boast . . to the people of Macedo'nia, saying †
10:11 Let such people understand •
11:26 danger from robbers, danger from my own people 21
Gal 1:14 many of my own age among my people 21
Php 3: 5 of the people of Israel, of the tribe of Benjamin 21
1Th 5: 3 When people say, "There is peace and security •
2Ti 2:16 it will lead people into more and more ungodliness •
3: 5 Avoid such people. •
4: 3 when people will not endure sound teaching •
Tit 2:14 to purify for himself a people of his own 26
3:14 let our people learn . . •
Heb 2:17 to make expiation for the sins of the people. 26
4: 9 remains a sabbath rest for the people of God; 26
5: 3 as well as for those of the people. 26
7: 5 the people, that is, from their brethren 26
11 (for under it the people received the law) 26
27 for his own sins and then for those of the people 26
8:10 I will be their God, and they shall be my people. 26
9: 7 for himself and for the errors of the people. 26
19 had been declared by Moses to all the people 26
19 sprinkled both the book itself and all the people 26
10:30 And again, "The Lord will judge his people. 26
11:14 For people who speak thus make it clear •
25 share ill-treatment with the people of God 26
29 By faith the people crossed the Red Sea •
13:12 sanctify the people through his own blood. 26
1Pe 2: 9 you are . . a holy nation, God's own people 26
10 Once you were no people but now you are God's 26
10 but now you are God's people; 26
2Pe 2: 1 false prophets also arose among the people 26
Jde 1: 5 he who saved a people out of the land of Egypt 26
16 boasters, flattering people to gain advantage. 30
Rev 3: 4 people who have not soiled their garments; •
5: 9 every tribe and tongue and people and nation 26
7: 9 from all tribes and peoples and tongues 26
10:11 prophesy about many peoples and nations 26
11: 9 the peoples and tribes and tongues and nations 26
13 7,000 people were killed in the earthquake 19
13: 7 every tribe and people and tongue and nation 26
14: 6 to every nation and tribe and tongue and people; 26
17:15 peoples and multitudes and nations and tongues 26
18: 4 Come out of her, my people 26
21: 3 and they shall be his people 26
1Es 1: 4 serve his people Israel 23
5 before your brethren the people of Israel 32
7 gave to the people who were present 30,000 lambs 26
7 the people and the priests and Levites. 26
11 before the people 26
13 carried them to all the people 26
19 people of Israel who were present at that time 32
24 beyond any other people or kingdom 23
49 Even the leaders of the people and of the priests 26
52 in his anger against his people 23
2: 5 If any one of you, therefore, is of his people 23
4:10 All his people and his armies obey him 26
15 Women gave birth to the king and to every people 26
41 then all the people shouted, and said 26
5:46 The priests, the Levites, and some of the people 26
50 joined them from the other peoples of the land. 23
50 all the peoples of the land were hostile to them 23
62 all the people sounded trumpets 26
65 that the people could not hear the trumpets 26
65 because of the weeping of the people 26
72 the peoples of the land 23
6:16 carried the people away captive to Babylon 26
7: 6 the people of Israel, the priests, the Levites 32
10 The people of Israel who came from the captivity 32
13 the people of Israel who came from the captivity 32
13 the abominations of the peoples of the land 23
8: 5 some of the people of Israel 32
67 these officials honored the people 23
69 The people of Israel and the leaders 23
69 the alien peoples of the land 23
70 sons have married the daughters of these people •
70 mixed with the alien peoples of the land 23
87 the uncleanness of the peoples of the land. 23
92 foreign women from the peoples of the land 23
9: 9 separate . . from the peoples of the land 23
53 the Levites commanded all the people, saying 22
2Es 1: 5 Go and declare to my people their evil deeds 38
8 they are a rebellious people. 38
11 the people of two provinces, Tyre and Sidon 38
29 you should be my people and I should be your God 38
35 I will give your houses to a people that will come 38
37 the gratitude of the people that is to come 38
38 and see the people coming from the east; 38
2: 1 I brought this people out of bondage 38
10 Thus says the Lord to Ezra: "Tell my people 38
24 Pause and be quiet, my people 38
41 that your people . . may be made holy. 38
48 tell my people how great and many are the wonders 38
3: 7 peoples and clans without number. 38
12 they produced children and peoples 38
22 the law was in the people's heart 38
30 and hast destroyed thy people 38
4:23 why the people whom you loved has been given over 38
5: 5 the peoples shall be troubled 38
16 Phaltiel, a chief of the people, came to me and said 38
27 from all the multitude of peoples 38
27 thou hast gotten for thyself one people 38
27 to this people, whom thou hast loved 38
30 If thou dost really hate thy people 38
35 and the exhaustion of the people of Israel? 35
40 the love that I have promised my people. 38
6:54 the people whom thou hast chosen. 38
58 thy people, whom thou hast called thy first-born 38
7:110 for the people in the days of Sennacherib 38
129 while he was alive, spoke to the people, saying 38
8:15 I will speak about thy people 38
26 O look not upon the sins of thy people 38
45 spare thy people and have mercy 38
9: 3 tumult of peoples, intrigues of nations 38
10:39 you have sorrowed continually for your people 38
12:34 he will deliver in mercy the remnant of my people 38
38 shall teach them to the wise among your people 38
40 When all the people heard that the seven days 38
50 the people went into the city, as I told them to do. 38
13:13 many people came to him, some of whom were joyful 36
31 people against people 35
31 people against people 35
36 Zion will come and be made manifest to all people •
48 those who are left of your people 38
49 he will defend the people who remain. 38
14: 3 when my people were in bondage in Egypt; 38
4 I sent him and led my people out of Egypt 38
13 reprove your people; comfort the lowly 38
20 I will reprove the people who are now living 38
23 He answered me and said, "Go and gather the people 38
27 I gathered all the people together, and said 38
46 to give them to the wise among your people. 38
15: 1 Behold, speak in the ears of my people the words 37
10 Behold, my people is led like a flock 38
18 and people shall be afraid. 36
53 If you had not always killed my chosen people •
56 As you will do to my chosen people," says the Lord •
57 all your people who are in the open country •
16:40 Hear my words, O my people; prepare for battle 37
Tob 1:17 if I saw any one of my people dead 21
2: 3 Father, one of our people has been strangled 21

4:13 the sons and daughters of your people 26
5:11 like to know . . your people and your name. 21
6:15 to take a wife from among your own people 21
8:15 let . . thy chosen people bless thee for ever. •
14: 7 his people will give thanks to God 26
7 the Lord will exalt his people 26
Jdt 1: 6 He was joined by all the people of the hill country 25
12 the people of Ammon, and all Judea 32
2:23 plundered all the people of Rassis 32
28 fear and terror of him fell upon all the people •
3: 7 these people and all in the country round about •
4: 1 the people of Israel living in Judea 32
3 all the people of Judea were newly gathered together 26
6 wrote to the people of Bethulia 25
8 the senate of the whole people of Israel 22
13 the people fasted many days throughout Judea 26
14 the vows and freewill offerings of the people. 26
5: 1 the people of Israel had prepared for war 32
3 what people is this 26
5 I will tell you the truth about this people 26
6 This people is descended from the Chaldeans. 26
14 and drove out all the people of the wilderness. 25
20 if there is any unwitting error in this people 26
23 a people with no strength or power for making war. 26
6: 2 not to make war against the people of Israel 21
16 they set Achior in the midst of all their people 26
18 Then the people fell down and worshiped God 26
19 and have pity on the humiliation of our people 21
7: 8 Then all the chieftains of the people of Esau 32
10 these people, the Israelites 26
13 where all the people of Bethulia get their water 25
13 We and our people will go up 26
19 The people of Israel cried out to the Lord their God 32
23 all the people, the young men, the women 26
32 he dismissed the people to their various posts 26
8: 9 heard the wicked words spoken by the people 26
11 Listen to me, rulers of the people of Bethulia! 25
11 What you have said to the people today 26
18 any tribe or family or people or city of ours 22
29 the people have recognized your understanding 26
30 the people were very thirsty 26
9:14 no other who protects the people of Israel 21
10: 8 the people of Israel may glory 32
12 To what people do you belong •
19 Who can despise these people 26
11: 2 your people who live in the hill country 26
13 it is not lawful for any of the people 26
14 the people living there have been doing this •
22 God has done well to send you before the people 26
12: 3 none of your people is here with us. 21
8 to direct her way for the raising up of her people. 26
13:17 All the people were greatly astonished 26
17 the enemies of thy people. 26
20 all the people said, "So be it, so be it! 26
14: 6 at the gathering of the people 26
8 in the presence of the people 26
9 the people raised a great shout 26
17 he rushed out to the people and shouted 26
15: 6 The rest of the people of Bethulia 25
8 the senate of the people of Israel 32
10 all the people said, "So be it! 26
11 the people plundered the camp for 30 days. 26
13 she went before all the people in the dance 26
16: 1 all the people loudly sang this song of praise. 26
3 brought me to his camp, in the midst of the people. 26
11 my oppressed people shouted for joy •
11 my weak people shouted and the enemy trembled; •
17 Woe to the nations that rise up against my people! 21
18 As soon as the people were purified 26
19 which the people had given her 26
20 the people continued feasting in Jerusalem 26
22 died and was gathered to his people. 26
25 spread terror among the people of Israel 32
AEs 10: 9 The Lord has saved his people 26
10 one for the people of God 26
12 God remembered his people. 26
13 for ever among his people Israel. 26
12: 6 he sought to injure Mordecai and his people 26
13: 4 there is scattered a certain hostile people 26
5 this people . . stands . . in opposition 23
15 spare thy people 26
16:21 made this day to be a joy to his chosen people 21
Wis 3: 8 They will govern nations and rule over peoples 26
4:15 Yet the peoples saw and did not understand 26
6:21 O monarchs over the peoples, honor wisdom 26
24 a sensible king is the stability of his people. 22
8:14 I shall govern peoples 26
15 among the people I shall show myself capable 29
9: 7 Thou hast chosen me to be king of thy people 26
12 I shall judge thy people justly 26
10:15 A holy people and blameless race 26
12:19 Through such works thou has taught thy people 26
15:14 all the enemies who oppressed thy people. 26
18 The enemies of thy people •
16: 2 thou didst show kindness to thy people 26
3 while thy people . . partake of delicacies. •
5 the terrible rage . . came upon thy people •
20 thou didst give thy people food of angels 26
18: 3 a guide for thy people's unknown journey •

7 were expected by thy people. 26
13 they acknowledged thy people to be God's son. 26
19: 2 though they . . permitted thy people to depart •
5 thy people might experience 26
22 thou hast exalted and glorified thy people 26
Sir 7: 7 do not disgrace yourself among the people. 28
9:17 so a people's leader is proved wise by his words. 26
10: 1 A wise magistrate will educate his people 26
2 Like the magistrate of the people 26
3 An undisciplined king will ruin his people 26
14: 8 he averts his face and disregards people. 33
16:17 Among so many people I shall not be known 26
19:25 people who distort kindness to gain a verdict. •
24: 1 will glory in the midst of her people. 26
6 in the whole earth, and in every people and nation 26
12 I took root in an honored people 26
31: 9 he has done wonderful things among his people. 26
33:18 Hear me, you who are great among the people 26
35:19 till he judges the case of his people 26
36: 8 let people recount thy mighty deeds. •
9 may those who harm thy people meet destruction. 26
12 the people called by thy name 26
17 the blessing of Aaron for thy people 26
37:23 A wise man will instruct his own people 26
26 He who is wise among his people 26
38:33 are not sought out for the council of the people 26
41:18 of iniquity, before a congregation or the people; 26
42:11 notorious among the people 26
44: 4 leaders of the people in their deliberations 26
4 in understanding of learning for the people 26
15 Peoples will declare their wisdom 26
45: 3 He gave him commands for his people 26
7 gave him the priesthood of the people 26
9 as a reminder to the sons of his people; 26
15 serve as priest and bless his people in his name. 26
16 to make atonement for the people. 26
22 in the land of the people he has no inheritance 26
22 he has no portion among the people 26
23 stood fast, when the people turned away 26
24 leader of the sanctuary and of his people 26
26 to judge his people in righteousness 26
46: 7 restrained the people from sin 26
13 anointed rulers over his people. 26
18 he wiped out the leaders of the people of Tyre †
20 to blot out the wickedness of the people. 26
47: 4 take away reproach from the people 26
5 to exalt the power of his people. 26
23 whose policy caused the people to revolt 26
48:15 For all this the people did not repent 26
15 the people were left very few in number 26
49: 2 He was led aright in converting the people 26
10 they comforted the people of Jacob •
50: 1 the pride of his people was Simon the high priest 15
4 He considered how to save his people from ruin 26
5 when the people gathered round him 26
17 all the people together made haste 26
19 the people besought the Lord Most High in prayer 26
26 the foolish people that dwell in Shechem. 26
Bar 1: 3 in the hearing of all the people who came to hear 26
4 in the hearing of all the people, small and great 26
7 people who were present with him in Jerusalem. 26
9 had carried away . . the people of the land 26
2: 4 desolation among all the surrounding peoples 26
11 didst bring thy people out of the land of Egypt 26
28 in the presence of the people of Israel, saying 32
30 for they are a stiff-necked people. 26
35 them to be their God and they shall be my people; 26
35 I will never again remove my people Israel 26
4: 3 Do not give . . advantages to an alien people. 23
5 Take courage, my people, O memorial of Israel! 26
LJr 1: 9 People take gold •
Sus 1: 5 two elders from the people were appointed 26
5 elders . . , who were supposed to govern the people. 26
7 When the people departed at noon 26
28 when the people gathered at the house 26
29 They said before the people, "Send for Susanna 26
34 the two elders stood up in the midst of the people 26
41 they were elders of the people and judges; 26
47 All the people turned to him, and said 26
50 Then all the people returned in haste. 26
64 Daniel had a great reputation among the people. 26
1Mc 1:13 some of the people eagerly went to the king 26
30 destroyed many people of Israel. 26
34 stationed there a sinful people, lawless men. 23
41 all should be one people 26
51 he appointed inspectors over all the people 26
52 Many of the people, every one who forsook the law 26
2: 7 the ruin of my people, the ruin of the holy city 26
66 and fight the battle against the peoples. 26
67 avenge the wrong done to your people. 26
3: 3 He extended the glory of his people 26
5 he burned those who troubled his people. 26
42 what the king had commanded to do to the people 26
43 Let us repair the destruction of our people 26
43 fight for our people and the sanctuary. 26
55 After this Judas appointed leaders of the people 26
4:17 he said to the people, "Do not be greedy for plunder 26
31 hem in this army by the hand of thy people Israel 26
55 All the people fell on their faces and worshiped 26

58 There was very great gladness among the people 26
61 so that the people might have a stronghold 26
5: 2 they began to kill and destroy among the people. 26
4 who were a trap and a snare to the people 26
6 many people with Timothy as their leader. 26
16 When Judas and the people heard these messages 26
18 Azariah, a leader of the people 26
19 Take charge of this people 26
42 the scribes of the people 26
53 encouraging the people all the way 26
60 as many as 2,000 of the people of Israel 26
61 Thus the people suffered a great rout 26
6:19 assembled all the people to besiege them. 26
24 the sons of our people besieged the citadel 26
44 So he gave his life to save his people 26
7: 6 they brought . . this accusation against the people 26
18 fear and dread of them fell upon all the people 26
19 seized . . some of the people 26
22 all who were troubling their people joined him. 26
26 he commanded him to destroy the people. 26
33 some of the elders of the people 26
37 for thy people a house of prayer 26
48 The people rejoiced greatly 26
8:15 constantly deliberate concerning the people 29
20 his brothers and the people of the Jews 29
29 the Romans make a treaty with the Jewish people. 22
9: 2 they took it and killed many people. 34
73 Jonathan began to judge the people 26
10: 7 read the letter in the hearing of all the people 26
46 When Jonathan and the people heard these words 26
11: 2 the people of the cities opened their gates to him •
14 because the people of that region were in revolt. •
51 all the people in his kingdom •
60 the people of the city met him and paid him honor. 27
62 Then the people of Gaza pleaded with Jonathan 27
12: 4 letters to the people in every place •
6 the rest of the Jewish people 22
35 he convened the elders of the people 26
44 Why have you wearied all these people 26
13: 2 he saw that the people were trembling 26
2 and gathering the people together 26
7 The spirit of the people was rekindled 26
17 great hostility among the people, who might say 26
42 the people began to write in their documents 26
14:14 He strengthened all the humble of his people 26
20 rest of the Jewish people, our brethren 22
21 The envoys who were sent to our people 22
23 It has pleased our people to receive these men 22
23 the people of the Spartans may have a record 22
25 When the people heard these things they said 22
28 the people and the rulers of the nation 26
30 was gathered to his people. 26
35 The people saw Simon's faithfulness 26
35 He sought in every way to exalt his people. 26
44 none of the people or priests shall be permitted 26
46 all the people agreed 26
15:17 sent . . by the people of the Jews 22
35 great damage among the people and to our land 26
39 to make war on the people 26
40 came to Jamnia and began to provoke the people 26
40 and invade Judea and take the people captive 26
2Mc 1:16 threw them to the people outside. •
26 on behalf of all thy people Israel 26
27 Gather together our scattered people •
29 Plant thy people in thy holy place, as Moses said. 26
36 by most people it is called naphtha. •
2: 7 until God gathers his people together again 26
15 send people to get them for you. •
17 It is God who has saved all his people 26
3:12 those people who had trusted . . •
18 People also hurried out of their houses •
4: 5 having in view the welfare . . of all the people. 29
30 the people of Tarsus and of Mallus revolted †
5:22 he left governors to afflict the people 21
6: 2 as did the people who dwelt in that place. •
12 not to destroy but to discipline our people. 21
16 he does not forsake his own people. 26
7: 6 which bore witness against the people to their faces •
16 do not think that God has forsaken our people. 21
8: 2 to look upon the people who were oppressed by all 26
36 the capture of the people of Jerusalem •
9: 2 the people rushed to the rescue with arms 29
24 the people throughout the realm •
10:21 he gathered the leaders of the people 26
11:16 Lysias to the people of the Jews, greeting 29
34 to the people of the Jews, greeting. 22
12: 9 he attacked the people of Jamnia by night †
11 to help his people in all other ways. •
26 slaughtered 25,000 people. 31
30 which the people of Scythopolis had shown them †
42 the noble Judas exhorted the people 29
13:10 he ordered the people to call upon the Lord 29
11 the people who had just begun to revive 26
22 the people in Beth-zur •
25 The people of Ptolemais were indignant †
14:15 who established his own people for ever 26
20 the leader had informed the people 29
23 the flocks of people that had gathered. 28

15:14 prays much for the people and the holy city 26
24 blasphemers who come against thy holy people 26
3Mc 1:27 they turned, together with our people •
2: 6 who had enslaved your holy people Israel. 26
16 bestowed your glory upon your people Israel 26
3: 5 the good deeds of upright people •
7 these people were loyal neither to the king 19
8 saw an unexpected tumult around these people 19
16 to honor the temple of those wicked people •
19 they become the only people among all nations •
24 these impious people behind our backs •
4: 4 the most miserable expulsion of these people. •
15 The registration of these people •
5: 5 and bound the hands of the wretched people •
34 and dismissed the assembled people •
47 destruction of the aforementioned people. •
6: 3 a people of your consecrated portion 26
11 the destruction of your beloved people •
7: 4 the ill-will which these people had •
4Mc 1:11 all people, even their torturers, marveled 19
4: 7 The people indignantly protested his words 23
12 he would praise . . before all people. 19
22 the people of Jerusalem . . rejoiced greatly †
24 to put an end to the people's observance of the law 23
26 his decrees were despised by the people 26
6:28 Be merciful to your people 23
16:23 people who have religious knowledge •
17: 8 a reminder to the people of our nation •
151 1: 7 removed reproach from the people of Israel. 32

people *See also* address, all, apply, arrogant, common, every, fill, good, lay, mass, more, multitude, number, old, other, rich, sick, some, stupid, thoughtful, worldly, young.

people clothed in white 1. candidatus
2Es 2:40 your people who are clothed in white 1

people of all nationalities 1. πάμφυλος
2Mc 12:27 a fortified city . . with . . people of all nationalities 1

people on foot 1. πεζός
Sir 46: 8 out of 600,000 people on foot 1

people there 1. ἐντόπιος
Act 21:12 we and the people there begged him not to go up 1

people to lead by the hand 1. χειραγωγός
Act 13:11 seeking people to lead him by the hand. 1

perceive 1. בין 2. טעם 3. ידע 4. ראה 5. שור
6. αἰσθάνομαι 7. γινώσκω 8. εἶδον 9. ἐπιγινώσκω
10. θεωρέω 11. καθοράω 12. καταλαμβάνω
13. κατανοέω 14. λαμβάνω 15. νοέω 16. οἶδα
17. ὁράω 18. συνοράω
Exd 20:18 when all the people perceived the thunderings 4
Jdg 6:22 Gideon perceived that he was the angel of the LORD 4
1Sm 3: 8 Eli perceived that the LORD was calling the boy. 1
2Sm 5:12 David perceived . . the LORD had established him 3
12:19 David perceived that the child was dead; 1
14: 1 Jo'ab . . perceived that the king's heart went out 3
19: 6 I perceive that if Ab'salom were . . then you would 3
1Kg 3:28 they perceived that the wisdom of God was in him 4
2Kg 4: 9 I perceive that this is a holy man of God 3
1Ch 14: 2 David perceived that the LORD had established 3
Neh 6:16 perceived that this work had been accomplished 3
Job 9:11 he moves on, but I do not perceive him. 1
14:21 they are brought low, and he perceives it not. 1
23: 8 backward, but I cannot perceive him; 1
33:14 though man does not perceive it. 5
Ps 73:17 then I perceived their end. 1
94: 7 does not see; the God of Jacob does not perceive. 1
Prv 7: 7 I have perceived among the youths 1
24:12 does not he who weighs the heart perceive it? 1
31:18 perceives that her merchandise is profitable. 2
Ecc 1:17 I perceived that this also is but a striving 3
2:14 yet I perceived that one fate comes to all of them. 3
Isa 6: 9 see and see, but do not perceive.' 3
43:19 now it springs forth, do you not perceive it? 3
Jer 23:18 of the LORD to perceive and to hear his word 4
Dan 9: 2 perceived in the books the number of years 1
Mat 13:14 and you shall indeed see but never perceive. 8
15 lest they should perceive with their eyes 17
16: 9 Do you not yet perceive? 15
11 How is it that you fail to perceive 15
21:45 they perceived that he was speaking about them. 7
Mrk 2: 8 immediately Jesus, perceiving in his spirit 9
4:12 so that they may indeed see but not perceive 17
5:30 perceiving in himself that power had gone forth 9
8:17 Do you not yet perceive or understand? 15
12:12 they perceived that he had told the parable 7
15:10 For he perceived that it was out of envy 7
Lke 1:22 perceived that he had seen a vision in the temple; 9
5:22 When Jesus perceived their questionings 9
8:46 I perceive that power has gone forth from me. 7
9:45 that they should not perceive it 6
47 Jesus perceived the thought of their hearts 16
20:19 they perceived that he had told this parable 7
23 he perceived their craftiness, and said to them 13
Joh 4:19 Sir, I perceive that you are a prophet. 10
6:15 Perceiving then that they were about to come 7
12:40 perceive with their heart 15
Act 4:13 perceived that they were uneducated, common men 12
10:34 Truly I perceive that God shows no partiality 12
17:22 I perceive that . . you are very religious 10
23: 6 when Paul perceived 7
27:10 I perceive that the voyage will be with injury 10
28:26 you shall indeed see but never perceive. 8
27 lest they should perceive with their eyes 17
Rom 1:20 clearly perceived in the things 11
Gal 2: 9 when they perceived the grace that was given 7
Eph 3: 4 perceive my insight into the mystery of Christ 15
Wis 8:21 I perceived that I would not possess wisdom 7
11:13 they perceived it was the Lord's doing. 6
13: 4 let them perceive from them 15
Sir 23:19 perceive even the hidden places. 13
LJr 1:42 Yet they themselves cannot perceive this 15
1Mc 1: 5 he fell sick and perceived that he was dying. 7
4:21 When they perceived this 18
2Mc 5:17 did not perceive that the Lord was angered 18
15:21 perceiving the hosts that were before him 18
3Mc 4: 4 perceiving the common object of pity 14

perceive by ear 1. אזן
Isa 64: 4 of old no one has heard or perceived by the ear 1

perception comes 1. θεωρέω
Wis 13: 5 created things comes a corresponding perception 1

perdition 1. בְּלִיַּעַל 2. ἀπώλεια 3. perditio
2Sm 22: 5 the torrents of perdition assailed me; 1
Ps 18: 4 the torrents of perdition assailed me; 1
Joh 17:12 none of them is lost but the son of perdition 2
2Th 2: 3 the son of perdition 2
Rev 17: 8 The beast . . is to ascend . . and go to perdition; 2
11 As for the beast . . it goes to perdition. 2
2Es 7:48 and has shown us the paths of perdition 3
10:10 and behold, almost all go to perdition 3

perfect 1. כָּלִיל 2. תַּכְלִית 3. תָּמִים 4. ἀκμή 5. ἅπας
6. ἐν παντί 7. ἴασις 8. πληρόω 9. τέλειος
10. τελειότης 11. τελειόω 12. τελέω 13. perficio
Lev 22:21 to be accepted it must be perfect 3
Deu 32: 4 The Rock, his work is perfect; for all his ways 3
2Sm 22:31 This God-his way is perfect; 3
Job 36: 4 one who is perfect in knowledge is with you. 3
37:16 the wondrous works of him who is perfect 3
Ps 18:30 This God-his way is perfect; 3
19: 7 The law of the LORD is perfect, reviving the soul; 3
139:22 I hate them with perfect hatred; 2
Isa 26: 3 Thou dost keep him in perfect peace †
Ezk 16:14 because of your beauty, for it was perfect 1
27: 3 O Tyre, you have said, 'I am perfect in beauty 1
28:12 full of wisdom and perfect in beauty. 1
Mat 5:48 You, therefore, must be perfect, as your heavenly 9
48 be perfect, as your heavenly Father is perfect. 9
19:21 If you would be perfect, go, sell what you possess 9
21:16 thou hast brought perfect praise'? •
Rom 12: 2 what is good and acceptable and perfect. 9
1Co 13:10 when the perfect comes 9
2Co 7:16 because I have perfect confidence in you. 6
Php 3:12 or am already perfect 11
Col 3:14 which binds everything together in perfect harmony. 10
1Ti 1:16 might display his perfect patience 5
Heb 9: 9 cannot perfect the conscience of the worshiper 11
10:14 perfected for all time those who are sanctified. 11
Jas 1: 4 that you may be perfect and complete 9
17 and every perfect gift is from above 9
25 he who looks into the perfect law 9
3: 2 he is a perfect man, able to bridle the whole body 9
1Jn 2: 5 in him truly love for God is perfected. 11
4:12 God abides in us and his love is perfected in us 11
17 In this is love perfected with us 11
18 but perfect love casts out fear. 9
18 and he who fears is not perfected in love. 11
Rev 3: 2 not found your works perfect in the sight of God. 8
2Es 8:52 and wisdom perfected beforehand. 13
9:22 because with much labor I have perfected them. 13
AEs 15: 5 She was radiant with perfect beauty 4
Wis 4:13 Being perfected in a short time 11
16 youth that is quickly perfected 12
6:15 perfect understanding 10
9: 6 for even if one is perfect among the sons of men 9
Sir 1:18 making peace and perfect health to flourish. 7
44:17 Noah was found perfect and righteous 9
4Mc 7:15 whom the faithful seal of death has perfected! 11

perfect *See also* courtesy, find, health, make.

more perfect 1. τέλειος
Heb 9:11 then through the greater and more perfect tent 1

perfect one 1. תָּם
Sng 5: 2 my sister, my love, my dove, my perfect one; 1
6: 9 My dove, my perfect one, is only one 1

perfecter 1. τελειωτής
Heb 12: 2 Jesus the pioneer and perfecter of our faith 1

perfection 1. כָּלִיל 2. מִכְלָל 3. תִּכְלָה 4. תָּכְנִית
5. συντέλεια 6. τελείωσις
Ps 50: 2 the perfection of beauty, God shines forth. 2
119:96 I have seen a limit to all perfection 3
Lam 2:15 city which was called the perfection of beauty 1
Ezk 28:12 You were the signet of perfection, full of wisdom 4
Heb 7:11 Now if perfection had been attainable 6
Sir 45: 8 He clothed him with superb perfection 5
50:11 clothed himself with superb perfection 5

perfectly 1. συντελέω 2. τέλειος 3. τελειόω
4. perfecte
Joh 17:23 that they may become perfectly one 3
2Es 7:89 might keep the law of the Lawgiver perfectly. 4
Sir 24:28 Just as the first man did not know her perfectly 1
3Mc 7:22 God perfectly performed great deeds 2

perfidy 1. ἀθεσία
2Mc 15:10 pointing out the perfidy of the Gentiles 1

perform 1. זבח 2. נתן 3. עבד 4. עמד 5. עשה
6. פעל 7. צבא 8. קום 9. שלם 10. שמר
11. ἀποδίδωμι 12. ἀποτελέω 13. γίνομαι 14. διεξάγω
15. ἐπιτελέω 16. κατεργάζομαι 17. ποιέω
18. πράσσω 19. τελέω 20. facio 21. perficio
Exd 18:18 you are not able to perform it alone. 5
Lev 8:35 performing what the LORD has charged 10
25:18 and keep my ordinances and perform them 5
Num 3: 7 They shall perform duties for him 10
8:24 shall go in to perform the work in the service 7
Deu 4:13 his covenant, which he commanded you to perform 5
23:23 be careful to perform what has passed your lips 5
Jos 22:27 that we do perform the service of the LORD 3
1Sm 12: 7 the saving deeds . . which he performed for you 5
15:11 and has not performed my commandments. 8
13 I have performed the commandment of the LORD. 8
2Sm 14:15 it may be that the king will perform the request 5
2Kg 23: 3 to perform the words of this covenant 8
1Ch 6:32 and they performed their service in due order. 4
29:19 he may keep thy commandments . . performing all 5
21 they performed sacrifices to the LORD 1
2Ch 34:31 to perform the words of the covenant 5
Neh 5:13 every man . . who does not perform this promise. 8
9:10 perform signs and wonders against Pharaoh 2
17 wonders which thou didst perform among them; 5
12:45 performed the service of their God 10
Est 1:15 she has not performed the command of King 5
Ps 44: 1 what deeds thou didst perform in their days 6
56:12 My vows to thee I must perform, O God; •
65: 1 to thee shall vows be performed 9
76:11 your vows to the LORD your God, and perform them; 9
111: 8 performed with faithfulness and uprightness. 5
119:112 I incline my heart to perform thy statutes 5
Isa 19:21 they will make vows to the LORD and perform them. 9
41: 4 Who has performed and done this 6
44:26 and performs the counsel of his messengers; 9
48:14 he shall perform his purpose on Babylon 5
Jer 1:12 for I am watching over my word to perform it. 5
11: 5 that I may perform the oath which I swore 8
44:25 We will surely perform our vows 5
25 Then confirm your vows and perform your vows! 5
Ezk 12:25 word which I will speak, and it will be performed. 5
25 I will speak the word and perform it, says the Lord 5
28 but the word which I speak will be performed 5
29:18 the labor that he had performed against it. 3
43:11 that they may observe and perform all its laws 5
Dan 11:17 shall bring terms of peace and perform them. 5
Mic 2: 1 When the morning dawns, they perform it 5
Mat 5:33 You shall not swear falsely, but shall perform 11
Lke 1:72 to perform the mercy promised to our fathers 17
2:39 when they had performed everything 19
13:32 I cast out demons and perform cures today 12
Joh 11:47 What are we to do? For this man performs many signs 17
Act 4:16 a notable sign has been performed through them 13
22 man on whom this sign of healing was performed 13
30 signs and wonders are performed 13
7:36 having performed wonders and signs in Egypt 17
8:13 seeing signs and great miracles performed 13
26:20 and perform deeds worthy of their repentance 18
2Co 12:12 The signs of a true apostle were performed among you 16
Heb 9: 6 priests . . performing their ritual duties; 15
Rev 16:14 for they are demonic spirits, performing signs 17
1Es 8:16 perform it in accordance with the will of your God; 15
2Es 7:24 and have not performed his works. 21
12:25 and perform his last actions. 21
13:44 For at that time the Most High performed signs 20
Tob 1: 3 I performed many acts of charity to my brethren 17
16 I performed many acts of charity to my brethren. 17
12: 9 perform deeds of charity and of righteousness 17
Jdt 15:12 some of them performed a dance for her 17
Sir 3:17 My son, perform your tasks in meekness 14
3Mc 7:22 God perfectly performed great deeds 17

perform duty of a brother-in-law 1. יבם
Gen 38: 8 Go in . . and perform the duty of a brother-in-law 1

perform duty of a husband's brother 1. יבם
Deu 25: 5 and perform the duty of a husband's brother to her 1
7 will not perform the duty of a husband's brother 1

perform work 1. *ἐργάζομαι*
Joh 6:30 What work do you perform? 1
Sir 7:20 a servant who performs his work faithfully 1

perfume 1. בֹּשֶׂם 2. נוף 3. נֶפֶשׁ 4. קטר 5. קְטֹרֶת 6. רִקּוּחַ 7. *ἥδυσμα* 8. *μύρον* 9. unguentum
Prv 7:17 perfumed my bed with myrrh, aloes, and cinnamon. 2
27: 9 Oil and perfume make the heart glad 5
Sng 3: 6 of smoke, perfumed with myrrh and frankincense 4
Isa 3:20 the perfume boxes, and the amulets; 3
24 Instead of perfume there will be rottenness; 1
57: 9 Molech with oil and multiplied your perfumes; 6
2Es 2:12 The tree . . shall give them fragrant perfume 9
AEs 14: 2 instead of costly perfumes 7
Wis 2: 7 Let us take our fill of costly wine and perfumes 8
perfume *See also* use.

perfumer 1. רקח 2. רַקָּח 3. רַקָּחָה 4. *μυρεψός*
Exd 30:25 anointing oil blended as by the perfumer; 1
35 make an incense blended as by the perfumer 1
37:29 fragrant incense, blended as by the perfumer. 1
1Sm 8:13 take your daughters to be perfumers and cooks 3
2Ch 16:14 kinds of spices prepared by the perfumer's art; 1
Neh 3: 8 Hanani'ah, one of the perfumers, repaired; 2
Ecc 10: 1 Dead flies make the perfumer's ointment . . evil 1
Sir 49: 1 prepared by the art of the perfumer 4

perhaps 1. אוּלַי 2. הֵן (A) 3. *εἰ τυγχάνω* 4. *ἴσος* 5. *ἴσως* 6. *καί* 7. *μή* 8. *μήποτε* 9. *πῶς* 10. *τάχα* 11. *τυγχάνω* 12. fortassis 13. forte
Gen 24: 5 Perhaps the woman may not be willing to follow me 1
39 'Perhaps the woman will not follow me.' 1
27:12 Perhaps my father will feel me, and I shall seem 1
32:20 shall see his face; perhaps he will accept me. 1
43:12 mouth of your sacks; perhaps it was an oversight. 1
Exd 32:30 perhaps I can make atonement for your sin. 1
Num22: 6 perhaps I shall be able to defeat them 1
11 curse them for me; perhaps I shall be able to fight 1
23: 3 perhaps the LORD will come to meet me; 1
27 perhaps it will please God that you may curse 1
Jos 9: 7 men of Israel said . . "Perhaps you live among us; 1
1Sm 6: 5 make images . . perhaps he will lighten his hand 1
9: 6 man of God . . perhaps he can tell us about 1
1Kg 18: 5 Go through the land . . perhaps we may find grass 1
27 or he is on a journey, or perhaps he is asleep 1
20:31 perhaps he will spare your life. 1
Isa 47:12 perhaps you may be able to succeed 1
12 able to succeed, perhaps you may inspire terror. 1
Jer 20:10 Perhaps he will be deceived, then we can overcome 1
21: 2 perhaps the LORD will deal with us 1
51: 8 Take balm for her pain; perhaps she may be healed. 1
Ezk 12: 3 Perhaps they will understand 1
Dan 4:27 perhaps be a lengthening of your tranquillity. 2
Jon 1: 6 Perhaps the god will give a thought to us 1
Zep 2: 3 perhaps you may be hidden on the day of the wrath 1
Mat 25: 9 Perhaps there will not be enough for us 8
Rom 2:15 thoughts accuse or perhaps excuse them 6
5: 7 perhaps for a good man one will dare even to die. 10
1Co 15:37 perhaps of wheat or of some other grain. 3
16: 6 perhaps I will stay with you 11
2Co 12:20 I fear that perhaps I may come and find you 9
20 perhaps there may be quarreling, jealousy, anger 9
2Ti 2:25 God may perhaps grant that . . 8
Phm 1:15 Perhaps this is why he was parted from you 10
2Es 4: 8 Perhaps you would have said to me 12
39 it is perhaps on account of us 13
7:69 perhaps it would have been better for us. 12
Tob 8:10 with the thought, "Perhaps he too will die. 7
Wis 13: 6 perhaps they go astray while seeking God 10
14:19 For he, perhaps wishing to please his ruler 10
Sir 19:13 Question a friend, perhaps he did not do it 8
14 Question a neighbor, perhaps he did not say it 8
4Mc 1: 5 Some might perhaps ask 5
7:17 Some perhaps might say 4
16: 5 she would have . . perhaps spoken as follows 4
perhaps *See also* except, whether.

peril 1. *θάνατος* 2. *κινδυνεύω* 3. *κίνδυνος* 4. periculum
1Ch 12:19 At peril to our heads he will desert to his master •
Rom 8:35 or famine, or nakedness, or peril, or sword? 3
1Co 15:30 Why am I in peril every hour? 2
2Co 1:10 he delivered us from so deadly a peril 1
2Es 9:20 and my earth, and behold, it was in peril 4
13:23 He who brings the peril at that time 4
23 will himself protect those who fall into peril 4
peril *See also* incur.

peril of life 1. נֶפֶשׁ
Lam 5: 9 We get our bread at the peril of our lives 1

period 1. יוֹם 2. *διάστημα* 3. *καιρός* 4. *χρόνος*
Est 2:12 was the regular period of their beautifying 1
Act 17:26 having determined allotted periods 3
18:20 When they asked him to stay for a longer period 4
2Es 5: 4 thrown into confusion after the third period; •
10:47 that was the period of residence in Jerusalem. •
Wis 7: 2 within the period of ten months 4
Sir 0: 3 using in that period of time great watchfulness 2
2Mc 4:23 After a period of three years 4
4Mc 13:20 and was shaped during the same period of time •

perish 1. אבד 2. גוע 3. דמה 4. דמם 5. כחד 6. כלה 7. כרת 8. נפל 9. ספה 10. עבר 11. שמד 12. שמם 13. תמם 14. אבד (A) 15. *ἀποθνῄσκω* 16. *ἀπόλλυμι* 17. *ἀπολλύω* 18. *ἀφανίζω* 19. *διόλλυμι* 20. *εἰς ἀπώλειαν* 21. *εἰς φθοράν* 22. *ἐξαπόλλυμι* 23. *ἐξολεθρεύω* 24. *ἐξολλύω* 25. *συναπόλλυμι* 26. corruptibilis 27. dispereo 28. extero 29. intereo 30. morior 31. pereo
Gen 41:36 that the land may not perish through the famine. 7
Exd 19:21 to the LORD to gaze and many of them perish. 8
Lev 26:38 you shall perish among the nations 1
Num16:33 they perished from the midst of the assembly. 1
17:12 Behold, we perish, we are undone, we are all undone. 2
13 Are we all to perish? 2
21:30 their posterity perished from Heshbon 1
Deu 2:14 men of war, had perished from the camp 13
15 to destroy them . . until they had perished. 13
16 when all the men of war had perished and were dead 13
4:26 that you will soon utterly perish from the land 1
8:19 warn you this day that you shall surely perish 1
20 Like the nations . . so shall you perish 1
11:17 perish quickly off the good land which the LORD 1
28:20 until you are destroyed and perish quickly 1
22 they shall pursue you until you perish. 1
30:18 I declare to you this day, that you shall perish; 1
Jos 5: 6 till all the nation, the men of war . . perished 13
22:20 And he did not perish alone for his iniquity. 2
23:13 till you perish from off this good land 1
16 you shall perish quickly from off the good land 1
Jdg 5:31 So perish all thine enemies, O LORD! 1
1Sm 26:10 or he shall go down into battle and perish. 9
27: 1 I shall now perish one day by the hand of Saul; 9
2Sm 1:27 How are . . and the weapons of war perished! 1
21: 9 and the seven of them perished together. 8
2Kg 7:13 multitude of Israel that have already perished; 13
9: 8 For the whole house of Ahab shall perish; 1
Est 4:14 but you and your father's house will perish. 1
16 I will go to the king . . and if I perish, I perish. 1
16 I will go to the king . . and if I perish, I perish. 1
Job 3: 3 Let the day perish wherein I was born 1
4: 7 Think now, who that was innocent ever perished? 1
9 By the breath of God they perish, and by the blast 1
11 The strong lion perishes for lack of prey 1
20 they perish for ever without any regarding it. 1
6:18 they go up into the waste, and perish. 1
8:13 the hope of the godless man shall perish. 1
18:17 His memory perishes from the earth 1
20: 7 he will perish for ever like his own dung; 1
29:13 blessing of him who was about to perish came upon 1
31:19 if I have seen any one perish for lack of clothing 1
33:18 his life from perishing by the sword. 10
34:15 all flesh would perish together 2
36:12 if they do not hearken, they perish by the sword 10
Ps 1: 6 but the way of the wicked will perish. 1
2:12 lest he be angry, and you perish in the way; 1
9: 3 enemies turned back, they stumbled and perished 1
6 the very memory of them has perished. 1
18 the hope of the poor shall not perish for ever. 1
10:16 the nations shall perish from his land. 1
37:20 But the wicked perish; the enemies of the LORD 1
41: 5 When will he die, and his name perish? 1
49:10 the fool and the stupid alike must perish 1
12 he is like the beasts that perish. 3
20 in his pomp, he is like the beasts that perish. 3
68: 2 as wax melts . . let the wicked perish before God! 1
73:27 For lo, those who are far from thee shall perish; 1
80:16 may they perish at the rebuke of thy countenance! 1
83:17 let them perish in disgrace. 1
92: 9 O LORD, for, lo, thy enemies shall perish; 1
102:26 They will perish, but thou dost endure; 1
119:92 I should have perished in my affliction. 1
146: 4 on that very day his plans perish. 1
Prv 11: 7 When the wicked dies, his hope perishes 1
10 wicked perish there are shouts of gladness. 1
19: 9 he who utters lies will perish. 1
21:28 A false witness will perish 1
28:28 but when they perish, the righteous increase. 1
31: 6 Give strong drink to him who is perishing 1
Ecc 7:15 a . . man who perishes in his righteousness 1
9: 6 their hate and their envy have already perished 1
Isa 29:14 the wisdom of their wise men shall perish 1
31: 3 fall, and they will all perish together. 6
41:11 those who strive against you shall . . perish. 1
57: 1 The righteous man perishes, and no one lays it 1
60:12 and kingdom that will not serve you shall perish; 1
Jer 6:21 together, neighbor and friend shall perish. 1
7:28 truth has perished; it is cut off from their lips. 1
8:14 let us go into the fortified cities and perish 4
14 for the LORD our God has doomed us to perish •
10:11 shall perish from the earth 14
15 the time of their punishment they shall perish. 1
16: 4 They shall perish by the sword and by famine 6
18:18 for the law shall not perish from the priest 1
27:10 and I will drive you out, and you will perish. 1
15 that I will drive you out and you will perish 1
40:15 scattered, and the remnant of Judah would perish? 1
47: 5 Ash'kelon has perished. 3
48: 8 the valley shall perish 1
36 therefore the riches they gained have perished. 1
49: 7 in Teman? Has counsel perished from the prudent? 1
51:18 the time of their punishment they shall perish. 1
Lam 1:19 my priests and elders perished in the city 2
4: 5 who feasted on dainties perish in the street; 12
Ezk 7:26 but the law perishes from the priest 1
13:14 when it falls, you shall perish in the midst of it; 6
31:17 its shadow among the nations shall perish. •
32:12 Egypt, and all its multitude shall perish. 11
Dan 2:18 might not perish with the rest of the wise men 14
Hos 10: 7 Sama'ria's king shall perish 3
Jol 1:11 because the harvest of the field has perished. 1
Ams 1: 8 and the remnant of the Philistines shall perish 1
2:14 Flight shall perish from the swift 1
3:15 and the houses of ivory shall perish 1
Jon 1: 6 give a thought to us, that we do not perish. 1
14 O LORD, let us not perish for this man's life 1
3: 9 turn from his fierce anger, so that we perish not? 1
4:10 into being in a night, and perished in a night. 1
Mic 4: 9 Has your counselor perished 1
7: 2 The godly man has perished from the earth 1
Zec 9: 5 The king shall perish from Gaza; 1
11:16 a shepherd who does not care for the perishing 5
13: 8 two thirds shall be cut off and perish 2
Mat 8:25 Save, Lord; we are perishing. 16
18:14 that one of these little ones should perish. 16
26:52 all who take the sword will perish by the sword. 16
Mrk 4:38 Teacher, do you not care if we perish? 16
Lke 8:24 Master, Master, we are perishing! 16
11:51 perished between the altar and the sanctuary. 16
13: 3 unless you repent you will all likewise perish. 16
5 unless you repent you will all likewise perish. 16
33 that a prophet should perish away from Jerusalem.' 16
15:17 I perish here with hunger! 16
21:18 not a hair of your head will perish. 16
Joh 3:16 that whoever believes in him should not perish 16
6:27 Do not labor for the food which perishes 16
10:28 they shall never perish 16
11:50 the whole nation should not perish. 16
Act 5:37 he also perished 16
8:20 Peter said to him, "Your silver perish with you 20
13:41 'Behold, you scoffers, and wonder, and perish 18
27:34 since not a hair is to perish from the head of any 16
Rom 2:12 will also perish without the law 16
1Co 1:18 folly to those who are perishing 16
15:18 who have fallen asleep in Christ have perished. 16
2Co 2:15 among those who are perishing 16
4: 3 it is veiled only to those who are perishing. 16
Col 2:22 things which all perish as they are used 21
2Th 2:10 those who are to perish 16
Heb 1:11 they will perish, but thou remainest 16
11:31 did not perish with those who were disobedient 25
Jas 1:11 its flower falls, and its beauty perishes 16
2Pe 3: 6 world . . was deluged with water and perished 16
9 not wishing that any should perish 16
Jde 1:11 and perish in Korah's rebellion. 16
1Es 4:27 Many have perished, or stumbled, or sinned 16
37 in their unrighteousness they will perish. 16
2Es 2:26 Not one . . will perish 29
7:15 seeing that you are to perish 26
17 but that the ungodly shall perish. 31
20 Let many perish who are now living 31
31 that which is corruptible shall perish. 30
61 the multitude of those who perish 31
64 because we perish and know it. 31
8:43 ruined by too much rain, it perishes. ‡
55 questions about the multitude . . who perish. 31
9:15 are more who perish than those who will be saved 31
22 let the multitude perish 31
32 yet the fruit of the law did not perish 31
33 Yet those who received it perished 31
36 who have received the law and sinned will perish 31
37 the law, however, does not perish but remains 31
12:21 two of them shall perish 31
15:58 shall perish of hunger 31
16:18 the beginning of famine, when many shall perish; 27
22 who live on the earth shall perish by famine 29
34 and their husbands shall perish of famine. 28
Tob 10: 4 his wife said to him, "The lad has perished 16
7 stop deceiving me; my child has perished 16
14:10 Nadab fell into the trap and perished. 16
Jdt 6: 8 will not die until you perish along with them. 23
16:12 they perished before the army of my Lord. 16
AEs 11: 9 were ready to perish. 16
Wis 3:16 the offspring of an unlawful union will perish. 18
4:19 the memory of them will perish. 16
10: 3 he perished because in rage he slew his brother. 25
6 when the ungodly were perishing 22
14: 6 when arrogant giants were perishing 16
17:10 they perished in trembling fear 19

18:19 not perish without knowing why they suffered. 17
Sir 3:26 whoever loves danger will perish by it. 16
5: 7 at the time of punishment you will perish. 24
8:15 through his folly you will perish with him. 25
41: 6 The inheritance . . will perish 16
44: 9 who have perished as though they had not lived; 16
Bar 2:25 They perished in great misery, by famine 15
3: 3 for ever, and we are perishing for ever. 17
28 so they perished because they had no wisdom 17
28 no wisdom, they perished through their folly. 17
1Mc 2:63 his plans will perish. 16
3: 9 he gathered in those who were perishing. 16
6:13 behold, I am perishing of deep grief 16
12:50 been seized and had perished along with his men 16
13: 4 By reason of this all my brothers have perished 16
18 he perished. 16
49 many of them perished from famine. 16
16:21 his father and brothers had perished 17
2Mc 7:20 she saw her seven sons perish within a single day 16
8:19 when 185,000 perished 16
3Mc 6: 3 perishing as foreigners in a foreign land. 16

cause to perish 1. אבד 2. *διαφθείρω*
Deu 28:51 until they have caused you to perish. 1
Sir 47:22 nor cause any of his works to perish 2

make perish 1. אבד
Deu 7:24 shall make their name perish from under heaven; 1
8:20 nations that the LORD makes to perish before you 1
9: 3 drive them out, and make them perish quickly 1
Ezk 25: 7 and will make you perish out of the countries; 1

perishable 1. *ἀπόλλυμι* 2. *εὔφθαρτος* 3. *φθαρτός* 4. *φθορά*
1Co 9:25 They do it to receive a perishable wreath 3
15:50 the perishable inherit the imperishable. 4
54 When the perishable puts on the imperishable 3
1Pe 1: 7 gold which though perishable is tested by fire 1
23 not of perishable seed but of imperishable 3
Wis 9:15 for a perishable body weighs down the soul 3
19:21 the flesh of perishable creatures that walked 2
perishable *See also* nature.

perishable thing 1. *φθαρτός*
1Pe 1:18 with perishable things such as silver or gold 1
Wis 14: 8 the perishable thing was named a god. 1

perjurer 1. *ἐπίορκος*
1Ti 1:10 sodomites, kidnapers, liars, perjurers 1

perjury 1. *ἐπιορκία*
Wis 14:25 corruption, faithlessness, tumult, perjury 1
perjury *See also* commit.

permanent 1. *αἰώνιος* 2. *εἰς μνημόσυνον* 3. *μένω* 4. permaneo
2Co 3:11 what is permanent must have much more splendor. 3
2Es 3:22 Thus the disease became permanent 4
AEs 12: 4 The king made a permanent record of these things 2
1Mc 13:29 suits of armor for a permanent memorial 1

permanently 1. *ἀπαράβατος*
Heb 7:24 he holds his priesthood permanently 1

permission 1. *ἄνεσις* 2. *ἄφεσις* 3. *ἐξουσία* 4. *ἐπιτρέπω*
Act 26: 1 You have permission to speak for yourself 4
1Es 4:62 because he had given them release and permission 2
Jdt 11:14 to bring back to them permission from the senate. 2
Sir 15:20 he has not given any one permission to sin. 1
Bel 1:26 if you, O king, will give me permission 3
26 The king said, "I give you permission. •
1Mc 9:35 and begged . . for permission to store with them •
14:44 to convene an assembly . . without his permission •
4Mc 5:15 When he had received permission to speak 3
permission *See also* give.

full permission 1. *ἄδεια*
2Mc 11:30 those . . will have . . full permission 1

permit 1. נטשׁ 2. נתן 3. *ἀφίημι* 4. *δίδωμι* 5. *ἐάω* 6. *ἔξεστι* 7. *ἐπιτρέπω* 8. *καθήκω* 9. permitto
Gen 31: 7 but God did not permit him to harm me. 2
28 why did you not permit me to kiss my sons 1
Num35: 6 where you shall permit the manslayer to flee 2
1Sm 24: 7 David . . did not permit them to attack Saul. 2
1Kg 15:17 permit no one to go out or come in to Asa 2
2Ch 16: 1 that he might permit no one to go out or come 2
Ps 55:22 he will never permit the righteous to be moved. 2
Hos 5: 4 deeds do not permit them to return to their God. 2
Mrk 1:34 he would not permit the demons to speak 3
7:12 then you no longer permit him to do anything 3
Lke 8:51 he permitted no one to enter with him 3
1Co 14:34 For they are not permitted to speak 7
16: 7 some time with you, if the Lord permits. 7
1Ti 2:12 I permit no woman to teach 7
Heb 6: 3 this we will do if God permits. 7
Rev 6: 4 rider was permitted to take peace from the earth 4
1Es 6:27 to permit Zerubbabel . . to build this house 5
2Es 5:13 the signs which I am permitted to tell you 9
Jdt 12: 6 command that your servant be permitted to go out 5
AEs 16:19 permit the Jews to live under their own laws. 5
Wis 19: 2 though they . . permitted thy people to depart 7
1Mc 5:42 Permit no man to encamp 3
12:40 He feared that Jonathan might not permit him 5
14:44 permitted to nullify any of these decisions 6
15: 6 I permit you to mint your own coinage 7
14 and permitted no one to leave or enter it. 5
3Mc 1:11 When they said that this was not permitted 8
4Mc 5:26 He has permitted us to eat 7

permit to live 1. חיה
Exd 22:18 You shall not permit a sorceress to live. 1

perpetrate 1. *συντελέω*
2Mc 3:32 some foul play had been perpetrated by the Jews 1

perpetual 1. נצח 2. נֵצַח 3. עוֹלָם 4. תָּמִיד 5. *αἰώνιος* 6. *διὰ παντός* 7. *ἐνδελεχής* 8. *ἐνδελεχίζω*
Exd 28:43 This shall be a perpetual statute for him 3
29: 9 priesthood . . theirs by a perpetual statute. 3
28 for Aaron and his sons as a perpetual due 3
30: 8 a perpetual incense before the LORD 4
31:16 their generations, as a perpetual covenant. 3
40:15 admit them to a perpetual priesthood 3
Lev 3:17 It shall be a perpetual statute 3
7:34 as a perpetual due from the people of Israel 3
36 it is a perpetual due throughout their 3
24: 9 offerings by fire to the LORD, a perpetual due 3
25:34 for that is their perpetual possession 3
Num10: 8 trumpets shall be to you for a perpetual statute 3
15:15 perpetual statute throughout 3
18: 8 as a portion, and to your sons as a perpetual due. 3
11 I have given them . . as a perpetual due; 3
19 I give to you . . as a perpetual due; 3
23 it shall be a perpetual statute 3
19:10 this shall be . . a perpetual statute. 3
21 it shall be a perpetual statute for them. 3
25:13 covenant of a perpetual priesthood 3
Ps 74: 3 Direct thy steps to the perpetual ruins; 2
Jer 5:22 a perpetual barrier which it cannot pass; 3
8: 5 people turned away in perpetual backsliding? 1
23:40 perpetual shame, which shall not be forgotten. 3
49:13 and all her cities shall be perpetual wastes. 3
51:26 you shall be a perpetual waste, says the LORD. 3
39 till they swoon away and sleep a perpetual sleep 3
57 they shall sleep a perpetual sleep and not wake 3
Ezk 35: 5 Because you cherished perpetual enmity 3
9 I will make you a perpetual desolation 3
1Es 6:24 where they sacrifice with perpetual fire; 7
Jdt 13:20 May God grant this to be a perpetual honor to you 5
AEs 16:13 Mordecai, our savior and perpetual benefactor 6
Sir 41: 6 on their posterity will be a perpetual reproach. 8

perpetually 1. לָעַד 2. *διὰ παντός*
Ams 1:11 his anger tore perpetually, and he kept his wrath 1
Sir 45:13 his sons and his descendants perpetually. 2

perpetuate 1. זרע 2. קום 3. קרא
Gen 48:16 in them let my name be perpetuated, 3
Deu 25: 7 My husband's brother refuses to perpetuate 2
Rut 4:10 to be my wife, to perpetuate the name of the dead 2
Nah 1:14 No more shall your name be perpetuated; 1

perpetuity 1. צְמִיתֻת
Lev 25:23 The land shall not be sold in perpetuity 1
30 be made sure in perpetuity to him who bought it 1

perplex 1. בוך 2. שׁבשׁ (A) 3. *ἀπορέω* 4. *διαπορέω* 5. *συγχέω*
Est 3:15 but the city of Susa was perplexed. 1
Dan 5: 9 his lords were perplexed. 2
Jol 1:18 The herds of cattle are perplexed 1
Mrk 6:20 When he heard him, he was much perplexed 3
Lke 9: 7 he was perplexed, because it was said by some 4
24: 4 While they were perplexed about this 3
Act 2:12 all were amazed and perplexed 4
10:17 Now while Peter was inwardly perplexed 4
2Co 4: 8 perplexed, but not driven to despair; 3
Gal 4:20 I am perplexed about you. 3
1Mc 3:31 He was greatly perplexed in mind 3
4:27 he was perplexed and discouraged 5

perplex much 1. *διαπορέω*
Act 5:24 they were much perplexed about them 1

perplexity 1. *ἀπορία* 2. *διαλογισμός* 3. complicatio 4. excessus
Lke 21:25 in perplexity at the roaring of the sea 1
2Es 7:93 because they see the perplexity 3
12: 3 Then I awoke in great perplexity of mind 4
Sir 40: 2 Their perplexities and fear of heart 2

persecute 1. רדף 2. שׂטם 3. *διώκτης* 4. *διώκω*
Deu 30: 7 your foes and enemies who persecuted you. 1
Job 30:21 with . . thy hand thou dost persecute me. 2
Ps 69:26 For they persecute him whom thou hast smitten 1
119:84 When wilt thou judge those who persecute me? 1
86 they persecute me with falsehood; help me! 1
150 They draw near who persecute me with evil 1
161 Princes persecute me without cause 1
Jer 17:18 Let those be put to shame who persecute me 1
Mat 5:10 Blessed are those who are persecuted 4
11 revile you and persecute you and utter all kinds 4
12 for so men persecuted the prophets who were 4
44 enemies and pray for those who persecute you 4
10:23 When they persecute you in one town 4
23:34 persecute from town to town 4
Lke 11:49 some of whom they will kill and persecute,' 4
21:12 lay their hands on you and persecute you 4
Joh 5:16 this was why the Jews persecuted Jesus 4
15:20 If they persecuted me, they will persecute you 4
20 If they persecuted me, they will persecute you 4
Act 7:52 did not your fathers persecute 4
9: 4 Saul, Saul, why do you persecute me? 4
5 he said, "I am Jesus, whom you are persecuting; 4
22: 4 I persecuted this Way to the death 4
7 'Saul, Saul, why do you persecute me?' 4
8 'I am Jesus of Nazareth whom you are persecuting.' 4
26:11 I persecuted them even to foreign cities. 4
14 Saul, Saul, why do you persecute me? 4
15 I am Jesus whom you are persecuting. 4
Rom 12:14 Bless those who persecute you; 4
1Co 4:12 When reviled, we bless; when persecuted, we endure; 4
15: 9 because I persecuted the church of God. 4
2Co 4: 9 persecuted, but not forsaken 4
Gal 1:13 how I persecuted the church of God violently 4
23 He who once persecuted us 4
4:29 who was born according to the flesh persecuted 4
5:11 why am I still persecuted 4
6:12 only in order that they may not be persecuted 4
1Ti 1:13 though I formerly blasphemed and persecuted 3
2Ti 3:12 Indeed all . . will be persecuted 4

persecution 1. מְרְדָּף 2. *διωγμός* 3. *θλῖψις*
Isa 14: 6 in anger with unrelenting persecution. 1
Mat 13:21 and when tribulation or persecution arises 2
Mrk 4:17 then, when tribulation or persecution arises 2
10:30 children and lands, with persecutions 2
Act 8: 1 a great persecution arose against the church 2
11:19 who were scattered because of the persecution 3
13:50 and stirred up persecution against Paul 2
Rom 8:35 Shall tribulation, or distress, or persecution 2
2Co 12:10 hardships, persecutions, and calamities 2
2Th 1: 4 in all your persecutions 2
2Ti 3:11 my persecutions, my sufferings 2
11 what persecutions I endured 2

persecutor 1. עָקֵב 2. רדף 3. *διώκω*
Ps 31:15 from the hand of my enemies and persecutors! 2
49: 5 the iniquity of my persecutors surrounds me 1
119:157 Many are my persecutors and my adversaries 2
142: 6 Deliver me from my persecutors; for they are too 2
Jer 15:15 and take vengeance for me on my persecutors. 2
20:11 therefore my persecutors will stumble 2
Php 3: 6 as to zeal a persecutor of the church 3

perseverance 1. *προσκαρτέρησις* 2. *ὑπομονή*
Eph 6:18 To that end keep alert with all perseverance 1
Heb 12: 1 let us run with perseverance the race 2

persevere 1. *διαμένω* 2. *ἐμμένω* 3. *παραμένω*
Jas 1:25 looks into the perfect law . . and perseveres 3
Sir 2:10 who ever persevered in the fear of the Lord 2
3Mc 3:11 persevere constantly in his same purpose 1

persist 1. יאל 2. עמד 3. *ἐνδελεχίζω* 4. *ἐπιμένω*
Deu 25: 8 if he persists, saying, 'I do not wish to take her,' 2
Jos 17:12 Canaanites persisted in dwelling in that land. 1
Jdg 1:27 Canaanites persisted in dwelling in that land. 1
35 the Amorites persisted in dwelling in Har-heres 1
Rom 11:23 if they do not persist in their unbelief 4
Sir 12: 3 No good will come to the man who persists in evil 3

persist in sin 1. *ἁμαρτάνω*
1Ti 5:20 those who persist in sin 1

persistently 1. שׁכם
2Ch 36:15 LORD . . sent persistently to them 1
Jer 7:13 when I spoke to you persistently 1
25 I have persistently sent all my servants 1
11: 7 warning them persistently, even to this day 1
25: 3 and I have spoken persistently to you 1
4 although the LORD persistently sent to you 1
29:19 which I persistently sent to you by my servants 1
32:33 and though I have taught them persistently 1
35:14 I have spoken to you persistently 1
15 the prophets, sending them persistently, saying 1
44: 4 Yet I persistently sent to you all my servants 1

person 1. אָדָם 2. אֶחָד 3. אִישׁ 4. נֶפֶשׁ 5. נֶפֶשׁ אָדָם 6. פָּנִים 7. ἄνθρωπος 8. ἑαυτοῦ 9. ὄνομα 10. πρόσωπον 11. σῶμα 12. τις 13. ψυχή 14. persona

Gen 12: 5 and the persons that they had gotten in Haran; 4
14:21 Give me the persons, but take the goods 4
46:18 and these she bore to Jacob–sixteen persons. 4
22 who were born to Jacob–fourteen persons in all. 4
25 and these she bore to Jacob–seven persons in all 4
26 All the persons belonging to Jacob 4
26 belonging to Jacob . . were 66 persons in all; 4
27 all the persons of the house of Jacob 4
Exd 1: 5 All the offspring of Jacob were 70 persons; 4
12: 4 shall take according to the number of persons; 4
15 that person shall be cut off from Israel. 4
19 that person shall be cut off 4
16:16 according to the number of the persons whom each 4
Lev 7:20 the person who eats of the flesh of the sacrifice 4
20 while an uncleanness is on him, that person shall 4
21 that person shall be cut off from his people 4
27 that person shall be cut off from his people 4
13:31 then the priest shall shut up the person *
33 shut up the person with the itching disease *
17:10 set my face against that person who eats blood 4
12 No person among you shall eat blood 4
15 every person that eats what dies of itself 4
18:29 the persons that do them shall be cut off 4
19: 8 that person shall be cut off from his people 4
20: 6 If a person turns to mediums and wizards 4
6 I will set my face against that person 4
22: 3 that person shall be cut off from my presence 4
6 the person who touches any such shall be unclean 4
23:30 that person I will destroy from among his people 4
27: 2 vow of persons to the LORD at your valuation 4
4 If the person is a female, your valuation shall be *
5 If the person is from five years old up to twenty *
6 If the person is from a month old up to five years *
7 if the person is 60 years old and upward *
8 then he shall bring the person before the priest *
Num 5: 6 When a man or woman . . that person is guilty 4
9:13 that person shall be cut off from his people 4
15:27 If one person sins unwittingly, he shall offer 4
28 for the person who commits an error, when he sins 4
30 person who does anything with a high hand 4
30 that person shall be cut off from among 4
31 that person shall be utterly cut off; 4
19:11 He who touches the dead body of any person 5
13 that person shall be cut off from Israel; 4
13 then a clean person shall take hyssop, and dip it 3
18 sprinkle it . . upon the persons who were there 4
20 that person shall be cut off from the midst 4
31:19 whoever of you has killed any person 4
28 tribute . . of the persons and of the oxen 1
30 take one drawn out of every 50, of the persons 1
35 32,000 persons in all, women who had not known man 4
40 persons were 16,000, of which the LORD'S tribute 5
40 of which the LORD'S tribute was 32 persons 4
46 16,000 persons 5
47 one of every 50, both of persons and of beasts 1
35:11 manslayer who kills any person without intent 4
15 that any one who kills any person without intent 4
30 If any one kills a person, the murderer shall 4
30 no person shall be put to death on the testimony *
Deu 10:22 Your fathers went down to Egypt 70 persons; 4
17: 6 person shall not be put to death on . . one witness. *
27:25 who takes a bribe to slay an innocent person.' 4
28:50 not regard the person of the old or show favor †
Jos 10:28 he utterly destroyed every person in it 4
30 smote it with the . . sword, and every person in it; 4
32 and smote it . . and every person in it 4
35 every person in it he utterly destroyed that day 4
37 and its king and its towns, and every person in it; 4
37 and utterly destroyed it with every person in it. 4
39 utterly destroyed every person in it. 4
20: 9 who killed a person without intent could flee 4
1Sm 9:22 those . . invited, who were about 30 persons. 3
22:18 Do'eg . . killed . . 85 persons who wore the linen 3
22 death of all the persons of your father's house. 4
2Sm 17:11 my counsel . . and that you go to battle in person. 6
2Kg 10: 6 the king's sons, 70 persons, were with the great men 3
7 took the king's sons, and slew them, 70 persons 3
14 slew them . . 42 persons, and he spared none of them. 3
12: 4 -the money from the assessment of persons- 4
Job 32:21 I will not show partiality to any person 3
Prv 6:12 A worthless person, a wicked man 1
19:15 idle person will suffer hunger. 4
Ecc 4: 8 a person who has no one, either son or brother 2
Jer 43: 6 and every person whom Nebu'zarad'an . . had left 4
52:29 carried away captive from Jerusalem . . 832 persons; 4
30 carried away captive of the Jews 745 persons; 4
30 all the persons were 4,600. 4
Ezk 13:18 veils for the heads of persons of every stature *
19 putting to death persons who should not die 4
19 and keeping alive persons who should not live 4
27:13 they exchanged the persons of men 4
44:25 defile themselves by going near to a dead person; 1
Jon 4:11 city, in which there are more than 120,000 persons 1
Act 1:15 the company of persons was in all about 100 9
4:34 There was not a needy person among them 12
27:37 We were in all 276 persons in the ship. 13
Rom 1:27 receiving in their own persons the due penalty 8
7: 1 law is binding on a person only during his life? 7
13: 1 Let every person be subject to the governing 13
1Co 2:11 what person knows a man's thoughts 7
7:26 it is well for a person to remain as he is. 7
1Th 2:17 in person not in heart 10
2Th 3:12 Now such persons we command and exhort *
Jas 1: 7 For that person must not suppose 7
14 each person is tempted when he is lured *
1Pe 3: 4 let it be the hidden person of the heart 7
20 in which a few, that is, eight persons, were saved 13
Jde 1: 4 ungodly persons who pervert the grace of our God *
1Es 3: 4 who kept guard over the person of the king 11
2Es 15:46 the glamour . . and the glory of her person- 14
16:47 their houses and possessions, and their persons 14
Tob 6: 7 that person will never be troubled again. *
AEs 16:11 the person second to the royal throne. 10
Sir 10: 5 confers his honor upon the person of the scribe. 10
13:15 every person his neighbor; 7
17:22 will keep a person's kindness 7
19:16 A person may make a slip without intending it. *
29: 4 Many persons regard a loan as a windfall *
27 Give place, stranger, to an honored person 10
37:28 not every person enjoys everything. 13
Bar 2:18 the person that is greatly distressed, that goes 13
18 person that hungers, will ascribe to thee glory 13
Sus 1:53 put to death an innocent and righteous person.' *
1Mc 2:38 to the number of 1,000 persons. 7
2Mc 1:35 with those persons whom the king favored *
3:37 what sort of person would be suitable 12
3Mc 5:14 the person who was in charge of the invitations *
4Mc 5: 4 when many persons had been rounded up *
7:20 when some persons appear to be dominated *

person *See also* any, certain, clean, contemptible, dead, defile, devout, diseased, employed, every, ill-bred, immoral, other, righteous, some, stiff-necked, such, uncircumcised, unclean, what, wicked.

personal *See* affair.

persons *See* many, seven.

persuade 1. נטה 2. פתה 3. ἀναπείθω 4. εὐπείθεια 5. πείθω 6. συμπείθω 7. persuadeo

1Sm 24: 7 David persuaded his men with these words *
Prv 7:21 With much seductive speech she persuades him; 1
25:15 With patience a ruler may be persuaded 2
Mat 27:20 elders persuaded the people to ask for Barab'bas 5
Act 12:20 persuaded Blastus, the king's chamberlain 5
14:19 having persuaded the people 5
17: 4 some of them were persuaded 5
18: 4 persuaded Jews and Greeks. 5
13 saying, "This man is persuading men to worship God 3
19:26 this Paul has persuaded 5
21:14 when he would not be persuaded, we ceased and said 5
26:26 I am persuaded 5
Rom 14:14 I know and am persuaded in the Lord Jesus 5
2Co 5:11 we persuade men 5
2Es 10:20 Do not say that, but let yourself be persuaded 7
Jdt 12:11 Go now and persuade the Hebrew woman 5
2Mc 4:34 Andronicus . . persuaded Onias to come out 5
7:26 she undertook to persuade her son. 5
11:14 and persuaded them to settle everything 5
14 promising that he would persuade the king 5
3Mc 1:11 the king was by no means persuaded. 5
7: 3 friends . . persuaded us to gather together the Jews 6
4Mc 5:16 persuaded to govern our lives by the divine law 5
8:12 to persuade them out of fear 5
12: 6 to influence her to persuade the surviving son 4
16:24 encouraged and persuaded each of her sons to die 5

persuade to change 1. μεταπείθω

4Mc 11:25 not been able to persuade us to change our mind 1

persuade to eat 1. ברה

2Sm 3:35 the people came to persuade David to eat bread 1

persuasion 1. παραμυθία 2. πεισμονή

Gal 5: 8 This persuasion is not from him who calls you. 2
AEs 16: 5 the persuasion of friends 1

persuasion *See also* yield.

persuasiveness 1. לֶקַח

Prv 16:21 pleasant speech increases persuasiveness. 1
23 adds persuasiveness to his lips. 1

pertain 1. דָּבָר 2. כְּלִי 3. ἀνήκω 4. πρός

Lev 11:46 This is the law pertaining to beast and bird *
Num 3:26 all the service pertaining to these. *
31 all the service pertaining to these. *
36 all the service pertaining to these; *
8:24 This is what pertains to the Levites; *
Deu 22: 5 woman . . not wear anything that pertains to a man 2
1Ch 26:32 oversight . . for everything pertaining to God 1
Dan 8:19 for it pertains to the appointed time of the end. *
26 vision, for it pertains to many days hence. *
Hos 5: 1 For the judgment pertains to you; *
2Pe 1: 3 all things that pertain to life and godliness 4
2Es 7:70 the things that pertain to the judgment. *
Sir 0: 1 write something pertaining to instruction 3

pervade 1. διηκέω

Wis 7:24 she pervades and penetrates all things. 1

perverse 1. הפך 2. ירט 3. עוה 4. עקשׁ 5. עִקֵּשׁ 6. תַּהְפֻּכָה 7. διαστρέφω 8. σκολιός 9. στρέβλη

Num 22:32 because your way is perverse before me; 2
Deu 32: 5 they are a perverse and crooked generation. 5
20 for they are a perverse generation 6
1Sm 20:30 You son of a perverse, rebellious woman, do I not 3
Prv 10:31 but the perverse tongue will be cut off. 6
32 but the mouth of the wicked, what is perverse. 6
11:20 Men of perverse mind are an abomination 5
12: 8 but one of perverse mind is despised. 3
16:28 A perverse man spreads strife 6
17:20 one with a perverse tongue falls into calamity. 1
19: 1 than a man who is perverse in speech, and is a fool. 5
22: 5 Thorns and snares are in the way of the perverse; 5
28: 6 than a rich man who is perverse in his ways. 5
18 who is perverse in his ways will fall into a pit. 4
Mat 17:17 O faithless and perverse generation 7
Lke 9:41 O faithless and perverse generation 7
Php 2:15 a crooked and perverse generation 7
Wis 1: 3 For perverse thoughts separate men from God 8
Sir 36:20 A perverse mind will cause grief 9

perverse *See also* prove.

perverse man 1. לוז 2. סוג

Prv 3:32 perverse man is an abomination to the LORD 1
14:14 perverse man . . filled with the fruit of his ways 2

show oneself perverse 1. פתל

2Sm 22:27 the crooked thou dost show thyself perverse. 1
Ps 18:26 thou dost show thyself perverse. 1

perverse thing 1. תַּהְפֻּכָה 2. διαστρέφω

Prv 16:30 He who winks his eyes plans perverse things 1
23:33 your mind utter perverse things. 1
Act 20:30 will arise men speaking perverse things 2

perversely 1. παραλλάσσω

AEs 13: 5 perversely following a strange manner of life 1

perversely *See also* deal.

act perversely 1. עוה

1Kg 8:47 'We have sinned, and have acted perversely 1
2Ch 6:37 'We have sinned, and have acted perversely 1

perverseness 1. לוז 2. סֶלֶף 3. עִקֵּשׁ

Ps 101: 4 Perverseness of heart shall be far from me; 3
Prv 15: 4 but perverseness in it breaks the spirit. 2
Isa 30:12 trust in oppression and perverseness 1

perversion 1. תֶּבֶל 2. תַּהְפֻּכָה 3. ἐναλλαγή

Lev 18:23 herself to a beast to lie with it: it is perversion 1
Prv 2:14 who . . delight in the perversions of evil; 2
Wis 14:26 sex perversion, disorder in marriage, adultery 3

perversion of justice 1. עַוְלָה

2Ch 19: 7 is no perversion of justice with the LORD our God 1

pervert 1. הפך 2. נטה 3. עוה 4. עות 5. עקל 6. עקשׁ 7. שׁנה 8. תַּהְפֻּכָה 9. ἀποστρέφω 10. διαστρέφω 11. ἐκκλίνω 12. ἐκστρέφω 13. μεταλλεύω 14. μεταστρέφω 15. μετατίθημι 16. μετατρέπω

Exd 23: 6 You shall not pervert the justice due 2
Deu 16:19 not pervert justice . . not show partiality; 2
24:17 not pervert the justice due to the sojourner 2
27:19 'Cursed be he who perverts the justice due 2
1Sm 8: 3 they took bribes and perverted justice. 2
Job 8: 3 Does God pervert justice? 4
3 Or does the Almighty pervert the right? 4
33:27 I sinned, and perverted what was right 3
34:12 the Almighty will not pervert justice. 4
Prv 2:12 delivering you from . . men of perverted speech 8
6:14 with perverted heart devises evil 8
8:13 way of evil and perverted speech I hate. 8
10: 9 but he who perverts his ways will be found out. 6
17:23 accepts a bribe . . to pervert the ways of justice. 2
31: 5 pervert the rights of all the afflicted. 7
Jer 3:21 because they have perverted their way 3
23:36 and you pervert the words of the living God 1
Mic 3: 9 Israel, who abhor justice and pervert all equity 6
Hab 1: 4 justice goes forth perverted. 5
Lke 23: 2 We found this man perverting our nation 10
14 as one who was perverting the people 9
Gal 1: 7 want to pervert the gospel of Christ. 14
Tit 3:11 such a person is perverted and sinful 12
Jde 1: 4 ungodly persons who pervert the grace of our God 15
Wis 4:12 roving desire perverts the innocent mind. 13
Sir 8: 2 gold . . has perverted the minds of kings. 11
Sus 1: 9 And they perverted their minds 10
56 and lust has perverted your heart. 10
4Mc 15:11 strong enough to pervert her reason. 16

pervert justice 1. נטה
Exd 23: 2 turning aside . . so as to pervert justice; 1

sexual pervert 1. *ἀρσενοκοίτης*
1Co 6: 9 nor adulterers, nor sexual perverts 1

pestilence 1. דֶּבֶר 2. מָוֶת 3. קֶטֶב 4. *ἀποστολή* 5. *θάνατος* 6. *λοιμός* 7. pestis
Exd 5: 3 fall upon us with pestilence or with the sword. 1
9:15 could have . . struck you . . with pestilence 1
Lev 26:25 I will send pestilence among you, and you shall be 1
Num14:12 I will strike them with the pestilence 1
Deu 28:21 LORD will make the pestilence cleave to you 1
32:24 devoured with . . heat and poisonous pestilence; 3
2Sm 24:13 there be three days' pestilence in your land? 1
15 the LORD sent a pestilence upon Israel 1
1Kg 8:37 famine . . pestilence or blight or mildew 1
1Ch 21:12 sword of the LORD, pestilence upon the land 1
14 the LORD sent a pestilence upon Israel; 1
2Ch 6:28 if there is pestilence or blight or mildew 1
7:13 When I . . or send pestilence among my people 1
20: 9 If evil comes upon us . . or pestilence, or famine 1
Job 27:15 Those who survive him the pestilence buries 2
Ps 91: 3 will deliver you . . from the deadly pestilence; 1
6 nor the pestilence that stalks in darkness 1
Jer 14:12 by the sword, by famine, and by pestilence. 1
15: 2 Those who are for pestilence, to pestilence 2
2 Those who are for pestilence, to pestilence 2
18:21 May their men meet death by pestilence 2
21: 6 they shall die of a great pestilence. 1
7 who survive the pestilence, sword, and famine 1
9 die by the sword, by famine, and by pestilence; 1
24:10 will send sword, famine, and pestilence upon them 1
27: 8 with the sword, with famine, and with pestilence 1
13 die by the sword, by famine, and by pestilence 1
28: 8 prophesied war, famine, and pestilence 1
29:17 I am sending on them sword, famine, and pestilence 1
18 pursue them with sword, famine, and pestilence 1
32:24 because of sword and famine and pestilence 1
36 given . . by sword, by famine, and by pestilence 1
34:17 liberty to the sword, to pestilence, and to famine 1
38: 2 die by the sword, by famine, and by pestilence; 1
42:17 die by the sword, by famine, and by pestilence; 1
22 die by the sword, by famine, and by pestilence 1
43:11 giving to the pestilence those who are doomed 2
11 those who are doomed to the pestilence 2
44:13 with the sword, with famine, and with pestilence 1
Ezk 5:12 A third part of you shall die of pestilence 1
17 pestilence and blood shall pass through you; 1
6:11 fall by the sword, by famine, and by pestilence. 1
12 He that is far off shall die of pestilence; 1
7:15 pestilence and famine are within; 1
15 in the city famine and pestilence devour. 1
12:16 from the sword, from famine and pestilence 1
14:19 Or if I send a pestilence into that land 1
21 sword, famine, evil beasts, and pestilence 1
28:23 for I will send pestilence into her, and blood 1
33:27 and in caves shall die by pestilence. 1
38:22 With pestilence . . I will enter into judgment 1
Ams 4:10 I sent among you a pestilence after the manner 1
Hab 3: 5 Before him went pestilence 1
Lke 21:11 in various places famines and pestilences 6
Rev 6: 8 kill . . with pestilence and by wild beasts 2
18: 8 plagues . . pestilence and mourning and famine 5
2Es 15:49 widowhood, poverty, famine, sword, and pestilence 7
Sir 39:29 Fire and hail and famine and pestilence 5
Bar 2:25 by famine and sword and pestilence. 4

pestilent 1. *λοιμός*
1Mc 10:61 A group of pestilent men from Israel, lawless men 1
pestilent *See also* behavior.

pestilent fellow 1. *λοιμός*
Act 24: 5 we have found this man a pestilent fellow 1

pestilent man 1. *λοιμός*
1Mc 15: 3 certain pestilent men have gained control 1
21 Therefore if any pestilent men have fled to you 1

pestle 1. עֱלִי
Prv 27:22 fool in a mortar with a pestle along with crushed 1

petition 1. מִשְׁאָלָה 2. שְׁאֵלָה 3. בעא (A) 4. בָּעוּ (A) 5. *δέησις* 6. *ἐντυγχάνω* 7. *ἐντυχία* 8. precatio
1Sm 1:17 Go . . and the God of Israel grant your petition 2
27 the LORD has granted me my petition which I made 2
Est 5: 6 What is your petition? It shall be granted you. 2
7 But Esther said, "My petition and my request is 2
8 to grant my petition and fulfil my request 2
7: 2 king again said to Esther, "What is your petition 2
3 let my life be given me at my petition 2
9:12 Now what is your petition? 2
Ps 20: 5 May the LORD fulfil all your petitions! 1
Dan 6: 7 whoever makes petition to any god or man 3
13 but makes his petition three times a day. 4
Act 25:24 about whom the whole Jewish people petitioned 6
2Es 8:24 and give ear to the petition of thy creature; 8
2Mc 13:12 When they had all joined in the same petition •
3Mc 2:10 you would listen to our petition 5
6:37 Then they petitioned the king 6
40 they made the petition for their dismissal. 7
petition *See also* grant, make.

petty 1. *μικρός*
4Mc 5:19 do not suppose that it would be a petty sin 1

phalanx 1. *φάλαγξ*
1Mc 6:35 distributed the beasts among the phalanxes; 1
38 while being themselves protected by the phalanxes 1
45 He . . ran into the midst of the phalanx to reach it 1
9:12 phalanx advanced to the sound of the trumpets 1
10:82 and engaged the phalanx in battle 1

phantom 1. צֶלֶם 2. *φάσμα*
Ps 73:20 on awaking you despise their phantoms. 1
Wis 17: 4 dismal phantoms with gloomy faces appeared. 2

pharmacist 1. *μυρεψός*
Sir 38: 8 the pharmacist makes of them a compound 1

phase 1. *ἀλλοιόω*
Sir 43: 8 increasing marvelously in its phases 1

philosopher 1. *φιλοσοφέω* 2. *φιλόσοφος*
Act 17:18 Epicurean and Stoic philosophers met him 2
4Mc 5: 7 it does not seem to me that you are a philosopher 1
7: 7 philosopher of divine life! 2
philosopher *See also* live.

philosophical 1. *φιλόσοφος*
4Mc 5:35 I will not put you to shame, philosophical reason 1

most philosophical 1. *φιλόσοφος*
4Mc 1: 1 The subject . . is most philosophical 1

philosophize 1. *φιλοσοφέω*
4Mc 5:11 philosophize according to the truth 1

philosophy 1. *φιλοσοφία*
Col 2: 8 makes a prey of you by philosophy and empty deceit 1
4Mc 1: 1 to pay earnest attention to philosophy. 1
5: 4 known to many . . because of his philosophy. ‡
11 not awaken from your foolish philosophy 1
22 You scoff at our philosophy 1
7: 9 you made your words of divine philosophy credible. 1
21 the whole rule of philosophy 1
philosophy *See also* follow, oppose.

phrase 1. *λέξις*
Heb 12:27 This phrase, "Yet once more," indicates . . •
Sir 0: 2 to have rendered some phrases imperfectly. 1
phrases *See* heap.

phylactery 1. *φυλακτήριον*
Mat 23: 5 they make their phylacteries broad 1

physical 1. *ἐν σαρκί* 2. *σωματικός* 3. *ψυχικός*
Rom 2:28 nor is true circumcision something . . physical 1
1Co 15:44 It is sown a physical body 3
44 If there is a physical body 3
46 the physical, and then the spiritual. 3
4Mc 1:32 Some desires are mental, others are physical 2

physically 1. *ἐκ φύσεως*
Rom 2:27 Then those who are physically uncircumcised 1

physician 1. רפא 2. *ἰατρός*
Gen 50: 2 commanded . . the physicians to embalm 1
2 the physicians embalmed Israel; 1
2Ch 16:12 but sought help from physicians. 1
Job 13: 4 worthless physicians are you all. 1
Jer 8:22 no balm in Gilead? Is there no physician there? 1
Mat 9:12 Those who are well have no need of a physician 2
Mrk 2:17 Those who are well have no need of a physician 2
5:26 who had suffered much under many physicians 2
Lke 4:23 Physician, heal yourself 2
5:31 Those who are well have no need of a physician 2
Col 4:14 Luke the beloved physician and Demas greet you. 2
Tob 2:10 I went to physicians, but they did not help me. 2
Sir 10:10 A long illness baffles the physician 2
38: 1 Honor the physician with the honor due him 2
3 The skill of the physician lifts up his head 2
12 give the physician his place 2
13 when success lies in the hands of physicians •
15 may he fall into the care of a physician. 2

pick 1. בחר 2. מִבְחָר 3. *ἐκλέγω* 4. *ἐκλεκτός* 5. *ἐπιλέγω* 6. *ἐπίλεκτος* 7. *κρίνω*
Exd 14: 7 and took 600 picked chariots 1
15: 4 his picked officers are sunk in the Red Sea. 2
Jdg 20:15 Gib'e-ah, who mustered 700 picked men. 1
16 were 700 picked men who were left-handed 1
34 came . . 10,000 picked men out of all Israel 1
2Ch 13: 3 army of valiant men of war, 400,000 picked men; 1
3 with 800,000 picked mighty warriors. 1
17 there fell slain of Israel 500,000 picked men. 1
Ezk 17:21 all the pick of his troops shall fall by the sword 2
Dan 11:15 shall not stand, or even his picked troops 2
Jdt 2:15 mustered the picked troops by divisions 4
19 horsemen and picked troops of infantry. 6
3: 6 took picked men from them as his allies. 6
1Mc 4: 1 and 1,000 picked cavalry 4
28 he mustered 60,000 picked infantrymen 6
6:35 500 picked horsemen 3
9: 5 with him were 3,000 picked men. 4
12:41 with 40,000 picked fighting men 5
15:26 Simon sent to Antiochus 2,000 picked men 4
2Mc 13:15 with a picked force of the bravest young men 7

pick (2) 1. חָרִיץ
2Sm 12:31 to labor with saws and iron picks and iron axes 1
1Ch 20: 3 to labor with saws and iron picks and axes; 1

pick (3) 1. קטף 2. *τρυγάω*
Job 30: 4 They pick mallow and the leaves of bushes 1
Lke 6:44 nor are grapes picked from a bramble bush. 2
pick *See* bird.

pick out 1. נקר 2. *ἐπισκέπτομαι*
Prv 30:17 The eye . . will be picked out by the ravens 1
Act 6: 3 pick out from among you 7 men of good repute 2

pick up 1. לקט 2. *αἴρω* 3. *ἀναιρέω* 4. *συναρπάζω*
Jdg 1: 7 kings . . used to pick up scraps under my table; 1
Mrk 16:18 they will pick up serpents 2
Sir 22: 2 any one that picks it up will shake it off his hand. 3
2Mc 4:41 some picked up stones, some blocks of wood 4

picked man 1. בָּחוּר 2. בחר
2Sm 10: 9 Jo'ab . . chose some of the picked men of Israel 2
1Ch 19:10 he chose some of the picked men of Israel 2
2Ch 25: 5 found that they were 300,000 picked men 2
Ps 78:31 and laid low the picked men of Israel. 1

picture 1. דְּמוּת 2. מַשְׂכִּית 3. imago
Ezk 8:12 in the dark, every man in his room of pictures? 2
23:15 looking like officers, a picture of Babylonians 1
2Es 5:37 or show me the picture of a voice 3

piece 1. אֲגוֹרָה 2. בָּדָל 3. גֶּזֶר 4. חֶלְקָה 5. נֵתַח 6. פֶּלַח 7. פַּת 8. פְּתוֹת 9. קֶרַע 10. שְׁבָבִים 11. *βῶλος* 12. *ἐπίβαλημα* 13. *ἐπίβλημα* 14. *μέρος* 15. *τις*
Gen 15:17 a flaming torch passed between these pieces. 3
20:16 I have given your brother 1,000 pieces of silver; •
33:19 bought . . the piece of land on which he had 4
Exd 25:36 one piece of hammered work of pure gold. •
29:17 Then you shall cut the ram into pieces, and wash 5
17 and put them with its pieces and its head 5
37:22 the whole of it was one piece of hammered work •
Lev 1: 6 flay the burnt offering and cut it into pieces 5
8 Aaron's sons the priests shall lay the pieces 5
12 he shall cut it into pieces, with its head 5
2: 6 you shall break it in pieces, and pour oil on it 7
6:21 in baked pieces like a cereal offering 7
8:20 when the ram was cut into pieces, Moses burned 5
20 Moses burned the head and the pieces and the fat 5
Jdg 5:30 two pieces . . embroidered for my neck †
9: 4 they gave him 70 pieces of silver out of the house •
16: 5 we will each give you 1,100 pieces of silver. •
17: 2 1,100 pieces of silver which were taken from you •
3 he restored the 1,100 pieces of silver •
4 his mother took 200 pieces of silver •
10 and I will give you ten pieces of silver a year •
19:29 he divided her, limb by limb, into twelve pieces 5
1Sm 2:36 shall come to implore him for a piece of silver 1
30:12 they gave him a piece of a cake of figs 6
2Sm 18:11 to give you ten pieces of silver and a girdle. •
12 if I felt in my hand . . 1,000 pieces of silver •
1Kg 11:30 laid hold . . and tore it into twelve pieces. 9
31 he said to Jerobo'am, "Take for yourself ten pieces; 9
2Kg 2:12 his own clothes and rent them in two pieces. 9
Job 33: 6 I too was formed from a piece of clay. •
Ps 119:72 than thousands of gold and silver pieces. •
Prv 28:21 but for a piece of bread a man will do wrong. 7
Sng 8:11 bring . . 1,000 pieces of silver. •
Ezk 13:19 for handfuls of barley and for pieces of bread 8
24: 4 put in it the pieces of flesh, all the good pieces 5
5 boil its pieces, seethe also its bones in it. 5
6 Take out of it piece after piece 5
6 Take out of it piece after piece 5
Hos 8: 6 The calf of Sama'ria shall be broken to pieces. 10
Ams 3:12 two legs, or a piece of an ear 2
Mat 9:16 no one puts a piece of unshrunk cloth 13
26:15 And they paid him 30 pieces of silver. •
27: 3 and brought back the 30 pieces of silver •
5 throwing down the pieces of silver in the temple •
6 the chief priests, taking the pieces of silver, said •
9 they took the 30 pieces of silver •
Mrk 2:21 sews a piece of unshrunk cloth on an old garment; 12
Lke 5:36 No one tears a piece from a new garment 13
36 the piece from the new will not match the old. 13
24:42 They gave him a piece of broiled fish 14
Act 19:19 and found it came to 50,000 pieces of silver. •
27:44 the rest on planks or on pieces of the ship 15

Wis 10: 4 steering . . by a paltry piece of wood. •
14: 1 one . . calls upon a piece of wood •
5 even to the smallest piece of wood •
Sir 22:15 Sand, salt, and a piece of iron are easier to bear 11
4Mc 9:20 pieces of flesh were falling off the axles •
piece *See also* castoff, one.

broken piece 1. κλάσμα
Mat 14:20 twelve baskets full of the broken pieces 1
15:37 baskets full of the broken pieces left over. 1
Mrk 6:43 took up twelve baskets full of broken pieces 1
8: 8 they took up the broken pieces left over 1
19 how many baskets full of broken pieces 1
20 how many baskets full of broken pieces 1
Lke 9:17 twelve baskets of broken pieces. 1

piece by piece 1. לִנְתָחִים
Lev 9:13 the burnt offering to him, piece by piece 1

fat piece 1. חֵלֶב
1Kg 8:64 and the fat pieces of the peace offerings. 1
64 and the fat pieces of the peace offerings. 1

piece of flesh 1. נֵתַח
Ezk 24: 4 put in it the pieces of flesh, all the good pieces 1

piece of land 1. אֶרֶץ 2. חֶלְקָה
Gen 23:15 a piece of land worth 400 shekels of silver 1
2Kg 3:19 and ruin every good piece of land with stones. 2
25 on every good piece of land every man threw 2

piece of money 1. קְשִׂיטָה
Gen 33:19 he bought for 100 pieces of money the . . land 1
Jos 24:32 Jacob bought . . for 100 pieces of money; 1
Job 42:11 each of them gave him a piece of money and a ring 1

piece of property 1. κτῆμα
Act 5: 1 Anani'as . . sold a piece of property 1

one piece 1. מִן
Exd 25:19 of one piece with the mercy seat shall you make 1
31 its flowers shall be of one piece with it; 1
35 a capital of one piece with it under each pair 1
36 shall be of one piece with it 1
27: 2 its horns shall be of one piece with it 1
30: 2 its horns shall be of one piece with it. 1
37:17 and its flowers were of one piece with it. 1
21 a capital of one piece with it under each pair 1
22 branches were of one piece with it; 1
25 its horns were of one piece with it. 1
38: 2 its horns were of one piece with it 1
1Kg 7:34 the supports were of one piece with the stands. •
35 its stays and its panels were of one piece with it. •

piecemeal 1. κατὰ μέρος
2Mc 15:33 said that he would give it piecemeal to the birds 1
pieces *See* beat, break, crush, cut, dash, hew, tear.

pierce 1. דקר 2. חלל 3. חלף 4. טען 5. יצא 6. מחק 7. נקב 8. פלח 9. ἀναπείρω 10. διαπείρω 11. διέρχομαι 12. διϊκνέομαι 13. ἐκκεντέω 14. νύσσω 15. ὀρύσσω 16. περιπείρω 17. πηρόω 18. σχίζω
Num 24: 8 pierce them through with his arrows. 6
25: 8 pierced both of them . . through her body. 1
Jdg 5:26 his head, she shattered and pierced his temple. 3
2Kg 9:24 shot Joram . . so that the arrow pierced his heart 5
18:21 which will pierce the hand of any man who leans 7
Job 26:13 his hand pierced the fleeing serpent. 2
40:24 with hooks, or pierce his nose with a snare? 7
41: 2 rope in his nose, or pierce his jaw with a hook? 7
Ps 22:16 they have pierced my hands and feet– 15
Prv 7:23 till an arrow pierces its entrails; 8
Isa 14:19 those pierced by the sword 4
36: 6 broken reed of a staff, which will pierce the hand 7
51: 9 cut Rahab in pieces, that didst pierce the dragon 2
Hab 3:14 Thou didst pierce with thy shafts the head 7
Zec 12:10 when they look on him whom they have pierced 1
13: 3 mother who bore him shall pierce him through 1
Joh 19:34 one of the soldiers pierced his side with a spear 14
37 They shall look on him whom they have pierced. 13
1Ti 6:10 pierced their hearts with many pangs. 16
Heb 4:12 piercing to the division of soul and spirit 12
Rev 1: 7 every one who pierced him; 13
Jdt 6: 6 shall pierce your sides 11
Wis 5:11 and pierced by the force of its rushing flight 18
Sir 35:17 The prayer of the humble pierces the clouds 11
2Mc 12:22 pierced by the points of their swords. 9
4Mc 11:19 pierced his ribs so that his entrails were burned 10
18:21 pierced the pupils of their eyes 17

pierce through 1. διέρχομαι 2. κατακεντέω
Lke 2:35 (and a sword will pierce through your own soul also) 1
Jdt 16:12 The sons of maidservants have pierced them through; 2

piety 1. δικαιοσύνη 2. εὐλαβῶς 3. εὐσέβεια
Mat 6: 1 Beware of practicing your piety before men 1
Act 3:12 by our own power or piety 3
2Mc 3: 1 because of the piety of the high priest Onias 3
6:11 their piety kept them from defending themselves 2
4Mc 5:18 to invalidate our reputation for piety. 3
24 it teaches us piety 3
31 to be young in reason on behalf of piety. 3
6: 2 the gracefulness of his piety. 3
7:16 If, therefore, because of piety 3
13:10 be cowardly in the demonstration of our piety. 3
17: 5 lighting the way . . to piety 3
7 to paint the history of your piety as an artist 3
piety *See also* exercise.

pigeon 1. יוֹנָה 2. περιστερά
Lev 1:14 offering of turtledoves or of young pigeons 1
5: 7 bring . . two turtledoves or two young pigeons 1
11 afford two turtledoves or two young pigeons 1
12: 6 a young pigeon or a turtledove for a sin offering 1
8 take two turtledoves or two young pigeons 1
14:22 also two turtledoves or two young pigeons 1
30 offer, of the turtledoves or young pigeons 1
15:14 take two turtledoves or two young pigeons 1
29 two turtledoves or two young pigeons 1
Num 6:10 bring two turtledoves or two young pigeons 1
Mat 21:12 and the seats of those who sold pigeons. 2
Mrk 11:15 the seats of those who sold pigeons; 2
Lke 2:24 a pair of turtledoves, or two young pigeons. 2
Joh 2:14 those who were selling . . sheep and pigeons 2
16 And he told those who sold the pigeons 2

young pigeon 1. גּוֹזָל
Gen 15: 9 a ram . . a turtledove, and a young pigeon. 1

pile 1. דּוּר 2. מְדוּרָה 3. ποιέω 4. σωρεύω
Ezk 24: 5 pile the logs under it; boil its pieces 1
9 I also will make the pile great. 2
Jdt 15:11 and piled the things on them. 4
1Mc 11: 4 they had piled them in heaps along his route. 3

pile up 1. יסד 2. כון 3. סלל 4. ערם
Exd 15: 8 At the blast of thy nostrils the waters piled up 4
2Ch 31: 7 In the third month they began to pile up the heaps 1
Job 27:16 silver like dust, and pile up clothing like clay; 2
17 he may pile it up, but the just will wear it 2
Jer 50:26 pile her up like heaps of grain, and destroy her 3

pilfer 1. νοσφίζω
Tit 2:10 nor to pilfer, but to show entire and true fidelity 1

pilgrimage 1. מָגוֹר 2. peregrinatio
Ps 119:54 have been my songs in the house of my pilgrimage. 1
2Es 8:39 I will rejoice . . over their pilgrimage also 2

pillage 1. חפש
Obd 1: 6 How Esau has been pillaged 1

pillar 1. מַצֵּבָה 2. מָצוּק 3. נְצִיב 4. עַמּוּד 5. στήλη 6. στῦλος 7. columna
Gen 19:26 looked back, and she became a pillar of salt. 3
28:18 set it up for a pillar and poured oil on the top 1
22 this stone, which I have set up for a pillar 1
31:13 I am the God of Bethel, where you anointed a pillar 1
45 Jacob took a stone, and set it up as a pillar. 1
49 the pillar Mizpah, for he said, "The LORD watch •
51 See this heap and the pillar, which I have set 1
52 This heap is a witness, and the pillar is a witness 1
52 pass over this heap and this pillar to me 1
35:14 Jacob set up a pillar in the place where he had 1
14 where he had spoken with him, a pillar of stone; 1
20 Jacob set up a pillar upon her grave; 1
20 it is the pillar of Rachel's tomb 1
Exd 13:21 the LORD went before them by day in a pillar 4
21 and by night in a pillar of fire to give them light 4
22 the pillar of cloud by day and the pillar of fire 4
22 the pillar of fire by night did not depart 4
14:19 and the pillar of cloud moved from before them 4
24 the LORD in the pillar of fire and of cloud looked 4
23:24 and break their pillars in pieces. 1
24: 4 built . . twelve pillars, according 1
26:32 you shall hang it upon four pillars of acacia 4
37 shall make for the screen five pillars of acacia 4
27:10 their pillars shall be twenty and their bases 4
10 the hooks of the pillars and their fillets 4
11 hangings . . their pillars twenty and their 4
11 the hooks of the pillars and their fillets shall 4
12 hangings . . with ten pillars and ten bases. 4
14 with three pillars and three bases. 4
15 with three pillars and three bases. 4
16 it shall have four pillars and . . four bases. 4
17 the pillars around the court shall be filleted 4
33: 9 When Moses entered the tent, the pillar of cloud 4
10 when all the people saw the pillar of cloud 4
34:13 You shall . . break their pillars, and cut down 1
35:11 its hooks and its frames, its bars, its pillars 4
17 the hangings of the court its pillars 4
36:36 for it he made four pillars of acacia 4
38 its five pillars with their hooks. 4
38:10 their pillars were twenty and their bases 4
10 the hooks of the pillars and their fillets were 4
11 their pillars twenty, their bases twenty 4
11 but the hooks of the pillars and their fillets 4
12 their pillars ten, and their sockets ten; 4
12 hooks of the pillars and their fillets were 4
14 hangings . . three pillars and three bases. 4
15 hangings . . three pillars and three bases. 4
17 the bases for the pillars were of bronze 4
17 the hooks of the pillars and their fillets were 4
17 and all the pillars of the court were filleted 4
19 their pillars were four; their four bases were 4
28 he made hooks for the pillars 4
39:33 frames, its bars, its pillars, and its bases; 4
40 the hangings of the court, its pillars 4
40:18 put in its poles, and raised up its pillars; 4
Lev 26: 1 and erect no graven image or pillar 1
Num 3:36 appointed charge . . the bars, the pillars 4
37 also the pillars of the court round about 4
4:31 frames . . with its bars, pillars, and bases 4
32 pillars of the court round about with their 4
12: 5 LORD came down in a pillar of cloud, and stood 4
14:14 thou goest before them, in a pillar of cloud by day 4
14 goest before . . in a pillar of fire by night. 4
Deu 7: 5 you shall . . dash in pieces their pillars 1
12: 3 you shall . . dash in pieces their pillars 1
16:22 not set up a pillar which the LORD your God hates. 1
31:15 LORD appeared in the tent in a pillar of cloud; 4
15 pillar of cloud stood by the door of the tent. 4
Jdg 9: 6 made . . king, by the oak of the pillar at Shechem. •
16:25 They made him stand between the pillars; 4
26 Let me feel the pillars on which the house rests 4
29 two middle pillars upon which the house rested 4
1Sm 2: 8 For the pillars of the earth are the LORD's 2
2Sm 18:18 set up . . the pillar which is in the King's Valley 1
18 he called the pillar after his own name 1
1Kg 7: 2 it was built upon three rows of cedar pillars 4
2 was built . . with cedar beams upon the pillars. 4
3 above the chambers that were upon the 45 pillars 4
6 he made the Hall of Pillars; its length was 50 cubits 4
6 there was a porch in front with pillars 4
15 He cast two pillars of bronze. 4
15 Eighteen cubits was the height of one pillar 4
16 capitals . . to set upon the tops of the pillars; 4
17 for the capitals upon the tops of the pillars; 4
18 the capital that was upon the top of the pillar; 4
19 capitals that were upon the tops of the pillars 4
20 The capitals were upon the two pillars and also 4
21 set up the pillars at the vestibule of the temple; 4
21 he set up the pillar on the south and called its 4
21 he set up the pillar on the north and called its 4
22 upon the tops of the pillars was lily-work. 4
22 Thus the work of the pillars was finished. 4
41 the two pillars, the two bowls 4
41 the capitals that were on the tops of the pillars; 4
41 the capitals that were on the tops of the pillars; 4
42 bowls of the capitals that were upon the pillars; 4
14:23 built . . high places, and pillars, and Ashe'rim 1
2Kg 3: 2 he put away the pillar of Ba'al 1
10:26 brought out the pillar that was in the house 1
27 they demolished the pillar of Ba'al 1
11:14 there was the king standing by the pillar 4
17:10 they set up for themselves pillars and Ashe'rim 1
18: 4 He removed the high places, and broke the pillars 1
23: 3 the king stood by the pillar and made a covenant 4
14 he broke in pieces the pillars, and cut down 1
25:13 the pillars of bronze . . the Chalde'ans broke 4
16 As for the two pillars, the one sea, and the stands 4
17 The height of the one pillar was eighteen cubits 4
17 And the second pillar had the like 4
1Ch 18: 8 Solomon made . . the pillars and the vessels 4
2Ch 3:15 he made two pillars 35 cubits high 4
16 chains . . and put them on the tops of the pillars; 4
17 He set up the pillars in front of the temple 4
4:12 the two pillars, the bowls, and the two capitals 4
12 the two capitals on the top of the pillars; 4
12 the capitals that were on the top of the pillars; 4
13 of the capitals that were upon the pillars. 4
14: 3 broke down the pillars 1
23:13 the king standing by his pillar at the entrance 4
31: 1 all Israel . . broke in pieces the pillars 1
Neh 9:12 pillar of cloud thou didst lead them in the day 4
12 by a pillar of fire in the night to light for them 4
19 pillar of cloud . . not depart from them by day 4
19 nor the pillar of fire by night which lighted 4
Est 1: 6 caught up . . to silver rings and marble pillars 4
Job 9: 6 earth out of its place, and its pillars tremble; 4
26:11 The pillars of heaven tremble, and are astounded 4
Ps 75: 3 it is I who keep steady its pillars. Selah 4
99: 7 He spoke to them in the pillar of cloud; 4
Prv 9: 1 Wisdom . . has set up her seven pillars. 4
Isa 19:10 the pillars of the land will be crushed •
19 of Egypt, and a pillar to the LORD at its border. 1
Jer 1:18 a fortified city, an iron pillar, and bronze walls 4
27:19 concerning the pillars, the sea, the stands 4
52:17 And the pillars of bronze that were in the house 4
20 As for the two pillars, the one sea 4
21 As for the pillars, the height of the one pillar 4
21 the height of the one pillar was eighteen cubits 4
22 And the second pillar had the like 4
Ezk 26:11 your mighty pillars will fall to the ground. 1
40:49 were pillars beside the jambs on either side. 4

42: 6 they had no pillars like the pillars of the outer 4
6 they had no pillars like the pillars of the outer 4
Hos 3: 4 dwell many days . . without sacrifice or pillar 1
10: 1 he improved his pillars. 1
2 break down . . altars, and destroy their pillars. 1
Mic 5:13 I will cut off your images and your pillars 1
Gal 2: 9 Cephas and John, who were reputed to be pillars 6
1Ti 3:15 the pillar and bulwark of the truth. 6
Rev 3:12 I will make him a pillar in the temple of my God; 6
10: 1 and his legs like pillars of fire. 6
2Es 1:14 I provided light for you from a pillar of fire 7
Wis 10: 7 a pillar of salt 5
18: 3 thou didst provide a flaming pillar of fire 6
Sir 24: 4 my throne was in a pillar of cloud. 6
26:18 Like pillars of gold on a base of silver 6
36:24 a helper fit for him and a pillar of support. 6
LJr 1:59 better also a wooden pillar in a palace 6
1Mc 14:27 and put it upon pillars on Mount Zion 5
3Mc 7:20 Then, after inscribing them as holy on a pillar 5
4Mc 17: 3 Nobly set like a roof on the pillars of your sons 6

pillar *See also* corner.

corner pillar 1. זָוִית

Ps 144:12 our daughters like corner pillars cut 1

pillow 1. כָּבִיר 2. προσκεφάλαιον

1Sm 19:13 and put a pillow of goats' hair at its head 1
16 with the pillow of goats' hair at its head. 1
1Es 3: 8 put them under the pillow of Darius the king 2

pilot 1. חֹבֵל 2. εὐθύνω 3. κυβερνήτης

Ezk 27: 8 men of Zemer were in you, they were your pilots. 1
27 your mariners and your pilots, your caulkers 1
28 At the sound of the cry of your pilots 1
29 all the pilots of the sea stand on the shore 1
Jas 3: 4 wherever the will of the pilot directs. 2
4Mc 7: 1 like a most skilful pilot 3

pim 1. פִּים

1Sm 13:21 the charge was a pim for the plowshares 1

pin 1. יָתֵד 2. נכה

Jdg 16:13 head with the web and make it tight with the pin •
14 she made them tight with the pin, and said to him 1
14 and pulled away the pin, the loom, and the web. 1
1Sm 18:11 he thought, "I will pin David to the wall. 2
19:10 Saul sought to pin David to the wall 2
26: 8 pin him to the earth with one stroke of the spear 2

pine 1. בְּרוֹת 2. תְּאַשּׁוּר

Sng 1:17 the beams . . are cedar, our rafters are pine. 1
Isa 41:19 the cypress, the plane and the pine together; 2
60:13 come to you, the cypress, the plane, and the pine 2
Ezk 27: 6 made your deck of pines from the coasts of Cyprus 2

pine away 1. זוב 2. מקק 3. רָזִי 4. τήκω

Lev 26:39 are left shall pine away in your enemies' lands 2
39 they shall pine away like them 2
Isa 24:16 But I say, "I pine away, I pine away. Woe is me! 3
16 But I say, "I pine away, I pine away. Woe is me! 3
Lam 4: 9 the victims of hunger, who pined away 1
Ezk 24:23 you shall pine away in your iniquities and groan 2
Wis 1:16 considering him a friend, they pined away 4

cause to pine away 1. דוב

Lev 26:16 that waste the eyes and cause life to pine away. 1

pinion 1. אֵבֶר 2. אֶבְרָה 3. ταρσός

Deu 32:11 catching them, bearing them on its pinions 2
Job 39:13 but are they the pinions and plumage of love? 2
Ps 68:13 with silver, its pinions with green gold. 2
91: 4 he will cover you with his pinions 2
Ezk 17: 3 A great eagle with great wings and long pinions 1
Wis 5:11 lashed by the beat of its pinions 3

pinnacle 1. שֶׁמֶשׁ 2. πτερύγιον

Isa 54:12 I will make your pinnacles of agate 1
Mat 4: 5 set him on the pinnacle of the temple 2
Lke 4: 9 set him on the pinnacle of the temple 2

pioneer 1. ἀρχηγός

Heb 2:10 make the pioneer of their salvation perfect 1
12: 2 Jesus the pioneer and perfecter of our faith 1

pious 1. εὐσεβής

2Mc 1:19 the pious priests of that time took some of the fire 1
12:45 it was a holy and pious thought 1
4Mc 10:15 by the everlasting life of the pious 1

piously *See* live.

pipe 1. חָלִיל 2. עוּגָב 3. צַנְתְּרוֹת 4. שְׁרִיקָה
5. מַשְׁרוֹקִי (A) 6. αὐλέω

Gen 4:21 the father of all those who play the lyre and pipe. 2
Jdg 5:16 the sheepfolds, to hear the piping for the flocks? 4
1Kg 1:40 went up after him, playing on pipes, and rejoicing 1
Job 21:12 and rejoice to the sound of the pipe. 2
30:31 and my pipe to the voice of those who weep. 2
Ps 150: 4 praise him with strings and pipe! 2
Dan 3: 5 hear the sound of the horn, pipe, lyre, trigon 5
7 heard the sound of the horn, pipe, lyre, trigon 5
10 hears the sound of the horn, pipe, lyre, trigon 5
15 hear the sound of the horn, pipe, lyre, trigon 5
Zec 4:12 trees, which are beside the two golden pipes 3
Mat 11:17 'We piped to you, and you did not dance 6
Lke 7:32 We piped to you, and you did not dance 6

pistachio nut 1. בָּטְנִים

Gen 43:11 honey, gum, myrrh, pistachio nuts, and almonds. 1

pit 1. בְּאֵר 2. באר 3. בּוֹר 4. גּוּמָּץ 5. מַהֲמֹרָה 6. מִכְרֶה
7. פַּחַת 8. שׁוּחָה 9. שְׁחוּת 10. שְׁחִית 11. שַׁחַת
12. שִׁיחָה 13. ἄβυσσος 14. βόθρος 15. βόθυνος
16. λίμνη 17. σιρός 18. φρέαρ 19. lacus

Gen 14:10 Now the Valley of Siddim was full of bitumen pits; 1
37:20 let us kill him and throw him into one of the pits; 3
22 cast him into this pit here in the wilderness 3
24 they took him and cast him into a pit. 3
24 The pit was empty, there was no water in it. 3
28 him out of the pit, and sold him to the Ish'maelites 3
29 When Reuben returned to the pit 3
29 Joseph was not in the pit, he rent his clothes 3
Exd 21:33 When a man leaves a pit open, or when a man digs 3
33 when a man digs a pit and does not cover it 3
34 the owner of the pit shall make it good; 3
2Sm 17: 9 even now he has hidden himself in one of the pits 7
18:17 they took Ab'salom, and threw him into a great pit 7
23:20 slew a lion in a pit on a day when snow had fallen. 2
2Kg 10:14 took them . . and slew them at the pit of Beth-eked 3
1Ch 11:22 slew a lion in a pit on a day when snow had fallen. 3
Job 9:31 yet thou wilt plunge me into a pit 11
17:14 if I say to the pit, 'You are my father,' 11
33:18 he keeps back his soul from the Pit 11
22 His soul draws near the Pit 11
24 Deliver him from going down into the Pit 11
28 has redeemed my soul from going down into the Pit 11
30 to bring back his soul from the Pit, 11
Ps 7:15 He makes a pit, digging it out, and falls 3
9:15 The nations have sunk in the pit which they made; 11
16:10 to Sheol, or let thy godly one see the Pit. 11
28: 1 I become like those who go down to the Pit. 3
30: 3 from among those gone down to the Pit. 3
9 profit is there in my death, if I go down to the Pit? 11
35: 7 without cause they dug a pit for my life. 11
40: 2 He drew me up from the desolate pit 3
49: 9 to live on for ever, and never see the Pit. 11
57: 6 They dug a pit in my way, but they have fallen 12
69:15 or the pit close its mouth over me. 1
88: 4 I am reckoned among those who go down to the Pit; 3
6 Thou hast put me in the depths of the Pit 3
94:13 until a pit is dug for the wicked. 11
103: 4 who redeems your life from the Pit 11
140:10 Let them be cast into pits, no more to rise! 5
143: 7 lest I be like those who go down to the Pit. 3
Prv 1:12 like those who go down to the Pit; 3
22:14 The mouth of a loose woman is a deep pit; 8
23:27 For a harlot is a deep pit; 8
26:27 He who digs a pit will fall into it 11
28:10 misleads the upright . . fall into his own pit; 9
18 who is perverse in his ways will fall into a pit. ‡
Ecc 10: 8 He who digs a pit will fall into it; 4
Isa 14:15 brought down to Sheol, to the depths of the Pit. 3
19 pierced . . who go down to the stones of the Pit 3
24:17 Terror, and the pit, and the snare are upon you 7
18 He who flees . . shall fall into the pit; 7
18 he who climbs out of the pit shall be caught 7
22 They will be gathered . . as prisoners in a pit; 3
38:17 held back my life from the pit of destruction 11
18 those who go down to the pit cannot hope 3
51:14 he shall not die and go down to the Pit 11
Jer 2: 6 in the wilderness, in a land of deserts and pits 8
18:20 Yet they have dug a pit for my life. 8
22 For they have dug a pit to take me, and laid snares 8
48:43 Terror, pit, and snare are before you 7
44 who flees from the terror shall fall into the pit 7
44 he who climbs out of the pit shall be caught 7
Lam 3:53 they flung me alive into the pit and cast stones 3
55 I called on thy name . . from the depths of the pit; 3
4:20 the LORD'S anointed, was taken in their pits 10
Ezk 19: 4 he was taken in their pit; and they brought him 11
8 their net over him; he was taken in their pit. 11
26:20 down with those who descend into the Pit 3
20 primeval ruins, with those who go down to the Pit 3
28: 8 They shall thrust you down into the Pit 11
31:14 among . . men, with those who go down to the Pit. 3
16 down to Sheol with those who go down to the Pit; 3
32:18 to those who have gone down to the Pit 3
23 graves are set in the uttermost parts of the Pit 3
24 their shame with those who go down to the Pit. 3
25 bear their shame with those who go down to the Pit; 3
29 uncircumcised, with those who go down to the Pit. 3
30 their shame with those who go down to the Pit. 3
Hos 5: 2 And they have made deep the pit of Shittim; •
Jon 2: 6 yet thou didst bring up my life from the Pit, O LORD 11
Zep 2: 9 a land possessed by nettles and salt pits 6
Zec 9:11 set your captives free from the waterless pit. 3
Mat 12:11 it falls into a pit on the sabbath 15
15:14 both will fall into a pit. 15
Lke 6:39 Will they not both fall into a pit? 15
2Pe 2: 4 God . . committed them to pits of nether gloom 17
Rev 20: 3 and threw him into the pit 13
2Es 7:36 Then the pit of torment shall appear 19
Sir 12:16 in his mind he will plan to throw you into a pit 14
21:10 at its end is the pit of Hades. 14
27:26 He who digs a pit will fall into it 14
1Mc 7:19 killed them and threw them into a great pit. 18
11:35 the salt pits and the crown taxes due to us 16

pit *See also* bottomless.

pit for the wine press 1. ὑπολήνιον

Mrk 12: 1 and dug a pit for the wine press 1

low pit 1. בְּאֵר שַׁחַת

Ps 55:23 thou, O God, wilt cast them down into the lowest pit; 1

pitch 1. חנה 2. נטה 3. נסע 4. תקע 5. ἵστημι
6. πήγνυμι 7. ποιέω

Gen 12: 8 east of Bethel, and pitched his tent 2
26:25 and pitched his tent there. 2
31:25 Jacob had pitched his tent in the hill country 4
33:19 piece of land on which he had pitched his tent. 2
35:21 Israel journeyed on, and pitched his tent beyond 2
Exd 33: 7 take the tent and pitch it outside the camp 2
Num 1:51 when the tabernacle is to be pitched, the Levites 1
Jdg 4:11 and had pitched his tent as far away as the oak 2
2Sm 6:17 inside the tent which David had pitched for it; 2
16:22 So they pitched a tent for Ab'salom upon the roof; 2
1Ch 15: 1 for the ark of God, and pitched a tent for it. 2
16: 1 inside the tent which David had pitched for it; 2
2Ch 1: 4 for he had pitched a tent for it in Jerusalem. 2
Jer 6: 3 they shall pitch their tents around her 4
Dan 11:45 pitch his palatial tents between the sea 3
Wis 11: 2 and pitched their tents in untrodden places. 6
Sir 14:25 he will pitch his tent near her 5
2Mc 13:14 he pitched his camp near Modein. 7

pitch (2) 1. זֶפֶת 2. כֹּפֶר 3. πίσσα 4. piceus

Gen 6:14 the ark, and cover it inside and out with pitch. 2
Exd 2: 3 a basket . . and daubed it with bitumen and pitch; 1
Isa 34: 9 the streams of Edom shall be turned into pitch 1
9 her land shall become burning pitch. 1
2Es 2: 9 lies in lumps of pitch and heaps of ashes 4
Sir 13: 1 Whoever touches pitch will be defiled 3
Aza 1:23 naphtha, pitch, tow, and brush. 3
Bel 1:27 Then Daniel took pitch, fat, and hair 3

pitch a tent 1. אהל 2. חנה

Num 1:52 The people of Israel shall pitch their tents 2
Deu 1:33 went . . to seek you out a place to pitch your tents 2
Isa 13:20 no Arab will pitch his tent there 1

pitcher 1. גָּבִיעַ 2. כַּד 3. κάλπη

Ecc 12: 6 or the pitcher is broken at the fountain 2
Jer 35: 5 set before the Re'chabites pitchers full of wine 1
4Mc 3:12 taking a pitcher 3

piteous 1. οἰκτρός

Wis 18:10 their piteous lament for their children 1

piteously 1. οἰκτρός

4Mc 15:18 the second in torments looked at you piteously 1

pitfall 1. פַּחַת 2. שְׂבָכָה 3. שִׁיחָה 4. σκάνδαλον

Job 18: 8 a net by his own feet, and he walks on a pitfall. 2
Ps 119:85 Godless men have dug pitfalls for me 3
Lam 3:47 panic and pitfall have come upon us 1
Rom 11: 9 become . . a pitfall and a retribution for them; 4

pitiable 1. ἐλεεινός

Rev 3:17 not knowing that you are wretched, pitiable, poor 1

most pitiable 1. οἴκτιστος

2Mc 9:28 a most pitiable fate 1

something pitiable 1. ἐλεέω

2Mc 3:21 There was something pitiable in the prostration 1

pitiful 1. ταλαίπωρος

3Mc 5:47 the grievous and pitiful destruction 1

most pitiful 1. οἰκτρός

3Mc 5:24 assembled for this most pitiful spectacle 1

pitiless 1. ἀνελεήμων 2. ἀνηλεής

Wis 19: 1 were assailed to the end by pitiless anger 1
3Mc 5:10 when he had drugged the pitiless elephants 2

pity 1. חוס 2. חמל 3. חֶמְלָה 4. חנן 5. נוד 6. נחם
7. רחם 8. רַחֲמִים 9. ἐλεάω 10. ἐλεέω 11. ἔλεος
12. οἰκτίρω 13. οἶκτος 14. σπλαγχνίζομαι 15. doleo
16. misereo 17. misereor

Deu 7:16 your eye shall not pity them; neither shall you 1
13: 8 nor shall your eye pity him, nor shall you spare 1
19:13 Your eye shall not pity him, but you shall purge 1
21 You eye shall not pity; it shall be life for life 1

25:12 cut off her hand; your eye shall have no pity. 1
2Sm 12: 6 because he did this . . and because he had no pity. 2
Job 19:21 Have pity on me, have pity on me, O you my friends 4
21 Have pity on me, have pity on me, O you my friends 4
Ps 17:10 They close their hearts to pity; *
69:20 I looked for pity, but there was none; 5
72:13 He has pity on the weak and the needy 1
90:13 O LORD! How long? Have pity on thy servants! 6
102:13 Thou wilt arise and have pity on Zion; 7
14 For thy servants . . have pity on her dust. 4
103:13 As a father pities his children 7
13 As a father . . so the LORD pities those who fear 7
106:46 He caused them to be pitied by all those who held 8
109:12 nor any to pity his fatherless children! 4
Isa 13:18 no mercy . . their eyes will not pity children. 1
49:10 for he who has pity on them will lead them 7
63: 9 in his love and in his pity he redeemed them; 3
Jer 13:14 I will not pity or spare or have compassion 2
15: 5 Who will have pity on you, O Jerusalem 2
20:16 cities which the LORD overthrew without pity; 6
21: 7 he shall not pity them, or spare them 1
Lam 2:17 as he ordained . . he has demolished without pity; 2
3:43 Thou hast . . and pursued us, slaying without pity; 2
Ezk 5:11 my eye will not spare, and I will have no pity. 2
7: 4 And my eye will not spare you, nor will I have pity; 2
9 And my eye will not spare, nor will I have pity; 2
8:18 my eye will not spare, nor will I have pity; 2
9: 5 shall not spare, and you shall show no pity; 2
10 As for me, my eye will not spare, nor will I have pity 2
16: 5 No eye pitied you, to do any of these things to you 1
Hos 1: 6 for I will no more have pity on the house of Israel 7
7 But I will have pity on the house of Judah 7
2: 4 Upon her children also I will have no pity 7
23 And I will have pity on Not pitied 7
Jol 2:18 jealous for his land, and had pity on his people. 2
Ams 1:11 and cast off all pity, and his anger tore 8
Jon 4:10 You pity the plant, for which you did not labor 1
11 And should not I pity Nin'eveh, that great city 1
Zec 11: 5 their own shepherds have no pity on them. 2
6 For I will no longer have pity on the inhabitants 2
Mat 20:34 Jesus in pity touched their eyes 14
Mrk 9:22 if you can do anything, have pity on us and help us. 14
2Es 1:19 I pitied your groanings 15
8:32 For if thou hast desired to have pity on us 17
15:19 A man shall have no pity upon his neighbors 16
Jdt 6:19 and have pity on the humiliation of our people 10
AEs 13: 6 destroyed . . without pity or mercy 13
Sir 12:13 Who will pity a snake charmer bitten by a serpent 10
14 So no one will pity a man *
36:13 Have pity on the city of thy sanctuary, Jerusalem 12
Bar 4:15 nation . . who . . had no pity for a child. 10
2Mc 4:37 grieved at heart and filled with pity 11
7:27 My son, have pity on me 10
8: 2 to have pity on the temple 12
3Mc 6:22 Then the king's anger was turned to pity and tears 13
4Mc 5:33 I do not so pity my old age 12
6:12 At that point, partly out of pity for his old age 9
9: 3 do not pity us more than we pity ourselves. 9
3 do not pity us more than we pity ourselves. *
4 this pity of yours which insures our safety 11

pity *See also* move, object, obtain, take.

pity most 1. ἐλεεινός

1Co 15:19 we are of all men most to be pitied. 1

out of pity 1. σπλαγχνίζομαι

Mat 18:27 out of pity for him the lord . . released him 1

show pity 1. ἐλεέω

Sir 16: 9 showed no pity for a nation 1

without pity 1. לֹא חמל

Job 27:22 It hurls at him without pity; 1

place 1. בַּיִת 2. היה 3. יָד 4. יעד 5. יצב 6. ישב 7. כון 8. כֵּן 9. מָכוֹן 10. מָלוֹן 11. מַעֲמָד* 12. מַצָּב 13. מָקוֹם 14. נוח 15. נתן 16. עַל כֵּן 17. עמד 18. עֹמֶד 19. שׂוּם 20. שׁית 21. שׁכן 22. שָׁם 23. תַּחַת 24. אֲתַר (A) 25. רמא (A) 26. ἀναβάλλω 27. ἀναπίπτω 28. ἀνίστημι 29. ἀντί 30. βάλλω 31. γέρας 32. ἐκεῖθεν 33. ἐκχέω 34. ἐμβάλλω 35. ἐπί 36. ἐπιτίθημι 37. ἵστημι 38. καθίστημι 39. κλῆρος 40. μέρος 41. μετέχω 42. ὅς 43. παράκειμαι 44. στάσις 45. τάξις 46. τίθημι 47. τόπος 48. ὑπέρ 49. χωρίον 50. ὧδε 51. constituo 52. impono 53. locus 54. sessio 55. sto

Gen 1: 9 waters . . be gathered together into one place 13
2:21 his ribs and closed up its place with flesh; 23
3:24 at the east . . of Eden he placed the cherubim 21
8: 9 the dove found no place to set her foot *
12: 6 to the place at Shechem, to the oak of Moreh. 13
13: 3 journeyed . . to the place where his tent had 13
4 to the place where he had made an altar 13
14 look from the place where you are 13
18:24 within the city; wilt thou then destroy the place 13
26 I will spare the whole place for their sake. 13
33 to Abraham; and Abraham returned to his place. 13
19:12 you have in the city, bring them out of the place; 13
13 for we are about to destroy this place 13
14 Up, get out of this place; 13
27 to the place where he had stood before the LORD; 13
20:11 There is no fear of God at all in this place 13
13 you must do me: at every place to which we come 13
21:31 Therefore that place was called Beer-sheba; 13
22: 3 went to the place of which God had told him. 13
4 lifted up his eyes and saw the place afar off. 13
9 When they came to the place 13
14 name of that place The LORD will provide; 13
24:31 prepared the house and a place for the camels. 13
26: 7 When the men of the place asked him about his wife 13
7 lest the men of the place should kill me 13
28:11 he came to a certain place, and stayed there 13
11 Taking one of the stones of the place 13
11 his head and lay down in that place to sleep. 13
16 LORD is in this place, and I did not know it. 13
17 was afraid, and said, "How awesome is this place! 13
19 He called the name of that place Bethel; 13
29: 3 and put the stone back in its place upon the mouth 13
22 Laban gathered together all the men of the place 13
30: 2 and he said, "Am I in the place of God 23
32: 2 he called the name of that place Mahana'im. 13
30 Jacob called the name of the place Peni'el 13
33:17 the name of the place is called Succoth. 13
35: 7 built an altar, and called the place El-bethel 13
13 went up from him in the place where he had spoken 13
14 a pillar in the place where he had spoken with him 13
15 Jacob called the name of the place where God 13
38:21 he asked the men of the place, "Where is the harlot 13
22 men of the place say, 'No harlot has been here.' 13
39:20 the prison, the place where the king's prisoners 13
40:11 Pharaoh's cup, and placed the cup in Pharaoh's 15
13 and you shall place Pharaoh's cup in his hand 15
21 and he placed the cup in Pharaoh's hand; 15
42:15 you shall not go from this place *
43:30 and he sought a place to weep. *
50:11 Therefore the place was named A'bel-mizraim; *
19 Fear not, for am I in the place of God? 23
Exd 2: 3 she . . placed it among the reeds 19
3: 5 for the place on which you are standing is holy 13
8 to the place of the Canaanites, the Hittites 13
10:23 nor did any rise from his place for three days; 23
13: 3 the LORD brought you out from this place; *
15:17 the place, O LORD, which thou has made 9
16:29 remain every man of you in his place, let no man go 23
29 let no man go out of his place on the seventh day. 13
33 a jar . . and place it before the LORD, to be kept 14
34 so Aaron placed it before the testimony 14
17: 7 he called the name of the place Massah 13
18:21 and place such men over the people as rulers 19
23 also will go to their place in peace. 13
20:24 in every place where I cause my name to be 13
21:13 appoint for you a place to which he may flee. 13
23:20 to bring you to the place which I have prepared. 13
29:30 The son who is priest in his place shall wear them 23
31 and boil its flesh in a holy place; 13
32:34 now go, lead the people to the place of which I have 47
33:21 the LORD said, "Behold, there is a place by me 13
40: 7 place the laver between the tent of meeting 15
Lev 1:16 on the east side, in the place for ashes 13
4:12 a clean place, where the ashes are poured out 13
24 kill it in the place where they kill the burnt 13
29 the sin offering in the place of burnt offering 13
33 kill it for a sin offering in the place 13
6:11 the ashes outside the camp to a clean place 13
16 it shall be eaten unleavened in a holy place 13
25 In the place where the burnt offering is killed 13
26 in a holy place it shall be eaten, in the court 13
27 on which it was sprinkled in a holy place 13
7: 2 in the place where they kill the burnt offering 13
6 it shall be eaten in a holy place; it is most holy 13
8: 8 he placed the breastpiece on him 19
26 placed them on the fat and on the right thigh 19
10:13 you shall eat it in a holy place 13
14 you shall eat in any clean place, you and your sons 13
17 sin offering in the place of the sanctuary 13
13:19 in the place of the boil . . comes a . . swelling 13
14:13 he shall kill the lamb in the place where 13
13 in the place . . in the holy place 13
28 in the place where the blood of the guilt 13
40 throw them into an unclean place outside the city 13
41 shall pour into an unclean place outside the city 13
42 stones and put them in the place of those stones 23
45 out of the city to an unclean place 13
16:24 he shall bathe his body in water in a holy place 13
32 and consecrated as priest in his father's place 23
24: 9 they shall eat it in a holy place 13
Num 5:18 place in her hands the cereal offering 15
9:17 in the place where the cloud settled down 13
10:29 We are setting out for the place of which the LORD 13
11: 3 name of that place was called Tab'erah 13
24 70 men . . and placed them round about the tent. 17
34 name of that place was called Kib'roth-hatta'avah 13
13:24 That place was called the Valley of Eshcol 13
14:40 go up to the place which the LORD has promised; 13
18:10 In a most holy place shall you eat of it; *
31 may eat it in any place, you and your households; 13
19: 9 deposit them outside the camp in a clean place; 13
20: 5 to bring us to this evil place? It is no place 13
5 It is no place for grain, or figs, or vines 13
21: 3 so the name of the place was called Hormah. 13
22:26 angel of the LORD . . stood in a narrow place 13
23:13 Balak said to him, "Come with me to another place 13
27 Come now, I will take you to another place; 13
24:11 Therefore now flee to your place; 13
25 Then Balaam rose, and went back to his place; 13
32: 1 behold, the place was a place for cattle. 13
1 behold, the place was a place for cattle. 13
17 until we have brought them to their place; 13
Deu 1:31 way that you went until you came to this place.' 13
33 went . . to seek you out a place to pitch your tents 13
9: 7 from . . until you came to this place 13
11: 5 did to you . . until you came to this place; 13
24 Every place on which the sole of your foot treads 13
12: 2 surely destroy all the places where the nations 13
3 destroy their name out of that place. 13
5 seek the place which the LORD . . will choose 13
11 then to the place which the LORD . . will choose 13
13 do not offer . . at every place that you see; 13
14 at the place which the LORD will choose 13
18 place which the LORD your God will choose 13
21 If the place which the LORD your God will choose 13
26 shall go to the place which the LORD will choose 13
14:23 place which he will choose, to make his name dwell 13
24 because the place is too far from you 13
25 go to the place which the LORD your God chooses 13
15:20 eat . . at the place which the LORD will choose. 13
16: 2 at the place which the LORD will choose 13
6 at the place which the LORD your God will choose 13
7 boil it and eat it at the place which the LORD 13
11 rejoice . . at the place which the LORD your God 13
15 feast . . at the place which the LORD will choose; 13
16 appear . . at the place which he will choose 13
17: 8 go up to the place which the LORD . . will choose 13
10 from that place which the LORD will choose; 13
18: 6 if a Levite comes . . to the place which the LORD 13
21:19 city at the gate of the place where he lives 13
23:12 place outside the camp and you shall go out to it; 3
16 dwell . . in the place which he shall choose 13
26: 2 basket, and . . go to the place which the LORD 13
9 brought us into this place and gave us this land 13
29: 7 when you came to this place, Sihon . . and Og 13
31:11 to appear . . at the place which he will choose 13
Jos 1: 3 Every place that . . I have given to you 13
3: 3 you shall set out from your place and follow it 13
4: 3 from the very place where the priests' feet stood 12
3 lay them . . in the place where you lodge tonight. 10
18 the waters of the Jordan returned to their place 13
5: 8 they remained in their places in the camp 23
9 And so the name of this place is called Gilgal 13
15 Put off . . for the place where you stand is holy. 13
7:26 name of that place is called the Valley of Achor. 13
8:19 And the ambush rose quickly out of their place 13
9:27 to this day, in the place which he should choose. 13
20: 4 shall take him into the city, and give him a place 13
Jdg 2: 5 And they called the name of that place Bochim; 13
7:21 stood every man in his place round about the camp 23
15:17 and that place was called Ra'math-le'hi. 13
16: 2 they surrounded the place and lay in wait for him *
17: 8 departed . . to live where he could find a place; *
9 and I am going to sojourn where I may find a place. *
18: 3 What are you doing in this place? *
10 God has given . . a place where there is no lack 13
12 that place is called Ma'haneh-dan to this day; 13
19:13 let us draw near to one of these places, and spend 13
16 Gib'e-ah; the men of the place were Benjaminites 13
20:22 battle line in the same place where they had 13
33 Israel rose up out of their place, and set 13
33 in ambush rushed out of their place west of Geba. 13
Rut 1: 7 she set out from the place where she was 13
3: 4 when he lies down, observe the place where he lies; 13
4:10 not be cut off . . from the gate of his native place; 13
1Sm 3: 2 At that time Eli . . was lying down in his own place; 13
9 So Samuel went and lay down in his place. 13
5: 3 So they took Dagon and put him back in his place. 13
11 Send away . . and let it return to its own place 13
6: 2 Tell us with what we shall send it to its place. 13
8 take the ark of the LORD and place it on the cart 15
7:16 and he judged Israel in all these places. 13
9:22 gave them a place at the head of those . . invited 13
10:12 And a man of the place answered, "And who is 22
12: 8 who brought . . and made them dwell in this place. 13
14: 9 we will stand still in our place, and we will not go 23
46 and the Philistines went to their own place. 13
20:19 then go to the place where you hid yourself 13
25 Abner sat by Saul . . but David's place was empty. 13
27 But on the second day . . David's place was empty. 13
37 And when the lad came to the place of the arrow 13
21: 2 made an appointment . . for such and such a place. 13
23:22 know and see the place where his haunt is 13
28 therefore that place was called the Rock of Escape 13
26: 5 and came to the place where Saul had encamped; 13
5 and David saw the place where Saul lay, with Abner 13
25 David went his way, and Saul returned to his place. 13
27: 5 let a place be given me in one of the country towns 13
29: 4 return to the place to which you . . assigned him; 13

30:31 all the places where David and his men . . roamed. 13
2Sm 2:16 that place was called Hel'kath-hazzu'rim 13
23 all who came to the place where As'ahel had fallen 13
5:20 the name of that place is called Ba'al-pera'zim. 13
6: 8 and that place is called Pe'rez-uz'zah, to this day. 13
17 they brought in the ark . . and set it in its place 13
7: 7 In all places where I have moved with . . Israel •
10 And I will appoint a place for my people Israel 13
10 that they may dwell in their own place 23
11:16 Jo'ab . . assigned Uri'ah to the place 13
12:30 the crown . . and it was placed on David's head. 2
16: 8 the house of Saul, in whose place you have reigned; 23
17: 9 in one of the pits, or in some other place. 13
12 come upon him in some place where he is to be found 13
19:13 commander of my army . . in place of Jo'ab.' 23
21: 5 so that we should have no place in all . . Israel 5
1Kg 2:24 has established me, and placed me on the throne 6
35 king put Benai'ah . . over the army in place of Jo'ab 23
35 king put Zadok . . in the place of Abi'athar. 23
3: 7 made thy servant king in place of David my father 23
4:28 they brought to the place where it was required 13
5: 1 they had anointed him king in place of his father; 23
5 whom I will set upon your throne in your place 23
9 rafts to go by sea to the place you direct 13
8: 6 the ark . . to its place, in the inner sanctuary 13
7 spread out their wings over the place of the ark 13
13 house, a place for thee to dwell in for ever. 9
20 I have risen in the place of David my father 23
21 I have provided a place for the ark, in which is 13
29 this house, the place of which thou hast said 13
29 which thy servant offers toward this place. 13
30 hearken . . when they pray toward this place; 13
30 hear thou in heaven thy dwelling place; 13
35 if they pray toward this place, and acknowledge 13
39 hear . . in heaven thy dwelling place, and forgive 9
43 hear thou in heaven thy dwelling place 9
49 hear thou in heaven thy dwelling place 9
12:32 he placed in Bethel the priests . . he had made. 17
13: 8 I will not eat bread or drink water in this place; 13
16 eat bread nor drink water with you in this place; 13
22 and drunk water in the place of which he said 13
19:16 Eli'sha . . to be prophet in your place. 23
20:24 remove . . and put commanders in their places; 23
21:19 In the place where dogs licked up the blood 13
2Kg 5:11 wave his hand over the place, and cure the leper. 13
6: 1 the place where we dwell . . is too small for us. 13
2 and let us make a place for us to dwell there. 13
6 When he showed him the place, he cut off a stick 13
8 At such and such a place shall be my camp. 13
9 Beware that you do not pass this place 13
10 the king of Israel sent to the place 13
16:14 from the place between his altar and the house •
17: 6 and placed them in Halah, and on the Habor 6
24 brought people . . and placed them in the cities 6
26 nations which you have carried away and placed 6
18:25 I have come up against this place to destroy it? 13
22:16 evil upon this place and upon its inhabitants 13
17 my wrath will be kindled against this place 13
19 you heard how I spoke against this place 13
20 all the evil which I will bring upon this place.' 13
23:14 and filled their places with the bones of men. 13
34 Neco made Eli'akim . . king in the place of Josi'ah 23
1Ch 4:41 exterminated them . . and settled in their place 23
5:22 And they dwelt in their place until the exile. 23
13:11 and that place is called Pe'rez-uz'za to this day. 13
14:11 the name of that place is called Ba'al-pera'zim. 13
15: 1 he prepared a place for the ark of God 13
3 to bring up the ark of the LORD to its place 13
12 to the place that I have prepared for it. •
16:27 strength and joy are in his place. 13
17: 6 In all places where I have moved with Israel •
9 I will appoint a place for my people Israel 13
9 plant them, that they may dwell in their own place 23
20: 2 the crown . . was placed on David's head. •
2Ch 1: 4 to the place that David had prepared for it •
2: 6 except as a place to burn incense before him? •
3: 1 at the place that David had appointed 13
8 And he made the most holy place; 1
10 In the most holy place he made two cherubim 1
4: 8 made ten tables, and placed them in the temple 14
5: 7 the priests brought the ark . . to its place 13
8 spread out their wings over the place of the ark 13
6: 2 exalted house, a place for thee to dwell 9
10 for I have risen in the place of David my father 23
20 place where thou hast promised to set thy name 13
20 which thy servant offers toward this place. 13
21 hearken . . when they pray toward this place; 13
21 yea, hear thou from heaven thy dwelling place; 13
26 if they pray toward this place, and acknowledge 13
30 then hear thou from heaven thy dwelling place 9
33 hear thou from heaven thy dwelling place, and do 9
39 hear thou from heaven thy dwelling place 9
40 thy ears attentive to a prayer of this place. 13
7:12 and have chosen this place for myself 13
15 to the prayer that is made in this place. 13
8:11 the places to which the ark of the LORD has come •
17: 2 He placed forces in all the fortified cities 15
19 king had placed in the fortified cities 15
20:26 therefore the name of that place has been called 13

24:11 take it and return it to its place. 13
34:24 I will bring evil upon this place 13
25 my wrath will be poured out upon this place 13
27 words against this place and its inhabitants 13
28 evil which I will bring upon this place 13
31 the king stood in his place and made a covenant 18
35:10 prepared for, the priests stood in their place 18
15 in their place according to the command of David 11
Ezr 1: 4 let each survivor, in whatever place he sojourns 13
4 survivor . . be assisted by the men of his place 13
7 carried . . and placed in the house of his gods. 15
3: 3 set the altar in its place, for fear was upon them 7
6: 3 place where sacrifices are offered 24
5 brought back to the temple . . each to its place; 24
8:17 Iddo, the leading man at the place Casiphi'a 13
17 temple servants at the place Casiphi'a 13
9: 8 to give us a secure hold within his holy place 13
Neh 1: 9 gather . . and bring them to the place 13
2: 3 when the city, the place of my fathers' sepulchres 1
14 there was no place for the beast that was under me 13
4:12 From all the places where they live 13
20 place where you hear the sound of the trumpet 13
8: 7 while the people remained in their places. 18
9: 3 stood up in their place and read from the book 18
12:27 sought the Levites in all their places 13
13: 6 While this was taking place I was not •
Est 7: 8 to the place where they were drinking wine 1
Job 2:11 they came each from his own place 13
6:17 when it is hot, they vanish from their place. 13
7:10 nor does his place know him any more. 13
8:18 If he is destroyed from his place 13
9: 6 who shakes the earth out of its place 13
14:18 the rock is removed from its place; 13
16: 4 I also could speak as you do, if you were in my place; 23
18: 4 or the rock be removed out of its place? 13
21 such is the place of him who knows not God. 13
20: 4 from of old, since man was placed upon earth 19
9 nor will his place any more behold him. 13
27:21 he is gone; it sweeps him out of his place. 13
23 hands at him, and hisses at him from its place. 13
28: 1 a place for gold which they refine. 13
6 Its stones are the place of sapphires 13
12 And where is the place of understanding? 13
20 where is the place of understanding? 13
23 God understands . . and he knows its place. 13
34:24 sets others in their place. 23
36:20 night, when peoples are cut off in their place. 23
37: 1 my heart trembles, and leaps out of its place. 13
38:12 caused the dawn to know its place 13
19 where is the place of darkness 13
24 way to the place where the light is distributed •
Ps 12: 5 I will place him in the safety for which he longs. 20
24: 3 And who shall stand in his holy place? 13
26: 8 thy house, and the place where thy glory dwells. 13
37:10 look well at his place, he will not be there. 13
44:19 shouldst have broken us in the place of jackals 13
66:12 yet hou hast brought us forth to a spacious place. •
103:16 it is gone, and its place knows it no more. 13
22 all his works, in all places of his dominion. 13
104: 8 to the place which thou didst appoint for them. 13
132: 5 until I find a place for the LORD, a dwelling place 13
Prv 4: 9 She will place on your head a fair garland; 15
15: 3 The eyes of the LORD are in every place 13
25: 6 Do not . . stand in the place of the great; 13
Ecc 1: 5 and hastens to the place where it rises. 13
7 to the place where the streams flow 13
3:16 in the place of justice, even there was 13
16 and in the place of righteousness, even there was 13
20 All go to one place . . and all turn to dust again. 13
4:15 youth, who was to stand in his place; 23
6: 6 though he should . . do not all go to the one place? 13
8:10 they used to go in and out of the holy place 13
10: 4 do not leave your place 13
11: 3 in the place where the tree falls, there it . . lie. 13
Isa 7:23 every place where there used to be 1,000 vines 13
25 will become a place where cattle are let loose •
13:13 and the earth will be shaken out of its place 13
14: 2 will take them and bring them to their place 13
18: 7 Zion, the place of the name of the LORD of hosts. 13
22:22 I will place on his shoulder the key of the house 15
23 I will fasten him like a peg in a sure place 13
25 the peg that was fastened in a sure place 13
25:10 and Moab shall be trodden down in his place 23
26:21 the LORD is coming forth out of his place 13
28: 8 full of vomit, no place is without filthiness. 13
30:28 and to place on the jaws of the peoples a bridle •
33:21 a place of broad rivers and streams 13
23 it cannot hold the mast firm in its place 8
46: 7 they set it in its place, and it stands there; 23
7 it stands there; it cannot move from its place. 13
49:20 say in your ears: 'The place is too narrow for me; 13
54: 2 Enlarge the place of your tent 13
60:13 the pine, to beautify the place of my sanctuary; 13
13 and I will make the place of my feet glorious. 13
66: 1 is the house . . and what is the place of my rest? 13
Jer 4: 7 he has gone forth from his place 13
5:22 I placed the sand as the bound for the sea 19
6: 3 around her, they shall pasture, each in his place. 3
7: 3 and I will let you dwell in this place. 13

6 or shed innocent blood in this place 13
7 then I will let you dwell in this place 13
12 Go now to my place that was in Shiloh 13
14 the place which I gave to you and to your fathers 13
20 and my wrath will be poured out on this place 13
8: 3 in all the places where I have driven them 13
13: 7 waistcloth from the place where I had hidden it. 13
14:13 but I will give you assured peace in this place. 13
16: 2 shall you have sons or daughters in this place. 13
3 the sons and daughters who are born in this place 13
9 Behold, I will make to cease from this place 13
17:12 throne . . is the place of our sanctuary. 13
26 Judah and the places round about Jerusalem •
19: 3 Behold, I am bringing such evil upon this place 13
4 and have profaned this place by burning incense 13
4 filled this place with the blood of innocents 13
6 when this place shall no more be called Topheth 13
7 in this place I will make void the plans of Judah 13
11 because there will be no place else to bury. 13
12 Thus will I do to this place, says the LORD 13
13 shall be defiled like the place of Topheth. 13
22: 3 nor shed innocent blood in this place. 13
11 and who went away from this place 13
12 in the place where they have carried him captive 13
24: 1 two baskets of figs placed before the temple 4
5 from Judah, whom I have sent away from this place 13
9 in all the places where I shall drive them. 13
27:22 bring them back and restore them to this place. 13
28: 3 Within two years I will bring back to this place 13
3 away from this place and carried to Babylon. 13
4 I will also bring back to this place Jeconi'ah 13
6 and bring back to this place from Babylon 13
13 but I will make in their place bars of iron. 23
29:10 my promise and bring you back to this place. 13
14 and all the places where I have driven you 13
14 and I will bring you back to the place 13
32:37 I will bring them back to this place 13
44 in the places about Jerusalem, and in the cities •
33:10 Thus says the LORD: In this place of which you say 13
12 In this place which is waste, without man or beast 13
40: 2 God pronounced this evil against this place; 13
12 then all the Jews returned from all the places 13
42:18 You shall see this place no more. 13
22 in the place where you desire to go to live. 13
44:29 says the LORD, that I will punish you in this place 13
45: 5 as a prize of war in all places to which you may go. 13
51:62 say, 'O LORD, thou hast said concerning this place 13
Ezk 3:12 and as the glory of the LORD arose from its place 13
25 O son of man, behold, cords will be placed upon you 15
4: 3 place it as an iron wall between you and the city; 15
12: 3 you shall go like an exile from your place 13
3 from your place to another place in their sight. 13
17: 5 he placed it beside abundant waters. •
16 the place where the king dwells who made him king 13
21:30 In the place where you were created 13
23:41 table . . on which you had placed my incense 19
26: 5 midst of the sea a place for the spreading of nets; •
14 you shall be a place for the spreading of nets; •
20 or have a place in the land of the living. 28
28:14 With an anointed guardian cherub I placed you; 15
31: 4 its rivers flow round the place of its planting •
32:25 they are placed among the slain. 15
34:12 from all places where they have been scattered 13
26 and the places round about my hill a blessing; •
36:36 I, the LORD, have rebuilt the ruined places, •
37:14 I will place you in your own land; 14
38:15 come from your place out of the uttermost parts 13
39:11 I will give to Gog a place for burial in Israel 13
42:13 and the guilt offering, for the place is holy. 13
43: 7 Son of man, this is the place of my throne 13
7 of my throne and the place of the soles of my feet 13
45: 4 it shall be a place for their houses 13
46:19 I saw a place at the extreme western end of them. 13
20 This is the place where the priests shall boil 13
47:10 it will be a place for the spreading of nets; •
Dan 7: 9 As I looked, thrones were placed 25
8:11 place of his sanctuary was overthrown. 9
22 in place of which four others arose 23
11: 7 branch from her roots shall arise in his place; 16
20 arise in his place one who shall send an exactor 16
21 In his place shall arise a contemptible person 16
Hos 1:10 and in the place where it was said to them 13
5:15 I will return again to my place 13
Jol 3: 7 up from the place to which you have sold them 13
Ams 2:13 Behold, I will press you down in your place 23
4: 6 and lack of bread in all your places 13
8: 3 in every place they shall be cast out in silence. 13
Mic 1: 3 behold, the LORD is coming forth out of his place 13
6 Sama'ria a heap . . a place for planting vineyards; •
Zep 1: 4 I will cut off from this place the remnant of Ba'al 13
2:11 and to him shall bow down, each in its place 13
Hag 2: 9 in this place I will give prosperity 13
15 Before a stone was placed upon a stone 19
Zec 6:12 for he shall grow up in his place 23
12: 6 Jerusalem shall still be inhabited in its place 23
14:10 Gate of Benjamin to the place of the former gate 13
Mal 1:11 in every place incense is offered to my name 13
Mat 2: 9 to rest over the place where the child was. •
22 in place of his father Herod, he was afraid to go 29

12:43 he passes through waterless places 47
14:15 This is a lonely place, and the day is now over 47
35 when the men of that place recognized him 47
24: 7 famines and earthquakes in various places 47
15 the prophet Daniel, standing in the holy place 47
25:33 he will place the sheep at his right hand 37
26:36 to a place called Gethsem'ane 49
52 Put your sword back into its place 47
27:33 when they came to a place called Gol'gotha 47
33 (which means the place of a skull) 47
28: 6 Come, see the place where he lay. 47
Mrk 1:35 he rose and went out to a lonely place 47
6:10 stay there until you leave the place. 32
11 if any place will not receive you 47
31 Come away by yourselves to a lonely place 47
32 in the boat to a lonely place by themselves. 47
35 This is a lonely place, and the hour is now late; 47
13: 8 there will be earthquakes in various places 47
14:32 they went to a place which was called Gethsem'ane; 49
15:22 they brought him to the place called Gol'gotha 47
22 Gol'gotha (which means the place of a skull). 47
16: 6 he is not here; see the place where they laid him. 47
Lke 2: 7 because there was no place for them in the inn. 47
4:17 found the place where it was written 47
37 reports of him went out into every place 47
42 he departed and went into a lonely place 47
6:17 he came down with them and stood on a level place 47
9:12 we are here in a lonely place. 47
10: 1 into every town and place 47
32 a Levite, when he came to the place and saw him 47
11: 1 He was praying in a certain place 47
24 he passes through waterless places seeking rest; 47
14: 9 'Give place to this man,' 47
9 will begin with shame to take the lowest place. 47
10 go and sit in the lowest place 47
16:28 lest they also come into this place of torment.' 47
19: 5 when Jesus came to the place, he looked up and said 47
21:11 in various places famines and pestilences 47
22:40 when he came to the place he said to them, "Pray 47
23: 5 from Galilee even to this place. 50
33 they came to the place which is called The Skull 47
Joh 4:20 in Jerusalem is the place . . to worship. 47
5:13 there was a crowd in the place. 47
6:10 Now there was much grass in the place 47
23 However, boats from Tiber'i-as came near the place 47
8: 3 placing her in the midst 37
10:40 to the place where John at first baptized 47
11: 6 he stayed two days longer in the place where he was. 47
30 still in the place where Martha had met him. 47
48 and destroy both our holy place and our nation. 47
13:12 taken his garments, and resumed his place 27
14: 2 I go to prepare a place for you? 47
3 when I go and prepare a place for you 47
18: 2 Now Judas, who betrayed him, also knew the place; 47
19:13 a place called The Pavement 47
17 to the place called the place of a skull •
17 to the place called the place of a skull 47
20 the place where Jesus was crucified 47
41 Now in the place where he was crucified 47
20: 7 and the napkin . . rolled up in a place by itself. 47
25 place my finger in the mark of the nails 30
25 place my hand in his side 30
27 and put out your hand, and place it in my side 30
Act 1:25 to take the place in this ministry 47
25 to go to his own place. 47
2: 1 they were all together in one place. •
4:31 the place in which they were gathered together 47
6:13 to speak words against this holy place and the law; 47
14 Jesus of Nazareth will destroy this place 47
7: 7 they shall come out and worship me in this place.' 47
33 the place where you are standing is holy ground. 47
49 what is the place of my rest? 47
12:17 Then he departed and went to another place. 47
16: 3 the Jews that were in those places 47
13 where we supposed there was a place of prayer; •
16 As we were going to the place of prayer •
21:28 against the people and the law and this place; 47
28 he has defiled this holy place. 47
26:18 a place among those who are sanctified by faith 39
27: 8 we came to a place called Fair Havens 47
28: 7 Now in the neighborhood of that place were lands 47
Rom 9:26 And in the very place where it was said to them 47
11:17 and you . . were grafted in their place •
1Co 1: 2 all those who in every place call on the name 47
11:18 in the first place, when you assemble as a church •
Eph 2:15 create in himself one new man in place of the two •
1Ti 2: 8 in every place the men should pray 47
Heb 4: 5 again in this place he said •
5: 6 as he says also in another place •
11: 8 a place which he was to receive as an inheritance; 47
2Pe 1:19 as to a lamp shining in a dark place 47
Rev 2: 5 and remove your lampstand from its place 47
6:14 mountain and island was removed from its place 47
11: 9 and refuse to let them be placed in a tomb 46
12: 6 wilderness, where she has a place prepared by God 47
8 there was no longer any place for them in heaven. 47
14 to the place where she is to be nourished 47
16:16 the place which is called in Hebrew Armaged'don. 47
20:11 and no place was found for them. 47
1Es 1: 2 having placed the priests 37
15 were in their place 45
2: 6 be helped by the men of his place with gold 47
16 living in Samaria and other places 47
4:34 returns to its place in one day. 47
5:50 they erected the altar in its place 47
6:26 to be placed where they had been. 46
27 Darius commanded . . to keep away from the place 47
8:45 the leading man at the place of the treasury 47
46 the treasurers at that place 47
78 to leave to us a root and a name in thy holy place 47
9:13 with the elders and judges of each place 47
2Es 2:16 I will raise up the dead from their places 53
23 give you the first place in my resurrection. 54
43 and on the head of each of them he placed a crown 52
46 Who is that young man who places crowns on them 52
4:19 to the sea is assigned a place to carry its waves. 53
29 if the place where the evil has been sown 53
42 these places hasten to give back those things •
5: 8 There shall be chaos also in many places 53
6: 1 before the portals of the world were in place 55
14 if the place where you are standing is . . shaken 53
22 Sown places shall suddenly appear unsown 53
29 the place where I was standing began to rock ‡
54 over these thou didst place Adam 51
7: 4 it has an entrance set in a narrow place 53
36 and opposite it shall be the place of rest 53
124 because we have lived in unseemly places? 53
10:27 and a place of huge foundations showed itself. 53
54 a place where the city . . was to be revealed. 53
11: 8 let each sleep in his own place 53
13 so that its place was not seen 53
24 but four remained in their place. 53
12:37 and put it in a hidden place; 53
41 that you have forsaken us and sit in this place? 53
42 and like a lamp in a dark place 53
48 but I have come to this place to pray 53
13: 7 or place from which the mountain was carved 53
31 city against city, place against place 53
31 city against city, place against place 53
15:40 shall pour out upon every high and lofty place 53
16:26 For in all places there shall be great solitude; 53
62 and searches out hidden things in hidden places. •
70 For in many places and in neighboring cities 53
Tob 1: 4 This was the place which had been chosen •
15 Sennacherib his son reigned in his place 29
21 Then Esarhaddon, his son, reigned in his place 29
4:17 Place your bread on the grave of the righteous 33
7:18 the Lord . . grant you joy in place of this sorrow 29
Jdt 6:14 placed him before the magistrates of their city 38
8:12 in the place of God among the sons of men? 48
13:10 who placed it in her food bag 34
AEs 13: 3 has attained the second place in the kingdom 31
16: 5 many of those who are set in places of authority 35
19 post . . this letter publicly in every place 47
Wis 3:14 a place of great delight in the temple of the Lord. 39
11: 2 and pitched their tents in untrodden places. •
19:22 to help them at all times and in all places. 47
Sir 4:13 the Lord will bless the place she enters. 42
10:14 has seated the lowly in their place. 29
15 has planted the humble in their place. 29
12:12 lest he overthrow you and take your place 47
14:26 he will place his children under her shelter 46
17: 4 He placed the fear of them in all living beings 46
22:18 Fences set on a high place will not stand firm •
23:19 perceive even the hidden places. 40
24: 4 I dwelt in high places •
7 Among all these I sought a resting place •
30:18 like offerings of food placed upon a grave. 43
33:12 he turned them out of their place. 44
36:13 Jerusalem, the place of thy rest. 47
38:12 give the physician his place 47
41:19 of theft, in the place where you live 47
47: 9 He placed singers before the altar 37
Bar 3:15 Who has found her place? And who has entered her 47
19 to Hades, and others have arisen in their place. 29
Aza 1:15 no place to make an offering before thee 47
Bel 1:11 set forth the food and mix and place the wine 46
39 returned Habakkuk to his own place. 47
1Mc 1: 8 his officers began to rule, each in his own place. 47
2:12 behold, our holy place, our beauty, and our glory •
3: 1 Then Judas his son . . took command in his place. 29
35 banish the memory of them from the place 47
46 Israel formerly had a place of prayer in Mizpah. 47
4:43 removed the defiled stones to an unclean place. 47
46 in a convenient place on the temple hill 47
51 They placed the bread on the table 36
6:54 they had been scattered, each to his own place. 47
57 the place against which we are fighting is strong 47
62 saw what a strong fortress the place was 47
8: 4 even though the place was far distant from them. 47
9:45 there is no place to turn. 47
51 he placed garrisons in them to harass Israel. 46
10:13 each left his place and departed to his own land. 47
40 from appropriate places. 47
73 where there is no stone or pebble, or place to flee. 47
11:37 and put up in a conspicuous place 47
38 each man to his own place 47
40 to become king in place of his father 29
69 Then the men in ambush emerged from their places 47
12: 2 to the Spartans and to other places. 47
13: 8 You are our leader in place of Judas 29
14 had risen up in place of Jonathan his brother 29
20 to every place he went. 47
32 and became king in his place 29
14:17 his brother had become high priest in his place 29
33 he placed there a garrison of Jews. 46
48 to put them up in a conspicuous place 47
15:29 taken possession of many places in my kingdom. 47
30 tribute money of the places . . you have conquered 47
16: 7 and placed the horsemen in the midst of the infantry •
2Mc 1:14 Antiochus came to the place 47
19 the place was unknown to any one. 47
29 Plant thy people in thy holy place, as Moses said. 47
33 in the place where . . 47
34 and enclosed the place and made it sacred. •
2: 7 The place shall be unknown 47
8 the place should be specially consecrated. 47
18 into his holy place 47
18 has purified the place. 47
3: 2 the kings themselves honored the place 47
12 had trusted in the holiness of the place 47
18 the holy place was . . brought into contempt. 47
30 acted marvelously for his own place 47
38 certainly is about the place some power of God. 47
39 he . . watches over that place himself 47
4:33 having first withdrawn to a place of sanctuary 47
34 to come out from the place of sanctuary •
38 led him about the whole city to that very place 47
5:10 he had . . no place in the tomb of his fathers. 41
16 to enhance the glory and honor of the place. 47
17 therefore he was disregarding the holy place. 47
19 the nation for the sake of the holy place 47
19 the place for the sake of the nation. 47
20 the place itself shared in the misfortunes 47
6: 2 as did the people who dwelt in that place. 47
8:17 against the holy place 47
31 stored them all carefully in strategic places 47
9:17 would visit every inhabited place 47
10: 7 the purifying of his own holy place. 47
17 they gained possession of the places 47
19 he himself set off for places where . . 47
34 relying on the strength of the place 47
11: 5 which was a fortified place 49
12: 2 some of the governors in various places 47
18 in one place he had left a very strong garrison. 47
21 a place called Carnaim •
21 that place was hard to besiege and difficult of access 49
13: 4 by the method which is the custom in that place. 47
5 there is a tower in that place, 50 cubits high 47
23 and showed generosity to the holy place. 47
14:22 armed men in readiness at key places 47
15:34 he who has kept his own place undefiled. 47
3Mc 1: 9 and did what was fitting for the holy place 47
9 Then, upon entering the place 47
23 created a considerable disturbance in the holy place 47
29 the profanation of the place. 47
2: 9 chose this city and sanctified this place 47
10 when we come to this place and pray. 47
14 undertakes to violate the holy place 47
16 you sanctified this place. 47
3: 1 all should promptly be gathered into one place •
29 Every place detected sheltering a Jew 47
4: 1 In every place, then, where this decree arrived •
3 or what habitable place at all 47
7 as far as the place of embarkation. •
11 men had been brought to the place called Schedia •
18 some at the place 47
5:44 the places in the city most favorable 47
6:30 in that same place in which they had expected 47
31 the place which had been prepared 47
7: 8 with no one in any place doing them harm at all 47
17 because of a characteristic of the place 47
20 dedicating a place of prayer •
20 brought safely . . each to his own place. •
4Mc 4: 9 to shield the holy place 47
12 would praise the blessedness of the holy place 47
5: 1 sitting in state . . on a certain high place 47
9:12 they placed him upon the wheel. 26
15:20 when you saw the place 49

place *See also* allotted, any, appointed, assign, bare, broad, burial, burning, burying, dark, deserted, desolate, dry, dwelling, every, find, forsaken, give, good, heavenly, hiding, high, hollow, holy, inhabited, lodging, lofty, lonely, low, lurking, market, meeting, one, open, parched, place, pleasant, precious, precipitous, priest's, proper, put, resting, rough, sacred, secret, set, slippery, standing, starting, steep, take, waste, watering.

place a seal upon 1. supersigno
2Es 6:20 when the seal is placed upon the age 1

place about 1. סָבִיב
Jer 33:13 the land of Benjamin, the places about Jerusalem 1

place before 1. παρατίθημι 2. προτίθημι
Sir 15:16 He has placed before you fire and water 1

LJr 1:27 gifts are placed before them 1
4Mc 8:13 when the guards had placed before them wheels 2

place in charge 1. καθίστημι
1Mc 7:20 He placed Alcimus in charge of the country 1

place of ambush 1. מַאֲרָב
Jos 8: 9 and they went to the place of ambush 1

place of appointed feast 1. מוֹעֵד
Lam 2: 6 laid in ruins the place of his appointed feasts; 1

place of burial 1. קְבֻרָה
Deu 34: 6 no man knows the place of his burial to this day. 1

place of captivity 1. αἰχμαλωσία
Tob 14: 5 they will return from the places of their captivity 1

place of defense 1. מִשְׂגָּב
Isa 33:16 his place of defense will be the fortresses 1

place of honor 1. προκάθημαι 2. πρωτοκλισία
Mat 23: 6 they love the place of honor at feasts 2
Mrk 12:39 and the places of honor at feasts 2
Lke 14: 7 when he marked how they chose the places of honor 2
8 do not sit down in a place of honor 2
20:46 and love . . the places of honor at feasts 2
1Es 9:45 he had the place of honor 1

place of judgment 1. κριτήριον
Sus 1:49 Return to the place of judgment. 1

place of refuge 1. φυγαδευτήριον
1Mc 1:53 hiding in every place of refuge they had. 1
10:14 it served as a place of refuge. 1

place of shelter 1. οἴκημα
Tob 2: 4 and removed the body to a place of shelter 1

place of springs 1. מַעְיָן
Ps 84: 6 valley of Baca they make it a place of springs; 1

place to lie down 1. רֵבֶץ
Isa 65:10 the Valley of Achor a place for herds to lie down 1

place to place 1. καθεξῆς
Act 18:23 went from place to place through the region 1

place to rest 1. מְנוּחָה
Mic 2:10 Arise and go, for this is no place to rest; 1

place to which scattered 1. διασπορά
Jdt 5:19 the places to which they were scattered 1

place where dwells 1. מוֹשָׁב
Num31:10 All their cities in the places where they dwelt 1

place where lives 1. גְּבוּל 2. παροικία
2Ch 11:13 from all places where they lived. 1
Jdt 5: 9 to leave the place where they were living 2

place where lodges 1. מָלוֹן
Jos 4: 8 carried them . . to the place where they lodged 1

place where stands 1. מַצָּב
Jos 4: 9 place where the feet of the priests . . had stood; 1
places *See* change, various.

plague 1. דֶּבֶר 2. מַגֵּפָה 3. מַכָּה 4. נֶגַע 5. נגף 6. נֶגֶף 7. רֶשֶׁף 8. θραῦσις 9. μάστιξ 10. πληγή 11. confractio 12. plaga
Gen 12:17 his house with great plagues because of Sar'ai 4
Exd 8: 2 behold, I will plague all your country with frogs; 5
9: 3 very severe plague upon your cattle which are 1
14 For this time I will send all my plagues upon 2
11: 1 Yet one plague more I will bring upon Pharaoh 4
12:13 no plague shall fall upon you to destroy you 6
30:12 that there be no plague among them 6
Lev 26:21 I will bring more plagues upon you, sevenfold 3
Num 8:19 there may be no plague among the people of Israel 6
11:33 LORD smote the people with a very great plague. 3
14:37 died by plague before the LORD. 2
16:46 wrath has gone forth . . the plague has begun. 6
47 plague had already begun among the people; 6
48 he stood between . . and the plague was stopped. 2
49 Now those who died by the plague were 14,700 2
50 Aaron returned . . when the plague was stopped. 2
25: 8 Thus the plague was stayed from the people 2
9 those that died by the plague were 24,000. 2
18 their sister, who was slain on the day of the plague 2
26: 1 After the plague the LORD said to Moses 2
31:16 plague came among the congregation of the LORD. 2
Jos 22:17 there came a plague upon the congregation 6
24: 5 I plagued Egypt with what I did in the midst of it; 5
1Sm 4: 8 smote the Egyptians with every sort of plague 3
6: 4 the same plague was upon all of you and upon 2
2Sm 24:21 build an altar . . that the plague may be averted 2
25 the LORD heeded . . and the plague was averted 2
1Kg 8:37 whatever plague, whatever sickness there is; 4
1Ch 21:17 but let not the plague be upon thy people. 2
22 that the plague may be averted from the people. 2
2Ch 6:28 whatever plague, whatever sickness there is; 4
21:14 LORD will bring a great plague on your people 2
Ps 38:11 companions stand aloof from my plague 4
78:50 but gave their lives over to the plague. 1
106:29 plague broke out among them. 2
30 interposed, and the plague was stayed. 2
Hos 13:14 O Death, where are your plagues? 1
Hab 3: 5 pestilence, and plague followed close behind. 7
Zec 14:12 the plague with which the LORD will smite 2
15 plague like this plague shall fall on the horses 2
15 plague like this plague shall fall on the horses 2
18 then upon them shall come the plague 2
Lke 7:21 he cured many of diseases and plagues 9
Rev 9:18 By . . three plagues a third of mankind was killed 10
20 rest of mankind, who were not killed by . . plagues 10
11: 6 and to smite the earth with every plague 10
15: 1 I saw . . seven angels with seven plagues 10
6 came the seven angels with the seven plagues 10
8 seven plagues of the seven angels were ended. 10
16: 9 God who had power over these plagues 10
21 till men cursed God for the plague of the hail 10
21 men cursed God . . so fearful was that plague. 10
18: 4 Come out of her . . lest you share in her plagues; 10
8 so shall her plagues come in a single day 10
21: 9 the seven bowls full of the seven last plagues 10
22:18 God will add to him the plagues 10
2Es 7:108and David for the plague 11
15:11 and will smite Egypt with plagues 12
12 for the plague of chastisement and punishment 12
16:19 Behold, famine and plague 12
Jdt 5:12 afflicted . . Egypt with incurable plagues 10
Wis 18:20 a plague came upon the multitude in the desert 8
Sir 40: 9 calamities, famine and affliction and plague. 9
2Mc 7:37 by afflictions and plagues 9
plague *See also* bring, send.

plain 1. אֶרֶץ עֵמֶק 2. בִּקְעָה 3. כִּכָּר 4. מִישׁוֹר 5. עֵמֶק 6. עֲרָבָה 7. בִּקְעָא (A) 8. γῆ πεδινός 9. πεδεινός 10. πεδίον 11. ταπεινός 12. campester 13. campus
Gen 11: 2 as men migrated from the east, they found a plain 2
Num22: 1 Israel set out, and encamped in the plains of Moab 6
26: 3 in the plains of Moab by the Jordan at Jericho 6
63 numbered . . Israel in the plains of Moab 6
31:12 at the camp on the plains of Moab by the Jordan 6
33:48 encamped in the plains of Moab by the Jordan 6
49 as far as Abel-shittim in the plains of Moab. 6
50 in the plains of Moab by the Jordan at Jericho 6
35: 1 said to Moses in the plains of Moab by the Jordan 6
36:13 in the plains of Moab by the Jordan at Jericho. 6
Deu 34: 1 Moses went up from the plains of Moab 6
3 Negeb, and the Plain, that is, the valley of Jericho 3
8 Israel wept for Moses in the plains of Moab 6
Jos 4:13 passed . . for battle, to the plains of Jericho. 6
5:10 kept the passover . . in the plains of Jericho. 6
13:32 which Moses distributed in the plains of Moab 6
17:16 all the Canaanites who dwell in the plain have 1
Jdg 1:19 could not drive out the inhabitants of the plain 5
34 they did not allow them to come down to the plain; 5
2Sm 18:23 Then Ahi'ma-az ran by the way of the plain 3
1Kg 7:46 In the plain of the Jordan the king cast them 3
20:23 let us fight against them in the plain 4
25 we will fight against them in the plain 4
2Kg 25: 5 and overtook him in the plains of Jericho; 6
2Ch 4:17 In the plain of the Jordan the king cast them 3
26:10 he had large herds . . in the plain 4
35:22 but joined battle in the plain of Megid'do. 2
Neh 3:22 priests, the men of the Plain, repaired. 3
6: 2 meet . . in one of the villages in the plain of Ono. 2
Isa 40: 4 become level, and the rough places a plain. 2
Jer 21:13 I am against you . . O rock of the plain 4
39: 5 and overtook Zedeki'ah in the plains of Jericho; 6
48: 8 the plain shall be destroyed 4
52: 8 and overtook Zedeki'ah in the plains of Jericho; 6
Ezk 3:22 and he said to me, "Arise, go forth into the plain 2
23 So I arose and went forth into the plain; 2
8: 4 like the vision that I saw in the plain. 2
Dan 3: 1 plain of Dura, in the province of Babylon. 7
Zec 4: 7 Before Zerub'babel you shall become a plain; 4
12:11 for Hadadrim'mon in the plain of Megid'do. 2
14:10 The whole land shall be turned into a plain 6
1Es 1:29 He joined battle with him in the plain of Megiddo 10
2Es 4:13 I went into a forest of trees of the plain 13
15 let us go up and subdue the forest of the plain 13
7: 6 There is a city built and set on a plain 12
Jdt 1: 5 the great plain which is on the borders of Ragae. 10
6 the plain where Arioch ruled the Elymaeans. 10
8 Upper Galilee and the great Plain of Esdraelon 10
2:21 from Nineveh to the plain of Bectileth 10
27 Then he went down into the plain of Damascus 10
4: 6 opposite the plain near Dothan 10
5: 1 and set up barricades in the plains 10
6:11 out of the camp into the plain 10
11 from the plain they went up into the hill country 9
7:18 rest of the Assyrian army encamped in the plain 10
14: 2 as if you were going down to the plain 10
15: 2 fled by every path across the plain 10
7 in the hill country and in the plain 9
Wis 19: 7 a grassy plain out of the raging waves 10
1Mc 3:24 They pursued them . . to the plain 10
40 they encamped near Emmaus in the plain. 8
4: 6 At daybreak Judas appeared in the plain 10
14 The Gentiles were crushed and fled into the plain 10
15 to the plains of Idumea, and to Azotus and Jamnia; 10
21 the army of Judas drawn up in the plain for battle 10
5:52 they crossed the Jordan into the large plain 10
6:40 some troops were on the plain 11
10:71 come down to the plain to meet us 10
73 my cavalry and such an army in the plain 10
77 At the same time he advanced into the plain 10
83 the cavalry was dispersed in the plain 10
11:67 they marched to the plain of Hazor 10
68 the army of the foreigners met him in the plain; 10
12:49 into Galilee and the Great Plain 10
13:13 Simon encamped in Adida, facing the plain. 10
14: 8 the trees of the plains their fruit. 10
16: 5 they arose and marched into the plain 10
11 appointed governor over the plain of Jericho 10
4Mc 18: 8 No seducer corrupted me on a desert plain 10

plain (2) 1. δῆλος 2. ἔκδηλος 3. φανερός 4. φανερόω
Rom 1:19 For what can be known about God is plain to them 3
1Co 15:27 it is plain that he is excepted 1
Gal 5:19 Now the works of the flesh are plain 3
2Ti 3: 9 their folly will be plain to all 2
1Jn 2:19 that it might be plain that they all are not of us. 4
plain *See* make.

plainly 1. באר 2. פרשׁ (A) 3. ὀρθῶς 4. παρρησία 5. πρόδηλος
Gen 26:28 They said, "We see plainly that the LORD is †
Exd 21: 5 if the slave plainly says, 'I love my master, my wife †
Deu 27: 8 write upon the stones . . this law very plainly. 1
1Sm 10:16 He told us plainly that the asses had been found. †
Ezr 4:18 letter which you sent to us has been plainly read 2
Mrk 7:35 tongue was released, and he spoke plainly. 3
8:32 he said this plainly 4
Joh 10:24 If you are the Christ, tell us plainly. 4
11:14 Jesus told them plainly, "Laz'arus is dead; 4
16:25 tell you plainly of the Father. 4
29 Ah, now you are speaking plainly, not in any figure! 4
2Mc 3:17 which plainly showed to those who looked at him 5

plait 1. πλέκω
Mat 27:29 plaiting a crown of thorns they put it on his head 1
Mrk 15:17 plaiting a crown of thorns they put it on him. 1
Joh 19: 2 the soldiers plaited a crown of thorns 1

plan 1. בוא עַל לֵב 2. דָּבָר 3. דמה 4. זִמָּה 5. זמם 6. חרשׁ 7. חשׁב 8. יעץ 9. יצר 10. יֵצֶר 11. מַחֲשָׁבָה 12. מַעֲרָךְ 13. מִשְׁפָּט 14. נטה 15. עֵצָה 16. עֶשְׁתּוֹן 17. שׂום 18. תַּבְנִית 19. עשׁת (A) 20. βουλεύω 21. βουλή 22. διαλογισμός 23. διανοέω 24. διάταξις 25. ἐνθυμέω 26. ἐπιβουλή 27. ἐπίκειμαι 28. ἐπινοέω 29. ἐπιτήδευμα 30. λογίζομαι 31. λογισμός 32. λόγος 33. οἰκονομία 34. ποιέω 35. πρᾶξις 36. τεκταίνω 37. cogitatio 38. cogitatus 39. cogito 40. consilium
Gen 27:42 Esau comforts himself by planning to kill you. •
Exd 26:30 erect the tabernacle according to the plan 13
2Sm 14:13 Why then have you planned . . against the people 7
21: 5 The man who consumed us and planned to destroy us 3
2Kg 19:25 I planned from days of old what now I bring to pass 9
1Ch 28: 9 LORD . . understands every plan and thought. 10
11 the plan of the vestibule of the temple 18
12 the plan of all that he had in mind for the courts 18
18 his plan for the golden chariot of the cherubim 18
19 all the work to be done according to the plan. 18
2Ch 7:11 all that Solomon had planned to do in the house 1
30: 4 the plan seemed right to the king 2
32: 3 he planned with his officers and his mighty men 8
Neh 4:15 heard . . that God had frustrated their plan 15
Job 17:11 My days are past, my plans are broken off 4
Ps 14: 6 You would confound the plans of the poor 15
20: 4 your heart's desire, and fulfil all your plans! 15
21:11 If they plan evil against you 14
33:10 LORD . . he frustrates the plans of the peoples. 11
55: 9 Destroy their plans, O Lord •
62: 4 They only plan to thrust him down 8
140: 2 who plan evil things in their heart 7
4 violent men, who have planned to trip up my feet. 7
146: 4 on that very day his plans perish. 16
Prv 3:29 Do not plan evil against your neighbor 6
6:18 a heart that devises wicked plans 11
12:20 but those who plan good have joy. 8
15:22 Without counsel plans go wrong 11
16: 1 The plans of the mind belong to man 12
3 your plans will be established. 11
9 A man's mind plans his way 7
30 He who winks his eyes plans perverse things 30
19:21 Many are the plans in the mind of a man 11
20:18 Plans are established by counsel; 11
21: 5 plans of the diligent lead surely to abundance 11
24: 8 plans to do evil will be called a mischief-maker. 7

Isa 14:24 LORD . . has sworn: "As I have planned, so shall it be 3
19: 3 emptied out, and I will confound their plans; 15
22:11 or have regard for him who planned it long ago. 9
25: 1 hast done wonderful things, plans formed of old 15
30: 1 who carry out a plan, but not mine; 15
37:26 I planned from days of old what now I bring to pass 9
Jer 9: 8 but in his heart he plans an ambush for him. 17
18:11 and devising a plan against you. 11
12 That is in vain! We will follow our own plans 11
19: 7 in this place I will make void the plans of Judah 15
29:11 For I know the plans I have for you, says the LORD 11
11 says the LORD, plans for welfare and not for evil 11
48: 2 In Heshbon they planned evil against her 7
49:20 Therefore hear the plan which the LORD has made 15
30 king of Babylon has made a plan against you 15
50:45 Therefore hear the plan which the LORD has made 15
51:12 the LORD has both planned and done what he spoke 5
Ezk 43:10 the temple and its appearance and plan 24
Dan 6: 3 king planned to set him over the whole kingdom. 19
11:24 shall devise plans against strongholds 11
Mic 4:12 of the LORD, they do not understand his plan 15
Joh 12:10 planned to put Laz'arus also to death 20
Act 2:23 delivered up according to the definite plan . . of God 21
4:28 whatever thy hand and thy plan had predestined 21
5:38 if this plan or this undertaking is of men 21
25: 3 planning an ambush to kill him on the way. 34
27:39 planned if possible to bring the ship ashore. 20
42 The soldiers' plan was to kill the prisoners 21
Eph 1:10 as a plan for the fulness of time 33
3: 9 to make all men see what is the plan of the mystery 33
2Es 4:13 and they made a plan 37
15 the waves of the sea also made a plan and said, 37
16 the plan of the forest was in vain 38
17 likewise also the plan of the waves of the sea 38
19 I answered and said, "Each has made a foolish plan 37
6: 6 then I planned these things 39
11:25 I looked, and behold, these little wings planned 39
28 the two . . were planning between themselves 39
29 while they were planning, behold, one of the heads 39
31 little wings which were planning to reign. 39
13:31 they shall plan to make war against one another 39
41 they formed this plan for themselves 40
Tob 4:19 all your paths and plans may prosper 21
6:12 Now listen to my plan •
Jdt 2: 2 and set forth to them his secret plan 21
4 When he had finished setting forth his plan 21
8:34 Only, do not try to find out what I plan 35
9: 9 give to me, a widow, the strength to do what I plan. 23
13 they have planned cruel things against thy covenant 20
10: 8 grant you favor and fulfil your plans 29
11:12 they have planned to kill their cattle 20
AEs 14:11 turn their plan against themselves 21
Wis 6: 3 inquire into your plans. 21
14: 2 it was desire for gain that planned that vessel 28
14 therefore their speedy end has been planned. 28
Sir 12:16 in his mind he will plan to throw you into a pit 20
27:22 Whoever winks his eye plans evil deeds 36
1Mc 2:63 his plans will perish. 22
5: 9 the Gentiles . . planned to destroy them •
6: 3 his plan became known to the men of the city 32
8 had not turned out for him as he had planned. 25
7:31 learned that his plan had been disclosed 21
8: 4 gained control . . by their planning 21
9 The Greeks planned to come and destroy them 20
9:60 unable to do it, because their plan became known. 21
68 his plan and his expedition had been in vain. 21
12:35 planned with them to build strongholds in Judea 20
2Mc 9:15 but had planned to throw out with their children •
3Mc 1:22 would not tolerate the completion of his plans 27
25 the plan that he had conceived. 26
26 to bring the aforesaid plan to a conclusion. •
3:14 it was brought to conclusion, according to plan 32
5:12 completely frustrated in his inflexible plan. 31

plan *See also* lay, make.

wickedly plan 1. *πονηρεύω*
Sus 1:62 as they had wickedly planned to do to their neighbor 1

plane 1. עַרְמוֹן 2. תִּדְהָר
Gen 30:37 took fresh rods of poplar and almond and plane 1
Isa 41:19 the cypress, the plane and the pine together; 2
60:13 come to you, the cypress, the plane, and the pine 2

plane (2) 1. מַקְצֻעָה
Isa 44:13 he fashions it with planes, and marks it 1

plane tree 1. עַרְמוֹן 2. *πλάτανος*
Ezk 31: 8 the plane trees were as nothing compared with its 1
Sir 24:14 like a plane tree I grew tall. 2

plank 1. לוּחַ 2. שְׂדֵרָה 3. *σανίς*
1Kg 6: 9 made the ceiling . . of beams and planks of cedar. 2
Ezk 27: 5 They made all your planks of fir trees from Senir; 1
Act 27:44 the rest on planks or on pieces of the ship 3

plant 1. חָצִיר 2. מַטָּע 3. נָטִיעַ 4. נטע 5. נֶטַע 6. נתן 7. עֵשֶׂב 8. צֶמַח 9. קִיקָיוֹן 10. שׂוּם 11. שִׂיחַ 12. שׁתל 13. *καταφυτεύω* 14. *περιφυτεύω* 15. *φυτεία* 16. *φυτεύω* 17. *φυτόν* 18. *χόρτος* 19. herba 20. plantatio 21. planto 22. semino
Gen 1:11 Let the earth put forth . . plants yielding seed 7
29 God said, "Behold, I have given you every plant 7
30 I have given every green plant for food. 7
2: 5 when no plant of the field was yet in the earth 11
8 the LORD God planted a garden in Eden, in the east; 4
3:18 and you shall eat the plants of the field. 7
9: 3 and as I gave you the green plants 7
20 tiller of the soil. He planted a vineyard; 4
21:33 Abraham planted a tamarisk tree in Beer-sheba 4
Exd 9:22 hail . . upon . . every plant of the field 7
25 the hail struck down every plant of the field 7
10:12 that they may . . eat every plant in the land 7
15 they ate all the plants in the land and all 7
15 neither tree nor plant of the field, through all 7
15:17 Thou wilt bring them in, and plant them on thy own 4
Lev 19:23 you come into the land and plant all kinds of trees 4
Num24: 6 like aloes that the LORD has planted 4
Deu 6:11 vineyards and olive trees, which you did not plant 4
16:21 not plant any tree as an Ashe'rah beside the altar 4
20: 6 what man is there that has planted a vineyard 4
28:30 plant a vineyard, and you shall not use the fruit 4
39 You shall plant vineyards and dress them 4
Jos 24:13 you eat the fruit . . which you did not plant.' 4
2Sm 7:10 I will appoint a place . . and will plant them 4
2Kg 19:26 and have become like plants of the field 7
29 sow, and reap, and plant vineyards, and eat 4
1Ch 17: 9 plant them, that they may dwell in their own place 4
Job 8:12 not cut down, they wither before any other plant. 1
12: 8 the plants of the earth, and they will teach you; 11
14: 9 bud and put forth branches like a young plant. 5
Ps 1: 3 He is like a tree planted by streams of water 12
44: 2 drive out the nations, but them thou didst plant; 4
80: 8 thou didst drive out the nations and plant it. 4
15 the stock which thy right hand planted. 4
92:13 They are planted in the house of the LORD 12
94: 9 He who planted the ear, does he not hear? 4
104:14 plants for man to cultivate 7
16 cedars of Lebanon which he planted. 4
107:37 sow fields, and plant vineyards 4
144:12 our sons in their youth be like plants full grown 3
Prv 31:16 fruit of her hands she plants a vineyard. 4
Ecc 2: 4 I built houses and planted vineyards for myself; 4
5 and planted in them all kinds of fruit trees. 4
3: 2 a time to plant, and a time to pluck up what is 4
2 to plant, and a time to pluck up what is planted; 4
Isa 5: 2 cleared it . . and planted it with choice vines; 4
17:10 therefore, though you plant pleasant plants 4
10 therefore, though you plant pleasant plants 5
11 you make them grow on the day that you plant them 4
37:27 and have become like plants of the field 7
30 and plant vineyards, and eat their fruit. 4
40:24 Scarcely are they planted, scarcely sown 4
44:14 he plants a cedar and the rain nourishes it. 4
60:21 the shoot of my planting, the work of my hands 2
61: 3 oaks of righteousness, the planting of the LORD 2
65:21 shall plant vineyards and eat their fruit. 4
22 they shall not plant and another eat; 4
Jer 1:10 and to overthrow, to build and to plant. 4
2:21 I planted you a choice vine, wholly of pure seed. 4
11:17 The LORD of hosts, who planted you 4
12: 2 Thou plantest them, and they take root; 4
17: 8 He is like a tree planted by water 12
18: 9 or a kingdom that I will build and plant it 4
24: 6 I will plant them, and not uproot them. 4
29: 5 plant gardens and eat their produce. 4
28 and plant gardens and eat their produce. 4
31: 5 Again you shall plant vineyards 4
5 planters shall plant, and shall enjoy the fruit. 4
28 so I will watch over them to build and to plant 4
32:41 I will plant them in this land in faithfulness 4
35: 7 you shall not plant or have a vineyard; 4
42:10 I will plant you, and not pluck you up; 4
45: 4 and what I have planted I am plucking up 4
Ezk 4: 2 plant battering rams against it round about. 10
16: 7 and grow up like a plant of the field. 8
17: 5 seed of the land and planted it in fertile soil; 6
7 From the bed where it was planted 2
22 will plant it upon a high and lofty mountain; 12
23 on the mountain height of Israel will I plant it 12
28:26 they shall build houses and plant vineyards. 4
31: 4 its rivers flow round the place of its planting 2
Hos 13:15 Though he may flourish as the reed plant •
Ams 5:11 you have planted pleasant vineyards 4
9:14 they shall plant vineyards and drink their wine 4
15 I will plant them upon their land 4
Jon 4: 6 the LORD God appointed a plant, and made it come up 9
6 was exceedingly glad because of the plant. 9
7 God appointed a worm which attacked the plant 9
9 to Jonah, "Do you do well to be angry for the plant? 9
10 You pity the plant, for which you did not labor 9
Mic 1: 6 Sama'ria a heap . . a place for planting vineyards; 2
Zep 1:13 though they plant vineyards, they shall not 4
Mat 13:26 when the plants came up and bore grain 18
15:13 Every plant which my heavenly Father has 15
13 which my heavenly Father has not planted 16
21:33 There was a householder who planted a vineyard 16
Mrk 12: 1 A man planted a vineyard 16
Lke 13: 6 A man had a fig tree planted in his vineyard 16
17: 6 'Be rooted up, and be planted in the sea,' 16
28 they sold, they planted, they built 16
20: 9 A man planted a vineyard, and let it out to tenants 16
1Co 3: 6 I planted, Apol'los watered 16
7 neither he who plants nor he who waters is 16
8 He who plants and he who waters are equal 16
9: 7 Who plants a vineyard without eating 16
1Es 4: 9 if he tells them to plant, they plant. 16
9 if he tells them to plant, they plant. 16
16 brought up the very men who plant the vineyards 16
2Es 3: 6 into the garden which thy right hand had planted 21
6:42 so that some of them might be planted 22
8:41 and plants a multitude of seedlings 21
41 not all that were planted will take root 21
52 paradise is opened, the tree of life is planted 21
9:21 and one plant out of a great forest. 20
22 but let my grape and my plant be saved 20
26 and ate of the plants of the field 19
12:51 and my food was of plants during those days. 19
Wis 7:20 the varieties of plants and the virtues of roots; 17
10: 7 plants bearing fruit that does not ripen 17
Sir 3:28 a plant of wickedness has taken root in him. 17
10:15 has planted the humble in their place. 16
24:14 like rose plants in Jericho 17
43:23 planted islands in it. 16
49: 7 likewise to build and to plant. 13
1Mc 3:56 were betrothed, or were planting vineyards 16
2Mc 1:29 Plant thy people in thy holy place, as Moses said. 13
4Mc 1:28 two plants growing from the body and the soul 17
28 there are many offshoots of these plants 17
2:21 he planted in him emotions and inclinations 14

plant *See also* lotus.

young plant 1. יוֹנֶקֶת
Isa 53: 2 For he grew up before him like a young plant 1

plantation 1. מַטָּע
Ezk 34:29 I will provide for them prosperous plantations 1

planter 1. נטע
Jer 31: 5 planters shall plant, and shall enjoy the fruit. 1

planting 1. נֶטַע
Isa 5: 7 the men of Judah are his pleasant planting; 1

plaster 1. טוח 2. עָפָר 3. שׂיד 4. שִׂיד 5. גִּיר (A)
Lev 14:41 the plaster that they scrape off they shall pour 2
42 and he shall take other plaster 2
42 shall take other plaster and plaster the house 1
43 scraped the house and plastered it 1
45 timber and all the plaster of the house 2
48 in the house after the house was plastered 1
Deu 27: 2 set up large stones, and plaster them with plaster; 3
2 set up large stones, and plaster them with plaster; 4
4 these stones . . plaster them with plaster. 3
4 these stones . . plaster them with plaster. 4
Dan 5: 5 appeared and wrote on the plaster of the wall 5

plate 1. מַחֲבַת 2. פַּח 3. צִיץ 4. קְעָרָה 5. *παροψίς*
Exd 25:29 you shall make its plates and dishes for incense 4
28:36 you shall make a plate of pure gold, and engrave 3
37:16 its plates and dishes for incense, and its bowls 4
39:30 they made the plate of the holy crown of pure gold 3
Lev 8: 9 on the turban, in front, he set the golden plate 3
Num 4: 7 cloth of blue, and put upon it the plates 4
7:13 his offering was one silver plate whose weight 4
19 he offered for his offering one silver plate 4
25 his offering was one silver plate 4
31 his offering was one silver plate whose weight 4
37 his offering was one silver plate 4
43 his offering was one silver plate, whose weight 4
49 his offering was one silver plate 4
55 his offering was one silver plate 4
61 his offering was one silver plate, whose weight 4
67 his offering was one silver plate, whose weight 4
73 his offering was one silver plate 4
79 his offering was one silver plate 4
84 dedication offering . . twelve silver plates 4
85 each silver plate weighing 130 shekels 4
16:38 let them be made into hammered plates 2
Ezk 4: 3 take an iron plate, and place it as an iron wall 1
Mat 23:25 the outside of the cup and of the plate 5
26 cleanse the inside of the cup and of the plate 5

plate (2) 1. אֲפֻדָּה
Isa 30:22 defile . . your gold-plated molten images. 1

gold plate 1. *χρύσωμα*
1Mc 11:58 he sent him gold plate and a table service 1
15:32 the sideboard with its gold and silver plate 1

silver plate 1. *ἀργύρωμα*
1Mc 15:32 the sideboard with its gold and silver plate 1

platform 1. כִּיּוֹר 2. βῆμα 3. χελώνις
2Ch 6:13 Solomon had made a bronze platform .. and set it 1
Ezk 41: 8 I saw also that the temple had a raised platform •
9 the part of the platform which was left free was •
9 Between the platform of the temple •
11 on the part of the platform that was left free •
1Es 9:42 stood on the wooden platform 2
Jdt 14:15 and found him thrown down on the platform dead 3

public platform 1. βῆμα
2Mc 13:26 Lysias took the public platform 1

platter 1. πίναξ
Mat 14: 8 she said, "Give me the head .. here on a platter. 1
11 his head was brought on a platter 1
Mrk 6:25 at once the head of John the Baptist on a platter. 1
28 brought his head on a platter 1

plausible 1. πειθός
1Co 2: 4 not in plausible words of wisdom 1

play 1. זמר 2. חלל 3. נגן 4. צחק 5. שׂחק 6. שׁעע 7. תפשׂ 8. αὐλέω ἢ κιθαρίζω 9. κιθαρίζω 10. παίζω 11. συμπαίζω
Gen 4:21 was the father of all those who play the lyre 7
21: 9 the son .. playing with her son Isaac. 4
Exd 32: 6 to eat and drink, and rose up to play. 4
1Sm 16:16 seek out a man who is skilful in playing the lyre; 3
16 when .. he will play it, and you will be well. 3
17 Provide for me a man who can play well, and bring 3
18 who is skilful in playing, a man of valor 3
23 David took the lyre and played it with his hand; 3
18:10 and he raved .. while David was playing the lyre 3
19: 9 as he sat in .. and David was playing the lyre. 3
2Sm 2:14 Let the young men arise and play before us. 5
1Kg 1:40 went up after him, playing on pipes, and rejoicing 2
2Kg 3:15 when the minstrel played, the power of the LORD 3
1Ch 15:16 who should play loudly on musical instruments •
20 were to play harps according to Al'amoth; •
16: 5 and Je-i'el, who were to play harps and lyres; •
Job 40:20 food for him where all the wild beasts play. 5
41: 5 Will you play with him as with a bird 5
Ps 144: 9 upon a ten-stringed harp I will play to thee 1
Isa 11: 8 sucking child .. play over the hole of the asp 6
Ezk 33:32 and plays well on an instrument, for they hear 3
Zec 8: 5 full of boys and girls playing in its streets. 5
1Co 14: 7 how will any one know what is played? 8
Rev 14: 2 like the sound of harpers playing on their harps 9
Sir 30: 9 play with him, and he will give you grief. 11
47: 3 He played with lions as with young goats 10
play *See also* cease.

play a timbrel 1. תפף
Ps 68:25 between them maidens playing timbrels 1

play false 1. ψεύδω
4Mc 5:34 I will not play false to you, O law that trained me 1

foul play 1. κακουργία
2Mc 3:32 some foul play had been perpetrated by the Jews 1

make play the harlot 1. זנה
Exd 34:16 make your sons play the harlot after their gods. 1

play on strings 1. נגן
Ps 33: 3 to him a new song, play skillfully on the strings 1

play the coward 1. δειλανδρέω 2. δειλιάζω
Sir 34:14 nor play the coward, for he is his hope. 2
4Mc 10:14 a fire hot enough to make me play the coward. 1

play the fool 1. סכל
1Sm 26:21 I .. played the fool, and have erred exceedingly. 1

play the great man 1. כבד
Prv 12: 9 than one who plays the great man but lacks bread. 1

play the judge 1. שׁפט
Gen 19: 9 came to sojourn, and he would play the judge! 1

play the harlot 1. זנה
Gen 38:24 Tamar your daughter-in-law has played the harlot 1
Exd 34:15 and when they play the harlot after their gods 1
16 their daughters play the harlot after their 1
Lev 17: 7 satyrs, after whom they play the harlot 1
20: 5 who follow him in playing the harlot after Molech 1
6 to mediums .. playing the harlot after them 1
21: 9 if she profanes herself by playing the harlot 1
Num25: 1 in Shittim the people began to play the harlot 1
Deu 22:21 wrought folly in Israel by playing the harlot 1
31:16 rise and play the harlot after the strange gods 1
Jdg 2:17 for they played the harlot after other gods 1
8:27 and all Israel played the harlot after it there 1
33 turned .. and played the harlot after the Ba'als 1
1Ch 5:25 played the harlot after the gods of the peoples 1
Ps 106:39 Thus they .. played the harlot in their doings. 1
Isa 23:17 Tyre .. will play the harlot with all 1
Jer 3: 1 You have played the harlot with many lovers; 1
6 under every .. tree, and there played the harlot? 1
8 but she too went and played the harlot. 1
Ezk 16:15 you trusted in your beauty, and played the harlot 1
16 decked shrines, and on them played the harlot; 1
17 images of men, and with them played the harlot; 1
26 You also played the harlot with the Egyptians 1
28 You played the harlot also with the Assyrians 1
28 yea, yu played the harlot with them 1
41 I will make you stop playing the harlot 1
23: 3 they played the harlot in Egypt; 1
3 they played the harlot in their youth; 1
5 Oho'lah played the harlot while she was mine; 1
19 when she played the harlot in the land of Egypt 1
30 because you played the harlot with the nations 1
Hos 2: 5 For their mother has played the harlot; 1
3: 3 you shall not play the harlot 1
4:10 they shall play the harlot, but not multiply; 1
12 and they have left their God to play the harlot. 1
13 Therefore your daughters play the harlot 1
14 punish your daughters when they play the harlot 1
15 Though you play the harlot, O Israel 1
5: 3 for now, O E'phraim, you have played the harlot 1
9: 1 you have played the harlot, forsaking your God. 1

play the host 1. ξενίζω
Sir 29:25 you will play the host 1

play the madman 1. שׁגע
1Sm 21:15 you have brought this fellow to play the madman 1

play the man 1. חזק
2Sm 10:12 play the man for our people, and for the cities 1
1Ch 19:13 let us play the man for our people 1

play the wanton 1. στρηνιάω
Rev 18: 7 As she glorified herself and played the wanton 1

flute player 1. αὐλητής
Mat 9:23 and saw the flute players, and the crowd 1
Rev 18:22 the sound .. of flute players and trumpeters 1

playmate 1. ἕτερος
Mat 11:16 and calling to their playmates 1

plea 1. דבר 2. קוֹל 3. תְּחִנָּה 4. δικαίωμα
Isa 32: 7 even when the plea of the needy is right. 1
59: 4 they rely on empty pleas, they speak lies •
Jer 18:19 Give heed to me, O LORD, and hearken to my plea. 4
37:20 lord the king: let my humble plea come before you 3
38:26 I made a humble plea to the king 3
Lam 3:56 thou didst hear my plea, 'Do not close thine ear 2

empty plea 1. תֹּהוּ
Isa 29:21 with an empty plea turn aside him .. in the right. 1

plead 1. דבר 2. פגע 3. ריב 4. רִיב 5. שׁפט 6. תַּחֲנוּן 7. ἀξιόω 8. ἐντυγχάνω 9. κατάστασις 10. λέγω 11. παρακαλέω 12. πείθω
1Sm 12: 7 stand .. that I may plead with you before the LORD 5
24:15 give sentence .. and see to it, and plead my cause 3
Job 13: 6 listen to the pleadings of my lips. 4
Ps 74:22 Arise, O God, plead thy cause; 3
119:154 Plead my cause and redeem me; give me life 3
Prv 22:23 for the LORD will plead their cause and despoil 3
23:11 Redeemer .. will plead their cause against you. 3
Isa 1:17 defend the fatherless, plead for the widow. 3
Jer 3:21 the weeping and pleading of Israel's sons 6
12: 1 yet I would plead my case before thee. 1
15:11 if I have not pleaded with thee 2
50:34 He will surely plead their cause 3
51:36 I will plead your cause and take vengeance 3
Hos 2: 2 Plead with your mother, plead- 3
2 Plead with your mother, plead- 3
Mic 7: 9 until he pleads my cause and executes judgment 3
Act 19: 8 arguing and pleading about the kingdom of God; 12
Rom11: 2 of Eli'jah, how he pleads with God against Israel? 8
Wis 12:12 who will come before thee to plead as an advocate 9
1Mc 11:62 Then the people of Gaza pleaded with Jonathan 7
2Mc 4:47 if they had pleaded even before Scythians. 10
4Mc 12: 6 When he had so pleaded 11

plead a case 1. ריב
Job 13: 8 will you plead the case for God? 1
Mic 6: 1 Arise, plead your case before the mountains 1

plead a cause 1. ריב
Isa 51:22 your God who pleads the cause of his people 1
pleading *See* win.

pleasant 1. חמד 2. חֶמֶד 3. חֶמְדָּה 4. טוֹב 5. מֶתֶק 6. נָעִים 7. נעם 8. נֹעַם 9. נַעֲמָן 10. עֹנֶג 11. ערב 12. שַׁעֲשֻׁעִים 13. תַּעֲנוּג 14. γλυκύς 15. ἡδύς 16. χαρά
Gen 2: 9 every tree that is pleasant to the sight and good 1
49:15 he saw .. that the land was pleasant; 7
2Sm 1:26 my .. Jonathan; very pleasant have you been to me; 7
19:35 can I discern what is pleasant and what is not? 4
2Kg 2:19 Behold, the situation of this city is pleasant 4
Ps 106:24 Then they despised the pleasant land 3
133: 1 how good and pleasant it is when brothers dwell 6
Prv 2:10 knowledge will be pleasant to your soul; 7
9:17 bread eaten in secret is pleasant. 7
16:21 pleasant speech increases persuasiveness. 5
24 Pleasant words are like a honeycomb 8
22:18 for it will be pleasant if you keep them within 6
23: 8 vomit .. and waste your pleasant words. 6
24: 4 filled with all precious and pleasant riches. 6
Ecc 11: 7 and it is pleasant for the eyes to behold the sun. 4
Sng 7: 6 How fair and pleasant you are, O loved one 7
Isa 5: 7 the men of Judah are his pleasant planting; 12
13:22 Hyenas .. and jackals in the pleasant palaces; 10
17:10 therefore, though you plant pleasant plants 9
27: 2 In that day: "A pleasant vineyard, sing of it! 2
32:12 Beat upon your breasts for the pleasant fields 2
Jer 3:19 and give you a pleasant land, a heritage 3
12:10 my pleasant portion a desolate wilderness. 3
31:26 I awoke and looked, and my sleep was pleasant to me 11
Ezk 26:12 your walls and destroy your pleasant houses; 3
Ams 5:11 you have planted pleasant vineyards 2
Mic 2: 9 people you drive out from their pleasant houses; 13
Zec 7:14 the pleasant land was made desolate. 3
Heb 12:11 discipline seems painful rather than pleasant; 16
Sir 6: 5 A pleasant voice multiplies friends 14
40:21 a pleasant voice is better than both. 15
3Mc 5:12 he was overcome by so pleasant and deep a sleep 15
pleasant *See also* make, odor.

most pleasant 1. ἡδύς
4Mc 8:23 Why do we banish .. from this most pleasant life 1

pleasant place 1. מַחְמָד 2. נָעִים
Ps 16: 6 The lines have fallen for me in pleasant places; 2
Isa 64:11 and all our pleasant places have become ruins. 1

pleasantness 1. נָעִים 2. נֹעַם
Job 36:11 in prosperity, and their years in pleasantness. 1
Prv 3:17 Her ways are ways of pleasantness 2

please 1. חפץ 2. חָפֵץ 3. טוב 4. טוֹב 5. טוֹב בְּעֵינַיִם 6. טוֹב לִפְנֵי 7. טוֹב עַל 8. יאל 9. יטב 10. יטב בְּעֵינַיִם 11. יטב לִפְנֵי 12. יָשָׁר בְּעֵינַיִם 13. ישׁר בְּעֵינַיִם 14. מַחְמָד 15. מצא חֵן בְּעֵינַיִם 16. נָא 17. נִיחֹחַ 18. נֹעַם 19. ערב 20. פאר 21. רַע בְּעֵינַיִם 22. רצה 23. רָצוֹן 24. נִיחוֹחַ (A) 25. שׁפר (A) 26. ἀγαθύνω 27. αἰσθάνομαι 28. ἀρεσκεία 29. ἄρεσκος 30. ἀρέσκω 31. ἀρεστά ἐνώπιον 32. ἀρεστός 33. ἀρέσω 34. βούλομαι 35. δοκέω 36. ἐθέλω 37. ἐπιχαίρω 38. εὐαρεστέω 39. εὐάρεστος 40. εὐδοκέω 41. εὐδοκία 42. εὐπρεπῶς 43. θέλημα 44. καλῶς 45. καλῶς ποιέω 46. κατὰ ψυχήν 47. μὴ ὀκνέω δή 48. ψυχαγωγία 49. placeo 50. video
Gen 8:21 when the LORD smelled the pleasing odor 17
16: 6 is in your power; do to her as you please. 5
19: 8 and do to them as you please; 5
20:15 land is before you; dwell where it pleases you. 5
28: 8 Canaanite women did not please Isaac his father 21
34:18 Their words pleased Hamor and Hamor's son 10
47:25 may it please my lord, we will be slaves 15
Exd 8: 9 Be pleased to command me when I am to entreat 20
21: 8 If she does not please her master 21
29:18 it is a pleasing odor, an offering by fire 17
25 burn them .. as a pleasing odor before the LORD; 17
41 for a pleasing odor, an offering by fire 17
Lev 1: 9 an offering by fire, a pleasing odor to the LORD 17
13 offering by fire, a pleasing odor to the LORD 17
17 offering by fire, a pleasing odor to the LORD 17
2: 2 an offering by fire, a pleasing odor to the LORD 17
9 an offering by fire, a pleasing odor to the LORD 17
12 be offered on the altar for a pleasing odor 17
3: 5 offering by fire, a pleasing odor to the LORD 17
16 as food offered by fire for a pleasing odor 17
4:31 upon the altar for a pleasing odor to the LORD 17
6:15 on the altar, a pleasing odor to the LORD 17
21 offer it for a pleasing odor to the LORD 17
8:21 burned .. as a burnt offering, a pleasing odor 17
28 a pleasing odor, an offering by fire to the LORD 17
17: 6 and burn the fat for a pleasing odor to the LORD 17
23:13 to be offered by fire to the LORD, a pleasing odor 17
18 an offering by fire, a pleasing odor to the LORD 17
26:31 I will not smell your pleasing odors 17
Num15: 3 to make a pleasing odor to the LORD 17
7 a pleasing odor to the LORD. 17
10 offering by fire, a pleasing odor to the LORD. 17
13 offering by fire, a pleasing odor to the LORD. 17
14 offering by fire, a pleasing odor to the LORD 17
24 a burnt offering, a pleasing odor to the LORD 17
18:17 offering by fire, a pleasing odor to the LORD; 17
23:27 perhaps it will please God that you may curse 13
24: 1 Balaam saw that it pleased the LORD to bless 4
28: 2 food for my offerings by fire, my pleasing odor 17
6 ordained at Mount Sinai for a pleasing odor 17
8 offering by fire, a pleasing odor to the LORD. 17
13 for a burnt offering of pleasing odor 17
24 offering by fire, a pleasing odor to the LORD; 17
27 burnt offering, a pleasing odor to the LORD; 17
29: 2 a burnt offering, a pleasing odor to the LORD 17

6 a pleasing odor, an offering by fire to the LORD. 17
8 burnt offering to the LORD, a pleasing odor 17
13 offering by fire, a pleasing odor to the LORD 17
36 offering by fire, a pleasing odor to the LORD 17
Deu 23:16 where it pleases him best; you shall not oppress 4
Jos 22:33 And the report pleased the people of Israel; 10
Jdg 16: 6 Please tell me wherein your great strength lies 16
10 me lies; please tell me how you might be bound. 16
19: 6 Be pleased to spend the night 8
1Sm 12:22 it has pleased the LORD to make you a people 8
18:20 and they told Saul, and the thing pleased him. 13
20:13 should it please my father to do you harm 9
2Sm 3:36 all the people took notice . . and it pleased them; 10
36 that the king did pleased all the people. 5
7:29 may it please thee to bless the house of thy 8
17: 4 the advice pleased Ab'salom and all the elders 13
19: 6 if Ab'salom were . . then you would be pleased. 12
1Kg 3:10 It pleased the Lord that Solomon had asked this. 10
9:12 they did not please him. 13
14:13 there is found something pleasing to the LORD 4
20: 6 and lay hands on whatever pleases them 14
21: 6 if it please you, I will give you another vineyard 1
2Kg 5:23 Na'aman said, "Be pleased to accept two talents. 8
6: 3 one . . said, "Be pleased to go with your servants. 8
1Ch 17:27 therefore may it please thee to bless the house 8
2Ch 10: 7 If you will be kind to this people and please them 22
Ezr 6:10 may offer pleasing sacrifices to the God 24
Neh 2: 5 If it pleases the king, and if your servant 3
6 it pleased the king to send me; and I set him a time. 9
7 If it pleases the king, let letters be given me 3
Est 1:19 If it please the king, let a royal order go forth 7
21 This advice pleased the king and the princes 10
2: 4 let the maiden who pleases the king be queen 10
4 This pleased the king, and he did so. 10
9 And the maiden pleased him and won his favor; 10
3: 9 If it please the king, let it be decreed 7
5: 4 If it please the king, let the king and Haman come 7
8 and if it please the king to grant my petition 7
14 This counsel pleased Haman, 11
7: 3 If I have found favor . . and if it please the king 7
8: 5 If it please the king, and if I have found favor 7
5 and if . . I be pleasing in his eyes 3
8 may write as you please with regard to the Jews 5
9: 5 and did as they pleased to those who hated them. 23
13 If it please the king, let the Jews . . be allowed 7
Job 6: 9 that it would please God to crush me 8
28 now, be pleased to look at me; 8
Ps 40:13 Be pleased, O LORD, to deliver me! 22
41:11 By this I know that thou art pleased with me 1
49:13 of those who are pleased with their portion. 22
51:16 a burnt offering, thou wouldst not be pleased. 22
69:31 This will please the LORD more than an ox or a bull 9
70: 1 Be pleased, O God, to deliver me! *
104:34 May my meditation be pleasing to him 19
115: 3 Our God . . does whatever he pleases. 1
135: 6 Whatever the LORD pleases he does 1
Prv 15:26 words of the pure are pleasing to him. 18
16: 7 When a man's ways please the LORD 22
Ecc 2:26 For to the man who pleases him God gives wisdom 6
26 he gives . . only to give to one who pleases God. 6
7:26 he who pleases God escapes her 6
8: 3 do not delay . . for he does whatever he pleases. 1
12:10 The Preacher sought to find pleasing words 2
Sng 2: 7 you stir not up nor awaken love until it please. 1
3: 5 stir not up nor awaken love until it please. 1
8: 4 stir not up nor awaken love until it please. 1
Isa 42:21 The LORD was pleased, for his righteousness' sake 1
56: 4 who choose the things that please me 1
Jer 6:20 nor your sacrifices pleasing to me. 19
Ezk 6:13 they offered pleasing odor to all their idols. 17
16:19 and honey–you set before them for a pleasing odor 17
20:41 As a pleasing odor I will accept you 17
Dan 6: 1 pleased Darius to set over the kingdom 120 25
8: 4 did as he pleased and magnified himself. 23
Hos 9: 4 shall not please him with their sacrifices. 19
Jon 1:14 for thou, O LORD, hast done as it pleased thee. 1
Mic 6: 7 Will the LORD be pleased with thousands of rams 22
Mal 1: 8 will he be pleased with you or show you favor? 22
3: 4 Judah and Jerusalem will be pleasing to the LORD 19
Mat 14: 6 Hero'di-as danced . . and pleased Herod 30
17:12 but did to him whatever they pleased. 36
Mrk 6:22 she pleased Herod and his guests 30
9:13 they did to him whatever they pleased 36
Lke 2:14 on earth peace among men with whom he is pleased! 41
Joh 8:29 I always do what is pleasing to him. 32
Act 6: 5 what they said pleased the whole multitude 30
9:38 Please come to us without delay. *
12: 3 when he saw that it pleased the Jews 32
Rom 8: 8 and those who are in the flesh cannot please God. 30
15: 1 and not to please ourselves; 30
2 let each of us please his neighbor for his good 30
3 For Christ did not please himself; 30
26 pleased to make some contribution for the poor 40
27 they were pleased to do it 40
1Co 1:21 it pleased God through the folly 40
7:32 how to please the Lord; 30
33 how to please his wife 30
34 how to please her husband. 30
10: 5 with most of them God was not pleased 40
33 just as I try to please all men in everything I do 30
2Co 5: 9 we make it our aim to please him. 39
Gal 1:10 Or am I trying to please men? 30
10 If I were still pleasing men 30
16 was pleased to reveal his Son to me 40
Eph 5:10 try to learn what is pleasing to the Lord. 39
Php 4:18 a sacrifice acceptable and pleasing to God. 39
Col 1:10 fully pleasing to him 28
19 in him all the fulness of God was pleased to dwell 40
3:20 this pleases the Lord. 39
1Th 2: 4 not to please men, but to please God 30
4 not to please men, but to please God *
4: 1 how you ought to live and to please God 30
Heb 11: 5 he was attested as having pleased God. 38
6 without faith it is impossible to please him. 38
13:16 such sacrifices are pleasing to God. 38
21 working . . that which is pleasing in his sight 39
Jas 2: 3 Have a seat here, please 44
1Jn 3:22 keep his commandments and do what pleases him. 31
2Es 12:39 whatever it pleases the Most High to show you. 50
15:47 to please and glory in your lovers 49
Tob 3:15 if it be not pleasing to thee to take my life 35
4: 3 do what is pleasing to her, and do not grieve her. 32
21 do what is pleasing in his sight. 32
Jdt 3: 3 do with them whatever you please. 30
7:16 These words pleased Holofernes 30
8:15 power to protect us within any time he pleases 36
17 he will hear our voice, if it pleases him. 32
11:20 Her words pleased Holofernes 30
12:13 This beautiful maidservant will please come 47
14 Surely whatever pleases him I will do at once 32
Wis 4:10 There was one who pleased God and was loved by him 39
14 for his soul was pleasing to the Lord 32
9: 9 who understand what is pleasing in thy sight 32
10 that I may learn what is pleasing to thee. 39
18 men were taught what pleases thee 32
13:11 with pleasing workmanship make a useful vessel 42
14:19 For he, perhaps wishing to please his ruler 30
Sir 7:26 you have a wife who pleases you, do not cast her out; 46
8:15 he will act as he pleases 43
9:12 Do not delight in what pleases the ungodly; 41
20:27 a sensible man will please great men. 33
28 whoever pleases great men 29
33:13 all his ways are as he pleases 41
34:19 The Most High is not pleased with the offerings 40
35: 3 To keep from wickedness is pleasing to the Lord 41
16 He whose service is pleasing to the Lord 41
39:18 At his command whatever pleases him is done 41
44:16 Enoch pleased the Lord, and was taken up 38
45:19 The Lord saw it and was not pleased 40
48:16 Some of them did what was pleasing to God 32
22 For Hezekiah did what was pleasing to the Lord 32
Bar 4: 4 for we know what is pleasing to God. 32
1Mc 1:12 This proposal pleased them 26
6:60 The speech pleased the king and the commanders 30
8:21 The proposal pleased them 30
11:49 gained control of the city as they pleased 34
12:18 now please send us a reply to this. 45
22 please write us concerning your welfare; 45
14: 4 his rule was pleasing to them 30
23 It has pleased our people to receive these men 30
2Mc 1:20 when it pleased God 35
2:16 Will you therefore please keep the days? 45
25 we have aimed to please those who wish to read 48
7:16 you do what you please 36
14:35 thou wast pleased that there be a temple 40
4Mc 8: 4 he was pleased with them 27
26 Why does . . such a fatal stubbornness please us 30
12: 9 Extremely pleased by the boy's declaration 37
151 1: 5 but the Lord was not pleased with them. 40

greatly please 1. εὐφραίνω
Jdt 12:20 Holofernes was greatly pleased with her 1

please well 1. יטב בְּעֵינַיִם 2. ישר בְּעֵינַיִם 3. εὐδοκέω
Gen 45:16 the report . . pleased Pharaoh . . well 1
Jos 22:30 When Phin'ehas . . heard . . it pleased them well. 1
Jdg 14: 3 Get her for me; for she pleases me well. 2
7 with the woman; and she pleased Samson well. 2
1Sm 18:26 it pleased David well to be the king's son-in-law. 2
Mat 17: 5 my beloved Son, with whom I am well pleased 3
Mrk 1:11 with thee I am well pleased. 3
Lke 3:22 my beloved Son; with thee I am well pleased. 3
2Pe 1:17 my beloved Son, with whom I am well pleased 3
Jdt 15:10 God is well pleased with it 3

well pleased 1. εὐδοκέω
Mat 3:17 my beloved Son, with whom I am well pleased. 1
12:18 my beloved with whom my soul is well pleased 1

pleasing *See* odor.

pleasure 1. חפץ 2. חֵפֶץ 3. חָפֵץ 4. טוֹב 5. טוֹב בְּעֵינַיִם 6. נָעִים 7. נֶפֶשׁ 8. עֶדְנָה 9. רצה 10. רָצוֹן 11. שִׂמְחָה 12. רְעוּ (A) 13. ἀπόλαυσις 14. ἀρεστός 15. δοκέω 16. εὐδοκέω 17. εὐδοκία 18. εὐφροσύνη 19. ἡδονή 20. χάρις
Gen 18:12 my husband is old, shall I have pleasure? 8
2Sm 15:26 'I have no pleasure in you,' behold, here I am 1
19:18 to bring over the king's . . and to do his pleasure. 5
1Ch 29:17 that thou . . hast pleasure in uprightness; 9
Ezr 5:17 let the king send us his pleasure in this matter. 12
Neh 9:37 power also over our bodies . . at their pleasure 10
Job 22: 3 Is it any pleasure to the Almighty if you are 2
Ps 16:11 in thy right hand are pleasures for evermore. 6
105:22 to instruct his princes at his pleasure 7
111: 2 studied by all who have pleasure in them. 3
147:10 nor his pleasure in the legs of a man; 9
Prv 10:23 but wise conduct is pleasure to a man *
21:17 He who loves pleasure will be a poor man; 11
Ecc 2: 1 I will make a test of pleasure; enjoy yourself. 11
2 I said . . and of pleasure, "What use is it? 11
10 I kept my heart from no pleasure 11
4: 8 For whom am I . . depriving myself of pleasure? 4
5: 4 do not delay . . for he has no pleasure in fools. 2
12: 1 when you will say, "I have no pleasure in them"; 2
Isa 58: 3 in the day of your fast you seek your own pleasure 2
13 from doing your pleasure on my holy day 2
13 going your own ways, or seeking your own pleasure 2
Ezk 18:23 Have I any pleasure in the death of the wicked 1
32 For I have no pleasure in the death of any one 1
33:11 I have no pleasure in the death of the wicked 1
Mal 1:10 I have no pleasure in you, says the LORD of hosts 2
Lke 8:14 the cares and riches and pleasures of life 19
2Co 1:15 so that you might have a double pleasure; 20
2Th 2:12 had pleasure in unrighteousness. 16
Tit 3: 3 slaves to various passions and pleasures 19
Heb 10:38 if he shrinks back, my soul has no pleasure in him. 16
11:25 to enjoy the fleeting pleasures of sin. 13
12:10 for a short time at their pleasure 15
2Pe 2:13 They count it pleasure to revel in the daytime. 19
Tob 3: 6 now deal with me according to thy pleasure; 14
Wis 7: 2 the seed of a man and the pleasure of marriage. 19
16:20 providing every pleasure 19
Sir 9:10 when it has aged you will drink it with pleasure. 18
18:31 allow your soul to take pleasure in base desire 17
4Mc 1:20 two . . types . . are pleasure and pain 19
21 The emotions of both pleasure and pain 19
22 desire precedes pleasure and delight follows 19
24 an emotion embracing pleasure and pain. 19
25 In pleasure . . exists . . malevolent tendency 19
28 Just as pleasure and pain are two plants 19
33 we abstain from the pleasure to be had from them 19
5:23 we master all pleasures and desires 19
6:35 also that it masters pleasures 19

pleasure *See also* find, live, lover, take.

good pleasure 1. רָצוֹן 2. εὐδοκέω 3. εὐδοκία
Ps 51:18 Do good to Zion in thy good pleasure; 1
Lke 12:32 it is your Father's good pleasure 2
Php 2:13 both to will and to work for his good pleasure. 3
Sir 41: 4 can you reject the good pleasure of the Most High? 3

pledge 1. אִסָּר 2. חבל 3. חֲבֹלָה 4. נתן 5. נתן יָד 6. עֲבוֹט 7. עַבְטִיט 8. עֵרָבוֹן 9. δεξιός 10. ἔγγυος 11. ἐπιβάλλω τὰς χεῖρας 12. ἵστημι 13. πίστιν δίδωμι 14. πίστις
Gen 38:17 And she said, "Will you give me a pledge 8
18 He said, "What pledge shall I give you? 8
20 Judah sent . . to receive the pledge 8
Num30: 2 swears an oath to bind himself by a pledge 1
3 Or when a woman . . binds herself by a pledge 1
4 her father hears of her vow and of her pledge 1
4 then . . every pledge . . shall stand. 1
5 no vow of hers, no pledge . . shall stand; 1
7 her pledges by which she has bound herself 1
10 if she . . bound herself by a pledge with an oath 1
11 not oppose her; then . . every pledge 1
12 her vows, or concerning her pledge of herself 1
14 then he establishes . . vows, or all her pledges 1
Deu 24:10 shall not go into his house to fetch his pledge. 6
11 man . . shall bring the pledge out to you. 6
12 if . . poor man, you shall not sleep in his pledge; 6
13 sun goes down, you shall restore to him the pledge 6
1Ch 29:24 pledged their allegiance to King Solomon. 4
Ezr 10:19 pledged themselves to put away their wives 5
Job 17: 3 Lay down a pledge for me with thyself; 8
Ezk 18: 7 but restores to the debtor his pledge 3
12 commits robbery, does not restore the pledge 2
33:15 if the wicked restores the pledge 2
Hab 2: 6 and loads himself with pledges! 7
1Ti 5:12 having violated their first pledge. 14
1Es 9:20 pledged themselves to put away their wives 11
1Mc 8: 1 they pledged friendship to those who came to them 12
2Mc 10:28 the one having as pledge of success and victory 10
12:12 after receiving his pledges 9
13:22 gave pledges, received theirs, withdrew 9
3Mc 3:10 already some . . were pledging to protect them 13

pledge *See also* exact, give, hold, offer, take.

pledge of friendship 1. δεξιός
2Mc 11:26 and give them pledges of friendship 1
30 those . . will have our pledge of friendship 1
12:11 to grant them pledges of friendship 1
14:19 to give and receive pledges of friendship. 1

plenteous 1.דָּשֵׁן 2.רבה 3.שָׂבָע
Gen 41:34 of Egypt during the seven plenteous years. 3
47 During the seven plenteous years the earth 3
Ps 130: 7 with him is plenteous redemption. 2
Isa 30:23 ground, which will be rich and plenteous. 1

plentiful 1.כַּרְמֶל 2.לָרֹב 3.ἄφθονος 4.πολύς 5.abundantia 6.abundo
2Ch 1:15 king . . made cedar as plentiful as the sycamore 2
9:27 king made . . cedar as plentiful as the sycamore 2
Jer 2: 7 I brought you into a plentiful land 1
Mat 9:37 The harvest is plentiful 4
Lke 10: 2 harvest is plentiful, but the laborers are few 4
2Es 7:58 what is plentiful is of less worth 6
59 rejoices more than he who has what is plentiful. 5
4Mc 3:10 although springs were plentiful there 3
plentiful *See also* make.

plentifully 1.רֹב
Job 26: 3 and plentifully declared sound knowledge! 1
plentifully *See also* bring.

plenty 1.דַּי 2.לָרֹב 3.רֹב 4.שׂבע 5.שָׂבָע 6.εἰς πλῆθος 7.πλησμονή 8.πολύς 9.χορτάζω 10.abundantia
Gen 27:28 of the earth, and plenty of grain and wine. 3
41:29 There will come seven years of great plenty 5
30 and all the plenty will be forgotten 5
31 the plenty will be unknown in the land by reason 5
48 years when there was plenty in the land of Egypt •
53 The seven years of plenty that prevailed 5
2Ch 31:10 we have eaten and had enough and have plenty left; 2
Est 1:18 and there will be contempt and wrath in plenty. 1
Prv 3:10 then your barns will be filled with plenty 5
12:11 He who tills his land will have plenty of bread 4
20:13 open your eyes, and you will have plenty of bread. 4
28:19 He who tills his land will have plenty of bread 4
19 pursuits will have plenty of poverty. 4
Jer 44:17 then we had plenty of food, and prospered 4
Jol 2:26 You shall eat in plenty and be satisfied •
Php 4:12 I have learned the secret of facing plenty and hunger 9
2Es 8:52 the age to come is prepared, plenty is provided 10
Jdt 2:18 also plenty of food for every man 6
Sir 18:25 In the time of plenty think of the time of hunger; 7
3Mc 5: 2 plenty of unmixed wine 8
pliable *See* make.

plight 1.רַע 2.καιρός
Exd 5:19 The foremen . . saw that they were in evil plight 1
Sir 51:12 rescue me from an evil plight 2

evil plight 1.רָעָה
Ps 107:26 their courage melted away in their evil plight; 1

plight troth 1.שׁבע
Ezk 16: 8 yea, I plighted my troth to you 1

plot 1.דבר 2.הגה 3.זמם 4.חָפֵשׂ 5.חרשׁ 6.חשׁב 7.כרה 8.מַחֲשָׁבָה 9.עֵצָה 10.עשׂה 11.קשׁר 12.רְכָס 13.βουλεύω 14.βουλή 15.ἔννοιας 16.ἐπιβουλή 17.κατεγχειρέω 18.λογίζομαι 19.συμβουλεύω 20.συστροφή 21.cogitatio
1Sm 23: 9 David knew . . Saul was plotting evil against him; 5
Neh 4: 8 they all plotted together to come and fight 11
Est 8: 3 evil design . . and the plot which he had devised 8
9:24 Haman . . had plotted against the Jews to destroy 6
25 his wicked plot . . should come upon his own head 8
Ps 2: 1 nations conspire, and the peoples plot in vain? 2
31:13 together against me, as they plot to take my life. 3
20 thou hidest them from the plots of men; 12
36: 4 He plots mischief while on his bed; 6
37:12 The wicked plots against the righteous 3
52: 2 you are plotting destruction. 6
64: 6 We have thought out a cunningly conceived plot. 4
119:23 Even though princes sit plotting against me 1
Prv 16:27 A worthless man plots evil 7
Isa 32: 6 speaks folly, and his mind plots iniquity 10
Jer 18:18 Come, let us make plots against Jeremiah 8
23 O LORD, knowest all their plotting to slay me. 9
Dan 11:25 not stand, for plots shall be devised against 8
Nah 1: 9 What do you plot against the LORD? 6
11 one . . who plotted evil against the LORD 6
Act 9:23 the Jews plotted to kill him 19
24 their plot became known to Saul 16
20: 3 when a plot was made against him by the Jews 16
19 which befell me through the plots of the Jews; 16
23:12 When it was day, the Jews made a plot 20
30 there would be a plot against the man 16
1Es 5:73 by plots and demagoguery and uprisings 16
2Es 15: 3 Do not fear the plots against you 21
Sus 1:28 their wicked plot to have Susanna put to death. 15
1Mc 3:52 thou knowest what they plot against us. 18
9:58 Then all the lawless plotted and said, "See! 13
3Mc 1: 2 determined to carry out the plot he had devised 16
6 Now that he had foiled the plot 16
21 because of what the king was profanely plotting. 17
5: 8 avert with vengeance the evil plot against them 14

plot (2) 1.חֶלְקָה
2Sm 23:11 where there was a plot of ground full of lentils; 1
12 But he took his stand in the midst of the plot 1
2Kg 9:25 Take him up, and cast him on the plot of ground 1
26 I will requite you on this plot of ground.' 1
26 take him up and cast him on the plot of ground 1
1Ch 11:13 There was a plot of ground full of barley 1
14 he took his stand in the midst of the plot 1
Ezk 45: 2 a square plot of 500 by 500 cubits •
plot *See* make.

plot against 1.ἐπιβουλεύω
AEs 16:23 for those who plot against us it may be a reminder 1

evil plot 1.זָמָם
Ps 140: 8 do not further his evil plot! Selah 1

garden plot 1.πρασιά
Sir 24:31 I will water my orchard and drench my garden plot 1

secret plot 1.סוֹד
Ps 64: 2 hide me from the secret plots of the wicked 1

treacherously plot 1.בגד
Ps 59: 5 spare none of those who treacherously plot 1

plotter against 1.ἐπιβούλος
2Mc 3:38 any enemy or plotter against your government 1
4: 2 to designate as a plotter against the government 1
50 the chief plotter against his fellow citizens. 1

plow 1.חָרִישׁ 2.חרשׁ 3.עבד 4.ἀροτριάω 5.ἄροτρον 6.ἐκδίδωμι
Gen 45: 6 there will be neither plowing nor harvest. 1
Deu 21: 4 valley . . which is neither plowed nor sown 3
22:10 You shall not plow with an ox and an ass together. 2
Jdg 14:18 If you had not plowed with my heifer, you would not 2
1Sm 8:12 he will appoint . . and some to plow his ground 2
1Kg 19:19 found Eli'sha . . who was plowing, with twelve yoke 2
Job 1:14 The oxen were plowing and the asses feeding 2
4: 8 those who plow iniquity and sow trouble 2
Ps 129: 3 The plowers plowed upon my back; 2
Prv 20: 4 The sluggard does not plow in the autumn; 2
Isa 28:24 Does he who plows for sowing plow continually? 2
24 Does he who plows for sowing plow continually? 2
Jer 26:18 Zion shall be plowed as a field; 2
Hos 10:11 Judah must plow, Jacob must harrow for himself. 2
13 You have plowed iniquity 2
Ams 6:12 Does one plow the sea with oxen? 2
Mic 3:12 because of you Zion shall be plowed as a field; 2
Lke 9:62 No one who puts his hand to the plow 5
17: 7 who has a servant plowing or keeping sheep 4
1Co 9:10 because the plowman should plow in hope 4
Sir 6:19 Come to her like one who plows and sows 4
38:25 How can he become wise who handles the plow 5
26 He sets his heart on plowing furrows 6

plower 1.חרשׁ
Ps 129: 3 The plowers plowed upon my back; 1
plowing *See* time.

plowman 1.אִכָּר 2.חרשׁ 3.יגב 4.ἀροτριάω
2Kg 25:12 the poorest . . to be vinedressers and plowmen. 3
Isa 61: 5 foreigners shall be your plowmen 1
Jer 52:16 the poorest of the land to be . . plowmen. 3
Ams 9:13 when the plowman shall overtake the reaper 2
1Co 9:10 because the plowman should plow in hope 4

plowshare 1.אֵת 2.מַחֲרֵשָׁה
1Sm 13:20 to sharpen his plowshare, his mattock, his axe 2
21 was a pim for the plowshares and for the mattocks 2
Isa 2: 4 they shall beat their swords into plowshares 1
Jol 3:10 Beat your plowshares into swords 1
Mic 4: 3 they shall beat their swords into plowshares 1

pluck 1.ארה 2.נסח 3.נצל 4.קָטַף 5.τίλλω
Deu 23:25 grain, you may pluck the ears with your hand 4
28:63 you shall be plucked off the land 2
Ps 80:12 so that all who pass along the way pluck its fruit? 1
Ezk 23:34 and pluck out your hair, and tear your breasts; ‡
Zec 3: 2 Is not this a brand plucked from the fire? 3
Mat 12: 1 they began to pluck heads of grain and to eat. 5
Mrk 2:23 his disciples began to pluck heads of grain. 5
Lke 6: 1 his disciples plucked and ate some heads of grain 5

pluck off 1.מרט (A)
Dan 7: 4 Then as I looked its wings were plucked off 1

pluck out 1.יצא 2.נצל 3.ἐκβάλλω 4.ἐξαιρέω 5.ἐξορύσσω
Ps 25:15 for he will pluck my feet out of the net. 1
Ams 4:11 and you were as a brand plucked out of the burning; 2
Mat 5:29 If your right eye causes you to sin, pluck it out 4
18: 9 if your eye causes you to sin, pluck it out 4
Mrk 9:46 if your eye causes you to sin, pluck it out 3
Gal 4:15 plucked out your eyes and given them to me. 5

pluck up 1.נסח 2.נתשׁ 3.עקר 4.ἐκριζόω 5.ἐκτίλλω
2Ch 7:20 will pluck you up from the land which I have given 2
Job 4:21 If their tent-cord is plucked up within them 1
Ecc 3: 2 to plant, and a time to pluck up what is planted; 3
Isa 33:20 tent, whose stakes will never be plucked up 1
38:12 My dwelling is plucked up and removed from me 1
Jer 1:10 to pluck up and to break down, to destroy 2
12:14 Behold, I will pluck them up from their land 2
14 will pluck up the house of Judah from among them. 2
15 And after I have plucked them up 2
17 then I will utterly pluck it up and destroy it 2
18: 7 that I will pluck up and break down and destroy it 2
31:28 watched over them to pluck up and break down 2
42:10 I will plant you, and not pluck you up; 2
45: 4 and what I have planted I am plucking up 2
Ezk 19:12 But the vine was plucked up in fury 2
Dan 11: 4 kingdom shall be plucked up and go to others 2
Ams 9:15 they shall never again be plucked up 2
Sir 10:15 The Lord has plucked up the roots of the nations 5
40:16 will be plucked up before any grass. 5
49: 7 to pluck up and afflict and destroy 4

pluck up by the roots 1.עקר (A)
Dan 7: 8 three . . horns were plucked up by the roots; 1

freshly plucked 1.טָרָף
Gen 8:11 and lo, in her mouth a freshly plucked olive leaf; 1

plumage 1.נוֹצָה
Job 39:13 but are they the pinions and plumage of love? 1
Ezk 17: 3 A great eagle . . rich in plumage of many colors 1
7 great eagle with great wings and much plumage; 1

plumb 1.εὑρίσκω
Jdt 8:14 You cannot plumb the depths of the human heart 1

plumb line 1.אֲנָךְ
Ams 7: 7 standing beside a wall built with a plumb line 1
7 the Lord . . with a plumb line in his hand. 1
8 the Lord said, "Behold, I am setting a plumb line 1

plummet 1.אֶבֶן 2.אֶבֶן בְּדִיל 3.מִשְׁקֶלֶת
2Kg 21:13 and the plummet of the house of Ahab; 3
Isa 28:17 justice the line, and righteousness the plummet; 3
34:11 and the plummet of chaos over its nobles. 1
Zec 4:10 shall see the plummet in the hand of Zerub'babel. 2

plump 1.בָּרִיא
Gen 41: 5 and behold, seven ears of grain, plump and good 1
7 swallowed up the seven plump and full ears. 1

plunder 1.בגד 2.בַּז 3.בִּזָּה 4.בזז 5.חלק 6.טֶרֶף 7.מְשִׁסָּה 8.שׁלל 9.שָׁלָל 10.שׁסה 11.שׁסס 12.ἁρπαγή 13.ἅρπαγμα 14.ἁρπάζω 15.διαρπαγή 16.διαρπάζω 17.λαμβάνω σκῦλα 18.λαφυρεύω 19.λάφυρον 20.λωποδυτέω 21.πορθέω 22.προνομεύω 23.προνομή 24.σκυλεία 25.σκυλεύω 26.σκυλεύω τὰ σκῦλα 27.σκῦλον 28.συλάω 29.diripio 30.rapina 31.rapio 32.spolio
Gen 34:27 sons of Jacob . . plundered the city 4
Jdg 2:14 gave them over to plunderers, who plundered them; 11
16 out of the power of those who plundered them. 10
1Sm 14:48 out of the hands of those who plundered them. 10
17:53 and they plundered their camp. 11
2Kg 7:16 went out, and plundered the camp of the Syrians. 4
2Ch 14:14 They plundered all the cities 4
14 for there was much plunder in them. 3
Ezr 9: 7 been given . . to plundering, and to utter shame 3
Neh 4: 4 give them up to be plundered in a land where 3
Est 3:13 to destroy . . and to plunder their goods. 4
8:11 to destroy, to slay . . and to plunder their goods 4
9:10 but they laid no hand on the plunder. 3
15 but they laid no hands on the plunder. 3
16 but they laid no hands on the plunder. 3
Ps 7: 4 with evil or plundered my enemy without cause 5
109:11 may strangers plunder the fruits of his toil! 4
Isa 10: 6 I command him, to take spoil and seize plunder 2
13 removed . . and have plundered their treasures; 10
11:14 they shall plunder the people of the east. 4
13:16 their houses will be plundered 11
17:14 portion . . and the lot of those who plunder us. 4
21: 2 the plunderer plunders, and the destroyer 1
42:22 this is a people robbed and plundered 10
Jer 20: 5 enemies, who shall plunder them, and seize them 4
50:10 Chalde'a shall be plundered; 9
10 all who plunder her shall be sated, says the LORD. 8
37 her treasures, that they may be plundered! 4
Ezk 29:19 its wealth and despoil it and plunder it 4
36: 5 that they might possess it and plunder it. 2
38:12 to seize spoil and carry off plunder; to assail 2
13 you assembled your hosts to carry off plunder 2
39:10 and plunder those who plundered them 4
10 and plunder those who plundered them 4
Dan 11:24 scattering among them plunder, spoil, and goods. 3
33 fall by sword and flame, by captivity and plunder 3
Ams 3:11 and your strongholds shall be plundered. 4
Nah 2: 9 Plunder the silver, plunder the gold! 4

9 Plunder the silver, plunder the gold! 4
3: 1 full of lies and booty–no end to the plunder! 6
Hab 2: 8 Because you have plundered many nations 8
8 all the remnant of the peoples shall plunder you 8
Zep 1:13 Their goods shall be plundered 7
2: 9 The remnant of my people shall plunder them 4
Zec 2: 8 glory sent me to the nations who plundered you 8
9 they shall become plunder for those who served 9
14: 2 the city shall be taken and the houses plundered 11
Mat 12:29 and plunder his goods 14
29 Then indeed he may plunder his house. 16
Mrk 3:27 enter a strong man's house and plunder his goods 16
27 then indeed he may plunder his house. 16
Heb 10:34 you joyfully accepted the plundering 12
1Es 4:24 when he steals and robs and plunders 20
8:77 to the sword and captivity and plundering 23
2Es 10:22 the ark of our covenant has been plundered 29
15:19 plunder their goods, because of hunger for bread 29
63 and shall plunder your wealth 32
16:46 gather their fruits, and plunder their goods 31
47 who conduct business, do it only to be plundered; 30
71 but plundering and destroying those 29
72 For they shall destroy and plunder their goods 29
Tob 3: 4 thou gavest us over to plunder, captivity, and death; 15
Jdt 1:14 plundered its markets 22
2: 7 and will hand them over to be plundered by my troops 15
11 hand them over to .. plunder 12
23 plundered all the people of Rassis 22
26 plundered their sheepfolds. 22
4: 1 how he had plundered .. all their temples; 25
7:26 surrender the whole city .. to be plundered. 23
8:19 were handed over .. to be plundered 15
21 our sanctuary will be plundered; and he will 22
15: 6 fell upon the Assyrian camp and plundered it 22
11 the people plundered the camp for 30 days. 18
Wis 10:20 Therefore the righteous plundered the ungodly; 25
Sir 16:13 The sinner will not escape with his plunder 13
36:25 the property will be plundered 16
LJr 1:18 they may not be plundered by robbers. 28
1Mc 1: 3 plundered many nations 17
19 he plundered the land of Egypt. 17
31 He plundered the city, burned it with fire 17
4:17 he said to the people, "Do not be greedy for plunder 27
18 afterward seize the plunder boldly. 27
23 Then Judas returned to plunder the camp 24
5:35 plundered it, and burned it with fire. 17
51 and razed and plundered the city 17
68 he plundered the cities 26
6: 3 he came and tried to take the city and plunder it 22
7:47 Then the Jews seized the spoils and the plunder 23
8:10 they plundered them, conquered the land 22
10:84 burned .. and plundered them 17
11:61 burned its suburbs .. and plundered them. 25
12:31 he crushed them and plundered them. 17
13:34 all that Trypho did was to plunder. 12
2Mc 8:30 they divided very much plunder 19
9:16 which he had formerly plundered 25
3Mc 5:41 in constant danger of being plundered. 16
4Mc 4:23 after he had plundered them he issued a decree 21

plunderer 1. בגד 2. בקק 3. שדד 4. שסה
Jdg 2:14 gave them over to plunderers, who plundered them; 4
Isa 21: 2 the plunderer plunders, and the destroyer 1
Jer 50:11 though you exult, O plunderers of my heritage 4
Obd 1: 5 If thieves came to you, if plunderers by night 3
Nah 2: 2 for plunderers have stripped them 2

plunge 1. טבל 2. נפל 3. βυθίζω 4. εἰμί 5. ὀλισθάνω
Job 9:31 yet thou wilt plunge me into a pit 1
Prv 13:17 A bad messenger plunges men into trouble 2
1Ti 6: 9 plunge men into ruin and destruction. 3
Sir 9: 9 in blood you be plunged into destruction. 5
1Mc 6:11 into what a great flood I now am plunged! 4

plunge headlong 1. שטף
Jer 8: 6 like a horse plunging headlong into battle. 1

ply a trade 1. סחר
Jer 14:18 For both prophet and priest ply their trade 1

pod 1. κεράτιον
Lke 15:16 the pods that the swine ate 1

poet 1. ποιητής
Act 17:28 as even some of your poets have said 1

point 1. לְ 2. מְעַט 3. ἐντεῦθεν 4. καιρός 5. μέλλω 6. μέχρι 7. ὅθεν 8. ὥστε
2Kg 20: 1 became sick and was at the point of death. 1
24:20 it came to the point in Jerusalem and Judah that •
Neh 3:16 Nehemi'ah .. repaired to a point opposite •
26 repaired to a point opposite the Water Gate •
Prv 5:14 point of utter ruin in the assembled congregation. 2
Isa 38: 1 became sick and was at the point of death. 1
Lke 7: 2 who was sick and at the point of death. 5
Joh 4:47 his son, for he was at the point of death. 5
2Co 7:11 At every point you have proved yourselves •
2Ti 4: 6 For I am already on the point of being sacrificed; •
Heb 12: 4 resisted to the point of shedding your blood. 6
Jas 2:10 whoever .. fails in one point has become guilty •
Rev 3: 2 strengthen what .. is on the point of death 5
Sir 18:21 when you are on the point of sinning, turn back. 4
2Mc 2:32 At this point therefore let us begin 3
13:10 who were on the point of being deprived of the law 5
4Mc 4:25 even to the point that .. 8
6:12 At that point, partly out of pity for his old age 7

point (2) 1. צִפֹּרֶן 2. ἀκμή 3. ἄκρος
Jer 17: 1 with a point of diamond it is engraved 1
Sir 43:19 when it freezes, it becomes pointed thorns. 3
2Mc 12:22 pierced by the points of their swords. 2

point (3) 1. ירה 2. שלח 3. προάγω
Prv 6:13 scrapes with his feet, points with his finger 1
Isa 58: 9 the pointing of the finger, and speaking 2
1Ti 1:18 the prophetic utterances which pointed to you 3
5:24 are conspicuous, pointing to judgment 3

point (4) 1. κεφάλαιον 2. σύνταξις
2Co 9: 6 The point is this: he who sows sparingly •
Heb 8: 1 Now the point in what we are saying is this 1
2Mc 15:38 If it is well told and to the point 2

glittering point 1. בָּרָק
Job 20:25 the glittering point comes out of his gall; 1

point in life 1. ἡλικία
2Mc 7:27 and brought you up to this point in your life 1

point of death 1. מות 2. ἐσχάτως
2Ch 32:24 Hezeki'ah .. was at the point of death 1
Mrk 5:23 My little daughter is at the point of death 2

point of dispute 1. ζήτημα
Act 25:19 they had certain points of dispute with him 1

point of view 1. κατά
2Co 5:16 we regard no one from a human point of view 1
16 once regarded Christ from a human point of view 1

point opposite 1. נֹכַח
Ezk 47:20 to a point opposite the entrance of Hamath. 1

point out 1. נכר 2. ἐπιδείκνυμι 3. παρεπιδείκνυμι 4. ὑποδείκνυμι
Gen 31:32 point out what I have that is yours, and take it. 1
Mat 24: 1 when his disciples came to point out to him 2
AEs 13: 4 pointed out to us that among all the nations 2
2Mc 15:10 pointing out the perfidy of the Gentiles 3
3Mc 5:15 he pointed out that .. 4
19 he .. pointed out that .. he had carried out 4
29 Hermon and all the king's friends pointed out 4

some point 1. μέρος
Rom 15:15 But on some points I have written to you 1

poison 1. חֵמָה 2. ראשׁ 3. ἰός 4. κακόω 5. φαρμακός
Deu 32:32 their grapes are grapes of poison 2
33 their wine is the poison of serpents 1
Job 6: 4 are in me; my spirit drinks their poison; 1
20:16 He will suck the poison of asps; 2
Ps 69:21 They gave me poison for food 2
140: 3 under their lips is the poison of vipers. Selah 1
Jer 8:14 and has given us poisoned water to drink 2
23:15 wormwood, and give them poisoned water to drink; 2
Ams 6:12 But you have turned justice into poison 2
Act 14: 2 poisoned their minds against the brethren. 4
Jas 3: 8 the tongue .. full of deadly poison. 3
Wis 1:14 there is no destructive poison in them 5
poison *See also* take.

poisonous 1. מְרִירִי 2. ראשׁ
Deu 32:24 devoured with .. heat and poisonous pestilence; 1
Jer 9:15 and give them poisonous water to drink. 2
poisonous *See also* fruit, weed.

pole 1. בַּד 2. בְּרִיחַ 3. מוט 4. מוֹטָה 5. נֵס
Exd 25:13 You shall make poles of acacia wood, and overlay 1
14 you shall put the poles into the rings 1
15 The poles shall remain in the rings of the ark; 1
27 as holders for the poles to carry the table. 1
28 You shall make the poles of acacia wood 1
27: 6 you shall make poles for the altar 1
6 make .. poles of acacia wood, and overlay them 1
7 the poles shall be put through the rings 1
7 so that the poles shall be upon the two sides 1
30: 4 holders for poles with which to carry it. 1
5 You shall make the poles of acacia wood 1
35:12 the ark with its poles, the mercy seat, and the veil 1
13 the table with its poles and all its utensils 1
15 the altar of incense, with its poles 1
16 with .. its poles, and all its utensils, the laver 1
37: 4 And he made poles of acacia wood 1
5 put the poles into the rings on the sides 1
14 as holders for the poles to carry the table. 1
15 He made the poles of acacia wood to carry 1
27 as holders for the poles with which to carry it. 1
28 he made the poles of acacia wood, and overlaid 1
38: 5 four rings .. as holders for the poles; 1
6 he made the poles of acacia wood, and overlaid 1
7 he put the poles through the rings on the sides 1
39:35 the ark of the testimony with its poles 1
39 grating of bronze, its poles, and all its utensils; 1
40:18 put in its poles, and raised up its pillars; 2
20 and put the poles on the ark, and set the mercy seat 1
Num 4: 6 shall put in its poles. 1
8 of goatskin, and shall put in its poles. 1
11 cover it .. and shall put in its poles; 1
14 shall put in its poles. 1
13:23 they carried it on a pole between two of them; 3
21: 8 Make a fiery serpent, and set it on a pole; 5
9 Moses made a bronze serpent, and set it on a pole; 5
1Kg 8: 7 made a covering above the ark and its poles. 1
8 the poles were so long that the ends .. were seen 1
8 ends of the poles were seen from the holy place 1
1Ch 15:15 ark of God upon their shoulders with the poles 4
2Ch 5: 8 cherubim made a covering above .. its poles. 1
9 the poles were so long that the ends of the poles 1
9 ends of the poles were seen from the holy place 1

police 1. ῥαβδοῦχος
Act 16:35 when it was day, the magistrates sent the police 1
38 police reported these words to the magistrates 1

policy 1. ἀγωγή 2. βουλή 3. πρᾶγμα 4. προαίρεσις
Sir 47:23 whose policy caused the people to revolt 2
2Mc 6: 8 should adopt the same policy toward the Jews 1
9:27 For I am sure that he will follow my policy 4
11:26 that they may know our policy and be of good cheer 4
3Mc 3:23 we may soon alter our policy. 3

polish 1. ברר 2. מרט 3. מרק 4. ἐκμάσσω 5. ξεστός
Isa 49: 2 he made me a polished arrow 1
Jer 46: 4 polish your spears, put on your coats of mail! 3
Ezk 21: 9 A sword, a sword is sharpened and also polished. 2
10 for slaughter, polished to flash like lightning! 2
11 the sword is given to be polished 2
11 sharpened and polished to be given into the hand 2
15 like lightning, it is polished for slaughter. •
28 it is polished to glitter and to flash 2
Sir 12:11 will be to him like one who has polished a mirror 4
1Mc 13:27 with polished stone at the front and back. 5
political *See* opponent.

pollute 1. גאל 2. חלל 3. חנף 4. טמא 5. עָדָה 6. שחת 7. ἀλισγέω 8. βδελύσσομαι 9. βεβηλόω 10. μιαίνω 11. μιαρός 12. μολύνω 13. contamino
Num 35:33 shall not thus pollute the land in which you live; 3
33 for blood pollutes the land 3
1Ch 5: 1 but because he polluted his father's couch 2
2Ch 36:14 polluted the house of the LORD which he had 4
Ps 106:38 land was polluted with blood. 3
Prv 25:26 Like a muddied spring or a polluted fountain 6
Isa 64: 6 all our righteous deeds are like a polluted garment. 5
Jer 3: 1 Would not that land be greatly polluted? 3
2 have polluted the land with your vile harlotry. 3
9 she polluted the land, committing adultery 3
16:18 because they have polluted my land 2
Ezk 20:43 doings with which you have polluted yourselves; 4
23:17 after she was polluted by them, she turned 4
30 and polluted yourself with their idols. 4
Mal 1: 7 By offering polluted food upon my altar. 1
7 upon my altar. And you say, 'How have we polluted it? 1
12 when you say that the LORD'S table is polluted 1
Rev 21: 8 as for the cowardly, the faithless, the polluted 8
1Es 1:49 polluted the temple of the Lord 10
8:83 a land polluted with the pollution of the aliens 12
2Es 10:22 our holy things have been polluted 13
15:25 Do not pollute my sanctuary. 13
Jdt 9: 2 polluted her womb to disgrace her 9
8 they intend .. to pollute the tabernacle 10
Sir 40:29 He pollutes himself with another man's food 7
2Mc 5:16 He took the holy vessels with his polluted hands 11
6: 2 also to pollute the temple in Jerusalem 12
polluted *See* lie.

pollution 1. טֻמְאָה 2. נִדָּה 3. ἀκαθαρσία 4. ἀλίσγημα 5. μίασμα 6. μιασμός 7. μολυσμός 8. μύσος
Ezr 6:21 separated .. from the pollutions 1
9:11 land unclean with the pollutions of the peoples 2
Act 15:20 abstain from the pollutions of idols 4
1Es 8:69 the alien peoples .. and their pollutions 3
83 a land polluted with the pollution of the aliens 7
Jdt 9: 4 abhorred the pollution of their blood 5
Wis 14:26 forgetfulness of favors, pollution of souls 6
1Mc 13:50 cleansed the citadel from its pollutions. 5
2Mc 6:19 rather than life with pollution 8

pomegranate 1. רִמּוֹן 2. ῥοΐσκος
Exd 28:33 On its skirts you shall make pomegranates 1
34 a golden bell and a pomegranate, a golden bell 1
34 a pomegranate, a golden bell and a pomegranate 1
39:24 they made pomegranates of blue and purple 1

25 bells between the pomegranates upon the skirts 1
25 the robe round about, between the pomegranates; 1
26 a bell and a pomegranate, a bell and a pomegranate 1
26 a bell and a pomegranate, a bell and a pomegranate 1
Num13:23 they brought also some pomegranates and figs. 1
20: 5 It is no place for . . or vines, or pomegranates; 1
Deu 8: 8 a land of . . vines and fig trees and pomegranates 1
1Kg 7:18 he made pomegranates; in two rows round about 1
20 200 pomegranates, in two rows round about; 1
42 400 pomegranates for the two networks 1
42 two rows of pomegranates for each network 1
2Kg 25:17 a network and pomegranates, all of bronze 1
2Ch 3:16 made 100 pomegranates, and put them 1
4:13 400 pomegranates for the two networks 1
13 two rows of pomegranates for each network 1
Sng 4: 3 Your cheeks are like halves of a pomegranate 1
13 Your shoots are an orchard of pomegranates 1
6: 7 Your cheeks are like halves of a pomegranate 1
11 see . . whether the pomegranates were in bloom. 1
7:12 whether . . and the pomegranates are in bloom. 1
8: 2 spiced wine . . the juice of my pomegranates. 1
Jer 52:22 a network and pomegranates, all of bronze 1
22 pillar had the like, with pomegranates. 1
23 There were 96 pomegranates on the sides; 1
23 pomegranates were 100 upon the network 1
Jol 1:12 Pomegranate, palm, and apple, all the trees 1
Hag 2:19 Do the vine, the fig tree, the pomegranate 1
Sir 45: 9 he encircled him with pomegranates 2

pomegranate tree 1. רִמּוֹן
1Sm 14: 2 Saul was staying . . under the pomegranate tree 1

pommel 1. ὑπωπιάζω
1Co 9:27 I pommel my body and subdue it 1

pomp 1. גָּאוֹן 2. יְקָר 3. תִּפְאָרָה 4. δόξα 5. φαντασία
Est 1: 4 he showed . . the splendor and pomp of his majesty 3
Ps 49:12 Man cannot abide in his pomp, he is like the beasts 2
20 Man cannot abide in his pomp, he is like the beasts 2
Isa 14:11 Your pomp is brought down to Sheol 1
Act 25:23 Agrippa and Berni'ce came with great pomp 5
1Mc 10:58 celebrated her wedding . . with great pomp 4
60 went with pomp to Ptolemais and met the two kings; 4
86 came out to meet him with great pomp. 4
11: 6 Jonathan met the king at Joppa with pomp 4

pond 1. אֲגַם
Exd 7:19 over their rivers, their canals, and their ponds 1

ponder 1. בין 2. הגה 3. שׂכל 4. διανοέω 5. διενθυμέομαι 6. ἐνθυμέομαι 7. ἐννοέω 8. συμβάλλω
Ps 64: 9 what God has wrought, and ponder what he has done. 3
Prv 15:28 The mind of the righteous ponders how to answer 2
Isa 14:16 who see you will stare at you, and ponder over you 1
Lke 2:19 pondering them in her heart. 8
Act 10:19 while Peter was pondering the vision 5
Sir 3:29 the intelligent man will ponder a parable 4
14:21 will also ponder her secrets. 7
16:20 Who will ponder his ways? 6
21:17 they will ponder his words in their minds. 4

ponder over 1. ἀντιβάλλω
2Mc 11:13 he pondered over the defeat which had befallen him 1

pool 1. אֲגַם 2. בְּרֵכָה 3. גֵּב 4. מַי 5. מִקְוֶה 6. κολυμβήθρα 7. κρήνη 8. λάκκος 9. συναγωγή 10. lacus
Exd 7:19 over . . all their pools of water, that they may 5
8: 5 the rivers, over the canals, and over the pools 1
2Sm 2:13 went out and met them at the pool of Gibeon; 2
13 they sat down, the one on the one side of the pool 2
13 one . . and the other on the other side of the pool. 2
4:12 killed them . . and hanged them beside the pool 2
1Kg 22:38 they washed the chariot by the pool of Sama'ria 2
2Kg 3:16 'I will make this dry stream-bed full of pools.' 3
18:17 came and stood by the conduit of the upper pool 2
20:20 how he made the pool and the conduit and brought 2
Neh 3:15 built the wall of the Pool of Shelah of the king's 2
16 repaired to . . the artificial pool 2
Ps 84: 6 early rain also covers it with pools. •
107:35 He turns a desert into pools of water 1
114: 8 who turns the rock into a pool of water 1
Ecc 2: 6 I made myself pools . . to water the forest 2
Sng 7: 4 Your eyes are pools in Heshbon, by the gate 2
Isa 7: 3 the conduit of the upper pool on the highway 2
14:23 a possession of the hedgehog, and pools of water 1
22: 9 you collected the waters of the lower pool 2
11 reservoir . . for the water of the old pool. 2
35: 7 the burning sand shall become a pool 1
36: 2 the upper pool on the highway to the Fuller's 2
41:18 I will make the wilderness a pool of water 1
42:15 the rivers into islands, and dry up the pools. 1
Jer 41:12 They came upon him at the great pool 4
Nah 2: 8 Nin'eveh is like a pool whose waters run away. 2
Joh 5: 2 Now there is in Jerusalem by the Sheep Gate a pool 6
7 I have no man to put me into the pool 6
9: 7 Go, wash in the pool of Silo'am" (which means Sent) 6
2Es 16:60 and pools on the tops of the mountains 10
Sir 43:20 it rests upon every pool of water 9
48:17 built pools for water. 7
1Mc 9:33 camped by the water of the pool of Asphar. 8

poor 1. אֶבְיוֹן 2. אִישׁ עָנִי 3. דַּל 4. דַּלָּה 5. זעף 6. ירשׁ 7. מוּךְ 8. מַחְסוֹר 9. מִסְכֵּן 10. עָנָו 11. עָנִי 12. רָאשׁ 13. רוּשׁ 14. רָזֶה 15. ἐλάσσων 16. πένης 17. πενιχρός 18. πτωχός
Gen 41:19 other cows came up after them, poor and very gaunt 3
Exd 22:25 to any of my people with you who is poor 11
23: 6 the justice due to your poor in his suit. 1
11 lie fallow, that the poor of your people may eat; 1
30:15 and the poor shall not give less 3
Lev 14:21 But if he is poor and cannot afford so much 3
19:10 leave them for the poor and for the sojourner 11
15 you shall not be partial to the poor 3
23:22 you shall leave them for the poor 11
27: 8 if a man is too poor to pay your valuation 7
Num13:20 whether the land is rich or poor 14
Deu 15: 4 there will be no poor among you (for the LORD 1
7 not . . shut your hand against your poor brother 1
9 your eye be hostile to your poor brother 1
11 For the poor will never cease out of the land; 1
11 wide your hand to . . the needy and to the poor 1
24:12 if . . poor man, you shall not sleep in his pledge; 11
14 not oppress a hired servant who is poor and needy 11
15 (for he is poor, and sets his heart upon it); 11
Rut 3:10 not gone after young men, whether poor or rich. 3
1Sm 2: 8 He raises up the poor from the dust; 3
18:23 seeing that I am a poor man and of no repute? 13
2Sm 12: 1 two men . . the one rich and the other poor. 12
4 but he took the poor man's lamb, and prepared it 12
2Kg 24:14 none remained, except the poorest people 4
25:12 captain . . left some of the poorest of the land 4
Est 9:22 sending . . to one another and gifts to the poor. 1
Job 5:16 poor have hope, and injustice shuts her mouth. 3
20:10 His children will seek the favor of the poor 3
19 For he has crushed and abandoned the poor 3
24: 4 They thrust the poor off the road; 1
4 the poor of the earth all hide themselves. 11
9 and take in pledge the infant of the poor. 11
14 that he may kill the poor and needy; 11
29:12 because I delivered the poor who cried 11
16 I was a father to the poor 1
30:25 Was not my soul grieved for the poor? 1
31:16 I have withheld anything that the poor desired 3
34:19 nor regards the rich more than the poor 3
28 that they caused the cry of the poor to come to him 3
Ps 9:18 the hope of the poor shall not perish for ever. 11
10: 2 In arrogance the wicked hotly pursue the poor; 11
9 he lurks that he may seize the poor 11
9 he seizes the poor when he draws him into his net. 11
12: 5 Because the poor are despoiled 11
14: 6 You would confound the plans of the poor 11
37:14 bend their bows, to bring down the poor and needy 11
40:17 As for me, I am poor and needy; 11
41: 1 Blessed is he who considers the poor! 3
49: 2 both low and high, rich and poor together! 1
70: 5 I am poor and needy; hasten to me, O God! 11
72: 2 with righteousness, and thy poor with justice! 11
4 May he defend the cause of the poor of the people 11
12 he delivers . . the poor and him who has no helper. 11
74:19 do not forget the life of thy poor for ever. 11
21 let the poor and needy praise thy name. 11
86: 1 answer me, for I am poor and needy. 11
109:16 pursued the poor and needy . . to their death. 2
22 poor and needy, and my heart is stricken within 11
112: 9 has distributed freely, he has given to the poor; 1
113: 7 He raises the poor from the dust 3
132:15 I will satisfy her poor with bread. 1
Prv 10:15 the poverty of the poor is their ruin. 3
13:23 The fallow ground of the poor yields much food 13
14:20 The poor is disliked even by his neighbor 13
21 but happy is he who is kind to the poor. 10
16:19 better to be of a lowly spirit with the poor 10
17: 5 He who mocks the poor insults his Maker; 13
18:23 poor use entreaties . . rich answer roughly. 13
19:17 He who is kind to the poor lends to the LORD 3
21:13 He who closes his ear to the cry of the poor 3
17 He who loves pleasure will be a poor man; 8
22: 2 The rich and the poor meet together; 13
7 The rich rules over the poor 13
9 blessed, for he shares his bread with the poor. 3
16 oppresses the poor to increase his own wealth 3
22 Do not rob the poor, because he is poor 3
22 Do not rob the poor, because he is poor 3
28: 3 A poor man who oppresses the poor is a . . rain 13
3 A poor man who oppresses the poor is a . . rain 3
8 gathers it for him who is kind to the poor. 3
15 bear is a wicked ruler over a poor people. 3
27 He who gives to the poor will not want 13
29: 7 A righteous man knows the rights of the poor; 3
14 If a king judges the poor with equity his throne 3
30: 9 lest I be poor, and steal, and profane the name 6
14 to devour the poor from off the earth, the needy 11
31: 9 maintain the rights of the poor and needy. 11
20 She opens her hand to the poor 11
Ecc 4:13 Better is a poor and wise youth than an old 9
14 though . . in his own kingdom had been born poor. 13
5: 8 If you see in a province the poor oppressed 13
9:15 But there was found in it a poor wise man 9
15 Yet no one remembered that poor man. 9
Isa 3:14 the spoil of the poor is in your houses. 11
15 by crushing . . by grinding the face of the poor? 11
10: 2 and to rob the poor of my people of their right 11
11: 4 with righteousness he shall judge the poor 3
14:30 the first-born of the poor will feed 3
25: 4 For thou hast been a stronghold to the poor 3
26: 6 The foot tramples it, the feet of the poor 11
29:19 the poor among men shall exult in the Holy One 1
32: 7 wicked devices to ruin the poor with lying words 11
41:17 the poor and needy seek water, and there is none 11
58: 7 and bring the homeless poor into your house; 11
Jer 2:34 is found the lifeblood of guiltless poor; 1
5: 4 I said, "These are only the poor, they have no sense; 3
22:16 He judged the cause of the poor and needy; 11
39:10 left in the land of Judah some of the poor people 3
40: 7 of the poorest of the land who had not been taken 4
52:15 carried away . . some of the poorest of the people 3
16 the guard left some of the poorest of the land 3
Ezk 16:49 but did not aid the poor and needy. 11
18:12 oppresses the poor and needy, commits robbery 11
22:29 they have oppressed the poor and needy 11
Dan 1:10 poorer condition than the youths . . of your own age. 5
Ams 4: 1 Sama'ria, who oppress the poor, who crush the needy 3
5:11 Therefore because you trample upon the poor 3
8: 4 and bring the poor of the land to an end 11
6 that we may buy the poor for silver 3
Hab 3:14 rejoicing as if to devour the poor in secret. 11
Zec 7:10 widow, the fatherless, the sojourner, or the poor; 11
Mat 5: 3 Blessed are the poor in spirit, for theirs is 18
11: 5 and the poor have good news preached to them. 18
19:21 sell what you possess and give to the poor 18
26: 9 and given to the poor. 18
11 For you always have the poor with you 18
Mrk 10:21 go, sell what you have, and give to the poor 18
12:42 a poor widow came, and put in two copper coins 18
43 this poor widow has put in more than all 18
14: 5 given to the poor 18
7 For you always have the poor with you 18
Lke 4:18 he has anointed me to preach good news to the poor 18
6:20 and said: "Blessed are you poor 18
7:22 the poor have good news preached to them. 18
14:13 when you give a feast, invite the poor, the maimed 18
21 bring in the poor and maimed and blind and lame.' 18
18:22 Sell all that you have and distribute to the poor 18
19: 8 the half of my goods I give to the poor 18
21: 2 he saw a poor widow put in two copper coins. 17
3 this poor widow has put in more than all of them; 18
Joh 2:10 and when men have drunk freely, then the poor wine; 15
12: 5 sold for 300 denarii and given to the poor? 18
6 This he said, not that he cared for the poor 18
8 The poor you always have with you 18
13:29 that he should give something to the poor. 18
Rom 15:26 pleased to make some contribution for the poor 18
2Co 6:10 as poor, yet making many rich 18
9: 9 He scatters abroad, he gives to the poor 16
Gal 2:10 only they would have us remember the poor 18
Jas 2: 5 Has not God chosen those who are poor in the world 18
Rev 3:17 not knowing that you are wretched, pitiable, poor 18
13:16 all, both small and great, both rich and poor 18
1Es 3:19 of the slave and the free, of the poor and the rich. 16
Sir 4: 1 My son, deprive not the poor of his living 18
4 nor turn your face away from the poor. 18
8 Incline your ear to the poor 18
7:32 Stretch forth your hand to the poor 18
10:22 The rich, and the eminent, and the poor 18
13:19 likewise the poor are pastures for the rich. 18
26: 4 Whether rich or poor, his heart is glad 18
34:20 a sacrifice from the property of the poor. 16
21 The bread of the needy is the life of the poor; 18
LJr 1:28 give none to the poor or helpless. 18

poor *See also* make, pretend, wretch.

become poor 1. מוּךְ 2. πτωχεύω
Lev 25:25 If your brother becomes poor, and sells part 1
35 if your brother becomes poor 1
39 if your brother becomes poor beside you 1
47 If . . your brother beside him becomes poor 1
2Co 8: 9 yet for your sake he became poor 2
Tob 4:21 Do not be afraid . . because we have become poor 2

poor man 1. אֶבְיוֹן 2. דַּל 3. מִסְכֵּן 4. עָנִי 5. רוּשׁ 6. ἐνδεής 7. πένης 8. πτωχός
Exd 23: 3 nor shall you be partial to a poor man in his suit. 2
Deu 15: 7 there is among you a poor man, one of your brethren 1
2Sm 12: 3 the poor man had nothing but one little ewe lamb 5
Job 31:19 lack of clothing, or a poor man without covering; 1
Ps 34: 6 This poor man cried, and the LORD heard him 4
Prv 13: 8 but a poor man has no means of redemption. 5
14:31 He who oppresses a poor man insults his Maker 2
19: 1 Better is a poor man who walks in his integrity 5
4 but a poor man is deserted by his friend. 2
7 All a poor man's brothers hate him; 5
22 poor man is better than a liar. 5

28: 6 Better is a poor man who walks in his integrity 5
11 poor man who has understanding will find him 2
29:13 The poor man and the oppressor meet together; 5
Ecc 6: 8 what does the poor man have who knows 4
9:16 though the poor man's wisdom is despised 3
Lke 16:20 at his gate lay a poor man named Laz'arus 8
22 The poor man died 8
Jas 2: 2 a poor man in shabby clothing also comes in 8
3 while you say to the poor man, "Stand there 8
6 But you have dishonored the poor man. 8
Tob 2: 2 bring whatever poor man of our brethren you . . find 6
4: 7 Do not turn your face away from any poor man 8
Wis 2:10 Let us oppress the righteous poor man 7
Sir 10:23 is not right to despise an intelligent poor man 8
30 A poor man is honored for his knowledge 8
11:21 to enrich a poor man quickly and suddenly. 7
13: 3 a poor man suffers wrong 8
18 what peace between a rich man and a poor man? 7
20 a poor man is an abomination to a rich one. 8
23 When the poor man speaks 8
21: 5 The prayer of a poor man goes from his lips 8
29: 9 Help a poor man for the commandment's sake 7
22 Better is the life of a poor man 8
30:14 Better off is a poor man who is well and strong 8
31: 4 The poor man toils as his livelihood diminishes 8
35:13 will not show partiality in the case of a poor man; 8
38:19 the life of the poor man weighs down his heart. 8

do poorly 1. εὐτελῶς
2Mc 15:38 if it is poorly done and mediocre 1

poplar 1. לִבְנֶה
Gen 30:37 took fresh rods of poplar and almond and plane 1
Hos 4:13 make offerings upon the hills, under oak, poplar 1
14: 5 he shall strike root as the poplar, •

populace 1. πλῆθος
2Mc 3:21 the prostration of the whole populace 1
4:39 the populace gathered against Lysimachus 1

popular 1. רצה
Est 10: 3 and popular with the multitude of his brethren 1

population 1. עַם
Num15:26 whole population was involved in the error. 1

great population 1. πολυοχλία
Bar 4:34 take away her pride in her great population 1

populous 1. הָמוֹן 2. רַב
Deu 26: 5 became a nation, great, mighty, and populous. 2
Isa 32:14 will be forsaken, the populous city deserted; 1

porch 1. אוּלָם 2. πυλών
1Kg 7: 6 there was a porch in front with pillars 1
Ezk 8:16 of the temple . . between the porch and the altar 1
Mat 26:71 when he went out to the porch, another maid saw him 2

porcupine 1. קִפֹּד
Isa 34:11 But the hawk and the porcupine shall possess it 1

pork 1. κρέας ὕειον 2. ὕειος
4Mc 5: 2 to eat pork and food sacrificed to idols. 1
6 I would advise you to save yourself by eating pork 2
6:15 save yourself by pretending to eat pork. 2

porphyry 1. בַּהַט
Est 1: 6 a mosaic pavement of porphyry, marble 1

port 1. τόπος
Act 27: 2 about to sail to the ports along the coast of Asia 1

portal 1. פֶּתַח 2. exitus
Prv 8: 3 at the entrance of the portals she cries aloud 1
2Es 6: 1 before the portals of the world were in place 2

portent 1. מוֹפֵת 2. σημεῖον
Ps 71: 7 I have been as a portent to many; 1
Isa 8:18 the children . . are signs and portents in Israel 1
20: 3 barefoot . . as a sign and a portent against Egypt 1
Jol 2:30 I will give portents in the heavens 1
Rev 12: 1 a great portent appeared in heaven, a woman 2
3 another portent appeared in heaven; 2
15: 1 Then I saw another portent in heaven 2

portico 1. στοά
Joh 5: 2 a pool . . which has five porticoes. 1
10:23 in the temple, in the portico of Solomon. 1
Act 3:11 in the portico called Solomon's 1
5:12 they were all together in Solomon's Portico. 1

portion 1. דָּבָר 2. חֶבֶל 3. חֵלֶק 4. חֶלְקָה 5. מַחֲלֹקֶת 6. מֵן 7. מָנָה 8. מְנָת 9. מַשְׂאֵת 10. מָשְׁחָה 11. מִשְׁחָה 12. פֶּה 13. תְּרוּמָה 14. תְּרוּמִיָּה 15. ἀποστολή 16. ἐπιμελῶς 17. μέλος 18. μερίς 19. μέρος 20. assatura 21. pars 22. portio
Gen 31:14 Is there any portion or inheritance left to us 3
43:34 Portions were taken to them from Joseph's table 9
34 but Benjamin's portion was five times as much 9
Exd 16: 4 go out and gather a day's portion every day 1
29:26 and it shall be your portion. 7
27 consecrate . . the thigh of the priests' portion 13
28 for it is the priests' portion to be offered 13
Lev 6:17 I have given it as their portion of my offerings 3
7:33 shall have the right thigh for a portion 7
35 This is the portion of Aaron and of his sons 11
8:29 it was Moses' portion of the ram of ordination 7
Num18: 8 I have given them to you as a portion 10
20 neither shall you have any portion among them; 3
20 I am your portion and your inheritance 3
31:36 half, the portion of those who had gone out to war 3
Deu 10: 9 no portion or inheritance with his brothers; 3
12:12 since he has no portion or inheritance with you. 3
14:27 Levite . . has no portion or inheritance with you. 3
29 Levite, because he has no portion or inheritance 3
18: 1 Levi . . no portion or inheritance with Israel; 3
8 They shall have equal portions to eat 3
32: 9 For the LORD'S portion is his people 3
33:21 for there a commander's portion was reserved; 4
Jos 14: 4 no portion was given to the Levites in the land 3
15:13 he gave . . a portion among the people of Judah 3
17: 5 there fell to Manas'seh ten portions, besides 2
14 Why have you given me but one lot and one portion 2
18: 5 They shall divide it into seven portions 3
7 The Levites have no portion among you 3
10 apportioned the land . . to each his portion. 5
19: 9 the portion of the tribe of Judah was too large 3
22:25 you have no portion in the LORD. 3
27 You have no portion in the LORD. 3
24:32 buried at Shechem, in the portion of ground 4
1Sm 1: 4 give portions to Penin'nah . . and to all her sons 7
5 he would give Hannah only one portion 7
9:23 Bring the portion I gave you, of which I said to you 7
2Sm 6:19 to each a cake of bread, a portion of meat, and a cake 20
20: 1 We have no portion in David, and . . no inheritance 3
1Kg 12:16 What portion have we in David? 3
2Kg 25:30 a regular allowance . . every day a portion 1
1Ch 16: 3 loaf of bread, a portion of meat, and a cake •
18 Canaan, as your portion for an inheritance. 2
2Ch 10:16 What portion have we in David? 3
31: 4 to give the portion due to the priests 7
15 to distribute the portions to their brethren •
19 designated by name to distribute portions 7
Neh 2:20 no portion or right or memorial in Jerusalem. 3
8:10 send portions to him for whom nothing 7
12 send portions and to make great rejoicing 7
12:44 gather . . portions required by the law 8
47 gave the daily portions for the singers 8
13:10 portions of the Levites had not been given 8
Job 20:29 This is the wicked man's portion from God 3
24:18 their portion is cursed in the land; 4
27:13 This is the portion of a wicked man with God 3
31: 2 What would be my portion from God above 3
Ps 11: 6 wind shall be the portion of their cup. 7
16: 5 The LORD is my chosen portion and my cup; 3
17:14 from men whose portion in life is of the world. 3
49:13 of those who are pleased with their portion. 12
68:23 dogs may have their portion from the foe. 6
73:26 God is the strength of my heart and my portion 3
105:11 Canaan as your portion for an inheritance. 2
119:57 The LORD is my portion; 3
142: 5 my refuge, my portion in the land of the living. 3
Ecc 9: 9 that is your portion in life and in your toil 3
11: 2 Give a portion to seven, or even to eight 3
Isa 17:14 This is the portion of those who despoil us 3
53:12 I will divide him a portion with the great •
57: 6 Among the smooth . . of the valley is your portion 3
Jer 10:16 Not like these is he who is the portion of Jacob 3
12:10 they have trampled down my portion 4
10 my pleasant portion a desolate wilderness. 4
13:25 is your lot, the portion I have measured out to you 7
51:19 Not like these is he who is the portion of Jacob 3
Lam 3:24 The LORD is my portion," says my soul 3
Ezk 45: 1 you shall set apart for the LORD a portion 13
7 corresponding . . to one of the tribal portions 3
14 as the fixed portion of oil, one tenth of a bath •
47:13 Joseph shall have two portions. 2
48: 1 from the east side to the west, Dan, one portion. •
2 from the east side to the west, Asher, one portion. •
3 the east side to the west, Naph'tali, one portion. •
4 the east side to the west, Manas'seh, one portion. •
5 the east side to the west, E'phraim, one portion. •
6 from the east side to the west, Reuben, one portion. •
7 from the east side to the west, Judah, one portion. •
8 shall be the portion which you shall set apart 13
8 in length equal to one of the tribal portions 3
9 portion which you shall set apart for the LORD 13
10 shall be the allotments of the holy portion 13
12 it shall belong to them as a special portion 14
12 portion from the holy portion of the land 13
18 of the length alongside the holy portion 13
18 it shall be alongside the holy portion. 13
20 The whole portion which you shall set apart 13
20 the holy portion together with the property 13
21 What remains on both sides of the holy portion 13
21 from the 25,000 cubits of the holy portion 13
21 the west border, parallel to the tribal portions 3
21 The holy portion with the sanctuary 13
22 The portion of the prince shall lie between •
23 the east side to the west, Benjamin, one portion. •
24 from the east side to the west, Simeon, one portion •
25 the east side to the west, Is'sachar, one portion. •
26 the east side to the west, Zeb'ulun, one portion. •
27 from the east side to the west, Gad, one portion. •
29 these are their several portions, says the Lord 5
Dan 1: 5 assigned them a daily portion of the rich food 1
Mic 2: 4 ruined; he changes the portion of my people; 3
Zec 2:12 the LORD will inherit Judah as his portion 3
Lke 10:42 Mary has chosen the good portion 18
1Es 6:29 a portion be scrupulously given to these men 16
9:51 send portions to those who have none; 15
54 to give portions to those who had none 15
2Es 7:10 And he said to me, "So also is Israel's portion. 21
15:30 and shall devastate a portion of the land 22
60 and abolish a portion of your glory 21
AEs 13:16 Do not neglect thy portion 18
Wis 2: 9 because this is our portion, and this our lot. 18
Sir 7:31 give him his portion, as is commanded you 18
14: 9 A greedy man's eye is not satisfied with a portion 18
17:17 Israel is the Lord's own portion. 18
24:12 in the portion of the Lord 18
41:21 taking away some one's portion or gift 18
44:23 he determined his portions 18
45:22 he has no portion among the people 18
22 Lord himself is his portion and inheritance. 18
50:12 when he received the portions 17
2Mc 1:26 preserve thy portion and make it holy. 18
3Mc 5:11 the Lord sent upon the king a portion of sleep 19
17 make the present portion of the banquet joyful 19
6: 3 a people of your consecrated portion 18

portion *See also* receive.

allotted portion 1. חֹק
Ezk 16:27 and diminished your allotted portion 1

choice portion 1. מָנָה 2. רֵאשִׁית
Est 9:19 they send choice portions to one another. 1
22 days for sending choice portions to one another 1
Ezk 48:14 not alienate this choice portion of the land 2

chosen portion 1. מָנָה
Ps 16: 5 The LORD is my chosen portion and my cup; 1

double portion 1. מִשְׁנֶה 2. שְׁנַיִם
Deu 21:17 by giving him a double portion of all that he has 2
Isa 61: 7 you shall have a double portion 1
7 in your land you shall possess a double portion; 1

fat portion 1. חֵלֶב
Gen 4: 4 Abel brought . . of their fat portions. 1

holy portion 1. קֹדֶשׁ
Lev 24: 9 since it is for him a most holy portion 1
Num 6:20 they are a holy portion for the priest 1
Ezk 45: 4 It shall be the holy portion of the land; 1

memorial portion 1. אַזְכָּרָה 2. μνημόσυνον
Lev 2: 2 priest shall burn this as its memorial portion 1
9 from the cereal offering its memorial portion 1
16 as its memorial portion part of the crushed grain 1
5:12 a handful of it as its memorial portion 1
6:15 burn this as its memorial portion on the altar 1
24: 7 it may go with the bread as a memorial portion 1
Num 5:26 a handful . . as its memorial portion 1
Sir 38:11 a memorial portion of fine flour 2
45:16 incense . . as a memorial portion 2

portion of food 1. מָנָה 2. σιτομέτριον
Est 2: 9 provided . . ointments and her portion of food 1
Lke 12:42 to give them their portion of food 2

portion out 1. חלק 2. מדד
Ps 60: 6 and portion out the Vale of Succoth. 2
108: 7 I will . . portion out the Vale of Succoth. 2
Isa 34:17 his hand . . portioned it out to them with the line; 1

sacred portion 1. קֹדֶשׁ
Deu 26:13 I have removed the sacred portion out of my house 1

portion set apart 1. תְּרוּמָה
Ezk 45: 6 Alongside the portion set apart as the holy 1

portray 1. חקה 2. חקק 3. διαγράφω
Ezk 4: 1 and portray upon it a city, even Jerusalem; 2
8:10 and there, portrayed upon the wall round about 1
23:14 she saw men portrayed upon the wall, the images 1
14 images of the Chalde'ans portrayed in vermilion 2
43:11 portray the temple, its arrangement, its exits 3

publicly portray 1. προγράφω
Gal 3: 1 Christ was publicly portrayed as crucified? 1

position 1. יָד 2. ἀρχή 3. κεῖμαι 4. πρόσωπον 5. τόπος 6. χρεία
Num 2:17 each in position, standard by standard. 1

Mat 22:16 for you do not regard the position of men. 4
Mrk 12:14 for you do not regard the position of men 4
1Co 14:16 how can any one in the position of an outsider say 5
Jde 1: 6 the angels that did not keep their own position 2
1Mc 1:34 These strengthened their position; •
10:37 be put in positions of trust in the kingdom 6
2Mc 3:11 a man of very prominent position 3
8: 6 He captured strategic positions 5
13:18 The king . . tried strategy in attacking their positions. 5
4Mc 8: 7 have positions of authority in my government 2

position *See also* keep, put, take.

high position 1. *πρωτεύω* 2. *ὑπεροχή*

1Ti 2: 2 for kings and all who are in high positions 2
2Mc 6:18 Eleazar, one of the scribes in high position 1

man's position 1. *πρόσωπον*

2Co 5:12 those who pride themselves on a man's position 1

proud position 1. *ὑπερηφανία*

AEs 14:16 I abhor the sign of my proud position 1

possess 1. אחז 2. אֲחֻזָּה 3. היה לְ 4. ירש 5. לְ 6. מוֹרָשָׁה 7. מִמְשָׁק 8. נחל 9. חסן (A) 10. *ἐγκρατής* 11. *ἐν* 12. *ἐπιγινώσκω* 13. *ἔχω* 14. *κατάσχεσις* 15. *κατέχω* 16. *κληρονομέω* 17. *κτῆσις* 18. *λαμβάνω* 19. *περιέχω* 20. *συγγίνομαι* 21. *ὑπάρχω* 22. *φέρω* 23. possido

Gen 15: 7 to give you this land to possess. 4
8 how am I to know that I shall possess it? 4
22:17 your descendants shall possess the gate 4
24:60 may your descendants possess the gate of those 4
47: 1 my brothers, with . . all that they possess, 5
49:30 bought . . to possess as a burying place. 2
50:13 bought . . to possess as a burying place. 2
Exd 23:30 until you are increased and possess the land. 8
Lev 20:24 I will give it to you to possess, a land flowing 4
25:24 And in all the country you possess 2
Num14:24 his descendants shall possess it. 4
21:35 they slew him . . and they possessed his land. 4
27:11 to his kinsman . . and he shall possess it. 4
33:53 for I have given the land to you to possess it. 4
36: 8 every daughter who possesses an inheritance 4
8 may possess the inheritance of his fathers. 4
Deu 1:39 to them I will give it, and they shall possess it. 4
3:18 LORD your God has given you this land to possess; 4
4:14 land which you are going over to possess. 4
26 land . . you are going over the Jordan to possess; 4
5:31 do them in the land which I give them to possess.' 4
33 live long in the land which you shall possess. 4
6: 1 land to which you are going over, to possess it; 4
18 that you may . . go in and possess the land 4
9: 4 LORD has brought me in to possess this land'; 4
5 are you going in to possess their land; 4
6 LORD . . not giving you this good land to possess 4
10:11 that they may go in and possess the land 4
11: 8 the land which you are going over to possess 4
11 land which you are going over to possess is a land 4
31 when you possess it and live in it 4
12: 1 which the LORD . . has given you to possess 4
15: 4 gives you for an inheritance to possess) 4
17:14 come to the land . . possess it and dwell in it 4
19: 2 land which the LORD . . gives you to possess. 4
14 land that the LORD your God gives you to possess 4
21: 1 in the land . . LORD your God gives you to possess 4
25:19 LORD . . gives you for an inheritance to possess 4
28:42 trees and the fruit . . locust shall possess. 4
30: 5 into the land which your fathers possessed 4
5 land . . fathers possessed, that you may possess 4
18 land . . going over the Jordan to enter and possess. 4
31:13 land . . you are going over the Jordan to possess. 4
32:47 land . . going over the Jordan to possess. 4
33:23 O Naph'tali . . possess the lake and the south. 4
Jos 1:11 land . . the LORD your God gives you to possess. 4
15 the land of your possession, and shall possess it 4
13: 1 there remains yet very much land to be possessed. 4
17:18 shall clear it and possess it to its . . borders; 3
22: 9 land of which they had possessed themselves 1
23: 5 and you shall possess their land, as . . promised 4
24: 4 I gave Esau the hill country of Se'ir to possess 4
Jdg 11:24 Will you not possess what Chemosh your god gives 4
24 God has dispossessed before us, we will possess. 4
18: 7 lacking nothing . . and possessing wealth 4
9 be slow to go, and enter in and possess the land. 4
1Ch 28: 8 that you may possess this good land 4
Neh 9:15 thou didst tell them to go in to possess the land 4
23 told their fathers to enter and possess. 4
24 descendants went in and possessed the land 4
Job 22: 8 The man with power possessed the land •
Ps 25:13 his children shall possess the land. 4
37: 9 who wait for the LORD shall possess the land. 4
11 the meek shall possess the land 4
22 those blessed by the LORD shall possess the land 4
29 The righteous shall possess the land 4
34 he will exalt you to possess the land; 4
69:35 his servants shall dwell there and possess it; 4
Isa 14: 2 the house of Israel will possess them 8
21 lest they rise and possess the earth 4
34:11 But the hawk and the porcupine shall possess it 4
17 they shall possess it for ever 4
54: 3 and your descendants will possess the nations 4
57:13 he who takes refuge in me shall possess the land 8
60:21 they shall possess the land for ever 4
61: 7 in your land you shall possess a double portion; 4
63:18 Thy holy people possessed thy sanctuary 4
Ezk 33:24 the land is surely given us to possess. 6
25 and shed blood; shall you then possess the land? 4
26 shall you then possess the land? 4
36: 5 that they might possess it and plunder it. 4
12 they shall possess you 4
Dan 7:18 possess the kingdom for ever, for ever and ever.' 9
Hos 9: 6 Nettles shall possess their precious things 4
Ams 2:10 and led you . . to possess the land of the Amorite. 4
9:12 that they may possess the remnant of Edom 4
Obd 1:17 Jacob shall possess their own possessions. 4
19 Those of the Negeb shall possess Mount Esau 4
19 they shall possess the land of E'phraim 4
19 and Benjamin shall possess Gilead. •
20 the people of Israel shall possess Phoenicia 4
20 exiles . . shall possess the cities of the Negeb. 4
Zep 2: 9 like Gomor'rah, a land possessed by nettles 7
9 the survivors of my nation shall possess them. 8
Mat 19:21 If you would be perfect, go, sell what you possess 21
Mrk 3:22 He is possessed by Be-el'zebul 13
7:25 a woman, whose little daughter was possessed 13
Act 8: 7 spirits came out of many who were possessed 13
1Co 8: 1 we know that "all of us possess knowledge. 13
7 However, not all possess this knowledge 11
12:30 Do all possess gifts of healing? 13
2Co 6:10 having nothing, and yet possessing everything. 15
1Es 8: 7 For Ezra possessed great knowledge 19
2Es 6:59 why do we not possess our world as an inheritance? 23
Tob 3:17 because Tobias was entitled to possess her. 16
Jdt 8:10 who was in charge of all she possessed 21
9:13 the house possessed by thy children. 14
12:16 he was moved with great desire to possess her 20
Wis 11:12 for a twofold grief possessed them 18
Sir 25: 4 for the aged to possess good counsel! 12
27:30 the sinful man will possess them. 10
Bar 3:24 And how vast the territory that he possesses! 17
LJr 1: 5 to let fear for these gods possess you 18
Sus 1:11 their lustful desire to possess her. 20
1Mc 5:23 all they possessed •
2Mc 2: 9 being possessed of wisdom 13
4:25 possessing no qualification for the high priesthood 22
3Mc 5:20 possessed by a savagery worse than . . Phalaris 13
7:21 They also possessed greater prestige 13

possess *See also* give.

possess a spirit 1. *πνευματικός*

1Co 2:13 to those who possess the Spirit. 1

cause to possess 1. נחל

Zec 8:12 I will cause the remnant of this people to possess 1

possess wisdom 1. *εἰμὶ ἐγκρατής*

Wis 8:21 I perceived that I would not possess wisdom 1

possessed by a demon 1. *δαιμονίζομαι*

Mat 15:22 my daughter is severely possessed by a demon. 1

thing possessed 1. *ὑπάρχω*

Act 4:32 any of the things which he possessed 1

possessed with a demon 1. *δαιμονίζομαι*

Mat 8:16 many who were possessed with demons 1
Mrk 1:32 all who were sick or possessed with demons. 1
5:18 the man who had been possessed with demons 1
Lke 8:36 he who had been possessed with demons 1

possession 1. אחז 2. אֲחֻזָּה 3. יְבוּל 4. יָד 5. יְרֻשָּׁה 6. יֵשׁ לְ 7. מוֹרָשׁ 8. מוֹרָשָׁה 9. מִקְנֶה 10. מִקְנָה 11. נַחֲלָה 12. נֶכֶס 13. סְגֻלָּה 14. עֹשֶׁר 15. קִנְיָן 16. רְכוּשׁ 17. חֵלֶק (A) 18. *ἐγκρατής* 19. *κατάσχεσις* 20. *κληροδοσία* 21. *κρατέω* 22. *κτῆμα* 23. *παρά* 24. *περιποίησις* 25. *ὕπαρξις* 26. *ὑπάρχος* 27. *ὑπάρχω* 28. possessio 29. sors

Gen 12: 5 brother's son, and all their possessions 16
13: 6 for their possessions were so great 16
15:14 they shall come out with great possessions. 16
17: 8 for an everlasting possession; 2
23: 9 give it to me . . as a possession for a burying 2
18 to Abraham as a possession in the presence 10
20 to Abraham as a possession for a burying place 2
26:14 He had possessions of flocks and herds 9
31:18 cattle in his possession which he had acquired 15
36: 7 For their possessions were too great for them 16
43 in the land of their possession. 2
47:11 and gave them a possession in the land of Egypt 2
48: 4 this land . . for an everlasting possession. 2
Exd 6: 8 I will give it to you for a possession. 8
19: 5 you shall be my own possession among all peoples; 13
21:16 found in possession of him, shall be put to death. 4
22: 4 stolen beast is found alive in his possession 4
Lev 14:34 land of Canaan, which I give you for a possession 2
34 in a house in the land of your possession 2
25:32 the houses in the cities of their possession 2
33 house that was sold in a city of their possession 2
33 houses . . of the Levites are their possession 2
34 for that is their perpetual possession 2
41 return to the possession of his fathers 2
46 your sons . . to inherit as a possession for ever 2
27:21 the priest shall be in possession of it 2
22 is not a part of his possession by inheritance 2
Num27: 4 Give to us a possession among our father's 2
7 give them possession of an inheritance 2
32: 5 land be given to your servants for a possession; 2
22 land shall be your possession before the LORD 2
29 give them the land of Gilead for a possession; 2
30 shall have possessions among you in . . Canaan. 1
32 possession of our inheritance shall remain 2
35: 2 from the inheritance of their possession 2
8 give from the possession of the people of Israel 2
28 manslayer may return to . . his possession. 2
Deu 2: 5 I have given Mount Se'ir to Esau as a possession. 5
9 not give you any of their land for a possession 5
9 have given Ar to the sons of Lot for a possession.' 5
12 as Israel did to the land of their possession 5
19 not give you any of the land . . as a possession 5
19 given it to the sons of Lot for a possession.' 5
3:20 then you shall return every man to his possession 5
4:20 be a people of his own possession, as at this day. 11
7: 6 chosen you to be a people for his own possession 13
14: 2 chosen you to be a people for his own possession 13
21:16 assigns his possessions as an inheritance •
26:18 you are a people for his own possession 13
32:49 give to the people of Israel for a possession; 2
33: 4 law, as a possession for the assembly of Jacob. 8
Jos 1:15 you shall return to the land of your possession 5
12: 6 gave . . land for a possession to the Reubenites 5
7 Joshua gave their land to . . as a possession 5
21:12 had been given to Caleb . . as his possession. 2
41 in the midst of the possession of the people 2
22: 4 your home in the land where your possession lies 2
7 Moses had given a possession in Bashan; •
7 to the other half Joshua had given a possession •
1Ch 7:28 possessions and settlements were Bethel 2
9: 2 the first to dwell again in their possessions 2
2Ch 1:11 you have not asked possessions, wealth, honor 14
12 will also give you riches, possessions, and honor 12
20:11 by coming to drive us out of thy possession 5
21:14 bring a great plague on . . all your possessions 16
17 carried away all the possessions they found 16
31: 1 every man to his possession. 2
3 contribution . . from his own possessions 16
32:29 God had given him very great possessions. 16
35: 7 these were from the king's possession. 16
Ezr 4:16 you will then have no possession in the province 17
Job 1:10 his possessions have increased in the land. 9
20:28 possessions of his house will be carried away 3
Ps 2: 8 and the ends of the earth your possession. 2
78:55 he apportioned them for a possession 11
105:21 he made him . . ruler of all his possessions 15
135: 4 chosen Jacob . . Israel as his own possession. 13
Ecc 2: 7 I had also great possessions of herds and flocks 9
5:19 given wealth and possessions and power to enjoy 12
6: 2 to whom God gives wealth, possessions, and honor 12
Isa 14:23 I will make it a possession of the hedgehog 7
Jer 32: 8 the right of possession and redemption is yours; 5
Ezk 11:15 to us this land is given for a possession. 8
25: 4 over to the people of the East for a possession 8
10 to the people of the East as a possession 8
36: 2 The ancient heights have become our possession, 8
3 became the possession of the rest of the nations 8
5 gave my land to themselves as a possession 8
44:28 you shall give them no possession in Israel; 2
28 no possession in Israel; I am their possession. 2
45: 1 When you allot the land as a possession 11
5 as their possession for cities to live in. 2
6 you shall assign for the possession of the city 2
Obd 1:17 Jacob shall possess their own possessions. 7
Zep 2: 7 shall become the possession of the remnant •
Zec 13: 5 the land has been my possession since my youth. •
Mal 3:17 my special possession on the day when I act 13
Mat 19:22 for he had great possessions. 22
24:47 he will set him over all his possessions. 27
Mrk 10:22 he had great possessions. 22
Lke 12:15 not consist in the abundance of his possessions 27
33 Sell your possessions, and give alms 27
44 he will set him over all his possessions. 27
Act 2:45 they sold their possessions and goods 22
7: 5 promised to give it to him in possession 19
Eph 1:14 until we acquire possession of it 24
Heb 10:34 a better possession and an abiding one. 25
2Es 14:31 to you for a possession in the land of Zion 29
16:47 their houses and possessions, and their persons 28
Tob 4: 7 Give alms from your possessions 27
8 If you have many possessions 27
Wis 8: 5 If riches are a desirable possession in life 22
13:17 When he prays about possessions 22
Sir 4:16 descendants will remain in possession of her. 19
25:21 do not desire a woman for her possessions. 6
36:24 He who acquires a wife gets his best possession 15
41: 1 one who lives at peace among his possessions 26

51:21 therefore I have gained a good possession. 22
1Mc 1:57 the book . . was found in the possession of any one 23
10:89 Ekron and all its environs as his possession. 20
11:34 We have confirmed as their possession •
13:38 let the strongholds . . be your possession. 27
2Mc 2:14 they are in our possession. 23
10:17 they gained possession of the places 18
13:13 and get possession of the city. 18
15:37 the city has been in the possession of the Hebrews 21

possession *See also* gain, get, give, put, strip, take.

possession by inheritance 1. אֲחֻזָּה
Lev 27:24 the land belongs as a possession by inheritance 1

king's possession 1. βασιλικός
1Es 1: 7 these were given from the king's possessions 1

valuable possession 1. מִגְדָּנָה
2Ch 21: 3 gifts, of silver, gold, and valuable possessions 1

possessor 1. בַּעַל 2. κτήτωρ
Prv 1:19 it takes away the life of its possessors. 1
Act 4:34 as many as were possessors of lands or houses 2

possible 1. ἀρά 2. δύναμαι 3. δυνατός 4. εἰμί 5. ἐνδέχομαι 6. ἔξεστι 7. μήποτε 8. πῶς 9. capax 10. possibilis
Mat 19:26 but with God all things are possible. 3
24:24 to lead astray, if possible, even the elect. 3
26:39 My father, if it be possible, let this cup pass 3
Mrk 9:23 All things are possible to him who believes. 3
10:27 for all things are possible with God. 3
13:22 to lead astray, if possible, the elect. 3
14:35 if it were possible, the hour might pass from him. 3
36 Abba, Father, all things are possible to thee 3
Lke 18:27 impossible with men is possible with God. 3
Act 2:24 it was not possible for him to be held by it. 3
8:22 if possible, the intent . . may be forgiven you. 1
20:16 at Jerusalem, if possible, on the day of Pentecost 3
27:39 planned if possible to bring the ship ashore. 2
Rom 12:18 If possible . . live peaceably with all. 3
Gal 4:15 I bear you witness that, if possible 3
Php 3:11 that if possible I may attain the resurrection 8
2Es 4:44 and if it is possible, and if I am worthy 10
10:55 as far as it is possible for your eyes to see it 9
Tob 10: 2 he said, "Is it possible that he has been detained? 7
2 is it possible that Gabael has died 7
Sir 18: 6 It is not possible to diminish or increase them 4
6 nor is it possible to trace the wonders 4
22:21 a renewal of friendship is possible. 4
22 do not worry, for reconciliation is possible 4
2Mc 3: 6 it was possible for them 3
11:18 he has agreed to what was possible. 5
14:29 Since it was not possible to oppose the king 4
4Mc 17: 7 If it were possible for us 6

possible *See also* best, quickly, soon.

post 1. מָקוֹם 2. מִשְׁמֶרֶת 3. עֹמֶד 4. שׂוּם 5. διάταξις 6. διατάσσω 7. ἐκτίθημι 8. παρεμβολή
1Kg 20:24 do this: remove the kings, each from his post 1
2Kg 11:18 And the priest posted watchmen over the house 4
2Ch 7: 6 priests stood at their posts; the Levites also 2
23:18 Jehoi'ada posted watchmen 4
30:16 They took their accustomed posts 3
Isa 21: 8 and at my post I am stationed whole nights. 2
Jdt 7:32 he dismissed the people to their various posts 8
8:36 went to their posts. 5
AEs 16:19 Therefore post a copy of this letter publicly 7
2Mc 14:22 Judas posted armed men in readiness 6
3Mc 5:44 they confidently posted the armed forces 6

post (2) 1. מְזוּזָה 2. עַמּוּד 3. κανών 4. πάσσαλος 5. στῦλος
Jdg 16: 3 took hold of the doors . . and the two posts 1
Sng 3:10 He made its posts of silver, its back of gold 2
Ezk 45:19 and the posts of the gate of the inner court. 1
46: 2 shall take his stand by the post of the gate. 1
Jdt 13: 6 She went up to the post at the end of the bed 3
9 and pulled down the canopy from the posts 5
Sir 26:12 so will she sit in front of every post 4

post *See* leave.

posterity 1. אַחֲרִית 2. זֶרַע 3. נֶכֶד 4. σπέρμα 5. generatio
Gen 21:23 deal falsely . . with my posterity 3
Num 21:30 their posterity perished from Heshbon 4
Ps 22:30 Posterity shall serve him; 2
37:37 there is posterity for the man of peace. 1
38 the posterity of the wicked shall be cut off. 1
102:28 their posterity . . established before thee. 2
109:13 May his posterity be cut off; 1
Isa 14:22 cut off from Babylon . . offspring and posterity 3
Dan 11: 4 not to his posterity, 1
Lke 1:55 to Abraham and to his posterity for ever. 4
Act 3:25 saying to Abraham, 'And in your posterity 4
7: 5 to him . . and to his posterity after him 4
6 his posterity would be aliens 4
13:23 Of this man's posterity 4
2Es 3:19 thy commandment to the posterity of Israel. 5
12:32 who will arise from the posterity of David ‡
Tob 4:12 their posterity will inherit the land. 4
Sir 41: 6 on their posterity will be a perpetual reproach. 4
44:13 Their posterity will continue for ever 4
21 nations would be blessed through his posterity; 4
21 exalt his posterity like the stars 4
47:20 defiled your posterity 4
22 nor destroy the posterity of him who loved him 4
Man 1: 1 God . . of their righteous posterity; 4

postpone 1. ὑπερβάλλω
Sir 5: 7 nor postpone it from day to day 1

posture 1. στάσις
3Mc 1:23 resorted to the same posture of supplication 1

pot 1. דּוּד 2. כִּיּוֹר 3. נֵבֶל 4. סִיר 5. עָצָב 6. פָּרוּר 7. תַּנּוּר 8. ξέστης 9. σκεύη 10. χαλκεῖον
Gen 15:17 behold, a smoking fire pot and a flaming torch 7
Exd 27: 3 You shall make pots for it to receive its ashes 4
38: 3 he made all the utensils of the altar, the pots 4
Num 11: 8 people . . boiled it in pots, and made cakes of it; 6
Jdg 6:19 meat he put in a basket, and the broth he put in a pot 6
1Sm 2:14 thrust it into the pan, or kettle, or caldron, or pot; 6
1Kg 7:40 Hiram also made the pots, the shovels 2
45 the pots, the shovels, and the basins, all these 4
2Kg 4:38 Set on the great pot, and boil pottage 4
39 and came and cut them up into the pot of pottage 4
40 cried out, "O man of God, there is death in the pot! 4
41 Then bring meal." And he threw it into the pot 4
41 And there was no harm in the pot. 4
25:14 they took away the pots, and the shovels 4
2Ch 4:11 Huram also made the pots, the shovels 4
16 pots, the shovels, the forks, and all the equipment 4
35:13 boiled the holy offerings in pots, in caldrons 4
Job 41:20 smoke, as from a boiling pot and burning rushes. 1
31 He makes the deep boil like a pot; 4
Ps 58: 9 Sooner than your pots can feel the heat of thorns 4
Ecc 7: 6 For as the crackling of thorns under a pot, 4
Jer 1:13 What do you see?" And I said, "I see a boiling pot 4
22:28 Is this man Coni'ah a despised, broken pot 5
52:18 they took away the pots, and the shovels 4
19 the firepans, and the basins, and the pots 4
Lam 4: 2 they are reckoned as earthen pots 3
Ezk 24: 3 Set on the pot, set it on, pour in water also; 4
6 to the pot whose rust is in it 4
Zec 12: 6 I will make the clans of Judah like a blazing pot 2
14:20 pots in the house of the LORD shall be as the bowls 4
21 every pot in Jerusalem and Judah shall be sacred 4
Mrk 7: 4 washing of cups and pots and vessels of bronze.) 8
Rev 2:27 as when earthen pots are broken in pieces 9
1Es 1:12 they boiled the sacrifices in brass pots 10
Sir 13: 2 The pot will strike against it •

clay pot 1. χύτρα
Sir 13: 2 can the clay pot associate with the iron kettle? 1

pot of ointment 1. מֶרְקָחָה
Job 41:31 he makes the sea like a pot of ointment. 1

potsherd 1. חֲרָסִית 2. חֶרֶשׂ 3. ὄστρακον
Job 2: 8 he took a potsherd with which to scrape himself 2
41:30 His underparts are like sharp potsherds; 2
Ps 22:15 my strength is dried up like a potsherd 2
Jer 19: 2 at the entry of the Potsherd Gate, and proclaim 1
Sir 22: 7 like one who glues potsherds together 3

pottage 1. נָזִיד 2. ἕψεμα
Gen 25:29 Once when Jacob was boiling pottage, Esau came 1
34 Jacob gave Esau bread and pottage of lentils 1
2Kg 4:38 and boil pottage for the sons of the prophets. 1
39 and came and cut them up into the pot of pottage 1
40 while they were eating of the pottage, they cried 1
Hag 2:12 and touches with his skirt bread, or pottage 1
Bel 1:33 He had boiled pottage 2

red pottage 1. אָדֹם
Gen 25:30 eat some of that red pottage, for I am famished! 1

potter 1. יצר 2. פֶּחָר (A) 3. κεραμεύς
1Ch 4:23 the potters and inhabitants of Neta'im 1
Ps 2: 9 dash them in pieces like a potter's vessel. 1
Isa 29:16 Shall the potter be regarded as the clay; 1
30:14 its breaking is like that of a potter's vessel 1
41:25 as on mortar, as the potter treads clay. 1
45: 9 with his Maker, an earthen vessel with the potter! •
64: 8 we are the clay, and thou art our potter; 1
Jer 18: 2 Arise, and go down to the potter's house 1
3 I went down to the potter's house 1
4 vessel . . of clay was spoiled in the potter's hand 1
4 as it seemed good to the potter to do. 1
6 can I not do with you as this potter has done? 1
6 Behold, like the clay in the potter's hand 1
19: 1 Thus said the LORD, "Go, buy a potter's earthen flask 1
11 this city, as one breaks a potter's vessel 1
Lam 4: 2 reckoned as . . pots, the work of a potter's hands! 1
Dan 2:41 toes partly of potter's clay and partly of iron 2
Mat 27: 7 and bought with them the potter's field 3
10 and they gave them for the potter's field 3
Rom 9:21 Has the potter no right over the clay 3
Wis 15: 7 when a potter kneads the soft earth 3
Sir 27: 5 The kiln tests the potter's vessels 3
33:13 As clay in the hand of the potter 3
38:29 So too is the potter sitting at his work 3

poultice 1. μάλαγμα
Wis 16:12 For neither herb nor poultice cured them 1

pound 1. λίτρα 2. μνᾶ
Lke 19:13 he gave them ten pounds 2
16 'Lord, your pound has made ten pounds more.' 2
16 'Lord, your pound has made ten pounds more.' 2
18 Lord, your pound has made five pounds.' 2
18 Lord, your pound has made five pounds.' 2
20 'Lord, here is your pound 2
24 Take the pound from him 2
24 give it to him who has the ten pounds.' 2
25 they said to him, 'Lord, he has ten pounds!') 2
Joh 12: 3 Mary took a pound of costly ointment of pure nard 1
19:39 about a 100 pounds' weight. 1

pour 1. יצק 2. נגר 3. נסך 4. נתך 5. סוך 6. ערה 7. שׁפך 8. βάλλω 9. ἐκχέω 10. ἐπιχέω 11. καταχέω 12. κεράννυμι 13. χέω
Gen 28:18 for a pillar and poured oil on the top of it. 1
35:14 drink offering on it, and poured oil on it. 1
Exd 4: 9 from the Nile and pour it upon the dry ground; 7
9:33 the rain no longer poured upon the earth. 4
29: 7 and pour it on his head and anoint him. 1
30: 9 and you shall pour no libation thereon. 3
32 It shall not be poured upon the bodies 5
Lev 2: 1 he shall pour oil upon it, and put frankincense 1
6 you shall break it in pieces, and pour oil on it 1
8:12 he poured some of the anointing oil on Aaron's 1
14:15 pour it into the palm of his own left hand 1
26 the priest shall pour some of the oil 1
41 shall pour into an unclean place outside the city 7
21:10 upon whose head the anointing oil is poured 1
Num 5:15 shall pour no oil upon it and put no frankincense 1
1Sm 10: 1 Samuel took a vial of oil and poured it on his head 1
1Kg 18:33 with water, and pour it on the burnt offering 1
2Kg 3:11 Eli'sha . . is here, who poured water on the hands 1
4: 4 shut the door . . and pour into all these vessels; 1
5 as she poured they brought the vessels to her. 1
9: 3 Then take the flask of oil, and pour it on his head 1
6 and the young man poured the oil on his head 1
16:13 and poured his drink offering 3
Job 12:21 He pours contempt on princes 7
Ps 45: 2 grace is poured upon your lips; 1
75: 8 he will pour a draught from it 2
107:40 he pours contempt upon princes 7
Isa 32:15 until the Spirit is poured upon us from on high 6
42:25 he poured upon him the heat of his anger 7
44: 3 For I will pour water on the thirsty land 1
3 I will pour my Spirit upon your descendants 1
Ezk 24: 3 Set on the pot, set it on, pour in water also; 1
7 she did not pour it upon the ground 7
30:15 I will pour my wrath upon Pelusium 7
Hos 9: 4 They shall not pour libations of wine to the LORD; 3
Mat 26: 7 she poured it on his head 11
12 In pouring this ointment on my body 8
Lke 10:34 bound up his wounds, pouring on oil and wine 10
Joh 13: 5 Then he poured water into a basin 8
Rom 5: 5 God's love has been poured into our hearts 9
Rev 12:15 The serpent poured water . . out of his mouth 8
16 river which the dragon had poured from his mouth 8
14:10 poured unmixed into the cup of his anger 12
16: 2 first angel went and poured his bowl on the earth 9
3 The second angel poured his bowl into the sea 9
4 The third angel poured his bowl into the rivers 9
8 The fourth angel poured his bowl on the sun 9
10 The fifth angel poured his bowl on the throne 9
12 angel poured his bowl on the river Euphra'tes 9
17 The seventh angel poured his bowl into the air 9
Sir 43:19 He pours the hoarfrost upon the earth like salt 13
4Mc 6:25 poured stinking liquids into his nostrils. 11

pour a libation 1. נסך 2. σπένδω
Exd 25:29 bowls with which to pour libations; 1
37:16 bowls and flagons with which to pour libations. 1
Sir 50:15 poured a libation of the blood of the grape 2

pour as a libation 1. σπένδω
Php 2:17 Even if I am to be poured as a libation 1

pour down 1. ירד 2. נגר 3. נזל 4. ריק 5. immitto
Job 36:28 which the skies pour down, and drop upon man 3
Jol 2:23 he has poured down for you abundant rain 1
Mic 1: 4 like waters poured down a steep place. 2
6 and I will pour down her stones into the valley 2
Mal 3:10 and pour down for you an overflowing blessing. 4
2Es 4:49 and poured down a heavy and violent rain 5

pour down rain 1. נטף
Ps 68: 8 earth quaked, the heavens poured down rain 1

pour forth 1. נבע 2. נתך 3. פוק 4. *ἀνομβρέω*
5. *βρύω* 6. eructo
Job 40:11 Pour forth the overflowings of your anger 3
Ps 19: 2 Day to day pours forth speech 1
119:171 My lips will pour forth praise 1
145: 7 pour forth the fame of thy abundant goodness 1
Jer 44: 6 my wrath and my anger were poured forth 2
Jas 3:11 Does a spring pour forth . . fresh water 5
2Es 14:40 my heart poured forth understanding 6
Sir 18:29 pour forth apt proverbs. 4
39: 6 he will pour forth words of wisdom 4
50:27 who out of his heart poured forth wisdom. 4

pour oil 1. *λιπαίνω*
Sir 38:11 pour oil on your offering 1

pour out 1. זרם 2. יצק 3. ירד 4. נבע 5. נסך 6. נתך
7. ערה 8. פוק 9. צוק 10. ריק 11. שפך 12. שְׁפַךְ
13. *ἐκπορεύομαι* 14. *ἐκχέω* 15. *ἐξομβρέω* 16. effundo
17. fundo
Gen 35:14 and he poured out a drink offering on it 5
Exd 29:12 the rest of the blood you shall pour out 11
Lev 4: 7 the rest of the blood of the bull he shall pour out 11
12 a clean place, where the ashes are poured out 12
12 where the ashes are poured out it shall be burned 12
18 the rest of the blood he shall pour out at the base 11
25 pour out the rest of its blood at the base 11
30 pour out the rest of its blood at the base 11
34 pour out the rest of its blood at the base 11
8:15 purified the altar, and poured out the blood 2
9: 9 poured out the blood at the base of the altar 2
17:13 shall pour out its blood and cover it with dust 11
Num28: 7 you shall pour out a drink offering 5
Deu 12:16 the blood; you shall pour it out upon the earth 11
24 you shall pour it out upon the earth like water. 11
27 the blood of your sacrifices shall be poured out 11
15:23 blood . . pour it out on the ground like water. 11
1Sm 1:15 I have been pouring out my soul before the LORD. 11
7: 6 and drew water and poured it out before the LORD 11
2Sm 23:16 would not drink of it; he poured it out to the LORD 5
1Kg 13: 3 the ashes that are upon it shall be poured out.' 11
5 and the ashes poured out from the altar 11
2Kg 4:40 And they poured out for the men to eat. 2
41 and said, "Pour out for the men, that they may eat. 2
1Ch 11:18 would not drink of it; he poured it out to the LORD 5
2Ch 12: 7 my wrath shall not be poured out upon Jerusalem 6
34:21 great is the wrath of the LORD that is poured out 6
25 my wrath will be poured out upon this place 6
Job 3:24 my groanings are poured out like water. 6
10:10 Didst thou not pour me out like milk and curdle me 6
16:13 he pours out my gall on the ground. 11
29: 6 the rock poured out for me streams of oil! 9
30:16 now my soul is poured out within me; 11
Ps 16: 4 their libations of blood I will not pour out 5
22:14 I am poured out like water 11
42: 4 These things I remember, as I pour out my soul 11
62: 8 O people; pour out your heart before him; 11
69:24 Pour out thy indignation upon them 11
77:17 The clouds poured out water; the skies gave forth 1
79: 3 poured out their blood like water round about 11
6 Pour out thy anger on the nations that do not know 11
94: 4 They pour out their arrogant words, they boast 4
102: 0 when he is faint and pours out his complaint 11
106:38 poured out innocent blood, the blood of their 11
142: 2 I pour out my complaint before him 11
Prv 1:23 behold, I will pour out my thoughts to you; 4
15: 2 but the mouths of fools pour out folly. 4
28 mouth of the wicked pours out evil things. 4
Sng 1: 3 oils are fragrant, your name is oil poured out; 10
Isa 26:16 they poured out a prayer when thy chastening was 9
29:10 the LORD has poured out upon you a spirit 5
53:12 because he poured out his soul to death 7
57: 6 to them you have poured out a drink offering 11
58:10 if you pour yourself out for the hungry 8
63: 6 and I poured out their lifeblood on the earth. 3
Jer 6:11 Pour it out upon the children in the street 11
7:18 they pour out drink offerings to other gods 5
20 and my wrath will be poured out on this place 6
10:25 Pour out thy wrath upon the nations 11
14:16 For I will pour out their wickedness upon them. 11
19:13 have been poured out to other gods 5
32:29 offerings have been poured out to other gods 5
42:18 As my anger and my wrath were poured out 6
18 so my wrath will be poured out on you when you go 6
44:17 burn incense to the queen . . pour out libations 5
18 left off burning . . and pouring out libations 5
19 burned incense . . and poured out libations to her 5
19 and poured out libations to her? 5
25 burn incense . . and to pour out libations to her. 5
Lam 2: 4 he has poured out his fury like fire. 11
11 soul is in tumult; my heart is poured out in grief 11
12 their life is poured out on their mothers' bosom. 11
19 Pour out your heart like water before 11
4:11 full vent to his wrath, he poured out his hot anger; 11
Ezk 7: 8 Now I will soon pour out my wrath upon you 11
14:19 and pour out my wrath upon it with blood 11
20: 8 Then I thought I would pour out my wrath upon them 11
13 Then I thought I would pour out my wrath upon them 11
21 Then I thought I would pour out my wrath upon them 11
28 there they poured out their drink offerings. 5
33 and with wrath poured out, I will be king over you. 11
34 an outstretched arm, and with wrath poured out; 11
21:31 I will pour out my indignation upon you; 11
22:22 I the LORD have poured out my wrath upon you. 11
31 I have poured out my indignation upon them; 11
23: 8 and poured out their lust upon her. 11
36:18 I poured out my wrath upon them for the blood 11
39:29 when I pour out my Spirit upon the house of Israel 11
Dan 9:11 curse and oath . . been poured out upon us 6
27 decreed end is poured out on the desolator. 6
Hos 5:10 upon them I will pour out my wrath like water. 11
Jol 2:28 that I will pour out my spirit on all flesh; 11
29 in those days, I will pour out my spirit. 11
Ams 5: 8 the waters of the sea, and pours them out upon 11
9: 6 and pours them out upon the surface of the earth- 11
Nah 1: 6 His wrath is poured out like fire 6
Zep 1:17 their blood shall be poured out like dust 11
3: 8 to pour out upon them my indignation 11
Zec 4:12 two golden pipes from which the oil is poured out? 10
12:10 I will pour out on the house of David 11
Mat 26:28 my blood . . which is poured out for many 14
Mrk 14:24 my blood . . which is poured out for many. 14
Lke 22:20 This cup which is poured out for you 14
Joh 2:15 and he poured out the coins of the money-changers 14
Act 2:17 I will pour out my Spirit upon all flesh 14
18 in those days I will pour out my Spirit 14
33 he has poured out this which you see and hear. 14
10:45 Holy Spirit had been poured out even on the Gentiles 14
Tit 3: 6 which he poured out upon us richly 14
Rev 11: 5 fire pours out from their mouth and consumes 13
16: 1 pour out on the earth the seven bowls of the wrath 14
2Es 15:35 shall pour out a heavy tempest upon the earth 16
40 shall pour out upon every high and lofty place 17
44 they shall pour out the tempest and all its wrath 16
Sir 1: 9 he poured her out upon all his works. 14
10:13 the man who clings to it pours out abominations. 15
16:11 he is mighty to forgive, and he pours out wrath. 14
18:11 pours out his mercy upon them. 14
24:33 I will again pour out teaching like prophecy 14
30:18 Good things poured out upon a mouth 14
32: 4 do not pour out talk 14
35:14 nor the widow when she pours out her story. 14
36: 7 Rouse thy anger and pour out thy wrath 14
39:28 they will pour out their strength 14
50:15 he poured it out at the foot of the altar 14
1Mc 7:17 their blood they poured out round about Jerusalem 14

pour out as an offering 1. *σπένδω*
4Mc 3:16 he poured out the drink as an offering to God. 1

pour out tears 1. דלף
Job 16:20 My friends scorn me; my eye pours out tears to God 1

pour over 1. שפך 2. *καταχέω*
Jdg 6:20 put them on this rock, and pour the broth over them. 1
Ps 92:10 thou hast poured over me fresh oil. ‡
Mrk 14: 3 she broke the flask and poured it over his head. 2

pour upon 1. *καταχέω*
2Mc 1:31 the liquid . . be poured upon large stones. 1

poverty 1. רָאשׁ 2. רִישׁ 3. *ἔνδεια* 4. *πτωχεία*
5. *ὑστέρημα* 6. *ὑστέρησις* 7. paupertas
Prv 6:11 poverty will come upon you like a vagabond 2
10: 4 A slack hand causes poverty 1
15 the poverty of the poor is their ruin. 2
13:18 Poverty and disgrace come to him who ignores 2
24:34 poverty will come upon you like a robber 2
28:19 pursuits will have plenty of poverty. 2
30: 8 give me neither poverty nor riches; 2
31: 7 let them drink and forget their poverty 2
Mrk 12:44 out of her poverty has put in everything she had 6
Lke 21: 4 she out of her poverty put in all the living 5
2Co 8: 2 their extreme poverty 4
9 so that by his poverty you might become rich. 4
Rev 2: 9 'I know your tribulation and your poverty 4
2Es 15:49 I will send evils upon you, widowhood, poverty 7
Sir 10:31 A man honored in poverty, how much more in wealth! 4
31 how much more in poverty! 4
11:12 who lacks strength and abounds in poverty 4
14 poverty and wealth, come from the Lord. 4
13:24 poverty is evil in the opinion of the ungodly. 4
18:25 in the days of wealth think of poverty and need. 4
20:21 may be prevented from sinning by his poverty 3
22:23 Gain the trust of your neighbor in his poverty 4
26:28 a warrior in want through poverty 3

poverty *See also* come.

powder 1. אָבָק 2. דַּק 3. דקק
Exd 32:20 burnt it with fire, and ground it to powder 2
Deu 28:24 will make the rain of your land powder and dust; 1
2Ch 34: 7 beat the Ashe'rim and the images into powder 3

fragrant powder 1. אֲבָקָה
Sng 3: 6 with all the fragrant powders of the merchant? 1

power 1. אוֹן 2. אֵל 3. אֵל יָד 4. גְבוּרָה 5. זְרוֹעַ 6. חַיִל
7. יָד 8. יכל 9. כֹּחַ 10. כַּף 11. משל 12. עַז 13. עֹז
14. עָצְמָה 15. קֶרֶן 16. שַׁלִּיט 17. תֹּקֶף 18. חֵסֶן (A)
19. יַד (A) 20. שלט (A) 21. *ἀλκή* 22. *βία* 23. *δύναμαι*
24. *δύναμις* 25. *δυναστεία* 26. *δυνατός* 27. *ἐνέργεια*
28. *ἐξισχύω* 29. *ἐξουσία* 30. *ἔργον* 31. *ἰσχύς*
32. *ἰσχύω* 33. *κέρας* 34. *κρατέω* 35. *κράτος*
36. *πάρειμι* 37. *πύλη* 38. *σθένος* 39. *χείρ*
40. imperium 41. manus 42. potentatus 43. potestas
44. principatus 45. sensus 46. virtus
Gen 16: 6 Behold, your maid is in your power; 7
31:29 It is in my power to do you harm; 2
49: 3 pre-eminent in pride and pre-eminent in power. 12
Exd 4:21 all the miracles which I have put in your power; 7
9:16 to show you my power, so that my name may be 9
15: 6 Thy right hand, O LORD, glorious in power 9
32:11 with great power and with a mighty hand? 9
Lev 26:19 I will break the pride of your power 13
Num14:17 let the power of the LORD be as great as thou hast 9
22:38 Have I now any power at all to speak anything? 8
Deu 4:37 brought you out of Egypt . . by his great power 9
8:17 My power and the might of my hand have gotten me 9
18 LORD . . who gives you power to get wealth; 9
9:29 whom thou didst bring out by thy great power 9
28:32 not be in the power of your hand to prevent it. 2
32:36 when he sees that their power is gone 7
34:11 for all the mighty power and all the great 7
Jos 8:20 and they had no power to flee this way or that 7
17:17 You are a numerous people, and have great power; 9
Jdg 2:14 sold them into the power of their enemies round 7
16 out of the power of those who plundered them. 7
23 he did not give them into the power of Joshua. 7
1Sm 2:10 LORD will . . and exalt the power of his anointed. 15
4: 3 come . . and save us from the power of our enemies. 10
8 deliver us from the power of these mighty gods? 7
2Sm 8: 3 he went to restore his power at the river 7
18:19 has delivered him from the power of his enemies. 7
31 delivered you . . from the power of all who rose up 7
2Kg 3:15 the power of the LORD came upon him. 7
17:36 brought you out . . with great power 9
18:20 that mere words are strategy and power for war? 4
1Ch 29:11 Thine, O LORD, is the greatness, and the power 4
12 In thy hand are power and might; 9
2Ch 13:20 Jerobo'am did not recover his power 9
20: 6 In thy hand are power and nmight 9
25: 8 for God has power to help or to cast down. 9
26:13 307,500, who could make war with mighty power 9
Ezr 4:23 and by force and power made them cease 6
8:22 power of his wrath is against all that forsake 13
Neh 1:10 people . . thou hast redeemed by thy great power 9
5: 5 but it is not in our power to help it, for other men 3
9:37 power also over our bodies and over our cattle 11
Est 10: 2 the acts of his power and might, and . . account 17
Job 1:12 Behold, all that he has is in your power; 7
2: 6 the LORD said to Satan, "Behold, he is in your power; 7
5:20 from death, and in war from the power of the sword. 7
8: 4 into the power of their transgression. 7
21: 7 live, reach old age, and grow mighty in power? 6
22: 8 The man with power possessed the land 5
23: 6 he contend with me in the greatness of his power? 9
24:22 God prolongs the life of the mighty by his power; 9
26: 2 How you have helped him who has no power! 9
12 By his power he stilled the sea; 9
14 But the thunder of his power who can understand? 4
27:22 he flees from its power in headlong flight. 7
36:22 Behold, God is exalted in his power; 9
37:23 he is great in power and justice 9
40:16 his power in the muscles of his belly. 1
Ps 21:13 We will sing and praise thy power. 4
22:20 Deliver . . my life from the power of the dog! 7
37:33 The LORD will not abandon him to his power 7
49:15 God will ransom my soul from the power of Sheol 7
59:11 make them totter by thy power, and bring them down 6
62:11 I heard this: that power belongs to God; 13
63: 2 in the sanctuary, beholding thy power and glory. 13
10 they shall be given over to the power of the sword 7
66: 3 So great is thy power that thy enemies cringe 13
68:34 Ascribe power to God, whose majesty 13
34 over Israel, and his power is in the skies. 13
35 God . . gives power and strength to his people. 13
71:18 to all the generations to come. Thy power 4
78:26 by his power he led out the south wind; 13
42 They did not keep in mind his power 7
61 delivered his power to captivity 13
79:11 according to thy great power preserve 5
89:48 Who can deliver his soul from the power of Sheol? 7
90:11 Who considers the power of thy anger 13
106:10 delivered them from the power of the enemy. 7
42 brought into subjection under their power. 7
111: 6 He has shown his people the power of his works 9
145:11 glory of thy kingdom, and tell of thy power 4
147: 5 Great is our LORD, and abundant in power; 9
Prv 3:27 when it is in your power to do it. 7
6: 3 for you have come into your neighbor's power 10

18:21 Death and life are in the power of the tongue 7
Ecc 4: 1 On the side of their oppressors there was power 9
8: 8 No man has power to retain the spirit 16
Isa 36: 5 that mere words are strategy and power for war? 4
40:26 because he is strong in power not one is missing. 9
29 He gives power to the faint 9
47: 9 and the great power of your enchantments. 14
14 deliver themselves from the power of the flame. 7
50: 2 cannot redeem? Or have I no power to deliver? 9
Jer 10:12 It is he who made the earth by his power 9
16:21 I will make them know my power and my might 7
18:21 give them over to the power of the sword 7
27: 5 I who by my great power and my outstretched arm 9
32:17 made the heavens and the earth by thy great power 9
51:15 It is he who made the earth by his power 9
Ezk 22: 6 every one according to his power, have been bent 5
24:21 profane my sanctuary, the pride of your power 13
35: 5 the people of Israel to the power of the sword 7
Dan 2:37 given the kingdom, the power, and the might 18
3:27 fire had not had any power over the bodies 20
4:30 Babylon, which I have built by my mighty power 18
6:27 who has saved Daniel from the power of the lions 19
8: 4 there was no one who could rescue from his power; 7
7 ram had no power to stand before him 9
7 no one who could rescue the ram from his power. 7
22 four kingdoms shall arise . . not with his power. 9
24 His power shall be great, and he shall cause 9
11:16 glorious land, and all of it shall be in his power. 7
25 he shall stir up his power and his courage 9
12: 7 shattering of the power of the holy people 7
Hos 13:14 Shall I ransom them from the power of Sheol? 7
Mic 2: 1 because it is in the power of their hand. 2
3: 8 But as for me, I am filled with power 9
Hab 3: 4 from his hand; and there he veiled his power. 13
Zec 4: 6 Not by might, nor by power, but by my Spirit 9
Mat 14: 2 that is why these powers are at work in him. 24
16:18 powers of death shall not prevail against it. 37
22:29 neither the scriptures nor the power of God. 24
24:29 the powers of the heavens will be shaken; 24
30 with power and great glory; 24
26:64 the Son of man seated at the right hand of Power 24
Mrk 5:30 perceiving in himself that power had gone forth 24
6:14 that is why these powers are at work in him. 24
9: 1 the kingdom of God has come with power. 24
12:24 you know neither the scriptures nor the power of God 24
13:25 the powers in the heavens will be shaken. 24
26 coming in clouds with great power and glory. 24
14:62 the Son of man seated at the right hand of Power 24
Lke 1:17 go before him in the spirit and power of Eli'jah 24
35 the power of the Most High will overshadow you; 24
4:14 in the power of the Spirit 24
36 with authority and power he commands 24
5:17 the power of the Lord was with him to heal. 24
6:19 for power came forth from him and healed them all. 24
8:46 I perceive that power has gone forth from me. 24
9: 1 gave them power and authority over all demons 24
10:19 authority . . over all the power of the enemy 24
12: 5 who . . has power to cast into hell 29
21:26 the powers of the heavens will be shaken. 24
27 coming in a cloud with power and great glory. 24
22:53 this is your hour, and the power of darkness. 29
69 seated at the right hand of the power of God. 24
24:49 until you are clothed with power from on high. 24
Joh 1:12 he gave power to become children of God; 29
10:18 I have power to lay it down 29
18 I have power to take it again 29
14:30 He has no power over me; •
17: 2 since thou hast given him power over all flesh 29
19:10 Do you not know that I have power to release you 29
10 I have . . power to crucify you? 29
11 You would have no power over me 29
Act 1: 8 you shall receive power 24
3:12 by our own power or piety 24
4: 7 By what power or by what name did you do this? 24
33 with great power 24
6: 8 Stephen, full of grace and power 24
8:10 that power of God which is called Great. 24
19 saying, "Give me also this power 29
10:38 with the Holy Spirit and with power 24
26:18 turn . . from the power of Satan to God 29
Rom 1: 4 designated Son of God in power 24
16 it is the power of God for salvation to every one 24
20 namely, his eternal power and deity 24
3: 9 both Jews and Greeks, are under the power of sin •
8:38 nor things present, nor things to come, nor powers 24
9:17 for the very purpose of showing my power in you 24
22 What if God, desiring . . to make known his power 26
11:23 for God has the power to graft them in again. 26
15:13 by the power of the Holy Spirit you may abound 24
19 by the power of signs and wonders 24
19 by the power of the Holy Spirit 24
1Co 1:17 lest the cross of Christ be emptied of its power. •
18 to us who are being saved it is the power of God. 24
24 Christ the power of God and the wisdom of God. 24
2: 4 in demonstration of the Spirit and of power 24
5 in the power of God. 24
4:19 but their power. 24
20 God does not consist in talk but in power. 24
5: 4 with the power of our Lord Jesus 24
6:14 will also raise us up by his power. 24
14:13 should pray for the power to interpret. •
15:24 every rule and every authority and power. 24
43 It is sown in weakness, it is raised in power. 24
56 the power of sin is the law. 24
2Co 4: 7 to show that the transcendent power belongs to God 24
6: 7 truthful speech, and the power of God 24
10: 4 divine power to destroy strongholds 26
12: 9 for my power is made perfect in weakness 24
9 that the power of Christ may rest upon me. 24
13: 4 lives by the power of God 24
4 we shall live with him by the power of God. 24
Eph 1:19 what is the immeasurable greatness of his power 24
21 rule and authority and power and dominion 24
2: 2 following the prince of the power of the air 29
3: 7 which was given me by the working of his power. 24
10 the principalities and powers 29
18 may have power to comprehend with all the saints 28
20 the power at work within us 24
6:12 against the principalities, against the powers 29
Php 3:10 know him and the power of his resurrection 24
21 by the power which enables him 27
Col 1:11 May you be strengthened with all power 24
2:15 He disarmed the principalities and powers 29
1Th 1: 5 also in power and in the Holy Spirit 24
2Th 1:11 may fulfil every . . work of faith by his power 24
2: 9 will be with all power and with pretended signs 24
2Ti 1: 7 a spirit of power and love and self-control. 24
8 in the power of God 24
3: 5 denying the power of it 24
Heb 1: 3 upholding the universe by his word of power 24
2:14 him who has the power of death, that is, the devil. 35
6: 5 the powers of the age to come 24
7:16 by the power of an indestructible life. 24
11:11 By faith Sarah . . received power to conceive 24
Jas 5:16 The prayer of a righteous man has great power 32
1Pe 1: 5 who by God's power are guarded through faith 24
3:22 angels, authorities, and powers subject to him. 24
2Pe 1: 3 His divine power has granted to us all things 24
16 made known to you the power and coming of our Lord 24
2:11 angels, though greater in might and power 24
1Jn 5:19 the whole world is in the power of the evil one. •
Rev 2:26 I will give him power over the nations 29
27 as I myself have received power from my Father; •
3: 8 I know that you have but little power 24
4:11 Lord and God, to receive glory and honor and power 24
5:12 to receive power and wealth and wisdom and might 24
6: 8 they were given power over a fourth of the earth 29
7: 2 angels who had been given power to harm earth •
12 honor and power and might be to our God for ever 24
9: 3 were given power like the power of scorpions 29
3 were given power like the power of scorpions 29
10 power of hurting men . . lies in their tails. 29
19 For the power of the horses is in their mouths 29
11: 3 I will grant my two witnesses power to prophesy •
6 They have power to shut the sky, that no rain 29
6 power over the waters to turn them into blood 29
17 hast taken thy great power and begun to reign. 24
12:10 salvation . . power and the kingdom of our God 24
13: 2 to it the dragon gave his power and his throne 24
14:18 the angel who has power over fire 29
15: 8 smoke from the glory of God and from his power 24
16: 9 God who had power over these plagues 29
17:13 give over their power and authority to the beast; 24
19: 1 Salvation and glory and power belong to our God 24
20: 6 Over such the second death has no power 29
1Es 4:28 Is not the king great in his power? 29
40 the strength and the kingship and the power 29
8:52 power of our Lord will be with those who seek him 31
2Es 2:41 beseech the Lord's power 40
4:22 been endowed with the power of understanding? 45
5:18 his flock in the power of cruel wolves. 41
6: 3 before the powers of movement were established 46
11:19 they wielded power one after another 44
32 and it had greater power over the world than all 42
15:30 and with great power they shall come 46
31 if they combine in great power and turn to pursue 46
32 be disorganized and silenced by their power 46
50 the glory of your power shall wither 46
16:12 and before the glory of his power. 46
18 when the powers shall be terrified 43
Tob 13: 6 I show his power and majesty 31
Jdt 2:12 as I live, and by the power of my kingdom 35
5: 3 in what does their power or strength consist? 35
23 a people with no strength or power for making war. 35
8:15 power to protect us within any time he pleases 29
9: 8 and bring down their power in thy anger 24
11 For thy power depends not upon numbers 35
14 thou art God, the God of all power and might 24
11: 7 as his power endures 35
7 will live by your power under Nebuchadnezzar 31
13:11 to show his power in Israel 31
19 they remember the power of God. 31
AEs 13: 9 the universe is in thy power 29
Wis 1: 3 when his power is tested, it convicts the foolish; 24
7:20 the powers of spirits . . and the virtues of roots; 22
25 For she is a breath of the power of God 24
11:20 scattered by the breath of thy power 24
21 it is always in thy power to show great strength 36
12:15 deeming it alien to thy power 24
17 when men doubt the completeness of thy power 24
18 thou hast power to act 36
13: 4 if men were amazed at their power and working 24
9 for if they had the power to know so much 32
14:31 not the power of the things by which men swear 24
15: 2 For even if we sin we are thine, knowing thy power; 35
3 to know thy power is the root of immortality. 35
16:13 For thou hast power over life and death 29
23 the fire . . even forgot its native power. 24
17: 5 no power of fire was able to give light 22
19:20 Fire even in water retained its normal power 24
Sir 9:13 Keep far from a man who has the power to kill 29
15:14 he left him in the power of his own inclination. 39
18 he is mighty in power and sees everything; 25
18: 5 Who can measure his majestic power? 35
28:23 who forsake the Lord will fall into its power •
29:18 it has driven men of power into exile 26
31:10 the power to transgress and did not transgress 23
33:19 do not give power over yourself 29
38: 5 in order that his power might be known? 31
43:29 marvelous is his power. 25
44: 3 men renowned for their power 24
46: 6 hailstones of mighty power 24
47: 5 to exalt the power of his people. 33
7 he crushed their power even to this day. 33
11 took away his sins, and exalted his power for ever; 33
49: 5 for they gave their power to others 33
Bar 2:11 with great power and outstretched arm 24
3: 5 in this crisis remember thy power and thy name. 39
4:21 deliver you from the power and hand of the enemy. 25
LJr 1:63 be compared with them in appearance or power. 24
Aza 1:21 deprived of all power and dominion 24
39 Bless the Lord, all powers 24
Man 1: 4 all things shudder, and tremble before thy power 24
1Mc 6:11 I was kind and beloved in my power.' 29
10:71 for I have with me the power of the cities. 24
2Mc 3:24 were astounded by the power of God 24
28 recognized clearly the sovereign power of God. 25
34 report to all men the majestic power of God. 35
38 certainly is about the place some power of God. 24
4:50 because of the cupidity of those in power 34
7:17 see how his mighty power will torture you 35
9: 8 making the power of God manifest to all. 24
17 to proclaim the power of God. 35
11: 4 He took no account whatever of the power of God 35
12:28 with power shatters the might of his enemies 35
3Mc 1:27 they turned . . to call upon him who has all power 35
2: 2 puffed up in his audacity and power. 38
6 You made known your mighty power 24
3:15 not rule . . by the power of the spear 22
18 they were spared the exercise of our power 21
5: 7 the Almighty Lord and Ruler of all power 24
51 imploring the Ruler over every power 24
6: 5 showing your power to many nations. 35
12 you, O Eternal One, who have all might and all power 25
13 who have power to save the nation of Jacob. 24
7: 9 not man but the Ruler over every power 24
4Mc 1:30 the restraining power of self-control. 30
5:13 some power watching over this religion of yours 24
6:33 we properly attribute to it the power to govern. 29
14:10 the power of fire is intense and swift 24

power *See also* give, hold, lust, regain.

beyond power 1. *ἰσχυρός*
Sir 3:21 nor investigate what is beyond your power. 1

glorious power 1. הָדָר
Ps 90:16 thy glorious power to their children. 1

great power 1. *μεγαλοκράτωρ*
3Mc 6: 2 King of great power 1

mighty power 1. גְּבוּרָה
Ps 106: 8 that he might make known his mighty power. 1

no power 1. *ἀδύνατος*
LJr 1:54 for they have no power 1

power over 1. *δυναστεύω*
Sir 5: 3 Do not say, "Who will have power over me? 1

prophetic power 1. *προφητεία*
1Co 13: 2 And if I have prophetic powers 1

royal power 1. מַמְלָכָה 2. *βασιλεία*
2Kg 14: 5 as soon as the royal power was firmly in his hand 1
15:19 help him to confirm his hold of the royal power. 1
2Ch 25: 3 as soon as the royal power was firmly in his hand 1
Rev 17:12 ten kings who have not yet received royal power 2
17 and giving over their royal power to the beast 2

saving power 1. יְשׁוּעָה 2. *σωτήριος*
Ps 67: 2 upon earth, thy saving power among all nations. 1
78:22 and did not trust his saving power. 1
Sir 39:18 none can limit his saving power. 2

terrifying power 1. מַעֲרָצָה
Isa 10:33 will lop the boughs with terrifying power; 1

power to stand 1. תְּקוּמָה
Lev 26:37 have no power to stand before your enemies 1

powerful 1. גָּדוֹל 2. כֹּחַ 3. עָצוּם 4. שַׁלִּיט (A)
5. δυνάστης 6. δυνατέω 7. δυνατός 8. ἰσχυρός
Est 9: 4 the man Mor′decai grew more and more powerful. 1
Ps 29: 4 The voice of the LORD is powerful 2
Dan 2:10 no great and powerful king has asked such a thing 4
Jol 1: 6 against my land, powerful and without number; 3
2: 2 upon the mountains a great and powerful people; 3
5 like a powerful army drawn up for battle. 3
11 he that executes his word is powerful. 3
1Co 1:26 not many were powerful 7
2Co 13: 3 is powerful in you. 6
Sir 8: 1 Do not contend with a powerful man 5
4Mc 9:17 your wheel is not so powerful 8
powerful *See also* contender.

all powerful 1. μεγαλοσθενής 2. παντοδύναμος
Wis 7:23 sure, free from anxiety, all-powerful 2
11:17 thy all-powerful hand, which created the world 2
18:15 thy all-powerful word leaped from heaven 2
3Mc 5:13 to show the might of his all-powerful hand 1

powerful man 1. δυνάστης
Sir 7: 6 lest you be partial to a powerful man 1
13: 9 When a powerful man invites you, be reserved 1

more powerful 1. βίαιος 2. δυνατός
Wis 10:12 godliness is more powerful than anything. 2
13: 4 how much more powerful is he who formed them. 2
4Mc 5:16 no compulsion more powerful than our obedience 1
7:10 O aged man, more powerful than tortures 1
16:14 you have proved more powerful than a man. 2

powerfully 1. εὐτόνως
Act 18:28 for he powerfully confuted the Jews in public 1

powerless 1. אֵין כֹּחַ 2. ἀδύνατος 3. invalidus
2Ch 20:12 we are powerless against this great multitude 1
2Es 10:22 and our strong men made powerless. 3
Wis 17:14 which was really powerless 2
14 beset them from the recesses of powerless Hades 2
4Mc 11:26 and your violence powerless. 2

render powerless 1. ἀκυρόω
4Mc 2: 1 desires of the mind . . are rendered powerless 1
18 to correct some, and to render others powerless. 1

practice 1. דָּבָר 2. מעל 3. מַעֲלָל 4. עשה 5. ἀσκητός
6. διώκω 7. ἕξις 8. ἐπιτηδεύω 9. ἐργάζομαι
10. ἐργασία 11. μελετάω 12. περιπατέω 13. ποιέω
14. πρᾶγμα 15. πρᾶξις 16. πράσσω 17. συνήθεια
18. χράω 19. exerceo 20. habeo
Lev 18:30 to practice any of these abominable customs 4
30 abominable customs which were practiced before 4
Jdg 2:19 they did not drop any of their practices 3
Ezr 9:14 peoples who practice these abominations? *
Est 9:32 Queen Esther fixed these practices of Purim 1
Ps 111:10 good understanding have all those who practice 4
Ecc 4: 1 oppressions that are practiced under the sun. 4
Isa 32: 6 to practice ungodliness, to utter error 4
Jer 9:24 that I am the LORD who practice steadfast love 4
22:17 for practicing oppression and violence. 4
Ezk 23: 8 not give up her harlotry which she had practiced *
39:26 the treachery they have practiced against me 2
Dan 4:27 off your sins by practicing righteousness *
Mat 6: 1 Beware of practicing your piety before men 13
23: 3 so practice and observe whatever they tell you 13
3 for they preach, but do not practice. 13
Act 16:21 not lawful for us Romans to accept or practice. 13
19:18 confessing and divulging their practices. 15
19 a number of those who practiced magic arts 16
Rom 1:32 but approve those who practice them. 16
10: 5 the man who practices the righteousness 13
12:13 practice hospitality. 6
1Co 11:16 we recognize no other practice 17
2Co 4: 2 we refuse to practice cunning 12
12:21 which they have practiced. 16
Eph 4:19 greedy to practice every kind of uncleanness. 10
Col 3: 9 put off the old nature with its practices 15
1Ti 4:15 Practice these duties, devote yourself to them 11
Heb 5:14 their faculties trained by practice 7
Jas 3:16 there will be disorder and every vile practice. 14
Rev 21:27 nor any one who practices abomination 13
22:15 every one who loves and practices falsehood. 13
2Es 7:125 the faces of those who practiced self-control 20
15: 8 will I tolerate their wicked practices 19
Tob 4:11 for all who practice it 3
Jdt 9: 3 was ashamed of the deceit they had practiced *
Wis 12: 4 thou didst hate for their detestable practices 16
19:13 practiced a more bitter hatred of strangers. 8
Sir 27: 9 truth returns to those who practice it. 9
38:34 their prayer is in the practice of their trade. 10
4Mc 9: 2 we should practice ready obedience to the law 18
12:11 those who practice religion? 5

abominable practice 1. תּוֹעֵבָה
Deu 18: 9 not learn to follow the abominable practices 1
12 because of these abominable practices the LORD 1
20:18 not teach you . . their abominable practices 1
32:16 with abominable practices they provoked him 1
2Kg 16: 3 the abominable practices of the nations 1
21: 2 the abominable practices of the nations 1
2Ch 28: 3 according to the abominable practices 1
33: 2 abominable practices of the nations 1

practice augury 1. נחש
Lev 19:26 You shall not practice augury or witchcraft 1
2Kg 21: 6 and practiced soothsaying and augury 1
2Ch 33: 6 practiced soothsaying and augury and sorcery 1

practice divination 1. קסם
Deu 18:10 any one who practices divination, a soothsayer 1
Ezk 13:23 see delusive visions nor practice divination; 1

practice extortion 1. עשק
Ezk 18:18 his father, because he practiced extortion 1
22:29 The people of the land have practiced extortion 1

practice harlotry 1. זנה
Ezk 23:43 commit adultery when they practice harlotry 1

practice hospitality 1. φιλόξενος
1Pe 4: 9 Practice hospitality ungrudgingly 1

practice immorality 1. πορνεύω
Rev 2:14 that they might . . practice immorality. 1
20 beguiling my servants to practice immorality 1

practice magic 1. μαγεύω
Act 8: 9 who had previously practiced magic in the city 1

practice soothsaying 1. ענן
2Kg 21: 6 and practiced soothsaying and augury 1
2Ch 33: 6 practiced soothsaying and augury and sorcery 1

practice sorcery 1. כשף
2Ch 33: 6 practiced soothsaying and augury and sorcery 1

practice witchcraft 1. ענן
Lev 19:26 You shall not practice augury or witchcraft 1
practices *See* follow, man.
praetorian *See* guard.

praetorium 1. πραιτώριον
Mat 27:27 the governor took Jesus into the praetorium 1
Mrk 15:16 the palace (that is, the praetorium) 1
Joh 18:28 from the house of Ca′iaphas to the praetorium 1
28 They themselves did not enter the praetorium 1
33 Pilate entered the praetorium again 1
19: 9 he entered the praetorium again and said 1
Act 23:35 to be guarded in Herod's praetorium. 1

praise 1. הלל 2. זכר 3. זמר 4. ידה 5. מַהֲלָל 6. נוה
7. פֶּה 8. רנן 9. שבח 10. תְּהִלָּה 11. תּוֹדָה
12. שבח (A) 13. αἴνεσις 14. αἰνετός 15. αἰνέω
16. αἶνος 17. ἀρετή 18. δίδωμι ἐξομολόγησιν 19. δόξα
20. δοξάζω 21. ἐξαίρω 22. ἐξομολογέω 23. ἐπαινέω
24. ἔπαινος 25. εὐλογέω 26. εὐλογία 27. εὔλογος
28. εὐφημέω 29. σεμνολογέω 30. ὑμνέω 31. conlaudo
32. magnifico
Gen 12:15 they praised her to Pharaoh. 1
29:35 This time I will praise the LORD"; 4
49: 8 Judah, your brothers shall praise you; 4
Exd 15: 2 this is my God, and I will praise him 6
Deu 10:21 He is your praise; he is your God 10
26:19 praise and in fame and in honor 10
32:43 Praise his people, O you nations; for he avenges 8
Jos 7:19 give glory to the LORD . . and render praise to him; 11
Jdg 16:24 when the people saw him, they praised their god; 1
2Sm 14:25 there was no one so much to be praised 1
1Ch 16: 4 to invoke, to thank, and to praise the LORD 1
25 For great is the LORD, and greatly to be praised 1
35 give thanks . . and glory in thy praise. 10
36 all the people said "Amen!" and praised the LORD. 1
23: 5 the instruments which I have made for praise. 1
30 every morning, thanking and praising the LORD 1
25: 3 in thanksgiving and praise to the LORD. 1
29:13 thank thee, our God, and praise thy glorious name 1
2Ch 5:13 in unison in praise and thanksgiving to the LORD 1
13 when the song was raised . . in praise to the LORD 1
8:14 for their offices of praise and ministry 1
20:19 the Levites . . stood up to praise the LORD 1
21 to sing to the LORD and praise him in holy array 1
22 when they began to sing and praise 10
23:12 noise of the people running and praising 1
30:21 Levites and the priests praised the LORD 1
31: 2 minister . . and to give thanks and praise. 1
Ezr 3:10 came forward . . to praise the LORD 1
11 praising and giving thanks to the LORD 1
11 great shout, when they praised the LORD 1
Neh 5:13 all the assembly said "Amen" and praised the LORD. 1
9: 5 name . . exalted above all blessing and praise. 10
12:24 praise and to give thanks, 1
46 there were songs of praise and thanksgiving 10
Ps 9:14 that I may recount all thy praises 10
18: 3 I call upon the LORD, who is worthy to be praised 1
21:13 We will sing and praise thy power. 3
22: 3 art holy, enthroned on the praises of Israel. 10
22 the midst of the congregation I will praise thee 1
23 You who fear the LORD, praise him! 1
25 From thee comes my praise in the . . congregation; 10
26 those who seek him shall praise the LORD! 1
30: 9 Will the dust praise thee? 4
12 that my soul may praise thee and not be silent. 3
33: 1 O you righteous! Praise befits the upright. 10
2 Praise the LORD with the lyre, make melody to him 4
34: 1 his praise shall continually be in my mouth. 10
35:18 in the mighty throng I will praise thee. 1
28 and of thy praise all the day long. 10
42: 5 Hope in God; for I shall again praise him, my help 4
11 Hope in God; for I shall again praise him 4
43: 4 I will praise thee with the lyre, O God, my God. 4
5 for I shall again praise him, my help and my God. 4
45:17 the peoples will praise you for ever and ever. 4
48: 1 Great is the LORD and greatly to be praised 1
10 so thy praise reaches to the ends of the earth. 10
51:15 my mouth shall show forth thy praise. 10
56: 4 In God, whose word I praise, in God I trust 1
10 In God, whose word I praise 1
10 in the LORD, whose word I praise 1
63: 3 my lips will praise thee. 9
5 my mouth praises thee with joyful lips 1
65: 1 Praise is due to thee, O God, in Zion; 10
66: 2 give to him glorious praise! 10
8 O peoples, let the sound of his praise be heard 10
67: 3 Let the peoples praise thee, O God; 4
3 O God; let all the peoples praise thee! 4
5 Let the peoples praise thee, O God; 4
5 O God; let all the peoples praise thee! 4
69:30 I will praise the name of God with a song; 1
34 Let heaven and earth praise him 1
71: 6 My praise is continually of thee. 10
8 My mouth is filled with thy praise 10
14 and will praise thee yet more and more. 10
16 I will praise thy righteousness, thine alone. 2
22 I will also praise thee with the harp 4
73:10 Therefore the people turn and praise them; *
74:21 let the poor and needy praise thy name. 1
76:10 Surely the wrath of men shall praise thee; 4
79:13 generation we will recount thy praise. 10
88:10 Do the shades rise up to praise thee? Selah 4
89: 5 Let the heavens praise thy wonders, O LORD 4
96: 4 For great is the LORD, and greatly to be praised; 1
99: 3 praise thy great and terrible name! Holy is he! 4
100: 4 Enter . . his courts with praise! 10
102:18 so that a people yet unborn may praise the LORD 1
21 that men may declare . . in Jerusalem his praise 10
104:35 Bless the LORD, O my soul! Praise the LORD! 1
105:45 Praise the LORD! 1
106: 1 Praise the LORD! O give thanks to the LORD 1
2 Who can utter . . or show forth all his praise? 10
12 believed his words; they sang his praise. 10
47 that we may . . glory in thy praise. 10
48 let all the people say, "Amen!" Praise the LORD! 1
107:32 praise him in the assembly of the elders. 1
109: 1 Be not silent, O God of my praise! 10
30 I will praise him in the midst of the throng. 1
111: 1 Praise the LORD. I will give thanks to the LORD 1
10 His praise endures for ever! 10
112: 1 Praise the LORD. Blessed is the man who fears 1
113: 1 Praise the LORD! Praise, O servants of the LORD 1
1 Praise, O servants of the LORD, praise the name 1
1 O servants of the LORD, praise the name of the LORD! 1
3 name of the LORD is to be praised! 1
9 Praise the LORD! 1
115:17 The dead do not praise the LORD 1
18 Praise the LORD! 1
116:19 Praise the LORD! 1
117: 1 Praise the LORD, all nations! 1
2 Praise the LORD! 1
119: 7 I will praise thee with an upright heart 4
62 At midnight I rise to praise thee 4
108 Accept my offerings of praise, O LORD, and teach me 7
164 I praise thee for thy righteous ordinances. 1
171 My lips will pour forth praise 10
175 Let me live, that I may praise thee 1
135: 1 Praise the LORD. Praise the name of the LORD 1
1 Praise the name of the LORD, give praise 1
3 Praise the LORD, for the LORD is good; 1
21 Praise the LORD! 1
138: 4 kings of the earth shall praise thee, O LORD 4
139:14 praise thee, for thou art fearful and wonderful. 4
145: 2 bless thee, and praise thy name for ever and ever. 1
3 Great is the LORD, and greatly to be praised 1
21 My mouth will speak the praise of the LORD 10
146: 1 Praise the LORD! Praise the LORD, O my soul! 1
1 Praise the LORD! Praise the LORD, O my soul! 1
2 I will praise the LORD as long as I live; 1

10 Praise the LORD! 1
147: 1 Praise the LORD! For it is good to sing praises 1
12 Praise the LORD, O Jerusalem! 9
12 LORD, O Jerusalem! Praise your God, O Zion! 1
20 Praise the LORD! 1
148: 1 Praise the LORD! Praise the LORD from the heavens 1
1 Praise the LORD from the heavens, praise him 1
1 LORD from the heavens, praise him in the heights! 1
2 Praise him, all his angels, praise him, all his host! 1
2 Praise him, all his angels, praise him, all his host! 1
3 Praise him, sun and moon 1
3 sun and moon, praise him, all you shining stars! 1
4 Praise him, you highest heavens 1
5 Let them praise the name of the LORD! 1
7 Praise the LORD from the earth, you sea monsters 1
13 Let them praise the name of the LORD 1
14 horn for his people, praise for all his saints 10
14 Praise the LORD! 1
149: 1 Praise the LORD! Sing to the LORD a new song 1
1 song, his praise in the assembly of the faithful! 10
3 Let them praise his name with dancing 1
9 Praise the LORD! 1
150: 1 Praise the LORD! Praise God in his sanctuary; 1
1 Praise the LORD! Praise God in his sanctuary; 1
1 praise him in his mighty firmament! 1
2 Praise him for his mighty deeds; praise him 1
2 praise him according to his exceeding greatness! 1
3 Praise him with trumpet sound; 1
3 praise him with lute and harp! 1
4 Praise him with timbrel and dance; 1
4 praise him with strings and pipe! 1
5 Praise him with sounding cymbals; 1
5 praise him with loud clashing cymbals! 1
6 Let everything that breathes praise the LORD! 1
6 Praise the LORD! 1
Prv 27: 2 Let another praise you, and not your own mouth; 1
21 man is judged by his praise. 5
28: 4 Those who forsake the law praise the wicked 1
31:28 her husband also, and he praises her; 1
30 but a woman who fears the LORD is to be praised. 1
31 let her works praise her in the gates. 1
Ecc 8:10 they used to go . . and were praised in the city 23
Sng 6: 9 queens and concubines . . and they praised her. 1
Isa 25: 1 my God; I will exalt thee, I will praise thy name; 4
38:18 Sheol cannot thank . . death cannot praise thee; 1
42: 8 give to no other, nor my praise to graven images. 10
10 a new song, his praise from the end of the earth! 10
12 and declare his praise in the coastlands. 10
43:21 I formed . . that they might declare my praise. 10
48: 9 for the sake of my praise I restrain it for you 10
60: 6 and shall proclaim the praise of the LORD. 10
18 your walls Salvation, and your gates Praise. 10
61: 3 the mantle of praise instead of a faint spirit; 10
11 cause righteousness and praise to spring forth 10
62: 7 Jerusalem and makes it a praise in the earth. 10
9 who garner it shall eat it and praise the LORD 1
63: 7 love of the LORD, the praises of the LORD 10
64:11 Our holy . . house, where our fathers praised thee 1
Jer 13:11 might be for me a people, a name, a praise, and a glory 10
17:14 save me, and I shall be saved; for thou art my praise. 10
20:13 Sing to the LORD; praise the LORD! 1
33: 9 And this city shall be to me a name of joy, a praise 10
51:41 Babylon . . the praise of the whole earth seized! 10
Dan 2:23 O God of my fathers, I give thanks and praise 12
4:34 praised and honored him who lives for ever; 12
37 Now I, Nebuchadnez'zar, praise and extol 12
5: 4 praised the gods of gold and silver, bronze, iron 12
23 praised the gods of silver and gold, of bronze 12
Jol 2:26 and praise the name of the LORD your God 1
Hab 3: 3 and the earth was full of his praise. Selah 10
Zep 3:19 and I will change their shame into praise 10
20 yea, I will make you renowned and praised 10
Mat 6: 2 that they may be praised by men. Truly, I say to you 20
21:16 thou hast brought perfect praise'?• 16
Lke 2:13 praising God and saying 15
20 glorifying and praising God 15
13:13 she was made straight, and she praised God. 20
17:15 turned back, praising God with a loud voice; 20
18 Was no one found to return and give praise to God 19
18:43 all the people, when they saw it, gave praise to God. 16
19:37 began to rejoice and praise God with a loud voice 15
23:47 he praised God, and said 20
Joh 9:24 Give God the praise 19
12:43 for they loved the praise of men 19
43 more than the praise of God. 19
Act 2:47 praising God and having favor 15
3: 8 walking and leaping and praising God. 15
9 all the people saw him walking and praising God 15
4:21 all men praised God for what had happened. 20
Rom 2:29 His praise is not from men but from God. 24
15: 9 Therefore I will praise thee among the Gentiles 22
11 and again, "Praise the Lord, all Gentiles 15
11 and let all the peoples praise him"; 23
Eph 1: 6 to the praise of his glorious grace 19
12 to live for the praise of his glory. 19
14 to the praise of his glory. 24
Php 1:11 to the glory and praise of God. 24
Heb 2:12 I will praise thee. 30
13:15 offer up a sacrifice of praise to God 13
1Pe 1: 7 faith . . may redound to praise and glory 24
2:14 sent by him . . to praise those who do right. 24
Rev 19: 5 Praise our God, all you his servants 15
1Es 4:58 praised the King of heaven, saying 25
62 they praised the God of their fathers 25
5:60 praising the Lord and blessing him 30
62 praising the Lord for the erection of the house 30
2Es 2:42 they all were praising the Lord with songs. 31
47 I began to praise those who had stood valiantly 32
10:16 and will be praised among women. 31
Tob 3:11 May all thy works praise thee for ever. 25
11: 1 Tobias went on his way, praising God 27
16 rejoicing and praising God 27
12: 6 Praise God and give thanks to him 25
6 It is good to praise God and to exalt his name 25
17 But praise God for ever. 25
18 Therefore praise him for ever. 25
13: 6 Praise the Lord of righteousness 25
10 praise the King of the ages 25
13 will praise the Lord of the righteous. 25
15 Let my soul praise God the great King. 25
14: 2 continued to fear the Lord God and to praise him. 22
7 All the Gentiles will praise the Lord 25
Jdt 6:20 they consoled Achior, and praised him greatly. 23
13:14 Then she said to them with a loud voice, "Praise God 15
14 Praise God, O praise him! Praise God 15
14 Praise God, O praise him! Praise God 15
AEs 13:17 not destroy the mouth of those who praise thee. 15
14: 9 to stop the mouths of those who praise thee 15
10 the praise of vain idols 17
Wis 10:20 and praised with one accord thy defending hand 15
15:19 escaped both the praise of God and his blessing 24
18: 9 they were singing the praises of the fathers. 16
19: 9 praising thee, O Lord, who didst deliver them. 15
Sir 0: 1 should praise Israel for instruction and wisdom; 23
9:17 will be praised for the skill of the craftsmen 23
11: 2 Do not praise a man for his good looks 15
17:10 they will praise his holy name 15
18:28 he praises the one who finds her. 18
21:15 he will praise it and add to it 15
24: 1 Wisdom will praise herself 15
27: 7 Do not praise a man before you hear him reason 23
31:23 Men will praise the one who is liberal with food 25
37: 7 Every counselor praises counsel 21
24 A wise man will have praise heaped upon him 26
39: 9 Many will praise his understanding 15
10 the congregation will proclaim his praise; 24
15 give thanks to him with praise 13
35 now sing praise with all your heart and voice •
43:11 Look upon the rainbow, and praise him who made it 25
28 Where shall we find strength to praise him? 20
30 When you praise the Lord 20
30 you cannot praise him enough. •
44: 1 Let us now praise famous men 15
8 so that men declare their praise. 24
15 the congregation proclaims their praise. 24
47: 6 praised him for the blessings of the Lord 20
10 while they praised God's holy name 15
50:18 the singers praised him with their voices 15
51: 1 will praise thee as God my Savior 15
11 I will praise thy name continually 15
12 I will give thanks to thee and praise thee 15
22 I will praise him with it. 15
29 may you not be put to shame when you praise him. 13
Bar 2:32 they will praise me in the land of their exile 15
3: 6 Lord our God, and thee, O Lord, will we praise. 15
7 we will praise thee in our exile, for we have put 15
Aza 1:28 praised and glorified and blessed God 20
29 to be praised and highly exalted for ever; 14
32 to be praised and highly exalted for ever. 14
Sus 1:63 Hilkiah and his wife praised God 15
Man 1:15 I will praise thee continually 15
1Mc 4:24 they sang hymns and praises to Heaven 25
33 let all who know thy name praise thee with hymns. 15
56 offered a sacrifice of deliverance and praise. 13
5:64 Men gathered to them and praised them. 28
13:47 then entered it with hymns and praise. 27
51 the Jews entered it with praise and palm branches 13
2Mc 3:30 they praised the Lord who had acted marvelously 25
11: 9 they all together praised the merciful God 25
3Mc 2: 8 they praised you, the Almighty. 15
20 put praises in the mouth of those . . downcast 13
4:16 praising speechless things 24
5:13 Then the Jews . . praised their holy God 15
35 praised the manifest Lord God, King of kings 15
6:11 Let not the vain-minded praise their vanities 25
29 the Jews . . praised their holy God and Savior 25
32 praising God, their Savior 15
4Mc 1: 2 it includes the praise of the highest virtue 24
10 it is fitting for me to praise for their virtues 23
2: 2 the temperate Joseph is praised 23
4: 4 he praised Simon for his service to the king 23
12 would praise the blessedness of the holy place 30
7: 9 did not abandon the holiness which you praised 29
13: 3 by reason, which is praised before God 23
17 all the fathers will praise us. 23
18:13 He praised Daniel in the den of the lions 20

praise *See also* get, give, hymn, offer, offering, sing, song, word, worthy.

high praise 1. רוֹמָם
Ps 149: 6 Let the high praises of God be in their throats 1

highly praise 1. ὑπεραινετός
Aza 1:30 to be highly praised and highly exalted for ever. 1

joyful praise 1. ἀγαλλίαμα
Tob 13:11 Generations . . will give you joyful praise. 1

joyously praise 1. רנן
Ps 89:12 Tabor and Hermon joyously praise thy name. 1

praised *See* worthy.

praiseworthy 1. mirabilis
2Es 8:48 you will be praiseworthy before the Most High 1

prance 1. רעל
Nah 2: 3 the chargers prance. 1

prate 1. שָׂפָה
Prv 10: 8 but a prating fool will come to ruin. 1

prate against 1. φλυαρέω
3Jn 1:10 he is . . prating against me with evil words. 1

prattle 1. ἀδολεσχέω
Sir 7:14 Do not prattle in the assembly of the elders 1

pray 1. אמר 2. אָנָּא 3. בִּי 4. נָא 5. עתר 6. פגע 7. פלל 8. שׁאל 9. תְּפִלָּה 10. צלא (A) 11. ἀξιόω 12. δέησις 13. δέομαι 14. ἐντυγχάνω 15. ἐπικαλέω 16. ἐπὶ προσευχήν 17. ἐρωτάω 18. εὔχομαι 19. κατεύχομαι 20. λέγω 21. λιτανεύω 22. ποιέω τὴν δέησιν 23. προσευχή 24. προσεύχομαι 25. deprecor 26. exoro 27. oratio 28. oro 29. rogo
Gen 19: 2 said, "My lords, turn aside, I pray you 4
20: 7 he is a prophet, and he will pray for you, and you 7
17 Abraham prayed to God; and God healed Abim'elech 7
24:12 O LORD . . grant me success today, I pray thee 4
14 'Pray let down your jar that I may drink,' 4
17 and said, "Pray give me a little water 4
43 Pray give me a little water from your jar to drink 4
45 I said to her, 'Pray let me drink.' 4
25:21 Isaac prayed to the LORD for his wife 5
30:14 Give me, I pray, some of your son's mandrakes. 4
32:11 Deliver me, I pray thee, 4
29 Then Jacob asked him, "Tell me, I pray, your name. 4
33:10 Jacob said, "No, I pray you, if I have found favor 4
11 Accept, I pray you, my gift that is brought to you 4
34: 8 I pray you, give her to him in marriage. 4
37:16 tell me, I pray you, where they are pasturing 4
38:25 And she said, "Mark, I pray you, whose these are 4
40: 8 Tell them to me, I pray you. 4
14 and do me the kindness, I pray you, to make mention 4
44:18 O my lord, let your servant, I pray you 4
33 Now therefore, let your servant, I pray you 4
45: 4 Come near to me, I pray you." And they came near. 4
47: 4 and now, we pray you, let your servants dwell 4
48: 9 And he said, "Bring them to me, I pray you, 4
50: 4 speak, I pray you, in the ears of Pharaoh, saying 4
5 let me go up, I pray you, and bury my father; 4
17 And now, we pray you, forgive the transgression 4
Exd 3:18 and now, we pray you, let us go a three days' journey 4
4:13 he said, "Oh, my Lord, send, I pray, some other person. 4
18 Let me go back, I pray, to my kinsmen in Egypt 4
5: 3 let us go, we pray, a three days' journey 4
8:29 Behold, I am going out from you and I will pray 5
30 Moses went out . . and prayed to the LORD. 5
10:17 Now therefore, forgive my sin, I pray you 4
32:32 forgive their sin-and if not, blot me, I pray thee, out 4
33:13 Now therefore, I pray thee, if I have found favor 4
18 Moses said, "I pray thee, show me thy glory. 4
34: 9 let the Lord, I pray thee, go in the midst of us 4
Num10:31 he said, "Do not leave us, I pray you, for you know 4
11: 2 Moses prayed to the LORD, and the fire abated. 7
14:17 now, I pray thee, let the power of the LORD be 4
19 Pardon the iniquity of this people, I pray thee 4
16:26 Depart, I pray you, from the tents of these wicked 4
21: 7 We have sinned . . pray to the LORD 7
7 So Moses prayed for the people. 7
22:19 Pray, now, tarry here this night also 4
Deu 3:25 Let me go over, I pray, and see the good land 4
9:20 I prayed for Aaron also at the same time. 7
26 I prayed to the LORD, 'O Lord GOD, destroy not 7
Jdg 1:24 Pray, show us the way into the city 4
4:19 he said to her, "Pray, give me a little water to drink; 4
6:13 Gideon said to him, "Pray, sir, if the LORD is with us 3
15 he said to him, "Pray, Lord, how can I deliver Israel? 3
18 Do not depart from here, I pray thee, until I come 4
39 pray, let me make trial only this once 4
39 with the fleece; pray, let it be dry only 4
8: 5 Pray, give loaves of bread to the people who 4
10:15 to thee; only deliver us, we pray thee, this day. 4
11:17 Let us pass, we pray, through your land'; but the king 4

19 Let us pass, we pray, through your land to our 4
13: 8 O LORD, I pray thee, let the man of God whom thou 4
15 Pray, let us detain you, and prepare a kid for you. 4
15: 2 sister fairer than she? Pray take her instead. 4
16:28 O Lord GOD, remember me, I pray thee, 4
28 remember me . . and strengthen me, I pray thee 4
18: 5 Inquire of God, we pray thee, that we may know 4
19: 9 now the day has waned . . pray tarry all night. 4
Rut 2: 7 Pray, let me glean and gather among the sheaves 4
1Sm 1:10 She was deeply distressed and prayed to the LORD 7
12 As she continued praying before the LORD 7
26 woman who was standing . . praying to the LORD. 7
27 For this child I prayed; 7
2: 1 Hannah also prayed and said, "My heart exults 7
36 Put me, I pray you, in one of the priest's places 4
7: 5 Gather . . and I will pray to the LORD for you. 7
8: 6 And Samuel prayed to the LORD. 7
10:15 Saul's uncle said, "Pray, tell me what Samuel said 4
12:19 Pray for your servants to the LORD . . that we may 7
23 sin against the LORD by ceasing to pray for you; 7
15:25 Now therefore, I pray, pardon my sin, and return 4
22: 3 Pray let my father and my mother stay with you 4
25: 8 Pray, give whatever you have . . to your servants 4
24 pray let your handmaid speak in your ears 4
28 Pray forgive the trespass of your handmaid; 4
2Sm 7:27 has found courage to pray this prayer to thee. 7
13: 6 Pray let my sister Tamar come and make . . cakes 4
13 Now therefore, I pray you, speak to the king; 4
24 pray let the king and his servants go 4
26 If not, pray let my brother Amnon go with us. 4
14:11 Pray let the king invoke the LORD your God 4
12 Pray let your handmaid speak a word to my lord 4
15: 7 Pray let me go and pay my vow, which I have vowed 4
31 O LORD, I pray thee, turn the counsel of Ahith'ophel 4
19:37 Pray let your servant return, that I may die 4
24:10 But now, O LORD, I pray thee, take away the iniquity 4
17 Let thy hand, I pray thee, be against me 4
1Kg 2:17 Pray ask King Solomon–he will not refuse you– 4
8:28 the prayer which thy servant prays before thee 7
30 hearken . . when they pray toward this place; 7
33 if they turn . . and pray and make supplication 7
35 if they pray toward this place, and acknowledge 7
42 when he comes and prays toward this house 7
44 thy people go out . . and they pray to the LORD 7
48 repent . . and pray to thee toward their land 7
13: 6 Entreat now . . and pray for me, that my hand may be 7
20:32 Your servant Ben-ha'dad says, 'Pray, let me live.' 4
35 Strike me, I pray." But the man refused 4
37 he found another man, and said, "Strike me, I pray. 4
2Kg 1:13 O man of God, I pray you, let my life . . be precious 4
2: 2 Eli'jah said to Eli'sha, "Tarry here, I pray you; 4
4 Eli'jah said to him, "Eli'sha, tarry here, I pray you; 4
6 Then Eli'jah said to him, "Tarry here, I pray you; 4
9 Eli'sha said, "I pray you, let me inherit 4
16 strong men; pray, let them go, and seek your master; 4
4:33 and shut the door . . and prayed to the LORD. 7
5:17 I pray you, let there be given to your servant 4
22 There have just now come . . pray, give them 4
6:17 Then Eli'sha prayed, and said, "O LORD, I pray thee 7
17 O LORD, I pray thee, open his eyes that he may see. 4
18 when the Syrians . . Eli'sha prayed to the LORD 7
18 Strike this people, I pray thee, with blindness. 4
18:26 Pray, speak to your servants in the Aramaic 4
19:15 Hezeki'ah prayed before the LORD, and said: 7
20: 2 Hezeki'ah turned . . and prayed to the LORD, saying 7
1Ch 17:25 servant has found courage to pray before thee. 7
21: 8 I pray thee, take away the iniquity of thy servant; 4
17 Let thy hand, I pray thee, O LORD my God, 4
2Ch 6:19 the prayer which thy servant prays before thee; 7
21 hearken . . when they pray toward this place; 7
24 when they . . pray and make supplication to thee 7
26 if they pray toward this place, and acknowledge 7
32 when he comes and prays toward this house 7
34 and they pray to thee toward this city which thou 7
38 if they repent . . and pray toward their land 7
7:14 if my people . . humble themselves, and pray 7
30:18 Hezeki'ah had prayed for them, saying 7
32:20 Then Hezeki'ah . . and Isaiah . . , prayed 7
24 Hezeki'ah became sick . . he prayed to the LORD 7
33:13 He prayed to him, and God received his entreaty 7
Ezr 6:10 may . . pray for the life of the king and his sons. 10
10: 1 While Ezra prayed and made confesssion 7
Neh 1: 4 I continued fasting and praying before the God 7
6 prayer . . I now pray before thee day and night 7
2: 4 I prayed to the God of heaven. 7
4: 9 we prayed to our God, and set a guard 7
Job 6:29 Turn, I pray, let no wrong be done. 4
8: 8 For inquire, I pray you, of bygone ages 4
21:15 what profit do we get if we pray to him? 6
33:26 then man prays to God, and he accepts him 5
42: 8 my servant Job shall pray for you 7
10 Job, when he had prayed for his friends; 7
Ps 5: 2 my King and my God, for to thee do I pray. 7
35:13 I prayed with head bowed on my bosom 9
38:16 For I pray, "Only let them not rejoice over me 1
122: 6 Pray for the peace of Jerusalem! 8
Isa 5: 3 judge, I pray you, between me and my vineyard. 4
16:12 when he comes to his sanctuary to pray 7
36:11 Pray, speak to your servants in Aramaic 4
37:15 Hezeki'ah prayed to the LORD 7
21 you have prayed to me concerning Sennach'erib 7
38: 2 turned his face to the wall, and prayed to the LORD 7
44:17 prays to it and says, "Deliver me, for thou art my god! 7
45:20 and keep on praying to a god that cannot save. 7
Jer 7:16 As for you, do not pray for this people 7
11:14 Therefore do not pray for this people 7
14:11 Do not pray for the welfare of this people. 7
29: 7 and pray to the LORD on its behalf 7
12 Then you will call upon me and come and pray to me 7
32:16 I prayed to the LORD, saying 7
37: 3 saying, "Pray for us to the LORD our God. 7
20 Now hear, I pray you, O my lord the king 4
42: 2 and pray to the LORD your God for us 7
4 behold, I will pray to the LORD your God 7
20 Pray for us to the LORD your God 7
Dan 6:10 prayed and gave thanks before his God 10
9: 4 prayed to the LORD my God and made confession 7
20 While I was speaking and praying, confessing 7
Jon 2: 1 Then Jonah prayed to the LORD his God 7
4: 2 he prayed to the LORD and said, "I pray thee, LORD 7
2 to the LORD and said, "I pray thee, LORD 2
Hag 2:15 Pray now, consider what will come to pass •
Mat 5:44 enemies and pray for those who persecute you 24
6: 5 when you pray, you must not be like the hypocrites; 24
5 for they love to stand and pray in the synagogues 24
6 when you pray, go into your room and shut the door 24
6 shut the door and pray to your Father who is 24
7 in praying do not heap up empty phrases 24
9 Pray then like this: Our Father who art in heaven 24
9:38 pray therefore the Lord of the harvest 13
14:23 he went up on the mountain by himself to pray 24
19:13 that he might lay his hands on them and pray 24
24:20 Pray that your flight may not be in winter 24
26:36 Sit here, while I go yonder and pray. 24
39 he fell on his face and prayed 24
41 Watch and pray that you may not enter 24
42 Again, for the second time, he went away and prayed 24
44 he went away and prayed for the third time 24
Mrk 1:35 there he prayed 24
6:46 he went up on the mountain to pray. 24
11:25 whenever you stand praying, forgive 24
13:18 Pray that it may not happen in winter. 24
14:32 he said to his disciples, "Sit here, while I pray. 24
35 he fell on the ground and prayed 24
38 pray that you may not enter into temptation 24
39 again he went away and prayed 24
Lke 1:10 praying outside at the hour of incense 24
3:21 Jesus also had been baptized and was praying 24
5:16 he withdrew to the wilderness and prayed. 24
6:12 In these days he went out to the mountain to pray; 24
28 pray for those who abuse you. 24
9:18 Now it happened that as he was praying alone 24
28 and went up on the mountain to pray. 24
29 as he was praying 24
10: 2 pray therefore the Lord of the harvest 13
11: 1 He was praying in a certain place 24
1 teach us to pray, as John taught his disciples. 24
2 he said to them, "When you pray, say: "Father 24
14:18 I pray you, have me excused.' 17
19 I pray you, have me excused.' 17
18: 1 they ought always to pray and not lose heart. 24
10 Two men went up into the temple to pray 24
11 The Pharisee stood and prayed thus with himself 24
21:36 praying that you may have strength 13
22:32 I have prayed for you that your faith may not fail; 13
40 Pray that you may not enter into temptation. 24
41 and knelt down and prayed 24
46 pray that you may not enter into temptation. 24
Joh 14:16 I will pray the Father 17
16:26 I do not say to you that I shall pray the Father 17
17: 9 I am praying for them 17
9 I am not praying for the world 17
15 I do not pray that . . 17
20 I do not pray for these only 17
Act 1:24 they prayed and said, "Lord, who knowest the hearts 24
4:31 when they had prayed 13
6: 6 they prayed and laid their hands upon them. 24
7:59 as they were stoning Stephen, he prayed 15
8:15 who came down and prayed for them 24
22 pray to the Lord 13
24 Simon answered, "Pray for me to the Lord 13
34 About whom, pray, does the prophet say this 13
9:11 behold, he is praying 24
40 Peter . . knelt down and prayed 24
10: 2 prayed constantly to God. 13
9 Peter went up on the housetop to pray 24
11: 5 I was in the city of Joppa praying 24
12:12 many were gathered together and were praying. 24
13: 3 Then after fasting and praying 24
16:25 Paul and Silas were praying and singing hymns 24
20:36 he knelt down and prayed with them all. 24
21: 5 we prayed and bade one another farewell. 24
22:17 was praying in the temple 24
27:29 prayed for day to come. 18
28: 8 Paul visited him and prayed 24
Rom 8:26 for we do not know how to pray as we ought 24
1Co 11: 4 Any man who prays or prophesies with his head 24
5 any woman who prays or prophesies with her head 24
13 for a woman to pray to God with her head uncovered? 24
14:13 who speaks in a tongue should pray for the power 24
14 For if I pray in a tongue, my spirit prays 24
14 my spirit prays but my mind is unfruitful. 24
15 What am I to do? I will pray with the spirit 24
15 I will pray with the mind also 24
2Co 9:14 while they long for you and pray for you 12
13: 7 we pray God that you may not do wrong 18
9 What we pray for is your improvement. 18
Eph 6:18 Pray at all times in the Spirit 24
Col 1: 3 when we pray for you 24
9 we have not ceased to pray for you 24
4: 3 pray for us also 24
1Th 3:10 praying earnestly night and day that we may see 13
5:17 pray constantly 24
25 Brethren, pray for us. 24
2Th 1:11 To this end we always pray for you 24
3: 1 Finally, brethren, pray for us 24
1Ti 2: 8 in every place the men should pray 24
Phm 1: 6 I pray that . . •
Heb 13:18 Pray for us 24
Jas 5:13 Is any one among you suffering? Let him pray. 24
14 let them pray over him, anointing him with oil 24
16 and pray for one another, that you may be healed. 18
17 he prayed fervently 24
18 Then he prayed again and the heaven gave rain 24
1Jn 5:16 I do not say that one is to pray for that. 17
3Jn 1: 2 Beloved, I pray that all may go well with you 18
Jde 1:20 pray in the Holy Spirit; 24
1Es 4:46 I pray therefore that you fulfil the vow 13
8:53 again we prayed to our Lord about these things 13
91 Ezra was praying and making his confession 24
2Es 2:13 pray that your days may be few 29
4:51 Then I prayed and said, "Do you think 28
5:13 and if you pray again, and weep as you do now 28
6:31 If therefore you will pray again 29
7:46 what of those for whom I prayed? 27
105 no one shall ever pray for another on that day 29
106 first Abraham prayed for the people of Sodom 29
110 and many others prayed for many? •
111 the righteous have prayed for the ungodly now 26
112 those who were strong prayed for the weak. 28
8: 6 grant to thy servant that we may pray before thee 28
17 Therefore I will pray before thee for myself 28
9:25 pray to the Most High continually 25
12:48 to pray on account of the desolation of Zion 25
Tob 3: 1 in my grief I wept, and I prayed in anguish, saying 24
11 she prayed by her window and said 13
8: 4 let us pray that the Lord may have mercy upon us. 24
5 Tobias began to pray 20
12:12 when you and your daughter-in-law Sarah prayed 24
Jdt 4:12 praying earnestly to the God of Israel •
8:31 pray for us, since you are a devout woman 13
11:17 I will pray to God and he will tell me 24
12: 6 permitted to go out and pray. 16
8 prayed the Lord God of Israel to direct her way 13
AEs 13: 8 Then Mordecai prayed to the Lord 13
14: 3 she prayed to the Lord God of Israel, and said 13
Wis 7: 7 Therefore I prayed 18
13:17 When he prays about possessions 24
18 for life he prays to a thing that is dead 11
16:28 and must pray to thee at the dawning of the light; 14
Sir 3: 5 when he prays he will be heard. 23
17:25 pray in his presence and lessen your offenses. 13
21: 1 Do so no more, but pray about your former sins. 13
28: 2 then your sins will be pardoned when you pray. 13
4 yet pray for his own sins? 13
34:24 When cne prays and another curses 18
37:15 besides all this pray to the Most High 13
38: 9 pray to the Lord, and he will heal you. 18
14 for they too will pray to the Lord 13
51: 9 prayed for deliverance from death. 13
Bar 1: 5 they wept, and fasted, and prayed before the Lord; 18
11 pray for the life of Nebuchadnezzar king 24
13 And pray for us to the Lord our God 24
LJr 1:41 they bring him and pray Bel that the man may speak 11
1Mc 3:44 to pray and ask for mercy and compassion. 24
4:30 When he saw that the army was strong, he prayed 24
7:40 Then Judas prayed and said 24
11:71 put dust on his head, and prayed. 24
2Mc 1: 6 We are now praying for you here. 24
2:10 Just as Moses prayed to the Lord 24
10 so also Solomon prayed 24
5: 4 Therefore all men prayed 11
12:44 superfluous and foolish to pray for the dead 18
14:15 prayed to him who established his own people 21
15:12 was praying with outstretched hands 19
14 loves the brethren and prays much for the people 24
27 praying to God in their hearts 18
3Mc 2: 1 the high priest Simon . . prayed as follows 22
10 when we come to this place and pray. 13
5: 7 called upon the Almighty Lord . . praying 13
6: 1 Then a certain Eleazar . . prayed as follows 24
4Mc 4:11 with tears besought the Hebrews to pray for him 24
13 Onias . . prayed for him 18

prayer 1. אֲשֶׁר פלל 2. דָּבָר 3. לַחַשׁ 4. פלל 5. פָּנִים
6. תְּפִלָּה 7. *δέησις* 8. *δέομαι* 9. *ἔντευξις* 10. *εὐχή*

11. ἱκετεία 12. προσευχή 13. προσεύχομαι 14. φωνή
15. deprecatio 16. oratio

2Sm 7:27 has found courage to pray this prayer to thee. 6
1Kg 8:28 Yet have regard to the prayer of thy servant 6
28 the cry and to the prayer which thy servant prays 6
29 hearken to the prayer which thy servant offers 6
38 whatever prayer, whatever supplication is made 6
45 hear . . their prayer and their supplication 6
49 hear . . their prayer and their supplication 6
54 offering all this prayer and supplication 6
9: 3 I have heard your prayer and your supplication 6
2Kg 6:18 in accordance with the prayer of Eli'sha. 2
19: 4 lift up your prayer for the remnant that is left. 6
20 Your prayer to me . . I have heard. 1
20: 5 I have heard your prayer, I have seen your tears; 6
2Ch 6:19 Yet have regard to the prayer of thy servant 6
19 hearkening to the cry and to the prayer 6
20 hearken to the prayer which thy servant offers 6
29 whatever prayer, whatever supplication is made 6
35 hear . . their prayer and their supplication 6
39 hear . . their prayer and their supplications 6
40 thy ears attentive to the prayer of this place. 6
7: 1 When Solomon had ended his prayer, fire came down 4
12 I have heard your prayer, and have chosen this 6
15 eyes . . open and my ears attentive to the prayer 6
30:27 their prayer came to his holy habitation 6
33:18 acts of Manas'seh, and his prayer to his God 6
19 his prayer, and how God received his entreaty 6
Neh 1: 6 to hear the prayer of thy servant which I now pray 6
11 ear be attentive to the prayer of thy servant 6
11 attentive . . to the prayer of thy servants 6
11:17 leader to begin the thanksgiving in prayer 6
Job 16:17 no violence in my hands, and my prayer is pure. 6
24:12 yet God pays no attention to their prayer. 6
42: 8 I will accept his prayer not to deal with you 5
9 the LORD accepted Job's prayer. 5
Ps 4: 1 Be gracious to me, and hear my prayer. 6
6: 9 The LORD has heard . . the LORD accepts my prayer. 6
17: 0 A Prayer of David. 6
1 Give ear to my prayer from lips free of deceit! 6
39:12 Hear my prayer, O LORD, and give ear to my cry; 6
42: 8 his song is with me, a prayer to the God of my life. 6
54: 2 Hear my prayer, O God; 6
55: 1 Give ear to my prayer, O God; and hide not thyself 6
61: 1 Hear my cry, O God, listen to my prayer; 6
65: 2 O thou who hearest prayer! 6
66:19 he has given heed to the voice of my prayer. 6
20 because he has not rejected my prayer 6
69:13 But as for me, my prayer is to thee, O LORD. 6
72:20 The prayers of David, the son of Jesse, are ended. 6
80: 4 how long . . be angry with thy people's prayers? 6
84: 8 O LORD God of hosts, hear my prayer; 6
86: 0 A Prayer of David. 6
6 Give ear, O LORD, to my prayer; 6
88: 2 prayer come before thee, incline thy ear to my cry! 6
13 in the morning my prayer comes before thee. 6
90: 0 A Prayer of Moses, the man of God. 6
102: 0 A prayer of one afflicted, when he is faint 6
1 Hear my prayer, O LORD; let my cry come to thee! 6
17 he will regard the prayer of the destitute 6
109: 4 accuse me, even as I make prayer for them. 6
7 tried, let . . his prayer be counted as sin! 6
141: 2 Let my prayer be counted as incense before thee 6
5 for my prayer is continually against their 6
142: 0 A Maskil of David . . A Prayer. 6
143: 1 Hear my prayer, O LORD; give ear 6
Prv 15: 8 but the prayer of the upright is his delight. 6
29 but he hears the prayer of the righteous. 6
28: 9 even his prayer is an abomination. 6
Isa 1:15 though you make many prayers, I will not listen; 6
26:16 they poured out a prayer when thy chastening was 3
37: 4 therefore lift up your prayer for the remnant 6
38: 5 I have heard your prayer, I have seen your tears; 6
56: 7 and make them joyful in my house of prayer; 6
7 be called a house of prayer for all peoples. 6
Jer 7:16 for this people, or lift up cry or prayer for them 6
11:14 or lift up a cry or prayer on their behalf 6
Lam 3: 8 though I call and cry . . he shuts out my prayer; 6
44 wrapped . . so that no prayer can pass through. 6
Dan 9: 3 seeking him by prayer and supplications 6
17 hearken to the prayer of thy servant 6
21 while I was speaking in prayer, the man Gabriel 6
Jon 2: 7 my prayer came to thee, into thy holy temple. 6
Hab 3: 1 A prayer of Habak'kuk the prophet 6
Mat 21:13 'My house shall be called a house of prayer' 12
22 whatever you ask in prayer, you will receive 12
Mrk 9:29 cannot be driven out by anything but prayer. 12
11:17 a house of prayer for all the nations 12
Lke 1:13 for your prayer is heard 7
2:37 worshiping with fasting and prayer 7
5:33 disciples of John fast often and offer prayers 7
6:12 and all night he continued in prayer to God. 12
19:46 'My house shall be a house of prayer'; 12
22:45 when he rose from prayer, he came to the disciples 12
Act 1:14 these with one accord devoted themselves to prayer 12
2:42 the breaking of bread and the prayers. 12
3: 1 going up . . at the hour of prayer, the ninth hour. 12
6: 4 we will devote ourselves to prayer 12
10: 4 Your prayers and your alms have ascended 12
30 I was keeping the ninth hour of prayer in my house; 13
31 saying, 'Cornelius, your prayer has been heard 12
12: 5 earnest prayer for him was made to God 12
14:23 with prayer and fasting 13
16:13 where we supposed there was a place of prayer; 12
16 As we were going to the place of prayer 12
Rom 1: 9 I mention you always in my prayers 12
10: 1 Brethren, my heart's desire and prayer to God 7
12:12 be constant in prayer. 12
15:30 with me in your prayers to God on my behalf 12
1Co 7: 5 that you may devote yourselves to prayer 12
2Co 1:11 You also must help us by prayer 7
11 granted us in answer to many prayers. •
Eph 1:16 remembering you in my prayers 12
6:18 with all prayer and supplication 12
Php 1: 4 always in every prayer of mine for you all 7
4 making my prayer with joy 7
9 it is my prayer that your love may abound more 13
19 For I know that through your prayers 7
4: 6 in everything by prayer and supplication 12
Col 4: 2 Continue steadfastly in prayer 12
12 remembering you earnestly in his prayers 12
1Th 1: 2 constantly mentioning you in our prayers 12
1Ti 2: 1 supplications, prayers, intercessions 12
4: 5 is consecrated by the word of God and prayer. 9
5: 5 continues in supplications and prayers 12
2Ti 1: 3 when I remember you constantly in my prayers. 7
Phm 1: 4 when I remember you in my prayers 12
22 through your prayers to be granted to you. 12
Heb 5: 7 In the days of his flesh, Jesus offered up prayers 7
Jas 5:15 the prayer of faith will save the sick man 10
16 The prayer of a righteous man has great power 7
1Pe 3: 7 in order that your prayers may not be hindered. 12
12 and his ears are open to their prayer. 7
4: 7 therefore keep sane and sober for your prayers. 12
Rev 5: 8 bowls . . which are the prayers of the saints; 12
8: 3 given much incense to mingle with the prayers 12
4 the smoke of the incense rose with the prayers 12
2Es 8:19 The beginning of the words of Ezra's prayer 16
24 hear, O Lord, the prayer of thy servant 16
10:28 and my prayer a reproach. 16
12: 7 if my prayer has indeed come up before thy face 15
13:14 and hast deemed me worthy to have my prayer heard 15
Tob 3:16 The prayer of both was heard 12
12: 8 Prayer is good when accompanied by fasting 12
12 I brought a reminder of your prayer 12
15 who present the prayers of the saints 12
13: 1 Then Tobit wrote a prayer of rejoicing, and said 12
Jdt 4:13 the Lord heard their prayers 14
9:12 King of all thy creation, hear my prayer! 7
13: 3 she said she would be going out for her prayers. 12
10 as they were accustomed to go for prayer 12
AEs 13:17 Hear my prayer, and have mercy 7
15: 1 On the third day, when she ended her prayer 13
Wis 18:21 prayer and propitiation by incense 12
Sir 4: 6 his Creator will hear his prayer. 7
7:10 Do not be fainthearted in your prayer 13
14 nor repeat yourself in your prayer. 13
21: 5 The prayer of a poor man goes from his lips 7
34:26 who will listen to his prayer? 12
35:13 will listen to the prayer of one who is wronged. 7
16 his prayer will reach to the clouds. 7
17 The prayer of the humble pierces the clouds 12
36:17 Hearken, O Lord, to the prayer of thy servants 7
38:34 their prayer is in the practice of their trade. 7
39: 5 he will open his mouth in prayer 13
6 give thanks to the Lord in prayer. 13
50:19 the people besought the Lord Most High in prayer 12
51:11 My prayer was heard 7
13 I sought wisdom openly in my prayer. 13
Bar 2:14 Hear, O Lord, our prayer and our supplication 12
19 bring before thee our prayer for mercy, O Lord •
3: 4 O Lord Almighty, God of Israel, hear now the prayer 12
1Mc 3:46 Israel formerly had a place of prayer in Mizpah. 12
5:33 and cried aloud in prayer. 13
7:37 a house of prayer and supplication. 12
12:11 in our prayers 12
2Mc 1: 5 May he hear your prayers and be reconciled to you 7
23 the priests offered prayer 12
24 The prayer was to this effect 12
10:27 rising from their prayer 7
12:42 they turned to prayer 11
15:24 With these words he ended his prayer. •
26 with invocation to God and prayers. 10
3Mc 1:24 the crowd, as before, was engaged in prayer 8
6:16 Just as Eleazar was ending his prayer 12
7:20 dedicating a place of prayer 12

prayer *See also* ask, grant, make, offer.

pre-eminence 1. יתר
Gen 49: 4 you shall not have pre-eminence 1

pre-eminent 1. יֶתֶר 2. προηγέομαι
Gen 49: 3 you are . . pre-eminent in pride and . . in power. 1
3 pre-eminent in pride and pre-eminent in power. 1
3Mc 1:11 only the high priest who was pre-eminent over all 2

preach 1. נטף 2. εὐαγγελίζω 3. κήρυγμα
4. κηρύσσω 5. λαλέω 6. λέγω 7. λόγος
8. παράκλησις 9. προκηρύσσω 10. ῥῆμα

Ezk 20:46 face toward the south, preach against the south 1
21: 2 and preach against the sanctuaries; 1
Ams 7:16 and do not preach against the house of Isaac.' 1
Mic 2: 6 Do not preach"-thus they preach 1
6 Do not preach"-thus they preach 1
6 one should not preach of such things; 1
11 I will preach to you of wine and strong drink 1
Mat 3: 1 John the Baptist, preaching in the wilderness 4
4:17 From that time Jesus began to preach, saying 4
23 in their synagogues and preaching the gospel 4
9:35 teaching in their synagogues and preaching 4
10: 7 preach as you go, saying 4
11: 1 to teach and preach in their cities. 4
12:41 for they repented at the preaching of Jonah 3
23: 3 for they preach, but do not practice. 6
24:14 this gospel of the kingdom will be preached 4
26:13 wherever this gospel is preached 4
Mrk 1: 4 preaching a baptism of repentance 4
7 he preached, saying 4
14 preaching the gospel of God 4
38 that I may preach there also 4
39 preaching in their synagogues 4
2: 2 he was preaching the word to them. 5
3:14 he appointed twelve . . to be sent out to preach 4
6:12 and preached that men should repent. 4
13:10 gospel must first be preached to all nations. 4
14: 9 the gospel is preached in the whole world 4
16:15 Go into all the world and preach the gospel 4
20 they went forth and preached everywhere 4
Lke 3: 3 preaching a baptism of repentance 4
4:44 he was preaching in the synagogues of Judea. 4
8: 1 preaching and bringing the good news 4
9: 2 he sent them out to preach the kingdom of God 4
11:32 they repented at the preaching of Jonah 3
24:47 preached in his name to all nations 4
Act 5:42 preaching Jesus as the Christ. 2
6: 2 that we should give up preaching the word of God •
8: 4 those . . went about preaching the word. 2
10:37 after the baptism which John preached 4
42 he commanded us to preach to the people 4
11:20 preaching the Lord Jesus. 2
13:24 Before his coming John had preached 9
15:21 Moses has had in every city those who preach him 4
35 teaching and preaching the word of the Lord 2
17:18 because he preached Jesus and the resurrection. 2
18: 5 Paul was occupied with preaching 7
19:13 I adjure you by the Jesus whom Paul preaches. 4
20:25 among whom I have gone preaching the kingdom 4
28:31 preaching the kingdom of God 4
Rom 2:21 While you preach against stealing, do you steal? 4
10: 8 (that is, the word of faith which we preach); 4
15 And how can men preach unless they are sent? 4
17 what is heard comes by the preaching of Christ. 10
16:25 my gospel and the preaching of Jesus Christ 3
1Co 1:21 through the folly of what we preach to save 3
23 we preach Christ crucified 4
9:18 Just this: that in my preaching 2
27 lest after preaching to others 4
15:11 so we preach and so you believed. 4
12 Now if Christ is preached as raised from the dead 4
14 then our preaching is in vain 3
2Co 1:19 Jesus Christ, whom we preached among you 4
2:12 to preach the gospel of Christ •
4: 5 For what we preach is not ourselves, but Jesus 4
8:18 for his preaching of the gospel; •
11: 4 For if some one comes and preaches another Jesus 4
4 preaches another Jesus than the one we preached 4
7 because I preached God's gospel without cost 2
Gal 1: 8 a gospel contrary to that which we preached 2
11 the gospel which was preached by me is not man's 2
16 I might preach him among the Gentiles 2
23 now preaching the faith he once tried to destroy 2
2: 2 the gospel which I preach among the Gentiles 4
5:11 if I, brethren, still preach circumcision 4
Eph 2:17 he came and preached peace to you who were far off 2
3: 8 to preach to the Gentiles 2
Php 1:15 Some indeed preach Christ from envy and rivalry 4
Col 1:23 which has been preached to every creature 4
1Th 2: 9 while we preached to you the gospel of God. 4
1Ti 3:16 preached among the nations 4
4:13 reading of scripture, to preaching, to teaching. 8
5:17 those who labor in preaching and teaching; 7
2Ti 2: 8 descended from David, as preached in my gospel •
4: 2 preach the word 4
Tit 1: 3 the preaching with which I have been entrusted 3
1Pe 3:19 he went and preached to the spirits in prison 4

preach a gospel 1. εὐαγγελίζω
Gal 1: 8 preach to you a gospel contrary to that 1
9 If any one is preaching to you a gospel 1

preach boldly 1. παρρησιάζομαι
Act 9:27 he had preached boldly in the name of Jesus. 1
29 preaching boldly in the name of the Lord. 1

preach fully 1. πληρόω
Rom 15:19 I have fully preached the gospel of Christ 1

preach good news 1. εὐαγγελίζω
Mat 11: 5 and the poor have good news preached to them. 1
Lke 3:18 he preached good news to the people. 1
4:18 he has anointed me to preach good news to the poor 1
43 I must preach the good news of the kingdom of God 1
7:22 the poor have good news preached to them. 1
16:16 the good news of the kingdom of God is preached 1
Act 8:12 as he preached good news about the kingdom of God 1
10:36 preaching good news of peace by Jesus Christ 1
Rom 10:15 the feet of those who preach good news! 1
1Pe 1:12 by those who preached the good news to you 1
25 That word is the good news which was preached 1

preach the gospel 1. εὐαγγελίζω
Lke 9: 6 preaching the gospel and healing everywhere. 1
20: 1 he was teaching . . and preaching the gospel 1
Act 8:25 preaching the gospel to many villages 1
40 he preached the gospel to all the towns 1
14: 7 there they preached the gospel. 1
21 When they had preached the gospel to that city 1
16:10 God had called us to preach the gospel to them. 1
Rom 1:15 I am eager to preach the gospel to you 1
15:20 thus making it my ambition to preach the gospel 1
1Co 1:17 not send me to baptize but to preach the gospel 1
9:16 For if I preach the gospel 1
16 Woe to me if I do not preach the gospel! 1
15: 1 in what terms I preached to you the gospel 1
2Co 10:16 that we may preach the gospel in lands beyond you 1
Gal 4:13 preached the gospel to you at first; 1
1Pe 4: 6 the gospel was preached even to the dead 1

preach the gospel beforehand 1. προευαγγελίζομαι
Gal 3: 8 preached the gospel beforehand to Abraham 1

preacher 1. נטף 2. קֹהֶלֶת 3. καταγγελεύς 4. κῆρυξ 5. κηρύσσω
Ecc 1: 1 The words of the Preacher, the son of David 2
2 Vanity of vanities, says the Preacher 2
12 I the Preacher have been king over Israel 2
7:27 Behold, this is what I found, says the Preacher 2
12: 8 Vanity of vanities, says the Preacher; 2
9 the Preacher also taught the people knowledge 2
10 The Preacher sought to find pleasing words 2
Mic 2:11 he would be the preacher for this people! 1
Act 17:18 He seems to be a preacher of foreign divinities 3
Rom 10:14 And how are they to hear without a preacher? 5
1Ti 2: 7 For this I was appointed a preacher and apostle 4
2Ti 1:11 For this gospel I was appointed a preacher 4

precautions *See* take.

precede 1. היה לִפְנֵי 2. εἰμὶ πρό 3. ἔμπροσθεν 4. πρό 5. προέρχομαι 6. πρόκειμαι 7. φθάνω
Jer 28: 8 The prophets who preceded you and me 1
1Th 4:15 shall not precede those who have fallen asleep. 7
AEs 11: 1 brought to Egypt the preceding Letter of Purim 6
Sir 22:24 vapor and smoke of the furnace precede the fire; 4
24 so insults precede bloodshed. 4
32:10 approval precedes a modest man. 5
37:16 counsel precedes every undertaking. 4
1Mc 3:30 give more lavishly than preceding kings. 3
4Mc 1:22 desire precedes pleasure and delight follows 2
23 Fear precedes pain and sorrow comes after. 2

precedence *See* take.

precept 1. לֶקַח 2. מִצְוָה 3. פִּקּוּד 4. צַו 5. δικαίωμα 6. ἔνταλμα 7. praecipio
Ps 19: 8 the precepts of the LORD are right 3
111: 7 all his precepts are trustworthy 3
119: 4 Thou hast commanded thy precepts to be kept 3
15 I will meditate on thy precepts 3
27 Make me understand the way of thy precepts 3
40 Behold, I long for thy precepts; 3
45 walk at liberty, for I have sought thy precepts. 3
56 This blessing . . that I have kept thy precepts. 3
63 all who fear thee, of those who keep thy precepts. 3
69 with my whole heart I keep thy precepts; 3
78 as for me, I will meditate on thy precepts. 3
87 but I have not forsaken thy precepts. 3
93 I will never forget thy precepts; 3
94 I am thine, save me; for I have sought thy precepts. 3
100 more than the aged, for I keep thy precepts. 3
104 Through thy precepts I get understanding; 3
110 I do not stray from thy precepts. 3
128 Therefore I direct my steps by all thy precepts; 3
134 Redeem me . . that I may keep thy precepts. 3
141 yet I do not forget thy precepts. 3
159 Consider how I love thy precepts! 3
168 I keep thy precepts and testimonies 3
173 help me, for I have chosen thy precepts. 3
Prv 4: 2 for I give you good precepts 1
Isa 28:10 For it is precept upon precept 4
10 For it is precept upon precept 4
10 is precept upon precept, precept upon precept 4
10 is precept upon precept, precept upon precept 4
13 will be to them precept upon precept 4
13 will be to them precept upon precept 4
13 precept upon precept, precept upon precept 4
13 precept upon precept, precept upon precept 4
Jer 35:18 and kept all his precepts 2
Mat 15: 9 teaching as doctrines the precepts of men.' 6
Mrk 7: 7 teaching as doctrines the precepts of men.' 6
Rom 2:26 uncircumcised keeps the precepts of the law 5
Col 2:22 according to human precepts and doctrines 6
2Es 16:76 You who keep my commandments and precepts 7

precinct 1. פַּרְוָר 2. ὅριον 3. περίβολος 4. σηκός
2Kg 23:11 by the chamber of . . which was in the precincts; 1
1Mc 10:43 in any of its precincts 2
14:48 in the precincts of the sanctuary 3
2Mc 6: 4 within the sacred precincts 3
14:33 I will level this precinct of God to the ground 4

sacred precinct 1. τέμενος
1Mc 1:47 to build altars and sacred precincts and shrines 1
5:43 and fled into the sacred precincts at Carnaim. 1
44 and burned the sacred precincts with fire 1
2Mc 1:15 inside the wall of the sacred precinct 1
10: 2 and also destroyed the sacred precincts. 1

precious 1. גדל 2. חמד 3. חֶמְדָּה 4. חֲמוּדָה 5. חֵפֶץ 6. טוֹב 7. יקר 8. יְקָר 9. יָקָר 10. מַחְמַד 11. מֶכֶר 12. תּוֹעָפָה 13. ἀντάλλαγμα 14. ἔντιμος 15. παχύς 16. πολυτελής 17. τιμή 18. τίμιος 19. electus 20. pretiosus
1Sm 26:21 my life was precious in your eyes this day; 7
24 as your life was precious this day in my sight 1
24 so may my life be precious in the sight of the LORD 1
2Sm 12:30 was a talent of gold, and in it was a precious stone; 9
1Kg 10: 2 with . . very much gold, and precious stones; 9
10 gold, and . . spices, and precious stones; 9
11 from Ophir . . almug wood and precious stones. 9
2Kg 1:13 let my life, and the life of these . . be precious 7
14 but now let my life be precious in your sight. 7
20:13 silver, the gold, the spices, the precious oil, his 6
1Ch 20: 2 crown . . and in it was a precious stone 9
29: 2 quantities of . . all sorts of precious stones 9
8 whoever had precious stones gave them *
2Ch 3: 6 He adorned the house with . . precious stones. 9
9: 1 camels bearing spices and . . precious stones. 9
9 she gave the king . . spices, and precious stones 9
10 brought algum wood and precious stones. 9
20:25 found cattle . . clothing, and precious things 4
32:27 made . . treasuries . . , for precious stones 9
36:10 precious vessels of the house of the LORD 3
19 destroyed all its precious vessels. 10
Ezr 8:27 fine bright bronze as precious as gold. 4
Job 22:25 Almighty is your gold, and your precious silver; 12
28:16 the gold of Ophir, in precious onyx or sapphire. 9
Ps 36: 7 How precious is thy steadfast love, O God! 9
72:14 precious is their blood in his sight. 7
116:15 Precious in the sight of the LORD is the death 9
133: 2 It is like the precious oil upon the head 6
139:17 How precious to me are thy thoughts, O God! 7
Prv 1:13 we shall find all precious goods 9
3:15 She is more precious than jewels 9
12:27 but the diligent man will get precious wealth. 9
20:15 but the lips of knowledge are a precious jewel. 8
21:20 Precious treasure remains in a wise man's 2
24: 4 filled with all precious and pleasant riches. 9
31:10 good wife . . is far more precious than jewels. 11
Ecc 7: 1 A good name is better than precious ointment; 6
Isa 28:16 a tested stone, a precious cornerstone 9
39: 2 silver, the gold, the spices, the precious oil 6
43: 4 Because you are precious in my eyes, and honored 7
54:12 and all your wall of precious stones. 5
Jer 15:19 If you utter what is precious 9
Lam 4: 2 The precious sons of Zion, worth their weight 9
Ezk 27:22 spices, and all precious stones, and gold. 9
28:13 every precious stone was your covering 9
Dan 11: 8 molten images and with their precious vessels 3
38 honor with . . precious stones and costly gifts. 9
Hos 13:15 strip his treasury of every precious thing. 3
Nah 2: 9 of treasure, or wealth of every precious thing. 3
Act 20:24 not . . of any value nor as precious to myself 18
1Co 3:12 with gold, silver, precious stones, wood, hay, straw- 18
Jas 5: 7 farmer waits for the precious fruit of the earth 18
1Pe 1:19 with the precious blood of Christ 18
2: 4 in God's sight chosen and precious; 14
6 in Zion . . a cornerstone chosen and precious 14
7 To you therefore who believe, he is precious 17
2Pe 1: 4 his precious and very great promises 18
2Es 7:52 If you have just a few precious stones 19
57 which things are precious and desirable 20
Tob 13:16 her walls with precious stones 14
Jdt 10: 3 anointed herself with precious ointment 15
21 gold and emeralds and precious stones. 16
AEs 15: 6 all covered with gold and precious stones 16
Sir 6:15 nothing so precious as a faithful friend 13
26:14 nothing so precious as a disciplined soul. 13
45:11 with precious stones engraved like signets 16
50: 9 adorned with all kinds of precious stones; 16

precious *See also* stone.

more precious 1. πολύτιμος 2. pretiosus
1Pe 1: 7 faith, more precious than gold 1
2Es 7:58 for what is more rare is more precious. 2

most precious 1. τίμιος
Wis 12: 7 the land most precious of all to thee 1

precious place 1. צפן
Ezk 7:22 that they may profane my precious place; 1

precious thing 1. חֲמוּדָה 2. יְקָר 3. מִגְדָּנָה 4. מַחְמַד
2Ch 32:23 many brought . . precious things to Hezeki'ah 3
Job 28:10 his eye sees every precious thing. 2
Lam 1: 7 Jerusalem remembers . . all the precious things 4
10 stretched out . . over all her precious things; 4
Ezk 22:25 they have taken treasure and precious things; 2
Dan 11:43 ruler of . . all the precious things of Egypt; 1
Hos 9: 6 shall possess their precious things of silver; 4

very precious 1. πολυτελής
1Pe 3: 4 spirit, which in God's sight is very precious. 1

precipitous 1. ἀπορρωγάς
4Mc 14:16 building in precipitous chasms 1

precipitous place 1. praecipitium
2Es 7: 7 is narrow and set in a precipitous place 1

precipitously *See* incline.

precisely 1. ἐπιμελῶς
3Mc 4:13 these men be dealt with in precisely the same fashion 1

predecessor 1. ὁ πρό
1Mc 11:26 treated him as his predecessors had treated him; 1

predestine 1. προορίζω
Act 4:28 whatever . . thy plan had predestined to take place. 1
Rom 8:29 For those whom he foreknew he also predestined 1
30 And those whom he predestined he also called; 1

predict 1. ידע 2. קרא 3. προεῖπον 4. προμαρτύρομαι 5. praedico
2Kg 23:16 the man of God . . who had predicted these things. 2
17 man of God who came . . and predicted these things 2
Isa 47:13 who at the new moons predict what shall befall 1
Rom 9:29 And as Isaiah predicted, "If the Lord of hosts had 3
1Pe 1:11 when predicting the sufferings of Christ 4
2Es 9: 1 a certain part of the predicted signs are past 5
8 survive the dangers that have been predicted 5

predicted thing 1. praedico
2Es 8:59 For just as the things which I have predicted 1

prediction 1. προεῖπον ῥῆμα
2Pe 3: 2 remember the predictions of the holy prophets 1
Jde 1:17 predictions of the apostles of our Lord Jesus 1

preeminence 1. נֹהַּ
Ezk 7:11 neither shall there be preeminence among them. 1

preeminent 1. πρωτεύω
Col 1:18 that in everything he might be preeminent. 1

preface 1. πρὸ ἱστορίας
2Mc 2:32 it is foolish to lengthen the preface 1

prefect 1. סְגַן (A) 2. ὕπατος
Dan 2:48 chief prefect over all the wise men of Babylon. 1
3: 2 assemble the satraps, the prefects 1
3 Then the satraps, the prefects, and the governors 1
27 satraps, the prefects, the governors 1
6: 7 presidents . . the prefects and the satraps 1
1Es 3:14 satraps and generals and governors and prefects 2

prefer 1. בחר 2. αἱρετίζω 3. αἱρετίζω μᾶλλον ἤ 4. ἀλλάσσω 5. ἐθέλω 6. μᾶλλον 7. πλείονα λογίζομαι 8. προαιρέω 9. προκρίνω 10. προτιμάω
Jer 8: 3 Death shall be preferred to life 1
Phm 1: 9 yet for love's sake I prefer to appeal to you–I, Paul 6
14 I preferred to do nothing without your consent 5
1Es 4:19 all prefer her to gold or silver 3
Wis 7: 8 I preferred her to scepters and thrones 9
17:13 prefers ignorance of what causes the torment. 7
2Mc 11:24 but prefer their own way of living 2
14:42 preferring to die nobly 5
3Mc 1:29 because indeed all at that time preferred death 4
2:30 if any of them prefer 8
4Mc 1:15 with sound logic prefers the life of wisdom. 10

preferable 1. αἱρετός 2. λυσιτελὴς μᾶλλον
Sir 20:25 A thief is preferable to a habitual liar 1
28:21 Hades is preferable to it. 2

preference 1. עַל פָּנִים 2. διαφορά
Deu 21:16 not . . in preference to the son of the disliked 1
1Es 4:39 With her there is no partiality or preference 2

pregnancy 1. בֶּטֶן 2. δεκάμηνος 3. κυοφορία
Hos 9:11 no birth, no pregnancy, no conception! 1
4Mc 15: 6 In seven pregnancies 3
16: 7 seven profitless pregnancies 2

pregnant 1. הָרָה 2. ἔγκυος
Ps 7:14 conceives evil, and is pregnant with mischief 1
Sir 42:10 become pregnant in her father's house 2

pregnant woman 1. הָרִיָּה
Hos 13:16 and their pregnant women ripped open. 1

premature 1. immaturus
2Es 6:21 premature children at three and four months 1

preparation 1. παρασκευή
Mat 27:62 Next day, that is, after the day of Preparation 1
Lke 23:54 was the day of Preparation 1
Jdt 4: 5 and stored up food in preparation for war 1
3Mc 5:10 to report to the king about these preparations. *

preparation *See also* make.

prepare 1. אסר 2. זבח 3. חצב 4. כון 5. ערך 6. עשׂה 7. עָתִיד 8. פנה 9. קדשׁ 10. קום 11. רקח 12. שׁית 13. שָׁלֵם 14. γίνομαι 15. διατάσσω 16. ἑτοιμάζω 17. ἑτοιμασία 18. ἕτοιμος 19. καταρτίζω 20. κατασκευάζω 21. κατεργάζομαι 22. κοσμέω 23. παρασκευάζω 24. ποιέω 25. προετοιμάζω 26. προκατασκευάζω 27. σκευάζω 28. στέλλω 29. συνίστημι 30. paro 31. praeparo
Gen 18: 7 gave it to the servant, who hastened to prepare it 6
8 took . . the calf which he had prepared 6
24:31 For I have prepared the house and a place 8
27: 4 prepare for me savory food, such as I love 6
7 'Bring me game, and prepare for me savory food 6
9 that I may prepare from them savory food 6
14 and his mother prepared savory food 6
17 savory food and the bread, which she had prepared 6
31 He also prepared savory food, and brought it 6
Exd 12:16 one must eat, that only may be prepared by you. 6
39 neither had they prepared for themselves any 6
16: 5 sixth day, when they prepare what they bring 4
23:20 to bring you to the place which I have prepared. 4
39: 6 onyx stones were prepared, enclosed in settings 6
Lev 7: 9 all that is prepared on a pan or a griddle 6
Num15: 5 you shall prepare with the burnt offering 6
6 for a ram, you shall prepare for a cereal offering 6
8 when you prepare a bull for a burnt offering 6
12 According to the number that you prepare 6
23: 4 I have prepared the seven altars 5
Deu 19: 3 prepare the roads, and divide into three parts 4
Jos 1:11 command the people, 'Prepare your provisions; 4
Jdg 6:19 Gideon . . prepared a kid, and unleavened cakes 6
13:15 Pray, let us detain you, and prepare a kid for you. 6
19: 5 arose early in the morning, and he prepared to go; 10
1Sm 6: 7 take and prepare a new cart and two milch cows 6
2Sm 12: 4 take one of his own . . to prepare for the wayfarer 6
4 but he took the poor man's lamb, and prepared it 6
13: 5 give me bread . . and prepare the food in my sight 6
7 Go to . . Amnon's house, and prepare food for him. 6
1Kg 1: 5 he prepared for himself chariots and horsemen 6
5:18 and prepared the timber and the stone to build 4
6: 7 it was with stone prepared at the quarry; 13
19 inner sanctuary he prepared in the innermost 4
17:12 I may go in and prepare it for myself and my son 6
18:23 I will prepare the other bull 6
25 Choose for yourselves one bull and prepare it 6
26 they took the bull . . and they prepared it 6
44 Go up, say to Ahab, 'Prepare your chariot and go down 1
2Kg 7:12 what the Syrians have prepared against us. 6
1Ch 9:30 Others . . prepared the mixing of the spices. 11
32 the showbread, to prepare it every sabbath. 4
15: 1 he prepared a place for the ark of God 4
3 to its place, which he had prepared for it. 4
12 to the place that I have prepared for it. 4
22: 2 he set stonecutters to prepare dressed stones 3
2Ch 1: 4 to the place that David had prepared for it 4
2: 9 to prepare timber for me in abundance 4
16:14 kinds of spices prepared by the perfumer's art; 11
26:14 Uzzi'ah prepared for all the army shields, spears 4
31:11 Hezeki'ah commanded them to prepare chambers 4
11 commanded them . . and they prepared them. 4
35: 4 Prepare yourselves according to your fathers' 4
6 sanctify . . and prepare for your brethren 4
10 When the service had been prepared 4
14 prepared for themselves and for the priests 4
14 Levites prepared for themselves 4
15 their brethren the Levites prepared for them. 4
16 all the service of the LORD was prepared that day 4
20 when Josi'ah had prepared the temple 4
Neh 5:18 Now that which was prepared for one day was one ox 6
18 fowls likewise were prepared for me 6
8:10 portions to him for whom nothing is prepared; 4
13: 5 prepared for Tobi'ah a large chamber 6
7 preparing for him a chamber in the courts 6
Est 5: 4 to a dinner that I have prepared for the king. 6
5 came to the dinner that Esther had prepared. 6
8 to the dinner which I will prepare for them 6
12 let no one come . . to the banquet she prepared 6
6: 4 on the gallows that he had prepared for him. 4
14 to the banquet that Esther had prepared. 6
7: 9 gallows which Haman has prepared for Mor'decai 6
10 hanged Haman on the gallows . . he had prepared 4
Job 13:18 Behold, I have prepared my case; 5
15:24 against him, like a king prepared for battle. 7
35 their heart prepares deceit. 4
29: 7 when I prepared my seat in the square 4
Ps 5: 3 in the morning I prepare a sacrifice for thee 5
7:13 he has prepared his deadly weapons 4
23: 5 Thou preparest a table before me 5
65: 9 providest their grain, for so thou hast prepared 4
132:17 I have prepared a lamp for my anointed. 5
147: 8 he prepares rain for the earth 4
Prv 6: 8 she prepares her food in summer 4
24:27 Prepare your work outside, get everything ready 4
Isa 14:21 Prepare slaughter for his sons 4
21: 5 They prepare the table, they spread the rugs 5
30:33 For a burning place has long been prepared; 5
40: 3 In the wilderness prepare the way of the LORD 8
57:14 shall be said, "Build up, build up, prepare the way 8
62:10 through the gates, prepare the way for the people; 8
Jer 6: 4 Prepare war against her; up, and let us attack 9
22: 7 I will prepare destroyers against you 9
46: 3 Prepare buckler and shield, and advance 5
14 Say, 'Stand ready and be prepared 4
19 Prepare yourselves baggage for exile 6
51:12 set up watchmen; prepare the ambushes; 4
27 prepare the nations for war against her 9
28 Prepare the nations for war against her 9
39 I will prepare them a feast and make them drunk 12
Ezk 4:15 dung, on which you may prepare your bread. 6
12: 3 prepare for yourself an exile's baggage 6
28:13 day that you were created they were prepared. 4
35: 6 I will prepare you for blood 6
39:17 sacrificial feast which I am preparing for you 2
19 sacrificial feast which I am preparing for you. 2
Jol 3: 9 Prepare war, stir up the mighty men. 9
Ams 4:12 do this to you, prepare to meet your God, O Israel! 4
Zep 1: 7 the LORD has prepared a sacrifice 4
Zec 5:11 when this is prepared, they will set the ephah 4
Mal 3: 1 I send my messenger to prepare the way before me 8
Mat 3: 3 one crying in the wilderness: Prepare the way 16
11:10 who shall prepare thy way before thee.' 20
20:23 for whom it has been prepared by my Father. 16
25:34 inherit the kingdom prepared for you 16
41 into the eternal fire prepared for the devil 16
26:17 Where will you have us prepare for you 16
19 they prepared the passover. 16
Mrk 1: 2 who shall prepare thy way; 20
3 Prepare the way of the Lord 16
10:40 is for those for whom it has been prepared. 16
14:12 prepare for you to eat the passover? 16
15 there prepare for us. 16
16 they prepared the passover. 16
Lke 1:17 to make ready for the Lord a people prepared. 20
76 you will go before the Lord to prepare his ways 16
2:31 which thou hast prepared in the presence of all 16
3: 4 Prepare the way of the Lord 16
7:27 who shall prepare thy way before thee.' 20
12:20 the things you have prepared, whose will they be?' 16
17: 8 Prepare supper for me 16
22: 8 prepare the passover for us, that we may eat it. 16
9 They said to him, "Where will you have us prepare it? 16
13 they prepared the passover. 16
23:56 they returned, and prepared spices 16
24: 1 taking the spices which they had prepared. 16
Joh 14: 2 I go to prepare a place for you? 16
3 when I go and prepare a place for you 16
Act 10:10 while they were preparing it, he fell into a trance 23
1Co 2: 9 what God has prepared for those who love him 16
2Co 4:17 preparing for us an eternal weight of glory 21
5: 5 He who has prepared us for this very thing is God 21
Phm 1:22 At the same time, prepare a guest room for me 16
Heb 9: 2 a tent was prepared, the outer one 20
10: 5 a body hast thou prepared for me; 19
11:16 he has prepared for them a city. 16
1Pe 3:15 Always be prepared to make a defense to any one 18
Rev 12: 6 wilderness, where she has a place prepared by God 16
16:12 to prepare the way for the kings of the east. 16
21: 2 prepared as a bride adorned for her husband; 16
1Es 1: 4 prepare yourselves by your families and kindred 16
6 prepare the sacrifices for your brethren 16
13 they prepared the passover for themselves 16
14 the Levites prepared it for themselves 16
16 the Levites prepared the passover for them. 16
5:48 prepared the altar of the God of Israel 16
9:42 the wooden platform which had been prepared; 20
2Es 2:11 which I had prepared for Israel. 31
13 The kingdom is already prepared for you; watch! 30
18 I have consecrated and prepared for you 30
7:70 he first prepared the judgment 31
8:52 the age to come is prepared, plenty is provided 31
59 and torment which are prepared await them 31
60 ungrateful to him who prepared life for them. 31
9:18 when I was preparing for those who now exist 30
13:11 multitude which was prepared to fight 30
36 prepared and built, as you saw the mountain 30
14:24 prepare for yourself many writing tablets 31
16:40 Hear my words, O my people; prepare for battle 30
Tob 2: 1 a good dinner was prepared for me 14
11: 3 run ahead of your wife and prepare the house. 16
Jdt 2: 7 Tell them to prepare earth and water 16
5: 1 the people of Israel had prepared for war 23
9: 6 all they ways are prepared in advance 18
12:19 drank before him what her maid had prepared. 16
AEs 11: 7 at their roaring every nation prepared for war 16
12: 2 preparing to lay hands upon Artaxerxes the king; 16
Wis 9: 8 which thou didst prepare from the beginning. 25
13:12 to prepare his food 17
14: 1 Again, one preparing to sail 28
16: 2 thou didst prepare quails to eat 16
Sir 0: 3 prepared . . to live according to the law. 26
2: 1 prepare yourself for temptation. 16
17 who fear the Lord will prepare their hearts 16
18:23 Before making a vow, prepare yourself 16
26:28 the Lord will prepare him for the sword! 16
29:26 Come here, stranger, prepare the table 22
33: 4 Prepare what to say, and thus you will be heard; 16
45:20 he prepared bread of first fruits in abundance; 16
47:13 prepare a sanctuary to stand for ever. 16
49: 1 prepared by the art of the perfumer 27
12 prepared for everlasting glory. 16
Bar 1:10 prepare a cereal offering, and offer them 24
3:32 He who prepared the earth for all time filled it 20
1Mc 2:32 prepared for battle against them 29
5:11 They are preparing to come 16
12:28 Jonathan and his men were prepared for battle 16
15: 7 All the weapons which you have prepared 20
2Mc 2:27 one who prepares a banquet 23
3Mc 1:19 bridal chambers prepared for wedded union 15
5: 8 rescue them from the fate now prepared for them. 18
20 tomorrow without delay prepare the elephants 16
31 I would have prepared them to be a rich feast 27
6:31 prepared for their destruction and burial. 16

prepare a feast 1. כרה
2Kg 6:23 So he prepared for them a great feast; 1

prepare beforehand 1. προετοιμάζω
Rom 9:23 vessels . . which he has prepared beforehand 1
Eph 2:10 for good works, which God prepared beforehand 1

prepare for burial 1. ἐνταφιάζω
Mat 26:12 she has done it to prepare me for burial. 1

prescribe 1. כתב 2. מִשְׁפָּט 3. פקד 4. שׁבר 5. כְּתָב (A) 6. κατά
2Ch 4: 7 he made ten golden lampstands as prescribed 2
20 burn before the inner sanctuary, as prescribed; 2
30: 5 had not kept it in great numbers as prescribed. 1
18 ate the passover otherwise than as prescribed. 1
Ezr 7:22 oil, and salt without prescribing how much. 5
Job 36:23 Who has prescribed for him his way, 3
38:10 prescribed bounds for it, and set bars and doors 4
1Es 6:34 done with all diligence as here prescribed. 6
8:21 all things prescribed in the law of God 6

prescribed order 1. constitutio
2Es 7:44 This is my judgment and its prescribed order 1

presence 1. לְנֶגֶד 2. לִפְנֵי 3. מִלִּפְנֵי 4. מֵעַל 5. מִפְּנֵי 6. נֶגֶד 7. נֶגְדָּה לְ 8. עַיִן 9. עַל 10. עַל פָּנִים 11. עִם 12. פָּנִים 13. שֵׁם 14. תּוֹךְ 15. קֳדָם (A) 16. ἀπέναντι 17. ἀπέναντι τῶν ὀφθαλμῶν 18. ἔμπροσθεν 19. ἔναντι 20. ἐναντίον 21. ἐνώπιον 22. κατέναντι 23. μέσος 24. ὄψις 25. παρά 26. παρουσία 27. πρόθεσις 28. πρόσοψις προσώπου 29. πρόσωπον 30. coram 31. facies
Gen 3: 8 hid themselves from the presence of the LORD God 12
4:16 Cain went away from the presence of the LORD 2
23: 9 let him give it to me in your presence 14
11 in the presence of the sons of my people I give it 8
18 a possession in the presence of the Hittites 8
27:30 gone out from the presence of Isaac his father 12
31:32 In the presence of our kinsmen point out 6
41:46 Joseph went out from the presence of Pharaoh 2
45: 3 for they were dismayed at his presence. 12
47:10 Jacob . . went out from the presence of Pharaoh. 2
Exd 10:11 they were driven out from Pharaoh's presence. 12
25:30 you shall set the bread of the Presence 12
33:14 he said, "My presence will go with you, and I will 12
15 he said to him, "If thy presence will not go with me 12
35:13 its utensils, and the bread of the Presence; 12
20 Israel departed from the presence of Moses. 12
39:36 its utensils, and the bread of the Presence; 12
Lev 10: 2 fire came forth from the presence of the LORD 2
22: 3 that person shall be cut off from my presence 12
Num 4: 7 over the table of the bread of the Presence 12
20: 6 Moses . . went from the presence of the assembly 12

Deu 4:37 brought you out of Egypt with his own presence 12
25: 2 beaten in his presence with a number of stripes 2
9 go up to him in the presence of the elders, and pull 8
Jos 8:32 there, in the presence of the people . . he wrote 2
22:27 perform the service of the LORD in his presence 2
Jdg 3:19 all his attendants went out from his presence. 4
Rut 4: 4 Buy it in the presence of those sitting here 6
4 and in the presence of the elders of my people. 6
1Sm 1:22 that he may appear in the presence of the LORD 12
26 the woman who was standing here in your presence 11
2:11 the boy ministered . . in the presence of Eli 12
21 the boy Samuel grew in the presence of the LORD. 11
18:13 Saul removed him from his presence, and made him 11
19: 7 and he was in his presence as before. 2
21: 6 was no bread there but the bread of the Presence 12
15 this fellow to play the madman in my presence? 9
26:20 away from the presence of the LORD; 12
2Sm 3:26 When Jo'ab came out from David's presence 11
11:13 he ate in his presence and drank 2
14:24 dwell apart . . he is not to come into my presence. 12
24 Ab'salom . . did not come into the king's presence. 12
28 without coming into the king's presence. 12
32 therefore let me go into the presence of the king; 12
24: 4 Jo'ab and . . went out from the presence of the king 12
1Kg 7:48 the golden table for the bread of the Presence 12
8:22 stood . . in the presence of all the assembly 6
10:24 the whole earth sought the presence of Solomon 12
21:13 brought a charge . . in the presence of the people 6
2Kg 5:27 So he went out from his presence a leper 12
6:32 the king had dispatched a man from his presence; 12
13:23 nor has he cast them from his presence until now. 10
24:20 he cast them out from his presence. 10
1Ch 16:11 and his strength, seek his presence continually! 12
24: 6 in the presence of the king, and the princes 2
31 in the presence of King David, Zadok, Ahim'elech 2
29:10 blessed . . in the presence of all the assembly; 8
2Ch 4:19 altar, the tables for the bread of the Presence 12
6:12 in the presence of all the assembly of Israel 6
13 in the presence of all the assembly of Israel 6
9:23 all the kings . . sought the presence of Solomon 12
26:19 in the presence of the priests 2
29:11 LORD has chosen you to stand in his presence 2
34: 4 broke down the altars . . in his presence 2
Neh 2: 1 Now I had not been sad in his presence. 12
4: 2 said in the presence of his brethren 12
6:19 Also they spoke of his good deeds in my presence 2
8: 3 read . . in the presence of the men and the women 6
Est 1:16 Then Memu'can said in presence of the king 2
2:23 recorded in . . the presence of the king. 2
7: 8 Will he even assault the queen in my presence 11
8:15 Mor'decai went out from the presence of the king 2
Job 1:12 Satan went forth from the presence of the LORD. 12
2: 7 Satan went forth from the presence of the LORD 12
21: 8 children are established in their presence 12
23:15 Therefore I am terrified at his presence; 12
30:11 they have cast off restraint in my presence. 12
33:26 he comes into his presence with joy. 12
Ps 16:11 in thy presence there is fulness of joy 12
21: 6 make him glad with the joy of thy presence. 12
23: 5 a table before me in the presence of my enemies; 6
31:20 In the covert of thy presence thou hidest them 12
39: 1 so long as the wicked are in my presence. 1
41:12 set me in thy presence for ever. 2
51:11 Cast me not away from thy presence 12
52: 9 for it is good, in the presence of the godly. 6
68: 8 heavens poured down rain, at the presence of God; 12
8 yon Sinai quaked at the presence of God 5
95: 2 Let us come into his presence with thanksgiving; 12
100: 2 Come into his presence with singing! 12
101: 7 no man . . lies shall continue in my presence. 1
105: 4 seek his presence continually! 12
114: 7 Tremble, O earth, at the presence of the LORD 3
7 Tremble . . at the presence of the God of Jacob 3
116:14 pay my vows . . in the presence of all his people. 7
18 pay my vows . . in the presence of all his people 7
139: 7 Or whither shall I flee from thy presence? 12
140:13 upright shall dwell in thy presence. 12
Prv 14: 7 Leave the presence of a fool, for there you do not 6
17:18 becomes surety in the presence of his neighbor. 2
25: 5 away the wicked from the presence of the king 12
6 not put yourself forward in the king's presence 12
7 than to be put lower in the presence of the prince. 12
Ecc 8: 3 go from his presence, do not delay 12
Isa 1: 7 in your very presence aliens devour your land; 1
3: 8 the LORD, defying his glorious presence. 8
19: 1 the idols of Egypt will tremble at his presence 12
63: 9 and the angel of his presence saved them; 12
64: 1 that the mountains might quake at they presence– 12
2 that the nations might tremble at thy presence! 12
3 the mountains quaked at thy presence. 12
Jer 3:17 to the presence of the LORD in Jerusalem 13
4: 1 abominations from my presence, and do not waver 12
23:39 lift you up and cast you away from my presence 12
28: 1 in the presence of the priests and all the people 8
5 Jeremiah spoke . . in the presence of the priests 8
11 Hanani'ah spoke in the presence of all the people 8
32:12 in the presence of Han'amel my cousin 8
12 in the presence of the witnesses who signed 8
12 in the presence of all the Jews who were sitting 8
13 I charged Baruch in their presence, saying 8
33:18 a man in my presence to offer burnt offerings 3
52: 3 that he cast them out from his presence. 12
Lam 2:19 Pour out . . before the presence of the Lord! 12
3:35 to turn aside . . in the presence of the Most High 12
Ezk 28: 9 I am a god,' in the presence of those who slay you 12
38:20 the face of the earth, shall quake at my presence 12
Dan 5:24 Then from his presence the hand was sent 15
Jon 1: 3 flee to Tarshish from the presence of the LORD. 12
3 to Tarshish, away from the presence of the LORD. 12
10 he was fleeing from the presence of the LORD 12
2: 4 Then I said, 'I am cast out from thy presence; 8
Mal 2: 3 I will put you out of my presence. •
Mat 12: 4 and ate the bread of the Presence 27
Mrk 2:26 ate the bread of the Presence 27
Lke 1:19 I am Gabriel, who stand in the presence of God 21
2:31 hast prepared in the presence of all peoples 29
6: 4 took and ate the bread of the Presence 27
8:47 declared in the presence of all the people 21
13:26 We ate and drank in your presence 21
14:10 then you will be honored in the presence of all 21
20:26 they were not able in the presence of the people 20
Joh 17: 5 now, Father, glorify thou me in thy own presence 25
20:30 many other signs in the presence of the disciples 21
Act 2:28 make me full of gladness with thy presence.' 29
3:13 denied in the presence of Pilate 29
16 in the presence of you all. 16
19 may come from the presence of the Lord 29
5:41 Then they left the presence of the council 29
27:35 giving thanks to God in the presence of all 21
Rom 4:17 –in the presence of the God in whom he believed 22
1Co 1:29 boast in the presence of God. 21
2Co 2:10 has been for your sake in the presence of Christ. 29
10:10 his bodily presence is weak 26
Php 2:12 as in my presence but much more in my absence 26
2Th 1: 9 and exclusion from the presence of the Lord 29
1Ti 5:20 rebuke them in the presence of all 21
21 In the presence of God and of Christ Jesus 21
6:12 in the presence of many witnesses. 21
13 In the presence of God 21
2Ti 4: 1 I charge you in the presence of God 21
Heb 9: 2 the table and the bread of the Presence 27
24 now to appear in the presence of God on our behalf. 29
Rev 7:15 he . . will shelter them with his presence. •
13:12 the authority of the first beast in its presence 21
14 it is allowed to work in the presence of the beast 21
14:10 tormented . . in the presence of the holy angels 21
10 and in the presence of the Lamb. 21
19:20 false prophet who in its presence had worked 21
20:11 from his presence earth and sky fled away 29
1Es 3:15 the writing was read in their presence. 21
8:90 we can no longer stand in thy presence 18
9:41 in the presence of both men and women 21
45 the place of honor in the presence of all. 21
2Es 1:30 I will cast you out from my presence. 31
3: 5 and he was made alive in thy presence. 30
5:22 to speak words in the presence of the Most High. 30
6:36 I began to speak in the presence of the Most High. 30
14:19 Let me speak in thy presence, Lord. 30
16:11 will not be utterly shattered at his presence? 31
12 be troubled at the presence of the Lord 31
Tob 3:16 in the presence of the glory of the great God. 21
4:11 in the presence of the Most High. 21
12: 6 exalt him . . in the presence of all the living 21
13: 4 exalt him in the presence of all the living; 21
Jdt 2: 5 When you leave my presence 29
14 Holofernes left the presence of his master 29
5: 8 they drove them out from the presence of their gods 29
6: 1 in the presence of all the foreign contingents 20
17 had said in the presence of the Assyrian leaders 23
8:15 even to destroy us in the presence of our enemies. 29
10:13 I am on my way to the presence of Holofernes 29
15 hurrying down to the presence of our lord 29
23 Judith came into the presence of Holofernes 29
11: 5 let your maidservant speak in your presence 29
13 priests who minister in the presence of our God 29
12:13 Bagoas went out from the presence of Holofernes 29
13 come to my lord and be honored in his presence 29
13: 1 shut out . . from his master's presence 29
14: 8 in the presence of the people 23
16:15 at thy presence the rocks shall melt like wax 29
Wis 5: 1 in the presence of those who have afflicted him 29
8:10 and honor in the presence of the elders 25
14:17 men could not honor monarchs in their presence 24
Sir 6:12 will hide himself from your presence. 29
8:18 In the presence of a stranger do nothing 21
17:25 pray in his presence and lessen your offenses. 29
23:14 lest you be forgetful in their presence 21
24: 2 in the presence of his host she will glory. 19
27:23 In your presence his mouth is all sweetness 17
30: 3 will glory in him in the presence of friends. 19
38: 3 in the presence of great men he is admired. 19
45: 3 the Lord glorified him in the presence of kings. 29
Bar 2:28 in the presence of the people of Israel, saying 20
Bel 1:14 in the presence of the king alone 21
1Mc 11:26 he exalted him in the presence of all his friends 20
2Mc 6:18 a man now advanced in age and of noble presence 28
10: 3 and set out the bread of the Presence. 27
14:24 he kept Judas always in his presence 29
3Mc 3:17 They accepted our presence by word 26

presence *See also* bread, bring.

before the presence 1. κατενώπιον

Jde 1:24 present you . . before the presence of his glory 1

good presence 1. תֹּאַר

1Sm 16:18 prudent in speech, and a man of good presence; 1

into the presence 1. לִפְנֵי 2. ἐνώπιον

1Kg 1:28 So she came into the king's presence, and stood 1
Tob 12:15 enter into the presence of the glory of the Holy 2

out of the presence 1. מֵעַל הַחוּצָה

2Sm 13:17 Put this woman out of my presence, and bolt 1

present 1. בְּרָכָה 2. מִנְחָה 3. מַשְׂאָה 4. מַשְׂאֵת 5. שֹׁחַד 6. תְּשׁוּרָה 7. ἀποστολή 8. δωρεάν 9. δῶρον 10. ξένια

Gen 32:13 had with him a present for his brother Esau 2
18 they are a present sent to my lord Esau; 2
20 appease him with the present that goes before me 2
21 the present passed on before him; 2
33:10 in your sight, then accept my present from my hand; 2
43:11 and carry down to the man a present, a little balm 2
15 the men took the present, and they took double 2
25 they made ready the present for Joseph's coming 2
26 they brought into the house to him the present 2
Jos 15:19 Give me a present; since you . . give me also 1
Jdg 1:15 Give me a present; since you have set me in the land 1
6:18 come to thee, and bring out my present, and set it 2
1Sm 9: 7 there is no present to bring to the man of God. 6
10:27 they despised him, and brought him no present. 2
25:27 this present which your servant has brought 1
30:26 Here is a present for you from the spoil 1
2Sm 11: 8 there followed him a present from the king. 4
1Kg 10:25 Every one of them brought his present 2
15:19 I am sending to you a present of silver and gold; 5
2Kg 5:15 accept now a present from your servant. 1
8: 8 Take a present with you and go to meet the man 2
9 Haz'ael went . . and took a present with him 2
16: 8 and sent a present to the king of Assyria. 5
20:12 sent envoys with letters and a present 2
2Ch 9:24 Every one of them brought his present 2
17:11 Philistines brought Jehosh'aphat presents 2
Isa 39: 1 envoys with letters and a present to Hezeki'ah 2
Jer 40: 5 guard gave him an allowance of food and a present 3
Rev 11:10 rejoice . . make merry and exchange presents 9
Sir 20:29 Presents and gifts blind the eyes of the wise; 10
2Mc 3: 2 glorified the temple with the finest presents 7
4:30 because their cities had been given as a present 8

present (2) 1. בוא 2. יָד 3. יצב 4. יצג 5. נגשׁ 6. נפל 7. נצב 8. נתן 9. עלה 10. עמד 11. עשׂה 12. קרב 13. ראה 14. רום 15. קרב (A) 16. ἀναφέρω 17. ἵστημι 18. λαλέω 19. πάρειμι 20. παρίστημι 21. ποιέω 22. προσάγω 23. προσαναφέρω 24. προσφέρω 25. συνίστημι 26. τιμάω

Gen 46:29 he presented himself to him, and fell on his neck 13
47: 2 he took five men and presented them to Pharaoh. 4
Exd 34: 2 present yourself there to me on the top 7
Lev 1: 5 Aaron's sons the priests shall present the blood 12
2: 8 when it is presented to the priest 12
7:35 the day they were presented to them as priests 12
8:18 Then he presented the ram of the burnt offering 12
22 Then he presented the other ram 12
9: 9 the sons of Aaron presented the blood to him 12
15 Then he presented the people's offering 12
16 he presented the burnt offering, and offered it 12
17 he presented the cereal offering 12
16: 9 Aaron shall present the goat on which the lot fell 12
10 goat . . shall be presented alive before the LORD 10
11 Aaron shall present the bull as a sin offering 12
20 he shall present the live goat 12
22:18 WHen any one . . presents his offering, whether 12
23 too short you may present for a freewill offering 11
23: 8 you shall present an offering by fire to the LORD 12
16 then you shall present a cereal offering 12
18 you shall present with the bread seven lambs 12
25 you shall present an offering by fire to the LORD 12
27 you shall . . present an offering by fire 12
36 Seven days you shall present offerings by fire 12
36 you shall . . present an offering by fire 12
37 for presenting to the LORD offerings by fire 12
Num 6:16 the priest shall present them before the LORD 12
8: 9 present the Levites before the tent of meeting 12
10 When you present the Levites before the LORD 12
15:19 when you eat . . you shall present an offering 14
20 meal you shall present a cake as an offering; 14
20 so shall you present it. 14
18:19 which the people of Israel present to the LORD 14
24 tithe . . they present as an offering to the LORD 14
26 you shall present an offering from it to the LORD 14
28 shall you also present an offering to the LORD 14
29 you shall present every offering due to the LORD 14
Deu 12: 6 bring . . the offering that you present 2
11 bring . . the offering that you present 2
17 not eat . . the offering that you present; 2

31:14 present yourselves in the tent of meeting 3
14 Moses and Joshua went and presented themselves 3
Jos 24: 1 and they presented themselves before God. 3
Jdg 3:17 he presented the tribute to Eglon king of Moab. 12
18 when Ehud had finished presenting the tribute 12
6:19 Gideon . . brought them . . and presented them. 5
20: 2 the chiefs . . presented themselves 3
1Sm 10:19 present yourselves before the LORD by . . tribes 3
1Ch 21:26 presented burnt offerings and peace offerings 9
Job 1: 6 when the sons of God came to present themselves 3
2: 1 when the sons of God came to present themselves 3
1 Satan also came among them to present himself 3
Isa 16:12 when Moab presents himself 13
45:21 Declare and present your case; 5
66: 3 he who presents a cereal offering, 9
Jer 41: 5 and incense to present at the temple of the LORD. 1
42: 9 to whom you sent me to present your supplication 6
Ezk 20:28 presented the provocation of their offering; 8
43:24 You shall present them before the LORD 12
Dan 7:13 Ancient of Days and was presented before him. 15
9:18 not present our supplications before thee 6
20 presenting my supplication before the LORD 6
Hos 13:13 for now he does not present himself at the mouth 10
Zec 6: 5 after presenting themselves before the LORD 3
14:18 of Egypt do not go up and present themselves 1
Mal 1: 8 Present that to your governor; will he be pleased 12
3: 3 till they present right offerings to the LORD. 5
Lke 2:22 to present him to the Lord. 20
Act 1: 3 he presented himself alive after his passion 20
9:41 he presented her alive. 20
17:19 what this new teaching is which you present? 18
21:26 the offering presented for every one of them. 24
23:33 they presented Paul also before him. 20
28:10 They presented many gifts to us 26
Rom 12: 1 to present your bodies as a living sacrifice 20
2Co 11: 2 to present you as a pure bride to her one husband. 20
Eph 5:27 might present the church to himself in splendor 20
Col 1:22 in order to present you holy . . before him 20
28 that we may present every man mature in Christ. 20
2Ti 2:15 Do your best to present yourself to God as . . 20
Jde 1:24 and to present you without blemish 17
Tob 12:15 who present the prayers of the saints 23
Jdt 9: 6 the things . . presented themselves and said 20
Sir 14:11 present worthy offerings to the Lord. 22
18:15 cause grief . . when you present a gift. *
2Mc 1:21 materials for the sacrifices were presented 16
4:24 he, when presented to the king, extolled him 25
44 three men . . presented the case before him. 21
14: 4 presenting to him a crown of gold and a palm 22
3Mc 5:10 Hermon . . presented himself at the courtyard 19

present (3) 1. ἄρτι 2. εἰμί 3. ἐνίστημι 4. νῦν 5. νυνί 6. οὗτος 7. παρίστημι 8. σήμερον 9. τὸ νῦν ἔχω 10. praesens

2Ch 28:13 in addition to our present sins and guilt. *
Lke 12:56 do you not know how to interpret the present time? 6
Act 24:25 Go away for the present 9
Rom 3:26 prove at the present time that he . . is righteous 4
8:18 the sufferings of this present time are not worth 4
11: 5 So too at the present time there is a remnant 4
15:25 At present, however, I am going to Jerusalem 5
1Co 3:22 the present or the future, all are yours; 3
4:11 To the present hour we hunger and thirst 1
7:26 I think that in view of the present distress 3
2Co 8:14 your abundance at the present time 4
Gal 1: 4 to deliver us from the present evil age 3
4:25 she corresponds to the present Jerusalem 4
Eph 6:12 against the world rulers of this present darkness *
1Ti 4: 8 as it holds promise for the present life 4
2Ti 4:10 Demas, in love with this present world 4
Heb 9: 9 (which is symbolic for the present age). 3
2Es 6: 5 before the present years were reckoned 10
7:112This present world is not the end 10
8: 2 so is the course of the present world. 10
Tob 7:11 But for the present be merry 4
Jdt 8:18 nor in these present days 8
AEs 13: 6 of the twelfth month, Adar, of this present year 3
2Mc 9:26 to maintain your present good will, each of you 2
3Mc 1:16 to aid in the present situation 3
5:18 to remain alive through the present day. 7
4Mc 3:19 The present occasion now invites us *
12:18 he will take vengeance both in this present life 4

present (4) 1. היה 2. מצא 3. נִמְצָא 4. εὑρίσκω 5. παραγίνομαι 6. πάρειμι 7. συμπάρειμι 8. praesens

Num16:16 to Korah, "Be present, you and all your company 1
1Sm 13:15 Saul numbered the people . . present with him 3
16 people who were present with them, stayed in Geba 2
1Ch 29:17 I have seen thy people, who are present here 3
2Ch 5:11 priests . . present had sanctified themselves 3
29:29 king and all who were present with him bowed 3
30:21 people of Israel that were present at Jerusalem 3
31: 1 Israel who were present went out to the cities 3
34:32 made all who were present . . stand to it. 2
35: 7 as passover offerings for all that were present 2
17 people of Israel . . present kept the passover 3
18 by . . all Judah and Israel who were present 2
Ezr 8:25 all Israel there present had offered; 2
Est 1: 5 for all the people present in Susa the capital 3
Ps 46: 1 God . . a very present help in trouble. 2
Lke 13: 1 There were some present at that very time 6
Act 21:18 all the elders were present. 5
25:24 King Agrippa and all who are present with us 7
1Co 5: 3 For though absent in body I am present in spirit 6
3 as if present 6
4 When you are assembled, and my spirit is present *
2Co 10: 2 I beg of you that when I am present 6
11 we do when present. 6
13: 2 as I did when present on my second visit 6
Gal 4:18 not only when I am present with you. 6
20 I could wish to be present with you now 6
1Es 1: 7 gave to the people who were present 30,000 lambs 4
19 people of Israel who were present at that time 4
2Es 5:45 to support all of them present at one time. 8
7:16 rather than what is now present? 8
Tob 12:12 I was likewise present with you. 7
Wis 4: 2 When it is present, men imitate it 6
9: 9 was present when thou didst make the world 6
11:11 Whether absent or present 6
14:17 they might flatter the absent one as though present. 6
Bar 1: 7 people who were present with him in Jerusalem. 4
2Mc 4:18 the king was present 6
6:26 even if for the present 6
7: 9 you dismiss us from this present life 6
3Mc 1:27 to defend them in the present trouble 6
3:11 the king, boastful of his present good fortune 6
5:16 those present for the banquet 5
17 make the present portion of the banquet joyful 6
21 all those present . . gave their approval 6
31 Were your parents or children present 6

present *See* case, give, here.

marriage present 1. מֹהַר

Gen 34:12 Ask of me ever so much as marriage present 1
Exd 22:17 pay money equivalent to the marriage present 1
1Sm 18:25 The king desires no marriage present except 1

thing present 1. ἐνίστημι 2. praesens

Rom 8:38 nor things present, nor things to come, nor powers 1
2Es 8:46 Things that are present are for those who live now 2

more presentable part 1. εὐσχήμων

1Co 12:24 which our more presentable parts do not require 1

preserve 1. חיה 2. יתר 3. נצל 4. נצר 5. שׂום 6. שׁמר 7. διαμένω 8. διατηρέω 9. διαφυλάσσω 10. ἵστημι 11. συντηρέω 12. σωτηρία 13. τηρέω 14. φυλάσσω 15. conservo

Gen 19:32 lie with him, that we may preserve offspring 1
34 lie with him, that we may preserve offspring 1
32:30 God face to face, and yet my life is preserved. 3
45: 7 sent me . . to preserve for you a remnant 5
Deu 6:24 that he might preserve us alive, as at this day. *
Jos 24:17 and preserved us in all the way that we went 6
1Sm 30:23 he has preserved us and given into our hand 6
Neh 9: 6 thou hast made . . and thou preservest all 1
Job 10:12 thy care has preserved my spirit. 6
Ps 16: 1 Preserve me, O God, for in thee I take refuge. 6
25:21 May integrity and uprightness preserve me 4
31:23 The LORD preserves the faithful 4
32: 7 thou preservest me from trouble; 4
37:28 The righteous shall be preserved for ever 6
40:11 let . . thy faithfulness ever preserve me! 4
64: 1 preserve my life from dread of the enemy 4
79:11 thy great power preserve those doomed to die! 2
86: 2 Preserve my life, for I am godly; 6
97:10 LORD . . preserves the lives of his saints; 6
116: 6 The LORD preserves the simple; 6
140: 1 preserve me from violent men 4
4 preserve me from violent men, who have planned 4
145:20 LORD preserves all who love him; 6
Prv 2: 8 preserving the way of his saints. 6
6:24 to preserve you from the evil woman 6
7: 5 to preserve you from the loose woman 6
13: 3 He who guards his mouth preserves his life; 6
14: 3 but the lips of the wise will preserve them. 6
16:17 he who guards his way preserves his life. 6
20:28 Loyalty and faithfulness preserve the king 4
Isa 49: 6 of Jacob and to restore the preserved of Israel; 4
Ezk 6:12 he that is left and is preserved shall die 4
Hos 12:13 and by a prophet he was preserved. 6
Mat 9:17 and so both are preserved. 11
Gal 2: 5 the truth of the gospel might be preserved 7
2Pe 2: 5 preserved Noah, a herald of righteousness 14
2Es 3:30 and hast preserved thy enemies 15
8: 8 what thou hast created is preserved 15
Wis 10: 5 and preserved him blameless before God 13
11:25 how would anything . . have been preserved? 8
16:26 thy word preserves those who trust in thee. 8
Sir 39: 2 he will preserve the discourse of notable men 11
1Mc 14:29 their sanctuary and the law might be preserved; 10
2Mc 1:26 preserve thy portion and make it holy. 9
4Mc 15: 2 preserving her seven sons for a time 12

preserve alive 1. salvo

2Es 7:67 we shall be preserved alive 1

preserve life 1. חיה 2. מִחְיָה 3. ἐμβίωσις

Gen 45: 5 for God sent me before you to preserve life. 2
Ps 119:149O LORD, in thy justice preserve my life. 1
159Preserve my life according to thy steadfast 1
138: 7 midst of trouble, thou dost preserve my life; 1
143:11 For thy name's sake, O LORD, preserve my life! 1
Ecc 7:12 that wisdom preserves the life of him who has it. 1
Sir 38:14 for the sake of preserving life. 3

preserve with salt 1. ταριχεύω

LJr 1:28 likewise their wives preserve some with salt 1

president 1. סָרַךְ (A)

Dan 6: 2 over them three presidents, 1
3 distinguished above all the other presidents 1
4 presidents and the satraps sought to find 1
6 these presidents and satraps came by agreement 1
7 presidents of the kingdom, the prefects 1

press 1. אוץ 2. יָקֶב 3. כֹּבֶד 4. לחץ 5. מִיץ 6. מעך 7. פצר 8. פרק 9. רדף 10. שׁחט 11. ἀνετάζω 12. διώκω 13. ἐνέχω 14. ἐπείγω 15. θλίβω 16. ποιέω 17. σπεύδω 18. στερεόω

Gen 19: 9 Then they pressed hard against the man Lot 7
40:11 I took the grapes and pressed them into Pharaoh's 10
Num22:25 ass . . pressed Balaam's foot against the wall; 4
2Sm 13:25 He pressed him, but he would not go 8
27 Ab'salom pressed him until he let Amnon . . go 8
Prv 30:33 For pressing milk produces curds 5
33 pressing the nose produces blood 5
33 pressing anger produces strife. 5
Isa 16:10 no treader treads out wine in the presses; 2
21:15 from the bent bow, and from the press of battle. 3
Jer 17:16 I have not pressed thee to send evil 1
Ezk 23: 3 there their breasts were pressed 6
21 your bosom and pressed your young breasts. *
Hos 6: 3 Let us know, let us press on to know the LORD; 9
Lke 11:53 the Pharisees began to press him hard 13
Php 3:12 I press on to make it my own 12
14 I press on toward the goal for the prize 12
1Es 5:58 the Levites, as one man pressing forward the work †
Sir 11:11 There is a man who works, and toils, and presses on 17
46: 5 when enemies pressed him on every side 15
16 when his enemies pressed him on every side 15
Sus 1:14 and when each pressed the other for the reason 11
Bel 1:30 The king saw that they were pressing him hard 14
1Mc 10:50 He pressed the battle strongly until the sun set 18
2Mc 12:23 Judas pressed the pursuit with the utmost vigor 16

press *See also* outflow, pit, wine.

press around 1. συνθλίβω

Mrk 5:31 You see the crowd pressing around you 1

press back 1. לחץ

Jdg 1:34 Amorites pressed the Danites back into the hill 1

press down 1. עוק 2. שׁקע 3. πιέζω

Job 41: 1 or press down his tongue with a cord? 2
Ams 2:13 Behold, I will press you down in your place 1
13 as a cart full of sheaves presses down. 1
Lke 6:38 good measure, pressed down, shaken together 3

press hard 1. כבד 2. נגשׂ 3. צוק 4. ἀπορέω 5. θλίβω 6. συνέχω

Jdg 14:17 he told her, because she pressed him hard. 3
16:16 when she pressed him hard with her words day 3
1Sm 13: 6 were in straits (for the people were hard pressed) 2
31: 3 The battle pressed hard upon Saul 1
1Ch 10: 3 The battle pressed hard upon Saul 1
Php 1:23 I am hard pressed between the two. 6
1Mc 15:14 he pressed the city hard from land and sea 5
2Mc 8:20 when the Macedonians were hard pressed 4
11: 5 he approached Beth-zur . . and pressed it hard. 5

press hard upon 1. ἐπίκειμαι

1Es 5:72 pressed hard upon those in Judea 1

press heavily 1. σκληρύνω

1Mc 2:30 because evils pressed heavily upon them. 1

press out 1. זור

Isa 1: 6 they are not pressed out, or bound up, or softened 1

press proudly 1. פושׁ

Hab 1: 8 their horsemen press proudly on. 1

press round 1. συμπνίγω

Lke 8:42 As he went, the people pressed round him. 1

press the siege 1. צור

Ezk 4: 3 and press the siege against it. 1

press upon 1. ἀποθλίβω 2. ἐπίκειμαι 3. ἐπιπίπτω

Mrk 3:10 all who had diseases pressed upon him to touch him. 3
Lke 5: 1 While the people pressed upon him 2
8:45 the multitudes surround you and press upon you! 1

press urgently upon 1. ἐπίκειμαι
1Mc 6:57 affairs of the kingdom press urgently upon us. 1

pressure 1. אֶכֶף 2. ἐπίστασις
Job 33: 7 my pressure will not be heavy upon you. 1
2Co 11:28 there is the daily pressure upon me 2
pressure *See also* exert.

prestige 1. ἐξουσία
3Mc 7:21 They also possessed greater prestige 1
prestige *See also* form.

presume 1. זיד 2. מלא לב 3. עפל 4. δοκέω
5. ἑαυτοῦ ἀξιόω 6. τολμάω
Num14:44 presumed to go up to the heights of the hill 3
Deu 18:20 prophet who presumes to speak a word in my name 1
Est 7: 5 Who is he . . that would presume to do this? 2
Mat 3: 9 do not presume to say to yourselves, 'We have 4
Lke 7: 7 therefore I did not presume to come to you 5
Jde 1: 9 not presume to pronounce a reviling judgment 6

presume upon 1. καταφρονέω
Rom 2: 4 Or do you presume upon the riches of his kindness 1

presumption 1. זָדוֹן 2. θράσος
1Sm 17:28 I know your presumption . . the evil of your heart; 1
AEs 13: 2 not elated with presumption of authority 2

presumptuous 1. זיד
Deu 1:43 rebelled . . and were presumptuous and went up 1
presumptuous *See also* sin.

presumptuously 1. בְּזָדוֹן 2. זָדוֹן
Deu 17:12 The man who acts presumptuously, by not obeying 1
18:22 prophet has spoken it presumptuously 2

act presumptuously 1. זיד
Deu 17:13 people shall . . not act presumptuously again. 1
Neh 9:16 they and our fathers acted presumptuously 1
29 Yet they acted presumptuously and did not obey 1

pretend 1. ὑποκρίνομαι 2. ψευδής 3. ὡς
Prv 18:24 There are friends who pretend to be friends •
Lke 20:20 sent spies, who pretended to be sincere 1
2Th 2: 9 with pretended signs and wonders 2
Sir 12:17 while pretending to help you, he will trip you 3
2Mc 5:25 he pretended to be peaceably disposed 1
6:21 pretend that he was eating the flesh 1
4Mc 6:15 save yourself by pretending to eat pork. 1

pretend not to hear 1. ἐθελοκωφόω
Sir 19:27 He hides his face and pretends not to hear 1

pretend to be a mourner 1. אבל
2Sm 14: 2 Pretend to be a mourner, and put on mourning 1

pretend to be another 1. נכר
1Kg 14: 5 When she came, she pretended to be another woman. 1
6 wife of Jerobo'am; why do you pretend to be another? 1

pretend to be ill 1. חלה
2Sm 13: 5 Lie down on your bed, and pretend to be ill; 1
6 Amnon lay down, and pretended to be ill; 1

pretend to be poor 1. רוש
Prv 13: 7 another pretends to be poor, yet has great wealth. 1

pretend to be rich 1. עשר
Prv 13: 7 One man pretends to be rich, yet has nothing; 1

pretense 1. שֶׁקֶר 2. πρόφασις 3. ὑποκρίνομαι
4. ὑπόκρισις
Jer 3:10 but in pretense, says the LORD. 1
Mrk 12:40 for a pretense make long prayers 2
Lke 20:47 and for a pretense make long prayers 2
Php 1:18 whether in pretense or in truth 2
2Mc 6:24 Such pretense is not worthy of our time of life 3
25 through my pretense 4
pretense *See also* make.

under pretense 1. πρόφασις
Act 27:30 under pretense of laying out anchors 1

pretension 1. ὑπόκρισις
1Ti 4: 2 through the pretensions of liars 1

pretext 1. ἀφορμή 2. ἐπικάλυμμα 3. πρόφασις
Prv 18: 1 He who is estranged seeks pretexts to break out 3
1Pe 2:16 without using your freedom as a pretext for evil; 2
3Mc 3: 2 a pretext being given by a report 1

under pretext 1. ὡς
2Mc 1:14 For under pretext of intending to marry her 1

prevail 1. אמץ 2. גבר 3. היה 4. חזק 5. יכל 6. עזז
7. עצר 8. קום 9. יכל (A) 10. ἐνίστημι 11. ἐπικρατέω
12. ἰσχύω 13. κατισχύω 14. κρατέω 15. νικάω
16. περιγίνομαι 17. dominatio
Gen 7:18 The waters prevailed and increased greatly 2
19 the waters prevailed so mightily upon the earth 2
20 the waters prevailed above the mountains 2
24 the waters prevailed upon the earth 150 days. 2
30: 8 I have wrestled with my sister . . and prevailed 5
32:25 saw that he did not prevail against Jacob 5
28 with God and with men, and have prevailed. 5
41:53 The seven years of plenty that prevailed 3
Exd 17:11 Moses held up his hand, Israel prevailed; 2
11 whenever he lowered his hand, Am'alek prevailed. 2
Deu 19:15 A single witness shall not prevail against a man 8
Jdg 3:10 and his hand prevailed over Cu'shan-rishatha'im. 6
6: 2 And the hand of Mid'ian prevailed over Israel; 6
1Sm 2: 9 for not by might shall a man prevail. 2
17: 9 but if I prevail against him and kill him 5
50 David prevailed over the Philistine 4
2Sm 24: 4 But the king's word prevailed against Jo'ab 4
1Ch 21: 4 the king's word prevailed against Jo'ab. 4
2Ch 13:18 the men of Judah prevailed 1
14:11 O LORD . . let not man prevail against thee. 7
27: 5 the Ammonites and prevailed against them. 4
Est 6:13 you will not prevail against him but will . . fall 5
Ps 9:19 Arise, O LORD! Let not man prevail; 6
12: 4 those who say, "With our tongue we will prevail 2
65: 3 When our transgressions prevail over us 2
129: 2 yet they have not prevailed against me. 5
Isa 16:12 when he comes . . to pray, he will not prevail. 5
Jer 1:19 shall not prevail against you, for I am with you 5
5:22 though the waves toss, they cannot prevail 5
15:20 they shall not prevail over you, for I am with you 5
20: 7 art stronger than I, and thou hast prevailed. 5
38:22 have deceived you and prevailed against you; 5
Lam 1:16 are desolate, for the enemy has prevailed. 2
Dan 7:21 horn made war with the saints, and prevailed over 9
11: 7 shall deal with them and shall prevail. 4
12 tens of thousands, but he shall not prevail. 6
Hos 12: 4 He strove with the angel and prevailed 5
Obd 1: 7 your confederates have prevailed against you; 5
Mat 16:18 powers of death shall not prevail against it. 13
Lke 23:23 their voices prevailed. 13
Act 19:20 the word of the Lord grew and prevailed 13
Rom 3: 4 and prevail when thou art judged. 15
1Es 4:38 lives and prevails for ever and ever. 14
9: 6 because of the bad weather that prevailed. 10
2Es 7:60 they who have made my glory to prevail now 17
Jdt 11:10 nor can the sword prevail against them 13
4Mc 2:10 the law prevails even over affection for parents 14
14 reason . . can prevail even over enmity 11
6:32 if the emotions had prevailed over reason 14
13: 3 they prevailed over their emotions. 16

prevail against 1. תקף 2. κατισχύω
Job 14:20 Thou prevailest for ever against him 1
15:24 they prevail against him, like a king prepared 1
Ecc 4:12 a man might prevail against one who is alone 1
Wis 7:30 against wisdom evil does not prevail. 2

prevail over 1. יכל 2. ἐπικρατέω 3. κατακρατέω
4. νικάω 5. superelevo 6. superinvalesco
Ps 13: 4 lest my enemy say, "I have prevailed over him"; 1
2Es 15:39 the winds . . shall prevail over the cloud 6
16:76 or your iniquities prevail over you. 5
1Mc 6:54 because famine had prevailed over the rest 3
2Mc 3: 5 when he could not prevail over Onias 4
4Mc 8: 1 the very young . . have prevailed over . . torture 2

prevail upon 1. παραβιάζομαι
Act 16:15 And she prevailed upon us. 1

prevent 1. עצר 2. ἀναστέλλω 3. ἀποκωλύω
4. ἀφίστημι 5. διακωλύω 6. ἵνα μή 7. κωλύω 8. μή
9. μήποτε 10. προκαταλαμβάνω
Gen 16: 2 LORD has prevented me from bearing children; 1
Deu 28:32 not be in the power of your hand to prevent it. •
Neh 5: 9 walk in the fear of our God to prevent the taunts •
Mat 3:14 John would have prevented him, saying, "I need to be 5
Joh 19:31 to prevent the bodies from remaining on the cross 8
Act 8:36 What is to prevent my being baptized? 7
24:23 none . . should be prevented from attending . . needs 7
Rom 1:13 (but thus far have been prevented) 7
Gal 5:17 to prevent you from doing what you would. 6
Heb 7:23 because they were prevented by death 7
1Es 2:28 to prevent these men from building the city 3
5:73 they prevented the completion of the building 3
6: 6 they were not prevented from building 7
Sir 19:28 by lack of strength he is prevented from sinning 7
20:21 A man may be prevented from sinning 7
31: 2 Wakeful anxiety prevents slumber 4
1Mc 6:27 unless you quickly prevent them 10
7:24 he prevented those in the city from going out 2
13:49 prevented from going out to the country and back 7
2Mc 14:22 to prevent sudden treachery on the part of the enemy 9
4Mc 4: 7 did all that they could to prevent it. 7

previous 1. praecedo 2. praetereo
2Es 5:31 the angel who had come to me on a previous night 2
6:12 thou didst show me in part on a previous night. 1

previously 1. לְפָנִים 2. מִן קַדְמַת דְּנָה (A) 3. πρίν
4. προϋπάρχω 5. πρῶτος
Neh 13: 5 chamber where they had previously put 1
Dan 6:10 before his God, as he had done previously. 2
Act 8: 9 who had previously practiced magic in the city 4
1Mc 1: 1 (He had previously become king of Greece.) 5
3Mc 5:28 the things he had previously devised. 3
6:34 those who had previously believed 3
previously *See also* afflict, issue, mention, ratified, wronged.

prey 1. אֹכֶל 2. בַּז 3. בזז 4. טֶרֶף 5. מַלְקוֹחַ 6. מְנָה
7. מְצוּדָה 8. עַד 9. צַיִד 10. διαρπαγή 11. θήρα
12. κυνήγιον 13. προνομή
Gen 49: 9 from the prey, my son, you have gone up. 4
27 wolf, in the morning devouring the prey 8
Num14: 3 Our wives and our little ones will become a prey; 2
31 your little ones, who you said would become a prey 2
23:24 it does not lie down till it devours the prey 4
Deu 1:39 your little ones, who you said would become a prey 2
2Kg 21:14 become a prey and a spoil to all their enemies 2
Job 4:11 The strong lion perishes for lack of prey 4
9:26 They go by . . like an eagle swooping on the prey. 1
24: 5 seeking prey in the wilderness as food 4
29:17 and made him drop his prey from his teeth. 4
38:39 Can you hunt the prey for the lion 4
41 Who provides for the raven its prey 9
39:29 he spies out the prey; his eyes behold it afar off. 1
Ps 63:10 they shall be prey for jackals. 6
104:21 The young lions roar for their prey 4
124: 6 LORD, who has not given us as prey to their teeth! 4
Prv 12:27 A slothful man will not catch his prey 9
Isa 5:29 they growl and seize their prey, they carry it off 4
31: 4 As a lion or a young lion growls over his prey 4
33:23 Then prey and spoil in abundance will be divided; 8
23 even the lame will take the prey. 2
42:22 they have become a prey with none to rescue 2
49:24 Can the prey be taken from the mighty 5
25 be taken, and the prey of the tyrant be rescued 5
Jer 2:14 Why then has he become a prey? 2
30:16 all who prey on you I will make a prey. 3
16 all who prey on you I will make a prey. 2
Ezk 7:21 give it into the hands of foreigners for a prey 2
13:21 they shall be no more in your hand as prey; 7
19: 3 he learned to catch prey; he devoured men. 4
6 he learned to catch prey; he devoured men. 4
22:25 are like a roaring lion tearing the prey; 4
27 like wolves tearing the prey, shedding blood 4
34: 8 because my sheep have become a prey 2
22 I will save my flock, they shall no longer be a prey; 2
28 They shall no more be a prey to the nations 2
36: 4 cities, which have become a prey and derision 2
Hos 9:13 E'phraim's sons . . are destined for a prey; •
Ams 3: 4 Does a lion roar in the forest, when he has no prey? 4
Nah 2:11 where the lion brought his prey •
12 and strangled prey for his lionesses; •
12 he filled his cave with prey 4
13 I will cut off your prey from the earth 4
Jdt 4:12 praying . . not to give up their infants as prey 10
9: 4 thou gavest their wives for a prey 13
16: 5 and seize my children as prey 13
Sir 13:19 Wild asses . . are the prey of lions 12
27:10 A lion lies in wait for prey 11
1Mc 3: 4 like a lion's cub roaring for prey. 11
prey *See also* beast, bird, make, take.

prey upon 1. κατεσθίω
2Co 11:20 if a man . . preys upon you, or takes advantage of you 1

price 1. יְקָר 2. כֶּסֶף 3. מְחִיר 4. מִקְנָה 5. מֶשֶׁךְ 6. τιμή
Gen 23: 9 For the full price let him give it to me 2
13 I will give the price of the field; accept it 2
Exd 21:35 sell the live ox and divide the price of it; 2
Lev 5:18 valued by you at the price for a guilt offering •
6: 6 valued by you at the price for a guilt offering •
25:16 If the years are many you shall increase the price 4
16 if the years are few you shall diminish the price 4
50 the price of his release shall be according 2
51 refund out of the price paid for him 2
Num18:16 their redemption price . . you shall fix •
2Sm 3:14 I betrothed at the price of 100 foreskins •
24:24 king said . . "No, but I will buy it of you for a price; 3
1Kg 10:28 king's traders received them from Ku'e at a price. 3
1Ch 21:22 give it to me at its full price 2
24 to Ornan, "No, but I will buy it for the full price; 2
2Ch 1:16 traders received them from Ku'e for a price. 3
Job 28:15 silver cannot be weighed as its price. 3
18 the price of wisdom is above pearls. 5
Ps 44:12 for a trifle, demanding no high price for them. 3
Prv 17:16 fool have a price in his hand to buy wisdom 3
27:26 goats the price of a field; 3
Isa 45:13 and set my exiles free, not for price or reward 3
55: 1 wine and milk without money and without price. 3
Jer 15:13 treasures I will give as spoil, without price 3
17: 3 give for spoil as the price of your sin •
Dan 11:39 shall divide the land for a price. 3
Zec 11:13 the lordly price at which I was paid off by them. 1
Mat 27: 9 price of him on whom a price had been set 6

1Co 6:20 you were bought with a price 6
7:23 You were bought with a price 6

price for redemption 1. גְאֻלָּה
Lev 25:51 paid for him the price for his redemption 1

price of life 1. כֹּפֶר
Ps 49: 7 or give to God the price of his life 1

price set 1. τιμάω
Mat 27: 9 price of him on whom a price had been set 1

without price 1. δωρεάν
Rev 22:17 take the water of life without price. 1

priceless 1. ἀτίμητος
Wis 7: 9 Neither did I liken to her any priceless gem 1
3Mc 3:23 they not only spurn the priceless citizenship 1

prick 1. מאר 2. שֵׂךְ 3. שׁנן 4. νύσσω
Num33:55 be as pricks in your eyes and thorns in your sides 2
Ps 73:21 when I was pricked in heart 3
Ezk 28:24 no more a brier to prick or a thorn to hurt them 1
Sir 22:19 A man who pricks an eye will make tears fall 4
19 one who pricks the heart makes it show feeling. 4

pride 1. גֵּאָה 2. גַּאֲוָה 3. גָּאוֹן 4. גֹּבַהּ 5. גֵּוָה 6. זָדוֹן 7. מַחְמָד 8. רוּם 9. שְׂאֵת 10. שַׁחַץ 11. תִּפְאָרָה 12. גֵּוָה (A) 13. ἀγαλλίαμα 14. ἀλαζονεία 15. γαυρίαμα 16. δόξα 17. καύχημα 18. καύχησις 19. καύχομαι 20. ὕβρις 21. ὑπερηφανία 22. gloria 23. superbia
Gen 49: 3 you are . . pre-eminent in pride and pre-eminent 9
Lev 26:19 I will break the pride of your power 3
2Ch 32:26 humbled himself for the pride of his heart 4
Job 33:17 man aside from his deed, and cut off pride from man; 5
35:12 does not answer, because of the pride of evil men. 3
41:34 he is king over all the sons of pride. 10
Ps 10: 4 In the pride of his countenance the wicked does 4
31:18 against the righteous in pride and contempt. 2
47: 4 heritage for us, the pride of Jacob whom he loves. 3
59:12 let them be trapped in their pride. 3
73: 6 Therefore pride is their necklace; 2
Prv 8:13 Pride and arrogance and the way of evil 1
11: 2 When pride comes, then comes disgrace; 6
16:18 Pride goes before destruction 3
21:24 proud, haughty man who acts with arrogant pride. 6
29:23 A man's pride will bring him low 2
Isa 2:11 brought low, and the pride of men shall be humbled; 8
17 humbled, and the pride of men shall be brought low; 8
4: 2 the pride and glory of the survivors of Israel. 3
9: 9 who say in pride and in arrogance of heart 2
13:11 I will put an end to the pride of the arrogant 3
19 Babylon . . splendor and pride of the Chalde'ans 3
16: 6 heard of the pride of Moab, how proud he was 3
6 of his arrogance, his pride, and his insolence– 3
23: 9 has purposed it, to defile the pride of all glory 3
25:11 the LORD will lay low his pride 2
Jer 13: 9 Even so will I spoil the pride of Judah 3
9 pride of Judah and the great pride of Jerusalem. 3
17 my soul will weep in secret for your pride; 5
48:29 have heard of the pride of Moab–he is very proud 3
29 of his loftiness, his pride, and his arrogance 3
49:16 has deceived you, and the pride of your heart 6
Lam 2: 4 and he has slain all the pride of our eyes 7
Ezk 7:10 injustice has blossomed, pride has budded. 6
16:49 she and her daughters had pride, surfeit of food 3
56 a byword in your mouth in the day of your pride 3
24:21 profane my sanctuary, the pride of your power 3
32:12 They shall bring to nought the pride of Egypt 3
Dan 4:37 those who walk in pride he is able to abase. 12
Hos 5: 5 The pride of Israel testifies to his face; 3
7:10 The pride of Israel witnesses against him; 3
Ams 6: 8 I abhor the pride of Jacob, and hate his 3
8: 7 The LORD has sworn by the pride of Jacob 3
Obd 1: 3 The pride of your heart has deceived you 6
Zep 2:10 This shall be their lot in return for their pride 3
Zec 9: 6 I will make an end of the pride of Philistia. 3
10:11 The pride of Assyria shall be laid low 3
Mrk 7:22 envy, slander, pride, foolishness. 21
1Co 11:15 if a woman has long hair, it is her pride 16
15:31 I protest, brethren, by my pride in you which I have 18
2Co 5:12 those who pride themselves on a man's position 19
7: 4 I have great pride in you; I am filled with comfort 18
Heb 3: 6 hold fast our confidence and pride in our hope. 17
1Jn 2:16 the lust of the eyes and the pride of life 14
2Es 1:38 now, father, look with pride and see the people 22
8:50 because they have walked in great pride. 23
11:43 and your pride to the Mighty One. 23
15:18 because of their pride the cities 23
Tob 4:13 For in pride there is ruin and great confusion; 21
Jdt 9: 9 Behold their pride 21
15: 9 you are the great pride of our nation! 17
AEs 13:12 not in insolence or pride or for any love of glory 21
14 I will not do these things in pride. 21
Sir 10:12 The beginning of man's pride 21
13 For the beginning of pride is sin 21
18 Pride was not created for men 21
43: 1 The pride of the heavenly heights 15
50: 1 the pride of his people was Simon the high priest 11
Bar 4:34 take away her pride in her great population 13
1Mc 3:20 come against us in great pride and lawlessness 20
2Mc 1:28 who oppress and are insolent with pride. 21

pride *See also* express, man, mark, take.

haughty pride 1. תִּפְאָרָה
Isa 10:12 the king of Assyria and his haughty pride. 1

priest 1. כהן 2. כֹּהֵן 3. כָּהֵן (A) 4. ἅγιος 5. ἱερατικός 6. ἱερεύς 7. sacerdos
Gen 14:18 he was priest of God Most High. 2
41:45 As'enath, the daughter of Poti'phera priest of On. 2
50 As'enath, the daughter of Poti'phera priest of On 2
46:20 daughter of Poti'phera the priest of On, 2
47:22 Only the land of the priests he did not buy; 2
22 for the priests had a fixed allowance 2
26 the land of the priests alone did not become 2
Exd 2:16 Now the priest of Mid'ian had seven daughters; 2
3: 1 his father-in-law, Jethro, the priest of Mid'ian; 2
18: 1 Jethro, the priest of Mid'ian, Moses' father-in-law 2
19: 6 be to me a kingdom of priests and a holy nation. 2
22 also let the priests who come near to the LORD 2
24 but do not let the priests and the people break 2
29:27 consecrate . . the thigh of the priests' portion *
28 for it is the priests' portion to be offered *
30 The son who is priest in his place shall wear them 2
31:10 holy garments for Aaron the priest 2
35:19 the holy garments for Aaron the priest 2
38:21 Ith'amar the son of Aaron the priest. 2
39:41 the holy garments for Aaron the priest 2
Lev 1: 5 Aaron's sons the priests shall present the blood 2
7 the sons of Aaron the priest shall put fire 2
8 Aaron's sons the priests shall lay the pieces 2
9 the priest shall burn the whole on the altar 2
11 Aaron's sons the priests shall throw its blood 2
12 the priest shall lay them in order upon the wood 2
13 the priest shall offer the whole, and burn it 2
15 the priest shall bring it to the altar 2
17 the priest shall burn it on the altar 2
2: 2 bring it to Aaron's sons the priests 2
2 the priest shall burn this as its memorial 2
8 when it is presented to the priest 2
9 the priest shall take from the cereal offering 2
16 the priest shall burn as its memorial portion 2
3: 2 Aaron's sons the priests shall throw the blood 2
11 the priest shall burn it on the altar as food 2
16 the priest shall burn them on the altar as food 2
4: 3 if it is the anointed priest who sins 2
5 the anointed priest shall take some of the blood 2
6 the priest shall dip his finger in the blood 2
7 the priest shall put some of the blood 2
10 the priest shall burn them upon the altar 2
16 Then the anointed priest shall bring some 2
17 the priest shall dip his finger in the blood 2
20 the priest shall make atonement for them 2
25 Then the priest shall take some of the blood 2
26 so the priest shall make atonement for him 2
30 the priest shall take some of its blood 2
31 the priest shall burn it upon the altar 2
31 the priest shall make atonement for him 2
34 Then the priest shall take some of the blood 2
35 the priest shall burn it on the altar 2
35 the priest shall make atonement for him 2
5: 6 and the priest shall make atonement for him 2
8 He shall bring them to the priest, who shall offer 2
10 the priest shall make atonement for him 2
12 he shall bring it to the priest, and the priest 2
12 the priest shall take a handful of it 2
13 Thus the priest shall make atonement for him 2
13 the remainder shall be for the priest 2
16 shall add a fifth to it and give it to the priest 2
16 the priest shall make atonement for him 2
18 He shall bring to the priest a ram 2
18 the priest shall make atonement for him 2
6: 6 he shall bring to the priest his guilt offering 2
7 the priest shall make atonement for him 2
10 the priest shall put on his linen garment 2
12 the priest shall burn wood on it every morning 2
22 The priest from among Aaron's sons 2
23 Every cereal offering of a priest 2
26 The priest who offers it for sin shall eat it 2
29 Every male among the priests may eat of it 2
7: 5 the priest shall burn them on the altar 2
6 Every male among the priests may eat of it 2
7 the priest who makes atonement with it 2
8 the priest who offers any man's burnt offering 2
9 all . . shall belong to the priest who offers it 2
14 shall belong to the priest who throws the blood 2
31 The priest shall burn the fat on the altar 2
32 the right thigh you shall give to the priest 2
34 I . . have given them to Aaron the priest 2
35 were presented to them as priests of the LORD 1
12: 6 she shall bring to the priest at the door 2
8 the priest shall make atonement for her 2
13: 2 then he shall be brought to Aaron the priest 2
2 brought . . to one of his sons the priests 2
3 the priest shall examine the diseased spot 2
3 when the priest has examined him 2
4 the priest shall shut up the diseased person 2
5 the priest shall examine him on the seventh day 2
5 then the priest shall shut him up seven days more 2
6 the priest shall examine him again 2
6 then the priest shall pronounce him clean 2
7 after he has shown himself to the priest 2
7 he shall appear again before the priest 2
8 the priest shall make an examination 2
8 then the priest shall pronounce him unclean 2
9 he shall be brought to the priest 2
10 the priest shall make an examination 2
11 the priest shall pronounce him unclean 2
12 from head to foot, so far as the priest can see 2
13 then the priest shall make an examination 2
15 the priest shall examine the raw flesh 2
16 then he shall come to the priest 2
17 the priest shall examine him, and if the disease 2
17 then the priest shall pronounce the . . person 2
19 then it shall be shown to the priest 2
20 the priest shall make an examination 2
20 then the priest shall pronounce him unclean 2
21 if the priest examines it, and the hair on it 2
21 then the priest shall shut him up seven days 2
22 then the priest shall pronounce him unclean 2
23 and the priest shall pronounce him clean 2
25 the priest shall examine it 2
25 and the priest shall pronounce him unclean 2
26 if the priest examines it, and the hair in the spot 2
26 the priest shall shut him up seven days 2
27 the priest shall examine him the seventh day 2
27 then the priest shall pronounce him unclean 2
28 the priest shall pronounce him clean 2
30 the priest shall examine the disease 2
30 then the priest shall pronounce him unclean 2
31 if the priest examines the itching disease 2
31 then the priest shall shut up the person 2
32 the priest shall examine the disease 2
33 the priest shall shut up the person 2
34 on the seventh day the priest shall examine 2
34 then the priest shall pronounce him clean 2
36 then the priest shall examine him 2
36 the priest need not seek for the yellow hair 2
37 and the priest shall pronounce him clean 2
39 the priest shall make an examination 2
43 Then the priest shall examine him 2
44 the priest must pronounce him unclean 2
49 leprous disease and shall be shown to the priest 2
50 the priest shall examine the disease 2
53 if the priest examines, and the disease has not 2
54 then the priest shall command that they wash 2
55 the priest shall examine the diseased thing 2
56 if the priest examines, and the disease is dim 2
14: 2 leper . . He shall be brought to the priest 2
3 the priest shall go out of the camp, and the priest 2
3 the priest shall make an examination 2
4 the priest shall command them to take for him 2
5 the priest shall command them to kill one 2
11 the priest who cleanses him shall set the man 2
12 the priest shall take one of the male lambs 2
13 like the sin offering, belongs to the priest 2
14 The priest shall take some of the blood 2
14 the priest shall put it on the tip of the right ear 2
15 Then the priest shall take some of the log of oil 2
17 oil . . the priest shall put on the tip 2
18 the rest of the oil that is in the priest's hand 2
18 Then the priest shall make atonement for him 2
19 The priest shall offer the sin offering 2
20 the priest shall offer the burnt offering 2
20 Thus the priest shall make atonement for him 2
23 bring them . . to the priest, to the door 2
24 the priest shall take the lamb 2
24 the priest shall wave them for a wave offering 2
25 the priest shall take some of the blood 2
26 the priest shall pour some of the oil 2
28 the priest shall put some of the oil 2
29 the rest of the oil that is in the priest's hand 2
31 the priest shall make atonement before the LORD 2
35 come and tell the priest, 'There seems to me to be 2
36 Then the priest shall command that they empty 2
36 before the priest goes to examine the disease 2
36 afterward the priest shall go in to see the house 2
38 then the priest shall go out of the house 2
39 the priest shall come again on the seventh day 2
40 then the priest shall command that they take out 2
44 then the priest shall go and look 2
48 if the priest comes and makes an examination 2
48 then the priest shall pronounce the house clean 2
15:14 and give them to the priest 2
15 and the priest shall offer them 2
15 the priest shall make atonement for him 2
29 bring them to the priest, to the door of the tent 2
30 the priest shall offer one for a sin offering 2
30 the priest shall make atonement for her 2
16:32 the priest who is anointed and consecrated 2
32 who is anointed and consecrated as priest 1
33 he shall make atonement for the priests 2
17: 5 that they may bring them to the LORD, to the priest 2

6 the priest shall sprinkle the blood on the altar 2
19:22 the priest shall make atonement for him 2
21: 1 Speak to the priests, the sons of Aaron, and say 2
7 for the priest is holy to his God *
9 the daughter of any priest, if she profanes 2
10 The priest who is chief among his brethren 2
21 no man of the descendants of Aaron the priest 2
22:10 A sojourner of the priest's or a hired servant 2
11 if a priest buys a slave as his property for money 2
12 If a priest's daughter is married to an outsider 2
13 if a priest's daughter is a widow or divorced 2
14 and give the holy thing to the priest 2
15 The priests shall not profane the holy things *
23:10 the first fruits of your harvest to the priest 2
11 after the sabbath the priest shall wave it 2
20 the priest shall wave them with the bread 2
20 they shall be holy to the LORD for the priest 2
27: 8 before the priest, and the priest shall value him 2
8 before the priest, and the priest shall value him 2
8 him who vowed the priest shall value him 2
11 man shall bring the animal before the priest 2
12 the priest shall value it as either good or bad 2
12 as you, the priest, value it, so it shall be 2
14 the priest shall value it as either good or bad 2
14 as the priest values it, so it shall stand 2
18 then the priest shall compute the money-value 2
21 the priest shall be in possession of it 2
23 then the priest shall compute the valuation 2
Num 3: 3 anointed priests, whom he ordained to minister 2
6 set them before Aaron the priest, that they may 2
31 vessels . . with which the priests minister *
32 son of Aaron the priest was to be chief 2
4:16 Elea'zar the son of Aaron the priest 2
28 Ith'amar the son of Aaron the priest. 2
33 Ith'amar the son of Aaron the priest. 2
5: 8 restitution . . shall go . . the LORD for the priest 2
9 which they bring to the priest, shall be his; 2
10 whatever any man gives to the priest shall be his. 2
15 then the man shall bring his wife to the priest 2
16 the priest shall bring her near 2
17 priest shall take holy water in an earthen 2
18 the priest shall set the woman before the LORD 2
18 in his hand the priest shall have the water 2
19 the priest shall make her take an oath, saying 2
21 priest make the woman take the oath of the curse 2
23 the priest shall write these curses in a book 2
25 priest shall take the cereal offering 2
26 priest shall take a handful of the . . offering 2
30 the priest shall execute upon her all this law. 2
6:10 shall bring two . . to the priest to the door 2
11 the priest shall offer one for a sin offering 2
16 the priest shall present them before the LORD 2
17 priest shall offer also its cereal offering 2
19 the priest shall take the shoulder of the ram 2
20 the priest shall wave them for a wave offering 2
20 they are a holy portion for the priest 2
7: 8 Ith'amar the son of Aaron the priest. 2
10: 8 of Aaron, the priests, shall blow the trumpets. 2
15:25 the priest shall make atonement for all 2
28 the priest shall make atonement before the LORD 2
16:37 Elea'zar the son of Aaron the priest to take up 2
39 Elea'zar the priest took the bronze censers 2
40 so that no one who is not a priest *
18:28 give the LORD'S offering to Aaron the priest. 2
19: 3 you shall give her to Elea'zar the priest 2
4 Elea'zar the priest shall take some of her blood 2
6 priest shall take cedarwood and hyssop 2
7 priest shall wash his clothes and bathe his body 2
7 priest shall be unclean until evening. 2
25: 7 Phin'ehas . . of Elea'zar, son of Aaron the priest 2
11 Phin'ehas . . of Elea'zar, son of Aaron the priest 2
26: 1 Elea'zar the son of Aaron, the priest 2
3 Moses and Elea'zar the priest spoke with them 2
63 those numbered by Moses and Elea'zar the priest 2
64 of those numbered by Moses and Aaron the priest 2
27: 2 stood . . before Elea'zar the priest 2
19 cause him to stand before Elea'zar the priest 2
21 he shall stand before Elea'zar the priest 2
22 caused him to stand before Elea'zar the priest 2
31: 6 with Phin'ehas the son of Elea'zar the priest 2
12 brought . . to Moses, and to Elea'zar the priest 2
13 Moses, and Elea'zar the priest, and all the leaders 2
21 Elea'zar the priest said to the men of war 2
26 you and Elea'zar the priest and the heads 2
29 give it to Elea'zar the priest as an offering 2
31 Moses and Elea'zar the priest did as the LORD 2
41 Moses gave the tribute . . to Elea'zar the priest 2
51 Moses and Elea'zar the priest received from them 2
54 Moses and Elea'zar the priest received the gold 2
32: 2 came and said to Moses and to Elea'zar the priest 2
28 command concerning them to Elea'zar the priest 2
33:38 Aaron the priest went up Mount Hor at the command 2
34:17 Elea'zar the priest and Joshua the son of Nun. 2
35:25 live in it until the death of the high priest 2
28 city of refuge until the death of the high priest; 2
28 but after the death of the high priest 2
32 may return . . before the death of the high priest. 2
Deu 17: 9 coming to the Levitical priests, and to the judge 2
12 by not obeying the priest who stands to minister 2
18 which is in the charge of the Levitical priests; 2
18: 1 Levitical priests, that is, all the tribe of Levi 2
3 this shall be the priests' due from the people 2
3 give to the priest the shoulder 2
19:17 LORD, before the priests and the judges 2
20: 2 priest shall come forward and speak to the people 2
21: 5 priests the sons of Levi shall come forward 2
24: 8 all that the Levitical priests shall direct you; 2
26: 3 go to the priest who is in office at that time 2
4 priest shall take the basket from your hand 2
27: 9 Moses and the Levitical priests said to all 2
31: 9 Moses . . gave it to the priests the sons of Levi 2
Jos 3: 3 ark . . being carried by the Levitical priests 2
6 And Joshua said to the priests, "Take up the ark 2
8 you shall command the priests who bear the ark 2
13 soles of the feet of the priests who bear the ark 2
14 to pass over . . with the priests bearing the ark 2
15 feet of the priests bearing the ark were dipped 2
17 priests who bore the ark . . stood on dry ground 2
4: 3 from the very place where the priests' feet stood 2
9 place where the feet of the priests . . had stood; 2
10 the priests who bore the ark stood in the midst 2
11 the ark of the LORD and the priests passed over 2
16 the priests who bear the ark of the testimony 2
17 Joshua therefore commanded the priests, "Come up 2
18 when the priests bearing the ark of the covenant 2
18 and the soles of the priests' feet were lifted up 2
6: 4 And seven priests shall bear seven trumpets 2
4 march . . the priests blowing the trumpets. 2
6 Joshua the son of Nun called the priests and said 2
6 and let seven priests bear seven trumpets 2
8 the seven priests bearing . . went forward 2
9 And the armed men went before the priests 2
12 and the priests took up the ark of the LORD. 2
13 And the seven priests bearing . . passed 2
16 at the seventh time, when the priests had blown 2
8:33 the Levitical priests who carried the ark 2
14: 1 Elea'zar the priest, and Joshua the son of Nun 2
17: 4 They came before Elea'zar the priest and Joshua 2
19:51 Elea'zar the priest and Joshua the son of Nun 2
20: 6 remain . . until the death of him who is high priest 2
21: 1 Levites came to Elea'zar the priest and to Joshua 2
4 who were descendants of Aaron the priest 2
13 to the descendants of Aaron the priest they gave 2
19 cities of the descendants of Aaron, the priests 2
22:13 Phin'ehas the son of Elea'zar the priest 2
30 Phin'ehas the priest and the chiefs 2
31 Phin'ehas the son of Elea'zar the priest said 2
32 Then Phin'ehas the son of Elea'zar the priest 2
Jdg 17: 5 installed one of his sons, who became his priest. 2
10 be to me a father and a priest, and I will give you 2
12 young man became his priest, and was in the house 2
13 prosper me, because I have a Levite as priest. 2
18: 4 he has hired me, and I have become his priest. 2
6 the priest said to them, "Go in peace. The journey 2
17 entered and took . . while the priest stood 2
18 the priest said to them, "What are you doing? 2
19 and come with us, and be to us a father and a priest. 2
19 better . . to be priest to the house of one man 2
19 or to be priest to a tribe and family in Israel? 2
20 the priest's heart was glad; he took the ephod 2
24 You take my gods which I made, and the priest, and go 2
27 Micah had made, and the priest who belonged to him 2
30 Jonathan . . and his sons were priests 2
1Sm 1: 3 Hophni and Phin'ehas, were priests of the LORD. 2
9 Now Eli the priest was sitting on the seat beside 2
2:11 And the boy . . in the presence of Eli the priest. 2
13 The custom of the priests with the people was 2
13 the priest's servant would come, while the meat 2
14 all . . the fork brought up the priest would take 2
15 the priest's servant would come and say to the man 2
15 Give meat for the priest to roast; 2
28 I chose him out of all the tribes . . to be my priest 2
35 And I will raise up for myself a faithful priest 2
5: 5 the priests of Dagon . . do not tread 2
6: 2 called for the priests and the diviners and said 2
14: 3 son of Eli, the priest of the LORD in Shiloh 2
19 while Saul was talking to the priest 2
19 and Saul said to the priest, "Withdraw your hand. 2
36 the priest said, "Let us draw near hither to God. 2
21: 1 Then came David to Nob to Ahim'elech the priest; 2
2 And David said to Ahim'elech the priest 2
4 the priest answered David, "I have no common bread 2
5 And David answered the priest, "Of a truth 2
6 the priest gave him the holy bread; 2
9 the priest said, "The sword of Goliath . . is here 2
22:11 the king sent to summon Ahim'elech the priest 2
11 all his father's house, the priests who were at Nob; 2
17 king said . . "Turn and kill the priests of the LORD; 2
17 to fall upon the priests of the LORD. 2
18 king said . . "You turn and fall upon the priests. 2
18 And Do'eg . . turned and fell upon the priests 2
19 Nob, the city of the priests, he put to the sword; 2
21 that Saul had killed the priests of the LORD. 2
23: 9 he said to Abi'athar the priest, "Bring the ephod 2
30: 7 said to Abi'athar the priest, the son of Ahim'elech 2
2Sm 8:17 Ahim'elech the son of Abi'athar were priests; 2
18 and David's sons were priests. 2
15:27 The king also said to Zadok the priest 2
35 Are not Zadok and Abi'athar the priests with you 2
35 tell it to Zadok and Abi'athar the priests. 2
17:15 Hushai said to Zadok and Abi'athar the priests 2
19:11 David sent . . to Zadok and Abi'athar the priests 2
20:25 and Zadok and Abi'athar were priests; 2
26 and Ira the Ja'irite was also David's priest. 2
1Kg 1: 7 He conferred . . and with Abi'athar the priest; 2
8 Zadok the priest, and Benai'ah the son of Jehoi'ada 2
19 the sons of the king, Abi'athar the priest, and Jo'ab 2
25 the king's sons, Jo'ab . . and Abi'athar the priest; 2
26 me, your servant, and Zadok the priest, and Benai'ah 2
32 Call to me Zadok the priest, Nathan the prophet 2
34 let Zadok the priest and Nathan . . anoint him 2
38 Zadok the priest, Nathan . . and Benai'ah . . went 2
39 Zadok the priest took the horn of oil 2
42 Jonathan the son of Abi'athar the priest came; 2
44 sent . . Zadok the priest, Nathan . . and Benai'ah 2
45 Zadok the priest and Nathan . . have anointed him 2
2:22 on his side are Abi'athar the priest and Jo'ab 2
26 to Abi'athar the priest the king said, "Go 2
27 expelled Abi'athar from being priest to the LORD 2
35 the king put Zadok the priest in the place 2
4: 2 Azari'ah . . was the priest; 2
4 of the army; Zadok and Abi'athar were priests; 2
5 Zabud . . was priest and king's friend; 2
8: 3 elders . . came, and the priests took up the ark. 2
4 the priests and the Levites brought them up. 2
6 Then the priests brought the ark of the covenant 2
10 when the priests came out of the holy place 2
11 priests could not stand to minister 2
12:31 and appointed priests from among all the people 2
32 placed in Bethel the priests of the high places 2
13: 2 sacrifice . . the priests of the high places 2
33 Jerobo'am . . made priests for the high places 2
33 he consecrated to be priests of the high places. 2
2Kg 10:11 great men . . familiar friends, and his priests 2
19 of Ba'al, all his worshipers and all his priests; 2
11: 9 all that Jehoi'ada the priest commanded 2
9 each brought . . and came to Jehoi'ada the priest. 2
10 the priest delivered to the captains the spears 2
15 Jehoi'ada the priest commanded the captains 2
15 the priest said, "Let her not be slain in the house 2
18 and they slew Mattan the priest of Ba'al 2
18 And the priest posted watchmen over the house 2
12: 2 because Jehoi'ada the priest instructed him. 2
4 Jeho'ash said to the priests, "All the money 2
5 let the priests take, each from his acquaintance; 2
6 the priests had made no repairs on the house. 2
7 Jeho'ash summoned Jehoi'ada the priest 2
7 summoned Jehoi'ada . . and the other priests 2
8 the priests agreed that they should take no more 2
9 Jehoi'ada the priest took a chest, and bored a hole 2
9 the priests who guarded the threshold put in it 2
10 the king's secretary and the high priest came up 2
16 The money from . . it belonged to the priests. 2
16:10 Ahaz sent to Uri'ah the priest a model of the altar 2
11 And Uri'ah the priest built the altar; 2
11 in accordance with . . so Uri'ah the priest made it 2
15 King Ahaz commanded Uri'ah the priest, saying 2
16 Uri'ah the priest did all this 2
17:27 Send there one of the priests . . you carried away 2
28 one of the priests whom they had carried away 2
32 appointed . . as priests of the high places 2
19: 2 Shebna the secretary, and the senior priests 2
22: 4 Go up to Hilki'ah the high priest 2
8 And Hilki'ah the high priest said to Shaphan 2
10 Hilki'ah the priest has given me a book. 2
12 king commanded Hilki'ah the priest, and Ahi'kam 2
14 Hilki'ah the priest, and Ahi'kam, and Achbor 2
23: 2 men of Judah . . and the priests and the prophets 2
4 And the king commanded Hilki'ah the high priest 2
4 high priest, and the priests of the second order 2
8 he brought all the priests out of the cities 2
8 places where the priests had burned incense 2
9 the priests of the high places did not come up 2
20 And he slew all the priests of the high places 2
24 book that Hilki'ah the priest found in the house 2
25:18 the captain . . took Serai'ah the chief priest 2
18 took Serai'ah . . and Zephani'ah the second priest 2
1Ch 9: 2 the priests, the Levites, and the temple servants. 2
10 Of the priests: Jedai'ah, Jehoi'arib, Jachin 2
30 Others, of the sons of the priests 2
13: 2 priests and Levites in the cities 2
15:11 David summoned the priests . . and the Levites 2
14 priests and the Levites sanctified themselves 2
24 priests, should blow the trumpets before the ark 2
16: 6 Benai'ah and Jaha'ziel the priests were to blow 2
39 he left Zadok the priest and his brethren 2
39 Zadok the priest and his brethren the priests 2
18:16 Zadok . . and Ahim'elech . . were priests; 2
23: 2 assembled . . and the priests and the Levites. 2
24: 6 in the presence of . . Zadok the priest 2
6 the heads of the fathers' houses of the priests 2
31 heads of fathers' houses of the priests 2
27: 5 Benai'ah, the son of Jehoi'ada the priest, as chief; 2
28:13 the divisions of the priests and of the Levites 2
21 divisions of the priests and the Levites 2
29:22 anointed him as prince . . and Zadok as priest. 2
2Ch 4: 6 and the sea was for the priests to wash in. 2

9 made the court of the priests, and the great court 2
5: 5 the priests and the Levites brought them up. 2
7 the priests brought the ark . . to its place 2
11 Now when the priests came out of the holy place 2
11 priests . . present had sanctified themselves 2
12 stood . . with 120 priests who 2
14 priests could not stand to minister 2
6:41 Let thy priests . . be clothed with salvation 2
7: 2 the priests could not enter the house of the LORD 2
6 priests stood at their posts; the Levites also 2
6 opposite them the priests sounded trumpets; 2
8:14 he appointed the divisions of the priests 2
14 offices of . . ministry before the priests 2
15 commanded the priests and Levites concerning 2
11:13 priests and the Levites that were in all Israel 2
15 he appointed his own priests for the high places 2
13: 9 Have you not driven out the priests of the LORD 2
9 made priests for yourselves 2
9 becomes a priest of what are no gods. 2
10 We have priests ministering to the LORD 2
12 his priests with their battle trumpets 2
14 the priests blew the trumpets. 2
15: 3 Israel was . . and without a teaching priest 2
17: 8 with these Levites, the priests Eli'shama 2
19: 8 appointed certain Levites and priests 2
11 Amari'ah the chief priest is over you 2
22:11 Jeho-shab'e-ath . . wife of Jehoi'ada the priest 2
23: 4 of you priests and Levites who come off duty 2
6 priests and ministering Levites; they may enter 2
8 all that Jehoi'ada the priest commanded. 2
8 for Jehoi'ada the priest did not dismiss 2
9 Jehoi'ada the priest delivered to the captains 2
14 Jehoi'ada the priest brought out the captains 2
14 priest said, "Do not slay her in the house 2
17 slew Mattan the priest of Ba'al before the altars. 2
18 under the direction of the Levitical priests 2
24: 2 all the days of Jehoi'ada the priest. 2
5 he gathered the priests and the Levites 2
11 secretary and the officer of the chief priest 2
20 Zechari'ah the son of Jehoi'ada the priest; 2
25 blood of the son of Jehoi'ada the priest 2
26:17 Azari'ah the priest went in after him 2
17 80 priests of the LORD who were men of valor; 2
18 but for the priests the sons of Aaron 2
19 became angry with the priests leprosy broke out 2
19 in the presence of the priests 2
20 Azari'ah the chief priest, and all the priests 2
20 Azari'ah the chief priest, and all the priests 2
29: 4 He brought in the priests and the Levites 2
16 The priests went into the inner part of the house 2
21 commanded the priests the sons of Aaron to offer 2
22 priests received the blood and threw it against 2
24 the priests killed them and made a sin offering 2
26 and the priests with the trumpets. 2
34 the priests were too few and could not flay all 2
34 until other priests had sanctified themselves 2
34 more upright in heart than the priests 2
30: 3 priests had not sanctified themselves 2
15 priests and the Levites were put to shame 2
16 the priests sprinkled the blood 2
21 Levites and the priests praised the LORD 2
24 priests sanctified themselves in great 2
25 Judah, and the priests and the Levites 2
27 the priests and the Levites arose and blessed 2
31: 2 the divisions of the priests and of the Levites 2
2 priests and the Levites, for burnt offerings 2
4 to give the portion due to the priests 2
9 questioned the priests and the Levites 2
10 Azari'ah the chief priest . . answered him 2
15 assisting him in the cities of the priests 2
17 The enrollment of the priests was according 2
18 priests were enrolled with all their *
19 sons of Aaron, the priests 2
19 portions to every male among the priests 2
34: 5 burned the bones of the priests on their altars 2
9 came to Hilki'ah the high priest and delivered 2
14 Hilki'ah the priest found the book of the law 2
18 Hilki'ah the priest has given me a book. 2
30 king went up . . with . . priests and the Levites 2
35: 2 He appointed the priests to their offices 2
8 to the people, to the priests, and to the Levites. 2
8 gave to the priests for the passover offerings 2
10 prepared for, the priests stood in their place 2
11 priests sprinkled the blood 2
14 prepared for themselves and for the priests 2
14 priests the sons of Aaron . . busied in offering 2
14 Levites prepared . . for the priests 2
18 by Josi'ah, and the priests and the Levites 2
36:14 All the leading priests and the people likewise 2
Ezr 1: 5 rose up the . . priests and the Levites 2
2:36 priests: the sons of Jedai'ah, of the house 2
61 of the sons of the priests: the sons of Habai'ah 2
63 priest to consult Urim and Thummim. 2
69 gave to . . the work . . 100 priests' garments. 2
70 priests, the Levites, and some of the people lived 2
3: 2 Then arose Jeshua . . with his fellow priests 2
8 priests and the Levites and all who had come 2
10 priests . . came forward with trumpets 2
12 many of the priests and Levites and heads 2
6: 9 wine, or oil, as the priests at Jerusalem require- 3
16 people of Israel, the priests and the Levites 3
18 set the priests in their divisions 3
20 priests and the Levites had purified 2
20 for their fellow priests, and for themselves; 2
7: 5 son of Elea'zar, son of Aaron the chief priest- 2
7 went up . . some of the priests and Levites 2
11 letter . . Ar-ta-xerx'es gave to Ezra the priest 2
12 Ar-ta-xerx'es, king of kings, to Ezra the priest 3
13 Israel or their priests or Levites in my kingdom 3
16 freewill offerings of . . the priests 3
21 Whatever Ezra the priest . . requires of you 3
24 upon any one of the priests, the Levites 3
8:15 As I reviewed the people and the priests, I found 2
24 Then I set apart twelve of the leading priests 2
29 until you weigh them before the chief priests 2
30 priests and the Levites took over the weight 2
33 weighed into the hands of Mer'emoth the priest 2
9: 1 people of Israel and the priests and the Levites 2
7 for our iniquities we, our kings, and our priests 2
10: 5 made the leading priests . . take oath 2
10 Ezra the priest stood up and said to them, 2
16 Ezra the priest selected men, heads of fathers' 2
18 sons of the priests who had married foreign 2
Neh 2:16 I had not yet told the Jews, the priests, the nobles 2
3: 1 Then Eli'ashib the high priest rose up 2
1 rose up with his brethren the priests 2
20 door of the house of Eli'ashib the high priest. 2
22 After him the priests, the men of the Plain 2
28 Above the Horse Gate the priests repaired 2
5:12 I called the priests, and took an oath of them to do 2
7:39 priests: the sons of Jedai'ah . . 973. 2
63 Also, of the priests: the sons of Hobai'ah 2
65 until a priest with Urim and Thummim 2
70 governor gave . . 530 priests' garments. 2
72 rest . . gave . . 67 priests' garments. 2
73 priests, the Levites, the gatekeepers 2
8: 2 Ezra the priest brought the law before 2
9 Nehemi'ah . . and Ezra the priest and scribe 2
13 heads . . with the priests and the Levites, came 2
9:32 come upon . . our kings, our princes, our priests 2
34 kings, our princes, our priests, and our fathers 2
38 princes, our Levites, and our priests set 2
10: 8 Ma-azi'ah, Bil'gai, Shemai'ah; these are the priests. 2
28 The rest of the people, the priests, the Levites 2
34 cast lots, the priests, the Levites, and the people 2
36 also to bring to . . the priests who minister 2
37 bring . . to the priests, to the chambers 2
38 priest, the son of Aaron, shall be with the Levites 2
39 priests that minister, and the gatekeepers 2
11: 3 Israel, the priests, the Levites 2
10 Of the priests: Jedai'ah the son of Joi'arib, Jachin 2
20 rest of Israel, and of the priests and the Levites 2
12: 1 These are the priests and the Levites who came up 2
7 chiefs of the priests and of their brethren 2
12 days of Joi'akim were priests, heads of fathers' 2
22 priests until the reign of Darius the Persian. 2
26 days of Nehemi'ah . . of Ezra the priest the scribe. 2
30 priests and the Levites purified themselves; 2
35 certain of the priests' sons with trumpets 2
41 priests Eli'akim, Ma-asei'ah, Mini'amin, Micai'ah 2
44 required . . for the priests and for the Levites 2
44 Judah rejoiced over the priests and the Levites 2
13: 4 Eli'ashib the priest, who was appointed 2
5 previously put . . contributions for the priests. 2
13 appointed . . Shelemi'ah the priest, Zadok 2
28 Jehoi'ada, the son of Eli'ashib the high priest 2
30 duties of the priests and Levites 2
Job 12:19 He leads priests away stripped 2
Ps 78:64 Their priests fell by the sword 2
99: 6 Moses and Aaron were among his priests 2
110: 4 priest for ever after the order of Melchiz'edek. 2
132: 9 Let thy priests be clothed with righteousness 2
16 Her priests I will clothe with salvation 2
Isa 8: 2 witnesses, Uri'ah the priest and Zechari'ah 2
24: 2 it shall be, as with the people, so with the priest; 2
28: 7 the priest and the prophet reel with strong 2
37: 2 and Shebna the secretary, and the senior priests 2
61: 6 but you shall be called the priests of the LORD 2
66:21 some . . I will take for priests and for Levites 2
Jer 1: 1 Jeremiah . . of the priests who were in An'athoth 2
18 Judah . . its priests, and the people of the land. 2
2: 8 The priests did not say, 'Where is the LORD?' 2
26 they, their kings, their princes, their priests 2
4: 9 the priests shall be appalled 2
5:31 and the priests rule at their direction; 2
6:13 from prophet to priest, every one deals falsely. 2
8: 1 the bones of its princes, the bones of the priests 2
10 from prophet to priest every one deals falsely. 2
13:13 the kings who sit on David's throne, the priests 2
14:18 For both prophet and priest ply their trade 2
18:18 for the law shall not perish from the priest 2
19: 1 of the people and some of the senior priests 2
20: 1 Now Pashhur the priest, the son of Immer 2
21: 1 Zephani'ah the priest, the son of Ma-asei'ah, saying 2
23:11 Both prophet and priest are ungodly; 2
33 or a prophet, or a priest asks you 2
34 the prophet, priest, or one of the people who says 2
26: 7 The priests and the prophets and all the people 2
8 the priests and the prophets and all the people 2
11 Then the priests and the prophets said 2
16 the people said to the priests and the prophets 2
27:16 Then I spoke to the priests and to all this people 2
28: 1 in the presence of the priests and all the people 2
5 in the presence of the priests and all the people 2
29: 1 to the elders of the exiles, and to the priests 2
25 and to Zephani'ah the son of Ma-asei'ah the priest 2
25 the priest, and to all the priests, saying 2
26 The LORD has made you priest instead of Jehoi'ada 2
26 made you priest instead of Jehoi'ada the priest 2
29 Zephani'ah the priest read this letter 2
31:14 I will feast the soul of the priests 2
32:32 their princes, their priests and their prophets 2
33:18 and the Levitical priests shall never lack a man 2
21 and my covenant with the Levitical priests 2
22 and the Levitical priests who minister to me. *
34:19 the priests, and all the people of the land 2
37: 3 and Zephani'ah the priest, the son of Ma-asei'ah 2
48: 7 into exile, with his priests and his princes. 2
49: 3 For Milcom shall go into exile, with his priests 2
52:24 the guard took Serai'ah the chief priest 2
24 chief priest, and Zephani'ah the second priest 2
Lam 1: 4 all her gates are desolate, her priests groan; 2
19 my priests and elders perished in the city 2
2: 6 in . . indignation has spurned king and priest. 2
20 priest and prophet be slain in the sanctuary 2
4:13 the sins . . and the iniquities of her priests 2
16 no honor was shown to the priests 2
Ezk 1: 3 the word of the LORD came to Ezekiel the priest 2
7:26 but the law perishes from the priest 2
22:26 Her priests have done violence to my law 2
40:45 for the priests who have charge of the temple 2
46 is for the priests who have charge of the altar; 2
42:13 holy chambers, where the priests who approach 2
14 When the priests enter the holy place 2
43:19 to the Levitical priests of the family of Zadok 2
24 the priests shall sprinkle salt upon them 2
27 the priests shall offer upon the altar 2
44:15 But the Levitical priests, the sons of Zadok 2
21 No priest shall drink wine, when he enters 2
22 or a widow who is the widow of a priest. 2
30 all your offerings, shall belong to the priests; 2
30 you shall also give to the priests 2
31 The priests shall not eat of anything 2
45: 4 it shall be for the priests, who minister 2
19 The priest shall take some of the blood 2
46: 2 The priests shall offer his burnt offering 2
19 north row of the holy chambers for the priests; 2
20 This is the place where the priests shall boil 2
48:10 the priests shall have an allotment measuring 2
11 This shall be for the consecrated priests 2
13 alongside the territory of the priests 2
Hos 4: 4 for with you is my contention, O priest. 2
6 I reject you from being a priest to me. 1
9 And it shall be like people, like priest; 2
5: 1 Hear this, O priests! Give heed, O house of Israel! 2
6: 9 so the priests are banded together 2
Jol 1: 9 The priests mourn, the ministers of the LORD. 2
13 Gird on sackcloth and lament, O priests 2
2:17 let the priests, the ministers of the LORD, weep 2
Ams 7:10 Amazi'ah the priest of Bethel sent to Jerobo'am 2
Mic 3:11 its priests teach for hire 2
Zep 3: 4 her priests profane what is sacred 2
Hag 1: 1 to Joshua the son of Jehoz'adak, the high priest 2
12 Joshua the son of Jehoz'adak, the high priest 2
14 Joshua the son of Jehoz'adak, the high priest 2
2: 2 to Joshua the son of Jehoz'adak, the high priest 2
4 O Joshua, son of Jehoz'adak, the high priest; 2
11 Ask the priests to decide this question 2
12 does it become holy?'" The priests answered, "No 2
13 The priests answered, "It does become unclean. 2
Zec 3: 1 Then he showed me Joshua the high priest 2
8 Hear now, O Joshua the high priest 2
6:11 of Joshua, the son of Jehoz'adak, the high priest; 2
13 there shall be a priest by his throne 2
7: 3 to ask the priests of the house of the LORD 2
5 Say to all the people of the land and the priests 2
Mal 1: 6 says the LORD of hosts to you, O priests, 2
2: 1 now, O priests, this command is for you. 2
7 For the lips of a priest should guard knowledge 2
Mat 8: 4 but go, show yourself to the priest 6
12: 4 but only for the priests? 6
5 on the sabbath the priests in the temple profane 6
Mrk 1:44 go, show yourself to the priest 6
2:26 which it is not lawful for any but the priests 6
Lke 1: 5 there was a priest named Zechari'ah 6
5:14 tell no one; but "go and show yourself to the priest 6
6: 4 it is not lawful for any but the priests to eat 6
10:31 Now by chance a priest was going down that road; 6
17:14 Go and show yourselves to the priests. 6
Joh 1:19 Jews sent priests and Levites from Jerusalem 6
Act 4: 1 the priests and the captain of the temple 6
6: 7 the priests were obedient to the faith. 6
14:13 the priest of Zeus . . brought oxen and garlands 6
Heb 5: 6 a priest for ever, after the order of Melchiz'edek. 6
7: 1 king of Salem, priest of the Most High God 6
3 he continues a priest for ever. 6
11 need . . for another priest to arise 6

14 Moses said nothing about priests. 6
15 when another priest arises 6
16 who has become a priest •
17 a priest for ever, after the order of Melchiz'edek. 6
21 Those who formerly became priests 6
21 'Thou art a priest for ever.' 6
23 The former priests were many in number 6
8: 3 hence it is necessary for this priest also . . •
4 he would not be a priest at all •
4 since there are priests who offer gifts •
9: 6 the priests go continually into the outer tent 6
10:11 every priest stands daily at his service 6
21 since we have a great priest over the house of God 6
Rev 1: 6 made us a kingdom, priests to his God and Father 6
5:10 hast made them a kingdom and priests to our God 6
20: 6 but they shall be priests of God and of Christ 6
1Es 1: 2 having placed the priests 6
7 the people and the priests and Levites. 6
8 gave to the priests for the passover 2,600 sheep 6
10 The priests and the Levites 6
13 their brethren the priests, the sons of Aaron 6
14 the priests were offering the fat until night 6
14 their brethren the priests, the sons of Aaron. 6
21 the priests and Levites and the men of Judah 6
49 Even the leaders of the people and of the priests 6
2: 8 the priests and the Levites 6
4:53 their children and all the priests who came. 6
54 the priests' garments 5
5: 5 the priests, the sons of Phinehas, son of Aaron; 6
24 The priests: the sons of Jedaiah 6
38 Of the priests the following 6
45 100 priests' garments. 5
46 The priests, the Levites, and some of the people 6
48 Jeshua . . with his fellow priests 6
56 their brethren and the Levitical priests 6
59 the priests stood arrayed in their garments 6
63 Some of the Levitical priests 6
6:30 as the priests in Jerusalem may indicate 6
7: 6 the people of Israel, the priests, the Levites 6
9 the priests and the Levites stood 6
10 after the priests and the Levites were purified 6
12 for their brethren the priests 6
8: 2 son of Eleazar, son of Aaron the chief priest. 6
5 some of the priests and Levites 6
8 which was delivered to Ezra the priest 6
9 King Artaxerxes to Ezra the priest 6
10 the priests and Levites and others in our realm 6
19 Ezra the priest and reader of the law 6
22 to be laid on any of the priests or Levites 6
42 When I found there none of the sons of the priests 6
54 I set apart twelve of the leaders of the priests 6
59 the leaders of the priests and the Levites 6
60 the priests and the Levites who took the silver 6
62 Meremoth the priest, son of Uriah; 6
69 the leaders and the priests and the Levites 6
77 our brethren and our kings and our priests 6
96 leaders of the priests and Levites of all Israel 6
9:16 Ezra the priest chose 6
18 Of the priests those who were brought 6
37 The priests and the Levites and the men of Israel 6
40 for . . all the priests to hear the law 6
42 Ezra the priest and reader of the law 6
2Es 1:13 I gave you Moses as leader and Aaron as priest; 7
10:22 our priests have been burned to death 7
Tob 1: 6 I would give these to the priests 6
Jdt 4: 6 Joakim, the high priest 6
8 Joakim the high priest 6
14 Joakim the high priest 6
14 all the priests who stood before the Lord 6
11:13 they had consecrated and set aside for the priests 6
15: 8 Then Joakim the high priest . . came to witness 6
AEs 11: 1 who said that he was a priest and a Levite 6
Sir 7:29 fear the Lord, and honor his priests. 6
31 Fear the Lord and honor the priest 6
50: 1 Simon the high priest, son of Onias 6
12 received . . from the hands of the priests 6
Bar 1: 7 they sent it . . to the priests 6
16 our priests and our prophets and our fathers 6
LJr 1:10 sometimes the priests secretly take gold 6
18 so the priests make their temples secure 6
28 The priests sell the sacrifices 6
31 the priests sit with their clothes rent 6
33 The priests take some of the clothing of their gods 6
48 the priests consult together 6
55 their priests will flee and escape 6
Aza 1:62 Bless the Lord, you priests of the Lord 6
Bel 1: 8 he called his priests and said to them 6
10 Now there were 70 priests of Bel 6
11 the priests of Bel said, "Behold 6
15 In the night the priests came with their wives 6
21 seized the priests and their wives and children; 6
28 slain the dragon, and slaughtered the priests. 6
1Mc 1:46 to defile the sanctuary and the priests 4
2: 1 son of Simeon, a priest of the sons of Joarib 6
3:51 thy priests mourn in humiliation. 6
4:42 He chose blameless priests devoted to the law 6
5:67 some priests, who wished to do a brave deed, fell 6
7:14 A priest of the line of Aaron has come with the army 6
33 Some of the priests came out of the sanctuary 6
36 the priests went in and stood before the altar 6
10:42 it belongs to the priests who minister there. 6
11:23 he chose . . some of the priests 6
12: 6 the senate of the nation, the priests 6
14:20 to Simon the high priest and to the elders 6
20 the priests and the rest of the Jewish people 6
28 in Asaramel, in the great assembly of the priests 6
29 a priest of the sons of Joarib 6
41 Jews and their priests decided that Simon should 6
44 none of the people or priests shall be permitted 6
47 be commander and ethnarch of the Jews and priests 6
15: 1 sent a letter . . to Simon, the priest 6
2 Simon the high priest and ethnarch 6
2Mc 1:10 who is of the family of the anointed priests 6
13 a deception employed by the priests of Nanea. 6
15 the priests of the temple of Nanea 6
19 the pious priests of that time took some of the fire 6
20 sent the descendants of the priests 6
21 Nehemiah ordered the priests to sprinkle 6
23 the priests offered prayer 6
23 -the priests and every one 6
30 Then the priests sang the hymns. 6
33 the exiled priests had hidden the fire 6
3:15 priests prostrated themselves 6
4:14 priests . . no longer intent upon their service 6
14:31 while the priests were offering . . sacrifices 6
34 Then the priests stretched forth their hands 6
15:31 stationed the priests before the altar 6
3Mc 1:11 nor even all of the priests 6
16 the priests in all their vestments 6
6: 1 famous among the priests of the country 6
7:13 their priests and the whole multitude 6
4Mc 4: 9 the priests together with women and children 6
7: 6 O priest, worthy of the priesthood 6
17: 9 Here lie buried an aged priest and an aged woman 6

priest *See also* chamber, minister, serve, service.

become a priest 1. כהן

1Ch 24: 2 Elea'zar and Ith'amar became the priests. 1

chief priest 1. ἀρχιερεύς

Mat 2: 4 assembling all the chief priests and scribes 1
16:21 from the elders and chief priests and scribes 1
20:18 delivered to the chief priests and scribes 1
21:15 when the chief priests and the scribes saw 1
23 the chief priests and the elders of the people 1
45 When the chief priests and the Pharisees heard 1
26: 3 the chief priests and the elders . . gathered 1
14 Judas Iscariot, went to the chief priests 1
47 from the chief priests and the elders of the people. 1
59 the chief priests and the whole council sought 1
27: 1 all the chief priests and the elders of the people 1
3 to the chief priests and the elders 1
6 the chief priests, taking the pieces of silver, said 1
12 accused by the chief priests and elders 1
20 Now the chief priests and the elders persuaded 1
41 also the chief priests, with the scribes 1
62 the chief priests and the Pharisees gathered 1
28:11 told the chief priests all that had taken place. 1
Mrk 8:31 rejected by the elders and the chief priests 1
10:33 Son of man will be delivered to the chief priests 1
11:18 the chief priests and the scribes heard it 1
27 the chief priests and the scribes 1
14: 1 the chief priests and the scribes were seeking 1
10 went to the chief priests in order to betray him 1
43 the chief priests and the scribes and the elders 1
53 the chief priests and the elders and the scribes 1
55 Now the chief priests and the whole council 1
15: 1 the chief priests, with the elders and scribes 1
3 the chief priests accused him of many things. 1
10 the chief priests had delivered him up. 1
11 the chief priests stirred up the crowd 1
31 also the chief priests mocked him to one another 1
Lke 9:22 the elders and chief priests and scribes 1
19:47 The chief priests . . sought to destroy him 1
20: 1 the chief priests and the scribes with the elders 1
19 the chief priests tried to lay hands on him 1
22: 2 chief priests . . were seeking how to put him to death 1
4 and conferred with the chief priests and officers 1
52 the chief priests and officers of the temple 1
66 both chief priests and scribes 1
23: 4 Pilate said to the chief priests 1
10 The chief priests and the scribes stood by 1
13 Pilate then called together the chief priests 1
24:20 our chief priests and rulers delivered him up 1
Joh 7:32 the chief priests and Pharisees sent officers 1
45 The officers then went back to the chief priests 1
11:47 the chief priests . . gathered the council 1
57 Now the chief priests . . had given orders 1
12:10 the chief priests planned 1
18: 3 some officers from the chief priests 1
35 the chief priests have handed you over to me 1
19: 6 When the chief priests and the officers saw him 1
15 The chief priests answered, "We have no king 1
21 The chief priests of the Jews then said to Pilate 1
Act 4:23 reported what the chief priests . . had said 1
5:24 when . . the chief priests heard these words 1
9:14 here he has authority from the chief priests 1
21 to bring them bound before the chief priests. 1
22:30 and commanded the chief priests . . to meet 1
23:14 they went to the chief priests and elders, and said 1
25: 2 the chief priests and the principal men of the Jews 1
15 the chief priests and the elders of the Jews 1
26:10 by authority from the chief priests 1
12 the authority and commission of the chief priests. 1
1Es 9:39 Ezra the chief priest and reader 1
40 Ezra the chief priest brought the law 1
49 Ezra the chief priest and reader 1

high priest 1. ἀρχιεράομαι 2. ἀρχιερατεύω 3. ἀρχιερεύς 4. ἱερατεύω 5. ἱερεύς 6. ἱερεὺς μέγας 7. ἱερωσύνη

Mat 26: 3 people gathered in the palace of the high priest 3
51 and struck the slave of the high priest 3
57 led him to Ca'iaphas the high priest 3
58 as far as the courtyard of the high priest 3
62 the high priest stood up and said 3
63 Jesus was silent. And the high priest said to him 3
65 Then the high priest tore his robes, and said 3
Mrk 2:26 when Abi'athar was high priest 3
14:47 struck the slave of the high priest 3
53 they led Jesus to the high priest 3
54 right into the courtyard of the high priest 3
60 the high priest stood up in the midst 3
61 the high priest asked him, "Are you the Christ 3
63 the high priest tore his garments, and said 3
66 one of the maids of the high priest came; 3
Lke 22:50 one of them struck the slave of the high priest 3
54 bringing him into the high priest's house 3
Joh 11:49 Ca'iaphas, who was high priest that year, said 3
51 being high priest that year he prophesied 3
18:10 Simon Peter . . struck the high priest's slave 3
13 Ca'iaphas, who was high priest that year. 3
15 this disciple was known to the high priest 3
15 he entered the court of the high priest 3
16 the other disciple, who was known to the high priest 3
19 The high priest then questioned Jesus 3
22 Is that how you answer the high priest? 3
24 then sent him bound to Ca'iaphas the high priest. 3
26 One of the servants of the high priest . . asked 3
Act 4: 6 Annas the high priest and Ca'iaphas and John 3
5:17 the high priest rose up and all who were with him 3
21 the high priest came and those who were with him 3
27 the high priest questioned them 3
7: 1 the high priest said, "Is this so? 3
9: 1 Saul . . went to the high priest 3
19:14 Seven sons of a Jewish high priest named Sceva 3
22: 5 the high priest and the whole council of elders 3
23: 2 the high priest Anani'as commanded . . to strike him 3
4 Would you revile God's high priest? 3
5 I did not know, brethren, that he was the high priest; 3
24: 1 the high priest Anani'as came down with some elders 3
Heb 2:17 become a merciful and faithful high priest 3
3: 1 the apostle and high priest of our confession. 3
4:14 Since then we have a great high priest 3
15 a high priest who is unable to sympathize . . 3
5: 1 every high priest chosen from among men 3
5 did not exalt himself to be made a high priest 3
10 being designated by God a high priest 3
6:20 having become a high priest for ever 3
7:26 fitting that we should have such a high priest 3
27 He has no need, like those high priests 3
28 appoints men in their weakness as high priests 3
8: 1 we have such a high priest 3
3 every high priest is appointed to offer gifts 3
9: 7 into the second only the high priest goes 3
11 a high priest of the good things that have come 3
25 as the high priest enters the Holy Place yearly 3
13:11 is brought into the sanctuary by the high priest 3
1Es 5:40 until a high priest should appear 3
Bar 1: 7 son to Jehoiakim the high priest, the son of Hilkiah 5
1Mc 7: 5 were led by Alcimus, who wanted to be high priest. 4
9 the ungodly Alcimus, whom he made high priest 7
10:20 to be the high priest of your nation 3
32 give it to the high priest 3
38 obey no other authority but the high priest. 3
69 he sent the . . message to Jonathan the high priest 3
12: 3 Jonathan the high priest and the Jewish nation 3
6 Jonathan the high priest 3
7 to Onias the high priest from Arius 3
20 Arius . . to Onias the high priest, greeting. 6
13:36 Simon, the high priest and friend of kings 3
42 In the first year of Simon the great high priest 3
14:17 his brother had become high priest in his place 3
23 they have sent a copy of this to Simon the high priest.' 3
27 the third year of Simon the great high priest 3
30 and became their high priest 3
35 they made him their leader and high priest 3
41 Simon should be their . . high priest for ever 3
47 So Simon accepted and agreed to be high priest 2
15:17 They had been sent by Simon the high priest 3
21 hand them over to Simon the high priest 3
24 They also sent a copy . . to Simon the high priest. 3
16:12 for he was son-in-law of the high priest. 3
24 from the time that he became high priest 3
2Mc 3: 1 because of the piety of the high priest Onias 3

4 Simon . . had a disagreement with the high priest 3
9 been kindly welcomed by the high priest of the city 3
10 The high priest explained 3
16 To see the appearance of the high priest 3
21 the anxiety of the high priest 3
32 the high priest . . offered sacrifice 3
33 While the high priest was making the offering 3
33 Be very grateful to Onias the high priest 3
4:13 who was ungodly and no high priest 3
14: 3 who had formerly been high priest 3
13 to set up Alcimus as high priest 3
15:12 Onias, who had been high priest 3
3Mc 1:11 only the high priest who was pre-eminent over all 3
2: 1 the high priest Simon, facing the sanctuary 3
4Mc 4:13 Onias the high priest . . prayed for him 3
16 and appointed Onias's brother Jason as high priest. 3
18 the king appointed him high priest 1

idolatrous priest 1. כֹּמֶר

2Kg 23: 5 And he deposed the idolatrous priests 1
Hos 10: 5 and its idolatrous priests shall wail over it 1
Zep 1: 4 cut off . . the name of the idolatrous priests; 1

priest's place 1. כְּהֻנָּה

1Sm 2:36 Put me, I pray you, in one of the priest's places 1

priesthood 1. כהן 2. כְּהֻנָּה 3. ἀρχιερωσύνη 4. ἱερατεία 5. ἱεράτευμα 6. ἱερωσύνη

Exd 28: 3 to consecrate him for my priesthood. 1
29: 9 the priesthood shall be theirs by a perpetual 2
40:15 admit them to a perpetual priesthood 2
Num 3:10 they shall attend to their priesthood; 2
16:10 And would you seek the priesthood also? 2
18: 1 iniquity in connection with your priesthood. 2
7 sons with you shall attend to your priesthood 2
7 I give your priesthood as a gift, and any one else 2
25:13 covenant of a perpetual priesthood 2
Jos 18: 7 for the priesthood of the LORD is their heritage; 2
Ezr 2:62 were excluded from the priesthood as unclean 2
Neh 7:64 excluded from the priesthood as unclean; 2
13:29 because they have defiled the priesthood 2
29 defiled . . the covenant of the priesthood 2
Lke 1: 9 according to the custom of the priesthood 4
Heb 7:11 attainable through the Levit'ical priesthood 6
12 when there is a change in the priesthood 6
24 he holds his priesthood permanently 6
1Pe 2: 5 like living stones . . be a holy priesthood 5
9 you are a chosen race, a royal priesthood 5
1Es 5:38 the following had assumed the priesthood 6
Sir 45: 7 gave him the priesthood of the people 4
24 have the dignity of the priesthood for ever. 6
1Mc 2:54 the covenant of everlasting priesthood. 6
3:49 also brought the garments of the priesthood 6
2Mc 2:17 the kingship and priesthood and consecration 5
4Mc 4:16 who removed Onias from the priesthood 3
5:35 nor will I reject you, honored priesthood 6
7: 6 O priest, worthy of the priesthood 6

high priesthood 1. ἀρχιερεύς 2. ἀρχιερωσύνη

Lke 3: 2 in the high-priesthood of Annas and Ca'iaphas 1
1Mc 7:21 Alcimus strove for the high priesthood 2
11:27 He confirmed him in the high priesthood 2
57 I confirm you in the high priesthood 2
14:38 Demetrius confirmed him in the high priesthood 2
16:24 in the chronicles of his high priesthood 2
2Mc 4: 7 Jason . . obtained the high priesthood by corruption 2
24 and secured the high priesthood for himself 2
25 possessing no qualification for the high priesthood 2
29 as deputy in the high priesthood 2
11: 3 to put up the high priesthood for sale every year. 2
14: 7 I mean the high priesthood 2
4Mc 4: 1 who then held the high priesthood for life 2

priestly 1. ἱερατικός 2. ἱερεύς

2Mc 3:15 in their priestly garments 1
4Mc 5: 4 He was a man of priestly family, learned in the law 2

priestly *See also* office, service.

high priestly 1. ἀρχιερατικός

Act 4: 6 and all who were of the high-priestly family. 1

prime 1. ἀκμάζω 2. ἀκμαίας

3Mc 4: 8 in the prime of youth 2
4Mc 2: 3 in his prime for intercourse 1

primeval 1. מֵעוֹלָם 2. antiquus

Ezk 26:20 dwell in the nether world, among primeval ruins 1
2Es 7:30 turned back to primeval silence for seven days 2

prince 1. אַדִּיר 2. אִישׁ שַׂר 3. אֵל 4. מִנְזָר 5. נָגִיד 6. נָדִיב 7. נָזִיר 8. נָסִיךְ 9. נָשִׂיא 10. רָזוֹן 11. רזן 12. שַׂר 13. ἄρχων 14. ἀφηγέομαι 15. δυνάστης 16. τύραννος 17. υἱὸς τοῦ βασιλέως 18. princeps

Gen 12:15 when the princes of Pharaoh saw her 12
17:20 he shall be the father of twelve princes 9
23: 6 Hear us, my lord; you are a mighty prince among us. 9
25:16 twelve princes according to their tribes. 9
34: 2 son of Hamor the Hivite, the prince of the land 9
Exd 2:14 Who made you a prince and a judge over us? 2
Num21:18 well which the princes dug, which the nobles 12
22: 8 so the princes of Moab stayed with Balaam. 12
13 Balaam . . said to the princes of Balak 3
14 princes of Moab rose and went to Balak, and said 12
15 Once again Balak sent princes, more in number 12
21 Balaam . . went with the princes of Moab. 12
35 So Balaam went on with the princes of Balak. 12
40 Balak . . sent to Balaam and to the princes 12
23: 6 lo, he and all the princes of Moab were standing 12
17 standing . . and the princes of Moab with him. 12
25:18 Cozbi, the daughter of the prince of Mid'ian 9
Deu 33:16 head of him that is prince among his brothers. 7
Jos 13:21 and Zur and Hur and Reba, the princes of Sihon 8
Jdg 5: 3 Hear, O kings; give ear, O princes; to the LORD I will 11
15 the princes of Is'sachar came with Deb'orah 12
7:25 they took the two princes of Mid'ian, Oreb and Zeeb; 12
8: 3 has given into your hands the princes of Mid'ian 12
1Sm 2: 8 lifts the needy . . to make them sit with princes 6
9:16 anoint him to be prince over my people Israel. 5
10: 1 Has not the LORD anointed you to be prince 13
1 the LORD has anointed you to be prince over his 5
13:14 LORD has appointed him . . prince over his people 5
18:30 Then the princes of the Philistines came out 12
25:30 and has appointed you prince over Israel 5
2Sm 3:38 a prince and a great man has fallen this day 12
5: 2 and you shall be prince over Israel.' 5
6:21 who chose . . to appoint me as prince over Israel 5
7: 8 that you should be prince over my people Israel; 5
10: 3 But the princes of the Ammonites said to Hanun 12
2Kg 20: 5 and say to Hezeki'ah the prince of my people 5
24:12 mother, and his servants, and his princes, and his 12
14 carried away all Jerusalem, and all the princes 12
1Ch 2:10 Nahshon, prince of the sons of Judah. 9
4:38 these . . were princes in their families 9
5: 2 though . . a prince was from him 5
7:40 men of Asher . . chief of the princes. 9
11: 2 you shall be prince over my people Israel 5
12:27 prince Jehoi'ada, of the house of Aaron 5
17: 7 that you should be prince over my people Israel; 5
19: 3 the princes of the Ammonites said to Hanun 12
24: 6 in the presence of the king, and the princes 12
29:22 and they anointed him as prince for the LORD 5
2Ch 6: 5 I chose no man as prince over my people Israel; 5
11:22 Rehobo'am appointed Abi'jah . . as chief prince 5
12: 5 Shemai'ah . . came . . to the princes of Judah 12
6 Then the princes of Israel and the king 12
17: 7 In the third year of his reign he sent his princes 12
21: 4 he slew . . also some of the princes of Israel. 12
22: 8 Jehu . . met the princes of Judah 12
24:10 all the princes and all the people rejoiced 12
17 the princes of Judah came and did obeisance 12
23 destroyed all the princes of the people 12
28:14 before the princes and all the assembly. 12
21 Ahaz took from . . the house . . of the princes 12
29:30 Hezeki'ah the king and the princes commanded 12
30: 2 For the king and his princes and all the assembly 12
6 with letters from the king and his princes 12
12 give them one heart to do what the . . princes 12
24 princes gave the assembly 1,000 bulls and 10,000 12
31: 8 Hezeki'ah and the princes came and saw the heaps 12
32:31 matter of the envoys of the princes of Babylon 12
35: 8 princes contributed willingly to the people 12
36:18 treasures of the king and of his princes 12
Ezr 1: 8 out to Shesh-baz'zar the prince of Judah. 9
Neh 9:32 come upon . . our kings, our princes, our priests 12
34 kings, our princes, our priests, and our fathers 12
38 princes, our Levites, and our priests set 12
12:31 I brought up the princes of Judah upon the wall 12
32 went Hoshai'ah and half of the princes of Judah 12
Est 1: 3 gave a banquet for all his princes and servants 12
11 to show the peoples and the princes her beauty; 12
14 the seven princes of Persia and Media 12
16 said in presence of the king and the princes 12
16 but also to all the princes and all the peoples 12
18 will be telling it to all the king's princes 12
21 This advice pleased the king and the princes 12
2:18 a great banquet to all his princes and servants; 12
3: 1 set his seat above all the princes . . with him. 12
12 and to the princes of all the peoples 12
5:11 advanced him above the princes and the servants 12
6: 9 handed . . to one of the king's most noble princes; 12
8: 9 the governors and the princes of the provinces 12
9: 3 All the princes of the provinces and the satraps 12
Job 3:15 or with princes who had gold 12
12:21 He pours contempt on princes 6
21:28 For you say, 'Where is the house of the prince? 6
29: 9 the princes refrained from talking 12
31:37 like a prince I would approach him. 5
34:19 who shows no partiality to princes 12
Ps 45:16 you will make them princes in all the earth. 12
47: 9 The princes of the peoples gather 6
68:27 princes of Judah in their throng, the princes 12
27 princes of Zeb'ulun, the princes of Naph'tali. 12
27 princes of Zeb'ulun, the princes of Naph'tali. 12
76:12 who cuts off the spirit of princes 5
83:11 all their princes like Zebah and Zalmun'na 8
105:22 to instruct his princes at his pleasure 12
107:40 he pours contempt upon princes 6
113: 8 to make them sit with princes 6
8 make them sit with . . the princes of his people. 6
118: 9 better to . . than to put confidence in princes. 6
119:23 Even though princes sit plotting against me 12
161 Princes persecute me without cause 12
146: 3 Put not your trust in princes, in a son of man 6
148:11 princes and all rulers of the earth! 12
Prv 8:16 by me princes rule, and nobles govern the earth. 12
14:28 but without people a prince is ruined. 10
17: 7 still less is false speech to a prince. 6
19:10 much less for a slave to rule over princes. 12
25: 7 than to be put lower in the presence of the prince. 6
Ecc 10: 7 and princes walking on foot like slaves. 12
16 and your princes feast in the morning! 12
17 and your princes feast at the proper time 12
Sng 6:12 my fancy set me in a chariot beside my prince. 6
Isa 1:23 princes are rebels and companions of thieves. 12
3: 4 make boys their princes, and babes shall rule 12
14 judgment with the . . princes of his people 12
9: 6 Mighty God, Everlasting Father, Prince of Peace. 12
19:11 The princes of Zo'an are utterly foolish; 12
13 The princes of Zo'an have become fools 12
13 and the princes of Memphis are deluded; 12
21: 5 eat, they drink. Arise, O princes, oil the shield! 12
23: 8 Tyre . . whose merchants were princes 12
32: 1 and princes will rule in justice. 12
34:12 and all its princes shall be nothing. 12
40:23 who brings princes to nought 11
43:28 I profaned the princes of the sanctuary 12
49: 7 princes, and they shall prostrate themselves; 12
Jer 1:18 against the kings of Judah, its princes 12
2:26 they, their kings, their princes, their priests 12
4: 9 courage shall fail both king and princes; 12
8: 1 the bones of its princes, the bones of the priests 12
17:25 on horses, they and their princes, the men of Judah 12
24: 1 king of Judah, together with the princes of Judah 12
8 the king of Judah, his princes, the remnant 12
25:18 its kings and princes, to make them a desolation 12
19 Pharoah king of Egypt, his servants, his princes 12
26:10 When the princes of Judah heard these things 12
11 the priests and the prophets said to the princes 12
12 Then Jeremiah spoke to all the princes 12
16 Then the princes and all the people said 12
21 his warriors and all the princes, heard his words 12
29: 2 the eunuchs, the princes of Judah and Jerusalem 12
30:21 Their prince shall be one of themselves 1
32:32 their kings and their princes, their priests 12
34:10 they obeyed, all the princes and all the people 12
19 the princes of Judah, the princes of Jerusalem 12
19 the princes of Judah, the princes of Jerusalem 12
21 And Zedeki'ah king of Judah, and his princes 12
35: 4 which was near the chamber of the princes 12
36:12 and all the princes were sitting there 12
12 Zedeki'ah the son of Hanani'ah, and all the princes. 12
14 all the princes sent Jehu'di the son of Nethani'ah 12
19 Then the princes said to Baruch, "Go and hide 12
21 and Jehu'di read it to the king and all the princes 12
37:14 seized Jeremiah and brought him to the princes. 12
15 And the princes were enraged at Jeremiah 12
38: 4 Then the princes said to the king 12
17 If you will surrender to the princes of the king 12
18 if you do not surrender to the princes of the king 12
22 led out to the princes of the king of Babylon 12
25 If the princes hear that I have spoken with you 12
27 all the princes came to Jeremiah and asked him 12
39: 3 the princes of the king of Babylon came and sat 12
44:17 our kings and our princes, in the cities of Judah 12
21 you and your fathers, your kings and your princes 12
48: 7 into exile, with his priests and his princes. 12
49: 3 into exile, with his priests and his princes. 12
38 and destroy their king and princes, says the LORD. 12
50:35 and upon her princes and her wise men! 12
51:57 I will make drunk her princes and her wise men 12
52:10 and also slew all the princes of Judah at Riblah. 12
Lam 1: 6 Her princes have become like harts 12
2: 9 her king and princes are among the nations; 12
4: 7 Her princes were purer than snow 7
5:12 Princes are hung up by their hands; 12
Ezk 7:27 The king mourns, the prince is wrapped in despair 9
11: 1 I saw among them . . princes of the people. 12
12:10 This oracle concerns the prince in Jerusalem 9
12 prince who is among them shall lift his baggage 9
17:12 to Jerusalem, and took her king and her princes 12
19: 1 take up a lamentation for the princes of Israel 9
21:12 it is against all the princes of Israel; 9
25 you, O unhallowed wicked one, prince of Israel 9
22: 6 Behold, the princes of Israel in you, every one 9
25 Her princes in the midst of her are like a roaring 14
27 Her princes in the midst of her are like wolves 12
26:16 Then all the princes of the sea will step down 9
27:21 the princes of Kedar were your favored dealers 9
28: 2 Son of man, say to the prince of Tyre 5
30:13 shall no longer be a prince in the land of Egypt; 9
32:29 Edom is there, her kings and all her princes 9
30 The princes of the north are there, all of them 8
34:24 my servant David shall be prince among them; 9
37:25 David my servant shall be their prince for ever. 9
38: 2 of Magog, the chief prince of Meshech and Tubal 9
3 O Gog, chief prince of Meshech and Tubal; 9

39: 1 O Gog, chief prince of Meshech and Tubal; 9
18 and drink the blood of the princes of the earth 9
44: 3 Only the prince may sit in it to eat bread 9
45: 7 to the prince shall belong the land on both sides 9
8 my princes shall no more oppress my people; 9
9 Thus says the Lord GOD: Enough, O princes of Israel! 9
16 give this offering to the prince in Israel. 9
17 the prince's duty to furnish the burnt offerings 9
22 On that day the prince shall provide for himself 9
46: 2 prince shall enter by the vestibule of the gate 9
4 offering that the prince offers to the LORD 9
8 When the prince enters, he shall go 9
10 When they go in, the prince shall go in with them; 9
12 When the prince provides a freewill offering 9
16 If the prince makes a gift to any of his sons 9
17 then it shall revert to the prince; 9
18 The prince shall not take any of the inheritance 9
48:21 of the city shall belong to the prince. 9
21 it shall belong to the prince. 9
22 in the midst of that which belongs to the prince. 9
22 The portion of the prince shall lie between 9
Dan 8:11 magnified . . even up to the Prince of the host; 12
25 even rise up against the Prince of princes; 12
25 even rise up against the Prince of princes; 12
9: 6 spoke in thy name to our kings, our princes 12
8 our kings, to our princes, and to our fathers 12
25 to the coming of an anointed one, a prince 5
26 people of the prince who is to come shall destroy 5
10:13 prince of the kingdom of Persia withstood me 12
13 but Michael, one of the chief princes, came to help 12
13 left . . with the prince of the kingdom of Persia *
20 return to fight against the prince of Persia; 12
20 lo, the prince of Greece will come. 12
21 against these except Michael, your prince. 12
11: 5 but one of his princes shall be stronger than he 12
22 broken, and the prince of the covenant also. 5
12: 1 Michael, the great prince who has charge 12
Hos 3: 4 shall dwell many days without king or prince 12
5:10 The princes of Judah have become like those 12
7: 3 and the princes by their treachery. 12
5 On the day of our king the princes became sick 12
16 their princes shall fall by the sword 12
8:10 shall cease . . from anointing king and princes. 12
9:15 all their princes are rebels. 12
13:10 where are all your princes, to defend you– *
10 those of whom you said, "Give me a king and princes"? 12
Ams 1:15 exile, he and his princes together," says the LORD. 12
2: 3 will slay all its princes with him," says the LORD. 12
Mic 5: 5 we will raise against him . . eight princes of men; 8
7: 3 the prince and the judge ask for a bribe 12
Nah 3:17 Your princes are like grasshoppers 4
Mat 9:34 He casts out demons by the prince of demons. 13
12:24 It is only by Be-el'zebul, the prince of demons 13
Mrk 3:22 by the prince of demons he casts out the demons. 13
Lke 11:15 by Be-el'zebul, the prince of demons"; 13
Eph 2: 2 following the prince of the power of the air 13
2Es 9: 3 wavering of leaders, confusion of princes 18
Jdt 5: 2 he called together all the princes of Moab 13
9: 3 thou didst strike down slaves along with princes 15
3 strike down . . princes on their thrones; 15
10 strike down the slave with the prince 13
10 strike down . . the prince with his servant 13
Sir 41:17 Be ashamed . . of a lie, before a prince or a ruler; 15
Bar 1: 4 in the hearing of the mighty men and the princes 17
9 Jeconiah and the princes and the prisoners 13
16 to our kings and our princes and our priests 13
2: 1 against our kings and against our princes 13
3:16 Where are the princes of the nations, and those 13
Aza 1:15 at this time there is no prince, or prophet 13
1Mc 1: 4 and ruled over countries, nations, and princes 16
7:26 the king sent Nicanor, one of his honored princes 13
2Mc 9:25 the princes along the borders 15

prince *See also* make, set.

royal prince 1. בֶּן מֶלֶךְ
2Kg 10:13 and we came down to visit the royal princes 1

princess 1. בַּת מֶלֶךְ 2. שָׂרָה
1Kg 11: 3 He had 700 wives, princesses 2
Ps 45:13 The princess is decked in her chamber 1
Jer 43: 6 the men, the women, the children, the princesses 1
Lam 1: 1 She that was a princess . . has become a vassal. 2

principal 1. συνέχω
2Mc 10:10 the principal calamities of the wars. 1

principal man 1. ἡγέομαι 2. προηγέομαι 3. προκάθημαι 4. πρῶτος
Lke 19:47 scribes and the principal men of the people 4
Act 25: 2 the chief priests and the principal men of the Jews 4
1Es 1:32 the principal men, with the women 3
8:28 These are the principal men 2
68 the principal men came to me and said 1

principality 1. ἀρχή
Rom 8:38 nor principalities, nor things present 1
Eph 3:10 the principalities and powers 1
6:12 against the principalities, against the powers 1
Col 1:16 thrones or dominions or principalities 1
2:15 He disarmed the principalities and powers 1

principle 1. δικαίωμα 2. λογισμός 3. νόμος 4. στοιχεῖον
Rom 3:27 On what principle? On the principle of works? 3
27 On what principle? On the principle of works? *
27 No, but on the principle of faith. 3
Heb 5:12 teach you . . the first principles of God's word. 4
4Mc 5:38 you shall not dominate my religious principles 2
11:15 we ought likewise to die for the same principles. *
18: 6 expressed also these principles to her children 1

main principle 1. ὑπόθεσις
4Mc 1:12 I shall begin by stating my main principle 1

print 1. τύπος
Joh 20:25 Unless I see in his hands the print of the nails 1

prior 1. προγίνομαι
Wis 19:13 not come upon the sinners without prior signs 1

prison 1. בֵּית אֱסוּרִים 2. בֵּית כֶּלֶא 3. בֵּית כְּלוּא 4. בֵּית מִשְׁמַר 5. בֵּית סֹהַר 6. בֵּית פְּקֻדּוֹת 7. כֶּלֶא 8. מַסְגֵּר 9. מִשְׁמָר 10. δέσμιος 11. δεσμός 12. δεσμωτήριον 13. δέω 14. εἱρκτή 15. συνδέω 16. τηρέω 17. φυλακή
Gen 39:20 master took him and put him into the prison 5
20 were confined, and he was there in prison. 5
21 favor in the sight of the keeper of the prison. 5
22 the keeper of the prison committed to Joseph's 5
22 care all the prisoners who were in the prison; 5
23 the keeper of the prison paid no heed to anything 5
40: 3 put them . . in the prison where Joseph was 5
5 who were confined in the prison–each his own 5
42:17 put them all together in prison for three days. 9
19 remain confined in your prison, and let the rest 4
Jdg 16:21 fetters; and he ground at the mill in the prison. 1
25 they called Samson out of the prison 1
1Kg 22:27 Put this fellow in prison, and feed him 2
2Kg 17: 4 the king . . shut him up, and bound him in prison. 2
25:27 freed Jehoi'achin king of Judah from prison; 2
29 So Jehoi'achin put off his prison garments. 7
2Ch 16:10 put him in the stocks, in prison, for he was in a rage 17
18:26 say, 'Thus says the king, Put this fellow in prison 2
Ps 142: 7 Bring me out of prison, that I may give thanks 8
Ecc 4:14 even though he had gone from prison to the throne 1
Isa 24:22 they will be shut up in a prison 8
42: 7 from the prison those who sit in darkness. 2
22 trapped in holes and hidden in prisons; 2
61: 1 the opening of the prison to those who are bound; *
Jer 37: 4 for he had not yet been put in prison. 3
15 for it had been made a prison. 2
18 that you have put me in prison? 2
52:11 and put him in prison till the day of his death. 6
31 and brought him out of prison; 3
33 Jehoi'achin put off his prison garments. 7
Mat 5:25 the judge to the guard, and you be put in prison; 17
11: 2 when John heard in prison about the deeds 13
14: 3 bound him and put him in prison 17
10 he sent and had John beheaded in the prison 17
18:30 He refused and went and put him in prison 17
25:36 I was in prison and you came to me.' 17
39 did we see thee sick or in prison and visit thee?' 17
43 sick and in prison and you did not visit me.' 17
44 a stranger or naked or sick or in prison 17
Mrk 6:17 bound him in prison for the sake of Hero'di-as 17
27 He went and beheaded him in the prison 17
15: 7 among the rebels in prison 13
Lke 3:20 he shut up John in prison. 17
12:58 the officer put you in prison. 17
21:12 delivering you up to the synagogues and prisons 17
22:33 I am ready to go with you to prison and to death. 17
23:19 a man who had been thrown into prison 17
25 the man who had been thrown into prison 17
Joh 3:24 For John had not yet been put in prison. 17
Act 5:18 put them in the common prison. 16
19 an angel of the Lord opened the prison doors 17
21 sent to the prison to have them brought. 12
22 they did not find them in the prison 17
23 We found the prison securely locked 12
25 The men whom you put in prison 17
8: 3 committed them to prison. 17
12: 4 when he had seized him, he put him in prison 17
5 So Peter was kept in prison 17
6 sentries . . were guarding the prison; 17
17 how the Lord had brought him out of the prison 17
16:23 they threw them into prison 17
24 he put them into the inner prison 17
26 the foundations of the prison were shaken 12
27 woke and saw that the prison doors were open 17
37 have thrown us into prison 17
40 So they went out of the prison, and visited Lydia; 17
22: 4 delivering to prison both men and women 17
24:27 Felix left Paul in prison. 13
26:10 I not only shut up many of the saints in prison 17
Col 4: 3 on account of which I am in prison 13
Heb 13: 3 Remember those who are in prison 10
3 as though in prison with them 15
1Pe 3:19 he went and preached to the spirits in prison 17
Rev 2:10 devil is about to throw some of you into prison 17
20: 7 Satan will be loosed from his prison 17
Wis 10:14 when he was in prison she did not leave him 11
17:16 thus was kept shut up in a prison not made of iron; 14
4Mc 18:11 Joseph in prison. 17

prison *See also* put, remain.

prisoner 1. אַסִּיר 2. אָסִיר 3. אסר 4. δέσμιος 5. δεσμώτης 6. πεδήτης
Gen 39:20 the prison, the place where the king's prisoners 3
22 to Joseph's care all the prisoners who were 2
2Kg 24:12 The king of Babylon took him prisoner *
Job 3:18 There the prisoners are at ease together; 2
Ps 68: 6 God . . leads out the prisoners to prosperity; 2
79:11 Let the groans of the prisoners come before thee; 2
102:20 to hear the groans of the prisoners 2
107:10 prisoners in affliction and in irons 2
146: 7 The LORD sets the prisoners free; 3
Isa 10: 4 Nothing . . but to crouch among the prisoners 1
14:17 who did not let his prisoners go home?' 2
24:22 They will be gathered . . as prisoners in a pit; 1
42: 7 to bring out the prisoners from the dungeon 1
49: 9 saying to the prisoners, 'Come forth,' 3
Lam 3:34 To crush . . all the prisoners of the earth 2
Zec 9:12 Return to your stronghold, O prisoners of hope; 2
Mat 27:15 for the crowd any one prisoner whom they wanted. 4
16 they had then a notorious prisoner 4
Mrk 15: 6 he used to release for them one prisoner 4
Act 16:25 the prisoners were listening to them 4
27 supposing that the prisoners had escaped. 4
23:18 Paul the prisoner called me 4
25:14 There is a man left prisoner by Felix; 4
27 seems to me unreasonable, in sending a prisoner 4
27: 1 Paul and some other prisoners 5
42 The soldiers' plan was to kill the prisoners 5
28:17 yet I was delivered prisoner from Jerusalem 4
Eph 3: 1 Paul, a prisoner for Christ Jesus on behalf of you 4
4: 1 I therefore, a prisoner for the Lord, beg you 4
2Ti 1: 8 nor of me his prisoner 4
Phm 1: 1 Paul, a prisoner for Christ Jesus 4
9 I, Paul, an ambassador and now a prisoner also 4
Heb 10:34 For you had compassion on the prisoners 4
Wis 17: 2 prisoners of long night 6
Bar 1: 9 Jeconiah and the princes and the prisoners 5
2Mc 14:27 to send . . to Antioch as a prisoner without delay. 4
33 If you do not hand Judas over to me as a prisoner 4

fellow prisoner 1. συναιχμάλωτος
Rom 16: 7 my kinsmen and my fellow prisoners; 1
Col 4:10 Aristar'chus my fellow prisoner greets you 1
Phm 1:23 Ep'aphras, my fellow prisoner in Christ Jesus 1

private 1. לָט 2. ἰδιωτικός 3. κατ' ἰδίαν 4. κρυπτός
1Sm 18:22 Speak to David in private and say, 'Behold, the king 1
Joh 7:10 he also went up, not publicly but in private. 4
2Mc 4: 5 the welfare, both public and private, of all the people 3
9:26 the public and private services rendered to you 3
4Mc 4: 3 there are deposited tens of thousands in private funds 2
6 to seize the private funds in the treasury. 2

private *See also* room.

private part 1. מְבֻשׁ
Deu 25:11 out her hand and seizes him by the private parts 1

privately 1. בַּשְׁלִי 2. καθ' ἑαυτόν 3. κατ' ἰδίαν 4. κρυπτῶς 5. μυστικός
2Sm 3:27 took him aside . . to speak with him privately 1
Mat 17:19 Then the disciples came to Jesus privately 3
24: 3 the disciples came to him privately, saying 3
Mrk 4:34 privately to his own disciples he explained 3
7:33 taking him aside from the multitude privately 3
9:28 his disciples asked him privately 3
13: 3 James and John and Andrew asked him privately 3
Lke 10:23 Then turning to the disciples he said privately 3
Act 23:19 going aside asked him privately, "What is it 3
Gal 2: 2 privately before those who were of repute 3
Tob 12: 6 the angel called the two of them privately 4
2Mc 6:21 privately urged him 3
13:13 After consulting privately with the elders 2
3Mc 3:10 some . . had taken some of them aside privately 5

prize 1. ἆθλον 2. βραβεῖον 3. γέρας 4. καύχημα 5. νῖκος
1Co 9:24 only one receives the prize 2
Php 3:14 I press on toward the goal for the prize 2
Wis 2:22 nor discern the prize for blameless souls; 3
4: 2 in the contest for prizes that are undefiled. 1
Sir 45:12 a distinction to be prized, the work of an expert 4
2Mc 4:15 disdaining the honors prized by their fathers *
4Mc 9: 8 shall have the prize of virtue 1
17:12 The prize was immortality in endless life. 5

prize *See also* carry.

prize highly 1. סלל
Prv 4: 8 Prize her highly, and she will exalt you; 1

prize of war 1. שָׁלָל
Jer 21: 9 and shall have his life as a prize of war. 1
38: 2 he shall have his life as a prize of war, and live. 1
39:18 you shall have your life as a prize of war 1
45: 5 but I will give you your life as a prize of war 1

prized *See* belongings.

probably 1. fortassis
2Es 7:140 there would probably be left only very few 1

problem 1. קְטַר (A) 2. similitudo
Dan 5:12 explain riddles, and solve problems were found 1
16 can give interpretations and solve problems. 1
2Es 4: 3 and to put before you three problems. 2

procedure 1. דָּבָר 2. מִשְׁפָּט
1Ch 24:19 according to the procedure established 2
Est 1:13 this was the king's procedure toward all who 1

proceed 1. יצא 2. מוֹצָא 3. יסף 4. עשׂה 5. ἐκπορεύομαι 6. ἐξέρχομαι 7. καταντάω 8. πορεύω 9. προστίθημι 10. proficio
Gen 41:34 Let Pharaoh proceed to appoint overseers over 4
Num30: 2 according to all that proceeds out of his mouth. 1
Deu 8: 3 everything that proceeds out of the mouth 2
Ecc 10: 5 an evil . . an error proceeding from the ruler: 1
Isa 57:16 for from me proceeds the spirit 3
Jer 9: 3 for they proceed from evil to evil 1
Hab 1: 7 justice and dignity proceed from themselves. 1
Mat 4: 4 by every word that proceeds from the mouth 5
15:18 comes out of the mouth proceeds from the heart 6
Lke 19:11 he proceeded to tell a parable 9
Joh 8:42 I proceeded and came forth from God 6
15:26 who proceeds from the Father 5
Act 12: 3 he proceeded to arrest Peter also 9
Rom14:23 for whatever does not proceed from faith is sin. •
2Es 14:37 we proceeded to the field, and remained there. 10
Tob 6: 1 Now as they proceeded on their way 8
Jdt 11:15 and they proceed to do this •
2Mc 4:21 arriving at Joppa he proceeded to Jerusalem. 7
3Mc 5: 4 Hermon . . proceeded faithfully to carry out the orders. •
4Mc 4: 5 he proceeded quickly to our country •

proceed against 1. μετέρχομαι
1Mc 15: 4 so that I may proceed against those 1

proceed further 1. יסף
Job 40: 5 twice, but I will proceed no further. 1

proceed out 1. יצא 2. מוֹצָא 3. ἐκπορεύομαι
Num30:12 then whatever proceeds out of her lips 2
Deu 8: 3 that proceeds out of the mouth of the LORD. 1
Lke 4:22 the gracious words which proceeded out of his mouth; 3

proceedings 1. χορηγία
1Es 2:29 that such wicked proceedings go no further •
2Mc 4:14 to take part in the unlawful proceedings 1

proceeds 1. τιμή
Act 4:34 brought the proceeds of what was sold 1
5: 2 he kept back some of the proceeds 1
3 to keep back part of the proceeds of the land? 1
Tob 1: 7 and spend the proceeds each year at Jerusalem; •

process
1Es 6:20 although it has been in process of construction •

procession 1. הֲלִיכָה 2. תַּהֲלוּכָה
Neh 12:31 two great companies which . . went in procession. 2
Ps 68:24 processions of my God, my King, into the sanctuary- 1
Isa 60:11 the nations, with their kings led in procession. •

procession *See also* lead, walk.

festal procession 1. חַג
Ps 118:27 Bind the festal procession with branches 1

solemn procession 1. הֲלִיכָה
Ps 68:24 Thy solemn processions are seen, O God 1

tumultuous procession 1. θροῦς
1Mc 9:39 and saw a tumultuous procession with much baggage; 1

proclaim 1. אמר 2. בשׂר 3. זכר 4. ידע 5. נגד 6. עבר 7. עבר קוֹל 8. קרא 9. שׁמע 10. קרא (A) 11. ἀναγγέλλω 12. ἀνακηρύσσω 13. ἀπαγγέλλω 14. ἀποδείκνυμι 15. γίνομαι 16. γνωρίζω 17. διαγγέλλω 18. διηγέομαι 19. ἐξαγγέλλω 20. εὐαγγελίζω 21. εὔχομαι 22. καταγγέλλω 23. κηρύσσω 24. κράζω 25. praedico
Exd 33:19 will proclaim before you my name 'The LORD'; 8
34: 5 the LORD . . proclaimed the name of the LORD. 8
6 The LORD passed before him, and proclaimed 8
36: 6 word was proclaimed throughout the camp 6
Lev 23: 2 feasts . . which you shall proclaim as holy 8
4 feasts . . which you shall proclaim at the time 8
24 a memorial proclaimed with blast of trumpets •
37 appointed feasts . . which you shall proclaim 8
25:10 proclaim liberty throughout the land to all 8
Deu 15: 2 because the LORD'S release has been proclaimed 8
32: 3 For I will proclaim the name of the LORD. 8
Jdg 7: 3 proclaim in the ears of the people, saying 8
21:13 sent word . . and proclaimed peace to them. 8
1Kg 21: 9 Proclaim a fast, and set Naboth on high 8
12 they proclaimed a fast 8
2Kg 9:13 blew the trumpet, and proclaimed, "Jehu is king. 1
10:20 Jehu ordered, "Sanctify . . " So they proclaimed it. 8
23:16 word of the LORD which the man of God proclaimed 8
2Ch 20: 3 Jehosh'aphat . . proclaimed a fast 8
Ezr 8:21 Then I proclaimed a fast there, at the river Aha'va 8
Neh 6: 7 set up prophets to proclaim concerning you 8
8:15 publish and proclaim in all their towns 7
Est 1:20 the decree . . is proclaimed throughout all his 9
2: 8 when the king's order and his edict were proclaimed 9
6: 9 conduct the man . . proclaiming before him 8
11 and made him ride through . . proclaiming 8
Ps 19: 1 the firmament proclaims his handiwork. 5
22:31 proclaim his deliverance to a people yet unborn 5
40: 5 Were I to proclaim and tell of them 5
52: 9 I will proclaim thy name, for it is good •
71:17 I still proclaim thy wondrous deeds. 5
18 till I proclaim thy might to all the generations 5
89: 1 proclaim thy faithfulness to all generations. 4
97: 6 The heavens proclaim his righteousness; 5
145: 6 Men . . proclaim the might of thy terrible acts 1
Prv 12:23 but fools proclaim their folly. 8
20: 6 Many a man proclaims his own loyalty 8
Isa 3: 9 they proclaim their sin like Sodom 5
12: 4 make known . . proclaim that his name is exalted. 3
41:26 none who proclaimed, none who heard your words. 9
43:12 I declared and saved and proclaimed 9
44: 7 Who is like me? Let him proclaim it 8
48:20 with a shout of joy, proclaim it, send it forth 9
60: 6 and shall proclaim the praise of the LORD. 2
61: 1 to proclaim liberty to the captives 8
2 to proclaim the year of the LORD'S favor 8
62:11 the LORD has proclaimed to the end of the earth 9
Jer 2: 2 Go and proclaim in the hearing of Jerusalem 8
3:12 Go, and proclaim these words toward the north 8
4: 5 Declare in Judah, and proclaim in Jerusalem 9
15 from Dan and proclaims evil from Mount E'phraim. 9
5:20 in the house of Jacob, proclaim it in Judah 9
7: 2 and proclaim there this word, and say 8
11: 6 Proclaim all these words in the cities of Judah 8
19: 2 and proclaim there the words that I tell you. 8
23:22 then they would have proclaimed my words 9
31: 7 proclaim, give praise, and say, 'The LORD has saved 9
34:15 by proclaiming liberty, each to his neighbor 8
17 You have not obeyed me by proclaiming liberty 8
17 behold, I proclaim to you liberty to the sword 8
36: 9 Jerusalem proclaimed a fast before the LORD. 8
46:14 Declare in Egypt, and proclaim in Migdol; 9
14 proclaim in Memphis and Tah'panhes; 9
50: 2 Declare among the nations and proclaim 9
2 set up a banner and proclaim, conceal it not 9
Dan 3: 4 herald proclaimed aloud, "You are commanded 10
Jol 3: 9 Proclaim this among the nations: Prepare war 8
Ams 3: 9 Proclaim to the strongholds in Assyria 9
4: 5 and proclaim freewill offerings, publish them; 8
Jon 3: 2 proclaim to it the message that I tell you. 8
5 they proclaimed a fast, and put on sackcloth 8
Nah 1:15 who brings good tidings, who proclaims peace! 9
Zec 7: 7 the LORD proclaimed by the former prophets? 8
Mat 10:27 proclaim upon the housetops. 23
12:18 he shall proclaim justice to the Gentiles. 13
Mrk 5:20 began to proclaim in the Decap'olis 23
7:36 the more zealously they proclaimed it. 23
Lke 4:18 has sent me to proclaim release to the captives 23
19 to proclaim the acceptable year of the Lord. 23
8:39 proclaiming throughout the whole city 23
9:60 as for you, go and proclaim the kingdom of God.". 17
12: 3 shall be proclaimed upon the housetops. 23
Joh 7:28 Jesus proclaimed, as he taught in the temple 24
37 Jesus stood up and proclaimed, "If any one thirst 24
Act 3:24 also proclaimed these days. 22
4: 2 proclaiming in Jesus the resurrection 22
8: 5 proclaimed to them the Christ. 23
9:20 immediately he proclaimed Jesus, saying 23
10:37 word which was proclaimed throughout all Judea 15
13: 5 proclaimed the word of God in the synagogues 22
38 forgiveness of sins is proclaimed to you 22
15:36 in every city where we proclaimed the word 22
16:17 who proclaim to you the way of salvation. 22
17: 3 This Jesus, whom I proclaim to you, is the Christ. 22
13 the word of God was proclaimed by Paul at Beroe'a 22
23 this I proclaim to you. 22
26:23 he would proclaim light . . to the people 22
Rom 1: 8 your faith is proclaimed in all the world. 22
9:17 so that my name may be proclaimed in all the earth 17
1Co 2: 1 I did not come proclaiming to you 22
9:14 those who proclaim the gospel 22
11:26 you proclaim the Lord's death until he comes. 22
Eph 6:19 to proclaim the mystery of the gospel 16
Php 1:17 the former proclaim Christ out of partisanship 22
18 Christ is proclaimed; and in that I rejoice 22
Col 1:28 Him we proclaim 22
2Th 2: 4 proclaiming himself to be God. 14
Heb 2:12 saying, "I will proclaim thy name to my brethren 13
1Jn 1: 2 and proclaim to you the eternal life 13
3 we proclaim also to you 13
5 heard from him and proclaim to you 11
Rev 5: 2 a strong angel proclaiming with a loud voice 23
14: 6 another angel . . with an eternal gospel to proclaim 20
1Es 8:50 There I proclaimed a fast for the young men 21
2Es 2:32 and proclaim mercy to them 25
Sir 17:10 to proclaim the grandeur of his works. 18
18: 4 To none has he given power to proclaim his works; 19
39:10 the congregation will proclaim his praise; 19
44: 3 proclaiming prophecies; 13
15 the congregation proclaims their praise. 19
1Mc 10:63 proclaim that no one is to bring charges 23
14:28 the following was proclaimed to us 16
2Mc 8:36 proclaimed that the Jews had a Defender 22
9:17 to proclaim the power of God. 22
4Mc 17:23 proclaimed them to his soldiers as an example 12

proclaim fully 1. πληροφορέω
2Ti 4:17 gave me strength to proclaim the message fully 1

proclaim king 1. מלך
2Kg 11:12 and they proclaimed him king, and anointed him; 1
2Ch 23:11 they proclaimed him king 1

proclamation 1. גלה 2. קוֹל 3. κήρυγμα 4. κηρύσσω
2Ch 24: 9 proclamation was made throughout Judah 2
30: 5 to make a proclamation throughout all Israel 2
Ezr 10: 7 proclamation was made throughout Judah 2
Est 3:14 be issued . . in every province by proclamation 1
8:13 in every province, and by proclamation to all 1
1Es 9: 3 a proclamation was made throughout Judea 3
1Mc 10:64 in accordance with the proclamation 4

proclamation *See also* make.

proconsul 1. ἀνθύπατος
Act 13: 7 He was with the Proconsul, Sergius Paulus 1
8 to turn away the proconsul from the faith. 1
12 Then the proconsul believed 1
18:12 when Gallio was proconsul of Acha'ia 1
19:38 there are proconsuls 1

procure 1. λαμβάνω
2Ch 11:23 procured wives for them. •
Joh 18: 3 Judas, procuring a band of soldiers 1

produce 1. יְבוּל 2. יצא 3. מַעֲשֶׂה 4. עֲבוּר 5. עשׂה 6. פְּרִי 7. תְּבוּאָה 8. תְּנוּבָה 9. γένεσις 10. γένημα 11. γίνομαι 12. ἐργάζομαι 13. καρποφορέω 14. κατεργάζομαι 15. ποιέω 16. προφέρω 17. creo 18. do 19. facio 20. fio 21. genero 22. multiplico
Gen 41:34 and take the fifth part of the produce of the land •
Lev 23:39 when you have gathered in the produce of the land 7
25:22 you will be eating old produce; until the ninth 7
22 until the ninth year, when its produce comes 7
Num 6: 4 eat nothing that is produced by the grapevine 5
18:30 reckoned . . as produce of the threshing floor 7
30 reckoned . . as produce of the wine press; 7
Deu 14:28 bring forth all the tithe of your produce 7
16:15 LORD . . will bless you in all your produce 7
26:12 paying . . tithe of your produce in the third year 7
32:13 he ate the produce of the field; 8
Jos 5:11 they ate of the produce of the land 4
12 when they ate of the produce of the land; 4
Jdg 6: 4 they would . . destroy the produce of the land 1
2Sm 9:10 till the land . . and shall bring in the produce •
2Kg 8: 6 Restore . . all the produce of the fields 7
1Ch 27:27 over the produce of the vineyards for the wine •
2Ch 31: 5 first fruits . . of all the produce of the field; 7
Prv 3: 9 first fruits of all your produce; 7
30:33 For pressing milk produces curds 2
33 pressing the nose produces blood 2
33 pressing anger produces strife. 2
Isa 30:23 the produce of the ground, which will be rich 7
54:16 of coals, and produces a weapon for its purpose. 2
Jer 29: 5 plant gardens and eat their produce. 6
28 and plant gardens and eat their produce. 6
Ezk 48:18 Its produce shall be food for the workers 7
Hab 3:17 Though . . the produce of the olive fail 3
Hag 1:10 the earth has withheld its produce. 1
Mat 21:43 given to a nation producing the fruits of it. 15
Mrk 4:28 The earth produces of itself, first the blade 13
Lke 6:45 The good man . . produces good 16
45 the evil man out of his evil treasure produces evil; 16
Rom 5: 3 knowing that suffering produces endurance 14
4 and endurance produces character •
4 and character produces hope •
2Co 7:10 For godly grief produces a repentance 12
10 worldly grief produces death. 14
11 what earnestness this godly grief has produced 14
9:11 which through us will produce thanksgiving 14
1Ti 6: 4 disputes about words, which produce envy 11
Jas 1: 3 testing of your faith produces steadfastness. 14
2Es 3:12 they produced children and peoples 22
4:30 how much ungodliness it has produced until now 21

30 and will produce until the time of threshing 21
31 a grain of evil seed has produced. 21
5:46 Request it therefore to produce ten at one time. 18
6:48 lifeless water produced living creatures 19
7:55 Say to her, 'You produce gold and silver and brass 17
116better if the earth had not produced Adam, or else 18
116or else, when it had produced him 18
8: 6 so that fruit may be produced 20
Tob 1: 6 Taking the first fruits and the tithes of my produce 10
7 Of all my produce I would give a tenth 10
5:13 offered . . the tithes of our produce 10
Wis 19:10 instead of producing animals the earth brought forth 9
Sir 1:17 their storehouses with her produce. 10
6:19 soon you will eat of her produce. 10
24:19 eat your fill of my produce. 10

produce blossoms 1. צוץ
Num17: 8 rod of Aaron . . produced blossoms, and it bore 1

fine produce 1. ראשׁ
Deu 33:15 with the finest produce of the ancient mountains 1

product 1. מַעֲשֶׂה 2. ἔργον 3. καρπός 4. creatio
Hag 2:17 I smote you and all the products of your toil 1
2Es 9:17 as is the work, so is the product 4
Tob 2:12 She used to send the product to the owners •
Sir 11: 3 her product is the best of sweet things. 3
14:19 Every product decays and ceases to exist 2

production 1. γένεσις
Wis 16:26 it is not the production of crops that feeds man 1

profanation 1. βεβήλωσις
Jdt 4: 3 had been consecrated after their profanation. 1
3Mc 1:29 the profanation of the place. 1
2:17 or call us to account for this profanation 1

profane 1. חלל 2. חנף 3. נכר 4. תפשׂ 5. ἀνόσιος 6. βέβηλος 7. βεβηλόω 8. βεβήλωσις 9. κοινὸν ἡγέομαι 10. μιαροφαγία 11. profano
Exd 20:25 for if you wield your tool upon it you profane it. 1
31:14 every one who profanes it shall be put to death; 1
Lev 18:21 fire to Molech, and so profane the name of your God 1
19: 8 because he has profaned a holy thing of the LORD 1
12 and so profane the name of your God: I am the LORD 1
29 Do not profane your daughter 1
20: 3 defiling my sanctuary and profaning my holy name 1
21: 4 defile himself . . and so profane himself 1
6 shall . . not profane the name of their God 1
9 if she profanes herself by playing the harlot 1
9 profanes her father; she shall be burned 1
12 nor profane the sanctuary of his God 1
15 that he may not profane his children 1
23 that he may not profane my sanctuaries 1
22: 2 may not profane my holy name: I am the LORD 1
9 lest they . . die thereby when they profane it 1
15 The priests shall not profane the holy things 1
32 you shall not profane my holy name 1
Num18:32 shall not profane the holy things of . . Israel 1
Neh 13:17 evil thing . . profaning the sabbath day? 1
18 wrath upon Israel by profaning the sabbath. 1
Prv 30: 9 I be poor, and steal, and profane the name of my God. 4
Isa 43:28 I profaned the princes of the sanctuary 1
47: 6 was angry with my people, I profaned my heritage; 1
48:11 I do it, for how should my name be profaned? 1
56: 2 who keeps the sabbath, not profaning it 1
6 one who keeps the sabbath, and does not profane it 1
Jer 19: 4 and have profaned this place by burning incense 3
34:16 but then you turned around and profaned my name 1
Ezk 7:21 for a spoil; and they shall profane it. 1
22 that they may profane my precious place; 1
22 robbers shall enter and profane it 1
24 their holy places shall be profaned. 1
13:19 You have profaned me among my people 1
20: 9 the sake of my name, that it should not be profaned 1
13 and my sabbaths they greatly profaned. 1
14 not be profaned in the sight of the nations 1
16 not walk in my statutes, and profaned my sabbaths; 1
21 they profaned my sabbaths. 1
22 the sake of my name, that it should not be profaned 1
24 rejected my statutes and profaned my sabbaths 1
39 but my holy name you shall no more profane 1
22: 8 my holy things, and profaned my sabbaths. 1
16 I shall be profaned through you 1
26 and have profaned my holy things; 1
26 so that I am profaned among them. 1
23:38 on the same day and profaned my sabbaths. 1
39 they came into my sanctuary to profane it. 1
24:21 Behold, I will profane my sanctuary 1
25: 3 said, 'Aha!' over my sanctuary when it was profaned 1
28:16 I cast you as a profane thing from the mountain 1
18 you profaned your sanctuaries; 1
36:20 whereever they came, they profaned my holy name 1
22 name, which you have profaned among the nations 1
23 name, which has been profaned among the nations 1
23 and which you have profaned among them; 1
39: 7 I will not let my holy name be profaned any more; 1
44: 7 to be in my sanctuary, profaning it, when you offer 1
Dan 11:31 appear and profane the temple and fortress 1
Ams 2: 7 the same maiden, so that my holy name is profaned; 1
Mic 4:11 saying, "Let her be profaned 2
Zep 3: 4 her priests profane what is sacred 1
Mal 1:12 you profane it when you say that the LORD'S table 1
2:10 profaning the covenant of our fathers? 1
11 Judah has profaned the sanctuary of the LORD 1
Mat 12: 5 priests in the temple profane the sabbath 7
Act 24: 6 He even tried to profane the temple 7
1Co 11:27 be guilty of profaning the body and blood of the Lord. •
1Ti 1: 9 for the unholy and profane 6
Heb 10:29 profaned the blood of the covenant 9
2Es 10:22 the name by which we are called has been profaned; 11
Jdt 4:12 the sanctuary to be profaned and desecrated 8
1Mc 1:43 sacrificed to idols and profaned the sabbath. 7
45 to profane sabbaths and feasts 7
48 abominable by everything unclean and profane 8
63 to profane the holy covenant 7
2:12 the Gentiles have profaned it. 7
34 so profane the sabbath day. 7
3:51 Thy sanctuary is trampled down and profaned 7
4:38 the sanctuary desolate, the altar profaned 7
44 which had been profaned. 7
54 on the very day that the Gentiles had profaned it 7
2Mc 5:16 swept away with profane hands the votive offerings 6
8: 2 which had been profaned by ungodly men 7
10: 5 had been profaned by the foreigners 7
4Mc 7: 6 nor profaned your stomach 10
12:11 profane tyrant, most impious of all the wicked 5

cause to profane 1. חלל
Ezk 36:21 which the house of Israel caused to be profaned 1

profane man 1. βέβηλος 2. βεβηλόω 3. δύσφημος
2Mc 15:32 He showed them . . that profane man's arm 3
3Mc 2: 2 an impious and profane man 2
14 this audacious and profane man 1

profane thing 1. חלל
Ezk 28:16 I cast you as a profane thing from the mountain 1

profanely 1. ἀνοσίως
3Mc 1:21 because of what the king was profanely plotting. 1

profaner 1. βέβηλος
3Mc 7:15 since they had destroyed the profaners. 1

profess 1. ἐπαγγέλλομαι 2. ὁμολογέω
1Ti 2:10 as befits women who profess religion. 1
6:21 by professing it some have missed the mark 1
Tit 1:16 They profess to know God 2
Wis 2:13 He professes to have knowledge of God 1

proficiency 1. ἕξις
Sir 0: 1 acquiring considerable proficiency in them, 1

profit 1. בֶּצַע 2. חַיִל 3. יעל 4. מוֹתָר 5. מַרְבִּית 6. סכן 7. שׁוה 8. תְּבוּאָה 9. διάφορος 10. λυσιτελέω 11. ὀνίνημι 12. ὄφελος 13. ὠφέλεια 14. ὠφελέω 15. fructus 16. prosum
Gen 37:26 What profit is it if we slay our brother 1
Lev 25:37 nor give him your food for profit 5
1Sm 12:21 after vain things which cannot profit or save 3
Est 3: 8 is not for the king's profit to tolerate them. 7
Job 20:18 from the profit of his trading he will get 2
34: 9 For he has said, 'It profits a man nothing 6
Ps 30: 9 What profit is there in my death 1
Prv 3:14 its profit better than gold. 8
10: 2 Treasures gained by wickedness do not profit 3
11: 4 Riches do not profit in the day of wrath 3
14:23 In all toil there is profit 4
Isa 30: 5 shame through a people that cannot profit them 3
5 that brings neither help nor profit 3
6 to a people that cannot profit them. 3
44: 9 and the things they delight in do not profit; 3
48:17 I am the LORD your God, who teaches you to profit 3
Jer 2: 8 and went after things that do not profit. 3
11 changed . . glory for that which does not profit. 3
12:13 have tired themselves out but profit nothing. 3
16:19 worthless things in which there is no profit. 3
23:32 so they do not profit this people at all 3
Ezk 13:18 and keep other souls alive for your profit? •
Hab 2:18 What profit is an idol when its maker has shaped 3
Mat 16:26 For what will it profit a man 14
Mrk 8:36 what does it profit a man, to gain the whole world 14
Lke 9:25 what does it profit a man if he gains the whole world 14
Jas 2:14 What does it profit, my brethren 12
16 what does it profit? 12
2Es 7:67 For what does it profit us 16
16:42 be like one who will not make a profit 15
Wis 5: 8 What has our arrogance profited us? 14
6:25 you will profit. 14
Sir 20:10 There is a gift that profits you nothing 10
14 A fool's gift will profit you nothing 10
29:11 it will profit you more than gold. 10
30: 2 He who disciplines his son will profit by him 11
23 there is no profit in it. 13
42: 5 of profit from dealing with merchants 9
2Mc 2:25 to profit all readers. 13

profit *See also* get, hold.

profitable 1. טוֹב 2. יעל 3. סכן 4. συμφέρω 5. χρήσιμος 6. ὠφέλιμος
Job 22: 2 Can a man be profitable to God? 3
2 Surely he who is wise is profitable to himself. 3
Prv 31:18 perceives that her merchandise is profitable. 1
Isa 44:10 casts an image, that is profitable for nothing? 2
Act 20:20 declaring to you anything that was profitable 4
2Ti 3:16 inspired by God and profitable for teaching 6
Tit 3: 8 these are excellent and profitable to men. 6
Sir 7:22 if they are profitable to you, keep them. 5

more profitable 1. χρήσιμος
Wis 8: 7 nothing in life is more profitable for men 1

profitless 1. ἀνόνητος
4Mc 16: 7 seven profitless pregnancies 1

profligacy 1. ἀσωτία
1Pe 4: 4 do not now join them in the same wild profligacy 1

profligate 1. ἀκρατής 2. ἀσωτία
2Ti 3: 3 inhuman, implacable, slanderers, profligates 1
Tit 1: 6 not open to the charge of being profligate 2

profound 1. βαθύς 2. μέγας 3. magnus 4. multus
Eph 5:32 This mystery is a profound one 2
2Es 7:85 are guarded by angels in profound quiet. 3
95 and guarded by angels in profound quiet 4
4Mc 3:20 our fathers were enjoying profound peace 1

profoundly 1. toto corde
2Es 10:50 sincerely grieved and profoundly distressed 1

profuse 1. עתר
Prv 27: 6 profuse are the kisses of an enemy. 1

progress 1. προβαίνω 2. προκοπή
Php 1:25 for your progress and joy in the faith 2
1Ti 4:15 so that all may see your progress. 2
Sir 51:17 I made progress therein 2
2Mc 4: 3 When his hatred progressed to such a degree 1

progress *See also* make.

project 1. יצא
Neh 3:25 tower projecting from the upper house 1
26 Water Gate on the east and the projecting tower. 1
27 section opposite the great projecting tower 1

project upward 1. לְמַעְלָה 2. מַעַל
1Kg 7:31 within a crown which projected upward one cubit; 2
Ezk 43:15 from the altar hearth projecting upward 1

rounded projection 1. בֶּטֶן
1Kg 7:20 above the rounded projection which was beside 1

prolific 1. πολύγονος
Wis 4: 3 the prolific brood of the ungodly 1

prolong 1. ארך 2. יסף 3. משׁך 4. παρατείνω 5. πολυετής 6. προστίθημι
Deu 4:40 that you may prolong your days in the land 1
5:16 your days may be prolonged, and that it may go well 1
6: 2 that your days may be prolonged. 1
25:15 that your days may be prolonged in the land 1
Job 24:22 God prolongs the life of the mighty by his power; 3
Ps 61: 6 Prolong the life of the king; †
85: 5 Wilt thou prolong thy anger to all generations? 3
Prv 10:27 The fear of the LORD prolongs life 2
28:16 who hates unjust gain will prolong his days. 1
Ecc 7:15 a . . man who prolongs his life in his evil-doing. 1
8:12 a sinner does evil . . and prolongs his life 1
13 neither will he prolong his days like a shadow 1
Isa 13:22 at hand and its days will not be prolonged. 3
53:10 see his offspring, he shall prolong his days; 1
Dan 7:12 lives were prolonged for a season and a time. •
Act 20: 7 he prolonged his speech until midnight. 4
Wis 4:16 the prolonged old age of the unrighteous man. 5
Sir 37:31 he who is careful to avoid it prolongs his life. 6

prominent 1. κατ' ἐξοχήν
Act 25:23 the prominent men of the city 1

promise 1. אמר 2. אֹמֶר 3. אִמְרָה 4. דבר 5. דָּבָר 6. דָּבָר טוֹב 7. יצא מִפֶּה 8. εἶπον 9. ἐπαγγελία 10. ἐπαγγέλλομαι 11. ἐπάγγελμα 12. λαλέω 13. ὁμολογέω 14. πιστός 15. προεπαγγέλλω 16. ὑπισχνέομαι 17. ὑπόσχεσις 18. dico 19. praedico 20. promitto 21. repromitto 22. sponsio
Gen 18:19 bring to Abraham what he has promised him. 4
21: 1 and the LORD did to Sarah as he had promised. 4
47:29 and promise to deal loyally and truly with me. •
Exd 3:17 I promise that I will bring you up out 1
12:25 the LORD will give you, as he had promised 4
32:13 all this land that I have promised I will give 1

Num10:29 for the LORD has promised good to Israel. 4
14:17 be as great as thou hast promised, saying 4
40 go up to the place which the LORD has promised; 1
32:24 and do what you have promised 7
Deu 1:11 May the LORD . . bless you, as he has promised you! 4
6: 3 as the LORD, the God of your fathers, has promised 4
19 thrusting out . . as the LORD has promised. 4
9: 3 perish quickly, as the LORD has promised you. 4
28 bring them into the land which he promised them 4
11:25 as he promised you. 4
12:20 enlarges your territory, as he has promised you 4
15: 6 LORD your God will bless you, as he promised you 4
18: 2 LORD is their inheritance, as he promised them. 4
19: 8 all the land . . he promised to give to your fathers- 4
23:23 vowed . . what you have promised with your mouth. 4
26:18 people for his own possession, as he has promised 4
27: 3 as the LORD, the God of your fathers, has promised 4
28:68 journey which I promised that you should never 1
29:13 that he may be your God, as he promised you 4
Jos 1: 3 I have given to you, as I promised to Moses. 4
21:45 Not one of all the good promises . . had failed; 5
22: 4 God has given rest . . as he promised them; 4
23: 5 possess their land, as the LORD your God promised 4
10 the LORD . . fights for you, as he promised you. 4
14 good things which the LORD your God promised 4
15 good things which the LORD your God has promised 4
1Sm 2:30 I promised that your house . . should go in and out 1
2Sm 3:18 the LORD has promised David, saying, 'By the hand 1
7:21 Because of thy promise, and according to thy own 5
28 thou . . promised this good thing to thy servant; 4
22:31 the promise of the LORD proves true; 3
1Kg 2:24 father, and who has made me a house, as he promised 4
5:12 the LORD gave Solomon wisdom, as he promised him; 4
8:15 has fulfilled what he promised . . to David 4
20 the LORD has fulfilled his promise which he made; 5
20 sit on the throne of Israel, as the LORD promised 4
25 keep . . what thou hast promised him, saying 4
56 given rest . . according to all that he promised; 4
56 not one word has failed of all his good promise 5
9: 5 I will establish . . as I promised David 4
2Kg 8:19 he promised to give a lamp to him and to his sons 1
15:12 the promise of the LORD which he gave to Jehu 5
19:10 by promising that Jerusalem will not be given 1
20: 9 the LORD will do the thing that he has promised 4
1Ch 17:26 hast promised this good thing to thy servant; 4
25: 5 according to the promise of God to exalt him; 5
27:23 LORD had promised to make Israel as many 1
2Ch 1: 9 let thy promise to David . . be now fulfilled 5
6: 4 LORD . . who . . fulfilled what he promised 4
10 the LORD has fulfilled his promise which he made; 5
10 I sit on the throne of Israel, as the LORD promised 4
16 LORD . . keep . . what thou hast promised him 4
20 place where thou hast promised to set thy name 1
21: 7 promised to give a lamp to him and to his sons 1
Neh 5:12 took an oath of them to do as they had promised. 5
13 every man . . who does not perform this promise. 5
13 And the people did as they had promised. 5
9: 8 fulfilled thy promise, for thou art righteous. 5
Est 4: 7 exact sum of money that Haman had promised to pay 1
Ps 12: 6 promises of the LORD are promises that are pure 3
6 promises of the LORD are promises that are pure 3
18:30 the promise of the LORD proves true; he is a shield 3
66:14 that which my lips uttered and my mouth promised 4
77: 8 Are his promises at an end for all time? 2
105:42 For he remembered his holy promise, and Abraham 5
106:24 land, having no faith in his promise. 5
108: 7 God has promised in his sanctuary 4
119:38 Confirm to thy servant thy promise 3
41 O LORD, thy salvation according to thy promise; 3
50 in my affliction that thy promise gives me life. 3
57 LORD is my portion; I promise to keep thy words. 1
58 be gracious to me according to thy promise. 3
76 according to thy promise to thy servant. 3
82 My eyes fail with watching for thy promise; 3
116Uphold me according to thy promise 3
123for the fulfilment of thy righteous promise. 3
133Keep steady my steps according to thy promise 3
140Thy promise is well tried 3
148awake . . that I may meditate upon thy promise. 3
154redeem me; give me life according to thy promise! 3
Isa 37:10 deceive you by promising that Jerusalem will 1
38: 7 the LORD will do this thing that he has promised 4
Jer 29:10 I will fulfil to you my promise and bring you back 6
32:42 I will bring upon them all the good that I promise 4
33:14 when I will fulfil the promise I made to the house 6
Hag 2: 5 according to the promise that I made you 5
Mat 14: 7 so that he promised with an oath to give her 13
Mrk 14:11 they were glad, and promised to give him money. 10
Lke 1:72 to perform the mercy promised to our fathers *
24:49 behold, I send the promise of my Father upon you; 9
Act 1: 4 to wait for the promise of the Father 9
2:33 the promise of the Holy Spirit 9
39 For the promise is to you and to your children 9
7: 5 promised to give it to him in possession 10
17 as the time of the promise drew near 9
13:23 brought to Israel a Savior, Jesus, as he promised. 9
32 what God promised to the fathers 9
23:21 they are ready, waiting for the promise from you. 9
26: 6 here on trial for hope in the promise made by God 9

Rom 4:13 The promise to Abraham and his descendants 9
14 If . . faith is null and the promise is void. 9
16 in order that the promise may rest on grace 9
20 made him waver concerning the promise of God 9
21 that God was able to do what he had promised. 10
7:10 the very commandment which promised life *
9: 4 giving of the law, the worship, and the promises; 9
8 but the children of the promise are reckoned 9
9 For this is what the promise said, "About this time 9
15: 8 to confirm the promises given to the patriarchs 9
2Co 1:20 For all the promises of God find their Yes in him. 9
7: 1 Since we have these promises, beloved 9
9: 5 this gift you have promised 15
Gal 3:14 receive the promise of the Spirit through faith 9
16 Now the promises were made to Abraham 9
17 so as to make the promise void. 9
18 it is no longer by promise 9
18 God gave it to Abraham by a promise. 9
21 Is the law then against the promises of God? 9
22 what was promised to faith in Jesus Christ 9
29 Abraham's offspring, heirs according to promise. 9
4:23 the son of the free woman through promise. 9
28 we, brethren, like Isaac, are children of promise. 9
Eph 1:13 were sealed with the promised Holy Spirit 9
2:12 strangers to the covenants of promise 9
3: 6 partakers of the promise in Christ Jesus 9
6: 2 (this is the first commandment with a promise) 9
1Ti 4: 8 as it holds promise for the present life 9
2Ti 1: 1 God according to the promise 9
Tit 1: 2 which God, who never lies, promised ages ago 10
Heb 4: 1 while the promise of entering his rest remains 9
6:12 imitators of those who . . inherit the promises. 9
15 thus Abraham . . obtained the promise. 9
17 the heirs of the promise 9
7: 6 blessed him who had the promises. 9
8: 6 since it is enacted on better promises. 9
9:15 may receive the promised eternal inheritance 9
10:23 he who promised is faithful; 10
36 do the will of God and receive what is promised. 9
11: 9 By faith he sojourned in the land of promise 9
9 heirs with him of the same promise. 9
11 she considered him faithful who had promised. 10
13 not having received what was promised 9
17 he who had received the promises 9
33 enforced justice, received promises 9
39 did not receive what was promised 9
12:26 now he has promised 10
Jas 1:12 the crown of life which God has promised 10
2: 5 heirs of the kingdom which he has promised 10
2Pe 1: 4 his precious and very great promises 11
2:19 They promise them freedom 10
3: 4 and saying, "Where is the promise of his coming? 9
9 The Lord is not slow about his promise 9
13 according to his promise we wait for new heavens 10
1Jn 2:25 this is what he has promised us, eternal life. 10
1Es 1: 7 these were given . . as he promised 9
2Es 3:15 and promise him that thou wouldst never forsake 18
4:27 things that have been promised to the righteous 21
5:29 those who opposed thy promises 22
40 the love that I have promised my people. 20
7:60 also will be the judgment which I have promised; 21
66 salvation promised to them after death. 21
119if an eternal age has been promised to us 20
120that an everlasting hope has been promised to us 19
Jdt 8:11 promising to surrender the city to our enemies 8
30 to do for them what we have promised 12
33 promised to surrender the city to our enemies 8
AEs 14: 5 didst do for them all that thou didst promise. 12
Wis 12:21 oaths and covenants full of good promises! 17
17: 8 promised to drive off the fears . . of a sick soul 16
Aza 1:13 to whom thou didst promise 12
Man 1: 6 yet . . unsearchable is thy promised mercy 9
7 promised repentance and forgiveness 10
1Mc 10:15 all the promises which Demetrius had sent 9
24 and promise them honor and gifts *
11:28 and promised him 300 talents. 10
53 he broke his word about all that he had promised; 8
2Mc 2:18 as he promised through the law 10
4: 8 promising the king at an interview 10
9 he promised to pay 150 more 16
27 any of the money promised to the king. 10
45 promised a substantial bribe to Ptolemy 10
7:24 promised with oaths 14
8:11 and promising to hand over 90 slaves for a talent 16
11:14 promising that he would persuade the king *
12:11 promising to give him cattle 16
3Mc 1: 4 promising to give them each two minas of gold 10
2:10 you promised that . . you would listen 10
4Mc 15: 2 as the tyrant had promised. 17
3 for eternal life according to God's promise. *

promise *See also* make.

promise beforehand 1. προεπαγγέλλω
Rom 1: 2 he promised beforehand through his prophets 1

solemn promise 1. ὁρισμός
2Mc 12:25 when . . he had confirmed his solemn promise 1

sworn promise 1. שְׁבוּעָה
1Ch 16:16 his sworn promise to Isaac 1
Ps 105: 9 covenant . . Abraham, his sworn promise to Isaac 1

promise under oath 1. ὄμνυμι
Jdt 8: 9 how he promised them under oath to surrender . . 1

promote 1. גדל 2. יעל 3. צלח (A) 4. γίνομαι
5. ἐνεργής 6. παρέχω
Est 3: 1 King Ahasu-e'rus promoted Haman the Ag'agite 1
Job 30:13 They break up my path, they promote my calamity; 2
Dan 3:30 king promoted Shadrach, Meshach, and Abed'nego 3
1Co 7:35 but to promote good order *
Col 2:23 in promoting rigor of devotion *
1Ti 1: 4 genealogies which promote speculations 6
Phm 1: 6 may promote the knowledge of all the good 5
2Mc 11:19 to help promote your welfare. 4

promotion
Est 5:11 the promotions with which the king had honored *

prompt 1. עלה עַל 2. προβιβάζω 3. συμβιβάζω
2Kg 12: 4 the money which a man's heart prompts him to bring 1
Mat 14: 8 Prompted by her mother, she said 2
Act 19:33 Some of the crowd prompted Alexander 3

promptly 1. εἰς τὸν καιρόν 2. εὐκαίρως
3. παραχρῆμα 4. σπεύδω 5. ταχέως
Sir 18:22 nothing hinder you from paying a vow promptly 2
29: 2 in turn, repay your neighbor promptly. 1
2Mc 8: 9 Ptolemy promptly appointed Nicanor 5
11:36 send some one promptly 3
3Mc 3: 1 all should promptly be gathered into one place 4

prong 1. שֵׁן
1Sm 2:13 come . . with a three-pronged fork in his hand 1

pronounce 1. אמר 2. דבר 3. δίδωμι 4. κρίνω
5. λαλέω 6. λέγω 7. ὀνομάζω 8. φέρω
Deu 17:11 according to the decision which they pronounce 1
Jdg 12: 6 Sibboleth," for he could not pronounce it right; 2
Neh 6:12 but he had pronounced the prophecy against me 2
Jer 11:17 who planted you, has pronounced evil against you 2
16:10 Why has the LORD pronounced all this great evil 2
19:15 all the evil that I have pronounced against it 2
26:13 the evil which he has pronounced against you. 2
19 the evil which he had pronounced against them? 2
35:17 all the evil that I have pronounced against them; 2
36: 7 the anger and wrath that the LORD has pronounced 2
31 all the evil that I have pronounced against them 2
40: 2 The LORD your God pronounced this evil 2
Mat 7: 2 For with the judgment you pronounce 4
Act 19:13 undertook to pronounce the name of the Lord 7
Rom 4: 6 So also David pronounces a blessing upon the man 6
9 Is this blessing pronounced only upon the circumcised *
2Pe 2:11 do not pronounce a reviling judgment upon them 8
Jdt 8:11 you have even sworn and pronounced this oath 5
Sir 50:20 pronounce the blessing of the Lord with his lips 3
Sus 1:53 pronouncing unjust judgments 4

pronounce a blessing 1. ברך
Gen 48:20 By you Israel will pronounce blessings, saying 1
1Ch 23:13 and pronounce blessings in his name for ever. 1

pronounce clean 1. טהר
Lev 13: 6 then the priest shall pronounce him clean 1
13 he shall pronounce him clean of the disease 1
17 shall pronounce the diseased person clean 1
23 and the priest shall pronounce him clean 1
28 the priest shall pronounce him clean 1
34 then the priest shall pronounce him clean 1
37 and the priest shall pronounce him clean 1
14: 7 then he shall pronounce him clean 1
48 then the priest shall pronounce the house clean 1

pronounce judgment 1. שפט 2. κρίνω
1Kg 7: 7 he made . . where he was to pronounce judgment 1
1Co 4: 5 do not pronounce judgment before the time 2
5: 3 I have already pronounced judgment 2
Wis 9: 3 and pronounce judgment in uprightness of soul 2

pronounce unclean 1. טמא
Lev 13: 3 has examined him he shall pronounce him unclean 1
8 then the priest shall pronounce him unclean 1
11 the priest shall pronounce him unclean 1
15 priest shall . . pronounce him unclean 1
20 then the priest shall pronounce him unclean 1
22 then the priest shall pronounce him unclean 1
25 and the priest shall pronounce him unclean 1
27 then the priest shall pronounce him unclean 1
30 then the priest shall pronounce him unclean 1
44 the priest must pronounce him unclean 1

pronounce upon 1. ἐπιφέρω
Jde 1: 9 to pronounce a reviling judgment upon him 1

proof 1. עַצְמָה 2. δοκιμή 3. ἔνδειξις 4. μαρτύριον
5. τεκμήριον

Isa 41:21 bring your proofs, says the King of Jacob. 1
Mat 8: 4 for a proof to the people. 4
Mrk 1:44 for a proof to the people. 4
Lke 5:14 as Moses commanded, for a proof to the people. 4
Act 1: 3 presented himself alive . . by many proofs 5
2Co 8:24 So give proof, before the churches, of your love 3
13: 3 since you desire proof that Christ is speaking 2

proof *See also* put.

prop up 1. סמך
1Kg 22:35 the king was propped up in his chariot 1
2Ch 18:34 king of Israel propped himself up in his chariot 1

proper 1. ἀληθινός 2. ἄξιος 3. ἁρμόζω 4. ἴδιος 5. καθήκω 6. πρέπω 7. προσήκω
Lev 23:37 drink offerings, each on its proper day •
1Co 11:13 Judge for yourselves; is it proper 6
1Ti 2: 6 testimony to which was borne at the proper time. 4
6:15 this will be made manifest at the proper time 4
Tit 1: 3 at the proper time manifested in his word 4
Jde 1: 6 the angels that . . left their proper dwelling 4
1Es 5:51 offered the proper sacrifices every day 7
Sir 10:23 nor is it proper to honor a sinful man. 5
41:23 Then you will show proper shame 1
1Mc 12:11 as it is right and proper to remember brethren. 6
2Mc 6:21 of his own providing, proper for him to use 5
8:33 received the proper recompense 2
14:22 they held the proper conference. 3
3Mc 1:19 neglecting proper modesty 3
3:20 did as was proper 6
4Mc 17: 8 Indeed it would be proper 2

proper *See also* condition, reverence, time.

proper place 1. סמן
Isa 28:25 wheat in rows and barley in its proper place 1

properly 1. καλῶς 2. προσηκόντως
Tob 14:10 Bury me properly, and your mother with me 1
4Mc 6:33 we properly attribute to it the power to govern. 2

properly *See also* behave.

property 1. אֲחֻזָּה 2. חֶלְקָה 3. מְלָאכָה 4. עֹשֶׁר 5. קִנְיָן 6. רְכוּשׁ 7. ἑαυτοῦ 8. ἐπικοινωνέω 9. κτῆμα 10. οὐσία 11. ὕπαρξις 12. ὑπάρχω 13. χρῆμα
Gen 23: 4 a sojourner among you; give me property among you 1
31:16 All the property which God has taken away 4
34:23 Will not their cattle, their property 5
36: 6 Esau took . . and all his property which he had 5
Exd 22:11 has not put his hand to his neighbor's property; 3
Lev 22:11 if a priest buys a slave as his property for money 5
25:10 when each of you shall return to his property 1
13 each of you shall return to his property 1
25 If your brother . . sells part of his property 1
27 and he shall return to his property 1
28 and he shall return to his property 1
45 and they may be your property 1
2Kg 9:21 to meet Jehu, and met him at the property of Naboth 2
1Ch 27:31 these were stewards of King David's property. 6
28: 1 the stewards of all the property and cattle 6
Ezr 10: 8 by order . . all his property should be forfeited 6
Neh 11: 3 every one lived on his property in their towns 1
Job 17: 5 informs . . to get a share of their property •
Ezk 45: 7 the holy district and the property of the city 1
7 the holy district and the property of the city 1
8 It is to be his property in Israel. 1
46:16 to his sons, it is their property by inheritance. 1
18 the people, thrusting them out of their property; 1
18 sons their inheritance out of his own property 1
18 shall be dispossessed of his property. 1
48:20 together with the property of the city. 1
21 holy portion and of the property of the city 1
22 the property of the Levites and the property 1
22 of the Levites and the property of the city 1
Mat 25:14 entrusted to them his property; 12
Lke 15:12 give me the share of property that falls to me 10
13 he squandered his property in loose living. 10
Heb 10:34 the plundering of your property 12
1Es 6:32 his property should be forfeited to the king. 12
Tob 1:20 Then all my property was confiscated 12
8:21 then he should take half of Raguel's property 12
10:10 half of his property in slaves, cattle, and money. 12
14:13 He inherited their property 10
Jdt 16:24 Before she died she distributed her property 12
Sir 14: 3 man; and of what use is property to an envious man? 13
28:24 See that you fence in your property with thorns 9
33:19 do not give your property to another 13
34:20 a sacrifice from the property of the poor. 13
36:25 the property will be plundered 9
46:19 I have not taken any one's property 13
1Mc 10:43 and receive back all his property in my kingdom. •
12:23 your cattle and your property belong to us 11
2Mc 8:14 Others sold all their remaining property •
3Mc 3:28 property of the one who incurs the punishment 10
7:22 they all recovered all of their property 7
4Mc 2:14 one preserves the property of enemies •
4: 3 which are not the property of the temple 8

property *See also* get, piece.

foreign property 1. ἀλλότριος
1Mc 15:33 neither taken foreign land nor seized foreign property 1

prophecy 1. חָזוֹן 2. נְבוּאָה 3. προφητεία 4. προφητεύω 5. prophetia
2Ch 9:29 and in the prophecy of Ahi'jah the Shi'lonite 2
15: 8 the prophecy of Azari'ah the son of Oded 2
Neh 6:12 but he had pronounced the prophecy against me 2
Prv 29:18 Where there is no prophecy the people cast off 1
Mat 13:14 indeed is fulfilled the prophecy of Isaiah 3
Rom 12: 6 if prophecy, in proportion to our faith; 3
1Co 12:10 to another prophecy 3
13: 8 as for prophecies, they will pass away 3
9 our prophecy is imperfect; 4
14: 6 revelation or knowledge or prophecy 3
22 while prophecy is not for unbelievers 3
2Pe 1:20 no prophecy of scripture is a matter of one's own 3
21 no prophecy ever came by the impulse of man 3
Rev 1: 3 he who reads aloud the words of the prophecy 3
19:10 testimony of Jesus is the spirit of prophecy. 3
22: 7 Blessed is he who keeps the words of the prophecy 3
10 the words of the prophecy of this book 3
18 hears the words of the prophecy of this book 3
19 from the words of the book of this prophecy 3
2Es 15: 1 speak . . the words of the prophecy 5
Tob 2: 6 Then I remembered the prophecy of Amos 3
Sir 0: 2 even the law itself, the prophecies, and the rest 3
24:33 I will again pour out teaching like prophecy 3
36:15 fulfil the prophecies spoken in thy name. 3
39: 1 will be concerned with prophecies; 3
44: 3 proclaiming prophecies; 3
46:20 lifted up his voice out of the earth in prophecy 3

prophesy 1. חזה 2. נבא 3. נְבִיא 4. נבא (A) 5. נְבוּאָה (A) 6. προφητεία 7. προφητεύω
Num 11:25 when the spirit rested upon them, they prophesied. 2
26 so they prophesied in the camp. 2
27 Eldad and Medad are prophesying in the camp. 2
1Sm 10: 5 a band of prophets coming down . . prophesying. 2
6 you shall prophesy with them and be turned 2
10 spirit of God came . . upon him, and he prophesied 2
11 all . . saw how he prophesied with the prophets 2
13 When he had finished prophesying, he came 2
19:20 when they saw . . the prophets prophesying 2
20 the Spirit of God came . . they also prophesied. 2
21 other messengers, and they also prophesied. 2
21 sent messengers . . and they also prophesied. 2
23 Spirit of God came . . and as he went he prophesied 2
24 and he too prophesied before Samuel 2
1Kg 22: 8 I hate him, for he never prophesies good 2
10 all the prophets were prophesying before them. 2
12 all the prophets prophesied so, and said, "Go up 2
18 that he would not prophesy good concerning me 2
1Ch 25: 1 prophesy with lyres, with harps 2
2 who prophesied under the direction of the king. 2
3 Jedu'thun, who prophesied with the lyre 2
2Ch 18: 7 never prophesies good concerning me, but always 2
9 all the prophets were prophesying before them. 2
11 all the prophets prophesied so, and said 2
17 Did I not tell you that he would not prophesy good 2
20:37 Elie'zer . . prophesied against Jehosh'aphat 2
Ezr 5: 1 prophesied to the Jews . . in Judah and Jerusalem 4
6:14 through the prophesying of Haggai the prophet 5
Isa 30:10 to the prophets, "Prophesy not to us what is right; 1
10 speak to us smooth things, prophesy illusions 1
Jer 2: 8 the prophets prophesied by Ba'al 2
5:31 the prophets prophesy falsely 2
11:21 and say, "Do not prophesy in the name of the LORD 2
14:14 The prophets are prophesying lies in my name; 2
14 They are prophesying to you a lying vision 2
15 concerning the prophets who prophesy in my name 2
16 people to whom they prophesy shall be cast out 2
19:14 Topheth, where the LORD had sent him to prophesy 2
20: 1 heard Jeremiah prophesying these things. 2
6 friends, to whom you have prophesied falsely. 2
23:13 I saw an unsavory thing: they prophesied by Ba'al 2
16 words of the prophets who prophesy to you 2
21 I did not speak to them, yet they prophesied. 2
25 prophets have said who prophesy lies in my name 2
26 in the heart of the prophets who prophesy lies 2
26 and who prophesy the deceit of their own heart 3
32 I am against those who prophesy lying dreams 2
25:13 written in this book, which Jeremiah prophesied 2
30 You, therefore, shall prophesy against them 2
26: 9 Why have you prophesied in the name of the LORD 2
11 because he has prophesied against this city 2
12 The LORD sent me to prophesy against this house 2
18 Micah of Mo'resheth prophesied in the days 2
20 There was another man who prophesied 2
20 He prophesied against this city 2
27:10 For it is a lie which they are prophesying to you 2
14 for it is a lie which they are prophesying to you. 2
15 but they are prophesying falsely in my name 2
15 you and the prophets who are prophesying to you. 2
16 your prophets who are prophesying to you, saying 2
16 for it is a lie which they are prophesying to you. 2
28: 6 words which you have prophesied come true 2
8 from ancient times prophesied war, 2
9 As for the prophet who prophesies peace 2
29: 9 a lie which they are prophesying to you in my name; 2
21 who are prophesying a lie to you in my name 2
26 madman who prophesies, to put him in the stocks 2
27 Jeremiah of An'athoth who is prophesying to you? 2
31 Because Shemai'ah has prophesied to you 2
32: 3 Why do you prophesy and say, 'Thus says the LORD 2
37:19 Where are your prophets who prophesied to you 2
Ezk 4: 7 and you shall prophesy against the city. 2
6: 2 set your face . . and prophesy against them 2
11: 4 prophesy against them, prophesy, O son of man. 2
4 prophesy against them, prophesy, O son of man. 2
13 And it came to pass, while I was prophesying 2
12:27 and he prophesies of times far off. 2
13: 2 prophesy against the prophets of Israel 2
2 prophesy and say to those who prophesy 7
2 say to those who prophesy out of their own minds 3
16 the prophets of Israel who prophesied 2
17 your people, who prophesy out of their own minds; 2
17 out of their own minds; prophesy against them 2
20:46 and prophesy against the forest land in the Negeb 2
21: 2 prophesy against the land of Israel 2
9 Son of man, prophesy and say, Thus says the Lord, 2
14 Prophesy therefore, son of man; clap your hands 2
28 son of man, prophesy, and say, Thus says the Lord 2
25: 2 the Ammonites, and prophesy against them. 2
28:21 face toward Sidon, and prophesy against her 2
29: 2 and prophesy against him and against all Egypt; 2
30: 2 Son of man, prophesy, and say, Thus says the Lord 2
34: 2 prophesy against the shepherds of Israel 2
2 prophesy, and say to them, even to the shepherds 2
35: 2 face against Mount Se'ir, and prophesy against it 2
36: 1 son of man, prophesy to the mountains of Israel 2
3 therefore prophesy, and say, Thus says the Lord 2
6 prophesy concerning the land of Israel, 2
37: 4 Again he said to me, "Prophesy to these bones, 2
7 I prophesied as I was commanded; 2
7 and as I prophesied, there was a noise 2
9 Then he said to me, "Prophesy to the breath 2
9 Prophesy to the breath, prophesy, son of man, 2
10 I prophesied as he commanded me 2
12 prophesy, and say to them, Thus says the Lord GOD 2
38: 2 of Meshech and Tubal, and prophesy against him 2
14 Therefore, son of man, prophesy, and say to Gog 2
17 who in those days prophesied for years 2
39: 1 And you, son of man, prophesy against Gog, 2
Jol 2:28 your sons and your daughters shall prophesy 2
Ams 2:12 commanded . . saying, 'You shall not prophesy.' 2
3: 8 The Lord GOD has spoken; who can but prophesy? 2
7:12 eat bread there, and prophesy there; 2
13 but never again prophesy at Bethel 2
15 LORD said to me, 'Go, prophesy to my people Israel.' 2
16 You say, 'Do not prophesy against Israel 2
Zec 13: 3 shall pierce him through when he prophesies. 2
4 ashamed of his vision when he prophesies; 2
Mat 7:22 Lord, Lord, did we not prophesy in your name 7
11:13 the prophets and the law prophesied until John; 7
15: 7 You hypocrites! Well did Isaiah prophesy of you 7
26:68 saying, "Prophesy to us, you Christ! 7
Mrk 7: 6 Well did Isaiah prophesy of you hypocrites 7
14:65 to strike him, saying to him, "Prophesy! 7
Lke 1:67 filled with the Holy Spirit, and prophesied 7
22:64 Prophesy! Who is it that struck you? 7
Joh 11:51 being high priest that year he prophesied 7
Act 2:17 your sons and your daughters shall prophesy 7
18 they shall prophesy. 7
19: 6 they spoke with tongues and prophesied. 7
21: 9 four unmarried daughters, who prophesied. 7
1Co 11: 4 Any man who prays or prophesies with his head 7
5 any woman who prays or prophesies with her head 7
14: 1 especially that you may prophesy. 7
3 On the other hand, he who prophesies speaks to men 7
4 he who prophesies edifies the church. 7
5 to speak in tongues, but even more to prophesy 7
5 He who prophesies is greater than he who speaks 7
24 if all prophesy 7
31 For you can all prophesy one by one 7
39 So, my brethren, earnestly desire to prophesy 7
1Th 5:20 do not despise prophesying 6
1Pe 1:10 The prophets who prophesied of the grace 7
Jde 1:14 It was of these also that Enoch . . prophesied 7
Rev 10:11 You must again prophesy about many peoples 7
11: 3 I will grant my two witnesses power to prophesy 7
6 no rain . . during the days of their prophesying 6
1Es 6: 1 the prophets . . prophesied to the Jews 7
1 they prophesied to them in the name of the Lord •
7: 3 the prophets Haggai and Zechariah prophesied; 7
Jdt 6: 2 to prophesy among us as you have done today 7
Wis 14:28 prophesy lies, or live unrighteously 7
Sir 46: 1 the successor of Moses in prophesying 6
20 Even after he had fallen asleep he prophesied 7
47: 1 Nathan rose up to prophesy in the days of David. 7
48:13 when he was dead his body prophesied. 7

prophet 1. חֹזֶה 2. נָבִיא 3. נְבִיא (A) 4. προφητεύω 5. προφήτης 6. propheta
Gen 20: 7 he is a prophet, and he will pray for you, and you 2
Exd 7: 1 and Aaron your brother shall be your prophet. 2

Num11:29 Would that all the LORD'S people were prophets 2
12: 6 said, "Hear my words: If there is a prophet among you 2
Deu 13: 1 If a prophet arises among you, or a dreamer 2
3 you shall not listen to the words of that prophet 2
5 But that prophet . . shall be put to death 2
18:15 LORD . . will raise up for you a prophet like me 2
18 I will raise up for them a prophet like you 2
20 prophet who presumes to speak a word in my name 2
20 that same prophet shall die.' 2
22 when a prophet speaks in the name of the LORD 2
22 prophet has spoken it presumptuously 2
34:10 not arisen a prophet since in Israel like Moses 2
Jdg 6: 8 the LORD sent a prophet to the people of Israel; 2
1Sm 3:20 Samuel was established as a prophet of the LORD. 2
9: 9 who is now called a prophet was formerly . . seer. 2
10: 5 you will meet a band of prophets coming down 2
10 When they came . . a band of prophets met him; 2
11 all . . saw how he prophesied with the prophets 2
11 Is Saul also among the prophets? 2
12 became a proverb, "Is Saul also among the prophets? 2
19:20 when they saw . . the prophets prophesying 2
24 Hence it is said, "Is Saul also among the prophets? 2
22: 5 Then the prophet Gad said to David, "Do not remain 2
28: 6 either by dreams, or by Urim, or by prophets. 2
15 answers . . either by prophets or by dreams; 2
2Sm 7: 2 the king said to Nathan the prophet 2
12:25 LORD . . sent a message by Nathan the prophet; 2
24:11 the word of the LORD came to the prophet Gad 2
1Kg 1: 8 of Jehoi'ada, and Nathan the prophet, and Shim'e-i 2
10 but he did not invite Nathan the prophet 2
22 with the king, Nathan the prophet came in. 2
23 they told the king, "Here is Nathan the prophet. 2
32 Zadok the priest, Nathan the prophet, and Benai'ah 2
34 let Zadok . . and Nathan the prophet . . anoint 2
38 Zadok . . Nathan the prophet, and Benai'ah . . went 2
44 sent . . Zadok . . Nathan the prophet, and Benai'ah 2
45 Zadok . . and Nathan the prophet have anointed 2
11:29 the prophet Ahi'jah the Shi'lonite found him 2
13:11 there dwelt an old prophet in Bethel. 2
18 I am also a prophet as you are, and an angel spoke 2
20 the word of the LORD came to the prophet 2
23 he saddled the ass for the prophet 2
25 told it in the city where the old prophet dwelt. 2
26 when the prophet . . heard of it, he said 2
29 the prophet took up the body of the man of God 2
14: 2 go to Shiloh; behold, Ahi'jah the prophet is there 2
18 he spoke by his servant Ahi'jah the prophet. 2
16: 7 the word of the LORD came by the prophet Jehu 2
12 he spoke against Ba'asha by Jehu the prophet 2
18: 4 when Jez'ebel cut off the prophets of the LORD 2
4 Obadi'ah took 100 prophets and hid them 2
13 when Jez'ebel killed the prophets of the LORD 2
13 how I hid 100 men of the LORD's prophets 2
19 send and gather . . and the 450 prophets of Ba'al 2
19 gather . . and the 400 prophets of Ashe'rah 2
20 Ahab sent . . and gathered the prophets together 2
22 I, even I only, am left a prophet of the LORD; 2
22 Ba'al's prophets are 450 men. 2
25 Then Eli'jah said to the prophets of Ba'al, "Choose 2
36 Eli'jah the prophet came near and said, "O LORD 2
40 Eli'jah said to them, "Seize the prophets of Ba'al; 2
19: 1 he had slain all the prophets with the sword. 2
10 thrown down thy altars, and slain thy prophets 2
14 thrown down thy altars, and slain thy prophets 2
16 Eli'sha . . you shall anoint to be prophet 2
20:13 a prophet came near to Ahab . . and said, "Thus says 2
22 the prophet came near to the king of Israel 2
35 a certain man of the sons of the prophets said 2
38 the prophet departed, and waited for the king 2
41 the king . . recognized him as one of the prophets. 2
22: 6 the king of Israel gathered the prophets 2
7 Is there not here another prophet of the LORD 2
10 all the prophets were prophesying before them. 2
12 all the prophets prophesied so, and said, "Go up 2
13 the words of the prophets . . are favorable 2
22 a lying spirit in the mouth of all his prophets.' 2
23 lying spirit in the mouth of all . . your prophets; 2
2Kg 2: 3 the sons of the prophets . . came out to Eli'sha 2
5 The sons of the prophets . . drew near to Eli'sha 2
7 50 men of the sons of the prophets also went 2
15 when the sons of the prophets . . saw him 2
3:11 Is there no prophet of the LORD here 2
13 Go to the prophets of your father and . . mother. 2
13 Go to . . and the prophets of your mother. 2
4: 1 the wife of one of the sons of the prophets cried 2
38 as the sons of the prophets were . . before him 2
38 and boil pottage for the sons of the prophets. 2
5: 3 my lord were with the prophet who is in Sama'ria! 2
8 he may know that there is a prophet in Israel. 2
13 if the prophet had commanded . . some great thing 2
22 two young men of the sons of the prophets; 2
6: 1 Now the sons of the prophets said to Eli'sha, "See 2
12 Eli'sha, the prophet who is in Israel, tells 2
9: 1 Eli'sha the prophet called one of the sons 2
1 Eli'sha . . called one of the sons of the prophets 2
4 the young man, the prophet, went to Ramoth-gilead. 2
7 avenge . . the blood of my servants the prophets 2
10:19 Now therefore call to me all the prophets of Ba'al 2
14:25 his servant Jonah the son of Amit'tai, the prophet 2
17:13 the LORD warned Israel . . by every prophet 2
13 which I sent to you by my servants the prophets. 2
23 he had spoken by all his servants the prophets. 2
19: 2 he sent . . to the prophet Isaiah the son of Amoz. 2
20: 1 Isaiah the prophet . . came to him, and said to him 2
11 Isaiah the prophet cried to the LORD 2
14 Then Isaiah the prophet came to King Hezeki'ah 2
21:10 And the LORD said by his servants the prophets 2
23: 2 men of Judah . . and the priests and the prophets 2
18 let his bones alone, with the bones of the prophet 2
24: 2 which he spoke by his servants the prophets. 2
1Ch 16:22 Touch not my anointed ones, do my prophets no harm! 2
17: 1 David said to Nathan the prophet 2
29:29 and in the Chronicles of Nathan the prophet 2
2Ch 9:29 written in the history of Nathan the prophet 2
12: 5 Then Shemai'ah the prophet came to Rehobo'am 2
15 chronicles of Shemai'ah the prophet and of Iddo 2
13:22 written in the story of the prophet Iddo. 2
18: 5 king of Israel gathered the prophets together 2
6 Is there not here another prophet of the LORD 2
9 all the prophets were prophesying before them. 2
11 all the prophets prophesied so, and said 2
12 Behold, the words of the prophets with one accord 2
21 a lying spirit in the mouth of all his prophets.' 2
22 lying spirit in the mouth of these your prophets; 2
20:20 believe his prophets, and you will succeed. 2
21:12 letter came to him from Eli'jah the prophet 2
24:19 sent prophets . . to bring them back to the LORD; 2
25:15 LORD . . sent him a prophet, who said to him 2
16 the prophet stopped, but said, "I know that God 2
26:22 Isaiah the prophet the son of Amoz wrote. 2
28: 9 prophet of the LORD was there, whose name 2
29:25 commandment of . . Nathan the prophet; 2
25 from the LORD through his prophets. 2
32:20 Isaiah the prophet, the son of Amoz 2
32 written in the vision of Isaiah the prophet 2
35:18 since the days of Samuel the prophet; 2
36:12 not humble himself before Jeremiah the prophet 2
16 scoffing at his prophets 2
Ezr 5: 1 prophets, Haggai and Zechari'ah the son of Iddo 3
2 with them were the prophets of God, helping them. 3
6:14 through the prophesying of Haggai the prophet 3
9:11 thou didst command by thy servants the prophets 2
Neh 6: 7 set up prophets to proclaim concerning you 2
14 No-adi'ah and the rest of the prophets who wanted 2
9:26 law behind their back and killed thy prophets 2
30 warn them by thy Spirit through thy prophets; 2
32 come upon . . our prophets, our fathers, and all 2
Ps 51: 0 when Nathan the prophet came to him 2
74: 9 there is no longer any prophet 2
105:15 Touch not my anointed ones, do my prophets no harm! 2
Isa 3: 2 the judge and the prophet, the diviner 2
9:15 and the prophet who teaches lies is the tail; 2
28: 7 priest and the prophet reel with strong drink 2
29:10 and has closed your eyes, the prophets 2
30:10 to the prophets, "Prophesy not to us what is right; 1
37: 2 he sent . . to the prophet Isaiah the son of Amoz. 2
38: 1 Isaiah the prophet the son of Amoz came to him 2
39: 3 Then Isaiah the prophet came to King Hezeki'ah 2
Jer 1: 5 I appointed you a prophet to the nations. 2
2: 8 the prophets prophesied by Ba'al 2
26 their princes, their priests, and their prophets 2
30 your own sword devoured your prophets 2
4: 9 and the prophets astounded. 2
5:13 The prophets will become wind; 2
31 the prophets prophesy falsely 2
6:13 from prophet to priest, every one deals falsely. 2
7:25 sent all my servants the prophets to them 2
8: 1 bones of the priests, the bones of the prophets 2
10 from prophet to priest every one deals falsely. 2
13:13 the prophets, and all the inhabitants 2
14:13 Ah, Lord GOD, behold, the prophets say to them 2
14 The prophets are prophesying lies in my name; 2
15 concerning the prophets who prophesy in my name 2
15 By . . famine those prophets shall be consumed. 2
18 For both prophet and priest ply their trade 2
18:18 from the wise, nor the word from the prophet. 2
20: 2 Then Pashhur beat Jeremiah the prophet 2
23: 9 Concerning the prophets: My heart is broken 2
11 Both prophet and priest are ungodly; 2
13 In the prophets of Sama'ria I saw an unsavory 2
14 But in the prophets of Jerusalem I have seen 2
15 the LORD of hosts concerning the prophets 2
15 for from the prophets of Jerusalem ungodliness 2
16 Do not listen to the words of the prophets 2
21 I did not send the prophets, yet they ran; 2
25 I have heard what the prophets have said 2
26 shall there be lies in the heart of the prophets 2
28 Let the prophet who has a dream tell the dream 2
30 behold, I am against the prophets, says the LORD 2
31 Behold, I am against the prophets, says the LORD 2
33 or a prophet, or a priest asks you 2
34 the prophet, priest, or one of the people who says 2
37 Thus you shall say to the prophet 2
25: 2 which Jeremiah the prophet spoke to all 2
4 sent to you all his servants the prophets 2
26: 5 to heed the words of my servants the prophets 2
7 The priests and the prophets and all the people 2
8 the priests and the prophets and all the people 2
11 Then the priests and the prophets said 2
16 the people said to the priests and the prophets 2
27: 9 do not listen to your prophets, your diviners 2
14 Do not listen to the words of the prophets 2
15 you and the prophets who are prophesying to you. 2
16 Do not listen to the words of your prophets 2
18 If they are prophets 2
28: 1 Hanani'ah . . the prophet from Gibeon, spoke to me 2
5 Then the prophet Jeremiah spoke to Hanani'ah 2
5 Jeremiah spoke to Hanani'ah the prophet 2
6 prophet Jeremiah said, "Amen! May the LORD do so; 2
8 The prophets who preceded you and me 2
9 As for the prophet who prophesies peace 2
9 when the word of that prophet comes to pass 2
9 that the LORD has truly sent the prophet. 2
10 Then the prophet Hanani'ah took the yoke-bars 2
10 yoke-bars from the neck of Jeremiah the prophet 2
11 But Jeremiah the prophet went his way. 2
12 the prophet Hanani'ah had broken the yoke-bars 2
12 from off the neck of Jeremiah the prophet 2
15 And Jeremiah the prophet said to . . Hanani'ah 2
15 And Jeremiah . . said to the prophet Hanani'ah 2
17 in the seventh month, the prophet Hanani'ah died. 2
29: 1 the letter which Jeremiah the prophet sent 2
1 to the priests, the prophets, and all the people 2
8 Do not let your prophets and your diviners 2
15 The LORD has raised up prophets for us in Babylon, 2
19 sent to you by my servants the prophets 2
29 in the hearing of Jeremiah the prophet. 2
32: 2 and Jeremiah the prophet was shut up in the court 2
32 their princes, their priests and their prophets 2
34: 6 Then Jeremiah the prophet spoke all these words 2
35:15 I have sent to you all my servants the prophets 2
36: 8 did all that Jeremiah the prophet ordered him 2
26 Baruch the secretary and Jeremiah the prophet 2
37: 2 which he spoke through Jeremiah the prophet. 2
3 Zedeki'ah sent . . to Jeremiah the prophet, saying 2
6 the word of the LORD came to Jeremiah the prophet 2
13 seized Jeremiah the prophet, saying 2
19 Where are your prophets who prophesied to you 2
38: 9 in all that they did to Jeremiah the prophet 2
10 and lift Jeremiah the prophet out of the cistern 2
14 King Zedeki'ah sent for Jeremiah the prophet 2
42: 2 and said to Jeremiah the prophet 2
4 Jeremiah the prophet said to them, "I have heard 2
43: 6 also Jeremiah the prophet and Baruch 2
44: 4 sent to you all my servants the prophets, saying 2
45: 1 The word that Jeremiah the prophet spoke 2
46: 1 Jeremiah the prophet concerning the nations. 2
13 spoke to Jeremiah the prophet about the coming 2
47: 1 that came to Jeremiah the prophet 2
49:34 came to Jeremiah the prophet concerning Elam 2
50: 1 land of the Chalde'ans, by Jeremiah the prophet 2
51:59 The word which Jeremiah the prophet commanded 2
Lam 2: 9 and her prophets obtain no vision from the LORD. 2
14 Your prophets have seen . . false and deceptive 2
20 priest and prophet be slain in the sanctuary 2
4:13 This was for the sins of her prophets 2
Ezk 2: 5 know that there has been a prophet among them. 2
7:26 they seek a vision from the prophet 2
13: 2 prophesy against the prophets of Israel 2
3 says the Lord GOD, Woe to the foolish prophets 2
4 Your prophets have been like foxes among ruins 2
9 My hand will be against the prophets 2
10 a wall, these prophets daub it with whitewash; •
16 the prophets of Israel who prophesied 2
14: 4 yet comes to the prophet, I the LORD will answer 2
7 yet comes to a prophet to inquire for himself 2
9 if the prophet be deceived and speak a word 2
9 I, the LORD, have deceived that prophet 2
10 their punishment–the punishment of the prophet 2
22:28 prophets have daubed for them with whitewash 2
33:33 will know that a prophet has been among them. 2
38:17 by my servants the prophets of Israel 2
Dan 9: 2 word of the LORD to Jeremiah the prophet 2
6 have not listened to thy servants the prophets 2
10 set before us by his servants the prophets. 2
24 seal both vision and prophet, 2
Hos 4: 5 the prophet also shall stumble with you by night; 2
6: 5 Therefore I have hewn them by the prophets 2
9: 7 The prophet is a fool, the man of the spirit is mad 2
8 The prophet is the watchman of E'phraim 2
12:10 I spoke to the prophets; 2
10 and through the prophets gave parables. 2
13 By a prophet the LORD brought Israel up 2
13 and by a prophet he was preserved. 2
Ams 2:11 And I raised up some of your sons for prophets 2
12 and commanded the prophets, saying, 'You shall not 2
3: 7 his secret to his servants the prophets. 2
7:14 answered . . "I am no prophet, nor a prophet's son 2
14 answered . . "I am no prophet, nor a prophet's son 2
Mic 3: 5 the prophets who lead my people astray, who cry 2
6 The sun shall go down upon the prophets 2
11 its prophets divine for money; 2
Hab 1: 1 oracle of God which Habak'kuk the prophet saw. 2
3: 1 A prayer of Habak'kuk the prophet 2
Zep 3: 4 Her prophets are wanton, faithless men; 2
Hag 1: 1 the word of the LORD came by Haggai the prophet 2
3 the word of the LORD came by Haggai the prophet 2

12 Haggai the prophet, as the LORD their God had sent 2
2: 1 the word of the LORD came by Haggai the prophet 2
10 the word of the LORD came by Haggai the prophet 2
Zec 1: 1 came to Zechari'ah . . the prophet, saying 2
4 fathers, to whom the former prophets cried out 2
5 And the prophets, do they live for ever? 2
6 which I commanded my servants the prophets 2
7 the son of Berechi'ah, son of Iddo, the prophet; 2
7: 3 the house of the LORD of hosts and the prophets 2
7 the LORD proclaimed by the former prophets? 2
12 by his Spirit through the former prophets. 2
8: 9 these words from the mouth of the prophets 2
13: 2 also I will remove from the land the prophets 2
4 every prophet will be ashamed of his vision 2
5 he will say, 'I am no prophet, I am a tiller of the soil; 2
Mal 4: 5 Behold, I will send you Eli'jah the prophet 2
Mat 1:22 to fulfil what the Lord had spoken by the prophet 5
2: 5 Judea; for so it is written by the prophet 5
15 the Lord had spoken by the prophet, "Out of Egypt 5
17 what was spoken by the prophet Jeremiah 5
23 Nazareth, that what was spoken by the prophets 5
3: 3 spoken of by the prophet Isaiah when he said 5
4:14 that what was spoken by the prophet Isaiah 5
5:12 men persecuted the prophets who were before 5
17 come to abolish the law and the prophets 5
7:12 do so to them; for this is the law and the prophets. 5
8:17 to fulfil what was spoken by the prophet Isaiah 5
10:41 He who receives a prophet because he is a prophet 5
41 He who receives a prophet because he is a prophet 5
41 shall receive a prophet's reward 5
11: 9 Why then did you go out? To see a prophet? 5
9 Yes, I tell you, and more than a prophet. 5
13 For all the prophets and the law prophesied 5
12:17 to fulfil what was spoken by the prophet Isaiah 5
39 except the sign of the prophet Jonah. 5
13:17 I say to you, many prophets and righteous men 5
35 This was to fulfil what was spoken by the prophet 5
57 A prophet is not without honor 5
14: 5 because they held him to be a prophet. 5
16:14 others Jeremiah or one of the prophets. 5
21: 4 to fulfil what was spoken by the prophet, saying 5
11 This is the prophet Jesus from Nazareth 5
26 for all hold that John was a prophet. 5
46 because they held him to be a prophet. 5
22:40 all the law and the prophets. 5
23:29 you build the tombs of the prophets 5
30 in shedding the blood of the prophets.' 5
31 you are sons of those who murdered the prophets. 5
34 I send you prophets and wise men and scribes 5
37 O Jerusalem, Jerusalem, killing the prophets 5
24:15 sacrilege spoken of by the prophet Daniel 5
26:56 scriptures of the prophets might be fulfilled. 5
27: 9 what had been spoken by the prophet Jeremiah 5
Mrk 1: 2 As it is written in Isaiah the prophet 5
6: 4 Jesus said to them, "A prophet is not without honor 5
15 It is a prophet, like one of the prophets of old. 5
15 It is a prophet, like one of the prophets of old. 5
8:28 others say, Eli'jah; and others one of the prophets 5
11:32 for all held that John was a real prophet. 5
Lke 1:70 the mouth of his holy prophets from of old 5
76 you . . will be called the prophet of the Most High 5
3: 4 the book of the words of Isaiah the prophet 5
4:17 was given to him the book of the prophet Isaiah. 5
24 no prophet is acceptable in his own country. 5
27 lepers in Israel in the time of the prophet Eli'sha 5
6:23 for so their fathers did to the prophets. 5
7:16 A great prophet has arisen among us! 5
26 What then did you go out to see? A prophet? 5
26 Yes, I tell you, and more than a prophet. 5
39 he said to himself, "If this man were a prophet 5
9: 8 by others that one of the old prophets had risen. 5
19 others, that one of the old prophets has risen. 5
10:24 many prophets and kings desired to see 5
11:47 Woe to you! for you build the tombs of the prophets 5
49 I will send them prophets and apostles 5
50 the blood of all the prophets 5
13:28 Abraham and Isaac and Jacob and all the prophets 5
33 that a prophet should perish away from Jerusalem.' 5
34 O Jerusalem, Jerusalem, killing the prophets 5
16:16 The law and the prophets were until John 5
29 Abraham said, 'They have Moses and the prophets; 5
31 If they do not hear Moses and the prophets 5
18:31 written of the Son of man by the prophets 5
20: 6 they are convinced that John was a prophet. 5
24:19 Concerning Jesus of Nazareth, who was a prophet 5
25 to believe all that the prophets have spoken! 5
27 beginning with Moses and all the prophets 5
44 the prophets and the psalms 5
Joh 1:21 Are you the prophet?" And he answered, "No. 5
23 'Make straight . . ' as the prophet Isaiah said. 5
25 neither the Christ, nor Elijah, nor the prophet? 5
45 Moses in the law and also the prophets wrote 5
4:19 Sir, I perceive that you are a prophet. 5
44 that a prophet has no honor in his own country. 5
6:14 the prophet who is to come into the world! 5
45 It is written in the prophets 5
7:40 This is really the prophet. 5
52 no prophet is to rise from Galilee. 5
8:52 Abraham died, as did the prophets 5

53 And the prophets died! Who do you claim to be? 5
9:17 He said, "He is a prophet. 5
12:38 the word spoken by the prophet Isaiah 5
Act 2:16 this is what was spoken by the prophet Joel 5
30 Being therefore a prophet 5
3:18 foretold by the mouth of all the prophets 5
21 the mouth of his holy prophets from of old. 5
22 The Lord God will raise up for you a prophet 5
23 every soul that does not listen to that prophet 5
24 all the prophets who have spoken 5
25 the sons of the prophets and of the covenant 5
7:37 a prophet from your brethren as he raised me up.' 5
42 as it is written in the book of the prophets 5
48 as the prophet says 5
52 Which of the prophets 5
8:28 he was reading the prophet Isaiah. 5
30 heard him reading Isaiah the prophet 5
34 About whom, pray, does the prophet say this 5
10:43 To him all the prophets bear witness 5
11:27 in these days prophets came down from Jerusalem 5
13: 1 at Antioch there were prophets and teachers 5
15 After the reading of the law and the prophets 5
20 he gave them judges until Samuel the prophet. 5
27 nor understand the utterances of the prophets 5
40 what is said in the prophets 5
15:15 the words of the prophets agree, as it is written 5
32 Judas and Silas, who were themselves prophets 5
21:10 a prophet named Ag'abus came down from Judea. 5
24:14 written in the prophets 5
26:22 saying nothing but what the prophets . . said 5
27 King Agrippa, do you believe the prophets? 5
28:23 both from the law of Moses and from the prophets. 5
25 saying . . through Isaiah the prophet 5
Rom 1: 2 he promised beforehand through his prophets 5
3:21 the law and the prophets bear witness to it 5
11: 3 Lord, they have killed thy prophets 5
1Co 12:28 first apostles, second prophets, third teachers 5
29 Are all apostles? Are all prophets? 5
14:29 Let two or three prophets speak 5
32 the spirits of prophets are subject 5
32 prophets are subject to prophets. 5
37 If any one thinks that he is a prophet, or spiritual 5
Eph 2:20 the foundation of the apostles and prophets 5
3: 5 been revealed to his holy apostles and prophets 5
4:11 some prophets, some evangelists 5
1Th 2:15 who killed both the Lord Jesus and the prophets 5
Tit 1:12 One of themselves, a prophet of their own, said 5
Heb 1: 1 God spoke of old to our fathers by the prophets; 5
11:32 David and Samuel and the prophets– 5
Jas 5:10 As an example . . brethren, take the prophets 5
1Pe 1:10 The prophets who prophesied of the grace 5
2Pe 2:16 a dumb ass . . restrained the prophet's madness. 5
3: 2 remember the predictions of the holy prophets 5
Rev 10: 7 as he announced to his servants the prophets 5
11:10 because these two prophets had been a torment 5
18 rewarding thy servants, the prophets and saints 5
16: 6 men have shed the blood of saints and prophets 5
18:20 O heaven, O saints and apostles and prophets 5
24 And in her was found the blood of prophets 5
22: 6 the Lord, the God of the spirits of the prophets 5
9 you and your brethren the prophets 5
1Es 1:20 since the times of Samuel the prophet; 5
28 did not heed the words of Jeremiah the prophet 5
32 Jeremiah the prophet lamented for Josiah 5
47 words that were spoken by Jeremiah the prophet 5
51 they scoffed at his prophets 5
6: 1 the prophets Haggai and Zechariah the son of Iddo 4
2 with the help of the prophets of the Lord 5
7: 3 the prophets Haggai and Zechariah prophesied; 5
8:82 didst give by thy servants the prophets, saying 5
2Es 1: 1 The second book of the prophet Ezra 6
32 I sent to you my servants the prophets 6
36 They have seen no prophets 6
2: 1 through my servants the prophets 6
7:130did not believe him, or the prophets after him 6
12:42 For of all the prophets you alone are left to us 6
Tob 4:12 for we are the sons of the prophets 5
14: 4 I fully believe what Jonah the prophet said 5
5 just as the prophets said of it. 5
8 what the prophet Jonah said will surely happen. 5
Wis 7:27 makes them friends of God, and prophets; 5
11: 1 the hand of a holy prophet. 5
Sir 0: 1 given to us through the law and the prophets 5
1 the reading of the law and the prophets 5
36:16 let thy prophets be found trustworthy. 5
46:13 Samuel, beloved by his Lord, a prophet of the Lord 5
15 By his faithfulness he was proved to be a prophet 5
48: 1 Then the prophet Elijah arose like a fire 5
8 prophets to succeed you. 5
22 which Isaiah the prophet commanded 5
49: 7 he had been consecrated in the womb as prophet 5
10 May the bones of the twelve prophets revive 5
Bar 1:16 our priests and our prophets and our fathers 5
21 in all the words of the prophets whom he sent to us 5
2:20 thou didst declare by thy servants the prophets 5
24 thou didst speak by thy servants the prophets 5
Aza 1:15 at this time there is no prince, or prophet 5
Bel 1:33 Now the prophet Habakkuk was in Judea 5
1Mc 4:46 until there should come a prophet 5

9:27 since the time that prophets ceased to appear 5
54 He tore down the work of the prophets! 5
14:41 until a trustworthy prophet should arise 5
2Mc 2: 1 Jeremiah the prophet ordered . . 5
2 the prophet . . instructed those . . deported 5
4 the prophet . . ordered that . . 5
13 the books about the kings and prophets 5
15: 9 Encouraging them from the law and the prophets 5
14 Jeremiah, the prophet of God. 5
4Mc 18:10 he taught you the law and the prophets. 5

prophet *See also* appear.

false prophet 1. *ψευδοπροφήτης*

Mat 7:15 Beware of false prophets 1
24:11 many false prophets will arise 1
24 For false Christs and false prophets will arise 1
Mrk 13:22 False Christs and false prophets will arise 1
Lke 6:26 for their fathers did to the false prophets. 1
Act 13: 6 a certain magician, a Jewish false prophet 1
2Pe 2: 1 false prophets also arose among the people 1
1Jn 4: 1 many false prophets have gone out into the world 1
Rev 16:13 issuing . . from the mouth of the false prophet 1
19:20 beast was captured, and with it the false prophet 1
20:10 where the beast and the false prophet were 1

prophetess 1. אִשָּׁה נְבִיאָה 2. נְבִיאָה 3. *προφῆτις*

Exd 15:20 Then Miriam, the prophetess, the sister of Aaron 2
Jdg 4: 4 Now Deb'orah, a prophetess, the wife of Lapp'idoth 1
2Kg 22:14 So . . and Asai'ah went to Huldah the prophetess 2
2Ch 34:22 Hilki'ah . . went to Huldah the prophetess 2
Neh 6:14 Remember . . also the prophetess No-adi'ah 2
Isa 8: 3 I went to the prophetess, and she conceived 2
Lke 2:36 a prophetess, Anna, the daughter of Phan'uel 3
Rev 2:20 Jez'ebel, who calls herself a prophetess 3

prophetic 1. *προφητικός*

Rom 16:26 through the prophetic writings is made known 1
2Pe 1:19 we have the prophetic word made more sure. 1

prophetic *See also* power, utterance.

propitiate 1. *ἐξευμενίζομαι* 2. *ἐξιλάσκομαι*

Sir 16: 7 He was not propitiated for the ancient giants 2
34:19 he is not propitiated for sins 2
4Mc 4:11 and propitiate the wrath of the heavenly army. 1

propitiation 1. *ἐξιλασμός*

Wis 18:21 prayer and propitiation by incense 1

proportion 1. דַּי 2. כְּפָה 3. *ἀναλογία* 4. *κατά*

Num 35: 8 each, in proportion to the inheritance . . it inherits 2
Deu 25: 2 number of stripes in proportion to his offense. 1
Rom 12: 6 if prophecy, in proportion to our faith; 3
Tob 4: 8 make your gift from them in proportion 4
Sir 28:10 In proportion to the fuel for the fire 4
10 in proportion to the obstinacy of strife 4
10 in proportion to the strength of the man 4
10 in proportion to his wealth 4

proposal 1. דָּבָר 2. *λόγος*

Gen 41:37 This proposal seemed good to Pharaoh 1
Tob 7: 9 he communicated the proposal to Raguel 2
1Mc 1:12 This proposal pleased them 2
8:21 The proposal pleased them 2

proposal *See also* make.

propose 1. אמר 2. דָּבָר 3. זמם 4. *προθυμέομαι* 5. *προτίθημι* 6. propono

Gen 11: 6 nothing that they propose . . will now be impossible 3
2Ch 28:13 propose to bring upon us guilt against the LORD 1
Est 1:21 and the king did as Memu'can proposed; 2
2Es 7:23 proposed to themselves wicked frauds 6
3Mc 2:27 He proposed to inflict public disgrace 5
3:17 we proposed to enter their inner temple 4

propound a riddle 1. חוד

Ezk 17: 2 propound a riddle, and speak an allegory 1

proselyte 1. *προσήλυτος*

Mat 23:15 to make a single proselyte 1
15 when he becomes a proselyte •
Act 2:10 visitors from Rome, both Jews and proselytes 1
6: 5 Par'menas, and Nicola'us, a proselyte of Antioch. 1

prospect 1. *ἐκδοχή*

Heb 10:27 a fearful prospect of judgment, and a fury of fire 1

prosper 1. בנה 2. היה טוֹב 3. חול 4. טוֹב 5. יטב 6. כשר 7. מצא טוֹב 8. עשה חַיִל 9. צלח 10. שׂכל 11. שׁלה 12. צלח (A) 13. רַעֲנַן (A) 14. *ἀγαθός* 15. *εὔοδος γίνομαι* 16. *εὐοδόω* 17. *εὐπορέω* 18. *κατευοδόω* 19. *πληθύνω* 20. *πλουτέω* 21. *πράσσω καλῶς* 22. dirigo

Gen 24:21 whether the LORD had prospered his journey 9
40 angel with you and prosper your way; 9
42 if now thou wilt prosper the way which I go 9
56 since the LORD has prospered my way; let me go 9
Deu 28:29 not prosper in your ways; and you shall be only 9

29: 9 that you may prosper in all that you do. 10
30: 9 LORD will again take delight in prospering you 4
Jdg 17:13 LORD will prosper me, because I have a Levite 5
Rut 4:11 May you prosper in Eph'rathah and be renowned 8
1Kg 2: 3 that you may prosper in all that you do 10
2Kg 18: 7 wherever he went forth, he prospered. 10
1Ch 22:13 you will prosper if you are careful to observe 9
29:23 and he prospered, and all Israel obeyed him. 9
2Ch 14: 7 So they built and prospered. 9
24:20 transgress . . so that you cannot prosper? 9
31:21 every work . . he did with all his heart, and prospered. 9
32:30 Hezeki'ah prospered in all his works. 9
Ezr 5: 8 goes on diligently and prospers in their hands. 12
6:14 elders of the Jews built and prospered 12
Ps 1: 3 In all that he does, he prospers. 9
10: 5 His ways prosper at all times; 3
37: 7 fret not . . over him who prospers in his way 9
122: 6 May they prosper who love you! 11
Prv 16:20 He who gives heed to the word will prosper 7
17: 8 wherever he turns he prospers. 10
20 A man of crooked mind does not prosper 7
19: 8 he who keeps understanding will prosper. 7
28:13 conceals his transgressions will not prosper 9
Ecc 11: 6 you do not know which will prosper, this or that 6
Isa 48:15 I have brought him, and he will prosper in his way. 9
52:13 my servant shall prosper, he shall be exalted 10
53:10 the will of the LORD shall prosper in his hand; 9
54:17 weapon . . fashioned against you shall prosper 9
55:11 and prosper in the thing for which I sent it. 9
Jer 2:37 and you will not prosper by them. 9
10:21 therefore they have not prospered 10
12: 1 Why does the way of the wicked prosper? 9
44:17 had plenty of food, and prospered, and saw no evil. 2
Lam 1: 5 foes have become the head, her enemies prosper 11
Dan 4: 4 Nebuchadnez'zar . . prospering in my palace. 13
6:28 Daniel prospered during the reign of Darius 12
8:12 horn acted and prospered. 9
11:36 prosper till the indignation is accomplished; 9
Mal 3:15 evildoers not only prosper 1
1Co 16: 2 store it up, as he may prosper 16
Rev 3:17 For you say, I am rich, I have prospered 20
1Es 6:10 the work is prospering in their hands 16
7: 3 the holy work prospered 15
2Es 5:12 shall labor but their ways shall not prosper. 22
Tob 4:19 all your paths and plans may prosper 16
5:16 God who dwells in heaven will prosper your way 16
10:11 The God of heaven will prosper you, my children 16
Jdt 5: 9 There they settled, and prospered 19
17 they prospered 14
Wis 10:10 she prospered him in his labors 17
11: 1 Wisdom prospered their works 16
Sir 12: 9 A man's enemies are grieved when he prospers 14
15:10 the Lord will prosper it. 16
1Mc 2:47 the work prospered in their hands. 18
3: 6 deliverance prospered by his hand. 16
4:55 blessed Heaven, who had prospered them. 16
14:36 in his days things prospered in his hands 16
16: 2 things have prospered in our hands 16
4Mc 3:20 our fathers . . were prospering 21

prosper *See also* ways.

cause to prosper 1. צלח 2. צמח
Gen 39: 3 the LORD caused all that he did to prosper 1
2Sm 23: 5 will he not cause to prosper all my help 2

how prosper 1. לְשָׁלוֹם
2Sm 11: 7 how the people fared, and how the war prospered. 1

make prosper 1. צלח
Gen 39:23 and whatever he did, the LORD made it prosper. 1
2Ch 26: 5 as long as he sought the LORD, God made him prosper 1
Neh 2:20 The God of heaven will make us prosper 1
Jer 5:28 they judge not with justice . . to make it prosper 1
Dan 8:25 cunning . . make deceit prosper under his hand 1

prosperity 1. טוּב 2. טוֹב 3. טוֹבָה 4. יְשׁוּעָה 5. כּוֹשָׁרָה 6. עֶצֶם 7. צְדָקָה 8. שָׁלֵו 9. שָׁלוּ 10. שַׁלְוָה 11. שָׁלוֹם 12. ἀγαθός 13. εὐημερία 14. κόρος
Deu 23: 6 shall not seek their peace or their prosperity 3
28:11 LORD will make you abound in prosperity 2
1Sm 2:32 look with envious eye on all the prosperity *
1Kg 10: 7 your wisdom and prosperity surpass the report 2
Ezr 9:12 never seek their peace or prosperity 3
Job 15:21 in prosperity the destroyer will come upon him. 11
20:21 therefore his prosperity will not endure. 1
21:13 They spend their days in prosperity 2
16 Behold, is not their prosperity in their hand? 1
23 One dies in full prosperity, being wholly at ease 6
30:15 my prosperity has passed away like a cloud. 4
36:11 they complete their days in prosperity 2
Ps 25:13 He himself shall abide in prosperity 2
30: 6 I said in my prosperity, "I shall never be moved. 9
37:11 delight themselves in abundant prosperity. 11
68: 6 God . . leads out the prisoners to prosperity; 5
72: 3 the mountains bear prosperity for the people 11
73: 3 when I saw the prosperity of the wicked. 11
106: 5 that I may see the prosperity of thy chosen ones 3
128: 5 May you see the prosperity of Jerusalem 1
Prv 8:18 with me, enduring wealth and prosperity. 7
13:21 but prosperity rewards the righteous. 2
Ecc 7:14 In the day of prosperity be joyful 2
Isa 54:13 and great shall be the prosperity of your sons. 11
66:12 I will extend prosperity to her like a river 11
Jer 22:21 I spoke to you in your prosperity 10
33: 6 and reveal to them abundance of prosperity 11
9 the good and all the prosperity I provide for it. 11
Hag 2: 9 I will give prosperity, says the LORD of hosts.' 11
Zec 1:17 My cities shall again overflow with prosperity 2
7: 7 When Jerusalem was inhabited and in prosperity 8
AEs 16: 3 in their inability to stand prosperity 14
Sir 6:11 In prosperity he will make himself your equal 12
11:23 what prosperity could be mine in the future? 12
25 In the day of prosperity, adversity is forgotten 12
25 prosperity is not remembered. 12
12: 8 A friend will not be known in prosperity 12
22:23 rejoice with him in his prosperity; 12
29:16 will overthrow the prosperity of his surety 12
31:11 His prosperity will be established 12
44:11 prosperity will remain with their descendants 2
45:26 so that their prosperity may not vanish 12
2Mc 14:14 would mean prosperity for themselves. 13

prosperity *See also* wish.

prosperous 1. שַׁלְוָה 2. εἰρήνη 3. εὐοδόω 4. κατευθύνω
Ezk 16:49 had pride, surfeit of food, and prosperous ease 1
34:29 I will provide for them prosperous plantations 2
Sir 29:18 many men who were prosperous 4
41: 1 who is prosperous in everything 3

prosperous *See also* journey, make.

become prosperous 1. נשׂג יד
Lev 25:26 and then himself becomes prosperous 1

prostitute 1. תעב 2. πόρνη
Ezk 16:25 your lofty place and prostituted your beauty 1
1Co 6:15 make them members of a prostitute? Never! 2
16 who joins himself to a prostitute becomes one 2

cult prostitute 1. קָדֵשׁ 2. קְדֵשָׁה
Deu 23:17 no cult prostitute of the daughters of Israel 2
17 neither . . a cult prostitute of the sons of Israel. 1
Hos 4:14 and sacrifice with cult prostitutes 2

male cult prostitute 1. קָדֵשׁ
1Kg 14:24 were also male cult prostitutes in the land. 1
15:12 He put away the male cult prostitutes 1
22:46 the male cult prostitutes . . he exterminated 1
2Kg 23: 7 houses of the male cult prostitutes 1

prostrate 1. שחה 2. שחח 3. ἐπὶ κοιλίαν 4. πίπτω 5. πίπτω ἐπὶ πρόσωπον 6. προσπίπτω 7. ῥίπτω 8. ῥίπτω ἐμαυτόν
Ps 38: 6 I am utterly bowed down and prostrate; 2
Isa 49: 7 princes, and they shall prostrate themselves; 1
Jdt 4:11 prostrated themselves before the temple 4
10:23 she prostrated herself and made obeisance to him 5
2Mc 3:15 priests prostrated themselves 7
10: 4 they fell prostrate and besought the Lord 3
3Mc 1:16 Then the priests . . prostrated themselves 6
5:50 they prostrated themselves with one accord 8

prostrate *See also* lie.

prostration 1. πρόπτωσις
2Mc 3:21 the prostration of the whole populace 1

protect 1. גנן 2. חפר 3. סבב 4. עזר 5. שׂגב 6. שׁמר 7. διαφυλάσσω 8. ἐπαρήγω 9. ἐπισκιάζω 10. ἐπισκοπή 11. καταφράσσω 12. προασπίζω 13. σκεπάζω 14. συνασπίζω 15. ὑπέρ 16. ὑπερασπίζω 17. custodio 18. servo 19. tuto
2Sm 18:12 'For my sake protect the young man Ab'salom.' 6
Ezr 8:22 protect us against the enemy on our way; 4
Job 11:18 you will be protected and take your rest 2
Ps 12: 7 Do thou, O LORD, protect us, guard us ever 6
20: 1 The name of the God of Jacob protect you! 5
41: 2 the LORD protects him and keeps him alive; 6
59: 1 God, protect me from those who rise up against me 5
91:14 I will protect him, because he knows my name. 5
Prv 18:11 like a high wall protecting him. 9
Isa 31: 5 the LORD of hosts will protect Jerusalem; 1
5 he will protect and deliver it, he will spare 1
Jer 31:22 a new thing on the earth: a woman protects a man. 3
Zec 9:15 The LORD of hosts will protect them 1
2Es 2:21 do not ridicule a lame man, protect the maimed 19
22 Protect the old and the young within your walls; 18
13:23 will himself protect those who fall into peril 17
Jdt 5:21 their God will protect them 15
8:15 power to protect us within any time he pleases 13
9:14 no other who protects the people of Israel 16
13:16 who has protected me in the way I went 7
Wis 2:20 according to what he says, he will be protected. 10
10: 1 Wisdom protected the first-formed father 7
12 She protected him from his enemies 7
17: 4 the inner chamber that held them protected them 7
19: 8 those protected by thy hand 13
Sir 22:25 I will not be ashamed to protect a friend 13
28:19 Happy is the man who is protected from it 13
1Mc 3: 3 waged battles, protecting the host by his sword. 13
6:38 themselves protected by the phalanx 11
2Mc 10:30 protecting him with their own armor and weapons 13
13:17 because the Lord's help protected him. 8
3Mc 3:10 already some . . were pledging to protect them 14
4Mc 6:21 and not protect our divine law even to death. 12
9:15 because I protect the divine law. 12
14:15 the ones that are tame protect their young 12

protect from fear 1. ἄφοβος
Wis 17: 4 even the inner chamber . . protected them from fear 1

protected one 1. צפן
Ps 83: 3 consult together against thy protected ones. 1

protection 1. גֶּדֶר 2. מָעוֹז 3. מָעוֹז 4. סִתְרָה 5. צֵל 6. ἐπισκοπή 7. σκέπη 8. σκιά 9. τήρησις 10. ὑπερασπισμός 11. tutela
Num 14: 9 their protection is removed from them 5
Deu 32:38 rise up and help you, let them be your protection! 4
Ezr 9: 9 to give us protection in Judea and Jerusalem. 1
Neh 4: 9 set a guard as a protection against them day *
Ecc 7:12 For the protection of wisdom is like . . of money; 5
12 For . . wisdom is like the protection of money; 5
Isa 27: 5 Or let them lay hold of my protection 3
30: 2 to take refuge in the protection of Pharaoh 2
3 the protection of Pharaoh turn to your shame 2
2Es 1:15 I gave you camps for your protection 11
Sir 6:29 will become for you a strong protection 7
34:16 a mighty protection and strong support 10
Bar 1:12 we shall live under the protection 8
12 under the protection of Belshazzar his son 8
2Mc 3:40 Heliodorus and the protection of the treasury. 9
5: 9 in hope of finding protection 7
3Mc 5:42 the protection of the Jews 6

protection *See also* find.

protector 1. דַּיָּן 2. κηδεμών 3. προστατέω 4. σκεπαστής
Ps 68: 5 of the fatherless and protector of widows 1
Jdt 9:11 upholder of the weak, protector of the forlorn 4
Sir 51: 2 thou hast been my protector and helper 4
1Mc 14:47 to be protector of them all. 3
2Mc 4: 2 the protector of his fellow countrymen 2
3Mc 6: 9 all-merciful and protector of all 4

protest 1. ἀντιλέγω 2. νή
1Co 15:31 I protest, brethren, by my pride in you which I have 2
4Mc 4: 7 The people indignantly protested his words 1

protest indignantly 1. σχετλιάζω
4Mc 4: 7 The people indignantly protested his words 1

proud 1. גֵּאֶה 2. גָּאוֹן 3. גֵּאוּת 4. גַּאֲיוֹן 5. גבה 6. גָּבֹהַּ 7. גֵּוָה 8. דָּשֵׁן 9. הוֹד 10. רָהָב 11. רוּם 12. רָחָב 13. שַׁחַץ 14. ἀλαζών 15. καύχημα 16. καύχησις 17. ὑπερηφανεύω 18. ὑπερηφανία 19. ὑπερήφανος 20. ὕψωμα
2Ch 32:25 did not make return . . for his heart was proud 5
Job 22:29 For God abases the proud, but he saves the lowly. 7
28: 8 The proud beasts have not trodden it; 13
38:11 here shall your proud waves be stayed 2
40:11 look on every one that is proud, and abase him. 1
12 Look on every one that is proud, and bring him low; 1
Ps 22:29 to him shall all the proud of the earth bow down; 8
40: 4 the man . . who does not turn to the proud 10
94: 2 render to the proud their deserts! 1
123: 4 who are at ease, the contempt of the proud. 4
Prv 15:25 The LORD tears down the house of the proud 1
16:19 better . . than to divide the spoil with the proud. 1
21: 4 Haughty eyes and a proud heart 12
Ecc 7: 8 patient . . is better than the proud in spirit. 6
Isa 2:12 has a day against all that is proud and lofty 1
16: 6 have heard of the pride of Moab, how proud he was; 1
28: 1 the proud crown of the drunkards of E'phraim 3
3 The proud crown of the drunkards of E'phraim 3
Jer 13:15 give ear; be not proud, for the LORD has spoken. 5
48:29 have heard of the pride of Moab-he is very proud 1
Ezk 7:24 I will put an end to their proud might 2
28: 2 says the Lord GOD: "Because your heart is proud 5
5 your heart has become proud in your wealth 5
17 Your heart was proud because of your beauty; 5
30: 6 her proud might shall come down; 2
18 of Egypt, and her proud might shall come to an end; 2
31:10 its heart was proud of its height 11
33:28 her proud might shall come to an end; 2
Zec 10: 3 will make them like his proud steed in battle. 9
Lke 1:51 he has scattered the proud 19
Rom 15:17 I have reason to be proud of my work for God. 16
2Co 1:14 you can be proud of us as we can be of you 15
5:12 giving you cause to be proud of us 15
10: 5 every proud obstacle to the knowledge of God 20
Php 2:16 so that in the day of Christ I may be proud 15
2Ti 3: 2 lovers of self, lovers of money, proud, arrogant 14

Jas 4: 6 God opposes the proud, but gives grace 19
1Pe 5: 5 God opposes the proud, but gives grace 19
AEs 13:12 I . . refused to bow down to this proud Haman. 19
Sir 3:28 The affliction of the proud has no healing 19
10: 9 How can he who is dust and ashes be proud? 17
21: 4 thus the house of the proud will be laid waste. 19
25: 2 a beggar who is proud, a rich man who is a liar 19
27:15 The strife of the proud leads to bloodshed 19
31:26 so wine tests hearts in the strife of the proud. 19
32:12 do not sin through proud speech. 19
51:10 the time when there is no help against the proud. 18

proud *See also* grow, position.

become proud 1. ὑψηλὰ φρονέω 2. φρονέω
Rom 11:20 So do not become proud, but stand in awe. 1
AEs 16: 2 the more proud do many men become. 2

proud man 1. זֵד 2. ὑπερήφανος
Prv 21:24 Scoffer" is the name of the proud, haughty man 1
Sir 11:30 so is the mind of a proud man 2
13: 1 whoever associates with a proud man 2
20 Humility is an abomination to a proud man; 2
27:28 Mockery and abuse issue from the proud man 2
32:18 an insolent and proud man will not cower in fear. 2

proud one 1. זָדוֹן
Jer 50:31 Behold, I am against you, O proud one, says the Lord 1
32 The proud one shall stumble and fall 1

proudly 1. גַּאֲוָה 2. גָּבֹהַּ 3. מָרוֹם
1Sm 2: 3 Talk no more so very proudly 2
Ps 56: 2 for many fight against me proudly. 3
Isa 13: 3 execute my anger, my proudly exulting ones. 1
Zep 3:11 from your midst your proudly exultant ones 1

proudly *See also* deal, press, wave.

proudly defy 1. זיד
Jer 50:29 she has proudly defied the LORD, the Holy One 1

prove 1. בחן 2. נגד 3. נסה 4. ἀκριβάζω 5. ἀπαγγέλλω 6. ἀποδείκνυμι 7. ἀπόδειξις 8. γίνομαι 9. δείκνυμι 10. διότι 11. δοκιμάζω 12. ἐλέγχω 13. ἔνδειξις 14. ἐπιδείκνυμι 15. εὑρίσκω 16. παρατίθημι 17. παρίστημι 18. πείθω 19. πειρασμός 20. συμβιβάζω 21. συνίστημι 22. φαίνω
Exd 7: 9 Pharaoh says to you, 'Prove yourselves by working †
15:25 an ordinance and there he proved them 3
16: 4 that I may prove them, whether they will walk in my 3
20:20 Do not fear; for God has come to prove you 3
1Kg 1:52 If he prove to be a worthy man, not one of his hairs •
Ezr 2:59 could not prove their fathers' houses 2
Neh 7:61 but they could not prove their fathers' houses 2
Ps 26: 2 Prove me, O LORD, and try me; test my heart 1
Mat 13:22 and it proves unfruitful. 8
Mrk 4:19 it proves unfruitful. 8
Lke 10:36 proved neighbor to the man 8
Joh 15: 8 and so prove to be my disciples. 8
Act 9:22 by proving that Jesus was the Christ. 20
17: 3 explaining and proving that it was necessary 16
24:13 Neither can they prove to you 17
25: 7 serious charges which they could not prove. 6
Rom 3:26 it was to prove . . that he himself is righteous 13
7:10 the very commandment . . proved to be death to me. •
12: 2 that you may prove what is the will of God 11
2Co 7:11 proved yourselves guiltless in the matter. 21
14 so our boasting before Titus has proved true. 8
8: 8 to prove by the earnestness of others 11
Gal 2:18 then I prove myself a transgressor. 21
1Th 1: 5 You know what kind of men we proved to be 8
1Pe 4:12 fiery ordeal which comes upon you to prove you 19
1Es 5:37 though they could not prove . . 5
Tob 10: 4 The lad has perished; his long delay proves it. 10
Wis 2:11 what is weak proves itself to be useless. 12
12:13 prove that thou hast not judged unjustly; 9
Sir 9:17 so a people's leader is proved wise by his words. •
31:26 Fire and water prove the temper of steel 11
42:10 having a husband, lest she prove unfaithful •
46:15 By his faithfulness he was proved to be a prophet 4
Bel 1: 9 if you prove that Bel is eating them 9
2Mc 5: 4 the apparition might prove to have been a good omen. 8
7:29 prove worthy of your brother 8
3Mc 4:20 when they said and proved that . . 7
4Mc 1: 7 I could prove to you 14
2: 4 Not only is reason proved to rule 22
6 I could prove to you all the more 18
6:35 I have proved 14
16:14 you have proved more powerful than a man. 15

prove a coward 1. δειλιάζω
4Mc 14: 4 None of the seven youths proved coward 1

prove a liar 1. כזב
Job 24:25 If it is not so, who will prove me a liar 1

prove blameless 1. ἀνέγκλητος
1Ti 3:10 then if they prove themselves blameless 1

prove false 1. ψεύδομαι
Heb 6:18 it is impossible that God should prove false 1

prove good 1. εὐδοκιμέω
Sir 39:34 all things will prove good in their season. 1

prove perverse 1. עקשׁ
Job 9:20 though I am blameless, he would prove me perverse. 1

prove right 1. צדק
Isa 43:26 set forth your case, that you may be proved right. 1

prove true 1. צרף
2Sm 22:31 the promise of the LORD proves true; 1
Ps 18:30 the promise of the LORD proves true; he is a shield 1
Prv 30: 5 Every word of God proves true; 1

prove vain 1. κενόω
2Co 9: 3 so that our boasting about you may not prove vain 1

provender 1. בְּלִיל 2. מִסְפּוֹא
Gen 24:25 We have both straw and provender enough 2
32 gave him straw and provender for the camels 2
42:27 to give his ass provender at the lodging place 2
43:24 when he had given their asses provender 2
Jdg 19:19 We have straw and provender for our asses 2
Isa 30:24 asses that till . . will eat salted provender 1

provender *See also* give.

proverb 1. מָשָׁל 2. παραβολή 3. παροιμία
Deu 28:37 you shall become a horror, a proverb, and a byword 1
1Sm 10:12 Therefore it became a proverb, "Is Saul also among 1
24:13 As the proverb of the ancients says 1
1Kg 4:32 He also uttered 3,000 proverbs; 1
9: 7 Israel will become a proverb and a byword 1
2Ch 7:20 make it a proverb and a byword among all peoples. 1
Job 13:12 Your maxims are proverbs of ashes 1
Ps 49: 4 I will incline my ear to a proverb; 1
Prv 1: 1 proverbs of Solomon, son of David, king of Israel 1
6 to understand a proverb and a figure 1
10: 1 The proverbs of Solomon. 1
25: 1 These also are proverbs of Solomon 1
26: 7 proverb in the mouth of fools. 1
9 Like a thorn . . proverb in the mouth of fools. 1
Ecc 12: 9 weighing and studying and arranging proverbs 1
Ezk 12:22 what is this proverb that you have about the land 1
23 I will put an end to this proverb 1
23 they shall no more use it as a proverb in Israel. 1
18: 2 What do you mean by repeating this proverb 1
3 this proverb shall no more be used by you 1
Lke 4:23 Doubtless you will quote to me this proverb 2
2Pe 2:22 It has happened to them according to the true proverb 3
Sir 6:35 do not let wise proverbs escape you. 3
13:26 to devise proverbs requires painful thinking. 2
18:29 pour forth apt proverbs. 3
20:20 A proverb from a fool's lips will be rejected 2
38:33 they are not found using proverbs. 2
39: 3 he will seek out the hidden meanings of proverbs 3
47:17 your songs and proverbs and parables 3

proverb *See also* recount, use.

provide 1. היה ל 2. יהב 3. כול 4. כון 5. מסר 6. נתן 7. עשׂה 8. פוק 9. קום 10. ראה 11. שׂום 12. נתן (A) 13. διακονέω 14. δίδωμι 15. ἐπιχορηγέω 16. ἰσχύω 17. παρά 18. παρακαθίστημι 19. παρασκευάζω 20. παρέχω 21. παρίστημι 22. ποιέω 23. προνοέω 24. προπέμπω 25. προσάγω 26. τίθημι 27. χορηγέω 28. do 29. praeparo 30. praesto 31. provideo
Gen 22: 8 Abraham said, "God will provide himself the lamb 10
14 name of that place The LORD will provide; 10
14 On the mount of the LORD it shall be provided. 10
30:30 But now when shall I provide for my own household 7
45:11 there I will provide for you, for there are yet 3
47:12 Joseph provided his father, his brothers, 3
50:21 I will provide for you and your little ones. 3
Lev 25: 6 The sabbath of the land shall provide food 1
Num23: 1 provide for me here seven bulls and seven rams. 4
29 provide for me here seven bulls and seven rams. 4
31: 5 there were provided . . 12,000 armed for war. 5
Jos 18: 4 Provide three men from each tribe, and I will send 2
1Sm 16: 1 I have provided for myself a king among his sons. 10
17 Provide for me a man who can play well, and bring 10
2Sm 19:33 I will provide for you with me in Jerusalem. 3
20: 3 and provided for them, but did not go in to them. 3
1Kg 5: 9 meet my wishes by providing food for my 6
8:21 there I have provided a place for the ark 11
1Ch 22: 3 David also provided great stores of iron 4
5 David provided materials in great quantity 4
14 I have provided for the house of the LORD 4
14 timber and stone too I have provided. 4
29: 2 I have provided for the house of my God 4
3 Moreover, in addition to all that I have provided 4
16 abundance that we have provided for building 4
2Ch 2: 7 workers . . whom David my father provided. 4
32:29 likewise provided cities for himself 7
Ezr 7:20 which you have occasion to provide 12
20 may provide it out of the king's treasury. 12
Neh 13:31 provided for the wood offering, at appointed •
Est 2: 9 and he quickly provided her with her ointments 6
Job 38:41 Who provides for the raven its prey 4
Ps 65: 9 thou providest their grain 4
68:10 goodness, O God, thou didst provide for the needy. 4
78:20 also give bread, or provide meat for his people? 4
111: 5 He provides food for those who fear him; 6
144:13 garners be full, providing all manner of store; 8
Prv 27:26 the lambs will provide your clothing •
30:25 yet they provide their food in the summer; 4
31:15 yet night and provides food for her household 6
Jer 33: 9 the good and all the prosperity I provide for it. 7
Ezk 34:29 I will provide for them prosperous plantations 9
43:25 you shall provide daily a goat for a sin offering; 7
25 the flock, without blemish, shall be provided. 7
45:17 he shall provide the sin offerings 7
22 On that day the prince shall provide for himself 7
23 he shall provide as a burnt offering to the LORD 7
24 he shall provide as a cereal offering an ephah 7
46: 7 as a cereal offering he shall provide an ephah 7
12 When the prince provides a freewill offering 7
13 He shall provide a lamb a year old 7
13 morning by morning he shall provide it. 7
14 he shall provide a cereal offering with it 7
15 the oil shall be provided, morning by morning 7
Lke 8: 3 others, who provided for them out of their means. 13
10: 7 eating and drinking what they provide 17
12:33 provide yourselves with purses 22
Act 23:24 Also provide mounts for Paul to ride 21
1Co 10:13 will also provide the way of escape 22
1Ti 5: 8 If any one does not provide for his relatives 23
2Pe 1:11 so there will be richly provided for you 15
1Es 4:55 the support for the Levites should be provided 14
56 He wrote that land and wages should be provided 14
8:18 you may provide out of the royal treasury. 14
2Es 1:14 I provided light for you from a pillar of fire 30
5:26 thou hast provided for thyself one sheep 31
8: 2 it provides very much clay 28
52 the age to come is prepared, plenty is provided 29
Jdt 12: 2 provided from the things I have brought with me. 27
Wis 16:20 providing every pleasure 16
18: 3 thou didst provide a flaming pillar of fire 20
Sir 23:22 provides an heir by a stranger. 21
1Mc 12: 4 asking them to provide . . safe conduct 24
14:34 provided . . whatever was necessary 26
2Mc 4:49 provided magnificently for their funeral. 27
6:21 urged him to bring meat of his own providing 19
9:16 he would provide from his own revenues; 27
12: 3 to embark . . on boats which they had provided 18
43 to provide for a sin offering 25
3Mc 6:30 ordered him to provide to the Jews 27
40 provided with everything by the king 27
7:18 the king had generously provided all things to them 27
4Mc 3: 2 reason can provide a way for us not to be enslaved 20

provide a place of rest 1. נוח
Jos 1:13 The LORD your God is providing you a place of rest 1

provide drink 1. ποτίζω
Sir 29:25 provide drink without being thanked 1

provide food 1. כול
1Kg 4: 7 officers . . who provided food for the king 1

provide in abundance 1. περισσεύω
2Co 9: 8 provide you with every blessing in abundance 1
8 provide in abundance for every good work. 1

provide with drink 1. שׁקה
2Ch 28:15 provided them with food and drink, and anointed 1

provide with food 1. אכל 2. כול
2Sm 19:32 he had provided the king with food while he stayed 2
2Ch 28:15 provided them with food and drink, and anointed 1

provided 1. כִּי 2. ἐάν 3. εἰ
Deu 19: 9 provided you are careful to keep all this 1
Rom 8:17 heirs with Christ, provided we suffer with him 3
11:22 provided you continue in his kindness; 2
Col 1:23 provided that you continue in the faith 3

providence 1. ἐπισκοπή 2. πρόνοια
1Es 6: 5 the providence of the Lord was over the captives; 1
Wis 14: 3 thy providence, O Father, that steers its course 2
17: 2 exiles from eternal providence. 2
3Mc 4:21 an act of the invincible providence of him 2
4Mc 9:24 the just Providence of our ancestors 2
13:19 the divine and all-wise Providence 2
17:22 divine Providence preserved Israel 2

province 1. מְדִינָה 2. מְדִינָה (A) 3. ἐπαρχεία 4. σατραπεία 5. χώρα 6. provincia
Ezr 2: 1 Now these were the people of the province 1
4:10 rest of the province Beyond the River, and now •
11 servants . . of the province Beyond the River •
15 rebellious city, hurtful to kings and provinces 2
16 no possession in the province Beyond the River. •
17 live in Sama'ria and in the rest of the province •

20 ruled over the whole province Beyond the River *
5: 3 governor of the province Beyond the River *
6 governor of the province Beyond the River *
6 governors . . in the province Beyond the River *
8 went to the province of Judah, to the house 2
6: 2 capital which is in the province of Media 2
6 governor of the province Beyond the River *
6 governors . . in the province Beyond the River *
8 tribute of the province from Beyond the River. *
13 governor of the province Beyond the River *
7:16 find in the whole province of Babylonia 2
21 treasurers in the province Beyond the River *
25 judge . . people in the province Beyond the River *
8:36 governors of the province Beyond the River; *
Neh 1: 3 survivors there in the province who escaped 1
2: 7 governors of the province Beyond the River *
9 governors of the province Beyond the River *
3: 7 governor of the province Beyond the River. *
7: 6 These were the people of the province who came up 1
11: 3 chiefs of the province who lived in Jerusalem; 1
Est 1: 1 Ahasu-e'rus who reigned . . over 127 provinces 1
3 and the nobles and governors of the provinces 1
16 who are in all the provinces of King Ahasu-e'rus. 1
22 he sent letters to all the royal provinces 1
22 he sent . . to every province in its own script 1
2: 3 the king appoint officers in all the provinces 1
18 granted a remission of taxes to the provinces 1
3: 8 There is . . in all the provinces of your kingdom; 1
12 and to the governors over all the provinces 1
12 to every province in its own script 1
13 Letters were sent . . to all the king's provinces 1
14 be issued . . in every province by proclamation 1
4: 3 in every province . . there was great mourning 1
11 and the people of the king's provinces know 1
8: 5 the Jews who are in all the provinces of the king. 1
9 princes of the provinces from India to Ethiopia 1
9 provinces from India to Ethiopia, 127 provinces 1
9 an edict . . to every province in its own script 1
11 any armed force of any people or province 1
12 to destroy . . throughout all the provinces 1
13 was to be issued as a decree in every province 1
17 And in every province . . there was gladness 1
9: 2 in their cites throughout all the provinces 1
3 All the princes of the provinces and the satraps 1
4 his fame spread throughout all the provinces; 1
12 have they done in the rest of the king's provinces! 1
16 the other Jews who were in the king's provinces 1
20 who were in all the provinces of King Ahasu-e'rus 1
28 generation, in every family, province, and city 1
30 to the 127 provinces of the kingdom of Ahasu-e'rus 1
Ecc 2: 8 and gold and the treasure of kings and provinces; 1
5: 8 If you see in a province the poor oppressed 1
Dan 2:48 ruler over the whole province of Babylon 2
49 over the affairs of the province of Babylon. 2
3: 1 plain of Dura, in the province of Babylon. 2
2 assemble . . all the officials of the provinces 2
3 all the officials of the provinces 2
12 over the affairs of the province of Babylon 2
30 king promoted . . in the province of Babylon. 2
8: 2 Susa the capital, which is in the province of Elam; 1
11:24 come into the richest parts of the province; 1
Act 23:34 he asked to what province he belonged 3
25: 1 Now when Festus had come into his province 3
2Es 1:11 the people of two provinces, Tyre and Sidon 6
AEs 13: 1 the 127 provinces from India to Ethiopia 5
16: 1 rulers of the provinces from India to Ethiopia 5
1Mc 3:37 and went through the upper provinces. 5
6: 1 Antiochus was going through the upper provinces 5
7: 8 governor of the province Beyond the River *
8: 7 and surrender some of their best provinces 5
2Mc 9:25 when I hastened off to the upper provinces 4

province *See also* governor.

provision 1. אכל 2. דָּבָר 3. כול 4. לֶחֶם 5. לֶחֶם צַיִד 6. מַאֲכָל 7. מָזוֹן 8. צַיִד 9. צֵידָה 10. *βρῶμα* 11. *δαπάνη* 12. *διατροφή* 13. *ἐπισιτισμός* 14. *παρασκευή* 15. *πρόνοια* 16. annona

Gen 14:11 took . . all their provisions 1
42:25 money in his sack, and to give them provisions 9
45:21 and gave them provisions for the journey. 9
23 asses loaded with grain, bread, and provision 7
Exd 12:39 they prepared for themselves any provisions. 9
Deu 19: 4 This is the provision for the manslayer 2
Jos 1:11 command the people, 'Prepare your provisions; 9
9: 5 and all their provisions were dry and moldy. 5
11 Take provisions in your hand for the journey 9
14 the men partook of their provisions 8
Jdg 20:10 to bring provisions for the people 9
1Sm 17:20 David rose . . and took the provisions, and went *
22:10 inquired of the LORD . . and gave him provisions 9
1Kg 4:22 Solomon's provision for one day was 30 cors 4
20:27 people . . were mustered, and were provisioned 3
1Ch 12:40 abundant provisions of meal, cakes of figs 6
2Ch 11:23 he gave them abundant provisions 7
Ps 132:15 I will abundantly bless her provisions; 8
Ezk 45:25 he shall make the same provision for sin 6
Lke 9:12 to lodge and get provisions 13
Act 24: 2 by your provision . . reforms are introduced 15
Rom 13:14 and make no provision for the flesh 15
1Co 9:15 to secure any such provision *
2Es 16:21 Behold, provision will be so cheap upon earth 16
Jdt 2:17 sheep and oxen and goats for provision; 14
Bel 1: 8 tell me who is eating these provisions 11
13 to go in regularly and consume the provisions. *
1Mc 6:49 because they had no provisions there 12
2Mc 12:14 relying . . on their supply of provisions 10

provision *See also* buyer, make, supply.

settled provision 1. אֲמָנָה

Neh 11:23 was . . a settled provision for the singers, 1

provocation 1. כַּעַס 2. מרר 3. *ἐρεθισμός*

Deu 32:19 because of the provocation of his sons 1
27 had I not feared provocation by the enemy, lest 1
2Kg 23:26 provocations with which Manas'seh had provoked 1
Job 17: 2 my eye dwells on their provocation. 2
Prv 27: 3 but a fool's provocation is heavier than both. 1
Ezk 20:28 presented the provocation of their offering; 1
Sir 31:29 with provocation and stumbling. 3

provocation *See also* give.

provoke 1. גרה 2. כעח 3. כעס 4. מרץ 5. רגז 6. תוה 7. *ἐρεθίζω* 8. *παραπικραίνω* 9. *παροξύνω* 10. *προκαλέω* 11. *προσοχθίζω*

Deu 32:21 they have provoked me with their idols. 3
21 I will provoke them with a foolish nation. 3
1Sm 1: 6 rival used to provoke her sorely, to irritate her 3
7 as often as she went up . . she used to provoke her. 3
1Kg 15:30 the anger to which he provoked the LORD 3
21:22 for the anger to which you have provoked me 3
2Kg 14:10 why should you provoke trouble so that you fall 1
23:26 provocations with which Manas'seh had provoked 3
2Ch 25:19 why should you provoke trouble so that you fall 1
Job 12: 6 those who provoke God are secure 5
16: 3 what provokes you that you answer? 4
Ps 78:41 and provoked the Holy One of Israel. 6
Isa 65: 3 a people who provoke me to my face continually 3
Jer 7:19 Is it I whom they provoke? says the LORD. 2
Act 17:16 his spirit was provoked within him 9
Gal 5:26 have no self-conceit, no provoking of one another 10
Col 3:21 Fathers, do not provoke your children 7
Heb 3:10 Therefore I was provoked with that generation 11
17 And with whom was he provoked 40 years? 11
1Es 6:15 sinned against the Lord . . and provoked him 8
Bar 4: 7 For you provoked him who made you 9
1Mc 15:40 came to Jamnia and began to provoke the people 7
2Mc 14:27 provoked by the false accusations 7

provoke to anger 1. כעס 2. עבר 3. *παροργίζω*

Deu 4:25 act corruptly . . so as to provoke him to anger 1
9:18 doing what was evil . . to provoke him to anger. 1
31:29 provoking him to anger through the work 1
32:16 with . . practices they provoked him to anger. 1
Jdg 2:12 and they provoked the LORD to anger. 1
1Kg 14: 9 made . . molten images, provoking me to anger 1
15 made their Ashe'rim, provoking the LORD to anger. 1
16: 2 to sin, provoking me to anger with their sins 1
7 the evil that he did . . provoking him to anger 1
13 made Israel to sin, provoking the LORD . . to anger 1
26 provoking the LORD . . to anger by their idols. 1
33 Ahab did more to provoke the LORD . . to anger 1
22:53 and provoked the LORD, the God of Israel, to anger 1
2Kg 17:11 did wicked things, provoking the LORD to anger 1
17 sold themselves . . provoking him to anger. 1
21: 6 He did much evil . . provoking him to anger. 1
15 done what is evil . . and have provoked me to anger 1
22:17 they might provoke me to anger with all the work 1
23:19 which kings . . made, provoking the LORD to anger 1
2Ch 28:25 provoking to anger the LORD, the God 1
33: 6 did much evil . . provoking him to anger. 1
34:25 provoke me to anger with all the works 1
Neh 4: 5 provoked thee to anger before the builders. 1
Ps 78:58 For they provoked him to anger 1
106:29 provoked the LORD to anger with their doings 1
Prv 20: 2 he who provokes him to anger forfeits his life. 2
Jer 7:18 offerings to other gods, to provoke me to anger. 1
8:19 Why have they provoked me to anger 1
11:17 provoking me to anger by burning incense 1
25: 6 provoke me to anger with the work of your hands. 1
7 that you might provoke me to anger with the work 1
32:29 poured out to other gods, to provoke me to anger. 1
30 Israel have done nothing but provoke me to anger 1
32 the evil . . which they did to provoke me to anger 1
44: 3 provoking me to anger, in that they went to burn 1
8 Why do you provoke me to anger 1
Ezk 8:17 with violence, and provoke me further to anger? 1
16:26 your harlotry, to provoke me to anger. 1
Eph 6: 4 Fathers, do not provoke your children to anger 3
Jdt 8:14 do not provoke the Lord our God to anger. 3
11:11 they are about to provoke their God to anger 3

provoke to jealousy 1. קנא 2. *παραζηλόω*

1Kg 14:22 they provoked him to jealousy with their sins 1
Ezk 8: 3 image of jealousy, which provokes to jealousy. 1
1Co 10:22 Shall we provoke the Lord to jealousy? 2

provoke to speak 1. *ἀποστοματίζω*

Lke 11:53 and to provoke him to speak of many things 1

provoke to wrath 1. קצף

Deu 9: 7 how you provoked the LORD your God to wrath 1
8 Even at Horeb you provoked the LORD to wrath 1
22 At Tab'erah . . you provoked the LORD to wrath. 1
Zec 8:14 when your fathers provoked me to wrath 1

provoke wrath 1. *παροργίζω*

Man 1:10 I have provoked thy wrath 1

prowl 1. הלך

Ps 12: 8 On every side the wicked prowl 1
Lam 5:18 Zion . . lies desolate; jackals prowl over it. 1
Ezk 19: 6 He prowled among the lions; he became a young lion 1

prowl about 1. סבב

Ps 59: 6 howling like dogs and prowling about the city. 1
14 howling like dogs and prowling about the city. 1

prowl around 1. *περιπατέω*

1Pe 5: 8 the devil prowls around like a roaring lion 1

prudence 1. עָרְמָה 2. עֵטָא (A) 3. *πανοῦργος* 4. *φρόνησις*

Prv 1: 4 that prudence may be given to the simple 1
8: 5 O simple ones, learn prudence; 1
12 I, wisdom, dwell in prudence 1
Dan 2:14 Daniel replied with prudence and discretion 2
Wis 8: 7 she teaches self-control and prudence 4
Sir 19:22 nor is there prudence 4
22:27 a seal of prudence upon my lips 3

prudence *See also* learn.

prudent 1. בין 2. עָרוּם 3. ערם 4. שׂכל 5. *φρόνησις* 6. *φρόνιμος*

1Sm 16:18 of valor, a man of war, prudent in speech 1
Prv 10: 5 A son who gathers in summer is prudent 4
19 but he who restrains his lips is prudent. 4
12:23 A prudent man conceals his knowledge 2
14:15 but the prudent looks where he is going. 2
18 but the prudent are crowned with knowledge. 2
15: 5 but he who heeds admonition is prudent. 3
19:14 but a prudent wife is from the LORD. 4
Jer 49: 7 Has counsel perished from the prudent? 1
Ams 5:13 he who is prudent will keep silent in such a time; 4
Sir 1: 4 prudent understanding from eternity. 5
19:24 Better . . than the highly prudent man 5
21:25 the words of the prudent 6
4Mc 7:17 because not every one has prudent reason. 6

prudent man 1. עָרוּם

Prv 12:16 but the prudent man ignores an insult. 1
13:16 In everything a prudent man acts with knowledge 1
14: 8 The wisdom of a prudent man is to discern his way 1
22: 3 A prudent man sees danger and hides himself; 1
27:12 A prudent man sees danger and hides himself; 1

prune 1. זמר 2. *ἀποκνίζω* 3. *καθαίρω* 4. puto

Lev 25: 3 six years you shall prune your vineyard 1
4 shall not sow your field or prune your vineyard 1
Isa 5: 6 it shall not be pruned or hoed, and briers 1
Joh 15: 2 every branch that does bear fruit he prunes 3
2Es 16:43 also him that prunes the vines 4
4Mc 1:29 the master cultivator, reason, weeds and prunes 2

pruning *See* hook.

pry a limb 1. *ἀναμοχλεύω*

4Mc 10: 5 by prying his limbs from their sockets 1

psalm 1. מִזְמוֹר 2. מַשְׂכִּיל 3. *ψαλμός* 4. psalmus

Ps 3: 0 A Psalm of David, when he fled from Absalom 1
4: 0 with stringed instruments. A Psalm of David. 1
5: 0 for the flutes. A Psalm of David. 1
6: 0 according to The Sheminith. A Psalm of David. 1
8: 0 according to The Gittith. A Psalm of David. 1
9: 0 according to Muth-labben. A Psalm of David. 1
12: 0 according to The Sheminith. A Psalm of David. 1
13: 0 To the choirmaster. A Psalm of David. 1
15: 0 A Psalm of David. 1
18: 0 To the choirmaster. A Psalm of David *
19: 0 To the choirmaster. A Psalm of David. 1
20: 0 To the choirmaster. A Psalm of David. 1
21: 0 To the choirmaster. A Psalm of David. 1
22: 0 The Hind of the Dawn. A Psalm of David. 1
23: 0 A Psalm of David. 1
24: 0 A Psalm of David. 1
25: 0 A Psalm of David. 4
26: 0 A Psalm of David. 4
27: 0 A Psalm of David. 4
28: 0 A Psalm of David. 4
29: 0 A Psalm of David. 1
30: 0 A Psalm of David. 1
31: 0 To the choirmaster. A Psalm of David. 1
32: 0 A Psalm of David. A Maskil. *
34: 0 A Psalm of David, when he feigned madness *
35: 0 A Psalm of David. *

36: 0 To the choirmaster. A Psalm of David *
37: 0 A Psalm of David. 4
38: 0 A Psalm of David, for the memorial offering. 1
39: 0 To Jeduthun. A Psalm of David. 1
40: 0 To the choirmaster. A Psalm of David. 1
41: 0 To the choirmaster. A Psalm of David. 1
46: 0 To the choirmaster. A Psalm of the Sons of Korah. *
47: 0 To the choirmaster. A Psalm of the Sons of Korah. 1
7 sing praises with a psalm! 2
48: 0 A Song. A Psalm of the Sons of Korah. 1
49: 0 To the choirmaster. A Psalm of the Sons of Korah. 1
50: 0 A Psalm of Asaph. 1
51: 0 To the choirmaster. A Psalm of David 1
61: 0 with stringed instruments. A Psalm of David. *
62: 0 according to Jeduthun. A Psalm of David. 1
63: 0 A Psalm of David, when he was in the Wilderness 1
64: 0 To the choirmaster. A Psalm of David. 1
65: 0 To the choirmaster. A Psalm of David. A Song. 1
66: 0 To the choirmaster. A Song. A Psalm. 1
67: 0 with stringed instruments. A Psalm. A Song. 1
68: 0 To the choirmaster. A Psalm of David. A Song. 1
69: 0 according to Lilies. A Psalm of David. *
70: 0 A Psalm of David, for the memorial offering. 4
72: 0 A Psalm of Solomon. 4
73: 0 A Psalm of Asaph. 1
75: 0 Do Not Destroy. A Psalm of Asaph. A Song. 1
76: 0 A Psalm of Asaph. A Song. 1
77: 0 according to Jeduthun. A Psalm of Asaph. 1
79: 0 A Psalm of Asaph. 1
80: 0 A Testimony of Asaph. A Psalm. 1
81: 0 A Psalm of Asaph. 4
82: 0 A Psalm of Asaph. 1
83: 0 A Song. A Psalm of Asaph. 1
84: 0 A Psalm of the Sons of Korah. 1
85: 0 To the choirmaster. A Psalm of the Sons of Korah. 1
87: 0 A Psalm of the Sons of Korah. A Song. 1
88: 0 A Song. A Psalm of the Sons of Korah. 1
92: 0 A Psalm. A Song for the Sabbath. 1
98: 0 A Psalm. 1
100: 0 A Psalm for the thank offering. 1
101: 0 A Psalm of David. 1
103: 0 A Psalm of David. *
108: 0 A Song. A Psalm of David. 1
109: 0 To the choirmaster. A Psalm of David. 1
110: 0 A Psalm of David. 1
138: 0 A Psalm of David. *
139: 0 To the choirmaster. A Psalm of David. 1
140: 0 To the choirmaster. A Psalm of David. 1
141: 0 A Psalm of David. 1
143: 0 A Psalm of David. 1
144: 0 A Psalm of David. *
Lke 20:42 For David himself says in the Book of Psalms 3
24:44 the prophets and the psalms 3
Act 1:20 it is written in the book of Psalms 3
13:33 as also it is written in the second psalm 3
35 Therefore he says also in another psalm *
Eph 5:19 addressing one another in psalms and hymns 3
Col 3:16 sing psalms and hymns and spiritual songs 3
Jdt 16: 2 Raise to him a new psalm 3
3Mc 6:35 joyous thanksgiving and psalms. 3

psalmist 1. זָמִיר 2. *ὑμνογράφος*
2Sm 23: 1 oracle of David . . the sweet psalmist of Israel 1
4Mc 18:15 He sang to you songs of the psalmist David 2

public 1. *δῆμος* 2. *δημόσιος* 3. *κοινός* 4. *πλῆθος* 5. palam
Act 18:28 for he powerfully confuted the Jews in public 2
20:20 teaching you in public and from house to house 2
1Ti 4:13 attend to the public reading of scripture *
2Es 14:26 some things you shall make public 5
45 Make public the 24 books that you wrote first 5
Sir 7: 7 Do not offend against the public 4
1Mc 14:22 we have recorded in our public decrees, as follows 1
23 put a copy of their words in the public archives 1
2Mc 4: 5 the welfare, both public and private, of all the people 3
9:26 the public and private services rendered to you 3
10: 8 They decreed by public ordinance and vote 3
12: 4 this was done by public vote of the city 3
15: 6 a public monument of victory over Judas and his men 3
36 they all decreed by public vote 3
3Mc 2:27 to inflict public disgrace upon the Jewish community 2
6:36 when they had ordained a public rite 3
4Mc 3:21 a revolution against the public harmony 3

public *See also* adjuration, affair, appear, assembly, expense, platform, square, view.

public and shameful 1. *παραδειγματισμός*
3Mc 7:14 punished and put to a public and shameful death 1

publicly 1. *δημόσιος* 2. *μετὰ παρρησίας* 3. *φανερῶς* 4. palam
Joh 7:10 he also went up, not publicly but in private. 3
Act 16:37 beaten us publicly, uncondemned 1
2Es 2:36 I publicly call on my Savior to witness. 4
AEs 16:19 post . . this letter publicly in every place 2
2Mc 6:10 These . . they publicly paraded about the city 1

publicly *See also* expose, portray.

publish 1. אמר 2. בשר 3. שמע 4. *ἐκδίδωμι* 5. facio
2Sm 1:20 in Gath, publish it not in the streets of Ash'kelon; 2
Neh 8:15 publish and proclaim in all their towns 3
Isa 52: 7 who publishes peace, who brings good tidings 3
7 good tidings of good, who publishes salvation 3
Ams 4: 5 and proclaim freewill offerings, publish them; 3
Jon 3: 7 and published through Nin'eveh 1
2Es 14: 6 'These words you shall publish openly 5
Sir 0: 3 in order to complete and publish the book 4

puff 1. פוח
Ps 10: 5 as for all his foes, he puffs at them. 1

puff up 1. *φρυάζω* 2. *φυσιόω*
1Co 4: 6 that none of you may be puffed up in favor of one 2
8: 1 Knowledge" puffs up, but love builds up. 2
Col 2:18 puffed up without reason by his sensuous mind 2
2Mc 7:34 and puffed up by uncertain hopes 1
3Mc 2: 2 puffed up in his audacity and power. 1

puff up with conceit 1. *τυφόω*
1Ti 3: 6 he may be puffed up with conceit 1
6: 4 is puffed up with conceit, he knows nothing 1

pull 1. מרט 2. משך 3. נשא 4. נסח (A)
Deu 21: 3 heifer . . which has not pulled in the yoke. 2
Ezr 6:11 beam shall be pulled out of his house 4
9: 3 pulled hair from my head and beard 1
Ezk 17: 9 not take . . many people to pull it from its roots. 3

pull away 1. נסע
Jdg 16:14 he awoke . . and pulled away the pin, the loom 1

pull down 1. הרס 2. נתץ 3. *ἀφαιρέω* 4. *καθαιρέω* 5. praepondero
Jdg 6:25 pull down the altar of Ba'al which your father has 1
30 he has pulled down the altar of Ba'al and cut down 2
31 himself, because his altar has been pulled down. 2
32 Jerubba'al . . because he pulled down his altar. 2
2Kg 23:12 the altars . . he pulled down and broke in pieces 2
15 that altar with the high place he pulled down 2
Jer 42:10 then I will build you up and not pull you down; 1
Lke 12:18 I will pull down my barns, and build larger ones; 4
1Es 6:16 they pulled down the house, and burned it 4
2Es 16:76 do not let your sins pull you down 5
Jdt 13: 9 and pulled down the canopy from the posts 3

pull off 1. חלץ
Deu 25: 9 pull his sandal off his foot, and spit in his face 1
10 The house of him that had his sandal pulled off. 1

pull out 1. מרט 2. נתק 3. שלל 4. *ἀνασπάω* 5. *κατατίλλω* 6. excutio
Rut 2:16 And also pull out some from the bundles for her 3
Isa 50: 6 and my cheeks to those who pulled out the beard; 1
Jer 12: 3 Pull them out like sheep for the slaughter 2
Lke 14: 5 will not immediately pull him out on a sabbath day? 4
1Es 8:71 pulled out hair from my head and beard 5
2Es 1: 8 Pull out the hair of your head 6
Bel 1:42 he pulled Daniel out 4

pull out hair 1. מרט
Neh 13:25 beat some of them and pulled out their hair; 1

pull up 1. נסע 2. נתק
Jdg 16: 3 took hold of the doors . . and pulled them up 1
Job 19:10 I am gone, and my hope has he pulled up like a tree. 1
Ezk 17: 9 Will it thrive? Will he not pull up its roots 2

pulpit 1. מִגְדָּל
Neh 8: 4 Ezra the scribe stood on a wooden pulpit 1

punish 1. חשך 2. נקם 3. נתן עַל 4. ענש 5. פקד 6. פְּקֻדָּה 7. שית עַל 8. שפט 9. *διχοτομέω* 10. *ἐκδικέω* 11. *ἐκδίκησις* 12. *ἐλέγχω* 13. *ἐπισκέπτομαι* 14. *ἐπιτιμάω* 15. *ἔχω ἐπιτιμίαν* 16. *κολάζω* 17. *κόλασις* 18. *ὄφλησις* 19. *παιδεύω* 20. *περιπίπτω ἐπιτίμοις* 21. *τιμωρέω* 22. *τιμωρητής* 23. castigo 24. crucio
Exd 21:20 slave dies under his hand, he shall be punished. 2
21 he is not to be punished; for the slave is his 2
Lev 18:25 became defiled, so that I punished its iniquity 5
Num12:11 do not punish us because we have done foolishly 7
1Sm 3:13 I am about to punish his house for ever 8
15: 2 I will punish what Am'alek did to Israel 5
Ezr 9:13 punished us less than our iniquities deserved 1
Job 31:11 would be an iniquity to be punished by the judges; *
28 this also would be an iniquity to be punished
35:15 now, because his anger does not punish 5
Ps 59: 5 Awake to punish all the nations; 5
89:32 I will punish their transgression with the rod 5
Prv 21:11 scoffer is punished, the simple becomes wise; 4
Isa 10:12 he will punish the arrogant boasting of the king 5
13:11 I will punish the world for its evil 5
24:21 that day the LORD will punish the host of heaven 5
22 and after many days they will be punished. 5
26:21 to punish the inhabitants of the earth 5
27: 1 will punish Leviathan the fleeing serpent 5
Jer 5: 9 Shall I not punish them for these things? 5
29 Shall I not punish them for these things? 5
6: 6 This is the city which must be punished; 5
15 at the time that I punish them 5
8:12 when I punish them, they shall be overthrown 6
9: 9 Shall I not punish them for these things? 5
25 when I will punish all those who are circumcised 5
11:22 Behold, I will punish them; 5
14:10 remember their iniquity and punish their sins. 5
21:14 I will punish you according to the fruit 5
23:34 I will punish that man and his household. 5
25:12 I will punish the king of Babylon and that nation 5
27: 8 I will punish that nation with the sword 5
29:32 thus says the LORD: Behold, I will punish Shemai'ah 5
30:20 and I will punish all who oppress them. 5
36:31 I will punish him and his offspring 5
44:13 I will punish those who dwell in the land of Egypt 5
13 as I have punished Jerusalem, with the sword 5
29 says the LORD, that I will punish you in this place 5
49: 8 calamity of Esau . . the time when I punish him. 5
50:18 as I punished the king of Assyria. 5
31 your day has come, the time when I will punish you. 5
51:44 I will punish Bel in Babylon 5
47 when I will punish the images of Babylon; 5
Lam 4:22 your iniquity, O daughter of Edom, he will punish 5
Ezk 7: 3 I will punish you for all your abominations. 3
4 but I will punish you for your ways 3
8 I will punish you for all your abominations. 3
9 I will punish you according to your ways 3
Hos 1: 4 a little while, and I will punish the house of Jehu 5
2:13 I will punish her for the feast days of the Ba'als 5
4: 9 I will punish them for their ways 5
14 I will not punish your daughters 5
8:13 remember their iniquity, and punish their sins; 5
9: 9 he will punish their sins. 5
12: 2 and will punish Jacob according to his ways 5
Ams 3: 2 I will punish you for all your iniquities. 5
14 the day I punish Israel for his transgressions 5
14 I will punish the altars of Bethel 5
Zep 1: 8 I will punish the officials and the king's sons 5
9 On that day I will punish every one 5
12 and I will punish the men who are thickening upon 5
Zec 10: 3 I will punish the leaders; 5
Mat 24:51 will punish him, and put him with the hypocrites; 9
Lke 12:46 will punish him, and put him with the unfaithful. 9
Act 4:21 they let them go, finding no way to punish them 16
22: 5 and bring them in bonds to Jerusalem to be punished. 21
26:11 I punished them often in all the synagogues 21
2Co 6: 9 as punished, and yet not killed; 19
10: 6 being ready to punish every disobedience 10
Heb 12: 5 nor lose courage when you are punished by him. 12
1Pe 2:14 sent by him to punish those who do wrong 11
1Es 8:24 shall be strictly punished 18
2Es 5:30 they should be punished at thy own hands. 23
9:13 be curious as to how the ungodly will be punished; 24
Tob 3: 3 do not punish me for my sins 10
Jdt 7:28 who punishes us according to our sins 10
11:10 our nation cannot be punished 10
Wis 1: 8 justice, when it punishes, will not pass him by. 12
3: 4 For though in the sight of men they were punished 16
10 the ungodly will be punished 16
11: 5 very things by which their enemies were punished 16
8 how thou didst punish their enemies. 16
15 irrational creatures to punish them 11
16 punished by the very things by which he sins. 16
12:14 about those whom thou hast punished. 16
15 condemn him who does not deserve to be punished. 16
20 if thou didst punish with such great care 21
27 being punished by means of them 16
14:10 will be punished together with him who did it. 16
16: 1 deservedly punished through such creatures 16
9 they deserved to be punished by such things; 16
24 exerts itself to punish the unrighteous 17
18: 8 thou didst punish our enemies 21
11 The slave was punished with the same penalty 16
Sir 2:14 What will you do when the Lord punishes you? 13
5: 3 the Lord will surely punish you. 10
23:21 will be punished in the streets of the city 10
39:30 the sword that punishes the ungodly 10
Bar 3: 8 to be reproached and cursed and punished 18
1Mc 7: 7 let him punish them and all who help them. 10
15:21 punish them according to their law. 10
2Mc 4:16 became their enemies and punished them. 22
6:13 to punish them immediately 20
14 the Lord waits patiently to punish them 16
7: 7 rather than have your body punished limb by limb? 21
3Mc 2:17 Do not punish us for the defilement 10
24 though he had been punished 14
3:26 when these all have been punished 16
7: 3 to punish them with barbarous penalties 16
14 punished and put to a public and shameful death 16
4Mc 2:12 one punishes them for misdeeds. 16
8: 6 I am able to punish those who disobey my orders 16
17:21 the tyrant was punished 21
18: 5 The tyrant Antiochus was both punished on earth 21

punishable 1. מִשְׁפָּט

Deu 21:22 man has committed a crime punishable by death 1
22:26 woman there is no offense punishable by death •

punisher 1. κολάζω

Wis 18:22 by his word he subdued the punisher 1

punishment 1. חֵטְא 2. חַטָּאת 3. מוּסָרָה 4. מוּסָר 5. עָוֹן 6. פְּקֻדָּה 7. תּוֹכֵחָה 8. ἀνάγκη 9. δίκη 10. ἐκδίκησις 11. ἐλεγμός 12. ἔλεγχος 13. ἐπισκοπή 14. ἐπιτιμία 15. ἐπίτιμος 16. εὐθύνω 17. κόλασις 18. κρίσις 19. πρόστιμον 20. τιμωρία 21. castigatio 22. punio 23. punitio

Gen 4:13 My punishment is greater than I can bear. 5
19:15 be consumed in the punishment of the city. 5
1Sm 28:10 no punishment shall come upon you for this 5
2Kg 7: 9 if we are silent . . punishment will overtake us; 5
Job 19:29 for wrath brings the punishment of the sword 5
Ps 69:27 Add to them punishment upon punishment; 5
27 Add to them punishment upon punishment; 5
Isa 10: 3 What will you do on the day of punishment 6
30:32 every stroke of the staff of punishment 3
Jer 10:15 the time of their punishment they shall perish. 6
11:23 bring evil . . the year of their punishment. 6
23:12 evil upon them in the year of their punishment 6
30:14 of an enemy, the punishment of a merciless foe 4
46:21 come upon them, the time of their punishment. 6
48:44 in the year of their punishment, says the LORD. 6
50:27 their day has come, the time of their punishment. 6
51: 6 Be not cut off in her punishment 5
18 the time of their punishment they shall perish. 6
Lam 3:39 man complain . . about the punishment of his sins? 1
4: 6 has been greater than the punishment of Sodom 2
Ezk 4: 4 lay the punishment of the house of Israel upon 5
4 you shall bear their punishment. 5
5 the number of the years of their punishment; 5
5 so long shall you bear the punishment 5
6 and bear the punishment of the house of Judah; 5
17 and waste away under their punishment. 5
14:10 And they shall bear their punishment 5
10 their punishment-the punishment of the prophet 5
10 and the punishment of the inquirer shall be alike 5
21:25 day has come, the time of your final punishment 5
29 day has come, the time of their final punishment. 5
35: 5 at the time of their final punishment; 5
44:10 went astray, shall bear their punishment. 5
12 that they shall bear their punishment. 5
Hos 5: 9 become a desolation in the day of punishment; 7
9: 7 The days of punishment have come 6
Mic 7: 4 The day of their watchmen, of their punishment 6
Zec 14:19 This shall be the punishment to Egypt 2
19 punishment to all the nations that do not go up 2
Mat 25:46 they will go away into eternal punishment 17
2Co 2: 6 this punishment by the majority is enough; 14
7:11 what longing, what zeal, what punishment 10
2Th 1: 9 suffer the punishment of eternal destruction 9
Heb 10:29 How much worse punishment . . will be deserved 20
1Jn 4:18 For fear has to do with punishment 17
Jde 1: 7 serve as an example by undergoing a punishment 9
2Es 7:21 what they should observe to avoid punishment. 22
93 and the punishment that awaits them. 23
117 in sorrow now and expect punishment after death? 23
15:12 for the plague of chastisement and punishment 21
Jdt 2:10 hold them for me till the day of their punishment. 11
AEs 16:18 inflicted on him the punishment he deserved. 18
Wis 11:13 through their own punishments 17
16: 2 Instead of this punishment 17
18: 5 thou didst in punishment take away 12
19: 4 in order that they might fill up the punishment 17
13 The punishments did not come upon the sinners 20
15 punishment of some sort will come upon the former 13
Sir 5: 7 at the time of punishment you will perish. 10
7:17 the punishment of the ungodly is fire and worms. 10
8: 5 remember that we all deserve punishment. 10
12: 6 will inflict punishment on the ungodly. 10
23:24 punishment will fall on her children. 13
2Mc 4:38 repaid him with the punishment he deserved. 17
6:12 these punishments were designed not to destroy 20
26 I should avoid the punishment of men 20
7:36 receive just punishment for your arrogance. 19
3Mc 2: 6 inflicting many and varied punishments 20
23 the severe punishment that had overtaken him 16
3:28 property of the one who incurs the punishment 16
4: 4 at the sight of their unusual punishments 20
13 not omitting any detail of their punishment. 20
7:10 should receive the punishment they deserved. 17
4Mc 4:24 punishments were being disregarded 20
6: 9 he bore the pains and scorned the punishment 8
28 let our punishment suffice for them. 9
8: 9 to destroy . . with dreadful punishments 17
11: 3 incur punishment from the heavenly justice 20

punishment *See also* bring, liable.

punishment of iniquity 1. עָוֹן

Lam 4:22 punishment of your iniquity . . is accomplished 1

some other punishment 1. τιμωρία

1Es 8:24 whether by death or some other punishment 1

under punishment 1. κολάζω

2Pe 2: 9 and to keep the unrighteous under punishment 1

puny 1. modicus

2Es 11: 3 wings; but they became little, puny wings. 1

pupil 1. תַּלְמִיד 2. κόρη

1Ch 25: 8 they cast lots . . teacher and pupil alike. 1
4Mc 18:21 pierced the pupils of their eyes 2

purchase 1. מִקְנָה 2. מִקְנָה 3. קנה 4. שׁבר

Gen 25:10 the field which Abraham purchased 3
49:32 field and the cave . . were purchased 2
Exd 15:16 the people pass by whom thou hast purchased. 3
Deu 2: 6 purchase food from them for money, that you may eat 4
Jer 32: 7 the right of redemption by purchase is yours. 3
11 Then I took the sealed deed of purchase 1
12 and I gave the deed of purchase to Baruch 1
12 the witnesses who signed the deed of purchase 1
14 this sealed deed of purchase and this open deed 1
16 After I had given the deed of purchase to Baruch 1

purchase a slave 1. ἀργυρώνητος

Jdt 4:10 hired laborer and purchased slave 1

pure 1. אֱמֶת 2. בַּר 3. ברר 4. זַךְ 5. זכה 6. חַף 7. טָהוֹר 8. טהר 9. טוֹב 10. יָשָׁר 11. מִכְלָה 12. נִקָּיוֹן 13. סגר 14. נָקָא (A) 15. ἀγαθός 16. ἁγνός 17. ἁγνότης 18. ἄδολος 19. εἰλικρινής 20. ἐκλεκτός 21. καθαρός 22. πιστικός 23. caste

Exd 25:11 you shall overlay it with pure gold 7
17 Then you shall make a mercy seat of pure gold; 7
24 You shall overlay it with pure gold 7
29 of pure gold you shall make them. 7
31 you shall make a lampstand of pure gold. 7
36 one piece of hammered work of pure gold. 7
38 snuffers and their trays shall be of pure gold. 7
39 Of a talent of pure gold shall it be made, with all 7
27:20 that they bring to you pure beaten olive oil 4
28:14 two chains of pure gold, twisted like cords; 7
22 make . . twisted chains like cords, of pure gold; 7
36 you shall make a plate of pure gold, and engrave 7
30: 3 you shall overlay it with pure gold 7
34 Take . . sweet spices with pure frankincense 4
35 incense . . seasoned with salt, pure and holy; 7
31: 8 pure lampstand with all its utensils 7
37: 2 he overlaid it with pure gold within and without 7
6 he made a mercy seat of pure gold; 7
11 he overlaid it with pure gold, and made a molding 7
16 he made the vessels of pure gold which were to be 7
17 He also made the lampstand of pure gold. 7
22 was one piece of hammered work of pure gold. 7
23 its snuffers and its trays of pure gold. 7
24 all its utensils of a talent of pure gold. 7
26 He overlaid it with pure gold, its top 7
29 made . . the pure fragrant incense, blended 7
39:15 twisted chains like cords, of pure gold; 7
25 They also made bells of pure gold 7
30 they made the plate of the holy crown of pure gold 7
Lev 24: 2 to bring you pure oil from beaten olives 4
7 you shall put pure frankincense with each row 4
2Sm 22:27 with the pure thou dost show thyself pure 3
1Kg 6:20 sanctuary . . and he overlaid it with pure gold. 13
21 Solomon overlaid the inside . . with pure gold 13
7:49 the lampstands of pure gold, five on the south 13
50 basins, dishes . . and firepans, of pure gold; 13
10:21 all the vessels of the House . . were of pure gold; 13
1Ch 28:17 pure gold for the forks, the basins, and the cups; 7
2Ch 3: 4 He overlaid it on the inside with pure gold. 7
4:20 the lampstands and their lamps of pure gold 13
21 flowers, the lamps, and the tongs, of purest gold; 11
22 dishes for incense, and firepans, of pure gold; 13
9:17 ivory throne, and overlaid it with pure gold. 7
20 all the vessels of the House . . were of pure gold; 13
13:11 set out the showbread on the table of pure gold 7
Job 4:17 Can a man be pure before his Maker? 8
8: 6 if you are pure and upright 4
11: 4 For you say, 'My doctrine is pure, and I am clean 4
16:17 no violence in my hands, and my prayer is pure. 4
33: 9 I am pure, and there is no iniquity in me. 6
Ps 12: 6 promises of the LORD are promises that are pure 7
18:26 with the pure thou dost show thyself pure; 3
19: 8 the commandment of the LORD is pure 2
24: 4 He who has clean hands and a pure heart 2
73: 1 to the upright, to those who are pure in heart. 2
Prv 15:26 words of the pure are pleasing to him. 7
16: 2 All the ways of a man are pure in his own eyes 4
20: 9 Who can say, "I . . am pure from my sin"? 7
11 whether what he does is pure and right. 4
21: 8 but the conduct of the pure is right. 10
30:12 There are those who are pure in their own eyes 7
Jer 2:21 I planted you a choice vine, wholly of pure seed. 1
Lam 4: 1 gold has grown dim, how the pure gold is changed! 9
7 princes were purer than snow, whiter than milk; 5
Dan 7: 9 as snow, and the hair of his head like pure wool; 14
Hos 8: 5 How long will it be till they are pure 12
Hab 1:13 Thou who art of purer eyes than to behold evil 7
Zep 3: 9 change the speech of the peoples to a pure speech 3
Mal 1:11 incense is offered to my name, and a pure offering; 7
Mat 5: 8 Blessed are the pure in heart, for they shall see 21
Mrk 14: 3 ointment of pure nard, very costly 22
Joh 12: 3 Mary took a pound of costly ointment of pure nard 22
2Co 11: 2 to present you as a pure bride to her one husband. 16
3 from a sincere and pure devotion to Christ. 17
Php 1:10 pure and blameless for the day of Christ 19
4: 8 whatever is pure, whatever is lovely 16
1Ti 1: 5 that issues from a pure heart and a good conscience 21
5:22 keep yourself pure. 16
2Ti 2:22 those who call upon the Lord from a pure heart. 21
Tit 1:15 To the pure all things are pure 21
15 To the pure all things are pure 21
15 to the corrupt and unbelieving nothing is pure; 21
Heb 10:22 our bodies washed with pure water. 21
Jas 1:27 Religion that is pure and undefiled before God 21
3:17 wisdom from above is first pure, then peaceable 16
1Pe 2: 2 long for the pure spiritual milk 18
1Jn 3: 3 every one . . purifies himself as he is pure. 16
Rev 15: 6 seven angels . . robed in pure bright linen 21
19: 8 clothed with fine linen, bright and pure"- 21
14 arrayed in fine linen, white and pure 21
21:18 while the city was pure gold, clear as glass. 21
21 and the street of the city was pure gold 21
2Es 7:122 those who have led a pure life 23
Tob 8:15 with every pure and holy blessing 21
13:16 her towers and battlements with pure gold. 21
Wis 7:23 intelligent and pure and most subtle. 21
25 a pure emanation of the glory of the Almighty; 19
8:18 in friendship with her, pure delight 15
14:24 keep either their lives or their marriages pure 21
Bar 3:30 Who . . found her, and will buy her for pure gold? 20
4Mc 5:37 The fathers will receive me as pure 16
18: 7 I was a pure virgin 16
23 have received pure and immortal souls from God 16

pure *See also* gold, keep.

show oneself pure 1. ברר

2Sm 22:27 with the pure thou dost show thyself pure 1
Ps 18:26 with the pure thou dost show thyself pure; 1

pureness 1. καθαρότης

Wis 7:24 because of her pureness she pervades . . all things 1

purge 1. בער 2. חטא 3. טהר

Deu 13: 5 So you shall purge the evil from the midst of you. 1
17: 7 So you shall purge the evil from the midst of you. 1
12 so you shall purge the evil from Israel. 1
19:13 purge the guilt of innocent blood from Israel 1
19 you shall purge the evil from the midst of you. 1
21: 9 purge the guilt of innocent blood 1
21 so you shall purge the evil from your midst; 1
22:21 you shall purge the evil from the midst of you. 1
22 so you shall purge the evil from Israel. 1
24 so you shall purge the evil from the midst of you. 1
24: 7 so you shall purge the evil from the midst of you. 1
2Ch 34: 3 began to purge Judah and Jerusalem 3
5 purged Judah and Jerusalem. 3
8 when he had purged the land and the house 3
Ps 51: 7 Purge me with hyssop, and I shall be clean; 2

purge away 1. ἀποκαθαρίζω

Tob 12: 9 it will purge away every sin 1

purge out 1. ברר

Ezk 20:38 I will purge out the rebels from among you 1

purification 1. טָהֳרָה 2. ἁγνισμός 3. καθαρισμός 4. καθαρότης 5. καθάρσιος

Neh 12:45 performed the . . service of purification 1
Lke 2:22 when the time came for their purification 3
Joh 2: 6 jars . . for the Jewish rites of purification 3
Act 21:26 the days of purification would be fulfilled 2
Heb 1: 3 When he had made purification for sins 3
9:13 sanctifies for the purification of the flesh 4
Sir 51:20 through purification I found her 3
2Mc 1:18 shall celebrate the purification of the temple 3
36 called this "nephthar," which means purification 3
2:16 we are about to celebrate the purification 3
19 the purification of the great temple 3
10: 5 the purification of the sanctuary took place 3
4Mc 6:29 Make my blood their purification 5

purifier 1. טהר

Mal 3: 3 he will sit as a refiner and purifier of silver 1

purify 1. ברר 2. זקק 3. חטא 4. טהר 5. טֹהַר 6. טָהֳרָה 7. קדשׁ 8. ἁγνίζω 9. βαπτίζω 10. ἐκκαθαίρω 11. καθαρίζω 12. καθαρισμός

Gen 35: 2 and purify yourselves, and change your garments 4
Lev 8:15 purified the altar, and poured out the blood 3
12: 4 continue . . in the blood of her purifying 6
4 until the days of her purifying are completed 5
5 she shall continue in the blood of her purifying 6
6 when the days of her purifying are completed 5

Num31:19 purify yourselves and your captives 3
20 You shall purify every garment, every 3
23 also be purified with the water of impurity; 3
2Sm 11: 4 Now she was purifying herself 7
Ezr 6:20 priests . . had purified themselves together; 4
Neh 12:30 priests and the Levites purified themselves; 4
30 purified the people and the gates and the wall. 4
13:22 Levites that they should purify themselves 4
Ps 12: 6 in a furnace on the ground, purified seven times. 2
Isa 52:11 purify yourselves, you who bear the vessels 1
66:17 and purify themselves to go into the gardens 4
Ezk 43:26 they make atonement for the altar and purify it 4
Dan 12:10 Many shall purify themselves 1
Mal 3: 3 he will purify the sons of Levi and refine them 4
Mrk 7: 4 they do not eat unless they purify themselves 9
Joh 3:25 a discussion arose . . over purifying. 12
11:55 many went up . . to purify themselves. 8
Act 21:24 purify yourself along with them 8
26 the next day he purified himself with them 8
24:18 they found me purified in the temple 8
2Ti 2:21 If any one purifies himself from what is ignoble 10
Tit 2:14 to purify for himself a people of his own 11
Heb 9:14 purify your conscience from dead works 11
22 almost everything is purified with blood 11
23 to be purified with these rites 11
Jas 4: 8 purify your hearts, you men of double mind. 8
1Pe 1:22 Having purified your souls by your obedience 8
1Jn 3: 3 every one who thus hopes in him purifies himself 8
1Es 7:10 the Levites were purified together. 8
11 Not all of the returned captives were purified 8
11 the Levites were all purified together 8
Jdt 16:18 As soon as the people were purified 11
2Mc 2:18 has purified the place. 11
10: 3 They purified the sanctuary 11
7 the purifying of his own holy place. 11
12:38 they purified themselves according to the custom 8
14:36 this house that has been so recently purified. 11
4Mc 1:11 their native land was purified through them. 11
17:21 and the homeland purified 11

purify from sin 1. חטא
Num 8:21 the Levites purified themselves from sin 1

purity 1. טָהוֹר 2. *ἁγνεία* 3. *ἁγνός* 4. *ἁγνότης* 5. *καθαρισμός* 6. pudicitia
Prv 22:11 He who loves purity of heart, and whose speech 1
2Co 6: 6 by purity, knowledge, forbearance, kindness 4
1Ti 4:12 conduct, in love, in faith, in purity. 2
5: 2 younger women like sisters, in all purity. 2
2Es 6:32 and has also observed the purity 6
1Mc 14:36 do great damage to its purity. 2
4Mc 7: 6 which had room only for reverence and purity 5
18: 8 defile the purity of my virginity. 3

purple 1. אַרְגָּמָן 2. תּוֹלָע 3. תְּכֵלֶת 4. אַרְגְּוָן (A) 5. *πορφύρα* 6. *πορφυροῦς* 7. *ὑακίνθινος*
Exd 25: 4 blue and purple and scarlet stuff 1
26: 1 twined linen and blue and purple and scarlet 1
31 veil of blue and purple and scarlet stuff 1
36 a screen . . of blue and purple and scarlet stuff 1
27:16 a screen . . of blue and purple and scarlet stuff 1
28: 5 receive gold, blue and purple and scarlet stuff 1
6 gold, of blue and purple and scarlet stuff 1
8 of gold, blue and purple and scarlet stuff 1
15 of gold, blue and purple and scarlet stuff 1
33 shall make pomegranates of blue and purple 1
35: 6 blue and purple and scarlet stuff and fine 1
23 with whom was found blue or purple or scarlet 1
25 spun in blue and purple and scarlet stuff 1
35 by an embroiderer in blue and purple and scarlet 1
36: 8 linen and blue and purple and scarlet stuff 1
35 veil of blue and purple and scarlet stuff 1
37 screen . . of blue and purple and scarlet stuff 1
38:18 needlework in blue and purple and scarlet stuff 1
23 embroiderer in blue and purple and scarlet 1
39: 1 of the blue and purple and scarlet stuff 1
2 gold, blue and purple and scarlet stuff 1
3 into the blue and purple and the scarlet stuff 1
5 of gold, blue and purple and scarlet stuff 1
8 of gold, blue and purple and scarlet stuff 1
24 they made pomegranates of blue and purple 1
29 linen and of blue and purple and scarlet stuff 1
Num 4:13 the altar, and spread a purple cloth over it; 1
Jdg 8:26 the purple garments worn by the kings of Mid'ian 1
Est 1: 6 caught up with cords of fine linen and purple 1
8:15 crown and a mantle of fine linen and purple 1
Prv 31:22 her clothing is fine linen and purple. 1
Sng 3:10 he made its . . its back of gold, its seat of purple; 1
7: 5 and your flowing locks are like purple; 1
Jer 10: 9 their clothing is violet and purple; 1
Lam 4: 5 who were brought up in purple lie on ash heaps. 2
Ezk 23: 6 warriors clothed in purple, governors 3
27: 7 blue and purple from the coasts of Eli'shah was 1
16 they exchanged for your wares emeralds, purple 1
Dan 5: 7 clothed with purple, and have a chain of gold 4
16 clothed with purple, and have a chain of gold 4
29 Daniel was clothed with purple, a chain of gold 4
Mrk 15:17 they clothed him in a purple cloak 5
20 they stripped him of the purple cloak 5
Lke 16:19 who was clothed in purple and fine linen 5
Joh 19: 2 put it on his head, and arrayed him in a purple robe; 6
5 the crown of thorns and the purple robe 6
Rev 17: 4 The woman was arrayed in purple and scarlet 6
18:12 cargo of . . fine linen, purple, silk and scarlet 5
16 clothed in fine linen, in purple and scarlet 6
1Es 3: 6 He shall be clothed in purple 5
Jdt 10:21 under a canopy which was woven with purple 5
Sir 40: 4 the man who wears purple and a crown 7
45:10 with a holy garment, of gold and blue and purple 5
LJr 1:12 When they have been dressed in purple robes 6
72 By the purple and linen that rot upon them 5
1Mc 4:23 and cloth dyed blue and sea purple, and great riches. 5
8:14 or worn purple as a mark of pride 5
10:62 and to clothe him in purple, and they did so. 5
64 and saw him clothed in purple 5
11:58 dress in purple and wear a gold buckle. 5
14:43 he should be clothed in purple and wear gold. 5
44 to be clothed in purple or put on a gold buckle. 5

purple *See also* fabric, robe.

purport 1. *ὡς*
2Th 2: 2 by letter purporting to be from us 1

purpose 1. אמר 2. בַּעֲבוּר 3. דָּבָר 4. זמם 5. חפץ 6. חֵפֶץ 7. יעץ 8. יצר 9. יֵצֶר 10. לְמַעַן 11. מְזִמָּה 12. מַחֲשָׁבָה 13. מְלָאכָה 14. מַעַן 15. מַעֲשֶׂה 16. עִם 17. עֵצָה 18. *βουλεύω* 19. *βουλή* 20. *βούλημα* 21. *γίνομαι ἡ διάνοια* 22. *γνώμη* 23. *δαπάνη* 24. *διά* 25. *διανόημα* 26. *εἰς* 27. *ἐπί* 28. *ἐπιτήδευμα* 29. *εὐδοκία* 30. *ἴδιος* 31. *καρδία* 32. *μέριμνα* 33. *ὅπως* 34. *πρόθεσις* 35. *τέλος* 36. *ὥστε* 37. ut
Exd 9:16 for this purpose have I let you live, to show you 2
Lev 11:32 any vessel that is used for any purpose 13
Deu 31:21 I know the purposes . . they are already forming 9
1Kg 5: 5 I purpose to build a house for the name of the LORD 1
1Ch 29:18 keep for ever such purposes and thoughts 9
2Ch 2: 1 Solomon purposed to build a temple for . . LORD 1
Ezr 4: 5 hired counselors . . to frustrate their purpose 17
Neh 6:13 For this purpose he was hired, that I should be 10
8: 4 pulpit which they had made for the purpose; 3
Job 10:13 I know that this was thy purpose. 16
42: 2 no purpose of thine can be thwarted. 11
Ps 57: 2 to God who fulfils his purpose for me. •
64: 5 They hold fast to their evil purpose; 3
106:43 but they were rebellious in their purposes 17
Prv 16: 4 The LORD has made everything for its purpose 14
19:21 purpose of the LORD that will be established. 17
20: 5 The purpose in a man's mind is like deep water 17
Isa 5:19 the purpose of the Holy One of Israel draw near 17
14:24 and as I have purposed, so shall it stand 7
26 This is the purpose that is purposed concerning 17
26 This is the purpose that is purposed concerning 7
27 For the LORD of hosts has purposed 7
19:12 what the LORD . . has purposed against Egypt. 7
17 fear because of the purpose which the LORD . . has 17
17 the LORD of hosts has purposed against them. 7
23: 8 Who has purposed this against Tyre 7
9 The LORD of hosts has purposed it 7
44:28 my shepherd, and he shall fulfil all my purpose'; 6
46:10 and I will accomplish all my purpose,' 6
11 bring it to pass; I have purposed, and I will do it. 8
48:14 he shall perform his purpose on Babylon 6
54:16 of coals, and produces a weapon for its purpose. 15
55:11 but it shall accomplish that which I purpose 6
Jer 4:28 for I have spoken, I have purposed; 4
6:20 To what purpose does frankincense come to me •
49:20 and the purposes which he has formed 12
30 and formed a purpose against you. 12
50:45 and the purposes which he has formed 12
51:11 his purpose concerning Babylon is to destroy it 11
29 for the LORD'S purposes against Babylon stand 12
Lam 2:17 The LORD has done what he purposed 4
Zec 1: 6 As the LORD of hosts purposed to deal with us 4
8:14 I purposed to do evil to you, when your fathers 4
15 so again have I purposed in these days to do good 4
Lke 4:43 I was sent for this purpose. 27
7:30 the lawyers rejected the purpose of God 19
23:51 who had not consented to their purpose and deed 19
Joh 12:27 No, for this purpose I have come to this hour. 24
Act 9:21 he has come here for this purpose 26
11:23 remain faithful . . with steadfast purpose; 31
26:16 I have appeared to you for this purpose 26
27:13 supposing that they had obtained their purpose 34
43 kept them from carrying out their purpose 20
Rom 4:11 The purpose was to make him the father of all 26
8:28 who are called according to his purpose. 34
9:11 that God's purpose of election might continue 34
17 for the very purpose of showing my power in you 33
1Co 4: 5 and will disclose the purposes of the heart. 19
Eph 1: 5 according to the purpose of his will. 29
9 according to his purpose 29
11 according to the purpose of him 34
3:11 This was according to the eternal purpose 34
6:22 I have sent him to you for this very purpose 26
Col 4: 8 I have sent him to you for this very purpose 26
2Ti 1: 9 called us . . in virtue of his own purpose 34
Heb 6:17 the unchangeable character of his purpose 19
Jas 5:11 and you have seen the purpose of the Lord 35
Rev 17:17 to carry out his purpose by being of one mind 22
2Es 8:14 to what purpose was he made? 37
Jdt 8:16 Do not try to bind the purposes of the Lord our God; 19
11: 6 my lord will not fail to achieve his purposes. 28
AEs 10:10 For this purpose he made two lots •
12: 2 inquired into their purposes 32
Wis 2:22 they did not know the secret purposes of God •
4:17 not understand what the Lord purposed for him 18
6: 4 nor walk according to the purpose of God 19
Sir 22:18 so a timid heart with a fool's purpose 25
Bar 4:28 For just as you purposed to go astray from God 21
2Mc 3: 8 in fact to carry out the king's purpose. 34
4:19 to expend it for another purpose. 23
14: 5 an opportunity that furthered his mad purpose 30
3Mc 1:22 the fulfillment of his intended purpose. 34
2:26 intently observing the king's purpose 34
3:11 persevere constantly in his same purpose 19
5:12 he quite failed in his lawless purpose 34
29 O king, according to your eager purpose. 34
4Mc 1: 6 is not for the purpose of destroying them 36
4: 1 he fled . . with the purpose of betraying it. •

purpose *See also* frustrate, fulfil, singleness.

evil purpose 1. זִמָּה 2. רָעָה
Exd 10:10 Look, you have some evil purpose in mind. 2
Ps 119:150draw near who persecute me with evil purpose; 1

no purpose 1. *δωρεάν*
Gal 2:21 then Christ died to no purpose. 1

no good purpose 1. *καλῶς*
Gal 4:17 They make much of you, but for no good purpose 1

purse 1. כִּיס 2. *βαλλάντιον* 3. *μάρσιππος*
Prv 1:14 we will all have one purse"- 1
Isa 46: 6 Those who lavish gold from the purse 1
Lke 10: 4 Carry no purse, no bag, no sandals 2
12:33 purses that do not grow old 2
22:35 When I sent you out with no purse or bag or sandals 2
36 let him who has a purse take it, and likewise a bag. 2
Sir 18:33 when you have nothing in your purse. 3

purslane 1. חַלָּמוּת
Job 6: 6 or is there any taste in the slime of the purslane? 1

pursue 1. אַחֲרֵי 2. הלך אַחֲרֵי 3. כתת 4. רדף 5. רדף אַחַר 6. רדף אַחֲרֵי 7. *διώκω* 8. *ἐλαύνω* 9. *ἐξέρχομαι ὀπίσω* 10. *ἐπακολουθέω* 11. *ἐπεξέρχομαι* 12. *ἐπιδιώκω* 13. *καταδιώκω* 14. *μετέρχομαι* 15. *συνδιώκω* 16. *τρέχω ὀπίσω* 17. persequor
Gen 14:15 he and his servants, and routed them and pursued 4
31:23 he took his kinsmen with him and pursued him 4
35: 5 that they did not pursue the sons of Jacob. 4
Exd 14: 4 and he will pursue them and I will get glory 4
8 king of Egypt and he pursued the people of Israel 4
9 The Egyptians pursued them, all Pharaoh's horses 4
23 The Egyptians pursued, and went in after them 4
15: 9 The enemy said, 'I will pursue, I will overtake 4
Lev 26:17 you shall flee when none pursues you 4
36 sword, and they shall fall when none pursues 4
37 they shall stumble . . though none pursues 4
Num14:45 came down, and defeated them and pursued them 3
Deu 11: 4 overflow them as they pursued after you 4
19: 6 avenger of blood . . pursue the manslayer 6
28:22 they shall pursue you until you perish. 4
45 these curses shall come upon you and pursue you 4
Jos 2: 5 pursue them quickly, for you will overtake them. 6
7 men pursued after them on the way to the Jordan 6
8:16 people . . were called together to pursue them 6
16 and as they pursued Joshua they were drawn away 6
17 they left the city open, and pursued Israel. 6
24 in the open wilderness where they pursued them 4
10:19 pursue your enemies, fall upon their rear 6
20: 5 And if the avenger of blood pursues him 6
24: 6 and the Egyptians pursued your fathers 6
Jdg 1: 6 Ado'ni-be'zek fled; but they pursued him, and caught 4
4:16 Barak pursued the chariots and the army 6
22 behold, as Barak pursued Sis'era, Ja'el went out 4
7:23 called out . . and they pursued after Mid'ian. 4
25 at the wine press of Zeeb, as they pursued Mid'ian; 4
8: 4 300 men who were with him, faint yet pursuing. 4
5 for they are faint, and I am pursuing after Zebah 4
12 Zebah and Zalmun'na fled; and he pursued them 4
20:43 they pursued them and trod them down from Nohah 4
1Sm 7:11 went out of Mizpah and pursued the Philistines 4
14:46 Then Saul went up from pursuing the Philistines; 1
17:52 rose with a shout and pursued the Philistines 4
23:25 And when Saul heard that, he pursued after David 4
28 Saul returned from pursuing after David 4
24:14 After whom do you pursue? After a dead dog! 4
25:29 If men rise up to pursue you and to seek your life 4
26:18 he said, "Why does my lord pursue after his servant? 4
30: 8 Shall I pursue after this band? Shall I overtake 4
8 Pursue; for you shall surely overtake and shall 4

2Sm 2:19 As'ahel pursued Abner, and . . turned neither 6
24 But Jo'ab and Abi'shai pursued Abner; 6
28 all the men stopped, and pursued Israel no more 4
17: 1 and I will set out and pursue David tonight. 6
18:16 and the troops came back from pursuing Israel; 6
20: 6 take your lord's servants and pursue him 6
7 they went out . . to pursue Sheba the son of Bichri. 6
10 Then Jo'ab and Abi'shai his brother pursued Sheba 6
13 all the people went on after Jo'ab to pursue Sheba 6
22:38 I pursued my enemies and destroyed them 4
24:13 flee . . before your foes while they pursue you? 4
1Kg 20:20 the Syrians fled and Israel pursued them 4
22:33 they turned back from pursuing him. 1
2Kg 9:27 And Jehu pursued him, and said, "Shoot him also"; 6
25: 5 But the army of the Chalde'ans pursued the king 5
2Ch 13:19 Abi'jah pursued Jerobo'am, and took cities 6
14:13 pursued them as far as Gerar 4
18:32 they turned back from pursuing him. 1
Job 13:25 thou frighten a driven leaf and pursue dry chaff? 4
19:22 Why do you, like God, pursue me? 4
28 If you say, 'How we will pursue him!' 4
30:15 my honor is pursued as by the wind 4
Ps 7: 5 let the enemy pursue me and overtake me 4
18:37 I pursued my enemies and overtook them; 4
34:14 from evil, and do good; seek peace, and pursue it. 4
35: 6 with the angel of the LORD pursuing them! 4
71:11 and say, "God has forsaken him; pursue and seize him 4
83:15 do thou pursue them with thy tempest 4
109:16 pursued the poor and needy . . to their death. 4
143: 3 enemy has pursued me; he has crushed my life 4
Prv 11:19 but he who pursues evil will die. 4
13:21 Misfortune pursues sinners 4
15: 9 but he loves him who pursues righteousness. 4
19: 7 He pursues them with words, but does not have them. 4
21:21 He who pursues righteousness and kindness 4
28: 1 The wicked flee when no one pursues 4
Isa 41: 3 He pursues them and passes on safely 4
51: 1 Hearken to me, you who pursue deliverance 4
Jer 29:18 I will pursue them with sword, famine 4
39: 5 But the army of the Chalde'ans pursued them 4
48: 2 the sword shall pursue you. 2
52: 8 But the army of the Chalde'ans pursued the king 4
Lam 3:43 hast wrapped thyself with anger and pursued us 4
66 Thou wilt pursue them in anger and destroy them 4
Ezk 35: 6 prepare you for blood, and blood shall pursue you; 4
6 therefore blood shall pursue you. 4
Hos 2: 7 She shall pursue her lovers, but not overtake 4
8: 3 the enemy shall pursue him. 4
12: 1 and pursues the east wind all day long; 4
Ams 1:11 because he pursued his brother with the sword 4
Nah 1: 8 and will pursue his enemies into darkness. 4
Mrk 1:36 Simon and those who were with him pursued him 13
Rom 9:30 That Gentiles who did not pursue righteousness 7
31 but that Israel who pursued the righteousness 7
32 Why? Because they did not pursue it through faith *
14:19 Let us then pursue what makes for peace 7
1Pe 3:11 let him seek peace and pursue it. 7
Rev 12:13 he pursued the woman who had borne the male child. 7
2Es 15:31 combine in great power and turn to pursue them 17
Jdt 14: 4 shall pursue them and cut them down as they flee. 10
Wis 11:20 when pursued by justice 7
14:31 pursues the transgression of the unrighteous. 11
16:16 pursued by unusual rains and hail 7
18 they were being pursued by the judgment of God; 8
19: 2 they would change their minds and pursue them. 7
3 pursued as fugitives 7
Sir 11:10 if you pursue you will not overtake 7
14:22 Pursue wisdom like a hunter 9
27: 8 If you pursue justice, you will attain it 7
29:19 who has fallen into suretyship and pursues gain 7
31: 5 he who pursues money will be led astray by it. 7
34: 2 catches at a shadow and pursues the wind 7
1Mc 2:32 Many pursued them, and overtook them 16
3: 5 He searched out and pursued the lawless 7
24 They pursued them down the descent of Beth-horon 7
4: 9 when Pharaoh with his forces pursued them. 7
15 They pursued them to Gazara 7
16 Judas . . turned back from pursuing them 7
5:22 He pursued them to the gate of Ptolemais 7
60 were pursued to the borders of Judea 7
7:45 The Jews pursued them a day's journey 13
9:15 he pursued them as far as Mount Azotus. 7
10:49 Alexander pursued him and defeated them. 7
78 Jonathan pursued him to Azotus 13
12:30 Then Jonathan pursued them 13
15:11 Antiochus pursued him 7
39 the king pursued Trypho. 7
16: 9 John pursued them 13
2Mc 2:21 pursued the barbarian hordes 7
5: 8 pursued by all men 7
8:25 After pursuing them for some distance 15
3Mc 2: 7 when he pursued them with chariots 12
4Mc 18:22 divine justice pursued . . the accursed tyrant. 14
22 justice . . will pursue the accursed tyrant. 14

pursue hard 1. דבק
Jdg 20:45 they were pursued hard to Gidom, and 2,000 men 1

hotly pursue 1. דלק
Gen 31:36 What is my sin, that you have hotly pursued me? 1
Ps 10: 2 In arrogance the wicked hotly pursue the poor; 1

pursuer 1. רדף 2. רדף אַחֲרֵי 3. *διώκω* 4. *καταδιώκω*
Jos 2: 7 as soon as the pursuers had gone out, the gate was 2
16 Go into the hills, lest the pursuers meet you; 1
16 and hide . . until the pursuers have returned; 1
22 there three days, until the pursuers returned; 1
22 for the pursuers had made search all along the way 1
8:20 the people . . turned back upon the pursuers. 1
Neh 9:11 thou didst cast their pursuers into the depths 1
Ps 7: 1 save me from all my pursuers, and deliver me 1
35: 3 Draw the spear and javelin against my pursuers! 1
Isa 30:16 therefore your pursuers shall be swift. 1
Lam 1: 3 her pursuers have all overtaken her 1
6 they fled without strength before the pursuer. 1
4:19 Our pursuers were swifter than the vultures 1
Jdt 16: 3 he has delivered me out of the hands of my pursuers 4
1Mc 7:46 and drove them back to their pursuers *
12:51 When their pursuers saw that they would fight 3

pursuit 1. אַחֲרֵי 2. רדף 3. *διωγμός* 4. *διώκω* 5. *κατατρέχω* 6. *πορεία* 7. *πραγματεία*
1Sm 30:10 But David went on with the pursuit 2
2Sm 2:26 people turn from the pursuit of their brethren? 1
27 have given up the pursuit of their brethren 1
30 Jo'ab returned from the pursuit of Abner; 1
2Ti 2: 4 gets entangled in civilian pursuits 7
Jas 1:11 rich man fade away in the midst of his pursuits. 6
1Mc 11:73 returned to him and joined him in the pursuit 4
2Mc 8:26 they did not continue their pursuit. 5
12:23 Judas pressed the pursuit with the utmost vigor 3

pursuit *See also* go.

worthless pursuit 1. רֵיק
Prv 12:11 follows worthless pursuits has no sense. 1
28:19 follows worthless pursuits will have plenty 1

push 1. דחה 2. הדף 3. לחץ 4. נגח 5. *προσωθέω*
Num22:25 ass . . pushed against the wall 3
Deu 33:17 with them he shall push the peoples, all of them 4
1Kg 22:11 With these you shall push the Syrians 4
2Ch 18:10 With these you shall push the Syrians 4
Ps 118:13 I was pushed hard, so that I was falling 1
Ezk 34:21 Because you push with side and shoulder 2
2Mc 13: 6 There they all push to destruction any man 5

push ahead 1. *προβαίνω*
2Mc 8: 8 he was pushing ahead with more frequent successes 1

push back 1. הדף
Jos 23: 5 The LORD your God will push them back before you 1

push down 1. נגח
Ps 44: 5 Through thee we push down our foes; 1

push forward 1. *ἐμπίπτω*
Sir 13:10 Do not push forward, lest you be repulsed 1

put 1. אסף 2. בוא 3. הדה 4. היה 5. חגר 6. חוד 7. יצג 8. כסה 9. לבש 10. לקח 11. נגש 12. נוח 13. נוף 14. נכה 15. נשג 16. נתן 17. סגר 18. ספח 19. עלה 20. עשה 21. פקד 22. שום 23. שוב 24. שית 25. שלח 26. נחת (A) 27. *ἀναλαμβάνω* 28. *ἀποστέλλω* 29. *ἀποτίθημι* 30. *βάλλω* 31. *βλητέος* 32. *γίνομαι* 33. *δέω* 34. *διαζώννυμι* 35. *δίδωμι* 36. *εἰμί* 37. *εἰσφέρω* 38. *ἐμβάλλω* 39. *ἐμπορπόω* 40. *ἐνδύνω* 41. *ἐνδύω* 42. *ἐντίθημι* 43. *ἐπενδύομαι* 44. *ἐπιβάλλω* 45. *ἐπιτίθημι* 46. *ἡγέομαι* 47. *θέσις* 48. *ἵστημι* 49. *καθίστημι* 50. *κατάγω* 51. *κεῖμαι* 52. *λαμβάνω* 53. *λέγω* 54. *μεθίστημι* 55. *πέμπω* 56. *περιβάλλω* 57. *περιτίθημι* 58. *ποιέω* 59. *ῥίπτω* 60. *συνελαύνω* 61. *τίθημι* 62. *ὑποδέω* 63. *φέρω* 64. immitto 65. pono 66. sumo 67. suscipio 68. trado
Gen 2: 8 and there he put the man whom he had formed. 22
15 LORD God took the man and put him in the garden 12
3:15 I will put enmity between you and the woman 24
4:15 And the LORD put a mark on Cain 22
21:14 gave it to Hagar, putting it on her shoulder 22
24: 2 servant . . "Put your hand under my thigh 22
9 the servant put his hand under the thigh 22
47 I put the ring in her nose, and the bracelets 22
27:15 took the best garments . . and put them on Jacob 9
28:11 he put it under his head and lay down in that place 22
18 he took the stone which he had put under his head 22
30:35 that was black, and put them in charge of his sons; 16
40 he put his own droves apart 24
40 and did not put them with Laban's flock. 24
31:34 the household gods and put them in the camel's 22
32:16 Pass on before me, and put a space between drove 22
33: 2 he put the maids with their children in front 22
37:34 Then Jacob rent his garments, and put sackcloth 22
38:14 she put off her widow's garments, and put on a veil 8
19 she put on the garments of her widowhood. 9
39: 4 house and put him in charge of all that he had. 16
8 and he has put everything that he has in my hand; 16
20 master took him and put him into the prison 16
40: 3 he put them in custody in the house of the captain 16
15 done nothing that they should put me 22
41:10 and put me and the chief baker in custody 16
42 from his hand and put it on Joseph's hand 16
42 of fine linen, and put a gold chain about his neck; 22
42:37 put him in my hands, and I will bring him back 16
43:22 We do not know who put our money in our sacks. 22
23 God . . must have put treasure in your sacks 16
44: 1 and put each man's money in the mouth of his sack 22
2 put my cup, the silver cup, in the mouth of the sack 22
47: 6 able men among them, put them in charge 22
29 put your hand under my thigh, and promise to deal 22
48:18 the first-born; put your right hand upon his head. 22
20 and thus he put E'phraim before Manas'seh. 22
50:25 he was put in a coffin in Egypt. 22
Exd 2: 3 a basket . . she put the child in it 22
3:22 clothing, and you shall put them on your sons 22
4: 6 LORD said to him, "Put your hand into your bosom. 2
6 your bosom." And he put his hand into his bosom; 2
15 speak to him and put the words in his mouth; 22
21 all the miracles which I have put in your power; 22
5:21 because you . . have put a sword in their hand 16
8:23 Thus I will put a division between my people 22
12: 7 the blood, and put it on the two doorposts 16
15:26 I will put none of the diseases upon you which I 22
26 diseases upon you which I put upon the Egyptians; 22
16:33 Take a jar, and put an omer of manna in it, and place 16
17:12 so they took a stone and put it under him, and he sat 22
22: 8 to show whether or not he has put his hand to his 25
11 has not put his hand to his neighbor's property; 25
24: 6 Moses took half of the blood and put it in basins 22
25:12 four rings . . and put them on its four feet 16
14 you shall put the poles into the rings 2
16 you shall put into the ark the testimony 16
21 you shall put the mercy seat on the top of the ark; 16
21 in the ark you shall put the testimony 16
26:11 and put the clasps into the loops 2
34 You shall put the mercy seat upon the ark 16
35 you shall put the table on the north side. 16
27: 7 the poles shall be put through the rings 2
28:23 put the two rings on the two edges 16
24 you shall put the two cords of gold 16
26 rings of gold, and put them at the two ends 22
30 judgment you shall put the Urim and Thummim 16
29: 3 you shall put them in one basket and bring them 16
5 put on Aaron the coat and the robe of the ephod 9
6 put the holy crown upon the turban. 16
8 you shall bring his sons, and put coats on them 9
12 the blood . . put it upon the horns of the altar 16
17 and put them with its pieces and its head 16
20 blood and put it upon the tip of the right ear 16
24 you shall put all these in the hands of Aaron 22
30: 6 you shall put it before the veil that is by the ark 16
18 you shall put it between the tent of meeting 16
18 a laver . . and you shall put water in it 16
33 whoever puts any of it on an outsider shall be cut 16
36 put part of it before the testimony in the tent 16
32:27 Put every man his sword on his side, and go 22
33: 4 they mourned; and no man put on his ornaments. 24
22 while my glory passes by I will put you in a cleft 22
34:33 speaking with them, he put a veil on his face; 16
36: 1 every able man in whom the LORD has put ability 16
2 man in whose mind the LORD had put ability 16
37: 5 put the poles into the rings on the sides 2
38: 7 he put the poles through the rings on the sides 2
39:16 they made . . two gold rings, and put the two rings 16
17 they put the two cords of gold in the two rings 16
19 and put them at the two ends of the breastpiece 22
25 and put the bells between the pomegranates 16
40: 3 you shall put in it the ark of the testimony 22
5 you shall put the golden altar for incense 16
7 place the laver . . and put water in it. 16
14 bring his sons also and put coats on them 9
18 laid its bases, and set up its frames, and put in its 16
19 over the tabernacle, and put the covering 22
20 he took the testimony and put it into the ark 16
20 and put the poles on the ark, and set the mercy seat 16
22 he put the table in the tent of meeting 16
24 he put the lampstand in the tent of meeting 22
26 he put the golden altar in the tent of meeting 22
30 the laver . . and put water in it for washing 16
Lev 1: 7 Aaron the priest shall put fire on the altar 16
2: 1 he shall pour oil upon it, and put frankincense 16
15 you shall put oil upon it, and lay frankincense 16
4: 7 the priest shall put some of the blood 16
18 he shall put some of the blood on the horns 16
25 put it on the horns of the altar of burnt offering 16
30 blood . . and put it on the horns of the altar 16
34 blood . . with his finger and put it on the horns 16
5:11 he shall put no oil upon it 22
11 and shall put no frankincense on it 16
6:10 the priest shall put on his linen garment 9
10 the ashes . . and put them beside the altar 22
11 put on other garments, and carry forth the ashes 9
8: 7 he put on him the coat, and girded him 16
7 clothed him with the robe, and put the ephod upon 16

8 in the breastpiece he put the Urim and the Thummim 16
15 blood, and with his finger put it on the horns 16
23 blood and put it on the tip of Aaron's right ear 16
24 Moses put some of the blood on the tips 16
27 he put all these in the hands of Aaron 16
9: 9 in the blood and put it on the horns of the altar 16
20 they put the fat upon the breasts, and he burned 22
10: 1 each took his censer, and put fire in it 16
11:32 it must be put into water, and it shall be unclean 2
38 if water is put on the seed 16
14:14 the priest shall put it on the tip of the right ear 16
17 oil . . the priest shall put on the tip 16
18 oil . . he shall put on the head of him who is to be 16
25 put it on the tip of the right ear of him who is to be 16
28 the priest shall put some of the oil 16
28 where the blood of the guilt offering was put •
29 shall put on the head of him who is to be cleansed 16
34 and I put a leprous disease in a house 16
42 other stones and put them in the place of those 2
16: 4 He shall put on the holy linen coat 9
4 bathe his body in water, and then put them on. 9
13 put the incense on the fire before the LORD 16
18 blood . . and put it on the horns of the altar 16
21 he shall put them upon the head of the goat 16
23 shall put off the linen garments which he put 9
24 and put on his garments, and come forth 9
19:14 or put a stumbling block before the blind 16
24: 7 you shall put pure frankincense with each row 16
12 they put him in custody, till the will of the LORD 12
Num 4: 6 then they shall put on it a covering of goatskin 16
6 shall put in its poles. 22
7 cloth of blue, and put upon it the plates 16
8 of goatskin, and shall put in its poles. 22
10 shall put it with all its utensils in a covering 16
10 put it upon the carrying frame. 16
11 cover it . . and shall put in its poles; 22
12 put them in a cloth of blue, and cover them 16
12 put them on the carrying frame. 16
14 they shall put on it all the utensils of the altar 16
14 shall put in its poles. 22
5: 3 male and female, putting them outside the camp 25
15 no oil upon it and put no frankincense on it 16
17 some of the dust . . and put it into the water. 16
6:18 put it on the fire which is under the sacrifice 16
19 shall put them upon the hands of the Nazirite 16
27 shall they put my name upon the people of Israel 22
11:17 take some of the spirit . . and put it upon them; 22
25 the LORD came . . and put it upon the 70 elders; 16
29 that the LORD would put his spirit upon them! 16
15:34 They put him in custody 12
38 to put upon the tassel of each corner a cord of blue; 16
16: 7 put fire in them and put incense upon them 16
7 put fire in them and put incense upon them 22
17 take his censer, and put incense upon it 16
18 took his censer, and they put fire in them 16
46 censer, and put fire therein from off the altar 16
47 he put on the incense, and made atonement 16
22:38 word that God puts in my mouth, that must I speak. 22
23: 5 the LORD put a word in Balaam's mouth, and said 22
12 take heed to speak what the LORD puts in my mouth? 22
16 LORD met Balaam, and put a word in his mouth 22
Deu 2:25 This day I will begin to put the dread and fear 16
10: 2 you shall put them in the ark.' 22
5 put the tables in the ark which I had made; 22
12: 5 to put his name and make his habitation there; 22
21 place . . LORD . . will choose to put his name there 22
13:15 surely put the inhabitants . . to the sword 14
16: 9 first put the sickle to the standing grain. •
17:15 you may not put a foreigner over you 16
18:18 I will put my words in his mouth, and he shall speak 16
20:13 hand you shall put all its males to the sword 14
22: 5 nor shall a man put on a woman's garment; 9
23:24 you shall not put any in your vessel. 16
25 not put a sickle to your neighbor's standing grain. 13
24: 1 bill of divorce and puts it in her hand and sends 16
3 bill of divorce and puts it in her hand 16
26: 2 put it in a basket, and you shall go to the place 22
28:48 he will put a yoke of iron upon your neck, until 16
30: 7 LORD . . will put all these curses upon your foes 16
31:19 this song, and teach it . . put it in their mouths 22
26 put it by the side of the ark of the covenant 22
33:10 they shall put incense before thee 22
Jos 6:24 only the silver and . . they put into the treasury 16
7: 6 and they put dust upon their heads. 19
11 stolen . . and put them among their own stuff. 22
10:24 put your feet upon the necks of these kings. 22
24 they came near, and put their feet on their necks. 22
11:11 And they put to the sword all who were in it 14
17:13 they put the Canaanites to forced labor 16
19:47 after capturing it and putting it to the sword 14
24: 7 he put darkness between you and the Egyptians 22
Jdg 1:28 they put the Canaanites to forced labor, but did 22
5:26 She put her hand to the tent peg and her right hand 25
6:19 the meat he put in a basket, and the broth he put 22
19 meat he put in a basket, and the broth he put in a pot 22
20 the meat and . . cakes, and put them on this rock 12
7: 6 that lapped, putting their hands to their mouths •
16 and put trumpets into the hands of all of them 16
8:27 Gideon made an ephod of it and put it in his city 7

9:25 the men of Shechem put men in ambush against him 22
49 his bundle and . . put it against the stronghold 22
14:16 you have put a riddle to my countrymen 6
15: 4 and put a torch between each pair of tails. 22
16: 3 and put them on his shoulders and carried them 22
18:19 Keep quiet, put your hand upon your mouth, and come 22
21 and departed, putting the little ones 22
19:28 he put her upon the ass; and the man rose up 10
Rut 3: 3 anoint yourself, and put on your best clothes 22
1Sm 2:36 Put me, I pray you, in one of the priest's places 18
6: 8 put in a box at its side the figures of gold 22
11 And they put the ark of the LORD on the cart 22
8:16 take . . your asses, and put them to his work. 20
9:23 the portion . . of which I said to you, 'Put it aside.' 22
11: 2 gouge out . . eyes, and thus put disgrace upon all 22
11 Saul put the people in three companies; 22
14:26 honey was . . but no man put his hand to his mouth; 15
27 and dipped it in . . and put his hand to his mouth; 23
17:38 he put a helmet of bronze on his head 16
40 and put them in his shepherd's bag or wallet; 22
49 David put his hand in his bag and took out a stone 25
54 but he put his armor in his tent. 22
19:13 and put a pillow of goats' hair at its head 22
22:19 Nob, the city of the priests, he put to the sword; 14
19 both men and women . . he put to the sword. •
24:18 not kill me when the LORD put me into your hands. 17
28: 8 disguised himself and put on other garments 9
25 and she put it before Saul and his servants; 11
31:10 They put his armor in the temple of Ash'taroth; 22
2Sm 1:24 who put ornaments of gold upon your apparel. 19
8: 6 Then David put garrisons in Aram of Damascus; 22
14 And he put garrisons in Edom; throughout all Edom 22
14 throughout all Edom he put garrisons 22
10:10 the rest of his men he put in the charge of Abi'shai 16
13:19 Tamar put ashes on her head, and rent the long robe 10
14: 2 be a mourner, and put on mourning garments; 9
3 speak thus . . " So Jo'ab put the words in her mouth. 22
19 it was he who put all these words in the mouth 22
20: 3 took the ten . . and put them in a house under guard 16
1Kg 2: 5 putting innocent blood upon the girdle about my 16
35 king put Benai'ah . . over the army in place of Jo'ab 16
35 the king put Zadok the priest in the place 16
5: 3 the LORD put them under the soles of his feet. 16
6:27 He put the cherubim in the innermost part 16
8: 9 tables of stone which Moses put there at Horeb 12
9: 3 consecrated this house . . and put my name there 22
10:17 and the king put them in the House of the Forest 16
24 hear his wisdom, which God had put into his mind. 16
11:36 the city where I have chosen to put my name. 22
12: 9 'Lighten the yoke that your father put upon us'? 16
29 he set one in Bethel, and the other he put in Dan. 16
14:21 the LORD had chosen . . to put his name there. 22
18:23 and lay it on the wood, but put no fire to it; 22
23 and lay it on the wood, and put no fire to it. 22
25 call on the name of your god, but put no fire to it. 22
42 he bowed . . and put his face between his knees. 22
20:24 remove . . and put commanders in their places; 22
31 let us put sackcloth on our loins 22
32 girded sackcloth . . and put ropes on their heads •
21:27 and put sackcloth upon his flesh, and fasted 22
22:23 the LORD has put a lying spirit in the mouth 16
27 Put this fellow in prison, and feed him 22
2Kg 2:20 He said, "Bring me a new bowl, and put salt in it. 22
4:10 put there for him a bed, a table, a chair, and a lamp 22
34 lay upon the child, putting his mouth upon his 22
5:24 he took them . . and put them in the house; 21
9:13 every man . . took his garment, and put it under him 22
10: 7 slew them . . and put their heads in baskets 22
25 So when they put them to the sword 14
11: 2 and she put him and his nurse in a bedchamber. •
12 the king's son, and put the crown upon him 16
12: 9 and the priests . . put in it all the money 16
16:14 he removed . . and put it on the north side of his altar. 16
17 and put it upon a pediment of stone. 16
17:29 made gods . . and put them in the shrines 12
18:11 carried the Israelites . . and put them in Halah 12
19: 7 I will put a spirit in him, so that he shall hear 16
28 I will put my hook in your nose and my bit 22
21: 4 the LORD had said, "In Jerusalem will I put my name. 22
7 In this house . . I will put my name for ever; 22
1Ch 10:10 they put his armor in the temple of their gods 22
18: 6 Then David put garrisons in Syria of Damascus; 22
13 he put garrisons in Edom; 22
19:11 the rest of his men he put in the charge of Abi'shai 16
2Ch 3:16 chains . . and put them on the tops of the pillars; 16
16 pomegranates, and put them on the chains. 16
5:10 the two tables which Moses put there at Horeb 16
9:16 put them in the House of the Forest of Lebanon. 16
23 his wisdom, which God had put into his mind. 16
10: 9 'Lighten the yoke that your father put upon us'? 16
11:11 fortresses strong, and put commanders in them 16
12 he put shields and spears in all the cities •
12:13 the LORD had chosen . . to put his name there. 22
16:10 was angry with the seer, and put him in the stocks 16
18:22 LORD has put a lying spirit in the mouth of these 16
26 say, 'Thus says the king, Put this fellow in prison 22
22:11 she put him and his nurse in a bedchamber. 16
23:11 put the crown upon him, and gave him the testimony; 16
33: 7 In this house . . I will put my name for ever; 22

14 put commanders of the army in all the fortified 22
35: 3 Put the holy ark in the house which Solomon 16
36: 7 to Babylon and put them in his palace in Babylon. 16
22 proclamation . . and also put it in writing •
Ezr 5:15 Take these vessels, go and put them in the temple 26
6: 5 you shall put them in the house of God. 26
7:27 LORD . . who put such a thing as this 16
Neh 2:12 my God had put into my heart to do for Jerusalem. 16
3: 5 nobles did not put their necks to the work 2
7: 5 Then God put it into my mind to assemble 16
13: 5 chamber where they had previously put 16
Est 2: 8 Esther also was . . and put in custody of Hegai •
3: 9 that they may put it into the king's treasuries. 2
4: 1 rent his clothes and put on sackcloth and ashes 9
5: 1 Esther put on her royal robes and stood 9
Job 13:14 and put my life in my hand. 22
27 Thou puttest my feet in the stocks 22
28: 3 Men put an end to darkness 22
9 Man puts his hand to the flinty rock 25
29:14 I put on righteousness, and it clothed me; 9
33:11 he puts my feet in the stocks 22
38:36 Who has put wisdom in the clouds 24
41: 2 Can you put a rope in his nose, or pierce his jaw 22
Ps 4: 7 Thou hast put more joy in my heart than they have 16
8: 6 thou hast put all things under his feet 24
9:20 Put them in fear, O LORD! 24
33: 7 as in a bottle; he put the deeps in storehouses. 16
40: 3 He put a new song in my mouth, a song of praise 16
56: 8 put thou my tears in thy bottle! 22
78:66 he put his adversaries to rout; †
66 he put them to everlasting shame. 16
88: 6 Thou hast put me in the depths of the Pit 24
105:18 his neck was put in a collar of iron; 2
Prv 12:24 while the slothful will be put to forced labor. 4
23: 2 put a knife to your throat if you are a man 22
30:32 put your hand on your mouth. •
31:19 She puts her hands to the distaff 25
Ecc 3:11 also he has put eternity into man's mind 16
Sng 5: 3 I had put off my garment, how could I put it on? 9
4 My beloved put his hand to the latch 25
Isa 5:20 put darkness for light and light for darkness 22
20 who put bitter for sweet and sweet for bitter! 22
11: 8 weaned child . . put his hand on the adder's den. 3
28:25 put in wheat in rows and barley in its proper 22
31: 8 and his young men shall be put to forced labor. •
37: 7 put a spirit in him, so that he shall hear a rumor 16
29 I will put my hook in your nose 22
41:19 I will put in the wilderness the cedar 16
42: 1 I have put my Spirit upon him 16
46:13 I will put salvation in Zion, for Israel my glory. 16
49:18 you shall put them all on as an ornament 9
51: 9 Awake, awake, put on strength, O arm of the LORD; 9
16 I have put my words in your mouth, and hid you 22
23 I will put it into the hand of your tormentors 22
52: 1 Awake, awake, put on your strength, O Zion; 9
1 put on your beautiful garments, O Jerusalem 9
59:17 He put on righteousness as a breastplate 9
17 he put on garments of vengeance for clothing 9
21 and my words which I have put in your mouth 22
63:11 he who put in the midst of them his holy Spirit 22
Jer 1: 9 Behold, I have put my words in your mouth. 16
13: 1 buy a linen waistcloth, and put it on your loins 22
2 and put it on my loins. 22
20: 2 beat Jeremiah . . and put him in the stocks 16
25:31 the wicked he will put to the sword, says the LORD. 16
27: 2 thongs and yoke-bars, and put them on your neck. 16
8 and put its neck under the yoke of the king 16
28:14 I have put upon the neck of all these nations 16
29:26 madman who prophesies, to put him in the stocks 16
31:33 says the LORD: I will put my law within them 16
32:14 and put them in an earthenware vessel 16
40 and I will put the fear of me in their hearts 16
36:20 having put the scroll in the chamber of Eli'shama 21
37: 4 for he had not yet been put in prison. 16
18 that you have put me in prison? 16
38: 7 that they had put Jeremiah into the cistern 16
12 Put the rags and clothes between your armpits 22
46: 4 polish your spears, put on your coats of mail! 9
47: 6 Put yourself into your scabbard, rest and be still! 1
52:11 and put him in prison till the day of his death. 16
Lam 2:10 cast dust on their heads and put on sackcloth; 5
3: 7 he has put heavy chains on me; •
29 let him put his mouth in the dust 16
Ezk 4: 2 put siegeworks against it, and build a siege wall 16
8 And, behold, I will put cords upon you 16
9 and put them into a single vessel, and make bread 16
8:17 Lo, they put the branch to their nose. 25
10: 7 put it into the hands of the man clothed in linen 16
11:19 and put a new spirit within them; 16
14: 7 and putting the stumbling block of his iniquity 22
16:11 with ornaments, and put bracelets on your arms 16
12 I put a ring on your nose, and earrings in your ears 16
17:13 made a covenant with him, putting him under oath. 2
19: 9 With hooks they put him in a cage, and brought him 16
22:20 and I will put you in and melt you. 12
23:42 they put bracelets upon the hands of the women 16
24: 4 put in it the pieces of flesh, all the good pieces 1
7 she put it on the bare rock 22
17 Bind on your turban, and put . . shoes on your feet; 22

29: 4 I will put hooks in your jaws 16
30:13 I will put fear in the land of Egypt. 16
24 and put my sword in his hand; 16
25 I put my sword into the hand of the king of Babylon 16
32: 8 and put darkness upon your land, says the Lord 16
36:26 and a new spirit I will put within you; 16
27 I will put my spirit within you 16
37: 6 and put breath in you, and you shall live; 16
14 I will put my Spirit within you, and you shall live 16
38: 4 I will turn you about, and put hooks into your jaws 16
42:13 there they shall put the most holy offerings 12
14 they shall put on other garments before they go 9
43:20 its blood, and put it on the four horns of the altar 16
44:19 they shall put on other garments 9
45:19 and put it on the doorposts of the temple 16
Dan 5:29 purple, a chain of gold was put about his neck *
Hos 10: 6 E'phraim shall be put to shame 10
Jol 3:13 Put in the sickle, for the harvest is ripe. 25
Jon 3: 5 they proclaimed a fast, and put on sackcloth 9
Mic 3: 5 against him who puts nothing into their mouths. 16
Hab 3: 9 from thy bow, and put the arrows to the string. *
Hag 1: 6 earns wages to put them into a bag with holes. *
Zec 3: 5 I said, "Let them put a clean turban on his head. 22
5 they put a clean turban on his head 22
13: 4 he will not put on a hairy mantle 9
9 I will put this third into the fire 2
Mal 2: 3 I will put you out of my presence. *
Mat 5:15 Nor do men light a lamp and put it under a bushel 61
25 the judge to the guard, and you be put in prison; 30
6:25 do not be anxious about . . what you shall put on. 41
9:16 no one puts a piece of unshrunk cloth 44
17 Neither is new wine put into old wineskins 30
17 but new wine is put into fresh wineskins 30
12:18 I will put my Spirit upon him 61
14: 3 bound him and put him in prison 29
15:30 they put them at his feet, and he healed them 59
18: 2 calling to him a child, he put him in the midst 48
30 He refused and went and put him in prison 30
21: 7 and put their garments on them 45
22:44 till I put thy enemies under thy feet'? 61
24:51 will punish him, and put him with the hypocrites; 61
27: 6 It is not lawful to put them into the treasury 30
29 plaiting a crown of thorns they put it on his head 45
29 and put a reed in his right hand *
31 put his own clothes on him 41
37 over his head they put the charge against him 45
48 put it on a reed, and gave it to him to drink. 57
Mrk 2:22 no one puts new wine into old wineskins 30
4:21 Is a lamp brought in to be put under a bushel 61
29 at once he puts in the sickle 28
6: 9 to wear sandals and not put on two tunics. 41
7:33 he put his fingers into his ears, and he spat 30
9:36 he took a child, and put him in the midst of them; 48
12:36 till I put thy enemies under thy feet.' 61
41 the multitude putting money into the treasury. 30
41 Many rich people put in large sums. 30
42 a poor widow came, and put in two copper coins 30
43 this poor widow has put in more than all 30
44 out of her poverty has put in everything she had 30
13:34 he leaves home and puts his servants in charge 35
15:17 plaiting a crown of thorns they put it on him. 57
20 and put his own clothes on him 41
36 filling a sponge full of vinegar, put it on a reed 57
Lke 5:37 no one puts new wine into old wineskins 30
38 new wine must be put into fresh wineskins. 31
6:38 good measure . . will be put into your lap 35
8:16 puts it under a bed 61
16 puts it on a stand 61
9:47 he took a child and put him by his side 48
62 No one who puts his hand to the plow 44
11:33 No one after lighting a lamp puts it in a cellar 61
12:22 nor about your body, what you shall put on. 41
46 will punish him, and put him with the unfaithful. 61
58 the officer put you in prison. 30
13: 8 till I dig about it and put on manure. 30
15:22 Bring quickly the best robe, and put it on him; 40
22 put a ring on his hand, and shoes on his feet; 35
16: 4 when I am put out of the stewardship.' 54
19:23 Why then did you not put my money into the bank 35
21: 1 and saw the rich putting their gifts into the treasury; 30
2 he saw a poor widow put in two copper coins. 30
3 this poor widow has put in more than all of them; 30
4 put in all the living that she had. 30
Joh 3:24 For John had not yet been put in prison. 30
5: 7 I have no man to put me into the pool 30
9:15 he said to them, "He put clay on my eyes, 45
13: 2 when the devil had already put it into the heart 30
16: 2 They will put you out of the synagogues 58
18:11 Put your sword into its sheath 30
19: 2 and put it on his head 45
19 Pilate also wrote a title and put it on the cross; 61
29 they put a sponge full of the vinegar on hyssop 57
20:27 Then he said to Thomas, "Put your finger here 63
21: 7 he put on his clothes, for he was stripped for work 34
Act 4: 3 put them in custody until the morrow 61
5:18 put them in the common prison. 61
25 The men whom you put in prison 61
34 ordered the men to be put outside for a while. 58
12: 4 when he had seized him, he put him in prison 61

8 Dress yourself and put on your sandals. 62
21 On an appointed day Herod put on his royal robes 40
16:24 he put them into the inner prison 30
27: 3 The next day we put in at Sidon 50
28: 3 put them on the fire 45
8 putting his hands on him healed him. 45
12 Putting in at Syracuse, we stayed there 50
Rom 13:12 Let us . . put on the armor of light; 41
14 But put on the Lord Jesus Christ 40
14:13 put a stumbling block . . in the way of a brother. 61
1Co 9:12 we endure anything rather than put an obstacle 33
15:25 until he has put all his enemies under his feet. 61
53 perishable nature must put on the imperishable 40
53 this mortal nature must put on immortality. 40
54 When the perishable puts on the imperishable 41
54 the mortal puts on immortality 41
16: 2 each of you is to put something aside 61
10 When Timothy comes, see that you put him at ease 32
2Co 3:13 not like Moses, who put a veil over his face 61
5: 2 long to put on our heavenly dwelling 43
3 so that by putting it on we may not be found naked. 40
6: 3 We put no obstacle in any one's way 35
8:16 who puts the same earnest care for you 35
Gal 3:27 baptized into Christ have put on Christ. 41
Eph 4:24 put on the new nature 40
6:11 Put on the whole armor of God 40
14 put on the breastplate of righteousness 40
Php 1:16 I am put here for the defense of the gospel; 51
Col 3:10 and have put on the new nature 40
12 Put on then . . compassion 40
14 above all these put on love *
1Th 5: 8 put on the breastplate of faith and love 40
Heb 2:13 again, "I will put my trust in him. 36
8:10 I will put my laws into their minds 35
10:16 I will put my laws on their hearts 35
Jas 3: 3 If we put bits into the mouths of horses 30
Rev 2:14 put a stumbling block before the sons of Israel 30
14:15 Put in your sickle, and reap 55
18 Put in your sickle, and gather the clusters 55
17:17 for God has put it into their hearts 35
1Es 1: 3 put the holy ark of the Lord in the house 47
2: 2 also put it in writing 53
3: 8 put them under the pillow of Darius the king 61
4:30 put it on her own 45
6:19 put them in the temple at Jerusalem 29
8:25 who put this into the heart of the king 35
2Es 2:45 and have put on the immortal 66
46 and puts palms in their hands? 68
9:34 what was launched or what was put in is destroyed 67
12:37 and put it in a hidden place; 65
15: 1 the prophecy which I will put in your mouth 64
16:60 who has put springs of water in the desert 65
61 and put a heart in the midst of his body 65
Jdt 5:21 we shall be put to shame before the whole world. *
6: 7 put you in one of the cities beside the passes 61
9: 1 and put ashes on her head 45
2 and uncovered her thigh to put her to shame *
10: 3 and combed her hair and put on a tiara 45
4 she put sandals on her feet, and put on her anklets 52
4 she put sandals on her feet, and put on her anklets 57
16: 8 and put on a linen gown to deceive him. 52
AEs 14: 2 put on the garments of distress and mourning 41
13 Put eloquent speech in my mouth before the lion 35
Wis 5:18 he will put on righteousness as a breastplate 41
8:12 they will put their hands on their mouths. 45
18:21 put an end to the disaster 45
Sir 5:12 if not, put your hand on your mouth. 36
6:24 Put your feet into her fetters 37
31 put her on like a crown of gladness. 57
7: 6 thus put a blot on your integrity. 61
12:12 Do not put him next to you, lest he overthrow you 48
33:27 Put him to work, that he may not be idle 38
43:20 the water puts it on like a breastplate. 41
45:13 No outsider ever put them on 41
47:20 You put stain upon your honor 35
50:11 When he put on his glorious robe 27
Bar 3: 7 For thou hast put the fear of thee in our hearts 35
4:20 I . . put on the sackcloth of my supplication 41
5: 1 put on for ever the beauty of the glory from God. 41
2 Put on the robe of the righteousness from God 56
2 put on your head the diadem 45
1Mc 1: 9 They all put on crowns after his death 45
2:14 Mattathias . . put on sackcloth, and mourned greatly. 56
3: 3 Like a giant he put on his breastplate 41
47 put on sackcloth and sprinkled ashes on their head 56
8:14 Yet for all this not one of them has put on a crown 45
9:25 and put them in charge of the country. 49
52 in them he put troops and stores of food. 61
53 put them under guard in the citadel at Jerusalem. 61
10:21 So Jonathan put on the holy garments 41
11:13 entered Antioch and put on the crown of Asia. 57
23 put himself in danger 35
54 who began to reign and put on the crown. 45
71 put dust on his head, and prayed. 45
12:39 to become king in Asia and put on the crown 57
13:29 upon the columns he put suits of armor 58
32 putting on the crown of Asia 57
14: 3 took him to Arsaces, who put him under guard. 61
23 put a copy of their words in the public archives 61

27 and put it upon pillars on Mount Zion 61
44 to be clothed in purple or put on a gold buckle. 39
2Mc 3:27 his men took him up and put him on a stretcher 42
4:15 and putting the highest value upon . . 46
42 put them all to flight 60
12:37 put them to flight. 58
3Mc 2:20 put praises in the mouth of those . . downcast 35
4Mc 8:24 nor take hollow pride in being put to the rack. *
17: 1 she also was about to be seized and put to death *

put a hedge 1. שׂוך
Job 1:10 Hast thou not put a hedge about him and his house 1

put a mark 1. תוה
Ezk 9: 4 and put a mark upon the foreheads of the men 1

put a riddle 1. חוד
Jdg 14:12 Let me now put a riddle to you; if you can tell me 1
13 Put your riddle, that we may hear it. 1

put a seal upon 1. σφραγίζω
2Co 1:22 he has put his seal upon us 1

put a shield 1. גנן
Zec 12: 8 the LORD will put a shield about the inhabitants 1

put a stop 1. שׁבת
Ezk 34:10 and put a stop to their feeding the sheep; 1

put again 1. שׁוב
Exd 34:35 and Moses would put the veil upon his face again 1

put an end 1. נשׂא 2. צמת 3. שׁבת 4. תמם 5. ἀπωθέω 6. καταλύω
Job 32:22 else would my Maker soon put an end to me. 1
Ps 54: 5 in thy faithfulness put an end to them. 2
73:27 dost put an end to those who are false to thee. 2
Prv 18:18 The lot puts an end to disputes 3
Isa 13:11 I will put an end to the pride of the arrogant 3
Ezk 7:24 I will put an end to their proud might 3
12:23 I will put an end to this proverb 3
23:27 Thus I will put an end to your lewdness 3
48 Thus will I put an end to lewdness in the land 3
30:10 I will put an end to the wealth of Egypt 3
13 and put an end to the images, in Memphis; 3
Dan 9:24 finish the transgression, to put an end to sin 4
11:18 commander shall put an end to his insolence; 3
Hos 1: 4 and I will put an end to the kingdom 3
2:11 And I will put an end to all her mirth, her feasts 3
3Mc 6:32 Putting an end to all mourning and wailing 5
4Mc 4:24 to put an end to the people's observance of the law 6

put ashes 1. σποδόω
Jdt 4:11 and put ashes on their heads 1

put aside 1. μεθίστημι
Sus 1:56 Then he put him aside 1

put asunder 1. χωρίζω
Mat 19: 6 let not man put asunder. 1
Mrk 10: 9 let not man put asunder. 1

put away 1. בער 2. יצא 3. סוג 4. סור 5. עבר 6. פרר 7. שׁבת 8. שׁלח 9. ἀθέτησις 10. αἴρω 11. ἀπολύω 12. ἀποστρέφω 13. ἀποτίθημι 14. ἐκβάλλω 15. τίθημι 16. χωρίζω 17. dimitto
Gen 35: 2 Put away the foreign gods that are among you 4
Exd 12:15 you shall put away leaven out of your houses 7
Deu 22:19 be his wife; he may not put her away all his days. 8
29 he may not put her away all his days. 8
Jos 24:14 put away the gods which your fathers served 4
23 put away the foreign gods which are among you 4
Jdg 10:16 So they put away the foreign gods from among them 4
20:13 put them to death, and put away evil from Israel. 1
1Sm 1:14 How long will you . . Put away your wine from you. 4
7: 3 put away the foreign gods and the Ash'taroth 4
4 So Israel put away the Ba'als and the Ash'taroth 4
2Sm 7:15 took it from Saul, whom I put away from before you. 4
12:13 LORD also has put away your sin; you shall not die. 5
1Kg 15:12 He put away the male cult prostitutes 5
2Kg 3: 2 he put away the pillar of Ba'al 4
23:24 Josi'ah put away the mediums and the wizards 1
2Ch 15: 8 put away the abominable idols from all the land 5
Ezr 10: 3 to put away all these wives and their children 2
19 pledged themselves to put away their wives 2
44 put them away with their children. *
Job 27: 5 till I die I will not put away my integrity from me. 4
Ps 18:22 his statutes I did not put away from me. 4
85: 4 put away thy indignation toward us! 6
Prv 4:24 Put away from you crooked speech 4
Ecc 11:10 Remove . . and put away pain from your body; 5
Isa 49:21 I was bereaved and barren, exiled and put away 4
50: 1 bill of divorce, with which I put her away? 8
1 for . . transgressions your mother was put away. 8
Ezk 45: 9 Israel! Put away violence and oppression 4
Hos 2: 2 that she put away her harlotry from her face 4
Mic 6:14 you shall put away, but not save 3
Mat 19: 7 give a certificate of divorce, and to put her away? 11

Mrk 10: 4 a certificate of divorce, and to put her away. 11
Eph 4:25 Therefore, putting away falsehood 13
31 Let . . clamor and slander be put away from you 10
Col 3: 8 now put them all away: anger, wrath, malice, slander 13
Heb 9:26 to put away sin by the sacrifice of himself. 9
Jas 1:21 put away all filthiness and rank growth 13
1Pe 2: 1 So put away all malice and all guile 13
1Es 8:69 have not put away from themselves 16
93 we will put away all our foreign wives 14
9:20 pledged themselves to put away their wives 14
36 they put them away with their children. 11
2Es 14:14 put away from you mortal thoughts 17
Tob 6: 4 and put them away safely. 15
Bar 3: 7 we have put away from our hearts all the iniquity 12

put back 1. שׁוּב 2. ἀποστρέφω
Gen 29: 3 and put the stone back in its place upon the mouth 1
42:28 said to his brothers, "My money has been put back; 1
Exd 4: 7 Then God said, "Put your hand back into your bosom. 1
7 So he put his hand back into his bosom; 1
Num17:10 Put back the rod of Aaron before the testimony 1
1Sm 5: 3 So they took Dagon and put him back in his place. 1
1Ch 21:27 angel; and he put his sword back into its sheath. 1
Mat 26:52 Put your sword back into its place 2

put before 1. παρατίθημι 2. ὑποτίθημι 3. propono
Mat 13:24 Another parable he put before them, saying 1
31 Another parable he put before them, saying 1
1Ti 4: 6 If you put these . . before the brethren 2
2Es 4: 3 and to put before you three problems. 3

put confidence 1. בטח 2. ἐμπιστεύω 3. πείθω
Jdg 9:26 and the men of Shechem put confidence in him. 1
Ps 62:10 Put no confidence in extortion 1
118: 8 It is better to . . than to put confidence in man. 1
9 better to . . than to put confidence in princes. 1
Php 3: 3 put no confidence in the flesh. 3
1Mc 10:77 and put confidence in it. 3
3Mc 2: 7 those who had put their confidence in you 2

put down 1. שׁפל 2. שׁפל (A) 3. καθαιρέω
Ps 75: 7 putting down one and lifting up another. 1
Dan 5:19 he raised up, and whom he would he put down. 2
7:24 different . . and shall put down three kings. 2
Lke 1:52 he has put down the mighty from their thrones 3

put far 1. סור 2. רחק
Job 19:13 He has put my brethren far from me 2
Ps 119:29 Put false ways far from me; 1
Prv 4:24 put devious talk far from you. 2

put far away 1. נדה 2. רחק
Job 11:14 If iniquity is in your hand, put it far away 2
Ezk 43: 9 let them put away their idolatry . . far from me 2
Ams 6: 3 O you who put far away the evil day, and bring near 1

put fat 1. πιαίνω
Sir 26:13 her skill puts fat on his bones. 1

put forth 1. דשׁא 2. חנט 3. יצא 4. מִשְׁלוֹחַ 5. עשׂה 6. שׁלח 7. שׁלח (A) 8. ἀναθάλλω 9. ἐκφύω 10. ποιέω 11. φύω
Gen 1:11 God said, "Let the earth put forth vegetation 1
3:22 good and evil; and now, lest he put forth his hand 6
8: 9 he put forth his hand and took her 6
19:10 the men put forth their hands 6
22:10 Then Abraham put forth his hand 6
Exd 9:15 For by now I could have put forth my hand 6
Num17: 8 rod of Aaron . . had sprouted and put forth buds 3
1Sm 14:27 so he put forth the tip of the staff . . in his hand 6
22:17 servants . . would not put forth their hand 6
24: 6 do this thing . . to put forth my hand against him 6
10 I said, 'I will not put forth my hand against my lord; 6
26: 9 put forth his hand against the LORD's anointed 6
11 put forth my hand against the LORD's anointed; 6
23 put forth my hand against the LORD's anointed. 6
2Sm 1:14 to put forth your hand to destroy the . . anointed? 6
6: 7 because he put forth his hand to the ark; •
18:12 would not put forth my hand against the king's son; 6
1Ch 13:10 smote him because he put forth his hand to the ark; 6
Ezr 6:12 any . . people that shall put forth a hand 7
Job 1:11 put forth thy hand now, and touch all that he has 6
12 only upon himself do not put forth your hand. 6
2: 5 But put forth thy hand now, and touch his bone 6
14: 9 bud and put forth branches like a young plant. 5
Ps 125: 3 righteous put forth their hands to do wrong. 6
Sng 2:13 The fig tree puts forth its figs 2
Isa 11:14 They shall put forth their hand against Edom 4
Jer 1: 9 the LORD put forth his hand and touched my mouth; 6
Ezk 8: 3 He put forth the form of a hand, and took me 6
17: 6 brought forth branches and put forth foliage. 6
Mat 24:32 becomes tender and puts forth its leaves 9
Mrk 4:32 and puts forth large branches 10
13:28 becomes tender and puts forth its leaves 9
Wis 4: 4 For even if they put forth boughs for a while 8
Sir 14:18 which sheds some and puts forth others 11
50:10 like an olive tree putting forth its fruit 8

put forth a blossom 1. ἀνθέω
Sir 39:14 put forth blossoms like a lily 1

put forth a shoot 1. פרח
Isa 27: 6 Israel shall blossom and put forth shoots 1

put forth all 1. πληθύνω
Sir 43:30 When you exalt him, put forth all your strength 1

put forth many 1. πληθύνω
Sir 40:15 will not put forth many branches 1

put forth more 1. גבר
Ecc 10:10 he must put forth more strength; 1

put forward 1. הדר 2. ἵστημι 3. προβάλλω 4. προτίθημι
Prv 25: 6 not put yourself forward in the king's presence 1
Act 1:23 they put forward two, Joseph . . and Matthi'as 2
19:33 Alexander, whom the Jews had put forward 3
Rom 3:25 whom God put forward as an expiation by his blood 4

put hope 1. ἐλπίζω
Sir 34: 7 those who put their hope in them have failed. 1
Bar 4:22 I have put my hope in the Everlasting to save you 1

put in a position 1. καθίστημι
1Mc 10:37 be put in positions of trust in the kingdom 1

put in bonds 1. אסר
2Kg 23:33 Pharaoh Neco put him in bonds at Riblah 1

put in charge 1. עמד
1Ch 6:31 whom David put in charge of the service of song 1

put in execution 1. προσχράω
AEs 16:17 do well not to put in execution the letters 1

put in order 1. ערך 2. κοσμέω
1Kg 18:33 he put the wood in order, and cut the bull in pieces 1
Mat 12:44 he finds it empty, swept, and put in order. 2
Lke 11:25 when he comes he finds it swept and put in order. 2

put in place 1. חלף 2. שׂום
Exd 40:28 he put in place the screen for the door 2
Isa 9:10 cut down, but we will put cedars in their place. 1

put in possession 1. נחל
Deu 3:28 he shall put them in possession of the land 1
31: 7 you shall put them in possession of it. 1

put in prison 1. δέω 2. κατακλείω
1Es 1:38 Jehoiakim put the nobles in prison 1
2Mc 13:21 he was sought for, caught, and put in prison. 2

put in remembrance 1. זכר
Isa 43:26 Put me in remembrance, let us argue together; 1
62: 6 You who put the LORD in remembrance, take no rest 1

put in seed 1. זרע
Jdg 6: 3 For whenever the Israelites put in seed 1

put in subjection 1. ὑποτάσσω
1Co 15:27 For God has put all things in subjection 1
27 All things are put in subjection under him 1
Heb 2: 8 Now in putting everything in subjection to him 1
8 Now in putting everything in subjection to him 1

put in the wrong 1. עות 2. פרר מִשְׁפָּט
Job 19: 6 know then that God has put me in the wrong 1
40: 8 Will you even put me in the wrong? 2

put in writing 1. מִכְתָּב
Ezr 1: 1 proclamation . . and also put it in writing 1

put into 1. βάλλω
Joh 12: 6 he used to take what was put into it. 1

put low 1. שׁפל
Prv 25: 7 than to be put lower in the presence of the prince. 1

make put forth 1. צמח
Job 38:27 to make the ground put forth grass? 1

put new 1. חדשׁ
Ps 51:10 O God, and put a new and right spirit within me. 1

put off 1. גלה 2. ירד 3. נשׁל 4. סור 5. עזב 6. פשׁט 7. פתח 8. שׁנה 9. ἀναβάλλω 10. ἀπεκδύομαι 11. ἀπέκδυσις 12. ἀποτίθημι 13. depono
Gen 38:14 she put off her widow's garments, and put on a veil 4
Exd 3: 5 Do not come near; put off your shoes from your feet 3
33: 5 So now put off your ornaments from you 3
Lev 6:11 Then he shall put off his garments 6
16:23 Aaron . . shall put off the linen garments 6
Deu 21:13 shall put off her captive's garb, and shall remain 4
Jos 5:15 Put off your shoes from your feet; 3
1Sm 17:39 I am not used to them." And David put them off. 4
1Kg 20:11 Let not him . . boast himself as he that puts it off.' 7
2Kg 25:29 So Jehoi'achin put off his prison garments. 8
Job 9:27 I will put off my sad countenance 5
Sng 5: 3 I had put off my garment, how could I put it on? 6
Isa 47: 2 grind meal, put off your veil, strip off your robe 1
Jer 52:33 Jehoi'achin put off his prison garments. 8
Ezk 44:19 to the people, they shall put off the garments 6
Act 24:22 Felix . . put them off, saying 9
Eph 4:22 Put off your old nature 12
Col 2:11 putting off the body of flesh 11
3: 9 seeing that you have put off the old nature 10
2Pe 1:14 know that the putting off of my body will be soon 12
2Es 2:45 they who have put off mortal clothing 13

put on a leash 1. קשׁר
Job 41: 5 or will you put him on leash for your maidens? 1

put on airs 1. ἐπαίρω
2Co 11:20 if a man . . puts on airs, or strikes you in the face. 1

put on armor 1. חגר
2Kg 3:21 all who were able to put on armor . . were called 1

put on board 1. ἐμβιβάζω 2. ἐπιτίθημι
Act 27: 6 found a ship . . and put us on board. 1
28:10 they put on board whatever we needed. 2

put on bold 1. עזז
Prv 21:29 A wicked man puts on a bold face 1

put on full armor 1. καθοπλίζω
4Mc 13:16 let us put on the full armor of self-control 1

put out 1. ארך 2. דעך 3. יצא 4. כבה 5. נקר 6. נתן 7. סור 8. עור 9. שׁלח 10. ἐκβάλλω 11. ἐξαίρω 12. ἐπανάγω 13. προβάλλω 14. σβέννυμι 15. φέρω 16. everto 17. extinguo
Gen 38:28 when she was in labor, one put out a hand; 6
Exd 4: 4 the LORD said to Moses, "Put out your hand, and take 9
4 it by the tail"– so he put out his hand and caught it 9
Num 5: 2 put out of the camp every leper 9
3 you shall put out both male and female 9
16:14 Will you put out the eyes of these men? 5
Deu 25:11 puts out her hand and seizes him by the private 9
Jdg 15:15 found a . . jawbone . . and put out his hand 9
19:25 man seized his concubine, and put her out to them; 3
1Sm 28: 3 And Saul had put the mediums and the wizards out 7
2Sm 6: 6 Uzzah put out his hand to the ark . . and took hold 9
13:17 Put this woman out of my presence, and bolt 9
18 So his servant put her out, and bolted the door 3
15: 5 he would put out his hand, and take hold of him 9
2Kg 25: 7 slew the sons . . and put out the eyes of Zedeki'ah 8
1Ch 13: 9 Uzzah put out his hand to hold the ark 9
2Ch 29: 7 They also shut the doors . . and put out the lamps 4
Job 18: 5 Yea, the light of the wicked is put out 2
6 dark in his tent, and his lamp above him is put out. 2
21:17 often is it that the lamp of the wicked is put out? 2
Ps 15: 5 who does not put out his money at interest 6
Prv 13: 9 but the lamp of the wicked will be put out. 2
20:20 his lamp will be put out in utter darkness. 2
24:20 lamp of the wicked will be put out. 2
Isa 57: 4 you open your mouth wide and put out your tongue? 1
Jer 39: 7 He put out the eyes of Zedeki'ah 8
52:11 He put out the eyes of Zedeki'ah, and bound him 8
Lke 4:29 they rose up and put him out of the city 10
5: 3 he asked him to put out a little from the land. 12
4 he said to Simon, "Put out into the deep 12
Joh 20:27 and put out your hand, and place it in my side 15
3Jn 1:10 stops those . . and puts them out of the church. 10
2Es 10: 2 Then we all put out the lamps 16
22 the light of our lampstand has been put out 17
14:25 which shall not be put out 17
16:15 The fire is kindled, and shall not be put out 17
Sir 28:12 if you spit on it, it will be put out 14
23 it will burn among them and will not be put out 14
1Mc 14:36 so that the Gentiles were put out of the country 11
2Mc 7:10 he quickly put out his tongue 13

put out of joint 1. יקע 2. ἐκτρέπω
Gen 32:25 put out of joint as he wrestled with him. 1
Heb 12:13 so that what is lame may not be put out of joint 2

put out of the synagogue 1. ἀποσυνάγωγος
Joh 9:22 he was to be put out of the synagogue. 1
12:42 lest they should be put out of the synagogue 1

put out of the way 1. παρακλείω
2Mc 4:34 then . . he immediately put him out of the way. 1

put outside 1. ἐκβάλλω
Mat 9:25 But when the crowd had been put outside, he went 1
Mrk 5:40 But he put them all outside 1
Act 9:40 Peter put them all outside and knelt down 1

put to confusion 1. בושׁ 2. חפר
Ps 35:26 Let them be put to shame and confusion 2
40:14 Let them be put to shame and confusion 2

44: 7 hast put to confusion those who hate us. 1
70: 2 be put to shame and confusion who seek my life! 2

put to death 1. מות 2. נכה 3. רצח 4. ἀναιρέω 5. ἀπάγω 6. ἀποκτείνω 7. ἀπόλλυμι 8. ζῆν μεθίστημι 9. θανατόω 10. νεκρόω 11. παραδίδωμι 12. πατάσσω 13. προσαπόλλυμι 14. συγκόπτω 15. σφάζω 16. φονεύω

Gen 26:11 this man or his wife shall be put to death. 1
Exd 19:12 touches the mountain shall be put to death; 1
21:12 a man so that he dies shall be put to death. 1
15 father or his mother shall be put to death. 1
16 Whoever steals a man . . shall be put to death. 1
17 father or his mother shall be put to death. 1
29 and its owner also shall be put to death. 1
22:19 Whoever lies with a beast shall be put to death. 1
31:14 every one who profanes it shall be put to death; 1
15 work on the sabbath day shall be put to death. 1
35: 2 whoever does any work on it shall be put to death; 1
Lev 19:20 They shall not be put to death 1
20: 2 gives . . children to Molech shall be put to death 1
4 if the people . . do not put him to death 1
9 who curses his father . . shall be put to death 1
10 the adulteress shall be put to death 1
11 both of them shall be put to death 1
12 both of them shall be put to death 1
13 they shall be put to death, their blood is upon them 1
15 If a man lies with a beast, he shall be put to death 1
16 they shall be put to death, their blood is upon them 1
27 a medium or a wizard shall be put to death 1
24:16 He who blasphemes . . shall be put to death 1
16 when he blasphemes the Name, shall be put to death 1
17 He who kills a man shall be put to death 1
21 he who kills a man shall be put to death 1
27:29 he shall be put to death 1
Num 1:51 any one else comes near, he shall be put to death. 1
3:10 if any one else comes near, he shall be put to death. 1
38 any one else who came near was to be put to death. 1
15:35 LORD said to Moses, "The man shall be put to death; 1
18: 7 any one else who comes near shall be put to death. 1
35:16 the murderer shall be put to death. 1
17 the murderer shall be put to death. 1
18 the murderer shall be put to death. 1
19 avenger of blood . . put the murderer to death; 1
19 when he meets him, he shall put him to death. 1
21 then he who struck the blow shall be put to death; 1
21 avenger of blood shall put the murderer to death 1
30 the murderer shall be put to death on the evidence 3
30 no person shall be put to death on the testimony 1
31 but he shall be put to death. 1
Deu 13: 5 But that prophet . . shall be put to death 1
9 your hand shall be first . . to put him to death 1
17: 6 witnesses he that is to die shall be put to death; 1
6 person shall not be put to death on . . one witness. 1
7 witnesses shall be first . . to put him to death 1
21:22 if a man . . is put to death, and you hang him on a tree 1
24:16 fathers . . not be put to death for the children 1
16 nor . . children be put to death for the fathers; 1
16 every man shall be put to death for his own sin. 1
Jos 1:18 Whoever rebels against . . shall be put to death. 1
10:26 Joshua smote them and put them to death 1
11:17 and smote them, and put them to death. 1
Jdg 6:31 Whoever contends for him shall be put to death 1
20:13 that we may put them to death, and put away evil 1
21: 5 a great oath . . saying, "He shall be put to death. 1
1Sm 11:12 Bring the men, that we may put them to death. 1
13 Saul said, "Not a man shall be put to death this day 1
19: 6 As the LORD lives, he shall not be put to death. 1
20:32 Why should he be put to death? What has he done? 1
33 his father was determined to put David to death. 1
2Sm 8: 2 two lines he measured to be put to death 1
19:21 Shall not Shim'e-i be put to death for this 1
22 Shall any one be put to death in Israel this day? 1
21: 1 because he put the Gib'eonites to death. 1
4 neither is it for us to put any man to death 1
9 They were put to death in the first days 1
1Kg 2: 8 saying, 'I will not put you to death with the sword.' 1
24 Adoni'jah shall be put to death this day. 1
26 I will not at this time put you to death 1
2Kg 14: 6 not put to death the children of the murderers; 1
6 The fathers shall not be put to death 1
6 or the children be put to death for the fathers; 1
25:21 king . . smote them, and put them to death at Riblah 1
2Ch 15:13 would not seek the LORD . . should be put to death 1
22: 9 Ahazi'ah . . was brought to Jehu and put to death. 1
25: 4 he did not put their children to death 1
4 fathers . . not be put to death for the children 1
4 or the children be put to death for the fathers; 1
16 Stop! Why should you be put to death? 2
Est 4:11 there is . . one law; all alike are to be put to death 1
Jer 26:15 Only know for certain that if you put me to death 1
19 king of Judah and all Judah put him to death? 1
21 the king sought to put him to death; 1
24 given over to the people to be put to death. 1
38: 4 Let this man be put to death 1
15 will you not be sure to put me to death? 1
16 I will not put you to death or deliver you 1
25 and we will not put you to death, 1
52:27 smote them, and put them to death at Riblah 1
Ezk 13:19 putting to death persons who should not die 1
Mat 10:21 and have them put to death; 9
14: 5 though he wanted to put him to death 6
21:41 put those wretches to a miserable death 7
24: 9 deliver you up . . and put you to death 6
26:59 that they might put him to death 9
27: 1 counsel against Jesus to put him to death; 9
Mrk 13:12 against parents and have them put to death; 9
14:55 testimony against Jesus to put him to death 9
Lke 21:16 some of you they will put to death; 9
22: 2 the scribes were seeking how to put him to death; 4
23:32 Two others . . were led away to be put to death 4
Joh 11:53 they took counsel how to put him to death. 6
12:10 planned to put Laz'arus also to death 6
18:31 It is not lawful for us to put any man to death. 6
Act 10:39 They put him to death by hanging him on a tree; 4
12:19 and ordered that they should be put to death 5
26:10 when they were put to death 4
Rom 4:25 who was put to death for our trespasses 11
8:13 if . . you put to death the deeds of the body 9
Col 3: 5 Put to death therefore what is earthly in you 10
1Pe 3:18 Christ . . put to death in the flesh 9
Tob 1:18 if Sennacherib . . put to death any . . from Judea 6
18 in his anger he put many to death 6
2: 8 He is no longer afraid that he will be put to death 16
Jdt 2:27 and put to death all their young men 12
5:22 insisted that he must be put to death. 14
Sus 1:28 their wicked plot to have Susanna put to death. 9
45 And as she was being led away to be put to death 7
53 'Do not put to death an innocent . . person 6
62 they put them to death. 6
Bel 1:22 Therefore the king put them to death 6
1Mc 1: 2 and put to death the kings of the earth. 15
60 they put to death the women 9
6:24 they have put to death as many of us as they have 9
2Mc 13: 4 to put him to death 13
3Mc 2:28 to be taken by force and put to death; 8
3: 1 and put to death by the most cruel means. 8
7: 5 they tried . . to put them to death. 4
14 punished and put to a public and shameful death 4
15 In that day they put to death more than 300 men 4
4Mc 18:21 and put them to death with various tortures. 6

put to flight 1. ברח 2. נוס 3. רדף 4. שׁית שְׁכֶם 5. κλίνω 6. τροπόω 7. φυγαδεύω

Lev 26:36 sound of a driven leaf shall put them to flight 3
Deu 32:30 How should . . two put 10,000 to flight 2
Jos 23:10 One man of you puts to flight 1,000 3
1Ch 8:13 who put to flight the inhabitants of Gath 1
12:15 and put to flight all those in the valleys 1
Ps 21:12 For you will put them to flight; 4
Heb 11:34 put foreign armies to flight. 5
1Mc 4:20 They saw that their army had been put to flight 6
10:72 fathers were twice put to flight in their own land. 6
11:15 and put him to flight. 6
16: 8 Cendebeus and his army were put to flight 6
2Mc 8: 6 and put to flight not a few of the enemy. 6
9: 2 Antiochus was put to flight by the inhabitants 6
4 the injury done by those who had put him to flight; 7

put to grief 1. חלה

Isa 53:10 of the LORD to bruise him; he has put him to grief; 1

put to proof 1. נסה

Exd 17: 2 Why do you put the LORD to the proof? 1
7 and because they put the LORD to the proof 1
Num14:22 yet have put me to the proof these ten times 1

put to rout 1. נגף

1Sm 4: 3 LORD put us to rout today before the Philistines? 1

put to sea 1. ἀνάγω 2. ἐπιβαίνω

Act 27: 2 we put to sea, accompanied by Aristar'chus 1
4 putting to sea from there 1
12 the majority advised to put to sea from there 1
Wis 14: 4 even if a man lacks skill, he may put to sea. 2

put to shame 1. בושׁ 2. חפר 3. חרף 4. כלם 5. αἰσχύνω 6. δειγματίζω 7. ἐντρέπω 8. καταισχύνω 9. confundo

2Ch 30:15 priests and the Levites were put to shame 4
Ps 6:10 shall turn back, and be put to shame in a moment. 1
25: 2 O my God, in thee I trust, let me not be put to shame; 1
3 Yea, let none that wait for thee be put to shame; 1
20 let me not be put to shame, for I take refuge 1
31: 1 let me never be put to shame; 1
17 Let me not be put to shame, O LORD, for I call on thee; 1
17 let the wicked be put to shame 1
35: 4 Let them be put to shame and dishonor 1
26 Let them be put to shame and confusion 1
37:19 they are not put to shame in evil times 1
40:14 Let them be put to shame and confusion 1
53: 5 will be put to shame, for God has rejected them. 1
57: 3 he will put to shame those who trample upon me. 3
69: 6 Let not those who hope in thee be put to shame 1
70: 2 Let them be put to shame and confusion 1
71: 1 I take refuge; let me never be put to shame! 1
13 May my accusers be put to shame and consumed; 1
24 for they have been put to shame and disgraced 1
74:21 Let not the downtrodden be put to shame; 4
83:17 Let them be put to shame and dismayed for ever; 1
86:17 that those who hate me may see and be put to shame 1
97: 7 All worshipers of images are put to shame 1
109:28 Let my assailants be put to shame; 1
119: 6 I shall not be put to shame 1
31 O LORD; let me not be put to shame! 1
46 before kings, and shall not be put to shame; 1
78 Let the godless be put to shame 1
80 in thy statutes, that I may not be put to shame! 1
116let me not be put to shame in my hope! 1
127: 5 He shall not be put to shame when he speaks 1
129: 5 who hate Zion be put to shame and turned backward! 1
Prv 25: 8 do in the end, when your neighbor puts you to shame? 4
Isa 41:11 against you shall be put to shame and confounded; 1
42:17 be turned back and utterly put to shame 1
44: 9 see nor know, that they may be put to shame. 1
11 Behold, all his fellows shall be put to shame 1
11 terrified, they shall be put to shame together. 1
45:16 All of them are put to shame and confounded 1
17 you shall not be put to shame or confounded 1
49:23 those who wait for me shall not be put to shame. 1
50: 7 and I know that I shall not be put to shame; 1
54: 4 be not confounded, for you will not be put to shame; 2
65:13 shall rejoice, but you shall be put to shame; 1
66: 5 but it is they who shall be put to shame. 1
Jer 2:36 You shall be put to shame by Egypt 1
36 by Egypt as you were put to shame by Assyria. 1
8: 9 The wise men shall be put to shame 1
10:14 every goldsmith is put to shame by his idols; 1
17:13 all who forsake thee shall be put to shame; 1
18 Let those be put to shame who persecute me 1
18 but let me not be put to shame; 1
46:24 The daughter of Egypt shall be put to shame 1
48: 1 Kiriatha'im is put to shame, it is taken; 1
1 the fortress is put to shame and broken down; 1
20 Moab is put to shame, for it is broken; wail and cry! 1
50: 2 and say: 'Babylon is taken, Bel is put to shame 1
2 Her images are put to shame 1
51:17 every goldsmith is put to shame by his idols; 1
47 her whole land shall be put to shame 1
51 We are put to shame, for we have heard reproach; 1
Jol 2:26 And my people shall never again be put to shame. 1
27 And my people shall never again be put to shame. 1
Mic 3: 7 be disgraced, and the diviners put to shame; 2
Zep 3:11 On that day you shall not be put to shame 1
Mat 1:19 just man and unwilling to put her to shame 6
Lke 13:17 all his adversaries were put to shame 8
Rom 9:33 he who believes in him will not be put to shame. 8
10:11 No one who believes in him will be put to shame 8
2Co 7:14 I was not put to shame 8
10: 8 I shall not be put to shame. 5
Tit 2: 8 so that an opponent may be put to shame 7
1Pe 2: 6 he who believes in him will not be put to shame. 8
3:16 those who revile . . may be put to shame. 8
2Es 16:65 you shall be put to shame 9
Sir 2:10 who ever trusted in the Lord and was put to shame? 8
15: 4 he will rely on her and will not be put to shame. 8
24:22 Whoever obeys me will not be put to shame 5
42:11 put you to shame before the great multitude. 8
51:18 I shall never be put to shame. 5
29 may you not be put to shame when you praise him. 5
LJr 1:39 those who serve them will be put to shame. 8
Aza 1:19 Do not put us to shame 8
20 Let all who do harm to thy servants be put to shame; 7
4Mc 5:35 I will not put you to shame, philosophical reason 8
9: 2 we are obviously putting our forefathers to shame 5
13:18 Do not put us to shame, brother 8

put to silence 1. φιμόω

1Pe 2:15 put to silence the ignorance of foolish men. 1

put to the proof 1. בחן

Ps 95: 9 your fathers tested me, and put me to the proof 1

put to the sword 1. συγκεντέω 2. συνεκκεντέω

2Mc 5:26 He put to the sword all those 2
12:23 putting the sinners to the sword 1

put to the test 1. בחן 2. נסה 3. ἐκπειράζω 4. ἐξετάζω 5. πειράζω

Deu 6:16 You shall not put the LORD your God to the test 2
Ps 106:14 put God to the test in the desert; 2
Isa 7:12 not ask, and I will not put the LORD to the test. 2
Mal 3:10 thereby put me to the test, says the LORD of hosts 1
15 but when they put God to the test they escape. 1
Mat 22:18 Why put me to the test, you hypocrites? 5
Mrk 12:15 Why put me to the test? 5
Lke 10:25 behold, a lawyer stood up to put him to the test 3
1Co 10: 9 We must not put the Lord to the test, as some of them 3
Heb 3: 9 where your fathers put me to the test 5
Jdt 8:12 that have put God to the test this day 5
13 You are putting the Lord Almighty to the test 4
25 who is putting us to the test as he did our forefathers. 5
Wis 1: 2 he is found by those who do not put him to the test 5
4Mc 9: 7 Therefore, tyrant, put us to the test 5

put to the worse 1. רשע

1Sm 14:47 wherever he turned he put them to the worse. 1

put to the yoke 1. רכב

Hos 10:11 but I will put E'phraim to the yoke 1

put to use 1. עשה

Lev 7:24 The fat . . may be put to any other use 1

put together 1. אסף

Gen 42:17 put them all together in prison for three days. 1

put too severely 1. ἐπιβαρέω

2Co 2: 5 not to put it too severely- to you all. 1

put trust 1. אמן 2. בטח 3. ἐλπίζω 4. πείθω 5. πιστεύω 6. confido

Job 4:18 Even in his servants he puts no trust 1
15:15 Behold, God puts no trust in his holy ones 1
Ps 4: 5 sacrifices, and put your trust in the LORD. 2
9:10 those who know thy name put their trust in thee 2
40: 3 see and fear, and put their trust in the LORD. 2
56: 3 When I am afraid, I put my trust in thee. 2
115:10 O house of Aaron, put your trust in the LORD! 2
143: 8 thy steadfast love, for in thee I put my trust. 2
146: 3 Put not your trust in princes, in a son of man 2
Jer 9: 4 and put no trust in any brother; 2
39:18 you have put your trust in me, says the LORD. 2
Mic 7: 5 Put no trust in a neighbor 1
2Es 8:30 who have always put their trust in thy glory. 6
Wis 12: 2 and put their trust in thee, O Lord. 5
1Mc 2:61 none who put their trust in him will lack strength 3
2Mc 7:40 putting his whole trust in the Lord. 4

put under 1. ὑποτάσσω 2. ὑποτίθημι

1Co 15:27 he is excepted who put all things under him. 1
28 be subjected to him who put all things under him 1
Eph 1:22 he has put all things under his feet 1
Sir 6:25 Put your shoulder under her and carry her 2
51:26 Put your neck under the yoke 2
2Mc 8:22 to command a division, putting 1,500 men under each. 1

put under oath 1. שׁבע

2Kg 11: 4 made a covenant with them and put them under oath 1

put up 1. ἵστημι 2. ποιέω 3. τίθημι

1Mc 11:37 and put up in a conspicuous place 3
14:48 to put them up in a conspicuous place 1
2Mc 11: 3 to put up the high priesthood for sale every year. 2

put upon 1. לבשׁ 2. ἐπιβάλλω 3. ἐπιτίθημι 4. περιζώννυμι 5. περιτίθημι

Gen 27:16 the skins of the kids she put upon his hands 1
Exd 28:41 put them upon Aaron your brother, and upon his sons 1
40:13 put upon Aaron the holy garments 1
Lev 6:10 and put his linen breeches upon his body 1
Num20:26 garments, and put them upon Elea'zar his son; 1
28 garments, and put them upon Elea'zar his son; 1
Mat 27:28 they stripped him and put a scarlet robe upon him 5
Lke 5:36 and puts it upon an old garment 2
Act 15:10 by putting a yoke upon the neck of the disciples 3
Tob 8: 2 and put the heart and liver of the fish upon them 3
Sir 45: 7 put a glorious robe upon him. 4
1Mc 11:13 Thus he put two crowns upon his head 5

pyramid 1. πυραμίς

1Mc 13:28 He also erected seven pyramids 1
29 for the pyramids •

pyre 1. מְדֻרָה

Isa 30:33 its pyre made deep and wide, with fire and wood 1

Q

quadrennial 1. πενταετηρικός
2Mc 4:18 the quadrennial games were being held at Tyre 1

quail 1. שְׂלָו 2. ὀρτυγομήτρα 3. coturnix
Exd 16:13 quails came up and covered the camp; 1
Num 11:31 brought quails from the sea, and let them fall 1
32 people rose . . and gathered the quails; 1
Ps 105:40 They asked, and he brought quails 1
2Es 1:15 The quails were a sign to you 3
Wis 16: 2 thou didst prepare quails to eat 2
19:12 to give them relief, quails came up from the sea. 2

quake 1. געש 2. זלל 3. חרד 4. נוט 5. רגז 6. רעש
7. רַעַשׁ 8. σείω 9. tremo
Exd 19:18 and the whole mountain quaked greatly. 3
Jdg 5: 5 The mountains quaked before the LORD, yon Sinai 2
1Sm 14:15 and even the raiders trembled; the earth quaked; 5
2Sm 22: 8 foundations of the heavens trembled and quaked 1
Ps 18: 7 the mountains trembled and quaked 1
68: 8 earth quaked, the heavens poured down rain 6
8 yon Sinai quaked at the presence of God •
99: 1 enthroned upon the cherubim; let the earth quake! 4
Isa 5:25 smote them, and the mountains quaked; 5
64: 1 that the mountains might quake at they presence– 2
3 the mountains quaked at thy presence. 2
Jer 4:24 looked on the mountains, and lo, they were quaking 6
8:16 at . . their stallions the whole land quakes. 6
10:10 At his wrath the earth quakes 6
Ezk 12:18 "Son of man, eat your bread with quaking 7
38:20 the face of the earth, shall quake at my presence 6
Jol 2:10 The earth quakes before them 5
Nah 1: 5 The mountains quake before him, the hills melt; 6
1Es 4:36 All God's works quake and tremble 8
2Es 16:12 The earth and its foundations quake 9

make quake 1. רעש
Ps 60: 2 Thou hast made the land to quake 1
Ezk 31:16 I will make the nations quake at the sound 1

qualification 1. ἄξιος
2Mc 4:25 possessing no qualification for the high priesthood 1

qualify 1. בָּלָה 2. ἐπιτήδειος 3. ἱκανόω
1Ch 26: 8 able men qualified for the service; 62 of O'bed-e'dom 1
Col 1:12 has qualified us to share in the inheritance 3
1Mc 13:40 if any of you are qualified to be enrolled 2

tested quality 1. probatio
2Es 16:73 the tested quality of my elect shall be manifest 1

quantity 1. מְשׂוּרָה 2. רֹב 3. πλῆθος 4. πολύς
5. mensura
Lev 19:35 in measures of length or weight or quantity 1
1Kg 10:10 gold, and a very great quantity of spices •
1Ch 22: 3 as well as bronze in quantities beyond weighing 2
23:29 and all measures of quantity or size. 1
Joh 21: 6 not able to haul it in, for the quantity of fish. 3
2Es 4:50 so the quantity that passed was far greater 5
Jdt 12:20 drank a great quantity of wine 4
15: 7 there was a vast quantity of it. 3

great quantity 1. לָרֹב 2. רֹב
1Ch 22: 4 and Tyrians brought great quantities of cedar 1
5 David provided materials in great quantity 1
29: 2 besides great quantities of onyx and stones 1
2Ch 4:18 made all these things in great quantities 2
9: 9 she gave . . a very great quantity of spices 2

quarrel 1. גלע 2. דִּין 3. מָדוֹן 4. מְדָיָן 5. נצה 6. רגז
7. ריב 8. רִיב 9. διαλογισμός 10. ἐρίζω 11. ἔρις
12. κρίνω 13. μάχη 14. μάχομαι
Gen 26:20 the herdsmen of Gerar quarreled with Isaac's 7
21 Then they dug another well, and they quarreled 7
22 did not quarrel; so he called its name Reho'both 7
45:24 he said to them, "Do not quarrel on the way. 6
Exd 21:18 "When men quarrel and one strikes the other 7
Lev 24:10 woman's son and a man of Israel quarreled 5
2Sm 14: 6 had two sons, and they quarreled with one another 5
Prv 17:14 so quit before the quarrel breaks out. 8
18:19 but quarreling is like the bars of a castle. 4
19:13 wife's quarreling is a continual dripping 4
20: 3 but every fool will be quarreling. 1
22:10 quarreling and abuse will cease. 2
26:17 He who meddles in a quarrel not his own is like one 8
20 where there is no whisperer, quarreling ceases. 3
Isa 58: 4 you fast only to quarrel and to fight and to hit 7
Act 7:26 he appeared to them as they were quarreling 14
Rom 13:13 not in quarreling and jealousy. 11
1Co 1:11 there is quarreling among you, my brethren. 11
2Co 12:20 perhaps there may be quarreling, jealousy, anger 11
1Ti 2: 8 lifting holy hands without anger or quarreling; 9
2Ti 2:23 you know that they breed quarrels. 13
Tit 3: 9 dissensions, and quarrels over the law 13
Sir 6: 9 will disclose a quarrel to your disgrace. 13
8: 2 Do not quarrel with a rich man 10
27:14 their quarrels make a man stop his ears. 13
28:11 A hasty quarrel kindles fire 11
42: 8 the aged man who quarrels with the young 12

quarrel *See also* seek.
quarreling *See* avoid.

quarrelsome 1. מִדְיָן 2. ἄμαχος 3. μάχομαι
Prv 26:21 so is a quarrelsome man for kindling strife. 1
1Ti 3: 3 not quarrelsome, and no lover of money. 2
2Ti 2:24 the Lord's servant must not be quarrelsome 3

quarry 1. חצב 2. מַחְצֵב 3. מַסָּע 4. מַקֶּבֶת בּוֹר 5. נסע
1Kg 6: 7 it was with stone prepared at the quarry; 3
2Kg 12:12 as well as to buy timber and quarried stone 2
22: 6 for buying timber and quarried stone to repair 2
2Ch 2: 2 80,000 to quarry in the hill country 1
18 80,000 to quarry in the hill country 1
34:11 to buy quarried stone, and timber for binders 2
Ecc 10: 9 He who quarries stones is hurt by them; 5
Isa 51: 1 and to the quarry from which you were digged. 4

quarry out 1. נסע
1Kg 5:17 they quarried out great, costly stones 1
Sir 50: 3 In his days a cistern for water was quarried out •

quart 1. χοῖνιξ
Rev 6: 6 A quart of wheat for a denarius 1
6 and three quarts of barley for a denarius 1

quarter 1. מָקוֹם 2. קֵץ 3. קָצָה
2Kg 22:14 (now she dwelt in Jerusalem in the Second Quarter); •
Est 4:14 deliverance will rise . . from another quarter 1
Jer 49:36 the four winds from the four quarters of heaven; 3
50:26 Come against her from every quarter; 2

every quarter 1. πάντοθεν
Mrk 1:45 people came to him from every quarter. 1

quarter of a mile 1. στάδιοι δύο
2Mc 12:16 the adjoining lake, a quarter of a mile wide 1

second quarter 1. מִשְׁנֶה
2Ch 34:22 now she dwelt in Jerusalem in the Second Quarter 1
Zep 1:10 a wail from the Second Quarter 1

quartermaster 1. שַׂר מְנוּחָה
Jer 51:59 Serai'ah was the quartermaster. 1

queen 1. גְּבִירָה 2. מלך 3. מַלְכָּה 4. שָׂרָה 5. שֵׁגָל
6. מַלְכָּה (A) 7. βασίλισσα
1Kg 10: 1 the queen of Sheba heard of the fame of Solomon 3
4 when the queen of Sheba had seen all the wisdom 3
10 which the queen of Sheba gave to King Solomon. 3
13 King Solomon gave to the queen of Sheba 3
11:19 the sister of Tah'penes the queen. 1
2Ch 9: 1 the queen of Sheba heard of the fame of Solomon 3
3 queen of Sheba had seen the wisdom of Solomon 3
9 which the queen of Sheba gave to King Solomon. 3
12 King Solomon gave to the queen of Sheba 3
Neh 2: 6 king said to me (the queen sitting beside him) 5
Est 1: 9 Queen Vashti also gave a banquet for the women 3
11 to bring Queen Vashti before the king 3
12 But Queen Vashti refused to come 3
15 what is to be done to Queen Vashti, 3
16 Not only to the king has Queen Vashti done wrong 3
17 this deed of the queen will be made known to all 3
17 Ahasu-e'rus commanded Queen Vashti to be brought 3
18 ladies . . who have heard of the queen's behavior 3
2: 4 let the maiden . . be queen instead of Vashti. 2
22 Mor'decai, and he told it to Queen Esther 3
4: 4 When . . told her, the queen was deeply distressed; 3
5: 2 the king saw Queen Esther standing in the court 3
3 What is it, Queen Esther? What is your request? 3
12 Even Queen Esther let no one come . . but myself. 3
7: 1 and Haman went in to feast with Queen Esther. 3
2 What is your petition, Queen Esther? 3
3 Then Queen Esther answered, "If I have found favor 3
5 King Ahasu-e'rus said to Queen Esther, "Who is he 3
6 in terror before the king and the queen. 3
7 Haman stayed to beg his life from Queen Esther 3
8 Will he even assault the queen in my presence 3
8: 1 Ahasu-e'rus gave to Queen Esther the house 3
7 Ahasu-e'rus said to Queen Esther and to Mor'decai 3
9:12 And the king said to Queen Esther, "In Susa 3
29 Queen Esther, the daughter of Ab'ihail 3
31 as Mor'decai the Jew and Queen Esther enjoined 3
32 The command of Queen Esther fixed . . Purim •
Ps 45: 9 stands the queen in gold of Ophir. 5
Sng 6: 8 There are 60 queens and 80 concubines 3
9 the queens and concubines also, and they praised 3
Isa 49:23 and their queens your nursing mothers. 4
Jer 7:18 knead dough, to make cakes for the queen of heaven; 3
44:17 we have vowed, burn incense to the queen of heaven 3
18 left off burning incense to the queen of heaven 3
19 When we burned incense to the queen of heaven 3
25 to burn incense to the queen of heaven 3
Dan 5:10 queen . . came into the banqueting hall; 6
10 queen said, "O king, live for ever! 6
Mat 12:42 The queen of the South will arise at the judgment 7
Lke 11:31 The queen of the South will arise at the judgment 7
Act 8:27 the Can'dace, queen of the Ethiopians 7
Rev 18: 7 A queen I sit, I am no widow 7
AEs 10: 6 Esther, whom the king married and made queen. 7
14: 1 Esther the queen, seized with deathly anxiety 7
15: 7 the queen faltered, and turned pale and faint 7

queen *See also* make.

queen mother 1. גְּבִירָה
1Kg 15:13 also removed Ma'acah . . from being queen mother 1
2Kg 10:13 royal princes and the sons of the queen mother. 1
2Ch 15:16 King Asa removed from being queen mother 1
Jer 13:18 Say to the king and the queen mother 1
29: 2 King Jeconi'ah, and the queen mother, the eunuchs 1

queenly 1. נָדִיב
Sng 7: 1 How graceful are your feet . . O queenly maiden! 1

quench 1. כבה 2. שבר 3. שקק 4. κατασβέννυμι
5. σβέννυμι 6. extinguo
2Sm 14: 7 Thus they would quench my coal which is left 1
21:17 no more . . lest you quench the lamp of Israel. 1
2Kg 22:17 my wrath will be . . and it will not be quenched. 1
2Ch 34:25 my wrath will . . not be quenched. 1
Ps 104:11 wild asses quench their thirst. 2
Sng 8: 7 Many waters cannot quench love 1
Isa 1:31 shall burn together, with none to quench them. 1
29: 8 awakes faint, with his thirst not quenched 3
34:10 Night and day it shall not be quenched; 1
42: 3 and a dimly burning wick he will not quench; 1
43:17 they are extinguished, quenched like a wick 1
66:24 worm . . not die, their fire shall not be quenched 1
Jer 4: 4 go forth like fire, and burn with none to quench it 1
7:20 it will burn and not be quenched. 1

17:27 it shall devour .. and shall not be quenched. 1
21:12 go forth like fire, and burn with none to quench it 1
Ezk 20:47 the blazing flame shall not be quenched 1
48 LORD have kindled it; it shall not be quenched. 1
Ams 5: 6 and it devour, with none to quench it for Bethel 1
Mat 12:20 or quench a smoldering wick 5
Mrk 9:47 the fire is not quenched. 5
Eph 6:16 can quench all the flaming darts of the evil one. 5
1Th 5:19 Do not quench the Spirit 5
Heb 11:34 quenched raging fire 5
2Es 6:27 and deceit shall be quenched; 6
16: 4 and who is there to quench it? 6
6 or quench a fire in the stubble 6
9 and who is there to quench it? 6
AEs 14: 9 to quench thy altar and the glory of thy house 5
Wis 16:17 in the water, which quenches all things 5
Sir 23:16 will not be quenched until it is consumed 5
3Mc 6:34 boldness was ignominiously quenched. 5
4Mc 3:17 and quench the flames of frenzied desires; 5
9:20 was being quenched by the drippings of gore 5
16: 4 the mother quenched so many .. emotions 4
18:20 quenched fire with fire in his cruel caldrons 5

question 1. דָּבָר 2. דרשׁ 3. שׁאל 4. תּוֹרָה 5. *διαλογίζομαι* 6. *διαλογισμός* 7. *ἐλέγχω* 8. *ἐπερωτάω* 9. *ἐρωτάω* 10. *ζήτημα* 11. *λόγος* 12. *συζητέω*

Gen 43: 7 They replied, "The man questioned us carefully 3
7 What we told him was in answer to these questions; 1
Jdg 8:14 caught a young man of Succoth, and questioned him; 3
1Kg 10: 3 Solomon answered all her questions; 1
2Ch 9: 2 Solomon answered all her questions; 1
31: 9 Hezeki'ah questioned .. about the heaps. 2
Job 38: 3 Gird up your loins like a man, I will question you 3
40: 7 I will question you, and you declare to me. 3
42: 4 I will question you, and you declare to me. 3
Isa 45:11 Will you question me about my children 3
Jer 37:17 The king questioned him secretly in his house 3
38:14 king said to Jeremiah, "I will ask you a question; 1
Hag 2:11 Ask the priests to decide this question 4
Mat 21:24 I also will ask you a question 11
22:23 they asked him a question •
Mrk 1:27 so that they questioned among themselves 12
2: 6 questioning in their hearts 5
8 that they thus questioned within themselves 5
8 "Why do you question thus in your hearts? 5
9:10 questioning what the rising from the dead meant 12
11:29 Jesus said to them, "I will ask you a question; 11
12:18 they asked him a question, saying •
34 after that no one dared to ask him any question. •
Lke 3:15 all men questioned in their hearts concerning John 5
5:21 the scribes and the Pharisees began to question 5
22 When Jesus perceived their questionings 6
22 Why do you question in your hearts? 5
20: 3 I also will ask you a question; now tell me 11
22:23 they began to question one another 12
23: 9 he questioned him at some length 8
24:38 why do questionings rise in your hearts? 6
Joh 16:30 need none to question you 9
18:19 The high priest then questioned Jesus 9
Act 5:27 the high priest questioned them 8
15: 2 to go up to Jerusalem .. about this question. 10
18:15 a matter of questions about words and names 10
23:29 he was accused about questions of their law 10
25:20 Being at a loss how to investigate these questions •
Php 2:14 Do all things without grumbling or questioning 6
Col 2:16 in questions of food and drink •
1Es 6:12 we questioned them and asked them 8
Sir 19:13 Question a friend, perhaps he did not do it 7
14 Question a neighbor, perhaps he did not say it 7
15 Question a friend, for often it is slander 7
17 Question your neighbor before you threaten him; 7

question *See also* ask, raise.

cause to question 1. *αἰτία*

1Mc 9:10 and leave no cause to question our honor. 1

hard question 1. חִידָה

1Kg 10: 1 she came to test him with hard questions. 1
2Ch 9: 1 to Jerusalem to test him with hard questions 1

without quibbling 1. *ἀναμφισβητήτως*

1Es 6:30 regularly every year, without quibbling 1

quick 1. בהל בָּרוּחַ 2. מהר 3. מִחְיָה 4. קְצַר 5. *σπεύδω* 6. *ταχύς* 7. festino

Lev 13:10 if .. there is quick raw flesh in the swelling 3
Job 5:13 the schemes of the wily are brought to a quick end. 2
Prv 14:17 A man of quick temper acts foolishly 4
Ecc 7: 9 Be not quick to anger, for anger lodges 1
Jas 1:19 Let every man be quick to hear, slow to speak 6
2Es 6:34 Do not be quick to think vain thoughts 7
Wis 18:21 a blameless man was quick to act as their champion; 5
Sir 5:11 Be quick to hear, and be deliberate in answering. 6

quick-tempered 1. *ὀργίλος*

Tit 1: 7 he must not be arrogant or quick-tempered 1

quickly 1. בהל 2. בִּמְהֵרָה 3. בִּמְעַט 4. מהר 5. מְהֵרָה 6. *ἄφνω* 7. *διὰ τάχους* 8. *ἐν τάχει* 9. *κατασπεύδω* 10. *κατὰ σπουδήν* 11. *ὀξέως* 12. *σπουδάζω* 13. *ταχέως* 14. *τάχιον* 15. *τάχος* 16. *ταχύς*

Gen 18: 6 Make ready quickly three measures of fine meal 4
24:18 and she quickly let down her jar upon her hand 4
20 she quickly emptied her jar into the trough 4
46 She quickly let down her jar from her shoulder 4
27:20 How is it that you have found it so quickly, my son? 4
44:11 every man quickly lowered his sack to the ground 4
Exd 32: 8 they have turned aside quickly out of the way 4
Num16:46 carry it quickly to the congregation 5
Deu 7: 4 LORD .. would destroy you quickly. 4
9: 3 drive them out, and make them perish quickly 4
12 LORD said to me, 'Arise, go down quickly from here; 4
12 they have turned aside quickly out of the way 4
16 you had turned aside quickly from the way 4
11:17 perish quickly off the good land which the LORD 5
28:20 until you are destroyed and perish quickly 4
Jos 2: 5 pursue them quickly, for you will overtake them. 4
8:19 And the ambush rose quickly out of their place 5
10: 6 come up to us quickly, and save us, and help us; 5
23:16 you shall perish quickly from off the good land 5
1Sm 17:48 David ran quickly toward the battle line to meet 4
28:24 had a fatted calf .. and she quickly killed it 4
2Sm 15:14 lest he overtake us quickly, and bring down evil 4
17:16 Now therefore send quickly and tell David, 'Do not 5
18 so both of them went away quickly 5
21 Arise, and go quickly over the water; 5
1Kg 20:33 they quickly took it up from him and said, "Yes 4
22: 9 and said, "Bring quickly Micai'ah the son of Imlah. 5
2Kg 1:11 this is the king's order, 'Come down quickly!' 5
2Ch 18: 8 "Bring quickly Micai'ah the son of Imlah. 4
Est 2: 9 and he quickly provided her with her ointments 1
5: 5 Bring Haman quickly, that we may do as Esther 4
Ps 2:12 for his wrath is quickly kindled. 3
Ecc 4:12 A threefold cord is not quickly broken. 2
Mat 5:25 Make friends quickly with your accuser 16
28: 7 Then go quickly and tell his disciples 16
8 they departed quickly from the tomb with fear 16
Lke 14:21 Go out quickly to the streets and lanes of the city 13
15:22 Bring quickly the best robe, and put it on him; 16
16: 6 and sit down quickly and write 50' 13
Joh 11:29 when she heard it, she rose quickly and went 16
31 the Jews .. saw Mary rise quickly and go out 13
13:27 "What you are going to do, do quickly. 14
Act 12: 7 woke him, saying, "Get up quickly. 8
22:18 Make haste and get quickly out of Jerusalem 8
Gal 1: 6 astonished that you are so quickly deserting 13
2Th 2: 2 not to be quickly shaken in mind or excited 13
2Es 8:14 thou wilt suddenly and quickly destroy him ‡
Jdt 13: 1 When evening came, his slaves quickly withdrew 12
Wis 4:16 youth that is quickly perfected 13
16:11 then were quickly delivered 11
Sir 11:21 to enrich a poor man quickly and suddenly. 7
19: 4 who trusts others too quickly is lightminded 16
27: 3 his house will be quickly overthrown. 8
43:22 A mist quickly heals all things 10
48:20 the Holy One quickly heard them from heaven 16
1Mc 2:40 they will quickly destroy us from the earth. 14
5:28 Then Judas and his army quickly turned back 6
6:27 unless you quickly prevent them 7
57 So he quickly gave orders to depart 9
2Mc 3:31 Quickly some of Heliodorus' friends asked Onias 16
4:48 quickly suffered the unjust penalty. 13
6:23 he declared himself quickly 13
7:10 he quickly put out his tongue 13
14:11 the rest .. quickly inflamed Demetrius still more. 16
44 as they quickly drew back, a space opened 13
3Mc 2:23 quickly dragged him out 16
5:43 quickly render it forever empty 8
6: 9 reveal yourself quickly 15
4Mc 4: 5 he proceeded quickly to our country 16
14:10 it consumed their bodies quickly. 16

quickly *See also* carry, go, take, thrust.

quickly as possible 1. *ταχύς*

1Mc 11:22 to meet him .. as quickly as possible. 1

more quickly 1. velox

2Es 11:27 this disappeared more quickly than the first. 1

quiet 1. גמל 2. דמם 3. הס 4. הַס 5. נַחַת 6. רָגֵעַ 7. שַׁאֲנָן 8. שַׁלְוָה 9. שקט 10. שֶׁקֶט 11. שתק 12. תָּם 13. *ἀτάραχος* 14. *ἤρεμος* 15. *ἡσυχάζω* 16. *ἡσυχία* 17. *ἡσύχιος* 18. *ἥσυχος* 19. *καταστέλλω* 20. quiesco 21. silentium

Gen 25:27 Jacob was a quiet man, dwelling in tents. 12
Num13:30 Caleb quieted the people before Moses, and said 3
Jdg 18: 7 manner of the Sido'nians, quiet and unsuspecting 9
27 came to La'ish, to a people quiet and unsuspecting 9
2Kg 11:20 the city was quiet after Athali'ah had been slain 9
1Ch 4:40 the land was very broad, quiet, and peaceful; 9
22: 9 I will give peace and quiet to Israel in his days. 10
2Ch 20:30 the realm of Jehosh'aphat was quiet 9
23:21 city was quiet, after Athali'ah had been slain 9
Neh 8:11 "Be quiet, for this day is holy; 4
Job 3:13 For then I should have lain down and been quiet; 9
26 I am not at ease, nor am I quiet; I have no rest; 9
34:29 When he is quiet, who can condemn? 9
Ps 35:20 but against those who are quiet in the land they 6
107:30 Then they were glad because they had quiet 11
131: 2 I have calmed and quieted my soul 2
2 like a child quieted at its mother's breast; 1
2 like a child that is quieted is my soul. 1
Prv 15:18 but he who is slow to anger quiets contention. 9
17: 1 Better is a dry morsel with quiet 8
29: 9 fool only rages and laughs, and there is no quiet. 5
Ecc 9:17 words of the wise heard in quiet are better 5
Isa 7: 4 say to him, 'Take heed, be quiet, do not fear 9
14: 7 The whole earth is at rest and quiet; 9
32:18 in secure dwellings, and in quiet resting places. 7
33:20 Your eyes will see Jerusalem, a quiet habitation 7
Jer 30:10 Jacob shall return and have quiet and ease 9
46:27 Jacob shall return and have quiet and ease 9
47: 6 Ah, sword of the LORD! How long till you are quiet? 9
7 can it be quiet, when the LORD has given it a charge? 9
49:23 troubled like the sea which cannot be quiet. 9
Ezk 38:11 I will fall upon the quiet people who dwell 9
Act 19:35 when the town clerk had quieted the crowd, 19
36 you ought to be quiet and do nothing rash. 19
22: 2 they were the more quiet. And he said 16
1Ti 2: 2 we may lead a quiet and peaceable life 14
1Pe 3: 4 the imperishable jewel of a gentle and quiet spirit 17
2Es 2:24 Pause and be quiet, my people 20
10: 3 that I might be quiet, I got up in the night and fled 20
7:85 are guarded by angels in profound quiet. 21
95 and guarded by angels in profound quiet 21
AEs 16: 8 we will take care to render our kingdom quiet 13
Sir 25:20 such is a garrulous wife for a quiet husband. 18
1Mc 9:58 his men are living in quiet and confidence 16
11:38 the land was quiet before him 15
52 the land was quiet before him. 15
2Mc 14: 4 During that day he kept quiet. 16

quiet *See also* keep.

become quiet 1. *ἡσυχάζω*

1Mc 1: 3 When the earth became quiet before him 1

quiet down 1. שתק

Jon 1:11 What shall we do to you, that the sea may quiet down 1
12 then the sea will quiet down for you; 1

remain quiet 1. quiesco

2Es 10: 2 I remained quiet until evening of the second day 1

quietly 1. דוּמָם 2. שׁקט

Isa 18: 4 quietly look from my dwelling like clear heat 2
4 quietly look from my dwelling like clear heat 2
Lam 3:26 wait quietly for the salvation of the LORD. 1

quietly *See also* hold, live, wait.

quietness 1. נַחַת 2. שֶׁקֶט 3. *ἡσυχία*

Ecc 4: 6 Better is a handful of quietness than two 1
Isa 30:15 in quietness and in trust shall be 2
32:17 the result of righteousness, quietness 2
2Th 3:12 to do their work in quietness 3

quit 1. חדל 2. נטשׁ 3. שׁבת מן

Jdg 15: 7 be avenged upon you, and after that I will quit. 1
Prv 17:14 so quit before the quarrel breaks out. 2
Lam 5:14 The old men have quit the city gate 3

quite 1. *παντελῶς* 2. *πᾶς* 3. *πολύς* 4. *σφόδρα*

Mrk 12:27 you are quite wrong. 3
Act 28:31 teaching .. quite openly and unhindered. 2
AEs 16:10 quite devoid of our kindliness 3
2Mc 3:31 one who was lying quite at his last breath. 1
3Mc 5:12 he quite failed in his lawless purpose 3
4Mc 3: 8 he came, sweating and quite exhausted 4

quiver 1. אַשְׁפָּה 2. תְּלִי 3. *φαρέτρα*

Gen 27: 3 take your weapons, your quiver and your bow 2
Job 39:23 Upon him rattle the quiver, 1
Ps 127: 5 Happy is the man who has his quiver full of them! 1
Isa 22: 6 Elam bore the quiver with chariots and horsemen 1
49: 2 a polished arrow, in his quiver he hid me away. 1
Jer 5:16 Their quiver is like an open tomb 1
Lam 3:13 He drove into my heart the arrows of his quiver; 1
Sir 26:12 open her quiver to the arrow. 3

quiver (2) 1. צלל

Hab 3:16 my body trembles, my lips quiver at the sound; 1

quote 1. *εἶπον*

Lke 4:23 Doubtless you will quote to me this proverb 1

quoted *See* word.

R

rabbi 1. ῥαββί
Mat 23: 7 being called rabbi by men. 1
8 are not to be called rabbi 1
Joh 1:38 And they said to him, "Rabbi" (which means Teacher) 1
49 Rabbi, you are the Son of God! 1
3: 2 Rabbi, we know that you are a teacher come from God 1
26 And they came to John, and said to him, "Rabbi 1
4:31 the disciples besought him, saying, "Rabbi, eat. 1
6:25 they said to him, "Rabbi, when did you come here? 1
9: 2 his disciples asked him, "Rabbi, who sinned 1
11: 8 The disciples said to him, "Rabbi 1

rabble 1. אֲסַפְסֻף 2. פִּרְחַח 3. ἀγοραῖος
Num11: 4 rabble that was among them had a strong craving; 1
Job 30:12 On my right hand the rabble rise, 2
Act 17: 5 taking some wicked fellows of the rabble 3

race 1. זֶרַע 2. βίος 3. γένος 4. σάρξ 5. σπέρμα
6. φῦλον 7. genus
Ezr 9: 2 holy race has mixed itself with the peoples 1
Act 7:19 He dealt craftily with our race 3
Rom 9: 3 the sake of my brethren, my kinsmen by race. 4
5 and of their race, according to the flesh *
1Pe 2: 9 you are a chosen race, a royal priesthood 3
1Es 8:70 the holy race has been mixed 5
2Es 7:65 Let the human race lament 7
8:34 what is a corruptible race 7
Tob 8: 6 From them the race of mankind has sprung 5
Jdt 6: 5 take revenge on this race that came out of Egypt. 3
Wis 10:15 A holy people and blameless race 5
12:11 they were an accursed race from the beginning 5
Sir 10:19 What race is worthy of honor? The human race. 5
19 What race is worthy of honor? The human race. 5
19 What race is worthy of honor? Those who fear 5
19 What race is unworthy of honor? The human race. 5
19 What race is unworthy of honor? The human race. 5
19 What race is unworthy of honor? Those who 5
2Mc 8: 9 to wipe out the whole race of Judea 3
12:31 well disposed to their race in the future also. 3
3Mc 4:14 The entire race was to be registered 6
4Mc 17:14 the world and the human race were the spectators. 2

race (2) 1. מֵרוֹץ 2. רוץ 3. ἀγών 4. δρόμος
5. στάδιον
Ecc 9:11 saw that under the sun the race is not to the swift 1
Jer 12: 5 If you have raced with men on foot 2
1Co 9:24 in a race all the runners compete 5
2Ti 4: 7 I have finished the race, I have kept the faith. 4
Heb 12: 1 the race that is set before us 3

other race 1. ἀλλόφυλος
3Mc 3: 6 Nevertheless those of other races paid no heed 1

rack 1. στρέβλη 2. στρεβλωτήριον 3. τύμπανον
Sir 33:26 there are racks and tortures. 1
2Mc 6:19 he . . went up to the rack of his own accord 3
28 he went at once to the rack. 3
4Mc 7: 4 was consumed by tortures and racks 1
14 he rendered the many-headed rack ineffective. 1
8:11 nothing remains . . but to die on the rack? 1
13 rack and hooks and catapults and caldrons 2
24 nor take hollow pride in being put to the rack. 1

rack (2) 1. נקר
Job 30:17 The night racks my bones, and the pain 1

racking 1. στρέβλη
4Mc 9:22 he nobly endured the rackings. 1
14:12 the mother . . bore up under the rackings of each one 1
15:24 the ingenious and various rackings 1
25 the rackings of her children- 1

radiance 1. φέγγος 2. φωστήρ
Rev 21:11 its radiance like a most rare jewel, like a jasper 2
Wis 7:10 because her radiance never ceases. 1

radiant 1. נהר 2. צַח 3. ἐρυθριάω 4. λαμπρός
Ps 34: 5 Look to him, and be radiant; 1
Sng 5:10 My beloved is all radiant and ruddy 2
Isa 60: 5 Then you shall see and be radiant 1
Jer 31:12 shall be radiant over the goodness of the LORD 1
AEs 15: 5 She was radiant with perfect beauty 3
Wis 6:12 Wisdom is radiant and unfading 4
radiant *See also* appearance.

raft 1. דֹּבְרוֹת 2. רַפְסֹדָה 3. σχεδία
1Kg 5: 9 I will make it into rafts to go by sea to the place 1
2Ch 2:16 and bring it to you in rafts by sea to Joppa 2
1Es 5:55 convey them in rafts to the harbor of Joppa 3
Wis 14: 5 and passing through the billows on a raft 3
6 the hope of the world took refuge on a raft 3

rafter 1. רָהִיט 2. δοκός
1Kg 6:15 from the floor . . to the rafters of the ceiling 2
16 boards of cedar from the floor to the rafters 2
Sng 1:17 the beams . . are cedar, our rafters are pine. 1

rag 1. בְּלוֹאֵי סְחָבוֹת 2. סְחָבָה 3. קֶרַע 4. ῥάκος
Prv 23:21 drowsiness will clothe a man with rags. 3
Jer 38:11 and took from there old rags and worn-out clothes 2
12 Put the rags and clothes between your armpits 1
AEs 14:16 I abhor it like a menstruous rag 4

rage 1. גֵּאוּת 2. הלל 3. המה 4. זֵידוֹן 5. זעף 6. זַעַף
7. זֶרֶם 8. חול 9. חֵמָה 10. סעה 11. רגז 12. רְגַז
13. רְגַז (A) 14. ἀγανακτέω 15. ἄγριος 16. βίαιος
17. διοργίζω 18. δύναμις 19. ἔκθυμος 20. θηριόομαι
21. θυμός 22. θυμόω 23. κλύδων 24. ὀργή 25. ὀργίζω
26. περιπαθῶς 27. περισσῶς 28. συνάπτω
29. φρυάσσω 30. insanio
2Kg 5:12 So he turned and went away in a rage. 9
19:27 I know your . . and your raging against me. 11
28 you have raged against me and your arrogance has 11
2Ch 16:10 he was in a rage with him because of this. 6
28: 9 but you have slain them in a rage 6
Job 39:24 With fierceness and rage he swallows the ground; 12
Ps 46: 6 The nations rage, the kingdoms totter; 3
55: 8 a shelter from the raging wind and tempest. 10
89: 9 Thou dost rule the raging of the sea; 1
124: 5 then over us would have gone the raging waters. 4
Prv 19: 3 way to ruin, his heart rages against the LORD. 5
29: 9 fool only rages and laughs, and there is no quiet. 11
Isa 37:28 and coming in, and your raging against me. 11
29 Because you have raged against me 11
Jer 46: 9 Advance, O horses, and rage, O chariots! 2
Dan 3:13 Then Nebuchadnez'zar in furious rage commanded 13
Hos 11: 6 The sword shall rage against their cities 8
Jon 1:15 the sea ceased from its raging. 6
Nah 2: 4 The chariots rage in the streets 2
Hab 3:10 the raging waters swept on; 7
Mat 2:16 been tricked by the wise men, was in a furious rage 22
Lke 8:24 awoke and rebuked the wind and the raging waves 23
Act 4:25 Why did the Gentiles rage 29
26:11 in raging fury against them 27
Heb 11:34 quenched raging fire 18
Rev 11:18 The nations raged, but thy wrath came 25
2Es 15:30 the Carmonians, raging in wrath, shall go forth 30
Wis 5:22 the water of the sea will rage against them 14
10: 3 he perished because in rage he slew his brother. 21
11:18 or newly created unknown beasts full of rage 21
14: 1 and about to voyage over raging waves 15
16: 5 the terrible rage of wild beasts 21
19: 7 a grassy plain out of the raging waves 16
1Mc 9:13 the battle raged from morning till evening. 28
2Mc 4:25 the rage of a savage wild beast. 24
5:11 raging inwardly, he left Egypt 20
7: 3 The king fell into a rage 19
39 The king fell into a rage 19
9: 4 Transported with rage 21
7 breathing fire in his rage against the Jews 21
10:28 the other made rage their leader in the fight. 21
3Mc 4:13 ordered in his rage 17
5:47 he had filled his impious mind with a deep rage 24
4Mc 8: 2 then in violent rage he commanded 26
18:20 in his burning rage brought those seven sons 21

rage fiery 1. ἐκφλέγω
4Mc 16: 3 the raging fiery furnace of Mishael 1
raging *See* riot.

raid 1. גְּדוּד 2. גוד 3. לקח 4. פשט
Gen 49:19 Raiders shall raid Gad 2
19 raid Gad, but he shall raid at their heels. 2
Jdg 11: 3 round Jephthah, and went raiding with him. *
2Sm 3:22 servants of David arrived with Jo'ab from a raid 1
2Kg 5: 2 the Syrians on one of their raids had carried off 1
6:23 the Syrians came no more on raids into the land 1
1Ch 7:21 because they came down to raid their cattle. 3
Hos 7: 1 thief breaks in, and the bandits raid without. 4
raid *See also* band, make.

raider 1. גְּדוּד 2. שחת
Gen 49:19 Raiders shall raid Gad 1
1Sm 13:17 raiders came out of the camp of the Philistines 2
14:15 the garrison and even the raiders trembled; 2
raiders *See* band.

rail 1. עיט 2. פצה פִּי 3. βλασφημέω 4. λοιδορέω
1Sm 25:14 to salute our master; and he railed at them. 1
Lam 2:16 All your enemies rail against you; 2
3:46 All our enemies rail against us; 2
Lke 23:39 the criminals who were hanged railed at him 3
2Mc 12:14 railing at them and even blaspheming 4

raiment 1. בֶּגֶד 2. לְבוּשׁ 3. מַלְבּוּשׁ 4. לְבוּשׁ (A)
5. ἔνδυμα 6. ἱματισμός
Gen 24:53 jewelry of silver and of gold, and raiment 1
Ps 22:18 for my raiment they cast lots. 2
102:26 changest them like a raiment, and they pass away; 2
Isa 63: 3 and I have stained all my raiment. 3
Ezk 16:13 and your raiment was of fine linen, and silk 3
Dan 7: 9 raiment was white as snow, and the hair of his head 4
Mat 28: 3 his raiment white as snow. 5
Lke 9:29 his raiment became dazzling white. 6

soft raiment 1. μαλακός
Mat 11: 8 To see a man clothed in soft raiment? 1
8 those who wear soft raiment are in kings' houses. 1

rain 1. גֶּשֶׁם 2. זֶרֶם 3. ירה 4. מטר 5. מָטָר 6. מַי
7. βρέχω 8. βροχή 9. ὄμβρος 10. ὑετός 11. pluvia
Gen 7:12 rain fell upon the earth 40 days and 40 nights. 1
8: 2 the rain from the heavens was restrained 1
19:24 Then the LORD rained on Sodom and Gomor'rah 4
Exd 9:23 the LORD rained hail upon the land of Egypt; 4
33 the rain no longer poured upon the earth. 5
34 when Pharaoh saw that the rain and the hail 5
16: 4 Behold, I will rain bread from heaven for you; 4
Lev 26: 4 then I will give you your rains in their season 1
Deu 11:11 which drinks water by the rain from heaven 5
14 he will give the rain for your land in its season 5
17 he shut up the heavens, so that there be no rain 5
28:12 to give the rain of your land in its season 5
24 will make the rain of your land powder and dust; 5
32: 2 May my teaching drop as the rain, my speech distil 5
1Sm 12:17 call . . the LORD, that he may send thunder and rain; 5
18 and the LORD sent thunder and rain that day; 5
2Sm 1:21 Gilbo'a, let there be no dew or rain upon you 5
21:10 until rain fell upon them from the heavens; 6
23: 4 he dawns . . like rain that makes grass to sprout 5

1Kg 8:35 and there is no rain because they have sinned 5
36 forgive . . and grant rain upon thy land 5
17: 1 there shall be neither dew nor rain these years 5
7 dried up, because there was no rain in the land. 1
14 the day that the LORD sends rain upon the earth.' 1
18: 1 Go . . to Ahab; and I will send rain upon the earth. 5
41 there is a sound of the rushing of rain. 1
44 Prepare . . and go down, lest the rain stop you.' 1
45 heavens grew black . . and there was a great rain. 1
2Kg 3:17 You shall not see wind or rain, but that stream-bed 1
2Ch 6:26 When heaven is shut up and there is no rain 5
27 forgive the sin . . and grant rain upon thy land 5
7:13 When I shut up the heavens so that there is no rain 5
Job 5:10 he gives rain upon the earth and sends waters 5
20:23 rain it upon him as his food. 4
24: 8 They are wet with the rain of the mountains 2
28:26 when he made a decree for the rain 5
29:23 They waited for me as for the rain; 5
36:27 the drops of water, he distils his mist in rain 5
37: 6 to the shower and the rain, 'Be strong.' 5
38:25 Who has cleft a channel for the torrents of rain •
28 Has the rain a father 5
Ps 11: 6 On the wicked he will rain coals of fire 4
68: 9 Rain in abundance, O God, thou didst shed abroad; 1
72: 6 May he be like rain that falls on the mown grass 5
78:27 he rained flesh upon them like dust 4
105:32 He gave them hail for rain 1
135: 7 who makes lightnings for the rain 5
147: 8 he prepares rain for the earth 5
Prv 19:13 quarreling is a continual dripping of rain. •
25:14 Like clouds and wind without rain is a man 1
23 The north wind brings forth rain; 1
26: 1 Like snow in summer or rain in harvest 5
28: 3 beating rain that leaves no food. 5
Ecc 11: 3 If the clouds are full of rain 1
12: 2 and the clouds return after the rain; 1
Sng 2:11 lo, the winter is past, the rain is over and gone. 1
Isa 4: 6 a refuge and a shelter from the storm and rain. 5
5: 6 command the clouds that they rain no rain upon it. 4
6 command the clouds that they rain no rain upon it. 5
30:23 he will give rain for the seed with which you sow 5
44:14 he plants a cedar and the rain nourishes it. 1
55:10 For as the rain and the snow come down from heaven 1
Jer 5:24 the LORD our God, who gives the rain in its season 1
10:13 He makes lightnings for the rain 5
14: 4 since there is no rain on the land 1
51:16 He makes lightnings for the rain 5
Ezk 1:28 the bow that is in the cloud on the day of rain 1
13:11 There will be a deluge of rain 1
13 and there shall be a deluge of rain in my anger 1
38:22 I will rain upon him and his hordes 4
22 torrential rains and hailstones 1
Hos 10:12 that he may come and rain salvation upon you. 3
Ams 4: 7 I also withheld the rain from you when there were 1
7 and the field on which it did not rain withered; 4
Zec 10: 1 Ask rain from the LORD in the season of the spring 5
1 who gives men showers of rain, to every one 5
14:17 there will be no rain upon them. 1
Mat 7:25 rain fell, and the floods came, and the winds blew 8
27 rain fell, and the floods came, and the wind blew 8
Lke 17:29 fire and sulphur rained from heaven 7
Act 14:17 he . . gave you from heaven rains and fruitful seasons 10
28: 2 because it had begun to rain and was cold. 10
Heb 6: 7 land which has drunk the rain that . . falls 10
Jas 5: 7 until it receives the early and the late rain •
17 he prayed . . that it might not rain 7
17 it did not rain on the earth. 7
18 Then he prayed again and the heaven gave rain 10
Rev 11: 6 shut the sky, that no rain may fall during the days 10
2Es 4:49 and poured down a heavy and violent rain 11
50 for as the rain is more than the drops 11
7:41 winter or frost or cold or hail or rain or dew 11
109Elijah for those who received the rain 11
8:43 it has not received thy rain in due season 11
43 or if it has been ruined by too much rain 11
Jdt 8:31 the Lord will send us rain to fill our cisterns 10
Wis 16:16 unusual rains and hail and relentless storms 10
Sir 1: 2 The sand of the sea, the drops of rain 10
35:20 clouds of rain in the time of drought. 10
40:13 crash like a loud clap of thunder in a rain. 10
LJr 1:53 they cannot . . give rain to men. 10
Aza 1:42 Bless the Lord, all rain and dew 9

rain *See also* bring, pour, send, shower, spring.

abundant rain 1. גֶּשֶׁם
Jol 2:23 he has poured down for you abundant rain 1

autumn rain 1. יוֹרֶה
Jer 5:24 who gives . . the autumn rain and the spring rain 1

cause to rain 1. מטר
Gen 2: 5 God had not caused it to rain upon the earth 1

rain down 1. מטר 2. נזל 3. ἐξομβρέω
Ps 78:24 he rained down upon them manna to eat 1
Isa 45: 8 and let the skies rain down righteousness; 2
Sir 1:19 he rained down knowledge 3

early rain 1. יוֹרֶה 2. מוֹרֶה
Deu 11:14 he will give the . . early rain and the later rain 1
Ps 84: 6 early rain also covers it with pools. 2
Jol 2:23 he has given the early rain for your vindication 2
23 the early and the latter rain, as before. 2

gentle rain 1. שְׂעִירִים
Deu 32: 2 as the dew, as the gentle rain upon the tender grass 1

heavy rain 1. גֶּשֶׁם
Ezr 10: 9 trembling . . because of the heavy rain. 1
13 people are many, and it is a time of heavy rain; 1

later rain 1. מַלְקוֹשׁ
Deu 11:14 he will give the . . early rain and the later rain 1

latter rain 1. מַלְקוֹשׁ
Jol 2:23 the early and the latter rain, as before. 1

rain upon 1. גשם 2. מטר
Ezk 22:24 or rained upon in the day of indignation. 1
Ams 4: 7 one field would be rained upon 2

rainbow 1. ἶρις 2. τόξον
Rev 4: 3 a rainbow that looked like an emerald. 1
10: 1 mighty angel . . with a rainbow over his head 1
Sir 43:11 Look upon the rainbow, and praise him who made it 2
50: 7 like the rainbow gleaming in glorious clouds; 2

raindrop 1. gutta
2Es 5:36 and gather for me the scattered raindrops 1

rainstorm 1. impetus pluviae
2Es 4:49 and when the rainstorm had passed 1

rainy 1. סַגְרִיר
Prv 27:15 A continual dripping on a rainy day 1

raise 1. גָּבַהּ 2. נוף 3. נצב 4. נשׂא 5. נתן 6. עלה
7. עמד 8. ענה 9. קום 10. רום 11. שׂגב 12. αἴρω
13. ἀνίστημι 14. ἀνυψόω 15. ἐγείρω 16. ἐκτείνω
17. ἐναρμόζω 18. ἐξάρχω 19. ἐπαίρω 20. καρπός
21. κατάρχω 22. οἰκοδομέω 23. ποιέω 24. συνάγω
25. συνεγείρω 26. ὑψηλὸν ἀνατείνω 27. extruo
28. suscito
Gen 33: 5 when Esau raised his eyes and saw the women 4
Num14: 1 Then all the congregation raised a loud cry; 4
Jos 7:26 And they raised over him a great heap of stones 9
8:29 took his body . . and raised over it a great heap 9
1Sm 30: 4 and the people . . raised their voices and wept 4
2Sm 12:17 stood beside him, to raise him from the ground; 9
18:17 raised over him a very great heap of stones; 3
28 the men who raised their hand against my lord 4
23: 1 the oracle of the man who was raised on high 9
1Kg 5:13 King Solomon raised a levy of forced labor 6
2Kg 19:22 Against whom have you raised your voice 10
1Ch 15:16 on harps . . and cymbals, to raise sounds of joy. 10
2Ch 5:13 when the song was raised . . in praise to the LORD 10
32: 5 built up all the wall . . and raised towers 27
Job 2:12 they raised their voices and wept; 4
31:21 if I have raised my hand against the fatherless 2
Ps 81: 2 Raise a song, sound the timbrel 4
83: 2 those who hate thee have raised their heads. 4
106:26 Therefore he raised his hand and swore to them 4
107:25 For he commanded, and raised the stormy wind 7
113: 7 He raises the poor from the dust •
Prv 1:20 in the markets she raises her voice; 5
2: 3 if you . . raise your voice for understanding 5
8: 1 does not understanding raise her voice? 5
Isa 2: 2 mountains, and shall be raised above the hills; 4
5:26 He will raise a signal for a nation afar off 4
9:11 So the LORD raises adversaries against them 11
11:12 He will raise an ensign for the nations 4
13: 2 On a bare hill raise a signal, cry aloud to them; 4
14: 9 it raises from their thrones all who were kings 9
18: 3 when a signal is raised on the mountains, look! 4
29: 3 and I will raise siegeworks against you. 9
37:23 Against whom have you raised your voice 10
49:22 to the nations, and raise my signal to the peoples; 10
Jer 4: 6 Raise a standard toward Zion, flee for safety 4
6: 1 and raise a signal on Beth-hacche'rem; 4
7:29 raise a lamentation on the bare heights 4
9:18 let them make haste and raise a wailing over us 4
51:14 they shall raise the shout of victory over you. 8
55 the noise of their voice is raised; 5
Lam 2: 7 a clamor was raised in the house of the LORD 5
Ezk 26: 8 and raise a roof of shields against you. 9
17 they will raise a lamentation over you 4
27: 2 Now you, son of man, raise a lamentation over Tyre 4
32 they raise a lamentation for you 4
28:12 raise a lamentation over the king of Tyre, and say 4
32: 2 raise a lamentation over Pharaoh king of Egypt 4
37:12 open your graves, and raise you from your graves 6
13 and raise you from your graves, O my people. 6
41: 8 I saw also that the temple had a raised platform 1
Dan 8: 3 I raised my eyes and saw, and behold 4
11:11 raise a great multitude, but it shall be given 7
13 king of the north shall again raise a multitude 7
12: 7 raised his right hand and his left hand toward 10
Mic 5: 5 we will raise against him seven shepherds 9
Zec 1:21 scattered Judah, so that no man raised his head; 4
14:13 the hand of the one will be raised against 6
Mat 10: 8 Heal the sick, raise the dead, cleanse lepers 15
14: 2 he has been raised from the dead 15
16:21 and be killed, and on the third day be raised. 15
17: 9 until the Son of man is raised from the dead. 15
23 he will be raised on the third day 15
20:19 he will be raised on the third day. 15
27:52 saints who had fallen asleep were raised 15
Mrk 6:14 John the baptizer has been raised from the dead; 15
16 John, whom I beheaded, has been raised. 15
12:26 as for the dead being raised 15
Lke 9: 7 John had been raised from the dead 15
22 be killed, and on the third day be raised. 15
11:27 a woman in the crowd raised her voice and said 19
20:37 that the dead are raised, even Moses showed 15
21:28 look up and raise your heads 19
Joh 2:22 When therefore he was raised from the dead 15
5:21 as the Father raises the dead and gives them life 15
12: 1 whom Jesus had raised from the dead. 15
9 to see Laz'arus, whom he had raised from the dead. 15
17 raised him from the dead 15
21:14 after he was raised from the dead. 15
Act 3:15 the Author of life, whom God raised from the dead. 15
4:10 whom you crucified, whom God raised from the dead 15
5:30 God of our fathers raised Jesus whom you killed 15
10:40 God raised him on the third day 15
13:30 God raised him from the dead; 15
33 this he has fulfilled . . by raising Jesus 13
34 as for the fact that he raised him from the dead 13
17:31 given assurance . . by raising him from the dead 13
26: 8 thought incredible . . that God raises the dead? 15
Rom 4:24 him that raised from the dead Jesus our Lord 15
25 and raised for our justification. 15
6: 4 so that as Christ was raised from the dead 15
9 Christ being raised from the dead will never die 15
7: 4 belong . . to him who has been raised from the dead 15
8:11 the Spirit of him who raised Jesus from the dead 15
11 he who raised Christ Jesus from the dead 15
34 Jesus, who died, yes, who was raised from the dead 15
10: 9 and believe . . that God raised him from the dead 15
15:28 and have delivered to them what has been raised 20
1Co 6:14 God raised the Lord and will also raise us up 15
15: 4 that he was raised on the third day 15
12 Now if Christ is preached as raised from the dead 15
13 then Christ has not been raised; 15
14 if Christ has not been raised 15
15 we testified of God that he raised Christ 15
15 whom he did not raise if it is true 15
15 if it is true that the dead are not raised. 15
16 For if the dead are not raised 15
16 then Christ has not been raised. 15
17 If Christ has not been raised 15
20 in fact Christ has been raised from the dead 15
29 If the dead are not raised at all 15
32 If the dead are not raised, "Let us eat and drink 15
35 some one will ask, "How are the dead raised? 15
42 what is raised is imperishable. 15
43 It is sown in dishonor, it is raised in glory. 15
43 It is sown in weakness, it is raised in power. 15
44 it is raised a spiritual body 15
52 the dead will be raised imperishable 15
2Co 1: 9 not on ourselves but on God who raises the dead; 15
4:14 knowing that he who raised the Lord Jesus 15
14 will raise us also with Jesus 15
5:15 who for their sake died and was raised. 15
Gal 1: 1 God the Father, who raised him from the dead- 15
Eph 1:20 when he raised him from the dead 15
Col 2:12 in which you were also raised with him 25
12 who raised him from the dead. 15
3: 1 If then you have been raised with Christ 25
1Th 1:10 his Son from heaven, whom he raised from the dead 15
Heb 11:19 God was able to raise men even from the dead 15
1Pe 1:21 who raised him from the dead and gave him glory 15
1Es 8:81 raised Zion from desolation 15
2Es 15:39 the cloud that was raised in wrath 28
Tob 13:10 his tent may be raised for you again with joy. 22
Jdt 16: 2 Raise to him a new psalm 17
AEs 15:11 Then he raised the golden scepter 12
Sir 20:11 raised their heads from humble circumstances. 12
21:20 A fool raises his voice when he laughs 14
28:17 The blow of a whip raises a welt 23
48: 5 You who raised a corpse from death and from Hades 15
49:12 raised a temple holy to the Lord 14
13 he raised for us the walls that had fallen 15
Bar 2: 5 They were brought low and not raised up •
LJr 1:17 the dust raised by the feet of those who enter. •
1Mc 3:31 collect the revenues . . and raise a large fund. 24
9:39 They raised their eyes and looked 12
12:39 to raise his hand against Antiochus the king. 16
42 he was afraid to raise his hand against him. 16
2Mc 7:14 the hope . . of being raised again by him 13
34 when you raise your hand 19
12:37 he raised the battle cry, with hymns 21
3Mc 4: 6 raising a lament instead of a wedding song 18

5:48 the Jews saw the dust raised by the elephants •
4Mc 6: 6 yet while the old man's eyes were raised to heaven 26

raise a cry 1. עור 2. ἀνακράζω

Isa 15: 5 road to Horona'im they raise a cry of destruction; 1
3Mc 6:17 they raised great cries to heaven 2

raise a question 1. ἀνακρίνω

1Co 10:25 without raising any question 1
27 eat . . without raising any question 1

raise a shout 1. צהל 2. רוע 3. ἀλαλάζω

Jos 6:20 As soon as the . . the people raised a great shout 2
Isa 16:10 no songs are sung, no shouts are raised; 2
Jer 31: 7 and raise shouts for the chief of the nations; 1
50:15 Raise a shout against her round about 2
Jdt 14: 9 the people raised a great shout 3

raise from the dead 1. excito

2Es 7:37 the nations that have been raised from the dead 1

raise high 1. רום

Ps 131: 1 O LORD, my . . eyes are not raised too high; 1

raise the battle shout 1. רוע

2Ch 13:15 Then the men of Judah raised the battle shout. 1

raise to a great height 1. גבה

2Ch 33:14 round Ophel, and raised it to a very great height; 1

raise up 1. זקף 2. נשא 3. עלה 4. קום 5. רום 6. שגב 7. קום (A) 8. רום (A) 9. ἀναλαμβάνω 10. ἀνάστημα 11. ἀνίστημι 12. ἀνυψόω 13. ἐγείρω 14. ἐξανίστημι 15. ἐξεγείρω 16. συνεγείρω 17. levo 18. resuscito 19. suscito

Gen 38: 8 to her, and raise up offspring for your brother. 4
Exd 40:18 put in its poles, and raised up its pillars; 4
Deu 18:15 LORD . . will raise up for you a prophet like me 4
18 I will raise up for them a prophet like you 4
Jos 5: 7 their children, whom he raised up in their stead 4
Jdg 2:16 the LORD raised up judges, who saved them 4
18 Whenever the LORD raised up judges for them 4
3: 9 the LORD raised up a deliverer for the people 4
15 the LORD raised up for them a deliverer 4
1Sm 2: 6 The LORD . . he brings down to Sheol and raises up. 3
8 He raises up the poor from the dust; 4
35 And I will raise up for myself a faithful priest 4
2Sm 7:12 I will raise up your offspring after you 4
12:11 I will raise up evil against you out of your own 4
1Kg 11:14 the LORD raised up an adversary against Solomon 4
23 God also raised up as an adversary to him, Rezon 4
14:14 the LORD will raise up for himself a king 4
1Ch 17:11 I will raise up your offspring after you 4
Job 41:25 When he raises himself up the mighty are afraid; 2
Ps 41:10 do thou, O LORD, be gracious to me, and raise me up 4
107:41 he raises up the needy out of affliction 6
145:14 LORD . . raises up all who are bowed down. 1
148:14 He has raised up a horn for his people 5
Isa 44:26 be built, and I will raise up their ruins'; 4
49: 6 be my servant to raise up the tribes of Jacob 4
11 and my highways shall be raised up. 5
58:12 you shall raise up the foundations of many 4
61: 4 they shall raise up the former devastations; 4
Jer 23: 5 when I will raise up for David a righteous Branch 4
29:15 The LORD has raised up prophets for us in Babylon, 4
30: 9 and David their king, whom I will raise up for them. 4
50:32 shall stumble and fall, with none to raise him up 4
Dan 5:19 whom he would he raised up, and . . put down. 8
7: 5 raised up on one side; it had three ribs 7
Hos 6: 2 on the third day he will raise us up 4
Ams 2:11 And I raised up some of your sons for prophets 4
5: 2 forsaken on her land, with none to raise her up. 4
6:14 For behold, I will raise up against you a nation 4
9:11 I will raise up the booth of David that is fallen 4
11 and repair its breaches, and raise up its ruins 4
Mic 4: 1 and shall be raised up above the hills; 2
Zec 11:16 For lo, I am raising up in the land a shepherd 4
Mat 3: 9 from these stones to raise up children to Abraham. 13
11: 5 the dead are raised up, and the poor have good news 13
22:24 raise up children for his brother.' 11
26:32 But after I am raised up 13
Mrk 12:19 and raise up children for his brother. 14
14:28 after I am raised up, I will go before you 13
Lke 1:69 and has raised up a horn of salvation for us 13
3: 8 God is able from these stones to raise up children 13
7:22 the deaf hear, the dead are raised up 13
20:28 the man must take the wife and raise up children 14
Joh 2:19 this temple, and in three days I will raise it up. 13
20 and will you raise it up in 3 days? 13
6:39 but raise it up at the last day. 11
40 I will raise him up at the last day. 11
44 I will raise him up at the last day. 11
54 I will raise him up at the last day. 11
Act 2:24 But God raised him up 11
32 This Jesus God raised up 11
3: 7 he took him by the right hand and raised him up; 13
22 The Lord God will raise up for you a prophet 11
22 a prophet from your brethren as he raised me up. •
26 God, having raised up his servant 11
7:37 God will raise up for you a prophet 11
37 a prophet from your brethren as he raised me up.' •
13:22 he raised up David to be their king 13
37 he whom God raised up saw no corruption. 13
Rom 9:17 I have raised you up for the very purpose 15
1Co 6:14 God raised the Lord and will also raise us up 15
Eph 2: 6 raised us up with him, and made us sit with him 16
Jas 5:15 and the Lord will raise him up 13
2Es 2:16 I will raise up the dead from their places 18
3:23 thou didst raise up for thyself a servant 19
11:18 Then the third wing raised itself up 17
12:23 the Most High will raise up three kings 19
Jdt 10:23 his slaves raised her up. 13
12: 8 to direct her way for the raising up of her people. 10
14: 7 when they raised him up he fell at Judith's feet 9
Sir 10: 4 over it he will raise up the right man 13
11:13 raises up his head, so that many are amazed at him. 12
2Mc 7: 9 the King of the universe will raise us up 11

raisin 1. אֲשִׁישָׁה 2. עֵנָב

Sng 2: 5 Sustain me with raisins, refresh me with apples; 1
Hos 3: 1 they turn to other gods and love cakes of raisins. 2

raisin-cake 1. אֲשִׁישָׁה

Isa 16: 7 stricken, for the raisin-cakes of Kir-har'eseth. 1

raisins *See* bunch, cake, cluster.

rally 1. זעק 2. נוס 3. קבץ 4. ἀθροίζω 5. ἐπισυνάγω 6. συνέρχομαι

1Sm 14:20 Saul and all . . with him rallied and went 1
Neh 4:20 hear the sound of the trumpet, rally to us there. 3
Ps 60: 4 those who fear thee, to rally to it from the bow. 2
1Mc 5:53 Judas kept rallying the laggards 5
11:47 they all rallied about him 5
14:30 Jonathan rallied the nation 4
15:10 All the troops rallied to him 6

rally about 1. προσάγω

1Mc 2:67 You shall rally about you all who observe the law 1

ram 1. אַיִל 2. יוֹבֵל 3. דְּכַר (A) 4. κριός

Gen 15: 9 a she-goat three years old, a ram three years old 1
22:13 looked, and behold, behind him was a ram 1
13 and Abraham went and took the ram 1
31:38 I have not eaten the rams of your flocks. 1
32:14 200 ewes and twenty rams 1
Exd 25: 5 tanned rams' skins, goatskins, acacia wood 1
26:14 for the tent a covering of tanned rams' skins 1
29: 1 Take one young bull and two rams without blemish 1
3 and bring the bull and the two rams. 1
15 Then you shall take one of the rams 1
15 shall lay their hands upon the head of the ram 1
16 you shall slaughter the ram, and shall take 1
17 Then you shall cut the ram into pieces, and wash 1
18 burn the whole ram upon the altar; 1
19 You shall take the other ram; 1
19 shall lay their hands upon the head of the ram 1
20 you shall kill the ram, and take part of its blood 1
22 You shall also take the fat of the ram 1
22 (for it is a ram of ordination) 1
26 you shall take the breast of the ram 1
27 which is offered from the ram of ordination 1
31 You shall take the ram of ordination 1
32 Aaron and his sons shall eat the flesh of the ram 1
35: 7 tanned rams' skins, and goatskins; acacia wood 1
23 or goats' hair or tanned rams' skins or goatskins 1
36:19 made for the tent a covering of tanned rams' skins 1
39:34 the covering of tanned rams' skins and goatskins 1
Lev 5:15 bring . . a ram without blemish out of the flock 1
16 for him with the ram of the guilt offering 1
18 He shall bring to the priest a ram 1
6: 6 guilt offering to the LORD, a ram without blemish 1
8: 2 Take . . the two rams, and the basket 1
18 Then he presented the ram of the burnt offering 1
18 laid their hands on the head of the ram 1
20 when the ram was cut into pieces, Moses burned 1
21 Moses burned the whole ram on the altar 1
22 Then he presented the other ram 1
22 Then he presented . . the ram of ordination 1
22 laid their hands on the head of the ram 1
29 it was Moses' portion of the ram of ordination 1
9: 2 Take a bull calf for a sin offering, and a ram 1
4 an ox and a ram for peace offerings, to sacrifice 1
18 He killed the ox also and the ram 1
19 the fat of the ox and of the ram, the fat tail 1
16: 3 a sin offering and a ram for a burnt offering 1
5 a sin offering, and one ram for a burnt offering 1
19:21 shall bring . . a ram for a guilt offering 1
22 make atonement for him with the ram 1
23:18 present . . one young bull, and two rams 1
Num 5: 8 in addition to the ram of atonement 1
6:14 one ram without blemish as a peace offering 1
17 offer the ram as a sacrifice of peace offering 1
19 the priest shall take the shoulder of the ram 1
7:15 one young bull, one ram . . for a burnt offering; 1
17 sacrifice of peace offerings . . five rams 1
21 one young bull, one ram . . for a burnt offering; 1
23 peace offerings . . five rams, five male goats 1
27 one young bull, one ram . . for a burnt offering; 1
29 peace offerings . . five rams, five male goats 1
33 one young bull, one ram . . for a burnt offering; 1
35 peace offerings . . five rams, five male goats 1
39 one young bull, one ram . . for a burnt offering; 1
41 peace offerings . . five rams, five male goats 1
45 one young bull, one ram . . for a burnt offering; 1
47 peace offerings . . five rams, five male goats 1
51 one young bull, one ram . . for a burnt offering; 1
53 peace offerings . . five rams, five male goats 1
57 one young bull, one ram . . for a burnt offering; 1
59 peace offerings . . five rams, five male goats 1
63 one young bull, one ram . . for a burnt offering; 1
65 peace offerings . . five rams, five male goats 1
69 one young bull, one ram . . for a burnt offering; 1
71 peace offering . . five rams, five male goats 1
75 one young bull, one ram . . for a burnt offering; 1
77 peace offerings . . five rams, five male goats 1
81 one young bull, one ram . . for a burnt offering; 1
83 peace offerings . . five rams, five male goats 1
87 burnt offering . . twelve rams 1
88 sacrifice of peace offerings . . the rams 60 1
15: 6 for a ram, you shall prepare for a cereal offering 1
11 Thus it shall be done for each bull or ram 1
23: 1 provide for me here seven bulls and seven rams. 1
2 offered on each altar a bull and a ram. 1
4 I have offered upon each altar a bull and a ram. 1
14 offered a bull and a ram on each altar. 1
29 provide for me here seven bulls and seven rams. 1
30 Balak . . offered a bull and a ram on each altar. 1
28:11 burnt offering . . two young bulls, one ram 1
12 cereal offering . . for the one ram; 1
14 drink offerings . . a third of a hin for a ram 1
19 burnt offering . . two young bulls, one ram 1
20 offer for a bull, and two tenths for a ram; 1
27 burnt offering . . two young bulls, one ram 1
28 ephah for each bull, two tenths for one ram 1
29: 2 burnt offering . . one young bull, one ram 1
3 of an ephah for the bull, two tenths for the ram 1
8 burnt offering . . one young bull, one ram 1
9 ephah for the bull, two tenths for the one ram 1
13 burnt offering . . two rams, fourteen male lambs 1
14 two tenths for each of the two rams 1
17 On the second day twelve young bulls, two rams 1
18 cereal . . offerings for the bulls, for the rams 1
20 On the third day eleven bulls, two rams, fourteen 1
21 cereal . . offerings for the bulls, for the rams 1
23 On the fourth day ten bulls, two rams, fourteen 1
24 cereal . . offerings for the bulls, for the rams 1
26 On the fifth day nine bulls, two rams, fourteen 1
27 cereal . . offerings for the bulls, for the rams 1
29 On the sixth day eight bulls, two rams, fourteen 1
30 cereal . . offerings for the bulls, for the rams 1
32 On the seventh day seven bulls, two rams, fourteen 1
33 cereal . . offerings for the bulls, for the rams 1
36 burnt offering . . one bull, one ram, seven 1
37 cereal . . offerings for the bull, for the ram 1
Deu 32:14 fat of lambs and rams, herds of Bashan and goats 1
Jos 6: 5 when they make a long blast with the ram's horn 2
1Sm 15:22 is better . . to hearken than the fat of rams. 1
2Kg 3: 4 had to deliver . . and the wool of 100,000 rams. 1
1Ch 15:26 they sacrificed seven bulls and seven rams. 1
29:21 burnt offerings to the LORD, 1,000 bulls, 1,000 rams 1
2Ch 13: 9 to conscecrate himself with . . seven rams 1
17:11 also brought him 7,700 rams and 7,700 he-goats. 1
29:21 they brought seven bulls, seven rams, seven lambs 1
22 killed the rams and their blood was thrown 1
32 number of the burnt offerings . . 100 rams 1
Ezr 6: 9 young bulls, rams, or sheep for burnt offerings 3
17 offered . . 100 bulls, 200 rams 3
7:17 with all diligence buy bulls, rams, and lambs 3
8:35 96 rams, 77 lambs 1
10:19 their guilt offering was a ram of the flock 1
Job 42: 8 Now therefore take seven bulls and seven rams 1
Ps 66:15 fatlings, with the smoke of the sacrifice of rams; 1
114: 4 mountains skipped like rams 1
6 O mountains, that you skip like rams? 1
Isa 1:11 I have had enough of burnt offerings of rams 1
34: 6 with the fat of the kidneys of rams. 1
60: 7 the rams of Nebai'oth shall minister to you; 1
Jer 25:34 and you shall fall like choice rams. 4
51:40 lambs to the slaughter, like rams and he-goats. 1
Ezk 27:21 your favored dealers in lambs, rams, and goats; 1
34:17 I judge between sheep and sheep, rams and he-goats 1
39:18 of rams, of lambs, and of goats, of bulls, 1
43:23 and a ram from the flock without blemish. 1
25 a sin offering; also a bull and a ram from the flock 1
45:23 seven . . bulls and seven rams without blemish 1
24 an ephah for each ram, and a hin of oil to each ephah 1
46: 4 lambs without blemish and a ram without blemish; 1
5 cereal offering with the ram shall be an ephah 1
6 bull without blemish, and six lambs and a ram 1
7 an ephah with the bull and an ephah with the ram 1
11 bull shall be an ephah, and with a ram an ephah, 1
Dan 8: 3 behold, a ram standing on the bank of the river. 1
4 I saw the ram charging westward and northward 1
6 He came to the ram with the two horns 1
7 I saw him come close to the ram, and he was enraged 1

7 enraged against him and struck the ram 1
7 ram had no power to stand before him 1
7 no one who could rescue the ram from his power. 1
20 As for the ram which you saw with the two horns 1
Mic 6: 7 Will the LORD be pleased with thousands of rams 1
1Es 6:29 for bulls and rams and lambs 4
7: 7 They offered . . 100 bulls, 200 rams, 400 lambs 4
8:14 both gold and silver for bulls and rams and lambs 4
65 12 bulls for all Israel, 96 rams 4
9:20 to give rams in expiation of their error. 4
Tob 7: 8 they killed a ram from the flock 4
Aza 1:16 with burnt offerings of rams and bulls 4

battering ram 1. כַּר 2. קֹבֶל 3. κριός
Ezk 4: 2 plant battering rams against it round about. 1
21:22 to set battering rams against the gates 1
26: 9 He will direct the shock of his battering rams 2
2Mc 12:15 without battering-rams or engines of war 3

ram's horn 1. יוֹבֵל
Jos 6: 4 bear seven trumpets of rams' horns before the ark; 1
6 bear seven trumpets of rams' horns before the ark 1
8 priests bearing . . trumpets of rams' horns 1
13 priests bearing . . trumpets of rams' horns 1

rampart 1. חֵל 2. מָצוֹר 3. מְצוּרָה 4. χάραξ
2Sm 20:15 a mound . . and it stood against the rampart; 1
Ps 48:13 consider well her ramparts 1
Lam 2: 8 he caused rampart and wall to lament 1
Nah 2: 1 Man the ramparts; watch the road; gird your loins; 3
3: 8 Thebes . . her rampart a sea, and water her wall? 1
Zec 9: 3 Tyre has built herself a rampart 2
4Mc 3:12 soldiers . . climbed over the enemy's ramparts. 4

range 1. שׁוט 2. תור 3. νέμω
Job 39: 8 He ranges the mountains as his pasture 2
Zec 4:10 the eyes . . which range through the whole earth. 1
Wis 19: 9 they ranged like horses 3

range free 1. שלח
Isa 32:20 who let the feet of the ox and the ass range free. 1

rank 1. חצץ 2. מוֹעֵד 3. מַעֲרָכָה 4. שְׂדֵרָה 5. γίνομαι 6. τάξις
1Sm 17: 8 He stood and shouted to the ranks of Israel 3
10 I defy the ranks of Israel this day; give me a man 3
22 David left the things . . and ran to the ranks 3
23 came up out of the ranks of the Philistines 3
2Kg 11: 8 and whoever approaches the ranks is to be slain. 4
15 Bring her out between the ranks; 4
2Ch 23:14 Bring her out between the ranks; 4
Prv 30:27 locusts have no king, yet all of them march in rank; 1
Isa 14:31 the north, and there is no straggler in his ranks. 2
Joh 1:15 'He who comes after me ranks before me 5
30 'After me comes a man who ranks before me 5
2Mc 13:21 Rhodocus, a man from the ranks of the Jews 6
rank *See also* growth, man, next.

high rank 1. ἀξίωμα
2Mc 4:31 Andronicus, a man of high rank 1
ranks *See* form.

ransom 1. כֹּפֶר 2. כֹּפֶר נֶפֶשׁ 3. פדה 4. פִּדְיוֹן 5. ἀγοράζω 6. ἀντίλυτρον 7. ἀντιψύχω 8. λύτρον 9. λυτρόω
Exd 21:30 If a ransom is laid on him, then he shall give 1
30:12 each shall give a ransom for himself to the LORD 2
Lev 19:20 a woman . . not yet ransomed or given her freedom 3
27:29 No one devoted . . shall be ransomed 3
Num 35:31 shall accept no ransom for the life of a murderer 1
32 you shall accept no ransom for him who has fled 1
1Sm 14:45 the people ransomed Jonathan, that he . . not die. 3
Job 6:23 Or, 'Ransom me from the hand of oppressors'? 3
33:24 from going down into the Pit, I have found a ransom; 1
36:18 let not the greatness of the ransom turn you 1
Ps 49: 7 Truly no man can ransom himself 3
8 for the ransom of his life is costly 4
15 God will ransom my soul from the power of Sheol 3
Prv 13: 8 The ransom of a man's life is his wealth 1
21:18 The wicked is a ransom for the righteous 1
Isa 35:10 the ransomed of the LORD shall return 3
43: 3 I give Egypt as your ransom 1
51:11 And the ransomed of the LORD shall return 3
Jer 31:11 the LORD has ransomed Jacob, and has redeemed him 3
Hos 13:14 Shall I ransom them from the power of Sheol? 3
Mat 20:28 to give his life as a ransom for many. 8
Mrk 10:45 to give his life as a ransom for many. 8
1Ti 2: 6 who gave himself as a ransom for all 6
1Pe 1:18 you were ransomed from the futile ways 9
Rev 5: 9 and by thy blood didst ransom men for God 5
4Mc 17:21 a ransom for the sin of our nation. 7

rapacity 1. ἀκρασία
Mat 23:25 inside they are full of extortion and rapacity. 1

rapidly 1. διὰ τάχους 2. ἐπὶ σπουδῆς 3. velociter
1Es 6:10 These operations are going on rapidly 2
2Es 14:24 because they are trained to write rapidly; 3
3Mc 5:43 and rapidly level it to the ground 1

rare 1. יָקָר 2. rarus
1Sm 3: 1 And the word of the LORD was rare in those days; 1
2Es 7:57 those that are abundant or those that are rare? 2
rare *See also* make.

more rare 1. rarus
2Es 7:58 for what is more rare is more precious. 1

most rare 1. τίμιος
Rev 21:11 its radiance like a most rare jewel, like a jasper 1

rascal 1. πονηρεύω
Sir 19:26 There is a rascal bowed down in mourning 1

rase 1. ערה
Ps 137: 7 Rase it, rase it! Down to its foundations! 1
7 Rase it, rase it! Down to its foundations! 1

rash 1. בהל 2. בטא 3. לוע 4. מהר 5. προπετής
Lev 5: 4 Or if any one utters with his lips a rash oath 2
4 any sort of rash oath that men swear •
Job 6: 3 therefore my words have been rash. 3
Ecc 5: 2 Be not rash with your mouth, nor . . hasty to utter 1
Isa 32: 4 The mind of the rash will have good judgment 4
Act 19:36 you ought to be quiet and do nothing rash. 5
rash *See also* act, speak, word.
rashly *See* say.

rate
Lev 25:50 time . . shall be rated as the time of a hired •

rather 1. בחר 2. כִּי 3. לֹא כִּי 4. ἀλλά 5. ἀλλ' ἤ 6. δέ 7. εὐδοκέω 8. ἤ 9. μᾶλλον 10. μενοῦν 11. νῦν
Deu 29:20 rather the anger of the LORD and his jealousy 2
2Kg 20:10 It is an easy thing . . rather let the shadow go 3
Ps 84:10 would rather be a doorkeeper in the house 1
Ezk 18:23 and not rather that he should turn from his way •
Dan 3:28 rather than serve and worship any god except •
Mat 10: 6 go rather to the lost sheep 9
28 rather fear him who can destroy both soul and body 9
25: 9 go rather to the dealers and buy for yourselves.' 9
27:24 rather that a riot was beginning 9
Mrk 5:26 no better but rather grew worse. 9
Lke 11:28 Blessed rather are those who hear the word of God 10
12:51 No, I tell you, but rather division; 8
17: 8 Will he not rather say to him, 'Prepare supper 4
22:26 rather let the greatest among you 4
Joh 3:19 and men loved darkness rather than light 9
Act 4:19 to listen to you rather than to God 9
5:29 We must obey God rather than men. 9
Rom 14:13 but rather decide never to put a stumbling block 9
1Co 5: 2 you are arrogant! Ought you not rather to mourn? 9
11 rather I wrote to you 11
6: 7 Why not rather suffer wrong? 9
7 Why not rather be defrauded? 9
9:15 I would rather die than have any one deprive me 9
2Co 2: 7 so you should rather turn to forgive and comfort 9
5: 8 we would rather be away from the body and at home 9
Gal 4: 9 rather to be known by God 9
Eph 4:15 Rather, speaking the truth in love 6
28 rather let him labor 9
1Ti 1: 4 rather than the divine training that is in faith; 9
6: 2 rather they must serve all the better 4
2Ti 3: 4 lovers of pleasure rather than lovers of God 9
Heb 11:25 choosing rather to share ill-treatment 9
12:13 not be put out of joint but rather be healed. 9
2Jn 1:12 I would rather not use paper and ink •
3Jn 1:13 but I would rather not write with pen and ink; •
Wis 8:20 rather, being good, I entered an undefiled body. 9
Sir 25:16 I would rather dwell with a lion and a dragon 7
1Mc 9: 9 We are not able. Let us rather save our own lives 5
2Mc 6:19 rather than life with pollution 9
3Mc 1: 4 matters were turning out rather in favor of Antiochus 9
6:31 near to death, or rather, who stood at its gates 9
7: 5 as slaves, or rather as traitors 9
4Mc 16:24 die rather than violate God's commandment. 9
rather *See also* accurate.

how much rather 1. אַף
2Kg 5:13 How much rather, then, when he says to you 1

rather than 1. וְאַל 2. מִן 3. עַל 4. ἀλλά 5. ἀντί 6. ἤ 7. ἤπερ 8. ἵνα μή 9. καί οὐ 10. παρά 11. πρό 12. pro 13. quam 14. sed
Gen 48:22 I have given to you rather than to your brothers 3
Job 7:15 strangling and death rather than my bones. 2
32: 2 because he justified himself rather than God; 2
36:21 this you have chosen rather than affliction. 2
Ps 84:10 rather be a doorkeeper in the house of my God than 2
Prv 8:10 Take . . knowledge rather than choice gold; 2
16:16 understanding is to be chosen rather than silver. 2
17:12 rather than a fool in his folly. 1
22: 1 good name . . be chosen rather than great riches 2
Ecc 6: 5 yet it finds rest rather than he. 2
Hos 6: 6 knowledge of God, rather than burnt offerings. 2
Lke 18:14 this man . . rather than the other 10
Rom 1:25 served the creature rather than the Creator 10
1Co 9:12 we endure anything rather than put an obstacle 8
14:19 I would rather speak five words with my mind . . than 6
Heb 7:11 rather than one named after the order of Aaron? 9
12:11 discipline seems painful rather than pleasant; 4
2Es 7:16 rather than what is now present? 14
20 rather than that the law of God 13
135 because he would rather give than take away; 12
Tob 6:12 you rather than any other man 6
Wis 7:10 I chose to have her rather than light 5
Sus 1:23 rather than to sin in the sight of the Lord. 6
1Mc 1:63 They chose to die rather than to be defiled by food 8
2Mc 7: 7 Will you eat rather than have your body punished 11
14:42 rather than to fall into the hands of sinners 7
4Mc 9: 1 we are ready to die rather than transgress 6

previously ratified 1. προκυρόω
Gal 3:17 annul a covenant previously ratified by God 1

ratify 1. ἐγκαινίζω 2. κυπόω
Gal 3:15 or adds to it, once it has been ratified. 2
Heb 9:18 was not ratified without blood. 1
rational *See* judgment.

rattle 1. רנה 2. רַעַשׁ
Job 39:23 Upon him rattle the quiver, 1
41:29 he laughs at the rattle of javelins. 2
Ezk 37: 7 there was a noise, and behold, a rattling; 2

ravage 1. כרסם 2. מַשְׁחִית 3. נקה 4. שׁוֹא 5. שחת 6. שׁכל 7. צדא (A) 8. διακόπτω 9. ἐκλικμάω 10. ἐκπορθέω 11. λυμαίνω
1Sm 6: 5 and images of your mice that ravage the land 2
2Sm 11: 1 and they ravaged the Ammonites, and besieged 5
1Ch 20: 1 and ravaged the country of the Ammonites 5
Ps 35:17 Rescue me from their ravages 4
80:13 The boar from the forest ravages it 1
Isa 3:26 mourn; ravaged, she shall sit upon the ground. 3
Ezk 14:15 and they ravage it, and it be made desolate 6
19: 7 he ravaged their strongholds, and laid waste 7
Act 8: 3 Saul was ravaging the church 11
Jdt 2:23 ravaged Put and Lud 8
27 sacked their cities and ravaged their lands 9
4Mc 17:24 he ravaged and conquered all his enemies. 10
18: 4 reviving . . the law . . they ravaged the enemy. 10

ravager 1. חרב 2. שחת
Jdg 16:24 our enemy . . the ravager of our country 1
Isa 54:16 I have also created the ravager to destroy; 2

rave 1. נבא 2. μαίνομαι
1Sm 18:10 an evil spirit . . rushed upon Saul, and he raved 1
1Kg 18:29 they raved on until the time of the . . oblation 1
Wis 14:28 For their worshipers either rave in exultation 2

raven 1. עֹרֵב 2. κόραξ
Gen 8: 7 sent forth a raven; and it went to and fro 1
Lev 11:15 every raven according to its kind 1
Deu 14:14 every raven after its kind; 1
1Kg 17: 4 I have commanded the ravens to feed you there. 1
6 ravens brought him bread and meat in the morning 1
Job 38:41 Who provides for the raven its prey 1
Ps 147: 9 food, and to the young ravens which cry. 1
Prv 30:17 picked out by the ravens of the valley and eaten 1
Sng 5:11 his locks are wavy, black as a raven. 1
Isa 34:11 the owl and the raven shall dwell in it. 1
Zep 2:14 the raven croak on the threshold; 2
Lke 12:24 Consider the ravens: they neither sow nor reap 2

raven (2) 1. טרף 2. שחת
Ps 22:13 like a ravening and roaring lion. 1
Jer 2:30 devoured your prophets like a ravening lion. 2

ravenous 1. טרף 2. פָּרִיץ 3. ἅρπαξ
Gen 49:27 Benjamin is a ravenous wolf 1
Isa 35: 9 nor shall any ravenous beast come up on it; 2
Mat 7:15 but inwardly are ravenous wolves. 3

ravine 1. אָפִיק 2. גַּיְא 3. נַחַל
Jos 8:11 encamped on . . with a ravine between them and Ai. 2
Isa 7:19 settle in the steep ravines, and in the clefts 3
Ezk 6: 3 says the Lord . . to the ravines and the valleys; 1
35: 8 hills and in your valleys and in all your ravines 1
36: 4 and the hills, the ravines and the valleys, 1
6 and say to the mountains and hills, to the ravines 1

ravish 1. ענה 2. שׁגל 3. ἁρπάζω 4. ἐξίστημι 5. vim patior
Jdg 19:24 Ravish them and do with them what seems good 1
20: 5 meant to kill me, and they ravished my concubine 1
Isa 13:16 houses . . plundered and their wives ravished. 2
Lam 5:11 Women are ravished in Zion, virgins in . . Judah. 1
Zec 14: 2 the houses plundered and the women ravished; 2
2Es 10:22 and our wives have been ravished 5
Jdt 12:16 Holofernes' heart was ravished with her 4
16: 9 Her sandal ravished his eyes 3

ravish the heart 1. לבב
Sng 4: 9 You have ravished my heart, my sister, my bride 1
9 my sister, my bride, you have ravished my heart 1

raw 1. חַי 2. מִחְיָה 3. נָא
Exd 12: 9 Do not eat any of it raw or boiled with water 3
Lev 13:10 if . . there is quick raw flesh in the swelling 2
14 when raw flesh appears . . he shall be unclean 1
15 the priest shall examine the raw flesh 1
15 raw flesh is unclean, for it is leprosy 1
16 if the raw flesh turns again and is changed 1
1Sm 2:15 he will not accept boiled meat from you, but raw. 1
raw *See also* flesh.

ray 1. קֶרֶן 2. ἀκτίς 3. ἀστραπή 4. βολαί 5. lumen
Hab 3: 4 like the light, rays flashed from his hand; 1
Lke 11:36 as when a lamp with its rays gives you light. 3
2Es 6:40 that a ray of light be brought forth 5
Wis 2: 4 mist that is chased by the rays of the sun 2
16:27 when simply warmed by a fleeting ray of the sun 2
3Mc 5:26 The rays of the sun were not yet shed abroad 4

raze 1. נתץ 2. ערר 3. γίνομαι 4. ἐκριζόω
Jdg 9:45 and he razed the city and sowed it with salt. 1
Isa 23:13 they razed her palaces, they made her a ruin. 2
Jdt 5:18 the temple of their God was razed to the ground 3
1Mc 5:51 and razed and plundered the city 4

razor 1. מוֹרָה 2. תַּעַר
Num 6: 5 no razor shall come upon his head; 2
8: 7 let them go with a razor over all their body 2
Jdg 13: 5 bear a son. No razor shall come upon his head 1
16:17 A razor has never come upon my head; for I have been 1
1Sm 1:11 to the LORD . . and no razor shall touch his head. 1
Ps 52: 2 Your tongue is like a sharp razor 2
Isa 7:20 a razor which is hired beyond the River 2
Ezk 5: 1 take a sharp sword; use it as a barber's razor 2

re-establish 1. ἀνανεόω
AEs 13: 2 to re-establish the peace which all men desire. 1

reach 1. בוא 2. היה 3. הלך 4. חצה 5. כַּף 6. מחה
7. מצא 8. נגע 9. נשׂג 10. פגע 11. שׁלח 12. הלך (A)
13. מטא (A) 14. ἀφικνέομαι 15. γίνομαι 16. διατείνω
17. ἐγγίζω 18. εἰμί 19. εἰς 20. εἰσέρχομαι
21. ἐπίκτητος 22. ἐπισπάω 23. ἔρχομαι
24. ἔρχομαι εἰς 25. ἐφικνέομαι 26. ἵημι 27. καταντάω
28. κρίνω 29. λαμβάνω 30. προσβαίνω
31. προσπίπτω 32. συνάπτω 33. συνεγγίζω
34. συντυγχάνω 35. τυγχάνω 36. χωρέω
37. ingredior
Gen 28:12 and the top of it reached to heaven; 8
Exd 28:42 from the loins to the thighs they shall reach; 2
Num34:11 reach to the shoulder of the sea of Chin'nereth 6
35: 4 shall reach from the wall of the city outward *
Jos 9:17 Israel set out and reached their cities 1
15: 1 The lot . . reached southward to the boundary 2
17: 7 The territory of Manas'seh reached from Asher 2
10 on the north Asher is reached, and on the east 10
19:10 its inheritance reached as far as Sarid; 2
29 turns . . reaching to the fortified city of Tyre; *
Jdg 3:21 Ehud reached with his left hand, took the sword 11
2Sm 22:17 He reached from on high, he took me, he drew me out 11
2Kg 5: 6 When this letter reaches you, know that I have 1
9:18 The messenger reached them, but he is not coming 1
20 He reached them, but he is not coming back. 1
2Ch 28: 9 in a rage which has reached up to heaven. 8
Ezr 5: 5 not stop them till a report should reach Darius 12
Job 20: 6 to the heavens, and his head reach to the clouds 8
41:26 Though the sword reaches him, it does not avail; 9
Ps 18: 6 heard my voice, and my cry to him reached his ears. 1
16 He reached from on high, he took me, he drew me out 11
32: 6 rush of great waters, they shall not reach him. 8
48:10 so thy praise reaches to the ends of the earth. *
71:19 thy righteousness, O God, reach the high heavens. *
107: 7 straight way, till they reached a city to dwell 3
108: 4 thy faithfulness reaches to the clouds. *
Isa 8: 8 overflow and pass on, reaching even to the neck; 8
10:10 my hand has reached to the kingdoms of the idols 7
15: 8 the wailing reaches to Egla'im *
8 to Egla'im, the wailing reaches to Beer-e'lim. *
16: 8 struck down its branches, which reached to Jazer 8
30: 4 officials are at Zo'an and his envoys reach Ha'nes 8
28 overflowing stream that reaches up to the neck; 4
49: 6 my salvation may reach to the end of the earth. 2
Jer 4:10 whereas the sword has reached their very life. 8
18 it is bitter; it has reached your very heart. 8
48:32 Your branches . . reached as far as Jazer; 8
Dan 4:11 tree grew . . and its top reached to heaven 13
20 grew . . so that its top reached to heaven 13
22 Your greatness has grown and reaches to heaven 13
6:24 before they reached the bottom of the den 13
8:23 transgressors have reached their full measure *
Jon 3: 6 Then tidings reached the king of Nin'eveh 8
Mic 1: 9 it has reached to the gate of my people 8
Hab 2: 9 nest on high, to be safe from the reach of harm! 5
Mat 16: 5 When the disciples reached the other side 23
Lke 8:19 they could not reach him for the crowd. 34
Joh 20: 4 outran Peter and reached the tomb first; 23
8 the other disciple, who reached the tomb first 23
Act 16: 4 decisions . . reached by the apostles 28
27:12 they could reach Phoenix, a harbor of Crete 27
1Co 14:36 or are you the only ones it has reached? 27
2Co 10:13 to reach even to you. 25
14 as though we did not reach you 25
Jas 5: 4 cries . . have reached the ears of the Lord 20
2Pe 3: 9 but that all should reach repentance. 36
1Es 6:20 it has not yet reached completion.' 29
2Es 7: 5 If any one, then, wishes to reach the sea 37
Tob 7: 1 When they reached Ecbatana 24
Jdt 7:10 not easy to reach the tops of their mountains. 30
14 before the sword reaches them 23
Wis 8: 1 She reaches mightily from one end of the earth 16
19: 3 they reached another foolish decision 22
Sir 18: 9 is great if he reaches 100 years. *
35:16 his prayer will reach to the clouds. 32
17 he will not be consoled until it reaches the Lord; 33
47:16 Your name reached to far-off islands, and you were 14
1Mc 3:26 His fame reached the king 17
12:52 So they all reached the land of Judah safely 23
13:53 Simon saw that John his son had reached manhood 18
16: 9 John pursued them until Cendebeus reached Kedron 24
2Mc 1:13 when the leader reached Persia 15
4: 6 affairs could not again reach a peaceful settlement 35
5:11 When news of what had happened reached the king 31
6:14 they have reached the full measure of their sins; 27
15 when our sins have reached their height. 14
23 gray hairs . . he had reached with distinction 21
8:35 till he reached Antioch 26
12: 1 When this agreement had been reached 15
35 Gorgias escaped and reached Marisa. 19
reach *See also* fail, run, word.

reach a limit 1. adimpleo
2Es 15: 6 their harmful deeds have reached their limit. 1

reach an agreement 1. συλλύω
1Mc 13:47 So Simon reached an agreement with them 1

reach eventide 1. ערב
Isa 24:11 for lack of wine; all joy has reached its eventide; 1

reach old age 1. עתק
Job 21: 7 the wicked live, reach old age, and grow mighty 1

reach out 1. שׁלח 2. ἐκτείνω
Jdg 6:21 angel of the LORD reached out the tip of the staff 1
2Kg 6: 7 Take it up." So he reached out his hand and took it. 1
Prv 31:20 She . . reaches out her hands to the needy. 1
Mat 14:31 Jesus immediately reached out his hand 2
Sir 14:13 reach out and give to him as much as you can. 2
31:14 Do not reach out your hand for everything you see 2
18 do not reach out your hand before they do. 2
50:15 he reached out his hand to the cup 2

reach the end 1. ἀφικνέομαι
Sir 43:27 Though we speak much we cannot reach the end 1

reach the full 1. συντέλεια
Sir 43: 7 a light that wanes when it has reached the full. 1

reach up 1. נגע 2. עמד
Jer 51: 9 for her judgment has reached up to heaven 1
Ezk 31:14 that drink water may reach up to them in height; 2

read 1. אמר 2. ידע סֵפֶר 3. מִקְרָא 4. קרא 5. קרא (A)
6. ἀναγινώσκω 7. ἀνάγνωσιν ποιέω 8. ἀνάγνωσις
9. γράφω 10. ἐντυγχάνω 11. ἐπιγράφω 12. ἔχω
13. παραναγινώσκω 14. lego
Exd 24: 7 Then he took the book of the covenant, and read it 4
Deu 17:19 he shall read in it all the days of his life 4
31:11 read this law before all Israel in their hearing. 4
Jos 8:34 And afterward he read all the words of the law 4
35 Joshua . . read before all the assembly of Israel 4
2Kg 5: 6 he brought the letter . . which read 1
7 when the king of Israel read the letter 4
19:14 Hezeki'ah received the letter . . and read it; 4
22: 8 Hilki'ah gave the book to Shaphan, and he read it. 4
10 And Shaphan read it before the king. 4
16 of the book which the king of Judah has read. 4
23: 2 he read in their hearing all the words of the book 4
2Ch 34:18 Shaphan read it before the king. 4
24 book which was read before the king of Judah. 4
30 read in their hearing all the words of the book 4
Ezr 4:18 letter which you sent to us has been plainly read 4
23 the copy of King Ar-ta-xerx'es' letter was read 4
Neh 8: 3 read from it facing the square before the Water 4
8 read from the book, from the law of God, clearly 4
8 so that the people understood the reading. 3
18 by day . . he read from the book of the law of God. 4
9: 3 read from the book of the law of the LORD their God 4
13: 1 read from the book of Moses in the hearing 4
Est 6: 1 chronicles, and they were read before the king. 4
Isa 29:11 give it to one who can read, saying, "Read this 2
11 give it to one who can read, saying, "Read this 4
12 when they give the book to one who cannot read 2
12 to one who cannot read, saying, "Read this 4
12 saying, "Read this," he says, "I cannot read. 2
34:16 Seek and read from the book of the LORD 4
37:14 Hezeki'ah received the letter . . and read it; 4
Jer 29:29 Zephani'ah the priest read this letter 4
36: 6 in the LORD'S house you shall read the words 4
6 shall read them also in the hearing of all the men 4
8 ordered him about reading from the scroll 4
10 Then, in the hearing of all the people, Baruch read 4
13 that he had heard, when Baruch read the scroll 4
14 scroll that you read in the hearing of the people 4
15 And they said to him, "Sit down and read it. 4
15 Baruch read it to them. 4
21 and Jehu'di read it to the king and all the princes 4
23 As Jehu'di read three or four columns 4
51:61 see that you read all these words 4
63 When you finish reading this book 4
Dan 5: 7 Whoever reads this writing, and shows me its 5
8 could not read the writing or make known 5
15 brought in before me to read this writing 5
16 Now if you can read the writing and make known 5
17 nevertheless I will read the writing to the king 5
Hab 2: 2 upon tablets, so he may run who reads it. 4
Mat 12: 3 He said to them, "Have you not read what David did 6
5 Or have you not read in the law 6
19: 4 He answered, "Have you not read 6
21:16 Yes, have you never read 6
42 Have you never read in the scriptures 6
22:31 have you not read what was said to you by God 6
27:37 they put the charge against him, which read 9
Mrk 2:25 he said to them, "Have you never read what David did 6
12:10 Have you not read this scripture: 'The very stone 6
26 have you not read in the book of Moses 6
15:26 the inscription of the charge against him read 11
Lke 4:16 And he stood up to read; 6
6: 3 Jesus answered, "Have you not read what David did 6
10:26 What is written in the law? How do you read? 6
Joh 19:19 it read, "Jesus of Nazareth, the King of the Jews. 9
20 Many of the Jews read this title 6
Act 8:28 he was reading the prophet Isaiah. 6
30 heard him reading Isaiah the prophet 6
30 asked, "Do you understand what you are reading? 6
32 passage of the scripture which he was reading 6
13:15 After the reading of the law and the prophets 8
27 the prophets which are read every sabbath 6
15:21 he is read every sabbath in the synagogues. 6
31 when they read it 6
23:34 On reading the letter 6
2Co 1:13 nothing but what you can read and understand 6
3: 2 to be known and read by all men; 6
14 for to this day, when they read the old covenant 8
15 Yes, to this day whenever Moses is read 6
Eph 3: 4 When you read this you can perceive my insight 6
Col 4:16 when this letter has been read among you 6
16 have it read also in the church of the La-odice'ans; 6
16 see that you read also the letter from La-odice'a. 6
1Th 5:27 that this letter be read to all the brethren. 6
1Ti 4:13 attend to the public reading of scripture 8
1Es 2:26 I have read the letter which you sent me 6
30 when the letter from King Artaxerxes was read 6
3:13 took the writing and gave it to him, and he read it. 6
15 the writing was read in their presence. 6
9:41 he read aloud in the open square before the gate 6
48 at the same time explaining what was read. 8
2Es 14:45 and let the worthy and the unworthy read them; 14
Sir 0: 1 devoting himself . . to the reading of the law 8
2 You are urged therefore to read with good will 7
Bar 1: 3 Baruch read the words of this book in the hearing 6
14 you shall read this book which we are sending you 6
1Mc 5:14 While the letter was still being read 6
10: 7 read the letter in the hearing of all the people 6
14:19 read before the assembly in Jerusalem. 6
2Mc 2:25 we have aimed to please those who wish to read 6
6:12 Now I urge those who read this book 10
11:34 sent them a letter, which read thus 12
15:39 the ears of those who read the work 10
3Mc 1:12 Even after the law had been read to him 13
4Mc 18:11 He read to you about Abel slain by Cain 6

read aloud 1. ἀναγινώσκω 2. παραναγινώσκω
Rev 1: 3 he who reads aloud the words of the prophecy 1
2Mc 8:23 to read aloud from the holy book 2

reader 1. ἀναγινώσκω 2. ἀναγνώστης 3. ἐντυγχάνω
Mat 24:15 (let the reader understand) 1
Mrk 13:14 let the reader understand 1
1Es 8: 8 Ezra the priest and reader of the law of the Lord 2
9 Ezra the priest and reader of the law of the Lord 2
19 Ezra the priest and reader of the law 2
9:39 Ezra the chief priest and reader 2
42 Ezra the priest and reader of the law 2
49 Ezra the chief priest and reader 2
Sir 0: 1 it is necessary not only that the readers 1
2Mc 2:25 to profit all readers. 3

readily 1. מהר 2. ἄσμενος 3. εὐχερής 4. ταχύς
Isa 32: 4 the tongue of the stammerers will speak readily 1
Wis 14:28 or live unrighteously, or readily commit perjury; 4

3Mc 2:31 Now some, however . . readily gave themselves up 3
5:21 readily and joyfully . . gave their approval 2

readily enough 1. καλῶς
2Co 11: 4 you submit to it readily enough. 1

readiness 1. כון 2. עֲתִי 3. ἕτοιμος 4. προθυμία
Lev 16:21 by the hand of a man who is in readiness 2
Jos 8: 4 do not go . . but hold yourselves all in readiness; 1
2Co 8:11 so that your readiness in desiring it 4
12 For if the readiness is there, it is acceptable 4
9: 2 for I know your readiness 4
2Mc 14:22 armed men in readiness at key places 3

ready 1. יצא 2. כון 3. מָהִיר 4. ערך 5. עָתִיד
6. עָתִיד(A) 7. ἀπαρασκεύαστος 8. βούλομαι
9. δύναμαι 10. ἐγγύς 11. ἐθέλω 12. ἑτοιμάζω
13. ἕτοιμος 14. ἑτοίμως 15. εὐδοκέω 16. ἵνα
17. παρασκευάζω 18. προθυμία 19. προσκαρτερέω
20. paro
Gen 18: 6 Make ready quickly three measures of fine meal •
Exd 17: 4 this people? They are almost ready to stone me. •
19:11 be ready by the third day; 2
15 he said to the people, "Be ready by the third day; 2
34: 2 Be ready in the morning, and come up in the morning 2
Deu 9: 8 LORD was so angry . . he was ready to destroy you. •
19 LORD . . was ready to destroy you. •
20 so angry with Aaron that he was ready to destroy •
2Sm 15:15 your servants are ready to do whatever •
1Kg 5: 8 I am ready to do all you desire in the matter •
2Kg 10: 6 If you are on my side, and if you are ready to obey me •
1Ch 5:18 valiant men . . ready for service. 1
7:11 mighty warriors, 17,200, ready for service in war. •
12:36 Of Asher 40,000 seasoned troops ready for battle. 4
Neh 9:17 But thou art a God ready to forgive •
Est 3:14 proclamation to all . . to be ready for that day. 5
8:13 the Jews were to be ready . . to avenge themselves 5
Job 12: 5 it is ready for those whose feet slip. 2
15:23 He knows that a day of darkness is ready at his hand; 2
17: 1 my days are extinct, the grave is ready for me. •
18:12 calamity is ready for his stumbling. 2
32:19 like new wineskins, it is ready to burst. •
Ps 38:17 For I am ready to fall, and my pain is ever with me. 2
45: 1 my tongue is like the pen of a ready scribe. 3
119:76 Let thy steadfast love be ready to comfort me •
173Let thy hand be ready to help me •
Prv 19:29 Condemnation is ready for scoffers 2
22:18 pleasant . . if all of them are ready on your lips. 2
Isa 65: 1 I was ready to be sought by those who did not ask •
1 I was ready to be found by those who did not seek •
Ezk 38: 7 Be ready and keep ready, you and all the hosts 2
Dan 3:15 Now if you are ready when you hear the sound 6
9:14 Therefore the LORD has kept ready the calamity •
Mat 22: 4 everything is ready; come to the marriage feast.' 13
8 Then he said to his servants, 'The wedding is ready 13
24:44 Therefore you also must be ready 13
25:10 those who were ready went in with him 13
Mrk 3: 9 he told his disciples to have a boat ready for him 19
14:15 a large upper room furnished and ready 13
Lke 12:40 You also must be ready; for the Son of man is coming 13
14:17 'Come; for all is now ready.' 13
22:33 I am ready to go with you to prison and to death. 13
Act 21:13 am ready not only to be imprisoned but even to die 14
23:15 we are ready to kill him before he comes near. 13
21 they are ready, waiting for the promise from you. 13
1Co 3: 2 for you were not ready for it 9
2 even yet you are not ready 9
2Co 1:17 like a worldly man, ready to say Yes and No at once? 16
9: 2 Acha'ia has been ready since last year 17
3 so that you may be ready, as I said you would be; 17
4 if some . . find that you are not ready 7
5 so that it may be ready not as an exaction 13
12:14 Here for the third time I am ready to come to you. 14
1Th 2: 8 ready to share with you not only the gospel of God 15
2Ti 2:21 ready for any good work. 12
Tit 3: 1 to be obedient, to be ready for any honest work 13
Heb 8:13 is ready to vanish away. 10
11:17 he . . was ready to offer up his only son •
1Pe 1: 5 salvation ready to be revealed in the last time. 13
4: 5 give account to him who is ready to judge 14
2Es 2:35 Be ready for the rewards of the kingdom 20
Tob 5:16 Then he said to Tobias, "Get ready for the journey 13
11: 9 I have seen you, my child; now I am ready to die. •
AEs 11: 6 great dragons came forward, both ready to fight 13
9 were ready to perish. 12
Wis 16:20 supply them from heaven with bread ready to eat 13
Sir 6:35 Be ready to listen to every narrative 11
45:23 in the ready goodness of his soul 18
48:10 you who are ready . . to calm the wrath of God 2
1Mc 3:28 ordered them to be ready for any need. 13
44 congregation assembled to be ready for battle 13
58 Be ready early in the morning to fight 13
4:35 how ready they were either to live or to die nobly 13
5:39 ready to come and fight against you 13
7:29 the enemy were ready to seize Judas. 13
12:27 so as to be ready all night for battle 12
34 they were ready to hand over the stronghold 8
50 marching in close formation, ready for battle. 13
13:37 we are ready to make a general peace with you 13
2Mc 7: 2 we are ready to die 13
8:21 and made them ready to die for their laws 13
11: 9 ready to assail not only men 13
3Mc 5:26 what the king desired was ready for action. 13
29 the beasts and the armed forces were ready 12
4Mc 9: 1 we are ready to die rather than transgress 13
ready *See also* armed, dressed, get, hold, keep, make, obedience, stand.

reaffirm 1. κυρόω
2Co 2: 8 I beg you to reaffirm your love for him. 1

real 1. ἀληθής 2. γνήσιος 3. εἰμί 4. καθίστημι
5. ὄντως
Mrk 11:32 for all held that John was a real prophet. 5
Act 12: 9 not know that what was done by the angel was real 1
Rom 2:28 For he is not a real Jew who is one outwardly •
29 and real circumcision is a matter of the heart •
1Ti 5: 3 Honor widows who are real widows. 5
5 She who is a real widow, and is left all alone 5
16 it may assist those who are real widows. 5
Sir 7:18 a real brother for the gold of Ophir. 2
2Mc 4: 1 had been the real cause of the misfortune. 4
4Mc 5:24 we worship the only real God. 3
real *See also* reason.

reality 1. πρᾶγμα
Heb 10: 1 instead of the true form of these realities 1

realize 1. γινώσκω 2. ἐπιγινώσκω 3. ἐπίσταμαι
4. ποιέω 5. συννοέω 6. συνοράω
Act 12:12 When he realized this, he went to the house of Mary 6
22:29 he realized that Paul was a Roman citizen 2
24:10 Realizing that . . you have been judge 3
2Co 13: 5 realize that Jesus Christ is in you 2
Eph 3:11 which he has realized in Christ Jesus our Lord 4
Heb 6:11 in realizing the full assurance of hope •
1Es 4:22 Hence you must realize that women rule over you! 1
Sir 12:12 at last you will realize the truth of my words 2
23:19 he does not realize 1
1Mc 5:34 army of Timothy realized that it was Maccabeus 2
7:25 realized that he could not withstand them 1
12:50 they realized that Jonathan had been seized 2
2Mc 5: 6 not realizing . . success . . is . . misfortune 5
11:13 realized that the Hebrews were invincible 5
14: 3 realized that there was no way for him to be safe 5
3Mc 7: 6 Since we have come to realize 1

really 1. גַּם 2. זֶה 3. ἀλήθεια 4. ἀληθῶς 5. γε καί
6. καθώς 7. μᾶλλον 8. μέντοι 9. ὄντως 10. ὡς
Gen 16:13 of seeing"; for she said, "Have I really seen God 1
27:21 know whether you are really my son Esau or not. 2
24 He said, "Are you really my son Esau? 2
Jdg 15: 2 I really thought that you utterly hated her; †
Joh 7:26 Can it be that the authorities really know 4
40 This is really the prophet. 4
1Co 5: 7 as you really are unleavened 6
8: 7 some . . eat food as really offered to an idol 10
14:25 declare that God is really among you. 9
Gal 3: 4 if it really is in vain. 5
Php 1:12 really served to advance the gospel 7
1Th 2:13 but as what it really is, the word of God 4
Jas 2: 8 If you really fulfill the royal law 8
AEs 16:10 really an alien to the Persian blood 3
Wis 17:14 which was really powerless 9
2Mc 3: 9 inquired whether this really was the situation. 3
12:12 Judas, thinking that they might really be useful 4
really *See also* if, yield.

realm 1. מַלְכוּת 2. מֶמְשָׁלָה 3. מַלְכוּת(A) 4. βασιλεία
5. χώρα
2Kg 20:13 there was nothing in his house or in all his realm 2
2Ch 20:30 the realm of Jehosh'aphat was quiet 1
Ezr 7:23 lest his wrath be against the realm of the king 3
Isa 39: 2 There was nothing in his house or in all his realm 2
Dan 9: 1 became king over the realm of the Chalde'ans– 1
11: 9 come into the realm of the king of the south 1
1Es 8:10 the priests and Levites and others in our realm 4
2Mc 9:24 the people throughout the realm 5

reap 1. כלה 2. מצא 3. קצר 4. ἔχω 5. θερίζω
6. messem facio 7. meto
Gen 26:12 Isaac . . reaped in the same year a hundredfold. 2
Lev 19: 9 When you reap the harvest of your land 3
9 you shall not reap your field to its very border 1
23:10 When you . . reap its harvest, you shall bring 3
22 when you reap the harvest of your land 3
22 you shall not reap your field to its very border 3
25: 5 What grows of itself . . you shall not reap 3
11 neither sow, nor reap what grows of itself 3
Deu 24:19 When you reap your harvest in your field 3
Rut 2: 9 your eyes be upon the field . . they are reaping 3
1Sm 6:13 Beth-she'mesh were reaping their wheat harvest 3
8:12 some to plow his ground and to reap his harvest 3
2Kg 19:29 the third year sow, and reap, and plant vineyards 3
Job 4: 8 who plow iniquity and sow trouble reap the same. 3
Ps 126: 5 May those who sow in tears reap with shouts of joy! 3
Prv 22: 8 He who sows injustice will reap calamity 3
Ecc 11: 4 and he who regards the clouds will not reap. 3
Isa 37:30 then in the third year sow and reap 3
Jer 12:13 They have sown wheat and have reaped thorns 3
Hos 8: 7 and they shall reap the whirlwind. 3
10:12 reap the fruit of steadfast love; 3
13 you have reaped injustice 3
Mic 6:15 You shall sow, but not reap; 3
Mat 6:26 they neither sow nor reap nor gather into barns 5
25:24 reaping where you did not sow 5
26 You knew that I reap where I have not sowed 5
Lke 12:24 Consider the ravens: they neither sow nor reap 5
19:21 reap what you did not sow.' 5
22 reaping what I did not sow? 5
Joh 4:36 He who reaps receives wages 5
37 'One sows and another reaps.' 5
38 I sent you to reap that for which you did not labor; 5
Rom 1:13 in order that I may reap some harvest among you 4
1Co 9:11 is it too much if we reap your material benefits? 5
2Co 9: 6 he who sows sparingly will also reap sparingly 5
6 sows bountifully will also reap bountifully. 5
Gal 6: 7 whatever a man sows, that he will also reap. 5
8 will from the flesh reap corruption 5
8 will from the Spirit reap eternal life. 5
9 in due season we shall reap 5
Rev 14:15 Put in your sickle, and reap 5
15 reap, for the hour to reap has come 5
16 swung his sickle . . and the earth was reaped. 5
2Es 4:29 that which has been sown is not reaped 7
16:43 let him that sows be like one who will not reap 6
Sir 7: 3 you will not reap a sevenfold crop. 5

reap the harvest 1. θερίζω
1Es 4: 6 reap the harvest and bring some to the king 1

reaper 1. קצר 2. θερίζω 3. θεριστής
Rut 2: 3 went and gleaned in the field after the reapers; 1
4 Bo'az came . . and he said to the reapers 1
5 to his servant who was in charge of the reapers 1
6 the servant who was in charge of the reapers 1
7 let me glean and gather . . after the reapers. 1
14 she sat beside the reapers 1
2Kg 4:18 he went out . . to his father among the reapers. 1
Ps 129: 7 with which the reaper does not fill his hand 1
Isa 17: 5 as when the reaper gathers standing grain •
Jer 9:22 men shall fall . . like sheaves after the reaper 1
Ams 9:13 when the plowman shall overtake the reaper 1
Mat 13:30 at harvest time I will tell the reapers 3
39 and the reapers are angels. 3
Joh 4:36 so that sower and reaper may rejoice together. 2
Bel 1:33 was going into the field to take it to the reapers. 3

rear 1. גדל 2. קום 3. רבה 4. ἐκτρέφω 5. τρέφω
2Sm 24:18 rear an altar to the LORD on the threshing floor 2
1Ch 21:18 David should go up and rear an altar to the LORD 2
Job 31:18 for from his youth I reared him as a father •
Isa 1: 2 Sons have I reared and brought up 1
23: 4 I have neither reared young men nor brought up 1
Lam 2:22 those . . I dandled and reared my enemy destroyed. 3
Ezk 19: 2 in the midst of young lions, rearing her whelps. 3
Tob 14:10 what Nadab did to Ahikar who had reared him 5
Bar 4: 8 and you grieved Jerusalem, who reared you. 4
2Mc 7:27 have reared you and brought you up 4

rear (2) 1. אָחוֹר 2. אַחֲרוֹן 3. אַחֲרֵי 4. יַרְכָה 5. סוֹף
6. ἔσχατος 7. ὀπίσω
Exd 26:22 for the rear of the tabernacle westward 4
23 for corners of the tabernacle in the rear; 4
27 the side of the tabernacle at the rear westward. 4
36:27 for the rear of the tabernacle westward he made 4
28 frames for corners of the tabernacle in the rear 4
32 frames of the tabernacle at the rear westward. 4
1Sm 29: 2 and David and his men were passing on in the rear 2
2Sm 5:23 You shall not go up; go around to their rear 3
10: 9 was set against him both in front and in the rear 1
1Kg 6:16 He built . . the rear of the house with boards 4
1Ch 19:10 set against him both in front and in the rear 1
Jol 2:20 the eastern sea, and his rear into the western sea; 5
1Mc 4:15 all those in the rear fell by the sword 6
9:47 he eluded him and went to the rear. 7
rear *See* cut, fall, guard.

reason 1. בְּ 2. דָּבָר 3. כִּי 4. מִן 5. מִפְּנֵי 6. עַל
7. עַל כֵּן 8. αἰτία 9. ἀντί 10. διά 11. διὰ τοῦτο
12. εἰς τοῦτο 13. ἕνεκα 14. λόγος 15. χάρις
16. propter 17. sensus
Gen 41:31 plenty will be unknown . . by reason of . . famine 5
47:13 Canaan languished by reason of the famine. 5
Exd 8:24 the land was ruined by reason of flies. 5
Lev 17:11 blood . . makes atonement, by reason of the life 3
Num 6:11 because he sinned by reason of the dead body. 6
18:32 you shall bear no sin by reason of it 6
Deu 23:10 man who is not clean by reason of what chances 4
28:47 by reason of the abundance of all things 4
Jos 5: 4 this is the reason why Joshua circumcised them 2
1Sm 20:29 For this reason he has not come to the king's 7
1Kg 11:27 this was the reason why he lifted up his hand 2

Ps 90:10 or even by reason of strength fourscore; 1
Ezk 19:10 full of branches by reason of abundant water. 4
Dan 10:16 by reason of the vision pains have come upon me •
Mat 19: 5 'For this reason a man shall leave his father 13
Mrk 10: 7 'For this reason a man shall leave his father 13
Joh 10:17 For this reason the Father loves me 10
Act 10:21 what is the reason for your coming? 8
18:14 I should have reason to bear with you, O Jews; 14
26:21 For this reason the Jews seized me in the temple 13
28:18 no reason for the death penalty in my case. 8
20 For this reason therefore I have asked to see 8
Rom 1:26 For this reason God gave them up to dishonorable 11
14:22 happy is he who has no reason to judge himself •
15:17 I have reason to be proud of my work for God. •
Eph 1:15 For this reason, because I have heard 10
3: 1 For this reason I, Paul, a prisoner for Christ 15
14 For this reason I bow my knees before the Father 15
5:31 For this reason a man shall leave his father 9
1Th 3: 5 For this reason, when I could bear it no longer 10
7 for this reason, brethren, in all our distress 10
1Ti 1:16 I received mercy for this reason 10
2Pe 1: 5 For this very reason make every effort •
1Jn 3: 8 The reason the Son of God appeared 12
2Es 5: 9 then shall reason hide itself 17
7:50 For this reason the Most High has made not one 16
72 For this reason, therefore, those who dwell •
13:19 and for that very reason! 16
Sus 1:14 and when each pressed the other for the reason 8
1Mc 6:24 For this reason the sons of our people besieged 15
10:63 let no one annoy him for any reason. 14
13: 4 By reason of this all my brothers have perished 15
2Mc 4:16 For this reason heavy disaster overtook them 15
35 For this reason not only Jews . . were grieved 8
8:26 for that reason they did not continue 8
3Mc 3: 4 For this reason they appeared hateful to some; 8
4Mc 2: 2 It is for this reason, certainly •

reason (2) 1. יכח 2. מַנְדַּע (A) 3. *διαλέγω* 4. *λογίζομαι* 5. *λογισμός* 6. *λόγος*

Lev 19:17 but you shall reason with your neighbor 1
Job 23: 7 There an upright man could reason with him 1
Dan 4:34 lifted my eyes to heaven, and my reason returned 2
36 At the same time my reason returned to me; 2
1Co 13:11 I thought like a child, I reasoned like a child; 4
Wis 2: 1 they reasoned unsoundly, saying to themselves 4
2 reason is a spark 6
21 Thus they reasoned, but they were led astray 4
3:10 be punished as their reasoning deserves 4
17:12 surrender of the helps that come from reason; 5
Sir 14:20 the man . . who reasons intelligently. 3
27: 7 Do not praise a man before you hear him reason 5
37:16 Reason is the beginning of every work 6
4Mc 1: 1 whether devout reason is sovereign 5
3 reason rules over those emotions 5
5 If reason rules the emotions 5
6 For reason does not rule its own emotions 5
7 that reason is dominant over the emotions 5
9 reason controls the emotions. 5
13 whether reason is sovereign over the emotions. 5
14 We shall decide just what reason is 5
14 whether reason rules over all these. 5
15 Now reason is the mind 5
19 by means of it reason rules over the emotions 5
29 the master cultivator, reason, weeds and prunes 5
30 For reason is the guide of the virtues 5
32 reason obviously rules over both. 5
33 because reason is able to rule over appetites 5
34 we abstain because of domination by reason. 5
35 the impulses of the body are bridled by reason. 5
2: 3 by his reason he nullified . . the passions. 5
4 Not only is reason proved to rule 5
6 reason is able to control desires. 5
7 unless reason is clearly lord of the emotions? 5
9 he is ruled by the law through his reason 5
9 can recognize that reason rules the emotions. 5
14 when reason, through the law, can prevail 5
15 reason rules even the more violent emotions 5
17 controlled his anger by reason. 5
20 For if reason could not control anger 5
24 if reason is master of the emotions 5
3: 1 reason rules not over its own emotions 5
2 reason can provide a way for us not to be enslaved 5
3 reason can help to deal with anger. 5
4 reason can fight at our side 5
5 For reason does not uproot the emotions 5
16 opposing reason to desire 5
18 by nobility of reason spurn all domination 5
19 a narrative demonstration of temperate reason. 5
5:31 to be young in reason on behalf of piety. 5
35 I will not put you to shame, philosophical reason 6
6: 7 he kept his reason upright and unswerving. 5
30 by reason he resisted even to . . death 5
31 devout reason is sovereign over the emotions. 5
32 if the emotions had prevailed over reason 5
33 now that reason has conquered the emotions 5
34 to acknowledge the dominance of reason 5
35 not only that reason has mastered agonies 5
7: 1 the reason of our father Eleazar 5
4 the shield of his devout reason. 5
12 Eleazar . . remained unmoved in his reason. 5
14 in spirit through reason 5
14 by reason like that of Isaac 5
16 devout reason is governor of the emotions. 5
17 because not every one has prudent reason. 5
20 because of the weakness of their reason. 5
8: 1 in accordance with devout reason 5
9:17 to strangle my reason 5
10:19 you will not make our reason speechless. 5
11:27 therefore, unconquered, we hold fast to reason. 5
13: 1 devout reason is sovereign over the emotions. 5
3 by reason, which is praised before God 5
16 self-control, which is divine reason. 5
14: 2 O reason, more royal than kings 5
11 reason had full command over these men 5
15: 1 O reason of the children, tyrant over the emotions! 5
11 strong enough to pervert her reason. 5
23 devout reason, giving her heart a man's courage 5
16: 1 devout reason is sovereign over the emotions. 5
4 quenched so many . . by devout reason. 5
18: 2 devout reason is master of all emotions 5

reason *See* open.

reason for confidence 1. *πείθω* 2. *πεποίθησις*

Php 3: 4 Though I myself have reason for confidence 2
4 reason for confidence in the flesh also 1

no reason 1. חִנָּם

Prv 3:30 Do not contend with a man for no reason 1

real reason 1. *ἀσφαλής*

Act 22:30 to know the real reason why the Jews accused him 1

right reason 1. *εὐλογιστία*

4Mc 13: 5 confess the sovereignty of right reason over emotion 1
7 the seven-towered right reason of the youths 1

same reason 1. *διὰ τοῦτο*

Rom 13: 6 For the same reason you also pay taxes 1

reason to boast 1. *καύχημα*

Gal 6: 4 then his reason to boast will be in himself alone 1

reason together 1. יכח

Isa 1:18 Come now, let us reason together, says the LORD 1

reason why 1. *διά* 2. *διό*

Joh 8:47 the reason why you do not hear them is 1
12:18 The reason why the crowd went to meet him 1
Rom 15:22 the reason why I have so often been hindered 2
1Jn 3: 1 The reason why the world does not know us 1

without good reason 1. *διὰ κενῆς*

1Mc 6:12 I sent to destroy . . without good reason. 1

reasonable 1. *διανόημα*

Sir 22:16 so the mind firmly fixed on a reasonable counsel 1

reasonably 1. *ἐπιεικής*

AEs 13: 2 always acting reasonably and with kindness 1

reasoning 1. תּוֹכַחַת 2. *διαλογισμός* 3. *λογισμός*

Job 13: 6 Hear now my reasoning 1
Wis 7:20 the powers of spirits and the reasonings of men 2
9:14 For the reasoning of mortals is worthless 3
Sir 27: 5 the test of a man is in his reasoning. 2
2Mc 7:21 fired her woman's reasoning with a man's courage 3
4Mc 5:11 dispel your futile reasonings 3

right reasoning 1. *εὐλογιστία*

4Mc 8:15 their right reasoning nullified his tyranny. 1

reassure 1. נחם 2. *πείθω*

Gen 50:21 Thus he reassured them and comforted them. 1
1Jn 3:19 and reassure our hearts before him 2

rebel 1. בֶּן מְרִי 2. מרד 3. מרה 4. סור 5. סרר 6. פשע 7. *ἀποστάτης* 8. *ἀφίστημι* 9. *στασιάζω* 10. *στασιαστής*

Gen 14: 4 in the thirteenth year they rebelled. 2
Exd 23:21 hearken to his voice, do not rebel against him 3
Num 14: 9 Only do not rebel against the LORD; and do not fear 2
17:10 to be kept as a sign for the rebels 1
20:10 Hear now, you rebels; shall we bring forth water 3
24 because you rebelled against my command 3
27:14 because you rebelled against my word 3
Jos 1:18 Whoever rebels against your commandment 3
22:18 And if you rebel against the LORD today 2
19 do not rebel against the LORD, or make us as rebels 2
29 Far be it . . that we should rebel against the LORD 2
2Kg 1: 1 Moab rebelled against Israel. 6
3: 5 the king of Moab rebelled against . . Israel. 6
7 The king of Moab has rebelled against me; 6
18: 7 He rebelled against the king of Assyria 2
20 On whom . . rely, that you have rebelled against me? 2
24: 1 then he turned and rebelled against him. 2
20 Zedeki'ah rebelled against the king of Babylon. 2
2Ch 13: 6 rose up and rebelled against his lord; 2
36:13 He also rebelled against King Nebuchadnez'zar 2
Neh 2:19 Are you rebelling against the king? 2
6: 6 that you and the Jews intend to rebel; 2
9:26 disobedient and rebelled against thee 2
Job 24:13 There are those who rebel against the light 2
Ps 5:10 for they have rebelled against thee. 3
78:17 rebelling against the Most High in the desert. 3
105:28 they rebelled against his words. 3
106: 7 rebelled against the Most High at the Red Sea. 3
Isa 1: 2 Sons have I reared . . but they have rebelled 6
5 Why . . be smitten, that you continue to rebel? 4
20 if you refuse and rebel, you shall be devoured 3
23 princes are rebels and companions of thieves. 5
28 rebels and sinners shall be destroyed together 6
36: 5 that you have rebelled against me? 2
48: 8 and that from birth you were called a rebel. 6
63:10 But they rebelled and grieved his holy Spirit; 3
66:24 bodies of the men that have rebelled against me; 6
Jer 2:29 You have all rebelled against me, says the LORD. 6
3:13 that you rebelled against the LORD your God 6
4:17 she has rebelled against me, says the LORD. 3
52: 3 Zedeki'ah rebelled against the king of Babylon. 2
Lam 1:18 The LORD is in the right, for I have rebelled 3
3:42 We have transgressed and rebelled 3
Ezk 2: 3 a nation of rebels, who have rebelled against me; 2
3 a nation of rebels, who have rebelled against me; 2
17:15 he rebelled against him by sending ambassadors 2
20: 8 they rebelled against me and would not listen 3
13 But the house of Israel rebelled against me 3
21 But the children rebelled against me; 3
38 I will purge out the rebels from among you 2
Dan 9: 5 done wrong and acted wickedly and rebelled 2
9 because we have rebelled against him 2
Hos 7:13 for they have rebelled against me! 6
14 they gash themselves, they rebel against me. 4
9:15 all their princes are rebels. 5
13:16 guilt, because she has rebelled against her God; 3
Zep 3:11 the deeds by which you have rebelled against me; 6
Mrk 15: 7 among the rebels in prison 10
1Es 1:48 he broke his oath and rebelled 8
2:23 the Jews were rebels 7
Jdt 7:15 because they rebelled 9
Wis 3:10 and rebelled against the Lord; 8
Aza 1: 9 the hands of lawless enemies, most hateful rebels 7
2Mc 5: 8 hated as a rebel against the laws 7

rebel *See also* make.

rebel against 1. מרה

Deu 1:26 you . . rebelled against the command of the LORD 1
43 you rebelled against the command of the LORD 1
9:23 then you rebelled against the commandment 1
1Sm 12:14 not rebel against the commandment of the LORD 1
15 but rebel against the commandment of the LORD 1
Ps 78:40 they rebelled against him in the wilderness 1
56 they tested and rebelled against the Most High 1
107:11 for they had rebelled against the words of God 1
Ezk 5: 6 she has . . rebelled against my ordinances 1

rebellion 1. מֶרֶד 2. מְרִי 3. סרה 4. פשע 5. פֶּשַׁע 6. מְרַד (A) 7. *ἀντιλογία* 8. *ἀποστασία* 9. *ἀπόστασις* 10. *παραπικρασμός*

Deu 13: 5 taught rebellion against the LORD your God 3
Jos 22:16 building yourselves an altar . . in rebellion 1
22 If it was in rebellion or in breach of faith 1
1Sm 15:23 For rebellion is as the sin of divination 2
1Kg 12:19 So Israel has been in rebellion 4
2Ch 10:19 been in rebellion against the house of David 4
Ezr 4:19 rebellion and sedition have been made in it 6
Job 34:37 For he adds rebellion to his sin; 5
Prv 17:11 An evil man seeks only rebellion 2
Jer 28:16 you have uttered rebellion against the LORD. 3
29:32 for he has talked rebellion against the LORD. 3
33: 8 the guilt of their sin and rebellion against me. 4
2Th 2: 3 unless the rebellion comes first 8
Heb 3: 8 do not harden your hearts as in the rebellion 10
15 do not harden your hearts as in the rebellion. 10
Jde 1:11 and perish in Korah's rebellion. 7
1Es 2:27 that the men in it were given to rebellion and war 9

rebellious 1. מרא 2. מַרְדוּת 3. מרה 4. מְרִי 5. סרר 6. מְרָד (A) 7. *ἀποστάτις* 8. *παραπικραίνω* 9. indisciplinatus

Deu 9: 7 you have been rebellious against the LORD. 3
24 You have been rebellious against the LORD 3
21:18 If a man has a stubborn and rebellious son 3
20 This our son is stubborn and rebellious 3
31:27 For I know how rebellious and stubborn you are; 4
27 today you have been rebellious against the LORD; 3
1Sm 20:30 You son of a perverse, rebellious woman, do I not 2
Ezr 4:12 rebuilding that rebellious and wicked city; 6
15 learn that this city is a rebellious city 6
Ps 66: 7 let not the rebellious exalt themselves. Selah 5
68: 6 but the rebellious dwell in a parched land. 5
18 gifts among men, even among the rebellious 5
78: 8 fathers, a stubborn and rebellious generation 3
106:43 but they were rebellious in their purposes 3
Isa 30: 1 Woe to the rebellious children," says the LORD 5

9 For they are a rebellious people, lying sons 4
50: 5 I was not rebellious, I turned not backward. 3
65: 2 a rebellious people, who walk in a way 5
Jer 5:23 this people has a stubborn and rebellious heart; 3
6:28 They are all stubbornly rebellious 5
Lam 1:20 I am in . . because I have been very rebellious. 3
Ezk 2: 5 for they are a rebellious house 4
6 for they are a rebellious house. 4
7 for they are a rebellious house. 4
8 be not rebellious like that rebellious house; 4
8 be not rebellious like that rebellious house; 4
3: 9 for they are a rebellious house. 4
26 for they are a rebellious house. 4
27 for they are a rebellious house. 4
12: 2 you dwell in the midst of a rebellious house 4
3 for they are a rebellious house. 4
3 though they are a rebellious house. 4
9 has not the house of Israel, the rebellious house 4
25 in your days, O rebellious house, I will speak 4
17:12 Say now to the rebellious house, Do you not know 4
24: 3 utter an allegory to the rebellious house 4
44: 6 say to the rebellious house 4
Zep 3: 1 Woe to her that is rebellious and defiled 1
Heb 3:16 Who were they that heard and yet were rebellious? 8
1Es 2:18 are building that rebellious and wicked city 7
22 will learn that this city was rebellious 7
2Es 1: 8 they are a rebellious people. 9

rebellious woman 1. מַרְדּוּת
1Sm 20:30 You son of a perverse, rebellious woman, do I not 1

rebelliously *See* assemble.

rebirth *See* give.

rebuild 1. בנה 2. יסד 3. שוב ובנה 4. בנא (A)
5. ἀνεγείρω 6. ἀνοικοδομέω 7. οἰκοδομέω
Jos 6:26 the man that rises up and rebuilds this city 1
19:50 and he rebuilt the city, and settled in it. 1
Jdg 18:28 And they rebuilt the city, and dwelt in it. 1
21:23 went and returned . . and rebuilt the towns 1
1Kg 9:17 so Solomon rebuilt Gezer) 1
2Kg 21: 3 he rebuilt the high places . . he erected altars 1
2Ch 8: 2 Solomon rebuilt the cities which Huram had 1
24:27 the rebuilding of the house of God 2
33: 3 For he rebuilt the high places which his father 3
Ezr 1: 3 Jerusalem . . and rebuild the house of the LORD 1
5 stirred to go up to rebuild the house of the LORD 1
4:12 rebuilding that rebellious and wicked city; 4
13 if this city is rebuilt and the walls finished 4
16 if this city is rebuilt and its walls finished 4
21 make a decree . . that this city be not rebuilt 4
5: 2 arose and began to rebuild the house of God 4
11 rebuilding the house . . built many years ago 4
13 decree that this house of God should be rebuilt. 4
15 let the house of God be rebuilt on its site. 4
17 decree . . for the rebuilding of this house 4
6: 3 let the house be rebuilt, the place where 4
7 Jews rebuild this house of God on its site. 4
8 do . . for the rebuilding of this house of God; 4
Neh 2: 5 send me to Judah . . that I may rebuild it. 1
3:13 rebuilt . . set its doors, its bolts, and its bars 1
14 rebuilt . . set its doors, its bolts, and its bars. 1
15 rebuilt it and covered it and set its doors 1
Job 3:14 of the earth who rebuilt ruins for themselves 1
12:14 If he tears down, none can rebuild; 1
Ps 51:18 rebuild the walls of Jerusalem 1
69:35 will save Zion and rebuild the cities of Judah; 1
Isa 25: 2 is a city no more, it will never be rebuilt. 1
58:12 And your ancient ruins shall be rebuilt; 1
Jer 30:18 the city shall be rebuilt upon its mound 1
31:38 when the city shall be rebuilt for the LORD 1
33: 7 and rebuild them as they were at first. 1
Ezk 26:14 you shall never be rebuilt; 1
36:10 shall be inhabited and the waste places rebuilt 1
33 and the waste places shall be rebuilt 1
36 I, the LORD, have rebuilt the ruined places, 1
Ams 9:11 and rebuild it as in the days of old; 1
14 and they shall rebuild the ruined cities 1
Hag 1: 2 has not yet come to rebuild the house of the LORD. 1
Mal 1: 4 We are shattered but we will rebuild the ruins 3
Act 15:16 rebuild the dwelling of David, which has fallen 6
16 I will rebuild its ruins, and I will set it up 6
1Es 6:17 Cyrus wrote that this house should be rebuilt. 7
19 this temple . . should be rebuilt on its site. 7
Tob 14: 5 they will rebuild the house of God 7
5 and will rebuild Jerusalem in splendor 7
5 the house of God will be rebuilt there 7
Sir 49:13 rebuilt our ruined houses. 5
1Mc 4:48 They also rebuilt the sanctuary 7
9:62 rebuilt the parts of it that had been demolished 7
10:10 began to rebuild and restore the city. 7
44 Let the cost of rebuilding . . be paid 7
45 the cost of rebuilding the walls of Jerusalem 7
45 the cost of rebuilding the walls in Judea 7

rebuke 1. גער 2. גְּעָרָה 3. יכח 4. תּוֹכֵחָה 5. תּוֹכַחַת
6. ἀπελέγχω 7. ἐλεγμός 8. ἔλεγξιν ἔχω 9. ἔλεγχος
10. ἐλέγχω 11. ἐξελέγχω 12. ἐπίπληξις
13. ἐπιπλήσσω 14. ἐπιτιμάω 15. ἐπιτίμησις
16. μέμφομαι 17. ὀνειδίζω
Gen 31:42 labor of my hands, and rebuked you last night. 3
37:10 his father rebuked him, and said to him 1
Rut 2:16 leave it for her to glean, and do not rebuke her. 1
2Sm 22:16 were laid bare, at the rebuke of the LORD 2
2Kg 19: 3 a day of distress, of rebuke, and of disgrace; 4
4 your God has heard . . and will rebuke the words 3
1Ch 12:17 may the God of our fathers see and rebuke you. 3
16:21 he rebuked kings on their account 3
Job 13:10 He will surely rebuke you 3
26:11 tremble, and are astounded at his rebuke. 2
Ps 6: 1 O LORD, rebuke me not in thy anger, nor chasten me 3
9: 5 Thou hast rebuked the nations 1
18:15 of the world were laid bare, at thy rebuke, O LORD 2
38: 1 O LORD, rebuke me not in thy anger, nor chasten me 3
14 does not hear, and in whose mouth are no rebukes. 5
39:11 When thou dost chasten man with rebukes for sin 5
50:21 But now I rebuke you 3
68:30 Rebuke the beasts that dwell among the reeds 1
76: 6 At thy rebuke, O God of Jacob, both rider and horse 2
80:16 may they perish at the rebuke of thy countenance! 2
104: 7 At thy rebuke they fled; 2
105:14 he rebuked kings on their account 3
106: 9 He rebuked the Red Sea, and it became dry; 1
119:21 Thou dost rebuke the insolent, accursed ones 1
141: 5 Let a good man strike or rebuke me in kindness 3
Prv 13: 1 but a scoffer does not listen to rebuke. 2
17:10 A rebuke goes deeper into a man of understanding 2
24:25 those who rebuke the wicked have delight 3
27: 5 Better is open rebuke than hidden love. 5
28:23 who rebukes a man will afterward find more favor 3
30: 6 Do not add to his words, lest he rebuke you 3
Ecc 7: 5 better for a man to hear the rebuke of the wise 2
Isa 17:13 he will rebuke them, and they will flee far away 1
37: 3 day of distress, of rebuke, and of disgrace; 4
4 rebuke the words which the LORD . . has heard; 3
50: 2 Behold, by my rebuke I dry up the sea 2
51:20 the wrath of the LORD, the rebuke of your God. 2
54: 9 not be angry with you and will not rebuke you. 1
66:15 anger in fury, and his rebuke with flames of fire. 2
Jer 29:27 why have you not rebuked Jeremiah of An'athoth 1
Nah 1: 4 He rebukes the sea and makes it dry 1
Zec 3: 2 LORD said to Satan, "The LORD rebuke you, O Satan! 1
2 The LORD who has chosen Jerusalem rebuke you! 1
Mal 2: 3 Behold, I will rebuke your offspring 1
3:11 I will rebuke the devourer for you 1
Mat 8:26 Then he rose and rebuked the winds and the sea 14
16:22 Peter took him and began to rebuke him, saying 14
17:18 Jesus rebuked him, and the demon came out of him 14
19:13 The disciples rebuked the people; 14
20:31 The crowd rebuked them, telling them to be silent; 14
Mrk 1:25 Jesus rebuked him, saying, "Be silent, and come out 14
4:39 he awoke and rebuked the wind, and said to the sea 14
8:32 Peter took him, and began to rebuke him. 14
33 seeing his disciples, he rebuked Peter, and said 14
9:25 he rebuked the unclean spirit, saying to it 14
10:13 the disciples rebuked them. 14
48 many rebuked him, telling him to be silent 14
Lke 4:35 Jesus rebuked him, saying, "Be silent 14
39 he stood over her and rebuked the fever 14
41 But he rebuked them 14
8:24 awoke and rebuked the wind and the raging waves 14
9:42 But Jesus rebuked the unclean spirit 14
55 he turned and rebuked them. 14
17: 3 if your brother sins, rebuke him 14
18:15 when the disciples saw it, they rebuked them. 14
39 those who were in front rebuked him 14
19:39 Teacher, rebuke your disciples. 14
23:40 the other rebuked him, saying, "Do you not fear God 14
1Ti 5: 1 Do not rebuke an older man 13
20 rebuke them in the presence of all 10
2Ti 4: 2 convince, rebuke, and exhort 14
Tit 1:13 Therefore rebuke them sharply 10
2Pe 2:16 was rebuked for his own transgression; 8
Jde 1: 9 but said, "The Lord rebuke you. 14
Wis 11: 7 in rebuke for the decree to slay the infants 9
12:17 dost rebuke any insolence among those who know it. 11
26 who have not heeded the warning of light rebukes 15
17: 7 their boasted wisdom was scornfully rebuked. 9
Sir 18:13 He rebukes and trains and teaches them 9
43:17 The voice of his thunder rebukes the earth 17
48: 7 who heard rebuke at Sinai 7
2Mc 2: 7 he rebuked them and declared 16
7:33 to rebuke and discipline us 12
4Mc 2:11 one rebukes her when she breaks the law. 6
13 one rebukes friends when they act wickedly. 11

recall 1. זכר 2. שוב 3. μιμνήσκω 4. μνήμην ποιέω
5. memoro
Isa 46: 8 Remember this and consider, recall it to mind 2
Ezk 29:16 the house of Israel, recalling their iniquity 1
2Pe 1:15 you may be able at any time to recall these things. 4
2Es 1:36 yet will recall their former state. 5
Wis 19:10 they still recalled the events of their sojourn 3

recast a narrative 1. μετάφρασιν ποιέω
2Mc 2:31 the one who recasts the narrative 1

recede 1. שוב 2. recedo
Gen 8: 3 the waters receded from the earth continually. 1
2Es 4:14 that it may recede before us 2

receipt 1. χειρόγραφον
Tob 5: 3 Then Tobit gave him the receipt, and said to him 1
9: 5 He gave him the receipt 1

receive 1. בוא אֶל 2. היה לְ 3. כול 4. לקח 5. נחל
6. נכה 7. נשא 8. קבל 9. קדם 10. חסן (A)
11. קבל (A) 12. ἀναδέχομαι 13. ἀπαντάω 14. ἀπέχω
15. ἀποδέχομαι 16. ἀπολαμβάνω 17. ἀποφέρω
18. γίνομαι 19. δέχομαι 20. διαδέχομαι 21. δίδωμι
22. εἰσδέχομαι 23. ἐκδέχομαι 24. ἐπιδέχομαι
25. ἐπιτυγχάνω 26. εὑρίσκω 27. ἔχω 28. κομίζω
29. λαμβάνω 30. λῆμψις 31. μεταλαμβάνω
32. μετάλημψις 33. παραδέχομαι 34. παραλαμβάνω
35. προσδέχομαι 36. προσλαμβάνω 37. τυγχάνω
38. ὑποδέχομαι 39. χωρέω 40. accipio 41. consequor
42. excipio 43. percipio 44. receptio 45. recipio
46. suscipio
Gen 4:11 opened its mouth to receive your brother's blood 4
38:20 Judah sent . . to receive the pledge 4
43:23 I received your money. 1
Exd 25: 2 from every man . . you shall receive 4
3 offering which you shall receive from them 4
27: 3 You shall make pots for it to receive its ashes •
28: 5 They shall receive gold, blue and purple 4
32: 4 he received the gold at their hand, and fashioned 4
36: 3 they received from Moses all the freewill 4
Num 18:28 your tithes, which you receive from . . Israel; 4
23:20 Behold, I received a command to bless 4
31:51 Moses and Elea'zar . . received from them the gold 4
54 Moses and Elea'zar the priest received the gold 4
34:14 have received their inheritance 4
15 received their inheritance beyond the Jordan 4
Deu 9: 9 up the mountain to receive the tables of stone 4
18: 8 besides what he receives from the sale •
33: 3 receiving direction from thee 7
Jos 11:20 and should receive no mercy but be exterminated 2
13: 8 and the Gadites received their inheritance 4
14: 1 which . . Israel received in the land of Canaan 5
18: 7 Manas'seh have received their inheritance 4
21: 4 those Levites . . received by lot from the tribes 2
5 Ko'hathites received by lot from the families •
6 Gersonites received by lot . . thirteen cities. •
7 Merar'ites . . received from the tribe of Reuben •
1Sm 25:35 received from her hand what she had brought him; 4
39 avenged the insult I received at the hand •
1Kg 5: 9 go by sea to the place . . and you shall receive it; 7
8:64 too small to receive the burnt offering 3
10:28 the king's traders received them . . at a price. 4
2Kg 5:16 he said, "As the LORD lives . . I will receive none. 4
19:14 Hezeki'ah received the letter from the hand 4
1Ch 12:18 Then David received them, and made them officers 8
2Ch 1:16 and the king's traders received them from Ku'e 4
22: 6 healed . . of the wounds which he had received 6
29:22 priests received the blood and threw it against 8
30:16 blood which they received from . . the Levites. •
35:11 sprinkled the blood which they received •
Job 2:10 Shall we receive good at the hand of God 8
10 at the hand of God, and shall we not receive evil? 8
3:12 Why did the knees receive me? 9
4:12 stealthily, my ear received the whisper of it. 4
22:22 Receive instruction from his mouth 4
27:13 which oppressors receive from the Almighty 4
35: 7 what does he receive from your hand? 4
Ps 24: 5 He will receive blessing from the LORD 7
49:15 from the power of Sheol, for he will receive me. 4
68:18 receiving gifts among men 4
73:24 afterward thou wilt receive me to glory. 4
Prv 1: 3 receive instruction in wise dealing 4
2: 1 My son, if you receive my words 4
24:32 I looked and received instruction. 4
Isa 37:14 Hezeki'ah received the letter . . and read it; 4
40: 2 received from the LORD'S hand double 4
Jer 9:20 and let your ear receive the word of his mouth; 4
17:23 they might not hear and receive instruction. 4
32:33 they have not listened to receive instruction. 4
35:13 Will you not receive instruction and listen 4
37:17 King Zedeki'ah sent for him, and received him. 4
38:14 received him at the third entrance of the temple 4
Ezk 3:10 that I shall speak to you receive in your heart 4
16:32 Adulterous wife, who receives strangers 4
Dan 2: 6 receive . . gifts and rewards and great honor. 11
5:31 Darius the Mede received the kingdom, 11
7:18 saints . . shall receive the kingdom 11
22 time came when the saints received the kingdom. 10
Mat 6: 2 say to you, they have received their reward. 14
5 say to you, they have received their reward. 14
16 to you, they have received their reward. 14
7: 8 For every one who asks receives 29
10: 8 You received without paying, give without pay. 29
14 if any one will not receive you or listen 19
40 He who receives you receives me 19
40 He who receives you receives me 19
40 and he who receives me receives him who sent me. 19

40 and he who receives me receives him who sent me. 19
41 He who receives a prophet because he is a prophet 19
41 shall receive a prophet's reward 29
41 he who receives a righteous man 19
41 shall receive a righteous man's reward. 29
13:20 and immediately receives it with joy; 29
18: 5 Whoever receives one such child in my name 19
5 one such child in my name receives me; 19
19:11 Not all men can receive this saying 39
12 He who is able to receive this 39
12 let him receive it. 39
29 for my name's sake, will receive a hundredfold 29
20: 9 each of them received a denarius. 29
10 they thought they would receive more 29
10 each of them also received a denarius. 29
11 on receiving it 29
21:22 whatever you ask in prayer, you will receive 29
25:16 He who had received the five talents went at once 29
18 he who had received the one talent went 29
20 he who had received the five talents came forward 29
24 He also who had received the one talent came forward 29
27 at my coming I should have received 28
Mrk 4:16 immediately receive it with joy; 29
6:11 if any place will not receive you 19
9:37 Whoever receives one such child in my name 19
37 receives one such child in my name receives me; 19
37 whoever receives me, receives not me 19
37 whoever receives me, receives not me 19
10:15 receive the kingdom of God like a child 19
30 who will not receive a hundredfold now 29
11:24 believe that you have received it 29
12:40 They will receive the greater condemnation. 29
14:65 the guards received him with blows. 29
Lke 6:24 you have received your consolation. 14
34 if you lend to those from whom you hope to receive 29
8:13 who, when they hear the word, receive it with joy 19
9: 5 wherever they do not receive you 19
48 Whoever receives this child in my name 19
48 Whoever receives this child . . receives me 19
48 whoever receives me receives him who sent me 19
48 whoever receives me receives him who sent me 19
53 the people would not receive him 19
10: 8 Whenever you enter a town and they receive you 19
10 they do not receive you 19
38 a woman named Martha received him 38
11:10 every one who asks receives 29
15: 2 This man receives sinners and eats with them. 35
27 because he has received him safe and sound.' 16
16: 4 so that people may receive me into their houses 19
9 receive you into the eternal habitations. 19
25 you in your lifetime received your good things 16
18:17 whoever does not receive the kingdom of God 19
30 who will not receive manifold more in this time 16
19: 6 came down, and received him joyfully. 38
12 to receive a kingdom and then return. 29
15 When he returned, having received the kingdom 29
20:47 They will receive the greater condemnation. 29
23:41 we are receiving the due reward of our deeds 16
Joh 1:11 and his own people received him not. 34
12 to all who received him, who believed in his name 29
16 And from his fulness have we all received, grace 29
3:11 but you do not receive our testimony. 29
27 No one can receive anything except what is given 29
32 yet no one receives his testimony; 29
33 he who receives his testimony sets his seal 29
4:36 He who reaps receives wages 29
5:34 the testimony which i receive is from man 29
41 I do not receive glory from men. 29
43 you do not receive me 29
43 him you will receive. 29
44 who receive glory from one another 29
7:23 If on the sabbath a man receives circumcision 29
39 which those who believed in him were to receive; 29
10:18 this charge I have received from my Father. 29
12:48 He who rejects me and does not receive my sayings 29
13:20 he who receives any one whom I send receives me; 29
20 he who receives any one whom I send receives me; 29
20 he who receives me receives him who sent me. 29
20 he who receives me receives him who sent me. 29
30 after receiving the morsel 29
14:17 whom the world cannot receive 29
16:24 ask, and you will receive, that your joy may be full. 29
17: 8 they have received them 29
19:30 When Jesus had received the vinegar, he said 29
20:22 Receive the Holy Spirit. 29
Act 1: 8 you shall receive power 29
2:33 having received from the Father the promise 29
38 you shall receive the gift of the Holy Spirit. 29
41 So those who received his word were baptized 15
3: 5 expecting to receive something from them. 29
21 whom heaven must receive 19
7:38 he received living oracles to give to us. 19
53 you who received the law as delivered by angels 29
59 Lord Jesus, receive my spirit. 19
8:14 Sama'ria had received the word of God 19
15 they might receive the Holy Spirit; 29
17 they received the Holy Spirit. 29
19 may receive the Holy Spirit. 29
10:43 receives forgiveness of sins through his name. 29

47 who have received the Holy Spirit just as we have? 29
11: 1 the Gentiles also had received the word of God. 19
16:24 received this charge 29
17: 7 Jason has received them 38
11 they received the word with all eagerness 19
15 receiving a command 29
18:27 wrote to the disciples to receive him 15
19: 2 he said to them, "Did you receive the Holy Spirit 29
20:24 the ministry which I received from the Lord 29
35 'It is more blessed to give than to receive.' 29
21:17 the brethren received us gladly. 15
22: 5 From them I received letters to the brethren 19
26:18 they may receive forgiveness of sins 29
28: 7 who received us and entertained us hospitably 12
21 they said to him, "We have received no letters 19
Rom 1: 5 through whom we have received grace 29
27 receiving in their own persons the due penalty 16
3:25 expiation by his blood, to be received by faith. •
4:11 He received circumcision as a sign or seal 29
5:11 we have now received our reconciliation. 29
17 those who receive the abundance of grace 29
8:15 For you did not receive the spirit of slavery 29
15 but you have received the spirit of sonship. 29
13: 3 do what is good, and you will receive his approval 27
16: 2 receive her in the Lord as befits the saints 35
1Co 2:12 Now we have received not the spirit of the world 29
14 The unspiritual man does not receive the gifts 19
3: 8 each shall receive his wages 29
14 he will receive a reward. 29
4: 5 Then every man will receive his commendation 18
7 What have you that you did not receive? 29
7 If then you received it, why do you boast 29
9:24 only one receives the prize 29
25 They do it to receive a perishable wreath 29
11:23 For I received from the Lord 34
15: 1 which you received, in which you stand 34
3 what I also received 34
2Co 1: 9 felt that we had received the sentence of death 27
5:10 so that each one may receive good or evil 28
7:15 fear and trembling with which you received him. 19
11: 4 if you receive a different spirit 29
4 a different spirit from the one you received 29
24 I have received at the hands of the Jews 29
Gal 1: 9 a gospel contrary to that which you received 34
12 I did not receive it from man, nor was I taught it 34
3: 2 Did you receive the Spirit by works of the law 29
14 receive the promise of the Spirit through faith 29
4: 5 so that we might receive adoption as sons. 16
14 received me as an angel of God 19
Php 2:29 So receive him in the Lord with all joy 35
4: 9 What you have learned and received and heard 34
15 in giving and receiving except you only; 30
18 I have received full payment, and more; I am filled 14
18 I am filled, having received from Epaphrodi'tus 19
Col 2: 6 As therefore you received Christ Jesus the Lord 34
3:24 from the Lord you will receive the inheritance 16
4:10 you have received instructions 29
10 if he comes to you, receive him) 19
17 the ministry which you have received in the Lord. 34
1Th 1: 6 received the word in much affliction 19
2:13 when you received the word of God 34
2Th 3: 6 the tradition that you received from us. 34
1Ti 4: 3 to be received with thanksgiving 32
4 if it is received with thanksgiving; 29
Phm 1:17 receive him as you would receive me 36
17 receive him as you would receive me •
Heb 2: 2 received a just retribution 29
4:16 we may receive mercy and find grace 29
6: 7 receives a blessing from God. 31
7: 5 descendants of Levi who receive the priestly office 29
8 Here tithes are received by mortal men 29
9 Levi himself, who receives tithes, paid tithes 29
9:15 may receive the promised eternal inheritance 29
10:26 after receiving the knowledge of the truth 29
36 do the will of God and receive what is promised. 28
11: 8 a place which he was to receive as an inheritance; 29
11 By faith Sarah . . received power to conceive 29
13 not having received what was promised 28
17 he who had received the promises 12
33 enforced justice, received promises 25
35 Women received their dead by resurrection. 29
39 did not receive what was promised 28
12: 6 chastises every son whom he receives. 33
28 for receiving a kingdom that cannot be shaken 34
Jas 1: 7 will receive anything from the Lord. 29
12 he will receive the crown of life 29
21 receive with meekness the implanted word 19
2:25 when she received the messengers 38
4: 3 You ask and do not receive 29
5: 7 until it receives the early and the late rain 29
1Pe 4:10 As each has received a gift, employ it 29
2Pe 1:17 he received honor and glory from God the Father 29
1Jn 2:27 the anointing which you received from him 29
3:22 we receive from him whatever we ask 29
5: 9 If we receive the testimony of men 29
2Jn 1:10 do not receive him into the house 29
Rev 2:17 which no one knows except him who receives it.' 29
27 as I myself have received power from my Father; 29
3: 3 Remember then what you received and heard; 29

4:11 Lord and God, to receive glory and honor and power 29
5:12 to receive power and wealth and wisdom and might 29
14: 9 receives a mark on his forehead or on his hand 29
11 and whoever receives the mark of its name. 29
17:12 ten kings who have not yet received royal power 29
12 they are to receive authority as kings 29
19:20 those who had received the mark of the beast 29
20: 4 and had not received its mark on their foreheads 29
2Es 2:13 Ask and you will receive 40
33 I, Ezra, received a command from the Lord 40
36 receive the joy of your glory 40
37 Receive what the Lord has entrusted to you 40
39 have received glorious garments from the Lord. 40
45 now they are being crowned, and receive palms. 40
7: 9 how will the heir receive his inheritance 40
14 they can never receive those things 45
72 and though they received the commandments 40
72 dealt unfaithfully with what they received. 40
91 with great joy the glory of him who receives them 46
96 the spacious liberty which they are to receive 45
98 to receive their reward when glorified. 45
109 Elijah for those who received the rain 40
128 he shall receive what I have said. 45
8:33 the righteous . . shall receive their reward 45
39 and their receiving their reward. 44
43 because it has not received thy rain 40
56 For they also received freedom 40
9:10 although they received my benefits 41
32 though our fathers received the law 40
33 Yet those who received it perished 40
34 when the ground has received seed 40
36 who have received the law and sinned will perish 40
36 as well as our heart which received it; 46
14:30 received the law of life, which they did not keep 40
15: 9 and will receive to myself all the . . blood 40
51 so that you cannot receive your mighty lovers. 46
55 therefore you shall receive your recompense. 43
16:36 Behold the word of the Lord, receive it 42
Tob 7: 8 They received them very warmly 38
Jdt 12:15 the soft fleeces which she had received from Bagoas 29
Wis 5:16 Therefore they will receive a glorious crown 29
7:15 have thought worthy of what I have received 21
12: 7 receive a worthy colony of the servants of God. 19
16: 6 received a token of deliverance 27
17:21 the darkness that was destined to receive them; 20
19:14 Others had refused to receive strangers 19
16 after receiving them with festal celebrations 22
Sir 4:31 Let not your hand be extended to receive 29
12: 5 you will receive twice as much evil 26
13:22 he speaks sensibly, and receives no attention. 21
16:14 will receive in accordance with his deeds. 26
32: 2 receive a wreath for your excellent leadership. 29
38: 2 he will receive a gift from the king. 29
41:19 surliness in receiving and giving 30
50:12 when he received the portions 19
21 to receive the blessing from the Most High. 24
51:16 I inclined my ear a little and received her 19
26 let your souls receive instruction 24
Bar 4:32 the city which received your sons. 19
Sus 1:55 angel of God has received the sentence from God 29
Bel 1: 1 Cyrus the Persian received his kingdom. 34
1Mc 2:51 receive great honor and an everlasting name. 19
54 Phinehas . . received the covenant 29
56 Caleb . . received an inheritance in the land. 29
8:26 without receiving any return. 29
10:30 the half of the fruit . . that I should receive 29
42 which my officials have received every year 29
11:34 royal taxes which the king formerly received 29
12: 8 received the letter 29
43 So he received him with honor 24
13:37 received the gold crown and the palm branch 28
14:23 It has pleased our people to receive these men 24
40 Romans had received the envoys of Simon with honor. 13
15:27 But he refused to receive them 19
16:15 The son of Abubus received them treacherously 38
2Mc 2: 4 the prophet, having received an oracle 18
4:25 After receiving the king's orders he returned 29
7:36 receive just punishment for your arrogance. 17
8:33 received the proper recompense 28
10:15 they received those who were banished 36
20 on receiving 70,000 drachmas 29
12:12 after receiving his pledges 29
13:22 gave pledges, received theirs, withdrew 29
24 He received Maccabeus 15
14:19 to give and receive pledges of friendship. 29
3Mc 3:28 will receive the property 29
5:26 while the king was receiving his friends 23
27 upon receiving the report 15
35 this also was his aid which they had received. 37
50 help which they had received before from heaven 18
7:10 Upon receiving this letter 29
10 should receive the punishment they deserved. 37
16 had received the full enjoyment of deliverance 29
4Mc 4: 5 On receiving authority to deal with this matter 29
5:15 When he had received permission to speak 29
37 The fathers will receive me as pure 22
12:11 received good things and also your kingdom 29
18:23 have received pure and immortal souls from God 16

receive a beating 1. δέρω
Lke 12:47 that servant . . shall receive a severe beating. 1
48 he . . shall receive a light beating 1

receive a portion 1. חלק
Jer 37:12 to receive his portion there among the people. 1

receive a tithe 1. עשׂר 2. δεκατόω
Neh 10:38 with . . when the Levites receive the tithes; 1
Heb 7: 6 received tithes from Abraham 2

receive a wound 1. נכה
Zec 13: 6 The wounds I received in the house of my friends. 1

receive again 1. ἀπολαμβάνω 2. κομίζω
Lke 6:34 to receive as much again. 1
Eph 6: 8 he will receive the same again from the Lord 2

receive an inheritance 1. נחל
Jos 17: 6 daughters of Manas'seh received an inheritance 1

receive approval 1. μαρτυρέω
Heb 11: 4 he received approval as righteous 1

receive ash 1. דשׁן
Exd 27: 3 You shall make pots for it to receive its ashes 1

receive back 1. κομίζω 2. recipio
Heb 11:19 figuratively speaking, he did receive him back. 1
2Es 10:16 you will receive your son back in due time 2
1Mc 10:43 and receive back all his property in my kingdom. •

receive benefit 1. εὐεργετέω
Wis 11: 5 they themselves received benefit in their need. 1
13 the righteous had received benefit 1

receive circumcision 1. περιτέμνω
Gal 5: 2 if you receive circumcision 1
3 to every man who receives circumcision 1
6:13 For even those who receive circumcision 1

receive divine approval 1. μαρτυρέω
Heb 11: 2 the men of old received divine approval. 1

receive entreaty 1. עתר
2Ch 33:13 He prayed to him, and God received his entreaty 1
19 his prayer, and how God received his entreaty 1

receive glory 1. glorifico
2Es 8:49 in order to receive the greatest glory. 1

receive good 1. εὐεργετέω
Wis 3: 5 they will receive great good 1

receive help 1. עזר
1Ch 5:20 when they received help against them 1
Dan 11:34 When they fall, they shall receive a little help. 1

receive inheritance 1. נחל 2. κατακληρονομέω
Jos 16: 4 The people . . received their inheritance. 1
Sir 24: 8 in Israel receive your inheritance.' 2

receive into one's home 1. ἐνοικίζω
Sir 11:34 Receive a stranger into your home 1

receive mercy 1. ἐλεέω
Rom 11:30 received mercy because of their disobedience 1
31 they also may receive mercy. 1
1Ti 1:13 I received mercy because I had acted ignorantly 1
16 I received mercy for this reason 1
1Pe 2:10 once you had not received mercy 1
10 but now you have received mercy. 1

receive payment 1. ἀποδίδωμι
Tob 4:14 if you serve God you will receive payment 1

receive repayment 1. ἀποδίδωμι
Tob 14:10 the other received repayment 1

receive sight 1. ἀναβλέπω
Mat 11: 5 the blind receive their sight and the lame walk 1
20:34 immediately they received their sight 1
Mrk 10:51 Master, let me receive my sight. 1
52 immediately he received his sight 1
Lke 7:22 the blind receive their sight, the lame walk 1
18:41 He said, "Lord, let me receive my sight. 1
42 Jesus said to him, "Receive your sight 1
43 immediately he received his sight and followed 1
Joh 9:11 so I went and washed and received my sight. 1
15 again asked him how he had received his sight. 1
18 he had been blind and had received his sight 1
18 the parents of the man who had received his sight 1
Act 22:13 'Brother Saul, receive your sight.' 1
13 in that very hour I received my sight and saw him. 1

receive the good news 1. εὐαγγελίζω
Heb 4: 6 those who formerly received the good news 1

receive the law 1. νομοθετέω
Heb 7:11 (for under it the people received the law) 1

receive up 1. ἀνάλημψις
Lke 9:51 When the days drew near for him to be received up 1

receive with favor 1. רצה
Gen 33:10 face of God, with such favor have you received me. 1

recent *See* convert.

recently 1. הַיּוֹם 2. προσαρτίως 3. προσφάτως 4. πρὸ τούτων τῶν ἡμερῶν 5. nunc
Jer 34:15 You recently repented and did what was right 1
Act 21:38 who recently stirred up a revolt 4
2Es 5:52 Why are those whom you have borne recently 5
Jdt 4: 3 they had only recently returned from the captivity 3
5 since their fields had recently been harvested. 3
2Mc 14:36 this house that has been so recently purified. 3
3Mc 1:19 who had recently been arrayed for marriage 2

reception 1. προσδέχομαι
Wis 19:15 their hostile reception of the aliens; 1

recess 1. אטם 2. חֵקֶר 3. μυχός
1Kg 6: 4 he made . . windows with recessed frames. 1
Job 38:16 or walked in the recesses of the deep? 2
Ezk 41:16 all three had windows with recessed frames. •
26 there were recessed windows and palm trees 1
Wis 17:14 beset them from the recesses of powerless Hades 3

far recess 1. יַרְכָה
2Kg 19:23 I have gone up . . to the far recesses of Lebanon; 1
Isa 37:24 I have gone up . . to the far recesses of Lebanon; 1

recite 1. דבר 2. ספר 3. סֵפֶר
Exd 17:14 in a book and recite it in the ears of Joshua, that I 3
Deu 32:44 Moses came and recited all the words of this song 1
Ps 50:16 What right have you to recite my statutes 2

reckless 1. פחז 2. θρασύς 3. προπετής 4. τολμηρός
Jdg 9: 4 hired worthless and reckless fellows 1
2Ti 3: 4 treacherous, reckless, swollen with conceit 3
Sir 4:29 Do not be reckless in your speech 2
9:18 the man who is reckless in speech will be hated. 3
19: 3 the reckless soul will be snatched away. 4

very reckless 1. τολμηρός
Sir 19: 2 who consorts with harlots is very reckless. 1

recklessness 1. פַּחֲזוּת
Jer 23:32 astray by their lies and their recklessness 1

reckon 1. חשׁב 2. שׁער 3. תמם 4. ἀναρίθμητος 5. λογίζομαι 6. συναίρω 7. ψηφίζω 8. investigo
Gen 15: 6 and he reckoned it to him as righteousness. 1
Lev 25:27 let him reckon the years since he sold it and pay 1
31 the houses . . shall be reckoned with the fields 1
50 He shall reckon with him who bought him 1
Num 3:47 reckoning by the shekel of the sanctuary •
50 took . . 1,365 shekels, reckoned by . . the sanctuary; •
18:27 your offering shall be reckoned to you as though 1
30 then the rest shall be reckoned to the Levites 1
23: 9 alone, and not reckoning itself among the nations 1
Jos 13: 3 from . . it is reckoned as Canaanite; 1
2Sm 4: 2 for Be-er'oth also is reckoned to Benjamin; 1
2Kg 22: 4 Go up . . that he may reckon the amount of the money 3
Ps 88: 4 I am reckoned among those who go down to the Pit; 1
106:31 that has been reckoned to him as righteousness 1
Prv 23: 7 for he is like one who is inwardly reckoning. 2
Lam 4: 2 they are reckoned as earthen pots 1
Mat 18:24 When he began the reckoning 6
Lke 22:37 'And he was reckoned with transgressors' 5
Rom 4: 3 and it was reckoned to him as righteousness. 5
4 his wages are not reckoned as a gift but as his due. 5
5 his faith is reckoned as righteousness. 5
6 the man to whom God reckons righteousness 5
8 the man . . whom the Lord will not reckon his sin. 5
9 faith was reckoned to Abraham as righteousness. 5
10 How then was it reckoned to him? 5
11 who thus have righteousness reckoned to them 5
22 his faith was "reckoned to him as righteousness. 5
23 the words, "it was reckoned to him 5
24 It will be reckoned to us who believe in him 5
9: 8 of the promise are reckoned as descendants. 5
Gal 3: 6 it was reckoned to him as righteousness. 5
Jas 2:23 and it was reckoned to him as righteousness"; 5
Rev 13:18 let him . . reckon the number of the beast 7
2Es 6: 5 before the present years were reckoned 8
1Mc 2:52 it was reckoned to him as righteousness? 5
2Mc 3: 6 the amount of the funds could not be reckoned 4

can not reckon 1. ἀναρίθμητος
2Mc 3: 6 the amount of the funds could not be reckoned 1

reckon genealogy 1. יחשׂ
1Ch 5: 7 when the genealogy . . was reckoned 1

reckon up 1. συλλογισμός
Wis 4:20 come with dread when their sins are reckoned up 1

reckoning 1. פְּקֻדָּה
1Ch 23:11 they became a father's house in one reckoning 1

reckoning *See also* make.

reckoning come 1. דרשׁ
Gen 42:22 now there comes a reckoning for his blood. 1

recline 1. ἀνάκειμαι 2. ἀνακλίνω 3. κατακλίνω
1Es 4:10 he reclines, he eats and drinks and sleeps 1
Jdt 12:15 that she might recline on them when she ate. 3
3Mc 5:16 to recline opposite him. 2

recognition *See* give.

recognize 1. נכר 2. ἀγνοέω 3. ἀποδέχομαι 4. γινώσκω 5. ἐπιγινώσκω 6. ἔχω 7. λογίζομαι 8. συνοράω 9. φανερός 10. cognosco
Gen 27:23 he did not recognize him, because his hands were 1
37:33 he recognized it, and said, "It is my son's robe; 1
Jdg 18: 3 they recognized the voice of the young Levite; 1
Rut 3:14 but arose before one could recognize another; 1
1Sm 26:17 Saul recognized David's voice, and said 1
1Kg 18: 7 Eli'jah met him; and Obadi'ah recognized him 1
20:41 the king . . recognized him as one of the prophets. 1
Job 2:12 when they saw him from afar, they did not recognize 1
Lam 4: 8 they are not recognized in the streets; 1
Mat 14:35 when the men of that place recognized him 5
Mrk 6:54 immediately the people recognized him 5
Lke 24:16 their eyes were kept from recognizing him. 5
31 their eyes were opened and they recognized him; 5
Act 3:10 recognized him as the one who sat for alms 5
4:13 they recognized that they had been with Jesus. 5
12:14 Recognizing Peter's voice 5
13:27 because they did not recognize him 2
19:34 when they recognized that he was a Jew 5
27:39 when it was day, they did not recognize the land 5
1Co 11:16 we recognize no other practice 6
19 who are genuine among you may be recognized. 9
14:38 If any one does not recognize this 2
38 he is not recognized. 2
2Es 2:16 because I recognize my name in them. 10
Jdt 8:29 the people have recognized your understanding 4
14: 5 let him see and recognize . . 5
Wis 10: 5 Wisdom also . . recognized the righteous man 4
8 not only . . hindered from recognizing the good 4
12:27 they saw and recognized as the true God 5
13: 1 nor did they recognize the craftsman 5
Sir 18:12 sees and recognizes that their end will be evil; 5
23:27 will recognize that nothing is better 5
2Mc 3:28 recognized clearly the sovereign power of God. 5
4: 4 Onias recognized that the rivalry was serious 8
6:12 to recognize that . . 7
7:28 recognize that God did not make them 4
15:28 they recognized Nicanor, lying dead 5
4Mc 2: 9 can recognize that reason rules the emotions. 5
3:20 recognized their commonwealth- 3

recoil 1. הפך
Hos 11: 8 My heart recoils within me, my compassion grows 1

recommendation 1. συστατικός
2Co 3: 1 do we need, as some do, letters of recommendation 1
2 our letter of recommendation •

recompense 1. גְּמוּל 2. גְּמוּלָה 3. גמל 4. פְּעֻלָּה 5. שׁוּב 6. שִׁלּוּם 7. שׁלם 8. שִׁלְמָה 9. תְּמוּרָה 10. ἀνταπόδομα 11. μισθός 12. opus 13. redditio
Deu 32:35 Vengeance is mine, and recompense 7
Rut 2:12 The LORD recompense you for what you have done 7
2Sm 19:36 should the king recompense me with such a reward? 3
22:21 to the cleanness of my hands he recompensed me. 5
25 the LORD has recompensed me according to my 5
Job 15:31 for emptiness will be his recompense. 9
21:19 Let him recompense it to themselves 7
Ps 18:20 the cleanness of my hands he recompensed me. 5
24 Therefore the LORD has recompensed me 5
56: 7 recompense them for their crime; •
91: 8 look . . and see the recompense of the wicked. 8
Isa 34: 8 a year of recompense for the cause of Zion. 6
35: 4 come with vengeance, with the recompense of God. 1
40:10 and his recompense before him. 4
49: 4 is with the LORD, and my recompense with my God. 4
61: 8 I will faithfully give them their recompense 4
62:11 is with him, and his recompense before him. 4
66: 6 of the LORD, rendering recompense to his enemies! 1
Jer 16:18 And I will doubly recompense their iniquity 7
18:20 Is evil a recompense for good? 7
25:14 I will recompense them according to their deeds 7
51:56 the LORD is a God of recompense 2
Ezk 29:20 Egypt as his recompense for which he labored 4
Hos 9: 7 the days of recompense have come; 6
Rev 22:12 Behold, I am coming soon, bringing my recompense 11
2Es 7:35 recompense shall follow 12
15:55 therefore you shall receive your recompense. 13

Sir 17:23 will bring their recompense on their heads. 10
2Mc 8:33 received the proper recompense 11

reconcile 1. רצה 2. ἀποκαταλλάσσω 3. διαλλάσσω 4. καταλλάσσω 5. συναλλάσσω εἰς εἰρήνην
1Sm 29: 4 could this fellow reconcile himself to his lord? 1
Mat 5:24 first be reconciled to your brother 3
Act 7:26 would have reconciled them, saying 5
Rom 5:10 while we were enemies we were reconciled to God 4
10 now that we are reconciled, shall we be saved 4
1Co 7:11 or else be reconciled to her husband 4
2Co 5:18 who through Christ reconciled us to himself 4
19 in Christ God was reconciling the world 4
20 on behalf of Christ, be reconciled to God. 4
Eph 2:16 might reconcile us both to God in one body 2
Col 1:20 through him to reconcile to himself all things 2
22 now reconciled in his body of flesh by his death 2
1Es 4:31 that she may be reconciled to him. 3
2Mc 1: 5 May he hear your prayers and be reconciled to you 4
7:33 again be reconciled with his own servants. 4
8:29 to be wholly reconciled with his servants 4

reconcile easily 1. εὐκατάλλακτος
3Mc 5:13 and again begged him who is easily reconciled 1

become reconciled 1. καταλλαγή
2Mc 5:20 when the great Lord became reconciled. 1

reconciliation 1. διαλλαγή 2. καταλλαγή
Rom 5:11 we have now received our reconciliation. 2
11:15 if their rejection means the reconciliation 2
2Co 5:18 gave us the ministry of reconciliation; 2
19 the message of reconciliation. 2
Sir 22:22 do not worry, for reconciliation is possible 1
27:21 there is reconciliation after abuse 1

reconvene 1. συνίστημι
3Mc 5:36 reconvened the party in the same manner 1

record 1. דְּבָר 2. דִּכְרָן 3. כתב 4. ספר 5. עלה 6. דִּכְרוֹן (A) 7. ἀναγραφή 8. ἀναγράφω 9. ἀπογραφή 10. βιβλίον 11. γραφή 12. γράφω 13. ἱστορέω 14. ἱστορία 15. καταγράφω 16. μνημόσυνον 17. ὑπομνηματίζομαι 18. ὑπομνηματισμός
Deu 28:61 affliction which is not recorded in . . this law 3
1Ch 4:22 (now the records are ancient). 1
24: 6 Shemai'ah . . recorded them in the presence 3
2Ch 20:34 which are recorded in the Book of the Kings 5
Ezr 4:15 search . . book of the records of your fathers. 2
15 You will find in the book of the records and learn 2
6: 2 scroll . . on which this was written: "A record. 6
8:34 weight of everything was recorded. 3
Neh 12:22 there were recorded the heads of fathers' houses; 3
Est 2:23 And it was recorded in the Book of the Chronicles 3
9:20 And Mor'decai recorded these things 3
32 Esther fixed . . and it was recorded in writing. 3
Ps 87: 6 LORD records as he registers the peoples 4
102:18 Let this be recorded for a generation to come 3
Isa 4: 3 one who has been recorded for life in Jerusalem 3
1Es 1:24 The events . . have been recorded in the past 8
33 recorded in the book of the kings of Israel 13
2:21 search may be made in the records of your fathers. 10
6:23 a scroll was found in which this was recorded 17
8:64 the weight . . was recorded at that very time. 12
AEs 16: 7 the more ancient records which we hand on 14
Sir 42: 7 make a record of all that you give out or take in. 11
1Mc 9:22 have not been recorded, for they were very many. 15
14:22 what they said we have recorded 8
23 the people of the Spartans may have a record 16
2Mc 2: 1 One finds in the records that . . 9
13 The same things are reported in the records 7
4:23 to complete the records of essential business. 18

record *See also* make.

recorder 1. זכר 2. γράφω τὰ προσπίπτοντα 3. προσπίπτω
2Sm 8:16 Jehosh'aphat the son of Ahi'lud was recorder; 1
20:24 Jehosh'aphat the son of Ahi'lud was the recorder; 1
1Kg 4: 3 Jehosh'aphat the son of Ahi'lud was recorder; 1
2Kg 18:18 and Jo'ah the son of Asaph, the recorder. 1
37 Eli'akim . . and Shebna.., and Jo'ah..the recorder 1
1Ch 18:15 Jehosh'aphat the son of Ahi'lud was recorder; 1
2Ch 34: 8 he sent . . Jo'ah the son of Jo'ahaz, the recorder 1
Isa 36: 3 and Jo'ah the son of Asaph, the recorder. 1
22 Jo'ah the son of Asaph, the recorder 1
1Es 2:17 Rehum the recorder and Shimshai the scribe 3
25 Rehum the recorder and Beltethmus and Shimshai 2

recount 1. זכר 2. ספר 3. ἐκδιηγέομαι
Jdg 6:13 deeds which our fathers recounted to us, saying 2
Est 5:11 Haman recounted to them the splendor of his 2
Job 33:26 He recounts to men his salvation *
Ps 9:14 that I may recount all thy praises 2
75: 1 call on thy name and recount thy wondrous deeds. ‡
79:13 generation we will recount thy praise. 2
118:17 I shall live, and recount the deeds of the LORD. 2
Isa 63: 7 I will recount the steadfast love of the LORD 1
Sir 18: 5 who can fully recount his mercies? 3
36: 8 let people recount thy mighty deeds. 3
42:17 to recount all his marvelous works 3

recount a proverb 1. παροιμιάζω
4Mc 18:16 He recounted to you Solomon's proverb 1

recount fully 1. συντελέω
Jdt 2: 2 and recounted fully . . the wickedness of the region; 1

recover 1. גדל 2. חזק 3. חיה 4. נצל 5. עצר 6. קנה 7. שׁוב 8. ἀνακομίζω 9. ἀναλέγω 10. γίνομαι 11. ἐκφεύγω 12. καλῶς ἔχω 13. κομίζω 14. σῴζω 15. resumo
Jdg 11:26 why did you not recover them within that time? 4
1Sm 20:41 and wept . . until David recovered himself. 1
30:18 David recovered all . . the Amal'ekites had taken; 4
22 give . . any of the spoil which we have recovered 4
2Kg 1: 2 whether I shall recover from this sickness. 3
8: 8 'Shall I recover from this sickness?' 3
9 saying, 'Shall I recover from this sickness?' 3
10 Go, say to him, 'You shall certainly recover'; 3
14 He told me that you would certainly recover. 3
13:25 Jo'ash defeated him and recovered the cities 7
14:28 how he recovered for Israel Damascus and Hamath 7
16: 6 the king of Edom recovered Elath for Edom 7
20: 1 for you shall die, you shall not recover.' 3
7 take and lay it on the boil, that he may recover. 3
2Ch 13:20 Jerobo'am did not recover his power 5
Isa 11:11 to recover the remnant . . left of his people 6
38: 1 for you shall die, you shall not recover. 3
9 been sick and had recovered from his sickness 3
21 apply it to the boil, that he may recover. 3
39: 1 he heard that he had been sick and had recovered. 2
Mrk 16:18 and they will recover. 12
Joh 11:12 Lord, if he has fallen asleep, he will recover. 14
1Es 3:23 when they recover from the wine 10
2Es 5:22 my soul recovered the spirit of understanding 15
2Mc 2:22 recovered the temple 8
9:22 I have good hope of recovering from my illness 11
10: 1 recovered the temple and the city; 13
3Mc 2:24 After a while he recovered 9
7:22 they all recovered all of their property 13

recovering of sight 1. ἀνάβλεψις
Lke 4:18 to proclaim . . recovering of sight to the blind 1

recovery 1. σωτηρία
2Mc 3:29 deprived of any hope of recovery 1
32 offered sacrifice for the man's recovery. 1

recruit 1. ξενολογέω 2. συνάγω
1Mc 10: 6 Demetrius gave him authority to recruit troops 2
8 had given him authority to recruit troops. 2
21 he recruited troops 2
11:38 recruited from the islands of the nations 1
15: 3 and have recruited a host of mercenary troops 1

red 1. אדם 2. אָדֹם 3. אַדְמוֹנִי 4. חַכְלִילִי 5. סוּף 6. πυρράζω 7. πυρρός 8. φῦκος
Gen 25:25 The first came forth red, all his body like a hairy 3
49:12 his eyes shall be red with wine 4
Num19: 2 to bring you a red heifer without defect 2
33:10 they set out from Elim, and encamped by the Red Sea 5
11 they set out from the Red Sea, and encamped 5
Deu 1:40 wilderness in the direction of the Red Sea.' 5
2: 1 the wilderness in the direction of the Red Sea 5
11: 4 how he made the water of the Red Sea overflow them 5
2Kg 3:22 the Moabites saw the water . . as red as blood. 2
Neh 9: 9 thou didst . . hear their cry at the Red Sea 5
Ps 106: 7 rebelled against the Most High at the Red Sea. 5
9 He rebuked the Red Sea, and it became dry; 5
22 terrible things by the Red Sea. 5
136:13 to him who divided the Red Sea in sunder 5
15 overthrew Pharaoh and his host in the Red Sea 5
Prv 23:31 Do not look at wine when it is red 1
Isa 1:18 though they are red like crimson 1
63: 2 Why is thy apparel red, and thy garments 2
Jer 49:21 their cry shall be heard at the Red Sea. 5
Nah 2: 3 The shield of his mighty men is red 1
Zec 1: 8 behold, a man riding upon a red horse! 2
8 behind him were red, sorrel, and white horses. 2
6: 2 The first chariot had red horses 2
Mat 16: 2 for the sky is red.' 6
3 for the sky is red and threatening 6
Rev 12: 3 great red dragon, with seven heads and ten horns 7
Wis 13:14 and coloring its surface red 8

red *See also* color, paint, pottage.

bright red 1. πυρρός
Rev 6: 4 And out came another horse, bright red; 1

red with weeping 1. חמר
Job 16:16 My face is red with weeping 1

reddish 1. אֲדַמְדָּם
Lev 13:19 there comes . . a reddish-white spot 1
24 flesh . . becomes . . reddish-white or white 1
42 if there is . . a reddish-white diseased spot 1
43 if the diseased swelling is reddish-white 1
49 disease shows . . reddish in the garment 1
14:37 walls of the house with greenish or reddish spots 1

redeem 1. גאל 2. גְּאֻלָּה 3. פדה 4. פְּדוּת 5. ἀγοράζω 6. ἀπολύτρωσις 7. ἐξαγοράζω 8. λυτρόω 9. ποιέω λύτρωσιν
Gen 48:16 the angel who has redeemed me from all evil, 1
Exd 6: 6 I will redeem you with an outstretched arm 1
13:13 firstling of an ass you shall redeem with a lamb 3
13 if you will not redeem it you shall break 3
13 first-born . . among your sons you shall redeem. 3
15 but all the first-born of my sons I redeem.' 3
15:13 led . . the people whom thou hast redeemed 1
21: 8 then he shall let her be redeemed; 3
34:20 an ass you shall redeem with a lamb 3
20 will not redeem it you shall break its neck. 3
20 All the first-born of your sons you shall redeem. 3
Lev 25:25 kin shall come and redeem what his brother has 1
26 If a man has no one to redeem it 1
26 and finds sufficient means to redeem it 2
29 he may redeem it within a whole year 2
30 If it is not redeemed within a full year 1
31 they may be redeemed, and they shall be released 2
32 houses . . the Levites may redeem at any time 2
48 then after he is sold he may be redeemed 2
48 one of his brothers may redeem him 1
49 or his uncle, or his cousin may redeem him 1
49 a near kinsman . . may redeem him 1
49 if he grows rich he may redeem himself 1
54 if he is not redeemed by these means 1
27:13 if he wishes to redeem it, he shall add a fifth 1
15 if he who dedicates it wishes to redeem his house 1
19 if he who dedicates the field wishes to redeem it 1
20 if he does not wish to redeem the field 1
20 it shall not be redeemed any more 1
27 if it is not redeemed, it shall be sold 1
28 no devoted thing . . shall be sold or redeemed 1
31 If a man wishes to redeem any of his tithe 1
33 it . . shall be holy; it shall not be redeemed 1
Num 3:48 by which the excess number of them is redeemed 3
49 over and above those redeemed by the Levites; 3
18:15 the first-born of man you shall redeem 3
15 firstling of unclean beasts you shall redeem. 3
16 (at a month old you shall redeem them) 3
17 firstling of . . you shall not redeem; 3
Deu 7: 8 LORD . . redeemed you from the house of bondage 3
9:26 whom thou hast redeemed through thy greatness 3
13: 5 LORD . . redeemed you out of the house of bondage 3
15:15 LORD your God redeemed you; therefore I command 3
21: 8 thy people Israel, whom thou hast redeemed 3
24:18 the LORD your God redeemed you from there; 3
Rut 4: 4 If you will redeem it, redeem it; 1
4 If you will redeem it, redeem it; 1
4 there is no one besides you to redeem it 1
4 And he said, "I will redeem it. 1
6 I cannot redeem it for myself, lest I impair my own 1
6 Take my right . . for I cannot redeem it. 1
7 custom . . concerning redeeming and exchanging 2
2Sm 4: 9 As the LORD lives, who has redeemed my life 3
7:23 Israel, whom God went to redeem to be his people 3
1Kg 1:29 who has redeemed my soul out of every adversity 3
1Ch 17:21 Israel, whom God went to redeem to be his people 3
21 thy people whom thou didst redeem from Egypt? 3
Neh 1:10 people . . thou hast redeemed by thy great power 3
Job 5:20 In famine he will redeem you from death 3
33:28 has redeemed my soul from going down into the Pit 3
Ps 25:22 Redeem Israel, O God, out of all his troubles. 3
26:11 redeem me, and be gracious to me. 3
31: 5 thou hast redeemed me, O LORD, faithful God. 3
34:22 The LORD redeems the life of his servants; 3
69:18 Draw near to me, redeem me, set me free 1
72:14 From oppression . . he redeems their life; 1
74: 2 thy congregation . . which thou hast redeemed 1
77:15 Thou didst with thy arm redeem thy people 1
78:42 or the day when he redeemed them from the foe; 3
103: 4 who redeems your life from the Pit 1
107: 2 Let the redeemed of the LORD say so 1
2 whom he has redeemed from trouble 1
119:134 Redeem me from man's oppression 3
154 Plead my cause and redeem me; give me life 1
130: 8 he will redeem Israel from all his iniquities. 3
Isa 1:27 Zion shall be redeemed by justice 3
29:22 thus says the LORD, who redeemed Abraham 3
35: 9 but the redeemed shall walk there. 1
43: 1 Fear not, for I have redeemed you; 1
44:22 return to me, for I have redeemed you. 1
23 For the LORD has redeemed Jacob 1
48:20 say, "The LORD has redeemed his servant Jacob! 1
50: 2 Is my hand shortened, that it cannot redeem? 4
51:10 of the sea a way for the redeemed to pass over? 1
52: 3 and you shall be redeemed without money. 1
9 his people, he has redeemed Jerusalem. 1
62:12 called The holy people, The redeemed of the LORD; 1
63: 9 in his love and in his pity he redeemed them; 1
Jer 15:21 and redeem you from the grasp of the ruthless. 3

31:11 has redeemed him from hands too strong for him. 1
Lam 3:58 taken up my cause . . thou has redeemed my life. 1
Hos 7:13 I would redeem them, but they speak lies 3
13:14 Shall I redeem them from Death? 1
Mic 4:10 will redeem you from the hand of your enemies. 1
6: 4 and redeemed you from the house of bondage; 3
Zec 10: 8 I have redeemed them, and they shall be as many 3
Lke 1:68 he has visited and redeemed his people 9
24:21 we had hoped that he was the one to redeem Israel. 8
Gal 3:13 Christ redeemed us from the curse of the law 7
4: 5 to redeem those who were under the law 7
Tit 2:14 who gave himself for us to redeem us 8
Heb 9:15 since a death has occurred which redeems them 6
Rev 14: 3 144,000 who had been redeemed from the earth. 5
4 redeemed from mankind as first fruits for God 5
AEs 13:16 which thou didst redeem for thyself 8
1Mc 4:11 there is one who redeems and saves Israel. 8

redeemer 1. גאל
Job 19:25 For I know that my Redeemer lives 1
Ps 19:14 in thy sight, O LORD, my rock and my redeemer. 1
78:35 was their rock, the Most High God their redeemer. 1
Prv 23:11 for their Redeemer is strong; 1
Isa 41:14 your Redeemer is the Holy One of Israel. 1
43:14 the LORD, your Redeemer, the Holy One of Israel 1
44: 6 says the LORD, the King of Israel and his Redeemer 1
24 your Redeemer, who formed you from the womb 1
47: 4 Our Redeemer–the LORD of hosts is his name 1
48:17 Thus says the LORD, your Redeemer, the Holy One 1
49: 7 Thus says the LORD, the Redeemer of Israel 1
26 and your Redeemer, the Mighty One of Jacob. 1
54: 5 and the Holy One of Israel is your Redeemer 1
8 compassion on you, says the LORD, your Redeemer. 1
59:20 And he will come to Zion as Redeemer 1
60:16 and your Redeemer, the Mighty One of Jacob. 1
63:16 O LORD . . our Redeemer from of old is thy name. 1
Jer 50:34 Their Redeemer is strong; 1

redemption 1. גְּאוּלִּים 2. גְּאֻלָּה 3. פדה 4. פְּדוּת 5. פִּדְיוֹם 6. פִּדְיֹן 7. ἀπολύτρωσις 8. λύτρωσις
Exd 21:30 then he shall give for the redemption of his life 6
Lev 25:24 you shall grant a redemption of the land 2
Num 3:46 for the redemption of the 273 of the first-born 3
49 Moses took the redemption money from those 5
51 gave the redemption money to Aaron and his sons 3
18:16 their redemption price . . you shall fix 3
Ps 111: 9 He sent redemption to his people; 4
130: 7 with him is plenteous redemption. 4
Prv 13: 8 but a poor man has no means of redemption. •
Isa 63: 4 and my year of redemption has come. 1
Jer 32: 7 the right of redemption by purchase is yours. 2
8 the right of possession and redemption is yours; 2
Lke 2:38 all who were looking for the redemption of Jerusalem 8
21:28 because your redemption is drawing near. 7
Rom 3:24 through the redemption which is in Christ Jesus 7
8:23 adoption as sons, the redemption of our bodies. 7
1Co 1:30 sanctification and redemption; 7
Eph 1: 7 In him we have redemption through his blood 7
4:30 you were sealed for the day of redemption. 7
Col 1:14 in whom we have redemption 7
Heb 9:12 thus securing an eternal redemption. 8
redemption *See also* exercise, money, price, right, take.

redness 1. חַכְלִילוּת
Prv 23:29 has wounds without cause? Who has redness of eyes? 1

redound 1. היה 2. εὑρίσκω
Ezk 39:13 it will redound to their honor 1
1Pe 1: 7 faith . . may redound to praise and glory 2

redress 1. מִשְׁפָּט
Ezk 22:29 extorted from the sojourner without redress. 1

reduce 1. ἐλαχύς 2. καταχωρίζω
Sir 31:30 reducing his strength and adding wounds. 1
3Mc 2:29 they shall . . be reduced to their former limited status. 2

reed 1. אֵבֶה 2. אַגְמֹן 3. אָחוּ 4. סוּף 5. קָנֶה 6. ἄχι 7. κάλαμος
Exd 2: 3 placed it among the reeds at the river's brink. 4
5 she saw the basket among the reeds and sent 4
1Kg 14:15 will smite Israel, as a reed is shaken in the water 5
2Kg 18:21 relying now on Egypt, that broken reed of a staff 5
Job 8:11 Can reeds flourish where there is no water? 3
9:26 They go by like skiffs of reed, like an eagle 1
40:21 in the covert of the reeds and in the marsh. 5
Ps 68:30 Rebuke the beasts that dwell among the reeds 5
Isa 9:14 cut off . . head and tail, palm branch and reed 2
19: 6 and dry up, reeds and rushes will rot away. 5
15 nothing . . palm branch or reed, may do. 2
35: 7 the grass shall become reeds and rushes. 5
36: 6 relying on Egypt, that broken reed of a staff 5
42: 3 a bruised reed he will not break 5
Ezk 29: 6 have been a staff of reed to the house of Israel; 5
40: 3 a line of flax and a measuring reed in his hand; 5
5 the length of the measuring reed in the man's hand 5
5 so he measured the thickness of the wall, one reed; 5
5 of the wall, one reed; and the height, one reed. 5
6 the threshold of the gate, one reed deep; 5
7 the side rooms, one reed long, and one reed broad; 5
7 the side rooms, one reed long, and one reed broad; 5
7 vestibule of the gate at the inner end, one reed. 5
41: 8 measured a full reed of six long cubits. 5
42:16 measured the east side with the measuring reed 5
16 500 cubits by the measuring reed. 5
17 500 cubits by the measuring reed. 5
18 500 cubits by the measuring reed. 5
19 500 cubits by the measuring reed. 5
Hos 13:15 Though he may flourish as the reed plant •
Mat 11: 7 A reed shaken by the wind? 7
12:20 he will not break a bruised reed 7
27:29 and put a reed in his right hand 7
30 took the reed and struck him on the head. 7
48 put it on a reed, and gave it to him to drink. 7
Mrk 15:19 they struck his head with a reed, and spat upon him 7
36 filling a sponge full of vinegar, put it on a reed 7
Lke 7:24 A reed shaken by the wind? 7
Sir 40:16 The reeds by any water or river bank 6
3Mc 2:22 as a reed is shaken by the wind 7
reed *See also* grass.

reel 1. געשׁ 2. חגג 3. רַעַל 4. שׁגה 5. תעה
2Sm 22: 8 Then the earth reeled and rocked; 1
Ps 18: 7 Then the earth reeled and rocked; 1
107:27 they reeled and staggered like drunken men 2
Isa 21: 4 My mind reels, horror has appalled me; 5
28: 7 These also reel with wine and stagger 4
7 priest and the prophet reel with strong drink 4
Zec 12: 2 Jerusalem a cup of reeling to all the peoples 3

make reel 1. רעל
Ps 60: 3 thou hast given us wine to drink that made us reel. 1

refer 1. εἰς 2. ἐπί 3. ὅς 4. προσαναφέρω
Gal 3:16 referring to many; but, referring to one 2
16 referring to many; but, referring to one 2
Eph 5:32 am saying that it refers to Christ and the church; 1
Col 2:22 referring to things which all perish 3
2Mc 11:36 which he decided are to be referred to the king 4

refine 1. זקק 2. צרף 3. πυρόω
1Ch 28:18 for the altar of incense made of refined gold 1
29: 4 and 7,000 talents of refined silver 1
Job 28: 1 a place for gold which they refine. 1
Ps 12: 6 silver refined in a furnace on the ground 2
Isa 25: 6 feast . . of wine on the lees well refined. 1
48:10 Behold, I have refined you, but not like silver; 2
Jer 6:29 in vain the refining goes on 2
9: 7 Behold, I will refine them and test them 2
Dan 11:35 refine and to cleanse them and to make them white 2
12:10 Many shall . . be refined 2
Zec 13: 9 and refine them as one refines silver 2
9 and refine them as one refines silver 2
Mal 3: 3 he will purify the sons of Levi and refine them 1
Rev 1:15 like burnished bronze, refined as in a furnace 3
3:18 I counsel you to buy from me gold refined by fire 3

woman of great refinement 1. τρυφερός
Sus 1:31 Now Susanna was a woman of great refinement 1

refiner 1. צרף
Mal 3: 2 he is like a refiner's fire and like fullers' soap 1
3 he will sit as a refiner and purifier of silver 1

reflect 1. בקר 2. ἀπαύγασμα 3. διανοέω 4. ἐννοέω 5. λογίζομαι
Prv 20:25 snare . . to reflect only after making his vows. 1
27:19 so the mind of man reflects the man. •
Heb 1: 3 He reflects the glory of God 2
Sir 6:37 Reflect on the statutes of the Lord 3
14:21 He who reflects in his mind on her ways 3
16:20 no mind will reflect on this 3
3Mc 4: 4 some . . reflected upon the uncertainty of life 5
4Mc 1:24 a man will see if he reflects on this experience 4

reflect upon 1. διανοέω
Sir 3:22 Reflect upon what has been assigned to you 1

reflection 1. ἀπαύγασμα 2. sermo
2Es 10: 5 the reflections with which I was still engaged 2
Wis 7:26 For she is a reflection of eternal light 1

reform 1. διόρθωμα
Act 24: 2 reforms are introduced on behalf of this nation 1

reformation 1. διόρθωσις
Heb 9:10 imposed until the time of reformation. 1

refractory 1. ἀντιλέγω
Tit 2: 9 they are not to be refractory 1

refrain 1. חדל 2. לְבִלְתִּי 3. עצר 4. רחק 5. רפה 6. ἀπέχω 7. ἀφίστημι 8. κωλύω 9. μή 10. οὐκέτι 11. τηρέω 12. φείδομαι
Exd 23: 5 you shall refrain from leaving him with it 1
Num 9:13 yet refrains from keeping the passover 1
Deu 23:22 if you refrain from vowing, it . . no sin in you. 1
Rut 1:13 Would you therefore refrain from marrying? 2
Job 29: 9 the princes refrained from talking 3
Ps 37: 8 Refrain from anger, and forsake wrath! 5
Ecc 3: 5 to embrace, and a time to refrain from embracing; 4
Jer 41: 8 he refrained and did not kill them 1
Dan 11: 8 for some years he shall refrain from attacking †
1Co 9: 6 have no right to refrain from working for a living? 9
2Co 1:23 it was to spare you that I refrained from coming 10
11: 9 So I refrained and will refrain from burdening 11
9 So I refrained and will refrain from burdening 11
12: 6 I refrain from it 12
Tob 4:21 fear God and refrain from every sin 7
Sir 4:23 Do not refrain from speaking at the crucial time 8
28: 8 Refrain from strife, and you will lessen sins 6

refrain from marriage 1. μὴ γαμίζω
1Co 7:38 he who refrains from marriage will do better. 1

refresh 1. דשׁן 2. נפשׁ 3. סעד 4. רוח 5. רפד 6. שׁוב 7. ἀνάπαυσις 8. ἀναπαύω 9. ἀνάψυξις 10. ἀναψύχω 11. ἱλαρόω 12. συναναπαύομαι 13. refrigero
Gen 18: 5 that you may refresh yourselves 3
Exd 23:12 your bondmaid, and the alien, may be refreshed. 2
31:17 on the seventh day he rested, and was refreshed.' 2
1Sm 16:23 so Saul was refreshed, and was well 4
2Sm 16:14 arrived . . and there he refreshed himself. 2
1Kg 13: 7 Come home with me, and refresh yourself 3
Prv 15:30 good news refreshes the bones. 1
25:13 faithful messenger . . refreshes the spirit 6
Sng 2: 5 Sustain me with raisins, refresh me with apples; 5
Act 3:19 times of refreshing may come 9
Rom 15:32 come . . and be refreshed in your company. 12
1Co 16:18 for they refreshed my spirit as well as yours. 8
2Ti 1:16 he often refreshed me 10
Phm 1: 7 the saints have been refreshed through you. 8
20 Refresh my heart in Christ. 8
2Es 11:46 whole earth . . may be refreshed and relieved 13
Sir 3: 6 whoever obeys the Lord will refresh his mother; 7
43:22 when the dew appears, it refreshes from the heat. 11

refreshment 1. שִׁקּוּי 2. ἀναψύχω
Prv 3: 8 It will be . . refreshment to your bones. 1
2Mc 4:46 taking the king aside . . as if for refreshment 2

refuge 1. מַחְסֶה 2. מָנוֹס 3. מְנוּס 4. מָעוֹז 5. מָעוֹז 6. סֵתֶר 7. מִקְלָט 8. מִשְׂגָּב 9. מָעוֹן
Num 35: 6 you give . . shall be the six cities of refuge 7
11 you shall select cities to be cities of refuge 7
12 cities shall be for you a refuge from the avenger 7
13 cities . . shall by your six cities of refuge. 7
14 shall give . . cities . ., to be cities of refuge. 7
15 cities . . for refuge for the people of Israel 7
25 congregation . . restore him to his city of refuge 7
26 go beyond the bounds of his city of refuge 7
27 outside the bounds of his city of refuge 7
28 For the man must remain in his city of refuge 7
32 for him who has fled to his city of refuge 7
Jos 20: 2 Appoint the cities of refuge, of which I spoke 7
3 shall be . . a refuge from the avenger of blood. 7
21:13 gave Hebron, the city of refuge for the slayer 7
21 given Shechem, the city of refuge for the slayer 7
27 Golan . . the city of refuge for the slayer 7
32 Kedesh . . the city of refuge for the slayer 7
38 Ramoth . . the city of refuge for the slayer 7
2Sm 22: 3 my God . . my stronghold and my refuge, my savior; 3
33 God is my strong refuge, and has made my way safe. 5
1Ch 6:57 they gave the cities of refuge 7
67 cities of refuge: Shechem . . Gezer 7
Ps 14: 6 the plans of the poor, but the LORD is his refuge. 1
28: 8 he is the saving refuge of his anointed. 4
31: 2 Be thou a rock of refuge for me, a strong fortress 4
4 for thou art my refuge. 5
37:39 he is their refuge in the time of trouble. 5
43: 2 For thou art the God in whom I take refuge; 5
46: 1 God is our refuge and strength 1
7 the God of Jacob is our refuge. Selah 8
11 the God of Jacob is our refuge. Selah 8
52: 7 See the man who would not make God his refuge 5
59:16 a fortress and a refuge in the day of my distress. 2
61: 3 thou art my refuge, a strong tower 1
62: 7 my mighty rock, my refuge is God. 1
8 God is a refuge for us. Selah 1
71: 3 Be thou to me a rock of refuge, a strong fortress 6
7 but thou art my strong refuge. 1
73:28 I have made the Lord GOD my refuge 1
91: 2 My refuge and my fortress; my God, in whom I trust. 1
9 Because you have made the LORD your refuge 1
94:22 my God the rock of my refuge. 1
104:18 rocks are a refuge for the badgers. 1
142: 4 no refuge remains to me, no man cares for me. 2
5 I say, Thou art my refuge, my portion in the land 1
Prv 14:26 his children will have a refuge. 1
Isa 4: 6 for a refuge and a shelter from the storm 1
16: 4 be a refuge to them from the destroyer. 9
17:10 and have not remembered the Rock of your refuge; 4
28:15 for we have made lies our refuge 1
17 hail will sweep away the refuge of lies 1

Jer 16:19 my stronghold, my refuge in the day of trouble 3
17:17 thou art my refuge in the day of evil. 1
25:35 No refuge will remain for the shepherds 2
Jol 3:16 But the LORD is a refuge to his people 1
Nah 3:11 you will seek a refuge from the enemy. 4

refuge *See also* find, flee, place, seek, take.

refund 1. שׁוּב
Lev 25:51 according to them he shall refund out 1
52 he shall refund the money for his redemption 1

refuse 1. חדל 2. לְבִלְתִּי 3. מאן 4. מאס 5. מנע 6. שׁוּב פָּנִים 7. ἀμύνω 8. ἀντερῶ 9. ἀντιλέγω 10. ἀπειθέω 11. ἀποστερέω 12. ἀποστρέφω 13. ἀρνέομαι 14. κατανωτίζομαι 15. μή 16. μηδέ 17. μὴ ἐθέλω 18. μὴ ὑπομένω 19. οὐ 20. οὐ βούλομαι 21. οὐ δέχομαι 22. οὐκ ἀφίημι 23. οὐκ ἐθέλω 24. οὔτε 25. παραιτέομαι 26. respuo
Gen 37:35 to comfort him; but he refused to be comforted 3
39: 8 he refused and said to his master's wife 3
48:19 his father refused, and said, "I know, my son, 3
Exd 4:23 if you refuse to let him go, behold, I will slay 3
7:14 Pharaoh . . refuses to let the people go. 3
8: 2 if you refuse to let them go, behold, I will plague 3
9: 2 For if you refuse to let them go and still hold 3
10: 3 says the LORD . . 'How long will you refuse 3
4 For if you refuse to let my people go, behold 3
16:28 How long do you refuse to keep my commandments 3
22:17 If her father utterly refuses to give her to him 3
Num20:21 Thus Edom refused to give Israel passage 3
22:13 for the LORD has refused to let me go with you. 3
14 to Balak, and said, "Balaam refuses to come with us. 3
Deu 25: 7 My husband's brother refuses to perpetuate 3
1Sm 8:19 But the people refused to listen to . . Samuel; 3
28:23 He refused, and said, "I will not eat. 3
2Sm 2:23 But he refused to turn aside; 3
13: 9 emptied it out before him, but he refused to eat. 3
1Kg 2:16 I have one request to make of you; do not refuse me. 6
17 ask King Solomon-he will not refuse you- 6
20 I have one small request . . do not refuse me. 6
20 Make your request . . for I will not refuse you. 6
20: 7 he sent to me for . . and I did not refuse him. 5
35 Strike me . . " But the man refused to strike him. 3
21:15 the vineyard . . which he refused to give you 3
2Kg 5:16 And he urged him to take it, but he refused. 3
Neh 9:17 refused to obey, and were not mindful 3
Est 1:12 Vashti refused to come at the king's command 3
Job 6: 7 My appetite refuses to touch them; 3
Ps 77: 2 my soul refuses to be comforted. 3
78:10 but refused to walk according to his law. 3
Prv 1:24 Because I have called and you refused to listen 3
21: 7 because they refuse to do what is just. 3
25 kills him for his hands refuse to labor. 3
Isa 1:20 if you refuse and rebel, you shall be devoured 3
7:15 knows how to refuse the evil and choose the good. 4
16 For before the child knows how to refuse the evil 4
8: 6 this people have refused the waters of Shilo'ah 4
Jer 3: 3 you have a harlot's brow, you refuse to be ashamed. 3
5: 3 but they refused to take correction. 3
3 they have refused to repent. 3
8: 5 They hold fast to deceit, they refuse to return. 3
9: 6 they refuse to know me, says the LORD. 3
11:10 their forefathers, who refused to hear my words; 3
13:10 This evil people, who refuse to hear my words 3
15:18 my wound incurable, refusing to be healed? 3
16:12 his stubborn evil will, refusing to listen to me; 2
19:15 stiffened their neck, refusing to hear my words. 2
25:28 if they refuse to accept the cup from your hand 3
31:15 she refuses to be comforted for her children 3
38:21 But if you refuse to surrender, this is the vision 3
50:33 have held them fast, they refuse to let them go. 3
Ezk 2: 5 whether they hear or refuse to hear 1
7 speak . . whether they hear or refuse to hear; 1
3:11 whether they hear or refuse to hear. 1
27 and he that will refuse to hear, let him refuse; 1
27 and he that will refuse to hear, let him refuse; 1
Dan 9:11 turned aside, refusing to obey thy voice. 2
Hos 11: 5 because they have refused to return to me. 3
Zec 7:11 But they refused to hearken 3
Mat 2:18 Rachel weeping . . she refused to be consoled 23
5:42 Give to him who begs from you, and do not refuse him 12
18:30 He refused and went and put him in prison 23
Mrk 5:19 he refused, and said to him 22
6:11 they refuse to hear you 16
Lke 15:28 he was angry and refused to go in 23
18: 4 For a while he refused 23
Joh 5:40 yet you refuse to come to me 23
Act 7:35 This Moses whom they refused, saying 13
39 Our fathers refused to obey him 23
18:15 I refuse to be a judge of these things. 20
1Co 7: 5 Do not refuse one another 11
2Co 4: 2 we refuse to practice cunning 15
2Th 2:10 because they refused to love the truth 21
3:14 If any one refuses to obey what we say 19
1Ti 5:11 But refuse to enrol younger widows 25
Heb 11:24 refused to be called the son of Pharaoh's daughter 13
35 Some were tortured, refusing to accept release 19
12:25 See that you do not refuse him who is speaking. 25
25 if they did not escape when they refused him 25
3Jn 1:10 he refuses himself to welcome the brethren 24
Rev 2:21 but she refuses to repent of her immorality. 23
11: 9 and refuse to let them be placed in a tomb 19
1Es 2:19 they will not only refuse to pay tribute 18
2Es 2:33 and refused the Lord's commandment. 26
Tob 4: 5 refuse to sin 17
13 by refusing to take a wife for yourself *
Jdt 1:11 refused to join him in the war 19
2:11 if they refuse, your eye shall not spare 10
5: 4 why have they . . refused to come out and meet me? 14
12:14 Judith said, "Who am I, to refuse my lord? 8
AEs 13:12 I . . refused to bow down to this proud Haman. 15
Wis 12:27 him whom they had before refused to know. 13
16:16 the ungodly, refusing to know thee 13
17:10 refusing to look even at the air 13
19:14 Others had refused to receive strangers 19
Sir 7:13 Refuse to utter any lie 17
29: 7 many have refused to lend 12
Sus 1:21 If you refuse, we will testify against you *
1Mc 2:40 refuse to fight with the Gentiles for our lives 15
5:48 they refused to open to him. 20
15:27 But he refused to receive them 20
2Mc 6:20 who have the courage to refuse things 7
4Mc 8: 2 if any were to refuse 9
11: 2 I will not refuse, tyrant 25

refuse (2) 1. מָאוֹס 2. מאס 3. מַפָּל 4. סוּחָה 5. κόπριον 6. περικάθαρμα 7. σκύβαλον
Isa 5:25 their corpses were as refuse in . . the streets. 4
Jer 6:30 Refuse silver they are called 2
Lam 3:45 Thou hast made us offscouring and refuse 1
Ams 8: 6 buy the poor . . and sell the refuse of the wheat? 3
1Co 4:13 we have become . . as the refuse of the world 6
Php 3: 8 loss of all things, and count them as refuse 7
Sir 27: 4 When a sieve is shaken, the refuse remains 5

stubbornly refuse 1. קשׁה
Exd 13:15 For when Pharaoh stubbornly refused to let us go 1

refuse to listen 1. παρακούω
Mat 18:17 If he refuses to listen to them 1
17 if he refuses to listen even to the church 1

regain 1. נשׂא 2. ἀναβλέπω
Prv 2:19 nor do they regain the paths of life. 1
Tob 14: 2 after eight years he regained it 2

regain power 1. iterum constituo
2Es 12:18 but shall regain its former power. 1

regain sight 1. ἀναβλέπω
Act 9:12 so that he might regain his sight. 1
17 that you may regain your sight 1
18 and he regained his sight 1

regal 1. מְלוּכָה
Ezk 16:13 You grew . . beautiful, and came to regal estate. 1

regal *See also* estate.

regard 1. בְּ 2. בין 3. דָּבָר 4. חשׁב 5. ידע 6. לְ 7. מִן 8. נבט 9. נכר 10. נשׂא פָּנִים 11. נתן לִפְנֵי 12. עַל 13. עַל דִּבְרָה 14. פנה 15. פָּנִים 16. פקד 17. ראה 18. שׂוּם 19. שׂוּם לֵב 20. שׂכל 21. שׁוּר 22. שׁמר 23. שׁעה 24. צַד (A) 25. αἰδέομαι 26. βλέπω 27. γινώσκω 28. δοκέω 29. δόξα 30. ἐντρέπω 31. ἐπιβλέπω 32. ἡγέομαι 33. κατά 34. λογίζομαι 35. μέρος 36. νομίζω 37. οἶδα 38. περί 39. στοχάζομαι 40. τίθημι 41. ὑπέρ 42. φέρω 43. φροντίζω 44. adtendo 45. in 46. respicio
Gen 4: 4 And the LORD had regard for Abel and his offering 23
5 for Cain and his offering he had no regard. 23
31:15 Are we not regarded by him as foreigners? 4
41:40 only as regards the throne will I be greater *
Exd 9:21 he who did not regard the word of the LORD 19
Lev 26: 9 I will have regard for you and make you fruitful 14
Num 4:26 do all that needs to be done with regard to them. *
Deu 9:27 do not regard the stubbornness of this people 14
28:50 not regard the person of the old or show favor 10
33: 9 of his father and mother, 'I regard them not'; 17
Jos 7: 1 broke faith in regard to the devoted things; 1
Jdg 15: 3 shall be blameless in regard to the Philistines 7
1Sm 1:16 Do not regard your maidservant as a base woman 11
2:12 they had no regard for the LORD. 5
25:25 Let not my lord regard this ill-natured fellow 19
1Kg 8:28 Yet have regard to the prayer of thy servant 14
2Kg 3:14 were it not that I have regard for Jehosh'aphat 15
22:18 Regarding the words which you have heard *
2Ch 5:11 without regard to their divisions; 22
6:19 Yet have regard to the prayer of thy servant 14
34:26 Thus says the LORD . . Regarding the words *
Ezr 6: 8 I make a decree regarding what you shall do *
Est 8: 8 may write as you please with regard to the Jews 12
9:31 they had laid down . . with regard to their fasts 3
Job 4:20 they perish for ever without any regarding it. 18
9:21 I regard not myself; I loathe my life. 5
34:19 nor regards the rich more than the poor 9
27 had no regard for any of his ways 20
35:13 an empty cry, nor does the Almighty regard it. 21
37:24 men fear him; he does not regard any who are wise 17
Ps 17: 4 With regard to the works of men, by the word 6
28: 5 they do not regard the works of the LORD 2
74:20 Have regard for thy covenant; 8
80:14 from heaven, and see; have regard for this vine 16
95:10 err in heart, and they do not regard my ways. 5
102:17 he will regard the prayer of the destitute 14
106:44 regarded their distress, when he heard their cry. 17
119:117 that I may . . have regard for thy statutes 23
138: 6 For though the LORD is high, he regards the lowly; 17
144: 3 O LORD, what is man that thou dost regard him 5
Prv 12:10 righteous man has regard for the life 5
Ecc 3:18 I said . . with regard to the sons of men that God is 13
11: 4 and he who regards the clouds will not reap. 17
Isa 5:12 they do not regard the deeds of the LORD 8
13:17 Medes . . who have no regard for silver 4
17: 7 In that day men will regard their Maker 23
8 they will not have regard for the altars 23
22:11 or have regard for him who planned it long ago. 17
29:16 Shall the potter be regarded as the clay; 4
17 the fruitful field shall be regarded as a forest? 4
33: 8 are despised, there is no regard for man. 4
Jer 24: 5 I will regard as good the exiles from Judah 9
Lam 4:16 has scattered them, he will regard them no more; 8
Dan 6: 4 against Daniel with regard to the kingdom; 24
Hos 8:12 they would be regarded as a strange thing. 4
Mal 2:13 because he no longer regards the offering 14
Mat 22:16 for you do not regard the position of men. 26
Mrk 12:14 for you do not regard the position of men 26
Lke 1:48 he has regarded the low estate of his handmaiden. 31
18: 2 a judge who neither feared God nor regarded man; 30
4 Though I neither fear God nor regard man 30
22:24 which of them was to be regarded as the greatest. 28
Act 25:20 be tried there regarding them. 38
28:22 with regard to this sect 38
Rom 2:26 uncircumcision be regarded as circumcision? 34
6:20 you were free in regard to righteousness. *
8:36 we are regarded as sheep to be slaughtered. 34
11:28 As regards the gospel they are enemies of God 33
28 but as regards election they are beloved 33
1Co 4: 1 This is how one should regard us 34
2Co 5:16 we regard no one from a human point of view 37
16 even though we once regarded Christ 27
16 we regard him thus no longer. 27
Col 2:16 with regard to a festival or a new moon 35
1Ti 6: 1 regard their masters as worthy of all honor 32
21 some have missed the mark as regards the faith. 38
1Pe 5:12 Silva'nus, a faithful brother as I regard him 34
2Es 4: 2 Your understanding . . regarding this world 45
8:27 Regard not the endeavors of those who act 44
29 regard those who have gloriously taught thy law. 46
Wis 2:10 nor regard the gray hairs of the aged. 30
9: 6 he will be regarded as nothing. 34
14:20 the multitude . . now regarded as an object of worship 34
Sir 29: 4 Many persons regard a loan as a windfall 36
6 will regard that as a windfall 34
41:12 Have regard for your name 43
Bar 4:13 They had no regard for his statutes 27
1Mc 11:27 to be regarded as one of his chief friends. 32
2Mc 3:32 some foul play . . with regard to Heliodorus 38
4:34 with no regard for justice 25
36 with regard to the unreasonable murder of Onias 41
6:11 in view of their regard for that most holy day. 29
7:12 for he regarded his sufferings as nothing. 40
8:35 he regarded as of the least account 36
11:15 Maccabeus, having regard for the common good 43
35 With regard to what Lysias . . has granted you 41
14: 8 I have regard also for my fellow citizens 39
3Mc 3:19 and are unwilling to regard any action as sincere. 42
5:30 in regard to these matters 38
4Mc 3:15 what was regarded as equivalent to blood. 34

regard *See also* pay.

regard as holy 1. קדשׁ
Isa 8:13 the LORD of hosts, him you shall regard as holy; 1

regard lightly 1. ὀλιγωρέω
Heb 12: 5 do not regard lightly the discipline of the Lord 1

regard with favor 1. דשׁן
Gen 31: 2 Laban did not regard him with favor †
5 your father does not regard me with favor †
Ps 20: 3 and regard with favor your burnt sacrifices! 1

regeneration 1. παλιγγενεσία
Tit 3: 5 by the washing of regeneration 1

region 1. גְּבוּל 2. גְּלִילָה 3. חֶבֶל 4. פָּנִים 5. שָׂדֶה 6. γῆ 7. ἔξωθεν 8. κλίμα 9. ὅριον 10. περίχωρος 11. τόπος 12. χώρα 13. regio
Num21:20 Bamoth to the valley lying in the region of Moab 5
Deu 3: 4 we took . . 60 cities, the whole region of Argob 3
13 kingdom of Og, that is, all the region of Argob 3
14 Ja'ir the Manas'site took all the region of Argob 3
Jos 13: 2 yet remains: all the regions of the Philistines 2

11 the region of the Gesh'urites and Ma-ac'athites 1
30 Their region extended from Mahana'im 1
24:15 the gods . . served in the region beyond the River •
Jdg 5: 4 from Se'ir . . march from the region of Edom 5
1Kg 4:13 he had the region of Argob, which is in Bashan 3
24 all the region west of the Euphra'tes •
1Ch 5:10 tents throughout all the region east of Gilead. 4
Neh 12:29 from the region of Geba and Az'maveth; 5
Ezk 47: 8 This water flows toward the eastern region 2
Jol 3: 4 O Tyre and Sidon, and all the regions of Philistia? 2
Mat 2:16 in all that region who were two years old or under 9
3: 5 Judea and all the region about the Jordan 10
4:16 who sat in the region and shadow of death light 12
14:35 they sent round to all that region 10
15:22 behold, a Canaanite woman from that region 9
39 and went to the region of Magadan. 9
19: 1 entered the region of Judea beyond the Jordan; 9
Mrk 7:24 he arose and went away to the region of Tyre 9
31 Then he returned from the region of Tyre 9
31 through the region of the Decap'olis. 9
10: 1 went to the region of Judea and beyond the Jordan 9
Lke 2: 8 in that region there were shepherds 12
3: 1 Philip tetrarch of the region of Iturae'a •
Act 8: 1 scattered throughout the region of Judea 12
13:49 spread throughout all the region. 12
16: 6 they went through the region of Phry'gia and Galatia 12
18:23 the region of Galatia and Phryg'ia 12
Rom 15:23 I no longer have any room for work in these regions 8
2Co 11:10 shall not be silenced in the regions of Acha'ia. 8
Gal 1:21 I went into the regions of Syria and Cili'cia. 8
2Es 5:24 thou hast chosen for thyself one region ‡
13: 7 I tried to see the region or place 13
41 and go to a more distant region 13
45 Through that region there was a long way to go 13
Tob 5: 5 Are you acquainted with that region? 11
Jdt 1:11 all who lived in the whole region 6
12 very angry with this whole region 6
2: 1 carrying out his revenge on the whole region 6
2 all the wickedness of the region; 6
11 throughout your whole region. 6
Bar 2:23 to cease . . from the region about Jerusalem 7
1Mc 3:31 collect the revenues from those regions 12
41 When the traders of the region heard 12
8: 4 how they had gained control of the whole region 11
11:14 because the people of that region were in revolt. 11
34 with all the region bordering them •
12:25 met them in the region of Hamath 12
32 and marched through all that region. 12
2Mc 4:36 the king returned from the region of Cilicia 11
9: 1 retreated . . from the region of Persia. 11
21 On my way back from the region of Persia 11
10:14 When Gorgias became governor of the region 11
12:18 They did not find Timothy in that region 11
18 departed from the region 11
15: 1 Judas and his men were in the region of Samaria 11
3Mc 1: 1 the regions which he had controlled 11
1 and marched out to the region near Raphia 11

region about 1. גְּלִילָה 2. *περίχωρος*
Jos 22:10 And when they came to the region about the Jordan 1
11 the land of Canaan, in the region about the Jordan 1
Lke 3: 3 he went into all the region about the Jordan 2

dark region 1. מַחֲשָׁךְ
Ps 88: 6 depths of the Pit, in the regions dark and deep. 1

deep region 1. מְצוֹלָה
Ps 88: 6 depths of the Pit, in the regions dark and deep. 1

surrounding region 1. *περίχωρος*
Mrk 1:28 fame spread . . throughout all the surrounding region 1
Lke 4:37 went out into every place in the surrounding region. 1

register 1. יחשׂ 2. ילד 3. כתב 4. כְּתָב 5. פקד
6. *ἀπογράφω* 7. *καταλοχισμός*
Num 1:18 congregation . . who registered themselves 2
11:26 they were among those registered 3
1Ch 4:41 These, registered by name 3
23:24 as they were registered according to the number 5
Ezr 8: 3 Zechari'ah, with whom were registered 150 men. 1
Ps 87: 6 LORD records as he registers the peoples 3
Ezk 13: 9 enrolled in the register of the house of Israel 4
1Es 5:38 were not found registered •
39 was sought in the register and was not found 7
3Mc 2:29 those who are registered are also to be branded 6
4:14 to be registered individually 6
6:34 had joyfully registered them 6

registration 1. כְּתָב 2. *ἀπογραφή* 3. *ἀπογράφω*
Ezr 2:62 These sought their registration among those 1
Neh 7:64 These sought their registration among those 1
3Mc 2:32 to save themselves from the registration. 3
4:15 The registration of these people 2
7:22 in accordance with the registration 2
registration *See also* carry.

registration involving a poll tax 1. *λαογραφία*
3Mc 2:28 a registration involving poll tax 1

regret 1. חֶמְדָּה 2. *μεταμέλομαι* 3. *μετάμελος*
2Ch 21:20 he departed with no one's regret. 1
2Co 7: 8 I do not regret it (though I did regret it) 2
8 I do not regret it (though I did regret it) 2
Sir 32:19 when you have acted, do not regret it. 3
1Mc 11:10 For I now regret that I gave him my daughter 2
regret *See also* bring.

regular 1. תָּמִיד 2. *ἀεί* 3. *ἔννομος*
Lev 6:20 fine flour as a regular cereal offering 1
15:19 blood which is her regular discharge •
2Kg 25:30 a regular allowance was given him by the king 1
Est 2:12 was the regular period of their beautifying •
Jer 52:34 a regular allowance was given him by the king 1
Act 19:39 it shall be settled in the regular assembly. 3
3Mc 3:21 participants in our regular religious rites. 2

regularly 1. תָּמִיד 2. *διόλου* 3. *ἐνδελεχῶς*
2Kg 25:29 he dined regularly at the king's table; 1
Jer 52:33 he dined regularly at the king's table; 1
1Es 6:30 regularly every year, without quibbling 3
Bel 1:13 through which they used to go in regularly 2
regularly *See also* pay.

regulation 1. דָּת 2. *δικαίωμα*
Est 2:12 being . . under the regulations for the women 1
Heb 9: 1 the first covenant had regulations for worship 2
10 regulations for the body 2
regulation *See also* submit.

reign 1. ישׁב 2. מלך 3. מַלְכוּת 4. מַמְלָכָה 5. מַמְלְכוּת
6. מַלְכוּת (A) 7. *ἄρχω* 8. *βασιλεία* 9. *βασιλεύς*
10. *βασιλεύω* 11. *ἡγεμονία* 12. *κατά*
13. *συμβασιλεύω* 14. regno 15. regnum
Gen 36:31 These are the kings who reigned in the land 2
31 before any king reigned over the Israelites. 2
32 Bela the son of Be'or reigned in Edom 2
33 son of Zerah of Bozrah reigned in his stead. 2
34 Husham . . reigned in his stead. 2
35 in the country of Moab, reigned in his stead 2
36 Samlah of Masre'kah reigned in his stead. 2
37 Reho'both on the Euphra'tes reigned in his stead 2
38 the son of Achbor reigned in his stead. 2
39 son of Achbor died, and Hadar reigned in his stead 2
37: 8 Are you indeed to reign over us? 2
Exd 15:18 The LORD will reign for ever and ever. 2
Jos 13:10 Sihon . . of the Amorites, who reigned in Heshbon 2
12 of Og . . who reigned in Ash'taroth and in Ed're-i 2
21 Sihon . . of the Amorites, who reigned in Heshbon 2
Jdg 4: 2 hand of Jabin king of Canaan, who reigned in Hazor; 2
9: 8 and they said to the olive tree, 'Reign over us.' 2
10 said to the fig tree, 'Come you, and reign over us.' 2
12 trees said to the vine, 'Come you, and reign over us.' 2
14 said to the bramble, 'Come you, and reign over us.' 2
1Sm 8: 9 the ways of the king who shall reign over them. 2
11 the ways of the king who will reign over you 2
10: 1 And you shall reign over the people of the LORD 7
11:12 Who is it that said, 'Shall Saul reign over us?' 2
12:12 you said to me, 'No, but a king shall reign over us,' 2
14 the king who reigns over you will follow the LORD 2
13: 1 Saul was . . years old when he began to reign; 2
1 and he reigned . . and two years over Israel. 2
2Sm 2:10 Ish-bo'shet . . was 40 years old when he began to reign 2
10 Ish-bo'sheth . . and he reigned two years. 2
3:21 you may reign over all that your heart desires. 2
5: 4 David was 30 years old when he began to reign 2
4 David was 30 years old . . and he reigned 40 years. 2
5 he reigned over Judah seven years and six months 2
5 he reigned over all Israel and Judah 2
8:15 David reigned over all Israel; 2
10: 1 and Hanun his son reigned in his stead. 2
16: 8 the house of Saul, in whose place you have reigned; 2
1Kg 1:13 Solomon . . shall reign after me, and he shall sit 2
17 Solomon . . shall reign after me, and he shall sit 2
24 Adoni'jah shall reign after me, and he shall sit 2
30 Solomon . . shall reign after me, and he shall sit 2
2:11 time that David reigned over Israel was 40 years; 2
11 he reigned seven years in Hebron 2
15 and that all Israel fully expected me to reign; 2
6: 1 in the fourth year of Solomon's reign over Israel 2
11:25 and he abhorred Israel, and reigned over Syria. 2
37 you shall reign over all that your soul desires 2
42 Solomon reigned in Jerusalem over all Israel 2
43 and Rehobo'am his son reigned in his stead. 2
12:17 But Rehobo'am reigned over the people of Israel 2
14:19 acts of Jerobo'am, how he warred and how he reigned 2
20 the time that Jerobo'am reigned was 22 years; 2
20 and Nadab his son reigned in his stead. 2
21 Rehobo'am the son of Solomon reigned in Judah. 2
21 Rehobo'am was 41 years old when he began to reign 2
21 and he reigned seventeen years in Jerusalem 2
31 And Abi'jam his son reigned in his stead. 2
15: 1 Abi'jam began to reign over Judah. 2
2 He reigned for three years in Jerusalem. 2
8 And Asa his son reigned in his stead. 2
9 Asa began to reign over Judah 2
10 he reigned 41 years in Jerusalem. 2
24 and Jehosh'aphat his son reigned in his stead. 2
25 Nadab . . began to reign over Israel 2
25 Nadab . . and he reigned over Israel two years. 2
28 Ba'asha killed him . . and reigned in his stead. 2
33 Ba'asha . . began to reign over all Israel 2
33 Ba'asha . . reigned 24 years. •
16: 6 and Elah his son reigned in his stead. 2
8 Elah . . began to reign over Israel in Tirzah 2
8 Elah . . began to reign . . and reigned two years. 2
10 and killed him . . and reigned in his stead. 2
11 When he began to reign . . he killed all the house 2
15 Zimri reigned seven days in Tirzah. 2
23 Omri began to reign over Israel 2
23 Omri . . reigned for twelve years; 2
23 Omri . . reigned . . six years he reigned in Tirzah. 2
28 and Ahab his son reigned in his stead. 2
29 Ahab the son of Omri began to reign over Israel 2
29 Ahab . . reigned over Israel in Sama'ria 22 years. 2
22:40 Ahazi'ah his son reigned in his stead. 2
41 Jehosh'aphat . . began to reign over Judah 2
42 Jehosh'aphat was 35 . . when he began to reign 2
42 and he reigned 25 years in Jerusalem. 2
50 and Jeho'ram his son reigned in his stead. 2
51 Ahazi'ah . . began to reign over Israel in Sama'ria 2
51 and he reigned two years over Israel. 2
2Kg 3: 1 and he reigned twelve years. 2
27 took his eldest son who was to reign in his stead 2
8:16 Jeho'ram the son of . . began to reign. 2
17 and he reigned eight years in Jerusalem. 2
24 and Ahazi'ah his son reigned in his stead. 2
25 Ahazi'ah the son of Jeho'ram . . began to reign. 2
26 Ahazi'ah was 22 years old when he began to reign 2
26 and he reigned one year in Jerusalem. 2
9:29 Ahazi'ah began to reign over Judah. 2
10:35 And Jeho'ahaz his son reigned in his stead. 2
36 time that Jehu reigned over Israel in Sama'ria 2
11: 3 while Athali'ah reigned over the land. 2
21 Jeho'ash was seven . . when he began to reign. 2
12: 1 seventh year of Jehu Jeho'ash began to reign 2
1 Jeho'ash . . reigned 40 years in Jerusalem. 2
21 and Amazi'ah his son reigned in his stead. 2
13: 1 Jeho'ahaz . . began to reign over Israel 2
1 Jeho'ahaz . . and he reigned seventeen years. •
9 and Jo'ash his son reigned in his stead. 2
10 Jeho'ash . . began to reign over Israel in Sama'ria 2
10 Jeho'ahaz began . . and he reigned sixteen years. •
14: 1 Amazi'ah . . king of Judah, began to reign. 2
2 He was 25 years old when he began to reign 2
2 and he reigned 29 years in Jerusalem. 2
16 and Jerobo'am his son reigned in his stead. 2
23 Jerobo'am . . began to reign in Sama'ria 2
23 began to reign in Sama'ria, and he reigned 41 years. •
29 and Zechari'ah his son reigned in his stead. 2
15: 1 Azari'ah the son of Amazi'ah . . began to reign. 2
2 He was sixteen years old when he began to reign 2
2 and he reigned 52 years in Jerusalem. 2
7 Azari'ah slept . . and Jotham his son reigned 2
8 Zechari'ah . . reigned over Israel in Sama'ria 2
10 and killed him, and reigned in his stead. 2
13 Shallum . . began to reign in the 39th year 2
13 Shallum . . and he reigned one month in Sama'ria. 2
14 struck down Shallum . . and reigned in his stead. 2
17 Men'ahem . . began to reign over Israel 2
17 Men'ahem . . and he reigned ten years in Sama'ria. •
22 Men'ahem slept . . and Pekahi'ah his son reigned 2
23 Pekahi'ah . . began to reign over Israel 2
23 Pekahi'ah . . and he reigned two years. •
25 Pekah . . he slew him, and reigned in his stead. 2
27 Pekah . . began to reign over Israel in Sama'ria 2
27 began to reign . . and reigned twenty years. •
30 struck . . and slew him, and reigned in his stead 2
32 Jotham the son of Uzzi'ah . . began to reign. 2
33 He was 25 years old when he began to reign 2
33 and he reigned sixteen years in Jerusalem. 2
38 and Ahaz his son reigned in his stead. 2
16: 1 Ahaz the son of Jotham . . began to reign. 2
2 Ahaz was twenty years old when he began to reign 2
2 and he reigned sixteen years in Jerusalem. 2
20 Ahaz slept . . and Hezeki'ah his son reigned 2
17: 1 Hoshe'a the son of Elah began to reign in Sama'ria 2
1 Hoshe'a . . and he reigned nine years. 2
18: 1 Hezeki'ah the son of Ahaz . . began to reign. 2
2 He was 25 years old when he began to reign 2
2 and he reigned 29 years in Jerusalem. 2
19:37 Esarhad'don his son reigned in his stead. 2
20:21 Manas'seh his son reigned in his stead. 2
21: 1 Manas'seh was twelve . . when he began to reign 2
1 and he reigned 55 years in Jerusalem. 2
18 Manas'seh slept . . and Amon his son reigned 2
19 Amon was 22 years old when he began to reign 2
19 Amon . . and he reigned two years in Jerusalem. 2
26 and Josi'ah his son reigned in his stead. 2
22: 1 Josi'ah was eight years old when he began to reign 2
1 Josi'ah was . . and he reigned 31 years 2
23:31 Jeho'ahaz was 23 years old when he began to reign 2
31 and he reigned three months in Jerusalem. 2
33 put him . . that he might not reign in Jerusalem 2
36 Jehoi'akim was 25 years old when he began to reign 2
36 and he reigned eleven years in Jerusalem. 2

24: 6 and Jehoi'achin his son reigned in his stead. 2
8 Jehoi'achin . . and he reigned three months 2
12 took him prisoner in the eighth year of his reign 2
18 Zedeki'ah was . . and he reigned eleven years 2
25: 1 in the ninth year of his reign, in the tenth month 2
27 in the year that he began to reign 2
1Ch 1:43 These are the kings who reigned in the land of Edom 2
43 the land of Edom before any king reigned over 2
44 Jobab the son of Zerah . . reigned in his stead. 2
45 Husham . . reigned in his stead. 2
46 Hadad the son of Bedad . . reigned in his stead 2
47 Samlah of Masre'kah reigned in his stead. 2
48 Sha'ul of Reho'both . . reigned in his stead. 2
49 Ba'al-ha'nan, the son of Achbor, reigned in his stead 2
50 When Ba'al-ha'nan died, Hadad reigned in his stead; 2
3: 4 where he reigned for seven years and six months. 2
4 And he reigned 33 years in Jerusalem. 2
4:31 These were their cities until David reigned. 2
16:31 let them say among the nations, "The LORD reigns! 2
18:14 David reigned over all Israel; 2
19: 1 Nahash . . died, and his son reigned in his stead. 2
26:31 In the 40th year of David's reign search was made 3
29:26 David the son of Jesse reigned over all Israel. 2
27 time that he reigned over Israel was 40 years; 2
27 he reigned seven years in Hebron 2
28 and Solomon his son reigned in his stead. 2
2Ch 1:13 And he reigned over Israel. 2
3: 2 the second month of the fourth year of his reign. 3
9:30 Solomon reigned in Jerusalem over all Israel 2
31 Rehobo'am his son reigned in his stead. 2
10:17 Rehobo'am reigned over the people of Israel 2
12:13 established himself in Jerusalem and reigned. 2
13 Rehobo'am was 41 . . when he began to reign 2
13 he reigned seventeen years in Jerusalem 2
16 Abi'jah his son reigned in his stead. 2
13: 1 Jerobo'am Abi'jah began to reign over Judah. 2
2 He reigned for three years in Jerusalem. 2
14: 1 Asa his son reigned in his stead. 2
15:10 month of the fifteenth year of the reign of Asa. 3
19 until the 35th year of the reign of Asa. 3
16: 1 In the 36th year of the reign of Asa 3
12 In the 39th year of his reign Asa 3
13 dying in the 41st year of his reign. 2
17: 1 Jehosh'aphat his son reigned in his stead 2
7 In the third year of his reign he sent his princes 2
20:31 Thus Jehosh'aphat reigned over Judah. 2
31 Jehosh'aphat . . was 35 . . when he began to reign 2
31 he reigned 25 years in Jerusalem. 2
21: 1 Jeho'ram his son reigned in his stead. 2
5 Jeho'ram . . reigned eight years in Jerusalem. 2
20 He was 32 years old when he began to reign 2
20 he reigned eight years in Jerusalem; 2
22: 1 Ahazi'ah the son of Jeho'ram . . reigned. 2
2 Ahazi'ah . . reigned one year in Jerusalem. 2
2 Ahazi'ah . . reigned one year in Jerusalem. 2
12 while Athali'ah reigned over the land. 2
23: 3 the king's son! Let him reign, as the LORD spoke 2
24: 1 Jo'ash was seven years old when he began to reign 2
1 Jo'ash . . reigned 40 years in Jerusalem; 2
27 And Amazi'ah his son reigned in his stead. 2
25: 1 25 years old when he began to reign 2
1 he reigned 29 years in Jerusalem. 2
26: 3 Uzzi'ah was sixteen . . when he began to reign 2
3 reigned 52 years in Jerusalem. 2
23 Jotham his son reigned in his stead. 2
27: 1 Jotham was 25 . . when he began to reign 2
1 Jotham . . reigned sixteen years in Jerusalem. 2
8 was 25 years old when he began to reign 2
8 he reigned sixteen years in Jerusalem. 2
9 Ahaz his son reigned in his stead. 2
28: 1 Ahaz was twenty years old when he began to reign 2
1 Ahaz . . reigned sixteen years in Jerusalem. 2
27 And Hezeki'ah his son reigned in his stead. 2
29: 1 Hezeki'ah began to reign when he was 25 2
1 Hezeki'ah . . reigned 29 years 2
3 In the first year of his reign, in the first month 2
19 Ahaz discarded in his reign when he was 3
32:33 Manas'seh his son reigned in his stead. 2
33: 1 Manas'seh was twelve . . when he began to reign 2
1 he reigned 55 years in Jerusalem. 2
20 Amon his son reigned in his stead. 2
21 Amon was 22 . . when he began to reign 2
21 Amon . . reigned two years in Jerusalem. 2
34: 1 Josi'ah was eight years old when he began to reign 2
1 Josi'ah . . reigned 31 years 2
3 eighth year of his reign, while he was yet a boy 2
8 Now in the eighteenth year of his reign 2
35:19 In the eighteenth year of the reign of Josi'ah 3
36: 2 23 years old when he began to reign; 2
2 he reigned three months in Jerusalem. 2
5 Jehoi'akim was 25 . . when he began to reign 2
5 he reigned eleven years in Jerusalem. 2
8 Jehoi'achin his son reigned in his stead. 2
9 Jehoi'achin was eight . . when he began to reign 2
9 reigned three months and ten days in Jerusalem. 2
11 Zedeki'ah was 21 . . when he began to reign 2
11 he reigned eleven years in Jerusalem. 2
Ezr 4: 5 even until the reign of Darius king of Persia. 3
6 reign of Ahasu-e'rus, in the beginning of his reign 3

6 reign of Ahasu-e'rus, in the beginning of his reign 3
24 second year of the reign of Darius king of Persia 6
6:15 in the sixth year of the reign of Darius the king. 6
7: 1 in the reign of Ar-ta-xerx'es king of Persia 3
8: 1 Babylonia, in the reign of Ar-ta-xerx'es the king 3
Neh 12:22 priests until the reign of Darius the Persian. 3
Est 1: 3 in the third year of his reign he gave a banquet 3
2:16 month of Tebeth, in the seventh year of his reign 3
Job 34:30 that a godless man should not reign 2
Ps 47: 8 God reigns over the nations; 2
93: 1 The LORD reigns; he is robed in majesty; 2
96:10 Say among the nations, "The LORD reigns! 2
97: 1 The LORD reigns; let the earth rejoice; 2
99: 1 The LORD reigns; let the peoples tremble! 2
146:10 The LORD will reign for ever, thy God, O Zion 2
Prv 8:15 By me kings reign, and rulers decree what is just; 2
Isa 24:23 for the LORD of hosts will reign on Mount Zion 2
32: 1 Behold, a king will reign in righteousness 2
37:38 E'sar-had'don his son reigned in his stead. 2
52: 7 salvation, who says to Zion, "Your God reigns. 2
Jer 1: 2 Josi'ah . . in the thirteenth year of his reign. 2
22:11 who reigned instead of Josi'ah his father 2
23: 5 and he shall reign as king and deal wisely 2
26: 1 In the beginning of the reign of Jehoi'akim 5
27: 1 In the beginning of the reign of Zedeki'ah 4
28: 1 at the beginning of the reign of Zedeki'ah 4
33:21 that he shall not have a son to reign on his throne 2
37: 1 reigned instead of Coni'ah the son of Jehoi'akim. 2
49:34 in the beginning of the reign of Zedeki'ah 3
51:59 to Babylon, in the fourth year of his reign. 2
52: 1 and he reigned eleven years in Jerusalem. 2
4 in the ninth year of his reign, in the tenth month 2
Lam 5:19 But thou, O LORD, dost reign for ever; 1
Dan 2: 1 second year of the reign of Nebuchadnez'zar 3
6:28 Daniel prospered during the reign of Darius 6
28 during the . . reign of Cyrus the Persian. 6
8: 1 third year of the reign of King Belshaz'zar 3
9: 2 first year of his reign, I, Daniel, perceived 2
Mic 4: 7 the LORD will reign over them in Mount Zion 2
Mat 2:22 when he heard that Archela'us reigned over Judea 10
Lke 1:33 he will reign over the house of Jacob for ever; 10
3: 1 fifteenth year of the reign of Tiber'ius Caesar 11
19:14 'We do not want this man to reign over us.' 10
27 who did not want me to reign over them 10
Rom 5:14 Yet death reigned from Adam to Moses 10
17 If, because of one man's trespass, death reigned 10
17 reign in life through the one man Jesus Christ. 10
21 so that, as sin reigned in death 10
21 grace also might reign through righteousness 10
6:12 Let not sin . . reign in your mortal bodies 10
1Co 4: 8 would that you did reign, so that we might share 10
15:25 For he must reign 10
2Ti 2:12 if we endure, we shall also reign with him 13
Rev 5:10 and they shall reign on the earth. 10
11:15 Christ, and he shall reign for ever and ever. 10
17 hast taken thy great power and begun to reign. 10
19: 6 For the Lord our God the Almighty reigns. 10
20: 4 and reigned with Christ a 1,000 years. 10
6 and they shall reign with him a 1,000 years. 10
22: 5 and they shall reign for ever and ever. 10
1Es 1:22 In the eighteenth year of the reign of Josiah 10
24 The events of his reign have been recorded 12
35 he reigned three months in Judah and Jerusalem. 10
35 deposed him from reigning in Jerusalem 10
39 when he began to reign in Judea and Jerusalem 10
44 reigned three months and ten days in Jerusalem. 10
46 he reigned eleven years. 10
57 until the Persians began to reign 10
2:30 until the second year of the reign of Darius 8
5: 6 in the second year of his reign 8
73 until the reign of Darius. 8
6: 1 Now in the second year of the reign of Darius 8
17 Cyrus reigned over the country of Babylonia 10
24 In the first year of the reign of Cyrus 10
8: 1 when Artaxerxes . . was reigning 10
6 in the seventh year of the reign of Artaxerxes 10
28 in the reign of Artaxerxes the king 8
2Es 1: 3 in the reign of Artaxerxes, king of the Persians. 15
5: 6 one shall reign whom those . . do not expect 14
11: 5 to reign over the earth 14
12 and it reigned over all the earth. 14
13 while it was reigning it came to its end 14
13 Then the next wing arose and reigned 14
13 and it continued to reign a long time. •
14 while it was reigning its end came also 14
28 planning between themselves to reign together 14
31 little wings which were planning to reign. 14
39 which I had made to reign in my world 14
12: 2 the two wings . . set themselves up to reign 14
2 and their reign was brief and full of tumult. 15
14 12 kings shall reign in it, one after another. 14
15 the second that is to reign shall hold sway 14
30 the reign which was brief and full of tumult 15
16:52 and righteousness will reign over us. 14
Tob 1:15 Sennacherib his son reigned in his place 10
21 Then Esarhaddon, his son, reigned in his place 10
Jdt 1: 1 the twelfth year of the reign of Nebuchadnezzar 8
AEs 11: 1 In the fourth year of the reign of Ptolemy 10
2 In the second year of the reign of Artaxerxes 10

Wis 3: 8 the Lord will reign over them for ever. 10
6:21 honor wisdom, that you may reign for ever. 10
Sir 0: 3 in the 38th year of the reign of Euergetes 9
47:13 Solomon reigned in days of peace 10
1Mc 1: 7 after Alexander had reigned twelve years 10
16 that he might reign over both kingdoms. 10
6: 2 the . . king who first reigned over the Greeks. 10
17 he set up Antiochus the king's son to reign 10
7: 1 and there began to reign. 10
8: 7 he and those who should reign after him 10
10: 1 They welcomed him, and there he began to reign. 10
11: 9 you shall reign over your father's kingdom. 10
54 who began to reign and put on the crown. 10
2Mc 1: 7 In the reign of Demetrius, in the 169th year 10

begin to reign 1. *βασιλεύω*

1Mc 1:10 He began to reign in the 137th year 1

reign over 1. מלך

Est 1: 1 Ahasu-e'rus who reigned . . over 127 provinces 1

rein *See* give.

rein about 1. הפך

2Kg 9:23 Joram reined about and fled, saying to Ahazi'ah 1

reinforce 1. *εἰς στήριγμα*

1Mc 2:43 joined them and reinforced them. 1

reinforcement *See* give.

reject 1. זנח 2. חדל 3. מאס 4. נטש 5. סור 6. עזב 7. *ἀθετέω* 8. *ἀνανεύω* 9. *ἀπαναινέω* 10. *ἀπεῖπον* 11. *ἀπόβλητος* 12. *ἀποδοκιμάζω* 13. *ἀποστρέφω* 14. *ἀποστροφή* 15. *ἀπωθέω* 16. *διασκεδάννυμι* 17. *ἐξαρνέομαι* 18. *ἐξουθενέω* 19. proicio 20. reprobo 21. repudio 22. separo

Num11:20 you have rejected the LORD who is among you 3
1Sm 8: 7 they have not rejected you, but . . rejected me 3
7 they have rejected me from being king over them. 3
10:19 you have this day rejected your God, who saves you 3
15:23 Because you have rejected the word of the LORD 3
23 LORD . . has also rejected you from being king. 3
26 for you have rejected the word of the LORD 3
26 and the LORD has rejected you from being king 3
16: 1 I have rejected him from being king over Israel? 3
7 Do not look on his . . because I have rejected him; 3
2Kg 17:20 the LORD rejected all the descendants of Israel 3
Job 8:20 Behold, God will not reject a blameless man 3
31:13 If I have rejected the cause of my manservant 3
34:33 make requital to suit you, because you reject it? 3
Ps 53: 5 will be put to shame, for God has rejected them. 3
60: 1 O God, thou hast rejected us, broken our defenses; 1
10 Hast thou not rejected us, O God? 1
66:20 because he has not rejected my prayer 5
78:59 full of wrath, and he utterly rejected Israel. 3
67 He rejected the tent of Joseph, he did not choose 3
89:38 now thou hast cast off and rejected 3
108:11 Hast thou not rejected us, O God? 1
118:22 The stone which the builders rejected 3
Prv 1: 8 reject not your mother's teaching; 4
10:17 but he who rejects reproof goes astray. 6
Isa 2: 6 thou hast rejected thy people, the house of Jacob 4
5:24 they have rejected the law of the LORD of hosts 3
53: 3 He was despised and rejected by men; 2
Jer 2:37 for the LORD has rejected those in whom you trust 3
6:19 as for my law, they have rejected it. 3
30 for the LORD has rejected them. 3
7:29 for the LORD has rejected and forsaken 3
8: 9 lo, they have rejected the word of the LORD 3
14:19 Hast thou utterly rejected Judah? 3
15: 6 You have rejected me, says the LORD 4
33:24 The LORD has rejected the two families 3
26 then I will reject the descendants of Jacob 3
Lam 5:22 Or hast thou utterly rejected us? 3
Ezk 5: 6 by rejecting my ordinances and not walking in my 3
20:13 walk in my statutes but rejected my ordinances 3
16 because they rejected my ordinances 3
24 but had rejected my statutes 3
Hos 4: 6 because you have rejected knowledge 3
6 I reject you from being a priest to me. 3
Ams 2: 4 because they have rejected the law of the LORD 3
Zec 10: 6 they shall be as though I had not rejected them; 1
Mat 21:42 The very stone which the builders rejected 12
Mrk 7: 9 a fine way of rejecting the commandment of God 7
8:31 rejected by the elders and the chief priests 12
12:10 The very stone which the builders rejected 12
Lke 7:30 the lawyers rejected the purpose of God 7
9:22 rejected by the elders and chief priests 12
10:16 he who rejects you rejects me 7
16 he who rejects you rejects me 7
16 he who rejects me rejects him who sent me. 7
16 he who rejects me rejects him who sent me. 7
17:25 be rejected by this generation. 12
20:17 The very stone which the builders rejected 12
Joh 12:48 He who rejects me and does not receive my sayings 7
Act 4:11 is the stone which was rejected by you builders 18
Rom11: 1 I ask, then, has God rejected his people? By no means! 15
2 God has not rejected his people 15

1Ti 1:19 By rejecting conscience 15
4: 4 nothing is to be rejected 11
Tit 1:14 commands of men who reject the truth. 13
Heb 12:17 he was rejected for he found no chance to repent 12
25 if we reject him who warns from heaven. 13
1Pe 2: 4 Come to him, to the living stone, rejected by men 12
7 The very stone which the builders rejected 12
Jde 1: 8 these men . . reject authority, and revile 7
2Es 1:31 for I have rejected your feast days, and new moons 21
2:33 When I came to them they rejected me 20
3:16 but Esau thou didst reject 22
9: 9 those who have rejected them with contempt 19
Wis 9: 4 do not reject me from among thy servants. 12
11:14 though they had mockingly rejected him 10
Sir 4: 4 Do not reject an afflicted suppliant 9
6:23 do not reject my counsel. 9
20:20 A proverb from a fool's lips will be rejected 12
41: 4 can you reject the good pleasure of the Most High? 9
21 rejecting the appeal of a kinsman 14
Man 1:10 so that I am rejected because of my sins 8
1Mc 2:31 men who had rejected the king's command 16
2Mc 1:27 look upon those who are rejected and despised 18
4Mc 5:35 nor will I reject you, honored priesthood 17

rejection 1. *ἀποβάλλω*

Rom 11:15 if their rejection means the reconciliation 1

rejoice 1. גיל 2. חדה 3. מָשׂוֹשׂ 4. מְשַׂחֶקֶת 5. עלז 6. עֲלִיצוּת 7. עלץ 8. רחב 9. רנן 10. שׂושׂ 11. שׂמח 12. שָׂמֵחַ 13. שִׂמְחָה 14. *ἀγαλλιάω* 15. *ἐπευθυμέω* 16. *ἐπιχαίρω* 17. *εὐφραίνω* 18. *ἥδομαι* 19. *καυχάομαι* 20. *πίμπλημι* 21. *συγχαίρω* 22. *χαίρω* 23. exulto 24. gaudeo 25. hilaris 26. iucundo

Exd 18: 9 Jethro rejoiced for all the good which the LORD 2
Lev 23:40 you shall rejoice before the LORD your God 11
Deu 12: 7 there you shall eat . . and you shall rejoice 11
12 rejoice before the LORD your God 11
18 rejoice before the LORD your God in all that you 11
14:26 eat there before the LORD your God and rejoice 11
16:11 rejoice before the LORD your God, you and your son 11
14 rejoice in your feast, you and your son 11
26:11 rejoice in all the good which the LORD your God 11
27: 7 you shall rejoice before the LORD your God. 11
33:18 Rejoice, Zeb'ulun, in your going out; and Is'sachar 11
Jdg 9:19 then rejoice in Abim'elech, and let him also 11
19 in Abim'elech, and let him also rejoice in you; 11
16:23 to offer a great sacrifice . . and to rejoice; 13
1Sm 2: 1 because I rejoice in thy salvation. 11
6:13 when they . . saw the ark, they rejoiced to see it. 11
11:15 Saul and all the men of Israel rejoiced greatly. 11
19: 5 You saw it, and rejoiced; why then will you sin 11
2Sm 1:20 lest the daughters of the Philistines rejoice 11
6:12 went and brought up the ark . . with rejoicing; 13
1Kg 1:40 playing on pipes, and rejoicing with great joy 12
45 gone up from there rejoicing, so that the city is 12
5: 7 When Hiram heard . . he rejoiced greatly, and said 11
2Kg 11:14 the people . . rejoicing and blowing trumpets. 12
20 So all the people of the land rejoiced; 11
1Ch 15:25 to bring up the ark . . with rejoicing. 13
16:10 let the hearts of those who seek the LORD rejoice! 11
31 Let the heavens be glad, and let the earth rejoice 1
29: 9 rejoiced because these had given willingly 11
9 David the king also rejoiced greatly. 11
2Ch 6:41 and let thy saints rejoice in thy goodness. 11
15:15 all Judah rejoiced over the oath; 11
23:13 all the people of the land rejoicing 12
18 with rejoicing and with singing 13
21 all the people of the land rejoiced; 11
24:10 all the princes and all the people rejoiced 11
29:36 Hezeki'ah and all the people rejoiced 11
30:25 whole assembly of Judah . . rejoiced. 11
Neh 8:12 send portions and to make great rejoicing 13
17 And there was very great rejoicing. 13
12:43 offered great sacrifices that day and rejoiced 11
43 women and children also rejoiced. 11
44 Judah rejoiced over the priests and the Levites 13
Est 8:15 while the city of Susa shouted and rejoiced. 11
Job 3: 6 let it not rejoice among the days of the year 2
22 who rejoice exceedingly, and are glad 11
21:12 and rejoice to the sound of the pipe. 11
31:25 if I have rejoiced because my wealth was great 11
29 If I have rejoiced at the ruin of him that hated me 11
Ps 5:11 But let all who take refuge in thee rejoice 11
9:14 I may rejoice in thy deliverance. 1
13: 4 lest my foes rejoice because I am shaken. 1
5 my heart shall rejoice in thy salvation. 1
14: 7 Jacob shall rejoice, Israel shall be glad. 1
16: 9 Therefore my heart is glad, and my soul rejoices; 1
19: 8 the precepts . . are right, rejoicing the heart; 11
21: 1 In thy strength the king rejoices, O LORD; 11
30: 1 and hast not let my foes rejoice over me. 11
31: 7 I will rejoice and be glad for thy steadfast love 1
32:11 Be glad in the LORD, and rejoice, O righteous 1
33: 1 Rejoice in the LORD, O you righteous! 9
35: 9 Then my soul shall rejoice in the LORD 1
19 those rejoice over me who are wrongfully my foes 11
24 let them not rejoice over me! 11
26 altogether who rejoice at my calamity! 12
38:16 For I pray, "Only let them not rejoice over me 11
40:16 may all who seek thee rejoice and be glad in thee; 10
48:11 Let the daughters of Judah rejoice 1
51: 8 let the bones which thou hast broken rejoice. 1
53: 6 Jacob will rejoice and Israel be glad. 1
58:10 The righteous will rejoice when he sees 11
63:11 the king shall rejoice in God; 11
64:10 Let the righteous rejoice in the LORD 11
66: 6 There did we rejoice in him 11
70: 4 May all who seek thee rejoice and be glad in thee! 10
75: 9 I will rejoice for ever, I will sing praises 14
85: 6 that thy people may rejoice in thee? 11
90:14 that we may rejoice and be glad all our days. 9
96:11 Let the heavens be glad, and let the earth rejoice; 1
97: 1 The LORD reigns; let the earth rejoice; 1
8 daughters of Judah rejoice 1
12 Rejoice in the LORD, O you righteous 11
104:31 may the LORD rejoice in his works 11
34 for I rejoice in the LORD. 11
105: 3 let the hearts of those who seek the LORD rejoice! 11
106: 5 that I may rejoice in the gladness of thy nation 11
118:24 let us rejoice and be glad in it. 1
119:74 Those who fear thee shall see me and rejoice 11
162I rejoice at thy word like one who finds 10
149: 2 let the sons of Zion rejoice in their King! 1
Prv 2:14 who rejoice in doing evil 12
5:18 rejoice in the wife of your youth 11
8:30 daily his delight, rejoicing before him always 4
31 rejoicing in his inhabited world 4
11:10 goes well with the righteous, the city rejoices; 7
13: 9 The light of the righteous rejoices 11
15:30 The light of the eyes rejoices the heart 11
23:16 My soul will rejoice when your lips speak 5
24 father of the righteous will greatly rejoice; 1
25 let her who bore you rejoice. 1
24:17 Do not rejoice when your enemy falls 11
29: 2 righteous are in authority, the people rejoice; 11
6 but a righteous man sings and rejoices. 11
Ecc 4:16 Yet those who come later will not rejoice in him. 11
11: 8 if a man lives . . years, let him rejoice in them all; 11
9 Rejoice, O young man, in your youth 11
Sng 1: 4 We will exult and rejoice in you; 11
Isa 9: 3 rejoice before thee as with joy at the harvest 11
3 as men rejoice when they divide the spoil. 1
17 the Lord does not rejoice over their young men 11
14: 8 The cypresses rejoice at you . . saying 11
29 Rejoice not, O Philistia, all of you 11
25: 9 let us be glad and rejoice in his salvation. 1
35: 1 the desert shall rejoice and blossom; 1
2 it shall blossom abundantly, and rejoice 1
41:16 And you shall rejoice in the LORD; 1
60: 5 be radiant, your heart shall thrill and rejoice; 8
61: 7 of dishonor you shall rejoice in your lot; 9
10 I will greatly rejoice in the LORD 10
62: 5 and as the bridegroom rejoices over the bride 3
5 over . . bride, so shall your God rejoice over you. 10
65:13 behold, my servants shall rejoice, 11
18 and rejoice for ever in that which I create; 1
19 I will rejoice in Jerusalem, and be glad 1
66:10 Rejoice with Jerusalem, and be glad for her 11
10 rejoice with her in joy, all you who mourn over her; 10
14 You shall see, and your heart shall rejoice; 10
Jer 15:17 in the company of merrymakers, nor did I rejoice; 5
31:13 Then shall the maidens rejoice in the dance 11
32:41 I will rejoice in doing them good 10
41:13 saw Joha'nan . . they rejoiced. 11
50:11 Though you rejoice, though you exult 11
Lam 4:21 Rejoice and be glad, O daughter of Edom 10
Ezk 7:12 Let not the buyer rejoice, nor the seller mourn 11
25: 6 and rejoiced with all the malice within you 11
35:14 For the rejoicing of the whole earth 11
15 As you rejoiced over the inheritance 13
Hos 9: 1 Rejoice not, O Israel! Exult not like the peoples; 11
Jol 2:21 Fear not, O land; be glad and rejoice 1
23 Be glad, O sons of Zion, and rejoice in the LORD 1
Ams 6:13 you who rejoice in Lo-debar, who say 12
Obd 1:12 you should not have rejoiced over the people 11
Mic 7: 8 Rejoice not over me, O my enemy; 11
Hab 1:15 he rejoices and exults. 11
3:14 rejoicing as if to devour the poor in secret. 6
18 yet I will rejoice in the LORD 5
Zep 3:14 Rejoice and exult with all your heart 11
17 he will rejoice over you with gladness 10
Zec 2:10 Sing and rejoice, O daughter of Zion; for lo, I come 11
4:10 shall rejoice, and shall see the plummet 11
9: 9 Rejoice greatly, O daughter of Zion! 1
10: 7 Their children shall see it and rejoice 11
Mat 2:10 star, they rejoiced exceedingly with great joy; 22
5:12 Rejoice and be glad, for your reward is great 22
18:13 if he finds it, truly, I say to you, he rejoices 22
Lke 1:14 many will rejoice at his birth; 22
47 my spirit rejoices in God my Savior 14
58 and they rejoiced with her. 21
6:23 Rejoice in that day, and leap for joy 22
10:20 Nevertheless do not rejoice in this 22
20 rejoice that your names are written in heaven. 22
21 In that same hour he rejoiced in the Holy Spirit 14
13:17 the people rejoiced at all the glorious things 22
15: 6 saying to them, 'Rejoice with me 21
9 saying, 'Rejoice with me 21
19:37 began to rejoice and praise God with a loud voice 22
Joh 3:29 friend of the bridegroom . . rejoices greatly 22
4:36 so that sower and reaper may rejoice together. 22
5:35 you were willing to rejoice for a while 14
8:56 Abraham rejoiced that he was to see my day 14
14:28 If you loved me, you would have rejoiced 22
16:20 the world will rejoice 22
22 our hearts will rejoice 22
Act 2:26 my heart was glad, and my tongue rejoiced; 14
7:41 rejoiced in the works of their hands. 17
15:31 they rejoiced at the exhortation. 22
16:34 he rejoiced with all his household 14
Rom 5: 2 we rejoice in our hope of sharing the glory of God. 19
3 More than that, we rejoice in our sufferings 19
11 rejoice in God through our Lord Jesus Christ 19
12:12 Rejoice in your hope, be patient in tribulation 22
15 Rejoice with those who rejoice 22
15 Rejoice with those who rejoice 22
15:10 Rejoice, O Gentiles, with his people"; 17
16:19 so that I rejoice over you 22
1Co 7:30 who rejoice as though they were not rejoicing 22
13: 6 it does not rejoice at wrong 22
6 but rejoices in the right. 21
16:17 I rejoice at the coming of Steph'anas 22
2Co 2: 3 from those who should have made me rejoice 22
7: 7 so that I rejoiced still more. 22
9 As it is, I rejoice, not because you were grieved 22
13 we rejoiced still more at the joy of Titus 22
16 I rejoice, because I have perfect confidence 22
Gal 4:27 Rejoice, O barren one who does not bear 17
Php 1:18 Christ is proclaimed; and in that I rejoice 22
19 Yes, and I shall rejoice. 22
2:17 I am glad and rejoice with you all. 21
18 you also should be glad and rejoice with me. 21
28 you may rejoice at seeing him again 22
3: 1 Finally, my brethren, rejoice in the Lord 22
4: 4 Rejoice in the Lord always 22
4 again I will say, Rejoice. 22
10 I rejoice in the Lord greatly 22
Col 1:24 Now I rejoice in my sufferings for your sake 22
1Th 5:16 Rejoice always 22
1Pe 1: 6 In this you rejoice 14
8 rejoice with unutterable and exalted joy. 14
4:13 rejoice in so far as you share Christ's 22
13 that you may also rejoice and be glad 22
2Jn 1: 4 I rejoiced greatly to find some of your children 22
3Jn 1: 3 For I greatly rejoiced 22
Rev 11:10 rejoice over them and make merry and exchange 22
12:12 Rejoice then, O heaven and you that dwell therein! 17
18:20 Rejoice over her, O heaven, O saints and apostles 17
19: 7 Let us rejoice and exult and give him the glory 22
2Es 1:37 whose children rejoice with gladness 23
2:27 you shall rejoice and have abundance. 25
30 Rejoice, O mother, with your sons 26
7:28 and those who remain shall rejoice 400 years. 26
59 rejoices more than he who has what is plentiful. 24
60 I will rejoice over the few who shall be saved 26
65 the four-footed beasts and the flocks rejoice! 26
96 they rejoice that they have now escaped 23
98 because they shall rejoice with boldness 23
8:39 will rejoice over the creation of the righteous 26
9:45 And I rejoiced greatly over him 26
Tob 10:12 that I may rejoice before the Lord 17
13: 7 my soul . . will rejoice in his majesty. 14
13 Rejoice and be glad for the sons of the righteous 22
14 They will rejoice in your peace. 22
14 will rejoice for you upon seeing all your glory 22
14: 7 all who love the Lord God . . will rejoice 22
15 Before his death he rejoiced over Nineveh. 22
Wis 7:12 I rejoiced in them all, because wisdom leads them; 17
18: 6 they might rejoice in sure knowledge 15
Sir 16: 1 nor rejoice in ungodly sons. 17
2 If they multiply , do not rejoice in them 17
19: 5 One who rejoices in wickedness 17
22:23 that you may rejoice with him in his prosperity; 20
26: 2 A loyal wife rejoices her husband 17
27:29 Those who rejoice in the fall of the godly 17
30: 1 he may rejoice at the way he turns out. 17
5 while alive he saw and rejoiced 17
37: 4 rejoice in the happiness of a friend 18
39:31 they will rejoice in his commands 17
51:29 May your soul rejoice in his mercy 17
Bar 4:31 afflicted you and rejoiced at your fall. 16
33 rejoiced at your fall and was glad for your ruin 22
1Mc 7:48 The people rejoiced greatly 17
10:26 we have heard of it and rejoiced. 22
11:44 the king rejoiced at their arrival. 17
12:12 we rejoice in your glory. 17
14:11 Israel rejoiced with great joy. 17
21 we rejoiced at their coming. 17
4Mc 4:22 the people of Jerusalem . . rejoiced greatly 22

make rejoice 1. שׂמח 2. *εὐφραίνω*

2Ch 20:27 LORD had made them rejoice over their enemies. 1
Neh 12:43 God had made them rejoice with great joy; 1
Ps 89:42 thou hast made all his enemies rejoice. 1
Lam 2:17 he has made the enemy rejoice over you 1
Sir 35:19 makes them rejoice in his mercy. 2

rejoice over 1. ἐπιχαίρω
Sir 8: 7 Do not rejoice over any one's death 1
23: 3 my enemy will not rejoice over me. 1
Bar 4:12 Let no one rejoice over me, a widow 1

rejoice together 1. συγχαίρω
1Co 12:26 if one member is honored, all rejoice together. 1

rejoicing 1. גִּילָה 2. ἀγαλλίαμα 3. ἀγαλλίασις 4. ἀγαλλιάω 5. εὐφραίνω 6. εὐφροσύνη 7. χαίρω 8. χαρά 9. exultatio
Isa 65:18 for behold, I create Jerusalem a rejoicing 1
Lke 15: 5 he lays it on his shoulders, rejoicing. 7
Act 5:41 rejoicing that they were counted worthy 7
8:39 went on his way rejoicing. 7
1Co 7:30 who rejoice as though they were not rejoicing 7
2Co 6:10 as sorrowful, yet always rejoicing 7
Col 2: 5 rejoicing to see your good order 7
Jde 1:24 before the presence of his glory with rejoicing 4
1Es 4:63 they feasted, with music and rejoicing 8
7:14 rejoicing before the Lord 5
2Es 10:22 and our rejoicing has been ended 9
Tob 11:15 his son went in rejoicing 7
16 rejoicing and praising God 7
17 rejoicing among all his brethren in Nineveh. 8
13: 1 Then Tobit wrote a prayer of rejoicing, and said 3
Sir 1:11 gladness and a crown of rejoicing. 2
15: 6 He will find gladness and a crown of rejoicing 2
25: 7 a man rejoicing in his children 5
30:22 the rejoicing of a man is length of days. 2
31:28 rejoicing of heart and gladness of soul. 2
Bar 4:37 they are . . rejoicing in the glory of God. 7
5: 5 rejoicing that God has remembered them. 7
1Mc 5:23 led them to Judea with great rejoicing. 6
13:52 celebrate this day with rejoicing 6
2Mc 10: 6 celebrated it for eight days with rejoicing 6
rejoicing *See also* day, make.

rekindle 1. ἀναζωπυρέω
2Ti 1: 6 Hence I remind you to rekindle the gift of God 1
1Mc 13: 7 The spirit of the people was rekindled 1

relate 1. ἐκδιηγέομαι 2. ἐξηγέομαι 3. προσεξηγέομαι
Act 10: 8 having related everything to them 2
15:12 as they related what signs . . God had done 2
14 Simeon has related how God first visited 2
21:19 he related one by one the things that God had done 2
Sir 31:11 the assembly will relate his acts of charity. 1
2Mc 15:11 he cheered them all by relating a dream 3

relation 1. ὁ πρός 2. χρῆσις
Rom 1:26 exchanged natural relations for unnatural 2
27 the men . . gave up natural relations with women 2
2:17 and boast of your relation to God •
Heb 5: 1 to act on behalf of men in relation to God 1
2Mc 10:12 attempted to maintain peaceful relations 1

relationship 1. συνήθεια
4Mc 2:13 It is sovereign over the relationship of friends 1

relative 1. קָרֹב 2. ἀδελφός 3. ἐκ γένους 4. ἴδιος 5. συγγενής 6. adfinis
Rut 2:20 The man is a relative of ours, one of our nearest 1
1Ti 5: 8 If any one does not provide for his relatives 4
16 If any believing woman has relatives who are widows •
2Es 7:103relatives for their kinsmen 6
Tob 1:10 my relatives ate the food of the Gentiles; 3
5:12 I am Azarias . . one of your relatives. 2
13 You are a relative of mine 2
6:10 He is your relative 5
7:12 You are her relative, and she is yours 2
2Mc 15:18 Their concern . . for brethren and relatives 5
3Mc 5:49 they kissed each other, embracing relatives 5

relax 1. רפה 2. ἀνίημι 3. ἐκλύω 4. λύω
Jos 10: 6 Do not relax your hand from your servants; 1
Mat 5:19 Whoever then relaxes one of the least of these 4
Wis 16:24 relaxes on behalf of those who trust in thee. 2
Sir 43:10 they never relax in their watches. 3

relay 1. חֲלִיפָה
1Kg 5:14 he sent them to Lebanon . . in relays; 1

release 1. חֲלִיפָה 2. יצא 3. מִמְכָּר 4. נתר 5. פתח 6. שׁמט 7. שְׁמִטָּה 8. ἄνεσις 9. ἀπαλλάσσω 10. ἀπολύτρωσις 11. ἀπολύω 12. ἄφεσις 13. ἀφίημι 14. δικαιόω 15. ἐλύθη ὁ δεσμός 16. λύω 17. παραδίδωμι
Lev 25:28 in the jubilee it shall be released 2
30 it shall not be released in the jubilee 2
31 they shall be released in the jubilee 2
33 the house . . shall be released in the jubilee 2
50 the price of his release shall be according 3
54 then he shall be released in the year of jubilee 2
27:21 the field, when it is released in the jubilee 2
Deu 15: 1 end of every seven years you shall grant a release. 7
2 this is the manner of the release: every creditor 7
2 every creditor shall release what he has lent 6
2 because the LORD'S release has been proclaimed. 7
3 your hand shall release. 6
9 The seventh year, the year of release is near,' 7
31:10 seven years, at the set time of the year of release 7
Job 14:14 I would wait, till my release should come. 1
Ps 105:20 The king sent and released him 4
Isa 51:14 He who is bowed down shall speedily be released; 5
Jer 20: 3 On the morrow, when Pashhur released Jeremiah 2
40: 4 Now, behold, I release you today from the chains 5
Mat 18:27 the lord of that servant released him 11
27:15 governor was accustomed to release for the crowd 11
17 Whom do you want me to release for you 11
21 Which of the two do you want me to release for you? 11
26 Then he released for them Barab'bas 11
Mrk 7:35 his ears were opened, his tongue was released 15
15: 6 he used to release for them one prisoner 11
9 you want me to release for you the King of the Jews? 11
11 to have him release for them Barab'bas instead. 11
15 to satisfy the crowd, released for them Barab'bas; 11
Lke 4:18 has sent me to proclaim release to the captives 12
23:16 I will therefore chastise him and release him. 11
18 release to us Barab'bas"- 11
20 desiring to release Jesus; 11
22 I will therefore chastise him and release him. 11
25 He released the man 11
Joh 18:39 you have a custom that I should release one man 11
39 release for you the King of the Jews? 11
19:10 Do you not know that I have power to release you 11
12 Upon this Pilate sought to release him 11
12 the Jews cried out, "If you release this man 11
Act 3:13 when he had decided to release him. 11
4:23 When they were released 11
Heb 11:35 Some were tortured, refusing to accept release 10
13:23 our brother Timothy has been released 11
Rev 9:14 Release the four angels who are bound 16
15 So the four angels were released 16
1Es 4: 7 if he tells them to release, they release 13
7 if he tells them to release, they release 13
62 because he had given them release and permission 8
Tob 3: 6 Command that I now be released from my distress 11
13 Command that I be released from the earth 11
Sir 18:22 do not wait until death to be released from it. 14
1Mc 10: 6 the hostages in the citadel should be released 17
9 the men in the citadel released the hostages 17
30 I release them from this day and henceforth 13
32 I release also my control of the citadel 13
34 let them all be days of immunity and release 12
43 let him be released 11
11:34 we have granted release from the royal taxes •
13:16 so that when released he will not revolt 13
16 we will release him. 13
19 broke his word and did not release Jonathan. 13
15: 5 and release from all the other payments •
5 payments from which they have released you. 13
3Mc 6:28 Release the sons of the almighty and living God 11
29 the Jews, immediately released, praised 16
4Mc 9:16 you may be released from the tortures 9
11:13 whether he was willing to eat and be released 11
release *See also* grant, obtain.

relent 1. נחם
Ps 106:45 relented according to the abundance of his 1
Jer 4:28 I have not relented nor will I turn back. 1
15: 6 and destroyed you;-I am weary of relenting. 1
Zec 8:14 I did not relent, says the LORD of hosts 1

relentless 1. ἀπαραίτητος
Wis 16:16 unusual rains and hail and relentless storms 1

relentlessly 1. ἀποτόμως 2. ἀφειδῶς
Wis 5:22 rivers will relentlessly overwhelm them; 1
2Mc 5: 6 Jason kept relentlessly slaughtering 2
12 to cut down relentlessly every one they met 2

reliable 1. אמן
Isa 8: 2 I got reliable witnesses, Uri'ah the priest 1

reliable man 1. πιστός
Tob 5: 8 and whether he is a reliable man to go with you. 1

reliance 1. מִבְטָח 2. καταφυγή
Ezk 29:16 it shall never again be the reliance of the house 1
2Mc 10:28 not only . . valor but their reliance upon the Lord 2

old relic 1. παλαιόω
Sus 1:52 You old relic of wicked days 1

relief 1. רְוָח 2. ἀναπαύω 3. ἄνεσις 4. ἄφεσις 5. διακονία 6. εἰς διακονίαν 7. παραμυθία 8. requietio
Est 4:14 relief and deliverance will rise for the Jews 1
Act 11:29 the disciples determined . . to send relief 6
2Co 8: 4 taking part in the relief of the saints- 5
2Es 10:24 a relief from your troubles. 8
Wis 19:12 to give them relief, quails came up from the sea. 7
Sir 31:21 you will have relief. 2
Man 1:10 I have no relief 3
1Mc 13:34 a request to grant relief to the country 4
relief *See also* bring, find, get.

no relief 1. ἀνήκεστος
2Mc 9: 5 for which there was no relief 1

relieve 1. סור 2. סכך רַגְלַיִם 3. רחב 4. ἐπαρκέω 5. adlevo 6. relevo
Jdg 3:24 He is only relieving himself in the closet 2
1Sm 24: 3 a cave; and Saul went in to relieve himself. 2
Ps 25:17 Relieve the troubles of my heart 3
81: 6 I relieved your shoulder of the burden; 1
1Ti 5:10 relieved the afflicted 4
2Es 7:138that those . . might be relieved of them 5
11:46 whole earth . . may be refreshed and relieved 6

religion 1. εὐσέβεια 2. θεοσέβεια 3. θρησκεία 4. λατρεία 5. νόμιμος
Act 26: 5 the strictest party of our religion 3
1Ti 2:10 as befits women who profess religion. 2
3:16 Great indeed . . is the mystery of our religion 1
2Ti 3: 5 holding the form of religion 1
Jas 1:26 this man's religion is vain. 3
27 Religion that is pure and undefiled before God 3
1Mc 1:43 Many . . gladly adopted his religion 4
2:19 departing . . from the religion of his fathers 4
22 by turning aside from our religion 4
2Mc 6:24 Eleazar . . has gone over to an alien religion •
3Mc 1: 3 a Jew by birth who later changed his religion 5
2:31 maintaining the religion of their city 1
32 did not depart from their religion 1
4Mc 5: 7 when you observe the religion of the Jews. 3
13 some power watching over this religion of yours 3
6:22 die nobly for your religion! 1
7: 1 steered the ship of religion over the sea 1
3 in no way did he turn the rudder of religion 1
18 as many as attend to religion with a whole heart 1
9: 6 because of their religion lived piously 1
7 if you take our lives because of our religion 1
24 Fight the sacred and noble battle for religion. 1
29 death for the religion of our fathers! 1
30 our endurance for the sake of religion? 1
11:20 summoned to an arena of sufferings for religion 1
12:11 those who practice religion? 1
13: 7 fortifying the harbor of religion 1
8 For they constituted a holy chorus of religion 1
12 being slain for the sake of religion. 1
26 with the aid of their religion 1
27 endured for the sake of religion 1
14: 3 harmonious concord . . on behalf of religion! 1
7 move in choral dance around religion 1
15: 1 O religion, more desirable to the mother 1
2 religion, and . . preserving her seven sons 1
3 She loved religion more 1
3 religion that preserves them for eternal life •
12 to death for the sake of religion. 1
14 because of religion 1
29 vindicator of the law and champion of religion 1
32 the wintry storms that assail religion. 1
16:13 urged them on to death for the sake of religion. 1
14 O mother, soldier of God in the cause of religion 1
17 endures such agonies for the sake of religion 1
17: 7 tortures to death for the sake of religion? 1
18: 3 suffering for the sake of religion 1

religious 1. εὐσέβεια 2. εὐσεβής 3. θεοσεβής 4. θρησκός
Jas 1:26 If any one thinks he is religious 4
Jdt 11:17 For your servant is religious 3
4Mc 5:38 you shall not dominate my religious principles 1
11:21 For religious knowledge, O tyrant, is 2
16:23 people who have religious knowledge 1
religious *See also* duty, rite.

reluctantly 1. ἐκ λύπης
2Co 9: 7 not reluctantly or under compulsion 1

rely 1. בטח 2. שׁען 3. εἰμί ἐκ 4. ἐμπιστεύω 5. ἐπαναπαύομαι 6. ἐπέχω 7. πείθω
2Kg 18:20 On whom do you now rely, that you have rebelled 1
21 Behold, you are relying now on Egypt 1
21 Such is Pharaoh . . to all who rely on him. 1
22 you say . . "We rely on the LORD our God," is it not he 1
24 you rely on Egypt for chariots and for horsemen? 1
19:10 Do not let your God on whom you rely deceive you 1
2Ch 13:18 because they relied upon the LORD 2
14:11 Help us, O LORD our God, for we rely on thee 2
16: 7 Because you relied on the king of Syria 2
7 did not rely on the LORD your God 2
8 Yet because you relied on the LORD 2
32:10 'On what are you relying, that you stand siege 1
Prv 3: 5 do not rely on your own insight. 2
Isa 30:12 oppression and perverseness, and rely on them; 2
31: 1 who go down to Egypt for help and rely on horses 2
36: 5 On whom do you now rely, that you have rebelled 1

6 Behold, you are relying on Egypt, that broken reed 1
6 Such is Pharaoh . . of Egypt to all who rely on him. 1
7 if you say to me, "We rely on the LORD our God 1
9 when you rely on Egypt for chariots 1
37:10 Do not let your God on whom you rely deceive you 1
50:10 trusts in the . . LORD and relies upon his God? 2
59: 4 they rely on empty pleas, they speak lies 1
2Co 1: 9 that was to make us rely not on ourselves 7
Gal 3:10 all who rely on works of the law are under a curse; 3
Jdt 7:10 the Israelites, do not rely on their spears 7
Sir 15: 4 he will rely on her and will not be put to shame. 6
16: 3 do not rely on their multitude 6
38:31 All these rely upon their hands 4
1Mc 8:12 with their friends and those who rely on them 5
2Mc 10:34 relying on the strength of the place 7
12:14 relying on the strength of the walls 7

make rely 1. בטח

2Kg 18:30 Do not let Hezeki'ah make you to rely on the LORD 1
Isa 36:15 Do not let Hezeki'ah make you rely on the LORD 1

rely upon 1. ἐπαναπαύομαι

Rom 2:17 if you call yourself a Jew and rely upon the law 1

remain 1. היה 2. ישב 3. יתר 4. יֶתֶר 5. כָּל יָמִים 6. לון 7. עדף 8. עמד 9. עמן 10. קום 11. שרד 12. שָׂרִיד 13. שאר 14. שְׁאֵרִית 15. שכן 16. ἀναμένω 17. ἀναπαύω 18. ἀπόκειμαι 19. ἀπολείπω 20. διαμένω 21. διατρίβω 22. εἰμί 23. ἐπίλοιπος 24. ἐπιμένω 25. ἵστημι 26. καθίζω 27. καθίστημι 28. καταλαμβάνω 29. καταλείπω 30. καταμένω 31. λοιπός 32. μένω 33. παραμένω 34. περιλείπω 35. προσμένω 36. ὑπολείπω 37. ὑπομένω 38. derelinquo 39. maneo 40. permaneo 41. persevero 42. relinquo 43. remaneo 44. supero

Gen 8:22 While the earth remains, seedtime and harvest 5
24:55 her mother said, "Let the maiden remain with us 2
38:11 his daughter-in-law, "Remain a widow 2
44:33 let your servant . . remain instead of the lad 2
49:24 yet his bow remained unmoved 2
Exd 7:22 so Pharaoh's heart remained hardened •
8:31 removed the . . flies . . not one remained. 13
10:15 not a green thing remained, neither tree nor 3
12:10 you shall let none of it remain until the morning 3
10 anything that remains until the morning 3
14:28 into the sea; not so much as one of them remained. 13
16:29 remain every man of you in his place, let no man go 2
23:18 fat of my feast remain until the morning. 6
25:15 The poles shall remain in the rings of the ark; 1
26:12 the part that remains of the curtains of the tent 7
12 the half curtain that remains, shall hang over 7
13 what remains in the length of the curtains 7
28:10 the names of the remaining six on the other stone 3
29:34 if any . . of the bread, remain until the morning 3
Lev 7:16 on the morrow what remains of it shall be eaten 3
17 what remains of the flesh of the sacrifice 3
8:32 what remains of the flesh and the bread 3
35 you shall remain day and night for seven days 2
10:12 cereal offering that remains of the offerings 3
11:11 They shall remain an abomination to you 1
13:23 if the spot remains in one place 8
28 if the spot remains in one place 8
14:17 some of the oil that remains in his hand 4
22:27 it shall remain seven days with its mother 1
25:28 then what he sold shall remain in the hand of him 1
52 If there remain but a few years until the year 13
27:18 the years that remain until the year of jubilee 3
19 and it shall remain his 10
Num 9:21 cloud remained from evening until morning; 1
11:26 Now two men remained in the camp, one named Eldad 13
35 people . . remained at Haze'roth. 1
31:32 booty remaining of the spoil that the men of war 4
32:26 shall remain there in the cities of Gilead; 1
32 inheritance shall remain with us beyond the Jordan. •
33:55 then those of them whom you let remain shall be 3
35:28 For the man must remain in his city of refuge 2
36:12 their inheritance remained in the tribe 1
Deu 1:46 you remained at Kadesh many days 2
46 many days, the days that you remained there. 2
2:34 destroyed every city . . we left none remaining; 12
3:19 shall remain in the cities which I have given you 2
29 we remained in the valley opposite Beth-pe'or. 2
9: 9 I remained on the mountain 40 days and 40 nights 2
21:13 shall remain in your house and bewail . . a full month; 2
28:54 last of the children who remain to him; 3
Jos 1:14 and your cattle shall remain in the land 2
2:22 into the hills, and remained there three days 2
5: 8 they remained in their places in the camp 2
7:26 a great heap of stones that remains to this day; •
10:20 the remnant which remained of them had entered 11
27 great stones . . which remain to this very day. •
28 he utterly destroyed . . he left none remaining; 12
30 and he smote it . . he left none remaining in it; 12
33 Joshua smote . . until he left none remaining. 12
37 he left none remaining . . and utterly destroyed 12
39 and utterly destroyed . . he left none remaining; 12
40 he left none remaining, but utterly destroyed 12
11: 8 they smote them, until they left none remaining. 12
22 in Gaza, in Gath, and in Ashdod, did some remain. 13
13: 1 there remains yet very much land to be possessed. 13
2 This is the land that yet remains: all the regions 13
18: 2 There remained among . . Israel seven tribes 3
20: 4 and he shall remain with them. 2
6 he shall remain in that city until he has stood 2
23: 4 I have allotted . . those nations that remain 13
Jdg 7: 3 tested them; 22,000 returned, and 10,000 remained 13
11:17 not consent. So Israel remained at Kadesh. 2
19: 4 made him stay, and he remained with him three days; 2
Rut 1: 2 They went into . . Moab and remained there. 1
3:13 Remain this night, and in the morning 6
1Sm 1:23 the woman remained and nursed her son 2
5: 7 ark of the God of Israel must not remain with us; 2
16:11 And he said, "There remains yet the youngest 13
20:19 go to . . and remain beside yonder stone heap. 2
22: 5 Do not remain in the stronghold; depart, and go 2
23:14 And David remained in the strongholds 2
18 David remained at Horesh, and Jonathan went home. 2
25:13 while 200 remained with the baggage. 2
26: 3 But David remained in the wilderness; 2
2Sm 1: 1 David remained two days in Ziklag; 2
6:11 ark of the LORD remained in the house 2
10: 5 Remain at Jericho until your beards have grown 2
11: 1 But David remained at Jerusalem. 2
12 Remain here today also, and tomorrow I will let 2
12 Uri'ah remained in Jerusalem that day 2
15:29 back to Jerusalem; and they remained there. 2
16: 3 he remains in Jerusalem; for he said 2
18 his I will be, and with him I will remain. 2
1Kg 11:16 Jo'ab and all Israel remained there six months 2
22:46 male cult prostitutes who remained in the days 13
2Kg 6:31 if the head of Eli'sha . . remains on his shoulders 8
7:13 Let some men take five of the remaining horses 13
10:11 Jehu slew all that remained of the house of Ahab 13
11 Jehu slew . . until he left him none remaining. 12
17 he slew all that remained to Ahab in Sama'ria 13
11: 3 he remained with her six years, hid in the house 1
13: 6 and the Ashe'rah also remained in Sama'ria.) 8
24:14 none remained, except the poorest people 13
25:22 over the people who remained in the land of Judah 13
1Ch 13: 2 our brethren who remain in all the land of Israel 13
14 the ark of God remained with the household 2
19: 5 Remain at Jericho until your beards have grown 2
20: 1 But David remained at Jerusalem. 2
2Ch 22:12 he remained with them six years 1
Ezr 8:32 came to Jerusalem . . remained three days. 2
Neh 8: 7 while the people remained in their places. •
11: 1 while nine tenths remained in the other towns. •
Job 19: 4 that I have erred, my error remains with myself. 6
37: 8 go into their lairs, and remain in their dens. 15
Ps 142: 4 no refuge remains to me, no man cares for me. †
Prv 2:21 men of integrity will remain in it; 3
21:20 treasure remains in a wise man's dwelling 17
Ecc 1: 4 A generation . . but the earth remains for ever. 8
2: 9 became great . . also my wisdom remained with me. 8
Isa 4: 3 he who . . remains in Jerusalem will be called 3
6:13 though a tenth remain in it, it will be burned •
10: 4 Nothing remains but to crouch •
66:22 earth which I will make shall remain before me 8
22 shall your descendants and your name remain. 8
Jer 8: 3 all the remnant that remains of this evil family 13
17: 8 for its leaves remain green 1
24: 8 the remnant of Jerusalem who remain in this land 13
27:22 shall be carried to Babylon and remain there 1
32: 5 and there he shall remain until I visit him 1
34: 7 only fortified cities of Judah that remained. 13
37:10 and there remained of them only wounded men 13
16 and remained there many days 2
21 Jeremiah remained in the court of the guard. 2
38:13 And Jeremiah remained in the court of the guard. 2
28 Jeremiah remained in the court of the guard 2
39: 9 had deserted to him, and the people who remained. 13
40: 5 If you remain, then return to Gedali'ah ‡
42:10 If you will remain in this land 2
12 mercy on you and let you remain in your own land. 2
13 if you say, 'We will not remain in this land,' 2
43: 4 to remain in the land of Judah. 2
47: 4 from Tyre and Sidon every helper that remains. 12
48:11 his taste remains in him, and his scent 8
51:30 they remain in their strongholds; 2
Ezk 7:11 none of them shall remain, nor their abundance •
9: 8 wilt thou destroy all that remains of Israel 14
17: 6 its roots remained where it stood. 1
19:14 so that there remains in it no strong stem 1
21:26 things shall not remain as they are; •
39:14 bury those remaining upon the face of the land 3
44: 2 And he said to me, "This gate shall remain shut; 1
2 therefore it shall remain shut. 1
48:21 What remains on both sides of the holy portion 3
Dan 2:49 but Daniel remained at the king's court. •
10:17 For now no strength remains in me, and no breath 8
Hos 9: 3 They shall not remain in the land of the LORD; 2
Ams 6: 9 if ten men remain in one house, they shall die. 3
Zec 1:11 behold, all the earth remains at rest.' 2
14:10 But Jerusalem shall remain aloft upon its site 2
Mat 2:13 flee to Egypt, and remain there till I tell you; 22
15 remained there until the death of Herod. 22
11:23 it would have remained until this day. 32
26:38 remain here, and watch with me. 32
Mrk 14:34 remain here, and watch. 32
Lke 1:22 he made signs to them and remained dumb. 20
56 Mary remained with her about three months 32
10: 7 remain in the same house, eating and drinking 32
Joh 1:32 the Spirit descend . . and it remained on him. 32
33 'He on whom you see the Spirit descend and remain 32
3:22 there he remained with them and baptized. 21
6:22 the people who remained on the other side of the sea 25
7: 9 So saying, he remained in Galilee. 32
9:41 now that you say, 'We see,' your guilt remains. 32
10:40 there he remained. 32
12:24 it remains alone 32
34 the Christ remains for ever 32
46 may not remain in darkness. 32
19:31 to prevent the bodies from remaining on the cross 32
21:22 If it is my will that he remain until I come 32
23 If it is my will that he remain until I come 32
Act 5: 4 While it remained unsold 32
4 did it not remain your own? 32
10:48 Then they asked him to remain for some days. 24
12:19 he went down . . and remained there. 21
14: 3 So they remained for a long time 21
28 remained no little time with the disciples. 21
15:35 Paul and Barnabas remained in Antioch 21
16:12 We remained in this city some days; 21
17:14 Silas and Timothy remained there. 37
27:41 the bow stuck and remained immovable 32
1Co 7: 8 it is well for them to remain single as I do. 32
11 if she does, let her remain single 32
20 Every one should remain in the state 32
24 there let him remain with God. 32
26 it is well for a person to remain as he is. •
40 she is happier if she remains as she is 32
2Co 3:14 that same veil remains unlifted 32
Gal 1:18 remained with him fifteen days. 24
Php 1:24 to remain in the flesh is more necessary 24
25 Convinced of this, I know that I shall remain, 32
1Ti 1: 3 remain at Ephesus 35
2Ti 2:13 if we are faithless, he remains faithful 32
4:20 Eras'tus remained at Corinth 32
Heb 1:11 they will perish, but thou remainest 20
4: 1 while the promise of entering his rest remains 29
6 Since therefore it remains for some to enter it 19
9 remains a sabbath rest for the people of God; 19
10:26 there no longer remains a sacrifice for sins 19
12:27 in order that what cannot be shaken may remain. 32
Rev 3: 2 Awake, and strengthen what remains 31
17:10 when he comes he must remain only a little while. 32
2Es 3:22 good departed, and the evil remained. 39
4:35 'How long are we to remain here? ‡
48 I looked, and behold, the smoke remained. 44
49 drops remained in the cloud. 44
50 but drops and smoke remained. 44
6:25 whoever remains after all that I have foretold 38
41 and the other part remain beneath. 39
7:28 and those who remain shall rejoice 400 years. 42
34 only judgment shall remain, truth shall stand 43
123 whose fruit remains unspoiled 41
9:35 the things that held them remain 39
37 does not perish but remains in its glory. 40
10:51 Therefore I told you to remain in the field 39
58 tomorrow night you shall remain here. 39
11:23 nothing remained on the eagle's body 44
24 and remained under the head 39
24 but four remained in their place. 39
28 the two that remained were planning 44
34 the two heads remained 44
39 not the one that remains of the four beasts 44
12: 2 behold, the remaining head disappeared 44
27 as for the two who remained 41
13:49 he will defend the people who remain. 44
14:12 so two of its parts remain 44
37 we proceeded to the field, and remained there. 39
15:27 and you shall remain in them 39
Jdt 3:10 and remained for a whole month 22
7: 5 they remained on guard all that night. 32
12 Remain in your camp 16
11:17 therefore, my lord, I will remain with you 32
12: 7 she remained in the camp for three days 33
14:10 remaining so to this day. •
15: 7 the Israelites . . took possession of what remained 31
16:20 Judith remained with them. 30
21 went to Bethulia, and remained on her estate 30
Wis 7:27 while remaining in herself 32
10: 7 Evidence of their wickedness still remains 27
19:18 while each note remains the same 32
Sir 4:16 descendants will remain in possession of her. 22
6:20 a weakling will not remain with her. 32
16:11 it will be a wonder if he remains unpunished •
21:23 a cultivated man remains outside. 25
23:11 if he offends, his sin remains on him •
27: 4 When a sieve is shaken, the refuse remains 20
4 so a man's filth remains in his thoughts. •
41:12 since it will remain for you longer 20
42:23 All these things live and remain for ever 32
44:11 prosperity will remain with their descendants 9
46: 9 which remained with him to old age 20

Bar 2:21 remain in the land which I gave to your fathers. 26
LJr 1: 3 you will remain there for many years 22
1Mc 3:37 the king took the remaining half of his troops 29
8:11 The remaining kingdoms and islands 23
22 sent to Jerusalem to remain with them there 22
10:14 Only in Beth-zur did some remain 36
47 they remained his allies all his days. •
12:45 the other strongholds and the remaining troops 31
13:11 he drove out its occupants and remained there. 32
30 This is the tomb . . it remains to this day. •
15: 7 the strongholds . . shall remain yours. 32
2Mc 4:50 remained in office, growing in wickedness 32
8:14 Others sold all their remaining property 34
15:19 those who had to remain in the city 28
3Mc 2:33 They remained resolutely hopeful of obtaining help 27
3:26 for the remaining time 23
4: 8 the remaining days of their marriage festival 23
4Mc 7:12 Eleazar . . remained unmoved in his reason. •
8:11 if you disobey, nothing remains for you but to die 18
18: 9 I remained with my husband 32

remain *See also* adorned, alive, behind, confined, faithful, hidden, quiet, silent, standing, unclean, valid.

remain in camp 1. חנה
Num 9:18 as the cloud rested . . they remained in camp. 1
20 command of the LORD they remained in camp; 1
22 the people of Israel remained in camp 1

remain in prison 1. אסר
Gen 42:16 Send one of you . . while you remain in prison 1

no remain 1. אבד
Jer 25:35 No refuge will remain for the shepherds 1

remainder 1. יתר 2. שְׁאָר
Exd 29:34 then you shall burn the remainder with fire; 1
Lev 5:13 the remainder shall be for the priest •
Jos 21:40 the remainder of the families of the Levites 1
Isa 21:17 the remainder of the archers . . will be few; 2
Ezk 48:15 The remainder, 5,000 cubits in breadth 1
18 The remainder of the length alongside the holy 1

remaining *See* leave.

none remaining 1. אֶפֶס
Deu 32:36 sees . . there is none remaining, bond or free. 1

remarkably 1. ἐκπρέπω
2Mc 3:26 remarkably strong, gloriously beautiful 1

remedy 1. מַרְפֵּא 2. ἴασις
2Ch 36:16 till there was no remedy. 1
Wis 2: 1 there is no remedy when a man comes to his end 2

remember 1. זכר 2. זָכָר 3. ראה 4. ἀναμιμνήσκω 5. εἰμὶ μνεία 6. ἐπιμιμνήσκομαι 7. μιμνήσκομαι 8. μνεία 9. μνείαν ἔχω 10. μνείαν ποιέω 11. μνημονεύω 12. memor 13. memoro
Gen 8: 1 God remembered Noah and all the beasts 1
9:15 I will remember my covenant which is between me 1
16 it and remember the everlasting covenant 1
19:29 God remembered Abraham, and sent Lot out 1
30:22 God remembered Rachel . . hearkened to her 1
31:50 remember, God is witness between you and me. 3
40:14 remember me, when it is well with you 1
23 Yet the chief butler did not remember Joseph 1
41: 9 said to Pharaoh, "I remember my faults today. 1
42: 9 Joseph remembered the dreams which he had 1
Exd 2:24 and God remembered his covenant with Abraham 1
3:15 thus I am to be remembered throughout all 2
6: 5 I have heard . . I have remembered my covenant. 1
13: 3 Moses said to the people, "Remember this day 1
20: 8 Remember the sabbath day, to keep it holy. 1
32:13 Remember Abraham, Isaac, and Israel, thy servants 1
Lev 26:42 then I will remember my covenant with Jacob 1
42 I will remember my covenant with Isaac 1
42 and I will remember the land 1
45 I will for their sake remember the covenant 1
Num10: 9 you may be remembered before the LORD your God 1
11: 5 We remember the fish we ate in Egypt for nothing 1
15:39 to look upon and remember all the commandments 1
40 you shall remember and do all my commandments 1
Deu 5:15 remember that you were a servant in . . Egypt 1
7:18 remember what the LORD your God did to Pharaoh 1
8: 2 you shall remember all the way which the LORD 1
18 You shall remember the LORD your God, for it is he 1
9: 7 Remember and do not forget how you provoked 1
27 Remember thy servants, Abraham, Isaac, and Jacob; 1
15:15 remember . . you were a slave in the land of Egypt 1
16: 3 all the days of your life you may remember the day 1
12 You shall remember that you were a slave in Egypt; 1
24: 9 Remember what the LORD your God did to Miriam 1
18 remember that you were a slave in Egypt 1
22 remember that you were a slave in the land of Egypt; 1
25:17 Remember what Am'alek did to you on the way 1
32: 7 Remember the days of old, consider the years 1
Jos 1:13 Remember the word which Moses . . commanded you 1
Jdg 8:34 the people of Israel did not remember the LORD 1
9: 2 Remember also that I am your bone and your flesh. 1
16:28 O Lord GOD, remember me, I pray thee, 1
1Sm 1:11 look on the affliction . . and remember me 1
19 knew Hannah . . and the LORD remembered her; 1
25:31 when the LORD . . then remember your handmaid. 1
2Sm 19:19 or remember how your servant did wrong 1
2Kg 9:25 remember . . how the LORD uttered this oracle 1
20: 3 Remember now, O LORD . . how I have walked before 1
1Ch 16:12 Remember the wonderful works that he has done 1
2Ch 6:42 Remember thy steadfast love for David 1
24:22 Jo'ash the king did not remember the kindness 1
Neh 1: 8 Remember the word which thou didst command 1
4:14 Remember the Lord, who is great and terrible 1
5:19 Remember for my good, O my God, all that I have done 1
6:14 Remember Tobi'ah and Sanbal'lat, O my God 1
13:14 Remember me, O my God, concerning this 1
22 Remember this also in my favor, O my God 1
29 Remember them, O my God, because they have defiled 1
31 Remember me, O my God, for good. 1
Est 2: 1 he remembered Vashti and what she had done 1
9:28 that these days should be remembered and kept 1
Job 7: 7 Remember that my life is a breath; 1
10: 9 Remember that thou hast made me of clay; 1
11:16 you will remember it as waters that have passed 1
14:13 appoint me a set time, and remember me! 1
24:20 their name is no longer remembered; 1
36:24 Remember to extol his work 1
Ps 20: 3 May he remember all your offerings 1
22:27 of the earth shall remember and turn to the LORD; 1
25: 7 Remember not the sins of my youth 1
7 according to thy steadfast love remember me 1
42: 4 These things I remember, as I pour out my soul 1
6 I remember thee from the land of Jordan 1
74: 2 Remember thy congregation 1
2 Remember Mount Zion, where thou hast dwelt. •
18 Remember this, O LORD, how the enemy scoffs 1
22 remember how the impious scoff at thee all the day! 1
77: 5 the days of old, I remember the years long ago. 1
11 yea, I will remember thy wonders of old. 1
78:35 They remembered that God was their rock 1
39 He remembered that they were but flesh 1
79: 8 not remember against us the iniquities 1
83: 4 let the name of Israel be remembered no more! 1
88: 5 like those whom thou dost remember no more 1
89:47 Remember, O Lord, what the measure of life is 1
50 Remember, O Lord, how thy servant is scorned; 1
98: 3 remembered his steadfast love 1
103:14 knows our frame; he remembers that we are dust. 1
18 covenant and remember to do his commandments. 1
105: 5 Remember the wonderful works that he has done 1
42 For he remembered his holy promise, and Abraham 1
106: 4 Remember me, O LORD, when thou showest favor 1
7 not remember the abundance of thy steadfast love 1
45 He remembered for their sake his covenant 1
109:14 iniquity of his . . remembered before the LORD 1
16 For he did not remember to show kindness 1
111: 4 caused his wonderful works to be remembered; 2
112: 6 righteous . . will be remembered for ever. 2
119:49 Remember thy word to thy servant 1
55 I remember thy name in the night, O LORD 1
132: 1 Remember, O LORD, in David's favor 1
136:23 It is he who remembered us in our low estate 1
137: 1 sat down and wept, when we remembered Zion. 1
6 if I do not remember you, if I do not set Jerusalem 1
7 Remember, O LORD, against the E'domites the day 1
143: 5 I remember the days of old, I meditate on all that 1
Prv 31: 7 drink and . . remember their misery no more. 1
Ecc 5:20 For he will not much remember the days of his life 1
9:15 Yet no one remembered that poor man. 1
11: 8 let him remember that the days of darkness will 1
12: 1 Remember also your Creator in . . your youth 1
Isa 17:10 and have not remembered the Rock of your refuge; 1
23:16 sing many songs, that you may be remembered. 1
38: 3 said, "Remember now, O LORD, I beseech thee 1
43:18 Remember not the former things 1
25 and I will not remember your sins. 1
44:21 Remember these things, O Jacob, and Israel 1
46: 8 Remember this and consider, recall it to mind 1
9 remember the former things of old; for I am God 1
47: 7 lay these things to heart or remember their end. 1
54: 4 of your widowhood you will remember no more. 1
57:11 fear, so that you lied, and did not remember me 1
63:11 Then he remembered the days of old, 1
64: 5 those that remember thee in thy ways. 1
9 O LORD, and remember not iniquity for ever. 1
65:17 and the former things shall not be remembered 1
Jer 2: 2 I remember the devotion of your youth 1
3:16 It shall not come to mind, or be remembered 1
11:19 that his name be remembered no more. 1
14:10 now he will remember their iniquity and punish 1
21 remember and do not break thy covenant with us. 1
15:15 O LORD, thou knowest; remember me and visit me 1
17: 2 while their children remember their altars 1
18:20 Remember how I stood before thee to speak good 1
31:20 I speak against him, I do remember him still. 1
34 and I will remember their sin no more. 1
44:21 did not the LORD remember it? 1
51:50 go, stand not still! Remember the LORD from afar 1
Lam 1: 7 Jerusalem remembers . . all the precious things 1
2: 1 he has not remembered his footstool 1
3:19 Remember my affliction and my bitterness 1
5: 1 Remember, O LORD, what has befallen us; 1
Ezk 3:20 deeds which he has done shall not be remembered; 1
6: 9 then those of you who escape will remember me 1
16:22 you did not remember the days of your youth 1
43 you have not remembered the days of your youth 1
60 yet I will remember my covenant with you 1
61 Then you will remember your ways, and be ashamed 1
63 that you may remember and be confounded 1
18:22 None . . shall be remembered against him; 1
24 deeds which he has done shall be remembered; 1
20:43 there you shall remember your ways 1
21:32 you shall be no more remembered; 1
23:19 her harlotry, remembering the days of her youth 1
27 to the Egyptians or remember them any more. 1
25:10 may be remembered no more among the nations 1
33:13 none of his righteous deeds shall be remembered; 1
16 has committed shall be remembered against him; 1
36:31 Then you will remember your evil ways 1
Hos 7: 2 that I remember all their evil works. 1
8:13 Now he will remember their iniquity 1
9: 9 he will remember their iniquity 1
Ams 1: 9 did not remember the covenant of brotherhood. 1
Jon 2: 7 my soul fainted within me, I remembered the LORD; 1
Mic 6: 5 remember what Balak king of Moab devised 1
Hab 3: 2 in wrath remember mercy. 1
Zec 10: 9 yet in far countries they shall remember me 1
13: 2 so that they shall be remembered no more; 1
Mal 4: 4 Remember the law of my servant Moses 1
Mat 5:23 the altar, and there remember that your brother 7
16: 9 Do you not remember the five loaves 11
26:75 Peter remembered the saying of Jesus 7
Mrk 8:18 do you not remember? 11
14:72 Peter remembered how Jesus had said to him 4
Lke 1:72 to remember his holy covenant 7
16:25 Abraham said, 'Son, remember 7
17:32 Remember Lot's wife. 11
23:42 remember me when you come into your kingdom. 7
24: 6 Remember how he told you 7
Joh 15:20 Remember the word that I said to you 11
16: 4 you may remember that I told you of them 11
21 she no longer remembers the anguish 11
Act 20:31 remembering that . . I did not cease night or day 11
35 remembering the words of the Lord Jesus 11
Rom 11:18 remember it is not you that support the root •
Gal 2:10 only they would have us remember the poor 11
Eph 1:16 remembering you in my prayers 10
2:11 Therefore remember that . . 11
12 remember that you were at that time separated •
Col 4:18 Remember my fetters. Grace be with you. 11
1Th 1: 3 remembering before our God and Father your work 11
2: 9 For you remember our labor and toil, brethren 11
3: 6 and reported that you always remember us kindly 9
2Th 2: 5 Do you not remember 11
2Ti 1: 3 when I remember you constantly in my prayers. 9
4 As I remember your tears 7
2: 8 Remember Jesus Christ, risen from the dead 11
Phm 1: 4 when I remember you in my prayers 10
Heb 13: 7 Remember your leaders 11
2Pe 3: 2 remember the predictions of the holy prophets 7
Jde 1:17 you must remember, beloved, the predictions 7
Rev 2: 5 Remember then from what you have fallen 11
3: 3 Remember then what you received and heard; 11
16:19 and God remembered great Babylon 7
18: 5 and God has remembered her iniquities. 11
1Es 3:23 they do not remember what they have done. 7
4:43 Remember the vow which you made 7
2Es 2: 8 O wicked nation, remember what I did to Sodom 13
31 Remember your sons that sleep 13
8:28 remember those who have willingly 13
15:31 then the dragons, remembering their origin 12
Tob 1:12 because I remembered God with all my heart. 7
2: 6 Then I remembered the prophecy of Amos 7
3: 3 Remember me and look favorably upon me 7
4: 1 On that day Tobit remembered the money 7
4 Remember, my son, that she faced many dangers 7
5 Remember the Lord our God all your days, my son 11
12 Remember, my son, that . . all took wives 7
19 So, my son, remember my commands 11
6:15 Do you not remember the words 7
8: 2 As he went he remembered the words of Raphael 7
Jdt 8:26 Remember what he did with Abraham 7
13:19 they remember the power of God. 11
AEs 10: 5 I remember the dream that I had 7
12 God remembered his people 7
14:12 Remember, O Lord; make thyself known in this time 7
Wis 2: 4 no one will remember our works 11
Sir 7:16 remember that wrath does not delay. 7
28 Remember . . through your parents you were born; 7
36 In all you do, remember the end of your life 7
8: 5 remember that we all deserve punishment. 7
7 remember that we all must die. 7
9:12 remember that they will not be held guiltless 7
11:25 prosperity is not remembered. 7
14:12 Remember that death will not delay 7
16:17 who from on high will remember me? 7
23:14 Remember your father and mother 7
28: 6 Remember the end of your life 7
6 remember destruction and death •

7 Remember the commandments 7
7 remember the covenant of the Most High •
31:13 Remember that a greedy eye is a bad thing 7
36: 8 Hasten the day, and remember the appointed time 7
38:20 drive it away, remembering the end of life. 7
22 Remember my doom, for yours is like it 7
41: 3 remember your former days and the end of life 7
49: 9 For God remembered his enemies with storm 7
51: 8 Then I remembered thy mercy, O Lord 7
Bar 2:32 land of their exile, and will remember my name 7
33 for they will remember the ways of their fathers 7
3: 5 Remember not the iniquities of our fathers 7
5 in this crisis remember thy power and thy name. 7
4:14 remember the capture of my sons and daughters 7
27 you will be remembered by him 5
5: 5 rejoicing that God has remembered them. 8
Sus 1: 9 or remembering righteous judgments. 11
Bel 1:38 Daniel said, "Thou hast remembered me, O God 7
1Mc 2:51 Remember the deeds of the fathers 7
4: 9 Remember how our fathers were saved 7
10 remember his covenant with our fathers 7
5: 4 He also remembered the wickedness of the sons 7
6:12 now I remember the evils I did in Jerusalem 7
7:38 remember their blasphemies 7
9:38 they remembered the blood of John their brother 7
10: 5 for he will remember all the wrongs which we did 7
46 because they remembered the great wrongs 6
12:11 We therefore remember you constantly 7
11 as it is right and proper to remember brethren. 11
2Mc 1: 2 may he remember his covenant with Abraham 7
8: 4 to remember also the lawless destruction of . . 7
9:21 I remember with affection your esteem 11
26 remember the public and private services 7
10: 6 remembering how . . they had been wandering 11
4Mc 13:12 reminded them, "Remember whence you came 7
15:28 she remembered his fortitude. 7
16:18 Remember that it is through God 4

cause to remember 1. זכר
Exd 20:24 place where I cause my name to be remembered 1

remember earnestly 1. *ἀγωνίζομαι*
Col 4:12 remembering you earnestly in his prayers 1

remember in favor 1. *ἀναμιμνήσκω*
Sir 3:15 it will be remembered in your favor 1

make remember 1. זכר
Ezk 21:24 you have made your guilt to be remembered 1

remembrance 1. זֵכֶר 2. זִכָּרוֹן 3. *ἀνάμνησις* 4. *μιμνήσκομαι* 5. *μνεία* 6. *μνήμη* 7. *μνημόσυνον* 8. memoria
Exd 17:14 I will . . blot out the remembrance of Am'alek 1
28:12 as stones of remembrance for the sons of Israel; 2
12 upon his two shoulders for remembrance. 2
29 them to continual remembrance before the LORD. 2
30:16 it may bring the people of Israel to remembrance 2
39: 7 to be stones of remembrance for the sons 2
Num 5:15 cereal offering of remembrance 2
18 in her hands the cereal offering of remembrance 2
10:10 shall serve you for remembrance before your God 2
Deu 25:19 blot out the remembrance of Am'alek from under 1
32:26 make the remembrance . . cease from among men 1
Ps 6: 5 For in death there is no remembrance of thee; 1
34:16 to cut off the remembrance of them from the earth. 1
Ecc 1:11 There is no remembrance of former things 2
11 nor will there be any remembrance of later 2
2:16 of the fool there is no enduring remembrance 2
Isa 26:14 and wiped out all remembrance of them. 1
Mal 3:16 a book of remembrance was written before him 2
Lke 1:54 in remembrance of his mercy 4
22:19 Do this in remembrance of me. 3
1Co 11:24 Do this in remembrance of me. 3
25 as often as you drink it, in remembrance of me. 3
Php 1: 3 I thank my God in all my remembrance of you 5
2Es 12:47 for the Most High has you in remembrance 8
Wis 5:14 the remembrance of a guest who stays but a day 5
8:13 leave an everlasting remembrance 6
Sir 24:20 For the remembrance of me is sweeter than honey 7
38:23 let his remembrance cease 7
50:16 heard for remembrance before the Most High. 7

remembrance *See also* bring, call, come, keep, put.

remind 1. *ἀνάμνησις* 2. *γνωρίζω* 3. *καταμιμνήσκομαι* 4. *λογίζομαι πάλιν* 5. *προσυπομιμνήσκω* 6. *ὑπομιμνήσκω* 7. *ὑπόμνησιν λαμβάνω* 8. *ὑπόμνησις*
1Co 15: 1 Now I would remind you, brethren 2
2Co 10: 7 let him remind himself 4
2Ti 1: 5 I am reminded of your sincere faith 7
Wis 12: 2 dost remind and warn them 6
16: 6 to remind them of thy law's command. 1
11 To remind them of thy oracles they were bitten 8
2Mc 15: 9 reminding them . . of the struggles they had won 5
4Mc 13:12 another reminded them, "Remember whence you 3
18:14 He reminded you of the scripture of Isaiah 6

reminder 1. זִכָּרוֹן 2. *ἀνάμνησις* 3. *μνεία* 4. *μνημόσυνον* 5. *ὑπόμνησις*
Num16:40 to be a reminder to the people of Israel 1
Zec 6:14 as a reminder to Heldai, Tobi'jah, Jedai'ah 1
Heb 10: 3 in these sacrifices there is a reminder of sin 2
Tob 12:12 I brought a reminder of your prayer 4
AEs 16:23 it may be a reminder of destruction. 4
Wis 10: 8 also left for mankind a reminder of their folly 4
Sir 41: 1 O death, how bitter is the reminder of you 4
45: 9 as a reminder to the sons of his people; 4
11 for a reminder, in engraved letters 4
2Mc 6:17 Let what we have said serve as a reminder 5
4Mc 17: 8 a reminder to the people of our nation 3

remiss 1. *παρίημι*
Sir 4:29 sluggish and remiss in your deeds. 1

remission of tax 1. הֲנָחָה
Est 2:18 granted a remission of taxes to the provinces 1

tax remission 1. *ἄφεμα*
1Mc 15: 5 now . . I confirm to you all the tax remissions 1

remnant 1. יֶתֶר 2. פְּלֵיטָה 3. שָׂרִיד 4. שאר 5. שְׁאָר 6. שְׁאֵרִית 7. *κατάλειμμα* 8. *λεῖμμα* 9. *ὑπόλειμμα* 10. residuus
Gen 45: 7 to preserve for you a remnant on earth 6
Deu 3:11 only Og . . was left of the remnant of the Reph'aim; 1
Jos 10:20 the remnant which remained of them had entered 3
12: 4 Og . . of Bashan, one of the remnant of the Reph'aim 1
13:12 he alone was left of the remnant of the Reph'aim 1
23:12 turn back, and join the remnant of these nations 1
Jdg 5:13 down marched the remnant of the noble; the people 3
2Sm 14: 7 leave . . neither name nor remnant upon the face 6
21: 2 the Gib'eonites . . of the remnant of the Amorites; 1
1Kg 22:46 the remnant of the male cult prostitutes 1
2Kg 19: 4 lift up your prayer for the remnant that is left. 6
30 the surviving remnant . . shall again take root 2
31 for out of Jerusalem shall go forth a remnant 6
21:14 I will cast off the remnant of my heritage 6
1Ch 4:43 they destroyed the remnant of the Amal'ekites 6
2Ch 30: 6 that he may turn again to the remnant of you 4
34: 9 collected . . from all the remnant of Israel 6
Ezr 9: 8 to leave us a remnant, and to give us a secure hold 2
13 hast given us such a remnant as this 2
14 that there should be no remnant, nor any to escape? 6
15 left a remnant that has escaped, as at this day. •
Isa 10:19 remnant of the trees of his forest will be so few 5
20 In that day the remnant of Israel 5
21 A remnant will return, the remnant of Jacob 5
21 will return, the remnant of Jacob, to the mighty 5
22 only a remnant of them will return. 5
11:11 to recover the remnant . . left of his people 5
16 for the remnant which is left of his people 5
14:22 and will cut off from Babylon name and remnant 5
30 kill your root . . and your remnant I will slay. 6
15: 9 a lion . . for the remnant of the land. 6
17: 3 the remnant of Syria will be like the glory 5
28: 5 a diadem of beauty, to the remnant of his people; 5
37: 4 therefore lift up your prayer for the remnant 6
31 the surviving remnant of the house of Judah 2
32 for out of Jerusalem shall go forth a remnant 6
46: 3 all the remnant of the house of Israel 6
Jer 6: 9 Glean thoroughly as a vine the remnant of Israel; 6
8: 3 all the remnant that remains of this evil family 6
23: 3 Then I will gather the remnant of my flock 6
24: 8 the remnant of Jerusalem who remain in this land 6
25:20 Gaza, Ekron, and the remnant of Ashdod); 6
31: 7 LORD has saved his people, the remnant of Israel. 6
40:11 heard that the king of Babylon had left a remnant 6
15 scattered, and the remnant of Judah would perish? 6
42: 2 to the LORD your God for us, for all this remnant 6
15 then hear the word of the LORD, O remnant of Judah. 6
17 they shall have no remnant or survivor 3
19 The LORD has said to you, O remnant of Judah 6
43: 5 the forces took all the remnant of Judah 6
44: 7 from the midst of Judah, leaving you no remnant? 6
12 I will take the remnant of Judah 6
14 so that none of the remnant of Judah who have come 6
28 the remnant of Judah, who came to the land of Egypt 6
47: 4 the remnant of the coastland of Caphtor. 6
5 O remnant of the Anakim, how long will you gash 6
50:20 for I will pardon those whom I leave as a remnant. •
Ezk 11:13 wilt thou make a full end of the remnant of Israel? 6
Ams 1: 8 and the remnant of the Philistines shall perish 6
5:15 will be gracious to the remnant of Joseph. 6
9:12 that they may possess the remnant of Edom 6
Mic 2:12 O Jacob, I will gather the remnant of Israel; 6
4: 7 and the lame I will make the remnant; 6
5: 7 the remnant of Jacob shall be in the midst of many 6
8 the remnant of Jacob shall be among the nations 6
7:18 pardoning . . for the remnant of his inheritance? 6
Hab 2: 8 all the remnant of the peoples shall plunder you 1
Zep 1: 4 I will cut off from this place the remnant of Ba'al 5
2: 7 possession of the remnant of the house of Judah 6
9 The remnant of my people shall plunder them 6
Hag 1:12 high priest, with all the remnant of the people 6
14 the spirit of all the remnant of the people; 6
2: 2 and to all the remnant of the people, and say 6
Zec 8: 6 If it is marvelous in the sight of the remnant 6
11 I will not deal with the remnant of this people 6
12 I will cause the remnant of this people to possess 6
9: 7 it too shall be a remnant for our God; 4
Rom 9:27 only a remnant of them will be saved; 9
11: 5 So too at the present time there is a remnant 8
2Es 12:34 he will deliver in mercy the remnant of my people 10
Sir 44:17 therefore a remnant was left to the earth 7
47:22 he gave a remnant to Jacob 7
1Mc 3:35 the remnant of Jerusalem 7

least remnant
Wis 16: 3 might lose the least remnant of appetite •

remonstrate 1. ריב 2. *προφέρω*
Neh 13:11 I remonstrated with the officials and said, "Why 1
17 I remonstrated with the nobles of Judah and said 1
3Mc 5:39 the officials . . remonstrated as follows 2

remorse *See* feel.

remote 1. קֵץ 2. *ἀνώτερος*
Isa 37:24 I came to its remotest height, its densest forest 1
Tob 8: 3 he fled to the remotest parts of Egypt 2

remote part 1. יַרְכָה
Jdg 19: 1 the remote parts of the hill country of E'phraim 1
18 to the remote parts of the hill country of E'phraim 1

removal 1. סור 2. *ἀποτίθημι* 3. *ἐκκομιδή* 4. *μετάθεσις*
Num19: 9 for the water for impurity, for the removal of sin. •
Isa 27: 9 the full fruit of the removal of his sin 1
Heb 12:27 indicates the removal of what is shaken 4
1Pe 3:21 not as a removal of dirt from the body 2
2Mc 3: 7 to effect the removal of the aforesaid money. 3

remove 1. אסף 2. בער 3. גלה 4. הגה 5. יצא 6. מוט 7. מוש 8. נתק 9. סוג 10. סור 11. עבר 12. עבר מֵעַל 13. עתק 14. קרב 15. רום 16. שבת 17. שלח 18. עדא (A) 19. *αἴρω* 20. *ἀναιρέω* 21. *ἀποστεγάζω* 22. *ἀποστρέφω* 23. *ἀφαιρέω* 24. *ἀφίστημι* 25. *ἐκβάλλω* 26. *ἐξαίρω* 27. *καταλύω* 28. *καταργέω* 29. *κινέω* 30. *μεθίστημι* 31. *μετάγω* 32. *μετοικίζω* 33. *παραφέρω* 34. *περιαιρέω* 35. *χωρίζω* 36. facio 37. tollo
Gen 8:13 Noah removed the covering of the ark, and looked 10
12: 8 Thence he removed to the mountain on the east 13
30:32 removing from it every speckled and spotted 10
35 that day Laban removed the he-goats 10
48:12 Then Joseph removed them from his knees 5
17 to remove it from E'phraim's head to Manas'seh's 10
Exd 8:31 the LORD . . removed the swarms of flies 10
10:17 entreat the LORD . . to remove this death 10
Lev 4:31 all its fat he shall remove 10
31 as the fat is removed from the peace offerings 10
35 all its fat he shall remove as the fat of the lamb 10
35 he shall remove as the fat of the lamb is removed 10
26: 6 I will remove evil beasts from the land 16
Num12:10 when the cloud removed from over the tent, behold 10
14: 9 their protection is removed from them 10
Deu 19:14 shall not remove your neighbor's landmark 9
26:13 I have removed the sacred portion out of my house 2
14 have not . . removed any of it while I was unclean 2
27:17 'Cursed . . who removes his neighbor's landmark.' 9
Jdg 9:29 under my hand! then I would remove Abim'elech 10
1Sm 18:13 Saul removed him from his presence, and made him 10
21: 6 which is removed from before the LORD 10
1Kg 15:12 removed all the idols that his fathers had made. 10
13 also removed Ma'acah . . from being queen mother 10
20:24 do this: remove the kings, each from his post 10
2Kg 14: 4 But the high places were not removed; 10
15:35 Nevertheless the high places were not removed; 10
16:14 the bronze altar . . before the LORD he removed 14
17 Ahaz cut off the frames . . and removed the laver 10
18 he removed from the house of the LORD •
17:18 and removed them out of his sight; 10
23 the LORD removed Israel out of his sight 10
18: 4 He removed the high places, and broke the pillars 10
22 high places and altars Hezeki'ah has removed 10
23:11 he removed the horses . . dedicated to the sun 16
19 And all the shrines also . . Josi'ah removed; 10
27 I will remove Judah also out of my sight 10
27 I will remove Judah . . as I have removed Israel 10
24: 3 to remove them out of his sight, for the sins 10
2Ch 15:16 King Asa removed from being queen mother 10
30:14 removed the altars that were in Jerusalem 10
33: 8 no more remove the foot of Israel from the land 10
Job 9: 5 he who removes mountains, and they know it not 13
14:18 the rock is removed from its place; 13
18: 4 or the rock be removed out of its place? 13
24: 2 Men remove landmarks; they seize flocks 9
Ps 39:10 Remove thy stroke from me; I am spent by the blows 10
66:20 or removed his steadfast love from me! 10
89:33 I will not remove from him my steadfast love 10
44 Thou hast removed the scepter from his hand 16
Prv 10:30 The righteous will never be removed 6

22:28 Remove not the ancient landmark 9
23:10 Do not remove an ancient landmark or enter 9
Ecc 11:10 Remove vexation from your mind, and put away pain 10
Isa 1:16 remove the evil of your doings from before my eyes 10
25 smelt away your dross . . and remove all your alloy. 10
5: 5 to my vineyard. I will remove its hedge 10
10:13 I have removed the boundaries of peoples 10
27: 8 he removed them with his fierce blast 4
36: 7 high places and altars Hezeki'ah has removed 10
38:12 My dwelling is plucked up and removed from me 3
54:10 mountains may depart and the hills be removed 6
10 and my covenant of peace shall not be removed 6
57:14 remove every obstruction from my people's way. 15
Jer 4: 1 If you remove your abominations 10
4 remove the foreskin of your hearts, O men of Judah 10
6:29 for the wicked are not removed. 8
28:16 I will remove you from the face of the earth. 17
32:31 so that I will remove it from my sight 10
Ezk 11:18 they will remove from it all its detestable 10
16:50 therefore I removed them, when I saw it. 10
21:26 Remove the turban, and take off the crown; 10
26:16 down from their thrones, and remove their robes 10
Dan 2:21 he removes kings and sets up kings; 18
Hos 2:17 will remove the names of the Ba'als from her mouth 10
5:10 have become like those who remove the landmark; 9
11: 7 appointed to the yoke, and none shall remove it. 15
Jon 3: 6 he arose from his throne, removed his robe 12
Mic 2: 3 evil, from which you cannot remove your necks; 7
4 portion of my people; how he removes it from me! 7
Zep 3:11 I will remove from your midst your proudly 10
18 I will remove disaster from you 1
Zec 3: 4 Remove the filthy garments from him. 10
9 I will remove the guilt of this land 7
13: 2 also I will remove from the land the prophets 11
Mrk 2: 4 they removed the roof above him 21
14:36 remove this cup from me 33
Lke 22:42 if thou art willing, remove this cup from me; 33
Act 7: 4 after his father died, God removed him from there 32
43 I will remove you beyond Babylon.' 32
13:22 when he had removed him 30
1Co 5: 2 Let him who has done this be removed 19
13: 2 if I have all faith, so as to remove mountains 30
2Co 3:16 when a man turns to the Lord the veil is removed. 34
Gal 5:11 stumbling block of the cross has been removed. 28
Rev 2: 5 and remove your lampstand from its place 29
6:14 mountain and island was removed from its place 29
1Es 1:45 Nebuchadnezzar sent and removed him to Babylon 31
2Es 7:48 and removed us far from life 36
16:52 and iniquity will be removed from the earth 37
Tob 2: 4 and removed the body to a place of shelter 20
Jdt 10: 3 she removed the sackcloth 34
Sir 7: 6 lest you be unable to remove iniquity 26
10:17 He has removed some of them and destroyed them 26
23: 5 remove from me evil desire. 22
30:23 remove sorrow far from you 24
31: 1 anxiety about it removes sleep. 24
47:24 so as to remove them from their land. 24
Bar 2:35 I will never again remove my people Israel 29
1Mc 4:43 removed the defiled stones to an unclean place. 19
58 the reproach of the Gentiles was removed. 22
11:41 that he remove the troops of the citadel 25
63 intending to remove him from office. 30
66 He removed them from there 25
13:41 the yoke of the Gentiles was removed from Israel 19
51 a great enemy had been . . removed from Israel. *
14: 7 he removed its uncleanness from it 26
3Mc 5:50 removing the babies from their breasts 35
4Mc 4:16 who removed Onias from the priesthood 27
10:18 he said, "Even if you remove my organ of speech 23
151 1: 7 removed reproach from the people of Israel. 19

remove far 1. רחק
Job 22:23 if you remove unrighteousness far 1
Ps 103:12 far does he remove our transgressions from us. 1
Prv 30: 8 Remove far from me falsehood and lying; 1
Jer 27:10 that you will be removed far from your land 1
Jol 2:20 I will remove the northerner far from you 1
3: 6 removing them far from their own border. 1

remove far away 1. רחק
Isa 6:12 the LORD removes men far away 1

remove far off 1. רחק
Ezk 11:16 Though I removed them far off among the nations 1

remove mark of circumcision 1. ἐπισπάομαι 2. ποιέω ἀκροβυστίαν
1Co 7:18 seek to remove the marks of circumcision 1
1Mc 1:15 and removed the marks of circumcision 2

rend 1. בקע 2. טרף 3. פרם 4. פרק 5. קרע 6. διαρρήγνυμι 7. discindo
Gen 37:29 Joseph was not in the pit, he rent his clothes 5
34 Then Jacob rent his garments, and put sackcloth 5
44:13 Then they rent their clothes 5
Lev 10: 6 do not rend your clothes, lest you die 3
21:10 The priest . . shall not . . nor rend his clothes 3
Num14: 6 Joshua . . and Caleb . . , rent their clothes 5
Jos 7: 6 Joshua rent his clothes, and fell to the earth 5
Jdg 11:35 when he saw her, he rent his clothes, and said, "Alas 5
1Sm 4:12 came to Shiloh . . with his clothes rent 5
2Sm 1: 2 with his clothes rent and earth upon his head. 5
11 Then David took hold of his clothes, and rent them; 5
3:31 Rend your clothes, and gird on sackcloth 5
13:19 put ashes . . and rent the long robe which she wore; 5
31 arose, and rent his garments, and lay on the earth; 5
31 and all his servants . . rent their garments. 5
15:32 came . . with his coat rent and earth upon his 5
1Kg 19:11 a great and strong wind rent the mountains 4
21:27 when Ahab heard those words, he rent his clothes 5
2Kg 2:12 took hold of his own clothes and rent them in two 5
5: 7 he rent his clothes and said, "Am I God 5
8 that the king of Israel had rent his clothes 5
8 Why have you rent your clothes? 5
6:30 When the king heard . . he rent his clothes 5
11:14 And Athali'ah rent her clothes, and cried, "Treason! 5
18:37 came to Hezeki'ah with their clothes rent 5
19: 1 he rent his clothes, and covered himself 5
22:11 when the king heard . . he rent his clothes. 5
19 and you have rent your clothes and wept before me 5
2Ch 23:13 Athali'ah rent her clothes, and cried, "Treason! 5
34:19 When the king heard . . he rent his clothes. 5
27 have rent your clothes and wept before me 5
Ezr 9: 3 When I heard this, I rent my garments and my mantle 5
5 I rose . . with my garments and my mantle rent 5
Est 4: 1 Mor'decai rent his clothes and put on sackcloth 5
Job 1:20 Job arose, and rent his robe, and shaved his head 5
2:12 they rent their robes and sprinkled dust 5
26: 8 the cloud is not rent under them. 1
Ps 7: 2 lest like a lion they rend me, dragging me away 2
50:22 lest I rend, and there be none to deliver! 2
Ecc 3: 7 a time to rend, and a time to sew; 5
Isa 36:22 came to Hezeki'ah with their clothes rent 5
37: 1 When King Hezeki'ah heard it, he rent his clothes 5
64: 1 O that thou wouldst rend the heavens 5
Jer 36:24 was afraid, nor did they rend their garments. 5
Hos 5:14 I, even I, will rend and go away, I will carry off 2
13: 8 as a wild beast would rend them. 1
Jol 2:13 and rend your hearts and not your garments. 5
1Es 8:71 I rent my garments and my holy mantle 6
73 with my garments and my holy mantle rent 6
2Es 9:38 her clothes were rent 7
Jdt 14:16 groaned and shouted, and rent his garments. 6
19 rent their tunics and were greatly dismayed 6
LJr 1:31 the priests sit with their clothes rent 6
1Mc 2:14 Mattathias and his sons rent their clothes 6
3:47 rent their clothes. 6
4:39 Then they rent their clothes 6
5:14 other messengers, with their garments rent, came 6
11:71 Jonathan rent his garments 6
13:45 went up on the wall with their clothes rent 6

rend asunder 1. פרר
Isa 24:19 the earth is rent asunder, the earth is violently 1

rend open 1. פצם
Ps 60: 2 made the land to quake, thou hast rent it open; 1

render 1. נתן 2. עשה 3. שוב 4. שלם 5. ἀνταποδίδωμι 6. ἀποδίδωμι 7. διακονία 8. καθίστημι 9. κατασκευάζω 10. προσέχω
Num18: 9 every offering . . which they render to me 3
Jos 7:19 give glory to the LORD . . and render praise to him; 1
1Kg 3:28 the wisdom of God was in him, to render justice. 2
8:39 and render to each . . according to all his ways 1
2Ch 6:30 hear thou . . and forgive, and render to each 1
Ps 28: 4 render them their due reward. 3
38:20 Those who render me evil for good 4
56:12 O God; I will render thank offerings to thee. 4
72:10 of Tarshish and of the isles render him tribute 3
94: 2 render to the proud their deserts! 3
116:12 What shall I render to the LORD for all his bounty 3
Isa 59:18 to the coastlands he will render requital. 4
66: 6 of the LORD, rendering recompense to his enemies! 4
15 like the stormwind, to render his anger in fury 3
Jer 51: 6 vengeance, the requital he is rendering her. 4
Hos 14: 2 and we will render the fruit of our lips. 4
Mat 22:21 Render therefore to Caesar 6
Mrk 12:17 Render to Caesar the things that are Caesar's 6
Lke 20:25 render to Caesar the things that are Caesar's 6
Rom 2: 6 will render to every man according to his works 6
2Co 9:12 the rendering of this service 7
1Th 3: 9 what thanksgiving can we render to God for you 5
1Pe 4:11 who renders it by the strength which God supplies *
Rev 18: 6 Render to her as she herself has rendered 6
6 Render to her as she herself has rendered 6
AEs 16: 8 we will take care to render our kingdom quiet 10
Sir 0: 2 seem to have rendered some phrases imperfectly *
42: 2 of rendering judgment to acquit the ungodly; *
3Mc 5:43 quickly render it forever empty 8
4Mc 13:26 they rendered their brotherly love more fervent. 9

render *See also* account, ineffective, judgment, powerless, service.

renew 1. חדש 2. חיה 3. חלף 4. ἀνακαινόω 5. ἀνανεόω 6. καινίζω 7. renovo
1Sm 11:14 let us go to Gilgal and there renew the kingdom. 1
Job 10:17 thou dost renew thy witnesses against me 1
Ps 90: 5 dream, like grass which is renewed in the morning 3
6 in the morning it flourishes and is renewed; 3
103: 5 so that your youth is renewed like the eagle's. 1
104:30 thou renewest the face of the ground. 1
Isa 40:31 who wait for the LORD shall renew their strength 3
41: 1 let the peoples renew their strength; 3
Lam 5:21 Restore us . . Renew our days as of old! 1
Hab 3: 2 In the midst of the years renew it; 2
Zep 3:17 he will renew you in his love; 6
2Co 4:16 our inner nature is being renewed every day. 4
Eph 4:23 be renewed in the spirit of your minds 5
Col 3:10 which is being renewed in knowledge 4
2Es 7:75 when thou wilt renew the creation 7
12:23 and they shall renew many things in it 7
Wis 7:27 she renews all things 6
1Mc 12: 1 to confirm and renew the friendship with them. 5
3 sent us to renew the former friendship 5
10 undertaken to send to renew our brotherhood 5
16 sent them to Rome to renew our former friendship 5
14:18 to renew with him the friendship and alliance 5
22 come to us to renew their friendship with us. 5
15:17 to renew our ancient friendship and alliance. 5

renewal 1. ἀναβιόω 2. ἀνακαίνωσις 3. ἀνανέωσις 4. ἐπάνοδος
Rom 12: 2 but be transformed by the renewal of your mind 2
Tit 3: 5 renewal in the Holy Spirit 2
Sir 22:21 a renewal of friendship is possible. 4
1Mc 12:17 concerning the renewal of our brotherhood. 3
2Mc 7: 9 an everlasting renewal of life 1

renounce 1. נאץ 2. נאר 3. ἀπεῖπον 4. ἀποτάσσομαι 5. ἀρνέομαι 6. ἐξόμνυμι 7. renuntio
Ps 10: 3 man greedy for gain curses and renounces the LORD. 1
13 Why does the wicked renounce God 1
89:39 hast renounced the covenant with thy servant; 2
Lke 14:33 whoever of you does not renounce all that he has 4
2Co 4: 2 renounced disgraceful, underhanded ways 3
Tit 2:12 training us to renounce irreligion 5
2Es 14:13 And now renounce the life that is corruptible 7
4Mc 4:26 to eat defiling foods and to renounce Judaism. 6
5:34 nor will I renounce you, beloved self-control. 6
8: 7 if you will renounce the ancestral tradition 5
9:23 renounce our courageous brotherhood. 6
10: 3 I do not renounce the noble kinship 6
15 I will not renounce our noble brotherhood. 5

renown 1. זֵכֶר 2. שֵׁם 3. תְּהִלָּה 4. εὔκλεια 5. ὄνομα
Gen 6: 4 that were of old, the men of renown. 2
Ps 135:13 thy renown, O LORD, throughout all ages. 1
Jer 48: 2 the renown of Moab is no more. 3
Ezk 16:14 your renown went forth among the nations 2
15 and played the harlot because of your renown 2
Zep 3:19 shame into praise and renown in all the earth. 2
20 yea, I will make you renowned and praised 2
Wis 8:18 renown in sharing her words 4
1Mc 14:10 till his renown spread to the ends of the earth. 5

renowned 1. הלל 2. כבד 3. קרא 4. קרא שֵׁם 5. εὐκλεής 6. ὀνομάζω 7. ὀνομαστός
Rut 4:11 May you prosper in Eph'rathah and be renowned 4
14 and may his name be renowned in Israel! 3
2Sm 23:19 He was the most renowned of the 30 2
23 He was renowned among the 30 2
1Ch 11:21 He was the most renowned of the 30 2
25 He was renowned among the 30 2
Ezk 26:17 O city renowned, that was mighty on the sea 1
Jdt 11:23 be renowned throughout the whole world. 7
Wis 3:15 For the fruit of good labors is renowned 5
Sir 44: 3 men renowned for their power 7
1Mc 3: 9 He was renowned to the ends of the earth 6

repair 1. אֲרוּכָה 2. בדק 3. בֶּדֶק 4. גדר 5. חדש 6. חזק 7. חזק בֶּדֶק 8. חיה 9. עמד 10. רפא 11. חוט (A) 12. ἀνίστημι 13. ἐπισκευάζω 14. θεραπεύω 15. ὑποράπτω
1Kg 18:30 he repaired the altar of the LORD 10
2Kg 12: 5 the priests take . . and let them repair the house 7
7 Why are you not repairing the house? 7
7 but hand it over for the repair of the house. 3
8 that they should not repair the house. 7
12 and for any outlay upon the repairs of the house. 6
14 workmen who were repairing the house of the LORD 6
22: 5 workmen who are at . . repairing the house 7
6 timber and quarried stone to repair the house. 6
1Ch 11: 8 and Jo'ab repaired the rest of the city. 8
2Ch 15: 8 he repaired the altar of the LORD 5
24: 5 money to repair the house of your God 6
12 workers . . to repair the house of the LORD. 6
13 the repairing went forward in their hands 1
29: 3 doors of the house of the LORD, and repaired them. 6
34: 8 to repair the house of the LORD his God. 6
10 gave it for repairing and restoring the house. 2
Ezr 4:12 walls and repairing the foundations. 11
9: 9 to repair its ruins, and to give us protection 9
Neh 3: 4 the son of Uri'ah, son of Hakkoz repaired. 6
4 son of Berechi'ah, son of Meshez'abel repaired. 6

4 next to them Zadok the son of Ba'ana repaired. 6
5 next to them the Teko'ites repaired; 6
6 Joi'ada . . Meshul'lam . . repaired the Old Gate; 6
7 next to them repaired Melati'ah the Gib'eonite 6
8 son of Harhai'ah, goldsmiths, repaired. 6
8 Hanani'ah, one of the perfumers, repaired; 6
9 Rephai'ah the son of Hur . . repaired. 6
10 Jedai'ah . . repaired opposite his house; 6
10 Hattush the son of Hashabnei'ah repaired. 6
11 repaired another section 6
12 Shallum . . repaired, he and his daughters. 6
13 Hanun and . . Zano'ah repaired the Valley Gate; 6
13 repaired 1,000 cubits of the wall •
14 Malchi'jah . . repaired the Dung Gate; 6
15 Shallum . . repaired the Fountain Gate; 6
16 Nehemi'ah . . repaired to a point opposite 6
17 After him the Levites repaired: Rehum the son 6
17 Hashabi'ah . . repaired for his district. 6
18 After him their brethren repaired: Bav'vai 6
19 Ezer . . repaired another section opposite 6
20 Baruch . . repaired another section 6
21 Mer'emoth . . repaired another section 6
22 priests, the men of the Plain, repaired. 6
23 Benjamin . . repaired opposite their house. 6
23 Azari'ah . . repaired beside his own house. 6
24 Bin'nui . . repaired another section 6
25 Palal . . repaired opposite the Angle •
26 temple servants . . repaired to a point opposite •
27 Teko'ites repaired another section opposite 6
28 Above the Horse Gate the priests repaired 6
29 Zadok . . repaired opposite his own house. 6
29 Shemai'ah the son of Shecani'ah . . repaired. 6
30 Hanani'ah . . Hanun . . repaired another section. 6
30 Meshul'lam . . repaired opposite his chamber. 6
31 Malchi'jah . . repaired as far as the house 6
32 goldsmiths and the merchants repaired. 6
4: 7 heard that the repairing of the walls 1
Ps 60: 2 repair its breaches, for it totters. 10
Isa 61: 4 they shall repair the ruined cities 5
Ams 9:11 booth . . that is fallen and repair its breaches 4
1Es 2:18 repairing its market places and walls 14
Sir 50: 1 who in his life repaired the house 15
1Mc 3:43 Let us repair the destruction of our people 12
12:37 he repaired the section called Chaphenatha. 13

repair *See also* need.

repairer 1. גדר
Isa 58:12 you shall be called the repairer of the breach 1

repairs *See* make.

repay 1. גמל 2. שוב 3. שלם 4. ἀνταποδίδωμι 5. ἀνταπόδομα 6. ἀποδίδωμι 7. ἀποτίνω 8. διπλόω 9. εὑρίσκω ἀνταπόδομα 10. reddo
1Sm 24:17 you have repaid me good, whereas I 1
17 good, whereas I have repaid you evil. 1
2Sm 16:12 the LORD will repay me with good for this cursing 2
Job 41:11 Who has given to me, that I should repay him? 3
Prv 19:17 he will repay him for his deed. 3
20:22 Do not say, "I will repay evil"; wait for the LORD 3
Isa 59:18 According to their deeds, so will he repay 3
65: 6 I will not keep silent, but I will repay 3
6 I will repay, yea, I will repay into their bosom 3
Mat 16:27 then he will repay every man for what he has done. 6
Lke 10:35 I will repay you when I come back.' 6
14:12 lest . . you be repaid. 5
14 you will be blessed, because they cannot repay 4
14 repaid at the resurrection of the just. 4
Rom 11:35 given a gift to him that he might be repaid? 4
12:17 Repay no one evil for evil 6
19 Vengeance is mine, I will repay, says the Lord. 4
1Th 5:15 See that none of you repays evil for evil 6
2Th 1: 6 to repay with affliction those who afflict you 4
Phm 1:19 I, Paul, write this with my own hand, I will repay 7
Heb 10:30 Vengeance is mine, I will repay. 4
Rev 18: 6 and repay her double for her deeds; 8
22:12 to repay every one for what he has done. 6
2Es 15:20 to turn and repay what they have given them. 10
21 so I will do, and will repay into their bosom 10
Tob 14:10 with what he repaid him 4
Sir 4:31 withdrawn when it is time to repay. 6
12: 2 Do good to a godly man, and you will be repaid 9
29: 2 in turn, repay your neighbor promptly. 6
6 he will repay him with curses and reproaches 6
6 instead of glory will repay him with dishonor. 6
30: 6 one to repay the kindness of his friends. 4
35:11 For the Lord is the one who repays 4
11 he will repay you sevenfold. 4
18 repays vengeance on the nations 4
19 till he repays the man according to his deeds 4
LJr 1:34 they will not be able to repay it 4
1Mc 10:27 repay you with good for what you do for us. 4
11:53 did not repay the favors which Jonathan had done 4
2Mc 4:38 repaid him with the punishment he deserved. 6

repayment 1. ἀνταπόδομα 2. ἀπόδοσις
Tob 14:10 the other received repayment 1
Sir 29: 5 at the time for repayment he will delay 2

repayment *See also* receive.

repeat 1. אמר 2. דבר 3. משל 4. נגד 5. שנה 6. תנה 7. δευτερόω 8. δευτέρωσις 9. πάλιν λέγω
Jdg 5:11 there they repeat the triumphs of the LORD 6
1Sm 8:21 all the words . . he repeated them in the ears 2
17:31 When the words . . they repeated them before Saul; 4
2Kg 4:43 So he repeated, "Give them to the men 1
Prv 17: 9 but he who repeats a matter alienates a friend. 5
26:11 dog . . to his vomit is a fool that repeats his folly. 5
Ezk 18: 2 What do you mean by repeating this proverb 3
2Co 11:16 I repeat, let no one think me foolish 9
Sir 7:14 nor repeat yourself in your prayer. 7
19: 7 Never repeat a conversation 7
41:23 repeating and telling what you hear 8

repeatedly 1. עוֹד 2. πολλάκις 3. πολύς
Ecc 7:28 my mind has sought repeatedly, but . . not found. 1
Heb 9:25 Nor was it to offer himself repeatedly 2
26 for then he would have had to suffer repeatedly 2
10:11 offering repeatedly the same sacrifices 2
4Mc 10: 1 many repeatedly urged him to save himself 3

repel 1. ἄμυνα 2. ἀπωθέω
Wis 5:17 and will arm all creation to repel his enemies; 1
4Mc 2:16 repels all these malicious emotions 2
16 just as it repels anger •

repent 1. נחם 2. שוב 3. שוב וְנחם 4. εἰς μετάμελον ἔρχομαι 5. ἐπιστρέφω 6. μεταμέλομαι 7. μετανοέω 8. μετάνοια
Exd 13:17 Lest the people repent when they see war 1
32:12 repent of this evil against thy people. 1
14 the LORD repented of the evil which he thought 1
Num 23:19 God is not . . a son of man, that he should repent. 1
1Sm 15:11 I repent that I have made Saul king; 1
29 the Glory of Israel will not lie or repent; 1
29 for he is not a man, that he should repent. 1
35 And the LORD repented that he had made Saul king 1
2Sm 24:16 the LORD repented of the evil, and said 1
1Kg 8:47 repent, and make supplication to thee in the land 2
48 if they repent with all their mind 2
1Ch 21:15 the LORD saw, and he repented of the evil; 1
2Ch 6:37 lay it to heart . . and repent, and make 2
38 if they repent with all their mind and . . heart 2
Job 42: 6 I despise myself, and repent in dust and ashes. 1
Ps 7:12 If a man does not repent, God will whet his sword; 2
78:34 they repented and sought God earnestly. 2
Isa 1:27 those in her who repent, by righteousness. 2
Jer 5: 3 they have refused to repent. 2
8: 6 no man repents of his wickedness 1
9: 5 they commit iniquity and are too weary to repent. •
18: 8 I will repent of the evil that I intended to do 1
10 I will repent of the good which I had intended 1
26: 3 that I may repent of the evil which I intend to do 1
13 and the LORD will repent of the evil 1
19 did not the LORD repent of the evil 1
31:19 For after I had turned away I repented; 1
34:15 You recently repented and did what was right 2
42:10 for I repent of the evil which I did to you. 1
Ezk 14: 6 Repent and turn away from your idols; 2
18:30 Repent and turn from all your transgressions 2
24:14 I will not spare, I will not repent; 1
Jol 2:13 in steadfast love, and repents of evil. 1
14 Who knows whether he will not turn and repent 1
Ams 7: 3 The LORD repented concerning this; 1
6 The LORD repented concerning this; 1
Jon 3: 9 God may yet repent and turn from his fierce anger 3
10 God repented of the evil which he had said 1
4: 2 in steadfast love, and repentest of evil. 1
Zec 1: 6 they repented and said, As the LORD of hosts 2
Mat 3: 2 Repent, for the kingdom of heaven is at hand. 7
4:17 Repent, for the kingdom of heaven is at hand. 7
11:20 because they did not repent. 7
21 they would have repented long ago in sackcloth 7
12:41 for they repented at the preaching of Jonah 7
21:29 but afterward he repented and went. 6
32 you did not afterward repent and believe him. 6
27: 3 he repented and brought back the 30 pieces 6
Mrk 1:15 repent, and believe in the gospel. 7
6:12 and preached that men should repent. 7
Lke 10:13 they would have repented long ago 7
11:32 they repented at the preaching of Jonah 7
13: 3 unless you repent you will all likewise perish. 7
5 unless you repent you will all likewise perish. 7
15: 7 more joy in heaven over one sinner who repents 7
10 there is joy . . over one sinner who repents. 7
16:30 they will repent.' 7
17: 3 if he repents, forgive him; 7
4 turns to you seven times, and says, 'I repent,' 7
Act 2:38 Repent, and be baptized every one of you 7
3:19 Repent therefore, and turn again 7
8:22 Repent therefore of this wickedness of yours 7
17:30 now he commands all men everywhere to repent 7
26:20 they should repent and turn to God 7
2Co 7: 9 because you were grieved into repenting 8
12:21 who sinned before and have not repented 7
2Ti 2:25 they will repent and come to know the truth 8
Heb 12:17 he was rejected for he found no chance to repent 8
Rev 2: 5 repent and do the works you did at first. 7
5 and remove your lampstand . . unless you repent 7
16 Repent then. If not, I will come to you soon and war 7
21 I gave her time to repent, but she refuses 7
21 but she refuses to repent of her immorality. 7
22 unless they repent of her doings; 7
3: 3 what you received . . keep that, and repent. 7
19 I reprove and chasten; so be zealous and repent. 7
9:20 did not repent of the works of their hands 7
21 nor did they repent of their murders 7
16: 9 and they did not repent and give him glory. 7
11 and did not repent of their deeds. 7
Wis 11:23 that they may repent. 8
12:10 thou gavest them a chance to repent 8
Sir 17:24 Yet to those who repent he grants a return 7
21: 6 he that fears the Lord will repent in his heart. 5
48:15 For all this the people did not repent 7
Man 1: 7 repentest over the evils of men. 7
13 thou, O Lord, art the God of those who repent 7
3Mc 2:24 he by no means repented 4

repentance 1. μετανοέω 2. μετάνοια 3. paenitentia 4. reversio
Mat 3: 8 Bear fruit that befits repentance 2
11 I baptize you with water for repentance, but he 2
Mrk 1: 4 preaching a baptism of repentance 2
Lke 3: 3 preaching a baptism of repentance 2
8 Bear fruits that befit repentance 2
5:32 sinners to repentance. 2
15: 7 who need no repentance. 2
24:47 repentance and forgiveness of sins 2
Act 5:31 give repentance to Israel 2
11:18 God has granted repentance unto life. 2
13:24 a baptism of repentance 2
19: 4 John baptized with the baptism of repentance 2
20:21 testifying . . of repentance to God 2
26:20 and perform deeds worthy of their repentance 2
Rom 2: 4 God's kindness is meant to lead you to repentance? 2
2Co 7:10 For godly grief produces a repentance 2
Heb 6: 1 not laying again a foundation of repentance 2
4 For it is impossible to restore to repentance 2
2Pe 3: 9 but that all should reach repentance. 2
2Es 7:82 because they cannot now make a good repentance 4
9:11 while an opportunity of repentance was . . open 3
Wis 5: 3 They will speak to one another in repentance 1
12:19 because thou givest repentance for sins. 2
Sir 44:16 an example of repentance to all generations. 2
Man 1: 7 promised repentance and forgiveness 2
7 thou hast appointed repentance for sinners 2
8 not appointed repentance for the righteous 2
8 appointed repentance for me, who am a sinner. 2

repentance *See also* turn.

replace 1. שום 2. שוב
Gen 42:25 gave orders . . to replace every man's money 2
43:18 the money, which was replaced in our sacks 2
1Sm 21: 6 which is removed . . to be replaced by hot bread 1

replant 1. נטע
Ezk 36:36 and replanted that which was desolate; 1

replenish 1. מלא
Jer 31:25 and every languishing soul I will replenish. 1
Ezk 26: 2 I shall be replenished, now that she is laid waste 1

reply 1. אמר 2. ענה 3. שוב 4. שוב דָּבָר 5. פִּתְגָם (A) 6. תוּב (A) 7. ἀνταποκρίνομαι 8. ἀποκρίνομαι 9. εἶπον 10. λέγω 11. ὑπολαμβάνω 12. φημί 13. respondeo
Gen 38:18 She replied, "Your signet and your cord 1
23 Judah replied, "Let her keep the things as her own 1
43: 7 They replied, "The man questioned us carefully 1
23 He replied, "Rest assured, do not be afraid; 1
Rut 3: 5 And she replied, "All that you say I will do. 1
18 She replied, "Wait, my daughter, until you learn 1
1Sm 20: 3 David replied, "Your father knows well that I have 8
1Kg 2:31 The king replied to him, "Do as he has said, strike 1
2Kg 4:29 and if any one salutes you, do not reply; 2
Ezr 5:11 this was their reply to us: 'We are the servants 5
Neh 2:20 Then I replied to them, "The God of heaven will make 4
Est 4:15 Then Esther told them to reply to Mor'decai 3
Job 13:22 or let me speak, and do thou reply to me. 3
Dan 2:14 Daniel replied with prudence and discretion 6
Mat 12:48 he replied to the man who told him 8
16:16 Simon Peter replied, "You are the Christ 8
17:11 He replied, "Eli'jah does come 8
19:27 Then Peter said in reply 8
20:13 he replied to one of them 8
25: 9 the wise replied 8
12 he replied, 'Truly, I say to you, I do not know you.' 8
Mrk 3:33 he replied, "Who are my mother and my brothers? 8
5: 9 He replied, "My name is Legion; for we are many. 10
Lke 10:30 Jesus replied, "A man was going down 11
14: 6 they could not reply to this. 7
Joh 7:52 They replied, "Are you from Galilee too? 8
Act 15:13 After they finished speaking, James replied 8
21:39 Paul replied, "I am a Jew, from Tarsus in Cili'cia 9
24:10 Paul replied 8
25: 4 Festus replied that Paul was being kept 8

2Es 4: 3 And he replied to me, "I have been sent to show you 13
5:44 He replied to me and said 13
51 He replied to me, "Ask a woman who bears children 13
7:62 I replied and said, "O earth 13
Tob 2:14 Then she replied to me 8
5: 6 The angel replied, "I will go with you 9
12 He replied, "I am Azarias 9
6: 7 He replied, "As for the heart and liver 9
7: 5 They replied, "He is alive and in good health. 9
10: 9 Tobias replied, "No, send me back to my father. 10
12: 2 He replied, "Father, it would do me no harm 9
Jdt 10:12 She replied, "I am a daughter of the Hebrews 9
11: 5 Judith replied to him 9
12: 4 Judith replied, "As your soul lives, my lord 9
1Mc 3:18 Judas replied, "It is easy 9
10:55 Ptolemy the king replied and said 8
13:35 sent him a favorable reply to this request 8
2Mc 3:37 When the king asked Heliodorus . . he replied 12
7: 8 He replied in the language of his fathers 8
15: 5 he replied, "And I am a sovereign also, on earth 12
4Mc 9:17 he replied, "You abominable lackeys 9

reply *See also* give, send, write.

report 1. בוא לִפְנֵי 2. דִּבָּה 3. דבר 4. דָּבָר 5. הַשְּׁמֻעוֹת 6. יצא 7. נגד 8. קוֹל 9. שׁוב 10. שׁוב דָּבָר 11. שְׁמוּעָה 12. שׁמע 13. שֵׁמַע 14. שֹׁמַע 15. טַעַם (A) 16. פִּתְגָם (A) 17. ἀκοή 18. ἀκούω 19. ἀναγγέλλω 20. ἀπαγγέλλω 21. δηλόω 22. διαβοάω 23. διαγγέλλω 24. διάθεσις 25. διασαφέω 26. διηγέομαι 27. ἐκδιηγέομαι 28. ἐξηγέομαι 29. ἦχος 30. ἱστορέω 31. λόγος 32. μηνύω 33. προσαγγέλλω 34. ῥῆμα 35. σημαίνω 36. φήμη

Gen 37: 2 and Joseph brought an ill report of them to their 2
45:16 When the report was heard in Pharaoh's house 8
Exd 19: 8 And Moses reported the words of the people 9
23: 1 You shall not utter a false report. 13
Num14:37 the men who brought up an evil report of the land 2
Deu 2:25 hear the report of you and shall tremble 13
Jos 9: 9 we have heard a report of him, and all that he did 14
22:33 And the report pleased the people of Israel; 4
Jdg 18: 8 their brethren said to them, "What do you report? *
1Sm 2:24 No, my sons; it is no good report that I hear 11
11: 4 they reported the matter in the ears 3
1Kg 10: 6 The report was true which I heard in my own land 4
7 I did not believe the reports until I came 4
7 prosperity surpass the report which I heard. 11
20:17 Ben-ha'dad sent . . scouts, and they reported to him 7
2Kg 9:18 And the watchman reported, saying 7
20 Again the watchman reported, "He reached them 7
22: 9 Shaphan . . reported to the king 10
1Ch 21: 2 Go, number Israel . . and bring me a report *
2Ch 9: 5 The report was true which I heard in my own land 4
6 I did not believe the reports until I came 4
6 you surpass the report which I heard. 11
34:16 Shaphan . . further reported to the king 10
Ezr 5: 5 not stop them till a report should reach Darius 15
7 sent him a report, in which was written as follows 16
Neh 6: 1 Now when it was reported to Sanbal'lat and Tobi'ah 12
6 It is reported among the nations, and Geshem also 12
6 become their king, according to this report. 4
7 reported to the king according to these words. 11
19 Also they . . reported my words to him. 6
Est 9:11 the number of . . was reported to the king. 1
Isa 23: 5 When the report comes to Egypt 13
5 Egypt . . in anguish over the report about Tyre. 13
Jer 6:24 We have heard the report of it 14
36:16 We must report all these words to the king. 7
20 and they reported all the words to the king. 7
50:43 The king of Babylon heard the report of them 13
51:46 be not fearful at the report heard in the land 11
46 when a report comes in one year 11
46 one year and afterward a report in another year 11
Ezk 24:26 will come to you to report to you the news. 5
Hab 3: 2 O LORD, I have heard the report of thee, and thy work 13
Mat 9:26 the report of this went through all 36
18:31 they went and reported to their lord 25
Mrk 2: 1 it was reported that he was at home. 18
5:27 She had heard the reports about Jesus *
Lke 4:14 and a report concerning him went out 36
37 reports of him went out into every place 29
5:15 so much the more the report went abroad 31
7:17 this report concerning him spread 31
14:21 So the servant came and reported this 20
Joh 12:38 Lord, who has believed our report 17
Act 4:23 reported what the chief priests . . had said 20
5:22 they returned and reported 20
15: 3 reporting the conversion of the Gentiles 27
16:36 the jailer reported the words to Paul, saying 20
38 police reported these words to the magistrates 20
28:21 none of the brethren coming here has reported 20
1Co 1:11 For it has been reported to me by Chlo'e's people 21
5: 1 It is actually reported 18
1Th 1: 9 report concerning us what a welcome we had 20
3: 6 and reported that you always remember us kindly *
1Es 1:42 the things that are reported about Jehoiakim 30
8:49 the list of all their names was reported. 35
Tob 10:12 Let me hear a good report of you 17
11:15 he reported to his father the great things 20
Jdt 10:13 to give him a true report 34
18 her arrival was reported from tent to tent 22
11: 8 it is reported throughout the whole world 19
Wis 1: 9 a report of his words will come to the Lord 17
Sir 19: 8 With friend or foe do not report it 26
1Mc 2:31 it was reported to the king's officers 19
3:27 When king Antiochus heard these reports 31
4:26 went and reported to Lysias 20
5:14 and made a similar report; 34
38 they reported to him 20
6: 5 reported that the armies . . had been routed; 20
9:37 was reported to Jonathan and Simon his brother 20
11:21 reported . . that Jonathan was besieging 20
40 He also reported to Imalkue what Demetrius had done 20
12:23 command that our envoys report to you 20
26 they returned and reported to him 20
15:32 He reported to him the words of the king 20
36 reported to him these words 20
16: 1 John went up from Gazara and reported to Simon 20
18 Then Ptolemy wrote a report about these things *
21 some one ran ahead and reported to John at Gazara 20
2Mc 1:20 when they reported to us 25
33 it was reported to the king of the Persians 23
2:13 The same things are reported in the records 28
3: 6 He reported to him that . . 33
34 report to all men the majestic power of God. 23
4:39 when report of them had spread abroad 36
3Mc 3: 2 a pretext being given by a report 24
5:10 to report to the king about these preparations. 33
27 upon receiving the report *
4Mc 4: 3 to report that . . there are deposited 32
14 went away to report to the king what had happened 21

report *See also* give, make.

evil report 1. דִּבָּה 2. δυσφημία

Num13:32 brought to the people of Israel an evil report 1
14:36 by bringing up an evil report against the land 1
3Mc 2:26 he framed evil reports in the various localities; 2

repose 1. מַרְגֵּעָה

Isa 28:12 and this is repose"; yet they would not hear. 1

represent 1. לְ 2. παρά

Exd 18:19 You shall represent the people before God 1
Num 1:44 twelve men, each representing his fathers' house. 1
1Es 1:15 and Eddinus, who represented the king. 2

representation 1. χάραγμα

Act 17:29 a representation by the art . . of man. 1

representative 1. ὁ παρά

2Mc 11:20 ordered these men and my representatives 1

reproach 1. חֶסֶד 2. חרף 3. חֶרְפָּה 4. כלם 5. כְּלִמָּה 6. ἐλεγμός 7. ἐμβριμάομαι 8. κακίζω 9. λοιδορία 10. μῶμος 11. ὀνειδίζω 12. ὀνειδισμός 13. ὄνειδος 14. προσεπιτιμάω 15. ὑβρίζω 16. ψόγος 17. improperium 18. impropero 19. opprobrium

Gen 30:23 and said, "God has taken away my reproach"; 3
Jos 5: 9 I . . rolled away the reproach of Egypt from you. 3
Rut 2:15 Let her glean . . and do not reproach her. 4
1Sm 17:26 and takes away the reproach from Israel? 3
Job 27: 6 my heart does not reproach me for any of my days. 2
Ps 15: 3 nor takes up a reproach against his neighbor; 3
69: 7 For it is for thy sake that I have borne reproach 3
10 my soul with fasting, it became my reproach. 3
19 Thou knowest my reproach, and my shame 3
119:39 Turn away the reproach which I dread; 3
Prv 14:34 but sin is a reproach to any people. 1
27:11 Be wise . . that I may answer him who reproaches 2
Isa 4: 1 called by your name; take away our reproach. 3
25: 8 the reproach of his people he will take away 3
51: 7 fear not the reproach of men, and be not dismayed 3
54: 4 of your youth, and the reproach of your widowhood 3
Jer 15:15 know that for thy sake I bear reproach. 3
20: 8 the word of the LORD has become for me a reproach 3
23:40 I will bring upon you everlasting reproach 3
24: 9 to be a reproach, a byword, a taunt, and a curse 3
25: 9 a horror, a hissing, and an everlasting reproach. 12
29:18 to be a curse, a terror, a hissing, and a reproach 3
51:51 We are put to shame, for we have heard reproach; 3
Ezk 5:14 make you a desolation and an object of reproach 3
15 You shall be a reproach and a taunt 3
16:57 you have become like her an object of reproach 3
21:28 the Ammonites, and concerning their reproach; 3
22: 4 I have made you a reproach to the nations 3
34:29 no longer suffer the reproach of the nations. 5
36: 6 you have suffered the reproach of the nations; 5
7 shall themselves suffer reproach. 5
15 let you hear any more the reproach of the nations 5
Hos 12:14 and will turn back upon him his reproaches. 3
Jol 2:17 and make not thy heritage a reproach, 3
19 no more make you a reproach among the nations. 3
Zep 3:18 that you will not bear reproach for it. 3
Mrk 14: 5 they reproached her. 7
Lke 1:25 to take away my reproach among men. 13
11:45 Teacher, in saying this you reproach us also. 15
Rom15: 3 The reproaches of those who reproached thee 12
3 The reproaches of those who reproached thee 11
1Ti 3: 7 fall into reproach and the snare of the devil. 12
Jas 1: 5 God, who gives to all . . without reproaching 11
1Pe 4:14 If you are reproached for the name of Christ 11
2Es 4:23 given over to the Gentiles as a reproach 19
10:28 and my prayer a reproach. 17
13:38 will reproach them to their face 18
Tob 3: 4 a byword of reproach in all the nations 12
6 because I have heard false reproaches 12
7 was reproached by her father's maids 11
13 Command . . that I hear reproach no more. 12
15 command . . that I hear reproach no more. 12
Jdt 8:22 we shall be an offense and a reproach 13
Wis 2:12 he reproaches us for sins against the law 11
5: 4 made a byword of reproach– we fools! 12
Sir 6: 1 a bad name incurs shame and reproach 13
8: 5 Do not reproach a man who is turning away from sin; 11
13:22 If a humble man slips, they even reproach him 14
18:15 My son, do not mix reproach with your good deeds 10
29: 6 he will repay him with curses and reproaches 9
28 the reproach of the moneylender. 12
31:31 speak no word of reproach to him 12
41: 6 on their posterity will be a perpetual reproach. 13
47: 4 take away reproach from the people 12
Bar 2: 4 to be a reproach and a desolation among all 12
3: 8 to be reproached and cursed and punished 12
LJr 1:47 They have left only lies and reproach 13
72 a reproach in the land. 13
73 he will be far from reproach. 12
1Mc 1:39 her sabbaths into a reproach 12
2:49 Arrogance and reproach have now become strong 6
4:45 lest it bring reproach upon them 13
58 the reproach of the Gentiles was removed. 12
10:70 I have become a laughingstock and reproach 12
3Mc 3: 7 they attached no ordinary reproach to them. 16
7: 8 reproaching them for the irrational things 11
4Mc 12: 2 had been fearfully reproached by the brothers 8
151 1: 7 removed reproach from the people of Israel. 13

reproach *See also* add, bring, even, free, suffer.

above reproach 1. ἀνεπίλημπτος

1Ti 3: 2 Now a bishop must be above reproach 1

without reproach 1. ἀνεπίλημπτος

1Ti 5: 7 so that they may be without reproach. 1

reproachful 1. ὀνειδίζω

2Mc 7:24 he was suspicious of her reproachful tone. 1

reprobate 1. מאס

Ps 15: 4 in whose eyes a reprobate is despised 1

reproof 1. יכח 2. תּוֹכַחַת 3. ἐλεγμός 4. ἔλεγχος

Job 6:25 But what does reproof from you reprove? 1
Prv 1:23 Give heed to my reproof; 2
25 would have none of my reproof 2
30 despised all my reproof 2
3:11 My son, do not . . be weary of his reproof 2
5:12 you say, "How . . my heart despised reproof! 2
6:23 reproofs of discipline are the way of life 2
10:17 but he who rejects reproof goes astray. 2
12: 1 but he who hates reproof is stupid. 2
13:18 but he who heeds reproof is honored. 2
15:10 he who hates reproof will die. 2
29:15 The rod and reproof give wisdom 2
2Ti 3:16 profitable . . for reproof, for correction 3
Wis 2:14 He became to us a reproof of our thoughts; 4
Sir 16:12 As great as his mercy, so great is also his reproof; 4
20: 1 There is a reproof which is not timely 4
29 like a muzzle on the mouth they avert reproofs. 3
21: 6 Whoever hates reproof 3
32:17 A sinful man will shun reproof 3

reprove 1. יכח 2. תּוֹכַחַת 3. ἐλέγχω 4. ἐπιτιμάω 5. arguo 6. corripio

Job 5:17 Behold, happy is the man whom God reproves; 1
6:25 But what does reproof from you reprove? 1
26 Do you think that you can reprove words 1
22: 4 Is it for your fear of him that he reproves you 1
Ps 50: 8 I do not reprove you for your sacrifices; 1
Prv 3:12 for the LORD reproves him whom he loves 1
9: 7 he who reproves a wicked man incurs injury. 1
8 Do not reprove a scoffer, or he will hate you; 1
8 reprove a wise man, and he will love you. 1
10:10 but he who boldly reproves makes peace. 3
15:12 A scoffer does not like to be reproved; 1
19:25 reprove a man of understanding, and he will gain 1
29: 1 He who is often reproved, yet stiffens his neck 2
Isa 29:21 lay a snare for him who reproves in the gate 1
Jer 2:19 and your apostasy will reprove you. 1
Ezk 3:26 you shall be dumb and unable to reprove them; 1
Ams 5:10 They hate him who reproves in the gate 1
Lke 3:19 Herod the tetrarch, who had been reproved by him 3
Tit 2:15 exhort and reprove with all authority 3
Rev 3:19 Those whom I love, I reprove and chasten; 3
2Es 8:12 and reproved him in thy wisdom. 6
12:31 and reproving him for his unrighteousness 5

33 and when he has reproved them 5
13:37 he, my Son, will reprove the assembled nations 5
14:13 reprove your people; comfort the lowly 6
20 I will reprove the people who are now living 6
Sir 11: 7 first consider, and then reprove. 4
20: 2 How much better it is to reprove 3
31:31 Do not reprove your neighbor at a banquet of wine 3

reprover 1. יכח
Prv 25:12 wise reprover to a listening ear. 1

reptile 1. רֶמֶשׂ 2. *ἑρπετόν*
1Kg 4:33 beasts, and of birds, and of reptiles, and of fish. 1
Act 10:12 animals and reptiles and birds of the air. 2
11: 6 beasts of prey and reptiles and birds of the air. 2
Rom 1:23 mortal man or birds or animals or reptiles. 2
Jas 3: 7 every kind . . of reptile and sea creature 2

repulse 1. שׁוב אֶת הַפָּנִים 2. *ἀπωθέω*
2Kg 18:24 How then can you repulse a single captain 1
Isa 36: 9 How then can you repulse a single captain 1
Sir 13:10 Do not push forward, lest you be repulsed 2
1Mc 14:26 they have fought and repulsed Israel's enemies •

repulsive 1. זור
Job 19:17 I am repulsive to my wife 1

reputation 1. *δόξα* 2. *εὔκλεια*
Sus 1:64 Daniel had a great reputation among the people. •
3Mc 2:31 they expected to enhance their reputation 2
4Mc 5:18 to invalidate our reputation for piety. 1
6:18 maintained . . the reputation of such a life 1

repute 1. *δοκέω* 2. deputo
Prv 3: 4 you will find favor and good repute •
Gal 2: 2 privately before those who were of repute 1
6 from those who were reputed to be something 1
6 those, I say, who were of repute added nothing to me; 1
9 Cephas and John, who were reputed to be pillars 1
2Es 6:57 these nations, which are reputed as nothing 2
repute *See also* give.

good repute 1. *εὐδόκιμος* 2. *εὐφημία* 3. *μαρτυρέω*
Act 6: 3 pick out from among you 7 men of good repute 3
2Co 6: 8 in ill repute and good repute 2
3Mc 3: 5 they were established in good repute among all men. 1

ill repute 1. דִּבָּה 2. *δυσφημία*
Prv 25:10 shame upon you, and your ill repute have no end. 1
2Co 6: 8 in ill repute and good repute 2

no repute 1. קלה
1Sm 18:23 seeing that I am a poor man and of no repute? 1

request 1. אֲרֶשֶׁת 2. בַּקָּשָׁה 3. דָּבָר 4. שׁאל 5. שְׁאֵלָה 6. *αἰτέω* 7. *αἴτημα* 8. *ἀξίωμα* 9. *λόγος* 10. *προσαξιόω* 11. rogo
Jdg 8:24 Let me make a request of you; 5
26 weight of the golden earrings that he requested 4
2Sm 14:15 king will perform the request of his servant. 3
22 the king has granted the request of his servant. 3
1Kg 2:16 I have one request to make of you; do not refuse me. 5
20 I have one small request to make of you; do not 5
Est 5: 3 What is it, Queen Esther? What is your request? 2
6 what is your request? . . it shall be fulfilled. 2
7 But Esther said, "My petition and my request is 2
8 to grant my petition and fulfil my request 2
7: 2 And what is your request? 2
3 let my life be . . and my people at my request. 2
9:12 what . . is your request? It shall be fulfilled. 2
Job 6: 8 O that I might have my request 5
Ps 21: 2 and hast not withheld the request of his lips. 1
Jer 42: 4 behold, I will pray . . according to your request 3
Php 4: 6 let your requests be made known to God. 7
1Jn 5:15 we have obtained the requests made of him. 7
1Es 4:46 now, O lord the king, this is what I ask and request 6
8: 4 found favor before the king in all his requests. 8
2Es 6:55 Request it therefore to produce ten at one time. 11
1Mc 11:41 Jonathan sent to Demetrius the king the request •
13:34 a request to grant relief to the country •
35 sent him a favorable reply to this request 9
2Mc 11:15 every request . . which Maccabeus delivered •
3Mc 7:10 they requested of the king 10
request *See also* make.

request payment 1. *ποιέω ἀπαίτησιν*
2Mc 4:28 When Sostratus . . kept requesting payment 1

require 1. בקשׁ 2. דָּבָר 3. דרשׁ 4. כְּמִשְׁפָּט 5. לְ 6. מלא 7. מִשְׁמֶרֶת 8. עַל 9. שׂוּם עַל 10. שׁאל 11. אמר (A) 12. חַשְׁחוּ (A) 13. שׁאל (A) 14. *ἀνήκω* 15. *ἀπαιτέω* 16. *ἐκζητέω* 17. *ἐπιζητέω* 18. *ἐπιτελέω* 19. *ἔργον* 20. *ζητέω* 21. *καθήκω* 22. *χρείαν ἔχω* 23. exquiro 24. inquiro 25. requiro
Gen 9: 5 I will surely require a reckoning; 3
5 of every beast I will require it and of man; 3
5 brother I will require the life of man. 3
31:39 of my hand you required it 1
43: 9 of my hand you shall require him. 1
50: 3 40 days were required for it 6
3 for so many are required for embalming. 6
Num 4:32 the objects which they are required to carry. 7
5:15 man shall . . bring the offering required of her 8
Deu 10:12 now, Israel, what does the LORD your God require 10
17: 8 If any case arises requiring decision 5
18:19 not give heed . . I myself will require it of him. 3
23:21 LORD your God will surely require it of you 3
2Sm 3:13 one thing I require of you; that is, you shall not 10
4:11 shall I not now require his blood at your hand 1
1Kg 4:28 they brought to the place where it was required •
8:59 may he maintain . . as each day requires; †
2Kg 18:14 the king . . required of Hezeki'ah king of Judah 9
1Ch 9:28 for they were required to count them •
16:37 minister . . before the ark as each day required 2
21: 3 Why then should my lord require this? 1
23:31 according to the number required of them 4
2Ch 8:13 as the duty of each day required •
14 he appointed . . as the duty of each day required •
24: 6 Why have you not required the Levites to bring 3
31:16 entered . . as the duty of each day required •
Ezr 3: 4 daily burnt offerings . . as each day required. 2
6: 9 wine, or oil, as the priests at Jerusalem require- 11
7:20 whatever else is required for the house 12
21 Whatever Ezra . . requires of you, be it done 13
Neh 5:12 We will restore these and require nothing 1
11:23 settled provision . . as every day required. 2
12:44 gather . . portions required by the law •
Ps 40: 6 sin offering thou hast not required. 10
137: 3 For there our captors required of us songs 10
Isa 1:12 who requires of you this trampling of my courts? 1
Ezk 3:18 but his blood I will require at your hand. 1
20 but his blood I will require at your hand. 1
20:40 there I will require your contributions 3
33: 6 his blood I will require at the watchman's hand. 3
8 but his blood I will require at your hand. 1
34:10 I will require my sheep at their hand 3
Mic 6: 8 does the LORD require of you but to do justice 3
Lke 11:50 the blood . . may be required of this generation 16
51 it shall be required of this generation. 16
12:20 This night your soul is required of you 15
48 of him will much be required 20
Rom 2:14 Gentiles . . do by nature what the law requires •
15 They show that what the law requires is written 19
1Co 4: 2 Moreover it is required of stewards 20
12:24 which our more presentable parts do not require 22
Phm 1: 8 to command you to do what is required 14
1Pe 5: 9 suffering is required of your brotherhood 18
1Es 1:12 roasted the passover lamb with fire, as required; 21
2Es 1:32 their blood I will require of you, says the Lord. 23
2:26 for I will require them from among your number. 25
6:19 when I require from the doers of iniquity 24
Wis 15: 8 when he is required to return the soul •
Sir 13:26 to devise proverbs requires painful thinking. •
LJr 1:35 they will not require it. 17

require haste 1. נחץ
1Sm 21: 8 because the king's business required haste. 1

requirement 1. *ἐντολή*
Heb 7:16 a legal requirement concerning bodily descent 1

just requirement 1. *δικαίωμα*
Rom 8: 4 the just requirement of the law might be fulfilled 1

requital 1. גְּמוּל
Isa 59:18 wrath to his . . requital to his enemies; 1
18 to the coastlands he will render requital. 1
Jer 51: 6 vengeance, the requital he is rendering her. 1
2Es 9: 6 and the end in requital and in signs. ‡
requital *See also* make.

requite 1. גמל 2. נתן 3. עשׂה כְּ 4. שׁוב 5. שׁוב גְּמוּל ל 6. שׁוה 7. שׁלם 8. *ἀνταποδίδωμι* 9. *ἀποδίδωμι*
Deu 7:10 and requites to their face those who hate him 7
10 not be slack . . he will requite him to his face. 7
32: 6 Do you thus requite the LORD, you foolish 1
41 I . . will requite those who hate me. 7
Jdg 1: 7 as I have done, so God has requited me." And they 7
9:56 Thus God requited the crime of Abim'elech 4
20:10 that . . they may requite Gib'e-ah of Benjamin 3
2Sm 3:39 The LORD requite the evildoer according to his 7
2Kg 9:26 I will requite you on this plot of ground.' 7
2Ch 6:23 requiting the guilty by bringing his conduct 4
Job 21:31 who requites him for what he has done? 7
33:27 I sinned . . and it was not requited to me. 6
34:11 according to the work of a man he will requite him 7
Ps 7: 4 if I have requited my friend with evil 1
28: 4 Requite them according to their work 2
4 requite them according to the work of their 2
31:23 but abundantly requites him who acts haughtily. 7
35:12 They requite me evil for good; my soul is forlorn. 7
41:10 raise me up, that I may requite them! 7
54: 5 He will requite my enemies with evil; 4
62:12 For thou dost requite a man according to his work. 7
103:10 nor requite us according to our iniquities. 1
137: 8 Happy shall he be who requites you with what you 7
Prv 11:31 If the righteous is requited on earth 7
24:12 will he not requite man according to his work? 4
Isa 57:18 I will lead him and requite him with comfort 7
Jer 32:18 but dost requite the guilt of fathers 7
50:29 Requite her according to her deeds 7
51:24 I will requite Babylon 7
56 a God of recompense, he will surely requite. 7
Lam 3:64 Thou wilt requite them, O LORD 5
Ezk 9:10 but I will requite their deeds upon their heads. 2
11:21 I will requite their deeds upon their own heads 2
16:43 behold, I will requite your deeds upon your head 2
17:19 which he broke, I will requite upon his head. 2
22:31 their way have I requited upon their heads 2
23:49 And your lewdness shall be requited upon you 2
Hos 4: 9 and requite them for their deeds. 4
12: 2 and requite him according to his deeds. 4
Jol 3: 4 If you are paying me back, I will requite your deed 4
7 and I will requite your deed upon your own head. 4
2Ti 4:14 the Lord will requite him for his deeds. 9
Sir 3:31 Whoever requites favors 8
17:23 Afterward he will arise and requite them 8

rescue 1. חלק 2. יכל 3. ישׁע 4. מלט 5. נצל 6. פדה 7. פלט 8. פצה 9. פרק 10. שׁוב 11. נצל (A) 12. *ἀντιλαμβάνω* 13. *βοήθεια* 14. *διασῴζω* 15. *ἐξαιρέω* 16. *ῥύομαι* 17. *σῴζω* 18. *σωτηρία* 19. *χρεία*
Gen 37:22 -that he might rescue him out of their hand 5
Num35:25 congregation shall rescue the manslayer 5
Deu 22:27 woman cried for help there was no one to rescue 3
25:11 near to rescue her husband from the hand of him 5
Jdg 8:34 the LORD . . who had rescued them from the hand 5
9:17 his life, and rescued you from the hand of Mid'ian; 5
1Sm 7:14 Israel rescued their territory from the hand 5
30: 8 you shall . . overtake and shall surely rescue. 5
18 and David rescued his two wives. 5
2Kg 16: 7 and rescue me from the hand of the king of Syria 3
Job 21:30 that he is rescued in the day of wrath? 2
Ps 7: 2 rend me, dragging me away, with none to rescue. 5
22: 8 let him deliver him, let him rescue him 5
31: 2 Incline thy ear to me, rescue me speedily! 5
35:17 Rescue me from their ravages 10
69:14 rescue me from sinking in the mire; 5
71: 2 In thy righteousness deliver me and rescue me; 7
4 Rescue me, O my God, from the hand of the wicked 7
23 my soul also, which thou hast rescued. 6
82: 4 Rescue the weak and the needy; 7
91:15 in trouble, I will rescue him and honor him. 1
136:24 rescued us from our foes, for his steadfast love 9
144: 7 rescue me and deliver me from the many waters 8
10 who rescuest David thy servant. 8
11 Rescue me from the cruel sword 8
Prv 24:11 Rescue those who are being taken away to death; 5
Isa 5:29 they carry it off, and none can rescue. 5
31: 5 and deliver it, he will spare and rescue it. 4
42:22 they have become a prey with none to rescue 5
49:24 or the captives of a tyrant be rescued? 4
25 be taken, and the prey of the tyrant be rescued 4
Ezk 34:10 I will rescue my sheep from their mouths 5
12 so will I seek out my sheep; and I will rescue them 5
Dan 6:14 labored till the sun went down to rescue him. 11
27 He delivers and rescues, he works signs 11
8: 4 there was no one who could rescue from his power; 5
7 no one who could rescue the ram from his power. 5
Hos 2:10 and no one shall rescue her out of my hand. 5
5:14 I will carry off, and none shall rescue. 5
Ams 3:12 the shepherd rescues from the mouth of the lion 5
12 people of Israel who dwell in Sama'ria be rescued 5
Mic 4:10 shall go to Babylon. There you shall be rescued 5
Act 7:10 rescued him out of all his afflictions 15
12:11 and rescued me from the hand of Herod 15
23:27 came upon them with the soldiers and rescued him 15
2Ti 3:11 yet from them all the Lord rescued me. 16
4:17 So I was rescued from the lion's mouth. 16
18 The Lord will rescue me from every evil 16
2Pe 2: 7 if he rescued the righteous Lot 16
9 the Lord knows how to rescue the godly from trial 16
Wis 10: 6 Wisdom rescued a righteous man 16
9 Wisdom rescued from troubles 16
18: 5 one child had been exposed and rescued 17
Sir 29:12 it will rescue you from all affliction; 15
40: 7 at the moment of his rescue he wakes up 19
24 almsgiving rescues better than both. 16
51:12 rescue me from an evil plight 15
LJr 1:36 rescue the weak from the strong. 15
37 they cannot rescue a man who is in distress. 15
Aza 1:66 he has rescued us from Hades 15
1Mc 2:48 rescued the law out of the hands of the Gentiles 12
5:12 Now then come and rescue us from their hands 15
17 go and rescue your brethren in Galilee 16
2Mc 1:25 who dost rescue Israel from every evil 14
2:18 he has rescued us from great evils 15
8:14 to rescue those who had been sold 16
9: 2 the people rushed to the rescue with arms 13
3Mc 2:12 rescued them from great evils 16
5: 8 in a glorious manifestation rescue them 16

6: 6 you rescued unharmed, even to a hair 16
10 rescue us from the hand of the enemy 16
11 'Not even their god has rescued them.' 16
30 celebrate their rescue with all joyfulness 18
33 the unexpected rescue which he had experienced. 18
39 and rescued them all together and unharmed. 16

rescuer 1. *ῥύομαι*
Sir 29:17 will abandon his rescuer. 1

resemble 1. כְּמַרְאֵה 2. כְּתֹאַר 3. *ἀφωμοιόω* 4. *ἐν ὁμοιώματι* 5. *ὅμοιος*
Jdg 8:18 every one . . they resembled the sons of a king. 2
Ezk 10: 1 like a sapphire, in form resembling a throne. 1
41:21 of the holy place was something resembling 1
Rom 1:23 for images resembling mortal man or birds 4
Heb 7: 3 resembling the Son of God 3
Tob 7: 2 How much the young man resembles my cousin Tobit! 5

resentful 1. סַר 2. *λογίζομαι τὸ κακόν*
1Kg 20:43 king . . went to his house resentful and sullen 1
1Co 13: 5 it is not irritable or resentful; 2

resentment 1. קֶצֶף
Ecc 5:17 in much vexation and sickness and resentment? 1

reserve 1. אצל 2. חשׂך 3. ספן 4. פִּקָּדוֹן 5. *τηρέω* 6. *ὑποχωρέω* 7. repono 8. servo
Gen 27:36 he said, "Have you not reserved a blessing for me? 1
41:36 That food shall be a reserve for the land 4
Num18: 9 most holy things, reserved from the fire; *
Deu 33:21 for there a commander's portion was reserved; 3
2Ch 31:14 the contribution reserved for the LORD *
Job 38:23 which I have reserved for the time of trouble 2
2Pe 2:17 the nether gloom of darkness has been reserved. 5
Jde 1:13 gloom of darkness has been reserved for ever. 5
2Es 7:14 those things that have been reserved for them. 7
121 healthful habitations have been reserved 7
11: 9 let the heads be reserved for the last. 8
13:18 what is reserved for the last days 7
Sir 13: 9 When a powerful man invites you, be reserved 6

reservoir 1. מִקְוָה 2. *ἀποδοχεῖον* 3. *λάκκος*
Isa 22:11 You made a reservoir between the two walls 1
Sir 39:17 reservoirs of water 2
50: 3 a reservoir like the sea in circumference. 3

reside 1. גור 2. *συνίστημι*
Ezk 47:22 for the aliens who reside among you 1
23 In whatever tribe the alien resides 1
3Mc 4:18 some still residing in their homes 2

residence 1. בַּיִת(A) 2. habitatio
Dan 4:30 built by my mighty power as a royal residence 1
2Es 10:47 that was the period of residence in Jerusalem. 2

resident 1. *ἐν* 2. *κατοικέω* 3. *κατοίκος*
Act 2: 9 E'lamites and residents of Mesopota'mia 2
9:35 all the residents of Lydda and Sharon saw him 2
19:10 the residents of Asia heard the word of the Lord 2
17 this became known to all residents of Ephesus 2
AEs 11: 1 one of the residents of Jerusalem. 1
1Mc 1:38 Because of them the residents of Jerusalem fled; 3
3:34 As for the residents of Judea and Jerusalem 2
resident *See also* alien.

residue 1. יֶתֶר 2. שְׁאֵרִית 3. שְׁאָר(A)
Ps 76:10 the residue of wrath thou wilt gird upon thee. 2
Isa 44:19 and shall I make the residue of it an abomination? 1
Dan 7: 7 stamped the residue with its feet. 3
19 pieces, and stamped the residue with its feet; 3

resist 1. *ἀνθίστημι* 2. *ἀντικαθίστημι* 3. *ἀντιπίπτω* 4. *ἀντιτάσσω* 5. *ὑφίστημι*
Mat 5:39 I say to you, do not resist one who is evil. But 1
Act 7:51 you always resist the Holy Spirit 3
Rom 9:19 For who can resist his will? 1
13: 2 Therefore he who resists the authorities 4
2 resists what God has appointed 1
2 and those who resist will incur judgment. 1
Heb 12: 4 not yet resisted to the point of . . blood 2
Jas 4: 7 Resist the devil and he will flee from you. 1
5: 6 the righteous man; he does not resist you. 4
1Pe 5: 9 Resist him, firm in your faith 1
1Es 2:19 will even resist kings. 1
Jdt 2:25 and killed every one who resisted him 1
6: 3 They cannot resist the might of our cavalry. 5
16:14 there is none that can resist thy voice. 1
AEs 13:11 is no one who can resist thee, who art the Lord. 4
Wis 12:12 will resist thy judgment 1
Sir 46: 6 he destroyed those who resisted 1
1Mc 5:40 we will not be able to resist him 5
14:29 resisted the enemies of their nation 1
4Mc 6:30 by reason he resisted even to . . death 1
resistance *See* offer.

resolute 1. חזק
1Ch 28: 7 if he continues resolute in keeping 1
resolutely *See* hopeful, work.

resolve 1. שׂוּם עַל לֵב 2. *βουλεύω* 3. *βούλημα* 4. *βούλομαι* 5. *διανοέω* 6. *λογισμός* 7. *ὀχυρόω* 8. *τίθημι*
Dan 1: 8 Daniel resolved that he would not defile 1
Mat 1:19 put her to shame, resolved to divorce her 4
Act 19:21 Paul resolved . . to pass through Macedo'nia 8
Wis 18: 5 had resolved to kill the babes of thy holy ones 2
Sir 51:18 For I resolved to live according to wisdom 5
1Mc 1:62 and were resolved . . not to eat unclean food. 7
14:35 glory which he had resolved to win for his nation 2
2Mc 6:23 making a high resolve, worthy of his years 6
4Mc 8:18 why do we take pleasure in vain resolves 3

good resolve 1. *εὐδοκία*
2Th 1:11 may fulfil every good resolve and work of faith 1

resort 1. דרשׁ 2. יצב 3. עמד 4. *πάρειμι* 5. *πείθω*
2Ch 11:13 resorted to him from all places 2
25:15 Why have you resorted to the gods of a people 1
Ezk 33:26 You resort to the sword, you commit abominations 3
2Mc 4:34 resorting to treachery 5
3Mc 1:23 resorted to the same posture of supplication 4

resound 1. בוא 2. הום 3. *ἠχέω* 4. *συνηχέω* 5. sono
1Sm 4: 5 gave a mighty shout, so that the earth resounded. 2
Jer 25:31 The clamor will resound to the ends of the earth 1
2Es 6:13 and you will hear a full, resounding voice. 5
Sir 47:10 the sanctuary resounded from early morning. 3
3Mc 6:17 even the nearby valleys resounded with them 4

resource 1. תּוּשִׁיָּה 2. *ἰσχύς* 3. *ὁλκή* 4. *σπόρος*
Job 6:13 no help in me, and any resource is driven from me. 1
2Co 9:10 supply and multiply your resources 4
Sir 8: 2 lest his resources outweigh yours 3
13: 5 he will drain your resources and he will not care. *
44: 6 rich men furnished with resources 2

respect 1. הדר 2. ירא 3. פנה 4. *αἰδέομαι* 5. *αἰσχύνω* 6. *δόξα* 7. *ἐντρέπω* 8. *εὐγενής* 9. *εὐσχημόνως* 10. *εὐσχήμων* 11. *καταιδέομαι* 12. *οἶδα* 13. *φοβέω* 14. *φόβος* 15. curo
Num16:15 Do not respect their offering. 3
Prv 13:13 who respects the commandment will be rewarded. 2
Lam 5:12 no respect is shown to the elders. 1
Mat 21:37 'They will respect my son.' 7
Mrk 12: 6 'They will respect my son.' 7
15:43 a respected member of the council 10
Lke 20:13 it may be they will respect him.' 7
Rom13: 7 respect to whom respect is due 14
7 respect to whom respect is due 14
Eph 5:33 let the wife see that she respects her husband. 13
1Th 4:12 that you may command the respect of outsiders 9
5:12 respect those who labor among you 12
Heb 12: 9 we respected them 7
1Pe 2:18 be submissive to your masters with all respect 14
2Es 15:16 in their might have no respect for their king 15
Bar 4:15 nation . . who had no respect for an old man 5
2Mc 10:13 Unable to command the respect due his office 8
13 Unable to command the respect due his office *
15: 2 show respect for the day 6
4Mc 3:12 respecting the king's desire 11
5: 7 for I respect your age and your gray hairs. 4

respect (2) 1. מִן 2. *ἐπί* 3. *κατά* 4. *περί* 5. *τρόπος*
Jos 2:17 We will be guiltless with respect to this oath 1
20 we shall be guiltless with respect to your oath 1
Act 23: 6 with respect to . . the resurrection of the dead 4
24:21 With respect to the resurrection of the dead 4
Tit 2: 7 in all respects a model of good deeds 4
9 to give satisfaction in every respect *
Heb 2:17 had to be made like his brethren in every respect 3
4:15 one who in every respect has been tempted 3
2Es 8:48 even in this respect you will be praiseworthy *
3Mc 3: 4 they kept their separateness with respect to foods. 2
4Mc 5:17 we should not transgress it in any respect. 5
6:35 and in no respect yields to them. *

greatly respect 1. *ὑπερτιμάω*
4Mc 8: 5 and greatly respect the beauty . . of such brothers 1

not to respect 1. *ἀδοξία*
Sir 3:11 a disgrace . . not to respect their mother. 1

show respect 1. *ἐντρέπω* 2. *ἐπιβλέπω*
Tob 3:15 command that respect be shown to me 2
Sir 41:16 Therefore show respect for my words 1

respectable 1. idoneus
2Es 16:49 Just as a respectable and virtuous woman abhors 1

respectful 1. *σεμνότης*
1Ti 2: 2 godly and respectful in every way. 1
3: 4 submissive and respectful in every way; 1

respectfully 1. *αἰσχύνω*
Sir 21:22 stands respectfully before it. 1

respective 1. *ἕκαστος*
Sir 46:11 The judges also, with their respective names 1

respite 1. הֲפוּגָה 2. רְוָחָה
Exd 8:15 Pharaoh saw that there was a respite, he hardened 2
Lam 3:49 eyes will flow without ceasing, without respite 1
respite *See also* give.

resplendent 1. *διαπρεπής*
2Mc 10:29 five resplendent men on horses 1

respond 1. ענה 2. *ἐπιφωνέω*
Hab 2:11 and the beam from the woodwork respond. 1
2Mc 1:23 Jonathan led, and the rest responded 2
response *See* make.

responsibility 1. *διακριβόω* 2. *πρός*
2Mc 2:28 leaving the responsibility for exact details 1
4:28 the collection . . was his responsibility 2

part responsible 1. *μεταίτιος*
AEs 16: 5 have been made in part responsible 1
responsively *See* sing.

rest 1. בטח 2. דוּמִיָּה 3. דֳּמִי 4. היה 5. ישׁב 6. כון 7. לון 8. מָנוֹחַ 9. מְנוּחָה 10. מַרְגּוֹעַ 11. מִשְׁכָּב 12. נוח 13. נַחַת 14. פוּגַת 15. רבץ 16. רגע 17. שׁבת 18. שׁכב 19. שׁכן 20. שָׁלֵו 21. שׁמט 22. שׁען 23. שׁקט 24. *ἀνάπαυσις* 25. *ἀναπαύω* 26. *ἄνεσις* 27. *εἰμί* 28. *ἐπισκηνόω* 29. *ἡσυχάζω* 30. *ἵστημι* 31. *καθίζω* 32. *κατά* 33. *κατάλυσις* 34. *κατάπαυμα* 35. *κατάπαυσις* 36. *καταπαύω* 37. *μένω* 38. quiescentia 39. quiesco 40. requies 41. requiesco 42. requietio
Gen 2: 2 God . . rested on the seventh day 17
3 and hallowed it, because on it God rested 17
18: 4 feet, and rest yourselves under the tree 22
Exd 16:30 So the people rested on the seventh day. 17
20:11 the LORD . . rested the seventh day; 12
23:11 the seventh year you shall let it rest and lie 21
12 do your work, but on the seventh day you shall rest; 17
12 that your ox and your ass may have rest 12
31:17 on the seventh day he rested, and was refreshed.' 17
34:21 but on the seventh day you shall rest; 17
21 in plowing time and in harvest you shall rest. 17
Lev 26:34 then the land shall rest, and enjoy its sabbaths 17
35 As long as it lies desolate it shall have rest 17
35 the rest which it had not in your sabbaths *
Num 9:18 as long as the cloud rested over the tabernacle 19
10:36 when it rested, he said, "Return, O LORD 12
11:25 when the spirit rested upon them, they prophesied. 12
26 Eldad . . Medad . . spirit rested upon them; 12
Deu 5:14 that your manservant . . may rest as well as you. 12
12: 9 not as yet come to the rest and to the inheritance 9
28:65 there shall be no rest for the sole of your foot; 8
Jos 3:13 soles . . shall rest in the waters of the Jordan 12
11:23 And the land had rest from war. 23
14:15 And the land had rest from war. 23
Jdg 3:11 the land had rest 40 years. Then Oth'ni-el the son 23
30 And the land had rest for 80 years. 23
5:31 And the land had rest for 40 years. 23
8:28 the land had rest 40 years in the days of Gideon 23
16:26 Let me feel the pillars on which the house rests 6
29 two middle pillars upon which the house rested 6
Rut 2: 7 she has . . without resting even for a moment. 36
3:18 the man will not rest, but will settle the matter 23
2Sm 4: 5 Ish-bo'sheth, as he was taking his noonday rest. 11
1Kg 8:56 the LORD who has given rest to his people Israel 9
2Kg 2:15 The spirit of Eli'jah rests on Eli'sha. 12
4:11 he turned into the chamber and rested there. 18
18:19 On what do you rest this confidence of yours? 1
1Ch 6:31 the house of the LORD, after the ark rested there. 8
28: 2 I had it in my heart to build a house of rest 9
2Ch 14: 1 In his days the land had rest for ten years. 23
5 And the kingdom had rest under him. 23
6 fortified cities in Judah, for the land had rest. 23
Neh 9:28 after they had rest they did evil again 12
Est 9:17 and on the fourteenth day they rested 12
18 gathered . . and rested on the fifteenth day 12
Job 3:13 then I should have been at rest 12
17 there the weary are at rest. 12
26 I have no rest; but trouble comes. 12
20:20 Because his greed knew no rest 20
Ps 22: 2 I cry by day . . and by night, but find no rest. 2
55: 6 wings like a dove! I would fly away and be at rest; 19
62: 7 On God rests my deliverance and my honor; *
95:11 swore in my anger that they . . not enter my rest. 9
116: 7 Return, O my soul, to your rest; 8
125: 3 scepter of wickedness shall not rest upon 12
127: 2 in vain that you rise up early and go late to rest 5
Prv 6:10 a little folding of the hands to rest 18
19:23 he who has it rests satisfied; 7
21:16 wanders . . will rest in the assembly of the dead. 12

24:33 slumber, a little folding of the hands to rest 18
Ecc 2:23 even in the night his mind does not rest. 18
Isa 11: 2 the Spirit of the LORD shall rest upon him 12
14: 7 The whole earth is at rest and quiet; 12
23:12 over to Cyprus, even there you will have no rest. 12
25:10 the hand of the LORD will rest on this mountain 12
28:12 This is rest; give rest to the weary; 9
30:15 In returning and rest you shall be saved; 13
36: 4 On what do you rest this confidence of yours? 1
57: 2 he enters into peace; they rest in their beds 12
20 for it cannot rest, and its waters toss up mire 23
62: 1 and for Jerusalem's sake I will not rest 23
6 You who put the LORD in remembrance, take no rest 3
7 give him no rest until he establishes Jerusalem 3
66: 1 is the house . . and what is the place of my rest? 9
Jer 6:16 and walk in it, and find rest for your souls. 10
31: 2 in the wilderness; when Israel sought for rest 16
33:12 shepherds resting their flocks. 15
45: 3 I am weary with my groaning, and I find no rest. 9
47: 6 Put yourself into your scabbard, rest and be still! 16
Lam 2:18 Give yourself no rest, your eyes no respite! 14
Ezk 9: 3 gone up from the cherubim on which it rested 4
44:30 that a blessing may rest on your house. 12
Dan 12:13 you shall rest, and shall stand in your . . place 12
Zec 1:11 behold, all the earth remains at rest.' 23
9: 1 The word of the LORD . . will rest upon Damascus. 9
Mat 2: 9 in the East went before them, till it came to rest 30
11:29 and you will find rest for your souls. 24
12:43 passes through waterless places seeking rest 24
Mrk 6:31 rest a while 25
Lke 11:24 he passes through waterless places seeking rest; 24
23:56 they rested according to the commandment. 29
Joh 3:36 but the wrath of God rests upon him. 37
Act 2: 3 distributed and resting on each one of them. 31
7:49 what is the place of my rest? 35
Rom 4:16 in order that the promise may rest on grace 32
1Co 2: 5 your faith might not rest in the wisdom of men 27
2Co 2:13 my mind could not rest 26
7: 5 our bodies had no rest 26
12: 9 that the power of Christ may rest upon me. 28
Gal 3:12 the law does not rest on faith 27
2Th 1: 7 to grant rest with us to you who are afflicted 26
Heb 3:11 'They shall never enter my rest.' 35
18 swear that they should never enter his rest 35
4: 1 while the promise of entering his rest remains 35
3 For we who have believed enter that rest 35
3 They shall never enter my rest 35
4 God rested on the seventh day from all his works. 36
5 They shall never enter my rest. 35
10 whoever enters God's rest 35
11 Let us therefore strive to enter that rest 35
1Pe 4:14 the spirit of glory and of God rests upon you. 25
Rev 6:11 they were each . . told to rest a little longer 25
14:11 and they have no rest, day or night 24
13 that they may rest from their labors 25
2Es 2:24 be quiet, my people, because your rest will come. 40
34 he will give you everlasting rest 40
7:36 and opposite it shall be the place of rest 42
38 here are delight and rest 40
75 we shall be kept in rest until those times come 40
91 for they shall have rest in seven orders. 41
95 they understand the rest which they now enjoy 40
8:52 a city is built, rest is appointed 40
10:24 and the Most High may give you rest 40
11: 4 But his heads were at rest; 38
4 but it also was at rest with them. 39
23 except the three heads that were at rest 39
29 behold, one of the heads that were at rest 39
12:22 As for your seeing three heads at rest 38
Jdt 9: 8 the tabernacle where thy glorious name rests 35
10:21 Holofernes was resting on his bed 25
Wis 4: 7 the righteous man . . will be at rest. 24
Sir 5: 6 his anger rests on sinners. 35
6:28 For at last you will find the rest she gives 24
11:19 I have found rest, and now I shall enjoy my goods! 24
20:21 when he rests he feels no remorse. 24
22:13 avoid him and you will find rest 24
24: 7 Among all these I sought a resting place 24
28:16 Whoever pays heed to slander will not find rest 24
30:17 and eternal rest than chronic sickness. 24
31: 3 when he rests he fills himself with his dainties. 24
4 when he rests he becomes needy. 24
33:25 Set your slave to work, and you will find rest; 24
36:13 Jerusalem, the place of thy rest. 34
38:23 When the dead is at rest 24
40: 5 when one rests upon his bed 24
6 He gets little or no rest 24
43:20 it rests upon every pool of water 33
47:23 Solomon rested with his fathers 25
51:27 have labored little and found myself much rest. 24
1Mc 7:50 the land of Judah had rest for a few days. 29
9:57 the land of Judah had rest for two years. 29
14: 4 The land had rest all the days of Simon 29
2Mc 15: 1 to attack them . . on the day of rest. 35

rest (2) 1. יתר 2. יֶתֶר 3. כֹּל 4. שאר 5. שְׁאָר 6. שְׁאֵרִית 7. שְׁאָר (A) 8. ἄλλος 9. ἐπίλοιπος 10. καταλείπω 11. κατάλοιπος 12. λοιπός 13. πᾶς 14. περισσός

Gen 14:10 into them, and the rest fled to the mountain. 4
30:36 and Jacob fed the rest of Laban's flock. 1
42:19 and let the rest go and carry grain for the famine •
44:10 and the rest of you shall be blameless. •
Exd 4: 7 it was restored like the rest of his flesh. •
29:12 the rest of the blood you shall pour out 3
20 throw the rest of the blood against the altar •
Lev 4: 7 the rest of the blood of the bull he shall pour out 3
18 the rest of the blood he shall pour out at the base 3
25 pour out the rest of its blood at the base •
30 pour out the rest of its blood at the base 3
34 pour out the rest of its blood at the base 3
5: 9 while the rest of the blood shall be drained out 4
6:16 the rest of it Aaron and his sons shall eat 1
14:18 the rest of the oil that is in the priest's hand 1
29 the rest of the oil that is in the priest's hand 1
Num 18:30 then the rest shall be reckoned to the Levites •
31: 8 slew the kings . . with the rest of their slain •
Deu 3:13 rest of Gilead, and all Bashan, the kingdom of Og 2
19:20 rest shall hear, and fear, and shall never again 4
Jos 13:22 Balaam also . . among the rest of their slain. •
27 the valley of . . the rest of the kingdom of Sihon 2
17: 2 And allotments were made to the rest of the tribe 1
6 was allotted to the rest of the Manas'sites. 1
21: 5 And the rest of the Ko'hathites received by lot 1
20 the rest of the Ko'hathites . . of the Levites 1
26 of the families of the rest of the Ko'hathites 1
34 And to the rest of the Levites . . were given 1
Jdg 7: 6 but all the rest of the people knelt down to drink 2
8 he sent all the rest of Israel every man to his •
1Sm 13: 2 the rest of the people he sent home 2
15:15 and the rest we have utterly destroyed. 1
2Sm 10:10 the rest of his men he put in the charge of Abi'shai 2
12:28 Now, then, gather the rest of the people together 2
1Kg 11:41 the rest of the acts of Solomon, and all that he did 2
12:23 Judah and Benjamin, and to the rest of the people 2
14:19 the rest of the acts of Jerobo'am . . are written 2
29 the rest of the acts of Rehobo'am, and all that he 2
15: 7 The rest of the acts of Abi'jam, and all that he did 2
23 the rest of all the acts of Asa, all his might 2
31 the rest of the acts of Nadab, and all that he did 2
16: 5 the rest of the acts of Ba'asha, and what he did 2
14 the rest of the acts of Elah, and all that he did 2
20 the rest of the acts of Zimri, and the conspiracy 2
27 the rest of the acts of Omri which he did 2
20:30 the rest fled into the city of Aphek; 1
22:39 the rest of the acts of Ahab, and all that he did 2
45 the rest of the acts of Jehosh'aphat, and his might 2
2Kg 1:18 Now the rest of the acts of Ahazi'ah which he did 2
4: 7 pay your debts, and you . . can live on the rest. 1
8:23 the rest of the acts of Joram, and all that he did 2
10:34 Now the rest of the acts of Jehu, and all that he did 2
12:19 the rest of the acts of Jo'ash, and all that he did 2
13: 8 the rest of the acts of Jeho'ahaz and all . . he did 2
12 the rest of the acts of Jo'ash, and all that he did 2
14:15 Now the rest of the acts of Jeho'ash which he did 2
18 Now the rest of the deeds of Amazi'ah 2
28 the rest of the acts of Jerobo'am and all . . he did 2
15: 6 the rest of the acts of Azari'ah, and all that he did 2
11 Now the rest of the deeds of Zechari'ah 2
15 Now the rest of the deeds of Shallum 2
21 the rest of the deeds of Men'aham, and all . . he did 2
26 the rest of the deeds of Pekahi'ah, and all . . he did 2
31 the rest of the acts of Pekah, and all that he did 2
36 the rest of the acts of Jotham, and all that he did 2
16:19 Now the rest of the acts of Ahaz which he did 2
20:20 The rest of the deeds of Hezeki'ah . . all his might 2
21:17 the rest of the acts of Manas'seh . . all that he did 2
25 Now the rest of the acts of Amon which he did 2
23:28 the rest of the acts of Josi'ah, and all that he did 2
24: 5 Now the rest of the deeds of Jehoi'akim 2
25:11 the rest of the people who were left in the city 2
11 together with the rest of the multitude 2
1Ch 6:61 To the rest of the Ko'hathites were given by lot 1
70 for the rest of the families of the Ko'hathites. 1
77 To the rest of the Merar'ites were allotted 1
11: 8 and Jo'ab repaired the rest of the city. 5
12:38 all the rest of Israel were of a single mind 6
16:41 the rest of those chosen and expressly named 5
19:11 the rest of his men he put in the charge of Abi'shai 2
24:20 And of the rest of the sons of Levi 1
2Ch 9:29 Now the rest of the acts of Solomon 5
13:22 The rest of the acts of Abi'jah 2
20:34 Now the rest of the acts of Jehosh'aphat 2
24:14 brought the rest of the money before the king 5
25:26 rest of the deeds of Amazi'ah, from first to last 2
26:22 the rest of the acts of Uzzi'ah, from first to last 2
27: 7 Now the rest of the acts of Jotham, and all his wars 2
28:26 Now the rest of his acts and all his ways 2
32:32 rest of the acts of Hezeki'ah, and his good deeds 2
33:18 the rest of the acts of Manas'seh, and his prayer 2
35:26 the rest of the acts of Josi'ah, and his good deeds 2
36: 8 Now the rest of the acts of Jehoi'akim 2
Ezr 3: 8 together with the rest of their brethren 5
4: 3 rest of the heads of fathers' houses in Israel 5
7 rest of their associates wrote to Ar-ta-xerx'es 5
9 rest of their associates, the judges 7
10 rest of the nations whom the great and noble 7
10 rest of the province Beyond the River, and now 7
17 rest of their associates who live in Sama'ria 7
17 live in Sama'ria and in the rest of the province 7
6:16 Levites, and the rest of the returned exiles 7
7:18 do with the rest of the silver and gold 7
Neh 2:16 I had not yet told the . . officials, and the rest 2
4:14 said to . . officials and to the rest of the people 2
19 said to . . officials and to the rest of the people 2
6: 1 to Geshem the Arab and to the rest of our enemies 2
14 No-adi'ah and the rest of the prophets who wanted 2
7:72 what the rest of the people gave was 20,000 darics 6
10:28 The rest of the people, the priests, the Levites 5
11: 1 rest of the people cast lots to bring one out 5
20 rest of Israel, and of the priests and the Levites 5
Est 9:12 have they done in the rest of the king's provinces! 5
Isa 38:10 consigned to . . Sheol for the rest of my years. 2
44:17 the rest of it he makes into a god, his idol; 6
Jer 15: 9 And the rest of them I will give to the sword 6
27:19 and the rest of the vessels which are left 2
39: 3 the rest of the officers of the king of Babylon. 6
9 the guard, carried into exile to Babylon the rest 2
41:10 Ish'mael took captive all the rest of the people 6
16 leaders of the forces with him took all the rest 6
52:15 the rest of the people who were left in the city 2
15 together with the rest of the artisans. 2
Ezk 25:16 and destroy the rest of the seacoast. 6
34:18 you must tread down . . the rest of your pasture; 2
18 that you must foul the rest with your feet? 1
36: 3 became the possession of the rest of the nations 6
4 derision to the rest of the nations round about; 6
5 my hot jealousy against the rest of the nations 6
48:23 As for the rest of the tribes: from the east side 2
Dan 2:18 might not perish with the rest of the wise men 7
7:12 As for the rest of the beasts, 7
19 beast, which was different from all the rest •
Mic 5: 3 then the rest of his brethren shall return 2
Zec 14: 2 the rest of the people shall not be cut off 2
Mat 22: 6 while the rest seized his servants 12
Mrk 16:13 they went back and told the rest 12
Lke 12:26 why are you anxious about the rest? 12
24: 9 told all this to the eleven and to all the rest. 12
Act 2:37 said to Peter and the rest of the apostles 12
5:13 None of the rest dared join them 12
15:17 the rest of men may seek the Lord 11
17: 9 they had taken security from Jason and the rest 12
27:44 the rest on planks or on pieces of the ship 12
28: 9 the rest of the people on the island 12
Rom 1:13 as well as among the rest of the Gentiles 12
11: 7 The elect obtained it, but the rest were hardened 12
1Co 7:12 To the rest I say, not the Lord 12
2Co 12:13 less favored than the rest of the churches 12
Gal 2:13 with him the rest of the Jews acted insincerely 12
Eph 2: 3 like the rest of mankind. 12
Php 1:13 to all the rest 12
4: 3 with Clement and the rest of my fellow workers 12
1Ti 5:20 so that the rest may stand in fear. 12
1Pe 4: 2 so as to live for the rest of the time in the flesh 9
Rev 2:24 But to the rest of you in Thyati'ra 12
9:20 rest of mankind, who were not killed by . . plagues 12
11:13 and the rest were terrified and gave glory 12
12:17 went off to make war on the rest of her offspring 12
19:21 And the rest were slain by the sword 12
20: 5 The rest of the dead did not come to life 12
1Es 2:16 the rest of their associates 12
5: 8 who returned to Jerusalem and the rest of Judea 12
7: 6 the rest of those from the captivity 12
Tob 8:21 the rest would be his "when my wife and I die. 12
Jdt 7:18 The rest of the Assyrian army 12
15: 6 The rest of the people of Bethulia 12
Sir 0: 2 the prophecies, and the rest of the books 12
1Mc 3:11 Many were wounded and fell, and the rest fled. 9
12 and used it in battle the rest of his life. 13
24 the rest fled into the land of the Philistines. 12
5:18 he left Joseph . . with the rest of the forces 9
6:38 The rest of the horsemen were stationed 9
54 because famine had prevailed over the rest •
7:32 the rest fled into the city of David. •
42 let the rest learn 9
8: 4 the rest paid them tribute every year. 9
9:18 Judas also fell, and the rest fled. 12
22 Now the rest of the acts of Judas 14
40 the rest fled to the mountain 9
12: 6 the rest of the Jewish people 12
14:20 the priests and the rest of the Jewish people 12
16: 8 the rest fled into the stronghold. 10
23 The rest of the acts of John and his wars 12
2Mc 1:23 Jonathan led, and the rest responded 12
7: 4 the rest of the brothers and the mother 12
8:28 and distributed the rest among themselves 12
31 carried the rest of the spoils to Jerusalem. 12
10:36 and let in the rest of the force 12
11:11 and forced all the rest to flee. •
14:11 the rest of the king's friends 12
4Mc 3: 9 Now all the rest were at supper 8

rest *See* arm, attain, day, enjoy, find, give, go, place, provide, set, take.

rest assured 1. שָׁלוֹם
Gen 43:23 He replied, "Rest assured, do not be afraid; 1

come to rest 1. נוח
Gen 8: 4 the ark came to rest upon the mountains 1

rest heavily 1. כבד
Jdg 1:35 hand . . of Joseph rested heavily upon them 1

make rest 1. שׁבת 2. καταπαύω
Exd 5: 5 you make them rest from their burdens! 1
Sir 44:23 he made to rest upon the head of Jacob 2

sabbath rest 1. σαββατισμός
Heb 4: 9 remains a sabbath rest for the people of God; 1

solemn rest 1. שַׁבָּתוֹן
Exd 31:15 seventh day is a sabbath of solemn rest, holy 1
35: 2 a holy sabbath of solemn rest to the LORD; 1
Lev 16:31 It is a sabbath of solemn rest to you 1
23: 3 on the seventh day is a sabbath of solemn rest 1
32 It shall be to you a sabbath of solemn rest 1
39 on the first day shall be a solemn rest 1
39 on the eighth day shall be a solemn rest 1
25: 4 shall be a sabbath of solemn rest for the land 1
5 it shall be a year of solemn rest for the land 1

rest upon 1. ἐπαναπαύομαι 2. ἐπιστηρίζω
Lke 10: 6 your peace shall rest upon him 1
Jdt 8:24 and the temple and the altar rest upon us. 2

resting place 1. נוּחַ 2. מְנוּחָה 3. מָקוֹם
Gen 49:15 he saw that a resting place was good 2
Num10:33 ark . . went . . to seek out a resting place for them. 2
2Ch 6:41 now arise, O LORD God, and go to thy resting place 2
Job 16:18 let my cry find no resting place. 3
Ps 132: 8 Arise, O LORD, and go to thy resting place 2
14 This is my resting place for ever; 2
Isa 32:18 in secure dwellings, and in quiet resting places. 2
34:14 alight, and find for herself a resting place. 1
Lam 1: 3 now among the nations, but finds no resting place; 1
restitution *See* make.

restitution for wrong 1. אָשָׁם
Num 5: 8 restitution may be made for the wrong 1
8 restitution for wrong shall go to the LORD 1

restive 1. קַל
Jer 2:23 a restive young camel interlacing her tracks 1

restless 1. ἀκατάστατος
Jas 3: 8 the tongue–a restless evil 1

restoration 1. ἐπανόρθωσις
1Mc 14:34 whatever was necessary for their restoration. 1

restore 1. בנה 2. חדשׁ 3. חזק 4. ישׁב 5. כון 6. עזב 7. עלה 8. עמד 9. קום 10. רפא 11. שׁוב 12. שׁלם 13. יהב (A) 14. ἀναδείκνυμι 15. ἀνακαινίζω 16. ἀποδίδωμι 17. ἀποκαθίστημι 18. ἐγκαινίζω 19. ἐπανορθόω 20. ἐπικαινίζω 21. ἐπιστρέφω 22. καθίστημι 23. καινίζω 24. καταρτίζω 25. περίστημι
Gen 20: 7 Now then restore the man's wife; 11
7 But if you do not restore her 11
14 to Abraham, and restored Sarah his wife to him. 11
37:22 out of their hand, to restore him to his father. 11
40:13 will lift up your head and restore you 11
21 He restored the chief butler to his butlership 11
41:13 I was restored to my office, and the baker was 11
Exd 4: 7 it was restored like the rest of his flesh. 11
22:26 you shall restore it to him before the sun goes 11
Lev 6: 4 he shall restore what he took by robbery 11
5 he shall restore it in full, and shall add a fifth 12
Num35:25 congregation shall restore him to his city 11
Deu 22: 2 your brother seeks it; then you shall restore it 11
24:13 sun goes down, you shall restore to him the pledge 11
28:31 your ass . . shall not be restored to you; 11
30: 3 LORD your God will restore your fortunes 11
Jdg 11:13 took away my land . . now therefore restore it 11
17: 3 he restored the 1,100 pieces of silver 11
3 now therefore I will restore it to you. 11
4 when he restored the money to his mother 11
Rut 4: 5 restore the name of the dead to his inheritance. 9
1Sm 7:14 The cities . . were restored to Israel, from Ekron 11
12: 3 Testify against me and I will restore it to you. 11
2Sm 8: 3 he went to restore his power at the river 11
9: 7 I will restore to you all the land of Saul 11
12: 6 and he shall restore the lamb fourfold 12
1Kg 12:21 to restore the kingdom to Rehobo'am 11
13: 6 pray for me, that my hand may be restored to me. 11
6 the king's hand was restored to him 11
20:34 The cities which my father took . . I will restore; 11
2Kg 5:10 Go and wash . . and your flesh shall be restored 4
14 and his flesh was restored like the flesh 11
8: 6 Restore all that was hers, together with all 11
14:22 He built Elath and restored it to Judah 11
25 He restored the border of Israel 11
2Ch 11: 1 to restore the kingdom to Rehobo'am. 11
24: 4 Jo'ash decided to restore the house of the LORD. 2
12 hired masons . . to restore the house of the LORD 2
13 they restored the house of God 8
26: 2 He built Eloth and restored it to Judah 11
29:35 service of the house of the LORD was restored. 5
33:16 He also restored the altar of the LORD 1
34:10 gave it for repairing and restoring the house. 3
Ezr 6: 5 be restored and brought back to the temple 13
Neh 3: 8 restored Jerusalem as far as the Broad Wall. 6
4: 2 Will they restore things? Will they sacrifice? 6
5:12 We will restore these and require nothing 11
Job 42:10 the LORD restored the fortunes of Job 11
Ps 14: 7 the LORD restores the fortunes of his people 11
23: 3 he restores my soul. He leads me in paths 11
51:12 Restore to me the joy of thy salvation 11
53: 6 When God restores the fortunes of his people 11
60: 1 thou hast been angry; oh, restore us. 11
68: 9 thou didst restore thy heritage as it languished; 5
69: 4 What I did not steal must I now restore? 11
80: 3 Restore us, O God; 11
7 Restore us, O God of hosts; let thy face shine 11
19 Restore us, O LORD God of hosts! let thy face shine 11
85: 1 thou didst restore the fortunes of Jacob. 11
126: 1 When the LORD restored the fortunes of Zion 11
4 Restore our fortunes, O LORD 11
Isa 1:26 I will restore your judges as at the first 11
42:22 a spoil with none to say, "Restore! 11
49: 6 of Jacob and to restore the preserved of Israel; 11
Jer 8:22 the daughter of my people not been restored? 7
15:19 says the LORD: "If you return, I will restore you 11
27:22 bring them back and restore them to this place. 11
29:14 and I will restore your fortunes and gather you 11
30: 3 when I will restore the fortunes of my people 11
17 For I will restore health to you 7
18 I will restore the fortunes of the tents of Jacob 11
31:18 bring me back that I may be restored 11
23 and in its cities, when I restore their fortunes 11
32:44 for I will restore their fortunes, says the LORD. 11
33: 7 I will restore the fortunes of Judah 11
11 For I will restore the fortunes of the land 11
26 For I will restore their fortunes 11
48:47 Yet I will restore the fortunes of Moab 11
49: 6 I will restore the fortunes of the Ammonites 11
39 I will restore the fortunes of Elam, says the LORD. 11
50:19 I will restore Israel to his pasture 11
Lam 2:13 For vast as the sea is your ruin; who can restore you? 10
14 exposed your iniquity to restore your fortunes 11
5:21 Restore us to thyself, O LORD 11
21 Restore us . . O LORD, that we may be restored! 11
Ezk 16:53 I will restore their fortunes 11
53 I will restore your own fortunes 11
18: 7 but restores to the debtor his pledge 11
12 commits robbery, does not restore the pledge 11
29:14 I will restore the fortunes of Egypt 11
33:15 if the wicked restores the pledge 11
38: 8 go against the land that is restored from war 11
39:25 Now I will restore the fortunes of Jacob 11
Dan 9:25 forth of the word to restore and build Jerusalem 11
Hos 6:11 When I would restore the fortunes of my people 11
Jol 2:25 I will restore to you the years 12
3: 1 when I restore the fortunes of Judah 11
Ams 9:14 I will restore the fortunes of my people Israel 11
Nah 2: 2 For the LORD is restoring the majesty of Jacob 11
Zep 2: 7 be mindful of them and restore their fortunes. 11
3:20 when I restore your fortunes before your eyes 11
Zec 9:12 today I declare that I will restore to you double. 11
Mat 12:13 and it was restored, whole like the other. 17
17:11 and he is to restore all things; 17
Mrk 3: 5 He stretched it out, and his hand was restored. 17
8:25 he looked intently and was restored 17
9:12 Eli'jah does come first to restore all things 17
Lke 6:10 he did so, and his hand was restored. 17
19: 8 I restore it fourfold. 16
Act 1: 6 Lord, will you at this time restore the kingdom 17
Gal 6: 1 you who are spiritual should restore him 24
Heb 6: 4 For it is impossible to restore to repentance 15
13:19 in order that I may be restored to you the sooner. 17
1Pe 5:10 will . . restore, establish, and strengthen you. 24
1Es 6:26 should be restored to the house in Jerusalem 17
Tob 2: 1 my wife Anna and my son Tobias were restored to me 16
Jdt 7:30 the Lord our God will restore to us his mercy 21
Sir 48:10 to restore the tribes of Jacob. 22
LJr 1:37 They cannot restore sight to a blind man 25
1Mc 4:57 they restored the gates 18
9:72 He restored to him the captives 16
10:10 began to rebuild and restore the city. 23
44 restoring the structures of the sanctuary 20
15: 3 so that I may restore it as it formerly was 17
2Mc 2:22 restored the laws 19
5:20 was restored again in all its glory 19
11:25 our decision is that their temple be restored 17
12:25 his solemn promise to restore them unharmed 17
3Mc 6: 8 restored unharmed to all his family. 14
7:22 those who held any restored it 16

restore again 1. שׁוב
Ps 85: 4 Restore us again, O God of our salvation 1

restore saltness 1. ἁλίζω 2. ἀρτύω
Mat 5:13 how shall its saltness be restored? 1
Lke 14:34 how shall its saltness be restored? 2

restore to health 1. חלם
Isa 38:16 Oh, restore me to health and make me live! 1

restore to life 1. חיה
2Kg 8: 1 to the woman whose son he had restored to life 1
5 how Eli'sha had restored the dead to life 1
5 the woman whose son he had restored to life 1
5 and here is her son whom Eli'sha restored to life. 1
Ps 30: 3 restored me to life from among those gone down 1

restore to rightful state 1. צדק
Dan 8:14 sanctuary . . restored to its rightful state. 1

restorer 1. שׁוב
Rut 4:15 He shall be to you a restorer of life 1
Isa 58:12 repairer . . the restorer of streets to dwell in. 1

restrain 1. אפק 2. חשׂם 3. חשׂך 4. כהה 5. כלא 6. מנע 7. עקב 8. צפן 9. שׁוב 10. ἀνέχω 11. ἀποτρέπω 12. ἡμερόομαι 13. καταπαύω 14. κατέχω 15. κρατέω 16. κωλυτικός 17. κωλύω 18. φέρω 19. coerceo
Gen 8: 2 the rain from the heavens was restrained 5
Exd 36: 6 So the people were restrained from bringing; 5
1Sm 3:13 blaspheming God, and he did not restrain them. 4
25:26 the LORD has restrained you from bloodguilt 6
34 LORD . . who has restrained me from hurting you 6
2Sm 18:16 troops came back . . for Jo'ab restrained them. 3
Est 5:10 Haman restrained himself, and went home; 1
Job 7:11 Therefore I will not restrain my mouth; 3
30:13 they promote my calamity; no one restrains them. •
37: 4 he does not restrain the lightnings 7
Ps 40: 9 lo, I have not restrained my lips, as thou knowest 5
78:38 he restrained his anger often 9
Prv 10:19 but he who restrains his lips is prudent. 3
17:27 He who restrains his words has knowledge 3
27:16 to restrain her is to restrain the wind 8
16 to restrain her is to restrain the wind 8
Isa 42:14 I have kept still and restrained myself; 1
48: 9 for the sake of my praise I restrain it for you 2
64:12 thou restrain thyself at these things, O LORD? 1
Jer 2:24 Who can restrain her lust? 9
14:10 they have not restrained their feet; 3
Lam 2: 8 he restrained not his hand from destroying; 9
Ezk 31:15 mourn for it, and restrain its rivers 6
Act 14:18 they scarcely restrained the people 13
2Th 2: 6 you know what is restraining him now 14
7 only he who now restrains it will do 14
2Pe 2:16 a dumb ass . . restrained the prophet's madness. 17
2Es 7:116or else . . had restrained him from sinning. 19
AEs 16:12 unable to restrain his arrogance 18
Wis 16:18 At one time the flame was restrained 12
Sir 18:30 restrain your appetites. 17
46: 7 restrained the people from sin 17
Bel 1:19 restrained the king from going in, and said 15
3Mc 1:23 and being barely restrained by the old men 11
4Mc 1:30 the restraining power of self-control. 16
35 the emotions of the appetites are restrained 10

restraint 1. מֵזַח 2. רֶסֶן 3. βρόχος
Job 30:11 they have cast off restraint in my presence. 2
Isa 23:10 Overflow . . there is no restraint any more. 1
1Co 7:35 not to lay any restraint upon you 3
restraint *See also* cast, keep, throw.

restrict 1. στενοχωρέω
2Co 6:12 You are not restricted by us 1
12 you are restricted in your own affections. 1

result 1. לְמַעַן 2. עֲבֹדָה 3. αἰτία 4. γίνομαι 5. εἰμί 6. εἰς 7. ἐκβαίνω 8. ὅθεν 9. συμβαίνω 10. τέλος 11. ὧν χάριν 12. ὥστε
Isa 32:17 the result of righteousness, quietness 2
Jer 27:10 with the result that you will be removed far 1
15 with the result that I will drive you out 1
Sir 20: 9 a windfall may result in a loss. 6
38:18 For sorrow results in death 7
2Mc 4:42 As a result, they wounded many of them 3
7:12 As a result the king himself and those with him 12
9: 2 with the result that . . 9
10:13 As a result he was accused before Eupator 8
3Mc 1: 4 When a bitter fight resulted 4
28 cry of the crowds resulted in an immense uproar; 5
5:41 As a result the city is in a tumult 11
4Mc 12: 3 You see the result of your brothers' stupidity 10

without result 1. κενός
Wis 1:11 because no secret word is without result 1

resume 1. πάλιν 2. ὑπολαμβάνω
Joh 13:12 taken his garments, and resumed his place 1
4Mc 8:13 the tyrant resumed speaking 2

resurrection 1. ἀνάστασις 2. ἔγερσις 3. ἐξανάστασις 4. resurrectio

Mat 22:23 who say that there is no resurrection 1
28 In the resurrection, therefore 1
30 For in the resurrection they neither marry 1
31 as for the resurrection of the dead 1
27:53 coming out of the tombs after his resurrection 2
Mrk 12:18 who say that there is no resurrection 1
23 In the resurrection whose wife will she be? 1
Lke 14:14 repaid at the resurrection of the just. 1
20:27 those who say that there is no resurrection 1
33 In the resurrection, therefore, whose wife 1
35 to the resurrection from the dead 1
36 sons of God, being sons of the resurrection. 1
Joh 5:29 who have done good, to the resurrection of life 1
29 to the resurrection of judgment. 1
11:24 rise again in the resurrection at the last day. 1
25 I am the resurrection and the life 1
Act 1:22 become with us a witness to his resurrection. 1
2:31 spoke of the resurrection of the Christ 1
4: 2 in Jesus the resurrection from the dead. 1
33 testimony to the resurrection of the Lord Jesus 1
17:18 because he preached Jesus and the resurrection. 1
32 when they heard of the resurrection of the dead 1
23: 6 the hope and the resurrection of the dead 1
8 the Sad'ducees say that there is no resurrection 1
24:15 a resurrection of both the just and the unjust. 1
21 With respect to the resurrection of the dead 1
Rom 1: 4 by his resurrection from the dead, Jesus Christ 1
6: 5 be united with him in a resurrection like his. 1
1Co 15:12 there is no resurrection of the dead? 1
13 if there is no resurrection of the dead 1
21 has come also the resurrection of the dead. 1
42 So is it with the resurrection of the dead. 1
Php 3:10 know him and the power of his resurrection 1
11 I may attain the resurrection from the dead. 3
2Ti 2:18 holding that the resurrection is past already. 1
Heb 6: 2 the resurrection of the dead 1
11:35 Women received their dead by resurrection. 1
1Pe 1: 3 the resurrection of Jesus Christ from the dead 1
3:21 through the resurrection of Jesus Christ 1
Rev 20: 5 This is the first resurrection. 1
6 holy is he who shares in the first resurrection! 1
2Es 2:23 give you the first place in my resurrection. 4
2Mc 7:14 there will be no resurrection to life! 1
12:43 taking account of the resurrection. 1

retain 1. אמץ 2. חזק 3. כלא 4. עצר 5. ἀνάλημμα 6. διαφυλάσσω 7. ἰσχύω 8. κρατέω 9. conservo

Jdg 7: 8 every man to his tent, but retained the 300 men; 2
Ecc 8: 8 No man has power to retain the spirit 3
Dan 10: 8 I retained no strength. 4
16 pains have come upon me, and I retain no strength. 4
11: 6 but she shall not retain the strength of her arm 4
Ams 2:14 and the strong shall not retain his strength 1
Mic 7:18 He does not retain his anger for ever 2
Joh 20:23 if you retain the sins of any, they are retained. 8
23 if you retain the sins of any, they are retained. 8
2Es 14:40 for my spirit retained its memory; 9
Wis 19:20 Fire even in water retained its normal power 7
Sir 41:16 it is good to retain every kind of shame 6
50: 2 high retaining walls for the temple enclosure. 5

retinue 1. חַיִל 2. παραδρομή

1Kg 10: 2 She came to Jerusalem with a very great retinue 1
2Ch 9: 1 having a very great retinue and camels 1
2Mc 3:28 with a great retinue and all his bodyguard 2
4Mc 6:13 some of the king's retinue came to him and said •

retort 1. λόγος

Act 7:29 At this retort Moses fled 1

retreat 1. ἀναζυγή 2. ἀναλύω

2Mc 9: 1 Antiochus had retreated in disorder 2
2 beat a shameful retreat. 1

retreat (2) 1. מָלוֹן

2Kg 19:23 I entered its farthest retreat, its densest 1

retribution 1. ἀνταπόδομα 2. μισθαποδοσία

Rom 11: 9 become . . a pitfall and a retribution for them; 1
Heb 2: 2 received a just retribution 2
Sir 14: 6 this is the retribution for his baseness; 1
48: 8 who anointed kings to inflict retribution 1

return 1. אסף 2. הלך 3. חֲלַף 4. ישב 5. כָּ 6. סור 7. שוב 8. שלם 9. תַּחַת 10. תוב (A) 11. ἀμοιβή 12. ἀναβαίνω 13. ἀναζεύγνυμι 14. ἀνακάμπτω 15. ἀνακομίζω 16. ἀναλύω 17. ἀναποδισμός 18. ἀναστρέφω 19. ἀντάλλαγμα 20. ἀνταποδίδωμι 21. ἀνταπόδομα 22. ἀντί 23. ἀντιμισθία 24. ἀπαιτέω 25. ἀπαλλάσσω 26. ἄπειμι 27. ἀπέρχομαι 28. ἀποδίδωμι 29. ἀποίχομαι 30. ἀποκαθίστημι 31. ἀποστρέφω 32. ἀποστροφή 33. ἀποτρέχω 34. εἰσέρχομαι 35. εἰσπορεύομαι 36. ἐπανάγω 37. ἐπανέρχομαι 38. ἐπανήκω 39. ἐπάνοδος 40. ἐπιστρέφω 41. ἐπιστροφή 42. ἔρχομαι 43. καρπός 44. πάλιν ἐξέρχομαι 45. παραγίνομαι 46. πορεύω 47. συνάγω 48. τρέπω 49. ὑποστρέφω 50. dimitto 51. reverto 52. revertor

Gen 3:19 you shall eat bread till you return to the ground 7
19 you are dust, and to dust you shall return. 7
8: 9 she returned to him to the ark 7
12 she did not return to him any more. 7
14:17 After his return from the defeat 7
16: 9 Return to your mistress, and submit to her. 7
18:10 The LORD said, "I will surely return to you 7
14 At the appointed time I will return to you 7
33 to Abraham; and Abraham returned to his place. 7
21:32 rose up and returned to the land 7
22:19 Abraham returned to his young men 7
29:27 you the other also in return for serving me •
31: 3 Then the LORD said to Jacob, "Return to the land 7
13 go forth from this land, and return to the land 7
55 then he departed and returned home. 7
32: 6 the messengers returned to Jacob, saying 7
9 O LORD who didst say to me, 'Return to your country 7
33:16 Esau returned that day on his way to Se'ir. 7
37:29 When Reuben returned to the pit 7
30 returned to his brothers, and said 7
38:22 he returned to Judah, and said, "I have not found 7
42:24 and he returned to them and spoke to them. 7
43:10 not delayed, we would now have returned twice. 7
12 the money that was returned to the mouth 7
44: 4 say to them, 'Why have you returned evil for good? 8
13 and they returned to the city. 7
50: 5 let me . . bury my father; then I will return. 7
14 Joseph returned to Egypt with his brothers 7
Exd 13:17 Lest the people repent . . and return to Egypt. 7
14:27 the sea returned to its wonted flow 7
28 The waters returned and covered the chariots 7
32:31 So Moses returned to the LORD and said 7
34:31 leaders of the congregation returned to him 7
Lev 22:13 daughter . . returns to her father's house 7
25:10 when each of you shall return to his property 7
10 each of you shall return to his family 7
13 each of you shall return to his property 7
27 and he shall return to his property 7
28 and he shall return to his property 7
41 return to the possession of his fathers 7
27:24 In the year of jubilee the field shall return 7
Num 10:36 Return, O LORD, to the ten thousand thousands 7
11:30 Moses and the elders . . returned to the camp. 1
13:25 they returned from spying out the land. 7
14:36 sent to spy out the land, and who returned 7
16:50 Aaron returned to Moses at the entrance 7
18:21 in return for their service which they serve 3
31 for it is your reward in return for your service 3
23: 5 Return to Balak, and thus you shall speak. 7
6 he returned to him, and lo, he and all the princes 7
16 Return to Balak, and thus shall you speak. 7
32:18 We will not return to our homes until 7
22 you shall return and be free of obligation 7
35:28 manslayer may return to . . his possession. 7
32 no ransom . . that he may return to dwell in the land 7
Deu 1:45 returned and wept before the LORD; 7
3:20 then you shall return every man to his possession 7
4:30 return to the LORD your God and obey his voice 7
5:30 Go and say to them, "Return to your tents. 7
17:16 You shall never return that way again.' 7
30: 2 return to the LORD your God, you and your children 7
Jos 1:15 you shall return to the land of your possession 7
2:16 and hide . . until the pursuers have returned; 7
22 there three days, until the pursuers returned; 7
4:18 the waters of the Jordan returned to their place 7
6:14 marched around . . and returned into the camp. 7
7: 3 And they returned to Joshua, and said to him 7
8:24 all Israel returned to Ai, and smote it 7
10:15 Joshua returned, and all Israel . . to the camp 7
21 the people returned safe to Joshua in the camp 7
43 Joshua returned, and all Israel with him 7
22: 9 the Reubenites and the Gadites . . returned home 7
32 Phin'ehas . . returned from the Reubenites 7
Jdg 6:18 And he said, "I will stay till you return. 7
7: 3 is fearful and trembling, let him return home.' 4
3 tested them; 22,000 returned, and 10,000 remained 7
15 worshiped; and he returned to the camp of Israel 7
8:13 Gideon the son of Jo'ash returned from the battle 7
35 show kindness . . in return for all the good 5
11:31 meet me, when I return victorious 7
39 the end of two months, she returned to her father 7
14: 8 And after a while he returned to take her; 7
15:19 he drank, his spirit returned . . and he revived. 7
20: 8 his tent, and none of us will return to his house. 6
21:14 Benjamin returned at that time; and they gave 7
23 they went and returned to their inheritance 7
Rut 1: 6 she started . . to return from the country of Moab 7
7 went on the way to return to the land of Judah. 7
8 Go, return each of you to her mother's house. 7
10 No, we will return with you to your people. 7
15 return after your sister-in-law. 7
16 not to leave you or to return from following you; 7
22 Na'omi returned, and Ruth . . with her 7
22 Ruth . . who returned from the country of Moab. 7
1Sm 2:20 so then they would return to their home. 2
5:11 Send away the ark . . and let it return to its own 4
6: 3 but by all means return him a guilt offering. 7
4 the guilt offering that we shall return to him? 7
8 which you are returning . . as a guilt offering. 7
16 they returned that day to Ekron. 7
17 Philistines returned as a guilt offering 7
21 The Philistines have returned the ark 7
7: 3 you are returning to the LORD with all your heart 7
15:25 I pray, pardon my sin, and return with me 7
26 I will not return with you, for you have rejected 7
30 and return with me, that I may worship the LORD 7
17:57 as David returned from the slaughter 7
18: 2 and would not let him return to his father's 7
6 David returned from slaying the Philistine 7
23:28 Saul returned from pursuing after David 7
24: 1 Saul returned from following the Philistines 7
25:21 and he has returned me evil for good. 7
39 LORD has returned the evil . . upon his own head. 7
26:21 Saul said, "I have done wrong; return, my son David 7
25 David went his way, and Saul returned to his place. 7
29: 4 return to the place to which you have assigned 4
11 to return to the land of the Philistines. 7
2Sm 1: 1 when David had returned from the slaughter 7
22 and the sword of Saul returned not empty. 7
2:30 Jo'ab returned from the pursuit of Abner; 7
3:16 Abner said to him, "Go, return"; and he returned. 7
16 Abner said to him, "Go, return"; and he returned. 4
27 when Abner returned . . Jo'ab took him aside 7
6:20 David returned to bless his household. 7
8:13 When he returned, he slew 18,000 E'domites 7
10: 5 Remain at Jericho until . . and then return. 7
14 Jo'ab returned from fighting . . the Ammonites 7
11: 4 Then she returned to her house. 7
12:23 I shall go to him, but he will not return to me. 7
31 David and all the people returned to Jerusalem. 7
15:34 But if you return to the city, and say to Ab'salom 7
17:20 could not find them, they returned to Jerusalem. 7
19:14 Return, both you and all your servants. 7
37 let your servant return, that I may die in my own 7
39 and he returned to his own home. 7
20:22 And Jo'ab returned to Jerusalem to the king. 7
23:10 men returned after him only to strip the slain. 7
24:13 and decide what answer I shall return to him 7
1Kg 2:41 that Shim'e-i had gone . . to Gath and returned 4
12: 2 then Jerobo'am returned from Egypt. 4
20 when all Israel heard that Jerobo'am had returned 7
24 Return every man to his home 7
27 they will kill me and return to Rehobo'am 7
13: 9 eat bread, nor drink water, nor return by the way 7
10 did not return by the way that he came to Bethel. 7
16 he said, "I may not return with you, or go in with you; 7
17 nor return by the way that you came.' 7
19:15 return on your way to the wilderness of Damascus; 7
21 he returned from following him, and took the yoke 7
22:17 let each return to his home in peace.' 7
28 If you return in peace, the LORD has not spoken 7
2Kg 1: 5 The messengers returned to the king 7
5 he said to them, "Why have you returned? 7
2:25 Mount Carmel, and thence he returned to Sama'ria. 7
3:27 they withdrew . . and returned to their own land. 7
4:31 he returned to meet him, and told him 7
5:15 Then he returned to the man of God 7
7:15 And the messengers returned, and told the king. 7
8: 3 when the woman returned . . she went forth 7
29 King Joram returned to be healed in Jezreel 7
9:15 King Joram had returned to be healed in Jezreel 7
14:14 he seized all the . . and he returned to Sama'ria. 7
19: 7 he shall hear a rumor and return to his own land; 7
8 The Rab'shakeh returned, and found the king 7
33 By the way that he came, by the same he shall return 7
23:20 Then he returned to Jerusalem. 7
1Ch 4:22 Saraph, who ruled in Moab and returned to Lehem 7
19: 5 until your beards have grown, and then return. 7
20: 3 David and all the people returned to Jerusalem. 7
21:12 decide what answer I shall return to him who sent 7
2Ch 10: 2 then Jerobo'am returned from Egypt. 7
11: 4 Return every man to his home 7
4 returned and did not go against Jerobo'am. 7
14:15 Then they returned to Jerusalem. 7
18:16 let each return to his home in peace.' 7
26 fellow in prison . . until I return in peace.' 7
27 If you return in peace, the LORD has not spoken 7
19: 1 Jehosh'aphat . . returned in safety to his house 7
20:27 returned, every man of Judah and Jerusalem 7
27 returning to Jerusalem with joy 7
22: 6 he returned to be healed in Jezreel of the wounds 7
24:11 empty the chest and take it and return it 7
25:10 returned home in fierce anger. 7
24 seized . . hostages, and he returned to Sama'ria. 7
28:15 Then they returned to Sama'ria. 7
30: 6 O people of Israel, return to the LORD 7
9 For if you return to the LORD 7
9 find compassion . . and return to this land. 7
9 will not turn away . . if you return to him. 7
31: 1 people of Israel returned to their cities 7
32:21 returned with shame of face to his own land. 7
34: 7 Then he returned to Jerusalem. 7
Ezr 2: 1 returned to Jerusalem and Judah, each to his own 7
4: 1 adversaries . . heard that the returned exiles •

5: 5 then answer be returned by letter concerning it. 10
6:16 Levites, and the rest of the returned exiles •
19 returned exiles kept the passover. •
20 passover lamb for all the returned exiles •
21 people of Israel who had returned from exile 7
8:35 come from captivity, the returned exiles •
9: 4 faithlessness of the returned exiles •
10: 7 proclamation . . to all the returned exiles •
16 Then the returned exiles did so. •
Neh 1: 9 if you return to me and keep my commandments 7
2: 6 How long will you be gone, and when will you return 7
15 I turned back and entered . . and so returned. 7
4:15 we all returned to the wall, each to his work. 7
5:11 Return to them this very day their fields 7
7: 6 returned to Jerusalem and Judah, each to his town. 7
8:17 all . . who had returned from the captivity 7
9:17 leader to return to their bondage in Egypt. 7
Est 4:13 Mor'decai told them to return answer to Esther 7
6:12 Then Mor'decai returned to the king's gate. 7
7: 8 And the king returned from the palace garden 7
Job 1:21 from my mother's womb, and naked shall I return; 7
7:10 he returns no more to his house 7
10:21 before I go whence I shall not return 7
15:22 not believe that he will return out of darkness 7
16:22 I shall go the way whence I shall not return. 7
22:23 If you return to the Almighty and humble 7
33:25 let him return to the days of his youthful vigor 7
34:15 man would return to dust. 7
36:10 commands that they return from iniquity. 7
39: 4 they go forth, and do not return to them. 7
12 Do you have faith in him that he will return 7
Ps 7:16 His mischief returns upon his own head 7
51:13 sinners will return to thee. 7
60: 0 when Joab on his return killed 12,000 7
79:12 Return sevenfold into the bosom 7
90:13 Return, O LORD! How long? Have pity on thy servants 7
94:15 for justice will return to the righteous 7
104:29 they die and return to their dust. 7
109: 4 In return for my love they accuse me 9
116: 7 Return, O my soul, to your rest; 7
146: 4 When his breath departs he returns to his earth; 7
Prv 17:13 If a man returns evil for good 7
26:11 Like a dog that returns to his vomit is a fool 7
Ecc 1: 6 and on its circuits the wind returns. 7
12: 2 and the stars are darkened and the clouds return 7
7 and the dust returns to the earth as it was 4
7 and the spirit returns to God who gave it. 7
Sng 6:13 Return, return, O Shu'lammite . . that we may look 7
13 Return, return, O Shu'lammite . . that we may look 7
13 return, return, that we may look upon you. 7
13 return, return, that we may look upon you. 7
Isa 10:21 A remnant will return, the remnant of Jacob 7
22 only a remnant of them will return. 7
19:22 they will return to the LORD, and he will heed 7
23:17 she will return to her hire, and will play 7
30:15 In returning and rest you shall be saved; 7
35:10 the ransomed of the LORD shall return 7
37: 7 he shall hear a rumor, and return to his own land; 7
8 The Rab'shakeh returned, and found the king 7
34 By the way that he came, by the same he shall return 7
43: 4 Because . . I love you, I give men in return for you 9
44:22 return to me, for I have redeemed you. 7
45:23 gone forth . . a word that shall not return 7
51:11 And the ransomed of the LORD shall return 7
52: 8 eye to eye they see the return of the LORD to Zion. 7
55: 7 let him return to the LORD 4
10 come down from heaven, and return not thither 7
11 from my mouth; it shall not return to me empty 7
63:17 Return for the sake of thy servants 7
Jer 3: 1 becomes another man's wife, will he return to her? 7
1 and would you return to me? says the LORD. 7
7 After she has done all this she will return to me'; 7
7 but she did not return 7
10 Yet . . her false sister Judah did not return to me 7
12 Return, faithless Israel, says the LORD. 7
14 Return, O faithless children, says the LORD; 7
22 Return, O faithless sons 7
4: 1 If you return, O Israel, says the LORD 7
1 to me you should return. 7
8: 4 If one turns away, does he not return? 7
5 They hold fast to deceit, they refuse to return. 7
14: 3 no water, they return with their vessels empty; 7
15:19 says the LORD: "If you return, I will restore you 7
18:11 Return, every one from his evil way 7
22:10 he shall return no more to see his native land. 7
11 away from this place: "He shall return here no more 7
27 to the land to which they will long to return 7
27 will long to return, there they shall not return. 7
24: 7 they shall return to me with their whole heart. 7
30:10 Jacob shall return and have quiet and ease 7
31: 8 a great company, they shall return here. 7
21 Return, O virgin Israel 7
21 O virgin Israel, return to these your cities. 7
37: 7 is about to return to Egypt, to its own land. 7
40: 5 then return to Gedali'ah the son of Ahi'kam 7
12 then all the Jews returned from all the places 7
43: 5 all the remnant of Judah who had returned to live 7
44:14 or survive or return to the land of Judah 7
14 Judah, to which they desire to return to dwell 7

14 they shall not return, except some fugitives. 7
28 And those who escape the sword shall return 7
46:27 Jacob shall return and have quiet and ease 7
50: 9 warrior who does not return empty-handed. 7
Lam 3:40 test and examine our ways, and return to the LORD! 7
Ezk 7:13 the seller shall not return to what he has sold 7
16:55 daughters shall return to their former estate; 7
55 daughters shall return to their former estate; 7
55 daughters shall return to your former estate. 7
21:30 Return it to its sheath. 7
46: 9 no one shall return by way of the gate by which he 7
Dan 4:34 lifted my eyes to heaven, and my reason returned 10
36 At the same time my reason returned to me; 10
36 my majesty and splendor returned to me. 10
10:20 return to fight against the prince of Persia; 7
11: 9 latter . . shall return into his own land. 7
28 he shall return to his land with great substance 4
28 shall work his will, and return to his own land. 7
29 shall return and come into the south; 7
Hos 2: 7 shall say, 'I will go and return to my first husband 7
3: 5 Afterward the children of Israel shall return 7
5: 4 deeds do not permit them to return to their God. 7
15 I will return again to my place 7
6: 1 Come, let us return to the LORD; 7
7:10 yet they do not return to the LORD their God 7
8:13 they shall return to Egypt. 7
9: 3 but E'phraim shall return to Egypt 7
11: 5 They shall return to the land of Egypt 7
5 because they have refused to return to me. 7
11 I will return them to their homes, says the LORD. 4
12: 6 return, hold fast to love and justice 7
14: 1 Return, O Israel, to the LORD your God 7
2 Take with you words and return to the LORD; 7
7 They shall return and dwell beneath my shadow 7
Jol 2:12 says the LORD, "return to me with all your heart 7
13 Return to the LORD, your God, for he is gracious 7
Ams 4: 6 yet you did not return to me," says the LORD. 7
8 yet you did not return to me," says the LORD. 7
9 yet you did not return to me," says the LORD. 7
10 yet you did not return to me," says the LORD. 7
11 yet you did not return to me," says the LORD. 7
Obd 1:15 your deeds shall return on your own head. 7
Mic 1: 7 and to the hire of a harlot they shall return. 7
5: 3 brethren shall return to the people of Israel. 7
Zep 2:10 This shall be their lot in return for their pride 9
Hag 2:17 yet you did not return to me, says the LORD. 40
Zec 1: 3 Return to me, says the LORD of hosts 7
3 and I will return to you, says the LORD of hosts. 7
4 Return from your evil ways and from your evil 7
16 I have returned to Jerusalem with compassion; 7
8: 3 Thus says the LORD: I will return to Zion 7
9:12 Return to your stronghold, O prisoners of hope; 7
10: 9 with their children they shall live and return. 7
Mal 3: 7 Return to me, and I will return to you, says the LORD 7
7 Return to me, and I will return to you, says the LORD 7
7 But you say, 'How shall we return?' 7
Mat 2:12 being warned in a dream not to return to Herod 14
10:13 if it is not worthy, let your peace return to you. 40
12:44 I will return to my house from which I came. 40
16:26 Or what shall a man give in return for his life? 19
21:18 In the morning, as he was returning to the city 36
Mrk 2: 1 when he returned to Caper'na-um after some days 34
6:30 The apostles returned to Jesus, and told him all 47
7:31 Then he returned from the region of Tyre 44
8:37 For what can a man give in return for his life? 19
Lke 1:56 returned to her home. 49
2:20 the shepherds returned 49
39 they returned into Galilee, to their own city 40
43 when the feast was ended, as they were returning 49
45 they returned to Jerusalem, seeking him. 49
4: 1 Jesus . . returned from the Jordan 49
14 Jesus returned . . into Galilee 49
7:10 those who had been sent returned to the house 49
8:37 so he got into the boat and returned. 49
39 Return to your home 49
40 Now when Jesus returned, the crowd welcomed him 49
55 her spirit returned, and she got up at once 40
9:10 On their return the apostles told him 49
10: 6 if not, it shall return to you. 14
17 The 70 returned with joy, saying, "Lord 49
11:24 finding none he says, 'I will return to my house 49
17:18 Was no one found to return and give praise to God 49
19:12 to receive a kingdom and then return. 49
15 When he returned, having received the kingdom 37
23:48 all . . returned home beating their breasts. 49
56 they returned, and prepared spices 49
24: 9 returning from the tomb they told all this 49
33 rose that same hour and returned to Jerusalem; 49
52 they returned to Jerusalem with great joy, 49
Act 1:12 Then they returned to Jerusalem from the mount 49
5:22 they returned and reported 18
8:25 they returned to Jerusalem 49
28 was returning 49
12:25 Barnabas and Saul returned from Jerusalem 49
13:13 John left them and returned to Jerusalem; 49
34 no more to return to corruption 49
14:21 returned to Lystra and to Ico'nium and to Antioch 49
15:16 'After this I will return, and I will rebuild 18
36 let us return and visit the brethren 40

18:21 I will return to you if God wills 14
20: 3 he determined to return through Macedo'nia. 49
21: 6 we went on board the ship, and they returned home. 49
22:17 When I had returned to Jerusalem 49
23:32 on the morrow they returned to the barracks 49
Rom 6:21 then what return did you get from the things 43
22 the return you get is sanctification 43
9: 9 I will return and Sarah shall have a son. 42
1Co 16:11 that he may return to me 42
2Co 6:13 In return-I speak as to children 23
Gal 1:17 again I returned to Damascus. 49
1Ti 5: 4 and make some return to their parents 11
Heb 7: 1 returning from the slaughter of the kings 49
11:15 they would have had opportunity to return. 14
1Pe 2:25 you . . have now returned to the Shepherd 40
3: 9 Do not return evil for evil 28
1Es 2:15 the returning exiles from Babylon to Jerusalem. •
4:34 returns to its place in one day. 33
5: 8 who returned to Jerusalem and the rest of Judea 40
67 those who had returned from captivity •
6:28 who have returned from the captivity of Judea •
7:11 Not all of the returned captives were purified •
12 for all the returned captives •
9: 3 to all who had returned from the captivity •
4 those who had returned from the captivity. •
15 those who had returned from the captivity •
2Es 7:78 leaves the body to return again to him who gave it 50
10: 4 I intend not to return to the city, but to stay here 51
12:40 I had not returned to the city 51
15:60 as they return from devastated Babylon. 52
16:14 are sent forth and shall not return 52
16 an arrow shot by a mighty archer does not return 52
16 the calamities . . shall not return. 52
Tob 1:22 I returned to Nineveh 42
2: 5 when I returned I washed myself 40
9 On the same night I returned from burying him 16
13 when she returned to me it began to bleat 42
13 Return it to the owners 28
14 told her to return it to the owners 28
3:17 At that very moment Tobit returned 40
5:15 if you both return safe and sound 40
20 he will return safe and sound 42
6:12 and as soon as we return from Rages 49
17 and will never again return 37
7: 1 They returned her greeting •
8:21 return in safety to his father 46
14: 5 they will return from the places of their captivity 40
12 Then Tobias returned with his wife 27
Jdt 1:16 Then he returned with them to Nineveh 18
4: 3 they had only recently returned from the captivity 12
5:19 now they have returned to their God 40
6: 6 shall fall among their wounded, when I return. 40
13 returned to their master. 29
7: 7 and then returned to his army. 13
8:36 they returned from the tent 31
12: 9 she returned clean and stayed in the tent 35
13:13 it was unbelievable that she had returned 42
15: 7 when they returned from the slaughter 18
Wis 2: 1 no one has been known to return from Hades. 16
5 there is no return from our death 17
11:15 In return for their foolish and wicked thoughts 22
15: 8 required to return the soul that was lent him. 24
Sir 16:30 to it they return. 32
17:24 Yet to those who repent he grants a return 39
26 Return to the Most High 36
20:10 there is a gift that brings a double return. 21
27: 9 truth returns to those who practice it. 38
35: 2 He who returns a kindness offers fine flour 20
40: 1 till the day they return to the mother of all. 41
11 what is from the waters returns to the sea. 14
41:10 Whatever is from the dust returns to dust 27
Bar 1: 8 to return them to the land of Judah-the silver 31
4:28 return with tenfold zeal to seek him. 40
Sus 1:49 Return to the place of judgment. 18
50 Then all the people returned in haste. 18
Bel 1:12 when you return in the morning 42
39 the angel of God immediately returned Habakkuk 30
1Mc 1:20 Antiochus returned in the 143rd year 40
2:63 because he has returned to the dust 40
3:33 until he returned. 40
56 each should return to his home 31
4:23 Then Judas returned to plunder the camp 18
24 On their return they sang hymns and praises 40
5: 8 then he returned to Judea. 18
19 do not engage in battle . . until we return. 40
54 before they returned in safety. 40
68 returned to the land of Judah. 40
6: 4 departed from there to return to Babylon. 31
56 returned from Persia and Media with the forces 31
63 he departed with haste and returned to Antioch. 31
7:25 he returned to the king 40
35 then if I return safely I will burn up this house. 40
8:26 without receiving any return. •
9:42 they returned to the marshes of the Jordan. 31
50 Bacchides then returned to Jerusalem 40
57 he returned to the king, and the land of Judah 40
10: 9 he returned them to their parents. 28
52 Since I have returned to my kingdom 18
55 you returned to the land of your fathers 40

66 Jonathan returned to Jerusalem in peace 40
68 he was greatly grieved and returned to Antioch. 49
87 returned to Jerusalem with much booty. 40
11: 7 then he returned to Jerusalem. 40
51 they returned to Jerusalem with much spoil. 40
54 After this Trypho returned 31
73 returned to him and joined him in the pursuit 40
74 Jonathan returned to Jerusalem. 40
12:24 the commanders of Demetrius had returned 40
26 they returned and reported to him 40
35 When Jonathan returned he convened the elders 40
46 they returned to the land of Judah. 27
15:36 returned in wrath to the king and reported to him 31
16:10 he returned to Judea safely. 31
17 returned evil for good. 28
2Mc 2:17 has returned the inheritance to all 28
4:25 After receiving the king's orders he returned 45
36 the king returned from the region of Cilicia 37
8:25 obliged to return because the hour was late. 16
12: 1 Lysias returned to the king 26
15:28 they were returning with joy 16
3Mc 1: 1 those who returned 15
5: 3 he returned to his feasting, together with . . his friends 48
16 The king . . returned to his drinking 48
36 king . . urged the guests to return to their celebrating. 48
6:30 when he had returned to the city 25
7: 8 every one to return to his own home 40

return *See also* expect, invite, make, revile.

cause to return 1. שׁוּב
Deu 17:16 must not . . cause the people to return to Egypt 1

return home 1. *ἀναζεύγνυμι* 2. *κατέρχομαι*
Jdt 16:21 every one returned home to his own inheritance 1
2Mc 11:29 you wish to return home 2

make return 1. *ἀποδίδωμι*
1Ti 5: 4 and make some return to their parents 1

reveal 1. גלה 2. גלה אֹזֶן 3. נגד 4. גלא (A)
5. גלה (A) 6. *ἀνακαλύπτω* 7. *ἀποκαλύπτω*
8. *ἀπὸ καλύψεως* 9. *ἀποκάλυψις* 10. *ἐκφαίνω*
11. *ἐνδείκνυμι* 12. *ἐπιφαίνω* 13. *ποιέω φανερός*
14. *ὑποδείκνυμι* 15. *φανερόω* 16. *χρηματίζω*
17. demonstro 18. ostendo 19. revelo
Gen 35: 7 there God had revealed himself to him when he 1
41:25 God has revealed to Pharaoh what he is about 3
1Sm 2:27 I revealed myself to the house of your father 1
3: 7 word of the LORD had not yet been revealed to him. 1
21 the LORD revealed himself to Samuel at Shiloh 1
9:15 before Saul came, the LORD had revealed to Samuel 2
1Ch 17:25 For thou, my God, hast revealed to thy servant that 2
Job 20:27 The heavens will reveal his iniquity 1
38:17 Have the gates of death been revealed to you 1
Ps 98: 2 revealed his vindication in the sight 1
Prv 11:13 who goes about as a talebearer reveals secrets 1
20:19 He who goes about gossiping reveals secrets; 1
Isa 22:14 The LORD of hosts has revealed himself in my ears 1
23: 1 From the land of Cyprus it is revealed to them. 1
40: 5 And the glory of the LORD shall be revealed 1
53: 1 to whom has the arm of the LORD been revealed? 1
56: 1 will come, and my deliverance be revealed. 1
Jer 33: 6 and reveal to them abundance of prosperity 1
Dan 2:19 mystery was revealed to Daniel in a vision 5
22 he reveals deep and mysterious things; 4
28 there is a God in heaven who reveals mysteries 4
29 who reveals mysteries made known to you what is 4
30 mystery been revealed to me, but in order that 4
47 for you have been able to reveal this mystery. 4
10: 1 third year . . a word was revealed to Daniel 1
Hos 7: 1 the corruption of E'phraim is revealed 1
Ams 3: 7 GOD does nothing, without revealing his secret 1
Mat 10:26 nothing is covered that will not be revealed 7
11:25 and revealed them to babes; 7
27 any one to whom the Son chooses to reveal him. 7
16:17 For flesh and blood has not revealed this to you 7
Lke 2:26 it had been revealed to him by the Holy Spirit 16
35 thoughts out of many hearts may be revealed. 7
10:21 revealed them to babes 7
22 and any one to whom the Son chooses to reveal him. 7
12: 2 Nothing is covered up that will not be revealed 7
17:30 on the day when the Son of man is revealed. 7
Joh 1:31 that he might be revealed to Israel. 15
12:38 to whom has the arm of the Lord been revealed? 7
21: 1 After this Jesus revealed himself again 15
1 and he revealed himself in this way. 15
14 Jesus was revealed to the disciples 15
Rom 1:17 righteousness of God is revealed through faith 7
18 For the wrath of God is revealed from heaven 7
2: 5 when God's righteous judgment will be revealed. 9
8:18 the glory that is to be revealed to us. 7
19 waits . . for the revealing of the sons of God; 9
1Co 1: 7 as you wait for the revealing of our Lord Jesus 9
2:10 God has revealed to us through the Spirit 7
3:13 because it will be revealed with fire 7
2Co 7:12 in order that your zeal for us might be revealed 15
Gal 1:16 was pleased to reveal his Son to me 7
3:23 until faith should be revealed. 7
Eph 3: 5 has now been revealed to his holy apostles 7
Php 3:15 God will reveal that also to you. 7
2Th 1: 7 when the Lord Jesus is revealed from heaven 9
2: 3 the man of lawlessness is revealed 7
6 so that he may be revealed in his time. 7
8 then the lawless one will be revealed 7
1Pe 1: 5 salvation ready to be revealed in the last time. 7
12 It was revealed to them that they were serving 7
4:13 and be glad when his glory is revealed. 9
5: 1 a partaker in the glory that is to be revealed. 7
Rev 15: 4 for thy judgments have been revealed. 15
2Es 3:14 to him only didst thou reveal the end of the times 17
6:28 the truth . . shall be revealed. 18
7:28 For my son the Messiah shall be revealed 19
33 shall be revealed upon the seat of judgment 19
123Or that a paradise shall be revealed 18
10:38 the Most High has revealed many secrets to you. 19
52 the Most High would reveal these things to you. 18
54 the city of the Most High was to be revealed. 18
13:32 then my Son will be revealed, whom you saw as a man 19
14: 3 Then he said to me, "I revealed myself in a bush 19
Tob 12: 7 gloriously to reveal the works of God 6
11 gloriously to reveal the works of God.' 6
Sir 1: 6 The root of wisdom–to whom has it been revealed? 7
30 The Lord will reveal your secrets 7
4:18 will reveal her secrets to him. 7
8:19 Do not reveal your thoughts to every one 10
11:27 his deeds will be revealed. 9
39: 8 He will reveal instruction in his teaching 10
41:23 revealing secrets 8
42:19 he reveals the tracks of hidden things. 7
46:20 he prophesied and revealed to the king his death 14
48:25 He revealed what was to occur to the end of time 14
LJr 1:26 revealing to mankind their worthlessness. 11
2Mc 12:41 who reveals the things that are hidden; 13
3Mc 2:19 reveal your mercy at this hour. 12
6: 9 reveal yourself quickly 12
18 revealed his holy face 12
39 the Lord of all most gloriously revealed his mercy 12

thing revealed 1. גלה
Deu 29:29 but the things that are revealed belong to us 1

revealer 1. גלא (A)
Dan 2:47 Truly, your God is . . a revealer of mysteries 1

revel 1. *ἐντρυφάω* 2. *εὐφραίνω* 3. *κῶμος*
4. *συμβολοκοπέω* 5. *τρυφή*
Rom 13:13 not in reveling and drunkenness 3
1Pe 4: 3 living in . . drunkenness, revels, carousing 3
2Pe 2:13 They count it pleasure to revel in the daytime. 5
13 They are . . reveling in their dissipation 1
Wis 14:23 hold frenzied revels with strange customs 3
Sir 9: 9 nor revel with her at wine 4
18:32 Do not revel in great luxury 2
2Mc 6: 4 filled with . . reveling by the Gentiles 3

revelation 1. *ἀποκάλυψις*
Lke 2:32 a light for revelation to the Gentiles 1
Rom 16:25 revelation of the mystery which was kept secret 1
1Co 14: 6 unless I bring you some revelation or knowledge 1
26 a hymn, a lesson, a revelation, a tongue 1
2Co 12: 1 go on to visions and revelations of the Lord. 1
7 too elated by the abundance of revelations 1
Gal 1:12 it came through a revelation of Jesus Christ. 1
2: 2 I went up by revelation 1
Eph 1:17 may give you a spirit of wisdom and of revelation 1
3: 3 the mystery was made known to me by revelation 1
1Pe 1: 7 and honor at the revelation of Jesus Christ. 1
13 coming to you at the revelation of Jesus Christ. 1
Rev 1: 1 The revelation of Jesus Christ, which God gave 1

revelation *See also* give, make.

reveler 1. *σπαταλάω*
Sir 21:15 when a reveler hears it, he dislikes it 1

revelry 1. מַרְזֵחַ 2. *ἀγερωχία* 3. *εὐωχία*
Ams 6: 7 and the revelry of those who stretch themselves 1
Wis 2: 9 Let none of us fail to share in our revelry 2
3Mc 5:17 he urged them to give themselves over to revelry 3

revenge 1. נְקָמָה
Jer 20:10 then we can overcome him, and take our revenge 1

revenge *See also* carry, take.

revengefully 1. בְּנָקָם 2. בִּנְקָמָה
Ezk 25:12 Because Edom acted revengefully 1
15 Because the Philistines acted revengefully 2

revenue 1. תְּבוּאָה 2. אַפְּתֹם (A) 3. נְכַס (A)
4. *διάφορος* 5. *λόγος* 6. *πρόσοδος* 7. *τέλος* 8. *φόρος*
Ezr 4:13 will not pay . . royal revenue will be impaired. 2
6: 8 in full and without delay from the royal revenue 3
Prv 16: 8 Better . . than great revenues with injustice. 1
Isa 23: 3 your revenue was the grain of Shihor 1
Rom 13: 7 revenue to whom revenue is due 7
7 revenue to whom revenue is due 7
1Mc 3:29 the revenues from the country were small 8
31 collect the revenues from those regions 8
10:31 let . . her tithes and her revenues, be holy 7
40 15,000 shekels of silver . . out of the king's revenues 5
44 paid from the revenues of the king. 5
45 also be paid from the revenues of the king. 5
2Mc 3: 3 defrayed from his own revenues all the expenses 6
4:28 the collection of the revenue 4
9:16 he would provide from his own revenues; 6
3Mc 3:16 we had granted very great revenues to the temples 6
6:30 summoned the official in charge of the revenues 6

revenue *See also* source.

revere 1. היה יָרֵא 2. ירא 3. נשׂא כַּף 4. *εὐσεβέω*
5. *σέβω* 6. *σεμνός*
Lev 19: 3 one of you shall revere his mother and father 2
1Kg 18: 3 Now Obadi'ah revered the LORD greatly; 1
12 I your servant have revered the LORD 2
Ps 119:48 I revere thy commandments, which I love 3
Bel 1: 4 The king revered it 5
5 Because I do not revere man-made idols 5
23 a great dragon, which the Babylonians revered. 5
2Mc 6:28 for the revered and holy laws 6
4Mc 8:14 whatever justice you revere will be merciful 5
11: 5 Is it because we revere the Creator of all things 4

revere as holy 1. קדשׁ
Deu 32:51 because you did not revere me as holy in the midst 1

reverence 1. ירא 2. *ἁγιάζω* 3. *εὐλάβεια*
4. *θεοσέβεια* 5. *φόβος*
Lev 19:30 keep my sabbaths and reverence my sanctuary 1
26: 2 keep my sabbaths and reverence my sanctuary 1
Eph 5:21 out of reverence for Christ. 5
Heb 12:28 acceptable worship, with reverence and awe; 3
1Pe 3:15 in your hearts reverence Christ as Lord. 2
15 yet do it with gentleness and reverence; 5
4Mc 7: 6 which had room only for reverence and purity 4

reverence *See also* pay.

reverence for God 1. *θεοσέβεια*
4Mc 17:15 Reverence for God was victor 1

proper reverence 1. *μεγαλοπρεπῶς*
4Mc 5:24 with proper reverence we worship . . God 1

reverent 1. *ἱεροπρεπής*
Tit 2: 3 older women likewise to be reverent in behavior 1

reverently 1. *σεμνῶς*
4Mc 1:17 by which we learn divine matters reverently 1

reverse 1. *ἀποστροφή*
3Mc 2:10 if we should have reverses 1

revert 1. שׁוּב
Ezk 46:17 then it shall revert to the prince; 1

review 1. בין
Ezr 8:15 As I reviewed the people and the priests, I found 1

revile 1. גִּדּוּפִים 2. גדף 3. חרף 4. נאץ 5. נֶאָצָה
6. קלל 7. *βλασφημέω* 8. *βλασφημία* 9. *βλάσφημος*
10. *ἐπηρεάζω* 11. *λοιδορέω* 12. *λοιδορία* 13. *ὀνειδίζω*
14. *ὀνειδισμός*
Exd 22:28 You shall not revile God, nor curse a ruler 6
Num 15:30 anything with a high hand . . reviles the LORD 2
Jdg 9:27 god, and ate and drank and reviled Abim'elech. 6
2Kg 19: 6 servants of the king of Assyria have reviled me. 2
22 Whom have you mocked and reviled? 2
Ps 74:10 Is the enemy to revile thy name for ever? 4
18 an impious people reviles thy name. 4
Isa 37: 6 servants of the king of Assyria have reviled me. 2
23 'Whom have you mocked and reviled? 2
43:28 I delivered . . Israel to reviling. 1
51: 7 of men, and be not dismayed at their revilings. 1
65: 7 upon the mountains and reviled me upon the hills 3
Ezk 35:12 have heard all the revilings which you uttered 5
Zep 2: 8 I have heard . . the revilings of the Ammonites 1
Mat 5:11 Blessed are you when men revile you 13
27:44 the robbers . . also reviled him in the same way. 13
Mrk 15:32 who were crucified with him also reviled him. 13
Lke 6:22 when they exclude you and revile you 13
22:65 many other words against him, reviling him. 7
Joh 9:28 they reviled him, saying, "You are his disciple 11
Act 13:45 contradicted . . and reviled him. 7
18: 6 when they opposed and reviled him 7
23: 4 Would you revile God's high priest? 11
1Co 4:12 When reviled, we bless; when persecuted, we endure; 11
1Ti 5:14 give the enemy no occasion to revile us. 12
1Pe 2:23 When he was reviled, he did not revile in return; 11
3: 9 Do not return . . reviling for reviling; 12
9 Do not return . . reviling for reviling; 12
16 those who revile your good behavior in Christ 10
2Pe 2: 2 because of them the way of truth will be reviled. 7
10 they are not afraid to revile the glorious ones 7
11 do not pronounce a reviling judgment upon them 9

12 reviling in matters of which they are ignorant 7
Jde 1: 8 reject authority, and revile the glorious ones. 7
9 not presume to pronounce a reviling judgment 8
10 men revile whatever they do not understand 7
Sir 22:20 one who reviles a friend 13
22 reviling, arrogance, disclosure of secrets 14

revile in return 1. ἀντιλοιδορέω
1Pe 2:23 When he was reviled, he did not revile in return; 1

reviler 1. גדף 2. λοίδορος
Ps 44:16 at the words of the taunters and revilers 1
1Co 5:11 if he . . is an idolater, reviler, drunkard 2
6:10 nor revilers, nor robbers 2
Sir 23: 8 the reviler and the arrogant are tripped by them. 2

revive 1. חיה 2. מִחְיָה 3. שׁוּב 4. שׁוּב אֶל 5. ἀναζάω
6. ἀναθάλλω 7. ἀνανεόω 8. ἀναψύχω
Gen 45:27 the spirit of their father Jacob revived; 1
Jdg 15:19 he drank, his spirit returned . . and he revived. 1
1Sm 30:12 when he had eaten, his spirit revived; 4
1Kg 17:22 soul . . came into him again, and he revived. 1
2Kg 13:21 as the man touched the bones of Eli'sha, he revived 1
Ezr 9: 8 grant us a little reviving in our bondage. 2
9 grant us some reviving to set up the house of our God 2
Neh 4: 2 Will they revive the stones out of the heaps 1
Ps 19: 7 The law of the LORD is perfect, reviving the soul; 3
69:32 you who seek God, let your hearts revive. 1
71:20 Thou . . wilt revive me again; 1
85: 6 Wilt thou not revive us again 3
119:25 revive me according to thy word! 1
Isa 57:15 to revive the spirit of the humble 1
15 and to revive the heart of the contrite. 1
Lam 1:11 treasures for food to revive their strength. 3
16 comforter is far from me, one to revive my courage; 3
19 they sought food to revive their strength. 3
Hos 6: 2 After two days he will revive us; 1
Rom 7: 9 when the commandment came, sin revived and I died; 5
Php 4:10 now at length you have revived your concern 6
Sir 46:12 May their bones revive from where they lie 6
49:10 May the bones of the twelve prophets revive 6
2Mc 13:11 the people who had just begun to revive 8
4Mc 18: 4 by reviving observance of the law in the homeland 7

revoke 1. שׁוּב 2. עדא (A) 3. ἐκ μεταβολῆς ἀναλύω
Num23:20 he has blessed, and I cannot revoke it. 1
Est 8: 5 order . . to revoke the letters devised by Haman 1
8 an edict written . . cannot be revoked. 1
Dan 6: 8 Medes and the Persians, which cannot be revoked. 2
12 law of the . . Persians, which cannot be revoked. 2
Ams 1: 3 for four, I will not revoke the punishment; 1
6 for four, I will not revoke the punishment; 1
9 for four, I will not revoke the punishment; 1
11 for four, I will not revoke the punishment; 1
13 for four, I will not revoke the punishment; 1
2: 1 for four, I will not revoke the punishment; 1
4 for four, I will not revoke the punishment; 1
6 for four, I will not revoke the punishment; 1
3Mc 5:40 again revoking your decree in the matter? 3

revolt 1. סרה 2. פשׁע 3. קֶשֶׁר 4. ἀπονοέω
5. ἀποστατέω 6. ἀφίστημι 7. στασιάζω
2Kg 8:20 In his days Edom revolted from the rule of Judah 2
22 Edom revolted from the rule of Judah to this day. 2
22 Then Libnah revolted at the same time. 2
2Ch 21: 8 In his days Edom revolted from the rule of Judah 2
10 Edom revolted from the rule of Judah to this day. 2
10 At that time Libnah also revolted from his rule 2
Isa 31: 6 Turn to him from whom you have deeply revolted 1
59:13 speaking oppression and revolt, 1
Jer 11: 9 There is revolt among the men of Judah 3
Sir 16: 7 the ancient giants who revolted in their might. 6
1Mc 11:14 because the people of that region were in revolt. 5
43 all my troops have revolted. 6
13:16 he will not revolt against us 5
2Mc 1: 7 after Jason and his company revolted 6
4:30 the people of Tarsus and of Mallus revolted 7
5:11 he took it to mean that Judea was in revolt 5
13:23 Philip . . had revolted in Antioch 4
revolt *See also* stir.

cause to revolt 1. ἀφίστημι
Sir 47:23 whose policy caused the people to revolt 1

revolution 1. νεωτερίζω
4Mc 3:21 just at that time certain men attempted a revolution 1
revulsion *See* feel.

reward 1. גְּמוּלָה 2. גמל 3. חֵלֶק 4. מַשְׂכֹּרֶת 5. מַתַּת
6. נתן 7. עֵקֶב 8. פְּעֻלָּה 9. פְּרִי 10. שׁוּם 11. שֶׂכֶר
12. שָׂכָר 13. שׁוּב 14. שֹׁחַד 15. שׁלם 16. נְבִזְבָּה (A)
17. ἀνταπόδοσις 18. ἀποδίδωμι 19. δίδωμι δόματα
20. δίδωμι μισθόν 21. ἐπίχειρον 22. μισθαποδοσία
23. μισθαποδότης 24. μισθός 25. χαριστήριος
26. merces 27. praemium
Gen 15: 1 I am your shield; your reward shall be very great. 12
Num18:31 for it is your reward in return for your service 12
Rut 2:12 and a full reward be given you by the LORD 4
1Sm 24:19 may the LORD reward you with good 15
26:23 LORD rewards every man for his righteousness 13
2Sm 4:10 and slew him . . which was the reward I gave him *
19:36 should the king recompense me with such a reward? 1
22:21 LORD rewarded me according to my righteousness; 2
1Kg 8:32 rewarding him according to his righteousness, 6
13: 7 Come home with me . . and I will give you a reward. 5
2Ch 6:23 vindicating the righteous by rewarding him 6
15: 7 for your work shall be rewarded. 12
20:11 behold, they reward us by coming to drive us 2
Job 8: 6 and reward you with a rightful habitation. 15
Ps 18:20 LORD rewarded me according to my righteousness; 2
19:11 in keeping them there is great reward. 7
58:11 Surely there is a reward for the righteous; 9
109: 5 reward me evil for good, and hatred for my love. 10
20 this be the reward of my accusers from the LORD 8
127: 3 fruit of the womb a reward. 12
Prv 11:18 one who sows righteousness gets a sure reward. 11
13:13 who respects the commandment will be rewarded. 15
21 but prosperity rewards the righteous. 15
22: 4 reward for humility and fear of the LORD is 7
25:22 for . . the LORD will reward you. 15
Ecc 2:10 this was my reward for all my toil. 3
4: 9 because they have a good reward for their toil. 12
9: 5 the dead know nothing, and . . have no more reward; 12
Isa 40:10 behold, his reward is with him 12
45:13 and set my exiles free, not for price or reward 14
62:11 behold, his reward is with him 12
Jer 31:16 for your work shall be rewarded, says the LORD 12
32:19 rewarding every man according to his ways 6
Dan 2: 6 receive . . gifts and rewards and great honor. 16
5:17 yourself, and give your rewards to another; 16
Mat 5:12 Rejoice and be glad, for your reward is great 24
46 you love those who love you, what reward have you? 24
6: 1 you will have no reward from your Father who is 24
2 say to you, they have received their reward. 24
4 your Father who sees in secret will reward you. 18
5 say to you, they have received their reward. 24
6 your Father who sees in secret will reward you. 18
16 to you, they have received their reward. 24
18 your Father who sees in secret will reward you. 18
10:41 shall receive a prophet's reward 24
41 shall receive a righteous man's reward. 24
42 truly, I say to you, he shall not lose his reward. 24
Mrk 9:41 will by no means lose his reward. 24
Lke 6:23 for behold, your reward is great in heaven 24
35 your reward will be great 24
23:41 we are receiving the due reward of our deeds *
Act 1:18 bought a field with the reward of his wickedness; 24
1Co 3:14 he will receive a reward. 24
9:17 For if I do this of my own will, I have a reward 24
18 What then is my reward? 24
Col 3:24 you will receive the inheritance as your reward; 17
Heb 10:35 your confidence, which has a great reward. 22
11: 6 he rewards those who seek him. 23
26 he looked to the reward. 22
2Jn 1: 8 that you may not lose . . but may win a full reward 24
Rev 11:18 for rewarding thy servants, the prophets 20
2Es 2:35 Be ready for the rewards of the kingdom 27
3:33 Yet their reward has not appeared 26
4:35 And when will come the harvest of our reward? 26
7:35 and the reward shall be manifested 26
83 they shall see the reward laid up for those 26
98 to receive their reward when glorified. 26
8:33 the righteous . . shall receive their reward 26
39 and their receiving their reward. 26
13:56 for there is a reward laid up with the Most High. 26
15:55 The reward of a harlot is in your bosom 26
AEs 12: 5 rewarded him for these things. 19
Wis 5:15 their reward is with the Lord 24
10:17 She gave holy men the reward of their labors 24
Sir 2: 8 trust in him, and your reward will not fail; 24
11:18 this is the reward allotted to him 24
22 blessing of the Lord is the reward of the godly 24
26 to reward a man on the day of death 18
36:16 Reward those who wait for thee 20
51:22 The Lord gave me a tongue as my reward 24
30 in God's time he will give you your reward. 24
2Mc 12:45 if he was looking to the splendid reward 25
15:33 and hang up these rewards of his folly 21

due reward 1. גְּמוּל
Ps 28: 4 render them their due reward. 1

reward for tidings 1. בְּשֹׂרָה
2Sm 18:22 you will have no reward for the tidings? 1

rework 1. שׁוּב וְעשׂה
Jer 18: 4 and he reworked it into another vessel 1

rhythm 1. ῥυθμός
Wis 17:18 the rhythm of violently rushing water 1
19:18 on a harp the notes vary the nature of the rhythm 1

rib 1. צֵלָע 2. עֲלַע (A) 3. πλευρά
Gen 2:21 and while he slept took one of his ribs 1
22 rib which the LORD God had taken from the man 1
Dan 7: 5 had three ribs in its mouth between its teeth; 2
4Mc 11:19 pierced his ribs so that his entrails were burned 3
18: 7 I guarded the rib from which woman was made. 3

rich 1. בָּרִיא 2. גָּדוֹל 3. טוֹב 4. כָּבֵד 5. מֶגֶד 6. מָלֵא
7. עָשִׁיר 8. עשׁר 9. עֹשֶׁר גָּדוֹל 10. רַב 11. רבה 12. שׁוֹעַ
13. שֶׁמֶן 14. שָׁמֵן 15. δαψιλῆ 16. μέγας 17. πλούσιος
18. πλουτέω 19. πλοῦτος 20. χρῆμα
Gen 13: 2 Now Abram was very rich in cattle 4
49:20 Asher's food shall be rich 14
Exd 30:15 The rich shall not give more, and the poor shall 7
Num13:20 whether the land is rich or poor 14
Deu 33:14 with the . . rich yield of the months 5
Rut 3:10 not gone after young men, whether poor or rich. 7
1Sm 25: 2 The man was very rich; he had 3,000 sheep 2
2Sm 12: 1 two men . . the one rich and the other poor. 7
4 Now there came a traveler to the rich man 7
1Ch 4:40 where they found rich, good pasture 14
Neh 9:25 captured fortified cities and a rich land 14
35 did not serve thee . . in the large and rich land 14
37 rich yield goes to the kings whom thou hast set 11
Job 15:29 he will not be rich, and his wealth will not endure 8
27:19 He goes to bed rich, but will do so no more; 7
34:19 nor regards the rich more than the poor 12
Ps 45:12 your favor with gifts, the richest of the people 7
49: 2 both low and high, rich and poor together! 7
Prv 11:24 One man gives freely, yet grows all the richer; *
14:20 but the rich has many friends. 7
18:23 poor use entreaties . . rich answer roughly. 7
21:17 he who loves wine and oil will not be rich. 8
22: 2 The rich and the poor meet together; 7
7 The rich rules over the poor 7
16 who . . gives to the rich, will only come to want. 7
28:11 A rich man is wise in his own eyes, but a poor man 7
20 he who hastens to be rich will not go unpunished. 8
Ecc 5:12 the surfeit of the rich will not let him sleep. 7
10: 6 and the rich sit in a low place. 7
20 nor in your bedchamber curse the rich; 7
Isa 28: 1 the rich valley of those overcome with wine! 13
4 beauty, which is on the head of the rich valley 13
30:23 ground, which will be rich and plenteous. 14
Jer 5:27 therefore they have become great and rich 8
51:13 O you who dwell by many waters, rich in treasures 10
Ezk 17: 3 A great eagle . . rich in plumage of many colors 6
Dan 11: 2 fourth shall be far richer than all of them; 9
Hos 12: 8 E'phraim has said, "Ah, but I am rich 8
Jol 3: 5 carried my rich treasures into your temples. 3
Hab 1:16 by them he lives in luxury, and his food is rich. 1
Mat 27:57 there came a rich man from Arimathe'a 17
Lke 1:53 the rich he has sent empty away. 18
6:24 woe to you that are rich 17
12:16 The land of a rich man brought forth plentifully; 17
21 is not rich toward God. 18
14:12 your brothers or your kinsmen or rich neighbors 17
16: 1 There was a rich man who had a steward 17
19 There was a rich man 17
18:23 he became sad, for he was very rich. 17
19: 2 he was a chief tax collector, and rich. 17
21: 1 and saw the rich putting their gifts into the treasury; 17
1Co 4: 8 Already you have become rich! 18
2Co 8: 9 though he was rich 17
Eph 2: 4 God, who is rich in mercy 17
1Ti 6: 9 those who desire to be rich fall into temptation 18
17 As for the rich in this world 17
18 They are to do good, to be rich in good deeds 18
Jas 1:10 and the rich in his humiliation 17
2: 5 be rich in faith and heirs of the kingdom 17
6 Is it not the rich who oppress you 17
5: 1 Come now, you rich, weep and howl for the miseries 17
Rev 2: 9 I know . . your poverty (but you are rich) 17
3:17 For you say, I am rich, I have prospered 17
18 buy from me gold . . that you may be rich 18
6:15 and the generals and the rich and the strong 17
13:16 all, both small and great, both rich and poor 17
1Es 3: 5 Darius the king will give rich gifts 16
19 of the slave and the free, of the poor and the rich. 17
21 It makes all hearts feel rich 17
Wis 8: 5 what is richer than wisdom who effects all things? 17
Sir 8: 2 Do not quarrel with a rich man 17
10:22 The rich, and the eminent, and the poor 17
11:18 There is a man who is rich through his diligence 19
13: 2 a man mightier and richer than you 17
19 likewise the poor are pastures for the rich. 17
26: 4 Whether rich or poor, his heart is glad 17
44: 6 rich men furnished with resources 17
Sus 1: 4 Joakim was very rich, and had a spacious garden 17
1Mc 6: 2 Its temple was very rich 17
3Mc 5:31 a rich feast for the savage beasts 15
4Mc 4: 4 to inform him of the rich treasure. 20
rich *See also* carpet, experience, food, get, grow, make, pretend, robe, setting.

rich apparel 1. מַחֲלָצָה
Zec 3: 4 I will clothe you with rich apparel. 1

become rich 1. גדל 2. נשׂג יַד 3. עשׁר 4. πλουτέω
5. πλουτίζω
Gen 26:13 the man became rich, and gained more and more 1
Lev 25:47 If a stranger or sojourner with you becomes rich 2

Ps 49:16 Be not afraid when one becomes rich 3
Zec 11: 5 'Blessed be the LORD, I have become rich'; 3
2Co 8: 9 so that by his poverty you might become rich. 4
Sir 19: 1 A workman who is a drunkard will not become rich; 5

rich man 1. עָשִׁיר 2. πλούσιος
2Sm 12: 2 The rich man had very many flocks and herds; 1
Prv 10:15 A rich man's wealth is his strong city; 1
18:11 A rich man's wealth is his strong city 1
28: 6 than a rich man who is perverse in his ways. 1
Isa 53: 9 with the wicked and with a rich man in his death 1
Jer 9:23 let not the rich man glory in his riches; 1
Mic 6:12 Your rich men are full of violence; 1
Mat 19:23 it will be hard for a rich man to enter 2
24 than for a rich man to enter the kingdom of God. 2
Mrk 10:25 than for a rich man to enter the kingdom of God. 2
Lke 16:21 fed with what fell from the rich man's table; 2
22 The rich man also died and was buried; 2
18:25 for a rich man to enter the kingdom of God. 2
Jas 1:11 So will the rich man fade away 2
Sir 10:30 while a rich man is honored for his wealth. 2
13: 3 A rich man does wrong, and he even adds reproaches; 2
4 A rich man will exploit you if you can be of use •
18 what peace between a rich man and a poor man? 2
21 When a rich man totters, he is steadied by friends 2
22 If a rich man slips, his helpers are many 2
23 When the rich man speaks all are silent 2
25: 2 a beggar who is proud, a rich man who is a liar 2
30:14 a rich man who is severely afflicted in body. 2
31: 3 The rich man toils as his wealth accumulates 2
8 Blessed is the rich man who is found blameless 2

rich one 1. πλούσιος
Sir 13:20 a poor man is an abomination to a rich one. 1

rich part 1. מִשְׁמָן
Dan 11:24 come into the richest parts of the province; 1

rich people 1. πλούσιος
Mrk 12:41 Many rich people put in large sums. 1

riches 1. הוֹן 2. חַיִל 3. חֹסֶן 4. יִתְרָה 5. כָּבוֹד 6. עֹשֶׁר 7. ὄλβος 8. πλοῦτος 9. χρῆμα
1Sm 17:25 the king will enrich with great riches 6
1Kg 3:11 long life or riches or the life of your enemies 6
13 what you have not asked, both riches and honor 6
10:23 Solomon excelled all . . in riches and in wisdom. 6
1Ch 29:12 riches and honor come from thee, and thou rulest 6
28 he died in a good old age, full of days, riches 6
2Ch 1:12 will also give you riches, possessions, and honor 6
9:22 Solomon excelled . . in riches and in wisdom. 6
17: 5 Jehosh'aphat; and he had great riches and honor. 6
18: 1 Now Jehosh'aphat had great riches and honor; 6
32:27 Hezeki'ah had very great riches and honor; 6
Est 1: 4 while he showed the riches of his royal glory 6
5:11 Haman recounted . . the splendor of his riches 6
Job 20:15 He swallows down riches and vomits them up again; 2
Ps 49: 6 boast of the abundance of their riches? 6
52: 7 but trusted in the abundance of his riches 6
62:10 if riches increase, set not your heart on them. 2
73:12 always at ease, they increase in riches. 2
112: 3 Wealth and riches are in his house; 6
119:14 I delight as much as in all riches. 1
Prv 3:16 in her left hand are riches and honor. 6
8:18 Riches and honor are with me 6
11: 4 Riches do not profit in the day of wrath 1
16 violent men get riches. 6
28 He who trusts in his riches will wither 6
22: 1 good name . . be chosen rather than great riches 6
4 reward . . is riches and honor and life. 6
24: 4 filled with all precious and pleasant riches. 1
27:24 for riches do not last for ever; 3
30: 8 give me neither poverty nor riches; 6
Ecc 4: 8 and his eyes are never satisfied with riches 6
5:13 riches were kept by their owner to his hurt 6
14 and those riches were lost in a bad venture; 6
9:11 bread to the wise, nor riches to the intelligent 6
Isa 30: 6 carry their riches on the backs of asses 2
61: 6 the nations, and in their riches you shall glory. 5
Jer 9:23 let not the rich man glory in his riches; 6
17:11 so is he who gets riches but not by right; 6
48:36 therefore the riches they gained have perished. 4
Ezk 26:12 They will make a spoil of your riches 2
27:27 Your riches, your wares, your merchandise 1
Dan 11: 2 when he has become strong through his riches 6
Hos 12: 8 but all his riches can never offset the guilt •
Mat 13:22 and the delight in riches choke the word 8
Mrk 4:19 the cares of the world, and the delight in riches 8
10:23 How hard it will be for those who have riches 9
Lke 8:14 the cares and riches and pleasures of life 8
16:11 who will entrust to you the true riches? •
18:24 How hard it is for those who have riches to enter 9
Rom 2: 4 Or do you presume upon the riches of his kindness 8
9:23 in order to make known the riches of his glory 8
11:12 Now if their trespass means riches for the world 8
12 if their failure means riches for the Gentiles 8
33 the riches and wisdom and knowledge of God! 8
Eph 1: 7 according to the riches of his grace 8
18 what are the riches of his glorious inheritance 8
2: 7 might show the immeasurable riches of his grace 8
3: 8 the unsearchable riches of Christ 8
16 according to the riches of his glory 8
Php 4:19 according to his riches in glory in Christ 8
Col 1:27 the riches of the glory of this mystery 8
2: 2 to have all the riches of assured understanding 8
1Ti 6:17 nor to set their hopes on uncertain riches 8
Jas 5: 2 Your riches have rotted 8
Wis 8: 5 If riches are a desirable possession in life 8
Sir 13:24 Riches are good if they are free from sin 8
14: 3 Riches are not seemly for a stingy man 8
5 He will not enjoy his own riches. 9
21: 4 Terror and violence will lay waste riches 8
30:15 and a robust body than countless riches 7
40:26 Riches and strength lift up the heart 9
1Mc 4:23 and cloth dyed blue and sea purple, and great riches. 8
riches *See also* bestow.

richly 1. πλουσίως
Col 3:16 Let the word of Christ dwell in you richly 1
1Ti 6:17 richly furnishes us with everything to enjoy. 1
Tit 3: 6 which he poured out upon us richly 1
2Pe 1:11 so there will be richly provided for you 1
Sir 45:12 the delight of the eyes, richly adorned. •
richly *See also* supply.

more richly 1. יסף
Lev 19:25 that they may yield more richly for you 1

richness 1. ῥίζα καὶ πιότης
Rom 11:17 to share the richness of the olive tree 1

riddle 1. חִידָה 2. אֲחִידָה (A) 3. αἴνιγμα
Jdg 14:12 Let me now put a riddle to you; if you can tell me 1
13 Put your riddle, that we may hear it. 1
14 And they could not . . tell what the riddle was. 1
15 Entice your husband to tell us what the riddle is 1
16 you have put a riddle to my countrymen 1
17 Then she told the riddle to her countrymen. 1
18 my heifer, you would not have found out my riddle. 1
19 festal garments to those who had told the riddle. 1
Ps 49: 4 I will solve my riddle to the music of the lyre. 1
Prv 1: 6 understand . . words of the wise and their riddles. 1
Ezk 17: 2 propound a riddle, and speak an allegory 1
Dan 5:12 interpret dreams, explain riddles, 2
8:23 king . . one who understands riddles 1
Wis 8: 8 she understands . . the solutions of riddles 3
Sir 47:15 you filled it with parables and riddles. 3
riddle *See also* propound, put.

ride 1. הלך 2. רכב 3. רִכְבָּה 4. ἐπιβιβάζω 5. σύνειμι
Gen 24:61 Rebekah . . arose, and rode upon the camels 2
Lev 15: 9 who has the discharge rides shall be unclean 2
Num 22:22 Now he was riding on the ass, and his two servants 2
30 your ass, upon which you have ridden all your life 2
Deu 33:26 who rides through the heavens to your help 2
Jdg 5:10 Tell of it, you who ride on tawny asses, you who sit 2
10: 4 he had 30 sons who rode on 30 asses; 2
12:14 40 sons and 30 grandsons, who rode on 70 asses; 2
1Sm 25:20 And as she rode on the ass . . David and his men came 2
2Sm 16: 2 The asses are for the king's household to ride on 2
18: 9 Ab'salom was riding upon his mule 2
19:26 that I may ride upon it and go with the king.' 2
22:11 He rode on a cherub, and flew . . upon the wings 2
1Kg 18:45 And Ahab rode and went to Jezreel. 2
2Kg 9:18 Turn round and ride behind me. •
19 Turn round and ride behind me. •
25 you and I rode side by side behind Ahab his father 2
10:16 Come with me . ." So he had him ride in his chariot. 2
Neh 2:12 no beast with me but the beast on which I rode. 2
Est 6: 8 and the horse which the king has ridden 2
8:10 sent by mounted couriers riding on swift horses 2
Ps 18:10 He rode on a cherub, and flew; he came swiftly 2
45: 4 In your majesty ride forth victoriously 2
66:12 thou didst let men ride over our heads; 2
68: 4 lift up a song to him who rides upon the clouds; 2
33 him who rides in the heavens, the ancient heavens; 2
104: 3 who ridest on the wings of the wind 1
Isa 19: 1 Behold, the LORD is riding on a swift cloud 2
30:16 We will ride upon swift steeds 2
Jer 6:23 they ride upon horses, set in array 2
17:25 kings . . riding in chariots and on horses 2
22: 4 riding in chariots and on horses 2
50:42 they ride upon horses, arrayed as a man for battle 2
Ezk 23: 6 desirable young men, horsemen riding on horses. 2
12 clothed in full armor, horsemen riding on horses 2
23 and warriors, all of them riding on horses. 2
27:20 traded with you in saddlecloths for riding. 3
38:15 peoples with you, all of them riding on horses 2
Hos 14: 3 we will not ride upon horses; 2
Ams 2:15 nor shall he who rides the horse save his life; 2
Hab 3: 8 when thou didst ride upon thy horses 2
Zec 1: 8 behold, a man riding upon a red horse! 2
9: 9 victorious is he, humble and riding on an ass 2
Act 23:24 Also provide mounts for Paul to ride 4
2Mc 9: 4 the judgment of heaven rode with him! 5

ride along 1. πορεύω
Lke 19:36 as he rode along 1

cause to ride 1. רכב
1Kg 1:33 cause Solomon my son to ride on my own mule 1
38 and caused Solomon to ride on King David's mule 1
44 they have caused him to ride on the king's mule; 1

make ride 1. רכב
Gen 41:43 he made him to ride in his second chariot; 1
Deu 32:13 He made him ride on the high places of the earth 1
Est 6:11 made him ride through the open square of the city 1
Job 30:22 me up on the wind, thou makest me ride on it 1
Isa 58:14 I will make you ride upon the heights of the earth; 1

ride out 1. יצא
Est 8:14 So the couriers . . rode out in haste 1

rider 1. רכב 2. רֶכֶב 3. רֶכֶב אִישׁ 4. ἀναβάτης 5. ἐπιβάτης 6. ἐπικάθημαι 7. κάθημαι 8. κατ᾽ οἰκίαν εἰμί
Gen 49:17 bites the horse's heels so that his rider falls 1
Exd 15: 1 the horse and his rider he has thrown into the sea. 1
21 the horse and his rider he has thrown 1
2Kg 18:23 if you are able . . to set riders upon them. 1
Job 39:18 she laughs at the horse and his rider. 1
Ps 76: 6 O God of Jacob, both rider and horse lay stunned. 2
Isa 21: 7 When he sees riders, horsemen in pairs 2
7 horsemen in pairs, riders on asses 2
7 riders on asses, riders on camels 2
9 And, behold, here come riders, horsemen in pairs! 3
36: 8 able on your part to set riders upon them. 1
Jer 51:21 with you I break in pieces the horse and his rider; 1
Ezk 39:20 be filled at my table with horses and riders 2
Hag 2:22 and overthrow the chariots and their riders; 1
22 the horses and their riders shall go down 1
Zec 10: 5 they shall confound the riders on horses. 1
12: 4 horse with panic, and its rider with madness. 1
Rev 6: 2 I saw . . a white horse, and its rider had a bow; 7
4 its rider was permitted to take peace 7
5 And I saw, and behold, a black horse, and its rider 7
8 a pale horse, and its rider's name was Death 7
9:17 the riders wore breastplates the color of fire 7
19:18 to eat . . the flesh of horses and their riders 7
Jdt 9: 7 they are exalted, with their horses and riders; 4
2Mc 3:25 a rider of frightening mien 5
25 Its rider was seen to have armor and weapons 6
13:15 He stabbed the leading elephant and its rider. 8

ridge 1. גְּדוּד 2. πρίων
Ps 65:10 settling its ridges, softening it with showers 1
Jdt 3: 9 fronting the great ridge of Judea; 2

ridicule 1. לעג 2. καταγελάω 3. irrideo
Neh 4: 1 Sanbal'lat . . ridiculed the Jews. 1
2Es 2:21 do not ridicule a lame man, protect the maimed 3
Sir 7:11 Do not ridicule a man who is bitter in soul 2
20:17 How many will ridicule him, and how often! 2

ridiculous 1. γελοῖος 2. καταγέλαστος
Wis 17: 8 were sick themselves with ridiculous fear. 2
4Mc 1: 5 Their attempt at argument is ridiculous! 1
3: 1 This notion is entirely ridiculous 1
6:34 It would be ridiculous to deny it. 1

right 1. אֱמֶת 2. בִּצְדָקָה 3. טוֹב 4. יכח 5. ישר 6. יָשָׁר 7. כון 8. כֵּן 9. כֵּן דבר 10. מֵישָׁר 11. מִשְׁפָּט 12. נָכֹחַ 13. צַדִּיק 14. צדק 15. צֶדֶק 16. צְדָקָה 17. קֹשְׁטְ 18. קְשֹׁט (A) 19. ἀγαθός 20. ἀλήθεια 21. ἀρεστός 22. δεῖ 23. δίκαιος 24. δικαιοσύνη 25. δικαίως 26. ἔξειμι 27. εὐθής 28. εὐθύς 29. θέμις 30. θεμιτός 31. καλός 32. καλῶς 33. ὀρθῶς 34. iustus
Gen 18:25 Shall not the Judge of all the earth do right? 11
20:16 and before every one you are righted. 4
24:48 the LORD . . who had led me by the right way to take 1
Exd 8:26 Moses said, "It would not be right to do so; 7
9:27 the LORD is in the right, and I and my people are 13
15:26 If you . . do that which is right in his eyes 6
23: 8 subverts the cause of those who are in the right. 13
Num 27: 7 The daughters of Zeloph'ehad are right; 9
36: 5 The tribe of the sons of Joseph is right. 9
Deu 6:18 do what is right and good in the sight of the LORD 6
12: 8 every man doing whatever is right in his own eyes; 6
25 when you do what is right in the sight of the LORD. 6
28 do what is good and right in the sight of the LORD 6
13:18 doing what is right in the sight of the LORD 6
21: 9 when you do what is right in the sight of the LORD. 6
32: 4 A God . . without iniquity, just and right is he. 6
33:19 mountain; there they offer right sacrifices; 15
Jos 9:25 do as it seems good and right in your sight to do 6
Jdg 12: 6 Sibboleth," for he could not pronounce it right; 8
17: 6 every man did what was right in his own eyes. 6
21:25 every man did what was right in his own eyes. 6
1Sm 12:23 I will instruct you in the good and the right way. 6
29: 6 it seems right that you should march . . with me 3
2Sm 15: 3 See, your claims are good and right; 12
1Kg 3:11 asked . . understanding to discern what is right 11

11:33 walked in my ways, doing what is right in my sight 6
38 do what is right in my eyes by keeping my statutes 6
14: 8 doing only that which was right in my eyes 6
15: 5 David did what was right in the eyes of the LORD 6
11 Asa did what was right in the eyes of the LORD 6
22:43 doing what was right in the sight of the LORD; 6
2Kg 7: 9 We are not doing right. This day is . . of good news; 8
10:30 done well in carrying out what is right in my eyes 6
12: 2 Jeho'ash did what was right in the eyes of the LORD 6
14: 3 And he did what was right in the eyes of the LORD 6
15: 3 he did what was right in the eyes of the LORD 6
34 And he did what was right in the eyes of the LORD 6
16: 2 he did not do what was right in the eyes of the LORD 6
17: 9 Israel did . . things that were not right. 8
18: 3 And he did what was right in the eyes of the LORD 6
22: 2 And he did what was right in the eyes of the LORD 6
1Ch 13: 4 the thing was right in the eyes of all the people. 5
2Ch 14: 2 Asa did what was good and right 6
20:32 did what was right in the sight of the LORD. 6
24: 2 Jo'ash did what was right in the eyes of the LORD 6
25: 2 he did what was right in the eyes of the LORD 6
26: 4 he did what was right in the eyes of the LORD 6
27: 2 he did what was right in the eyes of the LORD 6
28: 1 he did not do what was right in the eyes of the LORD 6
29: 2 he did what was right in the eyes of the LORD 6
30: 4 the plan seemed right to the king 5
31:20 he did what was good and right and faithful 6
34: 2 He did what was right in the eyes of the LORD 6
Neh 9:13 give them right ordinances and true laws 6
Job 8: 3 Or does the Almighty pervert the right? 15
32: 9 nor the aged that understand what is right. 11
33:12 in this you are not right. I will answer you. 14
23 to declare to man what is right for him; 5
27 I sinned, and perverted what was right 6
34: 4 Let us choose what is right; 11
42: 7 for you have not spoken of me what is right 7
8 for you have not spoken of me what is right 7
Ps 4: 5 Offer right sacrifices, and put your trust 15
15: 2 He who walks blamelessly, and does what is right 15
17: 2 my vindication come! Let thy eyes see the right! 10
19: 8 the precepts of the LORD are right 6
25: 9 He leads the humble in what is right, and teaches 11
45: 4 for the cause of truth and to defend the right; 15
51:10 O God, and put a new and right spirit within me. 7
19 then wilt thou delight in right sacrifices 15
58: 1 Do you indeed decree what is right, you gods? 15
119:75 I know, O LORD, that thy judgments are right 15
121I have done what is just and right; do not leave me 15
137O LORD, and right are thy judgments. 6
172of thy word, for all thy commandments are right. 15
Prv 8: 6 from my lips will come what is right; 10
9 They are all . . right to those who find knowledge. 6
12:15 The way of a fool is right in his own eyes 6
14:12 There is a way which seems right to a man 6
16:13 king, and he loves him who speaks what is right. 6
25 There is a way which seems right to a man 6
18:17 He who states his case first seems right 13
20:11 whether what he does is pure and right. 6
21: 2 Every way of a man is right in his own eyes 6
8 but the conduct of the pure is right. 6
22:21 to show you what is right and true 17
23:16 soul . . rejoice when your lips speak what is right. 10
24:26 He who gives a right answer kisses the lips. 12
Ecc 5: 8 see . . justice and right violently taken away 15
Isa 29:21 turn aside him who is in the right. 13
30:10 to the prophets, "Prophesy not to us what is right; 12
32: 7 even when the plea of the needy is right. 11
41:26 and beforetime, that we might say, "He is right"? 13
45:19 I . . speak the truth, I declare what is right. 10
48: 1 and confess . . but not in truth or right. 16
Jer 17:11 so is he who gets riches but not by right; 11
23:10 Their course is evil, and their might is not right. 8
26:14 Do with me as seems good and right to you. 6
27: 5 and I give it to whomever it seems right to me. 5
34:15 repented and did what was right in my eyes 6
40: 4 go wherever you think it good and right to go. 6
5 or go wherever you think it right to go. 6
Lam 1:18 The LORD is in the right, for I have rebelled 13
Ezk 16:52 they are more in the right than you. 14
18: 5 is righteous and does what is lawful and right 16
19 When the son has done what is lawful and right 16
21 all my statutes and does what is lawful and right 16
27 and does what is lawful and right, he shall save 16
33:14 from his sin and does what is lawful and right 16
16 he has done what is lawful and right 16
19 does what is lawful and right, he shall live by it. 16
Dan 4:37 for all his works are right and his ways are just; 18
Hos 14: 9 for the ways of the LORD are right 6
Ams 3:10 They do not know how to do right," says the LORD 12
Zec 11:12 If it seems right to you, give me my wages; 3
Mal 3: 3 till they present right offerings to the LORD. 2
Mat 20: 4 and whatever is right I will give you 23
Mrk 7:27 for it is not right to take the children's bread 31
12:32 the scribe said to him, "You are right, Teacher 32
Lke 10:28 You have answered right; do this, and you will live. 33
12:57 why do you not judge for yourselves what is right? 23
Joh 4:17 You are right in saying, 'I have no husband'; 32
7:24 judge with right judgment. 23
8:48 The Jews answered him, "Are we not right in saying 32
13:13 you are right, for so I am. 32
Act 4:19 Whether it is right in the sight of God 23
6: 2 It is not right that we should give up preaching 21
8:21 your heart is not right before God. 28
10:35 any one who fears him and does what is right 24
28:25 was right in saying to your fathers 32
Rom 7:18 I can will what is right, but I cannot do it. 31
21 when I want to do right, evil lies close at hand. 31
14:21 it is right not to eat meat or drink wine 31
1Co 13: 6 but rejoices in the right. 20
15:34 Come to your right mind, and sin no more 25
2Co 13: 7 that you may do what is right 31
Eph 5: 9 found in all that is good and right and true 24
6: 1 for this is right. 23
Php 1: 7 It is right for me to feel thus about you all 23
Jas 4:17 knows what is right to do and fails to do it 31
1Pe 3:11 let him turn away from evil and do right; 19
13 if you are zealous for what is right? 19
2Pe 1:13 I think it right, as long as I am in this body 23
2:15 Forsaking the right way they have gone astray; 28
1Jn 2:29 every one who does right is born of him. 24
3: 7 He who does right is righteous 24
10 whoever does not do right is not of God 24
Rev 22:11 Let . . the righteous still do right 23
2Es 5:11 or any one who does right 34
Tob 2:13 for it is not right to eat what is stolen. 30
13: 6 Turn back, you sinners, and do right before him 24
Jdt 8:11 What you have said . . is not right 27
29 your heart's disposition is right. 19
Wis 2:11 let our might be our law of right 24
9: 9 what is right according to thy commandments. 27
Sir 10:23 is not right to despise an intelligent poor man 23
Aza 1: 4 all thy works are true and thy ways right 28
1Mc 12:11 as it is right and proper to remember brethren. 22
2Mc 6:20 to refuse things that it is not right to taste 29
9:12 It is right to be subject to God 23
4Mc 1: 1 it is right for me to advise you 33
5:18 not even so would it be right for us 26
6:34 it is right for us to acknowledge 23
13:24 and brought up in right living 23

right (2) 1. יָמִין 2. ימן 3. יְמָנִי 4. δεξιός 5. dexter

Gen 48:17 his father laid his right hand upon the head 1
Exd 29:20 blood and put it upon the tip of the right ear 3
20 upon the tips of the right ears of his sons 3
20 upon the thumbs of their right hands 3
20 upon the great toes of their right feet 3
22 take . . the right thigh (for it is a ram 1
Lev 7:32 the right thigh you shall give to the priest 1
33 shall have the right thigh for a portion 1
8:23 blood and put it on the tip of Aaron's right ear 3
23 on the thumb of his right hand and on the great toe 3
23 right hand and on the great toe of his right foot 3
24 the blood on the tips of their right ears 3
24 blood . . on the thumbs of their right hands 3
24 blood . . on the great toes of their right feet 3
25 he took . . the right thigh 1
26 placed them on the fat and on the right thigh 1
9:21 the breasts and the right thigh Aaron waved 1
14:14 the priest shall put it on the tip of the right ear 3
14 on the thumb of his right hand, and on the great toe 3
14 on the great toe of his right foot 3
16 dip his right finger in the oil that is in his left 3
17 priest shall put on the tip of the right ear 3
17 the thumb of his right hand, and on the great toe 3
17 and on the great toe of his right foot 3
25 put it on the tip of the right ear of him who is to be 3
25 on the thumb of his right hand, and on the great toe 3
25 on the great toe of his right foot 3
27 shall sprinkle with his right finger 3
28 the tip of the right ear of him who is to be 3
28 on the thumb of his right hand, and the great toe 3
28 the great toe of his right foot 3
Num 18:18 as the breast that is waved and as the right thigh 1
22:26 no way to turn either to the right or to the left. 1
Deu 2:27 turn aside neither to the right nor to the left. 1
Jdg 3:16 girded it on his right thigh under his clothes. 1
21 his left hand, took the sword from his right thigh 1
7:20 and in their right hands the trumpets to blow; 1
1Sm 6:12 they turned neither to the right nor to the left 1
11: 2 condition . . that I gouge out all your right eyes 1
2Sm 20: 9 Jo'ab took Ama'sa by the beard with his right hand 1
1Kg 2:19 for the king's mother; and she sat on his right. 1
2Kg 22: 2 did not turn aside to the right hand or to the left. 1
2Ch 34: 2 he did not turn aside to the right or to the left. 1
Neh 12:31 One went to the right upon the wall to the Dung Gate; 1
Ps 73:23 thou dost hold my right hand. 1
121: 5 LORD is your shade on your right hand. 1
142: 4 I look to the right and watch, but there is none 1
Prv 4:27 Do not swerve to the right or to the left; 1
Ecc 10: 2 A wise man's heart inclines him toward the right 1
Isa 9:20 They snatch on the right, but are still hungry 1
54: 3 will spread abroad to the right and to the left 1
Jer 22:24 Coni'ah . . were the signet ring on my right hand 1
Ezk 1:10 the four had the face of a lion on the right side 1
4: 6 lie down a second time, but on your right side 1
21:16 Cut sharply to right and left 2
39: 3 make your arrows drop out of your right hand. 1
Zec 4: 3 olive trees by it, one on the right of the bowl 1
11 trees on the right and the left of the lampstand? 1
11:17 May the sword smite his arm and his right eye! 1
17 wholly withered, his right eye utterly blinded! 1
12: 6 they shall devour to the right and to the left 1
Mat 5:29 If your right eye causes you to sin, pluck it out 4
30 And if your right hand causes you to sin, cut it off 4
39 any one strikes you on the right cheek, turn to him 4
27:38 one on the right and one on the left. 4
Mrk 15:27 one on his right and one on his left. 4
Lke 6: 6 a man was there whose right hand was withered. 4
22:50 and cut off his right ear. 4
23:33 one on the right and one on the left. 4
Joh 18:10 and cut off his right ear 4
21: 6 Cast the net on the right side of the boat 4
Act 3: 7 he took him by the right hand and raised him up; 4
Rev 1:16 in his right hand he held seven stars 4
10: 2 And he set his right foot on the sea 4
5 the angel . . lifted up his right hand to heaven 4
13:16 to be marked on the right hand or the forehead 4
2Es 4:47 he said to me, "Stand at my right side 5
9:38 I lifted up my eyes and saw a woman on my right 5
11:12 behold, on the right side one wing arose 5
20 the wings . . also rose up on the right side 5
24 the head that was on the right side 5
35 the head on the right side devoured the one 5
12:29 to the head which was on the right side 5
Sir 12:12 do not have him sit at your right 4
21:19 like manacles on his right hand. 4
21 like a bracelet on the right arm. 4
36: 6 make thy hand and thy right arm glorious. 4
49:11 He was like a signet on the right hand 4
1Mc 5:46 they could not go round it to the right or to the left; 4
6:45 he killed men right and left 4
9: 1 and with them the right wing of the army. 4
12 Bacchides was on the right wing 4
14 the strength of his army were on the right 4
15 they crushed the right wing 4
16 the right wing was crushed 4

right (3) 1. דִּין 2. משל 3. מִשְׁפָּט 4. צֶדֶק 5. צְדָקָה 6. δεῖ 7. δίκαιος 8. ἐξουσία 9. καθήκω 10. κρίσις 11. ὀφειλή 12. πρεσβεῖον

Exd 21: 8 he shall have no right to sell her to a foreign 2
Deu 21:17 right of the first-born is his. 3
1Sm 10:25 told . . the rights and duties of the kingship; 3
2Sm 19:28 What further right have I, then, to cry to the king? 5
Neh 2:20 no portion or right or memorial in Jerusalem. 5
Job 27: 2 As God lives, who has taken away my right 3
34: 5 I am innocent, and God has taken away my right 3
6 in spite of my right I am counted a liar; 3
35: 2 Do you say, 'It is my right before God,' 4
36: 6 but gives the afflicted their right. 3
Ps 4: 1 Answer me when I call, O God of my right! 4
35:23 Bestir thyself, and awake for my right 3
37: 6 as the light, and your right as the noonday. 3
50:16 What right have you to recite my statutes •
Prv 29: 7 A righteous man knows the rights of the poor; 1
31: 5 pervert the rights of all the afflicted. 1
8 for the rights of all who are left desolate. 1
Isa 5:23 for a bribe, and deprive the innocent of his right! 5
10: 2 to rob the poor of my people of their right 3
40:27 and my right is disregarded by my God"? 3
49: 4 yet surely my right is with the LORD 3
Jer 5:28 they do not defend the rights of the needy. 3
11:15 What right has my beloved in my house •
32: 7 the right of redemption by purchase is yours. 3
8 the right of possession and redemption is yours; 3
Lam 3:35 to turn aside the right of a man 3
Ezk 21:27 until he comes whose right it is; 3
Zec 3: 7 I will give you the right of access •
Rom 9:21 Has the potter no right over the clay 8
1Co 7: 3 husband should give to his wife her conjugal rights 11
9: 4 Do we not have the right to our food and drink? 8
5 we not have the right to be accompanied by a wife 8
6 Or is it only Barnabas and I who have no right 8
12 Nevertheless, we have not made use of this right 8
15 I have made no use of any of these rights •
18 making full use of my right in the gospel. 8
2Th 3: 9 It was not because we have not that right 8
Tit 1:11 by teaching . . what they have no right to teach. 6
Heb 13:10 those who serve the tent have no right to eat. 8
Rev 22:14 they may have the right to the tree of life 8
Tob 7:10 for it is your right to take my child 9
Wis 19:16 those who had already shared the same rights. 7
Sir 3: 2 confirmed the right of the mother over her sons. 10
48: 4 who has the right to boast which you have? •
Sus 1:50 and inform us, for God has given you that right. 12
1Mc 8:32 we will defend their rights 10
11:58 and granted him the right to drink from gold cups 8
14:46 the right to act in accord with these decisions. •
2Mc 13:23 yielded and swore to observe all their rights 7

right (4) 1. αὐτός 2. ἕως ἔσω

Mrk 14:54 right into the courtyard of the high priest 2
2Mc 4:12 he founded a gymnasium right under the citadel 1

right *See* early, guard, hand, maintain, mind, moment, now, over, prove, reason, reasoning, say, side, time, turn, usurp, well.

do right 1. ἀγαθοποιέω 2. ἀγαθοποιΐα 3. ἀγαθοποιός

1Pe 2:14 sent by him . . to praise those who do right. 3
15 that by doing right you should put to silence 1
20 if when you do right and suffer for it you take it 1
3: 6 you are now her children if you do right 1
17 For it is better to suffer for doing right 1
4:19 let those who suffer . . do right 2

go right 1. ימן

Gen 13: 9 then I will go to the right; 1

legal right 1. דִּין

Deu 17: 8 between . . one kind of legal right and another 1

right man 1. χρήσιμος

Sir 10: 4 he will raise up the right man for the time. 1

marital right 1. עֹנָה

Exd 21:10 food, her clothing, or her marital rights. 1

right of redemption 1. גְּאֻלָּה

Lev 25:29 he shall have the right of redemption 1
Rut 4: 6 Take my right of redemption yourself 1

seem right 1. כשׁר

Est 8: 5 and if the thing seem right before the king 1

set right 1. διορθόω 2. εὐθύνω

Wis 9:18 thus the paths of those on earth were set right 1
Sir 2: 2 Set your heart right and be steadfast 2

righteous 1. יָשָׁר 2. צַדִּיק 3. צדק 4. צֶדֶק 5. צְדָקָה 6. δίκαιος 7. δικαίωμα 8. δικαίως 9. εὐθύτης 10. κατὰ τὸ κρίμα 11. iustus 12. rego

Gen 6: 9 Noah was a righteous man, blameless 2
7: 1 I have seen that you are righteous before me 2
18:23 Wilt thou indeed destroy the righteous 2
24 Suppose there are 50 righteous within the city; 2
24 not spare it for the 50 righteous who are in it? 2
25 to slay the righteous with the wicked 2
25 wicked, so that the righteous fare as the wicked! 2
26 If I find at Sodom 50 righteous in the city 2
28 Suppose five of the 50 righteous are lacking? 2
38:26 She is more righteous than I, inasmuch as I did not 3
Exd 23: 7 do not slay the innocent and righteous 2
Num23:10 Let me die the death of the righteous 1
Deu 4: 8 righteous as all this law which I set before you 2
16:18 judge the people with righteous judgment. 4
19 bribe . . subverts the cause of the righteous. 2
1Sm 24:17 He said to David, "You are more righteous than I; 2
2Sm 4:11 when wicked men have slain a righteous man 2
1Kg 2:32 slew . . two men more righteous and better 2
8:32 and vindicating the righteous by rewarding him 2
2Ch 6:23 vindicating the righteous by rewarding him 2
12: 6 said, "The LORD is righteous. 2
Neh 9: 8 fulfilled thy promise, for thou art righteous. 2
Job 4:17 Can mortal man be righteous before God? 3
10:15 If I am righteous, I cannot lift up my head 3
15:14 he that is born of a woman, that he can be righteous? 3
17: 9 Yet the righteous holds to his way 2
22: 3 pleasure to the Almighty if you are righteous 3
19 The righteous see it and are glad; 2
25: 4 How then can man be righteous before God? 3
32: 1 because he was righteous in his own eyes. 2
34:17 Will you condemn him who is righteous and mighty 2
35: 7 If you are righteous, what do you give to him; 3
36: 7 He does not withdraw his eyes from the righteous 2
Ps 1: 5 nor sinners in the congregation of the righteous; 2
6 for the LORD knows the way of the righteous 2
5:12 For thou dost bless the righteous, O LORD; 2
7: 9 come to an end, but establish thou the righteous 2
9 triest the minds and hearts, thou righteous God. 2
11 God is a righteous judge 2
9: 4 sat on the throne giving righteous judgment. 4
11: 3 are destroyed, what can the righteous do"? 2
5 The LORD tests the righteous and the wicked 2
7 the LORD is righteous, he loves righteous deeds; 2
14: 5 for God is with the generation of the righteous. 2
19: 9 the ordinances of the LORD are true, and righteous 3
31:18 which speak insolently against the righteous 2
32:11 Be glad in the LORD, and rejoice, O righteous 2
33: 1 Rejoice in the LORD, O you righteous! 2
34:15 The eyes of the LORD are toward the righteous 2
17 When the righteous cry for help, the LORD hears *
19 Many are the afflictions of the righteous; 2
21 those who hate the righteous will be condemned. 2
37:12 The wicked plots against the righteous 2
16 Better is a little that the righteous has 2
17 the LORD upholds the righteous. 2
21 but the righteous is generous and gives; 2
25 yet I have not seen the righteous forsaken 2
28 The righteous shall be preserved for ever *
29 The righteous shall possess the land 2
30 The mouth of the righteous utters wisdom 2
32 The wicked watches the righteous 2
39 The salvation of the righteous is from the LORD; 2
52: 6 The righteous shall see, and fear, and shall laugh 2
55:22 he will never permit the righteous to be moved. 2
58:10 The righteous will rejoice when he sees 2
11 Surely there is a reward for the righteous; 2
64:10 Let the righteous rejoice in the LORD 2
68: 3 righteous be joyful; let them exult before God; 2
69:28 let them not be enrolled among the righteous. 2
75:10 the horns of the righteous shall be exalted. 2
92:12 The righteous flourish like the palm tree 2
94:15 for justice will return to the righteous 4
21 band together against the life of the righteous 2
97:11 Light dawns for the righteous 2
12 Rejoice in the LORD, O you righteous 2
112: 4 LORD is gracious, merciful, and righteous. 2
6 For the righteous will never be moved; 2
116: 5 Gracious is the LORD, and righteous; 2
118:15 songs of victory in the tents of the righteous 2
20 righteous shall enter through it. 2
119: 7 when I learn thy righteous ordinances. 4
62 praise . . because of thy righteous ordinances. 4
106 an oath . . to observe thy righteous ordinances. 4
123 for the fulfilment of thy righteous promise. 4
137 Righteous art thou, O LORD 2
142 Thy righteousness is righteous for ever 4
144 Thy testimonies are righteous for ever; 4
160 every one of thy righteous ordinances endures 4
164 I praise thee for thy righteous ordinances. 4
125: 3 not rest upon the land allotted to the righteous 2
3 righteous put forth their hands to do wrong. 2
129: 4 The LORD is righteous; 2
140:13 Surely the righteous . . give thanks to thy name; 2
142: 7 The righteous will surround me; for thou wilt deal 2
143: 2 for no man living is righteous before thee. 3
146: 8 the LORD loves the righteous. 2
Prv 2:20 keep to the paths of the righteous. 2
3:33 but he blesses the abode of the righteous. 2
4:18 path of the righteous is like the light of dawn 2
8: 8 All the words of my mouth are righteous; 4
10: 3 The LORD does not let the righteous go hungry 2
6 Blessings are on the head of the righteous 2
7 The memory of the righteous is a blessing 2
11 The mouth of the righteous is a fountain of life 2
16 The wage of the righteous leads to life 2
20 The tongue of the righteous is choice silver; 2
21 The lips of the righteous feed many 2
24 but the desire of the righteous will be granted. 2
25 but the righteous is established for ever. 2
28 The hope of the righteous ends in gladness 2
30 The righteous will never be removed 2
31 The mouth of the righteous brings forth wisdom 2
32 lips of the righteous know what is acceptable 2
11: 8 The righteous is delivered from trouble 2
9 but by knowledge the righteous are delivered. 2
10 goes well with the righteous, the city rejoices; 2
21 but those who are righteous will be delivered. 2
23 desire of the righteous ends only in good; 2
28 righteous will flourish like a green leaf. 2
30 The fruit of the righteous is a tree of life 2
31 If the righteous is requited on earth 2
12: 3 root of the righteous will never be moved. 2
5 The thoughts of the righteous are just; 2
7 but the house of the righteous will stand. 2
12 but the root of the righteous stands firm. 2
13 but the righteous escapes from trouble. 2
21 No ill befalls the righteous 2
13: 9 The light of the righteous rejoices 2
21 but prosperity rewards the righteous. 2
22 sinner's wealth is laid up for the righteous. 2
25 righteous has enough to satisfy his appetite 2
14:19 the wicked at the gates of the righteous. 2
32 righteous finds refuge through his integrity. 2
15: 6 house of the righteous there is much treasure 2
28 The mind of the righteous ponders how to answer 2
29 but he hears the prayer of the righteous. 2
16:13 Righteous lips are the delight of a king 4
31 A hoary head . . is gained in a righteous life. 5
17:15 justifies . . and he who condemns the righteous 2
21:12 The righteous observes the house of the wicked; 2
15 When justice is done, it is a joy to the righteous 2
18 The wicked is a ransom for the righteous 2
26 but the righteous gives and does not hold back. 2
23:24 father of the righteous will greatly rejoice; 2
24:15 wicked man against the dwelling of the righteous; 2
28: 1 but the righteous are bold as a lion. 2
12 When the righteous triumph, there is great glory; 2
28 but when they perish, the righteous increase. 2
29: 2 righteous are in authority, the people rejoice; 2
16 but the righteous will look upon their downfall. 2
27 An unjust man is an abomination to the righteous 2
Ecc 3:17 God will judge the righteous and the wicked 2
7:16 Be not righteous overmuch 2
20 Surely there is not a righteous man on earth 2
8:14 according to the deeds of the righteous. 2
9: 1 the righteous and the wise . . are in the hand 2
2 one fate . . to all, to the righteous and the wicked 2
Isa 3:10 Tell the righteous that it shall be well 2
24:16 songs of praise, of glory to the Righteous One. 2
26: 2 that the righteous nation which keeps faith 2
7 The way of the righteous is level; 2
7 thou dost make smooth the path of the righteous. 2
45:21 god besides me, a righteous God and a Savior; 2
53:11 by his knowledge shall the righteous one 2
58: 2 they ask of me righteous judgments 4
60:21 Your people shall all be righteous; 2
Jer 12: 1 Righteous art thou, O LORD, when I complain to thee; 2
20:12 O LORD of hosts, who triest the righteous 2
23: 5 when I will raise up for David a righteous Branch 2
33:15 I will cause a righteous Branch to spring forth 5
Lam 4:13 priests, who shed . . the blood of the righteous. 2
Ezk 13:22 you have disheartened the righteous falsely 2
18: 5 If a man is righteous and does what is lawful 2
9 he is righteous, he shall surely live 2
20 the righteousness of the righteous shall be 2
24 But when a righteous man turns away from his 2
26 When a righteous man turns away from his 2
21: 3 will cut off from you both righteous and wicked. 2
4 I will cut off from you both righteous and wicked 2
23:45 But righteous men shall pass judgment on them 2
33:12 The righteousness of the righteous shall not 2
12 the righteous shall not be able to live 2
13 I say to the righteous that he shall surely live 2
18 the righteous turns from his righteousness 2
Dan 9:14 for the LORD our God is righteous in all the works 2
Ams 2: 6 because they sell the righteous for silver 2
5:12 you who afflict the righteous, who take a bribe 2
Hab 1: 4 the wicked surround the righteous 2
13 swallows up the man more righteous than he? 2
2: 4 but the righteous shall live by his faith. 2
Zep 3: 5 The LORD within her is righteous, he does no wrong; 2
Mal 3:18 between the righteous and the wicked 2
Mat 9:13 For I came not to call the righteous, but sinners. 6
13:43 Then the righteous will shine like the sun 6
49 and separate the evil from the righteous 6
23:28 So you also outwardly appear righteous to men 6
29 adorn the monuments of the righteous 6
35 all the righteous blood shed on earth 6
25:37 Then the righteous will answer him 6
46 but the righteous into eternal life. 6
Mrk 2:17 I came not to call the righteous, but sinners. 6
6:20 knowing that he was a righteous and holy man 6
Lke 1: 6 they were both righteous before God 6
2:25 this man was righteous and devout 6
5:32 I have not come to call the righteous, but sinners 6
18: 9 trusted in themselves that they were righteous 6
23:50 member of the council, a good and righteous man 6
Joh 17:25 O righteous Father, the world has not known thee 6
Rom 1:17 He who through faith is righteous shall live. 6
2:13 it is not the hearers of the law who are righteous 6
3:10 as it is written: "None is righteous, no, not one; 6
26 it was to prove . . that he himself is righteous 6
5:19 by one man's . . many will be made righteous. 6
Gal 3:11 He who through faith is righteous shall live"; 6
1Th 2:10 how holy and righteous and blameless 8
2Th 1: 5 is evidence of the righteous judgment of God 6
2Ti 4: 8 which the Lord, the righteous judge, will award 6
Heb 1: 8 the righteous scepter 9
11: 4 he received approval as righteous 6
1Pe 3:12 For the eyes of the Lord are upon the righteous 6
18 the righteous for the unrighteous 6
2Pe 2: 7 if he rescued the righteous Lot 6
8 he was vexed in his righteous soul day after day 6
1Jn 2: 1 an advocate . . Jesus Christ the righteous; 6
29 If you know that he is righteous, you may be sure 6
3: 7 who does right is righteous, as he is righteous. 6
7 who does right is righteous, as he is righteous. 6
12 deeds were evil and his brother's righteous. 6
Rev 22:11 Let . . the righteous still do right 6
1Es 4:39 she does what is righteous 6
2Es 3:11 all the righteous who have descended from him. 11
4:27 things that have been promised to the righteous 11
35 the souls of the righteous in their chambers 11
39 time of threshing is delayed for the righteous- 11
7:17 that the righteous shall inherit these things 11
18 The righteous therefore can endure 11
51 that the righteous are not many but few 11
99 This is the order of the souls of the righteous 11
102 the righteous will be able to intercede 11
111 the righteous have prayed for the ungodly now 11
8:33 For the righteous, who have many works laid up 11
39 will rejoice over the creation of the righteous 11
49 not deemed yourself to be among the righteous 11
9:13 but inquire how the righteous will be saved 11
10:39 For he has seen your righteous conduct 12
14:32 because he is a righteous judge 11
35 the names of the righteous will become manifest 11
15: 8 Behold, innocent and righteous blood cries out 11
8 the souls of the righteous cry out continually. 11
Tob 3: 2 Righteous art thou, O Lord 6
2 thou dost render true and righteous judgment 6
4:17 Place your bread on the grave of the righteous 6
13: 9 he will show mercy to the sons of the righteous. 6
13 Rejoice and be glad for the sons of the righteous 6
13 will praise the Lord of the righteous. 6
AEs 11: 7 to fight against the nation of the righteous 6
9 the whole righteous nation was troubled 6
14: 7 Thou art righteous, O Lord! 6
Wis 2:10 Let us oppress the righteous poor man 6
16 he calls the last end of the righteous happy 6
3: 1 the souls of the righteous are in the hand of God 6
5:15 the righteous live for ever 6

10:20 Therefore the righteous plundered the ungodly; 6
11:13 the righteous had received benefit *
14 their thirst was not like that of the righteous. 6
12: 9 the righteous in battle 6
15 Thou art righteous 6
16:17 the universe defends the righteous. 6
23 in order that the righteous might be fed 6
18: 7 The deliverance of the righteous 6
20 experience of death touched also the righteous 6
Sir 9:16 Let righteous men be your dinner companions 6
32:16 like a light they will kindle righteous deeds. 7
35: 7 The sacrifice of a righteous man is acceptable 6
17 does justice for the righteous 6
44:17 Noah was found perfect and righteous 6
Bar 2: 9 for the Lord is righteous in all his works 6
Aza 1:64 spirits and souls of the righteous 6
Sus 1: 3 Her parents were righteous 6
9 or remembering righteous judgments. 6
53 put to death an innocent and righteous person.' 6
Man 1: 1 God . . of their righteous posterity; 6
8 Therefore thou, O Lord, God of the righteous 6
8 not appointed repentance for the righteous 6
1Mc 2:24 He gave vent to righteous anger 10
2Mc 12: 6 calling upon God the righteous Judge 6
3Mc 2:22 since he was smitten by a righteous judgment. 6
4Mc 15:10 were righteous and self-controlled and brave 6
16:21 Daniel the righteous was thrown to the lions 6
18:15 'Many are the afflictions of the righteous.' 6

righteous *See also* account, declare, help, judge, judgment, make.

righteous act 1. צְדָקָה
Ps 71:15 My mouth will tell of thy righteous acts 1
Dan 9:16 O Lord, according to all thy righteous acts 1

righteous deed 1. צְדָקָה 2. δικαιοσύνη 3. δικαίωμα 4. iustitia
Ps 11: 7 the LORD is righteous, he loves righteous deeds; 1
Isa 64: 6 all our righteous deeds are like a polluted garment. 1
Ezk 3:20 his righteous deeds which he has done shall not be 1
18:24 None of the righteous deeds which he has done 1
33:13 none of his righteous deeds shall be remembered; 1
Rev 19: 8 fine linen is the righteous deeds of the saints. 3
2Es 7:35 righteous deeds shall awake 4
Tob 2:14 your charities and your righteous deeds 2
Sir 44:10 whose righteous deeds have not been forgotten; 2
Bar 2:19 any righteous deeds of our fathers or our kings 3

righteous man 1. צַדִּיק 2. δίκαιος 3. iustus
Prv 9: 9 teach a righteous man and he will increase 1
12:10 righteous man has regard for the life 1
26 A righteous man turns away from evil 1
13: 5 A righteous man hates falsehood 1
17:26 To impose a fine on a righteous man is not good; 1
18: 5 not good . . to deprive a righteous man of justice. 1
10 righteous man runs into it and is safe. 1
20: 7 A righteous man who walks in his integrity– 1
24:16 righteous man falls seven times, and rises again; 1
25:26 righteous man who gives way before the wicked. 1
29: 6 but a righteous man sings and rejoices. 1
7 A righteous man knows the rights of the poor; 1
Ecc 7:15 there is a righteous man who perishes 1
8:14 there are righteous men to whom it happens 1
Isa 57: 1 The righteous man perishes, and no one lays it 1
1 For the righteous man is taken away from calamity 1
Ezk 3:20 if a righteous man turns from his righteousness 1
21 if you warn the righteous man not to sin 1
Mat 10:41 he who receives a righteous man 2
41 because he is a righteous man 2
41 shall receive a righteous man's reward. 2
13:17 I say to you, many prophets and righteous men 2
27:19 Have nothing to do with that righteous man 2
Rom 5: 7 Why, one will hardly die for a righteous man 2
Jas 5: 6 you have killed the righteous man; 2
16 The prayer of a righteous man has great power 2
1Pe 4:18 If the righteous man is scarcely saved 2
2Pe 2: 8 what that righteous man saw and heard 2
2Es 10:22 our righteous men have been carried off 3
Wis 2:12 Let us lie in wait for the righteous man 2
18 for if the righteous man is God's son 2
3:10 who disregarded the righteous man 2
4: 7 the righteous man . . will be at rest. 2
16 The righteous man who had died 2
5: 1 the righteous man will stand 2
10: 4 steering the righteous man by a . . piece of wood 2
5 Wisdom also . . recognized the righteous man 2
6 Wisdom rescued a righteous man 2
10 When a righteous man fled 2
13 When a righteous man was sold 2
12:19 the righteous man must be kind 2
19:17 just as . . those at the door of the righteous man 2
Sir 35: 6 The offering of a righteous man 2

most righteous 1. δίκαιος
AEs 16:15 are governed by most righteous laws 1

righteous one 1. δίκαιος 2. iustus
Act 3:14 you denied the Holy and Righteous One 1
7:52 the coming of the Righteous One 1
Heb 10:38 my righteous one shall live by faith 1
2Es 8:57 they have even trampled upon his righteous ones 2

righteous person 1. δίκαιος
Lke 15: 7 99 righteous persons who need no repentance 1

righteously 1. צֶדֶק 2. צְדָקָה 3. δικαίως
Deu 1:16 'Hear the cases . . and judge righteously 1
Prv 31: 9 Open your mouth, judge righteously 1
Isa 33:15 He who walks righteously and speaks uprightly 2
Jer 11:20 But, O LORD of hosts, who judgest righteously 1
Wis 12:15 Thou . . rulest all things righteously 3

righteousness 1. צֶדֶק 2. צְדָקָה 3. צִדְקָה (A) 4. δικαιοσύνη 5. iustitia
Gen 15: 6 and he reckoned it to him as righteousness. 2
18:19 the LORD by doing righteousness and justice; 2
Lev 19:15 in righteousness shall you judge your neighbor 1
Deu 6:25 it will be righteousness for us, if we are careful 2
9: 4 Do not say . . 'It is because of my righteousness 2
5 Not because of your righteousness 2
6 not giving . . because of your righteousness; 2
24:13 righteousness to you before the LORD your God. 2
1Sm 26:23 LORD rewards every man for his righteousness 2
2Sm 22:21 LORD rewarded me according to my righteousness; 2
25 recompensed me according to my righteousness 2
1Kg 3: 6 before thee in faithfulness, in righteousness 2
8:32 rewarding him according to his righteousness. 2
10: 9 you may execute justice and righteousness. 2
2Ch 6:23 rewarding him according to his righteousness. 2
9: 8 you may execute justice and righteousness. 2
Job 27: 6 I hold fast my righteousness 2
29:14 I put on righteousness, and it clothed me; 1
35: 8 and your righteousness a son of man. 2
36: 3 ascribe righteousness to my Maker. 1
37:23 power and justice, and abundant righteousness 2
Ps 5: 8 Lead me, O LORD, in thy righteousness 2
7: 8 judge me, O LORD, according to my righteousness 1
17 to the LORD the thanks due to his righteousness 1
9: 8 he judges the world with righteousness 1
17:15 for me, I shall behold thy face in righteousness; 1
18:20 LORD rewarded me according to my righteousness; 1
24 recompensed me according to my righteousness 1
23: 3 He leads me in paths of righteousness 1
31: 1 be put to shame; in thy righteousness deliver me! 2
33: 5 He loves righteousness and justice; 2
35:24 O LORD, my God, according to thy righteousness; 1
28 Then my tongue shall tell of thy righteousness 1
36: 6 Thy righteousness is like the mountains of God 2
45: 7 you love righteousness and hate wickedness. 1
50: 6 The heavens declare his righteousness 1
71: 2 In thy righteousness deliver me and rescue me; 2
16 I will praise thy righteousness, thine alone. 2
19 thy righteousness, O God, reach the high heavens. 2
72: 1 O God, and thy righteousness to the royal son! 2
2 May he judge thy people with righteousness 1
3 for the people, and the hills, in righteousness! 2
7 In his days may righteousness flourish 4
85:10 righteousness and peace will kiss each other. 1
11 righteousness will look down from the sky. 1
13 Righteousness will go before him 1
89:14 Righteousness and justice are the foundation 1
16 who . . extol thy righteousness. 2
96:13 He will judge the world with righteousness 1
97: 2 righteousness and justice are the foundation 1
6 The heavens proclaim his righteousness; 1
98: 9 will judge the world with righteousness 1
99: 4 executed justice and righteousness in Jacob. 2
103:17 his righteousness to children's children 2
106: 3 Blessed . . who do righteousness at all times! 2
31 that has been reckoned to him as righteousness 2
111: 3 his righteousness endures for ever. 2
112: 3 his righteousness endures for ever. 2
9 his righteousness endures for ever; 2
118:19 Open to me the gates of righteousness 1
119:40 thy righteousness give me life! 2
138 appointed thy testimonies in righteousness 1
142 Thy righteousness is righteous for ever 2
132: 9 Let thy priests be clothed with righteousness 1
143: 1 faithfulness answer me, in thy righteousness! 2
11 In thy righteousness bring me out of trouble! 2
145: 7 shall sing aloud of thy righteousness. 2
Prv 1: 3 receive instruction in . . righteousness 1
2: 9 Then you will understand righteousness 1
8:20 I walk in the way of righteousness 2
10: 2 but righteousness delivers from death. 2
11: 4 but righteousness delivers from death. 2
5 righteousness of the blameless keeps his way 2
6 The righteousness of the upright delivers them 2
18 one who sows righteousness gets a sure reward. 2
19 He who is steadfast in righteousness will live 2
12:28 In the path of righteousness is life 2
13: 6 Righteousness guards him whose way is upright 2
14:34 Righteousness exalts a nation 2
15: 9 but he loves him who pursues righteousness. 2
16: 8 Better is a little with righteousness 2
12 throne is established by righteousness. 2
20:28 throne is upheld by righteousness. 4
21: 3 To do righteousness and justice is more 2
21 He who pursues righteousness and kindness 2
25: 5 throne will be established in righteousness. 1
Ecc 3:16 and in the place of righteousness, even there was 1
7:15 a . . man who perishes in his righteousness 1
Isa 1:21 Righteousness lodged in her, but now murderers. 1
26 you shall be called the city of righteousness 1
27 those in her who repent, by righteousness. 2
5: 7 he looked . . for righteousness, but behold, a cry! 2
16 the Holy God shows himself holy in righteousness 2
9: 7 to uphold it . . with righteousness 2
10:22 is decreed, overflowing with righteousness. 2
11: 4 with righteousness he shall judge the poor 1
5 Righteousness shall be the girdle of his waist 1
16: 5 seeks justice and is swift to do righteousness. 1
26: 9 inhabitants of the world learn righteousness. 1
10 If favor . . he does not learn righteousness; 1
28:17 justice the line, and righteousness the plummet; 2
32: 1 Behold, a king will reign in righteousness 1
16 and righteousness abide in the fruitful field. 2
17 the effect of righteousness will be peace 2
17 the result of righteousness, quietness 2
33: 5 fill Zion with justice and righteousness; 2
42: 6 I am the LORD, I have called you in righteousness 1
21 The LORD was pleased, for his righteousness' sake 1
45: 8 and let the skies rain down righteousness; 1
8 and let it cause righteousness to spring up also; 2
13 I have aroused him in righteousness 1
23 from my mouth has gone forth in righteousness 2
24 in the LORD . . are righteousness and strength; 2
48:18 and your righteousness like the waves of the sea; 2
51: 7 Hearken to me, you who know righteousness 1
54:14 In righteousness you shall be established; 2
56: 1 says the LORD: "Keep justice, and do righteousness 2
57:12 will tell of your righteousness and your doings 2
58: 2 as if they were a nation that did righteousness 2
8 your righteousness shall go before you 1
59: 9 and righteousness does not overtake us; 2
14 and righteousness stands afar off; 2
16 and his righteousness upheld him. 2
17 He put on righteousness as a breastplate 2
60:17 peace and your taskmasters righteousness. 2
61: 3 that they may be called oaks of righteousness 1
10 he has covered me with the robe of righteousness 2
11 cause righteousness and praise to spring forth 2
64: 5 meetest him that joyfully works righteousness 1
Jer 9:24 justice, and righteousness in the earth; 2
22: 3 Thus says the LORD: Do justice and righteousness 2
15 and do justice and righteousness? 2
23: 5 and shall execute justice and righteousness 2
6 he will be called: 'The LORD is our righteousness.' 1
31:23 LORD bless you, O habitation of righteousness 1
33:15 and he shall execute justice and righteousness 2
16 it will be called: 'The LORD is our righteousness 1
Ezk 3:20 if a righteous man turns from his righteousness 1
14:14 by their righteousness, says the Lord GOD. 2
20 their own lives by their righteousness. 2
18:20 the righteousness of the righteous shall be 2
22 for the righteousness which he has done 2
24 man turns away from his righteousness 2
26 man turns away from his righteousness 2
33:12 The righteousness of the righteous shall not 2
12 to live by his righteousness when he sins. *
13 yet if he trusts in his righteousness 2
18 the righteous turns from his righteousness 2
45: 9 and execute justice and righteousness; 2
Dan 4:27 off your sins by practicing righteousness 3
9: 7 To thee, O Lord, belongs righteousness, but to us 2
18 before thee on the ground of our righteousness 2
24 bring in everlasting righteousness 1
Hos 2:19 I will betroth you to me in righteousness 1
10:12 Sow for yourselves righteousness 2
Ams 5: 7 and cast down righteousness to the earth! 2
24 and righteousness like an ever-flowing stream. 2
6:12 and the fruit of righteousness into wormwood 2
Zep 2: 3 seek righteousness, seek humility; 1
Zec 8: 8 God, in faithfulness and in righteousness. 2
Mal 4: 2 the sun of righteousness shall rise 2
Mat 3:15 thus it is fitting for us to fulfil all righteousness. 4
5: 6 those who hunger and thirst for righteousness 4
10 those who are persecuted for righteousness' sake 4
20 tell you, unless your righteousness exceeds 4
6:33 seek first his kingdom and his righteousness 4
21:32 For John came to you in the way of righteousness 4
Lke 1:75 in holiness and righteousness before him 4
Joh 16: 8 concerning sin and righteousness and judgment 4
10 concerning righteousness 4
Act 13:10 you enemy of all righteousness 4
17:31 will judge the world in righteousness 4
Rom 1:17 For in it the righteousness of God is revealed 4
3:21 the righteousness of God has been manifested 4
22 the righteousness of God through faith in Jesus 4
25 This was to show God's righteousness 4
4: 3 and it was reckoned to him as righteousness. 4
5 his faith is reckoned as righteousness. 4
6 the man to whom God reckons righteousness 4
9 faith was reckoned to Abraham as righteousness. 4
11 righteousness which he had by faith 4
11 who thus have righteousness reckoned to them 4

13 but through the righteousness of faith. 4
22 his faith was "reckoned to him as righteousness. 4
5:17 who receive . . the free gift of righteousness 4
21 grace also might reign through righteousness 4
6:13 members to God as instruments of righteousness 4
16 or of obedience, which leads to righteousness? 4
18 have become slaves of righteousness. 4
19 so now yield your members to righteousness 4
20 you were free in regard to righteousness. 4
8:10 spirits are alive because of righteousness 4
9:30 That Gentiles who did not pursue righteousness 4
30 attained it . . righteousness through faith; 4
31 but that Israel who pursued the righteousness 4
10: 3 the righteousness that comes from God 4
3 they did not submit to God's righteousness. 4
5 the righteousness which is based on the law 4
6 But the righteousness based on faith says 4
14:17 kingdom of God is . . righteousness and peace 4
1Co 1:30 whom God made our wisdom, our righteousness 4
2Co 3: 9 the dispensation of righteousness 4
5:21 in him we might become the righteousness of God. 4
6: 7 with the weapons of righteousness 4
14 righteousness and iniquity 4
9: 9 his righteousness endures for ever. 4
10 increase the harvest of your righteousness. 4
11:15 as servants of righteousness 4
Gal 3: 6 it was reckoned to him as righteousness. 4
21 then righteousness would indeed be by the law. 4
5: 5 we wait for the hope of righteousness. 4
Eph 4:24 in true righteousness and holiness. 4
6:14 put on the breastplate of righteousness 4
Php 1:11 filled with the fruits of righteousness 4
3: 6 as to righteousness under the law blameless. 4
9 not having a righteousness of my own, based on law 4
9 righteousness from God that depends on faith 4
1Ti 6:11 aim at righteousness, godliness, faith, love 4
2Ti 2:22 aim at righteousness, faith, love, and peace 4
3:16 profitable . . for training in righteousness 4
4: 8 is laid up for me the crown of righteousness 4
Tit 3: 5 not because of deeds done by us in righteousness 4
Heb 1: 9 loved righteousness and hated lawlessness; 4
5:13 is unskilled in the word of righteousness 4
7: 2 He is first . . king of righteousness 4
11: 7 the righteousness which comes by faith. 4
12:11 it yields the peaceful fruit of righteousness 4
Jas 1:20 anger of man does not work the righteousness of God. 4
2:23 and it was reckoned to him as righteousness"; 4
3:18 the harvest of righteousness is sown in peace 4
1Pe 2:24 we might die to sin and live to righteousness. 4
3:14 even if you do suffer for righteousness' sake 4
2Pe 1: 1 the righteousness of our God and Savior Jesus 4
2: 5 preserved Noah, a herald of righteousness 4
21 to have known the way of righteousness 4
3:13 and a new earth in which righteousness dwells. 4
Rev 19:11 and in righteousness he judges and makes war. 4
2Es 5:11 Has righteousness . . passed through you? 5
7:105 his own righteousness and unrighteousness. 5
114 and righteousness has increased 5
8:12 Thou hast brought him up in thy righteousness 5
32 who have no works of righteousness 5
36 righteousness and goodness will be declared 5
16:50 righteousness shall abhor iniquity 5
52 and righteousness will reign over us. 5
Tob 1: 3 in the ways of truth and righteousness 4
12: 8 fasting, almsgiving, and righteousness 4
8 A little with righteousness is better 4
9 perform deeds of charity and of righteousness 4
13: 6 Praise the Lord of righteousness 4
14: 7 who love the Lord God in truth and righteousness 4
11 consider . . how righteousness delivers 4
Wis 1: 1 Love righteousness, you rulers of the earth 4
15 For righteousness is immortal. 4
5: 6 the light of righteousness did not shine on us 4
18 he will put on righteousness as a breastplate 4
8: 7 if any one loves righteousness 4
9: 3 rule the world in holiness and righteousness 4
12:16 For thy strength is the source of righteousness 4
14: 7 the wood by which righteousness comes. 4
15: 3 For to know thee is complete righteousness 4
Sir 26:28 a man who turns back from righteousness to sin 4
45:26 to judge his people in righteousness 4
Bar 1:15 Righteousness belongs to the Lord our God 4
2: 6 Righteousness belongs to the Lord our God 4
18 will ascribe to thee glory and righteousness 4
4:13 paths of discipline in his righteousness. 4
5: 2 Put on the robe of the righteousness from God 4
4 Peace of righteousness and glory of godliness. 4
9 mercy and righteousness that come from him. 4
1Mc 2:29 Then many who were seeking righteousness 4
52 it was reckoned to him as righteousness? 4

righteousness *See also* act, assert, turn.

rightful 1. צֶדֶק
Job 8: 6 and reward you with a rightful habitation. 1

rightful *See also* claim, due, state.

rightly 1. יטב 2. מֵישָׁר 3. καλῶς 4. κατὰ ἀλήθειαν 5. ὀρθῶς 6. bene 7. recte
Gen 27:36 Esau said, "Is he not rightly named Jacob? 4
Deu 5:28 they have rightly said all that they have spoken. 1
18:17 They have rightly said all that they have spoken. 1
Sng 1: 4 we will extol your . . rightly do they love you. 2
Lke 7:43 he said to him "You have judged rightly. 5
20:21 we know that you speak and teach rightly 5
Joh 18:23 if I have spoken rightly, why do you strike me? 3
Rom 2: 2 the judgment of God rightly falls upon those 4
2Es 4:20 He answered me and said, "You have judged rightly 6
8:37 Some things you have spoken rightly 7
Wis 6: 4 you did not rule rightly, nor keep the law 5

rightly *See also* handle.

rights *See* maintain.

become rigid 1. ξηραίνω
Mrk 9:18 he foams and grinds his teeth and becomes rigid; 1

rigor 1. פֶּרֶךְ 2. συντελέω
Exd 1:13 they made the people of Israel serve with rigor 1
14 all their work they made them serve with rigor. 1
Rom 9:28 Lord will execute . . with rigor and dispatch. 2

rigor of devotion 1. ἐθελοθρησκία
Col 2:23 in promoting rigor of devotion 1

rim 1. גַּב 2. גְּבוּל 3. ὄργανον
1Kg 7:33 their axles, their rims, their . . were all cast. 1
Ezk 1:18 The four wheels had rims and they had spokes; 1
18 and their rims were full of eyes round about. 1
10:12 And their rims, and their spokes, and the wheels 1
43:13 broad, with a rim of one span around its edge. 2
17 with a rim around it half a cubit broad 2
20 corners of the ledge, and upon the rim round about; 2
2Mc 13: 5 it has a rim running around it 3

ring 1. גָּלִיל 2. טַבַּעַת 3. נֶזֶם 4. δακτύλιος
Gen 24:22 the man took a gold ring weighing a half shekel 3
30 When he saw the ring, and the bracelets 3
47 I put the ring in her nose, and the bracelets 3
35: 4 gave . . he rings that were in their ears; 3
Exd 25:12 you shall cast four rings of gold for it 2
12 two rings on the one side of it, and two rings 2
12 and two rings on the other side of it. 2
14 you shall put the poles into the rings 2
15 The poles shall remain in the rings of the ark; 2
26 you shall make for it four rings of gold 2
26 and fasten the rings to the four corners 2
27 Close to the frame the rings shall lie, as holders 2
26:24 joined at the top, at the first ring; 2
29 shall make their rings of gold for holders 2
27: 4 make four bronze rings at its four corners. 2
7 the poles shall be put through the rings 2
28:23 shall make for the breastpiece two rings of gold 2
23 two rings on the two edges of the breastpiece. 2
24 the two cords of gold in the two rings at the edges 2
26 you shall make two rings of gold, and put them 2
27 you shall make two rings of gold, and attach them 2
28 they shall bind the breastpiece by its rings 2
28 bind . . to the rings of the ephod with a lace 2
28 bind . . to the rings of the ephod with a lace 2
30: 4 two golden rings shall you make for it; 2
32: 2 Aaron said to them, "Take off the rings of gold 3
3 people took off the rings of gold which were 3
36:29 but joined at the top, at the first ring; 2
34 and made their rings of gold for holders 2
37: 3 he cast for it four rings of gold 2
3 two rings on its one side and two rings on its 2
3 its one side and two rings on its other side. 2
5 put the poles into the rings on the sides 2
13 He cast for it four rings of gold, and fastened 2
13 rings of gold, and fastened the rings to the four 2
14 Close to the frame were the rings, as holders 2
27 made two rings of gold on it under its molding 2
38: 5 He cast four rings on the four corners 2
7 he put the poles through the rings on the sides 2
39:16 they made . . two gold rings, and put the two rings 2
16 put the two rings on the two edges 2
17 two cords of gold in the two rings at the edges 2
19 Then they made two rings of gold 2
20 they made two rings of gold, and attached them 2
21 they bound the breastpiece by its rings 2
21 its rings to the rings of the ephod with a lace 2
Est 1: 6 caught up with cords . . to silver rings 1
3:12 and sealed with the king's ring. 2
8: 8 you may write . . and seal it with the king's ring; 2
8 edict written . . and sealed with the king's ring 2
10 The writing was . . sealed with the king's ring 2
Job 42:11 gave him a piece of money and a ring of gold. 3
Prv 11:22 Like a gold ring in a swine's snout is a beautiful 3
25:12 Like a gold ring or an ornament of gold 3
Isa 3:21 the signet rings and nose rings; 3
Ezk 16:12 I put a ring on your nose, and earrings in your ears 3
Hos 2:13 and decked herself with her ring and jewelry 3
Lke 15:22 put a ring on his hand, and shoes on his feet; 4
Jdt 10: 4 put on her anklets and bracelets and rings 4

ring (2) 1. ἦχος
Sir 45: 9 to make their ringing heard in the temple 1

* **gold ring** 1. χρυσοδακτύλιος
Jas 2: 2 For if a man with gold rings and in fine clothing 1

ring out around 1. περικομπέω
Wis 17: 4 terrifying sounds rang out around them 1

signet ring 1. חֹתָם 2. טַבַּעַת
Gen 41:42 Then Pharaoh took his signet ring from his hand 2
Exd 35:22 earrings and signet rings and armlets, all sorts 2
Num31:50 armlets and bracelets, signet rings, earrings 2
Est 3:10 the king took his signet ring from his hand 2
8: 2 and the king took off his signet ring, 2
Isa 3:21 the signet rings and nose rings; 2
Jer 22:24 Coni'ah . . were the signet ring on my right hand 1
Hag 2:23 says the LORD, and make you like a signet ring; 1

ringleader 1. πρωτοστάτης
Act 24: 5 a ringleader of the sect of the Nazarenes. 1

rinse 1. שטף
Lev 6:28 that shall be scoured, and rinsed in water 1
15:11 touches without having rinsed his hands in water 1
12 every vessel of wood shall be rinsed in water 1

rinse off 1. דוח
2Ch 4: 6 In these they were to rinse off what was used 1

rinse out 1. דוח
Jer 51:34 an empty vessel . . he has rinsed me out. 1

riot 1. θόρυβος 2. στάσις
Mat 27:24 rather that a riot was beginning 1
Act 19:40 we are in danger of being charged with rioting today 2

raging riot 1. ἐπιμίξ
Wis 14:25 all is a raging riot of blood and murder 1

rip open 1. בקע
Hos 13:16 and their pregnant women ripped open. 1

rip up 1. בקע
2Kg 8:12 and rip up their women with child. 1
15:16 he ripped up all the women . . who were with child. 1
Ams 1:13 they have ripped up women with child in Gilead 1

ripe 1. בשל 2. ἀκμάζω 3. ἡλικία 4. παραδίδωμι
Jol 3:13 Put in the sickle, for the harvest is ripe. 1
Mrk 4:29 when the grain is ripe 4
Rev 14:18 gather the clusters . . for its grapes are ripe. 2
Wis 4: 9 a blameless life is ripe old age. 3
3Mc 6: 1 who had attained a ripe old age 3

ripe *See also* almond, fruit, grape.

ripe enough 1. ἄωρος
Wis 4: 5 their fruit will be useless, not ripe enough to eat 1

first ripe 1. בִּכּוּרָה
Jer 24: 2 had very good figs, like first-ripe figs 1

fully ripe 1. ξηραίνω
Rev 14:15 for the harvest of the earth is fully ripe. 1

ripen 1. בשל 2. גמל 3. ἀτελὴς ὥρα 4. περκάζω 5. trado ad vindemiam
Gen 40:10 and the clusters ripened into grapes. 1
Isa 18: 5 and the flower becomes a ripening grape 2
2Es 16:26 The grapes shall ripen, and who will tread them? 5
Wis 10: 7 plants bearing fruit that does not ripen 3
Sir 51:15 From blossom to ripening grape 4

rise 1. גאה 2. זרח 3. זֶרַח 4. יצא 5. מוֹצָא 6. מִזְרָח 7. מָצוֹק 8. נשא 9. עלה 10. עמד 11. קום 12. קִימָה 13. רבה 14. רום 15. נשא (A) 16. ἀναβαίνω 17. ἀνάστασις 18. ἀνατέλλω 19. ἀνατολή 20. ἀνίστημι 21. γίνομαι 22. διεγείρω 23. ἐγείρω 24. ἐξανίστημι 25. ἐξεγείρω 26. ἐξέρχομαι 27. ἐπανίστημι 28. ὀρθρίζω 29. πλεονάζω 30. exalto 31. exsurgo 32. surgo
Gen 7:17 the ark, and it rose high above the earth. 14
19: 1 When Lot saw them, he rose to meet them 11
23 sun had risen on the earth when Lot came to Zo'ar. 4
23: 7 Abraham rose and bowed to the Hittites 11
25:34 and he ate and drank, and rose and went his way. 11
31:35 I cannot rise before you, for the way of women 11
32:31 The sun rose upon him as he passed Penu'el 2
Exd 10:23 nor did any rise from his place for three days; 11
21:19 then if the man rises again and walks abroad 11
22: 3 if the sun has risen upon him, there shall be 2
24:13 So Moses rose with his servant Joshua 11
Num11:32 the people rose all that day, and all night 11
16:25 Then Moses rose and went to Dathan and Abi'ram; 11
22:13 Balaam rose in the morning, and said 11
14 princes of Moab rose and went to Balak, and said 11
20 If the men have come to call you, rise, go with them; 11
21 Balaam rose in the morning, and saddled his ass 11
23:18 Rise, Balak, and hear; hearken to me, O son of Zippor 11
24:17 scepter shall rise out of Israel; 11

25 Then Balaam rose, and went back to his place; 11
25: 7 When Phin'ehas . . saw it, he rose and left 11
32:14 behold, you have risen in your fathers' stead 11
Deu 6: 7 shall talk of them when . . you rise. 11
11:19 by the way, and when you lie down, and when you rise 11
19:16 If a malicious witness rises against any man 11
28: 7 LORD will cause your enemies who rise against 11
31:16 then this people will rise and play the harlot 11
33:11 crush the loins . . that they rise not again. 11
Jos 8:19 And the ambush rose quickly out of their place 11
11:17 lowland from Mount Halak, that rises toward Se'ir 9
12: 7 Ba'al-gad . . to Mount Halak, that rises toward Se'ir 9
Jdg 5:31 friends be like the sun as he rises in his might. 4
8:20 he said to Jether . . "Rise, and slay them. 11
21 Rise yourself, and fall upon us; for as the man is 11
9:35 Abim'elech and the men . . rose from the ambush. 11
43 and he rose against them and slew them. 11
20: 5 men of Gib'e-ah rose against me, and beset the house 11
19 the people of Israel rose in the morning 11
40 when the signal began to rise out of the city 9
Rut 2:15 When she rose to glean, Bo'az instructed his . . men 11
1Sm 1: 9 After they had eaten and drunk . . Hannah rose. 11
14: 5 one crag rose on the north in front of Michmash 7
17:52 And the men of Israel and Judah rose with a shout 11
20:34 And Jonathan rose from the table in fierce anger 11
41 David rose from beside the stone heap 11
42 And he rose and departed; and Jonathan went 11
21:10 And David rose and fled that day from Saul 11
22:13 he has risen against me, to lie in wait 11
23:16 Jonathan . . rose, and went to David at Horesh 11
25: 1 Then David rose and went down to the wilderness 11
41 And she rose and bowed with her face to the ground 11
42 Ab'igail made haste and rose and mounted on an ass 11
26: 5 David rose and came to . . where Saul had encamped; 11
28:25 Then they rose and went away that night. 11
2Sm 11:20 then, if the king's anger rises, and if he says to you 9
14: 7 whole family has risen against your handmaid 11
22:39 I thrust them through, so that they did not rise; 11
23:10 He rose and struck down the Philistines 11
1Kg 1:49 guests . . trembled, and rose, and each went his own 11
2:19 the king rose to meet her, and bowed down to her; 11
3:21 When I rose in the morning to nurse my child 11
8:20 I have risen in the place of David my father 11
18:44 a little cloud . . is rising out of the sea. 9
2Kg 3:24 the Israelites rose and attacked the Moabites 11
6:15 servant . . rose early in the morning and went out 11
7:12 the king rose in the night, and said 11
8:21 Joram passed over to Za'ir . . and rose by night 11
1Ch 28: 2 Then King David rose to his feet and said 11
2Ch 6:10 for I have risen in the place of David my father 11
20:23 rose against the inhabitants of Mount Se'ir 10
21: 9 Jeho'ram . . rose by night and smote the E'domites 11
28:15 the men . . rose and took the captives 11
36:16 till the wrath of the LORD rose against his people 9
Ezr 4:19 city . . has risen against kings 15
9: 5 at the evening sacrifice I rose from my fasting 11
6 our iniquities have risen higher than our heads 13
Est 4:14 relief and deliverance will rise for the Jews 10
5: 9 Haman saw . . that he neither rose nor trembled 11
7: 7 And the king rose from the feast in wrath 11
8: 5 and Esther rose and stood before the king. 11
Job 9: 7 who commands the sun, and it does not rise; 2
14:12 man lies down and rises not again; 11
19:18 when I rise they talk against me. 11
24:14 The murderer rises in the dark 11
29: 8 the aged rose and stood; 11
30:12 On my right hand the rabble rise, 11
Ps 3: 1 how many are my foes! Many are rising against me; 11
18:38 were not able to rise; they fell under my feet. 11
19: 6 Its rising is from the end of the heavens 5
20: 8 we shall rise and stand upright. 11
27:12 for false witnesses have risen against me 11
35: 2 Take hold of shield . . and rise for my help! 11
36:12 they are thrust down, unable to rise. 11
41: 8 he will not rise again from where he lies. 11
50: 1 from the rising of the sun to its setting. 6
54: 3 For insolent men have risen against me 11
78:31 the anger of God rose against them and he slew 9
89: 9 when its waves rise, thou stillest them. 8
104: 8 The mountains rose, the valleys sank down 9
22 When the sun rises, they get them away and lie down 2
112: 4 Light rises in the darkness for the upright; 2
113: 3 From the rising of the sun to its setting the name 6
119:62 At midnight I rise to praise thee 11
147I rise before dawn and cry for help; •
140:10 Let them be cast into pits, no more to rise! 11
Prv 24:16 righteous man falls seven times, and rises again; 11
22 for disaster from them will rise suddenly 11
28:12 but when the wicked rise, men hide themselves. 11
28 When the wicked rise, men hide themselves 11
31:15 She rises while it is yet night and provides food 11
Ecc 1: 5 The sun rises and the sun goes down 2
5 and hastens to the place where it rises. 2
10: 4 If the anger of the ruler rises against you 9
Sng 3: 2 I will rise now and go about the city 11
Isa 2:19 when he rises to terrify the earth. 11
21 his majesty, when he rises to terrify the earth. 11
8: 7 River . . it will rise over all its channels 9
13:10 the sun will be dark at its rising 4
14:21 lest they rise and possess the earth 11
24:20 upon it, and it falls, and will not rise again. 11
26:19 Thy dead shall live, their bodies shall rise. 11
34: 3 and the stench of their corpses shall rise; 9
41:25 and he has come, from the rising of the sun 6
43:17 they lie down, they cannot rise 11
45: 6 that men may know, from the rising of the sun 6
54:17 tongue that rises against you in judgment. 11
58:10 then shall your light rise in the darkness 2
59:19 and his glory from the rising of the sun; 6
60: 1 and the glory of the LORD has risen upon you. 2
3 and kings to the brightness of your rising. 3
Jer 8: 4 says the LORD: When men fall, do they not rise again? 11
25:27 Drink, be drunk and vomit, fall and rise no more 11
46: 7 Who is this, rising like the Nile 9
8 Egypt rises like the Nile 9
8 He said, I will rise, I will cover the earth 9
47: 2 Behold, waters are rising out of the north 9
51:64 say, 'Thus shall Babylon sink, to rise no more 11
Lam 3:63 Behold their sitting and their rising; 12
Ezk 1:19 when the living creatures rose from the earth 8
19 creatures rose from the earth, the wheels rose. 8
20 they went, and the wheels rose along with them; 8
21 when those rose from the earth, the wheels rose 8
21 when those rose from the earth, the wheels rose 8
41: 7 the side chambers became broader as they rose •
47: 5 I could not pass through, for the water had risen; 1
Dan 8:27 then I rose and went about the king's business; 11
11:14 many shall rise against the king of the south; 10
Hos 13:15 the LORD, shall come, rising from the wilderness; 9
Jol 2:20 the stench and foul smell of him will rise 9
Ams 5: 2 Fallen, no more to rise, is the virgin Israel; 11
7: 9 and I will rise against the house of Jerobo'am 11
8: 8 and all of it rise like the Nile, and be tossed 9
14 they shall fall, and never rise again. 11
9: 5 and all of it rises like the Nile, and sinks again 9
Obd 1: 1 Rise up! let us rise against her for battle! 11
Jon 1: 3 Jonah rose to flee to Tarshish 11
4: 8 When the sun rose, God appointed a sultry east 2
Mic 2: 8 But you rise against my people as an enemy; •
7: 8 when I fall, I shall rise; 11
Nah 3:17 when the sun rises, they fly away; 2
Mal 1:11 from the rising of the sun to its setting 6
4: 2 the sun of righteousness shall rise 2
Mat 2:13 Rise, take the child and his mother, and flee 23
14 he rose and took the child and his mother by night 23
20 Rise, take the child and his mother, and go 23
21 he rose and took the child and his mother, and went 23
8:15 fever left her, and she rose and served him. 23
26 Then he rose and rebuked the winds and the sea 23
9: 5 or to say, 'Rise and walk'? 23
6 Rise, take up your bed and go home. 23
7 he rose and went home. 23
9 Follow me." And he rose and followed him. 20
19 Jesus rose and followed him, with his disciples. 23
10:21 children will rise against parents 27
11:11 there has risen no one greater than John 23
13: 6 when the sun rose they were scorched 18
17: 7 Rise, and have no fear. 23
24: 7 For nation will rise against nation 23
25: 7 Then all those maidens rose 23
26:46 Rise, let us be going; see, my betrayer is at hand. 23
27:63 'After three days I will rise again.' 23
64 'He has risen from the dead,' 23
28: 6 He is not here; for he has risen, as he said 23
7 he has risen from the dead 23
Mrk 1:35 in the morning, a great while before day, he rose 20
2: 9 or to say, 'Rise, take up your pallet and walk'? 23
11 I say to you, rise, take up your pallet and go home. 23
12 he rose, and immediately took up the pallet 23
14 he rose and followed him. 20
4: 6 when the sun rose it was scorched 18
27 sleep and rise night and day 23
9: 9 until the Son of man should have risen 20
10 questioning what the rising from the dead meant 20
31 when he is killed, after three days he will rise. 20
10:34 after three days he will rise. 20
49 saying to him, "Take heart; rise, he is calling you. 23
12:25 For when they rise from the dead 20
13: 8 For nation will rise against nation 23
14:42 Rise, let us be going; see, my betrayer is at hand. 23
16: 2 they went to the tomb when the sun had risen. 18
6 He has risen, he is not here; 20
9 Now when he rose early on the first day of the week 20
14 those who saw him after he had risen. 23
Lke 2:34 the fall and rising of many in Israel 17
4:39 immediately she rose and served them. 20
5:23 or to say, 'Rise and walk'? 23
24 I say to you, rise, take up your bed and go home. 23
25 immediately he rose before them 20
28 he left everything, and rose and followed him. 20
6: 8 Come and stand here." And he rose and stood there. 20
9: 8 by others that one of the old prophets had risen. 20
19 others, that one of the old prophets has risen. 20
11: 8 yet because of his importunity he will rise 23
12:54 When you see a cloud rising in the west 18
16:31 if some one should rise from the dead.' 20
17:19 Rise and go your way; your faith has made you well. 20
18:33 on the third day he will rise. 20
21:10 he said to them, "Nation will rise against nation 23
22:45 when he rose from prayer, he came to the disciples 20
46 Rise and pray 20
24: 7 crucified, and on the third day rise. 20
33 rose that same hour and returned to Jerusalem; 20
34 who said, "The Lord has risen indeed 23
38 why do questionings rise in your hearts? 16
46 on the third day rise from the dead 20
Joh 5: 8 Rise, take up your pallet, and walk. 23
6:18 The sea rose because a strong wind was blowing. 22
7:52 no prophet is to rise from Galilee. 23
11:29 when she heard it, she rose quickly and went 23
31 the Jews . . saw Mary rise quickly and go out 20
13: 4 rose from supper, laid aside his garments 23
14:31 Rise, let us go hence. 23
20: 9 the scripture, that he must rise from the dead. 20
Act 5: 6 The young men rose and wrapped him up 20
8:26 Rise and go toward the south 20
27 he rose and went 20
9: 6 rise and enter the city 20
11 Rise and go to the street called Straight 20
18 Then he rose and was baptized 20
34 Jesus Christ heals you; rise and make your bed. 20
34 immediately he rose. 20
39 So Peter rose and went with them 20
40 then turning to the body he said, "Tabitha, rise. 20
10:13 there came a voice to him, "Rise, Peter; kill and eat. 20
20 Rise and go down 20
23 The next day he rose and went off with them 20
41 after he rose from the dead. 20
11: 7 'Rise, Peter; kill and eat.' 20
15: 7 Peter rose and said to them, "Brethren 20
17: 3 to suffer and to rise from the dead 20
22:10 the Lord said to me, 'Rise, and go into Damascus 20
16 now why do you wait? Rise and be baptized 20
26:16 rise and stand upon your feet 20
23 by being the first to rise from the dead 17
30 Then the king rose, and the governor and Berni'ce 20
Rom 15:12 he who rises to rule the Gentiles; 20
1Th 4:16 the dead in Christ will rise first; 20
2Ti 2: 8 Remember Jesus Christ, risen from the dead 23
Jas 1:11 For the sun rises with its scorching heat 18
2Pe 1:19 until the day dawns and the morning star rises 18
Rev 7: 2 I saw another angel ascend from the rising . . sun 19
8: 4 the smoke of the incense rose with the prayers 16
9: 2 and from the shaft rose smoke like the smoke 16
11: 1 Rise and measure the temple of God and the altar 23
13: 1 I saw a beast rising out of the sea 16
11 I saw another beast which rose out of the earth; 16
1Es 4:47 Darius the king rose, and kissed him 20
8:73 Then I rose from my fast 25
75 For our sins have risen higher than our heads 29
9: 1 Then Ezra rose 20
7 Then Ezra rose and said to them 20
2Es 2:38 Rise and stand, and see at the feast of the Lord 32
5:18 Rise therefore and eat some bread 31
6:13 He answered and said to me, "Rise to your feet 32
17 When I heard this, I rose to my feet and listened 32
7: 2 he said to me, "Rise, Ezra, and listen to the words 32
11: 7 and behold, the eagle rose upon his talons 32
14: 2 I said, "Here I am, Lord," and I rose to my feet. 32
15:40 mighty clouds . . shall rise 30
50 when the heat rises that is sent upon you. 31
Tob 12:13 did not hesitate to rise and leave your dinner 20
Jdt 10: 2 she rose from where she lay prostrate 20
14: 2 as soon as morning comes and the sun rises 26
AEs 11:11 light came, and the sun rose 18
Wis 5: 6 the sun did not rise upon us. 18
Sir 26:16 Like the sun rising in the heights of the Lord 18
31:20 he rises early, and feels fit 20
35: 6 its pleasing odor rises before the Most High. •
Sus 1:19 the two elders rose and ran to her, and said 20
61 And they rose against the two elders 20
Bel 1:16 Early in the morning the king rose and came 28
1Mc 4:53 they rose and offered sacrifice, as the law directs 28
6:33 the king rose and took his army by a forced march 28
9: 8 Let us rise and go up against our enemies 20
2Mc 10:27 rising from their prayer 21
14:45 Still alive and aflame with anger, he rose 24
3Mc 4:15 from the rising of the sun till its setting 19

rise *See also* bid.

rise again 1. *ἀνίστημι* 2. *τυγχάνω ἀναστάσεως*

Mrk 8:31 be killed, and after three days rise again. 1
Joh 11:23 Jesus said to her, "Your brother will rise again. 1
24 Martha said to him, "I know that he will rise again 1
1Th 4:14 since we believe that Jesus died and rose again 1
Heb 11:35 that they might rise again to a better life. 2
2Mc 12:44 those who had fallen would rise again 1

rise against 1. *ἀνθίστημι* 2. *ἐπανίστημι* 3. *ἐπεγείρω*

Mrk 13:12 children will rise against parents 2
Wis 5:23 a mighty wind will rise against them 1
Sir 46: 1 the enemies that rose against them 3

rise and depart 1. *ἀπανίστημι*

Wis 1: 5 and will rise and depart from foolish thoughts 1

rise before 1. *φθάνω*
Wis 16:28 to make it known that one must rise before the sun 1

rise early 1. שכם 2. *ὀρθρίζω*
Gen 20: 8 Abim'elech rose early in the morning 1
21:14 Abraham rose early in the morning 1
22: 3 Abraham rose early in the morning 1
26:31 In the morning they rose early and took oath 1
28:18 Jacob rose early in the morning 1
Exd 24: 4 he rose early in the morning, and built an altar 1
34: 4 he rose early in the morning and went up 1
Num14:40 rose early in the morning, and went up 1
Jos 3: 1 Early in the morning Joshua rose and set out 1
6:12 Then Joshua rose early in the morning 1
15 the seventh day they rose early at the dawn of day 1
7:16 Joshua rose early in the morning 1
Jdg 6:28 When the men of the town rose early in the morning 1
38 rose early next morning and squeezed the fleece 1
7: 1 Jerubba'al . . and all the people . . rose early 1
9:33 as the sun is up, rise early and rush upon the city; 1
21: 4 And on the morrow the people rose early 1
1Sm 1:19 They rose early in the morning and worshiped 1
5: 3 when the people of Ashdod rose early the next day 1
4 But when they rose early on the next morning 1
15:12 And Samuel rose early to meet Saul in the morning; 1
17:20 David rose early in the morning 1
29:10 rise early in the morning with the servants 1
2Sm 15: 2 Ab'salom used to rise early and stand beside 1
2Kg 3:22 they rose early in the morning, and the sun shone 1
2Ch 20:20 they rose early in the morning and went out 1
29:20 Then Hezeki'ah the king rose early and gathered 1
Job 1: 5 he would rise early in the morning 1
Prv 27:14 loud voice, rising early in the morning 1
Isa 5:11 Woe to those who rise early in the morning 1
Wis 6:14 He who rises early to seek her 2
Sir 32:14 those who rise early to seek him will find favor. 2
39: 5 will set his heart to rise early to seek the Lord 2

rise high 1. רום
Gen 7:17 the ark, and it rose high above the earth. 1

make rise 1. עלה 2. *ἀνατέλλω*
Ps 135: 7 who makes the clouds rise at the end of the earth 1
Jer 10:13 he makes the mist rise from the ends of the earth. 1
51:16 he makes the mist rise from the ends of the earth. 1
Mat 5:45 he makes his sun rise on the evil and on the good 2

make rise up 1. עלה
Jdg 20:38 when they made a great cloud of smoke rise up out 1

rise up 1. נשא 2. עמד 3. קום 4. קום (A) 5. *ἀνθίστημι* 6. *ἀνίστημι* 7. *ἐγείρω* 8. *ἐξανίστημι* 9. *ἐπαίρω* 10. erigo 11. exsurgo
Gen 4: 8 Cain rose up against his brother Abel 3
21:32 Phicol the commander of his army rose up 3
23: 3 Abraham rose up from before his dead 3
37:35 all his daughters rose up to comfort him; 3
Exd 12:30 And Pharaoh rose up in the night 3
31 and said, "Rise up, go forth from among my people 3
32: 6 to eat and drink, and rose up to play. 3
33: 8 all the people rose up, and every man stood 3
10 all the people would rise up and worship 3
Lev 19:32 You shall rise up before the hoary head 3
Num16: 2 took men; and they rose up before Moses 3
23:24 Behold, a people! As a lioness it rises up 3
Deu 2:13 'Now rise up, and go over the brook Zered.' 3
24 Rise up, take your journey, and go over the valley 3
29:22 your children who rise up after you 3
32:38 Let them rise up and help you, let them 3
Jos 3:16 the waters . . stood and rose up in a heap far off 3
6:26 the man that rises up and rebuilds this city 3
8: 7 you shall rise up from the ambush, and seize 3
Jdg 9:18 and you have risen up against my father's house 3
34 Abim'elech and all . . with him rose up by night 3
19: 7 when the man rose up to go, his father-in-law urged 3
9 the man and his concubine . . rose up to depart 3
10 he rose up and departed, and arrived opposite 3
27 her master rose up in the morning 3
28 and the man rose up and went away to his home. 3
20:33 all the men of Israel rose up out of their place 3
1Sm 16:13 And Samuel rose up, and went to Ramah. 3
24: 7 Saul rose up and left the cave, and went . . his way. 3
25:29 If men rise up to pursue you and to seek your life 3
2Sm 18:31 from the power of all who rose up against you. 3
32 and all who rise up against you for evil 3
2Ch 13: 6 rose up and rebelled against his lord; 3
Ezr 1: 5 Then rose up the heads of the fathers' houses 3
Neh 2:18 And they said, "Let us rise up and build. 3
3: 1 Eli'ashib . . rose up with his brethren 3
Job 16: 8 my leanness has risen up against me 3
20:27 the earth will rise up against him. 3
24:22 they rise up when they despair of life. 3
31:14 what then shall I do when God rises up? 3
Ps 35:11 Malicious witnesses rise up; 3
44:26 Rise up, come to our help! Deliver us 3
86:14 O God, insolent men have risen up against me; 3
88:10 Do the shades rise up to praise thee? Selah 3
94: 2 Rise up, O judge of the earth; 1
16 Who rises up for me against the wicked? 3
124: 2 when men rose up against us 3
127: 2 in vain that you rise up early and go late to rest 3
139: 2 Thou knowest when I sit down and when I rise up; 3
Prv 31:28 Her children rise up and call her blessed; 3
Ecc 12: 4 and one rises up at the voice of a bird 3
Isa 14:22 I will rise up against them," says the LORD of hosts 3
28:21 For the LORD will rise up as on Mount Pera'zim 3
32: 9 Rise up, you women who are at ease, hear my voice; 3
Jer 37:10 they would rise up and burn this city with fire. 3
41: 2 ten men with him rose up and struck down Gedali'ah 3
49:14 and come against her, and rise up for battle! 3
28 Thus says the LORD: "Rise up, advance against Kedar 3
31 Rise up, advance against a nation at ease 3
Dan 3:24 King . . was astonished and rose up in haste. 4
8:25 even rise up against the Prince of princes; 2
Obd 1: 1 Rise up! let us rise against her for battle! 3
Mic 7: 6 the daughter rises up against her mother 3
Mrk 3:26 if Satan has risen up against himself 6
Lke 4:29 they rose up and put him out of the city 6
13:25 the householder has risen up and shut the door 7
Act 5:17 the high priest rose up and all who were with him 6
14:20 he rose up and entered the city 6
15: 5 some believers . . rose up, and said 8
1Co 10: 7 sat down to eat and drink and rose up to dance. 6
1Es 1:24 the words of the Lord rose up against Israel. 6
2Es 11:20 the wings . . also rose up on the right side 10
21 others of them rose up, but did not hold the rule. 10
15:15 and nation shall rise up to fight against nation 11
Tob 6:17 when you approach her, rise up, both of you 7
Sir 47: 1 after him Nathan rose up to prophesy 6
12 After him rose up a wise son who fared amply 6
1Mc 9:44 Let us rise up now and fight for our lives 6
10:70 You are the only one to rise up against us 9
13:14 Simon had risen up in place of Jonathan 6
14:32 then Simon rose up and fought for his nation 5
16:16 Ptolemy and his men rose up, took their weapons 8

rise up against 1. קום 2. *ἐπαίρω* 3. *ἐπανίστημι*
Job 27: 7 let him that rises up against me be 1
Ps 59: 1 God, protect me from those who rise up against me 1
139:21 do I not loathe them that rise up against thee? 1
Jdt 13: 5 the enemies who have risen up against us. 3
16:17 Woe to the nations that rise up against my people! 3
1Mc 8: 5 the others who rose up against them 2

rise up early 1. שכם
Gen 19: 2 then you may rise up early and go on your way. 1
Exd 8:20 Rise up early in the morning and wait for Pharaoh 1
9:13 Rise up early in the morning and stand before 1
32: 6 they rose up early on the morrow, and offered 1

rising *See* smoke, sun.

risk 1. שלך מִנֶּגֶד 2. *παραβάλλω* 3. *παραβολεύομαι* 4. *παραδίδωμι* 5. *ὑποτίθημι*
Jdg 9:17 for my father fought for you, and risked his life 1
2Sm 23:17 of the men who went at the risk of their lives? •
Act 15:26 men who have risked their lives 4
Rom16: 4 who risked their necks for my life 5
Php 2:30 risking his life to complete your service to me. 3
2Mc 14:38 he had with all zeal risked body and life. 2

risk life 1. *διακινδυνεύω*
2Mc 11: 7 he urged the others to risk their lives with him 1

risk of life 1. נֶפֶשׁ
1Ch 11:19 For at the risk of their lives, they brought it. 1

rite 1. דָּבָר 2. מִשְׁמֶרֶת 3. *θεσμόν* 4. *τελετή*
Exd 12:24 You shall observe this rite as an ordinance 1
Num 3:38 having charge of the rites within the sanctuary 2
Joh 2: 6 jars . . for the Jewish rites of purification •
Heb 9:23 to be purified with these rites •
Wis 12: 4 their works of sorcery and unholy rites 4
3Mc 6:36 when they had ordained a public rite 3

religious rite 1. *ἱερός*
3Mc 3:21 make them participants in our regular religious rites. 1

secret rite 1. *μυστήριον*
Wis 14:15 and handed on to his dependents secret rites 1

ritual *See* duty.

rival 1. עמם 2. צָרָה 3. *ἀντίζηλος*
1Sm 1: 6 her rival used to provoke her sorely, to irritate 2
Ezk 31: 8 The cedars in the garden of God could not rival it 1
Sir 26: 6 when a wife is envious of a rival †
37:11 Do not consult with a woman about her rival 3

rival *See also* wife.

rivalry 1. *ἔρις* 2. *φιλονεικία*
Php 1:15 Some indeed preach Christ from envy and rivalry 1
2Mc 4: 4 Onias recognized that the rivalry was serious 2
4Mc 1:26 thirst for honor, rivalry, and malice; 2

river 1. אוּבַל 2. יְאֹר 3. נָהָר 4. נַחַל 5. פֶּלֶג 6. פְּלַגָּה 7. ראשׁ 8. נְהַר (A) 9. *ποταμός* 10. flumen 11. rivus
Gen 2:10 A river flowed out of Eden to water the garden 3
10 there it divided and became four rivers. 7
13 The name of the second river is Gihon; 3
14 the name of the third river is Tigris 3
14 And the fourth river is the Euphra'tes. 3
15:18 from the river of Egypt to the great river 3
18 of Egypt to the great river, the river Euphra'tes 3
18 of Egypt to the great river, the river Euphra'tes 3
Exd 2: 3 placed it among the reeds at the river's brink. 2
5 came down to bathe at the river, and her maidens 2
5 and her maidens walked beside the river; 2
7:15 Go to Pharaoh . . wait for him by the river's brink 2
19 stretch out your hand . . over their rivers 3
8: 5 Stretch out your hand . . over the rivers 3
Lev 11: 9 whether in the seas or in the rivers 4
10 anything in . . the rivers that has not fins 4
Num22: 5 at Pethor, which is near the River, in the land 3
24: 6 like gardens beside a river 3
Deu 1: 7 as far as the great river, the river Euphra'tes. 3
7 as far as the great river, the river Euphra'tes. 3
2:37 banks of the river Jabbok and the cities 4
3:16 as far over as the river Jabbok, the boundary •
11:24 from the River, the river Euphra'tes 3
24 from the River, the river Euphra'tes 3
Jos 1: 4 as far as the great river, the river Euphra'tes 3
4 as far as the great river, the river Euphra'tes 3
12: 2 from . . the valley as far as the river Jabbok 4
24: 3 I took your father Abraham from beyond the River 3
14 gods which your fathers served beyond the River 3
15 the gods . . served in the region beyond the River 3
Jdg 4: 7 to meet you by the river Kishon with his chariots 4
13 from Haro'sheth-ha-goiim to the river Kishon. 4
2Sm 8: 3 to restore his power at the river Euphra'tes. 3
2Kg 5:12 Are not Aba'na and Pharpar, the rivers of Damascus 3
17: 6 in Halah, and on the Habor, the river of Gozan 3
18:11 put them . . on the Habor, the river of Gozan 3
23:29 king of Egypt went up . . to the river Euphra'tes. 3
24: 7 from the Brook of Egypt to the river Euphra'tes. 3
1Ch 5:26 brought them to . . Hara, and the river Gozan 3
18: 3 to set up his monument at the river Euphra'tes. 3
Ezr 4:10 rest of the province Beyond the River, and now 8
11 servants . . of the province Beyond the River 8
16 no possession in the province Beyond the River. 8
17 rest of the province Beyond the River 8
20 ruled over the whole province Beyond the River 8
5: 3 governor of the province Beyond the River 8
6 governor of the province Beyond the River 8
6 governors . . in the province Beyond the River 8
6: 6 governor of the province Beyond the River 8
6 governors . . in the province Beyond the River 8
8 tribute of the province from Beyond the River. 8
13 governor of the province Beyond the River 8
7:21 treasurers in the province Beyond the River 8
25 judge . . people in the province Beyond the River 8
8:15 I gathered them to the river that runs to Aha'va 3
21 Then I proclaimed a fast there, at the river Aha'va 3
31 departed from the river Aha'va on the twelfth day 3
36 governors of the province Beyond the River; 3
Neh 2: 7 governors of the province Beyond the River 3
9 governors of the province Beyond the River 3
3: 7 governor of the province Beyond the River. 3
Job 14:11 a river wastes away and dries up 3
20:17 He will not look upon the rivers 6
40:23 if the river is turbulent he is not frightened; 3
Ps 24: 2 and established it upon the rivers. 3
36: 8 drink from the river of thy delights. 4
46: 4 a river whose streams make glad the city of God 3
65: 9 the river of God is full of water; 5
66: 6 men passed through the river on foot. 3
72: 8 to sea, and from the River to the ends of the earth! 3
78:16 caused waters to flow down like rivers. 3
44 He turned their rivers to blood 2
80:11 branches to the sea, and its shoots to the River. 3
83: 9 as to Sis'era and Jabin at the river Kishon 4
89:25 I will set . . his right hand on the rivers. 3
105:41 flowed through the desert like a river. 3
107:33 He turns rivers into a desert 3
Isa 7:20 a razor which is hired beyond the River 3
8: 7 the waters of the River, mighty and many 3
11:15 wave his hand over the River with his scorching 3
18: 1 whirring wings . . beyond the rivers of Ethiopia; 3
2 a nation . . whose land the rivers divide. 3
7 a nation . . whose land the rivers divide 3
19: 5 dried up, and the river will be parched and dry; 3
33:21 a place of broad rivers and streams 3
41:18 I will open rivers on the bare heights 3
42:15 I will turn the rivers into islands 3
43: 2 through the rivers, they shall not overwhelm you; 3
19 a way in the wilderness and rivers in the desert. 3
20 water in the wilderness, rivers in the desert 3
44:27 says to the deep, 'Be dry, I will dry up your rivers 3
47: 2 uncover your legs, pass through the rivers. 3
48:18 Then your peace would have been like a river 3
50: 2 I dry up the sea, I make the rivers a desert; 3
66:12 I will extend prosperity to her like a river 3
Jer 46: 2 which was by the river Euphra'tes at Car'chemish 3

7 like the Nile, like rivers whose waters surge? 3
8 like the Nile, like rivers whose waters surge. 3
10 in the north country by the river Euphra'tes. 3
Lam 3:48 my eyes flow with rivers of tears 5
Ezk 1: 1 as I was among the exiles by the river Chebar 3
3 in the land of the Chalde'ans by the river Chebar; 3
3:15 exiles at Tel-abib, who dwelt by the river Chebar. 3
23 the glory which I had seen by the river Chebar; 3
10:15 living creatures that I saw by the river Chebar. 3
20 underneath the God of Israel by the river Chebar; 3
22 whose appearance I had seen by the river Chebar. 3
31: 4 made it grow tall, making its rivers flow round 3
15 mourn for it, and restrain its rivers 3
32: 2 you burst forth in your rivers 3
2 the waters with your feet, and foul their rivers. 3
14 and cause their rivers to run like oil 3
43: 3 the vision which I had seen by the river Chebar; 3
47: 5 and it was a river that I could not pass through 4
5 a river that could not be passed through. 4
6 Then he led me back along the bank of the river. 4
7 I saw upon the bank of the river very many trees 4
9 wherever the river goes every living creature 9
9 everything will live where the river goes. 4
12 And on the banks, on both sides of the river 4
Dan 8: 2 saw in the vision, and I was at the river U'lai. 1
3 behold, a ram standing on the bank of the river. 1
6 ram . . seen standing on the bank of the river 1
10: 4 as I was standing on the bank of the great river 3
Mic 6: 7 pleased . . with ten thousands of rivers of oil? 4
7:12 and from Egypt to the River, from sea to sea 3
Nah 1: 4 he dries up all the rivers; 3
2: 6 The river gates are opened 3
Hab 3: 8 Was thy wrath against the rivers, O LORD? 3
8 Was thy anger against the rivers 3
9 Thou didst cleave the earth with rivers. 3
Zep 3:10 From beyond the rivers of Ethiopia 3
Zec 9:10 from the River to the ends of the earth. 3
Mat 3: 6 they were baptized by him in the river Jordan 9
Mrk 1: 5 and they were baptized by him in the river Jordan 9
Joh 7:38 shall flow rivers of living water.' 9
2Co 11:26 on frequent journeys, in danger from rivers 9
Rev 8:10 star fell . . and it fell on a third of the rivers 9
9:14 angels . . bound at the great river Euphra'tes. 9
12:15 The serpent poured water like a river 9
16 earth opened its mouth and swallowed the river 9
16: 4 The third angel poured his bowl into the rivers 9
12 angel poured his bowl on the river Euphra'tes 9
22: 1 Then he showed me the river of the water of life 9
2 on either side of the river, the tree 9
1Es 4:23 to sail the sea and rivers; 9
8:41 I assembled them at the river called Theras 9
61 We departed from the river Theras 9
2Es 5:25 thou hast filled for thyself one river 11
7: 4 so that it is like a river. 10
13:40 he took them across the river 10
43 the narrow passages of the Euphrates river. 10
44 and stopped the channels of the river 10
47 will stop the channels of the river again 10
14:47 and the river of knowledge. 10
16:60 to send rivers from the heights to water the earth; 10
Tob 6: 1 came . . to the Tigris river and camped there. 9
2 A fish leaped up from the river 9
Jdt 1: 9 Kadesh and the river of Egypt 9
2: 8 every brook and river 9
AEs 10: 6 The tiny spring which became a river 9
6 the river is Esther 9
11:10 there came a great river, with abundant water; 9
Wis 5:22 rivers will relentlessly overwhelm them; 9
11: 6 Instead of the fountain of an ever-flowing river 9
19:10 the river spewed out vast numbers of frogs. 9
Sir 4:26 do not try to stop the current of a river. 9
24:30 I went forth like a canal from a river 9
31 my canal became a river, and my river became a sea. 9
31 my canal became a river, and my river became a sea. 9
39:22 His blessing covers the dry land like a river 9
40:16 The reeds by any water or river bank 9
44:21 from the River to the ends of the earth. 9
47:14 You overflowed like a river with understanding. 9
Bar 1: 4 all who dwelt in Babylon by the river Sud. 9
Aza 1:56 Bless the Lord, seas and rivers 9
1Mc 3:32 from the river Euphrates to the borders of Egypt. 9
37 He crossed the Euphrates river 9
5:41 camps on the other side of the river 9
7: 8 governor of the province Beyond the River 9
11: 7 as far as the river called Eleutherus 9
60 traveled beyond the river 9
12:30 they had crossed the Eleutherus river. 9
3Mc 7:20 brought safely by land and sea and river 9

river *See also* Euphrates.

riverside 1. *παρὰ ποταμόν*
Act 16:13 we went outside the gate to the riverside 1

road 1. דֶּרֶךְ 2. מְסִלָּה 3. נְתִיבָה 4. שְׁבוּל 5. *ὁδός* 6. via
Gen 38:14 Enaim, which is on the road to Timnah; 1
Num22:23 ass saw the angel of the LORD standing in the road 1
23 the ass turned aside out of the road 1
23 Balaam struck the ass, to turn her into the road. 1
34 that thou didst stand in the road against me. 1
Deu 2: 8 from the Arabah road from Elath and E'zi-on-ge'ber. 1
27 pass through your land; I will go only by the road 1
11:30 beyond the Jordan, west of the road, toward 1
19: 3 prepare the roads, and divide into three parts 1
27:18 'Cursed be he who misleads a blind man on the road.' 1
Jdg 4: 9 nevertheless, the road on which you are going 1
1Sm 4:13 Eli was sitting upon his seat by the road 1
26: 3 Hachi'lah, which is beside the road on the east 1
2Sm 13:34 many people were coming from the Horona'im road 1
16:13 So David and his men went on the road 1
1Kg 11:29 the prophet Ahi'jah . . found him on the road. 1
13:24 a lion met him on the road and killed him. 1
24 his body was thrown in the road 1
25 and saw the body thrown in the road, and the lion 1
28 he went and found his body thrown in the road 1
1Ch 26:16 the gate of Shal'lecheth on the road that goes up. 2
18 for the parbar . . there were four at the road 2
Job 21:29 Have you not asked those who travel the roads 1
24: 4 They thrust the poor off the road; 1
Prv 7: 8 taking the road to her house 1
26:13 The sluggard says, "There is a lion in the road! 1
Ecc 10: 3 when the fool walks on the road, he lacks sense 1
Isa 15: 5 on the road to Horona'im they raise a cry 1
59: 8 they have made their roads crooked 3
Jer 6:16 Thus says the LORD: "Stand by the roads, and look 1
25 Go not forth into the field, nor walk on the road; 1
18:15 have stumbled in their ways, in the ancient roads 4
31:21 the highway, the road by which you went. 1
Lam 1: 4 The roads to Zion mourn, for none come to . . feasts; 1
Nah 2: 1 Man the ramparts; watch the road; gird your loins; 1
Mat 21: 8 the crowd spread their garments on the road 5
8 and spread them on the road. 5
Mrk 10:32 they were on the road, going up to Jerusalem 5
11: 8 many spread their garments on the road 5
Lke 9:57 As they were going along the road, a man said to him 5
10: 4 salute no one on the road. 5
31 Now by chance a priest was going down that road; 5
19:36 they spread their garments on the road. 5
24:32 while he talked to us on the road 5
35 Then they told what had happened on the road 5
Act 8:26 the road that goes down from Jerusalem to Gaza. 5
26 This is a desert road. •
36 as they went along the road 5
9:17 the Lord Jesus who appeared to you on the road 5
27 on the road he had seen the Lord, who spoke to him 5
2Es 16:32 its roads . . shall bring forth thorns 6
Tob 10: 7 every day to the road by which they had left 5
11: 5 looking intently down the road for her son. 5
Sir 8:15 Do not travel on the road with a foolhardy fellow 5
Bar 4:26 My tender sons have traveled rough roads 5
1Mc 5:28 Judas . . turned back by the wilderness road to Bozrah 5
46 This was a large and very strong city on the road 5
6:33 along the road to Beth-zechariah 5
9: 2 They went by the road which leads to Gilgal 5

road side 1. דֶּרֶךְ
Gen 38:16 He went over to her at the road side, and said 1

where no road 1. invius
2Es 1:13 safe highways for you where there was no road 1

roadside 1. *ὁδός*
Mat 20:30 behold, two blind men sitting by the roadside 1
Mrk 10:46 was sitting by the roadside. 1
Lke 18:35 a blind man was sitting by the roadside begging; 1

roam 1. הלך
1Sm 30:31 the places where David and his men had roamed. 1

roam about 1. נוע
Ps 59:15 They roam about for food, and growl 1

roam beyond 1. transmigro
2Es 5: 8 the wild beasts shall roam beyond their haunts 1

roar 1. דֳּבִי 2. המה 3. נהם 4. נְהָמָה 5. קוֹל 6. רעם 7. שׁאג 8. שְׁאָגָה 9. שׁאה 10. שָׁאוֹן 11. תְּשֻׁוָה 12. *ἐρεύγομαι* 13. *ἦχος* 14. *μυκάομαι* 15. *φωνή* 16. *ὠρύομαι* 17. mugio
Jdg 14: 5 And behold, a young lion roared against him; 7
1Ch 16:32 Let the sea roar, and all that fills it 6
Job 4:10 The roar of the lion, the voice of the fierce lion 8
30:22 thou tossest me about in the roar of the storm. 11
37: 4 After it his voice roars; 7
Ps 22:13 like a ravening and roaring lion. 7
46: 3 though its waters roar and foam 2
65: 7 who dost still the roaring of the seas 10
7 roaring of the seas, the roaring of their waves 10
74: 4 Thy foes have roared in the midst of thy holy place; 7
93: 3 floods lift up their roaring. 1
96:11 let the sea roar, and all that fills it; 6
98: 7 Let the sea roar, and all that fills it; 6
104:21 The young lions roar for their prey 7
Prv 28:15 roaring lion or a charging bear is a wicked ruler 3
Isa 5:29 Their roaring is like a lion, like young lions 8
29 like a lion, like young lions they roar; 7
30 growl . . like the roaring of the sea. 4
17:12 Ah, the roar of nations, they roar like the roaring 10
12 they roar like the roaring of mighty waters! 9
12 they roar like the roaring of mighty waters! 10
13 The nations roar like the roaring of many waters 9
13 The nations roar like the roaring of many waters 10
42:10 Let the sea roar and all that fills it •
51:15 God, who stirs up the sea so that its waves roar 2
Jer 2:15 The lions have roared against him 7
5:22 though they roar, they cannot pass over it. 2
6:23 the sound of them is like the roaring sea; 2
11:16 with the roar of a great tempest he will set fire 5
25:30 The LORD will roar from on high 7
30 he will roar mightily against his fold, and shout 7
31:35 who stirs up the sea so that its waves roar 2
50:42 The sound of them is like the roaring of the sea; 2
51:38 They shall roar together like lions; 7
55 Their waves roar like many waters 2
Ezk 19: 7 land was appalled . . at the sound of his roaring. 8
22:25 are like a roaring lion tearing the prey; 7
Hos 11:10 the LORD, he will roar like a lion; 7
10 he will roar, and his sons shall come trembling 7
Jol 3:16 And the LORD roars from Zion 7
Ams 1: 2 And he said: "The LORD roars from Zion 7
3: 4 Does a lion roar in the forest, when he has no prey? 7
8 The lion has roared; who will not fear? 7
Zep 3: 3 Her officials within her are roaring lions; 7
Zec 11: 3 Hark, the roar of the lions, for the jungle 8
Lke 21:25 in perplexity at the roaring of the sea 13
1Pe 5: 8 the devil prowls around like a roaring lion 16
Rev 10: 3 called out with a loud voice, like a lion roaring; 14
2Es 11:37 a creature like a lion was aroused . . roaring 17
12:31 and roaring and speaking to the eagle 17
AEs 11: 6 they roared terribly. 15
7 at their roaring every nation prepared for war 15
Wis 17:19 the sound of the most savage roaring beasts 16
1Mc 3: 4 like a lion's cub roaring for prey. 12

roar loudly 1. נתן קול
Jer 2:15 The lions . . they have roared loudly. 1

roast 1. בשׁל 2. צלה 3. צְלִי אֵשׁ 4. קלה 5. *ὀπτάω*
Exd 12: 8 They shall eat the flesh that night, roasted; 2
9 but roasted, its head with its legs and its inner 3
1Sm 2:15 Give meat for the priest to roast; 2
2Ch 35:13 they roasted the passover lamb with fire 1
Isa 44:16 he eats flesh, he roasts meat and is satisfied; 2
19 on its coals, I roasted flesh and have eaten; 2
Jer 29:22 Ahab, whom the king of Babylon roasted in the fire 4
1Es 1:12 roasted the passover lamb with fire, as required; 5
Tob 6: 5 they roasted and ate the fish. 5

roast from underneath 1. *ὑποκαίω*
4Mc 11:18 he was roasted from underneath. 1

rob 1. בזז 2. גזל 3. קבע 4. שְׁבוּל 5. שׁסה 6. *ἀποστερέω* 7. *ἁρπάζω* 8. *ἀφαιρέω* 9. *ἀφίστημι* 10. *συλάω*
Lev 19:13 You shall not oppress your neighbor or rob him 2
Deu 28:29 only oppressed and robbed continually 2
Jdg 9:25 they robbed all who passed by them along that way; 2
1Sm 23: 1 and are robbing the threshing floors. 5
2Sm 17: 8 like a bear robbed of her cubs in the field. 4
Prv 4:16 robbed of sleep unless they have made some one 2
17:12 Let a man meet a she-bear robbed of her cubs 4
22:22 Do not rob the poor, because he is poor 2
28:24 He who robs his father or his mother and says, "That 2
Isa 10: 2 and to rob the poor of my people of their right 2
42:22 this is a people robbed and plundered 1
Jer 21:12 from . . the oppressor him who has been robbed 2
22: 3 from . . the oppressor him who has been robbed. 2
Ezk 18:18 he practiced extortion, robbed his brother 2
Hos 13: 8 will fall upon them like a bear robbed of her cubs 4
Mal 3: 8 Will man rob God? Yet you are robbing me. 3
8 Will man rob God? Yet you are robbing me. 3
8 robbing me. But you say, 'How are we robbing thee?' 3
9 You are cursed with a curse, for you are robbing me; 3
2Co 11: 8 I robbed other churches by accepting support 10
1Es 4:24 when he steals and robs and plunders 7
Sir 9:13 lest he rob you of your life 8
29: 6 the borrower has robbed him of his money 6
42: 9 worry over her robs him of sleep 9

rob a temple 1. *ἱεροσυλέω*
Rom 2:22 You who abhor idols, do you rob temples? 1
2Mc 9: 2 and attempted to rob the temples 1

rob by violence 1. *διασείω*
Lke 3:14 Rob no one by violence or by false accusation 1

rob of a child 1. שׁכל
Lev 26:22 beasts . . which shall rob you of your children 1
Ezk 5:17 and they will rob you of your children; 1

robber 1. בזז 2. גְּדוּד 3. הלך 4. חֶתֶף 5. פָּרִיץ 6. שׁדד 7. *ἅρπαξ*
Job 12: 6 The tents of robbers are at peace 6
Prv 23:28 She lies in wait like a robber 4

24:34 poverty will come upon you like a robber 3
Isa 42:24 Jacob to the spoiler, and Israel to the robbers? 1
Jer 7:11 this house . . become a den of robbers in your eyes? 5
Ezk 7:22 robbers shall enter and profane it 5
18:10 If he begets a son who is a robber 5
Hos 6: 9 As robbers lie in wait for a man 2
1Co 5:10 the greedy and robbers, or idolaters 7
11 idolater, reviler, drunkard, or robber 7
6:10 nor revilers, nor robbers 7

temple robber 1. *ἱερόσυλος*

2Mc 4:42 the temple robber himself they killed 1

robbery 1. גָּזֵל 2. גְּזֵלָה 3. שֹׁד

Lev 6: 2 deposit or security, or through robbery 1
Ps 62:10 in extortion, set no vain hopes on robbery; 1
Isa 61: 8 I the LORD love justice, I hate robbery and wrong; 1
Ezk 18: 7 commits no robbery, gives his bread to the hungry 2
12 oppresses the poor and needy, commits robbery 2
16 exacts no pledge, commits no robbery 2
22:29 practiced extortion and committed robbery; 1
33:15 gives back what he has taken by robbery 2
Ams 3:10 those who store up violence and robbery in their 3

robbery *See also* take.

robe 1. אֶדֶר 2. אַדֶּרֶת 3. בֶּגֶד 4. כָּנָף 5. כְּתֹנֶת 6. לְבוּשׁ 7. לבש 8. מַד 9. מְעִיל 10. שֹׁבֶל 11. *διπλοΐς* 12. *ἔνδυμα* 13. *ἐνδύω* 14. *ἐσθής* 15. *ἱμάτιον* 16. *ἱματισμός* 17. *περιστολή* 18. *ποδήρης* 19. *στολή* 20. *χλαμύς*

Gen 37:23 they stripped him of his robe 5
23 of his robe, the long robe with sleeves that he 5
31 Then they took Joseph's robe, and killed a goat 5
31 killed a goat, and dipped the robe in the blood; 5
32 they sent the long robe with sleeves 5
32 whether it is your son's robe or not. 5
33 he recognized it, and said, "It is my son's robe; 5
Exd 28: 4 they shall make: a breastpiece, an ephod, a robe 5
31 you shall make the robe of the ephod all of blue. 9
34 round about on the skirts of the robe. 9
29: 5 put on Aaron the coat and the robe of the ephod 9
39:22 He also made the robe of the ephod 9
23 the opening of the robe in it was like the opening 9
24 On the skirts of the robe they made pomegranates 9
25 upon the skirts of the robe round about 9
26 round about upon the skirts of the robe 9
Lev 8: 7 clothed him with the robe, and put the ephod upon 9
1Sm 2:19 his mother used to make for him a little robe 9
15:27 Saul laid hold upon the skirt of his robe 9
18: 4 Jonathan stripped himself of the robe 9
24: 4 David . . cut off the skirt of Saul's robe. 9
11 See, my father, see the skirt of your robe in my hand; 9
11 I cut off the skirt of your robe, and did not kill 9
28:14 An old man is coming up; and he is wrapped in a robe. 9
1Kg 22:10 sitting on their thrones, arrayed in their robes 3
30 I will disguise . . but you wear your robes. 3
1Ch 15:27 David was clothed with a robe of fine linen 9
2Ch 18: 9 sitting on their thrones, arrayed in their robes; 3
29 but you will wear your robes. 3
Est 6: 8 let royal robes be brought . . and the horse 6
9 let the robes and the horse be handed over to one 6
10 take the robes and the horse, as you have said 6
11 Haman took the robes and the horse 6
8:15 Mor'decai went . . in royal robes of blue and white 6
Job 1:20 Job arose, and rent his robe, and shaved his head 9
2:12 they rent their robes and sprinkled dust 9
29:14 my justice was like a robe and a turban. 9
Ps 45: 8 your robes are all fragrant with myrrh and aloes 3
13 decked in her chamber with gold-woven robes; 6
93: 1 The LORD reigns; he is robed in majesty; 7
1 LORD is robed, he is girded with strength. 7
133: 2 of Aaron, running down on the collar of his robes! 8
Isa 22:21 I will clothe him with your robe 5
47: 2 grind meal, put off your veil, strip off your robe 10
61:10 he has covered me with the robe of righteousness 9
Ezk 5: 3 and bind them in the skirts of your robe. •
26:16 down from their thrones, and remove their robes 9
Jon 3: 6 he arose from his throne, removed his robe 2
Mic 2: 8 you strip the robe from the peaceful 1
Zec 8:23 every tongue shall take hold of the robe of a Jew 4
Mat 26:65 Then the high priest tore his robes, and said 15
27:28 they stripped him and put a scarlet robe upon him 20
31 they stripped him of the robe 20
Mrk 16: 5 they saw a young man . . dressed in a white robe; 19
Lke 15:22 Bring quickly the best robe, and put it on him; 19
Joh 19: 2 put it on his head, and arrayed him in a purple robe; 15
5 the crown of thorns and the purple robe 15
Act 1:10 behold, two men stood by them in white robes 14
12:21 On an appointed day Herod put on his royal robes 14
Rev 1:13 clothed with a long robe and with a golden girdle †
6:11 Then they were each given a white robe and told 19
7: 9 clothed in white robes, with palm branches 19
13 Who are these, clothed in white robes 19
14 they have washed their robes and made them white 19
15: 6 seven angels . . robed in pure bright linen 13
19:13 He is clad in a robe dipped in blood 15
16 On his robe and on his thigh he has a name 15
22:14 Blessed are those who wash their robes 19
Wis 18:24 upon his long robe the whole world was depicted 12
Sir 6:29 her collar a glorious robe. 19
31 You will wear her like a glorious robe 19
27: 8 will attain it and wear it as a glorious robe. 18
45: 7 put a glorious robe upon him. 17
50:11 When he put on his glorious robe 19
Bar 4:20 I have taken off the robe of peace 19
5: 2 Put on the robe of the righteousness from God 11
LJr 1:12 When they have been dressed in purple robes 16
20 devour them and their robes 16
58 the robes they wear 16
1Mc 6:15 He gave him the crown and his robe and the signet 19

festal robe 1. מַחֲלָצָה

Isa 3:22 the festal robes, the mantles, the cloaks 1

long robe 1. כְּתֹנֶת 2. *ποδήρης* 3. *στολή*

Gen 37: 3 old age; and he made him a long robe with sleeves. 1
2Sm 13:18 Now she was wearing a long robe with sleeves; 1
19 put ashes . . and rent the long robe which she wore; 1
Mrk 12:38 who like to go about in long robes 3
Lke 20:46 the scribes, who like to go about in long robes 3
Sir 45: 8 the linen breeches, the long robe, and the ephod. 2

many-colored robe 1. רִקְמָה

Ps 45:14 in many-colored robes she is led to the king 1

purple robe 1. *πορφύρα*

1Mc 10:20 he sent him a purple robe and a golden crown 1
2Mc 4:38 he immediately stripped off the purple robe 1

rich robe 1. פְּתִיגִיל

Isa 3:24 instead of a rich robe, a girding of sackcloth; 1

royal robe 1. מַלְכוּת

Est 5: 1 Esther put on her royal robes and stood 1

robust 1. *εὔρωστος*

Sir 30:15 and a robust body than countless riches 1

rock 1. אֶבֶן 2. סֶלַע 3. צוּר 4. כֵּף (A) 5. *πέτρα* 6. *τραχὺς τόπος* 7. petra

Gen 49:24 by the name of the Shepherd, the Rock of Israel 1
Exd 17: 6 stand before you there on the rock at Horeb; 3
6 and you shall strike the rock, and water shall 3
33:21 by me where you shall stand upon the rock; 3
22 I will put you in a cleft of the rock 3
Num20: 8 tell the rock before their eyes to yield 2
8 so you shall bring water out of the rock for them; 2
10 gathered the assembly together before the rock 2
10 shall we bring forth water for you out of this rock? 2
11 Moses . . struck the rock with his rod twice; 2
24:21 your nest is set in the rock; 2
Deu 8:15 who brought you water out of the flinty rock 3
32: 4 The Rock, his work is perfect; for all his ways 3
13 he made him suck honey out of the rock, and oil 2
13 made him suck . . oil out of the flinty rock. 3
15 then he . . scoffed at the Rock of his salvation. 3
18 You were unmindful of the Rock that begot you 3
30 unless their Rock had sold them 3
31 For their rock is not as our Rock 3
31 For their rock is not as our Rock 3
37 'Where . . gods, the rock in which they took refuge 3
Jdg 6:20 the meat and . . cakes, and put them on this rock 2
21 there sprang up fire from the rock and consumed 3
7:25 they killed Oreb at the rock of Oreb, and Zeeb they 3
13:19 and offered it upon the rock to the LORD 3
15: 8 down and stayed in the cleft of the rock of Etam. 2
11 Judah went down to the cleft of the rock of Etam 2
13 they bound him . . and brought him up from the rock. 2
20:45 fled toward the wilderness to the rock of Rimmon; 2
47 fled toward the wilderness to the rock of Rimmon 2
47 and abode at the rock of Rimmon four months. 2
21:13 the Benjaminites who were at the rock of Rimmon 2
1Sm 2: 2 none besides thee; there is no rock like our God. 3
13: 6 hid . . in caves and in holes and in rocks 2
23:25 David was told; therefore he went down to the rock 2
28 therefore that place was called the Rock of Escape 2
24: 2 seek David . . in front of the Wildgoats' Rocks. 3
2Sm 21:10 sackcloth, and spread it for herself on the rock 3
22: 2 The LORD is my rock . . my fortress . . my deliverer 2
3 my God, my rock, in whom I take refuge, my shield 3
32 For who is God . . ? And who is a rock, except our God? 3
47 and blessed be my rock, and exalted be my God 3
47 and exalted be my God, the rock of my salvation 3
23: 3 the Rock of Israel has said to me: When one rules 3
1Kg 19:11 rent the mountains, and broke in pieces the rocks 2
1Ch 11:15 to the rock to David at the cave of Adullam 3
2Ch 25:12 took them to the top of a rock and threw them down 2
12 threw them down from the top of the rock; 2
Neh 9:15 water for them from the rock for their thirst 2
Job 8:17 about the stoneheap; he lives among the rocks. 1
14:18 the rock is removed from its place; 3
18: 4 or the rock be removed out of its place? 3
19:24 they were graven in the rock for ever! 3
24: 8 and cling to the rock for want of shelter. 3
28:10 He cuts out channels in the rocks 3
29: 6 the rock poured out for me streams of oil! 3
30: 6 must dwell, in holes of the earth and of the rocks. 4
39:28 On the rock he dwells and makes his home 2
Ps 18: 2 The LORD is my rock, and my fortress 2
2 my fortress, and my deliverer, my God, my rock 3
31 who is a rock, except our God?– 3
46 The LORD lives; and blessed be my rock 3
19:14 in thy sight, O LORD, my rock and my redeemer. 3
27: 5 he will set me high upon a rock. 3
28: 1 To thee, O LORD, I call; my rock, be not deaf to me 3
31: 2 Be thou a rock of refuge for me, a strong fortress 3
3 Yea, thou art my rock and my fortress; 2
40: 2 set my feet upon a rock, making my steps secure. 2
42: 9 I say to God, my rock: "Why hast thou forgotten me? 2
61: 2 Lead thou me to the rock that is higher than I; 3
62: 2 He only is my rock and my salvation, my fortress; 3
6 He only is my rock and my salvation, my fortress; 3
7 my mighty rock, my refuge is God. 3
71: 3 Be thou to me a rock of refuge, a strong fortress 3
3 a strong fortress, to save me, for thou art my rock 2
78:15 He cleft rocks in the wilderness 3
16 He made streams come out of the rock 2
20 He smote the rock so that water gushed out 3
35 They remembered that God was their rock 3
81:16 with honey from the rock I would satisfy you. 3
89:26 my Father, my God, and the Rock of my salvation.' 3
92:15 my rock, and there is no unrighteousness in him. 3
94:22 my God the rock of my refuge. 3
95: 1 make a joyful noise to the rock of our salvation! 3
104:18 rocks are a refuge for the badgers. 2
105:41 He opened the rock, and water gushed forth; 3
114: 8 who turns the rock into a pool of water 3
137: 9 little ones and dashes them against the rock! 2
141: 7 rock which one cleaves and shatters on the land •
144: 1 Blessed be the LORD, my rock, who trains my hands 3
2 my rock and my fortress, my stronghold •
Prv 30:19 way of a serpent on a rock, the way of a ship 3
26 yet they make their homes in the rocks; 2
Sng 2:14 O my dove, in the clefts of the rock, in the covert 2
Isa 2:10 Enter into the rock, and hide in the dust 3
19 shall enter the caves of the rocks and the holes 3
21 to enter the caverns of the rocks and the clefts 3
7:19 the steep ravines, and in the clefts of the rocks 2
8:14 a rock of stumbling to both houses of Israel 3
10:26 as when he smote Mid'ian at the rock of Oreb; 3
17:10 and have not remembered the Rock of your refuge; 3
22:16 carve a habitation for yourself in the rock? 2
26: 4 for ever, for the LORD GOD is an everlasting rock. 3
30:29 to the mountain of the LORD, to the Rock of Israel. 3
31: 9 His rock shall pass away in terror 2
32: 2 like the shade of a great rock in a weary land. 2
33:16 his . . defense will be the fortresses of rocks; 2
44: 8 a God besides me? There is no Rock; I know not any. 3
48:21 he made water flow for them from the rock; 3
21 he cleft the rock and the water gushed out. 3
51: 1 look to the rock from which you were hewn 3
57: 5 valleys, and under the clefts of the rocks? 2
Jer 4:29 they enter thickets; they climb among rocks; 4
5: 3 They have made their faces harder than rock; 2
13: 4 and hide it there in a cleft of the rock. 2
16:16 and every hill, and out of the clefts of the rocks. 2
21:13 I am against you . . O rock of the plain 3
23:29 and like a hammer which breaks the rock in pieces? 2
48:28 Leave the cities, and dwell in the rock 2
49:16 you who live in the clefts of the rock 2
Ezk 24: 7 she put it on the bare rock 2
8 I have set on the bare rock the blood she has shed 2
26: 4 scrape her soil from her, and make her a bare rock. 2
14 I will make you a bare rock; 2
Ams 6:12 Do horses run upon rocks? Does one plow the sea 2
Obd 1: 3 you who live in the clefts of the rock 2
Nah 1: 6 and the rocks are broken asunder by him. 3
Hab 1:12 O Rock, hast established them for chastisement. 3
Mat 7:24 like a wise man who built his house upon the rock; 5
25 because it had been founded on the rock. 5
16:18 on this rock I will build my church 5
27:51 the earth shook, and the rocks were split; 5
60 his own new tomb, which he had hewn in the rock; 5
Mrk 15:46 a tomb which had been hewn out of the rock 5
Lke 6:48 who dug deep, and laid the foundation upon rock; 5
8: 6 some fell on the rock 5
13 the ones on the rock 5
Act 27:29 fearing that we might run on the rocks 6
Rom 9:33 make men stumble, a rock that will make them fall; 5
1Co 10: 4 they drank from the supernatural Rock 5
4 the Rock was Christ. 5
1Pe 2: 8 a rock that will make them fall 5
Rev 6:15 hid . . among the rocks of the mountains 5
16 calling to the mountains and the rocks, "Fall on us 5
2Es 1:20 did I not cleave the rock 7
16:28 in thick groves and clefts in the rocks. 7
Jdt 16:15 at thy presence the rocks shall melt like wax 5
Wis 11: 4 water was given them out of flinty rock 5
17:19 the harsh crash of rocks hurled down 5
Sir 40:15 they are unhealthy roots upon sheer rock. 5
48:17 he tunneled the sheer rock with iron •
2Mc 14:45 standing upon a steep rock 5

rock (2) 1. רעשׁ
2Sm 22: 8 Then the earth reeled and rocked; 1
Ps 18: 7 Then the earth reeled and rocked; 1
2Es 6:29 where I was standing began to rock to and fro ‡
rock *See* flinty.

rock badger 1. שָׁפָן
Lev 11: 5 the rock badger, because it chews the cud 1
Deu 14: 7 not eat . . the camel, the hare, and the rock badger 1

rock-hewn 1. λαξευτός
Lke 23:53 and laid him in a rock-hewn tomb 1

rocky 1. סֶלַע
1Sm 14: 4 there was a rocky crag on the one side 1
4 on the one side and a rocky crag on the other side; 1
Job 39:28 makes his home in the fastness of the rocky crag. 1
rocky *See also* ground.

rod 1. חֹטֶר 2. מַטֶּה 3. מַקֵּל 4. שֵׁבֶט 5. κάλαμος 6. ῥάβδος
Gen 30:37 Then Jacob took fresh rods of poplar and almond 3
37 in them, exposing the white of the rods. 3
38 He set the rods which he had peeled in front 3
39 the flocks bred in front of the rods 3
41 Jacob laid the rods in the runnels 3
41 the flock, that they might breed among the rods 3
Exd 4: 2 What is that in your hand?" He said, "A rod. 2
4 caught it, and it became a rod in his hand– 2
17 take in your hand this rod, with which you shall do 2
20 and in his hand Moses took the rod of God. 2
7: 9 Take your rod and cast it down before Pharaoh 2
10 Aaron cast down his rod before Pharaoh 2
12 For every man cast down his rod, and they became 2
12 But Aaron's rod swallowed up their rods. 2
12 But Aaron's rod swallowed up their rods. 2
15 take . . the rod which was turned into a serpent. 2
17 strike . . the Nile with the rod that is in my hand 2
19 Say to Aaron, 'Take your rod and stretch out 2
20 he lifted up the rod and struck the water that was 2
8: 5 Stretch out your hand with your rod over 2
16 Say to Aaron, 'Stretch out your rod and strike 2
17 Aaron stretched out his hand with his rod 2
9:23 Moses stretched forth his rod toward heaven; 2
10:13 So Moses stretched forth his rod over the land 2
14:16 Lift up your rod, and stretch out your hand over 2
17: 5 take . . the rod with which you struck the Nile 2
9 I will stand . . with the rod of God in my hand. 2
21:20 strikes his slave . . with a rod and the slave 4
Num17: 2 get from them rods, one for each fathers' house 2
2 get from them . . twelve rods. 2
2 Write each man's name upon his rod 2
3 write Aaron's name upon the rod of Levi. 2
3 For there shall be one rod for the head of each 2
5 the rod of the man whom I choose shall sprout; 2
6 their leaders gave him rods, one for each leader 2
6 according to their fathers' houses, twelve rods; 2
6 the rod of Aaron was among their rods. 2
6 the rod of Aaron was among their rods. 2
7 Moses deposited the rods before the LORD 2
8 rod of Aaron . . had sprouted and put forth buds 2
9 Moses brought out all the rods from before 2
9 they looked, and each man took his rod. 2
10 Put back the rod of Aaron before the testimony 2
20: 8 Take the rod, and assemble the congregation 2
9 Moses took the rod from before the LORD 2
11 Moses . . struck the rock with his rod twice; 2
2Sm 7:14 I will chasten him with the rod of men 4
Job 9:34 Let him take his rod away from me 4
21: 9 safe from fear, and no rod of God is upon them. 4
Ps 2: 9 You shall break them with a rod of iron 4
23: 4 thy rod and thy staff, they comfort me. 4
89:32 I will punish their transgression with the rod 4
Prv 10:13 but a rod is for the back of him who lacks sense. 4
13:24 He who spares the rod hates his son 4
14: 3 The talk of a fool is a rod for his back 1
22: 8 rod of his fury will fail. 4
15 but the rod of discipline drives it far from him. 4
23:13 if you beat him with a rod, he will not die. 4
14 beat him with the rod . . save his life from Sheol. 4
26: 3 bridle for the ass, and a rod for the back of fools. 4
29:15 The rod and reproof give wisdom 4
Isa 9: 4 staff for his shoulder, the rod of his oppressor 4
10: 5 Ah, Assyria, the rod of my anger, the staff of my fury! 4
15 As if a rod should wield him who lifts it 4
24 the Assyrians when they smite with the rod 4
26 his rod will be over the sea, and he will lift it 2
11: 4 he shall smite the earth with the rod of his mouth 4
14:29 that the rod which smote you is broken 4
28:27 beaten out with a stick, and cummin with a rod. 2
30:31 the voice of the LORD, when he smites with his rod. 4
Jer 1:11 And I said, "I see a rod of almond. 3
Lam 3: 1 has seen affliction under the rod of his wrath; 4
Ezk 7:11 Violence has grown up into a rod of wickedness; 2
20:37 I will make you pass under the rod 4
21:10 we make mirth? You have despised the rod, my son 4
13 what could it do if you despise the rod? 4
Mic 5: 1 with a rod they strike upon the cheek the ruler 4
1Co 4:21 What do you wish? Shall I come to you with a rod 6
Heb 9: 4 Aaron's rod that budded 6
Rev 2:27 he shall rule them with a rod of iron 6
12: 5 one who is to rule all nations with a rod of iron 6
19:15 and he will rule them with a rod of iron; 6
21:15 And he who talked to me had a measuring rod of gold 5
16 and he measured the city with his rod 5
rod *See also* beat.

measuring rod 1. κάλαμος
Rev 11: 1 Then I was given a measuring rod like a staff 1

roebuck 1. יַחְמוּר
Deu 14: 5 the hart, the gazelle, the roebuck, the wild goat 1
1Kg 4:23 harts, gazelles, roebucks, and fatted fowl. 1

role 1. δρᾶμα
4Mc 6:17 out of cowardice we feign a role unbecoming to us! 1

roll 1. גלל 2. סבב 3. פלשׁ 4. προσκυλίω
Gen 29: 3 the shepherds would roll the stone from the mouth 1
8 the stone is rolled from the mouth of the well; 1
10 Jacob went up and rolled the stone from the well's 1
Jos 10:18 Roll great stones against the mouth of the cave 1
1Sm 14:33 roll a great stone to me here. 1
Job 30:14 they come; amid the crash they roll on. 1
Isa 9: 5 every garment rolled in blood will be burned 1
28:27 nor is a cart wheel rolled over cummin; 2
Jer 6:26 gird on sackcloth, and roll in ashes; 3
25:34 Wail, you shepherds, and cry, and roll in ashes 3
Mic 1:10 in Beth-le-aph'rah roll yourselves in the dust. 3
Mat 27:60 rolled a great stone to the door of the tomb 4
Mrk 15:46 he rolled a stone against the door of the tomb. 4

roll (2) 1. מְגִלָּה 2. κεφαλίς
Ps 40: 7 in the roll of the book it is written of me; 1
Heb 10: 7 as it is written of me in the roll of the book. 2

roll about 1. κυλίω
Mrk 9:20 he fell on the ground and rolled about 1

roll away 1. גלל 2. ἀποκυλίω
Jos 5: 9 This day I have rolled away the reproach of Egypt 1
Mrk 16: 3 Who will roll away the stone for us from the door 2
Lke 24: 2 they found the stone rolled away from the tomb 2

roll back 1. ἀνακυλίω 2. ἀποκυλίω 3. κυλίω
Mat 28: 2 came and rolled back the stone, and sat upon it. 2
Mrk 16: 4 looking up, they saw that the stone was rolled back 1
Sir 27:27 If a man does evil, it will roll back upon him 3

roll down 1. גלל
Jer 51:25 hand against you, and roll you down from the crags 1
Ams 5:24 But let justice roll down like waters 1

roll up 1. גלל 2. גלם 3. קפד 4. ἑλίσσω 5. ἐντυλίσσω
2Kg 2: 8 Eli'jah took his mantle, and rolled it up 2
Isa 34: 4 and the skies roll up like a scroll. 1
38:12 like a weaver I have rolled up my life; 3
Joh 20: 7 and the napkin . . rolled up in a place by itself. 5
Heb 1:12 like a mantle thou wilt roll them up 4
Rev 6:14 the sky vanished like a scroll that is rolled up 4

roll upward 1. אבך
Isa 9:18 and they roll upward in a column of smoke. 1
rolling *See* start.

roof 1. גַּג 2. מְקָרֶה 3. צֹהַר 4. קוֹרָה 5. δοκός 6. δῶμα 7. ὄροφος 8. στέγη
Gen 6:16 Make a roof for the ark, and finish it to a cubit 3
19: 8 for they have come under the shelter of my roof. 4
Deu 22: 8 new house, you shall make a parapet for your roof 1
Jos 2: 6 she had brought them up to the roof, and hid them 1
6 stalks . . which she had laid in order on the roof. 1
8 she came up to them on the roof 1
Jdg 9:51 and they went to the roof of the tower. 1
16:27 and on the roof there were about 3,000 men 1
1Sm 9:25 a bed was spread for Saul upon the roof, and he lay 1
26 Samuel called to Saul upon the roof 1
2Sm 11: 2 when David arose . . and was walking upon the roof 1
2 It happened . . that he saw from the roof a woman 1
16:22 So they pitched a tent for Ab'salom upon the roof; 1
18:24 and the watchman went up to the roof of the gate 1
2Kg 23:12 altars on the roof of the upper chamber of Ahaz 1
Neh 8:16 themselves, each on his roof, and in their courts 1
Ecc 10:18 Through sloth the roof sinks in 2
Jer 19:13 houses upon whose roofs incense has been burned 1
32:29 houses on whose roofs incense has been offered 1
Ezk 26: 8 and raise a roof of shields against you. •
Dan 4:29 walking on the roof of the royal palace of Babylon •
Zep 1: 5 bow down on the roofs to the host of the heavens; 1
Mat 8: 8 I am not worthy to have you come under my roof; 8
Mrk 2: 4 they removed the roof above him 8
Lke 5:19 they went up on the roof 6
7: 6 for I am not worthy to have you come under my roof; 8
1Es 6: 4 building this house and this roof 8
Jdt 8: 5 She set up a tent for herself on the roof of her house 6
Wis 17: 2 shut in under their roofs 7
Sir 29:22 a poor man under the shelter of his roof 5
4Mc 17: 3 Nobly set like a roof on the pillars of your sons 8
roof *See also* chamber.

roof of mouth 1. חֵךְ
Job 29:10 their tongue cleaved to the roof of their mouth. 1
Ps 137: 6 Let my tongue cleave to the roof of my mouth, if I do 1
Lam 4: 4 The tongue . . cleaves to the roof of its mouth 1
Ezk 3:26 make your tongue cleave to the roof of your mouth 1

room 1. בַּיִת 2. חֶדֶר 3. קֵן 4. תָּא 5. κοιτών 6. μονή 7. ταμεῖον 8. ταμιεῖον
Gen 6:14 ark of gopher wood; make rooms in the ark 3
1Kg 6:29 all the walls . . in the inner and outer rooms. •
30 The floor . . in the inner and outer rooms. •
1Ch 28:11 plan of . . and of the room for the mercy seat; 1
Prv 24: 4 by knowledge the rooms are filled with all 2
Ezk 8:12 in the dark, every man in his room of pictures? 5
40:12 the side rooms were six cubits on either side. 4
41: 3 Then he went into the inner room and measured •
4 he measured the length of the room, twenty cubits •
15 and the inner room and the outer vestibule •
17 to the space above the door, even to the inner room 1
17 on all the walls round about in the inner room •
Jol 2:16 Let the bridegroom leave his room 2
Mat 6: 6 when you pray, go into your room and shut the door 7
Joh 14: 2 In my Father's house are many rooms 6
Tob 7:16 Sister, make up the other room, and take her into it. 8

room (2) 1. מָקוֹם 2. τόπος 3. χωρέω
Gen 24:23 Is there room in your father's house for us 1
25 We have . . enough, and room to lodge in. 1
Isa 5: 8 add field to field, until there is no more room 1
Jer 7:32 bury in Topheth, because there is no room 1
Zec 10:10 and to Lebanon, till there is no room for them. •
Mrk 2: 2 so that there was no longer room for them 3
Lke 14:22 still there is room.' 2
Sir 16:14 He will make room for every act of mercy 2
4Mc 7: 6 which had room only for reverence and purity 3
room *See* give, guest, make, side, upper.

room for work 1. τόπος
Rom15:23 I no longer have any room for work in these regions 1

inner room 1. קֻבָּה 2. ταμεῖον
Num25: 8 went after the man of Israel into the inner room 1
2Kg 10:25 and went into the inner room of the house of Ba'al •
Mat 24:26 if they say, 'Lo, he is in the inner rooms' 2

private room 1. ταμεῖον
Lke 12: 3 what you have whispered in private rooms 1

upper room 1. עֲלִיָּה 2. ἀνάγαιον
1Ch 28:11 its houses, its treasuries, its upper rooms 1
Jer 22:13 and his upper rooms by injustice; 1
14 a great house with spacious upper rooms 1
Mrk 14:15 he will show you a large upper room 2
Lke 22:12 he will show you a large upper room furnished; 2

root 1. קֶצֶב 2. שׁרשׁ 3. שֹׁרֶשׁ 4. שֹׁרֶשׁ (A) 5. ῥίζα 6. ῥιζόω 7. radix
Deu 29:18 root bearing poisonous and bitter fruit 3
Job 8:17 His roots twine about the stoneheap; 3
14: 8 Though its root grow old in the earth 3
15:29 nor will he strike root in the earth; 7
18:16 His roots dry up beneath, and his branches wither 3
19:28 The root of the matter is found in him'; 3
28: 9 and overturns mountains by the roots. 3
29:19 my roots spread out to the waters 3
30: 4 to warm themselves the roots of the broom. 3
31:12 it would burn to the root all my increase. 2
36:30 about him, and covers the roots of the sea. 3
Prv 12: 3 root of the righteous will never be moved. 3
12 but the root of the righteous stands firm. 3
Isa 5:24 so their root will be as rottenness 3
11: 1 of Jesse, and a branch shall grow out of his roots. 3
10 the root of Jesse shall stand as an ensign 3
14:29 from the serpent's root will come forth an adder 3
30 but I will kill your root with famine 3
53: 2 a young plant, and like a root out of dry ground; 3
Jer 17: 8 like a tree . . that sends out its roots by the stream 3
Ezk 17: 6 its roots remained where it stood. 3
7 behold, this vine bent its roots toward him 3
9 Will it thrive? Will he not pull up its roots 3
9 not take . . many people to pull it from its roots. 3
31: 7 for its roots went down to abundant waters. 3
Dan 4:15 leave the stump of its roots in the earth 4
23 but leave the stump of its roots in the earth 4
26 to leave the stump of the roots of the tree 4
11: 7 branch from her roots shall arise in his place; 3
Hos 9:16 E'phraim is stricken, their root is dried up 3
14: 5 he shall strike root as the poplar, 3
Ams 2: 9 his fruit above, and his roots beneath. 3
Jon 2: 6 at the roots of the mountains. 1
Mal 4: 1 it will leave them neither root nor branch. 3
Mat 3:10 Even now the axe is laid to the root of the trees; 5
13: 6 since they had no root they withered away. 5

21 yet he has no root in himself 5
Mrk 4: 6 since it had no root it withered away. 5
17 they have no root in themselves 5
11:20 they saw the fig tree withered away to its roots. 5
Lke 3: 9 Even now the axe is laid to the root of the trees; 5
8:13 but these have no root 5
Rom 11:16 and if the root is holy, so are the branches. 5
18 remember it is not you that support the root 5
18 but the root that supports you. 5
15:12 further Isaiah says, "The root of Jesse shall come 5
Eph 3:17 being rooted and grounded in love 6
Col 2: 7 rooted and built up in him 6
1Ti 6:10 For the love of money is the root of all evils 5
Heb 12:15 no "root of bitterness" spring up 5
Rev 5: 5 the Lion . . the Root of David, has conquered 5
22:16 I am the root and the offspring of David 5
1Es 8:78 to leave to us a root and a name in thy holy place 5
87 give us such a root as this 5
88 to destroy us without leaving a root or seed 5
89 we are left as a root to this day. 5
2Es 3:22 the law . . along with the evil root 7
5:28 and dishonored the one root beyond the others 7
8:53 The root of evil is sealed up from you 7
Wis 3:15 the root of understanding does not fail. 5
4: 3 will strike a deep root or take a firm hold. 5
7:20 the powers of spirits . . and the virtues of roots; 5
15: 3 to know thy power is the root of immortality. 5
Sir 1: 6 The root of wisdom–to whom has it been revealed? 5
20 To fear the Lord is the root of wisdom 5
10:15 The Lord has plucked up the roots of the nations 5
23:25 Her children will not take root 5
40:15 they are unhealthy roots upon sheer rock. 5
47:22 he gave . . to David a root of his stock. 5
1Mc 1:10 From them came forth a sinful root 5

root *See also* take.

root out 1.נסח 2.נתשׁ 3.שׁרשׁ 4.ἐκριζόω

Job 31: 8 let what grows for me be rooted out. 3
Ps 9: 6 their cities thou hast rooted out; 2
Prv 2:22 treacherous will be rooted out of it. 1
Mic 5:14 I will root out your Ashe'rim from among you 2
2Mc 12: 7 and root out the whole community of Joppa. 4

root up 1.נתשׁ 2.ἐκριζόω

1Kg 14:15 LORD will . . root up Israel out of this good land 1
Mat 13:29 lest in gathering the weeds you root up the wheat 2
15:13 Every plant . . will be rooted up. 2
Lke 17: 6 'Be rooted up, and be planted in the sea,' 2

roots *See* pluck.

rope 1.אַגְמֹן 2.חֶבֶל 3.נִקְפָּה 4.עֲבֹת 5.βρόχος 6.ζευκτηρία 7.σχοινίον

Jos 2:15 she let them down by a rope through the window 2
Jdg 15:13 they bound him with two new ropes, and brought him 4
14 the ropes . . became as flax that has caught fire 4
16:11 If they bind me with new ropes that have not been 4
12 Deli'lah took new ropes and bound him with them 4
12 he snapped the ropes off his arms like a thread. •
2Sm 17:13 all Israel will bring ropes to that city 2
1Kg 20:31 sackcloth on our loins and ropes upon our heads 2
32 girded sackcloth . . and put ropes on their heads 2
Job 18:10 A rope is hid for him in the ground 2
39:10 Can you bind him in the furrow with ropes 4
41: 2 Can you put a rope in his nose, or pierce his jaw 1
Isa 3:24 instead of a girdle, a rope; 3
5:18 Woe to those . . who draw sin as with cart ropes 4
Jer 38: 6 the guard, letting Jeremiah down by ropes. 2
11 he let down to Jeremiah in the cistern by ropes. 2
12 and clothes between your armpits and the ropes. 2
13 Then they drew Jeremiah up with ropes 2
Act 27:32 Then the soldiers cut away the ropes of the boat 7
40 loosening the ropes that tied the rudders 6
3Mc 4: 8 their necks encircled with ropes instead of garlands 5

rose 1.חֲבַצֶּלֶת 2.ἄνθος ῥόδων 3.ῥόδον 4.rosa

Sng 2: 1 I am a rose of Sharon, a lily of the valleys. 1
2Es 2:19 mighty mountains on which roses and lilies grow; 4
Sir 24:14 like rose plants in Jericho 3
39:13 bud like a rose growing by a stream of water; 3
50: 8 like roses in the days of the first fruits 2

rose-bearing 1.ῥοδοφόρον

3Mc 7:17 Ptolemais, called "rose-bearing 1

rosebud 1.ῥόδου κάλυξ

Wis 2: 8 Let us crown ourselves with rosebuds 1

rot 1.מקק 2.רקב 3.σήπω

Prv 10: 7 but the name of the wicked will rot. 2
14:30 but passion makes the bones rot. 2
Isa 40:20 chooses for an offering wood that will not rot; 2
Zec 14:12 their flesh shall rot 1
12 their eyes shall rot in their sockets 1
12 their tongues shall rot in their mouths. 1
Jas 5: 2 Your riches have rotted 3
LJr 1:72 By the purple and linen that rot upon them 3

rot *See also* dry.

rot away 1.מקק 2.קמל 3.διαπίπτω

Isa 19: 6 and dry up, reeds and rushes will rot away. 2
34: 4 All the host of heaven shall rot away 1
2Mc 9: 9 his flesh rotted away 3

rote

Isa 29:13 fear of me is a commandment of men learned by rote; •

rotten 1.רִקָּבוֹן

Job 41:27 counts iron as straw, and bronze as rotten wood. 1

rotten thing 1.רָקָב

Job 13:28 Man wastes away like a rotten thing 1

rottenness 1.מַק 2.רָקָב

Prv 12: 4 brings shame is like rottenness in his bones. 2
Isa 3:24 Instead of perfume there will be rottenness; 1
5:24 so their root will be as rottenness 1
Hab 3:16 rottenness enters into my bones, my steps totter 2

rough 1.τραχύς

Bar 4:26 My tender sons have traveled rough roads 1

rough place 1.מַעֲקָשׁ 2.רֶכֶס

Isa 40: 4 become level, and the rough places a plain. 2
42:16 turn . . the rough places into level ground. 1

rough way 1.τραχύς

Lke 3: 5 the rough ways shall be made smooth; 1

roughly 1.עַז 2.קָשֶׁה

Gen 42: 7 like strangers and spoke roughly to them. 2
30 The man, the lord of the land, spoke roughly to us 2
1Sm 20:10 tell me if your father answers you roughly? 2
Prv 18:23 poor use entreaties . . rich answer roughly. 1

round 1.גָּלִיל 2.חַמּוּק 3.סַהַר 4.עָגוֹל סָבִיב 5.עָגֹל

1Kg 7:23 it was round, ten cubits from brim to brim 5
31 its opening was round, as a pedestal is made 5
31 and its panels were square, not round. 5
35 on the top . . was a round band half a cubit high; 5
2Ch 4: 2 molten sea; it was round, ten cubits from brim 4
Sng 5:14 His arms are rounded gold, set with jewels. 1
7: 1 Your rounded thighs are like jewels 2
2 Your navel is a rounded bowl that never lacks 3

round (2) 1.אֶל 2.סבב 3.סָבִיב 4.εἰς τὰ ὀπίσω 5.κυκλόθεν 6.κύκλος 7.περί 8.πρός

Exd 40:33 he erected the court round the tabernacle 3
Jdg 11: 3 worthless fellows collected round Jephthah 1
1Kg 6: 5 running round the walls of the house 3
Ezr 9: 4 gathered round me while I sat appalled 1
Neh 12:28 gathered . . from the circuit round Jerusalem 3
Ecc 1: 6 round and round goes the wind, and on its circuits 2
6 round and round goes the wind, and on its circuits 2
Ezk 31: 4 its rivers flow round the place of its planting 3
37: 2 he led me round among them; 3
Mat 14:35 they sent round to all that region •
18: 6 have a great millstone fastened round his neck 7
Mrk 9:42 if a great millstone were hung round his neck 7
Lke 17: 2 if a millstone were hung round his neck 7
Joh 20:14 Saying this, she turned round 4
Rom 15:19 from Jerusalem and as far round as Illyr'icum 6
Rev 4: 3 and round the throne was a rainbow 5
4 Round the throne were 24 thrones 5
6 And round the throne, on each side of the throne 6
7:11 all the angels stood round the throne 6
11 round the elders and the four living creatures 6
1Es 8:72 gathered round me, as I mourned 8

round *See* all, bend, carry, come, gather, girdle, go, hang, lead, look, press, round, run, shine, turn, whirl, wrap.

round about 1.כַּדּוּר 2.מֵסַב 3.מְסִבִּיב 4.סבב 5.סָבִיב 6.κυκλόθεν 7.κύκλος 8.κυκλόω

Gen 35: 5 fell upon the cities that were round about them 5
Exd 7:24 Egyptians dug round about the Nile for water 5
16:13 in the morning dew lay round about the camp. 5
19:12 you shall set bounds for the people round about 5
25:11 make upon it a molding of gold round about. 5
28:34 a pomegranate, round about on the skirts 5
29:16 throw it against the altar round about. 5
20 the blood against the altar round about. 5
30: 3 its top and its sides round about and its horns; 5
3 make for it a molding of gold round about. 5
37:26 with pure gold, its top, and its sides round about 5
26 and he made a molding of gold round about it 5
38:16 hangings round about the court were of . . linen. 5
20 pegs . . for the court round about were of bronze. 5
31 the bases round about the court, and the bases 5
31 and all the pegs round about the court. 5
39:25 upon the skirts of the robe round about 5
26 a pomegranate round about upon the skirts 5
40: 8 you shall set up the court round about, and hang up 5
Lev 1: 5 throw the blood round about against the altar 5
11 throw its blood against the altar round about 5
3: 2 throw the blood against the altar round about 5
8 throw its blood against the altar round about 5
13 throw its blood against the altar round about 5
7: 2 its blood shall be thrown on the altar round about 5
8:15 put it on the horns of the altar round about 5
19 threw the blood upon the altar round about 5
24 Moses threw the blood upon the altar round about 5
9:12 he threw it on the altar round about 5
18 blood, which he threw upon the altar round about 5
14:41 inside of the house to be scraped round about 5
16:18 and put it on the horns of the altar round about 5
25:44 from among the nations that are round about you 5
Num 3:37 also the pillars of the court round about 5
4:32 pillars of the court round about with their 5
11:24 70 men . . and placed them round about the tent. 5
31 let them fall . . round about the camp 5
16:34 all Israel that were round about them fled 5
22: 4 horde will now lick up all that is round about us 5
35: 2 the Levites pasture lands round about the cities 5
Deu 6:14 the gods of the peoples who are round about you 5
12:10 gives you rest from all your enemies round about 5
13: 7 gods of the people that are round about you 5
17:14 king over me, like all the nations . . round about 5
25:19 given you rest from all your enemies round about 5
Jos 15:12 This is the boundary round about the people 5
18:20 inheritance . . boundary by boundary round about. 5
19: 8 with all the villages round about these cities 5
21:11 They gave . . with the pasture lands round about 5
42 cities had each its pasture lands round about it; 5
23: 1 given rest . . from all their enemies round about 3
Jdg 2:12 the gods of the peoples who were round about them 5
14 the power of their enemies round about 3
7:21 stood every man in his place round about the camp 5
20:29 Israel set men in ambush round about Gib'e-ah. 5
1Sm 10: 1 save them from . . their enemies round about. 6
2Sm 5: 9 David built the city round about from the Millo 5
7: 1 given him rest from all his enemies round about 3
1Kg 4:24 and he had peace on all sides round about him. 3
31 his fame was in all the nations round about. 5
6:29 He carved all the walls of the house round about 2
7:12 court had three courses of hewn stone round about 5
18 in two rows round about upon the one network 5
20 200 pomegranates, in two rows round about; 5
24 were gourds . . compassing the sea round about; 5
36 he carved . . with wreaths round about. 5
18:35 the water ran round about the altar 5
2Kg 6:15 an army . . was round about the city. 4
17 horses and chariots of fire round about Eli'sha. 5
17:15 followed the nations that were round about them 5
23: 5 at the cities of Judah and round about Jerusalem; 2
25: 1 they built siegeworks against it round about. 5
17 a network . . upon the capital round about. 5
1Ch 4:33 were round about these cities as far as Ba'al. 5
9:27 they lodged round about the house of God; 5
11: 8 he built the city round about from the Millo 3
22: 9 give him peace from all his enemies round about; 3
2Ch 4: 3 gourds . . compassing the sea round about; 5
14:14 they smote all the cities round about Gerar 5
15:15 the LORD gave them rest round about. 5
17:10 lands that were round about Judah 5
20:30 for his God gave him rest round about. 5
34: 6 as far as Naph'tali, in their ruins round about 5
Neh 6:16 all the nations round about us were afraid 5
Job 19:12 against me, and encamp round about my tent. 5
22:10 Therefore snares are round about you 5
41:14 Round about his teeth is terror. 5
Ps 3: 6 who have set themselves against me round about. 5
22:16 Yea, dogs are round about me; 4
27: 6 be lifted up above my enemies round about me; 5
50: 3 round about him a mighty tempest. 5
79: 3 blood like water round about Jerusalem 5
4 mocked and derided by those round about us. 5
89: 7 great . . above all that are round about him? 5
8 O LORD, with thy faithfulness round about thee? 5
97: 2 Clouds and thick darkness are round about him; 5
3 Fire . . burns up his adversaries round about. 5
125: 2 As the mountains are round about Jerusalem 5
2 so the LORD is round about his people 5
Isa 29: 3 I will encamp against you round about 1
42:25 heat of his anger . . set him on fire round about 3
49:18 Lift up your eyes round about and see; 5
60: 4 Lift up your eyes round about, and see; 5
Jer 1:15 against all its walls round about 5
4:17 are they against her round about 3
12: 9 Are the birds of prey against her round about? 5
17:26 Judah and the places round about Jerusalem 5
21:14 and it shall devour all that is round about her. 5
25: 9 and against all these nations round about; 5
46:14 for the sword shall devour round about you. 5
48:17 Bemoan him, all you who are round about him 5
39 a horror to all that are round about him. 5
49: 5 from all who are round about you 5
50:14 Set . . in array against Babylon round about 5
15 Raise a shout against her round about 5
29 Encamp round about her; let no one escape. 5
32 it will devour all that is round about him. 5
52: 4 and built siegeworks against it round about. 5
7 while the Chalde'ans were round about the city. 5
14 broke down all the walls round about Jerusalem. 5
22 all of bronze, were upon the capital round about. 5
23 pomegranates . . upon the network round about. 5
Ezk 1: 4 a great cloud, with brightness round about it 5

18 and their rims were full of eyes round about. 5
27 the appearance of fire enclosed round about; 5
27 and there was brightness round about him. 5
28 the appearance of the brightness round about. 5
4: 2 plant battering rams against it round about. 5
5: 2 and strike with the sword round about the city; 5
5 the center . . with countries round about her. 5
6 more than the countries round about her 5
7 than the nations that are round about you 5
7 the nations that are round about you; 5
12 a third . . shall fall by the sword round about you; 5
14 of reproach among the nations round about you 5
15 a warning and a horror, to the nations round about 5
6: 5 scatter your bones round about your altars. 5
13 among their idols round about their altars 5
8:10 and there, portrayed upon the wall round about 5
10:12 the wheels were full of eyes round about 5
11:12 of the nations that are round about you. 5
12:14 toward every wind all who are round about him 5
16:57 Philistines, those round about who despise you. 5
27:11 and Helech were upon your walls round about 5
11 hung their shields upon your walls round about; 5
32:22 all her company, their graves round about her 5
23 the Pit, and her company is round about her grave; 5
25 all her multitude, their graves round about her 5
26 their multitude, their graves round about them 5
34:26 and the places round about my hill a blessing; 5
36: 4 derision to the rest of the nations round about; 5
7 I swear that the nations that are round about you 3
36 Then the nations that are left round about you 5
40:14 and round about the vestibule of the gateway was 5
16 the gateway had windows round about 5
16 the vestibule had windows round about inside 5
17 and a pavement, round about the court; 5
25 there were windows round about in it 5
29 there were windows round about in it 5
30 there were vestibules round about 5
33 there were windows round about in it 5
36 as the others; and it had windows round about; 5
43 hooks . . were fastened round about within. 5
41: 5 the side chambers . . round about the temple. 5
7 from story to story round about the temple; 5
8 the temple had a raised platform round about; 5
10 round about the temple on every side. 5
11 that was left free was five cubits round about. 5
12 the building was five cubits thick round about 5
16 and round about all three had windows 5
16 the temple was paneled with wood round about 5
17 on all the walls round about in the inner room 5
19 They were carved on the whole temple round about; 5
42:15 and measured the temple area round about. 5
43:12 the whole territory round about upon the top 5
17 and its base one cubit round about. 5
20 corners of the ledge, and upon the rim round about; 5
46:23 made at the bottom of the rows round about. 5
Dan 9:16 become a byword among all who are round about us. 5
Jol 3:11 Hasten and come, all you nations round about 3
12 I will sit to judge all the nations round about. 3
Obd 1:16 all the nations round about shall drink; 5
Jon 2: 3 heart of the seas, and the flood was round about me; 4
5 waters closed in . . the deep was round about me; 4
Zec 2: 5 For I will be to her a wall of fire round about 5
7: 7 in prosperity, with her cities round about her 5
12: 2 a cup of reeling to all the peoples round about; 5
6 right and to the left all the peoples round about 5
14:14 the wealth of all the nations round about 5
Mrk 6:36 to go into the country and villages round about 7
Lke 9:12 to go into the villages and country round about 7
Sir 45: 9 with very many golden bells round about 6
1Mc 1:11 make a covenant with the Gentiles round about us 7
3:25 terror fell upon the Gentiles round about them. 7
4: 7 with cavalry round about it 8
60 with high walls and strong towers round about 6
5: 1 When the Gentiles round about heard 6
65 and burned its towers round about. 6
7:17 their blood they poured out round about Jerusalem 7
46 men came out of all the villages of Judea round about 6
10:45 and fortifying it round about 6
12:13 the kings round about us have waged war against us. 7
53 all the nations round about them 7

round and round 1. מֵסַב
Job 37:12 They turn round and round by his guidance 1

round off 1. נקף
Lev 19:27 You shall not round off the hair on your temples 1

round up 1. *συναρπάζω*
4Mc 5: 4 when many persons had been rounded up 1

rounded *See* projection.

rouse 1. עור 2. עלה 3. קום 4. *διατίθημι* 5. *διεγείρω* 6. *ἐγείρω* 7. *ἐξεγείρω* 8. excito
Job 8: 6 surely then he will rouse himself for you 1
14:12 he will not awake, or be roused out of his sleep. 1
39:18 When she rouses herself to flee, she laughs *
Ps 44:23 Rouse thyself! Why sleepest thou, O Lord? Awake! 1
59: 4 Rouse thyself, come to my help, and see! 1
76: 7 stand before thee when once thy anger is roused? *
Isa 14: 9 when you come, it rouses the shades to greet you 1
51:17 Rouse yourself, rouse yourself, stand up 1
17 rouse yourself, stand up, O Jerusalem 1
Ezk 23:22 Behold, I will rouse against you your lovers 1
24: 8 To rouse my wrath, to take vengeance 2
38:18 says the Lord GOD, my wrath will be roused. 2
Hab 1: 6 For lo, I am rousing the Chalde'ans 3
Zec 2:13 he has roused himself from his holy dwelling. 1
2Es 7:31 the world . . shall be roused 8
Jdt 14: 3 rouse the officers of the Assyrian army 6
Sir 22: 7 who rouses a sleeper from deep slumber. 7
36: 7 Rouse thy anger and pour out thy wrath 6
3Mc 5:15 when he had with difficulty roused him 5
4Mc 8: 9 if by disobedience you rouse my anger 4

rouse up 1. עור 2. קום 3. evigilo
Gen 49: 9 as a lioness; who dares rouse him up? 2
Num24: 9 and like a lioness; who will rouse him up? 2
Job 3: 8 who are skilled to rouse up Leviathan. 1
2Es 12:31 the lion whom you saw rousing up out of the forest 3

rout 1. המם 2. נגף 3. נכה 4. נצר 5. *διαφθείρω* 6. *τροπή* 7. *τροπόω*
Gen 14:15 he and his servants, and routed them and pursued 3
Exd 14:27 the LORD routed the Egyptians in the midst 4
Jdg 4:15 the LORD routed Sis'era and all his chariots 1
20:32 said, "They are routed before us, as at the first. 2
1Sm 7:10 and they were routed before Israel. 2
2Sm 22:15 And he sent out . . lightning, and routed them. 1
2Ch 20:22 had come against Judah, so that they were routed. 2
Ps 18:14 he flashed forth lightnings, and routed them. 1
78:66 he put his adversaries to rout; †
144: 6 send out thy arrows and rout them! 1
1Mc 4:35 when Lysias saw the rout of his troops 6
5:60 Then Joseph and Azariah were routed 7
61 Thus the people suffered a great rout 6
6: 5 reported that the armies . . had been routed; 7
11:55 he fled and was routed. 7
72 he . . routed them, and they fled. 7
2Mc 12:27 After the rout and destruction of these 6
3Mc 1: 5 the enemy was routed in the action 5

rout *See also* put.

route 1. דֶּרֶךְ 2. *ὁδός*
Jdg 8:11 went up by the caravan route east of Nobah 1
1Mc 11: 4 they had piled them in heaps along his route. 2

rove 1. *ῥεμβασμός*
Wis 4:12 roving desire perverts the innocent mind. 1

row 1. אָפִיק 2. טוּר 3. טִירָה 4. מִלֻּאָה 5. מַעֲרֶכֶת 6. פנה 7. שׂוּרָה
Exd 28:17 you shall set in it four rows of stones. 4
17 A row of sardius, topaz, and carbuncle shall be 2
17 topaz, and carbuncle shall be the first row; 2
18 the second row an emerald, a sapphire 2
19 the third row a jacinth, an agate, and an amethyst; 2
20 the fourth row a beryl, an onyx, and a jasper; 2
39:10 they set in it four rows of stones. 2
10 A row of sardius, topaz, and carbuncle 2
10 of sardius, topaz, and carbuncle was the first row; 2
11 the second row, an emerald, a sapphire 2
12 the third row, a jacinth, an agate, and an amethyst; 2
13 the fourth row, a beryl, an onyx, and a jasper; 2
Lev 24: 6 you shall set them in two rows, six in a row 5
6 set them . . six in a row, upon the table 5
7 you shall put pure frankincense with each row 5
1Kg 7: 2 it was built upon three rows of cedar pillars 2
3 upon the 45 pillars, fifteen in each row. 2
4 There were window frames in three rows 2
18 in two rows round about upon the one network 2
20 200 pomegranates, in two rows round about; 2
24 the gourds were in two rows, cast with it 2
42 two rows of pomegranates for each network 2
2Ch 4: 3 gourds were in two rows, cast with it when it was 2
13 two rows of pomegranates for each network 2
Job 41:15 His back is made of rows of shields 1
Isa 28:25 put in wheat in rows and barley in its proper 7
Ezk 46:19 north row of the holy chambers for the priests; 6
23 a row of masonry, with hearths made at the bottom 2
23 with hearths made at the bottom of the rows 3

row (2) 1. חתר 2. *ἐλαύνω*
Jon 1:13 the men rowed hard to bring the ship back to land 1
Joh 6:19 When they had rowed about three or four miles 2

olive row 1. שׂוּרָה
Job 24:11 among the olive rows of the wicked they make oil; 1

rower 1. שׁוט
Ezk 27: 8 inhabitants of Sidon and Arvad were your rowers; 1
26 rowers have brought you out into the high seas. 1

royal 1. לַמֶּלֶךְ 2. מְלָאכָה 3. מְלוּכָה 4. מֶלֶךְ 5. מַלְכוּת 6. מַמְלָכָה 7. מֶלֶךְ (A) 8. מַלְכוּ (A) 9. מַלְכוּת (A) 10. *βασιλεία* 11. *βασίλειος* 12. *βασιλεύς* 13. *βασιλικός*
Gen 49:20 be rich, and he shall yield royal dainties. 4
Jos 10: 2 Gibeon was a . . city, like one of the royal cities 6
1Sm 27: 5 why should . . dwell in the royal city with you? 6
2Sm 12:26 Jo'ab fought against . . and took the royal city. 3
1Kg 1: 9 he invited . . and all the royal officials of Judah 4
46 Solomon sits upon the royal throne. 3
9: 5 I will establish your royal throne over Israel 6
11:14 Hadad . . he was of the royal house in Edom. 4
2Kg 11: 1 she arose and destroyed all the royal family. 6
25:25 Ish'mael the son of . . of the royal family, came 3
1Ch 22:10 I will establish his royal throne in Israel 5
29:25 and bestowed upon him such royal majesty 5
2Ch 2: 1 to build a temple . . and a royal palace 5
12 who will build . . a royal palace for himself. 5
7:18 then I will establish your royal throne 5
22:10 destroyed all the royal family of . . Judah. 6
23:20 And they set the king upon the royal throne 6
25:16 Have we made you a royal counselor? 1
Ezr 4:13 will not pay . . royal revenue will be impaired. 7
5:17 let search be made in the royal archives there 7
6: 4 let the cost be paid from the royal treasury. 7
8 in full and without delay from the royal revenue 7
Est 1: 2 when . . Ahasu-e'rus sat on his royal throne in Susa 5
4 while he showed the riches of his royal glory 5
7 and the royal wine was lavished 5
11 to bring Queen Vashti . . with her royal crown 5
19 let a royal order go forth from him 5
19 let the king give her royal position to another 5
22 he sent letters to all the royal provinces 4
2:16 Esther was taken . . into his royal palace 5
17 he set the royal crown on her . . and made her queen 5
18 He also . . and gave gifts with royal liberality. 4
5: 1 The king was sitting on his royal throne inside 5
6: 8 let royal robes be brought . . and the horse 5
8 and on whose head a royal crown is set; 5
8:15 Mor'decai went . . in royal robes of blue and white 5
9: 3 governors and the royal officials also helped 2
Ps 45: 6 Your royal scepter is a scepter of equity; 5
72: 1 O God, and thy righteousness to the royal son! 4
Isa 62: 3 and a royal diadem in the hand of your God. 3
Jer 41: 1 son of Eli'shama, of the royal family 3
Ezk 17:13 he took one of the seed royal and made a covenant 3
Dan 4:29 walking on the roof of the royal palace of Babylon 9
30 built by my mighty power as a royal residence 8
6:26 all my royal dominion men tremble and fear 9
11:21 contemptible person to whom royal majesty 5
Zec 6:13 and shall bear royal honor, and shall sit and rule *
Act 12:21 On an appointed day Herod put on his royal robes 13
Jas 2: 8 If you really fulfill the royal law 13
1Pe 2: 9 you are a chosen race, a royal priesthood 11
1Es 1:54 treasure chests of the Lord, and the royal stores 13
6:21 let search be made in the royal archives 13
23 royal archives that were deposited in Babylon. 13
8:18 you may provide out of the royal treasury. 13
67 to the royal stewards and to the governors 13
Jdt 2:18 gold and silver from the royal palace. 12
AEs 15: 6 He was seated on his royal throne 10
16:11 the person second to the royal throne. 13
Wis 18:15 from heaven, from the royal throne 11
Bar 5: 6 carried in glory, as on a royal throne. 10
1Mc 3:32 Lysias, a distinguished man of royal lineage 10
6:43 one of the beasts was equipped with royal armor. 13
47 when the Jews saw the royal might 10
7: 2 he was entering the royal palace of his fathers 10
15: 8 Every debt you owe to the royal treasury 13
2Mc 4:11 He set aside the existing royal concessions 13
3Mc 3:28 2,000 drachmas from the royal treasury 13
7:12 freely and without royal authority 13
4Mc 3: 8 he came . . to the royal tent 11

royal *See also* authority, canopy, power, prince, robe, stud, tax, treasury.

more royal 1. *βασιλικός*
4Mc 14: 2 O reason, more royal than kings 1

rub 1. *διατρίβω* 2. *ψώχω*
Lke 6: 1 rubbing them in their hands. 2
Tob 11: 8 when they smart he will rub them 1
12 when his eyes began to smart he rubbed them 1

rub bare 1. מרט
Ezk 29:18 was made bald and every shoulder was rubbed bare; 1

rub with salt 1. מלח
Ezk 16: 4 nor rubbed with salt, nor swathed with bands. 1

rubbish 1. עָפָר 2. *περίψημα*
Neh 4: 2 revive the stones out of the heaps of rubbish 1
10 strength . . is failing, and there is much rubbish; 1
Tob 5:18 consider it as rubbish as compared to our child. 2

ruby 1. *ἄνθραξ*
Tob 13:17 beryl and ruby and stones of Ophir; 1
Sir 32: 5 A ruby seal in a setting of gold 1

rudder 1. *οἴαξ* 2. *πηδάλιον*
Act 27:40 loosening the ropes that tied the rudders 2

Jas 3: 4 they are guided by a very small rudder 2
4Mc 7: 3 in no way did he turn the rudder of religion 1

ruddy 1. אדם 2. אָדֹם 3. אַדְמוֹנִי
1Sm 16:12 Now he was ruddy, and had beautiful eyes, and was 3
17:42 was but a youth, ruddy and comely in appearance. 3
Sng 5:10 My beloved is all radiant and ruddy 2
Lam 4: 7 their bodies were more ruddy than coral 1

rude 1. *ἀσχημονέω*
1Co 13: 5 it is not arrogant or rude 1

more rudely 1. *ἄγροικος*
2Mc 14:30 meeting him more rudely than had been his custom 1

rue 1. *πήγανον*
Lke 11:42 you tithe mint and rue and every herb 1

rug 1. צָפִית 2. שְׂמִיכָה
Jdg 4:18 into the tent, and she covered him with a rug. 2
Isa 21: 5 They prepare the table, they spread the rugs 1

rugged 1. בֶּתֶר
Sng 2:17 or a young stag upon rugged mountains. 1

ruin 1. אבד 2. בלק 3. הַוָּה 4. הרס 5. חבל 6. חֹרֶב 7. חָרְבָּה 8. יצת 9. ישם 10. כאב 11. כשל 12. מִדְחֶה 13. מְחִתָּה 14. מִכְשׁוֹל 15. מַפֵּלָה 16. מַפֶּלֶת 17. מַשּׁוּאוֹת 18. נכה 19. עַוָּה 20. פִּיד 21. רַע 22. רָעָה 23. שֶׁבֶר 24. שדד 25. שׁוֹאָה 26. שחת 27. שמם 28. *ἀπόλλυμι* 29. *ἀπώλεια* 30. *ἐξολέθρευσις* 31. *καταστροφή* 32. *ὄλεθρος* 33. *πτῶμα* 34. *πτῶσις* 35. *ῥῆγμα* 36. *σύντριμμα* 37. *φθείρω* 38. confringo 39. corrumpo 40. direptio 41. vasto
Exd 8:24 the land was ruined by reason of flies. 26
9:31 The flax and the barley were ruined 18
32 the wheat and the spelt were not ruined 18
10: 7 do you not yet understand that Egypt is ruined? 1
2Sm 16: 8 See, your ruin is on you; for you are a man of blood. 22
2Kg 3:19 and ruin every good piece of land with stones. 10
2Ch 28:23 But they were the ruin of him, and of all Israel. 11
Job 31:29 If I have rejoiced at the ruin of him that hated me 20
Ps 35: 8 Let ruin come upon them unawares! 25
8 let them fall therein to ruin! 25
38:12 those who seek my hurt speak of ruin 3
55:11 ruin is in its midst; 3
73:18 thou dost make them fall to ruin. 17
Prv 3:25 Do not be afraid . . of the ruin of the wicked •
5:14 point of utter ruin in the assembled congregation. 21
10:14 but the babbling of a fool brings ruin near. 13
15 the poverty of the poor is their ruin. 13
13: 3 he who opens wide his lips comes to ruin. 13
15 but the way of the faithless is their ruin. •
14:28 but without people a prince is ruined. 13
18: 7 A fool's mouth is his ruin 13
19:13 A foolish son is ruin to his father 3
21:12 wicked are cast down to ruin. 21
24:22 who knows the ruin that will come from them both? 20
26:28 flattering mouth works ruin. 12
29: 4 but one who exacts gifts ruins it. 4
Isa 23:13 they razed her palaces, they made her a ruin. 15
25: 2 made the city a heap, the fortified city a ruin; 15
32: 7 he devises wicked devices to ruin the poor 5
47:11 ruin shall come on you suddenly 25
61: 4 they shall repair the ruined cities 6
Jer 4:13 woe to us, for we are ruined! 24
9:12 Why is the land ruined and laid waste 1
19 How we are ruined! We are utterly shamed 24
25:11 This whole land shall become a ruin and a waste 7
46:19 For Memphis shall become a waste, a ruin 8
Lam 2: 9 he has ruined and broken her bars; 1
13 For vast as the sea is your ruin; who can restore you? 23
Ezk 6: 6 your cities . . waste and your high places ruined 9
6 so that your altars will be waste and ruined 38
18:30 Repent and turn . . lest iniquity be your ruin. 14
21:27 A ruin, ruin, ruin I will make it; 19
27 A ruin, ruin, ruin I will make it; 19
27 A ruin, ruin, ruin I will make it; 19
27:27 into the heart of the seas on the day of your ruin. 16
31:13 Upon its ruin will dwell all the birds of the air 16
36:35 the waste and desolate and ruined cities 4
36 I, the LORD, have rebuilt the ruined places, 4
Jol 1:17 the granaries are ruined 4
Ams 6: 6 but are not grieved over the ruin of Joseph! 23
9:14 and they shall rebuild the ruined cities 27
Obd 1:12 the people of Judah in the day of their ruin; 1
Mic 2: 4 We are utterly ruined; he changes the portion 24
Nah 2: 2 have stripped them and ruined their branches. 26
10 Desolate! Desolation and ruin! Hearts faint 2
Zep 1:15 a day of ruin and devastation, a day of darkness 25
Zec 11: 2 for the glorious trees are ruined! 24
Lke 6:49 the ruin of that house was great. 35
Rom 3:16 in their paths are ruin and misery 36
1Co 15:33 Bad company ruins good morals. 37
1Ti 6: 9 plunge men into ruin and destruction. 32
2Ti 2:14 which does no good, but only ruins the hearers. 31
2Es 2: 6 and bring their mother to ruin 40
8:43 or if it has been ruined by too much rain 39
15:13 and their trees shall be ruined by blight 41
Tob 4:13 For in pride there is ruin and great confusion; 29
Jdt 13:20 have avenged our ruin 33
Sir 1:22 a man's anger tips the scale to his ruin. 34
4:19 hand him over to his ruin. 34
8: 2 gold has ruined many 28
10: 3 An undisciplined king will ruin his people 28
20:25 the lot of both is ruin. 29
29:18 Being surety has ruined many men 28
31: 6 Many have come to ruin because of gold 33
50: 4 He considered how to save his people from ruin 34
Bar 4:33 rejoiced at your fall and was glad for your ruin 33
1Mc 2: 7 the ruin of my people, the ruin of the holy city 36
7 the ruin of my people, the ruin of the holy city 36
49 it is a time of ruin and furious anger. 31
7: 7 see all the ruin which Judas has brought upon us 30

ruin *See also* bring, come, go.

cause ruin 1. *ἀπόλλυμι*
Rom 14:15 Do not let what you eat cause the ruin of one 1

ruined *See* house.

ruins 1. הֲרִיסָה 2. חָרֵב 3. חָרְבָּה 4. יצת 5. מְחִתָּה 6. מַפָּלָה 7. מַשּׁוּאוֹת 8. נצה 9. עִי 10. שְׁאִיָּה 11. שמם 12. שְׁמָמָה 13. נְוָלוּ (A) 14. *ἔρημος* 15. *καθαιρέω* 16. *κατασκάπτω*
Jos 8:28 burned Ai, and made it for ever a heap of ruins 12
2Kg 19:25 you . . turn fortified cities into heaps of ruins 8
2Ch 34: 6 as far as Naph'tali, in their ruins round about 3
Ezr 9: 9 to repair its ruins, and to give us protection 3
Job 3:14 of the earth who rebuilt ruins for themselves 3
Ps 9: 6 The enemy have vanished in everlasting ruins; 3
74: 3 Direct thy steps to the perpetual ruins; 7
79: 1 heathen . . have laid Jerusalem in ruins. 9
89:40 thou hast laid his strongholds in ruins. 5
109:10 may they be driven out of the ruins they inhabit! 3
Isa 5:17 fatlings and kids shall feed among the ruins. 3
17: 1 cease to be a city, and will become a heap of ruins. 6
24:12 in the city, the gates are battered into ruins. 10
37:26 make fortified cities crash into heaps of ruins 8
44:26 be built, and I will raise up their ruins'; 3
58:12 And your ancient ruins shall be rebuilt; 3
61: 4 They shall build up the ancient ruins 3
64:11 and all our pleasant places have become ruins. 3
Jer 2:15 his cities are in ruins, without inhabitant. 4
4: 7 your cities will be ruins without inhabitant. 8
Ezk 13: 4 Your prophets have been like foxes among ruins 3
26:20 dwell in the nether world, among primeval ruins 3
Dan 2: 5 torn . . and your houses shall be laid in ruins. 13
3:29 limb from limb, and their houses laid in ruins; 13
Ams 9:11 and repair its breaches, and raise up its ruins 1
Zep 3: 6 their battlements are in ruins; 11
Hag 1: 4 while this house lies in ruins? 2
9 Because of my house that lies in ruins 2
Mal 1: 4 We are shattered but we will rebuild the ruins 3
Act 15:16 I will rebuild its ruins, and I will set it up 16
Tob 14: 4 will be in ruins for a time. 14
1Mc 4:38 They saw also the chambers of the priests in ruins. 15

ruins *See also* heap, lay, lie.

rule 1. בעל 2. דין 3. יָד 4. מַלְכוּת 5. מֶמְשָׁלָה 6. מִשְׁטָר 7. משל 8. מֹשֶׁל 9. עצר 10. רדה 11. רעה 12. שׂרר 13. שפט 14. שלט (A) 15. שַׁלִּיט (A) 16. *ἀνίστημι* 17. *ἀρχή* 18. *ἄρχω* 19. *βασιλεία* 20. *βασιλεύς* 21. *βασιλεύω* 22. *βραβεύω* 23. *δεσποτεύω* 24. *διέπω* 25. *διοικέω* 26. *δυναστεύω* 27. *ἐξουσία* 28. *ἡγεμονία* 29. *κρατέω* 30. *κράτος* 31. *κρίνω* 32. *κυριεύω* 33. *ποιμαίνω* 34. *προΐστημι* 35. *προκάθημαι* 36. *πρύτανις* 37. dominor 38. principatus 39. regno 40. teneo 41. teneo principatum
Gen 1:16 the greater light to rule the day 5
16 the lesser light to rule the night; 5
18 to rule over the day and over the night 7
Lev 25:43 You shall not rule over him with harshness 10
46 you shall not rule, one over another 10
26:17 those who hate you shall rule over you 10
Deu 15: 6 rule over many nations, but they shall not rule 7
6 rule . . nations, but they shall not rule over you. 7
Jos 12: 2 who dwelt at Heshbon, and ruled from Aro'er 7
5 and ruled over Mount Hermon and Sal'ecah 7
Jdg 8:22 Then the men of Israel said to Gideon, "Rule over us 7
23 Gideon said to them, "I will not rule over you 7
23 not rule over you, and my son will not rule over you; 7
23 not rule over you; the LORD will rule over you. 7
9: 2 that all 70 of the sons of Jerubba'al rule over you 7
2 70 . . rule over you, or that one rule over you?' 7
22 Abim'elech ruled over Israel three years. 12
Rut 1: 1 In the days when the judges ruled 13
1Sm 9:17 He it is who shall rule over my people. 9
2Sm 23: 3 When one rules justly over men 7
3 When one rules justly . . ruling in the fear of God 7
1Kg 4:21 Solomon ruled over all the kingdoms 7
2Kg 8:20 In his days Edom revolted from the rule of Judah 3
22 Edom revolted from the rule of Judah to this day. 3
1Ch 4:22 Saraph, who ruled in Moab and returned to Lehem 1
29:12 and thou rulest over all. 7
30 with accounts of all his rule and his might 4
2Ch 1:10 who can rule this thy people, that is so great? 13
11 may rule my people over whom I have made you king 13
7:18 'There shall not fail you a man to rule Israel.' 7
9:26 he ruled over all the kings from the Euphra'tes 7
12: 1 rule of Rehobo'am was established and was strong 4
20: 6 not rule over all the kingdoms of the nations? 7
21: 8 In his days Edom revolted from the rule of Judah 3
10 Edom revolted from the rule of Judah to this day. 3
10 At that time Libnah also revolted from his rule 3
22: 9 had no one able to rule the kingdom. •
Ezr 4:20 ruled over the whole province Beyond the River 15
Job 38:33 Can you establish their rule on the earth? 6
Ps 22:28 to the LORD, and he rules over the nations. 7
59:13 that men may know that God rules over Jacob 7
66: 7 who rules by his might for ever 7
89: 9 Thou dost rule the raging of the sea; 7
103:19 his kingdom rules over all. 7
106:41 so that those who hated them ruled over them. 7
110: 2 Rule in the midst of your foes! 10
136: 8 the sun to rule over the day 5
9 the moon and stars to rule over the night 5
Prv 8:16 by me princes rule, and nobles govern the earth. 12
12:24 The hand of the diligent will rule 7
16:32 he who rules his spirit than he who takes a city. 7
17: 2 A slave who deals wisely will rule over a son 7
19:10 much less for a slave to rule over princes. 7
22: 7 The rich rules over the poor 7
29: 2 but when the wicked rule, the people groan. 7
Isa 3: 4 boys . . princes, and babes shall rule over them. 7
6 this heap of ruins shall be under your rule"; 3
12 are their oppressors, and women rule over them. 7
14: 2 captors, and rule over those who oppressed them. 10
6 that ruled the nations in anger 10
19: 4 a fierce king will rule over them 7
28:14 you scoffers, who rule this people in Jerusalem! 7
32: 1 and princes will rule in justice. 12
40:10 GOD comes with might, and his arm rules for him; 7
51: 5 has gone forth, and my arms will rule the peoples; 13
63:19 like those over whom thou hast never ruled 7
Jer 5:31 and the priests rule at their direction; 10
22:30 on the throne of David, and ruling again in Judah. 7
33:26 will not choose one of his descendants to rule 7
Lam 5: 8 Slaves rule over us; there is none to deliver us 7
Ezk 29:15 they will never again rule over the nations. 10
34: 4 with force and harshness you have ruled them. 10
Dan 2:39 kingdom of bronze . . rule over all the earth. 14
4:17 know that the Most High rules the kingdom of men 15
25 know that the Most High rules the kingdom of men 15
26 from the time that you know that Heaven rules. 15
32 Most High rules the kingdom of men 15
5:21 knew . . Most High God rules the kingdom of men 15
8:23 at the latter end of their rule 4
9:12 against us and against our rulers who ruled us 13
11: 3 rule with great dominion and do according 7
4 nor according to the dominion with which he ruled 8
Obd 1:21 shall go up to Mount Zion to rule Mount Esau; 13
Mic 5: 6 they shall rule the land of Assyria 11
Zec 3: 7 and keep my charge, then you shall rule my house 2
6:13 and shall sit and rule upon his throne. 7
Mrk 10:42 those who are supposed to rule over the Gentiles 18
Rom 15:12 he who rises to rule the Gentiles; 18
1Co 15:24 after destroying every rule 17
Eph 1:21 far above all rule and authority and power 17
Col 2:10 the head of all rule and authority. 17
3:15 let the peace of Christ rule in your hearts 22
1Ti 5:17 the elders who rule well 34
Rev 2:27 he shall rule them with a rod of iron 33
12: 5 one who is to rule all nations with a rod of iron 33
19:15 and he will rule them with a rod of iron; 33
1Es 2:27 mighty and cruel kings ruled in Jerusalem 32
9: 4 the decision of the ruling elders 35
2Es 5: 3 the land which you now see ruling 39
11:16 Hear me, you who have ruled the earth all this time; 40
17 After you no one shall rule as long as you 40
18 and held the rule like the former ones 38
20 also rose up . . in order to rule 41
20 There were some of them that ruled 40
21 others of them rose up, but did not hold the rule. 38
25 to set themselves up and hold the rule. 38
34 also ruled over the earth and its inhabitants. 39
12:23 and shall rule the earth 37
Jdt 1: 1 who ruled over the Assyrians 21
1 who ruled over the Medes in Ecbatana– 21
6 the plain where Arioch ruled the Elymaeans. 20
5: 3 Who rules over them as king, leading their army? 16
AEs 13: 9 O Lord, Lord, King who rulest over all things 30
16:21 God, who rules over all things 26
Wis 6: 4 Because . . you did not rule rightly 31
9: 3 rule the world in holiness and righteousness 24
10: 2 and gave him strength to rule all things. 29
12:15 Thou . . rulest all things righteously 24
13: 2 the gods that rule the world. 36
15: 1 patient, and ruling all things in mercy. 25
Sir 10: 1 the rule of an understanding man 28
37:18 it is the tongue that continually rules them. 32
44: 3 There were those who ruled in their kingdoms 32

Bar 2:34 they will rule over it; and I will increase them 32
1Mc 1: 4 and ruled over countries, nations, and princes 18
2:19 the nations that live under the rule of the king 19
8:16 They trust one man each year to rule over them 18
10:52 established my rule 17
14: 4 his rule was pleasing to them 27
3Mc 3:15 we should not rule the nations •
5:28 This was the act of God who rules over all things 23
4Mc 1: 5 If reason rules the emotions 29
6 For reason does not rule its own emotions 29
2: 9 he is ruled by the law through his reason 29
9 can recognize that reason rules the emotions. 30
15 reason rules even the more violent emotions 29
23 will rule a kingdom that is temperate, just, good 21

rule (2) 1. מִשְׁפָּט 2. *διατάσσω* 3. *κανών* 4. consuetudo
Exd 21:31 shall be dealt with according to this same rule. 1
1Co 7:17 This is my rule in all the churches. 2
Gal 6:16 Peace and mercy be upon all who walk by this rule 3
1Ti 5:21 I charge you to keep these rules without favor •
2Es 9:34 behold, it is the rule that . . 4
4Mc 7:21 the whole rule of philosophy 3

rule *See* share.

rule a household 1. *οἰκοδεσποτέω*
1Ti 5:14 bear children, rule their households 1

begin to rule 1. *ἐπικρατέω*
1Mc 1: 8 his officers began to rule, each in his own place. 1

make rule 1. שלט (A)
Dan 2:38 making you rule over them all–you are the head 1

rule of cleanness 1. טָהֳרָה
2Ch 30:19 the sanctuary's rules of cleanness. 1

rule over 1. בעל 2. משל 3. *ἐξουσιάζω* 4. *ἐπικρατέω* 5. *κατακρατέω* 6. *κρατέω* 7. *κυριεύω* 8. impero
Gen 3:16 your husband, and he shall rule over you. 2
Isa 26:13 other lords besides thee have ruled over us 1
1Co 7: 4 For the wife does not rule over her own body 3
4 the husband does not rule over his own body 3
1Es 4: 2 who rule over land and sea and all that is in them? 5
15 to every people that rules over sea and land. 7
22 Hence you must realize that women rule over you! 7
2Es 14:34 If you, then, will rule over your minds 8
AEs 16:18 God, who rules over all things 4
Wis 3: 8 They will govern nations and rule over peoples 6
6: 2 Give ear, you that rule over multitudes 6
Bar 3:16 and those who rule over the beasts on earth; 7
1Mc 14: 7 he ruled over Gazara and Beth-zur and the citadel 7
17 he was ruling over the country and the cities in it 4
4Mc 1: 3 reason rules over those emotions 4
14 whether reason rules over all these. 4
19 by means of it reason rules over the emotions. 4
32 reason obviously rules over both. 4
33 because reason is able to rule over appetites 4
2: 4 to rule over the frenzied urge of sexual desire 4
3: 1 reason rules not over its own emotions 4
16: 2 not only that men have ruled over the emotions 6
17:20 our enemies did not rule over our nation 4

ruler 1. חקק 2. כִּסֵּא 3. משל 4. נָגִיד 5. נגש 6. נָשִׂיא 7. סָגָן 8. סֶרֶן 9. קָצִין 10. רזן 11. רעה 12. שַׂר 13. שַׁלִּיט 14. שפט 15. שלט (A) 16. שַׁלִּיט (A) 17. *ἄνθρωπος κριτής* 18. *ἀρχή* 19. *ἀρχισυνάγωγος* 20. *ἄρχω* 21. *ἄρχων* 22. *ἀφηγέομαι* 23. *δεσπόζω* 24. *δεσπότης* 25. *δυναστεύω* 26. *δυνάστης* 27. *ἡγεμών* 28. *ἡγέομαι* 29. *κρατέω* 30. *κρίνω* 31. *τύραννος* 32. dux
Gen 45: 8 made me . . ruler over all the land of Egypt. 3
26 Joseph is . . ruler over all the land of Egypt. 3
Exd 18:21 and place such men over the people as rulers 12
25 Moses . . made them . . rulers of thousands 12
22:28 nor curse a ruler of your people. 6
Lev 4:22 When a ruler sins, doing unwittingly 6
Jos 13: 3 there are five rulers of the Philistines 8
Jdg 9:30 When Zebul the ruler of the city heard the words 12
15:11 not know that the Philistines are rulers over us? 3
1Kg 1:35 I have appointed him to be ruler over Israel 4
11:34 I will make him ruler all the days of his life 6
2Kg 10: 1 sent them to Sama'ria, to the rulers of the city 12
1Ch 9:20 Phin'ehas . . was the ruler over them in time past; 4
12:19 for the rulers of the Philistines took counsel 8
26: 6 Shemai'ah were sons born who were rulers 3
Neh 3: 9 ruler of half the district of Jerusalem 12
12 ruler of half the district of Jerusalem 12
14 ruler of the district of Beth-hacche'rem 12
15 Shallum . . ruler of the district of Mizpah 12
16 ruler of half the district of Beth-zur 12
17 Hashabi'ah, ruler of half the district of Kei'lah 12
18 Bav'vai . . ruler of half the district of Kei'lah; 12
19 next to him Ezer the son of Jeshua, ruler of Mizpah 12
11:11 Merai'oth, son of Ahi'tub, ruler of the house of God 4
Ps 2: 2 the rulers take counsel together 10
10 O kings, be wise; be warned, O rulers of the earth. 14
94:20 Can wicked rulers be allied with thee 2
105:20 the ruler of the peoples set him free; 3
21 he made him . . ruler of all his possessions 3
148:11 princes and all rulers of the earth! 14
Prv 6: 7 Without having any chief, officer or ruler 3
8:15 By me kings reign, and rulers decree what is just; 10
23: 1 When you sit down to eat with a ruler 3
25:15 With patience a ruler may be persuaded 9
28: 2 When a land transgresses it has many rulers; 12
15 bear is a wicked ruler over a poor people. 3
16 A ruler who lacks understanding is a cruel 4
29:12 ruler listens to falsehood, all his officials 3
26 Many seek the favor of a ruler 3
31: 4 it is not . . for rulers to desire strong drink; 10
Ecc 7:19 Wisdom gives . . more than ten rulers that are 13
9:17 better than the shouting of a ruler among fools. 3
10: 4 If the anger of the ruler rises against you 3
5 an evil . . an error proceeding from the ruler: 13
Isa 1:10 Hear the word of the LORD, you rulers of Sodom! 9
14: 5 The LORD has broken . . the scepter of rulers 3
16: 1 They have sent lambs to the ruler of the land 3
22: 3 All your rulers have fled together 9
33:22 For the LORD is our judge, the LORD is our ruler 1
40:23 and makes the rulers of the earth as nothing. 14
41:25 he shall trample on rulers as on mortar 7
49: 7 abhorred by the nations, the servant of rulers 3
52: 5 Their rulers wail, says the LORD 3
Jer 2: 8 the rulers transgressed against me; 11
30:21 their ruler shall come forth from their midst; 3
51:46 and ruler is against ruler. 3
46 and ruler is against ruler. 3
Lam 2: 2 has brought down . . the kingdom and its rulers. 12
Ezk 19:11 Its strongest stem became a ruler's scepter; 3
14 in it no strong stem, no scepter for a ruler. 3
Dan 5: 7 shall be the third ruler in the kingdom. 15
16 shall be the third ruler in the kingdom. 15
29 that he should be the third ruler in the kingdom. 16
9:12 words . . spoke against us and against our rulers 14
Hos 7: 7 and they devour their rulers. 14
Ams 2: 3 I will cut off the ruler from its midst 14
Mic 3: 1 Hear, you . . rulers of the house of Israel! 9
9 Hear this, you . . rulers of the house of Israel 9
5: 1 they strike upon the cheek the ruler of Israel. 14
2 for me one who is to be ruler in Israel 3
Hab 1:10 kings they scoff, and of rulers they make sport. 10
14 like crawling things that have no ruler. 3
Zec 10: 4 of them the battle bow, out of them every ruler. 5
Mat 2: 6 are by no means least among the rulers of Judah; 27
6 from you shall come a ruler who will govern my 28
9:18 behold, a ruler came in and knelt before him 21
23 when Jesus came to the ruler's house 21
20:25 the rulers of the Gentiles lord it over them 21
Mrk 5:35 there came from the ruler's house 19
Lke 8:41 Ja'irus, who was a ruler of the synagogue 21
49 a man from the ruler's house came and said 19
12:11 bring you before the synagogues and the rulers 18
14: 1 when he went to dine at the house of a ruler 21
18:18 a ruler asked him, "Good Teacher, what shall I do 21
23:13 chief priests and the rulers and the people 21
35 the rulers scoffed at him, saying, "He saved others; 21
24:20 our chief priests and rulers delivered him up 21
Joh 3: 1 Nicode'mus, a ruler of the Jews. 21
12:31 now shall the ruler of this world be cast out; 21
14:30 the ruler of this world is coming 21
16:11 because the ruler of this world is judged. 21
Act 3:17 you acted in ignorance, as did also your rulers. 21
4: 5 their rulers and elders and scribes 21
8 Rulers of the people and elders 21
26 the rulers were gathered together 21
7:27 Who made you a ruler and a judge over us? 21
35 Who made you a ruler and a judge? 21
35 God sent as both ruler and deliverer 21
13:27 For those who live in Jerusalem and their rulers 21
14: 5 both Gentiles and Jews, with their rulers 21
16:19 dragged them . . before the rulers; 21
23: 5 shall not speak evil of a ruler of your people.' 21
Rom 13: 3 For rulers are not a terror to good conduct 21
1Co 2: 6 rulers of this age, who are doomed to pass away. 21
8 None of the rulers of this age understood this; 21
Tit 3: 1 to be submissive to rulers and authorities 18
Rev 1: 5 Jesus Christ . . the ruler of kings on earth. 21
2Es 6:54 as ruler over all the works which thou hadst made; 32
Jdt 7:23 gathered about Uzziah and the rulers of the city 21
8: 9 words spoken by the people against the ruler 21
11 Listen to me, rulers of the people of Bethulia! 21
35 Uzziah and the rulers said to her, "Go in peace 21
9: 3 thou gavest up their rulers to be slain 21
AEs 13: 1 to the rulers of the 127 provinces 20
16: 1 rulers of the provinces from India to Ethiopia 20
Wis 1: 1 Love righteousness, you rulers of the earth 30
5:23 evil-doing will overturn the thrones of rulers. 26
8:11 in the sight of rulers I shall be admired. 26
14:19 For he, perhaps wishing to please his ruler 29
Sir 4:27 nor show partiality to a ruler. 26
10: 2 like the ruler of the city 28
3 grow through the understanding of its rulers. 26
14 The Lord has cast down the thrones of rulers 20
24 The nobleman, and the judge, and the ruler 26
11: 6 Many rulers have been greatly disgraced 26
17:17 He appointed a ruler for every nation 28
23: 1 O Lord, Father and Ruler of my life 24
36:10 Crush the heads of the rulers of the enemy, who say 20
39: 4 serve among great men and appear before rulers; 28
41:17 Be ashamed . . of a lie, before a prince or a ruler; 28
46:13 established the kingdom and anointed rulers 20
18 all the rulers of the Philistines. 20
48:12 all his days he did not tremble before any ruler 21
15 with rulers from the house of David. 21
LJr 1:14 Like a local ruler the god holds a scepter 17
1Mc 1:26 rulers and elders groaned 20
9:30 to take his place as our ruler and leader 21
10:38 they are considered to be under one ruler •
11:62 took the sons of their rulers as hostages 21
14:20 The rulers and the city of the Spartans 21
28 the people and the rulers of the nation 21
2Mc 5: 8 Accused before Aretas the ruler of the Arabs 31
3Mc 2: 3 For you . . are a just Ruler 26
7 the Ruler over the whole creation. 25
5: 7 the Almighty Lord and Ruler of all power 25
51 imploring the Ruler over every power 26
6: 4 the former ruler of this Egypt 26
7: 9 not man but the Ruler over every power 23
4Mc 4:18 high priest and ruler of the nation. 22

ruler *See also* make.

become ruler 1. משל 2. *ἐπάρχω*
Dan 11:43 become ruler of the treasures of gold . . silver 1
AEs 13: 2 Having become ruler of many nations 2

local ruler 1. *ἡγεμών*
1Es 6: 7 the local rulers in Syria and Phoenicia 1
27 appointed as local rulers in Syria and Phoenicia 1

ruler of the synagogue 1. *ἀρχισυνάγωγος*
Mrk 5:22 Then came one of the rulers of the synagogue 1
36 Jesus said to the ruler of the synagogue 1
38 came to the house of the ruler of the synagogue 1
Lke 13:14 the ruler of the synagogue . . said 1
Act 13:15 the rulers of the synagogue sent to them 1
18: 8 Crispus, the ruler of the synagogue 1
17 they all seized Sos'thenes, the ruler of the synagogue 1

only ruler 1. *μόναρχος*
3Mc 2: 2 holy among the holy ones, the only ruler, almighty 1

world ruler 1. *κοσμοκράτωρ*
Eph 6:12 against the world rulers of this present darkness 1

ruler's *See* staff.

rules *See* according.

rumble 1. הֶגֶה 2. הָמוֹן 3. קוֹל 4. קוֹל רַעַשׁ 5. vox
Job 37: 2 the rumbling that comes from his mouth. 1
Jer 47: 3 at the rumbling of their wheels the fathers look 2
Jol 2: 5 As with the rumbling of chariots, 3
Nah 3: 2 The crack of whip, and rumble of wheel 4
2Es 6: 2 before the rumblings of thunder sounded 5

rumor 1. שְׁמוּעָה 2. שֵׁמַע 3. *ἀγγελία* 4. *ἀκοή* 5. *λαλιά* 6. *φήμη*
2Kg 19: 7 he shall hear a rumor and return to his own land; 1
Job 28:22 Abaddon and Death say, 'We have heard a rumor of it 2
Isa 37: 7 put a spirit in him, so that he shall hear a rumor 1
Jer 10:22 Hark, a rumor! Behold, it comes!–a great commotion 1
Ezk 7:26 Disaster . . upon disaster, rumor follows rumor; 1
26 Disaster . . upon disaster, rumor follows rumor; 1
Mat 24: 6 you will hear of wars and rumors of wars 4
Mrk 13: 7 when you hear of wars and rumors of wars 4
Wis 5: 9 like a rumor that passes by; 3
2Mc 5: 5 When a false rumor arose that Antiochus was dead 5
3Mc 3: 2 a hostile rumor was circulated 6
4Mc 4:22 he heard that a rumor of his death had spread 6

run 1. בוא 2. היה 3. הלך 4. חַי 5. יָבָל 6. יצק 7. מְרוּצָה 8. צעד 9. רוץ 10. ריר 11. *διατρέχω* 12. *δρόμος* 13. *εἰστρέχω* 14. *ἐκπίπτω* 15. *ἐπιτρέχω* 16. *περιέχω* 17. *προστρέχω* 18. *προτρέχω* 19. *συντρέχω* 20. *τρέχω*
Gen 18: 2 When he saw them, he ran from the tent door 9
7 Abraham ran to the herd, and took a calf 9
24:17 Then the servant ran to meet her, and said 9
20 she . . ran again to the well to draw 9
28 the maiden ran and told her mother's household 9
29 and Laban ran out to the man, to the spring. 9
29:12 Rebekah's son; and she ran and told her father. 9
13 Laban . . ran to meet him, and embraced him 9
33: 4 Esau ran to meet him, and embraced him 9
49:22 his branches run over the wall. 8
Exd 9:23 thunder and hail, and fire ran down to the earth. 3
Lev 14: 5 kill . . one of the birds . . over running water 4
6 the bird that was killed over the running water 4
50 in an earthen vessel over running water 4
51 dip them in the blood . . and in the running water 4
52 cleanse the house . . with the running water 4
15: 3 whether his body runs with his discharge 10
13 he shall bathe his body in running water 4
Num 11:27 a young man ran and told Moses, "Eldad and Medad 9

16:47 ran into the midst of the assembly and behold 9
19:17 running water shall be added in a vessel; 4
Jos 7:22 Joshua sent messengers, and they ran to the tent; 9
8:19 they ran and entered the city and took it; 9
15: 2 south boundary ran from the end of the Salt Sea 2
5 the boundary . . runs from the bay of the sea •
19:33 its boundary ran from Heleph, from the oak 2
Jdg 1:36 the border of the Amorites ran from the ascent •
7:21 and all the army ran; they cried out and fled. 9
13:10 the woman ran in haste and told her husband 9
1Sm 3: 5 and ran to Eli, and said, "Here I am 9
4:12 A man of Benjamin ran from the battle line 9
8:11 to be his horsemen, and to run before his chariots; 9
10:23 Then they ran and fetched him from there; 9
17:22 David left the things . . and ran to the ranks 9
48 David ran quickly toward the battle line to meet 9
51 Then David ran and stood over the Philistine 9
20: 6 David . . asked leave of me to run to Bethlehem 9
36 Run and find the arrows which I shoot. 9
36 As the lad ran, he shot an arrow beyond him. 9
2Sm 15: 1 a chariot and horses, and 50 men to run before him. 9
18:19 Let me run, and carry tidings to the king 9
21 The Cushite bowed before Jo'ab, and ran. 9
22 Come what may, let me also run after the Cushite. 9
22 And Jo'ab said, "Why will you run, my son 9
23 Come what may," he said, "I will run. 9
23 I will run." So he said to him, "Run. 9
23 Then Ahi'ma-az ran by the way of the plain 9
24 when he . . looked, he saw a man running alone. 9
26 And the watchman saw another man running; 9
26 watchman . . said, "See, another man running alone! 9
27 the running of the foremost is like . . Ahi'ma-az 7
27 of the foremost is like the running of Ahi'ma-az 7
1Kg 1: 5 prepared . . and 50 men to run before him. 9
6: 5 running round the walls of the house •
18:35 the water ran round about the altar 3
46 Eli'jah . . girded up his loins and ran before Ahab 9
19:20 he left the oxen, and ran after Eli'jah, and said 9
2Kg 4:26 run at once to meet her, and say to her, Is it well 9
5:20 I will run after him, and get something 9
21 when Na'aman saw some one running after him 9
2Ch 23:12 noise of the people running and praising 9
Ezr 8:15 I gathered them to the river that runs to Aha'va 1
Job 15:26 running stubbornly against him 9
16:14 he runs upon me like a warrior. 9
38:38 when the dust runs into a mass 6
Ps 19: 5 like a strong man runs its course with joy. 9
59: 4 for no fault of mine, they run and make ready. 9
119:32 I will run in the way of thy commandments 9
147:15 command to the earth; his word runs swiftly. 9
Prv 1:16 for their feet run to evil 9
4:12 if you run, you will not stumble. 9
6:18 feet that make haste to run to evil 9
18:10 righteous man runs into it and is safe. 9
Ecc 1: 7 All streams run to the sea, but the sea is not full; 3
Isa 30:25 there will be brooks running with water 5
40:31 they shall run and not be weary 9
55: 5 and nations that knew you not shall run to you 9
59: 7 Their feet run to evil, and they make haste 9
Jer 23:21 I did not send the prophets, yet they ran; 9
51:31 One runner runs to meet another 9
Ezk 40:18 the pavement ran along the side of the gates •
47:17 the boundary shall run from the sea to Hazar-e'non 2
18 the boundary shall run from Hazar-e'non •
19 it shall run from Tamar as far as the waters •
48:28 the boundary shall run from Tamar to the waters 2
Dan 8: 6 ran at him in his mighty wrath. 9
Jol 2: 4 and like war horses they run. 9
9 They leap upon the city, they run upon the walls; 9
Ams 6:12 Do horses run upon rocks? Does one plow the sea 9
Hab 2: 2 upon tablets, so he may run who reads it. 9
Zec 2: 4 and said to him, "Run, say to that young man 9
Mat 27:48 one of them at once ran and took a sponge 20
28: 8 ran to tell his disciples. 20
Mrk 5: 6 when he saw Jesus from afar, he ran and worshiped 20
6:33 they ran there on foot from all the towns 19
15:36 one ran and, filling a sponge full of vinegar 20
Lke 15:20 ran and embraced him and kissed him. 20
19: 4 So he ran on ahead 18
Joh 20: 2 she ran, and went to Simon Peter 20
4 They both ran 20
Act 8:30 Philip ran to him, and heard him reading Isaiah 17
12:14 she did not open the gate but ran in and told 13
27:17 then, fearing that they should run on the Syr'tis 14
26 we shall have to run on some island. 14
29 fearing that we might run on the rocks 14
1Co 9:24 So run that you may obtain it. 20
26 Well, I do not run aimlessly 20
Gal 2: 2 somehow I should be running or had run in vain. 20
2 somehow I should be running or had run in vain. 20
5: 7 You were running well 20
Php 2:16 I did not run in vain or labor in vain. 20
Heb 12: 1 let us run with perseverance the race 20
Tob 11:10 his son ran to him 17
Jdt 6:16 their young men and their women ran to the assembly 19
Wis 3: 7 will run like sparks through the stubble. 11
17:19 the unseen running of leaping animals 12
Sus 1:19 the two elders rose and ran to her, and said 15
25 And one of them ran and opened the garden doors. 20
38 and when we saw this wickedness we ran to them. 20
1Mc 2:24 he ran and killed him upon the altar. 20
2Mc 11:22 The king's letter ran thus 16
14:45 he ran through the crowd 12
4Mc 7:11 Aaron . . ran through the multitude of the people 15
12:10 Running to the nearest of the braziers 20
14: 5 running the course toward immortality 20

run a course 1. נקף
Job 1: 5 when the days of the feast had run their course 1

run about 1. περιτρέχω
Mrk 6:55 and ran about the whole neighborhood 1

run after 1. רדף 2. καταδιώκω
Isa 1:23 Every one loves a bribe and runs after gifts. 1
5:11 rise . . that they may run after strong drink 1
Sir 27:17 if you betray his secrets, do not run after him. 2

run aground 1. ἐπικέλλω
Act 27:41 striking a shoal they ran the vessel aground 1

run ahead 1. προτρέχω
Tob 11: 3 Let us run ahead of your wife 1
1Mc 16:21 some one ran ahead and reported to John at Gazara 1

run around 1. περιφερής
2Mc 13: 5 it has a rim running around it 1

run away 1. ברח 2. הלך 3. נוס 4. ἀποδράω 5. φεύγω
Jdg 9:21 Jotham ran away and fled, and went to Beer 3
1Kg 2:39 two of Shim'e-i's slaves ran away to Achish, son 1
Ps 58: 7 Let them vanish like water that runs away; 2
Nah 2: 8 Nin'eveh is like a pool whose waters run away. 3
Mrk 14:52 he left the linen cloth and ran away naked. 5
Tob 2: 8 he once ran away 4
Sir 33:31 If you ill-treat him, and he leaves and runs away 4

cause to run 1. הלך
Ezk 32:14 and cause their rivers to run like oil 1

run down 1. בוא 2. ירד 3. καταβαίνω 4. κατατρέχω
1Sm 21:13 and let his spittle run down his beard. 2
Ps 133: 2 precious oil . . running down upon the beard 2
2 of Aaron, running down on the collar of his robes! 2
Jer 9:18 that our eyes may run down with tears 2
13:17 will weep bitterly and run down with tears 2
14:17 Let my eyes run down with tears night and day 2
Ezk 24:16 not mourn or weep nor shall your tears run down. 1
Act 21:32 and ran down to them 4
Sir 35:15 Do not the tears of the widow run down her cheek 3

run dry
Jer 18:14 Do the mountain waters run dry •

make run 1. רוץ
Jer 49:19 I will suddenly make them run away from her; 1
50:44 I will suddenly make them run away from her; 1

run off 1. διαδιδράσκω
2Mc 8:13 those . . ran off and got away. 1

run out 1. ἀμερής 2. ἀπέρχομαι 3. ἐκλείπω
Jdt 6:12 they caught up their weapons and ran out of the city 2
12: 3 If your supply runs out, where can we get more 3
3Mc 5:25 at their last gasp, since the time had run out 1

run over 1. κατάρρυτος 2. ὑπερεκχύνω 3. exubero
Lke 6:38 pressed down, shaken together, running over 2
2Es 2:32 because my springs run over 3
2Mc 12:16 the . . lake . . appeared to be running over with blood. 1

run round 1. נקף
Isa 29: 1 Add year to year; let the feasts run their round. 1

run through 1. διέρχομαι
2Mc 14:45 he ran through the crowd 1

run to and fro 1. שׁוט
2Ch 16: 9 the eyes of the LORD run to and fro 1
Jer 5: 1 Run to and fro through the streets of Jerusalem 1
49: 3 lament, and run to and fro among the hedges! 1
Dan 12: 4 Many shall run to and fro 1
Ams 8:12 they shall run to and fro, to seek the word 1

run to meet 1. προστρέχω
Tob 11: 9 Then Anna ran to meet them, and embraced her son 1

run to reach 1. ἐπιτρέχω
1Mc 6:45 He . . ran into the midst of the phalanx to reach it 1

run together 1. συνδρομή 2. συντρέχω
Act 3:11 all the people ran together to them 2
21:30 and the people ran together 1
Jdt 13:13 They all ran together, both small and great 2
2Mc 3:19 Some of the maidens . . ran together to the gates 2

run under the lee 1. ὑποτρέχω
Act 27:16 running under the lee of a small island 1

run up 1. ἀνατρέχω 2. προστρέχω
Mrk 9:15 greatly amazed, and ran up to him and greeted him. 2
10:17 a man ran up and knelt before him, and asked him 2
2Mc 14:43 He bravely ran up on the wall 1

runaway *See* slave.

runnel 1. רַהַט
Gen 30:38 the flocks in the runnels, that is, the watering 1
41 rods in the runnels before the eyes of the flock 1

runner 1. רוץ 2. τρέχω
Job 9:25 My days are swifter than a runner; they flee away 1
Jer 51:31 One runner runs to meet another 1
1Co 9:24 in a race all the runners compete 2

running *See* water.

come running together 1. ἐπισυντρέχω
Mrk 9:25 Jesus saw that a crowd came running together 1

rural 1. עֲבֹדָה
Neh 10:37 Levites . . collect the tithes in all our rural towns. 1

rush 1. גיח 2. הָמוֹן 3. מהר 4. פשׁט 5. צלח 6. צַר 7. רַעַשׁ 8. שֶׁטֶף 9. δρόμος 10. εἰσβάλλω 11. εἰσπηδάω 12. ἐνάλλομαι 13. ἐξανίστημι 14. ὁρμάω 15. πορεύω 16. συντρέχω 17. ταχύς 18. τρέχω 19. φέρω
Jdg 9:33 as the sun is up, rise early and rush upon the city; 4
44 the company that was with him rushed forward 4
44 two companies rushed upon all who were in the fields 4
20:33 men . . in ambush rushed out of their place west 1
37 men in ambush made haste and rushed upon Gib'e-ah 4
1Sm 18:10 an evil spirit from God rushed upon Saul 5
1Kg 18:41 there is a sound of the rushing of rain. 2
Job 40:23 though Jordan rushes against his mouth. 1
Ps 32: 6 rush of great waters, they shall not reach him. 8
Prv 7:23 as a bird rushes into a snare; 3
Isa 59:19 for he will come like a rushing stream 6
Jer 47: 3 at the rushing of his chariots 7
Mat 8:32 behold, the whole herd rushed down the steep bank 14
Mrk 5:13 rushed down the steep bank into the sea 14
Lke 8:33 the herd rushed down the steep bank into the lake 14
Act 2: 2 a sound . . like the rush of a mighty wind 19
7:57 stopped their ears and rushed together upon him. 14
16:29 And he called for lights and rushed in 11
19:29 they rushed together into the theater 14
Rev 9: 9 noise of many chariots . . rushing into battle. 18
Jdt 14: 3 they will rush into the tent of Holofernes 16
Wis 17:18 the rhythm of violently rushing water 15
Sir 21:22 The foot of a fool rushes into a house 17
Sus 1:26 they rushed in at the side door 11
1Mc 3:23 he rushed suddenly against Seron and his army 12
9:40 Then they rushed upon them from the ambush 13
2Mc 3:25 it rushed furiously at Heliodorus 19
9: 2 the people rushed to the rescue with arms 14
10:16 rushed to the strongholds of the Idumeans. 14
14:43 the crowd was now rushing in through the doors 10
3Mc 1:19 in a disorderly rush 9
4Mc 6: 8 One of the cruel guards rushed at him 12

rush (2) 1. אַגְמֹן 2. גֹּמֶא 3. סוּף
Job 41:20 smoke, as from a boiling pot and burning rushes. 1
Isa 19: 6 and dry up, reeds and rushes will rot away. 3
35: 7 the grass shall become reeds and rushes. 2
58: 5 Is it to bow down his head like a rush 1

rush down 1. צלח
2Sm 19:17 Ziba . . rushed down to the Jordan before the king 1

rush forth 1. שׁלח
Jdg 5:15 into the valley they rushed forth at his heels. 1

rush in against 1. ἐπεισέρχομαι
1Mc 16:16 and rushed in against Simon in the banquet hall 1

rush into 1. εἰστρέχω
2Mc 5:26 then rushed into the city with his armed men 1

rush like a whirlwind 1. שׂער
Dan 11:40 king . . shall rush upon him like a whirlwind 1

rush off 1. ἐξορμάω 2. ὁρμάω
2Mc 11: 7 Then they eagerly rushed off together. 1
12:22 they rushed off in flight 2

rush out 1. ἐκπηδάω 2. ἐκχέω 3. ἐξορμάω
Act 14:14 and rushed out among the multitude, crying 1
Jdt 14:17 he rushed out to the people and shouted 1
15: 2 with one impulse all rushed out and fled 2
3 the men of Israel . . rushed out upon them. 2
3Mc 1:18 virgins . . rushed out with their mothers 3
5:47 he . . rushed out in full force along with the beasts 3

rush out upon 1. *ἐπεκχέω*

Jdt 15: 4 to urge all to rush out upon their enemies 1

rush to and fro 1. שׁקק

Nah 2: 4 they rush to and fro through the squares; 1

rush upon 1. *ἐνσείω*

2Mc 12:15 his men . . rushed furiously upon the walls. 1

rushing *See* flight, sound.

rust 1. חֶלְאָה 2. טֻמְאָה 3. *βρῶσις* 4. *ἰόομαι* 5. *ἰός* 6. *κατιόω*

Ezk 24: 6 to the pot whose rust is in it 1
6 rust is in it, and whose rust has not gone out of it! 1
11 filthiness . . melted in it, its rust consumed. 1
12 its thick rust does not go out of it by fire. 1
13 Its rust is your filthy lewdness. 2
Mat 6:19 treasures on earth, where moth and rust consume 3
20 in heaven, where neither moth nor rust consumes 3
Jas 5: 3 Your gold and silver have rusted 6
3 and their rust will be evidence against you 5
Sir 12:10 like the rusting of copper, so is his wickedness. 4
29:10 do not let it rust under a stone and be lost. 4
LJr 1:12 which cannot save themselves from rust 5
24 will not shine unless some one wipes off the rust; 5

ruthless 1. עָרִיץ 2. *ἀνελεήμων* 3. *ἄνοικτος*

Job 15:20 all the years that are laid up for the ruthless. 1
Isa 13:11 and lay low the haughtiness of the ruthless. 1
25: 3 cities of ruthless nations will fear thee. 1
4 for the blast of the ruthless is like a storm 1
5 the song of the ruthless is stilled. 1
29: 5 the multitude of the ruthless like . . chaff. 1
20 For the ruthless shall come to nought 1
Jer 15:21 and redeem you from the grasp of the ruthless. 1
Rom 1:31 foolish, faithless, heartless, ruthless. 2
3Mc 4: 4 with such a harsh and ruthless spirit 3

ruthless man 1. עָרִיץ

Ps 54: 3 ruthless men seek my life; 1
86:14 band of ruthless men seek my life 1

ruthlessly 1. לֹא חמל

Isa 30:14 a potter's vessel which is smashed so ruthlessly 1

S

sabachthani 1. σαβαχθανι
Mat 27:46 Eli, Eli, la'ma sabach-tha'ni? 1
Mrk 15:34 E'lo-i, E'lo-i, la'ma sabach-tha'ni? 1

sabbath 1. יוֹם הַשַּׁבָּת 2. שַׁבָּת
3. ἡμέρα τοῦ σαββάτου 4. σάββατον
Exd 16:23 Tomorrow is a day of solemn rest, a holy sabbath 2
25 Eat it today, for today is a sabbath to the LORD; 2
26 but on the seventh day, which is a sabbath 2
29 See! The LORD has given you the sabbath, therefore 2
20: 8 Remember the sabbath day, to keep it holy. 2
10 the seventh day is a sabbath to the LORD your God; 2
11 therefore the LORD blessed the sabbath day 2
31:13 'You shall keep my sabbaths, for this is a sign 2
14 keep the sabbath, because it is holy for you; 2
15 seventh day is a sabbath of solemn rest, holy 2
15 whoever does any work on the sabbath day shall be 2
16 people of Israel shall keep the sabbath 2
16 observing the sabbath throughout 2
35: 2 on the seventh day you shall have a holy sabbath 2
3 in all your habitations on the sabbath day. 2
Lev 16:31 It is a sabbath of solemn rest to you 2
19: 3 you shall keep my sabbaths: I am the LORD your God 2
30 You shall keep my sabbaths 2
23: 3 on the seventh day is a sabbath of solemn rest 2
3 you shall do no work; it is a sabbath to the LORD 2
11 on the morrow after the sabbath the priest shall 2
15 after the sabbath, from the day that you brought 2
16 50 days to the morrow after the seventh sabbath 2
32 It shall be to you a sabbath of solemn rest 2
38 besides the sabbaths of the LORD 2
24: 8 Every sabbath day Aaron shall set it in order 2
25: 2 the land shall keep a sabbath to the LORD 2
4 in the seventh year there shall be a sabbath 2
4 solemn rest for the land, a sabbath to the LORD 2
6 The sabbath of the land shall provide food 2
26: 2 You shall keep my sabbaths and reverence my 2
34 Then the land shall enjoy its sabbaths 2
34 then the land shall rest, and enjoy its sabbaths 2
35 in your sabbaths when you dwelt upon it 2
43 land shall . . enjoy its sabbaths while it lies 2
Num15:32 found a man gathering sticks on the sabbath day. 2
28: 9 On the sabbath day two male lambs a year old 2
10 this is the burnt offering of every sabbath 2
Deu 5:12 'Observe the sabbath day, to keep it holy 2
14 seventh day is a sabbath to the LORD your God; 2
15 God commanded you to keep the sabbath day. 2
2Kg 4:23 Why . . today? It is neither new moon nor sabbath. 2
11: 5 those who come off duty on the sabbath 2
7 two . . which come on duty in force on the sabbath 2
9 his men who were to go off duty on the sabbath 2
9 with those who were to come on duty on the sabbath 2
16:18 the covered way for the sabbath . . he removed 2
1Ch 9:32 the showbread, to prepare it every sabbath. 2
23:31 to the LORD on sabbaths, new moons, and feast days 2
2Ch 2: 4 offerings . . on the sabbaths and the new moons 2
8:13 comandment . . for the sabbaths, the new moons 2
23: 4 who come off duty on the sabbath 2
8 men, who were to go off duty on the sabbath 2
8 with those who were to come on duty on the sabbath; 2
31: 3 burnt offerings for the sabbaths, the new moons 2
36:21 until the land had enjoyed its sabbaths. 2
Neh 9:14 thou didst make known to them thy holy sabbath 2
10:31 wares or any grain on the sabbath day to sell 2
31 not buy from them on the sabbath or on a holy day; 2
33 sabbaths, the new moons, the appointed feasts 2
13:15 saw . . men treading wine presses on the sabbath 2
15 brought into Jerusalem on the sabbath day; 2
16 sold them on the sabbath to the people of Judah 2
17 evil thing . . profaning the sabbath day? 2
18 wrath upon Israel by profaning the sabbath. 2
19 When it began to be dark . . before the sabbath 2
19 should not be opened until after the sabbath. 2
19 no burden might be brought in on the sabbath day. 2
21 time on they did not come on the sabbath. 2
22 guard the gates, to keep the sabbath day holy. 2
Ps 92: 0 A Psalm. A Song for the Sabbath. 1
Isa 1:13 New moon and sabbath and . . assemblies 2
56: 2 who keeps the sabbath, not profaning it 2
4 "To the eunuchs who keep my sabbaths 2
6 his servants, every one who keeps the sabbath 2
58:13 If you turn back your foot from the sabbath 2
13 and call the sabbath a delight and the holy day 2
66:23 new moon to new moon, and from sabbath to sabbath 2
23 new moon to new moon, and from sabbath to sabbath 2
Jer 17:21 and do not bear a burden on the sabbath day 2
22 out of your houses on the sabbath or do any work 2
22 or do any work, but keep the sabbath day holy 2
24 by the gates of this city on the sabbath day 2
24 but keep the sabbath day holy and do no work on it 2
27 do not listen to me, to keep the sabbath day holy 2
27 by the gates of Jerusalem on the sabbath day 2
Lam 2: 6 brought to an end . . appointed feast and sabbath 2
Ezk 20:12 Moreover I gave them my sabbaths, as a sign 2
13 and my sabbaths they greatly profaned. 2
16 not walk in my statutes, and profaned my sabbaths; 2
20 hallow my sabbaths that they may be a sign 2
21 they profaned my sabbaths. 2
24 rejected my statutes and profaned my sabbaths 2
22: 8 my holy things, and profaned my sabbaths. 2
26 they have disregarded my sabbaths 2
23:38 on the same day and profaned my sabbaths. 2
44:24 they shall keep my sabbaths holy. 2
45:17 at the feasts, the new moons, and the sabbaths 2
46: 1 but on the sabbath day it shall be opened 2
3 the LORD on the sabbaths and on the new moons. 2
4 prince offers to the LORD on the sabbath day 2
12 as he does on the sabbath day. Then he shall go out 2
Hos 2:11 her mirth, her feasts, her new moons, her sabbaths 2
Ams 8: 5 And the sabbath, that we may offer wheat for sale 2
Mat 12: 1 went through the grainfields on the sabbath 4
2 what is not lawful to do on the sabbath. 4
5 on the sabbath the priests in the temple profane 4
5 priests in the temple profane the sabbath 4
8 For the Son of man is lord of the sabbath. 4
10 they asked him, "Is it lawful to heal on the sabbath? 4
11 it falls into a pit on the sabbath 4
12 So it is lawful to do good on the sabbath. 4
24:20 in winter or on a sabbath. 4
28: 1 Now after the sabbath 4
Mrk 1:21 immediately on the sabbath 4
2:23 One sabbath he was going 4
24 what is not lawful on the sabbath? 4
27 sabbath was made for man, not man for the sabbath; 4
27 sabbath was made for man, not man for the sabbath; 4
28 the Son of man is lord even of the sabbath. 4
3: 2 whether he would heal him on the sabbath 4
4 he said to them, "Is it lawful on the sabbath 4
6: 2 on the sabbath he began to teach in the synagogue; 4
16: 1 when the sabbath was past 4
Lke 4:16 as his custom was, on the sabbath day 4
31 he was teaching them on the sabbath; 4
6: 1 On a sabbath 4
2 doing what is not lawful to do on the sabbath? 4
5 The Son of man is lord of the sabbath. 4
6 On another sabbath 4
7 to see whether he would heal on the sabbath 4
9 is it lawful on the sabbath to do good or to do harm 4
13:10 in one of the synagogues on the sabbath. 4
14 Jesus had healed on the sabbath 4
14 not on the sabbath day. 4
15 Does not each of you on the sabbath untie his ox 4
16 be loosed from this bond on the sabbath day? 4
14: 1 One sabbath when he went to dine 4
3 Is it lawful to heal on the sabbath, or not? 4
5 will not immediately pull him out on a sabbath day? 4
23:54 the sabbath was beginning. 4
56 On the sabbath they rested 4
Joh 5: 9 Now that day was the sabbath. 4
10 It is the sabbath 4
16 because he did this on the sabbath. 4
18 because he not only broke the sabbath 4
7:22 you circumcise a man upon the sabbath. 4
23 If on the sabbath a man receives circumcision 4
23 on the sabbath I made a man's whole body well? 4
9:14 Now it was a sabbath day when Jesus made the clay 4
16 for he does not keep the sabbath 4
19:31 remaining on the cross on the sabbath 4
31 (for that sabbath was a high day) 4
Act 1:12 is near Jerusalem, a sabbath day's journey away; 4
13:14 on the sabbath day they went into the synagogue 4
27 the prophets which are read every sabbath 4
42 might be told them the next sabbath. 4
44 The next sabbath almost the whole city gathered 4
15:21 he is read every sabbath in the synagogues. 4
16:13 on the sabbath day we went outside the gate 4
18: 4 he argued in the synagogue every sabbath 4
Col 2:16 a festival or a new moon or a sabbath. 4
1Es 1:58 Until the land has enjoyed its sabbaths 4
5:52 on sabbaths and at new moons 4
Jdt 8: 6 day before the sabbath and the sabbath itself 4
10: 2 on sabbaths and on her feast days; 3
1Mc 1:39 her sabbaths into a reproach 4
43 sacrificed to idols and profaned the sabbath. 4
45 to profane sabbaths and feasts 4
2:32 on the sabbath day. 4
34 so profane the sabbath day. 4
38 So they attacked them on the sabbath 4
41 who comes to attack us on the sabbath day 4
9:34 Bacchides found this out on the sabbath day 4
43 he came with a large force on the sabbath day 4
10:34 all the feasts and sabbaths and new moons 4
2Mc 5:25 waited until the holy sabbath day 4
8:26 For it was the day before the sabbath 4
27 they kept the sabbath 4
28 After the sabbath 4
12:38 they kept the sabbath there. 4
15: 3 who had commanded the keeping of the sabbath day. 4

sabbath *See also* day, keep, rest.

sabbatical *See* year.

sack 1. נכה 2. σκυλεύω
2Kg 15:16 Men'ahem sacked Tappuah and all who were in it 1
16 they did not open it to him, therefore he sacked it 1
Jdt 2:27 sacked their cities and ravaged their lands 2

sack (2) 1. אַמְתַּחַת 2. כְּלִי 3. צִקָּלֹן 4. שַׂק
Gen 42:25 money in his sack, and to give them provisions 4
27 opened his sack to give his ass provender 4
27 he saw his money in the mouth of his sack; 1
28 has been put back; here it is in the mouth of my sack 1
35 As they emptied their sacks 4
35 every man's bundle of money was in his sack; 4
43:12 that was returned to the mouth of your sacks; 1
18 which was replaced in our sacks the first time 1
21 came to the lodging place we opened our sacks 1
21 in the mouth of his sack, our money in full weight; 1
22 We do not know who put our money in our sacks. 1
23 God . . must have put treasure in your sacks 1
44: 1 Fill the men's sacks with food, as much as they can 1
1 and put each man's money in the mouth of his sack 1
2 my cup . . in the mouth of the sack of the youngest 1
8 money which we found in the mouth of our sacks 1
11 every man quickly lowered his sack to the ground 1
11 to the ground, and every man opened his sack. 1
12 and the cup was found in Benjamin's sack. 1
Lev 11:32 a garment or a skin or a sack, any vessel 4
Jos 9: 4 and took worn-out sacks upon their asses 4
1Sm 9: 7 the bread in our sacks is gone, and there is no 2
2Kg 4:42 loaves . . and fresh ears of grain in his sack. 3

sackcloth 1. שַׂק 2. σάκκος 3. saccus
Gen 37:34 put sackcloth upon his loins, and mourned for his 1

2Sm 3:31 Rend your clothes, and gird on sackcloth 1
21:10 Then Rizpah the daughter of Ai'ah took sackcloth 1
1Kg 20:31 sackcloth on our loins and ropes upon our heads 1
32 they girded sackcloth on their loins 1
21:27 and put sackcloth upon his flesh, and fasted 1
27 rent his clothes . . fasted and lay in sackcloth 1
2Kg 6:30 he had sackcloth beneath upon his body– 1
19: 1 his clothes, and covered himself with sackcloth 1
2 and the senior priests, covered with sackcloth 1
1Ch 21:16 David and the elders, clothed in sackcloth 1
Neh 9: 1 assembled with fasting and in sackcloth 1
Est 4: 1 rent his clothes and put on sackcloth and ashes 1
2 enter the king's gate clothed with sackcloth. 1
3 and most of them lay in sackcloth and ashes. 1
4 garments . . so that he might take off his sackcloth 1
Job 16:15 I have sewed sackcloth upon my skin 1
Ps 30:11 thou hast loosed my sackcloth 1
35:13 But I, when they were sick–I wore sackcloth 1
69:11 When I made sackcloth my clothing 1
Isa 3:24 instead of a rich robe, a girding of sackcloth; 1
15: 3 in the streets they gird on sackcloth; 1
20: 2 Go, and loose the sackcloth from your loins 1
22:12 to baldness and girding with sackcloth; 1
32:11 make . . bare, and gird sackcloth upon your loins. *
37: 1 and covered himself with sackcloth 1
2 the senior priests, clothed with sackcloth 1
50: 3 and make sackcloth their covering. 1
58: 5 and to spread sackcloth and ashes under him? 1
Jer 4: 8 For this gird you with sackcloth, lament and wail; 1
6:26 O daughter of my people, gird on sackcloth 1
48:37 and on the loins is sackcloth. 1
49: 3 Gird yourselves with sackcloth, lament, and run 1
Lam 2:10 cast dust on their heads and put on sackcloth; 1
Ezk 7:18 They gird themselves with sackcloth 1
27:31 bald for you, and gird themselves with sackcloth 1
Dan 9: 3 with fasting and sackcloth and ashes. 1
Jol 1: 8 Lament like a virgin girded with sackcloth *
13 Gird on sackcloth and lament, O priests 1
13 pass the night in sackcloth, O ministers of my God! 1
Ams 8:10 I will bring sackcloth upon all loins 1
Jon 3: 5 they proclaimed a fast, and put on sackcloth 1
6 covered himself with sackcloth, and sat in ashes. 1
8 but let man and beast be covered with sackcloth 1
Mat 11:21 repented long ago in sackcloth and ashes. 2
Lke 10:13 sitting in sackcloth and ashes. 2
Rev 6:12 and the sun became black as sackcloth 2
11: 3 power to prophesy . . clothed in sackcloth. 2
2Es 16: 2 Gird yourselves with sackcloth and haircloth 3
Jdt 4:10 they all girded themselves with sackcloth. 2
11 and spread out their sackcloth before the Lord. 2
12 They even surrounded the altar with sackcloth 2
14 with their loins girded with sackcloth 2
8: 5 girded sackcloth about her loins 2
9: 1 uncovered the sackcloth she was wearing 2
10: 3 she removed the sackcloth 2
Bar 4:20 I . . put on the sackcloth of my supplication 2
1Mc 2:14 Mattathias . . put on sackcloth, and mourned greatly. 2
3:47 put on sackcloth and sprinkled ashes on their head 2
2Mc 3:19 girded with sackcloth under their breasts 2
10:25 girded their loins with sackcloth 2

sacred 1. אֱלֹהִים 2. יְהוָה 3. קֹדֶשׁ 4. ἅγιος 5. ἱερός

Exd 30:25 you shall make of these a sacred anointing oil 3
Jos 6:19 all silver and gold, and . . are sacred to the LORD; 3
1Sm 20: 8 brought your servant into a sacred covenant 2
1Ch 16:42 the music and instruments for sacred song. 1
Ecc 8: 2 and because of your sacred oath be not dismayed; 1
Jer 31:40 Gate toward the east, shall be sacred to the LORD. 3
Ezk 20:40 your gifts, with all your sacred offerings. 3
Zep 3: 4 her priests profane what is sacred 3
Zec 14:21 every pot in Jerusalem and Judah shall be sacred 3
2Ti 3:15 have been acquainted with the sacred writings 5
1Es 5:45 would give to the sacred treasury for the work 5
Tob 2: 1 which is the sacred festival of the seven weeks 4
Jdt 4: 3 the sacred vessels and the altar and the temple *
2Mc 1:34 and enclosed the place and made it sacred. 5
6: 4 within the sacred precincts 5
8:33 burned those who had set fire to the sacred gates 5
4Mc 2:22 as a sacred governor over them all. 5
4: 7 committed deposits to the sacred treasury 5
5:29 the sacred oaths of my ancestors 5
7: 4 his sacred life was consumed by tortures 5
6 you neither defiled your sacred teeth 5
9:24 Fight the sacred and noble battle for religion. 5
14: 3 O sacred and harmonious concord 5
15:13 O sacred nature and affection of parental love 5
16:12 the sacred and God-fearing mother did not wail 5

sacred *See also* area, enclosure, grove, make, portion, precinct, stone, token.

sacred place 1. τέμενος

2Mc 11: 3 as he did on the sacred places of the other nations 1

sacred thing 1. קֹדֶשׁ

Ezk 44:13 nor come near any of my sacred things 1
13 nor come near . . the things that are most sacred; 1

sacrifice 1. זבח 2. זֶבַח 3. זֶבַח שֶׁלֶם 4. מִנְחָה 5. עבר 6. עשׂה 7. דְּבַח (A) 8. ἐπιθύω 9. θυσία 10. θυσιάζω 11. θυσιαστήριον 12. θύω 13. κάρπωμα 14. σπένδω 15. σπλαγχνισμός 16. σφαγιάζω 17. occido

Gen 31:54 Jacob offered a sacrifice on the mountain 2
46: 1 came to Beer-sheba, and offered sacrifices 2
Exd 3:18 the wilderness, that we may sacrifice to the LORD 1
5: 3 let us . . sacrifice to the LORD our God 1
17 'Let us go and sacrifice to the LORD,' 1
8: 8 I will let the people go to sacrifice to the LORD. 1
25 Go, sacrifice to your God within the land. 1
27 into the wilderness and sacrifice to the LORD 1
28 will let you go, to sacrifice to the LORD your God 1
29 letting the people go to sacrifice to the LORD. 1
10:25 let us have sacrifices and burnt offerings 2
25 that we may sacrifice to the LORD our God. 6
12:27 It is the sacrifice of the LORD'S passover 2
13:15 Therefore I sacrifice to the LORD all the males 1
18:12 offered a burnt offering and sacrifices to God; 2
20:24 and sacrifice on it your burnt offerings 1
22:20 Whoever sacrifices to any god, save to the LORD 1
23:18 You shall not offer the blood of my sacrifice 2
24: 5 who . . sacrificed peace offerings of oxen 1
32: 8 have worshiped it and sacrificed to it 1
34:15 when they . . sacrifice to their gods 1
15 when . . one invites you, you eat of his sacrifice 2
25 You shall not offer the blood of my sacrifice 2
25 neither shall the sacrifice of the feast 2
Lev 3: 1 offering is a sacrifice of peace offering 2
3 from the sacrifice of the peace offering 2
6 If his offering for a sacrifice of peace 2
9 Then from the sacrifice of the peace offering 2
4:10 the ox of the sacrifice of the peace offerings) 2
26 like the fat of sacrifice of peace offerings 2
35 fat . . is removed from the sacrifice of peace 2
7:11 the law of the sacrifice of peace offerings 2
13 With the sacrifice of his peace offerings 2
15 the flesh of the sacrifice of his peace 2
16 if the sacrifice of his offering is a votive 2
16 on the day that he offers his sacrifice 2
17 the flesh of the sacrifice on the third day 2
18 If any of the flesh of the sacrifice of his peace 2
20 the person who eats of the flesh of the sacrifice 2
21 the sacrifice of the LORD'S peace offerings 2
29 He that offers the sacrifice of his peace 2
29 from the sacrifice of his peace offerings 2
32 from the sacrifice of your peace offerings 2
34 out of the sacrifices of their peace offerings 2
9: 4 an ox and a ram for peace offerings, to sacrifice 1
18 the sacrifice of peace offerings for the people 2
10:14 from the sacrifices of the peace offerings 2
17: 5 the people of Israel may bring their sacrifices 2
5 slay them as sacrifices of peace offerings 2
7 shall no more slay their sacrifices for satyrs 2
8 who offers a burnt offering or sacrifice 2
9 bring it . . to sacrifice it to the LORD 6
19: 5 When you offer a sacrifice of peace offerings 2
22:21 any one offers a sacrifice of peace offerings 2
24 you shall not . . sacrifice within your land 6
29 when you sacrifice a sacrifice of thanksgiving 1
29 when you sacrifice a sacrifice of thanksgiving 2
29 sacrifice it so that you may be accepted 1
23:19 two lambs . . as a sacrifice of peace offerings 2
37 sacrifices and drink offerings 2
Num 6:17 offer the ram as a sacrifice of peace offering 2
18 under the sacrifice of the peace offering. 2
7:17 for the sacrifice of peace offerings, two oxen 2
23 for the sacrifice of peace offerings, two oxen 2
29 for the sacrifice of peace offerings, two oxen 2
35 for the sacrifice of peace offerings, two oxen 2
41 for the sacrifice of peace offerings, two oxen 2
47 for the sacrifice of peace offerings, two oxen 2
53 for the sacrifice of peace offerings, two oxen 2
59 for the sacrifice of peace offerings, two oxen 2
65 for the sacrifice of peace offerings, two oxen 2
71 for the sacrifice of peace offerings, two oxen 2
77 for the sacrifice of peace offerings, two oxen 2
83 for the sacrifice of peace offerings, two oxen 2
88 cattle for the sacrifice of peace offerings 2
10:10 over the sacrifices of your peace offerings; 2
15: 3 offer . . a burnt offering or a sacrifice 2
5 you shall prepare . . for the sacrifice 2
8 when you prepare a bull for . . a sacrifice 2
22:40 Balak sacrificed oxen and sheep, and sent 1
25: 2 people to the sacrifices of their gods 2
Deu 12: 6 thither you shall bring . . your sacrifices 2
11 bring . . your sacrifices, your tithes 2
27 the blood of your sacrifices shall be poured out 2
15:21 you shall not sacrifice it to the LORD your God. 1
16: 4 flesh which you sacrifice on the evening 1
17: 1 not sacrifice to the LORD your God an ox or a sheep 1
18: 3 priests' due . . from those offering a sacrifice 2
27: 7 sacrifice peace offerings, and shall eat there; 1
32:17 They sacrificed to demons which were no gods 1
38 who ate the fat of their sacrifices, and drank 2
33:19 mountain; there they offer right sacrifices; 2
Jos 8:31 and sacrificed peace offerings. 1
22:26 altar, not for burnt offering, nor for sacrifice 2
27 with our burnt offerings and sacrifices 2
28 made, not for burnt offerings, nor for sacrifice 2
29 burnt offering, cereal offering, or sacrifice 2
Jdg 2: 5 Bochim; and they sacrificed there to the LORD. 1
16:23 gathered to offer a great sacrifice to Dagon 2
1Sm 1: 3 to worship and to sacrifice to the LORD of hosts 1
4 when Elka'nah sacrificed, he would give portions 1
21 went up to offer to the LORD the yearly sacrifice 2
2:13 The custom . . when any man offered sacrifice 2
15 and say to the man who was sacrificing, "Give meat 1
19 she went up . . to offer the yearly sacrifice. 2
29 look with . . at my sacrifices and my offerings 2
3:14 shall not be expiated by sacrifice or offering 2
6:15 burnt offerings and sacrificed sacrifices 1
15 burnt offerings and sacrificed sacrifices 2
9:12 the people have a sacrifice . . on the high place. 2
13 till he comes, since he must bless the sacrifice; 2
10: 8 to offer . . and to sacrifice peace offerings. 1
11:15 sacrificed peace offerings before the LORD 1
15:15 spared the best . . to sacrifice to the LORD 1
21 people took . . to sacrifice to the LORD your God 1
22 delight in burnt offerings and sacrifices 2
22 to obey is better than sacrifice, and to hearken 2
16: 2 and say, 'I have come to sacrifice to the LORD.' 1
3 invite Jesse to the sacrifice, and I will show you 2
5 I have come to sacrifice to the LORD; 1
5 consecrate . . and come with me to the sacrifice. 2
5 and invited them to the sacrifice. 2
20: 6 there is a yearly sacrifice there for all 2
29 our family holds a sacrifice in the city 2
2Sm 6:13 he sacrificed an ox and a fatling. 1
15:12 And while Ab'salom was offering the sacrifices 2
1Kg 1: 9 Adoni'jah sacrificed sheep, oxen, and fatlings 1
19 He has sacrificed oxen, fatlings, and sheep 1
25 and has sacrificed oxen, fatlings, and sheep 1
3: 2 The people were sacrificing at the high places 1
3 he sacrificed and burnt incense at the high 1
4 the king went to Gibeon to sacrifice there 1
8: 5 Solomon and all . . sacrificing so many sheep 1
62 Israel . . offered sacrifice before the LORD. 2
11: 8 wives, who burned incense and sacrificed 1
12:27 go up to offer sacrifices in the house of the LORD 2
32 and he offered sacrifices upon the altar; *
32 so he did in Bethel, sacrificing to the calves 1
13: 2 Josi'ah . . shall sacrifice upon you the priests 1
22:43 the people still sacrificed and burned incense 1
2Kg 3:20 about the time of offering the sacrifice, behold 4
5:17 will not offer burnt offering or sacrifice 2
10:19 I have a great sacrifice to offer to Ba'al; 2
24 to offer sacrifices and burnt offerings. 2
12: 3 people continued to sacrifice and burn incense 1
14: 4 the people still sacrificed and burned incense 1
15: 4 the people still sacrificed and burned incense 1
35 the people still sacrificed and burned incense 1
16: 4 And he sacrificed and . . on the high places 1
15 throw upon it . . all the blood of the sacrifice; 2
17:32 priests . . who sacrificed for them in the shrines 6
35 fear other gods or bow . . or sacrifice to them; 1
36 you shall bow . . and to him you shall sacrifice. 1
1Ch 15:26 they sacrificed seven bulls and seven rams. 1
29:21 they performed sacrifices to the LORD 2
21 sacrifices in abundance for all Israel; 2
2Ch 5: 6 the ark, sacrificing so many sheep and oxen 1
7: 1 fire . . consumed . . and the sacrifices 2
4 the king and all the people offered sacrifice 2
5 King Solomon offered as a sacrifice 2
12 chosen this place . . as a house of sacrifice. 2
11:16 came . . to Jerusalem to sacrifice to the LORD 1
15:11 They sacrificed to the LORD on that day 1
28: 4 sacrificed and burned incense 1
23 For he sacrificed to the gods of Damascus 1
23 I will sacrifice to them that they may help me. 1
29:31 come near, bring sacrifices and thank offerings 2
31 assembly brought sacrifices and thank 2
30:22 sacrificing peace offerings and giving thanks 1
33:16 offered upon it sacrifices of peace offerings 2
17 people still sacrificed at the high places 1
22 Amon sacrificed to all the images that Manas'seh 1
34: 4 graves of those who had sacrificed to them. 1
Ezr 4: 2 we have been sacrificing to him ever since 1
6: 3 place where sacrifices are offered 7
9: 4 sat appalled until the evening sacrifice. 4
5 at the evening sacrifice I rose from my fasting 4
Neh 4: 2 Will they restore things? Will they sacrifice? 1
12:43 offered great sacrifices that day and rejoiced 2
Ps 4: 5 Offer right sacrifices, and put your trust 2
5: 3 in the morning I prepare a sacrifice for thee *
27: 6 I will offer in his tent sacrifices with shouts 2
40: 6 Sacrifice and offering thou dost not desire; 2
50: 5 who made a covenant with me by sacrifice! 2
8 I do not reprove you for your sacrifices; 2
51:16 For thou hast no delight in sacrifice, 2
17 sacrifice acceptable to God is a broken spirit; 2
19 then wilt thou delight in right sacrifices 2
54: 6 a freewill offering I will sacrifice to thee; 1
66:15 fatlings, with the smoke of the sacrifice of rams; *
106:28 ate sacrifices offered to the dead; 2
37 They sacrificed their sons and their daughters 1
38 sons and daughters, whom they sacrificed 1

107:22 let them offer sacrifices of thanksgiving 2
116:17 offer to thee the sacrifice of thanksgiving 2
141: 2 lifting up of my hands as an evening sacrifice! 4
Prv 7:14 I had to offer sacrifices 3
15: 8 sacrifice of the wicked is an abomination 2
21: 3 more acceptable to the LORD than sacrifice. 2
27 The sacrifice of the wicked is an abomination; 2
Ecc 5: 1 is better than to offer the sacrifice of fools; 2
9: 2 to him who sacrifices and him who does not 1
2 who sacrifices and him who does not sacrifice. 1
Isa 1:11 What to me is the multitude of your sacrifices? 2
19:21 Egyptians will . . worship with sacrifice 2
34: 6 For the LORD has a sacrifice in Bozrah 2
43:23 or honored me with you sacrifices. 2
24 or satisfied me with the fat of your sacrifices. 2
56: 7 their burnt offerings and their sacrifices 2
57: 7 and thither you went up to offer sacrifice. 2
65: 3 sacrificing in gardens and burning incense 1
66: 3 he who sacrifices a lamb, 1
Jer 6:20 nor your sacrifices pleasing to me. 2
7:21 Add your burnt offerings to your sacrifices 2
22 concerning burnt offerings and sacrifices. 2
17:26 bringing burnt offerings and sacrifices 2
33:18 and to make sacrifices for ever. 2
46:10 Lord GOD of hosts holds a sacrifice in the north 2
48:35 him who offers sacrifice in the high place •
Ezk 16:20 these you sacrificed to them to be devoured. 1
20:28 there they offered their sacrifices 2
31 offer your gifts and sacrifice your sons by fire 5
23:39 had slaughtered their children in sacrifice •
36:38 Like the flock for sacrifices †
40:41 on which the sacrifices were to be slaughtered. •
42 and the sacrifices were slaughtered. 2
44:11 burnt offering and the sacrifice for the people 2
46:24 shall boil the sacrifices of the people. 2
Dan 9:21 came . . at the time of the evening sacrifice. 4
27 shall cause sacrifice and offering to cease; 2
Hos 3: 4 dwell many days . . without sacrifice or pillar 2
4:13 They sacrifice on the tops of the mountains 1
14 and sacrifice with cult prostitutes 1
6: 6 For I desire steadfast love and not sacrifice 2
8:13 They love sacrifice; 2
13 they sacrifice flesh and eat it; 1
9: 4 shall not please him with their sacrifices. 2
12:11 if in Gilgal they sacrifice bulls 1
13: 2 Sacrifice to these, they say. Men kiss calves! 1
Ams 4: 4 bring your sacrifices every morning 2
5:25 Did you bring to me sacrifices and offerings 2
Jon 1:16 they offered a sacrifice to the LORD 2
2: 9 voice of thanksgiving will sacrifice to thee; 1
Hab 1:16 Therefore he sacrifices to his net 1
Zep 1: 7 the LORD has prepared a sacrifice 2
8 And on the day of the LORD'S sacrifice– 2
Zec 14:21 that all who sacrifice may come and take of them 1
21 take of them and boil the flesh of the sacrifice •
Mal 1: 8 When you offer blind animals in sacrifice 1
14 and yet sacrifices to the LORD what is blemished; 1
Mat 9:13 'I desire mercy, and not sacrifice.' 9
12: 7 'I desire mercy, and not sacrifice,' 9
Mrk 12:33 all whole burnt offerings and sacrifices. 9
14:12 when they sacrificed the passover lamb 12
Lke 2:24 to offer a sacrifice 9
13: 1 Pilate had mingled with their sacrifices. 9
22: 7 day . . on which the passover lamb had to be sacrificed. 12
Act 7:41 offered a sacrifice to the idol 9
42 Did you offer to me slain beasts and sacrifices 9
Rom12: 1 to present your bodies as a living sacrifice 9
1Co 5: 7 Christ, our paschal lamb, has been sacrificed. 12
10:18 who eat the sacrifices 9
20 No, I imply that what pagans sacrifice 12
Eph 5: 2 a fragrant offering and sacrifice to God. 9
Php 4:18 a sacrifice acceptable and pleasing to God. 9
2Ti 4: 6 For I am already on the point of being sacrificed; 14
Heb 5: 1 to offer gifts and sacrifices for sins. 9
7:27 He has no need . . to offer sacrifices daily 9
8: 3 is appointed to offer gifts and sacrifices; 9
9: 9 gifts and sacrifices are offered 9
23 purified . . with better sacrifices than these. 9
26 to put away sin by the sacrifice of himself. 9
10: 1 same sacrifices which are continually offered 9
3 in these sacrifices there is a reminder of sin •
5 Sacrifices and offerings thou hast not desired 9
8 in sacrifices and offerings and burnt offerings 9
11 offering repeatedly the same sacrifices 9
12 offered for all time a single sacrifice for sins 9
26 there no longer remains a sacrifice for sins 9
11: 4 a more acceptable sacrifice than Cain 9
13:11 as a sacrifice for sin •
15 offer up a sacrifice of praise to God 9
16 such sacrifices are pleasing to God. 9
1Pe 2: 5 offer spiritual sacrifices acceptable to God 9
1Es 1: 6 prepare the sacrifices for your brethren 9
12 they boiled the sacrifices in brass pots 9
17 the things that had to do with the sacrifices 9
18 sacrifices were offered on the altar of the Lord 9
5:50 they offered sacrifices at the proper times 9
51 offered the proper sacrifices every day 9
52 the continual offerings and sacrifices 9
53 began to offer sacrifices to God 9
69 we have been sacrificing to him 8
6:24 where they sacrifice with perpetual fire; 8
29 for sacrifices to the Lord 9
7:12 they sacrificed the passover lamb 12
8:15 to offer sacrifices upon the altar of their Lord 9
65 offered sacrifices to the Lord, the God of Israel 9
66 all as a sacrifice to the Lord. 9
72 I sat . . until the evening sacrifice. 9
2Es 16:68 and shall feed you what was sacrificed to idols. 17
Tob 1: 4 where all the tribes should sacrifice 10
5 All the tribes . . used to sacrifice to the calf Baal 12
Jdt 16:16 every sacrifice as a fragrant offering 9
Sir 7:31 the sacrifice of sanctification 9
34:18 If one sacrifices 10
19 a multitude of sacrifices. 9
20 the man who offers a sacrifice 9
35: 1 sacrifices a peace offering. 10
2 he who gives alms sacrifices a thank offering. 10
7 The sacrifice of a righteous man is acceptable 9
12 do not trust to an unrighteous sacrifice; 9
45:14 His sacrifices shall be wholly burned 9
16 to offer sacrifice to the Lord 13
21 for they eat the sacrifices to the Lord 9
Bar 4: 7 by sacrificing to demons and not to God. 12
LJr 1:28 The priests sell the sacrifices 9
29 Sacrifices to them may be touched by women 9
Aza 1:15 no burnt offering, or sacrifice, or oblation 9
17 such may our sacrifice be in thy sight this day 9
1Mc 1:43 sacrificed to idols and profaned the sabbath. 12
45 to forbid . . sacrifices and drink offerings 9
47 to sacrifice swine and unclean animals 12
2:25 king's officer who was forcing them to sacrifice 12
4:53 they rose and offered sacrifice, as the law directs 9
56 offered a sacrifice of deliverance and praise. 12
12:11 at the sacrifices which we offer 9
2Mc 1: 8 we offered sacrifice and cereal offering 9
18 when Nehemiah . . offered sacrifices. 11
21 materials for the sacrifices were presented 9
23 while the sacrifice was being consumed 9
26 accept this sacrifice 9
31 the materials of the sacrifice were consumed 9
33 Nehemiah . . had burned the materials of the sacrifice 9
2: 9 Solomon offered sacrifice 9
10 fire . . devoured the sacrifices 9
3: 3 the service of the sacrifices. 9
6 did not belong to the account of the sacrifices 9
32 offered sacrifice for the man's recovery. 9
35 Then Heliodorus offered sacrifice to the Lord 9
4:14 neglecting the sacrifices 9
19 to carry 300 silver drachmas for the sacrifice 9
19 Those . . thought best not to use it for sacrifice 9
20 intended . . for the sacrifice to Hercules 9
6: 4 things for sacrifice that were unfit. •
21 who were in charge of that unlawful sacrifice 15
9:16 the expenses incurred for the sacrifices 9
10: 3 they offered sacrifices, after a lapse of two years 9
13:23 settled with them and offered sacrifice 9
14:31 were offering the customary sacrifices 9
3Mc 2:28 None of those who do not sacrifice 12
5:43 empty of those who offered sacrifices there. 9
4Mc 16:20 Abraham was zealous to sacrifice his son Isaac 16

sacrifice *See also* altar, bring, burn, eat, make, offer, partake, seize.

sacrifice an offering 1. זבח
Exd 8:26 shall sacrifice . . offerings abominable 1
26 If we sacrifice offerings abominable 1

burnt sacrifice 1. עֹלָה
Ps 20: 3 and regard with favor your burnt sacrifices! 1

passover sacrifice 1. פֶּסַח
Deu 16: 2 offer the passover sacrifice to the LORD 1
5 not offer the passover sacrifice within any 1
6 there you shall offer the passover sacrifice 1

sweet-smelling sacrifice 1. *εὐωδία*
Sir 38:11 Offer a sweet-smelling sacrifice 1

sacrifice to idol 1. *εἰδωλόθυτος*
Act 15:29 you abstain from what has been sacrificed to idols 1
21:25 should abstain from what has been sacrificed to idols 1

sacrificial 1. זֶבַח 2. קֹדֶשׁ 3. *θυσία*
Ps 69:22 let their sacrificial feasts be a trap. ‡
Jer 11:15 Can vows and sacrificial flesh avert your doom? 2
Ezk 39:17 gather from all sides to the sacrificial feast 1
17 a great sacrificial feast upon the mountains 1
19 at the sacrificial feast which I am preparing 1
Php 2:17 upon the sacrificial offering of your faith 3
Wis 3: 6 like a sacrificial burnt offering 3

sacrificial *See also* feasting, meal, offering.

keep sacrificing 1. זבח
Hos 11: 2 they kept sacrificing to the Ba'als 1

sacrilege 1. *βδέλυγμα* 2. *ἱεροσυλία*
Mat 24:15 So when you see the desolating sacrilege 1
Mrk 13:14 when you see the desolating sacrilege set up 1
1Mc 1:54 they erected a desolating sacrilege 1
2Mc 13: 6 any man guilty of sacrilege 2

sacrilege *See also* act, commit.

sacrilegious 1. *ἱερόσυλος*
Act 19:37 neither sacrilegious nor blasphemers 1

sad 1. כאב 2. רַע 3. רעע 4. *περίλυπος* 5. tristis
1Sm 1: 8 And why do you not eat? And why is your heart sad? 3
18 and ate, and her countenance was no longer sad. •
Neh 2: 1 Now I had not been sad in his presence. 2
2 Why is your face sad, seeing you are not sick? 2
3 Why should not my face be sad, when the city 3
Job 9:27 I will put off my sad countenance •
Prv 14:13 Even in laughter the heart is sad 1
Lke 18:23 when he heard this he became sad 4
2Es 5:16 Where have you been? And why is your face sad? 5
7:80 ever grieving and sad, in seven ways. 5
8:16 and about Israel, for whom I am sad 5
13:17 For those who are not left will be sad 5

sad *See also* look.

saddle 1. חבש 2. כַּר 3. מֶרְכָּב 4. *ἐπισάσσω*
Gen 22: 3 saddled his ass, and took two of his young men 1
31:34 put them in the camel's saddle, and sat upon them. 2
Lev 15: 9 saddle on which he who has the discharge rides 3
Num22:21 Balaam rose in the morning, and saddled his ass 1
Jdg 19:10 He had with him a couple of saddled asses 1
2Sm 16: 1 Ziba . . met him, with a couple of asses saddled 1
17:23 he saddled his ass, and went off . . to his own city. 1
19:26 Saddle an ass for me, that I may ride upon it and go 4
1Kg 2:40 Shim'e-i arose and saddled an ass, and went to Gath 1
13:13 he said to his sons, "Saddle the ass for me. 1
13 Saddle the ass for me." So they saddled the ass 1
23 he saddled the ass for the prophet 1
27 Saddle the ass for me." And they saddled it. 1
27 Saddle the ass for me." And they saddled it. 1
2Kg 4:24 she saddled the ass, and she said to her servant 1

saddlecloth 1. בֶּגֶד חֹפֶשׁ
Ezk 27:20 Dedan traded with you in saddlecloths 1

sadly 1. *στενάζω*
Heb 13:17 Let them do this joyfully, and not sadly 1

sadness 1. רֹעַ 2. maestitia 3. tristitia
Neh 2: 2 This is nothing else but sadness of the heart. 1
Ecc 7: 3 by sadness of countenance the heart is made glad. 1
2Es 4:27 this age is full of sadness and infirmities. 2
10:24 Therefore shake off your great sadness 3

safe 1. בְּשָׁלוֹם 2. חסה 3. טוֹב 4. ישע 5. נצל 6. שגב 7. שָׁלוֹם 8. תָּמִים 9. *ἀσφαλής* 10. *εἰρήνη* 11. *σῶος* 12. *σωτηρία* 13. munitus 14. securitas 15. securus
Deu 29:19 I shall be safe, though I walk in the stubbornness 7
Jos 10:21 the people returned safe to Joshua in the camp 1
1Sm 20:21 it is safe for you and there is no danger. 7
24:19 a man finds his enemy, will he let him go away safe? 3
Job 5:24 You shall know that your tent is safe 7
21: 9 Their houses are safe from fear 7
Ps 18:32 girded me with strength, and made my way safe. 8
61: 4 Oh to be safe under the shelter of thy wings! Selah 2
119:117 Hold me up, that I may be safe 4
Prv 18:10 righteous man runs into it and is safe. 6
29:25 but he who trusts in the LORD is safe. 6
Jer 12: 5 And if in a safe land you fall down 7
Hab 2: 9 nest on high, to be safe from the reach of harm! 5
Php 3: 1 is not irksome to me, and is safe for you. 9
2Es 1:13 and made safe highways for you 13
7:13 the entrances . . are broad and safe 15
121 safe and healthful habitations 14
Tob 12:17 he said to them, "Do not be afraid; you will be safe. 10
Wis 14: 3 a safe way through the waves 9
2Mc 3:15 keep them safe for those who had deposited them. 11
22 keep what had been entrusted safe and secure 11
14: 3 realized that there was no way for him to be safe 12

safe *See also* conduct, hold, keep, make.

safe and sound 1. *ὑγιαίνω*
Lke 15:27 because he has received him safe and sound.' 1
Tob 5:15 if you both return safe and sound 1
20 he will return safe and sound 1
21 he will come back safe and sound 1

safekeeping 1. מִשְׁמֶרֶת
1Sm 22:23 Stay . . with me you shall be in safekeeping. 1

safely 1. בְּשָׁלוֹם 2. שָׁלוֹם 3. שָׁלֵם 4. *ἀσφαλῶς* 5. *μετ' εἰρήνης* 6. *σῶος* 7. *ὑγιής*
Gen 33:18 Jacob came safely to the city of Shechem 3
2Sm 19:30 since my lord the king has come safely home. 1
Isa 41: 3 He pursues them and passes on safely 2
Act 16:23 charging the jailer to keep them safely. 4
Tob 6: 4 and put them away safely. 4
12: 3 he has led me back to you safely, he cured my wife 7
Bar 5: 7 so that Israel may walk safely in the glory of God 4

1Mc 12:52 So they all reached the land of Judah safely 5
16:10 he returned to Judea safely. 5
3Mc 2: 7 but carried through safely those who . . 6

safely *See also* bring.

safety 1. בֶּטַח 2. יֵשַׁע 3. שָׁלוֹם 4. תְּשׁוּעָה 5. ἀσφάλεια 6. εἰρήνη 7. σῶος 8. σωτηρία 9. ὑγίεια

Deu 12:10 gives you rest . . so that you live in safety 1
33:12 The beloved of the LORD, he dwells in safety by him; 1
28 Israel dwelt in safety, the fountain of Jacob 1
1Sm 12:11 and delivered you . . and you dwelt in safety. 1
20:13 and send you away, that you may go in safety. 3
2Sm 19:24 from . . until the day he came back in safety. 3
1Kg 4:25 Judah and Israel dwelt in safety, from Dan even 1
2Ch 19: 1 Jehosh'aphat . . returned in safety to his house 3
Job 5: 4 His sons are far from safety 2
11 those who mourn are lifted to safety. 2
11:18 will be protected and take your rest in safety. 1
Ps 4: 8 for thou alone, O LORD, makest me dwell in safety. 1
12: 5 I will place him in the safety for which he longs. 2
55:18 He will deliver my soul in safety from the battle 3
78:53 He led them in safety, so that they were not afraid; 1
Prv 11:14 in an abundance of counselors there is safety. 4
Isa 14:30 the poor . . and the needy lie down in safety; 1
Jer 32:37 and I will make them dwell in safety. 1
Hos 2:18 and I will make you lie down in safety. 1
Zec 8:10 neither was there any safety from the foe 3
1Es 5: 2 to take them back to Jerusalem in safety 6
Tob 8:21 return in safety to his father 9
Jdt 11: 3 since you have come to safety. 8
1Mc 5:54 before they returned in safety. 6
14:37 fortified it for the safety of the country 7
2Mc 12:24 he besought them to let him go in safety 7
15: 1 to attack them with complete safety 5
4Mc 9: 4 this pity of yours which insures our safety 8
15: 8 disdained the temporary safety of her children. 8

safety *See also* find, flee.

saffron 1. כַּרְכֹּם

Sng 4:14 nard and saffron, calamus and cinnamon 1

sage 1. σοφός

Sir 8: 8 Do not slight the discourse of the sages 1

sail 1. מִפְרָשׂ 2. נֵס 3. ἀναβαίνω 4. ἀνάγω 5. ἀποπλέω 6. ἐκπλέω 7. πλέω 8. πλωτός

Isa 33:23 it cannot . . keep the sail spread out. 2
Ezk 27: 7 fine embroidered linen from Egypt was your sail 1
Lke 8:23 as they sailed he fell asleep 7
Act 13: 4 from there they sailed to Cyprus. 5
14:26 from there they sailed to Antioch 5
18:18 took leave of the brethren and sailed for Syria 6
20:15 sailing from there we came . . opposite Chi'os 5
21: 3 leaving it on the left we sailed to Syria 7
27: 1 when it was decided that we should sail for Italy 5
2 about to sail to the ports along the coast of Asia 7
6 a ship of Alexandria sailing for Italy 7
24 lo, God has granted you all those who sail with you.' 7
28:10 when we sailed 4
1Es 4:23 to sail the sea and rivers; 7
Wis 14: 1 Again, one preparing to sail 7
Sir 43:24 Those who sail the sea tell of its dangers 7
1Mc 7: 1 sailed with a few men to a city by the sea 3
13:29 so that they could be seen by all who sail the sea. 7
2Mc 5:21 he could sail on the land and walk on the sea 8
4Mc 7: 3 until he sailed into the haven of . . victory. 7

sail *See also* set.

sail across 1. διαπλέω

Act 27: 5 when we had sailed across the sea 1

sail along 1. παραλέγομαι

Act 27:13 sailed along Crete, close inshore. 1

sail away 1. ἐκπλέω

Act 15:39 Barnabas . . sailed away to Cyprus 1
20: 6 we sailed away from Philip'pi 1

sail into 1. εἰσπλέω

2Mc 14: 1 Demetrius . . had sailed into the harbor of Tripolis 1
4Mc 13: 6 those who sail into the inner basin 1

sail past 1. παραπλέω

Act 20:16 Paul had decided to sail past Ephesus 1

sail slowly 1. βραδυπλοέω

Act 27: 7 We sailed slowly for a number of days 1

sail through 1. διέρχομαι

Wis 5:10 like a ship that sails through the billowy water 1

sail under the lee 1. ὑποπλέω

Act 27: 4 we sailed under the lee of Cyprus 1
7 we sailed under the lee of Crete 1

sailor 1. ναύτης

Act 27:27 sailors suspected that they were nearing land. 1
30 the sailors were seeking to escape from the ship 1
Rev 18:17 And all shipmasters and seafaring men, sailors 1

saint 1. חָסִיד 2. קָדוֹשׁ 3. קַדִּישׁ (A) 4. ἁγιάζω 5. ἅγιος 6. ὅσιος

2Ch 6:41 and let thy saints rejoice in thy goodness. 1
Ps 16: 3 As for the saints in the land, they are the noble 2
30: 4 Sing praises to the LORD, O you his saints 1
31:23 Love the LORD, all you his saints! 1
34: 9 O fear the LORD, you his saints 2
37:28 he will not forsake his saints. 1
79: 2 flesh of thy saints to the beasts of the earth. 1
85: 8 will speak peace to his people, to his saints 1
97:10 LORD . . preserves the lives of his saints; 1
116:15 Precious . . of the LORD is the death of his saints. 1
132: 9 let thy saints shout for joy. 1
16 her saints will shout for joy. 1
145:10 O LORD, and all thy saints shall bless thee! 1
148:14 horn for his people, praise for all his saints 1
Prv 2: 8 preserving the way of his saints. 1
Dan 7:18 saints of the Most High shall receive 3
21 horn made war with the saints, and prevailed over 3
22 judgment . . given for the saints of the Most High 3
22 time came when the saints received the kingdom. 3
25 shall wear out the saints of the Most High 3
27 given to the people of the saints of the Most High; 3
8:24 destroy mighty men and the people of the saints. 2
Mat 27:52 many bodies of the saints who had fallen asleep 5
Act 9:13 evil he has done to thy saints at Jerusalem; 5
32 he came down also to the saints that lived at Lydda. 5
41 Then calling the saints and widows 5
26:10 I not only shut up many of the saints in prison 5
Rom 1: 7 God's beloved in Rome, who are called to be saints 5
8:27 because the Spirit intercedes for the saints 5
12:13 Contribute to the needs of the saints 5
15:25 I am going to Jerusalem with aid for the saints. 5
26 for the poor among the saints at Jerusalem; 5
31 my service . . be acceptable to the saints 5
16: 2 receive her in the Lord as befits the saints 5
15 and Olym'pas, and all the saints who are with them. 5
1Co 1: 2 called to be saints 5
6: 1 instead of the saints? 5
2 know that the saints will judge the world 5
14:33 As in all the churches of the saints 5
16: 1 Now concerning the contribution for the saints 5
15 devoted themselves to the service of the saints; 5
2Co 1: 1 with all the saints who are in the whole of Acha'ia 5
8: 4 taking part in the relief of the saints– 5
9: 1 to write to you about the offering for the saints 5
12 not only supplies the wants of the saints 5
13:13 All the saints greet you. 5
Eph 1: 1 the saints who are also faithful in Christ Jesus 5
15 your love toward all the saints 5
18 his glorious inheritance in the saints 5
2:19 you are fellow citizens with the saints 5
3: 8 To me, though I am the very least of all the saints 5
18 may have power to comprehend with all the saints 5
4:12 to equip the saints for the work of ministry 5
5: 3 as is fitting among saints. 5
6:18 making supplication for all the saints 5
Php 1: 1 To all the saints in Christ Jesus 5
4:21 Greet every saint in Christ Jesus 5
22 All the saints greet you 5
Col 1: 2 To the saints and faithful brethren in Christ 5
4 the love which you have for all the saints 5
12 the inheritance of the saints in light. 5
26 now made manifest to his saints. 5
1Th 3:13 the coming of our Lord Jesus with all his saints. 5
2Th 1:10 comes on that day to be glorified in his saints 5
1Ti 5:10 washed the feet of the saints 5
Phm 1: 5 toward the Lord Jesus and all the saints. 5
7 the hearts of the saints have been refreshed 5
Heb 6:10 in serving the saints, as you still do. 5
13:24 Greet all your leaders and all the saints 5
Jde 1: 3 faith . . once for all delivered to the saints. 5
Rev 5: 8 bowls . . which are the prayers of the saints; 5
8: 3 prayers of all the saints upon the golden altar 5
4 the smoke . . rose with the prayers of the saints 5
11:18 rewarding thy servants, the prophets and saints 5
13: 7 Also it was allowed to make war on the saints 5
10 a call for the endurance and faith of the saints. 5
14:12 Here is a call for the endurance of the saints 5
16: 6 men have shed the blood of saints and prophets 5
17: 6 I saw the woman, drunk with the blood of the saints 5
18:20 O heaven, O saints and apostles and prophets 5
24 was found the blood of prophets and of saints 5
19: 8 fine linen is the righteous deeds of the saints. 5
20: 9 and surrounded the camp of the saints 5
Tob 8:15 Let thy saints and all thy creatures bless thee; 5
12:15 who present the prayers of the saints 5
Wis 5: 5 why is his lot among the saints? 5
18: 9 the saints would share alike the same things 5
1Mc 7:17 The flesh of thy saints and their blood 6
3Mc 6: 3 look . . upon the children of the sainted Jacob 4

saintly 1. ἱεροπρεπής

4Mc 9:25 the saintly youth broke the thread of life. 1

sake 1. אוֹדָה 2. בִּגְלַל 3. בַּעֲבוּר 4. לְ 5. לְמַעַן 6. מִן 7. מִפְּנֵי 8. עַל 9. תַּחַת 10. διά 11. ἕνεκα 12. ἐπί 13. ὄνομα 14. περί 15. ὑπέρ 16. χάρις 17. per 18. propter

Gen 12:16 for her sake he dealt well with Abram; 3
18:26 I will spare the whole place for their sake. 3
29 He answered, "For the sake of 40 I will not do it. 3
31 He answered, "For the sake of twenty I will not 3
32 answered, "For the sake of ten I will not destroy 3
26: 7 the men . . should kill me for the sake of Rebekah 8
24 your descendants for my servant Abraham's sake. 3
39: 5 blessed the Egyptian's house for Joseph's sake; 2
Exd 18: 8 Pharaoh and to the Egyptians for Israel's sake 1
21:26 he shall let the slave go free for the eye's sake. 9
27 shall let the slave go free for the tooth's sake. 9
Lev 26:45 I will for their sake remember the covenant •
Num 11:29 Moses said to him, "Are you jealous for my sake? •
Jos 23: 3 has done to all these nations for your sake 7
Rut 1:13 it is exceedingly bitter to me for your sake 6
1Sm 12:22 not cast away his people, for his great name's sake 3
2Sm 5:12 exalted his kingdom for the sake of his people 3
9: 1 that I may show him kindness for Jonathan's sake? 3
7 show you kindness for the sake of your father 3
18: 5 Deal gently for my sake with the young man •
12 'For my sake protect the young man Ab'salom.' •
1Kg 8:41 comes from a far country for thy name's sake 5
11:12 for the sake of David your father I will not do it 5
13 I will give one tribe . . for the sake of David 5
13 I will give one tribe . . for the sake of Jerusalem 5
32 he shall have . . for the sake of my servant David 5
32 he shall have . . for the sake of Jerusalem 5
34 make him ruler . . for the sake of David 5
15: 4 for David's sake the LORD his God gave him a lamp 5
2Kg 8:19 would not destroy Judah for the sake of David 5
19:34 save it, for my own sake and for the sake of my 5
34 to save it . . for the sake of my servant David. 5
20: 6 I will defend this city for my own sake and for my 5
6 for my own sake and for my servant David's sake. 5
1Ch 14: 2 exalted for the sake of his people Israel. 3
17:19 For thy servant's sake, O LORD 3
2Ch 6:32 from a far country for the sake of thy great name 5
Ps 6: 4 deliver me for the sake of thy steadfast love. 5
23: 3 in paths of righteousness for his name's sake. 5
25: 7 remember me, for thy goodness' sake, O LORD! 5
11 For thy name's sake, O LORD, pardon my guilt 5
31: 3 for thy name's sake lead me and guide me 5
44:22 Nay, for thy sake we are slain all the day long 8
26 Deliver us for the sake of thy steadfast love! 5
69: 7 For it is for thy sake that I have borne reproach 8
79: 9 deliver us, and forgive our sins, for thy name's sake! 5
106: 8 Yet he saved them for his name's sake 5
45 He remembered for their sake his covenant 4
109:21 my Lord, deal on my behalf for thy name's sake; 5
115: 1 for the sake of thy steadfast love and thy faithfulness 8
122: 8 For my brethren and companions' sake I will say 5
9 For the sake of the house of the LORD our God 5
132:10 For thy servant David's sake do not turn away 3
143:11 For thy name's sake, O LORD, preserve my life! 5
Isa 37:35 for my own sake and for the sake of my servant 5
35 and for the sake of my servant David. 5
42:21 The LORD was pleased, for his righteousness' sake 5
43:14 For your sake I will send to Babylon 5
25 blots out your transgressions for my own sake 5
45: 4 For the sake of my servant Jacob 5
48: 9 For my name's sake I defer my anger 5
9 for the sake of my praise I restrain it for you •
11 For my own sake, for my own sake, I do it 5
11 For my own sake, for my own sake, I do it 5
62: 1 For Zion's sake I will not keep silent 5
1 and for Jerusalem's sake I will not rest 5
63:17 Return for the sake of thy servants 5
65: 8 I will do for my servants' sake, 5
66: 5 who hate you and cast you out for my name's sake 5
Jer 14: 7 act, O LORD, for thy name's sake; 5
21 Do not spurn us, for thy name's sake; 5
15:15 know that for thy sake I bear reproach. 8
17:21 says the LORD: Take heed for the sake of your lives •
Ezk 20: 9 I acted for the sake of my name 5
14 But I acted for the sake of my name 5
22 withheld my hand, and acted for the sake of my name 5
44 the LORD, when I deal with you for my name's sake 5
28:17 corrupted . . for the sake of your splendor. 8
36:22 It is not for your sake, O house of Israel 5
22 I am about to act, but for the sake of my holy name •
32 It is not for your sake that I will act 5
Dan 9:17 for thy own sake, O Lord, cause thy face to shine 5
19 delay not, for thy own sake, O my God 5
Mat 5:10 those who are persecuted for righteousness' sake 11
10:18 before governors and kings for my sake 11
22 you will be hated by all for my name's sake 10
39 he who loses his life for my sake will find it. 11
14: 3 for the sake of Hero'di-as 10
15: 3 for the sake of your tradition? 10
6 for the sake of your tradition 10
16:25 whoever loses his life for my sake will find it. 11
19:12 for the sake of the kingdom of heaven 10
29 for my name's sake, will receive a hundredfold 11
24: 9 hated by all nations for my name's sake. 10

22 for the sake of the elect 10
Mrk 6:17 bound him in prison for the sake of Hero'di-as 10
8:35 whoever loses his life for my sake 11
10:29 for my sake and for the gospel 11
13: 9 stand before governors and kings for my sake 11
13 you will be hated by all for my name's sake 10
20 for the sake of the elect, whom he chose 10
Lke 9:24 whoever loses his life for my sake, he will save it. 11
18:29 left house . . for the sake of the kingdom of God 11
21:12 before kings and governors for my name's sake. 11
17 you will be hated by all for my name's sake. 10
Joh 11:15 for your sake I am glad that I was not there 10
12:30 Jesus answered, "This voice has come for your sake 10
14:11 believe me for the sake of the works themselves. 10
17:19 for their sake I consecrate myself 15
Act 9:16 how much he must suffer for the sake of my name. 15
15:26 risked their lives for the sake of our Lord 15
Rom 1: 5 for the sake of his name among all the nations 15
4:23 the words . . were written not for his sake alone 10
8:36 For thy sake we are being killed all the day 11
9: 3 cut off from Christ for the sake of my brethren 15
11:28 they are enemies of God, for your sake; 10
28 beloved for the sake of their forefathers. 10
13: 5 but also for the sake of conscience. 10
14:20 Do not, for the sake of food, destroy the work 11
1Co 4:10 We are fools for Christ's sake, but you are wise 10
9:10 Does he not speak entirely for our sake? 10
10 It was written for our sake 10
23 I do it all for the sake of the gospel 10
10:28 for conscience' sake– •
2Co 2:10 has been for your sake in the presence of Christ. 10
4: 5 with ourselves as your servants for Jesus' sake. 10
11 always being given up to death for Jesus' sake 10
15 For it is all for your sake 10
5:15 who for their sake died and was raised. 15
21 For our sake he made him to be sin who knew no sin 15
8: 9 yet for your sake he became poor 10
12:10 For the sake of Christ, then, I am content 15
Php 1:29 granted to you that for the sake of Christ 15
29 also suffer for his sake 10
3: 7 I counted as loss for the sake of Christ. 15
8 For his sake I have suffered the loss of all 10
Col 1:24 Now I rejoice in my sufferings for your sake 15
24 for the sake of his body . . the church 15
1Th 1: 5 among you for your sake. 10
3: 9 which we feel for your sake before our God 10
1Ti 5:23 use a little wine for the sake of your stomach 10
2Ti 2:10 everything for the sake of the elect 10
Phm 1: 9 yet for love's sake I prefer to appeal to you–I, Paul 10
Heb 1:14 for the sake of those who are to obtain salvation? 10
6: 7 useful to those for whose sake it is cultivated 10
10 the love which you showed for his sake 13
1Pe 1:20 made manifest at the end . . for your sake. 10
2:13 Be subject for the Lord's sake 10
3:14 even if you do suffer for righteousness' sake 10
1Jn 2:12 because your sins are forgiven for his sake. 10
3Jn 1: 7 For they have set out for his sake 13
Jde 1:11 and abandon themselves for the sake of gain •
Rev 2: 3 and bearing up for my name's sake 10
2Es 1:10 For their sake I have overthrown many kings 18
7:11 For I made the world for their sake 18
74 not for their sake, but because of the times 18
8: 1 Most High made this world for the sake of many 18
1 but the world to come for the sake of few. 18
44 and for whose sake thou hast formed all things 17
9:13 and for whose sake the age was made. ‡
Sir 29: 9 Help a poor man for the commandment's sake 16
10 Lose your silver for the sake of a brother 10
31:17 first to stop eating, for the sake of good manners 16
37: 5 help a friend for their stomach's sake 16
38:14 for the sake of preserving life. 16
44:12 their children also, for their sake. 10
22 for the sake of Abraham his father. 10
Bar 2:14 for thy own sake deliver us, and grant us favor 11
Aza 1:11 For thy name's sake do not give us up utterly 10
12 for the sake of Abraham thy beloved 10
12 for the sake of Isaac thy servant 10
1Mc 13: 4 perished for the sake of Israel 16
2Mc 3:33 for his sake the Lord has granted you your life. 10
5:19 the nation for the sake of the holy place 10
19 the place for the sake of the nation. 10
6:25 for the sake of living a brief moment longer 10
7:23 forget yourselves for the sake of his laws. 10
8:15 if not for their own sake 10
15 yet for the sake of the covenants 10
12:25 for the sake of saving their brethren. 11
13: 3 not for the sake of his country's welfare 12
3Mc 7:11 for the belly's sake 11
4Mc 1: 8 those who died for the sake of virtue 15
10 for the sake of nobility and goodness 15
2:10 virtue is not abandoned for their sakes. 10
6:27 I am dying . . for the sake of the law. 10
30 he resisted . . for the sake of the law. 10
7:22 to endure any suffering for the sake of virtue 10
9:30 our endurance for the sake of religion? 10
10:20 Gladly, for the sake of God 15
11: 2 to be tortured for the sake of virtue. 15
13: 9 let us die . . for the sake of the law 14
12 being slain for the sake of religion. 10
27 endured for the sake of religion 10
14: 6 those holy youths . . agreed to go to death for its sake. 15
15:12 to death for the sake of religion. •
16:13 urged them on to death for the sake of religion. 15
17 endures such agonies for the sake of religion 10
19 to endure any suffering for the sake of God. 10
20 For his sake also our father Abraham was zealous 10
21 and endured it for the sake of God. 10
25 those who die for the sake of God live in God 10
17: 7 tortures to death for the sake of religion? 10
20 who have been consecrated for the sake of God 10
18: 3 suffering for the sake of religion 10

sale 1. מִמְכָּר 2. *πρατός*
Lev 25:29 redeem it within a whole year after its sale 1
Deu 18: 8 besides . . receives from the sale of his patrimony. 1
2Mc 11: 3 to put up the high priesthood for sale every year. 2
sale *See also* offer.

sally forth 1. *ἐκπορεύομαι*
1Mc 14:36 a citadel from which they used to sally forth 1

sally out 1. *ἐξέρχομαι*
1Mc 6:31 the Jews sallied out and burned these with fire 1
9:67 Simon and his men sallied out from the city 1

salt 1. חָמִיץ 2. מֶלַח 3. מְלַח (A) 4. *ἅλας* 5. *ἁλίζω* 6. *ἅλμη* 7. *ἅλς* 8. *ἁλυκός* 9. salsus
Gen 14: 3 valley of Siddim (that is, the Salt Sea). 2
19:26 looked back, and she became a pillar of salt. 2
Lev 2:13 not season all your cereal offerings with salt 2
13 salt of the covenant with your God be lacking 2
13 with all your offerings you shall offer salt 2
Num18:19 it is a covenant of salt for ever before the LORD 2
34: 3 boundary shall be from the end of the Salt Sea 2
12 to the Jordan, and its end shall be at the Salt Sea. 2
Deu 3:17 as far as the sea of the Arabah, the Salt Sea 2
29:23 whole land brimstone and salt, and a burnt-out 2
Jos 3:16 flowing . . toward the sea of Arabah, the Salt Sea 2
12: 3 to the sea of the Arabah, the Salt Sea, southward 2
15: 2 south boundary ran from the end of the Salt Sea 2
5 the east boundary is the Salt Sea 2
62 Nibshan, the City of Salt, and En-ge'di 2
18:19 boundary ends at the northern bay of the Salt Sea 2
Jdg 9:45 and he razed the city and sowed it with salt. 2
2Sm 8:13 he slew . . E'domites in the Valley of Salt. 2
2Kg 2:20 He said, "Bring me a new bowl, and put salt in it. 2
21 he went to the spring of water and threw salt in it 2
14: 7 He killed . . E'domites in the Valley of Salt 2
1Ch 18:12 slew 18,000 E'domites in the Valley of Salt. 2
2Ch 13: 5 to David and his sons by a covenant of salt? 2
25:11 went to the Valley of Salt and smote 10,000 men 2
Ezr 4:14 Now because we eat the salt of the palace 3
6: 9 wheat, salt, wine, or oil, as the priests at Jerusalem 3
7:22 oil, and salt without prescribing how much. 3
Job 6: 6 that which is tasteless be eaten without salt 2
Ps 60: 0 12,000 of Edom in the Valley of Salt. 2
Isa 30:24 asses that till . . will eat salted provender 1
Ezk 43:24 the priests shall sprinkle salt upon them 2
47:11 not become fresh; they are to be left for salt. 2
Zep 2: 9 a land possessed by nettles and salt pits 2
Mat 5:13 You are the salt of the earth; but if salt has lost 4
13 the earth; but if salt has lost its taste, how shall 4
Mrk 9:48 For every one will be salted with fire. 5
49 Salt is good 4
49 if the salt has lost its saltness 4
49 Have salt in yourselves 7
Lke 14:34 Salt is good 4
34 if salt has lost its taste 4
Col 4: 6 always be gracious, seasoned with salt 4
Jas 3:12 No more can salt water yield fresh. 8
1Es 6:30 likewise wheat and salt and wine and oil 7
8:20 100 baths of wine, and salt in abundance. 7
2Es 5: 9 salt waters shall be found in the sweet 9
Wis 10: 7 a pillar of salt 7
Sir 22:15 Sand, salt, and a piece of iron are easier to bear 7
39:23 just as he turns fresh water into salt. 6
26 water and fire and iron and salt and wheat flour 7
43:19 He pours the hoarfrost upon the earth like salt 7
1Mc 10:29 payment of tribute and salt tax and crown levies 7
11:35 the salt pits and the crown taxes due to us 7
salt *See also* eat, land, preserve, rub, season, seasoned.
saltness *See* lose.
salty *See* waste.

salutation 1. *ἀσπασμός*
Mat 23: 7 salutations in the market places 1
Mrk 12:38 to have salutations in the market places 1
Lke 11:43 and salutations in the market places. 1
20:46 and love salutations in the market places 1

salute 1. אמר לְחַי 2. ברך 3. שאל לְשָׁלוֹם 4. *ἀσπάζομαι*
1Sm 13:10 and Saul went out to meet him and salute him. 2
25: 6 And thus you shall salute him: 'Peace be to you 1
14 David sent messengers . . to salute our master; 2
30:21 when David drew near . . he saluted them. 3
2Kg 4:29 If you meet any one, do not salute him; 2
29 and if any one salutes you, do not reply; 2
Mat 5:47 And if you salute only your brethren, what more 4
10:12 As you enter the house, salute it. 4
Mrk 15:18 they began to salute him, "Hail, King of the Jews! 4
Lke 10: 4 salute no one on the road. 4

salvation 1. יְשׁוּעָה 2. יֵשַׁע 3. מוֹשָׁעָה 4. צֶדֶק 5. צְדָקָה 6. תְּשׁוּעָה 7. *σωτηρία* 8. *σωτήριος* 9. salus 10. saluto 11. salvatio
Gen 49:18 I wait for thy salvation, O LORD. 1
Exd 14:13 stand firm, and see the salvation of the LORD 1
15: 2 and he has become my salvation; this is my God 1
Deu 32:15 then he . . scoffed at the Rock of his salvation. 1
1Sm 2: 1 because I rejoice in thy salvation. 1
2Sm 22: 3 my God . . my shield and the horn of my salvation 2
36 Thou hast given me the shield of thy salvation 2
47 and exalted be my God, the rock of my salvation 2
1Ch 16:23 Tell of his salvation from day to day. 1
35 Deliver us, O God of our salvation, and gather 2
2Ch 6:41 Let thy priests . . be clothed with salvation 6
Job 13:16 This will be my salvation 1
33:26 He recounts to men his salvation 5
Ps 13: 5 my heart shall rejoice in thy salvation. 1
18: 2 my shield, and the horn of my salvation 2
35 Thou hast given me the shield of thy salvation 2
46 exalted be the God of my salvation 2
24: 5 and vindication from the God of his salvation. 2
25: 5 teach me, for thou art the God of my salvation; 2
27: 1 The LORD is my light and my salvation; 2
9 forsake me not, O God of my salvation! 2
36:10 thy salvation to the upright of heart! 5
37:39 The salvation of the righteous is from the LORD; 6
38:22 Make haste to help me, O Lord, my salvation! 6
40:10 spoken of thy faithfulness and thy salvation; 6
16 those who love thy salvation say continually 6
50:23 I will show the salvation of God! 2
51:12 Restore to me the joy of thy salvation 2
14 O God, thou God of my salvation 6
62: 1 from him comes my salvation. 1
2 He only is my rock and my salvation, my fortress; 1
6 He only is my rock and my salvation, my fortress; 1
65: 5 O God of our salvation, who art the hope of all 2
68:19 Lord . . bears us up; God is our salvation. Selah 1
20 Our God is a God of salvation; 3
69:29 let thy salvation, O God, set me on high! 1
70: 4 May those who love thy salvation say evermore 1
74:12 working salvation in the midst of the earth. 1
79: 9 Help us, O God of our salvation 2
85: 4 Restore us again, O God of our salvation 2
7 O LORD, and grant us thy salvation. 2
9 Surely his salvation is at hand 2
89:26 my Father, my God, and the Rock of my salvation.' 2
91:16 satisfy him, and show him my salvation. 1
95: 1 make a joyful noise to the rock of our salvation! 2
96: 2 tell of his salvation from day to day. 1
116:13 I will lift up the cup of salvation 1
118:14 LORD . . has become my salvation. 1
21 hast answered me and hast become my salvation. 1
119:41 O LORD, thy salvation according to thy promise; 6
81 My soul languishes for thy salvation; 6
123My eyes fail with watching for thy salvation 1
155Salvation is far from the wicked 1
166I hope for thy salvation, O LORD 1
174I long for thy salvation, O LORD 1
132:16 Her priests I will clothe with salvation 2
Isa 12: 2 Behold, God is my salvation; 1
2 the LORD GOD . . and he has become my salvation. 1
3 you will draw water from the wells of salvation. 1
17:10 For you have forgotten the God of your salvation 2
25: 9 let us be glad and rejoice in his salvation. 1
26: 1 he sets up salvation as walls and bulwarks. 1
33: 2 Be . . our salvation in the time of trouble. 1
6 abundance of salvation, wisdom, and knowledge; 1
45: 8 the earth open, that salvation may sprout forth 2
17 saved by the LORD with everlasting salvation; 6
46:13 it is not far off, and my salvation will not tarry; 6
13 I will put salvation in Zion, for Israel my glory. 6
49: 6 my salvation may reach to the end of the earth. 1
8 in a day of salvation I have helped you; 1
51: 5 draws near speedily, my salvation has gone forth 2
6 but my salvation will be for ever 1
8 for ever, and my salvation to all generations. 1
52: 7 good tidings of good, who publishes salvation 1
10 the earth shall see the salvation of our God. 1
56: 1 righteousness, for soon my salvation will come 1
59:11 is none; for salvation, but it is far from us. 1
17 and a helmet of salvation upon his head; 1
60:18 you shall call your walls Salvation 1
61:10 he has clothed me with the garments of salvation 2
62: 1 and her salvation as a burning torch. 1
11 Behold, your salvation comes; 2
Jer 3:23 in the LORD our God is the salvation of Israel. 6
Lam 3:26 wait quietly for the salvation of the LORD. 6
Hos 10:12 that he may come and rain salvation upon you. 4
Mic 7: 7 I will wait for the God of my salvation; 2
Hab 3:13 wentest forth for the salvation of thy people 2
13 forth . . for the salvation of thy anointed. 2

18 I will joy in the God of my salvation. 2
Lke 1:69 and has raised up a horn of salvation for us 7
77 to give knowledge of salvation to his people 7
2:30 for mine eyes have seen thy salvation 8
3: 6 all flesh shall see the salvation of God. 8
19: 9 Today salvation has come to this house 7
Joh 4:22 for salvation is from the Jews. 7
Act 4:12 there is salvation in no one else 7
13:26 sent the message of this salvation. 7
47 you may bring salvation 7
16:17 who proclaim to you the way of salvation. 7
28:28 salvation of God has been sent to the Gentiles; 8
Rom 1:16 it is the power of God for salvation to every one 7
11:11 salvation has come to the Gentiles 7
13:11 For salvation is nearer to us now 7
2Co 1: 6 it is for your comfort and salvation 7
6: 2 helped you on the day of salvation. 7
2 behold, now is the day of salvation. 7
7:10 that leads to salvation and brings no regret 7
Eph 1:13 the word of truth, the gospel of your salvation 7
6:17 take the helmet of salvation 8
Php 1:28 of your salvation, and that from God. 7
2:12 work out your own salvation with fear 7
1Th 5: 8 for a helmet the hope of salvation. 7
9 to obtain salvation through our Lord Jesus 7
2Ti 2:10 they also may obtain salvation in Christ Jesus 7
3:15 which are able to instruct you for salvation 7
Tit 2:11 has appeared for the salvation of all men 8
Heb 1:14 for the sake of those who are to obtain salvation? 7
2: 3 if we neglect such a great salvation 7
10 make the pioneer of their salvation perfect 7
5: 9 he became the source of eternal salvation 7
6: 9 better things that belong to salvation. 7
1Pe 1: 5 salvation ready to be revealed in the last time. 7
9 you obtain the salvation of your souls. 7
10 searched and inquired about this salvation 7
2: 2 that by it you may grow up to salvation; 7
2Pe 3:15 count the forbearance of our Lord as salvation. 7
Jde 1: 3 eager to write to you of our common salvation 7
Rev 7:10 Salvation belongs to our God who sits upon 7
12:10 salvation . . power and the kingdom of our God 7
19: 1 Salvation and glory and power belong to our God 7
2Es 6:25 shall see my salvation and the end of my world. 10
7:66 salvation promised to them after death. 9
131 joy over those to whom salvation is assured. 9
8:39 over their pilgrimage also, and their salvation 11
9: 8 and will see my salvation in my land 10
AEs 16:23 may mean salvation for us and the loyal Persians 7
Wis 5: 2 will be amazed at his unexpected salvation. 7
6:24 the salvation of the world 7
Bar 4:24 so they soon will see your salvation by God 7
29 bring you everlasting joy with your salvation. 7

salvation *See also* deed.

salve 1. *κολλούριον*

Rev 3:18 salve to anoint your eyes, that you may see. 1

same 1. אֶחָד 2. אֶחָד לְכֹל 3. אֵלֶּה 4. הוּא 5. הִיא 6. זֶה 7. כְּ 8. כֹּל 9. כֵּן 10. עֶצֶם 11. *αὐτός* 12. *ἑαυτοῦ* 13. *εἷς* 14. *ἐκεῖνος* 15. *ἴσος* 16. *κατά* 17. *ὅμοιος* 18. *ὅς* 19. *ὅσος* 20. *οὗτος* 21. *ὡσαύτως* 22. ipse 23. unus

Gen 26:12 Isaac . . reaped in the same year a hundredfold. 5
24 the LORD appeared to him the same night and said 4
32 That same day Isaac's servants came and told him 4
32:19 You shall say the same thing to Esau 6
22 The same night he arose and took his two wives 4
39:17 she told him the same story, saying 7
41:11 we dreamed on the same night, he and I 1
Exd 5: 6 The same day Pharaoh commanded the taskmasters 4
7:11 the magicians of Egypt, did the same by their 9
22 magicians . . did the same by their secret arts; 9
8: 7 the magicians did the same by their secret arts 9
12:42 so this same night is a night of watching kept 4
21:31 shall be dealt with according to this same rule. 6
26: 8 the eleven curtains shall have the same measure. 1
28: 8 shall be of the same workmanship and materials 7
36: 9 all the curtains had the same measure. 1
15 the eleven curtains had the same measure. 1
Lev 19: 6 It shall be eaten the same day you offer it •
22:30 be eaten on the same day, you shall leave none of it 4
23: 6 fifteenth day of the same month is the feast 6
14 you shall eat neither . . until this same day 10
21 you shall make proclamation on the same day 10
28 you shall do no work on this same day; for it is a day 10
29 For whoever is not afflicted on this same day 10
30 whoever does any work on this same day 10
Num 4: 8 and cover the same with a covering of goatskin •
6:11 And he shall consecrate his head that same day. •
10:32 good the LORD will do . . same will we do to you. •
Deu 9:20 I prayed for Aaron also at the same time. 5
14:28 all the tithe of your produce in the same year 5
18:20 that same prophet shall die.' •
21:23 bury him the same day, for a hanged man is accursed 4
27:11 Moses charged the people the same day, saying 4
31:22 Moses wrote this song the same day, and taught it 4
Jos 6:15 and marched around the city in the same manner 6
18:13 to the shoulder of Luz (the same is Bethel) 5
Jdg 7: 9 That same night the LORD said to him, "Arise, •
20:22 again formed the battle line in the same place •
1Sm 2:34 the sign . . both of them shall die on the same day. 1
4:12 and came to Shiloh the same day 4
6: 4 the same plague was upon all of you and upon 1
17:23 came up . . and spoke the same words as before. 3
27 And the people answered him in the same way 6
30 he turned . . and spoke in the same way; 6
31: 6 Saul died . . and all his men, on the same day 4
2Sm 7: 4 But that same night the word of the LORD came 4
1Kg 3:17 my lord, this woman and I dwell in the same house; 1
6:25 both cherubim had the same measure and . . form. 1
25 cherubim had the same measure and the same form. 1
7:18 he did the same with the other capital. 9
37 cast alike, of the same measure and the same form. 1
37 cast alike, of the same measure and the same form. 1
8:64 The same day the king consecrated the . . court 4
13: 3 he gave a sign the same day, saying, "This is the sign 4
2Kg 8:22 Then Libnah revolted at the same time. 5
19:33 By the way that he came, by the same he shall return •
1Ch 17: 3 same night the word of the LORD came to Nathan •
2Ch 16:10 upon some of the people at the same time. 5
28:22 more faithless to the LORD-this same King Ahaz. •
32:12 this same Hezeki'ah taken away his high places 4
30 This same Hezeki'ah closed the upper outlet •
Ezr 5: 3 At the same time Tat'tenai the governor •
Neh 6: 4 I answered them in the same manner. •
5 In the same way Sanbal'lat for the fifth time sent •
Est 9: 1 month of Adar, on the thirteenth day of the same •
21 keep . . and also the fifteenth day of the same •
Job 4: 8 who plow iniquity and sow trouble reap the same. •
Ps 102:27 thou art the same, and thy years have no end. •
Ecc 3:19 fate of . . men and the fate of beasts is the same; 2
19 They all have the same breath 1
Isa 37:34 By the way that he came, by the same he shall return •
Jer 28: 1 In that same year, at the beginning of the reign •
17 In that same year, in the seventh month •
39:10 gave them vineyards and fields at the same time. 4
Ezk 1:16 and the four had the same likeness 1
10:10 the four had the same likeness 1
18:24 iniquity and does the same abominable things 8
21:19 both of them shall come forth from the same land. 1
23:13 that she was defiled; they both took the same way. 1
38 they have defiled my sanctuary on the same day 4
39 on the same day they came into my sanctuary 4
40:10 the three were of the same size; 1
10 the jambs on either side were of the same size. 1
21 its jambs and its vestibule were of the same size 7
22 were of the same size as those of the gate 7
24 they had the same size as the others. 7
28 it was of the same size as the others. •
29 its vestibule were of the same size as the others; 7
32 it was of the same size as the others. 7
33 its vestibule were of the same size as the others; 7
35 he measured it; it had the same size as the others. 7
36 its vestibule were of the same size as the others; •
42:11 similar . . of the same length and breadth, †
11 with the same exits and arrangements and doors. •
44: 3 and shall go out by the same way. •
45:11 ephah and the bath shall be of the same measure 1
20 You shall do the same on the seventh day 9
25 he shall make the same provision for sin •
46: 8 he shall go out by the same way. •
22 the four were of the same size. 1
Dan 4:36 At the same time my reason returned to me; •
11:27 shall speak lies at the same table, but to no avail; 1
Zec 6:10 and go the same day to the house of Josi'ah 4
Mat 5:46 Do not even the tax collectors do the same? 11
47 than others? Do not even the Gentiles do the same? 11
13: 1 That same day Jesus went out of the house and sat •
18:28 that same servant, as he went out •
20: 5 he did the same. 21
21:30 he went to the second and said the same 21
36 they did the same to them. 11
22:23 The same day Sad'ducees came to him 14
26:44 for the third time, saying the same words. 11
27:44 the robbers . . also reviled him in the same way. 11
Mrk 14:31 they all said the same. 21
39 went away and prayed, saying the same words. 11
Lke 6:33 even sinners do the same. 11
10: 7 remain in the same house, eating and drinking 11
21 In that same hour he rejoiced in the Holy Spirit 11
23:40 you are under the same sentence of condemnation? 11
24:33 rose that same hour and returned to Jerusalem; 11
Act 1:11 Jesus . . will come in the same way as you saw him go •
11:17 If then God gave the same gift to them 15
16:33 he took them the same hour of the night 11
Rom 9:21 to make out of the same lump one vessel for beauty 11
10:12 the same Lord is Lord of all 11
12: 4 and all the members do not have the same function 11
1Co 1:10 be united in the same mind and the same judgment. 11
10 united in the same mind and the same judgment. 11
9: 8 Does not the law say the same? 20
10: 3 all ate the same supernatural food 11
4 all drank the same supernatural drink 11
11: 5 it is the same as if her head were shaven. 11
12: 4 there are varieties of gifts, but the same Spirit; 11
5 there are varieties of service, but the same Lord; 11
6 the same God who inspires them all in every one. 11
8 according to the same Spirit 11
9 to another faith by the same Spirit 11
11 All these are inspired by one and the same Spirit 11
25 members may have the same care for one another. 11
2Co 1: 6 when you patiently endure the same sufferings 11
3:14 that same veil remains unlifted 11
4:13 Since we have the same spirit of faith 11
8:16 who puts the same earnest care for you 11
12:18 Did we not act in the same spirit? 11
18 Did we not take the same steps? 11
Eph 6: 8 he will receive the same again from the Lord 20
9 Masters, do the same to them 11
Php 1:30 engaged in the same conflict which you saw 11
2: 2 complete my joy by being of the same mind 11
2 having the same love, being in full accord 11
Heb 1:12 thou art the same, and thy years will never end. 11
2:14 he himself likewise partook of the same nature 11
4:11 no one fall by the same sort of disobedience. 11
6:11 to show the same earnestness 11
10: 1 same sacrifices which are continually offered 11
11 offering repeatedly the same sacrifices 11
11: 9 heirs with him of the same promise. 11
29 the Egyptians, when they attempted to do the same 18
13: 8 Jesus Christ is the same yesterday and today 11
Jas 3:10 From the same mouth come blessing and cursing. 11
11 Does a spring pour forth from the same opening 11
1Pe 4: 1 arm yourselves with the same thought 11
4 do not now join them in the same wild profligacy 11
5: 9 the same experience of suffering is required 11
2Pe 2:12 these . . will be destroyed in the same destruction •
3: 7 But by the same word the heavens and earth 11
Rev 21:16 its length the same as its breadth; 19
1Es 6: 3 At the same time Sisinnes . . came to them and said 11
2Es 3:10 the same fate befell them: as death came upon Adam 23
13:12 I saw the same man come down from the mountain 22
Tob 2: 9 On the same night I returned from burying him 11
3: 7 On the same day, at Ecbatana in Media 11
4: 4 bury her beside me in the same grave. 13
Jdt 13: 3 she had said the same thing to Bagoas. 16
Wis 15: 7 he fashions out of the same clay 11
8 he forms a futile god from the same clay 11
17:14 they all slept the same sleep 11
18: 8 by the same means by which thou didst punish •
11 was punished with the same penalty as the master 17
11 the common man suffered the same loss as the king; 11
19:16 those who had already shared the same rights. 11
18 while each note remains the same •
Sir 44:22 To Isaac also he gave the same assurance 20
LJr 1:71 In the same way, their gods of wood 11
1Mc 8:27 In the same way, if war comes first 11
12: 2 sent letters to the same effect to the Spartans 11
2Mc 3:33 the same young men appeared again to Heliodorus 11
33 dressed in the same clothing 11
6: 8 should adopt the same policy toward the Jews 11
10: 5 on the same day 11
5 on the 25th day of the same month 11
12: 8 meant in the same way to wipe out the Jews 11
13:12 When they had all joined in the same petition 11
3Mc 1:23 resorted to the same posture of supplication 11
3:11 persevere constantly in his same purpose 11
4:13 these men be dealt with in precisely the same fashion 11
5:20 prepare the elephants in the same way 17
36 reconvened the party in the same manner 11
6:30 in that same place in which they had expected •
4Mc 8: 5 not to display the same madness 11
10: 2 the same father begot me and those who died 12
2 the same mother bore me 11
2 I was brought up on the same teachings? 11
13 do not give way to the same insanity 11
11:15 we ought likewise to die for the same principles. 11
12:13 are made of the same elements as you 11
13:20 the brothers dwelt the same length of time 15
20 and was shaped during the same period of time 11
20 growing from the same blood 11
20 growing . . through the same life 11
21 they drank milk from the same fountains 11
24 Since they had been educated by the same law 11
24 trained in the same virtues 11
15:19 gazing boldly at the same agonies 11
16:22 You too must have the same faith in God 11

same *See also* amount, effect, mind, number, ordeal, reason, sense, spring, term, time, trade.

same thing 1. *αὐτός*

Act 15:27 who . . will tell you the same things by word of mouth. 1
Rom 2: 1 you, the judge, are doing the very same things. 1
Php 3: 1 To write the same things to you is not irksome 1
1Th 2:14 you suffered the same things 1
Wis 18: 9 the saints would share alike the same things 1
Sir 34:26 goes again and does the same things 1
1Mc 15:22 The consul wrote the same thing to Demetrius 1
2Mc 2:13 The same things are reported in the records 1

very same 1. עֶצֶם

Gen 7:13 On the very same day Noah and his sons 1

same way 1. זֶה 2. כָּאֵלֶּה 3. *καθώς* 4. *ὁμοίως* 5. *οὗτος* 6. *ὡσαύτως*

Num28:24 In the same way you shall offer daily 2

Jdg 8: 8 up to Penu'el, and spoke to them in the same way; 1
1Co 9:14 In the same way, the Lord commanded 5
11:25 In the same way also the cup, after supper, saying 6
Heb 9:21 in the same way he sprinkled with the blood 4
Jas 2:25 in the same way was not also Rahab . . justified 4
1Jn 2: 6 ought to walk in the same way in which he walked. 3
2Mc 2:14 In the same way Judas also collected . . books 6
7:13 they . . tortured the fourth in the same way. 6
10:36 Others who came up in the same way 4

sanctification 1. ἁγιασμός

Rom 6:19 yield . . members to righteousness for sanctification. 1
22 the return you get is sanctification 1
1Co 1:30 righteousness and sanctification 1
1Th 4: 3 For this is the will of God, your sanctification 1
2Th 2:13 through sanctification by the Spirit 1
Sir 7:31 the sacrifice of sanctification 1

sanctify 1. קדשׁ 2. ἁγιάζω 3. sanctifico

Exd 29:43 it shall be sanctified by my glory; 1
31:13 that you may know that I, the LORD, sanctify you. 1
Lev 20: 8 do them; I am the LORD who sanctify you 1
21: 8 for I the LORD, who sanctify you, am holy 1
15 for I am the LORD who sanctify him 1
23 for I am the LORD who sanctify them 1
22: 9 they profane it: I am the LORD who sanctify them 1
16 holy thing: for I am the LORD who sanctify them 1
32 I am the LORD who sanctify you 1
Num20:12 did not . . sanctify me in the eyes of the people 1
27:14 to sanctify me at the waters before their eyes. 1
Jos 3: 5 Joshua said to the people, "Sanctify yourselves; 1
7:13 Up, sanctify the people, and say 1
13 and say, 'Sanctify yourselves for tomorrow; 1
2Kg 10:20 Sanctify a solemn assembly for Ba'al. 1
1Ch 15:12 sanctify yourselves, you and your brethren 1
14 priests and the Levites sanctified themselves 1
2Ch 5:11 priests . . present had sanctified themselves 1
29: 5 Hear me, Levites! Now sanctify yourselves 1
5 sanctify the house of the LORD, the God 1
15 They . . sanctified themselves, and went 1
17 began to sanctify on the first day of the first 1
17 eight days they sanctified the house of the LORD 1
19 we have made ready and sanctified; 1
34 until other priests had sanctified themselves 1
34 than the priests in sanctifying themselves. 1
30: 3 priests had not sanctified themselves 1
8 his sanctuary, which he has sanctified for ever 1
15 so that they sanctified themselves 1
17 were many . . who had not sanctified themselves; 1
24 priests sanctified themselves in great 1
35: 6 kill the passover lamb, and sanctify yourselves 1
Job 1: 5 Job would send and sanctify them 1
Isa 29:23 his children . . they will sanctify my name; 1
23 they will sanctify the Holy One of Jacob 1
66:17 Those who sanctify and purify themselves 1
Ezk 20:12 they might know that I the LORD sanctify them. 1
37:28 will know that I the LORD sanctify Israel 1
Jol 1:14 Sanctify a fast, call a solemn assembly. 1
2:15 Blow the trumpet in Zion; sanctify a fast; 1
16 gather the people. Sanctify the congregation; 1
Joh 17:17 Sanctify them in the truth; thy word is truth. 2
Act 20:32 among all those who are sanctified. 2
26:18 among those who are sanctified by faith in me.' 2
Rom15:16 be acceptable, sanctified by the Holy Spirit. 2
1Co 1: 2 to those sanctified in Christ Jesus 2
6:11 you were washed, you were sanctified 2
Eph 5:26 he might sanctify her 2
1Th 5:23 May the God of peace himself sanctify you wholly; 2
Heb 2:11 he who sanctifies and those who are sanctified 2
11 those who are sanctified have all one origin. 2
9:13 sanctifies for the purification of the flesh 2
10:10 by that will we have been sanctified through 2
14 perfected for all time those who are sanctified. 2
29 the blood . . by which he was sanctified 2
13:12 in order to sanctify the people 2
1Es 1: 3 they should sanctify themselves to the Lord 2
2Es 9: 8 have sanctified for myself from the beginning. 3
Sir 36: 4 us thou hast been sanctified before them 2
45: 4 He sanctified him through faithfulness 2
3Mc 2: 9 chose this city and sanctified this place 2
16 you sanctified this place. 2

sanctity 1. σεμνότης

2Mc 3:12 the sanctity and inviolability of the temple 1

sanctuary 1. דְּבִיר 2. מִקְדָּשׁ 3. קֹדֶשׁ 4. ἁγίασμα 5. ἁγιασμός 6. ἅγιος 7. ἱερός 8. ναός 9. νεώς 10. οἶκος 11. sanctificatio

Exd 15:17 the sanctuary, O LORD, which thy hands have 2
25: 8 let them make me a sanctuary, that I may dwell 2
30:13 shekel according to the shekel of the sanctuary 3
24 according to the shekel of the sanctuary 3
36: 1 any work in the construction of the sanctuary 3
3 had brought for doing the work on the sanctuary. 3
4 every sort of task on the sanctuary came 3
6 more for the offering for the sanctuary. 3
38:24 in all the construction of the sanctuary 3
24 730 shekels, by the shekel of the sanctuary. 3
25 by the shekel of the sanctuary 3
26 half a shekel, by the shekel of the sanctuary) 3
27 were for casting the bases of the sanctuary 3
Lev 4: 6 in front of the veil of the sanctuary 3
5:15 silver, according to the shekel of the sanctuary 3
10: 4 carry your brethren from before the sanctuary 3
17 sin offering in the place of the sanctuary 3
18 brought into the inner part of the sanctuary 3
18 eaten it in the sanctuary, as I commanded 3
12: 4 she shall not . . nor come into the sanctuary 2
16:33 he shall make atonement for the sanctuary 2
19:30 keep my sabbaths and reverence my sanctuary 2
20: 3 defiling my sanctuary and profaning my holy name 2
21:12 neither shall he go out of the sanctuary 2
12 nor profane the sanctuary of his God 2
23 that he may not profane my sanctuaries 2
26: 2 keep my sabbaths and reverence my sanctuary 2
31 I will . . make your sanctuaries desolate 2
27: 3 according to the shekel of the sanctuary 3
25 according to the shekel of the sanctuary 3
Num 3:28 8,600, attending to the duties of the sanctuary. 3
31 vessels of the sanctuary with which the priests 3
32 those who had charge of the sanctuary. 3
38 having charge of the rites within the sanctuary 2
47 reckoning by the shekel of the sanctuary 3
50 took . . 1,365 shekels, reckoned by . . the sanctuary; 3
4:12 the vessels . . which are used in the sanctuary 3
15 have finished covering the sanctuary 3
15 covering . . the furnishing of the sanctuary 3
16 oversight . . of the sanctuary and its vessels. 3
7:13 70 shekels, according to the shekel of the sanctuary 3
19 70 shekels, according to the shekel of the sanctuary 3
25 130 shekels, according to the shekel of the sanctuary 3
31 70 shekels, according to the shekel of the sanctuary 3
37 70 shekels, according to the shekel of the sanctuary 3
43 70 shekels, according to the shekel of the sanctuary 3
49 70 shekels, according to the shekel of the sanctuary 3
55 70 shekels, according to the shekel of the sanctuary 3
61 70 shekels, according to the shekel of the sanctuary 3
67 70 shekels, according to the shekel of the sanctuary 3
73 70 shekels, according to the shekel of the sanctuary 3
79 70 shekels, according to the shekel of the sanctuary 3
85 according to the shekel of the sanctuary 3
86 according to the shekel of the sanctuary 3
8:19 people . . should come near the sanctuary. 3
18: 1 bear iniquity in connection with the sanctuary; 2
3 not come near to the vessels of the sanctuary 3
5 you shall attend to the duties of the sanctuary 3
16 according to the shekel of the sanctuary 3
19:20 since he has defiled the sanctuary of the LORD; 2
31: 6 sent them . . with the vessels of the sanctuary 3
Jos 24:26 and set it up there under the oak in the sanctuary 2
1Ch 22:19 Arise and build the sanctuary of the LORD God 2
23:32 they shall keep charge of . . the sanctuary 3
24: 5 there were officers of the sanctuary 3
28:10 has chosen you to build a house for the sanctuary; 2
2Ch 20: 8 built thee in it a sanctuary for thy name, saying 2
26:18 Go out of the sanctuary; for you have done wrong 2
29:21 for a sin offering for . . the sanctuary 2
30: 8 come to his sanctuary, which he has sanctified 2
19 the sanctuary's rules of cleanness. 3
36:17 with the sword in the house of their sanctuary 2
Neh 10:39 chambers, where are the vessels of the sanctuary 2
Ps 20: 2 May he send you help from the sanctuary 3
28: 2 lift up my hands toward thy most holy sanctuary. 1
60: 6 God has spoken in his sanctuary 3
63: 2 I have looked upon thee in the sanctuary 3
68:24 processions of my God, my King, into the sanctuary– 3
35 Terrible is God in his sanctuary 2
73:17 until I went into the sanctuary of God; 2
74: 3 has destroyed everything in the sanctuary! 3
7 They set thy sanctuary on fire; 2
78:69 He built his sanctuary like the high heavens 2
96: 6 strength and beauty are in his sanctuary. 2
108: 7 God has promised in his sanctuary 3
114: 2 Judah became his sanctuary 3
150: 1 Praise the LORD! Praise God in his sanctuary; 3
Isa 8:14 he will become a sanctuary, and a stone of offense 2
16:12 when he comes to his sanctuary to pray 2
43:28 I profaned the princes of the sanctuary 3
60:13 the pine, to beautify the place of my sanctuary; 2
62: 9 shall drink it in the courts of my sanctuary. 3
63:18 Thy holy people possessed thy sanctuary 2
Jer 17:12 throne . . is the place of our sanctuary. 2
Lam 1:10 the nations invade her sanctuary 2
2: 7 has scorned his altar, disowned his sanctuary; 2
20 priest . . be slain in the sanctuary of the Lord? 2
Ezk 5:11 surely, because you have defiled my sanctuary 2
8: 6 to drive me far from my sanctuary? 2
9: 6 And begin at my sanctuary. 2
11:16 yet I have been a sanctuary to them for a while 2
21: 2 and preach against the sanctuaries; 2
23:38 they have defiled my sanctuary on the same day 2
39 they came into my sanctuary to profane it. 2
24:21 Behold, I will profane my sanctuary 2
25: 3 said, 'Aha!' over my sanctuary when it was profaned 2
28:18 you profaned your sanctuaries; 2
37:26 and will set my sanctuary in the midst of them 2
28 when my sanctuary is in the midst of them 2
44: 1 me back to the outer gate of the sanctuary 2
5 those who are to be excluded from the sanctuary. 2
7 to be in my sanctuary, profaning it, when you offer 2
8 foreigners to keep my charge in my sanctuary. 2
9 No foreigner . . shall enter my sanctuary. 2
11 They shall be ministers in my sanctuary 2
15 sons of Zadok, who kept the charge of my sanctuary 2
16 they shall enter my sanctuary 2
45: 2 500 cubits shall be for the sanctuary 3
3 in which shall be the sanctuary, the most holy 2
4 for the priests, who minister in the sanctuary 2
4 it shall be . . a holy place for the sanctuary. 2
18 without blemish, and cleanse the sanctuary. 2
47:12 the water for them flows from the sanctuary. 2
48: 8 to the west, with the sanctuary in the midst of it. 2
10 with the sanctuary of the LORD in the midst of it. 2
21 with the sanctuary of the temple in its midst 2
Dan 8:11 place of his sanctuary was overthrown. 2
13 giving over of the sanctuary 3
14 sanctuary . . restored to its rightful state. 3
9:17 cause thy face to shine upon thy sanctuary 2
26 prince . . destroy the city and the sanctuary. 3
Ams 7: 9 the sanctuaries of Israel shall be laid waste 2
13 never . . at Bethel, for it is the king's sanctuary 2
Mal 2:11 Judah has profaned the sanctuary of the LORD 3
Mat 23:35 murdered between the sanctuary and the altar. 8
Lke 11:51 perished between the altar and the sanctuary. 10
Heb 8: 2 a minister in the sanctuary and the true tent 6
5 a copy and shadow of the heavenly sanctuary •
9: 1 worship and an earthly sanctuary. 6
8 the way into the sanctuary is not yet opened 6
24 not into a sanctuary made with hands 6
10:19 we have confidence to enter the sanctuary 6
13:11 is brought into the sanctuary by the high priest 6
2Es 7:108 and Solomon for those in the sanctuary 11
10:21 you see that our sanctuary has been laid waste 11
12:48 on account of the humiliation of our sanctuary. 11
15:25 Do not pollute my sanctuary. 11
Jdt 4:12 the sanctuary to be profaned and desecrated 6
13 in Jerusalem before the sanctuary of the Lord 6
5:19 occupied Jerusalem, where their sanctuary is 4
8:21 our sanctuary will be plundered; and he will 6
24 the sanctuary and the temple and the altar 6
9: 8 they intend to defile thy sanctuary 6
16:20 before the sanctuary for three months 6
Sir 36:13 Have pity on the city of thy sanctuary, Jerusalem 4
45:24 leader of the sanctuary and of his people 6
47:10 the sanctuary resounded from early morning. 4
13 prepare a sanctuary to stand for ever. 4
49: 6 who set fire to the chosen city of the sanctuary 4
50:11 he made the court of the sanctuary glorious. 4
1Mc 1:21 He arrogantly entered the sanctuary 4
36 It became an ambush against the sanctuary 4
37 On every side of the sanctuary 4
37 they even defiled the sanctuary. 4
39 Her sanctuary became desolate as a desert 4
45 to forbid . . sacrifices . . in the sanctuary 4
46 to defile the sanctuary and the priests 4
2: 7 the sanctuary given over to aliens? 4
3:43 fight for our people and the sanctuary. 6
45 The sanctuary was trampled down 4
51 Thy sanctuary is trampled down and profaned 6
58 to destroy us and our sanctuary. 6
59 misfortunes of our nation and of the sanctuary. 6
4:36 go up to cleanse the sanctuary and dedicate it. 6
38 they saw the sanctuary desolate 4
41 until he had cleansed the sanctuary. 6
43 they cleansed the sanctuary 6
48 They also rebuilt the sanctuary 6
5: 1 the sanctuary dedicated as it was before 4
6: 7 had surrounded the sanctuary with high walls 4
18 kept hemming Israel in around the sanctuary. 6
26 have fortified both the sanctuary and Beth-zur; 4
51 he encamped before the sanctuary for many days. 4
54 Few men were left in the sanctuary 6
7:33 Some of the priests came out of the sanctuary 6
42 has spoken wickedly against the sanctuary 6
9:54 the wall of the inner court of the sanctuary 6
10:39 the sanctuary in Jerusalem 6
39 to meet the necessary expenses of the sanctuary. 6
44 restoring the structures of the sanctuary 6
13: 3 done for the laws and the sanctuary 6
6 I will avenge my nation and the sanctuary 6
14:15 He made the sanctuary glorious 6
15 added to the vessels of the sanctuary. 6
29 their sanctuary and the law might be preserved; 6
31 lay hands on their sanctuary 6
36 defile the environs of the sanctuary 6
42 that he should take charge of the sanctuary 6
42 that he should take charge of the sanctuary 6
48 in the precincts of the sanctuary 6
15: 7 I grant freedom to Jerusalem and the sanctuary. 6
2Mc 4:14 Despising the sanctuary 9
9:16 the holy sanctuary 9
10: 3 They purified the sanctuary 9
5 on which the sanctuary had been profaned 9
5 the purification of the sanctuary took place 8
13:23 honored the sanctuary 9
14:33 toward the sanctuary 9

15:17 the city and the sanctuary and the temple 6
18 first fear was for the consecrated sanctuary. 8
33 hang up . . opposite the sanctuary. 8
3Mc 2: 1 the high priest Simon, facing the sanctuary 8
18 We have trampled down the house of the sanctuary 5
28 shall enter their sanctuaries 7

sanctuary (2) 1. ἄσυλος
2Mc 4:33 having first withdrawn to a place of sanctuary 1
34 to come out from the place of sanctuary 1
sanctuary *See* forfeit.

inner sanctuary 1. דְּבִיר 2. οἶκος καταπετάσματος 3. oraculum
1Kg 6: 5 the house, both the nave and the inner sanctuary; 1
16 as an inner sanctuary, as the most holy place. 1
17 the nave in front of the inner sanctuary 3
19 The inner sanctuary he prepared 1
20 The inner sanctuary was twenty cubits long 1
21 he drew chains . . in front of the inner sanctuary 1
22 altar that belonged to the inner sanctuary 1
23 In the inner sanctuary he made two cherubim 1
31 For the entrance to the inner sanctuary he made 1
7:49 lampstands . . before the inner sanctuary; 1
8: 6 its place, in the inner sanctuary of the house 1
8 from the holy place before the inner sanctuary; 1
2Ch 4:20 lamps . . to burn before the inner sanctuary 1
5: 7 to its place, in the inner sanctuary of the house 1
9 from the holy place before the inner sanctuary; 1
Sir 50: 5 as he came out of the inner sanctuary! 2

sand 1. חוֹל 2. ἄμμος 3. ψάμμος 4. harena
Gen 22:17 as the sand which is on the seashore. 1
32:12 make your descendants as the sand of the sea 1
41:49 great abundance, like the sand of the sea 1
Exd 2:12 he killed the Egyptian and hid him in the sand. 1
Deu 33:19 they suck . . the hidden treasures of the sand. 1
Jos 11: 4 in number like the sand that is upon the seashore 1
Jdg 7:12 number, as the sand which is upon the seashore 1
1Sm 13: 5 and troops like the sand on the seashore 1
2Sm 17:11 all Israel . . as the sand by the sea for multitude 1
1Kg 4:20 and Israel were as many as the sand by the sea; they 1
29 largeness of mind like the sand on the seashore 1
Job 6: 3 then it would be heavier than the sand of the sea; 1
29:18 I shall multiply my days as the sand 1
Ps 78:27 like dust, winged birds like the sand of the seas; 1
139:18 If I would count them, they are more than the sand. 1
Prv 27: 3 A stone is heavy, and sand is weighty 1
Isa 10:22 though your people . . be as the sand of the sea 1
48:19 your offspring would have been like the sand 1
Jer 5:22 I placed the sand as the bound for the sea 1
15: 8 widows more in number than the sand of the seas; 1
33:22 and the sands of the sea cannot be measured 1
Hos 1:10 people of Israel shall be like the sand of the sea 1
Hab 1: 9 They gather captives like sand. 1
Mat 7:26 a foolish man who built his house upon the sand; 2
Rom 9:27 the sons of Israel be as the sand of the sea 2
Rev 12:17 And he stood on the sand of the sea. 2
20: 8 their number is like the sand of the sea. 2
2Es 4:17 for the sand stood firm and stopped them. 4
Wis 7: 9 because all gold is but a little sand in her sight 3
Sir 1: 2 The sand of the sea, the drops of rain 2
18:10 Like . . a grain of sand 2
22:15 Sand, salt, and a piece of iron are easier to bear 2
Aza 1:13 as many . . as the sand on the shore of the sea. 2
Man 1: 9 more in number than the sand of the sea 3
1Mc 11: 1 great forces, like the sand by the seashore 2
sand *See also* grain.

burning sand 1. שָׁרָב
Isa 35: 7 the burning sand shall become a pool 1

sand lizard 1. חֹמֶט
Lev 11:30 the lizard, the sand lizard, and the chameleon 1

sandal 1. נַעַל 2. σανδάλιον 3. ὑπόδημα
Gen 14:23 that I would not take a thread or a sandal-thong 1
Exd 12:11 your loins girded, your sandals on your feet 1
Deu 25: 9 pull his sandal off his foot, and spit in his face 1
10 The house of him that had his sandal pulled off. 1
29: 5 your sandals have not worn off your feet; 1
Jos 9: 5 with worn-out, patched sandals on their feet 1
Rut 4: 7 the custom . . the one drew off his sandal and gave 1
8 when the next of kin . . he drew off his sandal. 1
1Kg 2: 5 about my loins, and upon the sandals on my feet. 1
Sng 7: 1 How graceful are your feet in sandals 1
Isa 5:27 is loose, not a sandal-thong broken; 1
Mat 3:11 mightier than I, whose sandals I am not worthy 3
10:10 nor two tunics, nor sandals, nor a staff 3
Mrk 1: 7 the thong of whose sandals 3
6: 9 to wear sandals and not put on two tunics. 2
Lke 3:16 thong of whose sandals I am not worthy to untie 3
10: 4 Carry no purse, no bag, no sandals 3
22:35 When I sent you out with no purse or bag or sandals 3
Joh 1:27 the thong of whose sandal I am not worthy to untie. 3
Act 12: 8 Dress yourself and put on your sandals. 2
13:25 the sandals of whose feet I am not worthy to untie.' 3
Jdt 10: 4 she put sandals on her feet, and put on her anklets 2
16: 9 Her sandal ravished his eyes 2
sandals *See* give, pair.

sandy 1. ἀμμώδης
Sir 25:20 A sandy ascent for the feet of the aged 1
sane *See* keep.

sap 1. κάμπτω
Sir 38:18 sorrow of heart saps one's strength. 1
sap *See also* full.

sapphire 1. אֶבֶן סַפִּיר 2. סַפִּיר 3. σάπφιρος 4. ὑακίνθινος
Exd 24:10 under his feet . . a pavement of sapphire stone 2
28:18 second row an emerald, a sapphire, and a diamond; 2
39:11 an emerald, a sapphire, and a diamond; 2
Job 28: 6 Its stones are the place of sapphires 2
16 the gold of Ophir, in precious onyx or sapphire. 2
Sng 5:14 body is ivory work, encrusted with sapphires. 2
Isa 54:11 and lay your foundations with sapphires. 2
Lam 4: 7 the beauty of their form was like sapphire. 2
Ezk 1:26 of a throne, in appearance like sapphire; 1
10: 1 appeared above them something like a sapphire 1
28:13 chrysolite, beryl, and onyx, sapphire, carbuncle 2
Rev 9:17 the color of fire and of sapphire and of sulphur 4
21:19 every jewel . . the second sapphire 3
Tob 13:16 will be built with sapphires and emeralds 3

sardius 1. אֹדֶם
Exd 28:17 A row of sardius, topaz, and carbuncle shall be 1
39:10 A row of sardius, topaz, and carbuncle 1

sash 1. קִשֻּׁרִים
Isa 3:20 headdresses, the armlets, the sashes, the perfume 1

sate 1. מלא 2. רוה 3. שׂבע 4. שָׂבֵעַ
Ps 78:30 before they had sated their craving †
123: 4 Too long our soul has been sated with the scorn 3
Prv 1:31 be sated with their own devices. 3
25:16 only enough . . lest you be sated with it and vomit 3
27: 7 He who is sated loathes honey 4
Isa 34: 6 The LORD has a sword; it is sated with blood 1
Jer 46:10 The sword shall devour and be sated 3
50:10 all who plunder her shall be sated, says the LORD. 3
Lam 3:15 he has sated me with wormwood. 2
Hab 2:16 You will be sated with contempt 3

satiate 1. μεστάω
3Mc 5:10 satiated with frankincense 1

satisfaction 1. μακαρισμός
Gal 4:15 What has become of the satisfaction you felt? 1
satisfaction *See also* give.

satisfy 1. מלא 2. נוח 3. נחם 4. רוה 5. רִיק 6. שׂבע 7. שָׂבֵעַ 8. שֹׂבַע 9. שָׂבְעָה 10. ἀρέσκω 11. ἀρκέω 12. ἐμπίμπλημι 13. ἰάομαι 14. ἱκανὸν ποιέω 15. ἱκανόω 16. μεθύσκω 17. πείθω 18. χορτάζω 19. saturitas
Lev 26:26 you shall eat, and not be satisfied 6
Deu 33:23 O Naph'tali, satisfied with favor, and full 7
Rut 2:14 and she ate until she was satisfied 6
18 food she had left over after being satisfied. 8
Job 19:22 Why are you not satisfied with my flesh? 6
38:27 to satisfy the waste and desolate land 6
39 or satisfy the appetite of the young lions 1
Ps 17:15 I shall be satisfied with beholding thy form. 6
22:26 The afflicted shall eat and be satisfied; 6
65: 4 We shall be satisfied with the goodness 6
81:16 with honey from the rock I would satisfy you. 6
90:14 Satisfy us in the morning with thy . . love 6
91:16 With long life I will satisfy him 6
103: 5 who satisfies you with good as long as you live 6
104:13 earth is satisfied with the fruit of thy work. 6
107: 9 For he satisfies him who is thirsty 6
132:15 I will satisfy her poor with bread. 6
145:16 satisfiest the desire of every living thing. 6
Prv 6:30 if he steals to satisfy his appetite 1
12:14 fruit of his words a man is satisfied with good 6
13:25 righteous has enough to satisfy his appetite 8
18:20 From the fruit of his mouth a man is satisfied; 6
20 man . . is satisfied by the yield of his lips. 6
19:23 he who has it rests satisfied; 7
27:20 Sheol and Abaddon are never satisfied 6
20 never satisfied are the eyes of man. 6
30:15 Three things are never satisfied; 6
Ecc 1: 8 the eye is not satisfied with seeing 6
4: 8 and his eyes are never satisfied with riches 6
5:10 who loves money will not be satisfied with money; 6
6: 7 the toil . . yet his appetite is not satisfied. 1
Isa 9:20 and they devour on the left, but are not satisfied; 6
29: 8 awakes with his hunger not satisfied 5
43:24 or satisfied me with the fat of your sacrifices. 4
44:16 he eats flesh, he roasts meat and is satisfied; 6
53:11 fruit of the travail of his soul and be satisfied; 6
55: 2 and your labor for that which does not satisfy? 9
58:10 and satisfy the desire of the afflicted 6
11 and satisfy your desire with good things 6
66:11 and be satisfied with her consoling breasts; 6
Jer 31:14 my people shall be satisfied with my goodness 6
25 For I will satisfy the weary soul 4
50:19 shall be satisfied on the hills of E'phraim 6
Ezk 5:13 I will vent my fury upon them and satisfy myself; 3
7:19 they cannot satisfy their hunger 6
16:28 and still you were not satisfied. 6
29 and even with this you were not satisfied. 6
42 will I satisfy my fury on you 2
21:17 also will clap my hands, and I will satisfy my fury; 2
24:13 till I have satisfied my fury upon you. 2
27:33 came from the seas, you satisfied many peoples; 6
Hos 4:10 They shall eat, but not be satisfied; 6
Jol 2:19 and you will be satisfied; 6
26 You shall eat in plenty and be satisfied 6
Ams 4: 8 one city to drink water, and were not satisfied; 6
Mic 6:14 You shall eat, but not be satisfied 6
Mat 5: 6 righteousness, for they shall be satisfied. 18
14:20 they all ate and were satisfied 18
15:37 they all ate and were satisfied 18
28:14 we will satisfy him and keep you out of trouble. 17
Mrk 6:42 they all ate and were satisfied. 18
8: 8 they ate, and were satisfied 18
15:15 So Pilate, wishing to satisfy the crowd 14
Lke 6:21 you shall be satisfied 18
9:17 all ate and were satisfied 18
Joh 14: 8 we shall be satisfied. 11
Act 14:17 satisfying your hearts with food and gladness. 12
Rom 15:14 I myself am satisfied about you, my brethren 17
2Ti 2: 4 to satisfy the one who enlisted him. 10
1Es 3: 3 when they were satisfied they departed 12
2Es 9:26 the nourishment they afforded satisfied me. 19
AEs 14: 8 now they are not satisfied 15
Wis 16: 2 a delicacy to satisfy the desire of appetite; *
Sir 1:16 she satisfies men with her fruits; 16
14: 9 A greedy man's eye is not satisfied with a portion 12
32:13 satisfies you with his good gifts. 16
4Mc 3:10 he could not satisfy his thirst from them. 13

satrap 1. אֲחַשְׁדַּרְפְּנִים 2. אֲחַשְׁדַּרְפַּן (A) 3. σατράπης
Ezr 8:36 king's commissions to the king's satraps 1
Est 3:12 an edict . . was written to the king's satraps 1
8: 9 to the satraps and the governors and the princes 1
9: 3 the princes . . and the satraps and the governors 1
Dan 3: 2 assemble the satraps, the prefects 2
3 Then the satraps, the prefects, and the governors 2
27 satraps, the prefects, the governors 2
6: 1 Darius to set over the kingdom 120 satraps 2
2 to whom these satraps should give account 2
3 above all the other presidents and satraps 2
4 presidents and the satraps sought to find 2
6 these presidents and satraps came by agreement 2
7 presidents . . the prefects and the satraps 2
1Es 3: 2 all the satraps and generals and governors 3
14 satraps and generals and governors and prefects 3
21 forgets kings and satraps 3
4:47 governors and generals and satraps 3
49 no officer or satrap or governor or treasurer 3

satrapy 1. σατραπεία
1Es 3: 2 the 127 satrapies from India to Ethiopia. 1
AEs 16: 1 127 satrapies 1

satyr 1. שָׂעִיר
Lev 17: 7 shall no more slay their sacrifices for satyrs 1
2Ch 11:15 appointed his own priests . . for the satyrs 1
Isa 13:21 ostriches . . dwell, and there satyrs will dance. 1
34:14 the satyr shall cry to his fellow; 1

savage 1. ἄγριος 2. βάρβαρος 3. θηριώδης
2Mc 4:25 the rage of a savage wild beast. 2
10:35 and with savage fury cut down every one they met. 3
3Mc 5:31 a rich feast for the savage beasts 1
4Mc 16: 3 The lions surrounding Daniel were not so savage 1
savage *See also* beast.

more savage 1. ἄγριος
3Mc 7: 5 a cruelty more savage than that of Scythian custom 1

most savage 1. ἀπηνής 2. ὠμός
Wis 17:19 the sound of the most savage roaring beasts 1
4Mc 9:30 Do you not think, you most savage tyrant 2

savage of mind 1. ὠμόφρων
4Mc 9:15 enemy of heavenly justice, savage of mind 1

savagely 1. ἀγρίως
2Mc 15: 2 Do not destroy so savagely and barbarously 1

savagery 1. ἀγριότης 2. ὠμότητα
2Mc 15:21 the savagery of the elephants 1
3Mc 5:20 possessed by a savagery worse than . . Phalaris 2

save 1. חיה 2. חלץ 3. טוֹב עַל 4. יְשׁוּעָה 5. ישׁע 6. מלט 7. נצל 8. פלט 9. שׁמר 10. שׁוּב (A) 11. ἀπολύω 12. διασῴζω 13. ἐξαιρέω 14. ῥύομαι

15. σῴζω 16. σωτηρία 17. σωτήριος 18. salvo
19. salvus 20. servo

Gen 19:19 shown me great kindness in saving my life; 1
20 a little one?-and my life will be saved! 1
Exd 14:30 Thus the LORD saved Israel that day from the hand 5
Num10: 9 you shall be saved from your enemies. 5
Deu 23:14 to save you and to give up your enemies before you 7
33:29 O Israel! Who is like you, a people saved by the LORD 5
Jos 10: 6 come up to us quickly, and save us, and help us; 5
22:31 you have saved the people of Israel from the hand 7
Jdg 2:16 raised up judges, who saved them out of the power 5
18 he saved them from the hand of their enemies 5
1Sm 4: 3 come . . and save us from the power of our enemies. 5
7: 8 cry to the LORD our God for us, that he may save us 5
9:16 He shall save my people from . . the Philistines; 5
10: 1 you will save them from the hand of their enemies 15
19 your God, who saves you from all your calamities 5
27 But some . . said, "How can this man save us? 5
11: 3 if there is no one to save us, we will give . . up 5
12:21 after vain things which cannot profit or save 7
14: 6 hinder the LORD from saving by many or by few. 5
39 as the LORD lives who saves Israel . . he shall 5
17:47 know that the LORD saves not with sword and spear; 5
19:11 If you do not save your life tonight, tomorrow you 6
23: 2 Go and attack the Philistines and save Kei'lah. 5
2Sm 3:18 I will save my people Israel from . . Philistines 5
19: 5 your servants, who have this day saved your life 6
9 and saved us from the hand of the Philistines; 6
22: 3 my God . . my savior; thou savest me from violence. 5
4 I call upon . . and I am saved from my enemies. 5
42 They looked, but there was none to save; 5
1Kg 1:12 that you may save your own life and the life 6
2Kg 6:10 he saved himself there more than once or twice. 9
14:27 so he saved them by the hand of Jerobo'am the son 5
19:19 LORD our God, save us, I beseech thee, from his hand 5
34 I will defend this city to save it, for my own sake 5
1Ch 11:14 and the LORD saved them by a great victory. 5
16:35 O God of our salvation, and gather and save us 7
2Ch 20: 9 cry to thee . . and thou wilt hear and save.' 5
32:22 LORD saved Hezeki'ah and the inhabitants 5
Neh 9:27 give them saviors who saved them from the hand 5
Est 7: 9 prepared for Mor'decai, whose word saved the king 3
Job 5:15 he saves the fatherless from their mouth 5
20:20 he will not save anything in which he delights. 6
22:29 For God abases the proud, but he saves the lowly. 5
26: 2 How you have saved the arm that has no strength! 5
Ps 6: 4 Turn, O LORD, save my life; deliver me 2
7: 1 save me from all my pursuers, and deliver me 5
10 with God, who saves the upright in heart. 5
18: 3 I am saved from my enemies. 5
41 They cried for help, but there was none to save 5
22: 5 To thee they cried, and were saved; 6
21 Save me from the mouth of the lion 5
28: 8 he is the saving refuge of his anointed. 4
9 O save thy people, and bless thy heritage; 5
31: 2 refuge for me, a strong fortress to save me! 5
16 save me in thy steadfast love! 5
33:16 A king is not saved by his great army; 5
17 by its great might it cannot save. 6
34: 6 heard him, and saved him out of all his troubles. 5
18 The LORD . . saves the crushed in spirit. 5
36: 6 man and beast thou savest, O LORD. 5
37:40 he delivers them from the wicked, and saves them 5
44: 6 not in my bow do I trust, nor can my sword save me. 5
7 thou hast saved us from our foes 5
54: 1 Save me, O God, by thy name, and vindicate me 5
55:16 I call upon God; and the LORD will save me. 5
57: 3 He will send from heaven and save me 5
59: 2 save me from bloodthirsty men. 5
69: 1 Save me, O God! For the waters have come up 5
35 God will save Zion and rebuild the cities 5
71: 2 incline thy ear to me, and save me! 5
3 a strong fortress, to save me, for thou art my rock 5
72:13 He has pity . . and saves the lives of the needy. 5
76: 9 to establish judgment to save all the oppressed 5
80: 2 Stir up thy might, and come to save us! 4
3 let thy face shine, that we may be saved! 5
7 let thy face shine, that we may be saved! 5
19 let thy face shine, that we may be saved! 5
86: 2 save thy servant who trusts in thee. 5
16 save the son of thy handmaid. 5
106: 8 Yet he saved them for his name's sake 5
10 he saved them from the hand of the foe 5
47 Save us, O LORD our God, and gather us from among 5
109:26 Save me according to thy steadfast love! 5
31 to save him from those who condemn him to death. 5
116: 4 O LORD, I beseech thee, save my life! 6
6 when I was brought low, he saved me. 5
118:25 Save us, we beseech thee, O LORD! 5
119:94 I am thine, save me; for I have sought thy precepts. 5
146save me, that I may observe thy testimonies. 5
145:19 all who fear him, he also hears their cry, and saves 5
Prv 2:16 You will be saved from the loose woman 7
6: 3 then do this, my son, and save yourself 7
5 save yourself like a gazelle from the hunter 7
14:25 A truthful witness saves lives 7
23:14 beat him with the rod . . save his life from Sheol. 7
Isa 25: 9 God; we have waited for him, that he might save us. 5
30:15 In returning and rest you shall be saved; 5
33:22 the LORD is our king; he will save us. 5
35: 4 He will come and save you. 5
37:20 now, O LORD our God, save us from his hand 5
35 For I will defend this city to save it 5
38:20 The LORD will save me, and we will sing 5
43:12 I declared and saved and proclaimed 5
45:17 Israel is saved by the LORD with everlasting 5
20 and keep on praying to a god that cannot save. 5
22 Turn to me and be saved, all the ends of the earth! 5
46: 2 they cannot save the burden 6
4 I will bear; I will carry and will save. 6
7 it does not answer or save him from his trouble. 5
47:13 let them . . save you, those who divide the heavens 5
15 they wander about . . there is no one to save you. 5
49:25 I will contend . . and I will save your children. 5
59: 1 LORD'S hand is not shortened, that it cannot save 5
63: 1 It is I, announcing vindication, mighty to save. 5
9 and the angel of his presence saved them; 5
64: 5 sins we have been a long time, and shall we be saved 5
Jer 2:27 time of their trouble they say, 'Arise and save us!' 5
28 Let them arise, if they can save you 5
4:14 wash your heart . . that you may be saved. 5
8:20 the summer is ended, and we are not saved. 5
11:12 cannot save them in the time of their trouble. 5
14: 9 a man confused, like a mighty man who cannot save? 5
15:20 I am with you to save you and deliver you 5
17:14 save me, and I shall be saved; for thou art my praise. 5
14 and I shall be saved; for thou art my praise. 5
23: 6 In his days Judah will be saved 5
30: 7 yet he shall be saved out of it. 5
10 O Israel; for lo, I will save you from afar 5
11 For I am with you to save you, says the LORD; 5
31: 7 give praise, and say, 'The LORD has saved his people 5
33:16 In those days Judah will be saved 5
39:18 For I will surely save you 6
42:11 to save you and to deliver you from his hand. 5
46:27 for lo, I will save you from afar 5
48: 6 Flee! Save yourselves! Be like a wild ass 6
51: 6 the midst of Babylon, let every man save his life! 6
45 Let every man save his life from the fierce anger 6
Lam 4:17 we watched for a nation which could not save. 5
Ezk 3:19 but you will have saved your life. 7
21 you will have saved your life. 7
18:27 and does what is . . right, he shall save his life. 1
33: 5 had taken warning, he would have saved his life. 6
9 but you will have saved your life. 7
34:22 I will save my flock, they shall no longer be a prey; 5
37:23 I will save them from all the backslidings 5
Dan 6:27 who has saved Daniel from the power of the lions 10
Hos 13:10 Where now is your king, to save you; 5
14: 3 Assyria shall not save us 5
Ams 2:14 nor shall the mighty save his life; 6
15 and he who is swift of foot shall not save himself 6
15 nor shall he who rides the horse save his life; 6
Jon 4: 6 over his head, to save him from his discomfort. 7
Mic 6:14 you shall put away, but not save 8
14 and what you save I will give to the sword. 8
Hab 1: 2 Or cry to thee "Violence!" and thou wilt not save? 5
Zep 3:19 And I will save the lame and gather the outcast 5
Zec 8: 7 I will save my people from the east country 5
13 so will I save you and you shall be a blessing. 5
9:16 On that day the LORD their God will save them 5
10: 6 I will save the house of Joseph. 5
Mat 1:21 Jesus, for he will save his people from their 15
8:25 they went and woke him, saying, "Save, Lord 15
10:22 But he who endures to the end will be saved. 15
14:30 beginning to sink he cried out, "Lord, save me. 15
24:13 he who endures to the end will be saved. 15
27:40 save yourself! If you are the Son of God 15
49 let us see whether Eli'jah will come to save him. 15
Mrk 8:35 whoever loses his life . . will save it. 15
13:13 he who endures to the end will be saved. 15
15:30 save yourself, and come down from the cross! 15
16:16 He who believes and is baptized will be saved 15
Lke 1:71 that we should be saved from our enemies 16
8:12 that they may not believe and be saved. 15
9:24 whoever loses his life for my sake, he will save it. 15
13:23 Lord, will those who are saved be few? 15
23:35 He saved others; let him save himself 15
37 If you are the King of the Jews, save yourself! 15
39 saying, "Are you not the Christ? Save yourself and us! 15
Joh 3:17 but that the world might be saved through him. 15
5:34 I say this that you may be saved. 15
10: 9 if any one enters by me, he will be saved 15
12:27 'Father, save me from this hour'? 15
47 not . . to judge the world but to save the world. 15
Act 2:21 whoever calls on the name . . shall be saved.' 15
40 Save yourselves from this crooked generation. 15
47 those who were being saved. 15
11:14 a message by which you will be saved 15
16:30 Men, what must I do to be saved? 15
31 you will be saved, you and your household. 15
27:20 all hope of our being saved was . . abandoned. 15
43 the centurion, wishing to save Paul 12
Rom 5: 9 much more shall we be saved by him from the wrath 15
10 much more . . shall we be saved by his life. 15
9:27 only a remnant of them will be saved; 15
10: 1 prayer to God for them is that they may be saved. 16
9 if you confess . . you will be saved. 15
10 and he confesses with his lips and so is saved. 16
13 who calls upon the name of the Lord will be saved. 15
11:14 to make . . jealous, and thus save some of them. 15
26 so all Israel will be saved; as it is written 15
1Co 1:18 to us who are being saved it is the power of God. 15
3:15 though he himself will be saved 15
5: 5 his spirit may be saved in the day of the Lord 15
7:16 whether you will save your husband 15
16 how do you know whether you will save your wife? 15
9:22 that I might by all means save some. 15
10:33 that they may be saved. 15
15: 2 by which you are saved, if you hold it fast 15
2Co 2:15 among those who are being saved 15
1Th 2:16 that they may be saved 15
2Th 2:13 God chose you from the beginning to be saved 16
1Ti 2:15 woman will be saved through bearing children 15
4:16 by so doing you will save . . yourself 15
2Ti 1: 9 who saved us and called us with a holy calling 15
4:18 save me for his heavenly kingdom 15
Heb 9:28 to save those who are eagerly waiting for him. 16
11: 7 an ark for the saving of his household 16
Jas 5:15 the prayer of faith will save the sick man 15
20 will save his soul from death 15
1Pe 3:21 Baptism, which corresponds to this, now saves you 15
4:18 If the righteous man is scarcely saved 15
Jde 1:23 save some, by snatching them out of the fire; 15
2Es 6:25 whoever remains . . shall himself be saved 18
7:60 I will rejoice over the few who shall be saved 18
8: 3 Many have been created, but few shall be saved. 18
41 those . . sown in the world will not all be saved. 18
9: 7 every one who will be saved 19
13 but inquire how the righteous will be saved 18
15 are more who perish than those who will be saved 18
21 and saved for myself one grape out of a cluster 18
22 but let my grape and my plant be saved 20
12:34 those who have been saved throughout my borders 18
42 and like a haven for a ship saved from a storm. 18
13:48 those who are left . . shall be saved. ‡
Jdt 10:15 You have saved your life 15
AEs 10: 9 Israel, who cried out to God and were saved 15
9 The Lord has saved his people 15
13: 9 if it is thy will to save Israel. 15
13 kiss the soles of his feet, to save Israel! 16
14:14 save us by thy hand, and help me, who am alone 14
19 save us from the hands of evildoers 14
19 save me from my fear! 14
Wis 9:18 were saved by wisdom. 15
10: 4 wisdom again saved it 15
14: 4 showing that thou canst save from every danger 15
16: 7 For he who turned toward it was saved 15
Sir 50: 4 He considered how to save his people from ruin •
Bar 4:22 I have put my hope in the Everlasting to save you 16
LJr 1:15 it cannot save itself from war and robbers. 13
36 They cannot save a man from death 14
Aza 1:66 saved us from the hand of death 15
Man 1: 7 they may be saved. 16
14 unworthy as I am, thou wilt save me 15
1Mc 4: 9 how our fathers were saved at the Red Sea 15
11 there is one who redeems and saves Israel. 15
6:44 So he gave his life to save his people 15
2Mc 1:11 Having been saved by God out of grave dangers 15
2:17 It is God who has saved all his people 15
6:22 that by doing this he might be saved from death 11
30 though I might have been saved from death 11
7:25 urged her to advise the youth to save himself. 16
11: 6 to send a good angel to save Israel. 16
12:25 for the sake of saving their brethren. 16
3Mc 2:32 they confidently attempted to save themselves 14
6:13 who have power to save the nation of Jacob. 16
4Mc 12: 6 to obey and save himself. 17

save (2) 1. בִּלְתִּי
Exd 22:20 sacrifices to any god, save to the LORD only 1

save alive 1. חיה
Deu 20:16 you shall save alive nothing that breathes 1
Jos 2:13 and save alive my father and mother, my brothers 1
6:25 Rahab the harlot, and her . . Joshua saved alive; 1
Jdg 8:19 if you had saved them alive, I would not slay you. 1
21:14 whom they had saved alive of the women 1
1Sm 27:11 And David saved neither man nor woman alive 1
1Kg 18: 5 find grass and save the horses and mules alive 1

save life 1. חיה
Gen 47:25 they said, "You have saved our lives; 1
Deu 4:42 fleeing to one of these cities he might save his life 1
19: 4 manslayer, who by fleeing there may save his life. 1
5 may flee to one of these cities and save his life; 1
Ezk 3:18 from his wicked way, in order to save his life 1
13:22 not turn from his wicked way to save his life 1

saving *See* help, power.

saving act 1. צְדָקָה
Mic 6: 5 that you may know the saving acts of the LORD. 1

saving deed 1. צְדָקָה
1Sm 12: 7 the saving deeds of the LORD which he performed 1

savior 1. ישׁע 2. περιποιέω 3. σωτήρ 4. σωτηρία 5. salvator

2Sm 22: 3 my God . . my stronghold and my refuge, my savior; 1
2Kg 13: 5 Therefore the LORD gave Israel a savior 1
Neh 9:27 give them saviors who saved them from the hand 1
Ps 17: 7 Wondrously show thy steadfast love, O savior 1
106:21 forgot God, their Savior, who had done great 1
Isa 19:20 when they cry . . he will send them a savior 1
43: 3 your God, the Holy One of Israel, your Savior. 1
11 I, I am the LORD, and besides me there is no savior. 1
45:15 who hidest thyself, O God of Israel, the Savior. 1
21 god besides me, a righteous God and a Savior; 1
49:26 flesh shall know that I am the LORD your Savior 1
60:16 and you shall know that I, the LORD, am your Savior 1
63: 8 not deal falsely; and he became their Savior. 1
Jer 14: 8 thou hope of Israel, its savior in time of trouble 1
Hos 13: 4 and besides me there is no savior. 1
Obd 1:21 Saviors shall go up to Mount Zion to rule 1
Lke 1:47 my spirit rejoices in God my Savior 3
2:11 born this day in the city of David a Savior 3
Joh 4:42 this is indeed the Savior of the world. 3
Act 5:31 God exalted him . . as Leader and Savior 3
13:23 brought to Israel a Savior, Jesus, as he promised. 3
Eph 5:23 Christ . . is himself its Savior. 3
Php 3:20 from it we await a Savior, the Lord Jesus Christ 3
1Ti 1: 1 by command of God our Savior 3
2: 3 it is acceptable in the sight of God our Savior 3
4:10 the living God, who is the Savior of all men 3
2Ti 1:10 the appearing of our Savior Christ Jesus 3
Tit 1: 3 by command of God our Savior; 3
4 God the Father and Christ Jesus our Savior. 3
2:10 they may adorn the doctrine of God our Savior. 3
13 glory of our great God and Savior Jesus Christ 3
3: 4 loving kindness of God our Savior appeared 3
6 through Jesus Christ our Savior 3
2Pe 1: 1 righteousness of our . . Savior Jesus Christ 3
11 kingdom of our Lord and Savior Jesus Christ. 3
2:20 knowledge of our Lord and Savior Jesus Christ 3
3: 2 the commandment of the Lord and Savior 3
18 knowledge of our Lord and Savior Jesus Christ. 3
1Jn 4:14 Father has sent his Son as the Savior of the world 3
Jde 1:25 to the only God, our Savior through Jesus Christ 3
2Es 2:36 I publicly call on my Savior to witness. 5
Jdt 9:11 savior of those without hope. 3
AEs 15: 2 invoking the aid of the all-seeing God and Savior 3
16:13 Mordecai, our savior and perpetual benefactor 3
Wis 16: 7 not by what he saw, but by thee, the Savior of all. 3
Sir 46: 1 He became . . a great savior of God's elect 4
51: 1 will praise thee as God my Savior 3
Bar 4:22 mercy . . from your everlasting Savior. 3
1Mc 4:30 Blessed art thou, O Savior of Israel 3
2Mc 3:35 and made very great vows to the Savior of his life 2
3Mc 6:29 the Jews . . praised their holy God and Savior 3
32 God, their Savior and worker of wonders 3
7:16 the eternal Savior of Israel 3

savory *See* food.

saw 1. גרר 2. מְגֵרָה 3. πρίω

2Sm 12:31 set them to labor with saws and iron picks 2
1Kg 7: 9 costly stones . . sawed with saws, back and front 1
9 costly stones . . sawed with saws, back and front 1
1Ch 20: 3 to labor with saws and iron picks and axes; 2
Sus 1:59 angel . . waiting with his sword to saw you in two 3

saw down 1. ἐκπρίω

Wis 13:11 A skilled woodcutter may saw down a tree 1

saw in two 1. πρίζω

Heb 11:37 They were stoned, they were sawn in two 1

say 1. אמר 2. אִמְרָה 3. בְּפִי 4. דבר 5. דָּבָר 6. דבר לֵאמֹר 7. יסף 8. פִּי 9. מִלָּה 10. מלל 11. נאם 12. נְאֻם 13. עוד 14. ענה 15. קרא 16. אמר (A) 17. מלל (A) 18. ἀγγέλλω 19. ἀντιλέγω 20. ἀπαγγέλλω 21. ἀποκρίνομαι 22. γάρ 23. διαλογίζομαι 24. εἶπον 25. ἐκδιηγέομαι 26. ἐκλαλέω 27. ἐκ τοῦ στόματος 28. ἐλέγχω 29. λαλέω 30. λαλιά 31. λέγω 32. λόγος 33. ὄνομα 34. ὁ παρά 35. ὅτι 36. προσεῖπον 37. ῥῆμα 38. συλλαλέω 39. φημί 40. φωνή 41. dico 42. facio sermonem 43. loquor

Gen 1: 3 God said, "Let there be light"; and there was light 1
6 God said, "Let there be a firmament 1
9 God said, "Let the waters under the heavens 1
11 God said, "Let the earth put forth vegetation 1
14 God said, "Let there be lights in the firmament 1
20 God said, "Let the waters bring forth swarms 1
22 God blessed them, saying, "Be fruitful 1
24 God said, "Let the earth bring forth living 1
26 God said, "Let us make man in our image 1
28 God blessed them, and God said to them, "Be fruitful 1
29 God said, "Behold, I have given you every plant 1
2:16 the LORD God commanded the man, saying 1
18 the LORD God said, "It is not good that the man 1
23 the man said, "This at last is bone of my bones 1
3: 1 He said to the woman, "Did God say, 'You shall not eat 1
1 He said to the woman, "Did God say, 'You shall not eat 1
2 the woman said to the serpent, "We may eat 1
3 God said, 'You shall not eat of the fruit of the tree 1
4 the serpent said to the woman, "You will not die. 1
9 to the man, and said to him, "Where are you? 1
10 he said, "I heard the sound of thee in the garden 1
11 He said, "Who told you that you were naked? 1
12 The man said, "The woman whom thou gavest 1
13 the LORD God said to the woman 1
13 The woman said, "The serpent beguiled me, and I ate. 1
14 The LORD God said to the serpent 1
16 To the woman he said, "I will greatly multiply 1
17 to Adam he said, "Because you have listened 1
22 the LORD God said, "Behold, the man has become 1
4: 1 she conceived and bore Cain, saying, "I have gotten 1
6 The LORD said to Cain, "Why are you angry 1
8 Cain said to Abel his brother, "Let us go out 1
9 the LORD said to Cain, "Where is Abel your brother? 1
9 He said, "I do not know; 1
10 the LORD said, "What have you done? 1
13 Cain said to the LORD, "My punishment is greater 1
15 Then the LORD said to him, "Not so! If any one slays 1
23 Lamech said to his wives: "Adah and Zillah 1
23 hearken to what I say: I have slain a man 2
25 name Seth, for she said, "God has appointed for me 16
5:29 called his name Noah, saying, "Out of the ground 1
6: 3 Then the LORD said, "My spirit shall not abide 1
7 the LORD said, "I will blot out man 1
13 God said to Noah, "I have determined to make an end 1
7: 1 Then the LORD said to Noah, "Go into the ark 1
8:15 Then God said to Noah 4
21 the LORD said in his heart, "I will never again 1
9: 1 God blessed Noah and his sons, and said to them 1
8 Then God said to Noah and to his sons with him 1
12 God said, "This is the sign of the covenant 1
17 God said to Noah, "This is the sign of the covenant 1
25 he said, "Cursed be Canaan; 1
26 He also said, "Blessed by the LORD my God be Shem; 1
10: 9 therefore it is said, "Like Nimrod a mighty hunter 1
11: 3 they said to one another, "Come, let us make bricks 1
4 Then they said, "Come, let us build ourselves a city 1
6 the LORD said, "Behold, they are one people 1
12: 1 Now the LORD said to Abram, "Go from your country 1
7 Then the LORD appeared to Abram, and said 1
11 he said to Sar'ai his wife 1
12 when the Egyptians see you, they will say 1
13 Say you are my sister, that it may go well with me 1
18 Pharaoh called Abram, and said, "What is this 1
19 Why did you say, 'She is my sister,' 1
13: 8 Then Abram said to Lot, "Let there be no strife 1
14 The LORD said to Abram, after Lot had separated 1
14:19 he blessed him and said, "Blessed be Abram by God 1
21 the king of Sodom said to Abram 1
22 Abram said to the king of Sodom 1
23 lest you should say, 'I have made Abram rich.' 1
15: 2 Abram said, "O Lord GOD, what wilt thou give me 1
3 Abram said, "Behold, thou hast given me 1
5 he brought him outside and said 1
5 Then he said to him, "So shall your descendants be. 1
7 he said to him, "I am the LORD who brought you 1
8 he said, "O Lord GOD, how am I to know 1
9 He said to him, "Bring me a heifer three years old 1
13 Then the LORD said to Abram, "Know of a surety 1
18 a covenant with Abram, saying 1
16: 2 Sar'ai said to Abram, "Behold now, the LORD has 1
5 Sar'ai said to Abram, "May the wrong done to me be 1
6 Abram said to Sar'ai 1
8 he said "Hagar, maid of Sar'ai, where have you 1
8 She said, "I am fleeing from my mistress Sar'ai. 1
9 The angel of the LORD said to her 1
10 The angel of the LORD also said to her 1
11 the angel of the LORD said to her 1
13 of seeing"; for she said, "Have I really seen God 1
17: 1 the LORD appeared to Abram, and said to him 1
3 Then Abram fell on his face; and God said to him 4
9 God said to Abraham, "As for you 1
15 God said to Abraham, "As for Sar'ai your wife 1
17 and laughed, and said to himself, "Shall a child be 1
18 Abraham said to God, "O that Ish'mael might live 1
19 God said, "No, but Sarah your wife shall bear 1
23 foreskins that very day, as God had said to him. 4
18: 3 said, "My lord, if I have found favor 1
5 your servant." So they said, "Do as you have said. 1
5 your servant." So they said, "Do as you have said. 4
6 Abraham hastened into the tent to Sarah, and said 1
9 They said to him, "Where is Sarah your wife? 1
9 your wife?" And he said, "She is in the tent. 1
10 The LORD said, "I will surely return to you 1
12 Sarah laughed to herself, saying 1
13 The LORD said to Abraham, "Why did Sarah laugh 1
13 said to Abraham, "Why did Sarah laugh, and say 1
15 Sarah denied, saying, "I did not laugh"; 1
15 she was afraid. He said, "No, but you did laugh. 1
17 The LORD said, "Shall I hide from Abraham 1
20 Then the LORD said, "Because the outcry 1
23 Then Abraham drew near, and said 1
26 the LORD said, "If I find at Sodom 50 righteous 1
28 And he said, "I will not destroy it if I find 1
29 Again he spoke to him, and said 1
30 Then he said, "Oh let not the Lord be angry 1
31 He said, "Behold, I have taken upon myself to speak 1
32 Then he said, "Oh let not the Lord be angry 1
19: 2 said, "My lords, turn aside, I pray you 1
2 They said, "No; we will spend the night 1
7 said, "I beg you, my brothers 1
9 they said, "Stand back! 1
9 Stand back!" And they said, "This fellow came 1
12 the men said to Lot, "Have you any one else here? 1
14 Lot went out and said to his sons-in-law 4
15 angels urged Lot, saying, "Arise, take your wife 1
17 when they had brought them forth, they said 1
18 Lot said to them, "Oh, no, my lords; 1
21 He said to him, "Behold, I grant you this favor 1
31 the first-born said to the younger 1
34 on the next day, the first-born said to the younger 1
20: 2 Abraham said of Sarah his wife, "She is my sister. 1
3 Abim'elech in a dream by night, and said to him 1
4 Now Abim'elech had not approached her, so he said 1
5 Did he not himself say to me, 'She is my sister'? 1
5 And she herself said, 'He is my brother.' 1
6 Then God said to him in the dream 1
9 Then Abim'elech called Abraham, and said to him 1
10 Abim'elech said to Abraham, "What were you 1
11 Abraham said, "I did it because I thought 1
13 I said to her, 'This is the kindness you must do me 1
13 say of me, He is my brother.' 1
15 Abim'elech said, "Behold, my land is before you; 1
16 Sarah he said, "Behold, I have given your brother 1
21: 1 The LORD visited Sarah as he had said 1
6 Sarah said, "God has made laughter for me; 1
7 she said, "Who would have said to Abraham 1
7 she said, "Who would have said to Abraham 10
10 she said to Abraham, "Cast out this slave woman 1
12 God said to Abraham, "Be not displeased 1
12 whatever Sarah says to you, do as she tells you 1
16 for she said, "Let me not look upon the death 1
17 the angel of God . . said to her, "What troubles 1
22 commander of his army said to Abraham 1
24 And Abraham said, "I will swear. 1
26 Abim'elech said, "I do not know who has done this 1
29 Abim'elech said to Abraham, "What is the meaning 1
30 He said, "These seven ewe lambs you will take 1
22: 1 God tested Abraham, and said to him, "Abraham! 1
1 God tested Abraham, and said to him, "Abraham! 1
2 He said, "Take your son, your only son Isaac 1
5 Then Abraham said to his young men, "Stay here 1
7 Isaac said to his father Abraham, "My father! 1
7 My father!" And he said, "Here am I, my son. 1
7 He said, "Behold, the fire and the wood; 1
8 Abraham said, "God will provide himself the lamb 1
11 called to him from heaven, and said, "Abraham 1
11 Abraham, Abraham!" And he said, "Here am I. 1
12 He said, "Do not lay your hand on the lad 1
14 The LORD will provide; as it is said to this day 1
16 said, "By myself I have sworn 1
16 By myself I have sworn, says the LORD 12
23: 3 Abraham . . said to the Hittites 4
8 he said to them, "If you are willing that I should 4
13 he said to Ephron in the hearing of the people 4
24: 2 Abraham said to his servant 1
5 servant said to him, "Perhaps the woman may not 1
6 Abraham said to him, "See to it that you do not take 1
12 he said, "O LORD, God of my master Abraham 1
14 Let the maiden to whom I shall say 1
14 maiden . . who shall say, 'Drink, and I will water 1
17 and said, "Pray give me a little water 1
18 She said, "Drink, my lord"; 1
19 she said, "I will draw for your camels also 1
23 said, "Tell me whose daughter you are. 1
24 She said to him, "I am the daughter of Bethu'el 1
27 said, "Blessed be the LORD, the God of my master 1
31 He said, "Come in, O blessed of the LORD; 1
33 but he said, "I will not eat until I have told 1
33 have told my errand." He said, "Speak on. 1
34 he said, "I am Abraham's servant. 1
37 My master made me swear, saying 1
39 I said to my master, 'Perhaps the woman will not 1
40 he said to me, 'The LORD, before whom I walk 1
42 I came today to the spring, and said 1
43 young woman . . to whom I shall say, "Pray give me 1
44 who will say to me, "Drink, and I will draw 1
45 I said to her, 'Pray let me drink.' 1
46 She . . said, 'Drink, and I will give your camels 1
47 She said, The daughter of Bethu'el, Nahor's son 1
54 When they arose in the morning, he said, "Send me 1
55 Her brother and her mother said, "Let the maiden 1
56 he said to them, "Do not delay me, since the LORD has 1
57 They said, "We will call the maiden, and ask her. 1
58 they called Rebekah, and said to her 1
58 Will you go with this man?" She said, "I will go. 1
60 they blessed Rebekah, and said to her 1
65 said to the servant, "Who is the man yonder 1
65 The servant said, "It is my master. 1
25:22 and she said, "If it is thus, why do I live? 1
23 the LORD said to her, "Two nations are in your womb 1
30 Esau said to Jacob, "Let me eat some of that red 1
31 Jacob said, "First sell me your birthright. 1
32 Esau said, "I am about to die; 1
33 Jacob said, "Swear to me first. 1

26: 2 the LORD appeared to him and said, Do not go down 1
7 about his wife, he said, "She is my sister"; 1
7 She is my sister"; for he feared to say, "My wife 1
9 Abim'elech called Isaac, and said 1
9 Behold, she is your wife; how then could you say 1
9 you say, 'She is my sister'?" Isaac said to him 1
10 Abim'elech said, "What is this you have done to us 1
11 Abim'elech warned all the people, saying 1
16 Abim'elech said to Isaac, "Go away from us; 1
20 quarreled . . saying, "The water is ours. 1
22 called its name Reho'both, saying 1
24 the LORD appeared to him the same night and said 1
27 Isaac said to them, "Why have you come to me 1
28 They said, "We see plainly that the LORD is 1
28 LORD is with you; so we say, let there be an oath 1
32 they had dug, and said to him, "We have found water 1
27: 1 called Esau his older son, and said to him 1
2 He said, "Behold, I am old; I do not know the day 1
6 Rebekah said to her son Jacob, "I heard your father 1
11 Jacob said to Rebekah his mother 1
13 mother said to him, "Upon me be your curse, my son; 1
18 and said, "My father"; and he said, "Here I am; 1
18 and he said, "Here I am; who are you, my son? 1
19 Jacob said to his father, "I am Esau 1
20 Isaac said to his son, "How is it 1
21 Isaac said to Jacob, "Come near, that I may feel 1
22 who felt him and said, "The voice is Jacob's voice 1
24 He said, "Are you really my son Esau? 1
25 Then he said, "Bring it to me, that I may eat 1
26 Then his father Isaac said to him, "Come near 1
27 blessed him, and said, "See, the smell of my son 1
31 he said to his father, "Let my father arise 1
32 His father Isaac said to him, "Who are you? 1
33 Isaac trembled violently, and said, "Who was it 1
34 and said to his father, "Bless me, even me also 1
35 he said, "Your brother came with guile 1
36 Esau said, "Is he not rightly named Jacob? 1
36 he said, "Have you not reserved a blessing for me? 1
38 Esau said to his father, "Have you but one 1
41 Esau said to himself, "The days of mourning 1
42 her younger son, and said to him 1
46 Rebekah said to Isaac, "I am weary of my life 1
28:13 behold, the LORD stood above it and said 1
16 Then Jacob awoke from his sleep and said 1
17 was afraid, and said, "How awesome is this place! 1
20 Jacob made a vow, saying, "If God will be with me 1
29: 4 Jacob said to them, "My brothers 1
4 you come from?" They said, "We are from Haran. 1
5 said to them, "Do you know Laban the son of Nahor? 1
5 the son of Nahor?" They said, "We know him. 1
6 He said to them, "Is it well with him? 1
6 They said, "It is well; and see, Rachel 1
7 He said, "Behold, it is still high day 1
8 they said, "We cannot until all the flocks are 1
14 Laban said . . "Surely you are my bone and flesh! 1
15 Laban said to Jacob, "Because you are my kinsman 1
18 Jacob loved Rachel; and he said 1
19 Laban said, "It is better that I give her to you 1
21 Then Jacob said to Laban, "Give me my wife 1
25 Jacob said to Laban, "What is this you have done 1
26 Laban said, "It is not so done in our country 1
32 she called his name Reuben; for she said 1
33 bore a son, and said, "Because the LORD has heard 1
34 Again she conceived and bore a son, and said 1
35 she conceived again and bore a son, and said 1
30: 1 Rachel . . envied her sister; she said to Jacob 1
2 and he said, "Am I in the place of God 1
3 Then she said, "Here is my maid Bilhah; go in to her 1
6 Then Rachel said, "God has judged me 1
8 Then Rachel said, "With mighty wrestlings 1
11 And Leah said, "Good fortune! 1
13 Leah said, "Happy am I! For the women will call me 1
14 Then Rachel said to Leah, "Give me, I pray 1
15 she said to her, "Is it a small matter 1
15 Rachel said, "Then he may lie with you tonight 1
16 Leah went out to meet him, and said 1
18 Leah said, "God has given me my hire 1
20 Then Leah said, "God has endowed me 1
23 She conceived and bore a son, and said 1
24 name Joseph, saying, "May the LORD add to me 1
25 When Rachel had borne Joseph, Jacob said to Laban 1
27 Laban said to him, "If you will allow me to say so 1
27 Laban said to him, "If you will allow me to say so •
29 Jacob said to him, "You yourself know how I have 1
31 He said, "What shall I give you? 1
31 I give you?" Jacob said, "You shall not give me 1
34 Laban said, "Good! Let it be as you have said. 1
34 Laban said, "Good! Let it be as you have said. 5
31: 1 Jacob heard that the sons of Laban were saying 1
3 Then the LORD said to Jacob, "Return to the land 1
5 said to them, "I see that your father does not 1
8 If he said, 'The spotted shall be your wages,' 1
8 and if he said, 'The striped shall be your wages,' 1
11 the angel of God said to me in the dream, 'Jacob,' 1
11 in the dream, 'Jacob,' and I said, 'Here I am!' 1
12 he said, 'Lift up your eyes and see, all the goats 1
16 now then, whatever God has said to you, do. 1
24 dream by night, and said to him, "Take heed 1
26 Laban said to Jacob, "What have you done 1
29 spoke . . saying, 'Take heed that you speak 1
35 she said to her father, "Let not my lord be angry 1
36 Jacob said to Laban, "What is my offense? 1
43 Then Laban answered and said to Jacob 1
46 Jacob said to his kinsmen, "Gather stones 1
48 Laban said, "This heap is a witness 1
49 the pillar Mizpah, for he said, "The LORD watch 1
51 Then Laban said to Jacob, "See this heap 1
32: 2 when Jacob saw them he said, "This is God's army! 1
4 instructing them, "Thus you shall say to my lord 1
4 Thus says your servant Jacob, 'I have sojourned 1
6 the messengers returned to Jacob, saying 1
9 Jacob said, "O God of my father Abraham 1
9 O LORD who didst say to me, 'Return to your country 1
12 thou didst say, 'I will do you good 1
16 Jacob . . said to his servants, "Pass on before me 1
18 then you shall say, 'They belong to your servant 1
19 You shall say the same thing to Esau 4
20 you shall say, 'Moreover your servant Jacob is 1
26 Then he said, "Let me go, for the day is breaking. 1
26 But Jacob said, "I will not let you go 1
27 he said to him, "What is your name? 1
27 and he said, "Jacob. 1
28 he said, "Your name shall no more be called Jacob 1
29 But he said, "Why is it that you ask my name? 1
30 saying, "For I have seen God face to face •
33: 5 and children, he said, "Who are these with you? 1
5 Jacob said, "The children whom God has graciously 1
8 Esau said, "What do you mean by all his company 1
9 Esau said, "I have enough, my brother; 1
10 Jacob said, "No, I pray you, if I have found favor 1
12 Then Esau said, "Let us journey on our way 1
13 Jacob said to him, "My lord knows that the children 1
15 Esau said, "Let me leave with you some of the men 1
15 But he said, "What need is there? 1
34: 4 spoke to his father Hamor, saying, "Get me this 1
8 Hamor spoke with them, saying, "The soul of my son 1
11 Shechem also said to her father 1
11 and whatever you say to me I will give. 1
12 and I will give according as you say to me; 1
14 They said to them, "We cannot do this thing 1
20 spoke to the men of their city, saying 1
30 Then Jacob said to Simeon and Levi 1
31 they said, "Should he treat our sister as a harlot? 1
35: 1 God said to Jacob, "Arise, go up to Bethel 1
2 Jacob said to his household 1
10 God said to him, "Your name is Jacob; 1
11 God said to him, "I am God Almighty 1
17 midwife said to her, "Fear not; for now you will 1
37: 6 He said to them, "Hear this dream 1
8 His brothers said to him, "Are you indeed to reign 1
9 told it to his brothers, and said, "Behold, I have 1
10 his father rebuked him, and said to him 1
13 Israel said to Joseph, "Are not your brothers 1
13 And he said to him, "Here I am. 1
14 he said to him, "Go now, see if it is well 1
16 I am seeking my brothers," he said, "tell me 1
17 the man said, "They have gone away 1
17 away, for I heard them say, 'Let us go to Dothan.' 1
19 They said to one another, "Here comes this 1
20 then we shall say that a wild beast has devoured 1
21 he delivered him out of their hands, saying 1
22 Reuben said to them, "Shed no blood; 1
26 Then Judah said to his brothers, "What profit is it 1
30 returned to his brothers, and said 1
32 to their father, and said, "This we have found; see 1
33 he recognized it, and said, "It is my son's robe; 1
35 refused to be comforted, and said, "No, I shall go 1
38: 8 Judah said to Onan, "Go in to your brother's wife 1
11 Then Judah said to Tamar his daughter-in-law 1
16 He went over to her at the road side, and said 1
16 She said, "What will you give me 1
17 And she said, "Will you give me a pledge 1
18 He said, "What pledge shall I give you? 1
21 And they said, "No harlot has been here. 1
22 he returned . . and said, "I have not found her; 1
22 men of the place say, 'No harlot has been here.' 1
24 And Judah said, "Bring her out, and let her be 1
25 And she said, "Mark, I pray you, whose these are 1
26 Judah acknowledged them and said, "She is more 1
28 hand a scarlet thread, saying, "This came out 1
29 and she said, "What a breach you have made 1
39: 7 cast her eyes upon Joseph, and said, "Lie with me. 1
8 he refused and said to his master's wife 1
12 caught him by his garment, saying, "Lie with me 1
14 she called to the men of her household and said 1
17 she told him the same story, saying 1
40: 8 They said to him, "We have had dreams 1
8 And Joseph said to them, "Do not 1
9 told his dream to Joseph, and said to him 1
12 Then Joseph said to him, "This is its 1
16 that the interpretation was favorable, he said 1
41: 9 Then the chief butler said to Pharaoh 4
15 Pharaoh said to Joseph, "I have had a dream 1
15 I have heard it said of you that when you hear 1
17 Then Pharaoh said to Joseph, "Behold, in my dream 4
25 Joseph said to Pharaoh, "The dream of Pharaoh 1
38 Pharaoh said to his servants, "Can we find such 1
39 Pharaoh said to Joseph, "Since God has shown you 1
41 Pharaoh said to Joseph, "Behold, I have set you 1
44 Moreover Pharaoh said to Joseph, "I am Pharaoh 1
51 For," he said, "God has made me to forget all my •
54 years of famine began to come, as Joseph had said. 1
55 and Pharaoh said to all the Egyptians 1
55 Egyptians, "Go to Joseph; what he says to you, do. 1
42: 1 he said to his sons, "Why do you look at one another 1
2 he said, "Behold, I have heard that there is grain 1
7 Where do you come from?" he said. 1
7 They said, "From the land of Canaan, to buy food. 1
9 he said to them, "You are spies, you have come 1
10 They said to him, "No, my lord, but to buy food 1
12 He said to them, "No, it is the weakness of the land 1
13 said, "We, your servants, are twelve brothers 1
14 Joseph said to them, "It is as I said to you 1
14 Joseph said to them, "It is as I said to you 4
18 On the third day Joseph said to them 1
21 Then they said to one another, "In truth we are 1
28 said to his brothers, "My money has been put back; 1
28 turned trembling to one another, saying 1
29 they told him all that had befallen them, saying 1
31 we said to him, 'We are honest men, we are not spies 1
33 Then the man, the lord of the land, said to us 1
36 Jacob their father said to them 1
37 Reuben said to his father, "Slay my two sons if I do 1
38 he said, "My son shall not go down with you 1
43: 2 their father said to them, "Go again 1
3 Judah said to him, "The man solemnly warned us 1
3 solemnly warned us, saying, 'You shall not see 1
5 we will not go down, for the man said to us 1
6 Israel said, "Why did you treat me so ill 1
7 questioned us . . saying, 'Is your father still 1
7 could we in any way know that he would say 1
8 Judah said to Israel his father, "Send the lad 1
11 Then their father Israel said to them 1
16 When Joseph saw . . he said to the steward 1
18 and they said, "It is because of the money 1
20 said, "Oh, my lord, we came down the first time 1
27 he inquired about their welfare, and said 1
28 They said, "Your servant our father is well 1
29 saw his brother Benjamin . . and said 1
31 and controlling himself he said 1
44: 4 Joseph said to his steward, "Up, follow after 1
4 and when you overtake them, say to them, 'Why have 1
7 said to him, "Why does my lord speak such words 1
10 He said, "Let it be as you say 1
10 He said, "Let it be as you say 5
15 Joseph said to them, "What deed is this that you 1
16 Judah said, "What shall we say to my lord? 1
16 Judah said, "What shall we say to my lord? 1
17 he said, "Far be it from me that I should do so! 1
18 Then Judah went up to him and said, "O my lord 1
19 My lord asked his servants, saying 1
20 we said to my lord, 'We have a father, an old man 1
21 Then you said to your servants, 'Bring him down 1
22 said to my lord, 'The lad cannot leave his father 1
23 Then you said to your servants 1
25 when our father said, 'Go again, buy us a little food 1
26 we said, 'We cannot go down. 1
27 Then your servant my father said to us 1
28 one left me, and I said, Surely he has been torn 1
32 became surety for the lad to my father, saying 1
45: 3 Joseph said to his brothers, "I am Joseph; 1
4 Joseph said to his brothers, "Come near to me 1
4 And he said, "I am your brother, Joseph 1
9 to my father and say to him, 'Thus says your son 1
9 Thus says your son Joseph, God has made me lord 1
17 Pharaoh said to Joseph, "Say to your brothers 1
17 Pharaoh said to Joseph, "Say to your brothers 1
24 as they departed, he said to them 1
27 all the words of Joseph, which he had said to them 4
28 Israel said, "It is enough; Joseph my son is still 1
46: 2 God spoke . . and said, "Jacob, Jacob. 1
2 said, "Jacob, Jacob." And he said, "Here am I. 1
3 Then he said, "I am God, the God of your father; 1
30 Israel said to Joseph, "Now let me die 1
31 Joseph said to his brothers and to his father's 1
31 I will go up and tell Pharaoh, and will say to him 1
33 When Pharaoh calls you, and says, 1
34 you shall say, 'Your servants have been keepers 1
47: 3 Pharaoh said to his brothers, "What is 1
3 is your occupation?" And they said to Pharaoh 1
4 They said to Pharaoh, "We have come to sojourn 1
5 Then Pharaoh said to Joseph, "Your father 1
8 Pharaoh said to Jacob, "How many are the days 1
9 Jacob said to Pharaoh, "The days of the years of my 1
15 all the Egyptians came to Joseph, and said, 1
18 they came to him the following year, and said 1
23 Joseph said to the people, "Behold, I have 1
25 they said, "You have saved our lives; 1
29 called his son Joseph and said to him, 1
30 He answered, "I will do as you have said. 5
31 he said, "Swear to me"; and he swore to him. 1
48: 3 Jacob said to Joseph, "God Almighty appeared 1
4 said to me, 'Behold, I will make you fruitful 1
8 Israel saw Joseph's sons, he said, "Who are these 1
9 Joseph said to his father, "They are my sons 1
9 And he said, "Bring them to me, I pray you, 1
11 Israel said to Joseph, "I had not thought to see 1

15 he blessed Joseph, and said, "The God before 1
18 Joseph said to his father, "Not so, my father; 1
19 his father refused, and said, "I know, my son, 1
20 he blessed them that day, saying, "By you Israel 1
20 By you Israel will pronounce blessings, saying 1
21 Israel said to Joseph, "Behold, I am about to die 1
49: 1 Jacob called his sons, and said, "Gather 1
28 and this is what their father said to them 4
29 Then he charged them, and said to them, 1
50: 4 Joseph spoke . . saying, "If now I have found favor 1
4 speak, I pray you, in the ears of Pharaoh, saying 1
5 My father made me swear, saying, 'I am about to die 1
11 they said, "This is a grievous mourning 1
15 their father was dead, they said, "It may be that 1
16 sent a message to Joseph, saying, "Your father 1
17 'Say to Joseph, Forgive, I pray you 1
18 fell down before him, and said, "Behold, we are 1
19 Joseph said to them, "Fear not, 1
24 Joseph said to his brothers, "I am about to die; 1
25 took an oath . . saying, "God will visit you, 1
Exd 1: 9 he said to his people, "Behold, the people of Israel 1
15 the king of Egypt said to the Hebrew midwives 1
18 the king of Egypt called the midwives, and said 1
19 The midwives said to Pharaoh, "Because the Hebrew 1
2: 6 took pity on him and said, "This is one 1
7 his sister said to Pharaoh's daughter, "Shall I go 1
8 Pharaoh's daughter said to her, "Go. 1
9 Pharaoh's daughter said to her, "Take this child 1
10 named him Moses, for she said, "Because I drew him 1
13 and he said to the man that did the wrong, 1
18 father Reu'el, he said, "How is it that you have come 1
19 They said, "An Egyptian delivered us out 1
20 He said to his daughters, "And where is he? 1
22 name Gershom; for he said, "I have been a sojourner 1
3: 3 Moses said, "I will turn aside and see this 1
4 Moses, Moses!" And he said, "Here am I. 1
5 Then he said, "Do not come near; put off your shoes 1
6 he said, "I am the God of your father 1
7 Then the LORD said, "I have seen the affliction 1
11 Moses said to God, "Who am I that I should go 1
12 He said, "But I will be with you; 1
13 Moses said to God, "If I come to the people of Israel 1
13 to the people of Israel and say to them, 'The God 1
13 'What is his name?' what shall I say to them? 1
14 God said to Moses, "I AM WHO I AM." And he said, 1
14 And he said, "Say this to the people of Israel, 'I AM 1
14 And he said, "Say this to the people of Israel, 'I AM 1
15 God also said to Moses, "Say this to the people 1
15 Say this to the people of Israel, 'The LORD 1
16 Go . . and say to them, 'The LORD, the God 1
16 LORD . . has appeared to me, saying, "I have 1
18 you . . shall go to the king of Egypt and say to him 1
4: 1 for they will say, 'The LORD did not appear to you.' 1
2 The LORD said to him, "What is that in your hand? 1
2 What is that in your hand?" He said, "A rod. 1
3 he said, "Cast it to the ground." So he cast it 1
4 the LORD said to Moses, "Put out your hand, and take 1
6 Again, the LORD said to him, "Put your hand 1
7 Then God said, "Put your hand back into your bosom. 1
8 If they will not believe you," God said, "or heed *
10 Moses said . . "Oh, my Lord, I am not eloquent 1
11 Then the LORD said . . "Who has made man's mouth? 1
13 he said, "Oh, my Lord, send, I pray, some other person. 1
14 and he said, "Is there not Aaron, your brother 1
18 father-in-law and said to him, "Let me go back, I pray 1
18 And Jethro said to Moses, "Go in peace. 1
19 the LORD said to Moses in Mid'ian, "Go back to Egypt; 1
21 the LORD said to Moses, "When you go back to Egypt 1
22 you shall say to Pharaoh, 'Thus says the LORD 1
22 you shall say to Pharaoh, 'Thus says the LORD 1
23 I say to you, "Let my son go that he may serve me"; 1
25 and touched Moses' feet with it, and said, "Surely 1
26 Then it was that she said, "You are a bridegroom 1
27 The LORD said to Aaron, "Go into the wilderness 1
5: 1 Aaron went to Pharaoh and said, "Thus says 1
1 Thus says the LORD, the God of Israel 1
2 Pharaoh said, "Who is the LORD, that I should heed 1
3 they said, "The God of the Hebrews has met with us; 1
4 the king of Egypt said to them, "Moses and Aaron 1
5 Pharaoh said, "Behold, the people of the land 1
10 taskmasters . . went out and said to the people 1
10 Thus says Pharaoh, 'I will not give you straw. 1
13 The taskmasters were urgent, saying, "Complete 1
16 No straw . . yet they say to us, 'Make bricks!' 1
17 he said, "You are idle, you are idle; 1
17 you are idle; therefore you say, 'Let us go 1
19 they were in evil plight, when they said, "You shall 1
21 they said to them, "The LORD look upon you 1
22 Moses . . said, "O LORD, why hast thou done evil 1
6: 1 the LORD said to Moses, "Now you shall see what I 1
2 God said to Moses, "I am the LORD. 1
6 Say therefore to the people of Israel 1
10 the LORD said to Moses 4
12 Moses said to the LORD, "Behold, the people 4
26 to whom the LORD said: "Bring out the people 1
29 the LORD said to Moses, "I am the LORD; tell Pharaoh 4
29 tell Pharaoh king of Egypt all that I say to you. 4
30 Moses said to the LORD, "Behold, I am 1
7: 1 the LORD said to Moses, "See, I make you as God 1
8 the LORD said to Moses and Aaron 1
9 When Pharaoh says to you, 'Prove yourselves 4
9 by working a miracle,' then you shall say to Aaron 1
13 would not listen to them; as the LORD had said. 4
14 LORD said to Moses, "Pharaoh's heart is hardened 1
16 you shall say to him, 'The LORD, the God 1
16 LORD . . sent me to you, saying, "Let my people go 1
17 Thus says the LORD, "By this you shall know that 1
19 the LORD said to Moses, "Say to Aaron, 'Take your rod 1
19 the LORD said to Moses, "Say to Aaron, 'Take your rod 1
22 would not listen to them; as the LORD had said. 4
8: 1 Then the LORD said to Moses, "Go in to Pharaoh 1
1 to Pharaoh and say to him, 'Thus says the LORD 1
1 say to him, 'Thus says the LORD, "Let my people go 1
5 the LORD said to Moses, "Say to Aaron, 'Stretch out 1
5 the LORD said to Moses, "Say to Aaron, 'Stretch out 1
8 Then Pharaoh called Moses and Aaron, and said 1
9 Moses said to Pharaoh, "Be pleased to command me 1
10 he said, "Tomorrow." Moses said, "Be it as you say 1
10 he said, "Tomorrow." Moses said, "Be it as you say 1
10 Moses said, "Be it as you say, that you may know that 5
15 would not listen to them; as the LORD had said. 4
16 Then the LORD said to Moses, "Say to Aaron, 'Stretch 1
16 Then the LORD said to Moses, "Say to Aaron, 'Stretch 1
19 the magicians said to Pharaoh, "This is the finger 1
19 would not listen to them; as the LORD had said. 4
20 Then the LORD said to Moses, "Rise up early 1
20 say to him, 'Thus says the LORD, "Let my people go 1
20 say to him, 'Thus says the LORD, "Let my people go 1
25 Then Pharaoh called Moses and Aaron, and said, "Go 1
26 Moses said, "It would not be right to do so; 1
28 So Pharaoh said, "I will let you go, to sacrifice 1
29 Then Moses said, "Behold, I am going out from you 1
9: 1 Then the LORD said to Moses, "Go in to Pharaoh 1
1 Go in to Pharaoh, and say to him, 'Thus says 4
1 Thus says the LORD, the God of the Hebrews 1
5 the LORD set a time, saying, "Tomorrow the LORD 1
8 the LORD said to Moses and Aaron, "Take handfuls 1
13 Then the LORD said to Moses, "Rise up early 1
13 Rise up . . and stand before Pharaoh, and say 1
13 Thus says the LORD, the God of the Hebrews 1
22 the LORD said to Moses, "Stretch forth your hand 1
27 Pharaoh . . said to them, "I have sinned this time; 1
29 Moses said to him, "As soon as I have gone out 1
10: 1 Then the LORD said to Moses, "Go in to Pharaoh; 1
3 Moses and Aaron went in to Pharaoh, and said to him 1
3 Thus says the LORD, the God of the Hebrews, 1
7 Pharaoh's servants said to him, "How long shall 1
8 Pharaoh; and he said to them, "Go, serve the LORD 1
9 Moses said, "We will go with our young and our old; 1
10 he said to them, "The LORD be with you, if ever I let 1
12 Then the LORD said to Moses, "Stretch out your hand 1
16 Pharaoh . . said, "I have sinned against the LORD 1
21 Then the LORD said to Moses, "Stretch out your hand 1
24 Pharaoh called Moses, and said, "Go, serve the LORD; 1
25 Moses said, "You must also let us have sacrifices 1
28 Then Pharaoh said to him, "Get away from me; 1
29 Moses said, "As you say! I will not see your face 1
29 Moses said, "As you say! I will not see your face 4
11: 1 The LORD said to Moses, "Yet one plague more I will 1
4 Moses said, "Thus says the LORD: About midnight 1
4 Moses said, "Thus says the LORD: About midnight 1
8 shall . . and bow down to me, saying, 'Get you out 1
9 the LORD said to Moses, "Pharaoh will not listen 1
12: 1 The LORD said to Moses and Aaron in the land 1
21 Moses called all the elders of Israel, and said 1
26 when your children say to you, 'What do you mean 1
27 you shall say, 'It is the sacrifice of the LORD'S 1
31 and said, "Rise up, go forth from among my people 1
31 go, serve the LORD, as you have said. 4
32 flocks and your herds, as you have said, and be gone; 4
33 haste; for they said, "We are all dead men. 1
43 the LORD said to Moses and Aaron, "This is 1
13: 1 The LORD said to Moses 4
3 Moses said to the people, "Remember this day 1
14 you shall say to him, 'By strength of hand the LORD 1
17 for God said, "Lest the people repent when they see 1
19 solemnly sworn . . saying, "God will visit you; 1
14: 1 Then the LORD said to Moses 4
3 For Pharaoh will say of the people of Israel 1
5 and they said, "What is this we have done 1
11 they said to Moses, "Is it because there are no 1
12 Is not this what we said to you in Egypt 4
13 Moses said to the people, "Fear not, stand firm 1
15 The LORD said to Moses, "Why do you cry to me? 1
25 the Egyptians said, "Let us flee 1
26 Then the LORD said to Moses, "Stretch out your hand 1
15: 1 Israel sang this song to the LORD, saying 1
9 The enemy said, 'I will pursue, I will overtake 1
24 against Moses, saying, "What shall we drink? 1
26 saying, "If you will diligently hearken 1
16: 3 said to them, "Would that we had died by the hand 1
4 Then the LORD said to Moses, "Behold, I will rain 1
6 Moses and Aaron said to all the people of Israel 1
8 Moses said, "When the LORD gives you in the evening 1
9 Moses said to Aaron, "Say to the whole 1
9 Moses said to Aaron, "Say to the whole 1
11 the LORD said to Moses 4
12 the people of Israel; say to them, 'At twilight 4
15 Israel saw it, they said to one another, "What is it? 1
15 And Moses said to them, "It is the bread 1
19 Moses said to them, "Let no man leave any of it till 1
23 he said to them, "This is what the LORD has 1
25 Moses said, "Eat it today, for today is a sabbath 1
28 the LORD said to Moses, "How long do you refuse 1
32 Moses said, "This is what the LORD has commanded 1
33 Moses said to Aaron, "Take a jar, and put an omer 1
17: 2 the people . . said, "Give us water to drink. 1
2 And Moses said to them, "Why do you find fault 1
3 murmured against Moses, and said, "Why did you 1
5 the LORD said to Moses, "Pass on before the people 1
7 LORD to the proof by saying, "Is the LORD among us 1
9 Moses said to Joshua, "Choose for us men, and go out 1
14 the LORD said to Moses, "Write this as a memorial 1
16 saying, "A hand upon the banner of the LORD! 1
18: 3 was Gershom (for he said, "I have been a sojourner 1
4 for he said, "The God of father was my help *
10 Jethro said, "Blessed be the LORD, who has 1
14 he said, "What is this that you are doing 1
15 Moses said to his father-in-law, "Because 1
17 Moses' father-in-law said to him, "What you are doing 1
24 So Moses . . did all that he had said. 1
19: 3 LORD called to him out of the mountain, saying 1
3 Thus you shall say to the house of Jacob, and tell 1
8 all the people answered together and said 1
9 the LORD said to Moses, "Lo, I am coming to you 1
10 the LORD said to Moses, "Go to the people 1
12 set bounds . . saying, 'Take heed that you do not 1
15 he said to the people, "Be ready by the third day; 1
21 LORD said to Moses, "Go down and warn the people 1
23 Moses said to the LORD, "The people cannot come up 1
23 thou thyself didst charge us, saying 1
24 the LORD said to him, "Go down, and come up 1
20: 1 God spoke all these words, saying 1
19 said to Moses, "You speak to us, and we will hear; 1
20 Moses said to the people, "Do not fear; for God has 1
22 the LORD said to Moses, "Thus you shall say 1
22 Moses, "Thus you shall say to the people of Israel 1
21: 5 if the slave plainly says, 'I love my master, my wife 1
22: 9 lost thing, of which one says, 'This is it,' 1
23:13 Take heed to all that I have said to you; 1
22 if you . . and do all that I say 4
24: 1 he said to Moses, "Come up to the LORD, 1
3 all the people answered with one voice, and said 1
7 they said, "All that the LORD has spoken we will do 1
8 Moses . . said, "Behold the blood of the covenant 1
12 The LORD said to Moses, "Come up to me 1
14 he said to the elders, "Tarry here for us 1
25: 1 The LORD said to Moses 4
30:11 The LORD said to Moses 4
17 The LORD said to Moses 4
22 Moreover, the LORD said to Moses 4
31 you shall say to the people of Israel, 'This shall 4
34 the LORD said to Moses, "Take sweet spices, stacte 1
31: 1 LORD said to Moses 4
12 LORD said to Moses 1
13 Say to the people of Israel 4
32: 1 together to Aaron, and said to him, "Up, make us gods 1
2 Aaron said to them, "Take off the rings of gold 1
4 they said, "These are your gods, O Israel, who 1
5 and Aaron made proclamation and said, "Tomorrow 1
7 the LORD said to Moses, "Go down; for your people 4
8 and said, 'These are your gods, O Israel, who brought 1
9 the LORD said to Moses, "I have seen this people 1
11 Moses besought the LORD his God, and said, "O LORD 1
12 Why should the Egyptians say, 'With evil intent 1
13 and didst say to them, 'I will multiply 4
17 as they shouted, he said to Moses, "There is a noise 1
18 he said, "It is not the sound of shouting 1
21 Moses said to Aaron, "What did this people do to you 1
22 Aaron said, "Let not the anger of my lord burn hot; 1
23 For they said to me, 'Make us gods, who shall go 1
24 I said to them, 'Let any who have gold take it off'; 1
26 then Moses stood in the gate of the camp, and said 1
27 he said to them, "Thus says the LORD God of Israel 1
27 he said to them, "Thus says the LORD God of Israel 1
29 Moses said, "Today you have ordained yourselves 1
30 On the morrow Moses said to the people, "You have 1
31 So Moses returned to the LORD and said 1
33 the LORD said to Moses, "Whoever has sinned 1
33: 1 The LORD said to Moses, "Depart, go up hence 4
1 I swore to Abraham, Isaac, and Jacob, saying 1
5 For the LORD had said to Moses, "Say to the people 1
5 For the LORD had said to Moses, "Say to the people 1
12 Moses said to the LORD, "See, thou sayest to me 1
12 Moses said to the LORD, "See, thou sayest to me 1
12 Yet thou hast said, 'I know you by name 1
14 he said, "My presence will go with you, and I will 1
15 he said to him, "If thy presence will not go with me 1
17 the LORD said to Moses, "This very thing 1
18 Moses said, "I pray thee, show me thy glory. 1
19 he said, "I will make all my goodness pass before 1
20 But," he said, "you cannot see my face; 1
21 the LORD said, "Behold, there is a place by me 1
34: 1 The LORD said to Moses, "Cut two tables of stone 1
9 he said, "If now I have found favor in thy sight 1
10 he said, "Behold, I make a covenant. 1
27 the LORD said to Moses, "Write these words; 1

35: 1 the people of Israel, and said to them 1
4 Moses said to all the congregation of the people 1
30 Moses said to the people of Israel, "See, the LORD 1
36: 5 said to Moses, "The people bring much more 1
40: 1 The LORD said to Moses 4
Lev 1: 1 spoke to him from the tent of meeting, saying 1
2 Speak to the people of Israel, and say to them 1
4: 1 the LORD said to Moses 4
2 Say to the people of Israel, If any one sins 4
5:14 The LORD said to Moses 4
6: 1 The LORD said to Moses 4
8 The LORD said to Moses 4
9 Command Aaron and his sons, saying, This is the law 1
19 The LORD said to Moses 4
24 The LORD said to Moses 4
25 Say to Aaron and his sons, This is the law 4
7:22 The LORD said to Moses 4
23 Say to the people of Israel, You shall eat no fat 4
28 The LORD said to Moses 4
29 Say to the people of Israel, He that offers 4
8: 1 The LORD said to Moses 4
5 Moses said to the congregation, "This is the thing 1
31 Moses said to Aaron and his sons, "Boil the flesh 1
31 eat it . . as I commanded, saying, 'Aaron and his 1
9: 2 he said to Aaron, "Take a bull calf 1
3 say to the people of Israel, 'Take a male goat 4
6 Moses said, "This is the thing which the LORD 1
7 Then Moses said to Aaron, "Draw near to the altar 1
10: 3 Then Moses said to Aaron, "This is what the LORD 1
3 This is what the LORD has said, 'I will show myself 4
4 Moses called . . and said to them, "Draw near, 1
5 carried them . . as Moses had said 4
6 Moses said to Aaron and to Elea'zar and Ith'amar 1
8 the LORD spoke to Aaron, saying 1
12 Moses said to Aaron and to Elea'zar and Ith'amar 4
16 the sons of Aaron who were left, saying 1
19 Aaron said to Moses, "Behold, today they have 4
11: 1 the LORD said to Moses and Aaron 4
2 Say to the people of Israel 4
12: 1 The LORD said to Moses 4
2 Say to the people of Israel, If a woman conceives 4
13: 1 The LORD said to Moses and Aaron 4
14: 1 The LORD said to Moses 4
33 The LORD said to Moses and Aaron 4
15: 1 The LORD said to Moses and Aaron 4
2 Say to the people of Israel 4
16: 2 the LORD said to Moses, "Tell Aaron your brother 1
17: 1 the LORD said to Moses 4
2 Say to Aaron and his sons, and to all the people 4
8 And you shall say to them 1
12 Therefore I have said to the people of Israel 1
14 therefore I have said to the people of Israel 1
18: 1 the LORD said to Moses 4
2 Say to the people of Israel, I am the LORD your God 4
19: 1 And the LORD said to Moses 4
2 Say to all the congregation of the people 4
20: 1 The LORD said to Moses 4
2 Say to the people of Israel, Any man of the people 1
24 I have said to you, 'You shall inherit their land 1
21: 1 the LORD said to Moses, "Speak to the priests 1
1 say to them that none of them shall defile 1
16 And the LORD said to Moses 4
17 Say to Aaron, None of your descendants 4
22: 1 And the LORD said to Moses 4
3 Say to them, 'If any one . . approaches the holy 1
17 And the LORD said to Moses 4
18 Say to Aaron and to his sons and all the people 4
26 And the LORD said to Moses 4
23: 1 The LORD said to Moses 4
2 Say to the people of Israel, The appointed feasts 4
9 And the LORD said to Moses 4
10 Say to the people of Israel, When you come 4
23 And the LORD said to Moses 4
24 Say to the people of Israel, In the seventh month 4
26 And the LORD said to Moses 4
33 And the LORD said to Moses 4
34 Say to the people of Israel, On the fifteenth day 4
24: 1 The LORD said to Moses 4
13 And the LORD said to Moses 4
15 say to the people of Israel, Whoever curses 4
25: 1 The LORD said to Moses on Mount Sinai 4
2 Say to the people of Israel, When you come 4
20 if you say, 'What shall we eat in the seventh year 1
27: 1 The LORD said to Moses 4
2 Say to the people of Israel 4
Num 1: 1 The LORD spoke to Moses . . saying 1
48 For the LORD said to Moses 4
2: 1 The LORD said to Moses and Aaron 4
3: 5 the LORD said to Moses 4
11 the LORD said to Moses 4
14 the LORD said to Moses in the wilderness of Sinai 4
40 LORD said to Moses, "Number all the first-born 1
44 the LORD said to Moses 4
4: 1 The LORD said to Moses and Aaron 4
17 The LORD said to Moses and Aaron 4
21 The LORD said to Moses 4
5: 1 The LORD said to Moses 4
4 as the LORD said to Moses, so . . Israel did. 4
5 the LORD said to Moses 4
6 Say to the people of Israel, When a man or woman 4
11 the LORD said to Moses 4
12 Say to the people of Israel, If any man's wife 4
19 the priest shall make her take an oath, saying 1
21 (let the priest . . say to the woman) 1
22 And the woman shall say, 'Amen, Amen.' 1
6: 1 the LORD said to Moses 4
2 Say to the people of Israel, When either a man 4
22 The LORD said to Moses 4
23 Say to Aaron and his sons, Thus you shall bless 4
23 bless the people of Israel: you shall say to them 1
7: 4 Then the LORD said to Moses 1
11 LORD said to Moses, "They shall offer 1
8: 1 Now the LORD said to Moses 4
2 Say to Aaron, When you set up the lamps 4
5 the LORD said to Moses 4
23 the LORD said to Moses 4
9: 1 after they had come out of the land of Egypt, saying 1
7 those men said to him, "We are unclean 1
8 Moses said to them, "Wait, that I may hear 1
9 The LORD said to Moses 4
10 Say to the people of Israel, If any man of you 4
10: 1 The LORD said to Moses 4
29 Moses said to Hobab the son of Reu'el 1
29 place of which the LORD said, 'I will give it to you'; 1
30 he said to him, "I will not go; I will depart 1
31 he said, "Do not leave us, I pray you, for you know 1
35 whenever the ark set out, Moses said, "Arise, O LORD 1
36 when it rested, he said, "Return, O LORD 1
11: 4 Israel . . said, "O that we had meat to eat!. 1
11 Moses said to the LORD, "Why has thou dealt ill 1
12 Did I bring them forth, that thou shouldst say to me 1
13 For they weep before me and say, 'Give us meat 1
16 the LORD said to Moses, "Gather for me 70 men 1
18 say to the people, 'Consecrate yourselves 1
18 you have wept in the hearing of the LORD, saying 1
20 rejected . . and have wept before him, saying 1
21 Moses said, "The people among whom I am number 1
21 thou hast said, 'I will give them meat 1
23 LORD said to Moses, "Is the LORD'S hand shortened? 1
28 Joshua . . one of his chosen men, said 1
29 Moses said to him, "Are you jealous for my sake? 1
12: 2 they said, "Has the LORD indeed spoken only 1
4 suddenly the LORD said to Moses and to Aaron 1
6 said, "Hear my words: If there is a prophet among you 1
11 Aaron said to Moses, "Oh, my lord, do not punish us 1
14 LORD said to Moses, "If her father had but spit 1
13: 1 The LORD said to Moses 4
17 Moses sent them to spy . . and said to them 1
30 Caleb quieted the people before Moses, and said 1
31 Then the men who had gone up with him said 1
32 they brought . . an evil report . . , saying 1
14: 2 whole congregation said to them, "Would that we 1
4 they said to one another, "Let us choose a captain 1
7 said to all the congregation of the people 1
10 congregation said to stone them with stones. 1
11 LORD said to Moses, "How long will this people 1
13 Moses said to the LORD, "Then the Egyptians 1
15 then the nations who have heard thy fame will say 1
17 be as great as thou hast promised, saying 1
20 Then the LORD said, "I have pardoned 1
26 the LORD said to Moses and to Aaron 4
28 Say to them, 'As I live,' says the LORD 4
28 Say to them, 'As I live,' says the LORD 12
28 'what you have said in my hearing I will do to you 4
31 your little ones, who you said would become a prey 1
40 went up to the heights of the hill country, saying 1
41 Moses said, "Why now are you trangressing 1
15: 1 Then the LORD said to Moses 4
2 Say to the people of Israel, When you come 4
17 The LORD said to Moses 4
18 Say to the people of Israel, When you come 4
35 LORD said to Moses, "The man shall be put to death; 1
37 The LORD said to Moses 1
16: 3 against Moses and . . Aaron, and said to them 1
5 said to Korah and all his company, "In the morning 4
8 Moses said to Korah, "Hear now, you sons of Levi 1
12 Dathan and Abi'ram . . said, "We will not come up. 1
15 Moses was very angry, and said to the LORD 1
16 Moses said to Korah, "Be present, you and all 1
20 the LORD said to Moses and to Aaron 4
22 they fell on their faces, and said, "O God, the God 1
23 the LORD said to Moses 4
24 Say to the congregation, Get away from about 4
26 said to the congregation, "Depart, I pray you 4
28 Moses said, "Hereby you shall know that the LORD 1
34 for they said, "Lest the earth swallow us up! 1
36 Then the LORD said to Moses 4
40 as the LORD said to Elea'zar through Moses. 4
41 murmured against Moses and against Aaron, saying 1
44 the LORD said to Moses 4
46 Moses said to Aaron, "Take your censer, and put fire 1
47 Aaron took it as Moses said, and ran into the midst 4
17: 1 The LORD said to Moses 4
10 the LORD said to Moses, "Put back the rod of Aaron 1
12 people of Israel said to Moses, "Behold, we perish 1
18: 1 LORD said to Aaron, "You and your sons 1
8 Then the LORD said to Aaron, "And behold 4
20 LORD said to Aaron, "You shall have no inheritance 1
24 therefore I have said of them that 1
25 the LORD said to Moses 4
26 Moreover you shall say to the Levites, 'When you 4
30 Therefore you shall say to them, 'When you have 1
19: 1 Now the LORD said to Moses and to Aaron 4
20: 3 people contended with Moses, and said, "Would that 1
7 the LORD said to Moses 4
10 Moses and Aaron . . said to them, "Hear now 1
12 LORD said to Moses and Aaron, "Because you did not 1
14 Thus says your brother Israel: You know 1
18 Edom said to him, "You shall not pass through 1
19 people of Israel said to him, "We will go up 1
20 but he said, "You shall not pass through. 1
23 the LORD said to Moses and Aaron at Mount Hor 1
21: 2 Israel vowed a vow to the LORD, and said 1
7 people came to Moses, and said, "We have sinned 1
8 the LORD said to Moses, "Make a fiery serpent 1
14 Where it is said in the Book of the Wars of the LORD 1
16 Beer . . the well of which the LORD said to Moses 1
21 sent messengers to Sihon . . saying 1
27 Therefore the ballad singers say, "Come 1
34 the LORD said to Moses, "Do not fear him; 1
22: 4 Moab said to the elders of Mid'ian, "This horde 1
5 sent messengers to Balaam . . to call him, saying 1
8 said to them, "Lodge here this night 1
9 God came to Balaam and said, "Who are these men 1
10 Balaam said to God, "Balak the son of Zippor 1
10 Balak . . king of Moab, has sent to me, saying 31
12 God said to Balaam, "You shall not go with them; 1
13 Balaam . . said to the princes of Balak 1
14 princes of Moab rose and went to Balak, and said 1
16 came to Balaam and said to him, "Thus says Balak 1
16 Thus says Balak the son of Zippor: 'Let nothing 1
17 whatever you say to me I will do; 1
18 Balaam . . said to the servants of Balak 1
19 that I may know what more the LORD will say to me. 4
20 God came to Balaam at night and said to him 1
28 opened the mouth of the ass, and she said to Balaam 1
29 Balaam said to the ass, "Because you have 1
30 ass said to Balaam, "Am I not your ass 1
30 I ever accustomed to do so to you?" And he said, "No. 1
32 angel of the LORD said to him, "Why have you struck 1
34 Balaam said to the angel of the LORD, "I have sinned 1
35 angel of the LORD said to Balaam, "Go with the men; 1
37 Balak said to Balaam, "Did I not send to you to call 1
38 Balaam said to Balak, "Lo, I have come to you! 1
23: 1 Balaam said to Balak, "Build for me here 1
2 Balak did as Balaam had said; and Balak and Balaam 4
3 Balaam said to Balak 1
4 God met Balaam; and Balaam said to him 1
5 the LORD put a word in Balaam's mouth, and said 1
7 Balaam took up his discourse, and said 1
11 Balak said to Balaam, "What have you done to me? 1
13 Balak said to him, "Come with me to another place 1
15 Balaam said to Balak, "Stand here 1
16 LORD . . put a word in his mouth, and said, "Return 1
17 Balak said to him, "What has the LORD spoken? 1
18 Balaam took up his discourse, and said, "Rise, Balak 1
19 Has he said, and will he not do it? 1
23 be said of Jacob and Israel, 'What has God wrought!' 1
25 Balak said to Balaam, "Neither curse them at all 1
26 All that the LORD says, that I must do'? 4
27 Balak said to Balaam, "Come now, I will take you 1
29 Balaam said to Balak, "Build for me here 1
30 Balak did as Balaam had said, and offered 1
24: 3 took up his discourse, and said, "The oracle 1
10 Balak said to Balaam, "I called you 1
11 I said, 'I will certainly honor you,' 1
12 Balaam said to Balak, "Did I not tell 1
15 he took up his discourse, and said, "The oracle 1
20 took up his discourse, and said 1
21 took up his discourse, and said 1
23 And he took up his discourse, and said 1
25: 4 LORD said to Moses, "Take all the chiefs 1
5 Moses said to the judges of Israel, "Every one 1
10 the LORD said to Moses 4
12 Therefore say, 'Behold, I give to him my covenant 1
16 the LORD said to Moses 4
26: 1 LORD said to Moses and to Elea'zar the son of Aaron 1
3 spoke with them . . at Jericho, saying 1
52 The LORD said to Moses 4
65 For the LORD had said of them, "They shall die 1
27: 2 at the door of the tent of meeting, saying 1
6 the LORD said to Moses 1
8 you shall say to the people of Israel, 'If a man dies 4
12 LORD said to Moses, "Go up into this mountain 1
15 Moses said to the LORD 4
18 LORD said to Moses, "Take Joshua the son of Nun 1
28: 1 The LORD said to Moses 4
2 Command the people of Israel, and say to them 1
3 you shall say to them, This is the offering by fire 1
30: 1 Moses said to the heads of the tribes 4
31: 1 The LORD said to Moses 4
3 Moses said to the people, "Arm men from among you 4
15 Moses said to them, "Have you let all the women live? 1
21 Elea'zar the priest said to the men of war 1
25 The LORD said to Moses 1
49 said to Moses, "Your servants have counted 1
32: 2 sons of Gad and the sons of Reuben came and said 1

5 they said, "If we have found favor in your sight 1
6 Moses said to the sons of Gad and . . of Reuben 1
10 LORD'S anger was kindled . . and he swore, saying 1
16 Then they came near to him, and said, "We will build 1
20 Moses said to them, "If you will do this 1
25 sons of Gad and the sons of Reuben said to Moses 1
29 Moses said to them, "If the sons of Gad 1
31 As the LORD has said to your servants, so we will do. 4
33:50 LORD said to Moses in the plains of Moab 4
51 Say to the people of Israel, When you pass over 4
34: 1 The LORD said to Moses 4
2 Command the people of Israel, and say to them 1
13 Moses commanded the people of Israel, saying 1
16 The LORD said to Moses 4
35: 1 LORD said to Moses in the plains of Moab 4
9 the LORD said to Moses 4
10 Say to the people of Israel, When you cross 4
36: 2 they said, "The LORD commanded my lord to give 1
5 Israel according to the word of the LORD, saying 1
Deu 1: 5 Moses undertook to explain this law, saying 1
6 LORD our God said to us in Horeb, 'You have stayed 4
9 At that time I said to you, 'I am not able 1
20 I said to you, 'You have come to the hill country 1
22 Then all of you came near me, and said, 'Let us send 1
25 brought us word again, and said, 'It is a good land 1
27 murmured in your tents, and said, 'Because the LORD 1
28 Our brethren have made our hearts melt, saying 1
29 Then I said to you, 'Do not be in dread or afraid 1
37 The LORD was angry with me also . . and said 1
39 your little ones, who you said would become a prey 1
42 the LORD said to me, 'Say to them, Do not go up 1
42 the LORD said to me, 'Say to them, Do not go up 1
2: 2 Then the LORD said to me 1
9 LORD said to me, 'Do not harass Moab or contend 1
17 the LORD said to me 4
26 sent . . to Sihon . . , with words of peace, saying 1
31 LORD said to me, 'Behold, I have begun to give Sihon 1
3: 2 LORD said to me, 'Do not fear him; for I have given 1
18 I commanded you at that time, saying, 'The LORD 1
23 I besought the LORD at that time, saying 1
26 LORD said to me, 'Let it suffice you; speak no more 1
4: 6 when they hear all these statutes, will say 1
10 LORD said to me, 'Gather the people to me 1
5: 1 Moses summoned all Israel, and said to them, "Hear 1
5 you did not go up into the mountain. He said 1
24 said, 'Behold, the LORD our God has shown us 1
27 Go near, and hear all that the LORD our God will say; 1
28 LORD said to me, 'I have heard the words 1
28 rightly said all that they have spoken. 4
30 Go and say to them, "Return to your tents. 1
6:21 then you shall say to your son, 'We were Pharaoh's 1
7:17 If you say in your heart, 'These nations 1
8:17 Beware lest you say in your heart, 'My power 1
9: 2 sons of the Anakim . . of whom you have heard it said *
4 Do not say in your heart, after the LORD your God 1
12 Then the LORD said to me, 'Arise, go down quickly 1
13 Furthermore the LORD said to me, 'I have seen 1
23 the LORD sent you from Ka'desh-bar'nea, saying 1
25 because the LORD had said he would destroy you. 1
28 lest the land from which thou didst bring us say 1
10: 1 At that time the LORD said to me, 'Hew two tables 1
9 as the LORD your God said to him.) 4
11 LORD said to me, 'Arise, go on your journey 1
12:20 and you say, 'I will eat flesh,' 1
30 that you do not inquire about their gods, saying 1
13: 2 if he says, 'Let us go after other gods,' 1
6 entices you secretly, saying, 'Let us go and serve 1
13 saying, 'Let us go and serve other gods,' 1
15: 9 be a base thought in your heart, and you say 1
16 if he says to you, 'I will not go out from you,' 1
17:14 then say, 'I will set a king over me, 1
16 since the LORD has said to you, 'You shall never 1
18:16 just as you desired of the LORD . . when you said 1
17 LORD said to me, 'They have rightly said all 1
17 have rightly said all that they have spoken. *
21 if you say in your heart, 'How may we know the word 1
20: 3 say to them, 'Hear, O Israel, you draw near this day 1
5 officers shall speak to the people, saying, 'What 1
8 officers shall speak further . . and say, 'What 1
21:20 shall say to the elders of his city, 'This our son 1
22:14 brings an evil name upon her, saying, 'I took 1
16 father of the young woman shall say to the elders 1
17 he has made shameful charges against her, saying 1
25: 7 brother's wife shall go . . to the elders, and say 1
8 if he persists, saying, 'I do not wish to take her,' 1
9 she shall answer and say, 'So shall it be done 1
26: 3 go to the priest who is in office . . and say to him 1
13 then you shall say before the LORD your God, 'I have 1
27: 1 Moses . . commanded the people, saying, "Keep all 1
9 Moses and the . . priests said to all Israel 4
11 Moses charged the people the same day, saying 1
15 all the people shall answer and say, 'Amen.' 1
16 all the people shall say, 'Amen.' 1
17 all the people shall say, 'Amen.' 1
18 all the people shall say, 'Amen.' 1
19 all the people shall say, 'Amen.' 1
20 all the people shall say, 'Amen.' 1
21 all the people shall say, 'Amen.' 1
22 all the people shall say, 'Amen.' 1
23 all the people shall say, 'Amen.' 1
24 all the people shall say, 'Amen.' 1
25 all the people shall say, 'Amen.' 1
26 all the people shall say, 'Amen.' 1
28:67 morning you shall say, 'Would it were evening!' 1
67 at evening you shall say, 'Would it were morning!' 1
29: 2 Moses summoned all Israel and said to them 1
19 blesses . . in his heart, saying, 'I shall be safe 1
22 would say, when they see the sicknesses 1
24 yea, all the nations would say, 'Why has the LORD 1
25 Then men would say, 'It is because they forsook 1
30:12 is not in heaven, that you should say, 'Who will go up 1
13 Neither is it beyond the sea, that you should say 1
31: 2 said to them, "I am 120 years old this day; 1
2 LORD has said to me, 'You shall not go over 1
7 Joshua, and said to him in the sight of all Israel 1
14 LORD said to Moses, "Behold, the days approach 1
16 LORD said to Moses, "Behold, you are about to sleep 1
17 so that they will say in that day, 'Have not 1
23 LORD commissioned Joshua the son of Nun and said 1
32:20 said, 'I will hide my face from them, I will see 1
26 I would have said, "I will scatter them afar 1
27 lest they should say, "Our hand is triumphant 1
37 Then he will say, 'Where are their gods 1
46 said to them, "Lay to heart all the words which I 1
48 LORD said to Moses that very day 4
33: 2 said, "The LORD came from Sinai, and dawned 1
7 this he said of Judah: "Hear, O LORD, the voice 1
8 of Levi he said, "Give to Levi thy Thummim 1
9 who said of his father and mother, 'I regard . . not'; 1
12 Of Benjamin he said, "The beloved of the LORD 1
13 of Joseph he said, "Blessed by the LORD be his land 1
18 of Zeb'ulun he said, "Rejoice, Zeb'ulun 1
20 of Gad he said, "Blessed be he who enlarges Gad! 1
22 of Dan he said, "Dan is a lion's whelp 1
23 of Naph'tali he said, "O Naph'tali, satisfied 1
24 of Asher he said, "Blessed above sons be Asher; 1
27 And he thrust out the enemy . . and said, Destroy. 1
34: 4 LORD said to him, "This is the land of which I swore 1
Jos 1: 1 the LORD said to Joshua the son of Nun 1
12 to . . and the half-tribe of Manas'seh Joshua said 1
13 the word which Moses . . commanded you, saying 1
2: 1 sent two men . . saying, "Go, view the land 1
3 Then the king of Jericho sent to Rahab, saying 1
4 But the woman had . . hidden them; and she said 1
9 and said to the men, "I know that the LORD has given 1
14 And the men said to her, "Our life for yours! 1
16 And she said to them, "Go into the hills 1
17 The men said to her, "We will be guiltless 1
21 And she said, "According to your words, so be it. 1
24 And they said to Joshua, "Truly the LORD has given 1
3: 5 Joshua said to the people, "Sanctify yourselves; 1
6 And Joshua said to the priests, "Take up the ark 1
7 And the LORD said to Joshua, "This day I will begin 1
9 Joshua said to the people of Israel, "Come hither 1
10 And Joshua said, "Hereby you shall know 1
4: 1 When all the nation had . . the LORD said to Joshua 1
5 and Joshua said to them, "Pass on before the ark 1
15 And the LORD said to Joshua 1
21 And he said to the people of Israel 1
5: 2 the LORD said to Joshua, "Make flint knives 1
9 And the LORD said to Joshua, "This day I have rolled 1
13 and Joshua went to him and said to him, "Are you 1
14 And he said, "No; but as commander . . I have now 1
14 fell on his face . . and worshiped, and said to him 1
15 the commander of the LORD's army said to Joshua 1
6: 2 LORD said to Joshua, "See, I have given . . Jericho 1
6 Joshua . . called the priests and said to them 1
7 And he said to the people, "Go forward; 1
16 Joshua said to the people, "Shout; 1
22 Joshua said to the two men . . "Go into the harlot's 1
26 Joshua laid an oath upon them at that time, saying 1
7: 2 Joshua sent men . . and said to them, "Go up and spy 1
3 And they returned to Joshua, and said to him 1
7 And Joshua said, "Alas, O Lord GOD, why hast thou 1
8 O Lord, what can I say, when Israel has turned 1
10 The LORD said to Joshua, "Arise 1
13 Up, sanctify the people, and say 1
13 Sanctify yourselves . . for thus says the LORD 1
19 Joshua said to Achan, "My son, give glory to the LORD 1
25 And Joshua said, "Why did you bring trouble on us? 1
8: 1 the LORD said to Joshua, "Do not fear or be dismayed; 1
6 they will say, 'They are fleeing from us, as before.' 1
18 the LORD said to Joshua, "Stretch out the javelin 1
9: 6 And they went to Joshua . . and said to him 1
7 But the men of Israel said to the Hivites 1
8 They said to Joshua, "We are your servants. 1
8 We are your servants." And Joshua said to them 1
9 They said to him, "From a very far country 1
11 all the inhabitants of our country said to us 1
11 and go to meet them, and say to them 1
19 But all the leaders said to all the congregation 1
21 And the leaders said to them, "Let them live. 1
21 they became . . as the leaders had said of them. 4
22 Joshua summoned them, and he said to them 4
22 Why did you deceive us, saying, 'We are very far 1
10: 3 Ado'ni-ze'dek king of Jerusalem sent to . . saying 1
6 And the men of Gibeon sent to Joshua . . saying 1
8 And the LORD said to Joshua, "Do not fear them 1
12 spoke Joshua . . and he said in the sight of Israel 1
18 And Joshua said, "Roll great stones against 1
22 Then Joshua said, "Open the mouth of the cave 1
24 Joshua . . and said to the chiefs of the men of war 1
25 Joshua said to them, "Do not be afraid or dismayed; 1
11: 6 the LORD said to Joshua, "Do not be afraid of them 1
13: 1 Joshua was old . . and the LORD said to him 1
14 are their inheritance, as he said to him. 4
33 LORD . . is their inheritance, as he said to them. 4
14: 6 and Caleb . . said to him, "You know what the LORD 1
6 know what the LORD said to Moses the man of God 4
9 And Moses swore on that day, saying 1
10 And now . . the LORD has kept me alive, as he said 4
12 and I shall drive them out as the LORD said. 4
15:16 And Caleb said, "Whoever smites Kir'iath-se'pher 1
18 she alighted from her ass, and Caleb said to her 1
19 She said to him, "Give me a present; 1
17: 4 They came before . . the leaders, and said 1
14 And the tribe of Joseph spoke to Joshua, saying 1
15 Joshua said to them, "If you are a numerous people 1
16 The tribe of Joseph said, "The hill country is not 1
17 Then Joshua said to the house of Joseph 1
18: 3 Joshua said to the people of Israel, "How long 1
8 and Joshua charged those who went . . saying, "Go up 1
20: 1 Then the LORD said to Joshua 4
2 Say to the people of Israel, 'Appoint the cities 4
21: 2 they said to them at Shiloh in the land of Canaan 4
22: 2 said to them, "You have kept all that Moses 1
8 he said to them, "Go back to your homes with much 1
11 And the people of Israel heard say 1
15 came to the Reubenites . . and they said to them 4
16 Thus says the whole congregation of the LORD 1
21 the Reubenites, the Gadites . . said in answer 4
24 your children might say to our children 1
26 Therefore we said, 'Let us now build an altar 1
27 your children say to our children in time to come 1
28 If this should be said to us or to our descendants 1
28 If this should be said to us . . we should say 1
31 Phin'ehas . . said to the Reubenites 1
34 For," said they, "it is a witness between us *
23: 2 Joshua summoned all Israel . . and said to them 1
24: 2 Joshua said to all the people, "Thus says the LORD 1
2 Thus says the LORD, the God of Israel, 'Your fathers 1
19 But Joshua said to the people, "You cannot serve 1
21 the people said to Joshua, "Nay; but we will serve 1
22 Then Joshua said to the people, "You are witnesses 1
22 And they said, "We are witnesses. 1
23 He said, "Then put away the foreign gods *
24 And the people said to Joshua, "The LORD our God 1
27 Joshua said to all the people, "Behold, this stone 1
Jdg 1: 2 The LORD said, "Judah shall go up; behold, I have 1
3 Judah said to Simeon his brother, "Come up with me 1
7 Ado'ni-be'zek said, "70 kings with their thumbs 1
12 Caleb said, "He who attacks Kir'iath-se'pher 1
14 and Caleb said to her, "What do you wish? 1
15 She said to him, "Give me a present; since you have 1
20 Hebron was given to Caleb, as Moses had said; 4
24 and they said to him, "Pray, show us the way 1
2: 1 And he said, "I brought you up from Egypt 1
1 I said, 'I will never break my covenant with you 1
3 So now I say, I will not drive them out before you; 1
20 and he said, "Because this people have transgressed 1
3:19 and said, "I have a secret message for you, O king. 1
20 And Ehud said, "I have a message from God for you. 1
28 he said to them, "Follow after me; for the LORD has 1
4: 6 She . . said to him, "The LORD, the God of Israel 1
8 Barak said to her, "If you will go with me, I will go; 1
9 she said, "I will surely go with you; nevertheless 1
14 Deb'orah said to Barak, "Up! For this is the day 1
18 Ja'el came out to meet Sis'era, and said to him 1
19 he said to her, "Pray, give me a little water to drink; 1
20 he said to her, "Stand at the door of the tent 1
20 man comes and asks you, 'Is any one here?' say, No. 1
22 Ja'el went out to meet him, and said to him 1
5:23 Curse Meroz, says the angel of the LORD 1
6: 8 prophet . . and he said to them, "Thus says the LORD 1
8 Thus says the LORD, the God of Israel: I led you up 1
10 I said to you, 'I am the LORD your God; you shall not 1
12 angel . . appeared to him and said to him, "The LORD 1
13 Gideon said to him, "Pray, sir, if the LORD is with us 1
13 fathers recounted to us, saying, 'Did not the LORD 1
14 the LORD turned to him and said, "Go in this might 1
15 he said to him, "Pray, Lord, how can I deliver Israel? 1
16 the LORD said to him, "But I will be with you 1
17 he said to him, "If now I have found favor with thee 1
18 And he said, "I will stay till you return. 1
20 the angel of God said to him, "Take the meat 1
22 Gideon said, "Alas, O Lord GOD! For now I have seen 1
23 the LORD said to him, "Peace be to you; do not fear 1
25 night the LORD said to him, "Take your father's bull 1
29 they said to one another, "Who has done this thing? 1
29 after they . . inquired, they said, "Gideon the son 1
30 men of the town said to Jo'ash, "Bring out your son 1
31 Jo'ash said to all who were arrayed against him 1
32 called Jerubba'al, that is to say, "Let Ba'al contend 1
36 Gideon said to God, "If thou wilt deliver Israel 1
36 wilt deliver Israel by my hand, as thou hast said 4
37 wilt deliver Israel by my hand, as thou hast said. 4
39 Gideon said to God, "Let not thy anger burn against 1

7: 2 The LORD said to Gideon, "The people with you are 1
2 lest Israel vaunt themselves against me, saying 1
3 proclaim . . saying, 'Whoever is fearful 1
4 LORD said to Gideon, "The people are still too many; 1
4 he of whom I say to you, 'This man shall go with you,' 1
4 and any of whom I say to you, 'This man shall not go 1
5 and the LORD said to Gideon, "Every one that laps 1
7 the LORD said to Gideon, "With the 300 men 1
9 That same night the LORD said to him, "Arise, 1
11 you shall hear what they say, and afterward 4
13 telling a dream . . and he said, "Behold, I dreamed 1
15 he returned . . and said, "Arise; for the LORD has 1
17 And he said to them, "Look at me, and do likewise; 1
24 sent messengers . . saying, "Come down against 1
8: 1 the men of E'phraim said to him, "What is this 1
2 he said to them, "What have I done now in comparison 1
3 their anger . . was abated, when he had said this. 4
5 he said to the men of Succoth, "Pray, give loaves 1
6 the officials of Succoth said, "Are Zebah 1
7 Gideon said, "Well then, when the LORD has given 1
9 he said to the men of Penu'el, "When I come again 1
15 he came . . and said, "Behold Zebah and Zalmun'na 1
15 you taunted me, saying, 'Are Zebah and Zalmun'na 1
18 he said to Zebah and Zalmun'na, "Where are the men 1
19 he said, "They were my brothers, the sons of my 1
20 he said to Jether his first-born, "Rise, and slay 1
21 Zebah and Zalmun'na said, "Rise yourself, and fall 1
22 Then the men of Israel said to Gideon, "Rule over us 1
23 Gideon said to them, "I will not rule over you 1
24 Gideon said to them, "Let me make a request of you; 1
9: 1 mother's kinsmen and said to them and to the whole 4
2 Say in the ears of all the citizens of Shechem 4
3 Abim'elech, for they said, "He is our brother. 1
7 cried aloud and said to them, "Listen to me, you men 1
8 and they said to the olive tree, 'Reign over us.' 1
9 olive tree said to them, 'Shall I leave my fatness 1
10 the trees said to the fig tree, 'Come you, and reign 1
11 fig tree said to them, 'Shall I leave my sweetness 1
12 the trees said to the vine, 'Come you, and reign over 1
13 the vine said to them, 'Shall I leave my wine 1
14 all the trees said to the bramble, 'Come you 1
15 the bramble said to the trees, 'If in good faith you 1
28 Ga'al the son of Ebed said, "Who is Abim'elech 1
29 would remove Abim'elech, I would say to Abim'elech 1
31 sent . . saying, "Behold, Ga'al the son of Ebed 1
36 when Ga'al saw the men, he said to Zebul, "Look, 1
36 And Zebul said to him, "You see the shadow 1
37 Ga'al spoke again and said, "Look, men are coming 1
38 Zebul said to him, "Where is your mouth now 1
38 Where is your mouth now, you who said, 'Who is 1
48 he said to the men that were with him 1
54 his armor-bearer, and said to him, "Draw your sword 1
54 kill me, lest men say of me, 'A woman killed him.' 1
10:10 Israel cried to the LORD, saying, "We have sinned 1
11 the LORD said to the people of Israel, "Did I not 1
15 the people of Israel said to the LORD, "We have 1
18 people, the leaders of Gilead, said one to another 1
11: 2 thrust Jephthah out, and said to him, "You shall not 1
6 they said to Jephthah, "Come and be our leader 1
7 Jephthah said to the elders of Gilead, "Did you not 1
8 the elders of Gilead said to Jephthah, "That is why 1
9 Jephthah said to the elders of Gilead 1
10 the elders of Gilead said to Jephthah, "The LORD 1
10 witness between us; we will surely do as you say. 5
12 Jephthah sent messengers . . and said, "What have 1
15 sent messengers . . and said to him, "Thus says 1
15 Thus says Jephthah: Israel did not take away 1
17 Israel then sent messengers . . saying, 'Let us 1
19 Israel said to him, 'Let us pass, we pray, through 1
30 Jephthah made a vow to the LORD, and said, "If thou 1
35 when he saw her, he rent his clothes, and said, "Alas 1
36 she said to him, "My father, if you have opened 1
37 she said to her father, "Let this thing be done 1
38 And he said, "Go." And he sent her away 1
12: 1 and they crossed to Zaphon and said to Jephthah 1
2 Jephthah said to them, "I and my people had a great 1
4 they said, "You are fugitives of E'phraim 1
5 the fugitives of E'phraim said, "Let me go over 1
5 men of Gilead said to him, "Are you an E'phraimite? 1
5 Are you an E'phraimite?" When he said, "No 1
6 he said, "No," they said to him, "Then say Shibboleth 1
6 he said, "No," they said to him, "Then say Shibboleth 1
6 Then say Shibboleth," and he said, "Sibboleth 1
13: 3 angel . . appeared to the woman and said to her 1
7 he said to me, 'Behold, you shall conceive and bear 1
8 Mano'ah entreated the LORD, and said, "O LORD, 1
11 Mano'ah . . said to him, "Are you the man who spoke 1
11 spoke to this woman?" And he said, "I am. 1
12 Mano'ah said, "Now when your words come true 1
13 the angel of the LORD said to Mano'ah, "Of all that I 1
13 Of all that I said to the woman let her beware. 1
15 Mano'ah said to the angel of the LORD, "Pray, let us 1
16 the angel of the LORD said to Mano'ah, "If you detain 1
17 Mano'ah said to the angel of the LORD, "What is 1
18 angel of the LORD said to him, "Why do you ask 1
22 Mano'ah said to his wife, "We shall surely die 1
23 his wife said to him, "If the LORD had meant to kill 1
14: 3 his father and mother said to him, "Is there not 1
3 But Samson said to his father, "Get her for me; 1
12 Samson said to them, "Let me now put a riddle to you; 1
13 they said to him, "Put your riddle, that we may hear 1
14 he said to them, "Out of the eater came something 1
15 On the fourth day they said to Samson's wife 1
16 Samson's wife wept before him, and said, "You only 1
16 And he said to her, "Behold, I have not told 1
18 the men of the city said to him on the seventh day 1
18 And he said to them, "If you had not plowed 1
15: 1 and he said, "I will go in to my wife in the chamber. 1
2 her father said, "I really thought that you 1
3 Samson said to them, "This time I shall be 1
6 the Philistines said, "Who has done this? 1
6 And they said, "Samson, the son-in-law 1
7 Samson said to them, "If this is what you do, I swear 1
10 the men of Judah said, "Why have you come up 1
10 They said, "We have come up to bind Samson 1
11 men of Judah went down . . and said to Samson 1
11 And he said to them, "As they did to me, so have I 1
12 they said to him, "We have come down to bind you 1
12 Samson said to them, "Swear to me that you will not 1
13 They said to him, "No; we will only bind you and give 1
16 Samson said, "With the jawbone of an ass 1
18 he called on the LORD and said, "Thou hast granted 1
16: 2 They kept quiet all night, saying, "Let us wait till 1
5 the Philistines came to her and said to her 1
6 Deli'lah said to Samson, "Please tell me wherein 1
7 Samson said to her, "If they bind me with seven 1
9 she said to him, "The Philistines are upon you 1
10 Deli'lah said to Samson, "Behold, you have mocked 1
11 he said to her, "If they bind me with new ropes 1
12 Deli'lah . . bound him . . and said to him 1
13 Deli'lah said to Samson, "Until now you have mocked 1
13 he said to her, "If you weave the seven locks of my 1
14 she made them tight with the pin, and said to him 1
15 she said to him, "How can you say, 'I love you,' 1
15 How can you say, 'I love you,' when your heart is not 1
17 he told her all his mind, and said to her, "A razor has 1
18 called the lords of the Philistines, saying 1
20 she said, "The Philistines are upon you, Samson! 1
20 he awoke from his sleep, and said, "I will go out 1
23 and to rejoice; for they said, "Our god has given 1
24 praised their god; for they said, "Our god has given 1
25 when their hearts were merry, they said, "Call 1
26 Samson said to the lad who held him by the hand 1
28 Samson called to the LORD and said, "O Lord GOD 1
30 Samson said, "Let me die with the Philistines. 1
17: 2 he said to his mother, "The 1,100 pieces of silver 1
2 his mother said, "Blessed be my son by the LORD. 1
3 restored the . . silver . . ; and his mother said 1
9 Micah said to him, "From where do you come? 1
9 And he said to him, "I am a Levite 1
10 Micah said to him, "Stay with me, and be . . a father 1
13 Then Micah said, "Now I know that the LORD will 1
18: 2 they said to them, "Go and explore the land. 1
3 they turned aside and said to him, "Who brought you 1
4 he said to them, "Thus and thus has Micah dealt 1
5 they said to him, "Inquire of God, we pray thee 1
6 the priest said to them, "Go in peace. The journey 1
8 their brethren said to them, "What do you report? 1
9 They said, "Arise, and let us go up against them; 1
14 the five men . . said to their brethren, "Do you 1
18 the priest said to them, "What are you doing? 1
19 they said to him, "Keep quiet, put your hand upon 1
23 Danites, who turned round and said to Micah 1
24 he said, "You take my gods which I made 1
25 the Danites said to him, "Do not let your voice be 1
19: 5 to go; but the girl's father said to his son-in-law 1
6 the girl's father said to the man, "Be pleased 1
8 the girl's father said, "Strengthen your heart 1
9 father-in-law, the girl's father, said to him, "Behold 1
11 and the servant said to his master, "Come now, let us 1
12 his master said to him, "We will not turn aside 1
13 he said to his servant, "Come and let us draw near 1
17 the old man said, "Where are you going? and whence 1
18 he said to him, "We are passing from Bethlehem 1
20 the old man said, "Peace be to you; I will care for all 1
22 they said to the old man, the master of the house 1
23 the man . . went out to them and said to them, "No 1
28 He said to her, "Get up, let us be going. 1
30 all who saw it said, "Such a thing has never 1
20: 3 the people of Israel said, "Tell us, how was this 1
4 the Levite . . answered and said, "I came to Gib'e-ah 1
8 all the people arose as one man, saying, "We will not 1
12 tribes of Israel sent men . . saying, "What 1
18 And the LORD said, "Judah shall go up first. 1
23 And the LORD said, "Go up against them. 1
28 Israel inquired of the LORD . . saying, "Shall we 1
28 And the LORD said, "Go up; for tomorrow 1
32 the Benjaminites said, "They are routed before us 1
32 the men of Israel said, "Let us flee, and draw them 1
39 they said, "Surely they are smitten down before us 1
21: 3 they said, "O LORD, the God of Israel, why has this 1
5 the people of Israel said, "Which of all the tribes 1
5 they had taken a great oath . . saying, "He shall be 1
6 Israel . . said, "One tribe is cut off from Israel 1
8 they said, "What one is there of the tribes 1
16 the elders . . said, "What shall we do for wives 1
17 they said, "There must be an inheritance 1
19 they said, "Behold, there is the yearly feast 1
20 they commanded the Benjaminites, saying, "Go 1
22 we will say to them, 'Grant them graciously to us; 1
Rut 1: 8 Na'omi said to her two daughters-in-law, "Go, return 1
10 And they said to her, "No, we will return with you 1
11 Na'omi said, "Turn back, my daughters, 1
12 If I should say I have hope, even . . have a husband 1
15 And she said, "See, your sister-in-law has gone back 1
16 Ruth said, "Entreat me not to leave you or to return 1
18 when Na'omi saw that she was . . she said no more. 4
19 and the women said, "Is this Na'omi? 1
20 She said . . "Do not call me Na'omi, call me Mara 1
2: 2 And Ruth the Moabitess said to Na'omi, "Let me go 1
2 And she said to her, "Go, my daughter. 1
4 Bo'az came . . and he said to the reapers 1
5 Bo'az said to his servant who was in charge 1
7 She said, 'Pray, let me glean and gather 1
8 Then Bo'az said to Ruth, "Now, listen, my daughter 1
10 she fell on her face, bowing to the ground, and said 1
13 Then she said, "You are most gracious to me, my lord 1
14 And at mealtime Bo'az said to her, "Come here 1
15 Bo'az instructed his young men, saying 1
19 her mother-in-law said to her, "Where did you glean 1
19 she told her mother-in-law . . and said 1
20 Na'omi said to her daughter-in-law, "Blessed be he 1
20 Na'omi also said to her, "The man is a relative 1
21 And Ruth the Moabitess said, "Besides, he said to me 1
21 And Ruth the Moabitess said, "Besides, he said to me 1
22 Na'omi said to Ruth, her daughter-in-law, "It is well 1
3: 1 Then Na'omi her mother-in-law said to her 1
5 And she replied, "All that you say I will do. 1
9 He said, "Who are you?" And she answered, 1
10 he said, "May you be blessed by the LORD, 1
14 he said, "Let it not be known that the woman came 1
15 And he said, "Bring the mantle you are wearing 1
16 she said, "How did you fare, my daughter? 1
17 saying, "These six measures of barley he gave to me 1
17 six measures of barley he gave to me, for he said 1
4: 1 Bo'az said, "Turn aside, friend; sit down here"; 1
2 he took ten men of the elders of the city, and said 1
3 Then he said to the next of kin 1
4 I thought I would tell you of it, and say, Buy it 1
4 And he said, "I will redeem it. 1
5 Bo'az said, "The day you buy the field from . . Na'omi 1
6 the next of kin said, "I cannot redeem it for myself 1
8 when the next of kin said to Bo'az, "Buy it 1
9 Then Bo'az said to the elders and all the people 1
11 all the people . . and the elders, said 1
14 the women said to Na'omi, "Blessed be the LORD 1
17 And the women . . gave him a name, saying 1
1Sm 1: 8 Elka'nah, her husband, said to her, "Hannah, why 1
11 And she vowed a vow and said, "O LORD of hosts, 1
14 Eli said to her, "How long will you be drunken? 1
18 And she said, "Let your maidservant find favor 1
20 and she called his name Samuel, for she said •
22 Hannah did not go up, for she said to her husband 1
23 Elka'nah her husband said to her, "Do what seems 1
26 And she said, "Oh, my lord! As you live, my lord 1
2: 1 Hannah also prayed and said, "My heart exults 1
15 the priest's servant would come and say to the man 1
16 if the man said to him, "Let them burn the fat first 1
16 if the man said . . he would say, "No, you must give it 1
20 Then Eli would bless Elka'nah and his wife, and say 1
23 And he said to them, "Why do you do such things? 1
27 And there came a man of God to Eli, and said to him 1
27 Thus the LORD has said, 'I revealed myself 1
36 come to implore . . and shall say, "Put me, I pray you 1
3: 4 called, "Samuel! Samuel!" and he said, "Here I am! 1
5 ran to Eli, and said, "Here I am, for you called me. 1
5 But he said, "I did not call; lie down again. 1
6 Samuel arose and went to Eli, and said, "Here I am 1
6 you called me." But he said, "I did not call, my son; 1
8 And he arose and went to Eli, and said, "Here I am 1
9 Therefore Eli said to Samuel, "Go, lie down; 1
9 if he calls you, you shall say, 'Speak, LORD 1
10 And Samuel said, "Speak, for thy servant hears. 1
11 the LORD said to Samuel, "Behold, I am about to do 1
16 But Eli called Samuel and said, "Samuel, my son. 1
16 and said, "Samuel, my son." And he said, "Here I am. 1
17 Eli said, "What was it that he told you? Do not hide it 1
18 And he said, "It is the LORD; 1
4: 3 the elders of Israel said, "Why has the LORD 1
6 when the Philistines heard . . they said 1
7 they said, "A god has come into the camp. 1
7 And they said, "Woe to us! 1
14 When Eli heard . . he said, "What is this uproar? 1
16 the man said to Eli, "I . . come from the battle; 1
16 And he said, "How did it go, my son? 1
17 He who brought the tidings answered and said 1
20 the women attending her said to her, "Fear not 4
21 named . . Ich'abod, saying, "The glory has departed 1
22 And she said, "The glory has departed from Israel 1
5: 7 the men of Ashdod saw how things were, they said 1
8 they sent and gathered . . and said 1
11 and gathered together all the lords . . and said 1
6: 2 called for the priests and the diviners and said 1
3 They said, "If you send away the ark . . do not send it 1
4 And they said, "What is the guilt offering 1
20 the men of Beth-she'mesh said, "Who is able to stand 1
21 sent messengers to . . Kir'iath-je'arim, saying 1

7: 3 Then Samuel said to all the house of Israel 1
5 Then Samuel said, "Gather all Israel at Mizpah 1
6 gathered . . and fasted on that day, and said there 1
8 the people of Israel said to Samuel, "Do not cease 1
12 Ebene'zer; for he said, " . . the LORD has helped us. 1
8: 5 came to Samuel at Ramah, and said to him, "Behold 1
6 But the thing displeased Samuel when they said 1
7 the LORD said to Samuel, "Hearken to the . . people 1
7 Hearken . . in all that they say to you; 1
11 He said, "These will be the ways of the king 1
19 the people refused to listen . . and they said, "No! 1
22 the LORD said to Samuel, "Hearken to their voice 1
22 Samuel then said to the men of Israel 1
9: 3 asses . . were lost. So Kish said to Saul his son 1
5 Saul said to his servant who was with him, "Come 1
6 But he said to him, "Behold, there is a man of God 1
6 a man of God . . all that he says comes true. 4
7 Then Saul said to his servant, "But if we go, what can 1
9 when a man went to inquire of God, he said, "Come 1
10 Saul said to his servant, "Well said; come, let us go. 1
10 Saul said to his servant, "Well said; come, let us go. 5
11 they met young maidens coming . . and said to them 1
18 Then Saul approached Samuel in the gate, and said 1
23 Samuel said to the cook, "Bring the portion 1
23 the portion . . of which I said to you, 'Put it aside.' 1
24 Samuel said, "See, what was kept is set before you. 1
27 Samuel said to Saul, "Tell the servant to pass 1
10: 1 and poured it on his head, and kissed him and said 1
2 they will say to you, 'The asses . . you went to seek 1
2 your father . . is anxious . . saying, "What shall I do 1
11 the people said to one another, "What has come over 1
14 Saul's uncle said to him . . "Where did you go? 1
14 Where did you go?" And he said, "To seek the asses; 1
15 Saul's uncle said, "Pray, tell me what Samuel said 1
15 Pray, tell me what Samuel said to you. 1
16 Saul said to his uncle, "He told us plainly that 1
18 he said to the people of Israel, "Thus says the LORD 1
18 Thus says the LORD, the God of Israel, 'I brought up 1
19 and you have said, 'No! but set a king over us.' 1
22 the LORD said, "Behold, he has hidden himself 1
24 Samuel said to all the people, "Do you see him 1
27 some worthless fellows said, "How can this man 1
11: 1 all the men of Jabesh said to Nahash, "Make a treaty 1
2 Nahash . . said to them, "On this condition I will 1
3 The elders of Jabesh said . . "Give us seven days 1
5 and Saul said, "What ails the people 1
7 sent them throughout . . saying, "Whoever does not 1
9 they said to the messengers . . "Thus shall you say 1
9 Thus shall you say to the men of Ja'besh-gil'ead 1
10 Therefore the men of Jabesh said 1
12 Then the people said to Samuel, "Who is it that said 1
12 Who is it that said, 'Shall Saul reign over us?' 1
13 Saul said, "Not a man shall be put to death this day 1
14 Samuel said to the people, "Come, let us go to Gilgal 1
12: 1 Samuel said to all Israel, "Behold, I have 1
1 I have hearkened . . in all that you have said to me 1
4 They said, "You have not defrauded us or oppressed 1
5 he said to them, "The LORD is witness against you 1
5 And they said, "He is witness. 1
6 Samuel said to the people, "The LORD is witness 1
10 they cried to the LORD, and said, "We have sinned 1
12 you said to me, 'No, but a king shall reign over us,' 1
19 the people said to Samuel, "Pray for your servants 1
20 And Samuel said to the people, "Fear not; 1
13: 3 Saul blew the trumpet . . saying, "Let the Hebrews 1
4 Israel heard it said that Saul had defeated 1
9 Saul said, "Bring the burnt offering here to me 1
11 Samuel said, "What have you done? 1
11 Saul said, "When I saw that the people were 1
12 I said, 'Now the Philistines will come down upon me 1
13 Samuel said to Saul, "You have done foolishly; 1
19 the Philistines said, "Lest the Hebrews make 1
14: 1 Jonathan . . said to the young man who bore his armor 1
6 Jonathan said to the young man who bore his armor 1
7 And his armor-bearer said to him, "Do all that 1
8 Then said Jonathan, "Behold, we will cross over 1
9 If they say to us, 'Wait until we come to you,' 1
10 But if they say, 'Come up to us,' then we will go up; 1
11 the Philistines said, "Look, Hebrews are coming 1
12 the garrison hailed Jonathan . . and said, "Come up 1
12 Jonathan said to his armor-bearer, "Come up 1
17 Then Saul said to the people who were with him 1
18 Saul said to Ahi'jah, "Bring hither the ark of God. 1
19 and Saul said to the priest, "Withdraw your hand. 1
24 Saul laid an oath on the people, saying, "Cursed be 1
28 Then one of the people said, "Your father 14
28 charged the people with an oath, saying, 'Cursed be 1
29 Jonathan said, "My father has troubled the land; 1
33 And he said, "You have dealt treacherously; 1
34 Saul said, "Disperse yourselves among the people 1
34 Disperse . . among the people, and say to them 1
36 Saul said, "Let us go down after the Philistines 1
36 And they said, "Do whatever seems good to you. 1
36 the priest said, "Let us draw near hither to God. 1
38 Saul said, "Come hither . . leaders of the people; 1
40 Then he said to all Israel, "You shall be on one side 1
40 the people said to Saul, "Do what seems good to you. 1
41 Saul said, "O LORD God of Israel, why hast thou not 1
42 Then Saul said, "Cast the lot between me and my son 1
43 Saul said to Jonathan, "Tell me what you have done. 1
44 Saul said, "God do so to me and more also; 1
45 Then the people said to Saul, "Shall Jonathan die 1
15: 1 Samuel said to Saul, "The LORD sent me to anoint you 1
2 Thus says the LORD of hosts, 'I will punish 1
6 Saul said to the Ken'ites, "Go, depart, go down 1
13 Samuel came to Saul, and Saul said to him 1
14 And Samuel said, "What then is this bleating 1
15 Saul said, "They have brought them 1
16 Then Samuel said to Saul, "Stop! I will tell you 1
16 tell you what the LORD said to me on this night. 1
16 And he said to him, "Say on. 1
16 And he said to him, "Say on. 4
17 Samuel said, "Though you are little in your . . eyes 1
18 And the LORD sent you on a mission, and said 1
20 Saul said to Samuel, "I have obeyed the . . LORD 1
22 Samuel said, "Has the LORD as great delight 1
24 And Saul said to Samuel, "I have sinned; 1
26 And Samuel said to Saul, "I will not return with you 1
28 Samuel said to him, "The LORD has torn the kingdom 1
30 Then he said, "I have sinned; yet honor me now 1
32 Then Samuel said, "Bring here to me Agag the king 1
32 Agag said, "Surely the bitterness . . is past. 1
33 Samuel said, "As your sword has made women 1
16: 1 The LORD said to Samuel, "How long will you grieve 1
2 And Samuel said, "How can I go? 1
2 And the LORD said, "Take a heifer with you, and say 1
2 Take a heifer . . and say, 'I have come to sacrifice 1
4 The elders . . and said, "Do you come peaceably? 1
5 And he said, "Peaceably; I have come to sacrifice 1
7 But the LORD said to Samuel, "Do not look on his 1
8 And he said, "Neither has the LORD chosen this one. 1
9 And he said, "Neither has the LORD chosen this one. 1
10 And Samuel said to Jesse, "The LORD has not chosen 1
11 And Samuel said to Jesse, "Are all your sons here? 1
11 And he said, "There remains yet the youngest 1
11 And Samuel said to Jesse, "Send and fetch him; 1
12 And the LORD said, "Arise, anoint him; for this is he. 1
15 Saul's servants said to him, "Behold now 1
17 Saul said to his servants, "Provide for me a man 1
19 Saul sent messengers to Jesse, and said, "Send me 1
22 And Saul sent to Jesse, saying, "Let David remain 1
17:10 the Philistine said, "I defy the ranks of Israel 1
17 And Jesse said to David his son, "Take 1
25 And the men of Israel said, "Have you seen this man 1
26 And David said to the men who stood by him 1
28 Eli'ab's anger was kindled . . and he said. 1
29 And David said, "What have I done now? 1
32 David said to Saul, "Let no man's heart fail 1
33 And Saul said to David, "You are not able to go 1
34 But David said to Saul, "Your servant used to keep 1
37 David said, "The LORD who . . will deliver me 1
37 Saul said to David, "Go, and the LORD be with you! 1
39 Then David said to Saul, "I cannot go with these; 1
43 And the Philistine said to David, "Am I a dog 1
44 The Philistine said to David, "Come to me 1
45 Then David said to the Philistine 1
55 When Saul saw David go forth . . he said to Abner 1
55 Abner said, "As your soul lives . . I cannot tell. 1
56 And the king said, "Inquire whose son 1
58 Saul said to him, "Whose son are you, young man? 1
18: 8 Saul was very angry . . he said, "They have ascribed 1
17 Saul said to David, "Here is my elder daughter Merab; 1
18 David said to Saul, "Who am I . . who are my kinsfolk 1
21 Therefore Saul said to David a second time 1
22 Speak to David in private and say, 'Behold, the king 1
23 And David said, "Does it seem to you a little thing 1
25 Then Saul said, "Thus shall you say to David 1
25 Thus shall you say to David, 'The king desires no 1
19: 4 Jonathan spoke . . and said to him, "Let not the king 1
14 when Saul . . to take David, she said, "He is sick. 1
15 Saul sent . . to see David, saying, "Bring him up to me 1
17 Saul said to Michal, "Why have you deceived me thus 1
17 He said to me, 'Let me go; why should I kill you?' 1
22 And one said, "Behold, they are at Nai'oth in Ramah. 1
24 Hence it is said, "Is Saul also among the prophets? 1
20: 1 David fled . . and came and said before Jonathan 1
2 he said to him, "Far from it! You shall not die. 1
4 Then said Jonathan to David, "Whatever . . I will do 1
4 Whatever you say, I will do for you. 1
5 David said to Jonathan, "Behold, tomorrow is 1
6 If your father misses me at all, then say 1
7 If he says, 'Good!' it will be well with your servant; 1
9 And Jonathan said, "Far be it from you! 1
10 Then said David to Jonathan, "Who will tell me 1
11 Jonathan said to David, "Come, let us go out 1
12 Jonathan said to David, "The LORD . . be witness! 1
18 Jonathan said to him, "Tomorrow is the new moon; 1
21 I will send the lad, saying, 'Go, find the arrows.' •
21 If I say to the lad, 'Look, the arrows are 1
22 if I say to the youth, 'Look, the arrows are beyond 1
26 Saul did not say anything that day; for he thought 4
27 Saul said to Jonathan his son, "Why has not the son 1
29 he said, 'Let me go; for our family holds a sacrifice 1
30 Saul's anger was kindled . . and he said to him 1
36 And he said to his lad, "Run and find the arrows 1
37 Jonathan called after the lad and said 1
40 Jonathan gave his weapons . . and said to him, "Go 1
42 Then Jonathan said to David, "Go in peace 1
42 we have sworn . . saying, 'The LORD shall be between 1
21: 1 Ahim'elech came to meet David . . and said to him 1
2 And David said to Ahim'elech the priest 1
2 The king has charged me . . and said to me, 'Let no one 1
8 David said to Ahim'elech, "And have you . . a spear 1
9 the priest said, "The sword of Goliath . . is here 1
9 David said, "There is none like that; give it to me. 1
11 And the servants of A'chish said to him 1
14 said A'chish to his servants, "Lo . . the man is mad; 1
22: 3 David went . . and he said to the king of Moab 1
5 Then the prophet Gad said to David, "Do not remain 1
7 Saul said to his servants who stood about him 1
12 Saul said, "Hear now, son of Ahi'tub." 1
13 Saul said . . "Why have you conspired against me 1
16 And the king said, "You shall surely die, Ahim'elech 1
17 the king said to the guard who stood about him 1
18 the king said to Do'eg, "You turn and fall upon 1
22 And David said to Abi'athar, "I knew on that day 1
23: 2 And the LORD said to David, "Go and attack 1
3 David's men said to him, "Behold, we are afraid here 1
7 And Saul said, "God has given him into my hand; 1
9 he said to Abi'athar the priest, "Bring the ephod 1
10 Then said David, "O LORD, the God of Israel 1
11 And the LORD said, "He will come down. 1
12 Then said David, "Will the men . . surrender me 1
12 And the LORD said, "They will surrender you. 1
17 And he said to him, "Fear not; 1
19 the Ziphites went up to Saul at Gib'e-ah, saying 1
21 And Saul said, "May you be blessed by the LORD; 1
27 a messenger came to Saul, saying, "Make haste 1
24: 4 And the men of David said to him, "Here is the day 1
4 Here is the day of which the LORD said to you 1
6 He said to his men, "The LORD forbid that I . . do this 1
9 David said to Saul, "Why do you listen 1
9 men who say, 'Behold, David seeks your hurt'? 1
10 I said, 'I will not put forth my hand against my lord; 1
13 As the proverb of the ancients says 1
16 Saul said, "Is this your voice, my son David? 1
17 He said to David, "You are more righteous than I; 1
25: 5 and David said to the young men, "Go up to Carmel 1
9 they said all this to Nabal in the name of David; 4
13 David said to his men, "Every man gird on his sword! 1
19 And she said to her young men, "Go on before me; 1
21 Now David had said, "Surely in vain have I guarded 1
24 She fell at his feet and said, "Upon me alone 1
32 David said to Ab'igail, "Blessed be the LORD 1
35 and he said to her, "Go up in peace to your house; 1
39 When David heard that Nabal was dead, he said 1
40 they said to her, "David has sent us to you 4
41 she rose and bowed . . and said, "Behold 1
26: 1 Then the Ziphites came to Saul at Gib'e-ah, saying 1
6 Then David said to Ahim'elech the Hittite 1
6 And Abi'shai said, "I will go down with you. 1
8 Then said Abi'shai to David, "God has given 1
9 But David said to Abi'shai, "Do not destroy him; 1
10 David said, "As the LORD lives, the LORD will smite 1
14 David called . . saying, "Will you not answer 1
15 And David said to Abner, "Are you not a man? 1
17 Saul recognized David's voice, and said 1
17 And David said, "It is my voice, my lord, O king. 1
18 he said, "Why does my lord pursue after his servant? 1
19 driven me out . . saying, 'Go, serve other gods.' 1
21 Saul said, "I have done wrong; return, my son David 1
25 Saul said to David, "Blessed be you, my son David! 1
27: 1 David said in his heart, "I shall now perish one day 1
5 Then David said to A'chish, "If I have found favor 1
10 David would say, "Against the Negeb of Judah 1
11 Lest they should . . and say, 'So David has done.' 1
28: 1 And A'chish said to David 1
2 David said to A'chish, "Very well, you shall know 1
2 And A'chish said to David, "Very well 1
7 Saul said to his servants, "Seek out . . a medium 1
7 his servants said to him, "Behold, there is a medium 1
8 And he said, "Divine for me by a spirit 1
9 The woman said to him, "Surely you know what Saul 1
11 the woman said, "Whom shall I bring up for you? 1
11 He said, "Bring up Samuel for me. 1
12 the woman said to Saul, "Why have you deceived me? 1
13 The king said to her, "Have no fear; what do you see? 1
13 the woman said to Saul, "I see a god coming up 1
14 He said to her, "What is his appearance? 1
14 What is his appearance?" And she said, "An old man 1
15 Samuel said to Saul, "Why have you disturbed me 1
16 And Samuel said, "Why then do you ask me 1
21 when she saw that he was terrified, she said to him 1
21 I . . have hearkened to what you have said to me. 4
23 He refused, and said, "I will not eat. 1
29: 3 the commanders of the Philistines said 1
3 And A'chish said to the commanders 1
4 the commanders of the Philistines said to him 1
6 Then A'chish called David and said to him 1
8 And David said to A'chish, "But what have I done? 1
9 the commanders of the Philistines have said 1
30: 7 David said to Abi'athar . . "Bring me the ephod. 1
13 And David said to him, "To whom do you belong? 1
13 He said, "I am a young man of Egypt, servant 1
15 David said to him, "Will you take me down to this 1
15 he said, "Swear to me by God, that you will not kill me 1
20 people drove those cattle before him, and said 1

22 Then all the wicked and base fellows . . said 1
23 But David said, "You shall not do so, my brothers 1
26 he sent part of the spoil . . saying, "Here is 1
31: 4 Saul said to his armor-bearer, "Draw your sword 1
2Sm 1: 3 David said to him, "Where do you come from? 1
3 And he said to him, "I have escaped from the camp 1
4 David said to him, "How did it go? Tell me. 1
5 Then David said to the young man who told him 1
6 And the young man who told him said, "By chance I 1
8 And he said to me, 'Who are you?' 1
9 And he said to me, 'Stand beside me and slay me; 1
13 And David said to the young man who told him 1
14 David said to him, "How is it you were not afraid 1
15 Then David called one of the young men and said, "Go 1
16 David said to him, "Your blood be upon your head; 1
16 your own mouth has testified against you, saying 1
18 he said it should be taught to the people of Judah; 1
18 it is written in the Book of Jashar. He said •
2: 1 And the LORD said to him, "Go up. 1
1 Go up." David said, "To which shall I go up? 1
1 To which shall I go up?" And he said, "To Hebron. 1
5 David sent . . and said to them, "May you be blessed 1
14 Abner said to Jo'ab, "Let the young men arise 1
14 And Jo'ab said, "Let them arise. 1
20 Abner looked behind him and said, "Is it you, As'ahel? 1
21 Abner said to him, "Turn aside . . and seize one 1
22 And Abner said again to As'ahel, "Turn aside 1
27 Jo'ab said, "As God lives, if you had not spoken 1
3: 7 and Ish-bo'sheth said to Abner, "Why have you gone 1
8 Abner was very angry . . and said, "Am I a dog's head 1
12 Abner sent messengers to David at Hebron, saying 1
13 And he said, "Good; I will make a covenant with you; 1
14 David sent messengers to Ish-bo'sheth . . saying 1
16 Abner said to him, "Go, return"; and he returned. 1
17 Abner conferred with the elders . . saying 1
18 the LORD has promised David, saying, 'By the hand 1
21 And Abner said to David, "I will arise and go 1
24 Jo'ab went to the king and said, "What have you done 1
28 Afterward, when David heard of it, he said 1
31 Then David said to Jo'ab and to all the people 1
33 And the king lamented for Abner, saying 1
35 but David swore, saying, "God do so to me and more 1
38 the king said to his servants 1
4: 8 And they said to the king, "Here is the head 1
5: 1 the tribes . . came to David at Hebron, and said 1
2 the LORD said to you, 'You shall be shepherd 1
6 Jeb'usites . . who said to David, "You will not come 1
8 David said on that day, "Whoever would smite 1
8 Therefore it is said, "The blind and the lame shall 1
19 And the LORD said to David, "Go up; for I will 1
20 he said, "The LORD has broken through my enemies 1
23 And when David inquired of the LORD, he said 1
6: 9 he said, "How can the ark of the LORD come to me? 1
20 But Michal . . came out to meet David, and said 1
21 And David said to Michal, "It was before the LORD 1
7: 2 the king said to Nathan the prophet 1
3 Nathan said to the king, "Go, do all . . in your heart; 1
5 Thus says the LORD: Would you build me a house 1
7 judges of Israel, whom I commanded . . saying 1
8 therefore thus you shall say to my servant David 1
8 Thus says the LORD of hosts, I took you 1
18 David went in and sat before the LORD, and said 1
20 And what more can David say to thee? 4
26 and thy name will be magnified for ever, saying 1
27 hast made this revelation to thy servant, saying 1
9: 1 And David said, "Is there still any one left 1
2 and the king said to him, "Are you Ziba? 1
2 Are you Ziba?" And he said, "Your servant is he. 1
3 And the king said, "Is there not still some one 1
3 Ziba said to the king, "There is still a son 1
4 The king said to him, "Where is he? 1
4 Ziba said to the king, "He is in the house of Machir 1
6 And David said, "Mephib'osheth! 1
7 David said to him, "Do not fear; 1
8 And he did obeisance, and said 1
9 the king called Ziba . . and said to him 1
11 Then Ziba said to the king, "According to all 1
10: 2 And David said, "I will deal loyally with Hanun 1
3 But the princes of the Ammonites said to Hanun 1
5 And the king said, "Remain at Jericho until 1
11 And he said, "If the Syrians are too strong for me 1
11: 3 And one said, "Is not this Bathshe'ba, the daughter 1
8 Then David said to Uri'ah, "Go down to your house 1
10 David said to Uri'ah, "Have you not come 1
11 Uri'ah said to David, "The ark and Israel and Judah 1
12 Then David said to Uri'ah, "Remain here today also 1
20 then, if the king's anger rises, and if he says to you 1
21 you shall say, 'Your servant Uri'ah . . is dead also.' 1
23 The messenger said to David, "The men gained 1
25 David said to the messenger, "Thus shall you say 1
25 David said . . "Thus shall you say to Jo'ab 1
12: 1 came to him, and said to him, "There were two men 1
5 and he said to Nathan, "As the LORD lives 1
7 Nathan said to David, "You are the man. 1
7 Thus says the LORD, the God of Israel, 'I anointed 1
11 Thus says the LORD, 'Behold, I will raise up evil 1
13 David said to Nathan, "I have sinned 1
13 Nathan said to David, "The LORD . . put away 1
18 they said, "Behold, while the child was yet alive 1
18 how then can we say to him the child is dead? 1
19 and David said to his servants, "Is the child dead? 1
19 Is the child dead?" They said, "He is dead. 1
21 Then his servants said to him, "What is this thing 1
22 He said, "While the child was still alive, I fasted 1
22 I fasted and wept; for I said, 'Who knows whether 1
27 Jo'ab sent messengers to David, and said 1
13: 4 he said to him, "O son of the king 1
4 Amnon said to him, "I love Tamar 1
5 Jon'adab said to him, "Lie down on your bed 1
5 when your father comes . . say to him, 'Let my sister 1
6 when the king came to see him, Amnon said 1
7 Then David sent home to Tamar, saying, "Go 1
9 Amnon said, "Send out every one from me. 1
10 Then Amnon said to Tamar, "Bring the food 1
11 took hold of her, and said to her, "Come, lie with me 1
15 And Amnon said to her, "Arise, be gone. 1
16 But she said to him, "No, my brother; 1
17 He called the young man who served him and said 1
20 And her brother Ab'salom said to her 1
24 And Ab'salom came to the king, and said, "Behold 1
25 But the king said to Ab'salom, "No, my son 1
26 Then Ab'salom said, "If not, pray let . . Amnon go 1
26 the king said to him, "Why should he go with you? 1
28 and when I say to you, 'Strike Amnon,' then kill him. 1
32 Jon'adab the son of Shim'e-ah, David's brother, said 1
35 Jon'adab said to the king, "Behold, the king's sons 1
35 as your servant said, so it has come about. 5
14: 2 fetched from there a wise woman, and said to her 1
4 and did obeisance, and said, "Help, O king. 1
5 And the king said to her, "What is your trouble? 1
7 whole family has risen against . . and they say 1
8 Then the king said to the woman, "Go to your house 1
9 And the woman of Teko'a said to the king 1
10 The king said, "If any one says anything to you 1
10 If any one says anything to you, bring him to me 4
11 Then she said, "Pray let the king invoke the LORD 1
11 He said, "As the LORD lives, not one hair of your son 1
12 Then the woman said, "Pray let your handmaid speak 1
12 let your handmaid speak . . " He said, "Speak. 1
13 woman said, "Why then have you planned such 1
15 Now I have come to say this to my lord the king 4
18 And the woman said, "Let my lord the king speak. 1
19 The king said, "Is the hand of Jo'ab with you 1
19 The woman answered and said, "As surely as you live 1
19 from anything that my lord the king has said. 4
21 Then the king said to Jo'ab, "Behold now, I grant this; 1
22 and Jo'ab said, "Today your servant knows 1
24 the king said, "Let him dwell apart in his own house; 1
30 Then he said to his servants, "See, Jo'ab's field 1
31 Jo'ab arose and went to Ab'salom . . and said to him 1
15: 2 Ab'salom would call to him, and say, "From what city 1
2 And when he said, "Your servant is of such and such 1
3 Ab'salom would say to him, "See, your claims are good 1
4 Ab'salom said moreover, "Oh that I were judge 1
7 Ab'salom said to the king, "Pray let me go 1
8 vowed a vow while I dwelt at Geshur in Aram, saying 1
9 The king said to him, "Go in peace." So he arose 1
10 Ab'salom sent . . saying, "As soon as you hear 1
10 As soon as . . then say, 'Ab'salom is king at Hebron!' 1
13 And a messenger came to David, saying 1
14 David said to all his servants who were with him 1
15 And the king's servants said to the king 1
19 Then the king said to It'tai the Gittite 1
22 And David said to It'tai, "Go then, pass on. 1
25 Then the king said to Zadok, "Carry the ark of God 1
26 if he says, 'I have no pleasure in you,' 1
27 The king also said to Zadok the priest 1
31 David said, "O LORD, I pray thee, turn the counsel 1
33 David said to him, "If you go on with me, you will be 1
34 But if you return to the city, and say to Ab'salom 1
16: 2 the king said to Ziba, "Why have you brought these? 1
3 And the king said, "And where is your master's son? 1
3 Ziba said to the king, "Behold, he remains 1
3 he said, 'Today the house of Israel will give me 1
4 Then the king said to Ziba 1
4 And Ziba said, "I do obeisance; let me ever find 1
7 Shim'e-i said as he cursed, "Begone, begone, you man 1
9 Then Abi'shai the son of Zeru'iah said to the king 1
10 But the king said, "What have I to do with you 1
10 because the LORD has said to him, 'Curse David,' 1
10 who then shall say, 'Why have you done so?' 1
11 David said to Abi'shai and to all his servants 1
16 Hushai said to Ab'salom, "Long live the king! 1
17 And Ab'salom said to Hushai, "Is this your loyalty 1
18 And Hushai said to Ab'salom, "No; 1
20 Ab'salom said to Ahith'ophel, "Give your counsel; 1
21 Ahith'ophel said to Ab'salom, "Go in to your father's 1
17: 1 Moreover Ahith'ophel said to Ab'salom 1
5 Then Ab'salom said, "Call Hushai the Archite also 1
5 Call Hushai . . and let us hear what he has to say. 3
6 when Hushai came to Ab'salom, Ab'salom said to him 1
7 Then Hushai said to Ab'salom 1
8 Hushai said moreover, "You know that 1
9 when some . . fall.., whoever hears it will say 1
14 And Ab'salom and all the men of Israel said 1
15 Hushai said to Zadok and Abi'athar the priests 1
20 they said, "Where are Ahim'a-az and Jonathan? 1
20 And the woman said to them, "They have gone over 1
21 They said to David, "Arise, and go quickly over 1
29 they said, "The people are hungry and weary 1
18: 2 And the king said to the men, "I myself will also go 1
3 But the men said, "You shall not go out. 1
4 The king said to them, "Whatever seems best to you 1
11 Jo'ab said to the man . . "What, you saw him! 1
12 But the man said to Jo'ab, "Even if I felt in my hand 1
14 Jo'ab said, "I will not waste time like this 1
18 for he said, "I have no son to keep my name 1
19 Then said Ahi'ma-az the son of Zadok, "Let me run 1
20 Jo'ab said to him, "You are not to carry tidings 1
21 Then Jo'ab said to the Cushite, "Go, tell the king 1
22 Then Ahi'ma-az the son of Zadok said again to Jo'ab 1
22 And Jo'ab said, "Why will you run, my son 1
23 Come what may," he said, "I will run. 1
23 I will run." So he said to him, "Run. 1
25 And the king said, "If he is alone, there are tidings 1
26 and the watchman called to the gate and said 1
26 The king said, "He also brings tidings. 1
27 And the watchman said, "I think the running 1
27 the king said, "He is a good man, and comes with good 1
28 And he bowed . . with his face to the earth, and said 1
29 And the king said, "Is it well with the young man 1
30 And the king said, "Turn aside, and stand here. 1
31 and the Cushite said, "Good tidings for my lord 1
32 The king said to the Cushite, "Is it well 1
33 he said, "O my son Ab'salom, my son, 1
19: 5 Then Jo'ab came into the house to the king, and said 1
9 And all the people were at strife . . saying 1
11 Say to the elders of Judah, 'Why should you be 4
13 And say to Ama'sa, 'Are you not my bone 1
19 And Shim'e-i . . said to the king, "Let not my lord 1
22 But David said, "What have I to do with you 1
23 And the king said to Shim'e-i, "You shall not die. 1
25 he came . . the king said to him, "Why did you not 1
26 for your servant said to him, 'Saddle an ass for me 1
29 And the king said to him, "Why speak any more 1
30 Mephib'osheth said to the king, "Oh, let him take it 1
33 the king said to Barzil'lai, "Come over with me 1
34 But Barzil'lai said to the king, "How many years 1
41 all . . Israel came to the king, and said to the king 1
20: 1 and he blew the trumpet, and said, "We have no 1
4 Then the king said to Ama'sa, "Call the men of Judah 1
6 And David said to Abi'shai, "Now Sheba . . will do 1
9 Jo'ab said to Ama'sa, "Is it well with you, my brother? 1
11 one of Jo'ab's men took his stand by Ama'sa, and said 1
17 came near her; and the woman said, "Are you Jo'ab? 1
17 she said to him, "Listen to . . your maidservant. 1
18 Then she said, "They were wont to say in old time 1
18 They were wont to say in old time, 'Let them but ask 4
21 the woman said to Jo'ab, "Behold, his head shall be 1
21: 1 And the LORD said, "There is bloodguilt on Saul 1
3 And David said to the Gib'eonites, "What shall I do 1
4 The Gib'eonites said to him, "It is not a matter 1
4 And he said, "What do you say that I shall do for you? 1
4 And he said, "What do you say that I shall do for you? 1
5 They said to the king, "The man who consumed us 1
6 And the king said, "I will give them. 1
22: 2 He said, "The LORD is my rock, and my fortress 1
23: 3 the Rock of Israel has said to me: When one rules 4
15 And David said longingly, "O that some one would 1
17 he poured it out . . and said, "Far be it from me, 1
24: 1 and he incited David against them, saying, "Go 1
2 the king said to Jo'ab and the commanders 1
3 Jo'ab said to the king, "May the LORD your God add 1
10 And David said to the LORD, "I have sinned greatly 1
11 word of the LORD came to the prophet Gad . . saying 1
12 Go and say to David, 'Thus says the LORD 4
12 Thus says the LORD, Three things I offer you; 1
13 Gad came to David and told him, and said to him 1
14 Then David said to Gad, "I am in great distress 1
16 the LORD repented . . and said to the angel 1
17 Then David spoke to the LORD . . and said 1
18 Gad came that day to David, and said to him, "Go up 1
21 And Arau'nah said, "Why has my lord the king come 1
21 David said, "To buy the threshing floor of you 1
22 Arau'nah said to David, "Let my lord the king take 1
23 And Arau'nah said to the king, "The LORD your God 1
24 But the king said to Arau'nah, "No, but I will buy it 1
1Kg 1: 2 his servants said to him, "Let a young maiden be 1
5 Adoni'jah . . exalted himself, saying, "I will be 1
11 Nathan said to Bathshe'ba the mother of Solomon 1
13 Go in at once to King David, and say to him, 'Did you 1
13 Did you not . . swear to your maidservant, saying 1
16 and the king said, "What do you desire? 1
17 She said to him, "My lord, you swore 1
17 you swore . . by the LORD your God, saying, 'Solomon 8
24 Nathan said, "My lord the king, have you said 1
24 My lord the king, have you said, 'Adoni'jah shall 1
25 eating and drinking before him, and saying, 'Long 1
29 the king swore, saying, "As the LORD lives, who has 1
30 as I swore . . saying, 'Solomon your son shall 1
31 did obeisance to the king, and said, "May my lord 1
32 King David said, "Call to me Zadok the priest 1
33 the king said to them, "Take with you the servants 1
34 the trumpet, and say, 'Long live King Solomon! 1
36 Amen! May the LORD, the God of my lord . . say so. 1
39 and all the people said, "Long live King Solomon! 1
41 heard the sound of the trumpet, he said, "What does 1

42 Adoni'jah said, "Come in, for you are a worthy man 1
47 to congratulate our lord King David, saying, 'Your 1
48 the king also said, 'Blessed be the LORD, the God 1
51 he has laid hold of the horns of the altar, saying 1
52 Solomon said, "If he prove to be a worthy man, not one 1
53 and Solomon said to him, "Go to your house. 1
2: 1 drew near, he charged Solomon his son, saying 1
4 his word which he spoke concerning me, saying, 'If 1
8 I swore . . saying, 'I will not put you to death 1
13 she said, "Do you come peaceably? 1
13 Do you come peaceably?" He said, "Peaceably. 1
14 Then he said, "I have something to say to you. 1
14 I have something to say to you." She said, "Say on. •
14 I have something to say to you." She said, "Say on. 1
14 I have something to say to you." She said, "Say on. 4
15 He said, "You know that the kingdom was mine 1
16 do not refuse me." She said to him, "Say on. 1
16 do not refuse me." She said to him, "Say on. 4
17 he said, "Pray ask King Solomon–he will not refuse 1
18 Bathshe'ba said, "Very well; I will speak for you 1
20 she said, "I have one small request to make of you 1
20 the king said to her, "Make your request, my mother; 1
21 She said, "Let Ab'ishag the Shu'nammite be given 1
23 Solomon swore by the LORD, saying, "God do so to me 1
26 to Abi'athar the priest the king said, "Go 1
29 Solomon sent Benai'ah . . saying, "Go, strike him 1
30 Benai'ah came . . and said to him, "The king 1
30 The king commands, 'Come forth.'" But he said, "No 1
30 Benai'ah brought the king word again, saying, "Thus 1
30 saying, "Thus said Jo'ab, and thus he answered me. 4
31 Do as he has said, strike him down and bury him; 4
36 king . . summoned Shim'e-i, and said to him, "Build 1
38 Shim'e-i said to the king, "What you say is good; 1
38 What you say is good; as my lord the king has said 5
38 as my lord the king has said, so will your servant 4
42 the king sent and summoned Shim'e-i, and said to him 1
42 and solemnly admonish you, saying, 'Know 1
42 And you said to me, 'What you say is good; I obey.' 1
42 And you said to me, 'What you say is good; I obey.' 5
44 The king also said to Shim'e-i, "You know in your own 1
3: 5 in a dream by night; and God said, "Ask what I shall 1
6 Solomon said, "Thou hast shown great 1
11 God said to him, "Because you have asked this 1
17 The one woman said, "Oh, my lord, this woman and I 1
22 the other woman said, "No, the living child is mine 1
22 The first said, "No, the dead child is yours 1
23 the king said, "The one says, 'This is my son that is 1
23 the king said, "The one says, 'This is my son that is 1
23 the other says, 'No; but your son is dead, and my son is 1
24 the king said, "Bring me a sword." So a sword was 1
25 the king said, "Divide the living child in two 1
26 the woman . . said to the king, because her heart 1
26 the other said, "It shall be neither mine nor yours; 1
27 the king answered and said, "Give the living child 1
5: 5 to build a house . . as the LORD said to David 4
7 When Hiram heard . . he rejoiced greatly, and said 1
8 Hiram sent to Solomon, saying, "I have heard 1
8:12 Then Solomon said, "The LORD has set the sun 1
12 The LORD . . has said that he would dwell 1
15 he said, "Blessed be the LORD, the God of Israel 1
15 what he promised . . to David my father, saying 1
18 the LORD said to David my father, 'Whereas 1
23 and said, "O LORD, God of Israel 1
25 thou hast promised him, saying, 'There shall never 1
29 house, the place of which thou hast said, 'My name 1
47 make supplication . . saying, 'We have sinned 1
55 blessed . . Israel with a loud voice, saying 1
9: 3 the LORD said to him, "I have heard 1
5 as I promised David your father, saying 1
8 astonished, and will hiss; and they will say 1
9 they will say, 'Because they forsook the LORD 1
13 Therefore he said, "What kind of cities are these 1
10: 6 she said to the king, "The report was true 1
11: 2 the nations concerning which the LORD had said 1
11 Therefore the LORD said to Solomon 1
21 Hadad said to Pharaoh, "Let me depart 1
22 Pharaoh said to him, "What have you lacked with me 1
22 And he said to him, "Only let me go. 1
31 he said to Jerobo'am, "Take for yourself ten pieces; 1
31 Take . . ten pieces; for thus says the LORD 1
12: 3 Jerobo'am . . came and said to Rehobo'am 4
5 He said to them, "Depart for three days, then come 1
6 Rehobo'am took counsel . . saying, "How do you 1
7 they said to him, "If you will be a servant 4
9 he said to them, "What do you advise that we answer 1
9 this people who have said to me, 'Lighten the yoke 4
10 young men who had grown up with him said to him 4
10 speak to this people who said to you 4
10 thus shall you say to them 4
12 and all the people came . . as the king said, "Come 4
14 he spoke to them . . saying, "My father 1
23 Say to Rehobo'am the son of Solomon, king of Judah 1
24 'Thus says the LORD, You shall not go up or fight 1
26 Jerobo'am said in his heart 1
28 he said to the people, "You have gone up 1
13: 2 the man cried against the altar . . and said 1
2 thus says the LORD: 'Behold, a son shall be born 1
3 he gave a sign the same day, saying, "This is the sign 1
4 Jerobo'am stretched out his hand . . saying 1
6 the king said to the man of God, "Entreat now 1
7 the king said to the man of God, "Come home with me 4
8 the man of God said to the king 1
9 commanded me by the word of the LORD, saying 1
12 their father said to him, "Which way did he go? 4
13 he said to his sons, "Saddle the ass for me. 1
14 he said to him, "Are you the man of God who came 1
14 Are you the man of God . . ?" And he said, "I am. 1
15 he said to him, "Come home with me and eat bread. 1
16 he said, "I may not return with you, or go in with you; 1
17 it was said to me by the word of the LORD 5
18 he said to him, "I am also a prophet as you are 1
18 an angel spoke to me . . saying, "Bring him back 1
21 Thus says the LORD, 'Because you have disobeyed 1
22 in the place of which he said to you, "Eat no bread 4
26 when the prophet . . heard of it, he said 1
27 he said to his sons, "Saddle the ass for me. 4
30 they mourned over him, saying, "Alas, my brother! •
31 after he had buried him, he said to his sons 1
14: 2 Jerobo'am said to his wife, "Arise 1
2 Ahi'jah . . who said of me that I should be king 4
5 the LORD said to Ahi'jah, "Behold 1
5 Thus and thus shall you say to her. 4
6 when Ahi'jah heard . . he said, "Come in 1
7 Go, tell Jerobo'am, 'Thus says the LORD 1
15:18 Asa sent them to Ben-ha'dad . . saying 1
16: 1 the word of the LORD came to Jehu . . saying 1
16 the troops . . heard it said, "Zimri has conspired 1
17: 1 Now Eli'jah the Tishbite . . said to Ahab 1
10 he called to her and said, "Bring me a little water 1
11 as she was going . . he called to her and said 1
12 she said, "As the LORD your God lives, I have nothing 1
13 Eli'jah said to her, "Fear not; go and do 1
13 Fear not; go and do as you have said; 5
14 For thus says the LORD the God of Israel 1
15 she went and did as Eli'jah said; 5
18 she said to Eli'jah, "What have you against me 1
19 he said to her, "Give me your son. 1
23 and Eli'jah said, "See, your son lives. 1
24 the woman said to Eli'jah, "Now I know 1
18: 1 the word of the LORD came to Eli'jah . . saying, "Go 1
5 Ahab said to Obadi'ah, "Go through the land 1
7 Obadi'ah recognized him . . and said, "Is it you 1
9 he said, "Wherein have I sinned 1
10 when they would say, 'He is not here,' 1
11 now you say, 'Go, tell your lord 1
14 now you say, 'Go, tell your lord 1
15 Eli'jah said, "As the LORD of hosts lives 1
17 Ahab said to him, "Is it you, you troubler of Israel? 1
21 Eli'jah came near to all the people, and said 1
22 Eli'jah said to the people, "I, even I only, am left 1
25 Then Eli'jah said to the prophets of Ba'al, "Choose 1
26 called on . . Ba'al from morning until noon, saying 1
27 at noon Eli'jah mocked them, saying, "Cry aloud 1
30 Then Eli'jah said to all the people, "Come near to me"; 1
31 Jacob, to whom the word of the LORD came, saying 1
33 he said, "Fill four jars with water 1
34 he said, "Do it a second time"; and they did 1
34 he said, "Do it a third time"; and they did 1
36 Eli'jah the prophet came near and said, "O LORD 1
39 they said, "The LORD, he is God; the LORD, he is God. 1
40 Eli'jah said to them, "Seize the prophets of Ba'al; 1
41 Eli'jah said to Ahab, "Go up, eat and drink; 1
43 he said to his servant, "Go up now, look 1
43 he went up and looked, and said, "There is nothing. 1
43 And he said, "Go again seven times. 1
44 at the seventh time he said, "Behold, a little cloud 1
44 he said, "Go up, say to Ahab, 'Prepare your chariot 1
44 Go up, say to Ahab, 'Prepare your chariot and go down 1
19: 2 Then Jez'ebel sent a messenger to Eli'jah saying 1
4 and he asked that he might die, saying, "It is enough; 1
5 an angel touched him, and said to him, "Arise 1
7 the angel . . touched him, and said 1
9 the word of the LORD came to him, and he said to him 1
10 He said, "I have been very jealous for the LORD 1
11 he said, "Go forth, and stand upon the mount 1
13 And behold, there came a voice to him, and said 1
14 He said, "I have been very jealous for the LORD 1
15 the LORD said to him, "Go, return on your way 1
20 ran after Eli'jah, and said, "Let me kiss my father 1
20 he said to him, "Go back again; for what have I done 1
20: 2 sent messengers . . and said to him, "Thus says 1
2 Thus says Ben-ha'dad 1
4 As you say, my lord, O king, I am yours 5
5 The messengers came again, and said, "Thus says 1
5 Thus says Ben-ha'dad: 'I sent to you, saying 1
5 'I sent to you, saying, "Deliver to me your silver 1
7 the king of Israel called . . and said, "Mark now 1
8 all the elders and all the people said to him 1
9 So he said to the messengers of Ben-ha'dad 1
10 Ben-ha'dad sent to him and said 1
12 When Ben-ha'dad heard . . he said to his men 1
13 a prophet came near to Ahab . . and said, "Thus says 1
13 Thus says the LORD, Have you seen all this 1
14 Ahab said, "By whom?" He said, "Thus says the LORD 1
14 Ahab said, "By whom?" He said, "Thus says the LORD 1
14 Thus says the LORD, By the servants 1
14 Then he said, "Who shall begin the battle? 1
18 He said, "If they have come out for peace 1
22 the prophet came near . . and said to him, "Come 1
23 the servants of the king of Syria said to him 1
28 a man of God came near and said to the king 1
28 Thus says the LORD, 'Because the Syrians have said 1
28 Because the Syrians have said, "The LORD is a god 1
31 his servants said to him, "Behold now, we have heard 1
32 and went to the king of Israel and said 1
32 Your servant Ben-ha'dad says, 'Pray, let me live.' 1
32 And he said, "Does he still live? He is my brother. 1
33 they quickly took it up from him and said, "Yes 1
33 Then he said, "Go and bring him. 1
34 And Ben-ha'dad said to him, "The cities 1
34 And Ahab said, "I will let you go on these terms. •
35 a certain man . . said to his fellow 1
36 he said to him, "Because you have not obeyed 1
37 he found another man, and said, "Strike me, I pray. 1
39 as the king passed, he cried to the king and said 1
39 and brought a man to me, and said, 'Keep this man; 1
40 The king of Israel said to him 1
42 he said to him, "Thus says the LORD 1
42 Thus says the LORD, 'Because you have let go 1
21: 2 Ahab said to Naboth, "Give me your vineyard 4
3 Naboth said to Ahab, "The LORD forbid that I should 1
4 sullen because of what Naboth . . had said to him; 1
4 he had said, "I will not give you the inheritance 1
5 Jez'ebel his wife came to him, and said to him 4
6 he said to her, "Because I spoke to Naboth 4
6 I spoke to Naboth the Jezreelite, and said to him 1
7 Jez'ebel . . said to him, "Do you now govern Israel? 1
10 let them bring a charge against him, saying 1
13 brought a charge . . saying, "Naboth cursed God 1
14 sent to Jez'ebel, saying, "Naboth has been stoned; 1
15 Jez'ebel said to Ahab, "Arise, take possession 1
17 the word of the LORD came to Eli'jah . . saying 1
19 And you shall say to him, 'Thus says the LORD 4
19 'Thus says the LORD, "Have you killed, and also taken 1
19 And you shall say to him, 'Thus says the LORD 4
19 'Thus says the LORD: "In the place where dogs licked 1
20 Ahab said to Eli'jah, "Have you found me, 1
23 And of Jez'ebel the LORD also said 4
28 the word of the LORD came to Eli'jah . . saying 1
22: 3 the king of Israel said to his servants 1
4 he said to Jehosh'aphat, "Will you go with me 1
4 Jehosh'aphat said to the king of Israel, "I am as you 1
5 Jehosh'aphat said to the king of Israel 1
6 gathered the prophets . . and said to them 1
6 they said, "Go up; for the Lord will give it 1
7 Jehosh'aphat said, "Is there not here another 1
8 the king of Israel said to Jehosh'aphat, "There is 1
8 Jehosh'aphat said, "Let not the king say so. 1
8 Jehosh'aphat said, "Let not the king say so. 1
9 the king of Israel summoned an officer and said 1
11 Zedeki'ah . . and said, "Thus says the LORD 1
11 Thus says the LORD, 'With these you shall push 1
12 all the prophets prophesied so, and said, "Go up 1
13 the messenger . . said to him, "Behold, the words 4
14 Micai'ah said, "As the LORD lives . . that I will 1
14 what the LORD says to me, that I will speak. 1
15 when he had come to the king, the king said to him 1
16 the king said to him, "How many times shall I adjure 1
17 he said, "I saw all Israel scattered 1
17 the LORD said, 'These have no master; 1
18 the king of Israel said to Jehosh'aphat 1
19 Micai'ah said, "Therefore hear the word of the LORD 1
20 the LORD said, 'Who will entice Ahab 1
20 And one said one thing, and another said another. 1
20 And one said one thing, and another said another. 1
21 spirit came forward . . saying, 'I will entice him.' 1
22 the LORD said to him, 'By what means?' 1
22 he said, 'I will go forth, and will be a lying spirit 1
22 he said, 'You are to entice him 1
24 Zedeki'ah . . said, "How did the Spirit of the LORD go 1
25 Micai'ah said, "Behold, you shall see on that day 1
26 the king of Israel said, "Seize Micai'ah 1
27 and say, 'Thus says the king, 1
27 'Thus says the king, "Put this fellow in prison 1
28 Micai'ah said, "If you return . . the LORD has not 1
28 And he said, "Hear, all you peoples! 1
30 the king of Israel said to Jehosh'aphat 1
32 when the captains . . saw Jehosh'aphat, they said 1
34 he said to the driver of his chariot, "Turn about 1
49 Ahazi'ah the son of Ahab said to Jehosh'aphat, "Let 1
2Kg 1: 3 the angel of the LORD said to Eli'jah the Tishbite 4
3 meet the messengers . . and say to them 4
4 thus says the LORD, 'You shall not come down 1
5 returned to the king, and he said to them, "Why 1
6 they said to him, "There came a man to meet us 1
6 There came a man to meet us, and said to us, 'Go back 1
6 Go back to the king who sent you, and say to him 4
6 Thus says the LORD, Is it because there is no God 1
7 He said to them, "What kind of man was he who came 4
8 And he said, "It is Eli'jah the Tishbite. 1
9 He went up to Eli'jah . . and said to him, "O man of God 4
9 O man of God, the king says, 'Come down.' 4
11 And he went up and said to him, "O man of God 4
15 the angel of the LORD said to Eli'jah, "Go down 4
16 and said to him, "Thus says the LORD 1
16 Thus says the LORD, 'Because you have sent 1
2: 2 Eli'jah said to Eli'sha, "Tarry here, I pray you; 1

2 Eli'sha said, "As the LORD lives, and as you yourself 1
3 prophets . . came out to Eli'sha, and said to him 1
3 And he said, "Yes, I know it; hold your peace. 1
4 Eli'jah said to him, "Eli'sha, tarry here, I pray you; 1
4 But he said, "As the LORD lives, and as you yourself 1
5 prophets . . drew near to Eli'sha, and said to him 1
6 Then Eli'jah said to him, "Tarry here, I pray you; 1
6 But he said, "As the LORD lives, and as you yourself 1
9 Eli'jah said to Eli'sha, "Ask what I shall do for you 1
9 Eli'sha said, "I pray you, let me inherit 1
10 he said, "You have asked a hard thing; 1
14 took the mantle . . and struck the water, saying 1
15 the sons of the prophets . . said 1
16 And they said to him, "Behold now 1
16 And he said, "You shall not send. 1
17 when they urged him . . he said, "Send. 1
18 they came back to him . . and he said to them 1
18 he said to them, "Did I not say to you, Do not go? 1
19 Now the men of the city said to Eli'sha, "Behold 1
20 He said, "Bring me a new bowl, and put salt in it. 1
21 and threw salt in it, and said, "Thus says the LORD 1
21 Thus says the LORD, I have made this 1
23 boys came out . . and jeered at him, saying, "Go up 1
3: 7 And he said, "I will go; I am as you are 1
8 Then he said, "By which way shall we march? 1
10 Then the king of Israel said, "Alas! 1
11 Jehosh'aphat said, "Is there no prophet 1
12 Jehosh'aphat said, "The word of the LORD is 1
13 Eli'sha said to the king of Israel 1
13 But the king of Israel said to him, "No; it is the LORD 1
14 Eli'sha said, "As the LORD of hosts lives 1
16 he said, "Thus says the LORD, 'I will 1
16 Thus says the LORD, 'I will make this dry stream-bed 1
17 For thus says the LORD, 'You shall not see wind 1
23 they said, "This is blood; 1
4: 2 Eli'sha said to her, "What shall I do for you? Tell me; 1
2 And she said, "Your maidservant has nothing 1
3 Then he said, "Go outside, borrow vessels 1
6 When the vessels were full, she said to her son 1
6 And he said to her, "There is not another. 1
7 She came and told the man of God, and he said, "Go 1
9 she said to her husband, "Behold now, I perceive 1
12 he said to Geha'zi his servant 1
13 he said to him, "Say now to her, See, you have taken 1
13 Say now to her, See, you have taken all this trouble 1
14 he said, "What then is to be done for her? 1
15 He said, "Call her." And . . she stood in the doorway. 1
16 he said, "At this season . . you shall embrace a son. 1
16 she said, "No, my lord, O man of God; do not lie 1
17 she bore a son . . as Eli'sha had said to her. 4
19 he said to his father, "Oh, my head, my head! 1
19 The father said to his servant, "Carry him 1
22 she called to her husband, and said, "Send me one 1
23 he said, "Why will you go to him today? 1
23 She said, "It will be well. 1
24 she saddled the ass, and she said to her servant 1
25 he said to Geha'zi his servant, "Look 1
26 run at once to meet her, and say to her, Is it well 1
27 But the man of God said, "Let her alone 1
28 Then she said, "Did I ask my lord for a son? 1
28 Did I ask . . for a son? Did I not say, Do not deceive me? 1
29 He said to Geha'zi, "Gird up your loins 1
30 the mother of the child said, "As the LORD lives 1
36 summoned Geha'zi and said, "Call this Shu'nammite. 1
36 when she came to him, he said, "Take up your son. 1
38 he said to his servant, "Set on the great pot 1
41 He said, "Then bring meal. 1
41 he threw it into the pot, and said, "Pour out 1
42 Eli'sha said, "Give to the men, that they may eat. 1
43 his servant said, "How am I to set this 1
43 that they may eat, for thus says the LORD 1
5: 3 She said to her mistress, "Would that my lord 1
5 the king of Syria said, "Go now 1
7 he rent his clothes and said, "Am I God 1
8 when Eli'sha . . he sent to the king, saying, "Why 1
10 Eli'sha sent a messenger to him, saying, "Go and wash 1
11 Na'aman was angry, and went away, saying, "Behold 1
13 his servants came near and said to him, "My father 4
13 How much rather, then, when he says to you 1
15 he returned to the man of God . . and he said, "Behold 1
16 he said, "As the LORD lives . . I will receive none. 1
17 Then Na'aman said, "If not . . let there be given 1
19 He said to him, "Go in peace. 1
20 Geha'zi . . said, "See, my master has spared 1
21 he alighted from the chariot to meet him, and said 1
22 he said, "All is well. My master has sent me to say 1
22 he said, "All is well. My master has sent me to say 1
23 Na'aman said, "Be pleased to accept two talents. 1
25 Eli'sha said to him, "Where have you been, Geha'zi? 1
25 And he said, "Your servant went nowhere. 1
26 he said to him, "Did I not go with you in spirit 1
6: 1 Now the sons of the prophets said to Eli'sha, "See 1
3 Then one of them said, " . . go with your servants. 1
6 Then the man of God said, "Where did it fall? 1
7 he said, "Take it up." So he reached out his hand 1
8 he took counsel with his servants, saying 1
11 he called his servants and said to them 1
12 one of his servants said, "None, my lord, O king; 1
13 he said, "Go and see where he is 1
15 the servant said, "Alas, my master! What shall we do? 1
16 He said, "Fear not, for those . . with us are more 1
17 Then Eli'sha prayed, and said, "O LORD, I pray thee 1
18 Eli'sha prayed . . and said, "Strike this people 1
19 Eli'sha said to them, "This is not the way 1
20 Eli'sha said, "O LORD, open the eyes of these men 1
21 When the king of Israel saw them he said to Eli'sha 1
26 a woman cried out to him, saying, "Help, my lord, 1
27 he said, "If the LORD will not help . . whence shall I 1
28 She answered, "This woman said to me, 'Give your son 1
29 I said to her, 'Give your son, that we may eat him'; 1
31 he said, "May God do so to me . . if the head of Eli'sha 1
32 Eli'sha said to the elders, "Do you see 1
33 the king came down to him and said, "This trouble is 1
7: 1 Eli'sha said, "Hear the word of the LORD 1
1 thus says the LORD, Tomorrow about this time 1
2 the captain . . said to the man of God, "If the LORD 14
2 But he said, "You shall see it with your own eyes 1
3 they said to one another, "Why do we sit here 1
4 If we say, 'Let us enter the city,' . . we shall die 1
6 so that they said to one another, "Behold, the king 1
9 they said to one another, "We are not doing right. 1
12 the king rose . . and said to his servants 1
13 one of his servants said, "Let some men take five 1
14 the king sent them . . saying, "Go and see. 1
17 so that he died, as the man of God had said 4
18 when the man of God had said to the king 4
19 And he had said, "You shall see it with your own eyes 1
8: 1 Now Eli'sha had said to the woman . . "Arise 4
4 the king was talking with Geha'zi . . saying 1
5 And Geha'zi said, "My lord, O king, here is the woman 1
6 So the king appointed an official for her, saying 1
8 the king said to Haz'ael, "Take a present with you 1
8 inquire of the LORD . . saying, 'Shall I recover 1
9 When he came and stood before him, he said 1
9 Ben-ha'dad king of Syria has sent me to you, saying 1
10 Eli'sha said to him, "Go, say to him, 'You shall 1
10 Go, say to him, 'You shall certainly recover'; 1
12 Haz'ael said, "Why does my lord weep? 1
13 Haz'ael said, "What is your servant, who is but a dog 1
14 and came to his master, who said to him 1
14 said to him, "What did Eli'sha say to you? 1
9: 1 Eli'sha . . said to him, "Gird up your loins 1
3 take the . . oil, and pour it on his head, and say 1
3 'Thus says the LORD, I anoint you king over Israel.' 1
5 and he said "I have an errand to you, O commander. 1
5 And Jehu said, "To which of us all?" And he said, 1
5 which of us all?" And he said, "To you, O commander. 1
6 the young man poured . . saying to him, "Thus says 1
6 Thus says the LORD the God of Israel, I anoint you 1
11 Jehu came out to the servants . . they said to him 1
11 he said to them, "You know the fellow and his talk. 1
12 they said, "That is not true; tell us now. 1
12 And he said, "Thus and so he spoke to me, saying 1
12 he spoke to me, saying, 'Thus says the LORD 1
12 Thus says the LORD, I anoint you king over Israel.' 1
15 Jehu said, "If this is your mind, then let no one slip 1
17 he spied the company . . and said, "I see a company. 1
17 Joram said, "Take a horseman, and send to meet them 1
17 and send to meet them, and let him say, 'Is it peace?' 1
18 went to meet him, and said, "Thus says the king 1
18 and said, "Thus says the king, 'Is it peace?' 1
18 And Jehu said, "What have you to do with peace? 1
18 And the watchman reported, saying 1
19 a second horseman, who came to them, and said 1
19 and said, "Thus the king has said, 'Is it peace?' 1
21 Joram said, "Make ready." And they made ready 1
22 when Joram saw Jehu, he said, "Is it peace, Jehu? 1
23 Joram reined about and fled, saying to Ahazi'ah 1
25 Jehu said to Bidkar his aide, "Take him up 1
26 As surely as I saw . . –says the LORD–I will requite 12
27 And Jehu pursued him, and said, "Shoot him also"; 1
31 as Jehu entered the gate, she said, "Is it peace 1
32 he lifted up his face to the window, and said 1
33 He said, "Throw her down." So they threw her down; 1
34 and he said, "See now to this cursed woman 1
36 When they came back and told him, he said 1
37 so that no one can say, This is Jez'ebel.' 1
10: 1 Jehu wrote letters, and sent them . . saying 1
4 they were exceedingly afraid, and said, "Behold 1
5 sent to Jehu, saying, "We are your servants 1
6 he wrote to them a second letter, saying, "If you are 1
8 the messenger came . . he said, "Lay them in two 1
9 when he went . . he stood, and said to all the people 1
10 the LORD has done what he said by his servant 4
13 Jehu met the kinsmen of Ahazi'ah . . and he said 1
14 He said, "Take them alive." And they took them alive 1
15 he greeted him, and said to him, "Is your heart true 1
15 Jehu said, "If it is, give me your hand. 1
16 And he said, "Come with me, and see my zeal 1
18 Jehu assembled all the people, and said to them 1
22 He said to him who was in charge of the wardrobe 1
23 Jehu went . . and he said to the worshipers of Ba'al 1
24 Jehu had stationed 80 men outside, and said 1
25 Jehu said to the guard and to the officers, "Go 1
30 the LORD said to Jehu, "Because you have done well 1
11:12 and they clapped their hands, and said, "Long live 1
15 the priest said, "Let her not be slain in the house 1
12: 4 Jeho'ash said to the priests, "All the money 1
7 Jeho'ash summoned . . and said to them, "Why are you 1
13:15 Eli'sha said to him, "Take a bow and arrows"; 1
16 Then he said to the king of Israel, "Draw the bow"; 1
17 he said, "Open the window eastward"; and he opened 1
17 he opened it. Then Eli'sha said, "Shoot"; and he shot. 1
17 And he said, "The LORD'S arrow of victory 1
18 And he said, "Take the arrows"; and he took them. 1
18 he said to the king of Israel, "Strike the ground 1
19 and said, "You should have struck five or six times; 1
14: 8 Amazi'ah sent messengers to Jeho'ash . . saying 1
9 A thistle . . sent to a cedar on Lebanon, saying 1
27 the LORD had not said . . he would blot out the name 4
16: 7 Ahaz sent messengers . . saying, "I am your servant 1
15 King Ahaz commanded Uri'ah the priest, saying 1
17:12 served idols, of which the LORD had said to them 1
13 the LORD warned Israel and Judah . . saying 1
18:14 Hezeki'ah king of Judah sent to the king . . saying 1
19 the Rab'shakeh said to them, "Say to Hezeki'ah, 1
19 Rab'shakeh said to them, "Say to Hezeki'ah, 'Thus 1
19 Say to Hezeki'ah, 'Thus says the great king 1
22 if you say to me, "We rely on the LORD . . " is it not he 1
22 has removed, saying to Judah and to Jerusalem 1
25 The LORD said to me, Go up against this land 1
26 Eli'akim . . and Shebnah.., said to the Rab'shakeh 1
27 the Rab'shakeh said to them, "Has my master sent me 1
29 Thus says the king: 'Do not let Hezeki'ah deceive 1
30 Do not let . . make you to rely on the LORD by saying 1
31 thus says the king of Assyria: 'Make your peace 1
32 do not listen . . when he misleads you by saying 1
19: 3 They said to him, "Thus says Hezeki'ah, This day is 1
3 Thus says Hezeki'ah, This day is a day of distress 1
6 Isaiah said to them, "Say to your master, 'Thus says 1
6 Say to your master, 'Thus says the LORD: Do not be 1
6 Thus says the LORD: Do not be afraid 1
9 he sent messengers again to Hezeki'ah, saying 1
15 Hezeki'ah prayed . . and said: "O LORD the God 1
20 Amoz sent to Hezeki'ah, saying, "Thus says the LORD 1
20 Thus says the LORD, the God of Israel 1
23 you have mocked the LORD, and you have said 1
32 thus says the LORD concerning the king 1
33 he shall not come into this city, says the LORD. 12
20: 1 Isaiah the prophet . . came to him, and said to him 1
1 Thus says the LORD, 'Set your house in order; 1
2 Hezeki'ah turned . . and prayed to the LORD, saying 1
5 and say to Hezeki'ah the prince of my people 1
5 Thus says the LORD, the God of David your father 1
7 Isaiah said, "Bring a cake of figs. 1
8 Hezeki'ah said to Isaiah, "What shall be the sign 1
9 Isaiah said, "This is the sign to you from the LORD 1
14 Isaiah . . came to King Hezeki'ah, and said to him 1
14 What did these men say? And whence did they come 1
14 Hezeki'ah said, "They have come from a far country 1
15 He said, "What have they seen in your house? 1
16 Isaiah said to Hezeki'ah, "Hear the word of the LORD 1
17 carried to Babylon; nothing shall be left, says 1
19 Then said Hezeki'ah to Isaiah, "The word . . is good. 1
21: 4 the house of the LORD, of which the LORD had said 1
7 the LORD said to David and to Solomon his son 1
10 And the LORD said by his servants the prophets 4
12 thus says the LORD, the God of Israel 1
22: 3 the king sent . . to the house of the LORD, saying 1
8 And Hilki'ah the high priest said to Shaphan 1
12 the king commanded . . saying 1
15 And she said to them, "Thus says the LORD 1
15 said to them, "Thus says the LORD, the God of Israel 1
16 Thus says the LORD, Behold, I will bring evil 1
18 as to the king of Judah . . thus shall you say to him 1
18 Thus says the LORD, the God of Israel 1
19 I also have heard you, says the LORD. 12
23:17 Then he said, "What is yonder monument that I see? 1
18 And he said, "Let him be; let no man move his bones. 1
27 the LORD said, "I will remove Judah also 1
27 Jerusalem, and the house of which I said 1
25:24 Gedali'ah swore to them and their men, saying 1
1Ch 4: 9 his name Jabez, saying, "Because I bore him in pain. 1
10 Jabez . . saying, "Oh that thou wouldst bless me 1
10: 4 Then Saul said to his armor-bearer 1
11: 1 and said, "Behold, we are your bone and flesh. 1
2 LORD your God said to you, 'You shall be shepherd 1
5 The inhabitants of Jebus said to David 1
6 David said, "Whoever shall smite the Jeb'usites 1
17 David said longingly, "O that some one 1
19 said, "Far be it from me before my God 1
12:17 David went out to meet them and said to them 1
18 Ama'sai . . said, "We are yours, O David; and with you •
19 saying, "At peril to our heads he will desert 1
13: 2 David said to all the assembly of Israel 1
12 he said, "How can I bring the ark of God home to me? 1
14:10 LORD said to him, "Go up, and I will give them 1
11 David said, "God has broken through my enemies 1
14 when David again inquired of God, God said to him 1
15: 2 Then David said, "No one but the Levites may carry 1
12 said to them, "You are the heads 1
16:18 saying, "To you I will give the land of Canaan 1
22 saying, "Touch not my anointed ones •
31 let them say among the nations, "The LORD reigns! 1
35 Say also: "Deliver us, O God of our salvation 1
36 all the people said "Amen!" and praised the LORD. 1
17: 1 David said to Nathan the prophet 1

2 Nathan said to David, "Do all that is in your heart 1
4 Thus says the LORD: You shall not build me a house 1
6 saying, "Why have you not built me a house of cedar? 1
7 therefore thus shall you say to my servant David 1
7 Thus says the LORD of hosts 1
16 said, "Who am I, O LORD God, and what is my house 1
18 can David say to thee for honoring thy servant? 7
24 saying, 'The LORD of hosts, the God of Israel 1
19: 2 David said, "I will deal loyally with Hanun 1
3 the princes of the Ammonites said to Hanun 1
5 the king said, "Remain at Jericho 1
12 he said, "If the Syrians are too strong for me 1
21: 2 David said to Jo'ab and the commanders of the army 1
3 Jo'ab said, "May the LORD add to his people 1
8 David said to God, "I have sinned greatly 1
9 the LORD spoke to Gad, David's seer, saying 1
10 Go and say to David, 'Thus says the LORD 4
10 'Thus says the LORD, Three things I offer you; 1
11 Gad came to David and said . . "Thus says the LORD 1
11 Thus says the LORD, 'Take which you will 1
13 Then David said to Gad, "I am in great distress; 1
15 he said to the destroying angel, "It is enough; 1
17 David said to God, "Was it not I who gave command 1
18 angel of the LORD commanded Gad to say to David 1
22 David said to Ornan, "Give me the site 1
23 Ornan said to David, "Take it; and let my lord 1
24 King David said to Ornan, "No, but I will buy it 1
22: 1 David said, "Here shall be the house of the LORD God 1
5 For David said, "Solomon my son is young 1
7 David said to Solomon, "My son, I had it in my heart 1
8 the word of the LORD came to me, saying 1
17 leaders of Israel to help Solomon his son, saying 31
23: 4 24,000 of these," David said, "shall have charge •
25 For David said, "The LORD, the God of Israel 1
28: 2 and said: "Hear me, my brethren and my people. 1
3 God said to me, 'You may not build a house 1
6 said to me, 'It is Solomon your son who shall build 1
20 David said to Solomon . . "Be strong and of good 1
29: 1 David the king said to all the assembly 1
10 David said: "Blessed art thou, O LORD 1
20 David said to all the assembly, "Bless the LORD 1
2Ch 1: 7 God appeared . . and said to him 1
8 Solomon said to God, "Thou hast shown great 1
2:12 Huram also said, "Blessed be the LORD God of Israel 1
6: 1 Then Solomon said, "The LORD has said that he 1
1 The LORD has said that he would dwell in thick 1
4 he said, "Blessed be the LORD, the God of Israel, who 1
4 promised with his mouth to David . . saying 1
8 the LORD said to David my father, 'Whereas it was 1
14 said, "O LORD, God of Israel, there is no God like thee 1
16 promised him, saying, 'There shall never fail you 1
37 repent, and make supplication to thee . . saying 1
7: 3 worshiped and gave thanks to the LORD, saying •
12 LORD appeared to Solomon . . and said to him 1
18 as I covenanted with David your father, saying 1
21 every one passing by will be astonished, and say 1
22 Then they will say, 'Because they forsook the LORD 1
8:11 to the house which he had built for her, for he said 1
9: 5 she said to the king, "The report was true 1
10: 3 and all Israel came and said to Rehobo'am. 4
5 He said to them, "Come to me again in three days. 1
6 took counsel with the old men . . saying 1
7 they said to him, "If you will be kind to this people 4
9 he said to them, "What do you advise 1
9 this people who have said to me, 'Lighten the yoke 4
10 young men who had grown up with him said to him 4
10 Thus shall you speak to the people who said to you 4
10 thus shall you say to them 1
12 as the king said, "Come to me again the third day. 4
14 according to the counsel of the young men, saying 1
11: 3 Say to Rehobo'am the son of Solomon king of Judah 1
4 'Thus says the LORD, You shall not go up or fight 1
12: 5 Shemai'ah the prophet came . . and said to them 1
5 Thus says the LORD, 'You abandoned me 1
6 said, "The LORD is righteous. 1
13: 4 Abi'jah . . said, "Hear me, O Jerobo'am and all Israel! 1
14: 7 he said to Judah, "Let us build these cities 1
15: 2 he went out to meet Asa, and said to him, "Hear me, 1
16: 2 sent them to Ben-ha'dad, king of Syria . . saying 1
7 Hanani the seer came to Asa . . and said to him 1
18: 3 Ahab king of Israel said to Jehosh'aphat 1
4 Jehosh'aphat said to the king of Israel 1
5 gathered the prophets . . and said to them 1
5 they said, "Go up; for God will give it into the hand 1
6 Jehosh'aphat said, "Is there not here another 1
7 the king of Israel said to Jehosh'aphat 1
7 Jehosh'aphat said, "Let not the king say so. 1
7 Jehosh'aphat said, "Let not the king say so. 1
8 the king of Israel summoned an officer and said 1
10 Zedeki'ah . . made . . horns of iron, and said 1
10 Zedekiah . . said, "Thus says the LORD 1
11 all the prophets prophesied so, and said 1
12 messenger who went to summon Micai'ah said to him 4
13 Micai'ah said, "As the LORD lives, what my God says 1
13 what my God says, that I will speak. 1
14 when he had come to the king, the king said to him 1
15 king said to him, "How many times shall I adjure you 1
16 he said, "I saw all Israel scattered 1
16 LORD said, 'These have no master; 1
17 the king of Israel said to Jehosh'aphat 1
18 Micai'ah said, "Therefore hear the word of the LORD 1
19 LORD said, 'Who will entice Ahab the king of Israel 1
19 And one said one thing and another said another. 1
19 And one said one thing and another said another. 1
20 a spirit . . stood before the LORD, saying 1
20 And the LORD said to him, 'By what means?' 1
21 he said, 'I will go forth, and will be a lying spirit 1
21 said, 'You are to entice him, and you shall succeed; 1
23 Zedeki'ah . . struck Micai'ah . . , and said 1
24 Micai'ah said, "Behold, you shall see on that day 1
25 the king of Israel said, "Seize Micai'ah 1
26 say, 'Thus says the king, Put this fellow in prison 1
26 say, 'Thus says the king, Put this fellow in prison 1
27 Micai'ah said, "If you return in peace 1
27 Micai'ah . . said, "Hear, all you peoples! 1
29 the king of Israel said to Jehosh'aphat 1
31 when the captains . . saw Jehosh'aphat, they said 1
33 therefore he said to the driver of his chariot 1
19: 2 Jehu . . said to King Jehosh'aphat 1
6 said to the judges, "Consider what you do 1
20: 6 said, "O LORD . . art thou not God in heaven? 1
8 built thee in it a sanctuary for thy name, saying 1
15 said, "Hearken, all Judah and inhabitants 1
15 Thus says the Lord to you, 'Fear not 1
20 as they went out, Jehosh'aphat stood and said 1
21 as they went before the army, and say 1
37 prophesied against Jehosh'aphat, saying 1
21:12 a letter came to him from Eli'jah . . saying 1
12 Thus says the LORD, the God of David your father 1
22: 9 They buried him, for they said 1
23: 3 Jehoi'ada said to them, "Behold, the king's son! 1
11 anointed him, and they said, "Long live the king. 1
14 brought out the captains . . saying to them 1
14 priest said, "Do not slay her in the house 1
24: 5 the priests and the Levites, and said to them 1
6 king summoned Jehoi'ada the chief, and said to him 1
20 Zechari'ah . . stood above the people, and said 1
20 Thus says God, 'Why do you transgress 1
22 he was dying, he said, "May the LORD see and avenge! 1
25: 7 a man of God came to him and said 1
9 Amazi'ah said to the man of God 1
15 LORD . . sent him a prophet, who said to him 1
16 as he was speaking the king said to him 1
16 the prophet stopped, but said, "I know that God 1
17 Amazi'ah . . sent to Jo'ash . . saying, 1
18 A thistle on Lebanon sent to a cedar . . saying 1
19 You say, 'See, I have smitten Edom,' 1
26:18 they withstood King Uzzi'ah, and said to him 1
23 for they said, "He is a leper. 1
28: 9 went out to meet the army . . and said to them 1
13 said . . "You shall not bring the captives in here 1
23 sacrificed to the gods of Damascus . . and said 1
29: 5 said to them, "Hear me, Levites! 1
18 Then they went in to Hezeki'ah the king and said 1
31 Then Hezeki'ah said, "You have now consecrated 1
30: 6 as the king had commanded, saying 1
18 Hezeki'ah had prayed for them, saying 1
32: 4 stopped all the springs and the brook . . saying 1
6 spoke encouragingly to them, saying 1
9 Sennach'erib . . sent his servants . . , saying 1
10 Thus says Sennach'erib king of Assyria 1
16 servants said still more against the Lord GOD 4
17 he wrote letters . . to speak against him, saying 1
33: 4 house of the LORD, of which the LORD had said 1
7 house of God, of which God said to David 1
34:15 Then Hilki'ah said to Shaphan the secretary 1
20 king commanded . . saying 1
23 she said to them, "Thus says the LORD 1
23 Thus says the LORD, the God of Israel: 'Tell the man 1
24 Thus says the LORD, Behold, I will bring evil 1
26 to the king of Judah . . thus shall you say to him 1
26 Thus says the LORD . . Regarding the words 1
27 I also have heard you, says the LORD 12
35: 3 he said to the Levites who taught all Israel 1
21 he sent envoys to him, saying, "What have we to do 1
23 king said to his servants, "Take me away 1
36:23 Thus says Cyrus king of Persia, 'The LORD, the God 1
Ezr 1: 2 Thus says Cyrus king of Persia: The LORD 1
4: 2 said to them, "Let us build with you; for we worship 1
3 Zerub'babel, Jeshua . . said to them 1
5:15 said to him, "Take these vessels 16
8:17 telling them what to say to Iddo and his brethren 4
28 I said to them, "You are holy to the LORD 1
9: 1 officials approached me and said, "The people 1
6 saying: "O my God, I am ashamed and blush to lift 1
10 now, O our God, what shall we say after this? 1
11 which thou didst command . . saying, 'The land 1
10: 5 take oath that they would do as had been said. •
10 Ezra the priest stood up and said to them, 1
12 It is so; we must do as you have said. •
Neh 1: 3 said to me, "The survivors there in the province 1
5 I said, "O LORD God of heaven, the great and terrible 1
8 word . . didst command thy servant Moses, saying 1
2: 2 king said to me, "Why is your face sad 1
3 I said to the king, "Let the king live for ever! 1
4 king said to me, "For what do you make request? 1
5 I said to the king, "If it pleases the king 1
6 king said to me (the queen sitting beside him) 1
7 I said to the king, "If it pleases the king 1
17 Then I said to them, "You see the trouble we are 1
18 And they said, "Let us rise up and build. 1
19 derided us and despised us and said, "What is this 1
4: 2 said in the presence of his brethren 1
3 Tobi'ah the Ammonite was by him, and he said 1
10 Judah said, "The strength of the burden-bearers 1
11 our enemies said, "They will not know or see 1
12 When the Jews . . came they said to us ten times 1
14 I looked, and arose, and said to the nobles 1
19 I said to the nobles and to the officials 1
22 I also said to the people at that time, "Let every 1
5: 2 For there were those who said, "With our sons 1
3 There were also those who said, "We are mortgaging 1
4 there were those who said, "We have borrowed money 1
7 I said to them, "You are exacting interest 1
8 said to them, "We, as far as we are able, have bought 1
8 They were silent, and could not find a word to say. •
9 I said, "The thing that you are doing is not good. 1
12 Then they said, "We will restore these and require 1
12 We will restore these . . We will do as you say. 1
13 I also shook out my lap and said, "So may God shake 1
13 all the assembly said "Amen" and praised the LORD. 1
6: 2 Sanbal'lat and Geshem sent to me, saying, "Come 1
3 I sent messengers to them, saying, "I am doing 1
6 reported among the nations, and Geshem also says 1
8 Then I sent to him, saying, "No such things as you say 1
8 No such things as you say have been done 1
10 house of Shemai'ah . . who was shut up, he said 1
11 I said, "Should such a man as I flee? 1
7: 3 I said to them, "Let not the gates of Jerusalem 1
8: 9 taught the people said to all the people, "This day 1
10 Then he said to them, "Go your way, eat the fat 1
11 Levites stilled all the people, saying, "Be quiet 1
9: 5 Then the Levites . . said, "Stand up and bless 1
6 Ezra said: "Thou art the LORD, thou alone; •
18 Even when they had made . . a molten calf and said 1
13:11 I remonstrated with the officials and said, "Why 1
17 I remonstrated with the nobles of Judah and said 1
21 I warned them and said to them, "Why do you lodge 1
25 I made them take oath in the name of God, saying •
Est 1:13 the king said to the wise men who knew the times– 1
16 Then Memu'can said in presence of the king 1
17 causing them to . . since they will say 1
2: 2 Then the king's servants who attended him said 1
3: 3 Then the king's servants . . said to Mor'decai 1
8 Then Haman said to King Ahasu-e'rus 1
11 the king said to Haman, "The money is given to you 1
4: 9 went and told Esther what Mor'decai had said. 5
10 and gave him a message for Mor'decai, saying •
12 And they told Mor'decai what Esther had said. 5
5: 3 And the king said to her, "What is it, Queen Esther? 1
4 And Esther said, "If it please the king, 1
5 Then said the king, "Bring Haman quickly 1
6 the king said to Esther, "What is your petition? 1
7 But Esther said, "My petition and my request is 1
8 and tomorrow I will do as the king has said. 5
14 his wife Zeresh and all his friends said to him 1
6: 3 And the king said, "What honor or dignity has been 1
3 The king's servants who attended him said 1
4 And the king said, "Who is in the court? 1
5 And the king said, "Let him come in. 1
6 Haman came in, and the king said to him 1
6 And Haman said to himself, "Whom would the king 1
7 Haman said to the king, "For the man whom the king 1
10 Then the king said to Haman, "Make haste 1
10 take the robes and the horse, as you have said 4
13 Then his wise men and his wife Zeresh said to him 1
7: 2 king again said to Esther, "What is your petition 1
5 King Ahasu-e'rus said to Queen Esther, "Who is he 1
6 Esther said, "A foe and enemy! This wicked Haman! 1
8 and the king said, "Will he even assault the queen 1
9 Then said Harbo'na, one of the eunuchs 1
10 And the king said, "Hang him on that. 1
8: 5 And she said, "If it please the king 1
7 Ahasu-e'rus said to Queen Esther and to Mor'decai 1
9:12 And the king said to Queen Esther, "In Susa 1
13 And Esther said, "If it please the king, let the Jews 1
Job 1: 5 for Job said, "It may be that my sons have sinned 1
7 The LORD said to Satan, "Whence have you come? 1
8 the LORD said to Satan, "Have you considered 1
12 the LORD said to Satan, "Behold, all that he has 1
14 messenger to Job, and said, "The oxen were plowing 1
16 another, and said, "The fire of God fell from heaven 1
17 there came another, and said, "The Chalde'ans 1
18 there came another, and said, "Your sons 1
21 he said, "Naked I came from my mother's womb 1
2: 2 the LORD said to Satan, "Whence have you come? 1
3 the LORD said to Satan, "Have you considered 1
6 the LORD said to Satan, "Behold, he is in your power; 1
9 Then his wife said to him, "Do you still hold fast 1
10 he said to her, "You speak as one of the foolish 1
3: 2 Job said 1
3 the night which said, 'A man-child is conceived.' 1
6:22 Have I said, 'Make me a gift'? 1
7: 4 When I lie down I say, 'When shall I arise?' 1
13 When I say, 'My bed will comfort me 1
8: 2 How long will you say these things 10
18 it will deny him, saying, 'I have never seen you.' •

9:12 Who will say to him, 'What doest thou'? 1
22 It is all one; therefore I say, he destroys both 1
27 If I say, 'I will forget my complaint 1
10: 2 I will say to God, Do not condemn me; 1
11: 4 For you say, 'My doctrine is pure, and I am clean 1
15:23 He wanders abroad for bread, saying, 'Where is it?' •
17:12 The light,' they say, 'is near to the darkness.' 1
14 if I say to the pit, 'You are my father,' 15
19:28 If you say, 'How we will pursue him!' 1
20: 7 those who have seen him will say, 'Where is he?' 1
21:14 They say to God, 'Depart from us! 1
19 You say, 'God stores up their iniquity •
28 For you say, 'Where is the house of the prince? 1
22:13 Therefore you say, 'What does God know? 1
17 They said to God, 'Depart from us,' 1
20 saying, 'Surely our adversaries are cut off •
23: 5 and understand what he would say to me. 1
24:15 waits for the twilight, saying, 'No eye will see 1
18 You say, 'They are swiftly carried away •
25 and show that there is nothing in what I say? 9
27: 1 Job again took up his discourse, and said 1
28:14 The deep says, 'It is not in me,' 1
14 and the sea says, 'It is not with me.' 1
22 Abaddon and Death say, 'We have heard a rumor of it 1
28 he said to man, 'Behold, the fear of the Lord 1
29: 1 Job again took up his discourse, and said 1
31:31 if the men of my tent have not said, 1
32: 7 I said, 'Let days speak, and many years teach 1
10 Therefore I say, 'Listen to me; 1
11 while you searched out what to say. 9
13 Beware lest you say, 'We have found wisdom; 1
15 they answer no more; they have not a word to say. •
33: 9 You say, 'I am clean, without transgression; •
13 Why do you contend against him, saying •
24 he is gracious to him, and says, 'Deliver him 1
27 he sings before men, and says: 'I sinned 1
32 If you have anything to say, answer me; 9
34: 1 Then Eli'hu said 1
5 For Job has said, 'I am innocent 1
9 For he has said, 'It profits a man nothing 1
16 hear this; listen to what I say. 9
18 who says to a king, 'Worthless one,' 1
31 any one said to God, 'I have borne chastisement; 1
34 Men of understanding will say to me 1
34 the wise man who hears me will say •
35: 1 Eli'hu said 1
2 Do you say, 'It is my right before God,' 1
10 But none says, 'Where is God my Maker 1
14 How much less when you say that you do not see him 1
36: 1 Eli'hu continued, and said 1
2 for I have yet something to say on God's behalf. 9
23 or who can say, 'Thou hast done wrong'? 1
37: 6 For to the snow he says, 'Fall on the earth'; 1
19 Teach us what we shall say to him; 1
38:11 and said, 'Thus far shall you come, and no farther 1
35 that they may go and say to you, 'Here we are'? 1
39:25 When the trumpet sounds, he says 'Aha!' 1
40: 1 the LORD said to Job 1
42: 7 the LORD said to Eli'phaz the Te'manite 1
Ps 2: 2 against the LORD and his anointed, saying •
5 in his wrath, and terrify them in his fury, saying •
7 I will tell of the decree of the LORD: He said to me 1
3: 2 saying of me, there is no help for him in God. Selah 1
4: 6 many who say, "O that we might see some good! 1
10:13 does the wicked renounce God, and say in his heart 1
11: 1 how can you say to me, "Flee like a bird 1
12: 4 those who say, "With our tongue we will prevail 1
5 I will now arise," says the LORD; 1
13: 4 lest my enemy say, "I have prevailed over him"; 1
14: 1 The fool says in his heart, "There is no God. 1
16: 2 I say to the LORD, "Thou art my Lord; 1
18: 0 from the hand of Saul. He said 1
27: 8 Thou hast said, "Seek ye my face. •
8 My heart says to thee, "Thy face, LORD, do I seek. 1
30: 6 I said in my prosperity, "I shall never be moved. 1
31:14 I trust in thee, O LORD, I say, "Thou art my God. 1
22 I had said in my alarm, "I am driven far 1
32: 5 not hide my iniquity; I said, "I will confess 1
35: 3 Say to my soul, "I am your deliverance! 1
10 All my bones shall say, "O LORD, who is like thee 1
21 they say, "Aha, Aha! our eyes have seen it! 1
25 Let them not say to themselves, "Aha 1
25 Let them not say, "We have swallowed him up. 1
27 be glad, and say evermore, "Great is the LORD 1
39: 1 I said, "I will guard my ways, that I may not sin 1
40: 7 Then I said, "Lo, I come; 1
15 because of their shame who say to me, "Aha, Aha! 1
16 those who love thy salvation say continually 1
41: 4 As for me, I said, "O LORD, be gracious to me; 1
5 My enemies say of me in malice: "When will he die 1
8 They say, "A deadly thing has fastened upon him; •
42: 3 while men say to me continually, "Where is your God? 1
9 I say to God, my rock: "Why hast thou forgotten me? 1
10 my adversaries taunt me, while they say to me 1
50:16 But to the wicked God says: "What right have you 1
52: 6 see, and fear, and shall laugh at him, saying •
53: 1 The fool says in his heart, "There is no God. 1
55: 6 I say, "O that I had wings like a dove! I would fly away 1
58:11 Men will say, "Surely there is a reward 1
66: 3 Say to God, "How terrible are thy deeds! 1
68:22 The Lord said, "I will bring them back from Bashan 1
70: 3 appalled because of their shame who say, "Aha, Aha! 1
4 May those who love thy salvation say evermore 1
71:11 and say, "God has forsaken him; pursue and seize him 1
73:11 they say, "How can God know? 1
15 If I had said, "I will speak thus 1
74: 8 They said to themselves, "We will utterly subdue 1
75: 4 I say to the boastful, "Do not boast 1
77:10 I say, "It is my grief 1
78:19 They spoke against God, saying 1
79:10 Why should the nations say, "Where is their God? 1
82: 6 I say, "You are gods, sons of the Most High, all of you; 1
83: 4 They say, "Come, let us wipe them out as a nation; 1
12 who said, "Let us take possession for ourselves 1
87: 4 Ethiopia-"This one was born there," they say. •
5 of Zion it shall be said, "This one and that one 1
7 Singers and dancers alike say, "All my springs •
89: 3 Thou hast said, "I have made a covenant •
19 speak in a vision to thy faithful one, and say 1
90: 3 Thou . . sayest, "Turn back, O children of men! 1
91: 2 will say to the LORD, "My refuge and my fortress; 1
94: 7 they say, "The LORD does not see; the God of Jacob 1
95:10 40 years I loathed that generation and said 1
96:10 Say among the nations, "The LORD reigns! 1
102:24 O my God," I say, "take me not hence in the midst 1
105:11 saying, "To you I will give the land of Canaan 1
15 saying, "Touch not my anointed ones •
19 until what he had said came to pass 5
106:23 Therefore he said he would destroy them- 1
48 let all the people say, "Amen!" Praise the LORD! 1
107: 2 Let the redeemed of the LORD say so 1
110: 1 LORD says to my lord: "Sit at my right hand 12
115: 2 Why should the nations say, "Where is their God? 1
116:10 I kept my faith, even when I said 4
11 I said in my consternation, "Men are all a vain 1
118: 2 Israel say, "His steadfast love endures for ever. 1
3 house of Aaron say, "His steadfast love endures 1
4 who fear the LORD say, "His steadfast love endures 1
122: 1 I was glad when they said to me, "Let us go 1
8 For my brethren and companions' sake I will say 4
124: 1 If . . the LORD who was on our side, let Israel now say- 1
126: 2 then they said among the nations, "The LORD 1
129: 1 let Israel now say- 1
8 while those who pass by do not say, "The blessing 1
137: 3 saying, "Sing us one of the songs of Zion! •
7 how they said, "Rase it, rase it! 1
139:11 If I say, "Let only darkness cover me 1
140: 6 I say to the LORD, Thou art my God; give ear 1
142: 5 I say, Thou art my refuge, my portion in the land 1
Prv 1:11 If they say, "Come with us, let us lie in wait 1
3:28 Do not say to your neighbor, "Go, and come again 1
4: 4 taught me, and said to me, "Let your heart hold fast 1
5:12 you say, "How I hated discipline 1
7: 4 Say to wisdom, "You are my sister 1
13 with impudent face she says to him 1
9: 4 To him who is without sense she says 1
16 to him who is without sense she says 1
20: 9 Who can say, "I have made my heart clean; 1
14 It is bad, it is bad," says the buyer; 1
22 Do not say, "I will repay evil"; wait for the LORD 1
22:13 The sluggard says, "There is a lion outside! 1
20 Have I not written for you 30 sayings •
23: 7 Eat and drink!" he says to you; but his heart is not 1
35 They struck me," you will say, "but I was not hurt; •
24:12 If you say, "Behold, we did not know this, 1
23 These also are sayings of the wise. •
24 He who says to the wicked, "You are innocent 1
29 Do not say, "I will do to him as he has done to me; 1
26:13 The sluggard says, "There is a lion in the road! 1
19 deceives his neighbor and says, "I am only joking! 1
28:24 He who robs his father or his mother and says, "That 1
30: 1 The man says to Ith'i-el, to Ith'i-el and Ucal 12
9 and deny thee, and say, "Who is the LORD? 1
15 never satisfied; four never say, "Enough 1
16 fire which never says, "Enough. 1
20 adulteress . . says, "I have done no wrong. 1
Ecc 1: 2 Vanity of vanities, says the Preacher 1
10 Is there a thing of which it is said, "See, this is new"? 1
16 I said to myself, "I have acquired great wisdom 4
2: 1 I said to myself, " . . I will make a test of pleasure; 1
2 I said of laughter, "It is mad 1
15 Then I said to myself, "What befalls the fool will 1
15 And I said to myself that this also is vanity. 4
3:17 I said in my heart, God will judge the righteous 1
18 I said in my heart with regard to . . men that God is 1
5: 6 do not say before the messenger that it was 1
6: 3 I say that an untimely birth is better off than he 1
7:10 Say not, "Why were the former days better 1
21 Do not give heed to all the things that men say 4
23 I said, "I will be wise"; but it was far from me. 1
27 Behold, this is what I found, says the Preacher 1
8: 4 and who may say to him, "What are you doing? 1
14 I said that this also is vanity. 1
9:16 But I say that wisdom is better than might 1
10: 3 and he says to every one that he is a fool. 1
12: 1 and the years draw nigh, when you will say 1
8 Vanity of vanities, says the Preacher; 1
11 The sayings of the wise are like goads 5
Sng 2:10 My beloved speaks and says to me: "Arise, my love 1
7: 8 I say I will climb the palm tree and lay hold of its 1
Isa 1:11 What to me is . . your sacrifices? says the LORD; 1
18 Come now, let us reason together, says the LORD 1
24 Therefore the Lord says . . "Ah, I will vent my wrath 12
2: 3 many peoples shall come, and say: "Come, let us go up 1
3: 6 a man takes hold . . saying: "You have a mantle; •
7 he will speak out, saying: "I will not be a healer; 1
15 What do you mean . . ?" says the Lord GOD of hosts. 12
16 The LORD said: Because the daughters of Zion are 1
4: 1 seven women . . saying, "We will eat our own bread 1
5:19 who say: "Let him make haste, let him speed his work 1
6: 3 one called to another and said: "Holy, holy, holy 1
5 I said: "Woe is me! For I am lost; for I am a man 1
7 he touched my mouth, and said: "Behold 1
8 the voice of the Lord saying, "Whom shall I send 1
8 who will go for us?" Then I said, "Here am I! Send me. 1
9 he said, "Go, and say to this people: 'Hear and hear 1
9 he said, "Go, and say to this people: 'Hear and hear 1
11 Then I said, "How long, O Lord? 1
11 How long, O Lord?" And he said: "Until cities lie waste 1
7: 3 the LORD said to Isaiah, "Go forth to meet Ahaz 1
4 say to him, 'Take heed, be quiet, do not fear 1
5 Remali'ah, has devised evil against you, saying 1
7 thus says the Lord GOD: It shall not stand 1
12 Ahaz said, "I will not ask 1
13 he said, "Hear then, O house of David! 1
8: 1 the LORD said to me, "Take a large tablet and write 1
3 conceived and bore a son. Then the LORD said to me 1
11 not to walk in the way of this people, saying 1
19 when they say to you, "Consult the mediums 1
9: 9 who say in pride and in arrogance of heart 1
10: 8 for he says: "Are not my commanders all kings? 1
13 he says: "By the strength of my hand I have done it 1
24 Therefore thus says the Lord, the LORD of hosts 1
12: 1 You will say in that day 1
4 you will say in that day: "Give thanks to the LORD 1
14: 8 cypresses rejoice . . saying, 'Since you were laid •
10 All of them will speak and say to you 1
13 You said in your heart, 'I will ascend to heaven; 1
22 I will rise up against them," says the LORD of hosts 12
22 remnant, offspring and posterity, says the LORD. 12
23 I will sweep it . . says the LORD of hosts. 12
16:14 now the LORD says, "In three years 6
17: 3 of the children of Israel, says the LORD of hosts. 12
6 of a fruit tree, says the LORD God of Israel. 12
18: 4 For thus the LORD said to me: "I will quietly look 1
19: 4 rule over them, says the Lord, the LORD of hosts. 12
11 How can you say to Pharaoh, "I am a son of the wise 1
25 whom the LORD of hosts has blessed, saying 1
20: 2 LORD had spoken by Isaiah . . saying 1
3 the LORD said, "As my servant Isaiah has walked 1
6 coastland will say in that day, 'Behold, this 1
21: 6 For thus the Lord said to me: "Go, set a watchman 1
12 The watchman says: "Morning comes 1
16 For thus the Lord said to me, "Within a year 1
22: 4 Therefore I said: "Look away from me, let me weep 1
14 forgiven . . till you die." says the Lord GOD 1
15 Thus says the Lord GOD of hosts, "Come, go to this 1
15 Come, go to this steward . . and say to him •
25 In that day, says the LORD of hosts 12
23: 4 sea has spoken . . saying 1
12 he said: "You will no more exult 1
24:16 But I say, "I pine away, I pine away. Woe is me! 1
25: 9 It will be said on that day, "Lo, this is our God; 1
28:12 to whom he has said, "This is rest; 1
15 you have said, "We have made a covenant with death 1
16 thus says the Lord GOD, "Behold, I am laying in Zion 1
29:11 give it to one who can read, saying, "Read this 1
11 he says, "I cannot, for it is sealed. 1
12 to one who cannot read, saying, "Read this 1
12 saying, "Read this," he says, "I cannot read. 1
13 the Lord said: "Because this people draw near 1
15 and who say, "Who sees us? Who knows us 1
16 that the thing made should say of its maker 1
16 the thing formed say of him who formed it 1
22 thus says the LORD, who redeemed Abraham 1
30: 1 Woe to the rebellious children," says the LORD 12
10 who say to the seers, "See not"; 1
12 Therefore thus says the Holy One of Israel 1
15 For thus said the Lord GOD, the Holy One of Israel 1
16 you said, "No! We will speed upon horses 1
21 behind you, saying, "This is the way, walk in it 1
22 unclean things; you will say to them, "Begone! 1
31: 4 For thus the LORD said to me, As a lion 1
9 says the LORD, whose fire is in Zion 12
32: 5 nor the knave said to be honorable. 1
33:10 Now I will arise," says the LORD 1
24 no inhabitant will say, "I am sick"; 1
35: 4 Say to those who are of a fearful heart, "Be strong 1
36: 4 the Rab'shakeh said to them, "Say to Hezeki'ah 1
4 the Rab'shakeh said to them, "Say to Hezeki'ah 1
4 Thus says the great king, the king of Assyria 1
7 if you say to me, "We rely on the LORD our God 1
7 Hezeki'ah . . saying to Judah and to Jerusalem 1
10 The LORD said to me, Go up against this land 1
11 Eli'akim, Shebna, and Jo'ah said to the Rab'shakeh 1
12 the Rab'shakeh said, "Has my master sent me 1
14 says the king: 'Do not let Hezeki'ah deceive you 1

15 by saying, "The LORD will surely deliver us; 1
16 for thus says the king of Assyria 1
18 Beware lest Hezeki'ah mislead you by saying 1
37: 3 They said to him, "Thus says Hezeki'ah 1
3 Thus says Hezeki'ah, 'This day is a day of distress 1
6 Isaiah said to them, "Say to your master 1
6 Isaiah said to them, "Say to your master 1
6 Say to your master, 'Thus says the LORD 1
9 he sent messengers to Hezeki'ah, saying 1
21 Isaiah the son of Amoz sent to Hezeki'ah, saying 1
21 Thus says the LORD, the God of Israel 1
24 you have said, With my many chariots 1
33 says the LORD concerning the king of Assyria 1
34 he shall not come into this city, says the LORD. 12
38: 1 Isaiah . . came to him, and said to him 1
1 Thus says the LORD: Set your house in order; 1
3 said, "Remember now, O LORD, I beseech thee 1
5 Go and say to Hezeki'ah, Thus says the LORD 1
5 Thus says the LORD, the God of David your father 1
10 I said, In the noontide of my days I must depart; 1
11 I said, I shall not see the LORD in the land 1
15 But what can I say? For he has spoken to me 4
21 Now Isaiah had said, "Let them take a cake of figs 1
22 Hezeki'ah also had said, "What is the sign 1
39: 3 and said to him, "What did these men say? 1
3 and said to him, "What did these men say? 1
3 Hezeki'ah said, "They have come to me from a far 1
4 He said, "What have they seen in your house? 1
5 Isaiah said to Hezeki'ah, "Hear the word of the LORD 1
6 nothing shall be left, says the LORD. 1
8 Then said Hezeki'ah to Isaiah, "The word of the LORD 1
40: 1 Comfort, comfort my people, says your God. 1
6 A voice says, "Cry!" And I said, "What shall I cry? 1
6 A voice says, "Cry!" And I said, "What shall I cry? 1
9 say to the cities of Judah, "Behold your God! 1
25 that I should be like him? says the Holy One. 1
27 Why do you say, O Jacob, and speak, O Israel 1
41: 6 and says to his brother, "Take courage! 1
7 saying of the soldering, "It is good"; 1
9 called from its farthest corners, saying to you 1
13 it is I who say to you, "Fear not, I will help you. 1
14 I will help you, says the LORD; 12
21 Set forth your case, says the LORD; 1
21 bring your proofs, says the King of Jacob. 1
26 and beforetime, that we might say, "He is right"? 1
42: 5 Thus says God, the LORD, who created the heavens 1
17 who say to molten images, "You are our gods. 1
22 a spoil with none to say, "Restore! 1
43: 1 now thus says the LORD, he who created you 1
6 I will say to the north, Give up 1
9 and let them hear and say, It is true. 1
10 You are my witnesses," says the LORD 12
12 and you are my witnesses," says the LORD. 12
14 Thus says the LORD, your Redeemer 1
16 Thus says the LORD, who makes a way in the sea 1
44: 2 Thus says the LORD who made you, who formed you 1
5 This one will say 'I am the LORD'S,' 1
6 Thus says the LORD, the King of Israel 1
16 also he warms himself and says, "Aha, I am warm 1
17 prays to it and says, "Deliver me, for thou art my god! 1
19 nor is there knowledge or discernment to say 1
20 cannot deliver himself or say, "Is there not a lie 1
24 Thus says the LORD, your Redeemer, who formed you 1
26 who says of Jerusalem, 'She shall be inhabited,' 1
27 says to the deep, 'Be dry, I will dry up your rivers 1
28 who says of Cyrus, 'He is my shepherd 1
28 saying of Jerusalem, 'She shall be built,' 1
45: 1 Thus says the LORD to his anointed, to Cyrus 1
9 Does the clay say to him who fashions it 1
10 who says to a father, 'What are you begetting?' 1
11 Thus says the LORD, the Holy One of Israel 1
13 not for price or reward," says the LORD of hosts. 1
14 Thus says the LORD: "The wealth of Egypt 1
14 They will make supplication to you, saying •
18 For thus says the LORD, who created the heavens 1
19 I did not say to . . Jacob, 'Seek me in chaos.' 1
24 Only in the LORD, it shall be said of me 1
46:10 from ancient times things not yet done, saying 1
47: 7 You said, "I shall be mistress for ever 1
8 say in your heart, "I am, and there is no one 1
10 in your wickedness, you said, "No one sees me"; 1
10 led you astray, and you said in your heart 1
48: 5 lest you should say, 'My idol did them 1
7 lest you should say, 'Behold, I knew them.' 1
17 Thus says the LORD, your Redeemer, the Holy One 1
20 say, "The LORD has redeemed his servant Jacob! 1
22 There is no peace," says the LORD, "for the wicked. 1
49: 3 he said to me, "You are my servant, Israel 1
4 But I said, "I have labored in vain 1
5 now the LORD says, who formed me from the womb 1
6 he says: "It is too light a thing 1
7 Thus says the LORD, the Redeemer of Israel 1
8 Thus says the LORD: "In a time of favor 1
9 saying to the prisoners, 'Come forth,' 1
14 But Zion said, "The LORD has forsaken me 1
18 As I live, says the LORD, you shall put them 12
20 The children . . of your bereavement will yet say 1
21 will say in your heart: 'Who has borne me these? 1
22 says the Lord GOD: "Behold, I will lift up my hand 1

25 Surely, thus says the LORD: "Even the captives 1
50: 1 Thus says the LORD: "Where is your mother's bill 1
51:16 and saying to Zion, 'You are my people.' 1
22 thus says your Lord, the LORD, your God 1
23 your tormentors, who have said to you, 'Bow down 1
52: 3 For thus says the LORD: "You were sold for nothing 1
4 For thus says the Lord GOD: My people went down 1
5 Now therefore what have I here, says the LORD 12
5 Their rulers wail, says the LORD 12
7 salvation, who says to Zion, "Your God reigns. 1
54: 1 children of her that is married, says the LORD. 1
6 a wife of youth when she is cast off, says your God. 1
8 compassion on you, says the LORD, your Redeemer. 1
10 not be removed, says the LORD, who has compassion 1
17 and their vindication from me, says the LORD. 12
55: 8 neither are your ways my ways, says the LORD. 12
56: 1 Thus says the LORD: "Keep justice 1
3 Let not the foreigner . . say, "The LORD will 1
3 let not the eunuch say, "Behold, I am a dry tree. 1
4 thus says the LORD: "To the eunuchs who keep my 1
8 Thus says the Lord GOD, who gathers the outcasts 12
12 Come," they say, "let us get wine •
57:10 but you did not say, "It is hopeless"; 1
14 shall be said, "Build up, build up, prepare the way 1
15 For thus says the high and lofty One who inhabits 1
19 peace, to the far and to the near, says the LORD; 1
21 There is no peace, says my God, for the wicked. 1
58: 9 you shall cry, and he will say, Here I am. 1
59:20 who turn from transgression, says the LORD. 12
21 this is my covenant with them, says the LORD 1
21 of your children's children, says the LORD 1
62:11 Say to the daughter of Zion, "Behold 1
63: 8 For he said, Surely they are my people 1
65: 1 I said, "Here am I, here am I," to a nation 1
5 who say, "Keep to yourself, do not come near me 1
7 fathers' iniquities together, says the LORD; 1
8 Thus says the LORD: "As the wine is found 1
8 in the cluster, and they say, 'Do not destroy it 1
13 says the Lord GOD: "Behold, my servants shall eat 1
25 in all my holy mountain, says the LORD. 1
66: 1 Thus says the LORD: "Heaven is my throne 1
2 all these things are mine, says the LORD. 12
5 cast you out for my name's sake have said, 1
9 and not cause to bring forth? says the LORD; 1
9 I, who . . bring forth, shut the womb? says your God. 1
12 For thus says the LORD: "Behold, I will extend 1
17 shall come to an end together, says the LORD. 12
20 to my holy mountain Jerusalem, says the LORD 1
21 take for priests and for Levites, says the LORD. 1
22 shall remain before me, says the LORD; 12
23 shall come to worship before me, says the LORD. 1
Jer 1: 4 Now the word of the LORD came to me saying 1
6 Then I said, "Ah, Lord GOD! 1
7 the LORD said to me, "Do not say, 'I am only a youth' 1
7 the LORD said to me, "Do not say, 'I am only a youth' 1
8 for I am with you to deliver you, says the LORD. 12
9 the LORD said to me, "Behold, I have put my words 1
11 the word of the LORD came to me, saying, "Jeremiah 1
11 And I said, "I see a rod of almond. 1
12 Then the LORD said to me, "You have seen well 1
13 word of the LORD came to me a second time, saying 1
13 What do you see?" And I said, "I see a boiling pot 1
14 Then the LORD said to me 1
15 tribes of the kingdoms of the north, says the LORD; 12
17 and say to them everything that I command you. 4
19 for I am with you, says the LORD, to deliver you. 12
2: 1 The word of the LORD came to me, saying 1
2 Thus says the LORD, I remember the devotion 1
3 evil came upon them, says the LORD. 12
5 Thus says the LORD 1
6 They did not say, 'Where is the LORD 1
8 The priests did not say, 'Where is the LORD?' 1
9 Therefore I still contend with you, says the LORD 12
12 be shocked, be utterly desolate, says the LORD 12
19 says the Lord GOD of hosts. 12
20 and you said, 'I will not serve.' 1
22 guilt is still before me, says the Lord GOD. 12
23 How can you say, 'I am not defiled 1
25 But you said, 'It is hopeless 1
27 who say to a tree, 'You are my father,' 1
27 But in the ti[illegible] of their trouble they say 1
29 You have all rebelled against me, says the LORD. 12
31 Why then do my people say, 'We are free 1
35 you say, 'I am innocent; surely his anger has turned 1
35 you to judgment for saying, 'I have not sinned.' 1
3: 1 and would you return to me? says the LORD. 12
6 The LORD said to me in the days of King Josi'ah 1
10 but in pretense, says the LORD. 12
11 And the LORD said to me 1
12 proclaim these words toward the north, and say 1
12 Return, faithless Israel, says the LORD. 12
12 for I am merciful, says the LORD; 12
13 that you have not obeyed my voice, says the LORD. 12
14 Return, O faithless children, says the LORD; 12
16 in those days, says the LORD, they shall no more say 12
16 in those days, says the LORD, they shall no more say 1
20 faithless to me, O house of Israel, says the LORD.' 12
4: 1 If you return, O Israel, says the LORD 12
3 For thus says the LORD to the men of Judah 1

5 proclaim in Jerusalem, and say, "Blow the trumpet 1
5 cry aloud and say, 'Assemble, and let us go 1
9 In that day, says the LORD, courage shall fail 12
10 Then I said, "Ah, Lord GOD 1
10 deceived this people and Jerusalem, saying 1
11 At that time it will be said to this people 1
17 she has rebelled against me, says the LORD. 12
27 For thus says the LORD 1
5: 2 Though they say, "As the LORD lives 1
4 Then I said, "These are only the poor 1
9 not punish them for these things? says the LORD; 12
11 have been utterly faithless to me, says the LORD. 12
12 and have said, 'He will do nothing; no evil will come 1
14 Therefore thus says the LORD, the God of hosts 1
15 upon you a nation from afar . . says the LORD. 12
15 nor can you understand what they say. 4
18 But even in those days, says the LORD 12
19 when your people say, 'Why has the LORD our God 1
19 you shall say to them, 'As you have forsaken me 1
22 Do you not fear me? says the LORD; 12
24 They do not say in their hearts, 'Let us fear 1
29 not punish them for these things? says the LORD 12
6: 6 thus says the LORD of hosts: "Hew down her trees; 1
9 Thus says the LORD of hosts 1
12 hand against the inhabitants . . " says the LORD. 12
14 saying, 'Peace, peace,' when there is no peace. 1
15 they shall be overthrown," says the LORD. 1
16 Thus says the LORD: "Stand by the roads, and look 1
16 But they said, 'We will not walk in it.' 1
17 I set watchmen over you, saying, 'Give heed •
17 But they said, 'We will not give heed.' 1
21 Therefore thus says the LORD: 'Behold 1
22 Thus says the LORD: "Behold, a people is coming 1
7: 2 and proclaim there this word, and say 1
3 Thus says the LORD of hosts, the God of Israel 1
10 in this house, which is called by my name, and say 1
11 Behold, I myself have seen it, says the LORD. 12
13 you have done all these things, says the LORD 12
19 Is it I whom they provoke? says the LORD. 12
20 Therefore thus says the Lord GOD: Behold, my anger 1
21 Thus says the LORD of hosts, the God of Israel 1
28 And you shall say to them 1
30 Judah have done evil in my sight, says the LORD; 12
32 behold, the days are coming, says the LORD 12
8: 1 At that time, says the LORD 12
3 where I have driven them, says the LORD of hosts. 12
4 You shall say to them, Thus says the LORD 1
4 You shall say to them, Thus says the LORD 1
6 no man repents . . saying, 'What have I done? 1
8 How can you say, 'We are wise 1
11 saying, 'Peace, peace,' when there is no peace. 1
12 they shall be overthrown, says the LORD. 1
13 When I would gather them, says the LORD 12
17 and they shall bite you," says the LORD. 12
9: 3 they do not know me, says the LORD. 12
6 they refuse to know me, says the LORD. 12
7 Therefore thus says the LORD of hosts: "Behold 1
9 not punish them for these things? says the LORD; 12
13 the LORD says: "Because they have forsaken my law 1
15 Therefore thus says the LORD of hosts 1
17 Thus says the LORD of hosts: "Consider, and call 1
22 Speak, "Thus says the LORD 12
23 Thus says the LORD: "Let not the wise man glory 1
24 for in these things I delight, says the LORD. 12
25 Behold, the days are coming, says the LORD 12
10: 2 Thus says the LORD 1
11 Thus shall you say to them 16
18 For thus says the LORD 1
19 But I said, "Truly this is an affliction 1
11: 3 You shall say to them, Thus says the LORD 1
3 You shall say to them, Thus says the LORD 1
4 from the iron furnace, saying, Listen to my voice 1
6 And the LORD said to me, "Proclaim all these words 1
7 even to this day, saying, Obey my voice. 1
9 Again the LORD said to me 1
11 Therefore, thus says the LORD, Behold 1
19 devised schemes, saying, "Let us destroy the tree •
21 Therefore thus says the LORD 1
21 the men of An'athoth, who seek your life, and say 1
22 therefore thus says the LORD of hosts: "Behold 1
12: 4 because men said, "He will not see our latter end. 1
14 Thus says the LORD 1
17 utterly pluck it up and destroy it, says the LORD. 12
13: 1 Thus said the LORD to me 1
6 And after many days the LORD said to me 1
9 Thus says the LORD: Even so will I spoil the pride 1
11 whole house of Judah cling to me, says the LORD 12
12 Thus says the LORD, the God of Israel 1
12 And they will say to you, 'Do we not indeed know that 1
13 Then you shall say to them, 'Thus says the LORD 1
13 Then you shall say to them, 'Thus says the LORD 1
14 fathers and sons together, says the LORD. 12
18 Say to the king and the queen mother 1
21 What will you say when they set as head over you 1
22 And if you say in your heart 1
25 portion I have measured out to you, says the LORD 12
14:10 Thus says the LORD concerning this people 1
11 The LORD said to me: "Do not pray for the welfare 1
13 Then I said: "Ah, Lord GOD, behold, the prophets 1

13 the prophets say to them, 'You shall not see the sword 1
14 And the LORD said to me 1
15 Therefore thus says the LORD 1
15 and who say, 'Sword and famine shall not come 1
17 You shall say to them this word 1
15: 1 Then the LORD said to me 1
2 you shall say to them, 'Thus says the LORD 1
2 you shall say to them, 'Thus says the LORD 1
3 over them four kinds of destroyers, says the LORD 12
6 You have rejected me, says the LORD 12
9 before their enemies, says the LORD. 12
19 Therefore thus says the LORD: "If you return 1
20 to save you and deliver you, says the LORD. 12
16: 3 For thus says the LORD concerning the sons 1
5 says the LORD: Do not enter the house of mourning 1
5 my peace from this people, says the LORD 12
9 For thus says the LORD of hosts, the God of Israel 1
10 and they say to you, 'Why has the LORD pronounced 1
11 then you shall say to them 1
11 your fathers have forsaken me, says the LORD 12
14 behold, the days are coming, says the LORD 12
14 says the LORD, when it shall no longer be said 1
16 I am sending for many fishers, says the LORD 12
19 nations come from the ends of the earth and say 1
17: 5 Thus says the LORD 1
15 they say to me, "Where is the word of the LORD? 1
19 Thus said the LORD to me 1
20 say: 'Hear the word of the LORD, you kings of Judah 1
21 Thus says the LORD 1
24 But if you listen to me, says the LORD 12
18: 6 do with you as this potter has done? says the LORD. 12
11 Now, therefore, say to the men of Judah 1
11 Thus says the LORD, Behold, I am shaping evil 1
12 But they say, 'That is in vain! 1
13 thus says the LORD: Ask among the nations 1
18 Then they said, "Come, let us make plots 1
19: 1 Thus said the LORD, "Go, buy a potter's earthen flask 1
3 You shall say, 'Hear the word of the LORD 1
3 Thus says the LORD of hosts, the God of Israel 1
6 therefore, behold, days are coming, says the LORD 12
11 and shall say to them, 'Thus says the LORD of hosts 1
11 and shall say to them, 'Thus says the LORD of hosts 1
12 Thus will I do to this place, says the LORD 12
14 Then Jeremiah . . said to all the people 1
15 Thus says the LORD of hosts, the God of Israel 1
20: 3 Jeremiah said to him, "The LORD does not call 1
4 thus says the LORD: Behold, I will make you a terror 1
9 If I say, "I will not mention him 1
10 Let us denounce him!" say all my familiar friends •
21: 1 Zephani'ah the priest, the son of Ma-asei'ah, saying 1
3 Then Jeremiah said to them 1
4 Thus you shall say to Zedeki'ah, 'Thus says the LORD 1
4 Thus you shall say to Zedeki'ah, 'Thus says the LORD 1
7 Afterward, says the LORD, I will give Zedeki'ah 12
8 to this people you shall say: 'Thus says the LORD 1
8 to this people you shall say: 'Thus says the LORD 1
10 for evil and not for good, says the LORD 12
11 to . . Judah say, 'Hear the word of the LORD •
12 O house of David! Thus says the LORD 1
13 against you . . O rock of the plain, says the LORD; 12
13 you who say, 'Who shall come down against us 1
14 the fruit of your doings, says the LORD; 12
22: 1 says the LORD: "Go down to the house of the king 1
2 and say, 'Hear the word of the LORD, O King of Judah 1
3 Thus says the LORD: Do justice and righteousness 1
5 I swear by myself, says the LORD 12
6 For thus says the LORD concerning the house 1
8 and every man will say to his neighbor 1
11 For thus says the LORD concerning Shallum 1
14 who says, 'I will build myself a great house 1
16 Is not this to know me? says the LORD. 12
18 thus says the LORD concerning Jehoi'akim 1
18 shall not lament for him, saying, 'Ah my brother!' •
18 They shall not lament for him, saying, 'Ah lord!' •
21 but you said, 'I will not listen.' 1
24 As I live, says the LORD 12
30 Thus says the LORD: "Write this man down 1
23: 1 the sheep of my pasture!" says the LORD. 12
2 Therefore thus says the LORD, the God of Israel 1
2 attend to you for your evil doings, says the LORD. 12
4 neither shall any be missing, says the LORD. 12
5 Behold, the days are coming, says the LORD 12
7 behold, the days are coming, says the LORD 12
7 when men shall no longer say, 'As the LORD lives 1
11 I have found their wickedness, says the LORD. 12
12 in the year of their punishment, says the LORD. 12
15 Therefore thus says the LORD of hosts 1
16 Thus says the LORD of hosts 1
17 They say continually to those who despise 1
17 they say, 'No evil shall come upon you. 1
23 a God at hand, says the LORD, and not a God afar off? 12
24 places so that I cannot see him? says the LORD. 12
24 Do I not fill heaven and earth? says the LORD. 12
25 I have heard what the prophets have said 1
25 prophesy lies in my name, saying, 'I have dreamed 1
28 has straw in common with wheat? says the LORD. 12
29 Is not my word like fire, says the LORD 12
30 behold, I am against the prophets, says the LORD 12
31 Behold, I am against the prophets, says the LORD 12
31 who use their tongues and say, 'Says the LORD.' 11
31 who use their tongues and say, 'Says the LORD.' 12
32 those who prophesy lying dreams, says the LORD 12
32 not profit this people at all, says the LORD. 12
33 you shall say to them, 'You are the burden 1
33 and I will cast you off, says the LORD. 12
34 the prophet, priest, or one of the people who says 1
35 Thus shall you say, every one to his neighbor 1
37 Thus you shall say to the prophet 1
38 But if you say, 'The burden of the LORD,' 1
38 says the LORD, 'Because you have said these words 1
38 says the LORD, 'Because you have said these words 1
38 when I sent to you, saying, "You shall not say 1
38 saying, "You shall not say, 'The burden of the LORD,' 1
24: 3 the LORD said to me, "What do you see, Jeremiah? 1
3 I said, "Figs, the good figs very good 1
5 Thus says the LORD, the God of Israel 1
8 But thus says the LORD 1
25: 5 saying, 'Turn now, every one of you, 1
7 Yet you have not listened to me, says the LORD 12
8 Therefore thus says the LORD of hosts: 1
9 send for all the tribes of the north, says the LORD 12
12 punish . . for their iniquity, says the LORD 12
15 Thus the LORD, the God of Israel, said to me 1
27 you shall say to them, 'Thus says the LORD of hosts 1
27 you shall say to them, 'Thus says the LORD of hosts 1
28 you shall say to them, 'Thus says the LORD of hosts 1
28 you shall say to them, 'Thus says the LORD of hosts 1
29 inhabitants of the earth, says the LORD of hosts. 12
30 against them all these words, and say to them 1
31 the wicked he will put to the sword, says the LORD. 12
32 Thus says the LORD of hosts 1
26: 2 Thus says the LORD: Stand in the court of the LORD'S 1
4 You shall say to them, 'Thus says the LORD 1
4 You shall say to them, 'Thus says the LORD 1
8 the people laid hold of him, saying, "You shall die! 1
9 the LORD, saying, 'This house shall be like Shiloh 1
11 Then the priests and the prophets said 1
12 to all the princes and all the people, saying 1
16 all the people said to the priests 1
17 and spoke to all the assembled people, saying 1
18 and said to all the people of Judah 1
18 Thus says the LORD of hosts, Zion shall be plowed 1
27: 2 Thus the LORD said to me: "Make yourself thongs 1
4 Thus says the LORD of hosts, the God of Israel 1
4 This is what you shall say to your masters 1
8 with famine, and with pestilence, says the LORD 12
9 or your sorcerers, who are saying to you 1
11 to till it and dwell there, says the LORD. 12
14 the words of the prophets who are saying to you 1
15 I have not sent them, says the LORD 12
16 to all this people, saying, "Thus says the LORD 1
16 Thus says the LORD: Do not listen to the words 1
16 your prophets who are prophesying to you, saying 1
19 For thus says the LORD of hosts 1
21 thus says the LORD of hosts, the God of Israel 1
22 when I give attention to them, says the LORD. 12
28: 1 of the priests and all the people, saying 1
2 Thus says the LORD of hosts, the God of Israel 1
4 from Judah who went to Babylon, says the LORD 12
6 prophet Jeremiah said, "Amen! May the LORD do so; 1
11 spoke in the presence of all the people, saying 1
11 Thus says the LORD: Even so will I break the yoke 1
13 Go, tell Hanani'ah, 'Thus says the LORD 1
14 For thus says the LORD of hosts, the God of Israel 1
15 And Jeremiah the prophet said to . . Hanani'ah 1
16 Therefore thus says the LORD 1
29: 3 Nebuchadnez'zar king of Babylon. It said 1
4 Thus says the LORD of hosts, the God of Israel 1
8 For thus says the LORD of hosts, the God of Israel 1
9 I did not send them, says the LORD. 12
10 For thus says the LORD 1
11 For I know the plans I have for you, says the LORD 12
14 I will be found by you, says the LORD 12
14 the places where I have driven you, says the LORD 12
15 you have said, 'The LORD has raised up prophets 1
16 Thus says the LORD concerning the king 1
17 Thus says the LORD of hosts, Behold 1
19 because they did not heed my words, says the LORD 12
19 but you would not listen, says the LORD. 12
21 Thus says the LORD of hosts, the God of Israel 1
23 and I am witness, says the LORD. 12
24 To Shemai'ah of Nehel'am you shall say 1
25 Thus says the LORD of hosts, the God of Israel 1
26 the priest, and to all the priests, saying 1
28 For he has sent to us in Babylon, saying 1
31 Send to all the exiles, saying, 'Thus says the LORD 1
31 Send to all the exiles, saying, 'Thus says the LORD 1
32 thus says the LORD: Behold, I will punish Shemai'ah 1
32 the good that I will do to my people, says the LORD 12
30: 2 Thus says the LORD, the God of Israel 1
3 For behold, days are coming, says the LORD 12
3 my people, Israel and Judah, says the LORD 12
5 Thus says the LORD: We have heard a cry of panic 1
8 come to pass in that day, says the LORD of hosts 12
10 Then fear not, O Jacob my servant, says the LORD 12
11 For I am with you to save you, says the LORD; 12
12 For thus says the LORD: Your hurt is incurable 1
17 and your wounds I will heal, says the LORD 12
18 Thus says the LORD: Behold, I will restore 1
21 dare of himself to approach me? says the LORD. 12
31: 1 says the LORD, I will be the God of all the families 12
2 Thus says the LORD 1
7 For thus says the LORD: "Sing aloud with gladness 1
7 proclaim, give praise, and say, 'The LORD has saved 1
10 say, 'He who scattered Israel will gather him 1
14 be satisfied with my goodness, says the LORD. 12
15 Thus says the LORD: "A voice is heard in Ramah 1
16 Thus says the LORD: "Keep your voice from weeping 1
16 for your work shall be rewarded, says the LORD 12
17 There is hope for your future, says the LORD 12
20 I will surely have mercy on him, says the LORD. 12
23 Thus says the LORD of hosts, the God of Israel 1
27 Behold, the days are coming, says the LORD 12
28 to build and to plant, says the LORD. 12
29 In those days they shall no longer say 1
31 Behold, the days are coming, says the LORD 12
32 though I was their husband, says the LORD. 12
33 the covenant which I will make . . says the LORD 12
34 and each his brother, saying, 'Know the LORD,' 1
34 from the least . . to the greatest, says the LORD; 12
35 Thus says the LORD, who gives the sun for light 1
36 fixed order departs from before me, says the LORD 12
37 Thus says the LORD 1
37 for all that they have done, says the LORD. 12
38 Behold, the days are coming, says the LORD 12
32: 3 had imprisoned him, saying, "Why do you prophesy 1
3 Why do you prophesy and say, 'Thus says the LORD 1
3 Why do you prophesy and say, 'Thus says the LORD 1
5 shall remain until I visit him, says the LORD; 12
6 Jeremiah said, "The word of the LORD came to me 1
7 son of Shallum your uncle will come to you and say 1
8 and said to me, 'Buy my field which is at An'athoth 1
13 I charged Baruch in their presence, saying 1
14 Thus says the LORD of hosts, the God of Israel 1
15 For thus says the LORD of hosts, the God of Israel 1
16 I prayed to the LORD, saying 1
25 Yet thou, O Lord GOD, hast said to me, "Buy the field 1
28 Therefore, thus says the LORD 1
30 to anger by the work of their hands, says the LORD. 12
36 therefore thus says the LORD, the God of Israel 1
36 concerning this city of which you say, 'It is given 1
42 For thus says the LORD 1
43 land of which you are saying, It is a desolation 1
44 for I will restore their fortunes, says the LORD. 12
33: 2 Thus says the LORD who made the earth 1
4 For thus says the LORD, the God of Israel 1
10 Thus says the LORD: In this place of which you say 1
10 Thus says the LORD: In this place of which you say 1
11 fortunes of the land as at first, says the LORD. 1
12 Thus says the LORD of hosts 1
13 hands of the one who counts them, says the LORD. 1
14 Behold, the days are coming, says the LORD 12
17 For thus says the LORD 1
20 Thus says the LORD: If you can break my covenant 1
24 you not observed what these people are saying 4
25 Thus says the LORD 1
34: 2 Thus says the LORD, the God of Israel: Go and speak 1
2 speak to Zedeki'ah king of Judah and say to him 1
2 Thus says the LORD: Behold, I am giving this city 1
4 O Zedeki'ah . . ! Thus says the LORD concerning you 1
5 and lament for you, saying, "Alas, lord! •
5 For I have spoken the word, says the LORD. 12
13 Thus says the LORD, the God of Israel 1
13 out of the house of bondage, saying 1
17 Therefore, thus says the LORD: You have not obeyed 1
17 to pestilence, and to famine, says the LORD 12
22 Behold, I will command, says the LORD 12
35: 5 wine, and cups; and I said to them, "Drink wine. 1
11 king of Babylon came up against the land, we said 1
13 Thus says the LORD of hosts, the God of Israel 1
13 Go and say to the men of Judah 1
13 and listen to my words? says the LORD. 12
15 the prophets, sending them persistently, saying 1
17 Therefore, thus says the LORD, the God of hosts 1
18 to the house of the Re'chabites Jeremiah said 1
18 Thus says the LORD of hosts, the God of Israel 1
19 therefore thus says the LORD of hosts 1
36: 5 And Jeremiah ordered Baruch, saying 1
14 to say to Baruch, "Take in your hand the scroll 1
15 And they said to him, "Sit down and read it. 1
16 they said to Baruch, "We must report all these 1
19 Then the princes said to Baruch, "Go and hide 1
29 concerning Jehoi'akim . . you shall say 1
29 Thus says the LORD, You have burned this scroll 1
29 says the LORD, You have burned this scroll, saying 1
30 thus says the LORD concerning Jehoi'akim king 1
37: 3 Zedeki'ah sent . . to Jeremiah the prophet, saying 1
7 Thus says the LORD, God of Israel 1
7 Thus shall you say to the king of Judah 1
9 Thus says the LORD, Do not deceive yourselves 1
9 Do not deceive yourselves, saying 1
13 seized Jeremiah the prophet, saying 1
14 And Jeremiah said, "It is false; I am not deserting 1
17 and said, "Is there any word from the LORD? 1
17 any word from the LORD?" Jeremiah said, "There is. 1
17 Then he said, "You shall be delivered into the hand 1
18 Jeremiah also said to King Zedeki'ah 1

19 your prophets who prophesied to you, saying 1
38: 1 words that Jeremiah was saying to all the people 4
2 Thus says the LORD 1
3 Thus says the LORD, This city shall . . be given 1
4 Then the princes said to the king 1
5 King Zedeki'ah said, "Behold, he is in your hands; 1
8 went from the king's house and said to the king 4
12 Then E'bed-mel'ech the Ethiopian said to Jeremiah 1
14 The king said to Jeremiah 1
15 Jeremiah said to Zedeki'ah, "If I tell you 1
17 Then Jeremiah said to Zedeki'ah 1
17 Thus says the LORD, the God of hosts 1
19 King Zedeki'ah said to Jeremiah 1
20 Jeremiah said, "You shall not be given to them. 1
20 Obey now the voice of the LORD in what I say to you 4
22 saying, 'Your trusted friends have deceived you 1
24 Then Zedeki'ah said to Jeremiah, "Let no one know 1
25 have spoken with you and come to you and say to you 1
25 and say to you, 'Tell us what you said to the king 4
25 you said to the king and what the king said to you; 4
26 then you shall say to them, 'I made a humble plea 1
39:11 Nebu'zarad'an, the captain of the guard, saying 1
16 Go, and say to E'bed-mel'ech the Ethiopian 1
16 Thus says the LORD of hosts, the God of Israel 1
17 But I will deliver you on that day, says the LORD 12
18 you have put your trust in me, says the LORD. 12
40: 2 The captain of the guard took Jeremiah and said 1
3 has brought it about, and has done as he said. 4
9 Gedali'ah . . swore to them and their men, saying 1
14 and said to him, "Do you know that Ba'alis the king 1
16 But Gedali'ah the son of Ahi'kam said to Joha'nan 1
41: 6 he met them, he said to them, "Come in to Gedali'ah 1
8 there were ten men among them who said to Ish'mael 1
42: 2 and said to Jeremiah the prophet 1
4 Jeremiah the prophet said to them, "I have heard 1
5 Then they said to Jeremiah 1
9 said to them, "Thus says the LORD, the God of Israel 1
9 said to them, "Thus says the LORD, the God of Israel 1
11 do not fear him, says the LORD, for I am with you 12
13 if you say, 'We will not remain in this land,' 1
14 saying, 'No, we will go to the land of Egypt 1
15 Thus says the LORD of hosts, the God of Israel 1
18 For thus says the LORD of hosts, the God of Israel 1
19 The LORD has said to you, O remnant of Judah 4
20 sent me to the LORD your God, saying, 'Pray for us 1
20 whatever the LORD our God says declare to us 1
43: 2 and all the insolent men said to Jeremiah 1
2 The LORD our God did not send you to say 1
10 and say to them, 'Thus says the LORD of hosts 1
10 Thus says the LORD of hosts, the God of Israel 1
44: 2 Thus says the LORD of hosts, the God of Israel 1
4 sent to you all my servants the prophets, saying 1
7 thus says the LORD God of hosts, the God of Israel 1
11 thus says the LORD of hosts, the God of Israel 1
19 And the women said, "When we burned incense *
20 Then Jeremiah said to all the people 1
24 Jeremiah said to all the people and all the women 1
25 Thus says the LORD of hosts, the God of Israel 1
25 and have fulfilled it with your hands, saying 1
26 I have sworn by my great name, says the LORD 1
26 of any man of Judah in all the land of Egypt, saying 1
29 This shall be the sign to you, says the LORD 12
30 Thus says the LORD 1
45: 2 Thus says the LORD, the God of Israel, to you 1
3 You said, 'Woe is me! for the LORD has added sorrow 1
4 Thus shall you say to him, Thus says the LORD 1
4 Thus shall you say to him, Thus says the LORD 1
5 I am bringing evil upon all flesh, says the LORD; 12
46: 5 terror on every side! says the LORD. 12
8 He said, I will rise, I will cover the earth 1
14 Say, 'Stand ready and be prepared 1
16 they said one to another, 'Arise, and let us go back 1
18 As I live, says the King, whose name is the LORD 12
23 They shall cut down her forest, says the LORD 12
25 The LORD of hosts, the God of Israel, said: "Behold 1
26 as in the days of old, says the LORD. 12
28 Fear not, O Jacob my servant, says the LORD 12
47: 2 Thus says the LORD: Behold, waters are rising 1
48: 1 Concerning Moab. Thus says the LORD of hosts 1
12 behold, the days are coming, says the LORD 12
14 How do you say, 'We are heroes and mighty men 1
15 men have gone down to slaughter, says the King 12
17 say, 'How the mighty scepter is broken 1
19 Ask him who flees . . say, 'What has happened?' 1
25 his arm is broken, says the LORD. 12
30 I know his insolence, says the LORD; 12
35 I will bring to an end in Moab, says the LORD 12
38 a vessel for which no one cares, says the LORD. 12
40 For thus says the LORD: "Behold, one shall fly 1
43 before you, O inhabitant of Moab! says the LORD. 12
44 in the year of their punishment, says the LORD. 12
47 of Moab in the latter days, says the LORD. 12
49: 1 Concerning the Ammonites. Thus says the LORD 1
2 behold, the days are coming, says the LORD 12
2 those who dispossessed him, says the LORD. 1
4 daughter, who trusted in her treasures, saying *
5 Behold, I will bring terror upon you, says the Lord 12
6 the fortunes of the Ammonites, says the LORD. 12
7 Concerning Edom. Thus says the LORD of hosts 1
12 thus says the LORD: "If those who did not deserve 1
13 For I have sworn by myself, says the LORD 12
16 I will bring you down from there, says the LORD. 12
18 neighbor cities were overthrown, says the LORD 1
26 destroyed in that day, says the LORD of hosts. 12
28 says the LORD: "Rise up, advance against Kedar! 1
30 O inhabitants of Hazor! says the LORD. 12
31 at ease, that dwells securely, says the LORD 12
32 calamity from every side of them, says the LORD. 12
35 says the LORD of hosts: "Behold, I will break the bow 1
37 evil upon them, my fierce anger, says the LORD. 12
38 and destroy their king and princes, says the LORD. 12
39 I will restore the fortunes of Elam, says the LORD. 12
50: 2 proclaim, conceal it not, and say: 'Babylon is taken 1
4 In those days and in that time, says the LORD 12
5 saying, 'Come, let us join ourselves to the LORD *
7 and their enemies have said, 'We are not guilty 1
10 all who plunder her shall be sated, says the LORD. 12
18 Therefore, thus says the LORD of hosts 1
20 In those days and in that time, says the LORD 12
21 and utterly destroy after them, says the LORD 12
30 be destroyed on that day, says the LORD. 12
31 Behold, I am against you, O proud one, says the Lord 12
33 Thus says the LORD of hosts: The people of Israel 1
35 A sword upon the Chalde'ans, says the LORD 12
40 Sodom . . and their neighbor cities, says the LORD 12
51: 1 Thus says the LORD: "Behold, I will stir up 1
24 that they have done in Zion, says the LORD. 12
25 against you, O destroying mountain, says the LORD 12
26 you shall be a perpetual waste, says the LORD. 12
33 For thus says the LORD of hosts, the God of Israel 1
35 be upon Babylon," let the inhabitant of Zion say. 1
35 My blood be upon . . Chalde'a," let Jerusalem say. 1
36 Therefore thus says the LORD: "Behold, I will plead 1
39 a perpetual sleep and not wake, says the LORD. 12
48 come against them out of the north, says the LORD. 12
52 behold, the days are coming, says the LORD 12
53 would come from me upon her, says the LORD. 12
57 a perpetual sleep and not wake, says the King 12
58 Thus says the LORD of hosts 1
61 And Jeremiah said to Serai'ah 1
62 say, 'O LORD, thou hast said concerning this place 1
62 say, 'O LORD, thou hast said concerning this place 4
64 say, 'Thus shall Babylon sink, to rise no more 1
Lam 2:13 What can I say for you, to what compare you 13
3:18 I say, "Gone is my glory, and my expectation 1
24 The LORD is my portion," says my soul 1
54 water closed over my head; I said, 'I am lost.' 1
57 thou didst say, 'Do not fear!' 1
4:15 men said among the nations, "They shall stay 1
20 the LORD'S anointed . . he of whom we said 1
Ezk 2: 1 And he said to me, "Son of man, stand upon your feet 1
3 he said to me, "Son of man, I send you to the people 1
4 I send you to them; and you shall say to them 1
4 you shall say to them, 'Thus says the Lord GOD.' 1
8 But you, son of man, hear what I say to you; 4
3: 1 he said to me, "Son of man, eat what is offered to you; 1
3 he said to me, "Son of man, eat this scroll 1
4 he said to me, "Son of man, go 1
10 Moreover he said to me, "Son of man 1
11 to the exiles, to your people, and say to them 1
11 say to them, 'Thus says the Lord GOD' 1
18 If I say to the wicked, 'You shall surely die,' 1
22 and he said to me, "Arise, go forth into the plain 1
24 and he spoke with me and said to me 1
27 and you shall say to them, 'Thus says the Lord GOD' 1
27 and you shall say to them, 'Thus says the Lord GOD' 1
4:13 the LORD said, "Thus shall the people of Israel eat 1
14 Then I said, "Ah Lord GOD! 1
15 Then he said to me, "See, I will let you have 1
16 Moreover he said to me, "Son of man, behold 1
5: 5 Thus says the Lord GOD: This is Jerusalem; 1
7 Therefore thus says the Lord GOD 1
8 therefore thus says the Lord GOD: Behold, I, even I 1
11 Wherefore, as I live, says the Lord GOD 12
6: 3 and say, You mountains of Israel, hear the word 1
3 Thus says the Lord GOD to the mountains 1
10 I have not said in vain that I would do this evil 4
11 Thus says the Lord GOD: "Clap your hands 1
11 Clap your hands, and stamp your foot, and say, Alas! 1
7: 2 thus says the Lord GOD to the land of Israel: An end! 1
5 Thus says the Lord GOD: Disaster after disaster! 1
8: 5 Then he said to me, "Son of man, lift up your eyes now 1
6 And he said to me, "Son of man, do you see 1
8 Then said he to me, "Son of man, dig in the wall"; 1
9 he said to me, "Go in, and see the vile abominations 1
12 Then he said to me, "Son of man, have you seen 1
12 For they say, 'The LORD does not see us 1
13 He said also to me, "You will see still greater 1
15 he said to me, "Have you seen this, O son of man? 1
17 he said to me, "Have you seen this, O son of man? 1
9: 1 Then he cried in my ears with a loud voice, saying 1
4 And the LORD said to him, "Go through the city 1
5 to the others he said in my hearing, "Pass through 1
7 Then he said to them, "Defile the house 1
9 Then he said to me, "The guilt of the house of Israel 1
9 for they say, 'The LORD has forsaken the land 1
11 brought back word, saying, "I have done 1
10: 2 And he said to the man clothed in linen 1
11: 2 And he said to me, "Son of man, these are the men 1
3 who say, 'The time is not near to build houses; 1
5 Spirit of the LORD fell upon me, and he said to me 1
5 and he said to me, "Say, Thus says the LORD 1
5 Thus says the LORD: So you think, O house of Israel; 1
7 Therefore thus says the Lord GOD 1
8 I will bring the sword upon you, says the Lord GOD. 12
13 and said, "Ah Lord GOD! wilt thou make a full end 1
15 of whom the inhabitants of Jerusalem have said 1
16 Therefore say, 'Thus says the Lord GOD 1
16 Therefore say, 'Thus says the Lord GOD 1
17 Therefore say, 'Thus says the Lord GOD: 1
17 Therefore say, 'Thus says the Lord GOD: 1
21 upon their own heads, says the Lord GOD. 12
12: 9 house, said to you, 'What are you doing?' 1
10 Say to them, 'Thus says the Lord GOD: This oracle 1
10 Say to them, 'Thus says the Lord GOD: This oracle 1
11 Say, 'I am a sign for you 1
19 say of the people of the land, Thus says the Lord 1
19 say of the people of the land, Thus says the Lord 1
22 saying, 'The days grow long, and every vision comes 1
23 Tell them therefore, 'Thus says the Lord GOD 1
23 But say to them, The days are at hand 4
25 speak the word and perform it, says the Lord GOD. 12
27 Son of man, behold, they of the house of Israel say 1
28 Therefore say to them, Thus says the Lord GOD 1
28 Therefore say to them, Thus says the Lord GOD 1
28 will be performed, says the Lord GOD. 12
13: 2 say to those who prophesy out of their own minds 1
3 Thus says the Lord GOD, Woe to the foolish 1
6 they say, 'Says the LORD,' when the LORD has not 1
6 they say, 'Says the LORD,' when the LORD has not 12
7 a lying divination, whenever you have said 1
7 whenever you have said, 'Says the LORD,' 12
8 Therefore thus says the Lord God 1
8 behold, I am against you, says the Lord GOD. 12
10 they have misled my people, saying, 'Peace,' 1
11 say to those who daub it with whitewash 1
12 when the wall falls, will it not be said to you 1
13 Therefore thus says the Lord GOD 1
15 and I will say to you, The wall is no more 1
16 when there was no peace, says the Lord GOD. 12
18 and say, Thus says the Lord GOD 1
18 and say, Thus says the Lord GOD 1
20 Wherefore thus says the Lord GOD 1
14: 4 Therefore speak to them, and say to them 1
4 and say to them, Thus says the Lord GOD 1
6 Therefore say to the house of Israel 1
6 Thus says the Lord GOD: Repent and turn away 1
11 and I may be their God, says the Lord GOD. 12
14 by their righteousness, says the Lord GOD. 12
16 as I live, says the Lord GOD, they would deliver 12
17 and say, Let a sword go through the land; 1
18 as I live, says the Lord GOD, they would deliver 12
20 as I live, says the Lord GOD, they would deliver 12
21 For thus says the Lord GOD 1
23 all that I have done in it, says the Lord GOD. 12
15: 6 Therefore thus says the Lord GOD 1
8 they have acted faithlessly, says the Lord GOD. 12
16: 3 and say, Thus says the Lord GOD to Jerusalem 1
3 and say, Thus says the Lord GOD to Jerusalem 1
6 I said to you in your blood, 'Live 1
8 into a covenant with you, says the Lord GOD 12
14 which I had bestowed upon you, says the Lord GOD. 12
19 for a pleasing odor, says the Lord GOD. 12
23 woe, woe to you! says the Lord GOD 12
30 How lovesick is your heart, says the Lord GOD 12
36 Thus says the Lord GOD, Because your shame was 1
43 your deeds upon your head, says the Lord GOD. 12
48 As I live, says the Lord GOD 12
58 You bear the penalty . . says the LORD. 12
59 Yea, thus says the Lord GOD: I will deal with you 1
63 all that you have done, says the Lord GOD. 12
17: 3 say, Thus says the Lord GOD 1
3 say, Thus says the Lord GOD 1
9 Say, Thus says the Lord GOD: Will it thrive? 1
9 Say, Thus says the Lord GOD: Will it thrive? 1
12 Say now to the rebellious house, Do you not know 1
16 As I live, says the Lord GOD 12
19 Therefore thus says the Lord GOD: As I live, surely 1
22 Thus says the Lord GOD: "I myself will take a sprig 1
18: 3 As I live, says the Lord GOD 12
9 he shall surely live, says the Lord GOD. 12
19 Yet you say, 'Why should not the son suffer 1
23 in the death of the wicked, says the Lord GOD 12
25 Yet you say, 'The way of the Lord is not just.' 1
29 Yet the house of Israel says, 'The way of the Lord is 1
30 every one according to his ways, says the Lord 12
32 says the Lord GOD; so turn, and live. 12
19: 2 say: What a lioness was your mother among lions! 1
20: 3 and say to them, Thus says the Lord GOD 1
3 and say to them, Thus says the Lord GOD 1
3 As I live, says the Lord GOD 12
5 and say to them, Thus says the Lord GOD 1
5 and say to them, Thus says the Lord GOD 1
5 I swore to them, saying, I am the LORD your God. 1
7 I said to them, Cast away the detestable things 1
18 I said to their children in the wilderness 1
27 and say to them, Thus says the Lord GOD 1

27 and say to them, Thus says the Lord GOD 1
29 I said to them, What is the high place to which you 1
30 Wherefore say to the house of Israel 1
30 Thus says the Lord GOD: Will you defile 1
31 As I live, says the Lord GOD 12
33 As I live, says the Lord GOD 12
36 enter into judgment with you, says the Lord GOD. 12
39 As for you, O house of Israel, thus says the Lord GOD 1
40 mountain height of Israel, says the Lord GOD 12
44 O house of Israel, says the Lord GOD. 12
47 say to the forest of the Negeb, Hear the word 1
47 Hear the word of the LORD: Thus says the Lord GOD 1
49 Then I said, "Ah Lord GOD! 1
49 they are saying of me, 'Is he not a maker 1
21: 3 say to the land of Israel, Thus says the LORD 1
3 say to the land of Israel, Thus says the LORD 1
7 when they say to you, 'Why do you sigh?' 1
7 when they say to you, 'Why do you sigh?' 1
7 it will be fulfilled,'" says the Lord GOD. 12
9 Son of man, prophesy and say, Thus says the Lord, 1
9 prophesy and say, Thus says the Lord, Say 1
9 prophesy and say, Thus says the Lord, Say 1
13 if you despise the rod?" says the Lord GOD. 12
24 Therefore thus says the Lord GOD 1
26 thus says the Lord GOD: Remove the turban 1
28 son of man, prophesy, and say, Thus says the Lord 1
28 son of man, prophesy, and say, Thus says the Lord 1
28 say, A sword, a sword is drawn for the slaughter 1
22: 1 Moreover the word of the LORD came to me, saying 1
3 You shall say, Thus says the Lord GOD 1
3 You shall say, Thus says the Lord GOD 1
12 you have forgotten me, says the Lord GOD. 12
19 Therefore thus says the Lord GOD 1
24 say to her, You are a land that is not cleansed 1
28 divining lies for them, saying, 'Thus says the Lord 1
28 divining lies for them, saying, 'Thus says the Lord 1
31 requited upon their heads, says the Lord GOD. 12
23:22 Therefore, O Ohol'ibah, thus says the Lord GOD 1
28 For thus says the Lord GOD: Behold, I will deliver 1
32 Thus says the Lord GOD: "You shall drink 1
34 for I have spoken, says the Lord GOD. 12
35 Therefore thus says the Lord GOD 1
36 The LORD said to me: "Son of man, will you judge 1
43 Then I said, Do not men now commit adultery 1
46 thus says the Lord GOD: "Bring up a host 1
24: 3 say to them, Thus says the Lord GOD: Set on the pot 1
3 say to them, Thus says the Lord GOD: Set on the pot 1
6 Therefore thus says the Lord GOD 1
9 Therefore thus says the Lord GOD 1
14 I will judge you, says the Lord GOD. 12
19 the people said to me, "Will you not tell us 1
20 I said to them, "The word of the LORD came to me 1
21 Say to the house of Israel, Thus says the Lord GOD 1
21 Say to the house of Israel, Thus says the Lord GOD 1
25: 3 Say to the Ammonites, Hear the word of the Lord GOD 1
3 Thus says the Lord GOD, Because you said, 'Aha!' 1
3 Because you said, 'Aha!' over my sanctuary 1
6 For thus says the Lord GOD 1
8 Thus says the Lord GOD: Because Moab said, Behold 1
8 Thus says the Lord GOD: Because Moab said, Behold 1
12 Thus says the Lord GOD: Because Edom acted 1
13 therefore thus says the Lord GOD 1
14 they shall know my vengeance, says the Lord GOD. 12
15 Thus says the Lord GOD: Because the Philistines 1
16 therefore thus says the Lord GOD, Behold 1
26: 2 because Tyre said concerning Jerusalem 1
3 therefore thus says the Lord GOD 1
5 for I have spoken, says the Lord GOD; 12
7 For thus says the Lord GOD: Behold, I will bring 1
14 for I the LORD have spoken, says the Lord GOD. 12
15 Thus says the Lord GOD to Tyre 1
17 and say to you, 'How you have vanished from the seas 1
19 For thus says the Lord GOD: When I make you a city 1
21 you will never be found again, says the Lord GOD. 12
27: 3 say to Tyre, who dwells at the entrance to the sea 1
3 thus says the Lord GOD: "O Tyre, you have said 1
3 O Tyre, you have said, 'I am perfect in beauty 1
28: 2 Son of man, say to the prince of Tyre 1
2 to the prince of Tyre, Thus says the Lord GOD 1
2 you have said, 'I am a god, I sit in the seat 1
6 therefore thus says the Lord GOD 1
9 Will you still say, 'I am a god,' 1
10 for I have spoken, says the Lord GOD. 12
12 king of Tyre, and say to him, Thus says the Lord GOD 1
12 king of Tyre, and say to him, Thus says the Lord GOD 1
22 say, Thus says the Lord GOD: "Behold, I am against 1
22 Thus says the Lord GOD: "Behold, I am against you 1
25 Thus says the Lord GOD 1
29: 3 speak, and say, Thus says the Lord GOD 1
3 Thus says the Lord GOD: "Behold, I am against you 1
3 dragon . . that says, 'My Nile is my own; I made it 1
8 thus says the Lord GOD: Behold, I will bring a sword 1
9 Because you said, 'The Nile is mine, and I made it 31
13 thus says the Lord GOD: At the end of 40 years 1
19 thus says the Lord GOD: Behold, I will give the land 1
20 because they worked for me, says the Lord GOD. 12
30: 2 Son of man, prophesy, and say, Thus says the Lord 1
2 Son of man, prophesy, and say, Thus says the Lord 1
6 says the LORD: Those who support Egypt shall fall 1

6 fall within her by the sword, says the Lord GOD. 12
10 says the Lord GOD: I will put an end to the wealth 1
13 Thus says the Lord GOD: I will destroy the idols 1
22 Therefore thus says the Lord GOD: Behold, I am 1
31: 2 say to Pharaoh king of Egypt and to his multitude 1
10 Therefore thus says the Lord GOD 1
15 Thus says the Lord GOD: When it goes down to Sheol 1
18 Pharaoh and all his multitude, says the Lord GOD. 12
32: 2 over Pharaoh king of Egypt, and say to him 1
3 Thus says the Lord GOD: I will throw my net over you 1
8 put darkness upon your land, says the Lord GOD. 12
11 For thus says the Lord GOD: The sword of the king 1
14 their rivers to run like oil, says the Lord GOD. 12
16 shall they chant it, says the Lord GOD. 12
31 all his army, slain by the sword, says the Lord GOD. 12
32 Pharaoh and all his multitude, says the Lord GOD. 12
33: 2 Son of man, speak to your people and say to them 1
8 If I say to the wicked, O wicked man 1
10 And you, son of man, say to the house of Israel 1
10 say to the house of Israel, Thus have you said 1
11 Say to them, As I live, says the Lord GOD 1
11 Say to them, As I live, says the Lord GOD 12
12 And you, son of man, say to your people 1
13 I say to the righteous that he shall surely live 1
14 though I say to the wicked, 'You shall surely die 1
17 Yet your people say, 'The way of the Lord is not just 1
20 Yet you say, 'The way of the Lord is not just.' 1
21 came to me and said, "The city has fallen. 1
24 waste places in the land of Israel keep saying 1
25 Therefore say to them, Thus says the Lord GOD 1
25 Therefore say to them, Thus says the Lord GOD 1
27 Say this to them, Thus says the Lord GOD: As I live 1
27 Say this to them, Thus says the Lord GOD: As I live 1
30 say to one another, each to his brother 4
31 they hear what you say but they will not do it; 5
32 for they hear what you say, but they will not do it. 5
34: 2 prophesy, and say to them, even to the shepherds 1
2 Thus says the Lord GOD: Ho, shepherds of Israel 1
8 As I live, says the Lord GOD 12
10 Thus says the Lord GOD, Behold 1
11 For thus says the Lord GOD: Behold 1
15 I will make them lie down, says the Lord GOD. 12
17 As for you, my flock, thus says the Lord GOD: Behold 1
20 Therefore, thus says the Lord GOD to them: Behold 1
30 house of Israel, are my people, says the Lord GOD. 12
31 and I am your God, says the Lord GOD. 12
35: 3 and say to it, Thus says the Lord GOD: Behold 1
3 and say to it, Thus says the Lord GOD: Behold 1
6 therefore, as I live, says the Lord GOD 12
10 Because you said, 'These two nations 1
11 as I live, says the Lord GOD, I will deal with you 12
12 uttered against the mountains of Israel, saying 1
14 says the Lord GOD: For the rejoicing of the whole 1
36: 1 and say, O mountains of Israel, hear the word 1
2 Thus says the Lord GOD: Because the enemy said 1
2 Because the enemy said of you, 'Aha!' 1
3 therefore prophesy, and say, Thus says the Lord 1
3 therefore prophesy, and say, Thus says the Lord 1
4 Thus says the Lord GOD to the mountains 1
5 thus says the Lord GOD: I speak in my hot jealousy 1
6 and say to the mountains and hills, to the ravines 1
6 Thus says the Lord GOD: Behold, I speak 1
7 thus says the Lord GOD: I swear that the nations 1
13 Thus says the Lord GOD: Because men say to you 1
13 Because men say to you, 'You devour men 1
14 bereave your nation of children, says the Lord 12
15 cause your nation to stumble, says the Lord GOD. 12
20 men said of them, 'These are the people of the LORD 1
22 Therefore say to the house of Israel 1
22 Thus says the Lord GOD: It is not for your sake 1
23 nations will know that I am the LORD, says the Lord 12
32 not for your sake that I will act, says the Lord GOD; 12
33 Thus says the Lord GOD: On the day that I cleanse 1
35 they will say, 'This land that was desolate 1
37 Thus says the Lord GOD: This also I will let 1
37: 3 he said to me, "Son of man, can these bones live? 1
4 Again he said to me, "Prophesy to these bones, 1
4 Prophesy to these bones, and say to them 1
5 Thus says the Lord GOD to these bones 1
9 Then he said to me, "Prophesy to the breath 1
9 and say to the breath, Thus says the Lord GOD 1
9 and say to the breath, Thus says the Lord GOD 1
11 Then he said to me, "Son of man 1
11 Behold, they say, 'Our bones are dried up 1
12 prophesy, and say to them, Thus says the Lord GOD 1
12 prophesy, and say to them, Thus says the Lord GOD 1
14 have spoken, and I have done it, says the LORD. 12
18 when your people say to you, 'Will you not show us 1
19 say to them, Thus says the Lord GOD 4
19 say to them, Thus says the Lord GOD 1
21 then say to them, Thus says the Lord GOD 4
21 then say to them, Thus says the Lord GOD 1
38: 3 say, Thus says the Lord GOD: Behold, I am against 1
3 Thus says the Lord GOD: Behold, I am against you 1
10 says the Lord GOD: On that day thoughts will come 1
11 say, 'I will go up against the land of unwalled 1
13 Tarshish and all its villages will say to you 1
14 Therefore, son of man, prophesy, and say to Gog 1
14 Thus says the Lord GOD: On that day when my people 1

17 Thus says the Lord GOD: Are you he of whom I spoke 1
18 says the Lord GOD, my wrath will be roused. 12
21 kind of terror against Gog, says the Lord GOD; 12
39: 1 prophesy against Gog, and say, Thus says the Lord 1
1 says the Lord GOD: Behold, I am against you, O Gog 1
5 for I have spoken, says the Lord GOD. 12
8 and it will be brought about, says the Lord GOD. 12
10 those who plundered them, says the Lord GOD. 12
13 on the day that I show my glory, says the Lord GOD. 12
17 As for you, son of man, thus says the Lord GOD 1
20 men and all kinds of warriors,' says the Lord GOD. 12
25 Therefore thus says the Lord GOD 1
29 upon the house of Israel, says the Lord GOD. 12
40: 4 the man said to me, "Son of man, look with your eyes 4
45 he said to me, This chamber which faces south 4
41: 4 And he said to me, This is the most holy place. 1
22 He said to me, "This is the table 4
42:13 he said to me, "The north chambers and the south 1
43: 7 he said to me, "Son of man, this is the place 1
18 he said to me, "Son of man, thus says the Lord GOD 1
18 he said to me, "Son of man, thus says the Lord GOD 1
19 says the Lord GOD, a bull for a sin offering. 12
27 I will accept you, says the Lord GOD. 12
44: 2 And he said to me, "This gate shall remain shut; 1
5 And the LORD said to me, "Son of man, mark well 1
6 say to the rebellious house 1
6 Thus says the Lord GOD: O house of Israel 1
9 Therefore thus says the Lord GOD: No foreigner 1
12 I have sworn concerning them, says the Lord GOD 12
15 to offer me the fat and the blood, says the Lord GOD; 12
27 he shall offer his sin offering, says the Lord GOD 12
45: 9 Thus says the Lord GOD: Enough, O princes of Israel! 1
9 your evictions of my people, says the Lord GOD. 12
15 to make atonement for them, says the Lord GOD. 12
18 Thus says the Lord GOD: In the first month 1
46: 1 Thus says the Lord GOD: The gate of the inner court 1
16 Thus says the Lord GOD: If the prince makes a gift 1
20 he said to me, "This is the place where the priests 1
24 he said to me, "These are the kitchens where those 1
47: 6 And he said to me, "Son of man, have you seen this? 1
8 he said to me, "This water flows toward the eastern 1
13 Thus says the Lord GOD: "These are the boundaries 1
23 assign him his inheritance, says the Lord GOD. 12
48:29 are their several portions, says the Lord GOD. 12
Dan 1:10 chief of the eunuchs said to Daniel, "I fear lest my 1
11 Then Daniel said to the steward whom the chief 1
2: 3 king said to them, "I had a dream, and my spirit 1
4 Then the Chalde'ans said to the king, "O king 4
15 said to Ar'ioch, the king's captain 16
20 Daniel said: "Blessed be the name of God for ever 16
24 Daniel . . went and said thus to him 16
25 before the king in haste, and said thus to him 16
26 king said to Daniel, whose name was Belteshaz'zar 16
47 king said to Daniel, "Truly, your God is God of gods 16
3: 9 said to King Nebuchadnez'zar, "O king 16
14 Nebuchadnez'zar said to them, "Is it true 16
24 said to his counselors, "Did we not cast three men 16
26 door of the burning fiery furnace and said 16
28 Nebuchadnez'zar said, "Blessed be the God 16
4: 8 Daniel came in . . -and I told him the dream, saying •
14 cried aloud and said thus, 'Hew down the tree 16
19 king said, "Belteshaz'zar, let not the dream 16
23 holy one, coming down from heaven and saying, 16
30 king said, "Is not this great Babylon, 16
35 none can stay his hand or say to him, "What doest 16
5: 7 king said to the wise men of Babylon, 16
10 queen said, "O king, live for ever! 16
13 king said to Daniel, "You are that Daniel 16
6: 5 Then these men said, "We shall not find any ground 16
6 came by agreement to the king and said to him, 16
12 said before the king, concerning the interdict 16
15 came by agreement to the king, and said to the king 16
16 king said to Daniel, "May your God, 16
20 cried out in a tone of anguish and said to Daniel 16
21 Then Daniel said to the king, "O king, live for ever 17
7: 2 Daniel said, "I saw in my vision by night, 16
23 Thus he said: 'As for the fourth beast, there 16
8:13 another holy one said to the one that spoke 1
14 said to him, "For 2,300 evenings and mornings; 1
17 said to me, "Understand, O son of man, 1
19 said, "Behold, I will make known to you what shall be 1
9: 4 I prayed . . and made confession, saying, "O Lord 1
22 came and he said to me, "O Daniel, 1
10:11 said to me, "O Daniel, man greatly beloved, give heed 1
12 Then he said to me, "Fear not, Daniel 1
16 said to him who stood before me, "O my lord, 1
19 said, "O man greatly beloved, fear not, 1
19 when he spoke to me, I was strengthened and said 1
20 Then he said, "Do you know why I have come to you? 1
12: 6 I said to the man clothed in linen, who was above 1
8 Then I said, "O my lord, what shall be the issue 1
9 He said, "Go your way, Daniel, for the words 1
Hos 1: 2 the LORD said to Hose'a, "Go, take to yourself a wife 1
4 And the LORD said to him, "Call his name Jezreel; 1
6 the LORD said to him, "Call her name Not pitied 1
9 And the LORD said, "Call his name Not my people 1
10 and in the place where it was said to them 1
10 it shall be said to them, "Sons of the living God. 1
2: 1 Say to your brother, "My people," and to your sister 1

5 For she said, 'I will go after my lovers 1
7 Then she shall say, 'I will go and return 1
12 her fig trees, of which she said, 'These are my hire 1
13 after her lovers, and forgot me, says the LORD. 12
16 says the LORD, you will call me, 'My husband,' 12
21 that day, says the LORD, I will answer the heavens 12
23 and I will say to Not my people, 'You are my people'; 1
23 and he shall say 'Thou art my God.' 1
3: 1 And the LORD said to me, "Go again, love a woman 1
3 I said to her, "You must dwell as mine for many days; 1
5:15 and in their distress they seek me, saying *
10: 3 For now they will say: "We have no king 1
8 and they shall say to the mountains, Cover us 1
11:11 I will return them to their homes, says the LORD. 12
12: 8 E'phraim has said, "Ah, but I am rich 1
13: 2 Sacrifice to these, they say. Men kiss calves! 1
10 those of whom you said, "Give me a king and princes"? 1
14: 2 say to him, "Take away all iniquity; 1
3 will say no more, 'Our God,' to the work of our hands. 1
Jol 2:12 Yet even now," says the LORD, "return to me 12
17 weep and say, "Spare thy people, O LORD 1
17 Why should they say among the peoples 1
19 The LORD answered and said to his people 1
32 those who escape, as the LORD has said 1
3:10 let the weak say, "I am a warrior. 1
Ams 1: 2 And he said: "The LORD roars from Zion 1
3 Thus says the LORD: "For three transgressions 1
5 shall go into exile to Kir," says the LORD. 1
6 Thus says the LORD: "For three transgressions 1
8 the Philistines shall perish," says the Lord GOD 1
9 says the LORD: "For three transgressions of Tyre 1
11 says the LORD: "For three transgressions of Edom 1
13 Thus says the LORD: "For three transgressions 1
15 exile, he and his princes together," says the LORD. 1
2: 1 says the LORD: "For three transgressions of Moab 1
3 will slay all its princes with him," says the LORD. 1
4 says the LORD: "For three transgressions of Judah 1
6 Thus says the LORD: "For three transgressions 1
11 it not indeed so, O people of Israel?" says the LORD. 12
12 and commanded the prophets, saying, 'You shall not 1
16 shall flee naked in that day," says the LORD. 12
3: 9 to the strongholds in the land of Egypt, and say 1
10 They do not know how to do right," says the LORD 12
11 thus says the Lord GOD: "An adversary shall 1
12 Thus says the LORD: "As the shepherd rescues 1
13 against the house of Jacob," says the Lord GOD 12
15 houses shall come to an end," says the LORD. 12
4: 1 who say to their husbands, 'Bring, that we may drink 1
3 be cast forth into Harmon," says the LORD. 12
5 O people of Israel!" says the Lord GOD. 12
6 yet you did not return to me," says the LORD. 12
8 yet you did not return to me," says the LORD. 12
9 yet you did not return to me," says the LORD. 12
10 yet you did not return to me," says the LORD. 12
11 yet you did not return to me," says the LORD. 12
5: 3 For thus says the Lord GOD: "The city that went 1
4 thus says the LORD to the house of Israel 1
14 the God of hosts, will be with you, as you have said. 1
16 thus says the LORD, the God of hosts, the Lord 1
16 and in all the streets they shall say, 'Alas! Alas!' 1
17 will pass through the midst of you," says the LORD. 1
27 you into exile beyond Damascus," says the LORD 1
6: 8 The Lord GOD has sworn by himself (says the LORD 12
10 and shall say to him who is in the innermost parts 1
10 Is there still any one with you?" he shall say, "No"; 1
10 he shall say, "Hush! We must not mention the name 1
13 you who rejoice in Lo-debar, who say 1
14 O house of Israel," says the LORD, the God of hosts; 12
7: 2 I said, "O Lord GOD, forgive, I beseech thee! 1
3 concerning this; "It shall not be," said the LORD. 1
5 Then I said, "O Lord GOD, cease, I beseech thee! 1
6 This also shall not be," said the Lord GOD. 1
10 Amazi'ah . . to Jerobo'am king of Israel, saying 1
11 Amos has said, 'Jerobo'am shall die by the sword 1
12 Amazi'ah said to Amos, "O seer, go, flee away 1
15 and the LORD said to me, 'Go, prophesy to my people 1
16 You say, 'Do not prophesy against Israel 1
17 thus says the LORD: 'Your wife shall be a harlot 1
8: 2 he said, "Amos, what do you see? 1
2 And I said, "A basket of summer fruit. 1
2 the LORD said to me, "The end has come upon 1
3 become wailings in that day," says the Lord GOD; 12
5 saying, "When will the new moon be over 1
9 And on that day," says the Lord GOD 12
11 Behold, the days are coming," says the Lord GOD 12
14 Those who swear by Ash'imah of Sama'ria, and say 1
9: 1 the LORD standing beside the altar, and he said 1
7 O people of Israel?" says the LORD. 12
8 not . . destroy the house of Jacob," says the LORD. 12
10 who say, 'Evil shall not overtake or meet us.' 1
12 called by my name," says the LORD who does this. 12
13 Behold, the days are coming," says the LORD 12
15 which I have given them," says the LORD your God. 1
Obd 1: 1 Thus says the Lord GOD concerning Edom 1
3 whose dwelling is high, who say in your heart 1
4 thence I will bring you down, says the LORD. 12
8 Will I not on that day, says the LORD, destroy 12
Jon 1: 1 the LORD came to Jonah the son of Amit'tai, saying 1
6 the captain came and said to him, "What do you mean 1
7 they said to one another, "Come, let us cast lots 1
8 Then they said to him, "Tell us, on whose account 1
9 And he said to them, "I am a Hebrew; 1
10 the men were exceedingly afraid, and said to him 1
11 Then they said to him, "What shall we do to you 1
12 He said to them, "Take me up and throw me 1
2: 2 saying, "I called to the LORD, out of my distress 1
4 Then I said, 'I am cast out from thy presence; 1
3: 1 of the LORD came to Jonah the second time, saying 1
10 repented of the evil which he had said he would do 4
4: 2 he prayed to the LORD and said, "I pray thee, LORD 1
2 LORD, is not this what I said 5
4 the LORD said, "Do you do well to be angry? 1
8 he asked that he might die, and said 1
9 God said to Jonah, "Do you do well to be angry 1
9 he said, "I do well to be angry, angry enough to die. 1
10 the LORD said, "You pity the plant 1
Mic 2: 3 Therefore thus says the LORD 1
4 and wail with bitter lamentation, and say 1
7 Should this be said, O house of Jacob? 1
11 utter wind and lies, saying, "I will preach to you *
3: 1 And I said: Hear, you heads of Jacob 1
5 Thus says the LORD concerning the prophets 1
11 yet they lean upon the LORD and say 1
4: 2 many nations shall come, and say: "Come, let us go up 1
6 In that day, says the LORD, I will assemble the lame 12
11 many nations are assembled against you, saying 1
5:10 And in that day, says the LORD 12
6: 1 Hear what the LORD says: Arise, plead your case 1
7:10 and shame will cover her who said to me 1
Nah 1:12 says the LORD, "Though they be strong and many 1
2:13 Behold, I am against you, says the LORD of hosts 12
3: 5 Behold, I am against you, says the LORD of hosts 12
7 all who look on you will shrink from you and say 1
Hab 2: 1 and look forth to see what he will say to me 4
6 and say, "Woe to him who heaps up what is not his 1
19 Woe to him who says to a wooden thing, Awake; 1
Zep 1: 2 sweep away everything . . says the LORD. 12
3 I will cut off mankind . . says the LORD. 12
10 On that day," says the LORD, "a cry will be heard 12
12 who say in their hearts, 'The LORD will not do good 1
2: 9 Therefore, as I live," says the LORD of hosts 12
15 city that dwelt secure, that said to herself 1
3: 7 I said, 'Surely she will fear me 1
8 Therefore wait for me," says the LORD 12
16 On that day it shall be said to Jerusalem 1
20 when I restore your fortunes . . says the LORD. 1
Hag 1: 2 Thus says the LORD of hosts: This people say 1
2 This people say the time has not yet come 1
5 Now therefore thus says the LORD of hosts 1
7 Thus says the LORD of hosts: Consider how you have 1
8 that I may appear in my glory, says the LORD. 1
9 Why? says the LORD of hosts. Because of my house 12
13 the LORD's message, "I am with you, says the LORD. 12
2: 2 and to all the remnant of the people, and say 1
4 Yet now take courage, O Zerub'babel, says the LORD; 12
4 courage, all you people of the land, says the LORD; 12
4 work, for I am with you, says the LORD of hosts 12
6 For thus says the LORD of hosts 1
7 will fill this house with splendor, says the LORD 1
8 the gold is mine, says the LORD of hosts. 12
9 greater than the former, says the LORD of hosts; 1
9 I will give prosperity, says the LORD of hosts.' 12
11 Thus says the LORD of hosts: Ask the priests 1
13 Then said Haggai, "If one who is unclean by contact 1
14 Then Haggai said, "So is it with this people 1
14 and with this nation before me, says the LORD; 12
17 yet you did not return to me, says the LORD. 12
21 Speak to Zerub'babel, governor of Judah, saying 1
23 On that day, says the LORD of hosts, I will take you 12
23 says the LORD, and make you like a signet ring; 12
23 for I have chosen you, says the LORD of hosts. 12
Zec 1: 1 came to Zechari'ah . . the prophet, saying 1
3 Therefore say to them, Thus says the LORD of hosts 1
3 Therefore say to them, Thus says the LORD of hosts 1
3 Return to me, says the LORD of hosts 12
3 and I will return to you, says the LORD of hosts. 1
4 Thus says the LORD of hosts, Return from your evil 1
4 But they did not hear or heed me, says the LORD. 12
6 they repented and said, As the LORD of hosts 1
7 and Zechari'ah said 1
9 Then I said, 'What are these, my lord?' 1
9 The angel who talked with me said to me 1
12 Then the angel of the LORD said, 'O LORD of hosts 1
14 the angel who talked with me said to me, 'Cry out 1
14 Thus says the LORD of hosts: I am exceedingly 1
16 Therefore, thus says the LORD, I have returned 1
16 my house shall be built in it, says the LORD 12
17 Cry again, Thus says the LORD of hosts 1
19 I said to the angel who talked with me 1
21 I said, "What are these coming to do?" He answered 1
2: 2 Then I said, "Where are you going?" And he said to me 1
2 he said to me, "To measure Jerusalem 1
4 and said to him, "Run, say to that young man 1
4 and said to him, "Run, say to that young man 4
5 says the LORD, and I will be the glory within her. 12
6 ho! Flee from the land of the north, says the LORD; 12
6 as the four winds of the heavens, says the LORD. 12
8 thus said the LORD of hosts, after his glory sent 1
10 I will dwell in the midst of you, says the LORD. 12
3: 2 the LORD said to Satan, "The LORD rebuke you, 1
4 angel said to those who were standing before him 1
4 to him he said, "Behold, I have taken your iniquity 1
5 I said, "Let them put a clean turban on his head. 1
7 Thus says the LORD of hosts: If you will walk 1
9 I will engrave its inscription, says the LORD 12
10 In that day, says the LORD of hosts 12
4: 2 And he said to me, "What do you see? 1
2 I said, "I see, and behold, a lampstand all of gold 1
4 I said to the angel who talked with me 1
5 Do you not know what these are?" I said, "No, my lord. 1
6 Then he said to me, "This is the word of the LORD 1
6 by my Spirit, says the LORD of hosts. 1
8 Moreover the word of the LORD came to me, saying 1
11 Then I said to him, "What are these two olive trees 1
12 I said to him, "What are these two branches 1
13 He said to me, "Do you not know what these are? 1
13 He said to me, "Do you not know what these are? 1
14 Then he said, "These are the two anointed who stand 1
5: 2 he said to me, "What do you see? 1
3 Then he said to me, "This is the curse that goes out 1
4 I will send it forth, says the LORD of hosts 12
5 who talked with me came forward and said to me 1
6 I said, "What is it?" He said, "This is the ephah 1
6 He said, "This is the ephah that goes forth. 1
6 he said, "This is their iniquity in all the land. 1
8 he said, "This is Wickedness. 1
10 Then I said to the angel who talked with me 1
11 He said to me, "To the land of Shinar, to build a house 1
6: 4 Then I said to the angel who talked with me 1
7 he said, "Go, patrol the earth." So they patrolled 1
12 say to him, 'Thus says the LORD of hosts 1
12 say to him, 'Thus says the LORD of hosts 1
7: 5 Say to all the people of the land and the priests 1
8 the word of the LORD came to Zechari'ah, saying 1
9 says the LORD of hosts, Render true judgments 1
13 I would not hear," says the LORD of hosts 1
8: 1 the word of the LORD of hosts came to me, saying 1
2 Thus says the LORD of hosts: I am jealous for Zion 1
3 Thus says the LORD: I will return to Zion 1
4 Thus says the LORD of hosts: Old men and old women 1
6 Thus says the LORD of hosts: If it is marvelous 1
6 marvelous in my sight, says the LORD of hosts? 12
7 Thus says the LORD of hosts: Behold, I will save 1
9 says the LORD of hosts: "Let your hands be strong 1
11 as in the former days, says the LORD of hosts. 12
14 For thus says the LORD of hosts: "As I purposed to do 1
14 I did not relent, says the LORD of hosts 1
17 for all these things I hate, says the LORD. 12
18 the word of the LORD of hosts came to me, saying 1
19 Thus says the LORD of hosts: The fast of the fourth 1
20 says the LORD of hosts: Peoples shall yet come 1
21 city shall go to another, saying, 'Let us go at once 1
23 Thus says the LORD of hosts: In those days ten men 1
23 hold of the robe of a Jew, saying, 'Let us go with you 1
10:12 they shall glory in his name," says the LORD. 12
11: 4 said the LORD my God: "Become shepherd of the flock 1
5 those who sell them say, 'Blessed be the LORD 1
6 on the inhabitants of this land, says the LORD. 12
9 I said, "I will not be your shepherd. 1
12 Then I said to them, "If it seems right to you 1
13 Then the LORD said to me, "Cast it into the treasury 1
15 Then the LORD said to me, "Take once more 1
12: 1 Thus says the LORD, who stretched out the heavens 12
4 On that day, says the LORD, I will strike 12
5 Then the clans of Judah shall say to themselves 1
13: 2 says the LORD of hosts, I will cut off the names 12
3 his father and mother who bore him will say to him 1
5 he will say, 'I am no prophet, I am a tiller of the soil; 1
6 he will say, 'The wounds I received in the house 1
7 who stands next to me," says the LORD of hosts. 12
8 says the LORD, two thirds shall be cut off 12
9 I will say, 'They are my people'; 1
9 they will say, 'The LORD is my God.' 1
Mal 1: 2 I have loved you," says the LORD. 1
2 But you say, "How hast thou loved us? 1
2 Is not Esau Jacob's brother?" says the LORD. 12
4 If Edom says, "We are shattered but we will rebuild 1
4 the LORD of hosts says, "They may build 1
5 Your own eyes shall see this, and you shall say 1
6 if I am a master, where is my fear? says the LORD 1
6 You say, 'How have we despised thy name?' 1
7 upon my altar. And you say, 'How have we polluted it? 1
8 or show you favor? says the LORD of hosts. 1
9 show favor to any of you? says the LORD of hosts. 1
10 I have no pleasure in you, says the LORD of hosts 1
11 my name is great among the nations, says the LORD 1
12 when you say that the LORD'S table is polluted 1
13 What a weariness this is,' you say 1
13 you say, and you sniff at me, says the LORD of hosts. 1
13 Shall I accept that from your hand? says the LORD. 1
14 I am a great King, says the LORD of hosts 1
2: 2 to give glory to my name, says the LORD of hosts 1
4 my covenant . . may hold, says the LORD of hosts. 1
8 the covenant of Levi, says the LORD of hosts 1
16 For I hate divorce, says the LORD the God of Israel 1
16 garment with violence, says the LORD of hosts. 1
17 Yet you say, "How have we wearied him? 1

17 By saying, "Every one who does evil is good 1
3: 1 behold, he is coming, says the LORD of hosts. 1
5 and do not fear me, says the LORD of hosts. 1
7 Return to me, and I will return to you, says the LORD 1
7 But you say, 'How shall we return?' 1
8 robbing me. But you say, 'How are we robbing thee?' 1
10 thereby put me to the test, says the LORD of hosts 1
11 shall not fail to bear, says the LORD of hosts. 1
12 a land of delight, says the LORD of hosts. 1
13 words have been stout against me, says the LORD. 1
13 Yet you say, 'How have we spoken against thee?' 1
14 You have said 'It is vain to serve God. 1
17 They shall be mine, says the LORD of hosts 1
4: 1 shall burn them up, says the LORD of hosts 1
3 on the day when I act, says the LORD of hosts. 1
Mat 1:20 in a dream, saying, "Joseph, son of David, do not fear 31
2: 1 wise men from the East came to Jerusalem, saying 31
8 he sent them to Bethlehem, saying, "Go and search 24
13 angel of the Lord appeared to Joseph . . and said 31
19 in a dream to Joseph in Egypt, saying 31
3: 3 prophet Isaiah when he said, "The voice of one 31
7 coming for baptism, he said to them, "You brood 24
9 do not presume to say to yourselves, 'We have 31
14 John would have prevented him, saying, "I need to be 31
17 a voice from heaven, saying, "This is my beloved Son 31
4: 3 the tempter came and said to him, "If you are the Son 24
6 said to him, "If you are the Son of God, throw 31
7 Jesus said to him, "Again it is written, 'You shall 39
9 he said to him, "All these I will give you, if you will 31
10 Jesus said to him, "Begone, Satan! for it is written 31
17 From that time Jesus began to preach, saying 31
19 he said to them, "Follow me, and I will make you 31
5: 2 he opened his mouth and taught them, saying 31
18 For truly, I say to you, till heaven and earth pass 31
21 You have heard that it was said to the men of old 24
22 But I say to you that every one who is angry 31
22 whoever says, 'You fool!' shall be liable to the hell 31
26 truly, I say to you, you will never get out till you 31
27 You have heard that it was said, 'You shall not 24
28 I say to you that every one who looks at a woman 31
31 It was also said, 'Whoever divorces his wife 24
32 I say to you that every one who divorces his wife 31
33 Again you have heard that it was said to the men 24
34 I say to you, Do not swear at all, either by heaven 31
37 Let what you say be simply 'Yes' or 'No'; 32
38 heard that it was said, 'An eye for an eye and a tooth 24
39 I say to you, do not resist one who is evil. But 31
43 You have heard that it was said, 'You shall love 24
44 I say to you, Love your enemies and pray for those 31
6: 2 that they may be praised by men. Truly, I say to you 31
5 that they may be seen by men. Truly, I say to you 31
16 by men. Truly, I say to you, they have received 31
31 do not be anxious, saying, 'What shall we eat?' 31
7: 4 Or how can you say to your brother 24
21 Not every one who says to me, 'Lord, Lord,' shall enter 31
22 On that day many will say to me, 'Lord, Lord 24
8: 2 saying, "Lord, if you will, you can make me clean. 31
3 saying, "I will; be clean. 31
4 Jesus said to him, "See that you say nothing 24
4 Jesus said to him, "See that you say nothing 24
6 saying, "Lord, my servant is lying paralyzed 31
7 he said to him, "I will come and heal him. 31
8 but only say the word 24
9 and I say to one, 'Go,' and he goes, and to another, 31
10 he marveled, and said to those who followed him 24
10 Truly, I say to you, not even in Israel have I found 31
13 to the centurion Jesus said, "Go; be it done for you 24
19 a scribe came up and said to him 24
20 Jesus said to him, "Foxes have holes 31
21 Another of the disciples said to him 24
22 Jesus said to him, "Follow me, and leave the dead 31
25 they went and woke him, saying, "Save, Lord 31
26 he said to them, "Why are you afraid 31
27 the men marveled, saying, "What sort of man is this 31
32 he said to them, "Go." So they came out 24
9: 2 he said to the paralytic, "Take heart, my son 24
3 behold, some of the scribes said to themselves 24
4 Jesus, knowing their thoughts, said 24
5 For which is easier, to say, 'Your sins are forgiven,' 31
5 or to say, 'Rise and walk'? 31
6 he then said to the paralytic-"Rise 31
9 and he said to him, "Follow me. 31
11 Pharisees saw this, they said to his disciples 31
12 But when he heard it, he said 24
14 Then the disciples of John came to him, saying 31
15 Jesus said to them, "Can the wedding guests mourn 24
18 saying, "My daughter has just died 31
21 for she said to herself, "If I only touch 31
22 Jesus turned, and seeing her he said, "Take heart 24
24 he said, "Depart; for the girl is not dead 31
28 the blind men came to him; and Jesus said to them 31
28 They said to him, "Yes, Lord. 31
29 Then he touched their eyes, saying 31
33 the crowds marveled, saying 31
34 But the Pharisees said, "He casts out demons 31
37 Then he said to his disciples 31
10: 7 preach as you go, saying 31
15 Truly, I say to you, it shall be more tolerable 31
19 for what you are to say will be given to you 29
19 for what you are to say will be given to you 29
23 for truly, I say to you, you will not have gone 31
42 truly, I say to you, he shall not lose his reward. 31
11: 3 said to him, "Are you he who is to come 24
11 Truly, I say to you, among those born of women 31
18 and they say, 'He has a demon'; 31
19 and they say, 'Behold, a glutton and a drunkard 31
12: 2 when the Pharisees saw it, they said to him, "Look 24
3 He said to them, "Have you not read what David did 24
11 He said to them, "What man of you, if he has one 24
13 Then he said to the man, "Stretch out your hand. 31
23 all the people were amazed, and said 31
24 when the Pharisees heard it they said 24
25 Knowing their thoughts, he said to them 24
32 whoever says a word against the Son of man 31
38 Then some of the scribes and Pharisees said 21
44 Then he says, 'I will return 31
49 he said, "Here are my mother and my brothers! 24
13: 3 he told them many things in parables, saying 31
10 the disciples came and said to him 24
14 the prophecy of Isaiah which says 31
17 I say to you, many prophets and righteous men 31
24 Another parable he put before them, saying 31
27 the servants of the householder came and said 24
28 He said to them, 'An enemy has done this.' 39
28 The servants said to him 31
29 he said, 'No, lest in gathering the weeds you root up 39
31 Another parable he put before them, saying 31
34 All this Jesus said to the crowds in parables; 29
34 he said nothing to them without a parable. 29
36 And his disciples came to him, saying 31
51 They said to him, "Yes. 31
52 he said to them 24
54 so that they were astonished, and said 31
57 But Jesus said to them 24
14: 2 he said to this servants, "This is John the Baptist 24
4 because John said to him 31
8 she said, "Give me the head of John the Baptist 39
15 the disciples came to him and said 31
16 Jesus said, "They need not go away 24
17 They said to him, "We have only five loaves here 31
18 he said, "Bring them here to me. 24
26 they were terrified, saying, "It is a ghost! 31
27 immediately he spoke to them, saying 31
29 He said, "Come." So Peter got out of the boat 24
31 reached out his hand and caught him, saying to him 31
33 those in the boat worshiped him, saying 31
15: 1 scribes came to Jesus from Jerusalem and said 31
5 you say, 'If any one tells his father or his mother 31
7 when he said 31
10 he called the people to him and said to them 24
12 Then the disciples came and said to him 31
15 Peter said to him, "Explain the parable to us. 24
16 he said 24
23 And his disciples came and begged him, saying 31
25 she came and knelt before him, saying 31
27 She said, "Yes, Lord, yet even the dogs eat the crumbs 24
32 Jesus called his disciples to him and said 24
33 the disciples said to him 31
34 Jesus said to them, "How many loaves have you? 31
34 They said, "Seven, and a few small fish. 24
16: 2 When it is evening, you say, 'It will be fair weather; 31
6 Jesus said to them 24
7 they discussed it among themselves, saying 31
8 Jesus, aware of this, said 24
13 Who do men say that the Son of man is? 31
14 they said 24
14 Some say John the Baptist, others say Eli'jah •
14 Some say John the Baptist, others say Eli'jah •
15 He said to them, "But who do you say that I am? 31
15 He said to them, "But who do you say that I am? 31
22 Peter took him and began to rebuke him, saying 31
23 he turned and said to Peter, "Get behind me, Satan! 24
28 Truly, I say to you, there are some standing here 31
17: 4 Peter said to Jesus 24
5 and a voice from the cloud said 31
7 Jesus came and touched them, saying 24
10 Then why do the scribes say 31
14 a man came up to him and kneeling before him said 31
19 disciples came to Jesus privately and said 24
20 He said to them, "Because of your little faith. 31
20 For truly I say to you, if you have faith as a grain 31
20 you will say to this mountain 24
22 Jesus said to them 24
24 the collectors . . went up to Peter and said 24
25 He said "Yes. 31
25 when he came home, Jesus spoke to him first, saying 31
26 when he said, "From others 24
26 Jesus said to him, "Then the sons are free. 39
18: 1 At that time the disciples came to Jesus, saying 31
3 said, "Truly, I say to you 24
3 said, "Truly, I say to you 31
13 if he finds it, truly, I say to you, he rejoices 31
18 Truly, I say to you, whatever you bind on earth 31
19 Again I say to you, if two of you agree on earth 31
21 Then Peter came up and said to him 24
22 Jesus said to him, "I do not say to you seven times 31
22 Jesus said to him, "I do not say to you seven times 31
28 and seizing him by the throat he said 31
32 Then his lord summoned him and said to him 31
19: 5 said, 'For this reason a man shall leave his father 24
7 They said to him 31
8 He said to them, "For your hardness of heart 31
9 I say to you: whoever divorces his wife 31
10 The disciples said to him, "If such is the case 31
11 he said to them, "Not all men can receive 24
14 Jesus said, "Let the children come to me 24
16 behold, one came up to him, saying 24
17 said to him, "Why do you ask me about what is good? 24
18 He said to him, "Which? 31
18 And Jesus said, "You shall not kill 24
20 The young man said to him 31
21 Jesus said to him, "If you would be perfect 39
23 Jesus said to his disciples, "Truly, I say to you 24
23 Jesus said to his disciples, "Truly, I say to you 31
25 they were greatly astonished, saying 31
26 Jesus looked at them and said to them 24
27 Then Peter said in reply 24
28 Jesus said to them, "Truly, I say to you 24
28 Jesus said to them, "Truly, I say to you 31
20: 4 to them he said, 'You go into the vineyard too 24
6 and he said to them, 'Why do you stand here idle 31
7 They said to him, 'Because no one has hired us.' 31
7 He said to them, 'You go into the vineyard too.' 31
8 the owner of the vineyard said to his steward 31
12 saying, 'These last worked only one hour 31
17 and on the way he said to them 24
21 he said to her, "What do you want?" She said to him 24
21 he said to her, "What do you want?" She said to him 24
22 They said to him, "We are able. 31
23 He said to them, "You will drink my cup 31
25 Jesus called them to him and said 24
32 Jesus stopped and called them, saying 24
33 They said to him, "Lord, let our eyes be opened. 31
21: 2 saying to them, "Go into the village opposite you 31
3 If any one says anything to you, you shall say, 'The 31
3 If any one says anything to you, you shall say, 'The 24
4 to fulfil what was spoken by the prophet, saying 31
10 all the city was stirred, saying 31
11 the crowds said, "This is the prophet Jesus 31
13 He said to them, "It is written 31
16 they said to him, "Do you hear what these are saying? 24
16 they said to him, "Do you hear what these are saying? 31
16 Jesus said to them, "Yes 31
19 And he said to it, "May no fruit ever come from you 31
20 When the disciples saw it they marveled, saying 31
21 Jesus answered them, "Truly, I say to you 31
21 but even if you say to this mountain 24
23 came up to him as he was teaching, and said 31
25 If we say, 'From heaven,' he will say to us 31
25 If we say, 'From heaven,' he will say to us 24
26 if we say, 'From men,' we are afraid of the multitude; 24
27 he said to them, "Neither will I tell you 24
28 he went to the first and said 24
30 he went to the second and said the same 24
31 They said, "The first." Jesus said to them 31
31 They said, "The first." Jesus said to them 31
31 Truly, I say to you 31
37 Afterward he sent his son to them, saying 31
38 the tenants saw the son, they said to themselves 24
41 They said to him 31
42 Jesus said to them, "Have you never read 31
22: 1 again Jesus spoke to them in parables, saying 31
4 Again he sent other servants, saying 31
8 Then he said to his servants, 'The wedding is ready 31
12 and he said to him, 'Friend, how did you get in here 31
13 the king said to the attendants, 'Bind him 24
16 along with the Hero'dians, saying, "Teacher, 31
18 Jesus, aware of their malice, said 24
20 Jesus said to them 31
21 They said, "Caesar's." Then he said to them 31
21 They said, "Caesar's." Then he said to them 31
23 who say that there is no resurrection 31
24 saying, "Teacher, Moses said 31
24 saying, "Teacher, Moses said 24
31 have you not read what was said to you by God 24
37 he said to him, "You shall love the Lord your God 39
42 saying, "What do you think of the Christ? 24
42 They said to him, "The son of David. 31
43 He said to them, "How is it 31
43 inspired by the Spirit, calls him Lord, saying 31
44 'The Lord said to my Lord, Sit at my right hand 24
23: 1 Then said Jesus to the crowds 29
16 Woe to you, blind guides, who say 31
18 you say, 'If any one swears by the altar •
30 saying, 'If we had lived in the days of our fathers 31
36 Truly, I say to you 31
39 I tell you, you will not see me again, until you say 24
24: 2 Truly, I say to you 31
3 the disciples came to him privately, saying 31
5 For many will come in my name, saying 31
23 Then if any one says to you, 'Lo, here is the Christ!' 31
26 So, if they say to you, 'Lo, he is in the wilderness,' 24
26 if they say, 'Lo, he is in the inner rooms' •
34 Truly, I say to you 31
47 Truly, I say to you 31
48 if that wicked servant says to himself 31
25: 8 the foolish said to the wise 24

11 Afterward the other maidens came also, saying 31
12 he replied, 'Truly, I say to you, I do not know you.' 31
20 bringing five talents more, saying 31
21 His master said to him 39
22 who had the two talents came forward, saying 24
23 His master said to him 39
24 came forward, saying 24
34 Then the King will say to those at his right hand 24
40 the King will answer them, 'Truly, I say to you 31
41 Then he will say to those at his left hand 24
45 Then he will answer them, 'Truly, I say to you 31
26: 1 he said to his disciples 24
5 they said, "Not during the feast 31
8 they were indignant, saying, "Why this waste? 31
10 Jesus, aware of this, said to them 24
13 Truly, I say to you 31
15 said, "What will you give me if I deliver him to you? 24
17 the disciples came to Jesus, saying 31
18 He said, "Go into the city to a certain one 24
18 Go into the city to a certain one, and say to him 24
18 The Teacher says, My time is at hand 31
21 as they were eating, he said, "Truly, I say to you 24
21 as they were eating, he said, "Truly, I say to you 31
22 and began to say to him one after another 31
25 Judas, who betrayed him, said, "Is it I, Master? 24
25 He said to him, "You have said so. 24
25 He said to him, "You have said so. 24
26 broke it, and gave it to the disciples and said 24
27 when he had given thanks he gave it to them, saying 31
31 Then Jesus said to them, "You will all fall away 31
34 Jesus said to him, "Truly, I say to you 39
34 Jesus said to him, "Truly, I say to you 31
35 Peter said to him, "Even if I must die with you 31
35 so said all the disciples. 24
36 he said to his disciples 31
38 Then he said to them, "My soul is very sorrowful 31
40 he said to Peter 31
44 for the third time, saying the same words. 31
45 Then he came to the disciples and said to them 31
48 Now the betrayer had given them a sign, saying 31
49 he came up to Jesus at once and said, "Hail, Master! 24
50 Jesus said to him, "Friend, why are you here? 24
52 Then Jesus said to him, "Put your sword back 31
55 At that hour Jesus said to the crowds 24
61 said, "This fellow said, 'I am able to destroy 24
61 said, "This fellow said, 'I am able to destroy 24
62 the high priest stood up and said 24
63 Jesus was silent. And the high priest said to him 24
64 Jesus said to him, "You have said so. But I tell you 24
64 Jesus said to him, "You have said so. But I tell you 24
65 Then the high priest tore his robes, and said 31
68 saying, "Prophesy to us, you Christ! 31
69 a maid came up to him, and said 31
70 he denied it before them all, saying 31
71 she said to the bystanders 31
73 bystanders came up and said to Peter 24
27: 4 saying, "I have sinned 31
4 They said, "What is that to us? See to it yourself. 24
6 the chief priests, taking the pieces of silver, said 24
9 spoken by the prophet Jeremiah, saying 31
11 Jesus said, "You have said so. 39
11 Jesus said, "You have said so. 31
13 Then Pilate said to him, "Do you not hear 31
17 So when they had gathered, Pilate said to them 24
21 The governor again said to them 24
21 they said, "Barab'bas. 24
22 Pilate said to them, "Then what shall I do 31
22 They all said, "Let him be crucified. 31
23 he said, "Why, what evil has he done? 39
24 washed his hands before the crowd, saying 31
29 kneeling before him they mocked him, saying 31
40 saying, "You who would destroy the temple 31
41 with the scribes and elders, mocked him, saying 31
43 he said, 'I am the Son of God.' 24
47 some of the bystanders hearing it said 31
49 the others said, "Wait, let us see 31
54 they were filled with awe, and said 31
63 said, "Sir, we remember how that impostor said 31
63 said, "Sir, we remember how that impostor said 24
65 Pilate said to them, "You have a guard of soldiers; 39
28: 5 the angel said to the women, "Do not be afraid 24
6 He is not here; for he has risen, as he said 24
9 behold, Jesus met them and said, "Hail! 31
10 Then Jesus said to them, "Do not be afraid 31
13 said, "Tell people, 'His disciples came by night 24
18 Jesus came and said to them 29
Mrk 1: 7 he preached, saying 31
15 saying, "The time is fulfilled 31
17 Jesus said to them, "Follow me 24
25 Jesus rebuked him, saying, "Be silent, and come out 31
27 they questioned among themselves, saying 31
37 they found him and said to him 31
38 he said to them, "Let us go on to the next towns 31
40 kneeling said to him 31
41 stretched out his hand and touched him, and said 31
44 said to him, "See that you say nothing to any one 31
44 said to him, "See that you say nothing to any one 31
2: 5 he said to the paralytic 31
8 said to them, "Why do you question thus 31

9 Which is easier, to say to the paralytic 31
9 or to say, 'Rise, take up your pallet and walk'? 31
10 he said to the paralytic– 31
11 I say to you, rise, take up your pallet and go home. 31
12 saying, "We never saw anything like this! 31
14 he said to him, "Follow me. 31
16 said to his disciples 31
17 when Jesus heard it, he said to them 31
18 people came and said to him 31
19 Jesus said to them, "Can the wedding guests fast 24
24 the Pharisees said to him, "Look, why are they doing 31
25 he said to them, "Have you never read what David did 31
27 he said to them, "The sabbath was made for man 31
3: 3 he said to the man who had the withered hand 31
4 he said to them, "Is it lawful on the sabbath 31
5 said to the man, "Stretch out your hand. 31
21 for people were saying, "He is beside himself. 31
22 the scribes who came down from Jerusalem said 31
23 said to them in parables 31
28 Truly, I say to you, all sins will be forgiven 31
30 for they had said, "He has an unclean spirit. 31
32 a crowd was sitting about him; and they said to him 31
34 he said, "Here are my mother and my brothers! 31
4: 2 in his teaching he said to them 31
9 he said, "He who has ears to hear, let him hear. 31
11 he said to them, "To you has been given the secret 31
13 he said to them, "Do you not understand 31
21 he said to them, "Is a lamp brought 31
24 he said to them, "Take heed what you hear 31
26 he said, "The kingdom of God 31
30 he said, "With what can we compare 31
35 On that day, when evening had come, he said to them 31
38 they woke him and said to him 31
39 he awoke and rebuked the wind, and said to the sea 24
40 He said to them, "Why are you afraid? 24
41 and said to one another, "Who then is this 31
5: 7 crying out with a loud voice, he said 31
8 For he had said to him, "Come out of the man 31
19 he refused, and said to him 31
23 besought him, saying, "My little daughter 31
28 For she said, "If I touch even his garments 31
30 immediately turned about in the crowd, and said 31
31 his disciples said to him, "You see the crowd 31
31 yet you say, 'Who touched me?' 31
34 he said to her, "Daughter 24
35 from the ruler's house some who said 31
36 But ignoring what they said 32
36 Jesus said to the ruler of the synagogue 31
39 when he had entered, he said to them 31
41 her by the hand he said to her, "Tal'itha cu'mi"; 31
41 which means, "Little girl, I say to you, arise. 31
6: 2 many who heard him were astonished, saying 31
4 Jesus said to them, "A prophet is not without honor 31
10 he said to them, "Where you enter a house, stay there 31
14 Some said, "John the baptizer has been raised 31
15 others said, "It is Eli'jah. 31
15 others said, "It is a prophet 31
16 when Herod heard of it he said 31
18 For John said to Herod, "It is not lawful for you 31
22 and the king said to the girl 24
24 she went out, and said to her mother 24
24 she said, "The head of John the baptizer. 24
25 asked, saying, "I want you to give me at once the head 31
31 he said to them, "Come away by yourselves 31
35 it grew late, his disciples came to him and said 31
37 they said to him, "Shall we go and buy 31
38 he said to them, "How many loaves have you? 31
38 they said, "Five, and two fish. 31
50 But immediately he spoke to them and said 31
7: 6 he said to them, "Well did Isaiah prophesy of you 24
9 he said to them, "You have a fine way of rejecting 31
10 For Moses said, 'Honor your father and your mother'; 24
11 you say, 'If a man tells his father or his mother 31
14 he called the people to him again, and said 31
18 he said to them, "Then are you also 31
20 he said, "What comes out of a man is what defiles 31
27 he said to her, "Let the children first be fed 31
29 he said to her, "For this saying you may go your way 24
34 looking up to heaven, he sighed, and said 31
37 they were astonished beyond measure, saying 31
8: 1 he called his disciples to him, and said to them 31
5 They said, "Seven. 24
12 he sighed deeply in his spirit, and said 31
12 Truly, I say to you, no sign shall be given 31
15 he cautioned them, saying, "Take heed 31
16 they discussed it with one another, saying 35
17 being aware of it, Jesus said to them 31
19 They said to him, "Twelve. 31
20 they said to him, "Seven. 31
21 he said to them, "Do you not yet understand? 31
24 he looked up and said, "I see men 31
26 he sent him away to his home, saying 31
27 he asked his disciples, "Who do men say that I am? 31
28 others say, Eli'jah; and others one of the prophets •
29 he asked them, "But who do you say that I am? 31
32 he said this plainly 29
33 seeing his disciples, he rebuked Peter, and said 31
34 said to them, "If any man would come after me 24
9: 1 he said to them, "Truly, I say to you 31

1 he said to them, "Truly, I say to you 31
5 Peter said to Jesus, "Master, it is well 31
6 For he did not know what to say 21
11 they asked him, "Why do the scribes say 31
12 he said to them, "Eli'jah does come first to restore 39
21 he said, "From childhood. 24
23 Jesus said to him, "If you can! 24
24 cried out and said, "I believe; help my unbelief! 31
25 he rebuked the unclean spirit, saying to it 31
26 so that most of them said, "He is dead. 31
29 he said to them, "This kind cannot be driven out 24
31 for he was teaching his disciples, saying to them 31
35 he . . called the twelve; and he said to them 31
36 taking him in his arms, he said to them 24
38 John said to him, "Teacher, we saw a man 39
39 Jesus said, "Do not forbid him 24
41 truly, I say to you, whoever gives you a cup of water 31
10: 4 They said, "Moses allowed a man 24
5 Jesus said to them, "For your hardness of heart 24
11 he said to them, "Whoever divorces his wife 31
14 he was indignant, and said to them 24
15 Truly, I say to you, whoever does not receive 31
18 Jesus said to him, "Why do you call me good? 24
20 he said to him, "Teacher, all these I have observed 39
21 Jesus looking upon him loved him, and said to him 24
23 Jesus looked around and said to his disciples 31
24 Jesus said to them again 31
26 they were exceedingly astonished, and said 31
27 Jesus looked at them and said 31
28 Peter began to say to him, "Lo, we have left 31
29 Jesus said, "Truly, I say to you, there is no one 39
29 Jesus said, "Truly, I say to you, there is no one 31
33 saying, "Behold, we are going up to Jerusalem; 35
35 came forward to him, and said to him, "Teacher 31
36 he said to them, "What do you want me to do for you? 24
37 they said to him, "Grant us to sit 24
38 Jesus said to them, "You do not know 24
39 they said to him, "We are able. 24
39 Jesus said to them, "The cup that I drink 24
42 Jesus called them to him and said to them 31
47 he began to cry out and say, "Jesus, Son of David 31
49 Jesus stopped and said, "Call him. 24
49 saying to him, "Take heart; rise, he is calling you. 31
51 Jesus said to him, "What do you want me to do 24
51 the blind man said to him, "Master 24
52 Jesus said to him, "Go your way 24
11: 2 said to them, "Go into the village opposite you 31
3 If any one says to you, 'Why are you doing this?' 31
3 say, 'The Lord has need of it 24
5 those who stood there said to them 31
6 they told them what Jesus had said 24
14 he said to it, "May no one ever eat fruit from you 24
17 he taught, and said to them, "Is it not written 31
21 Peter remembered and said to him, "Master, look! 31
23 Truly, I say to you, whoever says to this mountain 31
23 Truly, I say to you, whoever says to this mountain 31
23 believes that what he says will come to pass 29
28 they said to him, "By what authority 31
29 Jesus said to them, "I will ask you a question; 24
31 If we say, 'From heaven,' he will say 24
31 he will say, 'Why then did you not believe him? 24
32 But shall we say, 'From men'? 24
33 Jesus said to them, "Neither will I tell you 31
12: 6 finally he sent him to them, saying 31
7 those tenants said to one another 24
14 they came and said to him, "Teacher 31
15 knowing their hypocrisy, he said to them 24
16 he said to them, "Whose likeness and inscription 31
16 They said to him, "Caesar's. 24
17 Jesus said to them, "Render to Caesar the things 24
18 who say that there is no resurrection 29
18 they asked him a question, saying 31
24 Jesus said to them, "Is not this why you are wrong 39
26 how God said to him, 'I am the God of Abraham 24
32 the scribe said to him, "You are right, Teacher 24
32 you have truly said that he is one 24
34 he said to him, "You are not far from the kingdom 24
35 as Jesus taught in the temple, he said 31
35 How can the scribes say that the Christ is the son 31
36 The Lord said to my Lord, Sit at my right hand 24
38 in his teaching he said, "Beware of the scribes 31
43 said to them, "Truly, I say to you 24
43 said to them, "Truly, I say to you 31
13: 1 one of his disciples said to him, "Look, Teacher 31
2 Jesus said to him, "Do you see 24
5 Jesus began to say to them, "Take heed 31
6 Many will come in my name, saying, 'I am he!' 31
11 not be anxious beforehand what you are to say 29
11 say whatever is given you in that hour 29
21 then if any one says to you, 'Look, here is the Christ!' 31
30 Truly, I say to you, this generation will not pass 31
37 what I say to you I say to all: Watch. 31
37 what I say to you I say to all: Watch. 31
14: 2 for they said, "Not during the feast 31
4 there were some who said to themselves indignantly •
6 Jesus said, "Let her alone; why do you trouble her? 24
9 truly, I say to you, wherever the gospel 31
12 his disciples said to him, "Where will you have us 31
13 he sent two of his disciples, and said to them, "Go 31

14 wherever he enters, say to the householder 24
14 'The Teacher says, Where is my guest room 31
18 as they were at table eating, Jesus said 24
18 Truly, I say to you, one of you will betray me 31
19 to say to him one after another, "Is it I? 31
20 He said to them, "It is one of the twelve 24
22 broke it, and gave it to them, and said, "Take 24
24 he said to them, "This is my blood of the covenant 24
25 Truly, I say to you, I shall not drink again 31
27 Jesus said to them, "You will all fall away 31
29 Peter said to him, "Even though they all fall away 39
30 Jesus said to him, "Truly, I say to you 31
30 Jesus said to him, "Truly, I say to you 31
31 he said vehemently, "If I must die with you 29
31 they all said the same. 31
32 he said to his disciples, "Sit here, while I pray. 31
34 he said to them, "My soul is very sorrowful 31
36 he said, "Abba, Father, all things are possible 31
37 he said to Peter, "Simon, are you asleep? 31
39 went away and prayed, saying the same words. 31
41 he came the third time, and said to them 31
44 Now the betrayer had given them a sign, saying 31
45 he went up to him at once, and said, "Master! 31
48 Jesus said to them, "Have you come out 24
57 bore false witness against him, saying 31
58 We heard him say, 'I will destroy this temple 31
62 Jesus said, "I am; and you will see the Son of man 24
63 the high priest tore his garments, and said 31
65 to strike him, saying to him, "Prophesy! 31
67 said, "You also were with the Nazarene, Jesus. 31
68 he denied it, saying, "I neither know 31
69 began again to say to the bystanders 31
70 again the bystanders said to Peter 31
72 Peter remembered how Jesus had said to him 24
15: 2 he answered him, "You have said so. 31
12 Pilate again said to them, "Then what shall I do 31
14 Pilate said to them, "Why, what evil has he done? 31
29 wagging their heads, and saying, "Aha! 31
31 saying, "He saved others; he cannot save himself. 31
35 some of the bystanders hearing it said, "Behold 31
36 gave it to him to drink, saying, "Wait 31
39 he said, "Truly this man was the Son of God! 24
16: 3 And they were saying to one another 31
6 And he said to them, "Do not be amazed 31
8 they said nothing to any one, for they were afraid. 24
15 he said to them, "Go into all the world and preach 24
Lke 1:13 the angel said to him, "Do not be afraid, Zechari'ah 24
18 Zechari'ah said to the angel, "How shall I know this? 24
24 for five months she hid herself, saying 31
28 he came to her and said, "Hail, O favored one 24
30 the angel said to her, "Do not be afraid, Mary 24
34 Mary said to the angel, "How shall this be 24
35 the angel said to her, "The Holy Spirit will come 24
38 Mary said, "Behold, I am the handmaid of the Lord 24
46 Mary said, "My soul magnifies the Lord 24
60 his mother said, "Not so, he shall be called John. 24
61 they said to her, "None of your kindred is called 24
66 saying, "What then will this child be? 31
67 prophesied, saying 31
2:10 the angel said to them, "Be not afraid 24
13 praising God and saying 31
15 the shepherds said to one another, "Let us go over 29
24 according to what is said in the law of the Lord 24
28 he took him up in his arms and blessed God and said 24
33 marveled at what was said about him; 29
34 Simeon blessed them and said to Mary his mother 24
48 his mother said to him, "Son, why have you treated us 24
49 he said to them, "How is it that you sought me? 24
3: 7 He said therefore to the multitudes 31
8 do not begin to say to yourselves 31
12 Tax collectors also came to be baptized, and said 24
13 he said to them, "Collect no more than is appointed 24
14 he said to them, "Rob no one by violence 24
4: 3 The devil said to him, "If you are the Son of God 24
6 said to him, "To you I will give all this authority 24
9 said to him, "If you are the Son of God 24
12 Jesus answered him, "It is said, 'You shall not tempt 24
21 he began to say to them, "Today this scripture 31
22 they said, "Is not this Joseph's son? 31
23 he said to them, "Doubtless you will quote to me 24
24 he said, "Truly, I say to you 24
24 he said, "Truly, I say to you 31
35 Jesus rebuked him, saying, "Be silent 31
36 they were all amazed and said to one another 38
43 he said to them, "I must preach the good news 24
5: 4 when he had ceased speaking, he said to Simon 24
8 he fell down at Jesus' knees, saying 31
10 Jesus said to Simon, "Do not be afraid 24
13 he stretched out his hand, and touched him, saying 31
20 when he saw their faith he said 24
21 Pharisees began to question, saying, "Who is this 31
23 Which is easier, to say, 'Your sins are forgiven you,' 31
23 or to say, 'Rise and walk'? 31
24 he said to the man who was paralyzed-"I say to you 24
24 he said to the man who was paralyzed-"I say to you 31
26 saying, "We have seen strange things today. 31
27 he said to him, "Follow me. 24
30 saying, "Why do you eat and drink 31
33 they said to him, "The disciples of John fast often 24
34 Jesus said to them, "Can you make wedding guests 24
39 for he says, 'The old is good.' 31
6: 2 some of the Pharisees said, "Why are you doing 24
5 he said to them, "The Son of man is lord 31
8 he said to the man who had the withered hand 24
9 Jesus said to them, "I ask you 24
10 said to him, "Stretch out your hand. 24
20 and said: "Blessed are you poor 31
27 I say to you that hear, Love your enemies 31
42 how can you say to your brother, 'Brother 31
7: 4 they besought him earnestly, saying, "He is worthy 31
6 the centurion sent friends to him, saying to him 31
7 But say the word, and let my servant be healed. 24
8 I say to one, 'Go,' and he goes 31
9 turned and said to the multitude that followed 24
13 compassion on her and said to her, "Do not weep. 24
14 he said, "Young man, I say to you, arise. 24
14 he said, "Young man, I say to you, arise. 31
16 they glorified God, saying, "A great prophet 31
19 sent them to the Lord, saying, "Are you he 31
20 when the men had come to him, they said 24
20 John the Baptist has sent us to you, saying 31
33 and you say, 'He has a demon.' 31
34 and you say, 'Behold, a glutton and a drunkard 31
39 he said to himself, "If this man were a prophet 24
40 Jesus answering said to him, "Simon 24
40 Simon, I have something to say to you. 31
43 he said to him "You have judged rightly. 24
44 Then turning toward the woman he said to Simon 39
48 he said to her, "Your sins are forgiven. 24
49 began to say among themselves 31
50 he said to the woman, "Your faith has saved you 24
8: 4 he said in a parable 24
8 As he said this, he called out, "He who has ears 31
10 he said, "To you it has been given to know 24
21 he said to them, "My mother and my brothers 24
22 he said to them, "Let us go across to the other side 24
24 they went and woke him, saying, "Master, Master 31
25 He said to them, "Where is your faith? 24
25 they marveled, saying to one another 31
28 fell down before him, and said with a loud voice 24
30 And he said, "Legion 24
38 he sent him away, saying 31
45 Jesus said, "Who was it that touched me? 24
45 When all denied it, Peter said, "Master 24
46 Jesus said, "Some one touched me 24
48 he said to her, "Daughter 24
49 a man from the ruler's house came and said 31
52 he said, "Do not weep 24
54 taking her by the hand he called, saying, "Child 31
9: 3 he said to them, "Take nothing for your journey 24
7 it was said by some that John had been raised 31
9 Herod said, "John I beheaded 24
12 the twelve came and said to him 24
13 he said to them, "You give them something to eat. 24
13 They said, "We have no more than five loaves 24
14 he said to his disciples, "Make them sit down 24
18 he asked them, "Who do the people say that I am? 31
19 others say, Eli'jah *
20 he said to them, "But who do you say that I am? 24
20 he said to them, "But who do you say that I am? 31
22 saying, "The Son of man must suffer many things 31
23 he said to all, "If any man would come after me 31
33 Peter said to Jesus, "Master, it is well 24
33 not knowing what he said. 31
34 As he said this, a cloud came 31
35 a voice came out of the cloud, saying, "This is my Son 31
43 he said to his disciples 24
48 said to them, "Whoever receives this child 24
50 Jesus said to him, "Do not forbid him 24
54 they said, "Lord, do you want us to bid fire come down 24
57 As they were going along the road, a man said to him 24
58 Jesus said to him, "Foxes have holes 24
59 To another he said, "Follow me. 24
59 he said, "Lord, let me first go and bury my father. 24
60 he said to him, "Leave the dead 24
61 Another said, "I will follow you, Lord 24
62 Jesus said to him, "No one 24
10: 2 he said to them, "The harvest is plentiful 31
5 Whatever house you enter, first say, 'Peace 31
9 heal the sick in it and say to them 31
10 go into its streets and say 24
17 The 70 returned with joy, saying, "Lord 31
18 he said to them, "I saw Satan fall like lightning 24
21 rejoiced in the Holy Spirit and said, "I thank thee 24
23 Then turning to the disciples he said privately 24
25 a lawyer stood up to put him to the test, saying 31
26 He said to him, "What is written in the law? 24
28 he said to him, "You have answered right 24
29 he, desiring to justify himself, said to Jesus 24
35 gave them to the innkeeper, saying 24
37 He said, "The one who showed mercy on him. 24
37 Jesus said to him "Go and do likewise. 24
40 she went to him and said, "Lord, do you not care 24
11: 1 when he ceased, one of his disciples said to him 24
2 he said to them, "When you pray, say: "Father 24
2 he said to them, "When you pray, say: "Father 31
5 he said to them, "Which of you who has a friend 24
5 go to him at midnight and say to him, 'Friend 31
15 some of them said, "He casts out demons 24
17 he, knowing their thoughts, said to them 24
18 you say that I cast out demons by Be-el'zebul. 31
24 finding none he says, 'I will return to my house 31
27 As he said this 31
27 a woman in the crowd raised her voice and said 24
28 he said, "Blessed rather are those who hear 24
29 When the crowds were increasing, he began to say 31
39 the Lord said to him, "Now you Pharisees cleanse 24
45 Teacher, in saying this you reproach us also. 31
46 he said, "Woe to you lawyers also! 24
49 the Wisdom of God said, 'I will send them prophets 24
54 to catch at something he might say. 27
12: 1 he began to say to his disciples first 31
3 whatever you have said in the dark shall be heard 24
11 what you are to answer or what you are to say; 24
12 what you ought to say. 31
13 One of the multitude said to him, "Teacher 24
14 he said to him, "Man, who made me a judge or divider 24
15 he said to them, "Take heed 24
16 he told them a parable, saying, "The land 31
18 he said, 'I will do this: I will pull down my barns 24
19 I will say to my soul, Soul, you have ample goods 24
20 God said to him, 'Fool! 24
22 he said to his disciples, "Therefore I tell you 24
37 truly, I say to you, he will gird himself 31
41 Peter said, "Lord, are you telling this parable 24
42 the Lord said, "Who then is the faithful and wise 24
44 Truly, I say to you, he will set him over all 31
45 if that servant says to himself 31
54 He also said to the multitudes 31
54 you say at once, 'A shower is coming' 31
55 when you see the south wind blowing, you say 31
13: 7 he said to the vinedresser, 'Lo, these three years 24
12 when Jesus saw her, he called her and said to her 24
14 ruler of the synagogue . . said to the people 31
17 As he said this 31
18 He said therefore, "What is the kingdom of God like? 31
20 again he said, "To what shall I compare the kingdom 24
23 some one said to him, "Lord 24
23 And he said to them 24
25 to knock at the door, saying, 'Lord, open to us.' 31
26 Then you will begin to say, 'We ate and drank 31
27 he will say, 'I tell you, I do not know 24
31 At that very hour some Pharisees came, and said 31
32 he said to them, "Go and tell that fox, 'Behold 24
35 I tell you, you will not see me until you say 24
14: 3 Jesus spoke to the lawyers and Pharisees, saying 31
5 he said to them, "Which of you, having a son or an ox 24
7 he told a parable . . saying to them 31
9 he who invited you both will come and say to you 24
10 so that when your host comes he may say to you 24
12 He said also to the man who had invited him 31
15 he said to him, "Blessed is he who shall eat bread 24
16 he said to him "A man once gave a great banquet 24
17 to say to those who had been invited, 'Come 31
18 The first said to him, 'I have bought a field 24
19 another said, 'I have bought five yoke of oxen 24
20 another said, 'I have married a wife 24
21 the householder in anger said to his servant 24
22 the servant said, 'Sir 24
23 the master said to the servant, 'Go out 24
25 he turned and said to them 24
30 saying, 'This man began to build 31
15: 2 the Pharisees and the scribes murmured, saying 31
6 saying to them, 'Rejoice with me 31
9 saying, 'Rejoice with me 31
11 he said, "There was a man who had two sons; 24
12 the younger of them said to his father, 'Father 24
17 when he came to himself he said 39
18 I will say to him, "Father, I have sinned 24
21 the son said to him, 'Father, I have sinned 24
22 the father said to his servants 24
27 he said to him, 'Your brother has come 24
31 he said to him, 'Son, you are always with me 24
16: 1 He also said to the disciples, "There was a rich man 31
2 he called him and said to him, 'What is this 24
3 the steward said to himself, 'What shall I do 24
5 he said to the first, 'How much . . owe my master?' 31
6 He said, 'A 100 measures of oil.' 24
6 he said to him, 'Take your bill 24
7 Then he said to another, 'And how much do you owe?' 24
7 Then he said to another, 'And how much do you owe?' 24
7 He said to him, 'Take your bill, and write 80.' 24
15 he said to them, "You are those who justify 24
25 Abraham said, 'Son, remember 24
27 he said, 'Then I beg you, father 24
29 Abraham said, 'They have Moses and the prophets; 31
30 he said, 'No, father Abraham 24
31 He said to him, 'If they do not hear Moses 24
17: 1 he said to his disciples, "Temptations to sin 24
4 turns to you seven times, and says, 'I repent,' 31
5 The apostles said to the Lord, "Increase our faith! 24
6 the Lord said, "If you had faith 24
6 you could say to this sycamine tree 31
7 say to him when he has come in from the field 24
8 Will he not rather say to him, 'Prepare supper 24
10 say, 'We are unworthy servants 31
13 lifted up their voices and said, "Jesus, Master 31

14 When he saw them he said to them, "Go 24
17 Then said Jesus, "Were not ten cleansed? 24
19 he said to him, "Rise and go your way 24
21 nor will they say, 'Lo, here it is!' or 'There!' 24
22 he said to the disciples, "The days are coming 24
23 they will say to you, 'Lo, there!' or 'Lo, here!' 24
37 they said to him, "Where, Lord? 31
37 He said to them, "Where the body is, there the eagles 24
18: 2 He said, "In a certain city there was a judge 31
3 saying, 'Vindicate me against my adversary.' 31
4 afterward he said to himself 24
6 the Lord said, "Hear 24
6 Hear what the unrighteous judge says. 31
13 beat his breast, saying, 'God, be merciful to me 31
16 Jesus called them to him, saying 31
17 Truly, I say to you, whoever does not receive 31
19 Jesus said to him, "Why do you call me good? 24
21 he said, "All these I have observed from my youth. 24
22 when Jesus heard it, he said to him, "One thing 24
24 Jesus looking at him said, "How hard it is for those 24
26 Those who heard it said, "Then who can be saved? 24
27 he said, "What is impossible with men 24
28 Peter said, "Lo, we have left our homes 24
29 he said to them, "Truly, I say to you, there is no man 24
29 he said to them, "Truly, I say to you, there is no man 31
31 taking the twelve, he said to them, "Behold 24
34 they did not grasp what was said. 31
41 He said, "Lord, let me receive my sight. 24
42 Jesus said to him, "Receive your sight 24
19: 5 when Jesus came to the place, he looked up and said 24
8 Zacchae'us stood and said to the Lord, "Behold 24
9 Jesus said to him, "Today salvation has come 24
12 He said therefore, "A nobleman went 24
13 said to them, 'Trade with these till I come.' 24
14 sent an embassy after him, saying, 'We do not want 31
16 The first came before him, saying, 'Lord 31
17 he said to him, 'Well done, good servant! 24
18 the second came, saying, 'Lord 31
19 he said . . 'And you are to be over five cities.' 24
20 Then another came, saying 31
22 He said to him, 'I will condemn you 31
24 he said to those who stood by, 'Take the pound 24
25 they said to him, 'Lord, he has ten pounds!') 24
28 when he had said this, he went on ahead 31
30 saying, "Go into the village opposite 31
31 you shall say this, 'The Lord has need of it.' 24
33 as they were untying the colt, its owners said 24
34 they said, "The Lord has need of it. 24
38 saying, "Blessed is the King who comes 31
39 some of the Pharisees in the multitude said 24
42 saying, "Would that even today you knew the things 31
46 saying to them, "It is written 31
20: 2 said to him, "Tell us 24
5 they discussed it with one another, saying 31
5 If we say, 'From heaven,' he will say 31
5 he will say, 'Why did you not believe him?' 24
6 if we say, 'From men,' all the people will stone us 24
8 Jesus said to them, "Neither will I tell you 24
13 the owner of the vineyard said, 'What shall I do? 24
14 when the tenants saw him, they said to themselves 23
16 When they heard this, they said, "God forbid! 24
17 he looked at them and said, "What then is this 24
20 that they might take hold of what he said 32
23 he perceived their craftiness, and said to them 24
24 They said, "Caesar's. 24
25 He said to them, "Then render to Caesar the things 24
26 to catch him by what he said 37
27 those who say that there is no resurrection 19
28 they asked him a question, saying, "Teacher 31
34 Jesus said to them, "The sons of this age marry 24
41 he said to them, "How can they say 24
41 How can they say that the Christ is David's son? 31
42 For David himself says in the Book of Psalms 31
42 The Lord said to my Lord, Sit at my right hand 24
45 he said to his disciples 24
21: 3 he said, "Truly I tell you 24
5 as some spoke of the temple . . he said 24
8 he said, "Take heed that you are not led astray 24
8 many will come in my name, saying, 'I am he!' 31
10 he said to them, "Nation will rise against nation 31
32 Truly, I say to you, this generation will not pass 31
22: 8 So Jesus sent Peter and John, saying, "Go 31
9 They said to him, "Where will you have us prepare it? 24
10 He said to them, "Behold 24
11 tell the householder, 'The Teacher says to you 31
15 he said to them, "I have earnestly desired to eat 24
17 he took a cup, and when he had given thanks he said 24
19 gave it to them, saying, "This is my body 31
20 likewise the cup after supper, saying, "This cup 31
25 he said to them, "The kings of the Gentiles 24
33 he said to him, "Lord, I am ready to go with you 24
34 He said, "I tell you, Peter, the cock will not crow 24
35 he said to them, "When I sent you out with no purse 24
35 did you lack anything?" They said, "Nothing. 24
36 He said to them, "But now 24
38 they said, "Look, Lord, here are two swords. 24
38 he said to them, "It is enough. 24
40 when he came to the place he said to them, "Pray 24
46 he said to them, "Why do you sleep? 24
48 Jesus said to him, "Judas 24
49 when those . . saw what would follow, they said 24
51 Jesus said, "No more of this! 24
52 Then Jesus said to the chief priests 24
56 Then a maid . . said, "This man also was with him. 24
57 he denied it, saying, "Woman, I do not know him. 31
58 a little later some one else saw him and said 39
58 Peter said, "Man, I am not. 39
59 still another insisted, saying, "Certainly 31
60 Peter said, "Man, I do not know what you are saying. 24
60 Peter said, "Man, I do not know what you are saying. 31
61 how he had said to him, "Before the cock crows today 24
66 they led him away to their council, and they said 31
67 he said to them, "If I tell you, you will not believe; 24
70 they all said, "Are you the Son of God, then? 24
70 he said to them, "You say that I am. 39
70 he said to them, "You say that I am. 31
71 they said, "What further testimony do we need? 24
23: 2 they began to accuse him, saying, "We found this man 31
2 saying that he himself is Christ a king. 31
3 he answered him, "You have said so. 31
4 Pilate said to the chief priests 24
5 they were urgent, saying, "He stirs up the people 31
14 said to them, "You brought me this man 24
22 A third time he said to them, "Why 24
28 Jesus turning to them said 24
29 For behold, the days are coming when they will say 24
30 they will begin to say to the mountains, 'Fall on us'; 31
34 Jesus said, "Father, forgive them 31
35 the rulers scoffed at him, saying, "He saved others; 31
37 saying, "If you are the King of the Jews 31
39 saying, "Are you not the Christ? Save yourself and us! 31
40 the other rebuked him, saying, "Do you not fear God 39
42 he said, "Jesus, remember me 31
43 he said to him, "Truly, I say to you 24
43 he said to him, "Truly, I say to you 31
46 Then Jesus, crying with a loud voice, said, "Father 24
46 having said this he breathed his last. 31
47 he praised God, and said 31
24: 5 the men said to them, "Why do you seek the living 24
17 he said to them, "What is this conversation 24
19 he said to him, "What things? 24
19 they said to him, "Concerning Jesus of Nazareth 24
23 came back saying that they had even seen a vision 31
23 a vision of angels, who said that he was alive. 31
24 and found it just as the women had said 24
25 he said to them, "O foolish men, and slow of heart 24
29 they constrained him, saying, "Stay with us 31
32 They said to each other, "Did not our hearts burn 24
34 who said, "The Lord has risen indeed 31
36 As they were saying this 29
38 he said to them, "Why are you troubled 24
41 he said to them, "Have you anything here to eat? 24
44 Then he said to them, "These are my words 24
46 said to them, "Thus it is written 24
Joh 1:15 This was he of whom I said, 'He who comes after me 31
21 Are you Elijah?" He said, "I am not. 31
22 They said to him then, "Who are you? 24
22 What do you say about yourself? 31
23 He said, "I am the voice of one crying 39
23 'Make straight . . ' as the prophet Isaiah said. 24
29 and said, "Behold, the Lamb of God 31
30 This is he of whom I said, 'After me comes a man 24
33 but he who sent me to baptize with water said to me 24
36 and he looked at Jesus as he walked, and said 31
37 The two disciples heard him say this 29
38 Jesus turned . . and said to them, "What do you seek? 31
38 And they said to him, "Rabbi" (which means Teacher) 24
39 He said to them, "Come and see." They came and saw 31
41 He first found his brother Simon, and said to him 31
42 Jesus looked at him, and said, "So you are Simon 24
43 And he found Philip and said to him, "Follow me. 31
45 Philip found Nathan'a-el, and said to him 31
46 Nathan'a-el said to him, "Can anything good come out 24
46 Philip said to him, "Come and see. 24
47 Jesus saw Nathan'a-el coming to him, and said of him 31
48 Nathan'a-el said to him, "How do you know me? 31
50 Because I said to you, I saw you under the fig tree 24
51 And he said to him, "Truly, truly, I say to you 31
51 truly, I say to you, you will see heaven opened 31
2: 3 When the wine failed, the mother of Jesus said 31
4 Jesus said to her, "O woman 31
5 His mother said to the servants 31
7 Jesus said to them, "Fill the jars with water. 31
8 He said to them, "Now draw some out 31
10 said to him, "Every man serves the good wine first; 31
18 The Jews then said to him, "What sign have you 24
20 The Jews then said, "It has taken 46 years to build 24
22 his disciples remembered that he had said this; 31
3: 2 This man came to Jesus by night and said to him 24
3 Jesus answered him, "Truly, truly, I say to you 31
4 Nicode'mus said to him, "How can a man be born 31
5 Jesus answered, "Truly, truly, I say to you 31
7 Do not marvel that I said to you 24
9 Nicode'mus said to him, "How can this be? 24
11 Truly, truly, I say to you, we speak of what we know 31
26 And they came to John, and said to him, "Rabbi 24
28 You yourselves bear me witness, that I said 24
4: 7 Jesus said to her, "Give me a drink. 31
9 The Samaritan woman said to him, "How is it that you 31
10 who it is that is saying to you, 'Give me a drink,' 31
11 The woman said to him, "Sir, you have nothing 31
13 Jesus said to her, "Every one who drinks 24
15 The woman said to him, "Sir, give me this water 31
16 Jesus said to her, "Go, call your husband 31
17 Jesus said to her, "You are right in saying 24
17 You are right in saying, 'I have no husband'; 24
18 this you said truly. 24
19 The woman said to him, "Sir, I perceive 31
20 and you say that in Jerusalem is the place 31
21 Jesus said to her, "Woman, believe me 31
25 The woman said to him, "I know that Messiah 31
26 Jesus said to her, "I who speak to you am he. 31
27 but none said, "What do you wish? 24
28 went away into the city, and said to the people 31
31 the disciples besought him, saying, "Rabbi, eat. 31
32 But he said to them, "I have food to eat 24
33 So the disciples said to one another 31
34 Jesus said to them, "My food is to do the will of him 31
35 Do you not say, 'There are yet four months 31
42 They said to the woman, "It is no longer 31
48 Jesus therefore said to him, "Unless you see signs 24
49 The official said to him, "Sir, come down 31
50 Jesus said to him, "Go; your son will live. 31
52 they said to him, "Yesterday at the seventh hour 24
53 knew that was the hour when Jesus had said to him 24
5: 6 he said to him, "Do you want to be healed? 31
8 Jesus said to him, "Rise, take up your pallet 31
10 the Jews said to the man who was cured 31
11 answered them, "The man who healed me said to me 24
12 They asked him, "Who is the man who said to you 31
14 Afterward, Jesus found him in the temple, and said 24
19 Jesus said to them, "Truly, truly, I say to you 31
19 Jesus said to them, "Truly, truly, I say to you 31
24 Truly, truly, I say to you 31
25 Truly, truly, I say to you, the hour is coming 31
34 I say this that you may be saved. 31
6: 5 Jesus said to Philip, "How are we to buy bread 31
6 This he said to test him 31
8 Andrew, Simon Peter's brother, said to him 31
10 Jesus said, "Make the people sit down. 24
14 they said, "This is indeed the prophet 31
20 he said to them, "It is I; do not be afraid. 31
25 they said to him, "Rabbi, when did you come here? 24
26 Jesus answered them, "Truly, truly, I say to you 31
28 they said to him, "What must we do 24
30 they said to him, "Then what sign do you do 24
32 Jesus then said to them, "Truly, truly, I say to you 24
32 Jesus then said to them, "Truly, truly, I say to you 31
34 They said to him, "Lord, give us this bread always. 24
35 Jesus said to them, "I am the bread of life 24
36 I said to you that you have seen me 24
41 because he said, "I am the bread 24
42 They said, "Is not this Jesus, the son of Joseph 31
42 does he now say, 'I have come down from heaven'? 31
47 Truly, truly, I say to you 31
52 The Jews then disputed among themselves, saying 31
53 Jesus said to them, "Truly, truly, I say to you 31
53 Jesus said to them, "Truly, truly, I say to you 31
59 This he said in the synagogue 24
60 Many of his disciples, when they heard it, said 24
61 Jesus . . said to them, "Do you take offense at this? 24
65 he said, "This is why I told you 31
67 Jesus said to the twelve 24
7: 3 his brothers said to him, "Leave here 24
6 Jesus said to them, "My time has not yet come 31
9 So saying, he remained in Galilee. 31
11 The Jews were . . saying, "Where is he? 31
12 While some said, "He is a good man 31
12 others said, "No, he is leading the people astray. 31
15 The Jews marveled at it, saying, "How is it 31
25 Some of the people of Jerusalem therefore said 31
26 here he is, speaking openly, and they say nothing 31
31 Yet many of the people believed in him; they said 31
33 Jesus then said, "I shall be with you 24
35 The Jews said to one another 24
36 What does he mean by saying, 'You will seek me 24
38 He who believes in me, as the scripture has said 24
39 Now this he said about the Spirit 24
40 some of the people said 31
41 Others said, "This is the Christ. 31
41 But some said, "Is the Christ to come from Galilee? 31
42 Has not the scripture said 24
45 who said to them, "Why did you not bring him? 24
50 Nicode'mus . . who was one of them, said to them 31
8: 4 they said to him, "Teacher 31
5 What do you say about her? 31
6 This they said to test him 31
7 he stood up and said to them 24
10 Jesus looked up and said to her, "Woman 24
11 She said, "No one, Lord. 24
11 Jesus said, "Neither do I condemn you 24
12 Again Jesus spoke to them, saying, "I am the light 31
13 The Pharisees then said to him 24
19 They said to him therefore, "Where is your Father? 31
21 he said to them, "I go away, and you will seek me 24
22 Then said the Jews, "Will he kill himself 31
22 since he says, 'Where I am going, you cannot come'? 31

23 He said to them, "You are from below, 31
25 They said to him, "Who are you? 31
25 Jesus said to them, "Even what I have told you 24
26 I have much to say about you and much to judge 29
28 Jesus said, "When you have lifted up the Son of man 24
31 Jesus then said to the Jews who had believed 31
33 How is it that you say, 'You will be made free'? 31
34 Jesus answered them, "Truly, truly, I say to you 31
39 Jesus said to them, "If you were Abraham's children 31
41 They said to him, "We were not born of fornication 24
42 Jesus said to them, "If God were your Father 24
43 Why do you not understand what I say? 30
48 The Jews answered him, "Are we not right in saying 31
51 Truly, truly, I say to you, if any one keeps my word 31
52 The Jews said to him, "Now we know 24
52 and you say, 'If any one keeps my word 31
54 of whom you say that he is your God. 31
55 If I said, I do not know him, I should be a liar 24
57 The Jews then said to him 24
58 Jesus said to them, "Truly, truly, I say to you 24
58 Jesus said to them, "Truly, truly, I say to you 31
9: 6 As he said this, he spat on the ground 31
7 saying to him, "Go, wash in the pool of Silo'am 24
8 those who had seen him before as a beggar, said 31
9 Some said, "It is he 31
9 others said, "No, but he is like him. 31
9 He said, "I am the man. 31
10 They said to him, "Then how were your eyes opened? 31
11 made clay and anointed my eyes and said to me 24
12 They said . . "Where is he?" He said, "I do not know 24
12 They said . . "Where is he?" He said, "I do not know 31
15 he said to them, "He put clay on my eyes, 24
16 Some of the Pharisees said 31
16 others said, "How can a man who is a sinner 31
17 they again said to the blind man 31
17 What do you say about him 31
17 He said, "He is a prophet. 24
19 Is this your son, who you say was born blind? 31
22 His parents said this 24
23 Therefore his parents said, "He is of age, ask him. 24
24 they called the man . . and said to him 24
26 They said to him, "What did he do to you? 24
28 they reviled him, saying, "You are his disciple 24
35 having found him he said 24
37 Jesus said to him, "You have seen him 24
38 He said, "Lord, I believe"; and he worshiped him. 39
39 Jesus said, "For judgment I came into this world 24
40 the Pharisees near him heard this, and they said 24
41 Jesus said to them, "If you were blind 24
41 now that you say, 'We see,' your guilt remains. 31
10: 1 Truly, truly, I say to you 31
6 they did not understand what he was saying 29
7 Jesus again said to them, "Truly, truly, I say to you 24
7 Jesus again said to them, "Truly, truly, I say to you 31
20 Many of them said, "He has a demon, and he is mad 31
21 Others said, "These are not the sayings 31
24 the Jews gathered round him and said to him 31
34 'I said, you are gods'? 24
36 do you say of him whom the Father consecrated 31
36 because I said, 'I am the Son of God'? 24
41 many came to him; and they said, "John did no sign 31
41 everything . . John said about this man was true 24
11: 3 the sisters sent to him, saying 31
4 when Jesus heard it he said 24
7 Then after this he said to the disciples 31
8 The disciples said to him, "Rabbi 31
11 Thus he spoke, and then he said to them 24
12 The disciples said to him, "Lord 24
16 Thomas . . said to his fellow disciples 31
21 Martha said to Jesus, "Lord if you had been here 24
23 Jesus said to her, "Your brother will rise again. 31
24 Martha said to him, "I know that he will rise again 31
25 Jesus said to her, "I am the resurrection 24
27 She said to him, "Yes, Lord; I believe 31
28 When she said this, she went and called her sister 24
28 went and called her sister Mary, saying quietly 24
32 Mary . . fell at his feet, saying to him, "Lord 31
34 he said, "Where have you laid him? 24
34 They said to him, "Lord, come and see. 31
36 the Jews said, "See how he loved him! 31
37 some of them said, "Could not he 24
39 Jesus said, "Take away the stone. 31
39 Martha, the sister of the dead man, said to him, "Lord 31
40 Jesus said to her, "Did I not tell you 24
41 Jesus lifted up his eyes and said, "Father 24
42 I have said this on account of the people 24
43 When he had said this, he cried with a loud voice 31
44 Jesus said to them, "Unbind him, and let him go. 31
47 the Pharisees gathered the council, and said 31
49 Ca'iaphas, who was high priest that year, said 24
51 He did not say this of his own accord 24
56 looking for Jesus and saying to one another 31
12: 4 (he who was to betray him), said 31
6 This he said, not that he cared for the poor 24
7 Jesus said, "Let her alone 24
19 The Pharisees then said to one another 24
21 these came to Philip . . and said to him 31
24 Truly, truly I say to you 31
27 Now is my soul troubled. And what shall I say? 24

29 heard it and said that it had thundered 31
29 Others said, "An angel has spoken to him. 31
33 He said this to show by what death he was to die. 31
34 How can you say . . the Son of man must be lifted up? 31
35 Jesus said to them, "The light is with you 24
36 When Jesus had said this 29
39 For Isaiah again said 24
41 Isaiah said this because he saw his glory 24
44 Jesus cried out and said, "He who believes in me 24
49 has himself given me commandment what to say 24
50 What I say, therefore 29
50 I say as the Father has bidden me. 29
13: 6 He came to Simon Peter; and Peter said to him, "Lord 31
8 Peter said to him, "You shall never wash my feet. 31
9 Simon Peter said to him, "Lord, not my feet only 31
10 Jesus said to him, "He who has bathed 31
11 that was why he said, "You are not all clean. 24
12 he said to them, "Do you know what I have done 24
16 Truly, truly, I say to you, a servant is not greater 31
20 Truly, truly, I say to you, he who receives any one 31
21 Truly, truly, I say to you, one of you will betray me. 31
24 Simon Peter beckoned to him and said, "Tell us •
25 lying thus, close to the breast of Jesus, he said 31
27 Jesus said to him, "What you are going to do 31
28 no one at the table knew why he said this to him. 24
31 When he had gone out, Jesus said 31
33 as I said to the Jews so now I say to you 24
33 as I said to the Jews so now I say to you 31
36 Simon Peter said to him, "Lord, where are you going? 31
37 Peter said to him, "Lord, why cannot I follow you 31
38 Truly, truly, I say to you, the cock will not crow 31
14: 5 Thomas said to him, "Lord, we do not know 24
6 Jesus said to him, "I am the way, and the truth 31
8 Philip said to him, "Lord, show us the Father 31
9 Jesus said to him, "Have I been with you so long 31
9 how can you say, 'Show us the Father'? 31
10 The words that I say to you 29
12 Truly, truly, I say to you 31
22 Judas (not Iscariot) said to him, "Lord, how is it 31
26 bring to your remembrance all . . I have said 31
28 You heard me say to you, 'I go away 24
15:20 Remember the word that I said to you 24
16: 1 I have said all this to you 29
4 I have said these things to you 29
4 not say these things to you from the beginning 24
6 because I have said these things to you 29
12 I have yet many things to say to you 31
15 therefore I said that he will take what is mine 24
17 Some of his disciples said to one another 24
17 What is this that he says to us 31
18 They said, "What does he mean by 'a little while'? 31
19 he said to them, "Is this what you are asking 24
19 what I meant by saying, 'A little while . . 24
20 Truly, truly, I say to you 31
23 Truly, truly, I say to you 31
25 I have said this to you in figures 29
26 I do not say to you that I shall pray the Father 31
29 His disciples said, "Ah 31
33 I have said this to you 29
17: 1 he lifted up his eyes to heaven and said 24
18: 4 Jesus . . came forward and said to them 31
5 Jesus said to them, "I am he. 31
6 When he said to them, "I am he 24
7 And they said, "Jesus of Nazareth. 24
11 Jesus said to Peter 24
17 The maid who kept the door said to Peter 31
17 He said, "I am not. 31
20 I have said nothing secretly. 29
21 Ask those who have heard me, what I said to them; 29
21 what I said to them; they know what I said. 24
22 When he had said this 24
22 one of the officers . . struck Jesus . . saying 24
25 They said to him, "Are not you also one 24
25 He denied it and said, "I am not. 24
29 Pilate went out to them and said 39
31 Pilate said to them, "Take him yourselves 24
31 The Jews said to him, "It is not lawful for us 24
33 Pilate . . called Jesus, and said to him 24
34 Jesus answered, "Do you say this of your own accord 31
34 did others say it to you about me? 31
37 Pilate said to him, "So you are a king? 24
37 Jesus answered, "You say that I am a king 31
38 Pilate said to him, "What is truth? 31
38 After he had said this, he went out to the Jews 31
19: 3 they came up to him, saying, "Hail, King of the Jews! 31
4 Pilate went out again, and said to them 31
5 Pilate said to them, "Behold the man! 31
6 Pilate said to them, "Take him yourselves 31
9 he . . said to Jesus, "Where are you from? 31
10 Pilate therefore said to him, "You will not speak 31
14 He said to the Jews, "Behold your King! 31
15 Pilate said to them, "Shall I crucify your King? 31
21 The chief priests of the Jews then said to Pilate 31
21 but 'This man said, I am King of the Jews.' 24
24 they said to one another, "Let us not tear it 24
26 he said to his mother, "Woman, behold, your son! 31
27 Then he said to the disciple, "Behold, your mother! 31
28 Jesus . . said (to fulfil the scripture), "I thirst. 31
30 he said, "It is finished 24

37 again another scripture says 31
20: 2 she ran . . and said to them 31
13 They said to her, "Woman, why are you weeping? 31
13 She said to them 31
14 Saying this, she turned round 24
15 Jesus said to her, "Woman, why are you weeping? 31
15 Supposing him to be the gardener, she said to him 31
16 Jesus said to her, "Mary. 31
16 She turned and said to him in Hebrew, "Rab-bo'ni! 31
17 Jesus said to her, "Do not hold me 31
17 go to my brethren and say to them 24
18 Mary Mag'dalene went and said to the disciples 18
18 she told them that he had said these things 24
19 Jesus came and stood among them and said to them 31
20 When he had said this, he showed them his hands 31
21 Jesus said to them again, "Peace be with you 24
22 when he had said this, he breathed on them, and said 31
22 when he had said this, he breathed on them, and said 31
25 But he said to them, "Unless I see 24
26 stood among them, and said, "Peace be with you. 24
27 Then he said to Thomas, "Put your finger here 31
29 Jesus said to him, "Have you believed 31
21: 3 Simon Peter said to them, "I am going fishing. 31
3 They said to him, "We will go with you. 31
5 Jesus said to them, "Children have you any fish? 31
6 He said to them, "Cast the net on the right side 24
7 That disciple whom Jesus loved said to Peter 31
10 Jesus said to them, "Bring some of the fish 31
12 Jesus said to them, "Come and have breakfast. 31
15 Jesus said to Simon Peter, "Simon, son of John 31
15 He said to him, "Yes, Lord; you know that I love you. 31
15 He said to him, "Feed my lambs. 31
16 A second time he said to him, "Simon, son of John 31
16 He said to him, "Yes, Lord; you know that I love you. 31
16 He said to him, "Tend my sheep. 31
17 He said to him the third time, "Simon, son of John 31
17 because he said to him the third time 24
17 he said to him, "Lord, you know everything 31
17 Jesus said to him, "Feed my sheep. 31
18 Truly, truly, I say to you 31
19 This he said to show 24
19 after this he said to him, "Follow me. 31
20 who . . had said, "Lord 24
21 When Peter saw him, he said to Jesus, "Lord 31
22 Jesus said to him, "If it is my will that he remain 31
23 yet Jesus did not say to him that he was not to die 24
Act 1: 4 which, he said, "you heard from me •
7 He said to them, "It is not for you to know 24
9 when he had said this, as they were looking 31
11 said, "Men of Galilee, why do you stand looking 24
15 Peter stood up . . and said 24
24 they prayed and said, "Lord, who knowest the hearts 24
2: 7 they were amazed and wondered, saying 31
12 were amazed and perplexed, saying to one another 31
13 others mocking said 31
25 David says concerning him, 'I saw the Lord 31
29 I may say to you confidently of the patriarch 31
34 he himself says, 'The Lord said to my Lord 31
34 The Lord said to my Lord, Sit at my right hand 24
37 said to Peter and the rest of the apostles 24
38 Peter said to them, "Repent, and be baptized •
40 exhorted them, saying, "Save yourselves 31
3: 4 Peter directed his gaze at him, with John, and said 24
6 Peter said, "I have no silver and gold 24
22 Moses said, 'The Lord God will raise up 24
25 saying to Abraham, 'And in your posterity 31
4: 8 Then Peter, filled with the Holy Spirit, said 24
16 saying, "What shall we do with these men? 31
23 what the chief priests and the elders had said 24
24 lifted their voices together to God and said 24
25 who . . didst say by the Holy Spirit 31
32 no one said that any of the things . . was his own 31
5: 3 Peter said, "Anani'as 24
8 Peter said to her, "Tell me 24
8 she said, "Yes, for so much. 24
9 Peter said to her, "How is it that you have agreed •
19 an angel . . brought them out and said 24
28 saying, "We strictly charged you not to teach 31
35 he said to them, "Men of Israel 24
6: 2 said, "It is not right 24
5 what they said pleased the whole multitude 32
11 Then they secretly instigated men, who said 31
13 and set up false witnesses who said 31
14 we have heard him say 31
7: 1 the high priest said, "Is this so? 24
2 Stephen said: "Brethren and fathers, hear me. 39
3 said to him, 'Depart from your land 24
7 I will judge the nation which they serve,' said God 24
26 would have reconciled them, saying 31
27 the man . . thrust him aside, saying 31
33 the Lord said to him, 'Take off the shoes 24
35 This Moses whom they refused, saying 24
37 This is the Moses who said to the Israelites 24
40 saying to Aaron, 'Make for us gods to go before us 24
48 as the prophet says 31
49 What house will you build for me, says the Lord 31
56 he said, "Behold, I see the heavens opened 24
60 when he had said this, he fell asleep. 31
8: 6 gave heed to what was said by Philip 31

9 saying that he himself was somebody great. 31
10 saying, "This man is that power of God 31
19 saying, "Give me also this power 31
20 Peter said to him, "Your silver perish with you 24
24 nothing of what you have said may come upon me. 24
26 an angel of the Lord said to Philip, "Rise and go 29
29 the Spirit said to Philip, "Go up 24
31 he said, "How can I, unless some one guides me? 24
34 the eunuch said to Philip 24
34 About whom, pray, does the prophet say this 31
36 the eunuch said, "See, here is water! 39
9: 4 he fell to the ground and heard a voice saying 31
5 he said, "Who are you, Lord? 24
5 he said, "I am Jesus, whom you are persecuting; •
10 The Lord said to him in a vision, "Anani'as. 24
10 he said, "Here I am, Lord. 24
11 the Lord said to him, "Rise and go •
15 the Lord said to him, "Go 24
17 laying his hands on him he said, "Brother Saul 24
20 immediately he proclaimed Jesus, saying 35
21 all who heard him were amazed, and said 31
34 Peter said to him, "Aene'as, Jesus Christ heals you; 24
40 then turning to the body he said, "Tabitha, rise. 24
10: 3 angel of God coming in and saying to him 24
4 stared at him in terror, and said, "What is it, Lord? 24
4 he said to him, "Your prayers and your alms 24
14 Peter said, "No, Lord 24
19 the Spirit said to him, "Behold 24
21 Peter went down to the men and said, "I am the one 24
22 they said, "Cornelius, a centurion 24
22 to hear what you have to say. 37
26 Peter lifted him up, saying, "Stand up; I too am a man. 31
28 he said to them, "You yourselves know 39
30 Cornelius said, "Four days ago, about this hour 39
31 saying, 'Cornelius, your prayer has been heard 39
34 Peter opened his mouth and said: "Truly I perceive 24
44 While Peter was still saying this 29
11: 3 saying, "Why did you go to uncircumcised men 31
7 I heard a voice saying to me, 'Rise, Peter 31
8 I said, 'No, Lord 24
13 the angel standing in his house and saying 24
16 I remembered the word of the Lord, how he said 31
18 they glorified God, saying 31
12: 7 he struck Peter on the side and woke him, saying 31
8 the angel said to him, "Dress yourself 24
8 And he did so. And he said to him 31
11 Peter came to himself, and said 24
15 They said to her, "You are mad. 24
15 They said, "It is his angel! 31
17 he said, "Tell this to James and to the brethren. 24
13: 2 the Holy Spirit said, "Set apart for me Barnabas 24
10 said, "You son of the devil 24
15 rulers of the synagogue sent to them, saying 31
15 word of exhortation for the people, say it. 31
16 So Paul stood up, and motioning with his hand said 24
22 of whom he testified and said 24
25 as John was finishing his course, he said 31
35 Therefore he says also in another psalm 31
40 what is said in the prophets 24
46 Paul and Barnabas spoke out boldly, saying 24
47 so the Lord has commanded us, saying •
14:10 said in a loud voice, "Stand upright on your feet. 24
11 they lifted up their voices, saying in Lycao'nian 31
22 saying that . . we must enter the kingdom of God. •
15: 5 some believers . . rose up, and said 31
7 Peter rose and said to them, "Brethren 24
18 says the Lord, who has made these things 31
36 after some days Paul said to Barnabas, "Come 24
16: 9 was standing beseeching him and saying 31
14 to give heed to what was said by Paul. 29
15 she besought us, saying 31
18 turned and said to the spirit 24
20 they said, "These men are Jews 24
30 brought them out and said 39
31 they said, "Believe in the Lord Jesus 24
35 sent the police, saying, "Let those men go. 31
36 the jailer reported the words to Paul, saying 35
37 Paul said to them, "they have beaten us publicly 39
17: 3 explaining and proving . . and saying 35
7 saying that there is another king, Jesus. 31
18 some said, "What would this babbler say? 31
18 some said, "What would this babbler say? 31
18 Others said, "He seems to be a preacher •
19 brought him to the Are-op'agus, saying 31
22 Paul . . said: "Men of Athens 39
28 as even some of your poets have said 24
32 some mocked; but others said, "We will hear you 24
18: 6 he shook out his garments and said to them 24
9 the Lord said to Paul one night in a vision 24
13 saying, "This man is persuading men to worship God 31
14 Gallio said to the Jews 24
21 but on taking leave of them he said 31
19: 2 he said to them, "Did you receive the Holy Spirit 24
2 they said, "No •
3 he said, "Into what then were you baptized? 24
3 They said, "Into John's baptism. 24
4 Paul said, "John baptized 24
13 saying, "I adjure you 31
21 resolved . . to . . go to Jerusalem, saying 31
25 said, "Men, you know 24
26 saying that gods made with hands are not gods. 31
35 when the town clerk had quieted the crowd, he said 39
41 when he had said this, he dismissed the assembly. 31
20:10 embracing him said, "Do not be alarmed 24
18 when they came to him, he said to them 24
35 the words of the Lord Jesus, how he said 24
21:11 bound his own feet and hands, and said 24
11 Thus says the Holy Spirit 31
14 when he would not be persuaded, we ceased and said 24
20 they said to him, "You see, brother 24
37 brought into the barracks, he said to the tribune 31
37 brought into the barracks, he said to the tribune 39
37 he said, "Do you know Greek? 31
40 he spoke to them in the Hebrew language, saying 31
22: 2 they were the more quiet. And he said 39
7 I fell to the ground and heard a voice saying to me 31
8 he said to me, 'I am Jesus of Nazareth 24
10 I said, 'What shall I do, Lord?' 24
10 the Lord said to me, 'Rise, and go into Damascus 24
13 came to me, and standing by me said to me 24
14 he said, 'The God of our fathers appointed you 24
18 saw him saying to me, 'Make haste 31
19 I said, 'Lord, they themselves know 24
21 he said to me, 'Depart 24
22 then they lifted up their voices and said 31
25 Paul said to the centurion who was standing by 24
26 he went to the tribune and said to him 20
27 So the tribune came and said to him 24
27 Tell me, are you a Roman citizen?" And he said, "Yes. 39
28 Paul said, "But I was born a citizen. 39
23: 1 Paul, looking intently at the council, said 24
3 Paul said to him, "God shall strike you 24
4 Those who stood by said 24
5 Paul said, "I did not know, brethren 39
7 when he had said this 24
8 the Sad'ducees say that there is no resurrection 31
11 the Lord stood by him and said, "Take courage 24
14 they went to the chief priests and elders, and said 24
17 Paul called one of the centurions and said 39
18 took him and brought him to the tribune and said 39
18 as he has something to say to you. 29
20 he said, "The Jews have agreed 24
23 Then he called two of the centurions and said 24
35 he said, "I will hear you 39
24: 2 Tertul'lus began to accuse him, saying 31
20 Or else let these men themselves say 24
22 Felix . . put them off, saying 24
25 Felix was alarmed and said 21
25: 5 So," said he, "let the men of authority . . go down 39
9 Festus, wishing to do the Jews a favor, said to Paul 24
10 Paul said, "I am standing before Caesar's tribunal 24
14 Festus laid Paul's case before the king, saying 31
22 Agrippa said to Festus, "I should like to hear •
22 Tomorrow," said he, "you shall hear him. 39
24 Festus said, "King Agrippa 39
26: 1 Agrippa said to Paul, "You have permission 39
14 heard a voice saying to me in the Hebrew language 31
15 And I said, 'Who are you, Lord?' And the Lord said, 24
15 'Who are you, Lord?' And the Lord said, 'I am Jesus 24
22 saying nothing but what the prophets . . said 31
22 what . . Moses said would come to pass 29
24 Festus said with a loud voice, "Paul, you are mad 39
25 Paul said, "I am not mad, most excellent Festus 39
28 Agrippa said to Paul •
29 Paul said, "Whether short or long, I would to God •
31 when they had withdrawn, they said to one another 29
32 Agrippa said to Festus 39
27:10 saying, "Sirs, I perceive that the voyage 31
11 what Paul said. 31
21 Paul then came forward among them and said, "Men 24
24 he said, 'Do not be afraid, Paul 31
31 Paul said to the centurion and the soldiers 24
33 Paul urged them all to take some food, saying 31
35 when he had said this, he took bread 24
28: 4 they said to one another 31
6 changed their minds and said that he was a god. 31
17 when they had gathered, he said to them, "Brethren 31
21 they said to him, "We have received no letters 24
24 some were convinced by what he said 31
25 was right in saying to your fathers 29
26 'Go to this people, and say, You shall indeed hear 24
Rom 2:22 You who say that one must not commit adultery 31
3: 5 what shall we say? 24
8 as some . . slanderously charge us with saying. 31
19 Now we know that whatever the law says 31
4: 1 What then shall we say about Abraham 24
3 For what does the scripture say? 31
9 We say that faith was reckoned to Abraham 31
6: 1 What shall we say then? Are we to continue in sin 24
7: 7 What then shall we say? That the law is sin? 24
7 if the law had not said, "You shall not covet. 31
8:31 What then shall we say to this? If God is for us, who 24
9: 9 For this is what the promise said, "About this time 32
14 What shall we say then? Is there injustice on God's 24
15 For he says to Moses, "I will have mercy 31
17 For the scripture says to Pharaoh 31
19 You will say to me then, "Why does he . . find fault? 24
20 Will what is molded say to its molder 24
25 As indeed he says in Hose'a 31
26 And in the very place where it was said to them 24
30 What shall we say, then? That Gentiles who did not 24
10: 6 But the righteousness based on faith says 31
6 Do not say in your heart, "Who will ascend 31
8 But what does it say? The word is near you 31
11 The scripture says, "No one who believes in him 31
16 for Isaiah says, "Lord, who has believed 31
19 First Moses says, "I will make you jealous of those 31
20 Then Isaiah is so bold as to say, "I have been found 31
21 But of Israel he says, "All day long I have held out 31
11: 2 Do you not know what the scripture says of Eli'jah 31
9 And David says, "Let their table become a snare 31
19 You will say, "Branches were broken off so that I 24
12:19 Vengeance is mine, I will repay, says the Lord. 31
14:11 As I live, says the Lord, every knee shall bow to me 31
15:10 and again it is said, "Rejoice, O Gentiles 31
12 further Isaiah says, "The root of Jesse shall come 31
1Co 1:12 What I mean is that each one of you says 31
15 lest any one should say that you were baptized 31
3: 4 For when one says, "I belong to Paul 31
6: 5 I say this to your shame 31
7: 6 I say this by way of concession, not of command. 31
8 To the unmarried and the widows I say 31
12 To the rest I say, not the Lord 31
35 I say this for your own benefit 31
9: 8 Do I say this on human authority? 29
8 Does not the law say the same? 31
10:15 judge for yourselves what I say. 31
28 if some one says to you 31
11:22 What shall I say to you? 24
24 when he had given thanks, he broke it, and said 24
25 In the same way also the cup, after supper, saying 31
12: 3 no one speaking by the Spirit of God ever says 31
3 no one can say "Jesus is Lord 31
15 If the foot should say, "Because I am not a hand 31
16 if the ear should say, "Because I am not an eye 31
21 The eye cannot say to the hand, "I have no need 31
14: 9 how will any one know what is said 29
16 say the "Amen" to your thanksgiving 24
16 when he does not know what you are saying? 31
21 they will not listen to me, says the Lord. 31
23 will they not say that you are mad? 24
29 let the others weigh what is said. •
34 be subordinate, as even the law says. 31
15:12 the dead, how can some of you say that there is no 31
27 when it says, "All things are put in subjection 31
34 I say this to your shame. 29
2Co 1:17 like a worldly man, ready to say Yes and No at once? †
4: 6 the God who said, "Let light shine out of darkness 31
6: 2 For he says, "At the acceptable time 31
16 For we are the temple of the living God; as God said 24
17 be separate from them, says the Lord 31
18 be my sons and daughters, says the Lord Almighty. 31
7: 3 I do not say this to condemn you 31
14 just as everything we said to you was true 29
8: 8 I say this not as a command 31
9: 2 I boast . . to the people of Macedo'nia, saying •
3 so that you may be ready, as I said you would be; 31
4 to say nothing of you 31
10:10 For they say, "His letters are weighty and strong 39
11 what we say by letter when absent 32
11:17 (What I am saying 29
17 I say not with the Lord's authority but as a fool 29
21 To my shame, I must say, we were too weak for that! 31
12: 9 he said to me, "My grace is sufficient for you 24
16 I was crafty, you say •
Gal 1: 9 As we have said before, so now I say again 31
23 they only heard it said 35
2: 6 those, I say, who were of repute added nothing to me; 22
14 I said to Cephas before them all 24
3: 8 saying, "In you shall all the nations be blessed. 35
16 It does not say, "And to offsprings 31
4:30 what does the scripture say? "Cast out the slave 31
5: 2 Now I, Paul, say to you 31
16 I say, walk by the Spirit 31
Eph 4: 8 Therefore it is said, "When he ascended on high 31
9 In saying, "He ascended," what does it mean •
5:14 Therefore it is said, "Awake, O sleeper 31
32 am saying that it refers to Christ and the church; 31
Php 4: 4 again I will say, Rejoice. 24
Col 2: 4 I say this in order that no one may delude you 31
4:17 say to Archip'pus 24
1Th 1: 8 so that we need not say anything. 29
5: 3 When people say, "There is peace and security 31
2Th 3:14 any one refuses to obey what we say in this letter 32
1Ti 1: 7 either what they are saying or . . 31
4: 1 Now the Spirit expressly says 31
5:13 saying what they should not. 29
18 for the scripture says, "You shall not muzzle an ox 31
2Ti 2: 7 Think over what I say 31
Tit 1:12 One of themselves, a prophet of their own, said 24
2: 8 having nothing evil to say of us. 31
Phm 1:19 to say nothing of your owing me 31
21 knowing that you will do even more than I say. 31
Heb 1: 5 For to what angel did God ever say, "Thou art my Son 24
6 he says, "Let all God's angels worship him. 31
7 Of the angels he says, "Who makes his angels winds 31
8 of the Son he says

13 to what angel has he ever said, "Sit at my right hand 24
2:12 saying, "I will proclaim thy name to my brethren 31
3: 7 Therefore, as the Holy Spirit says 31
10 I was provoked . . and said 24
4: 3 as he has said, "As I swore in my wrath . . 24
5 again in this place he said •
7 saying through David so long afterward 31
5: 5 but was appointed by him who said to him 29
6 as he says also in another place 31
11 About this we have much to say 32
6:14 saying, "Surely I will bless you and multiply you. 31
7: 9 One might even say . . 31
14 Moses said nothing about priests. 29
8: 1 in what we are saying is this: we have such a high 31
5 he was instructed by God, saying •
8 For he finds fault with them when he says 31
8 The days will come, says the Lord 31
9 so I paid no heed to them, says the Lord. 31
10 This is the covenant . . says the Lord 31
11 shall not teach . . every one his brother, saying 31
9:20 saying, "This is the blood of the covenant 31
10: 5 when Christ came into the world, he said 31
7 I said, 'Lo, I have come to do thy will, O God,' 24
8 When he said above 31
15 also bears witness to us; for after saying 24
16 after those days, says the Lord 31
30 we know him who said, "Vengeance is mine 24
11:18 of whom it was said 29
32 what more shall I say? 31
12:21 Moses said, "I tremble with fear. 24
13: 5 he has said, "I will never fail you nor forsake you. 24
6 Hence we can confidently say 31
Jas 1:13 Let no one say . . "I am tempted by God 31
2: 3 you pay attention . . and say 24
3 while you say to the poor man, "Stand there 24
11 For he who said, "Do not commit adultery 31
11 he . . said also, "Do not kill. 31
14 if a man says he has faith but has not works? 31
16 one of you says to them, "Go in peace 31
18 some one will say, "You have faith and I have works. 24
23 the scripture was fulfilled which says 31
3: 2 if any one makes no mistakes in what he says 32
4: 5 you suppose it is in vain that the scripture says 31
6 But he gives more grace; therefore it says 31
13 Come now, you who say, "Today or tomorrow we will 31
15 Instead you ought to say, "If the Lord wills 31
2Pe 3: 4 and saying, "Where is the promise of his coming? 31
1Jn 1: 6 If we say we have fellowship with him 24
8 If we say we have no sin, we deceive ourselves 24
10 If we say we have not sinned, we make him a liar 24
2: 4 He who says "I know him" but disobeys 31
6 he who says he abides in him ought to walk 31
9 He who says he is in the light 31
4: 5 therefore what they say is of the world 29
20 If any one says, "I love God," and hates his brother 31
5:16 I do not say that one is to pray for that. 31
Jde 1: 9 but said, "The Lord rebuke you. 24
14 Enoch . . prophesied, saying 31
18 they said to you, "In the last time there will be 31
Rev 1: 8 I am the Alpha and the Omega," says the Lord God 31
11 saying, "Write what you see in a book and send it 31
17 But he laid his right hand upon me, saying, "Fear not 31
2: 7 let him hear what the Spirit says to the churches 31
9 those who say that they are Jews and are not 31
11 let him hear what the Spirit says to the churches 31
17 He who has an ear, let him hear what the Spirit says 31
24 to you I say, I do not lay upon you any other burden; 31
29 He who has an ear, let him hear what the Spirit says 31
3: 6 He who has an ear, let him hear what the Spirit says 31
9 those . . who say that they are Jews and are not 31
13 He who has an ear, let him hear what the Spirit says 31
17 For you say, I am rich, I have prospered 31
22 He who has an ear, let him hear what the Spirit says 31
4: 1 the first voice . . said, "Come up hither 31
5: 5 Then one of the elders said to me, "Weep not; 31
9 they sang a new song, saying, "Worthy art thou 31
12 saying with a loud voice, "Worthy is the Lamb 31
13 every creature . . and all therein, saying 31
14 the four living creatures said, "Amen! 31
6: 1 and I heard one of the four living creatures say 31
3 I heard the second living creature say, "Come! 31
5 I heard the third living creature say, "Come! 31
6 a voice in the midst of the . . creatures saying 31
7 the voice of the fourth living creature say, "Come! 31
7: 3 saying, "Do not harm the earth or the sea 31
12 saying, "Amen! Blessing and glory and wisdom 31
13 Then one of the elders addressed me, saying 31
14 I said to him, "Sir, you know." And he said to me 24
14 I said to him, "Sir, you know." And he said to me 24
9:14 saying to the sixth angel who had the trumpet 31
10: 4 but I heard a voice from heaven saying 31
4 Seal up what the seven thunders have said 29
8 the voice . . spoke to me again, saying 31
9 and he said to me, "Take it and eat; 31
11:12 Then they heard a loud voice from heaven saying 31
15 and there were loud voices in heaven, saying 31
17 saying, "We give thanks to thee, Lord God Almighty 31
12:10 And I heard a loud voice in heaven, saying 31
13: 4 and they worshiped the beast, saying 31

14: 7 and he said with a loud voice, "Fear God 31
8 Another angel, a second, followed, saying 31
9 And another angel, a third, followed them, saying 31
13 And I heard a voice from heaven saying, "Write this 31
13 Blessed indeed," says the Spirit 31
15: 3 and the song of the Lamb, saying 31
16: 5 And I heard the angel of water say 31
17 voice came . . from the throne, saying, "It is done! 31
17: 1 one of the seven angels . . came and said to me 29
7 But the angel said to me, "Why marvel? I will tell you 24
15 And he said to me, "The waters that you saw 31
18: 4 Then I heard another voice from heaven saying 31
7 Since in her heart she says, 'A queen I sit 31
10 they will stand far off . . and say, "Alas! alas! 31
21 and threw it into the sea, saying 31
19: 4 worshiped God . . saying, "Amen. Hallelujah! 31
9 And the angel said to me, "Write this 31
9 And he said to me, "These are true words of God. 31
10 but he said to me, "You must not do that! 31
21: 3 I heard a loud voice from the throne saying 31
5 And he who sat upon the throne said, "Behold 24
5 Also he said, "Write this 31
6 And he said to me, "It is done! 24
9 one of the seven angels . . spoke to me, saying 31
22: 6 And he said to me, "These words are trustworthy 24
9 he said to me, "You must not do that! 31
10 And he said to me, "Do not seal up the words 31
17 The Spirit and the Bride say, "Come. 31
17 And let him who hears say, "Come. 24
19 He who testifies to these things says 31
1Es 1: 4 he said, "You need no longer carry it •
26 the king of Egypt sent word to him saying 31
30 the king said to his servants 24
2: 3 Thus says Cyrus king of the Persians 31
3: 4 the three young men . . said to one another 24
9 said, "When the king wakes 24
16 he said, "Call the young men 24
17 they said to them, "Explain to us 24
17 Then the first . . began and said 39
24 When he had said this, he stopped speaking 24
4: 3 whatever he says to them they obey. 31
41 then all the people shouted, and said 24
42 the king said to him, "Ask what you wish 24
43 he said to the king 24
58 praised the King of heaven, saying 31
5:68 they approached . . and said to them 31
70 the heads of the fathers' houses in Israel said 24
6: 3 Sathrabuzanes . . came to them and said 24
8:52 for we had said to the king 24
58 I said to them, "You are holy to the Lord 24
68 the principal men came to me and said 31
74 I said, "O Lord, I am ashamed and confounded 31
82 Lord, what shall we say, when we have these things? 24
82 didst give by thy servants the prophets, saying 31
92 Then Shecaniah . . called out, and said to Ezra 24
9: 7 Then Ezra rose and said to them 24
10 the multitude shouted and said with a loud voice 24
10 We will do as you have said. 24
49 Then Attharates said to Ezra the chief priest 24
53 the Levites commanded all the people, saying 31
2Es 1: 4 The word of the Lord came to me, saying 41
12 speak to them and say, Thus says the Lord 41
12 speak to them and say, Thus says the Lord 41
14 Yet you have forgotten me, says the Lord. 41
15 Thus says the Lord Almighty 41
18 saying, 'Why hast thou led us into this wilderness 41
21 What more can I do for you? says the Lord. 41
22 Thus says the Lord Almighty 41
27 you have forsaken yourselves, says the Lord. 41
28 Thus says the Lord Almighty 41
32 their blood I will require of you, says the Lord. 41
33 Thus says the Lord Almighty 41
37 they will believe the things I have said. 41
2: 1 Thus says the Lord 41
2 The mother who bore them says to them, 'Go 41
9 So will I do to those . . says the Lord Almighty. 41
10 Thus says the Lord to Ezra: "Tell my people 41
14 because I live, says the Lord. 41
15 because I have chosen you, says the Lord. 41
17 for I have chosen you, says the Lord. 41
28 to do anything against you, says the Lord. 41
30 because I will deliver you, says the Lord. 41
31 for I am merciful, says the Lord Almighty. 41
34 Therefore I say to you, O nations 41
45 He answered and said to me 41
46 Then I said to the angel, "Who is that young man 41
47 He answered and said to me, "He is the Son of God 41
48 Then the angel said to me, "Go, tell my people 41
3: 3 I began to speak . . and said 41
28 Then I said in my heart 41
4: 2 and said to me, "Your understanding 41
3 Then I said, "Yes, my lord. 41
5 I said, "Speak on, my lord. 41
5 he said to me, "Go, weigh for me the weight of fire 41
6 I answered and said, "Who of those 41
7 he said to me, "If I had asked you, 'How many 41
8 Perhaps you would have said to me 41
10 he said to me, "You cannot understand the things 41
12 and said to him, "It would be better for us 41

13 He answered me and said, "I went into a forest 41
14 and said, 'Come, let us go 41
15 the waves of the sea also made a plan and said, 'Come 41
19 I answered and said, "Each has made a foolish plan 41
20 He answered me and said, "You have judged rightly 41
22 Then I answered and said, "I beseech you, my lord 41
26 He answered me and said, "If you are alive 41
33 Then I answered and said, "How long 41
34 He answered me and said, "You do not hasten faster 41
35 ask about these matters, saying, 'How long 41
36 Jeremiel the archangel answered them and said 41
38 Then I answered and said, "O sovereign Lord 41
40 He answered me and said, "Go and ask a woman 41
41 I said, "No, lord, it cannot. 41
41 And he said to me, "In Hades 41
44 I answered and said, "If I have found favor 41
47 he said to me, "Stand at my right side 41
50 he said to me, "Consider it for yourself 41
51 Then I prayed and said, "Do you think 41
52 He answered me and said, "Concerning the signs 41
5:16 Phaltiel, a chief of the people, came to me and said 41
19 Then I said to him, "Depart from me 41
19 He heard what I said and left me. 41
23 I said, "O sovereign Lord 41
32 he said to me,"Listen to me 41
33 I said, "Speak, my lord." And he said to me 41
33 I said, "Speak, my lord." And he said to me 41
34 I said, "No, my lord 41
35 he said to me, "You cannot. 41
35 You cannot." And I said, "Why not, my lord? 41
36 He said to me, "Count up for me 41
38 I said, "O sovereign Lord, who is able to know 41
40 He said to me, "Just as you cannot do one 41
41 I said, "Yet behold, O Lord 41
42 He said to me, "I shall liken my judgment to a circle; 41
43 Then I answered and said, "Couldst thou not 41
44 He replied to me and said 41
45 I said, "How hast thou said to thy servant 41
45 I said, "How hast thou said to thy servant 41
46 He said to me, "Ask a woman's womb, and say to it 41
46 He said to me, "Ask a woman's womb, and say to it 41
47 I said, "Of course it cannot 41
48 He said to me, "Even so have I given the womb 41
50 Then I inquired and said 41
52 Say to her, "Why are those whom you have borne 41
56 I said, "O Lord, I beseech thee 41
6: 1 he said to me, "At the beginning 41
7 I answered and said, "What will be the dividing 41
8 He said to me, "From Abraham to Isaac 41
11 I answered and said, "O sovereign Lord 41
13 He answered and said to me, "Rise to your feet 41
18 it said, "Behold, the days are coming 41
30 he said to me, "I have come to show you these things 41
33 and to say to you: 'Believe and do not be afraid! 41
38 I said, "O Lord, thou didst speak at the beginning 41
38 and didst say on the first day 41
55 because thou hast said that it was for us 41
56 thou hast said that they are nothing 41
7: 2 he said to me, "Rise, Ezra, and listen to the words 41
3 I said, "Speak, my lord." And he said to me 41
3 I said, "Speak, my lord." And he said to me 41
10 I said, "He cannot, lord." And he said to me 41
10 And he said to me, "So also is Israel's portion. 41
17 Then I answered and said, "O sovereign Lord, behold 41
19 he said to me, "You are not a better judge than God 41
37 Then the Most High will say to the nations 41
45 I answered and said, "O sovereign Lord, I said ‡
45 O sovereign Lord, I said then and I say now 41
45 O sovereign Lord, I said then and I say now 41
49 He answered me and said, "Listen to me, Ezra 41
51 For whereas you have said that the righteous 41
53 I said, "Lord, how could that be? 41
54 he said to me, "Not only that, but ask the earth 41
55 Say to her, 'You produce gold and silver and brass 41
58 I said, "O sovereign Lord, what is plentiful 41
59 He answered me and said, "Weigh within yourself 41
62 I replied and said, "O earth 41
70 He answered me and said, "When the Most High made 41
71 for you have said that the mind grows with us. 41
73 What, then, will they have to say in the judgment 41
75 I answered and said, "If I have found favor 41
76 He answered me and said, "I will show you that also 41
100 I answered and said, "Will time therefore 41
101 He said to me, "They shall have freedom 41
102 I answered and said, "If I have found favor 41
104 He answered me and said, "Since you have found 41
106 I answered and said, "How then do we find 41
112 He answered me and said, "This present world 41
116 I answered and said, "This is my first and last word 41
127 He answered and said, "This is the meaning 41
128 he shall suffer what you have said 41
128 he shall receive what I have said. ‡
129 while he was alive, spoke to the people, saying 41
132 I answered and said, "I know, O Lord 41
8: 1 He answered me and said, "The Most High made 41
4 I answered and said, "Then drink your fill 41
19 before he was taken up. He said 41
37 He answered me and said, "Some things 41
42 I answered and said, "If I have found favor 41

46 He answered me and said, "Things that are present 41
58 said in their hearts that there is not God 41
62 Then I answered and said 41
9: 1 He answered me and said, "Measure carefully 41
14 I answered and said 41
15 I said before, and I say now, and will say it again 43
15 I said before, and I say now, and will say it again 41
15 I said before, and I say now, and will say it again 41
17 He answered me and said, "As is the field 41
28 I began to speak before the Most High, and said 41
30 thou didst say, 'Hear me, O Israel 41
38 When I said these things in my heart 43
40 said to her, "Why are you weeping 41
41 she said to me, "Let me alone, my lord, 41
42 I said to her, "What has happened to you? Tell me. 41
43 she said to me, "Your servant was barren 41
10: 5 and answered her in anger and said 41
12 if you say to me, 'My lamentation 41
14 then I say to you, 'As you brought forth in sorrow 41
18 She said to me, "I will not do so 41
19 I spoke again to her, and said 41
20 Do not say that, but let yourself be persuaded 42
27 I was afraid, and cried with a loud voice and said 41
30 and set me on my feet, and said to me 41
32 I said, "Because you have forsaken me! 41
33 He said to me, "Stand up like a man 41
34 I said, "Speak, my lord; only do not forsake me 41
38 He answered me and said, "Listen to me 41
48 as for her saying to you, 'When my son entered 41
11: 7 and uttered a cry to his wings, saying 41
15 behold, a voice sounded, saying to it. 41
36 Then I heard a voice saying to me, "Look before you 41
37 he uttered a man's voice . . and spoke, saying 41
38 The Most High says to you 41
12: 1 While the lion was saying these words 43
3 and I said to my spirit 41
7 I said, "O sovereign Lord, if I have found favor 41
10 He said to me, "This is the interpretation 41
40 and came to me and spoke to me, saying 41
45 Then I answered them and said 41
13:13 and I besought the Most High, and said 41
20 He answered me and said 41
22 As for what you said about those who are left 41
51 I said, "O sovereign Lord, explain this to me 41
52 He said to me, "Just as no one can explore 41
14: 1 a voice . . said, "Ezra, Ezra. 41
2 I said, "Here I am, Lord," and I rose to my feet. 41
3 Then he said to me, "I revealed myself in a bush 41
5 Then I commanded him, saying 41
7 now I say to you; 41
19 Then I answered and said, "Let me speak 41
23 He answered me and said, "Go and gather the people 41
27 I gathered all the people together, and said 41
38 on the next day, behold, a voice called me, saying 41
45 the Most High spoke to me, saying, "Make public 41
15: 1 The Lord says, "Behold, speak in the ears 41
5 Behold," says the Lord, "I bring evils upon the world 41
7 Therefore," says the Lord 41
9 I will surely avenge them," says the Lord 41
20 Behold," says God, "I call together all the kings 41
21 Thus says the Lord God 41
24 do not observe my commandments," says the Lord; 41
48 therefore God says 41
52 dealt with you so violently," says the Lord 41
56 As you will do to my chosen people," says the Lord 41
16:36 do not disbelieve what the Lord says. 41
48 the more angry I will be . . " says the Lord. 41
53 Let no sinner say that he has not sinned 41
53 coals of fire on the head of him who says 41
55 He said, "Let the earth be made," and it was made 41
74 Hear, my elect," says the Lord. 41
76 says the Lord God, "do not let your sins 41
Tob 2: 2 Upon seeing the abundance of food I said to my son 24
3 he came back and said 24
6 the prophecy of Amos, how he said 24
8 my neighbors laughed at me and said 31
13 So I said to her, "Where did you get the kid? 24
14 she said, "It was given to me as a gift 24
3: 1 in my grief I wept, and I prayed in anguish, saying 31
8 the maids said to her 24
10 But she said, "I am the only child of my father 24
11 she prayed by her window and said 24
4: 1 he said to himself; 24
3 he called him and said 24
5: 3 Then Tobit gave him the receipt, and said to him 24
5 Tobias said to him 24
7 Then Tobias said to him, "Wait for me 24
8 he said to him, "Go, and do not delay. 24
8 So he went in and said to his father 24
8 He said, "Call him to me 24
10 Then Tobit said to him, "My brother 24
11 Tobit said to him, "I should like to know, my brother 24
13 Tobit said to him, "You are welcome, my brother 24
16 Then he said to Tobias, "Get ready for the journey 24
16 his father said to him 24
17 Anna, his mother, began to weep, and said to Tobit 24
20 Tobit said to her, "Do not worry, my sister 24
6: 3 the angel said to him, "Catch the fish. 24
4 Then the angel said to him, "Cut open the fish 24
6 the young man said to the angel, "Brother Azarias 24
10 the angel said to the young man 24
13 the young man said to the angel, "Brother Azarias 24
15 the angel said to him 24
7: 2 Then Raguel said to his wife Edna 24
4 he said to them, "Do you know our brother Tobit? 24
4 they said, "Yes, we do. 24
5 Tobias said, "He is my father. 24
8 Then Tobias said to Raphael, "Brother Azarias 24
9 Raguel said to Tobias, "Eat, drink, and be merry; 24
11 Tobias said, "I will eat nothing here 24
12 Raguel said, "Take her right now 24
13 he gave her to Tobias to be his wife, saying 24
16 Raguel called his wife Edna and said to her 24
17 she did as he said, and took her there 24
17 comforted her daughter . . and said to her 24
8: 4 Tobias got up from the bed and said, "Sister, get up 24
6 Thou didst say, 'It is not good 24
8 she said with him, "Amen. 24
12 said to his wife Edna, "Send one of the maids 24
15 Then Raguel blessed God and said 31
9: 1 Then Tobias called Raphael and said to him 24
10: 2 he said, "Is it possible that he has been detained? 24
4 his wife said to him, "The lad has perished 24
4 Then she began to mourn for him, and said 24
6 Tobit said to her, "Be still and stop worrying 31
7 At that time Tobias said to Raguel, "Send me back 24
8 his father-in-law said to him, "Stay with me 24
11 when he had blessed them he sent them away, saying 31
12 He said also to his daughter 24
12 Edna said to Tobias 24
11: 2 Then Raphael said to Tobias 24
6 caught sight of him coming, and said to his father 24
7 Raphael said, "I know, Tobias 24
9 embraced her son, and said to him, "I have seen you 24
11 saying, "Be of good cheer, father. 31
14 he wept and said, "Blessed art thou, O God 24
17 he blessed her, saying, "Welcome, daughter! 31
12: 1 Tobit then called his son Tobias and said to him 24
4 The old man said, "He deserves it. 24
5 he called the angel and said to him 24
6 called the two of them privately and said to them 24
11 I have said, 'It is good . . 24
17 he said to them, "Do not be afraid; you will be safe. 24
13: 1 Then Tobit wrote a prayer of rejoicing, and said 24
18 and will give praise, saying, 'Blessed is God 31
14: 3 he called his son . . and said to him, "My son 24
4 what Jonah the prophet said about Nineveh 29
5 just as the prophets said of it. 29
8 what the prophet Jonah said will surely happen. 29
11 As he said this he died in his bed 31
Jdt 2: 1 carrying out his revenge . . just as he said. 29
4 called . . and said to him 24
5 Thus says the Great King 31
3: 1 they sent messengers to sue for peace, and said 31
5: 3 said to them, "Tell me, you Canaanites 24
5 Then Achior, the leader of all the Ammonites, said 24
22 When Achior had finished saying this 29
23 they said, "we will not be afraid of the Israelites; •
6: 1 Holofernes . . said to Achior 24
4 So says King Nebuchadnezzar 31
5 said these words on the day of your iniquity 29
17 all that he had said 29
18 cried out to him, and said 31
7: 4 and every one said to his neighbor 24
8 commanders of the coastland came to him and said 24
16 he gave orders to do as they had said. 29
23 said before all the elders 24
30 Uzziah said to them, "Have courage, my brothers! 24
31 I will do what you say. 37
8: 9 when she heard all that Uzziah said to them 29
11 They came to her, and she said to them 24
11 What you have said to the people today 29
28 Then Uzziah said to her 24
28 All that you have said 24
32 Judith said to them, "Listen to me 24
35 Uzziah and the rulers said to her, "Go in peace 24
9: 1 cried out . . with a loud voice, and said 24
2 thou hast said, 'It shall not be done' 24
6 the things . . presented themselves and said 24
10: 7 they greatly admired her beauty, and said to her 24
9 Then she said to them 24
9 to open the gate for her, as she had said. 29
14 they said to her 24
16 tell him just what you have said 37
19 and every one said to his neighbor 24
11: 1 Then Holofernes said to her, "Take courage, woman 24
9 Now as for the things Achior said in your council 29
9 he told them all he had said to you. 26
10 my lord and master, do not disregard what he said 32
20 they marveled at her wisdom and said 24
22 Holofernes said to her, "God has done well 24
23 if you do as you have said, your God shall be my God 29
12: 2 Judith said, "I cannot eat it, lest it be an offense; 24
3 Holofernes said to her 24
6 sent to Holofernes and said 31
11 he said to Bagoas 24
13 Bagoas . . approached her and said 24
14 Judith said, "Who am I, to refuse my lord? 24
17 Holofernes said to her. "Drink now 24
18 Judith said, "I will drink now, my lord 24
13: 3 she said she would be going out for her prayers. 39
3 she had said the same thing to Bagoas. 29
4 Then Judith . . said in her heart 24
7 She came close to his bed . . and said 24
14 Then she said to them with a loud voice, "Praise God 24
15 showed it to them, and said, "See 24
17 and said with one accord, "Blessed art thou, our God 24
18 Uzziah said to her, "O daughter . . 24
20 all the people said, "So be it, so be it! 24
14: 1 Then Judith said to them, "Listen to me, my brethren 24
7 knelt before her, and said 24
13 said to the steward 24
15: 9 all blessed her with one accord and said to her 24
10 all the people said, "So be it! 24
16: 2 Judith said, Begin a song to my God 24
AEs 10: 4 Mordecai said, "These things have come from God. 24
11: 1 Dositheus, who said that he was a priest 39
1 which they said was genuine 39
13: 8 He said 24
14: 3 she prayed to the Lord God of Israel, and said 24
15: 8 he comforted her with soothing words, and said 24
12 he embraced her, and said, "Speak to me. 24
13 she said to him, "I saw you, my lord 24
Wis 1: 7 and that . . knows what is said; 40
2: 1 they reasoned unsoundly, saying to themselves 24
20 according to what he says, he will be protected. 32
5: 3 in anguish of spirit they will groan, and say 24
8:21 with my whole heart I said 24
12:12 For who will say, "What hast thou done? 24
15:12 he says one must get money however one can 39
Sir 5: 1 nor say, "I have enough. 31
3 Do not say, "Who will have power over me? 31
4 Do not say, "I sinned, and what happened to me? 31
6 Do not say, "His mercy is great 31
7: 9 Do not say, "He will consider . . my gifts 31
11:19 when he says, "I have found rest 31
23 Do not say, "What do I need 31
24 Do not say, "I have enough 31
12:12 be stung by what I have said. 37
13: 6 will speak to you kindly and say, "What do you need? 24
23 they extol to the clouds what he says 32
23 they say, "Who is this fellow? 24
15:11 Do not say, "Because of the Lord I left the right way"; 31
12 Do not say, "It was he who led me astray 31
16:17 Do not say, "I shall be hidden from the Lord 31
17:14 he said to them, "Beware of all unrighteousness. 24
19:14 Question a neighbor, perhaps he did not say it 28
14 it; but if he said it, so that he may not say it again. 24
20:16 A fool will say, "I have no friend 24
22: 8 at the end he will say, "What is it? 24
23:18 A man who breaks his marriage vows says 31
24: 8 he said, 'Make your dwelling in Jacob 24
31 I said, "I will water my orchard 24
31:12 do not say, "There is certainly much upon it! 31
32: 8 Speak concisely, say much in few words •
33: 4 Prepare what to say, and thus you will be heard; 32
36:10 Crush the heads of the rulers of the enemy, who say 31
37: 1 Every friend will say, "I too am a friend 24
39:12 I have yet more to say, which I have thought upon 25
15 this you shall say in thanksgiving 24
17 No one can say, "What is this?" "Why is that? 31
21 No one can say, "What is this?" "Why is that? 31
34 no one can say, "This is worse than that 31
51:24 Why do you say you are lacking in these things 31
25 I opened my mouth and said 29
Bar 1:10 And they said: "Herewith we send you money; so buy 24
15 you shall say: 'Righteousness belongs to the Lord 24
2:20 by thy servants the prophets, saying 31
21 Thus says the Lord: Bend your shoulders and serve 24
28 in the presence of the people of Israel, saying 31
3:34 he called them, and they said, "Here we are! 24
4: 9 and she said: "Hearken, you neighbors of Zion 24
LJr 1: 6 say in your heart, "It is thou, O Lord 24
20 men say their hearts have melted 39
Aza 1: 2 he opened his mouth and said 24
28 glorified and blessed God in the furnace, saying 31
Sus 1: 5 Concerning them the Lord had said 29
13 They said to each other, "Let us go home 24
17 She said to her maids, "Bring me oil and ointments 24
18 They did as she said, shut the garden doors 24
19 the two elders rose and ran to her, and said 24
22 Susanna sighed deeply, and said, "I am hemmed 24
27 nothing like this had ever been said about Susanna. 24
29 They said before the people, "Send for Susanna 24
36 The elders said, "As we were walking in the garden 24
42 Then Susanna cried out with a loud voice, and said 24
47 All the people turned to him, and said 24
47 and said, "What is this that you have said? 29
48 Taking his stand in the midst of them, he said 24
50 And the elders said to him, "Come, sit among us 24
51 Daniel said to them, "Separate them 24
52 he summoned one of them and said to him 24
53 though the Lord said, 'Do not put to death 31
55 Daniel said, "Very well! You have lied 24
56 And he said to him, "You offspring of Canaan 24
59 Daniel said to him, "Very well! You also have lied 24
Bel 1: 5 the king said to him, "Why do you not worship Bel? 24

6 The king said to him 24
7 Then Daniel laughed, and said, "Do not be deceived 24
8 he called his priests and said to them 24
9 Daniel said to the king 24
9 Let it be done as you have said. 37
11 the priests of Bel said, "Behold 24
17 the king said, "Are the seals unbroken, Daniel? 24
19 restrained the king from going in, and said 24
20 The king said, "I see the footsteps of men and women 24
24 the king said to Daniel 24
25 Daniel said, "I will worship the Lord my God 24
26 The king said, "I give you permission. 24
27 Daniel said, "See what you have been worshiping! 24
28 conspired against the king, saying 24
29 Going to the king, they said, "Hand Daniel over to us 24
34 the angel of the Lord said to Habakkuk 24
35 Habakkuk said, "Sir, I have never seen Babylon 24
38 Daniel said, "Thou hast remembered me, O God 24
1Mc 1:11 lawless men . . misled many, saying 31
2: 7 said, "Alas! Why was I born to see this 24
19 Mattathias answered and said in a loud voice 24
27 cried out in the city with a loud voice, saying 31
33 they said to them, "Enough of this! 24
34 they said, "We will not come out 24
37 for they said, "Let us all die in our innocence; 31
40 each said to his neighbor 24
49 he said to his sons: "Arrogance and reproach 24
3:14 he said, "I will make a name for myself 24
17 they said to Judas, "How can we 24
41 traders of the region heard what was said to them 33
43 they said to one another 24
50 they cried aloud to Heaven, saying 31
56 he said to those who were building houses 24
58 Judas said, "Gird yourselves and be valiant 24
4: 5 because he said, "These men are fleeing from us. 24
8 Judas said to the men who were with him 24
17 he said to the people, "Do not be greedy for plunder 24
30 he prayed, saying, "Blessed art thou 24
36 Then said Judas and his brothers, "Behold 24
5:10 a letter which said 31
15 they said 31
17 Then Judas said to Simon his brother 24
32 he said to the men of his forces 24
40 Timothy said to the officers of his forces 24
57 So they said, "Let us also make a name for ourselves; 24
6:10 So he called all his friends and said to them 24
11 I said to myself, 'To what distress I have come! 24
22 They went to the king and said, "How long 24
23 to live by what he said and to follow his commands. 31
57 said to the king, to the commanders of the forces 24
7: 3 when this act became known to him, he said 24
14 they said, "A priest of the line of Aaron has come 24
18 they said, "There is no truth or justice in them 24
36 they wept and said 24
40 Then Judas prayed and said 24
9: 8 He became faint, but he said to those who were left 24
9 they tried to dissuade him, saying 31
10 Judas said, "Far be it from us 24
20 they mourned many days and said 24
28 assembled and said to Jonathan 24
44 Jonathan said to those with him 24
55 so that he could no longer say a word 29
58 Then all the lawless plotted and said, "See! 31
71 He agreed, and did as he said 32
10: 4 for he said, "Let us act first to make peace with him 24
16 So he said, "Shall we find another such man? 24
22 he was grieved and said 24
55 Ptolemy the king replied and said 31
56 as you have said. 24
63 he said to his officers 24
11: 9 He sent envoys to Demetrius the king, saying, "Come 31
31 so that you may know what it says. •
57 the young Antiochus wrote to Jonathan, saying 31
12: 3 entered the senate chamber and said 31
44 Then he said to Jonathan 24
46 Jonathan trusted him and did as he said 24
53 they said, "They have no leader or helper 24
13: 3 he encouraged them, saying to them 24
9 all that you say to us we will do. 24
14 so he sent envoys to him and said 31
17 great hostility among the people, who might say 31
46 they said, "Do not treat us 24
14:22 what they said we have recorded 24
25 When the people heard these things they said 24
44 to oppose what he says 24
15:28 He sent . . Athenobius . . to confer with him, saying 31
16: 2 Simon . . said to them 24
2Mc 1:29 Plant thy people in thy holy place, as Moses said. 24
2:11 Moses said, "They were consumed because . . 24
3:12 he said that it was utterly impossible •
13 said that this money must . . be confiscated 31
33 they stood and said 24
34 Having said this they vanished. 24
4: 1 saying that it was he who had incited Heliodorus •
6:17 Let what we have said serve as a reminder •
24 he said, "lest many of the young should suppose •
28 When he had said this 31
30 he groaned aloud and said 24
7: 2 One of them, acting as their spokesman, said 39
5 encouraged one another to die nobly, saying 31
6 when he said, 'And he will have compassion 31
8 and said to them, "No. 36
9 when he was at his last breath, he said 24
11 said nobly, "I got these from Heaven 24
14 when he was near death, he said 39
16 he looked at the king, and said 24
18 when he was about to die, he said 39
21 fired her woman's reasoning . . and said to them 31
30 speaking, the young man said, "What are you waiting 24
8:18 For they trust to arms and acts of daring," he said 39
9: 4 in his arrogance he said 24
12:14 even blaspheming and saying unholy things. 29
14:11 When he had said this 24
34 Having said this, he went away 31
15: 2 the Jews who were compelled to follow him said 31
14 Onias spoke, saying 31
33 said that he would give it piecemeal to the birds 39
34 blessed the Lord . . saying, "Blessed is he 31
3Mc 1:11 When they said that this was not permitted 31
12 did not cease to maintain . . saying 31
14 someone heedlessly said that it was wrong 39
15 since this has happened," the king said 39
2:17 exult in the arrogance of their tongue, saying 31
4:20 when they said and proved that . . 31
5:20 the king . . said that the Jews were benefited 39
30 with a threatening look he said 24
35 Then the Jews, upon hearing what the king had said 34
37 he said in a threatening tone 24
6:11 Let not the vain-minded praise . . saying 31
15 just as you have said 24
23 angrily threatened his friends, saying 31
29 These then were the things he said 31
7:12 approving the truth of what they said 31
4Mc 2: 5 Thus the law says, "You shall not covet 31
18 For, as I have said, the temperate mind is able 39
19 saying, "Cursed be their anger"? 31
24 How is it then, one might say 31
4: 2 he came to Apollonius . . and said 31
6 He said that he had come with the king's authority 31
12 For he said that he had committed a sin 31
5: 5 When Antiochus saw him he said 39
6:13 some of the king's retinue came to him and said 31
26 he lifted up his eyes to God and said 24
30 after he said this 31
7:17 Some perhaps might say 31
8: 4 summoned them nearer and said 39
12 When he had said these things 31
27 the youths . . neither said any of these things 24
29 all with one voice together, as from one mind, said 24
9:10 When they had said these things 31
14 he denounced the tyrant, saying 31
16 when the guards said 31
19 While he was saying these things 31
23 Imitate me, brothers," he said. 31
25 When he had said this 31
28 he steadfastly endured this agony and said 31
30 To the tyrant he said 39
10: 9 When he was about to die, he said 39
12 they dragged in the fourth, saying 31
14 he said to them, "You do not have a fire hot enough 39
18 he said, "Even if you remove my organ of speech 39
11: 1 the fifth leaped up, saying 31
9 While he was saying these things 31
12 he said, "Tyrant, they are splendid favors 31
13 When the tyrant inquired . . he said 39
17 When he had said this, they led him to the wheel. 31
20 While being tortured he said 31
12: 2 tried to console him, saying 31
8 he said, "Let me loose, let me speak to the king 39
11 he said, "You profane tyrant 39
15 Then because he too was about to die, he said 39
13: 2 we would say that they had been conquered 31
8 and encouraged one another, saying 31
11 While one said, "Courage, brother 31
12 another said, "Bear up nobly •
13 cheerful and undaunted, said 31
18 Those who were left behind said 31
16:15 said to your sons in the Hebrew language 31
17: 1 Some of the guards said 31
19 For Moses says 39
18:14 the scripture of Isaiah, which says 31
15 songs of the psalmist David, who said 31
18 the song that Moses taught, which says 31

say a word 1. דבר
Gen 31:24 Take heed that you say not a word to Jacob 1

say again 1. δευτερόω
Sir 19:14 it; but if he said it, so that he may not say it again. 1

say already 1. προεῖπον
2Mc 2:32 adding only so much to what has already been said; 1

say before 1. προεῖπον
2Co 7: 3 I said before that you are in our hearts 1
Gal 1: 9 As we have said before, so now I say again 1
3Mc 6:35 as we have said before 1

say boastfully 1. μεγαλορρημονέω
Jdt 6:17 all that Holofernes had said so boastfully 1

say farewell 1. ἀποτάσσομαι
Lke 9:61 let me first say farewell to those at my home. 1

say in defense 1. ἀπολογέομαι
Act 25: 8 Paul said in his defense 1

say in opposition 1. ἀντεῖπον
Act 4:14 they had nothing to say in opposition. 1

say nothing 1. חרשׁ
Num30: 4 her father hears . . and says nothing to her; 1
7 says nothing to her on the day that he hears; 1
11 her husband heard of it, and said nothing to her 1
14 if her husband says nothing to her from day to day 1
14 he said nothing to her on the day that he heard 1
2Sm 19:10 why do you say nothing about bringing the king 1

say one is right 1. צדק
Job 27: 5 Far be it from me to say that you are right; 1

say rashly 1. לוע
Prv 20:25 It is a snare for a man to say rashly, "It is holy 1

saying 1. אֵמֶר 2. דָּבָר 3. λέγω 4. λόγος 5. παραβολή 6. ῥῆμα
Gen 37:11 but his father kept the saying in mind. 2
1Sm 18: 8 Saul was . . angry, and this saying displeased him; 2
1Kg 13: 4 when the king heard the saying of the man of God 2
32 the saying which he cried by the word of the LORD 2
2Ch 13:22 the acts of Abi'jah, his ways and his sayings 2
Prv 4:20 incline your ear to my sayings. 1
Ecc 12:11 like nails firmly fixed are the . . sayings •
Mat 7:28 And when Jesus finished these sayings 4
15:12 when they heard this saying? 4
19: 1 Now when Jesus had finished these sayings 4
11 Not all men can receive this saying 4
26: 1 When Jesus had finished all these sayings 4
75 Peter remembered the saying of Jesus 6
Mrk 7:29 he said to her, "For this saying you may go your way; 4
9:32 they did not understand the saying 6
10:22 At that saying his countenance fell 4
Lke 1:29 she was greatly troubled at the saying 4
2:17 when they saw it they made known the saying 6
50 they did not understand the saying 6
7: 1 After he had ended all his sayings 6
9:28 Now about eight days after these sayings 4
45 they did not understand this saying 6
45 they were afraid to ask him about this saying. 6
18:34 this saying was hid from them 6
Joh 4:37 For here the saying holds true, 'One sows 4
6:60 This is a hard saying; who can listen to it? 4
10:21 These are not the sayings of one who has a demon. 3
12:47 If any one hears my sayings and does not keep them 6
48 He who rejects me and does not receive my sayings 6
21:23 The saying spread abroad among the brethren 4
1Co 15:54 then shall come to pass the saying that is written 4
1Ti 1:15 The saying is sure and worthy of full acceptance 4
3: 1 The saying is sure 4
4: 9 The saying is sure 4
2Ti 2:11 The saying is sure 4
Tit 3: 8 The saying is sure. 4
Sir 1:25 In the treasuries of wisdom are wise sayings 5
18:29 Those who understand sayings become skilled 4
21:15 When a man of understanding hears a wise saying 4
4Mc 18:17 He confirmed the saying of Ezekiel 3

dark saying 1. חִידָה
Ps 78: 2 I will utter dark sayings from of old 1

wise saying 1. תְּבוּנָה
Job 32:11 I listened for your wise sayings 1

scab 1. יַלֶּפֶת
Lev 21:20 an itching disease or scabs or crushed testicles 1
22:22 discharge or an itch or scabs, you shall not offer 1
scab *See also* smite.

scabbard 1. תַּעַר
Jer 47: 6 Put yourself into your scabbard, rest and be still! 1

scale 1. מאֹזְנַיִם 2. פֶּלֶס 3. קָנֶה 4. ζυγός 5. πλάστιγξ 6. σταθμός 7. punctum
Prv 16:11 A just balance and scales are the LORD'S; 1
20:23 false scales are not good. 1
Isa 40:12 weighed the mountains in scales 2
15 and are accounted as the dust on the scales; 1
46: 6 from the purse, and weigh out silver in the scales 3
Jer 32:10 got witnesses, and weighed the money on scales. 1
Mic 6:11 Shall I acquit the man with wicked scales 1
2Es 3:34 which way the turn of the scale will incline. 7
Wis 11:22 like a speck that tips the scales 5
Sir 6:15 no scales can measure his excellence. 6
28:25 make balances and scales for your words 6
42: 4 of accuracy with scales and weights 4

scale (2) 1. קַשְׂקֶשֶׂת 2. θώραξ 3. λεπίς
Lev 11: 9 Everything in the waters that has fins and scales 1
10 anything . . that has not fins and scales 1
12 Everything in the waters that has not . . scales 1
Deu 14: 9 whatever has fins and scales you may eat. 1
10 does not have fins and scales you shall not eat; 1
Ezk 29: 4 the fish of your streams stick to your scales; 1
4 fish of your streams which stick to your scales. 1
Act 9:18 something like scales fell from his eyes 3
Rev 9: 9 they had scales like iron breastplates 2

scale (3) 1. עלה
Prv 21:22 A wise man scales the city of the mighty 1
Jol 2: 7 they charge, like soldiers they scale the wall. 1
scale *See* armor, tip.

scale away 1. λεπίζω
Tob 3:17 to scale away the white films of Tobit's eyes 1

scale off 1. λεπίζω
Tob 11:13 the white films scaled off from . . his eyes 1

scalp 1. ἀποδειροτομέω 2. κεφαλῆς δορά
3. περισκυθίζω
2Mc 7: 4 they scalp him 3
4Mc 9:28 and tore away his scalp 2
15:20 scalped heads upon heads 1
scalp *See also* Scythian.

scant 1. רָזוֹן 2. ὀλίγος
Mic 6:10 and the scant measure that is accursed? 1
1Mc 6:57 We daily grow weaker, our food supply is scant 2

scant fare 1. לַחַץ
1Kg 22:27 and feed him with scant fare of bread and water 1
2Ch 18:26 in prison, and feed him with scant fare 1

scar 1. צָרֶבֶת
Lev 13:23 it is the scar of the boil 1
28 for it is the scar of the burn 1

scarcely 1. אַךְ 2. אַף כִּי 3. כִּמְעַט שֶׁ 4. μόλις
Gen 27:30 when Jacob had scarcely gone out 1
Sng 3: 4 Scarcely had I passed them, when I found him 3
Isa 40:24 Scarcely are they planted, scarcely sown 2
24 Scarcely are they planted, scarcely sown 2
24 scarcely has their stem taken root in the earth 2
Act 14:18 they scarcely restrained the people 4
1Pe 4:18 If the righteous man is scarcely saved 4

scarcity 1. מִסְכֵּנֻת
Deu 8: 9 in which you will eat bread without scarcity 1

scare 1. חתת 2. ἐκσοβέω
Job 7:14 then thou dost scare me with dreams 1
Wis 17: 9 yet, scared by the passing of beasts 2

scare away 1. ἀποσοβέω
Sir 22:20 One who throws a stone at birds scares them away 1

scarecrow 1. תֹּמֶר 2. προβασκάνιον
Jer 10: 5 idols are like scarecrows in a cucumber field 1
LJr 1:70 Like a scarecrow in a cucumber bed 2

scarf 1. רְעָלָה
Isa 3:19 the pendants, the bracelets, and the scarfs; 1

scarlet 1. שָׁנִי 2. תּוֹלַעַת שָׁנִי 3. κόκκινος 4. κόκκος
Num 4: 8 they shall spread over them a cloth of scarlet 2
Jos 2:18 you shall bind this scarlet cord in the window 1
21 and she bound the scarlet cord in the window. 1
2Sm 1:24 over Saul, who clothed you daintily in scarlet 1
Prv 31:21 for all her household are clothed in scarlet. 1
Sng 4: 3 Your lips are like a scarlet thread 1
Isa 1:18 sins are like scarlet, they shall be white as snow; 1
Jer 4:30 what do you mean that you dress in scarlet 1
Mat 27:28 they stripped him and put a scarlet robe upon him 3
Heb 9:19 with water and scarlet wool and hyssop 3
Rev 17: 3 and I saw a woman sitting on a scarlet beast 3
4 The woman was arrayed in purple and scarlet 3
18:12 cargo of . . fine linen, purple, silk and scarlet 3
16 clothed in fine linen, in purple and scarlet 3
Sir 45:11 with twisted scarlet, the work of a craftsman; 4
scarlet *See also* clothe, thread.

scarlet stuff 1. שָׁנִי תּוֹלַעָה 2. תּוֹלַעַת שָׁנִי
Exd 25: 4 blue and purple and scarlet stuff 2
26:31 veil of blue and purple and scarlet stuff 2
36 a screen . . of blue and purple and scarlet stuff 2
27:16 a screen . . of blue and purple and scarlet stuff 2
28: 5 receive gold, blue and purple and scarlet stuff 2
6 gold, of blue and purple and scarlet stuff 2
8 of gold, blue and purple and scarlet stuff 2
15 purple and scarlet stuff, and fine twined linen 2
33 of blue and purple and scarlet stuff 2
35: 6 blue and purple and scarlet stuff and fine 2
23 blue or purple or scarlet stuff or fine linen 2
25 purple and scarlet stuff and fine twined linen; 2
35 in blue and purple and scarlet stuff 2
36: 8 linen and blue and purple and scarlet stuff 2
35 veil of blue and purple and scarlet stuff 2
37 screen . . of blue and purple and scarlet stuff 2
38:18 blue and purple and scarlet stuff and fine 2
23 blue and purple and scarlet stuff and fine 2
39: 1 of the blue and purple and scarlet stuff 2
2 gold, blue and purple and scarlet stuff 2
3 into the blue and purple and the scarlet stuff 2
5 of gold, blue and purple and scarlet stuff 2
8 of gold, blue and purple and scarlet stuff 2
24 blue and purple and scarlet stuff 2
29 linen and of blue and purple and scarlet stuff 2
Lev 14: 4 take . . cedarwood and scarlet stuff and hyssop 1
6 take . . the scarlet stuff and the hyssop 1
49 with cedarwood and scarlet stuff and hyssop 1
51 cedarwood and the hyssop and the scarlet stuff 1
52 with the cedarwood and hyssop and scarlet stuff 1
Num19: 6 priest shall take . . hyssop and scarlet stuff 1

scatter 1. בזר 2. זרה 3. זרע 4. זרק 5. חלק 6. נפץ
7. פוץ 8. פוש 9. פזר 10. פרד 11. פרש 12. שגה
13. שטח 14. שלח 15. בדר (A) 16. ἀναμείγνυμι
17. βάλλω 18. διαδίδωμι 19. διασκεδάννυμι
20. διασκορπίζω 21. διασπείρω 22. διασπορά
23. διΐστημι 24. λικμάω 25. πάσσω 26. σκορπίζω
27. σπαίρω 28. dispergo 29. dissipo
Gen 49: 7 I will . . scatter them in Israel. 7
Exd 32:20 scattered it upon the water, and made the people 2
Lev 26:33 I will scatter you among the nations 2
Num10:35 Arise, O LORD, and let thy enemies be scattered; 7
16:37 scatter the fire far and wide. For they are holy 2
Deu 4:27 LORD will scatter you among the peoples 7
28:64 LORD will scatter you among all peoples 7
30: 3 peoples where the LORD your God has scattered 7
1Sm 11:11 and those who survived were scattered 7
13: 8 and the people were scattering from him. 7
11 I saw that the people were scattering from me 6
2Sm 17:19 spread a covering . . and scattered grain upon it; 13
22:15 And he sent out arrows, and scattered them; 7
1Kg 14:15 and scatter them beyond the Euphra'tes 2
22:17 I saw all Israel scattered upon the mountains 7
2Kg 25: 5 and all his army was scattered from him. 6
2Ch 18:16 I saw all Israel scattered upon the mountains 7
Neh 1: 8 unfaithful, I will scatter you among the peoples; 7
Est 3: 8 people scattered abroad and dispersed 9
Job 4:11 the whelps of the lioness are scattered. 10
18:15 brimstone is scattered upon his habitation. 2
36:30 Behold, he scatters his lightning about him 11
37:11 the clouds scatter his lightning. 7
38:24 where the east wind is scattered upon the earth? 7
Ps 18:14 he sent out his arrows, and scattered them; 7
44:11 hast scattered us among the nations. 2
53: 5 For God will scatter the bones of the ungodly; 9
68: 1 Let God arise, let his enemies be scattered; 7
14 When the Almighty scattered kings there 11
30 scatter the peoples who delight in war. 1
89:10 didst scatter thy enemies with thy mighty arm. 9
92: 9 all evildoers shall be scattered. 10
106:27 scattering them over the lands. 2
144: 6 Flash forth the lightning and scatter them 7
147:16 he scatters hoarfrost like ashes. 9
Prv 5:16 Should your springs be scattered abroad 7
Isa 16: 2 fluttering birds, like scattered nestlings 14
24: 1 twist its surface and scatter its inhabitants. 7
28:25 does he not scatter dill, sow cummin 7
30:22 You will scatter them as unclean things; 2
33: 3 lifting up of thyself nations are scattered; 6
41:16 and the tempest shall scatter them. 7
Jer 3:13 and scattered your favors among strangers 9
9:16 I will scatter them among the nations 7
10:21 and all their flock is scattered. 7
13:24 I will scatter you like chaff driven by the wind 7
18:17 Like the east wind I will scatter them 7
23: 1 who destroy and scatter the sheep of my pasture! 7
2 You have scattered my flock 7
30:11 of all the nations among whom I scattered you 7
31:10 say, 'He who scattered Israel will gather him 2
40:15 so that all the Jews . . would be scattered 6
49:32 I will scatter to every wind those who cut 2
36 and I will scatter them to all those winds 2
52: 8 and all his army was scattered from him. 6
Lam 4:16 has scattered them, he will regard them no more; 5
Ezk 5: 2 and a third part you shall scatter to the wind 2
10 you who survive I will scatter to all the winds. 2
12 and a third part I will scatter to all the winds 2
6: 5 I will scatter your bones round about 2
8 when you are scattered through the countries 2
10: 2 and scatter them over the city. 4
11:16 and though I scattered them among the countries 7
17 the countries where you have been scattered 7
12:14 I will scatter toward every wind all who are 2
15 when I . . scatter them through the countries. 2
17:21 the survivors shall be scattered to every wind; 11
20:23 that I would scatter them among the nations 7
34 you out of the countries where you are scattered 7
41 the countries where you have been scattered; 7
22:15 I will scatter you among the nations 7
28:25 from the peoples among whom they are scattered 6
29:12 I will scatter the Egyptians among the nations 7
13 from the peoples among whom they were scattered; 6
30:23 I will scatter the Egyptians among the nations 7
26 I will scatter the Egyptians among the nations 7
34: 5 were scattered, because there was no shepherd; 7
6 My sheep were scattered, they wandered 12
6 my sheep were scattered over all the face 6
12 when some of his sheep have been scattered •
12 from all places where they have been scattered 6
21 till you have scattered them abroad 7
36:19 I scattered them among the nations 7
Dan 4:14 strip off its leaves and scatter its fruit; 15
11:24 scattering among them plunder, spoil, and goods. 1
Jol 3: 2 because they have scattered them 9
Nah 3:18 Your people are scattered on the mountains 8
Hab 3: 6 then the eternal mountains were scattered 7
14 who came like a whirlwind to scatter me 7
Zec 1:19 These are the horns which have scattered Judah 2
21 These are the horns which scattered Judah 2
21 against the land of Judah to scatter it. 2
10: 9 Though I scattered them among the nations 3
13: 7 the shepherd, that the sheep may be scattered; 7
Mat 12:30 and he who does not gather with me scatters. 26
26:31 the sheep of the flock will be scattered.' 20
Mrk 4:26 as if a man should scatter seed upon the ground 17
14:27 the sheep will be scattered.' 20
Lke 1:51 he has scattered the proud 20
11:23 he who does not gather with me scatters. 26
Joh 10:12 the wolf snatches them and scatters them. 26
16:32 when you will be scattered, every man to his home 26
Act 5:37 all who followed him were scattered. 20
8: 1 scattered throughout the region of Judea and 21
4 those who were scattered went about preaching 21
11:19 who were scattered because of the persecution 21
2Es 1:11 and scattered in the east the people 29
2: 7 Let them be scattered among the nations 28
5:28 and scattered thine only one among the many? 28
36 and gather for me the scattered raindrops 28
Tob 13: 3 he has scattered us among them. 21
5 the nations among whom you have been scattered. 26
14: 4 Our brethren will be scattered over the earth 26
Jdt 5:19 the places to which they were scattered 21
AEs 13: 4 there is scattered a certain hostile people 16
Wis 2: 4 be scattered like mist 19
11:20 scattered by the breath of thy power 24
17: 3 they were scattered, terribly alarmed 26
Sir 28:14 scattered them from nation to nation 23
39:14 Scatter the fragrance, and sing a hymn of praise; 18
43:17 He scatters the snow like birds flying down 25
48:15 were scattered over all the earth 20
Bar 2: 4 peoples, where the Lord has scattered them. 21
13 among the nations where thou hast scattered us. 21
29 among the nations, where I will scatter them. 21
3: 8 today in our exile where thou hast scattered us 21
1Mc 6:54 they had been scattered, each to his own place. 26
2Mc 1:27 Gather together our scattered people 22
14:13 with orders to kill Judas and scatter his men 26
4Mc 15:15 their toes and fingers scattered on the ground 27

scatter abroad 1. פוץ 2. διασκορπίζω 3. σκορπίζω
Gen 11: 4 lest we be scattered abroad upon the . . earth. 1
8 the LORD scattered them abroad 1
9 the LORD scattered them abroad over . . the earth. 1
Exd 5:12 So the people were scattered abroad throughout 1
Joh 11:52 the children of God who are scattered abroad. 2
2Co 9: 9 He scatters abroad, he gives to the poor 3

scatter afar 1. פאה
Deu 32:26 I would have said, "I will scatter them afar 1

scatter with a whirlwind 1. סער
Zec 7:14 I scattered them with a whirlwind 1
scattered *See* lie, place.
scattering *See* wind.

scent 1. רֵיחַ 2. θύϊνος
Job 14: 9 yet at the scent of water it will bud 1
Sng 4:11 the scent of your garments is like . . Lebanon. 1
11 of your garments is like the scent of Lebanon. 1
7: 8 and the scent of your breath like apples 1
Jer 48:11 and his scent is not changed. 1
Rev 18:12 all kinds of scented wood, all articles of ivory 2

scepter 1. חקק 2. מַטֶּה 3. שֵׁבֶט 4. שַׁרְבִיט 5. ῥάβδος
6. σκῆπτρον
Gen 49:10 The scepter shall not depart from Judah 3
Num21:18 delved, with the scepter and with their staves. 1
24:17 scepter shall rise out of Israel; 3
Est 4:11 to whom the king holds out the golden scepter 4
5: 2 and he held out to Esther the golden scepter 4
2 Esther . . and touched the top of the scepter. 4
8: 4 the king held out the golden scepter to Esther 4
Ps 45: 6 Your royal scepter is a scepter of equity; 3
6 Your royal scepter is a scepter of equity; 3
60: 7 E'phraim is my helmet; Judah is my scepter. 1
89:44 Thou hast removed the scepter from his hand •

108: 8 E'phraim is my helmet; Judah my scepter. 1
110: 2 LORD sends forth from Zion your mighty scepter. 2
125: 3 scepter of wickedness shall not rest upon 3
Isa 14: 5 The LORD has broken . . the scepter of rulers 3
Jer 48:17 say, 'How the mighty scepter is broken 2
Ezk 19:11 Its strongest stem became a ruler's scepter; 3
14 in it no strong stem, no scepter for a ruler. 3
Ams 1: 5 and him that holds the scepter from Beth-eden; 3
8 and him that holds the scepter from Ash'kelon; 3
Zec 10:11 the scepter of Egypt shall depart. 3
Heb 1: 8 the righteous scepter 5
8 the scepter of thy kingdom. 5
AEs 14:11 do not surrender thy scepter to what has no being; 6
15:11 Then he raised the golden scepter 5
Wis 6:21 if you delight in thrones and scepters 6
7: 8 I preferred her to scepters and thrones 6
10:14 until she brought him the scepter of a kingdom 6
Sir 35:18 breaks the scepters of the unrighteous; 6
LJr 1:14 Like a local ruler the god holds a scepter 6

scheme 1.יסד 2.מְזִמָּה 3.מַחֲשָׁבָה 4.עֵצָה 5.רִגְשָׁה
Job 5:13 the schemes of the wily are brought to a quick end. 4
18: 7 his own schemes throw him down. 4
21:27 know your thoughts, and your schemes to wrong me. 2
Ps 10: 2 caught in the schemes which they have devised. 2
31:13 as they scheme together against me, as they plot 1
64: 2 hide me . . from the scheming of evildoers 5
Jer 11:19 not know it was against me they devised schemes 3
Ezk 38:10 you will devise an evil scheme 3

scheme against 1.μηχανάομαι
AEs 16: 3 to scheme against their own benefactors. 1

scheme to get 1.τεκταίνω
Bar 3:18 those who scheme to get silver, and are anxious 1

school 1.παιδείας οἶκος
Sir 51:23 lodge in my school. 1

scoff 1.חרף 2.חֶרְפָּה 3.ליץ 4.לַעַג 5.לָצוֹן 6.מוק 7.מְלִיצָה 8.נבל 9.קֶלֶס 10.שֶׂפֶק 11.תעע 12.ἐκμυκτηρίζω 13.ἐκπαίζω 14.ἐμπαιγμονή 15.χλευάζω
Deu 32:15 then he . . scoffed at the Rock of his salvation. 8
2Ch 36:16 scoffing at his prophets 11
Job 34: 7 man is like Job, who drinks up scoffing like water 4
36:18 Beware lest wrath entice you into scoffing; 10
Ps 73: 8 They scoff and speak with malice; 6
74:10 How long, O God, is the foe to scoff? 1
18 Remember this, O LORD, how the enemy scoffs 1
22 remember how the impious scoff at thee all the day! 2
Prv 1:22 How long will scoffers delight in their scoffing 5
9:12 if you scoff, you alone will bear it. 3
Isa 28:22 do not scoff, lest your bonds be made strong; 3
Hab 1:10 At kings they scoff, and of rulers they make sport. 9
2: 6 taunt against him, in scoffing derision of him 7
Zep 2:10 they scoffed and boasted against the people 1
Lke 16:14 they scoffed at him. 12
23:35 the rulers scoffed at him, saying, "He saved others; 12
2Pe 3: 3 scoffers will come . . with scoffing 14
1Es 1:51 they scoffed at his prophets 13
4Mc 5:22 You scoff at our philosophy 15

scoffer 1.אִישׁ לָצוֹן 2.ליץ 3.ἐμπαίκτης 4.καταφρονητής
Ps 1: 1 nor sits in the seat of scoffers; 2
Prv 1:22 How long will scoffers delight in their scoffing 2
9: 7 He who corrects a scoffer gets himself abuse 2
8 Do not reprove a scoffer, or he will hate you; 2
13: 1 but a scoffer does not listen to rebuke. 2
14: 6 A scoffer seeks wisdom in vain 2
15:12 A scoffer does not like to be reproved; 2
19:25 Strike a scoffer . . simple will learn prudence; 2
29 Condemnation is ready for scoffers 2
21:11 scoffer is punished, the simple becomes wise; 2
24 Scoffer" is the name of the proud, haughty man 2
22:10 Drive out a scoffer, and strife will go out 2
24: 9 scoffer is an abomination to men. 2
29: 8 Scoffers set a city aflame 1
Isa 28:14 Therefore hear the word of the LORD, you scoffers 1
29:20 ruthless . . come to nought and the scoffer cease 2
Act 13:41 'Behold, you scoffers, and wonder, and perish 4
2Pe 3: 3 scoffers will come in the last days 3
Jde 1:18 In the last time there will be scoffers 3

scold 1.ἐπιτίμησις
Sir 29:28 scolding about lodging 1

scorch 1.זַלְעָפָה 2.חרר 3.כוה 4.עַיִם 5.צרב 6.צָרָב 7.שׁוּף 8.καυματίζω
Ps 11: 6 scorching wind shall be the portion of their 1
Prv 6:28 walk upon hot coals and his feet not be scorched? 3
16:27 his speech is like a scorching fire. 6
Sng 1: 6 Do not gaze . . because the sun has scorched me. 7
Isa 11:15 hand over the River with his scorching wind 4
24: 6 the inhabitants of the earth are scorched 2
Ezk 20:47 all faces from south to north shall be scorched 5
Mat 13: 6 when the sun rose they were scorched 8
Mrk 4: 6 when the sun rose it was scorched 8
Rev 16: 8 and it was allowed to scorch men with fire; 8
9 men were scorched by the fierce heat 8

scorching *See* heat, wind.

scorn 1.בוז 2.זנח 3.חֶרְפָּה 4.ליץ 5.לעג 6.לַעַג 7.מָדוֹן 8.נאץ 9.קלס 10.קֶלֶס 11.שחק 12.ἐξουδενέω 13.ἐξουθενέω 14.μυκτηρισμός 15.περιφρονέω 16.fastidio 17.sperno
2Sm 12:14 by this deed you have utterly scorned the LORD 8
2Kg 19:21 She despises you, she scorns you 5
Job 16:20 My friends scorn me; my eye pours out tears to God 4
39: 7 He scorns the tumult of the city; 11
Ps 22: 6 scorned by men, and despised by the people. 3
31:11 I am the scorn of all my adversaries, a horror 3
39: 8 Make me not the scorn of the fool! 3
44:13 the derision and scorn of those about us. 10
71:13 with scorn and disgrace may they be covered 3
80: 6 Thou dost make us the scorn of our neighbors; 7
89:41 he has become the scorn of his neighbors. 3
50 Remember, O Lord, how thy servant is scorned; 3
119:22 take away from me their scorn and contempt 3
123: 4 sated with the scorn of those who are at ease 6
Prv 14: 9 God scorns the wicked, but the upright enjoy 4
30:17 eye . . mocks a father and scorns to obey a mother 1
Sng 8: 7 If a man offered . . it would be utterly scorned. 1
Isa 37:22 She despises you, she scorns you- 5
Lam 2: 7 The Lord has scorned his altar . . his sanctuary; 2
Ezk 16:31 were not like a harlot, because you scorned hire. 9
Mic 6:16 so you shall bear the scorn of the peoples. 3
Gal 4:14 you did not scorn or despise me 13
2Es 3: 8 did ungodly things before thee and scorned thee 17
7:24 They scorned his law, and denied his covenants; 17
81 they have scorned the law of the Most High. 17
9:11 as many as scorned my law 16
1Mc 3:14 who scorn the king's command. 12
2Mc 7:39 being exasperated at his scorn. 14
4Mc 6: 9 he bore the pains and scorned the punishment 15

scorn *See also* laugh, object.

show scorn 1.sperno
2Es 7:76 be associated with those who have shown scorn 1
79 if it is one of those who have shown scorn 1

scorner 1.ליץ
Prv 3:34 Toward the scorners he is scornful 1

scornful 1.ליץ
Prv 3:34 Toward the scorners he is scornful 1

scornfully 1.ἐφύβριστος
Wis 17: 7 their boasted wisdom was scornfully rebuked. 1

scorpion 1.עַקְרָב 2.σκορπίος
Deu 8:15 with its fiery serpents and scorpions 1
1Kg 12:11 but I will chastise you with scorpions.' 1
14 but I will chastise you with scorpions. 1
2Ch 10:11 but I will chastise you with scorpions.' 1
14 but I will chastise you with scorpions. 1
Ezk 2: 6 thorns are with you and you sit upon scorpions; 1
Lke 10:19 authority to tread upon serpents and scorpions 2
11:12 or if he asks for an egg, will give him a scorpion? 2
Rev 9: 3 like the power of scorpions of the earth; 2
5 their torture was like the torture of a scorpion 2
10 They have tails like scorpions, and stings 2
Sir 26: 7 taking hold of her is like grasping a scorpion. 2
39:30 scorpions and vipers 2
4Mc 11:10 he was completely curled back like a scorpion 2

scoundrel 1.בֶּן בְּלִיַּעַל 2.ἀλιτήριος 3.κακουργέω
2Ch 13: 7 certain worthless scoundrels gathered about 1
Sir 11:33 Beware of a scoundrel, for he devises evil 3
2Mc 13: 4 the anger of Antiochus against the scoundrel; 2

scour 1.מרק
Lev 6:28 that shall be scoured, and rinsed in water 1

scourge 1.נֶגַע 2.שׁוֹט 3.שֹׁטֵט 4.μαστιγόω 5.μαστίζω 6.μάστιξ 7.μάστιξιν καταικίζω 8.φραγελλόω 9.flagellum 10.plaga
Jos 23:13 a snare and a trap for you, a scourge on your sides 3
Job 5:21 You shall be hid from the scourge of the tongue 2
Ps 89:32 I will punish . . their iniquity with scourges; 1
91:10 no scourge come near your tent. 1
Isa 10:26 the LORD . . will wield against them a scourge 2
28:15 when the overwhelming scourge passes through 2
18 when the overwhelming scourge passes through 2
Mat 20:19 to be mocked and scourged and crucified 4
23:34 some you will scourge in your synagogues 4
27:26 having scourged Jesus 8
Mrk 10:34 mock him, and spit upon him, and scourge him 4
15:15 having scourged Jesus 8
Lke 18:33 they will scourge him and kill him 4
Joh 19: 1 Pilate took Jesus and scourged him. 4
Act 22:24 ordered him to be examined by scourging 6
25 lawful . . to scourge a man who is a Roman citizen 5
Heb 11:36 Others suffered mocking and scourging 6
2Es 16:19 tribulation and anguish are sent as scourges 9
20 nor be always mindful of the scourges. 10
Jdt 8:27 the Lord scourges those who draw near to him 4
Wis 12:22 while chastening us thou scourgest our enemies 4
16:16 were scourged by the strength of thy arm 4
Sir 23:11 the scourge will not leave his house 6
39:28 in their anger they scourge heavily 6
2Mc 3:26 scourged him continuously 4
34 you, who have been scourged by heaven 4
5:18 this man would have been scourged 4
9:11 to come to his senses under the scourge of God 6
3Mc 2:21 scourged him who had exalted himself 5
4Mc 6: 3 they scourged him 7
6 his flesh was being torn by scourges 6
9:12 beating him with scourges 6

scourge thoroughly 1.μαστιγόω
2Mc 3:38 for you will get him back thoroughly scourged 1

scout
1Kg 20:17 Ben-ha'dad sent out scouts, and they reported •

scrap
Jdg 1: 7 kings . . used to pick up scraps under my table; •

scrape 1.גרד 2.מלל 3.סחה 4.קצה
Lev 14:43 he has taken out the stones and scraped the house 4
Job 2: 8 he took a potsherd with which to scrape himself 1
Prv 6:13 winks with his eyes, scrapes with his feet 2
Ezk 26: 4 I will scrape her soil from her 3

cause to scrape 1.קצע
Lev 14:41 cause the inside of the house to be scraped 1

scrape off 1.קצה
Lev 14:41 the plaster that they scrape off they shall pour 1

scrape out 1.רדה
Jdg 14: 9 He scraped it out into his hands, and went on 1

screen 1.מָסָךְ 2.סכך
Exd 26:36 you shall make a screen for the door of the tent 1
37 shall make for the screen five pillars of acacia 1
27:16 there shall be a screen twenty cubits long 1
35:12 the mercy seat, and the veil of the screen; 1
15 the screen for the door, at the door 1
17 its bases, and the screen for the gate of the court; 1
36:37 He also made a screen for the door of the tent 1
38:18 the screen for the gate of the court was 1
39:34 goatskins, and the veil of the screen; 1
38 the screen for the door of the tent; 1
40 its bases, and the screen for the gate of the court 1
40: 3 and you shall screen the ark with the veil. 2
5 set up the screen for the door of the tabernacle. 1
8 hang up the screen for the gate of the court. 1
21 the tabernacle, and set up the veil of the screen 1
21 and screened the ark of the testimony; 2
28 he put in place the screen for the door 1
33 set up the screen of the gate of the court. 1
Num 3:25 the screen for the door of the tent of meeting 1
26 the hangings of the court, the screen for the door 1
31 their charge was . . and the screen; 1
4: 5 go in and take down the veil of the screen 1
25 carry . . the screen for the door of the tent 1
26 screen for the entrance of the gate of the court 1

scribe 1.מִסְפָּר 2.סֹפֵר 3.סָפַר (A) 4.γραμματεύς
1Ch 2:55 families also of the scribes that dwelt at Jabez 2
24: 6 the scribe Shemai'ah . . recorded them 2
27:32 being a man of understanding and a scribe; 2
2Ch 34:13 some of the Levites were scribes, and officials 2
Ezr 4: 8 Rehum the commander and Shim'shai the scribe 3
9 Rehum . . Shim'shai the scribe 3
17 To Rehum the commander and Shim'shai the scribe 3
23 Shim'shai the scribe and their associates 3
7: 6 Ezra . . was a scribe skilled in the law of Moses 2
11 Ezra the priest, the scribe, learned in matters 2
12 Ezra the priest, the scribe of the law of the God 3
21 Ezra the priest, the scribe of the law of the God 3
Neh 8: 1 told Ezra the scribe to bring the book of the law 2
4 Ezra the scribe stood on a wooden pulpit 2
9 Nehemi'ah . . and Ezra the priest and scribe 2
13 came . . to Ezra the scribe in order to study 2
12:26 days of Nehemi'ah . . of Ezra the priest the scribe. 2
36 Ezra the scribe went before them. 2
13:13 appointed . . Zadok the scribe, and Pedai'ah 2
Ps 45: 1 my tongue is like the pen of a ready scribe. 2
Jer 8: 8 the false pen of the scribes has made it into a lie. 2
36:32 another scroll and gave it to Baruch the scribe 2
Nah 3:17 your scribes like clouds of locusts 1
Mat 2: 4 assembling all the chief priests and scribes 4
5:20 exceeds that of the scribes and Pharisees 4
7:29 and not as their scribes. 4
8:19 a scribe came up and said to him 4
9: 3 behold, some of the scribes said to themselves 4
12:38 Then some of the scribes and Pharisees said 4
13:52 Therefore every scribe who has been trained 4
15: 1 Then Pharisees and scribes came to Jesus 4
16:21 from the elders and chief priests and scribes 4

17:10 Then why do the scribes say 4
20:18 delivered to the chief priests and scribes 4
21:15 when the chief priests and the scribes saw 4
23: 2 The scribes and the Pharisees sit on Moses' seat; 4
13 woe to you, scribes and Pharisees, hypocrites! 4
15 Woe to you, scribes and Pharisees, hypocrites! 4
23 Woe to you, scribes and Pharisees, hypocrites! 4
25 Woe to you, scribes and Pharisees, hypocrites! 4
27 Woe to you, scribes and Pharisees, hypocrites! 4
29 Woe to you, scribes and Pharisees, hypocrites! 4
34 I send you prophets and wise men and scribes 4
26:57 where the scribes and the elders had gathered. 4
27:41 chief priests, with the scribes and elders 4
Mrk 1:22 not as the scribes. 4
2: 6 Now some of the scribes were sitting there 4
16 the scribes of the Pharisees 4
3:22 the scribes who came down from Jerusalem said 4
7: 1 with some of the scribes 4
5 the Pharisees and the scribes asked him 4
8:31 chief priests and the scribes 4
9:11 they asked him, "Why do the scribes say 4
14 scribes arguing with them. 4
10:33 chief priests and the scribes 4
11:18 the chief priests and the scribes heard it 4
27 the chief priests and the scribes 4
12:28 one of the scribes came up and heard 4
32 the scribe said to him, "You are right, Teacher 4
35 How can the scribes say that the Christ is the son 4
38 in his teaching he said, "Beware of the scribes 4
14: 1 the chief priests and the scribes were seeking 4
43 the chief priests and the scribes and the elders 4
53 the chief priests and the elders and the scribes 4
15: 1 the chief priests, with the elders and scribes 4
31 mocked him to one another with the scribes 4
Lke 5:21 the scribes and the Pharisees began to question 4
30 the Pharisees and their scribes murmured 4
6: 7 the scribes and the Pharisees watched him 4
9:22 the elders and chief priests and scribes 4
11:53 the scribes and the Pharisees began to press him 4
15: 2 the Pharisees and the scribes murmured, saying 4
19:47 The chief priests and the scribes 4
20: 1 the chief priests and the scribes with the elders 4
19 The scribes and the chief priests 4
39 some of the scribes answered, "Teacher 4
46 Beware of the scribes 4
22: 2 the chief priests and the scribes were seeking 4
66 both chief priests and scribes 4
23:10 The chief priests and the scribes stood by 4
Joh 8: 3 The scribes and the Pharisees brought a woman 4
Act 4: 5 their rulers and elders and scribes 4
6:12 the elders and the scribes 4
23: 9 some of the scribes of the Pharisees' party 4
1Co 1:20 Where is the wise man? Where is the scribe? 4
1Es 2:16 Shimshai the scribe 4
17 Rehum the recorder and Shimshai the scribe 4
25 Shimshai the scribe and the others 4
30 Rehum and Shimshai the scribe 4
8: 3 a scribe skilled in the law of Moses 4
Sir 10: 5 confers his honor upon the person of the scribe. 4
38:24 The wisdom of the scribe 4
1Mc 5:42 he stationed the scribes . . at the stream 4
7:12 Then a group of scribes appeared in a body 4
2Mc 6:18 Eleazar, one of the scribes in high position 4
3Mc 4:17 the scribes declared to the king 4

script 1. כְּתָב

Est 1:22 he sent . . to every province in its own script 1
3:12 to every province in its own script 1
8: 9 an edict . . to every province in its own script 1
9 to the Jews in their script and their language. 1

scripture 1. γραφή 2. γράφω

Mat 21:42 Have you never read in the scriptures 1
22:29 neither the scriptures nor the power of God. 1
26:54 how then should the scriptures be fulfilled 1
56 scriptures of the prophets might be fulfilled. 1
Mrk 12:10 Have you not read this scripture: 'The very stone 1
24 you know neither the scriptures nor the power of God 1
14:49 let the scriptures be fulfilled. 1
Lke 4:21 Today this scripture has been fulfilled 1
22:37 I tell you that this scripture must be fulfilled 2
24:27 he interpreted to them in all the scriptures 1
32 while he opened to us the scriptures? 1
45 to understand the scriptures 1
Joh 2:22 and they believed the scripture and the word 1
5:39 You search the scriptures 1
7:38 He who believes in me, as the scripture has said 1
42 Has not the scripture said 1
10:35 (and scripture cannot be broken) 1
13:18 that the scripture may be fulfilled 1
17:12 that the scripture might be fulfilled. 1
19:24 This was to fulfil the scripture 1
28 Jesus . . said (to fulfil the scripture), "I thirst. 1
36 that the scripture might be fulfilled 1
37 again another scripture says 1
20: 9 for as yet they did not know the scripture 1
Act 1:16 Brethren, the scripture had to be fulfilled 1
8:32 passage of the scripture which he was reading 1
35 beginning with this scripture 1
17: 2 he argued with them from the scriptures 1
11 examining the scriptures daily 1
18:24 an eloquent man, well versed in the scriptures. 1
28 showing by the scriptures 1
Rom 1: 2 through his prophets in the holy scriptures 1
4: 3 For what does the scripture say? 1
9:17 For the scripture says to Pharaoh 1
10:11 The scripture says, "No one who believes in him 1
11: 2 Do you not know what the scripture says of Eli'jah 1
15: 4 by the encouragement of the scriptures 1
1Co 15: 3 Christ died . . in accordance with the scriptures 1
4 he was raised . . in accordance with the scriptures 1
Gal 3: 8 the scripture, foreseeing that God would justify 1
22 the scripture consigned all things to sin 1
4:30 what does the scripture say? "Cast out the slave 1
1Ti 4:13 attend to the public reading of scripture •
5:18 for the scripture says, "You shall not muzzle an ox 1
2Ti 3:16 All scripture is inspired by God 1
Jas 2: 8 fulfill the . . law, according to the scripture 1
23 the scripture was fulfilled which says 1
4: 5 you suppose it is in vain that the scripture says 1
1Pe 2: 6 For it stands in scripture 1
2Pe 1:20 no prophecy of scripture is a matter of one's own 1
3:16 as they do the other scriptures. 1
4Mc 18:14 He reminded you of the scripture of Isaiah 1

scroll 1. מְגִלָּה 2. מְגִלַּת סֵפֶר 3. סֵפֶר 4. מְגִלָּה (A) 5. βιβλίον 6. τόμος

Ezr 6: 2 scroll was found on which this was written 4
Isa 34: 4 and the skies roll up like a scroll. 3
Jer 36: 2 Take a scroll and write on it all the words 2
4 wrote upon a scroll at the dictation of Jeremiah 2
6 from the scroll which you have written 1
8 reading from the scroll the words of the LORD 3
10 read the words of Jeremiah from the scroll 3
11 heard all the words of the LORD from the scroll 3
13 that he had heard, when Baruch read the scroll 3
14 to say to Baruch, "Take in your hand the scroll 1
14 Baruch the son of Neri'ah took the scroll 1
18 while I wrote them with ink on the scroll. 3
20 having put the scroll in the chamber of Eli'shama 1
21 Then the king sent Jehu'di to get the scroll 1
23 until the entire scroll was consumed in the fire 1
25 Gemari'ah urged the king not to burn the scroll 1
27 Now, after the king had burned the scroll 1
28 Take another scroll and write on it 1
28 the former words that were in the first scroll 1
29 Thus says the LORD, You have burned this scroll 1
32 Then Jeremiah took another scroll 1
32 who wrote on it . . all the words of the scroll 3
Ezk 2: 9 a hand . . and, lo, a written scroll was in it; 1
3: 1 eat this scroll, and go, speak 1
2 I opened my mouth, and he gave me the scroll to eat. 1
3 Son of man, eat this scroll that I give you 1
Zec 5: 1 lifted my eyes and saw, and behold, a flying scroll! 1
2 What do you see?" I answered, "I see a flying scroll; 1
Rev 5: 1 I saw . . a scroll written within and on the back 5
2 Who is worthy to open the scroll and break 5
3 no one . . was able to open the scroll or to look 5
4 that no one was found worthy to open the scroll 5
5 so that he can open the scroll and its seven seals. 5
7 he went and took the scroll from the right hand •
8 when he had taken the scroll 5
9 Worthy . . to take the scroll and to open its seals 5
6:14 the sky vanished like a scroll that is rolled up 5
10: 8 the scroll which is open in the hand of the angel 5
1Es 6:23 a scroll was found in which this was recorded 6
Tob 7:14 and took a scroll and wrote out the contract 5

little scroll 1. βιβλαρίδιον

Rev 10: 2 He had a little scroll open in his hand. 1
9 angel and told him to give me the little scroll; 1
10 took the little scroll from the hand of the angel 1

scruples 1. εὐλαβέομαι 2. συνείδησις

1Co 10:29 be determined by another man's scruples? 2
4Mc 4:13 otherwise he had scruples about doing so 1

scrupulous 1. ἀκριβής

Sir 19:25 is a cleverness which is scrupulous but unjust 1

scrupulously 1. ἐπιμελῶς

1Es 6:29 a portion be scrupulously given to these men 1
8:21 scrupulously fulfilled for the Most High God 1

sculptured *See* stone.

scurvy 1. גָּרָב

Deu 28:27 smite you . . with the ulcers and the scurvy 1

scythe *See* arm.

sea 1. יָם 2. מַי 3. יָם (A) 4. ἄβυσσος 5. βυθός 6. θάλασσα 7. θαλάσσιος 8. παραθαλάσσιος 9. πέλαγος 10. mare

Gen 1:10 waters . . gathered together he called Seas 1
22 and multiply and fill the waters in the seas 1
26 let them have dominion over the fish of the sea 1
28 have dominion over the fish of the sea 1
9: 2 ground and all the fish of the sea; 1
14: 3 valley of Siddim (that is, the Salt Sea). 1
32:12 make your descendants as the sand of the sea 1
41:49 great abundance, like the sand of the sea 1
49:13 Zeb'ulun shall dwell at the shore of the sea; 1
Exd 10:19 locusts and drove them into the Red Sea; 1
13:18 the way of the wilderness toward the Red Sea. 1
14: 2 encamp . . between Migdol and the sea 1
2 you shall encamp over against it, by the sea. 1
9 his army, and overtook them encamped at the sea 1
16 stretch out your hand over the sea and divide it 1
16 Israel may go on dry ground through the sea. 1
21 Then Moses stretched out his hand over the sea; 1
21 the LORD drove the sea back by a strong east wind 1
21 the sea dry land, and the waters were divided. 1
22 people of Israel went into the midst of the sea 1
23 went in after them into the midst of the sea 1
26 Stretch out your hand over the sea, that the water 1
27 So Moses stretched forth his hand over the sea 1
27 the sea returned to its wonted flow 1
27 the Egyptians in the midst of the sea. 1
28 that had followed them into the sea; 1
29 walked on dry ground through the sea 1
15: 1 the horse and his rider he has thrown into the sea. 1
4 chariots and his host he cast into the sea; 1
4 his picked officers are sunk in the Red Sea. 1
8 the deeps congealed in the heart of the sea. 1
10 Thou didst blow with thy wind, the sea covered 1
19 chariots and his horsemen went into the sea 1
19 the LORD brought back the waters of the sea upon 1
19 on dry ground in the midst of the sea. 1
21 his rider he has thrown into the sea. 1
22 Then Moses led Israel onward from the Red Sea 1
20:11 heaven and earth, the sea, and all that is in them 1
23:31 I will set your bounds from the Red Sea to the sea 1
31 from the Red Sea to the sea of the Philistines 1
Lev 11: 9 whether in the seas or in the rivers 1
10 anything in the seas or the rivers 1
Num 11:22 Or shall all the fish of the sea be gathered 1
31 brought quails from the sea, and let them fall 1
13:29 Canaanites dwell by the sea, and along the Jordan. 1
14:25 out for the wilderness by the way to the Red Sea. 1
21: 4 From Mount Hor they set out . . to the Red Sea 1
33: 8 through the midst of the sea into the wilderness 1
10 they set out from Elim, and encamped by the Red Sea 1
11 they set out from the Red Sea, and encamped 1
34: 3 boundary shall be from the end of the Salt Sea 1
5 its termination shall be at the sea. 1
6 you shall have the Great Sea and its coast 1
7 from the Great Sea you shall mark out your line 1
11 reach to the shoulder of the sea of Chin'nereth 1
12 to the Jordan, and its end shall be at the Salt Sea. 1
Deu 1:40 wilderness in the direction of the Red Sea.' 1
2: 1 the wilderness in the direction of the Red Sea 1
3:17 from Chin'nereth as far as the sea of the Arabah 1
17 as far as the sea of the Arabah, the Salt Sea 1
4:49 as far as the Sea of the Arabah, under the slopes 1
11: 4 how he made the water of the Red Sea overflow them 1
24 from the . . river Euphra'tes, to the western sea. 1
30:13 Neither is it beyond the sea, that you should say 1
13 'Who will go over the sea for us, and bring it to us 1
33:19 for they suck the affluence of the seas 1
34: 2 all the land of Judah as far as the Western Sea 1
Jos 1: 4 all the land of the Hittites to the Great Sea 1
2:10 LORD dried up the water of the Red Sea before you 1
3:16 and those flowing down toward the sea of Arabah 1
16 flowing . . toward the sea of Arabah, the Salt Sea 1
4:23 as the LORD your God did to the Red Sea 1
5: 1 kings of the Canaanites that were by the sea 1
9: 1 the lowland all along the coast of the Great Sea 1
12: 3 and the Arabah to the Sea of Chin'neroth eastward 1
3 to the sea of the Arabah, the Salt Sea, southward 1
3 to the sea of the Arabah, the Salt Sea, southward 1
13:27 to the lower end of the Sea of Chin'nereth 1
15: 2 south boundary ran from the end of the Salt Sea 1
4 goes out by . . and comes to its end at the sea. 1
5 the east boundary is the Salt Sea 1
5 from the bay of the sea at the mouth of the Jordan; 1
11 then the boundary comes to an end at the sea. 1
12 And the west boundary was the Great Sea with its 1
46 from Ekron to the sea, all . . by the side of Ashdod 1
47 to . . and the Great Sea with its coast-line. 1
16: 3 it goes . . then to Gezer, and it ends at the sea. 1
6 and the boundary goes thence to the sea; 1
8 boundary goes westward to . . and ends at the sea. 1
17: 9 boundary of Manas'seh goes . . and ends at the sea; 1
10 Manas'seh's, with the sea forming its boundary; 1
18:19 boundary ends at the northern bay of the Salt Sea 1
19:29 the boundary turns to Hosah, and it ends at the sea; 1
23: 4 from the Jordan to the Great Sea in the west. 1
24: 6 I brought . . out of Egypt, and you came to the sea; 1
6 and the Egyptians pursued . . to the Red Sea. 1
7 he . . made the sea come upon them and cover them; 1
Jdg 5:17 Asher sat still at the coast of the sea 1
11:16 through the wilderness to the Red Sea and came 1
2Sm 17:11 all Israel . . as the sand by the sea for multitude 1
22:16 Then the channels of the sea were seen 1
1Kg 4:20 and Israel were as many as the sand by the sea; they 1
5: 9 servants . . bring it down to the sea from Lebanon; 1
9 rafts to go by sea to the place you direct 1

7:23 he made the molten sea; it was round, ten cubits 1
24 were gourds . . compassing the sea round about; 1
25 upon twelve oxen . . the sea was set upon them 1
39 he set the sea on the southeast corner 1
44 one sea, and the twelve oxen underneath the sea. 1
44 one sea, and the twelve oxen underneath the sea. 1
9:26 which is near Eloth on the shore of the Red Sea 1
27 seamen who were familiar with the sea 1
10:22 king had a fleet . . at sea with the fleet of Hiram. 1
18:43 he said . . "Go up now, look toward the sea. 1
44 a little cloud . . is rising out of the sea. 1
2Kg 14:25 from the . . as far as the Sea of the Arabah 1
16:17 and he took down the sea from off the bronze oxen 1
25:13 the pillars . . and the stands and the bronze sea 1
16 As for the two pillars, the one sea, and the stands 1
1Ch 16:32 Let the sea roar, and all that fills it 1
18: 8 with it Solomon made the bronze sea 1
2Ch 2:16 and bring it to you in rafts by sea to Joppa 1
4: 2 Then he made the molten sea; it was round 1
3 gourds . . compassing the sea round about; 1
4 upon twelve oxen . . the sea was set upon them 1
6 and the sea was for the priests to wash in. 1
10 set the sea at the southeast corner of the house. 1
15 the one sea, and the twelve oxen underneath it. 1
8:17 E'zion-ge'ber and Eloth on the shore of the sea 1
18 ships and servants familiar with the sea 1
20: 2 coming against you from Edom, from beyond the sea; 1
Ezr 3: 7 cedar trees from Lebanon to the sea, to Joppa 1
Neh 9: 6 thou hast made . . the seas and all that is in them; 1
9 thou didst . . hear their cry at the Red Sea 1
11 thou didst divide the sea before them 1
11 went through the midst of the sea on dry land; 1
Est 10: 1 laid tribute . . and on the coastlands of the sea. 1
Job 6: 3 then it would be heavier than the sand of the sea; 1
7:12 Am I the sea, or a sea monster 1
9: 8 trampled the waves of the sea; 1
11: 9 longer than the earth, and broader than the sea. 1
12: 8 the fish of the sea will declare to you. 1
26:12 By his power he stilled the sea; 1
28:14 and the sea says, 'It is not with me.' 1
36:30 about him, and covers the roots of the sea. 1
38: 8 who shut in the sea with doors 1
16 Have you entered into the springs of the sea 1
41:31 he makes the sea like a pot of ointment. 1
Ps 8: 8 the birds of the air, and the fish of the sea 1
8 whatever passes along the paths of the sea. 1
18:15 Then the channels of the sea were seen 1
24: 2 for he has founded it upon the seas 1
33: 7 He gathered the waters of the sea as in a bottle; 1
46: 2 though the mountains shake in the heart of the sea; 1
65: 5 all the ends of the earth, and of the farthest seas; 1
7 who dost still the roaring of the seas 1
66: 6 He turned the sea into dry land; 1
68:22 I will bring them back from the depths of the sea 1
69:34 the seas and everything that moves therein. 1
72: 8 May he have dominion from sea to sea 1
8 May he have dominion from sea to sea 1
74:13 Thou didst divide the sea by thy might; 1
77:19 Thy way was through the sea 1
78:13 He divided the sea and let them pass through it 1
27 like dust, winged birds like the sand of the seas; 1
53 but the sea overwhelmed their enemies. 1
80:11 it sent out its branches to the sea 1
89: 9 Thou dost rule the raging of the sea; 1
25 I will set his hand on the sea 1
93: 4 mightier than the waves of the sea 1
95: 5 The sea is his, for he made it; 1
96:11 let the sea roar, and all that fills it; 1
98: 7 Let the sea roar, and all that fills it; 1
104:25 Yonder is the sea, great and wide, which teems 1
106: 7 rebelled against the Most High at the Red Sea. 1
9 He rebuked the Red Sea, and it became dry; 1
22 terrible things by the Red Sea. 1
107:23 Some went down to the sea in ships, doing business 1
25 stormy wind, which lifted up the waves of the sea. •
29 waves of the sea were hushed. •
114: 3 The sea looked and fled, Jordan turned back. 1
5 What ails you, O sea, that you flee? 1
135: 6 in heaven and on earth, in the seas and all deeps. 1
136:13 to him who divided the Red Sea in sunder 1
15 overthrew Pharaoh and his host in the Red Sea 1
139: 9 dwell in the uttermost parts of the sea 1
146: 6 who made heaven and earth, the sea, and all that 1
Prv 8:29 when he assigned to the sea its limit 1
23:34 like one who lies down in the midst of the sea 1
30:19 way of a ship on the high seas, and the way of a man 1
Ecc 1: 7 All streams run to the sea, but the sea is not full; 1
7 All streams run to the sea, but the sea is not full; 1
Isa 5:30 growl . . like the roaring of the sea. 1
9: 1 he will make glorious the way of the sea 1
10:22 though your people . . be as the sand of the sea 1
26 his rod will be over the sea, and he will lift it 1
11: 9 of the knowledge . . as the waters cover the sea. 1
11 from Hamath, and from the coastlands of the sea. 1
15 utterly destroy the tongue of the sea of Egypt; 1
16: 8 its shoots spread abroad and passed over the sea. 1
17:12 they thunder like the thundering of the sea! 1
21: 1 oracle concerning the wilderness of the sea. 1
23: 2 your messengers passed over the sea 1

4 Be ashamed, O Sidon, for the sea has spoken 1
4 the sea has spoken, the stronghold of the sea 1
11 He has stretched out his hand over the sea 1
24:15 glory to the LORD; in the coastlands of the sea 1
27: 1 and he will slay the dragon that is in the sea. 1
42:10 Let the sea roar and all that fills it 1
43:16 Thus says the LORD, who makes a way in the sea 1
48:18 and your righteousness like the waves of the sea; 1
50: 2 Behold, by my rebuke I dry up the sea 1
51:10 Was it not thou that didst dry up the sea 1
10 that didst make the depths of the sea a way 1
15 God, who stirs up the sea so that its waves roar 1
57:20 But the wicked are like the tossing sea; 1
60: 5 the abundance of the sea shall be turned to you 1
63:11 up out of the sea the shepherds of his flock? 1
Jer 5:22 I placed the sand as the bound for the sea 1
6:23 the sound of them is like the roaring sea; 1
15: 8 widows more in number than the sand of the seas; 1
25:22 and the kings of the coastland across the sea; 1
27:19 concerning the pillars, the sea, the stands 1
31:35 who stirs up the sea so that its waves roar 1
33:22 and the sands of the sea cannot be measured 1
46:18 and like Carmel by the sea, shall one come. 1
48:32 vine of Sibmah! Your branches passed over the sea 1
49:21 their cry shall be heard at the Red Sea. 1
23 they melt in fear, they are troubled like the sea 1
50:42 The sound of them is like the roaring of the sea; 1
51:36 I will dry up her sea and make her fountain dry; 1
42 The sea has come up on Babylon; 1
52:17 the bronze sea that were in the house of the LORD 1
20 As for the two pillars, the one sea 1
20 the twelve bronze bulls which were under the sea 6
Lam 2:13 For vast as the sea is your ruin; who can restore you? 1
Ezk 26: 3 against you, as the sea brings up its waves. 1
5 She shall be in the midst of the sea 1
16 Then all the princes of the sea will step down 1
17 and say to you, 'How you have vanished from the seas 1
17 O city renowned, that was mighty on the sea 1
18 yea, the isles that are in the sea are dismayed 1
27: 3 say to Tyre, who dwells at the entrance to the sea 1
4 Your borders are in the heart of the seas; 1
9 ships of the sea with their mariners were in you 1
25 and heavily laden in the heart of the seas. 1
26 rowers have brought you out into the high seas. 2
26 wind has wrecked you in the heart of the seas. 1
27 into the heart of the seas on the day of your ruin. 1
29 all the pilots of the sea stand on the shore 1
32 destroyed like Tyre in the midst of the sea? 1
33 When your wares came from the seas 1
34 Now you are wrecked by the seas, in the depths 1
28: 2 sit in the seat of the gods, in the heart of the seas 1
8 the death of the slain in the heart of the seas. 1
32: 2 but you are like a dragon in the seas; 1
38:20 the fish of the sea, and the birds of the air 1
39:11 the Valley of the Travelers east of the sea; 1
47: 8 when it enters the stagnant waters of the sea •
9 that the waters of the sea may become fresh; •
10 Fishermen will stand beside the sea; •
10 of very many kinds, like the fish of the Great Sea. 1
15 from the Great Sea by way of Hethlon 1
17 the boundary shall run from the sea to Hazar-e'non 1
18 to the eastern sea and as far as Tamar. 1
19 thence along the Brook of Egypt to the Great Sea. 1
20 the Great Sea shall be the boundary to a point 1
48: 1 from the sea by way of Hethlon to the entrance •
28 thence along the Brook of Egypt to the Great Sea. 1
Dan 7: 2 four winds . . were stirring up the great sea. 3
3 four great beasts came up out of the sea 3
11:45 between the sea and the glorious holy mountain; 1
Hos 1:10 people of Israel shall be like the sand of the sea 1
4: 3 and even the fish of the sea are taken away. 1
Jol 2:20 drive . . his front into the eastern sea 1
20 the eastern sea, and his rear into the western sea; 1
Ams 5: 8 who calls for the waters of the sea, and pours them 1
8:12 They shall wander from sea to sea 1
12 They shall wander from sea to sea 1
9: 3 they hide from my sight at the bottom of the sea 1
6 who calls for the waters of the sea, and pours them 1
Jon 1: 4 the LORD hurled a great wind upon the sea 1
4 there was a mighty tempest on the sea 1
5 the wares that were in the ship into the sea 1
9 God of heaven, who made the sea and the dry land. 1
11 What shall we do to you, that the sea may quiet down 1
11 For the sea grew more and more tempestuous. 1
12 said to them, "Take me up and throw me into the sea; 1
12 then the sea will quiet down for you; 1
13 for the sea grew more and more tempestuous 1
15 they took up Jonah and threw him into the sea; 1
15 the sea ceased from its raging. 1
2: 3 cast me into the deep, into the heart of the seas 1
Mic 7:12 and from Egypt to the River, from sea to sea 1
12 and from Egypt to the River, from sea to sea 1
19 wilt cast all our sins into the depths of the sea. 1
Nah 1: 4 He rebukes the sea and makes it dry 1
3: 8 Thebes . . her rampart a sea, and water her wall? 1
Hab 1:14 For thou makest men like the fish of the sea 1
2:14 will be filled . . as the waters cover the sea. 1
3: 8 or thy indignation against the sea 1
15 Thou didst trample the sea with thy horses 1

Zep 1: 3 away the birds of the air and the fish of the sea. 1
Hag 2: 6 I will shake the heavens and the earth and the sea 1
Zec 9: 4 her possessions and hurl her wealth into the sea 1
10 his dominion shall be from sea to sea 1
10 his dominion shall be from sea to sea 1
10:11 They shall pass through the sea of Egypt 1
11 the waves of the sea shall be smitten 1
14: 8 from Jerusalem, half of them to the eastern sea 1
8 eastern sea and half of them to the western sea; 1
Mat 4:13 he went and dwelt in Caper'na-um by the sea 8
15 the land of Naph'tali, toward the sea 6
18 As he walked by the Sea of Galilee, he saw two 6
18 a net into the sea; for they were fishermen. 6
8:24 behold, there arose a great storm on the sea 6
26 Then he rose and rebuked the winds and the sea 6
27 that even winds and sea obey him? 6
32 down the steep bank into the sea, and perished 6
13: 1 went out of the house and sat beside the sea. 6
47 like a net which was thrown into the sea 6
14:25 he came to them, walking on the sea 6
26 when the disciples saw him walking on the sea 6
15:29 and passed along the Sea of Galilee 6
17:27 However, not to give offense to them, go to the sea 6
18: 6 and to be drowned in the depth of the sea. 6
21:21 'Be taken up and cast into the sea,' 6
23:15 you traverse sea and land 6
Mrk 1:16 And passing along by the Sea of Galilee 6
16 Simon and Andrew . . casting a net in the sea 6
2:13 He went out again beside the sea 6
3: 7 Jesus withdrew with his disciples to the sea 6
4: 1 Again he began to teach beside the sea 6
1 so that he got into a boat and sat in it on the sea; 6
1 the whole crowd was beside the sea on the land. 6
39 he awoke and rebuked the wind, and said to the sea 6
41 Who then is this, that even wind and sea obey him? 6
5: 1 They came to the other side of the sea 6
13 rushed down the steep bank into the sea 6
13 drowned in the sea. 6
21 he was beside the sea. 6
6:47 when evening came, the boat was out on the sea 6
48 he came to them, walking on the sea 6
49 when they saw him walking on the sea 6
7:31 went through Sidon to the Sea of Galilee 6
9:42 he were thrown into the sea. 6
11:23 'Be taken up and cast into the sea,' 6
Lke 17: 2 if . . he were cast into the sea 6
6 'Be rooted up, and be planted in the sea,' 6
21:25 at the roaring of the sea and the waves 6
Joh 6: 1 Jesus went to the other side of the Sea of Galilee 6
1 the Sea of Galilee, which is the Sea of Tiber'i-as. •
16 his disciples went down to the sea 6
17 started across the sea to Caper'na-um 6
18 The sea rose because a strong wind was blowing. 6
19 they saw Jesus walking on the sea 6
22 the people who remained on the other side of the sea 6
25 When they found him on the other side of the sea 6
21: 1 Jesus revealed himself . . by the Sea of Tibe'ri-as 6
7 and sprang into the sea. 6
Act 4:24 the earth and the sea and everything in them 6
7:36 wonders and signs in Egypt and at the Red Sea 6
14:15 the earth and the sea and all that is in them. 6
17:14 the brethren . . sent Paul off on his way to the sea 6
27: 5 when we had sailed across the sea 9
27 as we were drifting across the sea of A'dria •
30 had lowered the boat into the sea 6
38 throwing out the wheat into the sea. 6
40 they cast off the anchors and left them in the sea 6
28: 4 Though he has escaped from the sea 6
Rom 9:27 the sons of Israel be as the sand of the sea 6
1Co 10: 1 all passed through the sea 6
2 in the cloud and in the sea 6
2Co 11:25 a night and a day I have been adrift at sea; 5
26 danger at sea, danger from false brethren; 6
Heb 11:29 the people crossed the Red Sea as if on dry land 6
Jas 1: 6 wave of the sea . . driven and tossed by the wind. 6
Jde 1:13 wild waves of the sea, casting up the foam 6
Rev 4: 6 there is as it were a sea of glass, like crystal. 6
5:13 every creature . . under the earth and in the sea 6
7: 1 that no wind might blow on earth or sea 6
2 who had been given power to harm earth and sea 6
3 Do not harm the earth or the sea or the trees 6
8: 8 something like . . was thrown into the sea; 6
9 and a third of the sea became blood 6
9 a third of the living creatures in the sea died 6
10: 2 And he set his right foot on the sea 6
5 the angel whom I saw standing on sea and land 6
6 who created . . the sea and what is in it 6
8 angel who is standing on the sea and on the land. 6
12:12 woe to you, O earth and sea, for the devil has come 6
17 And he stood on the sand of the sea. 6
13: 1 I saw a beast rising out of the sea 6
14: 7 who made . . the sea and the fountains of water 6
15: 2 appeared to be a sea of glass mingled with fire 6
2 standing beside the sea of glass 6
16: 3 The second angel poured his bowl into the sea 6
3 and every living thing died that was in the sea. 6
18:17 sailors and all whose trade is on the sea 6
19 all who had ships at sea grew rich by her wealth! 6
21 took up a stone . . and threw it into the sea 6

20: 8 their number is like the sand of the sea. 6
13 And the sea gave up the dead in it 6
21: 1 earth had passed away, and the sea was no more. 6
1Es 4: 2 who rule over land and sea and all that is in them? 6
15 to every people that rules over sea and land. 6
23 to sail the sea and rivers; 6
2Es 1:13 Surely it was I who brought you through the sea 10
4: 7 How many dwellings are in the heart of the sea 10
14 Come, let us go and make war against the sea 10
15 the waves of the sea also made a plan and said, 'Come 10
17 likewise also the plan of the waves of the sea 10
19 to the sea is assigned a place to carry its waves. 10
21 and the sea to its waves 10
5: 7 the sea of Sodom shall cast up fish 10
25 from all the depths of the sea thou hast filled 10
7: 3 There is a sea set in a wide expanse 10
5 If any one, then, wishes to reach the sea 10
9:34 the sea a ship, or any dish food or drink 10
11: 1 and behold, there came up from the sea an eagle 10
12:11 The eagle which you saw coming up from the sea 10
13: 2 behold, a wind arose from the sea 10
3 a man come up out of the heart of the sea ‡
5 the man who came up out of the sea. 10
25 a man come up from the heart of the sea 10
32 whom you saw as a man coming up from the sea. ‡
51 the man coming up from the heart of the sea? 10
52 explore or know what is in the depths of the sea 10
16:12 the sea is churned up from the depths 10
57 who has measured the sea and its contents; 10
58 has enclosed the sea in the midst of the waters 10
Jdt 1:12 as far as the coasts of the two seas. 6
2:24 as far as the sea. 6
5:13 Then God dried up the Red Sea before them 6
Wis 5:22 the water of the sea will rage against them 6
10:18 She brought them over the Red Sea 6
19 and cast them up from the depth of the sea. 4
14: 3 because thou hast given it a path in the sea 6
19: 7 an unhindered way out of the Red Sea 6
12 to give them relief, quails came up from the sea. 6
Sir 1: 2 The sand of the sea, the drops of rain 6
18:10 Like a drop of water from the sea 6
24: 6 In the waves of the sea, in the whole earth 6
29 for her thought is more abundant than the sea 6
31 my canal became a river, and my river became a sea. 6
29:18 has shaken them like a wave of the sea 6
40:11 what is from the waters returns to the sea. 6
43:24 Those who sail the sea tell of its dangers 6
44:21 cause them to inherit from sea to sea 6
21 cause them to inherit from sea to sea 6
50: 3 a reservoir like the sea in circumference. 6
Bar 3:30 Who has gone over the sea, and found her, and will 6
Aza 1:13 as many . . as the sand on the shore of the sea. 6
56 Bless the Lord, seas and rivers 6
Man 1: 3 who hast shackled the sea by thy word of command 6
9 more in number than the sand of the sea 6
1Mc 4: 9 how our fathers were saved at the Red Sea 6
23 and cloth dyed blue and sea purple, and great riches. 7
6:29 came to him . . from islands of the seas. 6
7: 1 sailed with a few men to a city by the sea 8
8:23 May all go well . . at sea and on land for ever 6
32 fight you on sea and on land.' 6
11: 8 as far as Seleucia by the sea 8
13:29 so that they could be seen by all who sail the sea. 6
14: 5 opened a way to the isles of the sea. 6
34 He also fortified Joppa, which is by the sea 6
15: 1 sent a letter from the islands of the sea to Simon 6
11 he came in his flight to Dor, which is by the sea; 6
14 the ships joined battle from the sea 6
14 he pressed the city hard from land and sea 6
2Mc 5:21 he could sail on the land and walk on the sea 9
9: 8 he could command the waves of the sea 6
3Mc 2: 7 you overwhelmed him in the depths of the sea 6
7:20 brought safely by land and sea and river 6
4Mc 7: 1 steered . . over the sea of the emotions 9

sea *See also* creature, drown, monster, put, take.

sea gull 1. שַׁחַף
Lev 11:16 the ostrich, the nighthawk, the sea gull, the hawk 1
Deu 14:15 the ostrich, the nighthawk, the sea gull, the hawk 1

sea monster 1. תַּנִּין
Gen 1:21 God created the great sea monsters 1
Job 7:12 Am I the sea, or a sea monster 1
Ps 148: 7 Praise the LORD . . sea monsters and all deeps 1

sea-born 1. *βυθοτρεφής*
3Mc 6: 8 in the belly of a huge, sea-born monster 1

seacoast 1. חֶבֶל 2. חֶבֶל הַיָּם 3. חוֹף הַיָּם 4. *παραθαλάσσιος* 5. *παραλία* 6. *παράλιος*
Deu 1: 7 lowland, and in the Negeb, and by the seacoast 3
Ezk 25:16 and destroy the rest of the seacoast. 3
Zep 2: 5 Woe to you inhabitants of the seacoast 2
6 And you, O seacoast, shall be pastures 2
7 The seacoast shall become the possession 1
Lke 6:17 Jerusalem and the seacoast of Tyre and Sidon 6
Jdt 1: 7 all who lived along the seacoast 5
2:28 the people who lived along the seacoast 5
3: 6 Then he went down to the seacoast with his army 5
5:22 all the men from the seacoast and from Moab 5
2Mc 8:11 he immediately sent to the cities on the seacoast 4

seafaring man 1. *ἐπὶ τόπον πλέω*
Rev 18:17 And all shipmasters and seafaring men, sailors 1

seafood 1. *ἔνυδρος*
4Mc 1:34 when we crave seafood and fowl and animals 1

seal 1. חתם 2. חֹתָם 3. חתם (A) 4. *κατασφραγίζω* 5. *σφραγίζω* 6. *σφραγίς* 7. consigno 8. signaculum 9. signator 10. signo
1Kg 21: 8 wrote letters . . and sealed them with his seal 1
8 wrote letters . . and sealed them with his seal 2
Neh 10: 1 set their seal are Nehemi'ah the governor 9
Est 3:12 and sealed with the king's ring. 1
8: 8 you may write . . and seal it with the king's ring; 1
8 edict written . . and sealed with the king's ring 1
10 The writing was . . sealed with the king's ring 1
Job 38:14 It is changed like clay under the seal 2
41:15 rows of shields, shut up closely as with a seal. 2
Sng 4:12 my bride, a garden locked, a fountain sealed. 1
8: 6 Set me as a seal upon your heart . . upon your arm; 2
6 Set me . . upon your heart, as a seal upon your arm; 2
Isa 8:16 seal the teaching among my disciples. 1
29:11 like the words of a book that is sealed. 1
11 he says, "I cannot, for it is sealed. 1
Jer 32:10 I signed the deed, sealed it, got witnesses 1
11 Then I took the sealed deed of purchase 1
14 this sealed deed of purchase and this open deed 1
44 deeds shall be signed and sealed and witnessed 1
Dan 6:17 king sealed it with his own signet 3
9:24 seal both vision and prophet, 1
12: 4 Daniel, shut up the words, and seal the book 1
9 words are shut up and sealed until the . . end. 1
Mat 27:66 by sealing the stone and setting a guard. 5
Rom 4:11 He received circumcision as a sign or seal 6
1Co 9: 2 you are the seal of my apostleship in the Lord. 6
Eph 1:13 were sealed with the promised Holy Spirit 5
4:30 you were sealed for the day of redemption. 5
2Ti 2:19 God's firm foundation stands, bearing this seal 6
Rev 5: 1 a scroll . . sealed with seven seals; 4
1 a scroll . . sealed with seven seals; 6
2 to open the scroll and break its seals? 6
5 so that he can open the scroll and its seven seals. 6
9 Worthy . . to take the scroll and to open its seals 6
6: 1 I saw when the Lamb opened one of the seven seals 6
3 When he opened the second seal, I heard 6
5 When he opened the third seal, I heard 6
7 When he opened the fourth seal, I heard the voice 6
9 When he opened the fifth seal, I saw 6
12 When he opened the sixth seal, I looked, and behold 6
7: 2 another angel . . with the seal of the living God 6
3 till we have sealed the servants of our God 5
4 I heard the number of the sealed 5
4 144,000 sealed, out of every tribe 5
5 12,000 sealed out of the tribe of Judah 5
8 12,000 sealed out of the tribe of Benjamin. 5
8: 1 When the Lamb opened the seventh seal 6
9: 4 who have not the seal of God upon their foreheads; 6
20: 3 into the pit, and shut it and sealed it over him 5
1Es 3: 8 they sealed them 5
2Es 2:38 the number of those who have been sealed. 10
6: 5 who stored up treasures of faith were sealed- 7
7:104 and displays to all the seal of truth 8
10:23 And, what is more than all, the seal of Zion 8
Tob 9: 5 the money bags with their seals intact 6
Sir 22:27 a seal of prudence upon my lips 6
32: 5 A ruby seal in a setting of gold 6
6 A seal of emerald in a rich setting of gold 6
38:27 those who cut the signets of seals 6
42: 6 Where there is an evil wife, a seal is a good thing; 6
Bel 1:11 shut the door and seal it with your signet. 5
14 shut the door and sealed it with the king's signet 5
17 the king said, "Are the seals unbroken, Daniel? 6
Man 1: 3 sealed it with thy terrible and glorious name; 5
4Mc 7:15 whom the faithful seal of death has perfected! 6

seal *See also* lose, set.

seal up 1. חתם 2. חתם בְּעַד 3. סתם 4. *ἐμφράσσω* 5. *κατασφραγίζω* 6. *σφραγίζω* 7. signo
Deu 32:34 laid up in store . . sealed up in my treasuries? 1
Job 9: 7 who seals up the stars; 2
14:17 my transgression would be sealed up in a bag 1
37: 7 He seals up the hand of every man 1
Dan 8:26 seal up the vision, for it pertains to many days 3
Rev 10: 4 Seal up what the seven thunders have said 6
22:10 Do not seal up the words of the prophecy 6
2Es 8:53 The root of evil is sealed up from you 7
Wis 2: 5 because it is sealed up and no one turns back. 5
2Mc 2: 5 he sealed up the entrance. 4

seam 1. בֶּדֶק
Ezk 27: 9 her skilled men were in you, caulking your seams; 1

without seam 1. *ἄραφος*
Joh 19:23 the tunic was without seam 1

seaman 1. אִישׁ אֳנִיּוֹת
1Kg 9:27 Hiram sent . . his servants, seamen who were 1

sear 1. *καυστηριάζω*
1Ti 4: 2 liars whose consciences are seared 1

search 1. בקר 2. בקשׁ 3. דרשׁ 4. חפשׂ 5. חֹק 6. חקר 7. חֵקֶר 8. תור 9. בקר (A) 10. *ἀνερευνάω* 11. *ἐκζητέω* 12. *ἐξετάζω* 13. *ἐραυνάω* 14. *ἐρευνάω* 15. *ἐτασμός* 16. *ζητέω* 17. scrutor
Gen 31:35 he searched, but did not find the household 4
44:12 he searched, beginning with the eldest 4
Jdg 5:15 there were great searchings of heart 5
16 there were great searchings of heart. 7
2Sm 5:17 all the Philistines went up in search of David; 2
10: 3 sent his servants . . to search the city, and to spy 6
1Kg 20: 6 they shall search your house 4
2Kg 10:23 Search, and see that there is no servant 4
1Ch 14: 8 all the Philistines went up in search of David; 2
19: 3 to search and to overthrow and to spy out the land? 6
28: 9 LORD searches all hearts, and understands every 3
2Ch 22: 9 He searched for Ahazi'ah, and he was captured 2
Ezr 4:15 that search may be made in the book of the records 1
19 made a decree, and search has been made 1
6: 1 made a decree, and search was made in Babylonia 9
Job 10: 6 seek out my iniquity and search for my sin 3
39: 8 he searches after every green thing. 3
Ps 77: 6 in the night; I meditate and search my spirit ‡
139: 1 O LORD, thou hast searched me and known me! 6
23 Search me, O God, and know my heart! 6
Prv 2: 4 if you . . search for it as for hidden treasures; 4
11:27 but evil comes to him who searches for it. 3
20:27 searching all his innermost parts. 4
Ecc 2: 3 I searched with my mind how to cheer my body 8
Jer 5: 1 Search her squares to see if you can find a man 2
17:10 I the LORD search the mind and try the heart 6
Lam 1:11 All her people groan as they search for bread; 2
Ezk 34: 6 with none to search or seek for them. 3
8 my shepherds have not searched for my sheep 3
11 Behold, I, I myself will search for my sheep 3
39:14 they will make their search. 6
Zep 1:12 At that time I will search Jerusalem with lamps 4
Mat 2: 8 he sent them to Bethlehem, saying, "Go and search 12
13 Herod is about to search for the child, to destroy 16
13:45 like a merchant in search of fine pearls 16
18:12 and go in search of the one that went astray? 16
Mrk 1:37 Every one is searching for you. 16
Joh 5:39 You search the scriptures 13
7:52 Search and you will see 13
Rom 8:27 he who searches the hearts of men knows 13
1Co 2:10 the Spirit searches everything, even the depths 13
2Ti 1:17 he searched for me eagerly and found me- 16
1Pe 1:10 searched and inquired about this salvation 11
Rev 2:23 that I am he who searches mind and heart 13
2Es 16:30 who search carefully through the vineyard 17
31 those who search their houses with the sword. 17
57 It is he who searches the deep and its treasures 17
Jdt 8:27 to search their hearts 15
Sir 51:14 I will search for her to the last. 11
1Mc 9:26 They sought and searched for the friends of Judas 14
4Mc 3:13 went searching throughout the enemy camp 10

search *See also* make.

search after 1. דרשׁ
Deu 4:29 if you search after him with all your heart 1

search for 1. *ζητέω*
Tob 1:19 I was being searched for, to be put to death 1

search out 1. זרה 2. חפר 3. חפשׂ 4. חקר 5. תור 6. *ἐξερευνάω* 7. *ἐξετάζω* 8. *ἐξιχνεύω* 9. *ἐξιχνιάζω* 10. *ἐρευνάω* 11. exquiro 12. investigo 13. scrutino 14. scruto
Jos 2: 2 have come here tonight to search out the land. 2
3 they have come to search out all the land. 2
1Sm 23:23 search him out among all the thousands of Judah. 3
Job 5:27 Lo, this we have searched out; it is true. 4
13: 9 Will it be well with you when he searches you out? 4
28: 3 search out to the farthest bound the ore in gloom 4
27 he established it, and searched it out. 4
29:16 I searched out the cause of him whom I did not know. 4
32:11 while you searched out what to say. 4
Ps 64: 6 Who can search out our crimes? 3
139: 3 Thou searchest out my path and my lying down 1
Prv 25: 2 but the glory of kings is to search things out. 4
Ecc 1:13 to seek and to search out by wisdom all that is 5
7:25 to know and to search out and to seek wisdom 5
Ezk 20: 6 into a land that I had searched out for them 5
Ams 9: 3 from there I will search out and take them; 3
2Es 5:34 and to search out part of his judgment. 12
12: 4 because you search out the ways of the Most High. 14
13:54 and have searched out my law; 11
16:50 who searches out every sin on earth. 11
62 and searches out hidden things in hidden places. 13
Jdt 8:14 how do you expect to search out God 10
Wis 6: 3 who will search out your works 7
Sir 1: 3 the abyss, and wisdom-who can search them out? 9

6:27 Search out and seek 8
18: 4 who can search out his mighty deeds? 8
42:18 He searches out the abyss, and the hearts of men 8
1Mc 3: 5 He searched out and pursued the lawless 6

keep searching 1. διερευνάω
Wis 13: 7 as they live among his works they keep searching 1

seashore 1. חוֹף הַיָּם 2. שְׂפַת הַיָּם 3. χεῖλος τῆς θαλάσσης
Gen 22:17 as the sand which is on the seashore. 2
Exd 14:30 Israel saw the Egyptians dead upon the seashore. 2
Jos 11: 4 in number like the sand that is upon the seashore 2
Jdg 7:12 sand which is upon the seashore for multitude. 2
1Sm 13: 5 and troops like the sand on the seashore 2
1Kg 4:29 largeness of mind like the sand on the seashore 2
Jer 47: 7 against the seashore he has appointed it. 1
Heb 11:12 the innumerable grains of sand by the seashore. 3
1Mc 11: 1 great forces, like the sand by the seashore 3

seaside 1. θάλασσα
Act 10: 6 Simon, a tanner, whose house is by the seaside. 1
32 in the house of Simon, a tanner, by the seaside.' 1

season 1. זְמָן 2. יוֹם 3. מוֹעֵד 4. עֵת 5. זְמָן (A) 6. εὐκαίρως 7. καιρός 8. tempus
Gen 1:14 let them be . . for seasons and for days and years 3
17:21 Isaac, whom Sarah shall bear to you at this season 3
31:10 In the mating season of the flock I lifted up 4
Lev 26: 4 then I will give you your rains in their season 4
Num13:20 time was the season of the first ripe grapes. 2
Deu 11:14 he will give the rain for your land in its season 4
28:12 to give the rain of your land in its season 4
2Kg 4:16 At this season, when the time comes round 3
Job 5:26 comes up to the threshing floor in its season. 4
38:32 Can you lead forth the Maz'zaroth in their season 4
Ps 1: 3 a tree . . that yields its fruit in its season 4
Prv 15:23 word in season, how good it is! 4
Ecc 3: 1 For everything there is a season 1
Jer 5:24 the LORD our God, who gives the rain in its season 4
Ezk 34:26 I will send down the showers in their season; 4
46:11 At the feasts and the appointed seasons •
Dan 2:21 He changes times and seasons; 5
7:12 lives were prolonged for a season and a time. 5
Hos 2: 9 I will take back . . my wine in its season; 3
Zec 8:19 to the house of Judah seasons of joy and gladness •
10: 1 Ask rain from the LORD in the season of the spring 4
Mat 21:34 When the season of fruit drew near 7
41 who will give him the fruits in their seasons. 7
Mrk 11:13 it was not the season for figs. 7
Act 1: 7 not for you to know times or seasons 7
14:17 he . . gave you from heaven rains and fruitful seasons 7
1Co 7: 5 by agreement for a season 7
Gal 4:10 days, and months, and seasons, and years! 7
6: 9 in due season we shall reap 7
1Th 5: 1 as to the times and the seasons, brethren 7
2Ti 4: 2 be urgent in season and out of season, convince 6
2Es 13:58 whatever things come to pass in their seasons. 8
Wis 7:18 the changes of the seasons 7
8: 8 the outcome of seasons and times. 7
Sir 31:28 Wine drunk in season and temperately 7
33: 8 he appointed the different seasons and feasts; 7
39:34 all things will prove good in their season. 7
43: 6 made the moon . . to serve in its season 7
Bar 1:14 on the days of the feasts and at appointed seasons. 7
1Mc 4:54 At the very season and on the very day 7
59 every year at that season 7

season (2) 1. ἀρτύω
Mrk 9:49 how will you season it 1
Col 4: 6 always be gracious, seasoned with salt 1

season (3) 1. חַיִל
1Ch 28: 1 the mighty men, and all the seasoned warriors. 1
season *See* due, mark, troop.

appointed season 1. זְמָן
Est 9:31 Purim . . be observed at their appointed seasons 1

first season 1. רֵאשִׁית
Hos 9:10 first fruit on the fig tree, in its first season 1

out of season 1. ἀκαίρως
2Ti 4: 2 be urgent in season and out of season, convince 1
Sir 32: 4 do not display your cleverness out of season. 1

season with salt 1. מלח
Lev 2:13 not season all your cereal offerings with salt 1
Exd 30:35 incense . . seasoned with salt, pure and holy; 1

seat 1. יָשַׁב 2. כִּסֵּא 3. מוֹשָׁב 4. מְקוֹם שֶׁבֶת 5. מֶרְכָּב 6. שֶׁבֶת 7. תְּכוּנָה 8. ἀνάκειμαι 9. δίφρος 10. καθέδρα 11. κάθημαι 12. καθίζω 13. sedes
Num21:15 slope . . valleys that extends to the seat of Ar 6
Jdg 3:20 from God for you." And he arose from his seat. 2
1Sm 1: 9 Now Eli the priest was sitting on the seat beside 2
2: 8 to make them sit . . and inherit a seat of honor. 2
4:13 Eli was sitting upon his seat by the road 2
18 Eli fell . . from his seat by the side of the gate; 2
20:18 will be missed, because your seat will be empty. 3
25 The king sat upon his seat, as at other times 3
25 king sat upon his seat . . upon the seat by the wall; 3
1Kg 2:19 and had a seat brought for the king's mother; 2
10: 5 food of his table, the seating of his officials 3
19 on each side of the seat were arm rests 4
16:11 as soon as he had seated himself on his throne 1
2Kg 25:28 and gave him a seat above the seats of the kings 2
28 and gave him a seat above the seats of the kings 2
2Ch 9: 4 food of his table, the seating of his officials 3
18 on each side of the seat were arm rests 4
19: 8 They had their seat at Jerusalem. 1
Est 3: 1 promoted Haman . . and set his seat above all 2
Job 23: 3 that I might come even to his seat! 7
29: 7 when I prepared my seat in the square 3
Ps 1: 1 nor sits in the seat of scoffers; 3
7: 7 and over it take thy seat on high. •
113: 5 Who is like the LORD our God, who is seated on high 1
Prv 9:14 she takes a seat on the high places of the town 2
Sng 3:10 he made its . . its back of gold, its seat of purple; 5
Jer 52:32 and gave him a seat above the seats of the kings 2
32 and gave him a seat above the seats of the kings 2
Ezk 1:26 and seated above the likeness of a throne •
8: 3 where was the seat of the image of jealousy 3
28: 2 sit in the seat of the gods, in the heart of the seas 3
Ams 6: 3 and bring near the seat of violence? 6
Mat 21:12 and the seats of those who sold pigeons. 10
23: 2 The scribes and the Pharisees sit on Moses' seat; 10
26:64 the Son of man seated at the right hand of Power 11
Mrk 11:15 the seats of those who sold pigeons; 10
14:62 the Son of man seated at the right hand of Power 11
Lke 22:69 seated at the right hand of the power of God. 11
Joh 6:11 he distributed them to those who were seated 8
Act 8:28 seated in his chariot 11
Col 3: 1 where Christ is, seated at the right hand of God. 11
Heb 8: 1 one who is seated at the right hand of the throne 12
12: 2 seated at the right hand of the throne of God. 12
Jas 2: 3 Have a seat here, please 11
Rev 4: 2 in heaven, with one seated on the throne! 11
4 and seated on the thrones were 24 elders 11
9 thanks to him who is seated on the throne 11
10 fall down before him who is seated on the throne 11
5: 1 him who was seated on the throne 11
7 right hand of him who was seated on the throne. 11
6:16 hide us from . . him who is seated on the throne 11
14:14 and seated on the cloud one like a son of man 11
17: 1 the great harlot who is seated upon many waters 11
9 are seven mountains on which the woman is seated; 11
15 waters that you saw, where the harlot is seated 11
19: 4 worshiped God who is seated on the throne, saying 11
20: 4 Then I saw thrones, and seated on them were those 12
2Es 7:33 shall be revealed upon the seat of judgment 13
AEs 15: 6 He was seated on his royal throne 11
Sir 7: 4 nor the seat of honor from the king. 10
10:14 has seated the lowly in their place. 12
11: 1 will seat him among the great. 12
31:12 Are you seated at the table of a great man? 12
18 If you are seated among many persons 12
32: 1 take good care of them and then be seated; 12
38:33 They do not sit in the judge's seat 9
1Mc 10:63 The king also seated him at his side 12
seat *See also* mercy, take.

good seat 1. πρωτοκαθεδρία
Mat 23: 6 they love . . the best seats in the synagogues 1
Mrk 12:39 and the best seats in the synagogues 1
Lke 11:43 you love the best seat in the synagogues 1
20:46 and love . . the best seats in the synagogues 1

judgment seat 1. βῆμα 2. iudicium
Mat 27:19 while he was sitting on the judgment seat 1
Joh 19:13 and sat down on the judgment seat 1
Rom14:10 shall all stand before the judgment seat of God; 1
2Co 5:10 appear before the judgment seat of Christ 1
2Es 12:33 he will set them living before his judgment seat 2

seat of honor 1. δίφρος 2. καθέδρα
Sir 12:12 lest he try to take your seat of honor 2
2Mc 14:21 seats of honor were set in place; 1

second 1. אַחֵר 2. מִשְׁנֶה 3. שָׁנָה 4. שֵׁנִי 5. שְׁנַיִם 6. תִּנְיָן (A) 7. δευτεραῖος 8. δευτέριον 9. δεύτερος 10. ἕτερος 11. alius 12. secundus
Gen 1: 8 there was morning, a second day 4
2:13 The name of the second river is Gihon; 4
6:16 make it with lower, second, and third decks. 4
7:11 in the second month, on the seventeenth day 4
8:14 In the second month, on the 27th day of the month 4
30: 7 conceived again and bore Jacob a second son. 4
12 Leah's maid Zilpah bore Jacob a second son. 4
32:19 He likewise instructed the second and the third 4
41:43 he made him to ride in his second chariot; 2
52 The name of the second he called E'phraim 4
Exd 16: 1 on the fifteenth day of the second month 4
26: 4 edge of the outmost curtain in the second set. 4
5 the curtain that is in the second set; 4
10 the curtain which is outmost in the second set. 4
20 for the second side of the tabernacle 4
28:18 the second row an emerald, a sapphire 4
36:11 edge of the outmost curtain of the second set; 4
12 edge of the curtain that was in the second set; 4
25 for the second side of the tabernacle 4
39:11 the second row, an emerald, a sapphire 4
40:17 first month in the second year, on the first day 4
Lev 5:10 he shall offer the second for a burnt offering 4
Num 1: 1 on the first day of the second month 4
1 in the second year after they had come out 4
18 on the first day of the second month 4
2:16 They shall set out second. 4
7:18 On the second day Nethan'el . . made an offering; 4
9: 1 in the first month of the second year after 4
11 In the second month on the fourteenth day 4
10:11 In the second year, in the second month 4
11 In the second year, in the second month 4
29:17 On the second day twelve young bulls, two rams 4
Jos 6:14 the second day they marched around the city once 4
10:32 and he took it on the second day, and smote it 4
19: 1 The second lot came out for Simeon 4
Jdg 6:25 father's bull, the second bull seven years old 4
26 then take the second bull, and offer it as a burnt 4
28 and the second bull was offered upon the altar 4
20:24 against the Benjaminites the second day. 4
25 Benjamin went against them . . the second day 4
1Sm 8: 2 first-born . . and the name of his second, Abi'jah; 2
18:21 Therefore Saul said to David a second time •
20:27 on the second day, the morrow after the new moon 4
34 and ate no food the second day of the month 4
2Sm 3: 3 first-born . . and his second, Chil'e-ab, of Ab'igail 2
14:29 And he sent a second time, but Jo'ab would not come. 4
20:10 and shed his . . without striking a second blow; 3
1Kg 6: 1 in the month of Ziv, which is the second month 4
9: 2 the LORD appeared to Solomon a second time 4
15:25 to reign over Israel in the second year of Asa 5
19: 7 the angel of the LORD came again a second time 4
2Kg 1:17 became king . . in the second year of Jeho'ram 5
9:19 he sent out a second horseman, who came . . and said 4
10: 6 he wrote to them a second letter, saying, "If you are 4
14: 1 In the second year of Jo'ash the son of Jo'ahaz 5
15:32 In the second year of Pekah the son of Remali'ah 5
19:29 and in the second year what springs of the same; 4
22:14 (now she dwelt in Jerusalem in the Second Quarter); 2
23: 4 high priest, and the priests of the second order 2
25:17 And the second pillar had the like 4
18 took Serai'ah . . and Zephani'ah the second priest 2
1Ch 2:13 Jesse was the father of . . Abin'adab the second 4
3: 1 sons of David . . the second Daniel 4
15 sons of Josi'ah . . the second Jehoi'akim 4
5:12 Jo'el . . Shapham the second, Ja'nai, and Shaphat 2
6:28 sons of Samuel: Jo'el . . the second Abi'jah. 4
7:15 And the name of the second was Zeloph'ehad; 4
8: 1 Benjamin was the father of . . Ashbel the second 4
39 sons of Eshek his brother . . Je'ush the second 4
12: 9 Ezer the chief, Obadi'ah second, Eli'ab third 4
16: 5 second to him were Zechari'ah, Je-i'el, Shemi'ramoth 2
23:11 Jahath was the chief, and Zizah the second; 4
19 sons of Hebron: Jeri'ah . . Amari'ah the second 4
20 sons of Uz'ziel: Micah . . and Isshi'ah the second. 4
24: 7 The first lot fell to . . the second to Jedai'ah 4
23 sons of Hebron . . Amari'ah the second, Jaha'ziel 4
25: 9 second to Gedali'ah, to him and his brethren 4
26: 2 Meshelemi'ah had sons . . Jedi'a-el the second 4
4 O'bed-e'dom had sons . . Jehoz'abad the second, Jo'ah 4
11 Hilki'ah the second, Tebali'ah the third 4
27: 4 in charge of the division of the second month; 4
2Ch 3: 2 He began to build in the second month 4
27: 5 same amount in the second and the third years. 4
30: 2 to keep the passover in the second month 4
13 feast of unleavened bread in the second month 4
15 on the fourteenth day of the second month. 4
31:12 Conani'ah . . with Shim'e-i his brother as second; 2
35:24 servants . . carried him in his second chariot 2
Ezr 3: 8 second year of their coming to the house of God 4
8 in the second year . . in the second month 4
4:24 second year of the reign of Darius king of Persia 6
Neh 8:13 On the second day the heads of fathers' houses 4
11: 9 Judah . . of Hassen'u-ah was second over the city. 2
17 Bakbuki'ah, the second among his brethren; 2
Est 2:14 to the second harem in custody of Sha-ash'gaz 4
7: 2 on the second day . . the king again said to Esther 4
9:29 confirming this second letter about Purim. 4
Job 42:14 first Jemi'mah; and the name of the second Kezi'ah; 4
Ps 109:13 his name be blotted out in the second generation! 1
Isa 37:30 in the second year what springs of the same; 4
Jer 1:13 The word of the LORD came to me a second time 4
13: 3 the word of the LORD came to me a second time 4
33: 1 word of the LORD came to Jeremiah a second time 4
52:22 And the second pillar had the like 4
24 chief priest, and Zephani'ah the second priest 2
Ezk 4: 6 you shall lie down a second time 4
10:14 and the second face was the face of a man 4
43:22 on the second day you shall offer a he-goat 4
Dan 2: 1 second year of the reign of Nebuchadnez'zar 5
Jon 3: 1 word of the LORD came to Jonah the second time 4
Hag 1: 1 In the second year of Darius the king 5
15 In the second year of Darius the king 5

2:10 the ninth month, in the second year of Darius 5
20 The word of the LORD came a second time to Haggai 4
Zec 1: 1 In the eighth month, in the second year of Darius 5
7 the month of Shebat, in the second year of Darius 5
4:12 a second time I said to him, "What are these two 4
6: 2 chariot had red horses, the second black horses 4
11:14 Then I broke my second staff Union 4
Mat 21:30 he went to the second and said the same 10
22:26 So too the second and third, down to the seventh. 9
39 a second is like it, You shall love your neighbor 9
26:42 Again, for the second time, he went away and prayed 9
Mrk 12:21 the second took her, and died, leaving no children; 9
31 The second is this, 'You shall love your neighbor 9
14:72 immediately the cock crowed a second time. 9
Lke 12:38 If he comes in the second watch, or in the third 9
19:18 the second came, saying, 'Lord 9
20:30 the second 9
Joh 3: 4 Can he enter a second time into his mother's womb 9
4:54 This was now the second sign that Jesus did 9
9:24 for the second time they called the man 9
21:16 A second time he said to him, "Simon, son of John 9
Act 7:13 at the second visit 9
10:15 the voice came to him again a second time 9
11: 9 the voice answered a second time from heaven 9
12:10 they had passed the first and the second guard 9
13:33 as also it is written in the second psalm 9
28:13 on the second day we came to Pute'oli. 7
1Co 12:28 first apostles, second prophets, third teachers 9
15:47 the second man is from heaven. 9
2Co 13: 2 as I did when present on my second visit 9
Heb 8: 7 there would have been no occasion for a second. 9
9: 3 Behind the second curtain stood a tent 9
7 into the second only the high priest goes 9
28 will appear a second time, not to deal with sin 9
10: 9 in order to establish the second. 9
2Pe 3: 1 This is now the second letter that I have written 9
Rev 2:11 He . . shall not be hurt by the second death 9
4: 7 the second living creature like an ox 9
6: 3 When he opened the second seal, I heard 9
3 I heard the second living creature say, "Come! 9
8: 8 The second angel blew his trumpet 9
11:14 The second woe has passed; behold, the third woe 9
14: 8 Another angel, a second, followed, saying 9
16: 3 The second angel poured his bowl into the sea 9
20: 6 Over such the second death has no power 9
14 This is the second death, the lake of fire; 9
21: 8 the lake that burns . . which is the second death. 9
19 every jewel . . the second sapphire 9
1Es 1:31 he got into his second chariot 8
2:30 until the second year of the reign of Darius 9
3:11 The second wrote, "The king is strongest. 10
4: 1 Then the second . . began to speak 9
5: 6 in the second year of his reign 9
56 In the second year 9
56 in the second month 9
57 on the new moon of the second month 9
57 new moon of the second month in the second year 9
6: 1 Now in the second year of the reign of Darius 9
2Es 1: 1 The second book of the prophet Ezra 12
5:16 Now on the second night Phaltiel . . came to me 12
6:41 Again, on the second day, thou didst create 12
7:82 The second way, because they cannot now make 12
93 The second order, because they see 12
10: 2 I remained quiet until evening of the second day 11
11: 1 On the second night I had a dream 12
27 a second also, and this disappeared more quickly 12
12:15 the second that is to reign shall hold sway 12
Tob 1: 7 a second tenth I would sell 9
22 had appointed him second to himself 9
Jdt 2: 4 chief general of his army, second only to himself 9
7: 6 On the second day 9
AEs 11: 2 In the second year of the reign of Artaxerxes 9
13: 3 has attained the second place in the kingdom 9
6 is our second father 9
16:11 the person second to the royal throne. 9
Sir 23:23 second, she has committed an offense 9
1Mc 9: 1 sent . . into the land of Judah a second time 9
54 In the 153rd year, in the second month 9
13:51 the 23rd day of the second month, in the 171st year 9
2Mc 5: 1 Antiochus made his second invasion of Egypt. 9
7: 7 they brought forward the second for their sport 9
14: 8 second because I have regard also for . . 9
4Mc 15:18 nor when the second in torments looked at you 9

second *See also* order, quarter, time.

second one 1. תִּנְיָן (A)

Dan 7: 5 behold, another beast, a second one, like a bear. 1

secret 1. מִסְתָּר 2. סוֹד 3. סתם 4. סֵתֶר 5. עלם 6. תַּעֲלֻמָה 7. ἀπόκρυφος 8. κρύπτη 9. κρυπτός 10. κρύπτω 11. κρυφαῖος 12. κρύφιος 13. λαθραῖος 14. λόγος 15. λόγος κρύφιος 16. μυστήριον 17. absconse 18. mysterium 19. secretum

Deu 27:15 makes a graven . . image . . sets it up in secret.' 4
24 'Cursed be he who slays his neighbor in secret.' 4
Jdg 3:19 and said, "I have a secret message for you, O king. 4
16: 9 the secret of his strength was not known. *
Job 11: 6 and that he would tell you the secrets of wisdom! 6
13:10 rebuke you if in secret you show partiality. 4
Ps 10: 9 he lurks in secret like a lion in his covert; 1
44:21 For he knows the secrets of the heart. 6
90: 8 our secret sins in the light of thy countenance. 5
139:15 not hidden . . when I was being made in secret 4
Prv 9:17 bread eaten in secret is pleasant. 4
11:13 who goes about as a talebearer reveals secrets 2
20:19 He who goes about gossiping reveals secrets; 2
21:14 A gift in secret averts anger; 4
25: 9 do not disclose another's secret; 2
Isa 45:19 I did not speak in secret, in a land of darkness; 4
48:16 from the beginning I have not spoken in secret 4
Jer 13:17 if you will not listen, my soul will weep in secret 1
Ezk 28: 3 wiser than Daniel; no secret is hidden from you; 3
Ams 3: 7 without revealing his secret to his servants 2
Hab 3:14 rejoicing as if to devour the poor in secret. 1
Mat 6: 4 that your alms may be in secret; and your Father 9
4 your Father who sees in secret will reward you. 9
6 Father who is in secret; and your Father who sees 9
6 your Father who sees in secret will reward you. 9
18 Father who is in secret; and your Father who sees 11
18 your Father who sees in secret will reward you. 11
13:11 to know the secrets of the kingdom of heaven 16
Mrk 4:11 given the secret of the kingdom of God 16
22 nor is anything secret, except to come to light. 7
Lke 8:10 given to know the secrets of the kingdom of God; 16
17 nor anything secret that shall not be known 7
Joh 7: 4 For no man works in secret 9
Rom 2:16 God judges the secrets of men by Christ Jesus. 9
1Co 2: 7 we impart a secret and hidden wisdom of God 16
14:25 the secrets of his heart are disclosed 9
2Es 10:38 the Most High has revealed many secrets to you. 18
12:36 worthy to learn this secret of the Most High. 19
38 are able to comprehend and keep these secrets. 19
14: 5 and showed him the secrets of the times 19
26 and some you shall deliver in secret to the wise 17
Tob 12: 7 It is good to guard the secret of a king 16
11 It is good to guard the secret of a king 16
Jdt 2: 2 and set forth to them his secret plan 16
Wis 1:11 because no secret word is without result 13
2:22 they did not know the secret purposes of God 16
6:22 I will hide no secrets from you 16
7:21 both what is secret and what is manifest 9
14:23 or celebrate secret mysteries 12
17: 3 in their secret sins they were unobserved 11
Sir 1:30 The Lord will reveal your secrets 9
4:18 will reveal her secrets to him. 9
8:17 for he will not be able to keep a secret. 14
14:21 will also ponder her secrets. 7
22:22 reviling, arrogance, disclosure of secrets 16
27:16 Whoever betrays secrets destroys confidence 16
17 if you betray his secrets, do not run after him. 16
21 whoever has betrayed secrets is without hope. 16
39: 7 He will . . meditate on his secrets. 7
41:23 revealing secrets 15
Sus 1:42 O eternal God, who dost discern what is secret 9
Bel 1:21 they showed him the secret doors 9
2Mc 1:16 Opening the secret door in the ceiling 8
3Mc 4:12 the Jews' compatriots . . frequently went out in secret 10

secret *See also* art, heart, information, keep, learn, messenger, plot, rite.

secret part 1. פֹּת

Isa 3:17 the LORD will lay bare their secret parts. 1

secret place 1. מִסְתָּר 2. נצר 3. סֵתֶר

1Sm 19: 2 take heed . . stay in a secret place and hide 3
Ps 81: 7 I answered you in the secret place of thunder; 3
Isa 45: 3 I will give you . . the hoards in secret places 1
65: 4 sit in tombs, and spend the night in secret places; 2
Jer 23:24 Can a man hide himself in secret places 1

secret thing 1. סתר 2. עלם

Deu 29:29 secret things belong to the LORD our God; 1
Ecc 12:14 bring . . into judgment, with every secret thing 2

secretary 1. סֹפֵר

2Sm 8:17 Serai'ah was secretary; 1
20:25 Sheva was secretary; and Zadok and Abi'athar were 1
1Kg 4: 3 Elihor'eph and Ahi'jah . . were secretaries; 1
2Kg 12:10 the king's secretary and the high priest came up 1
18:18 there came out . . and Shebnah the secretary 1
37 Eli'akim . . and Shebna the secretary, and Jo'ah 1
19: 2 he sent Eli'akim . . and Shebna the secretary 1
22: 3 sent Shaphan the son of Azali'ah . . the secretary 1
8 And Hilki'ah . . said to Shaphan the secretary 1
9 And Shaphan the secretary came to the king 1
10 Then Shaphan the secretary told the king 1
12 Achbor the son of . . and Shaphan the secretary 1
25:19 and the secretary of the commander of the army 1
1Ch 18:16 and Shavsha was secretary; 1
2Ch 24:11 king's secretary . . would come and empty 1
26:11 in the muster made by Je-i'el the secretary 1
34:15 Then Hilki'ah said to Shaphan the secretary 1
18 Then Shaphan the secretary told the king 1
20 king commanded . . Shaphan the secretary 1
Est 3:12 Then the king's secretaries were summoned 1
8: 9 king's secretaries were summoned at that time 1
Isa 36: 3 Shebna the secretary, and Jo'ah the son of Asaph 1
22 Shebna the secretary, and Jo'ah the son of Asaph 1
37: 2 and Shebna the secretary, and the senior priests 1
Jer 36:10 of Gemari'ah the son of Shaphan the secretary 1
12 to the king's house, into the secretary's chamber; 1
12 were sitting there: Eli'shama the secretary 1
20 in the chamber of Eli'shama the secretary; 1
21 from the chamber of Eli'shama the secretary; 1
26 to seize Baruch the secretary and Jeremiah 1
37:15 in the house of Jonathan the secretary 1
20 back to the house of Jonathan the secretary 1
52:25 the secretary of the commander of the army 1

secretly 1. בַּסֵּתֶר 2. חבא 3. חֶרֶשׁ 4. סֵתֶר 5. ἀπόκρυφος 6. κλέπτω 7. κρύπτω 8. κρυπτῶς 9. λαθραίως 10. λεληθότως 11. secrete

Gen 31:27 Why did you flee secretly, and cheat me 2
Deu 13: 6 entices you secretly, saying, 'Let us go and serve 4
28:57 she will eat them secretly, for want of all things 4
Jos 2: 1 sent two men secretly from Shittim as spies 3
2Sm 12:12 For you did it secretly; but I will do this thing 1
Job 31:27 my heart has been secretly enticed 1
Ps 101: 5 Him who slanders his neighbors secretly 1
Jer 37:17 The king questioned him secretly in his house 1
38:16 Then King Zedeki'ah swore secretly to Jeremiah 1
40:15 Then Joha'nan the son of Kare'ah spoke secretly 1
Joh 19:38 was a disciple of Jesus, but secretly 7
Act 6:11 Then they secretly instigated men, who said *
2Es 3:14 the end of the times, secretly by night. 11
Tob 1:18 I buried them secretly 6
Sir 42: 9 A daughter keeps her father secretly wakeful 5
1Mc 10:79 Apollonius had secretly left 1,000 cavalry behind 8
2Mc 1:19 secretly hid it in the hollow of a dry cistern 9
6:11 to observe the seventh day secretly 10
8: 1 secretly entered the villages 10
3Mc 3:23 they secretly suspect *

secretly *See also* bring, gain, lay, take.

sect 1. αἵρεσις

Act 24: 5 a ringleader of the sect of the Nazarenes. 1
14 according to the Way, which they call a sect 1
28:22 with regard to this sect 1

section 1. מִדָּה

Neh 3:11 repaired another section 1
19 Ezer . . repaired another section opposite 1
20 repaired another section from the Angle 1
21 Mer'emoth . . repaired another section 1
24 of Hen'adad repaired another section 1
27 Teko'ites repaired another section opposite 1
30 Hanani'ah . . Hanun . . repaired another section. 1
Ezk 45: 3 a section 25,000 cubits long *
5 Another section, 25,000 cubits *
1Mc 12:37 he repaired the section called Chaphenatha. *

deserted section 1. ἔρημος

Sir 9: 7 nor wander about in its deserted sections. 1

secure 1. בטח 2. בֶּטַח 3. בַּטְחָה 4. יצק 5. לָבֶטַח 6. לָבֶטַח 7. מִבְטָח 8. שָׁלֵו 9. שמר 10. ἀσφάλεια 11. γίνομαι 12. ἐπισπάω 13. εὐπάρεδρος 14. εὑρίσκω 15. εὐσταθής 16. καταντάω 17. κατασφαλίζω 18. κατορθόω 19. λαμβάνω 20. πείθω 21. περικρατεῖς γίνομαι

2Sm 23: 5 covenant, ordered in all things and secure. 9
Job 11:15 you will be secure, and will not fear. 4
12: 6 those who provoke God are secure 3
21:23 full prosperity, being wholly at ease and secure 8
Ps 16: 9 my soul rejoices; my body also dwells secure. 5
Prv 1:33 he who listens to me will dwell secure 2
11:15 but he who hates suretyship is secure. 1
Isa 32:18 in secure dwellings, and in quiet resting places. 7
Ezk 34:27 they shall be secure in their land; 6
Mic 5: 4 And they shall dwell secure *
Zep 2:15 This is the exultant city that dwelt secure 2
Act 27:16 we managed with difficulty to secure the boat; 21
1Co 7:35 secure your undivided devotion to the Lord. 13
9:15 to secure any such provision 11
Heb 9:12 thus securing an eternal redemption. 14
AEs 13: 7 leave our government completely secure 15
Sir 4:15 whoever gives heed to her will dwell secure. 20
1Mc 14: 1 marched into Media to secure help 12
2Mc 1:14 to secure most of its treasures as a dowry. 19
2:27 However, to secure the gratitude of many *
3:22 keep . . safe and secure 10
4:11 secured through John the father of Eupolemus *
24 and secured the high priesthood for himself 16
8:36 had undertaken to secure tribute for the Romans 18
3Mc 4: 9 had their feet secured by unbreakable fetters 17

secure *See also* dwell, feel, hold, make.

secure justice 1. iudico

2Es 2:20 secure justice for the fatherless 1

set secure 1. עמד

2Sm 22:34 made my feet . . and set me secure on the heights. 1
Ps 18:33 like hinds' feet, and set me secure on the heights. 1

securely 1. בֶּטַח 2. לְבֶטַח 3. לָבֶטַח 4. *πάντοθεν*

Lev 25:18 so you will dwell in the land securely 2
19 you will eat your fill, and dwell in it securely 2
26: 5 you shall . . dwell in your land securely 2
Prv 3:23 Then you will walk on your way securely 3
10: 9 He who walks in integrity walks securely 1
Isa 47: 8 hear . . you lover of pleasures, who sit securely 3
Jer 23: 6 and Israel will dwell securely. 3
33:16 and Jerusalem will dwell securely. 3
49:31 a nation at ease, that dwells securely 3
Ezk 28:26 they shall dwell securely in it 3
26 They shall dwell securely, when I execute 3
34:25 that they may dwell securely in the wilderness 3
28 they shall dwell securely 3
38: 8 and now dwell securely, all of them. 3
11 fall upon the quiet people who dwell securely 3
14 when my people Israel are dwelling securely 3
39: 6 on those who dwell securely in the coastlands; 3
26 when they dwell securely in their land 3
3Mc 3:25 bound securely with iron fetters 4

security 1. אֱמוּנָה 2. אֱמֶת 3. בֶּטַח 4. ערב 5. שַׁלְוָה 6. תְּשׂוּמֶת יָד 7. *ἀσφάλεια* 8. *ἱκανός*

Lev 6: 2 in a matter of deposit or security 6
Jdg 18: 7 they dwelt in security, after the manner 3
2Kg 20:19 if there will be peace and security in my days? 2
Job 24:23 He gives them security, and they are supported; 3
Ps 37: 3 you will dwell in the land, and enjoy security. 1
122: 7 Peace . . walls, and security within your towers! 5
Isa 38:14 O Lord, I am oppressed; be thou my security! 4
39: 8 There will be peace and security in my days. 2
Jer 33: 6 to them abundance of prosperity and security. 2
Zec 14:11 Jerusalem shall dwell in security. 3
Act 17: 9 when they had taken security from Jason 8
1Th 5: 3 When people say, "There is peace and security 7
2Mc 4:21 he took measures for his own security. 7
9:21 to take thought for the general security of all. 7

sedition 1. אֶשְׁתַּדּוּר (A)

Ezr 4:15 sedition was stirred up in it from of old. 1
19 rebellion and sedition have been made in it. 1

sedition *See also* stir.

seduce 1. חנף 2. פתה 3. תעה

Exd 22:16 If a man seduces a virgin who is not betrothed 2
2Kg 21: 9 and Manas'seh seduced them to do more evil 3
2Ch 33: 9 Manas'seh seduced Judah and . . Jerusalem 3
Dan 11:32 shall seduce with flattery those who violate 1

seducer 1. *λυμεὼν φθορεύς*

4Mc 18: 8 No seducer corrupted me on a desert plain 1

seductive speech 1. לֶקַח

Prv 7:21 With much seductive speech she persuades him; 1

see 1. אַחֲרֵי 2. אֲשֶׁר 3. הִנֵּה 4. וְ 5. חזה 6. כִּי 7. מַרְאֶה 8. מָשׁוֹר 9. נבט 10. נכר 11. נשׂא עֵינַיִם 12. פקד 13. פִּקֵּחַ 14. ראה 15. רֳאִי 16. שֶׁ 17. שׁור 18. שׁזף 19. שׁמר 20. חזה (A) 21. חזה הוה (A) 22. *ἄδηλος* 23. *αἰσθάνομαι* 24. *ἀτενίζω* 25. *αὐγάζω* 26. *ἀφοράω* 27. *βλέμμα* 28. *βλέπω* 29. *γινώσκω* 30. *δείκνυμι* 31. *εἶδον* 32. *ἐμβλέπω* 33. *ἐνώπιον* 34. *ἐπεῖδον* 35. *ἐπιβλέπω* 36. *ἐπισκοπέω* 37. *ἐποπτεύω* 38. *ἐπόπτης* 39. *ἐφοράω* 40. *θεάομαι* 41. *θεωρέω* 42. *θεωρία* 43. *ἰδού* 44. *ἵνα* 45. *κατοπτεύω* 46. *νοέω* 47. *ὅρασις* 48. *ὁράω* 49. *ὅρος* 50. *ὄψις* 51. *περιβλέπω* 52. *ποιέω* 53. *σκοπέω* 54. *σπουδάζω* 55. *συνοράω* 56. *φαιδρός* 57. *φαίνω* 58. *φανερόω* 59. appareo 60. compareo 61. cum 62. video

Gen 1: 4 God saw that the light was good 14
10 And God saw that it was good 14
12 And God saw that it was good 14
18 And God saw that it was good 14
21 And God saw that it was good 14
25 And God saw that it was good 14
31 God saw everything that he had made 14
2:19 brought . . to the man to see what he would call them; 14
3: 6 when the woman saw that the tree was good for food 14
6: 2 the sons of God saw that the daughters of men 14
5 The LORD saw that the wickedness of man was great 14
12 God saw the earth, and behold, it was corrupt; 14
7: 1 I have seen that you are righteous before me 14
8: 5 of the month, the tops of the mountains were seen. 14
8 to see if the waters had subsided from the face 14
9:14 the earth and the bow is seen in the clouds 14
22 Ham . . saw the nakedness of his father 14
23 they did not see their father's nakedness. 14
11: 5 the LORD came down to see the city and the tower 14
12:12 when the Egyptians see you, they will say 14
14 When Abram entered Egypt the Egyptians saw that 14
15 when the princes of Pharaoh saw her 14
13:10 Lot lifted up his eyes, and saw that the Jordan 14
15 for all the land which you see I will give to you 14
16: 4 and when she saw that she had conceived 14
5 and when she saw that she had conceived 14
13 LORD who spoke to her, "Thou art a God of seeing"; 15
13 of seeing"; for she said, "Have I really seen God 14
13 seen God and remained alive after seeing him? •
18: 2 When he saw them, he ran from the tent door 14
18 seeing that Abraham shall become a great •
21 I will go down to see whether they have done 14
19: 1 When Lot saw them, he rose to meet them 14
21: 9 Sarah saw the son of Hagar the Egyptian 14
19 opened her eyes, and she saw a well of water; 14
22: 4 Abraham lifted up his eyes and saw the place afar 14
12 you fear God, seeing you have not withheld •
24: 6 See to it that you do not take my son back there. 19
30 When he saw the ring, and the bracelets 14
64 and when she saw Isaac, she alighted 14
26: 8 looked out of a window and saw Isaac 14
27 you come to me, seeing that you hate me •
28 They said, "We see plainly that the LORD is 14
27: 1 his eyes were dim so that he could not see 14
27 blessed him, and said, "See, the smell of my son 14
28: 6 Esau saw that Isaac had blessed Jacob 14
8 when Esau saw that the Canaanite women 14
29: 2 As he looked, he saw a well in the field 14
6 and see, Rachel his daughter is coming 3
10 Now when Jacob saw Rachel the daughter of Laban 14
31 When the LORD saw that Leah was hated 14
30: 1 When Rachel saw that she bore Jacob no children 14
9 Leah saw that she had ceased bearing children 14
31: 2 Jacob saw that Laban did not regard him 14
5 said to them, "I see that your father does not 14
10 the flock I lifted up my eyes, and saw in a dream 14
12 he said, 'Lift up your eyes and see, all the goats 14
12 for I have seen all that Laban is doing to you. 14
42 God saw my affliction and the labor of my hands 14
43 are my flocks, and all that you see is mine. 14
51 See this heap and the pillar, which I have set 3
32: 2 when Jacob saw them he said, "This is God's army! 14
20 and afterwards I shall see his face; 14
25 When the man saw that he did not prevail 14
30 saying, "For I have seen God face to face 14
33: 5 raised his eyes and saw the women and children 14
10 for truly to see your face is like seeing the face 14
10 to see your face is like seeing the face of God 14
34: 2 when Shechem . . saw her, he seized her and lay 14
37: 4 when his brothers saw that their father loved 14
14 Go now, see if it is well with your brothers 14
18 They saw him afar off, and before he came near 14
20 and we shall see what will become of his dreams. 14
25 looking up they saw a caravan of Ish'maelites 14
29 returned to the pit and saw that Joseph was not 3
32 This we have found; see now whether it is your son's 10
38: 2 Judah saw the daughter of a certain Canaanite 14
14 for she saw that Shelah was grown up 14
15 When Judah saw her, he thought her to be a harlot 14
23 you see, I sent this kid, and you could not find her 3
39: 3 his master saw that the LORD was with him 14
13 when she saw that he had left his garment 14
14 said to them, "See, he has brought among us a Hebrew 14
40: 6 in the morning and saw them, they were troubled. 14
16 chief baker saw that the interpretation was 14
41:19 such as I had never seen in all the land of Egypt. 14
22 I also saw in my dream seven ears growing 14
42: 7 Joseph saw his brothers, and knew them 14
9 you have come to see the weakness of the land. 14
12 weakness of the land that you have come to see. 14
21 we are guilty . . in that we saw the distress 14
27 he saw his money in the mouth of his sack; 14
35 and when they and their father saw their bundles 14
43: 3 You shall not see my face, unless your brother is 14
5 You shall not see my face, unless your brother is 14
16 When Joseph saw Benjamin with them, he said 14
29 he lifted up his eyes, and saw his brother 14
44:23 you shall see my face no more.' 14
26 for we cannot see the man's face unless our 14
28 torn to pieces; and I have never seen him since. 14
31 when he sees that the lad is not with us, he will die 14
34 I fear to see the evil that would come upon my 14
45:12 now your eyes see, and the eyes of my brother 14
12 eyes of my brother Benjamin see, that it is my •
13 You must tell . . of all that you have seen. 14
27 and when he saw the wagons which Joseph had sent 14
28 I will go and see him before I die. 14
46:30 Now let me die, since I have seen your face 14
48: 8 When Israel saw Joseph's sons, he said, 14
10 eyes . . were dim . . so that he could not see. 14
11 I had not thought to see your face; 14
11 and lo, God has let me see your children also. 14
17 Joseph saw that his father laid his right hand 14
49:15 he saw that a resting place was good 14
50:11 the Canaanites, saw the mourning 14
15 Joseph's brothers saw that their father was dead 14
23 Joseph saw E'phraim's children of the third 14
Exd 1:16 When you . . see them upon the birthstool 14
2: 2 and when she saw that he was a goodly child 14
5 she saw the basket among the reeds and sent 14
6 When she opened it she saw the child; 14
11 and he saw an Egyptian beating a Hebrew 14
12 He looked this way and that, and seeing no one 14
25 God saw the people of Israel 14
3: 3 I will turn aside and see this great sight 14
4 When the LORD saw that he turned aside to see 14
4 When the LORD saw that he turned aside to see 14
7 I have seen the affliction of my people 14
9 I have seen the oppression 14
4:11 Who makes him dumb, or deaf, or seeing, or blind? 13
14 and when he sees you he will be glad in his heart. 14
18 Let me . . see whether they are still alive. 14
21 see that you do before Pharaoh all the miracles 14
31 heard . . that he had seen their affliction 14
5:19 The foremen . . saw that they were in evil plight 14
6: 1 the LORD said to Moses, "Now you shall see what I 14
7: 1 the LORD said to Moses, "See, I make you as God 14
8:15 when Pharaoh saw that there was a respite 14
9:34 when Pharaoh saw that the rain and the hail 14
10: 5 cover . . the land, so that no one can see the land; 14
6 your fathers nor your grandfathers have seen 14
23 they did not see one another, nor did any rise 14
28 take heed to yourself; never see my face again; 14
28 for in the day you see my face you shall die. 14
29 I will not see your face again. 14
12:13 and when I see the blood, I will pass over you 14
23 and when he sees the blood on the lintel 14
13: 7 no leavened bread shall be seen with you 14
7 and no leaven shall be seen with you in all 14
17 Lest the people repent when they see war 14
14:13 Fear not, stand firm, and see the salvation 14
13 the Egyptians whom you see today, you shall never 14
13 Egyptians . . you shall never see again. 14
30 Israel saw the Egyptians dead upon the seashore. 14
31 Israel saw the great work which the LORD did 14
16: 7 in the morning you shall see the glory of the LORD 14
15 When the people of Israel saw it, they said to one 14
29 See! The LORD has given you the sabbath, therefore 14
32 that they may see the bread with which I fed you 14
18:14 When Moses' father-in-law saw all that he was doing 14
19: 4 You have seen what I did to the Egyptians 14
20:22 You have seen for yourselves that I have talked 14
22:10 or is driven away, without any one seeing it 14
11 between them both to see whether he has not put •
23: 5 If you see the ass of one who hates you lying under 14
24:10 they saw the God of Israel; 14
25:40 see that you make them after the pattern for them 14
31: 2 See, I have called by name Bez'alel and son of Uri 14
32: 1 When the people saw that Moses delayed to come 14
5 When Aaron saw this, he built an altar before it; 14
9 the LORD said to Moses, "I have seen this people 14
19 and saw the calf and the dancing, Moses' anger 14
25 when Moses saw that the people had broken loose 14
33:10 when all the people saw the pillar of cloud 14
12 Moses said to the LORD, "See, thou sayest to me 14
20 But," he said, "you cannot see my face; 14
20 for man shall not see me and live. 14
23 you shall see my back; but my face shall not be 14
23 my back; but my face shall not be seen. 14
34: 3 let no man be seen throughout all the mountain; 14
10 all the people . . shall see the work of the LORD; 14
30 when Aaron and all the people of Israel saw Moses 14
35 the people of Israel saw the face of Moses 14
35:30 Moses said to the people of Israel, "See, the LORD 14
39:43 Moses saw all the work, and behold, they had done it; 14
Lev 5: 1 whether he has seen or come to know the matter 14
9:24 when all the people saw it, they shouted 14
13:12 from head to foot, so far as the priest can see 7
14:36 afterward the priest shall go in to see the house 14
20:17 If a man . . sees her nakedness, and she sees his 14
17 If . . she sees his nakedness, it is a shameful 14
Num11:15 kill me . . that I may not see my wretchedness. 14
23 Now you shall see whether my word will come true 14
13:18 see what the land is, and whether the people 14
28 besides, we saw the descendants of Anak there. 14
32 people that we saw in it are men of great stature. 14
33 there we saw the Nephilim (the sons of Anak 14
14:14 for thou, O LORD, art seen face to face, and thy cloud 14
22 none of the men who have seen my glory and my signs 14
23 shall see the land which I swore to give 14
23 none of those who despised me shall see it. 14
40 See, we are here, we will go up to the place 3
20:29 all the congregation saw that Aaron was dead 14
21: 8 every one who is bitten when he sees it, shall live. 14
22: 2 Balak . . saw all that Israel had done 14
23 ass saw the angel of the LORD standing in the road 14
25 when the ass saw the angel of the LORD, she pushed 14
27 When the ass saw the angel of the LORD, she lay 14
31 he saw the angel of the LORD standing in the way 14
33 ass saw me, and turned aside before me these three 14
41 from there he saw the nearest of the people. 14
23: 9 For from the top of the mountains I see him 14
13 to another place, from which you may see them; 14
13 you shall see only the nearest of them 14
13 shall not see them all; 14
21 nor has he seen trouble in Israel. 14
24: 1 Balaam saw that it pleased the LORD to bless 14
2 Balaam . . saw Israel encamping tribe by tribe. 14
4 oracle of . . who sees the vision of the Almighty 5
16 who sees the vision of the Almighty 5
17 I see him, but not now; I behold him, but not nigh 14
25: 7 When Phin'ehas . . saw it, he rose and left 14
27:12 see the land which I have given to . . Israel. 14
13 when you have seen it, you also shall be gathered 14
28:19 see that they are without blemish; †

31 See that they are without blemish. †
32: 1 they saw the land of Jazer and the land of Gilead 14
8 sent them from Ka'desh-bar'nea to see the land. 14
9 went up to the Valley of Eshcol, and saw the land 14
11 shall see the land which I swore to give 14
35:23 stone . . and without seeing him cast it upon him 14
Deu 1:19 great and terrible wilderness which you saw 14
28 moreover we have seen the sons of the Anakim there. 14
31 wilderness, where you have seen how the LORD 14
35 Not one . . shall see the good land which I swore 14
36 Caleb . . shall see it, and to him and to his children 14
3:21 eyes have seen all that the LORD your God has done 14
25 Let me . . see the good land beyond the Jordan 14
28 possession of the land which you shall see.' 14
4: 3 eyes have seen what the LORD did at Ba'al-pe'or; 14
9 forget the things which your eyes have seen 14
12 you heard the sound of words, but saw no form; 14
15 Since you saw no form on the day that the LORD 14
19 when you see the sun and the moon and the stars 14
28 gods . . that neither see, nor hear, nor eat, nor smell. 14
36 on earth he let you see his great fire 14
5:24 day seen God speak with man and man still live. 14
7:19 great trials which your eyes saw, the signs 14
9:13 LORD said to me, 'I have seen this people, and behold 14
10:21 great . . things which your eyes have seen. 14
11: 2 children who have not known or seen it) 14
7 for your eyes have seen all the great work 14
12:13 do not offer . . at every place that you see; 14
16: 4 No leaven . . seen with you in all your territory 14
18:16 me not . . see this great fire any more, lest I die.' 14
20: 1 see horses and chariots and an army larger 14
21: 7 neither did our eyes see it shed. 14
11 see among the captives a beautiful woman 14
22: 1 not see your brother's ox or his sheep go astray 14
4 You shall not see your brother's ass or his ox 14
23:14 that he may not see anything indecent among you 14
26: 7 LORD . . saw our affliction, our toil 14
28:10 see that you are called by the name of the LORD; 14
34 driven mad by the sight which your eyes shall see. 14
67 because of . . sights which your eyes shall see. 14
29: 2 seen all that the LORD did before your eyes 14
3 great trials which your eyes saw 14
4 LORD has not given you . . eyes to see, or ears 14
17 have seen their detestable things, their idols 14
22 would say, when they see the sicknesses 14
30:15 See, I have set before you this day life and good 14
32:19 LORD saw it, and spurned them 14
20 hide my face . . I will see what their end will be 14
36 when he sees that their power is gone 14
39 'See now that I, even I, am he, and there is no god 14
52 For you shall see the land before you; 14
34: 4 I have let you see it with your eyes 14
Jos 3: 3 When you see the ark . . being carried 14
5: 6 LORD swore that he would not let them see the land 14
6: 2 See, I have given into your hand Jericho 14
7:21 when I saw among the spoil a beautiful mantle 14
8: 1 go up to Ai; see, I have given into your hand the king 14
8 when . . you shall..; see, I have commanded you. 14
14 when the king of Ai saw this he . . made haste 14
21 all Israel saw that the ambush had taken the city 14
23: 3 you have seen all that the LORD your God has done 14
24: 7 and your eyes saw what I did to Egypt; 14
Jdg 1:24 the spies saw a man coming out of the city 14
2: 7 elders who outlived Joshua, who had seen all 14
3:24 servants came; and when they saw that the doors 14
5: 8 Was shield or spear to be seen among . . Israel? 14
6:22 now I have seen the angel of the LORD face to face. 14
9:36 when Ga'al saw the men, he said to Zebul, "Look, 14
36 You see the shadow of the mountains as if they 14
43 he looked and saw the men coming out of the city 3
48 What you have seen me do, make haste to do 14
55 the men of Israel saw that Abim'elech was dead 14
11:35 when he saw her, he rent his clothes, and said, "Alas 14
12: 3 when I saw that you would not deliver me 14
13:18 Why do you ask my name, seeing it is wonderful? •
22 his wife, "We shall surely die, for we have seen God. 14
14: 1 and at Timnah he saw one of the daughters 14
2 I saw one of the daughters of the Philistines 14
8 he turned aside to see the carcass of the lion 14
11 And when the people saw him, they brought 30 14
16: 1 Samson went to Gaza, and there he saw a harlot 14
5 see wherein his great strength lies 14
18 When Deli'lah saw that he had told her all his mind 14
24 when the people saw him, they praised their god; 14
18: 7 came to La'ish, and saw the people who were there 14
9 go up against them; for we have seen the land 14
26 when Micah saw that they were too strong for him 14
19: 3 and when the girl's father saw him, he came with joy 14
17 he lifted up his eyes, and saw the wayfarer 14
23 seeing that this man has come into my house 1
30 all who saw it said, "Such a thing has never 14
30 Such a thing has never happened or been seen 14
20:36 the Benjaminites saw that they were defeated. 14
41 dismayed, for they saw that disaster was close 14
Rut 1:15 See, your sister-in-law has gone back to her people 3
18 Na'omi saw that she was determined to go with her 14
3: 2 See, he is winnowing barley tonight 3
1Sm 3: 2 had begun to grow dim, so that he could not see 14
4:15 and his eyes were set, so that he could not see. 14
5: 7 the men of Ashdod saw how things were, they said 14
6:13 when they lifted up their eyes and saw the ark 14
13 when they . . saw the ark, they rejoiced to see it. 14
16 when the five lords of the Philistines saw it 14
9:14 they saw Samuel coming out toward them on his way 3
16 I have seen the affliction of my people 14
17 When Samuel saw Saul, the LORD told him 14
24 Samuel said, "See, what was kept is set before you. 3
10:11 all . . saw how he prophesied with the prophets 14
14 we saw they were not to be found, we went to Samuel. 14
24 Do you see him whom the LORD has chosen? 14
12:12 when you saw that Nahash . . came against you 14
16 therefore stand still and see this great thing 14
17 shall know and see that your wickedness is great 14
13: 6 the men of Israel saw that they were in straits 14
11 I saw that the people were scattering from me 14
14:17 Saul said . . "Number and see who has gone from us. 14
29 see how my eyes have become bright 14
38 and know and see how this sin has arisen today. 14
52 when Saul saw any strong man, or any valiant man 14
15:35 Samuel did not see Saul again until . . his death 14
16: 1 How long will you . . seeing I have rejected him 4
7 for the LORD sees not as man sees; •
7 for the LORD sees not as man sees; 14
18 I have seen a son of Jesse the Bethlehemite 14
17:24 All . . Israel, when they saw the man, fled from him 14
25 Have you seen this man who has come up? 14
28 for you have come down to see the battle. 14
36 like one of them, seeing he has defied the armies 6
42 And when the Philistine looked, and saw David 14
51 the Philistines saw . . their champion was dead 14
55 Saul saw David go forth against the Philistine 14
18:15 And when Saul saw that he had great success 14
23 Does it seem . . seeing that I am a poor man 4
28 Saul saw and knew that the LORD was with David 14
19: 5 You saw it, and rejoiced; why then will you sin 14
15 Saul sent the messengers to see David, saying 14
20 when they saw the company of the prophets 14
20:29 let me get away, and see my brothers. 14
21:14 you see the man is mad; why . . have you brought him 14
22: 9 I saw the son of Jesse coming to Nob, to Ahim'elech 14
23:22 know and see the place where his haunt is 14
22 where his haunt is, and who has seen him there; 14
23 See therefore, and take note of . . where he hides 14
24: 6 LORD forbid . . seeing he is the LORD's anointed. 6
10 have seen how the LORD gave you today into my hand 14
11 See, my father, see the skirt of your robe in my hand; 14
11 See, my father, see the skirt of your robe in my hand; 14
11 know and see that there is no wrong 14
15 give sentence . . and see to it, and plead my cause 14
25:23 When Ab'igail saw David, she made haste 14
25 your handmaid did not see the young men of my lord 14
26 seeing the LORD has restrained you 2
35 Go up in peace to your house; see, I have hearkened 14
26: 3 when he saw that Saul came after him 14
5 and David saw the place where Saul lay, with Abner 14
12 No man saw it, or knew it, nor did any awake; 14
16 And now see where the king's spear is, and the jar 14
28: 5 When Saul saw the army of the Philistines 14
12 When the woman saw Samuel, she cried out 14
13 The king said to her, "Have no fear; what do you see? 14
13 I see a god coming up out of the earth. 14
21 when she saw that he was terrified, she said to him 14
31: 5 when his armor-bearer saw that Saul was dead 14
7 when the men . . saw that the men of Israel had fled 14
2Sm 1: 7 And when he looked behind him, he saw me, 14
3:13 you shall not see my face, unless you first bring 14
13 bring Michal . . when you come to see my face. 14
6:16 Michal . . saw King David leaping and dancing 14
7: 2 See now, I dwell in a house of cedar 14
10: 6 the Ammonites saw that they had become odious 14
9 When Jo'ab saw that the battle was set against him 14
14 when the Ammonites saw that the Syrians fled 14
15 when the Syrians saw that they had been defeated 14
19 all the kings . . saw that they had been defeated 14
11: 2 It happened . . that he saw from the roof a woman 14
12:19 David saw that his servants were whispering 14
13: 5 when your father comes to see you, say to him 14
5 and prepare the food in my sight, that I may see it 14
6 when the king came to see him, Amnon said 14
39 he was comforted about Amnon, seeing he was dead. 6
14:30 See, Jo'ab's field is next to mine, and he has barley 14
15: 3 See, your claims are good and right; 14
20 make you wander . . seeing I go I know not where? •
25 he will . . let me see both it and his habitation; 14
28 See, I will wait at the fords of the wilderness 14
16: 8 See, your ruin is on you; for you are a man of blood. 3
17:17 for they must not be seen entering the city. 14
18 But a lad saw them, and told Ab'salom; 14
23 Ahith'ophel saw that the counsel was not followed 14
18:10 And a certain man saw it, and told Jo'ab, "Behold, 14
10 Behold, I saw Ab'salom hanging in an oak. 14
11 What, you saw him! Why then did you not strike him 14
21 Jo'ab said . . "Go, tell the king what you have seen. 14
22 Why . . seeing that you will have no reward 4
24 when he . . looked, he saw a man running alone. 3
26 And the watchman saw another man running; 14
26 watchman . . said, "See, another man running alone! 3
29 When Jo'ab sent your servant, I saw a great tumult 14
20:12 And any one who came by, seeing him, stopped; 14
12 and when the man saw that all the people stopped 14
22:11 he was seen upon the wings of the wind. 14
16 Then the channels of the sea were seen 14
24: 3 while the eyes of my lord the king still see it; 14
17 when he saw the angel who was smiting the people 14
20 he saw the king and his servants coming 14
1Kg 1:48 to sit on my throne this day, my own eyes seeing it.' 14
6:18 all was cedar, no stone was seen. 14
8: 8 ends of the poles were seen from the holy place 14
8 but they could not be seen from outside; 14
9:12 came . . to see the cities which Solomon had given 14
10: 4 queen of Sheba had seen all the wisdom of Solomon 14
7 until I came and my own eyes had seen it; 14
12 no such almug wood has come or been seen, 14
11:28 Solomon saw that the young man was industrious 14
12:16 all Israel saw that the king did not hearken 14
13:25 and saw the body thrown in the road, and the lion 14
14: 4 Ahi'jah could not see, for his eyes were dim 14
16:18 when Zimri saw that the city was taken, he went 14
17:23 and Eli'jah said, "See, your son lives. 14
18:17 When Ahab saw Eli'jah, Ahab said to him, "Is it you 14
39 when . . the people saw it, they fell on their faces; 14
20: 7 Mark now, and see how this man is seeking trouble; 14
13 Have you seen all this great multitude? 14
21:29 Have you seen how Ahab has humbled himself 14
22:17 I saw all Israel scattered upon the mountains 14
19 I saw the LORD sitting on his throne 14
25 you shall see . . when you go into an inner chamber 14
32 when the captains . . saw Jehosh'aphat, they said 14
33 when the captains . . saw that it was not the king 14
2Kg 2:10 if you see me as I am being taken . . it shall be 14
10 but if you do not see me, it shall not be so. •
12 Eli'sha saw it and he cried, "My father, my father! 14
12 And he saw him no more. 14
15 when the sons of the prophets . . saw him 14
19 the situation . . is pleasant, as my lord sees; 14
24 when he saw them, he cursed them in the name 14
3:14 I would neither look at you, nor see you. 14
17 You shall not see wind or rain, but that stream-bed 14
22 the Moabites saw the water . . as red as blood. 14
26 Moab saw that the battle was going against him 14
4:13 See, you have taken all this trouble for us; 3
25 When the man of God saw her coming, he said 14
32 Eli'sha . . saw the child lying dead on his bed. 3
5: 7 see how he is seeking a quarrel with me. 14
20 See, my master has spared this Na'aman the Syrian 3
21 when Na'aman saw some one running after him 14
6: 1 See, the place where we dwell . . is too small 3
13 Go and see where he is, that I may send and seize 14
17 eyes that he may see." So the LORD opened the eyes 14
17 LORD opened the eyes of the young man, and he saw; 14
20 LORD, open the eyes of these men, that they may see. 14
20 So the LORD opened their eyes, and they saw; 14
21 When the king of Israel saw them he said to Eli'sha 14
32 see how this murderer has sent to take off my head? 14
7: 2 You shall see it with your own eyes, but . . not eat 14
10 there was no one to be seen or heard there, nothing •
13 Let some men . . seeing that those who are left 3
13 Let some men take . . let us send and see. 14
14 the king sent them . . saying, "Go and see. 14
19 You shall see it with your own eyes, but . . not eat 14
8:29 Ahazi'ah . . went down to see Joram the son of Ahab 14
9:17 he spied the company . . and said, "I see a company. 14
22 when Joram saw Jehu, he said, "Is it peace, Jehu? 14
26 As surely as I saw . . I will requite you 14
27 When Ahazi'ah the king of Judah saw this, he fled 14
34 See now to this cursed woman, and bury her; 12
10: 2 seeing your master's sons are with you •
16 Come with me, and see my zeal for the LORD. 14
23 see that there is no servant of the LORD here 14
11: 1 Now when Athali'ah . . saw that her son was dead 14
12:10 whenever they saw that there was much money 14
13: 4 for he saw the oppression of Israel 14
21 a marauding band was seen and the man was cast 14
14:26 the LORD saw that the affliction of Israel was 14
16:10 Ahaz . . he saw the altar that was at Damascus. 14
19:16 open thy eyes, O LORD, and see; and hear the words 14
20: 5 I have heard your prayer, I have seen your tears; 14
15 He said, "What have they seen in your house? 14
15 They have seen all that is in my house; 14
22:20 and your eyes shall not see all the evil 14
23:16 as Josi'ah turned, he saw the tombs . . on the mount; 14
17 Then he said, "What is yonder monument that I see? 14
24 abominations that were seen in the land of Judah 14
29 Neco slew him at Megid'do, when he saw him. 14
1Ch 10: 5 when his armor-bearer saw that Saul was dead 14
7 saw that the army had fled 14
12:17 may the God of our fathers see and rebuke you. 14
15:29 Michal . . saw King David dancing 14
19: 6 Ammonites saw that they had made themselves 14
10 When Jo'ab saw that the battle was set against him 14
15 when the Ammonites saw that the Syrians fled 14
16 when the Syrians saw that they had been defeated 14
19 when the servants of Hadade'zer saw that 14
21:15 when he was about to destroy it, the LORD saw 14
16 and saw the angel of the LORD standing between 14
20 Ornan . . he turned and saw the angel 14
21 Ornan looked and saw David and went forth 14

23 see, I give the oxen for burnt offerings 14
28 when David saw that the LORD had answered him 14
29:17 now I have seen thy people . . offering freely 14
2Ch 5: 9 ends of the poles were seen from the holy place 14
9 but they could not be seen from outside; 14
7: 3 all the children of Israel saw the fire come down 14
9: 3 queen of Sheba had seen the wisdom of Solomon 14
6 did not believe . . until my own eyes had seen it; 14
11 there never was seen the like of them before 14
10:16 Israel saw that the king did not hearken to them 14
12: 7 When the LORD saw that they humbled themselves 14
15: 9 when they saw that he LORD his God was with him. 14
18:16 I saw all Israel scattered upon the mountains 14
18 I saw the LORD sitting on his throne 14
24 Behold, you shall see on that day when you go 14
31 when the captains . . saw Jehosh'aphat, they said 14
32 saw that it was not the king of Israel 14
20:17 see the victory of the LORD on your behalf, O Judah 14
22: 6 Ahazi'ah . . went down to see Joram the son of Ahab 14
10 Now when Athali'ah . . saw that her son was dead 14
24: 5 see that you hasten the matter. •
11 when they saw that there was much money in it 14
22 he was dying, he said, "May the LORD see and avenge! 14
25:19 You say, 'See, I have smitten Edom,' 3
29: 8 as you see with your own eyes. 14
30: 7 so that he made them a desolation, as you see. 14
31: 8 Hezeki'ah and the princes came and saw the heaps 14
32: 2 when Hezeki'ah saw that Sennach'erib had come 14
34:28 your eyes shall not see all the evil which I will 14
Ezr 3:12 old men who had seen the first house 14
12 saw the foundation of this house being laid •
5:17 see whether a decree was issued by Cyrus the king •
9:13 seeing that thou, our God, hast punished us less •
Neh 2: 2 Why is your face sad, seeing you are not sick? •
17 You see the trouble we are in, how Jerusalem lies 14
4:11 not know or see till we come into the midst of them 14
6:12 I understood, and saw that God had not sent him 3
9: 9 didst see the affliction of our fathers in Egypt 14
13:15 saw in Judah men treading wine presses 14
23 days also I saw the Jews who had married women 14
Est 1:14 the seven princes of . . who saw the king's face 14
2:15 Esther found favor in the eyes of all who saw her. 14
3: 4 to see whether Mor'decai's words would avail; 14
5 Haman saw that Mor'decai did not bow down 14
5: 2 the king saw Queen Esther standing in the court 14
9 But when Haman saw Mor'decai in the king's gate 14
13 I see Mor'decai the Jew sitting at the king's gate. 14
7: 7 for he saw that evil was determined against him 14
8: 6 how can I endure to see the calamity . . coming 14
6 can I endure to see the destruction of my kindred? 14
Job 2:12 when they saw him from afar, they did not recognize 11
13 for they saw that his suffering was very great. 14
3: 9 nor see the eyelids of the morning; 14
16 as infants that never see the light? 14
4: 8 As I have seen, those who plow iniquity and sow 14
5: 3 I have seen the fool taking root 14
6:21 you see my calamity, and are afraid. 14
7: 7 my eye will never again see good. 14
8 The eye of him who sees me will behold me no more; 14
8:18 it will deny him, saying, 'I have never seen you.' 14
9:11 Lo, he passes by me, and I see him not; 14
25 they flee away, they see no good. 14
10: 4 Hast thou eyes of flesh? Dost thou see as man sees? 14
4 Hast thou eyes of flesh? Dost thou see as man sees? 14
18 Would that I had died before any eye had seen me 14
11:11 when he sees iniquity, will he not consider it? 14
13: 1 Lo, my eye has seen all this 14
15:17 what I have seen I will declare 5
17:15 where then is my hope? Who will see my hope? 17
19:26 thus destroyed, then from my flesh I shall see God 5
27 whom I shall see on my side 5
20: 7 those who have seen him will say, 'Where is he?' 14
9 The eye which saw him will see him no more 18
9 The eye which saw him will see him no more •
21:20 Let their own eyes see their destruction 14
22 seeing that he judges those that are on high? •
22:11 your light is darkened, so that you cannot see 14
12 See the highest stars, how lofty they are! 14
14 Thick clouds enwrap him, so that he does not see 14
19 The righteous see it and are glad; 14
23: 9 I turn to the right hand, but I cannot see him. 14
24: 1 why do those who know him never see his days? 5
15 waits for the twilight, saying, 'No eye will see 17
27:12 Behold, all of you have seen it yourselves; 5
28: 7 the falcon's eye has not seen it. 18
10 his eye sees every precious thing. 14
24 and sees everything under the heavens. 14
27 then he saw it and declared it; 14
29: 8 the young men saw me and withdrew 14
11 when the eye saw, it approved; 14
31: 4 Does not he see my ways, and number all my steps? 14
19 if I have seen any one perish for lack of clothing 14
21 because I saw help in the gate; 14
32: 5 when Eli'hu saw that there was no answer 14
33:21 His flesh is so wasted away that it cannot be seen; 15
21 his bones which were not seen stick out. 14
28 my life shall see the light. 14
30 from the Pit, that he may see the light of life. ‡
34:21 upon the ways of a man, and he sees all his steps. 14

32 teach me what I do not see; if I have done iniquity 5
35: 5 Look at the heavens, and see; and behold the clouds 14
14 How much less when you say that you do not see him 17
38:17 or have you seen the gates of deep darkness? 14
22 have you seen the storehouses of the hail 14
42: 5 by the hearing of the ear, but now my eye sees thee; 14
16 saw his sons, and his sons' sons, four generations. 14
Ps 4: 6 many who say, "O that we might see some good! 14
10:11 he has hidden his face, he will never see it. 14
14 Thou dost see; yea, thou dost note trouble 14
14: 2 to see if there are any that act wisely 14
16:10 to Sheol, or let thy godly one see the Pit. 14
17: 2 my vindication come! Let thy eyes see the right! 5
18:15 Then the channels of the sea were seen 14
22: 7 All who see me mock at me, they make mouths at me 14
27:13 believe that I shall see the goodness of the LORD 14
31: 7 because thou hast seen my affliction 14
11 those who see me in the street flee from me. 14
33:13 looks down from heaven, he sees all the sons of men; 14
34: 8 O taste and see that the LORD is good! 14
35:21 they say, "Aha, Aha! our eyes have seen it! 14
22 Thou hast seen, O LORD; be not silent! 14
36: 9 in thy light do we see light. 14
37:13 at the wicked, for he sees that his day is coming. 14
25 yet I have not seen the righteous forsaken 14
35 I have seen a wicked man overbearing 14
40: 3 a song of praise to our God. Many will see and fear 14
12 iniquities have overtaken me, till I cannot see; 14
41: 6 when one comes to see me, he utters empty words 14
48: 5 As soon as they saw it, they were astounded 14
8 so have we seen in the city of the LORD of hosts 14
49: 9 to live on for ever, and never see the Pit. 14
10 Yea, he shall see that even the wise die 14
19 his fathers, who will never more see the light. 14
50:18 If you see a thief, you are a friend of his; 14
52: 6 The righteous shall see, and fear, and shall laugh 14
7 See the man who would not make God his refuge 3
53: 2 to see if there are any that are wise 14
55: 9 for I see violence and strife in the city. 14
58: 8 like the untimely birth that never sees the sun. 5
10 will rejoice when he sees the vengeance; 5
59: 4 Rouse thyself, come to my help, and see! 14
64: 5 laying snares secretly, thinking, "Who can see us? 14
8 all who see them will wag their heads. 14
66: 5 Come and see what God has done 14
68:24 Thy solemn processions are seen, O God 14
69:23 their eyes be darkened, so that they cannot see; 14
32 Let the oppressed see it and be glad; 14
73: 3 when I saw the prosperity of the wicked. 14
74: 9 We do not see our signs; 14
77:16 When the waters saw thee, O God 14
16 O God, when the waters saw thee, they were afraid 14
80:14 Look down from heaven, and see; 14
84: 7 God of gods will be seen in Zion. 14
86:17 that those who hate me may see and be put to shame 14
89:48 What man can live and never see death? 14
90:15 as many years as we have seen evil. 14
91: 8 look . . and see the recompense of the wicked. 14
92:11 My eyes have seen the downfall of my enemies 9
94: 7 LORD does not see; the God of Jacob does not 14
9 He who formed the eye, does he not see? 9
95: 9 put me to the proof, though they had seen my work. 14
97: 4 earth sees and trembles. 14
98: 3 ends of the earth have seen the victory of our God. 14
106: 5 that I may see the prosperity of thy chosen ones 14
107:24 saw the deeds of the LORD, his wondrous works 14
42 The upright see it and are glad; 14
109:25 my accusers; when they see me, they wag their heads. 14
112: 8 until he sees his desire on his adversaries. 14
10 wicked man sees it and is angry; 14
115: 5 They have . . eyes, but do not see. 14
119:74 Those who fear thee shall see me and rejoice 14
96 I have seen a limit to all perfection 14
128: 5 May you see the prosperity of Jerusalem 14
6 May you see your children's children! 14
135:16 they have eyes, but they see not 14
139:24 see if there be any wicked way in me 14
Prv 7: 7 I have seen among the simple 14
20:12 hearing ear and the seeing eye, the LORD has made 14
22: 3 A prudent man sees danger and hides himself; 14
29 Do you see a man skilful in his work? 5
23:33 Your eyes will see strange things 14
24:18 lest the LORD see it, and be displeased 14
32 Then I saw and considered it; 5
25: 7 What your eyes have seen 14
26:12 Do you see a man who is wise in his own eyes? 14
27:12 A prudent man sees danger and hides himself; 14
29:20 Do you see a man who is hasty in his words? 5
Ecc 1: 8 the eye is not satisfied with seeing 14
10 Is there a thing of which it is said, "See, this is new"? 14
14 I have seen everything that is done under the sun; 14
2: 3 lay hold on folly, till I might see what was good 14
13 Then I saw that wisdom excels folly 14
18 I hated all my toil . . seeing that I must leave it 16
24 This also, I saw, is from the hand of God; 14
3:10 I have seen the business that God has given 14
16 I saw under the sun that in the place of justice 14
22 I saw that there is nothing better 14
22 who can bring him to see what will be after him? 14

4: 1 I saw all the oppressions that are practiced 14
3 and has not seen the evil deeds that are done 14
4 Then I saw that all toil . . come from a man's envy 14
7 Again, I saw vanity under the sun 14
15 I saw all the living who move about under the sun 14
5: 8 If you see in a province the poor oppressed 14
11 and what gain . . but to see them with his eyes? 14
13 a grievous evil which I have seen under the sun 14
18 what I have seen to be good and to be fitting is 14
6: 1 There is an evil which I have seen under the sun 14
5 it has not seen the sun or known anything; 14
7:11 Wisdom . . an advantage to those who see the sun. 14
15 In my vain life I have seen everything; 14
8:10 Then I saw the wicked buried; 14
16 and to see the business that is done on earth 14
16 how neither day nor night one's eyes see sleep; 14
17 then I saw all the work of God, that man cannot find 14
9:11 Again I saw that . . the race is not to the swift 14
13 I have also seen this example of wisdom 14
10: 5 There is an evil which I have seen under the sun 14
7 I have seen slaves on horses, and princes walking 14
Sng 2:14 let me see your face, let me hear your voice 14
3: 3 Have you seen him whom my soul loves? 14
6: 9 The maidens saw her and called her happy; 14
11 to . . see whether the vines had budded 14
7:12 let us go . . and see whether the vines have budded 14
Isa 1: 1 The vision of Isaiah the son of Amoz, which he saw 5
2: 1 The word which Isaiah . . saw concerning Judah 5
5:12 the deeds of the LORD, or see the work of his hands. 14
19 that we may see it; let the purpose of the Holy One 14
6: 1 In the year that King Uzzi'ah died I saw the Lord 14
5 for my eyes have seen the King, the LORD of hosts! 14
9 see and see, but do not perceive.' 14
9 see and see, but do not perceive.' 14
10 shut their eyes; lest they see with their eyes 14
9: 2 who walked in darkness have seen a great light; 14
10:15 the saw magnify itself against him who wields it? 8
11: 3 He shall not judge by what his eyes see 7
13: 1 oracle concerning Babylon which Isaiah . . saw. 5
14:16 Those who see you will stare at you, and ponder 14
21: 3 I cannot hear, I am dismayed so that I cannot see. 14
6 Go, set a watchman, let him announce what he sees. 14
7 When he sees riders, horsemen in pairs 14
8 Then he who saw cried: "Upon a watchtower I stand 14
22: 9 you saw that the breaches of the city . . were many 14
26:10 and does not see the majesty of the LORD. 14
11 O LORD, thy hand is lifted up, but they see it not 5
11 them see thy zeal for thy people, and be ashamed. 5
28: 4 when a man sees it, he eats it up 14
29:15 in the dark, and who say, "Who sees us? 14
18 out of . . darkness the eyes of the blind shall see. 14
23 For when he sees his children, the work of my hands 14
30:10 who say to the seers, "See not"; 14
20 but your eyes shall see your Teacher. 14
30 and the descending blow of his arm to be seen 14
32: 3 Then the eyes of those who see will not be closed 14
33:17 Your eyes will see the king in his beauty; 5
19 You will see no more the insolent people 14
20 Your eyes will see Jerusalem, a quiet habitation 14
35: 2 They shall see the glory of the LORD 14
37:17 open thy eyes, O LORD, and see; 14
38: 5 I have heard your prayer, I have seen your tears; 14
11 I shall not see the LORD in the land of the living; 14
39: 4 He said, "What have they seen in your house? 14
4 They have seen all that is in my house; 14
40: 5 be revealed, and all flesh shall see it together 14
26 and see: who created these? 14
41: 5 The coastlands have seen and are afraid 14
20 that men may see and know 14
42:18 Hear, you deaf; and look, you blind, that you may see! 14
20 He sees many things, but does not observe them; 14
44: 9 their witnesses neither see nor know 14
16 and says, "Aha, I am warm, I have seen the fire! 14
18 for he has shut their eyes, so that they cannot see 14
47: 3 shall be uncovered, and your shame shall be seen. 14
10 in your wickedness, you said, "No one sees me"; 14
48: 6 You have heard; now see all this; 5
49: 7 Kings shall see and arise; princes 14
18 Lift up your eyes round about and see; 14
52: 5 says the LORD, seeing that my people are taken •
8 eye to eye they see the return of the LORD to Zion. 14
10 the earth shall see the salvation of our God. 14
15 that which has not been told them they shall see 14
53:10 an offering for sin, he shall see his offspring 14
11 he shall see the fruit of the travail of his soul 14
57:18 I have seen his ways, but I will heal him; 14
58: 3 'Why have we fasted, and thou seest it not? 14
7 when you see the naked, to cover him 14
59:15 The LORD saw it, and it displeased him 14
16 He saw that there was no man 14
60: 2 and his glory will be seen upon you. 14
4 Lift up your eyes round about, and see; 14
5 Then you shall see and be radiant 14
61: 9 all who see them shall acknowledge them 14
62: 2 The nations shall see your vindication 14
63:15 Look down from heaven and see 14
64: 4 no eye has seen a God besides thee 14
66: 5 Let the LORD be glorified, that we may see your joy 14
8 Who . . heard such a thing? Who has seen such things? 14

14 You shall see, and your heart shall rejoice; 14
18 and they shall come and shall see my glory 14
19 that have not heard my fame or seen my glory; 14
Jer 1:10 See, I have set you this day over nations 14
11 came to me, saying, "Jeremiah, what do you see? 14
11 And I said, "I see a rod of almond. 14
12 Then the LORD said to me, "You have seen well 14
13 What do you see?" And I said, "I see a boiling pot 14
13 What do you see?" And I said, "I see a boiling pot 14
2:10 For cross to the coasts of Cyprus and see 14
10 see if there has been such a thing. 14
19 Know and see that it is evil and bitter for you 14
3: 2 Lift up your eyes to the bare heights, and see! 14
6 Have you seen what she did, that faithless one 14
7 and her false sister Judah saw it. 14
8 She saw that for all the adulteries of that 14
4:21 How long must I see the standard 14
5: 1 Search her squares to see if you can find a man •
12 nor shall we see sword or famine. 14
21 senseless people, who have eyes, but see not 14
7:11 Behold, I myself have seen it, says the LORD. 14
12 see what I did to it for the wickedness 14
17 Do you not see what they are doing in the cities 14
11:20 let me see thy vengeance upon them 14
12: 3 But thou, O LORD, knowest me; thou seest me 14
4 because men said, "He will not see our latter end. 14
13:20 and see those who come from the north. 14
26 and your shame will be seen. 14
27 I have seen your abominations, your adulteries 14
14:13 You shall not see the sword 14
17: 6 in the desert, and shall not see any good come. 14
20:12 O LORD . . who seest the heart and the mind 14
12 let me see thy vengeance upon them 14
18 Why did I come forth from the womb to see toil 14
22:10 he shall return no more to see his native land. 14
12 and he shall never see this land again. 14
23:13 In the prophets of Sama'ria I saw an unsavory 14
14 But in the prophets of Jerusalem I have seen 14
24 places so that I cannot see him? says the LORD. 14
24: 3 the LORD said to me, "What do you see, Jeremiah? 14
29:32 to see the good that I will do to my people 48
30: 6 Ask now, and see, can a man bear a child? 14
6 then do I see every man with his hands on his loins 14
32: 4 speak with him face to face and see him eye to eye; 14
24 has come to pass, and behold, thou seest it. 14
34: 3 you shall see the king of Babylon eye to eye 14
39: 4 king of Judah and all the soldiers saw them 14
40: 4 See, the whole land is before you; 14
41:13 all the people who were with Ish'mael saw Joha'nan 14
42: 2 for we are left but a few of many, as your eyes see us 14
14 go to the land of Egypt, where we shall not see war 14
18 You shall see this place no more. 14
44: 2 You have seen all the evil that I brought 14
17 had plenty of food, and prospered, and saw no evil. 14
46: 5 Why have I seen it? They are dismayed 14
51:61 see that you read all these words 14
Lam 1: 8 despise her, for they have seen her nakedness; 14
10 yea, she has seen the nations invade her 14
12 Look and see if there is any sorrow like my sorrow 14
2:16 the day we longed for; now we have it; we see it! 14
20 O LORD, and see! With whom hast thou dealt thus? 9
3: 1 I am the man who has seen affliction under the rod 14
50 until the LORD from heaven looks down and sees; 14
59 Thou hast seen the wrong done to me, O LORD; 14
60 Thou hast seen all their vengeance 14
5: 1 Remember, O LORD . . behold, and see our disgrace! 14
Ezk 1: 1 the heavens were opened, and I saw visions of God. 14
15 I saw a wheel upon the earth 3
27 I saw as it were gleaming bronze 14
27 I saw as it were the appearance of fire 14
28 And when I saw it, I fell upon my face 14
3:23 the glory which I had seen by the river Chebar; 14
4:15 See, I will let you have cow's dung 14
8: 4 like the vision that I saw in the plain. 14
6 Son of man, do you see what they are doing 14
6 you will see still greater abominations. 14
9 he said to me, "Go in, and see the vile abominations 14
10 I went in and saw; and there, portrayed 14
12 have you seen what the elders . . are doing 14
12 For they say, 'The LORD does not see us 14
13 You will see still greater abominations 14
15 he said to me, "Have you seen this, O son of man? 14
15 You will see still greater abominations 14
17 he said to me, "Have you seen this, O son of man? 14
9: 9 has forsaken the land, and the LORD does not see. 14
10:15 living creatures that I saw by the river Chebar. 14
20 These were the living creatures that I saw 14
22 whose appearance I had seen by the river Chebar. 14
11: 1 I saw among them Ja-azani'ah the son of Azzur 14
24 Then the vision that I had seen went up from me. 14
12: 2 rebellious house, who have eyes to see, but see not 14
2 rebellious house, who have eyes to see, but see not 14
6 cover your face, that you may not see the land; 14
12 that he may not see the land with his eyes. 14
13 yet he shall not see it; and he shall die there. 14
27 The vision that he sees is for many days hence 5
13: 3 follow their own spirit, and have seen nothing! 14
7 Have you not seen a delusive vision 5
8 you have uttered delusions and seen lies 5
9 against the prophets who see delusive visions 5
16 and saw visions of peace for her 5
23 you shall no more see delusive visions 5
14:22 and you see their ways and their doings 14
23 They will console you, when you see their ways 14
16: 6 passed by you, and saw you weltering in your blood 14
30 says the Lord GOD, seeing you did all these things •
37 to them, that they may see all your nakedness. 14
50 therefore I removed them, when I saw it. 14
18:14 son who sees all the sins which his father has 14
19: 5 When she saw that she was baffled 14
11 it was seen in its height with the mass of its 14
20:28 wherever they saw any high hill or any leafy tree 14
48 flesh shall see that I the LORD have kindled it; 14
21:29 while they see for you false visions 5
23:11 Ohol'ibah saw this, yet she was more corrupt 14
13 I saw that she was defiled; 14
14 she saw men portrayed upon the wall, the images 14
16 When she saw them she doted upon them 7
28:18 upon the earth in the sight of all who saw you. 14
32:31 When Pharaoh sees them, he will comfort himself 14
33: 3 if he sees the sword coming upon the land 14
6 if the watchman sees the sword coming 14
39:15 pass through the land and any one sees a man's bone 14
21 all the nations shall see my judgment 14
40: 4 declare all that you see to the house of Israel. 14
41: 8 I saw also that the temple had a raised platform 14
43: 3 vision I saw was like the vision which I had seen 14
3 vision I saw was like the vision which I had seen 14
3 the vision which I had seen by the river Chebar; 14
44: 5 see with your eyes, and hear with your ears 14
46:19 I saw a place at the extreme western end of them. 3
47: 6 And he said to me, "Son of man, have you seen this? 14
7 I saw upon the bank of the river very many trees 3
Dan 1:10 should see that you were in poorer condition 14
13 according to what you see deal with your servants. 14
15 seen that they were better in appearance 14
2: 8 because you see that the word from me is sure 20
26 make known to me the dream that I have seen 20
31 You saw, O king, and behold, a great image. 20
41 saw the feet and toes partly of potter's clay 20
41 just as you saw iron mixed with the miry clay. 20
43 As you saw the iron mixed with miry clay 20
45 just as you saw that a stone was cut 20
3:25 But I see four men loose, walking in the midst 20
27 saw that the fire had not had any power 20
4: 9 dream which I saw; tell me its interpretation. 20
10 I saw, and behold, a tree in the midst of the earth 21
13 I saw in the visions of my head as I lay in bed 21
18 This dream I, King Nebuchadnez'zar, saw. 20
20 tree you saw, which grew and became strong 20
23 king saw a watcher, a holy one, coming down 20
5: 5 king saw the hand as it wrote. 20
23 gods . . which do not see or hear or know 20
7: 2 Daniel said, "I saw in my vision by night, 20
7 After this I saw in the night visions, 20
13 I saw in the night visions, and behold 20
8: 2 I saw in the vision; and when I saw, I was in Susa 14
2 vision; and when I saw, I was in Susa the capital 14
2 saw in the vision, and I was at the river U'lai. 14
3 I raised my eyes and saw, and behold 14
4 I saw the ram charging westward and northward 14
6 ram . . seen standing on the bank of the river 14
7 I saw him come close to the ram, and he was enraged 14
15 Daniel, had seen the vision, I sought 14
20 As for the ram which you saw with the two horns 14
9:21 Gabriel, whom I had seen in the vision at the first 14
10: 7 I, Daniel, alone saw the vision, 14
7 men who were with me did not see the vision 14
8 I was left alone and saw this great vision 14
Hos 5:13 When E'phraim saw his sickness 14
6:10 In . . Israel I have seen a horrible thing; 14
9:10 in its first season, I saw your fathers. 14
13 E'phraim's sons, as I have seen, are destined 14
Jol 2:28 and your young men shall see visions. 14
Ams 1: 1 words of Amos . . which he saw concerning Israel 5
3: 9 of Sama'ria, and see the great tumults within her 14
6: 2 Pass over to Calneh, and see; 14
8: 2 he said, "Amos, what do you see? 14
9: 1 I saw the LORD standing beside the altar 14
Jon 3:10 When God saw what they did 14
4: 5 till he should see what would become of the city. 14
Mic 1: 1 to Micah . . which he saw concerning Sama'ria 5
7:10 Then my enemy will see, and shame will cover her 14
16 The nations shall see and be ashamed 14
Hab 1: 1 oracle of God which Habak'kuk the prophet saw. 5
5 Look among the nations, and see; 9
2: 1 and look forth to see what he will say to me 14
3: 7 I saw the tents of Cushan in affliction; 14
10 The mountains saw thee, and writhed; 14
Hag 2: 3 among you that saw this house in its former glory? 14
3 How do you see it now? Is it not in your sight 14
Zec 1: 8 I saw in the night, and behold, a man 14
18 I lifted my eyes and saw, and behold, four horns! 14
2: 1 I lifted my eyes and saw, and behold, a man 14
2 To measure Jerusalem, to see what is its breadth 14
4: 2 And he said to me, "What do you see? 14
2 I said, "I see, and behold, a lampstand all of gold 14
10 shall see the plummet in the hand of Zerub'babel. 14
5: 1 Again I lifted my eyes and saw 14
2 he said to me, "What do you see? 14
2 What do you see?" I answered, "I see a flying scroll; 14
5 see what this is that goes forth. 14
9 I lifted my eyes and saw, and behold, two women 14
6: 1 again I lifted my eyes and saw 14
9: 5 Ash'kelon shall see it, and be afraid; 14
8 for now I see with my own eyes. 14
10: 2 utter nonsense, and the diviners see lies; 5
7 Their children shall see it and rejoice 14
Mal 1: 5 Your own eyes shall see this, and you shall say 14
Mat 2: 2 For we have seen his star in the East, and have come 48
9 and lo, the star which they had seen in the East 48
10 When they saw the star, they rejoiced 31
11 going into the house they saw the child with Mary 48
16 Then Herod, when he saw that he had been tricked 48
3: 7 when he saw many of the Pharisees and Sad'ducees 48
16 heavens were opened and he saw the Spirit of God 48
4:16 the people who sat in darkness have seen a great 48
18 he saw two brothers, Simon who is called Peter 48
21 going on from there he saw two other brothers 48
5: 1 Seeing the crowds, he went up on the mountain 48
8 are the pure in heart, for they shall see God. 48
16 that they may see your good works and give glory 48
6: 1 in order to be seen by them; for then you will have 40
4 your Father who sees in secret will reward you. 28
5 that they may be seen by men. Truly, I say to you 57
6 your Father who sees in secret will reward you. 28
16 their faces that their fasting may be seen 57
18 fasting may not be seen by men but by your Father 57
18 your Father who sees in secret will reward you. 28
7: 3 do you see the speck that is in your brother's eye 28
8: 4 Jesus said to him, "See that you say nothing 48
14 he saw his mother-in-law lying sick with a fever; 48
18 Now when Jesus saw great crowds around him 48
34 and when they saw him, they begged him to leave 31
9: 2 and when Jesus saw their faith he said 48
8 When the crowds saw it, they were afraid 31
9 As Jesus passed on from there, he saw a man 48
11 when the Pharisees saw this, they said 31
22 Jesus turned, and seeing her he said, "Take heart 48
23 and saw the flute players, and the crowd 48
30 See that no one knows it. 48
33 Never was anything like this seen in Israel. 57
36 When he saw the crowds, he had compassion for them 48
11: 4 Go and tell John what you hear and see 28
8 To see a man clothed in soft raiment? 48
9 Why then did you go out? To see a prophet? 48
12: 2 when the Pharisees saw it, they said to him, "Look 31
22 he healed him, so that the dumb man spoke and saw. 28
38 Teacher, we wish to see a sign from you. 48
13:13 because seeing they do not see 28
13 because seeing they do not see 28
14 and you shall indeed see but never perceive. 28
16 blessed are your eyes, for they see 28
17 righteous men longed to see what you see 28
17 men longed to see what you see, and did not see it 28
17 men longed to see what you see, and did not see it 31
14:14 As he went ashore he saw a great throng 48
26 when the disciples saw him walking on the sea 31
30 when he saw the wind, he was afraid 28
15:17 Do you not see that whatever goes into the mouth 46
31 when they saw the dumb speaking 28
31 the lame walking, and the blind seeing 28
16:28 before they see the Son of man coming 48
17: 8 when they lifted up their eyes, they saw no one 48
18:10 See that you do not despise 48
31 When his fellow servants saw 31
20: 3 he saw others standing idle in the market place; 48
21:15 when the chief priests and the scribes saw 31
19 seeing a fig tree by the wayside he went to it 48
20 When the disciples saw it they marveled, saying 31
32 even when you saw it, you did not afterward repent 31
38 when the tenants saw the son 31
22:11 he saw there a man who had no wedding garment; 48
23: 5 They do all their deeds to be seen by men 40
39 I tell you, you will not see me again, until you say 31
24: 2 he answered them, "You see all these, do you not? 28
6 see that you are not alarmed 48
15 So when you see the desolating sacrilege 31
30 see the Son of man coming on the clouds of heaven 48
33 So also, when you see all these things 31
25:37 Lord, when did we see thee hungry and feed thee 48
38 when did we see thee a stranger and welcome thee 48
39 when did we see thee sick or in prison and visit 48
44 Lord, when did we see thee hungry or thirsty 48
26: 8 when the disciples saw it, they were indignant 31
46 Rise, let us be going; see, my betrayer is at hand. 43
58 he sat with the guards to see the end. 48
64 hereafter you will see the Son of man 48
71 when he went out to the porch, another maid saw him 48
27: 3 Judas, his betrayer, saw that he was condemned 48
4 They said, "What is that to us? See to it yourself. 48
24 So when Pilate saw that he was gaining nothing 48
24 see to it yourselves. 48
49 let us see whether Eli'jah will come to save him. 48
54 saw the earthquake and what took place 31
28: 1 the other Mary went to see the sepulchre. 41
6 Come, see the place where he lay. 31

7 there you will see him 48
10 there they will see me. 48
17 when they saw him they worshiped him 31
Mrk 1:10 immediately he saw the heavens opened 48
16 he saw Simon and Andrew the brother of Simon 48
19 he saw James the son of Zeb'edee 48
44 said to him, "See that you say nothing to any one 48
2: 5 when Jesus saw their faith 48
12 saying, "We never saw anything like this! 48
14 as he passed on, he saw Levi the son of Alphaeus 48
16 when they saw that he was eating with sinners 31
3: 2 they watched him, to see whether he would heal him •
4:12 so that they may indeed see but not perceive 28
5: 6 when he saw Jesus from afar, he ran and worshiped 48
14 people came to see what it was that had happened. 48
15 came to Jesus, and saw the demoniac sitting there 41
16 those who had seen it told what had happened 31
22 seeing him, he fell at his feet 48
31 You see the crowd pressing around you 28
32 he looked around to see who had done it. 51
38 he saw a tumult 41
6:33 Now many saw them going, and knew them 48
34 As he went ashore he saw a great throng 48
38 How many loaves have you? Go and see. 31
48 he saw that they were making headway painfully 48
49 when they saw him walking on the sea 31
50 for they all saw him, and were terrified. 48
7: 2 they saw that some of his disciples ate 31
18 Do you not see that whatever goes into a man 46
8:18 Having eyes do you not see 28
23 he asked him, "Do you see anything? 28
24 I see men; but they look like trees, walking. 28
25 was restored, and saw everything clearly. 32
33 turning and seeing his disciples 48
9: 1 before they see that the kingdom of God has come 48
8 they no longer saw any one with them but Jesus 48
9 he charged them to tell no one what they had seen 48
14 they saw a great crowd about them 48
15 the crowd, when they saw him, were greatly amazed 31
20 when the spirit saw him 48
25 Jesus saw that a crowd came running together 48
38 we saw a man casting out demons in your name 48
10:14 when Jesus saw it he was indignant 48
11:13 seeing in the distance a fig tree in leaf 48
13 he went to see if he could find anything on it. •
20 they saw the fig tree withered away to its roots. 48
12:28 seeing that he answered them well, asked him 48
34 when Jesus saw that he answered wisely 48
13: 2 Do you see these great buildings? 28
14 when you see the desolating sacrilege set up 31
26 then they will see the Son of man coming in clouds 48
29 So also, when you see these things taking place 31
14:42 Rise, let us be going; see, my betrayer is at hand. 43
62 Jesus said, "I am; and you will see the Son of man 48
67 seeing Peter warming himself, she looked at him 31
69 the maid saw him 31
15: 4 See how many charges they bring against you. 48
32 that we may see and believe 48
36 let us see whether Eli'jah will come 48
39 when the centurion, who stood facing him, saw 48
47 the mother of Joses saw where he was laid. 41
16: 4 And looking up, they saw that the stone 41
5 And entering the tomb, they saw a young man 48
6 he is not here; see the place where they laid him. 48
7 Galilee; there you will see him, as he told you. 48
11 heard that he was alive and had been seen by her 40
14 because they had not believed those who saw him 40
Lke 1:12 Zechari'ah was troubled when he saw him 48
22 perceived that he had seen a vision in the temple; 48
2:15 Let us go over to Bethlehem and see this thing 48
17 when they saw it they made known the saying 31
20 for all they had heard and seen 48
26 he should not see death 48
26 before he had seen the Lord's Christ. 31
30 for mine eyes have seen thy salvation 48
48 when they saw him they were astonished 31
3: 6 all flesh shall see the salvation of God. 48
5: 2 he saw two boats by the lake 48
8 when Simon Peter saw it 48
12 when he saw Jesus 48
20 when he saw their faith he said 48
26 saying, "We have seen strange things today. 48
27 he went out, and saw a tax collector, named Levi 40
6: 7 to see whether he would heal on the sabbath •
41 Why do you see the speck 28
42 you . . do not see the log that is in your own eye 28
7:13 when the Lord saw her 48
22 Go and tell John what you have seen and heard 31
25 What then did you go out to see? 48
26 What then did you go out to see? A prophet? 48
39 Now when the Pharisee who had invited him saw it 48
44 Do you see this woman? 28
8:10 so that seeing they may not see 28
10 so that seeing they may not see 28
16 that those who enter may see the light. 28
20 standing outside, desiring to see you. 48
28 When he saw Jesus, he cried out and fell down 48
34 When the herdsmen saw what had happened 31
35 Then people went out to see what had happened 48
36 those who had seen it told them 31
47 when the woman saw that she was not hidden 31
9: 9 he sought to see him. 48
27 before they see the kingdom of God. 48
32 when they wakened they saw his glory 48
36 told no one . . anything of what they had seen. 48
49 we saw a man casting out demons in your name 48
54 when his disciples James and John saw it 31
10:18 I saw Satan fall like lightning from heaven. 41
23 Blessed are the eyes which see what you see! 28
23 Blessed are the eyes which see what you see! 28
24 kings desired to see what you see, and did not see 28
24 kings desired to see what you see, and did not see 28
24 kings desired to see what you see, and did not see 28
31 when he saw him he passed by on the other side. 48
32 a Levite, when he came to the place and saw him 48
33 when he saw him, he had compassion 48
11:33 those who enter may see the light. 28
38 The Pharisee was astonished to see 48
44 you are like graves which are not seen 22
12:54 When you see a cloud rising in the west 31
55 when you see the south wind blowing, you say •
13:12 when Jesus saw her, he called her and said to her 48
28 when you see Abraham and Isaac and Jacob 48
35 I tell you, you will not see me until you say 31
14:18 I must go out and see it 48
29 all who see it begin to mock him 41
15:20 his father saw him and had compassion 48
16:23 he lifted up his eyes, and saw Abraham far off 48
17:14 When he saw them he said to them, "Go 48
15 Then one of them, when he saw that he was healed 48
22 will desire to see one of the days of the Son of man 48
22 and you will not see it. 48
18:15 when the disciples saw it, they rebuked them. 31
43 all the people, when they saw it, gave praise to God. 48
19: 3 he sought to see who Jesus was, but could not 48
4 climbed up into a sycamore tree to see him 31
7 when they saw it they all murmured 31
37 for all the mighty works that they had seen 48
41 when he drew near and saw the city he wept over it 48
20:14 when the tenants saw him, they said to themselves 31
21: 1 He looked up and saw the rich 48
2 he saw a poor widow put in two copper coins. 48
6 As for these things which you see 41
20 when you see Jerusalem surrounded by armies 31
27 then they will see the Son of man coming in a cloud 48
30 you see for yourselves 28
31 So also, when you see these things taking place 31
22:49 when those . . saw what would follow, they said 31
56 Then a maid, seeing him as he sat in the light 31
58 a little later some one else saw him and said 48
23: 8 When Herod saw Jesus, he was very glad 48
8 he had long desired to see him 48
8 he was hoping to see some sign done by him. 48
47 Now when the centurion saw what had taken place 48
48 the multitudes who assembled to see the sight •
48 when they saw what had taken place 41
49 stood at a distance and saw these things. 48
55 The women . . followed, and saw the tomb 40
24:23 saying that they had even seen a vision of angels 48
24 him they did not see. 48
37 supposed that they saw a spirit. 41
39 See my hands and my feet, that it is I myself 31
39 handle me, and see 31
39 not flesh and bones as you see that I have. 41
Joh 1:18 No one has ever seen God; 48
29 The next day he saw Jesus coming toward him 28
32 I saw the Spirit descend as a dove from heaven 40
33 'He on whom you see the Spirit descend and remain 31
34 And I have seen and have borne witness 48
38 Jesus turned, and saw them following, and said 40
39 He said to them, "Come and see." They came and saw 48
39 They came and saw where he was staying; 31
46 Philip said to him, "Come and see. 48
47 Jesus saw Nathan'a-el coming to him, and said of him 48
48 when you were under the fig tree, I saw you. 48
50 Because I said to you, I saw you under the fig tree 48
50 You shall see greater things than these. 48
51 truly, I say to you, you will see heaven opened 48
2:23 believed . . when they saw the signs which he did; 41
3: 3 he cannot see the kingdom of God. 48
11 and bear witness to what we have seen; 48
32 He bears witness to what he has seen and heard 48
36 he who does not obey the Son shall not see life 48
4:29 Come, see a man who told me all that I ever did. 31
35 see how the fields are already white for harvest 40
45 having seen all that he had done in Jerusalem 48
48 Unless you see signs and wonders 31
5: 6 When Jesus saw him 48
14 See, you are well! 48
19 only what he sees the Father doing 28
37 his form you have never seen; 48
6: 2 because they saw the signs which he did 41
5 seeing that a multitude was coming to him 40
14 When the people saw the sign which he had done 31
19 they saw Jesus walking on the sea 41
22 saw that there had been only one boat there 48
24 when the people saw that Jesus was not there 48
26 you seek me, not because you saw signs 31
30 what sign do you do, that we may see, and believe 48
36 I said to you that you have seen me 48
40 every one who sees the Son and believes in him 41
46 Not that any one has seen the Father 48
46 he has seen the Father. 48
62 what if you were to see the Son of man ascending 41
7: 3 your disciples may see the works you are doing. 41
52 Search and you will see 48
8:38 I speak of what I have seen with my Father 48
51 if any one keeps my word, he will never see death. 41
56 Abraham rejoiced that he was to see my day 31
56 he saw it and was glad. 48
57 and have you seen Abraham? 48
9: 1 As he passed by, he saw a man blind from his birth. 48
7 So he went and washed and came back seeing. 28
8 those who had seen him before as a beggar, said 41
15 I washed, and I see. 28
19 How then does he now see? 28
21 how he now sees we do not know 28
25 one thing I know, that though I was blind, now I see. 28
37 Jesus said to him, "You have seen him 48
39 that those who do not see may see 28
39 that those who do not see may see 28
39 that those who see may become blind. 28
41 now that you say, 'We see,' your guilt remains. 28
10:12 sees the wolf coming and leaves the sheep 41
11: 9 because he sees the light of this world. 28
31 the Jews . . saw Mary rise quickly and go out 31
32 Mary, when she came where Jesus was and saw him 31
33 When Jesus saw her weeping 48
34 They said to him, "Lord, come and see. 48
36 the Jews said, "See how he loved him! 48
40 if you would believe you would see the glory of God? 48
45 who had come with Mary and had seen what he did 40
12: 9 to see Laz'arus, whom he had raised from the dead. 48
19 You see that you can do nothing 41
21 Sir, we wish to see Jesus. 48
40 lest they should see with their eyes 48
41 Isaiah said this because he saw his glory 48
45 he who sees me sees him who sent me. 41
45 he who sees me sees him who sent me. 41
14: 7 henceforth you know him and have seen him. 48
9 He who has seen me has seen the Father 48
9 He who has seen me has seen the Father 48
17 because it neither sees him nor knows him 41
19 the world will see me no more 41
19 but you will see me 41
15:24 they have seen and hated both me and my Father. 48
16:10 you will see me no more; 41
16 A little while, and you will see me no more 41
16 again a little while, and you will see me. 48
17 A little while, and you will not see me 41
17 again a little while, and you will see me 48
19 A little while, and you will not see me 41
19 again a little while, and you will see me'? 48
22 you have sorrow now, but I will see you again 48
18:26 Did I not see you in the garden with him? 48
19: 4 See, I am bringing him out to you, that you may know 48
6 When the chief priests and the officers saw him 48
24 but cast lots for it to see whose it shall be •
26 When Jesus saw his mother 48
33 came to Jesus and saw that he was already dead 48
35 He who saw it has borne witness 48
20: 1 saw that the stone had been taken away 28
5 and stooping to look in, he saw the linen cloths 28
6 went into the tomb; he saw the linen cloths lying 41
8 also went in, and he saw and believed; 48
12 she saw two angels in white 41
14 she turned round and saw Jesus standing 41
18 I have seen the Lord 48
20 the disciples were glad when they saw the Lord. 31
25 We have seen the Lord. 48
25 Unless I see in his hands the print of the nails 48
27 Put your finger here, and see my hands 48
29 Have you believed because you have seen me? 48
29 Blessed are those who have not seen 31
21: 9 they saw a charcoal fire there 28
20 saw following them the disciple 28
21 When Peter saw him, he said to Jesus, "Lord 48
Act 1:11 Jesus . . will come in the same way as you saw him go 40
2:17 your young men shall see visions 48
27 nor let thy Holy One see corruption. 48
31 nor did his flesh see corruption. 48
33 he has poured out this which you see and hear. 28
3: 3 Seeing Peter and John about to go into the temple 48
9 all the people saw him walking and praising God 48
12 when Peter saw it he addressed the people 48
16 this man . . whom you see and know 41
4:13 Now when they saw the boldness of Peter and John 41
14 seeing the man that had been healed 28
20 cannot but speak of what we have seen and heard. 31
6:15 gazing at him, all who sat in the council saw 48
7:24 seeing one of them being wronged 48
31 When Moses saw it he wondered at the sight 48
34 I have surely seen the ill-treatment of my people 48
44 according to the pattern that he had seen. 48
55 saw the glory of God 48
56 he said, "Behold, I see the heavens opened 41
8: 6 when they heard him and saw the signs which he did. 28

13 seeing signs and great miracles performed 41
18 Now when Simon saw 48
23 For I see that you are in the gall of bitterness 48
36 the eunuch said, "See, here is water! 43
39 the eunuch saw him no more 48
9: 7 hearing the voice but seeing no one. 41
8 when his eyes were opened, he could see nothing 28
12 he has seen a man named Anani'as come 48
27 on the road he had seen the Lord, who spoke to him 48
35 all the residents of Lydda and Sharon saw him 31
40 when she saw Peter she sat up. 31
10: 3 he saw clearly in a vision an angel of God 48
11 saw the heaven opened, and something descending 41
17 as to what the vision which he had seen might mean 48
11: 5 in a trance I saw a vision, something descending 48
13 he told us how he had seen the angel standing 48
23 When he came and saw the grace of God, he was glad; 48
12: 3 when he saw that it pleased the Jews 48
9 thought he was seeing a vision. 28
16 when they opened, they saw him and were amazed. 31
13:11 you shall be blind and unable to see the sun for a time 28
12 when he saw what had occurred 48
35 Thou wilt not let thy Holy One see corruption. 48
36 was laid with his fathers, and saw corruption; 48
37 he whom God raised up saw no corruption. 48
45 when the Jews saw the multitudes 31
14: 9 and seeing that he had faith to be made well 48
11 when the crowds saw what Paul had done 31
15:36 see how they are. •
16:10 when he had seen the vision 48
19 her owners saw that their hope of gain was gone 31
27 woke and saw that the prison doors were open 48
40 when they had seen the brethren 31
17:11 to see if these things were so. •
16 as he saw that the city was full of idols. 41
18:15 see to it yourselves 48
19:21 After I have been there, I must also see Rome. 48
26 you see and hear 41
36 Seeing . . these . . cannot be contradicted •
20:25 all you . . will see my face no more. 48
38 that they should see his face no more 41
21:20 they said to him, "You see, brother 41
27 who had seen him in the temple 40
32 when they saw the tribune and the soldiers 31
22: 9 Now those who were with me saw the light 40
11 when I could not see 32
13 in that very hour I received my sight and saw him. •
14 to see the Just One and to hear a voice from his mouth 48
15 a witness . . of what you have seen and heard. 48
18 saw him saying to me, 'Make haste 48
25:24 you see this man 41
26:13 I saw on the way a light from heaven 48
16 the things in which you have seen me 48
28: 4 When the natives saw the creature 48
6 saw no misfortune come to him 41
15 On seeing them Paul thanked God 48
20 therefore I have asked to see you 48
26 you shall indeed see but never perceive. 28
Rom 1:11 For I long to see you 48
7:23 but I see in my members another law 28
8:24 Now hope that is seen is not hope. 28
24 For who hopes for what he sees? 28
25 if we hope for what we do not see, we wait for it 28
11: 8 eyes that should not see and ears that should not 28
10 their eyes be darkened so that they cannot see 28
15:21 They shall see who have never been told of him 48
24 I hope to see you in passing as I go to Spain 40
1Co 2: 9 What no eye has seen, nor ear heard 48
8:10 For if any one sees you, a man of knowledge, at table 31
9: 1 Have I not seen Jesus our Lord? 48
13:12 now we see in a mirror dimly, but then face to face. 28
16: 7 For I do not want to see you now just in passing 48
10 When Timothy comes, see that you put him at ease 28
2Co 3:13 see the end of the fading splendor. 24
4: 4 to keep them from seeing the light of the gospel 25
7: 8 I see that that letter grieved you 28
11 see what earnestness 43
8: 7 see that you excel in this gracious work also. 44
12: 6 no one may think more of me than he sees in me 28
13: 5 to see whether you are holding to your faith. •
Gal 1:19 I saw none of the other apostles 48
2: 7 but on the contrary, when they saw 31
14 when I saw that they were not straightforward 48
3: 7 So you see that it is men of faith who are the sons 29
6:11 See with what large letters I am writing to you 31
Eph 5:33 let the wife see that she respects her husband. 44
Php 1:27 so that whether I come and see you or am absent 48
30 engaged in the same conflict which you saw 31
2:23 just as soon as I see how it will go with me; 26
28 you may rejoice at seeing him again 31
4: 9 received and heard and seen in me, do 31
Col 2: 1 for all who have not seen my face 48
5 rejoicing to see your good order 28
8 See to it that no one makes a prey of you 28
3: 9 seeing that you have put off the old nature •
4:16 see that you read also the letter from La-odice'a. 52
17 See that you fulfil the ministry 28
1Th 2:17 we endeavored . . with great desire to see you 48
3: 6 and long to see us, as we long to see you- 48

6 and long to see us, as we long to see you- •
10 we may see you face to face 48
5:15 See that none of you repays evil for evil 48
1Ti 3:16 vindicated in the Spirit, seen by angels 48
4:15 so that all may see your progress. 56
6:16 whom no man has ever seen or can see 48
16 whom no man has ever seen or can see 48
2Ti 1: 4 I long night and day to see you 48
Tit 3:13 see that they lack nothing. 44
Heb 2: 8 do not yet see everything in subjection to him. 48
9 we see Jesus 28
3: 9 and saw my works for 40 years. 48
19 we see that they were unable to enter 28
7: 4 See how great he is! 41
8: 5 See that you make everything 48
10:25 all the more as you see the Day drawing near. 28
11: 1 faith is . . the conviction of things not seen. 28
3 what is seen 28
5 he should not see death 48
13 having seen it and greeted it from afar 31
23 because they saw that the child was beautiful 48
27 he endured as seeing him who is invisible. 48
12:14 holiness without which no one will see the Lord. 48
15 See to it that no one fail to obtain the grace 36
25 See that you do not refuse him who is speaking. 28
13:23 with whom I shall see you if he comes soon. 48
Jas 2:22 You see that faith was active . . with his works 28
24 You see that a man is justified by works 48
5:11 and you have seen the purpose of the Lord 31
1Pe 1: 8 Without having seen him you love him; 31
8 though you do not now see him you believe in him 48
2:12 they may see your good deeds and glorify God 37
3: 2 when they see your reverent and chaste behavior 37
10 He that would love life and see good days 48
2Pe 1:15 I will see to it that after my departure 54
2: 8 what that righteous man saw and heard 27
1Jn 1: 1 That . . which we have seen with our eyes 48
2 the life was made manifest, and we saw it 48
3 that which we have seen and heard we proclaim 48
3: 1 See what love the Father has given us 31
2 for we shall see him as he is. 48
6 no one who sins has either seen him or known him. 48
10 By this it may be seen who are the children of God 56
17 has the world's goods and sees his brother in need 41
4: 1 test the spirits to see whether they are of God; •
12 No man has ever seen God; 40
14 And we have seen and testify that 40
20 he who does not love his brother whom he has seen 48
20 cannot love God whom he has not seen. 48
5:16 If any one sees his brother committing . . sin 31
3Jn 1:11 he who does evil has not seen God. 48
14 I hope to see you soon 48
Rev 1: 2 bore witness . . even to all that he saw. 48
7 he is coming . . and every eye will see him 48
11 saying, "Write what you see in a book and send it 28
12 I turned to see the voice that was speaking to me 28
12 and on turning I saw seven golden lampstands 48
17 When I saw him, I fell at his feet as though dead. 48
19 Now write what you see 31
20 the seven stars which you saw in my right hand 31
3:18 salve to anoint your eyes, that you may see. 28
18 keep the shame of your nakedness from being seen 58
5: 1 And I saw in the right hand of him who was seated 48
2 I saw a strong angel proclaiming 48
6 I saw a Lamb standing, as though it had been slain 48
6: 1 I saw when the Lamb opened one of the seven seals 48
2 I saw, and behold, a white horse, and its rider 48
5 And I saw, and behold, a black horse, and its rider 48
8 I saw, and behold, a pale horse, and its rider 48
9 I saw under the altar the souls of those 48
7: 1 After this I saw four angels standing 48
2 I saw another angel ascend from the rising . . sun 48
8: 2 Then I saw the seven angels who stand before God 48
9: 1 and I saw a star fallen from heaven to earth 48
17 this was how I saw the horses in my vision 48
20 idols . . which cannot either see or hear or walk; 28
10: 1 Then I saw another mighty angel coming down 48
5 the angel whom I saw standing on sea and land 48
11:11 and great fear fell on those who saw them. 41
19 ark of his covenant was seen within his temple; 48
12:13 dragon saw that he had been thrown down to earth 48
13: 1 I saw a beast rising out of the sea 48
2 And the beast that I saw was like a leopard 48
11 I saw another beast which rose out of the earth; 48
14: 6 Then I saw another angel flying in midheaven 48
15: 1 Then I saw another portent in heaven 48
2 I saw what appeared to be a sea of glass 48
16:13 I saw, issuing from the mouth of the dragon 48
15 that he may not go naked and be seen exposed!") 28
17: 3 and I saw a woman sitting on a scarlet beast 48
6 I saw the woman, drunk with the blood of the saints 48
6 When I saw her I marveled greatly. 48
8 The beast that you saw was, and is not 31
12 And the ten horns that you saw are ten kings 31
15 The waters that you saw, where the harlot is 31
16 And the ten horns that you saw, they and the beast 31
18 And the woman that you saw is the great city 31
18: 1 I saw another angel coming down from heaven 48
7 I am no widow, mourning I shall never see,' 48

9 when they see the smoke of her burning; 28
18 and cried out as they saw the smoke of her burning 28
19:11 Then I saw heaven opened, and behold, a white horse! 48
17 Then I saw an angel standing in the sun 48
19 And I saw the beast and the kings of the earth 48
20: 1 Then I saw an angel coming down from heaven 48
4 Then I saw thrones, and seated on them were those 48
4 I saw the souls of those who had been beheaded •
11 I saw a great white throne and him who sat upon it; 48
12 And I saw the dead, great and small 48
21: 1 Then I saw a new heaven and a new earth; 48
2 I saw the holy city, new Jerusalem, coming down 48
22 And I saw no temple in the city 48
22: 4 they shall see his face 48
8 I John am he who heard and saw these things. 28
8 when I heard and saw them, I fell down to worship 28
1Es 4:18 then see a woman lovely in appearance and beauty 48
29 Yet I have seen him with Apame 41
5:63 old men who had seen the former house 48
2Es 1:36 They have seen no prophets 62
37 though they do not see me with bodily eyes 62
38 and see the people coming from the east; 62
2:29 that your sons may not see Gehenna. 62
38 Rise and stand, and see at the feast of the Lord 62
42 I, Ezra, saw on Mount Zion a great multitude 62
48 wonders of the Lord God which you have seen. 62
3: 2 because I saw the desolation of Zion 62
29 I saw ungodly deeds without number 62
29 my soul has seen many sinners 62
30 for I have seen how thou dost endure those who sin 62
33 and have seen that they abound in wealth 62
4: 4 I also will show you the way you desire to see 62
26 If you are alive, you will see, and if you live long 62
43 Then the things that you desire to see 62
5: 2 shall be increased beyond what you yourself see 62
3 the land which you now see ruling 62
3 and men shall see it desolate. 62
4 you shall see it thrown into confusion 62
35 that I might not see the travail of Jacob 62
6: 3 before the beautiful flowers were seen 62
20 and all shall see it together. 62
25 shall see my salvation and the end of my world. 62
26 they shall see the men who were taken up 62
32 for the Mighty One has seen your uprightness 62
7:15 seeing that you are to perish 61
15 why are you moved, seeing that you are mortal? 61
18 and will not see the easier ones. 62
26 that the city which now is not seen shall appear ‡
27 every one . . shall see my wonders. 62
42 by which all shall see what has been determined 62
47 now I see that the world to come 62
83 they shall see the reward laid up for those 62
85 they shall see how the habitations of the others 62
86 they shall see how some of them will pass over •
87 at seeing the glory of the Most High 62
91 they shall see with great joy the glory of him 62
93 because they see the perplexity 62
94 they see the witness which he who formed them 62
96 and besides they see the straits and toil 62
100 to see what you have described to me? 62
101 during these seven days they may see the things 62
8:17 I see the failings of us who dwell in the land 62
9: 1 when you see that a certain part . . are past 62
8 and will see my salvation in my land 62
21 I saw and spared some with great difficulty 62
38 I lifted up my eyes and saw a woman on my right 62
10: 3 and fled, and came to this field, as you see. 62
6 do you not see our mourning, and what has happened 62
21 you see that our sanctuary has been laid waste 62
32 and behold, I saw, and still see 62
32 I saw, and still see, what I am unable to explain. 62
35 For I have seen what I did not know 62
39 For he has seen your righteous conduct 62
41 whom you saw mourning and began to console- 62
42 you do not now see the form of a woman 62
44 This woman whom you saw, whom you now behold 62
49 behold, you saw her likeness, how she mourned 62
50 seeing that you are sincerely grieved 62
55 go in and see the splendor and vastness 62
55 as far as it is possible for your eyes to see it 62
11: 6 I saw how all things under heaven were subjected 62
13 so that its place was not seen 59
19 and then were never seen again. 60
30 I saw how it allied the two heads with itself 62
36 Look before you and consider what you see. 62
12:10 this vision which you have seen 62
11 The eagle which you saw coming up from the sea 62
16 the interpretation of the 12 wings which you saw. 62
19 As for your seeing eight little wings clinging 62
22 As for your seeing three heads at rest 62
26 your seeing that the large head disappeared 62
29 As for your seeing two little wings 62
30 brief and full of tumult, as you have seen. 62
31 the lion whom you saw rousing up out of the forest 62
35 This is the dream that you saw 62
37 write all . . that you have seen in a book 62
13: 7 I tried to see the region or place 62
9 he saw the onrush of the approaching multitude 62
10 I saw only how he sent forth from his mouth 62

11 suddenly nothing was seen of the . . multitude 62
11 When I saw it, I was amazed. 62
12 I saw the same man come down from the mountain 62
19 they shall see great dangers and much distress 62
20 and not to see what shall happen in the last days. 62
25 As for your seeing a man come up from . . the sea 62
27 as for your seeing wind and fire and a storm 62
32 whom you saw as a man coming up from the sea. 62
34 as you saw, desiring to come and conquer him. 62
36 as you saw the mountain carved out 62
39 as for your seeing him gather to himself 62
47 Therefore you saw the multitude 62
51 Why did I see the man coming up from . . the sea? 62
52 so no one on earth can see my Son 62
53 the interpretation of the dream which you saw. 62
14: 8 the dreams that you have seen 62
16 evils worse than those which you have now seen 62
18 the eagle which you saw in the vision 62
15:37 who see that wrath shall be horror-stricken 62
16:27 one man will long to see another 62
Tob 1:17 if I saw any one of my people dead 41
2: 2 Upon seeing the abundance of food I said to my son 40
3: 9 May we never see a son or daughter of yours! 48
5:20 your eyes will see him. 48
8:12 Send one of the maids to see whether he is alive 48
10: 7 have given up hope of ever seeing me again. 48
12 grant me to see your children by my daughter 48
12 See, I am entrusting my daughter to you 48
11: 8 he will see you. 48
9 I have seen you, my child; now I am ready to die. 48
14 Then he saw his son and embraced him 48
15 here I see my son Tobias! 28
16 Those who saw him as he went were amazed 41
16 Those who saw . . amazed because he could see. 28
12: 1 My son, see to the wages of the man who went 48
19 you were seeing a vision. 41
21 Then they stood up; but they saw him no more. 48
13: 6 see what he will do with you 40
14 will rejoice for you upon seeing all your glory 40
14:10 See, my son, what Nadab did to Ahikar 48
Jdt 6: 5 you shall not see my face again from this day 48
12 When the men of the city saw them 31
7: 4 When the Israelites saw their vast numbers 48
27 or see our wives . . draw their last breath. •
10: 4 to entice the eyes of all men who might see her. 48
7 When they saw her 48
10 and they could no longer see her. 41
12:16 ever since the day he first saw her. 48
13:15 showed it to them, and said, "See 43
14: 5 let him see and recognize . . 48
6 when he came and saw the head of Holofernes 48
10 Achior saw all that the God of Israel had done 48
12 when the Assyrians saw them 48
15: 8 to see Judith and to greet her. 48
12 Then all the women of Israel gathered to see her 48
AEs 11:12 Mordecai saw in this dream 48
15: 2 invoking the aid of the all-seeing God and Savior 38
13 I saw you, my lord, like an angel of God 48
16: 4 God, who always sees everything. 45
7 can be seen not so much from the . . records 53
Wis 2:17 Let us see if his words are true 48
4:15 Yet the peoples saw and did not understand 48
17 For they will see the end of the wise man 48
18 They will see, and will have contempt for him 48
5: 2 When they see him, they will be shaken 48
12:27 they saw and recognized as the true God 48
13: 1 the good things that are seen 48
7 they trust in what they see 50
15:15 these have neither the use of their eyes to see 47
16: 7 not by what he saw, but by thee, the Savior of all. 41
18 seeing this they might know 28
18: 1 Their enemies . . did not see their forms 48
19: 7 The cloud was seen overshadowing the camp 41
11 Afterward they saw also a new kind of birds 48
Sir 1: 9 he saw her and apportioned her 48
19 He saw her and apportioned her 48
2:10 Consider the ancient generations and see 48
6:36 If you see an intelligent man, visit him early 48
13: 7 Should he see you afterwards, he will forsake you 48
15: 7 sinful men will not see her. 48
18 he is mighty in power and sees everything; 28
16: 5 Many such things my eye has seen 48
21 Like a tempest which no man can see 48
17:13 Their eyes saw his glorious majesty 48
18:12 sees and recognizes that their end will be evil; 48
23:18 Who sees me? 48
18 no one sees me. Why should I fear? 48
25: 7 a man who lives to see the downfall of his foes; 28
28:24 See that you fence in your property with thorns 48
30: 5 while alive he saw and rejoiced 48
20 he sees with his eyes and groans 28
31:14 Do not reach out your hand for everything you see 35
34:11 I have seen many things in my travels 48
36: 3 let them see thy might. 48
37: 9 then stand aloof to see what will happen to you. 48
24 all who see him will call him happy. 48
27 see what is bad for it and do not give it that. 48
42:15 will declare what I have seen 48
22 how sparkling they are to see! 41
43:31 Who has seen him and can describe him? 48
32 we have seen but few of his works. 48
45:19 The Lord saw it and was not pleased 48
46:10 that all the sons of Israel might see 48
48:11 Blessed are those who saw you 48
24 By the spirit of might he saw the last things 48
49: 8 It was Ezekiel who saw the vision of glory 48
51:27 See with your eyes that I have labored little 48
Bar 2:17 open thy eyes, O Lord, and see; for the dead who are 48
3:20 Young men have seen the light of day, and have 48
22 She has not been heard of . . nor seen in Teman; 48
4: 9 For she saw the wrath that came upon you from God 48
10 I have seen the captivity of my sons 48
24 the neighbors of Zion have now seen your capture 48
24 so they soon will see your salvation by God 48
25 but you will soon see their destruction 50
36 see the joy that is coming to you from God! 48
5: 5 see your children gathered from west and east 48
LJr 1: 4 Now in Babylon you will see gods made of silver 48
5 you see the multitude before and behind them 48
19 though their gods can see none of them. 48
41 when they see a dumb man, who cannot speak 48
49 How then can one fail to see 23
Sus 1: 8 The two elders used to see her every day 41
12 they watched eagerly, day after day, to see her. 48
18 they did not see the elders 48
20 Look, the garden doors are shut, no one sees us 41
26 rushed in . . to see what had happened to her. 48
33 her family and friends and all who saw her wept. 48
38 and when we saw this wickedness we ran to them. 48
39 We saw them embracing 48
54 Now then, if you really saw her, tell me this 48
54 Under what tree did you see them being intimate 48
Bel 1: 6 see how much he eats and drinks every day? 48
20 The king said, "I see the footsteps of men and women 48
27 Daniel said, "See what you have been worshiping! 48
30 The king saw that they were pressing him hard 48
35 Habakkuk said, "Sir, I have never seen Babylon 48
Man 1: 9 am unworthy to look up and see the height of heaven 48
1Mc 1:16 Antiochus saw that his kingdom was established 33
2: 6 He saw the blasphemies being committed in Judah 48
7 said, "Alas! Why was I born to see this 48
24 When Mattathias saw it, be burned with zeal 48
3:17 when they saw the army coming to meet them 48
29 Then he saw 48
42 Judas . . saw that misfortunes had increased 48
59 to see the misfortunes of our nation 34
4: 7 they saw the camp of the Gentiles 48
10 to see whether he will favor us •
12 saw them coming against them 48
20 They saw that their army had been put to flight 48
20 the smoke that was seen 41
21 when they also saw the army of Judas 55
30 When he saw that the army was strong, he prayed 48
35 when Lysias saw the rout of his troops 48
38 they saw the sanctuary desolate 48
38 they saw bushes sprung up as in a thicket •
38 They saw also the chambers of the priests in ruins. •
5:31 So Judas saw that the battle had begun 48
6:43 Eleazar, called Avaran, saw 48
47 when the Jews saw the royal might 48
62 saw what a strong fortress the place was 48
7: 3 Do not let me see their faces! 30
7 let him go and see all the ruin 48
11 they saw that they had come with a large force. 48
23 Judas saw all the evil 48
25 When Alcimus saw that Judas . . had grown strong 48
28 I shall come . . to see you face to face in peace. 48
44 When his army saw that Nicanor had fallen 48
8:18 for they saw that the kingdom of the Greeks 48
9: 6 When they saw the huge number of the enemy forces 48
7 When Judas saw that his army had slipped away 48
14 Judas saw that the Bacchides 48
16 When those on the left wing saw 48
39 and saw a tumultuous procession with much baggage; 43
57 When Bacchides saw that Alcimus was dead 48
58 Then all the lawless plotted and said, "See! 43
10:56 so that we may see one another 48
64 when his accusers saw the honor that was paid him 48
64 and saw him clothed in purple •
11:38 Now when Demetrius the king saw 48
39 He saw that all the troops were murmuring 48
49 When the men of the city saw 48
73 When his men who were fleeing saw this 48
12: 1 Now when Jonathan saw that the time 48
29 they saw the fires burning. 28
42 Trypho saw that he had come with a large army 48
51 When their pursuers saw that they would fight 48
13: 2 he saw that the people were trembling 48
3 wars and the difficulties which we have seen. 48
27 he made it high that it might be seen 47
29 so that they could be seen by all who sail the sea. 41
53 Simon saw that John his son had reached manhood 48
14:35 The people saw Simon's faithfulness 48
15:32 when he saw the splendor of Simon 48
36 reported . . all that he had seen 48
16: 6 he saw that the soldiers were afraid 48
6 when his men saw him, they crossed over after him. 48
2Mc 1: 9 now see that you keep the feast of booths 44
2: 2 upon seeing the gold and silver statues 28
4 had seen the inheritance of God. 40
3:16 To see the appearance of the high priest 48
25 was seen to have armor and weapons of gold. 57
34 see that you . . report to all men •
36 which he had seen with his own eyes. 40
4: 6 he saw that without the king's attention 48
5:26 put to the sword all those who came out to see them 42
6: 9 One could see, therefore, the misery 48
7:17 see how his mighty power will torture you 41
20 Though she saw her seven sons perish 55
28 see everything that is in them 48
8: 8 When Philip saw that the man was gaining ground 55
12: 9 the glow of the light was seen in Jerusalem 57
22 who sees all things 39
42 they had seen with their own eyes 48
15: 2 he who sees all things 39
12 What he saw was this 42
3Mc 2: 8 when they had seen works of your hands 55
13 see now, O holy King, that because 48
23 seeing the severe punishment 48
3: 8 when they saw an unexpected tumult 41
4: 8 seeing death immediately before them. 48
5:14 seeing that the guests were assembled 48
48 the Jews saw the dust raised by the elephants 48
6:23 and saw them all fallen headlong to destruction 55
4Mc 1:24 a man will see if he reflects on this experience •
4:24 saw that . . threats . . were . . disregarded 48
5: 5 When Antiochus saw him he said 48
6:24 When they saw that he was so courageous 48
8: 4 When the tyrant saw them 48
15 and saw the dreadful devices 48
9:30 as you see . . your tyranny being defeated 49
10: 8 he saw his own flesh torn all around 48
19 See, here is my tongue; cut it off 48
12: 2 when he saw that he was already in fetters 49
3 You see the result of your brothers' stupidity 48
14: 9 they not only saw what was happening 48
15:14 who saw them tortured and burned one by one 48
19 and saw in their nostrils the signs •
20 When you saw the flesh of children 48
20 when you saw the place 48
25 she saw mighty advocates 48
16: 1 endured seeing her children tortured to death 48
3 inflamed as she saw her seven sons tortured 48
9 I shall not see your children 48
20 when Isaac saw his father's hand wielding a sword 49
17: 7 they saw the mother of the seven children 48
23 when he saw the courage of their virtue 26

see *See also* go, wait.

see a vision 1. חזה
Lam 2:14 Your prophets have seen . . deceptive visions; 1
Ezk 22:28 seeing false visions and divining lies for them 1

see an oracle 1. חזה
Lam 2:14 have seen for you oracles false and misleading. 1

see anything different 1. διακρίνω
1Co 4: 7 For who sees anything different in you? 1

see before 1. προοράω
Act 2:25 I saw the Lord always before me 1

see clearly 1. διαβλέπω 2. φανερόω
Mat 7: 5 and then you will see clearly to take the speck 1
Lke 6:42 then you will see clearly to take out the speck 1
Joh 3:21 that it may be clearly seen 2

come to see 1. γενέσθαι πρός
2Jn 1:12 I hope to come to see you and talk with you 1

see fit 1. δοκιμάζω
Rom 1:28 since they did not see fit to acknowledge God 1

see how 1. פקד לְ
1Sm 17:18 See how your brothers fare, and bring some token 1

make see 1. ראה 2. φωτίζω
Ps 71:20 Thou who hast made me see many sore troubles 1
Hab 1: 3 Why dost thou make me see wrongs 1
Eph 3: 9 to make all men see what is the plan of the mystery 2

see previously 1. προοράω
Act 21:29 they had previously seen Troph'imus . . with him 1

seed 1. זֶרַע 2. חַרְצַנִּים 3. פְּרֻדָה 4. σπέρμα 5. σπορά 6. σπόρος 7. semen
Gen 1:11 put forth vegetation, plants yielding seed 1
11 fruit in which is their seed 1
12 and trees bearing fruit in which is their seed 1
29 I have given . . every plant yielding seed 1
29 given . . every tree with seed in its fruit; 1
3:15 enmity . . between your seed and her seed; 1
15 enmity . . between your seed and her seed; 1
47:19 give us seed, that we may live, and not die 1
23 Now here is seed for you, and you shall sow 1
24 shall be your own, as seed for the field and as food 1

Exd 16:31 it was like coriander seed, white, and the taste 1
Lev 11:37 if any part . . falls upon the seed for sowing 1
38 if water is put on the seed 1
19:19 you shall not sow your field with two kinds of seed •
26:16 And you shall sow your seed in vain, 1
27:16 your valuation shall be according to the seed 1
30 tithe of the land, whether of the seed of the land 1
Num 6: 4 not even the seeds or the skins. 2
11: 7 Now the manna was like coriander seed 1
24: 7 his seed shall be in many waters 1
Deu 11:10 Egypt . . where you sowed your seed and watered 1
14:22 You shall tithe all the yield of your seed 1
22: 9 not sow your vineyard with two kinds of seed •
28:38 carry much seed into the field, and shall gather 1
1Kg 18:32 as great as would contain two measures of seed. 1
Ps 126: 6 goes forth weeping, bearing the seed for sowing 1
Ecc 11: 6 In the morning sow your seed 1
Isa 5:10 a homer of seed shall yield but an ephah. 1
6:13 The holy seed is its stump. 1
30:23 he will give rain for the seed with which you sow 1
55:10 giving seed to the sower and bread to the eater 1
Jer 2:21 I planted you a choice vine, wholly of pure seed. 1
31:27 with the seed of man and the seed of beast. 1
27 with the seed of man and the seed of beast. 1
33:26 to rule over the seed of Abraham, Isaac, and Jacob. 1
35: 7 you shall not build a house; you shall not sow seed; 1
9 We have no vineyard or field or seed; 1
Ezk 17: 5 Then he took of the seed of the land and planted it 1
13 he took one of the seed royal and made a covenant 1
20: 5 I swore to the seed of the house of Jacob 1
Jol 1:17 The seed shrivels under the clods 3
Ams 9:13 and the treader of grapes him who sows the seed; 1
Hag 2:19 Is the seed yet in the barn? 1
Mat 13: 4 as he sowed, some seeds fell along the path •
5 Other seeds fell on rocky ground •
7 Other seeds fell upon thorns •
8 Other seeds fell on good soil •
24 to a man who sowed good seed in his field; 4
27 Sir, did you not sow good seed in your field? 4
32 it is the smallest of all seeds 4
37 He who sows the good seed is the Son of man; 4
38 and the good seed means the sons of the kingdom 4
Mrk 4: 4 as he sowed, some seed fell along the path •
5 Other seed fell on rocky ground •
7 Other seed fell among thorns •
8 other seeds fell into good soil •
26 as if a man should scatter seed upon the ground 6
27 the seed should sprout and grow 6
31 the smallest of all the seeds on earth; 6
Lke 8: 5 A sower went out to sow his seed 6
11 the parable is this: The seed is the word of God. 6
1Co 15:38 to each kind of seed its own body. 4
2Co 9:10 He who supplies seed to the sower 4
1Pe 1:23 not of perishable seed but of imperishable 5
1Es 8:88 without leaving a root or seed or name? 4
2Es 4:30 For a grain of evil seed was sown in Adam's heart 7
31 a grain of evil seed has produced. 7
8: 6 give us seed for our heart 7
16 about the seed of Jacob, for whom I am troubled. 7
41 the farmer sows many seeds upon the ground 7
43 For if the farmer's seed does not come up 7
44 hast thou also made him like the farmer's seed? 7
9:17 As is the field, so is the seed 7
34 when the ground has received seed 7
15:13 because their seed shall fail 7
Wis 7: 2 compacted with blood, from the seed of a man 4
14: 6 left to the world the seed of a new generation. 4
4Mc 18: 1 offspring of the seed of Abraham 4

seed *See also* mustard, put, yield.

seedling 1. *μόσχευμα* 2. plantatio

2Es 8:41 and plants a multitude of seedlings 2
Wis 4: 3 none of their illegitimate seedlings 1

seedtime 1. זֶרַע

Gen 8:22 While the earth remains, seedtime and harvest 1

all seeing 1. *ἐπόπτης* 2. *παντεπόπτης*

2Mc 7:35 the judgment of the almighty, all-seeing God. 1
9: 5 the all-seeing Lord, the God of Israel 2

seeing that 1. בְּשֶׁ

Ecc 2:16 seeing that in the days to come all will have been 1

seek 1. בקר 2. בקש 3. דרש 4. הלך 5. מצא 6. פקד 7. שאל 8. שחר 9. בעא (A) 10. *ἀναζητέω* 11. *διώκω* 12. *ἐθέλω* 13. *εἰς* 14. *ἐκζητέω* 15. *ἐπιζητέω* 16. *ἐπιχειρέω* 17. *ζητέω* 18. *ζήτησις* 19. quaero 20. requiro

Gen 37:15 and the man asked him, "What are you seeking? 2
16 I am seeking my brothers," he said, "tell me 2
43:30 and he sought a place to weep. 2
Exd 2:15 When Pharaoh heard of it, he sought to kill Moses. 2
4:19 all the men who were seeking your life are dead. 2
24 on the way the LORD met him and sought to kill him. 2
33: 7 And every one who sought the LORD would go out 2
Lev 13:36 the priest need not seek for the yellow hair 1
Num16:10 And would you seek the priesthood also? 2
35:23 he was not his enemy, and did not seek his harm; 2
Deu 4:29 from there you will seek the LORD your God 2
12: 5 seek the place which the LORD . . will choose 3
13:10 because he sought to draw you away from the LORD 2
22: 2 shall be with you until your brother seeks it; 3
23: 6 shall not seek their peace or their prosperity 3
Jdg 4:22 and I will show you the man whom you are seeking. 2
14: 4 for he was seeking an occasion against 2
18: 1 of the Danites was seeking . . an inheritance 2
Rut 3: 1 should I not seek a home for you, that it may be well 2
1Sm 10: 2 The asses which you went to seek are found 2
14 Where did you go?" And he said, "To seek the asses; 2
21 But when they sought him, he could not be found. 2
14: 4 In the pass, by which Jonathan sought to go over 2
19: 2 Saul my father seeks to kill you; 2
10 Saul sought to pin David to the wall 2
20: 1 is my sin before your father, that he seeks my life? 2
22:23 he that seeks my life seeks your life; 2
23 he that seeks my life seeks your life; 2
23:10 Saul seeks to come to Kei'lah, to destroy the city 2
14 Saul sought him every day 2
15 Saul had come out to seek his life. 2
25 And Saul and his men went to seek him. 2
24: 2 Saul took . . and went to seek David and his men 2
9 men who say, 'Behold, David seeks your hurt'? 2
25:26 enemies and those who seek to do evil to my lord 2
29 If men rise up to pursue you and to seek your life 2
26: 2 Saul arose and went . . to seek David 2
20 the king of Israel has come out to seek my life 2
27: 1 Saul will despair of seeking me any longer 2
4 when it was told Saul . . he sought for him no more. 2
2Sm 3:17 you have been seeking David as king over you. 2
4: 8 Ish-bo'sheth . . your enemy, who sought your life; 2
16:11 my own son seeks my life; how much more now 2
17: 3 You seek the life of only one man 17
20 And when they had sought and could not find them 2
20:19 you seek to destroy a city which is a mother 2
21: 1 and David sought the face of the LORD. 2
2 Saul had sought to slay them in his zeal 2
1Kg 1: 2 Let a young maiden be sought for my lord the king 2
3 they sought for a beautiful maiden throughout 2
2:40 and went to Gath to Achish, to seek his slaves; 2
10:24 the whole earth sought the presence of Solomon 2
11:22 you are now seeking to go to your own country 2
40 Solomon sought therefore to kill Jerobo'am; 2
18:10 whither my lord has not sent to seek you; 2
19:10 I . . am left; and they seek my life, to take it away. 2
14 I . . am left; and they seek my life, to take it away. 2
20: 7 Mark now, and see how this man is seeking trouble; 2
2Kg 2:16 strong men; pray, let them go, and seek your master; 2
17 three days they sought him but did not find him. 2
6:19 I will bring you to the man whom you seek. 2
1Ch 4:39 to seek pasture for their flocks 2
16:10 let the hearts of those who seek the LORD rejoice! 2
11 Seek the LORD and his strength, seek his presence 3
11 and his strength, seek his presence continually! 2
22:19 set your mind and heart to seek the LORD your God. 3
28: 9 If you seek him, he will be found by you; 3
2Ch 1: 5 And Solomon and the assembly sought the LORD. 3
7:14 if my people . . and pray and seek my face 2
9:23 all the kings . . sought the presence of Solomon 2
11:16 those who had set their hearts to seek the LORD 2
12:14 for he did not set his heart to seek the LORD. 3
14: 4 commanded Judah to seek the LORD 3
7 because we have sought the LORD our God; 3
7 we have sought him, and he had given us peace 3
15: 2 If you seek him, he will be found by you 3
4 they turned to the LORD . . and sought him 2
12 they entered into a covenant to seek the LORD 3
13 whoever would not seek the LORD, the God of Israel 3
15 had sought him with their whole desire 2
16:12 yet even in his disease he did not seek the LORD 3
12 but sought help from physicians. •
17: 3 he did not seek the Ba'als 3
4 sought the God of his father 3
19: 3 have set your heart to seek God. 3
20: 3 Jehosh'aphat . . set himself to seek the LORD 3
4 Judah assembled to seek help from the LORD; 2
4 they came to seek the LORD. 2
22: 9 who sought the LORD with all his heart. 3
25:20 because they had sought the gods of Edom. 3
26: 5 set himself to seek God in the days of Zechari'ah 3
5 as long as he sought the LORD, God made him prosper 3
30:19 who sets his heart to seek God, the LORD 3
31:21 law and the commandments, seeking his God 3
34: 3 he began to seek the God of David his father; 3
Ezr 2:62 These sought their registration among those 2
8:21 to seek from him a straight way for ourselves 2
22 hand of our God is for good upon all that seek him 2
9:12 never seek their peace or prosperity 3
Neh 2:10 some one had come to seek the welfare 2
7:64 These sought their registration among those 2
12:27 dedication . . they sought the Levites 2
Est 2:21 angry and sought to lay hands on King Ahasu-e'rus. 2
3: 6 Haman sought to destroy all the Jews 2
6: 2 who had sought to lay hands upon King Ahasu-e'rus. 2
9: 2 to lay hands on such as sought their hurt. 2
10: 3 he sought the welfare of his people 2
Job 3: 4 Let that day be darkness! May God above not seek it 3
5: 8 I would seek God, and to God would I commit 3
7:21 in the earth; thou wilt seek me, but I shall not be. 8
8: 5 If you will seek God and make supplication 8
23: 9 on the left hand I seek him, but I cannot behold him; •
24: 5 seeking prey in the wilderness as food 8
Ps 9:10 O LORD, hast not forsaken those who seek thee. 3
10: 4 the wicked does not seek him; 3
22:26 those who seek him shall praise the LORD! 3
24: 6 Such is the generation of those who seek him 3
6 who seek him, who seek the face of the God of Jacob. 2
27: 8 Thou hast said, "Seek ye my face. 2
8 My heart says to thee, "Thy face, LORD, do I seek. 2
34: 4 I sought the LORD, and he answered me 3
10 but those who seek the LORD lack no good thing. 3
14 from evil, and do good; seek peace, and pursue it. 2
37:32 watches the righteous, and seeks to slay him. 2
36 though I sought him, he could not be found. 2
38:12 Those who seek my life lay their snares 2
12 those who seek my hurt speak of ruin 3
40:14 be put to shame . . who seek to snatch away my life; 2
16 may all who seek thee rejoice and be glad in thee; 2
54: 3 ruthless men seek my life; 2
63: 1 my God, I seek thee, my soul thirsts for thee; 8
9 those who seek to destroy my life shall go down 2
69: 6 those who seek thee be brought to dishonor 2
32 you who seek God, let your hearts revive. 3
70: 2 be put to shame and confusion who seek my life! 2
4 May all who seek thee rejoice and be glad in thee! 2
71:13 disgrace may they be covered who seek my hurt. 2
24 to shame and disgraced who sought to do me hurt. 2
77: 2 In the day of my trouble I seek the Lord; 3
78:34 When he slew them, they sought for him; 3
83:16 shame, that they may seek thy name, O LORD. 2
86:14 band of ruthless men seek my life 2
104:21 lions roar . . seeking their food from God. 2
105: 3 let the hearts of those who seek the LORD rejoice! 2
4 Seek the LORD and his strength 3
4 seek his presence continually! 2
119: 2 Blessed . . who seek him with their whole heart 3
10 With my whole heart I seek thee; let me not wander 3
45 walk at liberty, for I have sought thy precepts. 3
94 I am thine, save me; for I have sought thy precepts. 3
155 the wicked, for they do not seek thy statutes. 3
176 gone astray like a lost sheep; seek thy servant 2
122: 9 I will seek your good. 2
Prv 2: 4 if you seek it like silver 2
11:27 He who diligently seeks good seeks favor 2
14: 6 A scoffer seeks wisdom in vain 2
15:14 mind . . who has understanding seeks knowledge 2
17: 9 He who forgives an offense seeks love 2
11 An evil man seeks only rebellion 2
19 he who makes his door high seeks destruction. 2
18: 1 He who is estranged seeks pretexts to break out 2
15 the ear of the wise seeks knowledge. 2
20: 4 he will seek at harvest and have nothing. 7
23:35 When shall I awake? I will seek another drink. 2
28: 5 who seek the LORD understand it completely. 3
29:10 who is blameless, and the wicked seek his life. 2
26 Many seek the favor of a ruler 2
31:13 She seeks wool and flax, and works 3
Ecc 1:13 to seek and to search out by wisdom all that is 3
3: 6 a time to seek, and a time to lose; 2
15 and God seeks what has been driven away. 2
7:25 to know and to search out and to seek wisdom 2
28 my mind has sought . . but I have not found. 2
8:17 However much man may toil in seeking 2
12:10 The Preacher sought to find pleasing words 2
Sng 3: 1 by night I sought him whom my soul loves 2
1 I sought him, but found him not; 2
2 I will rise . . I will seek him whom my soul loves. 2
2 I sought him, but found him not. 2
5: 6 I sought him, but found him not; 2
6: 1 Whither . . that we may seek him with you? 2
Isa 1:17 seek justice, correct oppression; 3
9:13 did not turn . . nor seek the LORD of hosts. 3
11:10 ensign to the peoples; him shall the nations seek 3
16: 5 one who judges and seeks justice 3
26:16 O LORD, in distress they sought thee 6
34:16 Seek and read from the book of the LORD 3
41:12 You shall seek those who contend with you 2
17 the poor and needy seek water, and there is none 2
45:19 I did not say to . . Jacob, 'Seek me in chaos.' 2
51: 1 who pursue deliverance, you who seek the LORD; 2
55: 6 Seek the LORD while he may be found 3
58: 2 Yet they seek me daily and delight to know my ways 3
3 in the day of your fast you seek your own pleasure 5
13 going your own ways, or seeking your own pleasure 5
65: 1 I was ready to be sought by those who did not ask 3
1 was ready to be found by those who did not seek me. 2
10 to lie down, for my people who have sought me. 3
Jer 2:24 None who seek her need weary themselves; 2
33 How well you direct your course to seek lovers! 2
4:30 Your lovers despise you; they seek your life. 2
5: 1 find a man, one who does justice and seeks truth; 2
8: 2 and which they have sought and worshiped; 3
11:21 the men of An'athoth, who seek your life, and say 2
19: 7 and by the hand of those who seek their life. 2
9 and those who seek their life afflict them. 2
21: 7 into the hand of those who seek their lives. 2

22:25 give you into the hand of those who seek your life 2
26:21 the king sought to put him to death; 2
29: 7 seek the welfare of the city where I have sent you 3
13 You will seek me and find me; 2
13 when you seek me with all your heart 3
31: 2 in the wilderness; when Israel sought for rest 4
34:20 and into the hand of those who seek their lives. 2
21 and into the hand of those who seek their lives 2
38: 4 this man is not seeking . . welfare of this people 3
16 the hand of these men who seek your life. 2
44:30 and into the hand of those who seek his life 2
30 Babylon, who was his enemy and sought his life. 2
45: 5 And do you seek great things for yourself? 2
5 you seek great things for yourself? Seek them not; 2
46:26 into the hand of those who seek their life 2
49:37 and before those who seek their life; 2
50: 4 and they shall seek the LORD their God. 2
20 says the LORD, iniquity shall be sought in Israel 2
Lam 1:19 they sought food to revive their strength. 2
3:25 The LORD is good . . to the soul that seeks him. 3
Ezk 7:25 When anguish comes, they will seek peace 2
26 they seek a vision from the prophet 2
22:30 I sought for a man among them who should build up 2
26:21 though you be sought for, you will never be found 2
34: 4 the lost you have not sought 2
6 with none to search or seek for them. 2
16 I will seek the lost, and I will bring back 2
Dan 2:13 sought Daniel and his companions, to slay them. 9
18 told them to seek mercy of the God of heaven 9
4:36 counselors and my lords sought me 9
6: 4 presidents and the satraps sought to find 9
8:15 seen the vision, I sought to understand it; 2
9: 3 seeking him by prayer and supplications 2
Hos 2: 7 and she shall seek them, but shall not find them. 2
3: 5 Israel shall return and seek the LORD their God 2
5: 6 they shall go to seek the LORD 2
15 they acknowledge their guilt and seek my face 2
15 and in their distress they seek me, saying 8
7:10 nor seek him, for all this. 2
10:12 for it is the time to seek the LORD 3
Ams 5: 4 to the house of Israel: "Seek me and live; 3
5 do not seek Bethel, and do not enter into Gilgal 3
6 Seek the LORD and live, lest he break out like fire 3
14 Seek good, and not evil, that you may live; 3
8:12 run to and fro, to seek the word of the LORD 2
Nah 3: 7 whence shall I seek comforters for her? 2
11 you will seek a refuge from the enemy. 2
Zep 1: 6 who do not seek the LORD or inquire of him. 2
2: 3 Seek the LORD, all you humble of the land 2
3 seek righteousness, seek humility; 2
3 seek righteousness, seek humility; 2
Zec 8:21 to seek the LORD of hosts; I am going. 2
22 nations shall come to seek the LORD of hosts 2
11:16 not care for the perishing, or seek the wandering 2
12: 9 on that day I will seek to destroy all the nations 2
Mal 2: 7 men should seek instruction from his mouth 2
3: 1 the Lord whom you seek will suddenly come 2
Mat 2:20 of Israel, for those who sought the child's life 17
6:32 For the Gentiles seek all these things; 15
33 seek first his kingdom and his righteousness 17
7: 7 Ask, and it will be given you; seek, and you will find; 17
8 and he who seeks finds 17
12:39 evil and adulterous generation seeks for a sign; 15
43 passes through waterless places seeking rest 17
16: 4 evil and adulterous generation seeks for a sign 15
26:16 from that moment he sought an opportunity 17
59 the whole council sought false testimony 17
28: 5 I know that you seek Jesus who was crucified. 17
Mrk 8:11 seeking from him a sign from heaven, to test him. 17
12 Why does this generation seek a sign? 17
11:18 scribes heard it and sought a way to destroy him; 17
14: 1 the chief priests and the scribes were seeking 17
11 he sought an opportunity to betray him. 17
55 sought testimony against Jesus 17
16: 6 Do not be amazed; you seek Jesus of Nazareth 17
Lke 2:44 they sought him among their kinsfolk 10
45 they returned to Jerusalem, seeking him. 10
49 he said to them, "How is it that you sought me? 17
4:42 the people sought him and came to him 15
5:18 they sought to bring him in and lay him before Jesus; 17
6:19 all the crowd sought to touch him 17
9: 9 he sought to see him. 17
11: 9 seek, and you will find; knock, and it will be opened 17
10 he who seeks finds 17
16 while others, to test him, sought from him a sign 17
24 he passes through waterless places seeking rest; 17
29 it seeks a sign, but no sign shall be given to it 17
12:29 do not seek what you are to eat 17
30 all the nations of the world seek these things; 15
31 Instead, seek his kingdom 17
13: 6 he came seeking fruit on it and found none. 17
7 Lo, these three years I have come seeking fruit 17
24 many . . will seek to enter and will not be able. 17
15: 8 seek diligently until she finds it? 17
17:33 Whoever seeks to gain his life will lose it 17
19: 3 he sought to see who Jesus was, but could not 17
10 the Son of man came to seek and to save the lost. 17
47 principal men of the people sought to destroy 17
22: 2 the scribes were seeking how to put him to death; 17
6 sought an opportunity to betray him to them 17
24: 5 Why do you seek the living among the dead? 17
Joh 1:38 Jesus turned . . and said to them, "What do you seek? 17
4:23 for such the Father seeks to worship him. 17
5:18 why the Jews sought all the more to kill him 17
30 because I seek not my own will 17
44 do not seek the glory that comes from the only God?. 17
6:24 went to Caper'na-um, seeking Jesus. 17
26 you seek me, not because you saw signs 17
7: 1 because the Jews sought to kill him. 17
4 if he seeks to be known openly 17
18 He . . seeks his own glory 17
18 he who seeks the glory of him who sent him is true 17
19 Why do you seek to kill me? 17
20 Who is seeking to kill you? 17
25 Is not this the man whom they seek to kill? 17
30 they sought to arrest him 17
34 you will seek me and you will not find me 17
36 'You will seek me and you will not find me,' 17
8:21 you will seek me and die in your sin 17
37 yet you seek to kill me 17
40 now you seek to kill me 17
50 Yet I do not seek my own glory 17
50 there is One who seeks it and he will be the judge. 17
11: 8 the Jews were but now seeking to stone you 17
13:33 You will seek me 17
18: 4 Whom do you seek? 17
7 Again he asked them, "Whom do you seek? 17
8 I am he; so, if you seek me, let these men go. 17
19:12 Upon this Pilate sought to release him 17
20:15 Woman, why are you weeping? Whom do you seek? 17
Act 9:29 they were seeking to kill him. 16
12:19 Herod had sought for him and could not find him 15
13: 7 sought to hear the word of God. 15
8 seeking to turn away the proconsul 17
11 seeking people to lead him by the hand. 17
15:17 the rest of men may seek the Lord 14
16:10 immediately we sought to go on into Macedo'nia 17
17: 5 seeking to bring them out to the people. 17
27 that they should seek God 17
19:39 if you seek anything further 15
27:30 the sailors were seeking to escape from the ship 17
Rom 2: 7 who by patience in well-doing seek for glory 17
3:11 no one understands, no one seeks for God. 14
10: 3 and seeking to establish their own 17
20 I have been found by those who did not seek me; 17
11: 3 and I alone am left, and they seek my life. 17
7 Israel failed to obtain what it sought. 15
1Co 1:22 For Jews demand signs and Greeks seek wisdom 17
7:18 Let him not seek circumcision. •
18 Let him not seek circumcision. •
27 Are you bound to a wife? Do not seek to be free. 17
27 Are you free from a wife? Do not seek marriage. 17
10:24 Let no one seek his own good 17
33 not seeking my own advantage, but that of many 17
2Co 12:14 I seek not what is yours but you 17
Php 4:17 Not that I seek the gift 15
17 I seek the fruit which increases to your credit. 15
Col 3: 1 seek the things that are above, where Christ is 17
1Th 2: 6 nor did we seek glory from men 17
5:15 always seek to do good to one another and to all. 11
Heb 11: 6 he rewards those who seek him. 14
14 they are seeking a homeland. 15
12:17 though he sought it with tears. 14
13:14 we seek the city which is to come. 15
1Pe 3:11 let him seek peace and pursue it. 17
5: 8 the devil prowls . . seeking some one to devour. 17
Rev 9: 6 in those days men will seek death and will not find it; 17
1Es 5:39 when the genealogy of these men was sought 17
7:13 all those who . . sought the Lord. 17
8:50 to seek from him a prosperous journey 17
52 power of our Lord will be with those who seek him 15
85 do not seek ever to have peace with them 17
2Es 5:10 it shall be sought by many but shall not be found 19
6:10 seek for nothing else, Ezra! 19
12:48 and to seek mercy on account of the humiliation 19
14:23 and tell them not to seek you for 40 days. 19
36 and let no one seek me for 40 days. 20
Tob 1:18 When the bodies were sought by the king 17
4:18 Seek advice from every wise man 17
AEs 11:12 sought all day to understand it in every detail. 12
12: 6 he sought to injure Mordecai and his people 17
15:16 all his servants sought to comfort her. •
16: 3 They not only seek to injure our subjects 17
Wis 1: 1 seek him with sincerity of heart; 17
6:12 is found by those who seek her. 17
14 He who rises early to seek her †
16 she goes about seeking those worthy of her 17
8: 2 I loved her and sought her from my youth 14
18 I went about seeking how to get her for myself. 17
13: 6 perhaps they go astray while seeking God 17
Sir 2:16 Those who fear the Lord will seek his approval 17
3:21 Seek not what is too difficult for you 17
4:11 gives help to those who seek her. 17
12 those who seek her early will be filled with joy. †
6:27 Search out and seek 17
7: 4 not seek from the Lord the highest office 17
6 Do not seek to become a judge 17
21:17 The utterance of a sensible man will be sought 17
24: 7 Among all these I sought a resting place 17
7 I sought in whose territory I might lodge. •
34 for all who seek instruction. 14
27: 1 whoever seeks to get rich will avert his eyes. 17
28: 3 yet seek for healing from the Lord? 17
32:14 those who rise early to seek him will find favor. •
15 He who seeks the law will be filled with it 17
33:17 all who seek instruction. 17
25 leave his hands idle, and he will seek liberty. 18
31 which way will you go to seek him? 18
39: 5 to rise early to seek the Lord who made him †
40:26 with it there is no need to seek for help. 15
51: 3 from the hand of those who sought my life 17
13 I sought wisdom openly in my prayer. 17
21 My heart was stirred to seek her 14
Bar 3:23 sons . . who seek for understanding on the earth 14
4:28 return with tenfold zeal to seek him. 17
Aza 1:18 we fear thee and seek thy face. 17
1Mc 2:29 Then many who were seeking righteousness 17
7:13 first . . to seek peace from them 15
15 We will not seek to injure you or your friends. 14
9:26 They sought and searched for the friends of Judas 14
12:40 so he kept seeking to seize and kill him 17
14: 4 He sought the good of his nation 17
35 He sought in every way to exalt his people. 14
15:19 they should not seek their harm or make war 14
16:22 had found out that they were seeking to destroy him. 17
2Mc 2:27 seeks the benefit of others 17
13:21 he was sought for, caught, and put in prison. 10
14:32 did not know where the man was whom he sought 17
4Mc 1: 2 to everyone who is seeking knowledge 13

seek a quarrel 1. אנה

2Kg 5: 7 see how he is seeking a quarrel with me. 1

seek after 1. בקש 2. דרש 3. ζητέω

Ps 4: 2 will you love vain words, and seek after lies? 1
14: 2 any that act wisely, that seek after God. 2
27: 4 have I asked of the LORD, that will I seek after; 1
35: 4 put to shame and dishonor who seek after my life! 1
53: 2 any that are wise, that seek after God. 2
Sir 39:17 in God's time all things will be sought after 3

seek diligently 1. שחר

Prv 1:28 they will seek me diligently but will not find 1
8:17 those who seek me diligently find me. 1
11:27 He who diligently seeks good 1

seek eagerly 1. שחר

Prv 7:15 now I have come out to meet you, to seek you eagerly 1

seek earnestly 1. שחר

Ps 78:34 they repented and sought God earnestly. 1
Isa 26: 9 my spirit within me earnestly seeks thee. 1

seek favor 1. חלה 2. חנן 3. רצה 4. πείθω

Job 20:10 His children will seek the favor of the poor 3
Prv 19: 6 Many seek the favor of a generous man 1
Hos 12: 4 he wept and sought his favor. 2
Gal 1:10 Am I now seeking the favor of men, or of God? 4

seek guidance 1. דרש

1Ch 10:13 consulted a medium, seeking guidance 1
14 did not seek guidance from the LORD. 1

seek occasion 1. גלל

Gen 43:18 that he may seek occasion against us 1

seek out 1. בעה 2. בקר 3. בקש 4. דרש 5. תור 6. ἀνευρίσκω 7. ἐκζητέω 8. ζητέω

Lev 19:31 not turn to mediums or wizards; do not seek them out 3
Num10:33 ark . . went . . to seek out a resting place for them. 5
Deu 1:33 went . . to seek you out a place to pitch your tents 5
1Sm 13:14 the LORD has sought out a man after his own heart; 3
16:16 seek out a man who is skilful in playing the lyre; 3
28: 7 Seek out for me a woman who is a medium, 3
1Ch 28: 8 observe and seek out all the commandments 4
Est 2: 2 Let . . young virgins be sought out for the king. 3
Job 10: 6 that thou dost seek out my iniquity 3
Ps 10:15 seek out his wickedness till thou find none. 4
Ecc 7:29 but they have sought out many devices. 3
Isa 40:20 he seeks out a skilful craftsman 3
62:12 and you shall be called Sought out 4
Ezk 34:11 will search for my sheep, and will seek them out. 2
12 As a shepherd seeks out his flock 2
12 so will I seek out my sheep; and I will rescue them 2
Obd 1: 6 Esau has been pillaged, his treasures sought out! 1
Act 21: 4 having sought out the disciples, we stayed there 6
Sir 38:33 are not sought out for the council of the people 8
39: 1 will seek out the wisdom of all the ancients 7
3 he will seek out the hidden meanings of proverbs 7
47:25 For they sought out every sort of wickedness 7
1Mc 14:14 he sought out the law 7

seek refuge 1. חסה 2. עוז

Ps 17: 7 O savior of those who seek refuge 1
31: 1 In thee, O LORD, do I seek refuge; 1
52: 7 of his riches, and sought refuge in his wealth! 2

141: 8 in thee I seek refuge; leave me not defenseless! 1
Zep 3:12 They shall seek refuge in the name of the LORD 1

seek shelter 1. חסה

Isa 30: 2 and to seek shelter in the shadow of Egypt! 1

seek to escape 1. παραιτέομαι

Act 25:11 I do not seek to escape death 1

seek to injure 1. עצב

Ps 56: 5 All day long they seek to injure my cause; 1

seeker 1. ἐκζητητής

Bar 3:23 seekers for understanding, have not learned 1

seem 1. בְּעֵינַיִם 2. היה בְּעֵינַיִם 3. היה כְּ 4. חשׁב 5. ראה 6. חֲזוּ (A) 7. δοκέω 8. ἐν ὀφθαλμοῖς 9. ὁράω 10. τίθημι 11. φαίνω 12. ὡς 13. ὡς εἰμί

Gen 19:14 But he seemed to his sons-in-law to be jesting. 3
27:12 I shall seem to be mocking him, and bring a curse 2
29:20 and they seemed to him but a few days 2
Lev 14:35 seems to me to be some sort of disease in my house 5
Num13:33 we seemed to ourselves like grasshoppers 2
33 like grasshoppers, and so we seemed to them. 2
Deu 1:23 The thing seemed good to me, and I took twelve men 1
15:18 not seem hard to you, when you let him go free 1
Jos 9:25 do as it seems good and right in your sight to do •
Jdg 10:15 have sinned; do to us whatever seems good to thee; 1
19:24 Ravish . . and do with them what seems good to you; •
1Sm 1:23 Do what seems best to you, wait until you have 1
3:18 It is the LORD; let him do what seems good to him. 1
11:10 and you may do to us whatever seems good to you. 1
14:36 And they said, "Do whatever seems good to you. 1
40 the people said to Saul, "Do what seems good to you. 1
24: 4 you shall do to him as it shall seem good to you. 1
29: 6 it seems right that you should march . . with me 1
2Sm 10:12 and may the LORD do what seems good to him. 1
13: 2 it seemed impossible to Amnon to do anything 1
15:26 here I am, let him do to me what seems good to him. 1
18: 4 king said . . "Whatever seems best to you I will do. 1
19:27 do therefore what seems good to you. 1
37 and do for him whatever seems good to you. 1
38 and I will do for him whatever seems good to you; 1
24:22 my lord . . take and offer up what seems good to him; 1
1Kg 21: 2 or, if it seems good to you, I will give you . . money. 1
1Ch 13: 2 If it seems good to you, and if it is the will •
19:13 and may the LORD do what seems good to him. 1
21:23 let my lord the king do what seems good to him; 1
2Ch 30: 4 the plan seemed right to the king 1
Ezr 5:17 if it seem good to the king, let search be made •
Est 3:11 is given . . to do with them as it seems good to you. 1
Job 10: 3 Does it seem good to thee to oppress •
Ps 73:16 it seemed to me a wearisome task •
Prv 14:12 There is a way which seems right to a man 2
16:25 There is a way which seems right to a man 2
18:17 He who states his case first seems right •
Ecc 9:13 I have also seen this . . and it seemed great to me. •
Isa 5:28 their horses' hoofs seem like flint 4
Jer 26:14 Do with me as seems good and right to you. •
27: 5 and I give it to whomever it seems right to me. •
40: 4 If it seems good to you to come with me to Babylon •
4 if it seems wrong to you to come with me to Babylon •
Ezk 21:23 But to them it will seem like a false divination; 2
Dan 7:20 horn . . which seemed greater than its fellows. 6
Zec 11:12 If it seems right to you, give me my wages; 1
Lke 24:11 these words seemed to them an idle tale 11
Act 17:18 He seems to be a preacher of foreign divinities 7
25:27 it seems to me unreasonable 7
1Co 12:22 the parts of the body which seem to be weaker 7
16: 4 If it seems advisable that I should go also •
2Co 10: 9 seem to be frightening you with letters. 7
13: 7 though we may seem to have failed. 13
Heb 12:11 For the moment all discipline seems painful 7
Rev 6: 6 I heard what seemed to be a voice in the midst 12
13: 3 One of its heads seemed to have a mortal wound 12
19: 1 After this I heard what seemed to be a loud voice 12
6 Then I heard what seemed to be the voice 12
1Es 3: 5 to him whose statement seems wisest 11
Tob 2:14 You seem to know everything! 9
Jdt 3: 4 deal with them in any way that seems good to you. 8
Wis 3: 2 they seemed to have died 7
Sir 0: 2 seem to have rendered some phrases imperfectly 7
3 It seemed highly necessary that I should 10
6:20 She seems very harsh to the uninstructed 13
2Mc 1:13 a force that seemed irresistible 7
3Mc 1:29 for it seemed that . . 7
4Mc 5: 7 it does not seem to me that you are a philosopher 7
10 It seems to me 7

seem *See also* good, little, right, slow, wise.

seemly 1. נָאוֶה 2. καλός 3. κόσμιος

Ps 147: 1 for he is gracious, and a song of praise is seemly. 1
1Ti 2: 9 modestly and sensibly in seemly apparel 3
Sir 14: 3 Riches are not seemly for a stingy man 2

thing seen 1. βλέπω

2Co 4:18 because we look not to the things that are seen 1
18 for the things that are seen are transient 1
Wis 13: 7 because the things that are seen are beautiful. 1

widely seen 1. εὔοπτος

LJr 1:61 the lightning, when it flashes, is widely seen 1

seer 1. חֹזֶה 2. ראה 3. רֹאֶה 4. ὅρασις

1Sm 9: 9 to inquire of God, he said, "Come, let us go to the seer" 3
9 who is now . . prophet was formerly called a seer. 3
11 and said to them, "Is the seer here? 3
18 and said, "Tell me where is the house of the seer? 3
19 Samuel answered Saul, "I am the seer; 3
2Sm 24:11 the word . . came to the prophet Gad, David's seer 1
2Kg 17:13 the LORD warned Israel and Judah by . . every seer 1
1Ch 9:22 David and Samuel the seer established them 3
21: 9 the LORD spoke to Gad, David's seer, saying 1
25: 5 All these were the sons of Heman the king's seer 1
26:28 all that Samuel the seer, and Saul the son of Kish 3
29:29 are written in the Chronicles of Samuel the seer 3
29 and in the Chronicles of Gad the seer 1
2Ch 9:29 and in the visions of Iddo the seer 1
12:15 chronicles of Shemai'ah . . and of Iddo the seer? 1
16: 7 Hana'ni the seer came to Asa king of Judah 2
10 Then Asa was angry with the seer 3
19: 2 Jehu the son of Hana'ni the seer went out 1
29:25 commandment of David and of Gad the king's seer 1
30 praises . . with the words of . . Asaph the seer. 1
33:18 words of the seers who spoke to him 1
19 written in the Chronicles of the Seers. 1
35:15 command of David . . and Jedu'thun the king's seer 1
Isa 29:10 and covered your heads, the seers. 1
30:10 who say to the seers, "See not"; 3
Ams 7:12 Amazi'ah said to Amos, "O seer, go, flee away 1
Mic 3: 7 the seers shall be disgraced 1
Sir 46:15 he became known as a trustworthy seer. 4

thing which one sees 1. βλέπω

Wis 17: 6 they deemed the things which they saw to be worse 1

seethe 1. בשׁל

Ezk 24: 5 boil its pieces, seethe also its bones in it. 1

seine 1. מִכְמֶרֶת

Hab 1:15 he gathers them in his seine; 1
16 Therefore he . . burns incense to his seine; 1

seize 1. אחז 2. בזז 3. גזל 4. חזק 5. חטף 6. ירשׁ 7. לכד 8. לקח 9. נקשׁ 10. שׁלל 11. תמך 12. תפשׂ 13. ἀναλαμβάνω 14. ἁρπαγή 15. ἀφαίρεσις 16. διακατέχω 17. διαρπάζω 18. δίδωμι 19. ἐξαρπάζω 20. ἐπιλαμβάνω 21. ἐπισπάω 22. καταλαμβάνω 23. κληρονομέω 24. κρατέω 25. λαμβάνω 26. λεηλατέω 27. πιάζω 28. προκαταλαμβάνω 29. προλαμβάνω 30. συλλαμβάνω 31. συναρπάζω 32. συνέχω 33. apprehendo

Gen 19:16 he lingered; so the men seized him and his wife 4
21:25 water which Abim'elech's servants had seized 3
34: 2 when Shechem . . saw her, he seized her and lay 8
43:18 to make slaves of us and seize our asses. 8
Exd 15:14 pangs have seized on the inhabitants 1
15 the leaders of Moab, trembling seizes them; 1
Deu 22:25 open country . . man seizes her and lies with her 4
28 not betrothed, and seizes her and lies with her 12
25:11 out her hand and seizes him by the private parts 4
Jos 8: 7 rise up from the ambush, and seize the city; 6
Jdg 3:28 So they went down after him, and seized the fords 7
7:24 Mid'ianites and seize the waters against them 7
24 and they seized the waters as far as Beth-bar'ah 7
12: 6 then they seized him and slew him at the fords 1
15:15 of an ass, and put out his hand and seized it 8
16:21 Philistines seized him and gouged out his eyes 1
19:25 the man seized his concubine, and put her out 4
21:21 come out . . and seize each man his wife 5
2Sm 1: 9 Stand . . and slay me; for anguish has seized me 1
2:21 Turn aside . . and seize one of the young men 1
4:10 I seized him and slew him at Ziklag 1
1Kg 18:40 Eli'jah said to them, "Seize the prophets of Ba'al; 12
40 they seized them; and Eli'jah brought them down 12
22:26 Seize Micai'ah, and take him back to Amon 8
2Kg 6:13 and see where he is, that I may send and seize him. 8
14:14 he seized all the gold and silver 8
2Ch 18:25 Seize Micai'ah, and take him back to Amon 8
25:24 he seized all the gold and silver •
24 he seized also the treasuries of the king's house •
Job 3: 6 That night-let thick darkness seize it! 8
16:12 he seized me by the neck and dashed me to pieces; 1
18: 9 A trap seizes him by the heel, a snare lays hold 1
20 horror seizes them of the east. 1
20:19 he has seized a house which he did not build. 3
21: 6 I am dismayed, and shuddering seizes my flesh. 1
24: 2 they seize flocks and pasture them. 3
30:18 With violence it seizes my garment; 20
36:17 judgment and justice seize you. 11
Ps 10: 9 he lurks that he may seize the poor 5
9 he seizes the poor when he draws him into his net. 5
56: 0 David, when the Philistines seized him in Gath. 1
71:11 and say, "God has forsaken him; pursue and seize him 12
109: 8 May his days be few; may another seize his goods! 8
11 May the creditor seize all that he has; 9
119:53 Hot indignation seizes me because of the wicked 1
Prv 7:13 She seizes him and kisses him 4
Isa 5:29 they growl and seize their prey, they carry it off 1
10: 6 I command him, to take spoil and seize plunder 2
13: 8 Pangs and agony will seize them; 1
21: 3 pangs have seized me, like . . a woman in travail; 1
33:14 in Zion . . trembling has seized the godless 1
Jer 20: 5 enemies, who shall plunder them, and seize them 8
36:26 and Shelemi'ah the son of Abdeel to seize Baruch 8
37:13 seized Jeremiah the prophet, saying 12
14 and seized Jeremiah and brought him 12
38:23 but shall be seized by the king of Babylon; 12
48:41 shall be taken and the strongholds seized. 12
49:24 she turned to flee, and panic seized her; 4
50:43 anguish seized him, pain as of a woman in travail. 4
51:32 the fords have been seized 12
41 Babylon . . the praise of the whole earth seized! 12
Ezk 23:10 they seized her sons and her daughters; 8
25 They shall seize your sons and your daughters 8
38:12 to seize spoil and carry off plunder; to assail 10
13 will say to you, 'Have you come to seize spoil? 10
13 take away cattle and goods, to seize great spoil 10
Mic 2: 2 They covet fields, and seize them; 3
4: 9 that pangs have seized you like a woman in travail? 4
Hab 1: 6 who march . . to seize habitations not their own. 6
Mat 14: 3 For Herod had seized John and bound him 24
18:28 and seizing him by the throat he said 24
22: 6 while the rest seized his servants 24
26:48 The one I shall kiss is the man; seize him. 24
50 came up and laid hands on Jesus and seized him. 24
55 you did not seize me. 24
57 Then those who had seized Jesus 24
Mrk 3:21 they went out to seize him 24
6:17 For Herod had sent and seized John 24
9:18 wherever it seizes him, it dashes him down 22
14:44 seize him and lead him away under guard. 24
46 they laid hands on him and seized him. 24
49 you did not seize me 24
51 they seized him 24
Lke 5:26 amazement seized them all 25
7:16 Fear seized them all; and they glorified God 25
8:29 For many a time it had seized him 31
37 they were seized with great fear 32
9:39 a spirit seizes him, and he suddenly cries out 25
22:54 Then they seized him and led him away 30
23:26 they seized one Simon of Cyre'ne 20
Joh 18:12 officers of the Jews seized Jesus and bound him. 30
Act 6:12 they came upon him and seized him 31
12: 4 when he had seized him, he put him in prison 27
16:19 they seized Paul and Silas 20
18:17 they all seized Sos'thenes, the ruler of the synagogue 20
21:30 seized Paul and dragged him out of the temple 20
23:27 This man was seized by the Jews 30
24: 6 tried to profane the temple, but we seized him. 24
26:21 Jews seized me in the temple and tried to kill me. 30
2Co 11:32 guarded the city of Damascus in order to seize me 27
Heb 6:18 to seize the hope set before us. 24
Rev 3:11 hold fast . . so that no one may seize your crown. 25
20: 2 And he seized the dragon, that ancient serpent 24
1Es 1:38 seized his brother Zarius 30
2Es 5: 1 shall be seized with great terror 33
15:37 they shall be seized with trembling 33
Tob 6: 3 the young man seized the fish 24
Jdt 2:25 He also seized the territory of Cilicia 22
4: 7 to seize the passes up into the hills 16
6:10 to seize Achior and take him to Bethulia 30
7: 1 to seize the passes up into the hill country 28
7 seized them and set guards of soldiers over them 28
17 and seized the water supply 28
14: 3 they will seize their arms and go into the camp 13
16: 5 and seize my children as prey 18
AEs 14: 1 Esther the queen, seized with deathly anxiety •
Wis 17:17 he was seized, and endured the inescapable fate; 29
Sir 23:21 where he least suspects it, he will be seized. 27
Sus 1:40 So we seized this woman and asked her 20
Bel 1:21 seized the priests and their wives and children; 30
1Mc 1:32 seized the cattle. 23
2:10 What nation . . has not seized her spoils? 24
3:12 Then they seized their spoils 25
4:18 afterward seize the plunder boldly. 25
23 they seized much gold and silver 25
5:28 he seized all its spoils and burned it with fire. 25
6:12 I seized all her vessels of silver and gold 25
24 they have seized our inheritances. 17
7: 2 the army seized Antiochus and Lysias 30
16 he seized 60 of them and killed them in one day 30
19 seized many of the men who had deserted to him 30
29 the enemy were ready to seize Judas. 19
47 Then the Jews seized the spoils and the plunder 25
9:36 seized John and all that he had 30
60 telling them to seize Jonathan and his men 30
61 Jonathan's men seized about 50 of the men 30
11:46 Then the men of the city seized the main streets 22
48 seized much spoil on that day 25
12:40 so he kept seeking to seize and kill him 30
48 the men of Ptolemais closed the gates and seized him 30

50 they realized that Jonathan had been seized 30
14: 3 seized him and took him to Arsaces 30
15:30 hand over the cities which you have seized 22
33 neither taken foreign land nor seized foreign property 24
16:22 he seized the men who came to destroy him 30
2Mc 2:21 they seized the whole land 26
9: 5 he was seized with a pain in his bowels 25
3Mc 1: 1 the regions . . had been seized by Antiochus 15
4Mc 4: 6 to seize the private funds in the treasury. 25
10 going up with his armed forces to seize the money 14
5: 2 to seize each and every Hebrew 21
17: 1 she also was about to be seized and put to death 30

seize control 1. παραλαμβάνω
1Mc 6:56 he was trying to seize control of the government. 1

seize firm hold 1. עטה
Isa 22:17 He will seize firm hold on you 1

seize for sacrifice 1. ἀνιερόω
1Es 9: 4 their cattle should be seized for sacrifice 1

seize immediately 1. προκαταλαμβάνω
Jdt 4: 5 and immediately seized all the high hilltops 1

seize in advance 1. προκαταλαμβάνω
Jdt 2:10 and seize all their territory for me in advance 1

seize on every side 1. circumteneo
2Es 16:39 and pains will seize it on every side. 1

seldom 1. יקר
Prv 25:17 Let your foot be seldom in your neighbor's house 1

select 1. משך 2. קרה 3. ראה 4. ἀφορίζω 5. ἐπιλέγω
Gen 41:33 Now therefore let Pharaoh select a man discreet 3
Exd 12:21 said to them, "Select lambs for yourselves 1
Num35:11 you shall select cities to be cities of refuge 2
2Kg 10: 3 select the best and fittest of your master's sons 3
Ezr 10:16 Ezra . . selected men, heads of fathers' houses 5
Sir 47: 2 As the fat is selected from the peace offering 4
2 so David was selected from the sons of Israel. •

self 1. ἄνθρωπος 2. αὐτός 3. σεαυτοῦ 4. ψυχή
Act 20:30 from among your own selves will arise men 2
Rom 6: 6 We know that our old self was crucified with him 1
7:22 For I delight in the law of God, in my inmost self 1
1Th 2: 8 also our own selves 4
Phm 1:19 say nothing of your owing me even your own self. 3
self *See also* lover.

self-abasement 1. ταπεινοφροσύνη
Col 2:18 insisting on self-abasement 1
23 rigor of devotion and self-abasement 1

self-conceit 1. κενόδοξος
Gal 5:26 Let us have no self-conceit 1

self-condemned 1. αὐτοκατάκριτος
Tit 3:11 he is self-condemned. 1

self-control 1. מַעְצָר לְרוּחַ 2. ἐγκράτεια 3. παθοκράτεια 4. σωφρονισμός 5. σωφροσύνη 6. abstinentia
Prv 25:28 A man without self-control is like a city broken 1
Act 24:25 as he argued about justice and self-control 2
Gal 5:23 self-control; against such there is no law. 2
2Ti 1: 7 a spirit of power and love and self-control. 4
2Pe 1: 6 and knowledge with self-control 2
6 and self-control with steadfastness 2
2Es 7:125 the faces of those who practiced self-control 6
Wis 8: 7 she teaches self-control and prudence 5
4Mc 1: 3 those emotions that hinder self-control 5
6 opposed to justice, courage, and self-control 5
18 justice, courage, and self-control. 5
30 the restraining power of self-control. 5
31 Self-control, then, is dominance 5
5:23 it teaches us self-control 5
34 nor will I renounce you, beloved self-control. 2
13:16 let us put on the full armor of self-control 3
self-control *See also* exercise, lack.

self-controlled 1. ἐγκρατής 2. σώφρων
Tit 1: 8 upright, holy, and self-controlled; 1
4Mc 15:10 were righteous and self-controlled and brave 2

self-denial 1. σφιγγία
Sir 11:18 is rich through his diligence and self-denial 1

self-indulgent 1. σπαταλάω
1Ti 5: 6 whereas she who is self-indulgent is dead 1

self-kindled 1. αὐτόματος
Wis 17: 6 a dreadful, self-kindled fire 1

self-reliant 1. αὐτάρκης
Sir 40:18 Life is sweet for the self-reliant and the worker 1

selfish 1. πονηρός
Lke 6:35 he is kind to the ungrateful and the selfish. 1
selfish *See also* ambition, behavior.

selfishness 1. ἐριθεία
2Co 12:20 anger, selfishness, slander, gossip, conceit 1
Gal 5:20 anger, selfishness, dissension, party spirit 1
Php 2: 3 Do nothing from selfishness or conceit 1

sell 1. מכר 2. מִמְכָּר 3. משל 4. שׁבר 5. ἀποδίδωμι 6. ἀποπρατίζομαι 7. πιπράσκω 8. πρᾶσις 9. πράσσω 10. πωλέω 11. vendo
Gen 25:31 Jacob said, "First sell me your birthright. 1
33 So he swore to him, and sold his birthright 1
31:15 For he has sold us, and he has been using up 1
37:27 Come, let us sell him to the Ish'maelites 1
28 him out of the pit, and sold him to the Ish'maelites 1
36 Meanwhile the Mid'ianites had sold him in Egypt 1
41:56 Joseph . . sold to the Egyptians, for the famine 4
42: 6 he it was who sold to all the people of the land. 4
45: 4 Joseph, whom you sold into Egypt. 1
5 do not be distressed . . because you sold me here; 1
47:20 for all the Egyptians sold their fields 1
22 therefore they did not sell their land. 1
Exd 21: 7 When a man sells his daughter as a slave 1
8 have no right to sell her to a foreign people 3
16 Whoever steals a man, whether he sells him or is 1
35 then they shall sell the live ox and divide 1
22: 1 ox or a sheep, and kills it or sells it 1
1 he shall be sold for his theft. 1
Lev 25:14 if you sell to your neighbor or buy 1
15 years for crops he shall sell to you 1
16 the number of the crops that he is selling to you 1
23 The land shall not be sold in perpetuity 1
25 If your brother becomes poor, and sells part 1
25 come and redeem what his brother has sold 2
27 let him reckon the years since he sold it and pay 2
27 pay back . . to the man to whom he sold it 1
28 then what he sold shall remain in the hand of him •
29 If a man sells a dwelling house in a walled city 1
33 then the house that was sold in a city 2
34 fields . . to their cities may not be sold 1
39 if your brother . . sells himself to you 1
42 they shall not be sold as slaves 1
47 your brother . . sells himself to the stranger 1
48 then after he is sold he may be redeemed 1
50 reckon . . from the year when he sold himself 1
27:20 sold the field to another man, it shall not be 1
27 it shall be sold at your valuation 1
28 no devoted thing . . shall be sold or redeemed 1
Deu 2:28 You shall sell me food for money, that I may eat 4
14:21 give it . . or you may sell it to a foreigner; 1
15:12 Hebrew man, or a Hebrew woman, is sold to you 1
21:14 not sell her for money, you shall not treat her 1
24: 7 if he treats him as a slave or sells him 1
32:30 unless their Rock had sold them 1
Jdg 2:14 he sold them into the power of their enemies 1
3: 8 he sold them into the hand of Cu'shan-rishatha'im 1
4: 2 the LORD sold them into the hand of Jabin king 1
9 LORD will sell Sis'era into the hand of a woman. 1
10: 7 he sold them into the hand of the Philistines 1
Rut 4: 3 Na'omi . . is selling the parcel of land 1
1Sm 12: 9 and he sold them into the hand of Sis'era 1
1Kg 21:20 you have sold yourself to do what is evil 1
25 who sold himself to do what was evil 1
2Kg 4: 7 Go, sell the oil and pay your debts 1
6:25 an ass's head was sold for 80 shekels of silver •
7: 1 a measure of fine meal shall be sold for a shekel •
16 So a measure of fine meal was sold for a shekel •
18 Two measures of barley shall be sold for a shekel •
17:17 and sold themselves to do evil in the sight 1
Neh 5: 8 brethren who have been sold to the nations; 1
8 but you even sell your brethren that they may be 1
8 sell your brethren that they may be sold to us! 1
10:31 wares or any grain on the sabbath day to sell 1
13:15 warned them on the day when they sold food. 1
16 sold them on the sabbath to the people of Judah 1
Est 7: 4 For we are sold, I and my people, to be destroyed 1
4 If we had been sold merely as slaves, men and women 1
Ps 44:12 Thou hast sold thy people for a trifle 1
105:17 Joseph, who was sold as a slave. 1
Prv 11:26 but a blessing is on the head of him who sells it. 4
23:23 Buy truth, and do not sell it; 1
31:24 She makes linen garments and sells them; 1
Isa 50: 1 which of my creditors is it to whom I have sold you? 1
1 Behold, for your iniquities you were sold 1
52: 3 For thus says the LORD: "You were sold for nothing 1
Jer 34:14 the fellow Hebrew who has been sold to you 1
Ezk 7:13 the seller shall not return to what he has sold 2
30:12 and will sell the land into the hand of evil men; 1
48:14 They shall not sell or exchange any of it; 1
Jol 3: 3 and have sold a girl for wine, and have drunk it. 1
6 You have sold the people of Judah and Jerusalem 1
7 up from the place to which you have sold them 1
8 I will sell your sons and your daughters 1
8 and they will sell them to the Sabe'ans 1
Ams 2: 6 because they sell the righteous for silver 1
8: 5 will the new moon be over, that we may sell grain? 4
6 buy the poor . . and sell the refuse of the wheat? 4
Zec 11: 5 those who sell them say, 'Blessed be the LORD 1
Mat 10:29 Are not two sparrows sold for a penny? 10
13:44 in his joy he goes and sells all that he has 10
46 went and sold all that he had and bought it. 7
18:25 as he could not pay, his lord ordered him to be sold 7
19:21 If you would be perfect, go, sell what you possess 10
21:12 drove out all who sold and bought in the temple 10
12 and the seats of those who sold pigeons. 10
26: 9 this ointment might have been sold for a large sum 7
Mrk 10:21 go, sell what you have, and give to the poor 10
11:15 to drive out those who sold and those who bought 10
15 the seats of those who sold pigeons; 10
14: 5 For this ointment might have been sold 7
Lke 12: 6 Are not five sparrows sold for two pennies? 10
33 Sell your possessions, and give alms 10
17:28 they ate, they drank, they bought, they sold 10
18:22 Sell all that you have and distribute to the poor 10
19:45 began to drive out those who sold 10
22:36 who has no sword sell his mantle and buy one. 10
Joh 2:14 he found those who were selling oxen and sheep 10
16 And he told those who sold the pigeons 10
12: 5 Why was this ointment not sold for 300 denarii 7
Act 2:45 they sold their possessions and goods 7
4:34 as many as were possessors of lands . . sold them 10
34 brought the proceeds of what was sold 7
37 sold a field which belonged to him 10
5: 1 Anani'as . . sold a piece of property 10
4 after it was sold, was it not at your disposal? 7
8 Tell me whether you sold the land for so much. 5
7: 9 the patriarchs . . sold him into Egypt 5
Rom 7:14 but I am carnal, sold under sin. 7
1Co 10:25 Eat whatever is sold in the meat market 10
Heb 12:16 who sold his birthright for a single meal. 5
Rev 13:17 that no one can buy or sell unless he has the mark 10
2Es 16:41 Let him that sells be like one who will flee 11
Tob 1: 7 a second tenth I would sell 6
Jdt 7:25 God has sold us into their hands 9
Wis 10:13 When a righteous man was sold 7
Sir 27: 2 sin is wedged in between selling and buying. 8
37:11 with a buyer about selling 8
Bar 4: 6 you were sold to the nations 7
LJr 1:28 The priests sell the sacrifices 5
1Mc 1:15 sold themselves to do evil. 7
12:36 so that its garrison could neither buy nor sell. 10
13:49 to buy and sell 10
2Mc 4:32 other vessels, as it happened, he had sold to Tyre 7
5:14 as many were sold into slavery as were slain 7
24 to sell the women and boys as slaves. 10
8:10 by selling the captured Jews into slavery. •
14 Others sold all their remaining property 10
14 to rescue those who had been sold 7
10:21 and accused these men of having sold their brethren 7

seller 1. מכר
Neh 13:20 merchants and sellers of all kinds of wares 1
Isa 24: 2 as with the buyer, so with the seller; 1
Ezk 7:12 Let not the buyer rejoice, nor the seller mourn 1
13 the seller shall not return to what he has sold 1

seller of purple goods 1. πορφυρόπωλις
Act 16:14 Lydia . . a seller of purple goods 1

semblance 1. דְּמוּת
Ezk 10:21 and underneath . . the semblance of human hands. 1

human semblance 1. אִישׁ
Isa 52:14 appearance . . marred, beyond human semblance 1

semen 1. שִׁכְבַת זֶרַע
Gen 38: 9 he spilled the semen on the ground •
Lev 15:16 if a man has an emission of semen, he shall bathe 1
17 garment and every skin on which the semen comes 1
18 lies with a woman and has an emission of semen 1
32 and for him who has an emission of semen 1
22: 4 a man who has had an emission of semen 1

senate 1. γερουσία
Act 5:21 the council and all the senate of Israel 1
Jdt 4: 8 the senate of the whole people of Israel 1
11:14 to bring back to them permission from the senate. 1
15: 8 the senate of the people of Israel 1
1Mc 12: 6 the senate of the nation, the priests 1
2Mc 1:10 the senate and Judas 1
4:44 three men sent by the senate presented the case 1
11:27 King Antiochus to the senate of the Jews 1
senate *See also* chamber.

senator 1. βουλεύω 2. γέρων
1Mc 8:15 every day 320 senators constantly deliberate 1
2Mc 6: 1 the king sent an Athenian senator 2

send 1. בוא 2. הלך 3. יצא 4. לקח 5. מִשְׁלוֹחַ 6. נתן 7. עבר 8. שׁלח 9. שׁלח (A) 10. ἀναπέμπω 11. ἀποστέλλω 12. ἀπόστολος 13. γράφω 14. διαπέμπω 15. εἰσπέμπω 16. ἐνίημι 17. ἐξαποστέλλω 18. ἐπαποστέλλω 19. μεταπέμπω 20. παρά 21. παρίστημι 22. πέμπω 23. προπέμπω

24. προσαποστέλλω 25. συμπέμπω
26. συναποστέλλω 27. dimitto 28. do 29. emitto
30. immitto 31. mitto

Gen 19:13 and the LORD has sent us to destroy it. 8
29 God remembered Abraham, and sent Lot out 8
20: 2 And Abim'elech king of Gerar sent and took Sarah. 8
24: 7 he will send his angel before you 8
40 LORD . . will send his angel with you and prosper 8
27:42 she sent and called Jacob her younger son 8
45 then I will send, and fetch you from there. 8
31: 4 Jacob sent and called Rachel and Leah 8
32: 3 Jacob sent messengers before him to Esau 8
5 I have sent to tell my lord, in order that I may find 8
18 they are a present sent to my lord Esau; 8
37:13 Come, I will send you to them. 8
14 he sent him from the valley of Hebron 8
32 they sent the long robe with sleeves 8
38:17 He answered, "I will send you a kid from the flock. 8
17 Will you give me a pledge, till you send it? 8
20 When Judah sent the kid by his friend 8
23 you see, I sent this kid, and you could not find her 8
41: 8 and he sent and called for all the magicians 8
14 Then Pharaoh sent and called Joseph 8
42: 4 Jacob did not send Benjamin, Joseph's brother 8
16 Send one of you, and let him bring your brother 8
43: 4 If you will send our brother with us, we will go 8
5 if you will not send him, we will not go down 8
8 Judah said to Israel his father, "Send the lad 8
45: 5 for God sent me before you to preserve life. 8
7 God sent me before you to preserve for you 8
8 it was not you who sent me here, but God; 8
23 To his father he sent as follows: ten asses loaded 8
27 he saw the wagons which Joseph had sent to carry 8
46: 5 carried . . in the wagons which Pharaoh had sent 8
28 He sent Judah before him to Joseph, to appear 8
Exd 2: 5 saw the basket . . and sent her maid to fetch it. 8
3:10 Come, I will send you to Pharaoh that you may bring 8
12 this shall be the sign for you, that I have sent you 8
13 The God of your fathers has sent me to you,' 8
14 Say this . . 'I AM has sent me to you.' 8
15 God of Isaac, and the God of Jacob, has sent me to you 8
4:13 he said, "Oh, my Lord, send, I pray, some other person. 8
28 the words of the LORD with which he had sent him 8
5:22 O LORD . . Why didst thou ever send me? 8
7:16 The LORD, the God of the Hebrews, sent me to you 8
8:21 behold, I will send swarms of flies on you 8
9: 7 Pharaoh sent, and behold, not one of the cattle 8
14 For this time I will send all my plagues upon 8
19 therefore send, get your cattle and all that you 8
23 the LORD sent thunder and hail, and fire ran down 6
27 Then Pharaoh sent, and called Moses and Aaron 8
12:33 urgent . . to send them out of the land in haste; 8
23:20 Behold, I send an angel before you, to guard you 8
27 I will send my terror before you, and will throw 8
28 I will send hornets before you, which shall drive 8
24: 5 he sent young men of the people of Israel 8
33: 2 I will send an angel before you, and I will drive 8
12 know whom thou wilt send with me. Yet thou hast 8
Lev 26:25 I will send pestilence among you, and you shall be 8
36 I will send faintness into their hearts 1
Num13: 2 Send men to spy out the land of Canaan 8
2 each tribe of their fathers shall you send a man 8
3 Moses sent them from the wilderness of Paran 8
16 men whom Moses sent to spy out the land. 8
17 Moses sent them to spy out the land of Canaan 8
27 told him, "We came to the land to which you sent us; 8
14:36 men whom Moses sent to spy out the land 8
16:12 Moses sent to call Dathan and Abi'ram 8
28 Hereby you shall know that the LORD has sent me 8
29 then the LORD has not sent me. 8
20:14 Moses sent messengers from Kadesh to the king 8
16 sent an angel and brought us forth out of Egypt; 8
21: 6 LORD sent fiery serpents among the people 8
21 Then Israel sent messengers to Sihon king 8
32 Moses sent to spy out Jazer; 8
22: 5 sent messengers to Balaam the son of Be'or 8
10 Balak the son of Zippor, king of Moab, has sent to me 8
15 Once again Balak sent princes, more in number 8
37 Did I not send to you to call you? 8
40 Balak . . sent to Balaam and to the princes 8
24:12 Did I not tell your messengers whom you sent to me 8
31: 4 send 1,000 from each of the tribes of Israel to the war 8
6 Moses sent them to the war, 1,000 from each tribe 8
32: 8 your fathers when I sent them from Ka'desh-bar'nea 8
Deu 1:22 'Let us send men before us, that they may explore 8
2:26 I sent messengers from the wilderness 8
7:20 LORD your God will send hornets among them 8
9:23 when the LORD sent you from Ka'desh-bar'nea, 8
19:12 elders . . shall send and fetch him from there 8
24: 1 sends her out of his house, and she departs 8
3 dislikes her . . and sends her out of his house 8
28:20 LORD will send upon you curses, confusion 8
48 your enemies whom the LORD will send against you 8
32:24 I will send the teeth of beasts against them 8
34:11 signs . . which the LORD sent him to do in the land 8
Jos 1:16 and wherever you send us we will go. 8
2: 1 And Joshua . . sent two men secretly from Shittim 8
3 Then the king of Jericho sent to Rahab, saying 8
6:17 because she hid the messengers that we sent. 8
25 messengers whom Joshua sent to spy out Jericho. 8
7: 2 Joshua sent men from Jericho to Ai . . and said 8
22 Joshua sent messengers, and they ran to the tent; 8
10: 3 Ado'ni-ze'dek king of Jerusalem sent . . saying 8
6 And the men of Gibeon sent to Joshua . . in Gilgal 8
11: 1 When Jabin . . he sent to Jobab king of Madon 8
14: 7 Moses . . sent me from Ka'desh-bar'nea to spy out 8
11 as strong . . as I was in the day that Moses sent me; 8
22:13 Israel sent to the Reubenites . . Phin'ehas 8
24: 5 And I sent Moses and Aaron, and I plagued Egypt 8
9 and he sent and invited Balaam . . to curse you 8
12 I sent the hornet before you, which drove them out 8
Jdg 3:15 The people of Israel sent tribute by him to Eglon 8
4: 6 She sent and summoned Barak the son of Abin'o-am 8
6: 8 the LORD sent a prophet to the people of Israel; 8
14 Go . . and deliver Israel . . do not I send you? 8
35 And he sent messengers throughout all Manas'seh; 8
35 And he sent messengers to Asher, Zeb'ulun 8
7: 8 he sent all the rest of Israel every man to his 8
24 Gideon sent messengers throughout all the hill 8
9:23 God sent an evil spirit between Abim'elech 8
31 he sent messengers to Abim'elech at Aru'mah 8
11:12 Then Jephthah sent messengers to the king 8
14 Jephthah sent messengers again to the king 8
17 Israel then sent messengers to the king of Edom 8
17 And they sent also to the king of Moab, but he would 8
19 Israel then sent messengers to Sihon king 8
28 the message of Jephthah which he sent to him. 8
38 And he said, "Go." And he sent her away 8
13: 8 let the man of God whom thou didst send come again 8
16:18 When Deli'lah saw . . she sent and called 8
18: 2 the Danites sent five able men from the whole 8
19:29 divided her . . and sent her throughout all 8
20: 6 and sent her throughout all . . Israel; 8
12 tribes of Israel sent men through all the tribe 8
21:10 the congregation sent thither 12,000 8
13 the whole congregation sent word 8
1Sm 4: 4 the people sent to Shiloh, and brought . . the ark 8
5: 8 So they sent and gathered together all the lords 8
10 So they sent the ark of God to Ekron. 8
11 They sent . . and gathered together all the lords 8
6: 2 Tell us with what we shall send it to its place. 8
3 If you send away the ark . . do not send it empty 8
21 So they sent messengers to the inhabitants 8
9:16 I will send to you a man from the land of Benjamin 8
26 Up, that I may send you on your way. 8
11: 3 Give . . respite that we may send messengers 8
7 sent them through . . all the territory of Israel 8
12: 8 the LORD sent Moses and Aaron, who brought forth 8
11 the LORD sent Jerubba'al and Barak, and Jephthah 8
17 call . . the LORD, that he may send thunder and rain; 6
18 and the LORD sent thunder and rain that day; 6
15: 1 The LORD sent me to anoint you king over . . Israel; 8
18 And the LORD sent you on a mission, and said 8
20 have gone on the mission on which the LORD sent me 8
16: 1 and go; I will send you to Jesse the Bethlehemite 8
11 Send and fetch him; for we will not sit down till he 8
12 And he sent, and brought him in. Now he was ruddy 8
19 Saul sent messengers to Jesse, and said, "Send me 8
19 Send me David your son, who is with the sheep. 8
20 Jesse took . . and sent them by David his son 8
22 And Saul sent to Jesse, saying, "Let David remain 8
17:31 repeated them before Saul; and he sent for him. 4
18: 5 David . . was successful wherever Saul sent him; 8
19:11 Saul sent messengers to David's house to watch 8
14 when Saul sent messengers to take David, she said 8
15 Saul sent the messengers to see David, saying 8
20 Then Saul sent messengers to take David; 8
21 When it was told Saul, he sent other messengers 8
21 And Saul sent messengers again the third time 8
20:12 shall I not then send and disclose it to you? 8
21 I will send the lad, saying, 'Go, find the arrows.' 8
31 send and fetch him to me, for he shall surely die. 8
21: 2 no one know . . of the matter about which I send you 8
22:11 the king sent to summon Ahim'elech the priest 8
25: 5 David sent ten young men; 8
14 David sent messengers . . to salute our master; 8
25 did not see the young men of my lord, whom you sent. 8
32 the LORD . . who sent you this day to meet me! 8
39 David sent and wooed Ab'igail, to make her his wife. 8
40 David has sent us . . to take you to him as his wife. 8
30:26 David . . sent part of the spoil to his friends 8
31: 9 and sent messengers throughout the land 8
2Sm 2: 5 David sent messengers to . . Ja'besh-gil'ead 8
3:12 Abner sent messengers to David at Hebron, saying 8
14 David sent messengers to Ish-bo'sheth Saul's son 8
15 Ish-bo'sheth sent, and took her from her husband 8
26 When Jo'ab came . . he sent messengers after Abner 8
5:11 And Hiram king of Tyre sent messengers to David 8
8:10 To'i sent his son Joram to King David, to greet him 8
9: 5 Then King David sent and brought him 8
10: 2 David sent by his servants to console him 8
3 Do you think, because David has sent comforters 8
3 Has not David sent his servants to you to search 8
5 When it was told David, he sent to meet them 8
6 the Ammonites sent and hired the Syrians 8
7 when David heard . . he sent Jo'ab and all the host 8
16 Hadade'zer sent, and brought out the Syrians 8
11: 1 David sent Jo'ab, and his servants with him 8
3 And David sent and inquired about the woman. 8
4 David sent messengers, and took her; 8
5 and she sent and told David, "I am with child. 8
6 David sent word . . "Send me Uri'ah the Hittite. 8
6 Send me Uri'ah . . And Jo'ab sent Uri'ah to David. 8
14 David wrote . . and sent it by the hand of Uri'ah. 8
18 Jo'ab sent and told David . . about the fighting; 8
22 and told David all that Jo'ab had sent him to tell. 8
27 David sent and brought her to his house 8
12: 1 And the LORD sent Nathan to David. 8
25 LORD . . sent a message by Nathan the prophet; 8
27 Jo'ab sent messengers to David, and said 8
13: 7 Then David sent home to Tamar, saying, "Go 8
14: 2 Jo'ab sent to Teko'a, and fetched . . a wise woman 8
29 Then Ab'salom sent for Jo'ab, to send him to the king; 8
29 Then Ab'salom sent for Jo'ab, to send him to the king; 8
29 And he sent a second time, but Jo'ab would not come. 8
32 I sent word to you, 'Come here, that I may send you 8
32 Come here, that I may send you to the king 8
15:10 Ab'salom sent secret messengers throughout all 8
12 he sent for Ahith'opel the Gi'lonite 8
36 by them you shall send to me everything you hear. 8
17:16 Now therefore send quickly and tell David, 'Do not 8
18: 3 it is better that you send us help from the city. •
29 When Jo'ab sent your servant, I saw a great tumult 8
19:11 David sent this message to Zadok and Abi'athar 8
24:13 what answer I shall return to him who sent me. 8
15 the LORD sent a pestilence upon Israel 6
1Kg 1:44 the king has sent with him Zadok the priest 8
53 King Solomon sent, and they brought him down 8
2:25 So King Solomon sent Benai'ah the son of Jehoi'ada; 8
29 Solomon sent Benai'ah the son of Jehoi'ada, saying 8
36 the king sent and summoned Shim'e-i, and said to him 8
42 the king sent and summoned Shim'e-i, and said to him 8
5: 1 Hiram king of Tyre sent his servants to Solomon 8
2 Solomon sent word to Hiram 8
8 Hiram sent to Solomon, saying, "I have heard 8
8 I have heard the message which you have sent to me; 8
14 he sent them to Lebanon . . in relays; 8
7:13 King Solomon sent and brought Hiram from Tyre. 8
8:44 go . . by whatever way thou shalt send them 8
9:14 Hiram had sent to the king 120 talents of gold. 8
27 Hiram sent with the fleet his servants 8
12: 3 they sent and called him; and Jerobo'am . . came 8
18 Then King Rehobo'am sent Ador'am 8
20 they sent and called him to the assembly 8
15:18 Asa sent them to Ben-ha'dad the son of Tabrim'mon 8
19 I am sending to you a present of silver and gold; 8
20 Ben-ha'dad . . sent the commanders of his armies 8
17:14 until the day that the LORD sends rain 6
18: 1 Go . . to Ahab; and I will send rain upon the earth. 6
10 no nation or kingdom whither my lord has not sent 8
19 send and gather all Israel to me at Mount Carmel 8
20 So Ahab sent to all the people of Israel 8
19: 2 Then Jez'ebel sent a messenger to Eli'jah saying 8
20: 2 he sent messengers into the city to Ahab 8
5 'I sent to you, saying, "Deliver to me your silver 8
6 I will send my servants to you tomorrow 8
7 he sent to me for my wives and my children 8
10 Ben-ha'dad sent to him and said 8
21: 8 she sent the letters to the elders and the nobles 8
11 the men of his city . . did as Jez'ebel had sent word 8
11 written in the letters which she had sent to them 8
14 they sent to Jez'ebel, saying 8
2Kg 1: 2 he sent messengers, telling them, "Go, inquire 8
6 Go back to the king who sent you, and say to him 8
6 that you are sending to inquire of Ba'al-ze'bub 8
9 the king sent to him a captain of 50 men 8
11 the king sent to him another captain of 50 men 8
13 Again the king sent the captain of a third 50 8
16 Because you have sent messengers to inquire 8
2: 2 the LORD has sent me as far as Bethel. 8
4 tarry here . . the LORD has sent me to Jericho. 8
6 the LORD has sent me to the Jordan. 8
16 And he said, "You shall not send. 8
17 when they urged him . . he said, "Send. 8
17 he said, "Send." They sent therefore 50 men; 8
3: 7 he went and sent word to Jehosh'aphat 8
4:22 Send me one of the servants and one of the asses 8
5: 5 I will send a letter to the king of Israel. 8
6 know that I have sent to you Na'aman my servant 8
7 this man sends word to me to cure a man 8
8 when Eli'sha . . he sent to the king, saying, "Why 8
10 Eli'sha sent a messenger to him, saying, "Go and wash 8
22 he said, "All is well. My master has sent me to say 8
6: 9 the man of God sent word to the king of Israel 8
10 the king of Israel sent to the place 8
13 and see where he is, that I may send and seize him. 8
14 he sent . . horses and chariots and a great army; 8
32 see how this murderer has sent to take off my head? 8
7:13 Let some men take . . let us send and see. 8
14 the king sent them after the army of the Syrians 8
8: 9 Your son Ben-ha'dad king of Syria has sent me to you 8
9:17 and send to meet them, and let him say, 'Is it peace?' 8
10: 1 Jehu wrote letters, and sent them to Sama'ria 8
5 So he who was over the palace, and . . sent to Jehu 8
7 put their heads in baskets, and sent them to him 8
21 Jehu sent throughout all Israel; 8

11: 4 Jehoi'ada sent and brought the captains 8
12:18 king of Judah took . . and sent these to Haz'ael 8
14: 8 Then Amazi'ah sent messengers to Jeho'ash 8
9 Jeho'ash king of Israel sent word to Amazi'ah 8
9 A thistle on Lebanon sent to a cedar on Lebanon 8
19 But they sent after him to Lachish, and slew him 8
15:37 to send Rezin . . and Pekah . . against Judah. 8
16: 7 So Ahaz sent messengers to Tig'lath-pile'ser 8
8 and sent a present to the king of Assyria. 8
10 King Ahaz sent to Uri'ah . . a model of the altar 8
11 all that King Ahaz had sent from Damascus 8
17: 4 he had sent messengers to So, king of Egypt 8
13 all the law . . which I sent to you by my servants 8
25 the LORD sent lions among them, which killed some 8
26 therefore he has sent lions among them 8
27 Send there one of the priests . . you carried away 2
18:14 Hezeki'ah . . sent to the king of Assyria 8
17 the king of Assyria sent the Tartan, the Rab'saris 8
27 Has my master sent me to speak these words 8
19: 2 he sent Eli'akim . . and Shebna the secretary 8
4 whom his master . . has sent to mock the living God 8
9 when the king heard . . he sent messengers again 8
16 words of Sennach'erib, which he has sent to mock 8
20 Isaiah the son of Amoz sent to Hezeki'ah, saying 8
20:12 Mero'dach-bal'adan . . sent envoys with letters 8
22: 3 the king sent Shaphan . . to the house of the LORD 8
15 says the LORD . . 'Tell the man who sent you to me 8
18 king of Judah, who sent you to inquire of the LORD 8
23: 1 the king sent, and all . . were gathered to him. 8
16 and he sent and took the bones out of the tombs 8
24: 2 the LORD sent against him bands of the Chalde'ans 8
2 and sent them against Judah to destroy it 8
1Ch 10: 9 sent messengers throughout the land 8
14: 1 Hiram king of Tyre sent messengers to David 8
18:10 he sent his son Hador'am to King David, to greet him 8
10 he sent all sorts of articles of gold, of silver •
19: 2 David sent messengers to console him 8
3 because David has sent comforters to you 8
5 When David was told . . he sent to meet them 8
6 Hanun and the Ammonites sent 1,000 talents 8
8 he sent Jo'ab and all the army of the mighty men. 8
16 sent messengers and brought out the Syrians 8
21:12 what answer I shall return to him who sent me. 8
14 the LORD sent a pestilence upon Israel; 6
15 God sent the angel to Jerusalem to destroy it; 8
2Ch 2: 3 Solomon sent word to Huram the king of Tyre 8
3 dealt with David my father and sent him cedar 8
7 now send me a man skilled to work in gold, silver 8
8 Send me also cedar, cypress, and algum timber 8
11 answered in a letter which he sent to Solomon 8
13 Now I have sent a skilled man . . Huram-abi. 8
15 lord has spoken, let him send to his servants; 8
6:34 go out . . by whatever way thou shalt send them 8
7:13 When I . . or send pestilence among my people 8
8:18 Huram sent him . . ships and servants familiar 8
10: 3 they sent and called him; 8
18 Then King Rehobo'am send Hador'am 8
16: 2 sent them to Ben-ha'dad king of Syria 8
3 behold, I am sending to you silver and gold; 8
4 sent the commanders of his armies against 8
17: 7 In the third year of his reign he sent his princes 8
24:19 sent prophets . . to bring them back to the LORD; 8
23 sent all their spoil to the king of Damascus. 8
25:15 LORD . . sent him a prophet, who said to him 8
17 Amazi'ah . . took counsel and sent to Jo'ash 8
18 Jo'ash the king of Israel sent word to Amazi'ah 8
18 A thistle on Lebanon sent to a cedar on Lebanon 8
27 they sent after him to Lachish, and slew him there. 8
28:16 King Ahaz sent to the king of Assyria for help. 8
30: 1 Hezeki'ah sent to all Israel and Judah 8
32: 9 Sennach'erib . . sent his servants to Jerusalem 8
21 LORD sent an angel, who cut off all the mighty 8
31 sent to him to inquire about the sign 8
34: 8 sent Shaphan the son of Azali'ah, and Ma-asei'ah 8
22 Hilki'ah and those whom the king had sent went 31
23 Thus says the LORD . . 'Tell the man who sent you 8
26 king of Judah, who sent you to inquire of the LORD 8
29 king sent and gathered together all the elders 8
35:21 he sent envoys to him, saying, "What have we to do 8
36:10 Nebuchadnez'zar sent and brought him to Babylon 8
15 LORD . . sent persistently to them 8
Ezr 4:11 copy of the letter that they sent-"To Ar-ta-xerx'es 8
11 Your servants . . send greeting. And now •
14 therefore we send and inform the king 9
17 king sent an answer: "To Rehum the commander 9
18 letter which you sent to us has been plainly read 9
5: 6 copy of the letter . . sent to Darius the king; 9
7 sent him a report, in which was written as follows 9
17 let the king send us his pleasure in this matter. 9
6:13 according to the word sent by Darius the king 9
7:14 sent by the king and his seven counselors 9
8:16 Then I sent for Elie'zer, Ar'i-el, Shemai'ah, 8
17 sent them to Iddo, the leading man at . . Casiphi'a 3
17 to send us ministers for the house of our God. 1
Neh 2: 5 send me to Judah . . that I may rebuild it. 8
6 it pleased the king to send me; and I set him a time. 8
9 Now the king had sent with me officers of the army 8
6: 2 Sanbal'lat and Geshem sent to me, saying, "Come 8
3 I sent messengers to them, saying, "I am doing 8
4 sent to me four times in this way and I answered 8
5 Sanbal'lat for the fifth time sent his servant 8
8 Then I sent to him, saying, "No such things as you say 8
12 I understood, and saw that God had not sent him 8
17 nobles of Judah sent many letters to Tobi'ah 2
19 Tobi'ah sent letters to make me afraid. 8
8:10 send portions to him for whom nothing 8
12 send portions and to make great rejoicing 8
Est 1:22 he sent letters to all the royal provinces 8
3:13 Letters were sent by couriers to . . provinces 8
4: 4 she sent garments to clothe Mor'decai 8
5:10 and he sent and fetched his friends and his wife 8
8:10 and letters were sent by mounted couriers 8
9:19 they send choice portions to one another. 5
20 and sent letters to all the Jews who were 8
22 days for sending choice portions to one another 5
30 Letters were sent to all the Jews . . in words 8
Job 1: 4 they would send and invite their three sisters 8
5 Job would send and sanctify them 8
5:10 upon the earth and sends waters upon the fields; 8
20:23 God will send his fierce anger into him 8
Ps 20: 2 May he send you help from the sanctuary 8
57: 3 He will send from heaven and save me 8
59: 0 of David, when Saul sent men to watch his house 8
68:33 lo, he sends forth his voice, his mighty voice. 6
78:25 he sent them food in abundance. 8
45 He sent among them swarms of flies 8
105:17 he had sent a man ahead of them, Joseph 8
20 The king sent and released him 8
26 sent Moses his servant, and Aaron 8
28 He sent darkness, and made the land dark; 8
106:15 but sent a wasting disease among them. 8
111: 9 He sent redemption to his people; 8
135: 9 sent signs and wonders against Pharaoh 8
Prv 10:26 so is the sluggard to those who send him. 8
17:11 cruel messenger will be sent against him. 8
22:21 that you may give a true answer to those who sent 8
25:13 faithful messenger to those who send him 8
26: 6 He who sends a message by the hand of a fool 8
Isa 6: 8 the voice of the Lord saying, "Whom shall I send 8
8 who will go for us?" Then I said, "Here am I! Send me. 8
9: 8 The Lord has sent a word against Jacob 8
10: 6 Against a godless nation I send him 8
16 the LORD of hosts, will send wasting sickness 8
16: 1 They have sent lambs to the ruler of the land 8
18: 2 which sends ambassadors by the Nile 8
19:20 when they cry . . he will send them a savior 8
20: 1 the commander in chief, who was sent by Sargon 8
36: 2 the king of Assyria sent the Rab'shakeh 8
12 Has my master sent me to speak these words 8
37: 2 he sent Eli'akim, who was over the household 8
4 king of Assyria has sent to mock the living God 8
9 when he heard it, he sent messengers to Hezeki'ah 8
17 words . . which he has sent to mock the living God. 8
21 Isaiah the son of Amoz sent to Hezeki'ah, saying 8
39: 1 king of Babylon, sent envoys with letters 8
42:19 or deaf as my messenger whom I send? 8
43:14 I will send to Babylon and break down all the bars 8
48:16 And now the Lord GOD has sent me and his Spirit. 8
55:11 and prosper in the thing for which I sent it. 8
57: 9 you sent your envoys far off 8
61: 1 he has sent me to bind up the brokenhearted 8
66:19 from them I will send survivors to the nations 8
Jer 1: 7 for to all to whom I send you you shall go 8
2:10 or send to Kedar and examine with care; 8
7:25 I have persistently sent all my servants 8
8:17 For behold, I am sending among you serpents 8
9:16 and I will send the sword after them 8
17 send for the skilful women to come; 8
14: 3 Her nobles send their servants for water; 8
14 I did not send them, nor did I command them 8
15 prophesy in my name although I did not send them 8
15: 1 Send them out of my sight, and let them go! 8
16:16 I am sending for many fishers, says the LORD 8
16 and afterwards I will send for many hunters 8
17:16 I have not pressed thee to send evil •
19:14 Topheth, where the LORD had sent him to prophesy 8
21: 1 when King Zedeki'ah sent to him Pashhur 8
23:21 I did not send the prophets, yet they ran; 8
32 when I did not send them or charge them; 8
38 when I sent to you, saying, "You shall not say 8
24:10 will send sword, famine, and pestilence upon them 8
25: 4 although the LORD persistently sent to you 8
9 behold, I will send for all the tribes of the north 8
15 make all the nations to whom I send you drink it. 8
16 the sword which I am sending among them. 8
17 all the nations to whom the Lord sent me 8
27 because of the sword which I am sending among you. 8
26: 5 the prophets whom I send to you urgently 8
12 The LORD sent me to prophesy against this house 8
15 for in truth the LORD sent me to you to speak 8
22 Then King Jehoi'akim sent to Egypt certain men 8
27: 3 Send word to the king of Edom, the king of Moab 8
15 I have not sent them, says the LORD 8
28: 9 that the LORD has truly sent the prophet. 8
15 Listen, Hanani'ah, the LORD has not sent you 8
29: 1 the letter which Jeremiah the prophet sent 8
3 The letter was sent by the hand of Ela'sah 8
3 whom Zedeki'ah king of Judah sent to Babylon 8
9 I did not send them, says the LORD. 8
17 I am sending on them sword, famine, and pestilence 8
19 which I persistently sent to you by my servants 8
25 You have sent letters in your name 8
28 For he has sent to us in Babylon, saying 8
31 Send to all the exiles, saying, 'Thus says the LORD 8
31 has prophesied to you when I did not send him 8
35:15 I have sent to you all my servants the prophets 8
15 the prophets, sending them persistently, saying 8
36:14 all the princes sent Jehu'di the son of Nethani'ah 8
21 Then the king sent Jehu'di to get the scroll 8
37: 3 King Zedeki'ah sent Jehu'cal the son of Shelemi'ah 8
7 king of Judah who sent you to me to inquire of me. 8
17 King Zedeki'ah sent for him, and received him. 8
38:14 King Zedeki'ah sent for Jeremiah the prophet 8
39:14 sent and took Jeremiah from the court 8
40:14 Ba'alis . . has sent Ish'mael the son of Nethani'ah 8
42: 5 word with which the LORD your God sends you to us. 8
6 the LORD our God to whom we are sending you 8
9 to whom you sent me to present your supplication 8
20 you sent me to the LORD your God, saying, 'Pray 8
21 in anything that he sent me to tell you. 8
43: 1 with which the LORD their God had sent him to them 8
2 The LORD our God did not send you to say 8
10 I will send and take Nebuchadrez'zar the king 8
44: 4 Yet I persistently sent to you all my servants 8
48:12 when I shall send to him tilters who will tilt him 8
49:14 and a messenger has been sent among the nations 8
37 I will send the sword after them 8
51: 2 I will send to Babylon winnowers 8
Lam 1:13 From on high he sent fire; into my bones . . descend; 8
Ezk 2: 3 Son of man, I send you to the people of Israel 8
4 I send you to them; and you shall say to them 8
3: 5 For you are not sent to a people of foreign speech 8
6 if I sent you to such, they would listen to you. 8
5:17 I will send famine and wild beasts against you 8
13: 6 'Says the LORD,' when the LORD has not sent them 8
14:13 break its staff of bread and send famine upon it 8
19 Or if I send a pestilence into that land 8
21 I send upon Jerusalem my four sore acts 8
17:15 he rebelled against him by sending ambassadors 8
23:16 and sent messengers to them in Chalde'a. 8
40 They even sent for men to come from far 8
40 far, to whom a messenger was sent, and lo, they came. 8
28:23 for I will send pestilence into her, and blood 8
39: 6 I will send fire on Magog 8
Dan 3: 2 Nebuchadnez'zar sent to assemble the satraps 9
28 sent his angel and delivered his servants 9
5:24 Then from his presence the hand was sent 9
6:22 My God sent his angel and shut the lions' mouths 9
10:11 stand upright, for now I have been sent to you. 8
11:20 one who shall send an exactor of tribute 7
Hos 5:13 went to Assyria, and sent to the great king. 8
8:14 but I will send a fire upon his cities 8
Jol 2:19 Behold, I am sending to you grain, wine, and oil 8
25 my great army, which I sent among you. 8
Ams 1: 4 I will send a fire upon the house of Haz'ael 8
7 I will send a fire upon the wall of Gaza 8
10 I will send a fire upon the wall of Tyre 8
12 I will send a fire upon Teman 8
2: 2 I will send a fire upon Moab, and it shall devour 8
5 I will send a fire upon Judah 8
4:10 I sent among you a pestilence after the manner 8
7:10 Amazi'ah the priest of Bethel sent to Jerobo'am 8
8:11 when I will send a famine on the land; 8
Obd 1: 1 and a messenger has been sent among the nations 8
Mic 6: 4 and I sent before you Moses, Aaron, and Miriam. 8
Hag 1:12 the prophet, as the LORD their God had sent him; 8
Zec 1:10 These are they whom the LORD has sent to patrol 8
2: 8 after his glory sent me to the nations 8
9 you will know that the LORD of hosts has sent me. 8
11 know that the LORD of hosts has sent me to you. 8
4: 9 know that the LORD of hosts has sent me to you. 8
6:15 you shall know that the LORD of hosts has sent me 8
7: 2 Now the people of Bethel had sent Share'zer 8
12 law and the words which the LORD of hosts had sent 8
Mal 2: 2 then I will send the curse upon you 8
4 So shall you know that I have sent this command 8
3: 1 I send my messenger to prepare the way before me 8
4: 5 Behold, I will send you Eli'jah the prophet 8
Mat 2: 8 he sent them to Bethlehem, saying, "Go and search 22
16 furious rage, and he sent and killed all the male 11
10:40 and he who receives me receives him who sent me. 11
11: 2 he sent word by his disciples 22
10 'Behold, I send my messenger before thy face 11
13:41 The Son of man will send his angels 11
14:10 he sent and had John beheaded in the prison 22
35 they sent round to all that region 11
15:24 I was sent only to the lost sheep 11
20: 2 he sent them into his vineyard. 11
21: 1 then Jesus sent two disciples 11
3 he will send them immediately. 11
34 he sent his servants to the tenants 11
36 Again he sent other servants, more than the first; 11
37 Afterward he sent his son to them, saying 11
22: 3 sent his servants to call those who were invited 11
4 Again he sent other servants, saying 11
7 sent his troops and destroyed those murderers 22
16 And they sent their disciples to him 11

23:34 I send you prophets and wise men and scribes 11
37 stoning those who are sent to you! 11
26:53 he will at once send me more than twelve legions 21
27:19 his wife sent word to him 11
Mrk 1: 2 Behold, I send my messenger before thy face 11
3:31 standing outside they sent to him and called 11
5:10 not to send them out of the country. 11
12 Send us to the swine, let us enter them. 22
6:17 For Herod had sent and seized John 11
27 immediately the king sent a soldier of the guard 11
9:37 receives not me but him who sent me. 11
11: 1 he sent two of his disciples 11
3 will send it back here immediately.' 11
12: 2 he sent a servant to the tenants 11
4 Again he sent to them another servant 11
5 he sent another, and him they killed 11
6 finally he sent him to them, saying 11
13 they sent to him some of the Pharisees 11
14:13 he sent two of his disciples, and said to them, "Go 11
Lke 1:19 I was sent to speak to you 11
26 the angel Gabriel was sent from God 11
4:18 has sent me to proclaim release to the captives 11
26 Eli'jah was sent to none of them 22
43 I was sent for this purpose. 11
7: 3 he sent to him elders of the Jews 11
6 the centurion sent friends to him, saying to him 22
10 those who had been sent returned to the house 22
19 sent them to the Lord, saying, "Are you he 22
20 John the Baptist has sent us to you, saying 11
27 Behold, I send my messenger before thy face 11
9:48 whoever receives me receives him who sent me 11
52 he sent messengers ahead of him 11
10: 1 and sent them on ahead of him, 2 by 2 11
16 he who rejects me rejects him who sent me. 11
11:49 I will send them prophets and apostles 11
13:34 stoning those who are sent to you 11
14:17 at the time for the banquet he sent his servant 11
32 he sends an embassy and asks terms of peace. 11
15:15 who sent him into his fields to feed swine. 22
16:24 send Laz'arus to dip the end of his finger in water 22
27 I beg you, father, to send him to my father's house 22
19:14 sent an embassy after him, saying, 'We do not want 11
29 he sent two of the disciples 11
32 So those who were sent went away 11
20:10 he sent a servant to the tenants 11
11 he sent another servant 22
12 he sent yet a third 22
13 I will send my beloved son 22
20 So they watched him, and sent spies 11
22: 8 So Jesus sent Peter and John, saying, "Go 11
24:49 behold, I send the promise of my Father upon you; 11
Joh 1: 6 was a man sent from God, whose name was John. 11
19 Jews sent priests and Levites from Jerusalem 11
22 Let us have an answer for those who sent us. 22
24 Now they had been sent from the Pharisees. 11
33 but he who sent me to baptize with water said to me 22
3:17 For God sent the Son into the world 11
28 I am not the Christ, but I have been sent before him. 11
34 For he whom God has sent utters the words of God 11
4:34 My food is to do the will of him who sent me 22
38 I sent you to reap that for which you did not labor; 11
5:23 does not honor the Father who sent him. 22
24 he who hears my word and believes him who sent me 22
30 but the will of him who sent me. 22
33 You sent to John 11
36 bear me witness that the Father has sent me. 11
37 the Father who sent me has himself borne witness 22
38 for you do not believe him whom he has sent. 11
6:29 that you believe in him whom he has sent. 11
38 not . . own will, but the will of him who sent me; 22
39 this is the will of him who sent me 22
44 unless the Father who sent me draws him 22
57 As the living Father sent me 11
7:16 My teaching is not mine, but his who sent me; 22
18 he who seeks the glory of him who sent him is true 22
28 he who sent me is true, and him you do not know. 22
29 I know him, for I come from him, and he sent me. 11
32 the chief priests and Pharisees sent officers 11
33 then I go to him who sent me; 22
8:16 it is not I alone that judge, but I and he who sent me. 22
18 the Father who sent me bears witness to me. 22
26 he who sent me is true 22
29 he who sent me is with me; he has not left me alone 22
42 I came not of my own accord, but he sent me. 11
9: 4 work the works of him who sent me, while it is day; 22
7 Go, wash in the pool of Silo'am" (which means Sent) 11
10:36 the Father consecrated and sent into the world 11
11: 3 the sisters sent to him, saying 11
42 they may believe that thou didst send me. 11
12:44 believes not in me but in him who sent me. 22
45 he who sees me sees him who sent me. 22
49 the Father who sent me 22
13:16 nor is he who is sent greater than he who sent him. 12
16 nor is he who is sent greater than he who sent him. 22
20 he who receives any one whom I send receives me; 22
20 he who receives me receives him who sent me. 22
14:24 the word . . is not mine but the Father's who sent me. 22
26 Holy Spirit, whom the Father will send in my name 22
15:21 because they do not know him who sent me. 22
26 whom I shall send to you from the Father 22
16: 5 now I am going to him who sent me 22
7 if I go, I will send him to you. 22
17: 3 Jesus Christ whom thou hast sent. 11
8 they have believed that thou didst send me. 11
18 As thou didst send me into the world 11
18 so I have sent them into the world. 11
21 the world may believe that thou hast sent me. 11
23 so that the world may know that thou hast sent me 11
25 these know that thou hast sent me. 11
18:24 Annas then sent him bound to Ca'iaphas 11
20:21 As the Father has sent me, even so I send you. 11
21 As the Father has sent me, even so I send you. 22
Act 3:20 he may send the Christ appointed for you, Jesus 11
26 sent him to you first, to bless you 11
5:21 sent to the prison to have them brought. 11
7:14 Joseph sent and called to him Jacob his father 11
34 now come, I will send you to Egypt.' 11
35 God sent as both ruler and deliverer 11
8:14 they sent to them Peter and John 11
9:17 the Lord Jesus . . has sent me 11
38 the disciples . . sent two men to him entreating 11
10: 5 now send men to Joppa 22
8 he sent them to Joppa. 11
17 behold, the men that were sent by Cornelius 11
20 I have sent them. 11
22 Cornelius . . was directed . . to send for you 19
29 So when I was sent for, I came without objection 19
29 I ask then why you sent for me. 19
32 Send therefore to Joppa and ask for Simon 22
33 So I sent to you at once 22
36 You know the word which he sent to Israel 11
11:11 three men arrived . . sent to me from Caesare'a. 11
13 'Send to Joppa and bring Simon called Peter; 11
22 they sent Barnabas to Antioch. 17
29 the disciples determined . . to send relief 22
30 they did so, sending it to the elders 11
12:11 Now I am sure that the Lord has sent his angel 17
13:15 rulers of the synagogue sent to them, saying 11
26 sent the message of this salvation. 17
15:22 send them to Antioch with Paul and Barnabas 22
22 They sent Judas called Barsab'bas, and Silas •
25 to choose men and send them to you 22
27 We have therefore sent Judas and Silas 11
33 sent off . . to those who had sent them. 11
16:35 when it was day, the magistrates sent the police 11
36 The magistrates have sent to let you go 11
19:22 having sent into Macedo'nia two of his helpers 11
31 some of the A'si-archs . . sent to him 22
20: 1 Paul sent for the disciples 19
17 from Mile'tus he sent to Ephesus 22
23:30 I sent him to you at once 22
24:24 he sent for Paul 19
26 So he sent for him often and conversed with him. 19
25: 3 to have the man sent to Jerusalem 19
21 until I could send him to Caesar. 10
25 I decided to send him. 22
27 seems to me unreasonable, in sending a prisoner 22
26:17 from the Gentiles–to whom I send you 11
28:28 salvation of God has been sent to the Gentiles; 11
Rom 8: 3 sending his own Son in the likeness of sinful 22
10:15 And how can men preach unless they are sent? 11
1Co 1:17 For Christ did not send me to baptize 11
4:17 Therefore I sent to you Timothy 22
16: 3 when I arrive, I will send those whom you accredit 22
2Co 1:16 and have you send me on my way to Judea. 23
8:18 With him we are sending the brother who is famous 25
22 with them we are sending our brother 25
9: 3 I am sending the brethren 22
12:17 through any of those whom I sent to you? 11
18 I urged Titus to go, and sent the brother with him. 26
Gal 4: 6 God has sent the Spirit of his Son into our hearts 17
Eph 6:22 I have sent him to you for this very purpose 22
Php 2:19 hope in the Lord Jesus to send Timothy to you soon 22
23 I hope therefore to send him 22
25 I have thought it necessary to send to you 22
28 I am the more eager to send him, therefore 22
4:16 for even in Thessaloni'ca you sent me help once 22
18 having received from Epaphrodi'tus the gifts you sent 20
Col 4: 8 I have sent him to you for this very purpose 22
1Th 3: 2 we sent Timothy, our brother and God's servant 22
5 I sent that I might know your faith 22
2Th 2:11 Therefore God sends upon them a strong delusion 22
2Ti 4:12 Tych'icus I have sent to Ephesus. 11
Tit 3:12 When I send Artemas or Tych'icus to you 22
Phm 1:12 sending him back to you, sending my very heart. •
1Pe 1:12 through the Holy Spirit sent from heaven 11
2:14 or to governors as sent by him to punish 22
1Jn 4: 9 that God sent his only Son into the world 11
10 sent his Son to be the expiation for our sins. 11
14 Father has sent his Son as the Savior of the world 11
3Jn 1: 6 You will do well to send them on their journey 23
Rev 1: 1 he made it known by sending his angel 11
11 in a book and send it to the seven churches 22
22: 6 the Lord . . sent his angel to show his servants 11
16 I Jesus have sent my angel to you 22
1Es 1:27 I was not sent against you by the Lord God 17
45 Nebuchadnezzar sent and removed him to Babylon 11
50 the God of their fathers sent by his messenger 11
2:26 I have read the letter which you sent me 22
3:14 Then he sent and summoned all the nobles 17
4:57 to be done and to be sent to Jerusalem. 17
5: 2 Darius sent with them 1,000 horsemen 26
6: 7 wrote and sent to Darius 11
8:19 whatever Ezra . . sends for 11
43 I sent word to Eliezar, Iduel, Maasmas 11
46 to send us men to serve as priests 11
9:51 send portions to those who have none; 11
2Es 1:23 I did not send fire upon you for your blasphemies 28
32 I sent to you my servants the prophets 31
2:18 I will send you help 31
4: 1 Then the angel that had been sent to me 31
3 I have been sent to show you three ways 31
52 I was not sent to tell you concerning your life 31
5:31 the angel . . was sent to me 31
6:33 Therefore he sent me to show you all these things 31
7: 1 the angel who had been sent to me 31
1 the angel . . was sent to me again 31
104 Just as now a father does not send his son 31
14: 4 I sent him and led my people out of Egypt 31
22 send the Holy Spirit into me 30
15:50 when the heat rises that is sent upon you. 29
16: 8 The Lord God sends calamities 31
16 the calamities that are sent upon the earth 29
19 tribulation and anguish are sent as scourges 27
60 to send rivers from the heights to water the earth; 29
Tob 2:12 She used to send the product to the owners 11
3:17 Raphael was sent to heal the two of them 11
8:12 Send one of the maids to see whether he is alive 11
12:14 now God sent me to heal you 11
20 I am ascending to him who sent me 11
Jdt 1: 7 sent to all who lived in Persia 11
3: 1 they sent messengers to sue for peace, and said 11
4: 4 they sent to every district of Samaria 11
6: 3 He will send his forces and will destroy them 11
7:18 they sent some of their men toward the south 11
32 The women and children he sent home 11
8:10 she sent her maid 11
31 the Lord will send us rain to fill our cisterns 11
9: 9 send thy wrath upon their heads 11
11: 7 who had sent you to direct every living soul 11
14 They have sent men to Jerusalem 11
16 God has sent me to accomplish with you things 11
19 it was announced to me, and I was sent to tell you. 11
22 God has done well to send you before the people 11
12: 6 sent to Holofernes and said 11
14: 5 sent him to us as if to his death. 11
15: 4 Uzziah sent men to Betomasthaim and Bebai 11
AEs 16:17 letters sent by Haman the son of Hammedatha 11
Wis 9:10 from the throne of thy glory send her 22
17 and sent thy holy Spirit from on high? 22
12: 8 didst send wasps as forerunners of thy army 11
25 thou didst send thy judgment to mock them. 22
16: 3 because of the odious creatures sent to them 18
18 consume the creatures sent against the ungodly 11
Sir 15: 9 for it has not been sent from the Lord. 11
34: 6 Unless they are sent from the Most High 11
48:18 Sennacherib came up, and sent the Rabshakeh 11
Bar 1: 7 they sent it to Jerusalem to Jehoiakim the high 11
10 Herewith we send you money; so buy with the money 11
14 you shall read this book which we are sending you 11
21 in all the words of the prophets whom he sent to us 11
2:20 For thou hast sent thy anger and thy wrath upon us 16
LJr 1: 1 A copy of a letter which Jeremiah sent 11
63 the fire sent from above to consume mountains 17
Sus 1:29 Send for Susanna, the daughter of Hilkiah 11
30 So they sent for her. And she came 11
Bel 1:37 Take the dinner which God has sent you. 11
1Mc 1:29 the king sent . . a chief collector of tribute 11
44 the king sent letters by messengers to Jerusalem 11
3:27 sent and gathered all the forces of his kingdom 11
35 Lysias was to send a force against them 11
39 and sent with them 40,000 infantry 11
5:10 sent to Judas and his brothers a letter 11
38 Judas sent men to spy out the camp 11
48 Judas sent them this friendly message 11
6:12 I sent to destroy the inhabitants of Judah 17
60 he sent to the Jews an offer of peace 11
7: 7 Now then send a man whom you trust 11
9 he sent him, and with him the ungodly Alcimus 11
10 he sent messengers to Judas and his brothers 11
19 he sent and seized many of the men 11
26 the king sent Nicanor, one of his honored princes 11
27 treacherously sent . . this peaceable message 11
8:10 they sent a general against the Greeks 11
17 sent them to Rome to establish friendship 11
20 sent us to you to establish alliance and peace 11
22 sent to Jerusalem to remain with them there 11
9: 1 he sent Bacchides and Alcimus 11
35 Jonathan sent his brother as leader 11
60 secretly sent letters to all his allies in Judea 11
70 he sent ambassadors to him to make peace with him 11
10: 3 Demetrius sent Jonathan a letter 11
15 promises which Demetrius had sent to Jonathan 11
17 he wrote a letter and sent it to him 11
20 he sent him a purple robe and a golden crown 11
25 he sent a message to them in the following words 11
51 Then Alexander sent ambassadors to Ptolemy 11

69 Then he sent the following message to Jonathan 11
89 he sent to him a golden buckle 11
11: 9 He sent envoys to Demetrius the king, saying, "Come 11
17 sent it to Ptolemy. 11
41 Jonathan sent to Demetrius the king the request 11
42 Demetrius sent this message to Jonathan 11
43 you will do well to send me men who will help me 11
44 So Jonathan sent 3,000 stalwart men 11
58 he sent him gold plate and a table service 11
62 sent them to Jerusalem 17
12: 1 he chose men and sent them to Rome 11
2 He also sent letters to the same effect 11
3 sent us to renew the former friendship 11
7 Already in time past a letter was sent to Onias 11
10 undertaken to send to renew our brotherhood 11
10 since you sent your letter to us. 11
16 sent them to Rome to renew our former friendship 11
19 a copy of the letter which they sent to Onias 11
26 He sent spies to their camp 11
34 the men whom Demetrius had sent 20
49 Trypho sent troops and cavalry into Galilee 11
13:11 He sent Jonathan the son of Absalom to Joppa 11
14 so he sent envoys to him and said 11
16 Send now 100 talents of silver 11
17 he sent to get the money and the sons 22
18 Because Simon did not send him the money 11
19 So he sent the sons and the 100 talents 11
21 the men in the citadel kept sending envoys to Trypho 11
21 to send them food. 11
25 Simon sent and took the bones of Jonathan 11
34 Simon also chose men and sent them to Demetrius 11
35 Demetrius the king sent him a favorable reply 11
37 the palm branch which you sent 11
14: 2 he sent one of his commanders to take him alive. 11
20 a copy of the letter which the Spartans sent 11
21 The envoys who were sent to our people 11
23 they have sent a copy of this to Simon the high priest.' 13
24 After this Simon sent Numenius to Rome 11
15: 1 sent a letter from the islands of the sea to Simon 11
17 They had been sent by Simon the high priest 11
24 They also sent a copy of these things to Simon 13
26 Simon sent to Antiochus 2,000 picked men 11
28 He sent to him Athenobius, one of his friends 11
16:18 wrote a report . . and sent it to the king 11
18 asking him to send troops to aid him 11
19 He sent other men to Gazara to do away with John 11
19 he sent letters to the captains 11
20 he sent other men to take possession of Jerusalem 11
21 he has sent men to kill you also. 11
2Mc 1:20 sent the descendants of the priests 22
2:15 send people to get them for you. 11
3: 7 sent him with commands to effect the removal 11
38 send him there 22
4:19 the vile Jason sent envoys 11
21 When Apollonius . . was sent to Egypt 11
23 Jason sent Menelaus 11
44 three men sent by the senate presented the case 22
5:18 whom Seleucus . . sent to inspect the treasury. 22
24 Antiochus sent Apollonius 22
6: 1 the king sent an Athenian senator 17
23 telling them to send him to Hades. 23
8: 9 sent him, in command of no fewer than 20,000 11
11 he immediately sent to the cities on the seacoast 11
11: 6 to send a good angel to save Israel. 11
13 So he sent to them 24
17 John and Absalom, who were sent by you 22
32 I have also sent Menelaus to encourage you. 22
34 The Romans also sent them a letter 22
36 send some one promptly 22
37 Therefore make haste and send some men 22
12:43 sent it to Jerusalem 11
13:20 Judas sent in to the garrison whatever was necessary. 15
14:19 Therefore he sent Posidonius and Theodotus 22
27 to send Maccabeus to Antioch as a prisoner 17
39 sent more than 500 soldiers to arrest him; 11
15:22 thou didst send thy angel in the time of Hezekiah 11
23 now, O Sovereign of the heavens, send a good angel 11
31 he sent for those who were in the citadel. 19
3Mc 1: 8 Since the Jews had sent some of their council 14
3:25 you are to send to us those who live among you 11
5:11 the Lord sent upon the king a portion of sleep 11
42 he would send them to death without delay 22
4Mc 12: 6 he sent for the boy's mother 19
151 1: 4 It was he who sent his messenger and took me 17

send a letter 1. ἐπιστέλλω
Act 21:25 we have sent a letter with our judgment 1

send a message 1. צוה
Gen 50:16 they sent a message to Joseph 1

send a messenger 1. ἐξαποστέλλω
Tob 10: 8 I will send messengers to your father 1

send a plague 1. נגף
Exd 32:35 the LORD sent a plague upon the people 1

send a reply 1. ἀντιφωνέω
1Mc 12:18 now please send us a reply to this. 1

send abroad 1. עבר 2. שלח
Lev 25: 9 Then you shall send abroad the loud trumpet 1
9 on the day of atonement you shall send abroad 1
1Ch 13: 2 let us send abroad to our brethren 2

send across 1. עבר
Gen 32:23 He took them and sent them across the stream 1

send an order 1. παραγγέλλω
1Mc 9:63 and sent orders to the men of Judea. 1

send around 1. סבב
2Ch 13:13 sent an ambush around to come on them from behind; 1

send away 1. שִׁלּוּחִים 2. שלח 3. ἀπολύω 4. ἀποστέλλω 5. ἀποστρέφω 6. ἐκβάλλω 7. ἐκπέμπω 8. ἐξαποστέλλω
Gen 21:14 Abraham . . sent her away. And she departed 2
24:59 they sent away Rebekah their sister 2
25: 6 and while he was still living he sent them away 2
26:27 you hate me and have sent me away from you? 2
29 good and have sent you away in peace. 2
28: 5 Thus Isaac sent Jacob away; 2
6 blessed Jacob and sent him away to Paddan-aram 2
30:25 Send me away, that I may go to my own home 2
31:27 I might have sent you away with mirth and songs 2
42 you would have sent me away empty-handed. 2
44: 3 the men were sent away with their asses. 2
45:24 Then he sent his brothers away 2
Exd 18: 2 had taken Zippo'rah . . after he had sent her away 1
Lev 16:10 that it may be sent away into the wilderness 2
21 the goat, and send him away into the wilderness 2
Deu 24: 4 former husband, who sent her away, may not take her 2
Jos 2:21 Then she sent them away, and they departed; 2
22: 6 Joshua blessed them, and sent them away; 2
7 Joshua sent them away to their homes and blessed 2
24:28 Joshua sent the people away, every man to his 2
Jdg 3:18 he sent away the people that carried the tribute 2
1Sm 5:11 Send away the ark of the God of Israel 2
6: 3 If you send away the ark . . do not send it empty 2
10:25 Then Samuel sent all the people away 2
20:13 and send you away, that you may go in safety. 2
22 if I say . . then go; for the LORD has sent you away. 2
2Sm 3:21 David sent Abner away; and he went in peace. 2
22 he had sent him away, and he had gone in peace. 2
24 Abner came . . why is it that you have sent him away 2
10: 4 took David's servants . . and sent them away. 2
13:16 this wrong in sending me away is greater 2
1Kg 8:66 On the eighth day he sent the people away; 2
2Kg 5:24 and he sent the men away, and they departed. 2
6:23 when they had eaten and drunk, he sent them away 2
1Ch 8: 8 he had sent away Hushim and Ba'ara his wives. 2
12:19 Philistines took counsel and sent him away 2
19: 4 cut off their garments . . and sent them away. 2
2Ch 7:10 he sent the people away to their homes, joyful 2
Job 14:20 changest his countenance, and sendest him away. 2
22: 9 You have sent widows away empty 2
Jer 3: 8 I had sent her away with a decree of divorce; 2
24: 5 from Judah, whom I have sent away from this place 2
29:20 whom I sent away from Jerusalem to Babylon 2
Mat 8:31 cast us out, send us away into the herd of swine. 4
14:15 send the crowds away to go into the villages 3
15:23 Send her away, for she is crying after us. 3
32 I am unwilling to send them away hungry 3
39 sending away the crowds, he got into the boat 3
Mrk 1:43 sternly charged him, and sent him away at once 6
6:36 send them away, to go into the country 3
8: 3 if I send them away hungry to their homes 3
10 And he sent them away; 3
26 he sent him away to his home, saying 4
12: 3 beat him, and sent him away empty-handed. 4
Lke 1:53 the rich he has sent empty away. 8
8:38 but he sent him away 3
9:12 Send the crowd away, to go into the villages 3
20:10 the tenants . . sent him away empty-handed. 8
11 and sent him away empty-handed. 8
Act 17:10 The brethren immediately sent Paul and Silas away 7
22:21 I will send you far away to the Gentiles.' 8
Tob 5:17 Why have you sent our child away? 8
10:11 when he had blessed them he sent them away, saying 8
Sir 29: 9 because of his need do not send him away empty. 5
Bar 4:11 I sent them away with weeping and sorrow. 8
37 Behold, your sons are coming, whom you sent away; 8
Sus 1:21 and this was why you sent your maids away. 8
1Mc 12:46 he sent away the troops 8

send back 1. שוב 2. שלח 3. ἀναπέμπω 4. ἀναστρέφω 5. ἐκπέμπω 6. ἐξαποστέλλω
Gen 24:54 Send me back to my master. 2
43:14 may send back your other brother and Benjamin. 2
1Sm 29: 4 Send the man back, that he may return to the place 1
2Ch 25:13 the men of the army whom Amazi'ah sent back 1
28:11 send back the captives from your kinsfolk 1
Jer 37:20 do not send me back to the house of Jonathan 1
38:26 he would not send me back to the house of Jonathan 1
Lke 23:11 he sent him back to Pilate. 3
15 neither did Herod, for he sent him back to us. 3
Phm 1:12 I am sending him back to you 3
1Es 4:44 to send back all the vessels that were taken 5
44 vowed to send them back there. 6
57 he sent back from Babylon all the vessels 6
Tob 10: 7 At that time Tobias said to Raguel, "Send me back 6
9 Tobias replied, "No, send me back to my father. 6
Jdt 1:11 they sent back his messengers empty-handed 4
3Mc 6:27 Send them back to their homes in peace 6

send directions 1. προσφωνέω
1Es 6:22 let him send us directions 1

send down 1. ירד 2. שפל
Isa 57: 9 your envoys far off, and sent down even to Sheol. 2
Ezk 32:18 over the multitude of Egypt, and send them down 1
34:26 I will send down the showers in their season; 1

send driving 1. κατασπεύδω
Sir 43:13 By his command he sends the driving snow 1

send forth 1. יצא 2. שלח 3. ἀποστέλλω 4. ἐξαποστέλλω 5. ἠχέω 6. προπέμπω 7. emitto 8. mitto
Gen 3:23 the LORD God sent him forth from the garden 2
8: 7 sent forth a raven; and it went to and fro 2
8 Then he sent forth a dove from him 2
10 again he sent forth the dove out of the ark; 2
12 sent forth the dove; and she did not return 2
Exd 15: 7 thou sendest forth thy fury, it consumes them 2
Jos 8: 3 Joshua . . and sent them forth by night. 2
9 Joshua sent them forth; and they went to the place 2
2Sm 18: 2 And David sent forth the army 2
Job 21:11 They send forth their little ones like a flock 2
38:35 Can you send forth lightnings, that they may go 2
Ps 57: 3 God will send forth his steadfast love 2
104:30 thou sendest forth thy Spirit, they are created; 2
107:20 he sent forth his word, and healed them 2
110: 2 LORD sends forth from Zion your mighty scepter. 2
147:15 He sends forth his command to the earth; 2
18 He sends forth his word, and melts them; 2
Isa 48:20 proclaim it, send it forth to the end of the earth; 1
Ezk 31: 4 sending forth its streams to all the trees 2
Zec 5: 4 I will send it forth, says the LORD of hosts 1
Act 7:12 he sent forth our fathers the first time. 4
Gal 4: 4 God sent forth his Son 4
Heb 1:14 all ministering spirits sent forth to serve 3
2Es 13:10 I saw only how he sent forth from his mouth 7
16:14 Behold, calamities are sent forth 8
Jdt 16:14 Thou didst send forth thy Spirit 3
Wis 9:10 Send her forth from the holy heavens 4
19: 2 and hastily sent them forth 6
Sir 45: 9 to send forth a sound as he walked 5
Bar 3:33 he who sends forth the light, and it goes, called it 3
LJr 1:60 . . stars, shining and sent forth for service 3

send forth fragrance 1. εὐωδιάζω
Sir 39:14 send forth fragrance like frankincense 1

send greetings 1. ἀσπάζομαι 2. χαίρω
1Co 16:19 The churches of Asia send greetings 1
19 send you hearty greetings in the Lord. 1
20 All the brethren send greetings 1
2Ti 4:21 Eubu'lus sends greetings to you 1
Tit 3:15 All who are with me send greetings to you 1
Phm 1:23 Ep'aphras . . sends greetings to you 1
Heb 13:24 Those who come from Italy send you greetings. 1
1Pe 5:13 She who is at Babylon . . sends you greetings; 1
2Mc 9:19 Antiochus . . sends hearty greetings 2

send home 1. שלח
1Sm 13: 2 the rest of the people he sent home 1

send into exile 1. גלה
1Ch 6:15 the LORD sent Judah and Jerusalem into exile 1
Jer 29: 4 to all the exiles whom I have sent into exile 1
7 the city where I have sent you into exile 1
14 to the place from which I sent you into exile. 1
Ezk 39:28 because I sent them into exile among the nations 1

send off 1. שלח 2. ἀπολύω 3. ἐξαποστέλλω 4. προεξαποστέλλω
1Sm 6: 8 Then send it off, and let it go its way. 1
Act 9:30 and sent him off to Tarsus. 3
13: 3 they laid their hands on them and sent them off. 2
15:30 when they were sent off, they went down to Antioch; 2
33 they were sent off in peace by the brethren 2
17:14 the brethren . . sent Paul off on his way to the sea 3
2Mc 12:21 he sent off the women and the children 4
14:12 appointed him governor of Judea, and sent him off 3
3Mc 4: 4 were they being sent off, all together, by the generals 3

send on a mission 1. διαπέμπω
2Mc 3:37 to send on another mission to Jerusalem 1

send on one's way 1. προπέμπω
Act 15: 3 being sent on their way by the church 1

send out 1. יצא 2. שלח 3. ἀποστέλλω 4. ἐκβάλλω 5. ἐκπέμπω 6. ἐξαποστέλλω

Exd 6: 1 for with a strong hand he will send them out 2
Jos 18: 4 Provide three men . . and I will send them out 2
1Sm 26: 4 David sent out spies, and learned of a certainty 2
2Sm 13: 9 Amnon said, "Send out every one from me. 1
22:15 And he sent out arrows, and scattered them; 2
1Kg 20:17 Ben-ha'dad sent out scouts, and they reported 2
2Kg 9:19 Then he sent out a second horseman 2
Job 12:15 if he sends them out, they overwhelm the land. 2
Ps 18:14 he sent out his arrows, and scattered them; 2
43: 3 Oh send out thy light and thy truth; 2
80:11 it sent out its branches to the sea 2
144: 6 send out thy arrows and rout them! 2
Prv 9: 3 She has sent out her maids to call 2
Jer 17: 8 like a tree . . that sends out its roots by the stream 2
Mat 9:38 to send out laborers into his harvest. 4
10: 5 These twelve Jesus sent out, charging them 3
16 Behold, I send you out as sheep 3
24:31 he will send out his angels with a loud trumpet 3
Mrk 3:14 he appointed twelve . . to be sent out to preach 3
6: 7 began to send them out two by two 3
13:27 then he will send out the angels 3
Lke 9: 2 he sent them out to preach the kingdom of God 3
10: 2 to send out laborers into his harvest. 4
3 I send you out as lambs in the midst of wolves. 3
22:35 When I sent you out with no purse or bag or sandals 3
Act 13: 4 being sent out by the Holy Spirit 5
Jas 2:25 when she . . sent them out another way? 4
Rev 5: 6 seven spirits of God sent out into all the earth; 3
1Es 4: 4 if he sends them out against the enemy, they go 6
Bar 4:23 For I sent you out with sorrow and weeping 5

send out against 1. ἐπαποστέλλω
Sir 28:23 will be sent out against them like a lion 1

send over 1. ἀναπέμπω
Lke 23: 7 he sent him over to Herod 1

send rain 1. מטר 2. βρέχω
Gen 7: 4 For in seven days I will send rain upon the earth 1
Ams 4: 7 I would send rain upon one city, and send no rain 1
7 upon one city, and send no rain upon another city; 1
Mat 5:45 and sends rain on the just and on the unjust. 2

send to spy out 1. תור
Jdg 1:23 And the house of Joseph sent to spy out Bethel. 1

send up 1. שׂוּם 2. ἀνυψόω
Ezk 20:28 there they sent up their soothing odors 1
Sir 51: 9 I sent up my supplication from the earth 2

send upon 1. ἐπαποστέλλω 2. ἐπιπέμπω 3. immitto
2Es 15:49 I will send evils upon you, widowhood, poverty 3
16: 3 The sword has been sent upon you 3
4 A fire has been sent upon you 3
5 Calamities have been sent upon you 3
Wis 11:15 thou didst send upon them . . irrational creatures 1
17 to send upon them a multitude of bears 2

send word 1. שׁלח 2. διαπέμπω 3. ὑποσημαίνω
Gen 38:25 she sent word to her father-in-law 1
2Sm 11: 6 David sent word to Jo'ab, "Send me Uri'ah 1
19:14 they sent word to the king, "Return, both you and all 1
1Es 1:26 the king of Egypt sent word to him saying 2
6: 6 until word could be sent to Darius 3
Jdt 14:12 they sent word to their commanders 2
2Mc 11:26 You will do well, therefore, to send word to them 2

sender 1. ἀποστέλλω
2Mc 4:20 this money was intended by the sender for . . Hercules 1

senior 1. זָקֵן
2Kg 19: 2 Shebna the secretary, and the senior priests 1
Isa 37: 2 and Shebna the secretary, and the senior priests 1
Jer 19: 1 of the people and some of the senior priests 1

sense 1. לֵב 2. שֵׂכֶל 3. αἴσθησις 4. αἰσθητήριον 5. ἐπίγνωσις
Neh 8: 8 gave the sense, so that the people understood 2
Prv 6:32 He who commits adultery has no sense; 1
7: 7 I have seen . . a young man without sense 1
9: 4 To him who is without sense she says 1
16 to him who is without sense she says 1
10:13 but a rod is for the back of him who lacks sense. 1
21 but fools die for lack of sense. 1
11:12 He who belittles his neighbor lacks sense 1
12:11 follows worthless pursuits has no sense. 1
13:15 Good sense wins favor 2
15:21 Folly is a joy to him who has no sense 1
17:18 A man without sense gives a pledge, and becomes 1
24:30 I passed by . . the vineyard of a man without sense; 1
Ecc 10: 3 when the fool walks on the road, he lacks sense 1
Hos 7:11 E'phraim is like a dove, silly and without sense 1
LJr 1:42 they have no sense. 3
2Mc 9:11 to come to his senses under the scourge of God 5
4Mc 2:22 he enthroned the mind among the senses 4

good sense 1. שֵׂכֶל 2. σύνεσις 3. φρόνησις
Prv 12: 8 A man is commended according to his good sense 1
19:11 Good sense makes a man slow to anger 1
Sir 1:24 the lips of many will tell of his good sense. 2
25: 2 an adulterous old man who lacks good sense. 2
9 happy is he who has gained good sense 3

no sense 1. יאל
Jer 5: 4 I said, "These are only the poor, they have no sense; 1

sense of shame 1. αἰσχύνη
Sir 29:14 a man who has lost his sense of shame 1

sense of smell 1. ὄσφρησις
1Co 12:17 where would be the sense of smell? 1

same sense 1. ἰσοδυναμέω
Sir 0: 2 have exactly the same sense when translated 1

senseless 1. אֵין לֵב 2. לֹא חָכָם 3. נָבָל 4. ἀλόγιστος 5. ἀνόητος 6. ἀπαίδευτος 7. ἀσύνετος 8. ἀφρός
Deu 32: 6 requite . . you foolish and senseless people? 2
Job 30: 8 A senseless, a disreputable brood, 3
Jer 5:21 Hear this, O foolish and senseless people 1
Rom 1:21 and their senseless minds were darkened. 7
1Ti 6: 9 into many senseless and hurtful desires 5
2Ti 2:23 stupid, senseless controversies 6
Sir 16:23 a senseless and misguided man thinks foolishly. 8
3Mc 6:12 the senseless insolence of the lawless 4
4Mc 5: 9 It is senseless not to enjoy delicious things 5
8:17 O wretches that we are and so senseless! 5

senseless man 1. ἀνόητος
Sir 21:19 To a senseless man education is fetters 1

more senseless 1. ἀνόητος
4Mc 5:10 you will do something even more senseless 1

senselessly 1. ἄλογος
3Mc 6:25 senselessly gathered here 1

sensible 1. σώφρων 2. φρόνιμος
1Ti 3: 2 the husband of one wife, temperate, sensible 1
Tit 2: 2 Bid the older men be temperate, serious, sensible 1
5 to be sensible, chaste, domestic, kind 1
Tob 6:12 The girl is also beautiful and sensible 2
Wis 6:24 a sensible king is the stability of his people. 2
Sir 20:27 a sensible man will please great men. 2
22: 4 A sensible daughter obtains her husband 2
38: 4 a sensible man will not despise them. 2

sensible man 1. νοήμων 2. φρόνιμος
1Co 10:15 I speak as to sensible men; judge for yourselves 2
Sir 19:29 a sensible man is known by his face 1
21: 7 the sensible man, when he slips, is aware of it. 1
17 The utterance of a sensible man will be sought 2
21 To a sensible man education is like . . 2

sensibly 1. σύνεσις 2. σωφροσύνη
1Ti 2: 9 adorn themselves modestly and sensibly 2
Sir 13:22 he speaks sensibly, and receives no attention. 1

sensuous 1. σάρξ
Col 2:18 puffed up without reason by his sensuous mind 1

sentence 1. דָּבָר 2. מִשְׁפָּט 3. פִּתְגָם 4. דָּת פִּתְגָם (A) 5. פִּתְגָם (A) 6. ἀπάγω 7. ἀπόκριμα 8. διαθήκη 9. ἐπικρίνω 10. κρίμα 11. κρίσις 12. λόγος 13. φημί
2Kg 25: 6 king of Babylon . . who passed sentence upon him. 2
Ps 51: 4 so that thou art justified in thy sentence 1
Ecc 8:11 sentence against an evil deed is not executed 3
Jer 26:11 This man deserves the sentence of death 2
16 This man does not deserve the sentence of death 2
39: 5 and he passed sentence upon him. 2
52: 9 and he passed sentence upon him. 2
Ezk 23:45 on them with the sentence of adulteresses 2
45 and with the sentence of women that shed blood; 2
Dan 2: 9 dream known to me, there is but one sentence 4
4:17 The sentence is by the decree of the watchers 5
Mat 23:33 how are you to escape being sentenced to hell? 11
Rom 9:28 Lord will execute his sentence upon the earth 12
2Co 1: 9 felt that we had received the sentence of death 7
Sir 38:33 nor do they understand the sentence of judgment; 8
41: 2 O death, how welcome is your sentence 10
3 Do not fear the sentence of death 10
LJr 1:18 as though he were sentenced to death 6
Sus 1:55 angel of God has received the sentence from God 13
2Mc 4:47 while he sentenced to death those unfortunate men 9

sentence (2) 1. λόγος
Rom 13: 9 commandments . . are summed up in this sentence 1
sentence *See* give.

sentence against 1. καταδίκη
Act 25:15 asking for sentence against him. 1

sentence of condemnation 1. κρίμα
Lke 23:40 you are under the same sentence of condemnation? 1

sentinel 1. ἀκροφύλαξ
4Mc 3:13 Eluding the sentinels at the gates 1

sentry 1. בַּעַל פְּקִדוּת 2. φύλαξ
Jer 37:13 a sentry there named Iri'jah the son of Shelemi'ah 1
Act 5:23 the sentries standing at the doors 2
12: 6 sentries . . were guarding the prison; 2
19 he examined the sentries 2

separate 1. בדל 2. חָפְשִׁית 3. חצה 4. נָזִיר 5. נזר 6. פרד 7. תאם 8. תּוֹאַם 9. ἀποτέμνω 10. ἀποχωρέω 11. ἀποχωρίζω 12. ἀφορίζω 13. διαχωρίζω 14. χωρίζω 15. χωρίς 16. divido 17. divisio facio 18. separo
Gen 1: 4 and God separated the light from the darkness 1
6 firmament . . and let it separate the waters 1
7 God made the firmament and separated the waters 1
14 in . . the heavens to separate the day 1
18 to separate the light from the darkness. 1
13: 9 Separate yourself from me. 6
11 thus they separated from each other. 6
14 The LORD said to Abram, after Lot had separated 6
30:40 Jacob separated the lambs, and set the faces 6
49:26 brow of him who was separate from his brothers. 4
Exd 26:24 they shall be separate beneath, but joined 7
33 the veil shall separate for you the holy place 1
36:29 they were separate beneath, but joined at the top 8
Lev 20:24 your God, who have separated you from the peoples 1
26 I . . have separated you from the peoples 1
Num 6: 2 vow of a Nazirite, to separate himself to the LORD 5
3 separate himself from wine and strong drink; 5
5 for which he separates himself to the LORD 5
6 days that he separates himself to the LORD 5
12 separate himself to the LORD for the days 5
8:14 Thus you shall separate the Levites from among 1
16: 9 that the God of Israel has separated you 1
21 Separate yourselves from among this 1
31:42 Israel's half, which Moses separated from that 3
Deu 32: 8 when he separated the sons of men, he fixed 6
Jdg 4:11 Heber the Ken'ite had separated from the Ken'ites 6
1Kg 8:53 thou didst separate them from among all 1
2Kg 2:11 and horses of fire separated the two of them. 6
15: 5 he was a leper . . and he dwelt in a separate house. 2
2Ch 26:21 being a leper dwelt in a separate house 2
Ezr 6:21 every one who had . . separated himself 1
9: 1 not separated themselves from the peoples 1
10:11 separate yourselves from the peoples of the land 1
Neh 4:19 we are separated on the wall, far from one another. 6
9: 2 Israelites separated . . from all foreigners 1
10:28 separated themselves from the peoples 1
13: 3 separated from Israel all those of foreign 1
Job 41:17 they clasp each other and cannot be separated. 6
Prv 16:28 whisperer separates close friends. 6
Isa 56: 3 LORD will surely separate me from his people"; 1
Ezk 14: 7 who separates himself from me, taking his idols 5
Mat 13:49 and separate the evil from the righteous 12
25:32 he will separate them one from another 12
32 as a shepherd separates the sheep from the goats 12
Act 15:39 so that they separated from each other 11
Rom 8:35 Who shall separate us from the love of Christ? 14
39 will be able to separate us from the love of God 14
1Co 7:10 the wife should not separate from her husband 14
15 if the unbelieving partner desires to separate 14
2Co 6:17 come out from them, and be separate from them 12
Gal 2:12 when they came he drew back and separated 12
Eph 2:12 you were at that time separated from Christ 15
Heb 7:26 separated from sinners 14
1Es 7:13 all those who had separated themselves 14
9: 9 separate . . from the peoples of the land 14
2Es 6:41 command him to divide and separate the waters 17
50 thou didst separate one from the other 18
7:88 they shall be separated from their mortal body. 18
100after they have been separated from the bodies 18
11:24 behold, two little wings separated from the six 16
Wis 1: 3 For perverse thoughts separate men from God 14
Sir 12: 9 even his friend will separate from him. 13
25:26 separate her from yourself. 9
Sus 1:51 Separate them far from each other 13
52 When they were separated from each other 13
1Mc 1:11 since we separated from them 14
12:36 to separate it from the city 13
3Mc 2:33 those who separated themselves from them 10
separate *See also* keep.

separateness 1. χωρισμός
3Mc 3: 4 they kept their separateness with respect to foods. 1

separation 1. בדל 2. נֵזֶר 3. ἀμειξία
Num 6: 4 All the days of his separation he shall eat 2
5 All the days of his vow of separation no razor 2
7 because his separation to God is upon his head. 2
8 days of his separation he is holy to the LORD. 2
12 to the LORD for the days of his separation 2
12 be void, because his separation was defiled. 2
13 time of his separation has been completed 2
Isa 59: 2 a separation between you and your God 1

2Mc 14: 3 defiled himself in the times of separation 3
separation *See also* make.

sepulchre 1. קֶבֶר 2. *τάφος*
Gen 23: 6 Bury your dead in the choicest of our sepulchres; 1
6 none of us will withhold from you his sepulchre 1
Neh 2: 3 when the city, the place of my fathers' sepulchres 1
5 Judah, to the city of my fathers' sepulchres 1
3:16 point opposite the sepulchres of David 1
Ps 5: 9 their throat is an open sepulchre 1
Isa 14:19 you are cast out, away from your sepulchre 1
Mat 27:61 sitting opposite the sepulchre. 2
64 Therefore order the sepulchre to be made secure 2
66 So they went and made the sepulchre secure 2
28: 1 the other Mary went to see the sepulchre. 2
2Mc 12:39 the sepulchres of their fathers. 2

seraphim 1. שָׂרָף
Isa 6: 2 Above him stood the seraphim; each had six wings 1
6 flew one of the seraphim to me, having in his hand 1

serious 1. *βαρύς* 2. *σεμνός* 3. *χαλεπός*
Deu 15:21 blind, or has any serious blemish whatever •
Act 25: 7 bringing against him many serious charges 1
1Ti 3: 8 Deacons likewise must be serious 2
11 The women likewise must be serious 2
Tit 2: 2 Bid the older men be temperate, serious, sensible 2
2Mc 4: 4 Onias recognized that the rivalry was serious 3
seriously *See* consider.

equal seriousness 1. *ἰσοδύναμος*
4Mc 5:20 either small or great is of equal seriousness 1

serpent 1. זֹחֲלֵת 2. נָחָשׁ 3. שָׂרָף 4. תַּנִּין 5. *δράκων* 6. *ἑρπετόν* 7. *ὄφις*
Gen 3: 1 the serpent was more subtle 2
2 woman said to the serpent, "We may eat of the fruit 2
4 the serpent said to the woman, "You will not die. 2
13 The woman said, "The serpent beguiled me, and I ate. 2
14 The LORD God said to the serpent 2
49:17 Dan shall be a serpent in the way 2
Exd 4: 3 So he cast it on the ground, and it became a serpent; 2
7: 9 cast it down . . that it may become a serpent.' 4
10 cast down his rod . . and it became a serpent. 4
12 cast down his rod, and they became serpents. 4
15 take . . the rod which was turned into a serpent. 2
Num21: 6 LORD sent fiery serpents among the people 2
7 pray to the LORD, that he take away the serpents 2
8 Make a fiery serpent, and set it on a pole; 7
9 Moses made a bronze serpent, and set it on a pole; 2
9 if a serpent bit any man, he would look 2
9 man, he would look at the bronze serpent and live. 2
Deu 8:15 wilderness, with its fiery serpents 2
32:33 their wine is the poison of serpents 4
1Kg 1: 9 Adoni'jah sacrificed . . by the Serpent's Stone 1
2Kg 18: 4 broke . . the bronze serpent that Moses had made 2
Job 26:13 his hand pierced the fleeing serpent. 2
Ps 58: 4 They have venom like the venom of a serpent 2
91:13 young lion and the serpent you will trample 4
140: 3 They make their tongue sharp as a serpent's 2
Prv 23:32 At the last it bites like a serpent 2
30:19 way of a serpent on a rock, the way of a ship 2
Ecc 10: 8 a serpent will bite him who breaks through 2
11 If the serpent bites before it is charmed 2
Isa 14:29 from the serpent's root will come forth an adder 2
29 and its fruit will be a flying serpent. 3
27: 1 will punish Leviathan the fleeing serpent 2
1 Leviathan the twisting serpent 2
30: 6 the lion, the viper and the flying serpent 3
65:25 and dust shall be the serpent's food. 2
Jer 8:17 For behold, I am sending among you serpents 2
46:22 She makes a sound like a serpent gliding away; 2
Ams 5:19 hand against the wall, and a serpent bit him. 2
9: 3 I will command the serpent, and it shall bite 2
Mic 7:17 they shall lick the dust like a serpent 2
Mat 7:10 Or if he asks for a fish, will give him a serpent? 7
10:16 so be wise as serpents and innocent as doves. 7
23:33 You serpents, you brood of vipers 7
Mrk 16:18 they will pick up serpents 7
Lke 10:19 authority to tread upon serpents and scorpions 7
11:11 will instead of a fish give him a serpent; 7
Joh 3:14 as Moses lifted up the serpent in the wilderness 7
1Co 10: 9 destroyed by serpents; 7
2Co 11: 3 as the serpent deceived Eve by his cunning 7
Rev 9:19 their tails are like serpents, with heads 7
12: 9 ancient serpent, who is called the Devil 7
14 might fly from the serpent into the wilderness 7
15 The serpent poured water . . out of his mouth 7
20: 2 And he seized the dragon, that ancient serpent 7
Wis 11:15 led them astray to worship irrational serpents 6
16: 5 destroyed by the bites of writhing serpents 7
10 even by the teeth of venomous serpents 5
17: 9 the hissing of serpents 6
4Mc 18: 8 nor did the destroyer, the deceitful serpent 7
serpent *See also* bitten.

servant 1. אָמָה 2. נַעַר 3. עֶבֶד 4. עֲבֹדָה 5. צָעִיר 6. שִׁפְחָה 7. שׁרת 8. עֲבַד (A) 9. פלח (A) 10. *διάκονος* 11. *δουλεύω* 12. *δούλη* 13. *δοῦλος* 14. *θεραπεία* 15. *θεράπων* 16. *ἱερόδουλος* 17. *ἱκέτης* 18. *λειτουργός* 19. *οἰκέτης* 20. *παιδάριον* 21. *παῖς* 22. *συνεργός* 23. *ὑπηρέτης* 24. famula 25. puer 26. servus
Gen 14:15 he and his servants, and routed them and pursued 3
18: 3 favor in your sight, do not pass by your servant. 3
5 pass on-since you have come to your servant. 3
7 gave it to the servant, who hastened to prepare it 2
19: 2 I pray you, to your servant's house 3
19 behold, your servant has found favor 3
20: 8 Abim'elech . . called all his servants 3
21:25 water which Abim'elech's servants had seized 3
24: 2 Abraham said to his servant 3
5 servant said to him, "Perhaps the woman may not 3
9 the servant put his hand under the thigh 3
10 Then the servant took ten of his master's camels 3
14 thou hast appointed for thy servant Isaac. 3
17 Then the servant ran to meet her, and said 3
34 he said, "I am Abraham's servant. 3
52 When Abraham's servant heard their words 3
53 the servant brought forth jewelry of silver 3
59 sent away . . Abraham's servant and his men. 3
61 thus the servant took Rebekah, and went his way. 3
65 said to the servant, "Who is the man yonder 3
65 The servant said, "It is my master. 3
66 the servant told Isaac all the things 3
26:15 the wells which his father's servants had dug 3
19 when Isaac's servants dug in the valley 3
24 your descendants for my servant Abraham's sake. 3
25 And there Isaac's servants dug a well. 3
32 That same day Isaac's servants came and told him 3
27:37 all his brothers I have given to him for servants 3
32: 4 Thus says your servant Jacob, 'I have sojourned 3
10 which thou hast shown to thy servant 3
16 These he delivered into the hand of his servants 3
16 Jacob . . said to his servants, "Pass on before me 3
18 They belong to your servant Jacob; 3
20 you shall say, 'Moreover your servant Jacob is 3
33: 5 whom God has graciously given your servant. 3
14 Let my lord pass on before his servant 3
39:17 The Hebrew servant, whom you have brought 3
19 This is the way your servant treated me 3
40:20 made a feast for all his servants 3
20 head of the chief baker among his servants. 3
41:10 When Pharaoh was angry with his servants 3
12 with us, a servant of the captain of the guard; 3
37 seemed good to Pharaoh and to all his servants. 3
38 Pharaoh said to his servants, "Can we find such 3
42:10 lord, but to buy food have your servants come. 3
11 we are honest men, your servants are not spies. 3
13 said, "We, your servants, are twelve brothers 3
43:28 They said, "Your servant our father is well 3
44: 7 Far be it from your servants that they should do 3
9 With whomever of your servants it be found 3
16 God has found out the guilt of your servants; 3
18 O my lord, let your servant, I pray you 3
18 let not your anger burn against your servant; 3
19 My lord asked his servants, saying 3
21 you said to your servants, 'Bring him down to me 3
23 Then you said to your servants 3
24 When we went back to your servant my father 3
27 Then your servant my father said to us 3
30 when I come to your servant my father 3
31 and your servants will bring down the gray hairs 3
31 bring down the gray hairs of your servant 3
32 For your servant became surety for the lad 3
33 Now therefore, let your servant, I pray you 3
45:16 it pleased Pharaoh and his servants well. 3
46:34 you shall say, 'Your servants have been keepers 3
47: 3 said to Pharaoh, "Your servants are shepherds 3
4 for there is no pasture for your servants' flocks 3
4 let your servants dwell in the land of Goshen. 3
50: 2 Joseph commanded his servants the physicians 3
7 with him went up all the servants of Pharaoh 3
17 forgive the transgression of the servants 3
18 and said, "Behold, we are your servants. 3
Exd 4:10 since thou hast spoken to thy servant; 3
5:15 Why do you deal thus with your servants? 3
16 No straw is given to your servants, yet they say 3
16 And behold, your servants are beaten; 3
21 in the sight of Pharaoh and his servants 3
7:10 his rod before Pharaoh and his servants 3
20 Pharaoh and in the sight of his servants 3
8: 3 come up . . into the houses of your servants 3
4 you and on your people and on all your servants. 3
9 for you and your servants and for your people 3
11 depart from . . your servants and your people; 3
21 send swarms of flies on you and your servants 3
24 house of Pharaoh and into his servants' houses 3
29 swarms of flies may depart . . from his servants 3
31 removed the swarms of flies . . from his servants 3
9:14 plagues . . upon your servants and your people 3
20 word of the LORD among the servants of Pharaoh 3
30 as for you and your servants, I know that you do not 3
34 hardened his heart, he and his servants. 3
10: 1 hardened . . the heart of his servants 3
6 houses of all your servants and of all 3
7 Pharaoh's servants said to him, "How long shall 3
11: 3 in the sight of Pharaoh's servants 3
8 all these your servants shall come down to me 3
12:30 he, and all his servants, and all the Egyptians; 3
14: 5 the mind of Pharaoh and his servants was changed 3
31 they believed in the LORD and in his servant 3
24:13 So Moses rose with his servant Joshua 7
32:13 Remember Abraham, Isaac, and Israel, thy servants 3
33:11 his servant Joshua the son of Nun, a young man 7
Lev 25:42 For they are my servants, whom I brought forth 3
55 For to me the people of Israel are servants 3
55 they are my servants whom I brought forth 3
Num11:11 Why has thou dealt ill with thy servant? 3
12: 7 Not so with my servant Moses; he is entrusted 3
8 not afraid to speak against my servant Moses? 3
14:24 my servant Caleb . . I will bring into the land 3
22:18 Balaam . . said to the servants of Balak 3
22 his two servants were with him. 2
31:49 Your servants have counted the men of war 3
32: 4 land for cattle; and your servants have cattle. 3
5 land be given to your servants for a possession; 3
25 Your servants will do as my lord commands. 3
27 your servants will pass over, every man who 3
31 As the LORD has said to your servants, so we will do. 3
Deu 3:24 only begun to show thy servant thy greatness 3
5:15 remember that you were a servant in . . Egypt 3
9:27 Remember thy servants, Abraham, Isaac, and Jacob; 3
29: 2 LORD did . . to Pharaoh and to all his servants 3
32:36 LORD will . . have compassion on his servants 3
43 for he avenges the blood of his servants 3
34: 5 Moses the servant of the LORD died there 3
11 to do . . to Pharaoh and to all his servants 3
Jos 1: 1 After the death of Moses the servant of the LORD 3
2 Moses my servant is dead; now therefore arise 3
7 all the law which Moses my servant commanded you; 3
13 Moses the servant of the LORD commanded you 3
15 land which Moses the servant of the LORD gave you 3
5:14 What does my lord bid his servant? 3
8:31 as Moses the servant of the LORD had commanded 3
33 as Moses the servant of the LORD had commanded 3
9: 8 They said to Joshua, "We are your servants. 3
9 From a very far country your servants have come 3
11 We are your servants . . make a covenant with us. 3
24 it was told to your servants for a certainty 3
24 LORD . . had commanded his servant Moses to give 3
10: 6 Do not relax your hand from your servants; 3
11:12 as Moses the servant of the LORD had commanded. 3
15 As the LORD had commanded Moses his servant 3
12: 6 Moses, the servant of the LORD 3
6 and Moses the servant of the LORD gave their land 3
13: 8 as Moses the servant of the LORD gave them 3
14: 7 Moses the servant of the LORD sent me . . to spy out 3
18: 7 which Moses the servant of the LORD gave them. 3
22: 2 all that Moses the servant of the LORD commanded 3
4 which Moses the servant of the LORD gave you 3
5 which Moses the servant of the LORD commanded 3
24:29 Joshua the son of Nun, the servant of the LORD, died 3
Jdg 2: 8 Joshua the son of Nun, the servant of the LORD, died 3
3:24 When he had gone, the servants came; 3
6:27 Gideon took ten men of his servants, and did 3
7:10 down, go down to the camp with Purah your servant; 2
11 Then he went down with Purah his servant 2
15:18 great deliverance by the hand of thy servant; 3
19: 3 He had with him his servant and a couple of asses. 2
9 the man and his concubine and his servant rose up 2
11 and the servant said to his master, "Come now, let us 2
13 he said to his servant, "Come and let us draw near 2
19 and the young man with your servants; 3
Rut 2: 5 Bo'az said to his servant who was in charge 2
6 And the servant who was in charge . . answered 2
21 You shall keep close by my servants 2
1Sm 2:13 the priest's servant would come, while the meat 2
15 the priest's servant would come and say to the man 2
3: 9 you shall say, 'Speak, LORD, for thy servant hears.' 3
10 And Samuel said, "Speak, for thy servant hears. 3
8:14 take the best of . . and give them to his servants. 3
15 and give it to his officers and to his servants. 3
9: 3 Take one of the servants . . and arise, go and look 2
5 Saul said to his servant who was with him, "Come 2
7 Then Saul said to his servant, "But if we go, what can 2
8 The servant answered Saul again, "Here, I have 2
10 Saul said to his servant, "Well said; come, let us go. 2
22 took Saul and his servant and brought them 2
27 Tell the servant to pass on before us 2
10:14 said to him and to his servant, "Where did you go? 2
12:19 Pray for your servants to the LORD . . that we may 3
14:41 O LORD . . why hast thou not answered thy servant 26
16:15 Saul's servants said to him, "Behold now 3
16 command your servants, who are before you, to seek 3
17 Saul said to his servants, "Provide for me a man 3
17: 8 I . . a Philistine, and are you not servants of Saul? 3
9 If he is able to . . then we will be your servants; 3
9 you shall be our servants and serve us. 3
32 your servant will go and fight with this 3
34 Your servant used to keep sheep for his father; 3
36 Your servant has killed both lions and bears; 3
58 David answered, "I am the son of your servant Jesse 3
18: 5 and also in the sight of Saul's servants. 3
22 And Saul commanded his servants, "Speak to David 3
22 king has delight . . and all his servants love you; 3

23 Saul's servants spoke those words in the ears 3
24 And the servants of Saul told him 3
26 And when his servants told David these words 3
30 David had more . . than all the servants of Saul; 3
19: 1 Saul spoke to Jonathan . . and to all his servants 3
4 Let not the king sin against his servant David; 3
20: 7 If he says, 'Good!' it will be well with your servant; 3
8 Therefore deal kindly with your servant 3
8 you have brought your servant into a . . covenant 3
21: 7 a certain man of the servants of Saul was there 3
11 And the servants of A'chish said to him 3
14 said A'chish to his servants, "Lo . . the man is mad; 3
22: 6 and all his servants were standing about him. 3
7 Saul said to his servants who stood about him 3
8 that my son has stirred up my servant against me 3
9 Do'eg . . who stood by the servants of Saul 3
14 And who among all your servants is so faithful 3
15 Let not the king impute anything to his servant 3
15 your servant has known nothing of all this 3
17 But the servants of the king would not put forth 3
23:10 thy servant has surely heard that Saul seeks 3
11 Will Saul come down, as thy servant has heard? 3
11 O LORD . . I beseech thee, tell thy servant. 3
25: 8 give whatever you have at hand to your servants 3
10 Nabal answered David's servants, "Who is David? 3
10 There are many servants . . breaking away 3
27 this present which your servant has brought 6
39 has kept back his servant from evil; 3
40 the servants of David came to Ab'igail at Carmel 3
41 your handmaid is a servant to wash the feet 6
41 to wash the feet of the servants of my lord. 3
26:18 he said, "Why does my lord pursue after his servant? 3
19 let my lord . . hear the words of his servant. 3
27: 5 why should your servant dwell in the royal city 3
12 therefore he shall be my servant always. 3
28: 2 Very well, you shall know what your servant can 3
7 Saul said to his servants, "Seek out . . a medium 3
7 his servants said to him, "Behold, there is a medium 3
23 his servants, together with the woman, urged him; 3
25 put it before Saul and his servants; and they ate. 3
29: 3 this David, the servant of Saul, king of Israel 3
8 What have you found in your servant . . until now 3
10 rise early . . with the servants of your lord 3
30:13 I am a young man of Egypt, servant to an Amal'ekite; 3
2Sm 2:12 and the servants of Ish-bo'sheth the son of Saul 3
13 Jo'ab . . and the servants of David, went out and met 3
15 by number . . and twelve of the servants of David. 3
17 were beaten before the servants of David. 3
30 there were missing of David's servants nineteen 3
31 the servants of David had slain . . 360 . . men. 3
3:18 By the hand of my servant David I will save my 3
22 the servants of David arrived . . from a raid 3
38 the king said to his servants 3
6:20 today before the eyes of his servants' maids 3
7: 5 Go and tell my servant David, 'Thus says the LORD 3
8 therefore thus you shall say to my servant David 3
19 thou hast spoken also of thy servant's house 3
20 For thou knowest thy servant, O Lord GOD! 3
21 wrought all this . . to make thy servant know it. 3
25 the word . . spoken concerning thy servant 3
26 house of thy servant David will be established 3
27 hast made this revelation to thy servant, saying 3
27 therefore thy servant has found courage to pray 3
28 thou . . promised this good thing to thy servant; 3
29 it please thee to bless the house of thy servant 3
29 the house of thy servant be blessed for ever. 3
8: 2 And the Moabites became servants to David 3
6 the Syrians became servants to David 3
7 shields . . carried by the servants of Hadade'zer 3
14 and all the E'domites became David's servants. 3
9: 2 Now there was a servant of the house of Saul 3
2 Are you Ziba?" And he said, "Your servant is he. 3
6 And he answered, "Behold, your servant. 3
8 What is your servant, that you should look upon 3
9 Then the king called Ziba, Saul's servant 2
10 you and your sons and your servants shall till 3
10 Now Ziba had fifteen sons and twenty servants. 3
11 all that my lord the king commands his servant 3
11 According to all . . so will your servant do. 3
12 all who . . became Mephib'osheth's servants. 3
10: 2 David sent by his servants to console him 3
2 David's servants came into the land 3
3 Has not David sent his servants to you to search 3
4 Hanun took David's servants, and shaved off half 3
19 all the kings who were servants of Hadade'zer saw 3
11: 1 David sent Jo'ab, and his servants with him 3
9 Uri'ah slept . . with all the servants of his lord 3
11 Jo'ab and the servants of my lord are camping 3
13 to lie on his couch with the servants of his lord 3
17 and some of the servants of David . . fell. 3
21 say, 'Your servant Uri'ah the Hittite is dead also.' 3
24 the archers shot at your servants from the wall; 3
24 some of the king's servants are dead; 3
24 and your servant Uri'ah the Hittite is dead also. 3
12:18 And the servants of David feared to tell him 3
19 saw that his servants were whispering together 3
19 and David said to his servants, "Is the child dead? 3
21 Then his servants said to him, "What is this thing 3
13:18 So his servant put her out, and bolted the door 7
24 Behold, your servant has sheepshearers; 3
24 pray let the king and his servants go 3
24 the king and his servants go with your servant. 3
28 Then Ab'salom commanded his servants 2
29 So the servants of Ab'salom did to Amnon 2
31 and all his servants . . rent their garments. 3
35 as your servant said, so it has come about. 3
36 the king also and all his servants wept 3
14:15 king will perform the request of his servant. 1
16 and deliver his servant from the hand of the man 1
19 It was your servant Jo'ab who bade me; 3
20 to change . . affairs your servant Jo'ab did this. 3
22 Today your servant knows that I have found favor 3
22 the king has granted the request of his servant. 3
30 Then he said to his servants, "See, Jo'ab's field 3
30 Ab'salom's servants set the field on fire. 3
31 Why have your servants set my field on fire? 3
15: 2 Your servant is of such and such a tribe in Israel 3
8 your servant vowed a vow while I dwelt at Geshur 3
14 David said to all his servants who were with him 3
15 And the king's servants said to the king 3
15 your servants are ready to do whatever 3
18 And all his servants passed by him; 3
21 wherever . . there also will your servant be. 3
34 and say to Ab'salom, 'I will be your servant, O king; 3
34 as I have been your father's servant in time past 3
34 as I have been . . so now I will be your servant,' 3
16: 1 Ziba the servant of Mephib'osheth met him 2
6 he threw stones at David, and at all the servants 3
11 David said to Abi'shai and to all his servants 3
17:20 Ab'salom's servants came to the woman at the house 3
18: 7 were defeated there by the servants of David 3
9 Ab'salom chanced to meet the servants of David. 3
29 When Jo'ab sent your servant, I saw a great tumult 3
19: 5 covered . . the faces of all your servants 3
6 commanders and servants are nothing to you; 3
7 arise, go out and speak kindly to your servants; 3
14 Return, both you and all your servants. 3
17 Ziba the servant of the house of Saul . . rushed 2
17 sons and his twenty servants, rushed down 3
19 or remember how your servant did wrong 3
20 For your servant knows that I have sinned; 3
26 answered, "My lord, O king, my servant deceived me; 3
26 for your servant said to him, 'Saddle an ass for me 3
26 For your servant is lame. 3
27 He has slandered your servant to . . the king. 3
28 you set your servant among those who eat 3
35 Can your servant taste what he eats or . . drinks? 3
35 should your servant be an added burden to my lord 3
36 Your servant will go a little way over the Jordan 3
37 let your servant return, that I may die in my own 3
37 But here is your servant Chimham; let him go over 3
20: 6 take your lord's servants and pursue him 3
21:15 and David went down together with his servants 3
22 fell by . . David and by the hand of his servants. 3
24:10 I pray thee, take away the iniquity of thy servant; 3
20 he saw the king and his servants coming 3
21 Why has my lord the king come to his servant? 3
1Kg 1: 2 his servants said to him, "Let a young maiden be 3
19 but Solomon your servant he has not invited. 3
26 But me, your servant, and Zadok the priest 3
26 and your servant Solomon, he has not invited. 3
27 you have not told your servants who should sit 3
33 Take with you the servants of your lord, and cause 3
47 the king's servants came to congratulate our 3
51 that he will not slay his servant with the sword.' 3
2:38 as . . the king has said, so will your servant do. 3
3: 6 steadfast love to thy servant David my father 3
7 thou hast made thy servant king in place of David 3
8 thy servant is in the midst of thy people whom 3
9 Give thy servant . . an understanding mind 3
15 offerings, and made a feast for all his servants. 3
5: 1 Hiram king of Tyre sent his servants to Solomon 3
6 my servants will join your servants, and I will 3
6 my servants will join your servants, and I will 3
6 I will pay you for your servants such wages 3
9 My servants shall bring it down to the sea 3
8:23 love to thy servants who walk before thee 3
24 hast kept with thy servant David my father 3
25 keep with thy servant David my father what thou 3
26 thou hast spoken to thy servant David my father. 3
28 Yet have regard to the prayer of thy servant 3
28 the prayer which thy servant prays before thee 3
29 prayer which thy servant offers toward this 3
30 supplication of thy servant and of thy people 3
32 hear . . and act, and judge thy servants 3
36 forgive . . thy servants, thy people Israel 3
52 eyes be open to the supplication of thy servant 3
53 as thou didst declare through Moses, thy servant 3
56 promise, which he uttered by Moses his servant. 3
59 and may he maintain the cause of his servant 3
66 that the LORD had shown to David his servant 3
9:27 Hiram sent with the fleet his servants 3
27 seamen . . together with the servants of Solomon; 3
10: 5 the attendance of his servants, their clothing 7
8 Happy are these your servants 3
13 she turned and went back . . with her servants. 3
11:11 and will give it to your servant. 3
13 for the sake of David my servant 3
17 with certain E'domites of his father's servants 3
26 Jerobo'am the son of Nebat . . a servant of Solomon 3
32 he shall have . . for the sake of my servant David 3
34 for the sake of David my servant whom I chose 3
36 that David my servant may always have a lamp 3
38 do what is right . . as David my servant did 3
12: 7 be a servant to this people today and serve them 3
7 If you will . . then they will be your servants 3
14: 8 and yet you have not been like my servant David 3
18 he spoke by his servant Ahi'jah the prophet. 3
15:18 Asa . . gave them into the hands of his servants; 3
29 word . . which he spoke by his servant Ahi'jah 3
16: 9 his servant Zimri . . conspired against him. 3
18: 9 you would give your servant into the hand of Ahab 3
12 I your servant have revered the LORD 3
36 that thou art God . . and that I am thy servant 3
43 he said to his servant, "Go up now, look 2
19: 3 came to Beer-sheba . . and left his servant there. 2
20: 6 I will send my servants to you tomorrow 3
6 your house and the houses of your servants 3
9 All that you first demanded of your servant 3
14 By the servants of the governors 2
15 he mustered the servants of the governors 2
17 The servants of the governors . . went out 2
19 these went out . . the servants of the governors 2
23 the servants of the king of Syria said to him 3
31 his servants said to him, "Behold now, we have heard 3
32 Your servant Ben-ha'dad says, 'Pray, let me live.' 3
39 Your servant went out into the . . battle; 3
40 as your servant was busy . . he was gone. 3
22: 3 the king of Israel said to his servants 3
49 Let my servants go with your servants in the ships 3
49 Let my servants go with your servants in the ships 3
2Kg 1:13 the life of these 50 servants of yours 3
2:16 there are with your servants 50 strong men; 3
3:11 one of the king of Israel's servants answered 3
4: 1 Your servant my husband is dead; 3
1 you know that your servant feared the LORD 3
12 he said to Geha'zi his servant 2
19 The father said to his servant, "Carry him 2
22 Send me one of the servants and one of the asses 2
24 she saddled the ass, and she said to her servant 2
25 he said to Geha'zi his servant, "Look 2
38 he said to his servant, "Set on the great pot 2
43 his servant said, "How am I to set this 7
5: 6 know that I have sent to you Na'aman my servant 3
13 his servants came near and said to him, "My father 3
15 accept now a present from your servant. 3
17 let . . be given to your servant two mules' burden 3
17 your servant will not offer burnt offering 3
18 In this matter may the LORD pardon your servant 3
18 when I . . the LORD pardon your servant in this 3
20 Geha'zi, the servant of Eli'sha the man of God, said 2
23 and laid them upon two of his servants; 2
25 And he said, "Your servant went nowhere. 3
6: 3 one . . said, "Be pleased to go with your servants. 3
8 king of Syria . . took counsel with his servants 3
11 he called his servants and said to them 3
12 one of his servants said, "None, my lord, O king; 3
15 When the servant of the man of God rose early 7
15 the servant said, "Alas, my master! What shall we do? 2
7:12 the king rose . . and said to his servants 3
13 one of his servants said, "Let some men take five 3
8: 4 talking with Geha'zi the servant of the man of God 2
13 What is your servant . . that he should do this 3
19 LORD would . . for the sake of David his servant 3
9: 7 I may avenge on Jez'ebel the blood of my servants 3
7 and the blood of the all the servants of the LORD. 3
11 When Jehu came out to the servants of his master 3
28 His servants carried him . . to Jerusalem 3
36 he spoke by his servant Eli'jah the Tishbite 3
10: 5 We are your servants, and we will do all . . you bid 3
10 LORD has done what he said by his servant Eli'jah. 3
23 there is no servant of the LORD here among you 3
12:20 His servants arose and made a conspiracy 3
21 It was . . his servants, who struck him down 3
14: 5 he killed his servants who had slain the king 3
25 he spoke by his servant Jonah the son of Amit'tai 3
16: 7 I am your servant and your son. Come up, and rescue 3
17:13 which I sent to you by my servants the prophets. 3
23 he had spoken by all his servants the prophets. 3
18:12 all that Moses the servant of the LORD commanded; 3
24 captain among the least of my master's servants 3
26 speak to your servants in the Aramaic language 3
19: 5 When the servants of . . Hezeki'ah came to Isaiah 3
6 the servants of the king of Assyria have reviled 2
34 my own sake and for the sake of my servant David. 3
20: 6 for my own sake and for my servant David's sake. 3
21: 8 the law that my servant Moses commanded them. 3
10 And the LORD said by his servants the prophets 3
23 And the servants of Amon conspired against him 3
22: 9 Your servants have emptied out the money 3
12 and Shaphan . . and Asai'ah the king's servant 3
23:30 And his servants carried him dead in a chariot 3
24: 1 and Jehoi'akim became his servant three years; 3
2 which he spoke by his servants the prophets. 3
10 the servants of Nebuchadnez'zar . . came up 3
11 came to . . while his servants were besieging it; 3
12 his mother, and his servants, and his princes 3

25: 8 Nebu'zarad'an . . a servant of the king of Babylon 3
1Ch 6:49 all that Moses the servant of God had commanded. 3
16:13 O offspring of Abraham his servant 3
17: 4 Go and tell my servant David, 'Thus says the LORD 3
7 therefore thus shall you say to my servant David 3
17 O God; thou hast also spoken of thy servant's house 3
18 can David say to thee for honoring thy servant? 3
18 For thou knowest thy servant. 3
19 For thy servant's sake, O LORD 3
23 which thou hast spoken concerning thy servant 3
24 house of thy servant David will be established 3
25 For thou, my God, hast revealed to thy servant that 3
25 therefore thy servant has found courage to pray 3
26 hast promised this good thing to thy servant; 3
27 please thee to bless the house of thy servant 3
18: 2 the Mo'abites became servants to David 3
6 the Syrians became servants to David 3
7 which were carried by the servants of Hadade'zer 3
13 and all the E'domites became David's servants. 3
19: 2 David's servants came to Hanun . . to console 3
3 Have not his servants come to you to search 3
4 Hanun took David's servants, and shaved them 3
19 when the servants of Hadade'zer saw that 3
20: 8 they fell by . . the hand of his servants. 3
21: 3 my lord the king, all of them my lord's servants? 3
8 I pray thee, take away the iniquity of thy servant; 3
2Ch 1: 3 which Moses the servant of the LORD had made 3
2: 8 I know that your servants know how to cut timber 3
8 And my servants will be with your servants 3
8 And my servants will be with your servants 3
10 give for your servants . . 20,000 cors 3
15 lord has spoken, let him send to his servants; 3
6:14 to thy servants who walk before thee with all 3
15 who hast kept with thy servant David my father 3
16 O LORD . . keep with thy servant David my father 3
17 which thou hast spoken to thy servant David. 3
19 Yet have regard to the prayer of thy servant 3
19 the prayer which thy servant prays before thee; 3
20 hearken to the prayer which thy servant offers 3
21 to the supplications of thy servant 3
23 hear thou . . and act, and judge thy servants 3
27 then hear . . and forgive the sin of thy servants 3
42 thy steadfast love for David thy servant. 3
8:18 sent him by his servants ships and servants 3
18 Huram sent him . . ships and servants familiar 3
18 went to Ophir . . with the servants of Solomon 3
9: 4 attendance of his servants, and their clothing 7
7 Happy are your wives! Happy are . . your servants 3
10 servants of Huram and the servants of Solomon 3
10 servants of Huram and the servants of Solomon 3
12 went back to her own land, with her servants. 3
21 went to Tarshish with the servants of Huram; 3
10: 7 then they will be your servants for ever. 3
12: 8 Nevertheless they shall be servants to him 3
13: 6 Jerobo'am the son of Nebat, a servant of Solomon 3
24: 6 the tax levied by Moses, the servant of the LORD 3
9 tax that Moses the servant of God 3
25 his servants conspired against him 3
25: 3 he killed his servants who had slain the king 3
32: 9 Sennach'erib . . sent his servants to Jerusalem 3
16 servants said still more against the Lord GOD 3
16 said . . against his servant Hezeki'ah. 3
33:24 his servants conspired against him and killed 3
34:16 committed to your servants they are doing. 3
20 king commanded . . Asai'ah the king's servant 3
35:23 king said to his servants, "Take me away 3
24 his servants took him out of the chariot 3
36:20 became servants to him and to his sons 3
Ezr 2:55 sons of Solomon's servants: the sons of So'tai 3
58 servants and the sons of Solomon's servants 3
4:11 Your servants, the men of the province . . send 3
5:11 'We are the servants of the God of heaven and earth 8
7:24 temple servants, or other servants of this house 9
9:11 thou didst command by thy servants the prophets 3
Neh 1: 6 to hear the prayer of thy servant which I now pray 3
6 prayer . . for the people of Israel thy servants 3
7 which thou didst command thy servant Moses. 3
8 word . . didst command thy servant Moses, saying 3
10 servants and thy people, whom thou hast redeemed 3
11 ear be attentive to the prayer of thy servant 3
11 attentive . . to the prayer of thy servants 3
11 give success to thy servant today, and grant him 3
2: 5 if your servant has found favor in your sight 3
10 when Sanbal'lat . . and Tobi'ah the servant 3
19 when Sanbal'lat . . and Tobi'ah the servant 3
20 we his servants will arise and build; 3
4:16 half of my servants worked on construction 2
22 Let every man and his servant pass the night 2
23 neither I . . nor my servants nor the men of the guard 2
5:10 Moreover I and my brethren and my servants 2
15 Even their servants lorded it over the people. 2
16 my servants were gathered there for the work. 2
6: 5 Sanbal'lat for the fifth time sent his servant 2
7:57 sons of Solomon's servants: the sons of So'tai 3
60 servants and the sons of Solomon's servants 3
9:10 Pharaoh and all his servants and all the people 3
14 commandments . . and a law by Moses thy servant. 3
10:29 God's law . . given by Moses the servant of God 3
11: 3 descendants of Solomon's servants. 3
13:19 I set some of my servants over the gates 2
Est 1: 3 gave a banquet for all his princes and servants 3
2: 2 Then the king's servants who attended him said 2
18 a great banquet to all his princes and servants; 3
3: 2 all the king's servants . . did obeisance to Haman; 3
3 Then the king's servants . . said to Mor'decai 3
4:11 All the king's servants . . know that if any 3
5:11 advanced him above the princes and the servants 3
6: 3 The king's servants who attended him said 2
5 the king's servants told him, "Haman is there 2
Job 1: 3 500 she-asses, and very many servants; 4
8 Have you considered my servant Job 3
15 and slew the servants with the edge of the sword; 2
16 burned up the sheep and the servants 2
17 and slew the servants with the edge of the sword; 2
2: 3 said to Satan, "Have you considered my servant Job 3
4:18 Even in his servants he puts no trust 3
19:16 I call to my servant, but he gives me no answer; 3
41: 4 to take him for your servant for ever? 3
42: 7 spoken of me what is right, as my servant Job has. 3
8 go to my servant Job, and offer up for yourselves 3
8 my servant Job shall pray for you 3
8 spoken of me what is right, as my servant Job has. 3
Ps 18: 0 A Psalm of David the servant of the LORD 3
19:11 Moreover by them is thy servant warned; 3
13 Keep back thy servant also from presumptuous 3
27: 9 Turn not thy servant away in anger 3
31:16 Let thy face shine on thy servant; 3
34:22 The LORD redeems the life of his servants; 3
35:27 LORD, who delights in the welfare of his servant! 3
36: 0 A Psalm of David, the servant of the LORD. 3
69:17 Hide not thy face from thy servant; 3
35 his servants shall dwell there and possess it; •
36 the children of his servants shall inherit it 3
78:70 He chose David his servant 3
79: 2 given the bodies of thy servants to the birds 3
10 avenging of the outpoured blood of thy servants 3
86: 2 save thy servant who trusts in thee. 3
4 Gladden the soul of thy servant, for to thee, O Lord 3
16 give thy strength to thy servant 3
89: 3 I have sworn to David my servant 3
20 I have found David, my servant; 3
39 hast renounced the covenant with thy servant; 3
50 Remember, O Lord, how thy servant is scorned; 3
90:13 O LORD! How long? Have pity on thy servants! 3
16 Let thy work be manifest to thy servants 3
102:14 For thy servants hold her stones dear 3
28 The children of thy servants shall dwell secure; 3
105: 6 O offspring of Abraham, his servant 3
25 to deal craftily with his servants. 3
26 sent Moses his servant, and Aaron 3
42 For he remembered . . Abraham his servant. 3
109:28 may thy servant be glad! 3
113: 1 O servants of the LORD, praise the name of the LORD! 3
116:16 O LORD, I am thy servant; I am thy servant, the son 3
16 O LORD, I . . thy servant, the son of thy handmaid. 3
119:17 Deal bountifully with thy servant 3
23 thy servant will meditate on thy statutes. 3
38 Confirm to thy servant thy promise 3
49 Remember thy word to thy servant 3
65 Thou hast dealt well with thy servant, O LORD 3
76 according to thy promise to thy servant. 3
84 How long must thy servant endure? 3
91 all things are thy servants. 3
122 Be surety for thy servant for good; 3
124 Deal with thy servant according to thy 3
125 I am thy servant; give me understanding 3
135 Make thy face shine upon thy servant, and teach me 3
140 promise is well tried, and thy servant loves it. 3
176 gone astray like a lost sheep; seek thy servant 3
123: 2 eyes of servants look to the hand of their master 3
132:10 For thy servant David's sake do not turn away 3
134: 1 Come, bless the LORD, all you servants of the LORD 3
135: 1 give praise, O servants of the LORD 3
9 signs . . against Pharaoh and all his servants; 3
14 LORD will . . have compassion on his servants. 3
136:22 a heritage to Israel his servant 3
143: 2 Enter not into judgment with thy servant; 3
12 destroy all my adversaries, for I am thy servant. 3
144:10 who rescuest David thy servant. 3
Prv 11:29 fool will be servant to the wise. 3
14:35 A servant who deals wisely has the king's favor 3
29:19 By mere words a servant is not disciplined 3
21 He who pampers his servant from childhood 3
30:10 Do not slander a servant to his master 3
Ecc 7:21 lest you hear your servant cursing you; 3
Isa 20: 3 my servant Isaiah has walked naked and barefoot 3
22:20 I will call my servant Eli'akim the son of Hilki'ah 3
36: 9 captain among the least of my master's servants 3
11 Pray, speak to your servants in Aramaic 3
37: 5 the servants of King Hezeki'ah came to Isaiah 3
6 servants of the king of Assyria have reviled me. 2
24 By your servants you have mocked the Lord 3
35 and for the sake of my servant David. 3
41: 8 you, Israel, my servant, Jacob, whom I have chosen 3
9 You are my servant, I have chosen you 3
42: 1 Behold my servant, whom I uphold 3
19 Who is blind but my servant 3
19 or blind as the servant of the LORD? 3
43:10 and my servant whom I have chosen 3
44: 1 But now hear, O Jacob my servant 3
2 Fear not, O Jacob my servant 3
21 Israel, for you are my servant; I formed you 3
21 I formed you, you are my servant; 3
26 who confirms the word of his servant 3
45: 4 For the sake of my servant Jacob 3
48:20 say, "The LORD has redeemed his servant Jacob! 3
49: 3 my servant, Israel, in whom I will be glorified. 3
5 who formed me from the womb to be his servant 3
6 be my servant to raise up the tribes of Jacob 3
7 abhorred by the nations, the servant of rulers 3
50:10 fears the LORD and obeys the voice of his servant 3
52:13 my servant shall prosper, he shall be exalted 3
53:11 shall the righteous one, my servant 3
54:17 This is the heritage of the servants of the LORD 3
56: 6 love the name of the LORD, and to be his servants 3
63:11 remembered the days of old, of Moses his servant. 3
17 Return for the sake of thy servants 3
65: 8 I will do for my servants' sake, 3
9 inherit it, and my servants shall dwell there. 3
13 says the Lord GOD: "Behold, my servants shall eat 3
13 my servants shall drink, but you shall be thirsty; 3
13 behold, my servants shall rejoice, 3
14 my servants shall sing for gladness of heart 3
15 his servants he will call by a different name. 3
66:14 that the hand of the LORD is with his servants 3
Jer 2:14 Is Israel a slave? Is he a homeborn servant? •
7:25 I have persistently sent all my servants 3
14: 3 Her nobles send their servants for water; 5
21: 7 give Zedeki'ah king of Judah, and his servants 3
22: 2 your servants, and your people who enter 3
4 they, and their servants, and their people. 3
25: 4 sent to you all his servants the prophets 3
9 Nebuchadrez'zar the king of Babylon, my servant 3
19 Pharoah king of Egypt, his servants, his princes 3
26: 5 to heed the words of my servants the prophets 3
27: 6 Nebuchadnez'zar, the king of Babylon, my servant 3
29:19 sent to you by my servants the prophets 3
30:10 Then fear not, O Jacob my servant, says the LORD 3
33:21 my covenant with David my servant may be broken 3
22 multiply the descendants of David my servant 3
26 the descendants of Jacob and David my servant 3
35:15 I have sent to you all my servants the prophets 3
36:24 nor any of his servants who heard all these words 3
31 I will punish . . his servants for their iniquity; 3
37: 2 But neither he nor his servants nor the people 3
18 have I done to you or your servants or this people 3
43:10 Nebuchadrez'zar the king of Babylon, my servant 3
44: 4 Yet I persistently sent to you all my servants 3
46:27 But fear not, O Jacob my servant, nor be dismayed 3
28 Fear not, O Jacob my servant, says the LORD 3
Ezk 28:25 their own land which I gave to my servant Jacob. 3
34:23 shepherd, my servant David, and he shall feed them 3
24 my servant David shall be prince among them; 3
37:24 My servant David shall be king over them; 3
25 in the land . . that I gave to my servant Jacob; 3
25 David my servant shall be their prince for ever. 3
38:17 by my servants the prophets of Israel 3
46:17 out of his inheritance to one of his servants 3
Dan 1:12 Test your servants for ten days; let us be given 3
13 according to what you see deal with your servants. 3
2: 4 Tell your servants the dream, and we will show 8
7 Let the king tell his servants the dream 8
3:26 servants of the Most High God, come forth 8
28 sent his angel and delivered his servants 8
6:20 O Daniel, servant of the living God, 8
9: 6 have not listened to thy servants the prophets 3
10 set before us by his servants the prophets. 3
11 written in the law of Moses the servant of God 3
17 hearken to the prayer of thy servant 3
10:17 How can my lord's servant talk with my lord? 3
Ams 3: 7 his secret to his servants the prophets. 3
Hag 2:23 I will take you, O Zerub'babel my servant 3
Zec 1: 6 which I commanded my servants the prophets 3
3: 8 behold, I will bring my servant the Branch. 3
Mal 1: 6 A son honors his father, and a servant his master. 3
4: 4 Remember the law of my servant Moses 3
Mat 8: 6 saying, "Lord, my servant is lying paralyzed 21
8 say the word, and my servant will be healed. 21
13 And the servant was healed at that very moment. 21
10:24 nor a servant above his master; 13
25 and the servant like his master 13
12:18 Behold, my servant whom I have chosen, my beloved 21
13:27 the servants of the householder came and said 13
28 The servants said to him 13
14: 2 he said to this servants, "This is John the Baptist 21
18:23 to settle accounts with his servants. 13
26 So the servant fell on his knees, imploring him 13
27 the lord of that servant released him 13
28 that same servant, as he went out 13
32 'You wicked servant! I forgave you all that debt 13
20:26 whoever would be great . . must be your servant 10
21:34 he sent his servants to the tenants 13
35 the tenants took his servants and beat one 13
36 Again he sent other servants, more than the first; 13
22: 3 sent his servants to call those who were invited 13
4 Again he sent other servants, saying 13
6 while the rest seized his servants 13

8 Then he said to his servants, 'The wedding is ready 13
10 And those servants went out into the streets 13
23:11 shall be your servant; 10
24:45 Who then is the faithful and wise servant 13
46 Blessed is that servant 13
48 if that wicked servant says to himself 13
50 the master of that servant will come on a day 13
25:14 called his servants 13
19 the master of those servants came 13
21 Well done, good and faithful servant 13
23 Well done, good and faithful servant 13
26 You wicked and slothful servant! 13
30 cast the worthless servant 13
Mrk 9:35 he must be last of all and servant of all. 10
10:43 whoever would be great . . must be your servant 10
12: 2 he sent a servant to the tenants 13
4 Again he sent to them another servant 13
13:34 he leaves home and puts his servants in charge 13
Lke 1:54 He has helped his servant Israel 21
69 in the house of his servant David 21
2:29 now lettest thou thy servant depart in peace 13
7: 7 But say the word, and let my servant be healed. 21
12:37 those servants whom the master finds awake 13
38 and finds them so, blessed are those servants! •
43 Blessed is that servant 13
45 if that servant says to himself 13
46 the master of that servant will come 13
47 that servant who knew his master's will 13
14:17 at the time for the banquet he sent his servant 13
21 So the servant came and reported this 13
21 the householder in anger said to his servant 13
22 the servant said, 'Sir 13
23 the master said to the servant, 'Go out 13
15:22 the father said to his servants 13
26 he called one of the servants 21
16:13 No servant can serve two masters 19
17: 7 who has a servant plowing or keeping sheep 13
9 Does he thank the servant 13
10 say, 'We are unworthy servants 13
19:13 Calling ten of his servants 13
15 he commanded these servants 13
17 he said to him, 'Well done, good servant! 13
22 I will condemn you . . you wicked servant! 13
20:10 he sent a servant to the tenants 13
11 he sent another servant 13
Joh 2: 5 His mother said to the servants 10
9 though the servants who had drawn the water knew 10
4:51 As he was going down, his servants met him 13
12:26 where I am, there shall my servant be also 10
13:16 a servant is not greater than his master 13
15:15 No longer do I call you servants 13
15 servant does not know what his master is doing; 13
20 'A servant is not greater than his master.' 13
18:18 Now the servants and officers 13
26 One of the servants of the high priest . . asked 13
36 my servants would fight 23
Act 3:13 glorified his servant Jesus 21
26 God, having raised up his servant 21
4:25 by the mouth of our father David, thy servant 21
27 gathered together against thy holy servant 21
29 grant to thy servants to speak thy word 13
30 through the name of thy holy servant Jesus. 21
10: 7 called two of his servants and a devout soldier 19
16:17 These men are servants of the Most High God 13
Rom 1: 1 Paul, a servant of Jesus Christ 13
13: 4 for he is God's servant for your good. 10
4 he is the servant of God to execute his wrath 10
14: 4 to pass judgment on the servant of another? 19
15: 8 Christ became a servant to the circumcised 10
1Co 3: 5 Servants through whom you believed 10
4: 1 as servants of Christ 23
2Co 4: 5 with ourselves as your servants for Jesus' sake. 13
6: 4 as servants of God we commend ourselves 10
11:15 if his servants also disguise themselves 10
15 as servants of righteousness 10
23 Are they servants of Christ? I am a better one 10
Gal 1:10 I should not be a servant of Christ. 13
5:13 through love be servants of one another. 11
Eph 6: 6 as servants of Christ, doing the will of God 13
Php 1: 1 Paul and Timothy, servants of Christ Jesus 13
2: 7 emptied himself, taking the form of a servant 13
Col 4:12 Ep'aphras . . a servant of Christ Jesus 13
1Th 3: 2 we sent Timothy, our brother and God's servant 22
2Ti 2:24 the Lord's servant must not be quarrelsome 13
Tit 1: 1 Paul, a servant of God and an apostle of Jesus 13
Heb 1: 7 Who makes . . his servants flames of fire. 18
3: 5 Moses was faithful . . as a servant 15
Jas 1: 1 James, a servant of God and of the Lord Jesus 13
1Pe 2:16 but live as servants of God. 13
18 Servants, be submissive to your masters 19
2Pe 1: 1 Peter, a servant and apostle of Jesus Christ 13
Jde 1: 1 Jude, a servant of Jesus . . and brother of James 13
Rev 1: 1 which God gave him to show to his servants 13
1 by sending his angel to his servant John 13
2:20 beguiling my servants to practice immorality 13
7: 3 till we have sealed the servants of our God 13
10: 7 as he announced to his servants the prophets 13
11:18 for rewarding thy servants, the prophets 13
15: 3 And they sing the song of Moses, the servant of God 13
19: 2 he has avenged on her the blood of his servants. 13
5 Praise our God, all you his servants 13
22: 3 and his servants shall worship him; 13
6 the Lord . . sent his angel to show his servants 13
1Es 1: 3 told the Levites, the temple servants of Israel 16
30 the king said to his servants 21
30 his servants took him out of the line of battle. 21
57 they were servants to him and to his sons 21
2:17 Your servants Rehum the recorder and Shimshai 21
4:59 thine is the glory. I am thy servant. 19
5:33 The sons of Solomon's servants 21
35 the sons of Solomon's servants were 372. 21
6:13 the servants of the Lord who created the heaven 21
27 the servant of the Lord and governor of Judea 21
8:82 didst give by thy servants the prophets, saying 21
2Es 1:10 Pharaoh with his servants, and all his army. 25
32 I sent to you my servants the prophets 25
2: 1 I gave them commandments through my servants 25
18 send you help, my servants Isaiah and Jeremiah. 25
26 Not one of the servants whom I have given you 26
3:23 thou didst raise up for thyself a servant 26
5:45 I said, "How hast thou said to thy servant 26
56 show thy servant through whom thou dost visit 26
6:12 show thy servant the end of thy signs 26
7:75 show this also to thy servant 26
102show further to me, thy servant 26
104or a son his father, or a master his servant 26
8: 6 grant to thy servant that we may pray before thee 26
24 hear, O Lord, the prayer of thy servant 26
9:43 she said to me, "Your servant was barren 24
10:37 to give your servant an explanation of this 26
12: 8 and show me, thy servant, the interpretation 26
13:14 thou hast shown thy servant these wonders 26
16:35 and understand them, O servants of the Lord. 26
Tob 8:18 he ordered his servants to fill in the grave. 19
9: 2 Brother Azarias, take a servant and two camels 21
Jdt 3: 2 the servants of Nebuchadnezzar, the Great King 21
5: 5 a word from the mouth of your servant 13
5 No falsehood shall come from your servant's mouth. 13
6: 3 the king's servants will destroy them as one man. 13
6 the sword of my army and the spear of my servants 15
7:12 let your servants take possession of the spring 21
16 Holofernes and all his servants 15
9:10 strike down . . the prince with his servant 15
10:20 Holofernes' companions and all his servants 15
23 Holofernes and his servants 15
11: 4 the servants of my lord King Nebuchadnezzar. 13
5 Accept the words of your servant 12
16 Therefore, when I, your servant, learned all this 12
17 For your servant is religious 12
17 every night your servant will go out 12
20 Holofernes and all his servants 15
12: 4 your servant will not use up the things I have with me 12
5 Then the servants of Holofernes brought her 15
6 command that your servant be permitted to go out 12
AEs 14:17 thy servant has not eaten at Haman's table 12
18 Thy servant has had no joy 12
15:16 all his servants sought to comfort her. 14
Wis 6: 4 as servants of his kingdom 23
9: 4 do not reject me from among thy servants. 21
10:16 She entered the soul of a servant of the Lord 15
12: 7 receive a worthy colony of the servants of God. 21
20 the enemies of thy servants 21
18:21 showing that he was thy servant. 15
Sir 4:30 nor be a faultfinder with your servants. 19
6:11 be bold with your servants; 19
7:20 a servant who performs his work faithfully 19
21 Let your soul love an intelligent servant 19
10:25 Free men will be at the service of a wise servant 19
23:10 a servant who is continually examined 19
33:24 bread and discipline and work for a servant. 19
26 for a wicked servant there are racks 19
30 If you have a servant, let him be as yourself 19
31 If you have a servant, treat him as a brother 19
36:17 Hearken, O Lord, to the prayer of thy servants 17
37:11 with a lazy servant about a big task 19
42: 5 of whipping a wicked servant severely. 19
Bar 1:20 the Lord declared through Moses his servant 21
2:20 thou didst declare by thy servants the prophets 21
24 thou didst speak by thy servants the prophets 21
28 thou didst speak by thy servant Moses on the day 21
3:36 gave her to Jacob his servant and to Israel whom 21
Aza 1:10 shame and disgrace have befallen thy servants 13
12 for the sake of Isaac thy servant 13
20 Let all who do harm to thy servants be put to shame; 13
23 the king's servants who threw them 23
63 Bless the Lord, you servants of the Lord 13
Sus 1:27 the servants were greatly ashamed 13
Bel 1:14 Then Daniel ordered his servants to bring ashes 20
1Mc 4:30 by the hand of thy servant David 13
16:16 his two sons and some of his servants. 20
2Mc 1: 2 Isaac and Jacob, his faithful servants. 13
7: 6 'And he will have compassion on his servants.' 13
33 again be reconciled with his own servants. 13
8:29 to be wholly reconciled with his servants. 13
3Mc 5: 5 The servants in charge of the Jews went out 18
4Mc 12:11 were you not ashamed to murder his servants 15

servant *See also* make.

fellow servant 1. *σύνδουλος*

Mat 18:28 came upon one of his fellow servants 1
29 So his fellow servant fell down and besought him 1
31 When his fellow servants saw 1
33 you have had mercy on your fellow servant 1
24:49 begins to beat his fellow servants 1
Col 1: 7 Ep'aphras our beloved fellow servant 1
4: 7 Tych'icus . . fellow servant in the Lord. 1
Rev 6:11 until the number of their fellow servants 1
19:10 I am a fellow servant with you and your brethren 1
22: 9 I am a fellow servant with you and your brethren 1

hired servant 1. שָׂכִיר 2. *μίσθιος* 3. *μισθωτός*

Exd 12:45 No sojourner or hired servant may eat of it. 1
Lev 19:13 wages of a hired servant shall not remain with you 1
22:10 A sojourner of the priest's or a hired servant 1
25: 6 male and female slaves and for your hired servant 1
40 he shall be with you as a hired servant 1
50 shall be rated as the time of a hired servant 1
53 As a servant hired year by year shall he be 1
Deu 15:18 at half the cost of a hired servant he has served 1
24:14 not oppress a hired servant who is poor and needy 1
Mrk 1:20 Zeb'edee in the boat with the hired servants 3
Lke 15:17 How many of my father's hired servants have bread 2
19 treat me as one of your hired servants."' 2

household servant 1. *ὁ ἐκ τῆς οἰκίας*

Sus 1:26 When the household servants heard the shouting 1

temple servant 1. נְתִינִים 2. נְתִינִין (A) 3. *ἱερόδουλος*

1Ch 9: 2 the priests, the Levites, and the temple servants. 1
Ezr 2:43 temple servants: the sons of Ziha 1
58 temple servants and the sons of Solomon's 1
70 temple servants lived in their towns 1
7: 7 gatekeepers, and the temple servants. 1
24 singers, the doorkeepers, the temple servants 2
8:17 Iddo and his brethren the temple servants 1
20 besides 220 of the temple servants, whom David 1
Neh 3:26 temple servants living on Ophel repaired 1
31 as far as the house of the temple servants 1
7:46 temple servants: the sons of Ziha 1
60 All the temple servants and the sons of Solomon's 1
73 people, the temple servants, and all Israel 1
10:28 gatekeepers, the singers, the temple servants 1
11: 3 temple servants, and the descendants 1
21 temple servants lived on Ophel; 1
21 Ziha and Gishpa were over the temple servants. 1
1Es 5:29 The temple servants: the sons of Ziha 3
35 All the temple servants 3
8: 5 gatekeepers and temple servants. 3
22 gatekeepers or temple servants 3
49 of the temple servants 3
49 220 temple servants 3

serve 1. היה 2. היה לִפְנֵי 3. לִפְנֵי 4. עבד 5. עֲבֹדָה 6. עבד לִפְנֵי 7. עמד לִפְנֵי 8. צבא 9. שׂום 10. שׁרת 11. שׁרת פָּנִים 12. פלח (A) 13. שׁמשׁ (A) 14. *διακονέω* 15. *διακονία* 16. *δουλεύω* 17. *δοῦλος* 18. *εἰμί* 19. *εἶπον* 20. *εἰς* 21. *ἐργάζομαι* 22. *ἔρχομαι* 23. *θεραπεύω* 24. *λατρεύω* 25. *λειτουργέω* 26. *ὁ ἀπό* 27. *παρεδρεύω* 28. *παρίστημι* 29. *πίνω* 30. *πρόκειμαι* 31. *προσέχω* 32. *τίθημι* 33. *ὑπηρεσία* 34. *ὑπηρετέω* 35. *ὑπηρέτης* 36. *χρήσιμος* 37. deservio 38. servio

Gen 6:21 and store it up; and it shall serve as food for you 1
14: 4 Twelve years they had served Ched-or-lao'mer 4
15:14 bring judgment on the nation which they serve 4
25:23 the elder shall serve the younger. 4
27:29 Let peoples serve you, and nations bow down to you. 4
40 and you shall serve your brother; 4
29:15 you are my kinsman, should you therefore serve me 4
18 he said, "I will serve you seven years 4
20 Jacob served seven years for Rachel 4
25 Did I not serve with you for Rachel? 4
27 you the other also in return for serving me 5
30 he loved Rachel more than Leah, and served Laban 4
30:26 for whom I have served you, and let me go; 4
29 You yourself know how I have served you 4
31: 6 You know that I have served your father 4
41 I served you fourteen years for your two 4
43:31 controlling himself he said, "Let food be served. 9
32 They served him by himself 9
Exd 3:12 you shall serve God upon this mountain. 4
4:23 I say to you, "Let my son go that he may serve me"; 4
7:16 that they may serve me in the wilderness; 4
8: 1 Let my people go, that they may serve me. 4
20 Let my people go, that they may serve me. 4
9: 1 Let my people go, that they may serve me. 4
13 Let my people go, that they may serve me. 4
10: 3 Let my people go, that they may serve me. 4
7 that they may serve the LORD their God; 4
8 Go, serve the LORD your God; but who are to go? 4
11 No! Go, the men among you, and serve the LORD 4
24 Go, serve the LORD; your children also may go 4
26 cattle . . we must take of them to serve the LORD 4
26 with what we must serve the LORD until we arrive 4
12:31 go, serve the LORD, as you have said. 4
14: 5 that we have let Israel go from serving us? 4

12 Let us alone and let us serve the Egyptians'? 4
12 better for us to serve the Egyptians than to die 4
20: 5 you shall not bow down to them or serve them; 4
21: 2 you buy a Hebrew slave, he shall serve six years 4
6 and he shall serve him for life. 4
23:24 bow down to their gods, nor serve them 4
25 You shall serve the LORD your God, and I will bless 4
33 for if you serve their gods, it will surely be 4
Lev 25:40 He shall serve with you until the year 4
Num 4:24 service . . in serving and bearing burdens 4
37 all who served in the tent of meeting 4
41 Gershon, all who served in the tent of meeting 4
49 each to his task of serving or carrying; 5
8:25 withdraw from the work . . and serve no more 4
10:10 shall serve you for remembrance before your God 1
31 you will serve as eyes for us. 1
18: 7 you shall attend . . and you shall serve. 4
21 in return for their service which they serve 4
Deu 4:19 you be drawn away and worship them and serve them 4
28 there you will serve gods of wood and stone 4
5: 9 you shall not bow down to them or serve them; 4
6:13 you shall serve him, and swear by his name. 4
7: 4 turn away your sons . . to serve other gods; 4
16 serve their gods, for that would be a snare to you. 4
8:19 after other gods and serve them and worship them 4
10:12 require . . but . . , to serve the LORD your God 4
20 LORD . . you shall serve him and cleave to him 4
11:13 my commandments . . to serve him with all 4
16 turn aside and serve other gods and worship 4
12: 2 places where the nation . . served their gods 4
30 How did these nations serve their gods?-that I 4
13: 2 go after other gods . . let us serve them,' 4
4 you shall serve him and cleave to him. 4
6 entices . . saying, 'Let us go and serve other gods,' 4
13 go and serve other gods,' which you have not known 4
15:12 brother . . shall serve you six years 4
18 at half the cost . . he has served you six years. 4
17: 3 gone and served other gods and worshipped them 4
20:11 people . . do forced labor . . and shall serve you. 4
28:14 do not turn . . to go after other gods to serve 4
36 shall serve other gods, of wood and stone. 4
47 Because you did not serve the LORD your God 4
48 therefore you shall serve your enemies whom 4
64 there . . serve other gods, of wood and stone 4
29:18 turns . . to go and serve the gods of those nations; 4
26 went and served other gods and worshiped them 4
30:17 drawn away to worship other gods and serve them 4
31:20 they will turn to other gods and serve them 4
Jos 22: 5 and to serve him with all your heart and . . soul. 4
23: 7 their gods, or swear by them, or serve them, or bow 4
16 and go and serve other gods and bow down to them. 4
24: 2 and they served other gods. 4
14 fear the LORD, and serve him in sincerity 4
14 put away the gods which your fathers served 4
14 put away the gods . . and serve the LORD. 4
15 And if you be unwilling to serve the LORD 4
15 choose this day whom you will serve 4
15 the gods your fathers served in the region 4
15 but as for me and my house, we will serve the LORD. 4
16 that we . . forsake the LORD, to serve other gods; 4
18 we also will serve the LORD, for he is our God. 4
19 You cannot serve the LORD; for he is a holy God; 4
20 If you forsake the LORD and serve foreign gods 4
21 the people said . . "Nay; but we will serve the LORD. 4
22 that you have chosen the LORD, to serve him. 4
24 The LORD our God we will serve, and his voice we 4
31 And Israel served the LORD all the days of Joshua 4
Jdg 2: 7 the people served the LORD all the days of Joshua 4
11 evil in the sight of the LORD and served the Ba'als; 4
13 They forsook the LORD, and served the Ba'als 4
19 after other gods, serving them and bowing down 4
3: 6 to their sons; and they served their gods. 4
7 God, and serving the Ba'als and the Ashe'roth. 4
8 Israel served Cu'shan-rishatha'im eight years. 4
14 Israel served Eglon the king of Moab eighteen 4
9:28 Who is Abim'elech . . that we should serve him? 4
28 Zebul his officer serve the men of Hamor 4
28 father of Shechem? Why then should we serve him? 4
38 said, 'Who is Abim'elech, that we should serve him?' 4
10: 6 evil . . and served the Ba'als and the Ash'taroth 4
6 they forsook the LORD, and did not serve him. 4
10 have forsaken our God and have served the Ba'als. 4
13 Yet you have forsaken me and served other gods; 4
16 put away the foreign gods . . and served the LORD; 4
1Sm 2:22 the women who served at the entrance to the tent 8
7: 3 direct your heart to the LORD, and serve him only 4
4 Israel put away . . and they served the LORD only. 4
8: 8 done to me . . forsaking me and serving other gods 4
11: 1 Make a treaty with us, and we will serve you. 4
12:10 and have served the Ba'als and the Ash'taroth; 4
10 but now deliver us . . and we will serve thee.' 4
14 If you will fear the LORD and serve him 4
20 but serve the LORD with all your heart; 4
24 and serve him faithfully with all your heart; 4
17: 9 you shall be our servants and serve us. 4
26:19 driven me out . . saying, 'Go, serve other gods.' 4
2Sm 13:17 He called the young man who served him and said 10
16:19 whom should I serve? Should it not be his son? 4
19 As I have served your father, so I will serve you. 6

19 As I have served your father, so I will serve you. 2
22:44 people whom I had not known served me. 4
1Kg 4:21 brought tribute and served Solomon all the days 4
9: 6 if you . . go and serve other gods and worship them 4
9 other gods, and worshiped them and served them; 4
12: 4 lighten the . . yoke upon us, and we will serve you. 4
7 be a servant to this people today and serve them 4
16:31 took for wife Jez'ebel . . and went and served Ba'al 4
22:53 He served Ba'al and worshiped him 4
2Kg 3:14 As the LORD of hosts lives, whom I serve, were it not 7
5:16 As the LORD lives, whom I serve, I will receive 7
10:18 Ahab served Ba'al a little; 4
18 served Ba'al . . but Jehu will serve him much. 4
17:12 they served idols, of which the LORD had said 4
16 and worshiped all the host . . and served Ba'al. 4
33 feared the LORD but also served their own gods 4
35 fear other gods . . or serve them or sacrifice 4
41 and also served their graven images; 4
18: 7 He rebelled . . and would not serve him. 4
21: 3 all the host of heaven, and served them. 4
21 and served the idols that his father served 4
21 and served the idols that his father served 4
25:24 dwell in the land, and serve the king of Babylon 4
1Ch 27: 1 officers who served the king in all matters 10
28: 1 officers of the divisions that served the king 10
9 serve him with a whole heart 4
2Ch 7:19 turn aside . . and go and serve other gods 4
22 laid hold on other gods and . . served them; 4
10: 4 and we will serve you. 4
19:11 the Levites will serve you as officers. 3
24:18 served the Ashe'rim and the idols. 4
30: 8 serve the LORD your God, that his fierce anger may 4
33: 3 worshiped all the host of heaven, and served them. 4
16 commanded Judah to serve the LORD the God 4
22 Amon sacrificed . . and served them 4
35: 3 Now serve the LORD your God and his people Israel. 4
Neh 9:35 not serve thee in their kingdom, and in thy great 4
Est 1:10 the seven eunuchs who served King Ahasu-e'rus 11
Job 21:15 What is the Almighty, that we should serve him? 4
36:11 If they hearken and serve him 4
39: 9 Is the wild ox willing to serve you? 4
Ps 2:11 Serve the LORD with fear, with trembling 4
18:43 people whom I had not known served me. 4
22:30 Posterity shall serve him; 4
72:11 kings fall down before him, all nations serve him! 4
100: 2 Serve the LORD with gladness! 4
106:36 served their idols, which became a snare to them. 4
Isa 59: 6 Their webs will not serve as clothing; 1
60:12 and kingdom that will not serve you shall perish; 4
Jer 2:20 and you said, 'I will not serve.' 4
5:19 As you have forsaken me and served foreign gods 4
19 you shall serve strangers in a land . . not yours.' 4
8: 2 which they have loved and served 4
11:10 they have gone after other gods to serve them; 4
13:10 after other gods to serve them and worship them 4
16:11 other gods and have served and worshiped them 4
13 there you shall serve other gods day and night 4
22: 9 and worshiped other gods and served them. 4
25: 6 do not go after other gods to serve and worship 4
11 these nations shall serve the king of Babylon 4
27: 6 also the beasts of the field to serve him. 4
7 All the nations shall serve him and his son 4
8 But if any nation or kingdom will not serve 4
9 You shall not serve the king of Babylon. 4
11 under the yoke of the king of Babylon and serve 4
12 and serve him and his people, and live. 4
13 nation which will not serve the king of Babylon? 4
14 You shall not serve the king of Babylon, 4
17 Do not listen to them; serve the king of Babylon 4
28:14 king of Babylon, and they shall serve him 4
30: 9 But they shall serve the LORD their God and David 4
34:14 has been sold to you and has served you six years; 4
35:15 and do not go after other gods to serve them 4
40: 9 saying, "Do not be afraid to serve the Chalde'ans. 4
9 Dwell in the land, and serve the king of Babylon 4
44: 3 they went to burn incense and serve other gods 4
52:12 the bodyguard who served the king of Babylon 7
Ezk 20:39 Go serve every one of you his idols 4
40 Israel, all of them, shall serve me in the land; 4
27: 7 from Egypt was your sail, serving as your ensign; 1
41: 6 to serve as supports for the side chambers 1
44:11 gates of the temple, and serving in the temple; 10
11 they shall attend on the people, to serve them. 10
Dan 3:12 not serve your gods or worship the golden image 12
14 not serve my gods or worship the golden image 12
17 God whom we serve is able to deliver us 12
18 not serve your gods or worship the golden image 12
28 serve and worship any god except their own God. 12
6:16 God, whom you serve continually, deliver you! 12
20 has your God, whom you serve continually 12
7:10 1,000 thousands served him, 13
14 all peoples, nations, and languages should serve 12
27 all dominions shall serve and obey them.' 12
Zep 3: 9 and serve him with one accord. 4
Zec 2: 9 shall become plunder for those who served them. 4
Mal 3:14 You have said 'It is vain to serve God. 4
17 as a man spares his son who serves him. 4
18 between one who serves God and one who does not 4
18 one who serves God and one who does not serve him. 4

Mat 4:10 your God and him only shall you serve.' 24
6:24 No one can serve two masters; for either he will 16
24 the other. You cannot serve God and mammon. 16
8:15 fever left her, and she rose and served him. 14
20:28 the Son of man came not to be served but to serve 14
28 the Son of man came not to be served but to serve 14
Mrk 1:31 the fever left her; and she served them. 14
10:45 Son of man also came not to be served but to serve 14
45 Son of man also came not to be served but to serve 14
Lke 1:74 that we . . might serve him without fear 24
4: 8 him only shall you serve.' 24
39 immediately she rose and served them. 14
10:40 Martha was distracted with much serving 15
40 my sister has left me to serve alone 14
12:37 he will come and serve them. 14
15:29 Lo, these many years I have served you 16
16:13 No servant can serve two masters 16
13 You cannot serve God and mammon. 16
17: 8 gird yourself and serve me 14
22:26 the leader as one who serves. 14
27 one who sits at table, or one who serves 14
27 But I am among you as one who serves. 14
Joh 2:10 said to him, "Every man serves the good wine first; 32
12: 2 There they made him a supper; Martha served 14
26 If any one serves me, he must follow me 14
26 if any one serves me, the Father will honor him. 14
Act 6: 2 give up preaching the word of God to serve tables. 14
7: 7 I will judge the nation which they serve,' said God 16
13:36 served the counsel of God in his own generation 34
17:25 nor is he served by human hands 23
20:19 serving the Lord with all humility 16
26:16 to appoint you to serve and bear witness 35
Rom 1: 9 I serve with my spirit in the gospel of his Son 24
25 served the creature rather than the Creator 24
7: 6 so that we serve not under the old written code 16
25 I of myself serve the law of God with my mind 16
25 but with my flesh I serve the law of sin. •
9:12 she was told, "The elder will serve the younger. 16
12: 7 if service, in our serving; 15
11 be aglow with the Spirit, serve the Lord. 16
14:18 he who thus serves Christ is acceptable to God 16
16:18 For such persons do not serve our Lord Christ 16
1Co 9:13 those who serve at the altar 27
2Co 11: 8 accepting support from them in order to serve you. 15
Php 1:12 really served to advance the gospel 22
2:22 he has served with me in the gospel. 16
Col 3:23 work heartily, as serving the Lord and not men •
24 you are serving the Lord Christ. 16
1Th 1: 9 to serve a living and true God 16
1Ti 6: 2 rather they must serve all the better 16
2Ti 1: 3 I thank God whom I serve with a clear conscience 24
4:11 he is very useful in serving me. 15
Phm 1:13 in order that he might serve me on your behalf 14
Heb 1:14 all ministering spirits sent forth to serve 15
6:10 in serving the saints, as you still do. 14
7:13 from which no one has ever served at the altar. 31
8: 5 They serve a copy and shadow 24
9:14 to serve the living God. 24
13:10 those who serve the tent have no right to eat. 24
1Pe 1:12 they were serving not themselves but you 14
Jde 1: 7 serve as an example by undergoing a punishment 30
Rev 7:15 and serve him day and night within his temple; 24
1Es 1: 4 serve his people Israel 23
2Es 1:18 better for us to serve the Egyptians 38
6:46 thou didst command them to serve man 37
7:37 whom you have not served 38
89 they laboriously served the Most High 38
98 whom they served in life 38
8:26 at those who have served thee in truth. 38
15:45 those who survive shall serve those 38
Tob 4:14 if you serve God you will receive payment 16
Jdt 11: 1 any one who chose to serve Nebuchadnezzar 16
7 not only do men serve him because of you 16
17 serves the God of heaven day and night 23
12: 1 to serve her with his own wine. 29
13 who serve in the house of Nebuchadnezzar. 28
16:14 Let all thy creatures serve thee 16
AEs 11: 3 a great man, serving in the court of the king. 23
12: 5 the king ordered Mordecai to serve in the court 23
Wis 10: 9 rescued from troubles those who served her. 23
13:11 a useful vessel that serves life's needs 33
15: 7 both the vessels that serve clean uses 17
16:24 creation, serving thee who hast made it 34
25 it served thy all-nourishing bounty 34
Sir 2: 1 My son, if you come forward to serve the Lord 16
3: 7 he will serve his parents as his masters. 16
4:14 Those who serve her will minister to the Holy One; 24
7:13 the habit of lying serves no good. 20
8: 8 learn how to serve great men. 25
25: 8 he who has not served a man inferior to himself; 16
39: 4 serve among great men and appear before rulers; 34
43: 6 made the moon . . to serve in its season •
Bar 1:12 we shall serve them many days and find favor 16
21 by serving other gods and doing what is evil 21
2:21 serve the king of Babylon, and you will remain 21
22 obey . . and will not serve the king of Babylon 21
24 not obey thy voice, to serve the king of Babylon; 21
LJr 1:27 those who serve them are ashamed 23
39 those who serve them will be put to shame. 23

59 a household utensil that serves its owner's need 36
1Mc 6:23 We were happy to serve your father 16
10:14 it served as a place of refuge. 18
11:38 the troops who had served his fathers hated him. 26
2Mc 6:17 Let what we have said serve as a reminder 19
3Mc 6: 6 as not to serve vain things 24

serve *See also* man.

serve a drink 1. שקה
Est 1: 7 Drinks were served in golden goblets 1

serve a meal 1. παρατίθημι
LJr 1:30 Women serve meals for gods of silver and gold 1

serve as deacon 1. διακονέω
1Ti 3:10 let them serve as deacons. 1
13 those who serve well as deacons 1

serve as midwife 1. ילד
Exd 1:16 When you serve as midwife to the Hebrew women 1

serve as priest 1. כהן 2. ἱερατεύω
Exd 28: 1 to serve me as priests-Aaron and Aaron's sons 1
4 your brother and his sons to serve me as priests. 1
41 that they may serve me as priests. 1
29: 1 that they may serve me as priests. 1
44 I will consecrate, to serve me as priests. 1
30:30 that they may serve me as priests. 1
39:41 the garments of his sons to serve as priests. 1
40:13 consecrate him, that he may serve me as priest. 1
15 anoint them . . that they may serve me as priests 1
Num 3: 4 Elea'zar and Ith'amar served as priests 1
1Ch 6:10 Joha'nan . . who served as priest in the house 1
2Ch 11:14 cast them out from serving as priests of the LORD 1
Ezk 44:13 shall not come near to me, to serve me as priest 1
Lke 1: 8 Now while he was serving as priest before God 2
1Es 5:39 they were excluded from serving as priests. 2
8:46 to send us men to serve as priests 2
Sir 45:15 serve as priest and bless his people in his name. 2

serve as slave 1. δουλεύω
Jdt 8:22 wherever we serve as slaves 1
Bar 4:32 the cities which your children served as slaves; 1

serve as soldier 1. στρατεύω
1Co 9: 7 Who serves as a soldier at his own expense? 1

serve in army 1. στρατεύω
1Es 4: 6 who do not serve in the army or make war 1

make serve 1. עבד
Exd 1:13 they made the people of Israel serve with rigor 1
14 all their work they made them serve with rigor. 1
Lev 25:39 you shall not make him serve as a slave 1
2Ch 34:33 made all . . in Israel serve the LORD their God. 1
Isa 14: 3 hard service with which you were made to serve 1
Jer 15:14 I will make you serve your enemies 1
17: 4 and I will make you serve your enemies 1
22:13 who makes his neighbor serve him for nothing 1

serve to show 1. συνίστημι
Rom 3: 5 our wickedness serves to show the justice of God 1

serve with as judge 1. συμβραβεύω
1Es 9:14 served with them as judges. 1

service 1. יָד 2. יצא צָבָא 3. לִפְנֵי 4. מְלָאכָה 5. מִשְׁמָר 6. מִשְׁמֶרֶת 7. עֲבֹדָה 8. צבא 9. צָבָא 10. שרת 11. שָׁרֵת 12. עֲבִידָה (A) 13. פָּלְחָן (A) 14. διακονία 15. ἐργασία 16. ἔργον 17. εὐεργεσία 18. εὐσέβεια 19. θεραπεύω 20. κηδεμονία 21. λατρεία 22. λειτουργέω 23. λειτουργία 24. λειτουργός 25. ὁ πρός 26. ὑπηρεσία 27. χρεία 28. ministro
Gen 30:26 for you know the service which I have given you. 7
41:46 when he entered the service of Pharaoh king 3
Exd 1:14 made their lives bitter with hard service 7
12:25 when you come . . you shall keep this service. 7
26 'What do you mean by this service?' 7
13: 5 you shall keep this service in this month. 7
30:16 shall appoint it for the service of the tent 7
32:29 you have ordained yourselves for the service *
35:21 for all its service, and for the holy garments. 7
39:40 the utensils for the service of the tabernacle 7
Lev 25:52 according to the years of service due from him *
Num 3:26 all the service pertaining to these. 7
31 all the service pertaining to these. 7
36 all the service pertaining to these; 7
4: 3 all who can enter the service, to do the work 9
4 This is the service of the sons of Kohath 7
12 they shall take all the vessels of the service 11
14 utensils . . which are used for the service *
23 number them, all who can enter for service 8
24 This is the service of . . the Gershonites 7
26 cords, and all the equipment for their service; 7
27 All the service of the sons of the Gershonites 7
28 service of the families . . of the Gershonites 7
30 number them, every one that can enter the service 9
31 whole of their service in the tent of meeting 7
33 service of the families of the sons of Merar'i 7
33 whole of their service in the tent of meeting 7
35 every one that could enter the service, for work 9
39 enter the service, for work in the tent of meeting- 9
43 enter the service, for work in the tent of meeting- 9
47 could enter to do the work of service 7
7: 5 used in doing the service of the tent of meeting 7
5 give . . to each man according to his service. 7
7 sons of Gershon, according to their service; 7
8 to the sons of Merar'i, according to their service 7
8:11 may be theirs to do the service of the LORD. 7
19 to do the service for the people of Israel 7
22 Levites went in to do their service in the tent 7
24 work in the service of the tent of meeting; 7
25 they shall withdraw from the work of the service 7
26 minister . . and they shall do no service. 7
16: 9 to do service in the tabernacle of the LORD 7
18: 4 for all the service of the tent; 7
6 to do the service of the tent of meeting. 7
21 in return for their service which they serve 7
21 their service in the tent of meeting. 7
23 Levites shall do the service of the tent 7
31 for it is your reward in return for your service 7
31:14 officers . . who had come from service in the war. 9
Deu 20:18 which they have done in the service of their gods *
Jos 22:27 that we do perform the service of the LORD 7
1Sm 19: 4 and . . his deeds have been of good service to you; *
1Kg 12: 4 lighten the hard service of your father 7
2Kg 25:14 vessels of bronze used in the temple service *
1Ch 5:18 valiant men . . ready for service. 9
6:31 whom David put in charge of the service of song 1
32 and they performed their service in due order. 7
48 service of the tabernacle of the house of God. 7
7:11 mighty warriors, 17,200, ready for service in war. 2
40 Their number . . for service in war, was 26,000 men. 9
9:13 for the work of the service of the house of God. 7
19 were in charge of the work of the service 7
28 Some . . had charge of the utensils of service 7
33 the singers . . free from other service *
18:17 the chief officials in the service of the king. 1
23:24 the work for the service of the house of the LORD. 7
26 tabernacle or any of the things for its service 7
28 for the service of the house of the LORD 7
28 and any work for the service of the house of God; 7
32 for the service of the house of the LORD. 7
24: 3 to the appointed duties in their service. 7
19 had as their appointed duty in their service 7
25: 1 David and the chiefs of the service . . set apart 9
1 set apart for the service . . of the sons of Asaph 7
6 the music . . for the service of the house of God. 7
26: 8 able men qualified for the service; 62 of O'bed-e'dom 7
30 of the LORD and for the service of the king. 7
28:13 the work of the service in the house of the LORD; 7
13 vessels for the service in the house of the LORD 7
14 for all golden vessels for each service 7
14 weight of silver vessels for each service 7
15 the use of each lampstand in the service 7
20 work for the service of the house of the LORD 7
21 for all the service of the house of God; 7
21 willing man who has skill for any kind of service; 7
29: 7 They gave for the service of the house of God 7
2Ch 8:14 the divisions of the priests for their service 7
10: 4 lighten the hard service of your father 7
12: 8 that they may know my service 7
8 service of the kingdoms of the countries. 7
13:10 We have . . and Levites for their service. 4
17:16 a volunteer for the service of the LORD *
19 These were in the service of the king 10
24:14 both for the service and for the burnt offerings 11
29:35 service of the house of the LORD was restored. 7
30:22 showed good skill in the service of the LORD. *
31: 2 by division, each according to his service 7
16 for their service according to their offices 7
21 he undertook in the service of the house of God 7
34:13 all who did work in every kind of service; 7
35: 2 encouraged them in the service of the house 7
10 When the service had been prepared 7
15 did not need to depart from their service 7
16 all the service of the LORD was prepared that day 7
Ezr 6:18 set . . for the service of God at Jerusalem 12
7:19 given you for the service of the house of your God 13
Neh 10:32 third part of a shekel for the service 7
12: 9 stood opposite them in the service. 6
45 performed the service of their God 6
45 performed the . . service of purification 6
13:14 done for the house of my God and for his service. 5
Job 14:14 All the days of my service I would wait 9
Isa 14: 3 hard service with which you were made to serve 7
Jer 34:14 you must set him free from your service. *
52:18 the vessels of bronze used in the temple service; *
Ezk 44:14 keep charge of the temple, to do all its service 7
Lke 1:23 when his time of service was ended 23
Joh 16: 2 will think he is offering service to God. 21
Rom 12: 7 if service, in our serving; 14
15:27 they ought also to be of service to them 22
31 that my service for Jerusalem may be acceptable 14
1Co 12: 5 there are varieties of service, but the same Lord; 14
16:15 devoted themselves to the service of the saints; 14
2Co 8:23 my partner and fellow worker in your service; *
9:12 the rendering of this service 23
13 Under the test of this service 14
Php 2:30 risking his life to complete your service to me. 23
1Ti 1:12 by appointing me to his service 14
6: 2 those who benefit by their service 17
Heb 2:17 faithful high priest in the service of God 25
10:11 every priest stands daily at his service 22
3Jn 1: 6 to send them on . . as befits God's service. *
Rev 2:19 'I know your works, your love and faith and service 14
1Es 7: 9 for the services of the Lord God of Israel 16
15 for the service of the Lord God of Israel. 16
8:49 had given for the service of the Levites 15
2Es 6:42 and cultivated and be of service before thee. 28
Wis 15: 7 and laboriously molds each vessel for our service 26
Sir 6:19 in her service you will toil a little while 15
10:25 Free men will be at the service of a wise servant 22
35:16 He whose service is pleasing to the Lord 19
39:31 be made ready on earth for their service 27
50:14 Finishing the service at the altars 24
19 so they completed his service. 23
LJr 1:60 . . stars, shining and sent forth for service 27
1Mc 10:41 for the service of the temple. 16
42 from the income of the services of the temple 27
2Mc 3: 3 the service of the sacrifices. 23
4:14 no longer intent upon their service at the altar 23
8: 9 a man of experience in military service. 27
4Mc 4: 4 he praised Simon for his service to the king 20
20 also the temple service was abolished. 20
12:14 by dying nobly fulfilled their service to God 18

service *See also* enter, king's, soldier, use.

service as priest 1. כהן
Exd 31:10 Aaron . . his sons, for their service as priests 1
35:19 garments . . for their service as priests. 1

do service 1. עבד
Num 8:15 Levites shall go in to do service at the tent 1
Hos 12:12 land of Aram, there Israel did service for a wife 1

good service 1. εὐπραξία
3Mc 3: 6 their good service to their nation 1

hard service 1. צָבָא
Job 7: 1 Has not man a hard service upon earth 1

priestly service 1. ἱερουργέω
Rom 15:16 in the priestly service of the gospel of God 1

remain in service 1. עמד לִפְנֵי
1Sm 16:22 Let David remain in my service, for he has found 1

render service 1. διακονέω 2. δουλεύω 3. ἐργάζομαι 4. κοινός
Eph 6: 7 rendering service with a good will 2
2Ti 1:18 you well know all the service he rendered 1
1Pe 4:11 whoever renders service, as one who renders it 1
3Jn 1: 5 when you render any service to the brethren 3
2Mc 9:26 the public and private services rendered to you 4

table service 1. διακονία
1Mc 11:58 he sent him gold plate and a table service 1

temple service 1. ἱερός 2. ἱερουργία
1Co 9:13 who are employed in the temple service 1
4Mc 3:20 money . . for the temple service 2

serving of food 1. ὄψον
Tob 7: 8 and set large servings of food before them. 1

servitude 1. עבד 2. עֲבֹדָה 3. δουλεία
Neh 5:18 servitude was heavy upon this people. 2
Jer 28:14 an iron yoke of servitude to Nebuchadnez'zar 1
Lam 1: 3 exile because of affliction and hard servitude; 2
1Es 8:79 to give us food in the time of our servitude. 3

session 1. κάθημαι
Jdt 4: 8 the senate . . of Israel, in session at Jerusalem 1

session *See also* begin.

set 1. אמר 2. גבל 3. הות 4. היה 5. הלך 6. חשק 7. יהב 8. יסד 9. יצב 10. יצג 11. ירה 12. ישב 13. כון 14. מלא 15. מְלָאָה 16. מִלּוּא 17. מָנוֹחַ 18. מַעֲרָכָה 19. נוח 20. נַחַת 21. נסך 22. נצב 23. נשא 24. נתן 25. סות 26. עלה 27. עמד 28. ערך 29. עשה 30. פקד 31. קום 32. רבץ 33. רכב 34. שום 35. שוה 36. שית 37. שלח 38. שפה 39. שפת 40. שתת 41. קום (A) 42. שום (A) 43. αἴρω 44. ἀποστέλλω 45. ἀφίημι 46. γίνομαι 47. γνωρίζω 48. δίδωμι 49. ἐκβάλλω 50. ἐκτείνω 51. ἐν 52. ἐπιβιβάζω 53. ἐπιδίδωμι 54. ἐφίστημι 55. ἱδρύω 56. ἵστημι 57. καθίζω 58. καθίστημι 59. κατευθύνω 60. κεῖμαι 61. ὁρίζω 62. πήγνυμι 63. πορεύω 64. στηρίζω 65. συνίστημι 66. τάσσω 67. τίθημι 68. facio 69. pono 70. statuo
Gen 1:17 God set them in the firmament of the heavens 24
6:16 and set the door of the ark in its side; 34

8: 9 the dove found no place to set her foot 17
9:13 I set my bow in the cloud, and it shall be a sign 24
12:20 and they set him on the way, with his wife 37
18: 8 he had prepared, and set it before them; 24
19:16 brought him forth and set him outside the city. 19
21:28 Abraham set seven ewe lambs of the flock apart. 22
29 these seven ewe lambs which you have set apart? 22
24:33 Then food was set before him to eat; 34
30:36 he set a distance of three days' journey 34
38 He set the rods which he had peeled in front 10
40 Jacob separated the lambs, and set the faces 24
31:17 Jacob arose, and set his sons and his wives 23
21 and set his face toward the hill country 34
37 Set it here before my kinsmen and your kinsmen 34
51 pillar, which I have set between you and me. 11
41:33 let Pharaoh . . set him over the land of Egypt. 36
41 Behold, I have set you over all the land of Egypt. 24
43 Thus he set him over all the land of Egypt. 24
43: 9 If I do not bring him back to you and set him before 10
44:21 to me, that I may set my eyes upon him.' 34
47: 7 Jacob his father, and set him before Pharaoh 27
Exd 1:11 Therefore they set taskmasters over them 34
4:20 Moses . . set them on an ass, and went back 33
5:14 whom Pharaoh's taskmasters had set over them 34
9: 5 the LORD set a time, saying, "Tomorrow the LORD 34
19: 7 Moses . . set before them all these words 34
21: 1 ordinances which you shall set before them. 34
23:31 I will set your bounds from the Red Sea to the sea 36
25: 7 onyx stones, and stones for setting, for the ephod 15
30 you shall set the bread of the Presence 24
26:35 you shall set the table outside the veil 24
27: 5 you shall set it under the ledge of the altar 24
28:12 you shall set the two stones upon the shoulder- 34
17 you shall set in it four rows of stones. 14
29: 6 you shall set the turban on his head 34
31: 5 in cutting stones for setting 14
32:22 you know the people, that they are set on evil. •
35: 9 onyx stones and stones for setting, for the ephod 15
27 leaders brought onyx stones and stones to be set 15
33 cutting stones for setting, and in carving wood 14
39: 7 he set them on the shoulder-pieces of the ephod 34
10 they set in it four rows of stones. 14
37 its lamps with the lamps set and all its utensils 18
40: 6 You shall set the altar of burnt offering before 24
20 and set the mercy seat above on the ark; 24
29 he set the altar of burnt offering at the door 34
30 he set the laver between the tent of meeting 34
Lev 8: 9 he set the turban upon his head, and on the turban 34
9 on the turban, in front, he set the golden plate 34
14:11 the priest who cleanses him shall set the man 27
16: 7 take the two goats, and set them before the LORD 27
17:10 I will set my face against that person who eats 24
20: 3 I myself will set my face against that man 24
5 then I will set my face against that man 34
6 I will set my face against that person 24
24: 6 you shall set them in two rows, six in a row 34
26:17 I will set my face against you 24
Num 3: 6 Bring the tribe of Levi near, and set them before 27
5:16 priest shall . . set her before the LORD; 27
18 the priest shall set the woman before the LORD 27
30 then he shall set the woman before the LORD 27
21: 8 Make a fiery serpent, and set it on a pole; 34
9 Moses made a bronze serpent, and set it on a pole; 34
24: 1 Balaam . . set his face toward the wilderness. 36
21 your nest is set in the rock; 34
Deu 1: 8 Behold, I have set the land before you; go 24
15 set them as heads over you, commanders 24
21 LORD your God has set the land before you; go up 24
4: 8 as all this law which I set before you this day? 24
44 This is the law which Moses set before . . Israel; 34
10:15 LORD set his heart in love upon your fathers 6
11:26 I set before you this day a blessing and a curse 24
29 set the blessing on Mount Ger'izim and the curse 24
32 statutes and the ordinances which I set 24
14:24 which the LORD . . chooses, to set his name there 34
17:14 I will set a king over me, like all the nations 34
15 may indeed set as king over you him whom the LORD 34
15 your brethren you shall set as king over you; 34
19:14 neighbor's landmark, which the men of old have set. 2
21: 8 set not the guilt of innocent blood in the midst 24
24:15 (for he is poor, and sets his heart upon it); 23
26:19 that he will set you high above all nations 24
28: 1 LORD . . will set you high above all the nations 24
36 bring you, and your king whom you set over you 31
56 who would not venture to set the sole of her foot 10
30: 1 blessing and the curse, which I have set before 24
15 See, I have set before you this day life and good 24
19 set before you life and death, blessing and curse; 24
Jos 6:23 brought . . kindred, and set them outside the camp 19
8:12 and set them in ambush between Bethel and Ai 34
10:18 the cave, and set men by it to guard them; 30
27 and they set great stones against the . . cave 34
15:19 since you have set me in the land of the Negeb 24
Jdg 1:15 since you have set me in the land of the Negeb, give 24
6:18 and bring out my present, and set it before thee. 19
7: 5 Every one that laps . . you shall set by himself; 10
19 came . . when they had just set the watch; 31
22 the LORD set every man's sword against his fellow 34
20:29 Israel set men in ambush round about Gib'e-ah. 34
36 men in ambush whom they had set against Gib'e-ah. 34
1Sm 2: 8 the pillars . . and on them he has set the world. 36
4:15 and his eyes were set, so that he could not see. 31
6:15 took down the . . and set them upon the great stone; 34
9:20 As for your asses . . do not set your mind on them 34
24 took up the leg and . . and set them before Saul; 34
24 Samuel said, "See, what was kept is set before you. 34
10:19 and you have said, 'No! but set a king over us.' 34
12:13 behold, the LORD has set a king over you. 24
13:21 a third of a shekel for . . setting the goads. 22
18: 5 David . . so that Saul set him over the men of war. 34
28:22 let me set a morsel of bread before you; and eat 34
2Sm 6:17 they brought in the ark . . and set it in its place 10
10: 9 the battle was set against him both in front 4
11:15 Set Uri'ah in the forefront of the . . fighting 7
12:20 when he asked, they set food before him, and he ate. 34
31 brought forth the people . . and set them to labor 34
17:25 Ab'salom had set Ama'sa over the army instead 34
18: 1 David mustered . . and set over them commanders 34
19:28 you set your servant among those who eat 36
23:23 And David set him over his bodyguard. 34
1Kg 5: 5 whom I will set upon your throne in your place 24
6 I will pay you . . such wages as you set; 1
6:19 he prepared . . to set there the ark 24
7:16 capitals . . to set upon the tops of the pillars; 24
25 upon twelve oxen . . the sea was set upon them •
28 and the panels were set in the frames •
29 on the panels that were set in the frames were •
39 he set the stands, five on the south . . and five 24
39 he set the sea on the southeast corner 24
8:12 The LORD has set the sun in the heavens 47
9: 6 and my statutes which I have set before you 24
10: 9 who has delighted in you and set you on the throne 24
12:29 he set one in Bethel, and the other he put in Dan. 34
21: 9 Proclaim a fast, and set Naboth on high 12
10 set two base fellows opposite him 12
12 they proclaimed a fast, and set Naboth on high 12
2Kg 4:38 Set on the great pot, and boil pottage 38
43 How am I to set this before 100 men? 24
44 So he set it before them. And they ate 24
6:22 Set bread and water before them, that they may eat 34
10: 3 the best . . and set him on his father's throne 34
12: 9 priest took a chest . . and set it beside the altar 24
17 Haz'ael set his face to go up against Jerusalem 34
18:23 if you are able . . to set riders upon them. 24
21: 7 the graven image . . he set in the house 34
1Ch 11:25 And David set him over his bodyguard. 34
16: 1 brought the ark of God, and set it inside the tent 10
19:10 the battle was set against him both in front •
20: 3 set them to labor with saws and iron picks •
22: 2 he set stonecutters to prepare dressed stones 27
19 set your mind and heart to seek the LORD your God. 24
29: 2 great quantities of onyx and stones for setting 16
2Ch 4: 4 upon twelve oxen . . the sea was set upon them •
6 made ten lavers . . and set five on the south side 24
7 lampstands . . and set them in the temple 24
10 set the sea at the southeast corner of the house. 24
6:11 there I have set the ark, in which is the covenant 34
13 bronze platform . . and had set it in the court; 24
20 place where thou hast promised to set thy name 34
7:19 and my commandments which I have set before you 24
9: 8 LORD . . who has . . set you on his throne as king 24
11:16 those who had set their hearts to seek the LORD 24
12:14 for he did not set his heart to seek the LORD. 13
13:11 set out the showbread on the table of pure gold •
17: 2 set garrisons in the land of Judah 24
19: 3 have set your heart to seek God. 13
20: 3 Jehosh'aphat . . set himself to seek the LORD 24
22 LORD set an ambush against the men of Ammon, 24
33 people had not yet set their hearts upon the God 13
23:10 he set all the people as a guard for the king 27
14 the captains who were set over the army 30
20 And they set the king upon the royal throne 12
24: 8 set it outside the gate of the house of the LORD. 24
25: 5 Amazi'ah . . set them by fathers' houses 27
26: 5 set himself to seek God in the days of Zechari'ah 4
30:19 who sets his heart to seek God, the LORD 13
32: 6 he set combat commanders over the people 24
33: 7 the image of the idol . . he set in the house of God 34
34:12 Over them were set Jahath and Obadi'ah 30
Ezr 3: 3 set the altar in its place, for fear was upon them 13
6:18 set the priests in their divisions 41
7:10 Ezra had set his heart to study the law of the LORD 13
Neh 2: 6 it pleased the king to send me; and I set him a time. 24
3: 1 consecrated it and set its doors; 27
3 set its doors, its bolts, and its bars. 27
6 set its doors, its bolts, and its bars. 27
13 rebuilt . . set its doors, its bolts, and its bars 27
14 rebuilt . . set its doors, its bolts, and its bars. 27
15 covered . . set its doors, its bolts, and its bars; 27
4: 9 set a guard as a protection against them day 27
9:35 large and rich land which thou didst set before 24
37 goes to the kings whom thou hast set over us 24
13:11 gathered . . and set them in their stations. 27
19 I set some of my servants over the gates 27
Est 2:17 he set the royal crown on her . . and made her queen 34
3: 1 promoted Haman . . and set his seat above all 34
6: 8 and on whose head a royal crown is set; 24
8: 2 And Esther set Mor'decai over the house of Haman. 34
Job 5:11 he sets on high those who are lowly 34
7:12 a sea monster, that thou settest a guard over me? 34
17 that thou dost set thy mind upon him 36
19: 8 he has set darkness upon my paths. 34
30: 1 have disdained to set with the dogs of my flock. 36
34:24 sets others in their place. 27
36: 7 with kings upon the throne he sets them for ever 12
16 what was set on your table was full of fatness. 20
38:10 prescribed bounds for it, and set bars and doors 34
Ps 2: 2 The kings of the earth set themselves 9
6 I have set my king on Zion, my holy hill. 21
3: 6 people who have set themselves against me 36
17:11 they set their eyes to cast me to the ground. 36
19: 4 In them he has set a tent for the sun 34
21: 3 thou dost set a crown of fine gold upon his head. 36
31: 8 thou hast set my feet in a broad place. 27
36: 4 he sets himself in a way that is not good; 9
40: 2 set my feet upon a rock, making my steps secure. 31
41:12 set me in thy presence for ever. 22
54: 3 they do not set God before them. Selah 34
57: 6 They set a net for my steps; my soul was bowed down. 13
62: 3 How long will you set upon a man to shatter him 3
10 if riches increase, set not your heart on them. 36
73: 9 They set their mouths against the heavens 40
18 Truly thou dost set them in slippery places; 36
78: 7 that they should set their hope in God 34
86:14 they do not set thee before them. 34
89:19 I have set the crown upon one who is mighty 35
25 I will set his hand on the sea 34
90: 8 Thou hast set our iniquities before thee 36
101: 3 not set before my eyes anything that is base. 36
104: 5 Thou didst set the earth on its foundations 8
9 Thou didst set a bound which they should not pass 34
119:30 I set thy ordinances before me. 35
122: 5 There thrones for judgment were set 12
132:11 sons of your body I will set on your throne. 36
137: 6 if I do not set Jerusalem above my highest joy! 26
140: 5 by the wayside they have set snares for me. Selah 36
141: 3 Set a guard over my mouth, O LORD 36
Prv 9: 2 mixed her wine, she has also set her table. 28
17:24 understanding sets his face toward wisdom •
19:18 do not set your heart on his destruction. 23
22:28 ancient landmark which your fathers have set. 29
Ecc 8:11 the heart of the sons of men is fully set to do evil. •
10: 6 folly is set in many high places 24
Sng 5:12 His eyes are like . . bathed in milk, fitly set. 12
14 His arms are rounded gold, set with jewels. 14
15 His legs are alabaster . . set upon bases of gold. 8
6:12 my fancy set me in a chariot beside my prince. 34
8: 6 Set me as a seal upon your heart . . upon your arm; 34
Isa 14: 1 choose Israel, and will set them in their own land 19
21: 6 Go, set a watchman, let him announce what he sees. 27
36: 8 horses, if you are able on your part to set riders 24
41:19 I will set in the desert the cypress 34
46: 7 they set it in its place, and it stands there; 19
50: 7 therefore I have set my face like a flint 34
51:13 the oppressor, when he sets himself to destroy? 13
54:11 behold, I will set your stones in antimony 32
57: 7 Upon a . . lofty mountain you have set your bed 34
62: 6 Upon your walls, O Jerusalem, I have set watchmen; 30
65:11 who set a table for Fortune and fill cups 28
66:19 I will set a sign among them. 34
Jer 1:10 See, I have set you this day over nations 30
15 every one shall set his throne at the entrance 24
3:19 I thought how I would set you among my sons 36
5:26 lying in wait. They set a trap; they catch men. 22
6:17 I set watchmen over you, saying, 'Give heed 31
7:30 they have set their abominations in the house 34
9:13 they have forsaken my law which I set before them 24
13:21 What will you say when they set as head over you 30
17:12 A glorious throne set on high from the beginning •
21: 8 Behold, I set before you the way of life 24
10 For I have set my face against this city for evil 34
23: 4 I will set shepherds over them who will care 31
24: 6 I will set my eyes upon them for good 34
26: 4 to walk in my law which I have set before you 24
35: 5 Then I set before the Re'chabites pitchers 24
42:15 If you set your faces to enter Egypt 34
17 All the men who set their faces to go to Egypt 34
43: 3 Baruch the son of Neri'ah has set you against us 25
10 he will set his throne above these stones 34
44:10 in my law and my statutes which I set before you 24
11 Behold, I will set my face against you for evil 34
12 the remnant of Judah who have set their faces 34
49:38 I will set my throne in Elam 34
Lam 1:14 My transgressions . . they were set upon my neck; 26
2: 4 bent his bow . . with his right hand set like a foe; 22
3:12 he bent his bow and set me as a mark for his arrow. 22
Ezk 2: 2 the Spirit entered into me and set me upon my feet; 27
3:24 the Spirit entered into me, and set me upon my feet; 27
4: 2 set camps also against it 24
3 set your face toward it 13
7 you shall set your face toward the siege 13
5: 5 I have set her in the center of the nations 34
6: 2 set your face toward the mountains of Israel 34
13:17 son of man, set your face against the daughters 34
14: 3 and set the stumbling block of their iniquity 24
4 and sets the stumbling block of his iniquity 34
8 I will set my face against that man 24

15: 7 I will set my face against them; 24
7 I am the LORD, when I set my face against them. 34
16:18 and set my oil and my incense before them. 24
19 and honey–you set before them for a pleasing odor 24
17: 4 and set it in a city of merchants. 34
5 He set it like a willow twig 34
19: 8 the nations set against him snares on every side; 24
20:24 their eyes were set on their fathers' idols. 4
46 Son of man, set your face toward the south 34
21: 2 Son of man, set your face toward Jerusalem 34
22 to set battering rams against the gates 34
23:24 they shall set themselves against you 34
24: 3 Set on the pot, set it on, pour in water also; 39
3 Set on the pot, set it on, pour in water also; 39
8 I have set on the bare rock the blood she has shed 24
11 Then set it empty upon the coals 27
25: 2 Son of man, set your face toward the Ammonites 34
4 they shall set their encampments among you 12
28:21 Son of man, set your face toward Sidon 34
29: 2 set your face against Pharaoh king of Egypt 34
31:10 it towered high and set its top among the clouds 24
14 or set their tops among the clouds 24
32:23 graves are set in the uttermost parts of the Pit 24
33:31 but their heart is set on their gain. 5
35: 2 Son of man, set your face against Mount Se'ir 34
37:26 and will set my sanctuary in the midst of them 24
38: 2 set your face toward Gog, of the land of Magog 34
39:21 I will set my glory among the nations; 24
40: 4 and set your mind upon all that I shall show you 34
43: 8 by setting their threshold by my threshold 24
44: 8 you have set foreigners to keep my charge 34
Dan 4:17 sets over it the lowliest of men.' 41
5:21 kingdom of men, and sets over it whom he will. 41
6: 1 Darius to set over the kingdom 120 satraps 41
3 king planned to set him over the whole kingdom. 41
14 distressed, and set his mind to deliver Daniel; 42
8:18 but he touched me and set me on my feet. 27
9:10 laws, which he set before us by . . the prophets. 24
10:12 first day that you set your mind to understand 24
11:17 set his face to come with the strength 34
28 heart shall be set against the holy covenant. •
Hos 2: 3 like a wilderness, and set her like a parched land 36
8: 1 Set the trumpet to your lips •
Ams 7: 8 the Lord said, "Behold, I am setting a plumb line 34
9: 4 and I will set my eyes upon them for evil 34
Obd 1: 4 though your nest is set among the stars 34
7 your trusted friends have set a trap under you 34
Mic 2:12 I will set them together like sheep in a fold 34
Hab 2: 9 evil gain for his house, to set his nest on high 34
Zec 3: 9 upon the stone which I have set before Joshua 24
6:11 make a crown, and set it upon the head of Joshua 34
8:10 for I set every man against his fellow. 37
Mat 4: 5 the holy city, and set him on the pinnacle 56
5:14 A city set on a hill cannot be hid. 60
24:47 he will set him over all his possessions. 58
25:21 I will set you over much 58
23 I will set you over much 58
27:66 by sealing the stone and setting a guard. •
Lke 2:34 this child is set for the fall and rising of many 60
4: 9 set him on the pinnacle of the temple 56
18 to set at liberty those who are oppressed 44
7: 8 I am a man set under authority 66
9:51 he set his face to go to Jerusalem. 64
53 because his face was set toward Jerusalem. 63
10:34 then he set him on his own beast 52
12:42 whom his master will set over his household 58
44 he will set him over all his possessions. 58
Act 2:30 set one of his descendants upon his throne 57
4: 7 when they had set them in the midst, they inquired 56
5:27 they set them before the council 56
6: 6 These they set before the apostles 56
13:47 I have set you to be a light for the Gentiles 67
22:30 he brought Paul down and set him before them. 56
Rom 8: 6 To set the mind on the flesh is death •
6 to set the mind on the Spirit is life and peace. •
7 the mind that is set on the flesh is hostile to God; •
Col 2:14 this he set aside, nailing it to the cross. 43
1Ti 4:12 set the believers an example in speech 46
Heb 4: 7 again he sets a certain day, "Today 61
Rev 3: 8 Behold, I have set before you an open door 48
10: 2 And he set his right foot on the sea 67
2Es 5:15 held me and strengthened me and set me on my feet. 70
7: 3 There is a sea set in a wide expanse 69
4 it has an entrance set in a narrow place 69
6 There is a city built and set on a plain 69
7 is narrow and set in a precipitous place 69
9:47 I set a day for the marriage feast. 68
10:30 and set me on my feet, and said to me 70
12:33 he will set them living before his judgment seat 70
Tob 14:10 escaped the deathtrap which Nadab had set 62
Jdt 5:11 and set them to making bricks •
6:16 they set Achior in the midst of all their people 56
7: 7 seized them and set guards of soldiers over them 54
11:19 I will set your throne in the midst of it 67
14: 2 set a captain over them 48
AEs 16: 5 many of those who are set in places of authority 66
Wis 13:10 miserable, with their hopes set on dead things 51
15 sets it in the wall 67
Sir 17: 8 He set his eye upon their hearts 67
22:18 Fences set on a high place will not stand firm 60
27 O that a guard were set over my mouth 48
27:26 he who sets a snare will be caught in it. 56
33:28 Set him to work, as is fitting for him 58
38:26 He sets his heart on plowing furrows 48
27 he sets his heart on painting a lifelike image 48
28 He sets his heart on finishing his handiwork 48
30 he sets his heart to finish the glazing 53
39: 5 will set his heart to rise early to seek the Lord 53
49: 3 He set his heart upon the Lord 59
Bar 1:18 statutes of the Lord which he set before us. 48
2:10 statutes of the Lord which he set before us. 48
LJr 1:27 If any one sets one of them upright 56
1Mc 10:33 I set free without payment 45
11:57 set you over the four districts 58
66 set a garrison over it. 67
68 set an ambush against him in the mountains 49
2Mc 3:14 he set a day and went in to direct the inspection 66
12:20 Maccabeus . . set men in command of the divisions 58
14:21 the leaders set a day 66
3Mc 6:38 their destruction was set 65
4Mc 7: 5 in setting his mind firm like a jutting cliff 50
17: 3 Nobly set like a roof on the pillars of your sons 55

set (2) 1. חֹבֶרֶת 2. מַחְבֶּרֶת
Exd 26: 4 the outmost curtain in the first set; 1
4 edge of the outmost curtain in the second set. 2
5 the curtain that is in the second set; 2
10 the curtain that is outmost in one set 1
10 the curtain which is outmost in the second set. 1
36:11 edge of the outmost curtain of the first set; 2
11 edge of the outmost curtain of the second set; 2
12 edge of the curtain that was in the second set; 2
17 edge of the outmost curtain of the one set 2

set (3) 1. בּוֹא 2. מָבוֹא 3. δύνω 4. δυσμή 5. δύω
Gen 28:11 stayed there that night, because the sun had set. 1
Ps 50: 1 from the rising of the sun to its setting. 2
113: 3 From the rising of the sun to its setting the name 2
Mal 1:11 from the rising of the sun to its setting 2
Lke 4:40 Now when the sun was setting 3
Tob 2: 7 When the sun had set 5
1Mc 10:50 He pressed the battle strongly until the sun set 5
12:27 So when the sun set 5
3Mc 4:15 from the rising of the sun till its setting 4

set (4) 1. יצת 2. נתן 3. שׁלח
Jos 8: 8 you shall set the city on fire, doing as the LORD 1
Jdg 1: 8 took it, and smote it . . and set the city on fire. 3
9:49 they set the stronghold on fire over them 1
20:48 all the towns which they found they set on fire. 3
2Sm 14:30 See, Jo'ab's field . . go and set it on fire. 1
30 Ab'salom's servants set the field on fire. 1
31 Why have your servants set my field on fire? 1
Ps 74: 7 They set thy sanctuary on fire; 3
Isa 50:11 all you who kindle a fire, who set brands alight! ‡
Jer 11:16 with the roar of a great tempest he will set fire 1
Ezk 30: 8 when I have set fire to Egypt, and all her helpers 2
14 Pathros a desolation, and will set fire to Zo'an 2
16 I will set fire to Egypt; 2

set *See* ablaze, aflame, aright, date, free, price, right, time, trembling.

set a bound 1. גבל 2. חקה
Exd 19:23 Set bounds about the mountain, and consecrate 1
Job 13:27 thou settest a bound to the soles of my feet. 2

set a seal 1. חתם
Neh 9:38 princes . . and our priests set their seal to it. 1

set a snare 1. יקשׁ
Jer 50:24 I set a snare for you and you were taken, O Babylon 1

set a table 1. καταστρώννυμι
Jdt 12: 1 and ordered them to set a table for her 1

set above 1. ὑπεράνω
AEs 13:14 not set the glory of man above the glory of God 1

set against 1. ἀντιλέγω 2. διχάζω
Mat 10:35 For I have come to set a man against his father 2
Joh 19:12 every one . . sets himself against Caesar. 1

set an ambush 1. צפן
Prv 1:18 they set an ambush for their own lives. 1

set apart 1. בדל 2. נתן 3. עבר 4. פלה 5. קדשׁ 6. רום 7. ἀφορίζω 8. ἐκχωρίζω 9. χωρίζω 10. segrego
Exd 8:22 on that day I will set apart the land of Goshen 4
13:12 set apart to the LORD all that first opens 3
Lev 20:25 which I have set apart for you to hold unclean 1
Deu 4:41 Moses set apart three cities in the east 1
10: 8 At that time the LORD set apart the tribe of Levi 1
19: 2 set apart three cities for you in the land 1
7 command you, You shall set apart three cities. 1
Jos 16: 9 towns which were set apart for the E'phraimites 1
20: 7 they set apart Kedesh in Galilee 5
1Ch 23:13 Aaron was set apart to consecrate 1
25: 1 set apart for the service certain of the sons 1
Ezr 8:20 David . . had set apart to attend the Levites. 2
24 Then I set apart twelve of the leading priests 1
Neh 12:47 set apart that which was for the Levites; 5
47 Levites set apart that which was for the sons 5
Ps 4: 3 But know that the LORD has set apart the godly 4
Isa 65: 5 do not come near me, for I am set apart from you. 5
Jer 12: 3 and set them apart for the day of slaughter. 5
Ezk 39:14 They will set apart men to pass through the land 1
45: 1 you shall set apart for the LORD a portion 6
48: 8 shall be the portion which you shall set apart 6
9 portion which you shall set apart for the LORD 6
20 The whole portion which you shall set apart 6
Act 13: 2 Set apart for me Barnabas and Saul 7
Rom 1: 1 Paul . . set apart for the gospel of God 7
Gal 1:15 when he who had set me apart before I was born 7
1Es 4:44 which Cyrus set apart 8
57 all the vessels which Cyrus had set apart 8
8:54 Then I set apart twelve of the leaders 9
2Es 3:16 thou didst set apart Jacob for thyself 10

set around 1. περιτίθημι
Mat 21:33 set a hedge around it, and dug a wine press in it 1
Mrk 12: 1 and set a hedge around it 1

set aside 1. נסע 2. סור 3. ἀθέτησις 4. διαφυλάσσω 5. παρωθέω
2Kg 4: 4 pour into all . . and when one is full, set it aside. 1
2Ch 35:12 they set aside the burnt offerings 2
Heb 7:18 On the one hand, a former commandment is set aside 3
Jdt 11:13 they had consecrated and set aside for the priests 4
2Mc 4:11 He set aside the existing royal concessions 5

set at nought 1. שׁנא (A)
Dan 3:28 set at nought the king's command, and yielded up 1

set at rest 1. מְנוּחָה 2. נוח 3. ἀναπαύω
2Sm 14:17 The word of my lord the king will set me at rest'; 1
Zec 6: 8 have set my Spirit at rest in the north country. 2
2Co 7:13 because his mind has been set at rest by you all. 3

set back 1. אצל
Ezk 42: 6 the upper chambers were set back from the ground 1

set before 1. παράκειμαι 2. παρατίθημι 3. πρόκειμαι 4. antepono
Mrk 6:41 loaves . . to set before the people 2
8: 6 to his disciples to set before the people 2
6 and they set them before the crowd. 2
7 these also should be set before them. 2
Lke 9:16 and gave them . . to set before the crowd. 2
10: 8 eat what is set before you; 2
11: 6 I have nothing to set before him'; 2
Act 16:34 and set food before them 2
1Co 10:27 eat whatever is set before you 2
Heb 6:18 to seize the hope set before us. 3
12: 1 the race that is set before us 3
2 for the joy that was set before him 3
2Es 7: 9 he passes through the danger set before him? 4
20 the law of God which is set before them 4
Tob 7: 8 and set large servings of food before them. 2
Sir 31:16 Eat like a human being what is set before you 1
4Mc 6:15 We will set before you some cooked meat 2

set bounds 1. גבל
Exd 19:12 you shall set bounds for the people round about 1

set down 1. יצק 2. כתב 3. נוח 4. τίθημι
Deu 26: 4 set it down before the altar of the LORD your God. 3
10 set it down before the LORD your God, and worship 3
Jos 18: 9 the men . . set down in a book a description of it 2
1Sm 6:18 great stone, beside which they set down the ark 3
2Sm 15:24 and they set down the ark of God 1
Ezk 37: 1 and set me down in the midst of the valley; 3
40: 2 and set me down upon a very high mountain 3
Zec 5:11 they will set the ephah down there on its base. 3
Bel 1:36 lifted him by his hair and set him down in Babylon 4

set fire 1. בער 2. ἐμπιμπρημι 3. ἐμπίπρημι 4. ἐμπυρίζω 5. ὑφάπτω
Jdg 15: 5 And when he had set fire to the torches 1
Sir 49: 6 who set fire to the chosen city of the sanctuary 4
1Mc 9:67 and set fire to the machines of war. 4
11:48 They set fire to the city 4
2Mc 8: 6 he would set fire to towns and villages 3
33 burned those who had set fire to the sacred gates 2
10:36 and set fire to the towers 3
12: 6 He set fire to the harbor by night 2
9 and set fire to the harbor and the fleet 5

firmly set 1. στηρίζω
4Mc 17: 5 and are firmly set in heaven with them. 1

set foot 1. ἐπιβαίνω
Act 20:18 from the first day that I set foot in Asia 1

set forth 1. הלך 2. יצא 3. נסע 4. ספר 5. ערך 6. קרב 7. δηλόω 8. διηγέομαι 9. ἐξέρχομαι 10. παρατίθημι 11. προτίθημι 12. τίθημι

Gen 12: 5 and they set forth to go to the land of Canaan. 2
Jos 9:12 we took it . . on the day we set forth to come to you 2
Jdg 18:11 600 men . . set forth from Zorah and Esh'ta-ol 3
Rut 2: 3 she set forth and went and gleaned in the field 1
Isa 41:21 Set forth your case, says the LORD; 6
43:26 set forth your case, that you may be proved right. 4
44: 7 let him declare and set it forth before me. 5
Eph 1: 9 his purpose which he set forth in Christ 11
Jdt 2: 2 and set forth to them his secret plan 12
4 When he had finished setting forth his plan •
Sir 44: 5 set forth verses in writing; 8
Bel 1:11 you yourself, O king, shall set forth the food 10
14 the king set forth the food for Bel 10
1Mc 7: 1 Demetrius . . set forth from Rome 9
11:60 Then Jonathan set forth 9
2Mc 2:23 which has been set forth by Jason of Cyrene 7

set high 1. רום

Ps 27: 5 he will set me high upon a rock. 1
Isa 14:13 above the stars of God I will set my throne on high; 1

set in array 1. ערך 2. παρίστημι

Jdg 20:30 and set themselves in array against Gib'e-ah 1
33 Israel rose up . . and set themselves in array 1
1Ch 19:17 David set the battle in array against the Syrians 1
Jer 6:23 upon horses, set in array as a man for battle 1
50:14 Set yourselves in array against Babylon 1
Act 4:26 The kings of the earth set themselves in array 2

set in filigree 1. שבץ

Exd 28:20 they shall be set in gold filigree. 1

set in order 1. ערך 2. צוה אֶל 3. צוה לְ 4. διαρρυθμίζω 5. dispono

Exd 40: 4 in the table, and set its arrangements in order; 1
23 set the bread in order on it before the LORD; 1
Lev 24: 8 Every sabbath day Aaron shall set it in order 1
2Sm 17:23 And he set his house in order, and hanged himself; 2
2Kg 20: 1 Set your house in order; for you shall die 3
Job 33: 5 set your words in order before me; take your stand. 1
Isa 38: 1 Set your house in order; for you shall die 3
2Es 14:13 Now therefore, set your house in order 5
2Mc 7:22 nor I who set in order the elements 4

set in place 1. τίθημι

2Mc 14:21 seats of honor were set in place; 1

set off 1. χωρίζω

2Mc 10:19 he himself set off for places where . . 1

set on edge 1. קהה

Jer 31:30 eats sour grapes, his teeth shall be set on edge. 1
Ezk 18: 2 and the children's teeth are set on edge 1

set on fire 1. יצת 2. להט 3. תְּשַׁלַּח בָּאֵשׁ 4. φλογίζω 5. exardesco

Deu 32:22 sets on fire the foundations of the mountains. 2
Jos 8:19 and they made haste to set the city on fire. 1
2Kg 8:12 you will set on fire their fortresses 3
Isa 42:25 heat of his anger . . set him on fire round about 2
Jer 32:29 shall come and set this city on fire, and burn it 1
Jas 3: 6 setting on fire the cycle of nature 4
6 and set on fire by hell. 4
2Es 7:61 they are set on fire and burn hotly 5

set on high 1. שגב

Ps 69:29 let thy salvation, O God, set me on high! 1

set on the way 1. שלח

Gen 18:16 went with them to set them on their way. 1
26:31 and Isaac set them on their way, and they departed 1

set one's desire 1. ἐπιθυμέω

Wis 6:11 Therefore set your desire on my words 1

set one's heart 1. ἐπέχω

Sir 5: 1 Do not set your heart on your wealth 1

set one's hope 1. קוה 2. ἐλπίζω

Jer 14:22 We set our hope on thee, for thou doest all these 1
Joh 5:45 it is Moses . . on whom you set your hope. 2
2Co 1:10 on him we have set our hope 2
1Ti 4:10 because we have our hope set on the living God 2
5: 5 a real widow . . has set her hope on God 2
6:17 nor to set their hopes on uncertain riches 2
1Pe 1:13 set your hope fully upon the grace that is coming 2

set one's love 1. חשק

Deu 7: 7 that the LORD set his love upon you and chose you 1

set one's mind 1. φρονέω

Rom 8: 5 who . . set their minds on the things of the flesh 1
5 who . . set their minds on the things of the Spirit. •
Php 3:19 with minds set on earthly things. 1
Col 3: 2 Set your minds on things that are above 1

set out 1. הלך 2. זרע 3. יצא 4. נסע 5. נתן 6. פשע 7. קום 8. קוּם וְבוֹא 9. ἀνάγω 10. ἀναζεύγνυμι 11. ἐκπορεύομαι 12. ἐξέρχομαι 13. ποιέω 14. πρόθεσιν ποιέω 15. προτίθημι 16. iter

Gen 18:16 Then the men set out from there 7
46: 5 Then Jacob set out from Beer-sheba; 7
Exd 16: 1 They set out from Elim, and all the congregation 4
19: 2 when they set out from Reph'idim and came 4
Num 1:51 When the tabernacle is to set out, the Levites 4
2: 9 They shall set out first on the march. 4
16 They shall set out second. 4
17 Then the tent of meeting shall set out 4
17 as they encamp, so shall they set out 4
24 They shall set out third on the march. 4
31 They shall set out last, standard by standard. 4
34 so they set out, every one in his family 4
4: 5 When the camp is to set out, Aaron and his sons 4
15 as the camp sets out, after that the sons of Kohath 4
9:17 after that the people of Israel set out; 4
18 command of the LORD the people of Israel set out 4
19 kept the charge of the LORD, and did not set out. 4
20 according to the command of the LORD they set out. 4
21 cloud was taken up in the morning, they set out 4
21 when the cloud was taken up they set out. 4
22 Israel remained in camp and did not set out; 4
22 when it was taken up they set out. 4
23 at the command of the LORD they set out; 4
10: 5 camps that are on the east side shall set out. 4
6 camps that are on the south side shall set out. 4
6 alarm is to be blown whenever they are to set out. 4
13 They set out for the first time 4
14 men of Judah set out first by their companies; 4
17 sons . . who carried the tabernacle, set out. 4
18 camp of Reuben set out by their companies; 4
21 Ko'hathites set out, carrying the holy things 4
22 men of E'phraim set out by their companies; 4
25 men of Dan . . set out by their companies; 4
28 order of march . . when they set out. 4
29 We are setting out for the place of which the LORD 4
33 set out from the mount of the LORD three days' 4
34 whenever they set out from the camp. 4
35 whenever the ark set out, Moses said, "Arise, O LORD 4
12:15 the people did not set out on the march 4
16 After that the people set out from Haze'roth 4
14:25 turn tomorrow and set out for the wilderness 4
21: 4 From Mount Hor they set out . . to the Red Sea 4
10 people of Israel set out, and encamped in Oboth. 4
11 set out from Oboth, and encamped at I'ye-ab'arim 4
12 set out, and encamped in the Valley of Zered. 4
13 set out, and encamped on the other side 4
22: 1 Then the people of Israel set out, and encamped 4
33: 3 They set out from Ram'eses in the first month 4
5 the people of Israel set out from Ram'eses 4
6 they set out from Succoth, and encamped at Etham 4
7 they set out from Etham, and turned back 4
8 they set out from before Hahi'roth 4
9 they set out from Marah, and came to Elim; 4
10 they set out from Elim, and encamped by the Red Sea 4
11 they set out from the Red Sea, and encamped 4
12 set out from the wilderness of Sin, and encamped 4
13 they set out from Dophkah, and encamped at Alush. 4
14 they set out from Alush, and encamped at Reph'idim 4
15 they set out from Reph'idim, and encamped 4
16 they set out from the wilderness of Sinai 4
17 they set out from Kib'roth-hatta'avah, and encamped 4
18 set out from Haze'roth, and encamped at Rithmah. 4
19 set out from Rithmah, and encamped 4
20 they set out from Rim'mon-per'ez, and encamped 4
21 they set out from Libnah, and encamped at Rissah. 4
22 set out from Rissah, and encamped at Kehela'thah. 4
23 they set out from Kehela'thah, and encamped 4
24 set out from Mount Shepher, and encamped 4
25 set out from Hara'dah, and encamped at Makhe'loth. 4
26 set out from Makhe'loth, and encamped at Tahath. 4
27 they set out from Tahath, and encamped at Terah. 4
28 they set out from Terah, and encamped at Mithkah. 4
29 set out from Mithkah, and encamped at Hashmo'nah. 4
30 set out from Hashmo'nah, and encamped 4
31 set out from Mose'roth, and encamped 4
32 set out from Bene-ja'akan, and encamped 4
33 set out from Hor-haggid'gad, and encamped 4
34 set out from Jot'bathah, and encamped at Abro'nah. 4
35 they set out from Abro'nah, and encamped 4
36 they set out from E'zion-ge'ber, and encamped 4
37 set out from Kadesh, and encamped at Mount Hor 4
41 set out from Mount Hor, and encamped at Zalmo'nah. 4
42 set out from Zalmo'nah, and encamped at Punon. 4
43 they set out from Punon, and encamped at Oboth. 4
44 set out from Oboth, and encamped at I'ye-ab'arim 4
45 they set out from I'yim, and encamped at Dibon-gad. 4
46 set out from Dibon-gad, and encamped 4
47 set out from Al'mon-diblatha'im, and encamped 4
48 set out from the mountains of Ab'arim 4
Deu 1:19 And we set out from Horeb 4
Jos 3: 1 Early . . Joshua rose and set out from Shittim 4
3 you shall set out from your place and follow it 4
14 the people set out from their tents, to pass over 4
9:17 Israel set out and reached their cities 4
18: 4 I will send them out that they may set out 7
Jdg 5:14 From E'phraim they set out . . into the valley •
18: 5 the journey on which we are setting out will succeed. 1
Rut 1: 7 she set out from the place where she was 3
1Sm 9: 6 about the journey on which we have set out. 1
29:11 David set out with his men early in the morning 1
30: 9 David set out, and the 600 men who were with him 1
2Sm 4: 5 sons of Rimmon . . Rechab and Ba'anah, set out 1
17: 1 and I will set out and pursue David tonight. 7
1Kg 11:18 They set out from Mid'ian and came to Paran 7
2Kg 4:25 So she set out, and came to the man of God 1
9:21 Then Joram . . and Ahazi'ah king of Judah set out 3
10:12 Then he set out and went to Sama'ria. 8
19: 9 Behold, he has set out to fight against you 3
Isa 17:10 you plant . . and set out slips of an alien god 2
27: 4 I would set out against them, I would burn them up 6
30: 2 who set out to go down to Egypt 1
29 as when one sets out to the sound of the flute to go 1
37: 9 He has set out to fight against you. 3
Jer 4: 7 a destroyer of nations has set out; 4
37:12 Jeremiah set out from Jerusalem to go to the land 3
41:10 and set out to cross over to the Ammonites. 1
Ezk 17:22 from the lofty top of the cedar, and will set it out; 5
Mrk 10:17 as he was setting out on his journey 11
14:16 the disciples set out and went to the city 12
Lke 8:22 So they set out 9
3Jn 1: 7 For they have set out for his sake 12
2Es 15:29 and from the day that they set out 16
Jdt 2:19 he set out with his whole army 12
1Mc 10:57 So Ptolemy set out from Egypt 12
74 and set out from Jerusalem 12
11: 2 He set out for Syria with peaceable words 12
22 as soon as he heard it he set out 10
15:10 Antiochus set out and invaded the land of his fathers 12
2Mc 1: 8 we lighted the lamps and we set out the loaves. 15
15 When the priests . . had set out the treasures 15
3: 8 Heliodorus at once set out on his journey 13
10: 3 and set out the bread of the Presence. 14
12:29 Setting out from there 10
13:26 and set out for Antioch 10
14:16 they set out from there immediately 10

set out by stages 1. נסע

Num10:12 Israel set out by stages from the wilderness 1

set over 1. פקד 2. ἐφίστημι 3. καθίστημι 4. προΐστημι

2Kg 11:15 the captains who were set over the army 1
Mat 24:45 whom his master has set over his household 3
Sir 23: 2 O that whips were set over my thoughts 2
4Mc 11:27 those of the divine law that are set over us; 4

set sail 1. ἀνάγω

Act 13:13 Now Paul and his company set sail from Paphos 1
16:11 Setting sail therefore from Tro'as 1
18:21 and he set sail from Ephesus. 1
20: 3 as he was about to set sail for Syria 1
13 But going ahead to the ship, we set sail for Assos 1
21: 1 when we had parted from them and set sail 1
2 we went aboard, and set sail. 1
27:21 should not have set sail from Crete 1
28:11 After three months we set sail 1

set seal 1. σφραγίζω

Joh 3:33 he . . sets his seal to this 1
6:27 for on him has God the Father set his seal. 1
Tob 7:14 they set their seals to it. 1

set under a cloud 1. עוב

Lam 2: 1 the Lord in his anger has set . . Zion under a cloud! 1

set up 1. בנה 2. יצג 3. כון 4. נסך 5. נצב 6. נשא 7. נתן 8. עלה 9. עמד 10. קום 11. רום 12. שום 13. שית 14. שכן 15. קום (A) 16. ἀνίστημι 17. ἀνορθόω 18. ἵστημι 19. καθιδρύω 20. καθίστημι 21. καταβάλλω 22. πήγνυμι 23. ποιέω 24. συνίστημι 25. τίθημι 26. ὑπερείδω 27. erigo

Gen 28:12 there was a ladder set up on the earth 5
18 took the stone . . and set it up for a pillar 12
22 this stone, which I have set up for a pillar 12
31:45 Jacob took a stone, and set it up as a pillar. 11
35:14 Jacob set up a pillar in the place where he had 5
20 Jacob set up a pillar upon her grave; 5
Exd 25:37 the lamps shall be set up so as to give light 8
27:20 that a lamp may be set up to burn continually. 8
30: 8 when Aaron sets up the lamps in the evening 8
40: 4 bring in the lampstand, and set up its lamps. 8
5 set up the screen for the door of the tabernacle. 12
8 you shall set up the court round about, and hang up 12
18 he laid its bases, and set up its frames 12
21 set up the veil of the screen, and screened the ark 12
25 set up the lamps before the LORD; 8
33 set up the screen of the gate of the court. 7
Lev 26: 1 you shall not set up a figured stone in your land 7
Num 1:51 the Levites shall set it up. 10
7: 1 Moses had finished setting up the tabernacle 10
8: 2 When you set up the lamps, the seven lamps 8
3 Aaron . . set up its lamps to give light in front 8
9:15 On the day that the tabernacle was set up 10

10:21 tabernacle was set up before their arrival. 10
Deu 16:22 not set up a pillar which the LORD your God hates. 10
27: 2 set up large stones, and plaster them with plaster; 10
4 set up these stones, concerning which I command 10
15 makes a graven . . image . . sets it up in secret.' 12
Jos 4: 9 And Joshua set up twelve stones in the . . Jordan 10
20 those twelve stones . . Joshua set up in Gilgal. 10
6:26 at the cost of his . . son shall he set up its gates. 5
18: 1 at Shiloh, and set up the tent of meeting there; 14
24:26 took a . . stone, and set it up there under the oak 10
Jdg 18:30 the Danites set up the graven image 10
31 they set up Micah's graven image which he made 12
1Sm 5: 2 took the ark of God . . and set it up beside Dagon. 2
7:12 a stone and set it up between Mizpah and Jesha'nah 12
15:12 he set up a monument for himself and turned 5
2Sm 3:10 and set up the throne of David over Israel 10
18:18 Ab'salom . . set up for himself the pillar 5
1Kg 7:21 He set up the pillars at the vestibule 10
21 he set up the pillar on the south and called its 10
21 he set up the pillar on the north and called its 10
15: 4 a lamp in Jerusalem, setting up his son after him 10
16:34 and set up its gates at the cost of . . Segub 5
2Kg 17:10 they set up for themselves pillars and Ashe'rim 5
1Ch 18: 3 to set up his monument at the river Euphra'tes. 5
2Ch 3:17 He set up the pillars in front of the temple 10
25:14 gods . . of Se'ir . . , and set them up as his gods 9
33:19 sites on which he . . set up the Ashe'rim 9
Ezr 9: 9 grant us some reviving to set up the house of our God 11
Neh 6: 1 I had not set up the doors in the gates) 9
7 set up prophets to proclaim concerning you 9
7: 1 wall had been built and I had set up the doors 9
Job 16:12 he set me up as his target 10
Ps 60: 4 Thou hast set up a banner for those who fear thee 7
74: 4 they set up their own signs for signs. 12
Prv 8:23 Ages ago I was set up, at the first 4
9: 1 Wisdom . . has set up her seven pillars. 26
Isa 26: 1 he sets up salvation as walls and bulwarks. 13
40:20 a skilful craftsman to set up an image 3
57: 8 Behind the door . . you have set up your symbol; 12
Jer 10:20 to spread my tent again, and to set up my curtains. 10
11:13 the altars you have set up to shame 12
31:21 Set up waymarks for yourself 5
32:34 They set up their abominations in the house 12
50: 2 set up a banner and proclaim, conceal it not 6
51:12 Set up a standard against the walls of Babylon; 6
12 make the watch strong; set up watchmen; 10
27 Set up a standard on the earth, blow the trumpet 6
Ezk 26: 8 he will set up a siege wall against you 7
34:23 I will set up over them one shepherd 10
39:15 sees a man's bone, then he shall set up a sign by it 1
Dan 2:21 he removes kings and sets up kings; 15
44 God of heaven will set up a kingdom 15
3: 1 set it up on the plain of Dura, in the province 15
2 image which King Nebuchadnez'zar had set up. 15
3 image that King Nebuchadnez'zar had set up; 15
3 image that Nebuchadnez'zar had set up. 15
5 golden image . . King Nebuchadnez'zar has set up; 15
7 golden image . . King Nebuchadnez'zar had set up. 15
12 worship the golden image which you have set up. 15
14 worship the golden image which I have set up? 15
18 worship the golden image which you have set up. 15
11:31 set up the abomination that makes desolate. 7
12:11 abomination that makes desolate is set up 7
Nah 2: 5 they hasten to the wall, the mantelet is set up. 3
Mrk 13:14 when you see the desolating sacrilege set up 18
Act 6:13 and set up false witnesses who said 18
15:16 I will rebuild its ruins, and I will set it up 17
Heb 8: 2 the true tent which is set up not by man 22
1Es 2:23 kept setting up blockades in it from of old 24
2Es 11:25 wings planned to set themselves up 27
26 I looked, and behold, one was set up 27
12: 2 the two wings . . set themselves up to reign 27
Jdt 5: 1 and set up barricades in the plains 25
8: 5 She set up a tent for herself on the roof of her house 23
12 and are setting yourselves up in the place of God 18
Sir 49:13 set up the gates and bars 18
LJr 1:17 when they have been set up in the temples 19
34 They cannot set up a king or depose one. 20
53 they cannot set up a king over a country 16
Man 1:10 setting up abominations and multiplying offenses 18
1Mc 6:17 he set up Antiochus the king's son to reign 20
51 He set up siege towers 18
2Mc 5: 6 he was setting up trophies of victory 21
14:13 to set up Alcimus as high priest 20
3Mc 2:27 he set up a stone on the tower in the courtyard 16

set up a banner 1. דגל
Ps 20: 5 in the name of our God set up our banners! 1

set up a king 1. מלך
2Kg 8:20 Edom revolted . . and set up a king of their own. 1
2Ch 21: 8 Edom revolted . . and set up a king of their own. 1

set up a prince 1. שרר
Hos 8: 4 They set up princes, but without my knowledge. 1

set up as king 1. מלך
Isa 7: 6 set up the son of Ta'be-el as king in the midst of it 1

set up divisions 1. ἀποδιορίζω
Jde 1:19 It is these who set up divisions, worldly people 1

set upon 1. ἐπιβιβάζω 2. ἐπιτίθημι
Lke 19:35 they set Jesus upon it. 1
Jdt 16: 7 nor did tall giants set upon him 2

set vain hope 1. הבל
Ps 62:10 in extortion, set no vain hopes on robbery; 1

setting 1. מַשְׂכִּית 2. מִשְׁבְּצוֹת 3. תֹּף 4. δέσις 5. κόσμος
Exd 28:14 shall attach the corded chains to the settings. 2
2Ch 3: 6 the house with settings of precious stones. *
Prv 25:11 like apples of gold in a setting of silver. 1
Ezk 28:13 and wrought in gold were your settings 3
Sir 32: 5 A ruby seal in a setting of gold 5
45:11 in a setting of gold, the work of a jeweler 4

setting *See also* elaborate, time.

setting of filigree 1. מִשְׁבְּצוֹת
Exd 28:11 enclose them in settings of gold filigree. 1
13 you shall make settings of gold filigree 1
25 attach to the two settings of filigree 1
39: 6 enclosed in settings of gold filigree 1
13 they were enclosed in settings of gold filigree. 1
16 they made two settings of gold filigree 1
18 had attached to the two settings of filigree; 1

rich setting 1. κατασκεύασμα
Sir 32: 6 A seal of emerald in a rich setting of gold 1

settle 1. גור 2. חנה 3. ישב 4. נוח 5. נחת 6. נפל 7. רבץ 8. שכן 9. שקט 10. יתב (A) 11. ἑδράζω 12. καθίζω 13. καθίστημι 14. κατοικέω 15. κατοικίζω
Gen 11: 2 in the land of Shinar and settled there. 3
31 but when they came to Haran, they settled there. 3
25:18 he settled over against all his people. 6
47: 6 Egypt is before you; settle your father 3
11 Then Joseph settled his father and his brothers 3
Exd 10:14 locusts . . settled on the whole country 4
24:16 The glory of the LORD settled on Mount Sinai 8
Lev 26:32 your enemies who settle in it shall be astonished 3
Num21:25 Israel settled in all the cities of the Amorites 3
32:40 Moses gave Gilead to Machir . . and he settled in it. 3
33:53 take possession of the land and settle in it 3
Deu 2:12 sons of Esau . . settled in their stead; 3
21 dispossessed them, and settled in their stead; 3
22 dispossessed them, and settled in their stead 3
23 Caph'torim . . settled in their stead.) 3
21: 5 dispute and every assault shall be settled. *
29:20 curses written in this book would settle upon 7
Jos 19:47 they took possession of it and settled in it 3
50 and he rebuilt the city, and settled in it. 3
21:43 having taken possession . . they settled there. 3
22:33 the Reubenites and the Gadites were settled. 3
Jdg 1:16 Arad; and they went and settled with the people. 3
1Ch 4:41 exterminated them . . and settled in their place 3
2Ch 8: 2 and settled the people of Israel in them. 3
28:18 they settled there. 3
Ezr 4:10 Osnap'par deported and settled in the cities 10
Ps 65:10 settling its ridges, softening it with showers 5
78:55 settled the tribes of Israel in their tents. 8
Isa 7:19 will all come and settle in the steep ravines 4
23: 7 city . . whose feet carried her to settle afar? 1
Jer 48:11 Moab . . has settled on his lees; 9
49: 1 and his people settled in its cities? 3
Nah 3:17 like clouds of locusts settling on the fences 2
1Es 5:46 some of the people settled in Jerusalem 15
9:37 settled in Jerusalem and in the country 14
Jdt 5: 9 There they settled, and prospered 14
19 and have settled in the hill country 15
AEs 13: 2 to settle the lives of my subjects 13
Sir 22:17 A mind settled on an intelligent thought 11
1Mc 2: 1 moved from Jerusalem and settled in Modein. 12
3:36 settle aliens in all their territory 15
13:48 settled in it men who observed the law 15
14:34 He settled Jews there 15
37 He settled Jews in it 15

settle (2) 1. כלה 2. תמם 3. ἀπαλλάσσω 4. ἐπιλύω 5. καταστέλλω 6. συλλύω 7. συναίρω 8. τελέω 9. τίθημι
Rut 3:18 the man will not rest, but will settle the matter 1
2Sm 20:18 ask counsel at Abel'; and so they settled a matter. 2
Mat 18:23 to settle accounts with his servants. 7
25:19 settled accounts with them. 7
Lke 12:58 make an effort to settle with him on the way 3
21:14 Settle it therefore in your minds 9
Act 19:39 it shall be settled in the regular assembly. 4
Tob 7: 8 let the matter be settled. 8
2Mc 4:31 the king went hastily to settle the trouble 5
11:14 them to settle everything on just terms 6
13:23 settled with them and offered sacrifice 6

cause to settle 1. שכן
Ezk 32: 4 cause all the birds of the air to settle on you 1

settle down 1. שכן 2. εὐσταθέω 3. κατασκηνόω
Num 9:17 in the place where the cloud settled down 1
10:12 cloud settled down in the wilderness of Paran. 1
Jdg 5:17 Asher sat . . settling down by his landings. 1
Sir 28:16 nor will he settle down in peace. 3
2Mc 14:25 he . . settled down, and shared the common life. 2

settled *See* provision.

settlement 1. טִירָה 2. מוֹשָׁב 3. κατοικία
1Ch 4:33 These were their settlements 2
6:54 their settlements within their borders 1
7:28 possessions and settlements were Bethel 2
1Es 9:12 those in our settlements who have foreign wives 3
37 the sons of Israel were in their settlements 3

peaceful settlement 1. εἰρήνη
2Mc 4: 6 affairs could not again reach a peaceful settlement 1

seven 1. שֶׁבַע 2. שְׁבַע (A) 3. ἕβδομος 4. ἑπτά 5. septem
Gen 7: 2 Take with you seven pairs of all clean animals 1
3 seven pairs of the birds of the air also 1
4 For in seven days I will send rain upon the earth 1
10 after seven days the waters of the flood came 1
8:10 He waited another seven days 1
12 Then he waited another seven days 1
21:28 Abraham set seven ewe lambs of the flock apart. 1
29 What is the meaning of these seven ewe lambs 1
30 He said, "These seven ewe lambs you will take 1
29:18 he said, "I will serve you seven years 1
20 Jacob served seven years for Rachel 1
27 in return for serving me another seven years. 1
30 and served Laban for another seven years. 1
31:23 pursued him for seven days and followed close 1
33: 3 bowing himself to the ground seven times 1
41: 2 came up out of the Nile seven cows sleek and fat 1
3 behold, seven other cows, gaunt and thin, came up 1
4 thin cows ate up the seven sleek and fat cows. 1
5 and behold, seven ears of grain, plump and good 1
6 behold, after them sprouted seven ears 1
7 swallowed up the seven plump and full ears. 1
18 seven cows, fat and sleek, came up out of the Nile 1
19 seven other cows came up after them 1
20 gaunt cows ate up the first seven fat cows 1
22 saw in my dream seven ears growing on one stalk 1
23 seven ears, withered, thin, and blighted 1
24 the thin ears swallowed up the seven good ears. 1
26 The seven good cows are seven years 1
26 The seven good cows are seven years 1
26 good cows are seven years, and the seven good ears 1
26 and the seven good ears are seven years; 1
27 The seven lean and gaunt cows that came up after 1
27 cows that came up after them are seven years 1
27 and the seven empty ears blighted by the east 1
27 east wind are also seven years of famine. 1
29 There will come seven years of great plenty 1
30 after them there will arise seven years 1
34 of Egypt during the seven plenteous years. 1
36 a reserve for the land against the seven years 1
47 During the seven plenteous years the earth 1
48 he gathered up all the food of the seven years 1
53 The seven years of plenty that prevailed 1
54 the seven years of famine began to come 1
46:25 and these she bore to Jacob-seven persons in all 1
50:10 and he made a mourning for his father seven days. 1
Exd 2:16 Now the priest of Mid'ian had seven daughters; 1
7:25 Seven days passed after the LORD had struck 1
12:15 Seven days you shall eat unleavened bread; 1
19 For seven days no leaven shall be found 1
13: 6 Seven days you shall eat unleavened bread 1
7 Unleavened bread shall be eaten for seven days; 1
22:30 seven days it shall be with its dam; 1
23:15 you shall eat unleavened bread for seven days 1
25:37 you shall make the seven lamps for it; 1
29:30 The son . . shall wear them seven days 1
35 through seven days shall you ordain them 1
37 Seven days you shall make atonement 1
34:18 Seven days you shall eat unleavened bread 1
37:23 he made its seven lamps and its snuffers 1
Lev 4: 6 sprinkle part of the blood seven times 1
17 blood . . sprinkle it seven times before the LORD 1
8:11 he sprinkled some of it on the altar seven times 1
33 the door of the tent of meeting for seven days 1
33 for it will take seven days to ordain you 1
35 you shall remain day and night for seven days 1
12: 2 then she shall be unclean seven days 1
13: 4 shut up the diseased person for seven days 1
5 then the priest shall shut him up seven days more 1
21 then the priest shall shut him up seven days 1
26 the priest shall shut him up seven days 1
31 shut up the person . . for seven days 1
33 shut up the person . . for seven days more 1
50 priest shall shut up that . . for seven days 1
54 and he shall shut it up seven days more 1
14: 7 he shall sprinkle it seven times upon him 1
8 but shall dwell outside his tent seven days 1
16 sprinkle some oil with his finger seven times 1
27 sprinkle . . seven times before the LORD 1

38 go out . . and shut up the house seven days 1
51 and sprinkle the house seven times 1
15:13 then he shall count for himself seven days 1
19 she shall be in her impurity for seven days 1
24 impurity is on him, he shall be unclean seven days 1
28 she shall count for herself seven days 1
16:14 shall sprinkle the blood . . seven times 1
19 sprinkle . . with his finger seven times 1
22:27 it shall remain seven days with its mother 1
23: 6 seven days you shall eat unleavened bread 1
8 present an offering . . to the LORD seven days 1
15 seven full weeks shall they be 1
18 you shall present with the bread seven lambs 1
34 for seven days is the feast of booths to the LORD 1
36 Seven days you shall present offerings by fire 1
39 you shall keep the feast of the LORD seven days 1
40 rejoice before the LORD your God seven days 1
41 You shall keep it as a feast to the LORD seven days 1
42 You shall dwell in booths for seven days 1
25: 8 you shall count seven weeks of years, seven times 1
8 count . . weeks of years, seven times seven years 1
8 weeks . . seven times seven years 1
8 so that the time of the seven weeks of years shall 1
Num 8: 2 seven lamps shall give light in front 1
12:14 should she not be shamed seven days? 1
14 Let her be shut up outside the camp seven days 1
15 Miriam was shut up outside the camp seven days; 1
13:22 (Hebron was built seven years before Zo'an 1
19: 4 sprinkle some of her blood . . seven times. 1
11 He who touches . . shall be unclean seven days; 1
14 every one . . shall be unclean seven days. 1
16 shall be unclean seven days. 1
23: 1 said to Balak, "Build for me here seven altars 1
1 provide for me here seven bulls and seven rams. 1
1 provide for me here seven bulls and seven rams. 1
4 I have prepared the seven altars 1
14 built seven altars, and offered a bull and a ram 1
29 Build for me here seven altars 1
29 provide for me here seven bulls and seven rams. 1
29 provide for me here seven bulls and seven rams. 1
28:11 burnt offering . . seven male lambs a year old 1
17 seven days shall unleavened bread be eaten. 1
19 a burnt offering . . seven male lambs a year old; 1
21 tenth shall you offer for each of the seven lambs; 1
24 same way you shall offer daily, for seven days 1
27 a burnt offering . . seven male lambs a year old; 1
29 a tenth for each of the seven lambs; 1
29: 2 burnt offering . . seven male lambs a year old 1
4 one tenth for each of the seven lambs; 1
8 a burnt offering . . seven male lambs a year old; 1
10 a tenth for each of the seven lambs 1
12 you shall keep a feast to the LORD seven days; 1
32 On the seventh day seven bulls, two rams, fourteen 1
36 burnt offering . . seven male lambs a year old 1
31:19 Encamp outside the camp seven days; 1
Deu 7: 1 Jeb'usites, seven nations greater and mightier 1
15: 1 end of every seven years you shall grant a release. 1
16: 3 seven days . . eat it with unleavened bread 1
4 No leaven . . in all your territory for seven days; 1
9 count seven weeks; begin to count the seven weeks 1
9 begin to count the seven weeks from the time 1
13 You shall keep the feast of booths seven days 1
15 seven days you shall keep the feast to the LORD 1
28: 7 one way, and flee before you seven ways. 1
25 go out one way . . and flee seven ways before them; 1
31:10 At the end of every seven years, at the set time 1
Jos 6: 4 And seven priests shall bear seven trumpets 1
4 And seven priests shall bear seven trumpets 1
4 you shall march around the city seven times 1
6 and let seven priests bear seven trumpets 1
6 and let seven priests bear seven trumpets 1
8 the seven priests bearing . . went forward 1
8 priests bearing the seven trumpets of rams' 1
13 And the seven priests bearing . . passed 1
13 the seven priests bearing the seven trumpets 1
15 and marched around the city . . seven times 1
15 they marched around the city seven times. 1
18: 2 seven tribes whose inheritance had not yet been 1
5 They shall divide it into seven portions 1
6 you shall describe the land in seven divisions 1
9 a description of it by towns in seven divisions; 1
Jdg 6: 1 gave them into the hand of Mid'ian seven years. 1
25 father's bull, the second bull seven years old 1
12: 9 And he judged Israel seven years. 1
14:12 tell me . . within the seven days of the feast 1
17 wept . . the seven days that their feast lasted; 1
16: 7 bind me with seven fresh bowstrings which have 1
8 brought her seven fresh bowstrings which had 1
13 If you weave the seven locks of my head 1
14 Deli'lah took the seven locks of his head and wove •
19 and had him shave off the seven locks of his head. 1
Rut 4:15 who loves you, who is more to you than seven sons 1
1Sm 2: 5 The barren has borne seven, but she who has many 1
6: 1 in the country of the Philistines seven months. 1
10: 8 Seven days you shall wait, until I come to you 1
11: 3 Give us seven days respite that we may send 1
13: 8 He waited seven days, the time appointed 1
16:10 Jesse made seven of his sons pass before Samuel. 1
31:13 and buried them . . and fasted seven days. 1

2Sm 2:11 the time that . . was seven years and six months. 1
5: 5 he reigned over Judah seven years and six months 1
21: 6 let seven of his sons be given to us 1
9 and the seven of them perished together. 1
1Kg 2:11 he reigned seven years in Hebron 1
6: 6 and the third was seven cubits broad; 1
38 He was seven years in building it. 1
8:65 the feast . . before the LORD our God, seven days. 1
16:15 Zimri reigned seven days in Tirzah. 1
18:43 And he said, "Go again seven times. 1
20:29 they encamped opposite one another seven days. 1
2Kg 3: 9 when they had made a circuitous march of seven days 1
4:35 the child sneezed seven times 1
5:10 Go and wash in the Jordan seven times 1
14 and dipped himself seven times in the Jordan 1
8: 1 and it will come upon the land for seven years. 1
2 in the land of the Philistines seven years. 1
3 at the end of the seven years . . she went forth 1
11:21 Jeho'ash was seven years old when he began 1
1Ch 3: 4 where he reigned for seven years and six months. 1
24 sons of Eli-o-e'nai . . seven. 1
5:13 Michael . . Jo'rai, Jacan, Zi'a, and Eber, seven. 1
9:25 were obliged to come in every seven days 1
10:12 they . . fasted seven days. 1
15:26 they sacrificed seven bulls and seven rams. 1
26 they sacrificed seven bulls and seven rams. 1
29:27 reigned seven years in Hebron, and 33 in Jerusalem 1
2Ch 7: 8 Solomon held the feast for seven days 1
9 kept the dedication of the altar seven days 1
9 for they had kept . . and the feast seven days. 1
13: 9 comes to consecrate himself with . . seven rams 1
24: 1 Jo'ash was seven years old when he began to reign 1
29:21 they brought seven bulls, seven rams, seven lambs 1
21 they brought seven bulls, seven rams, seven lambs 1
21 they brought . . seven lambs, and seven he-goats 1
21 they brought . . seven lambs, and seven he-goats 1
30:21 kept the feast of unleavened bread seven days 1
22 ate the food of the festival for seven days 1
23 to keep the feast for another seven days; 1
23 kept it for another seven days with gladness. 1
35:17 kept . . feast of unleavened bread seven days. 1
Ezr 6:22 kept the feast . . seven days with joy; 1
7:14 sent by the king and his seven counselors 2
Neh 8:18 kept the feast seven days; and on the eighth day 1
Est 1: 5 the king gave . . a banquet lasting for seven days 1
10 he commanded . . the seven eunuchs who served 1
14 the seven princes of Persia and Media 1
2: 9 and with seven chosen maids from the king's 1
Job 1: 2 were born to him seven sons and three daughters. 1
2:13 on the ground seven days and seven nights 1
13 on the ground seven days and seven nights 1
5:19 in seven there shall no evil touch you. 1
42: 8 Now therefore take seven bulls and seven rams 1
8 Now therefore take seven bulls and seven rams 1
13 He had also seven sons and three daughters. 1
Prv 6:16 seven which are an abomination to him 1
9: 1 Wisdom . . has set up her seven pillars. 1
26:25 for there are seven abominations in his heart; 1
Ecc 11: 2 Give a portion to seven, or even to eight 1
Isa 4: 1 seven women shall take hold of one man in that day 1
11:15 smite it into seven channels that men may cross 1
30:26 sun will be sevenfold, as the light of seven days 1
Jer 15: 9 She who bore seven has languished; 1
52:25 the men of war, and seven men of the king's council 1
Ezk 3:15 I sat there overwhelmed among them seven days. 1
16 at the end of seven days, the word of the LORD came 1
39: 9 they will make fires of them for seven years; 1
12 For seven months the house of Israel will be 1
14 at the end of seven months they will make their 1
40:22 seven steps led up to it; 1
26 there were seven steps leading up to it 1
41: 3 and the sidewalls of the entrance, seven cubits. 1
43:25 For seven days you shall provide daily a goat 1
26 Seven days shall they make atonement 1
44:26 is defiled, he shall count for himself seven days 1
45:21 for seven days unleavened bread shall be eaten. 1
23 the seven days of the festival he shall provide 1
23 a burnt offering to the LORD seven young bulls 1
23 seven . . bulls and seven rams without blemish 1
23 rams without blemish, on each of the seven days; 1
25 for the seven days of the feast, he shall make 1
Dan 3:19 ordered the furnace heated seven times more 2
4:16 let seven times pass over him. 2
23 with the beasts . . till seven times pass over 2
25 seven times shall pass over you, 2
32 seven times shall pass over you, 2
9:25 there shall be seven weeks. 1
Mic 5: 5 we will raise against him seven shepherds 1
Zec 3: 9 upon a single stone with seven facets 1
4: 2 with a bowl on the top of it, and seven lamps on it 1
2 with seven lips on each of the lamps 1
10 These seven are the eyes of the LORD 1
Mat 12:45 he goes and brings with him seven other spirits 4
15:34 They said, "Seven, and a few small fish. 4
36 he took the seven loaves and the fish 4
37 and they took up seven baskets 4
16:10 Or the seven loaves of the 4,000 4
18:22 not . . seven times, but 70 times seven. 4
22:25 Now there were seven brothers among us 4

28 to which of the seven will she be wife 4
Mrk 8: 5 They said, "Seven. 4
6 he took the seven loaves 4
8 the broken pieces left over, seven baskets full. 4
20 And the seven for the 4,000 4
20 they said to him, "Seven. 4
12:20 There were seven brothers; the first took a wife 4
22 the seven left no children 4
23 the seven had her as wife. 4
16: 9 from whom he had cast out seven demons. 4
Lke 2:36 seven years from her virginity 4
8: 2 Mary . . from whom seven demons had gone out 4
11:26 seven other spirits more evil than himself 4
20:29 Now there were seven brothers 4
31 likewise all seven left no children and died. 4
33 the seven had her as wife. 4
Act 6: 3 pick out from among you seven men of good repute 4
13:19 when he had destroyed seven nations in the land 4
19:14 Seven sons of a Jewish high priest named Sceva 4
20: 6 Tro'as, where we stayed for seven days. 4
21: 4 we stayed there for seven days 4
8 Philip the evangelist, who was one of the seven 4
27 When the seven days were almost completed 4
28:14 were invited to stay with them for seven days 4
Heb 11:30 after they had been encircled for seven days. 4
Rev 1: 4 John to the seven churches that are in Asia 4
4 from the seven spirits who are before his throne 4
11 in a book and send it to the seven churches 4
12 and on turning I saw seven golden lampstands 4
16 in his right hand he held seven stars 4
20 the seven stars which you saw in my right hand 4
20 seven stars . . and the seven golden lampstands 4
20 seven stars are the angels of the seven churches 4
20 seven stars are the angels of the seven churches 4
20 the seven lampstands are the seven churches. 4
20 the seven lampstands are the seven churches. 4
2: 1 him who holds the seven stars in his right hand 4
1 who walks among the seven golden lampstands. 4
3: 1 The words of him who has the seven spirits of God 4
1 the seven spirits of God and the seven stars. 4
4: 5 before the throne burn seven torches of fire 4
5 torches . . which are the seven spirits of God; 4
5: 1 a scroll . . sealed with seven seals; 4
5 so that he can open the scroll and its seven seals. 4
6 a Lamb . . with seven horns and . . seven eyes 4
6 a Lamb . . with seven horns and . . seven eyes 4
6 seven spirits of God sent out into all the earth; 4
6: 1 I saw when the Lamb opened one of the seven seals 4
8: 2 Then I saw the seven angels who stand before God 4
2 and seven trumpets were given to them. 4
6 Now the seven angels who had the seven trumpets 4
6 Now the seven angels who had the seven trumpets 4
10: 3 when he called out, the seven thunders sounded. 4
4 when the seven thunders had sounded 4
4 Seal up what the seven thunders have said 4
12: 3 great red dragon, with seven heads and ten horns 4
3 and ten horns, and seven diadems upon his heads. 4
13: 1 I saw a beast . . with ten horns and seven heads 4
15: 1 I saw . . seven angels with seven plagues 4
1 I saw . . seven angels with seven plagues 4
6 out of the temple came the seven angels 4
6 came the seven angels with the seven plagues 4
7 the four living creatures gave the seven angels 4
7 seven golden bowls full of the wrath of God 4
8 seven plagues of the seven angels were ended. 4
8 seven plagues of the seven angels were ended. 4
16: 1 voice from the temple telling the seven angels 4
1 pour out . . the seven bowls of the wrath of God. 4
17: 1 one of the seven angels who had the seven bowls 4
1 one of the seven angels who had the seven bowls 4
3 and it had seven heads and ten horns. 4
7 and of the beast with seven heads and ten horns 4
9 the seven heads are seven mountains 4
9 the seven heads are seven mountains 4
10 seven kings, five of whom have fallen 4
11 it is an eighth but it belongs to the seven 4
21: 9 Then came one of the seven angels 4
9 the seven bowls full of the seven last plagues 4
9 the seven bowls full of the seven last plagues 4
1Es 1:19 kept the passover . . seven days. 4
4:63 they feasted . . for seven days. 4
7:14 kept the feast of unleavened bread seven days 4
8:11 I and the seven friends who are my counselors 4
2Es 2:19 seven mighty mountains on which roses . . grow 5
5:13 and fast for seven days 5
19 and do not come near me for seven days 5
20 I fasted seven days, mourning and weeping 5
21 after seven days the thoughts of my heart 5
6:31 will pray again and fast again for seven days 5
35 I wept again and fasted seven days as before 5
7:30 turned back to primeval silence for seven days 5
31 after seven days the world, which is not yet awake 5
80 ever grieving and sad, in seven ways. 5
91 for they shall have rest in seven orders. 5
101 They shall have freedom for seven days 5
101 during these seven days they may see the things 5
9:23 if you will let seven days more pass 5
27 after seven days, as I lay on the grass 5
12:39 wait here seven days more, so that you may be shown 5

40 people heard that the seven days were past 5
51 I sat in the field seven days 5
13: 1 After seven days I dreamed a dream in the night; 5
Tob 2: 1 which is the sacred festival of the seven weeks 4
3: 8 because she had been given to seven husbands 4
8 You already have had seven 4
15 Already seven husbands of mine are dead 4
6:13 the girl has been given to seven husbands 4
7:11 I have given my daughter to seven husbands 4
11:19 Tobias' marriage was celebrated for seven days 4
12:15 I am Raphael, one of the seven holy angels 4
Jdt 16:24 the house of Israel mourned for her seven days. 4
Sir 22:12 Mourning for the dead lasts seven days 4
37:14 seven watchmen sitting high on a watchtower. 4
LJr 1: 3 for a long time, up to seven generations 4
Bel 1:32 There were seven lions in the den 4
1Mc 13:28 He also erected seven pyramids 4
2Mc 7: 1 seven brothers and their mother 4
20 Though she saw her seven sons perish 4
3Mc 6:30 needed for a festival of seven days 4
7:17 the fleet waited for them . . for seven days. 4
4Mc 1: 8 Eleazar and the seven brothers and their mother. 4
8: 3 seven brothers–handsome, modest, noble 4
13: 1 seven brothers despised sufferings even unto death 4
14: 3 harmonious concord of the seven brothers 4
4 None of the seven youths proved coward 4
7 O most holy seven, brothers in harmony! 3
7 just as the seven days of creation 4
12 the mother of the seven young men 4
15: 2 preserving her seven sons for a time 4
6 The mother of the seven boys 4
6 In seven pregnancies 4
24 witnessed the destruction of seven children 4
27 preserve the seven sons for a short time 4
16: 1 advanced in years and mother of seven sons 4
3 inflamed as she saw her seven sons tortured 4
6 After bearing seven children 4
7 O seven childbirths all in vain 4
7 seven profitless pregnancies 4
17: 2 with your seven sons nullified . . the tyrant 4
5 lighting the way of your star-like seven sons 4
7 they saw the mother of the seven children 4
9 aged priest and an aged woman and seven sons 4
13 the mother of the seven sons 4
18: 6 The mother of seven sons 4
20 those seven sons of the daughter of Abraham 4

seven *See also* mother.

seven men 1. שֶׁבַע
Prv 26:16 than seven men who can answer discreetly. 1

seven miles 1. σταδίους ἑξήκοντα
Lke 24:13 Emma'us, about seven miles from Jerusalem 1

seven other persons 1. ὄγδοος
2Pe 2: 5 but preserved Noah . . with seven other persons 1

seven times 1. שֶׁבַע 2. שִׁבְעָתַיִם 3. ἑπτάκις 4. ἑπταπλάσιος
Ps 12: 6 in a furnace on the ground, purified seven times. 2
119:164 Seven times a day I praise thee 1
Prv 24:16 righteous man falls seven times, and rises again; 1
Mat 18:21 As many as seven times? 3
22 Jesus said to him, "I do not say to you seven times 3
Lke 17: 4 if he sins against you seven times in the day 3
4 turns to you seven times, and says, 'I repent,' 3
Sir 40: 8 upon sinners seven times more 4

seven times over 1. ἑπταπλάσιος
Sir 20:12 pays for it seven times over. 1

seven-towered 1. ἑπτάπυργος
4Mc 13: 7 the seven-towered right reason of the youths 1

sevenfold 1. שֶׁבַע 2. שִׁבְעָתַיִם 3. ἑβδομάς 4. ἑπταπλάσιος 5. ἑπταπλασίως
Gen 4:15 vengeance shall be taken on him sevenfold. 2
24 If Cain is avenged sevenfold 2
Lev 26:18 will chastise you again sevenfold for your sins 1
21 more plagues . . sevenfold as many as your sins 1
24 I myself will smite you sevenfold for your sins 1
28 chastise you myself sevenfold for your sins 1
Ps 79:12 Return sevenfold into the bosom 2
Prv 6:31 if he is caught, he will pay sevenfold; 2
Isa 30:26 and the light of the sun will be sevenfold 2
Sir 7: 3 you will not reap a sevenfold crop. 5
35:11 he will repay you sevenfold. 4
4Mc 14: 8 youths . . encircled the sevenfold fear of tortures 3

seventeen 1. שֶׁבַע וְעָשָׂר 2. שְׁבַע עֶשְׂרֵה 3. ἑπτακαίδεκα
Gen 37: 2 Joseph, being seventeen years old 2
47:28 Jacob lived in the land of Egypt seventeen years; 2
1Kg 14:21 and he reigned seventeen years in Jerusalem 2
2Kg 13: 1 Jeho'ahaz . . and he reigned seventeen years. 2
2Ch 12:13 he reigned seventeen years in Jerusalem 2
Jer 32: 9 the money to him, seventeen shekels of silver 1
1Es 4:52 the commandment to make seventeen offerings; 3

seventeenth 1. שְׁבַע עֶשְׂרֵה 2. ἑπτακαιδέκατος
Gen 7:11 on the seventeenth day of the month 1
8: 4 on the seventeenth day of the month 1
1Kg 22:51 in the seventeenth year of Jehosh'aphat 1
2Kg 16: 1 In the seventeenth year of Pekah the son 1
1Ch 24:15 the seventeenth to Hezir, the eighteenth 1
25:24 seventeenth, to Joshbekash'ah, his sons 1
Jdt 1:13 In the seventeenth year 2

seventh 1. שְׁבִיעִי 2. שֶׁבַע 3. ἑβδομάς 4. ἕβδομος 5. ἑπτά 6. septimus
Gen 2: 2 on the seventh day God finished his work 1
2 God . . rested on the seventh day 1
3 God blessed the seventh day and hallowed it 1
8: 4 in the seventh month, on the seventeenth day 1
Exd 12:15 from the first day until the seventh day 1
16 and on the seventh day a holy assembly; 1
13: 6 and on the seventh day there shall be a feast 1
16:26 but on the seventh day, which is a sabbath 1
27 On the seventh day some of the people went out 1
29 let no man go out of his place on the seventh day. 1
30 So the people rested on the seventh day. 1
20:10 the seventh day is a sabbath to the LORD your God; 1
11 the LORD . . rested the seventh day; 1
21: 2 years, and in the seventh he shall go out free 1
23:11 the seventh year you shall let it rest and lie 1
12 do your work, but on the seventh day you shall rest; 1
24:16 and on the seventh day he called to Moses 1
31:15 seventh day is a sabbath of solemn rest, holy 1
17 on the seventh day he rested, and was refreshed.' 1
34:21 but on the seventh day you shall rest; 1
35: 2 on the seventh day you shall have a holy sabbath 1
Lev 13: 5 the priest shall examine him on the seventh day 1
6 shall examine him again on the seventh day 1
27 the priest shall examine him the seventh day 1
32 on the seventh day the priest shall examine 1
34 on the seventh day the priest shall examine 1
51 he shall examine the disease on the seventh day 1
14: 9 on the seventh day he shall shave all his hair off 1
39 the priest shall come again on the seventh day 1
16:29 in the seventh month, on the tenth day of the month 1
23: 3 on the seventh day is a sabbath of solemn rest 1
8 on the seventh day is a holy convocation 1
16 50 days to the morrow after the seventh sabbath 1
24 In the seventh month, on the first day of the month 1
27 On the tenth day of this seventh month is the day 1
34 On the fifteenth day of this seventh month 1
39 On the fifteenth day of the seventh month 1
41 you shall keep it in the seventh month 1
25: 4 in the seventh year there shall be a sabbath 1
9 on the tenth day of the seventh month 1
20 if you say, 'What shall we eat in the seventh year 1
Num 6: 9 on the seventh day he shall shave it. 1
7:48 On the seventh day Eli'shama . . of E'phraim 1
19:12 cleanse himself . . day and on the seventh day 1
12 does not cleanse himself . . on the seventh day 1
19 sprinkle . . day and on the seventh day; 1
19 thus on the seventh day he shall cleanse him 1
28:25 seventh day you shall have a holy convocation; 1
29: 1 On the first day of the seventh month 1
7 On the tenth day of this seventh month 1
12 On the fifteenth day of the seventh month 1
32 On the seventh day seven bulls, two rams, fourteen 1
31:19 purify . . on the third day and on the seventh day. 1
24 You must wash your clothes on the seventh day 1
Deu 5:14 seventh day is a sabbath to the LORD your God; 1
15: 9 The seventh year, the year of release is near,' 2
12 in the seventh year you shall let him go free 1
16: 8 seventh day there shall be a solemn assembly 1
Jos 6: 4 and on the seventh day you shall march around 1
15 the seventh day they rose early at the dawn of day 1
16 at the seventh time . . Joshua said to the people 1
19:40 The seventh lot came out for the tribe of Dan 1
Jdg 14:17 on the seventh day he told her, because she 1
18 to him on the seventh day before the sun went down 1
2Sm 12:18 On the seventh day the child died. 1
1Kg 8: 2 the month Eth'anim, which is the seventh month. 1
18:44 at the seventh time he said, "Behold, a little cloud 1
20:29 on the seventh day the battle was joined; 1
2Kg 11: 4 in the seventh year Jehoi'ada sent and brought 1
12: 1 In the seventh year of Jehu Jeho'ash began 2
18: 9 which was the seventh year of Hoshe'a son of Elah 1
25: 8 In the fifth month, on the seventh day of the month 2
25 in the seventh month, Ish'mael . . came with ten men 1
1Ch 2:15 Ozem the sixth, David the seventh; 1
12:11 Attai sixth, Eli'el seventh 1
24:10 the seventh to Hakkoz, the eighth to Abi'jah 1
25:14 seventh to Jeshare'lah, his sons and his brethren 1
26: 3 Jehoha'nan the sixth, Eli-e-ho-e'nai the seventh. 1
5 Is'sachar the seventh, Pe-ul'lethai the eighth; 1
27:10 Seventh . . was Helez the Pel'onite 1
10 Seventh, for the seventh month, was Helez 1
2Ch 5: 3 at the feast which is in the seventh month. 1
7:10 On the 23rd day of the seventh month he 1
23: 1 in the seventh year Jehoi'ada took courage 1
31: 7 finished them in the seventh month. 1
Ezr 3: 1 When the seventh month came 1
6 From the first day of the seventh month 1
7: 7 went up . . in the seventh year of Ar-ta-xerx'es 2
8 which was in the seventh year of the king 1
Neh 7:73 seventh month had come, the children of Israel 1
8: 2 on the first day of the seventh month. 1
14 booths during the feast of the seventh month 1
10:31 forego the crops of the seventh year 1
Est 1:10 On the seventh day . . he commanded Mehu'man 1
2:16 month of Tebeth, in the seventh year of his reign 2
Jer 28:17 In that same year, in the seventh month 1
41: 1 In the seventh month, Ish'mael . . came 1
52:28 carried away captive: in the seventh year 2
Ezk 20: 1 In the seventh year, in the fifth month 1
30:20 the first month, on the seventh day of the month 2
45:20 You shall do the same on the seventh day 2
25 seventh month, on the fifteenth day of the month 1
Hag 2: 1 in the seventh month, on the 21st day of the month 1
Zec 7: 5 and mourned in the fifth month and in the seventh 1
8:19 the fast of the seventh, and the fast of the tenth 1
Mat 22:26 So too the second and third, down to the seventh. 5
Joh 4:52 Yesterday at the seventh hour the fever left him. 4
Heb 4: 4 has somewhere spoken of the seventh day 4
4 God rested on the seventh day from all his works. 4
Jde 1:14 Enoch in the seventh generation from Adam 4
Rev 8: 1 When the Lamb opened the seventh seal 4
10: 7 trumpet call to be sounded by the seventh angel 4
11:15 Then the seventh angel blew his trumpet 4
16:17 The seventh angel poured his bowl into the air 4
21:20 the sixth carnelian, the seventh chrysolite 4
1Es 5:47 When the seventh month came 4
53 from the new moon of the seventh month 4
8: 6 in the seventh year of the reign of Artaxerxes 4
6 the fifth month (this was the king's seventh year); 4
9:37 On the new moon of the seventh month 4
40 on the new moon of the seventh month. 4
2Es 6:42 in the seventh part of the earth 6
47 thou didst command the seventh part 6
50 the seventh part where the water had been 6
52 to Leviathan thou didst give the seventh part 6
7:87 The seventh way, which is worse than all the ways 6
98 The seventh order, which is greater than all 6
Bar 1: 2 in the fifth year, on the seventh day of the month 4
Bel 1:40 On the seventh day the king came to mourn 4
1Mc 6:53 because it was the seventh year 4
10:21 in the seventh month 4
2Mc 6:11 to observe the seventh day secretly 3
12:38 As the seventh day was coming on, they purified 3
15: 4 who ordered us to observe the seventh day 3
3Mc 6:38 was set for the fifth to the seventh of Epeiph 4
4Mc 2: 8 to cancel the debt when the seventh year arrives. 3
12: 1 the seventh and youngest of all came forward. 4

seventy-sevenfold 1. שִׁבְעִים וְשִׁבְעָה
Gen 4:24 truly Lamech seventy-sevenfold. 1

sever 1. בדל 2. ἀποτέμνω 3. ἀφαιρέω 4. διέρχομαι 5. καταργέω 6. περιτέμνω
Lev 5: 8 head from its neck, but shall not sever it 1
Gal 5: 4 You are severed from Christ 5
Jdt 13: 8 and severed it from his body. 3
16: 9 the sword severed his neck. 4
4Mc 9:21 the ligaments . . were already severed 6
15:20 severed hands upon hands 2

several 1. כֹּל 2. κατά 3. τίς
Jos 19:49 distributing the several territories •
21:33 The cities of the several families •
40 the cities of the several Merar'ite families •
2Ch 8:14 gatekeepers . . for the several gates; •
31:19 men in the several cities who were designated 1
Ezk 48:29 these are their several portions, says the Lord •
Act 9:19 For several days he was with the disciples 3
3Mc 4: 4 the generals in the several cities 2

severe 1. גָּדוֹל 2. חזק 3. חָזָק 4. חָזָק מְאֹד 5. כָּבֵד 6. עַד לְמַעְלָה 7. רַב 8. רַע 9. חצף (A) 10. ἀπότομος 11. ἀποτόμως 12. αὐστηρός 13. βαρύς 14. δυσχερής 15. μέγας 16. ὀξύς 17. πολύς 18. πονηρός
Gen 12:10 for the famine was severe in the land. 5
41:56 for the famine was severe in the land of Egypt. 2
57 to buy grain, because the famine was severe 2
43: 1 Now the famine was severe in the land. 5
47: 4 for the famine is severe in the land of Canaan; 5
13 for the famine was very severe, so that the land 5
20 because the famine was severe upon them. 2
Exd 9: 3 will fall with a very severe plague upon 5
Deu 28:59 afflictions severe and lasting, and sicknesses 1
1Kg 17:17 illness was so severe that there was no breath 4
18: 2 Now the famine was severe in Sama'ria. 3
2Kg 25: 3 the famine was so severe in the city that 2
2Ch 16:12 his disease became severe; 6
21:15 you yourself will have a severe sickness 7
Prv 15:10 severe discipline for him who forsakes the way; 8
Jer 52: 6 the famine was so severe in the city 2
Dan 2:15 Why is the decree of the king so severe? 9
Lke 12:47 that servant . . shall receive a severe beating. 17
19:21 I was afraid of you, because you are a severe man; 12
22 You knew that I was a severe man 12
2Co 8: 2 for in a severe test of affliction 17

13:10 not have to be severe in my use of the authority 11
Wis 6: 5 severe judgment falls on those in high places. 10
Sir 5:14 severe condemnation to the double-tongued. 18
31: 2 a severe illness carries off sleep. 13
1Mc 1:30 dealt it a severe blow, and destroyed many people 15
2Mc 14:45 his wounds were severe 14
3Mc 2:23 the severe punishment that had overtaken him 16
severe *See also* suffering.

severely 1. רַב 2. *κακῶς* 3. *σκληρός*
2Ch 24:25 departed from him, leaving him severely wounded 1
Mat 15:22 my daughter is severely possessed by a demon. 2
3Mc 4:19 After he had threatened them severely 3
severely *See also* afflict, whip.

very severely 1. *σκληρός*
3Mc 7: 6 we very severely threatened them for these acts 1

severity 1. *ἀποτομία* 2. *ἀφειδία*
Rom 11:22 Note then the kindness and the severity of God 1
22 severity toward those who have fallen 1
Col 2:23 self-abasement and severity to the body 2

sew 1. תפר 2. *ἐπιράπτω*
Job 16:15 I have sewed sackcloth upon my skin 1
Ecc 3: 7 a time to rend, and a time to sew; 1
Ezk 13:18 Woe to the women who sew magic bands 1
Mrk 2:21 sews a piece of unshrunk cloth on an old garment; 2

sew together 1. תפר
Gen 3: 7 they sewed fig leaves together 1

sex 1. *γένεσις* 2. *σκεῦος*
1Pe 3: 7 bestowing honor on the woman as the weaker sex 2
Wis 14:26 sex perversion, disorder in marriage, adultery 1

weaker sex 1. *ἀσθενόψυχος*
4Mc 15: 5 mothers are the weaker sex and give birth to many 1
sexual *See* desire, pervert.

shabby 1. *ῥυπαρός*
Jas 2: 2 a poor man in shabby clothing also comes in 1

shackle 1. *πεδάω* 2. *πέδη*
Man 1: 3 who hast shackled the sea by thy word of command 1
3Mc 6:19 binding them with immovable shackles. 2

shade 1. צֵל 2. צלל 3. *σκέπη* 4. *σκιά* 5. *σκιάζω*
Jdg 9:15 over you, then come and take refuge in my shade; 1
Job 40:22 For his shade the lotus trees cover him; 1
Ps 80:10 The mountains were covered with its shade 1
121: 5 LORD is your shade on your right hand. 1
Isa 4: 6 It will be for a shade by day from the heat 1
16: 3 make your shade like night at the height of noon; 1
25: 4 shelter from the storm and a shade from the heat 1
5 as heat by the shade of a cloud 1
32: 2 like the shade of a great rock in a weary land. 1
Ezk 17:23 in the shade of its branches birds of every sort 1
31: 3 a cedar . . with fair branches and forest shade 2
Hos 4:13 and terebinth, because their shade is good. 1
Jon 4: 5 He sat under it in the shade 1
6 that it might be a shade over his head 1
Mrk 4:32 the birds of the air can make nests in its shade. 4
Sir 34:16 a shade from noonday sun 3
Bar 5: 8 tree have shaded Israel at God's command. 5

shade (2) 1. רְפָאִים
Job 26: 5 The shades below tremble 1
Ps 88:10 Do the shades rise up to praise thee? Selah 1
Prv 2:18 her paths to the shades; 1
Isa 14: 9 when you come, it rouses the shades to greet you 1
26:14 they are shades, they will not arise; 1
19 on the land of the shades thou wilt let it fall. 1
shade *See* find.

shadow 1. צֵל 2. צֶלֶם 3. *ἀποσκίασμα* 4. *σκιά*
5. umbra
Jdg 9:36 You see the shadow of the mountains as if they 1
2Kg 20: 9 shall the shadow go forward ten steps, or go back 1
10 easy thing for the shadow to lengthen ten steps; 1
10 rather let the shadow go back ten steps. 1
11 the LORD, and he brought the shadow back ten steps 1
1Ch 29:15 our days on the earth are like a shadow 1
Job 7: 2 Like a slave who longs for the shadow 1
8: 9 know nothing, for our days on earth are a shadow. 1
14: 2 he flees like a shadow, and continues not. 1
17: 7 all my members are like a shadow. 1
Ps 17: 8 hide me in the shadow of thy wings 1
36: 7 men take refuge in the shadow of thy wings. 1
39: 6 Surely man goes about as a shadow! 2
57: 1 in the shadow of thy wings I will take refuge 1
63: 7 in the shadow of thy wings I sing for joy. 1
91: 1 who abides in the shadow of the Almighty 1
102:11 My days are like an evening shadow; 1
109:23 I am gone, like a shadow at evening; 1
144: 4 like a breath, his days are like a passing shadow. 1
Ecc 6:12 few days of . . life, which he passes like a shadow? 1
8:13 neither will he prolong his days like a shadow 1
Sng 2: 3 With great delight I sat in his shadow 1
17 Until the day breathes and the shadows flee 1
4: 6 Until the day breathes and the shadows flee 1
Isa 30: 2 and to seek shelter in the shadow of Egypt! 1
3 the shelter in the shadow of Egypt 1
34:15 lay and hatch and gather her young in her shadow; 1
38: 8 I will make the shadow cast by the declining sun 1
49: 2 in the shadow of his hand he hid me; 1
51:16 in your mouth, and hid you in the shadow of my hand 1
Jer 6: 4 for the shadows of evening lengthen! 1
48:45 In the shadow of Heshbon fugitives stop 1
Lam 4:20 Under his shadow we shall live among . . nations. 1
Ezk 31: 6 under its shadow dwelt all great nations. 1
12 the peoples of the earth will go from its shadow 1
17 who dwelt under its shadow among the nations 1
Hos 14: 7 They shall return and dwell beneath my shadow 1
Mat 4:16 who sat in the region and shadow of death light 4
Lke 1:79 who sit in darkness and in the shadow of death 4
Act 5:15 at least his shadow might fall on some of them. 4
Col 2:17 These are only a shadow of what is to come 4
Heb 8: 5 They serve a copy and shadow 4
10: 1 since the law has but a shadow of the good things 4
Jas 1:17 there is no variation or shadow due to change. 3
2Es 2:36 Flee from the shadow of this age 5
39 who have departed from the shadow of this age 5
Wis 2: 5 For our allotted time is the passing of a shadow 4
5: 9 All those things have vanished like a shadow 4
Sir 34: 2 As one who catches at a shadow 4

shadow fall 1. *ἐπισκιάζω*
Act 5:15 at least his shadow might fall on some of them. 1

shadow of death 1. צַלְמָוֶת
Ps 23: 4 I walk through the valley of the shadow of death 1

shaft 1. מַטֶּה 2. עֵץ 3. קָנֶה 4. *βολίς* 5. *δόρυ*
Exd 25:31 The base and the shaft of the lampstand shall be 3
37:17 The base and the shaft of the lampstand were made 3
1Sm 17: 7 And the shaft of his spear was like a weaver's beam 2
2Sm 21:19 the shaft of whose spear was like a weaver's beam. 2
23: 7 arms himself with iron and the shaft of a spear 2
1Ch 20: 5 the shaft of whose spear was like a weaver's beam. 2
Hab 3:14 pierce with thy shafts the head of his warriors 1
Wis 5:21 Shafts of lightning will fly with true aim 4
Sir 38:25 who glories in the shaft of a goad 5

shaft (2) 1. *φρέαρ*
Rev 9: 1 given the key of the shaft of the bottomless pit; 1
2 he opened the shaft of the bottomless pit 1
2 and from the shaft rose smoke like the smoke 1
2 were darkened with the smoke from the shaft. 1
shaft *See* open.

fiery shaft 1. דלק
Ps 7:13 deadly weapons, making his arrows fiery shafts. 1

water shaft 1. צִנּוֹר
2Sm 5: 8 get up the water shaft to attack the lame 1

shake 1. געשׁ 2. חול 3. מוט 4. נוד 5. נוע 6. נוף
7. נער 8. נתר 9. קלל 10. רגז 11. רחף 12. רעשׁ
13. רַעַשׁ 14. *ἀσάλευτος* 15. *κίνησις* 16. *κραδαίνω*
17. *σαλεύω* 18. *σεῖσμα* 19. *σείω* 20. *συσσείω*
21. *ταράσσω* 22. commoveo
1Kg 14:15 will smite Israel, as a reed is shaken in the water 4
Job 9: 6 who shakes the earth out of its place 10
16: 4 together against you, and shake my head at you. 5
34:20 at midnight the people are shaken and pass away 1
38:13 the wicked be shaken out of it? 7
Ps 13: 4 lest my foes rejoice because I am shaken. 3
29: 8 The voice of the LORD shakes the wilderness 2
8 LORD shakes the wilderness of Kadesh. 2
46: 2 though the mountains shake in the heart of the sea; 3
62: 6 my salvation, my fortress; I shall not be shaken. 3
77:18 the earth trembled and shook. 12
82: 5 all the foundations of the earth are shaken. 3
104: 5 so that it should never be shaken. 3
Isa 6: 4 the foundations of the thresholds shook 5
7: 2 heart . . shook as the trees of the forest shake 5
2 as the trees of the forest shake before the wind. 5
10:32 he will shake his fist at the mount of . . Zion 6
13:13 and the earth will be shaken out of its place 12
14:16 who made the earth tremble, who shook kingdoms 12
19:16 the hand . . the LORD of hosts shakes over them. 6
23:11 hand over the sea, he has shaken the kingdoms; 10
24:19 is rent asunder, the earth is violently shaken. 3
33:15 who shakes his hands, lest they hold a bribe 7
52: 2 Shake yourself from the dust, arise, O captive 7
Jer 18:16 Every one who passes by it . . shakes his head. 4
23: 9 My heart is broken within me, all my bones shake; 11
Ezk 21:21 he shakes the arrows, he consults the teraphim 9
26:10 your walls will shake at the noise 12
15 Will not the coastlands shake at the sound 12
27:28 of the cry of your pilots the countryside shakes 12
38:19 shall be a great shaking in the land of Israel; 13
Jol 3:16 and the heavens and the earth shake. 12
Ams 9: 1 Smite the capitals until the thresholds shake 12
9 shake the house of Israel among all the nations 5
9 and shake . . as one shakes with a sieve 5
Nah 3:12 if shaken they fall into the mouth of the eater. 5
Hab 3: 6 he looked and shook the nations; 8
Zep 2:15 Every one who passes . . hisses and shakes his fist 5
Hag 2: 6 I will shake the heavens and the earth and the sea 12
7 I will shake all nations, so that the treasures 12
21 I am about to shake the heavens and the earth 12
Zec 2: 9 Behold, I will shake my hand over them 6
Mat 11: 7 A reed shaken by the wind? 17
24:29 the powers of the heavens will be shaken; 17
27:51 the earth shook, and the rocks were split; 19
Mrk 13:25 the powers in the heavens will be shaken. 17
Lke 6:48 broke against that house, and could not shake it 17
7:24 A reed shaken by the wind? 17
21:26 the powers of the heavens will be shaken. 17
Act 2:25 he is at my right hand that I may not be shaken; 17
4:31 the place . . was shaken 17
16:26 so that the foundations . . were shaken 17
2Th 2: 2 not to be quickly shaken in mind or excited 17
Heb 12:26 His voice then shook the earth 17
26 Yet once more I will shake not only the earth 19
27 indicates the removal of what is shaken 17
27 in order that what cannot be shaken may remain. 17
28 for receiving a kingdom that cannot be shaken 14
Rev 6:13 sheds its winter fruit when shaken by a gale; 19
2Es 3:18 bend down the heavens and shake the earth ‡
6:14 where you are standing is greatly shaken 22
16 They will tremble and be shaken 22
10:26 so that the earth shook at the sound. 22
Jdt 16:15 mountains shall be shaken to their foundations 17
AEs 15:13 my heart was shaken with fear at your glory. 21
Wis 4: 4 they will be shaken by the wind 17
19 shake them from the foundations 17
5: 2 they will be shaken with dreadful fear 21
Sir 12:18 he will shake his head, and clap his hands 15
13: 7 will forsake you, and shake his head at you. 15
16:19 shake with trembling when he looks upon them. 20
27: 4 When a sieve is shaken, the refuse remains 18
28:14 Slander has shaken many 17
29:18 has shaken them like a wave of the sea 17
43:16 At his appearing the mountains are shaken 17
48:19 their hearts were shaken 17
1Mc 1:28 Even the land shook for its inhabitants 19
6: 8 he was astounded and badly shaken 17
9:13 The earth was shaken by the noise of the armies 17
3Mc 2:22 He shook him on this side and that 16
22 as a reed is shaken by the wind •

shake free 1. נער
Jdg 16:20 go out as at other times, and shake myself free. 1

make shake 1. פחד
Job 4:14 trembling, which made all my bones shake. 1
Ezk 29: 7 you broke, and made all their loins to shake; ‡

shake off 1. חמס 2. נער 3. *ἀποτινάσσω*
4. *ἐκτινάσσω* 5. *ἐντιναγμός* 6. excutio
Job 15:33 He will shake off his unripe grape, like the vine 1
Ps 109:23 I am shaken off like a locust. 2
Isa 33: 9 and Bashan and Carmel shake off their leaves. 2
Mat 10:14 shake off the dust from your feet as you leave 4
Mrk 6:11 shake off the dust that is on your feet 4
Lke 9: 5 shake off the dust from your feet 3
Act 13:51 they shook off the dust from their feet against them 4
28: 5 He, however, shook off the creature into the fire 3
2Es 10:24 Therefore shake off your great sadness 6
Sir 22: 2 any one that picks it up will shake it off his hand. 4
13 you will not be soiled when he shakes himself off; 5

shake out 1. נער 2. *ἐκτινάσσω*
Neh 5:13 I also shook out my lap and said, "So may God shake 1
13 So may God shake out every man from his house 1
13 may he be shaken out and emptied. 1
Act 18: 6 he shook out his garments and said to them 2

shake together 1. *σαλεύω*
Lke 6:38 good measure, pressed down, shaken together 1

shallow 1. *κενός*
Jas 2:20 Do you want to be shown, you shallow man 1

shame 1. בושׁ 2. בּוֹשָׁה 3. בָּשְׁנָה 4. בֹּשֶׁת 5. חֶרְפָּה
6. כלם 7. כְּלִמָּה 8. כְּלִמּוּת 9. מָעוֹר 10. נְחֹשֶׁת
11. עֶרְוָה 12. קִיקָלוֹן 13. קָלוֹן 14. שִׁמְצָה 15. *αἰσχρός*
16. *αἰσχύνη* 17. *αἰσχυντηρός* 18. *αἰσχύνω*
19. *ἀσχημοσύνη* 20. *ἀτιμία* 21. *ἐντροπή*
22. *καταισχύνω* 23. *ὀνειδισμός* 24. *ὄνειδος*
Exd 32:25 break loose, to their shame among their enemies) 14
Num 12:14 should she not be shamed seven days? 6
1Sm 20:30 you have chosen the son of Jesse to your own shame 4
30 and to the shame of your mother's nakedness? 4
2Sm 13:13 As for me, where could I carry my shame? 5
2Ch 32:21 returned with shame of face to his own land. 4
Ezr 9: 7 been given . . to plundering, and to utter shame 4
Neh 1: 3 escaped exile are in great trouble and shame; 5
Job 8:22 Those who hate you will be clothed with shame 4
11: 3 when you mock, shall no one shame you? 6
36:14 They die in youth, and their life ends in shame. •

Ps 4: 2 O men, how long shall my honor suffer shame? 7
35:26 Let them be clothed with shame and dishonor 4
40:15 Let them be appalled because of their shame 4
44:15 shame has covered my face 4
69: 7 shame has covered my face. 7
19 knowest my reproach, and my shame and 4
70: 3 appalled because of their shame who say, "Aha, Aha! 4
78:66 he put them to everlasting shame. 5
83:16 Fill their faces with shame, that they may seek 13
89:45 thou hast covered him with shame. Selah 2
109:29 be wrapped in their own shame as in a mantle! 4
132:18 His enemies I will clothe with shame 4
Prv 9:13 A foolish woman . . is wanton and knows no shame. 16
18:13 answer before he hears, it is his folly and shame. 7
28: 7 but a companion of gluttons shames his father. 6
Isa 3:24 instead of beauty, shame. 4
20: 4 with buttocks uncovered, to the shame of Egypt. 11
22:18 you shall die . . you shame of your master's house. 13
30: 3 the protection of Pharaoh turn to your shame 4
5 help nor profit, but shame and disgrace. 4
47: 3 shall be uncovered, and your shame shall be seen. 5
50: 6 I hid not my face from shame and spitting. 7
54: 4 for you will forget the shame of your youth 4
61: 7 Instead of your shame you shall have a double 4
Jer 2:26 As a thief is shamed when caught 4
26 the house of Israel shall be shamed 1
3:25 Let us lie down in our shame 4
9:19 How we are ruined! We are utterly shamed 1
11:13 the altars you have set up to shame 4
13:26 and your shame will be seen. 13
15: 9 she has been shamed and disgraced. 1
20:11 They will be greatly shamed 1
18 to see toil and sorrow, and spend my days in shame? 4
23:40 perpetual shame, which shall not be forgotten. 8
46:12 The nations have heard of your shame 13
48:39 they wail! How Moab has turned his back in shame! 1
50:12 your mother shall be utterly shamed 1
Ezk 7:18 horror covers them; shame is upon all faces 2
16:36 Because your shame was laid bare 10
63 never open your mouth again because of . . shame 7
32:24 they bear their shame with those who go down 7
25 bear their shame with those who go down to the Pit; 7
30 all the Sido'nians, who have gone down in shame 1
30 who are slain by the sword, and bear their shame 7
39:26 They shall forget their shame 7
44:13 they shall bear their shame 7
Dan 12: 2 some to everlasting life, and some to shame 5
Hos 4: 7 I will change their glory into shame. 13
18 they love shame more than their glory. 13
10: 6 E'phraim shall be put to shame 3
Obd 1:10 shame shall cover you, and you shall be cut off 2
Mic 1:11 inhabitants of Shaphir, in nakedness and shame; 4
7:10 and shame will cover her who said to me 2
Nah 3: 5 let nations look . . and kingdoms on your shame. 13
Hab 2:10 You have devised shame to your house 4
15 and makes them drunk, to gaze on their shame! 9
16 and shame will come upon your glory! 12
Zep 3: 5 but the unjust knows no shame. 4
19 and I will change their shame into praise 4
Lke 14: 9 will begin with shame to take the lowest place. 16
1Co 1:27 to shame the wise 22
27 to shame the strong 22
6: 5 I say this to your shame 21
15:34 I say this to your shame. 21
2Co 11:21 To my shame, I must say, we were too weak for that! 20
Eph 5:12 it is a shame even to speak of the things 15
Php 3:19 glory in their shame 16
Heb 12: 2 endured the cross, despising the shame 16
Jde 1:13 casting up the foam of their own shame 16
Rev 3:18 keep the shame of your nakedness from being seen 16
1Es 8:77 in shame until this day. 16
2Es 7:87 and be consumed with shame ‡
Jdt 1:14 turned its beauty into shame. 24
5:21 we shall be put to shame before the whole world. 23
9: 2 and uncovered her thigh to put her to shame 16
13:16 to defile and shame me. 16
Sir 4:21 For there is a shame which brings sin 16
21 there is a shame which is glory and favor. 16
5:14 shame comes to the thief 16
6: 1 a bad name incurs shame and reproach 16
13: 7 He will shame you with his foods 18
20:22 A man may lose his life through shame 16
23 A man may for shame make promises to a friend 16
26 his shame is ever with him. 16
26: 8 she will not hide her shame. 19
41:16 it is good to retain every kind of shame 16
23 Then you will show proper shame 17
Aza 1:10 shame and disgrace have befallen thy servants 16
17 will be no shame for those who trust in thee. 16
1Mc 1:28 all the house of Jacob was clothed with shame. 16

shame *See also* bring, come, cover, put, sense, shrink.

cause shame 1. בוש

Prv 19:26 son who causes shame and brings reproach. 1

shameful 1. אֱלִילָה 2. *αἰσχρός* 3. *ἀσχήμων* 4. *δυσκλεής* 5. *ὄνειδος*

Deu 22:14 charges her with shameful conduct, and brings 1
17 he has made shameful charges against her, saying 1
1Co 14:35 it is shameful for a woman to speak in church. 2
Wis 2:20 Let us condemn him to a shameful death 3
Sus 1:63 because nothing shameful was found in her. 3
2Mc 9: 2 beat a shameful retreat. 3
3Mc 3:25 sure and shameful death that befits enemies. 4
4Mc 5: 9 delicious things that are not shameful 5
6:20 It would be shameful if we should survive 2
16:17 it would be shameful 2

shameful *See also* gain, public.

shameful manner 1. *αἰδώς*

3Mc 4: 5 they were driven in such a shameful manner. 1

shameful thing 1. בֹּשֶׁת 2. חֶסֶד 3. נְבָלָה

Lev 20:17 it is a shameful thing, and they shall be cut off 2
Jos 7:15 because he has done a shameful thing in Israel 3
Jer 3:24 from our youth the shameful thing has devoured 1

shamefully *See* treat.

act shamefully 1. באשׁ 2. בושׁ 3. *καταισχύνω*

Prv 13: 5 wicked man acts shamefully and disgracefully. 1
14:35 but his wrath falls on one who acts shamefully. 2
17: 2 wisely will rule over a son who acts shamefully 2
Hos 2: 5 she that conceived them has acted shamefully. 2
Sir 22: 4 one who acts shamefully 3

shameless 1. לֹא כסף 2. *ἀναιδέομαι* 3. *ἀναιδής*

Zep 2: 1 and hold assembly, O shameless nation 1
Sir 23: 6 do not surrender me to a shameless soul. 2
40:30 In the mouth of the shameless begging is sweet 3
Bar 4:15 a shameless nation, of a strange language 3

shameless act 1. *ἀσχημοσύνη*

Rom 1:27 men committing shameless acts with men 1

shamelessly

2Sm 6:20 vulgar fellows shamelessly uncovers himself! *

shamelessness 1. *ἀσχημοσύνη*

Sir 30:13 you may not be offended by his shamelessness. 1

shape 1. טבע 2. יצר 3. עשה 4. פסל 5. *πλάσσω* 6. *τυπόω*

Prv 8:25 Before the mountains had been shaped 1
Isa 44:12 he shapes it with hammers, and forges it 2
13 he shapes it into the figure of a man 3
Jer 18:11 I am shaping evil against you and devising a plan 2
Hab 2:18 profit is an idol when its maker has shaped it 4
Wis 13:13 shapes it with skill gained in idleness 6
2Mc 7:23 who shaped the beginning of man 5
4Mc 13:20 and was shaped during the same period of time 5

shapely 1. *εὔμορφος*

Sir 9: 8 Turn away your eyes from a shapely woman 1

share 1. חָבֵר 2. חלק 3. חֵלֶק 4. יָד 5. נתן 6. ספח 7. ערב 8. פֶּה 9. פרס 10. *εἰς* 11. *ἔχω μέρος* 12. *κλῆρος* 13. *κοινωνέω* 14. *κοινωνία* 15. *κοινωνός* 16. *λαμβάνω* 17. *μερίς* 18. *μέρος* 19. *μεταδίδωμι* 20. *μεταλαμβάνω* 21. *μετέχω* 22. *μέτοχος* 23. *συγκληρονομέω* 24. *συγκοινωνέω* 25. *συγκοινωνός* 26. *συμμερίζω* 27. *συμμετέχω* 28. consors

Gen 14:24 the share of the men who went with me; 3
24 let Aner, Eshcol, and Mamre take their share. 3
1Sm 26:19 I should have no share in the heritage of the LORD 6
30:24 For as his share is who goes down into the battle 3
24 so shall his share be who stays by the baggage; 3
24 they shall share alike. 2
2Sm 19:43 We have ten shares in the king, and in David also 4
2Kg 2: 9 let me inherit a double share of your spirit. 8
Job 17: 5 informs . . to get a share of their property 3
39:17 and given her no share in understanding. 3
Prv 14:10 no stranger shares its joy. 7
17: 2 share the inheritance as one of the brothers. 2
21: 9 than in a house shared with a contentious woman. 1
22: 9 blessed, for he shares his bread with the poor. 5
25:24 than in a house shared with a contentious woman. 1
Ecc 9: 6 no more for ever any share in all that is done 3
Isa 58: 7 Is it not to share your bread with the hungry 9
Lke 3:11 let him share with him who has none 19
15:12 give me the share of property that falls to me 18
Act 1:17 allotted his share in this ministry. 12
Rom 4:16 but also to those who share the faith of Abraham *
5: 2 we rejoice in our hope of sharing the glory of God. *
11:17 to share the richness of the olive tree 25
15:27 the Gentiles . . share in their spiritual blessings 13
1Co 9:10 the thresher thresh in hope of a share in the crop. 21
12 If others share this rightful claim upon you 21
13 share in the sacrificial offerings? 26
23 that I may share in its blessings. 25
2Co 1: 5 as we share abundantly in Christ's sufferings 10
5 through Christ we share abundantly in comfort *
7 we know that as you share in our sufferings 15
7 you will also share in our comfort. *
Gal 6: 6 share all good things with him who teaches. 13
Php 3:10 share his sufferings 14
4:14 Yet it was kind of you to share my trouble. 24
Col 1:12 has qualified us to share in the inheritance 17
1Th 2: 8 ready to share with you not only the gospel of God 19
2Ti 2: 6 ought to have the first share of the crops. 20
Phm 1: 6 the sharing of your faith 14
Heb 2:14 Since . . the children share in flesh and blood 13
3: 1 holy brethren, who share in a heavenly call 22
14 we share in Christ 22
12:10 we may share his holiness. 20
13:16 to share what you have 14
1Pe 4:13 in so far as you share Christ's sufferings 13
2Jn 1:11 for he who greets him shares his wicked work. 13
Rev 1: 9 I John, your brother, who share with you in Jesus 25
18: 4 Come out of her . . lest you share in her plagues; 16
20: 6 holy is he who shares in the first resurrection! 11
22:19 God will take away his share in the tree of life 18
1Es 5:40 told them not to share in the holy things 21
8:70 the nobles have been sharing in this iniquity. 21
2Es 15:46 you, Asia, who share in the glamour of Babylon 28
Wis 8:18 renown in sharing her words 14
18: 9 the saints would share alike the same things 20
19:16 those who had already shared the same rights. 21
Sir 14:14 let not your share of desired good pass by you. 17
22:23 that you may share with him in his inheritance. 23
2Mc 5:20 the place itself shared in the misfortunes 27
27 that they might not share in the defilement. 21
14:25 he . . settled down, and shared the common life. 13
3Mc 4: 6 to share married life 14
4Mc 16:18 you have had a share in the world and have enjoyed 20
18: 3 were deemed worthy to share in a divine inheritance. *

share *See also* fail, ought.

share affliction 1. ענה

1Kg 2:26 you shared in all the affliction of my father. 1

equal share 1. *ἰσόμοιρος*

2Mc 8:30 also to the aged, shares equal to their own. 1

share hatred of crime 1. *συμμισοπονηρέω*

2Mc 4:36 the Greeks shared their hatred of the crime. 1

share in suffering 1. *συγκακοπαθέω*

2Ti 1: 8 share in suffering for the gospel 1
2: 3 Share in suffering as a good soldier 1

share the rule 1. *συμβασιλεύω*

1Co 4: 8 so that we might share the rule with you! 1

sharp 1. חַד 2. חַדּוּד 3. חָרוּץ 4. לטשׁ 5. שׁנן 6. *ὀξύς* 7. *πικρός* 8. *τομός* 9. acuo

Job 41:30 His underparts are like sharp potsherds; 2
Ps 45: 5 Your arrows are sharp in the heart of the king's 5
52: 2 Your tongue is like a sharp razor 4
57: 4 spears and arrows, their tongues sharp swords. 1
120: 4 A warrior's sharp arrows, with glowing coals 5
Prv 5: 4 in the end she is . . sharp as a two-edged sword. 1
25:18 like a war club, or a sword, or sharp arrow. 5
Isa 5:28 their arrows are sharp, all their bows bent 5
41:15 a threshing sledge, new, sharp, and having teeth; 3
49: 2 He made my mouth like a sharp sword 1
Ezk 5: 1 And you, O son of man, take a sharp sword; 1
Heb 4:12 sharper than any two-edged sword 8
Rev 1:16 from his mouth issued a sharp two-edged sword 6
2:12 The words of him who has the sharp two-edged sword. 6
14:14 crown on his head, and a sharp sickle in his hand. 6
17 another angel . . and he too had a sharp sickle. 6
18 called . . to him who had the sharp sickle 6
19:15 From his mouth issues a sharp sword 6
2Es 16:13 and his arrows that he shoots are sharp 9
Wis 18:16 the sharp sword of thy authentic command 6
2Mc 9: 5 with sharp internal tortures 7
3Mc 5:18 the king . . with sharp threats demanded to know why 7
4Mc 9:26 with iron gauntlets having sharp hooks 6
11:19 To his back they applied sharp spits 6

sharp *See also* contention, make.

sharpen 1. ברר 2. הדד 3. חוד 4. לטשׁ 5. *ὀξύνω*

1Sm 13:20 to sharpen his plowshare, his mattock, his axe 4
21 and a third of a shekel for sharpening the axes *
Job 16: 9 my adversary sharpens his eyes against me. 4
Prv 27:17 Iron sharpens iron, and one man sharpens 3
17 sharpens iron, and one man sharpens another. 3
Jer 51:11 Sharpen the arrows! Take up the shields! 1
Ezk 21: 9 A sword, a sword is sharpened and also polished. 2
10 sharpened for slaughter, polished to flash 2
11 it is sharpened and polished to be given 2
Wis 5:20 sharpen stern wrath for a sword 5

sharply 1. *ἀποτόμως*

Tit 1:13 Therefore rebuke them sharply 1

sharply *See also* cut.

shatter 1. בצע 2. בקע 3. מחץ 4. נפץ 5. קצץ 6. רעע 7. רעץ 8. רצח 9. רשׁשׁ 10. שׁבר 11. חשׁל (A) 12. *συντρίβω*

Exd 9:25 hail . . shattered every tree of the field. 10

15: 6 thy right hand, O LORD, shatters the enemy. 7
Jdg 5:26 his head, she shattered and pierced his temple. 3
Job 34:24 He shatters the mighty without investigation 6
Ps 46: 9 he breaks the bow, and shatters the spear 5
48: 7 thou didst shatter the ships of Tarshish. 10
62: 3 How long will you set upon a man to shatter him 8
68:21 But God will shatter the heads of his enemies 3
105:33 shattered the trees of their country. 10
107:16 For he shatters the doors of bronze 10
110: 5 shatter kings on the day of his wrath. 3
6 he will shatter chiefs over the wide earth. 3
141: 7 rock which one cleaves and shatters on the land 2
Isa 21: 9 her gods he has shattered to the ground. 10
Dan 2:40 iron breaks to pieces and shatters all things; 11
12: 7 shattering of the power of the holy people 4
Ams 9: 1 and shatter them on the heads of all the people; 1
Mal 1: 4 We are shattered but we will rebuild the ruins 9
Lke 9:39 it convulses him till he foams, and shatters him 12
2Mc 12:28 with power shatters the might of his enemies 12

shatter utterly 1. conterreo
2Es 16:11 will not be utterly shattered at his presence? 1

shatterer 1. פוץ
Nah 2: 1 The shatterer has come up against you. 1

shave 1. גזז 2. גלח 3. קָרְחָה 4. ξυράω
Gen 41:14 and when he had shaved himself and changed his 2
Lev 13:33 then he shall shave himself 2
33 himself, but the itch he shall not shave 2
14: 9 on the seventh day he shall shave all his hair off 2
Num 6: 9 shall shave his head on the day of his cleansing; 2
9 on the seventh day he shall shave it. 2
18 Nazirite shall shave his consecrated head 2
Deu 21:12 she shall shave her head and pare her nails. 2
Jdg 16:17 If I be shaved, then my strength will leave me 2
22 began to grow again after it had been shaved. 2
1Ch 19: 4 Hanun took David's servants, and shaved them 2
Job 1:20 Job arose, and rent his robe, and shaved his head 1
Isa 7:20 shave with a razor . . hired beyond the River 2
Jer 41: 5 with their beards shaved and their clothes torn 2
48:37 For every head is shaved and every beard cut off; 3
Ezk 44:20 They shall not shave their heads 2
Act 21:24 so that they may shave their heads 4
LJr 1:31 their heads and beards shaved 4

shave off 1. גלח
Lev 14: 8 shave off all his hair, and bathe himself in water 1
9 shall shave off his beard and his eyebrows 1
21: 5 nor shave off the edges of their beards 1
Jdg 16:19 and had him shave off the seven locks of his head. 1
2Sm 10: 4 and shaved off half the beard of each, and cut off 1

shave the hair 1. גלח
Num 6:19 after he has shaven the hair of his consecration 1

shaven 1. ξυράω
1Co 11: 5 it is the same as if her head were shaven. 1
6 is disgraceful for a woman to be shorn or shaven 1

she-ass 1. אָתוֹן
Gen 12:16 maidservants, she-asses, and camels. 1
32:15 bulls, twenty she-asses and ten he-asses. 1
45:23 sent . . ten she-asses loaded with grain, bread 1
1Ch 27:30 over the she-asses was Jehde'iah 1
Job 1: 3 500 she-asses, and very many servants; 1
42:12 1,000 yoke of oxen, and 1,000 she-asses. 1

she-bear 1. דֹּב
2Kg 2:24 And two she-bears came out of the woods 1
Prv 17:12 Let a man meet a she-bear robbed of her cubs 1

she-goat 1. עֵז
Gen 15: 9 a she-goat three years old, a ram three years old 1
30:35 all the she-goats that were speckled and spotted 1
31:38 your ewes and your she-goats have not miscarried 1
32:14 200 she-goats and twenty he-goats 1

sheaf 1. אֲלֻמָּה 2. עָמִיר 3. עֹמֶר 4. δράγμα
Gen 37: 7 behold, we were binding sheaves in the field 1
7 and lo, my sheaf arose and stood upright; 1
7 and behold, your sheaves gathered round it 1
7 gathered round it, and bowed down to my sheaf. 1
Lev 23:10 you shall bring the sheaf of the first fruits 3
11 he shall wave the sheaf before the LORD 3
12 on the day when you wave the sheaf, you shall offer 3
15 you brought the sheaf of the wave offering 3
Deu 24:19 reap . . and have forgotten a sheaf in the field 3
Rut 2: 7 Pray, let me glean and gather among the sheaves 3
15 Let her glean even among the sheaves 3
Job 24:10 hungry, they carry the sheaves; 3
Ps 126: 6 home with shouts of joy, bringing his sheaves 1
Jer 9:22 men shall fall . . like sheaves after the reaper 2
Ams 2:13 as a cart full of sheaves presses down. 2
Mic 4:12 he has gathered them as sheaves to the threshing 2
Zec 12: 6 Judah . . like a flaming torch among sheaves; 2
Jdt 8: 3 men who were binding sheaves in the field 4

shear 1. גזז 2. גרע
Gen 31:19 Laban had gone to shear his sheep 1
38:13 is going up to Timnah to shear his sheep 1
Deu 15:19 nor shear the firstling of your flock. 1
1Sm 25: 2 He was shearing his sheep in Carmel. 1
4 David heard . . Nabal was shearing his sheep. 1
Isa 15: 2 On every head is baldness, every beard is shorn; 2

shearer 1. גזז 2. κείρω
1Sm 25: 7 I hear that you have shearers; 1
11 my meat that I have killed for my shearers 1
Isa 53: 7 and like a sheep that before its shearers is dumb 1
Act 8:32 As . . a lamb before its shearer is dumb 2

first shearing 1. πρωτοκουρά
Tob 1: 6 the tithes of my produce and the first shearings 1

sheath 1. נָדָן 2. תַּעַר 3. θήκη
1Sm 17:51 and took his sword and drew it out of its sheath 2
2Sm 20: 8 and over it was a girdle with a sword in its sheath 2
1Ch 21:27 angel; and he put his sword back into its sheath. 1
Ezk 21: 3 and will draw forth my sword out of its sheath 2
4 therefore my sword shall go out of its sheath 2
5 I the LORD have drawn my sword out of its sheath; 2
30 Return it to its sheath. 2
Hab 3: 9 Thou didst strip the sheath from thy bow •
Joh 18:11 Put your sword into its sheath 3

sheathe 1. שׁוב
Ezk 21: 5 out of its sheath; it shall not be sheathed again. 1

sheaves *See* binder.

shed 1. ירד 2. שׁפך 3. βάλλω 4. ἐκχέω 5. καταβάλλω 6. effundo
Gen 9: 6 Whoever sheds the blood of man 2
6 by man shall his blood be shed; 2
37:22 Reuben said to them, "Shed no blood; 2
Lev 17: 4 he has shed blood; and that man shall be cut off 2
Num35:33 no expiation . . for the blood that is shed in it 2
33 except by the blood of him who shed it. 2
Deu 19:10 lest innocent blood be shed in your land 2
21: 7 Our hands did not shed this blood, neither did our 2
7 neither did our eyes see it shed. •
1Sm 25:31 pangs of conscience, for having shed blood 2
2Sm 20:10 Jo'ab struck . . and shed his bowels to the ground 2
1Kg 2: 5 in time of peace blood which had been shed in war •
31 for the blood which Jo'ab shed without cause. 2
2Kg 21:16 Manas'seh shed very much innocent blood 2
24: 4 and also for the innocent blood that he had shed; 2
1Ch 22: 8 have shed much blood and have waged great wars; 2
8 because you have shed so much blood before me 2
28: 3 for you are a warrior and have shed blood. 2
Ps 119:136 My eyes shed streams of tears 1
Prv 1:16 they make haste to shed blood. 2
6:17 hands that shed innocent blood 2
Isa 26:21 the earth will disclose the blood shed upon her •
59: 7 and they make haste to shed innocent blood; 2
Jer 7: 6 or shed innocent blood in this place 2
22: 3 nor shed innocent blood in this place. 2
17 dishonest gain, for shedding innocent blood 2
Lam 4:13 her priests, who shed in the midst of her the blood 2
Ezk 16:38 as women who break wedlock and shed blood 2
22: 3 A city that sheds blood in the midst of her 2
4 become guilty by the blood which you have shed 2
6 have been bent on shedding blood. 2
9 There are men in you who slander to shed blood 2
12 In you men take bribes to shed blood; 2
27 like wolves tearing the prey, shedding blood 2
23:45 and with the sentence of women that shed blood; 2
24: 7 the blood she has shed is still in the midst of her; •
8 I have set on the bare rock the blood she has shed •
33:25 and lift up your eyes to your idols, and shed blood; 2
36:18 for the blood which they had shed in the land 2
Jol 3:19 they have shed innocent blood in their land. 2
Mat 23:30 in shedding the blood of the prophets.' •
35 all the righteous blood shed on earth 4
Lke 11:50 blood . . shed from the foundation of the world 4
Act 22:20 when the blood of Stephen thy witness was shed 4
Rom 3:15 Their feet are swift to shed blood 4
Heb 12: 4 resisted to the point of shedding your blood. •
Rev 6:13 as the fig tree sheds its winter fruit 3
16: 6 men have shed the blood of saints and prophets 4
2Es 15:22 those who shed innocent blood on earth. 6
AEs 16: 5 the shedding of innocent blood •
Sir 11:32 a sinner lies in wait to shed blood. •
14:18 which sheds some and puts forth others 5
28:11 urgent strife sheds blood. 4
34:22 to deprive an employee . . is to shed blood. 4
1Mc 1:37 they shed innocent blood 4
2Mc 1: 8 burned the gate and shed innocent blood 4

shed abroad 1. נוף 2. κατασπείρω
Ps 68: 9 Rain in abundance, O God, thou didst shed abroad; 1
3Mc 5:26 The rays of the sun were not yet shed abroad 2

shed light 1. נגה
Isa 13:10 and the moon will not shed its light. 1

shed luster 1. צוץ
Ps 132:18 but upon himself his crown will shed its luster. 1

shed tears 1. δακρύω
Sir 31:13 Therefore it sheds tears from every face. 1
3Mc 4: 4 and shed tears at the most miserable expulsion 1
4Mc 15:20 you did not shed tears. 1

shedder 1. שׁפך
Ezk 18:10 a son who is a robber, a shedder of blood 1

shedding of blood 1. αἱματεκχυσία
Heb 9:22 without the shedding of blood 1

sheep 1. כֶּבֶשׂ 2. כֶּשֶׂב 3. צֹאן 4. צֹנֶה 5. רָחֵל 6. שֶׂה 7. שֵׂה כְשָׂבִים 8. אִמַּר (A) 9. μηλωτή 10. πρόβατον 11. ovis
Gen 4: 2 Abel was a keeper of sheep, and Cain a tiller 3
12:16 and he had sheep, oxen, he-asses, menservants 3
20:14 Then Abim'elech took sheep and oxen 3
21:27 Abraham took sheep and oxen and gave them 3
29: 2 lo, three flocks of sheep lying beside it; 3
3 shepherds would . . water the sheep 3
6 Rachel his daughter is coming with the sheep! 3
7 water the sheep, and go, pasture them. 3
8 mouth of the well; then we water the sheep. 3
9 Rachel came with her father's sheep; 3
10 saw . . the sheep of Laban his mother's brother 3
30:32 every speckled and spotted sheep 6
31:19 Laban had gone to shear his sheep 3
38:13 is going up to Timnah to shear his sheep 3
Exd 12: 5 you shall take it from the sheep or from the goats; 1
20:24 sacrifice . . your sheep and your oxen; 3
22: 1 If a man steals an ox or a sheep, and kills it 6
1 shall pay . . four sheep for a sheep. 3
1 shall pay . . four sheep for a sheep. 6
4 whether it is an ox or an ass or a sheep 6
9 whether it is for ox, for ass, for sheep 6
10 an ass or an ox or a sheep or any beast to keep 6
30 do likewise . . with your sheep 3
34:19 All . . the firstlings of cow and sheep. 6
Lev 1:10 from the flock, from the sheep or goats 2
7:23 You shall eat no fat, of ox, or sheep, or goat 2
22:19 a male . . of the bulls or the sheep or the goats 2
27 When a bull or sheep or goat is born 2
27:26 whether ox or sheep, it is the LORD'S 6
Num18:17 firstling of a sheep . . you shall not redeem; 2
22:40 Balak sacrificed oxen and sheep, and sent 3
27:17 congregation of the LORD may not be as sheep 3
31:32 booty remaining of the spoil . . 675,000 sheep 3
36 the half . . was in number 337,500 sheep 3
37 the LORD'S tribute of sheep was 675. 3
43 now the congregation's half was 337,500 sheep 3
32:24 Build cities . . and folds for your sheep; 4
36 fortified cities, and folds for sheep. 3
Deu 14: 4 animals you may eat: the ox, the sheep, the goat 7
26 whatever you desire, oxen, or sheep, or wine 3
17: 1 not sacrifice . . an ox or a sheep 6
18: 3 offering a sacrifice, whether it be ox or sheep 6
4 first of the fleece of your sheep, you shall give 3
22: 1 not see your brother's ox or his sheep go astray 6
28:31 your sheep shall be given to your enemies 3
Jos 6:21 men and women, young and old, oxen, sheep, and 6
7:24 and daughters, and his oxen and asses and sheep 3
Jdg 6: 4 leave no sustenance . . and no sheep or ox or ass. 6
1Sm 14:32 the people flew upon the spoil, and took sheep 3
34 Let every man bring his ox or his sheep 6
15: 3 infant and suckling, ox and sheep, camel and ass. 6
9 spared Agag, and the best of the sheep 3
14 What then is this bleating of the sheep in my ears 3
15 people spared the best of the sheep and . . oxen 3
21 But the people took of the spoil, sheep and oxen 3
16:11 the youngest, but behold, he is keeping the sheep. 3
19 Send me David your son, who is with the sheep. 3
17:15 went back and forth . . to feed his father's sheep 3
20 David rose . . and left the sheep with a keeper 3
28 with whom have you left those few sheep 3
34 Your servant used to keep sheep for his father; 3
22:19 oxen, asses and sheep, he put to the sword. 6
25: 2 The man was very rich; he had 3,000 sheep 3
2 He was shearing his sheep in Carmel. 3
4 David heard . . Nabal was shearing his sheep. 3
16 while we were with them keeping the sheep. 3
18 two skins of wine, and five sheep ready dressed 3
27: 9 took away the sheep, the oxen, the asses, the camels 3
2Sm 7: 8 I took you from . . from following the sheep 3
17:29 brought . . honey and curds and sheep and cheese 3
24:17 I have done . . but these sheep, what have they done? 3
1Kg 1: 9 Adoni'jah sacrificed sheep, oxen, and fatlings 3
19 He has sacrificed oxen, fatlings, and sheep 3
25 and has sacrificed oxen, fatlings, and sheep 3
4:23 twenty pasture-fed cattle, 100 sheep 3
8: 5 sacrificing so many sheep and oxen that 3
63 Solomon offered . . and 120,000 sheep. 3
22:17 scattered . . as sheep that have no shepherd; 3
2Kg 5:26 olive orchards and vineyards, sheep and oxen 3
1Ch 5:21 50,000 camels, 250,000 sheep, 2,000 asses 3
12:40 and wine and oil, oxen and sheep 3

17: 7 from the pasture, from following the sheep 3
21:17 But these sheep, what have they done? 3
2Ch 5: 6 sacrificing so many sheep and oxen that they 3
7: 5 as a sacrifice . . 120,000 sheep. 3
14:15 and carried away sheep in abundance and camels. 3
15:11 They sacrificed . . 700 oxen and 7,000 sheep. 3
18: 2 Ahab killed an abundance of sheep and oxen 3
16 as sheep that have no shepherd; 3
29:33 consecrated offerings were . . 3,000 sheep. 3
30:24 Hezeki'ah . . gave the assembly . . 7,000 sheep 3
24 princes gave the assembly . . 10,000 sheep. 3
31: 6 also brought in the tithe of cattle and sheep 3
Ezr 6: 9 young bulls, rams, or sheep for burnt offerings 8
Neh 5:18 one day was one ox and six choice sheep; 3
Job 1: 3 He had 7,000 sheep 3
16 fell from heaven and burned up the sheep 3
31:20 if he was not warmed with the fleece of my sheep; 1
42:12 had 14,000 sheep, 6,000 camels, 1,000 yoke of oxen 3
Ps 8: 7 sheep and oxen, and also the beasts of the field 4
44:11 Thou hast made us like sheep for slaughter 3
22 and accounted as sheep for the slaughter. 3
49:14 Like sheep they are appointed for Sheol; 3
74: 1 thy anger smoke against the sheep of thy pasture? 3
78:52 Then he led forth his people like sheep 3
95: 7 people of his pasture, and the sheep of his hand. 3
100: 3 we are his people, and the sheep of his pasture. 3
119:176I have gone astray like a lost sheep; 6
144:13 sheep bring forth thousands and ten thousands 3
Isa 7:21 a man will keep alive a young cow and two sheep; 3
25 cattle are let loose and where sheep tread. 6
13:14 or like sheep with none to gather them 3
22:13 behold . . slaying oxen and killing sheep 3
43:23 not brought me your sheep for burnt offerings 6
53: 6 All we like sheep have gone astray; 3
7 and like a sheep that before its shearers is dumb 5
Jer 12: 3 Pull them out like sheep for the slaughter 3
23: 1 who destroy and scatter the sheep of my pasture! 3
50: 6 My people have been lost sheep; 3
17 Israel is a hunted sheep driven away by lions. 6
Ezk 34: 2 Should not shepherds feed the sheep? 3
3 but you do not feed the sheep. 3
6 My sheep were scattered, they wandered 3
6 my sheep were scattered over all the face 3
8 because my sheep have become a prey 3
8 my sheep have become food for all the wild beasts 3
8 my shepherds have not searched for my sheep 3
8 have fed themselves, and have not fed my sheep; 3
10 I will require my sheep at their hand 3
10 and put a stop to their feeding the sheep; 3
10 I will rescue my sheep from their mouths 3
11 Behold, I, I myself will search for my sheep 3
12 when some of his sheep have been scattered 3
12 so will I seek out my sheep; and I will rescue them 3
15 I myself will be the shepherd of my sheep 3
17 I judge between sheep and sheep, rams and he-goats 6
17 I judge between sheep and sheep, rams and he-goats 6
19 And must my sheep eat what you have trodden 3
20 judge between the fat sheep and the lean sheep. 6
20 judge between the fat sheep and the lean sheep. 6
22 I will judge between sheep and sheep. 6
22 I will judge between sheep and sheep. 6
31 you are my sheep, the sheep of my pasture 3
31 you are my sheep, the sheep of my pasture 3
45:15 one sheep from every flock of 200 6
Hos 12:12 and for a wife he herded sheep.) *
Jol 1:18 even the flocks of sheep are dismayed. 3
Mic 2:12 I will set them together like sheep in a fold 3
5: 8 like a young lion among the flocks of sheep 3
Zec 10: 2 Therefore the people wander like sheep; 3
11: 7 slain for those who trafficked in the sheep. 3
7 I tended the sheep. 3
11 traffickers in the sheep, who were watching me 3
13: 7 the shepherd, that the sheep may be scattered; 3
Mat 7:15 who come to you in sheep's clothing 10
9:36 like sheep without a shepherd. 10
10: 6 to the lost sheep of the house of Israel. 10
16 I send you out as sheep in the midst of wolves 10
12:11 said to them, "What man of you, if he has one sheep 10
12 Of how much more value is a man than a sheep! 10
15:24 only to the lost sheep of the house of Israel. 10
18:12 If a man has a 100 sheep 10
25:32 as a shepherd separates the sheep from the goats 10
33 he will place the sheep at his right hand 10
26:31 the sheep of the flock will be scattered.' 10
Mrk 6:34 because they were like sheep without a shepherd; 10
14:27 the sheep will be scattered.' 10
Lke 15: 4 What man of you, having 100 sheep 10
6 I have found my sheep which was lost.' 10
Joh 2:14 he found those who were selling oxen and sheep 10
15 he drove them all, with the sheep and oxen, out 10
10: 2 the shepherd of the sheep. 10
3 the sheep hear his voice 10
3 he calls his own sheep by name and leads them out. 10
4 he goes before them, and the sheep follow him 10
7 I am the door of the sheep. 10
8 the sheep did not heed them. 10
11 lays down his life for the sheep. 10
12 not a shepherd, whose own the sheep are not 10
12 leaves the sheep and flees 10
13 is a hireling and cares nothing for the sheep. 10
15 I lay down my life for the sheep. 10
16 I have other sheep, that are not of this fold 10
26 because you do not belong to my sheep. 10
27 My sheep hear my voice, and I know them 10
21:16 He said to him, "Tend my sheep. 10
17 Jesus said to him, "Feed my sheep. 10
Act 8:32 As a sheep led to the slaughter 10
Rom 8:36 we are regarded as sheep to be slaughtered. 10
Heb 11:37 they went about in skins of sheep and goats 9
13:20 our Lord Jesus, the great shepherd of the sheep 10
1Pe 2:25 For you were straying like sheep 10
Rev 18:13 cattle and sheep, horses and chariots, and slaves 10
1Es 1: 8 gave to the priests for the passover 2,600 sheep 10
9 gave the Levites for the passover 5,000 sheep 10
2Es 5:26 thou hast provided for thyself one sheep 11
16:32 because no sheep will go along them. 11
Jdt 2:17 innumerable sheep and oxen and goats 10
8:26 while he was keeping the sheep of Laban 10
11:19 will lead them like sheep that have no shepherd 10
Bel 1: 3 40 sheep and 50 gallons of wine. 10
32 they had been given two human bodies and two sheep 10
151 1: 1 I tended my father's sheep. 10
4 and took me from my father's sheep 10

sheep *See also* breeder, keep.

sheepfold 1. גְּדֵרַת צֹאן 2. מִכְלְאַת צֹאן 3. מִשְׁפְּתַיִם 4. נָוֶה 5. שְׁפַתַּיִם 6. *αὐλὴ προβάτων* 7. *μάνδρα* 8. *μάνδρα εἰς τὰ ποίμνια*

Gen 49:14 a strong ass, crouching between the sheepfolds; 3
Num32:16 We will build sheepfolds here for our flocks 1
Jdg 5:16 tarry among the sheepfolds, to hear the piping 3
1Sm 24: 3 And he came to the sheepfolds by the way 1
2Ch 32:28 stalls for all kinds of cattle, and sheepfolds. 8
Ps 68:13 though they stay among the sheepfolds- 5
78:70 chose David . . and took him from the sheepfolds; 2
Jer 49:19 like a lion . . against a strong sheepfold 4
50:44 like a lion . . against a strong sheepfold 4
Joh 10: 1 he who does not enter the sheepfold by the door 6
Jdt 2:26 plundered their sheepfolds. 7
3: 3 all our sheepfolds with their tents 7

sheepshearer 1. גזז 2. גזז צאן

Gen 38:12 he went up to Timnah to his sheepshearers 2
2Sm 13:23 Ab'salom had sheepshearers at Ba'al-ha'zor 1
24 Behold, your servant has sheepshearers; 1

sheer 1. רַק 2. *ἀκρότομος*

Isa 28:19 it will be sheer terror to understand 1
Sir 40:15 they are unhealthy roots upon sheer rock. 2
48:17 he tunneled the sheer rock with iron 2

sheer *See also* madness.

sheet 1. *ὀθόνη*

Act 10:11 something descending, like a great sheet 1
11: 5 like a great sheet 1

shekel 1. מִשְׁקָל 2. שֶׁקֶל 3. *σίκλος* 4. *στατήρ*

Gen 23:15 a piece of land worth 400 shekels of silver 2
16 weighed out for Ephron . . 400 shekels of silver 2
24:22 bracelets . . weighing ten gold shekels *
37:28 sold him to the Ish'maelites for twenty shekels *
45:22 but to Benjamin he gave 300 shekels of silver *
Exd 21:32 the owner shall give to the master 30 shekels 2
30:13 Each . . shall give this: half a shekel according 2
13 shekel according to the shekel of the sanctuary 2
13 (the shekel is twenty gerahs) 2
13 half a shekel as an offering to the LORD. 2
15 shall not give less, than the half shekel 2
23 Take . . of liquid myrrh 500 shekels 2
24 according to the shekel of the sanctuary 2
38:24 gold . . 29 talents and 730 shekels 2
24 730 shekels, by the shekel of the sanctuary. 2
25 silver . . was 100 talents and 1,775 shekels 2
25 by the shekel of the sanctuary 2
26 a beka a head (that is, half a shekel, by the shekel 2
26 half a shekel, by the shekel of the sanctuary) 2
28 of the 1,775 shekels he made hooks *
29 the bronze . . was 70 talents, and 2,400 shekels; 2
Lev 5:15 a ram . . valued by you in shekels of silver 2
15 silver, according to the shekel of the sanctuary 2
27: 3 valuation . . shall be 50 shekels of silver 2
3 according to the shekel of the sanctuary 2
4 your valuation shall be 30 shekels 2
5 your valuation shall be for a male twenty shekels 2
5 twenty shekels, and for a female ten shekels 2
6 for a male five shekels of silver, and for a female 2
6 valuation shall be three shekels of silver 2
7 valuation for a male shall be fifteen shekels 2
7 fifteen shekels, and for a female ten shekels 2
16 barley shall be valued at 50 shekels of silver 2
25 according to the shekel of the sanctuary 2
25 twenty gerahs shall make a shekel 2
Num 3:47 you shall take five shekels apiece; 2
47 reckoning by the shekel of the sanctuary 2
47 of the sanctuary, the shekel of twenty gerahs 2
50 took . . 1,365 shekels, reckoned by . . the sanctuary; *
50 took . . 1,365 shekels, reckoned by . . the sanctuary; 2
7:13 one silver plate whose weight was 130 shekels *
13 one silver basin of 70 shekels 2
13 70 shekels, according to the shekel of the sanctuary 2
14 one golden dish of ten shekels, full of incense; *
19 one silver plate, whose weight was 130 shekels *
19 one silver basin of 70 shekels 2
19 70 shekels, according to the shekel of the sanctuary 2
20 one golden dish of ten shekels, full of incense; *
25 one silver plate, whose weight was 130 shekels *
25 one silver basin of 70 shekels 2
25 130 shekels, according to the shekel of the sanctuary 2
26 one golden dish of ten shekels, full of incense; *
31 one silver plate whose weight was 130 shekels *
31 one silver basin of 70 shekels 2
31 70 shekels, according to the shekel of the sanctuary 2
32 one golden dish of ten shekels, full of incense; *
37 one silver plate, whose weight was 130 shekels *
37 one silver basin of 70 shekels 2
37 70 shekels, according to the shekel of the sanctuary 2
38 one golden dish of ten shekels, full of incense; *
43 one silver plate, whose weight was 130 shekels *
43 one silver basin of 70 shekels 2
43 70 shekels, according to the shekel of the sanctuary 2
44 one golden dish of ten shekels, full of incense; *
49 one silver plate, whose weight was 130 shekels *
49 one silver basin of 70 shekels 2
49 70 shekels, according to the shekel of the sanctuary 2
50 one golden dish of ten shekels, full of incense; *
55 one silver plate, whose weight was 130 shekels *
55 one silver basin of 70 shekels 2
55 70 shekels, according to the shekel of the sanctuary 2
56 one golden dish of ten shekels, full of incense; *
61 one silver plate, whose weight was 130 shekels *
61 one silver basin of 70 shekels 2
61 70 shekels, according to the shekel of the sanctuary 2
62 one golden dish of ten shekels, full of incense; *
67 one silver plate, whose weight was 130 shekels *
67 one silver basin of 70 shekels 2
67 70 shekels, according to the shekel of the sanctuary 2
68 one golden dish of ten shekels, full of incense; *
73 one silver plate, whose weight was 130 shekels *
73 one silver basin of 70 shekels 2
73 70 shekels, according to the shekel of the sanctuary 2
74 one golden dish of ten shekels, full of incense; *
79 one silver plate, whose weight was 130 shekels *
79 one silver basin of 70 shekels 2
79 70 shekels, according to the shekel of the sanctuary 2
80 one golden dish of ten shekels, full of incense; *
85 each silver plate weighing 130 shekels *
85 all the silver of the vessels 2,400 shekels *
85 according to the shekel of the sanctuary 2
86 golden dishes . . weighing ten shekels apiece *
86 according to the shekel of the sanctuary 2
86 all the gold of the dishes being 120 shekels; *
18:16 you shall fix at five shekels in silver 2
16 according to the shekel of the sanctuary 2
31:52 gold of the offering . . was 16,750 shekels. 2
Deu 22:19 they shall fine him 100 shekels of silver *
29 give to the father . . 50 shekels of silver *
Jos 7:21 I saw . . and 200 shekels of silver 2
21 I saw . . and a bar of gold weighing 50 shekels 2
Jdg 8:26 the weight . . was 1,700 shekels of gold; *
1Sm 9: 8 I have . . the fourth part of a shekel of silver 2
13:21 and a third of a shekel for sharpening the axes *
17: 5 weight of the coat was 5,000 shekels of bronze. 2
7 and his spear's head weighed 600 shekels of iron; 2
2Sm 14:26 he weighed the hair of his head, 200 shekels 2
21:16 whose spear weighed 300 shekels of bronze 1
24:24 David bought . . for 50 shekels of silver. 2
1Kg 10:16 600 shekels of gold went into each shield. *
29 imported from Egypt for 600 shekels of silver *
2Kg 5: 5 taking with him . . silver, 6,000 shekels of gold *
6:25 an ass's head was sold for 80 shekels of silver *
25 of a kab of dove's dung for five shekels of silver. *
7: 1 a measure of fine meal shall be sold for a shekel 2
1 and two measures of barley for a shekel 2
16 So a measure of fine meal was sold for a shekel 2
16 and two measures of barley for a shekel 2
18 Two measures of barley shall be sold for a shekel 2
18 and a measure of fine meal for a shekel 2
15:20 exacted the money . . 50 shekels of silver 2
1Ch 21:25 David paid Ornan 600 shekels of gold by weight 2
2Ch 1:17 chariot . . for 600 shekels of silver *
3: 9 weight . . one shekel to 50 shekels of gold. *
9 weight . . one shekel to 50 shekels of gold. 2
9:15 600 shekels of . . gold went into each shield. *
16 300 shekels of gold went into each shield; *
Neh 5:15 food and wine, besides 40 shekels of silver. 2
10:32 charge . . yearly with the third part of a shekel 2
Isa 7:23 vines, worth 1,000 shekels of silver *
Jer 32: 9 the money to him, seventeen shekels of silver 2
Ezk 4:10 food . . shall be by weight, twenty shekels a day; 2
45:12 The shekel shall be twenty gerahs; 2
12 five shekels shall be five shekels 2
12 five shekels shall be five shekels *
12 ten shekels shall be ten shekels 3
12 ten shekels shall be ten shekels *
12 your mina shall be 50 shekels. 3
Hos 3: 2 So I bought her for fifteen shekels of silver *

Ams 8: 5 we may make the ephah small and the shekel great 2
Zec 11:12 they weighed out as my wages 30 shekels *
13 I took the 30 shekels of silver *
Mat 17:27 when you open its mouth you will find a shekel; 4
1Mc 10:40 I also grant 15,000 shekels of silver 3
42 Moreover, the 5,000 shekels of silver 3

shekel *See also* half.

shelter 1. חָסוּת 2. מַחְסֶה 3. מִסְתּוֹר 4. מִפְלָט 5. סֹךְ 6. סֻכָּה 7. סֵתֶר 8. צֵל 9. *σκεπάζω* 10. *σκέπης* 11. *σκηνόω*

Gen 19: 8 for they have come under the shelter of my roof. 8
Job 24: 8 and cling to the rock for want of shelter. 2
Ps 27: 5 he will hide me in his shelter 5
31:20 thou holdest them safe under thy shelter 6
55: 8 I would haste to find me a shelter from the raging 4
61: 4 Oh to be safe under the shelter of thy wings! Selah 7
91: 1 He who dwells in the shelter of the Most High 7
Isa 4: 6 a refuge and a shelter from the storm and rain. 3
25: 4 shelter from the storm and a shade from the heat 2
28:17 and waters will overwhelm the shelter. 7
30: 3 the shelter in the shadow of Egypt 1
Rev 7:15 he who sits upon the throne will shelter them 11
Wis 10:17 became a shelter to them by day 10
Sir 2:13 Therefore it will not be sheltered. 9
6:14 A faithful friend is a sturdy shelter 10
14:26 he will place his children under her shelter 10
27 he will be sheltered by her from the heat 9
29:22 a poor man under the shelter of his roof 10
34:16 a shelter from the hot wind 10
3Mc 3:27 whoever shelters any of the Jews 9
29 Every place detected sheltering a Jew 9

shelter *See also* get, place, seek, take.

shepherd 1. נֹקֵד 2. רעה 3. רעה צאן 4. *ποιμαίνω* 5. *ποιμήν* 6. pastor

Gen 29: 3 the shepherds would roll the stone from the mouth *
37: 2 Joseph . . was shepherding the flock 2
46:32 the men are shepherds, for they have been keepers 3
34 for every shepherd is an abomination 2
47: 3 Your servants are shepherds, as our fathers 3
49:24 by the name of the Shepherd, the Rock of Israel 2
Exd 2:17 The shepherds came and drove them away; 2
19 delivered us out of the hand of the shepherds 2
Num14:33 your children shall be shepherds 2
27:17 may not be as sheep which have no shepherd. 2
1Sm 17:40 and put them in his shepherd's bag or wallet; 2
25: 7 now your shepherds have been with us 2
2Sm 5: 2 You shall be shepherd of my people Israel 2
7: 7 whom I commanded to shepherd my people Israel 2
1Kg 22:17 scattered . . as sheep that have no shepherd; 2
2Kg 10:12 when he was at Beth-eked of the Shepherds 2
1Ch 11: 2 You shall be shepherd of my people Israel 2
17: 6 whom I commanded to shepherd my people 2
2Ch 18:16 as sheep that have no shepherd; 2
Ps 23: 1 The LORD is my shepherd, I shall not want; 2
28: 9 be thou their shepherd, and carry them for ever. 2
49:14 Death shall be their shepherd; 2
78:71 he brought him to be the shepherd of Jacob 2
80: 1 Give ear, O Shepherd of Israel 2
Ecc 12:11 the . . sayings which are given by one Shepherd. 2
Sng 1: 8 pasture your kids beside the shepherd's tents. 2
Isa 13:20 no shepherds will make their flocks lie down 2
31: 4 a band of shepherds is called forth against him 2
38:12 removed from me like a shepherd's tent; 2
40:11 He will feed his flock like a shepherd 2
44:28 who says of Cyrus, 'He is my shepherd 2
56:11 The shepherds also have no understanding; 2
63:11 up out of the sea the shepherds of his flock? 2
Jer 3:15 I will give you shepherds after my own heart 2
6: 3 Shepherds with . . flocks shall come against her; 2
10:21 For the shepherds are stupid 2
12:10 Many shepherds have destroyed my vineyard 2
22:22 The wind shall shepherd all your shepherds 2
22 The wind shall shepherd all your shepherds 2
23: 1 Woe to the shepherds who destroy and scatter 2
2 concerning the shepherds who care for my people 2
4 I will set shepherds over them who will care 2
25:34 Wail, you shepherds, and cry, and roll in ashes 2
35 No refuge will remain for the shepherds 2
36 the cry of the shepherds, and the wail of the lords 2
31:10 and will keep him as a shepherd keeps his flock. 2
33:12 there shall again be habitations of shepherds 2
43:12 as a shepherd cleans his cloak of vermin; 2
49:19 What shepherd can stand before me? 2
50: 6 lost sheep; their shepherds have led them astray 2
44 What shepherd can stand before me? 2
51:23 I break in pieces the shepherd and his flock; 2
Ezk 34: 2 prophesy against the shepherds of Israel 2
2 prophesy, and say to them, even to the shepherds 2
2 Thus says the Lord GOD: Ho, shepherds of Israel 2
2 Should not shepherds feed the sheep? 2
5 were scattered, because there was no shepherd; 2
7 you shepherds, hear the word of the LORD 2
8 since there was no shepherd; 2
8 my shepherds have not searched for my sheep 2
8 but the shepherds have fed themselves 2
9 you shepherds, hear the word of the LORD 2
10 Behold, I am against the shepherds; 2
10 no longer shall the shepherds feed themselves. 2
12 As a shepherd seeks out his flock 2
15 I myself will be the shepherd of my sheep 2
23 I will set up over them one shepherd 2
23 he shall feed them and be their shepherd. 2
37:24 they shall all hav· 2
Ams 1: 1 of Amos, who was among the shepherds of Teko'a 1
2 the pastures of the shepherds mourn 2
3:12 the shepherd rescues from the mouth of the lion 2
Mic 5: 5 we will raise against him seven shepherds 2
7:14 Shepherd thy people with thy staff 2
Nah 3:18 Your shepherds are asleep, O king of Assyria; 2
Zep 2: 6 shall be pastures, meadows for shepherds 2
Zec 10: 2 they are afflicted for want of a shepherd. 2
3 My anger is hot against the shepherds 2
11: 3 Hark, the wail of the shepherds, for their glory 2
5 their own shepherds have no pity on them. 2
6 men to fall each into the hand of his shepherd 2
8 In one month I destroyed the three shepherds. 2
9 I said, "I will not be your shepherd. 2
15 Take . . the implements of a worthless shepherd. 2
16 For lo, I am raising up in the land a shepherd 2
17 Woe to my worthless shepherd 2
13: 7 Awake, O sword, against my shepherd 2
7 Strike the shepherd 2
Mat 9:36 like sheep without a shepherd. 5
25:32 as a shepherd separates the sheep from the goats 5
26:31 it is written, 'I will strike the shepherd 5
Mrk 6:34 because they were like sheep without a shepherd; 5
14:27 it is written, 'I will strike the shepherd 5
Lke 2: 8 in that region there were shepherds 5
15 the shepherds said to one another, "Let us go over 5
18 wondered at what the shepherds told them. 5
20 the shepherds returned 5
Joh 10: 2 the shepherd of the sheep. 5
11 I am the good shepherd 5
11 The good shepherd lays down his life 5
12 He who is a hireling and not a shepherd 5
14 I am the good shepherd 5
16 there shall be one flock, one shepherd. 5
Heb 13:20 our Lord Jesus, the great shepherd of the sheep 5
1Pe 2:25 the Shepherd and Guardian of your souls. 5
Rev 7:17 For the Lamb . . will be their shepherd 4
2Es 2:34 Await your shepherd 6
5:18 like a shepherd who leaves his flock 6
Jdt 11:19 will lead them like sheep that have no shepherd 5
Wis 17:17 whether he was a farmer or a shepherd or a workman 5
Sir 18:13 turns them back, as a shepherd his flock. 5

become a shepherd 1. רעה

Zec 11: 4 said the LORD my God: "Become shepherd of the flock 1
7 I became the shepherd of the flock 1

chief shepherd 1. *ἀρχιποίμην*

1Pe 5: 4 when the chief Shepherd is manifested 1

sherd 1. חֶרֶשׂ

Isa 30:14 not a sherd is found with which to take fire 1

shield 1. מָגֵן 2. צִנָּה 3. שֶׁלֶט 4. *ἀσπίς* 5. *θυρεός* 6. *κάλυμμα* 7. *ὅπλον* 8. *ὑπερασπίζω*

Gen 15: 1 Fear not, Abram, I am your shield; 1
Deu 33:29 LORD, the shield of your help, and the sword 1
Jdg 5: 8 Was shield or spear to be seen among . . Israel? 1
1Sm 17:41 with his shield-bearer in front of him. 2
2Sm 1:21 For there the shield of the mighty was defiled 1
21 the mighty was defiled, the shield of Saul 1
8: 7 David took the shields of gold . . carried 3
22: 3 my God . . my shield and the horn of my salvation 1
31 he is a shield for all those who take refuge in him. 1
36 Thou hast given me the shield of thy salvation 1
1Kg 10:16 Solomon made . . large shields of beaten gold; 2
16 600 shekels of gold went into each shield. 2
17 he made 300 shields of beaten gold; 1
17 three minas of gold went into each shield; 1
14:26 He also took away all the shields of gold 1
27 Rehobo'am made in their stead shields of bronze 1
2Kg 11:10 the priest delivered . . the spears and shields 3
19:32 or come before it with a shield or cast up a siege 1
1Ch 5:18 valiant men, who carried shield and sword 1
12: 8 warriors, expert with shield and spear 2
24 The men of Judah bearing shield and spear were 2
34 were 37,000 men armed with shield and spear. 2
18: 7 David took the shields of gold 3
2Ch 9:15 600 shekels of . . gold went into each shield. 2
16 he made 300 shields of beaten gold; 1
16 300 shekels of gold went into each shield; 1
11:12 he put shields and spears in all the cities 2
12: 9 He also took away the shields of gold 1
10 Rehobo'am made in their stead shields of bronze 1
14: 8 280,000 men . . carried shields and drew bows; 1
17:17 with 200,000 men armed with bow and shield 1
25: 5 fit for war, able to handle spear and shield. 2
26:14 Uzzi'ah prepared for all the army shields, spears 1
32: 5 He also made weapons and shields in abundance. 1
27 made . . treasuries . . for spices, for shields 1
Neh 4:16 half held the spears, shields, bows 1
Job 15:26 against him with a thick-bossed shield; 1
41:15 His back is made of rows of shields 1
Ps 3: 3 But thou, O LORD, art a shield about me 1
5:12 thou dost cover him with favor as with a shield. 2
7:10 My shield is with God, who saves the upright 1
18: 2 my shield, and the horn of my salvation 1
30 he is a shield for all those who take refuge 1
35 Thou hast given me the shield of thy salvation 1
28: 7 The LORD is my strength and my shield; 1
33:20 soul waits for the LORD; he is our help and shield. 1
35: 2 Take hold of shield and buckler 1
47: 9 For the shields of the earth belong to God; 1
59:11 bring them down, O Lord, our shield! 1
76: 3 the shield, the sword, and the weapons of war. 1
84: 9 Behold our shield, O God; 1
11 For the LORD God is a sun and shield; 1
89:18 For our shield belongs to the LORD 1
91: 4 his faithfulness is a shield and buckler. 2
115: 9 He is their help and their shield. 1
10 He is their help and their shield. 1
11 He is their help and their shield. 1
119:114 Thou art my hiding place and my shield; 1
144: 2 my shield and he in whom I take refuge 1
Prv 2: 7 he is a shield to those who walk in integrity 1
30: 5 he is a shield to those who take refuge in him. 1
Sng 4: 4 bucklers, all of them shields of warriors. 3
Isa 21: 5 eat, they drink. Arise, O princes, oil the shield! 1
22: 6 bore the quiver . . and Kir uncovered the shield. 1
37:33 or come before it with a shield 1
Jer 46: 3 Prepare buckler and shield, and advance 2
9 men of Ethiopia and Put who handle the shield 1
51:11 Sharpen the arrows! Take up the shields! 3
Ezk 23:24 on every side with buckler, shield, and helmet 1
26: 8 and raise a roof of shields against you. 2
27:10 men of war; they hung the shield and helmet in you; 1
11 they hung their shields upon your walls 3
32:27 whose shields are upon their bones; *
38: 4 company, all of them with buckler and shield 1
5 are with them, all of them with shield and helmet; 1
39: 9 shields and bucklers, bows and arrows, handpikes 1
Nah 2: 3 The shield of his mighty men is red 1
Eph 6:16 besides all these, taking the shield of faith 5
Jdt 9: 7 they trust in shield and spear, in bow and sling 4
Wis 5:16 with his arm he will shield them. 8
19 he will take holiness as an invincible shield 4
18:21 he brought forward the shield of his ministry 7
Sir 29:13 more than a mighty shield 4
37: 5 in the face of battle take up the shield. 4
1Mc 6: 2 golden shields, breastplates, and weapons 6
39 the sun shone upon the shields of gold and brass 4
14:24 sent Numenius to Rome with a large gold shield 4
15:18 have brought a gold shield weighing 1,000 minas. 4
20 seemed good to us to accept the shield from them. 4
2Mc 5: 3 brandishing of shields, massing of spears 4
15:11 confidence in shields and spears 4
4Mc 4: 9 to shield the holy place 8
7: 4 the shield of his devout reason. 8
8 shielding it with their own blood 8

shield *See also* put.

large shield 1. מָגֵן 2. צִנָּה

2Ch 9:15 Solomon made 200 large shields of beaten gold; 2
23: 9 delivered . . the large and small shields 1

small shield 1. שֶׁלֶט 2. *ἀσπιδίσκη*

2Ch 23: 9 delivered . . the large and small shields 1
1Mc 4:57 golden crowns and small shields 2

shield-bearer 1. צִנָּה

1Sm 17: 7 and his shield-bearer went before him. 1

shift 1. *μεθίστημι* 2. *μετακινέω*

Col 1:23 not shifting from the hope of the gospel 2
2Mc 4:10 he at once shifted his countrymen over to . . 1

shiftlessness 1. *ἀχρειότης*

Tob 4:13 in shiftlessness there is loss and great want 1
13 because shiftlessness is the mother of famine. 1

shine 1. אור 2. אוֹר 3. הלל 4. זהר 5. זרח 6. יפע 7. נגה 8. נֹגַהּ 9. נסס 10. עַיִן 11. קרן 12. *ἐκλάμπω* 13. *ἐπιλάμπω* 14. *λαμπρός* 15. *λάμπω* 16. *λάμψις* 17. *στίλβω* 18. *φαίνω* 19. fulgeo 20. luceo 21. nitor 22. splendeo

Exd 34:29 Moses did not know that the skin of his face shone 11
30 Moses, behold, the skin of his face shone 11
35 saw . . that the skin of Moses' face shone; 11
2Kg 3:22 they rose . . and the sun shone upon the water 5
Job 3: 4 May God above not seek it, nor light shine upon it. 6
18: 5 the flame of his fire does not shine. 7
22:28 light will shine on your ways. 7
29: 3 when his lamp shone upon my head 3
31:26 if I have looked at the sun when it shone 3
41:32 Behind him he leaves a shining wake; 1
Ps 31:16 Let thy face shine on thy servant; 1
80: 3 let thy face shine, that we may be saved! 1
7 let thy face shine, that we may be saved! 1
19 let thy face shine, that we may be saved! 1

148: 3 sun and moon, praise him, all you shining stars! 2
Prv 4:18 light . . which shines brighter and brighter 1
Isa 4: 5 smoke and the shining of a flaming fire by night; 8
9: 2 of deep darkness, on them has light shined. 7
60: 1 Arise, shine; for your light has come 1
Ezk 1:22 likeness of a firmament, shining like crystal 10
43: 2 the earth shone with his glory. 1
Dan 12: 3 shine like the brightness of the firmament; 4
Jol 2:10 and the stars withdraw their shining. 7
3:15 and the stars withdraw their shining. 7
Zec 9:16 jewels of a crown they shall shine on his land. 9
Mat 5:16 Let your light so shine before men, that they may 15
13:43 Then the righteous will shine like the sun 12
17: 2 and his face shone like the sun 15
24:27 lightning . . shines as far as the west 18
Joh 1: 5 The light shines in the darkness 18
5:35 He was a burning and shining lamp 18
Act 12: 7 a light shone in the cell 15
2Co 4: 6 the God who said, "Let light shine out of darkness 15
6 who has shone in our hearts 15
Php 2:15 among whom you shine as lights in the world 18
2Pe 1:19 as to a lamp shining in a dark place 18
1Jn 2: 8 and the true light is already shining. 18
Rev 1:16 face was like the sun shining in full strength 18
8:12 a third of the day was kept from shining 18
18:23 and the light of a lamp shall shine in thee no more; 18
21:23 the city has no need of sun or moon to shine upon it 18
2Es 2:35 because the eternal light will shine upon you 20
6: 2 and before the flashes of lightning shone 22
7:42 night, or dawn or shining or brightness or light 21
97 how their face is to shine like the sun 19
125 the faces . . shall shine more than the stars 19
10:25 behold, her face suddenly shone exceedingly 19
Wis 5: 6 the light of righteousness did not shine on us 13
Sir 26:17 Like the shining lamp on the holy lampstand 12
50: 7 like the sun shining upon the temple 12
Bar 3:34 the stars shone in their watches, and were glad; 15
34 They shone with gladness for him who made them. 15
4: 2 take her; walk toward the shining of her light. 16
LJr 1:24 will not shine unless some one wipes off the rust; 17
60 . . stars, shining and sent forth for service 14
67 shine like the sun or give light like the moon. 15
1Mc 6:39 When the sun shone upon the shields of gold 17

shine about 1. περιαστράπτω
Act 22: 6 a great light from heaven suddenly shone about me 1

shine around 1. περιλάμπω
Lke 2: 9 the glory of the Lord shone around them 1

shine back 1. ἀντιλάμπω
2Mc 1:32 when the light from the altar shone back 1

cause to shine 1. אור 2. יפע
Job 37:15 causes the lightning of his cloud to shine? 2
Dan 9:17 cause thy face to shine upon thy sanctuary 1

shine forth 1. זרח 2. יפע 3. ἀναλάμπω 4. ἐκλάμπω 5. relucesco
Deu 33: 2 he shone forth from Mount Paran 2
2Sm 23: 4 the sun shining forth upon a cloudless morning 1
Ps 50: 2 the perfection of beauty, God shines forth. 2
80: 1 who art enthroned upon the cherubim, shine forth 2
94: 1 thou God of vengeance, shine forth! 2
2Es 5: 4 and the sun shall suddenly shine forth at night 5
Wis 3: 7 they will shine forth 3
Sir 43: 8 shining forth in the firmament of heaven. 4

make shine 1. אור 2. צהל 3. ἐκφαίνω
Num 6:25 The LORD make his face to shine upon you 1
Ps 67: 1 and bless us and make his face to shine upon us 1
104:15 oil to make his face shine 2
119:135 Make thy face shine upon thy servant, and teach me 1
Ecc 8: 1 A man's wisdom makes his face shine 1
Sir 24:32 I will make it shine afar; 3

make shine forth 1. ἐκφαίνω 2. φωτίζω
Sir 24:27 It makes instruction shine forth like light 1
32 again make instruction shine forth like the dawn 2

shine out 1. ἀναλάμπω
2Mc 1:22 the sun, which had been clouded over, shone out 1

shine round 1. περιλάμπω
Act 26:13 a light from heaven . . shining round me 1

shine through 1. διαφαίνω
Wis 17: 6 Nothing was shining through to them except . . 1

ship 1. אֳנִיָּה 2. סְפִינָה 3. צִי 4. ναῦς 5. πλοῖον 6. navis
Gen 49:13 he shall become a haven for ships 1
Num 24:24 ships shall come from Kittim and shall afflict 3
Deu 28:68 LORD will bring you back in ships to Egypt 1
Jdg 5:17 and Dan, why did he abide with the ships? Asher sat 1
1Kg 22:48 Jehosh'aphat made ships of Tarshish 1
48 the ships were wrecked at E'zion-ge'ber. 1
49 Let my servants go with your servants in the ships 1
2Ch 8:18 Huram sent him . . ships and servants familiar 1
9:21 king's ships went to Tarshish with the servants 1
21 ships of Tarshish used to come bringing gold 1
20:36 He joined him in building ships to go to Tarshish 1
36 they built the ships in E'zion-ge'ber. 1
37 the ships were wrecked and were not able to go 1
Ps 48: 7 thou didst shatter the ships of Tarshish. 1
104:26 There go the ships, and Leviathan which thou 1
107:23 Some went down to the sea in ships, doing business 1
Prv 30:19 way of a ship on the high seas, and the way of a man 1
31:14 She is like the ships of the merchant 1
Isa 2:16 against all the ships of Tarshish 1
23: 1 Wail, O ships of Tarshish, for Tyre is laid waste 1
14 Wail, O ships of Tarshish 1
33:21 with oars can go, nor stately ship can pass. 3
60: 9 the ships of Tarshish first, 1
Ezk 27: 9 ships of the sea with their mariners were in you 1
25 The ships of Tarshish traveled for you 1
29 from their ships come all that handle the oar. 1
Dan 11:30 For ships of Kittim shall come against him 3
40 with chariots and horsemen, and with many ships; 1
Jon 1: 3 to Joppa and found a ship going to Tarshish; 1
4 the ship threatened to break up. 1
5 they threw the wares that were in the ship 1
5 had gone down into the inner part of the ship 2
13 the men rowed hard to bring the ship back to land •
Act 20:13 But going ahead to the ship, we set sail for Assos 5
38 they brought him to the ship. 5
21: 2 having found a ship crossing to Phoeni'cia 5
3 there the ship was to unload its cargo. 5
6 we went on board the ship, and they returned home. 5
27: 2 embarking in a ship of Adramyt'tium 5
6 There the centurion found a ship of Alexandria 5
10 not only of . . the ship, but also of our lives. 5
15 the ship was caught and could not face the wind 5
17 they took measures to undergird the ship 5
19 they cast out . . the tackle of the ship. 5
22 no loss of life among you, but only of the ship. 5
30 the sailors were seeking to escape from the ship 5
31 Unless these men stay in the ship 5
37 We were in all 276 persons in the ship. 5
38 they lightened the ship 5
39 planned if possible to bring the ship ashore. 5
44 the rest on planks or on pieces of the ship 5
28:11 in a ship which had wintered in the island 5
11 a ship of Alexandria •
Jas 3: 4 Look at the ships also; though they are so great 5
Rev 8: 9 and a third of the ships were destroyed. 5
18:19 all who had ships at sea grew rich by her wealth! 5
2Es 9:34 the sea a ship, or any dish food or drink 6
12:42 and like a haven for a ship saved from a storm. 6
Wis 5:10 like a ship that sails through the billowy water 4
14: 1 the ship which carries him. 5
1Mc 8:26 not give or supply grain, arms, money, or ships 5
28 shall be given no grain, arms, money, or ships 5
11: 1 gathered great forces . . and many ships 5
13:29 beside the suits of armor carved ships 5
15:14 the ships joined battle from the sea 5
37 Trypho embarked on a ship and escaped 5
4Mc 7: 1 steered the ship of religion over the sea 4

ship *See also* owner.

shipmaster 1. κυβερνήτης
Rev 18:17 And all shipmasters and seafaring men, sailors 1

ships *See* fleet.

shipwreck 1. ναυαγέω
2Co 11:25 Three times I have been shipwrecked 1

shipwreck *See also* make.

shirt 1. χιτών
Lke 6:29 do not withhold even your shirt. 1

shiver 1. τρέμω
1Es 9: 6 shivering because of the bad weather 1

shoal 1. πλῆθος 2. τόπος διθάλασσος
Lke 5: 6 they enclosed a great shoal of fish 1
Act 27:41 striking a shoal they ran the vessel aground 2

shock 1. מְחִי 2. שער 3. ἐξίστημι
Jer 2:12 be shocked, be utterly desolate, says the LORD 2
Ezk 26: 9 He will direct the shock of his battering rams 1
1Mc 16:22 When he heard this, he was greatly shocked 3

shock (2) 1. גָּדִישׁ
Jdg 15: 5 and burned up the shocks and the standing grain 1

shock of grain 1. גָּדִישׁ
Job 5:26 as a shock of grain comes up to the threshing 1

shoe 1. נעל 2. נַעַל 3. ὑποδέω 4. ὑπόδημα
Exd 3: 5 Do not come near; put off your shoes from your feet 2
Jos 5:15 Put off your shoes from your feet; 2
9:13 and these garments and shoes of ours are worn out 2
Ps 60: 8 Moab is my washbasin; upon Edom I cast my shoe; 2
108: 9 Moab is my washbasin; upon Edom I cast my shoe; 2
Isa 20: 2 Go . . and take off your shoes from your feet 2
Ezk 16:10 and shod you with leather, I swathed you 1
24:17 Bind on your turban, and put . . shoes on your feet; 2
23 shall be on your heads and your shoes on your feet; 2
Lke 15:22 put a ring on his hand, and shoes on his feet; 4
Act 7:33 Take off the shoes from your feet 4
Eph 6:15 having shod your feet 3

shoes *See* pair.

shoot 1. ידה 2. ירא 3. ירה 4. נכה 5. רבב 6. שלח 7. βάλλω 8. ἐκτινάσσω 9. immitto 10. mitto
Gen 49:23 The archers . . attacked him, shot at him 5
Exd 19:13 he shall be stoned or shot; 3
1Sm 20:20 And I will shoot three arrows to the side of it 3
20 three arrows . . as though I shot at a mark. 6
36 he said . . "Run and find the arrows which I shoot. 3
36 As the lad ran, he shot an arrow beyond him. 3
37 the place of the arrow which Jonathan had shot 3
2Sm 11:20 Did you not know . . they would shoot from the wall? 3
24 the archers shot at your servants from the wall; 3
2Kg 9:24 Jehu . . and shot Joram between the shoulders 4
27 And Jehu pursued him, and said, "Shoot him also"; •
27 they shot him in the chariot at the ascent of Gur 4
13:17 he opened it. Then Eli'sha said, "Shoot"; and he shot. 3
17 he opened it. Then Eli'sha said, "Shoot"; and he shot. 3
19:32 not come into this city or shoot an arrow there 3
1Ch 12: 2 bowmen, and could shoot arrows and sling stones •
2Ch 26:15 engines . . to shoot arrows and great stones. 2
35:23 the archers shot King Josi'ah; 3
Ps 11: 2 to shoot in the dark at the upright in heart; 3
64: 4 shooting from ambush at the blameless 3
4 shooting at him suddenly and without fear. 3
7 God will shoot his arrow at them; 3
Isa 37:33 come into this city, or shoot an arrow there 3
Jer 50:14 shoot at her, spare no arrows 1
2Es 16: 7 Can one turn back an arrow shot by a strong archer? 9
13 and his arrows that he shoots are sharp 10
13 they begin to be shot to the ends of the world. 10
16 Just as an arrow shot by a mighty archer 10
Wis 5:12 when an arrow is shot at a target 7
1Mc 6:51 machines to shoot arrows, and catapults. 7
10:80 shot arrows at his men 8

shoot (2) 1. זַלְזַל 2. חֹטֶר 3. יוֹנֶקֶת 4. נֵצֶר 5. צֶמַח 6. שְׁלוּחָה 7. שֶׁלַח 8. שָׁתִיל
Job 8:16 his shoots spread over his garden. 3
14: 7 sprout again, and that its shoots will not cease. 3
15:30 the flame will dry up his shoots 3
Ps 80:11 branches to the sea, and its shoots to the River. 3
128: 3 your children will be like olive shoots 8
Sng 4:13 Your shoots are an orchard of pomegranates 7
Isa 11: 1 shall come forth a shoot from the stump of Jesse 2
16: 8 its shoots spread abroad and passed over the sea. 6
18: 5 he will cut off the shoots with pruning hooks 1
60:21 the shoot of my planting, the work of my hands 4
61:11 For as the earth brings forth its shoots 5
Ezk 31: 5 long, from abundant water in its shoots. 7
Hos 14: 6 his shoots shall spread out; 3
Rom 11:17 and you, a wild olive shoot, were grafted •

shoot *See* put.

shoot forth 1. נתן 2. עלה 3. שלח 4. emitto
Gen 40:10 as soon as it budded, its blossoms shot forth 2
Ezk 17: 7 and shot forth its branches toward him 3
36: 8 shall shoot forth your branches 1
2Es 13:10 from his tongue he shot forth a storm of sparks. 4

green shoot 1. βλαστός 2. χλόη
Sir 40:22 the green shoots of grain more than both. 2
50: 8 like a green shoot on Lebanon on a summer day; 1

shoot up 1. עלה
Ams 7: 1 beginning of the shooting up of the latter growth 1

shore 1. אֶרֶץ 2. חוֹף 3. שָׂפָה 4. χεῖλος
Gen 49:13 Zeb'ulun shall dwell at the shore of the sea; 2
1Kg 9:26 which is near Eloth on the shore of the Red Sea 3
2Ch 8:17 E'zion-ge'ber and Eloth on the shore of the sea 3
Ezk 27:29 all the pilots of the sea stand on the shore 1
Aza 1:13 as many . . as the sand on the shore of the sea. 4

shore *See also* moor.

shorn 1. קָצַר 2. κείρω
2Kg 19:26 inhabitants, shorn of strength, are dismayed 1
Isa 37:27 while their inhabitants, shorn of strength 1
1Co 11: 6 is disgraceful for a woman to be shorn or shaven 2

shorn ewe 1. קצב
Sng 4: 2 Your teeth are like a flock of shorn ewes 1

short 1. מִקָּרֹב 2. קלט 3. קצר 4. βραχύς 5. μικρός 6. ὀλίγος 7. ὥρα 8. levis 9. modicus
Lev 22:23 which has a part too long or too short 2
Job 20: 5 that the exulting of the wicked is short 1
Prv 10:27 but the years of the wicked will be short. 3
Isa 28:20 For the bed is too short to stretch oneself on it 3
Act 26:28 In a short time you think to make me a Christian! 6
1Th 2:17 for a short time 7

Heb 12:10 they disciplined us for a short time 6
Rev 12:12 because he knows that his time is short! 6
2Es 8: 5 for you have been given only a short time to live. 9
12:20 whose times shall be short and their years swift; 8
Wis 2: 1 Short and sorrowful is our life 6
4:13 Being perfected in a short time 6
15: 8 this man who was made of earth a short time before 5
16: 3 after suffering want a short time 6
4Mc 9: 5 a short time ago 4
15:27 preserve the seven sons for a short time 6

short *See also* come, cut, distance, fall, grow.

short-lived 1. ὀλιγοχρόνιος

Wis 9: 5 a man who is weak and short-lived 1

shorten 1. צרר 2. קצר 3. ἐλαττόω 4. κολοβόω 5. minoro

Num11:23 LORD said to Moses, "Is the LORD'S hand shortened? 2
Job 18: 7 His strong steps are shortened 1
Ps 102:23 he has shortened my days. 2
Isa 50: 2 Is my hand shortened, that it cannot redeem? 2
59: 1 Behold, the LORD'S hand is not shortened 2
Mat 24:22 if those days had not been shortened 4
22 those days will be shortened. 4
Mrk 13:20 if the Lord had not shortened the days 4
20 he shortened the days. 4
2Es 2:13 that they may be shortened 5
Sir 30:24 Jealousy and anger shorten life 3

shortly 1. מהר 2. מְהֵרָה 3. αὐτίκα 4. ἐν τάχει 5. ὀλίγος 6. ταχέως

Gen 41:32 and God will shortly bring it to pass. 1
Jer 27:16 will now shortly be brought back from Babylon, 2
Act 25: 4 he himself intended to go there shortly. 4
Php 2:24 shortly I myself shall come also. 6
Wis 14:20 the one whom shortly before they had honored 5
4Mc 1:12 shortly have an opportunity to speak of this 3

shortsighted 1. μυωπάζω

2Pe 1: 9 whoever lacks these things is . . shortsighted 1

shoulder 1. זְרוֹעַ 2. כָּתֵף 3. שְׁכֶם 4. βραχίων 5. ὦμος

Gen 9:23 garment, laid it upon both their shoulders 3
21:14 gave it to Hagar, putting it on her shoulder 3
24:15 came out with her water jar upon her shoulder. 3
45 came out with her water jar on her shoulder; 3
46 She quickly let down her jar from her shoulder *
49:15 he bowed his shoulder to bear 3
Exd 12:34 bound up in their mantles on their shoulders. 3
28:12 upon his two shoulders for remembrance. 2
Num 6:19 the priest shall take the shoulder of the ram 1
7: 9 things which had to be carried on the shoulder. 2
34:11 reach to the shoulder of the sea of Chin'nereth 2
Deu 18: 3 give to the priest the shoulder 1
33:12 makes his dwelling between his shoulders. 2
Jos 4: 5 and take up each of you a stone upon his shoulder 3
15: 8 goes . . at the southern shoulder of the Jeb'usite 2
10 along to the northern shoulder of Mount Je'arim 2
11 the boundary goes out to the shoulder of the hill 2
18:12 boundary goes up the shoulder north of Jericho 2
13 passes along southward . . to the shoulder of Luz 2
16 valley . . south of the shoulder of the Jeb'usites 2
18 to the north of the shoulder of Beth-arabah 2
19 passes . . north of the shoulder of Beth-hoglah; 2
Jdg 9:48 and took it up and laid it on his shoulder. 3
16: 3 and put them on his shoulders and carried them 2
1Sm 9: 2 from his shoulders upward he was taller than any 3
10:23 he was taller . . from his shoulders upward. 3
17: 6 a javelin of bronze . . between his shoulders. 2
2Kg 6:31 if the head of Eli'sha . . remains on his shoulders *
9:24 Jehu . . and shot Joram between the shoulders 1
1Ch 15:15 ark of God upon their shoulders with the poles 2
2Ch 35: 3 you need no longer carry it upon your shoulders. 2
Neh 9:29 turned a stubborn shoulder and stiffened 2
Job 31:22 then let my . . blade fall from my shoulder 3
36 Surely I would carry it on my shoulder; 3
Ps 81: 6 I relieved your shoulder of the burden; 3
Isa 9: 4 yoke of his burden, and the staff for his shoulder 3
6 the government will be upon his shoulder 3
10:27 his burden will depart from your shoulder 3
11:14 swoop down upon the shoulder of the Philistines 2
14:25 depart . . and his burden from their shoulder. 3
22:22 I will place on his shoulder the key of the house 3
46: 7 They lift it upon their shoulders, they carry it 2
49:22 daughters shall be carried on their shoulders. 2
Ezk 12: 6 you shall lift the baggage upon your shoulder 2
7 in the dark, carrying my outfit upon my shoulder 2
12 lift his baggage upon his shoulder in the dark 2
24: 4 all the good pieces, the thigh and the shoulder; 2
29: 7 you broke, and tore all their shoulders; 2
18 was made bald and every shoulder was rubbed bare; 2
34:21 Because you push with side and shoulder 2
Zec 7:11 to hearken, and turned a stubborn shoulder 2
Mat 23: 4 and lay them on men's shoulders 5
Lke 15: 5 when he has found it, he lays it on his shoulders 5
1Es 1: 4 You need no longer carry it upon your shoulders 5
Sir 6:25 Put your shoulder under her and carry her 5
7:31 the gift of the shoulders 4
Bar 2:21 Bend your shoulders and serve the king 5
LJr 1: 4 which are carried on men's shoulders 5
26 they are carried on men's shoulders 5

shoulder blade 1. כָּתֵף

Job 31:22 then let my shoulder blade fall from my shoulder 1

shoulder-piece 1. כָּתֵף

Exd 28: 7 It shall have two shoulder-pieces attached 1
12 set the two stones upon the shoulder-pieces 1
25 and so attach it in front to the shoulder-pieces 1
27 part of the two shoulder-pieces of the ephod 1
39: 4 They made for the ephod shoulder-pieces 1
7 he set them on the shoulder-pieces of the ephod 1
18 they attached it in front to the shoulder-pieces 1
20 to the lower part of the two shoulder-pieces 1

shout 1. אמר 2. הֵידָד 3. זְעָקָה 4. נתן קול 5. ענה 6. צהל 7. צוח 8. קול 9. קרא 10. רוע 11. רִנָּה 12. רנן 13. רֵעַ 14. שׁוַֹע 15. תְּרוּעָה 16. תְּשֻׁאָה 17. ἀλαλαγμός 18. ἀναβοάω 19. ἀνακράζω 20. βοάω 21. βοή 22. βοὴ ἰσχυρός 23. βοὴ μέγας σφόδρα 24. ἐπιφωνέω 25. κράζω 26. κραυγή 27. φωνέω 28. φωνή

Exd 32:17 heard the noise of the people as they shouted 13
18 It is not the sound of shouting for victory 5
Lev 9:24 they shouted, and fell on their faces 12
Num23:21 the shout of a king is among them. 15
Jos 6: 5 all the people shall shout with a great shout; 10
5 all the people shall shout with a great shout; 15
10 You shall not shout or let your voice be heard 10
10 shall not shout . . until the day I bid you shout; 10
10 until the day I bid you . . then you shall shout. 10
16 Shout; for the LORD has given you the city. 10
20 the people shouted, and the trumpets were blown. 10
20 As soon as the . . the people raised a great shout 15
Jdg 7:18 the camp, and shout, 'For the LORD and for Gideon.' 1
15:14 the Philistines came shouting to meet him; 10
18:23 they shouted to the Danites, who turned round 9
1Sm 4: 5 Israel gave a mighty shout, so that the earth 15
6 the Philistines heard the noise of the shouting 15
6 What does this great shouting . . mean? 15
10:24 And all the people shouted, "Long live the king! 10
17: 8 He stood and shouted to the ranks of Israel 9
20 the host was going forth . . shouting the war cry. 10
52 And the men of Israel and Judah rose with a shout 10
2Sm 6:15 brought up the ark of the LORD with shouting 15
1Ch 15:28 brought up the ark . . of the LORD with shouting 15
2Ch 13:15 when the men of Judah shouted, God defeated 10
15:14 took oath to the LORD . . with shouting 15
32:18 they shouted it with a loud voice in the language 9
Ezr 3:11 all the people shouted with a great shout 10
11 all the people shouted with a great shout 15
13 not distinguish the sound of the joyful shout 15
13 for the people shouted with a great shout 10
13 for the people shouted with a great shout 15
Est 8:15 while the city of Susa shouted and rejoiced. 6
Job 8:21 with laughter, and your lips with shouting. 15
30: 5 they shout after them as after a thief. 10
39: 7 he hears not the shouts of the driver. 16
25 the thunder of the captains, and the shouting. 15
Ps 47: 1 all peoples! Shout to God with loud songs of joy! 10
5 God has gone up with a shout 15
78:65 like a strong man shouting because of wine. 12
Ecc 9:17 better than the shouting of a ruler among fools. 3
Isa 12: 6 Shout, and sing for joy, O inhabitant of Zion 6
16: 9 upon your fruit . . the battle shout has fallen. 2
22: 2 you who are full of shoutings, tumultuous city 16
5 a day of . . a shouting to the mountains. 14
24:14 the majesty of the LORD they shout from the west. 6
31: 4 is not terrified by their shouting or daunted 8
42:11 let them shout from the top of the mountains. 7
43:14 the shouting of the Chalde'ans will be turned 11
44:23 shout, O depths of the earth; 10
48:20 declare this with a shout of joy, proclaim it 8
Jer 4:16 they shout against the cities of Judah. 4
20: 8 For whenever I speak, I cry out, I shout 9
25:30 and shout, like those who tread grapes 2
48:33 the shouting is not the shout of joy. 2
Ezk 21:22 with a cry, to lift up the voice with shouting 15
Ams 1:14 strongholds, with shouting in the day of battle 15
2: 2 amid shouting and the sound of the trumpet; 15
Zep 3:14 Sing aloud, O daughter of Zion; shout, O Israel! 10
Zec 4: 7 the top stone amid shouts of 'Grace, grace to it! 16
Mat 21: 9 shouted, "Hosanna to the Son of David! 25
27:23 they shouted all the more 25
Mrk 15:14 they shouted all the more, "Crucify him. 25
Act 12:22 people shouted, "The voice of a god, and not of man! 24
21:34 Some in the crowd shouted one thing, some another; 24
25:24 shouting that he ought not to live any longer. 20
Gal 4:27 break forth and shout, you who are not in travail; 20
1Es 4:41 then all the people shouted, and said 27
5:62 sounded trumpets and shouted with a great shout 20
62 sounded trumpets and shouted with a great shout 28
9:10 Then all the multitude shouted 27
Jdt 14: 9 the people raised a great shout 28
16 wept and groaned and shouted 22
17 he rushed out to the people and shouted 20
19 their loud cries and shouts arose 23
16:11 my weak people shouted and the enemy trembled; ‡
Sir 50:16 the sons of Aaron shouted 19
LJr 1:32 They howl and shout before their gods as some do 20
Sus 1:24 and the two elders shouted against her. 20
26 When the household servants heard the shouting 26
60 all the assembly shouted loudly and blessed God 18
Bel 1:18 looked at the table, and shouted in a loud voice 20
37 Then Habakkuk shouted, "Daniel, Daniel! 20
41 the king shouted with a loud voice 18
1Mc 3:54 they sounded the trumpets and gave a loud shout. 28
5:31 with trumpets and loud shouts 26
2Mc 4:22 with a blaze of torches and with shouts 21
15:29 Then there was shouting and tumult 26
3Mc 1:23 They shouted to their fellows to take arms 27
4: 1 was arranged . . with shouts and gladness 17
6:23 when he heard the shouting 26
7:13 shouted the Hallelujah and joyfully departed. 24
4Mc 10: 2 he shouted, "Do you not know 18

shout *See also* give, raise.

shout against 1. ἐπιφωνέω

Act 22:24 to find out why they shouted thus against him. 1

shout aloud 1. צרח 2. רום קול 3. רוע

Ezr 3:12 wept . . though many shouted aloud for joy; 2
Isa 42:13 he cries out, he shouts aloud 1
Zec 9: 9 Shout aloud, O daughter of Jerusalem! 3

festal shout 1. תְּרוּעָה

Ps 89:15 Blessed are the people who know the festal shout 1

shout for joy 1. רוע 2. רנן 3. ἀλαλάζω

Job 38: 7 all the sons of God shouted for joy? 1
Ps 20: 5 May we shout for joy over your victory 2
32:11 shout for joy, all you upright in heart! 2
35:27 those who desire my vindication shout for joy 2
65:13 they shout and sing together for joy. 1
71:23 My lips will shout for joy, when I sing praises 2
81: 1 shout for joy to the God of Jacob! 1
132: 9 let thy saints shout for joy. 2
16 her saints will shout for joy. 2
Jdt 16:11 my oppressed people shouted for joy 3

glad shout 1. רִנָּה

Ps 42: 4 with glad shouts and songs of thanksgiving 1

shout in triumph 1. רוע

Ps 60: 8 over Philistia I shout in triumph. 1
108: 9 over Philistia I shout in triumph. 1

loud shout 1. תְּרוּעָה

Ps 33: 3 skillfully on the strings, with loud shouts. 1

make shout for joy 1. רנן

Ps 65: 8 makest . . the morning and the evening to shout for joy. 1

shout of gladness 1. רִנָּה

Prv 11:10 wicked perish there are shouts of gladness. 1

shout of joy 1. הֵידָד 2. רִנָּה 3. תְּרוּעָה

Ps 27: 6 offer in his tent sacrifices with shouts of joy; 3
126: 2 our tongue with shouts of joy; 2
5 May those who sow in tears reap with shouts of joy! 2
6 come home with shouts of joy 2
Jer 48:33 no one treads them with shouts of joy; 1
33 the shouting is not the shout of joy. 1

shout of victory 1. הֵידָד

Jer 51:14 they shall raise the shout of victory over you. 1

shout out 1. ἐπιφωνέω

Lke 23:21 they shouted out, "Crucify, crucify him! 1

vintage shout 1. הֵידָד

Isa 16:10 no treader . . the vintage shout is hushed. 1

joyful shouting 1. הֵד

Ezk 7: 7 and not of joyful shouting upon the mountains. 1

shovel 1. יָע 2. רַחַת

Exd 27: 3 make . . shovels and basins and forks 1
38: 3 the pots, the shovels, the basins, the forks 1
Num 4:14 utensils . . the firepans, the forks, the shovels 1
1Kg 7:40 Hiram also made . . the shovels, and the basins. 1
45 the pots, the shovels, and the basins, all these 1
2Kg 25:14 they took away the pots, and the shovels 1
2Ch 4:11 Huram also made the pots, the shovels 1
16 pots, the shovels, the forks, and all the equipment 1
Isa 30:24 which has been winnowed with shovel and fork. 2
Jer 52:18 they took away the pots, and the shovels 1

show 1. גלה 2. היה 3. חוה 4. ידע 5. ירה 6. נגד 7. נטה 8. נתן 9. עשה 10. עשה עִמָּד 11. ראה 12. שום 13. שית 14. שמע 15. שמר 16. חוה (A) 17. ἀναγγέλλω 18. ἀναδείκνυμι 19. ἀπομερίζω 20. γίνομαι 21. γινώσκω 22. δείκνυμι

23. δείκνυμι ἔκδηλος 24. δηλόω 25. δίδωμι 26. εἰμί
27. ἐμφανὴς γίνομαι 28. ἐμφανίζω 29. ἐνδείκνυμι
30. ἔνδειξις 31. ἐπιδείκνυμι 32. ἔχω 33. λαμβάνω
34. μηνύω 35. παρέχω 36. ποιέω 37. πρόδηλος
38. πρόδηλος γίνομαι 39. πρόσωπον λαμβάνω
40. σημαίνω 41. συμβαίνω 42. συνίστημι
43. συντηρέω 44. τολμάω 45. ὑπέρ 46. ὑποδείκνυμι
47. ὑπόκειμαι 48. φαίνω 49. φανερόω 50. demonstro
51. facio 52. ostendo 53. significo

Gen 12: 1 house to the land that I will show you. 11
24:12 I pray thee, and show steadfast love to my master 9
14 thou hast shown steadfast love to my master. 9
32:10 faithfulness which thou hast shown 9
39:21 was with Joseph and showed him steadfast love 7
41:28 God has shown to Pharaoh what he is about to do. 11
39 Joseph, "Since God has shown you all this 4
Exd 9:16 for this purpose have I let you live, to show you 11
10: 1 that I may show these signs of mine among them 13
15:25 cried to the LORD; and the LORD showed him a tree 5
20: 6 showing steadfast love to thousands of those 9
22: 8 to show whether or not he has put his hand to his •
25: 9 According to all that I show you concerning 11
40 which is being shown you on the mountain. 11
26:30 which has been shown you on the mountain. 11
27: 8 as it has been shown you on the mountain, so shall 11
33:13 show me now thy ways, that I may know thee 4
18 Moses said, "I pray thee, show me thy glory. 11
Lev 13: 7 after he has shown himself to the priest 11
19 then it shall be shown to the priest 11
49 if the disease shows greenish or reddish 2
49 leprous disease and shall be shown to the priest 11
14:57 to show when it is unclean and when it is clean 5
Num 8: 4 pattern which the LORD had shown Moses 11
13:26 showed them the fruit of the land. 11
16: 5 In the morning the LORD will show who is his 4
23: 3 whatever he shows me I will tell you. 11
Deu 1:33 went . . to show you by what way you should go 11
3:24 only begun to show thy servant thy greatness 11
4:35 To you it was shown, that you might know 11
5:10 showing steadfast love to thousands 9
24 LORD our God has shown us his glory and greatness 11
6:22 LORD showed signs and wonders 8
13:17 show you mercy, and have compassion on you 8
32: 7 ask your father, and he will show you; your elders 6
34: 1 LORD showed him all the land. Gilead as far as Dan 11
Jdg 1:24 Pray, show us the way into the city, and we will deal 11
25 he showed them the way into the city; 11
4:22 and I will show you the man whom you are seeking. 11
6:17 If now I have found favor . . then show me a sign 9
8:35 they did not show kindness to the family 9
13:23 or shown us all these things, or now announced 11
Rut 2:18 she showed her mother-in-law what she had gleaned 11
1Sm 8: 9 and show them the ways of the king who shall reign 6
10: 8 until I come to you and show you what you shall do. 4
14: 8 and we will show ourselves to them. 1
11 both of them showed themselves to the garrison 1
12 Come up to us, and we will show you a thing. 4
15: 6 you showed kindness to all the people of Israel 9
16: 3 and I will show you what you shall do; 4
19: 7 and Jonathan showed him all these things. 6
20:14 show me the loyal love of the LORD 10
2Sm 2: 5 you showed this loyalty to Saul . . and buried him! 9
6 the LORD show steadfast love and faithfulness 9
3: 8 I keep showing loyalty to the house of Saul 9
7:19 and hast shown me future generations, O Lord GOD! •
9: 1 that I may show him kindness for Jonathan's sake? 9
3 that I may show the kindness of God to him? 9
7 Do not fear; for I will show you kindness 9
15:20 the LORD show steadfast love and faithfulness 36
22:51 he . . shows steadfast love to his anointed 9
1Kg 2: 2 Be strong, and show yourself a man 2
3: 6 Thou hast shown great and steadfast love to thy 9
8:23 keeping covenant and showing steadfast love 15
66 the goodness that the LORD had shown to David 9
13:12 his sons showed him the way which the man of God 11
16:27 acts of Omri . . and the might that he showed 9
18: 1 Go, show yourself to Ahab; and I will send rain 11
2 So Eli'jah went to show himself to Ahab. 11
15 I will surely show myself to him today. 11
22:45 acts of Jehosh'aphat, and his might that he showed 9
2Kg 6: 6 When he showed him the place, he cut off a stick 11
11 Will you not show me who of us is for . . Israel? 6
8:10 LORD has shown me that he shall certainly die. 11
13 The LORD has shown me that you are to be king 11
11: 4 and he showed them the king's son. 11
20:13 and he showed them all his treasure house 11
13 there was nothing . . Hezeki'ah did not show them. 11
15 there is nothing . . that I did not show them. 11
1Ch 17:17 and hast shown me future generations, O LORD God! •
2Ch 1: 8 Thou hast shown great and steadfast love 9
6:14 keeping covenant and showing steadfast love •
17:10 goodness that the LORD had shown to David 9
24:22 kindness which Jehoi'ada . . had shown him 9
Ezr 9: 8 favor has been shown by the LORD our God 2
Est 1: 4 while he showed the riches of his royal glory 11
11 to show the peoples and the princes her beauty; 11
4: 8 that he might show it to Esther and explain it 11

Job 15:17 I will show you, hear me; 3
24:25 and show that there is nothing in what I say? 12
36: 2 Bear with me a little, and I will show you 3
Ps 16:11 Thou dost show me the path of life; 4
18:50 and shows steadfast love to his anointed 9
48: 3 God has shown himself a sure defense. 4
50:23 I will show the salvation of God! 11
59:17 my fortress, the God who shows me steadfast love. •
78:11 the miracles that he had shown them. 11
85: 7 Show us thy steadfast love, O LORD 11
86:17 Show me a sign of thy favor, that those who hate me 9
91:16 satisfy him, and show him my salvation. 11
92:15 to show that the LORD is upright; 6
106: 4 me, O LORD, when thou showest favor to thy people; •
109:16 For he did not remember to show kindness 9
111: 6 He has shown his people the power of his works 6
Prv 3:34 but to the humble he shows favor. 8
22:21 to show you what is right and true 4
Ecc 3:18 I said . . that God is testing them to show them 11
Isa 39: 2 he showed them his treasure house 11
2 nothing . . that Hezeki'ah did not show them. 11
4 in my storehouses that I did not show them. 11
40:14 and showed him the way of understanding? 4
43: 9 can declare this, and show us the former things? 14
47: 6 gave them into your hand, you showed them no mercy 12
Jer 11:18 then thou didst show me their evil deeds. 11
16:13 for I will show you no favor. 8
18:17 I will show them my back, not my face 11
24: 1 the LORD showed me this vision 11
32:18 who showest steadfast love to thousands 9
20 hast shown signs and wonders in the land of Egypt 12
38:21 this is the vision which the LORD has shown to me 11
42: 3 that the LORD your God may show us the way 6
Lam 5:12 no respect is shown to the elders. •
Ezk 9: 5 shall not spare, and you shall show no pity; •
11:25 all the things that the LORD had showed me. 11
20:11 my statutes and showed them my ordinances 4
35:11 according to the anger and envy which you showed 9
37:18 Will you not show us what you mean by these? 6
40: 4 and set your mind upon all that I shall show you 11
4 brought here in order that I might show it to you; 11
Dan 2: 4 dream, and we will show the interpretation. 16
6 if you show the dream and its interpretation 16
6 show me the dream and its interpretation. 16
7 dream, and we will show its interpretation. 16
9 know that you can show me its interpretation. 16
11 none can show it to the king except the gods 16
16 might show to the king the interpretation. 16
24 I will show the king the interpretation. 16
27 can show to the king the mystery 16
4: 2 seemed good to me to show the signs and wonders 16
5: 7 this writing, and shows me its interpretation 16
12 and he will show the interpretation. 16
15 could not show the interpretation of the matter. 16
11: 2 now I will show you the truth. 6
Ams 7: 1 Thus the Lord GOD showed me 11
4 Thus the Lord GOD showed me 11
7 He showed me: behold, the Lord was standing beside 11
8: 1 GOD showed me: behold, a basket of summer fruit. 11
Mic 6: 8 He has showed you, O man, what is good; 6
7:15 I will show them marvelous things. 11
20 Thou wilt show faithfulness to Jacob 8
Zec 1: 9 said to me, 'I will show you what they are.' 11
20 Then the LORD showed me four smiths. 11
3: 1 Then he showed me Joshua the high priest 11
7: 9 show kindness and mercy each to his brother 9
Mat 4: 8 high mountain, and showed him all the kingdoms 22
8: 4 but go, show yourself to the priest 22
16: 1 to test him they asked him to show them a sign 31
21 From that time Jesus began to show his disciples 22
22:19 Show me the money for the tax. 31
24:24 false prophets will arise and show great signs 25
Mrk 1:44 go, show yourself to the priest 22
13:22 show signs and wonders 25
14:15 he will show you a large upper room 22
Lke 1:51 He has shown strength with his arm 36
58 the Lord had shown great mercy to her •
4: 5 showed him all the kingdoms of the world 22
5:14 tell no one; but "go and show yourself to the priest 22
6:47 I will show you what he is like 46
10:37 He said, "The one who showed mercy on him. 36
17:14 Go and show yourselves to the priests. 31
20:21 and show no partiality 33
24 Show me a coin 22
37 that the dead are raised, even Moses showed 34
22:12 he will show you a large upper room furnished; 22
Joh 2:18 What sign have you to show us for doing this? 22
4:25 when he comes, he will show us all things. 17
5:20 shows him all that he himself is doing 22
20 greater works than these will he show him 22
7: 4 If you do these things, show yourself to the world. 49
10:32 I have shown you many good works from the Father; 22
12:33 He said this to show by what death he was to die. 40
14: 8 Philip said to him, "Lord, show us the Father 22
9 how can you say, 'Show us the Father'? 22
18:32 to show by what death he was to die. 40
20:20 When he had said this, he showed them his hands 22
21:19 to show by what death he was to glorify God 40
Act 1:24 show which one of these two thou hast chosen 18

2:19 I will show wonders in the heaven above 25
7: 3 go into the land which I will show you.' 22
9:16 I will show him how much he must suffer 46
39 showing tunics and other garments 31
10:28 God has shown me that I should not call any man 22
34 Truly I perceive that God shows no partiality 26
18:28 showing by the scriptures 31
20:35 In all things I have shown you 46
28: 2 the natives showed us unusual kindness 35
Rom 1:19 plain to them, because God has shown it to them. 49
2:11 For God shows no partiality. 26
15 They show that what the law requires is written 29
3:25 This was to show God's righteousness 30
5: 8 But God shows his love for us 42
7:13 in order that sin might be shown to be sin 48
9:17 for the very purpose of showing my power in you 29
22 What if God, desiring to show his wrath 29
10:20 shown myself to those who did not ask for me. 27
11:31 by the mercy shown to you they . . receive mercy. •
12:10 outdo one another in showing honor. •
15: 8 to the circumcised to show God's truthfulness 45
1Co 12:31 I will show you a still more excellent way. 22
2Co 3: 3 you show that you are a letter from Christ 49
4: 7 to show that the transcendent power belongs to God •
8: 1 shown in the churches of Macedo'nia 25
19 for the glory of the Lord and to show our good will. •
10: 2 as I count on showing against some who suspect us 44
11:30 I will boast of the things that show my weakness. •
Gal 2: 6 God shows no partiality 39
Eph 2: 7 might show the immeasurable riches of his grace 29
Tit 2: 7 Show yourself . . a model of good deeds 35
7 in your teaching show integrity, gravity •
10 nor to pilfer, but to show entire and true fidelity 29
3: 2 to show perfect courtesy toward all men. 29
Heb 6:10 the love which you showed for his sake 29
11 to show the same earnestness 29
17 when God desired to show more convincingly 31
8: 5 the pattern which was shown you on the mountain. 22
Jas 2: 1 show no partiality as you hold the faith •
13 without mercy to one who has shown no mercy 36
18 Show me your faith apart from your works 22
18 and I by my works will show you my faith. 22
20 Do you want to be shown, you shallow man 21
3:13 let him show his works in the meekness of wisdom. 22
2Pe 1:14 will be soon, as our Lord Jesus Christ showed me. 24
Rev 1: 1 which God gave him to show to his servants 22
4: 1 I will show you what must take place after this. 22
17: 1 Come, I will show you the judgment 22
21: 9 Come, I will show you the Bride, the wife of the Lamb. 22
10 and showed me the holy city Jerusalem 22
22: 1 Then he showed me the river of the water of life 22
6 the Lord . . sent his angel to show his servants 22
8 at the feet of the angel who showed them to me; 22
1Es 8: 4 the king showed him honor 25
2Es 1:35 to whom I have shown no signs 52
2:31 and will show mercy to them 51
3:31 hast not shown to any one 53
4: 3 I have been sent to show you three ways 52
4 I also will show you the way you desire to see 50
45 show me this also: whether more time is to come 50
47 I will show you the interpretation of a parable. 50
5:37 or show me the picture of a voice 50
43 that thou mightest show thy judgment the sooner? 52
56 show thy servant through whom thou dost visit 50
6:12 show thy servant the end of thy signs 50
12 thou didst show me in part on a previous night. 50
20 then I will show these signs 51
30 he said to me, "I have come to show you these things 52
33 Therefore he sent me to show you all these things 50
7:44 and to you alone have I shown these things. 52
48 and has shown us the paths of perdition 52
75 show this also to thy servant 50
76 He answered me and said, "I will show you that also 52
77 it will not be shown to you until the last times. 50
97 The sixth order, when it is shown to them 52
102show further to me, thy servant 50
104I will show you this also 50
134patient, because he shows patience toward those 52
8:62 I have not shown this to all men 50
63 thou hast now shown me a multitude of the signs 50
63 thou hast not shown me when thou wilt do them. 50
9:29 O Lord, thou didst show thyself among us 52
10:27 and a place of huge foundations showed itself. 50
50 has shown you the brilliance of her glory 52
59 will show you in those dream visions 52
12: 8 and show me, thy servant, the interpretation 52
9 worthy to be shown the end of the times 52
39 that you may be shown whatever it pleases 52
39 whatever it pleases the Most High to show you. 52
13:14 thou hast shown thy servant these wonders 50
15 show me also the interpretation of this dream. 50
19 and much distress, as these dreams show. 52
32 and the signs occur which I showed you before 52
50 then he will show them very many wonders. 52
56 Therefore I have shown you this 52
14: 5 and showed him the secrets of the times 52
8 the signs that I have shown you 50
Tob 8:17 Show them mercy, O Lord 36
13: 6 I show his power and majesty 22

14: 7 showing mercy to our brethren. 36
Jdt 8:29 not the first time your wisdom has been shown 37
10:13 I will show him a way by which he can go 22
13:11 to show his power in Israel 36
15 Then she took the head out of the bag and showed it 22
Wis 3:14 special favor will be shown him 25
5:13 we had no sign of virtue to show 22
8:15 among the people I shall show myself capable 48
10:10 she showed him the kingdom of God 22
14 Those who accused him she showed to be false 22
11: 8 showing by their thirst at that time 22
12:17 thou dost show thy strength 29
14: 4 showing that thou canst save from every danger 22
16: 4 while to these it was merely shown 22
18:21 showing that he was thy servant. 22
Sir 3:13 show forbearance 32
23 matters . . have been shown you. 46
4:22 Do not show partiality, to your own harm 33
27 nor show partiality to a ruler. 33
14:12 the decree of Hades has not been shown to you. 46
17: 7 showed them good and evil. 46
8 to show them the majesty of his works. 22
12 showed them his judgments. 46
19:30 a man's manner of walking, show what he is. 17
26: 9 A wife's harlotry shows in her lustful eyes *
29: 1 He that shows mercy will lend to his neighbor 36
35:13 will not show partiality in the case of a poor man; 33
41:23 Then you will show proper shame 26
45: 3 showed him part of his glory. 22
49: 8 which God showed him 46
Bar 5: 3 For God will show your splendor everywhere 22
LJr 1:59 it is better to be a king who shows his courage 31
67 they cannot show signs in the heavens 22
Bel 1:21 they showed him the secret doors 22
1Mc 4:20 the smoke . . showed what had happened. 28
6:34 They showed the elephants the juice of grapes 22
7:33 came out . . to show him the burnt offering 22
11: 4 they showed him the temple of Dagon burned down 22
33 because of the good will they show toward us. *
12: 7 you are our brethren, as the appended copy shows. 47
14: 4 as was the honor shown him, all his days. *
2Mc 2: 7 until God gathers . . and shows his mercy. 20
8 as they were shown in the case of Moses 24
3:17 which plainly showed to those who looked at him 38
6:27 I will show myself worthy of my old age 48
7:37 appealing to God to show mercy soon to our nation 20
10:12 Ptolemy . . took the lead in showing justice to the Jews 43
12:24 and no consideration would be shown them. 41
30 which the people of Scythopolis had shown them 32
36 to show himself their ally and leader 48
13: 9 was coming to show the Jews things far worse 29
14: 9 the gracious kindness which you show to all. 32
15: 2 show respect for the day 19
32 He showed them the vile Nicanor's head 31
3Mc 5:13 to show the might of his all-powerful hand 22
6: 5 showing your power to many nations. 23
15 Let it be shown to all the Gentiles 22
4Mc 11:12 you give us an opportunity to show our endurance 31
17: 2 showed the courage of your faith! 22

show *See also* blameless, boldness, cheerful, compassion, deference, favor, fear, generosity, glory, great, greatness, holiness, holy, honor, hospitality, irreverence, kindness, loyal, mercy, might, mighty, partiality, perverse, pity, pure, respect, scorn, serve, skill, strength, sympathy, zeal.

show anew 1. *ἐγκαινίζω*
Sir 36: 6 Show signs anew, and work further wonders 1

show forth 1. נגד 2. נתן לְאוֹר 3. שמע
Ps 51:15 my mouth shall show forth thy praise. 1
106: 2 Who can utter . . or show forth all his praise? 3
Zep 3: 5 every morning he shows forth his justice 2

show how 1. ידע
Ezk 44:23 and show them how to distinguish between 1

make show 1. *ἐκφαίνω*
Sir 22:19 one who pricks the heart makes it show feeling. 1

wondrously show 1. פלא 2. פלה
Ps 17: 7 Wondrously show thy steadfast love, O savior 2
31:21 for he has wondrously shown his steadfast love 1

showbread 1. לֶחֶם הַמַּעֲרֶכֶת 2. מַעֲרֶכֶת 3. מַעֲרֶכֶת לֶחֶם
1Ch 9:32 had charge of the showbread, to prepare it 1
23:29 to assist also with the showbread 1
28:16 weight of gold for each table for the showbread 2
2Ch 2: 4 and for the continual offering of the showbread *
13:11 set out the showbread on the table of pure gold 3
29:18 the table for the showbread and all its utensils. 2
Neh 10:33 showbread, the continual cereal offering 1

shower 1. גֶּשֶׁם 2. רְבִיבִים 3. רעף 4. *ἐκρίπτω* 5. *ὄμβρος*
Deu 32: 2 speech distil . . as the showers upon the herb. 2
Job 37: 6 to the shower and the rain, 'Be strong.' 1
Ps 65:10 settling its ridges, softening it with showers 2
72: 6 like rain . . like showers that water the earth! 2
Isa 45: 8 Shower, O heavens, from above, and let the skies 3
Jer 3: 3 Therefore the showers have been withheld 2
14:22 Or can the heavens give showers? 2
Ezk 34:26 I will send down the showers in their season; 1
26 they shall be showers of blessing. 1
Hos 6: 3 he will come to us as the showers 1
Mic 5: 7 dew from the LORD, like showers upon the grass 2
Zec 10: 1 who gives men showers of rain, to every one 1
Lke 12:54 you say at once, 'A shower is coming' 5
2Mc 10:30 showered arrows and thunderbolts 4

shower of rain 1. *ὑετός*
Wis 16:22 the fire that . . flashed in the showers of rain; 1

showing *See* make.

shrewd 1. בין 2. בְּשֶׂכֶל 3. *πανοῦργος*
1Ch 26:14 Zechari'ah, a shrewd counselor 2
Isa 5:21 their own eyes, and shrewd in their own sight! 1
Sir 37:19 A man may be shrewd and the teacher of many 3

more shrewd 1. *φρόνιμος*
Lke 16: 8 the sons of this world are more shrewd 1

shrewdly *See* deal.

shrewdness 1. *φρονίμως*
Lke 16: 8 commended . . for his shrewdness 1

shrine 1. בַּיִת 2. בֵּית אֱלֹהִים 3. בָּמָה 4. *ναός*
Jdg 17: 5 the man Micah had a shrine, and he made an ephod 2
2Kg 17:29 made gods . . and put them in the shrines 1
32 sacrificed . . in the shrines of the high places. 1
23:19 And all the shrines also . . Josi'ah removed; 1
Ezk 16:16 and made for yourself gaily decked shrines 3
Act 17:24 God . . does not live in shrines made by man 4
19:24 a silversmith, who made silver shrines of Ar'temis 4
Heb 6:19 enters into the inner shrine behind the curtain *
Jdt 3: 8 he demolished all their shrines ‡

shrine for an idol 1. *εἰδώλιον*
1Mc 1:47 to build . . sacred precincts and shrines for idols 1

shrink 1. נדד 2. *ὀκνέω* 3. *ὑπευλαβέομαι* 4. *ὑποστέλλω*
Nah 3: 7 all who look on you will shrink from you and say 1
Act 20:20 how I did not shrink from declaring to you 4
27 I did not shrink from declaring to you 4
Sir 7:35 Do not shrink from visiting a sick man 2
2Mc 14:18 Nicanor . . shrank from deciding the issue by bloodshed 3
4Mc 14: 4 proved coward or shrank from death 2

shrink back 1. *συστέλλω* 2. *ὑποστέλλω* 3. *ὑποστολή*
Heb 10:38 if he shrinks back, my soul has no pleasure in him. 2
39 those who shrink back and are destroyed 3
1Mc 3: 6 Lawless men shrank back for fear of him 1

shrink in shame 1. *αἰσχύνομαι*
1Jn 2:28 and not shrink from him in shame at his coming 1

shrivel 1. עבשׁ 2. צפר
Lam 4: 8 their skin has shriveled upon their bones 2
Jol 1:17 The seed shrivels under the clods 1

shrivel up 1. קמט
Job 16: 8 he has shriveled me up, which is a witness 1

linen shroud 1. *σινδών*
Mat 27:59 and wrapped it in a clean linen shroud 1
Mrk 15:46 he bought a linen shroud 1
46 taking him down, wrapped him in the linen shroud 1
Lke 23:53 he took it down and wrapped it in a linen shroud 1

shrub 1. עֲרוֹעֵר 2. *λάχανον*
Jer 17: 6 He is like a shrub in the desert 1
Mat 13:32 when it has grown it is the greatest of shrubs 2
Mrk 4:32 becomes the greatest of all shrubs 2

shudder 1. פַּלָּצוּת 2. רגז 3. שׂער 4. *ὑπόφρικος* 5. *φρίσσω* 6. horreo
Job 21: 6 I am dismayed, and shuddering seizes my flesh. 1
Isa 32:10 In little more than a year you will shudder 2
11 who are at ease, shudder, you complacent ones; 2
Ezk 32:10 their kings shall shudder because of you 3
Jas 2:19 Even the demons believe–and shudder. 5
2Es 5:14 Then I awoke, and my body shuddered violently 6
Man 1: 4 at whom all things shudder 5
3Mc 6:20 Even the king began to shudder bodily 4
4Mc 14: 9 Even now, we ourselves shudder as we hear 5
17: 7 shuddered as they saw the mother 5

shun 1. ירא 2. *ἐκκλίνω* 3. *φεύγω*
Ecc 9: 2 and he who swears is as he who shuns an oath. 1
1Co 6:18 Shun immorality 3
10:14 Therefore, my beloved, shun the worship of idols. 3
1Ti 6:11 as for you, man of God, shun all this 3
2Ti 2:22 shun youthful passions 3
Sir 32:17 A sinful man will shun reproof 2

cause to shun 1. רחק
Ps 88: 8 Thou hast caused my companions to shun me; 1
18 Thou hast caused lover and friend to shun me; 1

shut 1. גוף 2. טחח 3. כלא 4. סגר 5. סוך 6. עצם 7. עצר 8. קפץ 9. שׁעה 10. סגר (A) 11. *ἀποκλείω* 12. *κατακλείω* 13. *κλείω* 14. *συγκλείω*
Gen 7:16 and the LORD shut him in. 4
19: 6 the door to the men, shut the door after him 4
10 into the house to them, and shut the door. 4
Exd 14: 3 in the land; the wilderness has shut them in.' 4
Deu 15: 7 not . . shut your hand against your poor brother 8
Jos 2: 7 as the pursuers had gone out, the gate was shut. 4
Jdg 9:51 of the city fled to it . . and shut themselves in; 4
1Sm 23: 7 he has shut himself in by entering a town 4
2Kg 4: 4 and shut the door upon yourself and your sons 4
5 and shut the door upon herself and her sons; 4
21 laid him on the bed . . and shut the door upon him 4
33 he went in and shut the door upon the two of them 4
6:32 shut the door, and hold the door fast against him. 4
2Ch 29: 7 They also shut the doors of the vestibule 4
Neh 7: 3 standing guard let them shut and bar the doors. 1
13:19 I commanded that the doors should be shut 4
Job 3:10 it did not shut the doors of my mother's womb 4
5:16 poor have hope, and injustice shuts her mouth. 8
12:14 if he shuts a man in, none can open. 4
38: 8 who shut in the sea with doors 5
Ps 88: 8 I am shut in so that I cannot escape; 3
Ecc 12: 4 and the doors on the street are shut; 4
Isa 6:10 shut their eyes; lest they see with their eyes 9
22:22 he shall open, and none shall shut; 4
22 and he shall shut, and none shall open. 4
26:20 enter your chambers, and shut your doors 4
33:15 who . . shuts his eyes from looking upon evil 6
44:18 for he has shut their eyes, so that they cannot see 2
52:15 kings shall shut their mouths because of him; 8
60:11 day and night they shall not be shut; 4
66: 9 shall I, who cause to bring forth, shut the womb? 7
Ezk 3:24 said to me, "Go, shut yourself within your house. 4
44: 1 the sanctuary, which faces east; and it was shut. 4
2 And he said to me, "This gate shall remain shut; 4
2 therefore it shall remain shut. 4
46: 1 The gate . . shall be shut on the six working days; 4
2 but the gate shall not be shut until evening. 4
12 after he has gone out the gate shall be shut. 4
Dan 6:22 My God sent his angel and shut the lions' mouths 10
Mal 1:10 there were one among you who would shut the doors 4
Mat 6: 6 when you pray, go into your room and shut the door 13
23:13 you shut the kingdom of heaven against men 13
25:10 the door was shut. 13
Lke 11: 7 door is now shut, and my children are with me in bed; 13
13:25 the householder has risen up and shut the door 11
Joh 20:19 the doors being shut where the disciples were 13
26 The doors were shut 13
Act 21:30 at once the gates were shut. 13
Rev 3: 7 the true one . . who opens and no one shall shut 13
7 the true one . . who shuts and no one opens. 13
8 an open door, which no one is able to shut; 13
11: 6 They have power to shut the sky, that no rain 13
20: 3 into the pit, and shut it and sealed it over him 13
21:25 and its gates shall never be shut by day- 13
Tob 8: 4 When the door was shut and the two were alone 14
Wis 17: 2 shut in under their roofs 12
Sus 1:17 and shut the garden doors so that I may bathe. 13
18 They did as she said, shut the garden doors 11
20 Look, the garden doors are shut, no one sees us 13
36 shut the garden doors, and dismissed the maids. 11
Bel 1:11 shut the door and seal it with your signet. 11
14 Then they went out, shut the door and sealed it 13

shut off 1. excludo
2Es 16:77 It is shut off and given up to be consumed by fire. 1

shut on every side 1. *περιφράσσω*
LJr 1:18 just as the gates are shut on every side upon a man 1

shut out 1. שׂתם 2. *ἀποκλείω* 3. *ἐκκλείω*
Lam 3: 8 though I call and cry . . he shuts out my prayer; 1
Gal 4:17 want to shut you out, that you may make much 3
Jdt 13: 1 shut out the attendants from his master's presence 2
1Mc 5:47 the men of the city shut them out 2
11:61 the men of Gaza shut him out 2

shut up 1. חתם 2. כלא 3. כלה 4. סגר 5. סתם 6. עצר 7. צרר 8. קפץ 9. *ἀνέχω* 10. *κατακλείω* 11. *κλείω* 12. *συγκλείω* 13. *συλλαμβάνω* 14. includo
Lev 13: 4 the priest shall shut up the diseased person 4
5 then the priest shall shut him up seven days more 4
11 he shall not shut him up, for he is unclean 4
21 then the priest shall shut him up seven days 4
26 the priest shall shut him up seven days 4
31 then the priest shall shut up the person 4
33 the priest shall shut up the person 4
50 and shut up that which has the disease 4
54 and he shall shut it up seven days more 4

14:38 go out . . and shut up the house seven days 4
46 he who enters the house while it is shut up 4
Num 12:14 Let her be shut up outside the camp seven days 4
15 Miriam was shut up outside the camp seven days; 4
Deu 11:17 he shut up the heavens, so that there be no rain 6
Jos 6: 1 Jericho was shut up from within and from without 4
1Sm 6:10 two milch cows . . and shut up their calves at home 3
2Sm 20: 3 they were shut up until the day of their death 7
1Kg 8:35 When heaven is shut up and there is no rain 6
2Kg 17: 4 the king of Assyria shut him up, and bound him 6
2Ch 6:26 When heaven is shut up and there is no rain 6
7:13 When I shut up the heavens so that there is no rain 6
28:24 Ahaz . . shut up the doors of the house of the LORD; 4
Neh 6:10 house of Shemai'ah . . who was shut up, he said 6
Job 24:16 by day they shut themselves up; 1
41:15 rows of shields, shut up closely as with a seal. 4
Ps 77: 9 Has he in anger shut up his compassion?" Selah 8
Isa 24:10 every house is shut up so that none can enter. 4
22 they will be shut up in a prison 4
Jer 13:19 The cities of Negeb are shut up, with none to open 4
20: 9 as it were a burning fire shut up in my bones 6
32: 2 and Jeremiah the prophet was shut up in the court 2
33: 1 while he was still shut up in the court of the guard 6
39:15 while he was shut up in the court of the guard 6
Dan 12: 4 Daniel, shut up the words, and seal the book 5
9 words are shut up and sealed until the . . end. 5
Lke 3:20 he shut up John in prison. 10
4:25 the heaven was shut up three years and six months 11
Act 26:10 I not only shut up many of the saints in prison 10
2Es 5:37 bring forth for me the winds shut up in them 14
Wis 17:16 thus was kept shut up in a prison not made of iron; 10
Sir 48: 3 By the word of the Lord he shut up the heavens 9
1Mc 5: 5 They were shut up by him in their towers 12
26 Many of them have been shut up in Bozrah and Bosor 13
27 some have been shut up in the other cities 13
15:25 he shut Trypho up and kept him from going out or in. 12

weaver's shuttle 1. אֶרֶג
Job 7: 6 My days are swifter than a weaver's shuttle 1

sick 1. דָּוֶה 2. דַּוַּי 3. חלה 4. חֳלִי 5. ἀρρώστημα 6. ἀρρωστία 7. ἄρρωστος 8. ἀσθενέω 9. ἀσθενής 10. ἐπὶ τὴν κοίτην 11. κακῶς ἔχω 12. νοσέω 13. συνέχω
Lev 15:33 also for her who is sick with her impurity 1
1Sm 19:14 when Saul . . to take David, she said, "He is sick. 3
1Kg 14: 5 inquire of you concerning her son; for he is sick. 3
2Kg 8: 7 Ben-ha'dad the king of Syria was sick; 3
29 went down to see Joram . . because he was sick. 3
20:12 for he heard that Hezeki'ah had been sick. 3
2Ch 22: 6 went down to see Joram . . because he was sick. 3
32:24 In those days Hezeki'ah became sick 3
Neh 2: 2 Why is your face sad, seeing you are not sick? 3
Ps 35:13 But I, when they were sick–I wore sackcloth 3
107:17 Some were sick through their sinful ways *
Sng 2: 5 refresh me with apples; for I am sick with love. 3
5: 8 my beloved, that you tell him I am sick with love. 3
Isa 1: 5 The whole head is sick, and the whole heart faint. 4
33:24 no inhabitant will say, "I am sick"; 3
38: 9 Hezeki'ah king of Judah, after he had been sick 3
39: 1 he heard that he had been sick and had recovered. 3
Jer 8:18 beyond healing, my heart is sick within me. 2
Lam 5:17 For this our heart has become sick 1
Ezk 34: 4 the sick you have not healed 3
Mal 1: 8 when you offer those that are lame or sick 3
13 what has been taken by violence or is lame or sick 3
Mat 4:24 they brought him all the sick, those afflicted 11
8:16 and healed all who were sick. 11
9:12 but those who are sick. 11
10: 8 Heal the sick, raise the dead, cleanse lepers 8
14:14 and healed their sick. 7
35 and brought to him all that were sick 11
25:36 I was sick and you visited me 8
39 did we see thee sick or in prison and visit thee?' 8
43 sick and in prison and you did not visit me.' 9
44 a stranger or naked or sick or in prison 9
Mrk 1:32 they brought to him all who were sick 11
34 healed many who were sick with various diseases 11
2:17 those who are sick 11
6:13 anointed with oil many that were sick 7
56 they laid the sick in the market places 8
16:18 they will lay their hands on the sick 7
Lke 4:40 all those who had any that were sick 8
5:31 those who are sick; 11
7: 2 who was sick and at the point of death. 11
10: 9 heal the sick in it and say to them 9
Act 5:15 they even carried out the sick into the streets 9
16 bringing the sick 9
9:37 In those days she fell sick and died 8
19:12 aprons were carried away from his body to the sick 8
28: 8 lay sick with fever and dysentery 13
Jas 5:14 Is any among you sick? Let him call for the elders 8
Wis 17: 8 the fears and disorders of a sick soul 12
8 were sick themselves with ridiculous fear. 12
Sir 7:35 Do not shrink from visiting a sick man 7
38: 9 My son, when you are sick do not be negligent 5
1Mc 1: 5 After this he fell sick 10

6: 8 He took to his bed and became sick from grief 6
sick *See also* fall, lie, make.

become sick 1. אנשׁ 2. חלה
2Sm 12:15 the LORD struck the child . . and it became sick. 1
2Kg 20: 1 Hezeki'ah became sick and was at the point 2
Isa 38: 1 became sick and was at the point of death. 2
Hos 7: 5 On the day of our king the princes became sick 2

sick man 1. נסס 2. ἀσθενέω 3. κάμνω
Isa 10:18 it will be as when a sick man wastes away. 1
Joh 5: 7 The sick man answered him, "Sir, I have no man 2
Jas 5:15 the prayer of faith will save the sick man 3

sick people 1. ἄρρωστος 2. κακῶς ἔχω
Mrk 6: 5 he laid his hands upon a few sick people 1
55 began to bring sick people on their pallets 2

sick with a fever 1. πυρέσσω
Mat 8:14 he saw his mother-in-law lying sick with a fever; 1
Mrk 1:30 Now Simon's mother-in-law lay sick with a fever 1

sickbed 1. עֶרֶשׂ דְּוָי 2. κλίνη
Ps 41: 3 The LORD sustains him on his sickbed; 1
Rev 2:22 Behold, I will throw her on a sickbed 2

sickle 1. חֶרְמֵשׁ 2. מַגָּל 3. δρέπανον
Deu 16: 9 first put the sickle to the standing grain. 1
23:25 not put a sickle to your neighbor's standing grain. 1
1Sm 13:20 sharpen his . . his mattock, his axe, or his sickle; 3
Jer 50:16 one who handles the sickle in time of harvest; 2
Jol 3:13 Put in the sickle, for the harvest is ripe. 2
Mrk 4:29 at once he puts in the sickle 3
Rev 14:14 crown on his head, and a sharp sickle in his hand. 3
15 Put in your sickle, and reap 3
16 he who sat upon the cloud swung his sickle 3
17 another angel . . and he too had a sharp sickle. 3
18 called . . to him who had the sharp sickle 3
18 Put in your sickle, and gather the clusters 3
19 So the angel swung his sickle on the earth 3

sickly 1. τήκω
Wis 6:23 travel in the company of sickly envy 1

sickness 1. דָּוֶה 2. חֳלִי 3. מַחֲלֶה 4. מַחֲלָה 5. תַּחֲלֻאִים 6. ἀρρώστημα 7. νόσος
Exd 23:25 I will take sickness away from the midst of you. 4
Lev 20:18 If a man lies with a woman having her sickness 1
Deu 7:15 LORD will take away from you all sickness; 2
28:59 bring . . sicknesses grievous and lasting. 2
61 Every sickness also, and every affliction 2
29:22 sicknesses with which the LORD has made it sick 5
1Kg 8:37 whatever plague, whatever sickness there is; 4
2Kg 1: 2 whether I shall recover from this sickness. 2
8: 8 'Shall I recover from this sickness?' 2
9 saying, 'Shall I recover from this sickness?' 2
2Ch 6:28 whatever plague, whatever sickness there is; 4
21:15 you yourself will have a severe sickness 2
Prv 18:14 A man's spirit will endure sickness; 3
Ecc 5:17 in much vexation and sickness and resentment? 2
Isa 38: 9 been sick and had recovered from his sickness 2
Jer 6: 7 sickness and wounds are ever before me. 2
Hos 5:13 When E'phraim saw his sickness 2
Sir 30:17 and eternal rest than chronic sickness. 6
31:22 no sickness will overtake you. 6
37:30 for overeating brings sickness 7

wasting sickness 1. רָזוֹן
Isa 10:16 the LORD of hosts, will send wasting sickness 1

side 1. אֵצֶל 2. אֵת 3. הֵנָּה 4. זֶה 5. יָד 6. יָרֵךְ 7. כָּתֵף 8. לְ 9. לְמִן 10. מִזֶּה 11. מֵעֵבֶר 12. מִפּוֹ 13. מָקוֹם 14. מָתְנַיִם 15. עֵבֶר 16. עִם 17. פֵּאָה 18. צַד 19. צֵלָע 20. קִיר 21. קָצֶה 22. רֶבַע 23. רוּחַ 24. רֹחַב 25. שְׂטַר (A) 26. εἰμί 27. κενεών 28. μέρος 29. μετά 30. πλάγιος 31. πλευρά 32. προσχωρέω 33. φρονέω τά 34. contra 35. pars
Gen 6:16 and set the door of the ark in its side; 18
31:42 If the God . . had not been on my side 8
Exd 17:12 held up his hands, one on one side, and the other *
12 one side, and the other on the other side; *
25:12 two rings on the one side of it, and two rings 19
12 and two rings on the other side of it. 19
14 poles into the rings on the sides of the ark 19
32 shall be six branches going out of its sides 18
32 branches of the lampstand out of one side of it 18
32 branches of the lampstand out of the other side 18
26:13 the cubit on the one side, and the cubit *
13 and the cubit on the other side, of what remains *
13 shall hang over the sides of the tabernacle 18
13 shall hang over . . on this side and that side *
13 shall hang over . . on this side and that side *
18 twenty frames for the south side; 17
20 for the second side of the tabernacle 19
20 the tabernacle, on the north side twenty frames 17
26 the frames of the one side of the tabernacle 19
27 the frames of the other side of the tabernacle 19
27 five bars for the frames of the side 19
35 lampstand on the south side of the tabernacle 19
35 you shall put the table on the north side. 19
27: 7 the poles shall be upon the two sides of the altar 19
9 On the south side the court shall have hangings 17
9 hangings . . 100 cubits long for one side; 17
11 on the north side there shall be hangings 17
12 for the breadth of the court on the west side 17
14 The hangings for the one side of the gate shall be 7
15 On the other side the hangings shall be fifteen 7
30: 3 its top and its sides round about and its horns; 20
4 on two opposite sides of it shall you make them 19
32:15 tables that were written on both sides; 15
15 on the one side and on the other were they written. *
26 Who is on the LORD'S side? Come to me. 8
27 Put every man his sword on his side, and go 6
36:23 made thus: twenty frames for the south side; 17
25 for the second side of the tabernacle 19
25 side of the tabernacle, on the north side 17
31 the frames of the one side of the tabernacle 19
32 the frames of the other side of the tabernacle 19
37: 3 two rings on its one side and two rings on its 19
3 its one side and two rings on its other side. 19
5 poles into the rings on the sides of the ark 19
18 there were six branches going out of its sides 18
18 three branches of the lampstand out of one side 18
18 branches . . out of the other side of it; 18
26 with pure gold, its top, and its sides round about 20
27 under its molding, on two opposite sides of it 18
38: 7 poles through the rings on the sides of the altar 19
9 for the south side the hangings of the court 17
11 for the north side 100 cubits, their pillars 20 17
12 for the west side were hangings of 50 cubits 17
14 hangings for one side of the gate were 15 cubits 7
15 so for the other side; on this hand and that hand 7
40:22 on the north side of the tabernacle 6
24 table on the south side of the tabernacle 6
Lev 1:11 he shall kill it on the north side of the altar 6
15 shall be drained out on the side of the altar 20
5: 9 blood of the sin offering on the side of the altar 20
Num 3:29 to encamp on the south side of the tabernacle 6
35 to encamp on the north side of the tabernacle. 6
11:31 about a day's journey on this side *
31 about . . a day's journey on the other side *
22:24 narrow path . . with a wall on either side. *
32:19 come to us on this side of the Jordan to the east. 11
33:55 be as pricks in your eyes and thorns in your sides 18
34: 3 south side shall be from the wilderness of Zin 17
3 from the wilderness of Zin along the side of Edom 5
35: 5 shall measure . . for the east side 2,000 cubits 17
5 shall measure . . for the south side 2,000 cubits 17
5 shall measure . . for the west side 2,000 cubits 17
5 shall measure . . for the north side 2,000 cubits 17
Deu 4:49 all the Arabah on the east side of the Jordan 15
31:26 put it by the side of the ark of the covenant 18
Jos 8:22 in the midst . . some on this side, and some on that *
22 some on this side, and some on that side; *
12: 7 Joshua . . defeated on the west side of the Jordan 15
15: 5 the boundary on the north side runs from the bay 17
46 from Ekron . . all that were by the side of Ashdod 5
18:12 On the north side their boundary began 17
14 goes . . turning on the western side southward 17
14 boundary goes . . This forms the western side. 17
15 the southern side begins at the outskirts 17
20 Jordan forms its boundary on the eastern side. 17
22:11 about the Jordan, on the side that belongs 15
23:13 a snare and a trap for you, a scourge on your sides 18
1Sm 4:18 Eli fell . . from his seat by the side of the gate; 5
6: 8 put in a box at its side the figures of gold 18
14: 1 go . . to the Philistine garrison on yonder side. 15
4 there was a rocky crag on the one side 15
4 on the one side and a rocky crag on the other side; 15
40 You shall be on one side, and I and Jonathan my son 15
40 I and Jonathan my son will be on the other side. 15
17: 3 stood on the mountain on the one side 4
20:20 And I will shoot three arrows to the side of it 18
21 'Look, the arrows are on this side of you, 3
25 The king sat . . and Abner sat by Saul's side 18
23:26 Saul went on one side of the mountain 18
26 David . . on the other side of the mountain; 18
2Sm 2:13 they sat down, the one on the one side of the pool 4
16 and thrust his sword in his opponent's side; 18
13:34 the Horona'im road by the side of the mountain. 18
18: 4 the king stood at the side of the gate 5
1Kg 2:22 on his side are Abi'athar the priest and Jo'ab 8
4:24 and he had peace on all sides round about him. *
6: 8 entrance . . was on the south side of the house; 7
7:30 supports . . with wreaths at the side of each. 11
39 set the stands, five on the south side of the house 7
39 stands . . and five on the north side of the house; 7
49 lampstands . . five on the south side and five *
10:19 on each side of the seat were arm rests †
2Kg 2: 8 water was parted to the one side and to the other 3
14 water was parted to the one side and to the other; 3
9:32 lifted up his face . . and said, "Who is on my side? 2
10: 6 If you are on my side, and if you are ready to obey me 8
11:11 from the south side of the house to the north side 7
11 from the south . . to the north side of the house 7
16:14 he removed . . and put it on the north side of his altar. 6

1Ch 5: 9 the desert this side of the Euphra'tes 9
9:24 The gatekeepers were on the four sides 23
2Ch 9:18 on each side of the seat were arm rests 13
23:10 from the south side of the house to the north side 7
10 from the south . . to the north side of the house 7
Neh 4:18 sword girded at his side while he built. 14
Job 19:27 whom I shall see on my side 8
Ps 91: 7 1,000 may fall at your side 18
118: 6 With the LORD on my side I do not fear. 8
7 The LORD is on my side to help me; 8
11 They surrounded me, surrounded me on every side; *
124: 1 If it had not been the LORD who was on our side 8
2 if it had not been the LORD who was on our side 8
Ecc 4: 1 On the side of their oppressors there was power 5
Jer 48:28 that nests in the sides of the mouth of a gorge. 15
49:32 I will bring their calamity from every side 15
51:31 that his city is taken on every side; 21
52:23 There were 96 pomegranates on the sides; 23
Ezk 1: 8 Under their wings on their four sides 22
10 the four had the face of a lion on the right side *
10 the four had the face of an ox on the left side *
4: 4 Then lie upon your left side 18
6 lie down a second time, but on your right side 18
8 so that you cannot turn from one side to the other 18
9 the number of days that you lie upon your side 18
9: 2 clothed in linen, with a writing case at his side. 14
3 the man . . who had the writing case at his side. 14
11 in linen, with the writing case at his side 14
10: 3 were standing on the south side of the house *
11:23 mountain which is on the east side of the city. *
34:21 Because you push with side and shoulder 18
40:18 the pavement ran along the side of the gates 7
32 he brought me to the inner court on the east side *
40 on the other side of the vestibule of the gate 7
41 four tables on the outside of the side of the gate 7
44 one at the side of the north gate facing south 7
44 at the side of the south gate facing north. 7
41: 7 on the side of the temple a stairway led upward 24
12 that was facing the temple yard on the west side *
19 face of a man toward the palm tree on the one side 12
42: 2 which was on the north side was 100 cubits *
9 an entrance on the east side, as one enters them *
12 was an entrance on the east side, where one enters *
16 He measured the east side with the measuring 23
17 Then he turned and measured the north side 23
18 Then he turned and measured the south side 23
19 Then he turned to the west side and measured 23
20 He measured it on the four sides. It had a wall 23
45: 7 to the prince shall belong the land on both sides *
46:19 the entrance, which was at the side of the gate 7
47: 2 the water was coming out on the south side. 7
7 very many trees on the one side and on the other. 10
12 And on the banks, on both sides of the river *
15 On the north side, from the Great Sea 17
17 This shall be the north side. 17
18 On the east side, the boundary shall run 17
18 This shall be the east side. 17
19 On the south side, it shall run from Tamar 17
19 This shall be the south side. 17
20 On the west side, the Great Sea 17
20 This shall be the west side. 17
48: 1 and extending from the east side to the west, 17
2 territory of Dan, from the east side to the west 17
3 territory of Asher, from the east side to the west 17
4 from the east side to the west, Manas'seh 17
5 of Manas'seh, from the east side to the west 17
6 from the east side to the west, Reuben, one portion. 17
7 from the east side to the west, Judah, one portion. 17
8 territory of Judah, from the east side to the west 17
8 tribal portions, from the east side to the west 17
10 measuring 25,000 cubits on the northern side *
10 10,000 cubits in breadth on the western side *
10 10,000 in breadth on the eastern side *
10 and 25,000 in length on the southern side *
16 its dimensions: the north side 4,500 cubits 17
16 the north side 4,500 cubits, the south side 4,500 17
16 the east side 4,500, and the west side 4,500. 17
16 the east side 4,500, and the west side 4,500. 17
21 What remains on both sides of the holy portion *
23 tribes: from the east side to the west, Benjamin 17
24 from the east side to the west, Simeon, one portion 17
25 from the east side to the west, Is'sachar 17
26 the east side to the west, Zeb'ulun, one portion. 17
27 from the east side to the west, Gad, one portion. 17
30 north side, which is to be 4,500 cubits by measure 17
32 On the east side, which is to be 4,500 cubits 17
33 south side, which is to be 4,500 cubits by measure 17
34 On the west side, which is to be 4,500 cubits 17
Dan 7: 5 raised up on one side; it had three ribs 25
10:21 none who contends by my side 16
Zec 14: 5 the valley of the mountains shall touch the side 1
Mat 16:23 are not on the side of God, but of men. 33
Mrk 8:33 you are not on the side of God, but of men. 33
Lke 9:47 he took a child and put him by his side *
17:24 and lights up the sky from one side to the other 31
Joh 19:34 one of the soldiers pierced his side with a spear 31
20:20 he showed them his hands and his side 31
25 place my hand in his side 31
27 and put out your hand, and place it in my side 31
21: 6 Cast the net on the right side of the boat 28
Act 12: 7 he struck Peter on the side and woke him, saying 31
14: 4 some sided with the Jews 26
2Es 4:47 he said to me, "Stand at my right side 35
7:38 Look on this side and on that 34
11:12 behold, on the right side one wing arose 35
20 the wings . . also rose up on the right side 35
24 the head that was on the right side 35
35 the head on the right side devoured the one 35
12:29 to the head which was on the right side 35
14:15 lay to one side the thoughts 35
Jdt 6: 6 shall pierce your sides 31
Sir 30:12 beat his sides while he is young 31
Sus 1:18 and went out by the side doors 30
26 they rushed in at the side door 30
1Mc 10:26 and have not sided with our enemies 32
63 The king also seated him at his side 29
2Mc 3:26 who stood on each side of him 28
4Mc 6: 6 his sides were being cut to pieces. 31
8 rushed at him and began to kick him in the side 27

side *See also* chamber, discuss, fight, flash, labor, pass, road, seize, shut, strive, take.

side by side 1. צָמֶד
2Kg 9:25 you and I rode side by side behind Ahab his father 1

each side 1. מִפּוֹ מִפּוֹ 2. *ἑκατέρωθεν*
Ezk 41: 1 on each side six cubits was the breadth 1
4Mc 6: 3 after they had tied his arms on each side 2
9:11 they bound his hands . . with thongs on each side. 2

east side 1. מִזְרַח הַשֶּׁמֶשׁ
Jdg 11:18 and arrived on the east side of the land of Moab 1

either side 1. מִפֹּה מִפֹּה 2. *ἔνθεν καὶ ἔνθεν* 3. *ἐντεῦθεν καὶ ἐκεῖθεν* 4. *ἐντεῦθεν καὶ ἐντεῦθεν*
Ezk 40:10 three side rooms on either side of the east gate; 1
10 the jambs on either side were of the same size. 1
12 before the side rooms, one cubit on either side; 1
12 the side rooms were six cubits on either side. 1
21 Its side rooms, three on either side, and its jambs 1
26 it had palm trees on its jambs, one on either side. 1
34 it had palm trees on its jambs, one on either side; 1
37 it had palm trees on its jambs, one on either side; 1
39 of the gate were two tables on either side 1
48 of the vestibule, five cubits on either side; 1
48 of the gate were three cubits on either side. 1
49 were pillars beside the jambs on either side. 1
41: 2 of the entrance were five cubits on either side; 1
15 and its walls on either side, 100 cubits. 1
26 recessed windows and palm trees on either side 1
Joh 19:18 and with him two others, one on either side 4
Rev 22: 2 on either side of the river, the tree 3
1Mc 6:38 the horsemen were stationed on either side 2

every side 1. מִסָּבִיב 2. סָבִיב 3. *κυκλόθεν* 4. *κύκλος* 5. *πανταχόθεν* 6. *πάντοθεν*
Num 2: 2 encamp facing the tent of meeting on every side. 2
Jos 21:44 And the LORD gave them rest on every side 1
Jdg 7:18 the trumpets also on every side of all the camp 2
8:34 from the hand of all their enemies on every side; 1
1Sm 12:11 delivered you . . of your enemies on every side; 1
14:47 he fought against all his enemies on every side 2
1Kg 5: 4 the LORD my God has given me rest on every side; 1
1Ch 22:18 has he not given you peace on every side? 2
2Ch 14: 7 he has given us peace on every side. 2
32:22 LORD . . gave them rest on every side. 2
Job 1:10 him and his house and all that he has, on every side? 2
18:11 Terrors frighten him on every side, and chase him 2
19:10 He breaks me down on every side, and I am gone 2
Ps 12: 8 On every side the wicked prowl 2
31:13 hear the whispering of many-terror on every side!- 2
Jer 6:25 for the enemy has a sword, terror is on every side. 2
20: 3 does not call . . Pashhur, but Terror on every side. 2
10 I hear many whispering. Terror is on every side! 2
46: 5 they look not back-terror on every side! 2
49:29 men shall cry to them: 'Terror on every side!' 2
51: 2 when they come against her from every side 2
Lam 2:22 Thou didst invite . . my terrors on every side; 1
Ezk 16:33 bribing them to come to you from every side 2
37 I will gather them against you from every side 2
19: 8 the nations set against him snares on every side; 2
23:22 I will bring them against you from every side 2
24 shall set themselves against you on every side 2
28:23 by the sword that is against her on every side. 2
41:10 round about the temple on every side. 2
Lke 19:43 surround you, and hem you in on every side 6
Sir 46: 5 when enemies pressed him on every side 3
16 when his enemies pressed him on every side 3
47: 7 For he wiped out his enemies on every side 3
13 God gave him rest on every side 3
51: 4 from choking fire on every side 3
7 They surrounded me on every side 6
Sus 1:22 I am hemmed in on every side. 6
1Mc 1:37 On every side of the sanctuary 4
13:10 he fortified it on every side. 3
3Mc 5: 7 they were forcibly confined on every side 6
4Mc 15:32 overwhelmed from every side 5

north side 1. צָפוֹן 2. שְׂמֹאל
Num 2:25 On the north side shall be the standard 1
Jos 8:11 drew near . . and encamped on the north side of Ai 1
17: 9 boundary . . goes on the north side of the brook 1
2Ch 4: 6 ten lavers . . and set . . five on the north side. 2

other side 1. בְּעֵבֶר 2. זֶה 3. מֵעֵבֶר 4. מִפּוֹ 5. עֵבֶר 6. *πέραν*
Num21:13 encamped on the other side of the Arnon 5
32:19 inherit with them on the other side of the Jordan 5
Jos 17: 5 Bashan, which is on the other side of the Jordan; 3
22: 4 land . . on the other side of the Jordan. 1
24: 8 who lived on the other side of the Jordan; 5
Jdg 11:18 and camped on the other side of the Arnon; 5
1Sm 17: 3 Israel stood on the mountain on the other side 2
26:13 Then David went over to the other side 5
31: 7 men of Israel . . on the other side of the valley 5
2Sm 2:13 one . . and the other on the other side of the pool. 2
1Kg 4:12 A'bel-meho'lah, as far as the other side of Jok'meam; 3
Ezk 41:19 toward the palm tree on the other side. 4
Mat 8:18 he gave orders to go over to the other side. 6
28 when he came to the other side 6
14:22 and go before him to the other side 6
16: 5 When the disciples reached the other side 6
Mrk 4:35 Let us go across to the other side. 6
5: 1 They came to the other side of the sea 6
21 Jesus had crossed again in the boat to the other side 6
6:45 go before him to the other side, to Beth-sa'ida 6
8:13 he departed to the other side. 6
Lke 8:22 Let us go across to the other side of the lake. 6
Joh 6: 1 Jesus went to the other side of the Sea of Galilee 6
22 the people who remained on the other side of the sea 6
25 When they found him on the other side of the sea 6
1Mc 5:37 on the other side of the stream. 6
41 camps on the other side of the river 6
9:48 and swam across to the other side 6

right side 1. יָמִין 2. *δεξιός*
2Kg 12: 9 beside the altar on the right side as one entered 1
Mrk 16: 5 they saw a young man sitting on the right side 2
Lke 1:11 standing on the right side of the altar 2

side room 1. תָּא
Ezk 40: 7 the side rooms, one reed long, and one reed broad; 1
7 and the space between the side rooms, five cubits; 1
10 there were three side rooms on either side 1
12 There was a barrier before the side rooms 1
13 back of the one side room to the back of the other 1
16 inwards into their jambs in the side rooms, 1
21 Its side rooms, three on either side, and its jambs 1
29 Its side rooms, its jambs, and its vestibule were 1
33 Its side rooms, its jambs, and its vestibule were 1
36 Its side rooms, its jambs, and its vestibule were 1

south side 1. יָמִין 2. נֶגֶב 3. תֵּימָן
Num 2:10 On the south side shall be the standard 3
10: 6 camps that are on the south side shall set out. 3
Jos 15: 7 Adum'mim . . on the south side of the valley; 2
2Ch 4: 6 made ten lavers . . and set five on the south side 1
7 set them in the temple, five on the south side 1
8 placed them in the temple, five on the south side 1

west side 1. אַחַר 2. יָם 3. מַעֲרָבָה
Exd 3: 1 flock to the west side of the wilderness 1
Num 2:18 On the west side shall be the standard of the camp 2
2Ch 32:30 directed them down to the west side of the city 3

sideboard 1. *κυλικεῖον*
1Mc 15:32 the sideboard with its gold and silver plate 1

all sides 1. סָבִיב 2. *πάντοθεν*
Ezk 36: 3 made you desolate, and crushed you from all sides 1
37:21 and will gather them from all sides 1
39:17 gather from all sides to the sacrificial feast 1
Heb 9: 4 the ark . . covered on all sides with gold 2
2Mc 13: 5 which on all sides inclines precipitously 2

both sides 1. *ἀλλήλων* 2. *ἐκ τούτου καὶ ἐκ τούτου* 3. *ἔνθα καὶ ἔνθα*
1Mc 4:34 Then both sides attacked 1
6:45 they parted before him on both sides. 3
9:17 many on both sides were wounded and fell. 2

opposite sides 1. מִזֶּה וּמִזֶּה
Jos 8:33 all Israel . . stood on opposite sides of the ark 1

sidewall 1. כָּתֵף 2. *ἐπωμίς*
Ezk 40:48 the sidewalls of the gate were three cubits 2
41: 2 the sidewalls of the entrance were five cubits 1
3 and the sidewalls of the entrance, seven cubits. 2
26 either side, on the sidewalls of the vestibule. 1

siege 1. מָצוֹר 2. *περικάθημαι* 3. *πολιορκήσις* 4. *πολιορκία* 5. *συγκλεισμός*
Deu 28:53 eat the offspring . . in the siege 1
55 nothing left him, in the siege and in the distress 1
57 want . . in the siege and in the distress 1
2Ch 32:10 that you stand siege in Jerusalem? 1

Jer 10:17 O you who dwell under siege! 1
19: 9 of his neighbor in the siege and in the distress 1
Ezk 4: 3 let it be in a state of siege, and press the siege 1
7 set your face toward the siege of Jerusalem 1
8 till you have completed the days of your siege. 1
5: 2 when the days of the siege are completed; 1
Mic 5: 1 siege is laid against us; with a rod they strike 1
Nah 3:14 Draw water for the siege, strengthen your forts; 1
Zec 12: 2 it will be against Judah also in the siege 1
Sir 50: 4 fortified the city to withstand a siege. 3
1Mc 6:21 some of the garrison escaped from the siege 5
11:22 he wrote Jonathan not to continue the siege 2
23 he gave orders to continue the siege 2
2Mc 10:18 well equipped to withstand a siege 4
4Mc 17:24 courageous for infantry battle and siege 4

siege *See also* engine, lay, mound, press, tower, wall, withstand.

siegework 1. דָּיֵק 2. דֶּרֶךְ 3. מָצוֹר 4. מְצוּרָה 5. סֹלְלָה

Deu 20:20 build siegeworks against the city that makes 3
2Kg 25: 1 they built siegeworks against it round about. 1
Job 19:12 they have cast up siegeworks against me 2
Ecc 9:14 and besieged it, building great siegeworks 3
Isa 29: 3 and I will raise siegeworks against you. 4
Jer 52: 4 and built siegeworks against it round about. 1
Ezk 4: 2 put siegeworks against it, and build a siege wall 3
Dan 11:15 king of the north shall . . throw up siegeworks 5

sieve 1. כְּבָרָה 2. נָפָה 3. *κόσκινον*

Isa 30:28 to sift . . with the sieve of destruction 2
Ams 9: 9 and shake . . as one shakes with a sieve 1
Sir 27: 4 When a sieve is shaken, the refuse remains 3

sift 1. נוף 2. *κατασείω* 3. *σινιάζω*

Isa 30:28 to sift the nations with the sieve 1
Lke 22:31 he might sift you like wheat 3
Bel 1:14 they sifted them throughout the whole temple 2

sigh 1. אנח 2. אֲנָחָה 3. אנק 4. הֶגֶה 5. *ἀναστενάζω* 6. *στεναγμός* 7. *στενάζω*

Job 3:24 For my sighing comes as my bread 2
Ps 31:10 is spent with sorrow, and my years with sighing; 2
38: 9 my sighing is not hidden from thee. 2
90: 9 our years come to an end like a sigh. 4
Isa 21: 2 all the sighing she has caused I bring to an end. 2
24: 7 vine languishes, all the merry-hearted sigh. 1
35:10 and sorrow and sighing shall flee away. 2
51:11 and sorrow and sighing shall flee away. 2
Ezk 9: 4 men who sigh and groan over all the abominations 1
21: 6 Sigh therefore, son of man; 1
6 sigh with breaking heart and bitter grief 1
7 when they say to you, 'Why do you sigh?' 1
24:17 Sigh, but not aloud; make no mourning for the dead. 3
Mrk 7:34 looking up to heaven, he sighed, and said 7
Rom 8:26 intercedes for us with sighs too deep for words. 6
2Co 5: 4 we sigh with anxiety 7
Sir 25:18 he cannot help sighing bitterly. 5
36:25 a man will wander about and sigh. 7

sigh deeply 1. *ἀναστενάζω*

Mrk 8:12 he sighed deeply in his spirit, and said 1
Sus 1:22 Susanna sighed deeply, and said, "I am hemmed 1

sight 1. אֵת פְּנֵי 2. לְ 3. לִפְנֵי 4. מִפְּנֵי 5. מַרְאֶה 6. נֶגֶד 7. נֶגֶד עַיִן 8. נֶגֶד פָּנִים 9. עַיִן 10. עַל פָּנִים 11. פָּנִים 12. ראה 13. *βλέπω* 14. *εἶδος* 15. *ἔναντι* 16. *ἐναντίον* 17. *ἐναντίος* 18. *ἐνώπιον* 19. *ἐπί* 20. *θεωρέω* 21. *θεωρία* 22. *κατέναντι* 23. *ὅραμα* 24. *ὅρασις* 25. *ὀφθαλμός* 26. *ὄψις* 27. *παρά* 28. *πρόσωπον* 29. *στόμα* 30. *φαντάζω* 31. conspectus 32. coram 33. oculus 34. visio

Gen 2: 9 every tree that is pleasant to the sight and good 5
6:11 Now the earth was corrupt in God's sight 3
17:18 O that Ish'mael might live in thy sight! 11
18: 3 found favor in your sight 9
19:19 your servant has found favor in your sight 9
23: 4 that I may bury my dead out of my sight. 11
8 I should bury my dead out of my sight, hear me 11
32: 5 in order that I may find favor in your sight.' 9
33: 8 To find favor in the sight of my lord. 9
10 No, I pray you, if I have found favor in your sight 9
15 Let me find favor in the sight of my lord. 9
38: 7 Er . . was wicked in the sight of the LORD; 9
10 he did was displeasing in the sight of the LORD 9
39: 4 Joseph found favor in his sight and attended him 9
21 LORD . . gave him favor in the sight of the keeper 9
44:32 I shall bear the blame in the sight of my father 2
47:18 there is nothing left in the sight of my lord 3
29 If now I have found favor in your sight, 9
Exd 3: 3 I will turn aside and see this great sight 5
21 give . . favor in the sight of the Egyptians; 9
4:30 did the signs in the sight of the people. 9
5:21 have made us offensive in the sight of Pharaoh 9
7:20 in the sight of Pharaoh and in the sight of his 9
20 Pharaoh and in the sight of his servants 9
9: 8 throw them . . in the sight of Pharaoh. 9
11: 3 the LORD gave the people favor in the sight 9
3 Moses was very great . . in the sight of Pharaoh's 9
3 in the sight of Pharaoh's servants 9
12:36 favor in the sight of the Egyptians, so that they 9
17: 6 did so, in the sight of the elders of Israel. 9
19:11 come down . . in the sight of all the people. 9
24:17 a devouring fire . . in the sight of the people 9
33:12 you have also found favor in my sight.' 9
13 I pray thee, if I have found favor in thy sight 9
13 that I may know thee and find favor in thy sight. 9
16 have found favor in thy sight, I and thy people? 9
17 for you have found favor in my sight, and I know you 9
34: 9 he said, "If now I have found favor in thy sight 9
40:38 by night, in the sight of all the house of Israel. 9
Lev 10:19 would it have been acceptable in he sight 9
20:17 they shall be cut off in the sight of the children 9
21:20 a man with a defect in his sight or an itching 9
25:53 rule with harshness over him in your sight 9
26:45 I brought forth . . in the sight of the nations 9
Num 11:11 why have I not found favor in thy sight 9
15 kill me at once, if I find favor in thy sight 9
19: 5 heifer shall be burned in his sight; 9
20:27 went up . . in the sight of all the congregation. 9
22:34 Now therefore, if it is evil in thy sight, I will go 9
25: 6 in the sight of Moses and in the sight of the whole 9
6 in the sight of the whole congregation 9
27:19 you shall commission him in their sight. 9
32: 5 they said, "If we have found favor in your sight 9
13 generation that had done evil in the sight of the LORD 9
33: 3 triumphantly in the sight of all the Egyptians 9
Deu 4: 6 will be your wisdom . . in the sight of the peoples 9
25 doing . . evil in the sight of the LORD your God 9
6:18 do what is right and good in the sight of the LORD 9
9:18 in doing what was evil in the sight of the LORD 9
12:25 when you do what is right in the sight of the LORD. 9
28 good and right in the sight of the LORD your God. 9
13:18 doing . . right in the sight of the LORD your God. 9
17: 2 does . . evil in the sight of the LORD your God 9
21: 9 when you do what is right in the sight of the LORD. 9
25: 3 lest . . your brother be degraded in your sight. 9
28:34 driven mad by the sight which your eyes shall see. 5
67 because of . . sights which your eyes shall see. 5
31: 7 Joshua, and said to him in the sight of all Israel 9
29 will do what is evil in the sight of the LORD 9
34:12 which Moses wrought in the sight of all Israel. 9
Jos 3: 7 I will begin to exalt you in the sight of Israel 9
4:14 LORD exalted Joshua in the sight of all Israel; 9
9:25 do as it seems good and right in your sight to do 9
10:12 spoke Joshua . . and he said in the sight of Israel 9
23: 5 push them back . . and drive them out of your sight; 11
24:17 and who did those great signs in our sight 9
Jdg 2:11 evil in the sight of the LORD and served the Ba'als; 9
3: 7 Israel did what was evil in the sight of the LORD 9
12 again did what was evil in the sight of the LORD; 9
12 had done what was evil in the sight of the LORD. 9
4: 1 again did what was evil in the sight of the LORD 9
6: 1 Israel did what was evil in the sight of the LORD; 9
21 the angel of the LORD vanished from his sight. 9
10: 6 Israel again did . . evil in the sight of the LORD 9
13: 1 Israel again did . . evil in the sight of the LORD; 9
Rut 2: 2 after him in whose sight I shall find favor. 9
1Sm 2:17 the sin . . was very great in the sight of the LORD; 1
12:17 which you have done in the sight of the LORD 9
15:19 and do what was evil in the sight of the LORD? 9
16:22 Let David . . for he has found favor in my sight. 9
18: 5 And this was good in the sight of all the people 9
5 and also in the sight of Saul's servants. 9
26:24 as your life was precious this day in my sight 9
24 so may my life be precious in the sight of the LORD 9
29: 9 you are as blameless in my sight as an angel of God; 9
2Sm 12: 9 you despised . . to do what is evil in his sight? 9
11 lie with your wives in the sight of this sun. 9
13: 5 give me bread . . and prepare the food in my sight 9
6 Tamar come and make a couple of cakes in my sight 9
8 kneaded it, and made cakes in his sight, and baked 9
14:22 I have found favor in your sight, my lord the king 9
16: 4 let me . . find favor in your sight, my lord the king. 9
22 Ab'salom went in to . . in the sight of all Israel. 9
22:25 according to my cleanness in his sight. 9
1Kg 8:50 compassion in the sight of those who carried 3
9: 7 the house . . I will cast out of my sight; 11
11: 6 Solomon did what was evil in the sight of the LORD 9
19 Hadad found great favor in the sight of Pharaoh 9
33 walked in my ways, doing what is right in my sight 9
14:22 Judah did what was evil in the sight of the LORD 9
15:26 He did what was evil in the sight of the LORD 9
34 He did what was evil in the sight of the LORD 9
16: 7 all the evil that he did in the sight of the LORD 9
19 his sins . . doing evil in the sight of the LORD 9
25 Omri did what was evil in the sight of the LORD 9
30 Ahab . . did evil in the sight of the LORD 9
21:20 to do what is evil in the sight of the LORD. 9
25 was evil in the sight of the LORD like Ahab, whom 9
22:43 doing what was right in the sight of the LORD; 9
52 He did what was evil in the sight of the LORD 9
2Kg 1:13 let my life . . be precious in your sight. 9
14 but now let my life be precious in your sight. 9
3: 2 He did what was evil in the sight of the LORD 9
18 This is a light thing in the sight of the LORD; 9
8:18 And he did what was evil in the sight of the LORD. 9
27 and did what was evil in the sight of the LORD 9
13: 2 He did what was evil in the sight of the LORD 9
11 He also did what was evil in the sight of the LORD; 9
14:24 And he did what was evil in the sight of the LORD; 9
15: 9 And he did what was evil in the sight of the LORD 9
18 And he did what was evil in the sight of the LORD; 9
24 And he did what was evil in the sight of the LORD; 9
28 And he did what was evil in the sight of the LORD; 9
17: 2 And he did what was evil in the sight of the LORD 9
17 to do evil in the sight of the LORD, provoking him 9
18 and removed them out of his sight; 10
20 until he had cast them out of his sight. 11
23 the LORD removed Israel out of his sight 10
20: 3 I have . . and have done what is good in thy sight. 9
21: 2 And he did what was evil in the sight of the LORD 9
6 He did much evil in the sight of the LORD 9
15 done what is evil in my sight and have provoked me 9
16 they did what was evil in the sight of the LORD. 9
20 And he did what was evil in the sight of the LORD 9
23:27 I will remove Judah also out of my sight 10
32 And he did what was evil in the sight of the LORD 9
37 And he did what was evil in the sight of the LORD 9
24: 3 to remove them out of his sight, for the sins 10
9 And he did what was evil in the sight of the LORD 9
19 And he did what was evil in the sight of the LORD 9
1Ch 2: 3 Er . . was wicked in the sight of the LORD 9
28: 8 Now therefore in the sight of all Israel 9
29:25 Solomon great repute in the sight of all Israel 9
2Ch 7:20 and this house . . I will cast out of my sight 11
20:32 did what was right in the sight of the LORD. 9
21: 6 And he did what was evil in the sight of the LORD. 9
22: 4 He did what was evil in the sight of the LORD 9
29: 6 done what was evil in the sight of the LORD our God; 9
32:23 he was exalted in the sight of all nations 9
33: 2 He did what was evil in the sight of the LORD 9
6 He did much evil in the sight of the LORD 9
22 He did what was evil in the sight of the LORD 9
36: 5 did what was evil in the sight of the LORD his God. 9
9 He did what was evil in the sight of the LORD. 9
12 did what was evil in the sight of the LORD his God. 9
Neh 1:11 grant him mercy in the sight of this man. 11
2: 5 if your servant has found favor in your sight 11
4: 5 let not their sin be blotted out from thy sight; 11
8: 5 opened the book in the sight of all the people 9
Est 2:17 and she found grace and favor in his sight 3
5: 2 when the king saw . . she found favor in his sight 9
8 If I have found favor in the sight of the king 9
7: 3 If I have found favor in your sight, O king 9
8: 5 and if I have found favor in his sight 3
Job 15:15 the heavens are not clean in his sight; 9
18: 3 Why are we stupid in your sight? 9
25: 5 the stars are not clean in his sight; 9
30:10 they do not hesitate to spit at the sight of me. 11
34:26 for their wickedness in the sight of men 12
41: 9 he is laid low even at the sight of him. 5
Ps 18:24 the cleanness of my hands in his sight. 9
19:14 my heart be acceptable in thy sight, O LORD, my rock 11
31:19 take refuge in thee, in the sight of the sons of men! 6
22 said in my alarm, "I am driven far from thy sight. 9
39: 5 my lifetime is as nothing in thy sight. 6
44:16 at the sight of the enemy and the avenger. 4
51: 4 sinned, and done that which is evil in thy sight 9
72:14 precious is their blood in his sight. 9
78:12 In the sight of their fathers he wrought marvels 6
90: 4 1,000 years in thy sight are but as yesterday 9
98: 2 his vindication in the sight of the nations. 9
116:15 Precious in the sight of the LORD is the death 9
Prv 1:17 For in vain is a net spread in the sight of any bird; 9
3: 4 favor and good repute in the sight of God and man. 9
21 let them not escape from your sight 9
4: 3 son . . the only one in the sight of my mother 11
21 Let them not escape from your sight; 9
Ecc 6: 9 Better is the sight of the eyes 5
11: 9 walk in the ways of . . and the sight of your eyes. 5
Isa 5:21 their own eyes, and shrewd in their own sight! 8
38: 3 and have done what is good in thy sight. 9
Jer 7:15 And I will cast you out of my sight 11
30 For the sons of Judah have done evil in my sight 9
15: 1 Send them out of my sight, and let them go! 11
18:10 and if it does evil in my sight 9
23 nor blot out their sin from thy sight. 11
19:10 you shall break the flask in the sight of the men 9
32:30 nothing but evil in my sight from their youth; 9
31 so that I will remove it from my sight 11
33:24 they are no longer a nation in their sight. 3
43: 9 in the sight of the men of Judah 9
52: 2 he did what was evil in the sight of the LORD 9
Ezk 4:12 cake, baking it in their sight on human dung. 9
5: 8 in the midst of you in the sight of the nations. 9
14 and in the sight of all that pass by. 9
6: 9 they will be loathsome in their own sight 11
10:19 and mounted up from the earth in my sight 9
12: 3 and go into exile by day in their sight; 9
3 from your place to another place in their sight. 9
4 bring out your baggage by day in their sight 9
4 go forth yourself at evening in their sight 9
5 Dig through the wall in their sight, and go out 9
6 In their sight you shall lift the baggage 9
7 carrying my outfit . . in their sight. 9

16:41 judgments upon you in the sight of many women; 9
20: 9 in the sight of the nations among whom they dwelt 9
9 in whose sight I made myself known to them 9
14 not be profaned in the sight of the nations 9
14 nations, in whose sight I had brought them out. 9
22 not be profaned in the sight of the nations 9
22 nations, in whose sight I had brought them out. 9
41 holiness among you in the sight of the nations. 9
22:16 profaned through you in the sight of the nations; 9
28:18 upon the earth in the sight of all who saw you. 9
25 my holiness in them in the sight of the nations 9
36:34 desolation that it was in the sight of all 9
39:27 my holiness in the sight of many nations. 9
43:11 write it down in their sight 9
Dan 1: 9 favor and compassion in the sight of the chief 11
Hos 2:10 uncover her lewdness in the sight of her lovers 9
Ams 9: 3 they hide from my sight at the bottom of the sea 7
Zep 3: 7 will not lose sight of all that I have enjoined 25
Hag 2: 3 do you see it now? Is it not in your sight as nothing? 9
Zec 8: 6 If it is marvelous in the sight of the remnant 9
6 should it also be marvelous in my sight 9
Mal 2:17 one who does evil is good in the sight of the LORD 9
Lke 7:21 on many that were blind he bestowed sight. 13
16:15 an abomination in the sight of God. 18
23:48 the multitudes who assembled to see the sight 21
Act 1: 9 a cloud took him out of their sight. 25
4:19 Whether it is right in the sight of God 18
7:31 When Moses saw it he wondered at the sight 23
46 who found favor in the sight of God 18
9: 9 for three days he was without sight 13
10:33 we are all here present in the sight of God 18
19:19 burned them in the sight of all 18
Rom 3:20 For no human being will be justified in his sight 18
12:17 take thought for what is noble in the sight of all 18
2Co 2:17 in the sight of God we speak in Christ. 22
4: 2 to every man's conscience in the sight of God. 18
5: 7 for we walk by faith, not by sight. 14
7:12 be revealed to you in the sight of God. 18
8:21 not only in the Lord's sight 18
21 also in the sight of men. 18
12:19 It is in the sight of God 22
Gal 1:22 I was still not known by sight 28
1Ti 2: 3 it is acceptable in the sight of God our Savior 18
5: 4 for this is acceptable in the sight of God. 18
Heb 12:21 Indeed, so terrifying was the sight 30
13:21 working . . that which is pleasing in his sight 18
1Pe 2: 4 in God's sight chosen and precious; 27
3: 4 spirit, which in God's sight is very precious. 18
Rev 3: 2 not found your works perfect in the sight of God. 18
11:12 in the sight of their foes they went up to heaven 20
13:13 making fire come down . . in the sight of men; 18
1Es 1:23 upright in the sight of the Lord 18
39 he did what was evil in the sight of the Lord. 18
44 He did what was evil in the sight of the Lord. 15
47 He also did what was evil in the sight of the Lord 18
8:26 who honored me in the sight of the king 15
9:45 in the sight of the multitude 18
2Es 1:34 and have done what is evil in my sight. 32
2: 3 and have done what is evil in my sight. 32
3:35 not sinned in thy sight 31
4:44 If I have found favor in your sight 33
5:56 if I have found favor in thy sight 33
6:11 if I have found favor in thy sight 33
7:75 If I have found favor in thy sight, O Lord 33
102If I have found favor in thy sight 33
104Since you have found favor in my sight 33
8:28 those who have lived wickedly in thy sight 31
12: 7 if I have found favor in thy sight 33
15:28 a terrifying sight, appearing from the east! 34
Tob 1:13 and good appearance in the sight of Shalmaneser 18
4:21 do what is pleasing in his sight. 18
7: 7 When he heard that Tobit had lost his sight 25
14: 2 He was 58 years old when he lost his sight 26
Jdt 5:12 the Egyptians drove them out of their sight. 28
Wis 2:15 the very sight of him is a burden to us 13
3: 4 For though in the sight of men they were punished 26
7: 9 because all gold is but a little sand in her sight 26
8:11 in the sight of rulers I shall be admired. 26
9: 9 who understand what is pleasing in thy sight 25
11:19 the mere sight of them could kill by fright. 26
19:18 inferred from the sight of what took place. 26
Sir 1:29 Be not a hypocrite in men's sight 29
3:18 so you will find favor in the sight of the Lord. 15
8:16 because blood is as nothing in his sight 25
11:21 easy in the sight of the Lord to enrich a poor man 25
26 it is easy in the sight of the Lord to reward a man 15
25: 1 are beautiful in the sight of the Lord and of men; 15
45: 1 found favor in the sight of all flesh 25
46: 6 he was fighting in the sight of the Lord 17
Bar 1:12 we shall . . find favor in their sight. 16
21 what is evil in the sight of the Lord our God. 25
2:14 deliver us, and grant us favor in the sight 28
LJr 1:37 They cannot restore sight to a blind man 24
Aza 1:17 such may our sacrifice be in thy sight this day 18
Sus 1:23 rather than to sin in the sight of the Lord. 18
Man 1:10 have done what is evil in thy sight 18
1Mc 2:23 a Jew came forward in the sight of all 25
3:18 in the sight of Heaven there is no difference 16
3Mc 4: 4 at the sight of their unusual punishments 19

sight *See also* come, gain, loss, receive, recovering, regain.

out of sight 1. מִנֶּגֶד 2. ἀπό

Ps 10: 5 thy judgments are on high, out of his sight; 1
Lke 24:31 he vanished out of their sight. 2

sign 1. אוֹת 2. כתב 3. מוֹפֵת 4. צִיּוּן 5. אָת (A) 6. רשם (A) 7. σημεῖον 8. σύμβολον 9. σύσσημον 10. τεκμήριον 11. ὑπογράφω 12. signum

Gen 1:14 let them be for signs and for seasons and for days 1
9:12 God said, "This is the sign of the covenant 1
13 I set my bow in the cloud, and it shall be a sign 1
17 God said to Noah, "This is the sign of the covenant 1
17:11 it shall be a sign of the covenant 1
Exd 3:12 this shall be the sign for you, that I have sent you 1
4: 8 not . . heed the first sign, they may believe 1
8 the first sign, they may believe the latter sign. 1
9 will not believe even these two signs or heed 1
17 this rod, with which you shall do the signs. 1
28 told Aaron . . all the signs which he had charged 1
30 did the signs in the sight of the people. 1
7: 3 and though I multiply my signs and wonders 1
8:23 By tomorrow shall this sign be. 1
10: 1 that I may show these signs of mine among them 1
2 tell . . what signs I have done among them; 1
12:13 The blood shall be a sign for you, upon the houses 1
13: 9 shall be to you as a sign on your hand 1
31:13 for this is a sign between me and you 1
17 sign for ever between me and the people of Israel 1
Num14:11 in spite of all the signs which I have wrought 1
22 none of the men who have seen my glory and my signs 1
16:38 Thus they shall be a sign to the people of Israel. 1
17:10 to be kept as a sign for the rebels 1
Deu 4:34 by trials, by signs, by wonders, and by war 1
6: 8 you shall bind them as a sign upon your hand 1
22 showed signs and wonders, great and grievous 1
7:19 eyes saw, the signs, the wonders, the mighty hand 1
11: 3 signs and his deeds which he did in Egypt 1
18 you shall bind them as a sign upon your hand 1
13: 1 prophet arises . . gives you a sign or a wonder 1
2 sign or wonder which he tells you comes to pass 1
26: 8 with great terror, with signs and wonders; 1
28:46 They shall be upon you as a sign and a wonder 1
29: 3 your eyes saw, the signs, and those great wonders; 1
34:11 none like him for all the signs and the wonders 1
Jos 2:12 swear to me by the LORD . . and give me a sure sign 1
4: 6 that this may be a sign among you 1
24:17 and who did those great signs in our sight 1
Jdg 6:17 show me a sign that it is thou who speakest 1
1Sm 2:34 this . . shall be the sign to you: both of them 1
10: 1 And this shall be the sign to you that the LORD has 7
7 when these signs meet you, do whatever your hand 1
9 and all these signs came to pass that day. 1
14:10 And this shall be the sign to us. 1
1Kg 13: 3 he gave a sign the same day, saying, "This is the sign 3
3 This is the sign that the LORD has spoken: 'Behold 3
5 the sign which the man of God had given 3
2Kg 19:29 And this shall be the sign for you 1
20: 8 What shall be the sign that the LORD will heal me 1
9 Isaiah said, "This is the sign to you from the LORD 1
2Ch 32:24 answered him and gave him a sign. 3
31 inquire about the sign that had been done 3
Neh 9:10 perform signs and wonders against Pharaoh 1
Ps 65: 8 earth's farthest bounds are afraid at thy signs; 1
74: 4 they set up their own signs for signs. 1
4 they set up their own signs for signs. 1
9 We do not see our signs; 1
78:43 when he wrought his signs in Egypt 1
86:17 Show me a sign of thy favor, that those who hate me 1
105:27 They wrought his signs among them, and miracles 1
135: 9 sent signs and wonders against Pharaoh 1
Isa 7:11 Ask a sign of the LORD your God; 1
14 Therefore the Lord himself will give you a sign. 1
8:18 the children . . are signs and portents in Israel 1
19:20 It will be a sign and a witness to the LORD of hosts 1
20: 3 barefoot . . as a sign and a portent against Egypt 1
37:30 this shall be the sign for you 1
38: 7 This is the sign to you from the LORD 1
22 sign that I shall go up to the house of the LORD 1
55:13 an everlasting sign which shall not be cut off. 1
66:19 I will set a sign among them. 1
Jer 10: 2 nor be dismayed at the signs of the heavens 1
32:10 I signed the deed, sealed it, got witnesses 2
12 the witnesses who signed the deed of purchase 2
20 hast shown signs and wonders in the land of Egypt 1
21 out of the land of Egypt with signs and wonders 1
44 deeds shall be signed and sealed and witnessed 2
44:29 This shall be the sign to you, says the LORD 1
Ezk 4: 3 This is a sign for the house of Israel. 1
12: 6 I have made you a sign for the house of Israel. 3
11 Say, 'I am a sign for you 3
14: 8 I will make him a sign and a byword and cut him off 1
20:12 Moreover I gave them my sabbaths, as a sign 1
20 hallow my sabbaths that they may be a sign 1
24:24 Thus shall Ezekiel be to you a sign; 3
27 you will be a sign to them; and they will know 3
39:15 sees a man's bone, then he shall set up a sign by it 4
Dan 4: 2 show the signs and wonders that the Most High God 5
3 How great are his signs, how mighty his wonders! 5
6: 8 establish the interdict and sign the document 6
9 King Darius signed the document and interdict. 6
10 Daniel knew that the document had been signed 6
12 O king! Did you not sign an interdict, 6
13 pays no heed to . . the interdict you have signed 6
27 works signs and wonders in heaven and on earth 5
Mat 12:38 Teacher, we wish to see a sign from you. 7
39 evil and adulterous generation seeks for a sign; 7
39 but no sign shall be given to it 7
39 except the sign of the prophet Jonah. 7
16: 1 they asked him to show them a sign from heaven. 7
3 but you cannot interpret the signs of the times. 7
4 evil and adulterous generation seeks for a sign 7
4 but no sign shall be given to it 7
4 except the sign of Jonah 7
24: 3 what will be the sign of your coming 7
24 false prophets will arise and show great signs 7
30 the sign of the Son of man in heaven 7
26:48 Now the betrayer had given them a sign, saying 7
Mrk 8:11 seeking from him a sign from heaven, to test him. 7
12 Why does this generation seek a sign? 7
12 Truly, I say to you, no sign shall be given 7
13: 4 Tell us, when will this be, and what will be the sign 7
22 show signs and wonders 7
14:44 Now the betrayer had given them a sign, saying 9
16:17 these signs will accompany those who believe 7
20 by the signs that attended it. Amen. 7
Lke 2:12 this will be a sign for you 7
34 this child is set . . for a sign that is spoken against 7
11:16 others . . sought from him a sign from heaven. 7
29 it seeks a sign, but no sign shall be given to it 7
29 it seeks a sign, but no sign shall be given to it 7
29 no sign . . except the sign of Jonah. 7
30 For as Jonah became a sign to the men of Nin'eveh 7
21: 7 the sign when this is about to take place? 7
11 terrors and great signs from heaven. 7
25 there will be signs in sun and moon and stars 7
23: 8 he was hoping to see some sign done by him. 7
Joh 2:11 This, the first of his signs, Jesus did at Cana 7
18 What sign have you to show us for doing this? 7
23 believed . . when they saw the signs which he did; 7
3: 2 for no one can do these signs that you do 7
4:48 Unless you see signs and wonders 7
54 This was now the second sign that Jesus did 7
6: 2 because they saw the signs which he did 7
14 When the people saw the sign which he had done 7
26 you seek me, not because you saw signs 7
30 what sign do you do, that we may see, and believe 7
7:31 will he do more signs than this man has done? 7
9:16 How can a man who is a sinner do such signs? 7
10:41 many came to him; and they said, "John did no sign 7
11:47 What . . to do? For this man performs many signs. 7
12:18 they heard he had done this sign. 7
37 Though he had done so many signs before them 7
20:30 Now Jesus did many other signs 7
Act 2:19 signs on the earth beneath 7
22 with mighty works and wonders and signs 7
43 many wonders and signs were done 7
4:16 a notable sign has been performed through them 7
22 man on whom this sign of healing was performed 7
30 signs and wonders are performed 7
5:12 Now many signs and wonders were done 7
6: 8 did great wonders and signs among the people. 7
7:36 having performed wonders and signs in Egypt 7
8: 6 when they heard him and saw the signs which he did. 7
13 seeing signs and great miracles performed 7
14: 3 granting signs . . to be done by their hands. 7
15:12 what signs and wonders God had done through them 7
Rom 4:11 He received circumcision as a sign or seal 7
15:19 by the power of signs and wonders 7
1Co 1:22 For Jews demand signs and Greeks seek wisdom 7
14:22 Thus, tongues are a sign not for believers 7
2Co 12:12 The signs of a true apostle were performed among you 7
12 with signs and wonders and mighty works. 7
2Th 2: 9 with pretended signs and wonders 7
Heb 2: 4 while God also bore witness by signs and wonders 7
Rev 13:13 It works great signs, even making fire come down 7
14 and by the signs which it is allowed to work 7
16:14 for they are demonic spirits, performing signs 7
19:20 worked the signs by which he deceived 7
2Es 1:15 The quails were a sign to you 12
35 to whom I have shown no signs 12
4:52 Concerning the signs about which you ask me 12
5: 1 Now concerning the signs 12
13 the signs which I am permitted to tell you 12
6:12 show thy servant the end of thy signs 12
20 then I will show these signs 12
7:26 when the signs which I have foretold to you 12
8:63 thou hast now shown me a multitude of the signs 12
9: 1 a certain part of the predicted signs are past 12
6 and the end in requital and in signs. 12
13:32 and the signs occur which I showed you before 12
44 For at that time the Most High performed signs 12
14: 8 the signs that I have shown you 12
AEs 10: 9 God has done great signs and wonders 7
14:16 I abhor the sign of my proud position 7
Wis 2: 9 everywhere let us leave signs of enjoyment 8

5:11 afterward no sign of its coming is found there; 7
13 we had no sign of virtue to show 7
8: 8 she has foreknowledge of signs and wonders 7
10:16 withstood dread kings with wonders and signs. 7
19:13 not come upon the sinners without prior signs 10
Sir 36: 6 Show signs anew, and work further wonders 7
42:18 he looks into the signs of the age. 7
43: 6 to mark the times and to be an everlasting sign. 7
7 From the moon comes the sign for feast days 7
45: 3 By his words he caused signs to cease 7
Bar 2:11 with signs and wonders and with great power 7
LJr 1:67 they cannot show signs in the heavens 7
2Mc 6:13 is a sign of great kindness. 7
11:17 have delivered your signed communication 11
15:35 a clear and conspicuous sign to every one 7
3Mc 6:32 formed choruses as a sign of peaceful joy. 7
sign *See also* make, observe, take.

sign of approach 1. προσημειόω
4Mc 15:19 the signs of the approach of death. 1

sign of life 1. קֶשֶׁב
2Kg 4:31 but there was no sound or sign of life. 1

signal 1. מַשְׂאֵת 2. נֵס 3. שׁרק 4. σημασία
Jdg 20:40 when the signal began to rise out of the city 1
Isa 5:26 He will raise a signal for a nation afar off 2
13: 2 On a bare hill raise a signal, cry aloud to them; 2
18: 3 when a signal is raised on the mountains, look! 2
30:17 like a flagstaff . . like a signal on a hill. 2
49:22 to the nations, and raise my signal to the peoples; 2
Jer 6: 1 and raise a signal on Beth-hacche'rem; 1
Zec 10: 8 I will signal for them and gather them 3
1Mc 4:40 and sounded the signal on the trumpets 4

appointed signal 1. מוֹעֵד
Jdg 20:38 the appointed signal between the men of Israel 1

signature 1. תָּו
Job 31:35 Here is my signature! let the Almighty answer me! 1

signet 1. חתם 2. חֹתָם 3. חֹתֶמֶת 4. עִזְקָה (A) 5. γλύμμα 6. δακτύλιος 7. σφραγίς
Gen 38:18 She replied, "Your signet and your cord 2
25 Mark . . the signet and the cord and the staff. 3
Exd 28:11 As a jeweler engraves signets, so shall you 2
21 they shall be like signets, each engraved 2
36 engrave on it, like the engraving of a signet 2
39: 6 engraved like the engravings of a signet 2
14 they were like signets, each engraved 2
30 the engraving of a signet, "Holy to the LORD. 2
Ezk 28:12 You were the signet of perfection, full of wisdom 1
Dan 6:17 king sealed it with his own signet 4
17 king sealed it . . with the signet of his lords 4
Tob 1:22 Now Ahikar was cupbearer, keeper of the signet 6
Sir 17:22 A man's almsgiving is like a signet with the Lord 7
38:27 those who cut the signets of seals 5
45:11 with precious stones engraved like signets 7
12 inscribed like a signet with "Holiness 7
49:11 He was like a signet on the right hand 7
Bel 1:11 shut the door and seal it with your signet. 6
14 shut the door and sealed it with the king's signet 6
1Mc 6:15 He gave him the crown and his robe and the signet 6
signet *See also* ring.

signpost 1. יָד
Ezk 21:19 And make a signpost, make it at the head of the way 1

silence 1. דּוּמָה 2. דּוּמִיָּה 3. דּוּמָם 4. דמם 5. דְּמָמָה 6. הַס 7. חרשׁ 8. ἐπιστομίζω 9. ἡσυχάζω 10. ἡσυχία 11. σιγή 12. σιωπή 13. φιμόω 14. φράσσω 15. conticesco 16. silentium 17. sileo
Gen 24:21 The man gazed at her in silence to learn 7
Jdg 3:19 O king." And he commanded, "Silence." And all his 6
Job 4:16 there was silence, then I heard a voice 5
11: 3 Should your babble silence men, and when you mock 7
13:13 Let me have silence, and I will speak 7
Ps 62: 1 For God alone my soul waits in silence; 2
115:17 nor do any that go down into silence. 1
Isa 47: 5 Sit in silence, and go into darkness 3
Lam 2:10 The elders of . . Zion sit on the ground in silence; 4
3:28 Let him sit alone in silence when he has laid it 4
Ams 8: 3 in every place they shall be cast out in silence. 6
Mat 22:34 that he had silenced the Sad'ducees 13
Act 11:18 When they heard this they were silenced 9
2Co 11:10 this boast of mine shall not be silenced 14
1Ti 2:11 Let a woman learn in silence 10
Tit 1:11 they must be silenced 8
Rev 8: 1 silence in heaven for about half an hour. 11
2Es 6:39 and darkness and silence embraced everything; 16
7:30 turned back to primeval silence for seven days 16
10:22 our song has been silenced 15
15:32 be disorganized and silenced by their power 17
Wis 18:14 For while gentle silence enveloped all things 11
Sir 41:20 of silence, before those who greet you 12
3Mc 3:23 both by speech and by silence 11
silence *See also* bring, keep, land, listen, put, wait.

silent 1. דּוּמִיָּה 2. דמם 3. הַס 4. חרשׁ 5. חשׁה 6. ἡσυχάζω 7. ἡσυχία 8. σιγάω 9. σιγηρός 10. σιωπάω 11. φιμόω 12. sileo 13. taceo
2Kg 7: 9 if we are silent and wait until the morning light 5
18:36 people were silent and answered him not a word 4
Neh 5: 8 They were silent, and could not find a word to say. 4
Job 6:24 Teach me, and I will be silent; 4
13:19 For then I would be silent and die. 4
33:31 O Job, listen to me; be silent, and I will speak. 4
33 If not, listen to me; be silent, 4
Ps 4: 4 with your own hearts on your beds, and be silent. 2
28: 1 lest, if thou be silent to me, I become like those 5
30:12 that my soul may praise thee and not be silent. 2
35:22 Thou hast seen, O LORD; be not silent! 4
39: 2 I was dumb and silent, I held my peace to no avail; 1
50:21 These things you have done and I have been silent; 4
109: 1 Be not silent, O God of my praise! 4
Isa 36:21 they were silent and answered him not a word 4
62: 6 day and all the night they shall never be silent. 5
Hab 1:13 and art silent when the wicked swallows up 4
Zep 1: 7 Be silent before the Lord GOD! 3
Zec 2:13 Be silent, all flesh, before the LORD; 3
Mat 20:31 The crowd rebuked them, telling them to be silent; 10
26:63 Jesus was silent. And the high priest said to him 10
Mrk 1:25 Be silent, and come out of him! 11
3: 4 they were silent. 10
9:34 they were silent 10
10:48 many rebuked him, telling him to be silent 10
14:61 he was silent and made no answer 10
Lke 1:20 behold, you will be silent and unable to speak 10
4:35 Be silent, and come out of him! 11
14: 4 they were silent. Then he took him and healed him 6
18:39 telling him to be silent 8
19:40 He answered, "I tell you, if these were silent 10
20:26 marveling at his answer they were silent. 8
Act 12:17 motioning to them with his hand to be silent 8
18: 9 Do not be afraid, but speak and do not be silent; 10
1Co 14:30 let the first be silent. 8
1Ti 2:12 she is to keep silent. 7
2Es 14:43 and was not silent at night. 13
15: 8 I will be silent no longer 12
Wis 8:12 When I am silent they will wait for me 8
Sir 13:23 When the rich man speaks all are silent 8
20: 7 A wise man will be silent until the right moment 8
26:14 A silent wife is a gift of the Lord 9
silent *See also* keep.

remain silent 1. חרשׁ
Prv 11:12 but a man of understanding remains silent. 1

silently 1. silentium
2Es 7:32 and the dust those who dwell silently in it 1

silk 1. מֶשִׁי 2. σιρικός
Ezk 16:10 in fine linen and covered you with silk. 1
13 and your raiment was of fine linen, and silk 1
Rev 18:12 cargo of . . fine linen, purple, silk and scarlet 2

silly 1. פתה 2. γραώδης
Hos 7:11 E'phraim is like a dove, silly and without sense 1
1Ti 4: 7 godless and silly myths 2
silly *See also* talk.

silver 1. כֶּסֶף 2. כְּסַף (A) 3. ἀργύριον 4. ἄργυρος 5. ἀργυροῦς 6. ἀργυροχόος 7. περιάργυρος 8. argentum
Gen 13: 2 was very rich in cattle, in silver, and in gold. 1
20:16 have given your brother 1,000 pieces of silver 1
23:15 a piece of land worth 400 shekels of silver 1
16 Abraham weighed out for Ephron the silver 1
16 weighed out for Ephron . . 400 shekels of silver 1
24:35 given him flocks and herds, silver and gold 1
53 brought forth jewelry of silver and of gold 1
37:28 sold him . . for twenty shekels of silver; 1
44: 2 put my cup, the silver cup, in the mouth of the sack 1
4 Why have you stolen my silver cup? 5
8 should we steal silver or gold from your lord's 1
45:22 but to Benjamin he gave 300 shekels of silver 1
Exd 3:22 ask of her . . jewelry of silver and of gold 1
11: 2 that they ask . . jewelry of silver and of gold. 1
12:35 asked . . jewelry of silver and of gold 1
20:23 You shall not make gods of silver to be with me 1
21:32 owner shall give . . 30 shekels of silver 1
25: 3 this is the offering . . gold, silver, and bronze 1
26:19 40 bases of silver you shall make 1
21 their 40 bases of silver, two bases under one 1
25 shall be eight frames, with their bases of silver 1
32 with hooks of gold, upon four bases of silver. 1
27:10 hooks . . and their fillets shall be of silver. 1
11 hooks . . and their fillets shall be of silver. 1
17 pillars . . shall be filleted with silver; 1
17 their hooks shall be of silver 1
31: 4 to work in gold, silver, and bronze 1
35: 5 bring the LORD'S offering: gold, silver, and bronze 1
24 who could make an offering of silver or bronze 1
32 to work in gold and silver and bronze 1
36:24 he made 40 bases of silver under the twenty frames 1
26 their 40 bases of silver, two bases under one 1
30 eight frames with their bases of silver 1
36 and he cast for them four bases of silver. 1
38:10 pillars and their fillets were of silver. 1
11 pillars and their fillets were of silver. 1
12 the pillars and their fillets were of silver. 1
17 the pillars and their fillets were of silver; 1
17 overlaying . . was also of silver 1
17 pillars . . were filleted with silver. 1
19 four bases were of bronze, their hooks of silver 1
19 their capitals and their fillets of silver. 1
25 the silver from those of the congregation 1
27 The 100 talents of silver were for casting 1
Lev 5:15 a ram . . valued by you in shekels of silver 1
27: 3 valuation . . shall be 50 shekels of silver 1
6 for a male five shekels of silver, and for a female 1
6 valuation shall be three shekels of silver 1
16 barley shall be valued at 50 shekels of silver 1
Num 7:13 his offering was one silver plate whose weight 1
13 one silver basin of 70 shekels 1
19 he offered for his offering one silver plate 1
19 one silver basin of 70 shekels 1
25 his offering was one silver plate 1
25 one silver basin of 70 shekels 1
31 his offering was one silver plate whose weight 1
31 one silver basin of 70 shekels 1
37 his offering was one silver plate 1
37 one silver basin of 70 shekels 1
43 his offering was one silver plate, whose weight 1
43 one silver basin of 70 shekels 1
49 his offering was one silver plate 1
49 one silver basin of 70 shekels 1
55 his offering was one silver plate 1
55 one silver basin of 70 shekels 1
61 his offering was one silver plate, whose weight 1
61 one silver basin of 70 shekels 1
67 his offering was one silver plate, whose weight 1
67 one silver basin of 70 shekels 1
73 his offering was one silver plate 1
73 one silver basin of 70 shekels 1
79 his offering was one silver plate 1
79 one silver basin of 70 shekels 1
84 dedication offering . . twelve silver plates 1
84 dedication offering . . twelve silver basins 1
85 each silver plate weighing 130 shekels 1
85 all the silver of the vessels 2,400 shekels 1
10: 2 Make two silver trumpets; of hammered work 1
18:16 you shall fix at five shekels in silver 1
22:18 were to give me his house full of silver and gold 1
24:13 should give me his house full of silver and gold 1
31:22 only the gold, the silver, the bronze, the iron 1
Deu 7:25 not covet the silver or the gold that is on them 1
8:13 when . . your silver and gold is multiplied 1
17:17 nor . . greatly multiply for himself silver and gold. 1
22:19 they shall fine him 100 shekels of silver 1
29 give to the father . . 50 shekels of silver 1
29:17 their idols of wood and stone, of silver and gold 1
Jos 6:19 all silver and gold, and vessels of . . are sacred 1
24 silver and gold, and the vessels of bronze 1
7:21 I saw . . and 200 shekels of silver 1
21 hidden . . with the silver underneath. 1
22 hidden in his tent with the silver underneath. 1
24 took Achan . . and the silver and the mantle 1
22: 8 with very many cattle, with silver, gold, bronze 1
Jdg 5:19 they got no spoils of silver. 1
9: 4 they gave him 70 pieces of silver out of the house 1
16: 5 we will each give you 1,100 pieces of silver. 1
17: 2 1,100 pieces of silver which were taken from you 1
2 behold, the silver is with me; I took it. 1
3 he restored the 1,100 pieces of silver 1
3 I consecrate the silver to the LORD from my hand 1
4 his mother took 200 pieces of silver 1
10 and I will give you ten pieces of silver a year 1
1Sm 2:36 implore . . for a piece of silver or a loaf of bread 1
9: 8 I have . . the fourth part of a shekel of silver 1
2Sm 8:10 Joram brought . . articles of silver, of gold 1
11 with the silver and gold which he dedicated 1
18:11 to give you ten pieces of silver and a girdle. 1
12 if I felt in my hand . . 1,000 pieces of silver 1
21: 4 not a matter of silver or gold between us and Saul 1
24:24 David bought . . for 50 shekels of silver. 1
1Kg 7:51 Solomon brought in . . the silver, the gold 1
10:21 all . . were of pure gold; none were of silver 1
22 bringing gold, silver, ivory, apes, and peacocks. 1
25 his present, articles of silver and gold 1
27 the king made silver as common . . as stone 1
29 imported from Egypt for 600 shekels of silver 1
15:15 his . . votive gifts, silver, and gold, and vessels. 1
18 Asa took all the silver and the gold 1
19 I am sending to you a present of silver and gold; 1
16:24 He bought the hill . . for two talents of silver; 1
20: 3 Your silver and your gold are mine; 1
5 Deliver to me your silver and your gold 1
7 he sent to me . . for my silver and my gold 1
39 his life, or else you shall pay a talent of silver.' 1
2Kg 5: 5 So he went, taking with him ten talents of silver 1
22 give them a talent of silver and two . . garments.' 1
23 and tied up two talents of silver in two bags 1
6:25 an ass's head was sold for 80 shekels of silver 1

25 of a kab of dove's dung for five shekels of silver. 1
7: 8 they carried off silver and gold and clothing 1
12:13 not made . . basins of silver, snuffers, bowls 1
13 trumpets, or any vessels of gold, or of silver 1
14:14 he seized all the gold and silver 1
15:19 Men'aham gave Pul 1,000 talents of silver 1
20 exacted the money . . 50 shekels of silver 1
16: 8 Ahaz . . took the silver and gold that was found 1
18:14 required of Hezeki'ah . . 300 talents of silver 1
15 Hezeki'ah gave him all the silver that was found 1
20:13 all his treasure house, the silver, the gold 1
23:33 laid upon the land a tribute of 100 talents of silver 1
35 gave the silver and the gold to Pharaoh 1
35 He exacted the silver and the gold of the people 1
25:15 took . . as gold, and what was of silver, as silver. 1
15 took . . as gold, and what was of silver, as silver. 1
1Ch 18:10 articles of gold, of silver, and of bronze; 1
11 the silver and gold which he had carried off 1
19: 6 sent 1,000 talents of silver to hire chariots 1
22:14 house of the LORD . . 1,000,000 talents of silver 1
16 gold, silver, bronze, and iron. Arise and be doing! 1
28:14 weight of silver vessels for each service 1
15 weight of silver for a lampstand and its lamps 1
16 the silver for the silver tables 1
16 the silver for the silver tables 1
17 for the silver bowls and the weight of each. 1
29: 2 the silver for the things of silver 1
3 I have a treasure of my own of gold and silver 1
4 and 7,000 talents of refined silver 1
5 of gold and silver for the things of silver. 1
7 10,000 talents of silver, 18,000 talents of bronze 1
2Ch 1:15 king made silver and gold as common . . as stone 1
17 chariot . . for 600 shekels of silver 1
2: 7 now send me a man skilled to work in gold, silver 1
14 He is trained to work in gold, silver, bronze, iron 1
5: 1 stored the silver, the gold, and all the vessels 1
9:14 brought gold and silver to Solomon. 1
20 silver was not considered as anything 1
21 ships . . used to come bringing gold, silver 1
24 his present, articles of silver and of gold 1
27 king made silver as common in Jerusalem as stone 1
15:18 votive gifts, silver, and gold, and vessels. 1
16: 2 Then Asa took silver and gold from the treasures 1
3 behold, I am sending to you silver and gold; 1
17:11 Philistines brought . . silver for tribute; 1
21: 3 gifts, of silver, gold, and valuable possessions 1
24:14 vessels of gold and silver. 1
25: 6 for 100 talents of silver. 1
24 he seized all the gold and silver 1
27: 5 gave him that year 100 talents of silver 1
32:27 made for himself treasuries for silver, for gold 1
36: 3 tribute of 100 talents of silver and a talent 1
Ezr 1: 4 be assisted . . with silver and gold, with goods 1
6 aided them with vessels of silver, with gold 1
9 number . . 1,000 basins of silver, 29 censers 1
10 30 bowls of gold, 2,410 bowls of silver 1
11 all the vessels of gold and of silver were 5,469. 1
2:69 gave to . . the work . . gold, 5,000 minas of silver 1
5:14 gold and silver vessels of the house of God 2
6: 5 gold and silver vessels of the house of God 2
7:15 also to convey the silver and gold which the king 2
16 with all the silver and gold which you shall find 2
18 do with the rest of the silver and gold 2
22 up to 100 talents of silver 2
8:25 weighed out . . silver and the gold and the vessels 1
26 I weighed out . . 650 talents of silver 1
26 silver vessels worth 100 talents 1
28 silver and the gold are a freewill offering 1
30 took over the weight of the silver and the gold 1
33 silver and the gold and the vessels were weighed 1
Neh 5:15 food and wine, besides 40 shekels of silver. 1
7:71 gave into the treasury . . 2,200 minas of silver. 1
72 rest of the people gave . . 2,000 minas of silver 1
Est 1: 6 caught up with cords . . to silver rings 1
6 and also couches of gold and silver 1
3: 9 I will pay 10,000 talents of silver 1
Job 3:15 princes . . who filled their houses with silver. 1
22:25 Almighty is your gold, and your precious silver; 1
27:16 Though he heap up silver like dust 1
17 the innocent will divide the silver. 1
28: 1 Surely there is a mine for silver 1
15 silver cannot be weighed as its price. 1
Ps 12: 6 silver refined in a furnace on the ground 1
66:10 thou hast tried us as silver is tried. 1
68:13 wings of a dove covered with silver, its pinions 1
105:37 Then he led forth Israel with silver and gold 1
115: 4 idols are silver and gold, the work of men's hands. 1
119:72 better . . than thousands of gold and silver 1
135:15 The idols of the nations are silver and gold 1
Prv 2: 4 if you seek it like silver 1
3:14 gain from it is better than gain from silver 1
8:10 Take my instruction instead of silver 1
19 my yield than choice silver. 1
10:20 The tongue of the righteous is choice silver; 1
16:16 understanding is to be chosen rather than silver. 1
17: 3 crucible is for silver, and the furnace 1
22: 1 favor is better than silver or gold. 1
25: 4 Take away the dross from the silver 1
11 like apples of gold in a setting of silver. 1

27:21 crucible is for silver . . furnace is for gold 1
Ecc 2: 8 I also gathered for myself silver and gold 1
12: 6 before the silver cord is snapped 1
Sng 1:11 make you ornaments of gold, studded with silver. 1
3:10 He made its posts of silver, its back of gold 1
8: 9 we will build upon her a battlement of silver; 1
11 bring . . 1,000 pieces of silver. 1
Isa 1:22 Your silver has become dross 1
2: 7 Their land is filled with silver and gold 1
20 men will cast forth their idols of silver 1
7:23 vines, worth 1,000 shekels of silver 1
13:17 no regard for silver and do not delight in gold. 1
30:22 defile your silver-covered graven images 1
31: 7 every one shall cast away his idols of silver 1
39: 2 his treasure house, the silver, the gold 1
40:19 with gold, and casts for it silver chains. 1
46: 6 from the purse, and weigh out silver in the scales 1
48:10 Behold, I have refined you, but not like silver; 1
60: 9 sons from far, their silver and gold with them 1
17 and instead of iron I will bring silver; 1
Jer 6:30 Refuse silver they are called 1
10: 4 Men deck it with silver and gold; 1
9 Beaten silver is brought from Tarshish 1
32: 9 the money to him, seventeen shekels of silver 1
52:19 as gold, and what was of silver, as silver. 1
19 as gold, and what was of silver, as silver. 1
Ezk 7:19 They cast their silver into the streets 1
19 silver and gold are not able to deliver them 1
16:13 Thus you were decked with gold and silver; 1
17 my gold and of my silver, which I had given you 1
22:18 silver and bronze and tin and iron and lead 1
20 As men gather silver and bronze and iron and lead 1
22 As silver is melted in a furnace, so you shall be 1
27:12 wealth of every kind; silver, iron, tin, and lead 1
28: 4 gathered gold and silver into your treasuries; 1
38:13 to carry away silver and gold, to take away cattle 1
Dan 2:32 head of . . gold, its breast and arms of silver 2
35 iron, the clay, the bronze, the silver, and the gold 2
45 broke in pieces the . . silver, and the gold. 2
5: 2 commanded that the vessels of gold and of silver 2
3 brought in the golden and silver vessels 5
4 praised the gods of gold and silver, bronze, iron 2
23 praised the gods of silver and gold, of bronze 2
11: 8 their precious vessels of silver and of gold; 1
38 honor with gold and silver, with precious stones 1
43 become ruler of the treasures of gold . . silver 1
Hos 2: 8 and who lavished upon her silver and gold 1
3: 2 So I bought her for fifteen shekels of silver 1
8: 4 With their silver and gold they made idols 1
9: 6 shall possess their precious things of silver; 1
13: 2 idols skilfully made of their silver 1
Jol 3: 5 For you have taken my silver and my gold 1
Ams 2: 6 because they sell the righteous for silver 1
8: 6 that we may buy the poor for silver 1
Nah 2: 9 Plunder the silver, plunder the gold! 1
Hab 2:19 Behold, it is overlaid with gold and silver 1
Zep 1:11 all who weigh out silver are cut off. 1
18 Neither their silver nor their gold shall be 1
Hag 2: 8 The silver is mine, and the gold is mine 1
Zec 6:11 Take from them silver and gold, and make a crown 1
9: 3 heaped up silver like dust, and gold like the dirt 1
11:12 weighed out as my wages 30 shekels of silver. 1
13 I took the 30 shekels of silver 1
13: 9 and refine them as one refines silver 1
14:14 shall be collected, gold, silver, and garments 1
Mal 3: 3 he will sit as a refiner and purifier of silver 1
3 sons of Levi and refine them like gold and silver 1
Mat 10: 9 Take no gold, nor silver, nor copper in your belts 4
26:15 And they paid him 30 pieces of silver. 3
27: 3 and brought back the 30 pieces of silver 3
5 throwing down the pieces of silver in the temple 3
6 the chief priests, taking the pieces of silver, said 3
9 they took the 30 pieces of silver 3
Act 3: 6 I have no silver and gold, but I give you what I have; 3
7:16 tomb that Abraham had bought for a sum of silver 3
8:20 Peter said to him, "Your silver perish with you 3
17:29 is like gold, or silver, or stone 4
19:19 and found it came to 50,000 pieces of silver. 3
24 a silversmith, who made silver shrines of Ar'temis 5
20:33 I coveted no one's silver or gold or apparel. 3
1Co 3:12 builds on the foundation with gold, silver 4
2Ti 2:20 there are not only vessels of gold and silver 5
Jas 5: 3 Your gold and silver have rusted 4
1Pe 1:18 with perishable things such as silver or gold 3
Rev 9:20 demons and idols of gold and silver and bronze 5
18:12 cargo of gold, silver, jewels and pearls 4
1Es 1:36 100 talents of silver and a talent of gold. 3
2: 6 be helped . . with gold and silver 3
9 with silver and gold, with horses and cattle 3
13 1,000 gold cups, 1,000 silver cups 5
13 29 silver censers, 30 gold bowls, 2,410 silver bowls 5
13 2,410 silver bowls, and 1,000 other vessels. 5
14 All the vessels were handed over, gold and silver 5
4:18 If men gather gold and silver 3
19 all prefer her to gold or silver 3
5:45 1,000 minas of gold, 5,000 minas of silver 3
6:18 the holy vessels of gold and of silver 5
26 the holy vessels . . both of gold and of silver 5
8:13 all the gold and silver that may be found 3

14 both gold and silver for bulls and rams and lambs 3
16 to do with the gold and silver 3
20 up to 100 talents of silver 3
55 I weighed out to them the silver and the gold 3
56 I weighed and gave to them 650 talents of silver 3
56 silver vessels worth a 100 talents 5
58 the silver and the gold are vowed to the Lord 3
60 the priests and the Levites who took the silver 3
62 the silver and the gold were weighed 3
2Es 7:55 Say to her, 'You produce gold and silver and brass 8
56 silver is more abundant than gold 8
56 and brass than silver, and iron than brass 8
Tob 1:14 I left ten talents of silver in trust with Gabael 3
4:20 explain to you about the ten talents of silver 3
Jdt 2:18 a huge amount of gold and silver 3
5: 9 settled, and prospered, with much gold and silver 3
8: 7 Manasseh had left her gold and silver 3
10:22 with silver lamps carried before him. 5
Wis 7: 9 silver will be accounted as clay before her. 4
13:10 gold and silver fashioned with skill 4
15: 9 he competes with workers in gold and silver 6
Sir 26:18 Like pillars of gold on a base of silver 5
28:24 lock up your silver and gold 3
29:10 Lose your silver for the sake of a brother 3
40:25 Gold and silver make the foot stand sure 3
47:18 amassed silver like lead. 3
51:28 Get instruction with a large sum of silver 3
Bar 1: 8 silver vessels which Zedekiah . . had made 5
3:17 who hoard up silver and gold, in which men trust 3
18 those who scheme to get silver, and are anxious 3
LJr 1: 4 you will see gods made of silver and gold and wood 5
8 they . . are overlaid with gold and silver 7
10 secretly take gold and silver from their gods 3
11 these gods of silver and gold and wood 5
30 serve meals for gods of silver and gold and wood; 5
39 and overlaid with gold and silver 7
50 and overlaid with gold and silver 7
55 wooden gods overlaid with gold or silver 7
58 strip them of their gold and silver 3
70 gods of wood, overlaid with gold and silver. 7
71 their gods of wood, overlaid with gold and silver 7
1Mc 1:23 He took the silver and the gold 3
2:18 your sons will be honored with silver and gold 3
3:41 they took silver and gold in immense amounts 3
4:23 they seized much gold and silver 3
6: 1 a city famed for its wealth in silver and gold. 3
12 I seized all her vessels of silver and gold 5
8: 3 to get control of the silver and gold mines there 3
10:40 I also grant 15,000 shekels of silver 3
42 Moreover, the 5,000 shekels of silver 3
60 he gave them and their friends silver and gold 3
11:24 taking silver and gold and clothing 3
13:16 Send now 100 talents of silver 3
15:26 silver and gold and much military equipment. 3
31 or else give me for them 500 talents of silver 3
16:11 he had much silver and gold 3
19 so that he might give them silver and gold 3
2Mc 2: 2 upon seeing the gold and silver statues 5
3:11 400 talents of silver and 200 of gold 3
4: 8 360 talents of silver 3
19 to carry 300 silver drachmas for the sacrifice 3
24 outbidding Jason by 300 talents of silver. 3
12:43 to the amount of 2,000 drachmas of silver 3

silver *See also* coin, dish, overlay, piece, plate.

thing of silver 1. כֶּסֶף
1Ch 29: 2 the silver for the things of silver 1
5 of gold and silver for the things of silver. 1

silversmith 1. צרף 2. *ἀργυροκόπος*
Jdg 17: 4 the silversmith, who made it into a graven image 1
Act 19:24 a man named Deme'trius, a silversmith 2

similar 1. כָּהֵמָּה 2. כְּמַרְאֶה 3. *κατά* 4. *τοιοῦτος* 5. adaequo
Jer 36:32 and many similar words were added to them. 1
Ezk 42:11 they were similar to the chambers on the north 2
2Es 7:61 and are similar to a flame and smoke 5
1Mc 5:14 and made a similar report; 3
2Mc 2: 3 with other similar words he exhorted them 4

simple 1. פתה 2. פֶּתִי
Job 5: 2 kills the fool, and jealousy slays the simple. 1
Ps 19: 7 the testimony . . is sure, making wise the simple; 2
116: 6 The LORD preserves the simple; 2
119:130 it imparts understanding to the simple. 2
Prv 1: 4 that prudence may be given to the simple 2
22 How long, O simple ones, will you love being simple? 2
32 For the simple are killed by their turning away 2
7: 7 I have seen among the simple 2
9: 4 Whoever is simple, let him turn in here! 2
16 Whoever is simple, let him turn in here! 2
14:15 The simple believes everything 2
18 The simple acquire folly, but the prudent 2
19:25 Strike a scoffer . . simple will learn prudence; 2
21:11 scoffer is punished, the simple becomes wise; 2
22: 3 but the simple go on, and suffer for it. 2
27:12 but the simple go on, and suffer for it. 2

simple one 1. פֶּתִי
Prv 1:22 How long, O simple ones, will you love being simple? 1
8: 5 O simple ones, learn prudence; 1

simple-minded 1. ἄκακος
Rom 16:18 they deceive the hearts of the simple-minded. 1

simpleness 1. פֶּתִי
Prv 9: 6 Leave simpleness, and live 1

simplicity 1. תֹּם
2Sm 15:11 they went in their simplicity, and knew nothing. 1

simply 1. ἁπλῶς 2. πλήν
Mat 5:37 Let what you say be simply 'Yes' or 'No'; *
Wis 16:27 when simply warmed by a fleeting ray of the sun 1
1Mc 5:48 we will simply pass by on foot 2

sin 1. אַשְׁמָה 2. חטא 3. חֵטְא 4. חַטָּאָה 5. חַטָּאָה 6. חַטָּאת 7. מעל 8. עָוֺן 9. חֲטָי (A) 10. ἁμαρτάνω 11. ἁμάρτημα 12. ἁμαρτία 13. ἐξαμαρτάνω 14. πλημμελέω 15. delictum 16. peccatum 17. pecco
Gen 4: 7 if you do not do well, sin is couching at the door; 6
18:20 is great and their sin is very grave 6
20: 6 it was I who kept you from sinning against me; 2
9 how have I sinned against you 2
9 brought on me and my kingdom a great sin? 4
31:36 What is my sin, that you have hotly pursued me? 6
39: 9 I do this great wickedness, and sin against God? 2
42:22 Did I not tell you not to sin against the lad? 2
50:17 Forgive . . their sin, because they did evil 6
Exd 9:27 Pharaoh . . said to them, "I have sinned this time; 2
34 Pharaoh . . sinned yet again, and hardened his 2
10:16 Pharaoh . . said, "I have sinned against the LORD 2
17 Now therefore, forgive my sin, I pray you 6
20:20 be before your eyes, that you may not sin. 2
32:21 that you have brought a great sin upon them? 4
30 You have sinned a great sin. And now I will go up 2
30 You have sinned a great sin. And now I will go up 4
30 perhaps I can make atonement for your sin. 6
31 said, "Alas, this people have sinned a great sin; 2
31 said, "Alas, this people have sinned a great sin; 4
32 now, if thou wilt forgive their sin–and if not, blot 6
33 the LORD said to Moses, "Whoever has sinned 2
34 I visit, I will visit their sin upon them. 6
34: 7 forgiving iniquity and transgression and sin 5
9 and pardon our iniquity and our sin 6
Lev 4: 2 If any one sins unwittingly in any of the things 2
3 if it is the anointed priest who sins 2
3 let him offer for the sin which he has committed 6
14 when the sin which they have committed 6
22 When a ruler sins, doing unwittingly 2
23 if the sin which he has committed is made known 6
26 shall make atonement for him for his sin 6
27 If any one of the common people sins unwittingly 2
28 when the sin which he has committed is made known 6
28 a goat . . for his sin which he has committed 6
35 atonement for the sin which he has committed 6
5: 1 If any one sins in that he hears 2
5 he shall confess the sin he has committed *
6 to the LORD for the sin which he has committed 6
6 shall make atonement for him for his sin 6
10 for him for the sin which he has committed 6
11 his offering for the sin which he has committed *
13 atonement for him for the sin 6
15 If any one . . sins unwittingly in any of the holy 2
17 If any one sins, doing any of the things 2
6: 2 If any one sins and commits a breach of faith 2
3 all the things which men do and sin therein 2
4 when one has sinned and become guilty 2
16:16 because of their transgressions, all their sins 6
21 and all their transgressions, all their sins 6
30 from all your sins you shall be clean 6
34 once in the year because of all their sins 6
19:17 your neighbor, lest you bear sin because of him 3
22 atonement . . for his sin which he has committed 6
22 the sin which he has committed shall be forgiven 6
20:20 they shall bear their sin, they shall die 3
22: 9 keep my charge, lest they bear sin for it and die 3
24:15 Whoever curses his God shall bear his sin 3
26:18 will chastise you again sevenfold for your sins 6
21 more plagues . . sevenfold as many as your sins 6
24 I myself will smite you sevenfold for your sins 6
28 chastise you myself sevenfold for your sins 6
Num 5: 6 When a man or woman commits any of the sins 6
7 he shall confess his sin which he has committed; 6
6:11 because he sinned by reason of the dead body. 2
9:13 shall be cut off . . that man shall bear his sin. 3
12:11 do not punish us because we have . . sinned. 2
14:40 we will go up . . for we have sinned. 2
15:27 If one person sins unwittingly, he shall offer 2
28 when he sins unwittingly, to make atonement 3
16:22 shall one man sin, and wilt thou be angry with all 2
26 lest you be swept away with all their sins. 6
18:22 lest they bear sin and die. 3
32 you shall bear no sin by reason of it 3
19: 9 for the water for impurity, for the removal of sin. 6
21: 7 We have sinned, for we have spoken against 2
22:34 I have sinned, for I did not know that thou 2
27: 3 Our father died . . but died for his own sin; 3
32:23 behold, you have sinned against the LORD; 2
23 and be sure your sin will find you out 6
Deu 1:41 'We have sinned against the LORD; we will go up 2
9:16 behold, you had sinned against the LORD your God; 2
18 because of all the sin which you had committed 6
27 do not regard . . their wickedness, or their sin 6
15: 9 cry to the LORD against you, and it be sin in you. 3
20:18 so to sin against the LORD your God. 2
23:21 it would be sin in you. 3
22 if you refrain from vowing, it . . no sin in you. 3
24:15 lest he cry against you to the LORD, and it be sin 3
16 every man shall be put to death for his own sin. 3
Jos 7:11 Israel has sinned; they have transgressed 2
20 I have sinned against the LORD God of Israel 2
22:17 Have we not had enough of the sin at Pe'or 8
24:19 not forgive your transgressions or your sins. 6
Jdg 10:10 cried to the LORD . . We have sinned against thee 2
15 We have sinned; do to us whatever seems good 2
11:27 I therefore have not sinned against you 2
1Sm 2:17 Thus the sin of the young men was very great 6
25 If a man sins against a man, God will mediate 2
25 if a man sins against the LORD, who can intercede 2
7: 6 and said there, "We have sinned against the LORD. 2
12:10 We have sinned, because we have forsaken the LORD 2
19 we have added to all our sins this evil 6
23 far be it . . that I should sin against the LORD 2
14:33 the people are sinning against the LORD 2
34 sin against the LORD by eating with the blood.' 2
38 and know and see how this sin has arisen today. 6
15:23 For rebellion is as the sin of divination 6
24 I have sinned . . transgressed the commandment 2
25 Now therefore, I pray, pardon my sin, and return 6
30 I have sinned; yet honor me now before the elders 2
19: 4 Let not the king sin against his servant David; 2
4 because he has not sinned against you 2
5 why then will you sin against innocent blood 2
20: 1 what is my sin before your father, that he seeks my 6
24:11 I have not sinned against you 2
2Sm 12:13 David said . . "I have sinned against the LORD. 2
13 LORD also has put away your sin; you shall not die. 6
19:20 For your servant knows that I have sinned; 2
24:10 I have sinned greatly in what I have done. 2
17 Lo, I have sinned, and I have done wickedly; 2
1Kg 8:31 If a man sins against his neighbor and is 2
33 the enemy because they have sinned against thee 2
34 hear . . and forgive the sin of thy people Israel 6
35 no rain because they have sinned against thee 2
35 acknowledge thy name, and turn from their sin 6
36 hear . . and forgive the sin of thy servants 6
46 If they sin against thee . . and thou art angry 2
46 for there is no man who does not sin 2
47 'We have sinned, and have acted perversely 2
50 forgive thy people who have sinned against thee 2
12:30 this thing became a sin, for the people went 6
13:34 this thing became sin to the house of Jerobo'am 6
14:16 give Israel up because of the sins of Jerobo'am 6
16 the sins of Jerobo'am, which he sinned 2
22 they provoked him to jealousy with their sins 6
15: 3 he walked in all the sins which his father did 6
26 and in his sin which he made Israel to sin. 6
30 it was for the sins of Jerobo'am which he sinned 6
30 the sins of Jerobo'am which he sinned and which he 2
34 and walked in the way of Jerobo'am and in his sin 6
16: 2 to sin, provoking me to anger with their sins 6
13 for all the sins of Ba'asha and the sins of Elah 6
13 the sins of Ba'asha and the sins of Elah his son 6
13 sins of Ba'asha and . . his son which they sinned 2
19 his sins which he committed, doing evil 6
19 his sin which he committed, making Israel to sin. 6
26 walked . . in the sins which he made Israel to sin 6
31 to walk in the sins of Jerobo'am the son of Nebat 6
17:18 You have come to me to bring my sin to remembrance 8
18: 9 he said, "Wherein have I sinned 2
2Kg 3: 3 he clung to the sin of Jerobo'am the son of Nebat 6
10:29 Jehu did not turn aside from the sins of Jerobo'am 6
31 he did not turn from the sins of Jerobo'am 6
13: 2 and followed the sins of Jerobo'am 6
6 depart from the sins of the house of Jerobo'am 6
11 he did not depart from all the sins of Jerobo'am 6
14: 6 but every man shall die for his own sin. 3
24 he did not depart from all the sins of Jerobo'am 6
15: 9 He did not depart from the sins of Jerobo'am 6
18 did not depart . . from all the sins of Jerobo'am 6
24 he did not turn away from the sins of Jerobo'am 6
28 he did not depart from the sins of Jerobo'am 6
17: 7 the people of Israel had sinned against the LORD 2
21 Jerobo'am . . and made them commit great sin. 4
22 Israel walked in all the sins which Jerobo'am did; 6
21:16 the sin which he made Judah to sin so that they did 6
17 and all that he did, and the sin that he committed 6
24: 3 to remove them . . for the sins of Manas'seh 6
1Ch 21: 8 I have sinned greatly in that I have done this 2
17 It is I who have sinned and done very wickedly. 2
2Ch 6:22 If a man sins . . and is made to take an oath 2
24 are defeated . . because they have sinned 2
25 hear . . and forgive the sin of thy people Israel 6
26 no rain because they have sinned against thee 2
26 and acknowledge thy name, and turn from their sin 6
27 then hear . . and forgive the sin of thy servants 6
36 If they sin against thee . . and thou art angry 2
36 If they sin . . –for there is no man who does not sin– 2
37 'We have sinned, and have acted perversely 2
39 forgive thy people who have sinned against 2
7:14 hear from heaven, and will forgive their sin 6
25: 4 but every man shall die for his own sin. 3
28:10 Have you not sins of your own against the LORD 1
13 in addition to our present sins and guilt. 6
33:19 all his sin and his faithlessness, and the sites 6
Neh 1: 6 confessing the sins of the people of Israel 6
6 confessing the sins . . we have sinned against thee. 2
6 Yea, I and my father's house have sinned. 2
4: 5 let not their sin be blotted out from thy sight; 6
6:13 that I should be afraid and act in this way and sin 2
9: 2 confessed their sins and the iniquities 6
29 not obey . . but sinned against thy ordinances 2
37 yield goes to the kings . . because of our sins; 6
13:26 Did not Solomon . . sin on account of such women? 2
Job 1: 5 for Job said, "It may be that my sons have sinned 2
22 Job did not sin or charge God with wrong. 2
2:10 In all this Job did not sin with his lips. 2
7:20 If I sin, what do I do to thee, thou watcher of men? 2
8: 4 If your children have sinned against him 2
10: 6 seek out my iniquity and search for my sin 6
14 If I sin, thou dost mark me 2
13:23 How many are my iniquities and my sins? 6
23 Make me know my transgression and my sin. 6
14:16 thou wouldest not keep watch over my sin; 6
24:19 does Sheol those who have sinned. 2
31:30 I have not let my mouth sin by asking for his life 2
33:27 I sinned, and perverted what was right 2
34:37 For he adds rebellion to his sin; 6
35: 3 How am I better off than if I had sinned? 6
6 If you have sinned, what do you accomplish 2
Ps 4: 4 Be angry, but sin not; commune with your own hearts 2
25: 7 Remember not the sins of my youth 6
18 Consider . . my trouble, and forgive all my sins. 6
32: 1 Blessed is he . . whose sin is covered. 4
3 When I declared not my sin, my body wasted away *
5 I acknowledged my sin to thee, and I did not hide 6
5 then thou didst forgive the guilt of my sin. 6
38: 3 there is no health in my bones because of my sin. 6
18 I confess my iniquity, I am sorry for my sin. 6
39: 1 guard my ways, that I may not sin with my tongue; 2
11 When thou dost chasten man with rebukes for sin 8
41: 4 heal me, for I have sinned against thee! 2
51: 2 from my iniquity, and cleanse me from my sin! 6
3 my transgressions, and my sin is ever before me. 6
4 Against thee, thee only, have I sinned 2
5 in iniquity, and in sin did my mother conceive me. 3
9 Hide thy face from my sins 3
59: 3 For no transgression or sin of mine, O LORD 6
12 the sin of their mouths, the words of their lips 6
65: 3 on account of sins. 8
78:17 Yet they sinned still more against him 2
32 In spite of all this they still sinned; 2
79: 9 deliver us, and forgive our sins, for thy name's sake! 6
85: 2 thou didst pardon all their sin. Selah 6
90: 8 our secret sins in the light of thy countenance. *
103:10 He does not deal with us according to our sins 3
106: 6 Both we and our fathers have sinned; 2
109: 7 tried, let . . his prayer be counted as sin! 4
14 let not the sin of his mother be blotted out! 6
119:11 in my heart, that I might not sin against thee. 2
Prv 5:22 he is caught in the coils of his sin. 6
10:16 leads to life, the gain of the wicked to sin. 6
13: 6 but sin overthrows the wicked. 6
14:34 but sin is a reproach to any people. 6
16:10 his mouth does not sin in judgment. 7
20: 9 Who can say, "I . . am pure from my sin"? 6
21: 4 heart, the lamp of the wicked, are sin. 6
24: 9 The devising of folly is sin 6
Ecc 7:20 not a . . man on earth who does good and never sins. 2
Isa 1:18 though your sins are like scarlet 6
3: 9 they proclaim their sin like Sodom 6
5:18 draw iniquity . . who draw sin as with cart ropes 5
6: 7 your guilt is taken away, and your sin forgiven. 6
27: 9 the full fruit of the removal of his sin 6
30: 1 but not of my spirit, that they may add sin to sin; 6
1 but not of my spirit, that they may add sin to sin; 6
38:17 for thou hast cast all my sins behind thy back. 3
40: 2 from the LORD'S hand double for all her sins. 6
42:24 Was it not the LORD, against whom we have sinned 2
43:24 But you have burdened me with your sins 6
25 and I will not remember your sins. 6
27 Your first father sinned 2
44:22 like a cloud, and your sins like mist; 6
53:12 yet he bore the sin of many, and made intercession 3
58: 1 declare . . to the house of Jacob their sins. 6
59: 2 your sins have hid his face from you 6
12 and our sins testify against us; 6
64: 5 Behold, thou wast angry, and we sinned; 2
5 in our sins we have been a long time, *
Jer 2:35 you to judgment for saying, 'I have not sinned.' 2
3:25 for we have sinned against the LORD our God 2
5:25 and your sins have kept good from you. 6
8:14 because we have sinned against the LORD. 2

14: 7 we have sinned against thee. 2
10 remember their iniquity and punish their sins. 6
20 for we have sinned against thee. 2
15:13 for all your sins, throughout all your territory. 6
16:10 What is the sin that we have committed 6
18 recompense their iniquity and their sin 6
17: 1 The sin of Judah is written with a pen of iron; 6
3 give for spoil as the price of your sin 6
18:23 nor blot out their sin from thy sight. 6
30:14 guilt is great, because your sins are flagrant. 6
15 guilt is great, because your sins are flagrant 6
31:30 But every one shall die for his own sin; 8
34 and I will remember their sin no more. 6
33: 8 from all the guilt of their sin against me 2
8 the guilt of their sin and rebellion against me. 2
36: 3 that I may forgive their iniquity and their sin. 6
40: 3 you sinned against the LORD, and did not obey 2
44:23 and because you sinned against the LORD 2
50: 7 for they have sinned against the LORD 2
14 for she has sinned against the LORD. 2
20 and sin in Judah, and none shall be found; 6
Lam 1: 8 Jerusalem sinned grievously 2
3:39 man complain . . about the punishment of his sins? 3
4:13 This was for the sins of her prophets 6
22 he will punish, he will uncover your sins. 6
5: 7 Our fathers sinned, and are no more; 2
16 crown has fallen . . woe to us, for we have sinned! 2
Ezk 3:20 he shall die for his sin 6
21 if you warn the righteous man not to sin 2
21 and he does not sin, he shall surely live 2
14:13 a land sins against me by acting faithlessly 2
16:51 Sama'ria has not committed half your sins; 6
52 your sins in which you acted more abominably 6
18: 4 the soul that sins shall die. 2
14 son who sees all the sins which his father has 6
20 The soul that sins shall die. 2
21 But if a wicked man turns away from all his sins 6
24 for . . the sin he has committed, he shall die. 6
21:24 so that in all your doings your sins appear 6
28:16 you were filled with violence, and you sinned; 2
33:10 Our transgressions and our sins are upon us 6
12 to live by his righteousness when he sins. 2
14 if he turns from his sin and does what is lawful 6
16 None of the sins that he has committed 6
37:23 all the backslidings in which they have sinned 2
Dan 4:27 off your sins by practicing righteousness 9
9: 5 sinned and done wrong and acted wickedly 2
8 because we have sinned against thee. 2
11 because we have sinned against him. 2
15 we have sinned, we have done wickedly. 2
16 because for our sins, and for the iniquities 3
20 confessing my sin and the sin of my people Israel 6
20 confessing my sin and the sin of my people Israel 6
24 finish the transgression, to put an end to sin 6
Hos 4: 7 The more they increased, the more they sinned 2
8 They feed on the sin of my people; 6
8:11 E'phraim has multiplied altars for sinning 2
11 they have become to him altars for sinning. 2
13 remember their iniquity, and punish their sins; 6
9: 9 he will punish their sins. 6
10: 8 The high places of Aven, the sin of Israel 6
9 From the days of Gib'e-ah, you have sinned, O Israel; 2
13: 2 And now they sin more and more 2
12 his sin is kept in store. 6
Ams 5:12 your transgressions, and how great are your sins 6
Mic 1: 5 this is . . for the sins of the house of Israel. 6
5 And what is the sin of the house of Judah? 12
13 were the beginning of sin to the daughter of Zion 6
3: 8 to declare . . to Israel his sin. 6
6: 7 give . . the fruit of my body for the sin of my soul? 6
13 making you desolate because of your sins. 6
7: 9 of the LORD because I have sinned against him 2
19 wilt cast all our sins into the depths of the sea. 6
Zep 1:17 because they have sinned against the LORD; 2
Zec 13: 1 to cleanse them from sin and uncleanness. 6
Mat 1:21 he will save his people from their sins. 12
3: 6 in the river Jordan, confessing their sins. 12
9: 2 Take heart, my son; your sins are forgiven. 12
5 For which is easier, to say, 'Your sins are forgiven,' 12
6 man has authority on earth to forgive sins 12
12:31 every sin and blasphemy will be forgiven men 12
18: 7 Woe to the world for temptations to sin! •
15 If your brother sins against you, go and tell him 10
21 Lord, how often shall my brother sin against me 10
26:28 for many for the forgiveness of sins. 12
27: 4 I have sinned in betraying innocent blood. 10
Mrk 1: 4 repentance for the forgiveness of sins. 12
5 confessing their sins. 12
2: 5 My son, your sins are forgiven. 12
7 Who can forgive sins but God alone? 12
9 'Your sins are forgiven,' 12
10 Son of man has authority on earth to forgive sins"- 12
3:28 Truly, I say to you, all sins will be forgiven 11
29 guilty of an eternal sin"- 11
Lke 1:77 in the forgiveness of their sins 12
3: 3 repentance for the forgiveness of sins. 12
5:20 Man, your sins are forgiven you. 12
21 Who can forgive sins but God only? 12
23 Which is easier, to say, 'Your sins are forgiven you,' 12
24 authority on earth to forgive sins 12
7:47 I tell you, her sins, which are many, are forgiven 12
48 he said to her, "Your sins are forgiven. 12
49 Who is this, who even forgives sins? 12
11: 4 forgive us our sins 12
15:18 I have sinned against heaven and before you; 10
21 I have sinned against heaven and before you 10
17: 3 if your brother sins, rebuke him 10
4 if he sins against you seven times in the day 10
24:47 repentance and forgiveness of sins 12
Joh 1:29 who takes away the sin of the world! 12
5:14 Sin no more, that nothing worse befall you. 10
8:11 go, and do not sin again. 10
21 you will seek me and die in your sin 12
24 I told you that you would die in your sins 12
24 for you will die in your sins 12
34 every one who commits sin is a slave to sin. 12
34 every one who commits sin is a slave to sin. 12
46 Which of you convicts me of sin? 12
9: 2 his disciples asked him, "Rabbi, who sinned 10
3 It was not that this man sinned, or his parents 10
34 You were born in utter sin, and would you teach us? 12
15:22 they would not have sin 12
22 now they have no excuse for their sin. 12
24 they would not have sin 12
16: 8 concerning sin and righteousness and judgment 12
9 concerning sin, because they do not believe in me; 12
19:11 who delivered me to you has the greater sin. 12
20:23 if you retain the sins of any, they are retained. •
23 If you forgive the sins of any, they are forgiven; 12
Act 2:38 for the forgiveness of your sins 12
3:19 that your sins may be blotted out 12
5:31 repentance to Israel and forgiveness of sins. 12
7:60 Lord, do not hold this sin against them. 12
10:43 receives forgiveness of sins through his name. 12
13:38 forgiveness of sins is proclaimed to you 12
22:16 and wash away your sins, calling on his name.' 12
26:18 they may receive forgiveness of sins 12
Rom 2:12 All who have sinned without the law 10
12 and all who have sinned under the law 10
3: 9 both Jews and Greeks, are under the power of sin 12
20 since through the law comes knowledge of sin. 12
23 since all have sinned and fall short of the glory 10
25 because . . he had passed over former sins; 11
4: 7 those . . whose sins are covered; 12
8 the man . . whom the Lord will not reckon his sin. 12
5:12 as sin came into the world through one man 12
12 sin came into the world . . death through sin 12
12 death spread to all men because all men sinned- 10
13 sin indeed was in the world before the law 12
13 but sin is not counted where there is no law. 12
14 sins . . not like the transgression of Adam 10
16 the free gift is not like . . that one man's sin. 10
20 where sin increased, grace abounded all the more 12
21 so that, as sin reigned in death 12
6: 1 Are we to continue in sin that grace may abound? 12
2 How can we who died to sin still live in it? 12
6 and we might no longer be enslaved to sin. 12
7 For he who has died is freed from sin. 12
10 The death he died he died to sin, once for all 12
11 you also must consider yourselves dead to sin 12
12 Let not sin . . reign in your mortal bodies 12
13 Do not yield your members to sin 12
14 For sin will have no dominion over you 12
15 Are we to sin because we are not under law 10
16 slaves . . either of sin, which leads to death 12
17 that you who were once slaves of sin 12
18 and, having been set free from sin 12
20 When you were slaves of sin 12
22 But now that you have been set free from sin 12
23 For the wages of sin is death 12
7: 7 What then shall we say? That the law is sin? 12
7 if it had not been . . I should not have known sin. 12
8 But sin, finding opportunity in the commandment 12
8 Apart from the law sin lies dead. 12
9 when the commandment came, sin revived and I died; 12
11 For sin, finding opportunity in the commandment 12
13 sin, working death in me through what is good 12
13 in order that sin might be shown to be sin •
13 in order that sin might be shown to be sin 12
14 but I am carnal, sold under sin. 12
17 no longer I . . but sin which dwells within me 12
20 no longer I . . but sin which dwells within me. 12
23 to the law of sin which dwells in my members. 12
25 but with my flesh I serve the law of sin. 12
8: 2 has set me free from the law of sin and death. 12
3 Son in the likeness of sinful flesh and for sin 12
3 he condemned sin in the flesh 12
10 although your bodies are dead because of sin 12
11:27 my covenant with them when I take away their sins. 12
14:23 for whatever does not proceed from faith is sin. 12
1Co 6:18 Every other sin which a man commits 11
18 the immoral man sins against his own body. 10
7:28 if you marry, you do not sin 10
28 if a girl marries she does not sin 10
36 let him do as he wishes: let them marry-it is no sin. 10
8:12 Thus, sinning against your brethren 10
12 you sin against Christ. 10
15: 3 Christ died for our sins 12
17 you are still in your sins. 12
34 Come to your right mind, and sin no more 10
56 The sting of death is sin 12
56 the power of sin is the law. 12
2Co 5:21 For our sake he made him to be sin who knew no sin 12
21 For our sake he made him to be sin who knew no sin 12
11: 7 Did I commit a sin in abasing myself 12
Gal 1: 4 who gave himself for our sins 12
2:17 is Christ then an agent of sin? Certainly not! 12
3:22 the scripture consigned all things to sin 12
Eph 2: 1 you were dead through the trespasses and sins 12
4:26 Be angry but do not sin 10
Col 1:14 we have redemption, the forgiveness of sins. 12
1Th 2:16 so as always to fill up the measure of their sins. 12
1Ti 5:22 nor participate in another man's sins 12
24 the sins of others appear later. •
24 The sins of some men are conspicuous 12
2Ti 3: 6 capture weak women, burdened with sins 12
Heb 1: 3 When he had made purification for sins 12
2:17 to make expiation for the sins of the people. 12
3:13 hardened by the deceitfulness of sin. 12
17 who sinned, whose bodies fell in the wilderness 10
4:15 who . . has been tempted as we are, yet without sin. 12
5: 1 to offer gifts and sacrifices for sins. 12
3 he is bound to offer sacrifice for his own sins 12
7:27 to offer sacrifices daily, first for his own sins 12
8:12 I will remember their sins no more. 12
9:22 there is no forgiveness of sins. •
26 to put away sin by the sacrifice of himself. 12
28 Christ . . offered once to bear the sins of many 12
28 will appear a second time, not to deal with sin 12
10: 2 would no longer have any consciousness of sin. 12
3 there is a reminder of sin year after year. 12
4 the blood of . . goats should take away sins. 12
6 in burnt offerings and sin offerings 12
8 burnt offerings and sin offerings 12
11 which can never take away sins. 12
12 offered for all time a single sacrifice for sins 12
17 remember their sins and their misdeeds no more. 12
18 there is no longer any offering for sin. 12
26 For if we sin deliberately 10
26 there no longer remains a sacrifice for sins 12
11:25 to enjoy the fleeting pleasures of sin. 12
12: 1 every weight, and sin which clings so closely 12
4 In your struggle against sin 12
13:11 as a sacrifice for sin 12
Jas 1:15 desire when it has conceived gives birth to sin; 12
15 sin when it is full-grown brings forth death. 12
2: 9 But if you show partiality, you commit sin 12
4:17 Whoever . . fails to do it, for him it is sin. 12
5:15 and if he has committed sins, he will be forgiven. 12
16 Therefore confess your sins to one another 12
20 and will cover a multitude of sins. 12
1Pe 2:22 He committed no sin; 12
24 He himself bore our sins in his body on the tree 12
24 we might die to sin and live to righteousness. 12
3:18 For Christ also died for sins once for all 12
4: 1 whoever has suffered . . has ceased from sin 12
8 since love covers a multitude of sins. 12
2Pe 1: 9 forgotten that he was cleansed from his old sins 12
2: 4 if God did not spare the angels when they sinned 10
14 eyes full of adultery, insatiable for sin. 12
1Jn 1: 7 blood of Jesus his Son cleanses us from all sin. 12
8 If we say we have no sin, we deceive ourselves 12
9 If we confess our sins, he is faithful and just 12
9 he is faithful and just, and will forgive our sins 12
10 If we say we have not sinned, we make him a liar 10
2: 1 I am writing this to you so that you may not sin 10
1 if any one does sin, we have an advocate 10
2 he is the expiation for our sins 12
2 but also for the sins of the whole world. •
12 because your sins are forgiven for his sake. 12
3: 4 Every one who commits sin is guilty 12
4 sin is lawlessness. 12
5 You know that he appeared to take away sins 12
5 and in him there is no sin. 12
6 No one who abides in him sins; 10
6 no one who sins has either seen him or known him. 10
8 He who commits sin is of the devil; 12
8 for the devil has sinned from the beginning. 10
9 No one born of God commits sin; 12
9 and he cannot sin because he is born of God. 10
4:10 sent his Son to be the expiation for our sins. 12
5:16 his brother committing what is not a mortal sin 12
16 give him life for those whose sin is not mortal. 10
16 There is sin which is mortal; 12
17 All wrongdoing is sin 12
17 but there is sin which is not mortal. 12
18 We know that any one born of God does not sin 10
Rev 1: 5 To him who . . freed us from our sins by his blood 12
18: 4 Come out of her . . lest you take part in her sins 12
5 for her sins are heaped high as heaven 12
1Es 1:24 concerning those who sinned and acted wickedly 10
4:27 Many have perished, or stumbled, or sinnec 10
6:15 when our fathers sinned against the Lord 10
7: 8 twelve he-goats for the sin of all Israel 12
8:75 For our sins have risen higher than our heads 12
76 we are in great sin to this day. 12
77 because of our sins and the sins of our fathers 12

77 because of our sins and the sins of our fathers •
86 because of our evil deeds and our great sins 12
86 thou, O Lord, didst lift the burden of our sins 12
92 We have sinned against the Lord 10
9: 7 have increased the sin of Israel. 12
11 we have sinned too much in these things. 10
2Es 1: 6 the sins of their parents have increased in them 16
2: 3 because you have sinned before the Lord God 17
3:30 for I have seen how thou dost endure those who sin 17
35 have the inhabitants of the earth not sinned 17
4:39 on account of the sins of those who dwell on earth. 16
6: 5 before the imaginations of those who now sin 17
7:46 that has not sinned 17
68 full of sins and burdened with transgressions. 16
87 before whom they sinned while they were alive 17
106 and Moses for our fathers who sinned in the desert 17
116 or else . . had restrained him from sinning. 17
118 For though it was you who sinned 17
134 he shows patience toward those who have sinned 17
139 and blot out the multitude of their sins ‡
8:26 O look not upon the sins of thy people 15
38 those who have sinned 17
9:36 who have received the law and sinned will perish 17
15:24 Woe to those who sin 17
27 because you have sinned against him. 17
16:48 the more angry I will be with them for their sins 16
50 who searches out every sin on earth. 16
53 Let no sinner say that he has not sinned 17
53 I have not sinned before God and his glory. 17
63 Woe to those who sin and want to hide their sins! 17
63 Woe to those who sin and want to hide their sins! 16
65 when your sins come out before men 16
66 Or how will you hide your sins before God 16
67 Cease from your sins, and forget your iniquities 16
76 do not let your sins pull you down 16
77 Woe to those who are choked by their sins 16
Tob 3: 3 do not punish me for my sins 12
5 are true in exacting penalty from me for my sins 12
14 I am innocent of any sin with man 12
4: 5 refuse to sin 10
21 fear God and refrain from every sin 12
12: 9 it will purge away every sin 12
Jdt 5:17 As long as they did not sin against their God 10
20 they sin against their God 10
7:28 who punishes us according to our sins 12
28 our sins and the sins of our fathers 12
11:10 unless they sin against their God. 10
11 a sin has overtaken them 11
17 tell me when they have committed their sins. 11
AEs 14: 6 now we have sinned before thee 10
Wis 1: 4 nor dwell in a body enslaved to sin. 12
2:12 he reproaches us for sins against the law 11
12 and accuses us of sins against our training. 11
4:20 come with dread when their sins are reckoned up 11
10:13 delivered him from sin 12
11:16 punished by the very things by which he sins. 10
23 thou dost overlook men's sins 11
12: 2 warn them of the things wherein they sin 10
11 didst leave them unpunished for their sins. 10
19 because thou givest repentance for sins. 11
14:31 the just penalty for those who sin 10
15: 2 For even if we sin we are thine, knowing thy power; 10
2 we will not sin 10
13 he sins when he makes . . fragile vessels 10
17: 3 in their secret sins they were unobserved 11
Sir 2:11 he forgives sins and saves in time of affliction. 12
3: 3 Whoever honors his father atones for sins 12
14 against your sins it will be credited to you; 12
15 as frost in fair weather, your sins will melt away. 12
27 the sinner will heap sin upon sin. 12
27 the sinner will heap sin upon sin. 12
30 so almsgiving atones for sin. 12
4:21 For there is a shame which brings sin 12
26 Do not be ashamed to confess your sins 12
5: 4 Do not say, "I sinned, and what happened to me? 10
5 so confident . . that you add sin to sin. 12
5 so confident . . that you add sin to sin. 12
6 he will forgive the multitude of my sins 12
7: 8 Do not commit a sin twice 12
36 then you will never sin. 10
8: 5 Do not reproach a man who is turning away from sin; 12
10:13 For the beginning of pride is sin 12
29 will justify the man that sins against himself? 10
12:14 becomes involved in his sins. 12
13:24 Riches are good if they are free from sin 12
14: 1 and need not suffer grief for sin. 12
15:20 he has not given any one permission to sin. 10
16: 9 those destroyed in their sins; 12
17:20 all their sins are before the Lord. 12
25 Turn to the Lord and forsake your sins 12
18:21 when you are on the point of sinning, turn back. 11
27 in days of sin he guards against wrongdoing. 12
19: 4 one who sins does wrong to himself. 10
8 unless it would be a sin for you, do not disclose it; 12
16 Who has never sinned with his tongue? 10
28 by lack of strength he is prevented from sinning 10
20:21 may be prevented from sinning by his poverty 10
21: 1 Have you sinned, my son? Do so no more 10
1 Do so no more, but pray about your former sins. •

2 Flee from sin as from a snake 12
2 for if you approach sin, it will bite you •
23: 2 that it may not pass by my sins; 11
3 in order that . . my sins may not abound 12
10 will not be cleansed from sin. 12
11 if he offends, his sin remains on him 12
11 if he disregards it, he sins doubly 10
12 they will not wallow in sins. 12
16 Two sorts of men multiply sins 12
18 The Most High will not take notice of my sins. 12
24:22 those who work with my help will not sin. 10
25:24 From a woman sin had its beginning 12
26:11 do not wonder if she sins against you. 14
28 a man who turns back from righteousness to sin 12
29 a tradesman will not be declared innocent of sin. 12
27: 2 sin is wedged in between selling and buying. 12
10 so does sin for the workers of iniquity. 12
28: 1 he will firmly establish his sins. 12
2 then your sins will be pardoned when you pray. 12
4 yet pray for his own sins? 12
5 who will make expiation for his sins? 12
8 Refrain from strife, and you will lessen sins 12
32:12 do not sin through proud speech. 10
34:19 he is not propitiated for sins 12
26 if a man fasts for his sins 12
38:10 cleanse your heart from all sin. 12
15 He who sins before his Maker 10
39: 5 make supplication for his sins. 12
42: 1 do not let partiality lead you to sin 10
46: 7 restrained the people from sin 12
47:11 The Lord took away his sins, and exalted his power 12
24 Their sins became exceedingly many 12
48:15 they did not forsake their sins 12
16 others multiplied sins. 12
Bar 1:13 for we have sinned against the Lord our God 10
17 because we have sinned before the Lord 10
2: 5 because we sinned against the Lord our God 10
12 we have sinned, we have been ungodly 10
33 their fathers, who sinned before the Lord. 10
3: 2 have mercy, for we have sinned before thee. 10
4 sons of those who sinned before thee, who did not 10
7 iniquity of our fathers who sinned before thee. 10
4:12 left desolate because of the sins of my children 12
LJr 1: 2 Because of the sins which you have committed 12
Aza 1: 5 thou hast brought all this upon us because of our sins. 12
6 and have sinned in all things 13
14 and are brought low . . because of our sins. 12
Sus 1:23 rather than to sin in the sight of the Lord. 10
52 your sins have now come home 12
Man 1: 7 those who have sinned against thee 10
8 Isaac and Jacob, who did not sin against thee 10
10 so that I am rejected because of my sins 12
12 I have sinned, O Lord, I have sinned 10
12 I have sinned, O Lord, I have sinned 10
2Mc 2:11 because the sin offering had not been eaten. 12
5:17 because of the sins of those who dwelt in the city 12
18 they were involved in many sins 11
6:14 they have reached the full measure of their sins; 12
15 when our sins have reached their height. 12
7:18 because of our sins against our own God. 10
32 For we are suffering because of our own sins. 12
10: 4 if they should ever sin 10
12:42 the sin which had been committed 11
42 because of the sin of those who had fallen. 12
43 to provide for a sin offering 12
45 they might be delivered from their sin. 12
13: 8 he had committed many sins against the altar 11
3Mc 2:13 because of our many and great sins 12
19 Wipe away our sins and disperse our errors 12
4Mc 5:19 do not suppose that it would be a petty sin 12
17:21 a ransom for the sin of our nation. 12

sin *See also* act, cause, commit, free, lead, man, offer, offering, persist, purify, temptation.

sin before 1. *προαμαρτάνω*

2Co 12:21 mourn over many of those who sinned before 1
13: 2 I warned those who sinned before 1

cause to sin 1. חטא 2. *ἐξαμαρτάνω* 3. *σκανδαλίζω*

Jer 32:35 this abomination, to cause Judah to sin. 1
Mat 5:29 If your right eye causes you to sin, pluck it out 3
30 And if your right hand causes you to sin, cut it off 3
18: 6 whoever causes one of these little ones . . to sin 3
8 if your hand or your foot causes you to sin 3
9 if your eye causes you to sin, pluck it out 3
Mrk 9:42 causes one of these little ones . . to sin 3
43 if your hand causes you to sin, cut it off 3
45 if your foot causes you to sin, cut it off 3
46 if your eye causes you to sin, pluck it out 3
Lke 17: 2 that he should cause one of these little ones to sin. 3
Sir 47:23 who caused Israel to sin 2

sin greatly 1. *πλημμέλειαν πλημμελέω*

Sir 49: 4 they all sinned greatly 1

make sin 1. חטא

Exd 23:33 lest they make you sin against me; 1
1Kg 14:16 sins of Jerobo'am . . which he made Israel to sin. 1
15:26 and in his sin which he made Israel to sin. 1
30 sins . . he sinned and which he made Israel to sin 1
34 and in his sin which he made Israel to sin. 1
16: 2 and have made my people Israel to sin 1
13 they sinned, and which they made Israel to sin 1
19 his sin which he committed, making Israel to sin. 1
26 walked . . in the sins which he made Israel to sin 1
21:22 I will . . and because you have made Israel to sin. 1
22:52 Jerobo'am the son of Nebat, who made Israel to sin. 1
2Kg 3: 3 the sin of Jerobo'am . . which he made Israel to sin; 1
10:29 the sins . . which he made Israel to sin 1
31 the sins of Jerobo'am, which he made Israel to sin. 1
13: 2 the sins of . . which he made Israel to sin; 1
6 sins . . of Jerobo'am, which he made Israel to sin 1
11 sins of Jerobo'am . . which he made Israel to sin 1
14:24 sins of Jerobo'am . . which he made Israel to sin. 1
15: 9 sins of Jerobo'am . . which he made Israel to sin. 1
18 sins of Jerobo'am . . which he made Israel to sin. 1
24 sins of Jerobo'am . . which he made Israel to sin. 1
28 sins of Jerobo'am . . which he made Israel to sin. 1
21:11 Manas'seh . . has made Judah also to sin 1
16 besides the sin which he made Judah to sin 1
23:15 Jerobo'am the son of Nebat, who made Israel to sin 1
Neh 13:26 nevertheless foreign women made even him to sin. 1

presumptuous sin 1. זֵד

Ps 19:13 Keep . . thy servant also from presumptuous sins; 1

sin through error 1. שׁגה

Ezk 45:20 for any one who has sinned through error 1

without sin 1. *ἀναμάρτητος*

Joh 8: 7 Let him who is without sin among you be the first 1

since 1. אַחֲרֵי 2. אַחֲרֵי אֲשֶׁר 3. אִם 4. בְּ 5. וְ 6. יַעַן אֲשֶׁר 7. כַּאֲשֶׁר 8. כִּי 9. כִּי עַל כֵּן 10. לְמִן 11. מֵאָז 12. מֵאֲשֶׁר 13. מִיּוֹם 14. מִן 15. מִן אָז 16. עַד 17. עַד הֵנָּה 18. עוֹד 19. תַּחַת אֲשֶׁר 20. *ἀπό* 21. *ἀφ' ἧς* 22. *ἀφ' οὗ* 23. *γάρ* 24. *δή* 25. *διά* 26. *διότι* 27. *εἰ* 28. *ἐπεί* 29. *ἐπειδή* 30. *καθότι* 31. *καθώς* 32. *κατά* 33. *ὅπου* 34. *ὅπου γε* 35. *ὅστις* 36. *ὅτε* 37. *ὅτι* 38. *οὖν* 39. *ὡς* 40. cum 41. quasi 42. quoniam

Gen 18: 5 pass on–since you have come to your servant. 9
24:56 since the LORD has prospered my way; let me go 5
41:39 Pharaoh said to Joseph, "Since God has shown you 1
44:28 torn to pieces; and I have never seen him since. 17
46:30 Now let me die, since I have seen your face 1
Exd 4:10 or since thou hast spoken to thy servant 14
5:23 For since I came to Pharaoh to speak 14
9:24 never been in . . Egypt since it became a nation. 11
21: 8 no right . . since he has dealt faithlessly 4
29:27 since it is for Aaron and for his sons. 12
Lev 10:17 since it is a thing most holy and has been given 8
22:25 Since there is a blemish in them, 14
24: 9 since it is for him a most holy portion 8
25:27 let him reckon the years since he sold it 14
Num 5:13 no witness . . since she was not taken in the act; 5
19:20 since he has defiled the sanctuary of the LORD 14
22: 6 curse this people . . since they are too mighty 8
Deu 4:15 Since you saw no form on the day that the LORD 8
32 since the day that God created man 14
11: 2 (since I am not speaking to your children who 8
12:12 since he has no portion or inheritance with you. 8
15:16 since he fares well with you 8
17:16 since the LORD has said to you, 'You shall never 5
19: 6 since he was not at enmity with his neighbor 8
21:14 since you have humiliated her. 19
34:10 not arisen a prophet since in Israel like Moses 18
Jos 10:14 There has been no day like it before or since 1
14:10 45 years since the time that the LORD spoke 14
15:19 since you have . . give me also springs of water. 8
17:14 I am . . since hitherto the LORD has blessed me? 16
15 go up . . since the hill country of E'phraim is too 8
21:10 the Levites; since the lot fell to them first. 14
23:10 since it is the LORD your God who fights for you 8
Jdg 1:15 Give me a present; since you have set me in the land 8
21:16 What shall we do . . since the women are destroyed 8
Rut 2:11 you have done . . since the death of your husband 1
1Sm 9:13 till he comes, since he must bless the sacrifice; 8
28:16 since the LORD has turned from you 14
29: 3 and since he deserted to me I have found no fault 13
2Sm 7: 6 since the day I brought up the people of Israel 10
19:30 let him take it all, since my lord the king has come 2
1Kg 8:16 Since the day that I brought my people 14
11:11 Since this has been your mind . . I will surely 6
16: 2 Since I exalted you out of the dust 6
2Kg 8:19 LORD would not . . since he promised to give a lamp 7
21:15 since the day their fathers came out of Egypt 14
23:22 since the days of the judges who judged Israel 14
1Ch 17: 5 not dwelt in a house since the day I led up Israel 14
24: 4 Since more chief men were found among the sons 5
2Ch 2: 6 since heaven . . cannot contain him? 8
6: 5 Since the day that I brought my people out 14
21: 7 since he had promised to give a lamp to him 7
30:26 for since the time of Solomon the son of David 14
31:10 Since they began to bring the contributions 14
35:18 in Israel since the days of Samuel the prophet 14
Ezr 8:22 I was ashamed to ask . . since we had told the king 8

Neh 9:32 since the time of the kings of Assyria 14
Est 1:17 since they will say, "King Ahasu-e'rus 4
2:12 after being . . since this was the regular period 8
Job 14: 5 Since his days are determined 3
17: 4 Since thou has closed their minds 8
20: 4 from of old, since man was placed upon earth 14
38:12 commanded the morning since your days began 14
Ps 22:10 from my birth, and since my mother bore me 14
45:11 Since he is your lord, bow to him; 8
Ecc 9: 2 since one fate comes to all, to the righteous 7
Isa 7:17 since the day that E'phraim departed from Judah 14
14: 8 Since you were laid low, no hewer comes up 14
Jer 14: 4 since there is no rain on the land 8
44:18 But since we left off burning incense 15
Ezk 23: 8 which she had practiced since her days in Egypt 14
34: 8 wild beasts, since there was no shepherd; 14
Dan 12: 1 such as never has been since there was a nation 14
Hag 2:18 Since the day that the foundation 14
Zec 8: 9 since the day that the foundation of the house 4
13: 5 the land has been my possession since my youth. 14
Mat 13: 5 since they had no depth of soil 25
6 since they had no root they withered away. 25
35 hidden since the foundation of the world. 20
27: 6 since they are blood money. 28
Mrk 4: 5 since it had no depth of soil; 25
6 since it had no root it withered away. 25
7:19 since it enters, not his heart but his stomach 37
15:42 since it was the day of Preparation 28
Lke 1:34 How shall this be, since I have no husband? 28
16: 3 since my master is taking the stewardship away 37
16 since then the good news . . is preached 20
19: 9 since he also is a son of Abraham. 30
23:40 since you are under the same sentence 37
24:21 it is now the third day since this happened. 22
Joh 8:22 since he says, 'Where I am going, you cannot come'? 37
9:17 since he has opened your eyes 37
32 Never since the world began has it been heard •
17: 2 since thou hast given him power over all flesh 31
19:31 Since it was the day of Preparation 28
Act 2:15 since it is only the third hour of the day; 23
9:38 Since Lydda was near Joppa •
13:46 Since you thrust it from you 29
15:24 Since we have heard 29
17:25 since he himself gives to all men life and breath •
18:15 since it is a matter of questions about words 27
24: 2 Since through you we enjoy much peace •
2 since . . reforms are introduced •
11 since I went up to worship at Jerusalem; 21
27:34 since not a hair is to perish from the head of any 23
28:20 since it is because of the hope of Israel 23
Rom 1:28 since they did not see fit to acknowledge God 31
3:20 since through the law comes knowledge of sin. 23
23 since all have sinned and fall short of the glory 23
30 since God is one; and he will justify 27
5: 1 since we are justified by faith, we have peace •
9 Since . . we are now justified by his blood •
6:14 since you are not under law but under grace. 23
14: 6 in honor of the Lord, since he gives thanks to God; 23
15:23 But now, since I no longer have any room for work •
23 since I have longed for many years to come to you •
1Co 1:21 since, in the wisdom of God, the world did not know 29
5:10 since then you would need to go out of the world. 28
11: 7 since he is the image and glory of God •
14:12 since you are eager 28
2Co 3:12 Since we have such a hope, we are very bold 38
4:13 Since we have the same spirit of faith •
7: 1 Since we have these promises, beloved 38
9: 2 Acha'ia has been ready since last year 20
11:18 since many boast of worldly things 28
13: 3 since you desire proof that Christ is speaking 28
1Th 2:17 since we were bereft of you, brethren •
4:14 since we believe that Jesus died and rose again 27
5: 8 But, since we belong to the day, let us be sober •
1Ti 6: 2 since those who benefit . . are believers 37
Tit 1:11 since they are upsetting whole families 35
Heb 2:14 Since . . the children share in flesh and blood 28
4: 6 Since therefore it remains for some to enter it 28
14 Since then we have a great high priest •
5: 2 since he himself is beset with weakness. 28
11 since you have become dull of hearing. 28
6: 6 since they crucify the Son of God •
13 since he had no one greater by whom to swear 28
7:25 since he always lives to make intercession •
8: 4 since there are priests who offer gifts •
6 since it is enacted on better promises. 35
9:15 since a death has occurred which redeems them •
17 since it is not in force as long as . . 28
26 since the foundation of the world 20
10: 1 since the law has but a shadow of the good things •
19 Therefore, brethren, since we have confidence •
21 since we have a great priest over the house of God •
34 since you knew •
11:11 since she considered him faithful 28
40 since God had foreseen something better for us •
12: 1 since we are surrounded by . . witnesses •
13: 3 since you also are in the body. 39
1Pe 1:16 since it is written, "You shall be holy, for I am 26
3: 7 since you are joint heirs of the grace of life 39
4: 1 Since therefore Christ suffered in the flesh •
8 since love covers a multitude of sins. 37
2Pe 1:14 since I know that the putting off . . will be soon 37
3:11 Since all these things are thus to be dissolved •
14 since you wait for these, be zealous •
Rev 16:18 such as had never been since men were on the earth 22
18: 7 Since in her heart she says, 'A queen I sit 37
11 since no one buys their cargo any more 37
1Es 1:20 since the times of Samuel the prophet; 20
2:20 since the building of the temple is now going on 28
3:24 since it forces men to do these things 37
4:12 since he is to be obeyed in this fashion? 37
32 are not women strong, since they do such things? 37
2Es 5:50 Since thou hast now given me the opportunity 40
7:104 Since you have found favor in my sight 42
134 since they are his own works; 41
Jdt 4: 5 since their fields had recently been harvested. 37
7 since by them Judea could be invaded 37
8:31 pray for us, since you are a devout woman 37
11: 3 since you have come to safety. 23
12 Since their food supply is exhausted 28
12:18 in all the days since I was born. •
20 in any one day since he was born. 22
AEs 14:18 since the day that I was brought here until now 20
Wis 12: 8 since they were but men 39
14:17 since they lived at a distance 25
15:17 since he has life, but they never have. •
18:12 since . . children had been destroyed. 28
Sir 0: 1 since it is necessary not only that the readers 39
17:30 since a son of man is not immortal. 37
37:21 since he is lacking in all wisdom. 37
41:12 since it will remain for you longer 23
LJr 1:29 Since you know . . that they are not gods 38
50 Since they are made of wood •
65 Since you know then that they are not gods •
1Mc 1:11 since we separated from them 37
6:49 since it was a sabbatical year for the land. 37
9:27 since the time that prophets ceased to appear 20
29 Since the death of your brother Judas 22
10:26 Since you have kept your agreement with us 28
52 Since I have returned to my kingdom 28
11: 2 since he was Alexander's father-in-law. 25
12: 9 since we have as encouragement the holy books •
10 since you sent your letter to us. 22
14:29 Since wars often occurred in the country 28
2Mc 1:18 Since . . we shall celebrate the purification •
2:16 Since . . we are about to celebrate •
3:33 since . . the Lord has granted you your life. 23
4:40 since the crowds were becoming aroused •
7:23 since you now forget yourselves 39
25 Since the young man would not listen to him at all •
11:25 Accordingly, since we choose that . . •
14: 9 Since you are acquainted, O king, with the details •
29 Since it was not possible to oppose the king 28
3Mc 1: 8 Since the Jews had sent some of their council •
2:22 since he was smitten by a righteous judgment. •
31 since they expected to enhance . . •
3: 5 since they adorned their style of life •
20 since we treat all nations with benevolence. •
22 Since they incline constantly to evil •
5:13 since they had escaped the appointed hour •
14 since it was nearly the middle of the tenth hour •
25 at their last gasp, since the time had run out 32
27 since he had been completely overcome •
35 since this also was his aid •
6:29 since they now had escaped death. •
7: 6 Since we have come to realize •
7 since we have taken into account •
15 since they had destroyed the profaners. •
20 since . . they had been brought safely by land •
4Mc 1:19 since by means of it reason rules 24
2: 6 In fact, since the law has told us not to covet 36
5:25 since we believe that the law was established •
7:19 since they believe •
8:17 Since the king has summoned and exhorted us •
10: 7 Since they were not able in any way •
11:15 Since to this end we were born and bred 23
25 Since you have not been able to persuade us 23
12:11 since you have received good things •
13: 1 Since, then, the 7 brothers despised sufferings 27
24 Since they had been educated by the same law 23
14:11 since the mind of woman despised . . agonies 33
19 since even bees . . defend themselves 34
18: 5 Since in no way whatever was he able 39

since *See also* ever.

since indeed 1. εἰ
2Th 1: 6 since indeed God deems it just 1

since one's aim 1. ἵνα
2Ti 2: 4 since his aim is to satisfy 1

sincere 1. ἀκέραιος 2. ἀνυπόκριτος 3. ἁπλότης 4. γνήσιος 5. δίκαιος 6. εἰλικρινής
Lke 20:20 sent spies, who pretended to be sincere 5
2Co 11: 3 from a sincere and pure devotion to Christ. 3
1Ti 1: 5 a good conscience and sincere faith. 2
2Ti 1: 5 I am reminded of your sincere faith 2
1Pe 1:22 your obedience to the truth for a sincere love 2
2Pe 3: 1 aroused your sincere mind by way of reminder; 6
AEs 16: 6 the sincere good will of their sovereigns. 1
3Mc 3:19 and are unwilling to regard any action as sincere. 4

most sincere 1. ἀληθής
Wis 6:17 the most sincere desire for instruction 1

sincerely 1. ברר 2. ἁγνός 3. γνήσιος 4. animus
Job 33: 3 what my lips know they speak sincerely. 1
Php 1:17 not sincerely but thinking to afflict me 2
2Es 10:50 seeing that you are sincerely grieved 4
3Mc 3:23 who are sincerely disposed toward us 3

sincerity 1. תָּמִים 2. ἀλήθεια 3. ἁπλότης 4. εἰλικρίνεια
Jos 24:14 and serve him in sincerity and in faithfulness; 1
1Co 5: 8 the unleavened bread of sincerity and truth. 4
2Co 1:12 with holiness and godly sincerity 4
2:17 as men of sincerity, as commissioned by God 4
Tob 8: 7 not . . because of lust, but with sincerity 2
Wis 1: 1 seek him with sincerity of heart; 3

sinew 1. גִּיד 2. νεῦρον 3. τένων
Gen 32:32 the Israelites do not eat the sinew of the hip 1
32 hollow of Jacob's thigh on the sinew of the hip. 1
Job 10:11 and knit me together with bones and sinews. 1
40:17 the sinews of his thighs are knit together. 1
Isa 48: 4 are obstinate, and your neck is an iron sinew 1
Ezk 37: 6 I will lay sinews upon you 1
8 as I looked, there were sinews on them, and flesh 1
4Mc 7:13 his muscles flabby, his sinews feeble 2
9:28 These leopard-like beasts tore out his sinews 3

sinful 1. חטא 2. חֵטְא 3. חַטָּא 4. פֶּשַׁע 5. ἁμαρτάνω 6. ἁμαρτία 7. ἁμαρτωλός 8. παράπτωμα
Num32:14 risen in your fathers' stead, a brood of sinful men 3
Ps 107:17 Some were sick through their sinful ways 4
Isa 1: 4 Ah, sinful nation, a people laden with iniquity 1
Ezk 23:49 shall bear the penalty for your sinful idolatry; 2
Ams 9: 8 eyes of the Lord GOD are upon the sinful kingdom 3
Mrk 8:38 in this adulterous and sinful generation 7
Lke 5: 8 Depart from me, for I am a sinful man, O Lord. 7
24: 7 must be delivered into the hands of sinful men 7
Rom 6: 6 so that the sinful body might be destroyed 6
7: 5 our sinful passions, aroused by the law 6
13 through the commandment might become sinful 7
8: 3 his own Son in the likeness of sinful flesh 6
Tit 3:11 such a person is perverted and sinful 5
Wis 3:13 who has not entered into a sinful union 8
Sir 10:23 nor is it proper to honor a sinful man. 7
15: 7 sinful men will not see her. 7
12 for he had no need of a sinful man. 7
23:13 it involves sinful speech. 6
27:13 their laughter is wantonly sinful. 6
30 the sinful man will possess them. 7
28: 9 a sinful man will disturb friends 7
32:17 A sinful man will shun reproof 7
47:23 gave Ephraim a sinful way. 6
1Mc 1:10 From them came forth a sinful root 7
34 stationed there a sinful people, lawless men. 7

sinful *See also* indulgence.

sinful thing 1. חַטָּאת
Deu 9:21 Then I took the sinful thing, the calf 1

sinfully 1. חֵטְא 2. ἁμαρτάνω
Isa 31: 7 idols . . your hands have sinfully made for you. 1
Aza 1: 6 have sinfully and lawlessly departed from thee 2

sing 1. אמר 2. זָמִיר 3. זמר 4. נגן 5. נשא 6. נתן קוֹל 7. ענה 8. רנה 9. רִנָּה 10. רנן 11. רְנָנָה 12. שיר 13. שִׁיר 14. שמע 15. ἀείδω 16. ἐπιψάλλω 17. λέγω 18. προαναμέλπω 19. ὑμνέω 20. ὑμνητός 21. φωνέω 22. ψάλλω
Exd 15: 1 Moses and the people of Israel sang this song 12
1 I will sing to the LORD, for he has triumphed 12
21 Miriam sang to them: "Sing to the LORD 7
21 Miriam sang to them: "Sing to the LORD 12
32:18 of defeat, but the sound of singing that I hear. 7
Num21:17 Israel sang this song: "Spring up, O well!–Sing to it!– 12
17 this song: "Spring up, O well!–Sing to it!– 7
Jdg 5: 1 Then sang Deb'orah and Barak . . on that day 12
3 to the LORD I will sing, I will make melody 12
1Sm 18: 6 the women came out . . singing and dancing, to meet 13
1Ch 16: 7 thanksgiving be sung to the LORD by Asaph •
9 Sing to him, sing praises to him 12
23 Sing to the Lord, all the earth! 12
25: 7 brethren, who were trained in singing to the LORD 13
2Ch 20:21 he appointed those who were to sing to the LORD 12
22 when they began to sing and praise 9
23:18 with rejoicing and with singing 13
29:28 whole assembly worshiped, and the singers sang 13
30:21 singing with all their might to the LORD. •
Neh 12:27 celebrate . . with singing, with cymbals, harps 13
42 singers sang with Jezrahi'ah as their leader. 14
Job 21:12 They sing to the tambourine and the lyre 5
33:27 he sings before men, and says: 'I sinned 12

36:24 to extol his work, of which men have sung. 12
38: 7 when the morning stars sang together 8
Ps 7: 0 A Shiggaion of David, which he sang to the LORD 12
13: 6 I will sing to the LORD 12
21:13 We will sing and praise thy power. 12
26: 7 singing aloud a song of thanksgiving 14
27: 6 I will sing and make melody to the LORD. 12
33: 3 Sing to him a new song, play skillfully 12
57: 7 my heart is steadfast! I will sing and make melody! 12
59:16 I will sing of thy might; 12
65:13 they shout and sing together for joy. 12
66: 2 sing the glory of his name; 3
68: 4 Sing to God, sing praises to his name; 12
32 Sing to God, O kingdoms of the earth; sing praises 12
89: 1 I will sing of thy steadfast love, O LORD, for ever; 12
95: 1 O come, let us sing to the LORD; 10
96: 1 O sing to the LORD a new song; 12
1 sing to the LORD, all the earth! 12
2 Sing to the LORD, bless his name; 12
98: 1 O sing to the LORD a new song 12
100: 2 Come into his presence with singing! 11
101: 1 sing of loyalty and of justice; to thee, O LORD 12
1 loyalty and of justice; to thee, O LORD, I will sing. 3
104:12 birds of the air . . sing among the branches. 6
33 I will sing to the LORD as long as I live; 12
105: 2 Sing to him, sing praises to him 12
43 led forth his . . chosen ones with singing. 9
106:12 believed his words; they sang his praise. 12
108: 1 I will sing and make melody! Awake, my soul! 12
119:172My tongue will sing of thy word 7
135: 3 sing to his name, for he is gracious! 3
137: 3 saying, "Sing us one of the songs of Zion! 12
4 How shall we sing the LORD'S song in a foreign land? 12
138: 5 they shall sing of the ways of the LORD 12
144: 9 I will sing a new song to thee, O God; 12
147: 7 Sing to the LORD with thanksgiving; make melody 7
149: 1 Sing to the LORD a new song, his praise 12
Prv 25:20 He who sings songs to a heavy heart is like one who 12
29: 6 but a righteous man sings and rejoices. 10
Sng 2:12 flowers appear . . the time of singing has come 2
Isa 5: 1 Let me sing for my beloved a love song concerning 12
14: 7 quiet; they break forth into singing. 9
24: 9 No more do they drink wine with singing; 13
26: 1 this song will be sung in the land of Judah 12
27: 2 In that day: "A pleasant vineyard, sing of it! 7
35: 2 blossom . . and rejoice with joy and singing. 10
10 shall return, and come to Zion with singing; 9
38:20 we will sing to stringed instruments 4
42:10 Sing to the LORD a new song 12
44:23 Sing, O heavens, for the LORD has done it; 10
23 break forth into singing, O mountains 9
49:13 break forth, O mountains, into singing! 9
51:11 shall return, and come to Zion with singing; 9
52: 9 Break forth together into singing 10
54: 1 Sing, O barren one, who did not bear; 10
1 break forth into singing and cry aloud 9
55:12 hills before you shall break forth into singing 9
65:14 my servants shall sing for gladness of heart 10
Jer 20:13 Sing to the LORD; praise the LORD! 12
33:11 those who sing, as they bring thank offerings 1
Ezk 33:32 lo, you are to them like one who sings love songs •
Zec 2:10 Sing and rejoice, O daughter of Zion; for lo, I come 10
Rom 15: 9 thee among the Gentiles, and sing to thy name"; 22
1Co 14:15 I will sing with the spirit 22
15 I will sing with the mind also. 22
Rev 4: 8 and day and night they never cease to sing 17
10 they cast their crowns before the throne, singing 17
1Es 5:61 they sang hymns, giving thanks to the Lord 21
Jdt 16: 2 sing to my Lord with cymbals 15
13 I will sing to my God a new song 19
Wis 18: 9 they were singing the praises of the fathers. 18
Sir 39:35 now sing praise with all your heart and voice 19
47: 8 he sang praise with all his heart 19
51:11 will sing praise with thanksgiving 19
Aza 1:34 to be sung and glorified for ever. 20
2Mc 1:30 Then the priests sang the hymns. 16

sing a hymn 1. ὑμνέω

Mat 26:30 And when they had sung a hymn 1
Mrk 14:26 when they had sung a hymn 1
Act 16:25 Paul and Silas were praying and singing hymns 1
Wis 10:20 they sang hymns, O Lord, to thy holy name 1
Aza 1: 1 singing hymns to God and blessing the Lord. 1
1Mc 4:24 they sang hymns and praises to Heaven 1

sing a song 1. רנן 2. שִׁיר

Isa 16:10 and in the vineyards no songs are sung 1
23:16 Make sweet melody, sing many songs 2

sing aloud 1. רנן

Ps 51:14 my tongue will sing aloud of thy deliverance. 1
59:16 I will sing aloud of thy steadfast love 1
81: 1 Sing aloud to God our strength; 1
145: 7 shall sing aloud of thy righteousness. 1
Jer 31: 7 Sing aloud with gladness for Jacob 1
12 shall come and sing aloud on the height of Zion 1
Zep 3:14 Sing aloud, O daughter of Zion; shout, O Israel! 1

sing an idle song 1. פרט

Ams 6: 5 who sing idle songs to the sound of the harp 1

cause to sing for joy 1. רנן

Job 29:13 I caused the widow's heart to sing for joy. 1

sing for joy 1. רנן

1Ch 16:33 the trees of the wood sing for joy before the LORD 1
Ps 5:11 let them ever sing for joy; and do thou defend them 1
63: 7 in the shadow of thy wings I sing for joy. 1
67: 4 Let the nations be glad and sing for joy 1
84: 2 my heart and flesh sing for joy to the living God. 1
92: 4 at the works of thy hands I sing for joy. 1
96:12 Then shall all the trees of the wood sing for joy 1
98: 8 let the hills sing for joy together 1
149: 5 faithful . . sing for joy on their couches. 1
Isa 12: 6 Shout, and sing for joy, O inhabitant of Zion 1
24:14 They lift up their voices, they sing for joy; 1
26:19 O dwellers in the dust, awake and sing for joy! 1
35: 6 and the tongue of the dumb sing for joy. 1
42:11 let the inhabitants of Sela sing for joy 1
49:13 Sing for joy, O heavens, and exult, O earth; 1
52: 8 lift up their voice, together they sing for joy; 1
Jer 51:48 the earth . . shall sing for joy over Babylon; 1

sing loudly 1. ὑπερφωνέω

Jdt 16: 1 all the people loudly sang this song of praise. 1

sing praise 1. הלל 2. זמר 3. αἰνέω 4. ὑμνέω 5. ψάλλω

2Sm 22:50 I will extol thee . . and sing praises to thy name. 2
1Ch 16: 9 Sing to him, sing praises to him 2
2Ch 29:30 Levites to sing praises to the LORD 1
30 sang praises with gladness, and they bowed down 1
Ps 7:17 I will sing praise to the name of the LORD 2
9: 2 I will sing praise to thy name, O Most High. 2
11 Sing praises to the LORD, who dwells in Zion! 2
18:49 among the nations, and sing praises to thy name. 2
30: 4 Sing praises to the LORD, O you his saints 2
47: 6 Sing praises to God, sing praises! 2
6 Sing praises to God, sing praises! 2
6 Sing praises to our King, sing praises! 2
6 Sing praises to our King, sing praises! 2
7 sing praises with a psalm! 2
57: 9 I will sing praises to thee among the nations. 2
59: 9 O my Strength, I will sing praises to thee; ‡
17 O my Strength, I will sing praises to thee 2
61: 8 So will I ever sing praises to thy name 2
66: 4 earth worships thee; they sing praises to thee 2
4 sing praises to thee, sing praises to thy name. 2
68: 4 Sing to God, sing praises to his name; 2
32 O kingdoms . . sing praises to the Lord, Selah 2
71:22 I will sing praises to thee with the lyre, O Holy One 2
23 shout for joy, when I sing praises to thee; 2
75: 9 for ever, I will sing praises to the God of Jacob. 2
84: 4 dwell in thy house, ever singing thy praise! Selah 1
92: 1 good to . . sing praises to thy name, O Most High; 2
98: 4 break forth into joyous song and sing praises! 2
5 Sing praises to the LORD with the lyre 2
104:33 I will sing praise to my God while I have being. 2
105: 2 Sing to him, sing praises to him 2
108: 3 I will sing praises to thee among the nations. 2
138: 1 before the gods I sing thy praise; 2
146: 2 I will sing praises to my God while I have being. 2
147: 1 For it is good to sing praises to our God; 2
Isa 12: 5 Sing praises to the LORD 2
Jas 5:13 Is any cheerful? Let him sing praise. 5
AEs 13:17 that we may live and sing praise to thy name, O Lord; 4
Sir 17:27 Who will sing praises to the Most High in Hades 3
28 he who is alive and well sings the Lord's praises. 3
39:14 Scatter the fragrance, and sing a hymn of praise; 3
47: 8 he sang praise with all his heart 4
51:11 will sing praise with thanksgiving 4
Aza 1:35 sing praise to him and highly exalt him for ever. 4
36 sing praise to him and highly exalt him for ever. 4
37 sing praise to him and highly exalt him for ever. 4
38 sing praise to him and highly exalt him for ever. 4
39 sing praise to him and highly exalt him for ever. 4
40 sing praise to him and highly exalt him for ever. 4
41 sing praise to him and highly exalt him for ever. 4
42 sing praise to him and highly exalt him for ever. 4
43 sing praise to him and highly exalt him for ever. 4
44 sing praise to him and highly exalt him for ever. 4
45 sing praise to him and highly exalt him for ever. 4
46 sing praise to him and highly exalt him for ever. 4
47 sing praise to him and highly exalt him for ever. 4
48 sing praise to him and highly exalt him for ever. 4
49 sing praise to him and highly exalt him for ever. 4
50 sing praise to him and highly exalt him for ever. 4
51 sing praise to him and highly exalt him for ever. 4
52 let it sing praise to him and highly exalt him 4
53 sing praise to him and highly exalt him for ever. 4
54 sing praise to him and highly exalt him for ever. 4
55 sing praise to him and highly exalt him for ever. 4
56 sing praise to him and highly exalt him for ever. 4
57 sing praise to him and highly exalt him for ever. 4
58 sing praise to him and highly exalt him for ever. 4
59 sing praise to him and highly exalt him for ever. 4
60 sing praise to him and highly exalt him for ever. 4
61 sing praise to him and highly exalt him for ever. 4
62 sing praise to him and highly exalt him for ever. 4
63 sing praise to him and highly exalt him for ever. 4
64 sing praise to him and highly exalt him for ever. 4
65 sing praise to him and highly exalt him for ever. 4
66 sing praise to him and highly exalt him for ever; 4
68 sing praise to him and give thanks to him 4
Man 1:15 all the host of heaven sings thy praise 4

sing responsively 1. ענה

Ezr 3:11 sang responsively, praising and giving thanks 1

sing to one another 1. ענה

1Sm 18: 7 the women sang to one another as they made merry 1
21:11 Did they not sing to one another of him in dances 1
29: 5 David, of whom they sing to one another in dances 1

singe 1. חרך(A)

Dan 3:27 hair of their heads was not singed 1

singer 1. שׁיר 2. זְמַר(A)

1Kg 10:12 king made . . lyres also and harps for the singers; 1
1Ch 6:33 Of the sons of the Ko'hathites: Heman the singer 1
9:33 the singers, the heads of fathers' houses 1
15:16 brethren as the singers who should play loudly 1
19 The singers . . were to sound bronze cymbals; 1
27 the singers, and Chenani'ah the leader 1
27 Chenani'ah the leader of the music of the singers 1
2Ch 5:12 Levitical singers, Asaph, Heman, and Jedu'thun 1
13 it was the duty of the trumpeters and singers 1
9:11 lyres also and harps for the singers; 1
23:13 singers with their musical instruments 1
29:28 whole assembly worshiped, and the singers sang 1
35:15 singers, the sons of Asaph, were in their place 1
Ezr 2:41 singers: the sons of Asaph, 128. 1
70 singers, the gatekeepers, and the temple servants 1
7: 7 singers and gatekeepers, and the temple 1
24 singers, the doorkeepers, the temple servants 2
10:24 Of the singers: Eli'ashib. 1
Neh 7: 1 gatekeepers, the singers, and the Levites 1
44 singers: the sons of Asaph, 148. 1
73 gatekeepers, the singers, some of the people 1
10:28 gatekeepers, the singers, the temple servants 1
39 priests . . the gatekeepers and the singers. 1
11:22 singers, over the work of the house of God. 1
23 settled provision for the singers, as every day 1
12:28 sons of the singers gathered together 1
29 singers had built for themselves villages 1
42 singers sang with Jezrahi'ah as their leader. 1
45 as did the singers and the gatekeepers 1
46 days of David . . there was a chief of the singers 1
47 portions for the singers and the gatekeepers; 1
13: 5 given by commandment to the Levites, singers 1
10 Levites and the singers, who did the work, 1
Ps 68:25 the singers in front, the minstrels last 1
87: 7 Singers and dancers alike say, "All my springs 1

ballad singer 1. משׁל

Num21:27 Therefore the ballad singers say, "Come 1

female singer 1. שׁיר

Ezr 2:65 7,337; and they had 200 male and female singers. 1
Neh 7:67 they had 245 singers, male and female. 1

male singer 1. שׁיר

Ezr 2:65 7,337; and they had 200 male and female singers. 1
Neh 7:67 they had 245 singers, male and female. 1

man singer 1. שׁיר

Ecc 2: 8 I got singers, both men and women 1

temple singer 1. ἱεροψάλτης

1Es 1:15 the temple singers, the sons of Asaph 1
5:27 The temple singers: the sons of Asaph, 128. 1
46 the temple singers, the gatekeepers 1
8: 5 temple singers and gatekeepers 1
22 temple singers or gatekeepers 1
9:24 Of the temple singers: Eliashib and Zaccur. 1

woman singer 1. שׁרה 2. ψάλλω

Ecc 2: 8 I got singers, both men and women 1
Sir 9: 4 Do not associate with a woman singer 2

loud singing 1. רִנָּה

Zep 3:17 he will exult over you with loud singing 1

singing man 1. שׁיר

2Sm 19:35 to the voice of singing men and singing women? 1
2Ch 35:25 all the singing men . . have spoken of Josi'ah 1

singing woman 1. שׁיר

2Sm 19:35 to the voice of singing men and singing women? 1
2Ch 35:25 all the . . singing women have spoken of Josi'ah 1

single 1. אֶחָד 2. גַּף 3. ἄγαμος 4. εἷς

Exd 10:19 not a single locust was left in all the country 1
21: 3 If he comes in single, he shall go out single; 2
3 If he comes in single, he shall go out single; 2

33: 5 if for a single moment I should go up among you 1
Num13:23 branch with a single cluster of grapes 1
Deu 19:15 A single witness shall not prevail against a man 1
1Kg 16:11 he did not leave him a single male of his kinsmen •
2Kg 18:24 How then can you repulse a single captain 1
1Ch 12:38 all the rest of Israel were of a single mind 1
Isa 36: 9 a single captain among the least of my master's 1
Ezk 4: 9 and put them into a single vessel, and make bread 1
Zec 3: 9 upon a single stone with seven facets 1
9 remove the guilt of this land in a single day. 1
Mat 23:15 to make a single proselyte 4
27:14 he gave him no answer, not even to a single charge; 4
1Co 7: 8 it is well for them to remain single as I do. •
11 if she does, let her remain single 3
10: 8 and 23,000 fell in a single day. 4
12:19 If all were a single organ, where would the body be? 4
Heb 10:12 offered for all time a single sacrifice for sins 4
14 by a single offering he has perfected 4
12:16 who sold his birthright for a single meal. 4
Rev 18: 8 so shall her plagues come in a single day 4
21:21 each of the gates made of a single pearl 4
Jdt 7:21 did not have enough .. for a single day 4
Wis 11:20 men could fall at a single breath 4
2Mc 2:23 we shall attempt to condense into a single book. 4
7:20 she saw her seven sons perish within a single day 4
8:18 is able with a single nod to strike down 4
3Mc 4:14 to be destroyed in the space of a single day. 4

single out 1. בדל
Deu 29:21 LORD would single him out .. for calamity 1

single-handed 1. *μόνος*
3Mc 1: 2 intending single-handed to kill him 1

singlehanded 1. *ἐν χειρί*
Jdt 15:10 You have done all this singlehanded 1

singleness 1. *ἁπλότης*
Eph 6: 5 with fear and trembling, in singleness of heart 1
Col 3:22 in singleness of heart, fearing the Lord. 1

singleness of purpose 1. לֹא לֵב וָלֵב
1Ch 12:33 to help David with singleness of purpose. 1

singly 1. *καθ' ἕνα*
4Mc 15:12 each child singly and all together 1

sink 1. טבע 2. כרע 3. מכך 4. נחת 5. נפל 6. צלל 7. שקע 8. *βυθίζω* 9. *καταποντίζω* 10. *καταφέρω* 11. *τίθημι*
Exd 15: 4 his picked officers are sunk in the Red Sea. 1
10 they sank as lead in the mighty waters. 6
Jdg 5:27 He sank, he fell, he lay still at her feet; 2
27 at her feet he sank, he fell; where he sank 2
27 at her feet .. where he sank, there he fell dead. 2
1Sm 17:49 the stone sank into his forehead, and he fell 1
2Kg 9:24 the arrow pierced .. and he sank in his chariot. 2
Job 38: 6 On what were its bases sunk 1
Ps 9:15 The nations have sunk in the pit which they made; 1
38: 2 thy arrows have sunk into me, and thy hand has come 4
69: 2 I sink in deep mire, where there is no foothold; 1
14 rescue me from sinking in the mire; 1
Ecc 10:18 Through sloth the roof sinks in 3
Jer 38: 6 and Jeremiah sank in the mire. 1
22 now that your feet are sunk in the mire 1
51:64 say, 'Thus shall Babylon sink, to rise no more 7
Lam 2: 9 Her gates have sunk into the ground; 1
Ezk 27:27 you .. sink into the heart of the seas 5
34 and all your crew have sunk with you. 5
Ams 8: 8 and be tossed about and sink again, like the Nile 7
9: 5 and all of it rises like the Nile, and sinks again 7
Mat 14:30 beginning to sink he cried out, "Lord, save me. 9
Lke 5: 7 so that they began to sink. 8
9:44 Let these words sink into your ears 11
Act 20: 9 He sank into a deep sleep 10

sink down 1. ירד 2. רפה 3. שוח 4. שחח
Ps 10:10 The hapless is crushed, sinks down, and falls 4
104: 8 The mountains rose, the valleys sank down 1
Prv 2:18 for her house sinks down to death 3
Isa 5:24 and as dry grass sinks down in the flame 2

sink into 1. נום
Ps 76: 5 stripped of their spoil; they sank into sleep; 1

sink low 1. שחח
Hab 3: 6 the everlasting hills sank low. 1

make sink 1. כרע
2Sm 22:40 thou didst make my assailants sink under me. 1
Ps 18:39 thou didst make my assailants sink under me. 1

sinner 1. חטא 2. חַטָּא 3. *ἀλιτήριος* 4. *ἁμαρτωλός* 5. *ἀνὴρ ἁμαρτωλός* 6. *ἄνθρωπος ἁμαρτωλός* 7. delinquo 8. peccator
Gen 13:13 were wicked, great sinners against the LORD. 2
1Sm 15:18 Go, utterly destroy the sinners, the Amal'ekites 2
Ps 1: 1 nor stands in the way of sinners 2
5 nor sinners in the congregation of the righteous; 2
25: 8 therefore he instructs sinners in the way. 2
26: 9 Sweep me not away with sinners 2
51:13 sinners will return to thee. 2
104:35 Let sinners be consumed from the earth 2
Prv 1:10 My son, if sinners entice you, do not consent. 2
11:31 how much more the wicked and the sinner! 1
13:21 Misfortune pursues sinners 2
22 sinner's wealth is laid up for the righteous. 1
14:21 He who despises his neighbor is a sinner 1
23:17 Let not your heart envy sinners 2
Ecc 2:26 to the sinner he gives the work of gathering 1
7:26 but the sinner is taken by her. 1
8:12 Though a sinner does evil 100 times 1
9: 2 As is the good man, so is the sinner; 1
18 but one sinner destroys much good. 1
Isa 1:28 rebels and sinners shall be destroyed together 2
13: 9 the LORD comes .. to destroy its sinners from it. 2
33:14 The sinners in Zion are afraid; 2
65:20 sinner 100 years old shall be accursed. 1
Ams 9:10 the sinners of my people shall die by the sword 2
Mat 9:10 behold, many tax collectors and sinners came 4
11 Why .. eat with tax collectors and sinners? 4
13 For I came not to call the righteous, but sinners. 4
11:19 a friend of tax collectors and sinners! 4
26:45 Son of man is betrayed into the hands of sinners. 4
Mrk 2:15 many tax collectors and sinners were sitting 4
16 he was eating with sinners and tax collectors 4
16 Why does he eat with tax collectors and sinners? 4
17 I came not to call the righteous, but sinners. 4
14:41 Son of man is betrayed into the hands of sinners. 4
Lke 5:30 Why do you .. drink with tax collectors and sinners? 4
32 sinners to repentance. 4
6:32 even sinners love those who love them. 4
33 even sinners do the same. 4
34 Even sinners lend to sinners 4
34 Even sinners lend to sinners 4
7:34 a friend of tax collectors and sinners!' 4
37 behold, a woman of the city, who was a sinner 4
39 who is touching him, for she is a sinner. 4
13: 2 worse sinners than all the other Galileans 4
15: 1 Now the tax collectors and sinners 4
2 This man receives sinners and eats with them. 4
7 more joy in heaven over one sinner who repents 4
10 there is joy .. over one sinner who repents. 4
18:13 'God, be merciful to me a sinner!' 4
19: 7 to be the guest of a man who is a sinner. 4
Joh 9:16 How can a man who is a sinner do such signs? 4
24 we know that this man is a sinner. 4
25 He answered, "Whether he is a sinner, I do not know; 4
31 We know that God does not listen to sinners 4
Rom 3: 7 why am I still being condemned as a sinner? 4
5: 8 while we were yet sinners Christ died for us. 4
19 by one man's disobedience many were made sinners 4
Gal 2:15 who are Jews by birth and not Gentile sinners 4
17 we ourselves were found to be sinners 4
1Ti 1: 9 for the ungodly and sinners 4
15 Jesus came into the world to save sinners 4
15 I am the foremost of sinners; •
Heb 7:26 separated from sinners 4
12: 3 endured from sinners such hostility 4
Jas 4: 8 Cleanse your hands, you sinners 4
5:20 brings back a sinner from the error of his way 4
1Pe 4:18 where will the impious and sinner appear? 4
Jde 1:15 harsh things which ungodly sinners have spoken 4
2Es 3:29 my soul has seen many sinners 7
8:31 thou, because of us sinners, are called merciful. 8
15:22 My right hand will not spare the sinners 8
23 and the sinners, like straw that is kindled. 8
16:53 Let no sinner say that he has not sinned 8
Tob 4:17 give none to sinners. 4
13: 6 I show his power .. to a nation of sinners 4
6 Turn back, you sinners, and do right before him 4
Wis 4:10 while living among sinners he was taken up. 4
19:13 not come upon the sinners without prior signs 4
Sir 1:25 godliness is an abomination to a sinner. 4
2:12 Woe .. to the sinner who walks along two ways! 4
3:27 the sinner will heap sin upon sin. 4
5: 6 his anger rests on sinners. 4
9 the double-tongued sinner does that. 4
6: 1 so fares the double-tongued sinner. 4
7:16 Do not count yourself among the crowd of sinners; 4
8:10 Do not kindle the coals of a sinner 4
9:11 Do not envy the honors of a sinner 4
11: 9 nor sit with sinners when they judge a case. 4
21 Do not wonder at the works of a sinner 4
32 a sinner lies in wait to shed blood. 6
12: 4 Give to the godly man, but do not help the sinner. 4
6 For the Most High also hates sinners 4
7 Give to the good man, but do not help the sinner. 4
14 will pity a man who associates with a sinner 5
13:17 No more has a sinner with a godly man. 4
15: 9 is not fitting on the lips of a sinner 4
16: 6 In an assembly of sinners a fire will be kindled 4
13 The sinner will not escape with his plunder 4
19:22 is there prudence where sinners take counsel. 4
21: 6 walks in the steps of the sinner 4
10 The way of sinners is smoothly paved with stones 4
23: 8 The sinner is overtaken through his lips 4
25:19 may a sinner's lot befall her! 4
29:16 A sinner will overthrow .. 4
19 The sinner who has fallen into suretyship 4
33:14 so the sinner is the opposite of the godly. 4
39:25 just as evil things for sinners. 4
27 just as they turn into evils for sinners. 4
40: 8 upon sinners seven times more 4
41: 5 The children of sinners are abominable 4
6 The inheritance of the children of sinners 4
11 the evil name of sinners will be blotted out. 4
Man 1: 5 wrath of thy threat to sinners is irresistible; 4
7 thou hast appointed repentance for sinners 4
8 appointed repentance for me, who am a sinner. 4
1Mc 2:44 and struck down sinners in their anger 4
48 they never let the sinner gain the upper hand. 4
62 Do not fear the words of a sinner 4
2Mc 12:23 putting the sinners to the sword 3
14:42 rather than to fall into the hands of sinners 3

sir 1. אָדוֹן 2. *ἀνήρ* 3. *κύριος*
Jdg 6:13 Gideon said to him, "Pray, sir, if the LORD is with us 1
Mat 13:27 Sir, did you not sow good seed in your field? 3
21:30 he answered, 'I go, sir,' but did not go. 3
27:63 said, "Sir, we remember how that impostor said 3
Lke 13: 8 he answered him, 'Let it alone, sir, this year also 3
14:22 Sir, what you commanded has been done 3
Joh 4:11 Sir, you have nothing to draw with, and the well 3
15 Sir, give me this water, that I may not thirst 3
19 Sir, I perceive that you are a prophet. 3
49 Sir, come down before my child dies. 3
5: 7 The sick man answered him, "Sir, I have no man 3
9:36 He answered, "And who is he, sir 3
12:21 Sir, we wish to see Jesus. 3
20:15 she said to him, "Sir, if you have carried him away 3
Act 27:10 saying, "Sirs, I perceive that the voyage 2
Rev 7:14 I said to him, "Sir, you know." And he said to me 3
Bel 1:35 Habakkuk said, "Sir, I have never seen Babylon 3

siren 1. *σειρήνιος*
4Mc 15:21 Neither the melodies of sirens nor .. swans 1

sister 1. אָחוֹת 2. *ἀδελφή*
Gen 4:22 The sister of Tubal-cain was Na'amah. 1
12:13 Say you are my sister, that it may go well with me 1
19 Why did you say, 'She is my sister,' 1
20: 2 Abraham said of Sarah his wife, "She is my sister. 1
5 Did he not himself say to me, 'She is my sister'? 1
12 Besides she is indeed my sister 1
24:30 he saw .. the bracelets on his sister's arms 1
30 when he heard the words of Rebekah his sister 1
59 sent away Rebekah their sister and her nurse 1
60 Our sister, be the mother of thousands 1
25:20 Rebekah .. the sister of Laban the Aramean. 1
26: 7 about his wife, he said, "She is my sister"; 1
9 you say, 'She is my sister'?" Isaac said to him 1
28: 9 Ma'halath .. the sister of Neba'ioth. 1
29:13 Laban heard the tidings of Jacob his sister's son 1
30: 1 Rachel .. envied her sister; she said to Jacob 1
8 I have wrestled with my sister .. and prevailed 1
34:13 because he had defiled their sister Dinah. 1
14 to give our sister to one who is uncircumcised 1
27 the city, because their sister had been defiled; 1
31 they said, "Should he treat our sister as a harlot? 1
36: 3 Ish'mael's daughter, the sister of Neba'ioth. 1
22 Hori and Heman; and Lotan's sister was Timna. 1
46:17 Ishvi, Beri'ah, with Serah their sister. 1
Exd 2: 4 his sister stood at a distance 1
7 his sister said to Pharaoh's daughter, "Shall I go 1
6:23 took .. the sister of Nahshon; 1
15:20 Then Miriam, the prophetess, the sister of Aaron 1
Lev 18: 9 shall not uncover the nakedness of your sister 1
11 begotten by your father, since she is your sister 1
12 not uncover the nakedness of your father's sister 1
13 not uncover the nakedness of your mother's sister 1
18 not take a woman as a rival wife to her sister 1
18 while her sister is yet alive •
20:17 If a man takes his sister, a daughter of his father 1
17 he has uncovered his sister's nakedness 1
19 uncover the nakedness of your mother's sister 1
19 nakedness .. of your father's sister 1
21: 3 or his virgin sister (who is near to him 1
Num 6: 7 Neither for .. nor for brother or sister 1
25:18 their sister, who was slain on the day of the plague 1
26:59 Aaron and Moses and Miriam their sister. 1
Deu 27:22 'Cursed be he who lies with his sister, whether 1
Jos 2:13 my father and mother, my brothers and sisters 1
Jdg 15: 2 Is not her younger sister fairer than she? 1
2Sm 13: 1 Now Ab'salom, David's son, had a beautiful sister 1
2 he made himself ill because of his sister Tamar; 1
4 I love Tamar, my brother Ab'salom's sister. 1
5 Let my sister Tamar come and give me bread to eat 1
6 Pray let my sister Tamar come and make .. cakes 1
11 and said to her, "Come, lie with me, my sister. 1
20 Now hold your peace, my sister; he is your brother; 1
22 because he had forced his sister Tamar. 1
32 determined from the day he forced his sister 1
17:25 of Nahash, sister of Zeru'iah, Jo'ab's mother. 1
1Kg 11:19 he gave him in marriage the sister of his own wife 1
19 gave him in marriage .. the sister of Tah'penes 1

20 the sister of Tah'penes bore him Genu'bath his son 1
2Kg 11: 2 Jehosh'eba . . sister of Ahazi'ah, took Jo'ash 1
1Ch 1:39 and Lotan's sister was Timna. 1
2:16 their sisters were Zeru'iah and Ab'igail. 1
3: 9 David's sons . . and Tamar was their sister. 1
19 and Hanani'ah, and Shel-o'mith was their sister; 1
4: 3 and the name of their sister was Hazzelelpo'ni. 1
19 The sons of the wife of Hodi'ah, the sister of Naham 1
7:15 The name of his sister was Ma'acah. 1
18 sister Hammo'lecheth bore Ishhod, Abi-e'zer 1
30 sons of Asher . . Beri'ah, and their sister Serah. 1
32 father of . . Hotham, and their sister Shu'a. 1
2Ch 22:11 because she was a sister of Ahazi'ah, hid him 1
Job 1: 4 they would send and invite their three sisters 1
17:14 if I say . . to the worm, 'My mother,' or 'My sister,' 1
42:11 Then came to him all his brothers and sisters 1
Prv 7: 4 Say to wisdom, "You are my sister 1
Sng 4: 9 You have ravished my heart, my sister, my bride 1
10 How sweet is your love, my sister, my bride! 1
12 A garden locked is my sister, my bride 1
5: 1 I come to my garden, my sister, my bride 1
2 Open to me, my sister, my love, my dove, 1
8: 8 We have a little sister, and she has no breasts. 1
8 What shall we do for our sister 1
Jer 3: 7 and her false sister Judah saw it. 1
8 yet her false sister Judah did not fear 1
10 Yet . . her false sister Judah did not return to me 1
22:18 lament . . saying, 'Ah my brother!' or 'Ah sister!' 1
Ezk 16:45 you are the sister of your sisters 1
45 your sisters, who loathed their husbands 1
46 your elder sister is Sama'ria 1
46 your younger sister, who lived to the south of you 1
48 your sister Sodom and her daughters have not 1
49 Behold, this was the guilt of your sister Sodom 1
51 and have made your sisters appear righteous 1
52 have made judgment favorable to your sisters; 1
52 you have made your sisters appear righteous. 1
55 As for your sisters, Sodom and her daughters 1
56 Was not your sister Sodom a byword in your mouth 1
61 and be ashamed when I take your sisters 1
22:11 defiles his sister, his father's daughter. 1
23: 4 and Ohol'ibah the name of her sister. 1
11 Her sister Ohol'ibah saw this 1
11 which was worse than that of her sister. 1
18 as I had turned from her sister. 1
31 You have gone the way of your sister; 1
32 You shall drink your sister's cup which is deep 1
33 desolation, is the cup of your sister Sama'ria; 1
44:25 for brother or unmarried sister they may defile 1
Hos 2: 1 and to your sister, "She has obtained pity. 1
Mat 12:50 is my brother, and sister, and mother. 2
13:56 are not all his sisters with us? 2
19:29 houses or brothers or sisters or father 2
Mrk 3:35 my brother, and sister, and mother. 2
6: 3 are not his sisters here with us? 2
10:29 house or brothers or sisters or mother or father 2
30 houses and brothers and sisters and mothers 2
Lke 10:39 she had a sister called Mary 2
40 Lord, do you not care that my sister has left me 2
14:26 wife and children and brothers and sisters 2
Joh 11: 1 the village of Mary and her sister Martha. 2
3 the sisters sent to him, saying 2
5 Jesus loved Martha and her sister and Laz'arus. 2
28 went and called her sister Mary, saying quietly 2
39 Martha, the sister of the dead man, said to him, "Lord 2
19:25 his mother's sister, Mary the wife of Clopas 2
Act 23:16 Now the son of Paul's sister heard of their ambush; 2
Rom 16: 1 I commend to you our sister Phoebe 2
15 Greet Philol'ogus, Julia, Nereus and his sister 2
1Co 7:15 in such a case the brother or sister is not bound. 2
1Ti 5: 2 younger women like sisters, in all purity. 2
Phm 1: 2 Ap'phia our sister and Archip'pus our fellow soldier 2
Jas 2:15 If a brother or sister is ill-clad 2
2Jn 1:13 The children of your elect sister greet you. 2
Tob 5:20 Tobit said to her, "Do not worry, my sister 2
7:16 Sister, make up the other room, and take her into it. 2
8: 4 Tobias got up from the bed and said, "Sister, get up 2
7 I am not taking this sister of mine because of lust 2
3Mc 1: 1 he . . took with him his sister Arsinoe 2

father's sister 1. דֹּדָה
Exd 6:20 Amram took to wife Joch'ebed his father's sister 1

sister-in-law 1. יְבֶמֶת
Rut 1:15 See, your sister-in-law has gone back to her people 1
15 return after your sister-in-law. 1

sit 1. ישׁב 2. רבץ 3. יתב (A) 4. ἀναπίπτω 5. διφρεύω 6. ἐπικάθημαι 7. ἐπικαθίζω 8. καθέζομαι 9. κάθημαι 10. καθίζω 11. παρακαθέζομαι 12. πάρεδρος 13. συγκάθημαι 14. συγκαθίζω 15. συνανάκειμαι 16. συνεδρεύω 17. sedeo
Gen 18: 1 as he sat at the door of his tent in the heat 1
19: 1 and Lot was sitting in the gate of Sodom. 1
21:16 as she sat over against him, the child 1
23:10 Now Ephron was sitting among the Hittites; 1
31:34 put them in the camel's saddle, and sat upon them. 1
38:14 she . . sat at the entrance to Enaim, which is 1
43:33 they sat before him, the first-born according 1
Exd 11: 5 first-born of Pharaoh who sits upon his throne 1
12:29 first-born of Pharaoh who sat on his throne 1
16: 3 in the land of Egypt, when we sat by the fleshpots 1
17:12 stone and put it under him, and he sat upon it 1
18:13 On the morrow Moses sat to judge the people 1
14 Why do you sit alone, and all the people stand 1
Lev 15: 4 everything on which he sits shall be unclean 1
6 on which he who has the discharge has sat 1
20 upon which she sits shall be unclean 1
22 whoever touches anything upon which she sits 1
23 the bed or anything upon which she sits 1
26 everything on which she sits shall be unclean 1
Num 32: 6 your brethren go to the war while you sit here? 1
Deu 6: 7 shall talk of them when you sit in your house 1
11:19 talking of them when you are sitting in your house 1
17:18 when he sits on the throne of his kingdom, he shall 1
22: 6 mother sitting upon the young or upon the eggs 2
Jdg 3:20 as he was sitting alone in his cool roof chamber. 1
4: 5 She used to sit under the palm of Deb'orah between 1
5:10 Tell of it . . you who sit on rich carpets 1
6:11 the angel . . came and sat under the oak at Ophrah 1
13: 9 came again to the woman as she sat in the field; 1
19: 6 the two men sat and ate and drank together; 1
20:26 they sat there before the LORD, and fasted 1
21: 2 to Bethel, and sat there till evening before God 1
Rut 2:14 she sat beside the reapers 1
4: 4 Buy it in the presence of those sitting here 1
1Sm 1: 9 Now Eli the priest was sitting on the seat beside 1
4:13 Eli was sitting upon his seat by the road 1
19: 9 as he sat in his house with his spear in his hand; 1
20: 5 and I should not fail to sit at table with the king; 1
25 The king sat upon his seat, as at other times 1
25 The king sat . . Jonathan sat opposite, and Abner •
25 The king sat . . and Abner sat by Saul's side 1
22: 6 Saul was sitting at Gib'e-ah, under the tamarisk 1
24: 3 David and his men were sitting in the . . cave. 1
28:23 he arose from the earth, and sat upon the bed. 1
2Sm 7:18 David went in and sat before the LORD, and said 1
18:24 Now David was sitting between the two gates; 1
19: 8 Behold, the king is sitting in the gate"; 1
1Kg 1:13 reign after me, and he shall sit upon my throne"? Why 1
17 reign after me, and he shall sit upon my throne.' 1
20 tell them who shall sit on the throne of my lord 1
24 reign after me, and he shall sit upon my throne'? 1
27 who should sit on the throne of my lord the king 1
30 reign after me, and he shall sit upon my throne 1
35 he shall come and sit upon my throne; for he shall 1
46 Solomon sits upon the royal throne. 1
48 granted one of my offspring to sit on my throne 1
2:12 Solomon sat upon the throne of David his father; 1
19 then he sat on his throne, and had a seat brought 1
19 for the king's mother; and she sat on his right. 1
3: 6 hast given him a son to sit on his throne this day. 1
8:20 I have risen . . and sit on the throne of Israel 1
25 a man before me to sit upon the throne of Israel 1
13:14 and found him sitting under an oak; 1
20 as they sat at the table, the word of the LORD came 1
21:13 the two base fellows came in and sat opposite him; 1
22:10 king of Israel and Jehosh'aphat . . were sitting 1
19 I saw the LORD sitting on his throne 1
2Kg 1: 9 to Eli'jah, who was sitting on the top of a hill 1
4:20 to his mother, the child sat on her lap till noon 1
38 the sons of the prophets were sitting before him 1
6:32 Eli'sha was sitting in his house 1
32 Eli'sha . . and the elders were sitting with him. 1
7: 3 said to one another, "Why do we sit here till we die? 1
4 we shall die there; and if we sit here, we die also. 1
10:30 your sons . . shall sit on the throne of Israel. 1
13:13 Jo'ash slept . . and Jerobo'am sat upon his throne; 1
15:12 Your sons shall sit upon the throne of Israel 1
18:27 and to you, and not to the men sitting on the wall 1
1Ch 13: 6 the LORD who sits enthroned above the cherubim. 1
17:16 Then King David went in and sat before the LORD 1
28: 5 Solomon . . to sit upon the throne of the kingdom 1
29:23 Then Solomon sat on the throne of the LORD as king 1
2Ch 6:10 I have risen . . and sit on the throne of Israel 1
16 never fail you a man . . to sit upon the throne 1
18: 9 sitting on their thrones, arrayed in their robes; 1
9 sitting at the threshing floor at the entrance 1
18 I saw the LORD sitting on his throne 1
Ezr 9: 3 pulled hair from my head . . and sat appalled. 1
4 sat appalled until the evening sacrifice. 1
10: 9 all the people sat in the open square 1
Neh 2: 6 king said to me (the queen sitting beside him) 1
Est 1: 2 when . . Ahasu-e'rus sat on his royal throne in Susa 1
14 saw the king's face, and sat first in the kingdom 1
2:19 Mor'decai was sitting at the king's gate. 1
21 as Mor'decai was sitting at the king's gate 1
5: 1 The king was sitting on his royal throne inside 1
13 I see Mor'decai the Jew sitting at the king's gate. 1
6:10 to Mor'decai the Jew who sits at the king's gate. 1
Job 2: 8 to scrape himself, and sat among the ashes. 1
13 they sat with him on the ground seven days 1
29:25 I chose their way, and sat as chief 1
Ps 1: 1 nor sits in the seat of scoffers; 1
2: 4 He who sits in the heavens laughs; 1
9: 4 sat on the throne giving righteous judgment. 1
10: 8 He sits in ambush in the villages; 1
26: 4 I do not sit with false men 1
5 I will not sit with the wicked. 1
47: 8 God sits on his holy throne. 1
50:20 You sit and speak against your brother; 1
69:12 I am the talk of those who sit in the gate 1
107:10 Some sat in darkness and in gloom, prisoners 1
110: 1 Sit at my right hand, till I make your enemies 1
119:23 Even though princes sit plotting against me 1
132:12 sons also for ever shall sit upon your throne. 1
Prv 9:14 She sits at the door of her house 1
20: 8 A king who sits on the throne of judgment 1
31:23 when he sits among the elders of the land. 1
Ecc 10: 6 and the rich sit in a low place. 1
Sng 2: 3 With great delight I sat in his shadow 1
Isa 3:26 mourn; ravaged, she shall sit upon the ground. 1
6: 1 I saw the Lord sitting upon a throne 1
14:13 sit on the mount of assembly in the far north; 1
16: 5 a throne . . and on it will sit in faithfulness 1
28: 6 a spirit of justice to him who sits in judgment 1
30: 7 therefore I have called her "Rahab who sits still. 1
36:12 to you, and not to the men sitting on the wall 1
40:22 It is he who sits above the circle of the earth 1
42: 7 from the prison those who sit in darkness. 1
47: 1 and sit in the dust, O virgin daughter of Babylon; 1
1 sit on the ground without a throne, O daughter 1
5 Sit in silence, and go into darkness 1
8 hear . . you lover of pleasures, who sit securely 1
8 I shall not sit as a widow or know the loss 1
14 No coal for warming . . no fire to sit before! 1
65: 4 who sit in tombs, and spend the night in secret 1
Jer 3: 2 By the waysides you have sat awaiting lovers 1
13:13 the kings who sit on David's throne, the priests 1
15:17 I did not sit in the company of merrymakers 1
17 I sat alone, because thy hand was upon me 1
16: 8 not go into the house of feasting to sit with them 1
17:25 kings who sit on the throne of David 1
22: 2 O King of Judah, who sit on the throne of David 1
4 kings who sit on the throne of David 1
30 shall succeed in sitting on the throne of David 1
29:16 the king who sits on the throne of David 1
32:12 Jews who were sitting in the court of the guard. 1
33:17 David shall never lack a man to sit on the throne 1
36:12 and all the princes were sitting there 1
22 the king was sitting in the winter house 1
30 He shall have none to sit upon the throne of David 1
38: 7 the king was sitting in the Benjamin Gate 1
39: 3 king of Babylon came and sat in the middle gate 1
48:18 from your glory, and sit on the parched ground 1
Lam 1: 1 How lonely sits the city that was full of people! 1
2:10 The elders of . . Zion sit on the ground in silence; 1
3:28 Let him sit . . in silence when he has laid it on him; 1
63 Behold their sitting and their rising; 1
Ezk 2: 6 thorns are with you and you sit upon scorpions; 1
3:15 I sat there overwhelmed among them seven days. 1
8: 1 on the fifth day of the month, as I sat in my house 1
1 sat . . with the elders of Judah sitting before me 1
14 and behold, there sat women weeping for Tammuz. 1
14: 1 the elders of Israel to me; and sat before me. 1
20: 1 came to inquire of the LORD, and sat before me. 1
23:41 you sat upon a stately couch 1
26:16 they will sit upon the ground 1
28: 2 you have said, 'I am a god, I sit in the seat 1
33:31 people come, and they sit before you as my people 1
44: 3 Only the prince may sit in it to eat bread 1
Dan 7:10 court sat in judgment, and the books were opened. 3
26 court shall sit in judgment, and his dominion 3
Jol 3:12 for there I will sit to judge all the nations 1
Jon 3: 6 covered himself with sackcloth, and sat in ashes. 1
4: 5 went out of the city and sat to the east of the city 1
5 He sat under it in the shade 1
Mic 4: 4 but they shall sit every man under his vine 1
7: 8 I sit in darkness, the LORD will be a light to me. 1
Nah 3: 8 Are you better than Thebes that sat by the Nile 1
Zec 3: 8 you and your friends who sit before you 1
5: 7 there was a woman sitting in the ephah! 1
6:13 and shall sit and rule upon his throne. 1
8: 4 old women shall again sit in the streets 1
Mal 3: 3 he will sit as a refiner and purifier of silver 1
Mat 4:16 the people who sat in darkness have seen a great 9
16 those who sat in the region and shadow of death 9
9: 9 a man called Matthew sitting at the tax office; 9
11:16 It is like children sitting in the market places 9
13: 1 went out of the house and sat beside the sea. 9
2 so that he got into a boat and sat there 9
19:28 the Son of man shall sit on his glorious throne 10
28 will also sit on twelve thrones 9
20:21 Command that these two sons of mine may sit 10
23 to sit at my right hand and at my left 10
30 behold, two blind men sitting by the roadside 9
21: 7 and he sat thereon. 7
22:44 'The Lord said to my Lord, Sit at my right hand 9
23: 2 The scribes and the Pharisees sit on Moses' seat; 10
22 by him who sits upon it. 9
24: 3 As he sat on the Mount of Olives 9
25:31 then he will sit on his glorious throne. 10
26:36 Sit here, while I go yonder and pray. 10
55 Day after day I sat in the temple teaching 8
58 he sat with the guards to see the end. 9
69 Now Peter was sitting outside in the courtyard. 9

27:19 while he was sitting on the judgment seat 9
61 sitting opposite the sepulchre. 9
28: 2 came and rolled back the stone, and sat upon it. 9
Mrk 2: 6 Now some of the scribes were sitting there 9
14 the son of Alphaeus sitting at the tax office 9
15 tax collectors and sinners were sitting with Jesus 15
3:32 a crowd was sitting about him; and they said to him 9
34 looking around on those who sat about him 9
4: 1 so that he got into a boat and sat in it on the sea; 9
5:15 came to Jesus, and saw the demoniac sitting there 9
10:37 Grant us to sit, one at your right hand 10
40 to sit at my right hand or at my left 10
46 was sitting by the roadside. 9
11: 2 a colt . . on which no one has ever sat 10
7 he sat upon it. 10
12:36 The Lord said to my Lord, Sit at my right hand 9
13: 3 as he sat on the Mount of Olives 9
14:32 he said to his disciples, "Sit here, while I pray. 10
54 he was sitting with the guards 13
16: 5 they saw a young man sitting on the right side 9
Lke 1:79 to give light to those who sit in darkness 9
2:46 sitting among the teachers 8
5:17 Pharisees and teachers of the law sitting 9
27 a tax collector . . sitting at the tax office; 9
7:32 They are like children sitting in the market place 9
8:35 sitting at the feet of Jesus 9
10:13 sitting in sackcloth and ashes. 9
39 a sister called Mary, who sat at the Lord's feet 11
14:10 go and sit in the lowest place 4
18:35 a blind man was sitting by the roadside begging; 9
19:30 a colt . . on which no one has ever yet sat 10
20:42 The Lord said to my Lord, Sit at my right hand 9
22:30 sit on thrones judging the twelve tribes 9
55 Peter sat among them. 9
56 seeing him as he sat in the light and gazing at him 9
Joh 9: 8 Is not this the man who used to sit and beg? 9
11:20 she went and met him, while Mary sat in the house. 8
12:14 Jesus found a young ass and sat upon it 10
15 behold, your king is coming, sitting on an ass's colt! 9
20:12 sitting where the body of Jesus had lain 8
Act 2: 2 it filled all the house where they were sitting. 9
34 The Lord said to my Lord, Sit at my right hand 9
3:10 the one who sat for alms at the Beautiful Gate 9
6:15 gazing at him, all who sat in the council saw 8
8:31 he invited Philip to come up and sit with him. 10
14: 8 Now at Lystra there was a man sitting 9
20: 9 Eu'tychus was sitting in the window 8
23: 3 Are you sitting to judge me according to the law 9
26:30 Berni'ce and those who were sitting with them; 13
1Co 14:30 If a revelation is made to another sitting 9
Heb 1:13 to what angel has he ever said, "Sit at my right hand 9
Jas 2: 3 Stand there," or "Sit at my feet 9
Rev 3:21 I will grant him to sit with me on my throne 10
4: 3 he who sat there appeared like jasper 9
5:13 To him who sits upon the throne and to the Lamb 9
7:10 Salvation . . to our God who sits upon the throne 9
15 he who sits upon the throne will shelter them 9
11:16 the 24 elders who sit on their thrones before God 9
14:15 calling . . to him that sat upon the cloud 9
16 he who sat upon the cloud swung his sickle 9
17: 3 and I saw a woman sitting on a scarlet beast 9
18: 7 A queen I sit, I am no widow 9
19:11 He who sat upon it is called Faithful and True 9
19 to make war against him who sits upon the horse 9
21 the sword of him who sits upon the horse 9
20:11 I saw a great white throne and him who sat upon it; 9
21: 5 And he who sat upon the throne said, "Behold 9
1Es 3: 7 because of his wisdom he shall sit next to Darius 10
4:29 she would sit at the king's right hand 9
42 you shall sit next to me, and be called my kinsman. 9
8:72 I sat grief-stricken 9
9: 6 all the multitude sat in the open square 14
2Es 9:26 and there I sat among the flowers 17
12:41 that you have forsaken us and sit in this place? 17
51 I sat in the field seven days 17
14: 1 On the third day, while I was sitting under an oak 17
42 They sat 40 days, and wrote during the daytime 17
Tob 11: 5 Now Anna sat looking intently down the road 9
Wis 6:14 he will find her sitting at his gates. 12
9: 4 give me the wisdom that sits by thy throne 12
Sir 1: 8 greatly to be feared, sitting upon his throne. 9
11: 5 Many kings have had to sit on the ground 10
9 nor sit with sinners when they judge a case. 16
12:12 do not have him sit at your right 10
26:12 so will she sit in front of every post 9
33: 6 he neighs under every one who sits on him. 6
37:14 seven watchmen sitting high on a watchtower. 9
38:28 So too is the smith sitting by the anvil 9
29 So too is the potter sitting at his work 9
33 They do not sit in the judge's seat 10
40: 3 the man who sits on a splendid throne 9
42:12 do not sit in the midst of women; 16
LJr 1:31 the priests sit with their clothes rent 5
71 a thorn bush in a garden, on which every bird sits 6
Aza 1:32 Blessed art thou, who sittest upon cherubim 9
Sus 1:50 And the elders said to him, "Come, sit among us 10
Bel 1:40 he looked in, and there sat Daniel. 9
1Mc 1:27 she who sat in the bridal chamber was mourning. 9
11:52 So Demetrius the king sat on the throne 10

14: 9 Old men sat in the streets 9
12 Each man sat under his vine and his fig tree 10

sit along 1. ἐγκάθημαι
LJr 1:43 the women . . sit along the passageways 1

sit among 1. συνεδρεύω
Sir 23:14 when you sit among great men 1

sit at table 1. ἀνάκειμαι 2. ἀνακλίνω 3. ἀναπίπτω 4. κατάκειμαι 5. συνανάκειμαι
Mat 8:11 and sit at table with Abraham 2
9:10 And as he sat at table in the house 1
26: 7 poured it on his head, as he sat at table. 1
20 he sat at table with the twelve disciples; 1
Mrk 2:15 as he sat at table in his house 4
14: 3 as he sat at table, a woman came 4
16:14 appeared to the eleven . . as they sat at table 1
Lke 5:29 and others sitting at table with them. 4
11:37 so he went in and sat at table. 3
12:37 he will gird himself and have them sit at table 2
13:29 and sit at table in the kingdom of God. 2
14:10 in the presence of all who sit at table with you. 5
15 When one of those who sat at table with him heard 5
22:14 he sat at table, and the apostles with him. 3
27 one who sits at table, or one who serves 1
27 Is it not the one who sits at table? 1

sit down 1. יָשַׁב 2. ἀνακλίνω 3. ἀναπίπτω 4. καθέζομαι 5. κάθημαι 6. καθίζω 7. κατακλίνω 8. συνανάκειμαι
Gen 21:16 Then she went, and sat down over against him 1
37:25 Then they sat down to eat; and looking up they saw 1
Exd 2:15 Moses fled . . and he sat down by a well. 1
32: 6 the people sat down to eat and drink, and rose up 1
Deu 23:13 when you sit down outside, you shall dig a hole 1
Jdg 19:15 he went in and sat down in the open square 1
Rut 4: 1 And Bo'az went up to the gate and sat down there; 1
1 Bo'az said, "Turn aside, friend; sit down here"; 1
1 and he turned aside and sat down. 1
2 And he took ten men . . and said, "Sit down here"; 1
2 Sit down here"; so they sat down. 1
1Sm 16:11 for we will not sit down till he comes here. 7
20:24 the new moon came, the king sat down to eat food. 1
2Sm 2:13 they sat down, the one on the one side of the pool 1
1Kg 19: 4 and came and sat down under a broom tree; 1
2Kg 19:27 I know your sitting down and your going out 1
Ezr 10:16 tenth month they sat down to examine the matter; 1
Neh 1: 4 When I heard these words I sat down and wept 1
Est 3:15 And the king and Haman sat down to drink; 1
Ps 137: 1 waters of Babylon, there we sat down and wept 1
139: 2 Thou knowest when I sit down and when I rise up; 1
Prv 3:24 If you sit down, you will not be afraid; 5
23: 1 When you sit down to eat with a ruler 1
Isa 37:28 I know your sitting down and your going out 1
Jer 36:15 And they said to him, "Sit down and read it. 1
Mat 5: 1 mountain, and when he sat down his disciples came 6
9:10 sinners came and sat down with Jesus 8
13:48 when it was full, men drew it ashore and sat down 6
14:19 he ordered the crowds to sit down on the grass 2
15:29 he went up on the mountain, and sat down there. 5
35 commanding the crowd to sit down on the ground 3
27:36 then they sat down and kept watch over him there. 5
Mrk 6:39 Then he commanded them all to sit down 2
40 So they sat down in groups 3
8: 6 he commanded the crowd to sit down on the ground; 3
9:35 he sat down and called the twelve; and he said 6
12:41 he sat down opposite the treasury 6
16:19 Jesus . . sat down at the right hand of God. 6
Lke 4:20 he closed the book . . and sat down 6
5: 3 he sat down and taught the people from the boat. 6
14: 8 do not sit down in a place of honor 7
28 which of you . . does not first sit down and count 6
31 what king . . will not sit down first and take counsel 6
16: 6 and sit down quickly and write 50' 6
Joh 4: 6 Jesus . . sat down beside the well. 4
6: 3 and there sat down with his disciples. 5
10 Jesus said, "Make the people sit down. 3
10 the men sat down, in number about 5,000. 3
8: 2 he sat down and taught them. 6
19:13 and sat down on the judgment seat 6
Act 13:14 they went into the synagogue and sat down. 6
16:13 we sat down and spoke to the women 6
1Co 10: 7 The people sat down to eat and drink 6
Heb 1: 3 he sat down at the right hand of the Majesty on high 6
10:12 he sat down at the right hand of God 6
Rev 3:21 and sat down with my Father on his throne. 6
1Es 8:71 sat down in anxiety and grief. 6
Tob 2: 1 I sat down to eat. 3

sit down at table 1. ἀναπίπτω
Lke 17: 7 'Come at once and sit down at table'? 1

sit down together 1. συγκαθίζω
Lke 22:55 and sat down together 1

sit enthroned 1. יָשַׁב
2Sm 6: 2 the LORD . . who sits enthroned on the cherubim. 1
Ps 9: 7 the LORD sits enthroned for ever 1
29:10 The LORD sits enthroned over the flood; 1
10 LORD sits enthroned as king for ever. 1
33:14 from where he sits enthroned he looks forth 1

sit enthroned upon 1. יָשַׁב
Ps 99: 1 sits enthroned upon the cherubim; 1

sit in state 1. προκαθίζω
4Mc 5: 1 sitting in state with his counselors 1

make sit 1. יָשַׁב 2. καθίζω 3. συγκαθίζω
1Sm 2: 8 lifts the needy . . to make them sit with princes 1
Ps 113: 8 to make them sit with princes 1
143: 3 has made me sit in darkness like those long dead. 1
Eph 1:20 made him sit at his right hand 2
2: 6 made us sit with him in the heavenly places 3

make sit down 1. κατακλίνω
Lke 9:14 he said to his disciples, "Make them sit down 1
15 And they did so, and made them all sit down. 1

sit on a throne 1. יָשַׁב
Isa 10:13 I have brought down those who sat on thrones. 1

sit still 1. יָשַׁב
Jdg 5:17 Asher sat still at the coast of the sea 1
Jer 8:14 Why do we sit still? Gather together 1

sit up 1. יָשַׁב 2. ἀνακαθίζω
Gen 27:19 now sit up and eat of my game 1
48: 2 Israel summoned his strength, and sat up in bed. 1
Lke 7:15 the dead man sat up, and began to speak 2
Act 9:40 when she saw Peter she sat up. 2

site 1. מָכוֹן 2. מָקוֹם 3. תַּחַת 4. אֲתַר (A) 5. τόπος
1Ch 21:22 to Ornan, "Give me the site of the threshing floor 2
25 600 shekels of gold by weight for the site. 2
2Ch 33:19 sites on which he built high places and set up 2
Ezr 2:68 freewill offerings . . to erect it on its site; 1
5:15 let the house of God be rebuilt on its site. 4
6: 7 Jews rebuild this house of God on its site. 4
Isa 4: 5 create over the whole site of Mount Zion 1
Zec 14:10 But Jerusalem shall remain aloft upon its site 3
1Es 5:44 vowed that they would erect the house on its site 5
6:19 this temple . . should be rebuilt on its site. 5
27 to build this house of the Lord on its site. 5
3Mc 7:20 at the site of the festival 5

whoever sits 1. יָשַׁב
Lev 15: 6 whoever sits on anything 1

situation 1. מוֹשָׁב 2. ὅς 3. οὕτως ἔχω
2Kg 2:19 Behold, the situation of this city is pleasant 1
Tob 7:10 let me explain the true situation to you. •
2Mc 3: 9 inquired whether this really was the situation. 3
3Mc 1:16 to aid in the present situation •
3: 1 When the impious king comprehended this situation 2
8 being grieved at the situation •
23 in every situation •
5:15 he gave him an account of the situation. •

six 1. שֵׁשׁ 2. שֵׁת (A) 3. ἕξ 4. sex
Gen 30:20 will honor me, because I have borne him six sons 1
31:41 served you . . six years for your flock 1
Exd 16:26 Six days you shall gather it; but on the seventh 1
20: 9 Six days you shall labor, and do all your work; 1
11 for in six days the LORD made heaven and earth 1
21: 2 you buy a Hebrew slave, he shall serve six years 1
23:10 For six years you shall sow your land 1
12 Six days you shall do your work, but on the seventh 1
24:16 Mount Sinai, and the cloud covered it six days; 1
25:32 there shall be six branches going out 1
33 so for the six branches going out of the lampstand; 1
35 under each pair of the six branches going out 1
26: 9 couple . . six curtains by themselves 1
22 tabernacle westward you shall make six frames. 1
28:10 six of their names on the one stone, and the names 1
10 the names of the remaining six on the other stone 1
31:15 Six days shall work be done, but the seventh day 1
17 in six days the LORD made heaven and earth 1
34:21 Six days you shall work, but on the seventh day 1
35: 2 Six days shall work be done, but on the seventh day 1
36:16 He coupled . . six curtains by themselves. 1
27 for . . the tabernacle westward he made six frames. 1
37:18 there were six branches going out of its sides 1
19 so for the six branches going out 1
21 each pair of the six branches going out of it. 1
Lev 23: 3 Six days shall work be done; but on the seventh day 1
24: 6 set them in two rows, six in a row, upon the table 1
25: 3 Six years you shall sow your field 1
3 six years you shall prune your vineyard 1
Num 7: 3 offering . . six covered wagons and twelve oxen 1
35: 6 you give . . shall be the six cities of refuge 1
13 cities . . shall by your six cities of refuge. 1
15 These six cities shall be for refuge 1
Deu 5:13 Six days you shall labor, and do all your work; 1
15:12 brother . . shall serve you six years 1

18 at half the cost . . he has served you six years. 1
16: 8 For six days you shall eat unleavened bread; 1
Jos 6: 3 Thus shall you do for six days. 1
14 And the second day . . So they did for six days. 1
15:59 six cities with their villages. 1
62 six cities with their villages. 1
Jdg 12: 7 Jephthah judged Israel six years. 1
Rut 3:15 and he measured out six measures of barley 1
17 saying, "These six measures of barley he gave to me 1
1Sm 17: 4 whose height was six cubits and a span. 1
2Sm 2:11 the time that . . was seven years and six months. 1
5: 5 he reigned over Judah seven years and six months 1
6:13 when those who bore the ark . . had gone six paces 1
21:20 man of . . stature, who had six fingers on each hand 1
20 who had six fingers . . and six toes on each foot 1
1Kg 6: 6 the middle one was six cubits broad 1
10:19 The throne had six steps 1
20 one on each end of a step on the six steps. 1
11:16 Jo'ab and all Israel remained there six months 1
16:23 Omri . . reigned . . six years he reigned in Tirzah. 1
2Kg 11: 3 he remained with her six years, hid in the house 1
13:19 and said, "You should have struck five or six times; 1
15: 8 reigned over Israel in Sama'ria six months. 1
1Ch 3: 4 six were born to him in Hebron 1
4 where he reigned for seven years and six months. 1
22 sons of Shemai'ah . . Neari'ah and Shaphat, six. 1
4:27 Shim'e-i had sixteen sons and six daughters; 1
8:38 Azel had six sons, and these are their names 1
9:44 Azel had six sons and these are their names 1
20: 6 who had six fingers on each hand, and six toes 1
6 who had six fingers . . and six toes on each foot 1
25: 3 sons of Jedu'thun . . and Mattithi'ah, six 1
26:17 On the east there were six each day 1
2Ch 9:18 The throne had six steps and a footstool of gold 1
19 one on each end of a step on the six steps. 1
22:12 he remained with them six years 1
Neh 5:18 one day was one ox and six choice sheep; 1
Est 2:12 six months with oil of myrrh and six . . with spices 1
12 six months with spices and ointments for women- 1
Job 5:19 He will deliver you from six troubles; 1
Isa 6: 2 Above him stood the seraphim; each had six wings 1
Jer 34:14 At the end of six years each of you must set free 3
14 has been sold to you and has served you six years; 1
Ezk 9: 2 six men came from the direction of the upper gate 1
40: 5 reed in the man's hand was six long cubits 1
12 the side rooms were six cubits on either side. 1
41: 1 six cubits was the breadth of the jambs. 1
3 and the breadth of the entrance, six cubits; 1
5 measured the wall of the temple, six cubits thick; 1
8 measured a full reed of six long cubits. 1
46: 1 The gate . . shall be shut on the six working days; 1
4 shall be six lambs without blemish and a ram 1
6 bull without blemish, and six lambs and a ram 1
Dan 3: 1 image of gold . . its breadth six cubits. 2
Mat 17: 1 after six days Jesus took with him Peter 3
Mrk 9: 2 And after six days Jesus took with him Peter 3
Lke 4:25 the heaven was shut up three years and six months 3
13:14 There are six days on which work ought to be done; 3
Joh 2: 6 Now six stone jars were standing there 3
12: 1 Six days before the Passover 3
Act 11:12 These six brethren also accompanied me 3
18:11 he stayed a year and six months 3
Jas 5:17 for three years and six months it did not rain 3
Rev 4: 8 four living creatures, each . . with six wings 3
2Es 6:42 six parts thou didst dry up 4
11:23 the three heads . . and six little wings. 4
24 behold, two little wings separated from the six 4
Jdt 1: 2 three cubits thick and six cubits long 3
Bel 1:31 he was there for six days. 3
4Mc 11:24 We six boys have paralyzed your tyranny! 3

six things 1. שֵׁשׁ
Prv 6:16 There are six things which the LORD hates 1

sixteen 1. שֵׁשׁ עֶשְׂרֵה
Gen 46:18 and these she bore to Jacob–sixteen persons. 1
Exd 26:25 with their bases of silver, sixteen bases; 1
36:30 sixteen bases, under every frame two bases. 1
Jos 15:41 sixteen cities with their villages. 1
19:22 sixteen cities with their villages. 1
2Kg 13:10 Jeho'ahaz began . . and he reigned sixteen years. 1
14:21 people . . took Azari'ah, who was sixteen years old 1
15: 2 He was sixteen years old when he began to reign 1
33 and he reigned sixteen years in Jerusalem. 1
16: 2 and he reigned sixteen years in Jerusalem. 1
1Ch 4:27 Shim'e-i had sixteen sons and six daughters; 1
24: 4 under sixteen heads of fathers' houses 1
2Ch 13:21 had 22 sons and sixteen daughters. 1
26: 1 Judah took Uzzi'ah, who was sixteen years old 1
3 Uzzi'ah was sixteen . . when he began to reign 1
27: 1 Jotham . . reigned sixteen years in Jerusalem. 1
8 he reigned sixteen years in Jerusalem. 1
28: 1 Ahaz . . reigned sixteen years in Jerusalem. 1

sixteenth 1. שֵׁשׁ עֶשְׂרֵה
1Ch 24:14 the fifteenth to Bilgah, the sixteenth to Immer 1
25:23 sixteenth, to Hanani'ah, his sons and his brethren 1
2Ch 29:17 on the sixteenth day of the first month 1

sixth 1. שֵׁשׁ 2. שִׁשִּׁי 3. שֵׁת (A) 4. ἕκτος 5. sextus
Gen 1:31 evening and there was morning, a sixth day. 2
30:19 conceived again, and she bore Jacob a sixth son. 2
Exd 16: 5 On the sixth day, when they prepare what they 2
22 On the sixth day they gathered twice as much 2
29 given you the sabbath, therefore on the sixth day 2
26: 9 the sixth curtain you shall double over 2
Lev 25:21 command my blessing upon you in the sixth year 2
Num 7:42 On the sixth day Eli'asaph . . of the men of Gad 2
29:29 On the sixth day eight bulls, two rams, fourteen 2
Jos 19:32 The sixth lot came out for the tribe of Naph'tali 2
2Sm 3: 5 and the sixth, Ith're-am, of Eglah, David's wife. 2
2Kg 18:10 In the sixth year of Hezeki'ah . . Sama'ria was 1
1Ch 2:15 Ozem the sixth, David the seventh; 2
3: 3 the sixth Ith'ream, by his wife Eglah; 2
12:11 Attai sixth, Eli'el seventh 2
24: 9 the fifth to Malchi'jah, the sixth to Mij'amin 2
25:13 sixth to Bukki'ah, his sons and his brethren 2
26: 3 Elam the fifth, Jehoha'nan the sixth, Eli-e-ho-e'nai 2
5 Am'mi-el the sixth, Is'sachar the seventh 2
27: 9 Sixth . . was Ira, the son of Ikkesh the Teko'ite; 2
9 Sixth, for the sixth month, was Ira, the son 2
Ezr 6:15 in the sixth year of the reign of Darius the king. 3
Neh 3:30 Hanani'ah . . and Hanun the sixth son of Zalaph 2
Ezk 4:11 shall drink by measure, the sixth part of a hin; 2
8: 1 In the sixth year, in the sixth month 2
1 In the sixth year, in the sixth month 2
Hag 1: 1 in the sixth month, on the first day of the month 2
15 day of the month, in the sixth month. 2
Mat 20: 5 Going out again about the sixth hour 4
27:45 Now from the sixth hour there was darkness 4
Mrk 15:33 when the sixth hour had come 4
Lke 1:26 In the sixth month the angel Gabriel was sent 4
36 the sixth month with her who was called barren. 4
23:44 It was now about the sixth hour 4
Joh 4: 6 It was about the sixth hour. 4
19:14 it was about the sixth hour 4
Act 10: 9 about the sixth hour. 4
Rev 6:12 When he opened the sixth seal, I looked, and behold 4
9:13 Then the sixth angel blew his trumpet, and I heard 4
14 saying to the sixth angel who had the trumpet 4
16:12 The sixth angel poured his bowl on the river 4
21:20 the fifth onyx, the sixth carnelian 4
1Es 7: 5 in the sixth year of King Darius 4
2Es 6:53 On the sixth day thou didst command the earth 5
7:86 The sixth way, they shall see how some of them 5
97 The sixth order, when it is shown to them 5
2Mc 7:18 After him they brought forward the sixth 4
4Mc 11:13 the sixth, a mere boy, was led 4

sixtyfold 1. ἑξήκοντα
Mrk 4: 8 thirtyfold and sixtyfold and a hundredfold. 1
20 thirtyfold and sixtyfold and a hundredfold. 1

size 1. מִדָּה 2. πλῆθος
Jos 22:10 an altar by the Jordan, an altar of great size. •
1Ch 23:29 and all measures of quantity or size. 1
Ezk 40:10 the three were of the same size; 1
10 the jambs on either side were of the same size. 1
21 its jambs and its vestibule were of the same size 1
22 were of the same size as those of the gate 1
24 they had the same size as the others. 1
28 it was of the same size as the others. 1
29 its vestibule were of the same size as the others; 1
32 it was of the same size as the others. 1
33 its vestibule were of the same size as the others; 1
35 he measured it; it had the same size as the others. 1
36 its vestibule were of the same size as the others; •
46:22 the four were of the same size. 1
1Mc 3:19 not on the size of the army 2

skiff 1. אֳנִיָּה
Job 9:26 They go by like skiffs of reed, like an eagle 1

skilful 1. בין 2. חָכָם 3. חָרָשׁ 4. ידע 5. מָהִיר 6. תְּבוּנָה 7. σοφίζω
Gen 25:27 When the boys grew up, Esau was a skilful hunter 4
1Sm 16:16 seek out a man who is skilful in playing the lyre; 4
18 who is skilful in playing, a man of valor 4
1Ch 25: 7 trained in singing . . all who were skilful 1
2Ch 34:12 Levites . . skilful with instruments of music 1
Ps 78:72 tended them, and guided them with skilful hand. 6
Prv 22:29 Do you see a man skilful in his work? 5
Isa 3: 3 the skilful magician and the expert in charms. 2
40:20 he seeks out a skilful craftsman 2
Ezk 21:31 into the hands of brutal men, skilful to destroy. 3
Sir 38:31 each is skilful in his own work. 7

skilful man 1. חשב
2Ch 26:15 he made engines, invented by skilful men 1

most skilful 1. ἀγαθός
4Mc 7: 1 like a most skilful pilot 1

skilful woman 1. חָכָם
Jer 9:17 send for the skilful women to come; 1

skilfully 1. חשב 2. תְּבוּנָה 3. εὐμαθῶς
Exd 26: 1 with cherubim skilfully worked shall you make 1
36: 6 of fine twined linen, skilfully worked. 1
36: 8 were made . . with cherubim skilfully worked. 1
35 with cherubim skilfully worked he made it. 1
Hos 13: 2 idols skilfully made of their silver 2
Wis 13:11 and skilfully strip off all its bark 3
14:19 For he . . skilfully forced the likeness •

skilfully woven band 1. חֵשֶׁב
Exd 28: 8 the skilfully woven band upon it, to gird it 1
27 at its joining above the skilfully woven band 1
28 that it may lie upon the skilfully woven band 1
29: 5 with the skilfully woven band of the ephod; 1
39: 5 the skilfully woven band upon it, to gird it 1
20 its joining above the skilfully woven band 1
21 that it should lie upon the skilfully woven band 1
Lev 8: 7 girded him with the skilfully woven band 1

skill 1. אֲרֻבָּה 2. דַּעַת 3. חָכְמָה 4. כִּשְׁרוֹן 5. שכל 6. שֵׂכֶל 7. תַּחְבֻּלָה 8. ἐπιστήμη 9. πανουργεύμα τῆς ψυχῆς 10. σύνεσις 11. τέχνη 12. χείρ
1Kg 7:14 wisdom, understanding, and skill, for making any 2
1Ch 28:21 willing man who has skill for any kind of service; 3
2Ch 30:22 the Levites who showed good skill in the service 6
Prv 1: 5 man of understanding acquire skill 7
Ecc 2:21 has toiled with wisdom and knowledge and skill 4
4: 4 all toil and all skill in work come from . . envy 4
Isa 25:11 his pride together with the skill of his hands. 1
Dan 1:17 God gave them learning and skill in all letters 5
Jdt 11: 8 For we have heard of your wisdom and skill 9
Wis 7:16 as are all understanding and skill in crafts. 8
13:10 gold and silver fashioned with skill 11
13 shapes it with skill gained in idleness 10
14: 4 even if a man lacks skill, he may put to sea. 11
Sir 0: 3 using . . great watchfulness and skill 8
9:17 will be praised for the skill of the craftsmen 12
26:13 her skill puts fat on his bones. 8
38: 3 The skill of the physician lifts up his head 8
6 he gave skill to men 8

skill *See also* man.

show skill 1. שכל
2Ch 30:22 the Levites who showed good skill in the service 1

skilled 1. חָכָם 2. חשב 3. ידע 4. מָהִיר 5. מַחֲשָׁבָה 6. עָתִיד 7. שכל 8. תפש 9. εὐφυής 10. σοφός 11. τέκτων
Exd 26:31 in skilled work shall it be made, with cherubim. 2
28:15 breastpiece of judgment, in skilled work; 2
35:33 in carving wood, for work in every skilled craft. 5
35 by any sort of workman or skilled designer. 2
39: 3 into the fine twined linen, in skilled design. 2
8 He made the breastpiece, in skilled work 2
1Ch 22:15 craftsmen without number, skilled in working 1
2Ch 2: 7 now send me a man skilled to work in gold, silver 1
13 Now I have sent a skilled man . . Huram-abi. 1
Ezr 7: 6 Ezra . . was a scribe skilled in the law of Moses 4
Job 3: 8 who are skilled to rouse up Leviathan. 6
Jer 4:22 They are skilled in doing evil 1
46: 9 men of Lud, skilled in handling the bow. 8
50: 9 Their arrows are like a skilled warrior 7
Ams 5:16 to wailing those who are skilled in lamentation 3
1Co 3:10 like a skilled master builder 10
1Es 8: 3 a scribe skilled in the law of Moses 9
Wis 13:11 A skilled woodcutter may saw down a tree 11

skilled *See also* worker.

become skilled 1. σοφίζω
Sir 18:29 Those who understand sayings become skilled 1

skilled man 1. חָכָם 2. σοφίζω
Jer 10: 9 they are all the work of skilled men. 1
Ezk 27: 8 skilled men of Zemer were in you 1
9 elders of Gebal and her skilled men were in you 1
Sir 37:20 A man skilled in words may be hated 2

skillfully 1. יטב
Ps 33: 3 to him a new song, play skillfully on the strings 1

skin 1. גֶּלֶד 2. זָג 3. חֵמֶת 4. נאד 5. נֵבֶל 6. עוֹר 7. ἀσκός 8. δέρμα
Gen 3:21 made . . garments of skins, and clothed them. 6
21:14 Abraham . . took bread and a skin of water 3
15 When the water in the skin was gone 3
19 she went, and filled the skin with water 3
27:16 the skins of the kids she put upon his hands 6
Exd 25: 5 tanned rams' skins, goatskins, acacia wood 6
26:14 for the tent a covering of tanned rams' skins 6
29:14 the flesh of the bull, and its skin, and its dung 6
34:29 Moses did not know that the skin of his face shone 6
30 Moses, behold, the skin of his face shone 6
35 saw . . that the skin of Moses' face shone; 6
35: 7 tanned rams' skins, and goatskins; acacia wood 6
23 or goats' hair or tanned rams' skins or goatskins 6

36:19 made for the tent a covering of tanned rams' skins 6
39:34 the covering of tanned rams' skins and goatskins 6
Lev 4:11 the skin of the bull and all its flesh 6
7: 8 have for himself the skin of the burnt offering 6
8:17 the bull, and its skin, and its flesh, and its dung 6
9:11 The flesh and the skin he burned with fire 6
11:32 a garment or a skin or a sack, any vessel 6
13: 2 When a man has on the skin of his body a swelling 6
2 a leprous disease on the skin of his body 6
3 examine the diseased spot on the skin of his body 6
3 the disease appears to be deeper than the skin 6
4 if the spot is white in the skin of his body 6
4 if the spot . . appears no deeper than the skin 6
5 if . . the disease has not spread in the skin 6
6 if . . the disease has not spread in the skin 6
7 if the eruption spreads in the skin 6
8 if the eruption has spread in the skin 6
10 if there is a white swelling in the skin 6
11 it is a chronic leprosy in the skin of his body 6
12 if the leprosy breaks out in the skin 6
12 covers all the skin of the diseased person 6
18 when there is in the skin of one's body a boil 6
20 if it appears deeper than the skin and its hair 6
21 if . . it is not deeper than the skin, but is dim 6
22 if it spreads in the skin 6
24 when the body has a burn on its skin 6
25 if . . it appears deeper than the skin 6
26 if . . it is no deeper than the skin, but is dim 6
27 if it is spreading in the skin 6
28 if the spot . . does not spread in the skin 6
30 if it appears deeper than the skin, and the hair 6
31 if . . it appears no deeper than the skin 6
32 the itch appears to be no deeper than the skin 6
34 if the itch has not spread in the skin 6
34 if . . it appears to be no deeper than the skin 6
35 itch spreads in the skin after his cleansing 6
36 if the itch has spread in the skin 6
38 has spots on the skin of the body, white spots 6
39 spots on the skin of the body are of a dull white 6
39 tetter . . has broken out in the skin; he is clean 6
43 the appearance of leprosy in the skin of the body 6
48 in warp or woof of linen or wool, or in a skin 6
48 in a skin or in anything made of skin 6
49 whether in warp or woof or in skin or in anything 6
49 in anything made of skin, it is a leprous disease 6
51 disease has spread in the garment . . in the skin 6
51 whatever be the use of the skin 6
52 woolen or linen, or anything of skin 6
53 garment in warp or woof or in anything of skin 6
56 shall tear the spot out of the garment or the skin 6
57 appears . . in anything of skin, it is spreading 6
58 anything of skin from which the disease departs 6
59 disease . . in anything of skin, to decide 6
15:17 every garment and every skin on which the semen 6
16:27 their skin and their flesh and their dung 6
Num 6: 4 not even the seeds or the skins. 2
19: 5 her skin, her flesh . . shall be burned; 6
31:20 purify every garment, every article of skin 6
Jdg 4:19 she opened a skin of milk and gave him a drink 4
1Sm 1:24 a . . bull, an ephah of flour, and a skin of wine; 5
10: 3 and another carrying a skin of wine. 5
16:20 Jesse took an ass . . and a skin of wine and a kid 4
25:18 and took 200 loaves, and two skins of wine 5
2Sm 16: 1 100 of summer fruits, and a skin of wine. 5
Neh 5:18 every ten days skins of wine in abundance; 5
Job 2: 4 Then Satan answered the LORD, "Skin for skin! 6
4 Then Satan answered the LORD, "Skin for skin! 6
7: 5 my skin hardens, then breaks out afresh. 6
10:11 Thou didst clothe me with skin and flesh 6
16:15 I have sewed sackcloth upon my skin 1
18:13 By disease his skin is consumed 6
19:20 My bones cleave to my skin and to my flesh 6
20 I have escaped by the skin of my teeth. 6
26 after my skin has been thus destroyed 6
30:30 My skin turns black and falls from me 6
41: 7 Can you fill his skin with harpoons 6
Jer 13:23 Can the Ethiopian change his skin 6
Lam 3: 4 He has made my flesh and my skin waste away 6
4: 8 their skin has shriveled upon their bones 6
5:10 Our skin is hot as an oven with . . heat of famine. 6
Ezk 37: 6 and cover you with skin, and put breath in you, 6
8 skin had covered them; but there was no breath 6
Mic 3: 2 who tear the skin from off my people 6
3 of my people, and flay their skin from off them 6
Mat 9:17 if it is, the skins burst, and the wine is spilled 7
17 the wine is spilled, and the skins are destroyed; 7
Mrk 2:22 if he does, the wine will burst the skins 7
22 the wine is lost, and so are the skins 7
22 new wine is for fresh skins. 7
Lke 5:37 if he does, the new wine will burst the skins 7
37 the skins will be destroyed. 7
Heb 11:37 they went about in skins of sheep and goats 8
2Mc 7: 7 They tore off the skin of his head with the hair 8

skip 1. רקד 2. ἀφάλλομαι
Ps 114: 4 mountains skipped like rams 1
6 O mountains, that you skip like rams? 1
Sir 36:26 a nimble robber that skips from city to city 2

make skip 1. רקד
Ps 29: 6 He makes Lebanon to skip like a calf 1

skirt 1. כָּנָף 2. שׁוּל
Exd 28:33 On its skirts you shall make pomegranates 2
33 make pomegranates . . around its skirts 2
34 round about on the skirts of the robe. 2
39:24 On the skirts of the robe they made pomegranates 2
25 bells between the pomegranates upon the skirts 2
26 round about upon the skirts of the robe 2
Rut 3: 9 spread your skirt over your maidservant 1
1Sm 15:27 Saul laid hold upon the skirt of his robe 1
24: 4 David . . cut off the skirt of Saul's robe. 1
5 because he had cut off Saul's skirt. 1
11 See, my father, see the skirt of your robe in my hand; 1
11 I cut off the skirt of your robe, and did not kill 1
Job 38:13 that it might take hold of the skirts of the earth 1
Jer 2:34 Also on your skirts is found the lifeblood 1
13:22 of your iniquity that your skirts are lifted up 2
26 I myself will lift up your skirts over your face 2
Lam 1: 9 Her uncleanness was in her skirts; 2
Ezk 5: 3 and bind them in the skirts of your robe. 1
16: 8 I spread my skirt over you 1
Nah 3: 5 and will lift up your skirts over your face; 2
Hag 2:12 carries holy flesh in the skirt of his garment 1
12 and touches with his skirt bread, or pottage 1

skull 1. גֻּלְגֹּלֶת 2. κρανίον
Jdg 9:53 upon Abim'elech's head, and crushed his skull. 1
2Kg 9:35 found . . the skull and the feet and the palms 1
Mat 27:33 (which means the place of a skull) 2
Mrk 15:22 Gol'gotha (which means the place of a skull). 2
Lke 23:33 they came to the place which is called The Skull 2
Joh 19:17 to the place called the place of a skull 2

sky 1. שַׁחַק 2. שָׁמַיִם 3. οὐρανός
Deu 33:26 who rides . . in his majesty through the skies. 1
Neh 1: 9 your dispersed be under the farthest skies 2
Job 36:28 which the skies pour down, and drop upon man 1
37:18 spread out the skies, hard as a molten mirror? 1
21 look on the light when it is bright in the skies 1
Ps 68:34 over Israel, and his power is in the skies. 1
77:17 the skies gave forth thunder; thy arrows flashed 1
78:23 Yet he commanded the skies above 1
85:11 righteousness will look down from the sky. 2
89: 6 For who in the skies can be compared to the LORD? 1
37 shall stand firm while the skies endure." Selah 1
Prv 8:28 when he made firm the skies above 1
30:19 the way of an eagle in the sky, the way of a serpent 2
Isa 34: 4 and the skies roll up like a scroll. 2
45: 8 and let the skies rain down righteousness; 1
Jer 51: 9 and has been lifted up even to the skies. 1
Mat 16: 2 for the sky is red.' 3
3 for the sky is red and threatening 3
3 how to interpret the appearance of the sky 3
Lke 12:56 to interpret the appearance of the earth and sky; 3
17:24 and lights up the sky from one side to the other 3
Rev 6:13 the stars of the sky fell to the earth 3
14 the sky vanished like a scroll that is rolled up 3
11: 6 They have power to shut the sky, that no rain 3
20:11 from his presence earth and sky fled away 3

sky *See also* fall.

slack 1. אחר 2. פוג 3. רְמִיָּה 4. רפה 5. שָׁלוּ (A)
6. παρίημι
Deu 7:10 he will not be slack with him who hates him 1
23:21 make a vow . . you shall not be slack to pay it; 1
Jos 18: 3 How long will you be slack to go in and take 4
Ezr 4:22 take care not to be slack in this matter; 5
Prv 10: 4 A slack hand causes poverty 3
18: 9 slack in his work is a brother to him who destroys. 4
Hab 1: 4 the law is slacked and justice never goes forth. 2
Sir 2:12 Woe to timid hearts and to slack hands 6

slacken 1. עצר
2Kg 4:24 do not slacken the pace for me unless I tell you. 1

slackness 1. רְמִיָּה
Jer 48:10 he who does the work of the LORD with slackness; 1

slain *See* lie, beast.

slain man 1. חָלָל
Deu 21: 3 elders of the city . . nearest to the slain man 1
6 elders of that city nearest to the slain man 1

slake 1. ἴαμα
Wis 11: 4 slaking of thirst from hard stone. 1

slander 1. דִּבָּה 2. לשׁן 3. נתן דֹּפִי 4. קרץ 5. רגל
6. רָכִיל 7. βλασφημία 8. γλωσσατρίτη 9. διαβάλλω
10. διαβολή 11. δυσφημέω 12. κακολογέω
13. καταλαλιά
2Sm 19:27 He has slandered your servant to . . the king. 5
Ps 15: 3 who does not slander with his tongue 5
27: 2 assail me, uttering slanders against me †
35:15 whom I knew not slandered me without ceasing; 4
50:20 you slander your own mother's son. 3
101: 5 Him who slanders his neighbors secretly 2
Prv 10:18 he who utters slander is a fool. 1
30:10 Do not slander a servant to his master 2
Jer 6:28 They are . . rebellious, going about with slanders; 6
Ezk 22: 9 There are men in you who slander to shed blood 6
Mat 15:19 fornication, theft, false witness, slander. 7
Mrk 7:22 envy, slander, pride, foolishness. 7
1Co 4:13 when slandered, we try to conciliate 11
2Co 12:20 anger, selfishness, slander, gossip, conceit 13
Eph 4:31 anger and clamor and slander be put away from you 7
Col 3: 8 wrath, malice, slander, and foul talk 7
1Ti 6: 4 dissension, slander, base suspicions 7
1Pe 2: 1 put away all . . envy and all slander. 13
Rev 2: 9 the slander of those who say that they are Jews 7
Wis 1:11 keep your tongue from slander 13
Sir 19:15 Question a friend, for often it is slander 10
26: 5 The slander of a city, the gathering of a mob 10
28:14 Slander has shaken many 8
15 Slander has driven away courageous women 8
16 Whoever pays heed to slander will not find rest •
51: 6 slander of an unrighteous tongue to the king 10
2Mc 4: 1 Simon . . slandered Onias 12
3Mc 6: 7 who through envious slanders was cast down 10
4Mc 4: 1 despite all manner of slander 9

slanderer 1. אִישׁ לָשׁוֹן 2. רָכִיל 3. διάβολος
4. κατάλαλος 5. ψίθυρος
Lev 19:16 You shall not go up and down as a slanderer 2
Ps 140:11 Let not the slanderer be established in the land; 1
Jer 9: 4 and every neighbor goes about as a slanderer. 2
Rom 1:30 slanderers, haters of God, insolent, haughty 4
1Ti 3:11 no slanderers, but temperate 3
2Ti 3: 3 inhuman, implacable, slanderers, profligates 3
Tit 2: 3 not to be slanderers or slaves to drink 3
Sir 5:14 Do not be called a slanderer 5

slanderous 1. διαβολή
Sir 51: 2 the snare of a slanderous tongue 1

slanderously 1. βλασφημέω
Rom 3: 8 as some . . slanderously charge us with saying. 1

slap 1. ῥαπίζω
Mat 26:67 some slapped him 1
1Es 4:30 slap the king with her left hand. 1

slash open 1. פלח
Job 16:13 He slashes open my kidneys, and does not spare; 1

slaughter 1. הרג 2. הֶרֶג 3. הֲרֵגָה 4. זבח 5. חָלָל
6. טבח 7. טֶבַח 8. טִבְחָה 9. מַאֲכָל 10. מַגֵּפָה
11. מַטְבֵּחַ 12. מַכָּה 13. מַפָּץ 14. נכה 15. קֶטֶל
16. שׁחט 17. שחט 18. ἀποσφάζω 19. κατασφάζω
20. κοπή 21. πληγή 22. ποιέω σφαγάς 23. σφαγή
24. φονεύς 25. φόνος 26. occisio
Gen 43:16 the men into the house, and slaughter an animal 6
Exd 29:16 you shall slaughter the ram, and shall take 17
Num11:22 Shall flocks and herds be slaughtered for them 17
19: 3 outside the camp and slaughtered before him; 17
Deu 12:15 However, you may slaughter and eat flesh 4
Jos 8:24 finished slaughtering all the inhabitants of Ai 1
10:10 who slew them with a great slaughter at Gibeon 12
20 slaying them with a very great slaughter 12
Jdg 11:33 he smote them . . with a very great slaughter. 12
15: 8 he smote them hip and thigh with great slaughter; 12
1Sm 4:10 and there was a very great slaughter 12
17 has also been a great slaughter among the people; 10
6:19 the LORD had made a great slaughter 12
14:14 that first slaughter . . was of about twenty men 12
30 now the slaughter . . has not been great. 12
17:57 returned from the slaughter of the Philistine 14
19: 8 and made a great slaughter among them 14
8 and made a great slaughter among them 12
23: 5 fought . . and made a great slaughter among them. 12
2Sm 1: 1 returned from the slaughter of the Amal'ekites 14
17: 9 There has been a slaughter among the people 10
18: 7 and the slaughter there was great on that day 10
1Kg 11:24 he gathered men . . after the slaughter by David; 1
20:21 and killed the Syrians with a great slaughter. 12
2Kg 3:24 they went forward, slaughtering the Moabites 14
2Ch 13:17 Abij'ah . . slew them with a great slaughter; 12
25:14 Amazi'ah came from the slaughter of the E'domites 14
28: 5 Israel, who defeated him with great slaughter. 12
Est 9: 5 the Jews smote . . slaughtering, and destroying 2
Ps 44:11 Thou hast made us like sheep for slaughter 9
22 and accounted as sheep for the slaughter. 8
Prv 7:22 follows her, as an ox goes to the slaughter 7
9: 2 She has slaughtered her beasts 6
24:11 hold back those . . stumbling to the slaughter. 2
Isa 13:18 Their bows will slaughter the young men; 16
14:21 Prepare slaughter for his sons 11
30:25 day of the great slaughter, when the towers fall. 2
34: 2 doomed them, has given them over for slaughter. 7
6 LORD has . . a great slaughter in the land of Edom. 7
53: 7 like a lamb that is led to the slaughter 7
65:12 and all of you shall bow down to the slaughter; 7
66: 3 He who slaughters an ox is like him who kills a man; 17
Jer 7:32 but the valley of Slaughter: for they will bury 3

11:19 But I was like a gentle lamb led to the slaughter. 6
12: 3 Pull them out like sheep for the slaughter 8
3 and set them apart for the day of slaughter. 3
19: 6 valley of . . Hinnom, but the valley of Slaughter. 3
25:34 your slaughter and dispersion have come 6
48:15 his young men have gone down to slaughter 7
50:27 all her bulls, let them go down to the slaughter. 7
51:40 will bring them down like lambs to the slaughter 6
Lam 2:21 hast slain them, slaughtering without mercy. 6
Ezk 9: 2 man with his weapon for slaughter in his hand 13
16:21 that you slaughtered my children 17
21:10 sharpened for slaughter, polished to flash 6
14 it is the sword for the great slaughter 5
15 like lightning, it is polished for slaughter. 7
28 say, A sword, a sword is drawn for the slaughter 7
23:39 For when they had slaughtered their children 17
26:15 when slaughter is made in the midst of you? 2
34: 3 you slaughter the fatlings; 4
40:39 and the guilt offering were to be slaughtered. 17
41 on which the sacrifices were to be slaughtered. 17
42 and the sacrifices were slaughtered. 17
Hos 9:13 E'phraim must lead forth his sons to slaughter. 1
Obd 1: 9 man from Mount Esau will be cut off by slaughter. 15
Zec 11: 4 shepherd of the flock doomed to slaughter. 3
Act 8:32 As a sheep led to the slaughter 23
Rom 8:36 we are regarded as sheep to be slaughtered. 23
Heb 7: 1 returning from the slaughter of the kings 20
Jas 5: 5 have fattened your hearts in a day of slaughter. 23
2Es 15:10 my people is led like a flock to the slaughter 26
26 he will hand them over to death and slaughter. 26
Jdt 2:11 you shall hand them over to slaughter 25
8:22 the slaughter of our brethren 25
15: 5 outflanked them with great slaughter 21
7 when they returned from the slaughter 20
Wis 12: 5 their merciless slaughter of children 24
Bel 1:28 slain the dragon, and slaughtered the priests. 19
2Mc 5: 6 Jason kept relentlessly slaughtering 22
13 slaughter of virgins and infants. 23
10:31 20,500 were slaughtered, besides 600 horsemen. 19
12:16 and slaughtered untold numbers 22
26 slaughtered 25,000 people. 19
4Mc 2:19 their irrational slaughter of the entire tribe 18

slaughter *See also* make.

slave 1. אָמָה 2. בֶּן בַּיִת 3. נֶפֶשׁ 4. עבד 5. עֶבֶד 6. עֶבֶד וְשִׁפְחָה 7. שִׁפְחָה 8. *δέσμιος* 9. *δουλεύω* 10. *δούλη* 11. *δοῦλος* 12. *δουλόω* 13. *οἰκέτης* 14. *οἰκετικός* 15. *παιδίσκη* 16. *παῖς* 17. *σῶμα*

Gen 9:25 a slave of slaves shall he be to his brothers 5
25 a slave of slaves shall he be to his brothers 5
26 and let Canaan be his slave. 5
27 tents of Shem; and let Canaan be his slave. 5
15: 3 and a slave born in my house will be my heir. 2
13 a land that is not theirs, and will be slaves there 4
17:23 all the slaves born in his house •
43:18 to make slaves of us and seize our asses. 5
44: 9 let him die, and we also will be my lord's slaves. 5
10 he with whom it is found shall be my slave 5
16 behold, we are my lord's slaves 5
17 Only the man . . shall be my slave; 5
33 remain instead of the lad as a slave to my lord; 5
47:19 we with our land will be slaves to Pharaoh; 5
25 my lord, we will be slaves to Pharaoh. 5
49:15 and became a slave at forced labor. 4
Exd 9:20 he who feared . . made his slaves and his cattle 5
21 left his slaves and his cattle in the field. 5
12:44 every slave that is bought for money may eat of it 5
21: 2 you buy a Hebrew slave, he shall serve six years 5
5 if the slave plainly says, 'I love my master, my wife 5
7 When a man sells his daughter as a slave 1
20 and the slave dies under his hand •
21 if the slave survives a day or two, he is not to be •
21 to be punished; for the slave is his money. •
26 he shall let the slave go free for the eye's sake. •
27 he shall let the slave go free for the tooth's •
Lev 19:20 If a man lies carnally with a woman who is a slave 7
22:11 if a priest buys a slave as his property for money 3
11 the slave may eat of it; and those that are born •
25:39 you shall not make him serve as a slave 5
42 they shall not be sold as slaves 5
26:13 you should not be their slaves 5
Deu 6:21 We were Pharaoh's slaves in Egypt; 5
15:15 remember . . you were a slave in the land of Egypt 5
16:12 You shall remember that you were a slave in Egypt; 5
23:15 not give up to his master a slave who has escaped 5
24:18 remember that you were a slave in Egypt 5
22 remember that you were a slave in the land of Egypt; 5
Jos 9:23 you are cursed, and some of you shall . . be slaves 5
16:10 but have become slaves to do forced labor. 4
1Sm 8:17 He will take . . and you shall be his slaves. 5
1Kg 2:39 two of Shim'e-i's slaves ran away to Achish, son 5
39 it was told Shim'e-i, "Behold, your slaves are in Gath 5
40 and went to Gath to Achish, to seek his slaves; 5
40 Shim'e-i went and brought his slaves from Gath. 5
9:21 Solomon made a forced levy of slaves 4
22 of the people of Israel Solomon made no slaves; 5
2Kg 4: 1 to take my two children to be his slaves. 5
1Ch 2:34 but Sheshan had an Egyptian slave, whose name was 5
35 gave his daughter . . to Jarha his slave; 5
2Ch 8: 9 of . . Israel Solomon made no slaves for his work; 5
Neh 5: 5 forcing our sons and our daughters to be slaves 5
9:36 Behold, we are slaves this day; 5
36 in the land . . behold, we are slaves. 5
Job 3:19 the slave is free from his master. 5
7: 2 Like a slave who longs for the shadow 5
Ps 105:17 Joseph, who was sold as a slave. 5
Prv 17: 2 A slave who deals wisely will rule over a son 5
19:10 much less for a slave to rule over princes. 5
22: 7 borrower is the slave of the lender. 5
30:22 a slave when he becomes king 5
Ecc 2: 7 and had slaves who were born in my house; •
10: 7 I have seen slaves on horses, and princes walking 5
7 and princes walking on foot like slaves. 5
Isa 24: 2 as with the slave, so with his master; 5
Jer 2:14 Is Israel a slave? Is he a homeborn servant? 5
34:11 and brought them into subjection as slaves. 6
16 brought them into subjection to be your slaves. 6
Lam 5: 8 Slaves rule over us; there is none to deliver us 5
Mat 8: 9 'Come,' and he comes, and to my slave, 'Do this,' 11
20:27 whoever would be first . . must be your slave; 11
26:51 and struck the slave of the high priest 11
Mrk 10:44 whoever would be first . . must be slave of all. 11
14:47 struck the slave of the high priest 11
Lke 7: 2 Now a centurion had a slave who was dear to him 11
3 asking him to come and heal his slave. 11
8 to my slave, 'Do this,' and he does it. 11
10 they found the slave well. 11
22:50 one of them struck the slave of the high priest 11
Joh 8:34 every one who commits sin is a slave to sin. 11
35 The slave does not continue in the house for ever; 11
18:10 Simon Peter . . struck the high priest's slave 11
10 The slave's name was Malchus. 11
Rom 6:16 if you yield . . to any one as obedient slaves 11
16 you are slaves of the one whom you obey 11
17 that you who were once slaves of sin 11
20 When you were slaves of sin 11
1Co 7:21 Were you a slave when called? Never mind. 11
22 who was called in the Lord as a slave is a freedman 11
22 who was free when called is a slave of Christ. 11
23 do not become slaves of men. 11
12:13 Jews or Greeks, slaves or free 11
Gal 3:28 there is neither slave nor free 11
4: 1 the heir . . is no better than a slave 11
3 slaves to the elemental spirits of the universe. 12
7 So through God you are no longer a slave but a son 11
9 whose slaves you want to be once more? 9
22 one by a slave and one by a free woman. 15
23 the son of the slave was born according to the flesh 15
30 Cast out the slave and her son 15
30 the son of the slave shall not inherit 15
31 So, brethren, we are not children of the slave 15
Eph 6: 5 Slaves, be obedient 11
8 whether he is a slave or free. 11
Col 3:11 barbarian, Scyth'ian, slave, free man 11
22 Slaves, obey in everything 11
4: 1 Masters, treat your slaves justly and fairly 11
Tit 2: 3 not to be slanderers or slaves to drink 12
9 Bid slaves to be submissive to their masters 11
3: 3 slaves to various passions and pleasures 9
Phm 1:16 no longer as a slave but more than a slave 11
16 no longer as a slave but more than a slave 11
2Pe 2:19 they themselves are slaves of corruption; 11
Rev 6:15 every one, slave and free, hid in the caves 11
13:16 both rich and poor, both free and slave 11
18:13 and chariots, and slaves, that is, human souls. 17
19:18 and the flesh of all men, both free and slave 11
1Es 3:19 of the slave and the free, of the poor and the rich. 13
4:26 Many men . . have become slaves because of them. 11
Tob 10:10 half of his property in slaves, cattle, and money. 17
Jdt 3: 4 their inhabitants are your slaves 11
5:11 humbled them and made slaves of them. 11
6: 7 Now my slaves are going to take you back 11
10 Then Holofernes ordered his slaves 11
11 the slaves took him and led him out of the camp 11
7:27 for we will be slaves, but our lives will be spared 11
9: 3 thou didst strike down slaves along with princes 11
10 strike down the slave with the prince 11
10:23 his slaves raised her up. 11
12:10 Holofernes held a banquet for his slave only 11
13: 1 When evening came, his slaves quickly withdrew 11
14:13 the slaves have been so bold as to come down 11
18 The slaves have tricked us! 11
Wis 9: 5 For I am thy slave and the son of thy maidservant 11
18:11 The slave was punished with the same penalty 11
Sir 33:25 Set your slave to work, and you will find rest; 16
1Mc 2:11 no longer free, she has become a slave. 10
3:41 to the camp to get the sons of Israel for slaves. 16
2Mc 1:27 set free those who are slaves among the Gentiles 9
5:24 to sell the women and boys as slaves. •
8:11 inviting them to buy Jewish slaves 17
11 and promising to hand over 90 slaves for a talent 17
25 those who had come to buy them as slaves •
3Mc 2:28 subjected . . to the status of slaves 14
7: 5 also led them out with harsh treatment as slaves 8
4Mc 13: 2 if they had been slaves to their emotions 12

slave *See also* make, man, purchase, serve, treat.

become a slave 1. עבד 2. *δουλόω*

1Sm 4: 9 lest you become slaves to the Hebrews 1
Rom 6:18 have become slaves of righteousness. 2
22 set free from sin and have become slaves of God 2

female slave 1. אָמָה 2. עֶבֶד 3. שִׁפְחָה

Gen 20:14 male and female slaves, and gave them to Abraham 3
17 female slaves so that they bore children. 1
Exd 21:20 man strikes his slave, male or female, with a rod 1
26 eye of his slave, male or female, and destroys it 1
27 tooth of his slave, male or female 1
32 If the ox gores a slave, male or female, the owner 1
Lev 25: 6 for yourself and for your male and female slaves 1
44 As for your male and female slaves whom you 1
44 you may buy male and female slaves from among 2
Deu 28:68 sale to your enemies as male and female slaves 3
2Ch 28:10 subjugate . . male and female, as your slaves. 3
Ecc 2: 7 I bought male and female slaves 3
Isa 14: 2 as male and female slaves; they will take captive 3
Jer 34: 9 set free his Hebrew slaves, male and female 3
10 every one would set free his slave, male or female 3
11 and took back the male and female slaves 3
16 each of you took back his male and female slaves 3

slave girl 1. *παιδίσκη*

Act 16:16 we were met by a slave girl 1

male slave 1. עֶבֶד

Gen 20:14 male and female slaves, and gave them to Abraham 1
Exd 21: 7 she shall not go out as the male slaves do. 1
20 man strikes his slave, male or female, with a rod 1
26 eye of his slave, male or female, and destroys it 1
27 tooth of his slave, male or female 1
32 If the ox gores a slave, male or female, the owner 1
Lev 25: 6 for yourself and for your male and female slaves 1
44 As for your male and female slaves whom you 1
44 you may buy male and female slaves from among 1
Deu 28:68 sale to your enemies as male and female slaves 1
2Ch 28:10 subjugate . . male and female, as your slaves. 1
Ecc 2: 7 I bought male and female slaves 1
Isa 14: 2 as male and female slaves; they will take captive 1
Jer 34: 9 set free his Hebrew slaves, male and female 1
10 every one would set free his slave, male or female 1
11 and took back the male and female slaves 1
16 when each of you took back his male . . slaves 1

man slave 1. עֶבֶד 2. *παῖς*

Est 7: 4 If we had been sold merely as slaves, men and women 1
Jdt 8: 7 gold and silver, and men and women slaves 2

runaway slave 1. *δραπέτης*

2Mc 8:35 and made his way alone like a runaway slave 1

slave woman 1. אָמָה

Gen 21:10 she said to Abraham, "Cast out this slave woman 1
10 for the son of this slave woman shall not be heir 1
12 Be not displeased . . because of your slave woman; 1
13 I will make a nation of the son of the slave woman 1

woman slave 1. שִׁפְחָה 2. *παιδίσκη*

Est 7: 4 If we had been sold merely as slaves, men and women 1
Jdt 8: 7 gold and silver, and men and women slaves 2

slavery 1. *δουλεία* 2. *δουλεύω* 3. *δοῦλος*

Rom 8:15 For you did not receive the spirit of slavery 1
Gal 4:24 bearing children for slavery; she is Hagar. 1
25 for she is in slavery with her children. 2
5: 1 do not submit again to a yoke of slavery. 1
1Ti 6: 1 all who are under the yoke of slavery 3
Jdt 8:23 For our slavery will not bring us into favor 1
AEs 14: 8 we are in bitter slavery 1
2Mc 5:14 as many were sold into slavery as were slain •
8:10 by selling the captured Jews into slavery. •

slay 1. הרג 2. הֲרֵגָה 3. זבח 4. חלל 5. חָלָל 6. חרב 7. טבח 8. מות 9. מָוֶת 10. נגף 11. נכה 12. נפל 13. נצה 14. קטל 15. רצח 16. שחט 17. שחת 18. קטל (A) 19. *ἀναιρέω* 20. *ἀποκτείνω* 21. *ἐξαίρω* 22. *θανατόω* 23. *καταστρώννυμι* 24. *κατασφάζω* 25. *πατάσσω* 26. *σφαγιάζω* 27. *σφάζω* 28. *φόνος* 29. interficio

Gen 4:14 on the earth, and whoever finds me will slay me. 1
15 If any one slays Cain, vengeance shall be taken 1
23 I have slain a man for wounding me 1
25 another child instead of Abel, for Cain slew him. 1
18:25 to slay the righteous with the wicked 8
20: 4 he said, "Lord, wilt thou slay an innocent people? 1
22:10 put forth his hand, and took the knife to slay 16
32:11 for I fear him, lest he come and slay us all 11
34:26 They slew Hamor and his son Shechem 1
27 the sons of Jacob came upon the slain 5
37:26 What profit is it if we slay our brother 1
38: 7 Er . . was wicked . . and the LORD slew him. 8
10 the sight of the LORD, and he slew him also. 8
42:37 Reuben said to his father, "Slay my two sons if I do 8
49: 6 for in their anger they slay men 1
Exd 4:23 behold, I will slay your first-born son.' 1

12:23 the LORD will pass through to slay the Egyptians; 10
23 destroyer to enter your houses to slay you. 10
27 when he slew the Egyptians but spared our 10
13:15 the LORD slew all the first-born in the land 1
23: 7 do not slay the innocent and righteous 1
32:12 With evil intent did he bring them forth, to slay 1
27 go . . and slay every man his brother 1
Lev 17: 5 sacrifices which they slay in the open field 3
5 slay them as sacrifices of peace offerings 3
7 shall no more slay their sacrifices for satyrs 3
Num 3:13 on the day that I slew all the first-born 11
8:17 day that I slew all the first-born in the land 11
14:16 therefore he has slain them in the wilderness.' 16
19:16 Whoever . . touches one who is slain with a sword 5
18 sprinkle it . . upon him who touched the . . slain 5
21:24 Israel slew him with the edge of the sword 11
35 they slew him, and his sons, and all his people 11
22:33 just now I would have slain you and let her live. 1
23:24 drinks the blood of the slain. 5
25: 5 Every one of you slay his men who have yoked 1
14 The name of the slain man of Israel . . was Zimri 13
14 man . . who was slain with the Mid'ianite woman 11
15 name of the Mid'ianite woman who was slain 11
18 sister, who was slain on the day of the plague 11
31: 7 warred against Mid'ian . . and slew every male. 1
8 slew the kings of Mid'ian with the rest of their 1
8 slew the kings . . with the rest of their slain 5
8 also slew Balaam the son of Be'or with the sword. 1
19 whoever has touched any slain 5
35:27 avenger of blood slays the manslayer 15
Deu 9:28 brought them out to slay them in the wilderness. 8
21: 1 any one is found slain, lying in the open country 5
2 cities which are around him that is slain; 5
27:24 'Cursed be he who slays his neighbor in secret.' 11
25 'Cursed be he who takes a bribe to slay an innocent 11
28:31 Your ox shall be slain before your eyes 7
32:42 with the blood of the slain and the captives 5
Jos 7: 5 and chased them . . and slew them at the descent. 11
10:10 Israel, who slew them with a great slaughter 11
20 Joshua and . . Israel had finished slaying them 11
11: 6 I will give over all of them, slain, to Israel; 5
13:22 Balaam also . . among the rest of their slain. 5
Jdg 8:17 the tower of Penu'el, and slew the men of the city. 1
18 Where are the men whom you slew at Tabor? 1
19 if you had saved them alive, I would not slay you. 1
20 he said to Jether . . "Rise, and slay them. 1
21 And Gideon arose and slew Zebah and Zalmun'na; 1
9: 5 and slew his brothers the sons of Jerubba'al 1
18 and have slain his sons, 70 men on one stone 1
24 blood be laid upon Abim'elech . . who slew them 1
24 who strengthened his hands to slay his brothers. 1
43 and he rose against them and slew them. 11
44 upon all who were in the fields and slew them. 11
12: 6 then they seized him and slew him at the fords 16
15:15 found a . . jawbone . . and with it he slew 1,000 men. 11
16 with the jawbone of an ass have I slain 1,000 men 11
16:24 ravager of our country, who has slain many of us. 5
30 the dead whom he slew at his death were more 8
30 more than those whom he had slain during his life. 8
20:45 to Gidom, and 2,000 men of them were slain. 11
1Sm 1:25 they slew the bull, and they brought the child 16
2:25 for it was the will of the LORD to slay them. 8
4: 2 defeated by the Philistines, who slew about 4,000 11
11 two sons of Eli, Hophni and Phin'ehas, were slain. 8
5:10 They have brought . . to slay us and our people. 8
11 Send . . that it may not slay us and our people. 8
6:19 And he slew some of the men of Beth-she'mesh 11
19 he slew 70 men of them, and the people mourned 11
14:32 took sheep and . . and slew them on the ground; 16
34 bring his ox or . . sheep, and slay them here, and eat; 16
34 the people brought his ox . . and slew them there. 16
18: 6 David returned from slaying the Philistine 11
7 Saul has slain his thousands 11
19: 5 he slew the Philistine, and the LORD wrought 11
20: 8 But if there is guilt in me, slay me yourself; 8
21:11 Saul has slain his thousands 11
29: 5 'Saul has slain his thousands 11
31: 1 Israel fled . . and fell slain on Mount Gilbo'a. 5
2 the Philistines slew Jonathan and Abin'adab 11
8 when the Philistines came to strip the slain 5
2Sm 1: 9 And he said to me, 'Stand beside me and slay me; 8
10 I stood beside him, and slew him 8
16 saying, 'I have slain the LORD's anointed.' 8
19 Thy glory, O Israel, is slain upon thy high places! 5
22 From the blood of the slain . . fat of the mighty 5
2:31 the servants of David had slain . . 360 . . men. 11
3:29 or who holds a spindle, or who is slain by the sword 12
30 Jo'ab and Abi'shai his brother slew Abner 1
37 it had not been the king's will to slay Abner 8
4: 7 they smote him, and slew him, and beheaded him. 8
10 I seized him and slew him at Ziklag 1
11 when wicked men have slain a righteous man 1
8: 5 David slew 22,000 men of the Syrians. 11
13 When he returned, he slew 18,000 E'domites 25
10:18 David slew of the Syrians the men of 700 chariots 1
11:17 Uri'ah the Hittite was slain also. 8
12: 9 have slain him with the sword of the Ammonites. 1
13:30 Ab'salom has slain all the king's sons 11
14: 7 kill him for the life of his brother whom he slew'; 1
11 that the avenger of blood slay no more 17
21: 2 Saul had sought to slay them in his zeal 11
18 then Sib'becai the Hu'shathite slew Saph 11
19 and Elha'nan . . slew Goliath the Gittite 11
21 Jonathan the son of Shim'e-i . . slew him. 11
23: 8 against 800 whom he slew at one time. 5
10 men returned after him only to strip the slain. •
12 But he took his stand . . and slew the Philistines; 11
18 wielded his spear against . . and slew them 5
20 He also went down and slew a lion in a pit 11
21 And he slew an Egyptian, a handsome man. 11
21 and slew him with his own spear. 1
1Kg 1:51 that he will not slay his servant with the sword.' 8
2:32 he attacked and slew with the sword two men more 1
3:26 give her the living child, and by no means slay it. 8
27 Give the living child . . and by no means slay it; 8
9:16 Pharaoh . . had slain the Canaanites who dwelt 1
11:15 Jo'ab the commander . . went up to bury the slain 5
15 Jo'ab the commander . . slew every male in Edom 11
13:26 the lion, which has torn him and slain him 8
17:20 hast thou brought calamity . . by slaying her son? 8
19: 1 he had slain all the prophets with the sword. 1
10 thrown down thy altars, and slain thy prophets 1
14 thrown down thy altars, and slain thy prophets 1
17 him who escapes from . . Haz'ael shall Jehu slay; 8
17 him who escapes from . . Jehu shall Eli'sha slay. 8
21 yokes of oxen, and slew them, and boiled their flesh 3
2Kg 3:23 kings . . fought together, and slain one another. 11
6:21 My father, shall I slay them? Shall I slay them? 11
21 My father, shall I slay them? Shall I slay them? 11
22 He answered, "You shall not slay them. 11
22 Would you slay those whom you have taken captive 11
8:12 you will slay their young men with the sword 1
10: 7 they took the king's sons, and slew them 16
9 I . . conspired against my master, and slew him; 1
11 Jehu slew all that remained of the house of Ahab 11
14 took them . . and slew them at the pit of Beth-eked 16
17 he slew all that remained to Ahab in Sama'ria 11
25 Go in and slay them; let not a man escape. 11
11: 2 among the king's sons who were about to be slain 8
2 she hid him from Athali'ah, so that he was not slain; 8
8 and whoever approaches the ranks is to be slain. 8
15 and slay with the sword any one who follows her. 8
15 Let her not be slain in the house of the LORD. 8
16 and she went . . and there she was slain. 8
18 and they slew Mattan the priest of Ba'al 1
20 Athali'ah had been slain with the sword 8
12:20 a conspiracy, and slew Jo'ash in the house of Millo 11
14: 5 he killed . . who had slain the king his father. 11
19 But they sent . . to Lachish, and slew him there. 8
15:14 he struck down Shallum . . in Sama'ria and slew him 8
25 Pekah . . and slew him in Sama'ria, in the citadel 11
25 Pekah . . he slew him, and reigned in his stead. 8
30 and struck him down, and slew him, and reigned 8
19:35 slew 185,000 in the camp of the Assyrians; 11
37 and Share'zer, his sons, slew him with the sword 11
21:24 the people of the land slew all those who had 11
23:20 And he slew all the priests of the high places 3
29 Josi'ah went to meet him; and Pharaoh Neco slew him 8
25: 7 They slew the sons of Zedeki'ah before his eyes 16
1Ch 2: 3 in the sight of the LORD, and he slew him. 8
5:22 For many fell slain, because the war was of God. 5
7:21 Ezer and E'le-ad, whom the men of Gath . . slew 1
10: 1 men of Israel . . fell slain on Mount Gilbo'a. 5
2 Philistines slew Jonathan and Abin'adab 11
8 when the Philistines came to strip the slain 5
14 Therefore the LORD slew him 8
11:11 his spear against 300 whom he slew at one time. 5
14 defended it, and slew the Philistines; 11
20 he wielded his spear against 300 men and slew them 5
22 slew a lion in a pit on a day when snow had fallen. 11
23 he slew an Egyptian, a man of great stature 11
23 Egyptian's hand, and slew him with his own spear. 1
18: 5 David slew 22,000 men of the Syrians. 11
12 Abi'shai, the son of Zeru'iah, slew 18,000 E'domites 11
19:18 David slew of the Syrians the men of 7,000 chariots 1
20: 4 then Sib'becai the Hu'shathite slew Sip'pai 11
5 Elha'nan the son of Ja'ir slew Lahmi 11
7 when he taunted Israel, Jonathan . . slew him. 11
2Ch 13:17 Abi'jah and his people slew them 11
17 there fell slain of Israel 500,000 picked men. 5
21: 4 slew all his brothers with the sword 1
22: 1 with the Arabs . . had slain all the older sons. 1
11 king's sons who were about to be slain 8
11 hid him from Athali'ah, so that she did not slay him; 8
23: 7 whoever enters the house shall be slain. 8
14 who follows her is to be slain with the sword. 8
14 Do not slay her in the house of the LORD. 8
15 and they slew her there. 8
17 slew Mattan the priest of Ba'al before the altars. 1
21 after Athali'ah had been slain with the sword. 8
24:25 conspired against him . . slew him on his bed. 1
25: 3 he killed his servants who had slain the king 11
27 they sent after him to Lachish, and slew him there. 8
28: 6 Pekah the son of Remali'ah slew 120,000 in Judah 1
7 Zichri . . slew Ma-asei'ah the king's son 1
9 but you have slain them in a rage 1
33:25 people of the land slew all . . who had conspired 11
36:17 slew their young men with the sword in the house 1
Est 3:13 to destroy, to slay, and to annihilate all Jews 1
7: 4 be destroyed, to be slain, and to be annihilated. 1
8:11 defend . . to destroy, to slay, and to annihilate 1
9: 6 the Jews slew and destroyed 500 men 1
7 also slew Par-shan-da'tha and Dalphon and Aspa'tha •
11 the number of those slain in Susa . . was reported 1
12 In Susa . . the Jews have slain 500 men 1
15 and they slew 300 men in Susa; 1
16 slew 75,000 of those who hated them 1
Job 1:15 and slew the servants with the edge of the sword; 11
17 and slew the servants with the edge of the sword; 11
5: 2 kills the fool, and jealousy slays the simple. 8
13:15 Behold, he will slay me; I have no hope; 14
39:30 suck up blood; and where the slain are, there is he. 5
Ps 34:21 Evil shall slay the wicked; 8
37:14 to slay those who walk uprightly; 7
32 watches the righteous, and seeks to slay him. 8
44:22 Nay, for thy sake we are slain all the day long 1
59:11 Slay them not, lest my people forget; 1
78:31 he slew the strongest of them 1
34 When he slew them, they sought for him; 1
88: 5 like the slain that lie in the grave 5
94: 6 They slay the widow and the sojourner 1
135:10 who smote many nations and slew mighty kings 1
136:18 slew famous kings 1
139:19 O that thou wouldst slay the wicked, O God 14
Prv 7:26 yea, all her slain are a mighty host. 1
22:13 lion outside! I shall be slain in the streets! 15
Isa 10: 4 among the prisoners or fall among the slain. 1
11: 4 with the breath of his lips . . slay the wicked. 8
14:19 clothed with the slain 1
20 destroyed your land, you have slain your people. 1
30 kill your root . . and your remnant I will slay. 1
22: 2 Your slain are not slain with the sword 5
2 Your slain are not slain with the sword 5
13 behold . . slaying oxen and killing sheep 1
26:21 disclose . . and will no more cover her slain. 1
27: 1 and he will slay the dragon that is in the sea. 1
7 Or have they been slain as their slayers were 1
7 have they been slain as their slayers were slain? 1
34: 3 Their slain shall be cast out 5
37:36 and slew 185,000 in the camp 11
38 his sons, slew him with the sword, and escaped 11
57: 5 who slay your children in the valleys 16
65:15 for a curse, and the Lord GOD will slay you; 8
66:16 and those slain by the LORD shall be many. 5
Jer 5: 6 Therefore a lion from the forest shall slay them 11
9: 1 weep . . for the slain of the daughter of my people! 5
14:18 into the field, behold, those slain by the sword! 5
15: 3 says the LORD: the sword to slay, the dogs to tear 1
18:21 their youths be slain by the sword in battle. 11
23 O LORD, knowest all their plotting to slay me. 9
20: 4 to Babylon, and shall slay them with the sword. 11
25:33 those slain by the LORD on that day 5
26:23 King Jehoi'akim, who slew him with the sword 11
29:21 and he shall slay them before your eyes. 11
39: 6 The king of Babylon slew the sons of Zedeki'ah 16
6 the king of Babylon slew all the nobles of Judah. 16
40:15 Let me go and slay Ish'mael the son of Nethani'ah 11
41: 3 Ish'mael also slew all the Jews 11
7 son of Nethani'ah and the men with him slew them 16
9 cast all the bodies of the men whom he had slain 11
9 the son of Nethani'ah filled it with the slain. 5
16 after he had slain Gedali'ah the son of Ahi'kam 11
18 Ish'mael the son of Nethani'ah had slain Gedali'ah 11
50:21 Slay, and utterly destroy after them 6
27 Slay all her bulls, let them go down 6
51: 4 fall down slain in the land of the Chalde'ans 5
47 and all her slain shall fall in the midst of her. 5
49 Babylon must fall for the slain of Israel 5
49 as for Babylon have fallen the slain of all 5
52:10 The king of Babylon slew the sons of Zedeki'ah 16
10 and also slew all the princes of Judah at Riblah. 16
Lam 2: 4 and he has slain all the pride of our eyes 1
20 priest . . be slain in the sanctuary of the Lord? 1
21 in the day of thy anger thou hast slain them 1
3:43 Thou hast . . and pursued us, slaying without pity; 1
Ezk 6: 4 I will cast down your slain before your idols. 5
7 And the slain shall fall in the midst of you 5
13 when their slain lie among their idols 5
9: 6 slay old men outright, young men and maidens 1
7 and fill the courts with the slain. Go forth. 5
11: 6 You have multiplied your slain in this city 5
6 and have filled its streets with the slain. 5
7 Your slain whom you have laid in the midst of it 5
21:14 twice, yea thrice, the sword for those to be slain; 5
23:10 and her they slew with the sword; 1
47 they shall slay their sons and their daughters 1
26: 6 her daughters on the mainland shall be slain 1
8 He will slay with the sword your daughters 1
11 he will slay your people with the sword; 1
28: 8 the death of the slain in the heart of the seas. 5
9 I am a god,' in the presence of those who slay you 1
23 the slain shall fall in the midst of her 5
30: 4 shall be in Ethiopia, when the slain fall in Egypt 5
11 against Egypt, and fill the land with the slain. 5
31:17 Sheol with it, to those who are slain by the sword; 5
18 with those who are slain by the sword. 5
32:20 shall fall amid those who are slain by the sword 5

21 lie still, the uncircumcised, slain by the sword 5
22 all of them slain, fallen by the sword; 5
23 all of them slain, fallen by the sword 5
24 all of them slain, fallen by the sword 5
25 They have made her a bed among the slain 5
25 all of them uncircumcised, slain by the sword; 5
25 they are placed among the slain. 5
26 all of them uncircumcised, slain by the sword; 4
28 with those who are slain by the sword. 5
29 are laid with those who are slain by the sword; 5
30 who have gone down in shame with the slain 5
30 they lie uncircumcised with those who are slain 5
31 Pharaoh and all his army, slain by the sword 5
32 with those who are slain by the sword 5
35: 8 I will fill your mountains with the slain; 5
8 those slain with the sword shall fall. 5
37: 9 breathe upon these slain, that they may live. 1
44:11 they shall slay the burnt offering 16
Dan 2:13 decree went forth . . wise men were to be slain 18
13 sought Daniel and his companions, to slay them. 18
14 who had gone out to slay the wise men of Babylon; 18
3:22 slew those men who took up Shadrach, Meshach 18
5:19 whom he would he slew, and . . kept alive; 18
30 night Belshaz'zar the Chalde'an king was slain. 18
7:11 looked, the beast was slain, and its body 18
11:26 army . . swept away, and many shall fall down slain 5
Hos 2: 3 like a parched land, and slay her with thirst. 8
6: 5 I have slain them by the words of my mouth 1
9:16 I will slay their beloved children. 8
Ams 2: 3 will slay all its princes with him," says the LORD. 1
4:10 I slew your young men with the sword; 1
9: 1 and what are left of them I will slay with the sword; 1
4 I will command the sword, and it shall slay them; 1
Nah 3: 3 hosts of slain, heaps of corpses, dead bodies 5
Hab 1:17 and mercilessly slaying nations for ever? 1
Zep 2:12 You also, O Ethiopians, shall be slain by my sword. 5
Zec 11: 5 Those who buy them slay them and go unpunished; 1
7 the shepherd of the flock doomed to be slain 2
Lke 19:27 bring them here and slay them before me.' 24
Act 5:36 but he was slain 19
2Th 2: 8 the Lord Jesus will slay him 19
Rev 5: 6 I saw a Lamb standing, as though it had been slain 27
9 for thou wast slain and by thy blood didst ransom 27
12 Worthy is the Lamb who was slain, to receive power 27
6: 4 so that men should slay one another; 27
9 the souls of those who had been slain for the word 27
13: 8 the book of life of the Lamb that was slain. 27
10 if any one slays with the sword 20
10 if any one slays . . with the sword must he be slain 20
15 those who would not worship . . to be slain. 20
18:24 the blood . . of all who have been slain on earth. 27
19:21 And the rest were slain by the sword 20
1Es 1:53 These slew their young men with the sword 20
2Es 1:11 I have slain all their enemies. 29
32 but you have taken and slain them 29
Tob 3: 8 the evil demon Asmodeus had slain each of them 20
Jdt 9: 3 thou gavest up their rulers to be slain 28
10:13 without losing one of his men, captured or slain. †
Sir 47: 5 to slay a man mighty in war 21
Bel 1:26 I will slay the dragon without sword or club. 20
28 he has destroyed Bel, and slain the dragon 20
1Mc 5:51 Then he passed through the city over the slain. 20
2Mc 5:12 to slay those who went into the house. 24
14 as many were sold into slavery as were slain 27
24 and commanded him to slay all the grown men 24
6: 9 slay those who did not choose to change over 24
8:24 they slew more than 9,000 of the enemy 24
10:17 slew those whom they encountered 24
22 he slew these men who had turned traitor 20
11:11 they . . slew 11,000 of them and 1,600 horsemen 23
13:15 slew as many as 2,000 men in the camp 19
15:22 he slew fully 185,000 19
4Mc 3: 7 had slain many of them. 20
8:25 would arbitrarily slay us 22
12:14 for having slain without cause the contestants 20
13:12 being slain for the sake of religion. 26
18:11 He read to you about Abel slain by Cain 19

slay a brother 1. *ἀδελφοκτόνος*

Wis 10: 3 he perished because in rage he slew his brother. 1

slay an infant 1. *νηπιοκτόνος*

Wis 11: 7 in rebuke for the decree to slay the infants 1

slayer 1. הרג 2. רצח

Jos 20: 5 they shall not give up the slayer into his hand; 2
6 the slayer may go again to his own town and . . home 2
21:13 gave Hebron, the city of refuge for the slayer 2
21 given Shechem, the city of refuge for the slayer 2
27 Golan . . the city of refuge for the slayer 2
32 Kedesh . . the city of refuge for the slayer 2
38 Ramoth . . the city of refuge for the slayer 2
Isa 27: 7 have they been slain as their slayers were slain? 1
Ezk 21:11 polished to be given into the hand of the slayer. 1

threshing sledge 1. חָרוּץ 2. מוֹרָג

2Sm 24:22 the threshing sledges and the yokes of the oxen 2
1Ch 21:23 I give . . the threshing sledges for the wood 2
Job 41:30 himself like a threshing sledge on the mire. 1
Isa 28:27 Dill is not threshed with a threshing sledge 1
41:15 Behold, I will make of you a threshing sledge 2
Ams 1: 3 threshed Gilead with threshing sledges of iron. 1

sleek 1. בָּרִיא 2. יָפֶה 3. יְפַת מַרְאֶה 4. יְפַת תֹּאַר 5. עשת

Gen 41: 2 came up out of the Nile seven cows sleek and fat 2
4 thin cows ate up the seven sleek and fat cows. 3
18 seven cows, fat and sleek, came up out of the Nile 4
Ps 73: 4 their bodies are sound and sleek. 1
Jer 5:28 they have grown fat and sleek. 5

become sleek 1. כשה

Deu 32:15 waxed fat, you grew thick, you became sleek; 1

sleep 1. ישן 2. יָשֵׁן 3. רדם 4. שכב 5. שֵׁנָה 6. שְׁנָה (A) 7. *καθεύδω* 8. *κοιμάω* 9. *κοίμησις* 10. *ὕπνος* 11. *ὑπνόω* 12. dormio

Gen 2:21 and while he slept took one of his ribs 1
28:11 his head and lay down in that place to sleep. •
16 Then Jacob awoke from his sleep and said 5
31:40 by night, and my sleep fled from my eyes. 5
Exd 22:27 in what else shall he sleep? 4
Deu 24:12 if . . poor man, you shall not sleep in his pledge; 4
13 restore . . pledge that he may sleep in his cloak 4
31:16 Behold, you are about to sleep with your fathers; 4
Jdg 16:14 while he slept, Deli'lah took the seven locks •
14 he awoke from his sleep, and pulled away the pin 5
20 he awoke from his sleep, and said, "I will go out 5
1Sm 9:25 a bed was spread . . and he lay down to sleep. •
26: 7 there lay Saul sleeping within the encampment 2
2Sm 4: 6 the doorkeeper . . but she grew drowsy and slept; 7
11: 9 Uri'ah slept at the door of the king's house 4
1Kg 1:21 when my lord the king sleeps with his fathers 4
2:10 David slept with his fathers, and was buried 4
3:20 took my son . . while your maidservant slept 2
11:21 Hadad heard . . that David slept with his fathers 4
43 Solomon slept with his fathers, and was buried 4
14:20 he slept with his fathers, and Nadab . . reigned 4
31 Rehobo'am slept with his fathers and was buried 4
15: 8 Abi'jam slept with his fathers; 4
24 Asa slept with his fathers, and was buried 4
16: 6 Ba'asha slept with his fathers, and was buried 4
28 Omri slept with his fathers, and was buried 4
19: 5 he lay down and slept under a broom tree; 1
22:40 So Ahab slept with his fathers; 4
50 Jehosh'aphat slept with his fathers 4
2Kg 8:24 So Joram slept with his fathers, and was buried 4
10:35 Jehu slept with his fathers, and they buried him 4
13: 9 So Jeho'ahaz slept with his fathers 4
13 So Jo'ash slept with his fathers, and Jerobo'am sat 4
14:16 Jeho'ash slept with his fathers, and was buried 4
22 after the king slept with his fathers. 4
29 And Jerobo'am slept with his fathers, the kings 4
15: 7 And Azari'ah slept with his fathers 4
22 And Men'ahem slept with his fathers 4
38 Jotham slept with his fathers, and was buried 4
16:20 And Ahaz slept with his fathers, and was buried 4
20:21 And Hezeki'ah slept with his fathers; 4
21:18 Manas'seh slept with his fathers, and was buried 4
24: 6 So Jehoi'akim slept with his fathers 4
2Ch 9:31 Solomon slept with his fathers, and was buried 4
12:16 Rehobo'am slept with his fathers 4
14: 1 Abi'jah slept with his fathers 4
16:13 Asa slept with his fathers 4
21: 1 Jehosh'aphat slept with his fathers 4
26: 2 after the king slept with his fathers. 4
23 Uzzi'ah slept with his fathers, and they buried him 4
27: 9 Jotham slept with his fathers 4
28:27 Ahaz slept with his fathers, and they buried him 4
32:33 Hezeki'ah slept with his fathers, and they buried 4
33:20 Manas'seh slept with his fathers and they buried 4
Est 6: 1 On that night the king could not sleep; 5
Job 3:13 I should have slept; 1
14:12 he will not awake, or be roused out of his sleep. 5
Ps 3: 5 I lie down and sleep; I wake again 1
4: 8 In peace I will both lie down and sleep; 1
13: 3 lighten my eyes, lest I sleep the sleep of death; 1
3 lighten my eyes, lest I sleep the sleep of death; •
44:23 Rouse thyself! Why sleepest thou, O Lord? Awake! 1
76: 5 stripped of their spoil; they sank into sleep; 5
78:65 Then the Lord awoke as from sleep 2
121: 4 keeps Israel will neither slumber nor sleep. 1
127: 2 for he gives to his beloved sleep. 5
132: 4 not give sleep to my eyes or slumber to my eyelids 5
Prv 3:24 when you lie down, your sleep will be sweet. 5
4:16 cannot sleep unless they have done wrong; •
16 robbed of sleep unless they have made some one 5
6: 4 Give your eyes no sleep 1
9 When will you arise from your sleep? 5
10 A little sleep, a little slumber 5
10: 5 but a son who sleeps in harvest brings shame. 3
20:13 Love not sleep, lest you come to poverty; 1
24:33 A little sleep, a little slumber, a little folding 5
Ecc 5:12 Sweet is the sleep of a laborer 5
12 the surfeit of the rich will not let him sleep. 1
8:16 how neither day nor night one's eyes see sleep; 1
Sng 5: 2 I slept, but my heart was awake. 2
Isa 5:27 none stumbles, none slumbers or sleeps 1
38:15 All my sleep has fled because of the bitterness •
Jer 31:26 I awoke and looked, and my sleep was pleasant to me 5
51:39 till they swoon away and sleep a perpetual sleep 1
39 till they swoon away and sleep a perpetual sleep 5
57 they shall sleep a perpetual sleep and not wake 1
57 they shall sleep a perpetual sleep and not wake 5
Ezk 34:25 in the wilderness and sleep in the woods. 1
Dan 2: 1 spirit was troubled, and his sleep left him. 5
6:18 no diversions . . and sleep fled from him. 6
12: 2 many of those who sleep in the dust of the earth 2
Zec 4: 1 like a man that is wakened out of his sleep. 5
Mat 1:24 When Joseph woke from sleep, he did as the angel 10
9:24 the girl is not dead but sleeping. 7
13:25 while men were sleeping, his enemy came and sowed 7
25: 5 they all slumbered and slept. 7
26:40 he came to the disciples and found them sleeping; 7
43 again he came and found them sleeping 7
45 Are you still sleeping and taking your rest? 7
Mrk 4:27 sleep and rise night and day 7
5:39 The child is not dead but sleeping. 7
14:37 he came and found them sleeping 7
40 again he came and found them sleeping 7
41 Are you still sleeping and taking your rest? 7
Lke 8:52 Do not weep; for she is not dead but sleeping. 7
9:32 were heavy with sleep 10
22:45 found them sleeping for sorrow 8
46 he said to them, "Why do you sleep? 7
Joh 11:13 they thought that he meant taking rest in sleep. 10
Act 12: 6 Peter was sleeping between two soldiers 8
20: 9 He sank into a deep sleep 10
9 overcome by sleep, he fell down 10
Rom 13:11 how it is full time now for you to wake from sleep. 10
1Co 15:51 We shall not all sleep 8
1Th 5: 6 So then let us not sleep, as others do 7
7 For those who sleep sleep at night 7
7 For those who sleep sleep at night 7
10 whether we wake or sleep we might live with him. 7
1Es 3: 6 sleep on a gold bed 7
4:10 he reclines, he eats and drinks and sleeps 7
2Es 2:31 Remember your sons that sleep 12
7:35 and unrighteous deeds shall not sleep. 12
104 to be ill or sleep or eat or be healed in his stead 12
10:59 So I slept that night and the following one 12
11: 8 let each sleep in his own place 12
Tob 2: 9 I slept by the wall of the courtyard 8
Jdt 12: 5 she slept until midnight 11
14:14 he supposed that he was sleeping with Judith. 7
Wis 17:14 they all slept the same sleep 8
14 they all slept the same sleep 10
Sir 31: 1 anxiety about it removes sleep. 10
2 a severe illness carries off sleep. 10
20 Healthy sleep depends on moderate eating 10
40: 5 his sleep at night confuses his mind. 10
6 afterward in his sleep, as though he were on watch 10
42: 9 worry over her robs him of sleep 10
46:19 Before the time of his eternal sleep 9
1Mc 6:10 Sleep departs from my eyes 10
3Mc 5:11 the Lord sent upon the king a portion of sleep 10
12 he was overcome by so pleasant and deep a sleep •
20 the Jews were benefited by today's sleep 10
22 employ the duration of the night in sleep 10

sleep *See also* arrange, awake, fall, go, loss.

deep sleep 1. רדם 2. תַּרְדֵּמָה

Gen 2:21 God caused a deep sleep to fall upon the man 2
15:12 a deep sleep fell on Abram; 2
1Sm 26:12 a deep sleep from the LORD had fallen upon them. 2
Job 4:13 of the night, when deep sleep falls on men 2
33:15 the night, when deep sleep falls upon men 2
Prv 19:15 Slothfulness casts into a deep sleep 2
Isa 29:10 poured out upon you a spirit of deep sleep 2
Dan 10: 9 I fell on my face in a deep sleep with my face 1

make sleep 1. ישן

Jdg 16:19 She made him sleep upon her knees; and she called 1

sleeper 1. רדם 2. *καθεύδω*

Jon 1: 6 and said to him, "What do you mean, you sleeper? 1
Eph 5:14 it is said, "Awake, O sleeper, and arise from the dead 2
Sir 22: 7 who rouses a sleeper from deep slumber. 2

sleepless *See* night.

sleeplessness 1. *ἀγρυπνία*

Sir 31:20 distress of sleeplessness . . nausea and colic 1

sleeves *See* long.

slight 1. *ἐλαφρός* 2. *παροράω* 3. *φαυλίζω*

2Co 4:17 this slight momentary affliction 1
Jdt 11: 2 even now, if your people . . had not slighted me 3
22 those who have slighted my lord. 3
Sir 8: 8 Do not slight the discourse of the sages 2

slight thing 1. קלל

Ezk 8:17 Is it too slight a thing for the house of Judah 1

slime 1. רִיר 2. תֶּמֶס
Job 6: 6 or is there any taste in the slime of the purslane? 1
Ps 58: 8 be like the snail which dissolves into slime 2

sling 1. מַרְגֵּמָה 2. קֶלַע 3. קָלַע 4. σφενδόνη
Jdg 20:16 every one could sling a stone at a hair, 2
1Sm 17: 6 and a javelin . . slung between his shoulders. •
40 his sling was in his hand, and he drew near 3
49 took out a stone, and slung it, and struck 2
50 David prevailed . . with a sling and with a stone 3
25:29 he shall sling out as from the hollow of a sling. 3
1Ch 12: 2 bowmen, and could shoot arrows and sling stones •
2Ch 26:14 prepared for all the army . . stones for slinging. 3
Prv 26: 8 Like one who binds the stone in the sling 1
Jdt 9: 7 they trust in shield and spear, in bow and sling 4
Sir 47: 4 when he lifted his hand with a stone in the sling 4

sling out 1. קלע
1Sm 25:29 and the lives of your enemies he shall sling out 1
Jer 10:18 I am slinging out the inhabitants of the land 1

slinger 1. בֶּן קֶלַע 2. קַלָּע 3. ἀνὴρ σφενδονήτης 4. σφενδονήτης
2Kg 3:25 and the slingers surrounded and conquered it. 2
Zec 9:15 they shall devour and tread down the slingers; 1
Jdt 6:12 all the slingers kept them from coming up 3
1Mc 9:11 the slingers and the archers went ahead 4

slingstone 1. אֶבֶן קֶלַע
Job 41:28 for him slingstones are turned to stubble. 1

slip 1. מוט 2. מעד 3. נשל 4. שפך 5. διαλανθάνω 6. ὀλισθάνω 7. ὀλίσθημα 8. παρεισέρχομαι 9. σφάλλω
Deu 19: 5 head slips from the handle and strikes 3
32:35 for the time when their foot shall slip; 1
2Sm 4: 6 so Rechab and Ba'anah his brother slipped in. 5
22:37 Thou didst give . . and my feet did not slip; 2
Job 12: 5 it is ready for those whose feet slip. 2
Ps 17: 5 held fast to thy paths, my feet have not slipped. 1
18:36 my feet did not slip. 2
37:31 God is in his heart; his steps do not slip. 2
38:16 who boast against me when my foot slips! 1
66: 9 us among the living, and has not let our feet slip. 1
73: 2 my steps had well nigh slipped. 4
94:18 When I thought, "My foot slips," thy steadfast love 1
Prv 25:19 like a bad tooth or a foot that slips. 2
Gal 2: 4 who slipped in to spy out our freedom 8
Sir 13:22 If a rich man slips, his helpers are many 9
22 If a humble man slips, they even reproach him 9
20:18 A slip on the pavement 7
18 better than a slip of the tongue •
21: 7 the sensible man, when he slips, is aware of it. 6

slip (2) 1. זְמוֹרָה
Isa 17:10 you plant . . and set out slips of an alien god 1
slip *See* make.

slip away 1. ἀπορρέω 2. διαρρέω 3. ἐκρέω 4. ὑπεκρέω
1Mc 9: 6 many slipped away from the camp 3
7 When Judas saw that his army had slipped away 1
2Mc 10:20 the men . . let some of them slip away. 2
3Mc 5:34 the . . friends one by one sullenly slipped away 4

slip by 1. παρατρέχω
3Mc 5:15 the hour of the banquet was already slipping by 1

cause to slip 1. ὀλισθάνω
Sir 3:24 wrong opinion has caused their thoughts to slip. 1

slip out 1. יצא
2Kg 9:15 let no one slip out of the city to go and tell 1

slippery 1. חֲלַקְלַקּוֹת
Ps 35: 6 Let their way be dark and slippery 1
slippery *See also* path.

slippery place 1. חֲלַקָּה
Ps 73:18 Truly thou dost set them in slippery places; 1

slope 1. אֶשֶׁד 2. אֲשֵׁדָה 3. הַר
Num21:15 slope of the valleys that extends to the seat 1
Deu 3:17 Salt Sea, under the slopes of Pisgah on the east. 2
4:49 Sea of the Arabah, under the slopes of Pisgah. 2
Jos 10:40 and the Negeb and the lowland and the slopes 2
12: 3 southward to the foot of the slopes of Pisgah; 2
8 in the Arabah, in the slopes, in the wilderness 2
13:20 and Beth-pe'or, and the slopes of Pisgah 2
Sng 4: 1 flock of goats, moving down the slopes of Gilead. 3
6: 5 flock of goats, moving down the slopes of Gilead. •

mountain slope 1. שְׁכֶם
Gen 48:22 I have given . . one mountain slope which I took 1

sloth 1. עַצְלָה
Ecc 10:18 Through sloth the roof sinks in 1

slothful 1. רְמִיָּה 2. ὀκνηρός
Prv 12:24 while the slothful will be put to forced labor. 1
Mat 25:26 You wicked and slothful servant! 2

slothful man 1. רְמִיָּה
Prv 12:27 A slothful man will not catch his prey 1

slothfulness 1. עַצְלָה
Prv 19:15 Slothfulness casts into a deep sleep 1

slow 1. אֶרֶךְ 2. כָּבֵד 3. עצל 4. βραδύνω 5. βραδύς 6. νωθρός 7. ὀκνέω 8. χρονίζω
Exd 4:10 but I am slow of speech and of tongue. 2
34: 6 a God merciful and gracious, slow to anger 1
Num14:18 LORD is slow to anger, and abounding in steadfast 1
Jdg 18: 9 Do not be slow to go, and enter in and possess 3
Neh 9:17 thou art a God . . slow to anger and abounding 1
Ps 86:15 slow to anger and abounding in steadfast love 1
103: 8 slow to anger and abounding in steadfast love. 1
145: 8 slow to anger and abounding in steadfast love. 1
Prv 14:29 He who is slow to anger has great understanding 1
15:18 but he who is slow to anger quiets contention. 1
16:32 He who is slow to anger is better than the mighty 1
Jol 2:13 for he is gracious and merciful, slow to anger 1
Jon 4: 2 a gracious God and merciful, slow to anger 1
Nah 1: 3 The LORD is slow to anger and of great might 1
Lke 24:25 slow of heart to believe 5
Jas 1:19 Let every man be quick to hear, slow to speak 5
19 Let every man be quick to hear . . slow to anger 5
2Pe 3: 9 The Lord is not slow about his promise 4
Tob 12: 6 Do not be slow to give him thanks. 7
Sir 6:21 he will not be slow to cast her off. 8
11:12 There is another who is slow and needs help 6
slow *See also* make.

seem slow 1. מהה
Hab 2: 3 If it seem slow, wait for it; it will surely come 1

slow to anger 1. μακρόθυμος
Sir 5: 4 the Lord is slow to anger. 1

slowly 1. לְאַט
Gen 33:14 I will lead on slowly, according to the pace 1
slowly *See also* sail.

slowness 1. βραδυτής 2. tarditas
2Pe 3: 9 The Lord is not slow . . as some count slowness 1
2Es 5:42 there is no slowness 2

sluggard 1. אִישׁ עָצֵל 2. עָצֵל
Prv 6: 6 Go to the ant, O sluggard; 2
9 How long will you lie there, O sluggard? 2
10:26 so is the sluggard to those who send him. 2
13: 4 The soul of the sluggard craves, and gets nothing 2
15:19 The way of a sluggard is overgrown with thorns 2
19:24 The sluggard buries his hand in the dish 2
20: 4 The sluggard does not plow in the autumn; 2
21:25 The desire of the sluggard kills him 2
22:13 The sluggard says, "There is a lion outside! 2
24:30 I passed by the field of a sluggard 1
26:13 The sluggard says, "There is a lion in the road! 2
14 door turns . . so does a sluggard on his bed. 2
15 The sluggard buries his hand in the dish; 2
16 sluggard is wiser in his own eyes than seven men 2

sluggish 1. νωθρός 2. νωθρότης ποδῶν
Heb 6:12 you may not be sluggish 1
Sir 4:29 sluggish and remiss in your deeds. 1
3Mc 4: 5 sluggish and bent with age 2

slumber 1. נום 2. שכן 3. תְּנוּמָה 4. νυσταγμός 5. νυστάζω 6. ὕπνος
Job 33:15 falls upon men, while they slumber on their beds 3
Ps 121: 3 he who keeps you will not slumber. 1
4 keeps Israel will neither slumber nor sleep. 1
132: 4 not give sleep to my eyes or slumber to my eyelids 3
Prv 6: 4 Give . . your eyelids no slumber; 3
10 A little sleep, a little slumber 3
24:33 A little sleep, a little slumber, a little folding 3
Isa 5:27 none stumbles, none slumbers or sleeps 1
56:10 dreaming, lying down, loving to slumber. 1
Nah 3:18 O king of Assyria; your nobles slumber. 2
Mat 25: 5 they all slumbered and slept. 5
Sir 22: 7 who rouses a sleeper from deep slumber. 6
31: 2 Wakeful anxiety prevents slumber 4

small 1. דַּק 2. מעט 3. מְעַט 4. מִצְעָר 5. צָעִיר 6. צער 7. צַר 8. קָטֹן 9. קָטָן 10. שֶׁמֶץ 11. ἐλαχύς 12. μικρός 13. μικρῶς 14. ὀλίγος 15. parvus
Gen 19:11 the men . . both small and great 9
Exd 12: 4 if the household is too small for a lamb, then a man 2
18:22 any small matter they shall decide themselves; 9
26 any small matter they decided themselves. 9
Num16: 9 is it too small a thing for you that the God 3
13 Is it a small thing that you have brought us up 3
26:56 divided . . between the larger and the smaller. 3
Deu 1:17 you shall hear the small and the great alike; 9
9:21 the calf . . and crushed it, grinding it very small •
25:13 not . . two kinds of weights, a large and a small. 8
14 not . . two kinds of measures, a large and a small. 8
1Sm 20: 2 my father does nothing either great or small 9
30: 2 taken . . all who were in it, both small and great; 9
19 Nothing was missing, whether small or great 9
1Kg 2:20 I have one small request to make of you; do not 8
8:64 the bronze altar . . was too small to receive 9
19:12 and after the fire a still small voice. 1
22:31 Fight with neither small nor great, but only 9
2Kg 2:23 while he was going . . some small boys came out 8
4:10 Let us make a small roof chamber with walls 8
6: 1 the place where we dwell . . is too small for us. 7
23: 2 all the people, both small and great; 9
25:26 all the people, both small and great . . arose 9
1Ch 25: 8 they cast lots for their duties, small and great 9
26:13 they cast lots . . small and great alike 9
2Ch 18:30 Fight with neither small nor great 9
34:30 all the people both great and small; 8
36:18 vessels of the house of God, great and small 8
Est 1: 5 all . . in Susa the capital, both great and small 8
Job 3:19 The small and the great are there 9
8: 7 though your beginning was small 4
15:11 Are the consolations of God too small for you 3
26:14 how small a whisper do we hear of him! 10
Ps 104:25 living things both small and great. 8
115:13 bless . . who fear the LORD, both small and great. 8
119:141 I am small and despised 5
Prv 24:10 If you faint . . your strength is small. 7
30:24 Four things on earth are small 8
Isa 22:24 small vessel, from the cups to all the flagons. 8
29: 5 your foes shall be like small dust 1
Jer 16: 6 Both great and small shall die in this land; 8
30:19 make them honored, and they shall not be small. 6
49:15 behold, I will make you small among the nations 9
52:19 also the small bowls, and the firepans •
Ezk 5: 3 And you shall take from these a small number 3
16:20 Were your harlotries so small a matter 3
43:14 and from the smaller ledge to the larger ledge 8
46:22 the four corners of the court were small courts 12
Dan 11:23 he shall become strong with a small people. 3
Ams 7: 2 How can Jacob stand? He is so small! 9
5 How can Jacob stand? He is so small"! 9
Obd 1: 2 Behold, I will make you small among the nations 9
Mat 13:32 it is the smallest of all seeds 12
Mrk 4:31 the smallest of all the seeds on earth; 12
Lke 19: 3 because he was small of stature. 12
Act 12:18 there was no small stir among the soldiers 14
15: 2 had no small dissension and debate with them 14
26:22 I stand here testifying both to small and great 12
27:20 no small tempest lay on us 14
Jas 3: 5 How great a forest is set ablaze by a small fire! 14
Rev 11:18 those who fear thy name, both small and great 12
13:16 all, both small and great, both rich and poor 12
19: 5 his servants, you who fear him, small and great. 12
18 and the flesh of all men . . both small and great. 12
20:12 dead, great and small, standing before the throne 12
1Es 1:54 all the holy vessels of the Lord, great and small 12
2Es 5:52 not like those . . but smaller in stature?' 15
54 your contemporaries are smaller in stature 15
55 those who come after you will be smaller than you 15
Jdt 13: 4 no one, either small or great, was left 12
13 They all ran together, both small and great 12
Wis 6: 7 because he himself made both small and great 12
14: 5 even to the smallest piece of wood 11
Sir 5:15 In great and small matters do not act amiss 12
11: 3 The bee is small among flying creatures 12
Bar 1: 4 in the hearing of all the people, small and great 12
1Mc 3:29 the revenues from the country were small 14
5:45 the small and the great 12
2Mc 14: 8 our whole nation is now in no small misfortune. 13
4Mc 5:20 in matters either small or great 12
15: 4 We impress upon the character of a small child 12
151 1: 1 I was small among my brothers 12
small *See also* account, beaten, bird, company, fish, give, island, make, matter, number, shield, tribe.

small one 1. צָעִיר
Isa 60:22 a clan, and the smallest one a mighty nation; 1

small thing 1. קטן 2. קָטֹן 3. ἐλάχιστος 4. μικρός 5. ὀλίγος
2Sm 7:19 yet this was a small thing in thy eyes, O Lord GOD; 1
1Ch 17:17 this was a small thing in thy eyes, O God; 1
Zec 4:10 For whoever has despised the day of small things 2
Lke 12:26 you are not able to do as small a thing as that 3
Jdt 16:16 every sacrifice . . is a small thing 4
Sir 19: 1 he who despises small things 5

very small 1. דקק 2. ἐλάχιστος
Exd 30:36 you shall beat some of it very small, and put part 1
Jas 3: 4 they are guided by a very small rudder 2

very small thing 1. ἐλάχιστος
1Co 4: 3 with me it is a very small thing 1

smart 1. רעע 2. δάκνω 3. συνδάκνω
Prv 11:15 He who gives surety for a stranger will smart 1

Tob 11: 8 when they smart he will rub them 2
12 when his eyes began to smart he rubbed them 3

smash 1. כתת 2. נפץ
Jdg 7:19 and they blew the trumpets and smashed the jars 2
Isa 30:14 a potter's vessel which is smashed so ruthlessly 1

smear 1. μολύνω
4Mc 9:20 The wheel was completely smeared with blood 1

smell 1. ריח 2. רֵיחַ 3. רֵיחַ (A) 4. ὀσφραίνομαι 5. odor
Gen 8:21 when the LORD smelled the pleasing odor 1
27:27 he came near and kissed him; and he smelled 1
27 he smelled the smell of his garments, and blessed 2
27 the smell of my son is as the smell of a field 2
27 the smell of a field which the LORD has blessed! 2
Lev 26:31 I will not smell your pleasing odors 1
Deu 4:28 that neither see, nor hear, nor eat, nor smell. 1
Job 39:25 he says 'Aha!' He smells the battle from afar 1
Ps 115: 6 have ears, but do not hear; noses, but do not smell. 1
Dan 3:27 no smell of fire had come upon them. 3
2Es 13:11 but only the dust of ashes and the smell of smoke. 5
Tob 6:17 Then the demon will smell it and flee away 4
8: 3 when the demon smelled the odor 4
Sir 30:19 it can neither eat nor smell 4
smell *See also* sense.

foul smell 1. צַחֲנָה
Jol 2:20 the stench and foul smell of him will rise 1

smelt 1. צוק
Job 28: 2 copper is smelted from the ore. 1

smelt away 1. צרף
Isa 1:25 I . . will smelt away your dross as with lye 1

smile 1. שחק 2. μειδιάω 3. προσγελάω 4. προσμειδιάω
Job 29:24 I smiled on them when they had no confidence; 1
1Es 4:31 If she smiles at him, he laughs 3
Sir 13: 6 he will smile at you and give you hope 3
11 while he smiles he will be examining you. 3
21:20 a clever man smiles quietly. 2
4Mc 8: 4 he smiled at them 4

smite 1. מחץ 2. נגע 3. נגף 4. נכה 5. ספק 6. שבר 7. מחא (A) 8. πατάσσω 9. περιπλήσσω 10. percutio
Exd 3:20 So I will stretch out my hand and smite Egypt 4
12:12 pass through . . that night, and I will smite 4
13 pass over you . . when I smite the land of Egypt. 4
29 At midnight the LORD smote all the first-born 4
Lev 26:17 you shall be smitten before your enemies 3
24 I myself will smite you sevenfold for your sins 4
Num 11:33 LORD smote the people with a very great plague. 4
25:17 Harass the Mid'ianites, and smite them; 4
32: 4 land which the LORD smote before . . Israel 4
Deu 3: 3 smote him until no survivor was left to him. 4
28:22 LORD will smite you with consumption . . fever 4
27 LORD will smite you with the boils of Egypt 4
28 LORD will smite you with madness and blindness 4
35 LORD will smite you on the knees and on the legs 4
Jos 8:21 then they turned back and smote the men of Ai. 4
22 and Israel smote them, until there was left none 4
24 returned to Ai, and smote it with the edge 4
10: 4 Come up to me, and help me, and let us smite Gibeon; 4
10 and smote them as far as Aze'kah and Makke'dah. 4
26 Joshua smote them and put them to death 4
28 Joshua took Makke'dah . . and smote it and its king 4
30 and he smote it with the edge of the sword 4
32 and smote it with the edge of the sword 4
33 and Joshua smote him and his people 4
35 took it . . and smote it with the edge of the sword; 4
37 and took it, and smote it with the edge of the sword 4
39 and they smote them with the edge of the sword 4
11: 8 smote them and chased them as far as Great Sidon 4
8 they smote them, until they left none remaining. 4
10 and took Hazor, and smote its king with the sword; 4
12 And all the cities . . Joshua took, and smote them 4
14 every man they smote with the edge of the sword 4
17 and smote them, and put them to death. 4
15:16 Whoever smites Kir'iath-se'pher, and takes it 4
Jdg 1: 8 and took it, and smote it with the edge of the sword 4
25 and they smote the city with the edge of the sword 4
6:16 and you shall smite the Mid'ianites as one man. 4
11:33 he smote them from Aro'er to the neighborhood 4
12: 4 and the men of Gilead smote E'phraim 4
15: 8 he smote them hip and thigh with great slaughter; 4
18:27 came to La'ish . . and smote them with the edge 4
20:31 they began to smite and kill some of the people 4
37 and smote all the city with the edge of the sword. 4
39 Benjamin had begun to smite and kill about 4
48 and smote them with the edge of the sword 4
21:10 Go and smite the inhabitants of Ja'besh-gil'ead 4
1Sm 4: 8 the gods who smote the Egyptians with every sort 4
7:11 men of Israel went out of Mizpah . . and smote them 4
14:48 And he did valiantly, and smote the Amal'ekites 4
15: 3 Now go and smite Am'alek, and utterly destroy all 4
17:35 I went after him and smote him and delivered it 4
35 I caught him . . and smote him and killed him. 4
20:33 But Saul cast his spear at him to smite him; 4
24: 5 David's heart smote him, because he had cut off 4
25:38 ten days later the LORD smote Nabal; and he died. 3
26:10 As the LORD lives, the LORD will smite him; 3
27: 9 David smote the land 4
30:17 David smote them from twilight until the evening 4
2Sm 1:15 Go, fall upon him." And he smote him so that he died. 4
2:22 Turn aside . . why should I smite you to the ground? 4
23 Abner smote him in the belly with . . his spear 4
3:27 and there he smote him in the belly, so that he died 4
4: 7 they smote him, and slew him, and beheaded him. 4
5: 8 Whoever would smite the Jeb'usites, let him get up 4
24 gone out . . to smite the army of the Philistines. 4
25 and smote the Philistines from Geba to Gezer. 4
6: 7 God smote him there because he put forth his hand 4
12: 9 You have smitten Uri'ah . . with the sword 4
15:14 and smite the city with the edge of the sword. 4
23:20 a doer of great deeds; he smote two ariels of Moab. 4
24:10 But David's heart smote him after he had numbered 4
17 when he saw the angel who was smiting the people 4
1Kg 14:15 the LORD will smite Israel, as a reed is shaken 4
20:29 the people of Israel smote . . 100,000 foot soldiers 4
37 And the man struck him, smiting and wounding him. 4
2Kg 8:21 and his chariot commanders smote the E'domites 4
14:10 You have indeed smitten Edom 4
15: 5 the LORD smote the king, so that he was a leper 2
18: 8 He smote the Philistines as far as Gaza and its 4
25:21 king of Babylon smote them, and put them to death 4
1Ch 11: 6 David said, "Whoever shall smite the Jeb'usites 4
22 doer of great deeds; he smote two ariels of Moab. 4
13:10 LORD . . smote him because he put forth his hand 4
14:15 before you to smite the army of the Philistines. 4
16 smote the Philistine army from Gibeon to Gezer. 4
20: 1 And Jo'ab smote Rabbah, and overthrew it. 4
21: 7 God was displeased . . and he smote Israel. 4
2Ch 13:20 the LORD smote him, and he died. 3
14:14 they smote all the cities round about Gerar 4
15 they smote the tents of those who had cattle 4
21: 9 Jeho'ram . . rose by night and smote the E'domites 4
18 after all this the LORD smote him in his bowels 3
25:11 to the Valley of Salt and smote 10,000 men of Se'ir. 4
19 You say, 'See, I have smitten Edom,' 4
26:20 to go out, because the LORD had smitten him. 2
Est 9: 5 the Jews smote all their enemies with the sword 4
Job 5:18 he smites, but his hands heal. 1
26:12 by his understanding he smote Rahab. 1
Ps 3: 7 For thou dost smite all my enemies on the cheek 4
69:26 For they persecute him whom thou hast smitten 4
78:20 He smote the rock so that water gushed out 4
51 He smote all the first-born in Egypt 4
102: 4 My heart is smitten like grass, and withered; 4
105:33 He smote their vines and fig trees 4
36 He smote all the first-born in their land 4
121: 6 The sun shall not smite you by day 4
135: 8 He it was who smote the first-born of Egypt 4
10 who smote many nations and slew mighty kings 4
136:10 to him who smote the first-born of Egypt 4
17 to him who smote the great kings 4
Isa 1: 5 Why will you still be smitten, that you continue 4
5:25 stretched out his hand . . and smote them 4
9:13 not turn to him who smote them, nor seek the LORD 4
10:20 Jacob will no more lean upon him that smote them 4
24 the Assyrians when they smite with the rod 4
26 as when he smote Mid'ian at the rock of Oreb; 4
11: 4 he shall smite the earth with the rod of his mouth 4
15 smite it into seven channels that men may cross 4
14: 6 that smote the peoples in wrath 4
29 that the rod which smote you is broken 4
19:22 the LORD will smite Egypt, smiting and healing 3
22 the LORD will smite Egypt, smiting and healing 3
27: 7 Has he smitten them as he smote those 4
7 smitten them as he smote those who smote them? 4
7 smitten them as he smote those who smote them? 4
30:31 the voice of the LORD, when he smites with his rod. 4
49:10 neither scorching wind nor sun shall smite them 4
53: 4 yet we esteemed him stricken, smitten by God 4
57:17 angry, I smote him, I hid my face and was angry; 4
60:10 for in my wrath I smote you 4
Jer 2:30 In vain have I smitten your children 4
5: 3 Thou hast smitten them, but they felt no anguish; 4
14:17 for the virgin daughter of my people is smitten 6
19 Why hast thou smitten us so . . there is no healing 4
18:18 Come, let us smite him with the tongue 4
21: 6 I will smite the inhabitants of this city 4
7 He shall smite them with the edge of the sword; 4
31:19 and after I was instructed, I smote upon my thigh; 5
33: 5 men whom I shall smite in my anger and my wrath 4
43:11 He shall come and smite the land of Egypt 4
46:13 king of Babylon to smite the land of Egypt 4
47: 1 the Philistines, before Pharaoh smote Gaza. 4
49:28 which Nebuchadrez'zar king of Babylon smote. 4
52:27 And the king of Babylon smote them 4
Ezk 7: 9 Then you will know that I am the LORD, who smite. 4
9: 5 Pass through the city after him, and smite; 4
7 they went forth, and smote in the city. 4
8 And while they were smiting, and I was left alone 4
21:12 Smite therefore upon your thigh. 5
32:15 when I smite all who dwell in it 4
Dan 2:34 smote the image on its feet of iron and clay 7
Ams 3:15 I will smite the winter house 4
4: 9 I smote you with blight and mildew; 4
6:11 the great house shall be smitten into fragments 4
9: 1 Smite the capitals until the thresholds shake 4
Mic 6:13 Therefore I have begun to smite you 4
Hag 2:17 I smote you and all the products of your toil 4
Zec 10:11 the waves of the sea shall be smitten 4
11:17 May the sword smite his arm and his right eye! •
14:12 LORD will smite all the peoples that wage war 3
Mal 4: 6 lest I come and smite the land with a curse. 4
Act 12:23 Immediately an angel of the Lord smote him 8
Rev 11: 6 and to smite the earth with every plague 8
19:15 a sharp sword with which to smite the nations 8
2Es 15:11 and will smite Egypt with plagues 10
Jdt 16: 7 nor did the sons of the Titans smite him 8
Sir 48:21 The Lord smote the camp of the Assyrians 8
3Mc 2:22 since he was smitten by a righteous judgment. 9

smite down 1. נגף
Jdg 20:39 they said, "Surely they are smitten down before us 1

smite with a scab 1. שפח
Isa 3:17 smite with a scab the heads of the daughters 1

smiter 1. נכה
Isa 50: 6 I gave my back to the smiters, and my cheeks 1
Lam 3:30 let him give his cheek to the smiter 1

smith 1. חָרָשׁ 2. מַסְגֵּר 3. צרף 4. χαλκεύς
1Sm 13:19 Now there was no smith . . throughout all the land 1
2Kg 24:14 and all the craftsmen and the smiths; 2
16 and the craftsmen and the smiths, 1,000 2
Prv 25: 4 dross . . and the smith has material for a vessel; 3
Isa 54:16 I . . created the smith who blows the fire of coals 1
Jer 24: 1 princes of Judah, the craftsmen, and the smiths 2
29: 2 and the smiths had departed from Jerusalem. 2
Zec 1:20 Then the LORD showed me four smiths. 1
Sir 38:28 So too is the smith sitting by the anvil 4

smoke 1. עשן 2. עָשָׁן 3. עָתָר 4. קְטֹרֶת 5. קִיטוֹר 6. ἀτμίς 7. καπνίζω 8. καπνός 9. fumus
Gen 15:17 behold, a smoking fire pot and a flaming torch 2
19:28 and beheld, and lo, the smoke of the land went up 5
28 land went up like the smoke of a furnace. 5
Exd 19:18 the smoke of it went up like the smoke of a kiln 2
18 the smoke of it went up like the smoke of a kiln 2
20:18 sound of the trumpet and the mountain smoking 2
Deu 29:20 anger of the LORD . . smoke against that man 1
Jos 8:20 behold, the smoke of the city went up to heaven; 2
21 saw . . and that the smoke of the city went up 2
Jdg 20:38 when they made a great cloud of smoke rise up out 2
40 began to rise out of the city in a column of smoke 2
40 the whole of the city went up in smoke to heaven. •
2Sm 22: 9 Smoke went up from his nostrils, and . . fire 2
Job 41:20 Out of his nostrils comes forth smoke 2
Ps 18: 8 Smoke went up from his nostrils 2
37:20 they vanish–like smoke they vanish away. 2
66:15 fatlings, with the smoke of the sacrifice of rams; 4
68: 2 As smoke is driven away, so drive them away; 2
74: 1 thy anger smoke against the sheep of thy pasture? 1
102: 3 For my days pass away like smoke 2
104:32 who touches the mountains and they smoke! 1
119:83 For I have become like a wineskin in the smoke 5
144: 5 Touch the mountains that they smoke! 1
Prv 10:26 Like vinegar to the teeth, and smoke to the eyes 2
Sng 3: 6 What is that coming . . like a column of smoke 2
Isa 4: 5 smoke and the shining of a flaming fire by night; 2
6: 4 and the house was filled with smoke. 2
9:18 and they roll upward in a column of smoke. 2
14:31 For smoke comes out of the north 2
34:10 its smoke shall go up for ever. 2
51: 6 for the heavens will vanish like smoke 2
65: 5 These are a smoke in my nostrils, 2
Ezk 8:11 and the smoke of the cloud of incense went up. 3
Hos 13: 3 they shall be . . like smoke from a window. 2
Jol 2:30 portents . . blood and fire and columns of smoke. 2
Nah 2:13 and I will burn your chariots in smoke 2
Act 2:19 blood, and fire, and vapor of smoke; 8
Rev 8: 4 the smoke of the incense rose with the prayers 8
9: 2 and from the shaft rose smoke like the smoke 8
2 rose smoke like the smoke of a great furnace 8
2 the sun and the air were darkened with the smoke 8
3 Then from the smoke came locusts on the earth 8
17 fire and smoke . . issued from their mouths. 8
18 killed, by the fire and smoke and sulphur 8
14:11 smoke of their torment goes up for ever and ever; 8
15: 8 and the temple was filled with smoke 8
18: 9 when they see the smoke of her burning; 8
18 and cried out as they saw the smoke of her burning 8
19: 3 The smoke from her goes up for ever and ever. 8
2Es 4:48 I looked, and behold, the smoke remained. 9
50 and the fire is greater than the smoke 9
50 but drops and smoke remained. 9
7:61 and are similar to a flame and smoke 9
13:11 but only the dust of ashes and the smell of smoke. 9
15:44 then the dust and smoke shall go up to heaven 9

Wis 2: 2 because the breath in our nostrils is smoke 8
5:14 it is dispersed like smoke before the wind 8
10: 7 a continually smoking wasteland 7
11:18 or belch forth a thick pall of smoke 8
Sir 22:24 vapor and smoke of the furnace precede the fire; 8
LJr 1:21 blackened by the smoke of the temple. 8
1Mc 4:20 the smoke . . showed what had happened. 8
2Mc 7: 5 The smoke from the pan spread widely 6
smoke *See also* make, wrap.

rising smoke 1.מַשָּׂאָה
Isa 30:27 burning with his anger, and in thick rising smoke; 1

smolder 1.יָשֵׁן 2.עָשֵׁן 3.τύφω
Isa 7: 4 these two smoldering stumps of firebrands 2
Hos 7: 6 all night their anger smolders; 1
Mat 12:20 or quench a smoldering wick 3

smooth 1.חלק 2.חֵלֶק 3.חַלָּק 4.חָלָק 5.חֶלְקָה 6.מרט 7.ἀπρόσκοπος 8.καταξύω 9.λεῖος
Gen 27:11 Esau is a hairy man, and I am a smooth man. 4
1Sm 17:40 and chose five smooth stones from the brook 3
Ps 55:21 His speech was smoother than butter 1
Prv 2:16 saved from . . adventuress with her smooth words 1
5: 3 her speech is smoother than oil; 4
6:24 from the smooth tongue of the adventuress. 5
7: 5 from the adventuress with her smooth words. 1
21 with her smooth talk she compels him. 2
26:23 smooth lips with an evil heart. 9
Isa 18: 2 swift messengers, to a nation, tall and smooth 6
7 to the LORD of hosts from a people tall and smooth 6
41: 7 he who smooths with the hammer him who strikes 1
57: 6 Among the smooth stones of the valley 4
Lke 3: 5 the rough ways shall be made smooth; 9
Sir 32:21 Do not be overconfident on a smooth way 7
LJr 1: 8 Their tongues are smoothed by the craftsman 8
smooth *See also* make.

smooth part 1.חֶלְקָה
Gen 27:16 his hands and upon the smooth part of his neck; 1

smooth thing 1.חֲלָקָה
Isa 30:10 speak to us smooth things, prophesy illusions 1

smoothly 1.לְמֵישָׁרִים 2.מֵישָׁר
Prv 23:31 sparkles in the cup and goes down smoothly. 2
Sng 7: 9 like the best wine that goes down smoothly 1
smoothly *See also* pave.

snail 1.שַׁבְּלוּל
Ps 58: 8 be like the snail which dissolves into slime 1

snake 1.ὄφις
Sir 12:13 Who will pity a snake charmer bitten by a serpent •
21: 2 Flee from sin as from a snake 1
25:15 There is no venom worse than a snake's venom 1

snap 1.נתק
Jdg 16: 9 But he snapped the bowstrings, as a string of tow 1
9 as a string of tow snaps when it touches the fire. 1
12 he snapped the ropes off his arms like a thread. 1
Ecc 12: 6 before the silver cord is snapped ‡

snare 1.בקשׁ 2.חֶבֶל 3.יקשׁ 4.מוֹקֵשׁ 5.מָצוֹד 6.מְצוּדָה 7.פַּח 8.צַמִּים 9.παγίς 10.σκάνδαλον
Exd 10: 7 How long shall this man be a snare to us? 4
23:33 gods, it will surely be a snare to you. 4
34:12 lest it become a snare in the midst of you. 4
Deu 7:16 serve their gods, for that would be a snare to you. 4
Jos 23:13 they shall be a snare and a trap for you, a scourge 7
Jdg 2: 3 their gods shall be a snare to you. 4
8:27 and it became a snare to Gideon and to his family. 4
1Sm 18:21 give her to him, that she may be a snare for him 4
2Sm 22: 6 the snares of death confronted me. 4
Job 18: 9 seizes him by the heel, a snare lays hold of him. 8
22:10 Therefore snares are round about you 7
40:24 with hooks, or pierce his nose with a snare? 4
Ps 9:16 wicked are snared in the work of their own hands. 3
18: 5 the snares of death confronted me. 4
69:22 Let their own table before them become a snare; 7
91: 3 he will deliver you from the snare of the fowler 7
106:36 served their idols, which became a snare to them. 4
116: 3 The snares of death encompassed me; 2
119:110 The wicked have laid a snare for me 7
124: 7 escaped as a bird from the snare of the fowlers; 7
7 snare is broken, and we have escaped! 7
140: 5 by the wayside they have set snares for me. Selah 4
141: 9 Keep me . . from the snares of evildoers! 4
Prv 6: 2 if you are snared in the utterance of your lips 3
7:23 as a bird rushes into a snare; 7
13:14 that one may avoid the snares of death. 4
14:27 that one may avoid the snares of death. 4
18: 7 A fool's . . lips are a snare to himself. 4
20:25 It is a snare for a man to say rashly, "It is holy 4
21: 6 fleeting vapor and a snare of death. 1
22: 5 Thorns and snares are in the way of the perverse; 7
25 learn his ways and entangle yourself in a snare. 4
29:25 The fear of man lays a snare 4
Ecc 7:26 the woman whose heart is snares and nets 5
9:12 and like birds which are caught in a snare 7
12 the sons of men are snared at an evil time 3
Isa 8:14 snare to the inhabitants of Jerusalem. 4
15 they shall be snared and taken. 3
24:17 Terror, and the pit, and the snare are upon you 7
18 he who climbs . . shall be caught in the snare. 7
28:13 be broken, and snared, and taken. 3
Jer 18:22 dug a pit to take me, and laid snares for my feet. 7
48:43 Terror, pit, and snare are before you 7
44 he who climbs out . . shall be caught in the snare. 7
Ezk 12:13 my net over him, and he shall be taken in my snare; 6
17:20 he shall be taken in my snare 6
19: 8 the nations set against him snares on every side; •
Hos 5: 1 for you have been a snare at Mizpah 7
9: 8 yet a fowler's snare is on all his ways 7
Ams 3: 5 Does a bird fall in a snare on the earth 7
5 Does a snare spring up from the ground 7
Lke 21:34 and that day come upon you suddenly like a snare; •
Rom 11: 9 Let their table become a snare and a trap, a pitfall 9
1Ti 3: 7 fall into reproach and the snare of the devil. 9
6: 9 into a snare, into many senseless . . desires 9
2Ti 2:26 they may escape from the snare of the devil 9
Wis 14:11 a snare to the feet of the foolish. 9
Sir 9: 3 lest you fall into her snares. 9
13 Know that you are walking in the midst of snares 9
27:20 has escaped like a gazelle from a snare. 9
26 he who sets a snare will be caught in it. 9
29 will be caught in a snare 9
51: 2 the snare of a slanderous tongue 9
1Mc 1:35 became a great snare. 9
5: 4 who were a trap and a snare to the people 10
snare *See also* lay, set.

snarl
Ps 59: 7 with their mouths, and snarling with their lips– •

snatch 1.גזל 2.גזר 3.חתה 4.ἁρπάζω
2Sm 23:21 Benai'ah went . . and snatched the spear out 1
1Ch 11:23 and snatched the spear out of the Egyptian's hand 1
Job 24: 9 There are those who snatch the fatherless child 1
Ps 52: 5 he will snatch and tear you from your tent; 3
Isa 9:20 They snatch on the right, but are still hungry 2
Joh 10:12 the wolf snatches them and scatters them. 4
28 no one shall snatch them out of my hand. 4
29 is able to snatch them out of the Father's hand. 4
Jde 1:23 save some, by snatching them out of the fire; 4

snatch away 1.גזל 2.חתף 3.ספה 4.קמט 5.ἁρπάζω 6.ἐξαίρω
Job 9:12 Behold, he snatches away; who can hinder him? 2
22:16 They were snatched away before their time; 4
24:19 Drought and heat snatch away the snow waters; 1
Ps 40:14 be put to shame . . who seek to snatch away my life; 3
Mat 13:19 the evil one comes and snatches away what is sown 5
Sir 19: 3 the reckless soul will be snatched away. 6

sneeze 1.זרר 2.עֲטִישָׁה
2Kg 4:35 the child sneezed seven times 1
Job 41:18 His sneezings flash forth light 2

sniff 1.נפח 2.שׁאף
Jer 2:24 a wild ass . . in her heat sniffing the wind! 2
Mal 1:13 you say, and you sniff at me, says the LORD of hosts. 1

snort 1.נַחַר 2.נַחֲרָה
Job 39:20 His majestic snorting is terrible. 1
Jer 8:16 The snorting of their horses is heard from Dan; 2

snout 1.אַף
Prv 11:22 gold ring in a swine's snout is a beautiful woman 1

snow 1.שֶׁלֶג 2.תְּלַג (A) 3.νιφετός 4.χιών
Exd 4: 6 behold, his hand was leprous, as white as snow. 1
Num 12:10 behold, Miriam was leprous, as white as snow. 1
2Sm 23:20 slew a lion in a pit on a day when snow had fallen. 1
2Kg 5:27 So he went out . . a leper, as white as snow. 1
1Ch 11:22 slew a lion in a pit on a day when snow had fallen. 1
Job 6:16 dark with ice, and where the snow hides itself. 1
9:30 If I wash myself with snow, and cleanse my hands 1
24:19 Drought and heat snatch away the snow waters; 1
37: 6 For to the snow he says, 'Fall on the earth'; 1
38:22 Have you entered the storehouses of the snow 1
Ps 51: 7 wash me, and I shall be whiter than snow. 1
147:16 He gives snow like wool; he scatters hoarfrost 1
148: 8 fire and hail, snow and frost, stormy wind 1
Prv 25:13 Like the cold of snow in the time of harvest 1
26: 1 Like snow in summer or rain in harvest 1
31:21 She is not afraid of snow for her household. 1
Isa 1:18 sins are like scarlet, they shall be white as snow; 1
55:10 For as the rain and the snow come down from heaven 1
Jer 18:14 Does the snow of Lebanon leave the crags 1
Lam 4: 7 princes were purer than snow, whiter than milk; 1
Dan 7: 9 raiment was white as snow, and the hair of his head 2
Mat 28: 3 his raiment white as snow. 4
Rev 1:14 his head and his hair were . . white as snow; 4
Wis 16:22 Snow and ice withstood fire without melting 4
Sir 43:13 By his command he sends the driving snow 4
17 He scatters the snow like birds flying down 4
Aza 1:46 Bless the Lord, dews and snows 3
50 Bless the Lord, frosts and snows 4
1Mc 13:22 that night a very heavy snow fell 4
22 he did not go because of the snow 4

snow fall 1.שׁלג
Ps 68:14 scattered kings there, snow fell on Zalmon. 1

snuffer 1.מְזַמֶּרֶת 2.מֶלְקָחַיִם
Exd 25:38 Its snuffers and their trays shall be of pure 2
37:23 seven lamps and its snuffers and its trays 2
Num 4: 9 with its lamps, its snuffers, its trays 2
1Kg 7:50 The cups, snuffers, basins, dishes for incense 1
2Kg 12:13 not made . . basins of silver, snuffers, bowls 1
25:14 the shovels, and the snuffers, and the dishes 1
2Ch 4:22 snuffers, basins, dishes . . of pure gold; 1
Jer 52:18 the shovels, and the snuffers, and the basins 1

so-called 1.λέγω
1Ch 4:14 so-called because they were craftsmen. •
1Co 8: 5 although there may be so-called gods in heaven 1
2Th 2: 4 every so-called god or object of worship 1

soak 1.בוא 2.רוה
Ps 109:18 may it soak into his body like water 1
Isa 34: 7 Their land shall be soaked with blood 2

soap 1.בֹּרִית
Jer 2:22 you wash yourself with lye and use much soap 1
Mal 3: 2 he is like a refiner's fire and like fullers' soap 1

soar 1.אבר
Job 39:26 Is it by your wisdom that the hawk soars 1

soar aloft 1.גבה
Obd 1: 4 Though you soar aloft like the eagle 1

sober 1.νήφω 2.σωφρόνως 3.σωφροσύνη
Act 26:25 I am speaking the sober truth. 3
1Th 5: 6 let us keep awake and be sober. 1
8 But, since we belong to the day, let us be sober 1
Tit 2:12 to live sober, upright, and godly lives in this world 2
1Pe 1:13 Therefore gird up your minds, be sober 1
5: 8 Be sober, be watchful. Your adversary the devil 1
sober *See also* keep, judgment.

socket 1.אֶדֶן 2.חר 3.פת 4.קָנֶה 5.ἁρμός
Exd 38:12 their pillars ten, and their sockets ten; 1
1Kg 7:50 the sockets of gold, for the doors 3
2Ch 4:22 sockets of the temple, for the inner doors •
Job 31:22 let my arm be broken from its socket. 4
Zec 14:12 their eyes shall rot in their sockets 2
4Mc 10: 5 by prying his limbs from their sockets 5

sodomite 1.ἀρσενοκοίτης
1Ti 1:10 immoral persons, sodomites, kidnapers, liars 1

soft 1.רַךְ 2.רכך 3.ἁπαλός 4.μαλακός
Ps 55:21 his words were softer than oil 2
Prv 15: 1 A soft answer turns away wrath 1
25:15 soft tongue will break a bone. 1
Lke 7:25 A man clothed in soft clothing? 4
Wis 15: 7 when a potter kneads the soft earth 3
soft *See also* fleece, raiment, word.

soften 1.מוג 2.רכך
Ps 65:10 settling its ridges, softening it with showers 1
Isa 1: 6 they are not pressed out . . or softened with oil. 2

softly 1.בַּלָּט
Jdg 4:21 took a hammer in her hand, and went softly to him 1
Rut 3: 7 Then she came softly, and uncovered his feet 1

soil 1.אֲדָמָה 2.טנף 3.עָפָר 4.שָׂדֶה 5.γῆ 6.μολύνω 7.χώρα
Gen 9:20 Noah was the first tiller of the soil. 1
1Ch 27:26 over those . . for tilling the soil was Ezri 1
2Ch 26:10 for he loved the soil. 1
Job 14:19 the torrents wash away the soil of the earth; 3
Sng 5: 3 I had bathed my feet, how could I soil them? 2
Isa 32:13 for the soil of my people growing up in thorns 1
34: 7 and their soil made rich with fat. 3
9 turned into pitch, and her soil into brimstone; 3
Ezk 17: 5 seed of the land and planted it in fertile soil; 4
8 he transplanted it to good soil 4
26: 4 I will scrape her soil from her 3
12 your stones and timber and soil they will cast 3
Mic 5: 5 when the Assyrian . . treads upon our soil 7
Zec 13: 5 he will say, 'I am no prophet, I am a tiller of the soil; 1
Mal 3:11 that it will not destroy the fruits of your soil; 1
Mat 13: 5 where they had not much soil 5
5 since they had no depth of soil 5
8 Other seeds fell on good soil 5
23 As for what was sown on good soil 5
Mrk 4: 5 where it had not much soil 5
5 since it had no depth of soil; 5
8 other seeds fell into good soil 5

20 those that were sown upon the good soil 5
Lke 8: 8 some fell into good soil and grew 5
15 as for that in the good soil 5
Rev 3: 4 people who have not soiled their garments; 6
1Es 4: 6 those who . . till the soil 5
Sir 20:28 Whoever cultivates the soil 5
22:13 you will not be soiled when he shakes himself off; 6

soil *See also* tiller.

sojourn 1. גור 2. מָגוֹר 3. παροικέω 4. παροικία

Gen 12:10 So Abram went down to Egypt to sojourn there 1
17: 8 give . . the land of your sojournings 2
19: 9 This fellow came to sojourn 1
20: 1 Kadesh and Shur; and he sojourned in Gerar. 1
21:23 and with the land where you have sojourned. 1
34 Abraham sojourned many days in the land 1
26: 3 Sojourn in this land, and I will be with you 1
28: 4 take possession of the land of your sojournings 2
32: 4 I have sojourned with Laban, and stayed until now 1
35:27 where Abraham and Isaac had sojourned. 1
36: 7 the land of their sojournings could not support 2
37: 1 dwelt in the land of his father's sojournings 2
47: 4 We have come to sojourn in the land; for there is no 1
9 The days of the years of my sojourning are 2
9 my fathers in the days of their sojourning. 2
Exd 3:22 shall ask . . of her who sojourns in her house 1
12:48 when a stranger shall sojourn with you and would 1
49 for the stranger who sojourns among you. 1
Lev 16:29 the native or the stranger who sojourns among you 1
17: 8 or of the strangers that sojourn among them 1
10 or of the strangers that sojourn among them 1
12 any stranger who sojourns among you 1
13 or of the strangers that sojourn among them 1
18:26 the native or the stranger who sojourns among you 1
19:33 When a stranger sojourns with you in your land 1
34 The stranger who sojourns with you shall be 1
20: 2 Any . . of the strangers that sojourn in Israel 1
25:45 from among the strangers who sojourn with you 1
Num 9:14 if a stranger sojourns among you 1
15:14 if a stranger is sojourning with you, or any one 1
15 you and for the stranger who sojourns with you 1
16 you and for the stranger who sojourns with you. 1
26 be forgiven, and the stranger who sojourns among 1
29 for the stranger who sojourns among them. 1
19:10 to the stranger who sojourns among them 1
Deu 26: 5 went down into Egypt and sojourned there 1
Jos 20: 9 and for the stranger sojourning among them 1
Jdg 17: 7 who was a Levite; and he sojourned there. 1
9 and I am going to sojourn where I may find a place. 1
19: 1 a certain Levite was sojourning in the remote 1
16 the man was from . . E'phraim, and he was sojourning 1
Rut 1: 1 went to sojourn in the country of Moab 1
1Kg 17:20 even upon the widow with whom I sojourn 1
2Kg 8: 1 Arise, and depart . . and sojourn wherever you can; 1
2 and sojourned in the land of the Philistines 1
2Ch 15: 9 those . . who were sojourning with them 1
Ezr 1: 4 let each survivor, in whatever place he sojourns 1
Ps 5: 4 evil may not sojourn with thee. 1
15: 1 O LORD, who shall sojourn in thy tent? 1
105:23 Jacob sojourned in the land of Ham. 1
120: 5 Woe is me, that I sojourn in Meshech 1
Isa 16: 4 let the outcasts of Moab sojourn among you; 1
52: 4 went down at the first into Egypt to sojourn 1
Jer 35: 7 may live many days in the land where you sojourn. 1
49:18 no man shall sojourn in her. 1
33 no man shall sojourn in her. 1
50:40 and no son of man shall sojourn in her. 1
Ezk 14: 7 or of the strangers that sojourn in Israel 1
20:38 bring them out of the land where they sojourn 2
Heb 11: 9 By faith he sojourned in the land of promise 3
1Es 5: 7 who came up out of their sojourn in captivity 4
Wis 19:10 they still recalled the events of their sojourn 4
Sir 38:32 men can neither sojourn nor live there. 3

sojourner 1. אִישׁ גֵּר 2. גור 3. גֵּר 4. תּוֹשָׁב 5. πάροικος

Gen 15:13 your descendants will be sojourners in a land 3
23: 4 I am a stranger and a sojourner among you; 4
Exd 2:22 he said, "I have been a sojourner in a foreign land. 3
6: 4 the land in which they dwelt as sojourners. 2
12:19 cut off . . whether he is a sojourner or a native 3
45 No sojourner or hired servant may eat of it. 4
18: 3 he said, "I have been a sojourner in a foreign land") 3
20:10 the sojourner who is within your gates; 3
Lev 17:15 whether he is a native or a sojourner 3
19:10 leave them for the poor and for the sojourner 3
22:10 A sojourner of the priest's or a hired servant 4
18 When any one . . of the sojourners in Israel 3
24:16 the sojourner as well as the native 3
22 have one law for the sojourner and for the native 3
25: 6 for your hired servant and the sojourner 4
23 you are strangers and sojourners with me 4
35 as a stranger and a sojourner he shall live 4
40 he shall be . . as a sojourner. He shall serve 4
47 If a stranger or sojourner with you becomes rich 4
47 sells . . to the stranger or sojourner with you 4
Num 9:14 both for the sojourner and for the native. 3
15:15 so shall the sojourner be before the LORD. 3
30 high hand, whether he is native or a sojourner 3
35:15 cities . . for refuge . . for the sojourner 4
Deu 5:14 or the sojourner who is within your gates 3
10:18 loves the sojourner, giving him food 3
19 Love the sojourner therefore; 3
19 for you were sojourners in the land of Egypt. 3
14:29 Levite . . and the sojourner, the fatherless 3
16:11 rejoice . . you and . . the sojourner 3
14 rejoice . . you and . . the Levite, the sojourner 3
23: 7 Egyptian . . you were a sojourner in his land. 3
24:14 or one of the sojourners who are in your land 3
17 not pervert the justice due to the sojourner 3
19 for the sojourner, the fatherless, and the widow; 3
20 for the sojourner, the fatherless, and the widow. 3
21 for the sojourner, the fatherless, and the widow. 3
26:11 rejoice . . you, and the Levite, and the sojourner 3
12 giving it to the Levite, the sojourner 3
13 given it to the Levite, the sojourner 3
27:19 who perverts the justice due to the sojourner 3
28:43 sojourner who is among you shall mount above you 3
29:11 your wives, and the sojourner who is in your camp 3
31:12 Assemble the people . . and the sojourner 3
Jos 8:33 And all Israel, sojourner as well as homeborn 3
35 and the sojourners who lived among them. 3
2Sm 1:13 I am the son of a sojourner, an Amal'ekite. 1
4: 3 have been sojourners there to this day 2
1Ch 16:19 and of little account, and sojourners in it 2
29:15 For we are strangers before thee, and sojourners 4
2Ch 30:25 sojourners who came out of the land of Israel 3
25 sojourners who dwelt in Judah •
Job 31:32 the sojourner has not lodged in the street; 3
Ps 39:12 passing guest, a sojourner, like all my fathers. 4
94: 6 They slay the widow and the sojourner 3
105:12 When they were . . sojourners in it 2
119:19 I am a sojourner on earth; 3
146: 9 The LORD watches over the sojourners 3
Ezk 22: 7 the sojourner suffers extortion in your midst; 3
29 and have extorted from the sojourner 3
Zec 7:10 widow, the fatherless, the sojourner, or the poor; 3
Mal 3: 5 against those who thrust aside the sojourner 3
Eph 2:19 you are no longer strangers and sojourners 5

solace 1. נִיד

Job 16: 5 the solace of my lips would assuage your pain. 1

soldering 1. דֶּבֶק

Isa 41: 7 saying of the soldering, "It is good"; 1

soldier 1. אִישׁ 2. אִישׁ חַיִל 3. אִישׁ מִלְחָמָה 4. גֶּבֶר אִישׁ מִלְחָמָה 5. עַם 6. עשה מִלְחָמָה 7. ἀνήρ πολεμιστής 8. λαός 9. ὁ παρά 10. πολεμιστής 11. στράτευμα 12. στρατεύω 13. στρατιώτης 14. στρατιῶτις

1Kg 9:22 they were the soldiers, they were his officials 3
20:39 a soldier turned and brought a man to me, and said 1
2Ch 8: 9 they were soldiers, and his officers 3
17:13 He had soldiers . . in Jerusalem. 3
26:11 Uzzi'ah had an army of soldiers, fit for war 6
Isa 3: 2 the mighty man and the soldier 3
Jer 38: 4 for he is weakening the hands of the soldiers 3
39: 4 king of Judah and all the soldiers saw them 3
41: 3 the Chalde'an soldiers who happened to be there. 3
16 soldiers, women, children, and eunuchs 4
46:21 soldiers in her midst are like fatted calves; •
49:26 all her soldiers shall be destroyed in that day 3
50:30 all her soldiers shall be destroyed on that day 3
51:32 burned with fire, and the soldiers are in panic. 3
Ezk 26: 7 with horsemen and a host of many soldiers. 5
Jol 2: 7 they charge, like soldiers they scale the wall. 3
Nah 2: 3 his soldiers are clothed in scarlet. 2
Mat 8: 9 I am a man under authority, with soldiers under me; 13
27:27 Then the soldiers of the governor took Jesus 13
28:12 counsel, they gave a sum of money to the soldiers 13
Mrk 15:16 the soldiers led him away inside the palace 13
Lke 3:14 Soldiers also asked him 12
7: 8 man set under authority, with soldiers under me 13
23:11 Herod with his soldiers 11
36 The soldiers also mocked him 13
Joh 19: 2 the soldiers plaited a crown of thorns 13
23 When the soldiers had crucified Jesus 13
23 made four parts, one for each soldier 13
25 So the soldiers did this. 13
32 the soldiers came and broke the legs of the first 13
34 one of the soldiers pierced his side with a spear 13
Act 10: 7 called two of his servants and a devout soldier 13
12: 4 four squads of soldiers to guard him 13
6 Peter was sleeping between two soldiers 13
18 there was no small stir among the soldiers 13
21:32 He at once took soldiers and centurions 13
32 when they saw the tribune and the soldiers 13
35 he was actually carried by the soldiers 13
23:10 the tribune . . commanded the soldiers to go down 11
23 200 soldiers with 70 horsemen 13
27 came upon them with the soldiers and rescued him 11
31 So the soldiers . . took Paul 13
27:31 Paul said to the centurion and the soldiers 13
32 Then the soldiers cut away the ropes of the boat 13
42 The soldiers' plan was to kill the prisoners 13
28:16 with the soldier that guarded him. 13
2Ti 2: 3 as a good soldier of Christ Jesus. 13
Jdt 7: 7 seized them and set guards of soldiers over them 7
15: 3 the men of Israel, every one that was a soldier 10
1Mc 6:47 The soldiers of the king's army went up to Jerusalem •
12:49 to destroy all Jonathan's soldiers. 9
16: 6 the soldiers were afraid to cross the stream 8
2Mc 5:12 he commanded his soldiers 13
14:39 Nicanor . . sent more than 500 soldiers to arrest him; 13
3Mc 3:12 his generals and soldiers in Egypt 13
4Mc 3: 7 together with the soldiers of his nation 13
12 two staunch young soldiers 13
5: 1 with his armed soldiers standing about him 11
16:14 O mother, soldier of God in the cause of religion 14
17:23 proclaimed them to his soldiers as an example 13

soldier *See also* foot, guard, serve.

soldier's *See* garment.

fellow soldier 1. συστρατιώτης

Php 2:25 my brother and fellow worker and fellow soldier 1
Phm 1: 2 Ap'phia our sister and Archip'pus our fellow soldier 1

soldier of the guard 1. σπεκουλάτωρ

Mrk 6:27 immediately the king sent a soldier of the guard 1

soldier on service 1. στρατεύω

2Ti 2: 4 No soldier on service gets entangled 1

soldiers *See* band.

sole 1. כַּף 2. שֹׁרֶשׁ 3. πέλμα

Deu 2: 5 not so much as for the sole of the foot to tread 1
11:24 place . . sole of your foot treads shall be yours; 1
28:35 sole of your foot to the crown of your head. 1
56 who would not venture to set the sole of her foot 1
65 there shall be no rest for the sole of your foot; 1
Jos 1: 3 Every place that the sole of your foot will tread 1
3:13 the soles of the feet of the priests who bear 1
4:18 and the soles of the priests' feet were lifted up 1
2Sm 14:25 from the sole of his foot to the crown of his head 1
1Kg 5: 3 the LORD put them under the soles of his feet. 1
2Kg 19:24 I dried up with the sole of my foot all the streams 1
Job 2: 7 from the sole of his foot to the crown of his head. 1
13:27 thou settest a bound to the soles of my feet. 2
Isa 1: 6 From the sole of the foot even to the head 1
37:25 I dried up with the sole of my foot all the streams 1
Ezk 1: 7 soles of their feet were like the sole of a calf's 1
7 of their feet were like the sole of a calf's foot 1
43: 7 of my throne and the place of the soles of my feet 1
Mal 4: 3 they will be ashes under the soles of your feet 1
AEs 13:13 willing to kiss the soles of his feet 3

solemn

Ezk 21:23 false divination; they have sworn solemn oaths; †

solemn *See also* assembly, procession, promise, rest, supplication.

solemnly 1. διαμαρτύρομαι

Gen 43: 3 Judah said to him, "The man solemnly warned us †
Exd 13:19 Joseph had solemnly sworn the people of Israel †
Deu 8:19 I solemnly warn you this day †
1Sm 8: 9 you shall solemnly warn them, and show them †
1Kg 2:42 make you swear . . and solemnly admonish you •
Jer 11: 7 For I solemnly warned your fathers †
1Th 4: 6 as we solemnly forewarned you. 1

solicit to play the harlot 1. זנה

Ezk 16:34 none solicited you to play the harlot; 1

solid 1. πυκνός 2. στερεός

Heb 5:12 You need milk, not solid food 2
14 solid food is for the mature 2
3Mc 4:10 they were confined under a solid deck 1

solid *See also* food.

solitary 1. בָּדָד 2. גְּזֵרָה

Lev 16:22 bear all their iniquities . . to a solitary land 2
Isa 27:10 For the fortified city is solitary 1

solitary *See also* gormandizer, gormandizing.

solitude 1. desertio

2Es 16:26 For in all places there shall be great solitude; 1

solstice 1. τροπή

Wis 7:18 the alternations of the solstices 1

solution 1. λύσις

Wis 8: 8 she understands . . the solutions of riddles 1

solve 1. פתח 2. שׁרא (A) 3. renuntio

Ps 49: 4 I will solve my riddle to the music of the lyre. 1
Dan 5:12 explain riddles, and solve problems were found 2
16 can give interpretations and solve problems. 2
2Es 4: 4 If you can solve one of them for me 3

some 1. אֶחָד 2. אִישׁ 3. אֵלֶּה 4. בְּ 5. היה 6. מִכֹּל 7. מִן 8. מְעַט 9. מִקְצָת 10. קֵץ 11. מִן (A) 12. ἄλλος 13. ἀπό 14. ἐκ 15. ἐν 16. ἔνιοι 17. ἕτερος 18. ἱκανός 19. ὁ δέ 20. ὁ μέν 21. ὅς 22. ὃς δέ 23. ὃς μέν 24. πολύς

25. πρὸς ὀλίγον 26. τις 27. aliqui 28. de 29. ex
30. quidam
Gen 3: 6 she also gave some to her husband, and he ate. •
14:10 Sodom and Gomor'rah fled, some fell into them •
25:30 Let me eat some of that red pottage 7
30:14 Give me, I pray, some of your son's mandrakes. 7
33:15 leave with you some of the men who are with me. 7
40: 1 Some time after this, the butler of the king •
43:11 do this: take some of the choice fruits of the land 7
Exd 4: 9 you shall take some water from the Nile and pour 7
13 he said, "Oh, my Lord, send, I pray, some other person. •
10:10 Look, you have some evil purpose in mind. •
12: 7 Then they shall take some of the blood, and put it 7
16:17 Israel did so; they gathered, some more, some less. •
17 Israel did so; they gathered, some more, some less. •
20 they did not listen to Moses; some left part of it 2
27 On the seventh day some of the people went out 7
17: 5 Pass on . . taking with you some of the elders 7
30:36 you shall beat some of it very small, and put part 7
Lev 4: 5 the anointed priest shall take some of the blood 7
7 the priest shall put some of the blood 7
16 priest shall bring some of the blood of the bull 7
18 he shall put some of the blood on the horns 7
25 take some of the blood of the sin offering 7
30 the priest shall take some of its blood 7
34 Then the priest shall take some of the blood 7
5: 9 sprinkle some of the blood of the sin offering 7
8:11 he sprinkled some of it on the altar seven times 7
12 he poured some of the anointing oil on Aaron's 7
23 Moses killed it, and took some of its blood 7
24 Moses put some of the blood on the tips 7
30 Then Moses took some of the anointing oil 7
14:14 The priest shall take some of the blood 7
15 Then the priest shall take some of the log of oil 7
16 sprinkle some oil with his finger seven times 7
17 some of the oil that remains in his hand 7
25 the priest shall take some of the blood 7
26 the priest shall pour some of the oil 7
27 sprinkle with his right finger some of the oil 7
28 shall put some of the oil that is in his hand 7
16:14 he shall take some of the blood of the bull 7
18 and shall take some of the blood of the bull 7
19 he shall sprinkle some of the blood upon it 7
Num 5:17 priest shall . . take some of the dust that is 7
20 some man other than your husband has lain with you •
11: 1 consumed some outlying parts of the camp. •
17 I will take some of the spirit which is upon you 7
25 LORD . . took some of the spirit that was upon him 7
13:20 bring some of the fruit of the land. 7
23 they brought also some pomegranates and figs. 7
19: 4 shall take some of her blood with his finger 7
4 sprinkle some of her blood toward the front 7
17 shall take some ashes of the burnt sin offering 7
21: 1 against Israel, and took some of them captive. 7
27:20 You shall invest him with some of your authority 7
Deu 1:25 took in their hands some of the fruit of the land 7
13: 7 some of the gods of the people that are round about 7
24: 1 no favor . . because he has found some indecency •
26: 2 take some of the first of all the fruit 7
Jos 7: 1 Achan . . of Judah, took some of the devoted things; 7
11 they have taken some of the devoted things; 7
8:22 in the midst . . some on this side, and some on that 3
22 some on this side, and some on that side; 3
9:23 you are cursed, and some of you shall . . be slaves •
11:22 in Gaza, in Gath, and in Ashdod, did some remain. •
Jdg 14: 9 father and mother, and gave some to them •
19: 2 at Bethlehem . . and was there some four months. •
20:31 they began to smite and kill some of the people •
Rut 2:14 Come here, and eat some bread, and dip your morsel 7
14 and she ate until . . and she had some left over. •
16 And also pull out some from the bundles for her 7
1Sm 6:19 And he slew some of the men of Beth-she'mesh 4
7: 2 From . . a long time passed, some twenty years 5
8:12 he will appoint . . and some to plow his ground •
10:27 some worthless fellows said, "How can this man •
17:18 See . . and bring some token from them. •
24:10 and some bade me kill you, but I spared you. •
2Sm 10: 9 Jo'ab . . chose some of the picked men of Israel 6
11:17 and some of the servants of David . . fell. 7
24 some of the king's servants are dead; 7
12:18 how then can we . . ? He may do himself some harm. •
17: 9 when some of the people fall at the first attack •
12 come upon him in some place where he is to be found 1
1Kg 14: 3 Take with you ten loaves, some cakes, and a jar •
18: 5 save . . alive, and not lose some of the animals. 7
2Kg 2: 7 also went, and stood at some distance from them •
16 cast him upon some mountain or into some valley. 1
16 cast him upon some mountain or into some valley. 1
23 while he was going . . some small boys came out •
4: 8 a wealthy woman . . who urged him to eat some food. •
43 says the LORD, 'They shall eat and have some left.' •
44 they ate, and had some left, according to the word •
5:13 prophet had commanded you to do some great thing •
7:13 Let some men take five of the remaining horses •
9:33 they threw her . . and some of her blood spattered •
17:25 the LORD sent lions . . which killed some of them. •
20:18 And some of your own sons . . shall be taken away; 7
25:12 captain . . left some of the poorest of the land 7
1Ch 4:42 some of them . . went to Mount Se'ir 7
6:66 some of the families of the sons of Kohath 7
9: 3 some of the people . . dwelt in Jerusalem 7
28 Some of them had charge of the utensils 7
32 Also some of their kinsmen of the Ko'hathites 7
12:16 some of the men of Benjamin and Judah 7
19 Some of the men of Manas'seh deserted to David 7
19:10 he chose some of the picked men of Israel 7
2Ch 11:23 some of his sons through all the districts 7
12: 7 but I will grant them some deliverance 8
16:10 Asa inflicted cruelties upon some of the people 7
17:11 Some of the Philistines brought Jehosh'aphat 7
18: 2 After some years he went down to Ahab in Sama'ria. •
19: 3 Nevertheless some good is found in you •
20: 1 with them some of the Me-u'nites 7
2 Some men came and told Jehosh'aphat •
21: 4 he slew . . also some of the princes of Israel. 7
32:21 some of his own sons struck him down there 7
34:13 some of the Levites were scribes, and officials 7
Ezr 2:68 Some of the heads of families, when they came 7
70 priests, the Levites, and some of the people lived 7
7: 7 went up . . some of the priests and Levites 7
7 went up . . some of the people of Israel 7
9: 2 taken some of their daughters to be wives 7
9 grant us some reviving to set up the house of our God •
Neh 5: 5 some of our daughters . . already been enslaved; •
7:70 Now some of the heads of fathers' houses gave 9
71 some of the heads of fathers' houses gave 7
73 gatekeepers, the singers, some of the people 7
11:25 some of the people of Judah lived in Kir'iath-ar'ba 7
13: 6 after some time I asked leave of the king 10
19 I set some of my servants over the gates 7
25 cursed them and beat some of them and pulled out 7
Ps 4: 6 many who say, "O that we might see some good! •
20: 7 Some boast of chariots, and some of horses; 3
7 Some boast of chariots, and some of horses; 3
107: 4 Some wandered in desert wastes, finding no way •
10 Some sat in darkness and in gloom, prisoners •
17 Some were sick through their sinful ways •
23 Some went down to the sea in ships, doing business •
Ecc 10:20 or some winged creature tell the matter. •
Isa 39: 7 some of your own sons . . shall be taken away; 7
66:21 And some of them also I will take for priests 7
Jer 19: 1 and take some of the elders of the people 7
1 of the people and some of the senior priests 7
39:10 left in the land of Judah some of the poor people 7
44:14 they shall not return, except some fugitives. •
52:15 carried away . . some of the poorest of the people •
16 the guard left some of the poorest of the land •
Ezk 5: 4 And of these again you shall take some •
6: 8 Yet I will leave some of you alive. •
8 have among the nations some who escape the sword •
10: 7 and took some of it, and put it into the hands •
16:16 You took some of your garments 7
34:12 when some of his sheep have been scattered •
43:20 you shall take some of its blood 7
45:19 The priest shall take some of the blood 7
Dan 2:41 some of the firmness of iron shall be in it 11
8:10 some of the host of the stars it cast down 7
27 I, Daniel, was overcome and lay sick for some days; •
11: 6 After some years they shall make an alliance •
8 for some years he shall refrain from attacking •
13 after some years he shall come on with a great •
33 though they shall fall . . for some days. •
35 some of those who are wise shall fall 7
12: 2 some to everlasting life, and some to shame 3
2 some to everlasting life, and some to shame 3
Ams 2:11 And I raised up some of your sons for prophets 7
11 and some of your young men for Nazirites. 7
4:11 I overthrew some of you, as when God overthrew 4
Mat 8:30 was feeding at some distance from them. 24
9: 3 behold, some of the scribes said to themselves 26
12:38 Then some of the scribes and Pharisees said 26
13: 4 as he sowed, some seeds fell along the path 23
8 grain, some a hundredfold, some 60, some 30. 23
8 grain, some a hundredfold, some 60, some 30. 22
8 grain, some a hundredfold, some 60, some 30. 22
16:14 Some say John the Baptist, others say Eli'jah 23
28 Truly, I say to you, there are some standing here 26
23:34 some of whom you will kill and crucify 14
34 some you will scourge in your synagogues 14
25: 8 'Give us some of your oil 14
26:67 some slapped him 22
27: 9 a price had been set by some of the sons of Israel •
47 some of the bystanders hearing it said 26
28:11 behold, some of the guard went into the city 26
17 they worshiped him; but some doubted. 22
Mrk 2: 1 when he returned to Caper'na-um after some days •
6 Now some of the scribes were sitting there 26
4: 4 as he sowed, some seed fell along the path 23
5:35 there came . . some who said •
6:14 Some said, "John the baptizer has been raised •
7: 1 with some of the scribes 26
2 they saw that some of his disciples ate 26
8: 3 some of them have come a long way. 26
22 some people brought to him a blind man •
9: 1 some standing here who will not taste death 26
12: 2 to get from them some of the fruit 13
5 some they beat and some they killed. 23
5 some they beat and some they killed. 22
13 some of the Pharisees and some of the Hero'di-ans 26
13 some of the Pharisees and some of the Hero'di-ans •
14: 4 there were some who said to themselves indignantly 26
57 some stood up and bore false witness against him 26
65 some began to spit on him, and to cover his face 26
15:35 some of the bystanders hearing it said, "Behold 26
Lke 6: 1 his disciples plucked and ate some heads of grain •
2 some of the Pharisees said, "Why are you doing 26
8: 2 also some women who had been healed 26
5 as he sowed, some fell along the path 23
6 some fell on the rock 17
7 some fell among thorns 17
8 some fell into good soil and grew 17
9: 7 it was said by some that John had been raised 26
8 by some that Eli'jah had appeared 26
27 are some standing here who will not taste death 26
11:15 some of them said, "He casts out demons 26
49 some of whom they will kill and persecute,' 14
13: 1 There were some present at that very time 26
30 behold, some are last who will be first •
30 some are first who will be last. •
31 At that very hour some Pharisees came, and said 26
18: 9 to some who trusted in themselves 26
19:39 some of the Pharisees in the multitude said 26
20:10 give him some of the fruit of the vineyard 13
27 There came to him some Sadducees 26
39 some of the scribes answered, "Teacher 26
21: 5 as some spoke of the temple, how it was adorned 26
16 some of you they will put to death; 14
23: 8 he was hoping to see some sign done by him. 26
9 he questioned him at some length 18
24:22 Moreover, some women of our company amazed us. 26
24 Some of those who were with us went to the tomb 26
Joh 2: 8 Now draw some out, and take it to the steward •
6:64 there are some of you that do not believe 26
7:12 While some said, "He is a good man 20
25 Some of the people of Jerusalem therefore said 26
40 some of the people said 14
41 But some said, "Is the Christ to come from Galilee? 19
44 Some of them wanted to arrest him 26
8: 6 they might have some charge to bring against him. •
9: 9 Some said, "It is he 12
16 Some of the Pharisees said 26
40 Some of the Pharisees near him heard this 14
11:37 some of them said, "Could not he 26
46 some of them went to the Pharisees 26
12:20 among those who went up . . were some Greeks. 26
13:29 Some thought that . . Jesus was telling him 26
16:17 Some of his disciples said to one another 14
18: 3 some officers from the chief priests •
21: 6 you will find some •
10 Bring some of the fish that you have just caught. 13
Act 5: 2 he kept back some of the proceeds 13
15 at least his shadow might fall on some of them. 26
37 and drew away some of the people after him •
6: 9 Then some of those who belonged to the synagogue 26
8:36 they came to some water 26
10:23 some of the brethren from Joppa accompanied him. 26
48 Then they asked him to remain for some days. 26
11:20 there were some of them, men of Cyprus and Cyre'ne 26
12: 1 Herod the king laid violent hands upon some 26
14: 4 some sided with the Jews 20
4 some with the apostles. 19
15: 2 Paul and Barnabas and some of the others 26
5 some believers . . rose up, and said 26
33 after they had spent some time •
36 after some days Paul said to Barnabas, "Come 26
16:12 We remained in this city some days; 26
17: 4 some of them were persuaded 26
5 taking some wicked fellows of the rabble 26
6 they dragged Jason and some of the brethren 26
18 Some . . Epicurean and Stoic philosophers 26
18 some said, "What would this babbler say? 26
20 you bring some strange things to our ears 26
28 as even some of your poets have said 26
32 some mocked; but others said, "We will hear you 20
34 some men joined him and believed 26
18:23 After spending some time there he departed 26
19: 1 There he found some disciples. 26
9 when some were stubborn and disbelieved 26
13 Then some of the itinerant Jewish exorcists 26
31 some of the A'si-archs also, who were friends of his 26
32 Now some cried one thing, some another 12
32 Now some cried one thing, some another †
33 Some of the crowd prompted Alexander 14
21:10 While we were staying for some days 24
16 some of the disciples from Caesare'a went with us •
34 Some in the crowd shouted one thing, some another; 12
34 Some in the crowd shouted one thing, some another; †
23: 9 some of the scribes of the Pharisees' party 26
24: 1 the high priest Anani'as came down with some elders 26
17 after some years I came to bring to my nation alms 24
18 some Jews from Asia- 26
23 but should have some liberty •
24 After some days Felix came with his wife 26
25:13 Now when some days had passed 26
27: 1 Paul and some other prisoners 26
26 we shall have to run on some island. 26

33 Paul urged them all to take some food, saying •
34 Therefore I urge you to take some food •
36 all were encouraged and ate some food themselves. •
28:24 some were convinced by what he said 20
Rom 1:11 that I may impart to you some spiritual gift 26
13 in order that I may reap some harvest among you 26
3: 3 What if some were unfaithful? 26
11:14 to make . . jealous, and thus save some of them. 26
17 But if some of the branches were broken off 26
15:26 pleased to make some contribution for the poor 26
1Co 4:18 Some are arrogant, as though I were not coming 26
6:11 such were some of you 26
8: 7 some, through being hitherto accustomed 26
9: 7 without getting some of the milk? 14
22 that I might by all means save some. 26
10: 7 Do not be idolaters as some of them were 26
8 We must not indulge in immorality as some of them 26
9 We must not put the Lord to the test, as some of them 26
10 nor grumble, as some of them did 26
11:30 many of you are weak and ill, and some have died 18
14: 6 unless I bring you some revelation or knowledge 15
15: 6 though some have fallen asleep. 26
12 the dead, how can some of you say that there is no 26
34 For some have no knowledge of God 26
37 perhaps of wheat or of some other grain. 26
16: 7 I hope to spend some time with you 26
2Co 2: 5 in some measure–not to put it too severely 13
3: 1 do we need, as some do, letters of recommendation 26
7:14 For if I have expressed to him some pride in you 26
9: 4 lest if some Macedo'nians come with me and find •
10: 2 as I count on showing against some who suspect us 26
12 class or compare ourselves with some of those 26
Gal 1: 7 there are some who trouble you 26
Eph 4:11 his gifts were that some should be apostles 20
11 some prophets, some evangelists 19
11 some prophets, some evangelists 19
11 some evangelists, some pastors and teachers 19
Php 1:15 Some indeed preach Christ from envy and rivalry 26
2Th 3:11 we hear that some of you are living in idleness 26
1Ti 4: 1 in later times some will depart from the faith 26
8 for while bodily training is of some value 25
5: 4 and make some return to their parents •
15 For some have already strayed after Satan. 26
24 The sins of some men are conspicuous 26
6:10 some have wandered away from the faith 26
21 some have missed the mark as regards the faith. 26
2Ti 2:18 They are upsetting the faith of some. 26
20 some for noble use, some for ignoble. 23
20 some for noble use, some for ignoble. 22
Phm 1:20 Yes, brother, I want some benefit from you •
Heb 4: 6 Since therefore it remains for some to enter it 26
10:25 as is the habit of some 26
11:35 Some were tortured, refusing to accept release 12
13: 2 thereby some have entertained angels unawares. 26
1Pe 3: 1 so that some . . may be won without a word 26
2Pe 3: 9 The Lord is not slow . . as some count slowness 26
2Jn 1: 4 to find some of your children following the truth 14
3Jn 1: 3 I greatly rejoiced when some of the brethren arrived •
Jde 1: 4 admission has been secretly gained by some 26
22 And convince some, who doubt; 21
23 save some, by snatching them out of the fire; 21
23 on some have mercy with fear 21
Rev 2:10 devil is about to throw some of you into prison 14
14 some there who hold the teaching of Balaam •
15 some who hold the teaching of the Nicola'itans. •
17 To him who conquers I will give some . . manna •
24 learned what some call the deep things of Satan •
1Es 1:41 Nebuchadnezzar also took some holy vessels 13
5:44 Some of the heads of families 14
46 The priests, the Levites, and some of the people 14
50 some . . from the other peoples of the land 14
63 Some of the Levitical priests 14
8: 5 some of the people of Israel 14
5 some of the priests and Levites •
78 now in some measure mercy has come to us from thee 26
2Es 5:18 Rise therefore and eat some bread 27
6:42 so that some of them might be planted 29
7:86 how some of them will pass over into torments. 28
9:21 I saw and spared some with great difficulty ‡
11:20 There were some of them that ruled 29
13:13 many people came to him, some of whom were joyful 30
13 some of whom were joyful and some sorrowful 30
13 some of them were bound 27
13 and some were bringing others as offerings. 27
14:26 and some you shall deliver in secret to the wise 30
16:30 some clusters may be left by those who search •
68 they shall carry off some of you 30
Tob 6:16 some of the heart and liver of the fish 13
Jdt 7:18 they sent some of their men toward the south 14
10:15 some of us will escort you and hand you over to him. 13
12: 1 to set a table for her with some of his own food 13
15:12 some of them performed a dance for her 14
Wis 13:14 or makes it like some worthless animal 26
Sir 0: 2 seem to have rendered some phrases imperfectly 26
3 I should myself devote some pains and labor 26
8: 6 some of us are growing old. 14
10:17 He has removed some of them and destroyed them 14
14:18 which sheds some and puts forth others 20
22:26 if some harm should happen to me because of him •
33: 9 some of them he exalted and hallowed 13
9 some of them he made ordinary days. 14
12 some of them he blessed and exalted 14
12 some of them he made holy 14
12 some of them he cursed and brought low 13
37: 1 some friends are friends only in name. •
4 Some companions rejoice •
5 Some companions help a friend •
7 some give counsel in their own interest. •
44: 8 There are some of them who have left a name •
9 there are some of them who have no memorial •
48:16 Some of them did what was pleasing to God 26
LJr 1:11 give some of it to the harlots in the brothel. 13
28 likewise their wives preserve some with salt 13
32 as some do at a funeral feast for a man who has died. 26
33 The priests take some of the clothing of their gods 13
1Mc 1:13 some of the people eagerly went to the king 26
5:27 some have been shut up in the other cities •
67 On that day some priests . . fell in battle •
6:21 some of the garrison escaped from the siege 14
21 some of the ungodly Israelites joined them. 26
40 some troops were on the plain 26
7:19 seized . . some of the people 26
33 Some of the priests came out of the sanctuary 13
33 some of the elders of the people 13
8: 7 and surrender some of their best provinces 13
10:14 Only in Beth-zur did some remain 26
37 Let some of them be stationed 14
37 let some of them be put in positions of trust 14
11:23 he chose some of the elders of Israel •
23 he chose . . some of the priests •
16:16 his two sons and some of his servants. 26
2Mc 1:19 took some of the fire of the altar 13
22 When this was done and some time had passed •
2: 1 to take some of the fire •
6 Some of those who followed him 26
3:10 some deposits belonging to widows and orphans •
11 also some money of Hyrcanus, son of Tobias 26
19 Some of the maidens who were kept indoors 20
19 Some . . ran together . . to the walls 19
31 Quickly some of Heliodorus' friends asked Onias 26
32 some foul play had been perpetrated by the Jews 26
38 certainly is about the place some power of God. 26
4:32 Menelaus . . stole some of the gold vessels 26
41 some picked up stones, some blocks of wood 20
41 some picked up stones, some blocks of wood 19
42 they wounded many of them, and killed some 26
8:25 After pursuing them for some distance 18
30 got possession of some exceedingly high strongholds •
33 Callisthenes and some others •
10:20 were bribed by some of those . . in the towers 26
20 the men . . let some of them slip away. 26
11:37 Therefore make haste and send some men 26
12: 2 some of the governors in various places •
3 some men of Joppa did so ungodly a deed as this •
24 because he held . . the brothers of some 22
14: 4 some of the customary olive branches •
3Mc 1: 8 Since the Jews had sent some of their council 13
20 some in houses and some in the streets 20
20 some in houses and some in the streets 19
2:31 Now some, however . . readily gave themselves up 16
3: 4 For this reason they appeared hateful to some; 16
10 some of their neighbors and friends 26
10 some . . had taken some of them aside privately 26
4: 4 even some of their enemies 26
9 some were fastened by the neck to the benches 20
18 some still residing in their homes 20
18 some at the place 19
5:18 After the party had been going on for some time 24
4Mc 1: 5 Some might perhaps ask 26
32 Some desires are mental, others are physical 20
2:18 to correct some, and to render others powerless. 20
5:13 some power watching over this religion of yours 26
6:13 some of the king's retinue came to him and said 26
15 We will set before you some cooked meat •
7:17 Some perhaps might say 26
20 when some persons appear to be dominated 26
8:16 if some of them had been cowardly and unmanly 26
16: 9 some unmarried, others married 20
17: 1 Some of the guards said 26

some *See also* bring, distance, give, point, time.

some man 1. τις

Act 15: 1 some men came down from Judea 1
2Mc 11:37 Therefore make haste and send some men 1

some one 1. אָדָם 2. אִישׁ 3. מִי 4. ὅς 5. τις

2Sm 9: 3 Is there not still some one of the house of Saul 2
23:15 O that some one would give me water to drink 3
2Kg 5:21 when Na'aman saw some one running after him •
1Ch 11:17 O that some one would give me water to drink 3
Neh 2:10 some one had come to seek the welfare 1
Prv 4:16 unless they have made some one stumble. •
Lke 8:46 Jesus said, "Some one touched me 5
13:23 And some one said to him 5
16:30 if some one goes to them from the dead 5
31 if some one should rise from the dead.' 5
Act 5:25 And some one came and told them 5
8:31 he said, "How can I, unless some one guides me? 5
34 does the prophet say this . . about some one else? 5
1Co 10:28 if some one says to you 5
14: 5 unless some one interprets •
15:35 some one will ask, "How are the dead raised? 5
2Co 11: 4 For if some one comes and preaches another Jesus •
Heb 3: 4 For every house is built by some one 5
5:12 you need some one to teach you again 5
Jas 2:18 some one will say, "You have faith and I have works. 5
5:19 and some one brings him back 5
1Pe 5: 8 the devil prowls . . seeking some one to devour. 5
Tob 5: 8 I have found some one to go with me 4
Sir 19: 9 for some one has heard you and watched you •
41:21 taking away some one's portion or gift •
LJr 1:24 will not shine unless some one wipes off the rust; 5
1Mc 6: 5 Then some one came to him in Persia 5
16:21 some one ran ahead and reported to John at Gazara 5
2Mc 11:36 send some one promptly 5

some other 1. אַחֵר

2Sm 17: 9 in one of the pits, or in some other place. 1

some people 1. τις

Rom 3: 8 as some people slanderously charge us 1

some person 1. τις

Act 15:24 some persons from us have troubled you with words 1

some sort 1. כְּ 2. τις

Lev 14:35 seems to me to be some sort of disease in my house 1
Wis 19:15 punishment of some sort will come upon the former 2

some things 1. τις 2. aliquis 3. quidam

2Pe 3:16 There are some things in them hard to understand 1
2Es 8:37 Some things you have spoken rightly 2
14:26 some things you shall make public 3

somebody 1. τις

Act 5:36 Theu'das arose, giving himself out to be somebody 1
8: 9 saying that he himself was somebody great. 1

somehow 1. πῶς

Act 27:12 somehow they could reach Phoenix 1
Rom 1:10 somehow by God's will I may now at last succeed 1
1Co 8: 9 somehow become a stumbling block to the weak. 1
Gal 2: 2 somehow I should be running or had run in vain. 1
1Th 3: 5 somehow the tempter had tempted you 1

someone 1. τις

3Mc 1:14 someone heedlessly said that it was wrong 1
4Mc 2: 7 someone who is . . a solitary gormandizer 1

something 1. דָּבָר 2. מְאוּמָה 3. מַרְאֶה 4. ὅς τις 5. πρᾶγμα 6. σκεῦός τις 7. τις

1Sm 20:26 Something has befallen him; he is not clean •
1Kg 2:14 Then he said, "I have something to say to you. 1
14:13 there is found something pleasing to the LORD 1
2Kg 5:20 run after him, and get something from him. 2
Job 36: 2 for I have yet something to say on God's behalf. •
Ezk 1:13 something that looked like burning coals •
10: 1 appeared above them something like a sapphire •
41:21 in front of the holy place was something 3
Jol 3: 4 Are you paying me back for something? •
Mat 5:23 that your brother has something against you 7
12: 6 something greater than the temple is here. •
41 behold, something greater than Jonah is here. •
42 behold, something greater than Solomon is here. •
14:16 you give them something to eat. •
20:20 she asked him for something. 7
Mrk 5:43 and told them to give her something to eat. •
6:36 buy themselves something to eat. 7
37 he answered them, "You give them something to eat. •
Lke 7:40 Simon, I have something to say to you. 7
8:55 he directed that something should be given her •
9:13 he said to them, "You give them something to eat. •
11:31 behold, something greater than Solomon is here. •
32 behold, something greater than Jonah is here. •
54 to catch at something he might say. 7
Joh 13:29 that he should give something to the poor. 7
Act 3: 5 expecting to receive something from them. 7
9:18 something like scales fell from his eyes •
10:10 he became hungry and desired something to eat; •
11 saw the heaven opened, and something descending 7
11: 5 in a trance I saw a vision, something descending 6
17:21 telling or hearing something new. 7
21:37 May I say something to you? 7
23:17 he has something to tell him. 7
18 as he has something to say to you. 7
25:26 I may have something to write. 7
Rom 2:28 nor is true circumcision something external •
1Co 8: 2 If any one imagines that he knows something 7
16: 2 each of you is to put something aside 4
Gal 2: 6 from those who were reputed to be something 7
6: 3 if any one thinks he is something 7
Heb 8: 3 also to have something to offer. 7
11:40 since God had foreseen something better for us 7
3Jn 1: 9 I have written something to the church; 7
Rev 8: 8 something like a great mountain, burning •

2Es 13: 3 this wind made something like the figure of a man ‡
14:39 it was full of something like water *
Jdt 11: 6 God will accomplish something through you 5
Sir 0: 1 write something pertaining to instruction 7
13: 5 If you own something, he will live with you *
4Mc 5:10 you will do something even more senseless *

something *See also* base, false, mysterious, new, over, pitiable, strange, sweet.

sometime

Jer 28:12 Sometime after the prophet Hanani'ah *

sometimes

1. יֵשׁ אֲשֶׁר 2. *ἐνίοτε* 3. *ἔστι καὶ ὅτε* 4. *τοῦτο δέ* 5. *τοῦτο μέν*

Num 9:20 Sometimes the cloud was a few days over 1
21 sometimes the cloud remained from evening 1
Ecc 2:21 sometimes a man who has toiled . . must leave all *
Heb 10:33 sometimes being publicly exposed to abuse 5
33 sometimes being partners with those so treated. 4
Sir 37:14 a man's soul sometimes keeps him better informed 2
LJr 1:10 sometimes the priests secretly take gold 3

somewhat

1. *τις*

Act 23:20 to inquire somewhat more closely about him. 1

somewhere

1. *ποῦ*

Heb 2: 6 It has been testified somewhere 1
4: 4 has somewhere spoken of the seventh day 1

son

1. אֲשֶׁר יצא מִמֵּעִים 2. בֵּן 3. בַּר 4. זָכָר 5. זֶרַע 6. זֶרַע אֲנָשִׁים 7. ילד 8. יֶלֶד 9. יְצִיא מֵעִים 10. נַעַר 11. פְּרִי 12. בַּר (A) 13. *γεννάω* 14. *ὁ* 15. *παιδάριον* 16. *παιδίον* 17. *παῖς* 18. *σπέρμα* 19. *τέκνον* 20. *υἱοθεσία* 21. *υἱός* 22. filius

Gen 4:17 name of the city after the name of his son, Enoch. 2
25 she bore a son and called his name Seth 2
26 To Seth also a son was born 2
5: 3 Adam . . became the father of a son in his own *
4 and he had other sons and daughters. 2
7 and had other sons and daughters. 2
10 and had other sons and daughters. 2
13 Kenan . . had other sons and daughters. 2
16 Ma-hal'alel . . had other sons and daughters. 2
19 and had other sons and daughters. 2
22 Enoch . . had other sons and daughters. 2
26 and had other sons and daughters. 2
28 Lamech . . became the father of a son 2
30 Lamech . . had other sons and daughters. 2
6: 2 the sons of God saw that the daughters of men 2
4 afterward, when the sons of God came 2
10 Noah had three sons, Shem, Ham, and Japheth. 2
18 you, your sons, your wife, and your sons' wives 2
18 you, your sons, your wife, and your sons' wives 2
7: 7 Noah and his sons and his wife and his sons' wives 2
7 Noah and his sons and his wife and his sons' wives 2
13 Noah and his sons, Shem and Ham and Japheth 2
13 three wives of his sons with them entered the ark 2
8:16 your wife, and your sons and your sons' wives 2
16 your sons and your sons' wives with you. 2
18 went forth, and his sons and his wife and his sons' 2
18 his wife and his sons' wives with him. 2
9: 1 God blessed Noah and his sons, and said to them 2
8 Then God said to Noah and to his sons with him 2
18 The sons of Noah who went forth from the ark 2
19 These three were the sons of Noah; 2
24 knew what his youngest son had done to him 2
10: 1 These are the generations of the sons of Noah 2
1 Japheth; sons were born to them after the flood. 2
2 sons of Japheth: Gomer, Magog, Madai, Javan 2
3 The sons of Gomer: Ash'kenaz, Riphath 2
4 The sons of Javan: Eli'shah, Tarshish, Kittim 2
5 These are the sons of Japheth in their lands *
6 The sons of Ham: Cush, Egypt, Put, and Canaan. 2
7 sons of Cush: Seba, Hav'ilah, Sabtah, Ra'amah 2
7 The sons of Ra'amah: Sheba and Dedan. 2
20 These are the sons of Ham, by their families 2
22 The sons of Shem: Elam, Asshur, Arpach'shad 2
23 The sons of Aram: Uz, Hul, Gether, and Mash. 2
25 To Eber were born two sons 2
29 and Jobab; all these were the sons of Joktan. 2
31 These are the sons of Shem, by their families 2
32 These are the families of the sons of Noah 2
11: 5 the tower, which the sons of men had built. 2
11 Shem lived . . and had other sons and daughters. 2
13 Arpach'shad . . had other sons and daughters. 2
15 Shelah . . had other sons and daughters. 2
17 Eber lived . . and had other sons and daughters. 2
19 Peleg . . had other sons and daughters. 2
21 Re'u lived . . and had other sons and daughters. 2
23 years, and had other sons and daughters. 2
25 and had other sons and daughters. 2
31 Terah took Abram his son and Lot the son of Haran 2
31 Terah took Abram his son and Lot the son of Haran 2
31 Sar'ai . . his son Abram's wife 2
12: 5 Sar'ai his wife, and Lot his brother's son 2
14:12 they also took Lot, the son of Abram's brother 2
15: 4 your own son shall be your heir. 1
16:11 and shall bear a son; you shall call his name 2
15 Hagar bore Abram a son; and Abram called the name 2
15 the name of his son, whom Hagar bore, Ish'mael. 2
17:16 moreover I will give you a son by her; 2
19 Sarah your wife shall bear you a son 2
23 Then Abraham took Ish'mael his son 2
25 Ish'mael his son was thirteen years old 2
26 That very day Abraham and his son Ish'mael 2
18:10 and Sarah your wife shall have a son. 2
14 to you, in the spring, and Sarah shall have a son. 2
19:12 Sons-in-law, sons, daughters, or any one 2
37 first-born bore a son, and called his name Moab; 2
38 The younger also bore a son, and called his name 2
21: 2 Sarah conceived, and bore Abraham a son 2
3 Abraham called the name of his son who was born 2
4 Abraham circumcised his son Isaac 2
5 Abraham was 100 . . when his son Isaac was born 2
7 Yet I have borne him a son in his old age. 2
9 Sarah saw the son of Hagar the Egyptian 2
9 the son . . playing with her son Isaac. 21
10 Cast out this slave woman with her son; 2
10 for the son of this slave woman shall not be heir 2
10 shall not be heir with my son Isaac. 2
11 displeasing to Abraham on account of his son. 2
13 I will make a nation of the son of the slave woman 2
22: 2 He said, "Take your son, your only son Isaac 2
2 your only son Isaac, whom you love *
3 Abraham . . took . . his son Isaac; 2
6 on Isaac his son and he took in his hand the fire 2
7 My father!" And he said, "Here am I, my son. 2
8 a burnt offering, my son." So they went both of them 2
9 Abraham . . bound Isaac his son 2
10 and took the knife to slay his son. 2
12 you have not withheld your son, your only son 2
13 up as a burnt offering instead of his son. 2
16 you . . have not withheld your son, your only son 2
23: 8 and entreat for me Ephron the son of Zohar 2
11 in the presence of the sons of my people I give it 2
24: 3 a wife for my son from the daughters 2
4 to my kindred, and take a wife for my son Isaac. 2
5 must I then take your son back to the land 2
6 See to it that you do not take my son back there. 2
7 you shall take a wife for my son from there. 2
8 only you must not take my son back there. 2
15 born to Bethu'el the son of Milcah 2
24 daughter of Bethu'el the son of Milcah 2
36 Sarah my master's wife bore a son to my master 2
37 a wife for my son from the daughters 2
38 to my kindred, and take a wife for my son.' 2
40 a wife for my son from my kindred 2
44 whom the LORD has appointed for my master's son.' 2
47 She said, The daughter of Bethu'el, Nahor's son 2
48 the daughter of my master's kinsman for his son. 2
51 wife of your master's son, as the LORD has spoken. 2
25: 3 The sons of Dedan were Asshu'rim, Letu'shim 2
4 sons of Mid'ian were Ephah, Epher, Hanoch 2
6 to the sons of his concubines Abraham gave gifts 2
6 he sent them away from his son Isaac 2
9 Isaac and Ish'mael his sons buried him in the cave 2
9 the field of Ephron the son of Zohar the Hittite 2
11 God blessed Isaac his son. 2
12 the descendants of Ish'mael, Abraham's son 2
13 These are the names of the sons of Ish'mael 2
16 These are the sons of Ish'mael 2
19 the descendants of Isaac, Abraham's son 2
27: 1 called Esau his older son, and said to him 2
1 said to him, "My son"; and he answered, "Here I am. 2
5 was listening when Isaac spoke to his son Esau. 2
6 Rebekah said to her son Jacob, "I heard your father 2
8 Now therefore, my son, obey my word as I command 2
13 mother said to him, "Upon me be your curse, my son; 2
15 the best garments of Esau her older son 2
15 and put them on Jacob her younger son; 2
17 had prepared, into the hand of her son Jacob. 2
18 and he said, "Here I am; who are you, my son? 2
20 Isaac said to his son, "How is it 2
20 How is it that you have found it so quickly, my son? 2
21 Come near, that I may feel you, my son 2
21 know whether you are really my son Esau or not. 2
24 He said, "Are you really my son Esau? 2
25 that I may eat of my son's game and bless you. 2
26 said to him, "Come near and kiss me, my son. 2
27 the smell of my son is as the smell of a field 2
29 may your mother's sons bow down to you. 2
31 eat of his son's game, that you may bless me. 2
32 Who are you?" He answered, I am your son 2
37 What then can I do for you, my son? 2
42 words of Esau her older son were told to Rebekah; 2
42 she sent and called Jacob her younger son 2
43 Now therefore, my son, obey my voice; 2
28: 5 went to Paddan-aram to Laban, the son of Bethu'el 2
9 the daughter of Ish'mael Abraham's son 2
29: 5 said to them, "Do you know Laban the son of Nahor? 2
12 he was Rebekah's son; and she ran and told her 2
13 Laban heard the tidings of Jacob his sister's son 2
32 Leah conceived and bore a son 2
33 She conceived again and bore a son 2
33 I am hated, he has given me this son also"; *
34 Again she conceived and bore a son, and said 2
34 because I have borne him three sons"; 2
35 she conceived again and bore a son, and said 2
30: 5 Bilhah conceived and bore Jacob a son. 2
6 God . . has also heard my voice and given me a son"; 2
7 conceived again and bore Jacob a second son. 2
10 Then Leah's maid Zilpah bore Jacob a son. 2
12 Leah's maid Zilpah bore Jacob a second son. 2
14 Give me, I pray, some of your son's mandrakes. 2
15 Would you take away my son's mandrakes also? 2
15 lie with you tonight for your son's mandrakes. 2
16 have hired you with my son's mandrakes." So he lay 2
17 she conceived and bore Jacob a fifth son. 2
19 conceived again, and she bore Jacob a sixth son. 2
20 will honor me, because I have borne him six sons 2
23 She conceived and bore a son, and said 2
24 saying, "May the LORD add to me another son! 2
35 that was black, and put them in charge of his sons; 2
31: 1 Jacob heard that the sons of Laban were saying 2
17 arose, and set his sons and his wives on camels; 2
28 to kiss my sons and my daughters farewell? 2
33:19 from the sons of Hamor, Shechem's father 2
34: 2 when Shechem the son of Hamor the Hivite 2
5 but his sons were with the cattle in the field 2
7 The sons of Jacob came in from the field 2
8 The soul of my son Shechem longs 2
13 The sons of Jacob answered Shechem 2
18 words pleased Hamor and Hamor's son Shechem. 2
20 Hamor and his son Shechem came to the gate 2
24 all . . hearkened to Hamor and his son Shechem; 2
25 when they were sore, two of the sons of Jacob 2
26 They slew Hamor and his son Shechem 2
27 the sons of Jacob came upon the slain 2
35: 5 that they did not pursue the sons of Jacob. 2
17 Fear not; for now you will have another son. 2
22 Now the sons of Jacob were twelve. 2
23 sons of Leah: Reuben (Jacob's first-born) 2
24 The sons of Rachel: Joseph and Benjamin. 2
25 The sons of Bilhah, Rachel's maid: Dan 2
26 The sons of Zilpah, Leah's maid: Gad and Asher. 2
26 These were the sons of Jacob who were born to him 2
29 and his sons Esau and Jacob buried him. 2
36: 2 daughter of Anah the son of Zib'eon the Hivite 21
5 These are the sons of Esau who were born 2
6 took his wives, his sons, his daughters, and all 2
10 These are the names of Esau's sons 2
10 Esau's sons: El'iphaz the son of Adah the wife 2
10 Reu'el the son of Bas'emath the wife of Esau. 2
11 The sons of El'iphaz were Teman, Omar, Zepho 2
12 (Timna was a concubine of El'iphaz, Esau's son; 2
12 These are the sons of Adah, Esau's wife. 2
13 are the sons of Reu'el: Nahath, Zerah, Shammah 2
13 These are the sons of Bas'emath, Esau's wife. 2
14 These are the sons of Oholiba'mah 2
14 daughter of Anah the son of Zib'eon, Esau's wife 21
15 These are the chiefs of the sons of Esau. 2
15 The sons of El'iphaz the first-born of Esau 2
16 the land of Edom; they are the sons of Adah. 2
17 These are the sons of Reu'el, Esau's son 2
17 These are the sons of Reu'el, Esau's son 2
17 Edom; they are the sons of Bas'emath, Esau's wife 2
18 These are the sons of Oholiba'mah, Esau's wife 2
19 These are the sons of Esau (that is, Edom) 2
20 These are the sons of Se'ir the Horite 2
21 the Horites, the sons of Se'ir in the land of Edom. 2
22 The sons of Lotan were Hori and Heman; 2
23 the sons of Shobal: Alvan, Man'ahath, Ebal 2
24 These are the sons of Zib'eon: A'iah and Anah; 2
26 These are the sons of Dishon: Hemdan, Eshban 2
27 These are the sons of Ezer: Bilhan, Za'avan 2
28 These are the sons of Dishan: Uz and Aran. 2
32 Bela the son of Be'or reigned in Edom 2
33 Bela died, and Jobab the son of Zerah of Bozrah 2
35 Husham died, and Hadad the son of Bedad 2
38 Shaul died, and Ba'al-ha'nan the son of Achbor 2
39 Ba'al-ha'nan the son of Achbor died 2
37: 2 he was a lad with the sons of Bilhah and Zilpah 2
3 loved Joseph . . because he was the son of his old 2
32 we have found; see now whether it is your son's robe 2
33 he recognized it, and said, "It is my son's robe; 2
34 Jacob . . mourned for his son many days. 2
35 All his sons and all his daughters rose up 2
35 No, I shall go down to Sheol to my son, mourning. 2
38: 3 she conceived and bore a son 2
4 Again she conceived and bore a son 2
5 Yet again she bore a son 2
11 Remain a widow . . till Shelah my son grows up 2
26 inasmuch as I did not give her to my son Shelah. 2
41:50 Joseph had two sons, whom As'enath 2
42: 1 he said to his sons, "Why do you look at one another 2
5 Thus the sons of Israel came to buy among 2
11 We are all sons of one man, we are honest men 2
13 twelve brothers, the sons of one man in the land 2
32 we are twelve brothers, sons of our father; 2
37 Slay my two sons if I do not bring him back to you; 2
38 he said, "My son shall not go down with you 2
43:29 and saw his brother Benjamin, his mother's son 2
29 God be gracious to you, my son! 2
45: 9 Thus says your son Joseph, God has made me lord 2
21 The sons of Israel did so; 2
28 It is enough; Joseph my son is still alive; 2

46: 5 and the sons of Israel carried Jacob their 2
7 his sons, and his sons' sons with him 2
7 his sons, and his sons' sons with him 2
7 his sons, and his sons' sons with him 2
7 his daughters, and his sons' daughters; all his 2
8 who came into Egypt, Jacob and his sons. 2
9 the sons of Reuben: Hanoch, Pallu, Hezron 2
10 The sons of Simeon: Jemu'el, Jamin, Ohad, Jachin 2
10 and Shaul, the son of a Canaanitish woman. 2
11 The sons of Levi: Gershon, Kohath, and Merar'i. 2
12 sons of Judah: Er, Onan, Shelah, Perez, and Zerah 2
12 and the sons of Perez were Hezron and Hamul. 2
13 sons of Is'sachar: Tola, Puvah, Iob, and Shimron 2
14 The sons of Zeb'ulun: Sered, Elon, and Jah'leel 2
15 these are the sons of Leah, whom she bore to Jacob 2
15 altogether his sons and his daughters numbered 2
16 sons of Gad: Ziph'ion, Haggi, Shuni, Ezbon, Eri 2
17 The sons of Asher: Imnah, Ishvah, Ishvi, Beri'ah 2
17 And the sons of Beri'ah: Heber and Mal'chi-el 2
18 these are the sons of Zilpah, whom Laban gave 2
19 The sons of Rachel, Jacob's wife: Joseph 2
21 the sons of Benjamin: Bela, Becher, Ashbel, Gera 2
22 these are the sons of Rachel, who were born 2
23 The sons of Dan: Hushim. 2
24 The sons of Naph'tali: Jahzeel, Guni, Jezer 2
25 these are the sons of Bilhah, whom Laban gave 2
26 own offspring, not including Jacob's sons' wives 2
27 the sons of Joseph, who were born to him in Egypt 2
47:29 Israel must die, he called his son Joseph 2
48: 1 with him his two sons, Manas'seh and E'phraim. 2
2 it was told to Jacob, "Your son Joseph has come 2
5 now your two sons, who were born to you in the land 2
8 Israel saw Joseph's sons, he said, "Who are these 2
9 They are my sons, whom God has given me here. 2
19 my son, I know; he also shall become a people 2
49: 1 Jacob called his sons, and said, "Gather 2
2 Assemble and hear, O sons of Jacob 2
8 your father's sons shall bow down before you. 2
9 from the prey, my son, you have gone up. 2
33 Jacob finished charging his sons, he drew up 2
50:12 Thus his sons did for him as he had commanded them; 2
13 for his sons carried him to the land of Canaan 2
23 children . . of Machir the son of Manas'seh were 2
25 Then Joseph took an oath of the sons of Israel 2
Exd 1: 1 the names of the sons of Israel who came to Egypt 2
16 if it is a son, you shall kill him; 2
22 Every son that is born to the Hebrews 2
2: 2 The woman conceived and bore a son; 2
10 child grew . . and he became her son; 2
22 She bore a son, and he called his name Gershom; 2
3:10 my people, the sons of Israel, out of Egypt. 2
11 that I should . . bring the sons of Israel out 2
22 put them on your sons and on your daughters; 2
4:20 So Moses took his wife and his sons and set them 2
22 Thus says the LORD, Israel is my first-born son 2
23 I say to you, "Let my son go that he may serve me"; 2
23 behold, I will slay your first-born son.' 2
25 took a flint and cut off her son's foreskin 2
6:14 the sons of Reuben, the first-born of Israel 2
15 The sons of Simeon: Jemu'el, Jamin, Ohad, Jachin 2
15 Zohar, and Shaul, the son of a Canaanite woman; 2
16 These are the names of the sons of Levi according 2
17 The sons of Gershon: Libni and Shim'e-i 2
18 The sons of Kohath: Amram, Izhar, Hebron, 2
19 The sons of Merar'i: Mahli and Mushi. 2
21 The sons of Izhar: Korah, Nepheg, and Zichri. 2
22 the sons of Uz'ziel: Mi'sha-el, Elza'phan, and Sithri. 2
24 The sons of Korah: Assir, Elka'nah, and Abi'asaph; 2
25 Elea'zar, Aaron's son, took to wife one 2
7: 4 bring forth . . my people the sons of Israel 2
10: 2 in the hearing of your son and of your son's son 2
2 in the hearing of your son and of your son's son 2
2 in the hearing of your son and of your son's son 2
9 we will go with our sons and daughters 2
12:24 ordinance for you and for your sons for ever. 2
13: 8 you shall tell your son on that day, 'It is 2
13 first-born . . among your sons you shall redeem. 2
14 when in time to come your son asks you, 'What does 2
15 but all the first-born of my sons I redeem.' 2
18: 3 her two sons, of whom the name of the one was 2
5 Jethro . . came with his sons and his wife 2
6 with your wife and her two sons with her 2
20:10 you, or your son, or your daughter, your manservant 2
21: 4 a wife and she bears him sons or daughters 2
9 If he designates her for his son, he shall deal 2
31 If it gores a man's son or daughter, he shall be 2
22:29 The first-born of your sons you shall give to me. 2
23:12 the son of your bondmaid, and the alien, may be 2
27:21 Aaron and his sons shall tend it from evening 2
28: 1 Aaron your brother, and his sons with him 2
1 to serve me as priests–Aaron and Aaron's sons 2
4 your brother and his sons to serve me as priests. 2
9 engrave on them the names of the sons of Israel 2
11 stones with the names of the sons of Israel; 2
12 as stones of remembrance for the sons of Israel; 2
21 according to the names of the sons of Israel; 2
29 Aaron shall bear all the names of the sons of Israel 2
40 for Aaron's sons you shall make coats and girdles 2
41 put them upon Aaron your brother, and upon his sons 2
43 they shall be upon Aaron, and upon his sons 2
29: 4 You shall bring Aaron and his sons to the door 2
8 you shall bring his sons, and put coats on them 2
9 Thus you shall ordain Aaron and his sons. 2
10 meeting. Aaron and his sons shall lay their 2
15 Aaron and his sons shall lay their hands upon 2
19 Aaron and his sons shall lay their hands upon 2
20 upon the tips of the right ears of his sons 2
21 upon his sons and his sons' garments with him; 2
21 upon his sons and his sons' garments with him; 2
21 his sons and his sons' garments with him. 2
21 his sons and his sons' garments with him. 2
24 the hands of Aaron and in the hands of his sons 2
27 since it is for Aaron and for his sons. 2
28 for Aaron and his sons as a perpetual due 2
29 The holy garments of Aaron shall be for his sons 2
30 The son who is priest in his place shall wear them 2
32 Aaron and his sons shall eat the flesh of the ram 2
35 Thus you shall do to Aaron and to his sons 2
44 Aaron also and his sons I will consecrate 2
30:19 with which Aaron and his sons wash 2
30 you shall anoint Aaron and his sons 2
31: 2 called by name Bez'alel and son of Uri, son of Hur 2
2 called by name Bez'alel and son of Uri, son of Hur 2
6 appointed with him Oho'liab, the son of Ahis'amach 2
10 Aaron the priest and the garments of his sons 2
32: 2 of your wives, your sons, and your daughters 2
26 Come to me." And all the sons of Levi gathered 2
28 the sons of Levi did according to the word of Moses; 2
29 each one at the cost of his son and of his brother 2
33:11 his servant Joshua the son of Nun, a young man 2
34:16 you take of their daughters for your sons 2
16 make your sons play the harlot after their gods. 2
20 All the first-born of your sons you shall redeem. 2
35:19 the garments of his sons, for their service 2
30 has called by name Bez'alel the son of Uri 2
30 the son of Uri, son of Hur, of the tribe of Judah; 2
34 Oho'liab the son of Ahis'amach of the tribe of Dan. 2
38:21 under the direction of Ith'amar the son of Aaron 2
22 Bez'alel the son of Uri, son of Hur, of the tribe 2
22 Bez'alel the son of Uri, son of Hur, of the tribe 2
23 with him was Oho'liab the son of Ahis'amach 2
39: 6 according to the names of the sons of Israel. 2
7 stones of remembrance for the sons of Israel; 2
14 according to the names of the sons of Israel; 2
27 coats, woven of fine linen, for Aaron and his sons 2
41 the garments of his sons to serve as priests. 2
40:12 you shall bring Aaron and his sons to the door 2
14 You shall bring his sons also and put coats 2
31 with which Moses and Aaron and his sons washed 2
Lev 1: 5 Aaron's sons the priests shall present the blood 2
7 the sons of Aaron the priest shall put fire 2
8 Aaron's sons the priests shall lay the pieces 2
11 Aaron's sons the priests shall throw its blood 2
2: 2 bring it to Aaron's sons the priests 2
3 cereal offering shall be for Aaron and his sons 2
10 cereal offering shall be for Aaron and his sons 2
3: 2 Aaron's sons the priests shall throw the blood 2
5 Then Aaron's sons shall burn it on the altar 2
8 Aaron's sons shall throw its blood 2
13 the sons of Aaron shall throw its blood 2
6: 9 Command Aaron and his sons, saying, This is the law 2
14 The sons of Aaron shall offer it before the LORD 2
16 the rest of it Aaron and his sons shall eat 2
20 which Aaron and his sons shall offer to the LORD 2
22 The priest from among Aaron's sons 2
25 Say to Aaron and his sons, This is the law 2
7:10 with oil or dry, shall be for all the sons of Aaron 2
31 but the breast shall be for Aaron and his sons 2
33 he among the sons of Aaron who offers the blood 2
34 given . . to his sons, as a perpetual due 2
35 This is the portion of Aaron and of his sons 2
8: 2 Take Aaron and his sons with him, and the garments 2
6 Moses brought Aaron and his sons, and washed them 2
13 Moses brought Aaron's sons, and clothed them 2
14 Aaron and his sons laid their hands upon the head 2
18 Aaron and his sons laid their hands on the head 2
22 Aaron and his sons laid their hands on the head 2
24 Aaron's sons were brought, and Moses put some 2
27 hands of Aaron and in the hands of his sons 2
30 upon his sons and his sons' garments 2
30 upon his sons and his sons' garments 2
30 his sons and his sons' garments with him 2
30 his sons and his sons' garments with him 2
31 Moses said to Aaron and his sons, "Boil the flesh 2
31 saying, 'Aaron and his sons shall eat it' 2
36 Aaron and his sons did all the things 2
9: 1 Aaron and his sons and the elders of Israel 2
9 the sons of Aaron presented the blood to him 2
12 Aaron's sons delivered to him the blood 2
18 Aaron's sons delivered to him the blood 2
10: 1 Now Nadab and Abihu, the sons of Aaron 2
4 Mish'a-el and Elza'phan, the sons of Uz'ziel 2
6 to Aaron and to Elea'zar and Ith'amar, his sons 2
9 Drink no wine nor strong drink, you nor your sons 2
12 Elea'zar and Ith'amar, his sons who were left 2
13 because it is your due and your sons' due 2
14 you and your sons and your daughters with you 2
14 for they are given as your due and your sons' due 2
15 it shall be yours, and your sons' with you, as a due 2
16 angry with Elea'zar and Ith'amar, the sons of Aaron 2
12: 6 days of her purifying . . whether for a son 2
13: 2 brought . . to one of his sons the priests 2
16: 1 after the death of the two sons of Aaron 2
17: 2 Say to Aaron and his sons, and to all the people 2
18:10 not uncover the nakedness of your son's daughter 2
15 your daughter-in-law; she is your son's wife 2
17 you shall not take her son's daughter 2
19:18 any grudge against the sons of your own people 2
21: 1 Speak to the priests, the sons of Aaron, and say 2
2 his father, his son, his daughter, his brother 2
24 to Aaron and to his sons and to all the people 2
22: 2 Tell Aaron and his sons to keep away from the holy 2
18 Say to Aaron and to his sons and all the people 2
24: 9 it shall be for Aaron and his sons 2
10 Now an Israelite woman's son, whose father was 2
10 woman's son and a man of Israel quarreled 2
11 the Israelite woman's son blasphemed the Name 2
25:46 You may bequeath them to your sons after you 2
26:29 You shall eat the flesh of your sons 2
Num 1: 5 From Reuben, Eli'zur the son of Shed'eur; 2
6 from Simeon, Shelu'mi-el the son of Zurishad'dai; 2
7 from Judah, Nahshon the son of Ammin'adab; 2
8 from Is'sachar, Nethan'el the son of Zu'ar; 2
9 from Zeb'ulun, Eli'ab the son of Helon; 2
10 from the sons of Joseph, from E'phraim, Eli'shama 2
10 from E'phraim, Eli'shama the son of Ammi'hud 2
10 from Manas'seh, Gama'liel the son of Pedah'zur; 2
11 from Benjamin, Abi'dan the son of Gideo'ni; 2
12 from Dan, Ahi-e'zer the son of Ammishad'dai; 2
13 from Asher, Pa'giel the son of Ochran; 2
14 from Gad, Eli'asaph the son of Deu'el; 2
15 from Naph'tali, Ahi'ra the son of Enan. 2
2: 3 leader . . being Nahshon the son of Ammin'adab 2
5 the leader . . being Nethan'el the son of Zu'ar 2
7 the leader . . being Eli'ab the son of Helon 2
10 the leader . . Eli'zur the son of Shed'eur 2
12 Simeon being Shelu'mi-el the son of Zurishad'dai 2
14 the leader . . Eli'asaph the son of Reu'el 2
18 the leader . . Eli'shama the son of Ammi'hud 2
20 the leader . . Gama'liel the son of Pedah'zur 2
22 the leader . . Abi'dan the son of Gideo'ni 2
25 the leader . . Ahi-e'zer the son of Ammishad'dai 2
27 the leader . . Pa'giel the son of Ochran 2
29 the leader . . being Ahi'ra the son of Enan 2
3: 2 These are the names of the sons of Aaron 2
3 these are the names of the sons of Aaron 2
9 you shall give the Levites to Aaron and his sons; 2
10 you shall appoint Aaron and his sons 2
15 Number the sons of Levi, by fathers' houses 2
17 these were the sons of Levi by their names 2
18 these are the names of the sons of Gershon 2
19 the sons of Kohath by their families 2
20 the sons of Merar'i by their families 2
24 son of La'el as head of the fathers' house 2
25 the charge of the sons of Gershon in the tent 2
29 The families of the sons of Kohath were to encamp 2
30 Eli-za'phan the son of Uz'ziel as head 2
32 Elea'zar the son of Aaron . . was to be chief 2
35 head . . was Zu'riel the son of Ab'ihail; 2
36 the appointed charge of the sons of Merar'i 2
38 Moses and Aaron and his sons, having charge 2
48 give the money . . to Aaron and his sons. 2
51 gave the redemption money to Aaron and his sons 2
4: 2 Take a census of the sons of Kohath 2
2 sons of Kohath from among the sons of Levi 2
4 This is the service of the sons of Kohath 2
5 Aaron and his sons shall go in and take down 2
15 when Aaron and his sons have finished covering 2
15 sons of Kohath shall come to carry these 2
15 things . . which the sons of Kohath are to carry. 2
16 Elea'zar the son of Aaron the priest 2
19 Aaron and his sons shall go in and appoint them 2
22 Take a census of the sons of Gershon also 2
27 All the service of the sons of the Gershonites 2
27 service . . at the command of Aaron and his sons 2
28 service of . . the sons of the Gershonites 2
28 Ith'amar the son of Aaron the priest. 2
29 As for the sons of Merar'i, you shall number them 2
33 service of the families of the sons of Merar'i 2
33 Ith'amar the son of Aaron the priest. 2
34 Moses . . numbered the sons of the Ko'hathites 2
38 number of the sons of Gershon, by their families 2
41 number of the families of the sons of Gershon 2
42 The number of the families of the sons of Merar'i 2
45 numbered of the families of the sons of Merar'i 2
6:23 Say to Aaron and his sons, Thus you shall bless 2
7: 7 gave to the sons of Gershon 2
8 gave to the sons of Merar'i 2
8 Ith'amar the son of Aaron the priest. 2
9 to the sons of Kohath he gave none 2
12 Nahshon the son of Ammin'adab, of . . Judah; 2
17 was the offering of Nahshon the son of Ammin'adab 2
18 Nethan'el the son of Zu'ar, the leader of Is'sachar 2
23 was the offering of Nethan'el the son of Zu'ar. 2
24 Eli'ab the son of Helon, the leader of the men 2
29 This was the offering of Eli'ab the son of Helon. 2
30 Eli'zur the son of Shed'eur, the leader of the men 2

35 was the offering of Eli'zur the son of Shed'eur. 2
36 Shelu'mi-el the son of Zurishad'dai, the leader 2
41 offering of Shelu'mi-el the son of Zurishad'dai. 2
42 Eli'asaph the son of Deu'el, the leader of the men 2
47 was the offering of Eli'asaph the son of Deu'el. 2
48 Eli'shama the son of Ammi'hud, the leader 2
53 was the offering of Eli'shama the son of Ammi'hud. 2
54 Gama'liel the son of Pedah'zur, the leader 2
59 offering of Gama'liel the son of Pedah'zur. 2
60 Abi'dan the son of Gideo'ni, the leader of the men 2
65 was the offering of Abi'dan the son of Gideo'ni. 2
66 Ahie'zer the son of Ammishad'dai, the leader 2
71 offering of Ahie'zer the son of Ammishad'dai. 2
72 Pa'giel the son of Ochran, the leader of the men 2
77 was the offering of Pa'giel the son of Ochran. 2
78 Ahi'ra the son of Enan, the leader of the men 2
83 This was the offering of Ahi'ra the son of Enan. 2
8:13 cause the Levites to attend Aaron and his sons 2
19 given the Levites as a gift to Aaron and his sons 2
22 in attendance upon Aaron and his sons; 2
10: 8 sons of Aaron . . shall blow the trumpets. 2
14 Nahshon the son of Ammin'adab. 2
15 over the host . . was Nethan'el the son of Zu'ar. 2
16 over the host . . was Eli'ab the son of Helon. 2
17 sons of Gershon and the sons of Merar'i 2
17 sons of Gershon and the sons of Merar'i 2
18 over their host was Eli'zur the son of Shed'eur. 2
19 Shelu'mi-el the son of Zurishad'dai. 2
20 over the host . . was Eli'asaph the son of Deu'el. 2
22 over their host was Eli'shama the son of Ammi'hud. 2
23 Gama'liel the son of Pedah'zur. 2
24 over the host . . was Abi'dan the son of Gideo'ni. 2
25 Ahie'zer the son of Ammishad'dai. 2
26 over the host . . was Pa'giel the son of Ochran. 2
27 over the host . . was Ahi'ra the son of Enan. 2
29 Hobab the son of Reu'el the Mid'ianite 2
11:28 Joshua the son of Nun, the minister of Moses 2
13: 4 tribe of Reuben, Sham'mu-a the son of Zaccur; 2
5 from the tribe of Simeon, Shaphat the son of Hori; 2
6 tribe of Judah, Caleb the son of Jephun'neh; 2
7 from the tribe of Is'sachar, Igal the son of Joseph; 2
8 from the tribe of E'phraim, Hoshe'a the son of Nun; 2
9 from the tribe of Benjamin, Palti the son of Raphu; 2
10 from the tribe of Zeb'ulun, Gad'diel the son of Sodi; 2
11 from the tribe of Joseph . . Gaddi the son of Susi; 2
12 from the tribe of Dan, Am'miel the son of Gemal'li; 2
13 from the tribe of Asher, Sethur the son of Michael; 2
14 tribe of Naph'tali, Nahbi the son of Vophsi; 2
15 from the tribe of Gad, Geu'el the son of Machi. 2
16 Moses called Hoshe'a the son of Nun Joshua. 2
33 (the sons of Anak, who come from the Nephilim); 2
14: 6 Joshua the son of Nun and Caleb . . of Jephun'neh 2
6 Joshua . . of Nun and Caleb the son of Jephun'neh 2
30 except Caleb the son of Jephun'neh and Joshua 2
30 except Caleb . . and Joshua the son of Nun. 2
38 Joshua the son of Nun and Caleb . . of Jephun'neh 2
38 Joshua . . of Nun and Caleb the son of Jephun'neh 2
16: 1 Korah the son of Izhar, son of Kohath, son of Levi 2
1 Korah the son of Izhar, son of Kohath, son of Levi 2
1 Korah the son of Izhar, son of Kohath, son of Levi 2
1 Dathan and Abi'ram the sons of Eli'ab, and On 2
1 Dathan and Abi'ram . . and On the son of Peleth 2
1 Dathan and Abi'ram . . and On . . , sons of Reuben 2
7 You have gone too far, sons of Levi! 2
8 Moses said to Korah, "Hear now, you sons of Levi 2
10 all your brethren the sons of Levi with you? 2
12 sent to call Dathan and Abi'ram the sons of Eli'ab; 2
27 together with their wives, their sons, and their 2
37 Elea'zar the son of Aaron the priest to take up 2
18: 1 You and your sons and your fathers' house with you 2
1 you and your sons with you shall bear iniquity 2
2 while you and your sons with you are before 2
7 sons with you shall attend to your priesthood 2
8 as a portion, and to your sons as a perpetual due. 2
9 shall be most holy to you and to your sons. 2
11 given . . to your sons and daughters with you 2
19 I give to you, and to your sons and daughters 2
20:25 Take Aaron and Elea'zar his son, and bring them up 2
26 garments, and put them upon Elea'zar his son; 2
28 garments, and put them upon Elea'zar his son; 2
21:29 He has made his sons fugitives, and his daughters 2
35 they slew him, and his sons, and all his people 2
22: 2 Balak the son of Zippor saw all that Israel 2
4 So Balak the son of Zippor, who was king of Moab 2
5 sent messengers to Balaam the son of Be'or 2
10 Balak the son of Zippor, king of Moab, has sent to me 2
16 Thus says Balak the son of Zippor: 'Let nothing 2
23:18 Rise, Balak, and hear; hearken to me, O son of Zippor 2
19 God is not . . a son of man, that he should repent. 2
24: 3 oracle of Balaam the son of Be'or 2
15 The oracle of Balaam the son of Be'or 2
17 it shall . . break down all the sons of Sheth. 2
25: 7 When Phin'ehas the son of Elea'zar . . saw it 2
7 Phin'ehas . . of Elea'zar, son of Aaron the priest 2
11 Phin'ehas the son of Elea'zar, son of Aaron 2
11 Phin'ehas . . of Elea'zar, son of Aaron the priest 2
14 Zimri the son of Salu, head of a fathers' house 2
26: 1 Elea'zar the son of Aaron, the priest 2
5 sons of Reuben: of Hanoch . . of Pallu 2
8 the sons of Pallu: Eli'ab. 2
9 The sons of Eli'ab: Nem'uel, Dathan, and Abi'ram. 2
11 Notwithstanding, the sons of Korah did not die. 2
12 The sons of Simeon according to their families 2
15 The sons of Gad according to their families 2
18 These are the families of the sons of Gad 2
19 The sons of Judah were Er and Onan; 2
20 sons of Judah according to their families were 2
21 the sons of Perez were: of Hezron . . of Hamul 2
23 sons of Is'sachar according to their families 2
26 The sons of Zeb'ulun, according to their families 2
28 The sons of Joseph according to their families 2
29 sons of Manas'seh 2
30 These are the sons of Gilead: of Ie'zer . . of Helek 2
33 Now Zeloph'ehad the son of Hepher had no sons 2
33 Now Zeloph'ehad the son of Hepher had no sons 2
35 sons of E'phraim according to their families 2
36 these are the sons of Shuthe'lah: of Eran 2
37 These are the families of the sons of E'phraim 2
37 sons of Joseph according to their families. 2
38 sons of Benjamin according to their families 2
40 the sons of Bela were Ard and Na'aman 2
41 sons of Benjamin according to their families; 2
42 sons of Dan according to their families 2
44 The sons of Asher according to their families 2
45 Of the sons of Beri'ah: of Heber . . of Mal'chi-el 2
47 These are the families of the sons of Asher 2
48 sons of Naph'tali according to their families 2
65 except Caleb the son of Jephun'neh 2
65 except Caleb . . and Joshua the son of Nun. 2
27: 1 daughters of Zeloph'ehad the son of Hepher 2
1 Hepher, son of Gilead, son of Machir 2
1 Hepher, son of Gilead, son of Machir 2
1 Gilead, son of Machir, son of Manas'seh 2
1 from the families of Manas'seh the son of Joseph. 2
3 died for his own sin; and he had no sons. 2
4 taken away from his family, because he had no son? 2
8 If a man dies, and has no son 2
18 Take Joshua the son of Nun . . and lay your hand 2
31: 6 with Phin'ehas the son of Elea'zar the priest 2
8 also slew Balaam the son of Be'or with the sword. 2
32: 1 sons of Reuben . . had a very great multitude of cattle; 2
1 sons of Gad had a very great multitude of cattle; 2
2 sons of Gad and the sons of Reuben came and said 2
2 sons of Gad and the sons of Reuben came and said 2
6 Moses said to the sons of Gad and . . of Reuben 2
6 Moses said to . . of Gad and to the sons of Reuben 2
12 except Caleb the son of Jephun'neh the Ken'izzite 2
12 none except Caleb . . and Joshua the son of Nun 2
25 the sons of Gad . . said to Moses 2
25 sons of Gad and the sons of Reuben said to Moses 2
28 command concerning them to . . Joshua the son of Nun 2
29 If the sons of Gad and the sons of Reuben 2
29 If the sons of Gad and the sons of Reuben 2
31 sons of Gad and the sons of Reuben answered, "As 2
31 sons of Gad and the sons of Reuben answered, "As 2
33 Moses gave to them, to the sons of Gad 2
33 Moses gave . . to the sons of Reuben 2
33 to the half-tribe of Manas'seh the son of Joseph 2
34 the sons of Gad built Dibon, At'aroth, Aro'er 2
37 sons of Reuben built Heshbon, Elea'leh, Kiriatha'im 2
39 sons of Machir the son of Manas'seh went to Gilead 2
39 sons of Machir the son of Manas'seh went to Gilead 2
40 Moses gave Gilead to Machir the son of Manas'seh 2
41 Ja'ir the son of Manas'seh went and took 2
34:14 tribe of the sons of Reuben by fathers' houses 2
14 tribe of the sons of Gad by their fathers' houses 2
17 Elea'zar the priest and Joshua the son of Nun. 2
19 Of the tribe of Judah, Caleb the son of Jephun'neh. 2
20 Of the tribe of the sons of Simeon, Shemu'el 2
20 tribe . . of Simeon, Shemu'el the son of Ammi'hud. 2
21 tribe of Benjamin, Eli'dad the son of Chislon. 2
22 Of the tribe of the sons of Dan a leader, Bukki 2
22 tribe . . of Dan a leader, Bukki the son of Jogli. 2
23 sons of Joseph: of the tribe of the sons of Manas'seh 2
23 of the tribe of the sons of Manas'seh a leader, 2
23 of Manas'seh a leader, Han'niel the son of Ephod. 2
24 of the tribe of the sons of E'phraim a leader, Kemu'el 2
24 of E'phraim a leader, Kemu'el the son of Shiphtan. 2
25 Of the tribe of the sons of Zeb'ulun a leader 2
25 of Zeb'ulun a leader, Eli-za'phan the son of Parnach. 2
26 Of the tribe of the sons of Is'sachar a leader 2
26 of Is'sachar a leader, Pal'tiel the son of Azzan. 2
27 of the tribe of the sons of Asher a leader 2
27 of Asher a leader, Ahi'hud the son of Shelo'mi. 2
28 Of the tribe of the sons of Naph'tali a leader 2
28 of Naph'tali a leader, Pedah'el the son of Ammi'hud. 2
36: 1 heads . . of the families of the sons of Gilead 2
1 sons of Gilead the son of Machir, son of Manas'seh 2
1 sons of Gilead the son of Machir, son of Manas'seh 2
1 of the fathers' houses of the sons of Joseph 2
3 married to any of the sons of the other tribes 2
5 The tribe of the sons of Joseph is right. 2
11 were married to sons of their father's brothers. 2
12 into the families of sons of Manas'seh 2
12 sons of Manas'seh the son of Joseph 2
Deu 1:28 moreover we have seen the sons of the Anakim there. 2
31 how the LORD . . bore you, as a man bears his son 2
36 except Caleb the son of Jephun'neh; he shall see it 2
38 Joshua the son of Nun . . he shall enter; 2
2: 4 territory of your brethren the sons of Esau 2
8 we went on, away from our brethren the sons of Esau 2
9 have given Ar to the sons of Lot for a possession.' 2
12 sons of Esau dispossessed them, and destroyed 2
19 when you approach the frontier of the sons of Ammon 2
19 not give you any of the land of the sons of Ammon 2
19 given it to the sons of Lot for a possession.' 2
22 he did for the sons of Esau, who live in Se'ir 2
29 as the sons of Esau who live in Se'ir . . did for me 2
33 we defeated him and his sons and all his people. 2
37 land of the sons of Ammon you did not draw near 2
5:14 not do any work, you, or your son, or your daughter 2
6: 2 fear the LORD . . you and your son and your son's son 2
2 fear the LORD . . you and your son and your son's son 2
2 fear the LORD . . you and your son and your son's son 2
20 When your son asks you in time to come, 'What is 2
21 then you shall say to your son, 'We were Pharaoh's 2
7: 3 not . . giving your daughters to their sons 2
3 not . . taking their daughters for your sons. 2
4 they would turn away your sons from following me 2
8: 5 as a man disciplines his son, the LORD your God 2
9: 2 people great and tall, the sons of the Anakim 2
2 said, 'Who can stand before the sons of Anak?' 2
10: 6 his son Elea'zar ministered as priest in his stead 2
11: 6 what he did to Dathan and Abi'ram the sons of Eli'ab 2
6 Dathan and Abi'ram the sons of Eli'ab, son of Reuben; 2
12:12 rejoice . . you and your sons and your daughters 2
18 eat . . you and your son and your daughter 2
31 burn their sons and their daughters in the fire 2
13: 6 If your brother, the son of your mother . . entices 2
6 If . . your son, or your daughter, . . , entices you 2
14: 1 You are the sons of the LORD your God; you shall not 2
16:11 rejoice . . you and your son and your daughter 2
14 rejoice . . you and your son and your daughter 2
18: 5 stand and minister . . him and his sons for ever. 2
10 any one who burns his son or his daughter 2
21: 5 priests the sons of Levi shall come forward 2
15 if the first-born son is hers that is disliked 2
16 possessions as an inheritance to his sons 2
16 not treat the son of the loved as the first-born 2
16 not . . in preference to the son of the disliked 2
17 first-born, the son of the disliked 2
18 If a man has a stubborn and rebellious son 2
20 This our son is stubborn and rebellious 2
23: 4 hired . . Balaam the son of Be'or from Pethor 2
17 neither . . a cult prostitute of the sons of Israel. 2
25: 5 dwell together, and one of them dies and has no son 2
28:32 Your sons and your daughters shall be given 2
41 You shall beget sons and daughters 2
53 eat the . . flesh of your sons and daughters 2
56 will grudge to . . her son and to her daughter 2
31: 9 Moses . . gave it to the priests the sons of Levi 2
23 LORD commissioned Joshua the son of Nun and said 2
32: 8 when he separated the sons of men, he fixed 2
8 according to the number of the sons of God. 2
19 provocation of his sons and his daughters. 2
44 Moses came and recited . . and Joshua the son of Nun. 2
33:24 of Asher he said, "Blessed above sons be Asher; 2
34: 9 Joshua the son of Nun was full of . . wisdom 2
Jos 1: 1 LORD said to Joshua the son of Nun, Moses' minister 2
2: 1 And Joshua the son of Nun sent two men secretly 2
23 and passed over and came to Joshua the son of Nun; 2
4:12 The sons of Reuben and the sons of Gad 2
12 The sons of Reuben and the sons of Gad 2
6: 6 Joshua the son of Nun called the priests and said 2
7: 1 Achan the son of Carmi, son of Zabdi, son of Zerah 2
1 Achan the son of Carmi, son of Zabdi, son of Zerah 2
1 Achan the son of Carmi, son of Zabdi, son of Zerah 2
18 Achan the son of Carmi, son of Zabdi, son of Zerah 2
18 Achan the son of Carmi, son of Zabdi, son of Zerah 2
18 son of Zabdi, son of Zerah, of the tribe of Judah 2
19 Joshua said to Achan, "My son, give glory to the LORD 2
24 Joshua . . took Achan the son of Zerah 2
24 took Achan . . and his sons and daughters 2
13:22 Balaam also, the son of Be'or, the soothsayer 2
31 were allotted to . . Machir the son of Manas'seh 2
14: 1 Elea'zar the priest, and Joshua the son of Nun 2
6 and Caleb the son of Jephun'neh the Ken'izzite 2
13 and he gave Hebron to Caleb the son of Jephun'neh 2
14 of Caleb the son of Jephun'neh the Ken'izzite 2
15: 6 goes up to the stone of Bohan the son of Reuben; 2
8 goes up by the valley of the son of Hinnom 2
13 he gave to Caleb the son of Jephun'neh a portion 2
14 Caleb drove out from there the three sons of Anak 2
17 Oth'ni-el the son of Kenaz, the brother of Caleb 2
17: 2 male descendants of Manas'seh the son of Joseph 2
3 Zeloph'ehad the son of Hepher, son of Gilead 2
3 Zeloph'ehad the son of Hepher, son of Gilead 2
3 son of Gilead, son of Machir, son of Manas'seh 2
3 son of Gilead, son of Machir, son of Manas'seh 2
3 Now Zeloph'ehad . . had no sons, but only daughters; 2
4 came before Elea'zar . . and Joshua the son of Nun 2
6 received an inheritance along with his sons. 2
8 Tap'puah . . belonged to the sons of E'phraim. 2
12 the sons of Manas'seh could not take possession 2
18:16 that overlooks the valley of the son of Hinnom 2
17 it goes down to the Stone of Bohan the son of Reuben; 2
19:49 gave an inheritance . . to Joshua the son of Nun. 2
51 Elea'zar the priest and Joshua the son of Nun 2

21: 1 to Elea'zar the priest and to Joshua the son of Nun 2
12 had been given to Caleb the son of Jephun'neh 2
22:13 Israel sent . . Phin'ehas the son of Elea'zar 2
20 Did not Achan the son of Zerah break faith 2
31 Phin'ehas the son of Elea'zar the priest said 2
32 Then Phin'ehas the son of Elea'zar the priest 2
24: 9 Balak the son of Zippor, king of Moab, arose 2
9 and invited Balaam the son of Be'or to curse you 2
29 Joshua the son of Nun, the servant of the LORD, died 2
32 ground which Jacob bought from the sons of Hamor 2
33 Elea'zar the son of Aaron died; and they buried him 2
33 the town of Phin'ehas his son, which had been given 2
Jdg 1:13 Oth'ni-el the son of Kenaz, Caleb's younger brother 2
20 and he drove out from it the three sons of Anak. 2
2: 8 Joshua the son of Nun, the servant of the LORD, died 2
3: 6 their own daughters they gave to their sons; 2
9 Oth'niel the son of Kenaz, Caleb's younger 2
11 40 years. Then Oth'ni-el the son of Kenaz died. 2
15 a deliverer, Ehud, the son of Gera, the Benjaminite 2
31 After him was Shamgar the son of Anath, who killed 2
4: 6 summoned Barak the son of Abin'o-am from Kedesh 2
12 told that Barak the son of Abin'o-am had gone up 2
5: 1 Then sang Deb'orah and Barak the son of Abin'o-am 2
6 In the days of Shamgar, son of Anath, in the days 2
12 lead away your captives, O son of Abin'o-am. 2
6:11 his son Gideon was beating out wheat in the wine 2
29 they said, "Gideon the son of Jo'ash has done this 2
30 said to Jo'ash, "Bring out your son, that he may die 2
7:14 no other than the sword of Gideon the son of Jo'ash 2
8:13 Gideon the son of Jo'ash returned from the battle 2
18 every one . . they resembled the sons of a king. 2
19 said, "They were my brothers, the sons of my mother; 2
22 Rule over us, you and your son and your grandson 2
23 not rule over you, and my son will not rule over you; 2
29 Jerubba'al the son of Jo'ash went and dwelt in his 2
30 Gideon had 70 sons, his own offspring 2
31 his concubine . . also bore him a son 2
32 Gideon the son of Jo'ash died in a good old age 2
9: 1 Abim'elech the son of Jerubba'al went to Shechem 2
2 that all 70 of the sons of Jerubba'al rule over you 2
5 and slew his brothers the sons of Jerubba'al 2
5 Jotham the youngest son of Jerubba'al was left 2
18 and have slain his sons, 70 men on one stone 2
18 made Abim'elech, the son of his maidservant 2
24 the violence done to the 70 sons of Jerubba'al 2
26 Ga'al the son of Ebed moved into Shechem 2
28 Ga'al the son of Ebed said, "Who is Abim'elech 2
28 Did not the son of Jerubba'al and Zebul 2
30 Zebul . . heard the words of Ga'al the son of Ebed 2
31 Ga'al the son of Ebed and his kinsmen have come 2
35 Ga'al the son of Ebed went out and stood 2
57 came the curse of Jotham the son of Jerubba'al. 2
10: 1 arose to deliver Israel Tola the son of Pu'ah 2
1 Tola the son of Pu'ah, son of Dodo, a man of Is'sachar 2
4 he had 30 sons who rode on 30 asses; 2
11: 1 a mighty warrior, but he was the son of a harlot. 2
2 Gilead's wife also bore him sons; 2
2 when his wife's sons grew up, they thrust Jephthah 2
2 for you are the son of another woman. 2
25 better than Balak the son of Zippor, king of Moab? 2
34 beside her he had neither son nor daughter. 2
12: 9 He had 30 sons; and 30 daughters he gave 2
9 30 daughters he brought in . . for his sons. 2
13 Abdon the son of Hillel the Pira'thonite judged 2
14 He had 40 sons and 30 grandsons, who rode 2
15 Abdon the son of Hillel the Pira'thonite died 2
13: 3 children; but you shall conceive and bear a son. 2
5 for lo, you shall conceive and bear a son. No razor 2
7 you shall conceive and bear a son; so then drink no 2
24 the woman bore a son, and called his name Samson; 2
17: 2 his mother said, "Blessed be my son by the LORD. 2
3 I consecrate the silver to the LORD . . for my son 2
5 and installed one of his sons, who became his 2
11 the young man became to him like one of his sons. 2
18:30 Jonathan the son of Gershom, son of Moses 2
30 Jonathan the son of Gershom, son of Moses 2
30 Jonathan . . and his sons were priests 2
20:28 Phin'ehas the son of Elea'zar, son of Aaron 2
28 Phin'ehas the son of Elea'zar, son of Aaron 2
Rut 1: 1 a certain man . . he and his wife and his two sons. 2
2 the names of his two sons were Mahlon and Chil'ion; 2
3 and she was left with her two sons. 2
5 woman was bereft of her two sons and her husband. 8
11 Have I yet sons in my womb that they may become 2
12 if I should have a husband . . and should bear sons 2
4:13 the LORD gave her conception, and she bore a son. 2
15 who loves you, who is more to you than seven sons 2
17 gave . . a name, saying, "A son has been born to Na'omi 2
1Sm 1: 1 whose name was Elka'nah the son of Jero'ham 2
1 of Jero'ham, son of Eli'hu, son of Tohu, son of Zuph 2
1 of Jero'ham, son of Eli'hu, son of Tohu, son of Zuph 2
1 of Jero'ham, son of Eli'hu, son of Tohu, son of Zuph 2
3 two sons of Eli, Hophni and Phin'ehas, were priests 2
4 to Penin'nah . . and to all her sons and daughters; 2
8 why do you . . ? Am I not more to you than ten sons? 2
11 but wilt give to thy maidservant a son 6
20 in due time Hannah conceived and bore a son 2
23 the woman remained and nursed her son 2
2:12 Now the sons of Eli were worthless men; 2
21 and bore three sons and two daughters. 2
22 Eli . . heard all that his sons were doing 2
24 No, my sons; it is no good report that I hear 2
29 and honor your sons above me by fattening 2
34 shall befall your two sons, Hophni and Phin'ehas 2
3: 6 But he said, "I did not call, my son; lie down again. 2
13 because his sons were blaspheming God 2
16 But Eli called Samuel and said, "Samuel, my son. 2
4: 4 the two sons of Eli . . were there with the ark 2
11 and the two sons of Eli . . were slain. 2
16 And he said, "How did it go, my son? 2
17 your two sons also, Hophni and Phin'ehas, are dead 2
20 said to her, "Fear not, for you have borne a son. 2
7: 1 they consecrated his son, Elea'zar, to have charge 2
8: 1 Samuel . . made his sons judges over Israel. 2
2 The name of his first-born son was Jo'el 2
3 his sons did not walk in his ways, but turned aside 2
5 you are old and your sons do not walk in your ways; 2
11 he will take your sons and appoint them to his 2
9: 1 whose name was Kish, the son of Abi'el, son of Zeror 2
1 whose name was Kish, the son of Abi'el, son of Zeror 2
1 son of Zeror, son of Beco'rath, son of Aphi'ah 2
1 son of Zeror, son of Beco'rath, son of Aphi'ah 2
2 he had a son whose name was Saul 2
3 asses . . were lost. So Kish said to Saul his son 2
10: 2 What shall I do about my son? 2
11 What has come over the son of Kish? 2
21 and Saul the son of Kish was taken by lot. 2
12: 2 I am old and gray, and behold, my sons are with you; 2
13:16 And Saul, and Jonathan his son . . stayed in Geba 2
22 but Saul and Jonathan his son had them. 2
14: 1 One day Jonathan the son of Saul said . . "Come 2
3 Ahi'jah the son of Ahi'tub, Ich'abod's brother 2
3 Ahi'tub . . son of Phin'ehas, son of Eli, the priest 2
3 Ahi'tub . . son of Phin'ehas, son of Eli, the priest 2
39 though it be in Jonathan my son, he shall . . die. 2
40 I and Jonathan my son will be on the other side. 2
41 If this guilt is in me or in Jonathan my son, O LORD 22
42 Cast the lot between me and my son Jonathan. 2
49 sons of Saul were Jonathan, Ishvi, and Mal'chishu'a; 2
50 commander of his army was Abner the son of Ner 2
51 and Ner the father of Abner was the son of Abi'el. 2
16: 1 I have provided for myself a king among his sons. 2
5 And he consecrated Jesse and his sons 2
10 Jesse made seven of his sons pass before Samuel. 2
11 And Samuel said to Jesse, "Are all your sons here? 10
18 I have seen a son of Jesse the Bethlehemite 2
19 Send me David your son, who is with the sheep. 2
20 and sent them by David his son to Saul. 2
17:12 David was the son of an Eph'rathite of Bethlehem 2
12 an Eph'rathite . . named Jesse, who had eight sons. 2
13 The three eldest sons of Jesse had followed Saul 2
13 the names of his three sons who went to the battle 2
17 And Jesse said to David his son, "Take 2
55 he said . . "Abner, whose son is this youth? 2
56 king said, "Inquire whose son the stripling is. 2
58 And Saul said to him, "Whose son are you, young man 2
58 David answered, "I am the son of your servant Jesse 2
19: 1 Saul spoke to Jonathan his son and to all his 2
1 But Jonathan, Saul's son, delighted much in David. 2
20:27 Saul said to Jonathan his son, "Why has not the son 2
27 Why has not the son of Jesse come to the meal 2
30 You son of a perverse, rebellious woman, do I not 2
30 do I not know that you have chosen the son of Jesse 2
31 as long as the son of Jesse lives upon the earth 2
22: 7 will the son of Jesse give every one of you fields 2
8 No one discloses to me when my son makes a league 2
8 when my son makes a league with the son of Jesse 2
8 that my son has stirred up my servant against me 2
9 I saw the son of Jesse coming to Nob, to Ahim'elech 2
9 coming to Nob, to Ahim'elech the son of Ahi'tub 2
11 summon Ahim'elech the priest, the son of Ahi'tub 2
12 Saul said, "Hear now, son of Ahi'tub." 2
13 Why have you conspired . . you and the son of Jesse 2
20 one of the sons of Ahim'elech the son of Ahi'tub 2
20 one of the sons of Ahim'elech the son of Ahi'tub 2
23: 6 When Abi'athar the son of Ahim'elech fled to David 2
16 Jonathan, Saul's son, rose, and went to David 2
24:16 Saul said, "Is this your voice, my son David? 2
25: 8 give . . to your servants and to your son David. 2
10 Who is David? Who is the son of Jesse? 2
44 Saul had given Michal . . to Palti the son of La'ish 2
26: 5 the place where Saul lay, with Abner the son of Ner 2
6 to Jo'ab's brother Abi'shai the son of Zeru'iah 2
14 David called . . to Abner the son of Ner 2
17 Saul . . said, "Is it your voice, my son David? 2
21 Saul said, "I have done wrong; return, my son David 2
25 Saul said to David, "Blessed be you, my son David! 2
27: 2 went . . to A'chish the son of Ma'och, king of Gath. 2
28:19 and tomorrow you and your sons shall be with me; 2
30: 3 wives and sons and daughters taken captive. 2
6 were bitter . . each for his sons and daughters. 2
7 said to Abi'athar the priest, the son of Ahim'elech 2
19 whether small or great, sons or daughters, spoil 2
31: 2 And the Philistines overtook Saul and his sons; 2
2 and Abin'adab and Mal'chishu'a, the sons of Saul. 2
6 Saul died, and his three sons, and his armor-bearer 2
7 saw that . . and that Saul and his sons were dead 2
8 they found Saul and his three sons fallen 2
12 took the body of Saul and the bodies of his sons 2
2Sm 1: 4 and Saul and his son Jonathan are also dead. 2
5 you know that Saul and his son Jonathan are dead? 2
12 mourned . . for Saul and for Jonathan his son 2
13 I am the son of a sojourner, an Amal'ekite. 2
17 David lamented . . over Saul and Jonathan his son 2
2: 8 Now Abner the son of Ner . . had taken Ish-bo'sheth 2
8 Abner . . had taken Ish-bo'sheth the son of Saul 2
10 Ish-bo'sheth, Saul's son, was 40 years old 2
12 Abner the son of Ner . . went out from Mahana'im 2
12 and the servants of Ish-bo'sheth the son of Saul 2
13 Jo'ab the son of Zeru'iah, and the servants . . went 2
15 for Benjamin and Ish-bo'sheth the son of Saul 2
18 And the three sons of Zeru'iah were there 2
3: 2 And sons were born to David at Hebron 2
3 Ab'salom the son of Ma'acah the daughter of Talmai 2
4 and the fourth, Adoni'jah the son of Haggith; 2
4 and the fifth, Shephati'ah the son of Abi'tal; 2
14 David sent messengers to Ish-bo'sheth Saul's son 2
15 and took her from . . Pal'ti-el the son of La'ish. 2
23 Abner the son of Ner came to the king 2
25 You know that Abner the son of Ner came to deceive 2
28 for the blood of Abner the son of Ner. 2
37 not . . the king's will to slay Abner the son of Ner. 2
39 these men the sons of Zeru'iah are too hard for me. 2
4: 1 Ish-bo'sheth, Saul's son, heard that Abner had died 2
2 Now Saul's son had two men who were captains 2
2 two men . . sons of Rimmon a man of Benjamin 2
4 Jonathan, the son of Saul, had a son 2
4 Jonathan . . had a son who was crippled 2
5 sons of Rimmon . . Rechab and Ba'anah, set out 2
8 Here is the head of Ish-bo'sheth, the son of Saul 2
9 Rechab and Ba'anah . . the sons of Rimmon 2
5:13 and more sons and daughters were born to David. 2
6: 3 Uzzah and Ahi'o, the sons of Abin'adab, were driving 2
7:14 I will be his father, and he shall be my son. 2
14 chasten him . . with the stripes of the sons of men; 2
8: 3 David also defeated Hadade'zer the son of Rehob 2
10 To'i sent his son Joram to King David, to greet him 2
12 of Hadade'zer the son of Rehob, king of Zobah. 2
16 Jo'ab the son of Zeru'iah was over the army; 2
16 Jehosh'aphat the son of Ahi'lud was recorder; 2
17 Zadok the son of Ahi'tub . . were priests; 2
17 Ahim'elech the son of Abi'athar were priests; 2
18 Benai'ah the son of Jehoi'ada was over 2
18 and David's sons were priests. 2
9: 3 There is still a son of Jonathan; he is crippled 2
4 He is in the house of Machir the son of Am'miel 2
5 from the house of Machir the son of Am'miel 2
6 Mephib'osheth the son of Jonathan, son of Saul 2
6 Mephib'osheth the son of Jonathan, son of Saul 2
9 I have given to your master's son. 2
10 you and your sons and your servants shall till 2
10 that your master's son may have bread to eat; 2
10 Mephib'osheth your master's son shall always eat 2
10 Now Ziba had fifteen sons and twenty servants. 2
11 Mephib'osheth ate . . like one of the king's sons. 2
12 Mephib'osheth had a young son, whose name was 2
10: 1 and Hanun his son reigned in his stead. 2
2 I will deal loyally with Hanun the son of Nahash 2
11:21 Who killed Abim'elech the son of Jerub'besheth? 2
27 and she became his wife, and bore him a son. 2
12:24 and she bore a son, and he called his name Solomon. 2
13: 1 Now Ab'salom, David's son, had a beautiful sister 2
1 after a time Amnon, David's son, loved her. 2
3 whose name was Jon'adab, the son of Shim'e-ah 2
4 O son of the king, why are you so haggard 2
23 and Ab'salom invited all the king's sons. 2
25 No, my son, let us not all go 2
27 he let Amnon and all the king's sons go with him. 2
29 Then all the king's sons arose, and each . . fled. 2
30 Ab'salom has slain all the king's sons 2
32 Jon'adab the son of Shim'e-ah, David's brother, said 2
32 have killed all the young men the king's sons 2
33 to suppose that all the king's sons are dead; 2
35 Jon'adab said . . "Behold, the king's sons have come; 2
36 the king's sons came, and lifted up their voice 2
37 went to Talmai the son of Ammi'hud, king of Geshur. 2
37 And David mourned for his son day after day. 2
14: 1 Jo'ab the son of Zeru'iah perceived that 2
6 your handmaid had two sons, and they quarreled 2
11 that . . slay no more, and my son be not destroyed. 2
11 not one hair of your son shall fall to the ground. 2
16 the man who would destroy me and my son together 2
27 were born to Ab'salom three sons, and one daughter 2
15:27 go back . . you and Abi'athar, with your two sons 2
27 your two sons, Ahim'a-az your son, and Jonathan 2
27 Ahi'ma-az . . and Jonathan the son of Abi'athar. 2
36 Behold, their two sons are with them there 2
36 their two sons . . Ahim'a-az, Zadok's son, *
36 their two sons . . and Jonathan, Abi'athar's son; *
16: 3 And the king said, "And where is your master's son? 2
5 a man . . whose name was Shim'e-i, the son of Gera; 2
8 the kingdom into the hand of your son Ab'salom. 2
9 Then Abi'shai the son of Zeru'iah said to the king 2
10 What have I to do with you, you sons of Zeru'iah? 2
11 my own son seeks my life; how much more now 2
19 whom should I serve? Should it not be his son? 2
17:25 Ama'sa was the son of a man named Ithra 2

27 Shobi the son of Nahash from Rabbah 2
27 and Machir the son of Am'miel from Lo'debar 2
18: 2 under the command of Abi'shai the son of Zeru'iah 2
12 would not put forth my hand against the king's son; 2
18 I have no son to keep my name in remembrance"; 2
19 Then said Ahi'ma-az the son of Zadok, "Let me run 2
20 carry no tidings, because the king's son is dead. 2
22 Then Ahi'ma-az the son of Zadok said again to Jo'ab 2
22 And Jo'ab said, "Why will you run, my son 2
27 is like the running of Ahi'ma-az the son of Zadok. 2
33 said, "O my son Ab'salom, my son, my son Ab'salom! 2
33 said, "O my son Ab'salom, my son, my son Ab'salom! 2
33 said, "O my son Ab'salom, my son, my son Ab'salom! 2
33 Would I . . instead of you, O Ab'salom, my son, my son! 2
33 Would I . . instead of you, O Ab'salom, my son, my son! 2
19: 2 people heard . . "The king is grieving for his son. 2
4 O my son Ab'salom, O Ab'salom, my son, my son! 2
4 O my son Ab'salom, O Ab'salom, my son, my son! 2
4 O my son Ab'salom, O Ab'salom, my son, my son! 2
5 saved your life, and the lives of your sons 2
16 Shim'e-i the son of Gera . . made haste to come down 2
17 Ziba . . with his fifteen sons and his twenty 2
18 Shim'e-i the son of Gera fell down before the king 2
21 Abi'shai the son of Zeru'iah answered 2
22 What have I to do with you, you sons of Zeru'iah 2
24 And Mephib'osheth the son of Saul came down 2
20: 1 a . . fellow, whose name was Sheba, the son of Bichri 2
1 and we have no inheritance in the son of Jesse; 2
2 men of Israel . . followed Sheba the son of Bichri; 2
6 Sheba the son of Bichri will do us more harm 2
7 they went out . . to pursue Sheba the son of Bichri. 2
10 Then Jo'ab and . . pursued Sheba the son of Bichri. 2
13 went on . . to pursue Sheba the son of Bichri. 2
21 a man of . . E'phraim, called Sheba the son of Bichri 2
22 they cut off the head of Sheba the son of Bichri 2
23 Benai'ah the son of Jehoi'ada was in command 2
24 Jehosh'aphat the son of Ahi'lud was the recorder; 2
21: 6 let seven of his sons be given to us 2
7 Mephib'osheth, the son of Saul's son Jonathan 2
7 Mephib'osheth, the son of Saul's son Jonathan 2
7 between David and Jonathan the son of Saul. 2
8 took the two sons of Rizpah the daughter of Ai'ah 2
8 and the five sons of Merab the daughter of Saul 2
8 to A'driel the son of Barzil'lai the Meho'lathite; 2
12 took . . the bones of his son Jonathan 2
13 bones of Saul and the bones of his son Jonathan; 2
14 buried the bones of Saul and his son Jonathan 2
17 But Abi'shai the son of Zeru'iah came to his aid 2
19 Elha'nan the son of Ja'areor'egim . . slew Goliath 2
21 Jonathan the son of Shim'e-i, David's brother 2
23: 1 The oracle of David, the son of Jesse 2
9 next . . was Elea'zar the son of Dodo, son of Aho'hi. 2
9 next . . was Elea'zar the son of Dodo, son of Aho'hi. 2
11 next . . was Shammah, the son of Agee the Har'arite. 2
18 Abi'shai, the brother of Jo'ab, the son of Zeru'iah 2
20 Benai'ah the son of Jehoi'ada was a valiant man 2
22 These things did Benai'ah the son of Jehoi'ada 2
24 As'ahel . . Elha'nan the son of Dodo of Bethlehem 2
26 Helez the Paltite, Ira the son of Ikkesh of Teko'a 2
29 Heleb the son of Ba'anah of Netoph'ah 2
29 It'tai the son of Ri'bai of Gib'e-ah 2
32 Eli'ahba of Sha-al'bon, the sons of Jashen, Jonathan 2
33 Shammah . . Ahi'am the son of Sharar the Har'arite 2
34 Eliph'elet the son of Ahas'bai of Ma'acah 2
34 Eli'am the son of Ahith'ophel of Gilo 2
36 Igal the son of Nathan of Zobah, Bani the Gadite 2
37 the armor-bearer of Jo'ab the son of Zeru'iah 2
1Kg 1: 5 Adoni'jah the son of Haggith exalted himself 2
7 He conferred with Jo'ab the son of Zeru'iah 2
8 Benai'ah the son of Jehoi'ada, and Nathan 2
9 and he invited all his brothers, the king's sons 2
11 that Adoni'jah the son of Haggith has become king 2
12 your own life and the life of your son Solomon. 2
13 Solomon your son shall reign after me 2
17 Solomon your son shall reign after me 2
19 and has invited all the sons of the king, Abi'athar 2
21 I and my son Solomon will be counted offenders. 2
25 and has invited all the king's sons, Jo'ab 2
26 Zadok the priest, and Benai'ah the son of Jehoi'ada 2
30 Solomon your son shall reign after me 2
32 the prophet, and Benai'ah the son of Jehoi'ada." So 2
33 cause Solomon my son to ride on my own mule 2
36 Benai'ah the son of Jehoi'ada answered the king 2
38 and Benai'ah the son of Jehoi'ada 2
42 Jonathan the son of Abi'athar the priest came; 2
44 Nathan . . and Benai'ah the son of Jehoi'ada 2
2: 1 drew near, he charged Solomon his son, saying 2
4 If your sons take heed to their way, to walk before 2
5 you know . . what Jo'ab the son of Zeru'iah did to me 2
5 commanders . . Abner the son of Ner, and Ama'sa 2
5 Abner the son of Ner, and Ama'sa the son of Jether 2
7 deal loyally with the sons of Barzil'lai 2
8 with you Shim'e-i the son of Gera, the Benjaminite 2
13 Adoni'jah the son of Haggith came to Bathshe'ba 2
22 Abi'athar the priest and Jo'ab the son of Zeru'iah. 2
25 So King Solomon sent Benai'ah the son of Jehoi'ada; 2
29 Solomon sent Benai'ah the son of Jehoi'ada, saying 2
32 slew . . Abner the son of Ner, commander of the army 2
32 Ama'sa the son of Jether, commander of the army 2
34 Benai'ah the son of Jehoi'ada went up, and struck 2
35 king put Benai'ah the son of Jehoi'ada over 2
39 ran away to Achish, son of Ma'acah, king of Gath. 2
46 the king commanded Benai'ah the son of Jehoi'ada; 2
3: 6 hast given him a son to sit on his throne this day. 2
19 this woman's son died in the night, because she lay 2
20 arose at midnight, and took my son from beside me 2
20 in her bosom, and laid her dead son in my bosom. 2
23 'This is my son that is alive, and your son is dead'; 2
23 'This is my son that is alive, and your son is dead'; 2
23 your son is dead, and my son is the living one.' 2
23 your son is dead, and my son is the living one.' 2
26 the woman whose son was alive said to the king 2
26 to the king, because her heart yearned for her son 2
4: 2 Azari'ah the son of Zadok was the priest; 2
3 Elihor'eph and Ahi'jah the sons of Shisha were 2
3 Jehosh'aphat the son of Ahi'lud was recorder; 2
4 Benai'ah the son of Jehoi'ada was in command 2
5 Azari'ah the son of Nathan was over the officers; 2
5 Zabud the son of Nathan was priest and king's 2
6 Adoni'ram the son of Abda was in charge 2
12 Ba'ana the son of Ahi'lud, in Ta'anach, Megid'do 2
13 he had the villages of Ja'ir the son of Manas'seh 2
14 Ahin'adab the son of Iddo, in Mahana'im; 2
16 Ba'ana the son of Hushai, in Asher and Bealoth; 2
17 Jehosh'aphat the son of Paru'ah, in Is'sachar; 2
18 Shim'e-i the son of Ela, in Benjamin; 2
19 Geber the son of Uri, in the land of Gilead 2
31 Heman, Calcol, and Darda, the sons of Mahol; and his 2
5: 5 Your son, whom I will set upon your throne 2
7 the LORD . . who has given to David a wise son 2
7:14 He was the son of a widow of the tribe of Naph'tali 2
8:19 your son who shall be born to you shall build 2
25 your sons take heed to their way, to walk before me 2
11:12 I will tear it out of the hand of your son. 2
13 I will give one tribe to your son 2
20 the sister of Tah'penes bore him Genu'bath his son 2
20 Genu'bath was in . . among the sons of Pharaoh. 2
23 as an adversary to him, Rezon the son of Eli'ada 2
26 Jerobo'am the son of Nebat, an E'phraimite 2
35 I will take the kingdom out of his son's hand 2
36 Yet to his son I will give one tribe 2
43 and Rehobo'am his son reigned in his stead. 2
12: 2 when Jerobo'am the son of Nebat heard of it 2
15 the LORD spoke . . to Jerobo'am the son of Nebat. 2
16 We have no inheritance in the son of Jesse. 2
21 the kingdom to Rehobo'am the son of Solomon. 2
23 Say to Rehobo'am the son of Solomon, king of Judah 2
13: 2 a son shall be born to the house of David, Josi'ah 2
11 his sons came and told him all that the man of God 21
12 Which way did he go?" And his sons showed him 2
13 he said to his sons, "Saddle the ass for me. 2
27 he said to his sons, "Saddle the ass for me. 2
31 he said to his sons, "When I die, bury me in the grave 2
14: 1 Abi'jah the son of Jerobo'am fell sick. 2
5 is coming to inquire of you concerning her son; 2
20 and Nadab his son reigned in his stead. 2
21 Rehobo'am the son of Solomon reigned in Judah. 2
31 And Abi'jam his son reigned in his stead. 2
15: 1 in the . . year of King Jerobo'am the son of Nebat 2
4 a lamp in Jerusalem, setting up his son after him 2
8 And Asa his son reigned in his stead. 2
18 Asa sent them to Ben-ha'dad the son of Tabrim'mon 2
18 Tabrim'mon, the son of He'zion, king of Syria 2
24 and Jehosh'aphat his son reigned in his stead. 2
25 Nadab the son of Jerobo'am began to reign 2
27 Ba'asha the son of Ahi'jah, of the house of Is'sachar 2
33 Ba'asha the son of Ahi'jah began to reign 2
16: 1 word of the LORD came to Jehu the son of Hana'ni 2
3 the house of Jerobo'am the son of Nebat. 2
6 and Elah his son reigned in his stead. 2
7 word of the LORD came by . . Jehu the son of Hana'ni 2
8 Elah the son of Ba'asha began to reign over Israel 2
13 the sins of Ba'asha and the sins of Elah his son 2
21 half . . followed Tibni the son of Ginath 2
22 the people who followed Tibni the son of Ginath; 2
26 walked in all the way of Jerobo'am the son of Nebat 2
28 and Ahab his son reigned in his stead. 2
29 Ahab the son of Omri began to reign over Israel 2
29 Ahab the son of Omri reigned over Israel 2
30 Ahab the son of Omri did evil 2
31 to walk in the sins of Jerobo'am the son of Nebat 2
34 word . . which he spoke by Joshua the son of Nun. 2
17:12 I may go in and prepare it for myself and my son 2
13 and afterward make for yourself and your son. 2
17 After this the son of the woman . . became ill; 2
18 You have come . . and to cause the death of my son! 2
19 he said to her, "Give me your son. 2
20 hast thou brought calamity . . by slaying her son? 2
23 and Eli'jah said, "See, your son lives. 2
18:31 the number of the tribes of the sons of Jacob 2
19:16 Jehu the son of Nimshi you shall anoint to be king 2
16 Eli'sha the son of Shaphat of A'bel-meho'lah 2
19 departed . . and found Eli'sha the son of Shaphat 2
20:35 a certain man of the sons of the prophets said 2
21:22 like the house of Jerobo'am the son of Nebat 2
22 and like the house of Ba'asha the son of Ahi'jah 2
29 but in his son's days I will bring the evil 2
22: 8 by whom we may inquire . . Micai'ah the son of Imlah; 2
9 and said, "Bring quickly Micai'ah the son of Imlah. 2
11 Zedeki'ah the son of Chena'anah made . . horns 2
24 Zedeki'ah the son of Chena'anah came near 2
26 take him back . . to Jo'ash the king's son; 2
40 Ahab slept . . and Ahazi'ah his son reigned 2
41 Jehosh'aphat the son of Asa began to reign 2
49 Ahazi'ah the son of Ahab said to Jehosh'aphat, "Let 2
50 and Jeho'ram his son reigned in his stead. 2
51 Ahazi'ah the son of Ahab began to reign 2
52 walked . . in the way of Jerobo'am the son of Nebat 2
2Kg 1:17 second year of Jeho'ram the son of Jehosh'aphat 2
17 became king . . because Ahazi'ah had no son. 2
2: 3 the sons of the prophets . . came out to Eli'sha 2
5 The sons of the prophets . . drew near to Eli'sha 2
7 50 men of the sons of the prophets also went 2
15 when the sons of the prophets . . saw him 2
3: 1 Jeho'ram the son of Ahab became king over Israel 2
3 he clung to the sin of Jerobo'am the son of Nebat 2
11 Eli'sha the son of Shaphat is here 2
27 took his eldest son who was to reign in his stead 2
4: 1 the wife of one of the sons of the prophets cried 2
4 and shut the door upon yourself and your sons 2
5 and shut the door upon herself and her sons; 2
6 When the vessels were full, she said to her son 2
7 you and your sons can live on the rest. 2
14 Well, she has no son, and her husband is old. 2
16 he said, "At this season . . you shall embrace a son. 2
17 conceived, and she bore a son about that time 2
28 Then she said, "Did I ask my lord for a son? 2
36 when she came to him, he said, "Take up your son. 2
37 then she took up her son and went out. 2
38 as the sons of the prophets were . . before him 2
38 and boil pottage for the sons of the prophets. 2
5:22 two young men of the sons of the prophets; 2
6: 1 Now the sons of the prophets said to Eli'sha, "See 2
28 woman said . . 'Give your son, that we may eat him 2
28 eat him today, and we will eat my son tomorrow.' 2
29 So we boiled my son, and ate him. 2
29 I said to her, 'Give your son, that we may eat him'; 2
29 'Give your son . . '; but she has hidden her son. 2
31 if the head of Eli'sha the son of Shaphat remains 2
8: 1 to the woman whose son he had restored to life 2
5 the woman whose son he had restored to life 2
5 O king, here is the woman, and here is her son 2
9 Your son Ben-ha'dad king of Syria has sent me to you 2
16 In the fifth year of Joram the son of Ahab 2
16 Jeho'ram the son of Jehosh'aphat, king of Judah 2
19 promised . . a lamp to him and to his sons for ever. 2
24 and Ahazi'ah his son reigned in his stead. 2
25 In the twelfth year of Joram the son of Ahab 2
25 Ahazi'ah the son of Jeho'ram . . began to reign. 2
28 went with Joram the son of Ahab to make war 2
29 Ahazi'ah the son of Jeho'ram king of Judah went 2
29 Ahazi'ah . . went down to see Joram the son of Ahab 2
9: 1 Eli'sha . . called one of the sons of the prophets 2
2 look there for Jehu the son of Jehosh'aphat 2
2 for Jehu the son of Jehosh'aphat, son of Nimshi; 2
9 like the house of Jerobo'am the son of Nebat 2
9 and like the house of Ba'asha the son of Ahi'jah. 2
14 Jehu the son of Jehosh'aphat the son of Nimshi 2
14 Jehu the son of Jehosh'aphat the son of Nimshi 2
20 is like the driving of Jehu the son of Nimshi; 2
26 I saw . . of Naboth and the blood of his sons 2
29 In the eleventh year of Joram the son of Ahab 2
10: 1 Now Ahab had 70 sons in Sama'ria. 2
1 sent . . and to the guardians of the sons of Ahab 21
2 your master's sons are with you, and there are 2
3 select the best and fittest of your master's sons 2
6 take the heads of your master's sons, and come to me 2
6 the king's sons . . were with the great men 2
7 they took the king's sons, and slew them 2
8 They have brought the heads of the king's sons 2
13 royal princes and the sons of the queen mother. 2
15 he met Jehon'adab the son of Rechab 2
23 Jehu went . . with Jehon'adab the son of Rechab; 2
29 turn . . from the sins of Jerobo'am the son of Nebat 2
30 your sons . . shall sit on the throne of Israel. 2
35 And Jeho'ahaz his son reigned in his stead. 2
11: 1 Now when Athali'ah . . saw that her son was dead 2
2 Jehosh'eba . . took Jo'ash the son of Ahazi'ah 2
2 and stole him away from among the king's sons 2
4 and he showed them the king's son. 2
12 he brought out the king's son, and put the crown 2
12:21 Jo'zacar the son of Shim'e-ath and Jeho'zabad 2
21 Jo'zacar . . and Jeho'zabad the son of Shomer 2
21 and Amazi'ah his son reigned in his stead. 2
13: 1 In the 23rd year of Jo'ash the son of Ahazi'ah 2
1 Jeho'ahaz the son of Jehu began to reign 2
2 the sins of Jerobo'am the son of Nebat 2
3 and into the hand of Ben-ha'dad the son of Haz'ael. 2
9 and Jo'ash his son reigned in his stead. 2
10 Jeho'ash the son of Jeho'ahaz began to reign 2
11 from all the sins of Jerobo'am the son of Nebat 2
24 When Haz'ael . . died, Ben-ha'dad his son became king 2
25 Jeho'ash the son of Jeho'ahaz took . . the cities 2
25 took again from Ben-ha'dad the son of Haz'ael 2
14: 1 In the second year of Jo'ash the son of Jo'ahaz 2
1 Amazi'ah the son of Jo'ash, king of Judah, began 2
8 sent messengers to Jeho'ash the son of Jeho'ahaz 2

8 to Jeho'ash the son of Jeho'ahaz, son of Jehu 2
9 saying, 'Give your daughter to my son for a wife'; 2
13 Amazi'ah . . the son of Jeho'ash, son of Ahazi'ah 2
13 Amazi'ah . . the son of Jeho'ash, son of Ahazi'ah 2
16 Jeho'ash slept . . and Jerobo'am his son reigned 2
17 Amazi'ah the son of Jo'ash, king of Judah, lived 2
17 death of Jeho'ash son of Jeho'ahaz, king of Israel. 2
23 In the fifteenth year of Amazi'ah the son of Jo'ash 2
23 Jerobo'am the son of Jo'ash, king of Israel, began 2
24 all the sins of Jerobo'am the son of Nebat 2
25 he spoke by his servant Jonah the son of Amit'tai 2
27 saved . . by the hand of Jerobo'am the son of Jo'ash. 2
29 Jerobo'am slept . . and Zechari'ah his son reigned 2
15: 1 Azari'ah the son of Amazi'ah . . began to reign. 2
5 And Jotham the king's son was over the household 2
7 Azari'ah slept . . and Jotham his son reigned 2
8 Zechari'ah the son of Jerobo'am reigned over 2
9 depart from the sins of Jerobo'am the son of Nebat 2
10 Shallum the son of Jabesh conspired against him 2
12 Your sons shall sit upon the throne of Israel 2
13 Shallum the son of Jabesh began to reign 2
14 Then Men'ahem the son of Gadi came up from Tirzah 2
14 and he struck down Shallum the son of Jabesh 2
17 Men'ahem the son of Gadi began to reign 2
18 from all the sins of Jerobo'am the son of Nebat 2
22 Men'ahem slept . . and Pekahi'ah his son reigned 2
23 Pekahi'ah the son of Men'ahem began to reign 2
24 away from the sins of Jerobo'am the son of Nebat 2
25 Pekah the son of Remali'ah . . conspired against 2
27 Pekah the son of Remali'ah began to reign over 2
28 depart from the sins of Jerobo'am the son of Nebat 2
30 Hoshe'a the son of Elah made a conspiracy against 2
30 a conspiracy against Pekah the son of Remali'ah 2
30 the twentieth year of Jotham the son of Uzzi'ah. 2
32 In the second year of Pekah the son of Remali'ah 2
32 Jotham the son of Uzzi'ah . . began to reign. 2
37 send Rezin . . and Pekah the son of Remali'ah 2
38 Jotham slept . . and Ahaz his son reigned 2
16: 1 seventeenth year of Pekah the son of Remali'ah 2
1 Ahaz the son of Jotham . . began to reign. 2
3 He even burned his son as an offering 2
5 Pekah the son of Remali'ah . . came up to wage war 2
7 I am your servant and your son. Come up, and rescue 2
20 Ahaz slept . . and Hezeki'ah his son reigned 2
17: 1 Hoshe'a the son of Elah began to reign in Sama'ria 2
17 burned their sons and . . daughters as offerings 2
21 When . . they made Jerobo'am the son of Nebat king. 2
18: 1 In the third year of Hoshe'a son of Elah 2
1 Hezeki'ah the son of Ahaz . . began to reign. 2
9 which was the seventh year of Hoshe'a son of Elah 2
18 there came out to them Eli'akim the son of Hilki'ah 2
18 and Jo'ah the son of Asaph, the recorder. 2
26 Eli'akim the son of Hilki'ah, and . . said 2
37 Eli'akim the son of Hilki'ah, who was over 2
37 Eli'akim . . and Shebna.., and Jo'ah the son of Asaph 2
19: 2 he sent . . to the prophet Isaiah the son of Amoz. 2
20 Isaiah the son of Amoz sent to Hezeki'ah, saying 2
37 Adram'melech and Share'zer, his sons, slew him 2
37 Esarhad'don his son reigned in his stead. 2
20: 1 Isaiah . . the son of Amoz came to him, and said 2
12 Mero'dach-bal'adan the son of Bal'adan, king 2
18 And some of your own sons . . shall be taken away; 2
21 Hezeki'ah slept . . and Manas'seh his son reigned 2
21: 6 And he burned his son as an offering 2
7 the LORD said to David and to Solomon his son 2
18 Manas'seh slept . . and Amon his son reigned 2
24 people . . made Josi'ah his son king in his stead. 2
26 and Josi'ah his son reigned in his stead. 2
22: 3 king sent Shaphan the son of Azali'ah, son 2
3 sent Shaphan the son of Azali'ah, son of Meshul'lam 2
12 Hilki'ah the priest, and Ahi'kam the son of Shaphan 2
12 Ahi'kam the son of . . and Achbor the son of Micai'ah 2
14 Huldah . . the wife of Shallum the son of Tikvah 2
14 wife of Shallum the son of Tikvah, son of Harhas 2
23:10 which is in the valley of the sons of Hinnom 2
10 burn his son or his daughter as an offering 2
15 high place erected by Jerobo'am the son of Nebat 2
30 the people . . took Jeho'ahaz the son of Josi'ah 2
34 Pharaoh Neco made Eli'akim the son of Josi'ah king 2
24: 6 and Jehoi'achin his son reigned in his stead. 2
25: 7 They slew the sons of Zedeki'ah before his eyes 2
22 he appointed Gedali'ah the son of Ahi'kam, son 2
22 Gedali'ah the son of Ahi'kam, son of Shaphan 2
23 they came . . namely, Ish'mael the son of Nethani'ah 2
23 namely, Ish'mael . . and Joha'nan the son of Kare'ah 2
23 namely, Ish'mael . . and Joha'nan the son of Kare'ah 2
23 and Ja-azani'ah the son of the Ma-ac'athite. 2
25 Ish'mael the son of Nethani'ah, son of Eli'shama 2
25 Ish'mael the son of Nethani'ah, son of Eli'shama 2
1Ch 1: 5 The sons of Japheth: Gomer, Magog, Madai, Javan 2
6 sons of Gomer: Ash'kenaz, Diphath, and To-gar'mah. 2
7 The sons of Javan: Eli'shah, Tarshish, Kittim 2
8 The sons of Ham: Cush, Egypt, Put, and Canaan. 2
9 sons of Cush: Seba, Hav'ilah, Sabta, Ra'ama 2
9 The sons of Ra'amah: Sheba and Dedan. 2
17 sons of Shem: Elam, Asshur, Arpach'shad, Lud 2
19 To Eber were born two sons: the name of the one was 2
23 Ophir, Hav'ilah, and Jobab . . the sons of Joktan 2
28 The sons of Abraham: Isaac and Ish'mael. 2
31 Ked'emah. These are the sons of Ish'mael. 2
32 The sons of Ketu'rah, Abraham's concubine 2
32 Shu'ah. The sons of Jokshan: Sheba and Dedan. 2
33 The sons of Mid'ian: Ephah, Epher, Hanoch, Abida 2
34 The sons of Isaac: Esau and Israel. 2
35 The sons of Esau: Eli'phaz, Reu'el, Je'ush 2
36 The sons of Eli'phaz: Teman, Omar, Zephi, Gatam 2
37 The sons of Reu'el: Nahath, Zerah, Shammah 2
38 The sons of Se'ir: Lotan, Shobal, Zib'eon, Anah 2
39 The sons of Lotan: Hori and Homam; and Lotan's 2
40 The sons of Shobal: Al'ian, Man'ahath, Ebal, Shephi 2
40 The sons of Zib'eon: Ai'ah and Anah. 2
41 The sons of Anah: Dishon. The sons of Dishon 2
41 The sons of Anah: Dishon. The sons of Dishon 2
42 The sons of Ezer: Bilhan, Za'avan, and Ja'akan. 2
42 The sons of Dishan: Uz and Aran. 2
43 Bela the son of Be'or . . whose city was Din'habah 2
44 When Bela died, Jobab the son of Zerah of Bozrah 2
46 When Husham died, Hadad the son of Bedad 2
49 Ba'al-ha'nan, the son of Achbor, reigned in his stead 2
2: 1 These are the sons of Israel: Reuben, Simeon, Levi 2
3 The sons of Judah: Er, Onan, and Shelah; 2
4 Judah had five sons in all. 2
5 The sons of Perez: Hezron and Hamul. 2
6 The sons of Zerah: Zimri, Ethan, Heman, Calcol 2
7 The sons of Carmi: Achar, the troubler of Israel 2
8 Ethan's son was Azari'ah. 2
9 The sons of Hezron, that were born to him 2
10 Nahshon, prince of the sons of Judah. 2
16 The sons of Zeru'iah: Abi'shai, Jo'ab, and As'ahel 2
18 Caleb the son of Hezron had children by his wife 2
18 these were her sons: Jesher, Shobab, and Ardon. 2
25 The sons of Jerah'meel, the first-born of Hezron 2
27 The sons of Ram, the first-born of Jerah'meel: Ma'az 2
28 The sons of Onam: Sham'mai and Jada. 2
28 The sons of Sham'mai: Nadab and Abi'shur. 2
30 sons of Nadab: Seled and Ap'pa-im; and Seled died 2
31 The sons of Ap'pa-im: Ishi. 2
31 The sons of Ishi: Sheshan. 2
31 The sons of Sheshan: Ahlai. 2
32 sons of Jada, Sham'mai's brother: Jether 2
33 The sons of Jonathan: Peleth and Zaza. 2
34 Now Sheshan had no sons, only daughters; 2
42 The sons of Caleb the brother of Jerah'meel 2
42 The sons of Mare'shah: Hebron. 2
43 sons of Hebron: Korah, Tap'puah, Rekem, and Shema. 2
45 The son of Sham'mai: Ma'on; 2
47 sons of Jah'dai: Regem, Jotham, Geshan, Pelet, 2
50 The sons of Hur . . Shobal the father 21
52 Shobal . . had other sons: Haro'eh, half 2
54 sons of Salma: Bethlehem, the Netoph'athites 2
3: 1 the sons of David that were born to him in Hebron 2
9 All these were David's sons 2
9 besides the sons of the concubines; 2
10 descendants of Solomon: Rehobo'am, Abi'jah his son 2
10 descendants of Solomon . . Asa his son 2
10 descendants of Solomon . . Jehosh'aphat his son 2
11 Joram his son, Ahazi'ah his son, Jo'ash his son 2
11 Joram his son, Ahazi'ah his son, Jo'ash his son 2
11 Joram his son, Ahazi'ah his son, Jo'ash his son 2
12 Amazi'ah his son, Azari'ah his son, Jotham his son 2
12 Amazi'ah his son, Azari'ah his son, Jotham his son 2
12 Amazi'ah his son, Azari'ah his son, Jotham his son 2
13 Ahaz his son, Hezeki'ah his son, Manas'seh his son 2
13 Ahaz his son, Hezeki'ah his son, Manas'seh his son 2
13 Ahaz his son, Hezeki'ah his son, Manas'seh his son 2
14 Amon his son, Josi'ah his son. 2
14 Amon his son, Josi'ah his son. 2
15 The sons of Josi'ah: Joha'nan the first-born 2
16 descendants of Jehoi'akim: Jeconi'ah his son 2
16 descendants of Jehoi'akim . . Zedeki'ah his son; 2
17 sons of Jeconi'ah, the captive: Sheal'tiel his son 2
17 sons of Jeconi'ah, the captive: Sheal'tiel his son 2
19 and the sons of Pedai'ah: Zerub'babel and Shim'e-i; 2
19 the sons of Zerub'babel: Meshul'lam and Hanani'ah 2
21 The sons of Hanani'ah: Pelati'ah and Jeshai'ah 2
21 sons of Hanani'ah . . Jeshai'ah, his son Rephai'ah 2
21 sons of Hanani'ah . . Rephai'ah, his son Arnan 21
21 sons of Hanani'ah . . Arnan, his son Obadi'ah 21
21 sons of Hanani'ah . . Obadi'ah, his son Shecani'ah. 21
22 The sons of Shecani'ah: Shemai'ah. 2
22 And the sons of Shemai'ah: Hattush, Igal, Bari'ah 2
23 sons of Neari'ah: Eli-o-e'nai, Hizki'ah, and Azri'kam 2
24 sons of Eli-o-e'nai: Hod'avi'ah, Eli'ashib, Pelai'ah 2
4: 1 sons of Judah: Perez, Hezron, Carmi, Hur, and Shobal. 2
2 Re-ai'ah the son of Shobal was the father of Jahath 2
3 the sons of Etam: Jezreel, Ishma, and Idbash; 21
4 the sons of Hur, the first-born of Eph'rathah 2
6 These were the sons of Na'arah. 2
7 The sons of Helah: Zereth, Izhar, and Ethnan. 2
8 the families of Ahar'hel the son of Harum. 2
13 The sons of Kenaz: Oth'ni-el and Serai'ah; 2
13 and the sons of Oth'ni-el: Hathath and Meo'nothai. 2
15 sons of Caleb . . Iru, Elah, and Na'am; 2
15 Caleb the son of Jephun'neh 2
15 and the sons of Elah: Kenaz. 2
16 sons of Jehal'lelel: Ziph, Ziphah, Tir'i-a 2
17 The sons of Ezrah: Jether, Mered, Epher, and Jalon. 2
17 These are the sons of Bith'i-ah 2
19 The sons of the wife of Hodi'ah, the sister of Naham 2
20 sons of Shimon: Amnon, Rinnah, Ben-ha'nan, 2
20 The sons of Ishi: Zoheth and Ben-zo'heth. 2
21 sons of Shelah . . Er the father of Lecah 2
21 sons of Shelah the son of Judah 2
24 sons of Simeon: Nem'uel, Jamin, Jarib, Zerah, Sha'ul; 2
25 Shallum was his son, Mibsam his son 2
25 Shallum . . Mibsam his son, Mishma his son. 2
25 Shallum . . Mibsam his son, Mishma his son. 2
26 sons of Mishma: Ham'mu-el his son, Zac'cur 2
26 sons of Mishma: Ham'mu-el his son, Zac'cur 2
26 sons of Mishma: Ham'mu-el . . Zac'cur his son 2
26 Ham'mu-el his son, Zac'cur his son, Shim'e-i his son. 2
27 Shim'e-i had sixteen sons and six daughters; 2
34 Mesho'bab, Jamlech, Joshah the son of Amazi'ah 2
35 Jo'el, Jehu the son of Joshibi'ah, son of Serai'ah 2
35 the son of Joshibi'ah, son of Serai'ah, son of As'i-el 2
35 the son of Joshibi'ah, son of Serai'ah, son of As'i-el 2
37 Ziza the son of Shiphi, son of Allon, son of Jedai'ah 2
37 Ziza the son of Shiphi, son of Allon, son of Jedai'ah 2
37 Ziza . . son of Jedai'ah, son of Shimri 2
37 Ziza . . son of Shimri, son of Shemai'ah 2
37 Ziza . . son of Shimri, son of Shemai'ah 2
42 Pelati'ah . . and Uz'ziel, the sons of Ishi; 2
5: 1 The sons of Reuben the first-born of Israel 2
1 his birthright was given to the sons of Joseph 2
1 sons of Joseph the son of Israel 2
3 the sons of Reuben, the first-born of Israel 2
4 sons of Jo'el: Shemai'ah his son, Gog his son, Shim'e-i 2
4 sons of Jo'el: Shemai'ah his son, Gog his son, Shim'e-i 2
4 sons of Jo'el: Shemai'ah his son, Gog his son, Shim'e-i 2
4 sons of Jo'el . . Gog his son, Shim'e-i his son 2
5 Micah his son, Re-ai'ah his son, Ba'al his son 2
5 Micah his son, Re-ai'ah his son, Ba'al his son 2
5 Micah his son, Re-ai'ah his son, Ba'al his son 2
6 Be-er'ah his son . . chieftain of the Reubenites. 2
8 Bela the son of Azaz, son of Shema, son of Jo'el 2
8 Bela the son of Azaz, son of Shema, son of Jo'el 2
8 Bela the son of Azaz, son of Shema, son of Jo'el 2
11 The sons of Gad dwelt . . in the land of Bashan 2
14 the sons of Ab'ihail the son of Huri, son of Jaro'ah 2
14 the sons of Ab'ihail the son of Huri, son of Jaro'ah 2
14 the sons of Ab'ihail the son of Huri, son of Jaro'ah 2
14 sons of Ab'ihail . . son of Jaro'ah, son of Gilead 2
14 sons of Ab'ihail . . son of Gilead, son of Michael 2
14 sons of Ab'ihail . . son of Jeshish'ai, son of Jahdo 2
14 sons of Ab'ihail . . son of Jeshish'ai, son of Jahdo 2
14 sons of Ab'ihail . . son of Jahdo, son of Buz; 2
15 Ahi the son of Ab'di-el, son of Guni 2
15 Ahi the son of Ab'di-el, son of Guni 2
6: 1 The sons of Levi: Gershom, Kohath, and Merar'i. 2
2 sons of Kohath: Amram, Izhar, Hebron, and Uz'ziel. 2
3 The sons of Aaron: Nadab, Abi'hu, Elea'zar 2
16 The sons of Levi: Gershom, Kohath, and Merar'i. 2
17 names of the sons of Gershom: Libni and Shim'e-i. 2
18 sons of Kohath: Amram, Izhar, Hebron, and Uz'ziel. 2
19 The sons of Merar'i: Mahli and Mushi. 2
20 Of Gershom: Libni his son, Jahath his son, Zimmah 2
20 Of Gershom: Libni his son, Jahath his son, Zimmah 2
20 Of Gershom: Libni . . Jahath . . , Zimmah his son 2
21 Jo'ah his son, Iddo . . Zerah . . Je-ath'erai 2
21 Jo'ah . . Iddo his son, Zerah . . Je-ath'erai 2
21 Jo'ah . . Iddo . . Zerah his son, Je-ath'erai 2
21 Jo'ah . . Iddo . . Zerah . . Je-ath'erai his son. 2
22 sons of Kohath: Ammin'adab . . Korah . . Assir 2
22 of Kohath: Ammin'adab his son, Korah . . Assir 2
22 of Kohath: Ammin'adab . . Korah his son, Assir 2
22 of Kohath: Aminn'adab . . Korah . . Assir his son 2
23 Elka'nah his son, Ebi'asaph his son, Assir his son 2
23 Elka'nah his son, Ebi'asaph his son, Assir his son 2
23 Elka'nah his son, Ebi'asaph his son, Assir his son 2
24 Tahath his son, Uri'el his son, Uzzi'ah 2
24 Tahath his son, Uri'el his son, Uzzi'ah 2
24 Uri'el his son, Uzzi'ah his son, and Sha'ul his son. 2
24 Uri'el his son, Uzzi'ah his son, and Sha'ul his son. 2
25 The sons of Elka'nah: Ama'sai and Ahi'moth 2
26 Elka'nah his son, Zophai his son, Nahath his son 2
26 Elka'nah his son, Zophai his son, Nahath his son 2
26 Elka'nah his son, Zophai his son, Nahath his son 2
27 Eli'ab his son, Jero'ham his son, Elka'nah his son. 2
27 Eli'ab his son, Jero'ham his son, Elka'nah his son. 2
27 Eli'ab his son, Jero'ham his son, Elka'nah his son. 2
28 sons of Samuel: Jo'el his first-born . . Abi'jah. 2
29 sons of Merar'i: Mahli, Libni his son, Shim'e-i 2
29 sons of Merar'i: Mahli, Libni his son, Shim'e-i 2
29 of Merar'i: Mahli, Libni . . Shim'e-i his son 2
29 of Merar'i . . Libni . . Shim'e-i . . Uzzah his son 2
30 Shim'e-a his son, Haggi'ah his son, and Asai'ah his 2
30 Shim'e-a his son, Haggi'ah his son, and Asai'ah his 2
30 Shim'e-a . . Haggi'ah his son, and Asai'ah his son. 2
33 These are the men who served and their sons. 2
33 Of the sons of the Ko'hathites: Heman the singer 2
33 Heman the singer the son of Jo'el, son of Samuel 2
33 Heman the singer the son of Jo'el, son of Samuel 2
34 son of Elka'nah, son of Jero'ham, son of Eli'el, son 2
34 Elka'nah, son of Jero'ham, son of Eli'el, son of To'ah 2
34 Elka'nah, son of Jero'ham, son of Eli'el, son of To'ah 2
34 Elka'nah, son of Jero'ham, son of Eli'el, son of To'ah 2
35 son of Zuph, son of Elka'nah, son of Mahath 2

35 son of Elka'nah, son of Mahath, son of Ama'sai 2
35 son of Elka'nah, son of Mahath, son of Ama'sai 2
35 son of Elka'nah, son of Mahath, son of Ama'sai 2
36 son of Elka'nah, son of Jo'el, son of Azari'ah 2
36 son of Jo'el, son of Azari'ah, son of Zephani'ah 2
36 son of Jo'el, son of Azari'ah, son of Zephani'ah 2
36 son of Jo'el, son of Azari'ah, son of Zephani'ah 2
37 son of Tahath, son of Assir, son of Ebi'asaph 2
37 son of Assir, son of Ebi'asaph, son of Korah 2
37 son of Assir, son of Ebi'asaph, son of Korah 2
37 son of Assir, son of Ebi'asaph, son of Korah 2
38 son of Izhar, son of Kohath, son of Levi 2
38 son of Kohath, son of Levi, son of Israel; 2
38 son of Kohath, son of Levi, son of Israel; 2
38 son of Kohath, son of Levi, son of Israel; 2
39 namely, Asaph the son of Berechi'ah, son of Shim'e-a 2
39 namely, Asaph the son of Berechi'ah, son of Shim'e-a 2
40 son of Michael, son of Ba-ase'iah, son of Malchi'jah 2
40 son of Michael, son of Ba-ase'iah, son of Malchi'jah 2
40 son of Michael, son of Ba-ase'iah, son of Malchi'jah 2
41 son of Ethni, son of Zerah, son of Adai'ah 2
41 son of Ethni, son of Zerah, son of Adai'ah 2
41 son of Ethni, son of Zerah, son of Adai'ah 2
42 son of Ethan, son of Zimmah, son of Shim'e-i 2
42 son of Ethan, son of Zimmah, son of Shim'e-i 2
42 son of Ethan, son of Zimmah, son of Shim'e-i 2
43 son of Jahath, son of Gershom, son of Levi. 2
43 son of Jahath, son of Gershom, son of Levi. 2
43 son of Jahath, son of Gershom, son of Levi. 2
44 their brethren the sons of Merar'i: Ethan 2
44 Ethan the son of Kishi, son of Abdi, son of Malluch 2
44 Ethan the son of Kishi, son of Abdi, son of Malluch 2
44 Ethan the son of Kishi, son of Abdi, son of Malluch 2
45 son of Hashabi'ah, son of Amazi'ah, son of Hilki'ah 2
45 son of Hashabi'ah, son of Amazi'ah, son of Hilki'ah 2
45 son of Hashabi'ah, son of Amazi'ah, son of Hilki'ah 2
46 son of Amzi, son of Bani, son of Shemer 2
46 son of Amzi, son of Bani, son of Shemer 2
46 son of Amzi, son of Bani, son of Shemer 2
47 son of Mahli, son of Mushi, son of Merar'i, son of Levi; 2
47 son of Mahli, son of Mushi, son of Merar'i, son of Levi; 2
47 son of Mahli, son of Mushi, son of Merar'i, son of Levi; 2
47 son of Mahli, son of Mushi, son of Merar'i, son of Levi; 2
49 Aaron and his sons made offerings upon the altar 2
50 sons of Aaron: Elea'zar his son, Phin'ehas his son 2
50 sons of Aaron: Elea'zar his son, Phin'ehas his son 2
50 sons of Aaron: Elea'zar his son, Phin'ehas his son 2
50 sons of Aaron . . Phin'ehas . . Abishu'a his son 2
51 Bukki his son, Uzzi his son, Zerahi'ah his son 2
51 Bukki his son, Uzzi his son, Zerahi'ah his son 2
51 Bukki his son, Uzzi his son, Zerahi'ah his son 2
52 Merai'oth his son, Amari'ah his son, Ahi'tub his son 2
52 Merai'oth his son, Amari'ah his son, Ahi'tub his son 2
52 Merai'oth his son, Amari'ah his son, Ahi'tub his son 2
53 Zadok his son, Ahim'a-az his son. 2
53 Zadok his son, Ahim'a-az his son. 2
54 sons of Aaron of the families of Ko'hathites 2
56 they gave to Caleb the son of Jephun'neh. 2
57 To the sons of Aaron they gave the cities 2
66 some of the families of the sons of Kohath 2
7: 1 sons of Is'sachar: Tola, Pu'ah, Jashub, and Shimron 2
2 sons of Tola: Uzzi, Rephai'ah, Je'ri-el, Jah'mai, Ibsam 2
3 The sons of Uzzi: Izrahi'ah. 2
3 sons of Izrahi'ah: Michael, Obadi'ah, Jo'el 2
4 36,000, for they had many wives and sons. 2
6 sons of Benjamin: Bela, Becher, and Jedi'a-el, three. 2
7 sons of Bela: Ezbon, Uzzi, Uz'ziel, Jer'imoth, and Iri 2
8 The sons of Becher: Zemi'rah, Jo'ash, Elie'zer 2
8 All these were the sons of Becher; 2
10 The sons of Jedi'a-el: Bilhan. 2
10 sons of Bilhan: Je'ush, Benjamin, Ehud, Chena'anah 2
11 All these were the sons of Jedi'a-el 2
12 And Shuppim and Huppim were the sons of Ir 2
12 Hushim the sons of Aher. 2
13 sons of Naph'tali: Jah'zi-el, Guni, Jezer, and Shallum 2
14 The sons of Manas'seh: As'ri-el 2
16 Ma'acah the wife of Machir bore a son 2
16 Peresh . . and his sons were Ulam and Rakem. 2
17 The sons of Ulam: Bedan. 2
17 These were the sons of Gilead the son of Machir 2
17 sons of Gilead the son of Machir, son of Manas'seh. 2
17 sons of Gilead the son of Machir, son of Manas'seh. 2
19 sons of Shemi'da were Ahi'an, Shechem, Likhi 2
20 The sons of E'phraim: Shuthe'lah, and Bered his son 2
20 Shuthe'lah, and Bered his son, Tahath his son 2
20 Bered his son, Tahath his son, Ele-a'dah his son 2
20 Tahath his son, Ele-a'dah his son, Tahath his son 2
20 Tahath his son, Ele-a'dah his son, Tahath his son 2
21 Zabad his son, Shuthe'lah his son, and Ezer 2
21 Shuthe'lah his son, and Ezer and E'le-ad 2
23 his wife, and she conceived and bore a son; 2
25 Rephah was his son, Resheph his son, Telah his son 2
25 Resheph his son, Telah his son, Tahan his son 2
25 Resheph his son, Telah his son, Tahan his son 2
25 Resheph his son, Telah his son, Tahan his son 2
26 Ladan his son, Ammi'hud his son, Eli'shama his son 2
26 Ladan his son, Ammi'hud his son, Eli'shama his son 2
26 Ladan his son, Ammi'hud his son, Eli'shama his son 2
27 Nun his son, Joshua his son. 2
27 Nun his son, Joshua his son. 2
29 In these dwelt the sons of Joseph 2
29 the sons of Joseph the son of Israel. 2
30 The sons of Asher: Imnah, Ishvah, Ishvi, Beri'ah 2
31 The sons of Beri'ah: Heber and Mal'chi-el 2
33 The sons of Japhlet: Pasach, Bimhal, and Ashvath. 2
33 These are the sons of Japhlet. 2
34 sons of Shemer . . Rohgah, Jehub'bah, and Aram. 2
35 sons of Helem . . Zophah, Imna, Shelesh, and Amal. 2
36 sons of Zophah: Su'ah, Har'nepher, Shu'al, Beri, 2
38 The sons of Jether: Jephun'neh, Pispa, and Ara. 2
39 The sons of Ulla: Arah, Han'niel, and Rizi'a. 2
8: 3 Bela had sons: Addar, Gera, Abi'hud 2
6 These are the sons of Ehud 2
8 Shahara'im had sons in the country of Moab 7
9 He had sons by Hodesh his wife: Jobab, Zib'i-a, 7
10 These were his sons, heads of fathers' houses. 2
11 He also had sons by Hushim: Abi'tub and Elpa'al. 7
12 The sons of Elpa'al: Eber, Misham, and Shemed 2
16 Michael, Ishpah, and Joha were sons of Beri'ah. 2
18 Ish'merai, Izli'ah, and Jobab . . sons of Elpa'al. 2
21 Adai'ah, Berai'ah, and Shimrath . . sons of Shim'e-i. 2
25 Iphdei'ah, and Penu'el were the sons of Shashak. 2
27 Eli'jah, and Zichri were the sons of Jero'ham. 2
30 His first-born son: Abdon, then Zur, Kish, Ba'al, 2
34 the son of Jonathan was Mer'ib-ba'al; 2
35 The sons of Micah: Pithon, Melech, Tare'a, and Ahaz. 2
37 Raphah was his son, Ele-a'sah his son, Azel his son. 2
37 Raphah was his son, Ele-a'sah his son, Azel his son. 2
37 Raphah was his son, Ele-a'sah his son, Azel his son. 2
38 Azel had six sons, and these are their names 2
38 All these were the sons of Azel. 2
39 The sons of Eshek his brother: Ulam his first-born 2
40 sons of Ulam were men who were mighty warriors 2
40 bowmen, having many sons and grandsons, 150. 2
9: 4 Uthai the son of Ammi'hud, son of Omri, son of Imri 2
4 son of Ammi'hud, son of Omri, son of Imri, son of Bani 2
4 son of Ammi'hud, son of Omri, son of Imri, son of Bani 2
4 son of Ammi'hud, son of Omri, son of Imri, son of Bani 2
4 from the sons of Perez the son of Judah. 2
4 from the sons of Perez the son of Judah. 2
5 of the Shi'lonites: Asai'ah . . and his sons. 2
6 Of the sons of Zerah: Jeu'el and their kinsmen, 690. 2
7 Of the Benjaminites: Sallu the son of Meshul'lam 2
7 Meshul'lam, son of Hodavi'ah, son of Hassenu'ah. 2
7 Meshul'lam, son of Hodavi'ah, son of Hassenu'ah. 2
8 Ibne'iah the son of Jero'ham, Elah the son of Uzzi 2
8 Elah the son of Uzzi, son of Michri 2
8 Elah the son of Uzzi, son of Michri 2
8 Meshul'lam the son of Shephati'ah, son of Reu'el 2
8 Shephati'ah, son of Reu'el, son of Ibni'jah; 2
8 Shephati'ah, son of Reu'el, son of Ibni'jah; 2
11 Azari'ah the son of Hilki'ah, son of Meshul'lam 2
11 Azari'ah the son of Hilki'ah, son of Meshul'lam 2
11 son of Zadok, son of Merai'oth, son of Ahi'tub 2
11 son of Zadok, son of Merai'oth, son of Ahi'tub 2
11 son of Ahi'tub, the chief officer 2
12 Adai'ah the son of Jero'ham, son of Pashhur 2
12 Jero'ham, son of Pashhur, son of Malchi'jah 2
12 Jero'ham, son of Pashhur, son of Malchi'jah 2
12 Ma'asai the son of Ad'i-el, son of Jah'zerah 2
12 Ad'i-el, son of Jah'zerah, son of Meshul'lam 2
12 Jah'zerah, son of Meshul'lam, son of Meshil'lemith 2
12 Jah'zerah, son of Meshul'lam, son of Meshil'lemith 2
12 Meshul'lam, son of Meshil'lemith, son of Immer; 2
14 Of the Levites: Shemai'ah the son of Hasshub 2
14 Hasshub, son of Azri'kam, son of Hashabi'ah 2
14 Hasshub, son of Azri'kam, son of Hashabi'ah 2
14 Azri'kam, son of Hashabi'ah, of the sons of Merar'i; 2
15 Mattani'ah the son of Mica, son of Zichri 2
15 the son of Mica, son of Zichri, son of Asaph; 2
15 the son of Mica, son of Zichri, son of Asaph; 2
16 Obadi'ah the son of Shemai'ah, son of Galal 2
16 Shemai'ah, son of Galal, son of Jedu'thun 2
16 Shemai'ah, son of Galal, son of Jedu'thun 2
16 Berechi'ah the son of Asa, son of Elka'nah 2
16 Berechi'ah the son of Asa, son of Elka'nah 2
19 Shallum the son of Ko're, son of Ebi'asaph 2
19 Shallum the son of Ko're, son of Ebi'asaph 2
19 Ko're, son of Ebi'asaph, son of Korah 2
20 Phin'ehas the son of Elea'zar 2
21 Zechari'ah the son of Meshelemi'ah 2
23 they and their sons were in charge of the gates 2
30 Others, of the sons of the priests 2
36 first-born son Abdon, then Zur, Kish, Ba'al, Ner, 2
40 the son of Jonathan was Mer'ib-ba'al; 2
41 sons of Micah: Pithon, Melech, Tahr'e-a, and Ahaz 2
43 Bin'e-a; and Rephai'ah was his son, Ele-a'sah his son 2
43 Rephai'ah . . Ele-a'sah his son, Azel his son. 2
43 Rephai'ah . . Ele-a'sah his son, Azel his son. 2
44 Azel had six sons and these are their names 2
44 these were the sons of Azel. 2
10: 2 the Philistines overtook Saul and his sons; 2
2 Jonathan . . and Mal'chishu'a, the sons of Saul. 2
6 he and his three sons and all his house died 2
7 saw . . that Saul and his sons were dead 2
8 found Saul and his sons fallen on Mount Gilbo'a. 2
12 took away . . Saul and the bodies of his sons 2
14 the kingdom over to David the son of Jesse. 2
11: 6 Jo'ab the son of Zeru'iah went up first 2
12 next to him . . was Elea'zar the son of Dodo 2
22 Benai'ah the son of Jehoi'ada was a valiant man 2
24 did Benai'ah the son of Jehoi'ada, and won a name 2
26 mighty men . . Elha'nan the son of Dodo 2
28 Ira the son of Ikkesh of Teko'a, Abi-e'zer 2
30 Heled the son of Ba'anah of Netoph'ah 2
31 Ithai the son of Ribai of Gib'e-ah 2
34 Jonathan the son of Shagee the Har'arite 2
35 Ahi'am the son of Sachar the Har'arite 2
35 Eli'phal the son of Ur 2
37 Hezro of Carmel, Na'arai the son of Ezbai 2
38 Mibhar the son of Hagri 2
39 the armor-bearer of Jo'ab the son of Zeru'iah 2
41 Uri'ah the Hittite, Zabad the son of Ahlai 2
42 Ad'ina the son of Shiza the Reubenite 2
43 Hanan the son of Ma'acah 2
44 Shama and Je-i'el the sons of Hotham the Aro'erite 2
45 Jedi'a-el the son of Shimri, and Joha his brother 2
46 Jer'ibai, and Joshavi'ah, the sons of El'na-am 2
12: 1 could not move . . because of Saul the son of Kish; 2
3 Ahi-e'zer, then Jo'ash, both sons of Shema'ah 2
3 also Je'zi-el and Pelet the sons of Az'maveth; 2
7 and Zebadi'ah, the sons of Jero'ham of Gedor. 2
18 We are yours, O David; and with you, O son of Jesse! 2
14: 3 and David begot more sons and daughters. 2
15: 4 together the sons of Aaron and the Levites 2
5 of the sons of Kohath, Uri'el the chief 2
6 of the sons of Merar'i, Asai'ah the chief 2
7 of the sons of Gershom, Jo'el the chief 2
8 of the sons of Eli-za'phan, Shemai'ah the chief 2
9 of the sons of Hebron, Eli'el the chief 2
10 of the sons of Uz'ziel, Ammin'adab the chief 2
17 the Levites appointed Heman the son of Jo'el; 2
17 of his brethren Asaph the son of Berechi'ah 2
17 of the sons of Merar'i, their brethren, Ethan 2
17 their brethren, Ethan the son of Kusha'iah 2
16:13 sons of Jacob, his chosen ones! 2
38 while O'bed-e'dom, the son of Jedu'thun, and Hosah 2
42 The sons of Jedu'thun were appointed to the gate. 2
17:11 raise up your offspring . . one of your own sons 2
13 I will be his father, and he shall be my son; 2
18:10 he sent his son Hador'am to King David, to greet him 2
12 Abi'shai, the son of Zeru'iah, slew 18,000 E'domites 2
15 Jo'ab the son of Zeru'iah was over the army; 2
15 Jehosh'aphat the son of Ahi'lud was recorder; 2
16 Zadok the son of Ahi'tub 2
16 Ahim'elech the son of Abi'athar 2
17 Benai'ah the son of Jehoi'ada 2
17 David's sons were the chief officials 2
19: 1 Nahash . . died, and his son reigned in his stead. 2
2 I will deal loyally with Hanun the son of Nahash 2
20: 5 Elha'nan the son of Ja'ir slew Lahmi 2
7 Jonathan the son of Shim'e-a . . slew him. 2
21:20 his four sons who were with him hid themselves. 2
22: 5 Solomon my son is young and inexperienced 2
6 called for Solomon his son, and charged him 2
7 My son, I had it in my heart to build a house 2
9 son shall be born to you; he shall be a man of peace. 2
10 He shall be my son, and I will be his father 2
11 Now, my son, the LORD be with you 2
17 leaders of Israel to help Solomon his son, saying 2
23: 1 David . . made Solomon his son king over Israel. 2
6 divisions corresponding to the sons of Levi 2
7 The sons of Gershom were Ladan and Shim'e-i. 22
8 sons of Ladan: Jehi'el . . and Zetham, and Jo'el 2
9 sons of Shim'e-i: Shelo'moth, Ha'zi-el, and Haran 2
10 sons of Shim'e-i: Jahath, Zina, and Je'ush 2
10 These four were the sons of Shim'e-i. 2
11 but Je'ush and Beri'ah had not many sons 2
12 sons of Kohath: Amram, Izhar, Hebron, and Uz'ziel 2
13 The sons of Amram: Aaron and Moses. 2
13 that he and his sons for ever should burn incense 2
14 sons of Moses . . named among the tribe of Levi. 2
15 The sons of Moses: Gershom and Elie'zer. 2
16 The sons of Gershom: Sheb'uel the chief. 2
17 The sons of Elie'zer: Rehabi'ah the chief; 2
17 Elie'zer had no other sons 2
17 but the sons of Rehabi'ah were very many. 2
18 The sons of Izhar: Shelo'mith the chief. 2
19 sons of Hebron: Jeri'ah the chief, Amari'ah 2
20 The sons of Uz'ziel: Micah the chief 2
21 The sons of Merar'i: Mahli and Mushi. 2
21 The sons of Mahli: Elea'zar and Kish. 2
22 Elea'zar died having no sons, but only daughters; 2
22 their kinsmen, the sons of Kish, married them. 2
23 The sons of Mushi: Mahli, Eder, and Jer'emoth, three. 2
24 were the sons of Levi by their fathers' houses 2
28 their duty shall be to assist the sons of Aaron 2
32 shall attend the sons of Aaron, their brethren 2
24: 1 The divisions of the sons of Aaron were these. 2
1 sons of Aaron: Nadab, Abi'hu, Elea'zar, and Ith'amar. 2
3 With the help of Zadok of the sons of Elea'zar 2
3 help of . . Ahim'elech of the sons of Ith'amar 2
4 chief men were found among the sons of Elea'zar 2
4 more . . than among the sons of Ith'amar 2
4 heads of fathers' houses of the sons of Elea'zar 2
4 and eight of the sons of Ith'amar. 2
5 officers . . among both the sons of Elea'zar 2

5 among both . . the sons of Ith'amar. 2
6 scribe Shemai'ah the son of Nethan'el, a Levite 2
6 Zadok . . and Ahim'elech the son of Abi'athar 2
20 And of the rest of the sons of Levi 2
20 sons of Levi: of the sons of Amram, Shu'ba-el; 2
20 of the sons of Shu'ba-el, Jehde'iah. 2
21 Of Rehabi'ah: of the sons of Rehabi'ah, Isshi'ah 2
22 of the sons of Shelo'moth, Jahath. 2
23 sons of Hebron: Jeri'ah the chief, Amari'ah 2
24 sons of Uz'ziel, Micah; of the sons of Micah, Shamir. 2
24 sons of Uz'ziel, Micah; of the sons of Micah, Shamir. 2
25 of the sons of Isshi'ah, Zechari'ah. 2
26 The sons of Merar'i: Mahli and Mushi. 2
26 The sons of Ja-azi'ah: Beno. 2
27 sons of Merar'i: of Ja-azi'ah, Beno, Shoham, Zaccur 2
28 Of Mahli: Elea'zar, who had no sons. 2
29 Of Kish, the sons of Kish: Jerah'meel. 2
30 The sons of Mushi: Mahli, Eder, and Jer'i-moth. 2
30 These were the sons of the Levites according 2
31 lots, just as their brethren the sons of Aaron 2
25: 1 set apart for the service . . of the sons of Asaph 2
2 sons of Asaph: Zaccur, Joseph, Nethani'ah 2
2 Zaccur . . and Ashare'lah, sons of Asaph 2
3 sons of Jedu'thun: Gedali'ah, Zeri, Jeshai'ah, 2
4 sons of Heman: Bukki'ah, Mattani'ah, Uz'ziel, 2
5 All these were the sons of Heman the king's seer 2
5 God had given Heman fourteen sons 2
9 to Gedali'ah . . and his brethren and his sons 2
10 third to Zaccur, his sons and his brethren, twelve; 2
11 fourth to Izri, his sons and his brethren, twelve; 2
12 fifth to Nethani'ah, his sons and his brethren 2
13 sixth to Bukki'ah, his sons and his brethren 2
14 seventh to Jeshare'lah, his sons and his brethren 2
15 eighth to Jeshai'ah, his sons and his brethren 2
16 ninth to Mattani'ah, his sons and his brethren 2
17 tenth to Shim'e-i, his sons and his brethren, twelve; 2
18 eleventh to Az'arel, his sons and his brethren 2
19 twelfth to Hashabi'ah, his sons and his brethren 2
20 thirteenth, Shu'ba-el, his sons and his brethren 2
21 Mattithi'ah, his sons and his brethren, twelve; 2
22 fifteenth, to Jer'emoth, his sons and his brethren 2
23 sixteenth, to Hanani'ah, his sons and his brethren 2
24 to Joshbekash'ah, his sons and his brethren 2
25 eighteenth, to Hana'ni, his sons and his brethren 2
26 to Mallo'thi, his sons and his brethren, twelve; 2
27 twentieth, to Eli'athah, his sons and his brethren 2
28 to Hothir, his sons and his brethren, twelve; 2
29 to Giddal'ti, his sons and his brethren, twelve; 2
30 to Maha'zi-oth, his sons and his brethren, twelve; 2
31 Romam'ti-e'zer, his sons and his brethren, twelve. 2
26: 1 of the Ko'rahites, Meshelemi'ah the son of Ko're 2
1 the son of Ko're, of the sons of Asaph. 2
2 Meshelemi'ah had sons: Zechari'ah the first-born 2
4 O'bed-e'dom had sons: Shemai'ah the first-born 2
6 Also to his son Shemai'ah were sons born who were 2
6 Shemai'ah were sons born who were leaders 2
7 sons of Shemai'ah: Othni, Reph'a-el, Obed, 2
8 sons of O'bed-e'dom with their sons and brethren 2
8 sons of O'bed-e'dom with their sons and brethren 2
9 Meshelemi'ah had sons and brethren, able men 2
10 Hosah, of the sons of Merar'i, had sons 2
10 Hosah . . of Merar'i, had sons: Shimri the chief 2
11 the sons and brethren of Hosah were thirteen. 2
14 They cast lots also for his son Zechari'ah 2
15 and to his sons was allotted the storehouse. 2
19 among the Ko'rahites and the sons of Merar'i. 2
21 The sons of Ladan, the sons of the Gershonites 2
21 sons of the Gershonites belonging to Ladan 2
22 The sons of Jehi'eli . . were in charge 2
24 Sheb'uel the son of Gershom, son of Moses 2
24 Sheb'uel the son of Gershom, son of Moses 2
25 His brethren: from Elie'zer were his son Rehabi'ah 2
25 from Elie'zer were . . his son Jeshai'ah 2
25 from Elie'zer were . . his son Joram 2
25 from Elie'zer were . . his son Zichri 2
25 from Elie'zer were . . his son Shelo'moth. 2
28 all that Samuel the seer, and Saul the son of Kish 2
28 Abner the son of Ner, and Jo'ab the son of Zeru'iah 2
28 Abner the son of Ner, and Jo'ab the son of Zeru'iah 2
29 Chenani'ah and his sons were appointed 2
27: 2 Jasho'beam the son of Zab'di-el was in charge 2
5 Benai'ah, the son of Jehoi'ada the priest, as chief; 2
6 Ammiz'abad his son was in charge of his division. 2
7 his son Zebadi'ah after him; in his division were 2
9 Sixth . . was Ira, the son of Ikkesh the Teko'ite; 2
10 Helez the Pel'onite, of the sons of E'phraim; 2
14 Benai'ah of Pira'thon, of the sons of E'phraim; 2
16 for the Reubenites Elie'zer the son of Zichri 2
16 for the Simeonites, Shephati'ah the son of Ma'acah; 2
17 for Levi, Hashabi'ah the son of Kem'uel; 2
18 for Is'sachar, Omri the son of Michael; 2
19 for Zeb'ulun, Ishma'iah the son of Obadi'ah; 2
19 for Naph'tali, Jer'emoth the son of Az'riel; 2
20 for the E'phraimites, Hoshe'a the son of Azazi'ah; 2
20 half-tribe of Manas'seh, Jo'el the son of Pedai'ah; 2
21 Manas'seh in Gilead, Iddo the son of Zechari'ah; 2
21 for Benjamin, Ja-a'si-el the son of Abner; 2
22 for Dan, Az'arel the son of Jero'ham. 2
24 Jo'ab the son of Zeru'iah began to number 2

25 Az'maveth the son of Ad'i-el; 2
25 treasuries . . was Jonathan the son of Uzzi'ah; 2
26 over those who . . was Ezri the son of Chelub; 2
29 in the valleys was Shaphat the son of Adlai. 2
32 he and Jehi'el the son of Hach'moni attended 2
32 and Jehi'el . . attended the king's sons. 2
34 was succeeded by Jehoi'ada the son of Benai'ah 2
28: 1 the property and cattle of the king and his sons 2
4 and among my father's sons he took pleasure in me 2
5 of all my sons . . he has chosen Solomon my son 2
5 of all my sons (for the LORD has given me many sons 2
5 of all my sons . . he has chosen Solomon my son 2
6 Solomon your son who shall build my house 2
6 chosen him to be my son, and I will be his father. 2
9 you, Solomon my son, know the God of your father 2
11 David gave Solomon his son the plan 2
20 said to Solomon his son, "Be strong and of good 2
29: 1 Solomon my son . . is young and inexperienced 2
19 Grant to Solomon my son that with a whole heart 2
22 Solomon the son of David king the second time 2
24 the mighty men, and also all the sons of King David 2
26 David the son of Jesse reigned over all Israel. 2
28 and Solomon his son reigned in his stead. 2
2Ch 1: 1 Solomon the son of David established himself 2
5 that Bez'alel the son of Uri, son of Hur, had made 2
5 that Bez'alel the son of Uri, son of Hur, had made 2
2:12 who has given King David a wise son 2
14 the son of a woman of the daughters of Dan 2
5:12 Levitical singers . . their sons and kinsmen 2
6: 9 your son . . shall build the house for my name.' 2
16 if only your sons take heed to their way, to walk 2
9:29 concerning Jerobo'am the son of Nebat? 2
31 Rehobo'am his son reigned in his stead. 2
10: 2 when Jerobo'am the son of Nebat heard of it 2
15 spoke by Ahi'jah . . to Jerobo'am the son of Nebat. 2
16 We have no inheritance in the son of Jesse. 2
11: 3 Say to Rehobo'am the son of Solomon king of Judah 2
14 Jerobo'am and his sons cast them out 2
17 they made Rehobo'am the son of Solomon secure 2
18 Jer'imoth the son of David 2
18 Ab'ihail the daughter of Eli'ab the son of Jesse; 2
19 she bore him sons, Je'ush, Shemari'ah, and Zaham. 2
21 had 28 sons and 60 daughters); 2
22 Abi'jah the son of Ma'acah as chief prince 2
23 some of his sons through all the districts 2
12:16 Abi'jah his son reigned in his stead. 2
13: 5 gave the kingship . . to David and his sons 2
6 Jerobo'am the son of Nebat, a servant of Solomon 2
6 son of Nebat, a servant of Solomon the son of David 2
7 defied Rehobo'am the son of Solomon 2
8 kingdom . . in the hand of the sons of David 2
9 the priests . . the sons of Aaron, and the Levites 2
10 We have priests . . who are sons of Aaron 2
12 O sons of Israel, do not fight against the LORD 2
21 took fourteen wives, and had 22 sons 2
14: 1 Asa his son reigned in his stead. 2
15: 1 Spirit of God came upon Azari'ah the son of Oded 2
8 the prophecy of Azari'ah the son of Oded *
17: 1 Jehosh'aphat his son reigned in his stead 2
16 next to him Amasi'ah the son of Zichri 2
18: 7 Micai'ah the son of Imlah; 2
8 Bring quickly Micai'ah the son of Imlah. 2
10 Zedeki'ah the son of Chena'anah 2
23 Zedeki'ah the son of Chena'anah came near 2
25 take him back . . to Jo'ash the king's son; 2
19: 2 Jehu the son of Hana'ni the seer went out 2
11 Zebadi'ah the son of Ish'mael 2
20:14 Jaha'ziel the son of Zechari'ah, son of Benai'ah 2
14 Jaha'ziel the son of Zechari'ah, son of Benai'ah 2
14 Benai'ah, son of Je-i'el, son of Mattani'ah, a Levite 2
14 Benai'ah, son of Je-i'el, son of Mattani'ah, a Levite 2
14 Mattani'ah, a Levite of the sons of Asaph 2
34 chronicles of Jehu the son of Hana'ni 2
37 Then Elie'zer the son of Do-dav'ahu of Mare'shah 2
21: 1 Jeho'ram his son reigned in his stead. 2
2 He had brothers, the sons of Jehosh'aphat 2
2 sons of Jehosh'aphat king of Judah. 2
7 promised to give a lamp to him and to his sons 2
17 carried away . . also his sons and his wives 2
17 so that no son was left to him except Jeho'ahaz 2
17 left to him except Jeho'ahaz, his youngest son. 2
22: 1 made Ahazi'ah his youngest son king in his stead; 2
1 Ahazi'ah the son of Jeho'ram . . reigned. 2
5 went with Jeho'ram the son of Ahab king of Israel 2
6 Ahazi'ah the son of Jeho'ram king of Judah 2
6 Ahazi'ah . . went down to see Joram the son of Ahab 2
7 with Jeho'ram to meet Jehu the son of Nimshi 2
8 Jehu . . met . . the sons of Ahazi'ah's brothers 2
10 Now when Athali'ah . . saw that her son was dead 2
11 Jeho-shab'e-ath . . took Jo'ash the son of Ahazi'ah 2
11 stole him away from among the king's sons 2
23: 1 commanders . . Azari'ah the son of Jero'ham 2
1 commanders . . Ish'mael the son of Jehoha'nan 2
1 commanders . . Azari'ah the son of Obed, Ma-asei'ah 2
1 commanders . . Ma-asei'ah the son of Adai'ah 2
1 commanders . . Elisha'phat the son of Zichri. 2
3 Behold, the king's son! Let him reign 2
3 as the LORD spoke concerning the sons of David. 2
11 Then he brought out the king's son 2

11 Jehoi'ada and his sons anointed him, 2
24: 3 for him two wives, and he had sons and daughters. 2
7 sons of Athali'ah . . had broken 2
20 Zechari'ah the son of Jehoi'ada the priest; 2
22 but killed his son 2
25 because of the blood of the son of Jehoi'ada 21
26 Zabad the son of Shim'e-ath the Ammonitess 2
26 Jeho'zabad the son of Shimrith the Moabitess. 2
27 Accounts of his sons, and of the many oracles 2
27 And Amazi'ah his son reigned in his stead. 2
25:17 Jo'ash the son of Jeho'ahaz, son of Jehu, 2
17 Jo'ash the son of Jeho'ahaz, son of Jehu, 2
18 Give your daughter to my son for a wife 2
23 Amazi'ah king of Judah, the son of Jo'ash 2
23 Amazi'ah . . son of Jo'ash, son of Ahazi'ah 2
25 Amazi'ah the son of Jo'ash king of Judah 2
25 after the death of Jo'ash the son of Jeho'ahaz 2
26:18 but for the priests the sons of Aaron 2
21 Jotham his son was over the king's household 2
22 Isaiah the prophet the son of Amoz wrote. 2
23 Jotham his son reigned in his stead. 2
27: 9 Ahaz his son reigned in his stead. 2
28: 3 burned incense in the valley of the son of Hinnom 2
3 burned his sons as an offering 2
6 Pekah the son of Remali'ah slew 120,000 in Judah 2
7 Zichri . . slew Ma-asei'ah the king's son 2
8 took captive 200,000 of their kinsfolk, women, sons 2
12 chiefs . . Azari'ah the son of Joha'nan, Berechi'ah 2
12 chiefs . . Berechi'ah the son of Meshil'lemoth 2
12 chiefs . . Jehizki'ah the son of Shallum 2
12 chiefs . . and Ama'sa the son of Had-lai 2
27 And Hezeki'ah his son reigned in his stead. 2
29: 9 our sons and our . . wives are in captivity 2
11 My sons, do not now be negligent 2
12 Then the Levites arose, Mahath the son of Ama'sai 2
12 Levites arose . . Jo'el the son of Azari'ah 2
12 of the sons of the Ko'hathites; 2
12 Levites arose . . of the sons of Merar'i, 2
12 Levites arose . . Kish the son of Abdi 2
12 Levites arose . . Azari'ah the son of Jehal'lelel; 2
12 Levites arose . . Jo'ah the son of Zimmah, 2
12 Levites arose . . Eden the son of Jo'ah; 2
13 of the sons of Eli-za'phan, Shimri and Jeu'el; 2
13 of the sons of Asaph, Zechari'ah and Mattani'ah; 2
14 of the sons of Heman, Jehu'el and Shim'e-i; 2
14 of the sons of Jedu'thun, Shemai'ah and Uz'ziel. 2
21 commanded the priests the sons of Aaron to offer 2
30:26 time of Solomon the son of David king of Israel 2
31:14 Ko're the son of Imnah the Levite 2
18 little children, their wives, their sons 2
19 sons of Aaron . . who were in the fields of common 2
32:20 Isaiah the prophet, the son of Amoz 2
21 some of his own sons struck him down there 9
32 written in the vision of Isaiah . . son of Amoz 2
33 the ascent of the tombs of the sons of David; 2
33 Manas'seh his son reigned in his stead. 2
33: 6 he burned his sons as an offering in the valley 2
6 as an offering in the valley of the son of Hinnom 2
7 God said to David and to Solomon his son 2
20 Amon his son reigned in his stead. 2
25 people of the land made Josi'ah his son king 2
34: 8 sent Shaphan the son of Azali'ah, and Ma-asei'ah 2
8 he sent . . Jo'ah the son of Jo'ahaz, the recorder 2
12 Jahath and Obadi'ah . . of the sons of Merar'i 2
12 of the sons of the Ko'hathites 2
20 king commanded . . Ahi'kam the son of Shaphan 2
20 king commanded . . Abdon the son of Micah 2
22 Huldah the . . wife of Shallum the son of Tokhath 2
22 Tokhath, son of Hasrah, keeper of the wardrobe 2
35: 3 house which Solomon the son of David . . built; 2
4 following . . directions of Solomon his son. 2
14 priests the sons of Aaron . . busied in offering 2
14 for the priests the sons of Aaron. 2
15 singers, the sons of Asaph, were in their place 2
36: 1 people . . took Jeho'ahaz the son of Josi'ah 2
8 Jehoi'achin his son reigned in his stead. 2
20 became servants to him and to his sons 2
Ezr 2: 3 sons of Parosh, 2,172. 2
4 sons of Shephati'ah, 372. 2
5 sons of Arah, 775. 2
6 sons of Pa'hath-moab, namely the sons of Jeshua 2
6 Pa'hath-moab, namely the sons of Jeshua and Jo'ab 2
7 sons of Elam, 1,254. 2
8 sons of Zattu, 945. 2
9 sons of Zac'cai, 760. 2
10 sons of Bani, 642. 2
11 sons of Be'bai, 623. 2
12 sons of Azgad, 1,222. 2
13 sons of Adoni'kam, 666. 2
14 sons of Bigva'i, 2,056. 2
15 sons of Adin, 454. 2
16 sons of Ater, namely of Hezeki'ah, 98. 2
17 sons of Be'zai, 323. 2
18 sons of Jorah, 112. 2
19 sons of Hashum, 223. 2
20 sons of Gibbar, 95. 2
21 sons of Bethlehem, 123. 2
24 sons of Az'maveth, 42. 2
25 sons of Kir'iathar'im, Chephi'rah, and Be-er'oth, 743. 2

26 sons of Ramah and Geba, 621. 2
29 sons of Nebo, 52. 2
30 sons of Magbish, 156. 2
31 sons of the other Elam, 1,254. 2
32 sons of Harim, 320. 2
33 sons of Lod, Hadid, and Ono, 725. 2
34 sons of Jericho, 345. 2
35 sons of Sena'ah, 3,630. 2
36 priests: the sons of Jedai'ah, of the house 2
37 sons of Immer, 1,052. 2
38 sons of Pashhur, 1,247. 2
39 sons of Harim, 1,017. 2
40 The Levites: the sons of Jeshua and Kad'mi-el 2
40 Kad'mi-el, of the sons of Ho-davi'ah, 74. 2
41 singers: the sons of Asaph, 128. 2
42 sons of the gatekeepers: the sons of Shallum 2
42 sons of the gatekeepers: the sons of Shallum 2
42 sons of the gatekeepers: the . . sons of Ater 2
42 sons of the gatekeepers: the . . sons of Talmon 2
42 sons of the gatekeepers: the . . sons of Akkub 2
42 sons of the gatekeepers: the . . sons of Hati'ta 2
42 sons of the gatekeepers: the . . sons of Sho'bai 2
43 temple servants: the sons of Ziha 2
43 temple servants: the . . sons of Hasu'pha 2
43 temple servants: the . . sons of Tabba'oth 2
44 sons of Keros, the sons of Si'aha, the sons of Padon 2
44 sons of Keros, the sons of Si'aha, the sons of Padon 2
44 sons of Keros, the sons of Si'aha, the sons of Padon 2
45 sons of Leba'nah, the sons of Hag'abah 2
45 sons of Leba'nah, the sons of Hag'abah 2
45 the sons of Hag'abah, the sons of Akkub 2
46 sons of Hagab, the sons of Shamlai 2
46 sons of Hagab, the sons of Shamlai 2
46 the sons of Shamlai, the sons of Hanan 2
47 sons of Giddel, the sons of Gahar 2
47 sons of Giddel, the sons of Gahar 2
47 the sons of Gahar, the sons of Re-ai'ah 2
48 sons of Rezin, the sons of Neko'da 2
48 sons of Rezin, the sons of Neko'da 2
48 the sons of Neko'da, the sons of Gazzam 2
49 sons of Uzza, the sons of Pase'ah, the sons of Besai 2
49 sons of Uzza, the sons of Pase'ah, the sons of Besai 2
49 sons of Uzza, the sons of Pase'ah, the sons of Besai 2
50 sons of Asnah, the sons of Me-u'nim 2
50 sons of Asnah, the sons of Me-u'nim 2
50 the sons of Me-u'nim, the sons of Nephi'sim 2
51 sons of Bakbuk, the sons of Haku'pha 2
51 sons of Bakbuk, the sons of Haku'pha 2
51 the sons of Haku'pha, the sons of Harhur 2
52 sons of Bazluth, the sons of Mehi'da 2
52 sons of Bazluth, the sons of Mehi'da 2
52 the sons of Mehi'da, the sons of Harsha 2
53 sons of Barkos, the sons of Sis'era 2
53 sons of Barkos, the sons of Sis'era 2
53 the sons of Sis'era, the sons of Temah 2
54 sons of Nezi'ah, and the sons of Hati'pha. 2
54 sons of Nezi'ah, and the sons of Hati'pha. 2
55 sons of Solomon's servants: the sons of So'tai 2
55 sons of Solomon's servants: the sons of So'tai 2
55 sons of Solomon's servants . . sons of Hasso'phereth 2
55 sons of Solomon's servants: the . . sons of Peru'da 2
56 sons of Ja'alah, the sons of Darkon 2
56 sons of Ja'alah, the sons of Darkon 2
56 the sons of Darkon, the sons of Giddel 2
57 sons of Shephati'ah, the sons of Hattil 2
57 sons of Shephati'ah, the sons of Hattil 2
57 the sons of Po'chereth-hazzeba'im 2
57 of Po'chereth-hazzeba'im, and the sons of Ami. 2
58 servants and the sons of Solomon's servants 2
60 sons of Delai'ah, the sons of Tobi'ah 2
60 sons of Delai'ah, the sons of Tobi'ah 2
60 the sons of Tobi'ah, and the sons of Neko'da 2
61 of the sons of the priests: the sons of Habai'ah 2
61 of the sons of the priests: the sons of Habai'ah 2
61 of the sons of the priests: the . . sons of Hakkoz 2
61 of the sons of the priests . . sons of Barzil'lai 2
3: 1 When the . . sons of Israel were in the towns 2
2 Then arose Jeshua the son of Jo'zadak 2
2 arose . . Zerub'babel the son of She-al'ti-el 2
8 Zerub'babel the son of She-al'ti-el and Jeshua 2
8 Zerub'babel . . and Jeshua the son of Jo'zadak 2
9 Jeshua with his sons and his kinsmen, and Kad'mi-el 2
9 Jeshua . . and Kad'mi-el and his sons 2
9 Kad'mi-el and his sons, the sons of Judah 2
9 along with the sons of Hen'adad and the Levites 2
9 Hen'adad and the Levites, their sons and kinsmen. 2
10 Levites, the sons of Asaph, with cymbals 2
5: 1 prophets, Haggai and Zechari'ah the son of Iddo 12
2 Then Zerub'babel the son of She-al'ti-el and Jeshua 12
2 Zerub'babel . . and Jeshua the son of Jo'zadak 12
6:10 may . . pray for the life of the king and his sons. 12
14 prophesying of . . Zechari'ah the son of Iddo. 12
7: 1 Ezra the son of Serai'ah, son of Azari'ah 2
1 son of Serai'ah, son of Azari'ah, son of Hilki'ah 2
1 son of Serai'ah, son of Azari'ah, son of Hilki'ah 2
2 son of Shallum, son of Za-dok, son of Ahi'tub 2
2 son of Shallum, son of Za-dok, son of Ahi'tub 2
2 son of Shallum, son of Za-dok, son of Ahi'tub 2
3 son of Amari'ah, son of Azari'ah, son of Merai'oth 2
3 son of Amari'ah, son of Azari'ah, son of Merai'oth 2
3 son of Amari'ah, son of Azari'ah, son of Merai'oth 2
4 son of Zerahi'ah, son of Uzzi, son of Bukki 2
4 son of Zerahi'ah, son of Uzzi, son of Bukki 2
4 son of Zerahi'ah, son of Uzzi, son of Bukki 2
5 son of Abi'shu-a, son of Phin'ehas 2
5 son of Abi'shu-a, son of Phin'ehas 2
5 Phin'ehas, son of Elea'zar, son of Aaron the chief 2
5 son of Elea'zar, son of Aaron the chief priest– 2
23 against the realm of the king and his sons. 12
8: 2 Of the sons of Phin'ehas, Gershom. 2
2 Of the sons of Ith'amar, Daniel. 2
2 Of the sons of David, Hattush 2
3 of the sons of Shecani'ah. 2
3 Of the sons of Parosh, Zechari'ah 2
4 Of the sons of Pa'hath-mo'ab, Eli-e-ho-e'nai the son 2
4 Eli-e-ho-e'nai the son of Zerahi'ah, and with him 200 2
5 Of the sons of Zattu, Shecani'ah 2
5 Shecani'ah the son of Jaha'ziel 2
6 Of the sons of Adin, Ebed the son of Jonathan 2
6 Of the sons of Adin, Ebed the son of Jonathan 2
7 Of the sons of Elam, Jeshai'ah the son of Athali'ah 2
7 Of the sons of Elam, Jeshai'ah the son of Athali'ah 2
8 Of the sons of Shephati'ah, Zebadi'ah the son 2
8 sons of Shephati'ah, Zebadi'ah the son of Michael 2
9 Of the sons of Jo'ab, Obadi'ah the son of Jehi'el 2
9 Of the sons of Jo'ab, Obadi'ah the son of Jehi'el 2
10 Of the sons of Bani, Shelo'mith the son 2
10 Shelo'mith the son of Josi-phi'ah, and with him 160 2
11 Of the sons of Be'bai, Zechari'ah, the son of Be'bai 2
11 Of the sons of Be'bai, Zechari'ah, the son of Be'bai 2
12 Of the sons of Azgad, Joha'nan the son of Hak'katan 2
12 Of the sons of Azgad, Joha'nan the son of Hak'katan 2
13 Of the sons of Adoni'kam, those who came later 2
14 Of the sons of Bigva'i, Uthai and Zaccur 2
15 I found there none of the sons of Levi. 2
18 man of discretion, of the sons of Mahli . . of Levi 2
18 sons of Mahli the son of Levi, son of Israel 2
18 sons of Mahli the son of Levi, son of Israel 2
18 Sherebi'ah with his sons and kinsmen, eighteen. 2
19 Hashabi'ah and . . Jeshai'ah of the sons of Merar'i 2
19 Hashabi'ah . . his kinsmen and their sons, twenty; 2
33 Mer'emoth the priest, son of Uri'ah 2
33 Mer'emoth . . Elea'zar the son of Phin'ehas 2
33 Levites, Jo'zabad the son of Jeshua and No-adi'ah 2
33 Levites . . No-adi'ah the son of Bin'nui. 2
9: 2 wives for themselves and for their sons; 2
12 Therefore give not your daughters to their sons 2
12 neither take their daughters for your sons 2
10: 2 Shecani'ah the son of Jehi'el, of the sons of Elam 2
2 Shecani'ah the son of Jehi'el, of the sons of Elam 2
6 Jehoha'nan the son of Eli'ashib 2
15 Only Jonathan the son of As'ahel and Jahzei'ah 2
15 Only Jonathan . . and Jahzei'ah the son of Tikvah 2
18 sons of the priests who had married foreign 2
18 of the sons of Jeshua the son of Jo'zadak 2
18 Jeshua the son of Jo'zadak and his brethren. 2
20 Of the sons of Immer: Hana'ni and Zebadi'ah. 2
21 Of the sons of Harim: Ma-asei'ah, Eli'jah, Shemai'ah 2
22 Of the sons of Pashhur: Eli-o-e'nai, Ma-asei'ah 2
25 of Israel: of the sons of Parosh: Rami'ah, Izzi'ah 2
26 Of the sons of Elam: Mattani'ah, Zechari'ah, Jehi'el 2
27 Of the sons of Zattu: Eli-o-e'nai, Eli'ashib 2
28 Of the sons of Be'bai were Jehoha'nan, Hanani'ah 2
29 Of the sons of Bani were Meshul'lam, Malluch 2
30 Of the sons of Pa'hath-mo'ab: Adna, Chelal, Benai'ah 2
31 Of the sons of Harim: Elie'zer, Isshi'jah, Malchi'jah 2
33 Of the sons of Hashum: Matte'nai, Mat'tattah, Zabad 2
34 Of the sons of Bani: Ma-ada'i, Amram, Uel 2
38 Of the sons of Bin'nui: Shim'e-i 21
43 Of the sons of Nebo: Je-i'el, Mattithi'ah, Zabad 2
Neh 1: 1 The words of Nehemi'ah the son of Hacali'ah. 2
3: 2 next to them Zaccur the son of Imri built. 2
3 sons of Hassena'ah built the Fish Gate; 2
4 the son of Uri'ah, son of Hakkoz repaired. 2
4 the son of Uri'ah, son of Hakkoz repaired. 2
4 next to them Meshul'lam the son of Berechi'ah 2
4 son of Berechi'ah, son of Meshez'abel repaired. 2
4 next to them Zadok the son of Ba'ana repaired. 2
6 Joi'ada the son of Pase'ah and Meshul'lam 2
6 Joi'ada . . and Meshul'lam the son of Besodei'ah 2
8 Uz'ziel the son of Harhai'ah, goldsmiths 2
9 Rephai'ah the son of Hur . . repaired. 2
10 Jedai'ah the son of Haru'maph repaired opposite 2
10 Hattush the son of Hashabnei'ah repaired. 2
11 Malchi'jah the son of Harim and Hasshub 2
11 Malchi'jah . . and Hasshub the son of Pa'hath-mo'ab 2
12 Next to him Shallum the son of Hallo'hesh 2
14 Malchi'jah the son of Rechab, ruler 2
15 Shallum the son of Colho'zeh, ruler 2
16 After him Nehemi'ah the son of Azbuk, ruler of half 2
17 Levites repaired: Rehum the son of Bani; 2
18 brethren repaired: Bav'vai the son of Hen'adad 2
19 next to him Ezer the son of Jeshua, ruler of Mizpah 2
20 After him Baruch the son of Zab'bai repaired 2
21 Mer'emoth the son of Uri'ah, son of Hakkoz repaired 2
21 Mer'emoth the son of Uri'ah, son of Hakkoz repaired 2
23 Azari'ah the son of Ma-asei'ah, son of Anani'ah 2
23 Azari'ah the son of Ma-asei'ah, son of Anani'ah 2
24 After him Bin'nui the son of Hen'adad repaired 2
25 Palal the son of Uzai repaired opposite 2
25 After him Pedai'ah the son of Parosh 2
29 Zadok the son of Immer repaired opposite his own 2
29 Shemai'ah the son of Shecani'ah . . repaired. 2
30 Hanani'ah the son of Shelemi'ah and Hanun 2
30 Hanani'ah . . and Hanun the sixth son of Zalaph 2
30 Meshul'lam the son of Berechi'ah repaired 2
4:14 fight for your brethren, your sons 2
5: 2 With our sons and our daughters, we are many; 2
5 forcing our sons and our daughters to be slaves 2
6:10 Shemai'ah the son of Delai'ah, son of Mehet'abel 2
10 Shemai'ah the son of Delai'ah, son of Mehet'abel 2
18 son-in-law of Shecani'ah the son of Arah 2
18 his son Jehoha'nan had taken the daughter 2
18 daughter of Meshul'lam the son of Berechi'ah 2
7: 8 sons of Parosh, 2,172. 2
9 sons of Shephati'ah, 372. 2
10 sons of Arah, 652. 2
11 sons of Pa'hath-mo'ab, namely the sons of Jeshua 2
11 Pa'hath-mo'ab, namely the sons of Jeshua and Jo'ab 2
12 sons of Elam, 1,254. 2
13 sons of Zattu, 845. 2
14 sons of Zac'cai, 760. 2
15 sons of Bin'nui, 648. 2
16 sons of Be'bai, 628. 2
17 sons of Azgad, 2,322. 2
18 sons of Adoni'kam, 667. 2
19 sons of Bigva'i, 2,067. 2
20 sons of Adin, 655. 2
21 sons of Ater, namely of Hezeki'ah, 98. 2
22 sons of Hashum, 328. 2
23 sons of Be'zai, 324. 2
24 sons of Hariph, 112. 2
25 sons of Gibeon, 95. 2
34 sons of the other Elam, 1,254. 2
35 sons of Harim, 320. 2
36 sons of Jericho, 345. 2
37 sons of Lod, Hadid, and Ono, 721. 2
38 sons of Sena'ah, 3,930. 2
39 sons of Jedai'ah, namely the house of Jeshua, 973. 2
40 sons of Immer, 1,052. 2
41 sons of Pashhur, 1,247. 2
42 sons of Harim, 1,017. 2
43 sons of Jeshua, namely of Kad'mi-el of the sons 2
43 Jeshua, namely of Kad'mi-el of the sons of Ho'devah 2
44 singers: the sons of Asaph, 148. 2
45 gatekeepers: the sons of Shallum, the sons of Ater 2
45 gatekeepers: the sons of Shallum, the sons of Ater 2
45 gatekeepers . . sons of Talmon, the sons of Akkub 2
45 gatekeepers . . sons of Talmon, the sons of Akkub 2
45 gatekeepers . . sons of Hati'ta 2
45 gatekeepers . . sons of Sho'bai 2
46 temple servants: the sons of Ziha 2
46 temple servants: the sons of Ziha 2
46 temple servants . . the sons of Tabba'oth 2
47 sons of Keros, the sons of Si'a, the sons of Padon 2
47 sons of Keros, the sons of Si'a, the sons of Padon 2
47 sons of Keros, the sons of Si'a, the sons of Padon 2
48 sons of Leba'na, the sons of Hag'aba 2
48 sons of Leba'na, the sons of Hag'aba 2
48 Leba'na, the sons of Hag'aba, the sons of Shalmai 2
49 sons of Hanan, the sons of Giddel, the sons of Gahar 2
49 sons of Hanan, the sons of Giddel, the sons of Gahar 2
49 sons of Hanan, the sons of Giddel, the sons of Gahar 2
50 sons of Re-ai'ah, the sons of Rezin 2
50 sons of Re-ai'ah, the sons of Rezin 2
50 Re-ai'ah, the sons of Rezin, the sons of Neko'da 2
51 sons of Gazzam, the sons of Uzza, the sons of Pase'ah 2
51 sons of Gazzam, the sons of Uzza, the sons of Pase'ah 2
51 sons of Gazzam, the sons of Uzza, the sons of Pase'ah 2
52 sons of Besai, the sons of Me-u'nim 2
52 sons of Besai, the sons of Me-u'nim 2
52 the sons of Me-u'nim, the sons of Nephush'esim 2
53 sons of Bakbuk, the sons of Haku'pha 2
53 sons of Bakbuk, the sons of Haku'pha 2
53 Bakbuk, the sons of Haku'pha, the sons of Harhur 2
54 sons of Bazlith, the sons of Mehi'da 2
54 sons of Bazlith, the sons of Mehi'da 2
54 Bazlith, the sons of Mehi'da, the sons of Harsha 2
55 sons of Barkos, the sons of Sis'era 2
55 sons of Barkos, the sons of Sis'era 2
55 Barkos, the sons of Sis'era, the sons of Temah 2
56 sons of Nezi'ah, the sons of Hati'pha. 2
56 sons of Nezi'ah, the sons of Hati'pha. 2
57 sons of Solomon's servants: the sons of So'tai 2
57 sons of So'tai, the sons of So'phereth 2
57 sons of So'tai, the sons of So'phereth 2
57 the sons of So'phereth, the sons of Peri'da 2
58 sons of Ja'ala, the sons of Darkon 2
58 sons of Ja'ala, the sons of Darkon 2
58 Ja'ala, the sons of Darkon, the sons of Giddel 2
59 sons of Shephati'ah, the sons of Hattil 2
59 sons of Shephati'ah, the sons of Hattil 2
59 sons of Hattil, the sons of Po'chereth-hazzeba'im 2
59 sons of Po'chereth-hazzeba'im, the sons of Amon. 2
60 servants and the sons of Solomon's servants 2
62 sons of Delai'ah, the sons of Tobi'ah 2
62 sons of Delai'ah, the sons of Tobi'ah 2

62 Delai'ah, the sons of Tobi'ah, the sons of Neko'da 2
63 priests: the sons of Hobai'ah, the sons of Hakkoz 2
63 priests: the sons of Hobai'ah, the sons of Hakkoz 2
63 priests . . sons of Hakkoz, the sons of Barzil'lai 2
8:17 from the days of Jeshua the son of Nun to that day 2
10: 1 Nehemi'ah the governor, the son of Hacali'ah 2
9 Levites: Jeshua the son of Azani'ah, Bin'nui 2
9 Levites: Jeshua . . Bin'nui of the sons of Hen'adad 2
28 wives, their sons, their daughters, all who have 2
30 not give . . or take their daughters for our sons; 2
36 bring . . first-born of our sons and of our cattle 2
38 priest, the son of Aaron, shall be with the Levites 2
39 For the people of Israel and the sons of Levi 2
11: 4 Jerusalem lived certain of the sons of Judah 2
4 Jerusalem lived certain . . of the sons of Benjamin. 2
4 Of the sons of Judah: Athai'ah the son of Uzzi'ah 2
4 Athai'ah the son of Uzzi'ah, son of Zechari'ah 2
4 Athai'ah the son of Uzzi'ah, son of Zechari'ah 2
4 Zechari'ah, son of Amari'ah, son of Shephati'ah 2
4 Zechari'ah, son of Amari'ah, son of Shephati'ah 2
4 Shephati'ah, son of Mahal'alel, of the sons of Perez; 2
4 Shephati'ah, son of Mahal'alel, of the sons of Perez; 2
5 Ma-asei'ah the son of Baruch, son of Col-ho'zeh 2
5 Ma-asei'ah the son of Baruch, son of Col-ho'zeh 2
5 Col-ho'zeh, son of Hazai'ah, son of Adai'ah 2
5 Hazai'ah, son of Adai'ah, son of Joi'arib 2
5 Adai'ah, son of Joi'arib, son of Zechari'ah 2
5 Joi'arib, son of Zechari'ah, son of the Shi'lonite. 2
5 Joi'arib, son of Zechari'ah, son of the Shi'lonite. 2
6 sons of Perez who lived in Jerusalem were 468 2
7 these are the sons of Benjamin: Sallu the son 2
7 Sallu the son of Meshul'lam, son of Jo'ed 2
7 Sallu the son of Meshul'lam, son of Jo'ed 2
7 Jo'ed, son of Pedai'ah, son of Ko-lai'ah 2
7 Jo'ed, son of Pedai'ah, son of Ko-lai'ah 2
7 Ko-lai'ah, son of Ma-asei'ah, son of I'thi-el 2
7 Ma-asei'ah, son of I'thi-el, son of Jeshai'ah. 2
7 Ma-asei'ah, son of I'thi-el, son of Jeshai'ah. 2
9 Jo'el the son of Zichri was their overseer; 2
9 Judah the son of Hassen'u-ah was second over 2
10 Of the priests: Jedai'ah the son of Joi'arib, Jachin 2
11 Serai'ah the son of Hilki'ah, son of Meshul'lam 2
11 Serai'ah the son of Hilki'ah, son of Meshul'lam 2
11 Meshul'lam, son of Zadok, son of Merai'oth 2
11 Meshul'lam, son of Zadok, son of Merai'oth 2
11 Merai'oth, son of Ahi'tub, ruler of the house of God 2
12 Adai'ah the son of Jero'ham, son of Pelali'ah 2
12 Adai'ah the son of Jero'ham, son of Pelali'ah 2
12 Pelali'ah, son of Amzi, son of Zechari'ah 2
12 Pelali'ah, son of Amzi, son of Zechari'ah 2
12 Zechari'ah, son of Pashhur, son of Malchi'jah 2
12 Zechari'ah, son of Pashhur, son of Malchi'jah 2
13 Amash'sai, the son of Az'arel, son of Ah'zai 2
13 Amash'sai, the son of Az'arel, son of Ah'zai 2
13 son of Ah'zai, son of Meshil'lemoth, son of Immer 2
13 son of Ah'zai, son of Meshil'lemoth, son of Immer 2
14 overseer was Zab'diel the son of Haggedo'lim. 2
15 Shemai'ah the son of Hasshub, son of Azri'kam 2
15 Shemai'ah the son of Hasshub, son of Azri'kam 2
15 son of Azri'kam, son of Hashabi'ah, son of Bunni; 2
15 son of Azri'kam, son of Hashabi'ah, son of Bunni; 2
17 Mattani'ah the son of Mica, son of Zabdi 2
17 Mattani'ah the son of Mica, son of Zabdi 2
17 Mattani'ah . . of Mica, son of Zabdi, son of Asaph 2
17 Abda the son of Sham'mua, son of Galal 2
17 son of Sham'mua, son of Galal, son of Jedu'thun. 2
17 son of Sham'mua, son of Galal, son of Jedu'thun. 2
22 overseer . . Uzzi the son of Bani 2
22 son of Bani, son of Hashabi'ah, son of Mattani'ah 2
22 son of Bani, son of Hashabi'ah, son of Mattani'ah 2
22 son of Mattani'ah, son of Mica, of the sons of Asaph 2
22 son of Mattani'ah, son of Mica, of the sons of Asaph 2
24 Pethahi'ah the son of Meshez'abel, of the sons 2
24 Pethahi'ah . . of the sons of Zerah the son of Judah 2
24 Pethahi'ah . . of the sons of Zerah the son of Judah 2
12: 1 who came up with Zerub'babel the son of She-al'ti-el 2
23 sons of Levi, heads of fathers' houses 2
23 until the days of Joha'nan the son of Eli'ashib. 2
24 Sherebi'ah, and Jeshua the son of Kad'mi-el 2
26 days of Joi'akim the son of Jeshua son of Jo'zadak 2
26 days of Joi'akim the son of Jeshua son of Jo'zadak 2
28 sons of the singers gathered together 2
35 certain of the priests' sons with trumpets 2
35 Zechari'ah the son of Jonathan, son of Shemai'ah 2
35 Zechari'ah the son of Jonathan, son of Shemai'ah 2
35 Shemai'ah, son of Mattani'ah, son of Micai'ah, 2
35 Shemai'ah, son of Mattani'ah, son of Micai'ah, 2
35 son of Micai'ah, son of Zaccur, son of Asaph; 2
35 son of Micai'ah, son of Zaccur, son of Asaph; 2
45 command of David and his son Solomon. 2
47 set apart that which was for the sons of Aaron. 2
13:13 as their assistant Hanan the son of Zaccur, 2
13 Hanan the son of Zaccur, son of Mattani'ah 2
25 You shall not give your daughters to their sons 2
25 not . . take their daughters for your sons 2
28 one of the sons of Jehoi'ada, the son of Eli'ashib 2
28 Jehoi'ada, the son of Eli'ashib the high priest 2
Est 2: 5 name was Mor'decai, the son of Ja'ir, son of Shim'e-i 2
5 the son of Ja'ir, son of Shim'e-i, son of Kish 2
5 the son of Ja'ir, son of Shim'e-i, son of Kish 2
3: 1 Haman the Ag'agite, the son of Hammeda'tha 2
10 to Haman the Ag'agite, the son of Hammeda'tha 2
5:11 riches, the number of his sons, all the promotions 2
8: 5 by Haman the Ag'agite, the son of Hammeda'tha 2
9:10 the ten sons of Haman the son of Hammeda'tha 2
10 the ten sons of Haman the son of Hammeda'tha 2
12 Jews have slain . . and also the ten sons of Haman. 2
13 let the ten sons of Haman be hanged 2
14 and the ten sons of Haman were hanged. 2
24 For Haman the Ag'agite, the son of Hammeda'tha 2
25 he and his sons should be hanged on the gallows. 2
Job 1: 2 were born to him seven sons and three daughters. 2
4 His sons used to go and hold a feast in the house 2
5 for Job said, "It may be that my sons have sinned 2
6 when the sons of God came to present themselves 2
13 his sons and daughters were eating and drinking 2
18 Your sons and daughters were eating 2
2: 1 Again there was a day when the sons of God came 2
5: 4 His sons are far from safety 2
14:21 His sons come to honor, and he does not know it; 2
19:17 loathsome to the sons of my own mother. 2
21:19 God stores up their iniquity for their sons.' 2
25: 6 and the son of man, who is a worm! 2
32: 2 Then Eli'hu the son of Bar'achel the Buzite 2
6 Eli'hu the son of Bar'achel the Buzite answered 2
35: 8 and your righteousness a son of man. 2
38: 7 all the sons of God shouted for joy? 2
41:34 he is king over all the sons of pride. 2
42:13 He had also seven sons and three daughters. 2
16 saw his sons, and his sons' sons, four generations. 2
16 saw his sons, and his sons' sons, four generations. 2
16 saw his sons, and his sons' sons, four generations. 2
Ps 2: 7 You are my son, today I have begotten you. 2
3: 0 David, when he fled from Absalom his son. 2
8: 4 and the son of man that thou dost care for him? 2
12: 1 have vanished from among the sons of men. 2
8 as vileness is exalted among the sons of men. 2
21:10 their children from among the sons of men. 2
22:23 all you sons of Jacob, glorify him, and stand in awe 5
23 stand in awe of him, all you sons of Israel! 5
31:19 take refuge in thee, in the sight of the sons of men! 2
33:13 looks down from heaven, he sees all the sons of men; 2
34:11 Come, O sons, listen to me, I will teach you 2
42: 0 A Maskil of the Sons of Korah. 2
44: 0 A Maskil of the Sons of Korah. 2
45: 0 A Maskil of the Sons of Korah; a love song. 2
2 You are the fairest of the sons of men; 2
16 Instead of your fathers shall be your sons; 2
46: 0 To the choirmaster. A Psalm of the Sons of Korah. 2
47: 0 To the choirmaster. A Psalm of the Sons of Korah. 2
48: 0 A Song. A Psalm of the Sons of Korah. 2
49: 0 To the choirmaster. A Psalm of the Sons of Korah. 2
50:20 you slander your own mother's son. 2
53: 2 God looks down from heaven upon the sons of men 2
57: 4 of lions that greedily devour the sons of men; 2
58: 1 you gods? Do you judge the sons of men uprightly? 2
69: 8 I have become . . an alien to my mother's sons. 2
72: 1 O God, and thy righteousness to the royal son! 2
20 The prayers of David, the son of Jesse, are ended. 2
77:15 redeem thy people, the sons of Jacob and Joseph. 2
80:17 son of man whom thou hast made strong for thyself! 2
82: 6 I say, "You are gods, sons of the Most High, all of you; 2
84: 0 A Psalm of the Sons of Korah. 2
85: 0 To the choirmaster. A Psalm of the Sons of Korah. 2
86:16 save the son of thy handmaid. 2
87: 0 A Psalm of the Sons of Korah. A Song. 2
88: 0 A Song. A Psalm of the Sons of Korah. 2
89:47 what vanity thou hast created all the sons of men! 2
105: 6 sons of Jacob, his chosen ones! 2
106:37 They sacrificed their sons and their daughters 2
38 poured out . . blood of their sons and daughters 2
107: 8 for his wonderful works to the sons of men! 2
15 for his wonderful works to the sons of men! 2
21 for his wonderful works to the sons of men! 2
31 for his wonderful works to the sons of men! 2
115:16 but the earth he has given to the sons of men. 2
116:16 O LORD, I . . thy servant, the son of thy handmaid. 2
127: 3 Lo, sons are a heritage from the LORD 2
4 Like arrows . . are the sons of one's youth. 2
132:11 One of the sons of your body I will set 11
12 If your sons keep my covenant and my testimonies 2
12 sons also for ever shall sit upon your throne. 2
144: 3 LORD, what is . . son of man that thou dost think 2
12 our sons in their youth be like plants full grown 2
145:12 to make known to the sons of men thy mighty deeds 2
146: 3 Put not your trust in princes, in a son of man 2
147:13 For he . . blesses your sons within you. 2
149: 2 let the sons of Zion rejoice in their King! 2
Prv 1: 1 proverbs of Solomon, son of David, king of Israel 2
8 Hear, my son, your father's instruction 2
10 My son, if sinners entice you, do not consent. 2
15 my son, do not walk in the way with them 2
2: 1 My son, if you receive my words 2
3: 1 My son, do not forget my teaching 2
11 My son, do not despise the LORD'S discipline 2
12 as a father the son in whom he delights. 2
21 My son, keep sound wisdom and discretion; 2
4: 1 Hear, O sons, a father's instruction 2
3 When I was a son with my father, tender 2
10 Hear, my son, and accept my words 2
20 My son, be attentive to my words; 2
5: 1 My son, be attentive to my wisdom 2
7 now, O sons, listen to me 2
20 Why . . be infatuated, my son, with a loose woman 2
6: 1 My son, if you have become surety 2
3 then do this, my son, and save yourself 2
20 My son, keep your father's commandment 2
7: 1 My son, keep my words 2
24 now, O sons, listen to me 2
8: 4 To you, O men, I call, and my cry is to the sons of men. 2
31 delighting in the sons of men. 2
32 now, my sons, listen to me 2
10: 1 A wise son makes a glad father 2
1 but a foolish son is a sorrow to his mother. 2
5 A son who gathers in summer is prudent 2
5 but a son who sleeps in harvest brings shame. 2
13: 1 A wise son hears his father's instruction 2
24 He who spares the rod hates his son 2
15:20 A wise son makes a glad father 2
17: 2 wisely will rule over a son who acts shamefully 2
6 glory of sons is their fathers. 2
25 A foolish son is a grief to his father 2
19:13 A foolish son is ruin to his father 2
18 Discipline your son while there is hope; 2
26 son who causes shame and brings reproach. 2
27 Cease, my son, to hear instructions only to stray 2
20: 7 blessed are his sons after him! 2
23:15 My son, if your heart is wise, my heart too 2
19 Hear, my son, and be wise, and direct your mind 2
26 My son, give me your heart 2
24:13 My son, eat honey, for it is good 2
21 My son, fear the LORD and the king 2
27:11 Be wise, my son, and make my heart glad 2
28: 7 He who keeps the law is a wise son 2
29:17 Discipline your son, and he will give you rest; 2
30: 1 The words of Agur son of Jakeh of Massa. 2
4 What is his name, and what is his son's name? 2
31: 2 What, my son? What, son of my womb? 12
2 What, son of my womb? What, son of my vows? 3
2 What, son of my womb? What, son of my vows? 3
Ecc 1: 1 The words of the Preacher, the son of David 2
13 God has given to the sons of men to be busy with. 2
2: 3 I might see what was good for the sons of men to do 2
3:10 the business that God has given to the sons of men 2
18 I said . . with regard to the sons of men that God is 2
19 the fate of the sons of men and the fate of beasts 2
4: 8 a person who has no one, either son or brother 2
5:14 he is father of a son, but . . nothing in his hand. 2
8:11 the heart of the sons of men is fully set to do evil. 2
9:12 the sons of men are snared at an evil time 2
10:17 Happy . . when your king is the son of free men 2
12:12 My son, beware of anything beyond these. 2
Sng 1: 6 My mother's sons were angry with me 2
Isa 1: 1 The vision of Isaiah the son of Amoz, which he saw 2
2 Sons have I reared and brought up 2
4 offspring of evildoers, sons who deal corruptly! 2
2: 1 The word which Isaiah the son of Amoz saw 2
7: 1 In the days of Ahaz the son of Jotham, son of Uzzi'ah 2
1 In the days of Ahaz the son of Jotham, son of Uzzi'ah 2
1 Pekah the son of Remali'ah the king of Israel came 2
3 to Isaiah . . you and She'ar-jash'ub your son 2
4 of Rezin and Syria and the son of Remali'ah. 2
5 Syria, with E'phraim and the son of Remali'ah 2
6 set up the son of Ta'be-el as king in the midst of it 2
9 the head of Sama'ria is the son of Remali'ah. 2
14 conceive and bear a son, and shall call his name 2
8: 2 the priest and Zechari'ah the son of Jeberechi'ah 2
3 the prophetess, and she conceived and bore a son. 2
6 melt in fear before Rezin and the son of Remali'ah; 2
9: 6 For to us a child is born, to us a son is given; 2
13: 1 oracle . . which Isaiah the son of Amoz saw. 2
14:12 O Day Star, son of Dawn! How you are cut down 2
21 Prepare slaughter for his sons 2
19:11 I am a son of the wise, a son of ancient kings"? 2
11 I am a son of the wise, a son of ancient kings"? 2
20: 2 the LORD had spoken by Isaiah the son of Amoz 2
21:17 archers of the mighty men of the sons of Kedar 2
22:20 I will call my servant Eli'akim the son of Hilki'ah 2
30: 9 For they are a rebellious people, lying sons 2
9 sons who will not hear the instruction 2
36: 3 there came out to him Eli'akim the son of Hilki'ah 2
3 and Jo'ah the son of Asaph, the recorder. 2
22 Then Eli'akim the son of Hilki'ah 2
22 Jo'ah the son of Asaph, the recorder 2
37: 2 he sent . . to the prophet Isaiah the son of Amoz. 2
21 Isaiah the son of Amoz sent to Hezeki'ah, saying 2
38 Adram'melech and Share'zer, his sons, slew him 2
38 E'sar-had'don his son reigned in his stead. 2
38: 1 Isaiah the prophet the son of Amoz came to him 2
39: 1 At that time Mer'odach-bal'adan the son of Bal'adan 2
7 some of your own sons . . shall be taken away; 2
43: 6 bring my sons from afar and my daughters 2
49:15 have no compassion on the son of her womb? 2
22 and they shall bring your sons in their bosom 2
51:12 who dies, of the son of man who is made like grass 2
18 none to guide her among all the sons she has borne 2
18 by the hand among all the sons she has brought up. 2

20 Your sons have fainted, they lie at the head 2
52:14 and his form beyond that of the sons of men– 2
54:13 All your sons shall be taught by the LORD 2
13 and great shall be the prosperity of your sons. 2
56: 2 and the son of man who holds it fast 2
5 a name better than sons and daughters; 2
57: 3 But you, draw near hither, sons of the sorceress 2
60: 4 your sons shall come from far, and your daughters 2
9 of Tarshish first, to bring your sons from far 2
14 The sons of those who oppressed you shall come 2
62: 5 man marries a virgin, so shall your sons marry you 2
63: 8 they are my people, sons who will not deal falsely; 2
66: 7 before her pain . . she was delivered of a son. 4
8 as Zion was in labor she brought forth her sons. 2
Jer 1: 1 The words of Jeremiah, the son of Hilki'ah 2
2 in the days of Josi'ah the son of Amon, king of Judah 2
3 days of Jehoi'akim the son of Josi'ah, king of Judah 2
3 year of Zedeki'ah, the son of Josi'ah, king of Judah 2
3:19 I thought how I would set you among my sons 2
21 the weeping and pleading of Israel's sons 2
22 Return, O faithless sons 2
24 and their herds, their sons and their daughters. 2
5:17 they shall eat up your sons and your daughters; 2
6:21 they shall stumble; fathers and sons together 2
7:30 For the sons of Judah have done evil in my sight 2
31 which is in the valley of the son of Hinnom 2
31 to burn their sons and their daughters 2
32 called Topheth, or the valley of the son of Hinnom 2
9:26 Egypt, Judah, Edom, the sons of Ammon, Moab 2
11:22 sons and their daughters shall die by famine; 2
13:14 one against another, fathers and sons together 2
14:16 their wives, their sons, and their daughters. 2
15: 4 Manas'seh the son of Hezeki'ah, king of Judah 2
16: 2 nor shall you have sons or daughters 2
3 For thus says the LORD concerning the sons 2
19: 2 the valley of the son of Hinnom at the entry 2
5 to burn their sons in the fire as burnt offerings 2
6 called Topheth, or the valley of the son of Hinnom 2
9 I will make them eat the flesh of their sons 2
20: 1 Now Pashhur the priest, the son of Immer 2
15 brought the news to my father, "A son is born to you 2
21: 1 Pashhur the son of Malchi'ah 2
1 Zephani'ah the priest, the son of Ma-asei'ah, saying 2
22:11 Shallum the son of Josi'ah, king of Judah 2
18 Jehoi'akim the son of Josi'ah, king of Judah 2
24 though Coni'ah the son of Jehoi'akim, king of Judah 2
24: 1 Jeconi'ah the son of Jehoi'akim, king of Judah 2
25: 1 in the fourth year of Jehoi'akim the son of Josi'ah 2
3 from the thirteenth year of Josi'ah the son of Amon 2
21 Edom, Moab, and the sons of Ammon; 2
26: 1 Jehoi'akim the son of Josi'ah, king of Judah 2
20 Uri'ah the son of Shemai'ah from Kir'iath-je'arim. 2
22 Elna'than the son of Achbor and others with him 2
24 the hand of Ahi'kam the son of Shaphan 2
27: 1 Zedeki'ah the son of Josi'ah, king of Judah 2
3 the king of the sons of Ammon, the king of Tyre 2
7 All the nations shall serve him and his son 2
20 Jeconi'ah the son of Jehoi'akim, king of Judah 2
28: 1 Hanani'ah the son of Azzur 2
4 Jeconi'ah the son of Jehoi'akim, king of Judah 2
29: 3 was sent by the hand of Ela'sah the son of Shaphan 2
3 son of Shaphan and Gemari'ah the son of Hilki'ah 2
6 Take wives and have sons and daughters; 2
6 have sons and daughters; take wives for your sons 2
6 marriage, that they may bear sons and daughters; 2
21 concerning Ahab the son of Kola'iah and Zedeki'ah 2
21 son of Kola'iah and Zedeki'ah the son of Ma-asei'ah 2
25 and to Zephani'ah the son of Ma-asei'ah the priest 2
31:20 Is E'phraim my dear son? Is he my darling child? 2
32: 7 Behold, Han'amel the son of Shallum your uncle 2
12 to Baruch the son of Neri'ah son of Mahsei'ah 2
12 to Baruch the son of Neri'ah son of Mahsei'ah 2
16 the deed of purchase to Baruch the son of Neri'ah 2
30 the sons of Israel . . have done nothing but evil 2
30 and the sons of Judah have done nothing but evil 2
30 the sons of Israel have done nothing but provoke 2
32 because of all the evil of the sons of Israel 2
32 evil of the sons of Israel and the sons of Judah 2
35 high places . . in the valley of the son of Hinnom 2
35 to offer up their sons and daughters to Molech 2
33:21 that he shall not have a son to reign on his throne 2
35: 1 in the days of Jehoi'akim the son of Josi'ah 2
3 So I took Ja-azani'ah the son of Jeremiah 2
3 the son of Jeremiah, son of Habazzini'ah 2
3 Habazzini'ah, and his brothers, and all his sons 2
4 into the chamber of the sons of Hanan 2
4 sons of Hanan the son of Igdali'ah, the man of God 2
4 above the chamber of Ma-asei'ah the son of Shallum 2
6 for Jon'adab the son of Rechab, our father 2
6 shall not drink wine, neither you nor your sons 2
8 the voice of Jon'adab the son of Rechab, our father 2
8 ourselves, our wives, our sons, or our daughters 2
14 which Jon'adab the son of Rechab gave to his sons 2
14 which Jon'adab the son of Rechab gave to his sons 2
16 The sons of Jon'adab the son of Rechab 2
16 The sons of Jon'adab the son of Rechab 2
19 Jon'adab the son of Rechab shall never lack a man 2
36: 1 In the fourth year of Jehoi'akim the son of Josi'ah 2
4 Then Jeremiah called Baruch the son of Neri'ah 2
8 Baruch the son of Neri'ah did all that 2
9 In the fifth year of Jehoi'akim the son of Josi'ah 2
10 of Gemari'ah the son of Shaphan the secretary 2
11 When Micai'ah the son of Gemari'ah, son of Shaphan 2
11 When Micai'ah the son of Gemari'ah, son of Shaphan 2
12 Delai'ah the son of Shemai'ah 2
12 Elna'than the son of Achbor 2
12 Gemari'ah the son of Shaphan 2
12 Zedeki'ah the son of Hanani'ah, and all the princes. 2
14 all the princes sent Jehu'di the son of Nethani'ah 2
14 son of Nethani'ah, son of Shelemi'ah, son of Cushi 2
14 son of Nethani'ah, son of Shelemi'ah, son of Cushi 2
14 Baruch the son of Neri'ah took the scroll 2
26 And the king commanded Jerah'meel the king's son 2
26 the king commanded . . Serai'ah the son of Az'ri-el 2
26 and Shelemi'ah the son of Abdeel to seize Baruch 2
32 and gave it to Baruch the scribe, the son of Neri'ah 2
37: 1 Zedeki'ah the son of Josi'ah whom Nebuchadrez'zar 2
1 reigned instead of Coni'ah the son of Jehoi'akim. 2
3 King Zedeki'ah sent Jehu'cal the son of Shelemi'ah 2
3 and Zephani'ah the priest, the son of Ma-asei'ah 2
13 a sentry there named Iri'jah the son of Shelemi'ah 2
13 Iri'jah the son of Shelemi'ah, son of Hanani'ah 2
38: 1 Now Shephati'ah the son of Mattan 2
1 Gedali'ah the son of Pashhur 2
1 Jucal the son of Shelemi'ah 2
1 and Pashhur the son of Malchi'ah heard the words 2
6 into the cistern of Malchi'ah, the king's son 2
23 All your wives and your sons shall be led out 2
39: 6 The king of Babylon slew the sons of Zedeki'ah 2
14 They entrusted him to Gedali'ah the son of Ahi'kam 2
14 Gedali'ah the son of Ahi'kam, son of Shaphan 2
40: 5 then return to Gedali'ah the son of Ahi'kam 2
5 Gedali'ah the son of Ahi'kam, son of Shaphan 2
6 Then Jeremiah went to Gedali'ah the son of Ahi'kam 2
7 had appointed Gedali'ah the son of Ahi'kam 2
8 Ish'mael the son of Nethani'ah 2
8 Joha'nan the son of Kare'ah 2
8 Serai'ah the son of Tanhu'meth 2
8 the sons of Ephai the Netoph'athite 2
8 Jezani'ah the son of the Ma-ac'athite 2
9 Gedali'ah the son of Ahi'kam, son of Shaphan, swore 2
9 Gedali'ah the son of Ahi'kam, son of Shaphan, swore 2
11 and had appointed Gedali'ah the son of Ahi'kam 2
11 Gedali'ah the son of Ahi'kam, son of Shaphan 2
13 Now Joha'nan the son of Kare'ah and all the leaders 2
14 Ba'alis . . has sent Ish'mael the son of Nethani'ah 2
14 But Gedali'ah the son of Ahi'kam would not believe 2
15 Then Joha'nan the son of Kare'ah spoke secretly 2
15 Let me go and slay Ish'mael the son of Nethani'ah 2
16 But Gedali'ah the son of Ahi'kam said to Joha'nan 2
16 But Gedali'ah . . said to Joha'nan the son of Kare'ah 2
41: 1 Ish'mael the son of Nethani'ah, son of Eli'shama 2
1 Ish'mael the son of Nethani'ah, son of Eli'shama 2
1 came . . to Gedali'ah the son of Ahi'kam, at Mizpah. 2
2 Ish'mael the son of Nethani'ah and the ten men 2
2 Gedali'ah the son of Ahi'kam, son of Shaphan 2
2 Gedali'ah the son of Ahi'kam, son of Shaphan 2
6 And Ish'mael the son of Nethani'ah came out 2
6 Come in to Gedali'ah the son of Ahi'kam. 2
7 Ish'mael the son of Nethani'ah and the men with him 2
9 the son of Nethani'ah filled it with the slain. 2
10 had committed to Gedali'ah the son of Ahi'kam. 2
10 Ish'mael the son of Nethani'ah took them captive 2
11 But when Joha'nan the son of Kare'ah . . heard 2
11 evil which Ish'mael the son of Nethani'ah had done 2
12 to fight against Ish'mael the son of Nethani'ah. 2
13 saw Joha'nan the son of Kare'ah and all the leaders 2
14 came back, and went to Joha'nan the son of Kare'ah. 2
15 But Ish'mael the son of Nethani'ah escaped 2
16 Then Joha'nan the son of Kare'ah 2
16 whom Ish'mael the son of Nethani'ah had carried 2
16 after he had slain Gedali'ah the son of Ahi'kam 2
18 Ish'mael the son of Nethani'ah had slain Gedali'ah 2
18 Ish'mael . . had slain Gedali'ah the son of Ahi'kam 2
42: 1 and Joha'nan the son of Kare'ah 2
1 Azari'ah the son of Hoshai'ah, and all the people 2
8 Then he summoned Joha'nan the son of Kare'ah 2
43: 2 Azari'ah the son of Hoshai'ah 2
2 Jona'nan the son of Kare'ah 2
3 Baruch the son of Neri'ah has set you against us 2
4 Joha'nan the son of Kare'ah and all the commanders 2
5 Joha'nan the son of Kare'ah and all the commanders 2
6 guard had left with Gedali'ah the son of Ahi'kam 2
6 Gedali'ah the son of Ahi'kam, son of Shaphan; 2
6 also Jeremiah . . and Baruch the son of Neri'ah. 2
45: 1 the prophet spoke to Baruch the son of Neri'ah 2
1 in the fourth year of Jehoi'akim the son of Josi'ah 2
46: 2 Jehoi'akim the son of Josi'ah, king of Judah 2
48:45 forehead of Moab, the crown of the sons of tumult. 2
46 for your sons have been taken captive 2
49: 1 says the LORD: "Has Israel no sons? Has he no heir? 2
50:40 and no son of man shall sojourn in her. 2
51:43 and through which no son of man passes. 2
59 the prophet commanded Serai'ah the son of Neri'ah 2
59 Serai'ah the son of Neri'ah, son of Mahsei'ah 2
52:10 The king of Babylon slew the sons of Zedeki'ah 2
Lam 3:33 he does not . . afflict or grieve the sons of men. 2
4: 2 The precious sons of Zion, worth their weight 2
Ezk 1: 3 came to Ezekiel the priest, the son of Buzi 2
2: 1 And he said to me, "Son of man, stand upon your feet 2
3 Son of man, I send you to the people of Israel 2
6 And you, son of man, be not afraid of them 2
8 But you, son of man, hear what I say to you; 2
3: 1 he said to me, "Son of man, eat what is offered to you; 2
3 Son of man, eat this scroll that I give you 2
4 Son of man, go, get you to the house of Israel 2
10 Son of man, all my words that I shall speak to you 2
17 Son of man, I have made you a watchman 2
25 O son of man, behold, cords will be placed upon you 2
4: 1 you, O son of man, take a brick and lay it before you 2
16 Son of man, behold, I will break the staff of bread 2
5: 1 And you, O son of man, take a sharp sword; 2
10 fathers shall eat their sons in the midst of you 2
10 and sons shall eat their fathers; 2
6: 2 Son of man, set your face toward the mountains 2
7: 2 And you, O son of man, thus says the Lord GOD 2
8: 5 Then he said to me, "Son of man, lift up your eyes now 2
6 Son of man, do you see what they are doing 2
8 Then said he to me, "Son of man, dig in the wall"; 2
11 with Ja-azani'ah the son of Shaphan standing among 2
12 Then he said to me, "Son of man, have you seen 2
15 he said to me, "Have you seen this, O son of man? 2
17 he said to me, "Have you seen this, O son of man? 2
11: 1 I saw among them Ja-azani'ah the son of Azzur 2
1 the son of Azzur, and Pelati'ah the son of Benai'ah 2
2 And he said to me, "Son of man, these are the men 2
4 prophesy against them, prophesy, O son of man. 2
13 Pelati'ah the son of Benai'ah died. 2
15 Son of man, your brethren, even your brethren 2
12: 2 Son of man, you dwell in the midst of a rebellious 2
3 son of man, prepare for yourself an exile's 2
9 Son of man, has not the house of Israel 2
18 Son of man, eat your bread with quaking 2
22 Son of man, what is this proverb that you have 2
27 Son of man, behold, they of the house of Israel say 2
13: 2 Son of man, prophesy against the prophets 2
17 son of man, set your face against the daughters 2
14: 3 Son of man, these men have taken their idols 2
13 Son of man, when a land sins against me by acting 2
16 they would deliver neither sons nor daughters; 2
18 they would deliver neither sons nor daughters 2
20 they would deliver neither son nor daughter; 2
22 any survivors to lead out sons and daughters 2
15: 2 Son of man, how does the wood of the vine surpass 2
16: 2 Son of man, make known to Jerusalem her 2
20 And you took your sons and your daughters 2
17: 2 Son of man, propound a riddle 2
18: 4 soul of the father as well as the soul of the son 2
10 If he begets a son who is a robber 2
14 if this man begets a son who sees all the sins 2
19 Why should not the son suffer for the iniquity 2
19 When the son has done what is lawful and right 2
20 The son shall not suffer for the iniquity 2
20 nor the father suffer for the iniquity of the son; 2
20: 3 Son of man, speak to the elders of Israel 2
4 Will you judge them, son of man, will you judge them? 2
27 Therefore, son of man, speak to the house of Israel 2
31 offer your gifts and sacrifice your sons by fire 2
46 Son of man, set your face toward the south 2
21: 2 Son of man, set your face toward Jerusalem 2
6 Sigh therefore, son of man; 2
9 Son of man, prophesy and say, Thus says the Lord, 2
10 despised the rod, my son, with everything of wood. 2
12 Cry and wail, son of man, for it is against my people; 2
14 Prophesy therefore, son of man; clap your hands 2
19 Son of man, mark two ways for the sword of the king 2
28 son of man, prophesy, and say, Thus says the Lord 2
22: 2 And you, son of man, will you judge 2
18 Son of man, the house of Israel has become dross 2
24 Son of man, say to her, You are a land that is not 2
23: 2 Son of man, there were two women, the daughters 2
4 they bore sons and daughters. 2
10 they seized her sons and her daughters; 2
25 They shall seize your sons and your daughters 2
36 Son of man, will you judge Oho'lah and Ohol'ibah? 2
37 have even offered up to them for food the sons 2
47 they shall slay their sons and their daughters 2
24: 2 Son of man, write down the name of this day 2
16 Son of man, behold, I am about to take the delight 2
21 your sons and your daughters whom you left 2
25 you, son of man, on the day when I take from them 2
25 heart's desire, and also their sons and daughters 2
25: 2 Son of man, set your face toward the Ammonites 2
26: 2 Son of man, because Tyre said concerning 2
27: 2 Now you, son of man, raise a lamentation over Tyre 2
28: 2 Son of man, say to the prince of Tyre 2
12 Son of man, raise a lamentation over the king 2
21 Son of man, set your face toward Sidon 2
29: 2 Son of man, set your face against Pharaoh 2
18 Son of man, Nebuchadrez'zar king of Babylon made 2
30: 2 Son of man, prophesy, and say, Thus says the Lord 2
21 Son of man, I have broken the arm of Pharaoh king 2
31: 2 Son of man, say to Pharaoh king of Egypt and to his 2
32: 2 Son of man, raise a lamentation over Pharaoh king 2
18 Son of man, wail over the multitude of Egypt 2
33: 2 Son of man, speak to your people and say to them 2
7 you, son of man, I have made a watchman 2

10 And you, son of man, say to the house of Israel 2
12 And you, son of man, say to your people 2
24 Son of man, the inhabitants of these waste places 2
30 son of man, your people who talk together 2
34: 2 Son of man, prophesy against the shepherds 2
35: 2 Son of man, set your face against Mount Se'ir 2
36: 1 son of man, prophesy to the mountains of Israel 2
17 Son of man, when the house of Israel dwelt 2
37: 3 he said to me, "Son of man, can these bones live? 2
9 Prophesy to the breath, prophesy, son of man, 2
11 Then he said to me, "Son of man 2
16 Son of man, take a stick and write on it, 'For Judah 2
38: 2 Son of man, set your face toward Gog 2
14 Therefore, son of man, prophesy, and say to Gog 2
39: 1 And you, son of man, prophesy against Gog, 2
17 As for you, son of man, thus says the Lord GOD 2
40: 4 the man said to me, "Son of man, look with your eyes 2
46 these are the sons of Zadok 2
46 sons of Zadok, who alone among the sons of Levi may 2
43: 7 Son of man, this is the place of my throne 2
10 And you, son of man, describe to the house of Israel 2
18 he said to me, "Son of man, thus says the Lord GOD 2
44: 5 And the LORD said to me, "Son of man, mark well 2
15 But the Levitical priests, the sons of Zadok 2
25 however, for father or mother, for son or daughter 2
46:16 a gift to any of his sons out of his inheritance 2
16 it shall belong to his sons, it is their property 2
17 his sons may keep a gift from his inheritance. 2
18 he shall give his sons their inheritance 2
47: 6 And he said to me, "Son of man, have you seen this? 2
22 They shall be to you as native-born sons of Israel; 2
48:11 for the consecrated priests, the sons of Zadok 2
Dan 2:38 given . . the sons of men, the beasts of the field 12
3:25 appearance of the fourth is like a son of the gods. 12
5:22 his son, Belshaz'zar, have not humbled your heart 12
7:13 clouds of heaven there came one like a son of man 12
8:17 said to me, "Understand, O son of man, 2
9: 1 In the first year of Darius the son of Ahasu-e'rus 2
10:16 likeness of the sons of men touched my lips; 2
11:10 His sons shall wage war and assemble a multitude 2
Hos 1: 1 The word . . that came to Hose'a the son of Be-e'ri 2
1 and in the days of Jerobo'am the son of Jo'ash 2
3 Gomer . . and she conceived and bore him a son. 2
8 Not pitied, she conceived and bore a son. 2
10 it shall be said to them, "Sons of the living God. 2
9:13 E'phraim's sons . . are destined for a prey; •
13 E'phraim must lead forth his sons to slaughter. 2
11: 1 and out of Egypt I called my son. 2
10 and his sons shall come trembling from the west; 2
13:13 but he is an unwise son; 2
Jol 1: 1 The word . . that came to Joel, the son of Pethu'el 2
12 and gladness fails from the sons of men. 2
2:23 Be glad, O sons of Zion, and rejoice in the LORD 2
28 your sons and your daughters shall prophesy 2
3: 8 I will sell your sons and your daughters 2
8 your daughters into the hand of the sons of Judah 2
Ams 1: 1 and in the days of Jerobo'am the son of Jo'ash, 2
2:11 And I raised up some of your sons for prophets 2
7:14 answered . . "I am no prophet, nor a prophet's son 2
17 sons and your daughters shall fall by the sword 2
Jon 1: 1 the LORD came to Jonah the son of Amit'tai, saying 2
Mic 5: 7 which tarry not . . nor wait for the sons of men. 2
6: 5 and what Balaam the son of Be'or answered him 2
7: 6 for the son treats the father with contempt 2
Zep 1: 1 Zephani'ah the son of Cushi, son of Gedali'ah 2
1 Zephani'ah the son of Cushi, son of Gedali'ah 2
1 son of Gedali'ah, son of Amari'ah, son of Hezeki'ah 2
1 son of Gedali'ah, son of Amari'ah, son of Hezeki'ah 2
1 Hezeki'ah, in the days of Josi'ah the son of Amon 2
8 I will punish the officials and the king's sons 2
Hag 1: 1 to Zerub'babel the son of She-al'ti-el, governor 2
1 to Joshua the son of Jehoz'adak, the high priest 2
12 Then Zerub'babel the son of She-al'ti-el 2
12 Joshua the son of Jehoz'adak, the high priest 2
14 spirit of Zerub'babel the son of She-al'ti-el 2
14 the spirit of Joshua the son of Jehoz'adak 2
2: 2 Speak now to Zerub'babel the son of She-al'ti-el 2
2 to Joshua the son of Jehoz'adak, the high priest 2
4 take courage, O Joshua, son of Jehoz'adak 2
23 O Zerub'babel my servant, the son of She-al'ti-el 2
Zec 1: 1 to Zechari'ah the son of Berechi'ah, son of Iddo 2
1 to Zechari'ah the son of Berechi'ah, the son of Iddo 2
7 the son of Berechi'ah, son of Iddo, the prophet; 2
7 the son of Berechi'ah, son of Iddo, the prophet; 2
6:10 to the house of Josi'ah, the son of Zephani'ah. 2
11 of Joshua, the son of Jehoz'adak, the high priest; 2
14 Jedai'ah, and Josi'ah the son of Zephani'ah. 2
9:13 I will brandish your sons, O Zion 2
13 brandish your sons, O Zion, over your sons, O Greece 2
Mal 1: 6 A son honors his father, and a servant his master. 2
3: 3 he will purify the sons of Levi and refine them 2
6 therefore you, O sons of Jacob, are not consumed. 2
17 I will spare them as a man spares his son 2
Mat 1: 1 Jesus Christ, the son of David, the son of Abraham. 21
1 Jesus Christ, the son of David, the son of Abraham. 21
20 in a dream, saying, "Joseph, son of David, do not fear 21
21 she will bear a son, and you shall call his name 21
23 virgin shall conceive and bear a son, and his name 21
25 she had borne a son; and he called his name Jesus. 21
2:15 the prophet, "Out of Egypt have I called my son. 21
3:17 my beloved Son, with whom I am well pleased. 21
4: 3 If you are the Son of God, command these stones 21
6 If you are the Son of God, throw yourself down; 21
21 other brothers, James the son of Zeb'edee and John 14
5: 9 for they shall be called sons of God. 21
45 so that you may be sons of your Father 21
7: 9 Or what man of you, if his son asks him for bread 21
8:12 while the sons of the kingdom will be thrown 21
20 but the Son of man has nowhere to lay his head. 21
29 What have you to do with us, O Son of God? 21
9: 2 Take heart, my son; your sins are forgiven. 19
6 you may know that the Son of man has authority 21
27 Have mercy on us, Son of David. 21
10: 2 James the son of Zeb'edee, and John his brother; 14
3 James the son of Alphaeus, and Thaddaeus; 14
23 before the Son of man comes. 21
37 and he who loves son or daughter more than me 21
11:19 the Son of man came eating and drinking 21
27 and no one knows the Son except the Father 21
27 and no one knows the Father except the Son 21
27 any one to whom the Son chooses to reveal him. 21
12: 8 For the Son of man is lord of the sabbath. 21
23 Can this be the Son of David? 21
27 by whom do your sons cast them out? 21
32 whoever says a word against the Son of man 21
40 so will the Son of man be three days 21
13:37 He who sows the good seed is the Son of man; 21
38 and the good seed means the sons of the kingdom 21
38 the weeds are the sons of the evil one 21
41 The Son of man will send his angels 21
55 Is not this the carpenter's son? 21
14:33 Truly you are the Son of God. 21
15:22 Have mercy on me, O Lord, Son of David 21
16:13 Who do men say that the Son of man is? 21
16 You are the Christ, the Son of the living God. 21
27 For the Son of man is to come with his angels 21
28 before they see the Son of man coming 21
17: 5 This is my beloved Son 21
9 until the Son of man is raised from the dead. 21
12 So also the Son of man will suffer at their hands. 21
15 Lord, have mercy on my son, for he is an epileptic 21
22 Son of man is to be delivered into the hands of men 21
25 From their sons or from others? 21
26 Jesus said to him, "Then the sons are free. 21
19:28 the Son of man shall sit on his glorious throne 21
20:18 the Son of man will be delivered 21
20 came up to him, with her sons 21
20 the mother of the sons of Zeb'edee came up to him 21
21 Command that these two sons of mine may sit 21
28 the Son of man came not to be served but to serve 21
30 Have mercy on us, Son of David! 21
31 Lord, have mercy on us, Son of David! 21
21: 9 shouted, "Hosanna to the Son of David! 21
15 Hosanna to the Son of David! 21
28 What do you think? A man had two sons 19
28 'Son, go and work in the vineyard today.' 19
37 Afterward he sent his son to them, saying 21
37 'They will respect my son.' 21
38 the tenants saw the son, they said to themselves 21
22: 2 to a king who gave a marriage feast for his son 21
42 What do you think of the Christ? Whose son is he? 21
42 They said to him, "The son of David. 14
45 If David thus calls him Lord, how is he his son? 21
23:31 you are sons of those who murdered the prophets. 21
35 to the blood of Zechari'ah the son of Barachi'ah 21
24:27 so will be the coming of the Son of man. 21
30 the sign of the Son of man in heaven 21
30 see the Son of man coming on the clouds of heaven 21
36 not even the angels of heaven, nor the Son 21
37 so will be the coming of the Son of man. 21
39 so will be the coming of the Son of man. 21
44 the Son of man is coming at an hour 21
25:31 When the Son of man comes in his glory 21
26: 2 the Son of man will be delivered up 21
24 The Son of man goes as it is written of him 21
24 woe to that man by whom the Son of man is betrayed! 21
37 taking with him Peter and the two sons of Zeb'edee 21
45 Son of man is betrayed into the hands of sinners. 21
63 tell us if you are the Christ, the Son of God. 21
64 hereafter you will see the Son of man 21
27: 9 a price had been set by some of the sons of Israel 21
40 If you are the Son of God, come down from the cross. 21
43 he said, 'I am the Son of God.' 21
54 Truly this was the Son of God! 21
56 the mother of the sons of Zeb'edee. 21
28:19 Father and of the Son and of the Holy Spirit 21
Mrk 1: 1 the Son of God. 21
11 a voice came from heaven, "Thou art my beloved Son; 21
19 he saw James the son of Zeb'edee •
2: 5 My son, your sins are forgiven. 19
10 Son of man has authority on earth to forgive sins"- 21
14 as he passed on, he saw Levi the son of Alphaeus •
28 the Son of man is lord even of the sabbath. 21
3:11 You are the Son of God. 21
17 James the son of Zeb'edee •
17 surnamed Bo-aner'ges, that is, sons of thunder; 21
18 and Thomas, and James the son of Alphaeus •
28 all sins will be forgiven the sons of men 21
5: 7 Jesus, Son of the Most High God? 21
6: 3 Is not this the carpenter, the son of Mary 21
8:31 the Son of man must suffer many things 21
38 of him will the Son of man also be ashamed 21
9: 7 This is my beloved Son; listen to him. 21
9 until the Son of man should have risen 21
12 how is it written of the Son of man 21
17 I brought my son to you, for he has a dumb spirit; 21
31 The Son of man will be delivered 21
10:33 Son of man will be delivered to the chief priests 21
35 James and John, the sons of Zeb'edee, came forward 21
45 Son of man also came not to be served but to serve 21
46 Bartimae'us, a blind beggar, the son of Timae'us 21
47 Jesus, Son of David, have mercy on me! 21
48 he cried out all the more, "Son of David, have mercy 21
12: 6 He had still one other, a beloved son 21
6 'They will respect my son.' 21
35 scribes say that the Christ is the son of David? 21
37 David himself calls him Lord; so how is he his son? 21
13:26 then they will see the Son of man coming in clouds 21
32 nor the Son, but only the Father. 21
14:21 For the Son of man goes as it is written of him 21
21 woe to that man by whom the Son of man is betrayed! 21
41 Son of man is betrayed into the hands of sinners. 21
61 Are you the Christ, the Son of the Blessed? 21
62 Jesus said, "I am; and you will see the Son of man 21
15:39 he said, "Truly this man was the Son of God! 21
Lke 1:13 your wife Elizabeth will bear you a son 21
16 he will turn many of the sons of Israel to the Lord 21
31 you will conceive in your womb and bear a son 21
32 He . . will be called the Son of the Most High 21
35 the child to be born will be called holy, the Son of God 21
36 Elizabeth in her old age has also conceived a son; 21
57 and she gave birth to a son. 21
2: 7 she gave birth to her first-born son 21
48 Son, why have you treated us so? 19
3: 2 the word of God came to John the son of Zechari'ah 21
22 my beloved Son; with thee I am well pleased. 21
23 being the son (as was supposed) of Joseph 21
23 Joseph, the son of Heli •
24 the son of Matthat, the son of Levi •
24 the son of Matthat, the son of Levi •
24 the son of Matthat, the son of Levi •
24 son of Melchi, the son of Jan'nai, the son of Joseph •
24 son of Melchi, the son of Jan'nai, the son of Joseph •
25 the son of Mattathi'as, the son of Amos •
25 the son of Mattathi'as, the son of Amos •
25 the son of Nahum, the son of Esli, the son of Nag'gai •
25 the son of Nahum, the son of Esli, the son of Nag'gai •
25 the son of Nahum, the son of Esli, the son of Nag'gai •
26 the son of Ma'ath, the son of Mattathi'as •
26 the son of Ma'ath, the son of Mattathi'as •
26 the son of Sem'ein, the son of Josech, the son of Joda •
26 the son of Sem'ein, the son of Josech, the son of Joda •
26 the son of Sem'ein, the son of Josech, the son of Joda •
27 the son of Joan'an, the son of Rhesa •
27 the son of Joan'an, the son of Rhesa •
27 the son of Zerub'babel, the son of She-al'ti-el •
27 the son of Zerub'babel, the son of She-al'ti-el •
27 the son of She-al'ti-el, the son of Neri •
28 the son of Melchi, the son of Addi, the son of Cosam •
28 the son of Melchi, the son of Addi, the son of Cosam •
28 the son of Melchi, the son of Addi, the son of Cosam •
28 son of Cosam, the son of Elma'dam, the son of Er •
28 son of Cosam, the son of Elma'dam, the son of Er •
29 the son of Joshua, the son of Elie'zer •
29 the son of Joshua, the son of Elie'zer •
29 son of Elie'zer, the son of Jorim, the son of Matthat •
29 son of Elie'zer, the son of Jorim, the son of Matthat •
29 the son of Matthat, the son of Levi •
30 the son of Simeon, the son of Judah •
30 the son of Simeon, the son of Judah •
30 the son of Joseph, the son of Jonam •
30 the son of Joseph, the son of Jonam •
30 the son of Jonam, the son of Eli'akim •
31 the son of Me'le-a, the son of Menna •
31 the son of Me'le-a, the son of Menna •
31 son of Menna, the son of Mat'tatha, the son of Nathan •
31 son of Menna, the son of Mat'tatha, the son of Nathan •
31 the son of Nathan, the son of David •
32 the son of Jesse, the son of Obed, the son of Bo'az •
32 the son of Jesse, the son of Obed, the son of Bo'az •
32 the son of Jesse, the son of Obed, the son of Bo'az •
32 son of Bo'az, the son of Sala, the son of Nahshon •
32 son of Bo'az, the son of Sala, the son of Nahshon •
33 the son of Ammin'adab, the son of Admin •
33 the son of Ammin'adab, the son of Admin •
33 the son of Arni, the son of Hezron, the son of Perez •
33 the son of Arni, the son of Hezron, the son of Perez •
33 son of Hezron, the son of Perez, the son of Judah •
33 son of Hezron, the son of Perez, the son of Judah •
34 the son of Jacob, the son of Isaac •
34 the son of Jacob, the son of Isaac •
34 son of Isaac, the son of Abraham, the son of Terah •
34 son of Isaac, the son of Abraham, the son of Terah •
34 son of Isaac, the son of Abraham, the son of Terah •
35 the son of Serug, the son of Re'u, the son of Peleg •
35 the son of Serug, the son of Re'u, the son of Peleg •
35 the son of Serug, the son of Re'u, the son of Peleg •

35 son of Peleg, the son of Eber, the son of Shelah •
35 son of Peleg, the son of Eber, the son of Shelah •
36 the son of Ca-i'nan, the son of Arphax'ad •
36 the son of Ca-i'nan, the son of Arphax'ad •
36 the son of Shem, the son of Noah, the son of Lamech •
36 the son of Shem, the son of Noah, the son of Lamech •
36 the son of Shem, the son of Noah, the son of Lamech •
37 the son of Methuselah, the son of Enoch •
37 the son of Methuselah, the son of Enoch •
37 the son of Jared, the son of Maha'lele-el •
37 the son of Jared, the son of Maha'lele-el •
37 the son of Maha'lele-el, the son of Ca-i'nan •
38 the son of Enos, the son of Seth, the son of Adam •
38 the son of Enos, the son of Seth, the son of Adam •
38 son of Seth, the son of Adam, the son of God. •
38 son of Seth, the son of Adam, the son of God. •
4: 3 The devil said to him, "If you are the Son of God 21
9 said to him, "If you are the Son of God 21
22 they said, "Is not this Joseph's son? 21
41 You are the Son of God! 21
5:10 so also were James and John, sons of Zeb'edee 21
24 you may know that the Son of man has authority 21
6: 5 The Son of man is lord of the sabbath. 21
15 and Thomas, and James the son of Alphaeus •
16 Judas the son of James, and Judas Iscariot •
22 revile you . . on account of the Son of man! 21
35 you will be sons of the Most High 21
7:12 the only son of his mother, and she was a widow 21
34 The Son of man has come eating and drinking; 21
8:28 Jesus, Son of the Most High God 21
9:22 saying, "The Son of man must suffer many things 21
26 of him will the Son of man be ashamed 21
35 This is my Son, my Chosen; listen to him! 21
38 I beg you to look upon my son, for he is my only child; 21
41 Bring your son here. 21
44 the Son of man is to be delivered 21
58 the Son of man has nowhere to lay his head. 21
10: 6 if a son of peace is there 21
22 who the Father is except the Son 21
22 and any one to whom the Son chooses to reveal him. 21
22 and any one to whom the Son chooses to reveal him. 21
11:11 What father among you, if his son asks for a fish 21
19 by whom do your sons cast them out? 21
30 so will the Son of man be to this generation. 21
12: 8 the Son of man also will acknowledge 21
10 every one who speaks a word against the Son of man 21
40 the Son of man is coming at an unexpected hour. 21
53 father against son and son against father 21
53 father against son and son against father 21
14: 5 a son or an ox that has fallen into a well 21
15:11 he said, "There was a man who had two sons; 21
13 Not many days later, the younger son gathered all 21
19 I am no longer worthy to be called your son 21
21 the son said to him, 'Father, I have sinned 21
21 I am no longer worthy to be called your son.' 21
24 this my son was dead, and is alive again 21
25 Now his elder son was in the field 21
30 when this son of yours came 21
31 he said to him, 'Son, you are always with me 19
16: 8 the sons of this world are more shrewd 21
8 more shrewd . . than the sons of light. 21
25 Abraham said, 'Son, remember 19
17:22 will desire to see one of the days of the Son of man 21
24 so will the Son of man be in his day. 21
26 so will it be in the days of the Son of man. 21
30 on the day when the Son of man is revealed. 21
18: 8 Nevertheless, when the Son of man comes 21
31 everything that is written of the Son of man 21
38 he cried, "Jesus, Son of David, have mercy on me! 21
39 Son of David, have mercy on me! 21
19: 9 since he also is a son of Abraham. 21
10 the Son of man came to seek and to save the lost. 21
20:13 I will send my beloved son 21
34 Jesus said to them, "The sons of this age marry 21
36 they are equal to angels and are sons of God 21
36 sons of God, being sons of the resurrection. 21
41 How can they say that the Christ is David's son? 21
44 David thus calls him Lord; so how is he his son? 21
21:27 then they will see the Son of man coming in a cloud 21
36 to stand before the Son of man. 21
22:22 For the Son of man goes as it has been determined; 21
48 would you betray the Son of man with a kiss? 21
69 from now on the Son of man shall be seated 21
70 they all said, "Are you the Son of God, then? 21
24: 7 the Son of man must be delivered 21
Joh 1:34 borne witness that this is the Son of God. 21
42 So you are Simon the son of John? 21
45 found him . . Jesus of Nazareth, the son of Joseph 21
49 Rabbi, you are the Son of God! 21
51 ascending and descending upon the Son of man. 21
3:13 but he who descended from heaven, the Son of man. 21
14 so must the Son of man be lifted up 21
16 God so loved the world that he gave his only Son 21
17 For God sent the Son into the world 21
18 not believed in the name of the only Son of God. 21
35 the Father loves the Son, and has given all things 21
36 He who believes in the Son has eternal life; 21
36 he who does not obey the Son shall not see life 21
4: 5 near the field that Jacob gave to his son Joseph. 21
12 drank from it himself, and his sons, and his cattle? 21
46 there was an official whose son was ill. 21
47 went and begged him to come down and heal his son 21
50 Jesus said to him, "Go; your son will live. 21
51 his servants . . told him that his son was living 17
53 Jesus had said to him, "Your son will live"; 21
5:19 the Son can do nothing of his own accord 21
19 whatever he does, that the Son does likewise. 21
20 For the Father loves the Son 21
21 so also the Son gives life to whom he will. 21
22 has given all judgment to the Son 21
23 that all may honor the Son 21
23 He who does not honor the Son 21
25 when the dead will hear the voice of the Son of God 21
26 he has granted the Son also to have life in himself 21
27 because he is the Son of man. 21
6:27 which the Son of man will give to you 21
40 every one who sees the Son and believes in him 21
42 They said, "Is not this Jesus, the son of Joseph 21
53 unless you eat the flesh of the Son of man 21
62 what if you were to see the Son of man ascending 21
71 He spoke of Judas the son of Simon Iscariot •
8:28 Jesus said, "When you have lifted up the Son of man 21
35 the son continues for ever. 21
36 if the Son makes you free, you will be free indeed. 21
9:19 Is this your son, who you say was born blind? 21
20 His parents answered, "We know that this is our son 21
35 Do you believe in the Son of Man? 21
10:36 because I said, 'I am the Son of God'? 21
11: 4 so that the Son of God may be glorified 21
27 I believe that you are the Christ, the Son of God 21
12:23 The hour . . for the Son of man to be glorified. 21
34 How can you say . . the Son of man must be lifted up? 21
34 Who is this Son of man? 21
36 that you may become sons of light 21
13: 2 the heart of Judas Iscariot, Simon's son •
26 he gave it to Judas, the son of Simon Iscariot. •
31 Now is the Son of man glorified 21
14:13 that the Father may be glorified in the Son; 21
17: 1 Father, the hour has come; glorify thy Son 21
1 glorify thy Son that the Son may glorify thee 21
12 none of them is lost but the son of perdition 21
19: 7 because he has made himself the Son of God. 21
26 he said to his mother, "Woman, behold, your son! 21
20:31 Jesus is the Christ, the Son of God 21
21: 2 Nathan'a-el of Cana in Galilee, the sons of Zeb'edee •
15 Jesus said to Simon Peter, "Simon, son of John •
16 A second time he said to him, "Simon, son of John •
17 Simon, son of John, do you love me? •
Act 1:13 James the son of Alphaeus and Simon the Zealot •
13 Simon the Zealot and Judas the son of James. •
2:17 your sons and your daughters shall prophesy 21
3:25 the sons of the prophets and of the covenant 21
4:36 Barnabas (which means, Son of encouragement) 21
7:16 bought . . from the sons of Hamor in Shechem. 21
21 and brought him up as her own son. 21
23 to visit his brethren, the sons of Israel. 21
29 Mid'ian, where he became the father of two sons. 21
56 the Son of man standing at the right hand of God. 21
9:15 Gentiles and kings and the sons of Israel; 21
20 He is the Son of God. 21
13:10 said, "You son of the devil 21
21 Saul the son of Kish, a man of the tribe of Benjamin 21
22 I have found in David the son of Jesse a man •
26 Brethren, sons of the family of Abraham 21
33 'Thou art my Son, today I have begotten thee.' 21
16: 1 the son of a Jewish woman who was a believer 21
19:14 Seven sons of a Jewish high priest named Sceva 21
20: 4 Sop'ater of Beroe'a, the son of Pyrrhus •
28 which he obtained with the blood of his own Son. •
23: 6 Brethren, I am a Pharisee, a son of Pharisees 21
16 Now the son of Paul's sister heard of their ambush; 21
Rom 1: 3 the gospel concerning his Son 21
4 designated Son of God in power 21
9 I serve with my spirit in the gospel of his Son 21
5:10 reconciled to God by the death of his Son 21
8: 3 his own Son in the likeness of sinful flesh 21
14 all who are led by the Spirit of God are sons of God 21
19 waits . . for the revealing of the sons of God; 21
29 to be conformed to the image of his Son 21
32 He who did not spare his own Son but gave him up 21
9: 9 I will return and Sarah shall have a son. 21
26 they will be called 'sons of the living God.' 21
27 Though the number of the sons of Israel be 21
1Co 1: 9 the fellowship of his Son, Jesus Christ our Lord. 21
15:28 then the Son himself will also be subjected 21
2Co 1:19 For the Son of God, Jesus Christ, whom we preached 21
6:18 you shall be my sons and daughters, says the Lord 21
Gal 1:16 was pleased to reveal his Son to me 21
2:20 I live by faith in the Son of God 21
3: 7 it is men of faith who are the sons of Abraham. 21
26 for in Christ Jesus you are all sons of God 21
4: 4 God sent forth his Son 21
6 because you are sons, God has sent the Spirit 21
6 God has sent the Spirit of his Son into our hearts 21
7 So through God you are no longer a slave but a son 21
7 if a son then an heir. 21
22 For it is written that Abraham had two sons 21
23 the son of the slave was born according to the flesh •
23 the son of the free woman through promise. •
30 Cast out the slave and her son 21
30 the son of the slave shall not inherit 21
30 not inherit with the son of the free woman. 21
Eph 1: 5 to be his sons through Jesus Christ 20
2: 2 is now at work in the sons of disobedience. 21
3: 5 the sons of men in other generations 21
4:13 the knowledge of the Son of God 21
5: 6 comes upon the sons of disobedience. 21
Php 2:22 how as a son with a father he has served with me 19
Col 1:13 transferred us to the kingdom of his beloved Son 21
1Th 1:10 to wait for his Son from heaven 21
5: 5 For you are all sons of light 21
5 of light and sons of the day; 21
2Th 2: 3 the son of perdition 21
1Ti 1:18 This charge I commit to you, Timothy, my son 19
2Ti 2: 1 You then, my son, be strong 19
Heb 1: 2 in these last days he has spoken to us by a Son 21
5 Thou art my Son, today I have begotten thee"? 21
5 he shall be to me a son"? 21
8 of the Son he says 21
2: 6 What is . . the son of man, that thou carest for him? 21
10 in bringing many sons to glory 21
3: 6 Christ was faithful over God's house as a son 21
4:14 a great high priest . . Jesus, the Son of God 21
5: 5 Thou art my Son, today I have begotten thee"; 21
8 Although he was a Son 21
6: 6 since they crucify the Son of God 21
7: 3 resembling the Son of God 21
28 appoints a Son who has been made perfect for ever. 21
10:29 the man who has spurned the Son of God 21
11:21 Jacob . . blessed each of the sons of Joseph 21
24 refused to be called the son of Pharaoh's daughter 21
12: 5 the exhortation which addresses you as sons 21
5 the exhortation which addresses you as sons 21
6 chastises every son whom he receives. 21
7 God is treating you as sons 21
7 what son is there 21
8 then you are illegitimate children and not sons. 21
Jas 2:21 when he offered his son Isaac upon the altar? 21
1Pe 5:13 sends you greetings; and so does my son Mark. 21
2Pe 1:17 my beloved Son, with whom I am well pleased 21
2:15 the way of Balaam, the son of Be'or •
1Jn 1: 3 with the Father and with his Son Jesus Christ. 21
7 blood of Jesus his Son cleanses us from all sin. 21
2:22 he who denies the Father and the Son. 21
23 No one who denies the Son has the Father. 21
23 He who confesses the Son has the Father also. 21
24 then you will abide in the Son and in the Father. 21
3: 8 The reason the Son of God appeared 21
23 believe in the name of his Son Jesus Christ 21
4: 9 that God sent his only Son into the world 21
10 sent his Son to be the expiation for our sins. 21
14 Father has sent his Son as the Savior of the world 21
15 Whoever confesses that Jesus is the Son of God 21
5: 5 he who believes that Jesus is the Son of God? 21
9 he has borne witness to his Son. 21
10 the testimony that God has borne to his Son. 21
10 He who believes in the Son of God 21
11 eternal life, and this life is in his Son. 21
12 He who has the Son has life; 21
12 he who has not the Son of God has not life. 21
13 to you who believe in the name of the Son of God 21
20 we are in him who is true, in his Son Jesus Christ. 21
20 we know that the Son of God has come 21
2Jn 1: 3 and from Jesus Christ the Father's Son 21
9 he who abides . . has both the Father and the Son. 21
Rev 1:13 in the midst of the lampstands one like a son 21
2:14 put a stumbling block before the sons of Israel 21
18 words of the Son of God, who has eyes like a flame 21
7: 4 sealed, out of every tribe of the sons of Israel 21
14:14 and seated on the cloud one like a son of man 21
21: 7 and I will be his God and he shall be my son. 21
12 names of the twelve tribes of the sons of Israel 21
1Es 1: 3 Solomon the king, the son of David •
5 the magnificence of Solomon his son 21
13 their brethren the priests, the sons of Aaron 21
14 their brethren the priests, the sons of Aaron. 21
15 the temple singers, the sons of Asaph 21
34 men of the nation took Jeconiah the son of Josiah 21
43 Jehoiachin his son became king in his stead 21
57 they were servants to him and to his sons 21
4:37 all the sons of men are unrighteous 21
5: 1 with their wives and sons and daughters 21
5 the priests, the sons of Phinehas, son of Aaron; 21
5 the priests, the sons of Phinehas, son of Aaron; 21
5 Jeshua the son of Jozadak, son of Seraiah 21
5 Jeshua the son of Jozadak, son of Seraiah •
5 Joakim the son of Zerubbabel, son of Shealtiel •
5 Joakim the son of Zerubbabel, son of Shealtiel •
9 the sons of Parosh, 2,172 21
9 The sons of Shephatiah, 472 21
10 The sons of Arah, 756 21
11 sons of Pahathmoab, of the sons of Jeshua and Joab 21
11 sons of Pahathmoab, of the sons of Jeshua and Joab 21
12 The sons of Elam, 1,254. The sons of Zattu, 945. 21
12 The sons of Zattu, 945. The sons of Chorbe, 705. 21
12 The sons of Chorbe, 705. The sons of Bani, 648. 21
12 The sons of Chorbe, 705. The sons of Bani, 648. 21

13 The sons of Bebai, 623 The sons of Azgad, 1,322 21
13 The sons of Bebai, 623 The sons of Azgad, 1,322 21
14 The sons of Adonikam, 667. 21
14 The sons of Bigvai, 2,066. The sons of Adin, 454 21
14 The sons of Bigvai, 2,066. The sons of Adin, 454 21
15 The sons of Ater, namely of Hezekiah, 92. 21
15 The sons of Kilan and Azetas, 67. 21
15 The sons of Azaru, 432 21
16 The sons of Annias,101. The sons of Arom. 21
16 The sons of Annias,101. The sons of Arom. 21
16 The sons of Bezai, 323. The sons of Jorah, 112. 21
16 The sons of Bezai, 323. The sons of Jorah, 112. 21
17 The sons of Baiterus, 3,005. 21
17 The sons of Bethlehem, 123. 21
21 The men of Bethel, 52. The sons of Magbish, 156. 21
22 The sons of the other Elam and Ono, 725. 21
22 The sons of Jericho, 345 21
23 The sons of Senaah, 3,330. 21
24 the sons of Jedaiah the son of Jeshua 21
24 the sons of Jedaiah the son of Jeshua 21
24 of the sons of Anasib, 972 21
24 The sons of Immer, 1,052. 21
25 The sons of Pashhur, 1,247. 21
25 The sons of Harim, 1,017. 21
26 sons of Jeshua and Kadmiel and Bannas and Sudias 21
27 The temple singers: the sons of Asaph, 128. 21
28 The gatekeepers: the sons of Shallum 21
28 the sons of Ater, the sons of Talmon 21
28 the sons of Ater, the sons of Talmon 21
28 the sons of Akkub, the sons of Hatita 21
28 the sons of Akkub, the sons of Hatita 21
28 sons of Hatita, the sons of Shobai, in all 139. 21
29 The temple servants: the sons of Ziha 21
29 the sons of Hasupha, the sons of Tabbaoth 21
29 the sons of Hasupha, the sons of Tabbaoth 21
29 the sons of Keros, the sons of Siaha 21
29 the sons of Keros, the sons of Siaha 21
29 the sons of Padon, the sons of Lebanah 21
29 the sons of Padon, the sons of Lebanah 21
29 the sons of Lebanah, the sons of Hagabah 21
30 the sons of Akkub, the sons of Uthai 21
30 the sons of Akkub, the sons of Uthai 21
30 sons of Uthai, the sons of Ketab, the sons of Hagab 21
30 sons of Uthai, the sons of Ketab, the sons of Hagab 21
30 sons of Hagab, the sons of Shamlai, the sons of Hana 21
30 sons of Hagab, the sons of Shamlai, the sons of Hana 21
30 sons of Hana, the sons of Cathua, the sons of Gahar 21
30 sons of Hana, the sons of Cathua, the sons of Gahar 21
31 sons of Reaiah, the sons of Rezin 21
31 sons of Reaiah, the sons of Rezin 21
31 the sons of Nekoda, the sons of Chezib 21
31 the sons of Nekoda, the sons of Chezib 21
31 sons of Chezib, the sons of Gazzam, the sons of Uzza 21
31 sons of Chezib, the sons of Gazzam, the sons of Uzza 21
31 sons of Uzza, the sons of Paseah, the sons of Hasrah 21
31 sons of Uzza, the sons of Paseah, the sons of Hasrah 21
31 the sons of Besai, the sons of Asnah 21
31 the sons of Besai, the sons of Asnah 21
31 the sons of the Meunites, the sons of Nephisim 21
31 the sons of the Meunites, the sons of Nephisim 21
31 the sons of Bakbuk, the sons of Hakupha 21
31 the sons of Bakbuk, the sons of Hakupha 21
31 the sons of Asur, the sons of Pharakim 21
31 the sons of Asur, the sons of Pharakim 21
31 the sons of Pharakim, the sons of Bazluth 21
32 the sons of Mehida, the sons of Cutha 21
32 the sons of Mehida, the sons of Cutha 21
32 the sons of Charea, the sons of Barkos 21
32 the sons of Charea, the sons of Barkos 21
32 the sons of Sisera, the sons of Temah 21
32 the sons of Sisera, the sons of Temah 21
32 the sons of Neziah, the sons of Hatipha. 21
32 the sons of Neziah, the sons of Hatipha. 21
33 The sons of Solomon's servants 21
33 the sons of Hassophereth, the sons of Peruda 21
33 the sons of Hassophereth, the sons of Peruda 21
33 the sons of Jaalah, the sons of Lozon 21
33 the sons of Jaalah, the sons of Lozon 21
33 the sons of Giddel, the sons of Shephatiah 21
33 the sons of Giddel, the sons of Shephatiah 21
34 the sons of Hattil 21
34 the sons of Pochereth-hazzebaim 21
34 the sons of Sarothie, the sons of Masiah 21
34 the sons of Sarothie, the sons of Masiah 21
34 the sons of Gas, the sons of Addus, the sons of Subas 21
34 the sons of Gas, the sons of Addus, the sons of Subas 21
34 the sons of Gas, the sons of Addus, the sons of Subas 21
34 the sons of Apherra, the sons of Barodis 21
34 the sons of Apherra, the sons of Barodis 21
34 the sons of Shaphat, the sons of Ami. 21
34 the sons of Shaphat, the sons of Ami. 21
35 the sons of Solomon's servants were 372. 21
37 the sons of Delaiah the son of Tobiah 21
37 the sons of Delaiah the son of Tobiah 21
37 the son of Tobiah, the sons of Nekoda, 652. 21
38 the sons of Habaiah, the sons of Hakkoz 21
38 sons of Habaiah, the sons of Hakkoz, the sons 21
38 the sons of Jaddus who had married Agia 21
47 the sons of Israel were each in his own home 21

48 Jeshua the son of Jozadak •
48 Zerubbabel the son of Shealtiel •
56 Zerubbabel the son of Shealtiel •
56 Jeshua the son of Jozadak •
58 Jeshua arose, and his sons and brethren 21
58 the sons of Jeshua Emadabun 21
58 the sons of Joda son of Iliadun 21
58 the sons of Joda son of Iliadun •
58 with their sons and brethren 21
59 the Levites, the sons of Asaph, with cymbals 21
6: 1 the prophets Haggai and Zechariah the son of Iddo •
2 Zerubbabel the son of Shealtiel •
2 Jeshua the son of Jozadak arose •
8: 1 Ezra came, the son of Seraiah, son of Azariah •
1 the son of Seraiah, son of Azariah, son of Hilkiah •
1 the son of Seraiah, son of Azariah, son of Hilkiah •
1 son of Azariah, son of Hilkiah, son of Shallum •
2 son of Zadok, son of Ahitub, son of Amariah •
2 son of Zadok, son of Ahitub, son of Amariah •
2 son of Zadok, son of Ahitub, son of Amariah •
2 son of Uzzi, son of Bukki, son of Abishua •
2 son of Uzzi, son of Bukki, son of Abishua •
2 son of Uzzi, son of Bukki, son of Abishua •
2 son of Phineas, son of Eleazar, son of Aaron •
2 son of Phineas, son of Eleazar, son of Aaron •
2 son of Eleazar, son of Aaron the chief priest. •
21 upon the kingdom of the king and his sons. 21
29 Of the sons of Phineas, Gershom 21
29 Of the sons of Ithamar, Gamael 21
29 Of the sons of David, Hattush 21
29 Hattush the son of Shecaniah. •
30 Of the sons of Parosh, Zechariah 21
31 Of the sons of Pahathmoab, Eliehoenai 21
31 Eliehoenai the son of Zerahiah •
32 Of the sons of Zattu, Shecaniah 21
32 Shecaniah the son of Jahaziel •
32 Of the sons of Adin, Obed the son of Jonathan 21
33 Of the sons of Elam, Jeshaiah the son of Gotholiah 21
33 Of the sons of Elam, Jeshaiah the son of Gotholiah •
34 Of the sons of Shephatiah, Zeraiah 21
34 Zeraiah the son of Michael •
35 Of the sons of Joab, Obadiah the son of Jehiel 21
35 Of the sons of Joab, Obadiah the son of Jehiel •
36 Of the sons of Bani, Shelomith 21
36 Shelomith the son of Josiphiah •
37 Of the sons of Bebai, Zechariah the son of Bebai 21
37 Of the sons of Bebai, Zechariah the son of Bebai •
38 Of the sons of Azgad, Johanan the son of Hakkatan 21
38 Of the sons of Azgad, Johanan the son of Hakkatan •
39 Of the sons of Adonikam, the last ones 21
40 Of the sons of Bigvai, Uthai the son of Istalcurus 21
40 Of the sons of Bigvai, Uthai the son of Istalcurus •
42 When I found there none of the sons of the priests 21
47 brought us competent men of the sons of Mahli 21
47 the son of Levi, son of Israel, namely Sherebiah •
47 the son of Levi, son of Israel, namely Sherebiah •
47 Sherebiah with his sons and kinsmen, eighteen; 21
48 of the sons of Hananiah 21
48 and their sons, twenty men; 21
62 Meremoth the priest, son of Uriah; •
63 with him was Eleazar the son of Phinehas •
63 with them were Jozabad the son of Jeshua •
63 Jozabad . . and Moeth the son of Binnui •
70 sons have married the daughters of these people 21
84 give . . in marriage to their sons 21
84 do not take their daughters for your sons 21
92 Shecaniah the son of Jehiel •
9: 1 the chamber of Jehohanan the son of Eliashib •
14 Jonathan the son of Asahel and Jahzeiah •
14 Jahzeiah the son of Tikvah •
19 of the sons of Jeshua the son of Jozadak 21
19 of the sons of Jeshua the son of Jozadak •
21 Of the sons of Immer: Hanani and Zebadiah 21
22 Of the sons of Pashhur: Elioenai, Maaseiah 21
26 Of Israel: of the sons of Parosh: Ramiah, Izziah 21
27 Of the sons of Elam: Mattaniah and Zechariah 21
28 Of the sons of Zattu: Elioenai, Eliashib, Othoniah 21
29 Of the sons of Bebai: Jehohanan and Hananiah 21
30 Of the sons of Bani: Meshullam, Malluch, Adaiah 21
31 Of the sons of Addi: Naathus and Moossias 21
32 Of the sons of Annan, Elionas and Asaias 21
33 Of the sons of Hashum: Mattenai and Mattattah 21
34 Of the sons of Bani: Jeremai, Maadai, Amram, Joel 21
34 Of the sons of Ezora: Shashai, Azarel, Azael 21
35 Of the sons of Nebo: Mattithiah, Zabad, Iddo, Joel 21
37 the sons of Israel were in their settlements 21
2Es 1: 1 the son of Seraiah, son of Azariah, son of Hilkiah 22
1 the son of Seraiah, son of Azariah, son of Hilkiah 22
1 the son of Seraiah, son of Azariah, son of Hilkiah 22
1 son of Hilkiah, son of Shallum, son of Zadok 22
1 son of Hilkiah, son of Shallum, son of Zadok 22
1 son of Shallum, son of Zadok, son of Ahitub 22
2 son of Ahijah, son of Phinehas, son of Eli 22
2 son of Ahijah, son of Phinehas, son of Eli 22
2 son of Ahijah, son of Phinehas, son of Eli 22
2 son of Eli, son of Amariah, son of Azariah 22
2 son of Eli, son of Amariah, son of Azariah 22
2 son of Meraioth, son of Arna, son of Uzzi 22
2 son of Meraioth, son of Arna, son of Uzzi 22

2 son of Meraioth, son of Arna, son of Uzzi 22
2 son of Borith, son of Abishua, son of Phinehas 22
2 son of Borith, son of Abishua, son of Phinehas 22
2 son of Borith, son of Abishua, son of Phinehas 22
2 son of Phinehas, son of Eleazar 22
3 son of Aaron, of the tribe of Levi 22
28 as a father entreats his sons 22
29 you should be my sons and I should be your father? 22
34 your sons will have no children 22
2:15 Mother, embrace your sons 22
17 Do not fear, mother of sons, for I have chosen you 22
25 Good nurse, nourish your sons 22
29 that your sons may not see Gehenna. 22
30 Rejoice, O mother, with your sons 22
31 Remember your sons that sleep 22
47 He answered and said to me, "He is the Son of God 22
7:28 For my son the Messiah shall be revealed 22
29 after these years my son the Messiah shall die 22
103fathers for sons or sons for parents 22
103fathers for sons or sons for parents 22
104Just as now a father does not send his son 22
104or a son his father, or a master his servant 22
9:45 and considered my distress, and gave me a son 22
10: 1 when my son entered his wedding chamber 22
8 you are sorrowing for one son 22
16 you will receive your son back in due time 22
43 her telling you about the misfortune of her son 22
46 then it was that the barren woman bore a son. 22
48 When my son entered his wedding chamber he died,' 22
49 you saw her likeness, how she mourned for her son 22
13:32 then my Son will be revealed, whom you saw as a man 22
37 he, my Son, will reprove the assembled nations 22
52 so no one on earth can see my Son 22
14: 9 and henceforth you shall live with my Son 22
Tob 1: 1 The book of the acts of Tobit the son of Tobiel •
1 son of Ananiel, son of Aduel, son of Gabael •
1 son of Ananiel, son of Aduel, son of Gabael •
1 son of Ananiel, son of Aduel, son of Gabael •
6 the priests, the sons of Aaron 21
7 I would give a tenth to the sons of Levi 21
15 Sennacherib his son reigned in his place 21
20 except my wife Anna and my son Tobias. 21
21 before two of Sennacherib's sons killed him 21
21 Then Esarhaddon, his son, reigned in his place 21
21 appointed Ahikar, the son of my brother Anael 21
2: 1 my wife Anna and my son Tobias were restored to me 21
2 Upon seeing the abundance of food I said to my son 21
3: 9 May we never see a son or daughter of yours! 21
15 he has . . no near kinsman or kinsman's son 21
17 give . . in marriage to Tobias the son of Tobit 21
4: 2 Why do I not call my son Tobias 21
3 My son, when I die, bury me 16
4 Remember, my son, that she faced many dangers 16
5 Remember the Lord our God all your days, my son 16
12 Beware, my son, of all immorality 16
12 for we are the sons of the prophets 21
12 Remember, my son, that . . all took wives 16
13 now, my son, love your brethren 16
13 the sons and daughters of your people 21
14 Watch yourself, my son, in everything you do 16
19 So, my son, remember my commands 16
20 Gabael the son of Gabrias at Rages in Media. •
21 Do not be afraid, my son 16
5:11 a man whom you will pay to go with your son 21
12 I am Azarias the son of the great Ananias •
13 Ananias and Jathan, the sons of . . Shemaiah 21
14 expenses for yourself as for my son? 21
16 his son made the preparations for the journey. 21
6:14 Now I am the only son my father has •
14 they have no other son to bury them. 21
7: 3 We belong to the sons of Naphtali 21
7 Son of that good and noble man! •
10: 7 she never stopped mourning for her son Tobias 21
11: 5 looking intently down the road for her son. 17
6 Behold, your son is coming 21
9 embraced her son, and said to him, "I have seen you 21
10 his son ran to him 21
14 Then he saw his son and embraced him 21
15 here I see my son Tobias! 21
15 his son went in rejoicing 21
12: 1 Tobit then called his son Tobias and said to him 21
1 My son, see to the wages of the man who went 21
13: 3 Acknowledge him . . O sons of Israel 21
9 he will afflict you for the deeds of your sons 21
9 he will show mercy to the sons of the righteous. 21
13 Rejoice and be glad for the sons of the righteous 21
14: 3 he called his son and grandsons 21
3 My son, take your sons 19
3 My son, take your sons 21
4 Go to Media, my son 19
8 now, my son, leave Nineveh 19
10 See, my son, what Nadab did to Ahikar 19
12 Tobias returned with . . his sons to Ecbatana 21
Jdt 6:15 Uzziah the son of Micah, of the tribe of Simeon •
15 Chabris the son of Gothoniel •
15 Charmis the son of Melchiel. 21
7:18 the sons of Esau and the sons of Ammon went up 21
18 the sons of Esau and the sons of Ammon went up 21
8: 1 the daughter of Merari the son of Ox, son of Joseph 21

1 the daughter of Merari the son of Ox, son of Joseph 21
1 son of Joseph, son of Oziel, son of Elkiah 21
1 son of Joseph, son of Oziel, son of Elkiah 21
1 son of Elkiah, son of Ananias, son of Gideon 21
1 son of Elkiah, son of Ananias, son of Gideon 21
1 son of Gideon, son of Raphaim, son of Ahitub 21
1 son of Gideon, son of Raphaim, son of Ahitub 21
1 son of Ahitub, son of Elijah, son of Hilkiah 21
1 son of Ahitub, son of Elijah, son of Hilkiah 21
1 son of Hilkiah, son of Eliab, son of Nathanael 21
1 son of Hilkiah, son of Eliab, son of Nathanael 21
1 son of Salamiel, son of Sarasadai, son of Israel. 21
1 son of Salamiel, son of Sarasadai, son of Israel. 21
1 son of Salamiel, son of Sarasadai, son of Israel. 21
12 in the place of God among the sons of men? 21
9: 4 their booty to be divided among thy beloved sons 21
16: 7 nor did the sons of the Titans smite him 21
12 The sons of maidservants have pierced them through; 21
AEs 11: 1 Dositheus . . and Ptolemy his son 21
1 translated by Lysimachus the son of Ptolemy •
2 Mordecai the son of Jair, son of Shimei, son of Kish •
2 Mordecai the son of Jair, son of Shimei, son of Kish •
2 Mordecai the son of Jair, son of Shimei, son of Kish •
12: 6 Haman, the son of Hammedatha, a Bougaean •
16:10 Haman, the son of Hammedatha, a Macedonian •
16 are sons of the Most High 21
17 letters sent by Haman the son of Hammedatha •
Wis 2:18 for if the righteous man is God's son 21
5: 5 Why has he been numbered among the sons of God? 21
9: 5 For I am thy slave and the son of thy maidservant 21
6 for even if one is perfect among the sons of men 21
7 to be judge over thy sons and daughters. 21
12:19 thou hast filled thy sons with good hope 21
21 with what strictness thou hast judged thy sons 21
16:10 thy sons were not conquered 21
26 thy sons, whom thou didst love, O Lord 21
18: 4 those who had kept thy sons imprisoned 21
13 they acknowledged thy people to be God's son. 21
Sir 2: 1 My son, if you come forward to serve the Lord 19
3: 2 confirmed the right of the mother over her sons. 21
12 O son, help your father in his old age 19
17 My son, perform your tasks in meekness 19
4: 1 My son, deprive not the poor of his living 19
10 you will then be like a son of the Most High 21
11 Wisdom exalts her sons and gives help 21
6:18 My son, from your youth up choose instruction 19
23 Listen, my son, and accept my judgment 19
32 If you are willing, my son, you will be taught 19
7: 3 My son, do not sow the furrows of injustice 21
10:28 My son, glorify yourself with humility 19
11:10 My son, do not busy yourself with many matters 19
14:11 My son, treat yourself well 19
16: 1 nor rejoice in ungodly sons. 21
24 Listen to me, my son, and acquire knowledge 19
17:30 since a son of man is not immortal. 21
18:15 My son, do not mix reproach with your good deeds 19
21: 1 Have you sinned, my son? Do so no more 19
22: 3 the father of an undisciplined son 13
30: 1 He who loves his son will whip him often 21
2 He who disciplines his son will profit by him 21
3 He who teaches his son 21
7 He who spoils his son will bind up his wounds 21
8 a son unrestrained turns out to be wilful. 21
13 Discipline your son and take pains with him 21
31:22 Listen to me, my son, and do not disregard me 19
33:19 To son or wife, to brother or friend 21
21 you should look to the hand of you sons. 21
34:20 Like one who kills a son before his father's eyes 21
37:27 My son, test your soul while you live 19
38: 9 My son, when you are sick do not be negligent 19
16 My son, let your tears fall for the dead 19
39:13 Listen to me, O you holy sons 21
40: 1 a heavy yoke is upon the sons of Adam 21
28 My son, do not lead the life of a beggar 19
45: 9 as a reminder to the sons of his people; 21
13 but only his sons and his descendants 21
23 Phinehas the son of Eleazar is the third in glory 21
25 David, the son of Jesse, of the tribe of Judah 21
25 the heritage of the king is from son to son only 21
25 the heritage of the king is from son to son only 21
46: 1 Joshua the son of Nun was mighty in war •
7 he and Caleb the son of Jephunneh 21
10 that all the sons of Israel might see 21
12 live again in their sons! 21
47: 2 so David was selected from the sons of Israel. 21
12 rose up a wise son who fared amply because of him; 21
23 left behind him one of his sons, ample in folly 18
23 Also Jeroboam the son of Nebat 21
48:10 to turn the heart of the father to the son 21
49:12 so was Jeshua the son of Jozadak 21
50: 1 Simon the high priest, son of Onias 21
13 all the sons of Aaron in their splendor 21
16 the sons of Aaron shouted 21
20 whole congregation of the sons of Israel 21
27 Jesus the son of Sirach, son of Eleazar 21
27 the son of Sirach, son of Eleazar, of Jerusalem 21
Bar 1: 1 Baruch the son of Neraiah, son of Mahseiah 21
1 son of Neraiah, son of Mahseiah, son of Zedekiah 21
1 son of Mahseiah, son of Zedekiah, son of Hasadiah 21

1 son of Zedekiah, son of Hasadiah, son of Hilkiah 21
1 son of Zedekiah, son of Hasadiah, son of Hilkiah 21
3 Jeconiah the son of Jehoiakim, king of Judah 21
7 Jehoiakim . . the son of Hilkiah, son of Shallum 21
7 Jehoiakim . . the son of Hilkiah, son of Shallum 21
8 Zedekiah the son of Josiah, king of Judah 21
11 pray . . for the life of Belshazzar his son 21
12 under the protection of Belshazzar his son 21
2: 3 we should eat, one the flesh of his son and another 21
3: 4 sons of those who sinned before thee, who did not 21
21 Their sons have strayed far from her way. 21
23 the sons of Hagar, who seek for understanding 21
4:10 I have seen the captivity of my sons 21
14 remember the capture of my sons and daughters 21
16 They led away the widow's beloved sons •
26 My tender sons have traveled rough roads •
32 the city which received your sons. 21
37 Behold, your sons are coming, whom you sent away; 21
Aza 1:60 Bless the Lord, you sons of men 21
Sus 1:48 Are you such fools, you sons of Israel? 21
1Mc 1: 1 After Alexander son of Philip, the Macedonian •
9 and so did their sons after them for many years 21
10 Antiochus Epiphanes, son of Antiochus the king; 21
48 to leave their sons uncircumcised 21
2: 1 Mattathias the son of John, son of Simeon 21
1 Mattathias the son of John, son of Simeon 21
1 son of Simeon, a priest of the sons of Joarib 21
2 He had five sons, John surnamed Gaddi 21
14 Mattathias and his sons rent their clothes 21
16 Mattathias and his sons were assembled. 21
17 supported by sons and brothers. 21
18 your sons will be numbered among the friends 21
18 your sons will be honored with silver and gold 21
20 I and my sons . . will live by the covenant 21
26 as Phinehas did against Zimri the son of Salu. 21
28 he and his sons fled to the hills 21
30 they, their sons, their wives, and their cattle 21
49 he said to his sons: "Arrogance and reproach 21
3: 1 Then Judas his son . . took command in his place. 21
15 to take vengeance on the sons of Israel. 21
33 Lysias was also to take care of Antiochus his son 21
38 Lysias chose Ptolemy the son of Dorymenes •
41 to the camp to get the sons of Israel for slaves. 21
45 the sons of aliens held the citadel 21
4:30 Jonathan, the son of Saul 21
5: 3 Judas made war on the sons of Esau in Idumea 21
4 remembered the wickedness of the sons of Baean 21
18 he left Joseph, the son of Zechariah •
56 Joseph, the son of Zechariah •
65 fought the sons of Esau in the land to the south 21
6: 2 Alexander, the son of Philip, the Macedonian king •
15 that he might guide Antiochus his son 21
17 he set up Antiochus the king's son to reign 21
24 the sons of our people besieged the citadel 21
55 had appointed to bring up Antiochus his son 21
7: 1 In the 151st year Demetrius the son of Seleucus •
9 take vengeance on the sons of Israel. 21
13 Hasideans were first among the sons of Israel 21
23 those with him had done among the sons of Israel 21
8:17 So Judas chose Eupolemus the son of John 21
17 Eupolemus the son of John, son of Accos 21
17 and Jason the son of Eleazar 21
9:36 the sons of Jambri from Medeba came out 21
37 sons of Jambri are celebrating a great wedding 21
53 he took the sons of the leading men of the land 21
66 the sons of Phasiron in their tents. 21
10: 1 Alexander Epiphanes, the son of Antiochus •
67 Demetrius the son of Demetrius came from Crete 21
11:62 took the sons of their rulers as hostages 21
70 Mattathias the son of Absalom •
70 Judas the son of Chalphi •
12:16 We . . have chosen Numenius the son of Antiochus •
16 Antipater the son of Jason •
13:11 He sent Jonathan the son of Absalom to Joppa •
16 two of his sons as hostages 21
17 he sent to get the money and the sons 15
18 the money and the sons 15
19 So he sent the sons and the 100 talents 15
53 Simon saw that John his son had reached manhood 21
14:22 Numenius the son of Antiochus •
22 Antipater the son of Jason •
25 How shall we thank Simon and his sons? 21
29 Simon the son of Mattathias . . and his brothers 21
29 a priest of the sons of Joarib 21
49 so that Simon and his sons might have them. 21
15: 1 Antiochus, the son of Demetrius the king 21
16: 2 Simon called in his two older sons Judas and John 21
11 Ptolemy the son of Abubus •
13 made treacherous plans against Simon and his sons 21
14 his sons, in the 177th year, in the eleventh month 21
15 The son of Abubus received them treacherously •
16 When Simon and his sons were drunk, Ptolemy 21
16 When Simon and his sons were drunk, Ptolemy 21
2Mc 2:20 Antiochus Epiphanes and his son Eupator 21
3:11 also some money of Hyrcanus, son of Tobias •
4: 4 Apollonius, the son of Menestheus •
21 Apollonius the son of Menestheus •
45 Ptolemy son of Dorymenes •
7:20 she saw her seven sons perish within a single day 21

26 she undertook to persuade her son. 21
27 My son, have pity on me 21
41 Last of all, the mother died, after her sons. 21
8: 9 appointed Nicanor the son of Patroclus •
9:25 I have appointed my son Antiochus to be king 21
26 good will . . toward me and my son. 21
29 fearing the son of Antiochus 21
10:10 who was the son of that ungodly man 21
12: 2 Timothy and Apollonius the son of Gennaeus •
14: 1 Demetrius, the son of Seleucus •
3Mc 1: 3 Dositheus, known as the son of Drimylus •
6:28 Release the sons of the almighty and living God 21
4Mc 4:15 his son Antiochus Epiphanes 21
25 because they had circumcised their sons 16
9:18 sons of the Hebrews alone are invincible 17
12: 6 who had been bereaved of so many sons 21
6 to influence her to persuade the surviving son •
15: 2 preserving her seven sons for a time 21
9 because of the nobility of her sons 21
22 her sons were tortured on the wheel 21
27 preserve the seven sons for a short time 21
32 the torture of your sons 21
16: 1 advanced in years and mother of seven sons 17
3 inflamed as she saw her seven sons tortured 21
8 In vain, my sons, I endured many birth-pangs for you 17
11 shall I have any of my sons to bury me. 21
13 the whole number of her sons 21
15 when you and your sons were arrested together 17
15 said to your sons in the Hebrew language 17
16 My sons, noble is the contest 17
20 Abraham was zealous to sacrifice his son Isaac 21
24 encouraged and persuaded each of her sons to die 21
17: 2 with your seven sons nullified . . the tyrant 17
3 Nobly set like a roof on the pillars of your sons 17
5 lighting the way of your star-like seven sons 17
9 aged priest and an aged woman and seven sons 17
13 the mother of the seven sons 17
18: 6 The mother of seven sons 17
9 when these sons had grown up their father died •
20 those seven sons of the daughter of Abraham 17
23 the sons of Abraham with their . . mother 17

son *See also* adoption, two.

first son 1. בְּכוֹר
Deu 25: 6 first son whom she bears shall succeed 1

first-born son 1. *πρωτόγονος*
Sir 36:12 whom thou hast likened to a first-born son. 1

old son 1. רִאשׁוֹן
2Ch 22: 1 with the Arabs . . had slain all the older sons. 1

only son 1. יָחִיד 2. *μονογενής*
Gen 22:12 withheld your son, your only son, from me. 1
16 you . . have not withheld your son, your only son 1
Jer 6:26 make mourning as for an only son 1
Ams 8:10 I will make it like the mourning for an only son 1
Joh 1:14 glory as of the only Son from the Father. 2
18 the only Son, who is in the bosom of the Father 2
Heb 11:17 he . . was ready to offer up his only son 2

stupid son 1. כְּסִיל
Prv 17:21 A stupid son is a grief to a father; 1

wise son 1. חָכָם
Prv 23:24 he who begets a wise son will be glad in him. 1

young son 1. צָעִיר 2. *παιδάριον*
Jos 6:26 at the cost of his youngest son 1
1Kg 16:34 set up its gates at the cost of his youngest son 1
1Mc 11:39 Antiochus, the young son of Alexander 2

son-in-law 1. חתן 2. חָתָן 3. *γαμβρός*
Gen 19:12 Sons-in-law, sons, daughters, or any one 2
14 Lot went out and said to his sons-in-law 2
14 But he seemed to his sons-in-law to be jesting. 2
Jdg 15: 6 they said, "Samson, the son-in-law of the Timnite 2
19: 5 to go; but the girl's father said to his son-in-law 2
1Sm 18:18 Who am I . . that I should be son-in-law to the king? 2
21 Saul said . . "You shall now be my son-in-law. 1
26 it pleased David well to be the king's son-in-law. 1
22:14 king's son-in-law, and captain over your bodyguard 2
2Kg 8:27 for he was son-in-law to the house of Ahab. 2
Neh 6:18 son-in-law of Shecani'ah the son of Arah 2
13:28 the son-in-law of Sanbal'lat the Hor'onite; 2
1Mc 16:12 for he was son-in-law of the high priest. 3

become a son-in-law 1. חתן 2. *ἐπιγαμβρεύω*
1Sm 18:22 now then become the king's son-in-law. 1
23 a little thing to become the king's son-in-law 1
27 that he might become the king's son-in-law. 1
1Mc 10:54 I will become your son-in-law 2

song 1. דִּבְרֵי שִׁיר 2. זָמִיר 3. זִמְרָה 4. מַנְגִּינָה 5. נְגִינָה 6. קוֹל 7. שִׁיר 8. שִׁירָה 9. *ὑμνέω* 10. *ὕμνος* 11. *φωνή* 12. canticum 13. hymnus
Gen 31:27 I might have sent you away with mirth and songs 7
Exd 15: 1 Israel sang this song to the LORD, saying 8

2 The LORD is my strength and my song, and he has 3
Num21:17 Israel sang this song: "Spring up, O well!–Sing to it!– 8
Deu 31:19 Now therefore write this song, and teach it 8
19 that this song may be a witness for me against 8
21 this song shall confront them as a witness 8
22 Moses wrote this song the same day, and taught it 8
30 Moses spoke the words of this song until they 8
32:44 Moses came and recited all the words of this song 8
Jdg 5:12 Awake, awake, Deb'orah! Awake, awake, utter a song 7
2Sm 22: 1 And David spoke to the LORD the words of this song 8
1Kg 4:32 and his songs were 1,005. 7
1Ch 6:31 whom David put in charge of the service of song 7
32 They ministered with song *
13: 8 making merry . . with song and lyres and harps 7
16:42 the music and instruments for sacred song. 7
2Ch 5:13 when the song was raised . . in praise to the LORD 6
29:27 burnt offering began, the song to the LORD began 7
Neh 12:46 there were songs of praise and thanksgiving 7
Job 30: 9 now I have become their song, I am a byword to them. 5
35:10 Where is God my Maker, who gives songs in the night 2
Ps 18: 0 David . . who addressed the words of this song 8
28: 7 with my song I give thanks to him. 7
30: 0 A Song at the dedication of the Temple. 7
33: 3 Sing to him a new song, play skillfully 7
40: 3 He put a new song in my mouth, a song of praise 7
42: 8 his song is with me, a prayer to the God of my life. 7
45: 0 A Maskil of the Sons of Korah; a love song. 7
46: 0 A Psalm . . According to Alamoth. A Song. 7
48: 0 A Song. A Psalm of the Sons of Korah. 7
65: 0 To the choirmaster. A Psalm of David. A Song. 7
66: 0 To the choirmaster. A Song. A Psalm. 7
67: 0 with stringed instruments. A Psalm. A Song. 7
68: 0 To the choirmaster. A Psalm of David. A Song. 7
4 lift up a song to him who rides upon the clouds; *
69:12 the drunkards make songs about me. 5
30 I will praise the name of God with a song; 7
75: 0 Do Not Destroy. A Psalm of Asaph. A Song. 7
76: 0 A Psalm of Asaph. A Song. 7
78:63 their maidens had no marriage song. †
81: 2 Raise a song, sound the timbrel 3
83: 0 A Song. A Psalm of Asaph. 7
87: 0 A Psalm of the Sons of Korah. A Song. 7
88: 0 A Song. A Psalm of the Sons of Korah. 7
92: 0 A Psalm. A Song for the Sabbath. 7
96: 1 O sing to the LORD a new song; 7
98: 1 O sing to the LORD a new song 7
108: 0 A Song. A Psalm of David. 7
118:14 The LORD is my strength and my song; 3
119:54 Thy statutes have been my songs 2
120: 0 A Song of Ascents. 7
121: 0 A Song of Ascents. 7
122: 0 A Song of Ascents. Of David. 7
123: 0 A Song of Ascents. 7
124: 0 A Song of Ascents. Of David. 7
125: 0 A Song of Ascents. 7
126: 0 A Song of Ascents. 7
127: 0 A Song of Ascents. Of Solomon. 7
128: 0 A song of Ascents. 7
129: 0 A Song of Ascents. 7
130: 0 A Song of Ascents. 7
131: 0 A Song of Ascents. Of David. 7
132: 0 A Song of Ascents. 7
133: 0 A Song of Ascents. 7
134: 0 A Song of Ascents. 7
137: 3 For there our captors required of us songs 1
3 saying, "Sing us one of the songs of Zion! 7
4 How shall we sing the LORD'S song in a foreign land? 7
144: 9 I will sing a new song to thee, O God; 7
149: 1 Sing to the LORD a new song, his praise 7
Prv 25:20 He who sings songs to a heavy heart is like one who 7
Ecc 7: 5 hear the rebuke . . than to hear the song of fools. 7
12: 4 and all the daughters of song are brought low; 7
Sng 1: 1 The Song of Songs, which is Solomon's. 7
1 The Song of Songs, which is Solomon's. 7
Isa 5: 1 my beloved a love song concerning his vineyard 8
12: 2 for the LORD GOD is my strength and my song 3
23:15 it will happen to Tyre as in the song of the harlot 8
25: 5 the song of the ruthless is stilled. 2
26: 1 this song will be sung in the land of Judah 8
30:29 a song as in the night when a holy feast is kept; 7
42:10 Sing to the LORD a new song 7
51: 3 found in her, thanksgiving and the voice of song. 3
Jer 30:19 Out of them shall come songs of thanksgiving *
Lam 3:14 the laughingstock . . the burden of their songs 5
63 I am the burden of their songs. 4
Ezk 26:13 I will stop the music of your songs 7
33:32 lo, you are to them like one who sings love songs *
Ams 5:23 Take away from me the noise of your songs; 7
8: 3 The songs of the temple shall become wailings 8
10 turn . . all your songs into lamentation; 7
2Es 2:42 they all were praising the Lord with songs. 12
10:22 our song has been silenced 13
Jdt 15:13 wearing garlands and with songs on their lips. 9
16: 2 Begin a song to my God with tambourines *
13 I will sing to my God a new song 10
3Mc 7:16 praise and all kinds of melodious songs. 10
4Mc 15:21 the melodies of sirens nor the songs of swans 11

song *See also* sing.

battle song 1. παιάν
2Mc 15:25 his men advanced with trumpets and battle songs; 1

glad song 1. רִנָּה
Ps 118:15 Hark, glad songs of victory in the tents 1

joyous song 1. רנן
Ps 98: 4 break forth into joyous song and sing praises! 1

song of joy 1. רִנָּה 2. שִׂמְחָה
1Sm 18: 6 to meet King Saul, with timbrels, with songs of joy 2
Ps 47: 1 all peoples! Shout to God with loud songs of joy! 1
107:22 let them . . tell of his deeds in songs of joy! 1

song of praise 1. זָמִיר 2. תְּהִלָּה 3. αἴνεσις
Ps 40: 3 a new song in my mouth, a song of praise to our God. 2
95: 2 make a joyful noise to him with songs of praise! 1
145: 0 A Song of Praise. Of David. 2
147: 1 for he is gracious, and a song of praise is seemly. 2
Isa 24:16 we hear songs of praise, of glory to the Righteous 1
Jdt 16: 1 all the people loudly sang this song of praise. 3

song of thanksgiving 1. הֻיְדוֹת 2. תּוֹדָה
Neh 12: 8 charge of the songs of thanksgiving. 1
Ps 26: 7 singing aloud a song of thanksgiving 2
42: 4 with glad shouts and songs of thanksgiving 2

taunt song 1. מָשָׁל
Mic 2: 4 they shall take up a taunt song against you 1

wedding song 1. ὑμέναιος
3Mc 4: 6 raising a lament instead of a wedding song 1

sonship 1. υἱοθεσία
Rom 8:15 but you have received the spirit of sonship. 1
9: 4 to them belong the sonship, the glory 1

soon 1. בְּ 2. בְּעוֹד 3. וְ 4. כְּ 5. כַּאֲשֶׁר 6. כִּמְעַט 7. לְ 8. מהר 9. מַהֵר 10. מְהֵרָה 11. מִקָּרֹב 12. עַד 13. פִּתְאֹם 14. קָרֹב 15. בֵּהּ זִמְנָא כְּדִי (A) 16. קרב (A) 17. ἅμα 18. ἅμα αὐθωρί 19. ἄρτι 20. αὐτίκα 21. διὰ τάχους 22. ἐν τάχει 23. εὐθέως 24. εὐθύς 25. ἡνίκα 26. ἡνίκα ἐάν 27. μετ᾽ ὀλίγον χρονίσκον 28. μετ᾽ οὐ πολύ 29. ὅταν 30. ὅταν ἤδη 31. παραχρῆμα 32. ταχέως 33. ταχινός 34. τάχιον 35. ταχύς 36. ὡς 37. celer 38. nunc
Gen 27:30 As soon as Isaac had finished blessing Jacob 5
39:18 as soon as I lifted up my voice and cried, he left 4
40:10 as soon as it budded, its blossoms shot forth 4
44: 3 As soon as the morning was light *
Exd 2:18 How is it that you have come so soon today? 8
9:29 As soon as I have gone out of the city, I will 4
32:19 as soon as he came near the camp and saw the calf 5
Deu 4:26 that you will soon utterly perish from the land 9
Jos 2: 7 as soon as the pursuers had . . the gate was shut. 5
11 And as soon as we heard it, our hearts melted 3
6: 5 as soon as you hear the sound of the trumpet 1
20 As soon as the people heard the sound 4
8:19 as soon as he had stretched out his hand, they ran 4
Jdg 2:17 they soon turned aside from the way 9
8:33 As soon as Gideon died, the people . . turned again 5
9:33 in the morning, as soon as the sun is up, rise early 5
1Sm 1:22 As soon as the child is weaned, I will bring him 12
9:13 As soon as you enter the city, you will find him 4
13:10 As soon as he had finished offering 4
20:41 as soon as the lad had gone, David rose from beside 3
29:10 and depart as soon as you have light. 3
2Sm 13:36 as soon as he had finished . . the king's sons came 4
15:10 As soon as you hear the sound of the trumpet 4
22:45 as soon as they heard of me, they obeyed me. 7
1Kg 15:29 as soon as he was king, he killed all the house 4
16:11 as soon as he had seated himself on his throne 4
18:12 as soon as I have gone from you *
20:36 as soon as you have gone . . a lion shall kill you. *
36 as soon as he had departed . . a lion met him *
21:15 As soon as Jez'ebel heard . . Jez'ebel said to Ahab 4
16 as soon as Ahab heard . . Ahab arose to go down 4
2Kg 6:20 As soon as they entered Sama'ria Eli'sha said 4
10: 2 Now then, as soon as this letter comes to you 1
25 So as soon as he had made an end of offering 4
13:21 and as soon as the man touched the bones of Eli'sha 3
14: 5 as soon as the royal power was firmly in his hand 5
2Ch 25: 3 as soon as the royal power was firmly in his hand 5
31: 5 As soon as the command was spread abroad 4
Job 32:22 else would my Maker soon put an end to me. 6
Ps 18:44 As soon as they heard of me they obeyed me; *
37: 2 For they will soon fade like the grass, and wither 10
48: 5 As soon as they saw it, they were astounded *
81:14 I would soon subdue their enemies 6
94:17 soul . . soon have dwelt in the land of silence. 6
106:13 they soon forgot his works; 8
Isa 28: 4 he eats it up as soon as it is in his hand. 2
56: 1 righteousness, for soon my salvation will come 14
66: 8 as soon as Zion was in labor she brought forth *
Ezk 7: 8 Now I will soon pour out my wrath upon you 11
36: 8 my people Israel; for they will soon come home. 16
Dan 3: 7 Therefore, as soon as all the peoples heard 15
Hos 8:10 I will soon gather them up. 13
Mat 24:32 as soon as its branch becomes tender 30
Mrk 13:28 as soon as its branch becomes tender 30
15: 1 And as soon as it was morning 24
Lke 21:30 as soon as they come out in leaf 30
Act 27:14 soon a tempestuous wind, called the northeaster 28
Rom16:20 God . . will soon crush Satan under your feet. 22
1Co 4:19 I will come to you soon, if the Lord wills 32
Php 2:19 hope in the Lord Jesus to send Timothy to you soon 32
1Ti 3:14 I hope to come to you soon 34
2Ti 4: 9 Do your best to come to me soon. 32
Heb 13:19 in order that I may be restored to you the sooner. 34
23 with whom I shall see you if he comes soon. 34
2Pe 1:14 know that the putting off of my body will be soon 33
3Jn 1:14 I hope to see you soon 23
Rev 1: 1 show to his servants what must soon take place; 22
2:16 Repent then. If not, I will come to you soon and war 35
3:11 I am coming soon; hold fast what you have 35
11:14 behold, the third woe is soon to come. 35
22: 6 to show his servants what must soon take place. 22
7 And behold, I am coming soon. 35
12 Behold, I am coming soon, bringing my recompense 35
19 Surely I am coming soon." Amen. Come, Lord Jesus! 35
1Es 8:71 As soon as I heard these things 17
2Es 5:43 that thou mightest show thy judgment the sooner? 37
7:75 as soon as every one of us yields up his soul 38
Tob 6:12 and as soon as we return from Rages 29
Jdt 14: 2 as soon as morning comes and the sun rises 26
11 As soon as it was dawn 25
16:18 As soon as the people were purified 25
Wis 5:13 we also, as soon as we were born, ceased to be *
6:15 he . . will soon be free from care 32
13: 9 how did they fail to find sooner the Lord 35
Sir 6:19 soon you will eat of her produce. 35
Bar 4:22 because of the mercy which soon will come to you 22
24 so they will soon see your salvation by God 22
25 but you will soon see their destruction 22
Bel 1:18 As soon as the doors were opened 17
1Mc 11:22 as soon as he heard it he set out 23
2Mc 1:15 they closed the temple as soon as he entered it. 36
2:18 he will soon have mercy upon us 32
5:18 as soon as he came forward 31
7:37 appealing to God to show mercy soon to our nation 35
8: 5 As soon as Maccabeus got his army organized *
9: 5 As soon as he ceased speaking 19
11: 1 Very soon after this 27
36 as soon as you have considered them *
3Mc 3:23 we may soon alter our policy. 21
25 as soon as this letter shall arrive 18
5:23 Then, as soon as the cock had crowed 19
4Mc 2: 8 as soon as a man adopts a way of life 20
8:29 as soon as the tyrant had ceased counseling them 17

soon *See also* just.

soon after 1. ταχύς
Mrk 9:39 will be able soon after to speak evil of me. 1

soon afterward 1. ἑξῆς 2. καθεξῆς
Lke 7:11 Soon afterward he went to a city called Na'in 1
8: 1 Soon afterward he went on through cities 2

soon as possible 1. ταχύς 2. ὡς ταχέως
Act 17:15 to come to him as soon as possible 2
3Mc 1: 8 to visit them as soon as possible. 1

too soon 1. πρὸ καιροῦ
Sir 30:24 anxiety brings on old age too soon. 1

sooner than 1. בְּטֶרֶם
Ps 58: 9 Sooner than your pots can feel the heat of thorns 1

soot 1. שְׁחוֹר
Lam 4: 8 Now their visage is blacker than soot 1

soothe 1. נִיחֹחַ 2. εἰρηνικός
Ezk 20:28 there they sent up their soothing odors 1
AEs 15: 8 he comforted her with soothing words, and said 2

soothsayer 1. ענן 2. קסם
Deu 18:10 divination, a soothsayer, or an augur, or a sorcerer 1
14 For these nations . . give heed to soothsayers 1
Jos 13:22 Balaam also, the son of Be'or, the soothsayer 2
Isa 2: 6 full . . of soothsayers like the Philistines 1
Jer 27: 9 your diviners, your dreamers, your soothsayers 1
Mic 5:12 and you shall have no more soothsayers; 1

soothsaying 1. μαντεύομαι
Act 16:16 brought her owners much gain by soothsaying. 1

soothsaying *See also* practice.

sorcerer 1. אִטִּי 2. כשׁף 3. כַּשָּׁף 4. φάρμακος
Exd 7:11 Pharaoh summoned the wise men and the sorcerers; 2
Deu 18:10 divination, a soothsayer, or an augur, or a sorcerer 2
Isa 19: 3 they will consult the idols and the sorcerers 1
Jer 27: 9 or your sorcerers, who are saying to you 3
Dan 2: 2 commanded that the . . sorcerers 2
Mal 3: 5 I will be a swift witness against the sorcerers 2

Rev 21: 8 as for murderers, fornicators, sorcerers 4
22:15 Outside are the dogs and sorcerers 4

sorceress 1. כשף 2. ענן
Exd 22:18 You shall not permit a sorceress to live. 1
Isa 57: 3 But you, draw near hither, sons of the sorceress 2

sorcery 1. כֶּשֶׁף 2. נחשׁ 3. *φαρμακεία* 4. *φάρμακον*
2Kg 9:22 the harlotries and the sorceries of your mother 1
17:17 and used divination and sorcery 2
Isa 47: 9 in spite of your many sorceries 1
12 in your enchantments and your many sorceries 1
Mic 5:12 I will cut off sorceries from your hand 1
Gal 5:20 idolatry, sorcery, enmity, strife, jealousy, anger 3
Rev 9:21 nor did they repent of . . their sorceries 4
18:23 and all nations were deceived by thy sorcery. 3
Wis 12: 4 their works of sorcery and unholy rites 3
sorcery *See also* practice.

sore 1. אֲבַעְבֻּעֹת 2. חַבּוּרָה 3. כאב 4. מְאֹד 5. רַע 6. שְׁחִין 7. *ἕλκος*
Gen 34:25 when they were sore, two of the sons of Jacob 3
Exd 9: 9 shall . . become boils breaking out in sores 1
10 and it became boils breaking out in sores on man 1
Jdg 2:15 and they were in sore straits. 4
Job 2: 7 Satan . . afflicted Job with loathsome sores 6
Ps 71:20 Thou who hast made me see many sore troubles 5
Ecc 6: 2 this is vanity; it is a sore affliction. 5
Isa 1: 6 but bruises and sores and bleeding wounds; 2
Ezk 14:21 upon Jerusalem my four sore acts of judgment 5
Lke 16:21 moreover the dogs came and licked his sores. 7
Rev 16: 2 and foul and evil sores came upon the men 7
11 cursed the God of heaven for their pain and sores 7
sore *See also* full.

sorely 1. כַּעַס 2. מְאֹד 3. עַד מְאֹד 4. רַב
Jdg 10: 9 so that Israel was sorely distressed. 2
1Sm 1: 6 rival used to provoke her sorely, to irritate her 1
Ps 6: 3 My soul also is sorely troubled. 2
10 my enemies shall be ashamed and sorely troubled; 2
118:18 The LORD has chastened me sorely †
119:107 I am sorely afflicted; give me life, O LORD 3
129: 1 Sorely have they afflicted me from my youth 4
2 Sorely have they afflicted me from my youth 4
Isa 64:12 Wilt thou keep silent, and afflict us sorely? 3
sorely *See also* harass, trouble.

sorrel 1. שָׂרֹק
Zec 1: 8 behind him were red, sorrel, and white horses. 1

sorrow 1. אֲבוֹי 2. חֵבֶל 3. יָגוֹן 4. כַּעַס 5. מַכְאוֹב 6. עֳנִי 7. עֶצֶב 8. עַצֶּבֶת 9. רָעָה 10. תּוּגָה 11. *λύπη* 12. *ὀδυνάω* 13. *ὀδύνη* 14. *πένθος* 15. *συναλγέω* 16. *συνοδυνάομαι* 17. contristo 18. dolor 19. gemitus 20. tristitia
Gen 42:38 bring down my gray hairs with sorrow to Sheol. 3
44:29 bring down my gray hairs in sorrow to Sheol.' 9
31 your servant our father with sorrow to Sheol. 3
48: 7 Rachel to my sorrow died in the land of Canaan •
2Ch 6:29 each knowing . . affliction and his own sorrow 5
Est 9:22 turned for them from sorrow into gladness 3
Ps 13: 2 in my soul, and have sorrow in my heart all the day? 3
16: 4 who choose another god multiply their sorrows; 8
31:10 my life is spent with sorrow 3
88: 9 my eye grows dim through sorrow. 6
107:39 low through oppression, trouble, and sorrow 3
119:28 My soul melts away for sorrow; 10
Prv 10: 1 but a foolish son is a sorrow to his mother. 10
22 makes rich, and he adds no sorrow with it. 7
15:13 but by sorrow of heart the spirit is broken. 8
23:29 Who has woe? Who has sorrow? Who has strife? 1
Ecc 1:18 he who increases knowledge increases sorrow. 5
7: 3 Sorrow is better than laughter 4
Isa 35:10 and sorrow and sighing shall flee away. 3
51:11 and sorrow and sighing shall flee away. 3
53: 3 a man of sorrows, and acquainted with grief; 5
4 he has borne our griefs and carried our sorrows; 5
Jer 20:18 to see toil and sorrow, and spend my days in shame? 3
31:13 comfort them, and give them gladness for sorrow. 3
45: 3 Woe is me! for the LORD has added sorrow to my pain; 3
49:24 anguish and sorrows have taken hold of her 2
Lam 1:12 Look and see if there is any sorrow like my sorrow 5
12 Look and see if there is any sorrow like my sorrow 5
Ezk 23:33 you will be filled with drunkenness and sorrow. 3
Lke 22:45 found them sleeping for sorrow 11
Joh 16: 6 sorrow has filled your hearts. 11
20 your sorrow will turn into joy. 11
21 When a woman is in travail she has sorrow 11
22 you have sorrow now, but I will see you again 11
Act 20:38 sorrowing most of all because of the word 12
Rom 9: 2 great sorrow and unceasing anguish in my heart. 11
2Co 2: 7 or he may be overwhelmed by excessive sorrow. 11
Php 2:27 lest I should have sorrow upon sorrow. 11
27 lest I should have sorrow upon sorrow. 11
1Es 3:20 forgets all sorrow and debt. 11
2Es 2: 3 but with mourning and sorrow I have lost you 20
7:117 For what good is it to all that they live in sorrow 20
8:54 sorrows have passed away 18
10: 8 and to be sorrowful, because we are all sorrowing; 17
8 you are sorrowing for one son 17
12 which I brought forth in pain and bore in sorrow; 18
14 then I say to you, 'As you brought forth in sorrow 18
15 Now, therefore, keep your sorrow to yourself 18
20 be consoled because of the sorrow of Jerusalem. 18
24 and lay aside your many sorrows 18
39 you have sorrowed continually for your people 17
16:18 The beginning of sorrows 19
Tob 2: 5 I washed myself and ate my food in sorrow. 11
3: 6 great is the sorrow within me 11
10 I shall bring his old age down in sorrow to the grave. 13
6:14 and bring . . to the grave in sorrow on my account 13
7:18 Lord . . grant you joy in place of this sorrow of yours 11
Sir 26: 6 There is grief of heart and sorrow 14
30:10 lest you have sorrow with him 16
12 you have sorrow of soul from him. •
21 Do not give yourself over to sorrow 11
23 remove sorrow far from you 11
23 sorrow has destroyed many 11
37:12 who will sorrow with you if you fail. 15
38:17 then be comforted for your sorrow. 11
18 For sorrow results in death 11
18 sorrow of heart saps one's strength. 11
19 In calamity sorrow continues 11
20 Do not give your heart to sorrow; drive it away 11
Bar 4: 9 God has brought great sorrow upon me; 14
11 I sent them away with weeping and sorrow. 14
23 For I sent you out with sorrow and weeping 14
5: 1 the garment of your sorrow and affliction 14
4Mc 1:23 Fear precedes pain and sorrow comes after. 11

sorrowful 1. כָּבֵד 2. *λυπέω* 3. *λυπηρός* 4. doleo 5. tristis 6. tristor
Gen 50:10 with a very great and sorrowful lamentation; 1
Mat 19:22 he went away sorrowful 2
26:22 they were very sorrowful, and began to say to him 2
37 he began to be sorrowful and troubled. 2
Mrk 10:22 he went away sorrowful 2
14:19 They began to be sorrowful 2
Joh 16:20 you will be sorrowful 2
2Co 6:10 as sorrowful, yet always rejoicing 2
1Es 9:52 do not be sorrowful, for the Lord will exalt you. 2
53 This day is holy; do not be sorrowful. 2
2Es 2:27 others shall weep and be sorrowful 5
7:12 were made narrow and sorrowful and toilsome; 4
10: 8 and to be sorrowful, because we are all sorrowing; 5
12:46 do not be sorrowful, O house of Jacob; 6
13:13 some of whom were joyful and some sorrowful 6
Wis 2: 1 Short and sorrowful is our life 3

very sorrowful 1. *περίλυπος*
Mat 26:38 My soul is very sorrowful, even to death 1
Mrk 14:34 My soul is very sorrowful, even to death 1

many sorrows 1. *πολύθρηνος*
4Mc 16:10 a widow and alone, with many sorrows. 1

sorry 1. דאג 2. חלה 3. נחם 4. *λυπέω*
Gen 6: 6 the LORD was sorry that he had made man 3
7 air, for I am sorry that I have made them. 3
1Sm 22: 8 none of you is sorry for me or discloses to me that 2
Ps 38:18 I confess my iniquity, I am sorry for my sin. 1
Mat 14: 9 the king was sorry 4
sorry *See also* make.

exceedingly sorry 1. *περίλυπος*
Mrk 6:26 And the king was exceedingly sorry; 1

sort 1. כָּנָף 2. *εἶδος* 3. *συλλέγω* 4. *τις* 5. *ὑπόδειγμα*
Gen 6:19 you shall bring two of every sort into the ark •
20 two of every sort shall come in to you •
21 take with you every sort of food that is eaten •
7:14 according to its kind, every bird of every sort. †
Exd 35:22 rings and armlets, all sorts of gold objects •
35 ability to do every sort of work done •
35 by any sort of workman or skilled designer. •
36: 4 able men who were doing every sort of task •
Lev 5: 3 touches human uncleanness, of whatever sort •
4 any sort of rash oath that men swear •
1Sm 4: 8 smote the Egyptians with every sort of plague •
2Kg 17:32 and appointed . . all sorts of people as priests •
1Ch 18:10 he sent all sorts of articles of gold, of silver •
29: 2 quantities of . . all sorts of precious stones •
Ezk 23:42 with men of the common sort drunkards were †
39: 4 I will give you to birds of prey of every sort 1
17 Speak to the birds of every sort and to all beasts 1
Mat 13:48 sat down and sorted the good into vessels 3
Heb 4:11 no one fall by the same sort of disobedience. 5
Sir 23:16 Two sorts of men multiply sins 2
47:25 For they sought out every sort of wickedness •
2Mc 7:31 who have contrived all sorts of evil •
15:11 a sort of vision, which was worthy of belief. 4
sort *See also* all, any, every, some, what.

soul 1. כָּבוֹד 2. כִּלְיָה 3. לֵבָב 4. מֵעֶה 5. נֶפֶשׁ 6. *ψυχή* 7. anima
Gen 34: 3 his soul was drawn to Dinah the daughter of Jacob; 5
8 Hamor spoke with them, saying, "The soul of my son 5
35:18 as her soul was departing (for she died) 5
42:21 we saw the distress of his soul, when he besought 5
49: 6 O my soul, come not into their council; 5
Exd 31:14 that soul shall be cut off from among his people. 5
Lev 17:11 upon the altar to make atonement for your souls 5
26:11 my soul shall not abhor you 5
15 if your soul abhors my ordinances 5
30 and my soul will abhor you 5
43 and their soul abhorred my statutes 5
Deu 4: 9 Only take heed, and keep your soul diligently 5
29 if you search after him with . . all your soul. 5
6: 5 love the LORD your God with . . all your soul 5
10:12 to serve the LORD your God . . with all your soul 5
11:13 to serve him with . . heart and with all your soul 5
18 lay up these words of mine . . in your soul; 5
13: 3 whether you love the LORD . . with all your soul. 5
6 If . . your friend who is as your own soul, entices 5
26:16 do . . with all your heart and with all your soul. 5
28:65 LORD will give you there . . a languishing soul; 5
30: 2 obey . . with all your heart and with all your soul; 5
6 love the LORD your God . . with all your soul 5
10 turn to the LORD your God . . with all your soul. 5
Jos 22: 5 with all your heart and with all your soul. 5
23:14 you know in your hearts and souls, all of you 5
Jdg 5:21 March on, my soul, with might! 5
16:16 and urged him, his soul was vexed to death. 5
1Sm 1:15 I have been pouring out my soul before the LORD. 5
17:55 As your soul lives, O king, I cannot tell. 5
18: 1 the soul of Jonathan was knit to the soul of David 5
1 the soul of Jonathan was knit to the soul of David 5
1 and Jonathan loved him as his own soul. 5
3 because he loved him as his own soul. 5
20: 3 as the LORD lives and as your soul lives 5
17 for he loved him as he loved his own soul. 5
25:26 as the LORD lives, and as your soul lives 5
30: 6 all the people were bitter in soul 5
2Sm 5: 8 lame and the blind, who are hated by David's soul. 5
11:11 As you live, and as your soul lives, I will not do 5
1Kg 1:29 who has redeemed my soul out of every adversity 5
2: 4 with all their heart and with all their soul 5
11:37 you shall reign over all that your soul desires 5
17:21 LORD . . let this child's soul come into him again. 5
22 the soul of the child came into him again 5
2Kg 23: 3 to keep his . . with all his heart and all his soul 5
25 all his heart and with all his soul and . . might 5
2Ch 15:12 to seek the LORD . . and with all their soul; 5
34:31 to keep . . with all his heart and all his soul 5
Job 3:20 that is in misery, and life to the bitter in soul 5
7:11 I will complain in the bitterness of my soul. 5
10: 1 I will speak in the bitterness of my soul. 5
21:25 Another dies in bitterness of soul 5
24:12 the soul of the wounded cries for help; 5
27: 2 the Almighty, who has made my soul bitter; 5
30:16 now my soul is poured out within me; 5
25 Was not my soul grieved for the poor? 5
33:18 he keeps back his soul from the Pit 5
22 His soul draws near the Pit 5
28 has redeemed my soul from going down into the Pit 5
30 to bring back his soul from the Pit, 5
Ps 6: 3 My soul also is sorely troubled. 5
7: 5 my life to the ground, and lay my soul in the dust. 1
11: 5 his soul hates him that loves violence. 5
13: 2 How long must I bear pain in my soul 5
16: 9 Therefore my heart is glad, and my soul rejoices; 1
19: 7 The law of the LORD is perfect, reviving the soul; 5
22:20 Deliver my soul from the sword 5
23: 3 he restores my soul. He leads me in paths 5
24: 4 who does not lift up his soul to what is false 5
25: 1 To thee, O LORD, I lift up my soul. 5
30: 3 O LORD, thou hast brought up my soul from Sheol 5
12 that my soul may praise thee and not be silent. 1
31: 9 eye is wasted from grief, my soul and my body also. 5
33:19 that he may deliver their soul from death 5
20 Our soul waits for the LORD; he is our help 5
34: 2 My soul makes its boast in the LORD; 5
35: 3 Say to my soul, "I am your deliverance! 5
9 Then my soul shall rejoice in the LORD 5
12 They requite me evil for good; my soul is forlorn. 5
42: 1 so longs my soul for thee, O God. 5
2 My soul thirsts for God, for the living God. 5
4 These things I remember, as I pour out my soul 5
5 Why are you cast down, O my soul 5
6 My soul is cast down within me 5
11 Why are you cast down, O my soul 5
43: 5 Why are you cast down, O my soul 5
44:25 For our soul is bowed down to the dust; 5
49:15 God will ransom my soul from the power of Sheol 5
55:18 He will deliver my soul in safety from the battle 5
56:13 For thou hast delivered my soul from death 5
57: 1 be merciful to me, for in thee my soul takes refuge; 5
6 They set a net for my steps; my soul was bowed down. 5
8 Awake, my soul! Awake, O harp and lyre! 1
62: 1 For God alone my soul waits in silence; 5
5 For God alone my soul waits in silence 5
63: 1 my God, I seek thee, my soul thirsts for thee; 5
5 My soul is feasted as with marrow and fat 5
8 My soul clings to thee; thy right hand upholds me. 5

69:10 When I humbled my soul with fasting 5
71:23 my soul also, which thou hast rescued. 5
73:21 When my soul was embittered 3
74:19 Do not deliver the soul of thy dove to the wild 5
77: 2 my soul refuses to be comforted. 5
84: 2 soul longs, yea, faints for the courts of the LORD; 5
86: 4 Gladden the soul of thy servant, for to thee, O Lord 5
4 for to thee, O Lord, do I lift up my soul. 5
13 hast delivered my soul from the depths of Sheol. 5
88: 3 For my soul is full of troubles 5
89:48 Who can deliver his soul from the power of Sheol? 5
94:17 soul . . soon have dwelt in the land of silence. 5
19 thy consolations cheer my soul. 5
103: 1 Bless the LORD, O my soul; and all that is within me 5
2 Bless the LORD, O my soul, and forget not 5
22 Bless the LORD, O my soul! 5
104: 1 Bless the LORD, O my soul! 5
35 Bless the LORD, O my soul! Praise the LORD! 5
107: 5 hungry and thirsty, their soul fainted within 5
108: 1 I will sing and make melody! Awake, my soul! 1
116: 7 Return, O my soul, to your rest; 5
8 For thou hast delivered my soul from death 5
119:20 My soul is consumed with longing 5
25 My soul cleaves to the dust; 5
28 My soul melts away for sorrow; 5
81 My soul languishes for thy salvation; 5
129 are wonderful; therefore my soul keeps them. 5
167 My soul keeps thy testimonies; I love them 5
123: 4 Too long our soul has been sated with the scorn 5
130: 5 for the LORD, my soul waits, and in his word I hope; 5
6 my soul waits for the LORD more than watchmen 5
131: 2 I have calmed and quieted my soul 5
2 like a child that is quieted is my soul. 5
138: 3 my strength of soul thou didst increase. 5
143: 6 my soul thirsts for thee like a parched land. 5
8 way I should go, for to thee I lift up my soul. 5
146: 1 Praise the LORD! Praise the LORD, O my soul! 5
Prv 2:10 knowledge will be pleasant to your soul; 5
3:22 life for your soul and adornment for your neck. 5
13: 4 The soul of the sluggard craves, and gets nothing 5
4 soul of the diligent is richly supplied. 5
19 A desire fulfilled is sweet to the soul; 5
16:24 sweetness to the soul and health to the body. 5
21:10 The soul of the wicked desires evil; 5
23:16 My soul will rejoice when your lips speak 2
24:12 Does not he who keeps watch over your soul know it 5
14 Know that wisdom is such to your soul; 5
25:25 Like cold water to a thirsty soul, so is good news 5
27: 9 but the soul is torn by trouble. 6
Sng 1: 7 Tell me, you whom my soul loves, where you pasture 5
3: 1 my bed by night I sought him whom my soul loves 5
2 I will rise . . I will seek him whom my soul loves. 5
3 Have you seen him whom my soul loves? 5
4 I found him whom my soul loves. 5
5: 6 My soul failed me when he spoke. 5
Isa 1:14 Your new moons and your . . feasts my soul hates; 5
10:18 the LORD will destroy, both soul and body 5
15: 4 of Moab cry aloud; his soul trembles. 5
16:11 Therefore my soul moans like a lyre for Moab 4
26: 8 thy memorial name is the desire of our soul. 5
9 My soul yearns for thee in the night 5
38:15 has fled because of the bitterness of my soul. 5
42: 1 my chosen, in whom my soul delights; 5
53:11 he shall see the fruit of the travail of his soul 5
12 because he poured out his soul to death 5
55: 3 come to me; hear, that your soul may live; 5
61:10 rejoice in the LORD, my soul shall exult in my God; 5
66: 3 and their soul delights in their abominations; 5
Jer 6:16 and walk in it, and find rest for your souls. 5
12: 7 I have given the beloved of my soul into the hands 5
13:17 if you will not listen, my soul will weep in secret 5
14:19 Does thy soul loathe Zion? 5
31:14 I will feast the soul of the priests 5
25 For I will satisfy the weary soul 5
25 and every languishing soul I will replenish. 5
32:41 faithfulness, with all my heart and all my soul. 5
38:16 to Jeremiah, "As the LORD lives, who made our souls 5
Lam 1:20 Behold . . for I am in distress, my soul is in tumult 4
2:11 My eyes are spent . . my soul is in tumult; 4
3:17 my soul is bereft of peace 5
20 My soul continually thinks of it and is bowed 5
24 The LORD is my portion," says my soul 5
25 The LORD is good . . to the soul that seeks him. 5
Ezk 13:18 persons of every stature, in the hunt for souls! 5
18 Will you hunt down souls belonging to my people 5
18 and keep other souls alive for your profit? 5
20 your magic bands with which you hunt the souls 5
20 I will let the souls that you hunt go free 5
18: 4 Behold, all souls are mine; 5
4 soul of the father as well as the soul of the son 5
4 soul of the father as well as the soul of the son 5
4 the soul that sins shall die. 5
20 The soul that sins shall die. 5
24:21 delight of your eyes, and the desire of your soul; 5
27:31 they weep over you in bitterness of soul 5
Jon 2: 7 my soul fainted within me, I remembered the LORD; 5
Mic 6: 7 give . . the fruit of my body for the sin of my soul? 5
7: 1 no first-ripe fig which my soul desires. 5
3 the great man utters the evil desire of his soul; 5

Hab 2: 4 he whose soul is not upright in him shall fail 5
Mat 10:28 kill the body but cannot kill the soul 6
28 who can destroy both soul and body in hell. 6
11:29 and you will find rest for your souls. 6
12:18 my beloved with whom my soul is well pleased 6
22:37 with all your heart, and with all your soul 6
26:38 My soul is very sorrowful, even to death 6
Mrk 12:30 with all your soul, and with all your mind 6
14:34 My soul is very sorrowful, even to death 6
Lke 1:46 Mary said, "My soul magnifies the Lord 6
2:35 (and a sword will pierce through your own soul also) 6
10:27 with all your soul, and with all your strength 6
12:19 I will say to my soul, Soul, you have ample goods 6
19 I will say to my soul, Soul, you have ample goods 6
20 This night your soul is required of you 6
Joh 12:27 Now is my soul troubled. And what shall I say? 6
Act 2:27 thou wilt not abandon my soul to Hades 6
41 there were added that day about 3,000 souls. 6
43 fear came upon every soul 6
3:23 every soul that does not listen to that prophet 6
4:32 who believed were of one heart and soul 6
7:14 all his kindred, 75 souls; 6
14:22 strengthening the souls of the disciples 6
2Co 12:15 most gladly spend and be spent for your souls 6
1Th 5:23 may your spirit and soul and body be kept sound 6
Heb 4:12 piercing to the division of soul and spirit 6
6:19 as a sure and steadfast anchor of the soul 6
10:38 if he shrinks back, my soul has no pleasure in him. 6
39 those who have faith and keep their souls. 6
13:17 for they are keeping watch over your souls 6
Jas 1:21 implanted word, which is able to save your souls. 6
5:20 will save his soul from death 6
1Pe 1: 9 you obtain the salvation of your souls. 6
22 Having purified your souls by your obedience 6
2:11 passions . . that wage war against your soul. 6
25 the Shepherd and Guardian of your souls. 6
4:19 and entrust their souls to a faithful Creator. 6
2Pe 2: 8 he was vexed in his righteous soul day after day 6
14 They entice unsteady souls. 6
3Jn 1: 2 I know that it is well with your soul. 6
Rev 6: 9 I saw under the altar the souls of those 6
18:13 and chariots, and slaves, that is, human souls. 6
14 The fruit for which thy soul longed has gone 6
20: 4 I saw the souls of those who had been beheaded 6
2Es 3:29 my soul has seen many sinners 7
4:35 the souls of the righteous in their chambers 7
41 the chambers of the souls are like the womb. 7
5:14 and my soul was so troubled that it fainted. 7
22 my soul recovered the spirit of understanding 7
6:37 and my soul was in distress. 7
7:32 and the chambers shall give up the souls 7
75 as soon as every one of us yields up his soul 7
93 in which the souls of the ungodly wander 7
99 This is the order of the souls of the righteous 7
100 Will time therefore be given to the souls 7
8: 4 Then drink your fill of understanding, O my soul 7
10:36 Or is my mind deceived, and my soul dreaming? 7
12: 8 that thou mayest fully comfort my soul. 7
15: 8 the souls of the righteous cry out continually. 7
Tob 13: 6 with all your heart and with all your soul 6
7 I exalt my God; my soul exalts the King of heaven 6
15 Let my soul praise God the great King. 6
Jdt 12: 4 Judith replied, "As your soul lives, my lord 6
Wis 1: 4 because wisdom will not enter a deceitful soul 6
11 a lying mouth destroys the soul. 6
2:22 nor discern the prize for blameless souls; 6
3: 1 the souls of the righteous are in the hand of God 6
13 she will have fruit when God examines souls. 6
4:11 lest . . guile deceive his soul. 6
14 for his soul was pleasing to the Lord 6
7:27 in every generation she passes into holy souls 6
8:19 a good soul fell to my lot; 6
9: 3 and pronounce judgment in uprightness of soul 6
15 for a perishable body weighs down the soul 6
10: 7 standing as a monument to an unbelieving soul. 6
16 She entered the soul of a servant of the Lord 6
14:11 and became traps for the souls of men 6
26 forgetfulness of favors, pollution of souls 6
15: 8 required to return the soul that was lent him. 6
11 formed him and inspired him with an active soul 6
16:14 nor set free the imprisoned soul. 6
17: 1 therefore unintructed souls have gone astray. 6
8 the fears and disorders of a sick soul 6
15 now were paralyzed by their souls' surrender 6
Sir 4: 6 in bitterness of soul 6
6: 2 not exalt yourself through your soul's counsel 6
2 lest your soul be torn in pieces like a bull. 6
4 An evil soul will destroy him who has it 6
26 Come to her with all your soul 6
7:11 Do not ridicule a man who is bitter in soul 6
21 Let your soul love an intelligent servant 6
29 With all your soul fear the Lord 6
14: 9 mean injustice withers the soul. 6
16:17 what is my soul in the boundless creation? 6
18:31 If you allow your soul to take pleasure 6
19: 3 the reckless soul will be snatched away. 6
21: 2 destroy the souls of men. 6
27 he curses his own soul. 6
28 A whisperer defiles his own soul 6

23: 6 do not surrender me to a shameless soul. 6
16 The soul heated like a burning fire 6
25: 1 My soul takes pleasure in three things •
2 My soul hates three kinds of men 6
26:14 nothing so precious as a disciplined soul. 6
15 no balance can weigh the value of a chaste soul. 6
30:12 you have sorrow of soul from him. •
23 Delight your soul and comfort your heart 6
31:28 rejoicing of heart and gladness of soul. 6
29 Wine drunk to excess is bitterness of soul 6
33:31 as your own soul you will need him 6
34:15 Blessed is the soul of the man who fears the Lord! 6
17 He lifts up the soul and gives light to the eyes 6
37:12 whose soul is in accord with your soul 6
12 whose soul is in accord with your soul 6
14 a man's soul sometimes keeps him better informed 6
27 My son, test your soul while you live 6
45:23 in the ready goodness of his soul 6
47:15 Your soul covered the earth 6
50:25 With two nations my soul is vexed 6
51: 6 My soul drew near to death 6
19 My soul grappled with wisdom 6
20 I directed my soul to her 6
24 why are your souls very thirsty? 6
26 let your souls receive instruction 6
29 May your soul rejoice in his mercy 6
Bar 3: 1 soul in anguish and the wearied spirit cry out 6
Aza 1:64 spirits and souls of the righteous 6
2Mc 3:16 disclosed the anguish of his soul. 6
6:30 in my soul I am glad to suffer these things 6
15:17 and awaking manliness in the souls of the young 6
30 the man who was ever in body and soul the defender 6
4Mc 1:20 by nature concerned with both body and soul. 6
26 In the soul it is boastfulness, covetousness 6
28 two plants growing from the body and the soul 6
3:15 an altogether fearful danger to his soul 6
13:15 for great is the struggle of the soul 6
21 brotherly-loving souls are nourished; 6
15:25 as in the council chamber of her own soul 6
18:23 have received pure and immortal souls from God 6

afflicted soul 1. *ταπείνωσις*

Ps 22:21 my afflicted soul from the horns of the wild oxen! 1

living soul 1. *ψυχή*

Jdt 11: 7 who had sent you to direct every living soul 1

sound 1. הֶמְיָה 2. חצצר 3. משך 4. נתן 5. פֶּה 6. קוֹל 7. שמע 8. שֶׁמַע 9. תקע 10. תֵּקַע 11. קוֹל (A) 12. *ἠχέω* 13. *ἦχος* 14. *θροῦς* 15. *λαλέω* 16. *λαλέω φωνάς* 17. *σημαίνω* 18. *φωνέω* 19. *φωνή* 20. cano 21. emitto 22. sono 23. sonus

Gen 3: 8 they heard the sound of the LORD God walking 6
10 he said, "I heard the sound of thee in the garden 6
Exd 19:13 When the trumpet sounds a long blast 3
19 as the sound of the trumpet grew louder 6
20:18 the lightnings and the sound of the trumpet 6
28:35 its sound shall be heard when he goes 6
32:18 It is not the sound of shouting for victory 6
18 or the sound of the cry of defeat, 6
18 of defeat, but the sound of singing that I hear. 6
Lev 26:36 sound of a driven leaf shall put them to flight 6
Deu 4:12 you heard the sound of words, but saw no form; 6
Jos 6: 5 as soon as you hear the sound of the trumpet 6
20 soon as the people heard the sound of the trumpet 6
Jdg 3:27 he sounded the trumpet in the hill country 9
5:11 To the sound of musicians at the watering places 6
6:34 of Gideon; and he sounded the trumpet 9
1Sm 4:14 When Eli heard the sound of the outcry, he said 6
2Sm 5:24 hear the sound of marching in the . . balsam trees 6
6:15 with shouting, and with the sound of the horn. 6
15:10 As soon as you hear the sound of the trumpet 6
1Kg 1:41 when Jo'ab heard the sound of the trumpet, he said 6
14: 6 when Ahi'jah heard the sound of her feet 6
18:41 there is a sound of the rushing of rain. 6
2Kg 4:31 but there was no sound or sign of life. 6
6:32 Is not the sound of his master's feet behind him? 6
7: 6 made the army . . hear the sound of chariots 6
6 chariots, and of horses, the sound of a great army 6
1Ch 14:15 sound of marching in the tops of the balsam trees 6
15:16 on harps . . and cymbals, to raise sounds of joy. 6
19 The singers . . were to sound bronze cymbals; 7
28 the sound of the horn, trumpets, and cymbals 6
16: 5 Asaph was to sound the cymbals 7
2Ch 29:28 singers sang, and the trumpeters sounded; 2
Ezr 3:13 not distinguish the sound of the joyful shout 6
13 from the sound of the people's weeping 6
13 with a great shout, and the sound was heard afar. 6
Neh 4:18 The man who sounded the trumpet was beside me. 9
20 place where you hear the sound of the trumpet 6
Job 15:21 Terrifying sounds are in his ears; 6
21:12 and rejoice to the sound of the pipe. 6
33: 8 I have heard the sound of your words. 6
39:24 he cannot stand still at the sound of the trumpet. 6
25 When the trumpet sounds, he says 'Aha!' 17
Ps 5: 2 Hearken to the sound of my cry, my King and my God 6
6: 8 for the LORD has heard the sound of my weeping. 6
47: 5 the LORD with the sound of a trumpet. 6

66: 8 O peoples, let the sound of his praise be heard 6
81: 2 sound the timbrel, the sweet lyre with the harp. 4
98: 5 praises . . with the lyre and the sound of melody! 6
6 With trumpets and the sound of the horn 6
104: 7 at the sound of thy thunder they took to flight. 6
150: 3 Praise him with trumpet sound; 10
5 Praise him with sounding cymbals; 8
Ecc 12: 4 when the sound of the grinding is low 6
Isa 14:11 brought down to Sheol, the sound of your harps; 1
24:18 He who flees at the sound of the terror shall fall 6
30:19 be gracious to you at the sound of your cry; 6
29 as when one sets out to the sound of the flute to go *
32 will be to the sound of timbrels and lyres; *
65:19 no more shall be heard in it the sound of weeping 6
Jer 4:19 I hear the sound of the trumpet, the alarm of war. 6
21 and hear the sound of the trumpet? 6
6:17 saying, 'Give heed to the sound of the trumpet!' 6
23 the sound of them is like the roaring sea; 6
8:16 at the sound of the neighing of their stallions 6
9:19 For a sound of wailing is heard from Zion 6
42:14 shall not see war, or hear the sound of the trumpet 6
46:22 She makes a sound like a serpent gliding away; 6
49:21 At the sound of their fall the earth shall 6
21 the sound of their cry shall be heard 6
50:42 The sound of them is like the roaring of the sea; 6
46 At the sound of the capture of Babylon 6
Ezk 1:24 when they went, I heard the sound of their wings 6
24 their wings like the sound of many waters 6
24 a sound of tumult like the sound of a host; 6
24 a sound of tumult like the sound of a host; 6
3:12 I heard behind me the sound of a great earthquake; 6
13 the sound of the wings of the living creatures 6
13 and the sound of the wheels beside them 6
13 wheels . . that sounded like a great earthquake. 6
10: 5 the sound of the wings of the cherubim was heard 6
19: 4 The nations sounded an alarm against him; 7
7 land was appalled . . at the sound of his roaring. 6
23:42 The sound of a carefree multitude was with her; 6
26:13 the sound of your lyres shall be heard no more. 6
15 Will not the coastlands shake at the sound 6
27:28 At the sound of the cry of your pilots 6
31:16 make the nations quake at the sound of its fall 6
33: 4 then if any one who hears the sound of the trumpet 6
5 He heard the sound of the trumpet 6
43: 2 the sound of his coming was like the sound of many 6
2 his coming was like the sound of many waters; 6
Dan 3: 5 hear the sound of the horn, pipe, lyre, trigon 11
7 heard the sound of the horn, pipe, lyre, trigon 11
10 made a decree, that every man who hears the sound 11
15 hear the sound of the horn, pipe, lyre, trigon 11
7:11 looked . . because of the sound of the great words 11
10: 6 sound of his words like the noise of a multitude. 6
9 Then I heard the sound of his words; 6
9 when I heard the sound of his words, I fell 6
Ams 2: 2 amid shouting and the sound of the trumpet; 6
6: 5 who sing idle songs to the sound of the harp 5
Hab 3:16 my body trembles, my lips quiver at the sound; 6
Zep 1:14 the sound of the day of the LORD is bitter 6
Zec 9:14 the Lord GOD will sound the trumpet, and march 9
Joh 3: 8 The wind blows . . and you hear the sound of it 19
Act 2: 2 suddenly a sound came from heaven 13
6 at this sound the multitude came together 19
1Co 14: 8 if the bugle gives an indistinct sound 19
Heb 12:19 the sound of a trumpet 13
Rev 1:15 and his voice was like the sound of many waters; 19
10: 3 when he called out, the seven thunders sounded. 16
4 when the seven thunders had sounded 15
14: 2 a voice from heaven like the sound of many waters 19
2 a voice . . like the sound of loud thunder; 19
2 like the sound of harpers playing on their harps 19
18:22 and the sound of harpers and minstrels 19
22 and the sound of the millstone shall be heard 19
19: 6 like the sound of many waters 19
6 like the sound of mighty thunderpeals, crying 19
1Es 5:65 the sound was heard afar; *
66 find out what the sound of the trumpets meant. 19
2Es 6: 2 before the rumblings of thunder sounded 22
17 its sound was like the sound of many waters. 23
17 its sound was like the sound of many waters. 23
23 the trumpet shall sound aloud 20
39 the sound of man's voice was not yet there. 23
10:26 so that the earth shook at the sound. 23
11:15 behold, a voice sounded, saying to it. 21
Wis 1:10 the sound of murmurings does not go unheard. 14
7: 3 my first sound was a cry, like that of all. 19
17: 4 terrifying sounds rang out around them 13
18 a melodious sound of birds 13
19 the sound of the most savage roaring beasts 19
Sir 38:28 he inclines his ear to the sound of the hammer 19
45: 9 to send forth a sound as he walked 19
46:17 made his voice heard with a mighty sound; 19
50:16 they sounded the trumpets of hammered work 12
1Mc 9:12 phalanx advanced to the sound of the trumpets 18

sound (2) 1. נצב 2. *ἀγαθός* 3. *ἁπλοῦς* 4. *ὀρθός* 5. *πονηρός* 6. *ὑγιαίνω* 7. *ὑγιής*
Ps 73: 4 have no pangs; their bodies are sound and sleek. *
Zec 11:16 or heal the maimed, or nourish the sound 1
Mat 6:22 if your eye is sound, your whole body will be full 3
23 your eye is not sound, your whole body will be full 5
7:17 So, every sound tree bears good fruit 2
18 A sound tree cannot bear evil fruit 2
Lke 11:34 when your eye is sound 3
34 when it is not sound, your body is full of darkness. 5
1Ti 1:10 whatever else is contrary to sound doctrine 6
6: 3 does not agree with the sound words of our Lord 6
2Ti 1:13 the sound words which you have heard from me 6
4: 3 when people will not endure sound teaching 6
Tit 1: 9 be able to give instruction in sound doctrine 6
13 that they may be sound in the faith 6
2: 1 as for you, teach what befits sound doctrine. 6
2 sound in faith, in love, and in steadfastness. 6
8 sound speech that cannot be censured 7
4Mc 1:15 with sound logic prefers the life of wisdom. 4

sound (3) 1. חקר 2. *βολίζω*
1Sm 20:12 When I have sounded my father, about this time 1
Act 27:28 So they sounded and found twenty fathoms 2
28 a little farther on they sounded again 2
sound *See* judgment, keep, knowledge, make, safe, wisdom.

sound a call to battle 1. רוע
2Ch 13:12 battle trumpets to sound the call to battle 1

sound a trumpet 1. חצצר 2. *σαλπίζω*
2Ch 7: 6 opposite them the priests sounded trumpets; 1
Mat 6: 2 when you give alms, sound no trumpet before you 2
1Es 5:62 all the people sounded trumpets 2
65 the multitude sounded the trumpets loudly 2
1Mc 3:54 they sounded the trumpets and gave a loud shout. 2
4:40 and sounded the signal on the trumpets 2
5:33 who sounded their trumpets 2
6:33 and sounded their trumpets. 2
16: 8 they sounded the trumpets 2

sound a trumpet call 1. *σαλπίζω*
Rev 10: 7 in the days of the trumpet call to be sounded 1

sound an alarm 1. רוע
Num10: 7 you shall blow, but you shall not sound an alarm. 1
9 then you shall sound an alarm with the trumpets 1
Hos 5: 8 Sound the alarm at Beth-a'ven; tremble, O Benjamin! 1
Jol 2: 1 sound the alarm on my holy mountain! 1

sound forth 1. *ἐξηχέω*
1Th 1: 8 sounded forth from you in Macedo'nia and Acha'ia 1

sound of a trumpet 1. *σάλπιγξ*
1Th 4:16 with the sound of the trumpet of God 1

sound on a trumpet 1. *σαλπίζω*
1Mc 7:45 Jews . . kept sounding the battle call on the trumpets. 1

rushing sound 1. *ῥοῖζος*
Bel 1:36 with the rushing sound of the wind itself. 1

soundness 1. מְתֹם 2. *εὐεξία*
Ps 38: 3 There is no soundness in my flesh 1
7 there is no soundness in my flesh. 1
Isa 1: 6 there is no soundness in it, but bruises and sores 1
Sir 30:15 Health and soundness are better than all gold 2
sour *See* grapes.

source 1. קָצֶה 2. *αἴτιος* 3. *ἀρχή* 4. *ἐκ* 5. principium
Isa 7:18 the fly . . at the sources of the streams of Egypt 1
1Co 1:30 He is the source of your life in Christ Jesus 4
Heb 5: 9 he became the source of eternal salvation 2
2Es 4: 7 or how many streams are at the source of the deep 5
Wis 12:16 For thy strength is the source of righteousness 3

source of revenue 1. *πρόσοδος*
2Mc 4: 8 from another source of revenue, 80 talents. 1

south 1. דָּרוֹם 2. יָמִין 3. יְמָנִי 4. מִיָּמִין 5. מִנֶּגֶב 6. נֶגֶב 7. נֶגֶב תֵּימָן 8. תֵּימָן 9. תֵּימָן נֶגֶב 10. *δεξιός* 11. *μεσημβρία* 12. *νότος* 13. meridianus 14. notus
Gen 28:14 to the east and to the north and to the south; 6
Exd 26:18 twenty frames for the south side; 8
35 the lampstand on the south side 8
27: 9 On the south side the court shall have hangings 8
36:23 made thus: twenty frames for the south side; 8
38: 9 for the south side the hangings of the court 8
40:24 opposite the table on the south side 6
Num 3:29 to encamp on the south side of the tabernacle 8
34: 3 south side shall be from the wilderness of Zin 6
3 your southern boundary shall be from the end 6
4 boundary shall turn south of the ascent of Akrab'bim 6
4 Zin, and its end shall be south of Ka'desh-bar'nea; 6
35: 5 shall measure . . for the south side 2,000 cubits 6
Deu 33:23 O Naph'tali . . possess the lake and the south. 1
Jos 11: 2 and in the Arabah south of Chin'neroth 6
13: 4 in the south, all the land of the Canaanites 8
15: 1 to the wilderness of Zin at the farthest south. 8
2 south boundary ran from the end of the Salt Sea 6
3 along to Zin, and goes up south of Ka'desh-bar'nea 6
4 This shall be your south boundary. 6
21 The cities . . of Judah in the extreme South 6
17: 9 The cities here, to the south of the brook 6
10 the land to the south being E'phraim's 6
18: 5 Judah continuing in his territory on the south 6
13 upon the mountain . . south of Lower Beth-hor'on. 6
14 turning . . from the mountain . . to the south 6
16 valley . . south of the shoulder of the Jeb'usites 6
19 the northern bay . . at the south end of the Jordan 6
19:34 goes . . to Hukkok, touching Zeb'ulun at the south 6
Jdg 21:19 is north of Bethel . . and south of Lebo'nah. 5
1Sm 14: 5 and the other on the south in front of Geba. 6
23:19 the hill of Hachi'lah, which is south of Jeshi'mon? 2
24 of Ma'on, in the Arabah to the south of Jeshi'mon. 2
1Kg 6: 8 entrance . . was on the south side of the house; 3
7:21 he set up the pillar on the south and called its 2
25 twelve oxen . . three facing south, and three 6
39 set the stands, five on the south side of the house 4
49 lampstands . . five on the south side and five 2
2Kg 11:11 from the south side of the house to the north side 3
23:13 east of Jerusalem, to the south of the mount 2
1Ch 9:24 on the four sides, east, west, north and south; 6
26:15 O'bed-e'dom's came out for the south 6
17 north four each day, on the south four each day 6
2Ch 3:17 one on the south, the other on the north; 2
17 pillars . . that on the south he called Jachin 2
4: 4 It stood upon twelve oxen . . three facing south 6
23:10 from the south side of the house to the north side 3
Job 9: 9 Orion, the Plei'ades and the chambers of the south; 8
39:26 soars, and spreads his wings toward the south? 8
Ps 89:12 The north and the south, thou hast created them; 2
107: 3 gathered in from . . north and from the south. *
Ecc 1: 6 wind blows to the south, and . . round to the north; 1
11: 3 and if a tree falls to the south or to the north 1
Isa 43: 6 north, Give up, and to the south, Do not withhold 8
Ezk 10: 3 Now the cherubim were standing on the south side 2
16:46 your younger sister, who lived to the south of you 2
20:46 Son of man, set your face toward the south 8
46 face toward the south, preach against the south 1
47 all faces from south to north shall be scorched 6
21: 4 against all flesh from south to north; 6
40:24 he led me toward the south 1
24 behold, there was a gate on the south; 1
27 there was a gate on the south of the inner court; 1
27 he measured from gate to gate toward the south 1
28 he brought me to the inner court by the south gate 1
28 he measured the south gate; it was of the same size 1
44 one at the side of the north gate facing south 1
44 at the side of the south gate facing north. 12
45 chamber which faces south is for the priests 1
41:11 and another door toward the south; 1
42:10 On the south also, opposite the yard 12
12 below the south chambers was an entrance *
13 The north chambers and the south chambers 1
18 Then he turned and measured the south side 1
46: 9 by the north gate . . shall go out by the south gate; 6
9 he who enters by the south gate 6
47: 1 water was flowing down from below the south end 3
1 the threshold of the temple, south of the altar. 6
2 the water was coming out on the south side. 3
19 On the south side, it shall run from Tamar 7
19 This shall be the south side. 9
48:16 the north side 4,500 cubits, the south side 4,500 6
17 on the south 250, on the east 250 6
28 And adjoining the territory of Gad to the south 7
33 south side, which is to be 4,500 cubits by measure 6
Dan 8: 9 grew exceedingly great toward the south, 6
11: 5 Then the king of the south shall be strong 6
6 daughter of the king of the south shall come 6
9 come into the realm of the king of the south 6
11 king of the south, moved with anger, shall come out 6
14 many shall rise against the king of the south; 6
15 forces of the south shall not stand 6
25 against the king of the south with a great army; 6
25 king of the south shall wage war 6
29 shall return and come into the south; 6
40 time of the end the king of the south shall attack 6
Zec 6: 6 and the dappled ones go toward the south country. 8
7: 7 the South and the lowland were inhabited 6
9:14 and march forth in the whirlwinds of the south. 8
14:10 a plain from Geba to Rimmon south of Jerusalem. 6
Mat 12:42 The queen of the South will arise at the judgment 12
Lke 11:31 The queen of the South will arise at the judgment 12
13:29 come from east and west, and from north and south 12
Act 8:26 Rise and go toward the south 11
Rev 21:13 on the south three gates 12
2Es 15:20 from the rising sun and from the south 14
34 from the east, and from the north to the south 13
38 stirred up from the south, and . . north 13
39 driven violently toward the south and west. 14
Tob 1: 2 which is to the south of Kedesh Naphtali 10
Jdt 2:23 south of the country of the Chelleans. 12
7:18 they sent some of their men toward the south 12
1Mc 3:57 encamped to the south of Emmaus. 12
5:65 fought the sons of Esau in the land to the south 12
south *See also* side, wind.

southeast 1. קֵדְמָה יָמִינָה 2. קֵדְמָה מִמּוּל נֶגְבָּה 3. *κατὰ χῶρον*

1Kg 7:39 set the sea on the southeast corner of the house. 1
2Ch 4:10 set the sea at the southeast corner of the house. 2
Act 27:12 looking northeast and southeast 3

southern 1. מִנֶּגֶב 2. נֶגֶב 3. *νότος*
Jos 15: 8 goes . . at the southern shoulder of the Jeb'usite 1
18:15 the southern side begins at the outskirts 2
19 the boundary . . this is the southern border. 2
Ezk 48:10 and 25,000 in length on the southern side 2
Jdt 2:25 came to the southern borders of Japheth 3

southward 1. אֶל הַיָּמִין 2. אֶל מִנֶּגֶב 3. מִתֵּימָן 4. נֶגֶב 5. תֵּימָן
Gen 13:14 place where you are, northward and southward 4
Deu 3:27 lift up your eyes . . southward and eastward 5
Jos 12: 3 southward to the foot of the slopes of Pisgah; 3
15: 1 The lot . . reached southward to the boundary 4
2 the Salt Sea, from the bay that faces southward 4
3 it goes out southward of the ascent of Akrab'bim 2
17: 7 then the boundary goes along southward 1
18:13 From there the boundary passes along southward 4
14 turning . . southward from the mountain 4
Dan 8: 4 charging westward and northward and southward; 4
Zec 14: 4 northward, and the other half southward. 4

sovereign 1. *αὐτοδέσποτος* 2. *αὐτοκράτωρ* 3. *δεσπόζω* 4. *δεσπότης* 5. *δυνάστης* 6. *ἐπικρατέω* 7. *καθίστημι* 8. *κύριος* 9. dominator
1Ti 6:15 the blessed and only Sovereign 5
2Es 3: 4 O sovereign Lord, didst thou not speak 9
4:38 Then I answered and said, "O sovereign Lord 9
5:23 I said, "O sovereign Lord 9
38 I said, "O sovereign Lord, who is able to know 9
6:11 I answered and said, "O sovereign Lord 9
7:17 Then I answered and said, "O sovereign Lord, behold 9
45 I answered and said, "O sovereign Lord, I said ‡
58 I said, "O sovereign Lord, what is plentiful 9
12: 7 I said, "O sovereign Lord, if I have found favor 9
13:51 I said, "O sovereign Lord, explain this to me 9
Jdt 2:13 to transgress any of your sovereign's commands 8
AEs 16: 6 the sincere good will of their sovereigns. 6
Wis 12:18 Thou who art sovereign in strength 3
2Mc 3:24 the Sovereign of spirits and of all authority 5
28 recognized clearly the sovereign power of God. 7
12:15 calling upon the great Sovereign of the world 5
28 the Jews called upon the Sovereign 5
15: 3 asked if there were a sovereign in heaven 5
4 the living Lord himself, the Sovereign in heaven 5
5 he replied, "And I am a sovereign also, on earth 5
23 now, O Sovereign of the heavens, send a good angel 5
29 they blessed the Sovereign Lord 5
3Mc 2: 2 and sovereign of all creation, holy 4
4Mc 1: 1 devout reason is sovereign over the emotions 1
5 why is it not sovereign over forgetfulness 3
13 whether reason is sovereign over the emotions. 2
30 over the emotions it is sovereign 2
30 is sovereign over the emotions 1
2:13 It is sovereign over the relationship of friends 3
16 for it is sovereign over even this. 3
6:31 devout reason is sovereign over the emotions. 4
8:28 they were . . sovereign over agonies 2
13: 1 that devout reason is sovereign over 1
16: 1 devout reason is sovereign over the emotions. 2
sovereign *See also* Lord.

sovereignty 1. מַלְכוּ (A) 2. *βασιλεία* 3. *δεσπόζω* 4. *δυναστεία* 5. *τυραννίς*
Dan 2:44 nor . . its sovereignty be left to another people. 1
Wis 6: 3 and your sovereignty from the Most High 4
12:16 sovereignty over all causes thee to spare all. 3
Sir 10: 8 Sovereignty passes from nation to nation 2
47:21 that the sovereignty was divided 5

sovereignty over emotion 1. *παθοκράτεια*
4Mc 13: 5 confess the sovereignty of right reason over emotion 1

sow 1. זֵרוּעַ 2. זרע 3. זֶרַע 4. זרק 5. מִזְרָע 6. משך 7. מֶשֶׁךְ 8. שלח 9. *βάλλω* 10. *ἐπισπείρω* 11. *σπεῖρα* 12. *σπείρω* 13. semino 14. sero
Gen 26:12 Isaac sowed in that land, and reaped 2
47:23 seed for you, and you shall sow the land. 2
Exd 23:10 For six years you shall sow your land 2
16 fruits of your labor, of what you sow in the field. 2
Lev 11:37 if any part . . falls upon the seed for sowing 1
37 seed for sowing that is to be sown, it is clean 2
19:19 you shall not sow your field with two kinds of seed 2
25: 3 Six years you shall sow your field 2
4 shall not sow your field or prune your vineyard 2
11 A jubilee . . in it you shall neither sow 2
20 we may not sow or gather in our crop?' 2
22 When you sow in the eighth year, you will be eating 2
26: 5 the vintage shall last to the time for sowing 3
16 And you shall sow your seed in vain, 2
27:16 a sowing of a homer of barley shall be valued 3
Deu 11:10 Egypt . . where you sowed your seed and watered 2
21: 4 valley . . which is neither plowed nor sown 2
22: 9 not sow your vineyard with two kinds of seed 2
9 crop which you have sown and the yield 2
Jdg 9:45 and he razed the city and sowed it with salt. 2
2Kg 19:29 the third year sow, and reap, and plant vineyards 2
Job 4: 8 who plow iniquity and sow trouble reap the same. 2
31: 8 then let me sow, and another eat; 2
Ps 107:37 sow fields, and plant vineyards 2
126: 5 May those who sow in tears reap with shouts of joy! 2
6 goes forth weeping, bearing the seed for sowing 7
Prv 6:14 continually sowing discord; 8
19 a man who sows discord among brothers. 8
11:18 one who sows righteousness gets a sure reward. 2
22: 8 He who sows injustice will reap calamity 2
Ecc 11: 4 He who observes the wind will not sow; 2
6 In the morning sow your seed 2
Isa 17:11 and make them blossom in the morning that you sow; 3
19: 7 all that is sown by the Nile will dry up 5
28:24 Does he who plows for sowing plow continually? 2
25 does he not scatter dill, sow cummin 4
30:23 rain for the seed with which you sow the ground 2
32:20 Happy are you who sow beside all waters 2
37:30 then in the third year sow and reap 2
40:24 Scarcely are they planted, scarcely sown 2
61:11 as a garden causes what is sown in it to spring up 1
Jer 2: 2 followed me in the wilderness, in a land not sown. 2
4: 3 and sow not among thorns. 2
12:13 They have sown wheat and have reaped thorns 2
31:27 says the LORD, when I will sow the house of Israel 2
35: 7 you shall not build a house; you shall not sow seed; 2
Ezk 36: 9 you shall be tilled and sown; 2
Hos 2:23 and I will sow him for myself in the land. 2
8: 7 For they sow the wind 2
10:12 Sow for yourselves righteousness 2
Ams 9:13 and the treader of grapes him who sows the seed; 6
Mic 6:15 You shall sow, but not reap; 2
Hag 1: 6 You have sown much, and harvested little; 2
Zec 8:12 For there shall be a sowing of peace; 3
Mat 6:26 of the air: they neither sow nor reap nor gather 12
13: 3 A sower went out to sow. 12
4 as he sowed, some seeds fell along the path 12
19 and snatches away what is sown in his heart 12
19 this is what was sown along the path. 12
20 As for what was sown on rocky ground 12
22 As for what was sown among thorns 12
23 As for what was sown on good soil 12
24 to a man who sowed good seed in his field; 12
25 his enemy came and sowed weeds among the wheat 10
27 Sir, did you not sow good seed in your field? 12
31 which a man took and sowed in his field; 12
37 He who sows the good seed is the Son of man; 11
39 the enemy who sowed them is the devil 11
25:24 reaping where you did not sow 12
26 You knew that I reap where I have not sowed 12
Mrk 4: 3 Listen! A sower went out to sow. 12
4 as he sowed, some seed fell along the path 12
14 The sower sows the word. 12
15 the ones along the path, where the word is sown; 12
15 takes away the word which is sown in them. 12
16 the ones sown upon rocky ground 12
18 others are the ones sown among thorns 12
20 those that were sown upon the good soil 12
31 which, when sown upon the ground, is the smallest 12
32 yet when it is sown it grows up 12
Lke 8: 5 A sower went out to sow his seed 12
5 as he sowed, some fell along the path 12
12:24 Consider the ravens: they neither sow nor reap 12
13:19 which a man took and sowed in his garden 9
19:21 reap what you did not sow.' 12
22 reaping what I did not sow? 12
Joh 4:37 'One sows and another reaps.' 11
1Co 9:11 If we have sown spiritual good among you 12
15:36 What you sow does not come to life unless it dies. 12
37 what you sow is not the body which is to be 12
42 What is sown is perishable 12
43 It is sown in dishonor, it is raised in glory. 12
43 It is sown in weakness, it is raised in power. 12
44 It is sown a physical body 12
2Co 9: 6 he who sows sparingly will also reap sparingly 11
6 he who sows bountifully will also reap 11
Gal 6: 7 whatever a man sows, that he will also reap. 12
8 For he who sows to his own flesh 11
8 he who sows to the Spirit 11
Jas 3:18 the harvest of righteousness is sown in peace 12
1Es 4: 6 whenever they sow, reap the harvest 12
2Es 4:28 For the evil about which you ask me has been sown 13
29 that which has been sown is not reaped 13
29 if the place where the evil has been sown 13
29 the field where the good has been sown 13
30 For a grain of evil seed was sown in Adam's heart 13
32 When heads of grain without number are sown 13
5:48 those who from time to time are sown in it. 13
6:22 Sown places shall suddenly appear unsown 13
8:41 just as the farmer sows many seeds 14
41 all that have been sown will come up in due season 13
41 those who have been sown in the world 13
9:31 For behold, I sow my law in you 13
33 they did not keep what had been sown in them. 13
34 when it happens that what was sown . . 13
16:24 shall be left to cultivate the earth or to sow it. 13
43 let him that sows be like one who will not reap 13
Sir 6:19 Come to her like one who plows and sows 12
7: 3 My son, do not sow the furrows of injustice 12

sow (2) 1. *ὗς*
2Pe 2:22 and the sow is washed only to wallow in the mire. 1

sower 1. זרע 2. *σπεῖρα* 3. *σπείρω*
Isa 55:10 giving seed to the sower and bread to the eater 1
Jer 50:16 Cut off from Babylon the sower 1
Mat 13: 3 A sower went out to sow. 2
18 Hear then the parable of the sower. 3
Mrk 4: 3 Listen! A sower went out to sow. 2
14 The sower sows the word. 2
Lke 8: 5 A sower went out to sow his seed 2
Joh 4:36 so that sower and reaper may rejoice together. 2
2Co 9:10 supplies seed to the sower and bread for food 3

space 1. מַעֲרֶה 2. מָקוֹם 3. עֵבֶר 4. רֶוַח 5. רָחֹק 6. *διάστημα* 7. *καιρός*
Gen 32:16 Pass on before me, and put a space between drove 4
Exd 25:37 to give light upon the space in front of it. 3
Jos 3: 4 Yet there shall be a space between you and it 5
1Sm 26:13 stood afar off . . with a great space between them; 2
1Kg 7:36 he carved . . according to the space of each 1
Neh 4:13 in the lowest parts of the space behind the wall 2
Ezk 40: 7 and the space between the side rooms, five cubits; •
41:17 to the space above the door, even to the inner room •
2Mc 14:44 as they quickly drew back, a space opened 6
3Mc 4:14 to be destroyed in the space of a single day. 7

empty space 1. *κενεών*
2Mc 14:44 he fell in the middle of the empty space. 1

open space 1. מִגְרָשׁ
Ezk 45: 2 with 50 cubits for an open space around it. 1

spacious 1. רוח 2. spatiosus
Ps 66:12 yet hou hast brought us forth to a spacious place. •
Jer 22:14 a great house with spacious upper rooms 1
2Es 7:96 the spacious liberty which they are to receive 2

spacious garden 1. *παράδεισος*
Sus 1: 4 and had a spacious garden adjoining his house; 1

span 1. זֶרֶת
Exd 28:16 It shall be square and double, a span its length 1
16 a span its length and a span its breadth. 1
39: 9 a span its length and a span its breadth 1
9 a span its length and a span its breadth 1
1Sm 17: 4 whose height was six cubits and a span. 1
Ps 90:10 yet their span is but toil and trouble; •
Isa 40:12 Who has . . marked off the heavens with a span 1
Ezk 43:13 broad, with a rim of one span around its edge. 1

span of life 1. *ἡλικία*
Mat 6:27 anxious can add one cubit to his span of life? 1
Lke 12:25 which of you . . can add a cubit to his span of life? 1

spare 1. חוס 2. חיה 3. חמל 4. חנן 5. חשך 6. ישע 7. לֹא כרת 8. נצל 9. נשא 10. עבר 11. פגע 12. פסח 13. שאר 14. שמר 15. תַּחְמֹל עָלָי 16. *ζάω* 17. *λείπω* 18. *περιποιέω* 19. *φείδομαι* 20. *χαρίζομαι* 21. parco
Gen 12:13 that my life may be spared on your account. 2
18:24 wilt thou then destroy the place and not spare it 9
26 I will spare the whole place for their sake. 9
Exd 12:27 slew the Egyptians but spared our houses.' 8
Deu 13: 8 nor shall your eye pity him, nor shall you spare 3
Jos 22:22 If it was in rebellion . . spare us not today 6
1Sm 2:33 The man . . shall be spared to weep out his eyes 7
15: 3 do not spare them, but kill both man and woman 15
9 But Saul and the people spared Agag, and the best 3
15 the people spared the best of the sheep 3
24:10 and some bade me kill you, but I spared you. 1
2Sm 8: 2 two . . put to death, and one full line to be spared. 2
21: 2 the people of Israel had sworn to spare them •
7 But the king spared Mephib'osheth 3
1Kg 20:31 perhaps he will spare your life. 2
2Kg 5:20 See, my master has spared this Na'aman the Syrian 5
10:14 and slew them . . and he spared none of them. 13
Neh 13:22 spare me according to the greatness 1
Job 2: 6 he is in your power; only spare his life. 14
16:13 He slashes open my kidneys, and does not spare; 3
21:30 the wicked man is spared in the day of calamity 5
Ps 59: 5 spare none of those who treacherously plot 4
78:50 He made a path for his anger; he did not spare them 5
Prv 6:34 he will not spare when he takes revenge. 3
13:24 He who spares the rod hates his son 5
25:27 so be sparing of complimentary words. •
Isa 9:19 like fuel for the fire; no man spares his brother. 3
31: 5 and deliver it, he will spare and rescue it. 12
47: 3 I will take vengeance, and I will spare no man. 11
58: 1 spare not, lift up your voice like a trumpet; 5
Jer 13:14 I will not pity or spare or have compassion 1
21: 7 he shall not pity them, or spare them 3
38:17 then your life shall be spared 2
20 be well with you, and your life shall be spared. 2
50:14 you that bend the bow; shoot at her, spare no arrows 3
51: 3 Spare not her young men; 3

Ezk 5:11 my eye will not spare, and I will have no pity. 1
7: 4 And my eye will not spare you, nor will I have pity; 1
9 And my eye will not spare, nor will I have pity; 1
8:18 my eye will not spare, nor will I have pity; 1
9: 5 and smite; your eye shall not spare 1
10 As for me, my eye will not spare, nor will I have pity 1
20:17 my eye spared them, and I did not destroy them 1
24:14 I will do it; I will not go back, I will not spare 1
Hos 10:11 and I spared her fair neck; 10
Jol 2:17 weep and say, "Spare thy people, O LORD 1
Mal 3:17 I will spare them as a man spares his son 3
17 I will spare them as a man spares his son 3
Act 20:29 fierce wolves . . not sparing the flock; 19
Rom 8:32 He who did not spare his own Son but gave him up 19
11:21 For if God did not spare the natural branches 19
21 neither will he spare you. 19
1Co 7:28 I would spare you that. 19
2Co 1:23 it was to spare you that I refrained from coming 19
13: 2 if I come again I will not spare them– 19
2Pe 2: 4 if God did not spare the angels when they sinned 19
5 if he did not spare the ancient world 19
1Es 1:50 because he would have spared them 19
53 did not spare young man or virgin 19
2Es 3:30 and hast spared those who act wickedly 21
8:45 spare thy people and have mercy 21
9:21 I saw and spared some with great difficulty 21
15:22 My right hand will not spare the sinners 21
25 I will not spare them 21
16:71 They shall be like mad men, sparing no one 21
Jdt 2:11 if they refuse, your eye shall not spare 19
7:27 for we will be slaves, but our lives will be spared 16
11: 9 the men of Bethulia spared him 18
13:20 because you did not spare your own life 19
AEs 13:15 spare thy people 19
Wis 2:10 let us not spare the widow 19
11:26 Thou sparest all things, for they are thine 19
12: 8 even these thou didst spare 19
16 sovereignty over all causes thee to spare all. 19
Sir 16: 8 He did not spare the neighbors of Lot 19
23: 2 That they may not spare me in my errors 19
1Mc 13: 5 now, far be it from me to spare my life 19
3Mc 3:18 they were spared the exercise of our power 17
7: 6 we barely spared their lives 20

spare *See also* enough.

spare life 1. חיה

2Kg 7: 4 if they spare our lives we shall live 1
Ps 119:88 In thy steadfast love spare my life 1

sparingly 1. *φειδομένως*

2Co 9: 6 he who sows sparingly will also reap sparingly 1
6 he who sows sparingly will also reap sparingly 1

spark 1. בֶּן רֶשֶׁף 2. כִּידוֹד 3. נִיצוֹץ 4. *σπινθήρ* 5. scintilla

Job 5: 7 man is born to trouble as the sparks fly upward. 1
41:19 Out of his mouth . . sparks of fire leap forth. 2
Isa 1:31 the strong shall become tow, and his work a spark 3
2Es 13:10 from his tongue he shot forth a storm of sparks. 5
Wis 2: 2 a spark kindled by the beating of our hearts. 4
3: 7 will run like sparks through the stubble. 4
11:18 flash terrible sparks from their eyes; 4
Sir 11:32 From a spark of fire come many burning coals 4
28:12 If you blow on a spark, it will glow 4

sparkle 1. נצץ 2. עין

Prv 23:31 not look at wine . . when it sparkles in the cup 2
Ezk 1: 7 and they sparkled like burnished bronze. 1
10: 9 of the wheels was like sparkling chrysolite. 2

sparkling 1. *σπινθήρ*

Sir 42:22 how sparkling they are to see! 1

sparrow 1. צִפּוֹר 2. *στρουθίον*

Ps 84: 3 Even the sparrow finds a home 1
Prv 26: 2 Like a sparrow in its flitting, like a swallow 1
Mat 10:29 Are not two sparrows sold for a penny? 2
31 you are of more value than many sparrows. 2
Lke 12: 6 Are not five sparrows sold for two pennies? 2
7 Fear not; you are of more value than many sparrows. 2
Tob 2:10 there were sparrows on the wall 2

spatter 1. נזה

2Kg 9:33 some of her blood spattered on the wall 1

speak 1. אמר 2. דבר 3. דָּבָר 4. חוה 5. מִלָּה 6. מלל 7. נְאֻם 8. נגד 9. ספר 10. ענה 11. פוח 12. שָׂפָה 13. אמר (A) 14. מלל (A) 15. *ἄλαλος* 16. *ἀποκρίνω* 17. *ἀποφθέγγομαι* 18. *γίνομαι* 19. *γλῶσσα* 20. *διαλέγω* 21. *διηγέομαι* 22. *εἶπον* 23. *ἐκδιηγέομαι* 24. *ἐν λόγοις* 25. *ἐπιφέρω ῥῆμα* 26. *καταλέγω* 27. *λαλέω* 28. *λαλιά* 29. *λαλιὰν προΐημι* 30. *λέγω* 31. *λόγος* 32. *παρά* 33. *προηγορέω* 34. *προσλαλέω* 35. *προσφωνέω* 36. *φημί* 37. *φθέγγομαι* 38. *φωνέω* 39. dico 40. loquor

Gen 16:13 she called the name of the LORD who spoke to her 2
18:27 taken upon myself to speak to the Lord 2
29 Again he spoke to him, and said 2
30 let not the Lord be angry, and I will speak. 2
31 I have taken upon myself to speak to the Lord. 2
32 be angry, and I will speak again but this once. 2
33 when he had finished speaking to Abraham; 2
19:21 overthrow the city of which you have spoken. 2
21: 2 at the time of which God had spoken to him. 2
24: 7 The LORD . . who spoke to me and swore to me 2
15 Before he had done speaking, behold, Rebekah 2
30 Thus the man spoke to me," he went to the man; 2
33 have told my errand." He said, "Speak on. 2
45 Before I had done speaking in my heart 2
50 from the LORD; we cannot speak to you bad or good. 2
51 wife of your master's son, as the LORD has spoken. 2
27: 5 was listening when Isaac spoke to his son Esau. 2
6 I heard your father speak to your brother Esau 2
28:15 have done that of which I have spoken to you. 2
29: 9 While he was still speaking with them 2
31:29 but the God of your father spoke to me last night 1
29 Take heed that you speak to Jacob neither good 2
34: 3 he loved the maiden and spoke tenderly to her. 2
4 Shechem spoke to his father Hamor, saying 1
6 Shechem went out to Jacob to speak with him. 2
8 Hamor spoke with them, saying, "The soul of my son 2
20 came to the gate of their city and spoke to the men 2
35:13 in the place where he had spoken with him. 2
14 a pillar in the place where he had spoken with him 2
15 name of the place where God had spoken with him 2
37: 4 hated him, and could not speak peaceably to him. 2
39:10 although she spoke to Joseph day after day 2
19 words which his wife spoke to him, "This is the way 2
42: 7 like strangers and spoke roughly to them. 2
24 and he returned to them and spoke to them. 2
30 The man, the lord of the land, spoke roughly to us 2
43:19 to the steward . . and spoke with him at the door 2
27 Is your father well, the old man of whom you spoke? 1
29 your youngest brother, of whom you spoke to me? 1
44: 6 he overtook them, he spoke to them these words. 2
7 said to him, "Why does my lord speak such words 2
16 shall we say to my lord? What shall we speak? 2
18 I pray you, speak a word in my lord's ears 2
45:12 see, that it is my mouth that speaks to you. 2
46: 2 God spoke to Israel in visions of the night 1
50: 4 Joseph spoke to the household of Pharaoh, saying 2
4 speak, I pray you, in the ears of Pharaoh, saying 2
17 Joseph wept when they spoke to him. 2
Exd 4:10 either heretofore or since thou hast spoken 2
12 I will . . teach you what you shall speak. 2
14 Aaron . . the Levite? I know that he can speak well; 2
15 you shall speak to him and put the words 2
16 He shall speak for you to the people; 2
30 Aaron spoke all the words which the LORD had 2
30 words which the LORD had spoken to Moses 2
5:23 For since I came to Pharaoh to speak in thy name 2
6: 9 Moses spoke thus to the people of Israel. 2
13 the LORD spoke to Moses and Aaron, and gave them 2
27 It was they who spoke to Pharaoh king of Egypt 2
28 when the LORD spoke to Moses in the land of Egypt 2
7: 2 You shall speak all that I command you; 2
7 was . . years old, when they spoke to Pharaoh. 2
9:12 as the LORD had spoken to Moses. 2
35 as the LORD had spoken through Moses. 2
11: 2 Speak now in the hearing of the people 2
16:10 as Aaron spoke to the whole congregation 2
19: 6 These are the words which you shall speak 2
8 All that the LORD has spoken we will do. 2
9 that the people may hear when I speak with you 2
19 Moses spoke, and God answered him in thunder. 2
20: 1 God spoke all these words, saying 2
19 said to Moses, "You speak to us, and we will hear; 2
19 but let not God speak to us, lest we die. 2
24: 3 the words which the LORD has spoken we will do. 2
7 they said, "All that the LORD has spoken we will do 2
25: 2 Speak to the people of Israel, that they take 2
22 I will speak with you of all that I will give you 2
28: 3 you shall speak to all who have ability 2
29:42 I will meet with you, to speak there to you. 2
31:18 made an end of speaking with him upon Mount Sinai 2
32:34 lead . . to the place of which I have spoken to you; 2
33: 9 the tent, and the LORD would speak with Moses. 2
11 Thus the LORD used to speak to Moses face to face 2
11 Moses face to face, as a man speaks to his friend. 2
17 This very thing that you have spoken I will do; 2
34:32 gave . . all that the LORD had spoken with him 2
33 when Moses had finished speaking with them 2
34 went in before the LORD to speak with him 2
35 until he went in to speak with him. 2
Lev 1: 1 and spoke to him from the tent of meeting 2
2 Speak to the people of Israel, and say to them 2
5: 1 yet does not speak, he shall bear his iniquity 8
10: 8 the LORD spoke to Aaron, saying 2
11 the statutes which the LORD has spoken to them 2
16: 1 The LORD spoke to Moses after the death of the two 2
21: 1 Speak to the priests, the sons of Aaron, and say 1
24 So Moses spoke to Aaron and to his sons 2
24:23 So Moses spoke to the people of Israel 2
Num 1: 1 The LORD spoke to Moses in the wilderness 2
3: 1 at the time when the LORD spoke with Moses 2
7:89 into the tent of meeting to speak with the LORD 2
89 Moses . . heard the voice speaking to him 2
89 voice speaking . . spoke to him. 2
9: 1 LORD spoke to Moses in the wilderness of Sinai 2
11:25 LORD came down in the cloud and spoke to him 2
12: 1 Miriam and Aaron spoke against Moses 2
2 Has the LORD indeed spoken only through Moses? 2
2 Has he not spoken through us also? 2
6 I the LORD . . speak with him in a dream. 2
8 With him I speak mouth to mouth, clearly 2
8 not afraid to speak against my servant Moses? 2
14:35 I, the LORD, have spoken; surely this will I do 2
15:22 commandments which the LORD has spoken to Moses 2
38 Speak to the people of Israel, and bid them to make 2
16:31 as he finished speaking all these words 2
17: 2 Speak to the people of Israel, and get from them 2
6 Moses spoke to the people of Israel; 2
21: 5 the people spoke against God and against Moses 2
7 we have spoken against the LORD and against you; 2
22: 8 bring back word to you, as the LORD speaks to me"; 2
35 the word which I bid you, that shall you speak 2
38 Have I now any power at all to speak anything? 2
38 word that God puts in my mouth, that must I speak. 2
23: 5 Return to Balak, and thus you shall speak. 2
12 Must I not take heed to speak what the LORD 2
16 Return to Balak, and thus shall you speak. 2
17 Balak said to him, "What has the LORD spoken? 2
19 Or has he spoken, and will he not fulfil it? 2
24:13 what the LORD speaks, that will I speak'? 2
13 what the LORD speaks, that will I speak'? 2
26: 3 spoke with them in the plains of Moab 2
36: 1 spoke before Moses and before the leaders 2
Deu 1: 1 words that Moses spoke to all Israel 2
3 Moses spoke to the people of Israel according 2
14 'The thing that you have spoken is good for us to do.' 2
43 I spoke to you, and you would not hearken; 2
3:26 suffice you; speak no more to me of this matter. 2
4:12 LORD spoke to you out of the midst of the fire; 2
15 day that the LORD spoke to you at Horeb 2
33 voice of a god speaking out of the midst of the fire 2
45 which Moses spoke to the children of Israel 2
5: 1 which I speak in your hearing this day 2
4 LORD spoke with you face to face at the mountain 2
22 These words the LORD spoke to all your assembly 2
24 day seen God speak with man and man still live. 2
26 living God speaking out of the midst of fire 2
27 speak to us all that the LORD our God will speak 2
27 speak to us all that the LORD our God will speak 2
28 LORD heard your words, when you spoke to me; 2
28 'I have heard the words . . which they have spoken 2
28 rightly said all that they have spoken. 2
9:10 all the words which the LORD had spoken with you 2
10: 4 commandments which the LORD had spoken to you 2
11: 2 (since I am not speaking to your children who •
18:17 have rightly said all that they have spoken. 2
18 he shall speak to them all that I command him. 2
19 my words which he shall speak in my name 2
20 prophet who presumes to speak a word in my name 2
20 not commanded him to speak, or who speaks 2
20 prophet . . who speaks in the name of other gods 2
21 we know the word which the LORD has not spoken? 2
22 when a prophet speaks in the name of the LORD 2
22 that is a word which the LORD has not spoken; 2
22 prophet has spoken it presumptuously 2
20: 2 priest shall come forward and speak to the people 2
5 officers shall speak to the people, saying, 'What 2
8 officers shall speak further to the people 2
9 made an end of speaking to the people 2
25: 8 elders of his city shall call him, and speak to him 2
26:19 people holy to the LORD your God, as he has spoken. 2
31: 1 Moses continued to speak these words 2
3 Joshua . . at your head, as the LORD has spoken. 2
28 that I may speak these words in their ears 2
30 Then Moses spoke the words of this song 2
32: 1 Give ear, O heavens, and I will speak; 2
45 Moses had finished speaking all these words 2
Jos 10:12 Then spoke Joshua to the LORD in the day 2
11:23 according to all . . the LORD had spoken to Moses; 2
14:10 the time that the LORD spoke this word to Moses 2
12 hill country of which the LORD spoke on that day; 2
17:14 And the tribe of Joseph spoke to Joshua, saying 2
20: 2 Appoint the cities of refuge, of which I spoke 2
22:30 heard the words that . . the Manas'sites spoke 2
33 Israel blessed God and spoke no more of . . war 1
24:27 it has heard all the words . . he spoke to us; 2
Jdg 2: 4 When the angel of the LORD spoke these words 2
6:17 a sign that it is thou who speakest with me. 2
39 Gideon said . . let me speak but this once; 2
8: 8 up to Penu'el, and spoke to them in the same way; 2
9: 3 his mother's kinsmen spoke all these words on his 2
37 Ga'al spoke again and said, "Look, men are coming 2
11:11 Jephthah spoke all his words before the LORD 2
13:11 Are you the man who spoke to this woman? 2
15:17 When he had finished speaking, he threw away 2
17: 2 you uttered a curse, and also spoke it in my ears 1
19: 3 went . . to speak kindly to her and bring her back. 2
30 this day; consider it, take counsel, and speak. 2
Rut 2:13 you have . . spoken kindly to your maidservant 2
4: 1 the next of kin, of whom Bo'az had spoken, came by. 2
1Sm 1:13 Hannah was speaking in her heart; 2

3: 9 you shall say, 'Speak, LORD, for thy servant hears.' 2
10 And Samuel said, "Speak, for thy servant hears. 2
12 I will fulfil against Eli all that I have spoken 2
9:17 told him, "Here is the man of whom I spoke to you! 1
21 Am I . . ? Why then have you spoken to me in this way? 2
10:16 matter of the kingdom, of which Samuel had spoken 1
17:23 came up . . and spoke the same words as before. 2
28 Now Eli'ab . . heard when he spoke to the men; 2
30 he turned . . and spoke in the same way; 1
31 When the words which David spoke were heard 2
18: 1 When he had finished speaking to Saul 2
22 Speak to David in private and say, 'Behold, the king 2
23 Saul's servants spoke those words in the ears 2
24 servants . . told him, "Thus and so did David speak. 2
19: 1 Saul spoke to Jonathan . . and to all his servants 2
3 and I will speak to my father about you; 2
4 Jonathan spoke well of David to Saul his father 2
20:23 as for the matter of which you and I have spoken 2
24:16 David had finished speaking these words to Saul 2
25:17 he is so ill-natured that one cannot speak to him. 2
24 pray let your handmaid speak in your ears 2
30 all the good that he has spoken concerning you 2
28:17 The LORD has done to you as he spoke by me; 2
30: 6 distressed; for the people spoke of stoning him 1
2Sm 2:27 if you had not spoken, surely the men would have 2
3:19 Abner also spoke to Benjamin; and then Abner went 2
27 took him aside . . to speak with him privately 2
6:22 by the maids of whom you have spoken . . I shall be 1
7: 7 did I speak a word with any of the judges of Israel 2
17 in accordance with all . . Nathan spoke to David. 2
19 thou hast spoken also of thy servant's house 2
25 confirm for ever the word which thou hast spoken 2
25 confirm for ever . . and do as thou hast spoken; 2
29 for thou, O Lord GOD, hast spoken 2
12:18 we spoke to him, and he did not listen to us; 2
13:13 speak to the king; for he will not withhold me 2
22 But Ab'salom spoke to Amnon neither good nor bad; 2
36 And as soon as he had finished speaking, behold 2
14: 3 and go to the king, and speak thus to him. 2
12 Pray let your handmaid speak a word to my lord 2
12 let your handmaid speak . . " He said, "Speak. 2
15 your handmaid thought, 'I will speak to the king; 2
18 And the woman said, "Let my lord the king speak. 2
17: 6 Ab'salom said to him, "Thus has Ahith'ophel spoken; 2
6 Thus . . shall we do as he advises? If not, you speak. 2
19: 7 arise, go out and speak kindly to your servants; 2
29 Why speak any more of your affairs? I have decided 2
43 the first to speak of bringing back our king? 3
20:16 Hear! Tell Jo'ab, 'Come here, that I may speak to you.' 2
22: 1 And David spoke to the LORD the words of this song 2
23: 2 The Spirit of the LORD speaks by me 2
3 The God of Israel has spoken, the Rock of Israel 1
24:17 Then David spoke to the LORD when he saw the angel 1
1Kg 1:14 while you are still speaking with the king, I also 2
22 While she was still speaking with the king 2
42 While he was still speaking, behold, Jonathan 2
2: 4 establish his word which he spoke concerning me 2
18 said, "Very well; I will speak for you to the king. 2
19 Bathshe'ba went . . to speak to him on behalf 2
27 word of the LORD which he had spoken concerning 2
3:22 child is mine." Thus they spoke before the king. 2
4:33 He spoke of trees . . of beasts, and of birds 2
33 he spoke also of beasts, and of birds 2
6:12 my word . . which I spoke to David your father. 2
8:24 thou didst speak with thy mouth, and with thy hand 2
26 thy word . . which thou hast spoken to thy servant 2
12: 7 serve them, and speak good words to them 2
10 Thus shall you speak to this people 1
14 he spoke to them according to the counsel 2
15 fulfil his word, which the LORD spoke by Ahi'jah 2
13: 3 This is the sign that the LORD has spoken: 'Behold 2
11 the words also which he had spoken to the king 2
18 an angel spoke to me by the word of the LORD, saying 2
26 the word which the LORD spoke to him. 2
14:11 the birds . . shall eat; for the LORD has spoken it."' 2
18 word of the LORD, which he spoke by his servant 2
15:29 word of the LORD which he spoke by his servant 2
16:12 word of the LORD, which he spoke against Ba'asha 2
34 the word of the LORD, which he spoke by Joshua 2
17:16 the word of the LORD which he spoke by Eli'jah. 2
18:24 And all the people answered, "It is well spoken. 3
21: 6 Because I spoke to Naboth the Jezreelite 2
22:13 let your word be . . and speak favorably. 2
14 what the LORD says to me, that I will speak. 2
16 that you speak to me nothing but the truth 2
23 the LORD has spoken evil concerning you. 2
24 How did the Spirit . . go from me to speak to you? 2
28 If you return . . the LORD has not spoken by me. 2
38 the word of the LORD which he had spoken. 2
2Kg 1:17 the word of the LORD which Eli'jah had spoken. 2
2:22 according to the word which Eli'sha spoke. 2
4:13 Would you have a word spoken on your behalf 2
5: 4 Thus and so spoke the maiden from . . Israel. 2
6:12 the words that you speak in your bedchamber. 2
33 while he was still speaking . . the king came down 2
9:12 he spoke to me, saying, 'Thus says the LORD 1
36 word of the LORD, which he spoke by his servant 2
10:10 the LORD spoke concerning the house of Ahab; 2
17 the word of the LORD which he spoke to Eli'jah. 2
14:25 word of the LORD . . which he spoke by his servant 2
17:23 he had spoken by all his servants the prophets. 2
18:26 speak to your servants in the Aramaic language 2
26 do not speak to us in the language of Judah 2
27 to speak these words to your master and to you 2
19:10 Thus shall you speak to Hezeki'ah king of Judah 1
21 This is the word that the LORD has spoken 2
20:19 The word of the LORD which you have spoken is good. 2
22:19 you heard how I spoke against this place 2
24: 2 word of the LORD which he spoke by his servants 2
25:28 he spoke kindly to him, and gave him a seat 2
1Ch 17: 6 did I speak a word with any of the judges of Israel 2
15 In accordance with . . Nathan spoke to David. 2
17 O God; thou hast also spoken of thy servant's house 2
23 now, O LORD, let the word which thou hast spoken 2
23 and do as thou hast spoken; 2
21: 9 the LORD spoke to Gad, David's seer, saying 2
19 David went up at Gad's word, which he had spoken 2
22:11 as he has spoken concerning you. 2
2Ch 1: 2 Solomon spoke to all Israel 1
2:15 of which my lord has spoken 1
6:15 yea, thou didst speak with thy mouth 2
17 word . . which thou hast spoken to . . David. 2
10: 7 If you will . . speak good words to them 2
10 Thus shall you speak to the people who said to you 1
14 Rehobo'am spoke to them according to the counsel 2
15 which he spoke by Ahi'jah the Shi'lonite 2
18:12 and speak favorably. 2
13 what my God says, that I will speak. 2
15 speak to me nothing but the truth 2
22 the LORD has spoken evil concerning you. 2
23 Spirit of the LORD go from me to speak to you? 2
27 If you return . . the LORD has not spoken by me. 2
23: 3 the king's son! Let him reign, as the LORD spoke 2
25:16 as he was speaking the king said to him 2
30:22 Hezeki'ah spoke encouragingly 2
32: 6 spoke encouragingly to them, saying 2
17 he wrote letters . . to speak against him, saying 1
19 spoke of the God of Jerusalem as . . the gods 2
19 as they spoke of the gods of the peoples •
33:10 The LORD spoke to Manas'seh and to his people 2
18 seers who spoke to him in the name of the LORD 2
34:22 went to Huldah . . spoke to her to that effect. 2
35:25 spoken of Josi'ah in their laments to this day. 1
36:12 Jeremiah . . spoke from the mouth of the LORD. •
Ezr 5: 3 came to them and spoke to them thus, "Who gave you 13
9 Then we asked those elders and spoke to them thus 13
Neh 2:18 also of the words which the king had spoken to me. 1
6:19 Also they spoke of his good deeds in my presence 1
9:13 Thou didst . . speak with them from heaven 2
13:24 half . . spoke the language of Ashdod 2
24 they could not speak the language of Judah 2
Est 1:22 speak according to the language of his people. 2
3: 4 spoke to him . . and he would not listen to them 1
4:10 Esther spoke to Hathach and gave him a message 1
6: 4 Haman had just entered . . to speak to the king 1
8: 3 Then Esther spoke again to the king; 2
10: 3 and spoke peace to all his people. 2
Job 1:16 While he was yet speaking, there came another 2
17 While he was yet speaking, there came another, 2
18 While he was yet speaking, there came another, 2
2:10 You speak as one of the foolish women would 2
10 as one of the foolish women would speak. 2
13 no one spoke a word to him 2
4: 2 Yet who can keep from speaking? 5
7:11 I will speak in the anguish of my spirit; 2
9:35 Then I would speak without fear of him 2
10: 1 I will speak in the bitterness of my soul. 2
11: 5 oh, that God would speak, and open his lips to you 2
13: 3 But I would speak to the Almighty 2
7 Will you speak falsely for God 2
7 falsely for God, and speak deceitfully for him? 2
13 Let me have silence, and I will speak 2
22 or let me speak, and do thou reply to me. 2
16: 4 I also could speak as you do, if you were in my place; 2
6 If I speak, my pain is not assuaged 2
18: 2 Consider, and then we will speak. 2
21: 3 Bear with me, and I will speak 2
3 I will speak, and after I have spoken, mock on. 2
27: 4 my lips will not speak falsehood 2
29:22 After I spoke they did not speak again 3
22 After I spoke they did not speak again •
32: 4 Now Eli'hu had waited to speak to Job 3
7 Let days speak, and many years teach wisdom. 2
16 And shall I wait, because they do not speak 2
20 I must speak, that I may find relief; 2
33: 2 I open my mouth; the tongue in my mouth speaks. 2
3 what my lips know they speak sincerely. 6
8 Surely, you have spoken in my hearing 1
14 For God speaks in one way, and in two 2
31 O Job, listen to me; be silent, and I will speak. 2
32 answer me; speak, for I desire to justify you. 2
34:35 Job speaks without knowledge 2
37:20 Shall it be told him that I would speak? 2
40: 5 I have spoken once, and I will not answer; 2
41: 3 Will he speak to you soft words? 2
42: 4 'Hear, and I will speak; I will question you 2
7 After the LORD had spoken these words to Job 2
7 for you have not spoken of me what is right 2
8 for you have not spoken of me what is right 2
Ps 2: 5 Then he will speak to them in his wrath 2
5: 6 Thou destroyest those who speak lies; 2
12: 2 with . . a double heart they speak. 2
15: 2 what is right, and speaks truth from his heart; 2
17:10 with their mouths they speak arrogantly. 2
28: 3 who speak peace with their neighbors 2
31:18 the lying lips be dumb, which speak insolently 2
33: 9 For he spoke, and it came to be; 1
34:13 from evil, and your lips from speaking deceit. 2
35:20 For they do not speak peace 2
36: 1 Transgression speaks to the wicked 7
37:30 utters wisdom, and his tongue speaks justice. 2
38:12 those who seek my hurt speak of ruin 2
39: 3 the fire burned; then I spoke with my tongue 2
40:10 I have spoken of thy faithfulness 1
49: 3 My mouth shall speak wisdom; 2
50: 1 the LORD, speaks and summons the earth 2
7 Hear, O my people, and I will speak 2
20 You sit and speak against your brother; 2
52: 3 lying more than speaking the truth. Selah 2
58: 3 they err from their birth, speaking lies. 2
60: 6 God has spoken in his sanctuary 2
62:11 Once God has spoken; twice have I heard this 2
71:10 For my enemies speak concerning me 1
73: 8 They scoff and speak with malice; 2
15 If I had said, "I will speak thus 9
75: 5 or speak with insolent neck. 2
77: 4 I am so troubled that I cannot speak. 2
78:19 They spoke against God, saying 2
85: 8 Let me hear what God the LORD will speak 2
8 will speak peace to his people, to his saints 2
87: 3 Glorious things are spoken of you, O city of God. 2
89:19 thou didst speak in a vision to thy faithful one 2
99: 7 He spoke to them in the pillar of cloud; 2
105:31 He spoke, and there came swarms of flies 1
34 He spoke, and the locusts came, and young locusts 1
109: 2 speaking against me with lying tongues. 2
20 of those who speak evil against my life! 2
115: 5 They have mouths, but do not speak; 2
119:46 will also speak of thy testimonies before kings 2
120: 7 I am for peace; but when I speak, they are for war! 2
127: 5 He shall not be put to shame when he speaks 2
135:16 They have mouths, but they speak not 2
144: 8 whose mouths speak lies, and whose right hand 2
11 aliens, whose mouths speak lies, and whose right 2
145:11 They shall speak of the glory of thy kingdom 1
21 My mouth will speak the praise of the LORD 2
Prv 1:21 at the entrance of the city gates she speaks 1
8: 6 Hear, for I will speak noble things 2
12:17 He who speaks the truth gives honest evidence 11
16:13 king, and he loves him who speaks what is right. 2
20:19 do not associate with one who speaks foolishly. 12
23: 9 Do not speak in the hearing of a fool 2
16 soul . . rejoice when your lips speak what is right. 2
25:11 A word fitly spoken is like apples of gold 2
26:25 when he speaks graciously, believe him not •
Ecc 3: 7 a time to keep silence, and a time to speak; 2
Sng 2:10 My beloved speaks and says to me: "Arise, my love 10
5: 6 My soul failed me when he spoke. 2
8: 8 What shall we . . on the day when she is spoken for? 2
Isa 1: 2 Hear . . for the LORD has spoken: "Sons have I reared 2
20 for the mouth of the LORD has spoken. 2
7:10 Again the LORD spoke to Ahaz 2
8: 5 The LORD spoke to me again 2
10 come to nought; speak a word, but it will not stand 2
11 For the LORD spoke thus to me with his strong hand 1
20 for this word which they speak there is no dawn. 1
9:17 and an evildoer, and every mouth speaks folly. 2
14:10 All of them will speak and say to you 10
16:13 the LORD spoke concerning Moab in the past. 2
19:18 cities . . which speak the language of Canaan 2
20: 2 the LORD had spoken by Isaiah the son of Amoz 2
21:17 for the LORD, the God of Israel, has spoken. 2
22:25 burden . . be cut off, for the LORD has spoken. 2
23: 4 Be ashamed, O Sidon, for the sea has spoken 1
24: 3 earth . . despoiled; for the LORD has spoken this 2
25: 8 all the earth; for the LORD has spoken. 2
28:11 alien tongue the LORD will speak to this people 2
29: 4 Then deep from the earth you shall speak 2
30:10 speak to us smooth things, prophesy illusions 2
32: 4 the tongue of the stammerers will speak readily 2
6 For the fool speaks folly 2
33:15 He who walks righteously and speaks uprightly 2
36:11 Pray, speak to your servants in Aramaic 2
11 do not speak to us in the language of Judah 2
12 Has my master sent me to speak these words 2
37:10 Thus shall you speak to Hezeki'ah king of Judah 1
22 the word that the LORD has spoken concerning him 2
38:15 he has spoken to me, and he himself has done it. 1
39: 8 word of the LORD which you have spoken is good. 2
40: 2 Speak tenderly to Jerusalem, and cry to her 2
5 together, for the mouth of the LORD has spoken. 2
27 Why do you say, O Jacob, and speak, O Israel 2
41: 1 let them approach, then let them speak; 2
45:19 I did not speak in secret, in a land of darkness; 2
19 I the LORD speak the truth 2
46:11 I have spoken, and I will bring it to pass; 2
48:15 have spoken and called him, I have brought him 2

16 from the beginning I have not spoken in secret 2
52: 6 in that day they shall know that it is I who speak; 2
58: 9 of the finger, and speaking wickedness 2
14 your father, for the mouth of the LORD has spoken. 2
59: 3 your lips have spoken lies, 2
4 they rely on empty pleas, they speak lies 2
13 speaking oppression and revolt, 2
61: 6 men shall speak of you as the ministers of our God; 1
65:12 you did not answer, when I spoke, you did not listen 2
24 while they are yet speaking I will hear. 2
66: 4 when I spoke they did not listen; 2
Jer 1: 6 "Ah, Lord GOD! Behold, I do not know how to speak 2
7 and whatever I command you you shall speak. 2
3: 5 Behold, you have spoken 2
4:12 Now it is I who speak in judgment upon them. 2
28 for I have spoken, I have purposed; 2
5: 5 I will go to the great, and will speak to them; 2
14 Because they have spoken this word 2
6:10 To whom shall I speak and give warning 2
7:13 when I spoke to you persistently 2
22 I did not speak to your fathers or command them 2
27 you shall speak all these words to them 2
8: 6 and listened, but they have not spoken aright; 2
9: 5 and no one speaks the truth; 2
5 they have taught their tongue to speak lies; 2
8 tongue is a deadly arrow; it speaks deceitfully; 2
8 each speaks peaceably to his neighbor 2
12 To whom has the mouth of the LORD spoken 2
22 Speak, "Thus says the LORD 2
10: 1 Hear the word which the LORD speaks to you 2
5 Their idols . . they cannot speak; 2
11: 2 and speak to the men of Judah 2
12: 6 believe them not, though they speak fair words 2
13:12 You shall speak to them this word 1
15 give ear; be not proud, for the LORD has spoken. 2
14:14 nor did I command them or speak to them. 2
18: 8 if that nation, concerning which I have spoken 2
20 how I stood before thee to speak good for them 2
20: 8 For whenever I speak, I cry out, I shout 2
9 not mention him, or speak any more in his name 2
22: 1 and speak there this word 2
21 I spoke to you in your prosperity 2
23:16 they speak visions of their own minds 2
21 I did not speak to them, yet they prophesied. 2
28 let him who has my word speak my word faithfully. 2
35 or 'What has the LORD spoken?' 2
37 LORD answered you?' or 'What has the LORD spoken? 2
25: 2 which Jeremiah the prophet spoke to all 2
3 and I have spoken persistently to you 2
26: 2 and speak to all the cities of Judah which come 2
2 all the words that I command you to speak to them; 2
7 the people heard Jeremiah speaking these words 2
8 And when Jeremiah had finished speaking 2
8 all that the LORD had commanded him to speak 2
12 Then Jeremiah spoke to all the princes 1
15 me to you to speak all these words in your ears. 2
16 he has spoken to us in the name of the LORD our God. 2
17 certain of the elders of the land arose and spoke 1
27:12 To Zedeki'ah king of Judah I spoke in like manner 2
13 and by pestilence, as the LORD has spoken 2
16 Then I spoke to the priests and to all this people 2
28: 1 Hanani'ah . . the prophet from Gibeon, spoke to me 1
5 Then the prophet Jeremiah spoke to Hanani'ah 1
7 hear now this word which I speak in your hearing 2
11 Hanani'ah spoke in the presence of all the people 1
29:23 and they have spoken in my name lying words 2
30: 2 Write in a book all the words that I have spoken 2
4 These are the words which the LORD spoke 2
31:20 For as often as I speak against him, I do remember 3
32: 4 and shall speak with him face to face 2
24 What thou didst speak has come to pass 2
34: 2 Go and speak to Zedeki'ah king of Judah 1
3 see . . eye to eye and speak with him face to face; 2
5 For I have spoken the word, says the LORD. 2
6 Then Jeremiah the prophet spoke all these words 2
35: 2 and speak with them, and bring them to the house 2
14 I have spoken to you persistently 2
17 I have spoken to them and they have not listened 2
36: 2 write on it all the words that I have spoken to you 2
2 from the day I spoke to you, from the days of Josi'ah 2
4 the words of the LORD which he had spoken to him. 2
37: 2 which he spoke through Jeremiah the prophet. 2
38: 4 weakening the hands . . by speaking such words 2
25 If the princes hear that I have spoken with you 2
40:15 Then Joha'nan the son of Kare'ah spoke secretly 1
16 for you are speaking falsely of Ish'mael. 2
43: 1 Jeremiah finished speaking to all the people 2
44:16 As for the word which you have spoken to us 2
45: 1 The word that Jeremiah the prophet spoke 2
46:13 The word which the LORD spoke to Jeremiah 2
48: 8 plain shall be destroyed, as the LORD has spoken. 1
27 whenever you spoke of him you wagged your head? 3
50: 1 word which the LORD spoke concerning Babylon 2
51:12 the LORD has both planned and done what he spoke 2
52:32 he spoke kindly to him, and gave him a seat 2
Ezk 1:28 and I heard the voice of one speaking. 2
2: 1 stand upon your feet, and I will speak with you. 2
2 when he spoke to me, the Spirit entered into me 2
2 and I heard him speaking to me. 2

7 you shall speak my words to them 2
3: 1 and go, speak to the house of Israel. 2
4 and speak with my words to them. 2
10 Son of man, all my words that I shall speak to you 2
18 nor speak to warn the wicked from his wicked way 2
22 into the plain, and there I will speak with you. 2
24 and he spoke with me and said to me 2
27 But when I speak with you, I will open your mouth 2
5:13 I, the LORD, have spoken in my jealousy 2
15 I, the LORD, have spoken 2
17 I, the LORD, have spoken. 2
10: 5 like the voice of God Almighty when he speaks. 2
12:25 I the LORD will speak the word which I will speak 2
25 I the LORD will speak the word which I will speak 2
25 I will speak the word and perform it, says the Lord 2
28 but the word which I speak will be performed 2
13: 6 They have spoken falsehood and divined a lie; 4
7 said, 'Says the LORD,' although I have not spoken? 2
14: 4 Therefore speak to them, and say to them 2
9 if the prophet be deceived and speak a word 2
17:21 you shall know that I, the LORD, have spoken. 2
24 I the LORD have spoken, and I will do it. 2
20: 3 Son of man, speak to the elders of Israel 2
27 Therefore, son of man, speak to the house of Israel 2
21:17 I will satisfy my fury; I the LORD have spoken. 2
32 no more remembered; for I the LORD have spoken. 2
22:14 I the LORD have spoken, and I will do it. 2
28 says the Lord GOD,' when the LORD has not spoken. 2
23:34 for I have spoken, says the Lord GOD. 2
24:14 I the LORD have spoken; it shall come to pass 2
18 I spoke to the people in the morning 2
27 you shall speak and be no longer dumb. 2
26: 5 for I have spoken, says the Lord GOD; 2
14 for I the LORD have spoken, says the Lord GOD. 2
28:10 for I have spoken, says the Lord GOD. 2
29: 3 speak, and say, Thus says the Lord GOD 2
30:12 by the hand of foreigners; I, the LORD, have spoken. 2
32:21 The mighty chiefs shall speak of them 2
33: 2 Son of man, speak to your people and say to them 2
8 and you do not speak to warn the wicked to turn 2
34:24 I, the LORD, have spoken. 2
36: 5 I speak in my hot jealousy against the rest 2
6 Behold, I speak in my jealous wrath 2
36 I, the LORD, have spoken, and I will do it. 2
37:14 then you shall know that I, the LORD, have spoken 2
38:17 Are you he of whom I spoke in former days 2
39: 5 You shall fall in the open field; for I have spoken 2
8 That is the day of which I have spoken. 2
17 Speak to the birds of every sort and to all beasts 1
43: 6 I heard one speaking to me out of the temple; 2
Dan 1:19 king spoke with them, and among them all 2
2: 9 agreed to speak lying and corrupt words 13
3:29 speaks anything against the God of Shadrach 13
4:31 O King Nebuchadnez'zar, to you it is spoken 13
7: 8 eyes of a man, and a mouth speaking great things. 14
11 great words which the horn was speaking. 14
20 had eyes and a mouth that spoke great things 14
25 He shall speak words against the Most High 14
8:13 Then I heard a holy one speaking; 2
13 another holy one said to the one that spoke 2
18 As he was speaking to me, I fell into a deep sleep 2
9: 6 prophets, who spoke in thy name to our kings 2
12 words, which he spoke against us and . . our rulers 2
20 While I was speaking and praying, confessing 2
21 while I was speaking in prayer, the man Gabriel 2
10:11 Daniel . . give heed to the words that I speak 2
11 While he was speaking this word to me, I stood up 2
15 When he had spoken to me according to these words 2
16 touched my lips; then I opened my mouth and spoke. 2
19 when he spoke to me, I was strengthened and said 2
19 Let my lord speak, for you have strengthened me. 2
11:27 shall speak lies at the same table, but to no avail; 2
36 speak astonishing things against the God 2
Hos 1: 2 When the LORD first spoke through Hose'a 2
2:14 into the wilderness, and speak tenderly to her. 2
7:13 but they speak lies against me. 2
12: 4 He met God at Bethel, and there God spoke with him- 2
10 I spoke to the prophets; 2
13: 1 When E'phraim spoke, men trembled; 2
Jol 3: 8 for the LORD has spoken. 2
Ams 3: 1 this word that the LORD has spoken against you 2
8 The Lord GOD has spoken; who can but prophesy? 2
5:10 and they abhor him who speaks the truth. 2
Obd 1:18 for the LORD has spoken. 2
Jon 2:10 the LORD spoke to the fish, and it vomited out 1
Mic 4: 4 for the mouth of the LORD of hosts has spoken. 2
6:12 your inhabitants speak lies 2
Hag 1:13 spoke to the people with the LORD's message 1
2: 2 Speak now to Zerub'babel the son of She-al'ti-el 1
21 Speak to Zerub'babel, governor of Judah, saying 1
Zec 8:16 that you shall do: Speak the truth to one another 2
13: 3 not live, for you speak lies in the name of the LORD 2
Mal 3:13 Yet you say, 'How have we spoken against thee?' 2
16 those who feared the LORD spoke with one another; 2
Mat 1:22 to fulfil what the Lord had spoken by the prophet 22
2:15 to fulfil what the Lord had spoken by the prophet 22
17 Then was fulfilled what was spoken 22
23 Nazareth, that what was spoken by the prophets 22
3: 3 For this is he who was spoken of by the prophet 22

4:14 that what was spoken by the prophet Isaiah 22
8:17 to fulfil what was spoken by the prophet Isaiah 22
9:18 While he was thus speaking to them 27
33 the dumb man spoke; and the crowds marveled 27
10:19 do not be anxious how you are to speak 27
20 it is not you who speak, but the Spirit 27
20 the Spirit of your Father speaking through you. 27
11: 7 they went away, Jesus began to speak to the crowds 30
12:17 to fulfil what was spoken by the prophet Isaiah 22
22 he healed him, so that the dumb man spoke and saw. 27
32 but whoever speaks against the Holy Spirit 30
34 You brood of vipers! how can you speak good 27
34 the abundance of the heart the mouth speaks. 27
46 While he was still speaking to the people 27
46 asking to speak to him. 27
13:10 Why do you speak to them in parables? 27
13 This is why I speak to them in parables 27
35 This was to fulfil what was spoken by the prophet 22
14:27 immediately he spoke to them, saying 27
15:31 when they saw the dumb speaking 27
16:11 that I did not speak about bread 22
17: 5 He was still speaking, when lo, a bright cloud 27
13 he was speaking to them of John the Baptist. 22
21: 4 to fulfil what was spoken by the prophet, saying 22
45 they perceived that he was speaking about them. 30
22: 1 again Jesus spoke to them in parables, saying 16
24:15 sacrilege spoken of by the prophet Daniel 22
26:47 While he was still speaking, Judas came 27
27: 9 what had been spoken by the prophet Jeremiah 22
Mrk 1:34 he would not permit the demons to speak 27
2: 7 Why does this man speak thus? It is blasphemy! 27
4:33 With many such parables he spoke the word to them 27
34 he did not speak to them without a parable 27
5:35 While he was still speaking 27
6:50 But immediately he spoke to them and said 27
7:35 tongue was released, and he spoke plainly. 27
37 he even makes the deaf hear and the dumb speak. 15
12: 1 he began to speak to them in parables 27
13:11 it is not you who speak, but the Holy Spirit. 27
14:43 while he was still speaking, Judas came 27
71 I do not know this man of whom you speak. 30
16:17 they will speak in new tongues; 27
19 So then the Lord Jesus, after he had spoken to them 27
Lke 1:19 I was sent to speak to you 27
20 behold, you will be silent and unable to speak 27
22 when he came out, he could not speak to them 27
45 fulfilment of what was spoken to her 27
55 as he spoke to our fathers 27
64 he spoke, blessing God. 27
70 as he spoke by the mouth of his holy prophets 27
2:38 spoke of him to all 27
50 the saying which he spoke to them. 27
4:41 would not allow them to speak 27
5: 4 when he had ceased speaking, he said to Simon 27
21 Who is this that speaks blasphemies? 30
6:26 Woe to you, when all men speak well of you 22
45 his mouth speaks. 27
7:15 the dead man sat up, and began to speak 27
24 he began to speak to the crowds concerning John 30
8:49 While he was still speaking 27
9:11 he welcomed them and spoke to them of the kingdom 27
31 who appeared in glory and spoke of his departure 30
36 when the voice had spoken, Jesus was found alone. 18
11:14 when the demon had gone out, the dumb man spoke 27
37 While he was speaking 27
12:10 every one who speaks a word against the Son of man 22
14: 3 Jesus spoke to the lawyers and Pharisees, saying 22
20:21 we know that you speak and teach rightly 30
39 Teacher, you have spoken well. 22
21: 5 as some spoke of the temple, how it was adorned 30
22:47 While he was still speaking, there came a crowd 27
60 immediately, while he was still speaking 27
65 they spoke many other words against him 30
24:25 to believe all that the prophets have spoken! 27
44 These are my words which I spoke to you 27
Joh 1:40 One of the two who heard John speak . . was Andrew 32
2:21 But he spoke of the temple of his body. 30
22 believed . . the word which Jesus had spoken. 27
3:11 Truly, truly, I say to you, we speak of what we know 27
31 belongs to the earth, and of the earth he speaks; 27
4:26 Jesus said to her, "I who speak to you am he. 30
50 The man believed the word that Jesus spoke to him 22
6:63 the words that I have spoken to you 27
71 He spoke of Judas the son of Simon Iscariot 30
7:13 Yet for fear of the Jews no one spoke openly 27
17 whether I am speaking on my own authority. 27
18 He who speaks on his own authority 27
26 here he is, speaking openly, and they say nothing 27
46 No man ever spoke like this man! 27
8:12 Again Jesus spoke to them, saying, "I am the light 27
20 These words he spoke in the treasury 27
27 he spoke to them of the Father. 30
28 speak thus as the Father taught me. 27
30 As he spoke thus, many believed in him. 27
38 I speak of what I have seen with my Father 27
44 When he lies, he speaks according to his own nature 27
9:21 Ask him; he is of age, he will speak for himself. 27
29 We know that God has spoken to Moses 27
37 it is he who speaks to you. 27

11:11 Thus he spoke, and then he said to them 22
13 Now Jesus had spoken of his death 22
12:29 Others said, "An angel has spoken to him. 27
38 the word spoken by the prophet Isaiah 22
41 because he saw his glory and spoke of him. 27
48 the word that I have spoken will be his judge 27
49 For I have not spoken on my own authority 27
49 commandment what to say and what to speak. 27
13:18 I am not speaking of you all 30
21 When Jesus had thus spoken 30
22 uncertain of whom he spoke. 30
24 Tell us who it is of whom he speaks. 30
14:10 I do not speak on my own authority 27
25 These things I have spoken to you 27
15: 3 made clean by the word which I have spoken to you. 27
11 These things I have spoken to you 27
22 If I had not come and spoken to them 27
16:13 for he will not speak on his own authority 27
13 whatever he hears he will speak 27
25 when I shall no longer speak to you in figures 27
29 Ah, now you are speaking plainly, not in any figure! 27
17: 1 When Jesus had spoken these words 27
13 these things I speak in the world 27
18: 1 When Jesus had spoken these words 30
9 This was to fulfil the word which he had spoken 22
16 went out and spoke to the maid who kept the door 22
20 I have spoken openly to the world 27
23 Jesus answered him, "If I have spoken wrongly 27
23 if I have spoken rightly, why do you strike me? •
32 to fulfil the word which Jesus had spoken 22
19:10 You will not speak to me? 27
Act 1: 3 speaking of the kingdom of God. 30
2: 4 began to speak in other tongues 27
6 each one heard them speaking in his own language. 27
7 Are not all these who are speaking Galileans? 27
16 this is what was spoken by the prophet Joel 22
31 spoke of the resurrection of the Christ 27
3:21 God spoke by the mouth of his holy prophets 27
24 all the prophets who have spoken 27
4: 1 as they were speaking to the people 27
17 let us warn them to speak no more to any one 27
18 not to speak or teach at all in the name of Jesus. 37
20 for we cannot but speak of what we have seen 27
29 grant to thy servants to speak thy word 27
31 spoke the word of God with boldness. 27
5:20 Go and stand in the temple and speak to the people 27
40 charged them not to speak in the name of Jesus 27
6:10 the wisdom and the Spirit with which he spoke. 27
11 We have heard him speak blasphemous words 30
13 to speak words against this holy place and the law; 27
7: 6 God spoke to this effect 27
38 the angel who spoke to him at Mount Sinai 27
44 even as he who spoke to Moses directed him 27
8:25 had testified and spoken the word of the Lord 27
9:27 on the road he had seen the Lord, who spoke to him 27
29 he spoke and disputed against the Hellenists; 27
10: 7 When the angel who spoke to him had departed 27
46 For they heard them speaking in tongues 27
11:15 As I began to speak, the Holy Spirit fell on them 27
19 speaking the word to none except Jews. 27
20 who on coming to Antioch spoke to the Greeks also 27
13:34 he spoke in this way 22
43 who spoke to them 34
45 contradicted what was spoken by Paul 27
46 the word of God should be spoken first to you. 27
14: 1 so spoke that a great company believed 27
9 He listened to Paul speaking 27
25 when they had spoken the word in Perga 27
16: 6 forbidden . . to speak the word in Asia. 27
13 and spoke to the women who had come together. 27
32 they spoke the word of the Lord to him 27
18: 9 Do not be afraid, but speak and do not be silent; 27
25 he spoke and taught accurately 27
19: 6 they spoke with tongues and prophesied. 27
20:30 will arise men speaking perverse things 27
36 when he had spoken thus, he knelt down and prayed 30
38 sorrowing . . because of the word he had spoken 22
21:39 I beg you, let me speak to the people. 27
40 he spoke to them in the Hebrew language, saying 35
22: 9 the voice of the one who was speaking to me. 27
23: 5 shall not speak evil of a ruler of your people.' 22
9 What if a spirit or an angel spoke to him? 27
24:10 when the governor had motioned to him to speak 30
24 and heard him speak upon faith in Christ Jesus. •
26: 1 You have permission to speak for yourself 30
25 I am speaking the sober truth. 17
26 to him I speak freely 27
28:20 to see you and speak with you 34
21 reported or spoken any evil about you. 27
Rom 3: 5 (I speak in a human way.) 30
19 the law . . speaks to those who are under the law 30
6:19 I am speaking in human terms 30
7: 1 for I am speaking to those who know the law- 27
9: 1 I am speaking the truth in Christ, I am not lying; 30
11:13 Now I am speaking to you Gentiles. 30
15:18 For I will not venture to speak of anything 27
1Co 9:10 Does he not speak entirely for our sake? 30
10:15 I speak as to sensible men; judge for yourselves 30
12: 3 no one speaking by the Spirit of God ever says 27
30 Do all speak with tongues? Do all interpret? 27
13: 1 If I speak in the tongues of men and of angels 27
11 When I was a child, I spoke like a child 27
14: 2 For one who speaks in a tongue speaks not to men 27
2 who speaks in a tongue speaks not to men but to God; 27
3 On the other hand, he who prophesies speaks to men 27
4 He who speaks in a tongue edifies himself 27
5 Now I want you all to speak in tongues 27
5 he who speaks in tongues 27
6 Now, brethren, if I come to you speaking in tongues 27
9 For you will be speaking into the air. 27
13 Therefore, he who speaks in a tongue should pray 27
18 I speak in tongues more than you all; 27
19 I would rather speak five words with my mind . . than 27
21 will I speak to this people 27
23 all speak in tongues 27
27 If any speak in a tongue 27
28 speak to himself and to God. 27
29 Let two or three prophets speak 27
34 For they are not permitted to speak 27
35 it is shameful for a woman to speak in church. 27
39 do not forbid speaking in tongues; 27
2Co 2:17 in the sight of God we speak in Christ. 27
4:13 as he had who wrote, "I believed, and so I spoke 27
13 we too believe, and so we speak 27
6:13 In return-I speak as to children 30
11: 6 Even if I am unskilled in speaking 31
21 I am speaking as a fool 30
12: 6 for I shall be speaking the truth 22
19 speaking in Christ, and all for your upbuilding 27
13: 3 you desire proof that Christ is speaking in me. 27
Eph 4:25 let every one speak the truth with his neighbor 27
5:12 it is a shame even to speak of the things 30
6:20 I may declare it boldly, as I ought to speak. 27
Php 1:14 bold to speak the word of God without fear. 27
Col 4: 4 that I may make it clear, as I ought to speak. 27
1Th 2: 4 entrusted with the gospel, so we speak 27
16 by hindering us from speaking to the Gentiles 27
Heb 1: 1 God spoke of old to our fathers by the prophets; 27
2 in these last days he has spoken to us by a Son 27
2: 5 the world to come, of which we are speaking. 27
4: 4 has somewhere spoken of the seventh day 22
8 God would not speak later of another day. 27
6: 9 Though we speak thus 27
7:13 the one of whom these things are spoken 30
8:13 In speaking of a new covenant 30
9: 5 Of these things we cannot now speak in detail. 30
11: 4 through his faith he is still speaking. 27
14 For people who speak thus make it clear 30
12:19 that no further messages be spoken to them •
24 that speaks more graciously than the blood of Abel. 27
25 See that you do not refuse him who is speaking. 27
13: 7 those who spoke to you the word of God 27
Jas 1:19 Let every man be quick to hear, slow to speak 27
2:12 So speak and so act as those who are to be judged 27
5:10 the prophets who spoke in the name of the Lord. 27
1Pe 3:10 let him keep . . his lips from speaking guile; 27
4:11 whoever speaks, as one who utters oracles of God; 27
2Pe 1:21 men moved by the Holy Spirit spoke from God. 27
2:16 a dumb ass spoke with human voice 37
3:16 speaking of this as he does in all his letters. 27
Jde 1:15 harsh things which ungodly sinners have spoken 27
Rev 1:12 I turned to see the voice that was speaking to me 27
4: 1 the first voice, which I had heard speaking to me 27
10: 8 the voice . . from heaven spoke to me again 27
13:11 and it spoke like a dragon. 27
15 so that the image of the beast should even speak 27
21: 9 one of the seven angels . . spoke to me, saying 27
1Es 1:47 the words that were spoken by Jeremiah 22
51 whenever the Lord spoke, they scoffed 27
2:21 to speak to our lord the king 35
3:17 the first, who had spoken of the strength of wine 22
4: 1 who had spoken of the strength of the king 22
1 Then the second . . began to speak 27
13 Zerubbabel, who had spoken of women and truth 22
13 Then the third . . began to speak 27
33 he began to speak about truth 27
5: 6 who spoke wise words before Darius 27
2Es 1:12 speak to them and say, Thus says the Lord 40
3: 3 I began to speak anxious words to the Most High 40
4 didst thou not speak at the beginning 39
4: 5 I said, "Speak on, my lord. 40
5:22 and I began once more to speak words 40
31 When I had spoken these words 40
33 I said, "Speak, my lord." And he said to me 40
34 but because of my grief I have spoken 40
39 and how can I speak concerning the things 39
50 let me speak before thee 40
6:15 while the voice is speaking, do not be terrified; 40
17 and behold, a voice was speaking 40
21 Infants a year old shall speak with their voices 40
29 While he spoke to me, behold, little by little 40
36 I began to speak in the presence of the Most High. 40
38 thou didst speak at the beginning of creation 40
55 All this I have spoken before thee, O Lord 39
7: 1 When I had finished speaking these words 40
2 the words that I have come to speak to you. 40
3 I said, "Speak, my lord." And he said to me 40
38 Thus he will speak to them on the day of judgment- 40
129 while he was alive, spoke to the people, saying 39
130 or even myself who have spoken to them. 40
8:15 I will speak about thy people •
19 and I will speak before thee. 40
25 For as long as I live I will speak 40
37 Some things you have spoken rightly 40
40 As I have spoken, therefore, so it shall be. 40
42 If I have found favor before thee, let me speak. 40
9: 4 of these that the Most High spoke 40
28 I began to speak before the Most High, and said 39
10:19 I spoke again to her, and said 40
29 As I was speaking these words, behold, the angel 40
34 I said, "Speak, my lord; only do not forsake me 40
11:37 he uttered a man's voice to the eagle, and spoke 39
38 Listen and I will speak to you 40
12:17 As for your hearing a voice that spoke 40
31 and roaring and speaking to the eagle 40
32 and will come and speak to them ‡
34 of which I spoke to you at the beginning. 40
40 and came to me and spoke to me, saying 39
14: 3 I revealed myself in a bush and spoke to Moses 40
19 Let me speak in thy presence, Lord. 40
43 As for me, I spoke in the daytime 40
45 the Most High spoke to me, saying, "Make public 40
15: 1 Behold, speak in the ears of my people the words 40
Tob 6:12 I will speak to her father 27
7: 8 speak of those things which you talked about 27
13: 8 Let all men speak 30
Jdt 2:12 what I have spoken my hand will execute. 27
6: 4 he has spoken; none of his words shall be in vain. 22
9 I have spoken and none of my words shall fail. 27
8: 8 No one spoke ill of her 25
9 heard the wicked words spoken by the people •
28 has been spoken out of a true heart 27
10: 9 accomplish the things about which you spoke 27
11: 5 let your maidservant speak in your presence 27
14: 8 until the moment of her speaking to them. 27
16:14 thou didst speak, and they were made 22
AEs 15:12 he embraced her, and said, "Speak to me. 27
15 as she was speaking, she fell fainting. 20
Wis 5: 3 They will speak to one another in repentance 22
7:15 May God grant that I speak with judgment 30
8:12 when I speak they will give heed 37
12 when I speak at greater length 27
Sir 0: 1 help the outsiders by both speaking and writing, 30
4:23 Do not refrain from speaking at the crucial time 31
5:13 Glory and dishonor come from speaking 28
13: 6 He will speak to you kindly and say, "What do you 27
22 he speaks unseemly words, and they justify him 27
22 he speaks sensibly, and receives no attention. 37
23 When the rich man speaks all are silent 27
23 When the poor man speaks 27
18:19 Before you speak, learn 27
20: 6 keeps silent because he knows when to speak. •
8 whoever usurps the right to speak will be hated. •
16 those who eat my bread speak unkindly. 19
27 He who speaks wisely will advance himself 24
21:25 The lips of strangers will speak of these things 21
25: 9 he who speaks to attentive listeners. 21
29: 5 in speaking of his neighbor's money •
31:31 speak no word of reproach to him 30
32: 3 Speak, you who are older 27
7 Speak, young man, if there is need of you 27
8 Speak concisely, say much in few words 31
9 when another is speaking, do not babble. 30
34: 9 will speak with understanding. 23
36:15 fulfil the prophecies spoken in thy name. •
43:27 Though we speak much we cannot reach the end 22
Bar 2: 1 confirmed his word, which he spoke against us 27
24 words, which thou didst speak by thy servants 27
28 thou didst speak by thy servant Moses on the day 27
LJr 1: 8 they are false and cannot speak. 27
41 when they see a dumb man, who cannot speak 27
41 they bring him and pray Bel that the man may speak 27
1Mc 1:24 spoke with great arrogance. 27
30 Deceitfully he spoke peaceable words to them 27
2:17 Then the king's officers spoke to Mattathias 22
23 When he had finished speaking these words 27
3:23 When he finished speaking 27
7:15 he spoke peaceable words . . and swore this oath 27
34 defiled them and spoke arrogantly 27
42 Nicanor has spoken wickedly 27
8:19 they entered the senate chamber and spoke as follows 22
10:47 he had been the first to speak peaceable words •
13:17 Simon knew that they were speaking deceitfully 27
2Mc 4:48 those who had spoken for the city 33
7:27 she spoke in their native tongue as follows 36
30 While she was still speaking, the young man said 26
9: 5 As soon as he ceased speaking 31
15:12 one who spoke fittingly 29
14 Onias spoke, saying 16
3Mc 2:22 he . . was unable even to speak 38
5:21 When the king had spoken 30
45 virtually to a state of madness, so to speak 30
6: 5 speaking grievous words with boasting 27
4Mc 1:12 shortly have an opportunity to speak of this 30
2:20 he would not have spoken thus. 22
5:15 When he had received permission to speak 30
8:13 the tyrant resumed speaking 36

12: 8 he said, "Let me loose, let me speak to the king 30
16: 5 she would have . . perhaps spoken as follows 22
speak *See also* cease, finish, leave, provoke, stop.

speak a word that is rash 1. בטא
Ps 106:33 spirit bitter, and he spoke words that were rash. 1

speak against 1. ἀντιλέγω 2. καταλαλέω 3. contradico
Lke 2:34 this child is set . . for a sign that is spoken against 1
Act 28:22 we know that everywhere it is spoken against. 1
1Pe 2:12 in case they speak against you as wrongdoers 2
2Es 7:22 they were not obedient, and spoke against him 3
11: 6 and no one spoke against him 3
Sir 4:25 Never speak against the truth 1

speak an allegory 1. משל
Ezk 17: 2 propound a riddle, and speak an allegory 1

speak beforehand 1. προεῖπον
Act 1:16 which the Holy Spirit spoke beforehand 1

speak blasphemy 1. δυσφημέω
1Mc 7:41 the messengers from the king spoke blasphemy 1

speak boldly 1. παρρησιάζομαι
Act 14: 3 speaking boldly for the Lord 1
18:26 He began to speak boldly in the synagogue 1
19: 8 and for three months spoke boldly 1

speak clearly 1. τρανός
Wis 10:21 and made the tongues of babes speak clearly. 1

speak evil 1. βλασφημέω 2. κακολογέω 3. καταλαλέω
Mat 15: 4 'He who speaks evil of father or mother 2
Mrk 7:10 'He who speaks evil of father or mother 2
9:39 will be able soon after to speak evil of me. 2
Act 19: 9 speaking evil of the Way before the congregation 2
Tit 3: 2 to speak evil of no one, to avoid quarreling 1
Jas 4:11 Do not speak evil against one another, brethren. 3
11 He that speaks evil against a brother 3
11 speaks evil against the law and judges the law. 3

speak falsely 1. כחש
Jer 5:12 They have spoken falsely of the LORD 1

speak first 1. προφθάνω
Mat 17:25 when he came home, Jesus spoke to him first, saying 1

speak humanly 1. κατὰ ἄνθρωπον
1Co 15:32 if, humanly speaking, I fought with beasts 1

speak of as evil 1. βλασφημέω
Rom 14:16 do not let your good be spoken of as evil. 1

speak out 1. דבר 2. נשא 3. dico
1Sm 1:16 I have been speaking out of my great anxiety 1
Isa 3: 7 he will speak out, saying: "I will not be a healer; 2
2Es 8:15 now I will speak out 3

speak out boldly 1. παρρησιάζομαι
Act 13:46 Paul and Barnabas spoke out boldly, saying 1

speak sweetly 1. γλυκαίνω
Sir 12:16 An enemy will speak sweetly with his lips 1

speak the truth 1. ἀληθεύω
Eph 4:15 Rather, speaking the truth in love 1

speak well 1. μαρτυρέω
Lke 4:22 And all spoke well of him 1
Act 10:22 who is well spoken of by the whole Jewish nation 1
16: 2 He was well spoken of by the brethren 1
22:12 well spoken of by all the Jews who lived there 1

speaker 1. λαλέω 2. λόγος
Act 14:12 because he was the chief speaker 2
1Co 12:28 speakers in various kinds of tongues. •
14:11 I shall be a foreigner to the speaker 1
11 the speaker a foreigner to me. 1
Sir 11: 8 nor interrupt a speaker in the midst of his words. •

spear 1. חֲנִית 2. כִּידוֹן 3. צִלְצַל 4. קַיִן 5. רֹמַח 6. γαῖσος 7. δόρυ 8. κάμαξ 9. λόγχη 10. framea
Num 25: 7 Phin'ehas . . took a spear in his hand 5
Jdg 5: 8 Was shield or spear to be seen among . . Israel? 5
1Sm 13:19 Lest the Hebrews make . . swords or spears"; 1
22 there was neither sword nor spear found 1
17: 7 And the shaft of his spear was like a weaver's beam 1
7 and his spear's head weighed 600 shekels of iron; 1
45 with a sword and with a spear and with a javelin; 1
47 know that the LORD saves not with sword and spear; 1
18:10 Saul had his spear in his hand; 1
11 and Saul cast the spear, for he thought, "I will pin 1
19: 9 as he sat in his house with his spear in his hand; 1
10 sought to pin David to the wall with the spear; 1
10 so that he struck the spear into the wall. 1
20:33 But Saul cast his spear at him to smite him; 1
21: 8 And have you not here a spear or a sword at hand? 1
22: 6 Saul was sitting . . with his spear in his hand 1
26: 7 with his spear stuck in the ground at his head; 1
8 pin him to the earth with one stroke of the spear 1
11 take now the spear that is at his head, and the jar 1
12 David took the spear and the jar of water 1
16 see where the king's spear is, and the jar of water 1
22 And David made answer, "Here is the spear, O king! 1
2Sm 1: 6 and there was Saul leaning upon his spear; 1
2:23 smote him in the belly with the butt of his spear 1
23 smote him . . so that the spear came out at his back; 1
21:16 whose spear weighed 300 shekels of bronze 4
19 the shaft of whose spear was like a weaver's beam. 1
23: 7 arms himself with iron and the shaft of a spear 1
8 he wielded his spear against 800 whom he slew •
18 he wielded his spear against 300 men 1
21 The Egyptian had a spear in his hand; 1
21 and snatched the spear out of the Egyptian's hand 1
21 and slew him with his own spear. 1
2Kg 11:10 the priest delivered . . the spears and shields 1
1Ch 11:11 he wielded his spear against 300 whom he slew 1
20 he wielded his spear against 300 men and slew them 1
23 Egyptian had in his hand a spear 1
23 and snatched the spear out of the Egyptian's hand 1
23 Egyptian's hand, and slew him with his own spear. 1
12: 8 warriors, expert with shield and spear 5
24 The men of Judah bearing shield and spear were 5
34 were 37,000 men armed with shield and spear. 1
20: 5 the shaft of whose spear was like a weaver's beam. 1
2Ch 11:12 he put shields and spears in all the cities 5
14: 8 an army . . armed with bucklers and spears 5
23: 9 delivered to the captains the spears 1
25: 5 fit for war, able to handle spear and shield. 5
26:14 Uzzi'ah prepared for all the army shields, spears 5
Neh 4:13 with their swords, their spears, and their bows. 5
16 half held the spears, shields, bows 5
21 held the spears from the break of dawn 5
Job 39:23 the flashing spear and the javelin. 1
41: 7 or his head with fishing spears? 3
26 not avail; nor the spear, the dart, or the javelin. 1
Ps 35: 3 Draw the spear and javelin against my pursuers! 1
46: 9 he breaks the bow, and shatters the spear 1
57: 4 their teeth are spears and arrows 1
Isa 2: 4 plowshares, and their spears into pruning hooks; 1
Jer 6:23 They lay hold on bow and spear, they are cruel 2
46: 4 polish your spears, put on your coats of mail! 5
50:42 They lay hold of bow and spear; they are cruel 2
Ezk 39: 9 bucklers, bows and arrows, handpikes and spears 5
Jol 3:10 into swords, and your pruning hooks into spears; 5
Mic 4: 3 shall beat . . their spears into pruning hooks; 1
Nah 3: 3 flashing sword and glittering spear 1
Hab 3:11 at the flash of thy glittering spear. 1
Joh 19:34 one of the soldiers pierced his side with a spear 9
2Es 13: 9 he neither lifted his hand nor held a spear 10
28 as for his not holding a spear or weapon of war 10
Jdt 6: 6 the sword of my army and the spear of my servants ‡
7:10 the Israelites, do not rely on their spears 7
9: 7 they trust in shield and spear, in bow and sling 6
11: 2 I would never have lifted my spear against them; 7
AEs 16:24 shall be destroyed in wrath with spear and fire. 7
Sir 29:13 more than a heavy spear 7
2Mc 5: 3 brandishing of shields, massing of spears 8
15:11 confidence in shields and spears 9
3Mc 3:15 not rule . . by the power of the spear 7
5:43 and rapidly level it . . with fire and spear 7
6: 5 gained control of the whole world by the spear 7

hunting spear 1. σιβύνη
Jdt 1:15 and struck him down with hunting spears 1

spearman 1. δεξιολάβος
Act 23:23 70 horsemen and 200 spearmen 1

special 1. יָד
Ezk 27:15 many coastlands were your own special markets 1
48:12 it shall belong to them as a special portion •
Mal 3:17 my special possession on the day when I act •
special *See also* favor, gift, harness, make.

specially 1. μεγάλως
2Mc 2: 8 the place should be specially consecrated. 1

species 1. γένος
Sir 13:16 all living beings associate by species 1

specification 1. מִשְׁפָּט
1Kg 6:38 and according to all its specifications. 1

speck 1. κάρφος
Mat 7: 3 do you see the speck that is in your brother's eye 1
4 'Let me take the speck out of your eye,' 1
5 and then you will see clearly to take the speck 1
Lke 6:41 do you see the speck that is in your brother's eye 1
42 let me take out the speck that is in your eye 1
42 take out the speck that is in your brother's eye. 1
Wis 11:22 like a speck that tips the scales †

speckle 1. נָקֹד 2. צָבוּעַ
Gen 30:32 removing from it every speckled and spotted 1
32 the spotted and speckled among the goats; 1
33 Every one that is not speckled and spotted 1
35 all the she-goats that were speckled and spotted 1
39 the flocks brought forth striped, speckled 1
Jer 12: 9 Is my heritage to me like a speckled bird of prey? 2

spectacle 1. θέατρον 2. θεωρία 3. ὅραμα
1Co 4: 9 because we have become a spectacle 1
Sir 43: 1 the appearance of heaven in a spectacle of glory. 3
3Mc 5:24 assembled for this most pitiful spectacle 2
spectacle *See also* make.

obvious spectacle 1. παραδειγματισμός
3Mc 4:11 well suited to make them an obvious spectacle 1

spectator 1. θεωρέω
4Mc 17:14 the world and the human race were the spectators. 1
spectators *See* filled.

specter 1. ἴνδαλμα 2. φάντασμα
Wis 17: 3 terribly alarmed, and appalled by specters. 1
15 now were driven by monstrous specters 2

speculation 1. ἐκζήτησις
1Ti 1: 4 genealogies which promote speculations 1

speech 1. אֹמֶר 2. אֵמֶר 3. אִמְרָה 4. דִּבֵּר 5. דָּבָר 6. חֵךְ 7. לָשׁוֹן 8. מִלָּה 9. עַל שָׂפָה 10. פֶּה 11. שָׂפָה 12. γλῶσσα 13. λόγος 14. στόμα 15. φωνή 16. χεῖλος 17. sermo
Gen 11: 7 they may not understand one another's speech. 11
Exd 4:10 but I am slow of speech and of tongue. 7
Deu 32: 2 May my . . speech distil as the dew, as the gentle 3
1Sm 16:18 of valor, a man of war, prudent in speech 5
Job 6:26 when the speech of a despairing man is wind? 1
12:20 He deprives of speech those who are trusted 11
32:14 I will not answer him with your speeches. 1
33: 1 now, hear my speech, O Job, and listen 8
Ps 19: 2 Day to day pours forth speech 2
3 There is no speech, nor are there words; 2
55:21 His speech was smoother than butter 10
Prv 2:12 delivering you from . . men of perverted speech 4
4:24 Put away from you crooked speech 10
5: 3 her speech is smoother than oil; 6
6:12 wicked man . . goes about with crooked speech 10
8:13 way of evil and perverted speech I hate. 10
16:21 pleasant speech increases persuasiveness. 11
23 The mind of the wise makes his speech judicious 10
27 his speech is like a scorching fire. 9
17: 7 Fine speech is not becoming to a fool; 11
7 still less is false speech to a prince. 11
19: 1 than a man who is perverse in speech, and is a fool. 11
22:11 purity of heart, and whose speech is gracious 11
Sng 5:16 His speech is most sweet, and he is . . desirable. 6
Isa 3: 8 has fallen; because their speech and their deeds 7
28:23 hear my voice; hearken, and hear my speech. 3
29: 4 and your speech shall whisper out of the dust. 3
32: 9 you complacent daughters, give ear to my speech. 3
33:19 the people of an obscure speech which you cannot 11
Ezk 3: 5 For you are not sent to a people of foreign speech 11
6 not to many peoples of foreign speech 11
Zep 3: 9 I will change the speech of the peoples •
9 change the speech of the peoples to a pure speech 11
Act 20: 7 he prolonged his speech until midnight. 13
1Co 1: 5 with all speech and all knowledge– 13
2: 4 my speech and my message 13
14: 9 if you in a tongue utter speech 13
2Co 6: 7 truthful speech, and the power of God 13
10:10 His letters are weighty . . his speech of no account. 13
Col 4: 6 Let your speech always be gracious 13
1Ti 4:12 set the believers an example in speech 13
Tit 2: 8 sound speech that cannot be censured 13
1Jn 3:18 let us not love in word or speech but in deed 12
2Es 6:16 that the speech concerns them 17
Jdt 11:21 either for beauty of face or wisdom of speech! 13
23 beautiful in appearance, but wise in speech 13
AEs 14:13 Put eloquent speech in my mouth before the lion 13
Wis 8: 8 she understands turns of speech 13
Sir 4:24 For wisdom is known through speech 13
29 Do not be reckless in your speech 12
5:10 let your speech be consistent. 13
9:18 the man who is reckless in speech will be hated. 13
21: 7 He who is mighty in speech is known from afar 12
16 be found in the speech of the intelligent. 16
23: 7 Listen . . to instruction concerning speech 14
13 it involves sinful speech. 13
27:23 later he will twist his speech 14
32:12 do not sin through proud speech. 13
36:23 If kindness and humility mark her speech 12
1Mc 4:19 Just as Judas was finishing this speech •
6:60 The speech pleased the king and the commanders 13
3Mc 3:23 both by speech and by silence 13
4Mc 10:18 he said, "Even if you remove my organ of speech 15
speech *See also* boldness, impediment, seductive.

beguiling speech 1. *πιθανολογία*
Col 2: 4 no one may delude you with beguiling speech. 1

dark speech 1. חִידָה
Num12: 8 mouth to mouth, clearly, and not in dark speech 1

speechless 1. *ἄφωνος* 2. *ἐνεός* 3. *φιμόω*
Mat 22:12 And he was speechless. 3
Act 9: 7 The men . . stood speechless 2
Wis 4:19 he will dash them speechless to the ground 1
2Mc 3:29 speechless because of the divine intervention 1
speechless *See also* make.

speechless thing 1. *κωφός*
3Mc 4:16 praising speechless things 1

speed 1. הלך 2. חוש 3. נוס 4. *κατασπεύδω*
5. *ταχύνω* 6. *τρέχω*
Isa 5:19 who say: "Let him make haste, let him speed his work 2
30:16 you said, "No! We will speed upon horses 3
Hab 3:11 at the light of thine arrows as they sped 1
2Th 3: 1 the word of the Lord may speed on and triumph 6
Sir 32:10 Lightning speeds before the thunder 4
43:13 speeds the lightnings of his judgment. 5

speed away 1. נוס
Isa 30:16 upon horses," therefore you shall speed away; 1

speed on a journey 1. *προπέμπω*
Rom15:24 and to be sped on my journey there by you 1
1Co 16: 6 so that you may speed me on my journey 1

speed on the way 1. *προπέμπω*
1Co 16:11 Speed him on his way in peace 1
Tit 3:13 speed Zenas the lawyer and Apol'los on their way 1

speedily 1. לְמַדְחֵפֹת 2. מהר 3. מַהֵר 4. מְהֵרָה 5. קַל
6. *διὰ τάχους* 7. *ἐν τάχει* 8. *κατὰ σπουδήν* 9. *ταχέως*
10. *ταχύς*
Ps 31: 2 Incline thy ear to me, rescue me speedily! 4
79: 8 let thy compassion come speedily to meet us 3
102: 2 answer me speedily in the day when I call! 3
140:11 let evil hunt down the violent man speedily! 1
Ecc 8:11 Because sentence . . is not executed speedily 4
Isa 5:26 and lo, swiftly, speedily it comes! 5
51: 5 My deliverance draws near speedily *
14 He who is bowed down shall speedily be released; 2
58: 8 and your healing shall spring up speedily; 4
Jol 3: 4 upon your own head swiftly and speedily. 4
Lke 18: 8 I tell you, he will vindicate them speedily. 7
AEs 16:18 has speedily inflicted on him the punishment 6
Sir 20:18 the downfall of the wicked will occur speedily. 8
21: 5 his judgment comes speedily. 8
3Mc 2:20 Speedily let your mercies overtake us 10
4Mc 4:22 He speedily marched against them 9

speedy 1. *σύντομος*
Wis 14:14 therefore their speedy end has been planned. 1

spellbind 1. miraculo
2Es 2:43 And I was held spellbound. 1

spelt 1. כֻּסֶּמֶת
Exd 9:32 the wheat and the spelt were not ruined 1
Isa 28:25 barley in its . . place, and spelt as the border? 1
Ezk 4: 9 and barley, beans and lentils, millet and spelt 1

spend 1. הלך 2. כלה 3. נתן 4. עמל 5. פוג 6. שקל
7. תמם 8. *γίνομαι* 9. *δαπανάω* 10. *διάγω*
11. *ἐκδαπανάω* 12. *ἐπιμένω* 13. *καταναλίσκω*
14. *κλίνω* 15. *ποιέω*
Gen 47:15 when the money was all spent in the land of Egypt 7
18 We will not hide . . that our money is all spent; 7
Lev 26:20 your strength shall be spent in vain 7
Deu 14:26 spend the money for whatever you desire, oxen 3
32:23 evils upon them; I will spend my arrows upon them; 2
Jos 8:13 But Joshua spent that night in the valley. 1
Jdg 19:11 When they were near Jebus, the day was far spent 14
1Kg 17:14 The jar of meal shall not be spent, and the cruse 2
16 The jar of meal was not spent 2
Job 21:13 They spend their days in prosperity 2
Ps 31:10 my life is spent with sorrow 2
38: 8 I am utterly spent and crushed; 5
39:10 I am spent by the blows of thy hand. 2
71: 9 forsake me not when my strength is spent. 2
Ecc 2:11 and the toil I had spent in doing it 4
5:17 and spent all his days in darkness and grief *
Isa 49: 4 I have spent my strength for nothing and vanity; 2
55: 2 Why do you spend your money for that which is not 6
Jer 20:18 to see toil and sorrow, and spend my days in shame? 2
Lam 2:11 My eyes are spent with weeping; 2
Ezk 5:13 Thus shall my anger spend itself 2
13 in my jealousy, when I spend my fury upon them. 2
6:12 Thus I will spend my fury upon them. 2
7: 8 my wrath upon you, and spend my anger against you 2
13:15 Thus will I spend my wrath upon the wall 2
20: 8 wrath upon them and spend my anger against them 2
21 and spend my anger against them 2
Mrk 5:26 spent all that she had 9
Lke 15:14 when he had spent everything 9
Act 15:33 after they had spent some time 15
18:23 After spending some time there he departed 15
20: 3 There he spent three months 15
26: 4 spent from the beginning among my own nation 8
1Co 16: 7 I hope to spend some time with you 12
2Co 12:15 most gladly spend and be spent for your souls 9
15 most gladly spend and be spent for your souls 11
Jas 4: 3 you ask wrongly, to spend it on your passions. 9
13 and spend a year there and trade and get gain"; 15
Tob 1: 7 and spend the proceeds each year at Jerusalem; 9
10: 7 fourteen days . . that he should spend there. 15
LJr 1:10 spend it upon themselves 13
Bel 1: 3 they spent on it twelve bushels of fine flour 9
1Mc 14:32 He spent great sums of his own money 9
3Mc 4: 8 spent the remaining days of their marriage 10

spend more 1. *προσδαπανάω*
Lke 10:35 whatever more you spend, I will repay you 1

spend the night 1. לון 2. בית (A) 3. *αὐλίζομαι*
4. *κοιμάω*
Gen 19: 2 to your servant's house and spend the night 1
2 we will spend the night in the street. 1
24:54 ate and drank, and they spent the night there. 1
Jos 6:11 they came into . . and spent the night in the camp. 1
8: 9 but Joshua spent that night among the people. 1
Jdg 19: 6 Be pleased to spend the night 1
10 the man would not spend the night; he rose up 1
11 let us turn aside . . and spend the night in it. 1
13 and spend the night at Gib'e-ah or at Ramah. 1
15 turned aside there, to go in and spend the night 1
15 no man took them in . . to spend the night. 1
20 only, do not spend the night in the square. 1
20: 4 I came . . I and my concubine, to spend the night. 1
2Sm 17: 8 he will not spend the night with the people. 1
Ezr 10: 6 where he spent the night, neither eating bread 3
Job 39: 9 Will he spend the night at your crib? 1
Isa 65: 4 sit in tombs, and spend the night in secret places; 1
Dan 6:18 went to his palace, and spent the night fasting; 2
1Es 9: 2 spent the night there 3
1Mc 11: 6 and spent the night there. 4

spend the winter 1. *παραχειμάζω*
1Co 16: 6 stay with you or even spend the winter 1
Tit 3:12 I have decided to spend the winter there. 1

spend time 1. *εὐκαιρέω* 2. *χρονοτριβέω*
Act 17:21 the Athenians . . spent their time in nothing 1
20:16 so that he might not have to spend time in Asia 2

far spent 1. *κλίνω*
Lke 24:29 it is toward evening and the day is now far spent 1

spew 1. *ἐμέω*
Rev 3:16 I will spew you out of my mouth. 1

spew out 1. *ἐξερεύγομαι*
Wis 19:10 the river spewed out vast numbers of frogs. 1

spice 1. בֹּשֶׂם 2. רֶקַח 3. *ἄμωμον* 4. *ἄρωμα*
Exd 25: 6 oil for the lamps, spices for the anointing oil 1
30:23 Take the finest spices: of liquid myrrh 1
35: 8 oil for the light, spices for the anointing oil 1
28 spices and oil for the light 1
1Kg 10: 2 a very great retinue, with camels bearing spices 1
10 gold, and a very great quantity of spices 1
10 never again came such an abundance of spices 1
25 garments, myrrh, spices, horses, and mules 1
2Kg 20:13 silver, the gold, the spices, the precious oil, his 1
1Ch 9:29 over . . the oil, the incense, and the spices. 1
30 Others . . prepared the mixing of the spices. 1
2Ch 9: 1 camels bearing spices and very much gold 1
9 she gave . . a very great quantity of spices 1
9 there were no spices such as those 1
24 his present . . garments, myrrh, spices, horses 1
16:14 filled with various kinds of spices prepared 1
32:27 made . . treasuries . . for spices, for shields 1
Est 2:12 six months with spices and ointments for women- 1
Sng 4:10 and the fragrance of your oils than any spice! 1
14 myrrh and aloes, with all chief spices- 1
5: 1 I gather my myrrh with my spice, I eat my honeycomb 1
13 His cheeks are like beds of spices 1
6: 2 has gone down to his garden, to the beds of spices 1
8: 2 I would give you spiced wine to drink 2
14 or a young stag upon the mountains of spices. 1
Isa 39: 2 silver, the gold, the spices, the precious oil 1
Jer 34: 5 And as spices were burned for your fathers *
5 so men shall burn spices for you and lament *
Ezk 27:22 for your wares the best of all kinds of spices 1
Mrk 16: 1 the mother of James, and Salo'me, bought spices 4
Lke 23:56 they returned, and prepared spices 4
24: 1 taking the spices which they had prepared. 4
Joh 19:40 and bound it in linen cloths with the spices 4
Rev 18:13 cinnamon, spice, incense, myrrh, frankincense 3
Sir 24:15 I gave forth the aroma of spices 4

sweet spice 1. סַם
Exd 30:34 the LORD said to Moses, "Take sweet spices, stacte 1
34 Take . . sweet spices with pure frankincense 1
2Ch 2: 4 burning of incense of sweet spices before him 1
13:11 offer to the LORD . . incense of sweet spices 1

spider 1. עַכָּבִישׁ
Job 8:14 his trust is a spider's web. 1
27:18 The house which he builds is like a spider's web *
Isa 59: 5 watch adders' eggs, they weave the spider's web; 1

spill 1. נגר 2. שחת 3. *ἐκχέω*
Gen 38: 9 went in to his brother's wife he spilled the semen 2
2Sm 14:14 we are like water spilt on the ground 1
Mat 9:17 the wine is spilled, and the skins are destroyed; 3
Lke 5:37 it will be spilled 3

spin 1. טוה 2. מַטְוֶה 3. *νήθω*
Exd 35:25 all women who had ability spun with their hands 1
25 brought what they had spun in blue and purple 2
26 women . . with ability spun the goats' hair. 1
Mat 6:28 how they grow; they neither toil nor spin; 3
Lke 12:27 they neither toil nor spin 3

spindle 1. פֶּלֶךְ
2Sm 3:29 is leprous, or who holds a spindle, or who is slain 1
Prv 31:19 her hands hold the spindle. 1

spirit 1. אוֹב 2. כָּבוֹד 3. לֵב 4. נֶפֶשׁ 5. נְשָׁמָה 6. רוּחַ
7. רוּחַ (A) 8. *διάνοια* 9. *καρδία* 10. *πνεῦμα*
11. *φρόνημα* 12. *ψυχή* 13. animus 14. inspiratio
15. sensus 16. spiramentum 17. spiritus
Gen 1: 2 and the Spirit of God was moving over the face 6
6: 3 the LORD said, "My spirit shall not abide in man 6
41: 8 in the morning his spirit was troubled; 6
38 such a man as this, in whom is the Spirit of God? 6
45:27 when he saw . . the spirit of their father Jacob 6
49: 6 O my spirit, be not joined to their company; 2
Exd 6: 9 because of their broken spirit and their cruel 6
31: 3 I have filled him with the Spirit of God 6
35:21 and every one whose spirit moved him 6
31 he has filled him with the Spirit of God 6
Num 5:14 or if the spirit of jealousy comes upon him 6
14 or if the spirit of jealousy comes upon him 6
30 or when the spirit of jealousy comes upon a man 6
11:17 I will take some of the spirit which is upon you 6
25 LORD . . took some of the spirit that was upon him 6
25 when the spirit rested upon them, they prophesied. 6
26 Eldad . . Medad . . spirit rested upon them; 6
29 that the LORD would put his spirit upon them! 6
14:24 Caleb, because he has a different spirit 6
16:22 said, "O God, the God of the spirits of all flesh 6
24: 2 And the Spirit of God came upon him 6
27:16 Let the LORD, the God of the spirits of all flesh 6
18 Joshua the son of Nun, a man in whom is the spirit 6
Deu 2:30 for the LORD your God hardened his spirit 6
34: 9 Joshua . . was full of the spirit of wisdom 6
Jos 5: 1 and there was no longer any spirit in them 6
Jdg 3:10 The Spirit of the LORD came upon him, and he judged 6
6:34 the Spirit of the LORD took possession of Gideon; 6
9:23 God sent an evil spirit between Abim'elech 6
11:29 the Spirit of the LORD came upon Jephthah 6
13:25 And the Spirit of the LORD began to stir him 6
14: 6 the Spirit of the LORD came mightily upon him 6
19 the Spirit of the LORD came mightily upon him 6
15:14 and the Spirit of the LORD came mightily upon him 6
19 he drank, his spirit returned . . and he revived. 6
1Sm 10: 6 the spirit of the LORD will come mightily upon 6
10 and the spirit of God came mightily upon him 6
11: 6 And the spirit of God came mightily upon Saul 6
16:13 the Spirit of the LORD came mightily upon David 6
14 Now the Spirit of the LORD departed from Saul 6
14 and an evil spirit from the LORD tormented him. 6
15 an evil spirit from God is tormenting you. 6
16 when the evil spirit from God is upon you 6
23 whenever the evil spirit from God was upon Saul 6
23 Saul was . . well, and the evil spirit departed 6
18:10 an evil spirit from God rushed upon Saul 6
19: 9 Then an evil spirit from the LORD came upon Saul 6
20 the Spirit of God came upon the messengers 6
23 and the Spirit of God came upon him also 6
28: 8 And he said, "Divine for me by a spirit 1
30:12 when he had eaten, his spirit revived; 6
2Sm 13:39 the spirit of the king longed to go . . to Ab'salom; 10
23: 2 The Spirit of the LORD speaks by me 6
1Kg 10: 5 there was no more spirit in her. 6
18:12 the Spirit of the LORD will carry you 6
21: 5 Why is your spirit so vexed that you eat no food? 6
22:21 a spirit came forward and stood before the LORD 6
22 I . . will be a lying spirit in the mouth 6
23 the LORD has put a lying spirit in the mouth 6
24 How did the Spirit of the LORD go from me 6
2Kg 2: 9 let me inherit a double share of your spirit. 6
15 The spirit of Eli'jah rests on Eli'sha. 6
16 the Spirit of the LORD has caught him up 6
5:26 Did I not go with you in spirit when the man turned 3
19: 7 I will put a spirit in him, so that he shall hear 6
1Ch 5:26 stirred up the spirit of Pul king of Assyria 6

26 the spirit of Til'gath-pilne'ser king of Assyria 6
12:18 Then the Spirit came upon Ama'sai, chief of the 30 6
2Ch 9: 4 there was no more spirit in her. 6
15: 1 Spirit of God came upon Azari'ah the son of Oded 6
18:20 a spirit came forward and stood before the LORD 6
21 a lying spirit in the mouth of all his prophets.' 6
22 LORD has put a lying spirit in the mouth of these 6
23 Which way did the Spirit of the LORD go 6
20:14 the Spirit of the LORD came upon Jaha'ziel 6
24:20 the Spirit of God took possession of Zechari'ah 6
36:22 LORD stirred up the spirit of Cyrus king 6
Ezr 1: 1 LORD stirred up the spirit of Cyrus king of Persia 6
5 every one whose spirit God had stirred to go up 6
Neh 9:20 Thou gavest thy good Spirit to instruct them 6
30 warn them by thy Spirit through thy prophets; 6
Job 4:15 A spirit glided past my face; 6
6: 4 are in me; my spirit drinks their poison; 6
7:11 I will speak in the anguish of my spirit; 6
10:12 thy care has preserved my spirit. 6
15:13 that you turn your spirit against God 6
17: 1 My spirit is broken, my days are extinct 6
20: 3 out of my understanding a spirit answers me. 6
26: 4 whose spirit has come forth from you? 5
27: 3 the spirit of God is in my nostrils; 6
32: 8 the spirit in a man, the breath of the Almighty 6
18 the spirit within me constrains me. 6
33: 4 The spirit of God has made me 6
34:14 If he should take back his spirit to himself 6
Ps 31: 5 Into thy hand I commit my spirit; 6
32: 2 in whose spirit there is no deceit. 6
34:18 The LORD . . saves the crushed in spirit. 6
51:10 O God, and put a new and right spirit within me. 6
11 take not thy holy Spirit from me. 6
12 uphold me with a willing spirit. 6
17 sacrifice acceptable to God is a broken spirit; 6
76:12 who cuts off the spirit of princes 6
77: 3 I moan; I meditate, and my spirit faints. 6
6 in the night; I meditate and search my spirit 6
78: 8 whose spirit was not faithful to God. 6
104:30 thou sendest forth thy Spirit, they are created; 6
106:33 made his spirit bitter, and he spoke words that 6
139: 7 Whither shall I go from thy Spirit? 6
142: 3 When my spirit is faint, thou knowest my way! 6
143: 4 Therefore my spirit faints within me; 6
7 Make haste to answer me, O LORD! My spirit fails! 6
10 Let thy good spirit lead me on a level path! 6
Prv 11:13 trustworthy in spirit keeps a thing hidden. 6
15: 4 but perverseness in it breaks the spirit. 6
13 but by sorrow of heart the spirit is broken. 6
16: 2 but the LORD weighs the spirit. 6
18 haughty spirit before a fall. 6
19 better to be of a lowly spirit with the poor 6
32 he who rules his spirit than he who takes a city. 6
17:22 but a downcast spirit dries up the bones. 6
27 who has a cool spirit is a man of understanding. 6
18:14 A man's spirit will endure sickness; 6
14 but a broken spirit who can bear? 6
20:27 The spirit of man is the lamp of the LORD 5
25:13 faithful messenger . . refreshes the spirit 4
29:23 but he who is lowly in spirit will obtain honor. 6
Ecc 3:21 Who knows whether the spirit of man goes upward 6
21 and the spirit of the beast goes down to the earth? 6
7: 8 and the patient in spirit is better 6
8 patient . . is better than the proud in spirit. 6
8: 8 No man has power to retain the spirit 6
11: 5 you do not know how the spirit comes to the bones 6
12: 7 and the spirit returns to God who gave it. 6
Isa 4: 4 cleansed . . by a spirit of judgment 6
4 spirit of judgment and by a spirit of burning. 6
11: 2 the Spirit of the LORD shall rest upon him 6
2 the spirit of wisdom and understanding 6
2 understanding, the spirit of counsel and might 6
2 the spirit of knowledge and the fear of the LORD. 6
19: 3 spirit of the Egyptians . . will be emptied out 6
14 LORD . . mingled within her a spirit of confusion; 6
26: 9 my spirit within me earnestly seeks thee. 6
28: 6 a spirit of justice to him who sits in judgment 6
29:10 poured out upon you a spirit of deep sleep 6
24 who err in spirit will come to understanding 6
30: 1 and who make a league, but not of my spirit 6
31: 3 their horses are flesh, and not spirit. 6
32:15 until the Spirit is poured upon us from on high 6
34:16 and his Spirit has gathered them. 6
37: 7 put a spirit in him, so that he shall hear a rumor 6
38:16 and in all these is the life of my spirit. 6
40:13 Who has directed the Spirit of the LORD 6
42: 1 I have put my Spirit upon him 6
5 who gives . . spirit to those who walk in it 6
44: 3 I will pour my Spirit upon your descendants 6
48:16 And now the Lord GOD has sent me and his Spirit. 6
54: 6 like a wife forsaken and grieved in spirit 6
57:15 with him who is of a contrite and humble spirit 6
15 to revive the spirit of the humble 6
16 for from me proceeds the spirit 6
59:21 says the LORD: my spirit which is upon you 6
61: 1 The Spirit of the Lord GOD is upon me 6
3 the mantle of praise instead of a faint spirit; 6
63:10 But they rebelled and grieved his holy Spirit; 6
11 he who put in the midst of them his holy Spirit 6
14 the Spirit of the LORD gave them rest. 6
65:14 cry out . . and shall wail for anguish of spirit. 6
66: 2 he that is humble and contrite in spirit 6
Jer 51: 1 Behold, I will stir up the spirit of a destroyer 6
11 The LORD has stirred up the spirit of the kings 6
Ezk 1:12 wherever the spirit would go, they went 6
20 Wherever the spirit would go, they went 6
20 the spirit of the . . creatures was in the wheels. 6
21 the spirit of the . . creatures was in the wheels. 6
2: 2 when he spoke to me, the Spirit entered into me 6
3:12 Then the Spirit lifted me up 6
14 The Spirit lifted me up and took me away 6
14 and I went in bitterness in the heat of my spirit 6
24 the Spirit entered into me, and set me upon my feet; 6
8: 3 the Spirit lifted me up between earth and heaven 6
10:17 the spirit of the living creatures was in them. 6
11: 1 The Spirit lifted me up, and brought me 6
5 Spirit of the LORD fell upon me, and he said to me 6
19 and put a new spirit within them; 6
24 Spirit lifted me up and brought me in the vision 6
24 and brought me in the vision by the Spirit of God 6
13: 3 foolish prophets who follow their own spirit 6
18:31 and get yourselves a new heart and a new spirit! 6
21: 7 all hands will be feeble, every spirit will faint 6
36:26 and a new spirit I will put within you; 6
27 I will put my spirit within you 6
37: 1 he brought me out by the spirit of the LORD 6
14 I will put my Spirit within you, and you shall live 6
39:29 when I pour out my Spirit upon the house of Israel 6
43: 5 the Spirit lifted me up, and brought me 6
Dan 2: 1 spirit was troubled, and his sleep left him. 6
3 spirit is troubled to know the dream. 6
4: 8 Daniel . . in whom is the spirit of the holy gods– 7
9 know that the spirit of the holy gods is in you 7
18 for the spirit of the holy gods is in you. 7
5:11 man in whom is the spirit of the holy gods. 7
12 excellent spirit, knowledge, and understanding 7
14 heard of you that the spirit of the holy gods 7
20 heart was lifted up and his spirit was hardened 7
6: 3 because an excellent spirit was in him; 7
7:15 As for me, Daniel, my spirit within me was anxious 7
Hos 4:12 For a spirit of harlotry has led them astray 6
5: 4 For the spirit of harlotry is within them 6
9: 7 The prophet is a fool, the man of the spirit is mad 6
Jol 2:28 that I will pour out my spirit on all flesh; 6
29 in those days, I will pour out my spirit. 6
Mic 2: 7 Is the Spirit of the LORD impatient? 6
3: 8 am filled with power, with the Spirit of the LORD 6
Hag 1:14 the LORD stirred up the spirit of Zerub'babel 6
14 the spirit of Joshua the son of Jehoz'adak 6
14 the spirit of all the remnant of the people; 6
2: 5 My Spirit abides among you; fear not. 6
Zec 4: 6 Not by might, nor by power, but by my Spirit 6
6: 8 have set my Spirit at rest in the north country. 6
7:12 by his Spirit through the former prophets. 6
12: 1 founded the earth and formed the spirit of man 6
10 I will pour out . . a spirit of compassion 6
13: 2 the land the prophets and the unclean spirit. 6
Mal 2:15 God made and sustained for us the spirit of life? 6
Mat 1:18 found to be with child of the Holy Spirit; 10
20 is conceived in her is of the Holy Spirit; 10
3:11 baptize you with the Holy Spirit and with fire. 10
16 heavens were opened and he saw the Spirit of God 10
4: 1 led up by the Spirit into the wilderness 10
5: 3 Blessed are the poor in spirit, for theirs is 10
8:16 and he cast out the spirits with a word 10
10: 1 and gave them authority over unclean spirits 10
20 the Spirit of your Father speaking through you. 10
12:18 I will put my Spirit upon him 10
28 if it is by the Spirit of God that I cast out demons 10
31 the blasphemy against the Spirit 10
32 but whoever speaks against the Holy Spirit 10
43 When the unclean spirit has gone out of a man 10
45 he goes and brings with him seven other spirits 10
22:43 How is it then that David, inspired by the Spirit 10
26:41 the spirit indeed is willing 10
27:50 Jesus cried . . and yielded up his spirit. 10
28:19 Father and of the Son and of the Holy Spirit 10
Mrk 1: 8 he will baptize you with the Holy Spirit 10
10 the Spirit descending upon him like a dove; 10
12 The Spirit immediately drove him out 10
23 in their synagogue a man with an unclean spirit; 10
26 the unclean spirit, convulsing him and crying 10
27 he commands even the unclean spirits 10
2: 8 immediately Jesus, perceiving in his spirit 10
3:11 whenever the unclean spirits beheld him 10
29 whoever blasphemes against the Holy Spirit 10
30 for they had said, "He has an unclean spirit. 10
5: 2 a man with an unclean spirit 10
8 Come out of the man, you unclean spirit! 10
13 unclean spirits came out, and entered the swine; 10
6: 7 and gave them authority over the unclean spirits. 10
7:25 possessed by an unclean spirit 10
8:12 he sighed deeply in his spirit, and said 10
9:17 I brought my son to you, for he has a dumb spirit; 10
20 when the spirit saw him 10
25 he rebuked the unclean spirit, saying to it 10
25 You dumb and deaf spirit, I command you 10
12:36 himself, inspired by the Holy Spirit, declared 10
13:11 it is not you who speak, but the Holy Spirit. 10
14:38 the spirit indeed is willing 10
Lke 1:15 he will be filled with the Holy Spirit 10
17 go before him in the spirit and power of Eli'jah 10
35 The Holy Spirit will come upon you 10
41 Elizabeth was filled with the Holy Spirit 10
47 my spirit rejoices in God my Savior 10
67 filled with the Holy Spirit, and prophesied 10
80 the child grew and became strong in spirit 10
2:25 the Holy Spirit was upon him. 10
26 it had been revealed to him by the Holy Spirit 10
27 inspired by the Spirit he came into the temple; 10
3:16 baptize you with the Holy Spirit and with fire. 10
22 Holy Spirit descended upon him in bodily form 10
4: 1 Jesus, full of the Holy Spirit, returned 10
1 Jesus . . was led by the Spirit 10
14 in the power of the Spirit 10
18 The Spirit of the Lord is upon me 10
33 a man who had the spirit of an unclean demon 10
36 he commands the unclean spirits, and they come out. 10
6:18 those who were troubled with unclean spirits 10
7:21 diseases and plagues and evil spirits 10
8: 2 been healed of evil spirits and infirmities 10
29 he had commanded the unclean spirit to come out 10
55 her spirit returned, and she got up at once 10
9:39 a spirit seizes him, and he suddenly cries out 10
42 But Jesus rebuked the unclean spirit 10
10:20 the spirits are subject to you 10
21 rejoiced in the Holy Spirit and said, "I thank thee 10
11:13 will the heavenly Father give the Holy Spirit 10
24 When the unclean spirit has gone out of a man 10
26 seven other spirits more evil than himself 10
12:10 he who blasphemes against the Holy Spirit 10
12 the Holy Spirit will teach you in that very hour 10
13:11 a woman who had had a spirit of infirmity 10
23:46 Father, into thy hands I commit my spirit! 10
24:37 supposed that they saw a spirit. 10
39 a spirit has not flesh and bones 10
Joh 1:32 I saw the Spirit descend as a dove from heaven 10
33 'He on whom you see the Spirit descend and remain 10
33 this is he who baptizes with the Holy Spirit.' 10
3: 5 unless one is born of water and the Spirit 10
6 and that which is born of the Spirit is spirit. 10
6 and that which is born of the Spirit is spirit. 10
8 so it is with every one who is born of the Spirit. 10
34 for it is not by measure that he gives the Spirit; 10
4:23 will worship the Father in spirit and truth 10
24 God is spirit, and those who worship him 10
24 must worship in spirit and truth. 10
6:63 It is the spirit that gives life 10
63 the words . . are spirit and life. 10
7:39 Now this he said about the Spirit 10
39 as yet the Spirit had not been given 10
11:33 he was deeply moved in spirit and troubled; 10
13:21 he was troubled in spirit, and testified 10
14:17 even the Spirit of truth 10
26 the Counselor, the Holy Spirit 10
15:26 even the Spirit of truth 10
16:13 When the Spirit of truth comes 10
19:30 he bowed his head and gave up his spirit. 10
20:22 Receive the Holy Spirit. 10
Act 1: 2 had given commandment through the Holy Spirit 10
5 you shall be baptized with the Holy Spirit. 10
8 when the Holy Spirit has come upon you 10
16 which the Holy Spirit spoke beforehand 10
2: 4 they were all filled with the Holy Spirit 10
4 as the Spirit gave them utterance. 10
17 I will pour out my Spirit upon all flesh 10
18 in those days I will pour out my Spirit 10
33 the promise of the Holy Spirit 10
38 you shall receive the gift of the Holy Spirit. 10
4: 8 Then Peter, filled with the Holy Spirit, said 10
25 who . . didst say by the Holy Spirit 10
31 they were all filled with the Holy Spirit 10
5: 3 filled your heart to lie to the Holy Spirit 10
9 have agreed together to tempt the Spirit of the Lord? 10
16 those afflicted with unclean spirits 10
32 so is the Holy Spirit 10
6: 3 full of the Spirit and of wisdom 10
5 Stephen, a man full of faith and of the Holy Spirit 10
10 the wisdom and the Spirit with which he spoke. 10
7:51 you always resist the Holy Spirit 10
55 he, full of the Holy Spirit, gazed into heaven 10
59 Lord Jesus, receive my spirit. 10
8: 7 unclean spirits came out of many 10
15 they might receive the Holy Spirit; 10
17 they received the Holy Spirit. 10
18 the Spirit was given 10
19 may receive the Holy Spirit. 10
29 the Spirit said to Philip, "Go up 10
39 the Spirit of the Lord caught up Philip 10
9:17 be filled with the Holy Spirit. 10
31 in the comfort of the Holy Spirit 10
10:19 the Spirit said to him, "Behold 10
38 anointed Jesus of Nazareth with the Holy Spirit 10
44 the Holy Spirit fell on all who heard the word. 10
45 the gift of the Holy Spirit had been poured out 10
47 who have received the Holy Spirit just as we have? 10
11:12 the Spirit told me to go with them 10

15 As I began to speak, the Holy Spirit fell on them 10
16 you shall be baptized with the Holy Spirit.' 10
10
10
10
10
10
10
10
us 10
10
10
10
10
10
10
10
10
10
10
10
m 10
10
10
10
10
10
10
10
10
10
10
10
10
10
10
10
10
10
10
10
10
10
10
10
10
10
10
10
10
10
10
23 we . . who have the first fruits of the Spirit 10
26 the Spirit himself intercedes for us with sighs 10
26 Likewise the Spirit helps us in our weakness; 10
27 knows what is the mind of the Spirit 10
27 because the Spirit intercedes for the saints *
9: 1 my conscience bears me witness in the Holy Spirit 10
11: 8 as it is written, "God gave them a spirit of stupor 10
12:11 Never flag in zeal, be aglow with the Spirit 10
14:17 and peace and joy in the Holy Spirit; 10
15:13 by the power of the Holy Spirit you may abound 10
16 be acceptable, sanctified by the Holy Spirit. 10
19 by the power of the Holy Spirit 10
30 I appeal to you . . by the love of the Spirit 10
1Co 2: 4 in demonstration of the Spirit and of power 10
10 God has revealed to us through the Spirit 10
10 the Spirit searches everything, even the depths 10
11 except the spirit of the man which is in him 10
11 except the Spirit of God. 10
12 Now we have received not the spirit of the world 10
12 the Spirit which is from God 10
13 taught by the Spirit 10
14 does not receive the gifts of the Spirit of God 10
3:16 God's Spirit dwells in you? 10
4:21 with love in a spirit of gentleness? 10
5: 3 For though absent in body I am present in spirit 10
4 When you are assembled, and my spirit is present 10
5 his spirit may be saved in the day of the Lord 10
6:11 in the Spirit of our God. 10
17 united to the Lord becomes one spirit with him. 10
19 a temple of the Holy Spirit within you 10
7:34 how to be holy in body and spirit 10
40 I think that I have the Spirit of God. 10
12: 3 no one speaking by the Spirit of God ever says 10
3 except by the Holy Spirit. 10
4 there are varieties of gifts, but the same Spirit; 10
7 To each is given the manifestation of the Spirit 10
8 To one is given through the Spirit the utterance 10
8 according to the same Spirit 10
9 to another faith by the same Spirit 10
9 to another gifts of healing by the one Spirit 10
10 the ability to distinguish between spirits 10
11 All these are inspired by one and the same Spirit 10
13 by one Spirit we were all baptized 10
13 all were made to drink of one Spirit. 10
14: 2 he utters mysteries in the Spirit. 10
14 my spirit prays but my mind is unfruitful. 10

15 What am I to do? I will pray with the spirit 10
15 I will sing with the spirit 10
16 Otherwise, if you bless with the spirit 10
32 the spirits of prophets are subject 10
15:45 the last Adam became a life-giving spirit. 10
16:18 for they refreshed my spirit as well as yours. 10
2Co 1:22 given us his Spirit in our hearts as a guarantee. 10
3: 3 not with ink but with the Spirit of the living God 10
6 not in a written code but in the Spirit 10
6 the written code kills, but the Spirit gives life. 10
8 will not the dispensation of the Spirit 10
17 Now the Lord is the Spirit 10
17 where the Spirit of the Lord is, there is freedom. 10
18 this comes from the Lord who is the Spirit. 10
4:13 Since we have the same spirit of faith 10
5: 5 who has given us the Spirit as a guarantee. 10
6: 6 kindness, the Holy Spirit, genuine love 10
7: 1 every defilement of body and spirit 10
11: 4 if you receive a different spirit 10
12:18 Did we not act in the same spirit? 10
13:14 fellowship of the Holy Spirit be with you all. 10
Gal 3: 2 Did you receive the Spirit by works of the law 10
3 Having begun with the Spirit 10
5 Does he who supplies the Spirit to you 10
14 receive the promise of the Spirit through faith 10
4: 6 God has sent the Spirit of his Son into our hearts 10
29 who was born according to the Spirit 10
5: 5 For through the Spirit, by faith, we wait 10
16 I say, walk by the Spirit 10
17 the desires of the flesh are against the Spirit 10
17 the desires of the Spirit are against the flesh; 10
18 if you are led by the Spirit 10
22 the fruit of the Spirit is love, joy, peace 10
25 If we live by the Spirit 10
25 let us also walk by the Spirit. 10
6: 1 restore him in a spirit of gentleness 10
8 he who sows to the Spirit 10
8 will from the Spirit reap eternal life. 10
18 Christ be with your spirit, brethren. Amen. 10
Eph 1:13 were sealed with the promised Holy Spirit 10
17 may give you a spirit of wisdom and of revelation 10
2: 2 the spirit that is now at work 10
18 both have access in one Spirit to the Father. 10
22 a dwelling place of God in the Spirit. 10
3: 5 has now been revealed . . by the Spirit; 10
16 through his Spirit in the inner man 10
4: 3 the unity of the Spirit in the bond of peace. 10
4 There is one body and one Spirit 10
23 be renewed in the spirit of your minds 10
30 do not grieve the Holy Spirit of God 10
5:18 be filled with the Spirit 10
6:17 the sword of the Spirit, which is the word of God. 10
18 Pray at all times in the Spirit 10
Php 1:19 the help of the Spirit of Jesus Christ 10
27 I may hear of you that you stand firm in one spirit 10
2: 1 any participation in the Spirit 10
3: 3 who worship God in spirit, and glory in Christ 10
4:23 the Lord Jesus Christ be with your spirit. 10
Col 1: 8 has made known to us your love in the Spirit. 10
2: 5 yet I am with you in spirit 10
1Th 1: 5 in the Holy Spirit and with full conviction 10
6 with joy inspired by the Holy Spirit; 10
4: 8 who gives his Holy Spirit to you. 10
5:19 Do not quench the Spirit 10
23 may your spirit and soul and body be kept sound 10
2Th 2: 2 either by spirit or by word, or by letter 10
13 through sanctification by the Spirit 10
1Ti 3:16 vindicated in the Spirit, seen by angels 10
4: 1 Now the Spirit expressly says 10
1 giving heed to deceitful spirits 10
2Ti 1: 7 for God did not give us a spirit of timidity 10
7 a spirit of power and love and self-control. 10
14 the Holy Spirit who dwells within us. 10
4:22 The Lord be with your spirit. Grace be with you. 10
Tit 3: 5 renewal in the Holy Spirit 10
Phm 1:25 the Lord Jesus Christ be with your spirit. 10
Heb 1:14 all ministering spirits sent forth to serve 10
2: 4 by gifts of the Holy Spirit 10
3: 7 Therefore, as the Holy Spirit says 10
4:12 piercing to the division of soul and spirit 10
6: 4 have become partakers of the Holy Spirit 10
9: 8 By this the Holy Spirit indicates 10
14 who through the eternal Spirit offered himself 10
10:15 the Holy Spirit also bears witness to us 10
29 outraged the Spirit of grace 10
12: 9 be subject to the Father of spirits and live? 10
23 to the spirits of just men made perfect 10
Jas 2:26 For as the body apart from the spirit is dead 10
4: 5 He yearns jealously over the spirit 10
1Pe 1: 2 sanctified by the Spirit for obedience 10
11 indicated by the Spirit of Christ within them 10
12 through the Holy Spirit sent from heaven 10
3: 4 the imperishable jewel of a gentle and quiet spirit 10
18 Christ . . made alive in the spirit; 10
19 he went and preached to the spirits in prison 10
4: 6 they might live in the spirit like God. 10
14 the spirit of glory and of God rests upon you. 10
2Pe 1:21 men moved by the Holy Spirit spoke from God. 10

1Jn 3:24 by the Spirit which he has given us. 10
4: 1 Beloved, do not believe every spirit 10
1 test the spirits to see whether they are of God; 10
2 By this you know the Spirit of God 10
2 every spirit which confesses that Jesus Christ 10
3 every spirit which does not confess Jesus 10
3 This is the spirit of the antichrist *
6 the spirit of truth and the spirit of error 10
6 the spirit of truth and the spirit of error 10
13 because he has given us of his own Spirit. 10
5: 7 the Spirit is the witness 10
7 because the Spirit is the truth. 10
8 three witnesses, the Spirit, the water . . blood 10
Jde 1:19 worldly people, devoid of the Spirit. 10
20 pray in the Holy Spirit; 10
Rev 1: 4 from the seven spirits who are before his throne 10
10 I was in the Spirit on the Lord's day, and I heard 10
2: 7 let him hear what the Spirit says to the churches 10
11 let him hear what the Spirit says to the churches 10
17 He who has an ear, let him hear what the Spirit says 10
29 He who has an ear, let him hear what the Spirit says 10
3: 1 The words of him who has the seven spirits of God 10
6 He who has an ear, let him hear what the Spirit says 10
13 He who has an ear, let him hear what the Spirit says 10
22 He who has an ear, let him hear what the Spirit says 10
4: 2 I was in the Spirit, and lo, a throne stood in heaven 10
5 torches . . which are the seven spirits of God; 10
5: 6 seven spirits of God sent out into all the earth; 10
14:13 Blessed indeed," says the Spirit 10
16:13 I saw . . three foul spirits like frogs; 10
14 for they are demonic spirits, performing signs 10
17: 3 And he carried me away in the Spirit 10
18: 2 a haunt of every foul spirit 10
19:10 testimony of Jesus is the spirit of prophecy. 10
21:10 And in the Spirit he carried me away 10
22: 6 the Lord, the God of the spirits of the prophets 10
17 The Spirit and the Bride say, "Come. 10
1Es 2: 2 the Lord stirred up the spirit of Cyrus 10
8 all whose spirit the Lord had stirred 10
2Es 1:37 yet with the spirit they will believe the things 17
3: 3 My spirit was greatly agitated 17
5:22 my soul recovered the spirit of understanding 17
6:26 and converted to a different spirit. 15
37 For my spirit was greatly aroused 17
39 then the Spirit was hovering 17
41 thou didst create the spirit of the firmament 17
7:78 as the spirit leaves the body to return again 14
80 such spirits shall not enter into habitations 14
9:41 I am greatly embittered in spirit 13
12: 3 and I said to my spirit 17
5 am still weary in mind and very weak in my spirit 17
14:22 send the Holy Spirit into me 17
40 for my spirit retained its memory; 17
16:62 the spirit of Almighty God 16
Tob 3: 6 command my spirit to be taken up 10
6: 7 if a demon or evil spirit gives trouble to any one 10
Jdt 14: 6 he fell down on his face and his spirit failed him. 10
16:14 Thou didst send forth thy Spirit 10
AEs 15: 8 God changed the spirit of the king to gentleness 10
Wis 1: 5 a holy and disciplined spirit 10
6 For wisdom is a kindly spirit 10
7 the Spirit of the Lord has filled the world 10
2: 3 the spirit will dissolve like empty air. 10
5: 3 in anguish of spirit they will groan, and say 10
7: 7 the spirit of wisdom came to me. 10
20 the powers of spirits . . and the virtues of roots; 10
22 a spirit that is intelligent, holy, unique 10
23 penetrating through all spirits 10
9:17 and sent thy holy Spirit from on high? 10
12: 1 For thy immortal spirit is in all things. 10
15:11 and breathed into him a living spirit. 10
16 one whose spirit is borrowed formed them 10
16:14 he cannot bring back the departed spirit 10
Sir 34:13 The spirit of those who fear the Lord will live 10
38:23 be comforted for him when his spirit is departed. 10
39: 6 will be filled with the spirit of understanding; 10
48:12 Elisha was filled with his spirit 10
24 By the spirit of might he saw the last things 10
Bar 2:17 whose spirit has been taken from their bodies 10
3: 1 soul in anguish and the wearied spirit cry out 10
Aza 1:16 with a contrite heart and a humble spirit 10
64 spirits and souls of the righteous 10
Sus 1:45 God aroused the holy spirit of a young lad 10
1Mc 9: 7 he was crushed in spirit 9
10:74 his spirit was aroused 8
13: 7 The spirit of the people was rekindled 10
2Mc 1: 3 a strong heart and a willing spirit. 12
3:24 the Sovereign of spirits and of all authority 10
5:17 Antiochus was elated in spirit 8
7:12 those . . were astonished at the young man's spirit 12
21 Filled with a noble spirit 11
14:46 calling upon the Lord of life and spirit 10
3Mc 2:20 those who are downcast and broken in spirit 12
32 acted firmly with a courageous spirit 12
3:22 they took this in a contrary spirit *
4: 4 with such a harsh and ruthless spirit 12
4Mc 7:14 in spirit through reason 10

14: 6 as though moved by an immortal spirit of devotion 12

spirit *See also* break, courageous, elemental, manifestation, possess, unity.

party spirit 1. αἵρεσις

Gal 5:20 anger, selfishness, dissension, party spirit 1

spiritual 1. λογικός 2. πνεῦμα 3. πνευματικός

Rom 1:11 that I may impart to you some spiritual gift 3
2:29 a matter of the heart, spiritual and not literal. 2
7:14 We know that the law is spiritual; but I am carnal 3
12: 1 which is your spiritual worship. 1
15:27 the Gentiles . . share in their spiritual blessings 3
1Co 14:37 If any one thinks that he is a prophet, or spiritual 3
15:44 it is raised a spiritual body 3
44 there is also a spiritual body. 3
46 it is not the spiritual which is first 3
46 the physical, and then the spiritual. 3
Gal 6: 1 you who are spiritual should restore him 3
Eph 1: 3 blessed us . . with every spiritual blessing 3
5:19 psalms and hymns and spiritual songs 3
Col 1: 9 in all spiritual wisdom and understanding 3
3:16 sing psalms and hymns and spiritual songs 3
1Pe 2: 2 long for the pure spiritual milk 1
5 be yourselves built into a spiritual house 3
5 offer spiritual sacrifices acceptable to God 3

spiritual *See also* gift, good, host, truth.

spiritual man 1. πνευματικός

1Co 2:15 The spiritual man judges all things 1
3: 1 could not address you as spiritual men 1

spiritually 1. πνευματικῶς

1Co 2:14 because they are spiritually discerned. 1

spit 1. ירק 2. רק 3. רקק 4. תֹּפֶת 5. ἐμπτύω 6. πτύω

Lev 15: 8 who has the discharge spits on one who is clean 3
Num12:14 If her father had but spit in her face 1
Deu 25: 9 pull his sandal off his foot, and spit in his face 1
Job 17: 6 I am one before whom men spit. 4
30:10 they do not hesitate to spit at the sight of me. 2
Isa 50: 6 I hid not my face from shame and spitting. 2
Mat 26:67 Then they spat in his face, and struck him 5
27:30 they spat upon him, and took the reed and struck 5
Mrk 7:33 he put his fingers into his ears, and he spat 6
8:23 when he had spit on his eyes 6
14:65 some began to spit on him, and to cover his face 5
Joh 9: 6 As he said this, he spat on the ground 6
Sir 28:12 if you spit on it, it will be put out 6

spit (2) 1. ὀβελίσκος

4Mc 11:19 To his back they applied sharp spits 1

spit out 1. προπτύω

2Mc 6:19 spitting out the flesh 1

spit upon 1. ἐμπτύω

Mrk 10:34 mock him, and spit upon him, and scourge him 1
15:19 they struck his head with a reed, and spat upon him 1
Lke 18:32 will be mocked and shamefully treated and spit upon; 1

spite 1. בְּ 2. עַד 3. עַל 4. καίπερ 5. παρά

Lev 26:18 if in spite of this you will not hearken to me 2
27 if in spite of this you will not hearken to me 1
Num14:11 in spite of all the signs which I have wrought 1
Deu 1:32 Yet in spite of this word you did not believe 1
Ezr 10: 2 there is hope for Israel in spite of this. 3
Job 23: 2 his hand is heavy in spite of my groaning. 3
34: 6 in spite of my right I am counted a liar; 3
Ps 78:32 In spite of all this they still sinned; 1
Isa 16:14 contempt, in spite of all his great multitude 1
47: 9 in spite of your many sorceries 1
Jer 2:34 Yet in spite of all these things 3
Jdt 8:25 In spite of everything let us give thanks 5
2Mc 4:34 in spite of his suspicion 4
4Mc 10:19 in spite of this 5

spittle 1. רִיר 2. רֹק 3. πτύσμα 4. saliva

1Sm 21:13 and let his spittle run down his beard. 1
Job 7:19 nor let me alone till I swallow my spittle? 2
Joh 9: 6 made clay of the spittle 3
2Es 6:56 that they are like spittle 4

splendid 1. כָּבוֹד 2. δόξα 3. δοξικός 4. ἔνδοξος 5. ἐπιφανής 6. καλός

Isa 22:18 and there shall be your splendid chariots 1
AEs 14: 2 she took off her splendid apparel 2
15: 1 arrayed herself in splendid attire. 2
Sir 40: 3 the man who sits on a splendid throne 4
2Mc 8:35 took off his splendid uniform 3
12:45 if he was looking to the splendid reward 6
14:33 will build here a splendid temple to Dionysus. 5
4Mc 11:12 they are splendid favors that you grant us 6

splendid *See also* vestment.

splendidly 1. διαπρέπω

2Mc 3:26 gloriously beautiful and splendidly dressed 1

splendor 1. הָדָר 2. הוֹד 3. יִפְעָה 4. יְקָר 5. יְקָר 6. כָּבוֹד 7. תִּפְאָרָה 8. זִיו (A) 9. δόξα 10. δοξάζω 11. ἔνδοξος 12. ἐντίμως 13. λαμπρός 14. λαμπρότης 15. μεγαλεῖος 16. claritas 17. splendor

Gen 45:13 tell my father of all my splendor in Egypt 6
Est 1: 4 he showed . . the splendor and pomp of his majesty 4
5:11 Haman recounted . . the splendor of his riches 6
Job 31:26 sun when it shone, or the moon moving in splendor 5
40:10 clothe yourself with glory and splendor. 1
Ps 21: 5 splendor and majesty thou dost bestow upon him. 2
145: 5 On the glorious splendor of thy majesty 1
12 make known . . glorious splendor of thy kingdom. 1
Isa 13:19 Babylon . . splendor and pride of the Chalde'ans 7
Lam 2: 1 has cast down . . to earth the splendor of Israel; 7
Ezk 16:14 it was perfect through the splendor 1
27:10 they gave you splendor. 1
28: 7 and defile your splendor. 3
17 corrupted . . for the sake of your splendor. 3
Dan 4:36 my majesty and splendor returned to me. 8
Hag 2: 7 I will fill this house with splendor 6
9 latter splendor of this house shall be greater 6
2Co 3: 7 if . . death . . came with such splendor 9
8 the Spirit be attended with greater splendor 9
9 For if there was splendor in the dispensation 9
9 the dispensation . . must far exceed it in splendor. 9
10 Indeed, in this case, what once had splendor 10
10 has come to have no splendor at all 10
10 because of the splendor that surpasses it. 9
11 For if what faded away came with splendor 9
11 what is permanent must have much more splendor. 9
13 see the end of the fading splendor. •
Eph 5:27 might present the church to himself in splendor 11
Rev 18: 1 and the earth was made bright with his splendor. 9
14 thy dainties and thy splendor are lost to thee 13
1Es 1:33 his splendor, and his understanding of the law 9
6:10 being completed with all splendor and care. 9
2Es 2:21 let the blind man have a vision of my splendor. 16
7:42 only the splendor of the glory of the Most High 17
10:55 see the splendor and vastness of the building 17
Tob 14: 5 and will rebuild Jerusalem in splendor 12
AEs 14:15 I hate the splendor of the wicked 9
15: 7 Lifting his face, flushed with splendor 9
Sir 42:21 He has ordained the splendors of his wisdom 15
50:13 all the sons of Aaron in their splendor 9
Bar 4:24 and with the splendor of the Everlasting. 14
5: 3 For God will show your splendor everywhere 14
Man 1: 5 for thy glorious splendor cannot be borne 9
1Mc 2:62 his splendor will turn into dung and worms. 9
15:32 when he saw the splendor of Simon 9
36 reported . . the splendor of Simon 9

golden splendor 1. זָהָב

Job 37:22 Out of the north comes golden splendor; 1

splinter 1. קְצָפָה

Jol 1: 7 and splintered my fig trees; 1

split 1. בקע 2. γίνομαι 3. σχίζω

1Kg 1:40 joy, so that the earth was split by their noise. 1
Ecc 10: 9 and he who splits logs is endangered by them. 1
Mat 27:51 the earth shook, and the rocks were split; 3
Rev 16:19 The great city was split into three parts 2

split asunder 1. בקע

Num16:31 the ground under them split asunder; 1

split in two 1. בקע

Zec 14: 4 the Mount of Olives shall be split in two 1

split open 1. בקע

Jdg 15:19 God split open the hollow place that is at Lehi 1

split up 1. בקע

1Sm 6:14 they split up the wood of the cart 1

spoil 1. בַּז 2. בִּזָּה 3. בֶּצַע 4. גְּזֵלָה 5. חֲלִיצָה 6. משׁסּ 7. שָׁלָל 8. ἀκροθίνιον 9. σκῦλον

Gen 49:27 wolf . . at even dividing the spoil. 7
Exd 15: 9 I will overtake, I will divide the spoil 7
Num31:11 took all the spoil and all the booty, both of man 7
12 brought the captives and the booty and the spoil 7
32 booty remaining of the spoil that the men of war 1
Deu 3: 7 cattle and the spoil of the cities we took 7
13:16 You shall gather all its spoil into the midst 7
16 burn the city and all its spoil with fire 7
20:14 everything else in the city, all its spoil 7
14 enjoy the spoil of your enemies, which the LORD 7
Jos 7:21 when I saw among the spoil a beautiful mantle 7
8: 2 its spoil and its cattle you shall take as booty 7
27 the cattle and the spoil of that city Israel took 7
11:14 And all the spoil . . the people of Israel took 7
22: 8 divide the spoil . . with your brethren. 7
Jdg 5:19 they got no spoils of silver. 3
30 Are they not . . dividing the spoil?–A maiden 7
30 spoil of dyed stuffs for Sis'era, spoil of dyed 7
30 for Sis'era, spoil of dyed stuffs embroidered 7
30 dyed work embroidered for my neck as spoil? 7
8:24 give me every man of you the earrings of his spoil. 7
25 every man cast in it the earrings of his spoil. 7
14:19 took their spoil and gave the festal garments 5
1Sm 14:30 had eaten . . of the spoil of their enemies 7
32 the people flew upon the spoil, and took sheep 7
15:19 Why did you swoop on the spoil, and do what was evil 7
21 But the people took of the spoil, sheep and oxen 7
30:16 because of all the great spoil they had taken 7
19 whether . . spoil or anything that had been taken; 7
20 and said, "This is David's spoil. 7
22 give . . any of the spoil which we have recovered 7
26 David . . sent part of the spoil to his friends 7
26 for you from the spoil of the enemies of the LORD"; 7
2Sm 2:21 and seize one of the young men, and take his spoil. 5
3:22 arrived . . from a raid, bringing much spoil 7
8:12 and from the spoil of Hadade'zer the son of Rehob 7
12:30 And he brought forth the spoil of the city 7
2Kg 3:23 Now then, Moab, to the spoil! 7
21:14 become a prey and a spoil to all their enemies 6
1Ch 20: 2 he brought forth the spoil of the city 7
26:27 From spoil won in battles they dedicated gifts 7
2Ch 15:11 from the spoil which they had brought 7
20:25 came to take the spoil from them 7
25 three days in taking the spoil, it was so much. 7
24:23 sent all their spoil to the king of Damascus. 7
25:13 killed 3,000 people in them, and took much spoil. 2
28: 8 they also took much spoil from them 7
8 and brought the spoil to Sama'ria. 7
14 the armed men left the captives and the spoil 2
15 with the spoil they clothed all that were naked 7
Ps 68:12 women at home divide the spoil 7
119:162I rejoice . . like one who finds great spoil. 7
Prv 1:13 we shall fill our houses with spoil; 7
16:19 better . . than to divide the spoil with the proud. 7
Isa 3:14 the spoil of the poor is in your houses. 4
8: 4 the wealth of Damascus and the spoil of Sama'ria 7
9: 3 as men rejoice when they divide the spoil. 7
10: 2 rob the poor . . that widows may be their spoil 7
33: 4 spoil is gathered as the caterpillar gathers; 7
23 Then prey and spoil in abundance will be divided; 7
42:22 a spoil with none to say, "Restore! 6
53:12 and he shall divide the spoil with the strong; 7
Jer 15:13 wealth and your treasures I will give as spoil 1
17: 3 and all your treasures I will give for spoil 1
30:16 those who despoil you shall become a spoil 6
49:32 become booty, their herds of cattle a spoil. 7
Ezk 7:21 a prey, and to the wicked of the earth for a spoil; 7
23:46 and make them an object of terror and a spoil. 1
25: 7 and will hand you over as spoil to the nations; 1
26: 5 she shall become a spoil to the nations; 1
38:12 to seize spoil and carry off plunder; to assail 7
13 will say to you, 'Have you come to seize spoil? 7
13 take away cattle and goods, to seize great spoil 7
Dan 11:24 scattering among them plunder, spoil, and goods. 7
Zec 14: 1 when the spoil taken from you will be divided 7
Lke 11:22 divides his spoil. 9
Heb 7: 4 Abraham . . gave him a tithe of the spoils. 8
1Mc 1:35 collecting the spoils of Jerusalem 9
2:10 What nation . . has not seized her spoils? 9
3:12 Then they seized their spoils 9
5:28 he seized all its spoils and burned it with fire. 9
6: 6 the arms, supplies, and abundant spoils 9
7:47 Then the Jews seized the spoils and the plunder 9
11:48 seized much spoil on that day 9
51 they returned to Jerusalem with much spoil. 9
2Mc 8:27 stripped them of their spoils 9
28 they gave some of the spoils to . . the widows 9
31 carried the rest of the spoils to Jerusalem. 9

spoil (2) 1. חבל 2. שׁחת 3. περιψύχω

Sng 2:15 foxes, the little foxes, that spoil the vineyards 1
Jer 13: 7 And behold, the waistcloth was spoiled; 2
9 Even so will I spoil the pride of Judah 2
18: 4 And the vessel he was making of clay was spoiled 2
Sir 30: 7 He who spoils his son will bind up his wounds 3

spoil *See* get, make, strip, take.

spoiler 1. שׁסה

2Kg 17:20 and gave them into the hand of spoilers 1
Isa 42:24 Who gave up Jacob to the spoiler 1

spoke 1. חִשּׁוּק 2. יָד

1Kg 7:33 rims, their spokes, and their hubs, were all cast. 1
Ezk 1:18 The four wheels had rims and they had spokes; •
10:12 And their rims, and their spokes, and the wheels 2

thing spoken later 1. λαλέω

Heb 3: 5 to testify to the things . . to be spoken later 1

spokesman 1. προήγορος 2. ῥήτωρ

Act 24: 1 some elders and a spokesman, one Tertul'lus 2
2Mc 7: 2 One of them, acting as their spokesman, said 1
4 that the tongue of their spokesman be cut out 1

sponge 1. σπόγγος

Mat 27:48 ran and took a sponge, filled it with vinegar 1
Mrk 15:36 filling a sponge full of vinegar, put it on a reed 1
Joh 19:29 they put a sponge full of the vinegar on hyssop 1

sport 1. שחק 2. שְׂחֹק 3. ἐμπαιγμός 4. ἐμπαίζω
Ps 104:26 Leviathan which thou didst form to sport in it. 1
Prv 10:23 It is like sport to a fool to do wrong 2
Bar 3:17 those who have sport with the birds of the air 4
2Mc 7: 7 they brought forward the second for their sport 3

sport *See also* make, victim.

spot 1. בַּהֶרֶת 2. חֲבַרְבֻּרָה 3. טלא 4. מאום 5. נָקֹד
6. שְׁקַעֲרוּרָה 7. σπίλος 8. σπιλόω
Gen 30:32 every speckled and spotted sheep 3
32 the spotted and speckled among the goats; 3
33 Every one that is not speckled and spotted 3
35 the he-goats that were striped and spotted 3
35 all the she-goats that were speckled and spotted 3
39 brought forth striped, speckled, and spotted. 3
31: 8 If he said, 'The spotted shall be your wages,' 5
8 be your wages,' then all the flock bore spotted; 5
10 the flock were striped, spotted, and mottled. 5
12 upon the flock are striped, spotted, and mottled; 5
Lev 13: 2 a spot, and it turns into a leprous disease 1
4 if the spot is white in the skin of his body 1
19 there comes . . a reddish-white spot 1
23 if the spot remains in one place 1
24 when . . the raw flesh of the burn becomes a spot 1
25 if the hair in the spot has turned white 1
26 if . . the hair in the spot is not white 1
28 if the spot remains in one place 1
38 a woman has spots on the skin of the body 1
38 has spots on the skin of the body, white spots 1
39 if the spots on the skin . . are of a dull white 1
55 the leprous spot is on the back or on the front *
56 shall tear the spot out of the garment or the skin *
14:37 walls of the house with greenish or reddish spots 6
56 for a swelling or an eruption or a spot 1
Job 31: 7 if any spot has cleaved to my hands; 4
Jer 13:23 change his skin or the leopard his spots? 2
Eph 5:27 without spot or wrinkle or any such thing 7
Jde 1:23 hating even the garment spotted by the flesh. 8

diseased spot 1. נֶגַע
Lev 13: 3 the priest shall examine the diseased spot 1
3 if the hair in the diseased spot has turned white 1
6 if the diseased spot is dim and the disease has 1
42 a reddish-white diseased spot, it is leprosy 1
55 if the diseased spot has not changed color 1

without spot 1. ἄσπιλος
1Pe 1:19 like that of a lamb without blemish or spot. 1
2Pe 3:14 to be found by him without spot or blemish 1

spotless 1. ἀκηλίδωτος 2. ἄμωμος
Rev 14: 5 no lie was found, for they are spotless. 2
Wis 7:26 a spotless mirror of the working of God 1

spread 1. היה 2. הלך 3. זרה 4. יצא 5. יצע 6. מִפְרָשׂ
7. משח 8. מִשְׁטוֹחַ 9. מִשְׁטָח 10. מתח 11. נטה
12. נטש 13. נסך 14. נפח 15. נתן 16. סרח 17. ערך
18. פוץ 19. פרד 20. פרח 21. פרש 22. פַּרְשֵׁז 23. פרש
24. פשה 25. פשט · 26. צפה 27. רדד 28. רפד 29. שטח
30. שלח 31. ἀπέρχομαι 32. δασύς 33. διαδίδωμι
34. διανέμω 35. διαφέρω 36. διαφημίζω 37. διέρχομαι
38. διηχέω 39. ἐξέρχομαι 40. ὀνομάζω 41. στρώννυμι
42. στρωννύω 43. ὑποστρωννύω 44. φανερόω
45. expando 46. fero 47. superpono
Gen 10: 5 From these the coastland peoples spread. 19
41:56 when the famine had spread over all the land 1
Exd 29: 2 and unleavened wafers spread with oil. 7
40:19 he spread the tent over the tabernacle 21
Lev 2: 4 unleavened wafers spread with oil 7
7:12 unleavened wafers spread with oil, and cakes 7
13: 5 if . . the disease has not spread in the skin 24
6 if . . the disease has not spread in the skin 24
7 if the eruption spreads in the skin 24
8 if the eruption has spread in the skin 24
22 if it spreads in the skin 24
23 if the spot . . does not spread, it is the scar 24
27 if it is spreading in the skin 24
28 if the spot . . does not spread in the skin 24
32 if the itch has not spread 24
34 if the itch has not spread in the skin 24
35 if the itch spreads in the skin 24
36 if the itch has spread in the skin 24
51 If the disease has spread in the garment, in warp 24
53 the disease has not spread in the garment in warp 24
55 though the disease has not spread, it is unclean 24
57 appears . . in anything of skin, it is spreading 20
14:39 if the disease has spread in the walls 24
44 if the disease has spread in the house 24
48 and the disease has not spread in the house 24
Num 4: 7 they shall spread a cloth of blue 23
8 they shall spread over them a cloth of scarlet 21
11 golden altar they shall spread a cloth of blue 21
13 the altar, and spread a purple cloth over it; 21
14 they shall spread upon it a covering of goatskin 21
6:15 unleavened wafers spread with oil 7
21:30 we laid waste until fire spread to Med'eba. 14
Deu 22:17 spread the garment before the elders of the city. 21
Jdg 8:25 And they spread a garment, and every man cast in it 21
Rut 3: 9 spread your skirt over your maidservant 21
1Sm 4: 2 and when the battle spread, Israel was defeated 12
2Sm 17:19 took and spread a covering over the well's mouth 21
18: 8 The battle spread over . . all the country; 18
21:10 sackcloth, and spread it for herself on the rock 11
1Kg 6:32 spread gold upon the cherubim and . . palm trees. 27
2Kg 8:15 dipped it in water and spread it over his face 21
19:14 Hezeki'ah went . . and spread it before the LORD. 21
1Ch 28:18 of the cherubim that spread their wings 21
2Ch 26: 8 his fame spread even to the border of Egypt 2
15 fame spread far, for he was marvelously helped 4
Est 9: 4 Mor'decai . . his fame spread throughout all 2
Job 8:16 his shoots spread over his garden. 4
17:13 Sheol as my house, if I spread my couch in darkness 28
26: 9 and spreads over it his cloud. 22
36:29 any one understand the spreading of the clouds 6
39:26 soars, and spreads his wings toward the south? 21
41:30 he spreads himself like a threshing sledge 28
Ps 78:19 Can God spread a table in the wilderness? 17
105:39 He spread a cloud for a covering 21
140: 5 trap for me, and with cords they have spread a net 21
Prv 1:17 For in vain is a net spread in the sight of any bird; 3
15: 7 The lips of the wise spread knowledge; 3
16:28 A perverse man spreads strife 30
29: 5 flatters his neighbor spreads a net for his feet. 21
Isa 19: 8 they . . languish who spread nets upon the water. 21
21: 5 They prepare the table, they spread the rugs 26
25: 7 the veil that is spread over all nations. 13
37:14 went up . . and spread it before the LORD. 21
40:22 and spreads them like a tent to dwell in; 10
58: 5 and to spread sackcloth and ashes under him? 5
Jer 8: 2 they shall be spread before the sun and the moon 29
10:20 there is no one to spread my tent again 11
43:10 he will spread his royal canopy over them. 11
48:40 like an eagle, and spread his wings against Moab; 21
49:22 an eagle, and spread his wings against Bozrah 21
Lam 1:13 he spread a net for my feet; he turned me back; 21
Ezk 2:10 he spread it before me; and it had writing 21
12:13 I will spread my net over him, and he shall be taken 21
16: 8 I spread my skirt over you 21
17: 6 it sprouted and became a low spreading vine 16
20 I will spread my net over him, and he shall be taken 21
19: 8 they spread their net over him; he was taken 21
23:41 a stately couch, with a table spread before it 17
26: 5 midst of the sea a place for the spreading of nets; 9
14 you shall be a place for the spreading of nets; 9
32:23 who spread terror in the land of the living. 15
24 who spread terror in the land of the living 15
25 terror . . was spread in the land of the living 15
26 they spread terror in the land of the living. 15
32 For he spread terror in the land of the living; 15
47:10 it will be a place for the spreading of nets; 8
Hos 5: 1 a snare at Mizpah, and a net spread upon Tabor. 21
7:12 As they go, I will spread over them my net; 21
Jol 2: 2 blackness there is spread upon the mountains 21
Nah 3:16 The locust spreads its wings and flies away. 25
Mal 2: 3 will rebuke . . and spread dung upon your faces 3
Mat 4:24 So his fame spread throughout all Syria 31
9:31 But they went away and spread his fame 36
21: 8 Most of the crowd spread their garments 42
8 and spread them on the road. 42
28:15 this story has been spread among the Jews 36
Mrk 1:28 And at once his fame spread everywhere 39
45 to spread the news 36
11: 8 many spread their garments on the road 42
8 and others spread leafy branches *
Lke 7:17 this report concerning him spread 39
19:36 they spread their garments on the road. 43
Act 4:17 it may spread no further among the people 34
13:49 spread throughout all the region. 35
Rom 5:12 death spread to all men because all men sinned- 37
2Co 2:14 spreads the fragrance of the knowledge of him 44
2Es 11: 2 and behold, he spread his wings over all the earth 45
15: 6 For iniquity has spread throughout every land 47
29 their hissing shall spread over the earth 46
Jdt 12:15 and spread on the ground for her . . the soft fleeces 41
Sir 14:18 Like flourishing leaves on a spreading tree 32
24:15 like choice myrrh I spread a pleasant odor 33
1Mc 14:10 till his renown spread to the ends of the earth. 40
2Mc 7: 5 The smoke from the pan spread widely 33
8: 7 talk of his valor spread everywhere. 38
4Mc 4:22 he heard that a rumor of his death had spread 33

spread a bed 1. διαστρώννυμι
1Sm 9:25 a bed was spread for Saul upon the roof, and he lay 1

spread abroad 1. נטש 2. נפץ 3. עבר 4. פרד 5. פרץ
6. פרש 7. διαδίδωμι 8. διαφέρω 9. ἐξέρχομαι
Gen 10:18 families of the Canaanites spread abroad. 2
32 the nations spread abroad on the earth 4
28:14 you shall spread abroad to the west 5
Exd 1:12 they multiplied and the more they spread abroad. 5
1Sm 2:24 no good report that I hear . . spreading abroad. 3
30:16 behold, they were spread abroad over all the land 1
2Ch 31: 5 As soon as the command was spread abroad 5
Isa 16: 8 its shoots spread abroad and passed over the sea. 1
54: 3 For you will spread abroad to the right 5
Zec 2: 6 I have spread you abroad as the four winds 6
Joh 21:23 The saying spread abroad among the brethren 9
Wis 18:10 lament for their children was spread abroad. 8
2Mc 4:39 when report of them had spread abroad 7

spread branches 1. נְטִישָׁה
Isa 18: 5 and the spreading branches he will hew away. 1

colored spread 1. חֲטֻבוֹת
Prv 7:16 colored spreads of Egyptian linen; 1

spread forth 1. פרש 2. רקע 3. ἐκπετάζω
1Kg 8:22 Solomon . . spread forth his hands toward heaven; 1
2Ch 6:12 before the altar . . and spread forth his hands. 1
13 and spread forth his hands toward heaven; 1
Ps 44:20 or spread forth our hands to a strange god 1
Isa 1:15 When you spread forth your hands, I will hide 1
42: 5 who spread forth the earth and what comes from it 2
Sir 48:20 spreading forth their hands toward him 3

spread out 1. הלך 2. טפח 3. נטה 4. נטש 5. פרד
6. פרש 7. פתח 8. רקע 9. שטח 10. διασπείρω
11. ἐκπετάζω 12. ἐκτείνω 13. καταστρατοπεδεύω
14. παρατείνω 15. extendo
Exd 25:20 The cherubim shall spread out their wings 6
37: 9 The cherubim spread out their wings above 6
Num11:32 they spread them out for themselves all around 9
Deu 32:11 spreading out its wings, catching them 6
2Sm 5:18 Philistines had come and spread out in the valley 4
22 spread out in the valley of Reph'aim. 4
1Kg 6:27 the wings of the cherubim were spread out 6
8: 7 cherubim spread out their wings over the place 6
2Ch 5: 8 cherubim spread out their wings over the . . ark 6
Ezr 9: 5 fell . . and spread out my hands to the LORD my God 6
Job 29:19 my roots spread out to the waters 7
37:18 spread out the skies, hard as a molten mirror? 8
Ps 88: 9 I spread out my hands to thee. 9
136: 6 to him who spread out the earth upon the waters 8
Isa 25:11 he will spread out his hands in the midst of it 6
11 as a swimmer spreads his hands out to swim; 6
33:23 it cannot . . keep the sail spread out. 6
44:24 who spread out the earth-Who was with me?- 8
48:13 and my right hand spread out the heavens; 2
65: 2 I spread out my hands all the day to a rebellious 6
Ezk 1:11 And their wings were spread out above; 5
22 firmament . . spread out above their heads. 3
Hos 14: 6 his shoots shall spread out; 1
2Es 16:59 who has spread out the heaven like an arch 15
Jdt 4:11 and spread out their sackcloth before the Lord. 12
7: 3 they spread out in breadth over Dothan 14
18 supply trains spread out in great number 13
Sir 24:16 Like a terebinth I spread out my branches 12
51:19 I spread out my hands to the heavens 11
1Mc 6:40 the king's army was spread out on the high hills 12
11:47 and then spread out through the city 10

spread over 1. פרש 2. ἐπιτείνω
3. καλύπτω τὸ πρόσωπον
Num 4: 6 spread over that a cloth all of blue 1
Jdt 5:10 When a famine spread over Canaan 3
Wis 17:21 over those men alone heavy night was spread 2

spread terror among 1. ἐκφοβέω
Jdt 16:25 no one ever again spread terror among the people 1

spread under 1. ὑποστρώννυμι
4Mc 9:19 they spread fire under him 1

widely spread 1. רָחָב
Neh 4:19 The work is great and widely spread 1

sprig
Ezk 17:22 I myself will take a sprig from the lofty top †

spring 1. יצא 2. צמח 3. ἀναπηδάω 4. βάλλω ἑαυτόν
5. γίνομαι 6. εἰμί 7. nascor
Gen 35:11 come from you, and kings shall spring from you. 1
Job 8:19 out of the earth others will spring. 2
Joh 21: 7 and sprang into the sea. 4
1Th 2: 3 our appeal does not spring from error *
2Es 3: 7 From him there sprang nations and tribes 7
Tob 8: 6 From them the race of mankind has sprung 5
AEs 15: 8 in alarm he sprang from his throne 3
2Mc 14:30 did not spring from the best motives 6

spring (2) 1. אָפִיק 2. גֻּלָּה 3. חַי 4. מַבּוּעַ 5. מוֹצָא
6. מַעְיָן 7. נֵבֶךְ 8. עַיִן 9. תְּהוֹם 10. תּוֹצָאָה 11. ἔξοδος
12. πηγή 13. fons 14. vena
Gen 16: 7 found her by a spring of water in the wilderness 8
7 in the wilderness, the spring on the way to Shur. 8
24:13 Behold, I am standing by the spring of water 8
16 She went down to the spring, and filled her jar 8
29 and Laban ran out to the man, to the spring. 8
30 he was standing by the camels at the spring. 8
42 I came today to the spring, and said 8
43 behold, I am standing by the spring of water; 8
45 and she went down to the spring, and drew. 8
26:19 found there a well of springing water 3

49:22 Joseph is . . a fruitful bough by a spring; 8
Exd 15:27 Elim, where there were twelve springs of water 8
Lev 11:36 Nevertheless a spring or a cistern 6
Num33: 9 at Elim there were twelve springs of water 8
Deu 8: 7 good land, a land of . . fountains and springs 9
Jos 15: 9 from . . to the spring of the Waters of Nephto'ah 6
19 since you have . . give me also springs of water. 2
19 gave . . the upper springs and the lower springs. 2
19 gave . . the upper springs and the lower springs. 2
18:15 to Ephron, to the spring of the Waters of Nephto'ah; 6
Jdg 1:15 me in the . . Negeb, give me also springs of water. 2
15 Caleb gave her the upper springs and the lower 2
15 gave her the upper . . and the lower springs. 2
7: 1 early and encamped beside the spring of Harod; 8
1Kg 18: 5 Go through the land to all the springs of water 6
2Kg 2:21 he went to the spring of water and threw salt in it 5
3:19 and stop up all springs of water 6
25 they stopped every spring of water 6
2Ch 32: 3 planned . . to stop the water of the springs 8
4 they stopped all the springs and the brook 6
Job 38:16 Have you entered into the springs of the sea 7
Ps 74:15 Thou didst cleave open springs and brooks; 6
87: 7 alike say, "All my springs are in you. 6
104:10 Thou makest springs gush forth in the valleys; 6
107:33 turns . . springs of water into thirsty ground 5
35 turns . . a parched land into springs of water. 5
114: 8 who turns the . . flint into a spring of water. 6
Prv 4:23 for from it flow the springs of life. 10
5:16 Should your springs be scattered abroad 6
8:24 when . . no springs abounding with water. 6
25:26 Like a muddied spring or a polluted fountain 6
Sng 5:12 His eyes are like doves beside springs of water 1
Isa 35: 7 a pool, and the thirsty ground springs of water; 4
41:18 a pool of water, and the dry land springs of water. 5
49:10 and by springs of water will guide them. 4
58:11 like a watered garden, like a spring of water 5
Hos 13:15 his spring shall be parched; 6
Joh 4:14 a spring of water welling up to eternal life. 12
Jas 3:11 Does a spring pour forth . . fresh water 12
2Pe 2:17 These are waterless springs and mists 12
Rev 7:17 and he will guide them to springs of living water; 12
2Es 2:19 the same number of springs 13
32 because my springs run over 13
6:24 the springs of the fountains shall stand still 14
14:47 in them is the spring of understanding 14
16:60 who has put springs of water in the desert 13
Jdt 6:11 came to the springs below Bethulia. 12
7: 3 near Bethulia, beside the spring 12
7 visited the springs that supplied their water 12
12 only . . take possession of the spring of water 12
17 the springs of the Israelites 12
12: 7 bathed at the spring in the camp. 12
8 When she came up from the spring *
AEs 10: 6 The tiny spring which became a river 12
11:10 from their cry, as though from a tiny spring 12
Sir 21:13 and his counsel like a flowing spring. 12
50: 8 like lilies by a spring of water 11
Aza 1:55 Bless the Lord, you springs 12
4Mc 3:10 although springs were plentiful there 12
14 found the spring 12

spring (3) 1. בוא 2. חַיָּה 3. עֵת חַיָּה 4. עֵת תְּשׁוּבָה 5. תְּשׁוּבָה 6. תְּשׁוּבַת הַשָּׁנָה 7. ἔαρ 8. ver

Gen 18:10 surely return to you in the spring 3
14 to you, in the spring, and Sarah shall have a son. 3
2Sm 11: 1 In the spring of the year . . David sent Jo'ab 5
1Kg 20:22 in the spring the king of Syria will come up 6
26 In the spring Ben-ha'dad mustered the Syrians 6
2Kg 4:17 bore a son about that time the following spring 2
13:20 used to invade the land in the spring of the year 1
1Ch 20: 1 In the spring of the year . . Jo'ab led out the army 4
2Ch 36:10 In the spring of the year King Nebuchadnez'zar 5
2Es 7:41 or summer or spring or heat or winter or frost 8
Wis 2: 7 let no flower of spring pass by us. 7

cause to spring forth 1. צמח

Isa 61:11 cause righteousness and praise to spring forth 1
Jer 33:15 I will cause a righteous Branch to spring forth 1
Ezk 29:21 On that day I will cause a horn to spring forth 1

cause to spring up 1. צמח

Isa 45: 8 and let it cause righteousness to spring up also; 1
61:11 as a garden causes what is sown in it to spring up 1

spring forth 1. צמח

Isa 42: 9 before they spring forth I tell you of them. 1
43:19 Behold, I am doing a new thing; now it springs forth 1

hot spring 1. יֵמִם

Gen 36:24 who found the hot springs in the wilderness 1

spring of the same 1. סָחִישׁ 2. שָׁחִים

2Kg 19:29 and in the second year what springs of the same; 1
Isa 37:30 in the second year what springs of the same; 2

spring rain 1. מַלְקוֹשׁ

Job 29:23 they opened their mouths as for the spring rain. 1
Prv 16:15 favor . . the clouds that bring the spring rain. 1

Jer 3: 3 and the spring rain has not come; 1
5:24 who gives . . the autumn rain and the spring rain 1
Hos 6: 3 as the spring rains that water the earth. 1
Zec 10: 1 in the season of the spring rain 1

spring up 1. עלה 2. פרח 3. צמח 4. ἅλλομαι 5. ἀναπηδάω 6. ἐξανατέλλω 7. ἐπιγίνομαι 8. φύω 9. superfloresco

Gen 2: 5 and no herb of the field had yet sprung up– 3
Num21:17 Israel sang this song: "Spring up, O well!–Sing to it!– 1
Jdg 6:21 there sprang up fire from the rock and consumed 1
Ps 85:11 Faithfulness will spring up from the ground 3
Isa 44: 4 They shall spring up like grass amid waters 3
58: 8 and your healing shall spring up speedily; 3
Hos 10: 4 so judgment springs up like poisonous weeds 2
Ams 3: 5 Does a snare spring up from the ground 1
Mat 13: 5 and immediately they sprang up 6
Mrk 4: 5 and immediately it sprang up 6
10:50 throwing off his mantle he sprang up 5
Act 14:10 he sprang up and walked. 4
28:13 after one day a south wind sprang up 7
Heb 12:15 no "root of bitterness" spring up 8
2Es 16:21 then the calamities shall spring up on the earth 9
Tob 2: 4 I sprang up and removed the body 5
7: 6 Then Raguel sprang up and kissed him and wept. 5
1Mc 4:38 they saw bushes sprung up as in a thicket 8

springs *See* place.

sprinkle 1. זרק 2. נזה 3. שׁלך 4. ἀποδίδωμι 5. ἐπιρραίνω 6. ἐπιτίθημι 7. καταπάσσω 8. προσπάσσω 9. πρόσχυσις 10. ῥαντίζω 11. ῥαντισμός 12. φύρω

Exd 29:21 sprinkle it upon Aaron and his garments 2
Lev 4: 6 sprinkle part of the blood seven times 2
17 dip his finger in the blood and sprinkle it 2
5: 9 he shall sprinkle some of the blood of the sin 2
6:27 when any of its blood is sprinkled on a garment 2
27 shall wash that on which it was sprinkled 2
8:11 he sprinkled some of it on the altar seven times 2
30 the blood which was on the altar, and sprinkled it 2
14: 7 he shall sprinkle it seven times upon him 2
16 sprinkle some oil with his finger seven times 2
27 shall sprinkle with his right finger 2
51 and sprinkle the house seven times 2
16:14 blood . . and sprinkle it with his finger 2
14 he shall sprinkle the blood with his finger 2
15 sprinkling it upon the mercy seat and before 2
19 he shall sprinkle some of the blood upon it 2
17: 6 the priest shall sprinkle the blood on the altar 1
Num 8: 7 sprinkle the water of expiation upon them 2
18:17 You shall sprinkle their blood upon the altar 1
19: 4 sprinkle some of her blood toward the front 2
18 dip it in the water, and sprinkle it upon the tent 2
19 clean person shall sprinkle upon the unclean 2
21 He who sprinkles the water for impurity 2
2Ch 30:16 the priests sprinkled the blood 1
35:11 priests sprinkled the blood 1
Job 2:12 sprinkled dust upon their heads toward heaven. 1
Isa 63: 3 their lifeblood is sprinkled upon my garments 2
Ezk 36:25 I will sprinkle clean water upon you 1
43:24 the priests shall sprinkle salt upon them 3
Hos 7: 9 gray hairs are sprinkled upon him 1
Heb 9:13 the sprinkling of defiled persons 10
19 sprinkled both the book itself and all the people 10
21 in the same way he sprinkled with the blood 10
10:22 our hearts sprinkled clean from an evil conscience 10
11:28 kept the Passover and sprinkled the blood 9
12:24 the sprinkled blood 11
1Pe 1: 2 Jesus Christ and for sprinkling with his blood 11
Tob 11:11 he sprinkled the gall upon his father's eyes 8
1Mc 3:47 and sprinkled ashes on their heads *
4:39 sprinkled themselves with ashes. 6
2Mc 1:21 to sprinkle the liquid on the wood 5
14:15 they sprinkled dust upon their heads 7
3Mc 1:18 sprinkled their hair with dust 4
4: 6 their myrrh-perfumed hair sprinkled with ashes 12

sprinkle upon 1. καταπάσσω

2Mc 10:25 his men sprinkled dust upon their heads 1

sprout 1. חלף 2. עלה 3. פרח 4. צמח 5. צֶמַח 6. βλαστάνω

Gen 41: 6 behold, after them sprouted seven ears 4
23 by the east wind, sprouted after them 4
Num17: 5 the rod of the man whom I choose shall sprout; 3
8 rod of Aaron . . had sprouted and put forth buds 3
Deu 29:23 growing nothing, where no grass can sprout 2
Job 5: 6 nor does trouble sprout from the ground; 4
14: 7 tree, if it be cut down, that it will sprout again 1
Ps 92: 7 though the wicked sprout like grass 3
Ezk 17: 6 it sprouted and became a low spreading vine 4
9 so that all its fresh sprouting leaves wither? 5
Mrk 4:27 the seed should sprout and grow 6

sprout forth 1. פרח

Isa 45: 8 the earth open, that salvation may sprout forth 1

make sprout 1. צמח

2Sm 23: 4 rain that makes grass to sprout from the earth. *
Ps 132:17 There I will make a horn to sprout for David; 1
Isa 55:10 water the earth, making it bring forth and sprout 1

spurn 1. זנח 2. מאס 3. נאץ 4. סלה 5. שׂנא 6. ἀποπτύω 7. ἀποστρέφω 8. καταπατέω

Lev 26:15 if you spurn my statutes 2
43 amends . . because they spurned my ordinances 2
44 I will not spurn them, neither will I abhor them 2
Deu 22:13 takes a wife, and goes in to her, and then spurns her 5
16 gave my daughter to this man . . and he spurns her; 5
32:19 LORD saw it, and spurned them 3
Ps 36: 4 in a way that is not good; he spurns not evil. 2
77: 7 Will the Lord spurn for ever 1
107:11 spurned the counsel of the Most High. 3
119:118 dost spurn all who go astray from thy statutes; 4
Jer 14:21 Do not spurn us, for thy name's sake; 3
Lam 2: 6 in . . indignation has spurned king and priest. 3
Hos 8: 3 Israel has spurned the good; 1
5 I have spurned your calf, O Sama'ria. 1
Heb 10:29 the man who has spurned the Son of God 8
3Mc 3:23 they not only spurn the priceless citizenship 7
4Mc 3:18 spurn all domination by the emotions. 6
5: 9 wrong to spurn the gifts of nature. 7

spy 1. רגל 2. שׁמר 3. ἐγκάθετος 4. κατάσκοπος

Gen 42: 9 he said to them, "You are spies, you have come 1
11 we are honest men, your servants are not spies. 1
14 It is as I said to you, you are spies. 1
16 by the life of Pharaoh, surely you are spies. 1
30 The man . . took us to be spies of the land. 1
31 we said to him, 'We are honest men, we are not spies 1
34 then I shall know that you are not spies 1
Jos 2: 1 sent two men secretly from Shittim as spies 1
6:23 the young men who had been spies went 1
Jdg 1:24 the spies saw a man coming out of the city 2
1Sm 26: 4 David sent out spies, and learned of a certainty 1
Lke 20:20 So they watched him, and sent spies 3
Heb 11:31 she had given friendly welcome to the spies. 4
Sir 11:30 like a spy he observes your weakness; 4
1Mc 12:26 He sent spies to their camp 4

spy (2) 1. ראה

2Kg 9:17 he spied the company of Jehu as he came, and said 1

spy out 1. חפר 2. רגל 3. תור 4. κατασκοπέω

Num13: 2 Send men to spy out the land of Canaan 3
16 men whom Moses sent to spy out the land. 3
17 Moses sent them to spy out the land of Canaan 3
21 So they went up and spied out the land 3
25 they returned from spying out the land. 3
32 an evil report of the land which they had spied out 3
32 The land, through which we have gone, to spy it out 3
14: 6 who were among those who had spied out the land 3
7 The land, which we passed through to spy it out 3
34 number of the days in which you spied out the land 3
36 men whom Moses sent to spy out the land 3
38 of those men who went to spy out the land. 3
21:32 Moses sent to spy out Jazer; 2
Deu 1:24 came to the Valley of Eshcol and spied it out. 2
Jos 6:22 Joshua said to the . . men who had spied out the land 2
25 messengers whom Joshua sent to spy out Jericho. 2
7: 2 Joshua . . said to them, "Go up and spy out the land 2
2 And the men went up and spied out Ai. 2
14: 7 Moses . . sent me . . to spy out the land; 2
Jdg 18: 2 sent . . to spy out the land and to explore it; 2
14 the five men who had gone to spy out the country 2
17 five men who had gone to spy out the land went up 2
2Sm 10: 3 David sent . . to search the city, and to spy it out 2
1Ch 19: 3 to search and to overthrow and to spy out the land? 2
Job 39:29 Thence he spies out the prey; his eyes behold it 1
Gal 2: 4 who slipped in to spy out our freedom 4
1Mc 5:38 Judas sent men to spy out the camp 4

squad 1. τετράδιον

Act 12: 4 delivered him to four squads of soldiers 1

squander 1. אבד 2. διασκορπίζω

Prv 29: 3 company with harlots squanders his substance. 1
Lke 15:13 he squandered his property in loose living. 2

square 1. רְבִיעִי 2. רבע 3. רבע אֶל אַרְבַּעַת רְבָעִים 4. τετράποδος

Exd 27: 1 the altar shall be square, and its height 2
28:16 It shall be square and double, a span its length 2
30: 2 it shall be square, and two cubits shall be its 2
37:25 it was square, and two cubits was its height; 2
38: 1 it was square, and three cubits was its height. 2
39: 9 It was square; the breastpiece was made double 2
1Kg 6:33 doorposts of olivewood, in the form of a square 1
7: 5 All the doorways and windows had square frames 2
31 and its panels were square, not round. 2
Job 24:20 The squares of the town forget them; *
Ezk 41:21 The doorposts of the nave were squared; 2
43:16 The altar hearth shall be square 3
17 The ledge also shall be square *
45: 2 a square plot of 500 by 500 cubits 2

48:20 set apart shall be 25,000 cubits square 1
1Mc 10:11 encircle Mount Zion with squared stones 4

square (2) 1. רְחוֹב 2. εὐρύχωρος
Jdg 19:20 only, do not spend the night in the square. 1
2Ch 29: 4 assembled them in the square on the east 1
32: 6 in the square at the gate of the city 1
Neh 8: 1 gathered . . into the square before the Water Gate; 1
3 read from it facing the square before the Water 1
16 made booths . . in the square at the Water Gate 1
16 booths . . in the square at the Gate of E'phraim. 1
Job 29: 7 when I prepared my seat in the square 1
Sng 3: 2 about the city, in the streets and in the squares; 1
Isa 15: 3 the housetops and in the squares every one wails 1
Jer 5: 1 Search her squares to see if you can find a man 1
9:21 and the young men from the squares. 1
48:38 On all the housetops of Moab and in the squares 1
49:26 Therefore her young men shall fall in her squares 1
50:30 her young men shall fall in her squares 1
Ezk 16:24 and made yourself a lofty place in every square; 1
31 and making your lofty place in every square. 1
Dan 9:25 built again with squares and moat 1
Ams 5:16 LORD, the God of hosts, the Lord: "In all the squares 1
Nah 2: 4 they rush to and fro through the squares; 1
1Es 5:47 in the square before the first gate 2

open square 1. רְחוֹב 2. εὐρύχωρος
Deu 13:16 spoil into the midst of its open square, and burn 1
Jdg 19:15 went in and sat down in the open square of the city; 1
17 saw the wayfarer in the open square of the city; 1
Ezr 10: 9 all the people sat in the open square 1
Est 4: 6 in the open square of the city in front 1
6: 9 conduct . . through the open square of the city 1
11 made him ride through the open square of the city 1
1Es 9: 6 sat in the open square before the temple 2
38 the open square before the east gate of the temple; 2
41 he read aloud in the open square before the gate 2

public square 1. רְחוֹב 2. ἀγορά
2Sm 21:12 stolen them from the public square of Beth-shan 1
Isa 59:14 for truth has fallen in the public squares 1
2Mc 10: 2 had been built in the public square by the foreigners 2

squeeze 1. זור
Jdg 6:38 rose early next morning and squeezed the fleece 1

stab 1. הדף 2. συγκεντέω
Num35:20 if he stabbed him from hatred, or hurled at him 1
22 But if he stabbed him suddenly without enmity 1
2Mc 13:15 He stabbed the leading elephant and its rider. 2

stab from beneath 1. ὑποτίθημι
1Mc 6:46 stabbed it from beneath, and killed it 1

stability 1. אֱמוּנָה 2. כֵּן 3. εὐστάθεια 4. στηριγμός
Prv 28: 2 with men . . its stability will long continue. 2
Isa 33: 6 he will be the stability of your times 1
2Pe 3:17 lest you . . lose your own stability. 4
AEs 13: 5 so that our kingdom may not attain stability. 3
Wis 6:24 a sensible king is the stability of his people. 3
3Mc 6:28 has granted an unimpeded and notable stability 3
stability *See also* give.

stable 1. θεμελιόω
Col 1:23 you continue in the faith, stable and steadfast 1
stable *See also* keep.
stacked *See* grain.

stacte 1. נָטָף 2. στακτή
Exd 30:34 Take sweet spices, stacte, and onycha 1
Sir 24:15 like galbanum, onycha, and stacte 2

stadium 1. στάδιον
Rev 14:20 blood flowed . . for 1,600 stadia 1
21:16 he measured the city with his rod, 12,000 stadia; 1

staff 1. מַטֶּה 2. מַקֵּל 3. מַקֵּל 4. מַשְׁעֵנָה 5. מִשְׁעֶנֶת 6. שֵׁבֶט 7. ῥάβδος
Gen 32:10 for with only my staff I crossed this Jordan; 3
38:18 your cord, and your staff that is in your hand. 1
25 Mark . . the signet and the cord and the staff. 1
Exd 12:11 sandals on your feet, and your staff in your hand; 3
21:19 rises again and walks abroad with his staff 5
Lev 26:26 When I break your staff of bread 1
Num22:27 he struck the ass with his staff. 3
Jdg 5:14 from Zeb'ulun those who bear the marshal's staff; 6
6:21 out the tip of the staff that was in his hand 5
1Sm 14:27 so he put forth the tip of the staff . . in his hand 1
43 I tasted a little honey with the tip of the staff 1
17:40 Then he took his staff in his hand 3
2Sm 23:21 but Benai'ah went down to him with a staff 6
2Kg 4:29 Gird up your loins, and take my staff . . and go. 5
29 and lay my staff upon the face of the child. 5
31 Geha'zi went on . . and laid the staff upon the face 5
18:21 relying now on Egypt, that broken reed of a staff 5
1Ch 11:23 but Benai'ah went down to him with a staff 6
Ps 23: 4 thy rod and thy staff, they comfort me. 5
105:16 When he . . broke every staff of bread 1
Isa 3: 1 stay and staff, the whole stay of bread . . water; 4
9: 4 yoke of his burden, and the staff for his shoulder 1
10: 5 Ah, Assyria, the rod of my anger, the staff of my fury! 1
15 or as if a staff should lift him who is not wood! 1
24 lift up their staff against you as the Egyptians 1
14: 5 The LORD has broken the staff of the wicked 1
30:32 every stroke of the staff of punishment 1
36: 6 relying on Egypt, that broken reed of a staff 5
Jer 48:17 mighty scepter is broken, the glorious staff. 3
Ezk 4:16 Son of man, behold, I will break the staff of bread 1
5:16 famine upon you, and break your staff of bread. 1
14:13 break its staff of bread and send famine upon it 1
29: 6 have been a staff of reed to the house of Israel; 5
Hos 4:12 and their staff gives them oracles. 3
Mic 7:14 Shepherd thy people with thy staff 6
Zec 8: 4 each with staff in hand for very age. 5
11: 7 I took two staffs; one I named Grace 2
10 I took my staff Grace, and I broke it 3
14 Then I broke my second staff Union 3
Mat 10:10 nor two tunics, nor sandals, nor a staff 7
Mrk 6: 8 nothing for their journey except a staff 7
Lke 9: 3 no staff, nor bag, nor bread, nor money 7
Heb 11:21 bowing in worship over the head of his staff. 7
Rev 11: 1 Then I was given a measuring rod like a staff 7
Tob 5:17 Is he not the staff of our hands 7

herdsman's staff 1. שֵׁבֶט
Lev 27:32 all that pass under the herdsman's staff 1

ruler's staff 1. חקק
Gen 49:10 nor the ruler's staff from between his feet 1

stag 1. אַיָּל
Prv 7:22 he follows her . . as a stag is caught fast *
Sng 2: 9 My beloved is like a gazelle, or a young stag. 1
17 or a young stag upon rugged mountains. 1
8:14 Make haste . . and be like a gazelle or a young stag 1

young stag 1. עֹפֶר
Sng 2: 9 My beloved is like a gazelle, or a young stag. 1
17 or a young stag upon rugged mountains. 1
8:14 Make haste . . and be like a gazelle or a young stag 1

stage 1. נסע
Exd 17: 1 Israel moved on . . by stages, according 1
Num33: 1 These are the stages of the people of Israel 1
2 these are their stages according 1
stage *See also* set.

stage by stage 1. לְמַסְּעֵיהֶם
Num33: 2 wrote down their starting places, stage by stage 1

stagger 1. געש 2. כשל 3. נוע 4. תעה 5. תַּרְעֵלָה
Ps 107:27 they reeled and staggered like drunken men 3
Isa 19:14 Egypt . . as a drunken man staggers in his vomit. 4
24:20 The earth staggers like a drunken man, it sways 3
28: 7 reel with wine and stagger with strong drink; 4
7 with wine, they stagger with strong drink; 4
29: 9 stagger, but not with strong drink! 3
51:17 have drunk to the dregs the bowl of staggering. 5
22 I have taken from your hand the cup of staggering; 5
Jer 25:16 They shall drink and stagger and be crazed 1
Lam 5:13 and boys stagger under loads of wood. 2
Obd 1:16 they shall drink, and stagger *
Hab 2:16 Drink, yourself, and stagger! *

make stagger 1. תעה
Job 12:25 he makes them stagger like a drunken man. 1
Isa 19:14 they have made Egypt stagger in all her doings 1

stagnant
Ezk 47: 8 when it enters the stagnant waters of the sea *

stain 1. גאל 2. כתם 3. μιαίνω 4. μολύνω 5. μῶμος 6. σπιλόω
Isa 63: 3 and I have stained all my raiment. 1
Jer 2:22 the stain of your guilt is still before me 2
Jas 3: 6 staining the whole body 6
Tob 3:15 I did not stain my name or the name of my father 4
Jdt 9: 3 their beds . . to be stained with blood *
Wis 15: 4 a figure stained with varied colors 6
Sir 33:22 bring no stain upon your honor. 5
47:20 You put stain upon your honor 5
4Mc 5:36 shall not stain the honorable mouth of my old age 3

stair 1. לוּל 2. מַעֲלֶה 3. מַעֲלָה
1Kg 6: 8 one went up by stairs to the middle story 1
Neh 3:15 as far as the stairs that go down from the City 3
9: 4 Upon the stairs of the Levites stood Jeshua, Bani 2
12:37 went up . . by the stairs of the city of David 3

stairway 1. מַעֲלֶה 2. מַעֲלָה
Ezk 40:31 its stairway had eight steps. 2
34 and its stairway had eight steps. 1
37 its stairway had eight steps. 1
41: 7 on the side of the temple a stairway led upward *

stake 1. יָתֵד 2. πάσσαλος
Job 6:29 Turn now, my vindication is at stake. *
Isa 33:20 tent, whose stakes will never be plucked up 1
54: 2 lengthen your cords and strengthen your stakes. 1
Sir 27: 2 As a stake is driven firmly into a fissure 2

stalk 1. עֵץ 2. קָנֶה
Gen 41: 5 plump and good, were growing on one stalk. 2
22 saw in my dream seven ears growing on one stalk 2
Jos 2: 6 and hid them with the stalks of flax 1

stalk (2) 1. הלך 2. צוד
Ps 91: 6 nor the pestilence that stalks in darkness 1
Prv 6:26 but an adulteress stalks a man's very life. 2

stall 1. אֻרְוָה 2. מַרְבֵּק 3. רֶפֶת
1Kg 4:26 Solomon also had 40,000 stalls of horses 1
2Ch 9:25 Solomon had 4,000 stalls for horses and chariots 1
32:28 stalls for all kinds of cattle, and sheepfolds. 1
Ams 6: 4 eat . . and calves from the midst of the stall; 2
Hab 3:17 Though . . there be no herd in the stalls 3
Mal 4: 2 go forth leaping like calves from the stall. 2

stallion 1. אַבִּיר 2. סוּס 3. ἵππος εἰς ὀχείαν
Jer 5: 8 They were well-fed lusty stallions 2
8:16 at the sound of the neighing of their stallions 1
47: 3 of the stamping of the hoofs of his stallions 1
50:11 as a heifer at grass, and neigh like stallions 1
Sir 33: 6 A stallion is like a mocking friend 3

stalwart 1. δυνατὸς ἰσχύς 2. ῥωμαλέος
1Mc 11:44 So Jonathan sent 3,000 stalwart men 1
2Mc 12:27 Stalwart young men took their stand 2

stammer 1. לעג
Isa 33:19 stammering in a tongue which you cannot 1

stammerer 1. עִלֵּג
Isa 32: 4 the tongue of the stammerers will speak readily 1

stamp 1. רקע 2. שְׁעָטָה 3. רפס (A)
Jer 47: 3 At the noise of the stamping of the hoofs 2
Ezk 6:11 Clap your hands, and stamp your foot, and say, Alas! 1
25: 6 clapped your hands and stamped your feet 1
Dan 7: 7 stamped the residue with its feet. 3
19 pieces, and stamped the residue with its feet; 3

stamp down 1. רקע
2Sm 22:43 stamped them down like the mire of the streets. 1

very stamp 1. χαρακτήρ
Heb 1: 3 and bears the very stamp of his nature 1

stand 1. יצב 2. ישב 3. נגשׁ 4. נצב 5. עמד 6. קוּם 7. שׁכן 8. קָאֵם (A) 9. קוּם (A) 10. βαίνω 11. διαμένω 12. εἰμί 13. ἐφίστημι 14. ἔχω 15. ἔχω στάσιν 16. ἵστημι 17. καθίστημι 18. καρτερέω 19. κεῖμαι 20. παραμένω 21. παρίστημι 22. περιέχω 23. περιΐστημι 24. στάσις 25. στήκω 26. συνίστημι 27. ὑφίστημι 28. sto
Gen 18: 2 behold, three men stood in front of him. 4
8 and he stood by them under the tree 5
22 Sodom; but Abraham still stood before the LORD. 5
19: 9 they said, "Stand back! 3
27 to the place where he had stood before the LORD; 5
24:13 Behold, I am standing by the spring of water 4
30 behold, he was standing by the camels 5
31 blessed of the LORD; why do you stand outside? 5
43 Behold, I am standing by the spring of water; 4
28:13 behold, the LORD stood above it and said 4
41: 1 Pharaoh dreamed that he was standing by the Nile 5
3 and stood by the other cows on the bank 5
17 Behold, in my dream I was standing on the banks 5
43:15 went down to Egypt, and stood before Joseph. 5
45: 1 himself before all those who stood by him; 4
47:26 a statute . . and it stands to this day *
Exd 2: 4 his sister stood at a distance 1
3: 5 place on which you are standing is holy ground. 5
8:21 and also the ground on which they stand. *
9:10 So they . . stood before Pharaoh, and Moses threw 5
11 the magicians could not stand before Moses 5
13 Rise up early in the morning and stand before 1
14:19 pillar of cloud . . stood behind them 5
17: 6 Behold, I will stand before you there on the rock 5
9 tomorrow I will stand on top of the hill 4
18:13 the people stood about Moses from morning till 5
14 you sit alone, and all the people stand about you 4
20:18 and they stood afar off 5
21 the people stood afar off, while Moses drew near 5
32:26 then Moses stood in the gate of the camp, and said 5
33: 8 every man stood at his tent door, and looked 4
9 cloud would descend and stand at the door 5
10 saw the pillar of cloud standing at the door 5
21 there is a place by me where you shall stand upon 4
34: 5 the LORD descended in the cloud and stood 1
Lev 9: 5 all the congregation drew near and stood 5
27:14 as the priest values it, so it shall stand 6

17 it shall stand at your full valuation 6
Num12: 5 LORD came . . and stood at the door of the tent 5
14:14 thy cloud stands over them and thou goest 5
16: 9 to stand before the congregation to minister 5
18 they stood at the entrance of the tent of meeting 5
27 came out and stood at the door of their tents 4
48 he stood between the dead and the living; 5
22:23 ass saw the angel of the LORD standing in the road 4
24 Then the angel of the LORD stood in a narrow path 5
26 angel of the LORD . . stood in a narrow place 5
31 he saw the angel of the LORD standing in the way 4
34 that thou didst stand in the road against me. 4
23: 3 Stand beside your burnt offering, and I will go; 1
6 Moab were standing beside his burnt offering. 4
15 Stand here beside your burnt offering 1
17 lo, he was standing beside his burnt offering 4
27: 2 stood before Moses, and before Elea'zar 5
21 he shall stand before Elea'zar the priest 5
30: 4 then all her vows shall stand 6
4 then . . every pledge . . shall stand. 6
5 no vow of hers, no pledge . . shall stand; 6
7 then her vows shall stand, and her pledges 6
7 her vows . . and her pledges . . shall stand. 6
9 any vow of a widow . . shall stand against her. 6
11 did not oppose her; then all her vows shall stand 6
11 then . . every pledge . . shall stand. 6
12 proceeds out of her lips . . shall not stand 6
35:12 not die until he stands before the congregation 5
Deu 1:38 Joshua . . who stands before you, he shall enter; 5
4:10 day that you stood before the LORD your God 5
11 came near and stood at the foot of the mountain 5
5: 5 I stood between the LORD and you at that time 5
31 stand here by me, and I will tell you all 5
7:24 not a man shall be able to stand against you 1
9: 2 said, 'Who can stand before the sons of Anak?' 1
10: 8 to stand before the LORD to minister to him 5
11:25 No man shall be able to stand against you; 1
17:12 by not obeying the priest who stands to minister 5
18: 5 chosen him . . to stand and minister in the name 5
7 who stand to minister there before the LORD. 5
24:11 stand outside, and the man to whom you make 5
27:12 these shall stand upon Mount Ger'izim to bless 5
13 these shall stand upon Mount Ebal for the curse 5
29:10 stand this day all of you before the LORD your God; 4
15 as well as with him who stands here with us 5
31:15 pillar of cloud stood by the door of the tent. 5
Jos 1: 5 No man shall be able to stand before you 1
3:13 waters coming down . . shall stand in one heap. 5
16 the waters . . stood and rose up in a heap far off 5
17 priests . . stood on dry ground in the midst 5
4: 3 from the very place where the priests' feet stood •
10 the priests . . stood in the midst of the Jordan 5
5:13 a man stood before him with his drawn sword 5
15 Put off . . for the place where you stand is holy. 5
7:12 Israel cannot stand before their enemies; 6
13 you cannot stand before your enemies 6
8:29 heap of stones, which stands there to this day. •
33 all Israel . . stood on opposite sides of the ark 5
10: 8 there shall not a man of them stand before you. 5
11:13 none of the cities that stood on mounds 5
20: 4 stand at the entrance of the gate of the city 5
6 has stood before the congregation for judgment 5
9 not . . till he stood before the congregation. 5
22:19 LORD's land where the LORD's tabernacle stands 7
29 the altar . . that stands before his tabernacle! •
Jdg 4:20 he said to her, "Stand at the door of the tent 5
6:24 To this day it still stands at Ophrah •
7:21 They stood every man in his place round about 5
9: 7 he went and stood on the top of Mount Ger'izim 5
35 Ga'al . . and stood in the entrance of the gate 5
44 rushed forward and stood at the entrance 5
18:16 600 men . . armed . . stood by the entrance 4
17 the priest stood by the entrance of the gate 4
1Sm 1:26 the woman who was standing here in your presence 4
6:20 Who is able to stand before the LORD, this holy God? 5
10:23 when he stood among the people, he was taller 1
17: 3 Philistines stood on the mountain on . . one side 5
3 Israel stood on the mountain on the other side 5
8 He stood and shouted to the ranks of Israel 5
26 And David said to the men who stood by him 5
51 Then David ran and stood over the Philistine 5
19: 3 and I will go out and stand beside my father 5
20 the prophets . . and Samuel standing as head 5
22: 6 and all his servants were standing about him. 4
7 Saul said to his servants who stood about him 4
9 Do'eg . . who stood by the servants of Saul 4
17 the king said to the guard who stood about him 4
26:13 and stood afar off on the top of the mountain 5
2Sm 1: 9 And he said to me, 'Stand beside me and slay me; 5
10 I stood beside him, and slew him 5
12:17 And the elders of his house stood beside him 6
13:31 and all his servants who were standing by 4
15: 2 rise early and stand beside the way of the gate; 5
18: 4 the king stood at the side of the gate 5
13 then you yourself would have stood aloof. 1
30 And the king said, "Turn aside, and stand here. 1
20:15 a mound . . and it stood against the rampart; 5
23: 5 Yea, does not my house stand so with God? •
1Kg 1:28 the king's presence, and stood before the king. 5

3:15 he came to Jerusalem, and stood before the ark 5
16 harlots came to the king, and stood before him. 5
7:25 It stood upon twelve oxen, three facing north 5
8:11 priests could not stand to minister 5
14 while all the assembly of Israel stood. 5
22 Then Solomon stood before the altar of the LORD 5
55 and he stood, and blessed all the assembly 5
10: 8 who continually stand before you and hear 5
19 and two lions standing beside the arm rests 5
20 twelve lions stood there, one on each end of a step 5
12: 6 the old men, who had stood before Solomon 5
8 young men who had . . and stood before him. 5
13: 1 Jerobo'am was standing by the altar 5
24 body was . . in the road, and the ass stood beside it; 5
24 the lion also stood beside the body. 5
25 the body . . in the road, and the lion standing 5
28 the ass and the lion standing beside the body. 5
17: 1 As the LORD . . lives, before whom I stand 5
18:15 As the LORD of hosts lives, before whom I stand 5
19:11 he said, "Go forth, and stand upon the mount 5
13 and went out and stood at the entrance 5
22:19 and all the host of heaven standing beside him 5
21 a spirit came forward and stood before the LORD 5
2Kg 2: 7 prophets also went, and stood at some distance 5
7 they both were standing by the Jordan. 5
13 and went back and stood on the bank 5
4:12 When he had called her, she stood before him. 5
15 when he had called her, she stood in the doorway. 5
5:11 come . . and stand, and call on the name of the LORD 5
15 he returned . . and he came and stood before him; 5
25 He went in, and stood before his master 5
8: 9 When he came and stood before him, he said 5
9:17 watchman was standing on the tower in Jezreel 5
10: 4 the two kings could not stand before him; 5
4 two kings could not . . how then can we stand? 5
9 when he went . . he stood, and said to all the people 5
11:11 guards stood . . around the altar and the house. 5
14 there was the king standing by the pillar 5
13:21 he revived, and stood on his feet. 6
18:17 they came and stood by the conduit of the upper 5
28 the Rab'shakeh stood and called . . in a loud voice 5
23: 3 the king stood by the pillar and made a covenant 5
1Ch 6:39 his brother Asaph, who stood on his right hand 5
21:15 the angel of the LORD was standing 5
16 of the LORD standing between earth and heaven 5
23:30 stand every morning, thanking and praising 5
2Ch 3:13 cherubim stood on their feet, facing the nave. 5
4: 4 It stood upon twelve oxen, three facing north 5
5:12 stood east of the altar with . . priests who were 5
14 priests could not stand to minister 5
6: 3 while all the assembly of Israel stood. 5
12 Then Solomon stood before the altar of the LORD 5
13 made a bronze platform . . and he stood upon it. 5
7: 6 priests stood at their posts; the Levites also 5
6 priests sounded trumpets; and all Israel stood. 5
9: 7 servants, who continually stand before you 5
18 two lions standing beside the arm rests 5
19 while twelve lions stood there, one on each end 5
10: 6 old men, who had stood before Solomon his father 5
8 who had grown up with him and stood before him. 5
13: 4 Then Abi'jah stood up on Mount Zemara'im 6
18:18 all the host of heaven standing on his right hand 5
20 a spirit came forward and stood before the LORD 5
20: 5 Jehosh'aphat stood in the assembly of Judah 5
9 we will stand before this house, and before thee 5
13 all the men of Judah stood before the LORD 5
20 as they went out, Jehosh'aphat stood and said 5
23:13 there was the king standing by his pillar 5
24:20 Zechari'ah . . he stood above the people, and said 5
29:11 LORD has chosen you to stand in his presence 5
26 The Levites stood with the instruments of David 5
34: 4 incense altars which stood above them; •
31 the king stood in his place and made a covenant 5
35: 5 stand in the holy place according 5
10 prepared for, the priests stood in their place 5
Ezr 9:15 none can stand before thee because of this. 5
10:13 we cannot stand in the open. 5
14 Let our officials stand for the whole assembly; 5
Neh 4:16 leaders stood behind all the house of Judah •
7: 3 still standing guard let them shut and bar 5
8: 4 Ezra the scribe stood on a wooden pulpit 5
4 beside him stood Mattithi'ah, Shema, Anai'ah, Uri'ah 5
5 when he opened it all the people stood. 5
9: 2 stood and confessed their sins 5
4 Upon the stairs of the Levites stood Jeshua, Bani 6
12: 9 Bakbuki'ah and Unno . . stood opposite them •
25 gatekeepers standing guard at the storehouses •
40 both companies . . stood in the house of God 5
Est 5: 1 and stood in the inner court of the king's palace 5
2 the king saw Queen Esther standing in the court 5
6: 5 Haman is there, standing in the court. 5
7: 9 the gallows . . is standing in Haman's house 5
8: 5 and Esther rose and stood before the king. 5
Job 4:16 It stood still, but I could not discern its 5
8:15 He leans against his house, but it does not stand; 5
19:25 at last he will stand upon the earth; 6
29: 8 the aged rose and stood; 5
30:20 I stand, and thou dost not heed me. 5
32:16 because they stand there, and answer no more? 5

41:10 Who then is he that can stand before me? 1
Ps 1: 1 nor stands in the way of sinners 5
5 the wicked will not stand in the judgment 6
5: 5 The boastful may not stand before thy eyes; 1
10: 1 Why dost thou stand afar off, O LORD? 5
24: 3 And who shall stand in his holy place? 6
26:12 My foot stands on level ground; 5
33:11 The counsel of the LORD stands for ever 5
38:11 companions stand aloof from my plague 5
11 my kinsmen stand afar off. 5
39: 5 Surely every man stands as a mere breath! Selah 4
45: 9 at your right hand stands the queen in gold 4
76: 7 Who can stand before thee when once thy anger is 5
87: 1 On the holy mount stands the city he founded; †
104: 6 waters stood above the mountains. 5
106:23 Moses, his chosen one, stood in the breach before 5
109:31 For he stands at the right hand of the needy 5
119:91 By thy appointment they stand this day; 5
122: 2 feet . . standing within your gates, O Jerusalem! 5
130: 3 LORD . . mark iniquities, Lord, who could stand? 5
134: 1 who stand by night in the house of the LORD! 5
135: 2 you that stand in the house of the LORD 5
147:17 who can stand before his cold? 5
Prv 12: 7 but the house of the righteous will stand. 5
22:29 skilful in his work? he will stand before kings; 1
29 he will not stand before obscure men. 1
25: 6 Do not . . stand in the place of the great; 5
27: 4 but who can stand before jealousy? 5
Ecc 4:15 living . . as well as that youth, who was to stand 5
Sng 2: 9 Behold, there he stands behind our wall, gazing 5
Isa 3:13 The LORD . . stands to judge his people. 5
6: 2 Above him stood the seraphim; each had six wings 5
7: 7 thus says the Lord GOD: It shall not stand 6
8:10 it will not stand, for God is with us. 6
11:10 the root of Jesse shall stand as an ensign 5
14:24 and as I have purposed, so shall it stand 6
21: 8 who saw cried: "Upon a watchtower I stand, O Lord 5
28:18 and your agreement with Sheol will not stand; 6
32: 8 and by noble things he stands. 6
36: 2 And he stood by the conduit of the upper pool 5
13 Then the Rab'shakeh stood and called out 5
40: 8 fades; but the word of our God will stand for ever. 6
46: 7 they set it in its place, and it stands there; 5
10 My counsel shall stand, and I will accomplish 6
59:14 and righteousness stands afar off; 5
61: 5 Aliens shall stand and feed your flocks 5
Jer 6:16 Thus says the LORD: "Stand by the roads, and look 5
7: 2 Stand in the gate of the LORD'S house, and proclaim 5
10 and then come and stand before me in this house 5
14: 6 The wild asses stand on the bare heights 5
15: 1 Though Moses and Samuel stood before me 5
19 I will restore you, and you shall stand before me. 5
17:19 Go and stand in the Benjamin Gate 5
18:20 how I stood before thee to speak good for them 5
19:14 and he stood in the court of the LORD'S house 5
23:18 For who . . has stood in the council of the LORD 5
22 But if they had stood in my council 5
26: 2 Stand in the court of the LORD'S house, and speak 5
28: 5 people who were standing in the house of the LORD; 5
30:18 the palace shall stand where it used to be. 2
35:19 shall never lack a man to stand before me. 5
36:21 all the princes who stood beside the king. 5
40:10 at Mizpah, to stand for you before the Chalde'ans 5
44:15 and all the women who stood by, a great assembly 5
28 shall know whose word will stand, mine or theirs. 6
29 my words will surely stand against you for evil 6
46:15 Why has Apis fled? Why did not your bull stand? 5
21 have turned and fled together, they did not stand; 5
48:19 Stand by the way and watch, O inhabitant of Aro'er! 5
49:19 What shepherd can stand before me? 5
50:44 What shepherd can stand before me? 5
51:29 for the LORD'S purposes against Babylon stand 6
50 escaped from the sword, go, stand not still! 5
Ezk 1:21 and when those stood, these stood; 5
21 and when those stood, these stood; 5
24 when they stood still, they let down their wings. 5
25 when they stood still, they let down their wings. 5
2: 1 And he said to me, "Son of man, stand upon your feet 5
3:23 and, lo, the glory of the LORD stood there 5
8:11 And before them stood 70 men of the elders 5
11 with Ja-azani'ah the son of Shaphan standing among 5
9: 2 they went in and stood beside the bronze altar. 5
10: 3 Now the cherubim were standing on the south side 5
6 he went in and stood beside a wheel. 5
17 When they stood still, these stood still 5
17 When they stood still, these stood still 5
18 went forth . . and stood over the cherubim. 5
19 they stood at the door of the east gate 5
11:23 and stood upon the mountain which is on the east 5
13: 5 it might stand in battle in the day of the LORD. 5
17: 6 its roots remained where it stood. •
14 that by keeping his covenant it might stand. 5
21:21 king of Babylon stands at the parting of the way 5
22:30 and stand in the breach before me for the land 5
27:29 all the pilots of the sea stand on the shore 5
37:10 and they lived, and stood upon their feet 5
40: 3 he was standing in the gateway. 5
43: 6 While the man was standing beside me, I heard one 5
47:10 Fishermen will stand beside the sea; 5

Dan 1: 5 end of that time .. were to stand before the king. 5
19 therefore they stood before the king. 5
2: 2 So they came in and stood before the king. 5
31 image .. stood before you, and its appearance 8
44 bring them to an end, and it shall stand for ever; 9
3: 3 stood before the image that Nebuchadnez'zar 9
7:10 10,000 times 10,000 stood before 9
16 approached one of those who stood there 9
8: 3 behold, a ram standing on the bank of the river. 5
4 no beast could stand before him, 5
6 ram .. seen standing on the bank of the river 5
7 ram had no power to stand before him 5
15 behold, there stood before me one having 5
17 came near where I stood; and when he came 5
10: 4 as I was standing on the bank of the great river •
11 stand upright, for now I have been sent to you. 5
16 said to him who stood before me, "O my lord, 5
11:15 forces of the south shall not stand 5
15 for there shall be no strength to stand. 5
16 none shall stand before him; 5
16 stand in the glorious land, and all of it 5
17 it shall not stand or be to his advantage. 5
25 not stand, for plots shall be devised against 5
12: 5 Then I Daniel looked, and behold, two others stood 5
13 rest, and shall stand in your allotted place 5
Ams 2:15 he who handles the bow shall not stand 5
7: 2 How can Jacob stand? He is so small! 6
5 How can Jacob stand? He is so small"! 6
7 behold, the Lord was standing beside a wall 4
9: 1 I saw the LORD standing beside the altar 4
Obd 1:11 On the day that you stood aloof 5
14 You should not have stood at the parting 5
Mic 5: 4 he shall stand and feed his flock 5
Nah 1: 6 Who can stand before his indignation? 5
Hab 3: 6 He stood and measured the earth; 5
11 The sun and moon stood still in their habitation 5
Zec 1: 8 He was standing among the myrtle trees 5
10 the man who was standing among the myrtle trees 5
11 angel .. who was standing among the myrtle trees 5
3: 1 priest standing before the angel of the LORD 5
1 Satan standing at his right hand to accuse him. 5
3 Now Joshua was standing before the angel 5
4 angel said to those who were standing before him 5
5 the angel of the LORD was standing by. 5
7 of access among those who are standing here. 5
4:14 These are the two anointed who stand by the Lord 5
14: 4 his feet shall stand on the Mount of Olives 5
Mal 3: 2 who can stand when he appears? 5
Mat 6: 5 for they love to stand and pray in the synagogues 16
12:25 house divided against itself will stand; 16
26 how then will his kingdom stand? 16
46 his mother and his brothers stood outside 16
13: 2 and the whole crowd stood on the beach. 16
16:28 Truly, I say to you, there are some standing here 16
20: 3 he saw others standing idle in the market place; 16
6 he went out and found others standing 16
6 he said to them, 'Why do you stand here idle all day? 16
24:15 the prophet Daniel, standing in the holy place 16
27:11 Now Jesus stood before the governor 16
Mrk 3:24 that kingdom cannot stand. 16
25 that house will not be able to stand. 16
26 he cannot stand, but is coming to an end. 16
31 standing outside they sent to him and called 25
9: 1 some standing here who will not taste death 16
11: 5 those who stood there said to them 16
25 whenever you stand praying, forgive 25
13: 9 stand before governors and kings for my sake 16
14:47 one of those who stood by drew his sword 21
15:39 when the centurion, who stood facing him, saw 21
Lke 1:11 standing on the right side of the altar 16
19 I am Gabriel, who stand in the presence of God 21
4:39 he stood over her and rebuked the fever 13
5: 1 he was standing by the lake of Gennes'aret. 16
6: 8 Come and stand here." And he rose and stood there. 16
8 Come and stand here." And he rose and stood there. 16
17 he came down with them and stood on a level place 16
7:14 the bearers stood still 16
38 standing behind him at his feet, weeping 16
8:20 your brothers are standing outside 16
9:27 are some standing here who will not taste death 16
32 his glory and the two men who stood with him. 26
11:18 how will his kingdom stand 16
13:25 begin to stand outside and to knock at the door 16
17:12 ten lepers, who stood at a distance 16
18:11 The Pharisee stood and prayed thus with himself 16
13 the tax collector, standing far off 16
19: 8 Zacchae'us stood and said to the Lord, "Behold 16
24 he said to those who stood by, 'Take the pound 21
21:36 to stand before the Son of man. 16
23:10 The chief priests and the scribes stood by 16
35 the people stood by, watching 16
49 stood at a distance and saw these things. 16
24: 4 behold, two men stood by them in dazzling apparel; 13
17 they stood still, looking sad. 16
36 Jesus himself stood among them 16
Joh 1:26 but among you stands one whom you do not know 16
35 John was standing with two of his disciples; 16
2: 6 Now six stone jars were standing there 19
3:29 the friend .. who stands and hears him, rejoices 16
8: 9 left alone with the woman standing before him. 12
11:42 said this on account of the people standing by 23
56 as they stood in the temple 16
12:29 The crowd standing by heard it and said 16
18: 5 Judas, who betrayed him, was standing with them. 16
16 while Peter stood outside at the door 16
18 they were standing and warming themselves 16
18 standing and warming himself. 16
22 one of the officers standing by struck Jesus 21
25 Simon Peter was standing and warming himself. 16
19:25 standing by the cross of Jesus were his mother 16
29 A bowl full of vinegar stood there 19
20:11 Mary stood weeping outside the tomb 16
14 she turned round and saw Jesus standing 16
19 Jesus came and stood among them and said to them 16
26 Jesus came and stood among them, and said 16
21: 4 Just as day was breaking, Jesus stood on the beach; 16
Act 1:10 behold, two men stood by them in white robes 21
11 why do you stand looking into heaven? 16
2:14 Peter, standing with the eleven 16
3: 8 stood and walked and entered the temple 16
4:14 seeing the man .. standing beside them 16
5:20 Go and stand in the temple and speak to the people 16
23 the sentries standing at the doors 16
25 standing in the temple and teaching the people. 16
7:33 the place where you are standing is holy ground. 16
55 Jesus standing at the right hand of God; 16
56 the Son of man standing at the right hand of God. 16
9: 7 The men .. stood speechless 16
10:17 stood before the gate 13
30 behold, a man stood before me in bright apparel 16
11:13 the angel standing in his house and saying 16
12:14 told that Peter was standing at the gate. 16
16: 9 a man of Macedo'nia was standing beseeching him 16
17:22 Paul, standing in the middle of the Are-op'agus 16
21:40 Paul, standing on the steps 16
22:13 came to me, and standing by me said to me 13
20 I also was standing by and approving 13
25 Paul said to the centurion who was standing by 16
23: 2 Anani'as commanded those who stood by him 21
4 Those who stood by said 21
11 the Lord stood by him and said, "Take courage 13
24:20 when I stood before the council 16
21 which I cried out while standing among them 16
25:10 Paul said, "I am standing before Caesar's tribunal 16
26: 6 now I stand here on trial for hope in the promise 16
16 rise and stand upon your feet 16
22 I stand here testifying both to small and great 16
27:23 this very night there stood by me an angel 21
Rom 5: 2 access to this grace in which we stand 16
11:20 but you stand fast only through faith. 16
20 So do not become proud, but stand in awe. •
14: 4 before his own master that he stands or falls. 25
1Co 10:12 Therefore let any one who thinks that he stands 16
15: 1 which you received, in which you stand 16
16:13 Be watchful, stand firm in your faith 25
Gal 2:11 because he stood condemned. 12
Eph 6:11 able to stand against the wiles of the devil. 16
13 and having done all, to stand. 16
14 Stand therefore, having girded your loins 16
Col 2:14 having canceled the bond which stood against us 12
4:12 may stand mature and fully assured 16
1Ti 5:20 so that the rest may stand in fear. 14
2Ti 2:19 God's firm foundation stands, bearing this seal 16
4:17 the Lord stood by me 21
Heb 9: 3 Behind the second curtain stood a tent •
8 as long as the outer tent is still standing 15
10:11 every priest stands daily at his service 16
Jas 2: 3 while you say to the poor man, "Stand there 16
5: 9 behold, the Judge is standing at the doors. 16
1Pe 2: 6 For it stands in scripture 22
Rev 3:20 Behold, I stand at the door and knock; 16
4: 2 I was in the Spirit, and lo, a throne stood in heaven 19
5: 6 I saw a Lamb standing, as though it had been slain 16
6:17 wrath has come, and who can stand before it? 16
7: 1 After this I saw four angels standing 16
9 standing before the throne and before the Lamb 16
11 all the angels stood round the throne 16
8: 2 Then I saw the seven angels who stand before God 16
3 another angel came and stood at the altar 16
10: 5 the angel whom I saw standing on sea and land 16
8 angel who is standing on the sea and on the land. 16
11: 4 two lampstands which stand before the Lord 16
12: 4 And the dragon stood before the woman 16
17 And he stood on the sand of the sea. 16
14: 1 Then I looked, and lo, on Mount Zion stood the Lamb 16
15: 2 standing beside the sea of glass 16
18:10 they will stand far off, in fear of her torment 16
15 merchants of these wares .. will stand far off 16
17 all whose trade is on the sea, stood far off 16
19:17 Then I saw an angel standing in the sun 16
20:12 dead, great and small, standing before the throne 16
1Es 1: 5 Stand in order in the temple 16
10 stood according to kindred 16
5:59 the priests stood arrayed in their garments 16
7: 9 the priests and the Levites stood 16
8:90 we can no longer stand in thy presence 16
9:11 we are not able to stand in the open air 16
42 stood on the wooden platform 16
43 beside him stood Mattathiah, Shema, Anaiah 16
46 when he opened the law, they all stood erect 16
2Es 2:38 Rise and stand, and see at the feast of the Lord 28
47 who had stood valiantly for the name of the Lord. 28
4:47 he said to me, "Stand at my right side 28
48 I stood and looked, and behold, a flaming furnace 28
6:14 if the place where you are standing is .. shaken 28
29 the place where I was standing began to rock 28
7:34 only judgment shall remain, truth shall stand 28
13:35 he shall stand on the top of Mount Zion. 28
16:65 shall stand as your accusers in that day. 28
Jdt 4:14 all the priests who stood before the Lord 21
8:33 Stand at the city gate tonight 16
10: 6 found Uzziah standing there with the elders 13
16 when you stand before him 16
13: 3 told her maid to stand outside the bedchamber 16
4 Then Judith, standing beside his bed, said 16
AEs 13: 5 stands constantly in opposition to all men 19
15: 6 she stood before the king 17
Wis 4: 4 standing insecurely they will be shaken 10
5: 1 the righteous man will stand 16
10: 7 standing as a monument to an unbelieving soul. 16
11 she stood by him and made him rich. 21
18:16 and stood and filled all things with death 16
16 and touched heaven while standing on the earth. 10
Sir 6: 8 will not stand by you in your day of trouble. 20
10 will not stand by you in your day of trouble. 20
34 Stand in the assembly of the elders. Who is wise? 16
11:20 Stand by your covenant and attend to it 16
12:15 if you falter, he will not stand by you. 18
21:22 stands respectfully before it. •
22:23 stand by him in time of affliction 11
37: 9 then stand aloof to see what will happen to you. 16
39:17 At his word the waters stood in a heap 16
40:12 good faith will stand for ever. 16
43:10 they stand as ordered 16
44:12 Their descendants stand by the covenants 16
47:13 prepare a sanctuary to stand for ever. •
50:12 as he stood by the hearth of the altar 16
51: 2 Before those who stood by thou wast my helper 21
Bar 5: 5 stand upon the height and look toward the east 16
Aza 1: 2 Then Azariah stood and offered this prayer 26
1Mc 4:18 stand now against our enemies and fight them 16
5:44 they could stand before Judas no longer. 27
7:36 the priests went in and stood before the altar 16
10:72 Men will tell you that you cannot stand before us 24
2Mc 3:26 who stood on each side of him 23
33 they stood and said 16
14:45 standing upon a steep rock 16
3Mc 5:51 they stood now at the gates of death. 17
6:31 near to death, or rather, who stood at its gates 10
4Mc 6: 1 the guards who were standing by dragged him 21
16:15 you stood and watched Eleazar being tortured 16
17: 5 does not stand so august as you 17

stand (2) 1. מְכוֹנָה 2. *λυχνία*

1Kg 7:27 He also made the ten stands of bronze; 1
27 stands of bronze; each stand was four cubits long 1
28 This was the construction of the stands 1
30 each stand had four bronze wheels and axles 1
32 the axles .. were of one piece with the stands; 1
34 four supports at the four corners of each stand; 1
34 the supports were of one piece with the stands. 1
35 on the top of the stand there was a round band 1
35 on the top of the stand its stays and its panels 1
37 After this manner he made the ten stands; 1
38 and there was a laver for each of the ten stands. 1
39 he set the stands, five on the south .. and five 1
43 the ten stands, and the ten lavers upon the stands; 1
43 the ten stands, and the ten lavers upon the stands; 1
2Kg 16:17 King Ahaz cut off the frames of the stands 1
25:13 the pillars .. and the stands and the bronze sea 1
16 As for the two pillars, the one sea, and the stands 1
2Ch 4:14 He made the stands also, and the lavers upon 1
14 stands also, and the lavers upon the stands 1
Jer 27:19 concerning the pillars, the sea, the stands 1
52:17 the stands .. that were in the house of the LORD 1
20 and the stands, which Solomon the king had made 1
Mat 5:15 under a bushel, but on a stand, and it gives light 2
Mrk 4:21 under a bushel, or under a bed, and not on a stand? 2
Lke 8:16 puts it on a stand 2
11:33 puts it in a cellar or under a bushel, but on a stand 2

stand (3) 1. בוא 2. ישב 3. *γίνομαι* 4. *φέρω*

Num31:23 everything that can stand the fire 1
23 whatever cannot stand the fire, you shall pass 1
2Ch 32:10 that you stand siege in Jerusalem? 2
Jas 1:12 when he has stood the test he will receive 3
AEs 16: 3 in their inability to stand prosperity 4

stand *See* make, power, take.

stand about 1. *παρίστημι* 2. *περιίστημι*

Act 25: 7 the Jews .. stood about him 2
4Mc 5: 1 with his armed soldiers standing about him 1

stand around 1. *κυκλόω* 2. *περιίστημι*

Jdt 5:22 all the men standing around the tent 2
10:18 they came and stood around her as she waited 1

stand aside 1. ἀφίστημι
1Es 1:27 Stand aside, and do not oppose the Lord. 1

stand before 1. καθίστημι 2. παρίστημι 3. προϋφίστημι 4. adsto
Act 4:10 by him this man is standing before you well. 2
27:24 you must stand before Caesar 2
Rom 14:10 shall all stand before the judgment seat of God; 2
2Es 8:21 before whom the hosts of angels stand trembling 4
Wis 19: 7 and dry land emerging where water had stood before 3
4Mc 17: 5 who . . stand in honor before God 1
18 they now stand before the divine throne 2

stand beside 1. παρίστημι
Act 9:39 All the widows stood beside him weeping 1

cause to stand 1. עמד
Num 27:19 cause him to stand before Elea'zar the priest 1
22 Joshua and caused him to stand before Elea'zar 1

stand fast 1. עמד 2. יַצִּיב (A) 3. ἵστημι 4. στήκω
Ps 119:90 hast established the earth, and it stands fast. 1
Isa 47:12 Stand fast in your enchantments 1
Dan 6:12 The thing stands fast, according to the law 2
Gal 5: 1 stand fast therefore, and do not submit 4
1Th 3: 8 for now we live, if you stand fast in the Lord. 4
1Pe 5:12 this is the true grace of God; stand fast in it. 3
Sir 45:23 stood fast, when the people turned away 3
1Mc 10:81 his men stood fast, as Jonathan commanded 3

stand firm 1. אמן 2. חזק 3. יצב 4. כון 5. ἵστημι 6. κραταιόω 7. στήκω 8. στηρίζω 9. ὑπομένω 10. sto
Exd 14:13 Fear not, stand firm, and see the salvation 3
1Ch 16:30 yea, the world stands firm, never to be moved. 4
Ps 89:28 my covenant will stand firm for him. 1
37 shall stand firm while the skies endure." Selah 1
Prv 12:12 but the root of the righteous stands firm. •
Dan 11:32 know their God shall stand firm and take action. 2
2Co 1:24 for you stand firm in your faith. 5
Php 1:27 I may hear of you that you stand firm in one spirit 7
4: 1 stand firm thus in the Lord, my beloved. 7
2Th 2:15 brethren, stand firm and hold to the traditions 7
2Es 4:17 for the sand stood firm and stopped them. 10
Sir 22:18 Fences set on a high place will not stand firm 9
18 will not stand firm against any fear. 9
42:17 the universe may stand firm in his glory. 8
46: 3 Who before him ever stood so firm? 5
1Mc 1:62 many in Israel stood firm 6
14:26 he and his brothers . . have stood firm 8

stand forth 1. יצב 2. עמד
Lev 19:16 you shall not stand forth against the life 2
1Sm 3:10 And the LORD came and stood forth, calling 1
Ps 33: 9 he commanded, and it stood forth. 2
Isa 44:11 let them all assemble, let them stand forth 2
47:13 let them stand forth and save you 2
48:13 when I call to them, they stand forth together. 2

stand in awe 1. גור 2. חתת 3. ירא 4. ירא מִפְּנֵי 5. ערץ 6. פחד 7. ὑποστέλλω πρόσωπον
Jos 4:14 they stood in awe of him, as they had . . of Moses 3
14 as they had stood in awe of Moses, all . . his life. 3
1Sm 18:15 when Saul saw . . he stood in awe of him. 1
1Kg 3:28 they stood in awe of the king 4
Ps 22:23 stand in awe of him, all you sons of Israel! 1
33: 8 the inhabitants of the world stand in awe of him! 1
119:161 my heart stands in awe of thy words. 6
Isa 29:23 and will stand in awe of the God of Israel. 5
Mal 2: 5 he feared me, he stood in awe of my name. 2
Wis 6: 7 For the Lord of all will not stand in awe of any one 7

stand in fear 1. ערץ
Job 31:34 because I stood in great fear of the multitude 1

stand in the way 1. ἐμποδιστικός
4Mc 1: 4 those that stand in the way of courage 1

make stand 1. נצב 2. עמד 3. קום 4. קום (A) 5. ἀνίστημι 6. ἵστημι
Jdg 16:25 They made him stand between the pillars; 2
2Ch 34:32 made all who were present . . stand to it. 2
Ps 78:13 and made the waters stand like a heap. 1
89:43 thou hast not made him stand in battle. 3
Dan 7: 4 made to stand upon two feet like a man; 4
Rom 14: 4 for the Master is able to make him stand. 6
LJr 1:27 through them these gods are made to stand 5

make stand on end 1. ἀνορθόω
Sir 27:14 makes one's hair stand on end 1

make stand sure 1. ἐφίστημι
Sir 40:25 Gold and silver make the foot stand sure 1

stand near 1. παρίστημι
Joh 19:26 and the disciple whom he loved standing near 1

stand next 1. עָמִית
Zec 13: 7 against the man who stands next to me 1

stand overseeing 1. ἐφίστημι
Jdt 8: 3 he stood overseeing the men 1

stand ready 1. יצב 2. παραγίνομαι
Jer 46:14 Say, 'Stand ready and be prepared 1
2Mc 13:12 exhorted them and ordered them to stand ready. 2

stand still 1. אמן 2. דמם 3. יצב 4. עמד 5. sto
Jos 3: 8 you shall stand still in the Jordan. 4
10:12 Sun, stand thou still at Gibeon, and thou Moon 2
13 And the sun stood still, and the moon stayed 2
1Sm 12: 7 Now therefore stand still, that I may plead 3
16 therefore stand still and see this great thing 3
14: 9 we will stand still in our place, and we will not go 4
2Sm 2:23 And all who came to the place . . stood still. 4
18:30 So he turned aside, and stood still. 4
2Ch 20:17 take your position, stand still, and see 4
Job 39:24 he cannot stand still at the sound of the trumpet. 1
2Es 6:24 the springs of the fountains shall stand still 5

stand up 1. יצב 2. נצב 3. סמר 4. עלה 5. עמד 6. קום 7. ἀνακύπτω 8. ἀνίστημι 9. ἵστημι 10. sto
Exd 2:17 but Moses stood up and helped them, and watered 6
15: 8 waters piled up, the floods stood up in a heap; 2
1Ch 21: 1 Satan stood up against Israel 5
2Ch 20:19 Levites . . stood up to praise the LORD 6
28:12 stood up against those . . coming from the war 6
Ezr 10:10 Ezra the priest stood up and said to them, 6
Neh 9: 3 stood up in their place and read from the book 6
5 Stand up and bless the LORD your God 6
Job 4:15 glided past my face; the hair of my flesh stood up. 3
30:28 I stand up in the assembly, and cry for help. 6
Ps 94:16 Who stands up for me against evildoers? 1
106:30 Phin'ehas stood up and interposed, and the plague 5
Isa 50: 8 will contend with me? Let us stand up together. 5
51:17 rouse yourself, stand up, O Jerusalem 6
Jer 51: 3 let him not stand up in his coat of mail. 4
Dan 10:11 speaking this word to me, I stood up trembling. 5
11: 1 stood up to confirm and strengthen him. 5
Mat 26:62 the high priest stood up and said 8
Mrk 14:57 some stood up and bore false witness against him 8
60 the high priest stood up in the midst 8
Lke 4:16 And he stood up to read; 8
10:25 behold, a lawyer stood up to put him to the test 8
Joh 7:37 Jesus stood up and proclaimed, "If any one thirst 9
8: 7 he stood up and said to them 7
Act 1:15 In those days Peter stood up among the brethren 8
5:34 Gama'li-el . . stood up and ordered the men 8
10:26 Peter lifted him up, saying, "Stand up; I too am a man. 8
11:28 one of them named Ag'abus stood up 8
13:16 So Paul stood up, and motioning with his hand said 8
23: 9 some of the scribes . . stood up and contended 8
25:18 When the accusers stood up 9
Rev 11:11 they stood up on their feet, and great fear fell 9
2Es 10:33 He said to me, "Stand up like a man 10
Tob 12:21 Then they stood up; but they saw him no more. 8
Sus 1:34 the two elders stood up in the midst of the people 8

stand upright 1. נצב 2. עוד 3. ἀνίστημι
Gen 37: 7 and lo, my sheaf arose and stood upright; 1
Ps 20: 8 we shall rise and stand upright. 2
Act 14:10 said in a loud voice, "Stand upright on your feet. 3

standard 1. דֶּגֶל 2. נֵס
Num 1:52 own camp and every man by his own standard; 1
2: 2 Israel shall encamp each by his own standard 1
3 of the standard of the camp of Judah 1
10 On the south side shall be the standard 1
18 On the west side shall be the standard of the camp 1
25 On the north side shall be the standard 1
34 so they encamped by their standards 1
10:14 standard of the camp of the men of Judah set out 1
18 standard of the camp of Reuben set out by their 1
22 standard of the camp of the men of E'phraim set out 1
25 Then the standard of the camp of the men of Dan 1
Isa 31: 9 and his officers desert the standard in panic 2
Jer 4: 6 Raise a standard toward Zion, flee for safety 2
21 How long must I see the standard 2
51:12 Set up a standard against the walls of Babylon; 2
27 Set up a standard on the earth, blow the trumpet 2
Ezk 45:11 the homer shall be the standard measure. •

standard (2) 1. מִדָּה 2. τύπος
2Ch 3: 3 length, in cubits of the old standard, was 60 1
Rom 6:17 obedient . . to the standard of teaching 2

standard by standard 1. לִדְגָלִים
Num 2:17 each in position, standard by standard. 1
31 They shall set out last, standard by standard. 1

worldly standard 1. σάρξ
1Co 1:26 wise according to worldly standards 1

standing 1. βαθμός 2. δόξα
1Ti 3:13 gain a good standing for themselves 1
Sir 8:14 because of his standing. 2

equal standing 1. ἰσότιμος
2Pe 1: 1 obtained a faith of equal standing with ours 1

standing grain 1. קָמָה
Exd 22: 6 stacked grain or the standing grain or the field 1
Deu 16: 9 first put the sickle to the standing grain. 1
23:25 When you go into your neighbor's standing grain 1
25 not put a sickle to your neighbor's standing grain. 1
Jdg 15: 5 go into the standing grain of the Philistines 1
5 and burned up the shocks and the standing grain 1
Isa 17: 5 as when the reaper gathers standing grain 1
Hos 8: 7 The standing grain has no heads 1

high standing 1. εὐσχήμων
Act 13:50 the Jews incited the devout women of high standing 1
17:12 with not a few Greek women of high standing 1

humble standing 1. קלה
Prv 12: 9 Better is a man of humble standing who works 1

standing place 1. עֶמְדָּה
Mic 1:11 shall take away from you its standing place. 1

remain standing 1. קום
Isa 6:13 whose stump remains standing when it is felled. •
27: 9 no . . incense altars will remain standing. 1

stands *See* place.

where one stands 1. תַּחַת
Job 40:12 tread down the wicked where they stand. 1

star 1. כּוֹכָב 2. ἀστήρ 3. ἄστρον 4. stella
Gen 1:16 he made the stars also. 1
15: 5 Look toward heaven, and number the stars 1
22:17 multiply your descendants as the stars of heaven 1
26: 4 I will multiply your descendants as the stars 1
37: 9 and eleven stars were bowing down to me. 1
Exd 32:13 your descendants as the stars of heaven 1
Num 24:17 star shall come forth out of Jacob, and a scepter 1
Deu 1:10 you are . . as the stars of heaven for multitude. 1
4:19 when you see the sun and the moon and the stars 1
10:22 made you as the stars of heaven for multitude. 1
28:62 you were as the stars of heaven for multitude 1
Jdg 5:20 From heaven fought the stars, from their courses 1
1Ch 27:23 to make Israel as many as the stars of heaven. 1
Neh 4:21 from the break of dawn till the stars came out. 1
9:23 descendants as the stars of heaven 1
Job 3: 9 Let the stars of its dawn be dark; 1
9: 7 who seals up the stars; 1
22:12 See the highest stars, how lofty they are! 1
25: 5 the stars are not clean in his sight; 1
38: 7 when the morning stars sang together 1
Ps 8: 3 moon and the stars which thou hast established; 1
136: 9 the moon and stars to rule over the night 1
147: 4 He determines the number of the stars 1
148: 3 sun and moon, praise him, all you shining stars! 1
Ecc 12: 2 the light and the moon and the stars are darkened 1
Isa 13:10 For the stars of the heavens 1
14:13 above the stars of God I will set my throne on high; 1
47:13 who divide the heavens, who gaze at the stars 1
Jer 31:35 fixed order of the moon and the stars for light 1
Ezk 32: 7 cover the heavens, and make their stars dark; 1
Dan 8:10 some of the host of the stars it cast down 1
12: 3 shine . . like the stars for ever and ever. 1
Jol 2:10 and the stars withdraw their shining. 1
3:15 and the stars withdraw their shining. 1
Ams 5:26 Sakkuth your king, and Kaiwan your star-god 1
Obd 1: 4 though your nest is set among the stars 1
Nah 3:16 merchants more than the stars of the heavens. 1
Mat 2: 2 For we have seen his star in the East, and have come 2
7 ascertained from them what time the star 2
9 and lo, the star which they had seen in the East 2
10 When they saw the star, they rejoiced 2
24:29 the stars will fall from heaven 2
Mrk 13:25 the stars will be falling from heaven 2
Lke 21:25 there will be signs in sun and moon and stars 3
Act 7:43 the star of the god Rephan 3
27:20 when neither sun nor stars appeared for many a day 3
1Co 15:41 another glory of the stars 2
41 star differs from star in glory. 2
41 star differs from star in glory. 2
Heb 11:12 as many as the stars of heaven 3
Jde 1:13 wandering stars for whom the nether gloom 2
Rev 1:16 in his right hand he held seven stars 2
20 the seven stars which you saw in my right hand 2
20 seven stars are the angels of the seven churches 2
2: 1 him who holds the seven stars in his right hand 2
28 I will give him the morning star. 2
3: 1 the seven spirits of God and the seven stars. 2
6:13 the stars of the sky fell to the earth 2
8:10 great star fell from heaven, blazing like a torch 2
11 The name of the star is Wormwood. 2
12 and a third of the moon, and a third of the stars 2
9: 1 and I saw a star fallen from heaven to earth 2
12: 1 and on her head a crown of twelve stars; 2
4 His tail swept down a third of the stars of heaven 2
22:16 the offspring of David, the bright morning star. 2
2Es 5: 5 and the stars shall fall. ‡

6:45 the arrangement of the stars to come into being; 4
7:39 a day that has no sun or moon or stars 4
97 how they are to be made like the light of the stars 4
125 the faces . . shall shine more than the stars 4
16:56 At his word the stars were fixed 4
56 and he knows the number of the stars. 4
Wis 7:19 the constellations of the stars 3
29 excels every constellation of the stars. 3
13: 2 the circle of the stars, or turbulent water 3
17: 5 nor did the brilliant flames of the stars avail 3
Sir 43: 9 The glory of the stars is the beauty of heaven 3
44:21 exalt his posterity like the stars 3
50: 6 Like the morning star among the clouds 2
Bar 3:34 the stars shone in their watches, and were glad; 2
LJr 1:60 sun and moon and stars . . are obedient. 3
Aza 1:13 as many as the stars of heaven 3
41 Bless the Lord, stars of heaven 3
2Mc 9:10 he could touch the stars of heaven. 3
4Mc 17: 5 The moon in heaven, with the stars 3

star *See also* day.

morning star 1. *φωσφόρος*
2Pe 1:19 until the day dawns and the morning star rises 1

star-like 1. *ἰσαστήρ*
4Mc 17: 5 lighting the way of your star-like seven sons 1

stare 1. נבט 2. שׂוּם 3. שׁגח 4. *ἀτενίζω* 5. *θεωρέω*
2Kg 8:11 And he fixed his gaze and stared at him 2
Ps 22:17 they stare and gloat over me; 1
Isa 14:16 who see you will stare at you, and ponder over you 3
Act 3:12 why do you stare at us 4
10: 4 he stared at him in terror, and said 4
1Es 4:19 with open mouths stare at her 5

starry 1. *ἄστρον*
Wis 10:17 a starry flame through the night. 1

start 1. קוּם 2. *ἀπαίρω* 3. *ἄρχω* 4. *γίνομαι* 5. *ἐξάρχω*
Rut 1: 6 she started with her daughters-in-law to return 1
Lke 23:19 an insurrection started in the city 4
Joh 6:17 started across the sea to Caper'na-um 3
Tob 11:10 Tobit started toward the door, and stumbled 5
1Mc 9:60 He started to come with a large force 2

start early 1. שׁכם
1Sm 29:10 start early in the morning, and depart as soon 1

start on the way 1. קוּם וְהלך
Jos 18: 8 So the men started on their way; 1

start rolling 1. גלל
Prv 26:27 come back upon him who starts it rolling. 1

starting place 1. מוֹצָא
Num33: 2 Moses wrote down their starting places 1
2 their stages according to their starting places. 1

startle 1. חרד 2. נזה 3. *πτοέω*
Rut 3: 8 At midnight the man was startled, and turned over 1
Isa 52:15 shall he startle many nations; 2
Lke 24:37 they were startled and frightened 3

state 1. *διασαφέω* 2. *εἶπον* 3. *λέγω* 4. *φάσκω*
Act 23:30 to state before you what they have against him. 3
1Es 3: 5 Let each of us state what one thing is strongest; 2
1Mc 12: 7 stating that you are our brethren *
2Mc 3: 9 stated why he had come 1
9:13 made a vow to the Lord . . stating 3
14:27 wrote to Nicanor, stating that . . 4
4Mc 1:12 I shall begin by stating my main principle *

state (2) 1. *διάθεσις* 2. *κατάστεμα* 3. *κλῆσις* 4. *ὅς*
Ezk 4: 3 let it be in a state of siege, and press the siege *
Lke 11:26 the last state of that man becomes worse *
1Co 7:20 Every one should remain in the state 3
24 So, brethren, in whatever state each was called 4
Php 4:11 I have learned, in whatever state I am, to be content. *
3Mc 3:26 in good order and in the best state. 1
5:45 had been brought virtually to a state of madness 2

state *See* sit.

state a case 1. רִיב
Prv 18:17 He who states his case first seems right 1

former state 1. antiquitas
2Es 1:36 yet will recall their former state. 1

last state 1. *ἔσχατος*
Mat 12:45 the last state of that man becomes worse 1
2Pe 2:20 the last state has become worse for them 1

state of affairs 1. *συνίστημι*
2Mc 4:30 While such was the state of affairs 1

stately 1. אַדִּיר 2. יטב 3. כָּבוֹד 4. קוֹמָה 5. *στάσιμος*
Prv 30:29 Three things are stately in their tread; 2
29 Three things . . four are stately in their stride 2
Sng 7: 7 You are stately as a palm tree 4
Isa 33:21 with oars can go, nor stately ship can pass. 1
Ezk 23:41 you sat upon a stately couch 3
Sir 26:17 so is a beautiful face on a stately figure. 5

statement 1. *λόγος* 2. *ῥῆμα*
Act 28:25 they departed, after Paul had made one statement 2
1Es 3: 5 to him whose statement seems wisest 2
8 each wrote his own statement 1
9 to the one whose statement . . judge to be wisest 1
16 they shall explain their statements 1

open statement 1. *φανερόω*
2Co 4: 2 by the open statement of the truth 1

station 1. יצב 2. מַעֲמָד 3. מִשְׁמָר 4. נוח 5. נצב 6. עמד 7. עֹמֶד 8. שׂוּם 9. *ἀποκαθίστημι* 10. *ἀποτάσσω* 11. *ἐκβάλλω* 12. *ἵστημι* 13. *καθίστημι* 14. *παρίστημι* 15. *τίθημι*
Jos 8:13 they stationed the forces 8
1Kg 10:26 whom he stationed in the chariot cities 4
2Kg 10:24 Now Jehu had stationed 80 men outside 8
1Ch 9:18 stationed hitherto in the king's gate *
2Ch 1:14 whom he stationed in the chariot cities 4
9:25 whom he stationed in the chariot cities 4
23:19 He stationed the gatekeepers at the gates 6
29:25 he stationed the Levites in the house of the LORD 6
Neh 4:13 I stationed the people according 6
7: 3 Appoint guards . . each to his station 3
13:11 gathered . . and set them in their stations. 7
Isa 21: 8 by day, and at my post I am stationed whole nights. 5
22:19 you will be cast down from your station. 2
Hab 2: 1 stand to watch, and station myself on the tower 1
1Mc 1:34 stationed there a sinful people, lawless men. 15
4:61 he stationed a garrison there to hold it 10
5:42 he stationed the scribes . . at the stream 12
6:35 with each elephant they stationed 1,000 men 14
38 the horsemen were stationed on either side 12
50 stationed a guard there to hold it. 10
10:32 station in it men of his own choice to guard it. 13
37 stationed in the great strongholds of the king 13
11: 3 he stationed forces as a garrison in each city. 10
12:27 he stationed outposts around the camp. 11
34 he stationed a garrison there to guard it. 15
15:41 He built up Kedron and stationed there horsemen 10
2Mc 15:20 the elephants strategically stationed 9
31 stationed the priests before the altar 12

station *See also* take.

station a garrison 1. *φρουρόω*
Jdt 3: 6 and stationed garrisons in the hilltop cities 1

statue 1. *ἄγαλμα*
2Mc 2: 2 upon seeing the gold and silver statues 1

stature 1. מִדָּה 2. קוֹמָה 3. *ἡλικία* 4. statura 5. status
1Sm 16: 7 Do not look on . . or on the height of his stature 2
Isa 45:14 the Sabe'ans, men of stature, shall come over to you 1
Ezk 13:18 veils for the heads of persons of every stature 2
Lke 2:52 Jesus increased in wisdom and in stature 3
19: 3 because he was small of stature. 3
Eph 4:13 measure of the stature of the fulness of Christ; 3
2Es 2:43 In their midst was a young man of great stature 4
5:52 not like those . . but smaller in stature?' 5
54 your contemporaries are smaller in stature 5

stature *See also* great, grow.

great stature 1. מִדָּה
Num13:32 people that we saw in it are men of great stature. 1
2Sm 21:20 war at Gath, where there was a man of great stature 1
1Ch 11:23 an Egyptian, a man of great stature, five cubits 1
20: 6 at Gath, where there was a man of great stature 1

status 1. *αὐθεντία* 2. *διάθεσις*
3Mc 2:28 subjected . . to the status of slaves 2
29 they shall . . be reduced to their former limited status. 1

statute 1. חֹק 2. חֻקָּה 3. חֻקָּה 4. *δικαίωμα* 5. *πρόσταγμα* 6. constitutio 7. legitimus
Gen 26: 5 Abraham obeyed . . my statutes, and my laws. 3
47:26 Joseph made it a statute concerning the land 1
Exd 15:25 There the LORD made for them a statute 1
26 If you . . keep all his statutes 1
18:16 I make them know the statutes of God 1
20 you shall teach them the statutes 1
27:21 It shall be a statute for ever to be observed 3
28:43 This shall be a perpetual statute for him 3
29: 9 priesthood . . theirs by a perpetual statute. 3
30:21 it shall be a statute for ever to them, even to him 1
Lev 3:17 It shall be a perpetual statute 3
10: 9 statute for ever throughout your generations 3
11 the statutes which the LORD has spoken to them 1
16:29 it shall be a statute to you for ever 3
31 shall afflict yourselves; it is a statute for ever 3
34 this shall be an everlasting statute for you 3
17: 7 This shall be a statute for ever to them 3
18: 3 You shall not walk in their statutes 3
4 You shall do my ordinances and keep my statutes 3
5 You shall therefore keep my statutes 3
26 you shall keep my statutes and my ordinances 3
19:19 You shall keep my statutes 3
37 observe all my statutes and all my ordinances 3
20: 8 Keep my statutes, and do them; I am the LORD 3
22 You shall therefore keep all my statutes 3
23:14 a statute for ever throughout your generations 3
21 it is a statute for ever in all your dwellings 3
31 You shall do no work: it is a statute for ever 3
41 it is a statute for ever throughout 3
24: 3 it shall be a statute for ever 3
25:18 Therefore you shall do my statutes 3
26: 3 walk in my statutes and observe my commandments 3
15 if you spurn my statutes 3
43 and their soul abhorred my statutes 3
46 These are the statutes and ordinances and laws 1
Num 9: 3 according to all its statutes 3
12 according to all the statute for the passover 3
14 according to the statute of the passover 3
14 you shall have one statute 3
10: 8 trumpets shall be to you for a perpetual statute 3
15:15 there shall be one statute for you 3
15 perpetual statute throughout 3
18:23 it shall be a perpetual statute 3
19: 2 statute of the law which the LORD has commanded 3
10 this shall be . . a perpetual statute. 3
21 it shall be a perpetual statute for them. 3
27:11 shall be to . . Israel a statute and ordinance 3
30:16 These are the statutes which the LORD commanded 1
31:21 This is the statute of the law which the LORD 3
35:29 these things shall be for a statute and ordinance 3
Deu 4: 1 give heed to the statutes and the ordinances 1
5 I have taught you statutes and ordinances 1
6 when they hear all these statutes, will say 1
8 that has statutes and ordinances so righteous 1
14 to teach you statutes and ordinances 1
40 shall keep his statutes and his commandments 1
45 testimonies, the statutes, and the ordinances 1
5: 1 Hear, O Israel, the statutes and the ordinances 1
31 tell you all the commandment and the statutes 1
6: 1 commandment, the statutes and the ordinances 1
2 keeping all his statutes and his commandments 3
17 commandments . . and his statutes 1
20 What is the meaning of . . the statutes 1
24 LORD commanded us to do all these statutes 1
7:11 be careful to do . . the statutes 1
8:11 by not keeping . . his statutes, which I command 3
10:13 keep the commandments and statutes of the LORD 3
11: 1 keep his charge, his statutes, his ordinances 3
32 shall be careful to do all the statutes 1
12: 1 These are the statutes and ordinances which you 1
16:12 you shall be careful to observe these statutes. 1
17:19 fear the LORD . . by keeping . . these statutes 1
26:16 you to do these statutes and ordinances; 1
17 keep his statutes and his commandments 1
27:10 keeping his commandments and his statutes 1
28:15 not . . be careful to do all his . . statutes 3
45 to keep his commandments and his statutes 3
30:10 keep his commandments and his statutes 3
16 by keeping his commandments and his statutes 3
Jos 24:25 and made statutes and ordinances for them 1
1Sm 30:25 he made it a statute and an ordinance for Israel 1
2Sm 22:23 and from his statutes I did not turn aside. 3
1Kg 2: 3 keeping his statutes, his commandments 3
3: 3 LORD, walking in the statutes of David his father; 3
14 my ways, keeping my statutes and my commandments 1
6:12 walk in my statutes and obey my ordinances 3
8:58 keep his commandments, his statutes 1
61 true to the LORD . . walking in his statutes 1
9: 4 and keeping my statutes and my ordinances 1
6 do not keep my commandments and my statutes 3
11:11 you have not kept my covenant and my statutes 3
33 and keeping my statutes and my ordinances 3
34 David . . kept my commandments and my statutes; 3
38 do what is right in my eyes by keeping my statutes 3
2Kg 17:13 Turn . . and keep my commandments and my statutes 3
15 They despised his statutes, and his covenant 1
34 follow the statutes or the ordinances or the law 3
37 the statutes and the ordinances and the law 1
23: 3 keep . . and his testimonies and his statutes 3
1Ch 16:17 which he confirmed as a statute to Jacob 1
22:13 to observe the statutes and the ordinances 1
29:19 he may keep . . thy testimonies, and thy statutes 1
2Ch 7:17 and keeping my statutes and my ordinances 1
19 and forsake my statutes and my commandments 3
19:10 concerning . . statutes or ordinance 1
33: 8 all the law, the statutes, and the ordinances 1
34:31 to keep his . . testimonies and his statutes 1
Ezr 7:10 to teach his statutes and ordinances in Israel. 1
11 learned in . . his statutes for Israel 1
Neh 1: 7 have not kept the commandments, the statutes 1
9:13 give them . . good statutes and commandments. 1
14 command them commandments and statutes 1
10:29 observe . . his ordinances and his statutes. 1
Ps 18:22 his statutes I did not put away from me. 3
50:16 What right have you to recite my statutes 1

81: 4 For it is a statute for Israel 1
89:31 if they violate my statutes 3
94:20 wicked rulers . . who frame mischief by statute? 1
99: 7 testimonies, and the statutes that he gave them. 1
105:10 which he confirmed to Jacob as a statute 1
45 to the end that they should keep his statutes 1
119: 5 may be steadfast in keeping thy statutes! 1
8 I will observe thy statutes; O forsake me not 1
12 Blessed be thou, O LORD; teach me thy statutes! 1
16 I will delight in thy statutes; 3
23 thy servant will meditate on thy statutes. 1
26 thou didst answer me; teach me thy statutes! 1
33 Teach me, O LORD, the way of thy statutes; 1
48 I will meditate on thy statutes. 1
54 Thy statutes have been my songs 1
64 teach me thy statutes! 1
68 teach me thy statutes. 1
71 I was afflicted, that I might learn thy statutes. 1
80 May my heart be blameless in thy statutes 1
83 yet I have not forgotten thy statutes. 1
112 I incline my heart to perform thy statutes 1
117 have regard for thy statutes continually! 1
118 dost spurn all who go astray from thy statutes; 1
124 teach me thy statutes. 1
135 teach me thy statutes. 1
145 answer me, O LORD! I will keep thy statutes. 1
155 the wicked, for they do not seek thy statutes. 1
171 praise that thou dost teach me thy statutes. 1
147:19 his statutes and ordinances to Israel. 1
Isa 24: 5 transgressed the laws, violated the statutes 1
Jer 44:10 in my law and my statutes which I set before you 3
23 or walk in his law and in his statutes 3
Ezk 5: 6 and against my statutes more than the countries 3
6 and not walking in my statutes. 3
7 and have not walked in my statutes 3
11:12 for you have not walked in my statutes 3
20 that they may walk in my statutes 3
18: 9 walks in my statutes 3
17 observes my ordinances, and walks in my statutes; 3
19 and has been careful to observe all my statutes 3
21 and keeps all my statutes and does what is lawful 2
20:11 I gave them my statutes 3
13 they did not walk in my statutes 3
16 my ordinances and did not walk in my statutes 3
18 Do not walk in the statutes of your fathers 1
19 I the LORD am your God; walk in my statutes 3
21 they did not walk in my statutes 3
24 but had rejected my statutes 3
25 Moreover I gave them statutes that were not good 1
33:15 and walks in the statutes of life 3
36:27 and cause you to walk in my statutes 1
37:24 and be careful to observe my statutes. 3
44:24 They shall keep my laws and my statutes 3
Ams 2: 4 and have not kept his statutes, but their lies 1
Mic 6:16 For you have kept the statutes of Omri 3
Zec 1: 6 But my words and my statutes, which I commanded 1
Mal 3: 7 you have turned aside from my statutes 1
4: 4 the statutes and ordinances that I commanded 1
2Es 1:24 that they may keep my statutes. 7
7:11 and when Adam transgressed my statutes 6
24 they have been unfaithful to his statutes 7
9:32 did not keep it, and did not observe the statutes; 7
13:42 there at least they might keep their statutes 7
Sir 6:37 Reflect on the statutes of the Lord 5
45:17 gave him authority and statutes and judgments 1
Bar 1:18 statutes of the Lord which he set before us. 5
2:10 to walk in the statutes of the Lord which he set 5
4:13 They had no regard for his statutes 4

staunch 1. *καρτερός*

4Mc 3:12 two staunch young soldiers 1

stave 1. מִשְׁעֶנֶת

Num21:18 delved, with the scepter and with their staves. 1

stay 1. אחר 2. גור 3. יָד 4. ישב 5. לון 6. מַשְׁעֵן 7. מִשְׁעָן 8. סמך 9. עמד 10. עצר 11. רפה 12. שִׁיבָה 13. שִׁית 14. שׁכב 15. שׁכן 16. מחא (A) 17. *αὐλίζομαι* 18. *διαμένω* 19. *διατρίβω* 20. *εἰμί* 21. *ἐνδελεχίζω* 22. *ἐπέχω* 23. *ἐπιμένω* 24. *ἵστημι* 25. *καθίζω* 26. *καταλύω* 27. *καταμένω* 28. *μένω* 29. *παραμένω* 30. *παροικία* 31. *προσμένω* 32. *συναλίζω* 33. consisto 34. sedeo

Gen 22: 5 Then Abraham said to his young men, "Stay here 4
27:44 stay with him a while, until your brother's fury 4
29:14 And he stayed with him a month. 4
19 give her to any other man; stay with me. 4
32: 4 I have sojourned with Laban, and stayed until now 1
45: 1 no one stayed with him when Joseph made 9
Exd 2:15 Moses fled . . and stayed in the land of Mid'ian; 4
9:28 I will let you go, and you shall stay no longer. 9
Num20: 1 people stayed in Kadesh; and Miriam died there 4
22: 8 so the princes of Moab stayed with Balaam. 4
25: 8 plague was stayed from the people of Israel. 10
Deu 1: 6 'You have stayed long enough at this mountain; 4
10:10 I stayed on the mountain, as at the first time 9
Jos 10:13 And the sun stood still, and the moon stayed 9
13 The sun stayed in the midst of heaven 9
19 but do not stay there yourselves, pursue 9
Jdg 5:17 Gilead stayed beyond the Jordan; 15
6:18 And he said, "I will stay till you return. 4
15: 8 he went down and stayed in the cleft of the rock 4
17:10 Stay with me, and be to me a father and a priest 4
1Sm 13:16 Saul, and Jonathan . . stayed in Geba of Benjamin; 4
14: 2 Saul was staying in the outskirts of Gib'e-ah 4
19: 2 take heed . . stay in a secret place and hide 4
20:38 Jonathan called . . "Hurry, make haste, stay not. 9
22: 3 Pray let my father and my mother stay with you ‡
4 they stayed with him all the time that David was 4
23 Stay with me, fear not; for he . . seeks your life; 4
30: 9 Besor, where those stayed who were left behind. 9
24 so shall his share be who stays by the baggage; 4
2Sm 15:19 Go back, and stay with the king; 4
19: 7 not a man will stay with you this night; 5
32 provided . . food while he stayed at Mahana'im 12
22:19 They came upon me . . but the LORD was my stay. 7
24:16 and said . . "It is enough; now stay your hand. 11
1Kg 7:35 its stays and its panels were of one piece with it. 3
36 on the surfaces of its stays . . he carved 3
2Kg 14:10 Be content with your glory, and stay at home; 4
15:20 turned back, and did not stay there in the land. 9
1Ch 21:15 It is enough; now stay your hand. 11
2Ch 25:19 now stay at home; why should you provoke trouble 4
Est 7: 7 Haman stayed to beg his life from Queen Esther 9
Job 24:13 with its ways, and do not stay in its paths. 4
38:11 here shall your proud waves be stayed 13
Ps 18:18 in the day of my calamity; but the LORD was my stay. 7
37:24 for the LORD is the stay of his hand. 8
68:13 though they stay among the sheepfolds- 14
106:30 interposed, and the plague was stayed. 10
Prv 7:11 her feet do not stay at home; 15
Isa 3: 1 stay and staff, the whole stay of bread . . water; 6
1 whole stay of bread, and the whole stay of water; 7
1 whole stay of bread, and the whole stay of water; 7
26: 3 in perfect peace, whose mind is stayed on thee 8
48: 2 and stay themselves on the God of Israel; 8
Jer 4: 6 stay not, for I bring evil from the north 9
21: 9 He who stays in this city shall die by the sword 4
38: 2 He who stays in this city shall die by the sword 4
41:17 and stayed at Geruth Chimham near Bethlehem 4
Lam 4:15 men said . . "They shall stay with us no longer. 2
Dan 4:35 none can stay his hand or say to him, "What doest 16
Mat 10:11 and stay with him until you depart. 28
Mrk 6:10 stay there until you leave the place. 28
Lke 9: 4 whatever house you enter, stay there 28
19: 5 I must stay at your house today. 28
24:29 they constrained him, saying, "Stay with us 28
29 So he went in to stay with them. 28
49 stay in the city, until you are clothed with power 25
Joh 1:38 they said to him, "Rabbi" . . "where are you staying? 28
39 They came and saw where he was staying; 28
39 and they stayed with him that day 28
2:12 and there they stayed for a few days. 28
4:40 they asked him to stay with them; 28
40 and he stayed there two days. 28
11: 6 he stayed two days longer in the place where he was. 28
54 there he stayed with the disciples. 28
Act 1: 4 while staying with them he charged them 32
13 where they were staying 27
9:43 he stayed in Joppa for many days with one Simon 28
13:17 during their stay in the land of Egypt 30
16:15 come to my house and stay. 28
18: 3 he stayed with them, and they worked 28
11 he stayed a year and six months 25
18 After this Paul stayed many days longer 31
20 When they asked him to stay for a longer period 28
19:22 he himself stayed in Asia for a while. 22
20: 6 Tro'as, where we stayed for seven days. 19
21: 4 we stayed there for seven days 23
7 stayed with them for one day. 28
8 we entered the house . . and stayed with him. 28
10 While we were staying for some days 23
25: 6 When he had stayed among them 19
14 as they stayed there many days 19
27:31 Unless these men stay in the ship 28
28:12 we stayed there for three days. 23
14 were invited to stay with them for seven days 23
16 Paul was allowed to stay by himself 28
1Co 16: 6 perhaps I will stay with you 29
8 I will stay in Ephesus until Pentecost 23
1Es 9:12 let the leaders of the multitude stay 24
2Es 10: 4 I intend not to return to the city, but to stay here 33
13:58 And I stayed there three days. 34
Tob 5: 6 I have stayed with our brother Gabael. 17
6:10 Brother, today we shall stay with Raguel 17
10: 8 his father-in-law said to him, "Stay with me 28
Jdt 12: 9 she returned clean and stayed in the tent 29
14:17 Then he went to the tent where Judith had stayed 26
Sir 12:15 He will stay with you for a time 18
27:12 among thoughtful people stay on. 21
1Mc 3:13 a body of faithful men who stayed with him •
11:40 he stayed there many days. 28
12:45 choose for yourself a few men to stay with you 20
2Mc 14:23 Nicanor stayed on in Jerusalem 19
3Mc 7:19 they decided . . during the time of their stay. 30

stay *See also* awake.

stay angry 1. *θυμόω*

Sir 20: 2 better it is to reprove than to stay angry! 1

stay away 1. הלך 2. *ἀφίστημι*

Jer 37: 9 The Chalde'ans will surely stay away from us 1
9 for they will not stay away. 1
Sir 7: 2 Stay away from wrong 2

stay behind 1. עמד 2. *ὑπομένω*

1Sm 30:10 200 stayed behind, who were too exhausted 1
Lke 2:43 the boy Jesus stayed behind in Jerusalem 2

stay but a day 1. *μονοήμερος*

Wis 5:14 the remembrance of a guest who stays but a day 1

come to stay 1. *ἐπιξενόομαι*

Sir 29:27 my brother has come to stay with me; 1

stay constantly 1. *ἐνδελεχίζω*

Sir 37:12 stay constantly with a godly man 1

stay for some time 1. *συγχρονίζω*

Sir 0: 3 came to Egypt . . and stayed for some time 1

make stay 1. חזק

Jdg 19: 4 father-in-law . . made him stay, and he remained 1

stay over night 1. *αὐλίζομαι*

Tob 9: 5 Raphael made the journey and stayed over night 1

stay the night 1. לון

Gen 28:11 came to a . . place, and stayed there that night 1

stead 1. תַּחַת 2. *ἀντί* 3. pro

Gen 36:33 son of Zerah of Bozrah reigned in his stead. 1
34 Husham . . reigned in his stead. 1
35 Hadad the son of Bedad . . reigned in his stead 1
36 Samlah of Masre'kah reigned in his stead. 1
37 Reho'both on the Euphra'tes reigned in his stead 1
38 the son of Achbor reigned in his stead. 1
39 son of Achbor died, and Hadar reigned in his stead 1
Num32:14 behold, you have risen in your fathers' stead 1
Deu 2:12 sons of Esau . . settled in their stead; 1
21 dispossessed them, and settled in their stead; 1
22 settled in their stead even to this day. 1
23 Caph'torim . . settled in their stead.) 1
10: 6 Elea'zar ministered as priest in his stead. 1
Jos 5: 7 their children, whom he raised up in their stead 1
2Sm 10: 1 and Hanun his son reigned in his stead. 1
1Kg 1:30 and he shall sit upon my throne in my stead'; 1
35 sit upon my throne; for he shall be king in my stead; 1
11:43 and Rehobo'am his son reigned in his stead. 1
14:20 and Nadab his son reigned in his stead. 1
27 Rehobo'am made in their stead shields of bronze 1
31 And Abi'jam his son reigned in his stead. 1
15: 8 And Asa his son reigned in his stead. 1
24 and Jehosh'aphat his son reigned in his stead. 1
28 Ba'asha killed him . . and reigned in his stead. 1
16: 6 and Elah his son reigned in his stead. 1
10 and killed him . . and reigned in his stead. 1
28 and Ahab his son reigned in his stead. 1
22:40 Ahazi'ah his son reigned in his stead. 1
50 and Jeho'ram his son reigned in his stead. 1
2Kg 1:17 Jeho'ram, his brother, became king in his stead 1
3:27 took his eldest son who was to reign in his stead 1
8:15 And Haz'ael became king in his stead. 1
24 and Ahazi'ah his son reigned in his stead. 1
10:35 And Jeho'ahaz his son reigned in his stead. 1
12:21 and Amazi'ah his son reigned in his stead. 1
13: 9 and Jo'ash his son reigned in his stead. 1
24 Ben-ha'dad his son became king in his stead. 1
14:16 and Jerobo'am his son reigned in his stead. 1
29 and Zechari'ah his son reigned in his stead. 1
15: 7 and Jotham his son reigned in his stead. 1
10 and killed him, and reigned in his stead. 1
14 struck down Shallum . . and reigned in his stead. 1
22 and Pekahi'ah his son reigned in his stead. 1
25 Pekah . . he slew him, and reigned in his stead. 1
30 struck . . and slew him, and reigned in his stead 1
38 and Ahaz his son reigned in his stead. 1
16:20 and Hezeki'ah his son reigned in his stead. 1
19:37 Esarhad'don his son reigned in his stead. 1
20:21 Manas'seh his son reigned in his stead. 1
21:18 and Amon his son reigned in his stead. 1
24 people . . made Josi'ah his son king in his stead. 1
26 and Josi'ah his son reigned in his stead. 1
23:30 and made him king in his father's stead. 1
24: 6 and Jehoi'achin his son reigned in his stead. 1
17 Mattani'ah, Jehoi'achin's uncle, king in his stead 1
1Ch 1:44 son of Zerah of Bozrah reigned in his stead. 1
45 Husham . . reigned in his stead. 1
46 Hadad the son of Bedad . . reigned in his stead 1
47 Samlah of Masre'kah reigned in his stead. 1
48 Sha'ul of Reho'both . . reigned in his stead. 1
49 Ba'al-ha'nan, the son of Achbor, reigned in his stead 1
50 When Ba'al-ha'nan died, Hadad reigned in his stead; 1
19: 1 Nahash . . died, and his son reigned in his stead. 1
29:28 and Solomon his son reigned in his stead. 1

2Ch 1: 8 Thou . . hast made me king in his stead. 1
9:31 Rehobo'am his son reigned in his stead. 1
12:10 Rehobo'am made in their stead shields of bronze 1
16 Abi'jah his son reigned in his stead. 1
14: 1 Asa his son reigned in his stead. 1
17: 1 Jehosh'aphat his son reigned in his stead 1
21: 1 Jeho'ram his son reigned in his stead. 1
22: 1 made Ahazi'ah his youngest son king in his stead; 1
24:27 And Amazi'ah his son reigned in his stead. 1
26:23 Jotham his son reigned in his stead. 1
27: 9 Ahaz his son reigned in his stead. 1
28:27 And Hezeki'ah his son reigned in his stead. 1
32:33 Manas'seh his son reigned in his stead. 1
33:20 Amon his son reigned in his stead. 1
25 made Josi'ah his son king in his stead. 1
36: 1 made him king in his father's stead in Jerusalem. 1
8 Jehoi'achin his son reigned in his stead. 1
Isa 37:38 E'sar-had'don his son reigned in his stead. 1
1Es 1:43 Jehoiachin his son became king in his stead 2
2Es 7:104 to be ill or sleep or eat or be healed in his stead 3

steadfast 1. חזק 2. כון 3. כֵּן 4. βέβαιος 5. ἑδραῖος 6. εὐσταθής 7. καρτερέω 8. κρατέω 9. πρόθεσις 10. στηρίζω 11. ὑπομένω

Jos 23: 6 be very steadfast to keep . . all that is written 1
Ps 57: 7 My heart is steadfast, O God, my heart is steadfast! 2
7 My heart is steadfast, O God, my heart is steadfast! 2
78: 8 a generation whose heart was not steadfast 2
37 Their heart was not steadfast toward him; 2
108: 1 My heart is steadfast, O God, my heart is steadfast! 2
1 My heart is steadfast, O God, my heart is steadfast! 2
119: 5 O that my ways may be steadfast 2
Prv 11:19 He who is steadfast in righteousness will live 3
Act 11:23 remain faithful . . with steadfast purpose; 9
1Co 15:58 my beloved brethren, be steadfast, immovable 5
Col 1:23 you continue in the faith, stable and steadfast 5
Heb 6:19 as a sure and steadfast anchor of the soul 4
Jas 5:11 Behold, we call those happy who were steadfast. 11
AEs 13: 3 unchanging good will and steadfast fidelity 4
Wis 7:23 beneficent, humane, steadfast, sure 4
Sir 2: 2 Set your heart right and be steadfast 7
5:10 Be steadfast in your understanding 10
26:18 so are beautiful feet with a steadfast heart. 6
27: 3 If a man is not steadfast and zealous 8

steadfast *See also* love.

steadfastly 1. βαρύς

4Mc 9:28 he steadfastly endured this agony and said 1

steadfastly *See also* continue, follow.

steadfastness 1. καρτερία 2. ὑπομονή

Rom 15: 4 that by steadfastness and by the encouragement 2
5 May the God of steadfastness and encouragement 2
1Th 1: 3 steadfastness of hope in our Lord Jesus Christ. 2
2Th 1: 4 your steadfastness and faith 2
3: 5 to the steadfastness of Christ. 2
1Ti 6:11 faith, love, steadfastness, gentleness. 2
2Ti 3:10 my patience, my love, my steadfastness 2
Tit 2: 2 sound in faith, in love, and in steadfastness. 2
Jas 1: 3 testing of your faith produces steadfastness. 2
4 let steadfastness have its full effect 2
5:11 You have heard of the steadfastness of Job 2
2Pe 1: 6 and self-control with steadfastness 2
6 and steadfastness with godliness 2
4Mc 15:30 O more noble than males in steadfastness 1
16:14 By steadfastness you have conquered 1

steadily 1. ἀσφαλῶς 2. constanter

2Ch 17:12 Jehosh'aphat grew steadily greater. †
2Es 15:43 they shall go on steadily to Babylon 2
1Mc 6:40 they advanced steadily and in good order. 1

steady 1. אֱמוּנָה 2. סמך 3. νήφω 4. στηρίζω

Exd 17:12 so his hands were steady until the going down 1
Ps 112: 8 His heart is steady, he will not be afraid 2
2Ti 4: 5 As for you, always be steady, endure suffering 3
Sir 13:21 When a rich man totters, he is steadied by friends 4

steady *See also* keep.

steal 1. גזל 2. גנב 3. διαφέρω 4. κλέπτω 5. κλεψιμαῖος 6. νοσφίζω

Gen 31:19 and Rachel stole her father's household gods. 2
30 father's house, but why did you steal my gods? 2
32 Jacob did not know that Rachel had stolen them. 2
39 whether stolen by day or stolen by night. 2
39 whether stolen by day or stolen by night. 2
40:15 For I was indeed stolen out of the land 2
44: 4 Why have you stolen my silver cup? 4
8 how then should we steal silver or gold 2
Exd 20:15 You shall not steal. 2
21:16 Whoever steals a man, whether he sells him or is 2
22: 1 If a man steals an ox or a sheep, and kills it 2
7 If . . it is stolen out of the man's house 2
12 if it is stolen from him, he shall make 2
Lev 19:11 You shall not steal, nor deal falsely 2
Deu 5:19 'Neither shall you steal. 2
24: 7 If a man is found stealing one of his brethren 2
Jos 7:11 they have stolen, and lied, and put them among 2
2Sm 15: 6 so Ab'salom stole the hearts of the men of Israel. 2
19: 3 And the people stole into the city that day 2
3 as people steal in who are ashamed when they flee 2
21:12 from the men of Ja'besh-gil'ead, who had stolen them 2
2Kg 11: 2 and stole him away from among the king's sons 2
Ps 69: 4 What I did not steal must I now restore? 1
Prv 6:30 if he steals to satisfy his appetite 2
9:17 Stolen water is sweet 2
30: 9 I be poor, and steal, and profane the name of my God. 2
Jer 7: 9 Will you steal, murder, commit adultery 2
23:30 prophets . . who steal my words from one another. 2
Hos 4: 2 there is swearing, lying, killing, stealing 2
Obd 1: 5 would they not steal only enough for themselves? 2
Zec 5: 3 every one who steals shall be cut off henceforth 2
Mat 6:19 consume and where thieves break in and steal 4
20 where thieves do not break in and steal. 4
19:18 You shall not steal 4
Mrk 10:19 Do not steal, Do not bear false witness 4
Lke 18:20 Do not commit adultery, Do not kill, Do not steal 4
Joh 10:10 thief comes only to steal and kill and destroy 4
Rom 2:21 While you preach against stealing, do you steal? 4
21 While you preach against stealing, do you steal? 4
13: 9 You shall not kill, You shall not steal 4
Eph 4:28 Let the thief no longer steal 4
1Es 4:23 goes out to travel and rob and steal 4
24 when he steals and robs and plunders 4
Tob 2:13 It is not stolen, is it? 5
13 for it is not right to eat what is stolen. 5
2Mc 4:32 Menelaus . . stole some of the gold vessels of the temple 6
39 many of the gold vessels had already been stolen. 3

steal away 1. גנב 2. κλέπτω

2Sm 19:41 Why have . . the men of Judah stolen you away 1
2Ch 22:11 took Jo'ash . . and stole him away from among 1
Mat 27:64 lest his disciples go and steal him away 2
28:13 and stole him away while we were asleep 2

stealth 1. δόλος

Mat 26: 4 in order to arrest Jesus by stealth and kill him. 1
Mrk 14: 1 how to arrest him by stealth, and kill him; 1

stealthily 1. בַּלָּט

1Sm 24: 4 David arose and stealthily cut off the skirt 1

stealthily *See also* bring, watch.

steed 1. אַבִּיר 2. אַמֹּץ 3. סוּס 4. רֶכֶשׁ

Jdg 5:22 hoofs with the . . galloping of his steeds. 1
Isa 30:16 We will ride upon swift steeds •
Mic 1:13 Harness the steeds to the chariots 4
Zec 6: 7 When the steeds came out, they were impatient 2
10: 3 will make them like his proud steed in battle. 3

swift steed 1. רֶכֶשׁ

1Kg 4:28 and swift steeds they brought to the place where 1

steel

Sir 31:26 Fire and water prove the temper of steel •

steep 1. בַּתָּה 2. ἀπορρώξ

Isa 7:19 settle in the steep ravines, and in the clefts 1
2Mc 14:45 standing upon a steep rock 2

steep *See also* bank.

steep place 1. מוֹרָד

Mic 1: 4 like waters poured down a steep place. 1

steer 1. διακυβερνάω 2. κυβερνάω 3. πηδαλιουχέω

Wis 10: 4 steering the righteous man by a . . piece of wood 2
14: 3 thy providence, O Father, that steers its course 1
4Mc 7: 1 steered the ship of religion over the sea 3

young steer 1. פַּר

Isa 34: 7 and young steers with the mighty bulls. 1

stem 1. גֶּזַע 2. מַטֶּה

Isa 40:24 scarcely has their stem taken root in the earth 1
Ezk 19:11 Its strongest stem became a ruler's scepter; 2
12 its strong stem was withered; the fire consumed 2
14 And fire has gone out from its stem, has consumed 2
14 so that there remains in it no strong stem 2

stench 1. בְּאֹשׁ 2. ὀσμή

Isa 34: 3 and the stench of their corpses shall rise; 1
Jol 2:20 the stench and foul smell of him will rise 1
Ams 4:10 I made the stench of your camp go up 1
2Mc 9: 9 because of his stench 2
10 Because of his intolerable stench 2
12 when he could not endure his own stench 2

step 1. אָשׁוּר 2. אשׁר 3. הָלִיךְ 4. מִצְעָד 5. עָקֵב 6. פַּעַם 7. פֶּשַׂע 8. צַעַד 9. רֶגֶל 10. βάσις 11. ἴχνος

Deu 33: 3 they followed in thy steps, receiving direction 9
1Sm 20: 3 there is but a step between me and death. 7
2Sm 22:37 Thou didst give a wide place for my steps under me 8
Job 14:16 For then thou wouldest number my steps 8
18: 7 His strong steps are shortened 8
23:11 My foot has held fast to his steps; 1
29: 6 when my steps were washed with milk 3
31: 4 Does not he see my ways, and number all my steps? 8
7 if my step has turned aside from the way 2
37 I would give him an account of all my steps; 8
34:21 upon the ways of a man, and he sees all his steps. 8
Ps 17: 5 My steps have held fast to thy paths 1
18:36 Thou didst give a wide place for my steps under me 8
37:23 The steps of a man are from the LORD 4
31 God is in his heart; his steps do not slip. 1
40: 2 set my feet upon a rock, making my steps secure. 1
44:18 nor have our steps departed from thy way 1
56: 6 together, they lurk, they watch my steps. 5
57: 6 They set a net for my steps; my soul was bowed down. 6
73: 2 my steps had well nigh slipped. 1
74: 3 Direct thy steps to the perpetual ruins; 6
119:133 Keep steady my steps according to thy promise 6
Prv 4:12 When you walk, your step will not be hampered; 8
5: 5 her steps follow the path to Sheol; 8
16: 9 but the LORD directs his steps. 8
20:24 A man's steps are ordered by the LORD; 4
Ecc 5: 1 Guard your steps when you go to the house of God; 9
Isa 26: 6 the feet of the poor, the steps of the needy. 6
41: 2 from the east whom victory meets at every step? 9
Jer 10:23 it is not in man who walks to direct his steps. 8
Lam 4:18 Men dogged our steps so that we could not walk 8
Hab 3:16 my steps totter beneath me. •
2Co 12:18 Did we not take the same steps? 11
1Pe 2:21 an example, that you should follow in his steps. 11
Wis 13:18 a thing that cannot take a step; 10
Sir 21: 6 walks in the steps of the sinner 11

step (2) 1. מַעֲלָה 2. ἀναβαθμός 3. ἀνάβασις 4. κρηπίς

Exd 20:26 you shall not go up by steps to my altar 1
1Kg 10:19 The throne had six steps 1
20 twelve lions stood there, one on each end of a step 1
20 one on each end of a step on the six steps. 1
2Kg 9:13 his garment, and put it under him on the bare steps 1
20: 9 shall the shadow go forward ten steps, or go back 1
9 shall the shadow go . . or go back ten steps? 1
10 easy thing for the shadow to lengthen ten steps; 1
10 rather let the shadow go back ten steps. 1
11 the LORD, and he brought the shadow back ten steps 1
2Ch 9:11 algum wood steps for the house of the LORD 3
18 The throne had six steps and a footstool of gold 1
19 one on each end of a step on the six steps. •
19 one on each end of a step on the six steps. 1
Isa 38: 8 make the shadow . . turn back ten steps. 1
8 back . . the ten steps by which it had declined. 1
Ezk 40: 6 into the gateway facing east, going up its steps 1
22 seven steps led up to it; 1
26 there were seven steps leading up to it 1
31 its stairway had eight steps. 1
34 and its stairway had eight steps. 1
37 its stairway had eight steps. 1
49 breadth twelve cubits; and ten steps led up to it; 1
43:17 The steps of the altar shall face east. 1
Act 21:35 when he came to the steps 2
40 Paul, standing on the steps 2
2Mc 10:26 Falling upon the steps before the altar 4

step *See* direct.

step down 1. ירד 2. καταβαίνω

Ezk 26:16 Then all the princes of the sea will step down 1
Joh 5: 7 while I am going another steps down before me. 2

step out 1. ἐξέρχομαι

Lke 8:27 And as he stepped out on land 1

steppe 1. מִדְבָּר 2. עֲרָבָה

1Ch 6:78 Bezer in the steppe with its pasture lands 1
Job 39: 6 to whom I have given the steppe for his home 2

steps *See* follow.

stern 1. עַז 2. קָשֶׁה 3. ἀπότομος

Deu 28:50 nation of stern countenance, who shall not 1
Isa 21: 2 A stern vision is told to me; 2
Wis 5:20 sharpen stern wrath for a sword 3
11:10 as a stern king does in condemnation. 3
12: 9 dread wild beasts or thy stern word. 3
18:15 a stern warrior 3

stern (2) 1. πρύμνα

Mrk 4:38 he was in the stern, asleep on the cushion 1
Act 27:29 they let out four anchors from the stern 1
41 the stern was broken up by the surf. 1

sternly 1. ἐμβριμάομαι

Mat 9:30 And Jesus sternly charged them 1

sternly *See also* charge.

steward 1. אִישׁ אֲשֶׁר עַל 2. אֲשֶׁר עַל 3. מֶלְצַר 4. סכן 5. שַׂר 6. ἐπίτροπος 7. οἰκονομέω 8. οἰκονόμος

Gen 43:16 When Joseph saw . . he said to the steward 2
19 they went up to the steward of Joseph's house 1
44: 1 Then he commanded the steward of his house 2
4 Joseph said to his steward, "Up, follow after 2

1Ch 27:31 these were stewards of King David's property. 5
28: 1 the stewards of all the property and cattle 5
Isa 22:15 Come, go to this steward, to Shebna 4
Dan 1:11 said to the steward whom the chief of the eunuchs 3
16 steward took away their rich food and the wine 3
Mat 20: 8 the owner of the vineyard said to his steward 6
Lke 8: 3 Joan'na, the wife of Chuza, Herod's steward 6
12:42 Who then is the faithful and wise steward 8
16: 1 There was a rich man who had a steward 8
2 you can no longer be steward.' 7
3 the steward said to himself, 'What shall I do 8
8 The master commended the dishonest steward 8
1Co 4: 1 stewards of the mysteries of God. 8
2 Moreover it is required of stewards 8
Tit 1: 7 For a bishop, as God's steward, must be blameless 8
1Pe 4:10 as good stewards of God's varied grace 8
1Es 8:67 to the royal stewards and to the governors 8
Jdt 14:13 the steward in charge of all his personal affairs •

steward of the feast 1. ἀρχιτρίκλινος
Joh 2: 8 and take it to the steward of the feast. 1
9 When the steward of the feast tasted the water 1
9 the steward of the feast called the bridegroom 1

stewardship 1. οἰκονομία
Lke 16: 2 Turn in the account of your stewardship 1
3 my master is taking the stewardship away from me? 1
4 when I am put out of the stewardship.' 1
Eph 3: 2 the stewardship of God's grace that was given to me 1

stick 1. יָתֵד 2. מַטֶּה 3. מַקֵּל 4. עֵץ 5. ξύλον 6. ῥάβδος 7. φρύγανον
Num15:32 found a man gathering sticks on the sabbath day. 4
33 those who found him gathering sticks 4
Deu 23:13 you shall have a stick with your weapons; 1
1Sm 17:43 Am I a dog, that you come to me with sticks? 3
1Kg 17:10 a widow was there gathering sticks; 4
12 I am gathering a couple of sticks, that I may go 4
2Kg 6: 6 he cut off a stick, and threw it in there 4
Isa 28:27 but dill is beaten out with a stick 2
Ezk 37:16 Son of man, take a stick and write on it, 'For Judah 4
16 then take another stick and write upon it 4
16 For Joseph (the stick of E'phraim) and all the house 4
17 join them together into one stick 4
19 Behold, I am about to take the stick of Joseph 4
19 I will join with it the stick of Judah 4
19 with it the stick of Judah, and make them one stick 4
20 When the sticks on which you write 4
Act 28: 3 Paul had gathered a bundle of sticks 7
Wis 13:13 a stick crooked and full of knots 5
Sir 33:24 Fodder and a stick and burdens for an ass 6

stick (2) 1. דבק 2. מעך 3. ἐρείδω 4. πήγνυμι
1Sm 26: 7 with his spear stuck in the ground at his head; 2
Ezk 29: 4 fish of your streams which stick to your scales. 1
Act 27:41 the bow stuck and remained immovable 3
Sir 19:12 Like an arrow stuck in the flesh of the thigh 4

stick close 1. דָּבֵק
Prv 18:24 friend who sticks closer than a brother. 1

make stick 1. דבק
Ezk 29: 4 and make the fish of your streams stick 1

stick out 1. שׂפה
Job 33:21 his bones which were not seen stick out. 1

stiff 1. קָשֶׁה
Exd 32: 9 and behold, it is a stiff-necked people; 1
33: 3 for you are a stiff-necked people. 1
5 You are a stiff-necked people; if for a single 1
34: 9 although it is a stiff-necked people; 1
stiff *See also* make.

stiff-necked 1. קשה ערף 2. σκληροτράχηλος
2Ch 30: 8 Do not now be stiff-necked as your fathers were 1
Act 7:51 You stiff-necked people 2
Bar 2:30 for they are a stiff-necked people. 2

stiff-necked person 1. σκληροτράχηλος
Sir 16:11 Even if there is only one stiff-necked person 1

stiffen 1. קשה 2. σκληρύνω
2Ch 36:13 stiffened his neck and hardened his heart 1
Neh 9:16 stiffened their neck and did not obey 1
17 stiffened their neck and appointed a leader 1
29 stubborn shoulder and stiffened their neck 1
Prv 29: 1 He who is often reproved, yet stiffens his neck 1
Jer 7:26 or incline their ear, but stiffened their neck. 1
17:23 or incline their ear, but stiffened their neck 1
19:15 because they have stiffened their neck 1
1Es 1:48 he stiffened his neck and hardened his heart 2

still 1. אַךְ 2. גַּם 3. עַד 4. עַד הֵנָּה 5. עֲדֶנָה 6. עוֹד 7. עמד 8. עוֹד (A) 9. ἀκμήν 10. ἐπί 11. ἔτι 12. ἕως ἄρτι 13. καί 14. λοιπός 15. μένω 16. μετὰ ταῦτα 17. adhuc 18. multo 19. usque
Gen 8: 9 the waters were still on the face •
12: 9 still going toward the Negeb. †
18:22 Sodom; but Abraham still stood before the LORD. 6
25: 6 and while he was still living he sent them away 6
29: 7 He said, "Behold, it is still high day 6
9 While he was still speaking with them 6
35:16 and when they were still some distance 6
41:21 for they were still as gaunt as at the beginning. •
43: 7 Is your father still alive? 6
27 Is your father well . . Is he still alive? 6
28 our father is well, he is still alive. 6
44:14 came to Joseph's house, he was still there; 6
45: 3 I am Joseph; is my father still alive? 6
26 they told him, "Joseph is still alive 6
28 It is enough; Joseph my son is still alive; 6
46:30 seen your face and know that you are still alive. 6
48: 7 there was still some distance to go to Ephrath; 6
Exd 4:18 Let me . . see whether they are still alive. 6
9: 2 refuse to let them go and still hold them 6
17 You are still exalting yourself against my 6
36: 3 They still kept bringing him freewill 6
Lev 25:51 If there are still many years, according to them 6
Num 9:10 he shall still keep the passover to the LORD. •
19:13 unclean; his uncleanness is still on him. 6
Deu 4:33 hear the voice of a god speaking . . and still live? •
5:24 day seen God speak with man and man still live. •
26 heard the voice . . as we have, and has still lived? •
Jos 9:12 it was still warm when we took it from our houses •
14:11 I am still as strong to this day as . . the day that 6
Jdg 3:25 still did not open the doors of the roof chamber •
6:24 To this day it still stands at Ophrah 6
7: 4 LORD said to Gideon, "The people are still too many; 6
8:20 for he was afraid, because he was still a youth. 6
1Sm 12:25 if you still do wickedly, you shall be swept away •
13: 7 Saul was still at Gilgal, and all the people 6
18:29 Saul was still more afraid of David. 6
20:14 If I am still alive, show me the . . love of the LORD 6
2Sm 1: 9 and yet my life still lingers.' 6
9: 1 Is there still any one left of the house of Saul 6
3 Is there not still some one of the house of Saul 6
3 There is still a son of Jonathan; he is crippled 6
12:22 While the child was still alive, I fasted and wept; 6
14:32 It would be better for me to be there still. 6
18:14 of Ab'salom, while he was still alive in the oak. 6
19:34 How many years have I still to live •
35 Can I still listen to the voice of singing men 6
24: 3 while the eyes of my lord the king still see it; •
1Kg 1:14 while you are still speaking with the king, I also 6
22 While she was still speaking with the king 6
42 While he was still speaking, behold, Jonathan 6
12: 2 he was still in Egypt, whither he had fled 6
20:32 And he said, "Does he still live? He is my brother. 6
22:43 the people still sacrificed and burned incense 6
2Kg 2:11 as they still went on and talked, behold, a chariot †
6:33 while he was still speaking . . the king came down 6
14: 4 the people still sacrificed and burned incense 6
15: 4 the people still sacrificed and burned incense 6
35 the people still sacrificed and burned incense 6
17:29 But every nation still made gods of its own •
23:26 Still the LORD did not turn from . . great wrath 1
2Ch 14: 7 the land is still ours 6
27: 2 the people still followed corrupt practices. 6
33:17 people still sacrificed at the high places 6
Neh 7: 3 still standing guard let them shut and bar •
Job 2: 3 He still holds fast his integrity 6
9 Do you still hold fast your integrity? 6
Ps 69:26 whom thou hast wounded, they afflict still more. †
71:17 I still proclaim thy wondrous deeds. 4
78:17 Yet they sinned still more against him 6
30 while the food was still in their mouths 6
32 In spite of all this they still sinned; 6
92:14 They still bring forth fruit in old age 6
139:18 When I awake, I am still with thee. 6
Prv 9: 9 instruction to a wise man . . will be still wiser; 6
Ecc 2: 3 my mind still guiding me with wisdom •
4: 2 more . . than the living who are still alive; 5
Isa 1: 5 Why will you still be smitten, that you continue 6
5:25 turned away and his hand is stretched out still. 6
9:12 For all this . . his hand is stretched out still. 6
17 turned away and his hand is stretched out still. 6
20 They snatch on the right, but are still hungry •
21 turned away and his hand is stretched out still. 6
10: 4 turned away and his hand is stretched out still. 6
Jer 2: 9 Therefore I still contend with you, says the LORD 6
22 the stain of your guilt is still before me •
31:20 I speak against him, I do remember him still. 6
33: 1 while he was still shut up in the court of the guard 6
37: 4 was still going in and out among the people •
Ezk 8: 6 you will see still greater abominations. 6
13 You will see still greater abominations 6
15 You will see still greater abominations 6
16:28 and still you were not satisfied. 2
24: 7 the blood she has shed is still in the midst of her; •
28: 9 Will you still say, 'I am a god,' †
Dan 4:31 While the words were still in the king's mouth 8
Hos 11:12 but Judah is still known by God, and is faithful 6
Ams 6:10 in . . the house, "Is there still any one with you? 6
Hab 2: 3 For still the vision awaits its time; 6
Hag 2:19 and the olive tree still yield nothing? 3
Zec 12: 6 Jerusalem shall still be inhabited in its place 6
14:12 flesh . . rot while they are still on their feet 7
Mat 12:46 While he was still speaking to the people 11
15:16 Are you also still without understanding? 9
17: 5 He was still speaking, when lo, a bright cloud 11
19:20 what do I still lack? 11
26:45 Are you still sleeping and taking your rest? 14
47 While he was still speaking, Judas came 11
65 Why do we still need witnesses? 11
27:63 how that impostor said, while he was still alive 11
Mrk 5:35 While he was still speaking 11
12: 6 He had still one other, a beloved son 11
14:41 Are you still sleeping and taking your rest? 14
43 while he was still speaking, Judas came 11
63 Why do we still need witnesses? 11
Lke 8:49 While he was still speaking 11
14:22 still there is room.' 11
18:22 One thing you still lack 11
22:47 While he was still speaking, there came a crowd 11
59 still another insisted, saying, "Certainly •
60 immediately, while he was still speaking 11
24: 6 while he was still in Galilee 11
41 while they still disbelieved for joy 11
44 while I was still with you 11
Joh 5:17 Jesus answered them, "My Father is working still 12
11:30 still in the place where Martha had met him. 11
14:25 while I am still with you. 15
20: 1 early, while it was still dark 11
Act 9: 1 Saul, still breathing threats and murder 11
10:44 While Peter was still saying this 11
20: 9 as Paul talked still longer 10
Rom 3: 7 why am I still being condemned as a sinner? 11
4:11 had by faith while he was still uncircumcised. •
5: 6 While we were still weak . . Christ died 11
6: 2 How can we who died to sin still live in it? 11
9:19 Why does he still find fault? 11
1Co 3: 3 for you are still of the flesh 11
9:12 do not we still more •
12:31 I will show you a still more excellent way. 11
15: 6 most of whom are still alive 12
17 you are still in your sins. 11
2Co 5: 4 while we are still in this tent •
7: 7 so that I rejoiced still more. •
Gal 1:10 If I were still pleasing men 11
22 I was still not known by sight •
5:11 if I, brethren, still preach circumcision 11
11 why am I still persecuted 11
2Th 2: 5 when I was still with you I told you this? 11
Heb 6:10 in serving the saints, as you still do. •
7:10 for he was still in the loins of his ancestor 11
9: 8 as long as the outer tent is still standing 11
11: 4 through his faith he is still speaking. 11
1Jn 2: 9 and hates his brother is in the darkness still. 12
Rev 3: 4 Yet you have still a few names in Sardis •
9:12 behold, two woes are still to come. 16
22:11 Let the evildoer still do evil 11
11 Let . . the filthy still be filthy 11
11 Let . . the righteous still do right 11
11 Let . . the holy still be holy. 11
2Es 1:16 but to this day you still complain. 19
5:50 Is our mother . . still young? 17
9:11 scorned my law while they still had freedom 17
11 an opportunity of repentance was still open 17
10: 5 the reflections with which I was still engaged 17
32 and behold, I saw, and still see •
12: 5 Behold, I am still weary in mind 17
13:16 And still more, alas for those who are not left! 18
Tob 1: 4 in the land of Israel, while I was still a young man •
Jdt 13:11 God, our God, is still with us, to show his power 11
Wis 10: 7 Evidence of their wickedness still remains 11
16:17 the fire had still greater effect •
17:21 still heavier than darkness •
19: 3 while they were still busy at mourning 11
4 which their torments still lacked •
10 they still recalled the events of their sojourn 11
Sir 33:20 While you are still alive and have breath in you 11
41: 1 still has the vigor to enjoy his food! 11
51:13 While I was still young 11
1Mc 1: 6 while he was still alive. 11
4: 4 the division was still absent from the camp. 11
5:14 While the letter was still being read 11
6:27 they will do still greater things •
55 King Antiochus while still living 11
10:27 now continue still to keep faith with us 11
88 he honored Jonathan still more; 11
2Mc 7: 5 to take him to the fire, still breathing •
24 The youngest brother being still alive 11
30 While she was still speaking, the young man said 11
9: 9 while he was still living in anguish and pain •
11: 8 while they were still near Jerusalem •
14:45 Still alive and aflame with anger, he rose 11
3Mc 3: 1 but was still more bitterly hostile toward those 13
4:18 although most of them were still in the country 11
18 some still residing in their homes 11
5:19 while it was still night 11
4Mc 18:10 While he was still with you 11

still (2) 1. אבר 2. דמם 3. דְּמָמָה 4. חרש 5. חשה 6. מְנוּחָה 7. ענה 8. רגע 9. רפה 10. שבח 11. שבת 12. שׁקט 13. κοπάζω 14. σιγάω 15. φιμόω

Exd 14:14 you have only to be still. 4
15:16 they are as still as a stone, till thy people 2
1Kg 19:12 and after the fire a still small voice. 3
Neh 8:11 Levites stilled all the people, saying, "Be quiet 5
Job 4:16 It stood still, but I could not discern its •
26:12 By his power he stilled the sea; 8
30:27 My heart is in turmoil, and is never still; 2
37:17 when the earth is still because of the south wind? 12
Ps 8: 2 a bulwark . . to still the enemy and the avenger. 11
23: 2 He leads me beside still waters; 6
37: 7 Be still before the LORD, and wait patiently 2
46:10 Be still, and know that I am God. 9
65: 7 who dost still the roaring of the seas 10
76: 8 the earth feared and was still 12
83: 1 do not hold thy peace or be still, O God! 12
89: 9 when its waves rise, thou stillest them. 10
107:29 he made the storm be still 3
Isa 23: 2 Be still, O inhabitants of the coast 2
24: 8 The mirth of the timbrels is stilled 11
8 has ceased, the mirth of the lyre is stilled. 11
25: 5 the song of the ruthless is stilled. 7
30: 7 therefore I have called her "Rahab who sits still. •
Jer 47: 6 Put yourself into your scabbard, rest and be still! 2
51:50 escaped from the sword, go, stand not still! •
55 laying . . waste, and stilling her mighty voice. 1
Ezk 1:24 when they stood still, they let down their wings. •
25 when they stood still, they let down their wings. •
10:17 When they stood still, these stood still •
17 When they stood still, these stood still •
Hab 3:11 The sun and moon stood still in their habitation •
Mrk 4:39 said to the sea, "Peace! Be still!" And the wind ceased 15
Lke 7:14 touched the bier, and the bearers stood still •
24:17 they stood still, looking sad. •
Tob 10: 6 Be still and stop worrying; he is well. 14
7 she answered him, "Be still and stop deceiving me; 14
Sir 43:23 By his counsel he stilled the great deep 13
46: 7 stilled their wicked murmuring. 13

still *See* belong, keep, lie, sit, stand, stronger.

still less 1. אַף כִּי

Prv 17: 7 still less is false speech to a prince. 1

still more 1. עוֹד 2. יָתִיר (A) 3. περισσοτέρως 4. περισσοτέρως μᾶλλον

Num32:14 increase still more the fierce anger of the LORD 1
2Ch 32:16 servants said still more against the Lord GOD 1
Dan 4:36 still more greatness was added to me. 2
2Co 1:12 and still more toward you 3
7:13 we rejoiced still more at the joy of Titus 4

sting 1. פרשׁ 2. κατανύσσομαι 3. κέντρον 4. παίω 5. πλήσσω

Prv 23:32 At the last it . . stings like an adder. 1
1Co 15:55 O death, where is thy sting? 3
56 The sting of death is sin 3
Rev 9: 5 the torture of a scorpion, when it stings a man. 4
10 They have tails like scorpions, and stings 3
Sir 12:12 be stung by what I have said. 2
4Mc 14:19 sting those who approach their hive 5

stingy 1. רַע עַיִן 2. μικρολόγος

Prv 23: 6 Do not eat the bread of a man who is stingy; 1
Sir 14: 3 Riches are not seemly for a stingy man 2

stingy man 1. πονηρός

Sir 14:10 A stingy man's eye begrudges bread 1

stink 1. באשׁ 2. δυσώδης

Exd 8:14 and the land stank. 1
Isa 50: 2 fish stink for lack of water, and die of thirst. 1
4Mc 6:25 poured stinking liquids into his nostrils. 2

stint 1. σμικρύνω

Sir 35: 8 do not stint the first fruits of your hands. 1

stir 1. הום 2. נשׂא 3. עור 4. פעם 5. ἀγείρω 6. σείω 7. ταράσσω 8. τάραχος 9. τρομέω

Exd 35:21 they came, every one whose heart stirred him 2
Jdg 13:25 Spirit . . began to stir him in Ma'haneh-dan 4
Rut 1:19 the whole town was stirred because of them; 1
Ezr 1: 5 every one whose spirit God had stirred to go up 3
Jer 6:22 a great nation is stirring 3
25:32 and a great tempest is stirring 3
50:41 many kings are stirring from the farthest parts 3
Hos 7: 4 a heated oven, whose baker ceases to stir the fire 3
Mat 21:10 all the city was stirred, saying 6
Act 12:18 there was no small stir among the soldiers 8
19:23 there arose no little stir concerning the Way. 8
1Es 2: 8 all whose spirit the Lord had stirred 5
9 from many whose hearts were stirred. 5
Sir 51:21 My heart was stirred to seek her 7
1Mc 2:24 burned with zeal and his heart was stirred 9

stir to jealousy 1. קנא

Deu 32:16 They stirred him to jealousy with strange gods; 1
21 have stirred me to jealousy with what is no god; 1
21 So I will stir them to jealousy with . . no people; 1

stir up 1. גור 2. גרה 3. נשׂא 4. סות 5. עור 6. עלה 7. צור 8. קום 9. רגז 10. רגע 11. שׂכך 12. גוח (A) 13. עבר (A) 14. ἀγείρω 15. ἀνασείω 16. ἐπεγείρω 17. ἐπίστασιν ποιέω 18. ἐρεθίζω 19. παροξυσμός 20. σαλεύω 21. συγκινέω 22. συγχέω 23. ταράσσω 24. conturbo 25. moveo

Exd 36: 2 every one whose heart stirred him up to come 3
Deu 32:11 Like an eagle that stirs up its nest 5
Jdg 9:31 and they are stirring up the city against you. 7
1Sm 22: 8 that my son has stirred up my servant against me 8
26:19 If it is the LORD who has stirred you up against me 4
1Ch 5:26 So the God of Israel stirred up the spirit of Pul 5
2Ch 21:16 LORD stirred up against Jeho'ram the anger 5
36:22 LORD stirred up the spirit of Cyrus king 5
Ezr 1: 1 LORD stirred up the spirit of Cyrus king of Persia 5
4:15 sedition was stirred up in it from of old. 13
Job 17: 8 innocent stirs himself up against the godless. 5
41:10 No one is so fierce that he dares to stir him up. 5
Ps 78:38 did not stir up all his wrath. 5
80: 2 Stir up thy might, and come to save us! 5
140: 2 stir up wars continually. 1
Prv 10:12 Hatred stirs up strife 5
15: 1 but a harsh word stirs up anger. 6
18 A hot-tempered man stirs up strife 2
28:25 A greedy man stirs up strife 2
29:22 A man of wrath stirs up strife 2
Sng 2: 7 I adjure . . that you stir not up nor awaken love 5
3: 5 stir not up nor awaken love until it please. 5
8: 4 I adjure . . that you stir not up nor awaken love 5
Isa 9:11 against them, and stirs up their enemies. 11
13:17 Behold, I am stirring up the Medes against them 5
14: 9 Sheol beneath is stirred up to meet you 9
19: 2 I will stir up Egyptians against Egyptians 11
41: 2 Who stirred up one from the east 5
25 I stirred up one from the north, and he has come 5
42:13 like a man of war he stirs up his fury; 5
51:15 God, who stirs up the sea so that its waves roar 10
54:15 If any one stirs up strife, it is not from me; 1
Jer 31:35 who stirs up the sea so that its waves roar 10
50: 9 I am stirring up and bringing against Babylon 5
51: 1 Behold, I will stir up the spirit of a destroyer 5
11 The LORD has stirred up the spirit of the kings 5
Dan 7: 2 four winds . . were stirring up the great sea. 12
11: 2 shall stir up all against the kingdom of Greece. 5
25 he shall stir up his power and his courage 5
Jol 3: 7 But now I will stir them up from the place 5
9 Prepare war, stir up the mighty men. 5
Hag 1:14 the LORD stirred up the spirit of Zerub'babel 5
Mrk 15:11 the chief priests stirred up the crowd 15
Lke 23: 5 they were urgent, saying, "He stirs up the people 15
Act 6:12 they stirred up the people and the elders 21
13:50 and stirred up persecution against Paul 16
14: 2 the unbelieving Jews stirred up the Gentiles 16
17:13 stirring up and inciting the crowds. 20
21:27 stirred up all the crowd, and laid hands on him 22
24:12 they did not find me . . stirring up a crowd 17
2Co 9: 2 your zeal has stirred up most of them. 18
Heb 10:24 let us consider how to stir up one another to love 19
1Es 2: 2 the Lord stirred up the spirit of Cyrus 14
2Es 13: 2 and stirred up all its waves. 24
15:38 heavy storm clouds shall be stirred up 25
Wis 11: 6 stirred up and defiled with blood 23
1Mc 3:49 they stirred up the Nazirites 14

stir up revolt 1. ἀναστατόω

Act 21:38 who recently stirred up a revolt 1

stir up sedition 1. στασιάζω

2Mc 14: 6 Those . . are keeping up war and stirring up sedition 1

stir up strife 1. גור

Isa 54:15 whoever stirs up strife with you shall fall 1

stock 1. זֶרַע 2. כַּנָּה 3. ῥίζα

Ps 80:15 the stock which thy right hand planted. 2
Ezk 44:22 a virgin of the stock of the house of Israel 1
Tob 5:13 My brother, you come of good stock. 3
Sir 47:22 he gave . . to David a root of his stock. •

stock *See also* laughing.

stocks 1. מַהְפֶּכֶת 2. סַד 3. ξύλον

2Ch 16:10 was angry with the seer, and put him in the stocks 1
Job 13:27 Thou puttest my feet in the stocks 2
33:11 he puts my feet in the stocks 2
Jer 20: 2 beat Jeremiah . . and put him in the stocks 1
3 Pashhur released Jeremiah from the stocks 1
29:26 madman who prophesies, to put him in the stocks 1
Act 16:24 fastened their feet in the stocks. 3

stolen *See* beast, count.

stomach 1. מֵעֶה 2. קֵבָה 3. γαστήρ 4. κοιλία 5. στόμαχος

Deu 18: 3 give to the priest . . two cheeks and the stomach. 2
Job 20:14 yet his food is turned in his stomach; 1
Ezk 3: 3 eat this scroll . . and fill your stomach with it. 1
7:19 not satisfy . . or fill their stomachs with it. 1
Mat 15:17 goes into the mouth passes into the stomach 4
Mrk 7:19 since it enters, not his heart but his stomach 4
1Co 6:13 Food is meant for the stomach 4
13 the stomach for food 4
1Ti 5:23 use a little wine for the sake of your stomach 5
Rev 10: 9 Take it and eat; it will be bitter to your stomach 4
10 when I had eaten it my stomach was made bitter. 4
Sir 36:18 The stomach will take any food 4
37: 5 help a friend for their stomach's sake 3
40:30 in his stomach a fire is kindled. 4
4Mc 7: 6 nor profaned your stomach 3

stone 1. אֶבֶן 2. לְבֵנָה 3. סקל 4. צור 5. רגם 6. אֶבֶן (A) 7. καταλιθάζω 8. λιθάζω 9. λίθινος 10. λιθοβολέω 11. λιθοβόλος 12. λίθος 13. πέτρος 14. στήλη 15. ψῆφος 16. lapis

Gen 2:12 land is good; bdellium and onyx stone are there. 1
11: 3 And they had brick for stone 1
28:11 Taking one of the stones of the place 1
18 he took the stone which he had put under his head 1
22 this stone, which I have set up for a pillar 1
29: 2 The stone on the well's mouth was large 1
3 the shepherds would roll the stone from the mouth 1
3 and put the stone back in its place upon the mouth 1
8 the stone is rolled from the mouth of the well; 1
10 Jacob . . rolled the stone from the well's mouth 1
31:45 Jacob took a stone, and set it up as a pillar. 1
46 Jacob said to his kinsmen, "Gather stones 1
46 and they took stones, and made a heap; 1
35:14 where he had spoken with him, a pillar of stone; 1
Exd 8:26 If we sacrifice . . will they not stone us? 3
15: 5 they went down into the depths like a stone. 1
16 they are as still as a stone, till thy people 1
17: 4 this people? They are almost ready to stone me. 3
12 so they took a stone and put it under him, and he sat 1
19:13 he shall be stoned or shot; 3
20:25 if you make me an altar of stone, you shall not 1
21:18 strikes the other with a stone or with his fist 1
28 the ox shall be stoned, and its flesh shall 3
29 the ox shall be stoned, and its owner also shall 3
32 and the ox shall be stoned. 3
24:10 under his feet . . a pavement of sapphire stone 2
12 I will give you the tables of stone, with the law 1
25: 7 onyx stones, and stones for setting, for the ephod 1
7 onyx stones, and stones for setting, for the ephod 1
28: 9 you shall take two onyx stones, and engrave 1
10 six of their names on the one stone, and the names 1
10 the names of the remaining six on the other stone 1
11 shall you engrave the two stones with the names 1
12 set the two stones upon the shoulder-pieces 1
12 as stones of remembrance for the sons of Israel; 1
17 you shall set in it four rows of stones. 1
21 There shall be twelve stones with their names 1
31: 5 in cutting stones for setting 1
18 tables of the testimony, tables of stone, written 1
34: 1 The LORD said to Moses, "Cut two tables of stone 1
4 Moses cut two tables of stone like the first; 1
4 and took in his hand two tables of stone. 1
35: 9 onyx stones and stones for setting, for the ephod 1
9 onyx stones and stones for setting, for the ephod 1
27 leaders brought onyx stones and stones to be set 1
27 leaders brought onyx stones and stones to be set 1
33 cutting stones for setting, and in carving wood 1
39: 6 The onyx stones were prepared 1
7 to be stones of remembrance for the sons 1
10 it four rows of stones. A row of sardius, topaz 1
14 There were twelve stones with their names 1
Lev 14:40 they take out the stones in which is the disease 1
42 shall take other stones and put them in the place 1
42 stones and put them in the place of those stones 1
43 after he has taken out the stones and scraped 1
45 its stones and timber and all the plaster 1
20: 2 people of the land shall stone him with stones 5
2 people of the land shall stone him with stones 1
27 they shall be stoned with stones, their blood 5
27 they shall be stoned with stones, their blood 1
24:14 and let all the congregation stone him 5
16 all the congregation shall stone him 5
23 and stoned him with stones 5
23 and stoned him with stones 1
26: 1 you shall not set up a figured stone in your land 1
Num14:10 congregation said to stone them with stones. 5
10 congregation said to stone them with stones. 1
15:35 all . . shall stone him with stones outside 5
35 all . . shall stone him with stones outside 1
36 stoned him to death with stones, as the LORD 5
36 stoned him to death with stones, as the LORD 1
35:17 if he struck him down with a stone in the hand 1
23 or used a stone, by which a man may die 1
Deu 4:13 wrote them upon two tables of stone. 1
28 there you will serve gods of wood and stone 1
5:22 wrote them upon two tables of stone, and gave them 1
8: 9 a land whose stones are iron, and out of whose hills 1
9: 9 up the mountain to receive the tables of stone 1

10 LORD gave me the two tables of stone written 1
11 at the end . . LORD gave me the two tables of stone 1
10: 1 Hew two tables of stone like the first, and come up 1
3 I made an ark . . and hewed two tables of stone 1
13:10 You shall stone him to death with stones 3
10 You shall stone him to death with stones 1
17: 5 stone that man or woman to death with stones. 3
5 stone that man or woman to death with stones. 1
21:21 men . . shall stone him to death with stones; 5
21 men . . shall stone him to death with stones; 1
22:21 men . . shall stone her to death with stones 3
21 men . . shall stone her to death with stones 1
24 you shall stone them to death with stones 3
24 you shall stone them to death with stones 1
27: 2 set up large stones, and plaster them with plaster; 1
4 set up these stones, concerning which I command 1
5 build an altar . . an altar of stones; 1
6 altar to the LORD your God of unhewn stones; 1
8 write upon the stones all the words of this law 1
28:36 shall serve other gods, of wood and stone. 1
64 there . . serve other gods, of wood and stone 1
29:17 their idols of wood and stone, of silver and gold 1
Jos 4: 3 Take twelve stones from here out of the . . Jordan 1
5 and take up each of you a stone upon his shoulder 1
6 'What do those stones mean to you?' 1
7 these stones shall be . . a memorial for ever. 1
8 and took up twelve stones out of the midst 1
9 And Joshua set up twelve stones in the . . Jordan 1
20 those twelve stones . . Joshua set up in Gilgal. 1
21 your children ask . . 'What do these stones mean?' 1
7:25 And all Israel stoned him with stones; 5
25 And all Israel stoned him with stones; 1
25 they burned them . . and stoned them with stones. 3
25 they burned them . . and stoned them with stones. 1
26 And they raised over him a great heap of stones 1
8:29 and raised over it a great heap of stones 1
31 an altar of unhewn stones, upon which no man has 1
32 he wrote upon the stones a copy of the law of Moses 1
10:11 the LORD threw down great stones from heaven 1
18 Roll great stones against the mouth of the cave 1
27 set great stones against the mouth of the cave 1
15: 6 goes up to the stone of Bohan the son of Reuben; 1
18:17 it goes down to the Stone of Bohan the son of Reuben; 1
24:26 and he took a great stone, and set it up there 1
27 this stone shall be a witness against us; 1
Jdg 6:26 build an altar . . with stones laid in due order; •
9: 5 slew his brothers . . 70 men, upon one stone; 1
18 and have slain his sons, 70 men on one stone 1
20:16 every one could sling a stone at a hair, and not 1
1Sm 6:14 A great stone was there; 1
15 took down the . . and set them upon the great stone; 1
18 The great stone, beside which they set . . the ark 12
7:12 Then Samuel took a stone and set it up 1
14:33 roll a great stone to me here. 1
17:40 and chose five smooth stones from the brook 1
49 David put his hand in his bag and took out a stone 1
49 the stone sank into his forehead, and he fell 1
50 David prevailed . . with a sling and with a stone 1
25:37 his heart died within . . and he became as a stone. 1
30: 6 distressed; for the people spoke of stoning him 3
2Sm 12:30 was a talent of gold, and in it was a precious stone; 1
16: 6 he threw stones at David, and at all the servants 1
13 cursed . . and threw stones at him and flung dust. 1
18:17 raised over him a very great heap of stones; 1
20: 8 they were at the great stone which is in Gibeon 1
1Kg 1: 9 Adoni'jah sacrificed . . by the Serpent's Stone 1
5:15 Solomon also had . . and 80,000 hewers of stone •
17 they quarried out great, costly stones 1
17 to lay the foundation . . with dressed stones. 1
18 and prepared the timber and the stone to build 1
6: 7 it was with stone prepared at the quarry; 1
18 all was cedar, no stone was seen. 1
7: 9 were made of costly stones, hewn according 1
10 The foundation was of costly stones, huge stones 1
10 huge stones, stones of eight and ten cubits. 1
10 huge stones, stones of eight and ten cubits. 1
11 costly stones, hewn according to measurement 1
8: 9 the two tables of stone which Moses put there 1
10: 2 with . . very much gold, and precious stones; 1
10 gold, and . . spices, and precious stones; 1
11 from Ophir . . almug wood and precious stones. 1
27 the king made silver as common . . as stone 1
12:18 and all Israel stoned him to death with stones. 5
18 and all Israel stoned him to death with stones. 1
15:22 carried away the stones of Ramah and its timber 1
18:31 Eli'jah took twelve stones 1
32 with the stones he built an altar 1
38 burnt offering, and the wood, and the stones 1
21:10 Then take him out, and stone him to death. 3
13 took him outside the city, and stoned him to death 3
13 and stoned him to death with stones. 1
14 saying, "Naboth has been stoned; he is dead. 3
15 Jez'ebel heard that Naboth had been stoned 3
2Kg 3:19 and ruin every good piece of land with stones. 1
25 on every . . piece of land every man threw a stone 1
25 only its stones were left in Kir-har'eseth 1
12:12 as well as to buy timber and quarried stone 1
16:17 and put it upon a pediment of stone. 1
19:18 no gods, but the work of men's hands, wood and stone; 1
22: 6 for buying timber and quarried stone to repair 1
23:15 he pulled down and he broke in pieces its stones 12
1Ch 12: 2 bowmen, and could shoot arrows and sling stones 1
20: 2 crown . . and in it was a precious stone 1
22: 2 he set stonecutters to prepare dressed stones 1
14 timber and stone too I have provided. 1
29: 2 great quantities of onyx and stones for setting 1
2 quantities of . . all sorts of precious stones 1
8 whoever had precious stones gave them 1
2Ch 1:15 king made silver and gold as common . . as stone 1
2:14 He is trained to work in gold, silver . . stone 1
3: 6 He adorned the house with . . precious stones. 1
9: 1 camels bearing spices and . . precious stones. 1
9 she gave the king . . spices, and precious stones 1
10 brought algum wood and precious stones. 1
27 king made silver as common in Jerusalem as stone 1
10:18 people of Israel stoned him to death 5
18 Israel stoned him to death with stones. 1
16: 6 carried away the stones of Ramah and its timber 1
24:21 stoned him with stones in the court of the house 5
21 stoned him with stones in the court of the house 1
26:14 prepared for all the army . . stones for slinging. 1
15 engines . . to shoot arrows and great stones. 1
32:27 made . . treasuries . . , for precious stones 1
34:11 to buy quarried stone, and timber for binders 1
Ezr 5: 8 It is being built with huge stones 6
6: 4 with three courses of great stones 6
Neh 4: 2 Will they revive the stones out of the heaps 1
3 fox goes up . . he will break down their stone wall! 1
9:11 into the depths, as a stone into mighty waters. 1
Job 5:23 in league with the stones of the field 1
6:12 Is my strength the strength of stones 1
14:19 the waters wear away the stones; 1
22:24 gold of Ophir among the stones of the torrent bed 4
28: 6 Its stones are the place of sapphires 1
38:30 The waters become hard like stone 1
41:24 His heart is hard as a stone 1
Ps 91:12 lest you dash your foot against a stone. 1
102:14 For thy servants hold her stones dear 1
118:22 The stone which the builders rejected 1
Prv 17: 8 A bribe is like a magic stone in the eyes of him 1
24:31 its stone wall was broken down. 1
26: 8 Like one who binds the stone in the sling 1
27 stone will come back upon him who starts it 1
27: 3 A stone is heavy, and sand is weighty 1
Ecc 3: 5 a time to cast away stones, and a time to gather 1
5 cast away . . and a time to gather stones together; 1
10: 9 He who quarries stones is hurt by them; 1
Isa 8:14 he will become a sanctuary, and a stone of offense 1
14:19 pierced . . who go down to the stones of the Pit 1
27: 9 when he makes all the stones of the altars 1
28:16 for a foundation a stone, a tested stone 1
16 for a foundation a stone, a tested stone 1
37:19 but the work of men's hands, wood and stone; 1
54:11 behold, I will set your stones in antimony 1
12 and all your wall of precious stones. 1
57: 6 Among the smooth stones of the valley •
60:17 instead of wood, bronze, instead of stones, iron. 1
62:10 build up, build up the highway, clear it of stones 1
Jer 2:27 and to a stone, 'You gave me birth.' 1
3: 9 committing adultery with stone and tree. 1
43: 9 Take in your hands large stones, and hide them 1
10 he will set his throne above these stones 1
51:26 No stone shall be taken from you for a corner 1
26 for a corner and no stone for a foundation 1
63 you finish reading this book, bind a stone to it 1
Lam 3:53 flung me . . into the pit and cast stones on me; 1
4: 1 holy stones lie scattered at . . every street. 1
Ezk 16:40 they shall stone you and cut you to pieces 5
20:32 and worship wood and stone. 1
23:47 the host shall stone them and dispatch them 5
26:12 your stones and timber and soil they will cast 1
27:22 spices, and all precious stones, and gold. 1
28:13 every precious stone was your covering 1
14 in the midst of the stones of fire you walked. 1
16 out from the midst of the stones of fire. 1
36:26 I will take out of your flesh the heart of stone 1
40:42 there were also four tables of hewn stone 1
Dan 2:34 As you looked, a stone was cut out by no human hand 6
35 stone that struck the image became a great 6
45 stone was cut from a mountain by no human hand 6
5: 4 praised the gods of . . wood, and stone. 6
23 gods of . . bronze, iron, wood, and stone 6
6:17 stone was brought and laid upon the mouth 6
11:38 honor with . . precious stones and costly gifts. 1
Mic 1: 6 and I will pour down her stones into the valley 1
Hab 2:11 For the stone will cry out from the wall 1
19 to a wooden thing, Awake; to a dumb stone, Arise! 1
Hag 2:15 Before a stone was placed upon a stone 1
15 Before a stone was placed upon a stone 1
Zec 3: 9 upon the stone which I have set before Joshua 1
9 upon a single stone with seven facets 1
4: 7 he shall bring forward the top stone amid shouts 1
5: 4 his house and consume it, both timber and stones. 1
12: 3 make Jerusalem a heavy stone for all the peoples; 1
Mat 3: 9 God is able from these stones to raise up 12
4: 3 command these stones to become loaves of bread. 12
6 lest you strike your foot against a stone.' 12
7: 9 asks him for bread, will give him a stone? 12
21:35 beat one, killed another, and stoned another. 10
42 The very stone which the builders rejected 12
23:37 stoning those who are sent to you! 10
24: 2 one stone upon another 12
27:60 rolled a great stone to the door of the tomb 12
66 by sealing the stone and setting a guard. 12
28: 2 came and rolled back the stone, and sat upon it. 12
Mrk 5: 5 bruising himself with stones. 12
12:10 The very stone which the builders rejected 12
13: 1 Look, Teacher, what wonderful stones 12
2 There will not be left here one stone upon another 12
15:46 he rolled a stone against the door of the tomb. 12
16: 3 Who will roll away the stone for us from the door 12
4 And looking up, they saw that the stone 12
Lke 3: 8 God is able from these stones to raise up children 12
4: 3 of God, command this stone to become bread. 12
11 lest you strike your foot against a stone.' 12
13:34 stoning those who are sent to you 10
19:40 the very stones would cry out. 12
44 they will not leave one stone upon another in you; 12
20: 6 if we say, 'From men,' all the people will stone us 7
17 The very stone which the builders rejected 12
18 Every one who falls on that stone 12
21: 5 it was adorned with noble stones and offerings 12
6 there shall not be left here one stone upon another 12
22:41 he withdrew from them about a stone's throw 12
24: 2 they found the stone rolled away from the tomb 12
Joh 2: 6 Now six stone jars were standing there 9
8: 5 Now in the law Moses commanded us to stone such. 8
7 Let him . . be the first to throw a stone at her. 12
59 they took up stones to throw at him 12
10:31 The Jews took up stones again to stone him. 12
31 The Jews took up stones again to stone him. 8
32 for which of these do you stone me? 8
33 It is not for a good work that we stone you 8
11: 8 the Jews were but now seeking to stone you 8
38 it was a cave, and a stone lay upon it. 12
39 Jesus said, "Take away the stone. 12
41 they took away the stone 12
20: 1 the stone had been taken away from the tomb. 12
Act 4:11 is the stone which was rejected by you builders 12
5:26 they were afraid of being stoned by the people. 8
7:58 Then they cast him out of the city and stoned him; 10
59 as they were stoning Stephen, he prayed 10
14: 5 to molest them and to stone them 10
19 they stoned Paul and dragged him out of the city 8
17:29 is like gold, or silver, or stone 12
Rom 9:32 They have stumbled over the stumbling stone 12
33 laying in Zion a stone that will make men stumble 12
1Co 3:12 with gold, silver, precious stones, wood, hay, straw- 12
2Co 3: 3 not on tablets of stone 9
7 carved in letters on stone 12
11:25 once I was stoned 8
Heb 11:37 They were stoned, they were sawn in two 8
12:20 it shall be stoned. 10
1Pe 2: 4 Come to him, to the living stone, rejected by men 12
5 like living stones be yourselves built 12
6 Behold, I am laying in Zion a stone, a cornerstone 12
7 The very stone which the builders rejected 12
8 A stone that will make men stumble 12
Rev 2:17 and I will give him a white stone 15
17 with a new name written on the stone 15
9:20 idols of . . silver and bronze and stone and wood 9
18:21 angel took up a stone like a great millstone 12
1Es 6: 9 of hewn stone 12
25 with three courses of hewn stone 9
2Es 5: 5 and the stone shall utter its voice 16
7:52 If you have just a few precious stones 16
Tob 13:16 her walls with precious stones 12
17 beryl and ruby and stones of Ophir; 12
Jdt 1: 2 hewn stones three cubits thick 12
6:12 kept them from coming up by casting stones 12
10:21 gold and emeralds and precious stones. 12
AEs 15: 6 all covered with gold and precious stones 12
Wis 11: 4 slaking of thirst from hard stone. 12
13:10 likenesses of animals, or a useless stone 12
14:21 men . . bestowed on objects of stone or wood the name 12
18:24 engraved on the four rows of stones 12
Sir 6:21 will weigh him down like a heavy testing stone 12
21: 8 like one who gathers stones for his burial mound. 12
10 The way of sinners is smoothly paved with stones 12
22: 1 The indolent may be compared to a filthy stone 12
20 One who throws a stone at birds scares them away 12
27: 2 driven firmly into a fissure between stones 12
25 Whoever throws a stone straight up 12
29:10 do not let it rust under a stone and be lost. 12
45:11 with precious stones engraved like signets 12
47: 4 when he lifted his hand with a stone in the sling 12
50: 9 adorned with all kinds of precious stones; 12
LJr 1:39 like stones from the mountain 12
1Mc 2:36 they did not answer them or hurl a stone at them 12
4:43 removed the defiled stones to an unclean place. 12
46 stored the stones in a convenient place 12
47 Then they took unhewn stones, as the law directs 12
5:47 and blocked up the gates with stones. 12
6:51 engines of war to throw fire and stones 11
10:11 encircle Mount Zion with squared stones 12
73 where there is no stone or pebble, or place to flee. 12
13:27 with polished stone at the front and back. 12

2Mc 1:16 they threw stones and struck down the leader 13
31 the liquid . . be poured upon large stones. 12
4:41 some picked up stones, some blocks of wood 13
3Mc 2:27 he set up a stone on the tower in the courtyard 14
stone *See also* clear, figured, throw, vessel.

colored stone 1. רִקְמָה
1Ch 29: 2 quantities of . . antimony, colored stones 1

costly stone 1. פְּנִינִים
Prv 20:15 There is gold, and abundance of costly stones; 1

dressed stone 1. גָּזִית
Isa 9:10 fallen, but we will build with dressed stones; 1

stone heap 1. גַּל 2. εργαβ
1Sm 20:19 go to . . and remain beside yonder stone heap. 2
41 David rose from beside the stone heap 2
Hos 12:11 their altars also shall be like stone heaps 1

hewn stone 1. גָּזִית
Exd 20:25 you shall not build it of hewn stones; 1
1Kg 6:36 He built the inner court with . . hewn stone 1
7:12 The great court had three courses of hewn stone 1
Lam 3: 9 he has blocked my ways with hewn stones 1
Ams 5:11 you have built houses of hewn stone 1

hot stone 1. רִצְפָּה
1Kg 19: 6 there was at his head a cake baked on hot stones 1

precious stone 1. סֹחֶרֶת
Est 1: 6 marble, mother-of-pearl and precious stones. 1

sacred stone
Act 19:35 and of the sacred stone that fell from the sky? •

sculptured stone 1. פָּסִיל
Jdg 3:19 back at the sculptured stones near Gilgal 1
26 and passed beyond the sculptured stones 1

stonecutter 1. חצב 2. חצב אֶבֶן
2Kg 12:12 the masons and the stonecutters 2
1Ch 22: 2 he set stonecutters to prepare dressed stones 1
15 stonecutters, masons, carpenters 1

stoneheap 1. גַּל
Job 8:17 His roots twine about the stoneheap; 1

stony 1. אֶבֶן
Ezk 11:19 I will take the stony heart out of their flesh 1
stony *See also* ground.

stool 1. ὑποπόδιον
Lke 20:43 till I make thy enemies a stool for thy feet.' 1
Act 2:35 till I make thy enemies a stool for thy feet.' 1
Heb 1:13 till I make thy enemies a stool for thy feet"? 1
10:13 his enemies should be made a stool for his feet. 1

stoop 1. קרס
Isa 46: 1 Bel bows down, Nebo stoops 1
2 They stoop, they bow down together 1

stoop down 1. כרע 2. κύπτω
Gen 49: 9 He stooped down, he couched as a lion 1
Mrk 1: 7 I am not worthy to stoop down and untie. 2

stoop to look 1. παρακύπτω
Joh 20: 5 and stooping to look in, he saw the linen cloths 1
11 as she wept she stooped to look into the tomb; 1

stop 1. אטם 2. חדל 3. חתם 4. כבד 5. כלא 6. כרת 7. סכר 8. סתם 9. עמד 10. עצר 11. קפץ 12. רפה 13. שׁבת 14. בטל (A) 15. ἀποφράσσω 16. βιάζω 17. διακωλύω 18. διαλιμπάνω 19. ἐμφραγμός 20. ἐμφράσσω 21. ἵστημι 22. κατέχω 23. κωλύω 24. λαμβάνω τὸ τέλος 25. λήγω 26. μή 27. οὐ 28. παῦλαν λαμβάνω 29. παύω 30. συνέχω 31. φράσσω 32. prohibeo 33. quiesco 34. statuo
Gen 19:17 do not look back or stop anywhere in the valley; 9
26:15 Now the Philistines had stopped and filled 8
18 for the Philistines had stopped them 8
Lev 15: 3 or his body is stopped from discharge 3
Num16:48 he stood between . . and the plague was stopped. 10
50 Aaron returned . . when the plague was stopped. 10
Jos 3:13 the Jordan shall be stopped from flowing 6
1Sm 6:14 cart came into the field . . and stopped there. 9
9:27 stop here yourself for a while, that I may 9
15:16 Then Samuel said to Saul, "Stop! I will tell you 12
2Sm 2:28 all the men stopped, and pursued Israel no more 9
20:12 And any one who came by, seeing him, stopped; 9
12 and when the man saw that all the people stopped 9
1Kg 15:21 when Ba'asha heard . . he stopped building Ramah 2
18:44 Prepare . . and go down, lest the rain stop you.' 10
2Kg 3:25 they stopped every spring of water 8
13:18 Strike . . "; and he struck three times, and stopped. 9
2Ch 16: 5 when Ba'asha heard . . he stopped building Ramah 2
25:16 Stop! Why should you be put to death? 2
16 the prophet stopped, but said, "I know that God 2
32: 3 planned . . to stop the water of the springs 8
4 they stopped all the springs and the brook 8
Ezr 4:24 the work on the house of God . . in Jerusalem stopped 14
5: 5 not stop them till a report should reach Darius 14
Neh 4:11 till we come . . and kill them and stop the work. 13
6: 3 Why should the work stop while I leave it 13
Job 37:14 stop and consider the wondrous works of God. 9
Ps 58: 4 a serpent, like the deaf adder that stops its ear 1
63:11 for the mouths of liars will be stopped. 7
107:42 all wickedness stops its mouth. 11
Isa 33:15 who stops his ears from hearing of bloodshed 1
Jer 48:45 In the shadow of Heshbon fugitives stop 9
Ezk 26:13 I will stop the music of your songs 13
31:15 many waters shall be stopped; 5
Zec 7:11 stopped their ears that they might not hear. 4
Mat 20:32 Jesus stopped and called them, saying 21
Mrk 10:49 Jesus stopped and said, "Call him. 21
Lke 18:40 Jesus stopped, and commanded him to be brought 21
Act 7:57 stopped their ears and rushed together upon him. 30
8:38 he commanded the chariot to stop 21
13:10 will you not stop making crooked 29
21:32 they stopped beating Paul. 29
Rom 3:19 so that every mouth may be stopped 31
Heb 11:33 received promises, stopped the mouths of lions 31
3Jn 1:10 and also stops those who want to welcome them 23
2Es 4:17 for the sand stood firm and stopped them. 32
10: 3 when they all had stopped consoling me 33
13:44 and stopped the channels of the river 34
47 the Most High will stop the channels of the river 34
Tob 5:21 So she stopped weeping. 29
10: 6 Be still and stop worrying; he is well. 26
7 she answered him, "Be still and stop deceiving me; 26
7 she never stopped mourning for her son Tobias 18
Jdt 4: 7 it was easy to stop any who tried to enter 17
AEs 14: 9 to stop the mouths of those who praise thee 20
Sir 4:26 do not try to stop the current of a river. 16
18: 7 when he stops, he will be at a loss. 29
27:14 their quarrels make a man stop his ears. 19
31:17 first to stop eating, for the sake of good manners 29
1Mc 6:27 you will not be able to stop them. 22
9:55 his mouth was stopped and he was paralyzed 15
13:47 and stopped fighting against them 27
2Mc 4: 6 Simon would not stop his folly. 28
9: 7 Yet he did not in any way stop his insolence 25
3Mc 1:13 no one there had stopped him. 23
4:15 though uncompleted it stopped after 40 days. 24
stop *See also* put.

stop flowing 1. עמד
2Kg 4: 6 Then the oil stopped flowing. 1

make stop 1. שׁבת 2. παύω
Ezk 16:41 I will make you stop playing the harlot 1
1Mc 11:50 and make the Jews stop fighting against us 2

stop speaking 1. σιγάω
1Es 3:24 When he had said this, he stopped speaking 1
4:12 he stopped speaking. 1

stop up 1. סתם
2Kg 3:19 and stop up all springs of water 1
Zec 14: 5 the valley of my mountains shall be stopped up 1

without stopping 1. ἀδιαλείπτως
2Mc 9: 4 to drive without stopping 1

storage 1. ἀγγεῖον
1Mc 6:53 they had no food in storage 1

store 1. אוֹצָר 2. אצר 3. זַן 4. מְלָאכָה 5. מִסְכְּנוֹת 6. נתן 7. פקד 8. שׂום 9. נחת (A) 10. ἀπερείδω 11. ἀποθήκη 12. ἀποτίθημι 13. εἰμί 14. ἐφίστημι 15. θησαυρός 16. παράθεσις 17. παρατίθημι 18. συνάγω 19. συντίθημι 20. τίθημι 21. substantia
1Kg 7:51 stored them in the treasuries of the house 6
1Ch 27:28 and over the stores of oil was Jo'ash. 1
2Ch 5: 1 stored the silver, the gold, and all the vessels 6
8: 4 all the store-cities which he built in Hamath. 5
6 Ba'alath, and all the store-cities . . Solomon had 5
11:11 and put . . in them, stores of food, oil, and wine. 1
16: 4 conquered . . all the store-cities of Naph'tali. 5
17:13 he had great stores in the cities of Judah. 4
Ezr 6: 1 archives where the documents were stored. 9
Neh 12:44 men . . appointed over the chambers for the stores 1
Ps 144:13 garners be full, providing all manner of store; 3
Isa 10:28 at Michmash he stores his baggage; 7
23:18 it will not be stored or hoarded 2
Jer 40:10 fruits and oil, and store them in your vessels 8
Lke 12:17 I have nowhere to store my crops?' 18
18 there I will store all my grain and my goods. 18
1Es 1:41 carried them away, and stored them in his temple 10
54 treasure chests of the Lord, and the royal stores 11
2:10 stored in his temple of idols. 10
6:18 stored in his own temple 10
2Es 8:36 to those who have no store of good works. 21
Wis 6: 8 a strict inquiry is in store for the mighty. 14
Sir 41:12 longer than 1,000 great stores of gold. 15
1Mc 1:35 they stored them there 12
4:46 stored the stones in a convenient place 12
6:53 had consumed the last of the stores. 16
9:35 to store with them the great amount of baggage 17
52 in them he put troops and stores of food. 16
13:33 he stored food in the strongholds. 20
14:33 where . . the arms of the enemy had been stored 13
2Mc 8:31 stored them all carefully in strategic places 19
12:27 great stores of war engines and missiles 16
store *See also* keep, lay.

great store 1. לָרֹב 2. רֹב
1Ch 22: 3 David also provided great stores of iron 1
2Ch 31:10 we have this great store left. 2

hidden store 1. מַטְמוֹן
Jer 41: 8 we have stores of wheat . . hidden in the fields. 1

old store 1. יָשָׁן
Lev 26:10 you shall eat old store long kept 1

store up 1. אסף 2. אצר 3. נתן 4. צבר 5. צפן 6. θησαυρίζω 7. παρατίθημι 8. συγκλείω
Gen 6:21 and store it up; and it shall serve as food for you 1
41:48 and stored up food in the cities; 3
48 he stored up in every city the food 3
49 Joseph stored up grain in great abundance 4
2Kg 20:17 which your fathers have stored up till this day 2
Job 21:19 God stores up their iniquity for their sons.' 5
Ps 17:14 filled with what thou hast stored up for them; 5
Prv 2: 7 he stores up sound wisdom for the upright; 5
Isa 39: 6 which your fathers have stored up till this day 2
Ams 3:10 those who store up violence and robbery in their 2
Rom 2: 5 storing up wrath for yourself on the day of wrath 6
1Co 16: 2 put something aside and store it up 6
2Pe 3: 7 and earth . . have been stored up for fire 6
Jdt 4: 5 and stored up food in preparation for war 7
Sir 29:12 Store up almsgiving in your treasury 8
1Mc 1:35 they stored up arms and food 7

store up treasure 1. thesaurizo
2Es 6: 5 before those who stored up treasures of faith 1

store-city 1. עִיר מִסְכְּנוֹת
Exd 1:11 and they built for Pharaoh store-cities 1
1Kg 9:19 build . . all the store-cities that Solomon had 1
2Ch 17:12 He built in Judah fortresses and store-cities 1

storehouse 1. אוֹצָר 2. אָסֹף 3. בֵּית אוֹצָר 4. בֵּית אֲסֻפִּים 5. מִסְכְּנוֹת 6. ἀποδοχεῖον 7. θησαυρός 8. σιτοβολών 9. ταμεῖον 10. promptuarius
Gen 41:56 Joseph opened all the storehouses 8
2Kg 20:13 his armory, all that was found in his storehouses; 1
15 nothing in my storehouses that I did not show 1
1Ch 26:15 and to his sons was allotted the storehouse. 4
17 as well as two and two at the storehouse; 2
2Ch 32:28 storehouses also for the yield of grain, wine 5
Neh 10:38 bring up . . to the chambers, to the storehouse. 3
12:25 standing guard at the storehouses of the gates. 2
13:12 brought the tithe . . into the storehouses. 1
13 I appointed as treasurers over the storehouses 1
Job 38:22 Have you entered the storehouses of the snow 1
22 have you seen the storehouses of the hail 1
Ps 33: 7 as in a bottle; he put the deeps in storehouses. 1
135: 7 brings forth the wind from his storehouses. 1
Isa 39: 2 all that was found in his storehouses. 1
4 nothing in my storehouses that I did not show 1
Jer 10:13 he brings forth the wind from his storehouses. 1
38:11 house of the king, to a wardrobe of the storehouse 1
51:16 he brings forth the wind from his storehouses. 1
Jol 1:17 the storehouses are desolate; 1
Mal 3:10 Bring the full tithes into the storehouse 3
Lke 12:24 they have neither storehouse nor barn 9
2Es 6:22 full storehouses shall suddenly be . . empty; 10
Sir 1:17 their storehouses with her produce. 6
43:14 Therefore the storehouses are opened 7
Bar 3:15 her place? And who has entered her storehouses? 7

stork 1. חֲסִידָה
Lev 11:19 the stork, the heron according to its kind 1
Deu 14:18 stork, the heron, after their kinds; 1
Ps 104:17 stork has her home in the fir trees. 1
Jer 8: 7 Even the stork in the heavens knows her times; 1
Zec 5: 9 they had wings like the wings of a stork 1

storm 1. זֶרֶם 2. מִלְחָמָה 3. סוּפָה 4. סַעַר 5. סְעָרָה 6. שְׂעָרָה 7. שׁוֹאָה 8. ἀπειλέω 9. δοριάλωτος 10. καταιγίς 11. λαῖλαψ 12. ὄμβρος 13. προσβάλλω 14. σεισμός 15. procella 16. tempestas
2Kg 14: 7 He killed 10,000 E'domites . . and took Sela by storm 2
Job 21:18 like chaff that the storm carries away? 3
30:22 thou tossest me about in the roar of the storm. *
Ps 107:29 he made the storm be still 5
Prv 1:27 when panic strikes you like a storm 7
Isa 4: 6 a refuge and a shelter from the storm and rain. 1
10: 3 in the storm which will come from afar? 7
17:13 the wind and whirling dust before the storm. 3

25: 4 shelter from the storm and a shade from the heat 1
4 for the blast of the ruthless is like a storm 1
28: 2 like a storm of hail, a destroying tempest 1
2 like a storm of mighty, overflowing waters 1
Jer 23:19 Behold, the storm of the LORD! Wrath has gone forth 4
30:23 Behold the storm of the LORD! Wrath has gone forth 4
Ezk 38: 9 You will advance, coming on like a storm 7
Hos 10:15 In the storm the king of Israel shall be utterly *
Nah 1: 3 His way is in whirlwind and storm 6
Mat 8:24 behold, there arose a great storm on the sea 14
Mrk 4:37 a great storm of wind arose 11
Lke 8:23 a storm of wind came down on the lake 11
2Pe 2:17 waterless springs and mists driven by a storm; 11
2Es 12:42 and like a haven for a ship saved from a storm. 16
13:10 from his tongue he shot forth a storm of sparks. 16
11 the flaming breath and the great storm 16
27 as for your seeing wind and fire and a storm 16
37 (this was symbolized by the storm) 16
15:34 very threatening, full of wrath and storm. 15
Wis 5:14 like a light hoarfrost driven away by a storm 11
16:16 unusual rains and hail and relentless storms 12
Sir 33: 2 like a boat in a storm. 10
49: 9 For God remembered his enemies with storm 12
2Mc 5:11 he left Egypt and took the city by storm. 9
10:24 He came on, intending to take Judea by storm. 9
35 bravely stormed the wall 13
4Mc 7: 2 though buffeted by the stormings of the tyrant 8

storm cloud 1. חֲזִיז 2. nimbus
Zec 10: 1 from the LORD who makes the storm clouds 1
2Es 15:38 heavy storm clouds shall be stirred up 2

storm of destruction 1. הַוָּה
Ps 57: 1 refuge, till the storms of destruction pass by. 1

wintry storm 1. *χειμών*
4Mc 15:32 endured nobly and withstood the wintry storms 1

storm-tossed 1. סער 2. *χειμάζω*
Isa 54:11 O afflicted one, storm-tossed, and not comforted 1
Act 27:18 As we were violently storm-tossed 2

stormwind 1. סוּפָה
Isa 66:15 come in fire, and his chariots like the stormwind 1

stormy 1. סְעָרָה 2. *χειμών*
Ps 107:25 For he commanded, and raised the stormy wind 1
148: 8 stormy wind fulfilling his command! 1
Ezk 1: 4 behold, a stormy wind came out of the north 1
13:11 hailstones will fall, and a stormy wind break out; 1
13 I will make a stormy wind break out in my wrath; 1
Mat 16: 3 It will be stormy today, for the sky is red 2

story 1. דָּבָר 2. מִדְרָשׁ 3. *διήγησις* 4. *λαλιά* 5. *λόγος* 6. *μῦθος* 7. *ὁ κατά*
Gen 39:17 she told him the same story, saying 1
2Ch 13:22 written in the story of the prophet Iddo. 2
Mat 28:15 this story has been spread among the Jews 5
Sir 20:19 like a story told at the wrong time 6
35:14 nor the widow when she pours out her story. 4
2Mc 2:19 The story of Judas Maccabeus and his brothers 7
6:17 we must go on briefly with the story. 3
15:37 So I too will here end my story. 5
39 so also the style of the story delights the ears 5
4Mc 1:12 then I shall turn to their story 5
3: 6 the story of King David's thirst. *

story (2) 1. יָצִיעַ 2. מַעֲלָה 3. פַּעַם 4. צֵלָע
1Kg 6: 6 The lowest story was five cubits broad 1
8 The entrance for the lowest story was 4
8 one went up by stairs to the middle story *
8 by stairs . . from the middle story to the third. *
10 He built . . each story five cubits high *
Ezk 41: 6 the side chambers were in three stories *
6 stories, one over another, 30 in each story. 3
7 became broader as they rose from story to story 2
7 became broader as they rose from story to story 2
7 from story to story round about the temple; 2
7 from story to story round about the temple; 2
7 thus one went up from the lowest story to the top *
7 to the top story through the middle story. *
7 to the top story through the middle story. *
42: 3 was gallery against gallery in three stories. *
6 For they were in three stories *

story *See* tell.

third story 1. *τρίστεγον*
Act 20: 9 he fell down from the third story 1

story-teller 1. *μυθολόγος*
Bar 3:23 story-tellers and the seekers 1

stout 1. אַמִּיץ 2. חזק
Ams 2:16 he who is stout of heart among the mighty shall 1
Mal 3:13 Your words have been stout against me 2

stout *See also* warrior.

stouthearted 1. אַבִּיר לֵב
Ps 76: 5 The stouthearted were stripped of their spoil; 1

stouthearted man 1. *εὔψυχος*
1Mc 9:14 then all the stouthearted men went with him 1

stoutly 1. *καρτερός*
4Mc 15:31 stoutly endured the waves 1

stove 1. כִּיר
Lev 11:35 whether oven or stove, it shall be broken 1

straggler 1. בדד
Isa 14:31 the north, and there is no straggler in his ranks. 1

straight 1. ישר 2. יָשָׁר 3. נֶגֶד 4. נָכֹחַ 5. *εἰς εὐθεῖαν* 6. *εὐθύς* 7. *εὐθύτης* 8. *κατ' εὐθεῖαν* 9. *ὀρθός*
Ezr 8:21 to seek from him a straight way for ourselves 2
Ps 49:14 straight to the grave they descend *
107: 7 he led them by a straight way, till they reached 2
Prv 4:25 your gaze be straight before you. 1
8: 9 They are all straight to him who understands 4
29:27 way is straight is an abomination to the wicked. 2
Jer 31: 9 a straight path in which they shall not stumble; 2
39 shall go out farther, straight to the hill Gareb 3
Ezk 1: 7 Their legs were straight 2
23 their wings were stretched out straight 2
Ams 4: 3 the breaches, every one straight before her; *
Mat 3: 3 way of the Lord, make his paths straight. 6
Mrk 1: 3 make his paths straight- 6
Lke 3: 4 make his paths straight. 6
5 the crooked shall be made straight 6
Act 9:11 Rise and go to the street called Straight 6
13:10 making crooked the straight paths of the Lord? 6
Heb 12:13 make straight paths for your feet 9
Tob 4:19 ask him that your ways may be made straight 6
Jdt 10:11 The women went straight on through the valley; 5
13:20 walking in the straight path before our God 6
Wis 10:10 she guided him on straight paths 6
Sir 4:18 Then she will come straight back to him 8
27:25 Whoever throws a stone straight up *
39:24 To the holy his ways are straight 6
51:15 my foot entered upon the straight path 7

straight *See also* course, go, keep, make.

straight ahead 1. נֹכַח
Ezk 46: 9 but each shall go out straight ahead. 1

straight before 1. לִפְנֵי 2. נֶגֶד
Jos 6: 5 and . . shall go up every man straight before him. 2
20 people went up . . every man straight before him 2
Neh 12:37 Fountain Gate they went up straight before 2
Jer 49: 5 driven out, every man straight before him 1

straight forward 1. אֶל עֵבֶר פָּנִים
Ezk 1: 9 they went every one straight forward 1
12 And each went straight forward; 1
10:22 They went every one straight forward. 1

straighten 1. *ἀνακύπτω* 2. *ὀρθόω*
Lke 13:11 could not fully straighten herself. 1
LJr 1:27 if it is tipped over, it cannot straighten itself; 2

straightforward 1. *ὀρθοποδέω*
Gal 2:14 when I saw that they were not straightforward 1

strain 1. רַעְיוֹן לֵב
Ecc 2:22 What has a man from all the toil and strain 1

strain forward 1. *ἐπεκτείνομαι*
Php 3:13 straining forward to what lies ahead 1

strain out 1. *διϋλίζω*
Mat 23:24 straining out a gnat and swallowing a camel! 1

straits 1. צַר לְ 2. צרר 3. angustus
Jdg 2:15 and they were in sore straits. 2
1Sm 13: 6 the men of Israel saw that they were in straits 1
Job 20:22 he will be in straits; all the force of misery will 2
2Es 7:96 and besides they see the straits and toil 3

strange 1. זור 2. לַעַג 3. נֵכָר 4. *ἀλλότριος* 5. *ἐξαλλάσσω* 6. *ἔξαλλος* 7. *μέγας* 8. *ξενίζω* 9. *ξένος* 10. *παράδοξος* 11. alienus
Deu 31:16 rise and play the harlot after the strange gods 3
Ps 44:20 or spread forth our hands to a strange god 1
81: 9 There shall be no strange god among you; 1
Isa 28:11 by men of strange lips and with an alien tongue 2
21 to do his deed-strange is his deed! 1
43:12 when there was no strange god among you; 1
2Co 11:15 So it is not strange 7
Heb 13: 9 led away by diverse and strange teachings 9
2Es 1: 6 have offered sacrifices to strange gods. 11
Wis 14:23 his ways are strange. 5
14:23 hold frenzied revels with strange customs 6
19: 5 they themselves might meet a strange death. 9
Sir 43:25 for in it are strange and marvelous works 10
1Mc 1:38 she became strange to her offspring 4
44 to follow customs strange to the land 4
6:13 I am perishing of deep grief in a strange land. 4
2Mc 9: 6 with many and strange infliction. 8

strange *See also* god, land, language.

something strange 1. *ξένος*
1Pe 4:12 as though something strange were happening 1

strange thing 1. זור 2. *ξενίζω* 3. *παράδοξος*
Prv 23:33 Your eyes will see strange things 1
Hos 8:12 they would be regarded as a strange thing. 1
Lke 5:26 saying, "We have seen strange things today. 3
Act 17:20 you bring some strange things to our ears 2

stranger 1. אִישׁ זָר 2. בֶּן תּוֹשָׁב 3. גֵּר 4. זור 5. נָכְרִי 6. *ἀγνοέω* 7. *ἀλλογενής* 8. *ἀλλότριος* 9. *ξένος* 10. *παροικέω* 11. *πάροικος* 12. *χωρίζω* 13. advena 14. alienigena
Gen 23: 4 I am a stranger and a sojourner among you; 3
Exd 12:48 when a stranger shall sojourn with you and would 3
49 for the native and for the stranger who sojourns 3
22:21 You shall not wrong a stranger or oppress him 3
21 for you were strangers in the land of Egypt. 3
23: 9 You shall not oppress a stranger; 3
9 you know the heart of a stranger 3
9 for you were strangers in the land of Egypt. 3
Lev 16:29 the native or the stranger who sojourns among you 3
17: 8 or of the strangers that sojourn among them 3
10 or of the strangers that sojourn among them 3
12 any stranger who sojourns among you 3
13 or of the strangers that sojourn among them 3
18:26 the native or the stranger who sojourns among you 3
19:33 When a stranger sojourns with you in your land 3
34 The stranger who sojourns with you shall be 3
34 for you were strangers in the land of Egypt 3
20: 2 Any . . of the strangers that sojourn in Israel 3
23:22 leave them for . . the stranger: I am the LORD 3
25:23 for the land is mine; for you are strangers 3
35 as a stranger and a sojourner he shall live 3
45 from among the strangers who sojourn with you 2
47 If a stranger or sojourner with you becomes rich 3
47 your brother . . sells himself to the stranger 3
47 sells . . to a member of the stranger's family 3
Num 9:14 if a stranger sojourns among you 3
15:14 if a stranger is sojourning with you, or any one 3
15 shall be one statute for you and for the stranger 3
16 you and for the stranger who sojourns with you. 3
26 be forgiven, and the stranger who sojourns among 3
29 for the stranger who sojourns among them. 3
19:10 be to the people of Israel, and to the stranger 3
35:15 cities . . for refuge . . for the stranger 3
Deu 25: 5 not be married outside the family to a stranger; 1
Jos 20: 9 for . . Israel, and for the stranger sojourning 3
1Ch 29:15 For we are strangers before thee, and sojourners 3
Job 15:19 no stranger passed among them). 4
19:15 my maidservants count me as a stranger; 4
Ps 69: 8 I have become a stranger to my brethren, an alien 4
109:11 may strangers plunder the fruits of his toil! 4
Prv 5:10 lest strangers take their fill of your strength 4
17 not for strangers with you. 4
6: 1 if you have . . given your pledge for a stranger; 4
11:15 He who gives surety for a stranger will smart 4
14:10 no stranger shares its joy. 4
20:16 garment when he has given surety for a stranger 4
27: 2 stranger, and not your own lips. 5
13 garment when he has given surety for a stranger 4
Ecc 6: 2 power to enjoy them, but a stranger enjoys them; 5
Jer 2:25 It is hopeless, for I have loved strangers 4
3:13 and scattered your favors among strangers 4
5:19 you shall serve strangers in a land . . not yours.' 4
14: 8 why shouldst thou be like a stranger in the land 3
30: 8 strangers shall no more make servants of them. 4
Lam 5: 2 inheritance has been turned over to strangers 4
Ezk 14: 7 or of the strangers that sojourn in Israel 3
16:32 Adulterous wife, who receives strangers 4
28: 7 behold, I will bring strangers upon you 4
Jol 3:17 and strangers shall never again pass through it. 4
Obd 1:11 on the day that strangers carried off his wealth 4
Mat 25:35 I was a stranger and you welcomed me 9
38 when did we see thee a stranger and welcome thee 9
43 I was a stranger and you did not welcome me 9
44 thirsty or a stranger or naked or sick 9
27: 7 the potter's field, to bury strangers in. 9
Joh 10: 5 A stranger they will not follow 8
5 for they do not know the voice of strangers. 8
Eph 2:12 strangers to the covenants of promise 9
19 you are no longer strangers and sojourners 9
Heb 11:13 having acknowledged that they were strangers 9
3Jn 1: 5 you render any service . . especially to strangers 9
2Es 16:40 be like strangers on the earth. 13
46 for strangers shall gather their fruits 14
Jdt 9: 2 gavest a sword to take revenge on the strangers 7
Wis 19:14 Others had refused to receive strangers 6
Sir 8:18 In the presence of a stranger do nothing 8
11:34 Receive a stranger into your home 8
21:25 The lips of strangers will speak of these things 8
23:22 provides an heir by a stranger. 8
29:24 where you are a stranger 10

26 Come here, stranger, prepare the table 11
27 Give place, stranger, to an honored person 11
1Mc 1:38 she became a dwelling of strangers 8
3Mc 2:25 who were strangers to everything just. 12

stranger *See also* hatred, hospitality, treat.

strangle 1. חנק 2. מַחֲנָק 3. *ἄγχω* 4. *ἀποπνίγω* 5. *πνικτός* 6. *στραγγαλόομαι*

Job 7:15 that I would choose strangling and death 2
Nah 2:12 and strangled prey for his lionesses; 1
Act 15:20 from what is strangled and from blood. 5
29 from blood and from what is strangled 5
21:25 from what is strangled and from unchastity. 5
Tob 2: 3 Father, one of our people has been strangled 6
3: 8 Do you not know that you strangle your husbands? 4
4Mc 9:17 not so powerful as to strangle my reason 3

stratagem 1. *στρατήγημα*

2Mc 14:29 to accomplish this by a stratagem. 1

strategic 1. *ἐπίκαιρος*

2Mc 8: 6 He captured strategic positions 1
31 stored them all carefully in strategic places 1

strategically 1. *ἐπὶ μέρος εὔκαιρον*

2Mc 15:20 the elephants strategically stationed 1

strategy 1. עֵצָה 2. *μέθοδος* 3. *στράτευμα*

2Kg 18:20 that mere words are strategy and power for war? 1
Isa 36: 5 you think . . mere words are strategy and power 1
Jdt 11: 8 you are . . marvelous in military strategy. 3
2Mc 13:18 tried strategy in attacking their positions. 2

straw 1. מַתְבֵּן 2. תֶּבֶן 3. *καλάμη* 4. stipula 5. stramen

Gen 24:25 We have both straw and provender enough 2
32 Laban ungirded the camels, and gave him straw 2
Exd 5: 7 no longer give the people straw to make bricks 2
7 let them go and gather straw for themselves. 2
10 Thus says Pharaoh, 'I will not give you straw. 2
11 get your straw wherever you can find it; 2
12 scattered . . to gather stubble for straw. 2
13 Complete your work . . as when there was straw. 2
16 No straw is given to your servants, yet they say 2
18 Go now, and work; for no straw shall be given you 2
Jdg 19:19 We have straw and provender for our asses 2
1Kg 4:28 Barley also and straw . . they brought 2
Job 21:18 That they are like straw before the wind 2
41:27 He counts iron as straw, and bronze as rotten 2
Isa 11: 7 and the lion shall eat straw like the ox. 2
25:10 as straw is trodden down in a dung-pit. 1
65:25 the lion shall eat straw like the ox; 2
Jer 23:28 What has straw in common with wheat? 2
1Co 3:12 with gold, silver, precious stones, wood, hay, straw– 3
2Es 1:33 I will drive you out as the wind drives straw; 4
15:23 and the sinners, like straw that is kindled. 5

straw *See also* gather.

stray 1. נדד 2. נדח 3. שׁגה 4. תעה 5. *γίνομαι* 6. *ἐκτρέπω* 7. *πλανάω*

Ps 119:110I do not stray from thy precepts. 4
Prv 7:25 do not stray into her paths; 4
19:27 only to stray from the words of knowledge. 3
27: 8 Like a bird that strays from its nest 1
8 from its nest, is a man who strays from his home. 1
Isa 16: 8 its branches, which . . strayed to the desert; 4
Ezk 34: 4 the strayed you have not brought back 2
16 I will bring back the strayed 2
Hos 7:13 Woe to them, for they have strayed from me! 1
1Ti 5:15 For some have already strayed after Satan. 6
1Pe 2:25 For you were straying like sheep 7
Wis 5: 6 it was we who strayed from the way of truth 7
Bar 3:21 Their sons have strayed far from her way. 5

streak 1. פְּצָלָה

Gen 30:37 fresh rods . . and peeled white streaks in them 1

stream 1. יְאֹר 2. יוּבַל 3. מַי 4. נָהָר 5. נזל 6. נַחַל 7. פֶּלֶג 8. תְּעָלָה 9. נָהָר (A) 10. *ποταμός* 11. *ῥεῦμα* 12. *χειμάρρους* 13. fluctus 14. flumen 15. rivus 16. vena

Gen 32:23 He took them and sent them across the stream 6
2Kg 19:24 I dried up . . all the streams of Egypt.' 1
Job 20:17 the streams flowing with honey and curds. 4
28:11 binds up the streams so that they do not trickle 4
29: 6 the rock poured out for me streams of oil! 7
Ps 1: 3 He is like a tree planted by streams of water 7
42: 1 As a hart longs for flowing streams 3
46: 4 a river whose streams make glad the city of God 7
74:15 thou didst dry up ever-flowing streams. 4
78:16 He made streams come out of the rock 5
20 that water gushed out and streams overflowed. 6
44 so that they could not drink of their streams. 5
119:136My eyes shed streams of tears 7
Prv 5:16 streams of water in the streets? 7
18: 4 fountain of wisdom is a gushing stream. 6
21: 1 heart is a stream of water in the hand of the LORD; 7
Ecc 1: 7 All streams run to the sea, but the sea is not full; 6
7 where the streams flow, there they flow again. 6
Isa 7:18 the fly . . at the sources of the streams of Egypt 1
30:28 his breath is like an overflowing stream 6
33 the breath of the LORD, like a stream of brimstone 6
32: 2 like streams of water in a dry place 7
33:21 a place of broad rivers and streams 1
34: 9 the streams of Edom shall be turned into pitch 6
35: 6 in the wilderness, and streams in the desert; 6
37:25 I dried up with . . my foot all the streams of Egypt. 1
44: 3 For I will pour . . streams on the dry ground; 5
4 like grass . . like willows by flowing streams. 3
59:19 for he will come like a rushing stream 4
66:12 of the nations like an overflowing stream; 6
Jer 17: 8 like a tree . . that sends out its roots by the stream 2
Ezk 29: 3 dragon that lies in the midst of his streams 1
4 the fish of your streams stick to your scales; 1
4 I will draw you up out of the midst of your streams 1
4 fish of your streams which stick to your scales. 1
5 you and all the fish of your streams; 1
10 I am against you, and against your streams 1
31: 4 sending forth its streams to all the trees 8
Dan 7:10 stream of fire issued and came forth from before 9
12: 5 one on this bank of the stream and one on that bank 1
5 one on this bank . . one on that bank of the stream. 1
6 man . . who was above the waters of the stream 1
7 man . . who was above the waters of the stream 1
Ams 5:24 and righteousness like an ever-flowing stream. 6
Lke 6:48 the stream broke against that house 10
49 a house . . against which the stream broke 10
2Es 1:22 in the wilderness, at the bitter stream 14
23 and made the stream sweet. 14
4: 7 or how many streams are at the source of the deep 16
7 or how many streams are above the firmament 16
13:10 from his mouth as it were a stream of fire 13
11 the stream of fire and the flaming breath 13
15:41 all the fields and all the streams may be filled 15
Sir 39:13 bud like a rose growing by a stream of water; 11
1Mc 5:37 on the other side of the stream. 12
39 they are encamped across the stream 12
40 his army drew near to the stream of water 12
42 When Judas approached the stream of water 12
42 he stationed the scribes . . at the stream 12
16: 5 a stream lay between them. 12
6 the soldiers were afraid to cross the stream 12

stream bed 1. אָפִיק

Jol 3:18 the stream beds of Judah shall flow with water; 1

stream down 1. ירד

Lam 2:18 tears stream down like a torrent day and night! 1

flowing stream 1. נזל

Sng 4:15 living water, and flowing streams from Lebanon. 1
Jer 18:14 waters run dry, the cold flowing streams? 1

stream out 1. *διαχέω*

Aza 1:24 the flame streamed out above the furnace 1

stream-bed 1. נַחַל

2Kg 3:17 that stream-bed shall be filled with water 1

dry stream-bed 1. נַחַל

2Kg 3:16 'I will make this dry stream-bed full of pools.' 1

street 1. דֶּרֶךְ 2. חוּץ 3. נְתִיבָה 4. רְחוֹב 5. שׁוּק 6. *ἀγυιά* 7. *ὁδός* 8. *πλατεῖα* 9. *πλατύς* 10. *ῥύμη*

Gen 19: 2 we will spend the night in the street. 4
Jos 2:19 If any one goes out . . into the street 2
1Sm 9:26 Saul . . and Samuel went out into the street. 2
2Sm 1:20 in Gath, publish it not in the streets of Ash'kelon; 2
22:43 stamped them down like the mire of the streets. 2
Job 18:17 he has no name in the street. 2
31:32 the sojourner has not lodged in the street; 2
Ps 18:42 I cast them out like the mire of the streets. 2
31:11 those who see me in the street flee from me. 2
144:14 there be no cry of distress in our streets! 4
Prv 1:20 Wisdom cries aloud in the street; 2
5:16 streams of water in the streets? 4
7: 8 passing along the street near her corner 5
12 now in the street, now in the market 2
22:13 lion outside! I shall be slain in the streets! 4
26:13 sluggard says, " . . There is a lion in the streets! 4
Ecc 12: 4 and the doors on the street are shut; 5
5 and the mourners go about the streets; 5
Sng 3: 2 about the city, in the streets and in the squares; 5
Isa 5:25 their corpses were as refuse in . . the streets. 2
10: 6 to tread them down like the mire of the streets. 2
15: 3 in the streets they gird on sackcloth; 2
24:11 There is an outcry in the streets for lack of wine; 2
42: 2 lift up his voice, or make it heard in the street; 2
51:20 at the head of every street like an antelope 2
23 and like the street for them to pass over. 2
58:12 repairer . . the restorer of streets to dwell in. 3
Jer 5: 1 Run to and fro through the streets of Jerusalem 2
6:11 Pour it out upon the children in the street 2
7:17 cities of Judah and in the streets of Jerusalem? 2
34 from the streets of Jerusalem the voice of mirth 2
9:21 cutting off the children from the streets 2
11: 6 cities of Judah, and in the streets of Jerusalem 2
13 as many as the streets of Jerusalem 2
14:16 shall be cast out in the streets of Jerusalem 2
33:10 and the streets of Jerusalem that are desolate 2
37:21 bread was given him daily from the bakers' street 2
44: 6 cities of Judah and in the streets of Jerusalem; 2
9 the land of Judah and in the streets of Jerusalem? 2
17 cities of Judah and in the streets of Jerusalem; 2
21 cities of Judah and in the streets of Jerusalem 2
51: 4 fall down slain . . and wounded in her streets. 2
Lam 1:20 In the street the sword bereaves; 2
2:11 and babes faint in the streets of the city. 4
12 faint like wounded men in the streets of the city 4
19 who faint for hunger at the head of every street. 2
21 In the dust of . . streets lie the young and the old; 2
4: 1 holy stones lie . . at the head of every street. 2
5 who feasted on dainties perish in the street; 2
8 they are not recognized in the streets; 2
14 They wandered, blind, through the streets 2
18 we could not walk in our streets; our end drew near; 4
Ezk 7:19 They cast their silver into the streets 2
11: 6 and have filled its streets with the slain. 2
16:25 at the head of every street you built your lofty 1
31 your vaulted chamber at the head of every street 1
26:11 With . . horses he will trample all your streets; 2
28:23 pestilence into her, and blood into her streets; 2
Ams 5:16 and in all the streets they shall say, 'Alas! Alas!' 2
Mic 7:10 be trodden down like the mire of the streets. 2
Nah 2: 4 The chariots rage in the streets 2
3:10 dashed in pieces at the head of every street; 2
Zep 3: 6 I have laid waste their streets 2
Zec 8: 4 shall again sit in the streets of Jerusalem 4
5 And the streets of the city shall be full of boys 4
5 full of boys and girls playing in its streets. 4
9: 3 like dust, and gold like the dirt of the streets. 2
10: 5 trampling the foe in the mud of the streets; 2
Mat 6: 2 in the synagogues and in the streets 10
5 pray in the synagogues and at the street corners 8
12:19 nor will any one hear his voice in the streets; 9
22:10 And those servants went out into the streets 7
Lke 10:10 go into its streets and say 8
13:26 you taught in our streets.' 9
14:21 Go out quickly to the streets and lanes of the city 8
Act 5:15 they even carried out the sick into the streets 8
9:11 Rise and go to the street called Straight 10
12:10 they went out and passed on through one street; 10
Rev 11: 8 their dead bodies will lie in the street 8
21:21 and the street of the city was pure gold 8
22: 2 through the middle of the street of the city; 8
Tob 13:17 The streets of Jerusalem will be paved 8
Jdt 7:14 strewn about in the streets where they live. 9
22 and fell down in the streets of the city 8
Sir 9: 7 Do not look around in the streets of a city 10
23:21 will be punished in the streets of the city 9
49: 6 made her streets desolate 7
1Mc 1:55 burned incense . . in the streets. 9
2: 9 Her babes have been killed in her streets 9
14: 9 Old men sat in the streets 9
2Mc 3:19 Women . . thronged the streets 7
3Mc 1:18 filled the streets with groans 9
20 some in houses and some in the streets 6
4: 3 what streets were not filled with mourning 6

main street 1. *δίοδος*

1Mc 11:46 the men . . seized the main streets of the city 1

open street 1. *ἄμφοδον*

Mrk 11: 4 at the door out in the open street; 1

strength 1. און 2. אֱיָל 3. אַמִּיץ 4. אַמְצָה 5. גְבוּרָה 6. דֹּבֶא 7. זְרוֹעַ 8. חֵזֶק 9. חֹזֶק 10. חַיִל 11. יָד 12. כֹּחַ 13. לֶשֶׁד 14. מָעוֹז 15. נֶפֶשׁ 16. עֹז 17. עֶצֶם 18. עָצְמָה 19. צוּר 20. קֶרֶן 21. תַּעֲצֻמָה 22. תֹּקֶף 23. גְּבוּרָה (A) 24. *βραχίων* 25. *δύναμις* 26. *ἐρυμνότης* 27. *εὐδράνεια* 28. *ἰσχύς* 29. *ἰσχύω* 30. *κατισχύω* 31. *κραταίωσις* 32. *κράτος* 33. *ὁ δύναμαι* 34. *ῥώμη* 35. *στερέωμα* 36. *σωτηρία* 37. fortitudo 38. virtus

Gen 4:12 it shall no longer yield to you its strength; 12
31: 6 I have served your father with all my strength; 12
49: 3 you are . . the first fruits of my strength 1
Exd 13: 3 for by strength of hand the LORD brought you out 9
14 By strength of hand the LORD brought us out 9
15: 2 The LORD is my strength and my song, and he has 16
13 guided them by thy strength to thy holy abode. 16
Lev 26:20 your strength shall be spent in vain 12
Num11: 6 now our strength is dried up, and there is nothing 15
Deu 21:17 first issue of his strength; the right 1
33:25 as your days, so shall your strength be. 6
Jos 14:11 my strength now is as my strength was then, for war 12
11 my strength now is as my strength was then, for war 12
Jdg 8:21 for as the man is, so is his strength. 5
16: 5 see wherein his great strength lies 12
6 Please tell me wherein your great strength lies 12
9 the secret of his strength was not known. 12
15 not told me wherein your great strength lies. 12
17 If I be shaved, then my strength will leave me 12
19 began to torment him, and his strength left him. 12

1Sm 2: 1 my strength is exalted in the LORD. 20
4 bows . . are broken, but the feeble gird on strength. 10
10 The LORD will . . he will give strength to his king 16
31 I will cut off your strength and the strength 7
31 cut off . . and the strength of your father's house 7
28:20 and there was no strength in him 12
22 you may have strength when you go on your way. 12
30: 4 and wept, until they had no more strength to weep. 12
2Sm 22:40 thou didst gird me with strength for the battle; 10
1Kg 19: 8 and went in the strength of that food 40 days 12
2Kg 9:24 Jehu drew his bow with his full strength 11
19: 3 and there is no strength to bring them forth. 12
26 inhabitants, shorn of strength, are dismayed 11
1Ch 16:11 Seek the LORD and his strength, seek his presence 16
27 strength and joy are in his place. 16
28 ascribe to the LORD glory and strength! 16
Neh 4:10 The strength of the burden-bearers is failing 12
8:10 for the joy of the LORD is your strength. 14
Job 6:11 What is my strength, that I should wait? 12
12 Is my strength the strength of stones 12
12 Is my strength the strength of stones 12
9: 4 He is wise in heart, and mighty in strength 12
19 If it is a contest of strength, behold him! 3
12:16 With him are strength and wisdom; 16
16:15 and have laid my strength in the dust. 20
18:12 His strength is hunger-bitten 1
26: 2 How you have saved the arm that has no strength! 16
30: 2 could I gain from the strength of their hands 12
36: 5 he is mighty in strength of understanding. 12
19 or all the force of your strength? 12
39:11 you depend on him because his strength is great 12
19 Do you clothe his neck with strength? •
21 He paws in the valley, and exults in his strength; 12
40:16 Behold, his strength in his loins, and his power 12
41:22 In his neck abides strength 16
Ps 18: 1 I love thee, O LORD, my strength. 8
32 the God who girded me with strength 10
39 thou didst gird me with strength for the battle; 10
21: 1 In thy strength the king rejoices, O LORD; 16
13 Be exalted, O LORD, in thy strength! 16
22:15 my strength is dried up like a potsherd 12
28: 7 The LORD is my strength and my shield; 16
8 The LORD is the strength of his people 16
29: 1 ascribe to the LORD glory and strength. 16
11 May the LORD give strength to his people! 16
31:10 my strength fails because of my misery 12
32: 4 my strength was dried up as by the heat of summer. 13
33:16 a warrior is not delivered by his great strength. 12
38:10 My heart throbs, my strength fails me; 12
46: 1 God is our refuge and strength 16
59: 9 O my Strength, I will sing praises to thee; 16
17 O my Strength, I will sing praises to thee 16
65: 6 by thy strength hast established the mountains 12
68:35 God . . gives power and strength to his people. 21
71: 9 forsake me not when my strength is spent. 12
73:26 God is the strength of my heart and my portion 19
78:51 first issue of their strength in the tents of Ham. 1
81: 1 Sing aloud to God our strength; 16
84: 5 Blessed are the men whose strength is in thee 16
7 They go from strength to strength; 10
7 They go from strength to strength; 10
86:16 give thy strength to thy servant 16
88: 4 I am a man who has no strength 2
89:17 For thou art the glory of their strength; 16
90:10 or even by reason of strength fourscore; 5
93: 1 LORD is robed, he is girded with strength. 16
96: 6 strength and beauty are in his sanctuary. 16
7 ascribe to the LORD glory and strength! 16
102:23 He has broken my strength in mid-course; 12
105: 4 Seek the LORD and his strength 16
36 smote . . first issue of all their strength. 1
118:14 The LORD is my strength and my song; 16
138: 3 my strength of soul thou didst increase. 16
147:10 His delight is not in the strength of the horse 5
Prv 5:10 lest strangers take their fill of your strength 12
8:14 I have insight, I have strength. 5
14: 4 abundant crops come by the strength of the ox. 12
20:29 The glory of young men is their strength 12
24: 5 man of knowledge than he who has strength; 12
10 If you faint . . your strength is small. 12
31: 3 Give not your strength to women 10
17 She girds her loins with strength 16
25 Strength and dignity are her clothing 16
Ecc 10:10 he must put forth more strength; 10
17 feast . . for strength, and not for drunkenness! 5
Isa 10:13 he says: "By the strength of my hand I have done it 12
12: 2 for the LORD GOD is my strength and my song 16
28: 6 strength to those who turn back the battle 5
30:15 trust shall be your strength." And you would not 5
37: 3 and there is no strength to bring them forth. 12
27 while their inhabitants, shorn of strength 11
40: 9 lift up your voice with strength, O Jerusalem 12
29 to him who has no might he increases strength. 18
31 who wait for the LORD shall renew their strength 12
41: 1 let the peoples renew their strength; 12
44:12 he becomes hungry and his strength fails 12
45:24 in the LORD . . are righteousness and strength; 16
49: 4 I have spent my strength for nothing and vanity; 12
5 the LORD, and my God has become my strength- 16
51: 9 Awake, awake, put on strength, O arm of the LORD; 16
52: 1 Awake, awake, put on your strength, O Zion; 16
57:10 you found new life for your strength 11
63: 1 marching in the greatness of his strength? 12
Jer 16:19 O LORD, my strength and my stronghold, my refuge 16
48:45 fugitives stop without strength; 12
51:30 strength has failed, they have become women; 5
Lam 1: 6 they fled without strength before the pursuer. 12
11 treasures for food to revive their strength. 15
14 he caused my strength to fail; the Lord gave me 12
19 they sought food to revive their strength. 15
Dan 2:23 for thou hast given me wisdom and strength 23
10: 8 great vision, and no strength was left in me; 12
8 I retained no strength. 12
16 pains have come upon me, and I retain no strength. 12
17 For now no strength remains in me, and no breath 12
11: 6 but she shall not retain the strength of her arm 12
15 for there shall be no strength to stand. 12
17 come with the strength of his whole kingdom 22
Hos 7: 9 Aliens devour his strength, and he knows it not; 12
Ams 2:14 and the strong shall not retain his strength 12
6:13 Have we not by our own strength taken Karnaim 9
Mic 5: 4 and feed his flock in the strength of the LORD 16
Nah 2: 1 gird your loins; collect all your strength. 12
3: 9 Ethiopia was her strength, Egypt too 17
Hab 3:19 GOD, the Lord, is my strength; 10
Hag 2:22 am about to destroy the strength of the kingdoms 9
Zec 12: 5 The inhabitants of Jerusalem have strength 4
Mrk 5: 4 no one had the strength to subdue him. 29
12:30 with all your mind, and with all your strength.' 28
33 with all the strength 28
Lke 1:51 He has shown strength with his arm 32
10:27 with all your soul, and with all your strength 28
21:36 praying that you may have strength 30
Act 27:34 it will give you strength 36
1Co 10:13 not let you be tempted beyond your strength 33
Eph 6:10 in the strength of his might. 32
1Pe 4:11 who renders it by the strength which God supplies 28
Rev 1:16 face was like the sun shining in full strength 25
1Es 3:17 the first, who had spoken of the strength of wine 28
4: 1 who had spoken of the strength of the king 28
40 To her belongs the strength . . of all the ages 28
2Es 5:53 Those born in the strength of youth 38
55 is aging and passing the strength of youth. 37
12: 5 and not even a little strength is left in me 38
Jdt 2: 5 take with you men confident in their strength 28
5: 3 in what does their power or strength consist? 28
23 a people with no strength or power for making war. 25
7:22 there was no strength left in them any longer. 31
9: 7 they glory in the strength of their foot soldiers; 24
8 Break their strength by thy might 28
9 give to me, a widow, the strength to do what I plan. 32
11:22 to lend strength to our hands 32
13:11 to show . . his strength against our enemies 32
16:13 wonderful in strength, invincible. 28
Wis 10: 2 and gave him strength to rule all things. 28
12:16 For thy strength is the source of righteousness 28
17 thou dost show thy strength 25
18 Thou who art sovereign in strength 28
13:19 he asks strength 27
16:16 were scourged by the strength of thy arm 28
18:22 He conquered the wrath not by strength of body 28
Sir 3:13 in all your strength do not despise him. 28
5: 2 Do not follow your inclination and strength 28
9: 2 so that she gains mastery over your strength. 28
11:12 who lacks strength and abounds in poverty 28
13: 2 Do not lift a weight beyond your strength •
17: 3 He endowed them with strength like his own 28
19:28 by lack of strength he is prevented from sinning 28
28:10 in proportion to the strength of the man 28
31:30 reducing his strength and adding wounds. 28
38:18 sorrow of heart saps one's strength. 28
39:28 they will pour out their strength 28
40:26 Riches and strength lift up the heart 28
41: 2 one who is in need and is failing in strength 28
43:30 put forth all your strength, and do not grow weary 28
46: 9 the Lord gave Caleb strength 28
47: 5 he gave him strength in his right hand 32
Bar 1:12 And the Lord will give us strength 28
3:14 Learn . . where there is strength, where there is 28
Aza 1:21 let their strength be broken. 28
1Mc 3:19 strength comes from Heaven. 28
35 to wipe out and destroy the strength of Israel 28
4:32 melt the boldness of their strength 28
9:14 Bacchides and the strength of his army 35
2Mc 10:34 relying on the strength of the place 26
12:14 relying on the strength of the walls 26
3Mc 2: 4 who trusted in their strength and boldness 34

strength *See also* find, give, increase, lack, man, match, summon, win.

main strength 1. εὐρώστως
2Mc 12:35 and . . was dragging him off by main strength 1

mighty strength 1. גְבוּרָה
Job 41:12 or his mighty strength, or his goodly frame. 1

no strength 1. ἀδρανής
Wis 13:19 a thing whose hands have no strength. 1

show strength 1. עזז 2. ἰσχύω
Ps 68:28 Summon thy might, O God; show thy strength, O God 1
Wis 11:21 it is always in thy power to show great strength 2

strengthen 1. אמץ 2. גבר 3. חזק 4. כון 5. מָעוֹז 6. סעד 7. קום 8. βεβαιόω 9. δυναμόω 10. ἐνδυναμόω 11. ἐνισχύω 12. ἐπιρρωνύω 13. ἐπιστηρίζω 14. ἐπισχύω 15. ἐπιτείνω 16. θεμελιόω 17. καθίστημι 18. κατισχύω 19. κραταιόω 20. κυρέω 21. στερεόω 22. στήριγμα 23. στηρίζω 24. confirmo 25. conforto
Deu 3:28 charge Joshua, and encourage and strengthen him; 1
Jdg 3:12 and the LORD strengthened Eglon the king of Moab 3
7:11 your hands shall be strengthened to go down 3
9:24 upon . . Shechem, who strengthened his hands 3
16:28 remember me . . and strengthen me, I pray thee 3
19: 5 Strengthen your heart with a morsel of bread 6
8 Strengthen your heart, and tarry until the day 6
1Sm 23:16 Jonathan . . and strengthened his hand in God. 3
30: 6 David strengthened himself in the LORD his God. 3
2Sm 11:25 strengthen your attack upon the city 3
16:21 all who are with you will be strengthened. 3
1Kg 20:22 Come, strengthen yourself, and consider well 3
2Ch 11:17 They strengthened the kingdom of Judah 3
17: 1 strengthened himself against Israel. 3
24:13 restored the house of God . . and strengthened 1
28:20 afflicted him instead of strengthening him. 3
32: 5 he strengthened the Millo in the city of David. 3
Neh 2:18 strengthened their hands for the good work. 3
6: 9 But now, O God, strengthen thou my hands. 3
Job 4: 3 you have strengthened the weak hands. 3
16: 5 I could strengthen you with my mouth 1
Ps 10:17 of the meek; thou wilt strengthen their heart 4
89:21 my arm also shall strengthen him. 1
104:15 bread to strengthen man's heart. 6
119:28 strengthen me according to thy word! 7
147:13 For he strengthens the bars of your gates; 3
Isa 35: 3 Strengthen the weak hands 3
41:10 I will strengthen you, I will help you 1
54: 2 lengthen your cords and strengthen your stakes. 3
Jer 23:14 they strengthen the hands of evildoers 3
Ezk 30:24 I will strengthen the arms of the king of Babylon 3
25 I will strengthen the arms of the king 3
34: 4 The weak you have not strengthened 3
16 and I will strengthen the weak 3
Dan 10:18 appearance of a man touched me and strengthened 3
19 when he spoke to me, I was strengthened and said 3
19 Let my lord speak, for you have strengthened me. 3
11: 1 stood up to confirm and strengthen him. 5
Hos 7:15 Although I trained and strengthened their arms 3
Nah 3:14 Draw water for the siege, strengthen your forts; 3
Zec 10: 6 I will strengthen the house of Judah 2
Lke 22:32 strengthen your brethren. 23
Act 9:19 took food and was strengthened 11
14:22 strengthening the souls of the disciples 13
15:32 exhorted . . and strengthened them. 13
41 strengthening the churches. 13
16: 5 So the churches were strengthened in the faith 21
18:23 strengthening all the disciples. 13
Rom 1:11 impart . . some spiritual gift to strengthen you 23
16:25 Now to him who is able to strengthen you 23
Eph 3:16 he may grant you to be strengthened with might 19
Php 4:13 I can do all things in him who strengthens me. 10
Col 1:11 May you be strengthened with all power 9
2Th 3: 3 he will strengthen you and guard you from evil. 23
Heb 12:12 and strengthen your weak knees •
13: 9 is well that the heart be strengthened by grace 8
1Pe 5:10 will . . restore, establish, and strengthen you. 16
Rev 3: 2 Awake, and strengthen what remains 23
1Es 7:15 to strengthen their hands 18
2Es 2:25 nourish your sons, and strengthen their feet. 24
5:15 held me and strengthened me and set me on my feet. 25
10:30 he grasped my right hand and strengthened me 25
12: 6 that he may strengthen me to the end. 25
8 strengthen me and show me, thy servant 25
Sir 3: 9 a father's blessing strengthens the houses 23
29: 1 he that strengthens him with his hand 14
45: 8 strengthened him with the symbols of authority 21
49: 3 he strengthened godliness. 18
1Mc 1:34 These strengthened their position; 11
6:18 strengthen the Gentiles. 22
10:23 to strengthen himself. 22
14:14 He strengthened all the humble of his people 23
2Mc 11: 9 were strengthened in heart 12
3Mc 1: 7 he strengthened the morale of his subjects. 17
4Mc 7: 9 You, father, strengthened our loyalty to the law 20
15:23 strengthened her to disregard 15

strengthen a fortification 1. προσοχυρόω
1Mc 13:48 also strengthened its fortifications 1
52 He strengthened the fortification 1

stress 1. χαλεπός
2Ti 3: 1 in the last days there will come times of stress. 1

stretch 1. גהר 2. מדד 3. נטה 4. סוח 5. סרח 6. שרע 7. τείνω
Num24: 6 Like valleys that stretch afar 3

1Kg 17:21 he stretched himself upon the child three times 2
2Kg 4:34 as he stretched himself upon him, the flesh 1
35 and went up, and stretched himself upon him; 1
21:13 I will stretch over Jerusalem the . . line 3
Job 38: 5 Or who stretched the line upon it? 3
Isa 28:20 For the bed is too short to stretch oneself on it 6
34:11 He shall stretch the line of confusion over it 3
44:13 The carpenter stretches a line, he marks it out 3
Ams 6: 4 and stretch themselves upon their couches 5
7 and the revelry of those who stretch themselves 4
3Mc 5:25 stretched their hands toward heaven 7

stretch afar 1. מֶרְחָק
Isa 33:17 they will behold a land that stretches afar. 1

stretch forth 1. נטה 2. שׁלח 3. *ἐκτείνω* 4. *κτείνω* 5. *προτείνω*
Exd 7: 5 when I stretch forth my hand upon Egypt and bring 1
9:22 the LORD said to Moses, "Stretch forth your hand 1
23 Moses stretched forth his rod toward heaven; 1
10:13 Moses stretched forth his rod over the land 1
14:27 Moses stretched forth his hand over the sea 1
2Sm 24:16 when the angel stretched forth his hand 2
Job 15:25 he has stretched forth his hand against God 1
Ps 144: 7 Stretch forth thy hand from on high 2
Ezk 10: 7 a cherub stretched forth his hand 2
1Es 8:73 stretching forth my hands to the Lord 3
Sir 7:32 Stretch forth your hand to the poor 4
2Mc 7:10 and courageously stretched forth his hands 5
14:34 Then the priests stretched forth their hands 5

stretch out 1. משׁך 2. נגר 3. נטה 4. נטע 5. פרשׂ 6. שׁלח 7. *ἀνατείνω* 8. *ἐκτείνω* 9. *ἐκτίθημι* 10. *κατατείνω* 11. *κτείνω* 12. *προπίπτω* 13. *προτείνω* 14. *τανύω*
Gen 48:14 Israel stretched out his right hand and laid it 6
Exd 3:20 So I will stretch out my hand and smite Egypt 6
7:19 stretch out your hand over the waters of Egypt 3
8: 5 Say to Aaron, 'Stretch out your hand with your rod 3
6 So Aaron stretched out his hand over the waters 3
16 Say to Aaron, 'Stretch out your rod and strike 3
17 they did so; Aaron stretched out his hand 3
9:29 I will stretch out my hands to the LORD; 5
33 Moses . . stretched out his hands to the LORD; 5
10:12 Then the LORD said to Moses, "Stretch out your hand 3
21 Stretch out your hand toward heaven 3
22 So Moses stretched out his hand toward heaven 3
14:16 Lift up your rod, and stretch out your hand over 3
21 Then Moses stretched out his hand over the sea; 3
26 Then the LORD said to Moses, "Stretch out your hand 3
15:12 Thou didst stretch out thy right hand 3
Jos 8:18 Stretch out the javelin that is in your hand 3
18 Joshua stretched out the javelin . . in his hand 3
19 as soon as he had stretched out his hand, they ran 3
26 his hand, with which he stretched out the javelin 3
1Kg 8:38 and stretching out his hands toward this house; 5
13: 4 Jerobo'am stretched out his hand from the altar 6
4 his hand, which he stretched out against him 6
1Ch 21:16 a drawn sword stretched out over Jerusalem. 3
2Ch 6:29 and stretching out his hands toward this house; 5
Job 9: 8 who alone stretched out the heavens 3
11:13 you will stretch out your hands toward him. 5
26: 7 He stretches out the north over the void 3
30:24 not one in a heap of ruins stretch out his hand 6
Ps 55:20 My companion stretched out his hand 6
77: 2 my hand is stretched out without wearying; 2
104: 2 who hast stretched out the heavens like a tent 3
138: 7 stretch out thy hand against the wrath of my 6
143: 6 I stretch out my hands to thee; my soul thirsts 5
Prv 1:24 stretched out my hand and no one has heeded 3
Isa 5:25 he stretched out his hand against them and smote 3
25 turned away and his hand is stretched out still. 3
9:12 For all this . . his hand is stretched out still. 3
17 turned away and his hand is stretched out still. 3
21 turned away and his hand is stretched out still. 3
10: 4 turned away and his hand is stretched out still. 3
14:26 the hand . . stretched out over all the nations. 3
27 His hand is stretched out, and who will turn it back? 3
23:11 He has stretched out his hand over the sea 3
31: 3 When the LORD stretches out his hand 3
40:22 who stretches out the heavens like a curtain 3
42: 5 who created the heavens and stretched them out 3
44:24 the LORD . . who stretched out the heavens alone 3
45:12 it was my hands that stretched out the heavens 3
51:13 your Maker, who stretched out the heavens 3
16 stretching out the heavens and laying 4
54: 2 curtains of your habitations be stretched out; 3
Jer 4:31 gasping for breath, stretching out her hands 5
6:12 for I will stretch out my hand 3
10:12 his understanding stretched out the heavens. 3
15: 6 I have stretched out my hand against you 3
51:15 by his understanding stretched out the heavens. 3
25 I will stretch out my hand against you 3
Lam 1:10 The enemy has stretched out his hands over all 5
17 Zion stretches out her hands 5
Ezk 1:23 their wings were stretched out straight •
2: 9 I looked, behold, a hand was stretched out to me 6
6:14 I will stretch out my hand against them 3
14: 9 I will stretch out my hand against him 3
13 I stretch out my hand against it 3
16:27 I stretched out my hand against you 3
25: 7 behold, I have stretched out my hand against you 3
13 I will stretch out my hand against Edom 3
16 Behold, I will stretch out my hand 3
30:25 he shall stretch it out against the land of Egypt; 3
35: 3 I will stretch out my hand against you 3
Dan 11:42 stretch out his hand against the countries 6
Hos 7: 5 he stretched out his hand with mockers. 1
Zep 1: 4 I will stretch out my hand against Judah 3
2:13 he will stretch out his hand against the north 3
Zec 1:16 line shall be stretched out over Jerusalem. 3
12: 1 Thus says the LORD, who stretched out the heavens 3
Mat 8: 3 And he stretched out his hand and touched him 8
12:13 Then he said to the man, "Stretch out your hand. 9
13 And the man stretched it out 8
49 stretching out his hand toward his disciples 8
26:51 one of those . . with Jesus stretched out his hand 8
Mrk 1:41 Moved with pity, he stretched out his hand 8
3: 5 said to the man, "Stretch out your hand. 9
5 He stretched it out, and his hand was restored. 8
Lke 5:13 he stretched out his hand, and touched him, saying 8
6:10 said to him, "Stretch out your hand. 9
Joh 21:18 when you are old, you will stretch out your hands 8
Act 4:30 while thou stretchest out thy hand to heal 9
26: 1 Paul stretched out his hand and made his defense 8
1Es 6:33 stretch out their hands to hinder . . that house 8
Jdt 13: 2 with Holofernes stretched out on his bed 12
Sir 15:16 stretch out your hand for whichever you wish. 8
43:12 the hands of the Most High have stretched it out. 14
46: 2 stretched out his sword against the cities! 8
1Mc 6:25 they stretched out their hands 8
7:47 the right hand which he so arrogantly stretched out 8
9:47 Jonathan stretched out his hand to strike Bacchides 8
2Mc 14:33 he stretched out his right hand 13
15:15 Jeremiah stretched out his right hand 13
21 Maccabeus . . stretched out his hands toward heaven 7
32 had been . . stretched out against the holy house 11
4Mc 4:11 Apollonius . . stretched out his hands toward heaven 8
9:13 the noble youth was stretched out around this 10

stretch tight 1. *κατατείνω*
4Mc 11:18 He was carefully stretched tight upon it 1

stretcher 1. *φορεῖον*
2Mc 3:27 his men took him up and put him on a stretcher 1

strew 1. זרק 2. נתן 3. פזר
2Ch 34: 4 made dust of them and strewed it over the graves 1
Ps 141: 7 their bones be strewn at the mouth of Sheol. 3
Ezk 32: 5 I will strew your flesh upon the mountains 2

strew about 1. *καταστρώννυμι*
Jdt 7:14 they will be strewn about in the streets 1

strew on the ground 1. *καταστρώννυμι*
Jdt 7:25 to strew us on the ground before them with thirst 1

strict 1. חצף (A) 2. *ἀκριβής* 3. *διακριβόω* 4. *ἰσχυρός*
Dan 3:22 king's order was strict and the furnace very hot 1
Act 26: 5 the strictest party of our religion 2
Wis 6: 8 a strict inquiry is in store for the mighty. 4
Sir 51:19 in my conduct I was strict 3

strict *See also* keep, manner.

strictly 1. אָסְפַּרְנָא (A) 2. *ἐπιμελῶς* 3. *πολύς*
1Sm 14:28 Your father strictly charged the people †
Ezr 7:26 let judgment be strictly executed upon him 1
Mrk 3:12 he strictly ordered them not to make him known. 3
5:43 he strictly charged them that no one should know 3
Act 5:28 We strictly charged you not to teach in this name †
23:14 We have strictly bound ourselves by an oath †
1Es 8:24 shall be strictly punished 2

strictly *See also* charge, command, examine.

strictness 1. *ἀκρίβεια*
Jas 3: 1 we . . shall be judged with greater strictness. •
Wis 12:21 with what strictness thou hast judged thy sons 1

stride 1. אַלְקוּם 2. הלך
Prv 30:29 four are stately in their stride 2
31 he-goat, and a king striding before his people. 1

strife 1. גור 2. דין 3. מָדוֹן 4. מַצָּה 5. מְרִיבָה 6. רִיב 7. *ἔρις* 8. *μάχη* 9. *πόλεμος*
Gen 13: 7 there was strife between the herdsmen of Abram's 6
8 Let there be no strife between you and me 5
Num27:14 during the strife of the congregation 5
Deu 1:12 How can I bear alone . . you and your strife? 6
2Sm 19: 9 the people were at strife throughout . . Israel 2
22:44 didst deliver me from strife with the peoples; 6
Job 33:19 with continual strife in his bones; 6
Ps 18:43 Thou didst deliver me from strife 6
31:20 under thy shelter from the strife of tongues. 6
55: 9 for I see violence and strife in the city. 6
Prv 10:12 Hatred stirs up strife 3
13:10 By insolence the heedless make strife 4
15:18 A hot-tempered man stirs up strife 3
16:28 A perverse man spreads strife 3
17: 1 quiet than a house full of feasting with strife. 6
14 beginning of strife is like letting out water; 3
19 He who loves transgression loves strife; 4
18: 6 A fool's lips bring strife 6
20: 3 It is an honor for a man to keep aloof from strife; 6
22:10 Drive out a scoffer, and strife will go out 3
23:29 Who has strife? Who has complaining? 3
26:21 so is a quarrelsome man for kindling strife. 6
28:25 A greedy man stirs up strife 3
29:22 A man of wrath stirs up strife 3
30:33 pressing anger produces strife. 6
Isa 54:15 If any one stirs up strife, it is not from me; 1
Jer 15:10 Woe is me . . that you bore me, a man of strife 6
Hab 1: 3 strife and contention arise. 6
Rom 1:29 Full of envy, murder, strife, deceit, malignity 7
1Co 3: 3 For while there is jealousy and strife among you 7
Gal 5:20 idolatry, sorcery, enmity, strife, jealousy, anger 7
Wis 14:22 they live in great strife due to ignorance 9
Sir 27:15 The strife of the proud leads to bloodshed 8
28: 8 Refrain from strife, and you will lessen sins 8
8 a man given to anger will kindle strife 8
10 in proportion to the obstinacy of strife 8
11 urgent strife sheds blood. 8
31:26 so wine tests hearts in the strife of the proud. 8
40: 5 fear of death, and fury and strife 7
9 are death and bloodshed and strife and sword 7

strife *See also* stir.

strike 1. בוא 2. דקר 3. הלם 4. חַבּוּרָה 5. חלל 6. מצא 7. נגע 8. נֶגַע 9. נגף 10. נטה 11. נָכָא 12. נכה 13. נצה 14. ספק 15. פגע 16. מחא (A) 17. *ἀποκτείνω* 18. *βάλλω* 19. *δέρω* 20. *δίδωμι* 21. *ἐκπλήσσω* 22. *ἐνσείω* 23. *καταπλήσσω* 24. *κολαφίζω* 25. *λαμβάνω* 26. *παίω* 27. *πατάσσω* 28. *περιπίπτω* 29. *πίπτω* 30. *πληγή* 31. *πλήσσω* 32. *προσκόπτω* 33. *ῥαπίζω* 34. *τραῦμα* 35. *τύπτω*
Gen 4:23 for wounding me, a young man for striking me. 4
19:11 they struck with blindness the men 12
Exd 2:13 Why do you strike your fellow? 12
7:17 I am the LORD: behold, I will strike the water 12
20 he lifted up the rod and struck the water that was 12
25 days passed after the LORD had struck the Nile. 12
8:16 your rod and strike the dust of the earth 12
17 Aaron . . struck the dust of the earth 12
9:15 I could have . . struck you and your people 13
17: 5 take . . the rod with which you struck the Nile 12
6 and you shall strike the rock, and water shall 12
21:12 Whoever strikes a man so that he dies shall be put 12
15 Whoever strikes his father or his mother shall 12
18 When men quarrel and one strikes the other 12
19 he that struck him shall be clear; 12
20 When a man strikes his slave, male or female 12
26 When a man strikes the eye of his slave 12
22: 2 a thief . . is struck so that he dies 12
Num14:12 I will strike them with the pestilence 12
20:11 Moses . . struck the rock with his rod twice; 12
22:23 Balaam struck the ass, to turn her into the road. 12
25 so he struck her again. 12
27 he struck the ass with his staff. 12
28 that you have struck me these three times? 12
32 Why have you struck your ass these three times? 12
35:21 then he who struck the blow shall be put to death; 12
Deu 19: 5 head slips . . and strikes his neighbor 6
Jdg 7:13 came to the tent, and struck it so that it fell 12
1Sm 5:12 the men who did not die were stricken with tumors 12
6: 9 we shall know that it is not his hand that struck us 7
17:49 and slung it, and struck the Philistine 12
50 David prevailed . . and struck the Philistine 12
19:10 so that he struck the spear into the wall. 12
26: 8 let me . . and I will not strike him twice. •
2Sm 12:15 the LORD struck the child . . and it became sick. 9
13:28 and when I say to you, 'Strike Amnon,' then kill him. 12
14: 6 and one struck the other and killed him. 12
7 Give up the man who struck his brother 12
18:11 Why . . did you not strike him there to the ground? 12
15 surrounded Ab'salom and struck him, and killed 12
20:10 so Jo'ab struck him with it in the body 12
10 and shed his . . without striking a second blow; •
1Kg 20:35 Strike me, I pray." But the man refused 12
35 Strike me . . " But the man refused to strike him. 12
37 he found another man, and said, "Strike me, I pray. 12
37 Strike me, I pray." And the man struck him, smiting 12
22:24 came near and struck Micai'ah on the cheek 12
34 drew his bow . . and struck the king of Israel 12
2Kg 2: 8 Eli'jah took his mantle . . and struck the water 12
14 took the mantle . . and struck the water, saying 12
14 when he had struck the water, the water was parted 12
6:18 Strike this people, I pray thee, with blindness. 12
18 he struck them . . in accordance with the prayer 12
13:18 he said to the king . . "Strike the ground with them"; 12
18 Strike the ground . . "; and he struck three times 12
19 and said, "You should have struck five or six times; 12
2Ch 18:23 Then Zedeki'ah . . came near and struck Micai'ah 12
33 struck the king of Israel between 12

Job 1:19 and struck the four corners of the house 7
15:29 nor will he strike root in the earth; 10
16:10 they have struck me insolently upon the cheek 12
34:26 He strikes them for their wickedness 14
36:32 lightning, and commands it to strike the mark. 15
Ps 73: 5 they are not stricken like other men. 7
14 For all the day long I have been stricken 7
109:22 poor and needy, and my heart is stricken within 5
141: 5 Let a good man strike or rebuke me in kindness 3
Prv 1:26 I will mock when panic strikes you 1
27 when panic strikes you like a storm 1
19:25 Strike a scoffer . . simple will learn prudence; 12
23:35 They struck me," you will say, "but I was not hurt; 12
Isa 16: 7 Mourn, utterly stricken, for the raisin-cakes 11
41: 7 him who strikes the anvil 3
53: 4 yet we esteemed him stricken, smitten by God 7
8 stricken for the transgression of my people? 8
Lam 4: 9 who pined away, stricken by want of the fruits 2
Ezk 5: 2 and strike with the sword round about the city; 12
17:10 utterly wither when the east wind strikes it 7
22:13 I strike my hands together at the dishonest gain 12
39: 3 then I will strike your bow from your left hand 12
Dan 2:35 stone that struck the image became a great 16
8: 7 enraged against him and struck the ram 12
Hos 6: 1 he has stricken, and he will bind us up. 12
9:16 E'phraim is stricken, their root is dried up 12
14: 5 he shall strike root as the poplar, 12
Mic 5: 1 they strike upon the cheek the ruler of Israel. 12
Zec 12: 4 I will strike every horse with panic 12
4 when I strike every horse of the peoples 12
13: 7 Strike the shepherd 12
Mat 4: 6 will bear you up, lest you strike your foot 32
5:39 But if any one strikes you on the right cheek, turn 33
26:31 it is written, 'I will strike the shepherd 27
51 and struck the slave of the high priest 27
67 Then they spat in his face, and struck him 24
68 Who is it that struck you? 26
27:30 took the reed and struck him on the head. 35
Mrk 14:27 it is written, 'I will strike the shepherd 27
47 struck the slave of the high priest 26
65 to cover his face, and to strike him, saying to him 24
15:19 they struck his head with a reed, and spat upon him 35
Lke 4:11 lest you strike your foot against a stone.' 32
6:29 To him who strikes you on the cheek 35
22:49 shall we strike with the sword? 27
50 one of them struck the slave of the high priest 27
64 Prophesy! Who is it that struck you? 26
Joh 18:10 Simon Peter . . struck the high priest's slave 26
23 if I have spoken rightly, why do you strike me? 19
Act 7:24 avenged him by striking the Egyptian. 27
12: 7 he struck Peter on the side and woke him, saying 27
23: 2 to strike him on the mouth. 35
3 God shall strike you, you whitewashed wall! 35
3 yet contrary to the law you order me to be struck? 35
27:14 a tempestuous wind . . struck down from the land; 18
41 striking a shoal they ran the vessel aground 28
2Co 11:20 if a man . . puts on airs, or strikes you in the face. 19
Rev 2:23 and I will strike her children dead. 17
7:16 sun shall not strike them, nor any scorching heat 29
8:12 blew his trumpet, and a third of the sun was struck 30
Jdt 13: 8 she struck his neck twice with all her might 27
18 guided you to strike the head of the leader 34
Wis 4: 3 will strike a deep root or take a firm hold. 20
19:17 They were stricken also with loss of sight 31
1Mc 5:65 He struck Hebron and its villages 27
9:47 Jonathan stretched out his hand to strike Bacchides 27
55 at that time Alcimus was stricken 30
2Mc 3:25 struck at him with its front hoofs 22
39 strikes and destroys those 35
9: 5 struck him an incurable and unseen blow 27
10: 3 striking fire out of flint 25
3Mc 5:27 being struck by the unusual invitation to come out 23
4Mc 8: 4 struck by their appearance and nobility 21

strike a blow 1. הלם
Jdg 5:26 she struck Sis'era a blow, she crushed his head 1

strike against 1. προσκρούω
Sir 13: 2 The pot will strike against it 1

strike down 1. הלם 2. נגף 3. נכה 4. נפל 5. פגע
6. θραύω 7. καταβάλλω 8. κατακοντίζω
9. καταπλήσσω 10. πατάσσω 11. συγκεραυνόω
12. percutio
Exd 9:25 The hail struck down everything that was 3
25 the hail struck down every plant of the field 3
Num14:42 Do not go up lest you be struck down before 2
33: 4 first-born, whom the LORD had struck down among 3
35:16 if he struck him down with an instrument of iron 3
17 if he struck him down with a stone in the hand 3
18 Or if he struck him down with a weapon of wood 3
21 or in enmity struck him down with his hand 3
1Sm 14:31 They struck down the Philistines that day 3
17:46 I will strike you down, and cut off your head; 3
2Sm 11:15 draw back . . that he may be struck down, and die. 3
17: 2 I will strike down the king only 3
23:10 He rose and struck down the Philistines 3
1Kg 2:25 Solomon sent Benai'ah . . and he struck him down 5
29 sent Benai'ah . . saying, "Go, strike him down. 5
31 Do as he has said, strike him down and bury him; 5
34 Benai'ah . . struck him down and killed him; 5
46 and he went out and struck him down, and he died 5
15:27 Ba'asha struck him down at Gib'bethon 3
16:10 Zimri came in and struck him down and killed him 3
2Kg 9: 7 you shall strike down the house of Ahab 3
10: 9 but who struck down all these? 3
12:21 his servants, who struck him down, so that he died. 3
13:19 then you would have struck down Syria until 3
19 now you will strike down Syria only three times. 3
15:10 Shallum . . and struck him down at Ibleam 3
14 and he struck down Shallum the son of Jabesh 3
30 and struck him down, and slew him, and reigned 3
2Ch 32:21 some of his own sons struck him down there 4
Ps 89:23 I will . . strike down those who hate him. 2
Isa 16: 8 lords of the nations . . struck down its branches 1
Jer 41: 2 ten men with him rose up and struck down Gedali'ah 3
2Co 4: 9 struck down, but not destroyed; 7
2Es 1:10 I struck down Pharaoh with his servants 12
Jdt 1:15 and struck him down with hunting spears 8
9: 3 thou didst strike down slaves along with princes 10
10 By the deceit of my lips strike down the slave 10
13:15 Lord has struck him down by the hand of a woman. 10
Sir 8:16 where no help is at hand, he will strike you down. 7
47: 4 struck down the boasting of Goliath? 7
1Mc 2:44 and struck down sinners in their anger 10
4:33 Strike them down with the sword 7
5: 7 he struck them down. 10
7:41 thy angel . . struck down 185,000 of the Assyrians. 10
9:66 He struck down Odomera and his brothers 10
2Mc 1:16 they threw stones and struck down the leader 11
8:18 to strike down those who are coming against us 7
15:16 you will strike down your adversaries. 6
24 may these blasphemers . . be struck down 9

strike fire out 1. πυρόω
2Mc 10: 3 striking fire out of flint 1

strike hands 1. ספק
Isa 2: 6 they strike hands with foreigners. 1

strike terror 1. ערץ
Ps 10:18 man who is of the earth may strike terror no more. 1

strike through 1. חלף
Job 20:24 a bronze arrow will strike him through. 1

strike together 1. ספק
Num24:10 Balak . . struck his hands together; 1

strike with grief 1. λυπέω
Tob 7: 7 he was stricken with grief and wept. 1

strike with the hand 1. δίδωμι ῥάπισμα
Joh 18:22 one of the officers . . struck Jesus with his hand 1
19: 3 and struck him with their hands. 1

thing more striking 1. ἰσχυρός
Sir 16: 5 has heard things more striking than these. 1

string 1. יֶתֶר 2. כון 3. מֵן 4. פְּתִיל
Jdg 16: 9 as a string of tow snaps when it touches the fire. 4
Ps 7:12 will whet his sword; he has bent and strung his bow; 2
11: 2 they have fitted their arrow to the string 1
33: 2 make melody to him with the harp of ten strings! *
144: 9 upon a ten-stringed harp I will play to thee *
150: 4 praise him with strings and pipe! 3
Hab 3: 9 from thy bow, and put the arrows to the string. *

navel string 1. שֹׁר
Ezk 16: 4 day you were born your navel string was not cut 1

string of jewels 1. חָרוּז
Sng 1:10 your neck with strings of jewels. 1

stringed instrument 1. מֵן 2. נְגִינָה 3. νάβλα
Ps 4: 0 To the choirmaster: with stringed instruments. 2
6: 0 To the choirmaster: with stringed instruments; 2
45: 8 stringed instruments make you glad; 1
54: 0 To the choirmaster: with stringed instruments. 2
55: 0 To the choirmaster: with stringed instruments. 2
61: 0 To the choirmaster: with stringed instruments. 2
67: 0 To the choirmaster: with stringed instruments. 2
76: 0 To the choirmaster: with stringed instruments. 2
Isa 38:20 we will sing to stringed instruments 2
Hab 3:19 To the choirmaster: with stringed instruments. 2
1Mc 13:51 cymbals and stringed instruments 3

strings *See* play.

strip 1. בקק 2. גלה 3. ישם 4. כלה 5. נצל 6. פשט
7. קצץ 8. שׁוֹלָל 9. שׁמם 10. שׁסה 11. γυμνός
12. ἐκδύω 13. περαιρέω 14. περιδύω
Gen 37:23 Joseph came to his brothers, they stripped him 6
Exd 33: 6 the people of Israel stripped themselves 5
Num20:26 strip Aaron of his garments, and put them upon 6
28 Moses stripped Aaron of his garments 6
1Sm 18: 4 Jonathan stripped himself of the robe 6
31: 8 when the Philistines came to strip the slain 6
2Sm 23:10 men returned after him only to strip the slain. 6
2Kg 18:16 Hezeki'ah stripped the gold from the doors 7
1Ch 10: 8 when the Philistines came to strip the slain 6
9 they stripped him and took his head and his armor 6
Job 12:17 He leads counselors away stripped 8
19 He leads priests away stripped 8
19: 9 He has stripped from me my glory 6
22: 6 and stripped the naked of their clothing. 6
Isa 27:10 there he lies down, and strips its branches. 4
32:11 strip, and make yourselves bare 6
Ezk 12:19 their land will be stripped of all it contains 3
16:39 they shall strip you of your clothes 6
23:26 They shall also strip you of your clothes 6
32:15 when the land is stripped of all that fills it 9
Hos 2: 3 lest I strip her naked 6
13:15 it shall strip his treasury of every precious 10
Mic 1: 8 will lament and wail; I will go stripped and naked; 8
2: 8 you strip the robe from the peaceful 6
Nah 2: 2 for plunderers have stripped them 1
7 its mistress is stripped, she is carried off 2
Hab 3: 9 Thou didst strip the sheath from thy bow *
Mat 27:28 they stripped him and put a scarlet robe upon him 12
31 they stripped him of the robe 12
Mrk 15:20 they stripped him of the purple cloak 12
Lke 10:30 robbers, who stripped him and beat him 12
Joh 21: 7 he put on his clothes, for he was stripped for work 11
LJr 1:58 Strong men will strip them of their gold 13
2Mc 8:27 stripped them of their spoils 12
11:12 Most of them got away stripped and wounded 11
4Mc 6: 2 First they stripped the old man 14

strip away 1. סור
Jer 5:10 strip away her branches 1

strip bare 1. חשף 2. עלל
Lev 19:10 you shall not strip your vineyard bare 2
Ps 29: 9 voice of the LORD . . strips the forests bare; 1
Jer 49:10 But I have stripped Esau bare 1

strip of possessions 1. ירש
Zec 9: 4 But lo, the Lord will strip her of her possessions 1

strip of spoil 1. שׁלל
Ps 76: 5 The stouthearted were stripped of their spoil; 1

strip off 1. גלה 2. חסף 3. פרק 4. פשט 5. נתר (A)
6. λεπίζω 7. περαιρέω 8. περιξύω
1Sm 19:24 And he too stripped off his clothes 4
31: 9 they cut off his head, and stripped off his armor 4
Job 41:13 Who can strip off his outer garment? 1
Isa 47: 2 grind meal, put off your veil, strip off your robe 2
Ezk 19:12 east wind dried it up; its fruit was stripped off; 3
26:16 and strip off their embroidered garments; 4
Dan 4:14 strip off its leaves and scatter its fruit; 5
Wis 13:11 and skilfully strip off all its bark 8
1Mc 1:22 he stripped it all off. 6
2Mc 4:38 he immediately stripped off the purple robe 7

strip off bark 1. חשף
Jol 1: 7 it has stripped off their bark and thrown it down; 1

strip oneself bare 1. ערה
Lam 4:21 you shall become drunk and strip yourself bare. 1

stripe 1. חַבּוּרָה 2. מַכָּה 3. נֶגַע 4. μώλωψ
Exd 21:25 burn for burn, wound for wound, stripe for stripe. 1
25 burn for burn, wound for wound, stripe for stripe. 1
Deu 25: 2 beaten in his presence with a number of stripes *
3 Forty stripes may be given him, but not more; *
3 go on to beat him with more stripes than these 2
2Sm 7:14 chasten him . . with the stripes of the sons of men; 3
Isa 53: 5 made us whole, and with his stripes we are healed. 1
Jdt 9:13 to be their wound and stripe 4

striped 1. עָקֹד
Gen 30:35 the he-goats that were striped and spotted 1
39 the flocks brought forth striped, speckled 1
40 toward the striped and all the black in the flock 1
31: 8 and if he said, 'The striped shall be your wages,' 1
8 your wages,' then all the flock bore striped. 1
10 which leaped upon the flock were striped 1
12 the goats that leap upon the flock are striped 1

stripling 1. עֶלֶם
1Sm 17:56 king said, "Inquire whose son the stripling is. 1

strive 1. גרה 2. הַצָּה 3. ריב 4. שׂרה 5. ἀγῶνα ἔχω
6. ἀγωνίζομαι 7. ἀνδραγαθέω 8. διώκω 9. ζητέω
10. μεταδιώκω 11. σπουδάζω 12. certo 13. quaero
Gen 32:28 Israel, for you have striven with God and with men 4
Deu 33: 8 whom thou didst strive at the waters of Mer'ibah; 3
Jdg 11:25 Did he ever strive against Israel, or did he ever 3
Ps 60: 0 he strove with Aram-naharaim and with Aram-zobah 2
Prv 28: 4 but those who keep the law strive against them. 1
Isa 45: 9 Woe to him who strives with his Maker 3
Jer 50:24 caught, because you strove against the LORD. 1
Hos 12: 3 and in his manhood he strove with God. 4

4 He strove with the angel and prevailed 4
Lke 13:24 Strive to enter by the narrow door 6
1Co 14:12 strive to excel in building up the church. 9
Col 1:29 striving with all the energy 6
2: 1 For I want you to know how greatly I strive for you 5
1Ti 4:10 For to this end we toil and strive 6
Heb 4:11 Let us therefore strive to enter that rest 11
12:14 Strive for peace with all men 8
2Es 5:34 I strive to understand the way of the Most High 13
7:92 because they have striven with great effort 12
Sir 4:28 Strive even to death for the truth 6
1Mc 7:21 Alcimus strove for the high priesthood 6
2Mc 2:21 those who strove zealously on behalf of Judaism 7
31 be allowed to strive for brevity of expression 10

strive after 1. רְעוּת 2. רַעְיוֹן
Ecc 1:14 behold, all is vanity and a striving after wind. 1
17 this also is but a striving after wind. 2
2:11 all was vanity and a striving after wind 1
17 for all is vanity and a striving after wind. 1
26 This also is vanity and a striving after wind. 1
4: 4 This also is vanity and a striving after wind. 1
6 two hands full of toil and a striving after wind. 1
16 this also is vanity and a striving after wind. 2
6: 9 this also is vanity and a striving after wind. 1

strive against 1. רִיב
Isa 41:11 those who strive against you shall be as nothing 1

strive side by side 1. *συναθλέω*
Php 1:27 with one mind striving side by side for the faith 1

strive together 1. נצה 2. *συναγωνίζομαι*
Exd 21:22 When men strive together, and hurt a woman 1
Rom 15:30 to strive together with me in your prayers 2

stroke 1. מַגֵּפָה 2. מַכָּה 3. מַעֲבָר 4. נֶגַע 5. פַּעַם
1Sm 26: 8 pin him to the earth with one stroke of the spear 5
Ps 39:10 Remove thy stroke from me; I am spent by the blows 4
Prv 20:30 strokes make clean the innermost parts. 2
Isa 30:32 every stroke of the staff of punishment 3
Ezk 24:16 the delight of your eyes away from you at a stroke; 1

strong 1. אַבִּיר 2. אוֹן 3. אַמִּיץ 4. אמץ 5. אֹמֶץ 6. אָפִיק 7. אֵיתָן 8. בֶּן חַיִל 9. גִּבּוֹר 10. גבר 11. גָּדוֹל 12. גֶּרֶם 13. חזק 14. חָזָק 15. חֹזֶק 16. חֶזְקָה 17. חַיִל 18. חָסֹן 19. כֹּחַ 20. מָעוֹז 21. מְצוּדָה 22. מִשְׁמָן 23. עַז 24. עֹז 25. עִזּוּז 26. עזז 27. עָצוּם 28. עצם 29. קשר 30. שָׁלֵם 31. שָׁמֵן 32. תַּקִּיף 33. תַּקִּיף (A) 34. *βαρύς* 35. *δυνατός* 36. *ἐνδυναμόω* 37. *ἐνέργεια* 38. *ἰσχυρός* 39. *ἰσχύς* 40. *ἰσχύω* 41. *καρτερός* 42. *κατισχύω* 43. *κραταιός* 44. *κραταιόω* 45. *μέγας* 46. *ὀχυρός* 47. *ῥώμη* 48. *σκληρός* 49. *σφοδρός* 50. *ὑπερισχύω* 51. fortis 52. possum
Gen 25:23 the one shall be stronger than the other 4
30:41 Whenever the stronger of the flock were breeding 29
42 feebler were Laban's, and the stronger Jacob's. 29
49:14 Is'sachar is a strong ass, crouching between 12
Exd 6: 1 for with a strong hand he will send them out 14
1 yea, with a strong hand he will drive them out 14
10:19 the LORD turned a very strong west wind 14
13: 9 for with a strong hand the LORD has brought you 14
16 for by a strong hand the LORD brought us out 15
14:21 the LORD drove the sea back by a strong east wind 23
Num 13:18 people who dwell in it are strong or weak 14
28 Yet the people who dwell in the land are strong 23
31 We are not able . . for they are stronger than we. 14
20:20 came out against them with . . a strong force. 14
Deu 11: 8 that you may be strong, and go 13
31: 6 Be strong and of good courage, do not fear 13
7 Be strong and of good courage; for you shall go 13
23 Be strong and of good courage; for you shall bring 13
Jos 1: 6 Be strong and of good courage; 13
7 Only be strong and very courageous 13
9 Be strong and of good courage; be not frightened 13
18 Only be strong and of good courage. 13
10:25 Do not be afraid . . be strong and of good courage; 13
14:11 I am still as strong to this day as . . the day that 14
17:18 you shall drive out . . though they are strong. 14
23: 9 driven out before you great and strong nations; 27
Jdg 3:29 of the Moabites, all strong, able-bodied men; 31
9:51 there was a strong tower within the city 24
14:14 Out of the strong came something sweet. 23
18 sweeter than honey? What is stronger than a lion? 23
18:26 when Micah saw that they were too strong for him 14
1Sm 14:52 when Saul saw any strong man, or any valiant man 9
2Sm 1:23 they were stronger than lions. 10
2: 7 Now . . let your hands be strong, and be valiant; 13
3: 1 and David grew stronger and stronger •
10:11 And he said, "If the Syrians are too strong for me 13
11 but if the Ammonites are too strong for you 13
13:14 and being stronger than she, he forced her 13
15:12 And the conspiracy grew strong 3
22:18 He delivered me from my strong enemy 23
33 God is my strong refuge, and has made my way safe. 17
1Kg 2: 2 Be strong, and show yourself a man 13
19:11 a great and strong wind rent the mountains 14
20:23 Their gods . . and so they were stronger than we; 13
23 surely we shall be stronger than they. 13
25 surely we shall be stronger than they. 13
2Kg 2:16 there are with your servants 50 strong men; 8
24:16 all of them strong and fit for war. 9
1Ch 19:12 he said, "If the Syrians are too strong for me 13
12 if the Ammonites are too strong for you 13
22:13 Be strong, and of good courage. 13
28:10 you to build a house . . be strong, and do it. 13
20 Be strong and of good courage, and do it. 13
2Ch 12: 1 rule of Rehobo'am was established and was strong 16
25: 8 if you suppose that . . you will be strong for war 42
26:15 he was marvelously helped, till he was strong. 14
16 when he was strong he grew proud 16
32: 7 Be strong and of good courage. Do not be afraid 13
Ezr 9:12 that you may be strong, and eat the good of the land 13
10: 4 it is your task . . be strong and do it. 13
Neh 1:10 redeemed by thy great power and by thy strong hand. 14
Job 4:11 The strong lion perishes for lack of prey •
12:21 and looses the belt of the strong. 6
17: 9 he that has clean hands grows stronger 5
9 has clean hands grows stronger and stronger. •
18: 7 His strong steps are shortened 2
37: 6 to the shower and the rain, 'Be strong.' 24
Ps 18:17 He delivered me from my strong enemy 23
22:12 strong bulls of Bashan surround me; 1
24: 8 the King of glory? The LORD, strong and mighty 25
27:14 be strong, and let your heart take courage; 13
30: 7 thou hadst established me as a strong mountain; 24
31: 2 refuge for me, a strong fortress to save me! 21
24 Be strong, and let your heart take courage 13
35:10 deliverest the weak from him who is too strong 14
61: 3 art my refuge, a strong tower against the enemy. 24
71: 3 Be thou to me a rock of refuge, a strong fortress 46
7 but thou art my strong refuge. 24
78:31 he slew the strongest of them 22
89:13 strong is thy hand, high thy right hand. 26
136:12 with a strong hand and an outstretched arm 14
140: 7 O LORD, my Lord, my strong deliverer 24
142: 6 from my persecutors; for they are too strong 4
Prv 10:15 A rich man's wealth is his strong city; 24
12:12 The strong tower of the wicked comes to ruin •
14:26 In the fear of the LORD one has strong confidence 24
18:10 The name of the LORD is a strong tower; 24
11 A rich man's wealth is his strong city 24
19 A brother helped is like a strong city 46
21:14 bribe in the bosom, strong wrath. 23
23:11 for their Redeemer is strong; 14
30:25 ants are a people not strong, yet they provide 23
Ecc 6:10 not able to dispute with one stronger than he. 32
9:11 nor the battle to the strong, nor bread to the wise 9
12: 3 keepers . . tremble, and the strong men are bent 17
Sng 8: 6 love is strong as death, jealousy is cruel 23
Isa 1:31 the strong shall become tow, and his work a spark 18
8:11 spoke thus to me with his strong hand upon me 16
17: 9 their strong cities will be like the deserted 20
25: 3 Therefore strong peoples will glorify thee; 23
26: 1 We have a strong city; he sets up salvation 24
27: 1 the LORD with his hard and great and strong sword 14
28: 2 Behold, the Lord has one who is mighty and strong; 3
31: 1 and in horsemen because they are very strong 28
35: 4 Be strong, fear not! Behold, your God will come 13
40:26 because he is strong in power not one is missing. 3
44:12 with hammers, and forges it with his strong arm; 19
53:12 and he shall divide the spoil with the strong; 27
Jer 20: 7 art stronger than I, and thou hast prevailed. 13
21: 5 with outstretched hand and strong arm, in anger 14
31:11 has redeemed him from hands too strong for him. 14
32:21 with a strong hand and outstretched arm 14
49:19 like a lion . . against a strong sheepfold 7
50:34 Their Redeemer is strong; 14
44 like a lion . . against a strong sheepfold 7
51:53 and though she should fortify her strong height 24
Ezk 3:14 the hand of the LORD being strong upon me; 13
17: 9 not take a strong arm or many people to pull it 11
19:11 Its strongest stem became a ruler's scepter; 24
12 its strong stem was withered; the fire consumed 24
14 so that there remains in it no strong stem 24
22:14 your courage endure, or can your hands be strong 13
30:22 both the strong arm and the one that was broken; 14
34:16 the fat and the strong I will watch over; 14
Dan 2:40 there shall be a fourth kingdom, strong as iron 33
42 kingdom shall be partly strong and partly brittle. 33
7: 7 terrible and dreadful and exceedingly strong; 33
8: 8 when he was strong, the great horn was broken 28
10:19 peace be with you; be strong and of good courage. 13
11: 5 Then the king of the south shall be strong 13
5 but one of his princes shall be stronger than he 13
39 He shall deal with the strongest fortresses 20
Ams 2: 9 and who was as strong as the oaks; 18
14 and the strong shall not retain his strength 14
5: 9 destruction flash forth against the strong 23
Mic 4: 3 and shall decide for strong nations afar off; 27
7 and those who were cast off, a strong nation; 27
Nah 1:12 says the LORD, "Though they be strong and many 30
Zec 8: 9 says the LORD of hosts: "Let your hands be strong 13
13 Fear not, but let your hands be strong. 13
22 Many peoples and strong nations shall come 27
Lke 11:22 when one stronger than he assails him 38
16: 3 I am not strong enough to dig 40
Joh 6:18 The sea rose because a strong wind was blowing. 45
Rom 15: 1 We who are strong ought to bear with the failings 35
1Co 1:25 the weakness of God is stronger than men. 38
27 to shame the strong 38
4:10 We are weak, but you are strong. 38
10:22 Are we stronger than he? 38
16:13 be courageous, be strong. 44
2Co 10:10 For they say, "His letters are weighty and strong 38
12:10 when I am weak, then I am strong. 35
13: 9 we are glad when we are weak and you are strong. 35
Eph 6:10 Finally, be strong in the Lord 36
2Th 2:11 Therefore God sends upon them a strong delusion 37
2Ti 2: 1 You then, my son, be strong 36
Heb 6:18 might have strong encouragement 38
Jas 3: 4 though they . . are driven by strong winds 48
1Jn 2:14 I write to you, young men, because you are strong 38
Rev 5: 2 a strong angel proclaiming with a loud voice 38
6:15 and the generals and the rich and the strong 38
1Es 3: 5 Let each of us state what one thing is strongest; 50
10 The first wrote, "Wine is strongest. 50
11 The second wrote, "The king is strongest. 50
12 The third wrote, "Women are strongest 50
18 Gentlemen, how is wine the strongest? 50
24 Gentlemen, is not wine the strongest 50
4: 2 Gentlemen, are not men strongest 50
3 the king is stronger; he is their lord and master 50
12 Gentlemen, why is not the king the strongest 50
14 is not wine strong? 40
32 Gentlemen, why are not women strong 38
34 Gentlemen, are not women strong? 38
35 truth is great, and stronger than all things. 38
38 truth endures and is strong for ever 40
5:50 were stronger than they 42
6:14 a king of Israel who was great and strong 38
8:85 in order that you may be strong 40
2Es 7:112 therefore those who were strong prayed 52
8:22 whose ordinance is strong 51
16: 7 Can one turn back an arrow shot by a strong archer? 51
13 For his right hand that bends the bow is strong 51
Wis 10: 5 kept him strong 38
Sir 6:29 will become for you a strong protection 39
8:12 Do not lend to a man who is stronger than you 38
28:14 destroyed strong cities 46
30:14 well and strong in constitution 39
34:16 a mighty protection and strong support 39
50:29 For if he does them, he will be strong 40
LJr 1:36 rescue the weak from the strong. 38
Sus 1:39 for he was too strong for us 40
1Mc 1: 4 He gathered a very strong army 38
17 So he invaded Egypt with a strong force 34
20 came to Jerusalem with a strong force. 34
33 fortified . . with a great strong wall 46
33 great strong wall and strong towers 46
3:15 again a strong army of ungodly men went up 38
17 fight against so great and strong a multitude 38
27 a very strong army. 38
4: 7 the camp of the Gentiles, strong and fortified 38
30 When he saw that the army was strong, he prayed 38
60 with high walls and strong towers round about 46
5: 6 where he found a strong band and many people 43
26 - all these cities were strong and large- 46
46 This was a large and very strong city on the road 46
6: 6 that Lysias had gone first with a strong force 38
37 wooden towers, strong and covered 46
41 the army was very large and strong. 38
57 the place against which we are fighting is strong 46
9:50 built strong cities in Judea 46
11:15 marched out and met him with a strong force 38
2Mc 1: 3 a strong heart and a willing spirit. 45
24 awe-inspiring and strong and just and merciful 38
3:26 remarkably strong, gloriously beautiful 47
10:18 9,000 took refuge in two very strong towers 46
12:18 in one place he had left a very strong garrison. 46
35 who was on horseback and was a strong man 41
13:19 Beth-zur, a strong fortress of the Jews 46
14: 1 a strong army and a fleet 38
4Mc 13:22 they grow stronger from this common nurture 49

strong *See also* arm, craving, drink, fortress, grow, make, measure, passion.

become strong 1. גבר 2. חזק 3. חֶזְקָה 4. חלם 5. עצם 6. תקף (A) 7. *κραταιόω* 8. *στηρίζω*
1Ch 5: 2 though Judah became strong among his brothers 1
2Ch 26: 8 his fame spread . . for he became very strong. 2
Job 39: 4 Their young ones become strong, they grow up 4
Ezk 30:21 that it may become strong to wield the sword. 2
Dan 4:11 tree grew and became strong, and its top reached 6
20 tree you saw, which grew and became strong 6
22 it is you, O king, who have grown and become strong 6
11: 2 when he has become strong through his riches 3
23 he shall become strong with a small people. 5
Lke 1:80 the child grew and became strong in spirit 7
2:40 And the child grew and became strong 7
1Mc 2:49 Arrogance and reproach have now become strong 8

strong enough 1. *ἰσχύω* 2. *σθένω*
3Mc 3: 8 The Greeks . . were not strong enough to help them 2
4Mc 15:11 strong enough to pervert her reason. 1

strong man 1. גִּבּוֹר 2. גֶּבֶר 3. *ἰσχυρός* 4. *ἰσχύω*
5. fortis
Ps 19: 5 like a strong man runs its course with joy. 1
78:65 like a strong man shouting because of wine. 1
Prv 24: 5 A wise man is mightier than a strong man 3
Isa 22:17 will hurl you away violently, O you strong man. 2
Mat 12:29 Or how can one enter a strong man's house 3
29 unless he first binds the strong man 3
Mrk 3:27 no one can enter a strong man's house 3
27 unless he first binds the strong man 3
Lke 11:21 a strong man, fully armed, guards his own palace 3
2Es 10:22 and our strong men made powerless. 5
LJr 1:58 Strong men will strip them of their gold 4

very strong 1. *βαρύς* 2. *δυνατὸς ἰσχύς*
1Mc 8: 1 they were very strong 2
2 they were very strong 2
4Mc 4: 5 a very strong military force. 1

become still stronger 1. supervalesco
2Es 15:31 the dragons . . shall become still stronger 1

strongest of all 1. *ὑπερισχύω*
1Es 4:41 Great is truth, and strongest of all! 1

stronghold 1. אַרְמוֹן 2. בִּצָּרוֹן 3. מִבְצָר 4. מִסְגֶּרֶת
5. מָעֹז 6. מָעוֹז 7. מְצָד 8. מְצוּדָה 9. מְצוּדָה 10. מִשְׂגָּב
11. עֹז 12. צְרִיחַ 13. בִּירַנְתָּא (A) 14. *ὀχύρωμα*
15. *στερέωμα*
Num13:19 dwell in are camps or strongholds 3
Jdg 6: 2 Israel made . . the caves and the strongholds. 7
26 build an altar . . on the top of the stronghold 6
9:46 they entered the stronghold of the house 12
49 his bundle and . . put it against the stronghold 12
49 they set the stronghold on fire over them 12
1Sm 22: 4 all the time that David was in the stronghold. 9
5 Do not remain in the stronghold; depart, and go 9
23:14 remained in the strongholds in the wilderness 7
19 David hide among us in the strongholds at Horesh 7
29 David . . dwelt in the strongholds of En-ge'di. 7
24:22 but David and his men went up to the stronghold. 9
2Sm 5: 7 Nevertheless David took the stronghold of Zion 9
9 And David dwelt in the stronghold 9
17 David heard . . and went down to the stronghold. 9
22: 3 my God . . my stronghold and my refuge, my savior; 10
23:14 David was then in the stronghold; 9
1Ch 11: 5 Nevertheless David took the stronghold of Zion 9
7 David dwelt in the stronghold; 7
16 David was then in the stronghold; 9
12: 8 to David at the stronghold in the wilderness 7
16 men of Benjamin and Judah came to the stronghold 7
Ps 9: 9 The LORD is a stronghold for the oppressed 10
9 The LORD is . . a stronghold in times of trouble. 10
18: 2 the horn of my salvation, my stronghold. 10
27: 1 The LORD is the stronghold of my life; 6
89:40 thou hast laid his strongholds in ruins. 3
94:22 the LORD has become my stronghold 10
144: 2 my fortress, my stronghold and my deliverer 10
Prv 10:29 LORD is a stronghold to him whose way is upright 6
21:22 wise man . . brings down the stronghold 11
Isa 23: 4 the sea has spoken, the stronghold of the sea 6
11 concerning Canaan to destroy its strongholds. 6
14 Wail . . for your stronghold is laid waste. 6
25: 4 For thou hast been a stronghold to the poor 6
4 a stronghold to the needy in his distress 6
29: 7 all that fight against her and her stronghold 8
34:13 Thorns shall grow over its strongholds 1
Jer 16:19 O LORD, my strength and my stronghold, my refuge 6
48: 7 because you trusted in your strongholds 14
18 he has destroyed your strongholds. 3
41 shall be taken and the strongholds seized. 7
49:27 it shall devour the strongholds of Ben-ha'dad. 1
51:30 they remain in their strongholds; 7
Lam 2: 2 in his wrath he has broken down the strongholds 3
5 The Lord has . . laid in ruins its strongholds; 3
Ezk 19: 7 he ravaged their strongholds, and laid waste 13
24:25 on the day when I take from them their stronghold 5
30:15 my wrath upon Pelusium, the stronghold of Egypt 6
33:27 those who are in strongholds . . shall die 7
Dan 11:24 shall devise plans against strongholds 3
Hos 8:14 and it shall devour his strongholds. 1
Jol 3:16 a stronghold to the people of Israel. 6
Ams 1: 4 it shall devour the strongholds of Ben-ha'dad. 1
7 fire . . and it shall devour her strongholds. 1
10 Tyre, and it shall devour her strongholds. 1
12 it shall devour the strongholds of Bozrah. 1
14 Rabbah, and it shall devour her strongholds 1
2: 2 and it shall devour the strongholds of Ker'ioth 1
5 it shall devour the strongholds of Jerusalem. 1
3: 9 Proclaim to the strongholds in Assyria 1
9 to the strongholds in the land of Egypt, and say 1
10 violence and robbery in their strongholds. 1
11 and your strongholds shall be plundered. 1
6: 8 the pride of Jacob, and hate his strongholds; 1
Mic 5:11 cut off . . and throw down all your strongholds; 3
7:17 shall come trembling out of their strongholds 4
Nah 1: 7 LORD is good, a stronghold in the day of trouble; 6
Zec 9:12 Return to your stronghold, O prisoners of hope; 2
2Co 10: 4 divine power to destroy strongholds 14
1Es 8:81 to give us a stronghold in Judea and Jerusalem. 15
1Mc 1: 2 He fought many battles, conquered strongholds 14
4:61 so that the people might have a stronghold 14
5: 9 they fled to the stronghold of Dathema 14
11 capture the stronghold to which we have fled 14
27 are getting ready to attack the strongholds 14
29 they went all the way to the stronghold of Dathema. 14
30 engines of war to capture the stronghold 14
65 and tore down its strongholds 14
6:61 the Jews evacuated the stronghold. 14
8:10 tore down their strongholds 14
10:12 Then the foreigners who were in the strongholds 14
37 stationed in the great strongholds of the king 14
11:18 his troops in the strongholds were killed 14
18 killed by the inhabitants of the strongholds. 14
41 that he remove . . the troops in the strongholds 14
12:33 Askalon and the neighboring strongholds 14
34 they were ready to hand over the stronghold 14
35 planned with them to build strongholds in Judea 14
45 the other strongholds and the remaining troops 14
13:33 Simon built up the strongholds of Judea 14
33 he stored food in the strongholds. 14
38 the strongholds that you have built 14
14:42 the country and the weapons and the strongholds 14
15: 7 the strongholds which you have built 14
16: 8 the rest fled into the stronghold. 14
2Mc 8:30 got possession of some exceedingly high strongholds 14
10:15 who had control of important strongholds 14
16 rushed to the strongholds of the Idumeans. 14
23 more than 20,000 in the two strongholds. 14
32 Timothy . . fled to a stronghold called Gazara 14
11: 6 Lysias was besieging the strongholds 14
12:19 whom Timothy had left in the stronghold 14

little stronghold 1. *ὀχυρωμάτιον*
1Mc 16:15 in the little stronghold called Dok 1

strongly 1. מְאֹד 2. *λίαν* 3. *ὀχυρός* 4. *πολύς*
5. *σφόδρα*
Gen 19: 3 he urged them strongly; 1
1Co 16:12 I strongly urged him to visit you 4
2Ti 4:15 he strongly opposed our message. 2
1Mc 10:50 He pressed the battle strongly until the sun set 5
2Mc 12:13 which was strongly fortified with earthworks 3
strongly *See also* hold.

structure 1. יָצִיעַ 2. מִבְנֶה 3. תַּבְנִית 4. אֻשַּׁרְנָא (A)
5. *ἔργον* 6. *οἰκοδομή* 7. *σύστασις*
1Kg 6: 5 built a structure against the wall of the house 1
10 He built the structure against the whole house 1
Ezr 5: 3 decree to . . finish this structure? 4
9 gave you a decree . . to finish this structure?' 4
Ps 144:12 corner pillars cut for the structure of a palace; 3
Ezk 40: 2 mountain, on which was a structure like a city 2
Eph 2:21 in whom the whole structure is joined together 6
1Es 6:11 laying the foundations of this structure?' 5
Wis 7:17 to know the structure of the world 7
1Mc 10:44 restoring the structures of the sanctuary 5

struggle 1. *ἀγών* 2. *ἄθλησις* 3. *ἀνταγωνίζομαι*
4. contentio
Heb 10:32 you endured a hard struggle with sufferings 2
12: 4 In your struggle against sin 3
2Es 12:18 great struggles shall arise 4
47 has not forgotten you in your struggle. 4
2Mc 14:43 in the heat of the struggle he did not hit exactly 1
15: 9 reminding them . . of the struggles they had won 1
4Mc 9:23 Do not leave your post in my struggle 1
13:15 for great is the struggle of the soul 1

struggle against 1. *βιάζω*
4Mc 8:24 Let us not struggle against compulsion 1

struggle together 1. נצה 2. רצץ
Gen 25:22 The children struggled together within her; 2
Exd 2:13 behold, two Hebrews were struggling together; 1

strut 1. הלך 2. *ἐμπεριπατέω*
Ps 73: 9 their tongue struts through the earth. 1
Prv 30:31 strutting cock, the he-goat, and a king striding 2

stubble 1. קַשׁ 2. *καλάμη* 3. stramen
Exd 5:12 scattered . . to gather stubble for straw. 1
15: 7 thy fury, it consumes them like stubble. 1
Job 41:28 for him slingstones are turned to stubble. 1
29 Clubs are counted as stubble; 1
Isa 5:24 as the tongue of fire devours the stubble 1
33:11 You conceive chaff, you bring forth stubble; 1
40:24 and the tempest carries them off like stubble. 1
41: 2 like dust . . like driven stubble with his bow. 1
47:14 they are like stubble, the fire consumes them; 1
Jol 2: 5 a flame of fire devouring the stubble 1
Obd 1:18 of Joseph a flame, and the house of Esau stubble; 1
Nah 1:10 they are consumed, like dry stubble. 1
Mal 4: 1 the arrogant and all evildoers will be stubble; 1
2Es 15:61 you shall be broken down by them like stubble 3
16: 6 or quench a fire in the stubble 3
Wis 3: 7 will run like sparks through the stubble. 2
stubble *See also* gather.

stubborn 1. אַבִּיר 2. חֲזַק לֵב 3. סרר 4. עֹרֶף קָשֶׁה
5. קָשֶׁה 6. קְשֵׁה עֹרֶף 7. קשה עֹרֶף 8. שְׁרִירוּת
9. *σκληρός* 10. *σκληρύνω*
Deu 9: 6 righteousness; for you are a stubborn people 6
13 seen . . and behold, it is a stubborn people; 6
10:16 be no longer stubborn. 7
21:18 If a man has a stubborn and rebellious son 3
20 This our son is stubborn and rebellious 3
31:27 For I know how rebellious and stubborn you are; 4
Jdg 2:19 their practices or their stubborn ways. 5
2Kg 17:14 they would not listen, but were stubborn 7
Neh 9:29 turned a stubborn shoulder and stiffened 3
Ps 78: 8 fathers, a stubborn and rebellious generation 3
81:12 I gave them over to their stubborn hearts 8
Isa 46:12 Hearken to me, you stubborn of heart 1
Jer 5:23 this people has a stubborn and rebellious heart; 3
16:12 every one of you follows his stubborn evil will 8
Ezk 2: 4 The people also are impudent and stubborn 2
3: 7 are of a hard forehead and of a stubborn heart. 5
Hos 4:16 Like a stubborn heifer, Israel is stubborn; 3
16 Like a stubborn heifer, Israel is stubborn; 3
Zec 7:11 to hearken, and turned a stubborn shoulder 3
Act 19: 9 when some were stubborn and disbelieved 10
Sir 3:26 A stubborn mind will be afflicted at the end 9
27 A stubborn mind will be burdened by troubles 9
30: 8 A horse that is untamed turns out to be stubborn 9

become stubborn 1. *σκληρύνω*
Sir 30:12 lest he become stubborn and disobey you 1

stubbornly 1. בְּצַוָּאר 2. בִּשְׁרִרוּת 3. סרר 4. שְׁרִירוּת
Job 15:26 running stubbornly against him 1
Jer 3:17 no more stubbornly follow their own evil heart. 4
6:28 They are all stubbornly rebellious 3
9:14 but have stubbornly followed their own hearts 4
13:10 who stubbornly follow their own heart 2
23:17 every one who stubbornly follows his own heart 4
stubbornly *See also* refuse.

stubbornness 1. פצר 2. קְשִׁי 3. שְׁרִירוּת 4. *καρτερία*
5. *νῶτον σκληρόν* 6. *σκληροκαρδία*
Deu 9:27 do not regard the stubbornness of this people 2
29:19 though I walk in the stubbornness of my heart.' 3
1Sm 15:23 and stubbornness is as iniquity and idolatry. 1
Jer 7:24 and the stubbornness of their evil hearts 3
11: 8 walked in the stubbornness of his evil heart. 3
18:12 according to the stubbornness of his evil heart. 3
Sir 16:10 assembled in their stubbornness. 6
Bar 2:33 from their stubbornness and their wicked deeds; 5
4Mc 8:26 Why does . . such a fatal stubbornness please us 4

stucco 1. *ψαμμωτός*
Sir 22:17 the stucco decoration on the wall of a colonnade. 1

stud 1. עִם נְקֻדּוֹת
Sng 1:11 make you ornaments of gold, studded with silver. 1

royal stud 1. רַמָּךְ
Est 8:10 on swift horses . . bred from the royal stud. 1

study 1. דרשׁ 2. חקר 3. לַהַג 4. שׂכל 5. *διανοέω*
6. *μανθάνω*
Ezr 7:10 Ezra had set his heart to study the law of the LORD 1
Neh 8:13 came . . in order to study the words of the law. 4
Ps 111: 2 studied by all who have pleasure in them. 1
Ecc 12: 9 weighing and studying and arranging proverbs 2
12 and much study is a weariness of the flesh. 3
Joh 7:15 this man has learning, when he has never studied? 6
Sir 39: 1 the study of the law of the Most High 5

stuff 1. כְּלִי 2. מְלָאכָה 3. שַׁעַטְנֵז 4. שֵׁשׁ
Exd 36: 7 for the stuff they had was sufficient to do all 2
39: 5 of gold, blue and purple and scarlet stuff 4
Lev 19:19 a garment of cloth made of two kinds of stuff 3
Jos 7:11 stolen . . and put them among their own stuff. 1
stuff *See also* colored, dyed, mingled, scarlet.

stumble 1. דְּחִי 2. כשׁל 3. מוט 4. מִכְשׁוֹל 5. נגף
6. נטה 7. פוק 8. צֶלַע 9. שׁמט 10. *ἀντίπτωμα*
11. *πρόσκομμα* 12. *προσκόπτω* 13. *πταίω*
14. *σκανδαλίζω* 15. *σφάλλω*
Lev 26:37 They shall stumble over one another 2
2Sm 6: 6 and took hold of it, for the oxen stumbled. 9
1Ch 13: 9 to hold the ark, for the oxen stumbled. 9
Job 4: 4 Your words have upheld him who was stumbling 2
18:12 calamity is ready for his stumbling. 8
Ps 9: 3 enemies turned back, they stumbled and perished 2
27: 2 foes, they shall stumble and fall. 2
35:15 But at my stumbling they gathered in glee 8
73: 2 But as for me, my feet had almost stumbled 6

105:37 there was none among his tribes who stumbled. 2
116: 8 thou hast delivered my . . feet from stumbling; 1
Prv 3:23 your foot will not stumble. 5
4:12 if you run, you will not stumble. 2
19 they do not know over what they stumble. 2
24:11 hold back those . . stumbling to the slaughter. 3
17 let not your heart be glad when he stumbles; 2
Isa 3: 8 For Jerusalem has stumbled, and Judah has fallen; 2
5:27 None is weary, none stumbles, none slumbers 2
8:14 a rock of stumbling to both houses of Israel 4
15 many shall stumble thereon; they shall fall 2
28: 7 err in vision, they stumble in giving judgment. 7
31: 3 the helper will stumble, and he who is helped will 2
59:10 we stumble at noon as in the twilight 2
63:13 Like a horse in the desert, they did not stumble. 2
Jer 6:21 blocks against which they shall stumble; 2
13:16 before your feet stumble on the . . mountains 5
18:15 they have stumbled in their ways 2
20:11 therefore my persecutors will stumble 2
31: 9 a straight path in which they shall not stumble; 2
46: 6 by the river Euphra'tes they have stumbled 2
12 for warrior has stumbled against warrior; 2
16 Your multitude stumbled and fell, and they said 2
50:32 The proud one shall stumble and fall 2
Dan 11:19 shall stumble and fall, and shall not be found. 2
Hos 4: 5 You shall stumble by day 2
5 the prophet also shall stumble with you by night; 2
5: 5 E'phraim shall stumble in his guilt; 2
5 Judah also shall stumble with them. 2
14: 1 for you have stumbled because of your iniquity. 2
9 but transgressors stumble in them. 2
Nah 2: 5 officers are summoned, they stumble as they go 2
3: 3 bodies without end–they stumble over the bodies 2
Joh 11: 9 If any one walks in the day, he does not stumble 12
10 if any one walks in the night, he stumbles 12
Rom 9:32 They have stumbled over the stumbling stone 12
32 They have stumbled over the stumbling stone 11
11:11 I ask, have they stumbled so as to fall? By no means! 13
1Pe 2: 8 they stumble because they disobey the word 12
1Es 4:27 Many have perished, or stumbled, or sinned 15
Tob 11:10 Tobit started toward the door, and stumbled 12
Sir 9: 5 lest you stumble and incur penalties for her. 14
13:23 should he stumble, they even push him down. 12
31: 7 a stumbling block to those who are devoted to it 11
29 with provocation and stumbling. 10
32:15 the hypocrite will stumble at it. 14
20 do not stumble over stony ground. 12
34:16 a guard against stumbling 11

cause to stumble 1. כשל
Ezk 36:15 and no longer cause your nation to stumble 1
Mal 2: 8 you have caused many to stumble 1

make stumble 1. כשל 2. מִכְשׁוֹל 3. πρόσκομμα 4. προσκόπτω 5. σκάνδαλον
Ps 119:165 who love thy law; nothing can make them stumble. 2
Prv 4:16 unless they have made some one stumble. 1
Rom 9:33 laying in Zion a stone that will make men stumble 5
14:21 or do anything that makes your brother stumble. 4
1Pe 2: 8 A stone that will make men stumble 3

stumbling *See* block, cause.

stump 1. גֶּזַע 2. זָנָב 3. מַצֵּבָה 4. עִקָּר (A)
Job 14: 8 and its stump die in the ground 1
Isa 6:13 whose stump remains standing when it is felled. 3
13 The holy seed is its stump. 3
7: 4 these two smoldering stumps of firebrands 2
11: 1 shall come forth a shoot from the stump of Jesse 1
Dan 4:15 leave the stump of its roots in the earth 4
23 but leave the stump of its roots in the earth 4
26 to leave the stump of the roots of the tree 4

stun 1. שׁמם
Lam 1:13 he turned me back; he has left me stunned, faint 1

stunned *See* lie.

stupefy 1. מהה
Isa 29: 9 Stupefy yourselves and be in a stupor 1

stupid 1. בער 2. בַּעַר 3. טמה 4. כְּסִיל 5. נבב 6. סָכָל 7. ἀνόητος 8. ἀσύνετος 9. μωρός
Job 11:12 a stupid man will get understanding 5
18: 3 Why are we stupid in your sight? 3
Ps 49:10 the fool and the stupid alike must perish 2
73:22 I was stupid and ignorant, I was like a beast 2
92: 6 the stupid cannot understand this 4
Prv 12: 1 but he who hates reproof is stupid. 1
30: 2 Surely I am too stupid to be a man. 2
Isa 19:11 counselors of Pharaoh give stupid counsel. 1
Jer 4:22 they know me not; they are stupid children 6
10: 8 They are both stupid and foolish; 1
14 Every man is stupid and without knowledge; 1
21 For the shepherds are stupid 1
51:17 Every man is stupid and without knowledge; 1
2Ti 2:23 stupid, senseless controversies 9
Tit 3: 9 avoid stupid controversies, genealogies 9
Sir 22:15 of iron are easier to bear than a stupid man. 8
42: 8 Do not be ashamed to instruct the stupid 7

stupid *See also* son.

stupid people 1. ἀσύνετος
Sir 27:12 Among stupid people watch for a chance to leave 1

stupidity 1. ἀπόνοια
4Mc 12: 3 You see the result of your brothers' stupidity 1

stupor 1. חמה 2. κατάνυξις
Isa 29: 9 Stupefy yourselves and be in a stupor 1
Rom 11: 8 as it is written, "God gave them a spirit of stupor 2

drunken stupor 1. μέθη
Jdt 13:15 he lay in his drunken stupor 1

sturdy 1. κραταιός
Sir 6:14 A faithful friend is a sturdy shelter 1

style 1. κατασκευή
2Mc 15:39 so also the style of the story delights the ears 1

style of life 1. συναναστροφή
3Mc 3: 5 they adorned their style of life with the good deeds 1

subdue 1. דבר 2. ינה 3. כבש 4. כנע 5. נכה 6. ענה 7. רדד 8. רדף 9. δαμάζω 10. δουλαγωγέω 11. δυναστεύω 12. ἐκπολεμέω 13. κατακρατέω 14. πατάσσω 15. συντρίβω 16. ὑποτάσσω 17. debello
Gen 1:28 and fill the earth and subdue it; 3
14: 5 with him came and subdued the Reph'aim 5
7 and subdued all the country of the Amal'ekites 5
Num 32:22 and the land is subdued before the LORD 3
29 the land shall be subdued before you 3
Deu 9: 3 LORD . . will destroy them and subdue them 4
Jdg 3:30 Moab was subdued that day under the hand 4
4:23 on that day God subdued Jabin the king of Canaan 4
8:28 Mid'ian was subdued before the people of Israel 4
11:33 the Ammonites were subdued before the people 4
16: 5 overpower him, that we may bind him to subdue him; 6
6 how you might be bound, that one could subdue you. 6
1Sm 7:13 the Philistines were subdued and did not again 4
2Sm 8: 1 defeated the Philistines and subdued them 4
11 the silver and . . from all the nations he subdued 3
1Ch 17:10 I will subdue all your enemies. 4
18: 1 defeated the Philistines and subdued them 4
20: 4 and the Philistines were subdued. 4
22:18 land is subdued before the LORD and his people. 3
2Ch 13:18 Thus the men of Israel were subdued at that time 4
Neh 9:24 thou didst subdue before them the inhabitants 4
Ps 18:47 gave me vengeance and subdued peoples under me; 1
47: 3 He subdued peoples under us, and nations 1
74: 8 said to themselves, "We will utterly subdue them 2
81:14 I would soon subdue their enemies 4
144: 2 who subdues the peoples under him. 8
Isa 25: 5 Thou dost subdue the noise of the aliens; 4
45: 1 to subdue nations before him and ungird 7
Mrk 5: 4 no one had the strength to subdue him. 9
1Co 9:27 I pommel my body and subdue it 10
2Es 4:15 let us go up and subdue the forest of the plain 17
Wis 18:22 by his word he subdued the punisher 16
Sir 12: 5 lest by means of it he subdue you 11
1Mc 1:20 After subduing Egypt, Antiochus returned 14
4:28 and 5,000 cavalry to subdue them. 12
8: 4 They also subdued the kings who came against them 15
12 They have subdued kings far and near 13

subdued *See* lie.

subject 1. ἄγω 2. ἐκ 3. ἔνοχος 4. κατά 5. ὑπεταγή 6. ὑποστρώννυμι 7. ὑποταγή 8. ὑποτάσσω 9. subicio
Jdg 1:30 among them, and became subject to forced labor. •
33 and of Beth-anath became subject to forced labor •
35 them, and they became subject to forced labor. •
1Sm 2:27 were in Egypt subject to the house of Pharaoh. •
Lke 10:17 even the demons are subject to us in your name! 8
20 the spirits are subject to you 8
Rom 8:20 for the creation was subjected to futility 5
20 by the will of him who subjected it in hope; 8
13: 1 be subject to the governing authorities. 8
5 Therefore one must be subject 8
1Co 14:32 the spirits of prophets are subject 8
15:28 When all things are subjected to him 7
28 then the Son himself will also be subjected 8
16:16 I urge you to be subject to such men 8
Eph 5:21 Be subject to one another 8
22 Wives, be subject to your husbands, as to the Lord. •
24 As the church is subject to Christ 8
24 let wives also be subject in everything •
Php 3:21 even to subject all things to himself. 8
Col 3:18 Wives, be subject to your husbands 8
Heb 2: 5 God subjected the world to come 8
15 those who . . were subject to lifelong bondage. 3
12: 9 be subject to the Father of spirits and live? 8
1Pe 2:13 Be subject . . to every human institution 8
3:22 angels, authorities, and powers subject to him. 8
5: 5 you that are younger be subject to the elders. 8
2Es 11: 6 all things under heaven were subjected to him 9
AEs 13: 2 to settle the lives of my subjects 8
16: 3 They not only seek to injure our subjects 8
Wis 8:14 nations will be subject to me; 8
Sir 4:27 Do not subject yourself to a foolish fellow 6
2Mc 9:12 It is right to be subject to God 8
11:23 the subjects of the kingdom be undisturbed 2
3Mc 1: 7 he strengthened the morale of his subjects. 8
2:13 subjected to our enemies 8
28 all Jews shall be subjected to a registration 1
7:21 they were not subject at all to confiscation •
4Mc 2:23 one who lives subject to this will rule a kingdom 4

subject (2) 1. λόγος
4Mc 1: 1 The subject that I am about to discuss 1
2 the subject is essential to everyone 1

subject *See* live.

become subject 1. עבד
2Sm 10:19 made peace with . . and became subject to them. 1
1Ch 19:19 made peace with David, and became subject to him. 1

subjection 1. ὑποτάσσω 2. ὑποχείριος
Heb 2: 8 do not yet see everything in subjection to him. 1
Bar 2: 4 he gave them into subjection to all the kingdoms 2

subjection *See also* bring, put.

subjugate 1. כבש
2Ch 28:10 now you intend to subjugate the people of Judah 1

submission 1. ὑποταγή
Gal 2: 5 we did not yield submission even for a moment 1

submissive 1. ὑποτάσσω
Tit 2: 5 submissive to their husbands 1
9 Bid slaves to be submissive to their masters 1
3: 1 Remind them to be submissive to rulers 1
1Pe 2:18 Servants, be submissive to your masters 1
3: 1 wives, be submissive to your husbands 1
5 women . . were submissive to their husbands 1

submissiveness 1. ὑποταγή
1Ti 2:11 learn in silence with all submissiveness. 1

submit 1. ענה 2. ἀνέχομαι 3. ἐνέχω 4. ὑπείκω 5. ὑπομένω 6. ὑποτάσσω
Gen 16: 9 Return to your mistress, and submit to her. 1
Rom 8: 7 it does not submit to God's law, indeed it cannot; 6
10: 3 they did not submit to God's righteousness. 6
2Co 11: 4 you submit to it readily enough. 2
Gal 5: 1 do not submit again to a yoke of slavery. 3
Heb 13:17 Obey your leaders and submit to them 4
Jas 4: 7 Submit yourselves therefore to God. 6
4Mc 13:12 Isaac would have submitted to being slain 5

submit to regulation 1. δογματίζω
Col 2:20 Why do you submit to regulations 1

subordinate 1. ὑποτάσσω
1Co 14:34 but should be subordinate 1

subsequent 1. μετὰ ταῦτα
1Pe 1:11 sufferings of Christ and the subsequent glory. 1

subside 1. קלל 2. שׁכך
Gen 8: 1 wind blow over the earth, and the waters subsided; 2
8 waters had subsided from the face of the ground; 1
11 that the waters had subsided from the earth. 1

substance 1. הוֹן 2. חַיִל 3. קִנְיָן 4. רְכוּשׁ 5. σῶμα
Deu 33:11 Bless, O LORD, his substance, and accept the work 2
Jos 14: 4 lands for their cattle and their substance. 3
Prv 3: 9 Honor the LORD with your substance 1
29: 3 company with harlots squanders his substance. 1
Dan 11:28 he shall return to his land with great substance 4
Col 2:17 the substance belongs to Christ. 5

unformed substance 1. גֹּלֶם
Ps 139:16 Thy eyes beheld my unformed substance; 1

substantial 1. ἱκανός
2Mc 4:45 promised a substantial bribe to Ptolemy 1

substitute 1. חלף
Lev 27:10 He shall not substitute anything for it 1

subtle 1. עָרוּם 2. λεπτός
Gen 3: 1 the serpent was more subtle 1
Wis 7:22 is intelligent, holy, unique, manifold, subtle 2

most subtle 1. λεπτός
Wis 7:23 intelligent and pure and most subtle. 1

subtlety 1. στροφή
Sir 39: 2 penetrate the subtleties of parables; 1

suburb 1. περιπόλιον
1Mc 11: 4 Azotus and its suburbs destroyed 1
61 burned its suburbs with fire 1

subvert 1. סלף 2. עות
Exd 23: 8 a bribe . . subverts the cause of those who are 1
Deu 16:19 bribe . . subverts the cause of the righteous. 1
Ps 119:78 shame, because they have subverted me with guile; 2
Lam 3:36 to subvert a man in his cause 2

succeed 1. אַחֲרֵי 2. ירשׁ 3. קום 4. תַּחַת 5. ἀντί 6. διαδέχομαι 7. διάδοχος 8. λαμβάνω διάδοχον 9. παραλαμβάνω
Lev 6:22 among Aaron's sons, who is anointed to succeed him 4
Deu 25: 6 first son . . succeed to the name of his brother 3
1Ch 27:34 Ahith'ophel was succeeded by Jehoi'ada 1
Prv 30:23 maid when she succeeds her mistress. 2
Act 24:27 Felix was succeeded by Porcius Festus; 8
Wis 7:30 for it is succeeded by the night 6
Sir 48: 8 prophets to succeed you. 7
1Mc 1: 1 he succeeded him as king 5
2Mc 4: 7 who was called Epiphanes succeeded 9
10:11 This man, when he succeeded to the kingdom 9
4Mc 4:15 Antiochus Epiphanes succeeded to the throne 6

succeed (2) 1. יכל 2. יעל 3. כשׁר 4. צלח 5. קום 6. שׂכל 7. שׁלם 8. εὐημερέω 9. εὐοδόω 10. κατέχω
Num 14:41 for that will not succeed? 4
Jdg 18: 5 may know whether the journey . . will succeed. 4
1Sm 26:25 You will do many things and will succeed in them. 1
1Kg 22:22 You are to entice him, and you shall succeed; 1
1Ch 22:11 so that you may succeed in building the house 4
2Ch 13:12 for you cannot succeed. 4
18:21 said, 'You are to entice him, and you shall succeed; 1
20:20 believe his prophets, and you will succeed. 4
Job 9: 4 hardened himself against him, and succeeded? 7
Ps 21:11 if they devise mischief, they will not succeed. 1
Prv 15:22 but with many advisers they succeed. 5
Ecc 10:10 but wisdom helps one to succeed. 3
Isa 47:12 perhaps you may be able to succeed 2
Jer 20:11 be greatly shamed, for they will not succeed. 6
22:30 childless, a man who shall not succeed in his days; 4
30 for none of his offspring shall succeed 4
32: 5 against the Chalde'ans, you shall not succeed'? 4
Ezk 17:15 Will he succeed? Can a man escape who does such 4
Dan 8:24 succeed in what he does, and destroy mighty men 4
Rom 1:10 I may now at last succeed in coming to you. 9
2Mc 8:35 having succeeded chiefly in the destruction 8
15: 5 he did not succeed in carrying out 10

succeed in fulfilling 1. φθάνω
Rom 9:31 Israel . . did not succeed in fulfilling that law 1

success 1. שׂכל 2. תּוּשִׁיָּה 3. ἐπιτυχία 4. εὐημερία 5. εὐοδία 6. εὐοδόω
1Sm 18:14 And David had success in all his undertakings; 1
15 And when Saul saw that he had great success 1
30 David had more success than all the servants 1
Job 5:12 that their hands achieve no success. 2
Wis 13:19 money-making and work and success with his hands 3
Sir 10: 5 The success of a man is in the hands of the Lord 5
11:17 what he approves will have lasting success. 6
38:13 when success lies in the hands of physicians 5
2Mc 5: 6 success at the cost of one's kindred 4
8: 8 he was pushing ahead with more frequent successes 4
10:23 Having success at arms in everything 6
28 the one having as pledge of success and victory 4
success *See also* give, grant, make.

good success 1. שׂכל 2. εὐοδόω
Jos 1: 7 that you may have good success wherever you go. 1
8 and then you shall have good success. 1
Tob 5:16 and good success to you both 2

successful 1. צלח 2. שׂכל 3. εὐοδόω
Gen 39: 2 with Joseph, and he became a successful man; 1
1Sm 18: 5 David . . was successful wherever Saul sent him; 2
Tob 5:21 his journey will be successful 3
successfully *See* accomplish.

succession 1. ἀντί
1Es 1:34 made him king in succession to Josiah his father. 1

successor 1. διαδέχομαι 2. διάδοχος
Sir 46: 1 the successor of Moses in prophesying 2
2Mc 9:23 my father . . appointed his successor 1
14:26 appointed . . Judas, to be his successor. 2

such 1. אֵלֶּה 2. אֲשֶׁר 3. הוּא 4. הִיא 5. הֵם 6. זֶה 7. כְּ 8. כַּאֲשֶׁר 9. כֹּה 10. כָּזֶה 11. כִּי 12. כָּכָה 13. כְּכֹל 14. כְּמוֹ 15. כֵּן 16. מֵאֲשֶׁר 17. מִן 18. כְּ (A) 19. βιωτικός 20. εἰ 21. καθώς 22. κατὰ πᾶν 23. οἷος 24. οἷος τοιοῦτος 25. ὅμοιος 26. ὅς 27. ὅστις 28. οὗτος 29. οὕτως 30. παρόμοιος τοιοῦτος 31. πᾶς οὗτος 32. πρόσωπον 33. τίς 34. τοιοῦτος 35. τοσοῦτος 36. ὡς 37. ὥστε 38. hic
Gen 6: 2 took to wife such of them as they chose. 17
18:25 Far be it from thee to do such a thing 7
27: 4 prepare for me savory food, such as I love 8
9 savory food for your father, such as he loves; 8
14 prepared savory food, such as his father loved. 8
46 one of the Hittite women such as these 7
30:32 among the goats; and such shall be my wages. •
33:10 face of God, with such favor have you received me. •
41:19 gaunt and thin, such as I had never seen in all 7
38 Pharaoh said to his servants, "Can we find such 7
44: 7 Why does my lord speak such words as these? 7
7 Far be it . . that they should do such a thing! 7
15 know that such a man as I can indeed divine? 7
Exd 9:18 heavy hail . . such as never has been in Egypt 7
24 very heavy hail, such as had never been in all 7
10:14 such a dense swarm of locusts as had never been 7
11: 6 a great cry . . such as there has never been 7
18:21 choose able men . . such as fear God •
21 and place such men over the people as rulers •
23:13 nor let such be heard out of your mouth. •
34:10 marvels, such as have not been wrought in all •
Lev 7:14 of such he shall offer one cake from each offering •
10: 1 such as he had not commanded them 2
19 yet such things as these have befallen me 7
11:34 drink which may be drunk from every such vessel •
14:22 or two young pigeons, such as he can afford 2
30 offer . . young pigeons such as he can afford 16
15:10 he who carries such a thing shall wash •
22: 6 the person who touches any such shall be unclean •
7 he may eat . . because such are his food 3
25 neither shall you offer . . any such animals 1
27: 9 If it is an animal such as men offer as an offering 2
9 all of such that any man gives to the LORD is holy 2
11 if it is an unclean animal such as is not offered 2
Deu 3:24 what god . . can do such works and mighty acts 7
4:32 ask . . whether such a great thing as this 7
5:29 Oh that they had such a mind as this always •
13:11 never again do any such wickedness as this among 7
14 true and certain that such an abominable thing 6
17: 4 true . . such an abominable thing has been done 6
19:20 never again commit any such evil among you. 6
33:17 such are the ten thousands of E'phraim 5
17 such are the thousands of Manas'seh. 5
Jos 16: 8 Such is the inheritance of the . . E'phraimites 6
Jdg 3: 2 teach war to such at least as had not known it 2
13:23 or now announced to us such things as these. •
18:23 What ails you that you come with such a company? •
1Sm 2:23 Why do you do such things? For I hear of your evil 1
27:11 Such was his custom all the while he dwelt 9
2Sm 9: 8 that you should look upon a dead dog such as I? 2
19:36 should the king recompense me with such a reward? 6
1Kg 2: 7 with such loyalty they met me when I fled 15
5: 6 I will pay you . . such wages as you set; 13
10:10 never again came such an abundance of spices 7
12 no such almug wood has come or been seen, 15
2Kg 7:19 If the LORD himself . . could such a thing be? 6
18:21 Such is Pharaoh . . to all who rely on him. 15
21:12 bringing . . such evil that the ears of every one •
23:22 no such passover had been kept since the days 7
1Ch 29:18 keep for ever such purposes and thoughts •
25 and bestowed upon him such royal majesty •
2Ch 1:12 such as none of the kings had who were before you 2
9: 9 there were no spices such as those 7
35:18 none . . kept such a passover as was kept 7
Ezr 7:25 all such as know the laws of your God; •
27 such a thing as this into the heart of the king •
9:13 hast given us such a remnant as this •
Neh 4:17 carried burdens were laden in such a way •
6: 8 No such things as you say have been done 7
11 I said, "Should such a man as I flee? 7
11 man such as I could go into the temple and live? 7
13:26 Did not Solomon . . sin on account of such women? •
Est 4:14 For if you keep silence at such a time as this •
14 have . . come to the kingdom for such a time as this? 7
9: 2 to lay hands on such as sought their hurt. •
Job 6:21 Such you have now become to me; you see 11
8:13 Such are the paths of all who forget God; 15
12: 3 Who does not know such things as these? 14
14: 3 dost thou open thy eyes upon such a one •
15:13 and let such words go out of your mouth? •
16: 2 I have heard many such things; 7
18:21 Surely such are the dwellings of the ungodly 1
21 such is the place of him who knows not God. 6
23:14 many such things are in his mind. 7
Ps 24: 6 Such is the generation of those who seek him 6
53: 5 in great terror, in terror such as has not been! •
139: 6 Such knowledge is too wonderful for me; it is high •
144:15 Happy the people to whom such blessings fall! 12
Prv 1:19 Such are the ways of all who get gain by violence; 15
24:14 Know that wisdom is such to your soul; 15
29: 7 wicked man does not understand such knowledge. •
Isa 7:17 bring . . such days as have not come •
36: 6 Such is Pharaoh . . of Egypt to all who rely on him. 15
47:15 Such to you are those with whom you have labored 15
58: 5 Is such the fast that I choose, a day for a man 10
66: 8 Who has heard such a thing? 7
8 Who . . heard such a thing? Who has seen such things? 7
Jer 2:10 see if there has been such a thing. 10
5: 9 shall I not avenge myself on a nation such as this? 2
29 shall I not avenge myself on a nation such as this? 2
9: 9 shall I not avenge myself on a nation such as this? 2
16:20 Can man make for himself gods? Such are no gods! 5
19: 3 Behold, I am bringing such evil upon this place •
38: 4 weakening the hands . . by speaking such words 1
52: 3 things came to such a pass in Jerusalem and Judah •
Ezk 1:11 Such were their faces. •
28 Such was the appearance of the likeness 3
3: 6 if I sent you to such, they would listen to you. 5
17:15 Can a man escape who does such things? 1
41:25 palm trees, such as were carved on the walls; 8
Dan 2:10 no . . king has asked such a thing of any magician 18
12: 1 such as never has been since there was a nation 2
Ams 5:13 he who is prudent will keep silent in such a time; 4
Mal 1: 9 With such a gift from your hand, will he show favor •
Mat 8:10 not even in Israel have I found such faith. 35
9: 8 they glorified God, who had given such authority 34
11:26 yea, Father, for such was thy gracious will. 28
18: 5 Whoever receives one such child in my name 34
19:10 If such is the case of a man with his wife 28
14 for to such belongs the kingdom of heaven. 34
24:21 such as has not been from the beginning 23
Mrk 4:33 With many such parables he spoke the word to them 34
7:13 many such things you do. 30
9:37 Whoever receives one such child in my name 34
10:14 to such belongs the kingdom of God. 34
13:19 such tribulation as has not been 24
Lke 7: 9 not even in Israel have I found such faith. 35
10:21 yea, Father, for such was thy gracious will. 28
18:16 to such belongs the kingdom of God. 34
Joh 4:23 for such the Father seeks to worship him. 34
6:58 not such as the fathers ate and died 21
8: 5 Now in the law Moses commanded us to stone such. 34
9:16 How can a man who is a sinner do such signs? 34
Act 25:18 such evils as I supposed; 26
26:29 might become such as I am–except for these chains. 34
Rom 15: 5 to live in such harmony with one another •
1Co 5: 4 on the man who has done such a thing •
6: 4 If then you have such cases 19
11 such were some of you 28
7:15 in such a case the brother or sister is not bound. 34
9:15 to secure any such provision 28
14: 7 instruments, such as the flute or the harp 20
2Co 3: 4 Such is the confidence that we have 34
7 if . . death . . came with such splendor •
12 Since we have such a hope, we are very bold 34
10: 2 not have to show boldness with such confidence •
11 Let such people understand 34
Gal 5:23 self-control; against such there is no law. 34
Eph 4:29 only such as is good for edifying 33
5:27 without spot or wrinkle or any such thing 34
2Th 3:12 Now such persons we command and exhort 34
2Ti 2:16 Avoid such godless chatter •
3: 5 Avoid such people. •
Heb 7:26 fitting that we should have such a high priest 34
8: 1 we have such a high priest 34
12: 3 who endured . . such hostility against himself 34
13:16 such sacrifices are pleasing to God. 34
Jas 3:15 This wisdom is not such as comes down from above •
4:16 All such boasting is evil. 34
1Pe 1:18 with perishable things such as silver or gold •
Jde 1:15 which they have committed in such an ungodly way •
Rev 16:18 such as had never been since men were on the earth 23
20: 6 Over such the second death has no power 28
1Es 1:21 none of the kings . . had kept such a passover 34
2:20 we think it best not to neglect such a matter 34
29 that such wicked proceedings go no further •
8:87 give us such a root as this 34
2Es 7:80 such spirits shall not enter into habitations 38
Jdt 11:21 There is not such a woman . . 34
12:12 it will be a disgrace if we let such a woman go 34
Wis 11:18 such as breathe out fiery breath •
12:19 Through such works thou has taught thy people 34
15: 6 and fit for such objects of hope 34
16: 1 deservedly punished through such creatures 25
Sir 6: 8 a friend who is such at his own convenience •
7:35 because for such deeds you will be loved. 34
19:11 With such a word a fool will suffer pangs 32
25:20 such is a garrulous wife for a quiet husband. 29
29: 7 Because of such wickedness, therefore •
34: 8 Without such deceptions •
45:13 there never were such beautiful things 34
Aza 1:17 such may our sacrifice be in thy sight this day 29
Sus 1:48 Are you such fools, you sons of Israel? 29
1Mc 1:51 In such words he wrote to his whole kingdom 31
3:30 He feared that he might not have such funds •
4: 6 armor and swords such as they desired. 36
9:10 to do such a thing as to flee from them 28
27 was great distress in Israel, such as had not been 27
10:16 So he said, "Shall we find another such man? 34
73 my cavalry and such an army in the plain 34
89 such as it is the custom to give 36
2Mc 1:19 they took such precautions that the place 37
2:29 such in my judgment is the case with us. 29
4: 3 When his hatred progressed to such a degree 35
13 There was such an extreme of Hellenization 29
30 While such was the state of affairs 34
6:12 not to be depressed by such calamities •
24 Such pretense is not worthy of our time of life •

8: 7 the nights most advantageous for such attacks. 34
9:28 such as he had inflicted on others 36
10: 4 they might never again fall into such misfortunes 34
9 Such then was the end of Antiochus 29
13: 7 By such a fate it came about that . . 34
3Mc 2:26 he also continued with such audacity 35
4: 4 with such a harsh and ruthless spirit •
5 they were driven in such a shameful manner. †
7: 9 as an antagonist to avenge such acts. Farewell. 22
4Mc 1: 4 the emotions . . such as malice 23
5:27 to eat in such a way that you may deride us •
28 you shall have no such occasion to laugh at me 28
7: 8 Such should be those who are administrators 34
8: 5 the beauty and the number of such brothers 35
26 Why does such contentiousness excite us 35
26 Why does . . such a fatal stubbornness please us •
13:21 For such embraces . . souls are nourished; •
16: 3 she saw her seven sons tortured in such varied ways. 28
12 did not wail with such a lament for any of them 28
17 while an aged man endures such agonies 28

such *See also* any, complete, great.

such a fellow 1. *τοιοῦτος*
Act 22:22 Away with such a fellow from the earth! 1

such a great 1. *τηλικοῦτος*
3Mc 3: 9 such a great community 1

such a man 1. *τοιοῦτος*
1Co 16:16 I urge you to be subject to such men 1
18 Give recognition to such men. 1
2Co 11:13 such men are false apostles, deceitful workmen 1
Php 2:29 receive him in the Lord . . and honor such men 1
3Jn 1: 8 So we ought to support such men 1

such a one 1. *οὗτος* 2. *τοιοῦτος*
1Co 5:11 not even to eat with such a one. 2
2Co 2: 6 For such a one this punishment . . is enough 2
2Jn 1: 7 such a one is the deceiver and the antichrist. 1
Sir 20:15 such a one is a hateful man. 2

such a person 1. *τοιοῦτος*
Rom 16:18 For such persons do not serve our Lord Christ 1
Tit 3:11 knowing that such a person is perverted 1

such a thing 1. אֵלֶּה 2. זֶה 3. כָּזֶה 4. כֵּן 5. *οὗτος* 6. *τοιοῦτος*
Gen 34: 7 for such a thing ought not to be done. 4
Deu 25:16 all who do such things, all who act dishonestly 1
Jdg 19:30 Such a thing has never happened or been seen 3
2Sm 13:12 for such a thing is not done in Israel; 4
14:13 planned such a thing against the people of God? 3
Ecc 8:10 in the city where they had done such things. 4
Jol 1: 2 Has such a thing happened in your days 2
Mic 2: 6 one should not preach of such things; 1
Lke 9: 9 who is this about whom I hear such things? 6
Rom 1:32 that those who do such things deserve to die 6
2: 2 judgment . . falls upon those who do such things 6
3 when you judge those who do such things 6
Gal 5:21 those who do such things 6
1Es 4:32 are not women strong, since they do such things? 5
37 works are unrighteous, and all such things. 6
Wis 4:15 nor take such a thing to heart 6
16: 9 they deserved to be punished by such things; 6
Sir 16: 5 Many such things my eye has seen 6

such an extent 1. *οὕτως*
2Mc 3:11 To such an extent . . Simon had misrepresented 1

such and such 1. אֶחָד 2. פְּלֹנִי אַלְמֹנִי 3. *ὅδε*
1Sm 21: 2 made an appointment . . for such and such a place. 2
2Sm 15: 2 Your servant is of such and such a tribe in Israel 1
2Kg 6: 8 At such and such a place shall be my camp. 2
Jas 4:13 tomorrow we will go into such and such a town 3

suck 1. חָלַב 2. ינק 3. *γαλαθηνός* 4. *θηλάζω*
Deu 33:19 for they suck the affluence of the seas 2
1Sm 7: 9 Samuel took a sucking lamb and offered it 1
Job 3:12 Or why the breasts, that I should suck? 2
20:16 He will suck the poison of asps; 2
Isa 60:16 You shall suck the milk of nations 2
16 you shall suck the breast of kings; 2
66:11 that you may suck and be satisfied 2
12 you shall suck, you shall be carried upon her hip 2
Lke 11:27 the breasts that you sucked! 4
Sir 46:16 he offered in sacrifice a sucking lamb. 3

suck *See also* give.

make suck 1. ינק
Deu 32:13 he made him suck honey out of the rock, 1

suck up 1. עלע
Job 39:30 His young ones suck up blood; 1

sucking *See* child.

suckle 1. ינק
Gen 21: 7 to Abraham that Sarah would suckle children? 1
Lam 4: 3 jackals give the breast and suckle their young 1

suckling 1. ינק 2. *θηλάζω*
1Sm 15: 3 kill both man and woman, infant and suckling, ox 1
22:19 men and women, children and sucklings, oxen, asses 1
Mat 21:16 Out of the mouth of babes and sucklings 2

sudden 1. בהל 2. פִּתְאֹם 3. *αἰφνίδιος* 4. *αἰφνιδίως*
Job 9:23 When disaster brings sudden death, he mocks 2
22:10 sudden terror overwhelms you; 2
Prv 3:25 Do not be afraid of sudden panic 2
Zep 1:18 sudden end he will make of all the inhabitants 1
1Th 5: 3 then sudden destruction will come upon them 3
Wis 17:15 sudden and unexpected fear overwhelmed them. 3
2Mc 14:17 because of the sudden consternation 3
22 to prevent sudden treachery on the part of the enemy 4
3Mc 3:24 a sudden disorder should later arise against us 3

sudden *See also* terror.

suddenly 1. בְּפֶתַע 2. לְפֶתַע 3. פִּתְאֹם 4. פֶּתַע 5. רגע 6. *αἰφνίδιος* 7. *αἰφνιδίως* 8. *ἀπρόσκοπος* 9. *ἄφνω* 10. *ἐξαίφνης* 11. *ἐξάπινα* 12. *ταχύς* 13. statim 14. subito
Num 6: 9 if any man dies very suddenly beside him 1
12: 4 suddenly the LORD said to Moses and to Aaron 3
35:22 But if he stabbed him suddenly without enmity 1
Jos 10: 9 Joshua came upon them suddenly 3
11: 7 Joshua came suddenly . . with all his people 3
2Ch 29:36 for the thing came about suddenly. 3
Job 5: 3 but suddenly I cursed his dwelling. 3
Ps 64: 4 shooting at him suddenly and without fear. 3
7 his arrow at them; they will be wounded suddenly. 3
Prv 6:15 therefore calamity will come upon him suddenly; 3
23: 5 for suddenly it takes to itself wings •
24:22 for disaster from them will rise suddenly 3
29: 1 suddenly be broken beyond healing. 4
Ecc 9:12 at an evil time, when it suddenly falls upon them. 3
Isa 29: 5 suddenly you will be visited by the LORD of hosts 2
30:13 whose crash comes suddenly, in an instant; 2
47:11 ruin shall come on you suddenly 3
48: 3 then suddenly I did them and they came to pass. 3
Jer 4:20 Suddenly my tents are destroyed 3
6:26 for suddenly the destroyer will come upon us. 3
15: 8 anguish and terror fall upon them suddenly. 3
18:22 thou bringest the marauder suddenly upon them! 3
49:19 I will suddenly make them run away from her; 5
50:44 I will suddenly make them run away from her; 5
51: 8 Suddenly Babylon has fallen and been broken; 3
Hab 2: 7 Will not your debtors suddenly arise 4
Mal 3: 1 the Lord whom you seek will suddenly come 3
Mrk 9: 8 suddenly looking around they no longer saw 11
13:36 lest he come suddenly and find you asleep. 10
Lke 2:13 suddenly there was with the angel a multitude 10
9:39 a spirit seizes him, and he suddenly cries out 10
21:34 and that day come upon you suddenly like a snare; 6
Act 2: 2 suddenly a sound came from heaven 9
9: 3 suddenly a light from heaven flashed about him. 10
16:26 suddenly there was a great earthquake 9
22: 6 a great light from heaven suddenly shone about me 10
28: 6 to swell up or suddenly fall down dead 9
2Es 5: 4 and the sun shall suddenly shine forth at night 14
6:22 Sown places shall suddenly appear unsown 14
22 full storehouses shall suddenly be . . empty; 14
23 they shall suddenly be terrified. 14
8:14 thou wilt suddenly and quickly destroy him ‡
10:25 behold, her face suddenly shone exceedingly 14
26 she suddenly uttered a loud and fearful cry 14
11:20 some . . that ruled, yet disappeared suddenly; 13
26 one was set up, but suddenly disappeared; 13
33 the middle head also suddenly disappeared 14
13:11 suddenly nothing was seen of the . . multitude 14
Wis 14:15 who had been suddenly taken from him 12
Sir 5: 7 suddenly the wrath of the Lord will go forth 11
11:21 to enrich a poor man quickly and suddenly. 11
1Mc 1:30 he suddenly fell upon the city 11
3:23 he rushed suddenly against Seron and his army 9
4: 2 attack them suddenly 9
2Mc 3:27 When he suddenly fell to the ground 9
5: 5 suddenly made an assault upon the city 7
3Mc 3: 8 the crowds that suddenly were forming 8
4: 2 that had suddenly been decreed for them. 10

sue 1. חלה 2. *κρίνω* 3. *λόγος*
Ps 45:12 the people of Tyre will sue your favor with gifts 1
Mat 5:40 if any one would sue you and take your coat, let him 2
Jdt 3: 1 they sent messengers to sue for peace, and said 3

suffer 1. כְּאֵב 2. מַכְאוֹב 3. נשא 4. ענש 5. עַצֶּבֶת 6. צָרָה 7. *ἀλγηδών* 8. *θλῖψις* 9. *κακοπάθεια* 10. *κακοπαθέω* 11. *πάθημα* 12. *παθητός* 13. *πάθος* 14. *πάσχω* 15. *πόνος* 16. *συμπάθεια* 17. *συμπάσχω* 18. patior
Exd 3: 7 I have seen . . I know their sufferings 2
Num 14:33 children . . suffer for your faithlessness 3
Neh 9:27 in the time of their suffering they cried to thee 6
Job 2:13 for they saw that his suffering was very great. 1
9:28 I become afraid of all my suffering 5
Prv 22: 3 but the simple go on, and suffer for it. 4
27:12 but the simple go on, and suffer for it. 4
Lam 1: 4 and she herself suffers bitterly. •
18 but hear, all you peoples, and behold my suffering; 2
Ezk 18:19 Why should not the son suffer for the iniquity 3
20 shall not suffer for the iniquity of the father 3
20 nor the father suffer for the iniquity of the son; 3
Mat 9:20 a woman who had suffered from a hemorrhage •
16:21 he must go to Jerusalem and suffer many things 14
17:12 So also the Son of man will suffer at their hands. 14
15 and he suffers terribly 14
27:19 for I have suffered much over him today 14
Mrk 5:26 who had suffered much under many physicians 14
8:31 the Son of man must suffer many things 14
9:12 suffer many things and be treated with contempt? 14
Lke 9:22 saying, "The Son of man must suffer many things 14
13: 2 because they suffered thus? 14
17:25 first he must suffer many things and be rejected 14
22:15 to eat this passover with you before I suffer; 14
24:26 necessary that the Christ should suffer 14
46 the Christ should suffer 14
Act 3:18 that his Christ should suffer, he thus fulfilled. 14
9:16 how much he must suffer for the sake of my name. 14
17: 3 necessary for the Christ to suffer and to rise 14
26:23 that the Christ must suffer 12
28: 5 shook off the creature . . and suffered no harm. 14
Rom 5: 3 More than that, we rejoice in our sufferings 8
3 knowing that suffering produces endurance 8
8:17 heirs with Christ, provided we suffer with him 17
18 the sufferings of this present time are not worth 11
1Co 12:26 If one member suffers, all suffer together 14
2Co 1: 5 as we share abundantly in Christ's sufferings 11
6 when you patiently endure the same sufferings 11
6 endure the same sufferings that we suffer. 14
7 we know that as you share in our sufferings 11
Eph 3:13 not to lose heart over what I am suffering for you 8
Php 1:29 also suffer for his sake 14
3:10 share his sufferings 11
Col 1:24 Now I rejoice in my sufferings for your sake 11
1Th 2:14 you suffered the same things 14
2Th 1: 5 the kingdom of God, for which you are suffering- 14
2Ti 1:12 therefore I suffer as I do 14
2: 9 for which I am suffering and wearing fetters 10
3:11 my persecutions, my sufferings 11
Heb 2: 9 because of the suffering of death 11
10 make . . perfect through suffering. 11
18 because he . . has suffered and been tempted 14
5: 8 he learned obedience through what he suffered; 14
9:26 for then he would have had to suffer repeatedly 14
10:32 you endured a hard struggle with sufferings 11
13:12 Jesus also suffered outside the gate 14
Jas 5:10 As an example of suffering and patience 9
13 Is any one among you suffering? Let him pray. 10
1Pe 1:11 sufferings of Christ and the subsequent glory. 11
2:19 he endures pain while suffering unjustly. 14
20 if when you do right and suffer for it you take it 14
21 because Christ also suffered for you 14
23 when he suffered, he did not threaten; 14
3:14 even if you do suffer for righteousness' sake 14
17 For it is better to suffer for doing right 14
4: 1 Since therefore Christ suffered in the flesh 14
1 whoever has suffered in the flesh 14
13 in so far as you share Christ's sufferings 11
15 let none of you suffer as a murderer, or a thief 14
16 yet if one suffers as a Christian •
19 let those who suffer according to God's will 14
5: 1 elder and witness of the sufferings of Christ 11
9 suffering is required of your brotherhood 11
10 after you have suffered a little while 14
Rev 2:10 Do not fear what you are about to suffer. 14
2Es 4:12 and to suffer and not understand why. 18
7:99 those who would not . . shall suffer hereafter. 18
Wis 12:27 when in their suffering they became incensed 14
18: 1 and counted them happy for not having suffered 14
11 the common man suffered the same loss as the king; 14
19 not perish without knowing why they suffered. 14
19:13 they justly suffered because of their wicked acts; 14
16 afflicted with terrible sufferings 15
Sir 38:16 as one who is suffering grievously 14
2Mc 6:30 I am enduring terrible sufferings in my body 7
30 in my soul I am glad to suffer these things 14
7:12 for he regarded his sufferings as nothing. 7
18 we are suffering these things on our own account 14
32 For we are suffering because of our own sins. 14
36 after enduring a brief suffering 15
9:18 when his sufferings did not in any way abate 15
4Mc 1: 9 by despising sufferings that bring death 15
5:23 we endure any suffering willingly; 15
7: 8 in sufferings even to death. 13
22 to endure any suffering for the sake of virtue 15
9: 8 shall be with God, for whom we suffer; 14
10:10 are suffering because of our godly training 14
11:12 through these noble sufferings 15
20 summoned to an arena of sufferings for religion 15
13: 1 despised sufferings even unto death 15
14: 9 but also bore the sufferings patiently 14
15:11 to suffer with them out of love for her children 16
13 nurture and indomitable suffering by mothers! 13
16:19 therefore you ought to endure any suffering 15

18: 2 reason is master . . not only of sufferings from within 15
3 those who gave over their bodies in suffering 15

suffer (2) 1. לקח 2. מצא 3. נשא 4. עֲנִי 5. עשׂה 6. ἀναγκάζω 7. γίνομαι 8. εἰμί ἐν 9. εὑρίσκω 10. ἔχω 11. κατανύσσομαι 12. λυπέω 13. πείθω 14. πεῖραν λαμβάνω 15. περιπίπτω 16. πίπτω 17. τίνω 18. ὑπέχω 19. ὑποφέρω 20. excipio 21. patior

Lev 22: 4 none . . suffers a discharge may eat of the holy •
Ps 4: 2 O men, how long shall my honor suffer shame? •
9:13 Behold what I suffer from those who hate me 4
88:15 I suffer thy terrors; I am helpless. 3
116: 3 I suffered distress and anguish. 2
144:14 suffering no mischance or failure in bearing; •
Ezk 22: 7 the sojourner suffers extortion in your midst; 5
34:29 no longer suffer the reproach of the nations. 3
36: 6 you have suffered the reproach of the nations; 3
7 shall themselves suffer reproach. 3
30 may never again suffer the disgrace of famine 1
2Co 2: 3 so that when I came I might not suffer pain 10
2Th 1: 9 suffer the punishment of eternal destruction 17
Heb 11:26 He considered abuse suffered for the Christ •
36 Others suffered mocking and scourging 14
1Pe 1: 6 you may have to suffer various trials 12
2Es 7:18 have suffered the difficult circumstances 21
126 consider what we should suffer after death. 21
128 he shall suffer what you have said 21
10:22 our free men have suffered abuse 21
15:59 you shall come and suffer fresh afflictions 20
Jdt 8:19 they suffered a great catastrophe 16
Wis 4:19 they will suffer anguish 8
Sir 14: 1 and need not suffer grief for sin. 11
28: 1 He that takes vengeance will suffer vengeance 9
1Mc 5:61 Thus the people suffered a great rout 7
2Mc 4:48 quickly suffered the unjust penalty. 18
9:21 I suffered an annoying illness 15
3Mc 3:25 to suffer the sure and shameful death •
5:33 suffered an unexpected and dangerous threat 19
4Mc 4:25 known beforehand that they would suffer this 13
15: 7 because of the many pains she suffered with each 6
16 the birth-pangs you suffered for them! •

suffer affliction 1. ענה 2. θλίβω
Ps 107:17 of their iniquities suffered affliction; 1
1Th 3: 4 we were to suffer affliction 2

suffer agony 1. torqueo
2Es 5:34 for every hour I suffer agonies of heart 1

suffer disgrace 1. חֶרְפָּה
Neh 2:17 that we may no longer suffer disgrace. 1

suffer dishonor 1. ἀτιμάζω
Act 5:41 were counted worthy to suffer dishonor for the name. 1

suffer for guilt 1. אשם
Isa 24: 6 and its inhabitants suffer for their guilt; 1

suffer grievously 1. καταπονέω
3Mc 2: 2 who are suffering grievously 1

suffer harm 1. כלם 2. רעע 3. ἀδικέω
1Sm 25:15 men were very good to us, and we suffered no harm 1
Prv 13:20 but the companion of fools will suffer harm. 2
Wis 14:29 swear wicked oaths and expect to suffer no harm. 3

suffer hunger 1. רעב
Ps 34:10 The young lions suffer want and hunger; 1
Prv 19:15 idle person will suffer hunger. 1

suffer loss 1. נזק (A) 2. ἐλαττόω 3. ζημιόω
Dan 6: 2 account, so that the king might suffer no loss. 1
1Co 3:15 If any man's work is burned up, he will suffer loss 3
2Co 7: 9 so that you suffered no loss through us. 3
Php 3: 8 I have suffered the loss of all things 3
Sir 32:24 he who trusts the Lord will not suffer loss. 2

make suffer 1. יגה 2. צרר 3. ראה
Neh 9:27 hand of their enemies, who made them suffer; 2
Ps 60: 3 Thou hast made thy people suffer hard things; 3
Lam 1: 5 LORD has made her suffer for . . transgressions 1

suffer outrage 1. ὑβρίζω
2Mc 14:42 and suffer outrages unworthy of his noble birth. 1

suffer pangs 1. ὠδίνω
Sir 19:11 With such a word a fool will suffer pangs 1

suffer reproach 1. ὀνειδίζω
Sir 41: 7 they suffer reproach because of him. 1

suffer the wrong 1. ἀδικέω
2Co 7:12 nor on account of the one who suffered the wrong 1

suffer thirst 1. צמא
Job 24:11 they tread the wine presses, but suffer thirst. 1

suffer together 1. συμπάσχω
1Co 12:26 If one member suffers, all suffer together 1

suffer torment 1. βασανίζω
4Mc 15:22 how many torments the mother then suffered 1

suffer torture 1. βασανίζω
4Mc 9:32 you suffer torture by the threats 1

suffer violence 1. חמס 2. βιάζω
Jer 13:22 and you suffer violence. 1
Mat 11:12 the kingdom of heaven has suffered violence 2

suffer want 1. חסר 2. מַחְסוֹר 3. רושׁ 4. ἐνδεής
Ps 34:10 The young lions suffer want and hunger; 3
Prv 11:24 another withholds . . and only suffers want. 2
13:25 but the belly of the wicked suffers want. 1
Wis 16: 3 after suffering want a short time 4

suffer wrong 1. ἀδικέω
1Co 6: 7 Why not rather suffer wrong? 1
2Pe 2:13 suffering wrong for their wrongdoing. 1
Sir 13: 3 a poor man suffers wrong 1

already suffered 1. προπάσχω
1Th 2: 2 though we had already suffered 1

suffering *See* crush, endure, share.

severe suffering 1. κακοπαθεία
4Mc 9: 8 through this severe suffering and endurance 1

suffice 1. דַּי 2. מצא 3. מצא כֵּן 4. רַב 5. שׂפק 6. ἀρκετός 7. ἀρκέω
Num 11:22 herds be slaughtered for them, to suffice them? 2
22 fish of the sea be gathered . . to suffice them? 2
Deu 3:26 suffice you; speak no more to me of this matter. 4
Jdg 21:14 but they did not suffice for them. 3
1Kg 20:10 the dust of Sama'ria shall suffice for handfuls 5
Isa 40:16 Lebanon would not suffice for fuel 1
1Pe 4: 3 Let the time that is past suffice 6
4Mc 6:28 let our punishment suffice for them. 7

never suffice 1. חדל לְעוֹלָם
Ps 49: 8 is costly, and can never suffice 1

sufficiency 1. שֶׂפֶק
Job 20:22 In the fulness of his sufficiency he will be 1

sufficient 1. דַּי 2. ἀρκετός 3. ἀρκέω 4. ἱκανός 5. sufficio
Exd 36: 7 for the stuff they had was sufficient to do all 1
Deu 15: 8 lend him sufficient for his need, whatever it may be. 1
Mat 6:34 day's own trouble be sufficient for the day. 2
2Co 2:16 Who is sufficient for these things? 4
12: 9 he said to me, "My grace is sufficient for you 3
2Es 12:43 Are not the evils . . sufficient? 5
Wis 18:12 the living were not sufficient even to bury them 4
2Mc 10:19 a force sufficient to besiege them 4

sufficient *See also* means, number.

suggest 1. λαλέω
Tob 6:10 I will suggest that she be given to you in marriage 1

suggestion 1. ὑποτίθημι
2Mc 6: 8 At the suggestion of Ptolemy a decree was issued 1

suit 1. טַעַם 2. עֵרֶךְ 3. רִיב 4. ἁρμόνιος 5. καθίστημι 6. κατά 7. πρός
Exd 23: 2 nor shall you bear witness in a suit 3
3 nor shall you be partial to a poor man in his suit. 3
6 the justice due to your poor in his suit. 3
Jdg 17:10 I will give you . . and a suit of apparel 2
2Sm 15: 2 when any man had a suit to come before the king 3
4 every man with a suit or cause might come to me 3
Job 34:33 Will he then make requital to suit you 1
2Ti 4: 3 teachers to suit their own likings 6
Wis 16:20 suited to every taste. 4
21 was changed to suit every one's liking. 7
3Mc 4:11 well suited to make them an obvious spectacle 5

suit *See also* enter.

suit at law 1. κρίνω
Sus 1: 6 and all who had suits at law came to them. 1

suit of armor 1. πανοπλία
1Mc 13:29 upon the columns he put suits of armor 1
29 beside the suits of armor carved ships 1

suitable 1. כְּ 2. ἐπιτήδειος 3. εὐφυής
Gen 49:28 each with the blessing suitable to him. 1
2Mc 2:29 only what is suitable for its adornment 2
3:37 what sort of person would be suitable 2
4:32 he had obtained a suitable opportunity 3

most suitable 1. οἰκειόω
4Mc 5:26 to eat what will be most suitable for our lives 1

not suitable 1. ἀνεύθετος
Act 27:12 because the harbor was not suitable to winter in 1

sullen 1. זָעֵף 2. βαρύθυμος
1Kg 20:43 king . . went to his house resentful and sullen 1
21: 4 Ahab went into his house vexed and sullen 1
3Mc 6:20 he forgot his sullen insolence. 2

sullenly 1. σκυθρωπός
3Mc 5:34 the . . friends one by one sullenly slipped away 1

sulphur 1. θεῖον 2. θειώδης
Lke 17:29 fire and sulphur rained from heaven 1
Rev 9:17 the color of fire and of sapphire and of sulphur 2
17 and smoke and sulphur issued from their mouths. 1
18 killed, by the fire and smoke and sulphur 1
14:10 he shall be tormented with fire and sulphur 1
19:20 the lake of fire that burns with sulphur. 1
20:10 thrown into the lake of fire and sulphur 1
21: 8 in the lake that burns with fire and sulphur 1
3Mc 2: 5 consumed with fire and sulphur the men of Sodom 1

sultry 1. חֲרִישִׁי
Jon 4: 8 the sun rose, God appointed a sultry east wind 1

sum 1. חֶשְׁבּוֹן 2. מִסְפָּר 3. פְּקוּדִים 4. ראשׁ 5. רֵאשׁ (A) 6. ἀριθμός 7. ἱκανός 8. κεφάλαιον 9. συντέλεια 10. τιμή
Exd 38:21 This is the sum of the things for the tabernacle 3
2Sm 24: 9 Jo'ab gave the sum of the numbering of the people 2
1Ch 21: 5 Jo'ab gave the sum of the numbering of the people 2
Ps 119:160 The sum of thy word is truth; 4
139:17 thy thoughts, O God! How vast is the sum of them! 4
Ecc 7:27 adding one thing to another to find the sum 1
Dan 7: 1 down the dream, and told the sum of the matter. 5
Mat 26: 9 this ointment might have been sold for a large sum •
28:12 counsel, they gave a sum of money to the soldiers 7
Act 7:16 tomb that Abraham had bought for a sum of silver 10
22:28 I bought this citizenship for a large sum. 8
Sir 43:27 the sum of our words is: "He is the all. 9
51:28 Get instruction with a large sum of silver 6

exact sum 1. פָּרָשָׁה
Est 4: 7 and the exact sum of money that Haman had 1

large sum 1. πολύς
Mrk 12:41 Many rich people put in large sums. 1

sum of money 1. χρῆμα
1Mc 14:32 He spent great sums of his own money 1
2Mc 3: 6 the treasury . . was full of untold sums of money 1

sum of things 1. חֶשְׁבּוֹן
Ecc 7:25 to know . . and to seek wisdom and the sum of things 1

sum up 1. ἀνακεφαλαιόω 2. recapitulo
Rom 13: 9 commandments . . are summed up in this sentence 1
2Es 12:25 they who shall sum up his wickedness 2

summary *See* give.

summer 1. קיץ 2. קַיִץ 3. קִיט (A) 4. θέρμη 5. θέρος 6. aestas
Gen 8:22 cold and heat, summer and winter, day and night 2
Ps 32: 4 my strength was dried up as by the heat of summer. 2
74:17 thou hast made summer and winter. 2
Prv 6: 8 she prepares her food in summer 2
10: 5 A son who gathers in summer is prudent 2
26: 1 Like snow in summer or rain in harvest 2
30:25 yet they provide their food in the summer; 2
Isa 18: 6 the birds of prey will summer upon them 1
28: 4 will be like a first-ripe fig before the summer 2
Jer 8:20 The harvest is past, the summer is ended 2
Dan 2:35 like the chaff of the summer threshing floors; 3
Ams 3:15 smite the winter house with the summer house; 2
Zec 14: 8 it shall continue in summer as in winter. 2
Mat 24:32 you know that summer is near. 4
Mrk 13:28 you know that summer is near. 4
Lke 21:30 know that the summer is already near. 4
2Es 7:41 or summer or spring or heat or winter or frost 6
Sir 50: 8 like a green shoot on Lebanon on a summer day; 5

summer *See also* fruit, heat.

summit 1. ראשׁ
2Sm 15:32 David came to the summit, where God was worshiped 1
16: 1 When David had passed a little beyond the summit 1
Jer 22: 6 You are as Gilead to me, as the summit of Lebanon 1

summon 1. זכר 2. זעק 3. יעד 4. מִקְרָא 5. צוה 6. קרא 7. קרה 8. שׁמע 9. καλέω 10. μετακαλέω 11. προσκαλέω
Exd 7:11 Pharaoh summoned the wise men and the sorcerers; 6
12:31 he summoned Moses and Aaron by night, and said 6
Num 10: 2 shall use them for summoning the congregation 4
Deu 5: 1 Moses summoned all Israel, and said to them, "Hear 6
29: 2 Moses summoned all Israel and said to them 6
31: 7 Then Moses summoned Joshua, and said to him 6
Jos 9:22 Joshua summoned them, and he said to them 6

10:24 Joshua summoned all the men of Israel, and said 6
22: 1 Joshua summoned the Reubenites, and the Gadites 6
23: 2 Joshua summoned all Israel, their elders 6
24: 1 and summoned the elders, the heads, the judges 6
Jdg 4: 6 She sent and summoned Barak the son of Abin'o-am 6
10 Barak summoned Zeb'ulun and Naph'tali to Kedesh; 2
1Sm 15: 4 Saul summoned the people, and numbered them 8
22:11 the king sent to summon Ahim'elech the priest 6
23: 8 And Saul summoned all the people to war 8
28:15 I have summoned you to tell me what I shall do. 7
2Sm 14:33 Then Jo'ab . . told him; and he summoned Ab'salom. 6
20: 5 Ama'sa went to summon Judah; but he delayed 2
1Kg 2:36 the king sent and summoned Shim'e-i, and said to him 6
42 the king sent and summoned Shim'e-i, and said to him 6
22: 9 the king of Israel summoned an officer and said 6
13 the messenger who went to summon Micai'ah said 6
2Kg 4:36 Then he summoned Geha'zi and said 6
12: 7 King Jeho'ash summoned Jehoi'ada . . and the other 6
1Ch 15:11 David summoned the priests . . and the Levites 6
2Ch 18: 8 the king of Israel summoned an officer and said 6
12 messenger who went to summon Micai'ah said to him 6
24: 6 king summoned Jehoi'ada the chief, and said to him 6
Est 2:14 unless the king . . and she was summoned by name. 6
3:12 Then the king's secretaries were summoned 6
8: 9 king's secretaries were summoned at that time 6
Job 9:16 If I summoned him and he answered me 6
19 If it is a matter of justice, who can summon him? 3
Ps 50: 1 the LORD, speaks and summons the earth 6
68:28 Summon thy might, O God; show thy strength, O God 5
105:16 When he summoned a famine on the land 6
Isa 13: 3 have summoned my mighty men to execute my anger 6
Jer 25:29 not go unpunished, for I am summoning a sword 6
42: 8 Then he summoned Joha'nan the son of Kare'ah 6
49:19 For who is like me? Who will summon me? 3
50:29 Summon archers against Babylon 8
44 For who is like me? Who will summon me? 3
51:27 war against her, summon against her the kingdoms 8
Lam 1:15 he summoned an assembly against me to crush my 6
Ezk 36:29 I will summon the grain and make it abundant 6
38:21 I will summon every kind of terror against Gog 6
Dan 2: 2 commanded that the . . Chalde'ans be summoned 6
Nah 2: 5 officers are summoned, they stumble as they go 1
Mat 2: 7 Then Herod summoned the wise men secretly 9
18:32 Then his lord summoned him and said to him 11
Mrk 15:44 summoning the centurion 11
Lke 16: 5 summoning his master's debtors one by one 11
Act 6: 2 the twelve summoned the body of the disciples 11
13: 7 who summoned Barnabas and Saul 11
24:25 when I have an opportunity I will summon you. 10
1Es 3:14 Then he sent and summoned all the nobles 9
16 they were summoned, and came in. 9
Jdt 8:10 to summon Chabris and Charmis 9
14: 6 they summoned Achior from the house of Uzziah. 9
Wis 1:16 men by their words and deeds summoned death 11
Sus 1:52 he summoned one of them and said to him 9
1Mc 1: 6 So he summoned his most honored officers 9
2Mc 4:28 the two of them were summoned by the king 11
8: 1 summoned their kinsmen 11
3Mc 5: 1 he summoned Hermon, keeper of the elephants 11
18 the king summoned Hermon 11
37 After summoning Hermon 11
6:30 king . . summoned the official in charge of . . revenues 11
4Mc 8: 4 summoned them nearer and said 9
17 Since the king has summoned and exhorted us 9
11:20 summoned to an arena of sufferings for religion 9

summon strength 1. חזק
Gen 48: 2 Israel summoned his strength, and sat up in bed. 1

summon to come 1. μεταπέμπω
4Mc 12: 2 He summoned him to come nearer 1

sumptuous 1. λαμπρός
Sir 29:22 sumptuous food in another man's house. 1

sumptuously 1. λαμπρῶς
Lke 16:19 and who feasted sumptuously every day. 1

sun 1. חַמָּה 2. חֶרֶס 3. שֶׁמֶשׁ 4. שֶׁמֶשׁ (A) 5. ἥλιος 6. sol
Gen 15:12 As the sun was going down, a deep sleep fell 3
17 When the sun had gone down and it was dark 3
19:23 sun had risen on the earth when Lot came to Zo'ar. 3
28:11 stayed there that night, because the sun had set. 3
32:31 The sun rose upon him as he passed Penu'el 3
37: 9 behold, the sun, the moon, and eleven stars were 3
Exd 16:21 but when the sun grew hot, it melted. 3
17:12 were steady until the going down of the sun. 3
22: 3 if the sun has risen upon him, there shall be 3
26 restore it to him before the sun goes down; 3
Lev 22: 7 When the sun is down he shall be clean 3
Num25: 4 hang them in the sun before the LORD 3
Deu 4:19 when you see the sun and the moon and the stars 3
11:30 west of the road, toward the going down of the sun 3
16: 6 evening at the going down of the sun 3
17: 3 worshipped . . sun or the moon or any of the host 3
23:11 when the sun is down, he may come within the camp. 3
24:13 when the sun goes down, you shall restore to him 3
15 hire . . day he earns it, before the sun goes down 3
33:14 with the choicest fruits of the sun 3
Jos 1: 4 to the Great Sea toward the going down of the sun 3
8:29 and at the going down of the sun Joshua commanded 3
10:12 Sun, stand thou still at Gibeon, and thou Moon 3
13 And the sun stood still, and the moon stayed 3
13 The sun stayed in the midst of heaven 3
27 at the time of the going down of the sun 3
Jdg 5:31 O LORD! But thy friends be like the sun as he rises 3
9:33 in the morning, as soon as the sun is up, rise early 3
14:18 to him on the seventh day before the sun went down 2
19:14 the sun went down on them near Gib'e-ah 3
1Sm 11: 9 Tomorrow, by the time the sun is hot, you shall have 3
2Sm 2:24 and as the sun was going down they came to the hill 3
3:35 if I taste bread or . . till the sun goes down! 3
12:11 lie with your wives in the sight of this sun. 3
12 do this . . before all Israel, and before the sun. 3
23: 4 like the sun shining . . upon a cloudless morning 3
1Kg 8:12 The LORD has set the sun in the heavens 5
2Kg 3:22 they rose . . and the sun shone upon the water 3
20:11 by which the sun had declined on the dial of Ahaz. ‡
23: 5 burned incense to Ba'al, to the sun, and the moon 3
11 horses that the kings . . had dedicated to the sun 3
11 and he burned the chariots of the sun with fire. 3
Neh 7: 3 not the gates . . be opened until the sun is hot; 3
Job 8:16 He thrives before the sun, and his shoots spread 3
9: 7 who commands the sun, and it does not rise; 2
30:28 I go about blackened, but not by the sun; 1
31:26 if I have looked at the sun when it shone 5
Ps 19: 4 In them he has set a tent for the sun 3
50: 1 from the rising of the sun to its setting. 3
58: 8 like the untimely birth that never sees the sun. 3
72: 5 May he live while the sun endures 3
17 for ever, his fame continue as long as the sun! 3
74:16 hast established the luminaries and the sun. 3
84:11 For the LORD God is a sun and shield; 3
89:36 his throne as long as the sun before me. 3
104:19 sun knows its time for setting. 3
22 When the sun rises, they get them away and lie down 3
113: 3 From the rising of the sun to its setting the name 3
121: 6 The sun shall not smite you by day 3
136: 8 the sun to rule over the day 3
148: 3 Praise him, sun and moon 3
Ecc 1: 3 gain by . . the toil at which he toils under the sun? 3
5 The sun rises and the sun goes down 3
5 The sun rises and the sun goes down 3
9 and there is nothing new under the sun. 3
14 I have seen everything that is done under the sun; 3
2:11 and there was nothing to be gained under the sun. 3
17 what is done under the sun was grievous to me; 3
18 all my toil in which I had toiled under the sun 3
19 which I toiled and used my wisdom under the sun. 3
20 all the toil of my labors under the sun 3
22 and strain with which he toils beneath the sun? 3
3:16 I saw under the sun that in the place of justice 3
4: 1 oppressions that are practiced under the sun. 3
3 the evil deeds that are done under the sun. 3
7 Again, I saw vanity under the sun 3
15 move about under the sun, as well as that youth, 3
5:13 a grievous evil which I have seen under the sun 3
18 one toils under the sun the few days of his life 3
6: 1 There is an evil which I have seen under the sun 3
5 it has not seen the sun or known anything; 3
12 tell man what will be after him under the sun? 3
7:11 Wisdom . . an advantage to those who see the sun. 3
8: 9 applying my mind to all that is done under the sun 3
15 no good thing under the sun but to eat and drink 3
15 days of life which God gives him under the sun. 3
17 find out the work that is done under the sun. 3
9: 3 This is an evil in all that is done under the sun 3
6 have no . . share in all that is done under the sun. 3
9 vain life which he has given you under the sun 3
9 and in your toil at which you toil under the sun. 3
11 saw that under the sun the race is not to the swift 3
13 also seen this example of wisdom under the sun 3
10: 5 There is an evil which I have seen under the sun 3
11: 7 and it is pleasant for the eyes to behold the sun. 3
12: 2 before the sun and the light . . are darkened 3
Sng 1: 6 Do not gaze . . because the sun has scorched me. 3
6:10 fair as the moon, bright as the sun 1
Isa 13:10 the sun will be dark at its rising 3
19:18 One of these will be called the City of the Sun. 2
24:23 moon will be confounded, and the sun ashamed; 1
30:26 light of the moon will be as the light of the sun 1
26 and the light of the sun will be sevenfold 1
38: 8 I will make the shadow cast by the declining sun 3
8 the sun turned back on the dial the ten steps 3
41:25 and he has come, from the rising of the sun 3
45: 6 that men may know, from the rising of the sun 3
49:10 neither scorching wind nor sun shall smite them 3
59:19 and his glory from the rising of the sun; 3
60:19 The sun shall be no more your light by day 3
20 Your sun shall no more go down 3
Jer 8: 2 they shall be spread before the sun and the moon 3
15: 9 her sun went down while it was yet day; 3
31:35 says the LORD, who gives the sun for light by day 3
Ezk 8:16 their faces toward the east, worshiping the sun 3
32: 7 I will cover the sun with a cloud 3
Dan 6:14 labored till the sun went down to rescue him. 4
Jol 2:10 The sun and the moon are darkened 3
31 The sun shall be turned to darkness 3
3:15 The sun and the moon are darkened 3
Ams 8: 9 I will make the sun go down at noon 3
Jon 4: 8 When the sun rose, God appointed a sultry east 3
8 the sun beat upon the head of Jonah 3
Mic 3: 6 The sun shall go down upon the prophets 3
Nah 3:17 when the sun rises, they fly away; 3
Hab 3:11 The sun and moon stood still in their habitation 3
Mal 1:11 from the rising of the sun to its setting 3
4: 2 the sun of righteousness shall rise 3
Mat 5:45 Father who is in heaven; for he makes his sun rise 5
13: 6 when the sun rose they were scorched 5
43 Then the righteous will shine like the sun 5
17: 2 and his face shone like the sun 5
24:29 the sun will be darkened 5
Mrk 4: 6 when the sun rose it was scorched 5
13:24 after that tribulation, the sun will be darkened 5
16: 2 they went to the tomb when the sun had risen. 5
Lke 4:40 Now when the sun was setting 5
21:25 there will be signs in sun and moon and stars 5
23:45 while the sun's light failed 5
Act 2:20 the sun shall be turned into darkness 5
13:11 you shall be blind and unable to see the sun for a time 5
26:13 a light from heaven, brighter than the sun 5
27:20 when neither sun nor stars appeared for many a day 5
1Co 15:41 one glory of the sun, and another glory of the moon 5
Eph 4:26 do not let the sun go down on your anger. 5
Jas 1:11 For the sun rises with its scorching heat 5
Rev 1:16 face was like the sun shining in full strength 5
6:12 and the sun became black as sackcloth 5
7: 2 I saw another angel ascend from the rising . . sun 5
16 sun shall not strike them, nor any scorching heat 5
8:12 blew his trumpet, and a third of the sun was struck 5
9: 2 the sun and the air were darkened with the smoke 5
10: 1 his face was like the sun, and his legs like 5
12: 1 a woman clothed with the sun 5
16: 8 The fourth angel poured his bowl on the sun 5
19:17 Then I saw an angel standing in the sun 5
21:23 the city has no need of sun or moon to shine upon it 5
22: 5 they need no light of lamp or sun 5
1Es 4:34 the sun is swift in its course 5
2Es 5: 4 and the sun shall suddenly shine forth at night 6
6:45 thou didst command the brightness of the sun 6
7:39 a day that has no sun or moon or stars 6
97 how their face is to shine like the sun 6
Tob 2: 7 When the sun had set 5
Jdt 14: 2 as soon as morning comes and the sun rises 5
AEs 10: 6 there was light and the sun and abundant water 5
11:11 light came, and the sun rose 5
Wis 2: 4 mist that is chased by the rays of the sun 5
5: 6 the sun did not rise upon us. 5
7:29 For she is more beautiful than the sun 5
16:27 when simply warmed by a fleeting ray of the sun 5
28 one must rise before the sun to give thee thanks 5
18: 3 a harmless sun for their glorious wandering. 5
Sir 17:19 All their works are as the sun before him 5
31 What is brighter than the sun? 5
23:19 10,000 times brighter than the sun 5
26:16 Like the sun rising in the heights of the Lord 5
33: 7 when all the daylight in the year is from the sun? 5
42:16 The sun looks down on everything with its light 5
43: 2 The sun, when it appears, making proclamation 5
4 the sun burns the mountains three times as much 5
46: 4 Was not the sun held back by his hand? 5
48:23 In his days the sun went backward 5
50: 7 like the sun shining upon the temple 5
LJr 1:60 sun and moon and stars . . are obedient. 5
67 shine like the sun or give light like the moon. 5
Aza 1:40 Bless the Lord, sun and moon 5
1Mc 6:39 When the sun shone upon the shields of gold 5
10:50 He pressed the battle strongly until the sun set 5
12:27 So when the sun set 5
2Mc 1:22 the sun, which had been clouded over, shone out 5
3Mc 4:15 from the rising of the sun till its setting 5
5:26 The rays of the sun were not yet shed abroad 5

noonday sun 1. μεσημβρία
Sir 34:16 a shade from noonday sun 1

rising sun 1. oriens
2Es 15:20 from the rising sun and from the south 1

sunder 1. גזר
Ps 136:13 to him who divided the Red Sea in sunder 1

sunder *See also* break.

sundown 1. δύνω ἥλιος
Mrk 1:32 That evening, at sundown 1

sunrise 1. מִזְרָח 2. מִזְרַח הַשֶּׁמֶשׁ
Num 2: 3 Those . . toward the sunrise shall be 1
3:38 before the tent of meeting toward the sunrise 1
21:11 wilderness . . opposite Moab, toward the sunrise. 2
34:15 at Jericho eastward, toward the sunrise. 1
Jos 1:15 land . . beyond the Jordan toward the sunrise. 2
19:12 eastward toward the sunrise to the boundary 2
13 it passes along on the east toward the sunrise 1

sunrising 1. מִזְרַח הַשֶּׁמֶשׁ
Jos 12: 1 land beyond the Jordan toward the sunrising 1
13: 5 and all Lebanon, toward the sunrising 1

sunset 1. בוא הַשֶּׁמֶשׁ 2. עֵת בוא הַשֶּׁמֶשׁ 3. *δύνω ὁ ἥλιος*
1Kg 22:36 about sunset a cry went through the army 1
2Ch 18:34 then at sunset he died. 2
Tob 2: 4 to a place of shelter until sunset. 3

sunshine 1. אור
Isa 18: 4 from my dwelling like clear heat in sunshine 1

superb 1. *καύχημα*
Sir 45: 8 He clothed him with superb perfection 1
50:11 clothed himself with superb perfection 1

superfluous 1. *περισσός*
2Co 9: 1 Now it is superfluous for me to write to you 1
2Mc 12:44 superfluous and foolish to pray for the dead 1

superhuman 1. *ὑπὲρ ἄνθρωπον*
2Mc 9: 8 in his superhuman arrogance 1

superior 1. *ἐπικρατέω* 2. *κρείττων* 3. *πρῶτος* 4. *ὑπέρ*
Heb 1: 4 having become as much superior to angels as . . 2
7: 7 the inferior is blessed by the superior. 2
Wis 7:29 she is found to be superior 3
Sir 25:10 no one superior to him who fears the Lord. 4
4Mc 2:11 It is superior to love for one's wife 1

superlative 1. *ὑπερλίαν*
2Co 11: 5 inferior to these superlative apostles. 1
12:11 inferior to these superlative apostles 1

supernatural 1. *πνευματικός*
1Co 10: 3 all ate the same supernatural food 1
4 all drank the same supernatural drink 1
4 they drank from the supernatural Rock 1

superstition 1. *δεισιδαιμονία*
Act 25:19 dispute . . about their own superstition 1

supervise 1. *ἐπιστατέω*
1Es 7: 2 supervised the holy work with very great care 1

supervision 1. *ἐπίσκεψις*
3Mc 7:12 without royal authority or supervision 1

supper 1. *δειπνέω* 2. *δεῖπνον*
Lke 17: 8 Prepare supper for me 1
22:20 likewise the cup after supper, saying, "This cup 1
Joh 12: 2 There they made him a supper; Martha served 2
13: 2 during supper 2
4 rose from supper, laid aside his garments 2
21:20 who had lain close to his breast at the supper 2
1Co 11:20 it is not the Lord's supper that you eat. 2
25 In the same way also the cup, after supper, saying 1
Rev 19: 9 invited to the marriage supper of the Lamb. 2
17 Come, gather for the great supper of God 2
4Mc 3: 9 Now all the rest were at supper 2

supplant 1. עקב 2. *ὑπονοθεύω*
Gen 27:36 Jacob? For he has supplanted me these two times. 1
2Mc 4:26 after supplanting his own brother 2
26 Jason . . was supplanted by another man 2

supplanter 1. עקב
Jer 9: 4 for every brother is a supplanter 1

supplement 1. *ἐπιχορηγέω*
2Pe 1: 5 to supplement your faith with virtue 1

suppliant 1. עָתָר 2. *ἱκέτης*
Zep 3:10 my suppliants, the daughter of my dispersed ones 1
Sir 4: 4 Do not reject an afflicted suppliant 2

supplication 1. חנה 2. תְּחִנָּה 3. תַּחֲנוּן 4. תְּפִלָּה 5. חנן (A) 6. *δέησις* 7. *ἱκετεία* 8. *ἱκετήριος* 9. *λιτανεία*
1Kg 8:28 prayer of thy servant and to his supplication 2
30 hearken thou to the supplication of thy servant 2
38 whatever prayer, whatever supplication is made 1
45 hear . . their prayer and their supplication 2
49 hear . . their prayer and their supplication 2
52 eyes be open to the supplication of thy servant 2
52 open . . to the supplication of thy people Israel 2
54 offering . . prayer and supplication to the LORD 1
9: 3 I have heard your prayer and your supplication 2
2Ch 6:19 regard to the prayer . . and to his supplication 2
21 hearken thou to the supplications of thy 3
29 whatever prayer, whatever supplication is made 1
35 hear . . their prayer and their supplication 2
39 hear . . their prayer and their supplications 2
33:13 God . . heard his supplication and brought him 2
Job 41: 3 Will he make many supplications to you? 3
Ps 6: 9 The LORD has heard my supplication; 2
28: 2 Hear the voice of my supplication, as I cry to thee 3
6 for he has heard the voice of my supplications. 3
31:22 But thou didst hear my supplications 3
55: 1 O God; and hide not thyself from my supplication! 2
86: 6 hearken to my cry of supplication. 3
102:17 will not despise their supplication. 4
116: 1 has heard my voice and my supplications. 3
119:170 Let my supplication come before thee; 2
130: 2 attentive to the voice of my supplications! 3
140: 6 give ear to the voice of my supplications, O LORD! 3
143: 1 O LORD; give ear to my supplications! 3
Jer 36: 7 their supplication will come before the LORD 2
42: 2 Let our supplication come before you 2
9 to whom you sent me to present your supplication 2
Dan 6:11 found Daniel making petition and supplication 5
9: 3 seeking him by prayer and supplications 3
17 hearken to the prayer . . to his supplications 3
18 not present our supplications before thee 3
20 presenting my supplication before the LORD 2
23 beginning of your supplications a word went 3
Zec 12:10 a spirit of compassion and supplication, 3
Eph 6:18 with all prayer and supplication 6
18 making supplication for all the saints 6
Php 4: 6 in everything by prayer and supplication 6
1Ti 2: 1 supplications, prayers, intercessions 6
5: 5 continues in supplications and prayers 6
Heb 5: 7 Jesus offered up prayers and supplications 8
Sir 35:14 not ignore the supplication of the fatherless 7
51: 9 I sent up my supplication from the earth 7
Bar 2:14 Hear, O Lord, our prayer and our supplication 6
4:20 I . . put on the sackcloth of my supplication 6
1Mc 7:37 a house of prayer and supplication. 6
2Mc 3:18 to make a general supplication 7
8:29 they made common supplication 7
9:18 in the form of a supplication 8
10:25 in supplication to God. 7
3Mc 1:21 Various were the supplications 6
23 resorted to the same posture of supplication 6
2:21 having heard the lawful supplication 9
5:25 with most tearful supplication and mournful dirges 7

supplication *See also* heed, make.

solemn supplication 1. *λιτανεία*
2Mc 10:16 after making solemn supplication 1

supply 1. היה 2. נהל 3. נשא 4. נתן 5. רְכוּשׁ 6. שׁרת 7. *ἀπαρτία* 8. *γίνομαι εἰς* 9. *δύναμις* 10. *εἰμί* 11. *εἰς* 12. *ἐπαρκέω* 13. *ἐπιχορηγέω* 14. *ἐπιχορηγία* 15. *καταρτίζω* 16. *παράθεσις* 17. *παρασκευή* 18. *παρέχω* 19. *πληρόω* 20. *προσαναπληρόω* 21. *χορηγέω* 22. paro 23. praebeo
Gen 47:17 and he supplied them with food in exchange 2
Num 4: 9 all the vessels for oil with which it is supplied 6
1Kg 5:10 So Hiram supplied Solomon with all the timber 4
9:11 Hiram . . had supplied Solomon with cedar 3
Isa 23:18 her merchandise will supply abundant food 1
Dan 11:13 come on with a great army and abundant supplies. 5
2Co 8:14 your abundance . . should supply their want 8
14 so that their abundance may supply your want 11
9:10 He who supplies seed to the sower 13
10 supply and multiply your resources 21
12 not only supplies the wants of the saints 20
11: 9 my needs were supplied by the brethren 20
Gal 3: 5 Does he who supplies the Spirit to you 13
Eph 4:16 every joint with which it is supplied 14
Php 4:19 my God will supply every need of yours 19
1Th 3:10 supply what is lacking in your faith? 15
1Pe 4:11 who renders it by the strength which God supplies 21
2Es 8:10 milk should be supplied 23
9:19 which is supplied both with an unfailing table 22
Jdt 3:10 in order to assemble all the supplies 7
7: 7 visited the springs that supplied their water •
12: 3 If your supply runs out, where can we get more 10
Wis 16:20 supply them from heaven with bread ready to eat 18
Sir 1:10 he supplied her to those who love him. 21
26 the Lord will supply it for you. 21
39:33 he will supply every need in its hour. 21
1Mc 6: 6 the arms, supplies, and abundant spoils 9
8:26 not give or supply grain, arms, money, or ships 12
14:10 He supplied the cities with food 21
2Mc 12:14 relying . . on their supply of provisions 16
15:21 the varied supply of arms 17

supply *See also* cut, train.

food supply 1. *βρῶμα* 2. *τροφή*
Jdt 11:12 Since their food supply is exhausted 1
1Mc 6:57 We daily grow weaker, our food supply is scant 2

supply provision 1. כול
1Kg 4:27 officers supplied provisions for King Solomon 1

richly supply 1. דשן
Prv 13: 4 soul of the diligent is richly supplied. 1

water supply 1. *ὕδωρ*
Jdt 7:17 and seized the water supply 1

support 1. אחז 2. כָּתֵף 3. מִסְעָד 4. מַשְׁעֵן 5. נטה אַחֲרֵי 6. נשׂא 7. סמך 8. סעד 9. עזר 10. שׁען 11. *βαστάζω* 12. *ἐπανόρθωσις* 13. *ἐπιχορηγέω* 14. *ἱστός* 15. *ὀψώνιον* 16. *στήριγμα* 17. *στηριγμός* 18. *στηρίζω* 19. *ὑπολαμβάνω* 20. *χορηγία* 21. porto
Gen 13: 6 that the land could not support both of them 6
36: 7 the land of their sojournings could not support 6
1Kg 2:28 Jo'ab had supported Adoni'jah 5
28 although he had not supported Ab'salom- 5
6: 6 the supporting beams should not be inserted •
7:30 at the four corners were supports for a laver. 2
30 The supports were cast, with wreaths at the side 2
34 There were four supports at the four corners 2
34 the supports were of one piece with the stands. 2
10:12 king made . . supports for the house of the LORD 3
Ezr 10:15 Meshul'lam and Shab'bethai the Levite supported 9
Job 24:23 He gives them security, and they are supported; 10
Ps 18:35 thy right hand supported me, and thy help made me 8
Ezk 30: 6 says the LORD: Those who support Egypt shall fall 7
41: 6 to serve as supports for the side chambers 1
6 so that they should not be supported by the wall 1
Rom 11:18 remember it is not you that support the root 11
18 but the root that supports you. •
2Co 11: 8 I robbed other churches by accepting support 15
3Jn 1: 8 So we ought to support such men 19
1Es 4:54 He wrote also concerning their support 20
55 the support for the Levites should be provided 20
8:52 will support them in every way. 12
2Es 5:45 it might even now be able to support all of them 21
Tob 8: 6 gavest him Eve his wife as a helper and support. 16
Sir 3:31 at the moment of his falling he will find support. 17
25:22 when a wife supports her husband. 13
34:15 To whom does he look? And who is his support? 16
16 a mighty protection and strong support 16
36:24 a helper fit for him and a pillar of support. 4
1Mc 2:17 supported by sons and brothers. 18
27 every one who . . supports the covenant 14

support *See also* give.

supporter 1. *ὁ παρά* 2. *ὁ περί*
1Mc 11:39 formerly . . one of Alexander's supporters 1
3Mc 1: 1 where Antiochus's supporters were encamped. 2

suppose 1. אוּלַי 2. אמר 3. *δοκέω* 4. *λογίζομαι* 5. *νομίζω* 6. *οἴομαι* 7. *τίθημι* 8. *ὑπολαμβάνω* 9. *ὑπονοέω*
Gen 18:24 Suppose there are 50 righteous within the city; 1
28 Suppose five of the 50 righteous are lacking? 1
29 Suppose 40 are found there. 1
30 Suppose 30 are found there. 1
31 Suppose twenty are found there. 1
32 again but this once. Suppose ten are found 1
2Sm 13:32 Let not my lord suppose that they have killed 2
33 to suppose that all the king's sons are dead; 2
2Ch 25: 8 if you suppose that in this way you will be strong 8
Mrk 10:42 those who are supposed to rule over the Gentiles 3
Lke 2:44 supposing him to be in the company 5
3:23 being the son (as was supposed) of Joseph 5
7:43 The one, I suppose, to whom he forgave more. 8
19:11 because they supposed 3
24:37 supposed that they saw a spirit. 3
Joh 11:31 supposing that she was going to the tomb to weep 3
20:15 Supposing him to be the gardener, she said to him 3
21:25 I suppose that the world . . could not contain 6
Act 2:15 these men are not drunk, as you suppose 8
7:25 He supposed that his brethren understood 5
13:25 What do you suppose that I am? 9
14:19 supposing that he was dead. 5
16:13 where we supposed there was a place of prayer; 5
27 supposing that the prisoners had escaped. 5
21:29 they supposed that Paul had brought him 5
25:18 such evils as I supposed; 9
27:13 supposing that they had obtained their purpose 3
Rom 2: 3 Do you suppose, O man, that when you judge 4
Jas 1: 7 For that person must not suppose 6
4: 5 you suppose it is in vain that the scripture says 3
Tob 6:17 I suppose that you will have children by her. 8
Jdt 14:14 he supposed that he was sleeping with Judith. 9
AEs 16: 4 they suppose that they will escape 8
Wis 13: 2 supposed that . . fire or wind . . were the gods 5
17: 2 when lawless men supposed 8
Sus 1: 5 elders . . , who were supposed to govern the people. 3
1Mc 6:43 he supposed that the king was upon it. 6
2Mc 6:24 he said, "lest many of the young should suppose 8
3Mc 1:17 hurried out, supposing that . . 7
4Mc 4:13 lest King Seleucus suppose 5
5:18 Even if, as you suppose, our law were not . . divine 8
19 do not suppose that it would be a petty sin 5
9: 7 do not suppose that you can injure us by torturing us. 5

suppress 1. *κατέχω*
Rom 1:18 men who by their wickedness suppress the truth. 1

supremacy 1. *ἡγεμονία*
4Mc 13: 4 The supremacy of the mind over these 1

supreme 1. שִׁלְטוֹן 2. *κύριος* 3. *μέγας* 4. *ὑπερέχω*
Ecc 8: 4 For the word of the king is supreme, and who may say 1
1Pe 2:13 whether it be to the emperor as supreme 4
2Mc 3:36 the deeds of the supreme God 3
3Mc 1: 9 he offered sacrifice to the supreme God 3
16 entreated the supreme God 3
3:11 not considering the might of the supreme God 3
4:16 improper words against the supreme God. 3
5:25 implored the supreme God to help them again 3
7:22 the supreme God . . performed great deeds 3
4Mc 1:19 Rational judgment is supreme over all of these 2
7:10 O supreme king over the passions, Eleazar! 3

sure 1. אֱמוּנָה 2. אמן 3. אֹמֶן 4. אֱמֶת 5. חזק 6. ידע
7. יסד 8. כון 9. אַזְדָּא (A) 10. אמן (A) 11. קַיָּם (A)
12. *ἀληθῶς* 13. *ἀνένδεκτος μή* 14. *ἀνήκεστος*
15. *ἀσφαλής* 16. *ἀσφαλῶς* 17. *γινώσκω*
18. *διαλαμβάνω* 19. *πείθω* 20. *πεποίθησις* 21. *πιστός*
22. verus
Num32:23 and be sure your sin will find you out 6
Deu 12:23 Only be sure that you do not eat the blood; 5
Jos 2:12 swear to me by the LORD . . and give me a sure sign 4
1Sm 2:35 and I will build him a sure house, and he shall go 2
23:23 See . . and come back to me with sure information. 8
25:28 the LORD will certainly make my lord a sure house 2
2Sm 1:10 I was sure . . he could not live after he had fallen; 6
1Kg 11:38 I will be with you, and will build you a sure house 2
Ps 19: 7 the testimony of the LORD is sure 2
93: 5 Thy decrees are very sure; 2
119:86 All thy commandments are sure; 1
132:11 The LORD swore to David a sure oath 4
Prv 4:26 then all your ways will be sure. 8
11:18 one who sows righteousness gets a sure reward. 4
Isa 22:23 I will fasten him like a peg in a sure place 2
25 the peg that was fastened in a sure place 2
25: 1 plans formed of old, faithful and sure. 3
28:16 a precious cornerstone, of a sure foundation 7
33:16 his bread will be given him, his water will be sure. 2
55: 3 covenant, my steadfast, sure love for David. 2
Jer 38:15 will you not be sure to put me to death? †
Dan 2: 5 The word from me is sure: if you do not make known 9
8 because you see that the word from me is sure 9
45 dream is certain, and its interpretation sure. 10
4:26 your kingdom shall be sure for you 11
Hos 5: 9 among . . Israel I declare what is sure. 2
6: 3 his going forth is sure as the dawn; 8
Lke 17: 1 Temptations to sin are sure to come 13
Act 12:11 Now I am sure that the Lord has sent his angel 12
13:34 give you the holy and sure blessings of David.' 21
Rom 2:19 if you are sure that you are a guide to the blind 19
8:38 For I am sure that neither death, nor life 19
2Co 1:15 Because I was sure of this, I wanted to come to you 20
Eph 5: 5 Be sure of this 17
Php 1: 6 I am sure that he who began a good work in you 19
1Ti 1:15 The saying is sure and worthy of full acceptance 21
3: 1 The saying is sure 21
4: 9 The saying is sure 21
2Ti 1: 5 now, I am sure, dwells in you. 19
2:11 The saying is sure 21
Tit 1: 9 he must hold firm to the sure word as taught 21
3: 8 The saying is sure. 21
Heb 6:19 as a sure and steadfast anchor of the soul 15
13:18 we are sure that we have a clear conscience 19
1Jn 2: 3 by this we may be sure that we know him 17
5 By this we may be sure that we are in him 17
29 you may be sure that every one who does right 17
2Es 8:22 whose word is sure 22
Wis 7:23 sure, free from anxiety, all-powerful 15
18: 6 they might rejoice in sure knowledge 16
2Mc 9:27 For I am sure that he will follow my policy 19
3Mc 3:25 to suffer the sure and shameful death 14
26 we are sure that . . 18

sure *See also* defense, feel, make, stand.

sure to carry out 1. *ἐπιτελέω*
Jdt 2:13 be sure to carry them out 1

surely 1. אוּלָם 2. אַךְ 3. אָכֵן 4. אִם 5. הִנֵּה 6. כִּי
7. כִּי אָז 8. כִּי אִם 9. רַק 10. *ἀσφαλής* 11. *δέ* 12. *δήπου*
13. *εἰ μήν* 14. *μέν* 15. *μήν* 16. *ναί* 17. *ὅτι* 18. *πᾶς*
19. certe 20. nempe
Gen 9: 5 I will surely require a reckoning; 2
18:10 The LORD said, "I will surely return to you †
20: 7 do not restore her, know that you shall surely die †
28:16 Surely the LORD is in this place 3
29:14 Laban said . . "Surely you are my bone and flesh! 2
32 surely now my husband will love me. 6
31:42 surely now you would have sent me away 6
42:16 by the life of Pharaoh, surely you are spies. 6
44:28 and I said, Surely he has been torn to pieces; 2
Exd 2:14 Moses . . thought, "Surely the thing is known. 3
4:25 Surely you are a bridegroom of blood to me! 6
22:23 cry out to me, I will surely hear their cry; †
23:33 if you serve their gods, it will surely be a snare 6
Num14:35 surely this will I do to all this wicked †
22:17 for I will surely do you great honor †
33 surely just now I would have slain you 6
32:11 Surely none of the men who came up out of Egypt †
Deu 4: 6 Surely this great nation is a wise . . people 9
8:19 warn you this day that you shall surely perish †
12: 2 You shall surely destroy all the places †
13:15 you shall surely put . . to the sword †
23:21 LORD your God will surely require it of you †
31:18 surely hide my face in that day on account of all †
29 after my death you will surely act corruptly †
Jos 14: 9 Surely the land . . shall be an inheritance †
Jdg 4: 9 she said, "I will surely go with you; nevertheless †
11:10 witness between us; we will surely do as you say. †
13:22 his wife, "We shall surely die, for we have seen God. †
20:39 said, "Surely they are smitten down before us 2
1Sm 14:39 For as the LORD lives . . he shall surely die. †
44 God do so to me . . you shall surely die, Jonathan. †
15:32 Surely the bitterness of death is past. 3
16: 6 Surely the LORD's anointed is before him. 2
17:25 Surely he has come up to defy Israel; 6
20:26 he is not clean, surely he is not clean. 6
31 send and fetch him to me, for he shall surely die. †
22:16 You shall surely die, Ahim'elech, you and all †
22 I knew . . that he would surely tell Saul. †
23:10 thy servant has surely heard that Saul seeks †
24:20 now, behold, I know that you shall surely be king †
25:21 Surely in vain have I guarded all that 2
34 For as surely as the LORD the God of Israel lives 1
28: 9 Surely you know what Saul has done 5
30: 8 you shall surely overtake and shall . . rescue. †
8 you shall . . overtake and shall surely rescue. †
2Sm 2:27 surely the men would have given up the pursuit 7
14:19 As surely as you live, my lord the king, one cannot •
1Kg 11: 2 surely they will turn away your heart 3
11 Since . . I will surely tear the kingdom from you †
13:32 the saying . . shall surely come to pass. †
18:15 I will surely show myself to him today. 6
20:23 let us fight . . and surely we shall be stronger †
25 we will fight . . and surely we shall be stronger †
22:32 they said, "It is surely the king of Israel. 2
2Kg 1: 4 'You shall not come . . but you shall surely die.' †
6 you shall not come . . but shall surely die.' †
16 you shall not come . . but you shall surely die.' †
3:23 the kings have surely fought together †
5:11 I thought that he would surely come out to me †
9:26 As surely as I saw . . I will requite you †
18:30 The LORD will surely deliver us †
24: 3 Surely this came . . at the command of the LORD 2
Est 6:13 not prevail . . but will surely fall before him. †
Job 5: 2 Surely vexation kills the fool 6
8: 6 surely then he will rouse himself for you 6
11:15 Surely then you will lift up your face without 6
13:10 He will surely rebuke you †
16: 7 Surely now God has worn me out; 2
17: 2 Surely there are mockers about me †
18:21 Surely such are the dwellings of the ungodly 2
22: 2 Surely he who is wise is profitable to himself. 6
20 saying, 'Surely our adversaries are cut off †
28: 1 Surely there is a mine for silver 6
31:36 Surely I would carry it on my shoulder; †
33: 8 Surely, you have spoken in my hearing 2
35:13 Surely God does not hear an empty cry 2
38: 5 its measurements–surely you know! 6
Ps 23: 6 Surely goodness and mercy shall follow me 2
39: 5 Surely every man stands as a mere breath! Selah 2
6 Surely man goes about as a shadow! 2
6 Surely for nought are they in turmoil; 2
11 surely every man is a mere breath! Selah 2
58:11 Surely there is a reward for the righteous; 2
11 surely there is a God who judges on earth. 2
76:10 Surely the wrath of men shall praise thee; 6
85: 9 Surely his salvation is at hand 2
140:13 Surely the righteous . . give thanks to thy name; 2
Prv 21: 5 plans of the diligent lead surely to abundance 2
23:18 Surely there is a future, and your hope 8
30: 2 Surely I am too stupid to be a man. 6
4 and what is his son's name? Surely you know! 6
Ecc 4:16 Surely this also is vanity and a striving after 6
7: 7 Surely oppression makes the wise man foolish 6
20 Surely there is not a righteous man on earth 6
Isa 5: 9 Surely many houses shall be desolate †
7: 9 surely you shall not be established.' 6
8:20 Surely for this word which they speak †
22:14 Surely this iniquity will not be forgiven you 4
30:19 He will surely be gracious to you at the sound †
36:15 by saying, "The LORD will surely deliver us; †
40: 7 The grass withers . . surely the people is grass. 3
49: 4 yet surely my right is with the LORD 3
19 Surely your waste and your desolate places 6
19 surely now you will be too narrow 6
25 Surely, thus says the LORD: "Even the captives 6
53: 4 Surely he has borne our griefs and carried our 3
56: 3 LORD will surely separate me from his people"; †
63: 8 For he said, Surely they are my people 2
Jer 2:35 I am innocent; surely his anger has turned from me.' 2
3:20 Surely, as a faithless wife leaves her husband 3
4:10 Ah, Lord GOD, surely thou hast utterly deceived 3
22: 6 yet surely I will make you a desert †
23:39 therefore, behold, I will surely lift you up †
31:20 I will surely have mercy on him, says the LORD. †
32: 4 shall surely be given into the hand of the king †
34: 3 but shall surely be captured and delivered †
37: 9 The Chalde'ans will surely stay away from us †
38: 3 This city shall surely be given into the hand †
39:18 For I will surely save you †
44:25 We will surely perform our vows †
29 my words will surely stand against you for evil †
49:20 surely their fold shall be appalled †
50:34 He will surely plead their cause †
45 Surely the little ones of their flock †
45 surely their fold shall be appalled †
51:14 Surely I will fill you with men, as many as locusts 8
56 a God of recompense, he will surely requite. †
52: 3 Surely because of the anger of the LORD 6
Lam 3: 3 surely against me he turns his hand 2
Ezk 3: 6 Surely, if I sent you to such, they would listen †
18 If I say to the wicked, 'You shall surely die,' †
21 he shall surely live, because he took warning; †
5:11 surely, because you have defiled my sanctuary †
17:16 surely in the place where the king dwells †
19 surely my oath which he despised, and my covenant †
18: 9 he shall surely live, says the Lord GOD. †
13 he shall surely die; †
17 he shall not die . . he shall surely live. †
19 to observe all my statutes, he shall surely live. †
21 he shall surely live; he shall not die. †
28 he shall surely live, he shall not die. †
20:33 says the Lord GOD, surely with a mighty hand †
31:11 surely deal with it as its wickedness deserves. †
33: 8 to the wicked, O wicked man, you shall surely die †
13 I say to the righteous that he shall surely live †
14 though I say to the wicked, 'You shall surely die †
15 he shall surely live, he shall not die. †
16 what is lawful and right, he shall surely live. †
24 the land is surely given us to possess. •
27 As I live, surely those who are in the waste places †
Hos 12:11 they shall surely come to nought; 2
Ams 3: 7 Surely the Lord GOD does nothing, 6
5: 5 for Gilgal shall surely go into exile †
7:17 shall surely go into exile away from its land.' †
8: 7 Surely I will never forget any of their deeds. 4
Mic 2:12 I will surely gather all of you, O Jacob †
Hab 2: 3 it will surely come, it will not delay. †
Zep 3: 7 I said, 'Surely she will fear me 2
Mat 15: 4 who speaks evil of father . . let him surely die. †
Mrk 7:10 who speaks evil of father . . let him surely die †
Act 7:34 I have surely seen the ill-treatment of my people †
2Co 1:18 As surely as God is faithful 11
Heb 2:16 surely it is not with angels that he is concerned 12
6:14 saying, "Surely I will bless you and multiply you. 13
Rev 22:19 Surely I am coming soon." Amen. Come, Lord Jesus! 16
2Es 1:13 Surely it was I who brought you through the sea 20
16:63 Surely he knows your imaginations 19
Tob 14: 8 what the prophet Jonah said will surely happen. 18
Jdt 1:12 he would surely take revenge 15
10:19 Surely not a man of them had better be left alive 17
12:14 Surely whatever pleases him I will do at once 17
Sir 5: 3 the Lord will surely punish you. †
Bar 2:29 multitude will surely turn into a small number 15
1Mc 5:40 he will surely defeat us. †
3Mc 7: 6 the God of heaven surely defends the Jews 10
4Mc 12:14 Surely they . . fulfilled their service to God 14

surely *See also* avenge.

surety 1. ערב 2. *ἐγγυάω* 3. *ἐγγύη* 4. *ἔγγυος*
Gen 15:13 Know of a surety that your descendants will be †
43: 9 I will be surety for him; of my hand 1
Ps 119:122 Be surety for thy servant for good; 1
Prv 22:26 Be not one of those who . . become surety for debts. 1
Heb 7:22 makes Jesus the surety of a better covenant. 4
Sir 29:14 A good man will be surety for his neighbor 2
15 Do not forget all the kindness of your surety 4
16 will overthrow the prosperity of his surety 4
18 Being surety has ruined many men 3

surety *See also* give.

become surety 1. ערב 2. ערב עֲרֻבָּה
Gen 44:32 For your servant became surety for the lad 1
Prv 6: 1 if you have become surety for your neighbor 1
17:18 becomes surety in the presence of his neighbor. 2

suretyship 1. תקע 2. *ἐγγύη*
Prv 11:15 but he who hates suretyship is secure. 1
Sir 29:19 The sinner who has fallen into suretyship 2

surf 1. *βία τῶν κυμάτων*
Act 27:41 the stern was broken up by the surf. 1

surface 1. לוּחַ 2. פָּנִים 3. קִיר 4. *πρόσωπον* 5. *χρόα*
Lev 14:37 if it appears to be deeper than the surface 3
1Kg 7:36 on the surfaces of its stays . . he carved 1
Isa 24: 1 waste the earth . . and he will twist its surface 2
28:25 When he has leveled its surface 2
Jer 8: 2 be as dung on the surface of the ground. 2
16: 4 shall be as dung on the surface of the ground. 2
25:33 they shall be dung on the surface of the ground. 2
Ams 5: 8 and pours them out upon the surface of the earth 2
9: 6 and pours them out upon the surface of the earth– 2
8 I will destroy it from the surface of the ground; 2

Wis 13:14 and coloring its surface red 5
Sir 16:30 he covered its surface 4

surfeit 1. שָׂבָע 2. שָׂבְעָה
Ecc 5:12 the surfeit of the rich will not let him sleep. 1
Ezk 16:49 she and her daughters had pride, surfeit of food 2

surge 1. געשׁ 2. חמר 3. מוג
1Sm 14:16 the multitude was surging hither and thither. 3
Jer 46: 7 like the Nile, like rivers whose waters surge? 1
8 like the Nile, like rivers whose waters surge. 1
Hab 3:15 trample the sea . . the surging of mighty waters. 2

surliness 1. *σκορακισμός*
Sir 41:19 surliness in receiving and giving 1

surname 1. כנה 2. *ἐπικαλέω* 3. *ἐπιτίθημι ὄνομα*
Isa 44: 5 and surname himself by the name of Israel. 1
45: 4 I call you by your name, I surname you 1
Mrk 3:16 Simon whom he surnamed Peter; 3
17 whom he surnamed Bo-aner'ges 3
Act 1:23 Joseph called Barsab'bas, who was surnamed Justus 2
4:36 Joseph who was surnamed . . Barnabas 2
1Mc 2: 2 He had five sons, John surnamed Gaddi 2

surpass 1. יסף 2. עַל 3. עלה 4. רבה מִן 5. *ὑπέρ* 6. *ὑπεράγω* 7. *ὑπερβαίνω* 8. *ὑπερβάλλω* 9. *ὑπερέχω*
1Kg 4:30 Solomon's wisdom surpassed the wisdom of all 4
10: 7 your wisdom and prosperity surpass the report 1
2Ch 9: 6 you surpass the report which I heard. 1
Prv 31:29 but you surpass them all. 3
Ecc 1:16 wisdom, surpassing all who were over Jerusalem 2
2: 9 and surpassed all who were before me 1
Ezk 15: 2 how does the wood of the vine surpass any wood *
2Co 3:10 because of the splendor that surpasses it. 8
9:14 because of the surpassing grace of God in you. 8
Eph 3:19 the love of Christ which surpasses knowledge 8
Sir 18:17 Indeed, does not a word surpass a good gift? 5
25:11 The fear of the Lord surpasses everything 8
36:22 surpasses every human desire. 6
43:30 he will surpass even that 9
2Mc 4:13 because of the surpassing wickedness of Jason 8
3Mc 6:24 surpassing tyrants in cruelty 7

surpass in beauty 1. נעם
Ezk 32:19 Whom do you surpass in beauty? 1
surpassing *See* worth.

surplus 1. *περισσεύω*
Tob 4:16 Give all your surplus to charity 1

surprise 1. *καταλαμβάνω* 2. *ξενίζω*
1Th 5: 4 for that day to surprise you like a thief. 1
1Pe 4: 4 They are surprised that you do not now join them 2
12 Beloved, do not be surprised at the fiery ordeal 2
surprise *See also* take.

surrender 1. יצא 2. נפל 3. נתן יָד 4. סגר 5. *διαστολή* 6. *δίδωμι* 7. *ἐκδίδωμι* 8. *παραδίδωμι* 9. *προδοσία*
1Sm 23:11 Will the men of Kei'lah surrender me into his hand? 4
12 Will the men of Kei'lah surrender me and my men 4
12 And the LORD said, "They will surrender you. 4
20 our part . . to surrender him into the king's hand. 4
Jer 21: 9 he who goes out and surrenders to the Chalde'ans 2
38:17 If you will surrender to the princes of the king 1
18 if you do not surrender to the princes of the king 1
21 But if you refuse to surrender, this is the vision 1
50:15 she has surrendered; her bulwarks have fallen 3
Jdt 7:26 Now call them in and surrender the whole city 7
8: 9 to surrender the city to the Assyrians 8
11 promising to surrender the city to our enemies 7
33 promised to surrender the city to our enemies 8
AEs 14:11 do not surrender thy scepter to what has no being; 8
Wis 17:12 surrender of the helps that come from reason; 9
15 now were paralyzed by their souls' surrender 9
Sir 23: 6 do not surrender me to a shameless soul. 8
1Mc 8: 7 and surrender some of their best provinces 5
3Mc 6: 6 had voluntarily surrendered their lives to the flames 6

surround 1. כתר 2. מֵסַב 3. נקף 4. נקף סָבִיב 5. סבב 6. סָבִיב 7. *ἔχω περίκειμαι* 8. *κυκλεύω* 9. *κύκλος* 10. *κυκλόω* 11. *μέσον λαμβάνω* 12. *περί* 13. *περιβάλλω* 14. *περιέχω* 15. *περικατάληπτος* 16. *περικυκλόω* 17. *συνέχω* 18. circueo
Gen 19: 4 to the last man, surrounded the house; 5
Jos 7: 9 will hear of it, and will surround us, and cut off 5
Jdg 16: 2 they surrounded the place and lay in wait for him 5
2Sm 18:15 ten young men . . surrounded Ab'salom and struck 5
1Kg 5: 3 warfare with which his enemies surrounded him 5
2Kg 3:25 and the slingers surrounded and conquered it. 5
6:14 and they came by night, and surrounded the city. 3
8:21 he . . smote the E'domites who had surrounded him; 5
11: 8 shall surround the king 4
1Ch 6:55 Hebron . . and its surrounding pasture lands 6
28:12 the plan of all . . all the surrounding chambers 6
2Ch 14: 7 surround them with walls and towers 5
21: 9 E'domites who had surrounded him and his chariot 5
23: 7 The Levites shall surround the king 3
Job 16:13 his archers surround me. 5
40:22 the willows of the brook surround him. 5
Ps 17: 9 despoil me, my deadly enemies who surround me. 3
11 They track me down; now they surround me; 5
22:12 strong bulls of Bashan surround me; 1
32:10 love surrounds him who trusts in the LORD. 5
49: 5 the iniquity of my persecutors surrounds me 5
88:17 They surround me like a flood all day long; 5
118:10 All nations surrounded me; in the name of the LORD 5
11 They surrounded me, surrounded me on every side; 5
11 They surrounded me, surrounded me on every side; 5
12 surrounded me like bees, they blazed like a fire 5
140: 9 Those who surround me lift up their head 2
142: 7 The righteous will surround me; for thou wilt deal 1
Ams 3:11 An adversary shall surround the land 6
Hab 1: 4 the wicked surround the righteous 1
Lke 8:45 the multitudes surround you and press upon you! 17
19:43 surround you, and hem you in on every side 16
21:20 when you see Jerusalem surrounded by armies 10
Heb 12: 1 surrounded by so great a cloud of witnesses 7
Jde 1: 7 Sodom and Gomor'rah and the surrounding cities 12
Rev 20: 9 and surrounded the camp of the saints 8
2Es 15:44 They shall come to her and surround her 18
Jdt 1: 9 who were in Samaria and its surrounding towns *
2:26 He surrounded all the Midianites 10
4:12 They even surrounded the altar with sackcloth 13
7:19 because all their enemies had surrounded them 10
Wis 19:17 surrounded by yawning darkness 13
Sir 23:18 Darkness surrounds me, and the walls hide me 9
50:12 they surrounded him like the trunks of palm trees 10
51: 7 They surrounded me on every side 14
Bar 2: 4 desolation among all the surrounding peoples 9
1Mc 1:31 and tore down its houses and its surrounding walls. 9
54 built altars in the surrounding cities of Judah 9
6: 7 had surrounded the sanctuary with high walls 10
10:80 they surrounded his army 10
84 burned Azotus and the surrounding towns 9
13:43 surrounded it with troops 10
15:14 He surrounded the city 10
2Mc 10:30 Surrounding Maccabeus 11
14:41 Being surrounded, Razis fell upon his own sword 15
4Mc 16: 3 The lions surrounding Daniel were not so savage 12
surrounding *See* country, region.

surrounding part 1. *ὅριον*
1Mc 7:24 Judas went out into all the surrounding parts of Judea 1

survival 1. *ζωή*
Sir 16: 3 Do not trust in their survival 1

survive 1. יתר 2. עמד 3. פְּלֵיטָה 4. שָׂרִיד 5. שׁאר 6. שְׁאָר 7. שְׁאֵרִית 8. *ἐπιβιόω* 9. *καταλείπω* 10. *μένω* 11. *περιλείπω* 12. relinquo 13. subremaneo 14. supero
Exd 21:21 if the slave survives a day or two, 2
Jos 8:22 there was left none that survived or escaped. 4
1Sm 11:11 and those who survived were scattered 5
2Kg 19:30 the surviving remnant . . shall again take root 5
Neh 1: 2 I asked them concerning the Jews that survived 3
Job 27:15 Those who survive him the pestilence buries 4
Isa 16:14 those who survive will be very few and feeble. 6
37:31 the surviving remnant of the house of Judah 5
Jer 21: 7 and the people in this city who survive 5
31: 2 The people who survived the sword found grace 4
44:14 or survive or return to the land of Judah 4
Lam 2:22 and on the day of . . none escaped or survived; 4
Ezk 5:10 and any of you who survive I will scatter 7
Zec 14:16 Then every one that survives of all the nations 1
1Co 3:14 built on the foundation survives 10
2Es 9: 8 survive the dangers that have been predicted 12
15:45 those who survive shall serve those 13
16:22 who survive the famine shall die by the sword. 14
Sir 23:27 Those who survive her 9
4Mc 6:20 if we should survive for a little while 8
12: 6 to influence her to persuade the surviving son 11

survivor 1. אַחֲרִית 2. יֶתֶר 3. פָּלִיט 4. פְּלִיט 5. פְּלֵיטָה 6. שָׂרִיד 7. שׁאר 8. *ἐπίλοιπος* 9. *λοιπός*
Gen 45: 7 sent me . . to keep alive for you many survivors. 5
Num21:35 until there was not one survivor left to him; 6
24:19 By Jacob . . survivors of cities be destroyed! 6
Deu 3: 3 smote him until no survivor was left to him. 6
Jdg 21:17 an inheritance for the survivors of Benjamin 5
Ezr 1: 4 let each survivor, in whatever place he sojourns 7
Neh 1: 3 survivors there in the province who escaped 7
Job 18:19 no survivor where he used to live. 6
Isa 1: 9 If the LORD . . had not left us a few survivors 6
4: 2 the pride and glory of the survivors of Israel. 5
10:20 of Israel and the survivors of the house of Jacob 5
37:32 and out of Mount Zion a band of survivors. 5
45:20 draw near together, you survivors of the nations! 4
66:19 from them I will send survivors to the nations 3
Jer 42:17 they shall have no remnant or survivor 4
Ezk 7:16 if any survivors escape 4
14:22 Yet, if there should be left in it any survivors 5
17:21 the survivors shall be scattered to every wind; 7
23:25 your survivors shall fall by the sword. 1
25 your survivors shall be devoured by fire. 1
Jol 2:32 the survivors shall be those whom the LORD calls. 6
Obd 1:14 you should not have delivered up his survivors 6
18 there shall be no survivor to the house of Esau; 6
Zep 2: 9 the survivors of my nation shall possess them. 2
1Es 1:56 The survivors he led away to Babylon 8
1Mc 2:44 the survivors fled to the Gentiles for safety. 9
survivors *See* band.

suspect 1. *λογίζομαι* 2. *ὑπονοέω* 3. *ὕποπτον ἔχω* 4. *ὑφοράω*
Act 27:27 sailors suspected that they were nearing land. 2
2Co 10: 2 who suspect us of acting in worldly fashion. 1
Sir 23:21 where he least suspects it, he will be seized. 2
2Mc 12: 4 because they . . suspected nothing 3
3Mc 3:23 they secretly suspect 4

suspend 1. suspendo
2Es 16:58 has suspended the earth over the water; 1

suspense 1. *προσδοκάω* 2. *προσδοκία*
Act 27:33 you have continued in suspense and without food 1
3Mc 5:49 the end of their most miserable suspense 2
suspense *See also* keep.

suspicion 1. *ὑπόνοια* 2. *ὑποψία*
1Ti 6: 4 dissension, slander, base suspicions 1
2Mc 4:34 in spite of his suspicion 2

suspicious 1. *ὑφοράω*
2Mc 7:24 he was suspicious of her reproachful tone. 1
suspiciously *See* look.

sustain 1. כול 2. סמך 3. סעד 4. עות 5. קום 6. *βεβαιόω* 7. *ἵστημι* 8. sustineo
Gen 27:37 and with grain and wine I have sustained him. 2
Deu 19:15 two . . three witnesses, shall a charge be sustained. 5
Neh 9:21 40 years . . sustain them in the wilderness 1
Ps 3: 5 I wake again, for the LORD sustains me. 2
41: 3 The LORD sustains him on his sickbed; 3
55:22 your burden on the LORD, and he will sustain you; 1
Sng 2: 5 Sustain me with raisins, refresh me with apples; 2
Isa 50: 4 know how to sustain with a word him that is weary. 4
Mal 2:15 God made and sustained for us the spirit of life? *
1Co 1: 8 who will sustain you to the end 6
2Co 13: 1 Any charge must be sustained 7
2Es 5:45 and the creation will sustain them 8

sustenance 1. מַאֲכָל 2. מִחְיָה 3. *ὑπόστασις*
Jdg 6: 4 they would . . leave no sustenance in Israel 2
Prv 6: 8 gathers her sustenance in harvest. 1
Wis 16:21 For thy sustenance manifested thy sweetness 3
swaddling *See* band, cloth.

swallow 1. בלע 2. בֶּלַע 3. גמא 4. *καταπίνω*
Exd 15:12 thy right hand, the earth swallowed them. 1
Job 7:19 nor let me alone till I swallow my spittle? 1
39:24 With fierceness and rage he swallows the ground; 3
Prv 1:12 like Sheol let us swallow them alive and whole 1
Jer 51:34 he has swallowed me like a monster; 1
44 and take out of his mouth what he has swallowed. 2
Mat 23:24 straining out a gnat and swallowing a camel! 4
Rev 12:16 earth opened its mouth and swallowed the river 4
Tob 6: 2 A fish . . would have swallowed the young man; 4

swallow (2) 1. דְּרוֹר 2. סוּס 3. *χελιδών*
Ps 84: 3 swallow a nest for herself 1
Prv 26: 2 in its flitting, like a swallow in its flying 1
Isa 38:14 Like a swallow or a crane I clamor 2
Jer 8: 7 swallow, and crane keep the time of their coming; 2
LJr 1:22 Bats, swallows, and birds light on their bodies 3

swallow down 1. בלע
Job 20:15 He swallows down riches and vomits them up again; 1
18 fruit of his toil, and will not swallow it down; 1

swallow up 1. בלע 2. *καταπίνω*
Gen 41: 7 the thin ears swallowed up the seven plump 1
24 the thin ears swallowed up the seven good ears. 1
Exd 7:12 But Aaron's rod swallowed up their rods. 1
Num16:30 ground opens its mouth, and swallows them up 1
32 earth opened its mouth and swallowed them up 1
34 for they said, "Lest the earth swallow us up! 1
26:10 earth . . swallowed them up together with Korah 1
Deu 11: 6 the earth opened its mouth and swallowed them up 1
2Sm 17:16 lest the king and all . . with him be swallowed up. 1
20:19 why will you swallow up the heritage of the LORD? 1
20 far be it, that I should swallow up or destroy! 1
Job 37:20 Did a man ever wish that he would be swallowed up? 1
Ps 21: 9 The LORD will swallow them up in his wrath; 1
35:25 Let them not say, "We have swallowed him up. 1
69:15 the flood sweep over me, or the deep swallow me up 1
106:17 earth opened and swallowed up Dathan 1
124: 3 then they would have swallowed us up alive 1
Isa 9:16 and those who are led by them are swallowed up. 1
25: 8 He will swallow up death for ever 1
49:19 and those who swallowed you up will be far away. 1

Hos 8: 8 Israel is swallowed up; 1
Jon 1:17 LORD appointed a great fish to swallow up Jonah; 1
Hab 1:13 the wicked swallows up the man more righteous 1
1Co 15:54 Death is swallowed up in victory. 2
2Co 5: 4 what is mortal may be swallowed up by life. 2

swamp 1. καλύπτω
Mat 8:24 so that the boat was being swamped by the waves; 1

swamp (2) 1. בִּצָּה
Isa 35: 7 the haunt of jackals shall become a swamp •
Ezk 47:11 its swamps and marshes will not become fresh; 1

swan 1. κύκνειος
4Mc 15:21 the melodies of sirens nor the songs of swans 1

swarm 1. עֵדָה 2. שׁרץ 3. שֶׁרֶץ 4. ἀναζέω
Gen 1:20 waters bring forth swarms of living creatures 3
21 creature that moves, with which the waters swarm 2
7:21 swarming creatures that swarm upon the earth 2
Exd 8: 3 the Nile shall swarm with frogs which shall come 2
10:14 such a dense swarm of locusts as had never been •
Lev 11:29 the swarming things that swarm upon the earth 2
31 These are unclean to you among all that swarm 3
41 Every swarming thing that swarms upon the earth 2
42 the swarming things that swarm upon the earth 2
43 abominable with any swarming thing that swarms 2
46 every living creature that swarms upon the earth 2
Jdg 14: 8 there was a swarm of bees in the body of the lion 1
Ps 105:30 Their land swarmed with frogs 2
Ezk 47: 9 every living creature which swarms will live 2
Jdt 2:20 a mixed crowd like a swarm of locusts •
2Mc 9: 9 so the ungodly man's body swarmed with worms 4

swarm of flies 1. עָרֹב
Exd 8:21 behold, I will send swarms of flies on you 1
21 houses . . shall be filled with swarms of flies 1
22 so that no swarms of flies shall be there; 1
24 there came great swarms of flies into the house 1
29 I will pray . . that the swarms of flies may depart 1
31 and removed the swarms of flies from Pharaoh 1
Ps 78:45 He sent among them swarms of flies 1
105:31 He spoke, and there came swarms of flies 1
swarming *See* creature, locust.

swarming thing 1. שֶׁרֶץ
Lev 5: 2 or a carcass of unclean swarming things 1
11:29 the swarming things that swarm upon the earth 1
41 Every swarming thing that swarms upon the earth 1
42 the swarming things that swarm upon the earth 1
43 abominable with any swarming thing that swarms 1
44 not defile yourselves with any swarming thing 1

swarthy 1. שְׁחַרְחֹר
Sng 1: 6 Do not gaze at me because I am swarthy 1

swathe 1. חבשׁ
Ezk 16:10 I swathed you in fine linen 1

swathe with bands 1. חתל
Ezk 16: 4 nor rubbed with salt, nor swathed with bands. 1

sway 1. נוד 2. נוע 3. נטה 4. ἄγω 5. μετακινέω 6. potentatus
Jdg 9: 9 leave my fatness . . and go to sway over the trees?' 2
11 and my good fruit, and go to sway over the trees?' 2
13 cheers gods and men, and go to sway over the trees?' 2
2Sm 19:14 he swayed the heart of all the men of Judah as one 3
Isa 24:20 The earth staggers . . it sways like a hut; 1
2Ti 3: 6 swayed by various impulses 4
2Es 11:40 have held sway over the world with much terror 6
4Mc 14:20 did not sway the mother of the young men 5
sway *See also* hold.

swear 1. אלה 2. אָלָה 3. אמר 4. בטא 5. נשׂא יָד 6. רום 7. שׁבע 8. ἵστημι 9. ὄμνυμι 10. ὀμνύω 11. ὁρίζω 12. ὅρκος
Gen 14:22 I have sworn to the LORD God Most High 6
21:23 now therefore swear to me here by God 7
24 And Abraham said, "I will swear. 7
22:16 By myself I have sworn, says the LORD 7
24: 7 The LORD . . who spoke to me and swore to me 7
9 thigh of Abraham his master, and swore to him 7
25:33 Jacob said, "Swear to me first. 7
33 he swore to him, and sold his birthright 7
26: 3 fulfil the oath which I swore to Abraham 7
31:53 Jacob swore by the Fear of his father Isaac 7
47:31 he said, "Swear to me"; and he swore to him. 7
31 he said, "Swear to me"; and he swore to him. 7
50:24 to the land which he swore to Abraham, 7
Exd 6: 8 the land which I swore to give to Abraham, to Isaac 5
13: 5 which he swore to your fathers to give you 7
11 brings you . . as he swore to you and your fathers 7
19 Joseph had solemnly sworn the people of Israel 7
32:13 Israel, thy servants, to whom thou didst swear 7
33: 1 go up . . to the land of which I swore to Abraham 7
Lev 5: 4 any sort of rash oath that men swear 4
6: 3 lied about it, swearing falsely- 7
5 or anything about which he has sworn falsely 7
19:12 you shall not swear by my name falsely 7
Num11:12 to the land which thou didst swear to give 7
14:16 into the land which he swore to give to them 7
23 land which I swore to give to their fathers; 7
30 land where I swore that I would make you dwell 5
30: 2 When a man . . swears an oath to bind himself 7
32:10 LORD'S anger was kindled on that day, and he swore 7
11 shall see the land which I swore to give 7
Deu 1: 8 land which the LORD swore to your fathers 7
34 heard your words, and was angered, and he swore 7
35 good land which I swore to give to your fathers 7
2:14 perished from the camp, as the LORD had sworn 7
4:21 LORD . . swore that I should not cross the Jordan 7
31 covenant with your fathers which he swore 7
6:10 into the land which he swore to your fathers 7
13 you shall serve him, and swear by his name. 7
18 land which the LORD swore to give to your fathers 7
23 land which he swore to give to our fathers. 7
7: 8 keeping the oath which he swore to your fathers 7
12 which he swore to your fathers to keep; 7
13 in the land which he swore to your fathers to give 7
8: 1 land . . the LORD swore to give to your fathers. 7
18 his covenant which he swore to your fathers 7
9: 5 word which the LORD swore to your fathers 7
10:11 land, which I swore to their fathers to give them.' 7
20 fear the LORD . . by his name you shall swear. 7
11: 9 LORD swore to your fathers to give to them 7
21 land which the LORD swore to your fathers to give 7
13:17 multiply you, as he swore to your fathers 7
19: 8 enlarges . . as he has sworn to your fathers 7
26: 3 land . . LORD swore to our fathers to give us.' 7
15 as thou didst swear to our fathers, a land flowing 7
28: 9 LORD will establish you . . as he has sworn to you 7
11 land which the LORD swore to your fathers to give 7
29:12 enter . . the sworn covenant of the LORD your God 2
13 as he swore to your fathers, to Abraham, to Isaac 7
14 with you only that I make this sworn covenant 2
30:20 land which the LORD swore to your fathers 7
31: 7 land . . LORD has sworn to their fathers to give 7
20 land . . which I swore to give to their fathers 7
21 brought them into the land that I swore to give. 7
23 Israel into the land which I swore to give them 7
32:40 I lift up my hand . . and swear, As I live for ever 3
34: 4 land . . I swore to Abraham, to Isaac, and to Jacob 7
Jos 1: 6 land which I swore to their fathers to give them. 7
2:12 swear to me by the LORD that as I have dealt kindly 7
5: 6 LORD swore that he would not let them see the land 7
6 land which the LORD had sworn to their fathers 7
6:22 bring out from it the woman . . as you swore to her. 7
9:15 the leaders of the congregation swore to them. 7
18 the leaders . . had sworn to them by the LORD 7
19 We have sworn to them by the LORD, the God 7
20 because of the oath which we swore to them. 7
14: 9 And Moses swore on that day, saying 7
21:43 the land which he swore to give to their fathers; 7
44 LORD gave . . just as he has sworn to their fathers; 7
23: 7 their gods, or swear by them, or serve them, or bow ‡
Jdg 2: 1 the land which I swore to give to your fathers. 7
15 had warned, and as the LORD had sworn to them; 7
15: 7 If this is what you do, I swear I will be avenged †
12 Swear to me that you will not fall upon me 7
21: 1 the men of Israel had sworn at Mizpah, "No one of us 7
7 we have sworn by the LORD that we will not give 7
18 the people of Israel had sworn, "Cursed be he who 7
1Sm 3:14 I swear to the house of Eli that the iniquity 7
19: 6 Saul swore, "As the LORD lives, he shall not be put 7
20:42 we have sworn both of us in the name of the LORD 7
24:21 Swear to me therefore by the LORD that you will 7
22 And David swore this to Saul. Then Saul went home; 7
28:10 But Saul swore to her by the LORD, "As the LORD 7
30:15 he said, "Swear to me by God, that you will not kill me 7
2Sm 3: 9 accomplish for David what the LORD has sworn 7
35 but David swore, saying, "God do so to me and more 7
19: 7 I swear by the LORD, if you do not go, not a man will 7
21: 2 the people of Israel had sworn to spare them 7
1Kg 1:13 Did you not . . swear to your maidservant, saying 7
17 My lord, you swore to your maidservant by the LORD 7
29 the king swore, saying, "As the LORD lives, who has 7
30 I swore to you by the LORD, the God of Israel, saying 7
51 Let King Solomon swear to me first that he will 7
2: 8 when he came . . I swore to him by the LORD, saying 7
23 King Solomon swore by the LORD, saying, "God do 7
2Kg 25:24 Gedali'ah swore to them and their men, saying 7
2Ch 15:15 for they had sworn with all their heart 7
Neh 9:15 possess the land which thou hadst sworn to give 5
Ps 15: 4 who swears to his own hurt and does not change; 7
24: 4 to what is false, and does not swear deceitfully. 7
63:11 all who swear by him shall glory; 7
89: 3 I have sworn to David my servant 7
35 Once for all I have sworn by my holiness; 7
49 by thy faithfulness thou didst swear to David? 7
95:11 swore in my anger that they . . not enter my rest. 7
106:26 Therefore he raised his hand and swore to them •
110: 4 The LORD has sworn and will not change his mind 7
119:106 I have sworn an oath and confirmed it 7
132: 2 swore to the LORD and vowed to the Mighty One 7
11 The LORD swore to David a sure oath 7
Ecc 9: 2 and he who swears is as he who shuns an oath. 7
Isa 5: 9 The LORD of hosts has sworn in my hearing •
14:24 The LORD of hosts has sworn: "As I have planned 7
45:23 By myself I have sworn, from my mouth 7
23 every knee shall bow, every tongue shall swear. 7
48: 1 who swear by the name of the LORD, and confess 7
54: 9 I swore that the waters of Noah should no more go 7
9 I have sworn that I will not be angry with you 7
62: 8 The LORD has sworn by his right hand 7
65:16 in the land shall swear by the God of truth; 7
Jer 4: 2 if you swear, 'As the LORD lives,' in truth, in justice 7
5: 2 As the LORD lives," yet they swear falsely. 7
7 and have sworn by those who are no gods. 7
7: 9 steal, murder, commit adultery, swear falsely 7
11: 5 the oath which I swore to your fathers 7
12:16 my people, to swear by my name, 'As the LORD lives 7
16 even as they taught my people to swear by Ba'al 7
22: 5 if you will not heed these words, I swear by myself 7
32:22 thou didst swear to their fathers to give them 7
38:16 Then King Zedeki'ah swore secretly to Jeremiah 7
40: 9 Gedali'ah the son of Ahi'kam, son of Shaphan, swore 7
44:26 I have sworn by my great name, says the LORD 7
49:13 For I have sworn by myself, says the LORD 7
51:14 The LORD of hosts has sworn by himself 7
Ezk 20: 5 I swore to the seed of the house of Jacob 5
5 I swore to them, saying, I am the LORD your God. 5
6 On that day I swore to them that I would bring them 5
15 Moreover I swore to them in the wilderness 5
23 Moreover I swore to them in the wilderness 5
28 into the land which I swore to give them 5
42 country which I swore to give to your fathers. 5
21:23 false divination; they have sworn solemn oaths; †
36: 7 I swear that the nations that are round about you 5
44:12 I have sworn concerning them, says the Lord GOD 5
47:14 I swore to give it to your fathers 5
Dan 12: 7 heard him swear by him who lives for ever 7
Hos 4: 2 there is swearing, lying, killing, stealing 1
15 and swear not, "As the LORD lives. 7
Ams 4: 2 The Lord GOD has sworn by his holiness 7
6: 8 The Lord GOD has sworn by himself (says the LORD 7
8: 7 The LORD has sworn by the pride of Jacob 7
14 Those who swear by Ash'imah of Sama'ria, and say 7
Mic 7:20 hast sworn to our fathers from the days of old 7
Zep 1: 5 those who bow down and swear to the LORD 7
5 those who bow . . and yet swear by Milcom; 7
Zec 5: 3 every one who swears falsely shall be cut off 7
4 the house of him who swears falsely by my name; 7
Mal 3: 5 against those who swear falsely 7
Mat 5:33 shall perform to the Lord what you have sworn.' 12
34 I say to you, Do not swear at all, either by heaven 10
36 do not swear by your head, for you cannot make one 10
23:16 If any one swears by the temple, it is nothing 10
16 if any one swears by the gold of the temple 10
18 If any one swears by the altar, it is nothing 10
18 if any one swears by the gift that is on the altar 10
20 So he who swears by the altar 10
20 swears by it and by everything on it; 10
21 he who swears by the temple 10
21 swears by it and by him who dwells in it; 10
22 he who swears by heaven 10
22 swears by the throne of God 10
26:74 he began to invoke a curse on himself and to swear 10
Mrk 14:71 he began to invoke a curse on himself and to swear 10
Lke 1:73 the oath which he swore to our father Abraham 9
Act 2:30 knowing that God had sworn with an oath to him 9
Heb 3:11 As I swore in my wrath 9
18 swear that they should never enter his rest 9
4: 3 as he has said, "As I swore in my wrath . . 9
6:13 since he had no one greater by whom to swear 10
13 he swore by himself 9
16 Men indeed swear by a greater than themselves 10
7:21 The Lord has sworn and will not change his mind 9
Jas 5:12 above all, my brethren, do not swear 10
Rev 10: 6 swore by him who lives for ever and ever 9
Tob 9: 3 For Raguel has sworn that I should not leave; 9
10: 7 which Raguel had sworn that he should spend 9
Jdt 1:12 swore by his throne and kingdom 9
8:11 you have even sworn and pronounced this oath 8
Wis 14:30 because in deceit they swore unrighteously 9
31 not the power of the things by which men swear 9
Sir 23:10 the man who always swears and utters the Name 10
11 if he has sworn needlessly 9
Bar 2:34 land which I swore to give to their fathers 9
1Mc 6:62 he broke the oath he had sworn 9
7:18 violated . . the oath which they swore. 9
9:71 he swore to Jonathan 9
2Mc 4:34 and . . offered him sworn pledges 12
13:23 yielded and swore to observe all their rights 9
14:33 and swore this oath 9
3Mc 5:42 he firmly swore an irrevocable oath 11

swear allegiance 1. שׁבע
Isa 19:18 swear allegiance to the LORD of hosts. 1

swear an oath 1. אלה 2. שׁבע 3. ὄμνυμι
Gen 21:31 because there both of them swore an oath. 2
1Kg 8:31 comes and swears his oath before thine altar 1
2Ch 6:22 made to take an oath, and comes and swears his oath 1
Wis 14:29 they swear wicked oaths 3

1Mc 7:15 he spoke peaceable words . . and swore this oath 3
35 in anger he swore this oath 3

swear falsely 1. ἐπιορκέω
Mat 5:33 to the men of old, 'You shall not swear falsely 1

make swear 1. שׁבע 2. ὁρκίζω
Gen 24: 3 I will make you swear by the LORD, the God 1
37 My master made me swear, saying 1
50: 5 My father made me swear, saying, 'I am about to die 1
6 bury your father, as he made you swear. 1
Jos 2:17 this oath of yours which you have made us swear. 1
20 to your oath which you have made us swear. 1
1Sm 20:17 Jonathan made David swear . . by his love for him; 1
1Kg 2:42 Did I not make you swear by the LORD, and solemnly 1
2Ch 36:13 Nebuchadnez'zar, who had made him swear by God; 1
1Es 1:48 though King Nebuchadnezzar had made him swear 2

swear many oaths 1. πολύορκος
Sir 23:11 A man who swears many oaths 1
swearing *See* given.

sweat 1. זֵעָה 2. יֶזַע 3. ἱδρόω 4. ἱδρώς
Gen 3:19 In the sweat of your face you shall eat bread 1
Ezk 44:18 not gird . . with anything that causes sweat. 2
2Mc 2:26 but calls for sweat and loss of sleep 4
4Mc 3: 8 he came, sweating and quite exhausted 3
7: 8 their own blood and noble sweat 4
sweat *See also* bathe.

sweep 1. חלף 2. עבר 3. קאקא 4. שׂער 5. σαρόω 6. φέρω
Job 27:21 he is gone; it sweeps him out of his place. 4
Ps 88:16 Thy wrath has swept over me; 2
Isa 8: 8 it will sweep on into Judah, it will overflow 1
14:23 I will sweep it with the broom of destruction 3
21: 1 As whirlwinds in the Negeb sweep on 1
Hab 1:11 they sweep by like the wind and go on, guilty men 1
3:10 the raging waters swept on; 2
Mat 12:44 he finds it empty, swept, and put in order. 5
Lke 11:25 when he comes he finds it swept and put in order. 5
15: 8 does not light a lamp and sweep the house and seek 5
2Mc 12:22 and were swept on, this way and that 6

sweep away 1. אסף 2. בער אַחֲרֵי 3. גרף 4. גרר 5. זרם 6. יעה 7. מחה 8. סוף 9. סור 10. ספה 11. שׂער 12. שׁטף 13. αἴρω 14. συσσύρω
Num16:26 lest you be swept away with all their sins. 10
Deu 29:19 lead to the sweeping away of moist and dry alike. 10
Jdg 5:21 The torrent Kishon swept them away 3
1Sm 12:25 if you still do wickedly, you shall be swept away 10
1Kg 16: 3 I will utterly sweep away Ba'asha and his house 2
Job 15:30 his blossom will be swept away by the wind. 9
Ps 26: 9 Sweep me not away with sinners 1
58: 9 whether green or ablaze, may he sweep them away! 11
73:19 swept away utterly by terrors! 10
90: 5 Thou dost sweep men away; 5
124: 4 then the flood would have swept us away 12
Prv 13:23 but it is swept away through injustice. 10
21: 7 The violence of the wicked will sweep them away 4
Isa 7:20 razor . . it will sweep away the beard also. 10
28:17 hail will sweep away the refuge of lies 6
44:22 I have swept away your transgressions 7
Jer 12: 4 the beasts and the birds are swept away 10
Dan 11:22 Armies shall be utterly swept away before him 12
26 army . . swept away, and many shall fall down slain 12
Zep 1: 2 I will utterly sweep away everything 8
3 I will sweep away man and beast; 8
3 I will sweep away the birds of the air 8
Mat 24:39 the flood came and swept them all away 13
2Mc 5:16 swept away with profane hands the votive offerings 14

sweep away with the flood 1. ποταμοφόρητον ποιέω
Rev 12:15 to sweep her away with the flood 1

sweep down 1. σύρω
Rev 12: 4 His tail swept down a third of the stars of heaven 1

sweep over 1. שׁטף
Ps 69: 2 into deep waters, and the flood sweeps over me. 1
15 Let not the flood sweep over me 1

utterly sweep away 1. בער
1Kg 16: 3 I will utterly sweep away Ba'asha and his house 1
21:21 I will bring evil . . I will utterly sweep you away 1

sweet 1. טוֹב 2. יפה 3. מלץ 4. מָתוֹק 5. מתק 6. נָעִים 7. סַם 8. ערב 9. עָרֵב 10. γλυκαίνω 11. γλύκασμα 12. γλυκύς 13. ἡδύς 14. dulcis
Lev 16:12 and two handfuls of sweet incense beaten small 7
Jdg 14:18 What is sweeter than honey? What is stronger 4
2Sm 23: 1 oracle of David . . the sweet psalmist of Israel 6
Job 20:12 Though wickedness is sweet in his mouth 5
21:33 The clods of the valley are sweet to him; 4
Ps 19:10 sweeter also than honey and drippings 4
81: 2 sound the timbrel, the sweet lyre with the harp. 6
119:103 How sweet are thy words to my taste 3
103 words to my taste, sweeter than honey to my mouth! *
Prv 3:24 when you lie down, your sleep will be sweet. 8
9:17 Stolen water is sweet 4
13:19 A desire fulfilled is sweet to the soul; 8
20:17 Bread gained by deceit is sweet to a man 9
24:13 drippings . . are sweet to your taste. 4
27: 7 one who is hungry everything bitter is sweet. 4
Ecc 5:12 Sweet is the sleep of a laborer 4
11: 7 Light is sweet, and it is pleasant . . to behold 4
Sng 2: 3 and his fruit was sweet to my taste. 4
14 your voice is sweet, and your face is comely. 9
4:10 How sweet is your love, my sister, my bride! 2
Isa 5:20 who put bitter for sweet and sweet for bitter! 4
20 who put bitter for sweet and sweet for bitter! 4
Jer 6:20 or sweet cane from a distant land? 1
Ezk 3: 3 I ate it; and it was in my mouth as sweet as honey. 4
Rev 10: 9 bitter . . but sweet as honey in your mouth. 12
10 it was sweet as honey in my mouth 12
1Es 9:51 go your way, eat the fat and drink the sweet 11
2Es 1:23 and made the stream sweet. 14
5: 9 salt waters shall be found in the sweet 14
Sir 23:17 To a fornicator all bread tastes sweet 13
27 nothing sweeter than to heed the commandments 12
24:20 For the remembrance of me is sweeter than honey 12
20 and my inheritance sweeter than the honeycomb. *
40:18 Life is sweet for the self-reliant and the worker 10
30 In the mouth of the shameless begging is sweet 10
49: 1 it is sweet as honey to every mouth 10
50:18 in sweet and full-toned melody. 10
2Mc 15:39 wine mixed with water is sweet and delicious 13
4Mc 9:29 How sweet is any kind of death 13
sweet *See also* cane, hold, make, spice, wine.

become sweet 1. מתק
Exd 15:25 and the water became sweet. There the LORD made 1

most sweet 1. מַמְתַקִּים
Sng 5:16 His speech is most sweet, and he is . . desirable. 1

something sweet 1. מָתוֹק
Jdg 14:14 Out of the strong came something sweet. 1

sweet thing 1. γλύκασμα
Sir 11: 3 her product is the best of sweet things. 1

sweet-smelling 1. בֹּשֶׂם
Exd 30:23 of sweet-smelling cinnamon half as much 1
sweet-smelling *See also* sacrifice.
sweetly *See* speak.

sweetness 1. מָתוֹק 2. γλυκαίνω 3. γλυκύτης
Jdg 9:11 Shall I leave my sweetness and my good fruit 1
Prv 16:24 sweetness to the soul and health to the body. 1
Wis 16:21 For thy sustenance manifested thy sweetness 3
Sir 27:23 In your presence his mouth is all sweetness 2

swell 1. בצק 2. צבה 3. שְׂאֵת
Lev 13: 2 When a man has . . a swelling or an eruption 3
10 if there is a white swelling in the skin 3
10 if . . there is quick raw flesh in the swelling 3
19 there comes a white swelling or a reddish-white 3
28 if the spot . . is dim, it is a swelling 3
43 if the diseased swelling is reddish-white 3
14:56 for a swelling or an eruption or a spot 3
Num 5:21 when the LORD makes . . your body swell; 2
27 body shall swell, and her thigh shall fall away 2
Deu 8: 4 your foot did not swell, these 40 years. 1
Neh 9:21 not wear out and their feet did not swell. 1

make swell 1. צבה
Num 5:22 make your body swell and your thigh fall away.' 1

swell out 1. יצא
Ps 73: 7 Their eyes swell out with fatness 1

swell up 1. πίμπρημι
Act 28: 6 They waited, expecting him to swell up 1

swell with conceit 1. τυφόω
2Ti 3: 4 treacherous, reckless, swollen with conceit 1

swerve 1. נטה 2. ἀστοχέω 3. ἐκκλίνω
Ps 119:157 I do not swerve from thy testimonies. 1
Prv 4:27 Do not swerve to the right or to the left; 1
Jol 2: 7 they do not swerve from their paths. 3
1Ti 1: 6 by swerving from these have wandered away 2
2Ti 2:18 swerved from the truth 2

swift 1. חושׁ 2. מָהִיר 3. מהר 4. מַהֵר 5. קַל 6. קלל 7. ὀξύς 8. σπεύδω 9. σύντομος 10. ταχινός 11. ταχύς 12. cito 13. impiger
Deu 28:49 bring a nation . . as swift as the eagle flies *
2Sm 1:23 they were swifter than eagles 6
2:18 Now As'ahel was as swift of foot as a wild gazelle; 5
1Ch 12: 8 who were swift as gazelles upon the mountains 4
Job 7: 6 My days are swifter than a weaver's shuttle 6
9:25 My days are swifter than a runner; they flee away 6
Ecc 9:11 saw that under the sun the race is not to the swift 5
Isa 16: 5 seeks justice and is swift to do righteousness. 2
18: 2 Go, you swift messengers, to a nation 5
19: 1 Behold, the LORD is riding on a swift cloud 5
30:16 We will ride upon swift steeds 5
16 therefore your pursuers shall be swift. 6
Jer 4:13 his horses are swifter than eagles 6
46: 6 The swift cannot flee away 5
Lam 4:19 Our pursuers were swifter than the vultures 5
Ezk 30: 9 that day swift messengers shall go forth from me 8
Dan 9:21 Gabriel . . came to me in swift flight at the time *
Ams 2:14 Flight shall perish from the swift 5
15 and he who is swift of foot shall not save himself 5
Hab 1: 8 Their horses are swifter than leopards 6
8 they fly like an eagle swift to devour. 1
Mal 3: 5 I will be a swift witness against the sorcerers 3
Rom 3:15 Their feet are swift to shed blood 7
2Pe 2: 1 bringing upon themselves swift destruction. 10
1Es 4:34 the sun is swift in its course 11
2Es 1:26 and your feet are swift to commit murder. 13
12:20 whose times shall be short and their years swift; 12
Wis 13: 2 either fire or wind or swift air 10
18:14 and night in its swift course was now half gone 11
4Mc 14:10 the power of fire is intense and swift 9
swift *See also* ass, horse, pace, steed.

swiftly 1. מְהֵרָה 2. קַל 3. ταχέως 4. ταχινός 5. ταχύς
Job 24:18 swiftly carried away upon the face of the waters; 2
Ps 147:15 command to the earth; his word runs swiftly. 1
Isa 5:26 and lo, swiftly, speedily it comes! 1
Jer 48:40 Behold, one shall fly swiftly like an eagle *
49:22 one shall mount up and fly swiftly like an eagle *
Jol 3: 4 upon your own head swiftly and speedily. 2
Wis 6: 5 he will come upon you terribly and swiftly 3
Sir 18:26 all things move swiftly before the Lord. 4
4Mc 10:21 God will visit you swiftly 5
swiftly *See also* come, hasten.

swiftness 1. celeritas
2Es 8:18 I have heard of the swiftness of the judgment 1

swim 1. שׂחה 2. κολυμβάω 3. νηκτός
Isa 25:11 as a swimmer spreads his hands out to swim; 1
Ezk 47: 5 the water had risen; it was deep enough to swim 1
Act 27:43 He ordered those who could swim 2
Wis 19:19 and creatures that swim moved over to the land. 3

swim across 1. διακολυμβάω
1Mc 9:48 and swam across to the other side 1

swim away 1. ἐκκολυμβάω
Act 27:42 lest any should swim away and escape; 1

swimmer 1. שׂחה
Isa 25:11 as a swimmer spreads his hands out to swim; 1

swine 1. חֲזִיר 2. ὕειος 3. χοῖρος
Lev 11: 7 the swine, because it parts the hoof and is cloven- 1
Deu 14: 8 swine, because it parts the hoof but does not chew 1
Prv 11:22 gold ring in a swine's snout is a beautiful woman 1
Isa 65: 4 who eat swine's flesh, and broth of abominable 1
66: 3 a cereal . . like him who offers swine's blood; 1
17 following one in the midst, eating swine's flesh 1
Mat 7: 6 and do not throw your pearls before swine 3
8:30 a herd of swine was feeding at some distance 3
31 cast us out, send us away into the herd of swine. 3
32 Go." So they came out and went into the swine; 3
Mrk 5:11 Now a great herd of swine was feeding there 3
12 Send us to the swine, let us enter them. 3
13 unclean spirits came out, and entered the swine; 3
16 to the demoniac and to the swine. 3
Lke 8:32 Now a large herd of swine was feeding there 3
33 the demons . . entered the swine 3
15:15 who sent him into his fields to feed swine. 3
16 the pods that the swine ate 3
1Mc 1:47 to sacrifice swine and unclean animals 2
2Mc 6:18 forced to open his mouth to eat swine's flesh. 2
7: 1 to partake of unlawful swine's flesh. 2

swing 1. נדה 2. סבב 3. βάλλω
Deu 19: 5 his hand swings the axe to cut down a tree 1
Ezk 26: 2 the gate . . is broken, it has swung open to me; 2
41:24 two swinging leaves for each door. 2
Rev 14:16 he who sat upon the cloud swung his sickle 3
19 So the angel swung his sickle on the earth 3

swing to and fro 1. נוע
Job 28: 4 they hang afar from men, they swing to and fro. 1

swirl 1. סער
Hos 13: 3 the chaff that swirls from the threshing floor 1

swoon away 1. נפח 2. καρόω
Jer 15: 9 She who bore seven . . she has swooned away; 1
51:39 till they swoon away and sleep a perpetual sleep 2

swoop 1. טוּשׂ 2. עִיט

1Sm 15:19 Why did you swoop on the spoil, and do what was evil 2
Job 9:26 They go by . . like an eagle swooping on the prey. 1

swoop down 1. עוּף

Isa 11:14 they shall swoop down upon the . . Philistines 1

sword 1. חֶרֶב 2. מְכֵרָה 3. פִּי חֶרֶב 4. שֶׁלַח 5. *ἀκινάκης* 6. *μάχαιρα* 7. *ξιφηφόρος* 8. *ξίφος* 9. *ῥομφαία* 10. *σίδηρος* 11. gladius 12. romphea

Gen 3:24 a flaming sword which turned every way 1
27:40 By your sword you shall live, and you shall serve 1
31:26 my daughters like captives of the sword? 1
34:25 Dinah's brothers, took their swords and came upon 1
26 his son Shechem with the sword, and took Dinah out 1
48:22 which I took . . with my sword and with my bow. 1
49: 5 weapons of violence are their swords. 2
Exd 5: 3 fall upon us with pestilence or with the sword. 1
21 you . . put a sword in their hand to kill us. 1
15: 9 I will draw my sword, my hand shall destroy them.' 1
17:13 Am'alek and his people with the edge of the sword. 1
18: 4 God . . delivered me from the sword of Pharaoh"). 1
22:24 I will kill you with the sword, and your wives 1
32:27 Put every man his sword on his side, and go 1
Lev 26: 6 the sword shall not go through your land 1
7 they shall fall before you by the sword 1
8 your enemies shall fall before you by the sword 1
25 I will bring a sword upon you, that shall execute 1
33 I will unsheathe the sword after you 1
36 they shall flee as one flees from the sword 1
37 stumble over one another, as if to escape a sword 1
Num14: 3 LORD bring us into this land, to fall by the sword? 1
43 shall fall by the sword; because you have turned 1
19:16 Whoever . . touches one who is slain with a sword 1
20:18 not pass through, lest I come out with the sword 1
21:24 Israel slew him with the edge of the sword 1
22:23 angel . . with a drawn sword in his hand; 1
29 I wish I had a sword in my hand, for then I would kill 1
31 saw the angel . . with his drawn sword in his hand; 1
31: 8 also slew Balaam the son of Be'or with the sword. 1
Deu 13:15 surely put the inhabitants . . to the sword 1
15 destroying it . . with the edge of the sword. 1
20:13 hand you shall put all its males to the sword 1
32:25 In the open the sword shall bereave 1
41 if I whet my glittering sword, and my hand 1
42 my arrows . . and my sword shall devour flesh 1
33:29 LORD, the shield . . and the sword of your triumph! 1
Jos 5:13 stood before him with his drawn sword in his hand; 1
6:21 destroyed all . . with the edge of the sword. 1
8:24 all of them . . had fallen by the edge of the sword 1
24 and smote it with the edge of the sword. 1
10:11 the men of Israel killed with the sword. 1
28 smote it and its king with the edge of the sword; 1
30 and he smote it with the edge of the sword 1
32 and smote it with the edge of the sword 1
35 took it . . and smote it with the edge of the sword; 1
37 and took it, and smote it with the edge of the sword 1
39 and they smote them with the edge of the sword 1
11:10 and took Hazor, and smote its king with the sword; 1
11 And they put to the sword all who were in it 3
12 took, and smote them with the edge of the sword 1
14 every man they smote with the edge of the sword 1
13:22 Balaam also . . Israel killed with the sword 1
19:47 after capturing it and putting it to the sword 3
24:12 I sent . . it was not by your sword or by your bow. 1
Jdg 1: 8 and took it, and smote it with the edge of the sword 1
25 and they smote the city with the edge of the sword 1
3:16 himself a sword with two edges, a cubit in length; 1
21 his left hand, took the sword from his right thigh 1
22 for he did not draw the sword out of his belly; 1
4:15 all his army before Barak at the edge of the sword; 1
16 the army of Sis'era fell by the edge of the sword; 1
7:14 This is no other than the sword of Gideon the son 1
20 they cried, "A sword for the LORD and for Gideon! 1
22 the LORD set every man's sword against his fellow 1
8:10 there had fallen 120,000 men who drew the sword. 1
20 the youth did not draw his sword; for he was afraid 1
9:54 Draw your sword and kill me, lest men say of me 1
18:27 came . . and smote them with the edge of the sword 1
20: 2 of God, 400,000 men on foot that drew the sword. 1
15 mustered . . 26,000 men that drew the sword 1
17 Israel . . mustered 400,000 men that drew sword 1
25 of Israel; all these were men who drew the sword. 1
35 25,100 . . all these were men who drew the sword. 1
37 and smote all the city with the edge of the sword. 1
46 fell . . 25,000 men that drew the sword 1
48 and smote them with the edge of the sword 1
21:10 Go and smite . . with the edge of the sword; 1
1Sm 2:33 all the increase . . shall die by the sword of men. 9
13:19 Lest the Hebrews make . . swords or spears"; 1
22 there was neither sword nor spear found 1
14:20 behold, every man's sword was against his fellow 1
15: 8 destroyed . . people with the edge of the sword. 1
33 As your sword has made women childless 1
17:39 And David girded his sword over his armor 1
45 You come to me with a sword and with a spear 1
47 know that the LORD saves not with sword and spear; 1
50 there was no sword in the hand of David. 1
51 and took his sword and drew it . . and killed him 1
18: 4 and even his sword and his bow and his girdle. 1
21: 8 And have you not here a spear or a sword at hand? 1
8 I have brought neither my sword nor my weapons 1
9 The sword of Goliath the Philistine . . is here 1
22:10 gave him the sword of Goliath the Philistine. 1
13 you have given him bread and a sword 1
19 Nob, the city of the priests, he put to the sword; 1
19 both men and women . . he put to the sword. 1
25:13 David said to his men, "Every man gird on his sword! 1
13 And every man of them girded on his sword; 1
13 David also girded on his sword; 1
31: 4 Draw your sword, and thrust me through with it 1
4 Saul took his own sword, and fell upon it. 1
5 armor-bearer . . also fell upon his sword, and died 1
2Sm 1:12 mourned . . because they had fallen by the sword. 1
22 and the sword of Saul returned not empty. 1
2:16 and thrust his sword in his opponent's side; 1
26 Abner called . . "Shall the sword devour for ever? 1
3:29 or who holds a spindle, or who is slain by the sword 1
11:25 for the sword devours now one and now another; 1
12: 9 You have smitten Uri'ah . . with the sword 1
9 have slain him with the sword of the Ammonites. 1
10 the sword shall never depart from your house 1
15:14 and smite the city with the edge of the sword. 1
18: 8 forest devoured more people . . than the sword. 1
20: 8 and over it was a girdle with a sword in its sheath 1
10 did not observe the sword which was in Jo'ab's hand; 1
21:16 Ish'bi-be'nob . . who was girded with a new sword •
23:10 hand was weary, and his hand cleaved to the sword; 1
24: 9 there were . . valiant men who drew the sword 1
1Kg 1:51 that he will not slay his servant with the sword.' 1
2: 8 saying, 'I will not put you to death with the sword.' 1
32 he attacked and slew with the sword two men more 1
3:24 king said, "Bring me a sword." So a sword was brought 1
24 So a sword was brought before the king. 1
18:28 cut themselves . . with swords and lances 1
19: 1 he had slain all the prophets with the sword. 1
10 and slain thy prophets with the sword; 1
14 and slain thy prophets with the sword; 1
17 who escapes from the sword of Haz'ael 1
17 who escapes from the sword of Jehu 1
2Kg 6:22 taken captive with your sword and with your bow? 1
8:12 you will slay their young men with the sword 1
10:25 So when they put them to the sword 3
11:15 and slay with the sword any one who follows her. 1
20 Athali'ah had been slain with the sword 1
19: 7 cause him to fall by the sword in his own land.' 1
37 and Share'zer, his sons, slew him with the sword 1
1Ch 5:18 valiant men, who carried shield and sword 1
10: 4 Draw your sword, and thrust me through with it 1
4 Saul took his own sword, and fell upon it. 1
5 he also fell upon his sword, and died. 1
21: 5 Israel there were 1,100,000 men who drew the sword 1
5 and in Judah 470,000 who drew the sword. 1
12 while the sword of your enemies overtakes you; 1
12 or else three days of the sword of the LORD 1
16 and in his hand a drawn sword stretched out 1
27 angel; and he put his sword back into its sheath. 1
30 afraid of the sword of the angel of the LORD. 1
2Ch 20: 9 If evil comes upon us, the sword, judgment 1
21: 4 slew all his brothers with the sword 1
23:14 who follows her is to be slain with the sword. 1
21 after Athali'ah had been slain with the sword. 1
29: 9 For lo, our fathers have fallen by the sword 1
32:21 sons struck him down there with the sword. 1
36:17 slew their young men with the sword in the house 1
20 exile . . those who had escaped from the sword 1
Ezr 9: 7 been given . . to the sword, to captivity 1
Neh 4:13 with their swords, their spears, and their bows. 1
18 builders had his sword girded at his side 1
Est 9: 5 the Jews smote all their enemies with the sword 1
Job 1:15 and slew the servants with the edge of the sword; 1
17 and slew the servants with the edge of the sword; 1
5:20 from death, and in war from the power of the sword. 1
15:22 he is destined for the sword. 1
19:29 be afraid of the sword 1
29 for wrath brings the punishment of the sword 1
27:14 his children are multiplied, it is for the sword; 1
33:18 his life from perishing by the sword. 4
36:12 if they do not hearken, they perish by the sword 4
39:22 he does not turn back from the sword. 1
40:19 let him who made him bring near his sword! 1
41:26 Though the sword reaches him, it does not avail; 1
Ps 7:12 If a man does not repent, God will whet his sword; 1
17:13 Deliver my life from the wicked by thy sword 1
22:20 Deliver my soul from the sword 1
37:14 The wicked draw the sword and bend their bows 1
15 their sword shall enter their own heart 1
44: 3 for not by their own sword did they win the land 1
6 not in my bow do I trust, nor can my sword save me. 1
45: 3 Gird your sword upon your thigh, O mighty one 1
57: 4 spears and arrows, their tongues sharp swords. 1
63:10 they shall be given over to the power of the sword 1
64: 3 who whet their tongues like swords 1
76: 3 the shield, the sword, and the weapons of war. 1
78:62 He gave his people over to the sword 1
64 Their priests fell by the sword 1
89:43 Yea, thou hast turned back the edge of his sword 1
144:11 Rescue me from the cruel sword 1
149: 6 Let . . two-edged swords in their hands 1
Prv 5: 4 in the end she is . . sharp as a two-edged sword. 1
12:18 one whose rash words are like sword thrusts 1
25:18 like a war club, or a sword, or sharp arrow. 1
30:14 whose teeth are swords, whose teeth are knives 1
Sng 3: 8 all girt with swords and expert in war 1
8 each with his sword at his thigh, against alarms 1
Isa 1:20 if you . . rebel, you shall be devoured by the sword; 1
2: 4 they shall beat their swords into plowshares 1
4 nation shall not lift up sword against nation 1
3:25 Your men shall fall by the sword . . in battle. 1
13:15 and whoever is caught will fall by the sword. 1
14:19 those pierced by the sword 1
21:15 For they have fled from the swords 1
15 swords, from the drawn sword, from the bent bow 1
22: 2 Your slain are not slain with the sword 1
27: 1 the LORD with his hard and great and strong sword 1
31: 8 the Assyrian shall fall by a sword, not of man; 1
8 and a sword, not of man, shall devour him; 1
8 he shall flee from the sword 1
34: 5 For my sword has drunk its fill in the heavens; 1
6 The LORD has a sword; it is sated with blood 1
37: 7 I will make him fall by the sword in his own land.' 1
38 his sons, slew him with the sword, and escaped 1
41: 2 he makes them like dust with his sword 1
49: 2 He made my mouth like a sharp sword 1
51:19 devastation and destruction, famine and sword; 1
65:12 I will destine you to the sword 1
66:16 execute judgment, and by his sword, upon all flesh; 1
Jer 2:30 your own sword devoured your prophets 1
4:10 whereas the sword has reached their very life. 1
5:12 nor shall we see sword or famine. 1
17 cities . . they shall destroy with the sword. 1
6:25 for the enemy has a sword, terror is on every side. 1
9:16 and I will send the sword after them 1
11:22 the young men shall die by the sword; 1
12:12 for the sword of the LORD devours from one end 1
14:12 but I will consume them by the sword, by famine 1
13 You shall not see the sword 1
15 Sword and famine shall not come on this land 1
15 By sword . . those prophets shall be consumed. 1
16 victims of famine and sword, with none to bury 1
18 into the field, behold, those slain by the sword! 1
15: 2 those who are for the sword, to the sword; 1
2 those who are for the sword, to the sword; 1
3 says the LORD: the sword to slay, the dogs to tear 1
9 And the rest of them I will give to the sword 1
16: 4 They shall perish by the sword and by famine 1
18:21 give them over to the power of the sword 1
21 their youths be slain by the sword in battle. 1
19: 7 and will cause their people to fall by the sword 1
20: 4 They shall fall by the sword of their enemies 1
4 to Babylon, and shall slay them with the sword. 1
21: 7 who survive the pestilence, sword, and famine 1
7 He shall smite them with the edge of the sword; 1
9 He who stays in this city shall die by the sword 1
24:10 will send sword, famine, and pestilence upon them 1
25:16 the sword which I am sending among them. 1
27 because of the sword which I am sending among you. 1
29 not go unpunished, for I am summoning a sword 1
31 the wicked he will put to the sword, says the LORD. 1
38 a waste because of the sword of the oppressor 1
26:23 King Jehoi'akim, who slew him with the sword 1
27: 8 I will punish that nation with the sword 1
13 Why will you and your people die by the sword 1
29:17 I am sending on them sword, famine, and pestilence 1
18 I will pursue them with sword, famine 1
31: 2 The people who survived the sword found grace 1
32:24 because of sword and famine and pestilence 1
36 given . . by sword, by famine, and by pestilence 1
33: 4 against the siege mounds and before the sword 1
34: 4 You shall not die by the sword. 1
17 behold, I proclaim to you liberty to the sword 1
38: 2 He who stays in this city shall die by the sword 1
39:18 you shall not fall by the sword; 1
41: 2 and struck down . . with the sword, and killed him 1
42:16 then the sword which you fear shall overtake you 1
17 to go to Egypt to live there shall die by the sword 1
22 know . . that you shall die by the sword, by famine 1
43:11 to the sword those who are doomed to the sword. 1
11 to the sword those who are doomed to the sword. 1
44:12 by the sword and by famine they shall be consumed; 1
12 they shall die by the sword and by famine; 1
13 as I have punished Jerusalem, with the sword 1
18 been consumed by the sword and by famine. 1
27 shall be consumed by the sword and by famine 1
28 And those who escape the sword shall return 1
46:10 The sword shall devour and be sated 1
14 for the sword shall devour round about you. 1
16 because of the sword of the oppressor. 1
47: 6 Ah, sword of the LORD! How long till you are quiet? 1
48: 2 the sword shall pursue you. 1
10 is he who keeps back his sword from bloodshed. 1
49:37 I will send the sword after them 1
50:16 because of the sword of the oppressor 1
35 A sword upon the Chalde'ans, says the LORD 1
36 A sword upon the diviners, that they may become 1
36 A sword upon her warriors, that they may be 1

37 A sword upon her horses and upon her chariots 1
37 A sword upon all her treasures 1
51:50 You that have escaped from the sword, go, stand not 1
Lam 1:20 In the street the sword bereaves; 1
2:21 maidens and . . young men have fallen by the sword; 1
4: 9 Happier were the victims of the sword 1
5: 9 because of the sword in the wilderness. 1
Ezk 5: 1 And you, O son of man, take a sharp sword; 1
2 and strike with the sword round about the city; 1
2 and I will unsheathe the sword after them. 1
12 a third . . shall fall by the sword round about you; 1
12 and will unsheathe the sword after them. 1
17 I will bring the sword upon you. 1
6: 3 Behold, I, even I, will bring a sword upon you 1
8 have among the nations some who escape the sword 1
11 for they shall fall by the sword, by famine 1
12 he that is near shall fall by the sword; 1
7:15 The sword is without 1
15 he that is in the field dies by the sword; 1
11: 8 You have feared the sword; 1
8 I will bring the sword upon you, says the Lord GOD. 1
10 You shall fall by the sword; 1
12:14 I will unsheathe the sword after them. 1
16 But I will let a few of them escape from the sword 1
14:17 Or if I bring a sword upon that land, and say 1
17 and say, Let a sword go through the land; 1
21 sword, famine, evil beasts, and pestilence 1
16:40 and cut you to pieces with their swords. 1
17:21 all the pick of his troops shall fall by the sword 1
21: 3 and will draw forth my sword out of its sheath 1
4 therefore my sword shall go out of its sheath 1
5 shall know that I the LORD have drawn my sword out 1
9 A sword, a sword is sharpened and also polished. 1
9 A sword, a sword is sharpened and also polished. 1
11 the sword is given to be polished 1
12 delivered over to the sword with my people. 1
14 clap your hands and let the sword come down twice 1
14 twice, yea thrice, the sword for those to be slain; 1
14 it is the sword for the great slaughter 1
15 I have given the glittering sword; 1
19 ways for the sword of the king of Babylon to come; 1
20 mark a way for the sword to come to Rabbah 1
28 say, A sword, a sword is drawn for the slaughter 1
28 say, A sword, a sword is drawn for the slaughter 1
23:10 and her they slew with the sword; 1
25 your survivors shall fall by the sword. 1
47 stone them and dispatch them with their swords; 1
24:21 whom you left behind shall fall by the sword. 1
25:13 Teman even to Dedan they shall fall by the sword. 1
26: 6 her daughters . . shall be slain by the sword. 1
8 He will slay with the sword your daughters 1
11 he will slay your people with the sword; 1
28: 7 they shall draw their swords against the beauty 1
23 by the sword that is against her on every side. 1
29: 8 I will bring a sword upon you, and will cut off 1
30: 4 A sword shall come upon Egypt 1
5 shall fall with them by the sword. 1
6 fall within her by the sword, says the Lord GOD. 1
11 and they shall draw their swords against Egypt 1
17 On and of Pibe'seth shall fall by the sword; 1
21 that it may become strong to wield the sword. 1
22 I will make the sword fall from his hand. 1
24 and put my sword in his hand; 1
25 I put my sword into the hand of the king of Babylon 1
31:17 Sheol with it, to those who are slain by the sword; 1
18 with those who are slain by the sword. 1
32:10 when I brandish my sword before them; 1
11 sword of the king of Babylon shall come upon you. 1
12 to fall by the swords of mighty ones, all of them 1
20 shall fall amid those who are slain by the sword 1
21 lie still, the uncircumcised, slain by the sword 1
22 all of them slain, fallen by the sword; 1
23 all of them slain, fallen by the sword 1
24 all of them slain, fallen by the sword 1
25 all of them uncircumcised, slain by the sword; 1
26 all of them uncircumcised, slain by the sword; 1
27 whose swords were laid under their heads 1
28 with those who are slain by the sword. 1
29 are laid with those who are slain by the sword; 1
30 who are slain by the sword, and bear their shame 1
31 Pharaoh and all his army, slain by the sword 1
32 with those who are slain by the sword 1
33: 2 and say to them, If I bring the sword upon a land 1
3 if he sees the sword coming upon the land 1
4 and the sword comes and takes him away 1
6 if the watchman sees the sword coming 1
6 and the sword comes, and takes any one of them; 1
26 You resort to the sword, you commit abominations 1
27 are in the waste places shall fall by the sword; 1
35: 5 the people of Israel to the power of the sword 1
8 those slain with the sword shall fall. 1
38: 4 with buckler and shield, wielding swords; 1
21 every man's sword will be against his brother. 1
39:23 they all fell by the sword. 1
Dan 11:33 though they shall fall by sword and flame 1
Hos 1: 7 I will not deliver them by bow, nor by sword 1
2:18 and I will abolish the bow, the sword, and war 1
7:16 their princes shall fall by the sword 1
11: 6 The sword shall rage against their cities 1
13:16 they shall fall by the sword 1
Jol 3:10 Beat your plowshares into swords 1
Ams 1:11 because he pursued his brother with the sword 1
4:10 I slew your young men with the sword; 1
7: 9 against the house of Jerobo'am with the sword. 1
11 Amos has said, 'Jerobo'am shall die by the sword 1
17 sons and your daughters shall fall by the sword 1
9: 1 and what are left of them I will slay with the sword; 1
4 I will command the sword, and it shall slay them; 1
10 the sinners of my people shall die by the sword 1
Mic 4: 3 they shall beat their swords into plowshares 1
3 nation shall not lift up sword against nation 1
5: 6 shall rule the land of Assyria with the sword 1
6:14 and what you save I will give to the sword. 1
Nah 2:13 and the sword shall devour your young lions; 1
3: 3 Horsemen charging, flashing sword 1
15 the fire devour you, the sword will cut you off. 1
Zep 2:12 You also, O Ethiopians, shall be slain by my sword. 1
Hag 2:22 go down every one by the sword of his fellow. 1
Zec 9:13 O Greece, and wield you like a warrior's sword. 1
11:17 May the sword smite his arm and his right eye! 1
13: 7 Awake, O sword, against my shepherd 1
Mat 10:34 I have not come to bring peace, but a sword. 6
26:47 with him a great crowd with swords and clubs 6
51 Jesus stretched out his hand and drew his sword 6
52 Put your sword back into its place 6
52 all who take the sword will perish by the sword. 6
52 all who take the sword will perish by the sword. 6
55 with swords and clubs to capture me 6
Mrk 14:43 with him a crowd with swords and clubs 6
47 one of those who stood by drew his sword 6
48 with swords and clubs to capture me? 6
Lke 2:35 (and a sword will pierce through your own soul also) 9
21:24 they will fall by the edge of the sword 6
22:36 let him who has no sword sell his mantle 6
38 they said, "Look, Lord, here are two swords. 6
49 shall we strike with the sword? 6
52 as against a robber, with swords and clubs? 6
Joh 18:10 Simon Peter, having a sword, drew it 6
11 Put your sword into its sheath 6
Act 12: 2 killed James the brother of John with the sword; 6
16:27 he drew his sword and was about to kill himself 6
Rom 8:35 or famine, or nakedness, or peril, or sword? 6
13: 4 be afraid, for he does not bear the sword in vain; 6
Eph 6:17 the sword of the Spirit, which is the word of God. 6
Heb 4:12 sharper than any two-edged sword 6
11:34 escaped the edge of the sword 6
37 they were killed with the sword 6
Rev 1:16 from his mouth issued a sharp two-edged sword 9
2:12 The words of him who has the sharp two-edged sword. 9
16 and war against them with the sword of my mouth. 9
6: 4 and he was given a great sword. 6
8 power . . to kill with sword and with famine 9
13:10 if any one slays with the sword 6
10 if any one slays . . with the sword must he be slain 6
14 the beast which was wounded by the sword 6
19:15 From his mouth issues a sharp sword 9
21 And the rest were slain by the sword 9
21 the sword that issues from his mouth; •
1Es 1:53 These slew their young men with the sword 9
56 he led away to Babylon with the sword 9
3:22 before long they draw their swords. 6
4:23 A man takes his sword, and goes out to travel 9
8:77 to the sword and captivity and plundering 9
2Es 12:27 the sword shall devour them. 11
28 the sword of one shall devour him who was with him; 11
28 he also shall fall by the sword in the last days. 11
15: 5 the sword and famine and death and destruction. 11
15 For the sword and misery draw near them 11
15 with swords in their hands. 12
19 an assault upon their houses with the sword 11
22 my sword will not cease from those 12
35 be blood from the sword as high as a horse's belly 11
41 hail and flying swords and floods of water 12
49 widowhood, poverty, famine, sword, and pestilence 11
57 and you shall fall by the sword 12
57 all your people . . shall fall by the sword. 11
16: 3 The sword has been sent upon you 11
21 earth–the sword, famine, and great confusion. 11
22 who survive the famine shall die by the sword. 11
31 those who search their houses with the sword. 12
Jdt 1:12 he would kill them by the sword 9
2:27 put to death . . with the edge of the sword. 9
6: 6 the sword of my army and the spear of my servants 10
7:14 before the sword reaches them 9
8:19 why our fathers were handed over to the sword 9
9: 2 gavest a sword to take revenge on the strangers 9
8 to cast down the horn of thy altar with the sword. 10
11:10 nor can the sword prevail against them 9
13: 6 and took down his sword that hung there. 5
16: 5 and kill my young men with the sword 9
9 the sword severed his neck. 5
AEs 13: 6 utterly destroyed by the sword of their enemies 6
Wis 5:20 sharpen stern wrath for a sword 9
18:16 the sharp sword of thy authentic command 8
Sir 21: 3 All lawlessness is like a two-edged sword 9
22:21 Even if you have drawn your sword 9
26:28 the Lord will prepare him for the sword! 9
28:18 Many have fallen by the edge of the sword 6
39:30 the sword that punishes the ungodly 9
40: 9 are death and bloodshed and strife and sword 9
46: 2 stretched out his sword against the cities! 9
Bar 2:25 by famine and sword and pestilence. 9
Sus 1:59 angel . . waiting with his sword to saw you in two 9
Bel 1:26 I will slay the dragon without sword or club. 6
1Mc 2: 9 her youths by the sword of the foe. 9
3: 3 waged battles, protecting the host by his sword. 9
12 Judas took the sword of Apollonius 6
4: 6 armor and swords such as they desired. 6
15 all those in the rear fell by the sword 9
33 the sword of those who love thee 9
5:28 killed every male by the edge of the sword 9
51 He destroyed every male by the edge of the sword 9
7:38 let them fall by the sword 9
46 so that they all fell by the sword 9
8:23 may sword and enemy be far from them. 9
9:73 Thus the sword ceased from Israel 9
10:85 The number of those who fell by the sword 6
12:48 they killed with the sword. 9
2Mc 5: 2 fully armed with lances and drawn swords– 6
12:22 pierced by the points of their swords. 8
14:41 Being surrounded, Razis fell upon his own sword 8
15:15 gave to Judas a golden sword 9
16 Take this holy sword, a gift from God 9
4Mc 16:20 when Isaac saw his father's hand wielding a sword 7
151 1: 7 I drew his own sword; I beheaded him 6

sword *See also* put.

drawn sword 1. פְּתִיחָה
Ps 55:21 were softer than oil, yet they were drawn swords. 1
Mic 5: 6 rule . . the land of Nimrod with the drawn sword; •

swordsman 1. אִישׁ שֹׁלֵף חֶרֶב
2Kg 3:26 he took with him . . swordsmen to break through 1

sworn *See* covenant, promise.

sycamine tree 1. συκάμινος
Lke 17: 6 you could say to this sycamine tree 1

sycamore 1. שִׁקְמָה
1Kg 10:27 he made cedar as plentiful as the sycamore 1
2Ch 1:15 as plentiful as the sycamore of the Shephe'lah. 1
9:27 king made . . cedar as plentiful as the sycamore 1
Ps 78:47 vines with hail, and their sycamores with frost. 1
Isa 9:10 the sycamores have been cut down 1

sycamore tree 1. שִׁקְמָה 2. συκομορέα
1Ch 27:28 Over the . . sycamore trees in the Shephe'lah was 1
Ams 7:14 I am a herdsman, and a dresser of sycamore trees 1
Lke 19: 4 and climbed up into a sycamore tree 2

symbol 1. זִכָּרוֹן 2. παράσημος 3. σκεῦος
Isa 57: 8 Behind the door . . you have set up your symbol; 1
Sir 45: 8 strengthened him with the symbols of authority 3
3Mc 2:29 the ivy-leaf symbol of Dionysus 2

symbolic 1. παραβολή
Heb 9: 9 (which is symbolic for the present age). 1

symbolize 1. appropinquo 2. assimilo
2Es 13:37 (this was symbolized by the storm) 1
38 (which were symbolized by the flames) 2
38 (which was symbolized by the fire). 2

more sympathetic 1. συμπαθής
4Mc 13:23 the brothers were the more sympathetic 1

sympathize 1. συμπαθέω
Heb 4:15 is unable to sympathize with our weaknesses 1

sympathy 1. οἰκτιρμός 2. συμπάθεια 3. συμπαθής
Php 2: 1 any affection and sympathy 1
1Pe 3: 8 Finally, all of you, have unity of spirit, sympathy 3
4Mc 6:13 partly out of sympathy 2
13:23 when sympathy . . had been so established 3
14:14 have a sympathy and parental love 2
18 to demonstrate sympathy for children 2
20 sympathy for her children 2
15: 7 she had sympathy for them; 2

deep sympathy 1. συμπαθής
4Mc 15: 4 have a deeper sympathy toward their offspring 1

show sympathy 1. נוּד 2. συμπαθέω
Job 42:11 they showed him sympathy and comforted him 1
4Mc 5:25 the Creator . . has shown sympathy toward us. 2

synagogue 1. συναγωγή
Mat 4:23 about all Galilee teaching in their synagogues 1
6: 2 as the hypocrites do in the synagogues 1
5 pray in the synagogues and at the street corners 1
9:35 teaching in their synagogues and preaching 1
10:17 and flog you in their synagogues 1
12: 9 and entered their synagogue. 1
13:54 he taught them in their synagogue 1
23: 6 they love . . the best seats in the synagogues 1

34 some you will scourge in your synagogues 1
Mrk 1:21 he entered the synagogue and taught. 1
23 immediately there was in their synagogue a man 1
29 immediately he left the synagogue 1
39 preaching in their synagogues 1
3: 1 Again he entered the synagogue 1
6: 2 on the sabbath he began to teach in the synagogue; 1
12:39 and the best seats in the synagogues 1
13: 9 you will be beaten in synagogues 1
Lke 4:15 he taught in their synagogues 1
16 he went to the synagogue, as his custom was 1
20 the eyes of all in the synagogue were fixed on him. 1
28 all in the synagogue were filled with wrath. 1
33 in the synagogue there was a man 1
38 he arose and left the synagogue 1
44 he was preaching in the synagogues of Judea. 1
6: 6 when he entered the synagogue and taught 1
7: 5 he loves our nation, and he built us our synagogue 1
8:41 Ja'irus, who was a ruler of the synagogue 1
11:43 you love the best seat in the synagogues 1
12:11 bring you before the synagogues and the rulers 1
13:10 in one of the synagogues on the sabbath. 1
20:46 and love . . the best seats in the synagogues 1
21:12 delivering you up to the synagogues and prisons 1
Joh 6:59 This he said in the synagogue 1
18:20 always taught in synagogues and in the temple 1
Act 6: 9 the synagogue of the Freedman 1
9: 2 letters to the synagogues at Damascus 1
20 in the synagogues . . he proclaimed Jesus 1
13: 5 proclaimed the word of God in the synagogues 1
14 they went into the synagogue and sat down. 1
43 when the meeting of the synagogue broke up 1
14: 1 entered together into the Jewish synagogue 1
15:21 he is read every sabbath in the synagogues. 1
17: 1 where there was a synagogue of the Jews. 1
10 they went into the Jewish synagogue. 1
17 he argued in the synagogue with the Jews 1
18: 4 he argued in the synagogue every sabbath 1
7 his house was next door to the synagogue. 1
19 went into the synagogue and argued with the Jews. 1
26 He began to speak boldly in the synagogue 1
19: 8 he entered the synagogue 1
22:19 in every synagogue I imprisoned and beat 1
24:12 in the temple or in the synagogues, or in the city. 1
26:11 I punished them often in all the synagogues 1
Rev 2: 9 but are a synagogue of Satan. 1
3: 9 I will make those in the synagogue of Satan 1

synagogue *See also* put, ruler.

out of the synagogue 1. ἀποσυνάγωγος
Joh 16: 2 They will put you out of the synagogues 1

T

tabernacle 1. מִשְׁכָּן 2. סֻכָּה 3. σκηνή 4. σκηνοπηγία 5. σκήνωμα

Exd 25: 9 concerning the pattern of the tabernacle 1
26: 1 you shall make the tabernacle with ten curtains 1
6 that the tabernacle may be one whole. 1
7 goats' hair for a tent over the tabernacle; 1
12 shall hang over the back of the tabernacle. 1
13 shall hang over the sides of the tabernacle 1
15 frames for the tabernacle of acacia wood. 1
17 for all the frames of the tabernacle. 1
18 You shall make the frames for the tabernacle 1
20 for the second side of the tabernacle 1
22 for the rear of the tabernacle westward 1
23 for corners of the tabernacle in the rear; 1
26 the frames of the one side of the tabernacle 1
27 the frames of the other side of the tabernacle 1
27 the side of the tabernacle at the rear westward. 1
30 you shall erect the tabernacle according 1
35 lampstand on the south side of the tabernacle 1
27: 9 You shall make the court of the tabernacle. 1
19 All the utensils of the tabernacle for every use 1
35:10 all that the LORD has commanded: the tabernacle 1
15 screen for the door, at the door of the tabernacle; 1
18 the pegs of the tabernacle and the pegs 1
36: 8 able men among the workmen made the tabernacle 1
13 so the tabernacle was one whole. 1
14 goats' hair for a tent over the tabernacle; 1
20 he made the upright frames for the tabernacle 1
22 he did this for all the frames of the tabernacle. 1
23 The frames for the tabernacle he made thus 1
25 for the second side of the tabernacle 1
27 for the rear of the tabernacle westward he made 1
28 made two frames for corners of the tabernacle 1
31 the frames of the one side of the tabernacle 1
32 the frames of the other side of the tabernacle 1
32 frames of the tabernacle at the rear westward. 1
38:20 all the pegs for the tabernacle and for the court 1
21 This is the sum of the things for the tabernacle 1
21 for the . . tabernacle of the testimony 1
31 gate of the court, all the pegs of the tabernacle 1
39:32 Thus all the work of the tabernacle of the tent 1
33 they brought the tabernacle to Moses 1
40 the utensils for the service of the tabernacle 1
40: 2 first month you shall erect the tabernacle 1
5 set up the screen for the door of the tabernacle. 1
6 altar . . before the door of the tabernacle 1
9 anoint the tabernacle and all that is in it 1
17 first month . . the tabernacle was erected. 1
18 Moses erected the tabernacle; he laid its bases 1
19 he spread the tent over the tabernacle 1
21 he brought the ark into the tabernacle 1
22 north side of the tabernacle, outside the veil 1
24 table on the south side of the tabernacle 1
28 the screen for the door of the tabernacle. 1
29 burnt offering at the door of the tabernacle 1
33 he erected the court round the tabernacle 1
34 the glory of the LORD filled the tabernacle. 1
35 the glory of the LORD filled the tabernacle. 1
36 the cloud was taken up from over the tabernacle 1
38 the cloud of the LORD was upon the tabernacle 1
Lev 8:10 Moses . . anointed the tabernacle and all that 1
15:31 by defiling my tabernacle that is in their midst 1
17: 4 bring it . . before the tabernacle of the LORD 1
Num 1:50 appoint the Levites over the tabernacle 1
50 they are to carry the tabernacle and all its 1
50 and shall encamp around the tabernacle. 1
51 When the tabernacle is to set out, the Levites 1
51 when the tabernacle is to be pitched, the Levites 1
53 the Levites shall encamp around the tabernacle 1
53 the Levites shall keep charge of the tabernacle 1
3: 7 as they minister at the tabernacle 1
8 attend . . as they minister at the tabernacle. 1
23 Gershonites . . encamp behind the tabernacle 1
25 the tabernacle, the tent with its covering 1
26 the court which is around the tabernacle 1
29 to encamp on the south side of the tabernacle 1
35 to encamp on the north side of the tabernacle. 1
36 charge . . was to be the frames of the tabernacle 1
38 to encamp before the tabernacle on the east 1
4:16 oversight of all the tabernacle and all that is 1
25 they shall carry the curtains of the tabernacle 1
26 court which is around the tabernacle 1
31 charged to carry . . frames of the tabernacle 1
5:17 dust that is on the floor of the tabernacle 1
7: 1 Moses had finished setting up the tabernacle 1
3 offered them before the tabernacle. 1
9:15 On the day that the tabernacle was set up 1
15 cloud covered the tabernacle, the tent 1
15 at evening it was over the tabernacle 1
18 as long as the cloud rested over the tabernacle 1
19 cloud continued over the tabernacle many days 1
20 cloud was a few days over the tabernacle 1
22 that the cloud continued over the tabernacle 1
10:11 from over the tabernacle of the testimony 1
17 when the tabernacle was taken down 1
17 sons . . who carried the tabernacle, set out. 1
21 tabernacle was set up before their arrival. 1
16: 9 to do service in the tabernacle of the LORD 1
17:13 Every one . . who comes near to the tabernacle 1
19:13 defiles the tabernacle of the LORD 1
31:30 Levites who have charge of the tabernacle 1
47 had charge of the tabernacle of the LORD; 1
Jos 22:19 LORD's land where the LORD's tabernacle stands 1
29 the altar . . that stands before his tabernacle! 1
1Ch 6:32 before the tabernacle of the tent of meeting 1
48 service of the tabernacle of the house of God. 1
16:39 tabernacle of the LORD in the high place 1
21:29 tabernacle of the LORD, which Moses had made 1
23:26 Levites no longer need to carry the tabernacle 1
2Ch 1: 5 was there before the tabernacle of the LORD. 1
8:13 annual feasts- . . and the feast of tabernacles. 2
Joh 7: 2 Now the Jews' feast of Tabernacles was at hand. 4
Jdt 9: 8 they intend . . to pollute the tabernacle 5
Sir 24:10 In the holy tabernacle I ministered before him 3
15 fragrance of frankincense in the tabernacle. 3
1Mc 10:21 at the feast of tabernacles 4

table 1. אכל 2. פָּנִים 3. שֻׁלְחָן 4. ἀνάκειμαι 5. κατάκειμαι 6. κατακλίνω 7. συνανάκειμαι 8. τράπεζα 9. mensa

Gen 43:34 Portions were taken to them from Joseph's table 2
Exd 25:23 you shall make a table of acacia wood; 3
27 as holders for the poles to carry the table. 3
28 and the table shall be carried with these. 3
30 bread of the Presence on the table before me 3
26:35 you shall set the table outside the veil 3
35 lampstand . . opposite the table; 3
35 you shall put the table on the north side. 3
30:27 the table and all its utensils, and the lampstand 3
31: 8 table and its utensils, and the pure lampstand 3
35:13 the table with its poles and all its utensils 3
37:10 He also made the table of acacia wood; 3
14 as holders for the poles to carry the table. 3
15 the poles of acacia wood to carry the table 3
16 vessels . . to be upon the table, and its plates 3
39:36 the table with all its utensils, and the bread 3
40: 4 you shall bring in the table, and set its 3
22 he put the table in the tent of meeting 3
24 opposite the table on the south side 3
Lev 24: 6 set them . . upon the table of pure gold 3
Num 3:31 their charge was to be the ark, the table 3
4: 7 over the table of the bread of the Presence 3
Jdg 1: 7 kings . . used to pick up scraps under my table; 3
1Sm 20: 5 and I should not fail to sit at table with the king; 1
29 For this . . he has not come to the king's table. 3
34 And Jonathan rose from the table in fierce anger 3
2Sm 9: 7 and you shall eat at my table always. 3
10 Mephib'osheth . . shall always eat at my table. 3
11 Mephib'osheth ate at David's table 3
13 for he ate always at the king's table. 3
19:28 but you set . . among those who eat at your table. 3
1Kg 2: 7 and let them be among those who eat at your table; 3
4:27 and for all who came to King Solomon's table, each 3
7:48 the golden table for the bread of the Presence 3
10: 5 the food of his table 3
13:20 as they sat at the table, the word of the LORD came 3
18:19 prophets of Ashe'rah, who eat at Jez'ebel's table. 3
2Kg 4:10 put there for him a bed, a table, a chair, and a lamp 3
25:29 he dined regularly at the king's table; •
1Ch 28:16 weight of gold for each table for the showbread 3
16 the silver for the silver tables 3
2Ch 4: 8 made ten tables, and placed them in the temple 3
19 altar, the tables for the bread of the Presence 3
9: 4 food of his table, the seating of his officials 3
13:11 set out the showbread on the table of pure gold 3
29:18 the table for the showbread and all its utensils. 3
Neh 5:17 there were at my table 150 men, Jews and officials 3
Job 36:16 what was set on your table was full of fatness. 3
Ps 23: 5 Thou preparest a table before me 3
69:22 Let their own table before them become a snare; 3
78:19 Can God spread a table in the wilderness? 3
128: 3 children . . olive shoots around your table. 3
Prv 9: 2 mixed her wine, she has also set her table. 3
Isa 21: 5 They prepare the table, they spread the rugs 3
28: 8 For all tables are full of vomit 3
65:11 who set a table for Fortune and fill cups 3
Jer 52:33 he dined regularly at the king's table; •
Ezk 23:41 a stately couch, with a table spread before it 3
39:20 And you shall be filled at my table with horses 3
40:39 And in the vestibule of the gate were two tables 3
40 the entrance of the north gate were two tables; 3
40 of the vestibule of the gate were two tables. 3
41 Four tables were on the inside 3
41 four tables on the outside of the side of the gate 3
41 eight tables, on which the sacrifices were to be 3
42 there were also four tables of hewn stone 3
43 on the tables the flesh of the offering was to be 3
41:22 This is the table which is before the LORD. 3
44:16 they shall approach my table, to minister to me 3
Dan 11:27 shall speak lies at the same table, but to no avail; 3
Mal 1: 7 By thinking that the LORD'S table may be despised. 3
12 when you say that the LORD'S table is polluted 3
Mat 15:27 crumbs that fall from their master's table. 8
21:12 and he overturned the tables of the money-changers 8
Mrk 7:28 Yes, Lord; yet even the dogs under the table eat 8
11:15 he overturned the tables of the money-changers 8
14:18 as they were at table eating, Jesus said 4
Lke 7:37 he was at table in the Pharisee's house 5
49 Then those who were at table with him began to say 7
16:21 fed with what fell from the rich man's table; 8
22:21 with me on the table. 8
30 you may eat and drink at my table in my kingdom 8
24:30 When he was at table with them, he took the bread 6
Joh 2:15 and overturned their tables 8
12: 2 Laz'arus was one of those at table with him. 4
13:28 no one at the table knew why he said this to him. 4
Act 6: 2 give up preaching the word of God to serve tables. 8
Rom 11: 9 Let their table become a snare and a trap, a pitfall 8
1Co 8:10 man of knowledge, at table in an idol's temple 5
10:21 You cannot partake of the table of the Lord 8
21 table of the Lord and the table of demons. 8
Heb 9: 2 in which were the lampstand and the table 8
2Es 9:19 which is supplied both with an unfailing table 9
AEs 14:17 thy servant has not eaten at Haman's table 8
Sir 6:10 there is a friend who is a table companion 8
14:10 it is lacking at his table. 8
29:26 Come here, stranger, prepare the table 8
31:12 Are you seated at the table of a great man? 8
40:29 When a man looks to the table of another 8
Bel 1:13 beneath the table 8
18 the king looked at the table 8
21 devour what was on the table. 8
1Mc 1:22 He took also the table for the bread of the Presence 8
4:49 the altar of incense, and the table 8

51 They placed the bread on the table 8
3Mc 5:39 the officials who were at table with him 7

table (2) 1. לוּחַ 2. πλάξ

Exd 24:12 I will give you the tables of stone, with the law 1
31:18 gave to Moses . . two tables of the testimony 1
18 tables of the testimony, tables of stone, written 1
32:15 with the two tables of the testimony in his hands 1
15 tables that were written on both sides; 1
16 the tables were the work of God, and the writing 1
16 the writing of God, graven upon the tables. 1
19 he threw the tables out of his hands and broke 1
34: 1 The LORD said to Moses, "Cut two tables of stone 1
1 I will write upon the tables the words 1
1 were on the first tables, which you broke. 1
4 Moses cut two tables of stone like the first; 1
4 and took in his hand two tables of stone. 1
28 he wrote upon the tables the words 1
29 with the two tables of the testimony in his hand 1
Deu 4:13 wrote them upon two tables of stone. 1
5:22 wrote them upon two tables of stone, and gave them 1
9: 9 up the mountain to receive the tables of stone 1
9 to receive . . the tables of the covenant 1
10 LORD gave me the two tables of stone written 1
11 at the end . . LORD gave me the two tables of stone 1
11 two tables of stone, the tables of the covenant. 1
15 two tables of the covenant were in my two hands. 1
17 I took hold of the two tables, and cast them out 1
10: 1 Hew two tables of stone like the first, and come up 1
2 I will write on the tables the words 1
2 write . . the words that were on the first tables 1
3 I made an ark . . and hewed two tables of stone 1
3 up the mountain with the two tables in my hand. 1
4 he wrote on the tables . . the ten commandments 1
5 put the tables in the ark which I had made; 1
1Kg 8: 9 the two tables of stone which Moses put there 1
2Ch 5:10 except the two tables which Moses put there 1
Heb 9: 4 the tables of the covenant; 2

table *See* service, set, sit, take.

tableland 1. אֶרֶץ מִישׁוֹר 2. מִישׁוֹר

Deu 3:10 all the cities of the tableland and all Gilead 2
4:43 Bezer in the wilderness on the tableland 2
Jos 13: 9 and all the tableland of Med'eba as far as Dibon; 2
16 and all the tableland by Med'eba; 2
17 Heshbon, and all its cities . . in the tableland; 2
21 that is, all the cities of the tableland 2
20: 8 Bezer in the wilderness on the tableland 2
Jer 48:21 Judgment has come upon the tableland, upon Holon 1

tablet 1. גִּלָּיוֹן 2. לוּחַ 3. δέλτος 4. πλάξ

Prv 3: 3 write them on the tablet of your heart. 2
7: 3 write them on the tablet of your heart. 2
Isa 8: 1 Take a large tablet and write upon it 1
30: 8 now, go, write it before them on a tablet 2
Jer 17: 1 it is engraved on the tablet of their heart 2
Hab 2: 2 Write the vision; make it plain upon tablets 2
2Co 3: 3 not on tablets of stone 4
3 but on tablets of human hearts. 4
1Mc 8:22 they wrote in reply, on bronze tablets 3
14:18 they wrote to him on bronze tablets 3
27 they made a record on bronze tablets 3
48 to inscribe this decree upon bronze tablets 3

writing tablet 1. πινακίς 2. buxum

Lke 1:63 he asked for a writing tablet, and wrote, "His name 1
2Es 14:24 prepare for yourself many writing tablets 2

tackle 1. חֶבֶל 2. σκευή

Isa 33:23 Your tackle hangs loose; 1
Act 27:19 they cast out . . the tackle of the ship. 2

tail 1. זָנָב 2. οὐρά

Exd 4: 4 Put out your hand, and take it by the tail 1
Deu 28:13 LORD will make you the head, and not the tail; 1
44 he shall be the head, and you shall be the tail. 1
Jdg 15: 4 he turned them tail to tail, and put a torch 1
4 he turned them tail to tail, and put a torch 1
4 and put a torch between each pair of tails. 1
Job 40:17 He makes his tail stiff like a cedar; 1
Isa 9:14 So the LORD cut off from Israel head and tail 1
15 and the prophet who teaches lies is the tail; 1
19:15 nothing for Egypt which head or tail . . may do. 1
Rev 9:10 They have tails like scorpions, and stings 2
10 power of hurting men . . lies in their tails. 2
19 power . . is in their mouths and in their tails; 2
19 their tails are like serpents, with heads 2
12: 4 His tail swept down a third of the stars of heaven 2

fat tail 1. אַלְיָה

Exd 29:22 take the fat of the ram, and the fat tail 1
Lev 3: 9 he shall offer its fat, the fat tail entire 1
7: 3 all its fat shall be offered, the fat tail 1
8:25 Then he took the fat, and the fat tail, and all 1
9:19 the fat of the ox and of the ram, the fat tail 1

take 1. אחז 2. אסף 3. אצל 4. בוא 5. בזז 6. בְּיַד
7. גוח 8. גזה 9. גרע 10. היה לְ 11. הלך 12. חזק
13. חלק 14. חצק 15. חשב 16. חתה 17. יצא 18. ישב
19. לכד 20. לקח 21. מִקָּח 22. נדר 23. נכה 24. נצל
25. נשא 26. נתן 27. סור 28. ספר 29. עבר 30. עלה
31. עמד 32. עשה 33. עַתִּיק 34. צעד 35. קבל 36. רדה
37. רום 38. שום 39. שבה 40. שְׁבִי 41. שׁוב 42. שית
43. תמך 44. תפש 45. נפק (A) 46. נשא (A)
47. עדא (A) 48. ἄγω 49. αἴρω 50. αἰχμαλωτεύω
51. ἀνάγω 52. ἀναλαμβάνω 53. ἀπάγω 54. ἀπαίρω
55. ἀποκαθίστημι 56. ἀποφέρω 57. ἀφαιρέω
58. ἀφίστημι 59. ἀφορίζω 60. βαστάζω 61. γίνομαι
62. δέχομαι 63 διά 64. διαδίδωμι 65. ἑδράζω
66. εἰσάγω 67. ἐκβάλλω 68. ἐκδέχομαι 69. ἐξαίρω
70. ἐπί 71. ἐπιλαμβάνω 72. ἐσθίω 73. ἔχω 74. ἵστημι
75. κατακρατέω 76. καταλαμβάνω 77. κατέχω
78. κομίζω 79. κρατέω 80. κτάομαι 81. λαμβάνω
82. λῆμψις 83. μετάθεσις 84. μεταλαμβάνω
85. μετατίθημι 86. παραλαμβάνω 87. πιάζω
88. πίπτω 89. ποιέω 90. προαιρέω
91. προκαταλαμβάνω 92. προσάγω 93. προσέρχομαι
94. προσλαμβάνω 95. προσφέρω 96. συλλαμβάνω
97. συμπαραλαμβάνω 98. τίθημι 99. τρέπω
100. ὑπολαμβάνω 101. φέρω 102. χράομαι
103. accipio 104. aufero 105. transfero

Gen 2:15 God took the man and put him in the garden 20
21 and while he slept took one of his ribs 20
22 rib which the LORD God had taken from the man 20
23 Woman, because she was taken out of Man. 20
3: 6 make one wise, she took of its fruit and ate; 20
19 return to the ground, for out of it you were taken; 20
22 put forth his hand and take also of the tree 20
23 sent . . to till the ground from which he was taken. 20
4:19 Lamech took two wives; the name of the one 20
5:24 with God; and he was not, for God took him. 20
6: 2 and they took to wife such of them 20
21 take with you every sort of food that is eaten 20
7: 2 Take with you seven pairs of all clean animals 20
8: 9 he put forth his hand and took her 20
20 Noah . . took of every clean animal 20
9:23 Then Shem and Japheth took a garment 20
11:29 Abram and Nahor took wives; 20
31 Terah took Abram his son and Lot the son of Haran 20
12: 5 Abram took Sar'ai his wife, and Lot 20
15 And the woman was taken into Pharaoh's house. 20
19 so that I took her for my wife? 20
19 Now then, here is your wife, take her, and be gone. 20
13: 9 If you take the left hand •
9 or if you take the right hand •
14:11 the enemy took all the goods of Sodom 20
12 they also took Lot, the son of Abram's brother 20
21 Give me the persons, but take the goods 20
23 that I would not take a thread or a sandal-thong 20
24 let Aner, Eshcol, and Mamre take their share. 20
24 let Aner, Eshcol, and Mamre take their share. 20
16: 3 Sar'ai, Abram's wife, took Hagar the Egyptian 20
17:23 Then Abraham took Ish'mael his son 20
18: 7 Abraham ran to the herd, and took a calf 20
8 Then he took curds, and milk, and the calf 20
19:15 angels urged Lot, saying, "Arise, take your wife 20
20: 2 And Abim'elech king of Gerar sent and took Sarah. 20
3 woman whom you have taken; for she is a man's wife. 20
14 Then Abim'elech took sheep and oxen 20
21:14 Abraham . . took bread and a skin of water 20
21 and his mother took a wife for him from the land 20
27 Abraham took sheep and oxen and gave them 20
30 These seven ewe lambs you will take from my hand 20
22: 2 He said, "Take your son, your only son Isaac 20
3 saddled his ass, and took two of his young men 20
6 Abraham took the wood of the burnt offering 20
6 on Isaac his son and he took in his hand the fire 20
10 put forth his hand, and took the knife to slay 20
13 and Abraham went and took the ram 20
24: 3 you will not take a wife for my son 20
4 to my kindred, and take a wife for my son Isaac. 20
7 the God of heaven, who took me from my father's 20
7 you shall take a wife for my son from there. 20
10 Then the servant took ten of his master's camels 20
10 departed, taking all sorts of choice gifts 6
22 the man took a gold ring weighing a half shekel 20
37 You shall not take a wife for my son 20
38 to my kindred, and take a wife for my son.' 20
40 and you shall take a wife for my son 20
48 the right way to take the daughter of my master's 20
51 Behold, Rebekah is before you, take her and go 20
61 thus the servant took Rebekah, and went his way. 20
65 she took her veil and covered herself. 20
67 Isaac brought her into the tent, and took Rebekah 20
25: 1 Abraham took another wife, whose name was 20
20 Isaac was 40 years old when he took to wife Rebekah 20
26:34 When Esau was 40 years old, he took to wife Judith 20
27: 3 Now then, take your weapons, your quiver 25
14 he went and took them and brought them 20
15 Then Rebekah took the best garments of Esau 20
28: 2 take as wife from there one of the daughters 20
6 away to Paddan-aram to take a wife from there 20
9 Esau went to Ish'mael and took to wife 20
11 Taking one of the stones of the place 20
18 he took the stone which he had put under his head 20
29:23 in the evening he took his daughter Leah 20
30: 9 she took her maid Zilpah and gave her to Jacob 20
37 Then Jacob took fresh rods of poplar and almond 20
31: 1 Jacob has taken all that was our father's; 20
23 he took his kinsmen with him and pursued him 20
32 point out what I have that is yours, and take it. 20
34 Rachel had taken the household gods 20
45 Jacob took a stone, and set it up as a pillar. 20
46 and they took stones, and made a heap; 20
50 or if you take wives besides my daughters 20
32:13 he lodged there that night, and took 20
22 The same night he arose and took his two wives 20
23 He took them and sent them across the stream 20
33:11 Thus he urged him, and he took it. 20
34: 9 and take our daughters for yourselves. 20
16 we will take your daughters to ourselves 20
17 then we will take our daughter 20
21 let us take their daughters in marriage 20
25 Dinah's brothers, took their swords and came upon 20
26 his son Shechem with the sword, and took Dinah out 20
28 they took their flocks and their herds 20
36: 2 Esau took his wives from the Canaanites 20
6 Then Esau took his wives, his sons, his daughters 20
37:21 saying, "Let us not take his life. 23
24 they took him and cast him into a pit. 20
28 shekels of silver; and they took Joseph to Egypt. 4
31 Then they took Joseph's robe, and killed a goat 20
38: 6 Judah took a wife for Er his first-born 20
28 a hand; and the midwife took and bound on his hand 20
39:20 Joseph's master took him and put him 20
40:11 Pharaoh's cup was in my hand; and I took the grapes 20
41:42 Then Pharaoh took his signet ring from his hand 27
42:24 he took Simeon from them and bound him before 20
30 The man . . took us to be spies of the land. 26
33 and take grain for the famine of your households 20
36 is no more, and now you would take Benjamin; 20
43:11 then do this: take some of the choice fruits 20
12 Take double the money with you; 20
13 Take also your brother, and arise, go again 20
15 the men took the present, and they took double 20
15 the present, and they took double the money 20
34 Portions were taken to them from Joseph's table 25
44:29 If you take this one also from me, and harm befalls 20
45:18 take your father and your households, and come 20
19 Do this: take wagons from the land of Egypt 20
46: 6 They also took their cattle and their goods 20
47: 2 from among his brothers he took five men 20
48: 1 he took with him his two sons 20
13 Joseph took them both, E'phraim in his right hand 20
17 he took his father's hand, to remove it 43
22 one mountain slope which I took from the hand 20
Exd 2: 3 she took for him a basket made of bulrushes 20
9 So the woman took the child and nursed him. 20
4: 4 Put out your hand, and take it by the tail 1
9 you shall take some water from the Nile and pour 20
9 and the water which you shall take from the Nile 20
17 you shall take in your hand this rod 20
20 So Moses took his wife and his sons and set them 20
20 and in his hand Moses took the rod of God. 20
25 Then Zippo'rah took a flint and cut off her son's 20
6: 7 I will take you for my people, and I will be your God; 20
20 Amram took to wife Joch'ebed his father's sister 20
23 Aaron took to wife Eli'sheba, the daughter 20
25 Elea'zar . . took to wife one of the daughters 20
7: 9 you shall say to Aaron, 'Take your rod and cast it 20
15 Go . . take in your hand the rod which was turned 20
19 Say to Aaron, 'Take your rod and stretch out 20
9: 8 to Moses and Aaron, "Take handfuls of ashes 20
10 So they took ashes from the kiln, and stood before 20
10:26 cattle . . we must take of them to serve the LORD 20
12: 3 they shall take every man a lamb according 20
4 neighbor next to his house shall take according 20
5 you shall take it from the sheep or from the goats; 20
7 Then they shall take some of the blood, and put it 20
22 Take a bunch of hyssop and dip it in the blood 20
32 Take your flocks and your herds, as you have said 20
34 So the people took their dough before it was 25
13:19 Moses took the bones of Joseph with him; 20
14: 6 his chariot and took his army with him 20
7 and took 600 picked chariots 20
15:20 Miriam . . took a timbrel in her hand; 20
16:16 you shall take an omer apiece, according 20
33 Moses said to Aaron, "Take a jar, and put an omer 20
17: 5 Pass on before the people, taking with you some 20
5 and take in your hand the rod with which you 20
12 so they took a stone and put it under him, and he sat 20
18: 2 Jethro, Moses' father-in-law, had taken Zippo'rah 20
20: 7 You shall not take the name of the LORD your God 25
7 hold him guiltless who takes his name in vain. 25
21:10 If he takes another wife to himself, he shall not 20
14 you shall take him from my altar, that he may die. 20
23: 8 you shall take no bribe, for a bribe blinds 20
24: 6 Moses took half of the blood and put it in basins 20
7 Then he took the book of the covenant, and read it 20
8 Moses took the blood and threw it upon the people 20
25: 2 Speak to the people of Israel, that they take 20
15 they shall not be taken from it. 27

28: 9 you shall take two onyx stones, and engrave 20
29: 1 Take one young bull and two rams without blemish 20
5 you shall take the garments, and put on Aaron 20
7 you shall take the anointing oil 20
12 shall take part of the blood of the bull and put it 20
13 you shall take all the fat that covers 20
15 Then you shall take one of the rams 20
16 you shall slaughter the ram, and shall take 20
19 You shall take the other ram; 20
20 you shall kill the ram, and take part of its blood 20
21 Then you shall take part of the blood 20
22 You shall also take the fat of the ram 20
25 Then you shall take them from their hands 20
26 you shall take the breast of the ram 20
31 You shall take the ram of ordination 20
30:16 you shall take the atonement money 20
23 Take the finest spices: of liquid myrrh 20
34 the LORD said to Moses, "Take sweet spices, stacte 20
32:20 he took the calf which they had made, and burnt it 20
33: 7 Now Moses used to take the tent and pitch it 20
34: 4 and took in his hand two tables of stone. 20
16 you take of their daughters for your sons 20
35: 5 Take from among you an offering to the LORD; 20
40: 9 Then you shall take the anointing oil, and anoint 20
20 he took the testimony and put it into the ark 20
Lev 2: 9 the priest shall take from the cereal offering 37
4: 5 the anointed priest shall take some of the blood 20
8 all the fat . . he shall take from it 37
10 just as these are taken from the ox 37
19 all its fat he shall take from it and burn 37
25 Then the priest shall take some of the blood 20
30 the priest shall take some of its blood 20
34 Then the priest shall take some of the blood 20
6:15 one shall take from it a handful of the fine flour 37
7:34 the thigh that is offered I have taken 20
8: 2 Take Aaron and his sons with him, and the garments 20
10 The Moses took the anointing oil, and anointed 20
15 Moses killed it, and took the blood 20
16 he took all the fat that was on the entrails 20
23 Moses killed it, and took some of its blood 20
25 Then he took the fat, and the fat tail, and all 20
26 he took one unleavened cake, and one cake of bread 20
28 Then Moses took them from their hands, and burned 20
29 Moses took the breast, and waved it for a wave 20
30 Then Moses took some of the anointing oil 20
33 for it will take seven days to ordain you •
9: 2 Take a bull calf for a sin offering, and a ram 20
3 say to the people of Israel, 'Take a male goat 20
15 took the goat of the sin offering 20
10: 1 the sons of Aaron, each took his censer 20
12 Take the cereal offering that remains 20
12: 8 then she shall take two turtledoves or two young 20
14: 4 the priest shall command them to take for him 20
6 He shall take the living bird with the cedarwood 20
10 on the eighth day he shall take two male lambs 20
12 the priest shall take one of the male lambs 20
14 The priest shall take some of the blood 20
15 Then the priest shall take some of the log of oil 20
21 shall take one male lamb for a guilt offering 20
24 priest shall take the lamb of the guilt offering 20
25 the priest shall take some of the blood 20
42 then they shall take other stones and put them 20
42 shall take other plaster and plaster the house 20
49 he shall take two small birds 20
51 shall take the cedarwood and the hyssop 20
15:14 on the eighth day he shall take two turtledoves 20
29 on the eighth day she shall take two turtledoves 20
16: 5 he shall take from the congregation 20
7 Then he shall take the two goats, and set them 20
12 he shall take a censer full of coals of fire 20
14 he shall take some of the blood of the bull 20
18 and shall take some of the blood of the bull 20
18:17 you shall not take her son's daughter 20
18 you shall not take a woman as a rival wife 20
20:14 If a man takes a wife and her mother also 20
17 If a man takes his sister, a daughter of his father 20
21 If a man takes his brother's wife, it is impurity 20
21:13 he shall take a wife in her virginity 20
14 but he shall take to wife a virgin 20
23:40 you shall take on the first day the fruit 20
24: 5 you shall take fine flour, and bake twelve cakes 20
25:36 Take no interest from him or increase 20
Num 1:17 Moses . . took these men who have been named 20
3:12 Behold, I have taken the Levites from among 20
40 taking their number by names. 25
41 you shall take the Levites for me–I am the LORD 20
45 Take the Levites instead of all the first-born 20
47 you shall take five shekels apiece; 20
47 by the shekel of the sanctuary . . you shall take 20
49 Moses took the redemption money from those 20
50 he took the money, 1,365 shekels 20
4: 9 take a cloth of blue, and cover the lampstand 20
12 they shall take all the vessels of the service 20
5:13 no witness . . since she was not taken in the act; 44
17 priest shall take holy water in an earthen 20
17 priest shall . . take some of the dust that is 20
25 priest shall take the cereal offering 20
6:18 shall take the hair from his consecrated head 20
19 the priest shall take the shoulder of the ram 20

21 in accordance with the vow which he takes 22
7: 6 Moses took the wagons and the oxen, and gave them 20
8: 6 Take the Levites from among the people of Israel 20
8 them take a young bull and its cereal offering 20
8 take another young bull for a sin offering. 20
16 I have taken them for myself. 20
18 taken the Levites instead of all the first-born 20
11:17 I will take some of the spirit which is upon you 3
25 LORD . . took some of the spirit that was upon him 3
16: 2 took men; and they rose up before Moses 20
6 Do this: take censers, Korah and all his company; 20
15 I have not taken one ass from them, and I have not 25
17 let every one of you take his censer 20
18 every man took his censer, and they put fire 20
39 Elea'zar the priest took the bronze censers 20
46 Take your censer, and put fire therein from off 20
47 Aaron took it as Moses said, and ran into the midst 20
17: 9 they looked, and each man took his rod. 20
18: 6 behold, I have taken your brethren the Levites 20
26 When you take from the people of Israel the tithe 20
19: 3 she shall be taken outside the camp 17
4 Elea'zar the priest shall take some of her blood 20
6 priest shall take cedarwood and hyssop 20
17 For the unclean they shall take some ashes 20
18 then a clean person shall take hyssop, and dip it 20
20: 8 Take the rod, and assemble the congregation 20
9 Moses took the rod from before the LORD 20
25 Take Aaron and Elea'zar his son, and bring them up 20
21:25 Israel took all these cities, and Israel settled 20
26 taken all his land out of his hand 20
32 sent to spy out Jazer; and they took its villages 19
22:41 on the morrow Balak took Balaam and brought him 20
23:11 I took you to curse my enemies, and behold 20
14 he took him to the field of Zophim, to the top 20
27 Come now, I will take you to another place; 20
28 Balak took Balaam to the top of Pe'or 20
25: 4 Take all the chiefs of the people, and hang them 20
7 Phin'ehas . . took a spear in his hand 20
26: 4 Take a census of the people, from twenty years old •
27:18 Take Joshua the son of Nun . . and lay your hand 20
22 took Joshua and caused him to stand 20
31:11 took all the spoil and all the booty, both of man 20
26 Take the count of the booty that was taken 25
26 Take the count of the booty that was taken 40
29 take it from their half, and give it to Elea'zar 20
30 from . . Israel's half you shall take one 20
32 remaining of the spoil that the men of war took 5
47 from . . Israel's half Moses took one of every fifty 20
32:39 sons of Machir . . went to Gilead and took it 19
41 Ja'ir . . of Manas'seh went and took their villages 19
42 Nobah went and took Kenath and its villages 19
34:18 You shall take one leader of every tribe 20
35: 8 from the larger tribes you shall take many •
36: 3 inheritance will be taken from the inheritance 9
4 inheritance will be taken from the inheritance 9
Deu 1:15 So I took the heads of your tribes 20
23 I took twelve men of you, one man for each tribe; 20
25 took in their hands some of the fruit of the land 20
3: 4 we took all his cities at that time . . 60 cities 19
4 there was not a city which we did not take 20
8 took the land at that time out of the hand 20
14 Ja'ir the Manas'site took all the region of Argob 20
4: 2 You shall not add to the word . . nor take from it; 9
20 LORD has taken you, and brought you forth 20
34 has any god ever attempted to go and take a nation 20
5:11 not take the name of the LORD your God in vain 25
11 not hold him guiltless who takes his name in vain. 25
7: 3 not . . taking their daughters for your sons. 20
25 not covet the silver or the gold . . or take it 20
9:21 Then I took the sinful thing, the calf 20
10:17 God, who is not partial and takes no bribe. 20
12:26 take, and you shall go to the place which the LORD 25
32 to do; you shall not add to it or take from it. 9
15:17 take an awl, and thrust it through his ear 20
16:19 not take a bribe, for a bribe blinds the eyes 20
20: 7 betrothed a wife and has not taken her? 20
7 die in the battle and another man take her.' 20
19 making war against it in order to take it 44
21: 3 elders of the city . . shall take a heifer 20
11 desire for her and would take her . . as wife 20
22: 6 you shall not take the mother with the young; 20
7 let the mother go, but the young you may take 20
13 If a man takes a wife, and goes in to her 20
14 I took this woman, and when I came near her 20
15 the father . . shall take and bring out 20
18 elders of that city shall take the man and whip 20
30 A man shall not take his father's wife 20
24: 1 When a man takes a wife and marries her 20
3 the latter husband dies, who took her to be his wife 20
4 husband . . may not take her again to be his wife 20
5 year, to be happy with his wife whom he has taken. 20
25: 5 husband's brother shall . . take her as his wife 20
7 if the man does not wish to take his brother's wife 20
8 if he persists, saying, 'I do not wish to take her,' 20
26: 2 take some of the first of all the fruit 20
4 priest shall take the basket from your hand 20
27:25 'Cursed be he who takes a bribe to slay an innocent 20
29: 8 took their land, and gave it for an inheritance 20
31:26 Take this book of the law, and put it by the side 20

32:41 I will take vengeance on my adversaries 41
43 for he . . takes vengeance on his adversaries 41
Jos 2: 4 the woman had taken the two men and hidden them; 20
3:12 Now . . take twelve men from the tribes of Israel 20
4: 2 Take twelve men from the people, from each . . a man 20
3 Take twelve stones from here out of the . . Jordan 25
20 twelve stones, which they took out of the Jordan 20
6:18 lest . . you take any of the devoted things 20
20 the people went up into . . and they took the city. 19
7: 1 Achan . . of Judah, took some of the devoted things; 20
11 they have taken some of the devoted things; 20
14 the tribe which the LORD takes shall come near 19
14 the family which the LORD takes shall come near 19
14 the household which the LORD takes shall come 19
15 he who is taken with the . . things shall be burned 19
16 and the tribe of Judah was taken; 19
17 and the family of the Zer'ahites was taken; 19
17 he brought near the family . . and Zabdi was taken; 19
18 and Achan the son of Carmi . . of Judah, was taken. 19
21 when I saw . . then I coveted them, and took them; 20
23 they took them out of the tent and brought them 20
24 Joshua . . took Achan the son of Zerah 20
8: 1 take all the fighting men with you, and arise 20
8 And when you have taken the city 44
12 he took about 5,000 men, and set them in ambush 20
19 they ran and entered the city and took it; 19
21 all Israel saw that the ambush had taken the city 19
23 But the king of Ai they took alive, and brought him 44
9: 4 and took worn-out sacks upon their asses 20
11 Take provisions in your hand for the journey 20
10: 1 When Ado'ni-ze'dek . . heard how Joshua had taken Ai 19
28 And Joshua took Makke'dah on that day, and smote it 19
32 and he took it on the second day, and smote it 19
35 and they took it on that day, and smote it 19
37 and took it, and smote it with the edge of the sword 19
39 and he took it with its king and all its towns; 19
42 And Joshua took all these kings and their land 19
11:10 Joshua turned back at that time, and took Hazor 19
12 all the cities . . and all their kings, Joshua took 19
16 Joshua took all that land 20
17 And he took all their kings, and smote them 19
19 was not a city that . . they took all in battle. 20
23 Joshua took the whole land 20
15:16 Whoever smites Kir'iath-se'pher, and takes it 19
17 And Oth'ni-el . . took it; and he gave him Achsah 19
24: 3 I took your father Abraham from beyond the River 20
26 and he took a great stone, and set it up there 20
Jdg 1: 8 Judah fought against Jerusalem, and took it 19
12 He who attacks Kir'iath-se'pher and takes it, I will 19
13 Oth'ni-el the son of Kenaz . . took it; and he gave 19
18 Judah also took Gaza with its territory 19
3: 6 they took their daughters to themselves for wives 20
21 his left hand, took the sword from his right thigh 20
25 roof chamber, they took the key and opened them; 20
4: 6 Go, gather your men at Mount Tabor, taking 10,000 20
21 Ja'el the wife of Heber took a tent peg 20
21 a tent peg, and took a hammer in her hand 38
6:20 to him, "Take the meat and the unleavened cakes 20
25 Take your father's bull . . and pull down 20
26 then take the second bull, and offer it as a burnt 20
27 Gideon took ten men of his servants, and did 20
7: 8 he took the jars of the people from their hands •
25 they took the two princes of Mid'ian, Oreb and Zeeb; 19
8:12 he pursued them and took the two kings of Mid'ian 19
16 he took the elders of the city and he took thorns 20
16 and he took thorns of the wilderness and briers 20
21 he took the crescents that were on the necks 20
9:43 He took his men and divided them into three 20
45 he took the city, and killed the people . . in it; 19
48 Abim'elech took an axe in his hand, and cut down 20
50 and encamped against Thebez, and took it. 19
12: 3 you would not deliver me, I took my life in my hand 38
5 the Gileadites took the fords of the Jordan 19
13:19 So Mano'ah took the kid with the cereal offering 20
14: 3 you must go to take a wife from the uncircumcised 20
8 And after a while he returned to take her; 20
9 that he had taken the honey from the carcass 36
19 took their spoil and gave the festal garments 20
15: 2 sister fairer than she? Pray take her instead. 10
4 Samson . . caught 300 foxes, and took torches; 20
6 because he has taken his wife and given her to his 20
16:12 Deli'lah took new ropes and bound him with them 20
14 Deli'lah took the seven locks of his head and wove •
31 family came down and took him and brought him up 25
17: 2 1,100 pieces of silver which were taken from you 20
2 behold, the silver is with me; I took it. 20
4 his mother took 200 pieces of silver 20
18:17 went up, and entered and took the graven image 20
18 these went . . and took the graven image, the ephod 20
20 he took the ephod, and the teraphim, and the graven 20
24 You take my gods which I made, and the priest, and go 20
27 taking what Micah had made, and the priest who 20
19: 1 who took to himself a concubine from Bethlehem 20
15 no man took them into his house to spend 2
18 to my home; and nobody takes me into his house. 2
29 he took a knife, and . . he divided her, limb by limb 20
20: 6 I took my concubine and cut her in pieces, and sent 1
10 we will take ten men of a 100 throughout all 20
21: 5 they had taken a great oath concerning him who •

22 we did not take for each man . . his wife in battle 20
23 the Benjaminites did so, and took their wives 25
Rut 1: 4 These took Moabite wives; 25
4: 2 he took ten men of the elders of the city, and said 20
13 Bo'az took Ruth and she became his wife; 20
16 Na'omi took the child and laid him in her bosom 20
1Sm 1:13 therefore Eli took her to be a drunken woman. 15
2:14 all . . the fork brought up the priest would take 20
16 burn the fat . . and then take as much as you wish 20
16 must give it now; and if not, I will take it by force. 20
19 make . . a little robe and take it to him each year 30
5: 2 the Philistines took the ark . . and set it up 20
3 So they took Dagon and put him back in his place. 20
6: 7 take and prepare a new cart and two milch cows 20
7 yoke the cows . . but take their calves home 41
8 take the ark of the LORD and place it on the cart 20
10 and took two milch cows and yoked them to the cart 20
7: 9 Samuel took a sucking lamb and offered it 20
12 Then Samuel took a stone and set it up 20
14 cities . . the Philistines had taken from Israel 20
8: 3 they took bribes and perverted justice. 20
11 he will take your sons and appoint them to his 20
13 He will take your daughters to be perfumers 20
14 He will take the best of your fields 20
16 He will take your menservants and maidservants 20
9: 3 Take one of the servants . . and arise, go and look 20
22 Samuel took Saul and his servant and brought 20
10: 1 Samuel took a vial of oil and poured it on his head 20
11: 7 He took a yoke of oxen, and cut them in pieces 20
12: 3 Whose ox have I taken? Or whose ass have I taken? 20
3 Whose ox have I taken? Or whose ass have I taken? 20
3 from whose hand have I taken a bribe 20
4 oppressed us or taken anything from any . . hand. 20
14:32 the people flew upon the spoil, and took sheep 20
41 Jonathan and Saul were taken, but the people 19
42 Saul said, "Cast the lot . . " And Jonathan was taken. 19
47 When Saul had taken the kingship over Israel 19
15: 8 And he took Agag the king of the Amal'ekites alive 44
21 But the people took of the spoil, sheep and oxen 20
16: 2 And the LORD said, "Take a heifer with you, and say 20
13 Then Samuel took the horn of oil, and anointed him 20
20 Jesse took an ass laden with bread 20
23 David took the lyre and played it with his hand; 20
17:17 Take for your brothers an ephah of this . . grain 20
18 also take these ten cheeses to the commander 4
20 David rose . . and took the provisions, and went 25
34 when there came a lion, or a bear, and took a lamb 25
40 Then he took his staff in his hand 20
49 David put his hand in his bag and took out a stone 20
51 and took his sword and drew it . . and killed him 20
54 David took the head of the Philistine 20
57 as David returned . . Abner took him, and brought 20
18: 2 Saul took him . . and would not let him return 20
19: 5 for he took his life in his hand and he slew 38
13 Michal took an image and laid it on the bed 20
14 when Saul sent messengers to take David, she said 20
20 Then Saul sent messengers to take David; 20
20:21 'Look, the arrows are on this side of you, take them,' 20
21: 9 if you will take that, take it 20
9 if you will take that, take it 20
12 And David took these words to heart 38
24: 2 Then Saul took 3,000 chosen men out of all Israel 20
11 though you hunt my life to take it. 20
25:11 Shall I take my bread and my water 20
18 Ab'igail made haste, and took 200 loaves 20
40 David has sent us . . to take you to him as his wife. 20
43 David also took Ahin'o-am of Jezreel; 20
26:11 but take now the spear that is at his head 20
12 David took the spear and the jar of water 20
28:21 I have taken my life in my hand, and have hearkened 38
24 killed it, and she took flour, and kneaded it 20
30:16 spoil they had taken from . . the Philistines 20
18 David recovered all . . the Amal'ekites had taken; 20
19 whether . . spoil or anything that had been taken; 20
31: 4 Saul took his own sword, and fell upon it. 20
12 took the body of Saul and the bodies of his sons 20
13 And they took their bones and buried them 20
2Sm 1:10 I took the crown which was on his head 20
2: 8 Abner . . had taken Ish-bo'sheth the son of Saul 20
21 and seize one of the young men, and take his spoil. 20
3:15 Ish-bo'sheth sent, and took her from her husband 20
4: 7 They took his head, and went by the . . Arabah 20
12 they took the head of Ish-bo'sheth, and buried it 20
5: 7 Nevertheless David took the stronghold of Zion 19
13 David took more concubines and wives 20
6:10 David was not willing to take the ark of the LORD 27
7: 8 I took you from the pasture, from following 20
15 but I will not take my steadfast love from him 58
15 take my steadfast love . . as I took it from Saul 27
8: 1 David took Meth'eg-am'mah out of the hand 20
4 David took from him 1,700 horsemen 19
7 David took the shields of gold . . carried 20
8 And from . . King David took very much bronze. 20
10: 4 Hanun took David's servants, and shaved off half 20
11: 4 David sent messengers, and took her; 20
12: 4 and he was unwilling to take one of his own flock 20
4 but he took the poor man's lamb, and prepared it 20
9 You have smitten Uri'ah . . and have taken his wife 20
10 have taken the wife of Uri'ah . . to be your wife. 20
11 and I will take your wives before your eyes 20
26 Jo'ab fought against . . and took the royal city. 19
27 moreover, I have taken the city of waters. 19
28 gather . . and encamp against the city, and take it; 19
28 lest I take the city, and it be called by my name. 19
29 went to Rabbah, and fought against it and took it. 19
30 And he took the crown of their king from his head; 20
13: 8 And she took dough, and kneaded it, and made cakes 20
9 she took the pan and emptied it out before him 20
10 And Tamar took the cakes she had made 20
20 he is your brother; do not take this to heart. 42
33 let . . the king so take it to heart as to suppose 38
15:20 Go back, and take your brethren with you; 41
17:19 And the woman took and spread a covering 20
18:14 he took three darts in his hand, and thrust them 20
17 they took Ab'salom, and threw him into a great pit 20
18 Ab'salom . . had taken and set up for himself 20
19:30 Mephib'osheth said . . "Oh, let him take it all 20
20: 3 the king took the ten concubines whom he had left 20
6 take your lord's servants and pursue him 20
9 Jo'ab took Ama'sa by the beard with his right hand 1
21: 8 The king took the two sons of Rizpah 20
10 Then Rizpah the daughter of Ai'ah took sackcloth 20
12 David went and took the bones of Saul 20
22:17 he took me, he drew me out of many waters. 20
23: 6 thorns . . for they cannot be taken with the hand; 20
16 drew water . . and took and brought it to David. 25
24:22 Let my lord . . take and offer up what seems good 20
1Kg 1:33 Take with you the servants of your lord, and cause 20
39 There Zadok . . took the horn of oil from the tent 20
3: 1 he took Pharaoh's daughter, and brought her 20
20 arose at midnight, and took my son from beside me 20
4:15 Ahi'ma-az . . (he had taken Bas'emath the daughter 20
7: 8 daughter whom he had taken in marriage. 20
11:18 took men with them from Paran and came to Egypt 20
31 he said to Jerobo'am, "Take for yourself ten pieces; 20
34 I will not take the whole kingdom out of his hand; 20
35 I will take the kingdom out of his son's hand 20
37 I will take you, and you shall reign 20
14: 3 Take with you ten loaves, some cakes, and a jar 20
15:18 Asa took all the silver and the gold 20
16:18 when Zimri saw that the city was taken, he went 19
31 he took for wife Jez'ebel the daughter of Ethba'al 20
17:19 And he took him from her bosom, and carried him up 20
23 Eli'jah took the child, and brought him down 20
18: 4 Obadi'ah took 100 prophets and hid them 20
26 they took the bull . . and they prepared it 20
31 Eli'jah took twelve stones 20
19:21 and took the yoke of oxen, and slew them, and boiled 20
20:18 If they have come out for peace, take them alive; 44
18 if they have come out for war, take them alive. 44
34 The cities which my father took . . I will restore; 20
21:13 So they took him outside the city, and stoned him 17
22: 3 do not take it out of the hand of the king of Syria? 20
2Kg 2: 8 Eli'jah took his mantle, and rolled it up 20
9 Ask what I shall do for you, before I am taken 20
10 if you see me as I am being taken from you 20
14 Then he took the mantle of Eli'jah that had fallen 20
3:26 he took with him 700 swordsmen to break through 20
27 he took his eldest son who was to reign 20
4: 1 the creditor has come to take my two children 20
29 Gird up your loins, and take my staff . . and go. 20
5: 5 So he went, taking with him ten talents of silver 20
16 And he urged him to take it, but he refused. 20
24 he took them from their hand, and put them 20
6: 7 Take it up." So he reached out his hand and took it. 20
7:12 When they come out . . we shall take them alive 44
13 Let some men take five of the remaining horses 20
14 they took two mounted men, and the king sent them 20
8: 8 Take a present with you and go to meet the man 20
9 Haz'ael went . . and took a present with him 20
15 he took the coverlet and dipped it in water 20
9: 1 Gird up your loins, and take this flask of oil 20
3 Then take the flask of oil, and pour it on his head 20
13 every man . . took his garment, and put it under him 20
17 Joram said, "Take a horseman, and send to meet them 20
10: 6 take the heads of your master's sons, and come to me 20
7 they took the king's sons, and slew them 20
14 they took them alive, and slew them at the pit 44
14 they took them alive, and slew them at the pit 44
11: 2 Jehosh'eba . . took Jo'ash the son of Ahazi'ah 20
19 he took the captains, the Carites, the guards 20
12: 5 let the priests take, each from his acquaintance; 20
7 take no more money from your acquaintances 20
8 priests agreed . . they should take no more money 20
9 priest took a chest, and bored a hole in the lid 20
17 Haz'ael . . fought against Gath, and took it. 19
18 Jeho'ash king of Judah took all the votive gifts 20
13:15 Eli'sha said to him, "Take a bow and arrows"; 20
15 Take a bow and arrows"; so he took a bow and arrows. 20
18 And he said, "Take the arrows"; and he took them. 20
18 And he said, "Take the arrows"; and he took them. 20
25 Jeho'ash the son of Jeho'ahaz took . . the cities 20
25 the cities which he had taken from Jeho'ahaz 20
14: 7 He killed 10,000 E'domites . . and took Sela by storm 44
21 the people . . took Azari'ah, who was sixteen 20
16: 8 Ahaz also took the silver and gold . . and sent 20
9 Assyria marched up against Damascus, and took it 44
18:10 and at the end of three years he took it. 19
10 the sixth year of Hezeki'ah . . Sama'ria was taken. 19
13 came up against all . . and took them. 44
20: 7 take and lay it on the boil, that he may recover. 20
23:16 and he sent and took the bones out of the tombs 20
30 the people . . took Jeho'ahaz the son of Josi'ah 20
24: 7 the king of Babylon had taken all that belonged 20
12 The king of Babylon took him prisoner 20
15 he took into captivity from Jerusalem 11
25: 7 and bound him in fetters, and took him to Babylon. 4
18 the captain of the guard took Serai'ah 20
19 from the city he took an officer . . and five men 20
20 Nebu'zarad'an . . took them, and brought them 20
1Ch 2:23 Geshur and Aram took . . Havvoth-ja'ir, Kenath 20
7:15 Machir took a wife for Huppim and for Shuppim. 20
10: 4 Saul took his own sword, and fell upon it. 20
9 they stripped him and took his head and his armor 25
11: 5 Nevertheless David took the stronghold of Zion 19
18 drew water . . and took and brought it to David. 25
12:19 for the rulers of the Philistines took counsel •
14: 3 David took more wives in Jerusalem 20
17: 7 I took you from the pasture 20
13 I will not take my steadfast love from him 27
13 as I took it from him who was before you 27
18: 1 he took Gath and its villages out of the hand 20
4 And David took from him a 1,000 chariots 19
7 David took the shields of gold 20
8 and from Cun . . David took very much bronze; 20
19: 4 Hanun took David's servants, and shaved them 20
20: 2 David took the crown of their king from his head; 20
21:11 Thus says the LORD, 'Take which you will 35
23 Take it; and let my lord the king do what seems good 20
24 I will not take for the LORD what is yours 25
2Ch 2:17 census of them which David his father had taken; 28
8: 3 Solomon went to Ma'math-zo'bah, and took it. 12
11:18 Rehobo'am took as wife Ma'halath 20
20 After her he took Ma'acah the daughter of Ab'salom 20
21 (he took eighteen wives and 60 concubines 25
12: 4 he took the fortified cities of Judah 19
13:19 pursued Jerobo'am, and took cities from him 19
21 took fourteen wives, and had 22 sons 25
15: 8 from the cities which he had taken 19
17 the high places were not taken out of Israel. 27
16: 2 Then Asa took silver and gold from the treasures 17
6 Then King Asa took all Judah 20
17: 2 cities . . which Asa his father had taken. 19
19: 7 or partiality, or taking bribes. 21
20:25 came to take the spoil from them 5
25 took for themselves until they could carry no 24
25 three days in taking the spoil, it was so much. 5
22:11 Jeho-shab'e-ath . . took Jo'ash . . and stole him away 20
23:20 he took the captains, the nobles, the governors 20
24:11 would come and empty the chest and take it 25
25:12 took them to the top of a rock and threw them down 4
13 killed 3,000 people in them, and took much spoil. 5
26: 1 all the people of Judah took Uzzi'ah 20
28: 8 they also took much spoil from them 5
11 captives from your kinsfolk whom you have taken 39
15 the men . . rose and took the captives 12
18 had taken Beth-she'mesh, Ai'jalon, Gede'roth 19
21 For Ahaz took from the house of the LORD 13
29:16 Levites took it and carried it out to the brook 35
30:16 They took their accustomed posts 31
32:18 in order that they might take the city. 19
33:11 who took Manas'seh with hooks and bound him 19
36: 1 people . . took Jeho'ahaz the son of Josi'ah 20
4 Neco took Jeho'ahaz . . and carried him to Egypt. 20
6 bound him in fetters to take him to Babylon. 11
Ezr 2:61 sons of Barzil'lai (who had taken a wife 20
3: 9 together took the oversight of the workmen 31
5:14 Nebuchadnez'zar had taken out of the temple 45
14 Cyrus the king took out of the temple of Babylon 45
15 Take these vessels, go and put them in the temple 46
6: 5 which Nebuchadnez'zar took out of the temple 45
9: 2 taken some of their daughters to be wives 25
12 neither take their daughters for your sons 25
10:14 all in our cities who have taken foreign wives 18
Neh 5:15 took from them food and wine 20
6:18 Jehoha'nan had taken the daughter of Meshul'lam 20
7:63 Barzil'lai (who had taken a wife of the daughters 20
10:30 not give . . or take their daughters for our sons; 20
13: 6 While this was taking place I was not •
25 not . . take their daughters for your sons 25
Est 2: 8 Esther also was taken into the king's palace 20
13 was given whatever she desired to take with her 4
16 And when Esther was taken to King Ahasu-e'rus 20
3:10 the king took his signet ring from his hand 27
6:10 take the robes and the horse, as you have said 20
11 Haman took the robes and the horse 20
8: 2 his signet ring, which he had taken from Haman 29
Job 1:15 the Sabe'ans fell upon them and took them 20
17 and made a raid upon the camels and took them 20
2: 8 he took a potsherd with which to scrape himself 20
5: 5 the hungry eat, and he takes it even out of thorns; 20
13 He takes the wise in their own craftiness; 19
8:20 nor take the hand of evildoers. 12
13:14 I will take my flesh in my teeth 25
19: 9 my glory, and taken the crown from my head. 27
23:10 But he knows the way that I take; •
28: 2 Iron is taken out of the earth 20

38:20 that you may take it to its territory 20
40:24 Can one take him with hooks, or pierce his nose 20
41: 4 Will he make a covenant with you to take him 20
42: 8 Now therefore take seven bulls and seven rams 20
Ps 7: 7 and over it take thy seat on high. *
10:14 vexation, that thou mayst take it into thy hands; 26
15: 5 and does not take a bribe against the innocent. 20
16: 4 not pour out or take their names upon my lips. 25
18:16 he took me, he drew me out of many waters. 20
22: 9 Yet thou art he who took me from the womb; 7
31:13 together against me, as they plot to take my life. 20
43: 2 For thou art the God in whom I take refuge; *
50:16 or take my covenant on your lips? 25
51:11 take not thy holy Spirit from me. 20
71: 6 thou art he who took me from my mother's womb. 8
78:70 chose David . . and took him from the sheepfolds; 20
119:43 take not the word of truth utterly out of my mouth 24
137: 9 Happy shall he be who takes your little ones 1
139: 9 If I take the wings of the morning and dwell 25
Prv 7: 8 taking the road to her house 34
20 he took a bag of money with him; 20
8:10 Take my instruction instead of silver 20
9:14 she takes a seat on the high places of the town *
16:32 he who rules his spirit than he who takes a city. 19
20:16 Take a man's garment when he has given surety 20
22:27 why should your bed be taken from under you? 20
23: 5 for suddenly it takes to itself wings 32
26:17 like one who takes a passing dog by the ears. 14
27:13 Take a man's garment when he has given surety 20
30:28 lizards you can take in your hands 44
Ecc 3:14 nothing . . added to it, nor anything taken from it; 9
5:15 he shall go . . and shall take nothing for his toil 25
7:26 but the sinner is taken by her. 19
9:12 Like fish which are taken in an evil net 1
Isa 6: 6 burning coal . . taken with tongs from the altar. 20
8: 1 Take a large tablet and write upon it 20
15 they shall be snared and taken. 19
14: 2 the peoples will take them . . to their place 20
20: 1 came to Ashdod and fought against it and took it,- 19
23:16 Take a harp, go about the city, O forgotten harlot! 20
28: 9 weaned from the milk, those taken from the breast? 33
13 be broken, and snared, and taken. 19
19 As often as it passes through it will take you; 20
30:14 sherd . . with which to take fire from the hearth 16
36: 1 all the fortified cities of Judah and took them. 44
38:21 Now Isaiah had said, "Let them take a cake of figs 25
41: 9 you whom I took from the ends of the earth 12
42: 6 I have taken you by the hand and kept you; 12
25 it burned him, but he did not take it to heart. 38
44:15 fuel . . he takes a part of it and warms himself 20
47: 2 Take the millstones and grind meal 20
3 I will take vengeance, and I will spare no man. 20
49:24 Can the prey be taken from the mighty 20
25 Even the captives of the mighty shall be taken 20
51:18 none to take her by the hand among all the sons 14
22 I have taken from your hand the cup of staggering; 20
62: 6 You who put the LORD in remembrance, take no rest *
66:21 some . . I will take for priests and for Levites 20
Jer 2:30 smitten your children, they took no correction; 20
3:14 for I am your master; I will take you, one from a city 20
5: 3 but they refused to take correction. 20
6:11 both husband and wife shall be taken 19
8: 9 be put to shame, they shall be dismayed and taken; 19
13: 4 Take the waistcloth which you have bought 20
6 and take from there the waistcloth 20
7 and dug, and I took the waistcloth from the place 20
16: 2 You shall not take a wife, nor shall you have sons 20
18:22 For they have dug a pit to take me, and laid snares 19
19: 1 and take some of the elders of the people *
20:10 then we can overcome him, and take our revenge 20
25:15 Take from my hand this cup of the wine of wrath 20
17 I took the cup from the LORD'S hand 20
28:10 Then the prophet Hanani'ah took the yoke-bars 20
29: 6 Take wives and have sons and daughters; 20
6 have sons and daughters; take wives for your sons 20
31:32 when I took them by the hand to bring them out 12
32: 3 the king of Babylon, and he shall take it; 19
5 and he shall take Zedeki'ah to Babylon 11
11 Then I took the sealed deed of purchase 20
14 Take these deeds 20
24 siege mounds have come up to the city to take it 19
28 king of Babylon, and he shall take it. 19
34:22 they will fight against it, and take it, and burn it 19
35: 3 So I took Ja-azani'ah the son of Jeremiah 20
36: 2 Take a scroll and write on it all the words 20
14 to say to Baruch, "Take in your hand the scroll 20
14 Baruch the son of Neri'ah took the scroll 20
21 he took it from the chamber of Eli'shama 20
28 Take another scroll and write on it 20
32 Then Jeremiah took another scroll 20
37: 8 they shall take it and burn it with fire. 19
38: 3 of the army of the king of Babylon and be taken. 19
6 they took Jeremiah and cast him into the cistern 20
10 Take three men with you from here 20
11 E'bed-mel'ech took the men with him and went 20
11 and took from there old rags and worn-out clothes 20
28 until the day that Jerusalem was taken. 19
39: 3 When Jerusalem was taken 19
5 when they had taken him, they brought him up 20
7 and bound him in fetters to take him to Babylon. 4
12 Take him, look after him well and do him no harm 20
14 and took Jeremiah from the court of the guard. 20
14 son of Shaphan, that he should take him home. 17
40: 1 when he took him bound in chains 20
2 The captain of the guard took Jeremiah and said 20
10 and dwell in your cities that you have taken. 44
14 has sent Ish'mael . . to take your life? 23
15 Why should he take your life 23
41:12 they took all their men and went to fight 20
16 leaders of the forces with him took all the rest 20
43: 5 the forces took all the remnant of Judah 20
9 Take in your hands large stones, and hide them 20
10 I will send and take Nebuchadrez'zar the king 20
44:12 I will take the remnant of Judah 20
46:11 and take balm, O virgin daughter of Egypt! 20
48: 1 Kiriatha'im is put to shame, it is taken; 19
7 you also shall be taken; 19
41 the cities shall be taken 19
46 for your sons have been taken captive 20
49:29 Their tents and their flocks shall be taken 20
50: 2 proclaim, conceal it not, and say: 'Babylon is taken 19
9 from there she shall be taken. 19
24 I set a snare for you and you were taken, O Babylon 19
51: 8 wail for her! Take balm for her pain; 20
26 No stone shall be taken from you for a corner 20
31 to tell the king of Babylon that his city is taken 19
41 How Babylon is taken 19
56 her warriors are taken, their bows are broken 19
52:11 and the king of Babylon took him to Babylon 4
24 And the captain of the guard took Serai'ah 20
25 from the city he took an officer 20
26 Nebu'zarad'an the captain of the guard took them 20
Lam 4:20 the LORD'S anointed, was taken in their pits 19
Ezk 4: 1 you, O son of man, take a brick and lay it before you 20
3 take an iron plate, and place it as an iron wall 20
9 you, take wheat and barley, beans and lentils 20
5: 1 And you, O son of man, take a sharp sword; 20
1 take balances for weighing, and divide the hair. 20
2 a third part you shall take and strike 20
3 And you shall take from these a small number 20
4 And of these again you shall take some 20
8: 3 the form of a hand, and took me by a lock of my head; 20
10: 6 Take fire from between the whirling wheels 20
7 and took some of it, and put it into the hands 25
7 man clothed in linen, who took it and went out. 20
11:19 I will take the stony heart out of their flesh 27
12:13 my net over him, and he shall be taken in my snare; 44
14: 3 men have taken their idols into their hearts 30
4 Any man . . who takes his idols into his heart 30
7 taking his idols into his heart 30
15: 3 Is wood taken from it to make anything? 20
3 Do men take a peg from it to hang any vessel on? 20
16:16 You took some of your garments 20
17 You also took your fair jewels of my gold 20
18 you took your embroidered garments to cover 20
20 And you took your sons and your daughters 20
39 and take your fair jewels, and leave you naked 20
61 and be ashamed when I take your sisters 20
17: 3 came to Lebanon and took the top of the cedar; 20
5 Then he took of the seed of the land and planted it 20
9 It will not take a strong arm . . to pull it from its *
12 to Jerusalem, and took her king and her princes 20
13 he took one of the seed royal and made a covenant 20
20 he shall be taken in my snare 44
22 I myself will take a sprig from the lofty top 20
18: 8 does not lend at interest or take any increase 20
13 lends at interest, and takes increase; 20
17 takes no interest or increase 20
19: 4 he was taken in their pit; and they brought him 44
5 she took another of her whelps 20
8 their net over him; he was taken in their pit. 44
21:24 you shall be taken in them. 44
22:12 In you men take bribes to shed blood; 20
12 you take interest and increase and make gain 20
25 they have taken treasure and precious things; 20
23:13 that she was defiled; they both took the same way. *
24: 5 Take the choicest one of the flock 20
25 on the day when I take from them their stronghold 20
27: 5 they took a cedar from Lebanon to make a mast 20
33: 2 the people of the land take a man from among them 20
6 and the sword comes, and takes any one of them; 20
15 gives back what he has taken by robbery *
36:24 For I will take you from the nations 20
37:16 Son of man, take a stick and write on it, 'For Judah 20
16 then take another stick and write upon it 20
19 Behold, I am about to take the stick of Joseph 20
21 I will take the people of Israel from the nations 20
39:10 they will not need to take wood out of the field 25
43:20 you shall take some of its blood 20
21 You shall also take the bull of the sin offering 20
45:18 you shall take a young bull without blemish, 20
19 The priest shall take some of the blood 20
46:18 The prince shall not take any of the inheritance 20
Dan 5: 2 vessels . . taken out of the temple in Jerusalem 45
3 vessels which had been taken out of the temple 45
20 deposed . . and his glory was taken from him; 47
11:12 when the multitude is taken, his heart shall be 25
15 siegeworks, and take a well-fortified city. 19
18 face to the coastlands, and shall take many 19
Hos 1: 2 the LORD said to Hose'a, "Go, take to yourself a wife 20
3 he went and took Gomer the daughter of Dibla'im 20
2: 9 Therefore I will take back my grain in its time 20
11: 3 taught E'phraim to walk, I took them up in my arms; 20
14: 2 Take with you words and return to the LORD; 20
Jol 3: 5 For you have taken my silver and my gold 20
Ams 3: 4 cry out from his den, if he has taken nothing? 19
5 a snare spring up . . when it has taken nothing? 19
5:11 the poor and take from him exactions of wheat 20
12 you who afflict the righteous, who take a bribe 20
6:13 Have we not by our own strength taken Karnaim 20
7:15 the LORD took me from following the flock 20
9: 2 dig into Sheol, from there shall my hand take them; 20
3 from there I will search out and take them; 20
Jon 4: 3 now, O LORD, take my life from me, I beseech thee 20
Hab 1:10 for they heap up earth and take it. 19
Hag 2:23 I will take you, O Zerub'babel my servant 20
Zec 5:10 Where are they taking the ephah? 11
6:10 Take from the exiles Heldai, Tobi'jah, and Jedai'ah 20
11 Take from them silver and gold, and make a crown 20
11: 7 I took two staffs; one I named Grace 20
10 I took my staff Grace, and I broke it 20
13 I took the 30 shekels of silver 20
15 Then the LORD said to me, "Take once more 20
14: 1 when the spoil taken from you will be divided *
2 the city shall be taken and the houses plundered 19
21 that all who sacrifice may come and take of them 20
Mat 1:20 do not fear to take Mary your wife, for that 86
24 of the Lord commanded him; he took his wife 86
2:13 Rise, take the child and his mother, and flee 86
14 he rose and took the child and his mother by night 86
20 Rise, take the child and his mother, and go 86
21 he rose and took the child and his mother, and went 86
4: 5 Then the devil took him to the holy city, and set 86
8 Again, the devil took him to a very high mountain 86
5:40 if any one would sue you and take your coat, let him 81
7: 4 'Let me take the speck out of your eye,' 67
5 hypocrite, first take the log out of your own eye 67
5 and then you will see clearly to take the speck 67
8:17 He took our infirmities and bore our diseases. 81
9:25 he went in and took her by the hand 79
10: 9 Take no gold, nor silver, nor copper in your belts 80
38 he who does not take his cross and follow me 81
11:29 Take my yoke upon you, and learn from me 49
12:14 and took counsel against him, how to destroy him. 81
13:31 which a man took and sowed in his field; 81
33 leaven which a woman took and hid 81
14:12 his disciples came and took the body 49
19 and taking the five loaves and the two fish 81
15:26 It is not fair to take the children's bread 81
36 he took the seven loaves and the fish 81
16:22 Peter took him and began to rebuke him, saying 94
17: 1 after six days Jesus took with him Peter 86
25 From whom do kings of the earth take toll 81
27 cast a hook, and take the first fish that comes up 49
27 take that and give it to them for me 81
20:14 Take what belongs to you, and go 49
17 he took the twelve disciples aside 86
21:35 the tenants took his servants and beat one 81
39 they took him and cast him out of the vineyard 81
22:15 Then the Pharisees went and took counsel 81
24:17 to take what is in his house; 49
18 to take his mantle. 49
40 one is taken and one is left. 86
41 one is taken and one is left. 86
25: 1 ten maidens who took their lamps 81
3 For when the foolish took their lamps 81
3 they took no oil with them; 81
4 the wise took flasks of oil with their lamps. 81
28 So take the talent from him 49
26:26 as they were eating, Jesus took bread, and blessed 81
26 Take, eat; this is my body. 81
27 he took a cup 81
37 taking with him Peter and the two sons of Zeb'edee 86
52 all who take the sword will perish by the sword. 81
27: 1 elders of the people took counsel against Jesus 81
6 the chief priests, taking the pieces of silver, said 81
7 So they took counsel 81
9 they took the 30 pieces of silver 81
24 took water and washed his hands before the crowd 81
27 Then the soldiers of the governor took Jesus 86
30 took the reed and struck him on the head. 81
48 one of them at once ran and took a sponge 81
59 Joseph took the body 81
28:12 assembled with the elders and taken counsel 81
15 they took the money and did as they were directed; 81
Mrk 1:31 he came and took her by the hand and lifted her up 79
4:36 leaving the crowd, they took him with them 86
5:40 and took the child's father and mother 86
41 Taking her by the hand he said to her, "Tal'itha 79
6: 8 charged them to take nothing for their journey 49
29 they came and took his body, and laid it in a tomb. 49
41 taking the five loaves and the two fish 81
7:27 for it is not right to take the children's bread 81
8: 6 he took the seven loaves 81
23 he took the blind man by the hand 71
32 Peter took him, and began to rebuke him. 94
9: 2 And after six days Jesus took with him Peter 86

27 Jesus took him by the hand and lifted him up 79
36 he took a child, and put him in the midst of them; 81
10:32 taking the twelve again, he began to tell them 86
12: 3 they took him and beat him, and sent him away 81
8 they took him and killed him 81
19 the man must take the wife, and raise up children 81
20 There were seven brothers; the first took a wife 81
21 the second took her, and died, leaving no children; 81
13:15 nor enter his house, to take anything away; 49
16 not turn back to take his mantle. 49
14:22 he took bread, and blessed, and broke it, and gave it 81
22 Take; this is my body. 81
23 he took a cup 81
33 he took with him Peter and James and John 86
15:23 he did not take it. 81
24 to decide what each should take. 49
Lke 4: 9 he took him to Jerusalem 48
5: 5 Master, we toiled all night and took nothing! 81
9 the catch of fish which they had taken; 96
6: 4 took and ate the bread of the Presence 81
8:54 taking her by the hand he called, saying, "Child 79
9: 3 he said to them, "Take nothing for your journey 49
10 he took them and withdrew apart to a city 86
16 taking the five loaves and the two fish 81
28 he took with him Peter and John and James 86
47 he took a child and put him by his side 71
13:19 which a man took and sowed in his garden 81
21 It is like leaven which a woman took and hid 81
14: 4 they were silent. Then he took him and healed him 71
9 will begin with shame to take the lowest place. 77
15:13 and took his journey into a far country *
16: 6 he said to him, 'Take your bill 62
7 He said to him, 'Take your bill, and write 80.' 62
17:34 one will be taken and the other left. 86
35 one will be taken and the other left. 86
18:31 taking the twelve, he said to them, "Behold 86
19:24 Take the pound from him 49
20:28 the man must take the wife and raise up children 81
29 the first took a wife, and died without children; 81
31 the third took her 81
22:17 he took a cup, and when he had given thanks he said 62
17 Take this, and divide it among yourselves; 81
19 he took bread 81
36 let him who has a purse take it, and likewise a bag. 49
24: 1 taking the spices which they had prepared. 101
30 When he was at table with them, he took the bread 81
43 he took it and ate before them. 81
Joh 2: 8 and take it to the steward of the feast. 101
8 to the steward of the feast." So they took it. 101
16 the pigeons, "Take these things away; 49
20 It has taken 46 years to build this temple *
6:11 Jesus then took the loaves 81
21 they were glad to take him into the boat 81
10:17 I lay down my life, that I may take it again. 81
18 No one takes it from me 49
18 I have power to take it again 81
12: 3 Mary took a pound of costly ointment of pure nard 81
6 he used to take what was put into it. 60
13 they took branches of palm trees 81
13:12 When he had . . and taken his garments 81
14: 3 I will come again and will take you to myself 86
16:14 he will take what is mine and declare it to you. 81
15 therefore I said that he will take what is mine 81
22 no one will take your joy from you. 49
17:15 that thou shouldst take them out of the world 49
18:31 Pilate said to them, "Take him yourselves 81
19: 1 Pilate took Jesus and scourged him. 81
6 Pilate said to them, "Take him yourselves 81
17 they took Jesus, and he went out 86
23 they took his garments and made four parts 81
27 the disciple took her to his own home. 81
40 They took the body of Jesus 81
20: 2 They have taken the Lord out of the tomb 49
21:13 Jesus came and took the bread and gave it to them 81
Act 1: 9 a cloud took him out of their sight. 100
20 'His office let another take.' 81
25 to take the place in this ministry 81
3: 7 he took him by the right hand and raised him up; 87
9:19 took food and was strengthened 81
25 his disciples took him by night 81
27 Barnabas took him 71
39 when he had come, they took him to the upper room. 51
15:14 to take out of them a people for his name. 81
37 Barnabas wanted to take with them John 97
38 Paul thought best not to take with them one 97
39 Barnabas took Mark with him 86
16: 3 he took him and circumcised him 81
33 he took them the same hour of the night 86
17: 5 taking some wicked fellows of the rabble 94
9 when they had taken security from Jason 81
18:26 they took him and expounded to him the way of God 94
19: 9 he withdrew . . taking the disciples with him 59
21:11 coming to us he took Paul's girdle 49
24 take these men and purify yourself 86
26 Then Paul took the men 86
32 He at once took soldiers and centurions 86
22: 5 to take those also who were there *
23:17 Take this young man to the tribune 53
18 took him and brought him to the tribune and said 86
19 The tribune took him by the hand 71
31 according to their instructions, took Paul 52
27:17 they took measures to undergird the ship 102
33 Paul urged them all to take some food, saying 84
33 without food, having taken nothing. 94
34 Therefore I urge you to take some food 84
35 when he had said this, he took bread 81
28:15 Paul thanked God and took courage. 81
1Co 6:15 Shall I therefore take the members of Christ 49
11:23 the night when he was betrayed took bread 81
2Co 11:20 if a man . . preys upon you, or takes advantage of you 81
12:18 Did we not take the same steps? *
Eph 6:13 Therefore take the whole armor of God 52
16 besides all these, taking the shield of faith 52
17 take the helmet of salvation 62
Php 2: 7 emptied himself, taking the form of a servant 81
1Th 4: 4 each one of you know how to take a wife for himself 80
Heb 5: 4 one does not take the honor upon himself 81
8: 9 on the day when I took them by the hand 71
9: 7 not without taking blood *
12 taking not the blood of goats and calves 63
19 he took the blood of calves and goats 81
11: 5 he was not found, because God had taken him 85
5 Now before he was taken 83
Jas 5:10 As an example . . brethren, take the prophets 81
Rev 5: 7 he went and took the scroll from the right hand 81
8 when he had taken the scroll 81
9 Worthy . . to take the scroll and to open its seals 81
6: 4 rider was permitted to take peace from the earth 81
8: 5 Then the angel took the censer and filled it 81
10: 8 Go, take the scroll which is open in the hand 81
9 Take it and eat; it will be bitter to your stomach 81
10 took the little scroll from the hand of the angel 81
11:17 hast taken thy great power and begun to reign. 81
22:17 let him who desires take the water of life 81
1Es 1:34 men of the nation took Jeconiah the son of Josiah 52
41 Nebuchadnezzar also took some holy vessels 81
54 they took and carried away to Babylon. 52
3:13 they took the writing and gave it to him 81
4:23 A man takes his sword, and goes out to travel 81
30 take the crown from the king's head 57
44 the vessels that were taken from Jerusalem 81
61 he took the letters, and went to Babylon 81
6:32 a beam should be taken out of his house 81
8:60 the priests and the Levites who took the silver 86
84 do not take their daughters for your sons 81
93 Let us take an oath to the Lord about this 61
95 we are with you to take strong measures. 89
2Es 1:32 but you have taken and slain them 103
9:47 when he grew up and I came to take a wife for him 103
13:40 and they were taken into another land. 105
14:24 and take with you Sarea, Dabria, Selemia, Ethanus 103
32 in due time he took from you what he had given. 104
37 I took the five men, as he commanded me 103
40 I took it and drank; and when I had drunk it 103
Tob 1: 6 Taking the first fruits and the tithes of my produce 73
4:12 First of all take a wife 81
12 all took wives from among their brethren 81
13 by refusing to take a wife for yourself 81
6: 4 take the heart and liver and gall 81
15 to take a wife from among your own people 81
16 you shall take live ashes of incense 81
7:10 for it is your right to take my child 81
12 Take her right now, in accordance with the law 78
13 taking her by the hand he gave her to Tobias 81
13 Here she is; take her according to the law of Moses 78
13 take her with you to your father. 53
14 and took a scroll and wrote out the contract 81
17 she did as he said, and took her there 66
8: 2 he took the live ashes of incense 81
7 I am not taking this sister of mine because of lust 81
21 then he should take half of Raguel's property 81
9: 2 Brother Azarias, take a servant and two camels 81
11: 4 take the gall of the fish with you 81
12: 5 Take half of all that you two have brought back. 81
14: 3 My son, take your sons 81
Jdt 2: 5 take with you men confident in their strength 81
22 From there Holofernes took his whole army 81
3: 6 took picked men from them as his allies. 81
6: 9 hope in your heart that they will not be taken 96
10 to seize Achior and take him to Bethulia 55
11 the slaves took him and led him out of the camp 96
21 took him from the assembly to his own house 86
8: 3 took to his bed and died in Bethulia his city 88
12:19 Then she took and ate and drank before him 81
13:15 Then she took the head out of the bag and showed it 90
14: 1 take this head and hang it upon the parapet 81
2 let every valiant man take his weapons and go out 52
11 every man took his weapons 52
15: 3 Those . . also took to flight 99
11 she took them and loaded her mule 81
12 she took branches in her hands 81
16:19 the canopy which she took for herself 81
AEs 14: 5 didst take Israel out of all the nations 81
15: 2 Then . . she took her two maids with her 86
8 took her in his arms until she came to herself 52
Wis 4: 3 will strike a deep root or take a firm hold. 65
15 nor take such a thing to heart 98
5:17 The Lord will take his zeal as his whole armor 81
19 he will take holiness as an invincible shield 81
8: 2 I desired to take her for my bride 48
9 I determined to take her to live with me 48
13:13 he takes and carves with care in his leisure 81
18 a thing that cannot take a step; 102
14:15 who had been suddenly taken from him 57
19 forced the likeness to take more beautiful form 70
15: 8 this man . . goes to the earth from which he was taken 81
16:21 ministering to the desire of the one who took it 95
Sir 12:12 lest he overthrow you and take your place 74
12 lest he try to take your seat of honor *
14:16 Give, and take, and beguile yourself 81
19:17 let the law of the Most High take its course. *
22 is there prudence where sinners take counsel. *
23:25 Her children will not take root 64
36:18 The stomach will take any food 72
37: 5 in the face of battle take up the shield. 81
42: 7 make a record of all that you give out or take in. 82
44:20 was taken into covenant with him 61
46:19 I have not taken any one's property 81
Bar 1: 2 at the time when the Chaldeans took Jerusalem 81
8 Baruch took the vessels of the house of the Lord 81
2:17 whose spirit has been taken from their bodies 81
3:29 Who has gone up into heaven, and taken her 81
4: 2 Turn, O Jacob, and take her 71
LJr 1: 1 those who were to be taken to Babylon as captives 48
2 you will be taken to Babylon as captives 48
9 People take gold 81
33 The priests take some of the clothing of their gods 57
Sus 1: 2 And he took a wife named Susanna 81
Bel 1:27 Then Daniel took pitch, fat, and hair 81
33 was going into the field to take it to the reapers. 56
34 Take the dinner which you have to Babylon 56
36 angel of the Lord took him by the crown of his head 71
37 Take the dinner which God has sent you. 81
1Mc 1:21 entered the sanctuary and took the golden altar 81
22 He took also the table for the bread of the Presence *
23 He took the silver and the gold 81
23 he took also the hidden treasures which he found. 81
24 Taking them all, he departed to his own land 81
3:12 Judas took the sword of Apollonius 81
15 to take vengeance on the sons of Israel. 89
37 the king took the remaining half of his troops 86
41 they took silver and gold in immense amounts 81
45 Joy was taken from Jacob 69
50 Where shall we take them? 53
4: 1 Now Gorgias took 5,000 infantry 86
47 Then they took unhewn stones, as the law directs 81
5: 8 He also took Jazer and its villages 91
23 Then he took the Jews of Galilee and Arbatta 86
27 take and destroy all these men in one day. 76
28 he took the city 76
35 fought against it and took it 76
36 From there he marched on and took Chaspho 91
44 he took the city 91
6: 3 he came and tried to take the city and plunder it 76
6 spoils which they had taken from the armies 81
8 He took to his bed and became sick from grief 88
26 encamped against the citadel . . to take it 76
33 and took his army by a forced march along the road 54
50 So the king took Beth-zur 76
63 took the city by force. 76
7:24 took vengeance on the men who had deserted 89
38 Take vengeance on this man and on his army 89
8: 7 they took him alive 81
8 took from him and gave to Eumenes the king. 81
9: 2 they took it and killed many people. 91
19 Jonathan and Simon took Judas their brother 49
40 they took all their goods. 81
53 he took the sons of the leading men of the land 81
72 the captives whom he had formerly taken 50
11:24 taking silver and gold and clothing 81
62 took the sons of their rulers as hostages 81
13:25 Simon sent and took the bones of Jonathan 81
14: 2 he sent one of his commanders to take him alive. 96
3 seized him and took him to Arsaces 96
5 To crown all his honors he took Joppa for a harbor 81
15:33 neither taken foreign land nor seized foreign property 81
33 unjustly taken by our enemies. 75
16:16 Ptolemy and his men rose up, took their weapons 81
2Mc 1:19 took some of the fire of the altar 81
2: 1 to take some of the fire 81
4:34 Menelaus, taking Andronicus aside 81
5: 5 Jason took no less than 1,000 men 86
5 at last the city was being taken 76
11 he left Egypt and took the city by storm. 81
16 He took the holy vessels with his polluted hands 81
6: 7 the Jews were taken, under bitter constraint 48
7: 5 the king ordered them to take him to the fire 92
24 he would take him for his friend 73
8:20 destroyed 120,000 and took much booty. 81
10:24 He came on, intending to take Judea by storm. 81
12:16 They took the city by the will of God 76
35 wishing to take the accursed man alive 81
13: 4 he ordered them to take him to Beroea 48
26 Lysias took the public platform 93
14:26 he took the covenant that had been made 81
46 he tore out his entrails, took them with both hands 81
15:16 Take this holy sword, a gift from God 81

3Mc 1: 1 he . . took with him his sister Arsinoe 97
2 Theodotus . . took with him the best of the Ptolemaic 86
5 many captives also were taken. 96
23 They shouted to their fellows to take arms 89
2:28 Those who object to this are to be taken by force 101
3:22 they took this in a contrary spirit 68
4:17 were no longer able to take the census of the Jews 89
6:25 Who . . has taken each man from his home 58
4Mc 3:12 taking a pitcher 81
6:29 take my life in exchange for theirs. 81
151 1: 4 and took me from my father's sheep 49

take *See also* allow.

take a census 1. נשא ראש 2. ספר

Exd 30:12 When you take the census of the people of Israel 1
Num 1: 2 Take a census of all the congregation 1
49 take a census of them among the people of Israel; 1
4: 2 Take a census of the sons of Kohath 1
22 Take a census of the sons of Gershon also 1
26: 2 Take a census of all the congregation 1
2Ch 2:17 Solomon took a census of all the aliens who were 2

take a fifth part 1. חמש

Gen 41:34 and take the fifth part of the produce of the land 1

take a handful 1. קמץ 2. *δράσσομαι*

Lev 2: 2 he shall take from it a handful of the fine flour 1
5:12 the priest shall take a handful of it 1
Num 5:26 priest shall take a handful of the . . offering 1
2Mc 4:41 others took handfuls of the ashes that were lying 2

take a journey 1. נסע

Gen 46: 1 Israel took his journey with all that he had 1
Deu 1: 7 turn and take your journey, and go to the hill 1
2:24 Rise up, take your journey, and go over the valley 1

take a life 1. *ἀποκτείνω* 2. *θανατόω*

Tob 3:15 if it be not pleasing to thee to take my life 1
4Mc 9: 7 if you take our lives because of our religion 2

take a meal 1. *ἀναπίπτω*

Sir 25:18 Her husband takes his meals among the neighbors 1

take a part 1. *παραγίνομαι* 2. *συμμαχέω*

2Ti 4:16 At my first defense no one took my part 1
3Mc 7: 6 always taking their part 2

take a position 1. יצב 2. שׂום 3. *εἰμί*

1Kg 20:12 he said to his men, "Take your positions. 2
12 And they took their positions against the city. 2
2Ch 20:17 take your position, stand still, and see 1
1Mc 6:36 These took their position beforehand 3

take a possession 1. אחז

Jos 22:19 and take for yourselves a possession among us; 1

take a rest 1. שׁכב 2. *ἀναπαύω* 3. *ἡσυχάζω*

2Sm 4: 5 Ish-bo'sheth, as he was taking his noonday rest. 1
Job 11:18 will be protected and take your rest in safety. 1
30:17 the pain that gnaws me takes no rest. 1
Mat 26:45 Are you still sleeping and taking your rest? 2
Mrk 14:41 Are you still sleeping and taking your rest? 2
AEs 12: 1 Now Mordecai took his rest in the courtyard 3

take a right of redemption 1. גאל

Rut 4: 6 Take my right of redemption yourself 1

take a seat 1. ישׁב 2. יתב (A) 3. *ἐγκαθίζω* 4. *καθίζω*

2Sm 19: 8 Then the king arose, and took his seat in the gate. 1
2Kg 11:19 And he took his seat on the throne of the kings. 1
Jer 13:18 to the king and the queen mother: "Take a lowly seat 1
26:10 to the house of the LORD and took their seat 1
Dan 7: 9 one that was ancient of days took his seat; 2
Act 12:21 Herod . . took his seat upon the throne 4
25: 6 the next day he took his seat on the tribunal 4
17 but on the next day took my seat on the tribunal 4
2Th 2: 4 he takes his seat in the temple of God 4
1Es 3:15 he took his seat in the council chamber 4
1Mc 7: 4 Demetrius took his seat upon the throne 4
10:52 and have taken my seat on the throne of my fathers 3
53 we have taken our seat on the throne of his kingdom 4
55 and took your seat on the throne of their kingdom. 4

take a side 1. *φρονέω τά*

1Mc 10:20 to take our side and keep friendship with us. 1
2Mc 1:11 for taking our side against the king. *

take a stand 1. יצב 2. נצב 3. עמד 4. שׁית 5. *ἐμβατεύω* 6. *ἵστημι* 7. *καθίστημι*

Exd 19:17 they took their stand at the foot 1
Num11:16 let them take their stand there with you. 1
22:22 the angel of the LORD took his stand in the way 1
1Sm 17:16 the Philistine came forward and took his stand 1
2Sm 2:25 and took their stand on the top of a hill. 3
20:11 And one of Jo'ab's men took his stand by Ama'sa 3
23:12 But he took his stand in the midst of the plot 1
1Ch 11:14 he took his stand in the midst of the plot 1
Job 33: 5 set your words in order before me; take your stand. 1
Prv 8: 2 in the paths she takes her stand; 2
Isa 22: 7 and the horsemen took their stand at the gates. 4
Ezk 46: 2 and shall take his stand by the post of the gate. 3
Hab 2: 1 I will take my stand to watch 3
Col 2:18 taking his stand on visions 5
Sus 1:48 Taking his stand in the midst of them, he said 6
1Mc 9:11 and took its stand for the encounter 6
2Mc 12:27 young men took their stand before the walls 7

take a station 1. יצב

Jer 46: 4 Take your stations with your helmets 1

take a tenth 1. עשׂר

1Sm 8:15 He will take the tenth of your grain 1
17 He will take the tenth of your flocks 1

take a tithe 1. *ἀποδεκατόω*

Heb 7: 5 to take tithes from the people 1

take a view 1. *φρονέω*

Gal 5:10 you will take no other view than mine 1

take a vow 1. נדר

Num 6:21 This is the law for the Nazirite who takes a vow. 1

take aboard 1. *ἀναλαμβάνω*

Act 20:13 intending to take Paul aboard there 1

take account 1. *διαλογίζομαι* 2. *ἐπιλογίζομαι* 3. *ἡγέομαι*

2Mc 11: 4 He took no account whatever of the power of God 2
12:43 taking account of the resurrection. 1
3Mc 5:42 the king . . took no account of the changes of mind 3

take across 1. עבר 2. transfero

Num32: 5 do not take us across the Jordan. 1
2Es 13:40 he took them across the river 2
40 he took them across the river 2

take action 1. עשׂה 2. *ἐπιτελέω*

Dan 11:30 enraged and take action against the holy 1
32 know their God shall stand firm and take action. 1
1Es 8:95 Arise and take action, for it is your task 2

take advantage 1. *κατασοφίζομαι* 2. *πλεονεκτέω*

2Co 7: 2 we have taken advantage of no one. 2
12:17 Did I take advantage of you 2
18 Did Titus take advantage of you? 2
Jdt 5:11 he took advantage of them 1

take advice 1. זהר 2. יעץ 3. *πείθω*

Prv 13:10 but with those who take advice is wisdom. 2
Ecc 4:13 and foolish king, who will no longer take advice 1
Act 5:40 So they took his advice 3

take again 1. recipio

2Es 2:40 Take again your full number, O Zion 1

take along 1. *παραλαμβάνω* 2. *συμπαραλαμβάνω*

Mat 18:16 if he does not listen, take one or two others along 1
Gal 2: 1 taking Titus along with me 2

take an oath 1. שׁבע 2. *ὄμνυμι* 3. *ὁρκίζω*

Gen 26:31 rose early and took oath with one another; 1
50:25 Then Joseph took an oath of the sons of Israel 1
1Kg 18:10 he would take an oath of the kingdom or nation 1
2Ch 15:14 They took oath to the LORD with a loud voice 1
Ezr 10: 5 So they took the oath. 1
Neh 5:12 took an oath of them to do as they had promised. 1
Isa 65:16 who takes an oath in the land shall swear 1
1Es 8:96 had the leaders . . take oath 3
96 And they took the oath. 2

take as a sign 1. *τερατεύομαι*

3Mc 1:14 it was wrong to take this as a sign in itself. 1

take as booty 1. בזז 2. *σκυλεύω*

Num31: 9 they took as booty all their cattle, their flocks 1
Deu 3: 7 the spoil of the cities we took as our booty 1
20:14 all its spoil, you shall take as booty 1
Jos 8: 2 its spoil and its cattle you shall take as booty 1
27 the spoil of that city Israel took as their booty 1
Jdt 16: 5 and take my virgins as booty. 2

take as captive 1. *αἰχμαλωτίζω*

1Mc 10:33 every one of the Jews taken as a captive 1

take as food 1. ציד

Jos 9:12 when we took it from our houses as our food 1

take as spoil 1. בזז

Deu 2:35 only the cattle we took as spoil for ourselves 1

take aside 1. נטה 2. *ἀπολαμβάνω* 3. *ἐπισπάομαι*

2Sm 3:27 Jo'ab took him aside . . to speak with him 1
6:10 but David took it aside into the house 1
1Ch 13:13 took it aside to the house of O'bed-e'dom 1
Mrk 7:33 taking him aside from the multitude privately 2
2Mc 4:46 taking the king aside into a colonnade 2
6:21 Those . . took the man aside 2
3Mc 3:10 some . . had taken some of them aside privately 3

take away 1. אכל 2. אסף 3. גזל 4. גלה 5. גרע 6. הגה 7. הלך 8. לקח 9. מִן 10. נצל 11. נשׂא 12. סור 13. עבר 14. פרע 15. רום 16. שׁלה 17. עדא (A) 18. *ἄγω* 19. *αἴρω* 20. *ἀνταναιρέω* 21. *ἀπάγω* 22. *ἀπαίρω* 23. *ἀφαίρεσις* 24. *ἀφαιρέω* 25. *ἀφίστημι* 26. *ἐλαττόω* 27. *ἐξαίρω* 28. *καταργέω* 29. *περιαιρέω* 30. *περιελαύνω* 31. aufero 32. exigo

Gen 27:35 Your brother . . has taken away your blessing. 8
36 He took away my birthright; 8
36 behold, now he has taken away my blessing. 8
30:15 a small matter that you have taken away my husband 8
15 Would you take away my son's mandrakes also? 8
23 and said, "God has taken away my reproach"; 2
31: 9 Thus God has taken away the cattle of your father 10
16 property . . God has taken away from our father 10
Exd 2: 9 said to her, "Take this child away, and nurse him 7
5: 4 why do you take the people away from their work? 14
8: 8 Entreat the LORD to take away the frogs from me 12
14:11 you have taken us away to die in the wilderness? 8
23:25 I will take sickness away from the midst of you. 12
33:23 then I will take away my hand, and you shall see 12
Lev 1:16 he shall take away its crop with the feathers 12
3: 4 appendage of the liver which he shall take away 12
9 fat tail . . taking it away close by the backbone 12
10 which he shall take away with the kidneys 12
15 appendage of the liver which he shall take away 12
4: 9 which he shall take away with the kidneys 12
7: 4 appendage of the liver which he shall take away 12
Num21: 7 pray to the LORD, that he take away the serpents 12
27: 4 name of our father be taken away from his family 5
36: 3 so it will be taken away from the lot 9
Deu 7:15 the LORD will take away from you all sickness 12
28:31 your ass shall be violently taken away 3
Jos 7:13 until you take away the devoted things 12
Jdg 11:13 Israel on coming from Egypt took away my land 8
15 Israel did not take away the land of Moab 8
1Sm 17:26 who kills this . . and takes away the reproach 12
21: 6 replaced by hot bread on the day it is taken away. 8
27: 9 but took away the sheep, the oxen, the asses 8
2Sm 14:14 but God will not take away the life of him 11
24:10 I pray thee, take away the iniquity of thy servant; 13
1Kg 2:31 thus take away from me and from my father's house 12
14:26 he took away the treasures of the house 8
26 of the king's house; he took away everything. 8
26 He also took away all the shields of gold 8
15:14 the high places were not taken away. 12
19: 4 It is enough; now, O LORD, take away my life; 8
10 I . . am left; and they seek my life, to take it away. 8
14 I . . am left; and they seek my life, to take it away. 8
20: 6 lay hands on whatever . . and take it away.' 8
41 made haste to take the bandage away from his eyes; 12
22:43 yet the high places were not taken away 12
2Kg 2: 3 the LORD will take away your master from over you? 8
5 the LORD will take away your master from over you? 8
12: 3 the high places were not taken away; 12
15: 4 the high places were not taken away; 12
18:32 I come and take you away to a land like your own 8
20:18 sons, who are born to you, shall be taken away; 8
23:34 But he took Jeho'ahaz away; and he came to Egypt 8
25:14 they took away the pots, and the shovels 8
15 What was of gold the captain . . took away as gold 8
1Ch 10:12 took away the body of Saul and . . of his sons 11
21: 8 I pray thee, take away the iniquity of thy servant; 13
2Ch 12: 9 took away the treasures of the house of the LORD 8
9 he took away everything. 8
9 He also took away the shields of gold 8
14: 3 took away the foreign altars and the high places 12
20:33 The high places, however, were not taken away; 12
30:14 the altars for burning incense they took away 12
32:12 this same Hezeki'ah taken away his high places 12
33:15 he took away the foreign gods and the idol 12
34:33 Josi'ah took away all the abominations 12
35:23 king said . . "Take me away, for I am badly wounded. 13
Job 1:21 the LORD gave, and the LORD has taken away; 8
7:21 thou not pardon . . and take away my iniquity? 13
9:34 Let him take his rod away from me 12
12:20 and takes away the discernment of the elders. 8
24 He takes away understanding from the chiefs 12
27: 2 As God lives, who has taken away my right 12
8 when God cuts him off, when God takes away his life? 16
34: 5 I am innocent, and God has taken away my right; 12
20 the mighty are taken away by no human hand. 12
Ps 104:29 when thou takest away their breath, they die 2
119:22 take away from me their scorn and contempt 4
Prv 1:19 it takes away the life of its possessors. 8
11:30 but lawlessness takes away lives. 8
24:11 Rescue those who are being taken away to death; 8
25: 4 Take away the dross from the silver 6
5 take away the wicked from the presence 6
Sng 5: 7 beat me, they wounded me, they took away my mantle 11
Isa 3: 1 the LORD of hosts, is taking away from Jerusalem 12
18 the Lord will take away the finery of the anklets 12
4: 1 called by your name; take away our reproach. 2
6: 7 your guilt is taken away, and your sin forgiven. 12

16:10 gladness are taken away from the fruitful field; 2
22: 8 He has taken away the covering of Judah. 4
25: 8 the reproach of his people he will take away 12
36:17 and take you away to a land like your own land 8
39: 7 own sons, who are born to you, shall be taken away; 8
52: 5 seeing that my people are taken away for nothing? 8
53: 8 By oppression and judgment he was taken away; 8
57: 1 devout men are taken away, while no one 2
1 For the righteous man is taken away from calamity 2
13 will carry them off, a breath will take them away. 8
58: 9 If you take away from the midst of you the yoke 12
64: 6 and our iniquities, like the wind, take us away. 11
Jer 15:15 In thy forbearance take me not away; 8
16: 5 for I have taken away my peace from this people 2
27:20 Babylon did not take away, when he took into exile 8
28: 3 which Nebuchadnez'zar king of Babylon took away 8
48:33 Gladness and joy have been taken away 2
52:18 they took away the pots, and the shovels 8
19 gold the captain of the guard took away as gold 8
Ezk 3:14 The Spirit lifted me up and took me away 8
17:13 The chief men of the land he had taken away 8
23:26 your clothes and take away your fine jewels. 8
29 and take away all the fruit of your labor 8
24:16 I am about to take the delight of your eyes away 8
33: 4 and the sword comes and takes him away 8
6 that man is taken away in his iniquity 8
38:13 to take away cattle and goods, to seize great 8
42: 5 for the galleries took more away from them 1
Dan 1:16 steward took away their rich food and the wine 11
7:12 rest of the beasts, their dominion was taken away 17
26 dominion shall be taken away, to be consumed 17
8:11 continual burnt offering was taken away 15
11:31 shall take away the continual burnt offering. 12
12:11 time that the . . burnt offering is taken away 12
Hos 2: 9 and I will take away my wool and my flax 10
4: 3 and even the fish of the sea are taken away. 2
11 Wine and new wine take away the understanding. 8
13:11 and I have taken them away in my wrath. 8
14: 2 say to him, "Take away all iniquity; 11
Ams 4: 2 when they shall take you away with hooks 11
5:23 Take away from me the noise of your songs; 12
Mic 1:11 the wailing of Beth-e'zel shall take away from you 8
2: 2 and seize them; and houses, and take them away; 11
9 from their young children you take away my glory 8
Zep 3:15 LORD has taken away the judgments against you 12
Zec 3: 4 Behold, I have taken your iniquity away from you 13
9: 7 I will take away its blood from its mouth 12
Mat 9:15 the bridegroom is taken away from them 22
13:12 even what he has will be taken away. 19
21:43 the kingdom of God will be taken away from you 19
25:29 even what he has will be taken away. 19
Mrk 2:20 when the bridegroom is taken away from them 22
4:15 takes away the word which is sown in them. 19
25 even what he has will be taken away. 19
Lke 1:25 to take away my reproach among men. 24
5:35 when the bridegroom is taken away from them 22
6:29 from him who takes away your coat 19
30 of him who takes away your goods 19
8:12 then the devil comes and takes away the word 19
18 what he thinks that he has will be taken away. 19
10:42 which shall not be taken away from her. 24
11:22 he takes away his armor in which he trusted 19
52 you have taken away the key of knowledge 19
16: 3 since my master is taking the stewardship away 24
17:31 let him . . not come down to take them away 19
19:26 even what he has will be taken away. 19
Joh 1:29 who takes away the sin of the world! 19
11:39 Jesus said, "Take away the stone. 19
41 they took away the stone 19
15: 2 Every branch . . he takes away 19
19:31 and that they might be taken away. 19
38 that he might take away the body of Jesus 19
38 So he came and took away his body. 19
20: 1 the stone had been taken away from the tomb. 19
13 Because they have taken away my Lord 19
15 and I will take him away. 19
Act 20:12 they took the lad away alive 18
Rom11:27 my covenant with them when I take away their sins. 24
2Co 3:14 because only through Christ is it taken away. 28
Heb 10: 4 the blood of . . goats should take away sins. 24
11 which can never take away sins. 29
1Jn 3: 5 You know that he appeared to take away sins 19
Rev 22:19 if any one takes away from the words of the book 24
19 God will take away his share in the tree of life 24
1Es 1:30 Take me away from the battle, for I am very weak. 25
40 took him away to Babylon. 21
2Es 3:20 didst not take away from them their evil heart 31
7:135because he would rather give than take away; 32
AEs 16: 4 not only take away thankfulness from among men 20
Wis 18: 5 thou didst . . take away a multitude of their children 24
Sir 34:22 To take away a neighbor's living is to murder him; 24
35:18 till he takes away the multitude of the insolent 27
38: 7 By them he heals and takes away pain; 19
41:21 taking away some one's portion or gift 23
42:21 Nothing can be added or taken away 26
47: 4 take away reproach from the people 27
11 The Lord took away his sins, and exalted his power 24
49: 2 took away the abominations of iniquity. 27
Bar 4:26 taken away like a flock carried off by the enemy. 19

34 I will take away her pride 30
1Mc 2:11 All her adornment has been taken away 24
11:12 So he took his daughter away from him 24

take away captive 1. שבה
Num24:22 How long shall Asshur take you away captive? 1

take away life 1. mortifico
2Es 8:13 Thou wilt take away his life 1

take away the ash 1. דשן
Num 4:13 they shall take away the ashes from the altar 1

take away violently 1. גזל 2. גָּזֵל
Deu 28:31 your ass shall be violently taken away 1
Ecc 5: 8 see . . justice and right violently taken away 2

take back 1. שים אל 2. שוב 3. ἀποκαθίστημι 4. ἀποφέρω 5. sumo
Gen 24: 5 must I then take your son back to the land 2
6 See to it that you do not take my son back there. 2
8 only you must not take my son back there. 2
Deu 22: 1 you shall take them back to your brother. 2
Jdg 11:35 opened my mouth . . and I cannot take back my vow. 2
1Kg 22:26 Seize Micai'ah, and take him back to Amon 2
2Ch 18:25 Seize Micai'ah, and take him back to Amon 2
Job 34:14 If he should take back his spirit to himself 1
Jer 34:11 and took back the male and female slaves 2
16 when each of you took back his male . . slaves 2
1Es 5: 2 to take them back to Jerusalem in safety 3
6:19 he should take all these vessels back 4
2Es 2:11 Moreover, I will take back to myself their glory 5
Jdt 6: 7 to take you back into the hill country 3

take booty 1. בזז
Num31:53 men of war had taken booty, every man for himself.) 1

take by force 1. גזל 2. ἁρπάζω
Gen 31:31 you would take your daughters . . by force 1
Mat 11:12 men of violence take it by force. 2
Joh 6:15 and take him by force to make him king 2
Act 23:10 go down and take him by force from among them 2

take by lot 1. לכד
1Sm 10:20 and the tribe of Benjamin was taken by lot. 1
21 the family of the Matrites was taken by lot; 1
21 and Saul the son of Kish was taken by lot. 1

take by robbery 1. גְּזֵלָה
Lev 6: 4 he shall restore what he took by robbery 1

take by surprise 1. προκαταλαμβάνω
1Mc 12:33 He turned aside to Joppa and took it by surprise 1

take by the heel 1. עקב
Hos 12: 3 In the womb he took his brother by the heel 1

take by violence 1. גזל
Mal 1:13 You bring what has been taken by violence 1

take captive 1. לכד 2. שבה 3. αἰχμαλωσία 4. αἰχμαλωτίζω 5. ἁλίσκω 6. captivo
Gen 14:14 his kinsman had been taken captive 2
Num21: 1 against Israel, and took some of them captive. 2
31: 9 Israel took captive the women of Mid'ian 2
Deu 21:10 into your hands, and you take them captive 2
1Sm 30: 2 and taken captive the women and all who were in it 2
3 wives and sons and daughters taken captive. 2
5 David's two wives also had been taken captive 2
2Kg 6:22 Would you slay those whom you have taken captive 2
2Ch 28: 5 king of Syria, who defeated him and took captive 2
8 The men of Israel took captive 200,000 2
Prv 11: 6 treacherous are taken captive by their lust. 1
Isa 14: 2 will take captive those who were their captors 2
Jer 13:17 because the LORD'S flock has been taken captive. 2
41:10 Then Ish'mael took captive all the rest 2
10 Ish'mael the son of Nethani'ah took them captive 2
50:33 all who took them captive have held them fast 2
2Co 10: 5 take every thought captive to obey Christ 4
Rev 13:10 If any one is to be taken captive 3
2Es 16:46 and take their children captive 6
Sir 31: 7 every fool will be taken captive by it. 5
1Mc 1:32 they took captive the women and children 4
15:40 and invade Judea and take the people captive 4

take care 1. שמר 2. זהר (A) 3. βλέπω 4. ἐπιμελέομαι 5. ἐπιμελῶς 6. εὐλαβέομαι 7. θάλπω 8. παρέχω 9. προνοέω 10. προσέχω 11. τρέφω 12. τροφοφορέω 13. φροντίς
Jos 22: 5 Take good care to observe the commandment 1
Jdg 2:22 whether they will take care to walk in the way 1
Ezr 4:22 take care not to be slack in this matter; 2
Lke 10:34 and brought him to an inn, and took care of him. 4
35 Take care of him 4
Act 5:35 take care what you do with these men. 10
1Co 3:10 Let each man take care how he builds upon it. 3
8: 9 Only take care lest this liberty of yours 3
1Th 2: 7 like a nurse taking care of her children. 7

Heb 3:12 Take care, brethren, lest . . 3
1Es 2:28 to take care that nothing more be done 9
8:19 they shall take care to give him 5
Tob 2:10 Ahikar, however, took care of me 11
Jdt 2:13 take care not to transgress any . . commands •
AEs 16: 8 we will take care to render our kingdom quiet 8
Wis 5:15 the Most High takes care of them. 13
Sir 13: 8 Take care not to be led astray 10
LJr 1: 5 take care not to become at all like the foreigners 6
1Mc 3:33 Lysias was also to take care of Antiochus his son 11
11:37 Now therefore take care to make a copy of this 4
2Mc 7:27 and have taken care of you. 12

take care of health 1. θεραπεύω
Sir 18:19 before you fall ill, take care of your health. 1

take charge 1. μέλω 2. προΐστημι
1Mc 5:19 Take charge of this people 2
14:42 that he should take charge of the sanctuary 1
42 that he should take charge of the sanctuary 1

take comfort 1. נחם
Ps 119:52 thy ordinances from of old, I take comfort, O LORD. 1

take command 1. ἀνίστημι
1Mc 3: 1 Then Judas his son . . took command in his place. 1

take confidence 1. סמך
2Ch 32: 8 people took confidence from the words 1

take counsel 1. יסד 2. יעץ 3. מלך 4. עוץ 5. βουλεύω
Jdg 19:30 this day; consider it, take counsel, and speak. 4
1Kg 12: 6 King Rehobo'am took counsel with the old men 2
8 took counsel with the young men who had grown up 2
28 the king took counsel, and made two calves 2
2Kg 6: 8 king of Syria . . took counsel with his servants 2
2Ch 10: 6 Then King Rehobo'am took counsel with the old men 2
8 took counsel with the young men 2
20:21 when he had taken counsel with the people 2
25:17 Amazi'ah . . took counsel and sent to Jo'ash 2
30: 2 had taken counsel to keep the passover 2
Neh 5: 7 I took counsel with myself, and I brought charges 3
6: 7 now come, and let us take counsel together. 2
Ps 2: 2 the rulers take counsel together 1
Isa 8:10 Take counsel together, but it will come to nought; 4
45:21 let them take counsel together! 2
Lke 14:31 what king . . will not sit down first and take counsel 5
Joh 11:53 they took counsel how to put him to death. 5

take counsel together 1. συμβουλεύω
Mat 26: 4 and took counsel together . . to arrest 1

take courage 1. אמץ 2. חזק 3. θαρρέω 4. θαρσέω 5. τολμάω 6. confido
Jdg 20:22 But the people, the men of Israel, took courage 2
1Sm 4: 9 Take courage, and acquit yourselves like men 2
2Ch 15: 7 But you, take courage! Do not let your hands be weak 2
8 When Asa heard these words . . he took courage 2
23: 1 in the seventh year Jehoi'ada took courage 2
25:11 Amazi'ah took courage, and led out his people 2
Ezr 7:28 I took courage, for the hand of the LORD my God 2
Ps 27:14 be strong, and let your heart take courage; 1
31:24 Be strong, and let your heart take courage 1
Isa 41: 6 and says to his brother, "Take courage!" 2
Hag 2: 4 Yet now take courage, O Zerub'babel, says the LORD; 2
4 take courage, O Joshua, son of Jehoz'adak 2
4 take courage, all you people of the land 2
Mrk 15:43 took courage and went to Pilate 5
Act 23:11 the Lord stood by him and said, "Take courage 4
2Es 12:46 Take courage, O Israel 6
Jdt 11: 1 Then Holofernes said to her, "Take courage, woman 4
AEs 15: 9 What is it, Esther? I am your brother. Take courage; 4
Bar 4: 5 Take courage, my people, O memorial of Israel! 3
21 Take courage, my children, cry to God 3
27 Take courage, my children, and cry to God 4
30 Take courage, O Jerusalem 4
4Mc 17: 4 Take courage, therefore, O holy-minded mother 4

take delight 1. ענג 2. ריח 3. רצה 4. שוש
Deu 28:63 as the LORD took delight in doing you good 4
63 LORD will take delight in bringing ruin upon you 4
30: 9 LORD will again take delight in prospering you 4
9 as he took delight in your fathers 4
Job 27:10 Will he take delight in the Almighty? 1
34: 9 that he should take delight in God 3
Ps 37: 4 Take delight in the LORD 1
Isa 58:14 then you shall take delight in the LORD 1
Ams 5:21 and I take no delight in your solemn assemblies. 2

take down 1. ירד 2. καθαιρέω
Gen 39: 1 Now Joseph was taken down to Egypt 1
Num 1:51 the Levites shall take it down; 1
4: 5 go in and take down the veil of the screen 1
10:17 when the tabernacle was taken down 1
Jos 8:29 Joshua commanded, and they took his body down 1
10:27 and they took them down from the trees 1
Jdg 7: 4 take them down to the water and I will test them 1

1Sm 6:15 And the Levites took down the ark of the LORD 1
30:15 David said . . "Will you take me down to this band? 1
15 Swear . . and I will take you down to this band. 1
16 And when he had taken him down 1
2Kg 16:17 Ahaz cut off . . and he took down the sea 1
Mrk 15:36 see whether Eli'jah will come to take him down. 2
46 taking him down, wrapped him in the linen shroud 2
Lke 23:53 he took it down and wrapped it in a linen shroud 2
Act 13:29 they took him down from the tree 2
Jdt 13: 6 and took down his sword that hung there. 2

take ease 1. ἀναπαύω
Lke 12:19 take your ease, eat, drink, be merry.' 1

take effect 1. βέβαιος
Heb 9:17 a will takes effect only at death 1

take few 1. מעט
Num35: 8 from the smaller tribes you shall take few; 1

take for a pledge 1. חבל
Job 24: 3 they take the widow's ox for a pledge. 1

take for booty 1. בזז
Jos 11:14 all the spoil . . Israel took for their booty; 1

take for inheritance 1. נחל
Exd 34: 9 and take us for thy inheritance. 1

take good care 1. φροντίζω
Sir 32: 1 take good care of them and then be seated; 1

take heart 1. εὐθυμέω 2. θαρρέω 3. θαρσέω
Mat 9: 2 he said to the paralytic, "Take heart, my son 3
22 Jesus turned, and seeing her he said, "Take heart 3
14:27 Take heart, it is I; have no fear. 2
Mrk 6:50 Take heart, it is I; have no fear. 2
10:49 saying to him, "Take heart; rise, he is calling you. 3
Act 27:22 I now bid you take heart 1
25 So take heart, men 1

take heed 1. ידע 2. פלס 3. ראה 4. שמר 5. βλέπω 6. ἐπέχω 7. εὐλαβέομαι 8. ὁράω 9. προσέχω
Gen 31:29 Take heed that you speak to Jacob neither good 4
Exd 10:28 Get away from me; take heed to yourself; 4
19:12 set bounds . . saying, 'Take heed that you do not 4
23:13 Take heed to all that I have said to you; 4
34:12 Take heed to yourself, lest you make a covenant 4
Num23:12 Must I not take heed to speak what the LORD 4
28: 2 My offering . . you shall take heed to offer to me 4
Deu 2: 4 they will be afraid of you. So take good heed; 4
4: 9 Only take heed, and keep your soul diligently 4
15 Therefore take good heed to yourselves. 4
23 Take heed to yourselves, lest you forget 4
6:12 then take heed lest you forget the LORD 4
8:11 Take heed lest you forget the LORD your God, by not 4
11:16 Take heed lest your heart be deceived 4
12:13 Take heed that you do not offer 4
19 Take heed that you do not forsake the Levite 4
30 take heed that you be not ensnared to follow them 4
15: 9 Take heed lest there be a base thought 4
24: 8 Take heed, in an attack of leprosy, to be very 4
Jos 23:11 Take good heed to yourselves, therefore, to love 4
1Sm 19: 2 take heed to yourself . . stay in a secret place 4
1Kg 2: 4 If your sons take heed to their way, to walk before 4
8:25 your sons take heed to their way, to walk before me 4
1Ch 28:10 Take heed now, for the LORD has chosen you to build 3
2Ch 6:16 if only your sons take heed to their way, to walk 4
19: 7 take heed what you do 4
Job 36:21 Take heed, do not turn to iniquity 4
Ps 31: 7 thou hast taken heed of my adversities 1
Prv 4:26 Take heed to the path of your feet 2
5: 6 she does not take heed to the path of life; 2
Isa 7: 4 say to him, 'Take heed, be quiet, do not fear 4
Jer 17:21 says the LORD: Take heed for the sake of your lives 4
Mal 2:15 So take heed to yourselves 4
16 take heed to yourselves and do not be faithless. 4
Mat 16: 6 Take heed and beware of the leaven 8
24: 4 Take heed that no one leads you astray. 5
Mrk 4:24 he said to them, "Take heed what you hear 5
8:15 Take heed, beware of the leaven of the Pharisees 8
13: 5 Take heed that no one leads you astray. 5
9 But take heed to yourselves 5
23 take heed; I have told you all things beforehand. 5
33 Take heed, watch; for you do not know 5
Lke 8:18 Take heed then how you hear 5
12:15 Take heed, and beware of all covetousness 8
17: 3 Take heed to yourselves 9
21: 8 he said, "Take heed that you are not led astray 5
34 But take heed to yourselves 9
Act 20:28 Take heed to yourselves and to all the flock 9
1Co 10:12 thinks that he stands take heed lest he fall. 5
Gal 5:15 if you bite and devour one another take heed 5
1Ti 4:16 Take heed to yourself and to your teaching 6
Heb 11: 7 Noah . . took heed and constructed an ark 7
Sir 29:20 take heed to yourself lest you fall. 9

take heed of nothing 1. πάντα παραπέμπω
3Mc 1:26 he, in his arrogance, took heed of nothing 1

take hence 1. עלה
Ps 102:24 I say, "take me not hence in the midst of my days 1

take hold 1. אחז 2. חזק 3. תפש 4. δράσσομαι 5. ἐπιλαμβάνω 6. κρατέω
Gen 25:26 his hand had taken hold of Esau's heel; 2
Deu 9:17 I took hold of the two tables, and cast them out 3
21:19 his father and his mother shall take hold of him 3
32:41 if . . my hand takes hold on judgment 1
Jdg 16: 3 he arose and took hold of the doors of the gate 1
2Sm 1:11 Then David took hold of his clothes, and rent them; 2
6: 6 put out his hand to the ark . . and took hold of it 1
13:11 he took hold of her, and said to her, "Come, lie 2
15: 5 put out his hand, and take hold of him, and kiss him. 2
2Kg 2:12 Then he took hold of his own clothes and rent them 2
Job 30:16 days of affliction have taken hold of me. 1
38:13 that it might take hold of the skirts of the earth 1
Ps 35: 2 Take hold of shield and buckler 2
48: 6 trembling took hold of them there 1
Ecc 7:18 It is good that you should take hold of this 1
Isa 3: 6 When a man takes hold of his brother in the house 3
4: 1 seven women shall take hold of one man in that day 2
64: 7 that bestirs himself to take hold of thee; 2
Jer 6:24 anguish has taken hold of us 2
8:21 I mourn, and dismay has taken hold on me. 2
13:21 Will not pangs take hold of you 1
49:24 anguish and sorrows have taken hold of her 1
Nah 3:14 tread the mortar, take hold of the brick mold! 2
Zec 8:23 ten men . . shall take hold of the robe of a Jew 2
Mat 28: 9 they came and took hold of his feet and worshiped 6
Lke 20:20 that they might take hold of what he said 5
Act 17:19 And they took hold of him 5
1Ti 6:12 take hold of the eternal life 5
19 take hold of the life which is life indeed. 5
Tob 11:11 and took hold of his father 5
Jdt 13: 7 and took hold of the hair of his head 4
Sir 26: 7 taking hold of her is like grasping a scorpion. 6

take hollow pride 1. κενοδοξέω
4Mc 8:24 nor take hollow pride in being put to the rack. 1

take home 1. סור 2. παρακομίζω
1Ch 13:13 David did not take the ark home into the city 1
2Mc 9:29 Philip, one of his courtiers, took his body home; 2

take in exchange 1. ἀντάλλαγμα
Sir 44:17 in the time of wrath he was taken in exchange; 1

take in hunting 1. צוד
Lev 17:13 who takes in hunting any beast or bird 1

take in one's arms 1. ἐναγκαλίζομαι
Mrk 9:36 taking him in his arms, he said to them 1
10:16 he took them in his arms and blessed them 1

take in pledge 1. חבל
Exd 22:26 If . . you take your neighbor's garment in pledge 1
Deu 24: 6 No man . . take a mill or an upper millstone in pledge; 1
6 for he would be taking a life in pledge. 1
17 not . . take a widow's garment in pledge; 1
Job 24: 9 and take in pledge the infant of the poor. 1
Ams 2: 8 lay . . down . . upon garments taken in pledge; 1

take into 1. אסף 2. εἰσάγω
Jos 20: 4 they shall take him into the city 1
Tob 7:16 Sister, make up the other room, and take her into it. 2

take into account 1. ἀναλογίζομαι
3Mc 7: 7 we have taken into account the friendly . . goodwill 1

take into captivity 1. αἰχμαλωτεύω
Tob 1: 2 who . . was taken into captivity from Thisbe 1

take into custody 1. συλλαμβάνω
Jdt 10:12 and took her into custody, and asked her 1

take into exile 1. גלה
2Kg 25:21 So Judah was taken into exile out of its land. 1
1Ch 9: 1 And Judah was taken into exile in Babylon 1
2Ch 36:20 took into exile in Babylon those who had escaped 1
Jer 13:19 all Judah is taken into exile 1
19 is taken into exile, wholly taken into exile. 1
24: 1 Babylon had taken into exile from Jerusalem 1
27:20 when he took into exile from Jerusalem 1
29: 1 whom Nebuchadnez'zar had taken into exile 1
40: 7 who had not been taken into exile to Babylon 1
43: 3 they may kill us or take us into exile in Babylon. 1
Ams 5:27 I will take you into exile beyond Damascus 1

take knowledge 1. ידע
Isa 58: 3 humbled ourselves, and thou takest no knowledge 1

take leave 1. ἀποτάσσομαι 2. ἀσπάζομαι
Mrk 6:46 after he had taken leave of them 1
Act 18:18 and then took leave of the brethren 1
21 but on taking leave of them he said 1
20: 1 and having exhorted them took leave of them 2
2Co 2:13 So I took leave of them and went on to Macedo'nia. 1

make take 1. נשא 2. ἐπάγω
1Kg 8:31 If a man sins . . and is made to take an oath 1
2Ch 6:22 If a man sins . . and is made to take an oath 1
Jdt 8:30 and made us take an oath which we cannot break. 2

make take an oath 1. שבע
Num 5:19 Then the priest shall make her take an oath 1
21 priest make the woman take the oath of the curse 1
Ezr 10: 5 made . . all Israel take oath that they would do 1
Neh 13:25 I made them take oath in the name of God, saying 1

take measures 1. φροντίζω
2Mc 4:21 he took measures for his own security. 1

take note 1. ידע 2. σκοπέω
1Sm 23:23 See therefore, and take note of . . where he hides 1
Jer 5: 1 Run to and fro . . look and take note! 1
Rom16:17 take note of those who create dissensions 2

take notice 1. נכר 2. μιμνήσκω
Rut 2:10 Why have I . . that you should take notice of me 1
19 Blessed be the man who took notice of you. 1
2Sm 3:36 all the people took notice . . and it pleased them; 1
Ps 142: 4 watch, but there is none who takes notice of me; 1
Sir 23:18 The Most High will not take notice of my sins. 2

take off 1. חלק 2. משך 3. סור 4. סור מֵעַל 5. עדה 6. פרק 7. פשט 8. רום 9. ἀποτίθημι 10. ἀφαιρέω 11. ἐκδύω 12. λύω
Gen 38:19 taking off her veil she put on the garments 3
Exd 32: 2 Aaron said to them, "Take off the rings of gold 6
3 So all the people took off the rings of gold 6
24 I said to them, 'Let any who have gold take it off'; 6
34:34 he took the veil off, until he came out; 3
2Sm 16: 9 Why should . . ? Let me go over and take off his head. 3
2Kg 6:32 see how this murderer has sent to take off my head? 3
Neh 4:23 none of us took off our clothes; 7
Est 4: 4 garments . . so that he might take off his sackcloth 4
8: 2 the king took off his signet ring . . and gave it 3
Ps 28: 3 Take me not off with the wicked 2
Prv 25:20 like one who takes off a garment on a cold day 5
Isa 20: 2 Go . . and take off your shoes from your feet 1
Ezk 21:26 Remove the turban, and take off the crown; 8
Act 7:33 Take off the shoes from your feet 12
Jdt 10: 3 and took off her widow's garments 11
16: 8 For she took off her widow's mourning 11
AEs 14: 2 she took off her splendid apparel 10
15: 1 took off the garments in which she had worshiped 11
Bar 4:20 I have taken off the robe of peace 11
5: 1 Take off the garment of your sorrow 11
1Mc 10:62 The king gave orders to take off Jonathan's garments 11
2Mc 8:35 took off his splendid uniform 9

take offense 1. σκανδαλίζω
Mat 11: 6 blessed is he who takes no offense at me. 1
13:57 they took offense at him 1
Mrk 6: 3 And they took offense at him. 1
Lke 7:23 blessed is he who takes no offense at me. 1
Joh 6:61 Jesus . . said to them, "Do you take offense at this? 1

take office
Heb 7:21 took their office without an oath •

take on board 1. ἀναλαμβάνω
Act 20:14 when he met us at Assos, we took him on board 1

take one's fill 1. רוה 2. שבע 3. ἐμπίμπλημι 4. πίμπλημι
Prv 5:10 lest strangers take their fill of your strength 2
7:18 Come, let us take our fill of love till morning; 1
Wis 2: 7 Let us take our fill of costly wine and perfumes 4
5: 7 We took our fill of the paths of lawlessness 3

take one's place 1. נצב 2. ἀλλάσσω 3. ἀναπίπτω 4. εἰμὶ ἀντί 5. καθίστημι
Ps 82: 1 God has taken his place in the divine council; 1
Isa 3:13 The LORD has taken his place to contend 1
1Es 5:48 took their places and prepared the altar 5
Sir 32: 2 take your place, that you may be merry 3
33:20 do not let any one take your place. 2
1Mc 9:30 to take his place as our ruler and leader 4

take one's place at table 1. κατακλίνω
Lke 7:36 and took his place at table 1

take out 1. חלק 2. יגה 3. יצא 4. סור 5. עבר 6. ἀφίστημι 7. ἐκβάλλω 8. ἐκφέρω 9. ἐξάγω
Exd 4: 6 and when he took it out, behold, his hand 3
7 and when he took it out, behold, it was restored 3
Lev 14:40 shall command that they take out the stones 1
43 after he has taken out the stones and scraped 1
2Sm 20:13 When he was taken out of the highway 2
1Kg 21:10 Then take him out, and stone him to death. 3
1Ch 9:28 when they were brought in and taken out. 3

2Ch 14: 5 He also took out . . the high places 4
17: 6 took the high places and the Ashe'rim out 4
35:24 his servants took him out of the chariot 5
Ps 31: 4 take me out of the net which is hidden for me 3
Jer 51:44 and take out of his mouth what he has swallowed. 3
Ezk 24: 6 Take out of it piece after piece 3
36:26 I will take out of your flesh the heart of stone 4
Lke 6:42 let me take out the speck that is in your eye 7
42 hypocrite, first take the log out of your own eye 7
42 then you will see clearly to take out the speck 7
10:35 the next day he took out two denarii 7
Act 16:37 No! let them come themselves and take us out. 9
39 And they took them out 9
1Ti 6: 7 we cannot take anything out of the world; 8
1Es 1:30 his servants took him out of the line of battle. 6
6:18 which Nebuchadnezzar had taken out of the house 8
18 these Cyrus the king took out again 8
26 which Nebuchadnezzar took out of the house 8

take out to sea 1. ἐπανάγω
2Mc 12: 4 the men . . took them out to sea and drowned them 1

take over 1. קבל
Ezr 8:30 priests and the Levites took over the weight 1

take pains 1. ἀσκέω 2. ἐργάζομαι
Act 24:16 I always take pains to have a clear conscience 1
Sir 30:13 Discipline your son and take pains with him 2

take part 1. κοινωνία 2. κοινωνός 3. μετέχω 4. συγκοινωνέω
Mat 23:30 we would not have taken part with them 2
2Co 8: 4 taking part in the relief of the saints- 1
Eph 5:11 Take no part in the unfruitful works of darkness 4
Rev 18: 4 Come out of her . . lest you take part in her sins 4
2Mc 4:14 to take part in the unlawful proceedings 3

take patiently 1. ὑπομένω
1Pe 2:20 when you . . are beaten . . you take it patiently? 1
20 if when you . . suffer . . you take it patiently 1

take pity 1. חמל 2. חנן 3. ἐλεέω 4. κατελεέω
Exd 2: 6 the babe was crying. She took pity on him 1
Ps 86:16 Turn to me and take pity on me; 2
Tob 3:15 command that . . pity be taken upon me 3
LJr 1:38 They cannot take pity on a widow 3
4Mc 8:10 Therefore take pity on yourselves 4
20 Let us take pity on our youth 3

take place 1. היה 2. עשה 3. ἀνίστημι ἀντί 4. γίνομαι 5. γίνομαι ἀντί 6. εἰμί 7. ῥῆμα 8. συντελέω
Jdg 20:12 What wickedness is this that has taken place 1
Ecc 8:14 There is a vanity which takes place on earth 2
Mat 1:18 the birth of Jesus Christ took place in this way. 6
22 All this took place to fulfil what the Lord had 4
18:31 his fellow servants saw what had taken place 4
31 reported to their lord all that had taken place. 4
21: 4 This took place to fulfil what was spoken 4
24: 6 this must take place, but the end is not yet. 4
34 not pass away till all these things take place. 4
26:56 But all this has taken place 4
27:54 saw the earthquake and what took place 4
28:11 told the chief priests all that had taken place. 4
Mrk 13: 7 do not be alarmed; this must take place 4
29 So also, when you see these things taking place 4
30 before all these things take place. 4
Lke 21: 7 the sign when this is about to take place? 4
9 this must first take place 4
28 Now when these things begin to take place, look up 4
31 So also, when you see these things taking place 4
32 till all has taken place. 4
36 to escape all these things that will take place 4
23:47 Now when the centurion saw what had taken place 4
48 when they saw what had taken place 4
Joh 1:28 This took place in Bethany beyond the Jordan 4
13:19 I tell you this now, before it takes place 4
19 when it does take place 4
14:29 now I have told you before it takes place 4
29 so that when it does take place, you may believe. 4
19:36 these things took place 4
Act 4:28 whatever . . thy plan had predestined to take place. 4
11:28 this took place in the days of Claudius. 4
28: 9 when this had taken place 4
Col 4: 9 everything that has taken place here. •
Rev 1: 1 show to his servants what must soon take place; 4
19 what is and what is to take place hereafter. 4
4: 1 I will show you what must take place after this. 4
22: 6 to show his servants what must soon take place. 4
1Es 1:10 this is what took place 4
Jdt 6:17 He answered and told them what had taken place 7
15: 4 to tell what had taken place 8
Wis 19:18 inferred from the sight of what took place. 4
1Mc 9:31 and took the place of Judas his brother. 3
16: 3 Take my place and my brother's 5
2Mc 8:20 that took place in Babylonia 4
10: 5 the purification of the sanctuary took place 4
3Mc 3:14 When our expedition took place in Asia 4

take place under 1. κατά
2Mc 10:10 tell what took place under Antiochus Eupator 1

take pleasure 1. אהב 2. חפץ 3. ראה טוב 4. רצה 5. εὐδοκέω 6. εὐφραίνω 7. placeo
1Ch 28: 4 and among my father's sons he took pleasure in me 4
Ps 62: 4 They take pleasure in falsehood. 4
147:11 the LORD takes pleasure in those who fear him 4
149: 4 For the LORD takes pleasure in his people; 4
Prv 18: 2 A fool takes no pleasure in understanding 2
Ecc 3:13 eat and drink and take pleasure in all his toil. 3
Jer 6:10 an object of scorn, they take no pleasure in it. 2
Ezk 16:37 all your lovers, with whom you took pleasure 1
Hag 1: 8 and build the house, that I may take pleasure in it 4
Heb 10: 6 thou hast taken no pleasure. 5
8 Thou hast neither desired nor taken pleasure in 5
Sir 25: 1 My soul takes pleasure in three things 7
4Mc 8:18 why do we take pleasure in vain resolves 6

take poison 1. φαρμακεύω
2Mc 10:13 he took poison and ended his life. 1

take possession 1. ירש 2. לבש 3. ἐπικρατέω 4. καταλαμβάνω 5. κληρονομέω 6. κρατέω 7. κυριεύω
Gen 28: 4 that you may take possession of the land 1
Num21:24 Israel . . took possession of his land 1
33:53 take possession of the land and settle in it 1
Deu 1: 8 go in and take possession of the land 1
21 go up, take possession, as the LORD . . has told you; 1
2:24 begin to take possession, and contend with him 1
31 begin to take possession, that you may occupy 1
3:12 When we took possession of this land at that time 1
4: 1 live, and go in and take possession of the land 1
5 land . . you are entering to take possession of it. 1
22 go over and take possession of that good land. 1
47 took possession of his land and the land of Og 1
6:18 that you may . . take possession of the good land 1
7: 1 land which you are entering to take possession 1
9:23 Go up and take possession of the land 1
11: 8 and go in and take possession of the land 1
10 land which you are entering to take possession 1
29 land which you are entering to take possession 1
31 pass over . . to go in to take possession of the land 1
23:20 land which you are entering to take possession 1
26: 1 taken possession of it, and live in it 1
28:21 land which you are entering to take possession 1
63 which you are entering to take possession of it. 1
30:16 land which you are entering to take possession 1
Jos 1:11 to go in to take possession of the land 1
15 and they also take possession of the land 1
12: 1 and took possession of their land 1
17:12 Yet . . Manas'seh could not take possession 1
18: 3 be slack to go in and take possession of the land 1
19:47 they took possession of it and settled in it 1
21:43 and having taken possession of it, they settled 1
24: 8 and you took possession of their land 1
Jdg 1:19 Judah, and he took possession of the hill country 1
2: 6 his inheritance to take possession of the land. 1
3:13 and they took possession of the city of palms. 1
6:34 the Spirit of the LORD took possession of Gideon; 2
11:21 Israel took possession of all the land 1
22 they took possession of all the territory 1
23 and are you to take possession of them? 1
1Kg 21:15 Arise, take possession of the vineyard of Naboth 1
16 Ahab arose to go . . to take possession of it. 1
18 where he has gone to take possession. 1
19 Have you killed, and also taken possession?"' 1
2Kg 17:24 they took possession of Sama'ria, and dwelt in its 1
2Ch 24:20 the Spirit of God took possession of Zechari'ah 2
Ezr 9:11 land which you are entering, to take possession 1
Neh 9:22 took possession of the land of Sihon king 1
25 took possession of houses full of all good 1
Ps 83:12 Let us take possession for ourselves 1
105:44 took possession of the fruit of the peoples' toil 1
Jer 30: 3 they shall take possession of it. 1
32:23 they entered and took possession of it. 1
Ezk 7:24 the nations to take possession of their houses; 1
35:10 we will take possession of them 1
1Es 8:83 you are entering to take possession of it 5
Jdt 1:14 Thus he took possession of his cities 7
5:15 they took possession of all the hill country. 5
7:12 let your servants take possession of the spring 3
15: 7 the Israelites . . took possession of what remained 7
1Mc 11:66 took possession of the city 4
15:29 you have taken possession of many places 7
16:20 he sent other men to take possession of Jerusalem 4
2Mc 14: 2 and had taken possession of the country 6

take precautions 1. κατασφαλίζομαι 2. προνοέω
2Mc 1:19 they took such precautions that . . 1
3Mc 3:24 we have taken precautions lest . . 2

take precedence 1. κυριεύω
4Mc 2:12 It takes precedence over love for children 1

take prey 1. בזז
Isa 33:23 even the lame will take the prey. 1

take quickly 1. σπεύδω
Wis 4:14 therefore he took him quickly 1

take refuge 1. חסה 2. עוז 3. καταφεύγω 4. συμφεύγω 5. φεύγω 6. φυγαδεύω
Deu 32:37 'Where . . gods, the rock in which they took refuge 1
Jdg 9:15 over you, then come and take refuge in my shade; 1
Rut 2:12 under whose wings you have come to take refuge! 1
2Sm 22: 3 my God, my rock, in whom I take refuge, my shield 1
31 he is a shield for all those who take refuge in him. 1
Ps 2:12 Blessed are all who take refuge in him. 1
5:11 But let all who take refuge in thee rejoice 1
7: 1 O LORD my God, in thee do I take refuge; 1
11: 1 In the LORD I take refuge; how can you say to me, 1
16: 1 Preserve me, O God, for in thee I take refuge. 1
18: 2 my God, my rock, in whom I take refuge 1
30 a shield for all those who take refuge in him. 1
25:20 me not be put to shame, for I take refuge in thee. 1
31:19 and wrought for those who take refuge in thee 1
34: 8 Happy is the man who takes refuge in him! 1
22 none . . who take refuge in him will be condemned. 1
36: 7 men take refuge in the shadow of thy wings. 1
37:40 saves them, because they take refuge in him. 1
57: 1 be merciful to me, for in thee my soul takes refuge; 1
1 in the shadow of thy wings I will take refuge 1
64:10 rejoice in the LORD, and take refuge in him! 1
71: 1 In thee O LORD, do I take refuge; 1
118: 8 It is better to take refuge in the LORD 1
9 better to take refuge in the LORD 1
144: 2 my shield and he in whom I take refuge 1
Prv 30: 5 he is a shield to those who take refuge in him. 1
Isa 30: 2 to take refuge in the protection of Pharaoh 2
57:13 he who takes refuge in me shall possess the land 1
Nah 1: 7 he knows those who take refuge in him. 1
Wis 14: 6 the hope of the world took refuge on a raft 3
1Mc 10:43 whoever takes refuge at the temple in Jerusalem 5
84 those who had taken refuge in it 4
2Mc 5: 5 Menelaus took refuge in the citadel. 6
10:18 no less than 9,000 took refuge in two . . strong towers 4
12: 6 massacred those who had taken refuge there. 4

take rest 1. κοίμησις
Joh 11:13 they thought that he meant taking rest in sleep. 1

take revenge 1. נָקַם 2. ἐκδικέω 3. ἐκδίκησις
Prv 6:34 he will not spare when he takes revenge. 1
Jdt 1:12 he would surely take revenge 2
6: 5 until I take revenge on this race 2
8:27 nor has he taken revenge upon us 2
35 to take revenge upon our enemies. 3
9: 2 gavest a sword to take revenge on the strangers 3

take root 1. שרש 2. שָׁרַשׁ 3. ῥιζόω 4. radico
2Kg 19:30 remnant . . shall again take root downward 2
Job 5: 3 I have seen the fool taking root 1
Ps 80: 9 it took deep root and filled the land. 1
Isa 27: 6 In days to come Jacob shall take root 1
37:31 house of Judah shall again take root downward 2
40:24 scarcely has their stem taken root in the earth 1
Jer 12: 2 Thou plantest them, and they take root; 1
2Es 8:41 not all that were planted will take root 4
Sir 3:28 a plant of wickedness has taken root in him. 3
24:12 I took root in an honored people 3

secretly take 1. ὑφαιρέω
LJr 1:10 sometimes the priests secretly take gold 1

take shelter 1. סתר
Isa 28:15 and in falsehood we have taken shelter"; 1

take spoil 1. שלל 2. προνομεύω
Isa 10: 6 I command him, to take spoil and seize plunder 1
1Es 4: 5 whatever spoil they take and everything else. 2

take the lead 1. פרע 2. προηγέομαι
Jdg 5: 2 That the leaders took the lead in Israel 1
2Mc 10:12 Ptolemy . . took the lead in showing justice to the Jews 2

take thought 1. זכר 2. חשב 3. βουλεύω 4. προνοέω 5. φροντίζω
Ps 40:17 poor and needy; but the Lord takes thought for me. 2
Lam 1: 9 she took no thought of her doom; 1
Rom12:17 take thought for what is noble in the sight of all 4
Wis 6: 7 he takes thought for all alike. 4
13:16 he takes thought for it, that it may not fall 4
Sir 37: 8 for he will take thought for himself 3
2Mc 9:21 to take thought for the general security of all. 5
14: 9 Since you . . deign to take thought for our country 4

take to flight 1. ברח 2. חפז
Ps 48: 5 they were in panic, they took to flight; 2
104: 7 at the sound of thy thunder they took to flight. 2
Jer 4:29 every city takes to flight; they enter thickets; 1

take to mean 1. διαλαμβάνω
2Mc 5:11 he took it to mean that Judea was in revolt 1

take to wife 1.לקח

Exd 2: 1 a man . . went and took to wife a daughter of Levi. 1

take trouble 1.חרד 2.πολυπραγμονέω

2Kg 4:13 See, you have taken all this trouble for us; 1
2Mc 2:30 to take trouble with details 2

take uncleanness 1.טמא

Lev 22: 5 or a man from whom he may take uncleanness 1

take up 1.אסף 2.חלט 3.מלא 4.נטל 5.נשׂא 6.עלה 7.רום 8.סלק (A) 9.αἴρω 10.ἀνάγω 11.ἀναλαμβάνω 12.βαστάζω 13.δέχομαι 14.λαμβάνω 15.μετατίθημι 16.ποιέω 17.συναρπάζω 18.assumo 19.recipio

Exd 40:36 the cloud was taken up from over the tabernacle 6
37 if the cloud was not taken up, then they did not go 6
37 go onward till the day that it was taken up. 6
Lev 6:10 he shall take up the ashes 7
Num 9:17 cloud was taken up from over the tent 6
21 cloud was taken up in the morning, they set out 6
21 when the cloud was taken up they set out. 6
22 when it was taken up they set out. 6
10:11 cloud was taken up from over the tabernacle 6
16:37 to take up the censers out of the blaze; 7
23: 7 Balaam took up his discourse, and said 5
18 Balaam took up his discourse, and said, "Rise, Balak 5
24: 3 and he took up his discourse, and said 5
15 And he took up his discourse, and said 5
20 he looked on Am'alek, and took up his discourse 5
21 he looked on the Ken'ite, and took up his discourse 5
23 And he took up his discourse, and said 5
Jos 3: 6 Take up the ark of the covenant 5
6 And they took up the ark of the covenant, and went 5
4: 5 and take up each of you a stone upon his shoulder 7
8 and took up twelve stones out of the midst 5
6: 6 Take up the ark of the covenant 5
12 and the priests took up the ark of the LORD. 5
Jdg 9:48 cut down a bundle of brushwood, and took it up 5
Rut 2:18 And she took it up and went into the city; 5
1Sm 1:24 when she had weaned him, she took him up with her 6
6:21 the ark . . Come down and take it up to you. 6
7: 1 the men . . came and took up the ark of the LORD 6
9:24 the cook took up the leg and the upper portion 7
2Sm 2:32 And they took up As'ahel, and buried him in the tomb 5
4: 4 and his nurse took him up, and fled; 5
1Kg 8: 3 elders . . came, and the priests took up the ark. 5
13:29 the prophet took up the body of the man of God 5
20:33 they quickly took it up from him and said, "Yes 2
2Kg 2: 1 the LORD was about to take Eli'jah up to heaven 6
13 he took up the mantle of Eli'jah that had fallen 7
4:36 And when she came to him, he said, "Take up your son 5
37 then she took up her son and went out. 5
6: 7 Take it up." So he reached out his hand and took it. 7
9:25 Take him up, and cast him on the plot of ground 5
26 take him up and cast him on the plot of ground 5
10:15 And Jehu took him up with him into the chariot. 6
2Ch 2:16 to Joppa, so that you may take it up to Jerusalem. 6
5: 4 and the Levites took up the ark. 5
Neh 2: 1 I took up the wine and gave it to the king. 5
Job 27: 1 Job again took up his discourse, and said 5
29: 1 Job again took up his discourse, and said 5
Ps 15: 3 nor takes up a reproach against his neighbor; 5
27:10 have forsaken me, but the LORD will take me up. 1
102:10 for thou hast taken me up and thrown me away. 5
Isa 14: 4 you will take up this taunt against . . Babylon 5
40:15 behold, he takes up the isles like fine dust. 4
Jer 9:10 Take up weeping and wailing for the mountains 14
51:11 Sharpen the arrows! Take up the shields! 3
Ezk 19: 1 take up a lamentation for the princes of Israel 5
Dan 3:22 slew those men who took up Shadrach, Meshach 8
6:23 commanded that Daniel be taken up out of the den. 8
23 Daniel was taken up out of the den, 8
Ams 5: 1 Hear this word which I take up over you 5
26 You shall take up Sakkuth your king, and Kaiwan 5
6:10 who burns him, shall take him up to bring the bones 5
Jon 1:12 said to them, "Take me up and throw me into the sea; 5
15 they took up Jonah and threw him into the sea; 5
Mic 2: 4 they shall take up a taunt song against you 5
Hab 2: 6 all these take up their taunt against him 5
Mat 9: 6 Rise, take up your bed and go home. 9
14:20 they took up twelve baskets 9
15:37 and they took up seven baskets 9
16:24 let him deny himself and take up his cross 9
21:21 'Be taken up and cast into the sea,' 9
Mrk 2: 9 or to say, 'Rise, take up your pallet and walk'? 9
11 I say to you, rise, take up your pallet and go home. 9
12 he rose, and immediately took up the pallet 9
6:43 they took up twelve baskets 9
8: 8 they took up the broken pieces left over 9
19 how many . . broken pieces did you take up 9
20 how many . . broken pieces did you take up 9
34 let him deny himself and take up his cross 9
11:23 'Be taken up and cast into the sea,' 9
16:19 Jesus . . was taken up into heaven 11
Lke 2:28 he took him up in his arms and blessed God and said 13
4: 5 And the devil took him up 10
5:24 I say to you, rise, take up your bed and go home. 9
25 and took up that on which he lay, and went home 9
9:17 they took up what was left over 9
23 let him deny himself and take up his cross daily 9
19:21 you take up what you did not lay down 9
22 a severe man, taking up what I did not lay down 9
Joh 5: 8 Rise, take up your pallet, and walk. 9
9 he took up his pallet and walked. 9
11 'Take up your pallet, and walk.' 9
12 'Take up your pallet, and walk'? 9
8:59 they took up stones to throw at him 9
10:31 The Jews took up stones again to stone him. 12
Act 1: 2 until the day when he was taken up 11
11 who was taken up from you into heaven 11
22 until the day when he was taken up from us 11
7:43 you took up the tent of Moloch 11
8:33 his life is taken up from the earth. 9
10:16 the thing was taken up at once to heaven. 11
20: 9 he fell down . . and was taken up dead. 9
1Ti 3:16 believed on in the world, taken up in glory. 11
Heb 11: 5 By faith Enoch was taken up 15
Rev 18:21 Then a mighty angel took up a stone 9
1Es 9:45 Then Ezra took up the book of the law 11
2Es 6:26 they shall see the men who were taken up 19
8:19 before he was taken up. He said 18
14: 9 you shall be taken up from among men 19
Tob 3: 6 command my spirit to be taken up 11
Jdt 7: 5 Then each man took up his weapons 11
Wis 4:10 while living among sinners he was taken up. 15
Sir 44:16 Enoch pleased the Lord, and was taken up 15
48: 9 You who were taken up by a whirlwind of fire 11
49:14 he was taken up from the earth. 11
1Mc 1:27 Every bridegroom took up the lament 11
2:58 Elijah . . was taken up into heaven. 11
2Mc 3:27 his men took him up and put him on a stretcher 17
10:27 they took up their arms 11
11: 7 Maccabeus himself was the first to take up arms 11
12:39 went to take up the bodies of the fallen •
43 He also took up a collection, man by man 16
15: 5 I command you to take up arms 9
3Mc 6:32 and took up the song of their fathers 11

take up a cause 1.ריב

Lam 3:58 Thou hast taken up my cause, O Lord 1

take up arms 1.חלץ

Num32:17 we will take up arms, ready to go before the people 1
20 if you will take up arms to go before the LORD 1

take upon 1.יאל 2.נשׂא 3.קבל

Gen 18:27 Behold, I have taken upon myself to speak 1
31 I have taken upon myself to speak to the Lord. 1
Exd 28:38 Aaron shall take upon himself any guilt 2
Est 9:27 the Jews ordained and took it upon themselves 3

take vengeance 1.בקשׁ 2.בקשׁ מִיַּד 3.ישׁע 4.נקם 5.ἐκδικάζω 6.ἐκδικέω 7.ἐκδίκησις 8.ποιέω ἐκδίκησιν 9.τιμωρέω

Gen 4:15 vengeance shall be taken on him sevenfold. 4
Lev 19:18 You shall not take vengeance or bear any grudge 4
Jos 10:13 the nation took vengeance on their enemies. 4
22:23 if we did . . may the LORD himself take vengeance. 1
1Sm 20:16 may the LORD take vengeance on David's enemies. 2
25:26 and from taking vengeance with your own hand 3
31 or for my lord taking vengeance himself. 3
Jer 15:15 and take vengeance for me on my persecutors. 4
50:15 take vengeance on her, do to her as she has done. 4
51:36 plead your cause and take vengeance for you. 4
Ezk 24: 8 To rouse my wrath, to take vengeance 4
25:12 has grievously offended in taking vengeance 4
15 and took vengeance with malice of heart 4
Nah 1: 2 the LORD takes vengeance on his adversaries 4
9 he will not take vengeance twice on his foes. 6
Jdt 16:17 The Lord Almighty will take vengeance on them 7
Sir 28: 1 He that takes vengeance will suffer vengeance 6
46: 1 to take vengeance on the enemies 5
1Mc 7: 9 he commanded him to take vengeance 8
9:26 he took vengeance on them and made sport of them. 6
2Mc 6:15 in order that he may not take vengeance on us 5
4Mc 9:24 and take vengeance on the accursed tyrant. 9
12:18 he will take vengeance both in this present life 9

take warning 1.זהר 2.יסר

Ezk 3:21 he shall surely live, because he took warning; 1
23:48 that all women may take warning 2
33: 4 one who hears the sound . . does not take warning 1
5 the sound of the trumpet, and did not take warning; 1
5 But if he had taken warning, he would have saved 1

tale 1.διήγησις 2.λόγος

Sir 22: 6 a tale told at the wrong time 1
Sus 1:27 And when the elders told their tale 2

idle tale 1.λῆρος

Lke 24:11 these words seemed to them an idle tale 1

talebearer 1.רָכִיל

Prv 11:13 who goes about as a talebearer reveals secrets 1

talent 1.כִּכָּר 2.כִּכַּר (A) 3.τάλαντον

Exd 25:39 Of a talent of pure gold shall it be made, with all 1
37:24 all its utensils of a talent of pure gold. 1
38:24 the gold from the offering, was 29 talents 1
25 silver . . was 100 talents and 1,775 shekels 1
27 The 100 talents of silver were for casting 1
27 100 bases for the 100 talents, a talent for a base. 1
27 100 bases for the 100 talents, a talent for a base. 1
29 the bronze that was contributed was 70 talents 1
2Sm 12:30 the weight of it was a talent of gold, and in it was 1
1Kg 9:14 Hiram had sent to the king 120 talents of gold. 1
28 gold, to the amount of 420 talents; 1
10:10 she gave the king 120 talents of gold 1
14 weight of gold . . was 666 talents of gold 1
16:24 He bought the hill . . for two talents of silver; 1
20:39 his life, or else you shall pay a talent of silver.' 1
2Kg 5: 5 So he went, taking with him ten talents of silver 1
22 give them a talent of silver and two . . garments.' 1
23 Na'aman said, "Be pleased to accept two talents. 1
23 and tied up two talents of silver in two bags 1
15:19 Men'ahem gave Pul 1,000 talents of silver 1
18:14 required of Hezeki'ah . . 300 talents of silver 1
14 300 talents of silver and 30 talents of gold. 1
23:33 laid upon the land a tribute of 100 talents of silver 1
33 a tribute of . . silver and a talent of gold. 1
1Ch 19: 6 sent 1,000 talents of silver to hire chariots 1
20: 2 he found that it weighed a talent of gold 1
22:14 for the house of the LORD 100,000 talents of gold 1
14 house of the LORD . . 1,000,000 talents of silver 1
29: 4 3,000 talents of gold, of the gold of Ophir 1
4 and 7,000 talents of refined silver 1
7 5,000 talents and 10,000 darics of gold 1
7 10,000 talents of silver, 18,000 talents of bronze 1
7 10,000 talents of silver, 18,000 talents of bronze 1
7 bronze, and 100,000 talents of iron. 1
2Ch 3: 8 he overlaid it with 600 talents of fine 1
8:18 there 450 talents of gold 1
9: 9 she gave . . 120 talents of gold 1
13 weight of gold . . was 666 talents of gold 1
25: 6 for 100 talents of silver. 1
9 But what shall we do about the 100 talents 1
27: 5 gave him that year 100 talents of silver 1
36: 3 tribute of 100 talents of silver and a talent 1
3 tribute of . . silver and a talent of gold. 1
Ezr 7:22 up to 100 talents of silver 2
8:26 I weighed out . . 650 talents of silver 1
26 silver vessels worth 100 talents 1
26 silver vessels . . and 100 talents of gold 1
Est 3: 9 I will pay 10,000 talents of silver 1
Mat 18:24 one was brought to him who owed him 10,000 talents; 3
25:15 to one he gave five talents, to another two 3
16 He who had received the five talents went at once 3
16 he made five talents more. •
17 he who had the two talents made two talents more. •
17 he who had the two talents made two talents more. •
18 he who had received the one talent went •
20 he who had received the five talents came forward 3
20 bringing five talents more, saying 3
20 Master, you delivered to me five talents 3
20 here I have made five talents more.' 3
22 who had the two talents came forward, saying 3
22 Master, you delivered to me two talents 3
22 here I have made two talents more.' 3
24 who had received the one talent came forward 3
25 I went and hid your talent in the ground 3
28 So take the talent from him 3
28 give it to him who has the ten talents. 3
1Es 1:36 fined the nation 100 talents of silver 3
36 100 talents of silver and a talent of gold. 3
4:51 that twenty talents a year should be given 3
52 an additional ten talents a year 3
8:20 up to 100 talents of silver 3
56 I weighed and gave to them 650 talents of silver 3
56 silver vessels worth a 100 talents 3
56 a 100 talents of gold 3
Tob 1:14 I left ten talents of silver in trust with Gabael 3
4:20 explain to you about the ten talents of silver 3
1Mc 11:28 and promised him 300 talents. 3
13:16 Send now 100 talents of silver 3
19 So he sent the sons and the 100 talents 3
15:31 or else give me for them 500 talents of silver 3
31 500 talents more 3
35 for them we will give you 100 talents. 3
2Mc 3:11 totaled in all 400 talents of silver 3
4: 8 360 talents of silver 3
8 from another source of revenue, 80 talents. 3
24 outbidding Jason by 300 talents of silver. 3
5:21 Antiochus carried off 1,800 talents 3
8:10 tribute due to the Romans, 2,000 talents 3
11 and promising to hand over 90 slaves for a talent 3
4Mc 4:17 he would pay the king 3,660 talents annually. 3

talitha 1.ταλιθά

Mrk 5:41 by the hand he said to her, "Tal'itha cu'mi"; 1

talk 1.דבר 2.דָּבָר 3.דְּבַר שְׂפָתַיִם 4.הגה 5.מִלָּה 6.ספר 7.פֶּה 8.שִׂיחַ 9.שִׂיחָה 10.שָׂפָה 11.שְׂפַת לָשׁוֹן 12.διαλέγομαι 13.διήγησις 14.ἐξηγέομαι

15. κηρύσσω 16. λαλέω 17. λαλιά 18. λέγω
19. λόγος 20. ὁμιλέω 21. συλλαλέω 22. συνομιλέω
23. dico 24. loquor

Gen 17:22 When he had finished talking with him 1
45:15 and after that his brothers talked with him. 1
Exd 20:22 You have seen for yourselves that I have talked 1
34:29 face shone because he had been talking with God. 1
31 returned to him, and Moses talked with them. 1
Num11:17 I will come down and talk with you there; 1
Deu 6: 7 shall talk of them when you sit in your house 1
11:19 talking of them when you are sitting in your house 1
Jdg 14: 7 he went down and talked with the woman; 1
1Sm 2: 3 Talk no more so very proudly 1
14:19 while Saul was talking to the priest 1
17:23 As he talked with them . . Goliath by name, came up 1
2Kg 2:11 as they still went on and talked, behold, a chariot 1
8: 4 Now the king was talking with Geha'zi the servant 1
9:11 he said to them, "You know the fellow and his talk. 9
22:14 went to Huldah . . and they talked with her. 1
Est 6:14 While they were yet talking with him, 1
Job 15: 3 Should he argue in unprofitable talk 2
19:18 when I rise they talk against me. 1
29: 9 the princes refrained from talking 5
Ps 64: 5 they talk of laying snares secretly 6
69:12 I am the talk of those who sit in the gate 8
71:24 my tongue will talk of thy righteous help 4
Prv 4:24 put devious talk far from you. 10
6:22 when you awake, they will talk with you. 8
7:21 with her smooth talk she compels him. 10
14: 3 The talk of a fool is a rod for his back 7
23 but mere talk tends only to want. 3
24: 2 for . . their lips talk of mischief. 1
Ecc 10:13 and the end of his talk is wicked madness. 7
Isa 58:13 seeking your own pleasure, or talking idly; 1
Jer 29:32 for he has talked rebellion against the LORD. 1
Ezk 36: 3 you became the talk and evil gossip of the people; 11
Dan 10:17 How can my lord's servant talk with my lord? 1
Zec 1: 9 The angel who talked with me said to me 1
13 words to the angel who talked with me. 1
14 the angel who talked with me said to me, 'Cry out 1
19 I said to the angel who talked with me 1
2: 3 behold, the angel who talked with me came forward 1
4: 1 the angel who talked with me came again 1
4 I said to the angel who talked with me 1
5 Then the angel who talked with me answered me 1
5: 5 Then the angel who talked with me came forward 1
10 Then I said to the angel who talked with me 1
6: 4 Then I said to the angel who talked with me 1
Mat 17: 3 Moses and Eli'jah, talking with him. 21
22:15 and took counsel how to entangle him in his talk. 19
Mrk 1:45 he went out and began to talk freely about it 15
9: 4 they were talking to Jesus. 21
Lke 9:30 behold, two men talked with him, Moses and Eli'jah 21
24:14 talking with each other about all these things 20
15 they were talking and discussing together, 20
32 while he talked to us on the road 16
Joh 4:27 They marveled that he was talking with a woman 16
27 What do you wish?" or, "Why are you talking with her 16
14:30 I will no longer talk much with you 16
Act 10:27 as he talked with him 22
20: 7 Paul talked with them 12
9 as Paul talked still longer 12
1Co 4:19 find out not the talk of these arrogant people 19
20 For the kingdom of God does not consist in talk 19
2Co 11:23 I am talking like a madman 16
Eph 4:29 Let no evil talk come out of your mouths 19
2Ti 2:17 their talk will eat its way like gangrene 19
2Jn 1:12 I hope to come to see you and talk with you 16
3Jn 1:14 and we will talk together face to face. 16
Rev 21:15 And he who talked to me had a measuring rod of gold 16
1Es 3:21 makes every one talk in millions. 16
2Es 5:15 the angel who had come and talked with me held me 24
9:25 then I will come and talk with you. 24
10:25 While I was talking to her, behold, her face 24
15:53 and talking about their death when you were drunk? 23
Tob 7: 8 speak of those things which you talked about 18
Jdt 2: 1 there was talk in the palace of Nebuchadnezzar 19
Sir 13:11 he will test you through much talk 17
21:18 knowledge of the ignorant is unexamined talk. 19
22:13 Do not talk much with a foolish man 19
27:11 The talk of the godly man is always wise 13
13 The talk of fools is offensive 13
14 The talk of men given to swearing 17
32: 4 do not pour out talk 17
38:25 whose talk is about bulls? 13
1Mc 3:26 the Gentiles talked of the battles of Judas. 14
2Mc 8: 7 talk of his valor spread everywhere. 17

talk *See also* entrap, full.

talk about 1. διαλαλέω
Lke 1:65 all these things were talked about 1

common talk 1. θρυλέω
3Mc 3: 6 which was common talk among all; 1

empty talk 1. הֶבֶל
Job 35:16 Job opens his mouth in empty talk 1

foul talk 1. αἰσχρολογία
Col 3: 8 malice, slander, and foul talk from your mouth. 1

silly talk 1. μωρολογία
Eph 5: 4 nor silly talk, nor levity, which are not fitting; 1

talk together 1. דבר 2. κοινολογέομαι
Ezk 33:30 your people who talk together about you 1
1Mc 14: 9 they all talked together of good things 2

talkative 1. λαλιά
Sir 20: 5 detested for being too talkative. 1

empty talker 1. ματαιολόγος
Tit 1:10 empty talkers and deceivers 1

tall 1. גבה 2. גָּבֹהַּ 3. משך 4. קוֹמָה 5. רום 6. μέγας
7. ὑπεράγω 8. ὑψηλός 9. eminens
Deu 1:28 The people are greater and taller than we; 5
2:10 Emim . . great and many, and tall as the Anakim; 5
21 a people great and many, and tall as the Anakim; 5
9: 2 people great and tall, the sons of the Anakim 5
1Sm 9: 2 he was taller than any of the people. 2
10:23 he was taller than any of the people 1
2Kg 19:23 I felled its tallest cedars, its choicest 4
1Ch 11:23 a man of great stature, five cubits tall. •
Isa 18: 2 swift messengers, to a nation, tall and smooth 3
7 to the LORD of hosts from a people tall and smooth 3
37:24 I felled its tallest cedars 4
2Es 2:43 of great stature, taller than any of the others 9
Jdt 16: 7 nor did tall giants set upon him 8
1Mc 6:43 It was taller than all the others 7
151 1: 5 My brothers were handsome and tall 6

tall *See also* grow.

become tall 1. גדל
Ezk 16: 7 And you grew up and became tall 1

talon 1. unguis
2Es 11: 7 and behold, the eagle rose upon his talons 1
45 and your most evil talons 1

tamarisk tree 1. אֶשֶׁל
Gen 21:33 Abraham planted a tamarisk tree in Beer-sheba 1
1Sm 22: 6 at Gib'e-ah, under the tamarisk tree on the height 1
31:13 buried them under the tamarisk tree in Jabesh 1

tambourine 1. תֹּף 2. τύμπανον
Gen 31:27 with mirth and songs, with tambourine and lyre? 1
1Sm 10: 5 prophets coming . . with harp, tambourine, flute 1
2Sm 6: 5 lyres and harps and tambourines and castanets 1
1Ch 13: 8 making merry . . with . . harps and tambourines 1
Job 21:12 They sing to the tambourine and the lyre 1
Jdt 3: 7 garlands and dances and tambourines. 2
16: 2 Begin a song to my God with tambourines 2
1Mc 9:39 came out . . to meet them with tambourines 2

tame 1. δαμάζω 2. ἐξημερόω 3. ἥμερα
Jas 3: 7 every . . creature, can be tamed 1
7 every kind . . has been tamed by humankind 1
8 no human being can tame the tongue 1
4Mc 1:29 so tames the jungle of habits and emotions. 2
14:15 the ones that are tame protect their young 3

tamper 1. δολόω
2Co 4: 2 practice cunning or to tamper with God's word 1

tan 1. אדם
Exd 25: 5 tanned rams' skins, goatskins, acacia wood 1
26:14 for the tent a covering of tanned rams' skins 1
35: 7 tanned rams' skins, and goatskins; acacia wood 1
23 or goats' hair or tanned rams' skins or goatskins 1
36:19 made for the tent a covering of tanned rams' skins 1
39:34 the covering of tanned rams' skins and goatskins 1

tangle 1. στρεπτός
AEs 14: 2 she covered with her tangled hair. 1

tanner 1. βυρσεύς
Act 9:43 in Joppa for many days with one Simon, a tanner. 1
10: 6 he is lodging with Simon, a tanner 1
32 in the house of Simon, a tanner, by the seaside.' 1

target 1. מַטָּרָה 2. σκοπός
Job 16:12 he set me up as his target 1
Wis 5:12 when an arrow is shot at a target 2
21 and will leap to the target as from a well-drawn bow 2

tarnish 1. κατιόω
Sir 12:11 will know that it was not hopelessly tarnished. 1

tarry 1. אחר 2. חכה 3. ישב 4. לון 5. מהה 6. עמד
7. קוה 8. χρονίζω
Gen 45: 9 come down to me, do not tarry; 6
Exd 12:39 thrust out of Egypt and could not tarry 5
24:14 he said to the elders, "Tarry here for us 3
Num22:19 Pray, now, tarry here this night also 3
Jdg 5:16 Why did you tarry among the sheepfolds, to hear 3
28 Why tarry the hoofbeats of his chariots?' 1
19: 8 and tarry until the day declines." So they ate 5
2Kg 2: 2 Eli'jah said to Eli'sha, "Tarry here, I pray you; 3
4 Eli'jah said to him, "Eli'sha, tarry here, I pray you; 3
6 Then Eli'jah said to him, "Tarry here, I pray you; 3
18 they came back to him, while he tarried at Jericho 3
9: 3 Then open the door and flee; do not tarry. 2
Ps 30: 5 Weeping may tarry for the night 4
40:17 my help and my deliverer; do not tarry, O my God! 1
70: 5 my help and my deliverer, O LORD, do not tarry! 1
Isa 46:13 it is not far off, and my salvation will not tarry; 1
Mic 5: 7 showers . . which tarry not for men nor wait 7
Heb 10:37 the coming one shall come and shall not tarry; 8

tarry all night 1. לון
Gen 31:54 ate bread and tarried all night on the mountain. 1
Jdg 19: 9 now the day has waned . . pray tarry all night. 1

tarry for a night 1. לון
Jer 14: 8 a wayfarer who turns aside to tarry for a night? 1

tarry late 1. אחר
Isa 5:11 who tarry late into the evening till wine 1

tarry long 1. אחר
Prv 23:30 Those who tarry long over wine 1

task 1. דָּבָר 2. חֹק 3. מְלָאכָה 4. עֲבֹדָה 5. ἐργασία
6. ἔργον 7. καθίστημι 8. ποιέω 9. πρός
Exd 5:13 Complete your work, your daily task 1
14 Why have you not done all your task of making 2
36: 4 able men who were doing every sort of task 3
4 able men . . came, each from the task that he was 3
Num 4:19 appoint them each to his task and to his burden 4
49 each to his task of serving or carrying; •
Ezr 10: 4 Arise, for it is your task, and we are with you; 1
Prv 31:15 provides food . . and tasks for her maidens. 2
Col 3:23 Whatever your task, work heartily 8
1Ti 3: 1 he desires a noble task. 6
1Es 8:95 Arise and take action, for it is your task 9
Sir 3:17 My son, perform your tasks in meekness 6
23 Do not meddle in what is beyond your tasks 6
7:25 you will have finished a great task 6
37:11 with a lazy servant about a big task 5
1Mc 14:42 and appoint men over its tasks and over the country 6
3Mc 4:18 the task was impossible for all the generals 7

wearisome task 1. עָמָל
Ps 73:16 it seemed to me a wearisome task 1

taskmaster 1. נגשׂ 2. שַׂר מִסִּים 3. שֹׁטֵר
Exd 1:11 Therefore they set taskmasters over them 2
3: 7 their cry because of their taskmasters; 1
5: 6 commanded the taskmasters of the people 1
10 the taskmasters and the foremen of the people 3
13 The taskmasters were urgent, saying, "Complete 1
14 whom Pharaoh's taskmasters had set over them 1
1Kg 12:18 Ador'am, who was taskmaster over the forced labor •
2Ch 10:18 Hador'am . . taskmaster over the forced labor •
Job 3:18 they hear not the voice of the taskmaster. 1
Isa 60:17 peace and your taskmasters righteousness. 1

tassel 1. גְּדִלִים 2. צִיצִת
Num15:38 bid them to make tassels on the corners 2
38 to put upon the tassel of each corner a cord of blue; 2
39 shall be to you a tassel to look upon and remember 2
Deu 22:12 make yourself tassels on the four corners 1

taste 1. אכל 2. חֵךְ 3. טעם 4. טַעַם 5. טְעֵם (A)
6. ἀπογεύω 7. γεῦμα 8. γεύομαι 9. γεῦσις 10. gusto
11. gustus
Exd 16:31 manna . . and the taste of it was like wafers 4
Num11: 8 taste of it was like the taste of cakes baked 4
8 taste of it was like the taste of cakes baked 4
1Sm 14:24 So none of the people tasted food. 3
29 because I tasted a little of this honey. 3
43 I tasted a little honey with the tip of the staff 3
2Sm 3:35 if I taste bread or anything else till the sun 3
19:35 Can your servant taste what he eats or . . drinks? 3
Job 6: 6 or is there any taste in the slime of the purslane? 4
30 Cannot my taste discern calamity? 2
12:11 the ear try words as the palate tastes food? 3
21:25 bitterness of soul, never having tasted of good. 1
34: 3 the ear tests words as the palate tastes food. 3
Ps 34: 8 O taste and see that the LORD is good! 3
119:103 How sweet are thy words to my taste 2
Prv 24:13 drippings . . are sweet to your taste. 2
Sng 2: 3 and his fruit was sweet to my taste. 2
Jer 48:11 his taste remains in him, and his scent 4
Dan 5: 2 Belshaz'zar, when he tasted the wine, 5
Jon 3: 7 man nor beast, herd nor flock, taste anything; 3
Mat 16:28 some standing here who will not taste death 8
27:34 when he tasted it, he would not drink it. 8
Mrk 9: 1 some standing here who will not taste death 8
Lke 9:27 are some standing here who will not taste death 8
14:24 who were invited shall taste my banquet.' 8
Joh 2: 9 the steward . . tasted the water now become wine 8
8:52 he will never taste death.' 8

Act 23:14 an oath to taste no food till we have killed Paul. 8
Col 2:21 Do not handle, Do not taste, Do not touch 8
Heb 2: 9 that by the grace of God he might taste death 8
6: 4 who have tasted the heavenly gift 8
5 have tasted the goodness of the word of God 8
1Pe 2: 3 for you have tasted the kindness of the Lord. 8
2Es 6:26 who from their birth have not tasted death 10
44 and of varied appeal to the taste 11
9:24 and taste no meat and drink no wine 10
Tob 2: 4 before I tasted anything 8
Wis 16:20 suited to every taste. 9
Sir 23:17 To a fornicator all bread tastes sweet *
36:19 As the palate tastes the kinds of game 8
2Mc 6:20 to refuse things that it is not right to taste 8
13:18 having had a taste of the daring of the Jews 7
4Mc 10: 1 to save himself by tasting the meat. 6

taste *See also* lose.

tasteless 1. תָּפֵל
Job 6: 6 Can that which is tasteless be eaten 1

tattoo 1. קַעֲקַע
Lev 19:28 or tattoo any marks upon you: I am the LORD 1

taught by God 1. *θεοδίδακτος*
1Th 4: 9 taught by God to love one another; 1

taunt 1. גְּדוּפָה 2. חרף 3. חֶרְפָּה 4. מָשָׁל 5. שְׁנִינָה
Jdg 8:15 Zebah and Zalmun'na, about whom you taunted me 2
2Sm 21:21 when he taunted Israel, Jonathan . . slew him. 2
1Ch 20: 7 when he taunted Israel, Jonathan . . slew him. 2
Neh 4: 4 turn back their taunt upon their own heads 3
5: 9 prevent the taunts of the nations our enemies? 3
6:13 could give me an evil name, in order to taunt me. 2
Ps 42:10 my adversaries taunt me, while they say to me 2
44:13 Thou hast made us the taunt of our neighbors 3
55:12 not an enemy who taunts me–then I could bear it; 2
79: 4 We have become a taunt to our neighbors 3
12 taunts with which they have taunted thee, O Lord! 3
12 taunts with which they have taunted thee, O Lord! 2
89:51 with which thy enemies taunt, O LORD 2
102: 8 All the day my enemies taunt me 2
119:42 then shall I have an answer for those who taunt me 2
Isa 14: 4 you will take up this taunt against . . Babylon 4
Jer 24: 9 to be a reproach, a byword, a taunt, and a curse 5
42:18 an execration, a horror, a curse, and a taunt. 3
44: 8 and a taunt among all the nations of the earth? 3
12 an execration, a horror, a curse, and a taunt. 3
49:13 shall become a horror, a taunt, a waste, and a curse; 3
Lam 3:61 Thou hast heard their taunts, O LORD 3
Ezk 5:15 You shall be a reproach and a taunt 1
Hab 2: 6 all these take up their taunt against him 4
Zep 2: 8 I have heard the taunts of Moab 3
8 how they have taunted my people 2

taunt *See also* song.

taunter 1. חרף
Ps 44:16 at the words of the taunters and revilers 1

tavern *See* Three Taverns.

tawny 1. צָחֹר
Jdg 5:10 Tell of it, you who ride on tawny asses, you who sit 1

tax 1. מִדָּה 2. מַשְׂאֵת 3. ערך 4. *δίδραχμον* 5. *ἐπιβολή* 6. *κῆνσος* 7. *τέλος* 8. *τιμή* 9. *φόρος*
2Kg 23:35 he taxed the land to give the money 3
2Ch 24: 6 bring in . . the tax levied by Moses 2
9 to bring in for the LORD the tax that Moses 2
10 princes and all the people . . brought their tax *
Neh 5: 4 We have borrowed money for the king's tax 1
Mat 17:24 the collectors of the half-shekel tax *
24 Does not your teacher pay the tax? 4
22:17 Is it lawful to pay taxes to Caesar, or not? 6
19 Show me the money for the tax. 6
Mrk 12:14 Is it lawful to pay taxes to Caesar, or not? 6
Rom 13: 6 For the same reason you also pay taxes 9
7 Pay . . their dues, taxes to whom taxes are due 9
7 Pay . . their dues, taxes to whom taxes are due 9
1Es 4: 6 they compel one another to pay taxes to the king. 9
8:22 no tribute or any other tax 5
22 no one has authority to impose any tax upon them. *
1Mc 10:29 payment of tribute and salt tax and crown levies 8
33 cancel also the taxes on their cattle. 9
11:35 the tithes, and the taxes due to us 7
13:39 and cancel the crown tax which you owe *

tax *See also* collect, collector, free, office, registration, remission.

crown tax 1. *στέφανος*
1Mc 11:35 the salt pits and the crown taxes due to us 1
13:39 and cancel the crown tax which you owe 1

royal tax 1. *βασιλικός*
1Mc 11:34 we have granted release from the royal taxes 1

teach 1. אלף 2. בין 3. דבר 4. זהר 5. ידע 6. יסר 7. ירה 8. למד 9. לִמֵּד 10. לֶקַח 11. ידע (A) 12. *διδακτός* 13. *διδασκαλία* 14. *διδάσκαλος* 15. *διδάσκω* 16. *διδαχή* 17. *ἐκδιδάσκω* 18. *κατηχέω* 19. *λαλέω* 20. *μανθάνω* 21. *παιδεύω* 22. doceo
Exd 4:12 I will . . teach you what you shall speak. 7
15 and will teach you what you shall do. 7
18:20 you shall teach them the statutes 4
35:34 he has inspired him to teach, both him and Oho'liab 7
Lev 10:11 you are to teach the people of Israel 7
Deu 4: 1 statutes and the ordinances which I teach you 8
5 I have taught you statutes and ordinances 8
10 that they may teach their children so.' 8
14 LORD commanded me at that time to teach you 8
5:31 tell you all . . which you shall teach them 8
6: 1 the LORD your God commanded me to teach you 8
11:19 you shall teach them to your children 8
13: 5 put to death, because he has taught rebellion 3
20:18 that they may not teach you to do according 8
31:19 this song, and teach it to the people of Israel; 8
22 song . . and taught it to the people of Israel. 8
32: 2 May my teaching drop as the rain, my speech distil 10
33:10 They shall teach Jacob thy ordinances 7
Jdg 3: 2 Israel might know war, that he might teach war 8
8:16 and briers and with them taught the men 5
13: 8 let the man . . teach us what we are to do 7
2Sm 1:18 he said it should be taught to the people of Judah; 8
1Kg 8:36 thou dost teach them the good way 7
2Kg 17:27 and teach them the law of the god of the land. 7
28 and dwelt . . and taught them how they should fear 7
2Ch 6:27 when thou dost teach them the good way 7
15: 3 Israel was . . and without a teaching priest 7
17: 7 to teach in the cities of Judah; 8
9 they taught in Judah, having the book of the law 8
9 they went about . . and taught among the people. 8
35: 3 he said to the Levites who taught all Israel 2
Ezr 7:10 to teach his statutes and ordinances in Israel. 8
25 those who do not know them, you shall teach. 11
Neh 8: 9 Nehemi'ah . . Ezra . . , and the Levites who taught 2
Job 6:24 Teach me, and I will be silent; 7
8:10 Will they not teach you, and tell you 7
12: 7 But ask the beasts, and they will teach you; 7
8 the plants of the earth, and they will teach you; 7
15: 5 For your iniquity teaches your mouth 1
21:22 Will any teach God knowledge 8
27:11 I will teach you concerning the hand of God; 7
32: 7 Let days speak, and many years teach wisdom. 5
33:33 be silent, and I will teach you wisdom. 1
34:32 teach me what I do not see; if I have done iniquity 7
35:11 who teaches us more than the beasts of the earth 1
37:19 Teach us what we shall say to him; 5
Ps 25: 4 to know thy ways, O LORD; teach me thy paths. 8
5 teach me, for thou art the God of my salvation; 8
9 in what is right, and teaches the humble his way. 8
27:11 Teach me thy way, O LORD; and lead me 7
32: 8 I will instruct you and teach you the way 7
34:11 listen to me, I will teach you the fear of the LORD. 8
45: 4 let your right hand teach you dread deeds! 7
51: 6 therefore teach me wisdom in my secret heart. 5
13 Then I will teach transgressors thy ways 8
71:17 O God, from my youth thou hast taught me 8
78: 5 our fathers to teach to their children; 5
86:11 Teach me thy way, O LORD, that I may walk 7
90:12 teach us to number our days that we may get 5
94:10 He who teaches men knowledge 8
12 O LORD, and whom thou dost teach out of thy law 8
119:12 Blessed be thou, O LORD; teach me thy statutes! 8
26 thou didst answer me; teach me thy statutes! 8
33 Teach me, O LORD, the way of thy statutes; 7
64 teach me thy statutes! 8
66 Teach me good judgment and knowledge 8
68 teach me thy statutes. 8
102 from thy ordinances, for thou hast taught me. 7
108 O LORD, and teach me thy ordinances. 8
124 teach me thy statutes. 8
135 teach me thy statutes. 8
171 praise that thou dost teach me thy statutes. 8
132:12 covenant and my testimonies which I shall teach 8
143: 8 Teach me the way I should go, for to thee I lift up 5
10 Teach me to do thy will, for thou art my God! 8
Prv 4: 4 taught me, and said to me, "Let your heart hold fast 7
11 I have taught you the way of wisdom; 7
9: 9 teach a righteous man and he will increase 5
31: 1 words of Lemuel . . which his mother taught him 6
Ecc 12: 9 the Preacher also taught the people knowledge 8
Isa 2: 3 that he may teach us his ways and that we may walk 7
9:15 and the prophet who teaches lies is the tail; 7
28: 9 Whom will he teach knowledge 7
26 For he is instructed aright; his God teaches him. 7
40:14 and who taught him the path of justice 8
14 and taught him knowledge, and showed him the way 8
48:17 I am the LORD your God, who teaches you to profit 8
50: 4 has given me the tongue of those who are taught 9
4 he wakens my ear to hear as those who are taught. 9
54:13 All your sons shall be taught by the LORD 9
Jer 2:33 even to wicked women you have taught your ways. 8
9: 5 they have taught their tongue to speak lies; 8
14 after the Ba'als, as their fathers taught them. 8
20 teach to your daughters a lament 8
12:16 even as they taught my people to swear by Ba'al 8
13:21 whom you yourself have taught to be friends 8
31:34 And no longer shall each man teach his neighbor 8
32:33 and though I have taught them persistently 8
Ezk 22:26 neither have they taught the difference 5
44:23 They shall teach my people the difference 7
Mic 3:11 its priests teach for hire 7
4: 2 that he may teach us his ways 7
Mat 4:23 about all Galilee teaching in their synagogues 15
5: 2 he opened his mouth and taught them, saying 15
19 and teaches men so, shall be called least 15
19 who does them and teaches them shall be called 15
7:29 for he taught them as one who had authority 15
9:35 teaching in their synagogues and preaching 15
11: 1 he went on from there to teach and preach 15
13:54 he taught them in their synagogue 15
15: 9 in vain do they worship me, teaching as doctrines 15
21:23 came up to him as he was teaching, and said 15
22:16 you are true, and teach the way of God truthfully 14
26:55 Day after day I sat in the temple teaching 15
28:20 teaching them to observe all 15
Mrk 1:21 he entered the synagogue and taught. 15
22 he taught them as one who had authority 15
2:13 the crowd gathered about him, and he taught them. 15
4: 1 Again he began to teach beside the sea 15
2 he taught them many things in parables 15
6: 2 on the sabbath he began to teach in the synagogue; 15
6 he went about among the villages teaching. 15
30 told him all that they had done and taught. 15
34 he began to teach them many things. 15
7: 7 teaching as doctrines the precepts of men.' 15
8:31 he began to teach them that the Son of man must 15
9:31 for he was teaching his disciples, saying to them 15
10: 1 again, as his custom was, he taught them. 15
11:17 he taught, and said to them, "Is it not written 15
12:14 truly teach the way of God 15
35 as Jesus taught in the temple, he said 15
14:49 I was with you in the temple teaching 15
Lke 4:15 he taught in their synagogues 15
31 he was teaching them on the sabbath; 15
5: 3 he sat down and taught the people from the boat. 15
17 On one of those days, as he was teaching 15
6: 6 when he entered the synagogue and taught 15
11: 1 teach us to pray, as John taught his disciples. 15
1 teach us to pray, as John taught his disciples. 15
12:12 the Holy Spirit will teach you in that very hour 15
13:10 Now he was teaching in one of the synagogues 15
22 teaching, and journeying toward Jerusalem. 15
26 you taught in our streets.' 15
19:47 he was teaching daily in the temple 15
20: 1 as he was teaching the people in the temple 15
21 we know that you speak and teach rightly 15
21 truly teach the way of God. 15
21:37 every day he was teaching in the temple 15
23: 5 teaching throughout all Judea 15
Joh 6:45 they shall all be taught by God 12
59 as he taught at Caper'na-um. 15
7:14 Jesus went up into the temple and taught. 15
28 Jesus proclaimed, as he taught in the temple 15
35 Does he intend to . . teach the Greeks? 15
8: 2 he sat down and taught them. 15
20 as he taught in the temple 15
28 speak thus as the Father taught me. 15
9:34 You were born in utter sin, and would you teach us? 15
14:26 he will teach you all things 15
18:20 always taught in synagogues and in the temple 15
Act 1: 1 dealt with all that Jesus began to do and teach 15
4: 2 annoyed because they were teaching the people 15
18 not to speak or teach at all in the name of Jesus. 15
5:21 they entered the temple at daybreak and taught 15
25 standing in the temple and teaching the people. 15
28 We strictly charged you not to teach in this name 15
42 they did not cease teaching 15
11:26 and taught a large company of people 15
15: 1 were teaching the brethren 15
35 teaching and preaching the word of the Lord 15
18:11 teaching the word of God among them. 15
25 and taught accurately the things concerning Jesus 19
20:20 teaching you in public and from house to house 15
21:21 you teach all the Jews who are among the Gentiles 15
28 This is the man who is teaching men everywhere 15
28:31 teaching about the Lord Jesus Christ 15
Rom 2:21 who teach others, will you not teach yourself? 15
21 who teach others, will you not teach yourself? 15
12: 7 he who teaches, in his teaching; 15
7 he who teaches, in his teaching; 15
16:17 to the doctrine which you have been taught; 20
1Co 2:13 in words not taught by human wisdom 12
13 taught by the Spirit 12
4:17 as I teach them everywhere in every church. 15
11:14 Does not nature itself teach you 15
Gal 1:12 I did not receive it from man, nor was I taught it 15
6: 6 Let him who is taught the word 18
6 share all good things with him who teaches. 18
Eph 4:21 have heard about him and were taught in him 15
Col 1:28 teaching every man in all wisdom 15
2: 7 just as you were taught 15
3:16 teach and admonish one another in all wisdom 15
2Th 2:15 hold to the traditions which you were taught 15
1Ti 2:12 I permit no woman to teach 15
4:11 Command and teach these things. 15

13 reading of scripture, to preaching, to teaching. 13
16 Take heed to yourself and to your teaching 13
5:17 those who labor in preaching and teaching; 13
6: 2 Teach and urge these duties. 15
2Ti 2: 2 who will be able to teach others also. 15
3:16 inspired by God and profitable for teaching 13
4: 2 be unfailing in patience and in teaching. 16
Tit 1: 9 he must hold firm to the sure word as taught 16
11 teaching for base gain 15
11 by teaching . . what they have no right to teach. *
2: 1 as for you, teach what befits sound doctrine. 19
Heb 5:12 you need some one to teach you again 15
8:11 they shall not teach every one his fellow 15
Jas 3: 1 for you know that we who teach shall be judged *
1Jn 2:27 and you have no need that any one should teach you; 15
27 as his anointing teaches you about everything 15
27 just as it has been taught you, abide in him. 15
Rev 2:14 Balaam, who taught Balak to put a stumbling block 15
20 Jez'ebel . . is teaching and beguiling 15
1Es 8: 7 taught all Israel all the ordinances 15
23 those who do not know it you shall teach. 15
9:48 the Levites, taught the law of the Lord 15
49 the Levites who were teaching the multitude 15
55 the words which they had been taught 15
2Es 4: 4 and will teach you why the heart is evil. 22
8:29 regard those who have gloriously taught thy law. 22
12:38 shall teach them to the wise among your people 22
Wis 6:10 who have been taught them will find a defense. 15
7:22 wisdom, the fashioner of all things, taught me 15
8: 7 she teaches self-control and prudence 17
9:18 men were taught what pleases thee 15
12:19 Through such works thou has taught thy people 15
Sir 6:32 If you are willing, my son, you will be taught 21
9: 1 do not teach her an evil lesson to your own hurt. 15
18:13 He rebukes and trains and teaches them 15
21:12 He who is not clever cannot be taught 21
22: 7 He who teaches a fool 15
30: 3 He who teaches his son 15
33:27 idleness teaches much evil. 15
39: 8 He will reveal instruction in his teaching 13
45: 5 to teach Jacob the covenant 15
17 to teach Jacob the testimonies 15
Sus 1: 3 had taught their daughter according to the law 15
4Mc 5:23 it teaches us self-control 17
24 it teaches us piety 17
18:10 he taught you the law and the prophets. 15
12 he taught you about Hananiah, Azariah, and Mishael 15
18 For he did not forget to teach you the song 15
18 the song that Moses taught, which says 15

teach different doctrine 1. ἑτεροδιδασκαλέω
1Ti 1: 3 not to teach any different doctrine 1

teach diligently 1. שנן
Deu 6: 7 you shall teach them diligently to your children 1

teach fully 1. καταρτίζω
Lke 6:40 when he is fully taught 1

teach otherwise 1. ἑτεροδιδασκαλέω
1Ti 6: 3 If any one teaches otherwise 1

teach to walk 1. רגל
Hos 11: 3 Yet it was I who taught E'phraim to walk 1

teach what is good 1. καλοδιδάσκαλος
Tit 2: 3 they are to teach what is good 1

teach wisdom 1. חכם
Ps 105:22 to teach his elders wisdom. 1

teacher 1. בין 2. ירה 3. למד 4. מוֹרֶה 5. διδάσκαλος 6. παιδευτής
1Ch 25: 8 they cast lots . . teacher and pupil alike. 1
Job 36:22 exalted in his power; who is a teacher like him? 4
Ps 119:99 I have more understanding than all my teachers 3
Prv 5:13 I did not listen to the voice of my teachers 2
Isa 30:20 yet your Teacher will not hide himself any more 4
20 but your eyes shall see your Teacher. 4
Hab 2:18 has shaped it, a metal image, a teacher of lies? 4
Mat 8:19 Teacher, I will follow you wherever you go. 5
9:11 Why does your teacher eat with tax collectors 5
10:24 A disciple is not above his teacher 5
25 the disciple to be like his teacher 5
12:38 Teacher, we wish to see a sign from you. 5
17:24 Does not your teacher pay the tax? 5
19:16 Teacher, what good deed must I do 5
22:16 Teacher, we know that you are true 5
24 saying, "Teacher, Moses said 5
36 Teacher, which is the great commandment 5
23: 8 you have one teacher, and you are all brethren. 5
26:18 The Teacher says, My time is at hand 5
Mrk 4:38 Teacher, do you not care if we perish? 5
5:35 Why trouble the Teacher any further? 5
9:17 Teacher, I brought my son to you 5
38 Teacher, we saw a man casting out demons 5
10:17 Good Teacher, what must I do 5
20 Teacher, all these I have observed from my youth. 5
35 came forward to him, and said to him, "Teacher 5
12:14 Teacher, we know that you are true 5
19 Teacher, Moses wrote for us 5
32 the scribe said to him, "You are right, Teacher 5
13: 1 one of his disciples said to him, "Look, Teacher 5
14:14 'The Teacher says, Where is my guest room 5
Lke 2:46 sitting among the teachers 5
3:12 Teacher, what shall we do? 5
6:40 A disciple is not above his teacher 5
40 every one . . will be like his teacher. 5
7:40 he answered, "What is it, Teacher? 5
8:49 do not trouble the Teacher any more. 5
9:38 behold, a man from the crowd cried, "Teacher 5
10:25 Teacher, what shall I do to inherit eternal life? 5
11:45 One of the lawyers answered him, "Teacher 5
12:13 One of the multitude said to him, "Teacher 5
18:18 a ruler asked him, "Good Teacher, what shall I do 5
19:39 Teacher, rebuke your disciples. 5
20:21 They asked him, "Teacher 5
28 they asked him a question, saying, "Teacher 5
39 some of the scribes answered, "Teacher 5
21: 7 they asked him, "Teacher, when will this be 5
22:11 tell the householder, 'The Teacher says to you 5
Joh 1:38 And they said to him, "Rabbi" (which means Teacher) 5
3: 2 we know that you are a teacher come from God; 5
10 Jesus answered him, "Are you a teacher of Israel 5
8: 4 they said to him, "Teacher 5
11:28 The Teacher is here and is calling for you. 5
13:13 You call me Teacher and Lord; and you are right 5
14 I . . your Lord and Teacher, have washed your feet 5
20:16 Rab-bo'ni!" (which means Teacher) 5
Act 13: 1 at Antioch there were prophets and teachers 5
Rom 2:20 a corrector of the foolish, a teacher of children 5
1Co 12:28 first apostles, second prophets, third teachers 5
29 Are all teachers? Do all work miracles? 5
Eph 4:11 some evangelists, some pastors and teachers 5
1Ti 2: 7 a teacher of the Gentiles in faith and truth. 5
2Ti 1:11 appointed a preacher and apostle and teacher 5
4: 3 will accumulate for themselves teachers 5
Heb 5:12 For though by this time you ought to be teachers 5
Jas 3: 1 Let not many of you become teachers, my brethren 5
Sir 37:19 A man may be shrewd and the teacher of many 6
2Mc 1:10 teacher of Ptolemy the king 5

apt teacher 1. διδακτικός
1Ti 3: 2 dignified, hospitable, an apt teacher 1
2Ti 2:24 kindly to every one, an apt teacher, forbearing 1

false teacher 1. ψευδοδιδάσκαλος
2Pe 2: 1 just as there will be false teachers among you 1

teacher of the law 1. νομοδιδάσκαλος
Lke 5:17 there were Pharisees and teachers of the law 1
Act 5:34 Gama'li-el, a teacher of the law 1
1Ti 1: 7 desiring to be teachers of the law 1

teaching 1. תּוֹרָה 2. διδασκαλία 3. διδαχή 4. δόγμα 5. λόγος 6. sermo
Ps 78: 1 Give ear, O my people, to my teaching; 1
Prv 1: 8 reject not your mother's teaching; 1
3: 1 My son, do not forget my teaching 1
4: 2 good precepts: do not forsake my teaching. 1
6:20 My son . . forsake not your mother's teaching. 1
23 commandment is a lamp and the teaching a light 1
7: 2 keep my teachings as the apple of your eye; 1
13:14 The teaching of the wise is a fountain of life 1
31:26 teaching of kindness is on her tongue. 1
Isa 1:10 Give ear to the teaching of our God . . Gomor'rah! 1
8:16 seal the teaching among my disciples. 1
20 To the teaching and to the testimony! 1
Mat 7:28 the crowds were astonished at his teaching 3
16:12 the teaching of the Pharisees and Sadducees. 3
22:33 they were astonished at his teaching. 3
Mrk 1:22 they were astonished at his teaching 3
27 What is this? A new teaching! 3
4: 2 in his teaching he said to them 3
11:18 the multitude was astonished at his teaching. 3
12:38 in his teaching he said, "Beware of the scribes 3
Lke 4:32 they were astonished at his teaching 3
10:39 listened to his teaching. 5
Joh 7:16 Jesus answered them, "My teaching is not mine 3
17 he shall know whether the teaching is from God 3
18:19 about his disciples and his teaching. 3
Act 2:42 devoted themselves to the apostles' teaching 3
5:28 you have filled Jerusalem with your teaching 3
13:12 he was astonished at the teaching of the Lord. 3
17:19 May we know what this new teaching is 3
Rom 6:17 obedient . . to the standard of teaching 3
1Co 14: 6 knowledge or prophecy or teaching? 3
1Ti 6: 1 name of God and the teaching may not be defamed. 2
3 the teaching which accords with godliness 2
2Ti 3:10 Now you have observed my teaching, my conduct 2
4: 3 when people will not endure sound teaching 2
Tit 2: 7 in your teaching show integrity, gravity 2
Heb 13: 9 led away by diverse and strange teachings 3
Rev 2:14 some there who hold the teaching of Balaam 3
15 some who hold the teaching of the Nicola'itans. 3
24 you in Thyati'ra, who do not hold this teaching 3
2Es 7:78 Now, concerning death, the teaching is 6
90 Therefore this is the teaching concerning them 6
Sir 0: 1 many great teachings have been given to us *
24:33 I will again pour out teaching like prophecy 2
4Mc 10: 2 I was brought up on the same teachings? 4

team 1. צֶמֶד
Jer 51:23 with you I break in pieces the farmer and his team; 1

tear 1. בקע 2. גזל 3. טרף 4. טְרֵפָה 5. נסח 6. נתק 7. סחב 8. פרם 9. קרע 10. שבר 11. שסע 12. עבר (A) 13. ἀποξαίνω 14. διαρρήγνυμι 15. καταρρήγνυμι 16. ῥήγνυμι 17. σπαράσσω 18. σχίζω 19. σχίσμα
Exd 22:13 not make restitution for what has been torn. 4
28:32 an opening . . that it may not be torn. 9
39:23 around the opening, that it might not be torn. 9
Lev 1:17 he shall tear it by its wings, but shall not divide 11
7:24 and the fat of one that is torn by beast 4
13:45 The leper . . shall wear torn clothes 8
56 shall tear the spot out of the garment or the skin 9
22:24 its testicles bruised or crushed or torn or cut 6
Deu 33:20 Gad . . tears the arm, and the crown of the head. 3
Jos 9: 4 took . . wineskins, worn-out and torn and mended 1
Jdg 14: 6 him, and he tore the lion asunder as one tears a kid; 11
1Sm 15:27 Saul laid hold upon . . his robe, and it tore. 9
28 The LORD has torn the kingdom of Israel from you 9
28:17 the LORD has torn the kingdom out of your hand 9
1Kg 11:11 Since . . I will surely tear the kingdom from you 9
12 I will tear it out of the hand of your son. 9
30 laid hold . . and tore it into twelve pieces. 9
31 to tear the kingdom from the hand of Solomon 9
13:26 the lion, which has torn him and slain him 10
28 The lion had not eaten the body or torn the ass. 10
14: 8 tore the kingdom away from the house of David 9
2Kg 2:24 two she-bears came . . and tore 42 of the boys. 1
17:21 When he had torn Israel from the house of David 9
Job 16: 9 He has torn me in his wrath, and hated me; 3
18: 4 You who tear yourself in your anger 3
14 He is torn from the tent in which he trusted 6
Ps 17:12 They are like a lion eager to tear, as a young lion 3
52: 5 he will snatch and tear you from your tent; 5
Prv 27: 9 but the soul is torn by trouble. 15
Jer 15: 3 says the LORD: the sword to slay, the dogs to tear 7
22:24 were the signet ring . . yet I would tear you off 6
41: 5 with their beards shaved and their clothes torn 9
Ezk 4:14 eaten what died of itself or was torn by beasts 4
13:20 I will tear them from your arms; 9
22:25 are like a roaring lion tearing the prey; 3
27 like wolves tearing the prey, shedding blood 3
23:34 and pluck out your hair, and tear your breasts; 6
29: 7 you broke, and tore all their shoulders; 1
44:31 bird or beast, that has died of itself or is torn. 4
Dan 2: 5 torn limb from limb, and your houses . . laid 12
3:29 against the God . . shall be torn limb from limb 12
Hos 6: 1 for he has torn, that he may heal us; 3
Ams 1:11 his anger tore perpetually, and he kept his wrath 3
Mic 3: 2 who tear the skin from off my people 2
Nah 2:12 The lion tore enough for his whelps 3
Mat 9:16 and a worse tear is made. 19
26:65 Then the high priest tore his robes, and said 14
27:51 behold, the curtain of the temple was torn in two 18
Mrk 2:21 the new from the old, and a worse tear is made. 19
14:63 the high priest tore his garments, and said 14
15:38 the curtain of the temple was torn in two 18
Lke 5:36 No one tears a piece from a new garment 18
36 if he does, he will tear the new 18
9:42 the demon tore him and convulsed him 16
23:45 the curtain of the temple was torn in two. 18
Joh 19:24 they said to one another, "Let us not tear it 18
21:11 although there were so many, the net was not torn. 18
Act 14:14 they tore their garments 14
3Mc 1:18 they were torn by the harsh treatment 17
4Mc 6: 6 his flesh was being torn by scourges 13

tear (2) 1. בכה 2. בְּכִי 3. דִּמְעָה 4. מַי 5. δάκρυον 6. κλαίω
2Kg 20: 5 I have heard your prayer, I have seen your tears; 3
Est 8: 3 she fell at his feet and besought him with tears 1
Ps 6: 6 every night I flood my bed with tears; 3
39:12 give ear to my cry; hold not thy peace at my tears! 3
42: 3 My tears have been my food day and night 3
56: 8 put thou my tears in thy bottle! 3
80: 5 Thou hast fed them with the bread of tears 3
5 given them tears to drink in full measure. 3
102: 9 mingle tears with my drink 2
116: 8 For thou hast delivered my . . eyes from tears 3
119:136 My eyes shed streams of tears 4
126: 5 May those who sow in tears reap with shouts of joy! 3
Ecc 4: 1 And behold, the tears of the oppressed 3
Isa 15: 3 in . . squares every one wails and melts in tears. 2
16: 9 I drench you with my tears, O Heshbon and Ele-a'leh; 3
25: 8 the Lord GOD will wipe away tears from all faces 3
38: 5 I have heard your prayer, I have seen your tears; 3
Jer 9: 1 head were waters, and my eyes a fountain of tears 3
18 that our eyes may run down with tears 3
13:17 will weep bitterly and run down with tears 3
14:17 Let my eyes run down with tears night and day 3
31:16 your voice from weeping, and your eyes from tears; 3

Lam 1: 2 She weeps . . in the night, tears on her cheeks; 3
16 For these things I weep; my eyes flow with tears; 4
2:18 tears stream down like a torrent day and night! 3
3:48 my eyes flow with rivers of tears 4
Ezk 24:16 not mourn or weep nor shall your tears run down. 3
Mal 2:13 You cover the LORD'S altar with tears 3
Lke 7:38 she began to wet his feet with her tears 5
44 she has wet my feet with her tears 5
Act 20:19 with all humility and with tears and with trials 5
31 not cease . . to admonish every one with tears. 5
2Co 2: 4 anguish of heart and with many tears 5
Php 3:18 now tell you even with tears 6
2Ti 1: 4 As I remember your tears 5
Heb 5: 7 with loud cries and tears 5
12:17 though he sought it with tears. 5
Rev 7:17 and God will wipe away every tear from their eyes. 5
21: 4 he will wipe away every tear from their eyes 5
Tob 7:17 the mother comforted her daughter in her tears 5
Sir 22:19 A man who pricks an eye will make tears fall 5
35:15 Do not the tears of the widow run down her cheek 5
38:16 My son, let your tears fall for the dead 5
2Mc 11: 6 with lamentations and tears, besought the Lord 5
3Mc 1: 4 went to the troops with wailing and tears 5
16 they filled the temple with cries and tears; 5
5: 7 with tears and a voice hard to silence 5
6:14 their parents entreat you with tears. 5
22 Then the king's anger was turned to pity and tears 5
4Mc 4:11 with tears besought the Hebrews to pray for him 5

tear *See* shed.

tear all around 1. *περιλακίζω*

4Mc 10: 8 he saw his own flesh torn all around 1

tear asunder 1. שסע

Jdg 14: 6 him, and he tore the lion asunder as one tears a kid; 1

tear away 1. קרע 2. *αἴρω*

1Kg 11:13 However I will not tear away all the kingdom; 1
Mat 9:16 for the patch tears away from the garment 2
Mrk 2:21 if he does, the patch tears away from it 2
4Mc 9:28 and tore away his scalp *

tear down 1. הרס 2. נסח 3. נתץ 4. קרע 5. *καθαίρεσις* 6. *καθαιρέω* 7. *καταίρω* 8. *καταλύω* 9. *κατασκάπτω*

Exd 34:13 You shall tear down their altars 3
Deu 12: 3 you shall tear down their altars 3
1Kg 13: 3 Behold, the altar shall be torn down 4
5 altar also was torn down, and the ashes poured out 4
2Kg 11:18 all . . went to the house of Ba'al, and tore it down; 3
2Ch 23:17 people went to the house of Ba'al, and tore it down; 3
Job 12:14 If he tears down, none can rebuild; 1
Prv 14: 1 but folly with her own hands tears it down. 1
15:25 The LORD tears down the house of the proud 2
Jer 24: 6 I will build them up, and not tear them down; 1
33: 4 houses of the kings of Judah which were torn down 3
Ezk 30: 4 her foundations are torn down. 1
Mal 1: 4 They may build, but I will tear down 1
2Co 13:10 for building up and not for tearing down. 5
Gal 2:18 if I build up again those things which I tore down 8
Sir 34:23 When one builds and another tears down 6
1Mc 1:31 and tore down its houses and its surrounding walls. 6
2:25 he tore down the altar. 6
45 Mattathias . . went about and tore down the altars; 6
4:45 they thought it best to tear it down 6
45 So they tore down the altar 6
5:65 and tore down its strongholds 6
68 he tore down their altars 6
6: 7 they had torn down the abomination 6
62 and gave orders to tear down the wall all around. 6
8:10 tore down their strongholds 6
9:54 Alcimus gave orders to tear down the wall 7
54 He tore down the work of the prophets! 6
55 he only began to tear it down 7
2Mc 10: 2 they tore down the altars 6
14:33 and tear down the altar 9

tear in pieces 1. טרף 2. *διαρπάζω* 3. *διασπάω* 4. lanio

Jer 5: 6 one who goes out of them shall be torn in pieces; 1
Mic 5: 8 it goes through, treads down and tears in pieces 1
Act 23:10 afraid that Paul would be torn in pieces by them 3
2Es 1:32 slain them and torn their bodies in pieces 4
Sir 6: 2 lest your soul be torn in pieces like a bull. 2

tear loose 1. *διαλύω*

Sir 22:16 will not be torn loose by an earthquake 1

tear off 1. פרק 2. קרע 3. *διαρρήγνυμι* 4. *περιρρήγνυμι* 5. *περισύρω*

Ezk 13:21 Your veils also I will tear off 2
Zec 11:16 devours the flesh . . tearing off even their hoofs. 1
Act 16:22 the magistrates tore the garments off them 4
2Mc 4:38 tore off his garments 4
7: 7 They tore off the skin of his head with the hair 5
4Mc 9:11 having torn off his tunic 3

tear open 1. קרע

Hos 13: 8 I will tear open their breast 1

tear out 1. נתץ 2. *ἀποσύρω* 3. *προβάλλω*

Ps 58: 6 tear out the fangs of the young lions, O LORD! 1
2Mc 14:46 he tore out his entrails, took them with both hands 3
4Mc 9:28 These leopard-like beasts tore out his sinews 2

tear to pieces 1. טרף 2. פשח 3. *κατασχίζω*

Gen 37:33 Joseph is without doubt torn to pieces. 1
44:28 and I said, Surely he has been torn to pieces; 1
Lam 3:11 he led me off my way and tore me to pieces; 2
1Mc 1:56 The books . . they tore to pieces and burned with fire. 3

tearful 1. *μετὰ δακρύων*

3Mc 4: 2 mourning, lamentation, and tearful cries 1

most tearful 1. *πολύδακρυν*

3Mc 5:25 with most tearful supplication and mournful dirges 1

tears *See* pour, shed, weep.

teem 1. רמשׂ

Lev 20:25 or by anything with which the ground teems 1

teem with things 1. רֶמֶשׂ

Ps 104:25 sea . . which teems with things innumerable 1

tell 1. אמר 2. בשׂר 3. גלה אֹזֶן 4. דבר 5. דָּבָר 6. דבר בְּאָזְנַיִם 7. הגה 8. ידע 9. מִסְפָּר 10. נגד 11. ספר 12. ענה 13. צוה 14. קוֹל 15. שׂיח 16. שׂים בְּפֶה 17. שׁמע 18. אמר (A) 19. *ἀναγγέλλω* 20. *ἀνατίθημι* 21. *ἀπαγγέλλω* 22. *ἀποκρίνω* 23. *ἄρρητος* 24. *γνωρίζω* 25. *δηλόω* 26. *διαλέγομαι* 27. *διηγέομαι* 28. *εἶπον* 29. *ἐκδιηγέομαι* 30. *ἐκλαλέω* 31. *ἐμφανίζω* 32. *ἐξηγέομαι* 33. *εὐθίκτως* 34. *ἵνα* 35. *κατηχέω* 36. *λαλέω* 37. *λέγω* 38. *λόγος* 39. *μεταδίδωμι* 40. *ὅπως* 41. *προσαγγέλλω* 42. *προσαναλέγω* 43. *προσαναφέρω* 44. *πυνθάνομαι* 45. *σημαίνω* 46. *ὑποδείκνυμι* 47. *φημί* 48. adnuntio 49. dico 50. enarro 51. loquor 52. nuntio 53. praedico

Gen 3:11 He said, "Who told you that you were naked? 10
9:22 of his father, and told his two brothers outside. 10
12: 4 Abram went, as the LORD had told him; 4
18 Why did you not tell me that she was your wife? 10
14:13 one . . came, and told Abram the Hebrew 10
20: 8 Abim'elech . . told them all these things; 4
21:12 whatever Sarah says to you, do as she tells you 14
26 who has done this thing; you did not tell me 10
22: 2 one of the mountains of which I shall tell you. 1
3 went to the place of which God had told him. 1
9 came to the place of which God had told him 1
20 Now after these things it was told Abraham 10
24:23 said, "Tell me whose daughter you are. 10
28 the maiden ran and told her mother's household 10
33 I will not eat until I have told my errand. 4
49 deal loyally and truly with my master, tell me; 10
49 tell me; and if not, tell me; that I may turn 10
66 the servant told Isaac all the things 11
26: 2 dwell in the land of which I shall tell you. 1
32 That same day Isaac's servants came and told him 10
27:19 I have done as you told me; now sit up and eat 4
42 words of Esau her older son were told to Rebekah; 10
29:12 Jacob told Rachel that he was her father's 10
12 Rebekah's son; and she ran and told her father. 10
13 Jacob told Laban all these things 11
15 Tell me, what shall your wages be? 10
31:20 that he did not tell him that he intended to flee. 10
22 When it was told Laban on the third day that Jacob 10
27 and did not tell me, so that I might have sent you 10
32: 5 I have sent to tell my lord, in order that I may find 10
29 Then Jacob asked him, "Tell me, I pray, your name. 10
37: 5 had a dream, and when he told it to his brothers 10
9 Then he dreamed another dream, and told it to his 11
10 when he told it to his father and to his brothers 11
16 I am seeking my brothers," he said, "tell me 10
38:13 when Tamar was told, "Your father-in-law is going up 10
24 Judah was told, "Tamar your daughter-in-law has 10
39:17 she told him the same story, saying 4
40: 8 Tell them to me, I pray you. 11
9 the chief butler told his dream to Joseph 11
41:12 and when we told him, he interpreted our dreams 11
24 And I told it to the magicians, but there was no one 1
28 It is as I told Pharaoh, God has shown to Pharaoh 4
42:22 Reuben answered them, "Did I not tell you 1
29 they told him all that had befallen them, saying 10
43: 6 so ill as to tell the man that you had another 10
7 What we told him was in answer to these questions; 10
44: 2 And he did as Joseph told him. 4
24 we told him the words of my lord. 10
45:13 You must tell my father of all my splendor 10
26 they told him, "Joseph is still alive 10
27 when they told him all the words of Joseph 4
46:31 I will go up and tell Pharaoh, and will say to him 10
47: 1 Joseph went in and told Pharaoh, 10
48: 1 Joseph was told, "Behold, your father is ill"; 1
2 it was told to Jacob, "Your son Joseph has come 10
49: 1 that I may tell you what shall befall you 10
Exd 4:28 Moses told Aaron all the words of the LORD 10
6:11 Go in, tell Pharaoh king of Egypt to let the people 4
29 I am the LORD; tell Pharaoh king of Egypt all that I 4
7: 2 Aaron . . shall tell Pharaoh to let the people 4
10: 2 that you may tell in the hearing of your son 11
12: 3 Tell all the congregation of Israel that 4
35 Israel had also done as Moses told them 5
13: 8 you shall tell your son on that day, 'It is 10
14: 2 Tell the people of Israel to turn back and encamp 4
5 When the king of Egypt was told that the people 10
15 Tell the people of Israel to go forward. 4
16:22 leaders of the congregation came and told Moses 10
17:10 So Joshua did as Moses told him, and fought 1
18: 6 when one told Moses, "Lo, your father-in-law Jethro 1
8 Moses told his father-in-law all that the LORD had 11
19: 3 Thus you shall . . tell the people of Israel 10
9 Moses told the words of the people to the LORD. 10
25 So Moses went down to the people and told them. 1
24: 3 Moses came and told the people all the words 11
34:34 told the people of Israel what he was commanded 4
Lev 14:35 come and tell the priest, 'There seems to me to be 10
16: 2 Tell Aaron your brother not to come at all times 4
22: 2 Tell Aaron and his sons to keep away from the holy 4
Num 9: 4 Moses told the people of Israel that they should 4
11:24 Moses . . told the people the words of the LORD; 4
27 a young man ran and told Moses, "Eldad and Medad 10
13:27 told him, "We came to the land to which you sent us; 1
14:14 they will tell the inhabitants of this land. 1
39 Moses told these words to all . . Israel 4
16:37 Tell Elea'zar . . to take up the censers 1
19: 2 Tell the people of Israel to bring you 4
20: 8 tell the rock before their eyes to yield 4
23: 3 whatever he shows me I will tell you. 10
26 Did I not tell you, 'All that the LORD says 4
24:12 Did I not tell your messengers whom you sent to me 4
29:40 Moses told the people of Israel everything 1
Deu 1:21 go up, take possession, as the LORD . . has told you; 4
2: 1 in the direction of the Red Sea, as the LORD told me 4
5:31 tell you all the commandment and the statutes 4
13: 2 sign or wonder which he tells you comes to pass 4
17: 4 told you and you hear of it; then you shall inquire 10
32: 7 ask your . . elders, and they will tell you. 1
Jos 2: 2 And it was told the king of Jericho, "Behold 1
14 If you do not tell this business of ours 10
20 But if you tell this business of ours 10
23 and they told him all that had befallen them. 11
4: 7 Then you shall tell them that the waters 1
8 took up twelve stones . . as the LORD told Joshua; 4
10 the LORD commanded Joshua to tell the people 4
7:19 give glory to . . and tell me now what you have done; 10
9:24 it was told to your servants for a certainty 10
10:17 it was told Joshua, "The five kings have been found 10
Jdg 4:12 When Sis'era was told that Barak the son 10
5:10 Tell of it, you who ride on tawny asses, you who sit 15
6:27 Gideon took . . and did as the LORD had told him; 4
7:13 behold, a man was telling a dream to his comrade; 11
15 When Gideon heard the telling of the dream 9
9: 7 When it was told to Jotham, he went and stood 10
25 by them along that way; and it was told Abim'elech. 10
42 men went out . . And Abim'elech was told. 10
47 Abim'elech was told that all the people 10
13: 6 woman came and told her husband, "A man of God 1
6 him whence he was, and he did not tell me his name; 10
10 the woman ran in haste and told her husband 10
14: 2 he came up, and told his father and mother, "I saw 10
6 he did not tell his father or his mother what he 10
9 he did not tell them that he had taken the honey 10
12 if you can tell me what it is . . then I will give 10
13 if you cannot tell me what it is, then you shall 10
14 And they could not . . tell what the riddle was. 10
15 Entice your husband to tell us what the riddle is 10
16 and you have not told me what it is. 10
16 Behold, I have not told my father nor my mother 10
16 told my father nor my mother, and shall I tell you? 10
17 on the seventh day he told her, because she 10
17 Then she told the riddle to her countrymen. 10
19 festal garments to those who had told the riddle. 10
16: 2 The Gazites were told, "Samson has come here 21
6 Please tell me wherein your great strength lies 10
10 you have mocked me, and told me lies; please tell me 4
10 me lies; please tell me how you might be bound. 10
13 Until now you have mocked me, and told me lies; 4
13 and told me lies; tell me how you might be bound. 10
15 mocked me . . and you have not told me wherein 10
17 he told her all his mind, and said to her, "A razor has 10
18 When Deli'lah saw that he had told her all his mind 10
18 Come up this once, for he has told me all his mind. 10
20: 3 Tell us, how was this wickedness brought to pass? 4
Rut 2:11 All that you have done . . has been fully told me 10
19 she told her mother-in-law with whom she had 10
3: 4 go . . and lie down; and he will tell you what to do. 10
6 and did just as her mother-in-law had told her. 13
16 Then she told her all that the man had done for her 10
4: 4 I thought I would tell you of it, and say, Buy it 3
4 but if you will not, tell me, that I may know 10
1Sm 3:13 And I tell him that I am about to punish his house 10
15 And Samuel was afraid to tell the vision to Eli. 10
17 What was it that he told you? Do not hide it from me. 4

17 if you hide anything . . of all that he told you. 4
18 Samuel told him everything and hid nothing 10
4:13 when the man came into the city and told the news 10
14 Then the man hastened and came and told Eli. 10
6: 2 Tell us with what we shall send it to its place. 8
8:10 Samuel told all the words of the LORD 1
9: 6 he can tell us about the journey on which we have 10
8 I will give it to the man of God, to tell us our way. 10
17 the LORD told him, "Here is the man of whom I spoke 12
18 and said, "Tell me where is the house of the seer? 10
19 go and will tell you all that is on your mind. 10
27 Tell the servant to pass on before us 1
10:15 Pray, tell me what Samuel said to you. 10
16 He told us plainly that the asses had been found. 10
25 Samuel told the people the rights and duties 4
11: 5 they told him the tidings of the men of Jabesh. 11
9 the messengers came and told the men of Jabesh 10
14: 1 But he did not tell his father. 10
33 they told Saul, "Behold, the people are sinning 10
43 Saul said to Jonathan, "Tell me what you have done. 10
43 Tell me what you have done." And Jonathan told him 10
15:12 and it was told Samuel, "Saul came to Carmel 10
16 Stop! I will tell you what the LORD said to me 10
17:55 As your soul lives, O king, I cannot tell. 8
18:20 and they told Saul, and the thing pleased him. 10
24 And the servants of Saul told him 10
26 And when his servants told David these words 10
19: 2 Jonathan told David, "Saul . . seeks to kill you; 10
3 and if I learn anything I will tell you. 10
11 But Michal, David's wife, told him, "If you do not save 10
18 and told him all that Saul had done to him. 10
19 And it was told Saul, "Behold, David is at Nai'oth 10
21 When it was told Saul, he sent other messengers 10
20: 9 If I knew that . . would I not tell you? 10
10 Who will tell me if your father answers you 10
22:21 Abi'athar told David that Saul had killed 10
22 I knew . . that he would surely tell Saul. 10
23: 1 Now they told David, "Behold, the Philistines are 10
7 it was told Saul that David had come to Kei'lah. 10
11 O LORD . . I beseech thee, tell thy servant. 10
13 Saul was told that David had escaped from Kei'lah 10
22 it is told me that he is very cunning. 1
25 David was told; therefore he went down to the rock 10
24: 1 When Saul returned . . he was told 10
25: 8 Ask your young men, and they will tell you. 10
12 came back and told him all this. 10
14 But one of the young men told Ab'igail, Nabal's wife 10
19 But she did not tell her husband Nabal. 10
36 she told him nothing at all until the morning 10
37 his wife told him these things, and his heart died 10
27: 4 when it was told Saul that David had fled to Gath 10
11 Lest they should tell about us 10
28:15 I have summoned you to tell me what I shall do. 8
2Sm 1: 4 David said to him, "How did it go? Tell me. 10
5 Then David said to the young man who told him 10
6 And the young man who told him said, "By chance I 10
13 And David said to the young man who told him 10
20 Tell it not in Gath, publish it not in . . Ash'kelon; 10
2: 4 they told David, "It was the men of Ja'besh-gil'ead 10
3:19 then Abner went to tell David at Hebron 6
23 it was told Jo'ab, "Abner . . came to the king 10
4:10 when one told me, 'Behold, Saul is dead,' 10
6:12 And it was told King David, "The LORD has blessed 10
7: 5 Go and tell my servant David, 'Thus says the LORD 1
10: 5 When it was told David, he sent to meet them 10
17 when it was told David, he gathered all Israel 10
11: 5 and she sent and told David, "I am with child. 10
10 When they told David . . David said to Uri'ah 10
18 Jo'ab sent and told David . . about the fighting; 10
19 When you have finished telling all the news 4
22 messenger . . told David all that Jo'ab had sent 10
22 and told David all that Jo'ab had sent him to tell. •
12:18 feared to tell him that the child was dead; 10
13: 4 why are you so haggard . . ? Will you not tell me? 10
14:33 Then Jo'ab went to the king, and told him; 10
15:31 And it was told David, "Ahith'ophel is among 10
35 tell it to Zadok and Abi'athar the priests. 10
17:16 Now therefore send quickly and tell David, 'Do not 10
17 a maidservant used to go and tell them 10
17 tell them, and they would go and tell King David; 10
18 But a lad saw them, and told Ab'salom; 10
21 the men came up . . and went and told King David. 10
18:10 a certain man saw it, and told Jo'ab, "Behold, I saw 10
11 said to the man who told him, "What, you saw him! 10
21 Jo'ab said . . "Go, tell the king what you have seen. 10
25 And the watchman called out and told the king. 10
19: 1 It was told Jo'ab, "Behold, the king is weeping 10
8 And the people were all told, "Behold, the king is 10
20:16 Hear! Tell Jo'ab, 'Come here, that I may speak to you.' 1
21:11 When David was told what Rizpah . . had done 10
24:13 Gad came to David and told him, and said to him 10
1Kg 1:20 eyes . . are upon you, to tell them who shall sit 10
23 they told the king, "Here is Nathan the prophet. 10
27 you have not told your servants who should sit 8
51 it was told Solomon, "Behold, Adoni'jah fears King 10
2:29 when it was told King Solomon, "Jo'ab has fled 10
39 it was told Shim'e-i, "Behold, your slaves are in Gath 10
41 Solomon was told that Shim'e-i had gone 10
10: 2 she told him all that was on her mind. 4
7 and behold, the half was not told me; 10
13:11 his sons came and told him all that the man of God 11
11 the words also . . they told to their father. 11
25 they came and told it in the city 4
14: 3 he will tell you what shall happen to the child. 10
7 Go, tell Jerobo'am, 'Thus says the LORD 1
18: 8 Go, tell your lord, 'Behold, Eli'jah is here.' 1
11 'Go, tell your lord, "Behold, Eli'jah is here."' 1
12 when I come and tell Ahab . . he will kill me 10
13 Has it not been told my lord what I did 10
14 'Go, tell your lord, "Behold, Eli'jah is here"'; 1
16 Obadi'ah went to meet Ahab, and told him; 10
19: 1 Ahab told Jez'ebel all that Eli'jah had done 10
20: 9 Tell my lord the king, 'All that you first demanded 1
11 Tell him, 'Let not him that girds on his armor boast 4
22:18 Did I not tell you that he would not prophesy good 1
2Kg 1: 2 he sent messengers, telling them, "Go, inquire 1
7 who came to meet you and told you these things? 4
4: 2 Tell me; what have you in the house? 10
7 She came and told the man of God, and he said, "Go 10
24 do not slacken the pace for me unless I tell you. 1
27 the LORD has hidden it from me, and has not told me. 10
31 he returned to meet him, and told him 10
5: 4 Na'aman went in and told his lord, "Thus and so 10
6:10 sent to the place of which the man of God told him. 1
12 Eli'sha . . tells the king of Israel the words 10
13 It was told him, "Behold, he is in Dothan. 10
7: 9 come, let us go and tell the king's household. 10
10 called to the gatekeepers . . and told them 10
11 and it was told within the king's household. 10
12 I will tell you what the Syrians have prepared 10
15 And the messengers returned, and told the king. 10
8: 4 Tell me all the great things . . Eli'sha has done. 11
5 he was telling the king how Eli'sha had restored 11
6 And when the king asked the woman, she told him. 11
7 when it was told him, "The man of God has come here 10
14 he answered, "He told me that you would . . recover. 1
9:12 they said, "That is not true; tell us now. 10
15 out of the city to go and tell the news in Jezreel. 10
36 When they came back and told him, he said 10
10: 8 the messenger came and told him, "They have 10
17:26 So the king of Assyria was told 1
18:37 came . . and told him the words of the Rab'shakeh. 10
22:10 Then Shaphan the secretary told the king 10
15 says the LORD . . 'Tell the man who sent you to me 1
23:17 And the men of the city told him, "It is the tomb 1
1Ch 16: 9 Sing to him . . tell of all his wonderful works! 15
23 Tell of his salvation from day to day. 2
17: 4 Go and tell my servant David, 'Thus says the LORD 1
19: 5 When David was told concerning the men 10
17 when it was told David, he gathered all Israel 10
2Ch 9: 1 to Solomon, she told him all that was on her mind. 4
6 half the greatness of your wisdom was not told me; 10
18:17 Did I not tell you that he would not prophesy good 1
20: 2 Some men came and told Jehosh'aphat 10
32:11 Is not Hezeki'ah misleading you . . when he tells 1
34:18 Then Shaphan the secretary told the king 10
23 Thus says the LORD . . 'Tell the man who sent you 1
Ezr 2:63 governor told them that they were not to partake 1
8:17 I . . sent them . . telling them what to say 16
22 since we had told the king, "The hand of our God 1
Neh 2:12 told no one what my God had put into my heart to do 10
16 I had not yet told the Jews, the priests, the nobles 10
18 I told them of the hand of my God which had been 10
7:65 governor told them that they were not to partake 1
8: 1 told Ezra the scribe to bring the book of the law 1
9:15 thou didst tell them to go in to possess the land 1
23 land which thou hadst told their fathers 1
Est 1:18 the ladies . . will be telling it to all the king's 1
2:22 Mor'decai, and he told it to Queen Esther 10
22 and Esther told the king in the name of Mor'decai. 1
3: 4 they told Haman, in order to see whether 10
4 for he had told them that he was a Jew. 10
4: 4 Esther's maids and her eunuchs came and told her 10
7 Mor'decai told him all that had happened to him 10
9 Hathach went and told Esther what Mor'decai had 10
12 And they told Mor'decai what Esther had said. 10
13 Mor'decai told them to return answer to Esther 1
15 Then Esther told them to reply to Mor'decai 1
5:14 tell the king to have Mor'decai hanged upon it; 1
6: 2 how Mor'decai had told about Bigthana and Teresh 10
5 the king's servants told him, "Haman is there 1
13 Haman told . . everything that had befallen him. 11
8: 1 Mor'decai . . for Esther had told what he was to her; 10
Job 1:15 I alone have escaped to tell you. 10
16 I alone have escaped to tell you. 10
17 I alone have escaped to tell you. 10
19 I alone have escaped to tell you. 10
8:10 Will they not teach you, and tell you 10
11: 6 and that he would tell you the secrets of wisdom! 10
12: 7 the birds of the air, and they will tell you; 10
15:18 what wise men have told 10
37:20 Shall it be told him that I would speak? 11
38: 4 Tell me, if you have understanding. 10
42: 9 went and did what the LORD had told them; 4
Ps 2: 7 I will tell of the decree of the LORD: He said to me 11
9: 1 I will tell of all thy wonderful deeds. 11
11 Tell among the peoples his deeds! 10
19: 1 The heavens are telling the glory of God; 11
22:22 I will tell of thy name to my brethren; 11
30 shall tell of the Lord to the coming generation 11
26: 7 and telling all thy wondrous deeds. 11
30: 9 Will it tell of thy faithfulness? 10
35:28 Then my tongue shall tell of thy righteousness 7
40: 5 Were I to proclaim and tell of them 4
41: 6 mischief; when he goes out, he tells it abroad. 4
44: 1 our fathers have told us, what deeds thou didst 11
48:13 that you may tell the next generation 11
50:12 If I were hungry, I would not tell you; 1
52: 0 when Doeg, the Edomite, came and told Saul 10
54: 0 when the Ziphites went and told Saul 1
64: 9 men will fear; they will tell what God has wrought 10
66:16 fear God, and I will tell what he has done for me. 11
71:15 My mouth will tell of thy righteous acts 11
73:28 GOD my refuge, that I may tell of all thy works. 11
78: 3 heard and known, that our fathers have told us. 11
4 but tell to the coming generation 11
6 arise and tell them to their children 11
96: 2 tell of his salvation from day to day. 2
105: 2 tell of all his wonderful works! 15
107:22 let them . . tell of his deeds in songs of joy! 11
119:26 When I told of my ways, thou didst answer me; 11
142: 2 complaint before him, I tell my trouble before 10
145:11 glory of thy kingdom, and tell of thy power 4
Prv 25: 7 for it is better to be told, "Come up here 1
Ecc 6:12 For who can tell man what will be after him 10
8: 7 for who can tell him how it will be? 10
10:14 and who can tell him what will be after him? 10
20 or some winged creature tell the matter. 10
Sng 1: 7 Tell me, you whom my soul loves, where you pasture 10
5: 8 my beloved, that you tell him I am sick with love. 10
Isa 3:10 Tell the righteous that it shall be well 1
5: 5 now I will tell you what I will do to my vineyard. 8
7: 2 the house of David was told, "Syria is in league 10
19:12 Let them tell you and make known 10
21: 2 A stern vision is told to me; 10
36:22 and told him the words of the Rab'shakeh. 10
40:21 Has it not been told you from the beginning? 10
41:22 Let them bring them, and tell us what is to happen. 10
22 Tell us the former things, what they are 10
23 Tell us what is to come hereafter, that we may know 10
42: 9 before they spring forth I tell you of them. 17
44: 7 Let them tell us what is yet to be. 10
8 have I not told you from of old and declared it? 17
45:21 Who told this long ago? Who declared it of old? 17
52:15 that which has not been told them they shall see 11
57:12 will tell of your righteousness and your doings 10
Jer 16:10 And when you tell this people all these words 10
19: 2 and proclaim there the words that I tell you. 4
23:27 by their dreams which they tell one another 11
28 Let the prophet who has a dream tell the dream 11
32 and who tell them and lead my people astray 11
28:13 Go, tell Hanani'ah, 'Thus says the LORD 1
33: 3 and will tell you great and hidden things 10
36:13 Micai'ah told them all the words that he had heard 10
17 Tell us, how did you write all these words? 10
38:15 If I tell you, will you not be sure to put me to death? 10
25 and say to you, 'Tell us what you said to the king 10
39:12 do him no harm, but deal with him as he tells you. 4
42: 4 and whatever the LORD answers you I will tell you; 10
21 in anything that he sent me to tell you. •
43: 2 men said to Jeremiah, "You are telling a lie. 4
48:20 Tell it by the Arnon, that Moab is laid waste. 10
51:31 to tell the king of Babylon that his city is taken 10
Ezk 11:25 I told the exiles all the things that the LORD had 4
12:23 Tell them therefore, 'Thus says the Lord GOD 1
17:12 Tell them, Behold, the king of Babylon came 1
24:19 Will you not tell us what these things mean for us 10
44: 5 with your ears all that I shall tell you 4
Dan 2: 2 summoned, to tell the king his dreams. 10
4 Tell your servants the dream, and we will show 18
7 Let the king tell his servants the dream 18
9 Therefore tell me the dream, and I shall know 18
18 told them to seek mercy of the God of heaven •
36 now we will tell the king its interpretation. 18
4: 7 told them the dream, but they could not make known 18
8 Daniel came in . . -and I told him the dream, saying 18
9 dream which I saw; tell me its interpretation. 18
7: 1 down the dream, and told the sum of the matter. 18
5 it was told, 'Arise, devour much flesh.' 18
16 told me, and made known to me the interpretation 18
8:26 vision . . which has been told is true; 1
9:23 come to tell it to you, for you are greatly beloved; 10
10:21 tell you what is inscribed in the book of truth 10
Jol 1: 3 Tell your children of it 11
3 and let your children tell their children •
Jon 1: 8 Tell us, on whose account this evil has come upon 10
10 because he had told them. 10
3: 2 proclaim to it the message that I tell you. 4
Mic 1:10 Tell it not in Gath, weep not at all; 10
Hab 1: 5 a work . . that you would not believe if told. 11
Zec 10: 2 the dreamers tell false dreams 4
Mat 2: 5 They told him, "In Bethlehem of Judea; 28
13 flee to Egypt, and remain there till I tell you; 28
3: 9 for I tell you, God is able from these stones 37
5:20 For I tell you, unless your righteousness 37
6:25 I tell you, do not be anxious about your life 37
29 yet I tell you, even Solomon in all his glory was not 37

8:11 I tell you, many will come from east and west 37
33 going into the city they told everything 21
10:27 What I tell you in the dark, utter in the light 37
11: 4 Jesus answered them, "Go and tell John 21
9 Yes, I tell you, and more than a prophet. 37
22 But I tell you, it shall be more tolerable 37
24 But I tell you that it shall be more tolerable 37
12: 6 I tell you, something greater than the temple 37
31 Therefore I tell you, every sin and blasphemy 37
36 I tell you, on the day of judgment 37
48 he replied to the man who told him 37
13: 3 he told them many things in parables, saying 36
30 at harvest time I will tell the reapers 28
33 He told them another parable 36
14:12 and they went and told Jesus. 21
15: 5 you say, 'If any one tells his father or his mother 37
16:12 he did not tell them to beware of the leaven 28
18 I tell you, you are Peter 37
20 strictly charged the disciples to tell no one 28
24 Then Jesus told his disciples 28
17: 9 Tell no one the vision 28
12 I tell you that Eli'jah has already come 37
18:10 I tell you that in heaven 37
17 tell it to the church 28
19:24 Again I tell you, it is easier for a camel 37
20:31 The crowd rebuked them, telling them to be silent; 34
21: 5 Tell the daughter of Zion 28
24 and if you tell me the answer 28
24 then I also will tell you by what authority 28
27 he said to them, "Neither will I tell you 37
43 I tell you, the kingdom of God will be taken away 37
22: 4 Tell those who are invited 28
17 Tell us, then, what you think. 28
23: 3 so practice and observe whatever they tell you 28
39 I tell you, you will not see me again, until you say 37
24: 3 Tell us, when will this be 28
26:13 what she has done will be told in memory of her. 36
29 I tell you I shall not drink again of this fruit 37
63 tell us if you are the Christ, the Son of God. 28
64 Jesus said to him, "You have said so. But I tell you 37
27:64 steal him away, and tell the people 28
28: 7 Then go quickly and tell his disciples 28
7 Lo, I have told you. 28
8 ran to tell his disciples. 21
10 go and tell my brethren to go to Galilee 21
11 told the chief priests all that had taken place. 21
13 said, "Tell people, 'His disciples came by night 28
Mrk 1:30 immediately they told him of her. 37
3: 9 he told his disciples to have a boat ready for him 28
5:14 told it in the city and in the country 21
16 those who had seen it told what had happened 27
19 tell them how much the Lord has done for you 28
33 told him the whole truth. 28
43 and told them to give her something to eat. 28
6:30 told him all that they had done and taught. 21
7:11 you say, 'If a man tells his father or his mother 37
36 he charged them to tell no one 37
8:28 they told him, "John the Baptist 28
30 he charged them to tell no one about him. 37
9: 9 he charged them to tell no one what they had seen 27
13 I tell you that Eli'jah has come 37
10:32 he began to tell them what was to happen to him 37
48 many rebuked him, telling him to be silent 34
11: 6 they told them what Jesus had said 28
24 Therefore I tell you, whatever you ask in prayer 37
29 tell you by what authority I do these things. 28
33 Neither will I tell you by what authority 37
12:12 he had told the parable against them 28
13: 4 Tell us, when will this be, and what will be the sign 28
14: 9 what she has done will be told in memory of her. 36
16 found it as he had told them 28
16: 7 But go, tell his disciples and Peter that he is going 28
7 Galilee; there you will see him, as he told you. 28
10 She went and told those who had been with him 21
13 they went back and told the rest 21
Lke 2:17 which had been told them concerning this child; 36
18 wondered at what the shepherds told them. 36
20 as it had been told them. 36
3: 8 I tell you, God is able from these stones to raise 37
4:25 in truth, I tell you, there were many widows 37
5:14 he charged him to tell no one 37
36 He told them a parable also 37
6:39 He also told them a parable 28
46 Why do you call me 'Lord, Lord,' and not do what I tell 37
7: 9 I tell you, not even in Israel 37
18 disciples of John told him of all these things. 21
22 Go and tell John what you have seen and heard 21
26 Yes, I tell you, and more than a prophet. 37
28 I tell you, among those born of women 37
47 Therefore I tell you, her sins, which are many 37
8:20 he was told, "Your mother and your brothers 21
34 told it in the city and in the country. 21
36 those who had seen it told them 21
56 he charged them to tell no one what had happened. 37
9:10 the apostles told him what they had done 27
21 he . . commanded them to tell this to no one 37
27 I tell you truly, there are some standing here 37
36 they kept silence and told no one in those days 21
10:12 I tell you, it shall be more tolerable on that day 37
24 I tell you that many prophets and kings desired 37
40 Tell her then to help me. 28
11: 8 I tell you, though he will not get up 37
9 I tell you, Ask, and it will be given you 37
51 Yes, I tell you, it shall be required 37
12: 4 I tell you, my friends, do not fear those who kill 37
5 yes, I tell you, fear him! 37
8 I tell you, every one who acknowledges me 37
16 he told them a parable, saying, "The land 28
22 he said to his disciples, "Therefore I tell you 37
27 yet I tell you, even Solomon in all his glory 37
41 are you telling this parable for us or for all? 37
51 No, I tell you, but rather division; 37
59 I tell you, you will never get out 37
13: 1 who told him of the Galileans 21
3 I tell you, No 37
5 I tell you, No 37
6 he told this parable: "A man had a fig tree planted 37
24 many, I tell you, will seek to enter 37
27 he will say, 'I tell you, I do not know 37
32 he said to them, "Go and tell that fox, 'Behold 28
35 I tell you, you will not see me until you say 37
14: 7 Now he told a parable to those who were invited 37
24 For I tell you, none of those men who were invited 37
15: 3 he told them this parable 28
7 Just so, I tell you, there will be more joy in heaven 37
10 Just so, I tell you, there is joy before the angels 37
16: 9 I tell you, make friends for yourselves 37
17:34 I tell you . . there will be two in one bed 37
18: 1 he told them a parable 37
8 I tell you, he will vindicate them speedily. 37
9 He also told this parable to some 28
14 I tell you, this man went down to his house 37
37 They told him, "Jesus of Nazareth is passing by. 21
39 telling him to be silent 34
19:11 he proceeded to tell a parable 28
26 'I tell you 37
32 went away and found it as he had told them. 28
40 He answered, "I tell you, if these were silent 37
20: 2 Tell us by what authority you do these things 28
3 I also will ask you a question; now tell me 28
8 Jesus said to them, "Neither will I tell you 37
9 he began to tell the people this parable 37
19 he had told this parable against them. 28
21: 3 he said, "Truly I tell you 37
29 he told them a parable 28
22:11 tell the householder, 'The Teacher says to you 28
13 they went, and found it as he had told them 28
16 I tell you I shall not eat it until it is fulfilled 37
18 I tell you that from now on I shall not drink 37
34 He said, "I tell you, Peter, the cock will not crow 37
37 I tell you that this scripture must be fulfilled 37
67 If you are the Christ, tell us. 28
67 he said to them, "If I tell you, you will not believe; 28
24: 6 Remember how he told you 36
9 returning from the tomb they told all this 21
10 who told this to the apostles; 37
35 Then they told what had happened on the road 32
Joh 2: 5 said to the servants, "Do whatever he tells you. 37
16 And he told those who sold the pigeons 28
3:12 told you earthly things and you do not believe 28
12 how can you believe if I tell you heavenly things? 28
4:29 Come, see a man who told me all that I ever did. 28
35 I tell you, lift up your eyes, and see how the fields 37
39 woman's testimony, "He told me all that I ever did. 28
51 his servants . . told him that his son was living 37
5:15 The man went away and told the Jews 19
6:12 he told his disciples, "Gather up the fragments 37
65 he said, "This is why I told you 28
8:24 I told you that you would die in your sins 28
25 Even what I have told you from the beginning. 36
40 a man who has told you the truth 36
45 because I tell the truth, you do not believe me. 37
46 If I tell the truth, why do you not believe me? 37
9:27 He answered them, "I have told you already 28
10:24 If you are the Christ, tell us plainly. 28
25 Jesus answered them, "I told you 28
11:14 Jesus told them plainly, "Laz'arus is dead; 28
40 Jesus said to her, "Did I not tell you 28
46 told them what Jesus had done. 28
12:22 Philip went and told Andrew 37
22 Andrew went with Philip and they told Jesus. 37
13:19 I tell you this now, before it takes place 37
24 Tell us who it is of whom he speaks. 44
29 Some thought that . . Jesus was telling him 37
14: 2 if it were not so, would I have told you 28
29 now I have told you before it takes place 28
16: 4 you may remember that I told you of them 28
7 Nevertheless I tell you the truth 37
25 tell you plainly of the Father. 21
18: 8 Jesus answered, "I told you that I am he 28
38 went out to the Jews again, and told them 37
19:35 he knows that he tells the truth 37
20:15 tell me where you have laid him 28
18 she told them that he had said these things •
25 the other disciples told him 37
Act 2:11 we hear them telling in our own tongues 36
3:22 You shall listen to him in whatever he tells you. 36
5: 8 Tell me whether you sold the land for so much. 28
25 And some one came and told them 21
38 So in the present case I tell you 37
9: 6 you will be told what you are to do. 36
11:12 the Spirit told me to go with them 28
13 he told us how he had seen the angel standing 21
12:14 told that Peter was standing at the gate. 21
17 he said, "Tell this to James and to the brethren. 21
13:42 begged that these things might be told them 36
15:27 who themselves will tell you the same things 21
17:21 telling or hearing something new. 37
19: 4 telling the people to believe 37
21: 4 they told Paul not to go on to Jerusalem. 37
21 they have been told about you 35
21 telling them not to circumcise their children 37
23 Do therefore what we tell you 37
24 is nothing in what they have been told about you 35
22:10 will be told all that is appointed for you to do.' 36
27 Tell me, are you a Roman citizen?" And he said, "Yes. 37
23:16 he went and entered the barracks and told Paul. 21
17 he has something to tell him. 21
19 What is it that you have to tell me? 21
22 Tell no one that you have informed me of this. 30
27:25 it will be exactly as I have been told. 36
Rom 4:18 as he had been told 28
9:12 she was told, "The elder will serve the younger. 28
15: 8 For I tell you that Christ became a servant 37
21 They shall see who have never been told of him 19
1Co 15:50 I tell you this, brethren 47
51 Lo! I tell you a mystery 37
2Co 7: 7 as he told us of your longing, your mourning 19
12: 4 he heard things that cannot be told 23
Gal 4:21 Tell me, you who desire to be under law 37
Eph 6:21 Tych'icus . . will tell you everything. 24
Php 1:22 Yet which I shall choose I cannot tell. 24
3:18 many, of whom I have often told you and now tell you 37
18 many, of whom I have often told you and now tell you 37
Col 4: 9 They will tell you of everything 24
2Th 2: 5 when I was still with you I told you this? 37
1Ti 2: 7 (I am telling the truth, I am not lying) 37
Heb 11:32 time would fail me to tell of Gideon, Barak, Samson 27
Rev 6:11 they were each . . told to rest a little longer 28
9: 4 they were told not to harm the grass of the earth 28
10: 9 So I went to the angel and told him to give me 37
11 I was told, "You must again prophesy 37
11: 1 and I was told: "Rise and measure the temple of God 37
16: 1 voice from the temple telling the seven angels 37
17: 7 I will tell you the mystery of the woman 28
1Es 1: 3 he told the Levites . . sanctify themselves 28
33 these that are now told •
4: 4 If he tells them to make war on one another 37
7 If he tells them to kill, they kill 37
7 if he tells them to release, they release 28
8 if he tells them to attack, they attack 28
8 if he tells them to lay waste, they lay waste 28
8 if he tells them to build, they build 28
9 if he tells them to cut down, they cut down 28
9 if he tells them to plant, they plant. 28
61 told this to all his brethren. 21
5:40 Nehemiah and Attharias told them . . 28
8:45 I told them to go to Iddo 28
46 ordered them to tell Iddo and his brethren 26
9:39 they told Ezra . . to bring the law of Moses 28
2Es 1: 5 so that they may tell their children's children 52
2:10 Thus says the Lord to Ezra: "Tell my people 48
48 tell my people how great and many are the wonders 48
4:52 I can tell you in part 49
52 I was not sent to tell you concerning your life 49
5:13 the signs which I am permitted to tell you 49
50 our mother, of whom thou hast told me 49
51 Ask . . and she will tell you. 49
6:35 complete the three weeks as I had been told. 49
7:54 but ask the earth and she will tell you 49
101 the things of which you have been told 53
8: 2 I tell you a parable, Ezra 49
2 Just as, when you ask the earth, it will tell you 49
9:42 I said to her, "What has happened to you? Tell me. 49
10: 9 Now ask the earth, and she will tell you 49
38 and tell you about the things which you fear 49
43 her telling you about the misfortune of her son 50
45 as for her telling you that she was barren 49
47 as for her telling you that she brought him up 49
51 Therefore I told you to remain in the field 49
53 Therefore I told you to go into the field 49
11:42 you have hated those who tell the truth 49
12:50 the people went into the city, as I told them to do. 49
13:21 I will tell you the interpretation of the vision 49
56 I will tell you other things 51
14: 5 I told him many wondrous things 50
23 and tell them not to seek you for 40 days. 49
Tob 2:14 told her to return it to the owners 37
5: 7 Wait for me, and I shall tell my father. 28
10 to what tribe and family do you belong? Tell me. 46
14 tell me, what wages am I to pay you–a drachma a day 28
6: 5 the young man did as the angel told him 28
8:14 she came out and told them that he was alive. 21
Jdt 2: 7 Tell them to prepare earth and water 21
3: 5 The men came to Holofernes and told him all this. 21
5: 3 said to them, "Tell me, you Canaanites 19
5 I will tell you the truth about this people 19

6: 2 tell us not to make war 28
17 He answered and told them what had taken place 21
8:34 for I will not tell you until I have finished 28
10:16 tell him just what you have said 19
18 she waited . . while they told him about her. 41
22 When they told him of her 19
11: 3 now tell me why you have fled from them 37
5 I will tell nothing false to my lord this night. 19
9 he told them all he had said to you. 19
17 tell me when they have committed their sins. 28
18 I will come and tell you 43
19 For this has been told me, by my foreknowledge 36
19 it was announced to me, and I was sent to tell you. 19
13: 3 Now Judith had told her maid . . 28
14: 8 Now tell me what you have done during these days. 19
15: 4 to tell what had taken place 21
5 they were told what had happened 19
Wis 6:22 will tell you what wisdom is and how she came to be 21
Sir 1:24 the lips of many will tell of his good sense. 29
20:19 like a story told at the wrong time •
20 for he does not tell it at its proper time. 37
22: 6 a tale told at the wrong time •
25: 7 a tenth I shall tell with my tongue 28
37: 9 tell you, "Your way is good," and then stand aloof 37
41:23 repeating and telling what you hear 38
43:24 Those who sail the sea tell of its dangers 27
Sus 1:10 they did not tell each other of their distress 19
27 And when the elders told their tale 28
40 but she would not tell us. 19
54 Now then, if you really saw her, tell me this 28
58 tell me: Under what tree did you catch them 37
Bel 1: 8 If you do not tell me who is eating these 28
1Mc 4:46 a prophet to tell what to do with them. 22
5:25 told them all that had happened 27
8: 2 Men told him of their wars and of the brave deeds 27
9:60 telling them to seize Jonathan and his men 40
10:15 men told him of the battles 27
72 Men will tell you that you cannot stand before us 37
11: 5 They also told the king what Jonathan had done 27
40 and told of the hatred •
14:21 told us about your glory and honor 21
2Mc 2: 1 as has been told 45
3: 7 he told him of the money 31
9 he told about the disclosure that had been made 20
6:23 telling them to send him to Hades. 37
8:12 when he told his companions 39
19 Moreover, he told them of the times when . . 42
10:10 tell what took place under Antiochus Eupator 25
14:26 He told him that Nicanor was disloyal 37
15:38 If it is well told and to the point 33
4Mc 2: 6 In fact, since the law has told us not to covet 28
12: 7 as we shall tell a little later 28
18:12 He told you of the zeal of Phineas 37

tell a fault 1. ἐλέγχω
Mat 18:15 go and tell him his fault 1

tell a lie 1. ψεύδομαι
Bel 1:12 who is telling lies about us. 1

tell a story 1. διηγέομαι
Sir 22: 8 He who tells a story to a fool 1
8 who tells a story to a fool tells it to a drowsy man 1

tell about 1. נגד 2. γνωρίζω
1Sm 10:16 about the matter . . he did not tell him 1
Col 4: 7 Tych'icus will tell you all about my affairs 2

tell beforehand 1. προεῖπον 2. προλέγω
Mat 24:25 Lo, I have told you beforehand. 1
Mrk 13:23 take heed; I have told you all things beforehand. 1
1Th 3: 4 For when we were with you, we told you beforehand 2

tell glad news 1. בשׂר
Ps 40: 9 I have told the glad news of deliverance 1

tell more 1. adicio
2Es 5:32 pay attention to me, and I will tell you more. 1

tell the good news 1. εὐαγγελίζω
Act 8:35 he told him the good news of Jesus. 1

tell the truth 1. ἀληθεύω
Gal 4:16 become your enemy by telling you the truth? 1

temper 1. אַף 2. רוּחַ 3. θυμός
Prv 14:17 A man of quick temper acts foolishly 1
29 but he who has a hasty temper exalts folly. 2
Wis 7:20 and the tempers of wild beasts 3

temper (2) 1. βαθή
Sir 31:26 Fire and water prove the temper of steel 1
temper *See* lose.

hot temper 1. θυμός
2Mc 4:25 having the hot temper of a cruel tyrant 1

temperate 1. νηφάλιος 2. σώφρων
1Ti 3: 2 the husband of one wife, temperate, sensible 1
11 no slanderers, but temperate 1
Tit 2: 2 Bid the older men be temperate, serious, sensible 1
4Mc 1:35 checked by the temperate mind 2
2: 2 the temperate Joseph is praised 2
16 the temperate mind repels all these 2
18 the temperate mind is able to get the better 2
23 temperate, just, good, and courageous. 2
3:17 the temperate mind can conquer the drives 2
19 a narrative demonstration of temperate reason. 2

temperately 1. αὐτάρκης
Sir 31:28 Wine drunk in season and temperately 1

hot tempered 1. חֵמָה
Prv 15:18 A hot-tempered man stirs up strife 1

tempest 1. הֲמֻלָּה 2. זֶרֶם 3. סוּפָה 4. סַעַר 5. סְעָרָה 6. שַׂעַר 7. שַׂעַר 8. שְׂעָרָה 9. ἀκολασία 10. θύελλα 11. καταιγίς 12. λαῖλαψ 13. χειμών 14. sidus
Job 9:17 For he crushes me with a tempest 8
Ps 50: 3 round about him a mighty tempest. 6
55: 8 a shelter from the raging wind and tempest. 4
83:15 do thou pursue them with thy tempest 4
Prv 10:25 When the tempest passes, the wicked is no more 3
Isa 28: 2 like a storm of hail, a destroying tempest 7
29: 6 with whirlwind and tempest, and the flame 5
30:30 with a cloudburst and tempest and hailstones. 2
32: 2 place from the wind, a covert from the tempest 2
40:24 and the tempest carries them off like stubble. 5
41:16 and the tempest shall scatter them. 5
Jer 11:16 with the roar of a great tempest he will set fire 1
23:19 Wrath has gone forth, a whirling tempest; 4
25:32 and a great tempest is stirring 4
30:23 Wrath has gone forth, a whirling tempest; 4
Ams 1:14 with a tempest in the day of the whirlwind; 4
Jon 1: 4 there was a mighty tempest on the sea 4
12 this great tempest has come upon you. 4
Act 27:20 no small tempest lay on us 13
Heb 12:18 darkness, and gloom, and a tempest 10
2Es 15:13 by blight and hail and by a terrible tempest. 14
35 shall pour out a heavy tempest upon the earth 14
35 shall pour out . . their own tempest 14
39 the tempest that was to cause destruction 14
40 full of wrath and tempest 14
40 and shall pour out . . a terrible tempest 14
44 they shall pour out the tempest and all its wrath 14
Wis 5:23 like a tempest it will winnow them away. 12
Sir 16:21 Like a tempest which no man can see 11
43:17 the tempest from the north and the whirlwind 11
4Mc 13: 7 conquered the tempest of the emotions. 9

tempestuous 1. סער 2. τυφωνικός
Jon 1:11 For the sea grew more and more tempestuous. 1
13 grew more and more tempestuous against them. 1
Act 27:14 soon a tempestuous wind, called the northeaster 2

temple 1. בַּיִת 2. הֵיכָל 3. מִקְדָּשׁ 4. הֵיכָל (A) 5. ἅγιος 6. ἱερεύς 7. ἱερόδουλος 8. ἱερός 9. ἱερουργία 10. ναός 11. νεώς 12. οἰκία 13. οἶκος 14. τέμενος 15. templum
1Sm 1: 9 beside the doorpost of the temple of the LORD. 2
3: 3 Samuel was lying . . within the temple of the LORD 2
31:10 They put his armor in the temple of Ash'taroth; 1
2Sm 22: 7 From his temple he heard my voice, and my cry came 2
1Kg 6: 7 axe nor any tool of iron was heard in the temple 1
7:21 set up the pillars at the vestibule of the temple; 2
50 and for the doors of the nave of the temple. 1
2Kg 18:16 the gold from the doors of the temple of the LORD 2
23: 4 to bring out of the temple of the LORD all 2
24:13 all the vessels of gold in the temple of the LORD 2
25:14 vessels of bronze used in the temple service •
1Ch 9:33 dwelling in the chambers of the temple •
10:10 they put his armor in the temple of their gods 1
10 and fastened his head in the temple of Dagon. 1
28:11 the plan of the vestibule of the temple 10
2Ch 2: 1 to build a temple for the name of the LORD 1
12 a wise son . . who will build a temple for the LORD 1
3:17 He set up the pillars in front of the temple 2
4: 7 lampstands . . and set them in the temple 2
8 made ten tables, and placed them in the temple 2
22 sockets of the temple, for the inner doors 1
22 and for the doors of the nave of the temple 2
7: 1 and the glory of the LORD filled the temple. 1
3 saw . . and the glory of the LORD upon the temple 1
26:16 entered the temple of the LORD to burn incense 2
27: 2 only he did not invade the temple of the LORD. 2
29:16 the uncleanness that they found in the temple 2
35:20 when Josi'ah had prepared the temple 1
Ezr 3: 6 foundation of the temple of the LORD was not yet 2
10 laid the foundation of the temple of the LORD 2
4: 1 exiles were building a temple to the LORD 2
5:14 Nebuchadnez'zar had taken out of the temple 4
14 taken . . and brought into the temple of Babylon 4
14 Cyrus the king took out of the temple of Babylon 4
15 Take these vessels, go and put them in the temple 4
6: 5 took out of the temple that is in Jerusalem 4
5 be restored and brought back to the temple 4
Neh 2: 8 beams for the gates of the fortress of the temple 1
6:10 together in the house of God, within the temple 2
10 meet . . and let us close the doors of the temple; 2
11 man such as I could go into the temple and live? 2
Ps 5: 7 I will worship toward thy holy temple 2
11: 4 The LORD is in his holy temple 2
18: 6 From his temple he heard my voice, and my cry to him 2
27: 4 of the LORD, and to inquire in his temple. 2
29: 9 in his temple all cry, "Glory! 2
30: 0 A Song at the dedication of the Temple. 1
48: 9 steadfast love, O God, in the midst of thy temple. 2
65: 4 the goodness of thy house, thy holy temple! 2
68:29 Because of thy temple at Jerusalem 2
79: 1 heathen . . have defiled thy holy temple; 2
138: 2 I bow down toward thy holy temple and give thanks 2
Isa 6: 1 saw the Lord . . and his train filled the temple. 2
44:28 and of the temple, 'Your foundation shall be laid.' 2
66: 6 an uproar from the city! A voice from the temple! 2
Jer 7: 4 deceptive words: 'This is the temple of the LORD 2
4 the temple of the LORD, the temple of the LORD.' 2
4 the temple of the LORD, the temple of the LORD.' 2
24: 1 two baskets of figs placed before the temple 2
38:14 received him at the third entrance of the temple 1
41: 5 and incense to present at the temple of the LORD. 1
43:12 He shall kindle a fire in the temples of the gods 1
13 the temples of the gods of Egypt he shall burn 1
50:28 vengeance of . . God, vengeance for his temple. 2
51:11 of the LORD, the vengeance for his temple. 2
52:18 the vessels of bronze used in the temple service; •
Ezk 8:16 and behold, at the door of the temple of the LORD 2
16 men, with their backs to the temple of the LORD 2
40: 5 a wall all around the outside of the temple area 1
45 for the priests who have charge of the temple 1
47 and the altar was in front of the temple. 1
48 Then he brought me to the vestibule of the temple 1
41: 5 Then he measured the wall of the temple 1
5 the side chambers . . round about the temple. 1
6 offsets all around the wall of the temple 1
6 not be supported by the wall of the temple. 1
7 from story to story round about the temple; 1
7 on the side of the temple a stairway led upward 1
8 I saw also that the temple had a raised platform 1
9 Between the platform of the temple 1
10 round about the temple on every side. 1
12 The building that was facing the temple yard •
13 he measured the temple, 100 cubits long; 1
14 also the breadth of the east front of the temple 1
15 The nave of the temple and the inner room 2
16 the temple was paneled with wood round about •
19 They were carved on the whole temple round about; 1
42: 8 those opposite the temple were 100 cubits 2
15 measuring the interior of the temple area 1
15 and measured the temple area round about. •
43: 4 glory of the LORD entered the temple by the gate 1
5 behold, the glory of the LORD filled the temple. 1
6 I heard one speaking to me out of the temple; 1
10 describe to the house of Israel the temple 1
11 portray the temple, its arrangement, its exits 1
12 This is the law of the temple 1
12 Behold, this is the law of the temple. 1
21 in the appointed place belonging to the temple 1
44: 4 by way of the north gate to the front of the temple; 1
4 glory of the LORD filled the temple of the LORD; 1
5 all the ordinances of the temple of the LORD 1
5 mark well those who may be admitted to the temple 1
11 having oversight at the gates of the temple, 1
11 gates of the temple, and serving in the temple; 1
14 I will appoint them to keep charge of the temple 1
45: 5 be for the Levites who minister at the temple 1
19 and put it on the doorposts of the temple 1
20 you shall make atonement for the temple. 1
46:24 those who minister at the temple shall boil 1
47: 1 Then he brought me back to the door of the temple; 1
1 issuing from below the threshold of the temple 1
1 temple toward the east (for the temple faced east); 1
1 the south end of the threshold of the temple 1
48:21 with the sanctuary of the temple in its midst 1
Dan 5: 2 vessels . . taken out of the temple in Jerusalem 4
3 vessels which had been taken out of the temple 4
11:31 appear and profane the temple and fortress 3
Jol 3: 5 carried my rich treasures into your temples. 2
Ams 7:13 and it is a temple of the kingdom. 1
8: 3 The songs of the temple shall become wailings 2
Jon 2: 4 how shall I again look upon thy holy temple? 2
7 my prayer came to thee, into thy holy temple. 2
Mic 1: 2 against you, the Lord from his holy temple. 2
Hab 2:20 But the LORD is in his holy temple; 2
Hag 2:15 was placed upon a stone in the temple of the LORD 2
18 that the foundation of the LORD'S temple was laid 2
Zec 6:12 he shall build the temple of the LORD. 2
13 It is he who shall build the temple of the LORD 2
14 the crown shall be in the temple of the LORD 2
15 come and help to build the temple of the LORD; 2
8: 9 was laid, that the temple might be built. 2
Mal 3: 1 whom you seek will suddenly come to his temple; 2
Mat 4: 5 set him on the pinnacle of the temple 8
12: 5 on the sabbath the priests in the temple profane 8
6 something greater than the temple is here. 8

21:12 Jesus entered the temple of God 8
12 drove out all who sold and bought in the temple 8
14 the blind and the lame came to him in the temple 8
15 the children crying out in the temple 8
23 when he entered the temple 8
23:16 If any one swears by the temple, it is nothing 10
16 if any one swears by the gold of the temple 10
17 which is greater, the gold or the temple 10
21 he who swears by the temple 10
24: 1 Jesus left the temple and was going away 8
1 point out to him the buildings of the temple. 8
26:55 Day after day I sat in the temple teaching 8
61 I am able to destroy the temple of God 10
27: 5 throwing down the pieces of silver in the temple 10
40 saying, "You who would destroy the temple 10
51 behold, the curtain of the temple was torn in two 10
Mrk 11:11 he entered Jerusalem, and went into the temple; 8
15 he entered the temple 8
15 those who sold and those who bought in the temple 8
16 to carry anything through the temple. 8
27 as he was walking in the temple 8
12:35 as Jesus taught in the temple, he said 8
13: 1 as he came out of the temple 8
3 on the Mount of Olives opposite the temple 8
14:49 I was with you in the temple teaching 8
58 will destroy this temple that is made with hands 10
15:29 You who would destroy the temple 10
38 the curtain of the temple was torn in two 10
Lke 1: 9 to enter the temple of the Lord and burn incense. 10
21 they wondered at his delay in the temple. 10
22 perceived that he had seen a vision in the temple; 10
2:27 inspired by the Spirit he came into the temple; 8
37 She did not depart from the temple 8
46 After three days they found him in the temple 8
4: 9 set him on the pinnacle of the temple 8
18:10 Two men went up into the temple to pray 8
19:45 he entered the temple 8
47 he was teaching daily in the temple 8
20: 1 as he was teaching the people in the temple 8
21: 5 as some spoke of the temple, how it was adorned 8
37 every day he was teaching in the temple 8
38 came to him in the temple to hear him. 8
22:52 officers of the temple and elders 8
53 I was with you day after day in the temple 8
23:45 the curtain of the temple was torn in two. 10
24:53 were continually in the temple blessing God. 8
Joh 2:14 In the temple he found those who were selling 8
15 he drove them all . . out of the temple; 8
19 Destroy this temple, and in three days I 10
20 It has taken 46 years to build this temple 10
21 But he spoke of the temple of his body. 10
5:14 Afterward, Jesus found him in the temple, and said 8
7:14 Jesus went up into the temple and taught. 8
28 Jesus proclaimed, as he taught in the temple 8
8: 2 Early in the morning he came again to the temple 8
20 as he taught in the temple 8
59 Jesus hid himself, and went out of the temple. 8
10:23 it was winter, and Jesus was walking in the temple 8
11:56 as they stood in the temple 8
18:20 always taught in synagogues and in the temple 8
Act 2:46 And day by day, attending the temple together 8
3: 1 Now Peter and John were going up to the temple 8
2 whom they laid daily at that gate of the temple 8
2 to ask alms of those who entered the temple. 8
3 Seeing Peter and John about to go into the temple 8
8 walked and entered the temple with them 8
10 at the Beautiful Gate of the temple 8
4: 1 the captain of the temple and the Sad'ducees 8
5:20 Go and stand in the temple and speak to the people 8
21 they entered the temple at daybreak and taught 8
24 the captain of the temple and the chief priests 8
25 standing in the temple and teaching the people. 8
42 every day in the temple and at home 8
14:13 whose temple was in front of the city •
19:27 the temple of the great goddess Ar'temis 8
21:26 and went into the temple 8
27 who had seen him in the temple 8
28 moreover he also brought Greeks into the temple 8
29 Paul had brought him into the temple. 8
30 seized Paul and dragged him out of the temple 8
22:17 was praying in the temple 8
24: 6 tried to profane the temple, but we seized him. 8
12 in the temple or in the synagogues, or in the city. 8
18 they found me purified in the temple 8
25: 8 nor against the temple, nor against Caesar 8
26:21 Jews seized me in the temple and tried to kill me. 8
1Co 3:16 Do you not know that you are God's temple 10
17 If any one destroys God's temple 10
17 God's temple is holy, and that temple you are. 10
17 God's temple is holy, and that temple you are. •
6:19 Do you not know that your body is a temple 10
9:13 get their food from the temple 8
2Co 6:16 What agreement has the temple of God with idols? 10
16 For we are the temple of the living God; as God said 10
Eph 2:21 grows into a holy temple in the Lord; 10
2Th 2: 4 he takes his seat in the temple of God 10
Rev 3:12 I will make him a pillar in the temple of my God; 10
7:15 and serve him day and night within his temple; 10
11: 1 Rise and measure the temple of God and the altar 10
2 do not measure the court outside the temple; 10
19 Then God's temple in heaven was opened 10
19 ark of his covenant was seen within his temple; 10
14:15 another angel came out of the temple, calling 10
17 another angel came out of the temple in heaven 10
15: 5 temple of the tent of witness in heaven was opened 10
6 out of the temple came the seven angels 10
8 and the temple was filled with smoke 10
8 and no one could enter the temple 10
16: 1 Then I heard a loud voice from the temple 10
17 and a loud voice came out of the temple 10
21:22 And I saw no temple in the city 10
22 for its temple is the Lord God the Almighty 10
1Es 1: 2 in the temple of the Lord. 6
3 told the Levites, the temple servants of Israel 7
5 Stand in order in the temple 8
8 the chief officers of the temple 8
41 stored them in his temple in Babylon. 10
49 polluted the temple of the Lord 8
53 slew . . with the sword around their holy temple 8
2: 7 votive offerings for the temple of the Lord 8
18 laying the foundations for a temple. 10
20 since the building of the temple is now going on 10
30 the building of the temple in Jerusalem ceased 8
4:45 You also vowed to build the temple 10
51 be given for the building of the temple 8
55 until the day when the temple should be finished 13
63 the temple which is called by his name 8
5:35 All the temple servants 7
44 when they came to the temple of God 8
53 though the temple of God was not yet built. 10
56 after their coming to the temple of God 8
57 they laid the foundation of the temple of God 10
58 So the builders built the temple of the Lord. 10
67 were building the temple for the Lord God 10
6:18 stored in his own temple 10
18 took out again from the temple in Babylon 10
19 put them in the temple at Jerusalem 10
19 this temple of the Lord should be rebuilt 10
7: 7 at the dedication of the temple of the Lord 8
8:14 the temple of their Lord which is in Jerusalem 8
17 given you for the use of the temple of your God 8
18 as necessary for the temple of your God 8
22 persons employed in this temple 8
60 carried them to the temple of the Lord. 8
67 the people and the temple of the Lord. 8
81 glorified the temple of our Lord 8
91 lying upon the ground before the temple 8
9: 1 went from the court of the temple 8
6 sat in the open square before the temple 8
38 the open square before the east gate of the temple; 8
41 in the open square before the gate of the temple 8
2Es 10:21 our altar thrown down, our temple destroyed; 15
Tob 1: 4 where the temple . . was consecrated 10
Jdt 4: 1 plundered and destroyed all their temples; 8
2 alarmed both for Jerusalem and for the temple 10
3 the altar and the temple had been consecrated 13
11 prostrated themselves before the temple 10
5:18 the temple of their God was razed to the ground 10
8:24 the sanctuary and the temple and the altar 13
Wis 3:14 a place of great delight in the temple of the Lord. 10
9: 8 Thou hast given command to build a temple 10
Sir 36:14 Fill . . thy temple with thy glory. 2
45: 9 to make their ringing heard in the temple 10
49:12 raised a temple holy to the Lord 10
50: 1 in his time fortified the temple. 10
2 high retaining walls for the temple enclosure. 8
7 the sun shining upon the temple of the Most High 10
51:14 Before the temple I asked for her 10
Bar 1: 8 which had been carried away from the temple 10
LJr 1:13 because of the dust from the temple 12
17 when they have been set up in the temples 13
18 so the priests make their temples secure 13
20 They are just like a beam of the temple 12
21 blackened by the smoke of the temple. 12
31 in their temples the priests sit 13
55 When fire breaks out in a temple of wooden gods 12
Aza 1:31 Blessed art thou in the temple of thy holy glory 10
Bel 1:10 the king went with Daniel into the temple of Bel. 13
14 they sifted them throughout the whole temple 10
22 destroyed it and its temple. 8
1Mc 1:22 the gold decoration on the front of the temple 10
2: 8 Her temple has become like a man without honor; 10
4:46 in a convenient place on the temple hill 13
48 the sanctuary and the interior of the temple 13
49 brought . . the table into the temple. 10
50 these gave light in the temple. 10
57 They decorated the front of the temple 10
6: 2 Its temple was very rich 8
7:36 stood before the altar and the temple 10
10:41 for the service of the temple. 13
42 from the income of the services of the temple 5
43 whoever takes refuge at the temple in Jerusalem 8
83 Beth-dagon, the temple of their idol •
84 the temple of Dagon 8
11: 4 they showed him the temple of Dagon burned down 8
13:52 the temple hill alongside the citadel 8
15: 9 upon you and your nation and the temple 8
16:20 Jerusalem and the temple hill. 8
2Mc 1:13 they were cut to pieces in the temple of Nanea 8
15 the priests of the temple of Nanea 6
15 they closed the temple as soon as he entered it. 8
18 shall celebrate the purification of the temple 8
18 Nehemiah, who built the temple and the altar 8
2: 9 the dedication and completion of the temple. 8
19 the purification of the great temple 8
22 the temple famous throughout the world 8
3: 2 glorified the temple with the finest presents 8
4 who had been made captain of the temple 8
12 the sanctity and inviolability of the temple 8
30 the temple, which . . was full of fear 8
4:32 Menelaus . . stole some of the gold vessels of the temple 8
5:15 to enter the most holy temple in all the world 8
21 1,800 talents from the temple 8
6: 2 also to pollute the temple in Jerusalem 11
2 and call it the temple of Olympian Zeus •
2 the temple of Zeus the Friend of Strangers •
4 the temple was filled with debauchery 8
8: 2 to have pity on the temple 10
10: 1 recovered the temple and the city; 8
11: 3 to levy tribute on the temple 8
25 our decision is that their temple be restored 8
12:26 Judas marched against . . the temple of Atargatis †
13:10 the law and their country and the holy temple 8
14 the laws, temple, city, country, and commonwealth 8
14: 4 the customary olive branches from the temple. 8
13 as high priest of the greatest temple. 8
31 he went to the great and holy temple 8
33 will build here a splendid temple to Dionysus. 8
35 a temple for thy habitation among us; 10
15:17 the city and the sanctuary and the temple 8
3Mc 1:10 he marveled at the good order of the temple 8
13 when he entered every other temple 14
16 they filled the temple with cries and tears; 8
20 they crowded together at the most high temple. 8
3:16 very great revenues to the temples in the cities 8
16 to honor the temple of those wicked people 8
17 we proposed to enter their inner temple 10
5:43 by burning . . the temple inaccessible to him 10
4Mc 3:20 money . . for the temple service 9
4: 3 which are not the property of the temple 8
8 Apollonius went on to the temple. 8
9 imploring God in the temple 8
11 half dead in the temple area that was open to all 8
20 also the temple service was abolished. 8

temple (2) 1. פְּאַת פָּנִים 2. פְּאַת רֹאשׁ 3. רֹאשׁ 4. רַקָּה
Lev 13:41 hair has fallen from his forehead and temples 1
19:27 You shall not round off the hair on your temples 2
27 You shall not round off the hair on your temples 3
Jdg 4:21 drove the peg into his temple, till it went down 4
22 lay Sis'era dead, with the tent peg in his temple. 4
5:26 his head, she shattered and pierced his temple. 4

temple *See* keeper, officer, rob, robber, servant, service, singer, yard.

idol's temple 1. εἰδωλεῖον
1Co 8:10 man of knowledge, at table in an idol's temple 1

temple of idols 1. εἰδωλεῖον
1Es 2:10 stored in his temple of idols. 1

temporal 1. πρόσκαιρος
4Mc 15:23 to disregard her temporal love for her children. 1

temporarily 1. βραδέως
2Mc 14:17 had been temporarily checked 1

temporary 1. πρόσκαιρος
4Mc 15: 8 disdained the temporary safety of her children. 1

tempt 1. ἀπείραστος 2. ἐκπειράζω 3. πειράζω
Mat 4: 1 the wilderness to be tempted by the devil. 3
7 written, 'You shall not tempt the Lord your God.' 2
Mrk 1:13 he was in the wilderness 40 days, tempted by Satan 3
Lke 4: 2 tempted by the devil 3
12 'You shall not tempt the Lord your God.' 2
Act 5: 9 have agreed together to tempt the Spirit of the Lord? 3
1Co 7: 5 then come together again, lest Satan tempt you 3
10:13 not let you be tempted beyond your strength 3
Gal 6: 1 Look to yourself, lest you too be tempted. 3
1Th 3: 5 somehow the tempter had tempted you 3
Heb 2:18 because he . . has suffered and been tempted 3
18 he is able to help those who are tempted. 3
4:15 one who in every respect has been tempted 3
Jas 1:13 Let no one say when he is tempted 3
13 Let no one say . . "I am tempted by God 3
13 for God cannot be tempted with evil 1
13 God cannot be tempted . . and . . tempts no one; 3
14 each person is tempted when he is lured 3
Sir 18:23 do not be like a man who tempts the Lord. 3

temptation 1. πειρασμός 2. σκάνδαλον
Mat 6:13 And lead us not into temptation, But deliver us 1
18: 7 Woe to the world for temptations to sin! 2
7 For it is necessary that temptations come 2
7 woe to the man by whom the temptation comes! 2

26:41 that you may not enter into temptation 1
Mrk 14:38 pray that you may not enter into temptation 1
Lke 4:13 when the devil had ended every temptation 1
8:13 and in time of temptation fall away. 1
11: 4 lead us not into temptation. 1
22:40 Pray that you may not enter into temptation. 1
46 pray that you may not enter into temptation. 1
1Co 7: 2 because of the temptation to immorality •
10:13 No temptation has overtaken you 1
13 with the temptation will also provide 1
1Ti 6: 9 those who desire to be rich fall into temptation 1
Sir 2: 1 prepare yourself for temptation. 1

temptation to sin 1. σκάνδαλον
Lke 17: 1 Temptations to sin are sure to come 1

tempter 1. πειράζω
Mat 4: 3 the tempter came and said to him, "If you are the Son 1
1Th 3: 5 somehow the tempter had tempted you 1

ten 1. עָשׂוֹר 2. עֶשֶׂר 3. עֶשֶׂר (A) 4. δέκα 5. δεκαδάρχος 6. decem
Gen 16: 3 after Abram had dwelt ten years in the land 2
18:32 Suppose ten are found there." He answered 2
32 For the sake of ten I will not destroy it. 2
24:10 Then the servant took ten of his master's camels 2
22 bracelets . . weighing ten gold shekels 2
55 remain with us a while, at least ten days; 1
31: 7 changed my wages ten times 2
41 flock, and you have changed my wages ten times. 2
32:15 40 cows and ten bulls, twenty she-asses 2
15 bulls, twenty she-asses and ten he-asses. 2
42: 3 ten of Joseph's brothers went down to buy grain 2
45:23 he sent as follows: ten asses loaded with the good 2
23 sent . . ten she-asses loaded with grain, bread 2
Exd 18:21 rulers . . of hundreds, of fifties, and of tens. 2
25 rulers . . of hundreds, of fifties, and of tens. 2
26: 1 you shall make the tabernacle with ten curtains 2
16 Ten cubits shall be the length of a frame 2
27:12 hangings . . with ten pillars and ten bases. 2
12 hangings . . with ten pillars and ten bases. 2
34:28 words of the covenant, the ten commandments. 2
36: 8 workmen made the tabernacle with ten curtains; 2
21 Ten cubits was the length of a frame 2
38:12 their pillars ten, and their sockets ten; 2
12 their pillars ten, and their sockets ten; 2
Lev 26:26 ten women shall bake your bread in one oven 2
27: 5 twenty shekels, and for a female ten shekels 2
7 fifteen shekels, and for a female ten shekels 2
Num 7:14 one golden dish of ten shekels, full of incense; 2
20 one golden dish of ten shekels, full of incense; 2
26 one golden dish of ten shekels, full of incense; 2
32 one golden dish of ten shekels, full of incense; 2
38 one golden dish of ten shekels, full of incense; 2
44 one golden dish of ten shekels, full of incense; 2
50 one golden dish of ten shekels, full of incense; 2
56 one golden dish of ten shekels, full of incense; 2
62 one golden dish of ten shekels, full of incense; 2
68 one golden dish of ten shekels, full of incense; 2
74 one golden dish of ten shekels, full of incense; 2
80 one golden dish of ten shekels, full of incense; 2
86 golden dishes . . weighing ten shekels apiece 2
11:19 You shall not eat . . ten days, or twenty days 2
32 he who gathered least gathered ten homers; 2
14:22 yet have put me to the proof these ten times 2
29:23 On the fourth day ten bulls, two rams, fourteen 2
Deu 1:15 heads over you, commanders . . of tens 2
4:13 to perform, that is, the ten commandments; 2
10: 4 he wrote on the tables . . the ten commandments 2
Jos 15:57 ten cities with their villages. 2
17: 5 there fell to Manas'seh ten portions, besides 2
21: 5 Ko'hathites received by lot from . . ten cities. 2
26 The cities of the families of . . were ten in all 2
22:14 and with him ten chiefs, one from each . . tribal 2
Jdg 6:27 Gideon took ten men of his servants, and did 2
12:11 Elon . . and he judged Israel ten years. 2
17:10 and I will give you ten pieces of silver a year 2
20:10 take ten men of a 100 throughout all the tribes 2
Rut 1: 4 They lived there about ten years; 2
4: 2 he took ten men of the elders of the city, and said 2
1Sm 1: 8 why do you . . ? Am I not more to you than ten sons? 2
17:17 an ephah of . . parched grain, and these ten loaves 2
18 also take these ten cheeses to the commander 2
25: 5 David sent ten young men; 2
38 And about ten days later the LORD smote Nabal; 2
2Sm 15:16 the king left ten concubines to keep the house. 2
18:11 to give you ten pieces of silver and a girdle. 2
15 ten young men . . surrounded Ab'salom and struck 2
19:43 We have ten shares in the king, and in David also 2
20: 3 the king took the ten concubines whom he had left 2
1Kg 4:23 ten fat oxen, and twenty . . cattle 2
6: 3 twenty cubits long . . and ten cubits deep 2
23 he made two cherubim . . each ten cubits high. 2
24 ten cubits from the tip of one wing to the tip 2
25 The other cherub also measured ten cubits; 2
26 The height of one cherub was ten cubits, and so was 2
7:10 huge stones, stones of eight and ten cubits. 2
23 it was round, ten cubits from brim to brim 2
27 He also made the ten stands of bronze; 2
37 After this manner he made the ten stands; 2
38 he made ten lavers of bronze; each laver held 2
38 and there was a laver for each of the ten stands. 2
43 the ten stands, and the ten lavers upon the stands; 2
43 the ten stands, and the ten lavers upon the stands; 2
11:31 he said to Jerobo'am, "Take for yourself ten pieces; 2
31 I am about to . . and will give you ten tribes 2
35 I will . . give it to you,ten tribes. 2
14: 3 Take with you ten loaves, some cakes, and a jar 2
2Kg 5: 5 So he went, taking with him ten talents of silver 2
5 taking . . gold, and ten festal garments. 2
13: 7 an army of more than 50 horsemen and ten chariots 2
15:17 Men'ahem . . and he reigned ten years in Sama'ria. 2
20: 9 shall the shadow go forward ten steps, or go back 2
9 shall the shadow go . . or go back ten steps? 2
10 easy thing for the shadow to lengthen ten steps; 2
10 rather let the shadow go back ten steps. 2
11 the LORD, and he brought the shadow back ten steps 2
25:25 Ish'mael . . came with ten men, and attacked 2
1Ch 6:61 the Ko'hathites were given by lot . . ten cities. 2
2Ch 4: 1 made an altar of bronze . . and ten cubits high. 2
2 molten sea . . round, ten cubits from brim to brim 2
6 He also made ten lavers in which to wash 2
7 he made ten golden lampstands as prescribed 2
8 made ten tables, and placed them in the temple 2
14: 1 In his days the land had rest for ten years. 2
36: 9 reigned three months and ten days in Jerusalem. 2
Ezr 8:24 Sherebi'ah, Hashabi'ah, and ten of their kinsmen 2
Neh 4:12 When the Jews . . came they said to us ten times 2
5:18 every ten days skins of wine in abundance; 2
11: 1 lots to bring one out of ten to live in Jerusalem 2
Est 9:10 the ten sons of Haman the son of Hammeda'tha 2
12 Jews have slain . . and also the ten sons of Haman. 2
13 let the ten sons of Haman be hanged 2
14 and the ten sons of Haman were hanged. 2
Job 19: 3 These ten times you have cast reproach upon me; 2
Ps 33: 2 make melody to him with the harp of ten strings! 1
144: 9 upon a ten-stringed harp I will play to thee 1
Ecc 7:19 Wisdom gives . . more than ten rulers that are 2
Isa 5:10 ten acres of vineyard shall yield but one bath 2
38: 8 make the shadow . . turn back ten steps. 2
8 back . . the ten steps by which it had declined. 2
Jer 41: 1 the chief officers of the king, came with ten men 2
2 Ish'mael the son of Nethani'ah and the ten men 2
8 there were ten men among them who said to Ish'mael 2
42: 7 At the end of ten days the word of the LORD came 2
Ezk 40:11 breadth of the opening of the gateway, ten cubits; 2
49 breadth twelve cubits; and ten steps led up to it; 4
41: 2 And the breadth of the entrance was ten cubits; 2
42: 4 was a passage inward, ten cubits wide 2
45:12 ten shekels shall be ten shekels 4
12 ten shekels shall be ten shekels 4
14 the cor, like the homer, contains ten baths 2
Dan 1:12 Test your servants for ten days; let us be given 2
14 hearkened . . and tested them for ten days. 2
15 end of ten days it was seen that they were better 2
20 found them ten times better than all 2
7: 7 It was different . . and it had ten horns. 3
20 concerning the ten horns that were on its head 3
24 As for the ten horns, out of this kingdom 3
24 horns, out of this kingdom ten kings shall arise 3
Ams 5: 3 which went forth 100 shall have ten left 2
6: 9 if ten men remain in one house, they shall die. 2
Hag 2:16 to a heap of twenty measures, there were but ten; 2
Zec 5: 2 is twenty cubits, and its breadth ten cubits. 2
8:23 In those days ten men from the nations 2
Mat 20:24 when the ten heard it 4
25: 1 ten maidens who took their lamps 4
28 give it to him who has the ten talents. 4
Mrk 10:41 when the ten heard it, they began to be indignant 4
Lke 15: 8 what woman, having ten silver coins 4
17:12 as he entered a village, he was met by ten lepers 4
17 Were not ten cleansed? Where are the nine? 4
19:13 Calling ten of his servants 4
13 he gave them ten pounds 4
16 'Lord, your pound has made ten pounds more.' 4
17 you shall have authority over ten cities.' 4
24 give it to him who has the ten pounds.' 4
25 they said to him, 'Lord, he has ten pounds!') 4
Act 25: 6 stayed among them not more than eight or ten days 4
Rev 2:10 and for ten days you will have tribulation. 4
12: 3 great red dragon, with seven heads and ten horns 4
13: 1 I saw a beast . . with ten horns and seven heads 4
1 a beast . . with ten diadems upon its horns 4
17: 3 and it had seven heads and ten horns. 4
7 and of the beast with seven heads and ten horns 4
12 And the ten horns that you saw are ten kings 4
12 And the ten horns that you saw are ten kings 4
16 And the ten horns that you saw, they and the beast 4
1Es 1:44 reigned three months and ten days in Jerusalem. 4
4:52 an additional ten talents a year 4
8:54 ten of their kinsmen with them; 4
2Es 5:46 If you bear ten children, why one after another?' ‡
46 Request it therefore to produce ten at one time. 6
13:40 these are the ten tribes 6
16:28 For out of a city, ten shall be left 6
Tob 1:14 I left ten talents of silver in trust with Gabael 4
4:20 explain to you about the ten talents of silver 4
Sir 41: 4 for ten or 100 or 1,000 years 4
1Mc 3:55 in charge of . . fifties and tens. 5
ten *See also* threescore.

ten thousand thousands 1. רִבְבוֹת אֲלָפִים
Num10:36 O LORD, to the ten thousand thousands of Israel. 1

ten thousands 1. רבב 2. רְבָבָה 3. רִבּוֹ 4. μυριάς
Gen 24:60 be the mother of thousands of ten thousands; 2
Deu 33: 2 he came from the ten thousands of holy ones 2
17 such are the ten thousands of E'phraim 2
1Sm 18: 7 Saul has slain . . and David his ten thousands. 2
8 They have ascribed to David ten thousands 2
21:11 'Saul has slain his . . and David his ten thousands'? 2
29: 5 'Saul has slain . . and David his ten thousands'? 2
Ps 3: 6 I am not afraid of ten thousands of people 2
144:13 sheep bring forth thousands and ten thousands 1
Hos 8:12 Were I to write for him my laws by ten thousands 3
Mic 6: 7 pleased . . with ten thousands of rivers of oil? 2
Sir 47: 6 they glorified him for his ten thousands 4
2Mc 11: 4 but was elated with his ten thousands of infantry 4

tenant 1. γεωργός
Mat 21:33 and let it out to tenants 1
34 he sent his servants to the tenants 1
35 the tenants took his servants and beat one 1
38 when the tenants saw the son 1
40 what will he do to those tenants? 1
41 and let out the vineyard to other tenants 1
Mrk 12: 1 built a tower, and let it out to tenants 1
2 he sent a servant to the tenants 1
7 those tenants said to one another 1
9 He will come and destroy the tenants 1
Lke 20: 9 A man planted a vineyard, and let it out to tenants 1
10 he sent a servant to the tenants 1
10 the tenants beat him 1
14 when the tenants saw him, they said to themselves 1
16 He will come and destroy those tenants 1

tend 1. נצר 2. ערך 3. רעה 4. שׁרת 5. ποιμαίνω 6. φυσάω
Exd 27:21 Aaron and his sons shall tend it from evening 2
Num 1:50 they shall tend it, and shall encamp around 4
Ps 78:71 from tending the ewes that had young •
72 With upright heart he tended them 3
Prv 27:18 He who tends a fig tree will eat its fruit 1
Zec 11: 7 I tended the sheep. 3
Joh 21:16 He said to him, "Tend my sheep. 5
1Co 9: 7 Who tends a flock 5
1Pe 5: 2 Tend the flock of God that is your charge 5
Sir 43: 4 A man tending a furnace works in burning heat 6
151 1: 1 I tended my father's sheep. 5

tend (2) 1. היה
Deu 28:13 you shall tend upward only, and not downward; 1
Ps 37: 8 Fret not yourself, it tends only to evil. •
Prv 14:23 but mere talk tends only to want. •

tendency 1. διάθεσις
4Mc 1:25 there exists even a malevolent tendency 1

tender 1. יָרָק 2. רַךְ 3. רֹךְ 4. ἁπαλός 5. σπλάγχνον 6. τρυφερός
Gen 18: 7 took a calf, tender and good 2
Deu 28:54 man who is the most tender and delicately bred 2
56 because she is so delicate and tender 3
2Kg 19:26 have become like plants . . and like tender grass 1
Prv 4: 3 When I was a son with my father, tender 2
Isa 47: 1 you shall no more be called tender and delicate. 2
Ezk 17:22 from the topmost of its young twigs a tender one 2
Mat 24:32 as soon as its branch becomes tender 4
Mrk 13:28 as soon as its branch becomes tender 4
Lke 1:78 through the tender mercy of our God 5
Bar 4:26 My tender sons have traveled rough roads 6
tender *See also* care, grass, grow, heart, love.

tender woman 1. רַךְ
Deu 28:56 most tender and delicately bred woman among you 1

tenderhearted 1. εὔσπλαγχνος
Eph 4:32 be kind to one another, tenderhearted 1

tenderly 1. עַל לֵב
Gen 34: 3 he loved the maiden and spoke tenderly to her. 1
Isa 40: 2 Speak tenderly to Jerusalem, and cry to her 1
Hos 2:14 into the wilderness, and speak tenderly to her. 1

tenderness 1. φιλοστοργία
4Mc 15: 9 she felt a greater tenderness toward them. 1

tenfold 1. δεκαπλασιάζω
Bar 4:28 return with tenfold zeal to seek him. 1

tenon 1. יָד
Exd 26:17 There shall be two tenons in each frame 1
19 two bases under one frame for its two tenons 1
19 two bases under another frame for its two tenons; 1
36:22 Each frame had two tenons, for fitting together; 1

24 two bases under one frame for its two tenons 1
24 bases under another frame for its two tenons. 1

tens of thousands 1. רִבּוֹ 2. *μυριάς*
3. *πολλαὶ μυριάδες*
Dan 11:12 shall cast down tens of thousands 1
41 tens of thousands shall fall, but these 1
Aza 1:16 with tens of thousands of fat lambs; 2
4Mc 4: 3 there are deposited tens of thousands in private funds 3

tense
4Mc 7:13 his body no longer tense and firm †

tent 1. אֹהֶל 2. יְרִיעָה 3. מִשְׁכָּן 4. *σκηνή* 5. *σκῆνος*
6. *σκήνωμα*
Gen 4:20 father of those who dwell in tents 1
9:21 became drunk, and lay uncovered in his tent. 1
27 Japheth, and let him dwell in the tents of Shem; 1
12: 8 east of Bethel, and pitched his tent 1
13: 3 Bethel, to the place where his tent had been 1
5 Lot . . also had flocks and herds and tents 1
18: 1 the door of his tent in the heat of the day. 1
2 When he saw them, he ran from the tent door 1
6 Abraham hastened into the tent to Sarah, and said 1
9 your wife?" And he said, "She is in the tent. 1
10 Sarah was listening at the tent door behind him 1
24:67 Isaac brought her into the tent, and took Rebekah 1
25:27 Jacob was a quiet man, dwelling in tents. 1
26:25 and pitched his tent there. 1
31:25 Jacob had pitched his tent in the hill country 1
33 Laban went into Jacob's tent, and into Leah's 1
33 Laban went into Jacob's tent, and into Leah's 1
33 into Leah's tent, and into the tent of the two 1
33 he did not find them. And he went out of Leah's tent 1
34 felt all about the tent, but did not find them. 1
33:19 piece of land on which he had pitched his tent. 1
35:21 and pitched his tent beyond the tower of Eder. 1
Exd 16:16 the persons whom each of you has in his tent.' 1
18: 7 and they . . went into the tent. 1
26: 7 curtains of goats' hair for a tent over 1
9 you shall double over at the front of the tent. 1
11 and couple the tent together that it may be one 1
12 the part that remains of the curtains of the tent 1
13 the curtains of the tent shall hang over 1
14 you shall make for the tent a covering of tanned 1
36 you shall make a screen for the door of the tent 1
27:21 In the tent of meeting, outside the veil 1
28:43 when they go into the tent of meeting 1
29: 4 to the door of the tent of meeting, and wash them 1
10 shall bring the bull before the tent of meeting. 1
11 at the door of the tent of meeting 1
30 when he comes into the tent of meeting 1
32 shall eat . . at the door of the tent of meeting. 1
42 offering . . at the door of the tent of meeting 1
44 I will consecrate the tent of meeting 1
30:16 appoint it for the service of the tent of meeting; 1
18 put it between the tent of meeting and the altar 1
20 When they go into the tent of meeting, or when they 1
26 you shall anoint with it the tent of meeting 1
36 before the testimony in the tent of meeting 1
31: 7 tent of meeting, and the ark of the testimony 1
7 all the furnishings of the tent 1
33: 7 Now Moses used to take the tent and pitch it 1
7 and he called it the tent of meeting. 1
7 every one . . would go out to the tent of meeting 1
8 went out to the tent, all the people rose up 1
8 every man stood at his tent door, and looked 1
8 Moses, until he had gone into the tent. 1
9 When Moses entered the tent, the pillar of cloud 1
9 descend and stand at the door of the tent 1
10 cloud standing at the door of the tent 1
10 rise up and worship, every man at his tent door. 1
11 Joshua . . did not depart from the tent. 1
35:11 its tent and its covering, its hooks 1
21 offering to be used for the tent of meeting 1
36:14 goats' hair for a tent over the tabernacle; 1
18 clasps . . to couple the tent together 1
19 he made for the tent a covering of tanned rams' 1
37 He also made a screen for the door of the tent 1
38: 8 ministered at the door of the tent of meeting. 1
30 with it he made the bases for the door of the tent 1
39:32 Thus all the work of the tabernacle of the tent 1
33 the tent and all its utensils, its hooks 1
38 the screen for the door of the tent; 1
40 of the tabernacle, for the tent of meeting; 1
40: 2 erect the tabernacle of the tent of meeting. 1
6 door of the tabernacle of the tent of meeting 1
7 place the laver between the tent of meeting 1
12 to the door of the tent of meeting 1
19 he spread the tent over the tabernacle 1
19 and put the covering of the tent over it 1
22 he put the table in the tent of meeting 1
24 he put the lampstand in the tent of meeting 1
26 he put the golden altar in the tent of meeting 1
29 door of the tabernacle of the tent of meeting 1
30 he set the laver between the tent of meeting 1
32 when they went into the tent of meeting 1
34 Then the cloud covered the tent of meeting 1
35 Moses was not able to enter the tent of meeting 1
Lev 1: 1 and spoke to him from the tent of meeting 1
3 offer it at the door of the tent of meeting 1
5 that is at the door of the tent of meeting 1
3: 2 kill it at the door of the tent of meeting 1
8 killing it before the tent of meeting 1
13 and kill it before the tent of meeting 1
4: 4 to the door of the tent of meeting before the LORD 1
5 blood . . and bring it to the tent of meeting 1
7 which is in the tent of meeting 1
7 which is at the door of the tent of meeting 1
14 and bring it before the tent of meeting 1
16 the blood of the bull to the tent of meeting 1
18 the altar which is in the tent of meeting 1
18 which is at the door of the tent of meeting 1
6:16 in the court of the tent of meeting they shall eat 1
26 in the court of the tent of meeting 1
30 any blood is brought into the tent of meeting 1
8: 3 congregation at the door of the tent of meeting 1
4 assembled at the door of the tent of meeting 1
31 Boil the flesh at the door of the tent of meeting 1
33 the door of the tent of meeting for seven days 1
35 At the door of the tent of meeting 1
9: 5 brought what Moses commanded before the tent 1
23 Moses and Aaron went into the tent of meeting 1
10: 7 do not go out from the door of the tent of meeting 1
9 no wine . . when you go into the tent of meeting 1
12: 6 the priest at the door of the tent of meeting 1
14: 8 but shall dwell outside his tent seven days 1
11 the LORD, at the door of the tent of meeting 1
23 bring them . . to the door of the tent of meeting 1
15:14 before the LORD to the door of the tent of meeting 1
29 to the priest, to the door of the tent of meeting 1
16: 7 before the LORD at the door of the tent of meeting 1
16 so he shall do for the tent of meeting 1
17 There shall be no man in the tent of meeting 1
20 holy place and the tent of meeting and the altar 1
23 Then Aaron shall come into the tent of meeting 1
33 he shall make atonement for the tent of meeting 1
17: 4 bring it to the door of the tent of meeting 1
5 to the priest at the door of the tent of meeting 1
6 altar of the LORD at the door of the tent of meeting 1
9 does not bring it to the door of the tent of meeting 1
19:21 to the LORD, to the door of the tent of meeting 1
24: 3 in the tent of meeting, Aaron shall keep it 1
Num 1: 1 in the wilderness of Sinai, in the tent of meeting 1
2: 2 they shall encamp facing the tent of meeting 1
17 Then the tent of meeting shall set out 1
3: 7 perform . . before the tent of meeting 1
8 all the furnishings of the tent of meeting 1
25 the charge . . in the tent of meeting was to be 1
25 the tabernacle, the tent with its covering 1
25 the screen for the door of the tent of meeting 1
38 before the tent of meeting toward the sunrise 1
4: 3 to do the work in the tent of meeting. 1
4 service of . . Kohath in the tent of meeting 1
15 things of the tent of meeting which the sons 1
23 for service, to do the work in the tent of meeting. 1
25 carry . . the tent of meeting with its covering 1
25 screen for the door of the tent of meeting 1
28 This is the service . . in the tent of meeting 1
30 service, to do the work of the tent of meeting. 1
31 whole of their service in the tent of meeting 1
33 whole of their service in the tent of meeting 1
35 enter the service, for work in the tent of meeting; 1
37 all who served in the tent of meeting 1
39 enter the service for work in the tent of meeting– 1
41 Gershon, all who served in the tent of meeting 1
43 enter the service, for work in the tent of meeting– 1
47 enter to do the work . . in the tent of meeting 1
6:10 to the priest to the door of the tent of meeting 1
13 be brought to the door of the tent of meeting 1
18 shave . . at the door of the tent of meeting 1
7: 5 used in doing the service of the tent of meeting 1
89 when Moses went into the tent of meeting to speak 1
8: 9 present the Levites before the tent of meeting 1
15 shall go in to do service at the tent of meeting 1
19 to do the service . . at the tent of meeting 1
22 to do their service in the tent of meeting 1
24 work in the service of the tent of meeting; 1
26 minister . . in the tent of meeting 1
9:15 cloud covered the . . tent of the testimony; 1
17 cloud was taken up from over the tent 1
10: 3 at the entrance of the tent of meeting. 1
11:10 weeping . . every man at the door of his tent; 1
16 bring them to the tent of meeting 1
24 70 men . . and placed them round about the tent. 1
26 they had not gone out to the tent 1
12: 4 Come out, you three, to the tent of meeting. 1
5 LORD came . . and stood at the door of the tent 1
10 when the cloud removed from over the tent, behold 1
14:10 glory . . appeared at the tent of meeting to all 1
16:18 they stood at the entrance of the tent of meeting 1
19 at the entrance of the tent of meeting. 1
26 Depart . . from the tents of these wicked men 1
27 came out and stood at the door of their tents 1
42 they turned toward the tent of meeting; 1
43 came to the front of the tent of meeting 1
50 to Moses at the entrance of the tent of meeting 1
17: 4 deposit them in the tent of meeting 1
7 rods before the LORD in the tent of the testimony. 1
8 morrow Moses went into the tent of the testimony; 1
18: 2 you . . are before the tent of the testimony. 1
3 attend you and attend to all duties of the tent; 1
4 shall join you, and attend to the tent of meeting 1
4 for all the service of the tent; 1
6 to do the service of the tent of meeting. 1
21 their service in the tent of meeting. 1
22 Israel shall not come near the tent of meeting 1
23 shall do the service of the tent of meeting 1
31 return for your service in the tent of meeting. 1
19: 4 toward the front of the tent of meeting 1
14 This is the law when a man dies in a tent 1
14 every one who comes into the tent 1
14 every one who is in the tent, shall be unclean 1
18 dip it in the water, and sprinkle it upon the tent 1
20: 6 went . . to the door of the tent of meeting 1
24: 5 how fair are your tents, O Jacob 1
25: 6 weeping at the door of the tent of meeting. 1
27: 2 stood . . at the door of the tent of meeting 1
31:54 gold . . and brought it into the tent of meeting 1
Deu 1:27 murmured in your tents, and said, 'Because the LORD 1
5:30 Go and say to them, "Return to your tents. 1
11: 6 with their households, their tents 1
16: 7 morning you shall turn and go to your tents. 1
31:14 present yourselves in the tent of meeting 1
14 presented themselves in the tent of meeting. 1
15 LORD appeared in the tent in a pillar of cloud; 1
15 pillar of cloud stood by the door of the tent. 1
33:18 Rejoice, Zeb'ulun . . and Is'sachar, in your tents. 1
Jos 3:14 the people set out from their tents, to pass over 1
7:21 they are hidden in the earth inside my tent 1
22 Joshua sent messengers, and they ran to the tent; 1
22 it was hidden in his tent with the silver 1
23 they took them out of the tent and brought them 1
24 asses and sheep, and his tent, and all that he had; 1
18: 1 at Shiloh, and set up the tent of meeting there; 1
19:51 before . . LORD, at the door of the tent of meeting. 1
Jdg 4:11 and had pitched his tent as far away as the oak 1
17 Sis'era fled away on foot to the tent of Ja'el 1
18 So he turned aside to her into the tent 1
20 Stand at the door of the tent, and if any man comes 1
21 Ja'el the wife of Heber took a tent peg 1
22 So he went in to her tent; and there lay Sis'era dead *
5:24 be Ja'el . . of tent-dwelling women most blessed. 1
6: 5 would come up with their cattle and their tents 1
7: 8 sent all the rest of Israel every man to his tent 1
13 camp of Mid'ian, and came to the tent, and struck it 1
13 turned it upside down, so that the tent lay flat. 1
20: 8 We will not any of us go to his tent, and none of us 1
1Sm 2:22 served at the entrance to the tent of meeting. 1
13: 2 the rest . . he sent home, every man to his tent. 1
17:54 but he put his armor in his tent. 1
2Sm 6:17 its place, inside the tent which David . . pitched 1
7: 2 I dwell . . but the ark of God dwells in a tent. 2
6 have been moving about in a tent for my dwelling. 1
16:22 So they pitched a tent for Ab'salom upon the roof; 1
20: 1 every man to his tents, O Israel! 1
1Kg 1:39 took the horn of oil from the tent, and anointed 1
2:28 Jo'ab fled to the tent of the LORD and caught hold 1
29 Jo'ab has fled to the tent of the LORD, and behold 1
30 Benai'ah came to the tent of the LORD, and said 1
8: 4 brought up the ark . . the tent of meeting, and all 1
4 and all the holy vessels that were in the tent; 1
12:16 To your tents, O Israel! Look now to your own house 1
16 So Israel departed to their tents. 1
2Kg 7: 7 and forsook their tents, their horses 1
8 they went into a tent, and ate and drank 1
8 then they came back, and entered another tent 1
10 the asses tied, and the tents as they were. 1
1Ch 4:41 These . . destroyed their tents and the Me-u'nim 1
5:10 they dwelt in their tents throughout all 1
6:32 before the tabernacle of the tent of meeting 1
9:19 keepers of the thresholds of the tent 1
21 at the entrance of the tent of meeting. 1
23 the house of the LORD, that is, the house of the tent 1
15: 1 for the ark of God, and pitched a tent for it. 1
16: 1 inside the tent which David had pitched for it; 1
17: 1 ark of the covenant of the LORD is under a tent. 2
5 but I have gone from tent to tent 1
5 but I have gone from tent to tent 1
23:32 they shall keep charge of the tent of meeting 1
2Ch 1: 3 at Gibeon; for the tent of meeting of God 1
4 for he had pitched a tent for it in Jerusalem. 1
6 which was at the tent of meeting 1
13 from before the tent of meeting 1
5: 5 they brought up the ark, the tent of meeting 1
5 all the holy vessels that were in the tent; 1
10:16 Each of you to your tents, O Israel! 1
16 So all Israel departed to their tents. 1
14:15 they smote the tents of those who had cattle 1
24: 6 tax levied . . for the tent of testimony? 1
Job 5:24 You shall know that your tent is safe 1
8:22 the tent of the wicked will be no more. 1
11:14 let not wickedness dwell in your tents. 1
12: 6 The tents of robbers are at peace 1
15:34 fire consumes the tents of bribery. 1
18: 6 The light is dark in his tent 1

14 He is torn from the tent in which he trusted 1
15 In his tent dwells that which is none of his; 1
19:12 against me, and encamp round about my tent. 1
20:26 what is left in his tent will be consumed. 1
21:28 Where is the tent in which the wicked dwelt?' 1
22:23 you remove unrighteousness far from your tents 1
29: 4 when the friendship of God was upon my tent; 1
31:31 if the men of my tent have not said, 1
Ps 15: 1 O LORD, who shall sojourn in thy tent? 1
19: 4 In them he has set a tent for the sun 1
27: 5 he will conceal me under the cover of his tent 1
6 I will offer in his tent sacrifices with shouts 1
52: 5 he will snatch and tear you from your tent; 1
61: 4 Let me dwell in thy tent for ever! 1
69:25 let no one dwell in their tents. 1
78:51 first issue of their strength in the tents of Ham. 1
55 settled the tribes of Israel in their tents. 1
60 at Shiloh, the tent where he dwelt among men 1
67 He rejected the tent of Joseph, he did not choose 1
83: 6 the tents of Edom and the Ish'maelites 1
84:10 than dwell in the tents of wickedness. 1
91:10 no scourge come near your tent. 1
104: 2 who hast stretched out the heavens like a tent 2
106:25 murmured in their tents, and did not obey 1
118:15 songs of victory in the tents of the righteous 1
120: 5 Woe is me, that . . I dwell among the tents of Kedar! 1
Prv 14:11 but the tent of the upright will flourish. 1
Sng 1: 5 I am very dark . . like the tents of Kedar 1
8 pasture your kids beside the shepherd's tents. 3
Isa 16: 5 sit in faithfulness in the tent of David 1
33:20 tent, whose stakes will never be plucked up 1
38:12 removed from me like a shepherd's tent; 1
40:22 and spreads them like a tent to dwell in; 1
54: 2 Enlarge the place of your tent 1
Jer 4:20 Suddenly my tents are destroyed 1
6: 3 they shall pitch their tents around her 1
10:20 My tent is destroyed, and all my cords are broken; 1
20 there is no one to spread my tent again 1
30:18 I will restore the fortunes of the tents of Jacob 1
35: 7 but you shall live in tents all your days 1
10 but we have lived in tents 1
37:10 only wounded men, every man in his tent 1
49:29 Their tents and their flocks shall be taken 1
Lam 2: 4 he has slain . . in the tent of the daughter of Zion; 1
Dan 11:45 pitch his palatial tents between the sea 1
Hos 9: 6 thorns shall be in their tents. 1
12: 9 I wili again make you dwell in tents 1
Hab 3: 7 I saw the tents of Cushan in affliction; 1
Zec 10: 4 out of them the tent peg, out of them the battle bow •
12: 7 the LORD will give victory to the tents of Judah 1
Mal 2:12 May the LORD cut off from the tents of Jacob 1
Act 7:43 you took up the tent of Moloch 4
44 Our fathers had the tent of witness 4
2Co 5: 1 For we know that if the earthly tent we live 5
4 while we are still in this tent 5
Heb 8: 2 a minister in the sanctuary and the true tent 4
5 when Moses was about to erect the tent 4
9: 2 a tent was prepared, the outer one 4
3 a tent called the Holy of Holies 4
6 the priests go continually into the outer tent 4
8 as long as the outer tent is still standing 4
11 then through the greater and more perfect tent 4
21 both the tent and all the vessels used in worship. 4
11: 9 living in tents with Isaac and Jacob 4
13:10 those who serve the tent have no right to eat. 4
Rev 15: 5 temple of the tent of witness in heaven was opened 4
Tob 13:10 his tent may be raised for you again with joy. 4
Jdt 2:26 burned their tents 6
3: 3 all our sheepfolds with their tents 4
5:22 all the men standing around the tent 4
6:10 his slaves, who waited on him in his tent 4
7:18 their tents and supply trains spread out 4
8: 5 She set up a tent for herself on the roof of her house 4
36 they returned from the tent 4
10:15 Go at once to his tent 4
17 they brought them to the tent of Holofernes. 4
18 she waited outside the tent of Holofernes 4
20 all his servants came out and led her into the tent. 4
12: 5 the servants . . brought her into the tent 4
9 she returned clean and stayed in the tent 4
13: 1 Bagoas closed the tent from outside 4
2 Judith was left alone in the tent 4
14: 3 they will rush into the tent of Holofernes 4
7 Blessed are you in every tent of Judah! 6
13 they came to Holofernes' tent 4
14 Bagoas went in and knocked at the door of the tent 4
17 Then he went to the tent where Judith had stayed 4
15: 1 When the men in the tents heard it 6
11 They gave Judith the tent of Holofernes 4
Wis 9: 8 a copy of the holy tent which thou didst prepare 4
15 this earthy tent burdens the thoughtful mind. 5
11: 2 and pitched their tents in untrodden places. 4
Sir 14:25 he will pitch his tent near her 4
24: 8 assigned a place for my tent 4
1Mc 9:66 the sons of Phasiron in their tents. 6
2Mc 2: 4 ordered that the tent and the ark should follow 4
5 he brought there the tent and the ark 4
12:12 they departed to their tents. 4
3Mc 1: 2 and crossed over by night to the tent of Ptolemy 4
3 and arranged that a . . man should sleep in the tent 4
4Mc 3: 8 he came . . to the royal tent 4

tent *See also* front, move, peg, pitch, tent.

tent to tent 1. *σκήνωμα*
Jdt 10:18 her arrival was reported from tent to tent 1

tent-cord 1. יֶתֶר
Job 4:21 If their tent-cord is plucked up within them 1

tenth 1. עָשׂוֹר 2. עֲשִׂירִי 3. *δέκατος*
Gen 8: 5 to abate until the tenth month; 2
5 to abate until the tenth month; 2
Exd 12: 3 on the tenth day of this month they shall take 1
Lev 16:29 in the seventh month, on the tenth day of the month 1
23:27 On the tenth day of this seventh month is the day 1
25: 9 send abroad the loud trumpet on the tenth day 1
27:32 every tenth animal of all that pass under 2
Num 7:66 On the tenth day Ahie'zer . . of the men of Dan 2
29: 7 On the tenth day of this seventh month 1
Deu 23: 2 even to the tenth generation none 2
3 even to the tenth generation none belonging 2
Jos 4:19 people came . . on the tenth day of the first month 1
2Kg 25: 1 in the ninth year of his reign, in the tenth month 2
1 in the tenth month, on the tenth day of the month 1
1Ch 12:13 Jeremiah tenth, Mach'bannai eleventh. 2
24:11 the ninth to Jeshua, the tenth to Shecani'ah 2
25:17 tenth to Shim'e-i, his sons and his brethren, twelve; 2
27:13 Tenth . . was Ma'harai of Netoph'ah 2
13 Tenth, for the tenth month, was Ma'harai 2
Ezr 10:16 On the first day of the tenth month they sat down 2
Est 2:16 taken . . into his royal palace in the tenth month 2
Jer 32: 1 in the tenth year of Zedeki'ah king of Judah 2
39: 1 Zedeki'ah king of Judah, in the tenth month 2
52: 4 in the ninth year of his reign, in the tenth month 2
4 tenth month, on the tenth day of the month 1
12 In the fifth month, on the tenth day 1
Ezk 20: 1 the fifth month, on the tenth day of the month 1
24: 1 In the ninth year, in the tenth month, on the tenth 2
1 in the tenth month, on the tenth day of the month 1
29: 1 In the tenth year, in the tenth month 2
1 In the tenth year, in the tenth month 2
33:21 in the tenth month, on the fifth day of the month 2
40: 1 on the tenth day of the month 1
Zec 8:19 the fast of the seventh, and the fast of the tenth 2
Joh 1:39 they stayed . . for it was about the tenth hour. 3
Rev 21:20 the ninth topaz, the tenth chrysoprase 3
1Es 9:16 on the new moon of the tenth month 3
Bar 1: 8 At the same time, on the tenth day of Sivan, Baruch 3
3Mc 5:14 since it was nearly the middle of the tenth hour 3

tenth *See also* give, take.

tentmaker 1. *σκηνοποιός*
Act 18: 3 by trade they were tentmakers. 1

teraphim 1. תְּרָפִים
Jdg 17: 5 had a shrine, and he made an ephod and teraphim 1
18:14 in these houses there are an ephod, teraphim 1
17 took the graven image, the ephod, the teraphim 1
18 took the graven image, the ephod, the teraphim 1
20 he took the ephod, and the teraphim, and the graven 1
2Kg 23:24 the wizards and the teraphim and the idols 1
Ezk 21:21 he shakes the arrows, he consults the teraphim 1
Hos 3: 4 dwell many days . . without ephod or teraphim. 1
Zec 10: 2 For the teraphim utter nonsense 1

terebinth 1. אֵיל 2. אֵלָה 3. *τερέμινθος*
Ps 56: 0 according to The Dove on Far-off Terebinths. 1
Isa 6:13 it will be burned again, like a terebinth or an oak 2
Hos 4:13 and terebinth, because their shade is good. 2
Sir 24:16 Like a terebinth I spread out my branches 3

term 1. אמר 2. בְּרִית 3. דָּבָר 4. מִצְוָה 5. שֵׁם 6. *διάσταλσις* 7. *εὐαγγέλιον* 8. *κατά* 9. *λόγος* 10. *τὰ πρός*
1Kg 20:34 And Ahab said, "I will let you go on these terms. 2
Est 9:26 they called these days Purim, after the term Pur. 5
Isa 62: 4 You shall no more be termed Forsaken 1
4 and your land shall no more be termed Desolate; 1
Jer 32:11 sealed deed of purchase, containing the terms 4
34:18 and did not keep the terms of the covenant 3
Lke 14:32 he sends an embassy and asks terms of peace. 10
1Co 15: 1 in what terms I preached to you the gospel 7
1Es 9:14 undertook the matter on these terms 8
Tob 5:15 So they agreed to these terms. •
1Mc 8:29 Thus on these terms the Romans make a treaty 9
30 If after these terms are in effect both parties 9
2Mc 13:25 so angry that they wanted to annul its terms. 6
14:20 When the terms had been fully considered •

human term 1. *ἀνθρώπινος*
Rom 6:19 I am speaking in human terms 1

just term 1. *δίκαιος*
1Mc 7:12 to ask for just terms. 1
2Mc 11:14 them to settle everything on just terms 1

same term 1. *καθώς*
2Co 11:12 they work on the same terms as we do. 1

termination 1. תּוֹצָאָה
Num34: 5 its termination shall be at the sea. 1

terms *See* come.

terms of peace 1. שָׁלוֹם 2. *δεξιός* 3. *συνθήκη*
Deu 20:10 city to fight against it, offer terms of peace 1
Dan 11:17 shall bring terms of peace and perform them. 3
1Mc 11:66 Then they asked him to grant them terms of peace 2

terrestrial 1. *ἐπίγειος*
1Co 15:40 there are terrestrial bodies 1
40 the glory of the terrestrial is another. 1

terrible 1. אָיֹם 2. אֵימָה 3. ירא 4. עָרִיץ 5. פֶּלֶא 6. דחל (A) 7. *δεινός* 8. *δεινῶς* 9. *σκληρός* 10. *φοβερός* 11. terribilis
Exd 15:11 terrible in glorious deeds, doing wonders? 3
Deu 1:19 through all that great and terrible wilderness 3
7:21 in the midst of you, a great and terrible God. 3
8:15 led you through the great and terrible wilderness 3
10:17 great, the mighty, and the terrible God 3
Jdg 13: 6 countenance of the angel of God, very terrible; 3
Neh 1: 5 O LORD God of heaven, the great and terrible God 3
4:14 Remember the Lord, who is great and terrible 3
9:32 our God, the great and mighty and terrible God 3
Job 37:22 God is clothed with terrible majesty. 3
39:20 His majestic snorting is terrible. 2
Ps 47: 2 the LORD, the Most High, is terrible, a great king 3
66: 3 Say to God, "How terrible are thy deeds! 3
5 he is terrible in his deeds among men. 3
68:35 Terrible is God in his sanctuary 3
76: 7 thou, terrible art thou! Who can stand before thee 3
12 who is terrible to the kings of the earth. 3
89: 7 great and terrible above all that are round 3
99: 3 praise thy great and terrible name! Holy is he! 3
111: 9 Holy and terrible is his name! 3
Sng 6: 4 terrible as an army with banners. 1
10 Who is this . . terrible as an army with banners? 1
Isa 21: 1 it comes from the desert, from a terrible land. 3
Lam 1: 9 her fall is terrible, she has no comforter. 5
Ezk 28: 7 upon you, the most terrible of the nations; 4
30:11 people with him, the most terrible of the nations 4
31:12 Foreigners, the most terrible of the nations 4
32:12 all of them most terrible among the nations. 4
Dan 7: 7 terrible and dreadful and exceedingly strong; 6
19 exceedingly terrible, with its teeth of iron 6
9: 4 O Lord, the great and terrible God 3
Jol 2:11 For the day of the LORD is great and very terrible; 3
31 before the great and terrible day of the LORD 3
Hab 1: 7 Dread and terrible are they; 3
Zep 2:11 The LORD will be terrible against them; 3
Mal 4: 5 before the great and terrible day of the LORD 3
Mat 8: 6 paralyzed at home, in terrible distress. 8
2Es 8:22 and whose command is terrible 11
15:13 by blight and hail and by a terrible tempest. 11
40 and shall pour out . . a terrible tempest 11
Wis 11:18 flash terrible sparks from their eyes; 7
16: 5 the terrible rage of wild beasts 7
19:16 afflicted with terrible sufferings 7
Sir 43:29 Terrible is the Lord and very great 10
Man 1: 3 sealed it with thy terrible and glorious name; 10
2Mc 6:30 I am enduring terrible sufferings in my body 9
4Mc 4:15 an arrogant and terrible man 7

terrible act 1. ירא
Ps 145: 6 Men . . proclaim the might of thy terrible acts 1

terrible deed 1. מוֹרָא
Deu 34:12 all the great and terrible deeds which Moses 1

terrible thing 1. ירא
Exd 34:10 it is a terrible thing that I will do with you. 1
Deu 10:21 done for you these great and terrible things 1
2Sm 7:23 and doing for them great and terrible things 1
1Ch 17:21 making . . a name for great and terrible things 1
Ps 106:22 terrible things by the Red Sea. 1
Isa 64: 3 didst terrible things which we looked not for 1

terribly 1. *δεινῶς* 2. *κακῶς* 3. *μέγας* 4. *πολύς* 5. *ὑπεράγαν* 6. *φρικτῶς*
Mat 17:15 and he suffers terribly 2
Mrk 9:26 after crying out and convulsing him terribly 4
AEs 11: 6 they roared terribly. 3
Wis 6: 5 he will come upon you terribly and swiftly 6
17: 3 they were scattered, terribly alarmed 1
2Mc 10:34 The men within . . blasphemed terribly 5

terrified 1. פחד
Isa 44:11 they shall be terrified, they shall be put to shame 1

terrify 1. בהל 2. בעת 3. חרד 4. חתת 5. ירא 6. ערץ 7. פַּחַד 8. קוץ 9. שׁמם 10. *ἐκταράσσω* 11. *ἐκφοβέω* 12. *ἔμφοβος* 13. *καταπλήσσω* 14. *πτήσσω* 15. *πτοέω* 16. *ταράσσω* 17. *φοβερός* 18. *φοβέω*

19. *φοβέω πτόησιν* 20. expavesco 21. horreo
22. horribilis 23. timeo
1Sm 5: 6 and he terrified and afflicted them with tumors 9
28:21 when she saw that he was terrified, she said 1
2Ch 32:18 they shouted it . . to frighten and terrify them 1
Job 3: 5 let the blackness of the day terrify it. 2
7:14 scare me with dreams and terrify me with visions 2
9:34 let not dread of him terrify me. 2
13:11 Will not his majesty terrify you 2
21 let not dread of thee terrify me. 2
15:21 Terrifying sounds are in his ears; 7
24 distress and anguish terrify him; 2
23:15 Therefore I am terrified at his presence; 1
16 the Almighty has terrified me; 1
31:34 the contempt of families terrified me 4
33: 7 Behold, no fear of me need terrify you; 2
16 then he opens the ears of men, and terrifies them 4
Ps 2: 5 in his wrath, and terrify them in his fury, saying 1
83:15 terrify them with thy hurricane! 1
Isa 2:19 when he rises to terrify the earth. 6
21 his majesty, when he rises to terrify the earth. 6
7: 6 Let us go up against Judah and terrify it 8
31: 4 is not terrified by their shouting or daunted 4
41:23 do harm, that we may be dismayed and terrified. 5
Jer 49:37 I will terrify Elam before their enemies 4
Ezk 30: 9 from me to terrify the unsuspecting Ethiopians; 3
Hab 2:17 the destruction of the beasts will terrify you 4
Zec 1:21 these have come to terrify them, to cast down 3
Mat 14:26 they were terrified, saying, "It is a ghost! 16
Mrk 6:50 for they all saw him, and were terrified. 16
Lke 21: 9 do not be terrified 15
Heb 12:21 Indeed, so terrifying was the sight 17
1Pe 3: 6 if you do right and let nothing terrify you. 19
Rev 11:13 and the rest were terrified and gave glory 12
2Es 6:15 while the voice is speaking, do not be terrified; 20
23 they shall suddenly be terrified. 20
24 those who inhabit it shall be terrified 20
10:25 and my heart was terrified ‡
55 do not let your heart be terrified 20
11:45 and your terrifying wings 22
12: 3 and the earth was exceedingly terrified 20
5 with which I have been terrified this night. 20
8 and meaning of this terrifying vision 22
15:28 a terrifying sight, appearing from the east! 22
16:10 He will thunder, and who will not be terrified? 21
18 when the powers shall be terrified 23
Jdt 4: 2 they were therefore very greatly terrified 18
7: 4 they were greatly terrified 16
AEs 15: 6 he was most terrifying. 17
Wis 17: 4 terrifying sounds rang out around them 10
1Mc 12:28 they were afraid and were terrified at heart 14
4Mc 9: 5 You are trying to terrify us by threatening us 11
16:17 to be terrified by tortures. 13

terrifying *See* power.

more terrifying 1. timoratior
2Es 12:13 it shall be more terrifying than all 1

territory 1. אֶרֶץ 2. גְּבוּל 3. גְּבוּלָה 4. חֶבֶל 5. חֵלֶק
6. *κληρονομία* 7. *ὅριον* 8. *παρά* 9. *τόπος* 10. regio
Gen 10:19 the territory of the Canaanites extended 2
30 The territory in which they lived extended *
20: 1 journeyed toward the territory of the Negeb 1
Exd 13: 7 be seen with you in all your territory. 2
Num20:16 in Kadesh, a city on the edge of your territory. 2
17 until we have passed through your territory. 2
21 to give Israel passage through his territory; 2
21:22 until we have passed through your territory. 2
23 not allow Israel to pass through his territory. 2
32:33 the land and its cities with their territories 3
33:44 encamped at I'ye-ab'arim, in the territory of Moab. 2
Deu 2: 4 territory of your brethren the sons of Esau 2
3:12 I gave . . the territory beginning at Aro'er *
16 I gave the territory from Gilead *
11:24 your territory shall be from the wilderness 2
12:20 When the LORD your God enlarges your territory 2
16: 4 No leaven . . in all your territory for seven days; 2
28:40 have olive trees throughout all your territory 2
Jos 1: 4 land of the Hittites . . shall be your territory. 2
13:16 their territory was from Aro'er . . and the city 2
25 Their territory was Jazer, and all the cities 2
26 from Mahana'im to the territory of Debir 2
16: 2 along to At'aroth, the territory of the Archites; 2
3 goes down . . to the territory of the Japh'letites 2
3 as far as the territory of Lower Beth-hor'on 2
5 The territory of the E'phraimites . . as follows 2
17: 7 The territory of Manas'seh reached from Asher 2
18: 5 Judah continuing in his territory on the south 2
5 house of Joseph in their territory on the north. 2
11 the territory allotted to it fell between 2
19: 9 formed part of the territory of Judah; 4
10 the territory of its inheritance reached as far 2
18 Its territory included Jezreel, Chesul'loth 2
25 Its territory included Helkath, Hali, Beten 2
41 the territory of its inheritance included Zorah 2
46 Rakkon with the territory over against Joppa. 2
47 the territory of the Danites was lost to them 2
49 distributing the several territories 2
Jdg 1:18 Judah also took Gaza with its territory 2
18 and Ash'kelon with its territory, and Ekron 2
18 its territory, and Ekron with its territory. 2
11:18 but they did not enter the territory of Moab 2
20 not trust Israel to pass through his territory; 2
22 possession of all the territory of the Amorites 2
19:29 her throughout all the territory of Israel. 2
1Sm 5: 6 and afflicted . . both Ashdod and its territory. 2
7:13 and did not again enter the territory of Israel. 2
14 Israel rescued their territory from the hand 2
10: 2 Rachel's tomb in the territory of Benjamin 2
11: 3 send . . through all the territory of Israel. 2
7 sent them through . . all the territory of Israel 2
2Sm 21: 5 have no place in all the territory of Israel 2
1Kg 1: 3 throughout all the territory of Israel 2
2Kg 9:10 dogs . . eat Jez'ebel in the territory of Jezreel 5
36 In the territory of Jezreel the dogs shall eat 5
37 shall be as dung . . in the territory of Jezreel 5
10:32 defeated . . throughout the territory of Israel 2
15:16 sacked Tappuah . . and its territory from Tirzah 2
18: 8 the Philistines as far as Gaza and its territory 2
1Ch 6:66 cities of their territory out of the tribe 2
21:12 destroying . . all the territory of Israel. 2
2Ch 34:33 territory that belonged to the people of Israel 1
Job 38:20 that you may take it to its territory 2
Jer 15:13 for all your sins, throughout all your territory. 2
17: 3 of your sin throughout all your territory. 2
Ezk 43:12 the whole territory round about upon the top 2
48: 2 Adjoining the territory of Dan, from the east 2
3 Adjoining the territory of Asher, from the east 2
4 Adjoining the territory of Naph'tali 2
5 Adjoining the territory of Manas'seh 2
6 Adjoining the territory of E'phraim 2
7 Adjoining the territory of Reuben, from the east 2
8 Adjoining the territory of Judah, from the east 2
12 adjoining the territory of the Levites. 2
13 alongside the territory of the priests 2
22 shall lie between the territory of Judah 2
22 of Judah and the territory of Benjamin. 2
24 Adjoining the territory of Benjamin 2
25 Adjoining the territory of Simeon, from the east 2
26 Adjoining the territory of Is'sachar 2
27 Adjoining the territory of Zeb'ulun 2
28 And adjoining the territory of Gad to the south 2
Ams 6: 2 is their territory greater than your territory 2
2 is their territory greater than your territory 2
Zep 2: 8 and made boasts against their territory. 2
Mat 4:13 Caper'na-um by the sea, in the territory of Zebulun 7
2Es 4:15 there also we may gain more territory 10
Jdt 1:12 take revenge on the whole territory of Cilicia 7
2:10 and seize all their territory for me in advance 7
25 He also seized the territory of Cilicia 7
16: 5 He boasted that he would burn up my territory 7
Sir 24: 7 I sought in whose territory I might lodge. 6
Bar 3:24 And how vast the territory that he possesses! 9
1Mc 3:36 settle aliens in all their territory 7
42 the forces were encamped in their territory. 7
5: 9 the Israelites who lived in their territory 7
9:72 came no more into their territory. 7
11:34 the territory of Judea 7
14: 2 heard that Demetrius had invaded his territory 7
15:29 You have devastated their territory 7
4Mc 3:11 the water in the enemy's territory 8

territory allotted 1. גּוֹרָל
Jdg 1: 3 with me into the territory allotted to me 1
3 with you into the territory allotted to you. 1

terror 1. אֵימָה 2. בֶּהָלָה 3. בַּלָּהָה 4. בִּעוּתִים 5. בעת
6. בְּעָתָה 7. דְּאָבָה 8. זְוָעָה 9. זַעֲוָה 10. חָגָּא 11. חַתְחַת
12. חִתִּית 13. חִתָּת 14. מָגוֹר 15. מגר 16. מוֹרָא
17. מְחִתָּה 18. פחד 19. פַּחַד 20. שַׁמָּה 21. *δειλία*
22. *δέος* 23. *ἐκδειματόω* 24. *ἐκφοβέω* 25. *ἔμφοβος*
26. *καταπληγμός* 27. *πτόη* 28. *τρόμος* 29. *φόβητρον*
30. *φόβος* 31. tremor
Gen 35: 5 as they journeyed, a terror from God fell upon 13
Exd 15:16 Terror and dread fall upon them; 1
23:27 I will send my terror before you, and will throw 1
Deu 4:34 by . . an outstretched arm, and by great terrors 16
26: 8 with great terror, with signs and wonders; 16
32:25 in the chambers shall be terror, destroying 1
Est 7: 6 Haman was in terror before the king and the queen. 5
Job 6: 4 the terrors of God are arrayed against me. 4
18:11 Terrors frighten him on every side, and chase him 3
14 he trusted, and is brought to the king of terrors. 3
20:25 terrors come upon him. 1
22:10 sudden terror overwhelms you; 19
24:17 are friends with the terrors of deep darkness. 3
27:20 Terrors overtake him like a flood; 3
30:15 Terrors are turned upon me; 3
31:23 For I was in terror of calamity from God 19
41:14 Round about his teeth is terror. 1
22 terror dances before him. 7
Ps 31:13 hear the whispering of many–terror on every side!– 15
53: 5 There they are, in great terror 18
5 in great terror, in terror such as has not been! 19
55: 4 the terrors of death have fallen upon me. 1
15 let them go away in terror into their graves. *
73:19 swept away utterly by terrors! 3
78:33 vanish like a breath, and their years in terror. 2
88:15 I suffer thy terrors; I am helpless. 1
91: 5 You will not fear the terror of the night 19
Ecc 12: 5 afraid also of what . . and terrors are in the way; 11
Isa 2:10 terror of the LORD . . the glory of his majesty. 19
19 from before the terror of the LORD 19
21 from before the terror of the LORD 19
17:14 At evening time, behold, terror! 3
19:17 Judah will become a terror to the Egyptians; 10
24:17 Terror, and the pit, and the snare are upon you 19
18 He who flees at the sound of the terror shall fall 19
28:19 be sheer terror to understand the message. 8
31: 9 His rock shall pass away in terror 15
33:18 Your mind will muse on the terror 1
54:14 and from terror, for it shall not come near you. 17
Jer 6:25 for the enemy has a sword, terror is on every side. 15
8:15 for a time of healing, but behold, terror. 6
14:19 for a time of healing, but behold, terror. 6
15: 8 I have made anguish and terror fall upon them 2
17:17 Be not a terror to me; thou art my refuge 17
20: 3 your name Pashhur, but Terror on every side. 15
4 Behold, I will make you a terror to yourself 15
10 I hear many whispering. Terror is on every side! 15
29:18 to be a curse, a terror, a hissing, and a reproach 20
30: 5 heard a cry of panic, of terror, and no peace. 19
32:21 hand and outstretched arm, and with great terror; 16
46: 5 they look not back–terror on every side! 15
48:43 Terror, pit, and snare are before you 19
44 He who flees from the terror shall fall 19
49: 5 Behold, I will bring terror upon you, says the Lord 19
29 men shall cry to them: 'Terror on every side!' 15
Lam 2:22 Thou didst invite . . my terrors on every side; 14
Ezk 23:46 and make them an object of terror and a spoil. 9
26:17 who imposed your terror on all the mainland! 12
32:23 who spread terror in the land of the living. 12
24 who spread terror in the land of the living 12
25 terror of them was spread in the land 12
26 they spread terror in the land of the living. 12
27 for the terror of the mighty men was in the land 12
30 all the terror which they caused by their might; 12
32 For he spread terror in the land of the living; 12
38:21 I will summon every kind of terror against Gog 30
Hab 1: 9 terror of them goes before them. *
Lke 21:11 terrors and great signs from heaven. 29
Act 10: 4 he stared at him in terror, and said 25
Rom13: 3 For rulers are not a terror to good conduct 30
2Es 5: 1 shall be seized with great terror ‡
11:40 have held sway over the world with much terror 31
Jdt 2:28 fear and terror of him fell upon all the people 28
Wis 17: 6 in terror they deemed the things . . to be worse 23
19 it paralyzed them with terror. 24
Sir 21: 4 Terror and violence will lay waste riches 26
1Mc 3:25 terror fell upon the Gentiles round about them. 27
2Mc 3:17 terror and bodily trembling 22
24 became faint with terror. 21
12:22 terror and fear came over the enemy 22
13:16 filled the camp with terror and confusion 22
15:23 to carry terror and trembling before us. 22
3Mc 6:17 and brought an uncontrollable terror upon the army. 27
19 filled them with confusion and terror 21

terror *See also* inspire, palsy, strike.

great terror 1. פחד
Ps 14: 5 There they shall be in great terror 1

sudden terror 1. בֶּהָלָה
Lev 26:16 I will appoint over you sudden terror, 1

terror-stricken 1. חתת
Isa 30:31 The Assyrians will be terror-stricken 1

test 1. בחן 2. בֹּחַן 3. ברר 4. חפש 5. נסה 6. צרף
7. *δοκιμάζω* 8. *δοκιμασία* 9. *δοκιμή* 10. *δοκίμιον*
11. *δόκιμος* 12. *ἐτάζω* 13. *πεῖρα* 14. *πειράζω*
15. *πειρασμός* 16. *πειράω* 17. probo
Gen 22: 1 After these things God tested Abraham 5
42:15 By this you shall be tested 1
16 your words may be tested, whether there is truth 1
Deu 6:16 as you tested him at Massah. 5
8: 2 testing you to know what was in your heart 5
16 that he might humble you and test you 5
13: 3 LORD your God is testing you, to know whether 5
33: 8 godly one, whom thou didst test at Massah 5
Jdg 2:22 that by them I may test Israel, whether they will 5
3: 1 the nations which the LORD left, to test Israel 5
4 They were for the testing of Israel, to know 5
7: 3 Gideon tested them; 22,000 returned *
4 take them down to the water and I will test them 6
1Kg 10: 1 she came to test him with hard questions. 5
2Ch 9: 1 to Jerusalem to test him with hard questions 5
Job 7:18 every morning, and test him every moment? 1
34: 3 the ear tests words as the palate tastes food. 1
Ps 11: 4 his eyes behold, his eyelids test 1
5 The LORD tests the righteous and the wicked 1
17: 3 if thou visitest me by night, if thou testest me 6
26: 2 O LORD, and try me; test my heart and my mind. 6
66:10 For thou, O God, hast tested us; thou hast tried us 1

78:18 tested God in their heart by demanding the food 5
41 They tested him again and again 5
56 Yet they tested and rebelled 5
81: 7 I tested you at the waters of Mer'ibah. Selah 1
95: 9 your fathers tested me, and put me to the proof 5
105:19 the word of the LORD tested him 6
Ecc 3:18 I said . . that God is testing them to show them 3
7:23 All this I have tested by wisdom; 5
Isa 28:16 for a foundation a stone, a tested stone 2
Jer 9: 7 Behold, I will refine them and test them 1
Lam 3:40 Let us test and examine our ways, and return 4
Ezk 21:13 For it will not be a testing 1
Dan 1:12 Test your servants for ten days; let us be given 5
14 hearkened . . and tested them for ten days. 5
Zec 13: 9 refines silver, and test them as gold is tested. 1
9 refines silver, and test them as gold is tested. 1
Mat 16: 1 to test him they asked him to show them a sign 14
19: 3 Pharisees came up to him and tested him by asking 14
22:35 a lawyer, asked him a question, to test him. 14
Mrk 8:11 seeking from him a sign from heaven, to test him. 14
10: 2 Pharisees came up and in order to test him asked 14
Lke 11:16 while others, to test him, sought from him a sign 14
Joh 6: 6 This he said to test him 14
8: 6 This they said to test him 14
1Co 3:13 fire will test what sort of work 7
2Co 2: 9 For this is why I wrote, that I might test you 9
8: 2 for in a severe test of affliction 9
22 whom we have often tested 7
9:13 Under the test of this service 9
13: 5 Test yourselves 7
Gal 6: 4 let each one test his own work 7
1Th 2: 4 to please God who tests our hearts. 7
5:21 test everything; hold fast what is good 7
1Ti 3:10 let them also be tested first 7
Heb 3: 8 on the day of testing in the wilderness 15
11:17 Abraham, when he was tested, offered up Isaac 14
Jas 1: 3 testing of your faith produces steadfastness. 10
12 when he has stood the test he will receive 11
1Pe 1: 7 gold which though perishable is tested by fire 7
1Jn 4: 1 test the spirits to see whether they are of God; 7
Rev 2: 2 tested those who call themselves apostles 14
10 throw . . you into prison, that you may be tested 14
2Es 16:73 as gold that is tested by fire. 17
Jdt 8:26 how he tested Isaac 14
Wis 1: 3 when his power is tested, it convicts the foolish; 7
2:17 let us test what will happen at the end of his life; 14
19 Let us test him with insult and torture 12
3: 5 God tested them and found them worthy of himself; 14
6: 6 mighty men will be mightily tested. 12
11:10 thou didst test them as a father does in warning 7
18:25 merely to test the wrath was enough. 13
Sir 2: 5 For gold is tested in the fire 7
4:17 she will test him with her ordinances. 16
6: 7 When you gain a friend, gain him through testing 15
21 will weigh him down like a heavy testing stone 8
13:11 he will test you through much talk 16
27: 5 The kiln tests the potter's vessels 7
5 the test of a man is in his reasoning. 15
7 this is the test of men. 15
31:10 Who has been tested by it and been found perfect? 7
26 so wine tests hearts in the strife of the proud. *
37:27 My son, test your soul while you live 16
39: 4 he tests the good and the evil among men. 14
44:20 when he was tested he was found faithful. 15
1Mc 2:52 Was not Abraham found faithful when tested 15
4Mc 17:12 tested them for their endurance 7

test *See also* fail, make, meet, put, quality.

tester 1. מִבְצָר
Jer 6:27 made you an assayer and tester among my people 1

testicle 1. אֶשֶׁךְ
Lev 21:20 an itching disease or scabs or crushed testicles 1
22:24 Any animal which has its testicles bruised *
Deu 23: 1 He whose testicles are crushed *

testify 1. אָלָה 2. עוד 3. ענה 4. *ἀποδίδωμι μαρτυρίαν* 5. *διαμαρτύρομαι* 6. *μαρτυρέω* 7. *μαρτύριον* 8. *μαρτύρομαι*
Lev 5: 1 he hears a public adjuration to testify 1
Deu 21: 7 they shall testify, 'Our hands did not shed 3
1Sm 12: 3 Here I am; testify against me before the LORD 3
3 Testify against me and I will restore it to you. 3
2Sm 1:16 your own mouth has testified against you, saying 3
2Ch 24:19 these testified against them 2
Job 15: 6 your own lips testify against you. 3
16: 8 risen up against me, it testifies to my face. 3
Ps 50: 7 I will testify against you. I am God, your God. 2
Isa 59:12 and our sins testify against us; 3
Jer 14: 7 Though our iniquities testify against us 3
Hos 5: 5 The pride of Israel testifies to his face; 3
Ams 3:13 Hear, and testify against the house of Jacob 2
Joh 4:44 For Jesus himself testified that a prophet 6
7: 7 because I testify of it that its works are evil. 6
13:21 he was troubled in spirit, and testified 6
Act 2:40 he testified with many other words and exhorted 5
8:25 Now when they had testified and spoken the word 5
10:42 to testify that he is the one ordained by God 5
13:22 of whom he testified and said 6
18: 5 testifying to the Jews that the Christ was Jesus. 5
20:21 testifying both to Jews and to Greeks 5
23 the Holy Spirit testifies to me in every city 5
24 testify to the gospel of the grace of God. 5
26 Therefore I testify to you this day 8
23:11 as you have testified about me at Jerusalem 5
26: 5 if they are willing to testify 6
22 I stand here testifying both to small and great 8
28:23 testifying to the kingdom of God 5
1Co 15:15 we testified of God that he raised Christ 6
2Co 8: 3 they gave according to their means, as I can testify 6
Gal 5: 3 I testify again to every man 8
Eph 4:17 Now this I affirm and testify in the Lord 8
2Ti 1: 8 Do not be ashamed then of testifying to our Lord 7
Heb 2: 6 It has been testified somewhere 5
3: 5 to testify to the things . . to be spoken later 7
7: 8 one of whom it is testified that he lives. 6
1Jn 1: 2 and we saw it, and testify to it 6
4:14 And we have seen and testify that 6
3Jn 1: 3 the brethren arrived and testified to the truth 6
6 testified to your love before the church. 6
12 I testify to him too 6
Rev 22:19 He who testifies to these things says 6
Sus 1:40 These things we testify. 6
1Mc 2:37 heaven and earth testify for us 6
56 Caleb, because he testified in the assembly 6
4Mc 6:32 we would have testified to their domination. 4

testify against 1. *καταμαρτυρέω*
Mat 26:62 What is it that these men testify against you? 1
27:13 hear how many things they testify against you? 1
Mrk 14:60 What is it that these men testify against you? 1
Sus 1:21 If you refuse, we will testify against you 1

testimony 1. אות 2. עֵדָה 3. עֵדוּת 4. תְּעוּדָה 5. *ἐπί* 6. *λόγος* 7. *μαρτυρέω* 8. *μαρτυρία* 9. *μαρτύριον* 10. *μάρτυς*
Exd 16:34 placed it before the testimony, to be kept. 3
25:16 you shall put into the ark the testimony 3
21 you shall put the testimony that I shall give 3
22 cherubim that are upon the ark of the testimony 3
26:33 bring the ark of the testimony in thither within 3
34 mercy seat upon the ark of the testimony 3
27:21 the veil which is before the testimony 3
30: 6 the veil that is by the ark of the testimony 3
6 before the mercy seat that is over the testimony 3
26 you shall anoint . . the ark of the testimony 3
36 put part of it before the testimony in the tent 3
31: 7 tent of meeting, and the ark of the testimony 3
18 gave to Moses . . two tables of the testimony 3
32:15 with the two tables of the testimony in his hands 3
34:29 with the two tables of the testimony in his hand 3
38:21 for the . . tabernacle of the testimony 3
39:35 the ark of the testimony with its poles 3
40: 3 you shall put in it the ark of the testimony 3
5 golden altar . . before the ark of the testimony 3
20 he took the testimony and put it into the ark 3
21 and screened the ark of the testimony; 3
Lev 16:13 cover the mercy seat which is upon the testimony 3
24: 3 Outside the veil of the testimony, in the tent 3
Num 1:50 over the tabernacle of the testimony 3
53 around the tabernacle of the testimony 3
53 keep charge of the tabernacle of the testimony. 3
4: 5 cover the ark of the testimony with it; 3
7:89 mercy seat that was upon the ark of the testimony 3
9:15 cloud covered the . . tent of the testimony; 3
10:11 from over the tabernacle of the testimony 3
17: 4 in the tent of meeting before the testimony 3
7 rods before the LORD in the tent of the testimony. 3
8 morrow Moses went into the tent of the testimony; 3
10 Put back the rod of Aaron before the testimony 3
18: 2 you . . are before the tent of the testimony. 3
35:30 no . . put to death on the testimony of one witness. *
Deu 4:45 testimonies, the statutes, and the ordinances 2
6:17 commandments . . and his testimonies 2
20 What is the meaning of the testimonies 2
Jos 4:16 the priests who bear the ark of the testimony 3
1Kg 2: 3 his ordinances, and his testimonies, as it is 2
2Kg 11:12 put the crown upon him, and gave him the testimony; 3
23: 3 to keep his commandments and his testimonies 2
1Ch 29:19 he may keep . . thy testimonies, and thy statutes 2
2Ch 23:11 put the crown upon him, and gave him the testimony; 3
24: 6 tax levied . . for the tent of testimony? 3
34:31 to keep his . . testimonies and his statutes 2
Job 21:29 do you not accept their testimony 1
Ps 19: 7 the testimony of the LORD is sure 3
25:10 who keep his covenant and his testimonies. 2
78: 5 He established a testimony in Jacob 3
56 did not observe his testimonies 2
80: 0 A Testimony of Asaph. A Psalm. 3
99: 7 kept his testimonies, and the statutes 2
119: 2 Blessed are those who keep his testimonies 2
14 In the way of thy testimonies I delight 2
22 for I have kept thy testimonies. 2
24 Thy testimonies are my delight 2
31 I cleave to thy testimonies, O LORD; 2
36 Incline my heart to thy testimonies 2
46 will also speak of thy testimonies before kings 2
59 I turn my feet to thy testimonies; 2
79 turn to me, that they may know thy testimonies. 2
88 that I may keep the testimonies of thy mouth. 3
95 but I consider thy testimonies. 2
99 for thy testimonies are my meditation. 2
111 Thy testimonies are my heritage for ever; 2
119 therefore I love thy testimonies. 2
125 understanding, that I may know thy testimonies! 2
129 Thy testimonies are wonderful; 2
138 Thou hast appointed thy testimonies 2
144 Thy testimonies are righteous for ever; 2
146 save me, that I may observe thy testimonies. 2
152 Long have I known from thy testimonies 2
157 I do not swerve from thy testimonies. 2
167 My soul keeps thy testimonies; I love them 2
168 I keep thy precepts and testimonies 2
132:12 If your sons keep my covenant and my testimonies 2
Isa 8:16 Bind up the testimony, seal the teaching 4
20 To the teaching and to the testimony! 4
Jer 44:23 law and in his statutes and in his testimonies 2
Mat 24:14 as a testimony to all nations 9
Mrk 6:11 for a testimony against them. 9
13: 9 to bear testimony before them. 9
14:55 sought testimony against Jesus 8
59 Yet not even so did their testimony agree. 8
Lke 9: 5 dust from your feet as a testimony against them. 9
21:13 This will be a time for you to bear testimony. 9
22:71 they said, "What further testimony do we need? 8
Joh 1: 7 He came for testimony, to bear witness 8
19 And this is the testimony of John 8
3:11 but you do not receive our testimony. 8
32 yet no one receives his testimony; 8
33 he who receives his testimony sets his seal 8
4:39 believed in him because of the woman's testimony 6
5:31 my testimony is not true; 8
32 the testimony which he bears to me is true. 8
34 the testimony which I receive is from man 8
36 the testimony which I have is greater 8
8:13 your testimony is not true. 8
14 my testimony is true, for I know whence I have come 8
17 the testimony of two men is true; 8
19:35 his testimony is true 8
21:24 we know that his testimony is true. 8
Act 4:33 testimony to the resurrection of the Lord Jesus 9
22:18 will not accept your testimony about me.' 8
1Co 1: 6 even as the testimony to Christ was confirmed 9
2: 1 the testimony of God in lofty words or wisdom. 9
2Co 1:12 the testimony of our conscience 9
2Th 1:10 because our testimony to you was believed. 9
1Ti 2: 6 testimony to which was borne at the proper time. 9
6:13 in his testimony before Pontius Pilate 7
Tit 1:13 This testimony is true 8
Heb 10:28 at the testimony of two or three witnesses. 5
1Jn 5: 9 If we receive the testimony of men 8
9 testimony of men, the testimony of God is greater; 8
9 for this is the testimony of God 8
10 He who believes . . has the testimony in himself 8
10 the testimony that God has borne to his Son. 8
11 the testimony, that God gave us eternal life 8
3Jn 1:12 Deme'trius has testimony from every one 7
12 and you know my testimony is true. 8
Rev 1: 2 bore witness . . to the testimony of Jesus Christ 8
9 on account of . . the testimony of Jesus. 8
11: 7 when they have finished their testimony 8
12:11 conquered him . . by the word of their testimony 8
17 and bear testimony to Jesus 8
19:10 your brethren who hold the testimony of Jesus. 8
10 testimony of Jesus is the spirit of prophecy. 8
20: 4 beheaded for their testimony to Jesus 8
22:16 to you with this testimony for the churches. 7
Wis 17:11 condemned by its own testimony 10
Sir 31:23 their testimony to his excellence 8
24 their testimony to his niggardliness 8
45:17 to teach Jacob the testimonies 8

testimony *See also* bear.

false testimony 1. *ψευδομαρτυρία*
Mat 26:59 council sought false testimony against Jesus 1

tetrarch 1. *τετραρχέω* 2. *τετράρχης*
Mat 14: 1 At that time Herod the tetrarch heard 2
Lke 3: 1 Herod being tetrarch of Galilee 1
1 Philip tetrarch of the region of Iturae'a 1
1 Lysa'nias tetrarch of Abile'ne 1
19 Herod the tetrarch, who had been reproved by him 2
9: 7 Now Herod the tetrarch heard of all that was done 2
Act 13: 1 a member of the court of Herod the tetrarch 2

tetter 1. בֹּהַק
Lev 13:39 it is tetter that has broken out in the skin 1

than 1. אִם 2. כִּי 3. כִּי אִם 4. מִן 5. עַל 6. מִן (A) 7. *ἀπό* 8. *ἤ* 9. *ἤπερ* 10. *καὶ μή* 11. *οὐ* 12. *παρά* 13. *πλήν* 14. *ὑπέρ* 15. prae 16. quam 17. super
Gen 4:13 My punishment is greater than I can bear. 4
19: 9 Now we will deal worse with you than with them. 4
25:23 the one shall be stronger than the other 4

26:16 for you are much mightier than we. 4
29:19 give her to you than that I should give 4
38:26 She is more righteous than I, inasmuch as I did not 4
39: 9 he is not greater in this house than I am; 4
41:40 the throne will I be greater than you. 4
48:19 his younger brother shall be greater than he 4
Exd 14:12 better for us to serve the Egyptians than to die 4
18:11 Now I know that the LORD is greater than all gods 4
30:15 shall not give less, than the half shekel 4
36: 5 The people bring much more than enough for doing 4
Lev 13: 3 the disease appears to be deeper than the skin 4
4 if the spot . . appears no deeper than the skin 4
20 if it appears deeper than the skin and its hair 4
21 if . . it is not deeper than the skin, but is dim 4
25 if . . it appears deeper than the skin 4
26 if . . it is no deeper than the skin, but is dim 4
30 if it appears deeper than the skin, and the hair 4
31 if . . it appears no deeper than the skin 4
32 the itch appears to be no deeper than the skin 4
34 if . . it appears to be no deeper than the skin 4
14:37 if it appears to be deeper than the surface 4
Num13:31 We are not able . . for they are stronger than we. 4
14:12 you a nation greater and mightier than they. 4
22:15 more in number and more honorable than they. 4
24: 7 his king shall be higher than Agag 4
Deu 1:28 The people are greater and taller than we; 4
4:38 nations greater and mightier than yourselves 4
7: 1 nations greater and mightier than yourselves 4
17 These nations are greater than I; how can I 4
9: 1 nations greater and mightier than yourselves 4
14 nation mightier and greater than they.' 4
11:23 nations greater and mightier than yourselves. 4
20: 1 see . . an army larger than your own 4
25: 3 go on to beat him with more stripes than these •
Jos 10: 2 it was greater than Ai, and all its men were mighty. 4
11 more who died . . than the men of Israel killed 4
Jdg 2:19 turned back and behaved worse than their fathers 4
7:14 This is no other than the sword of Gideon 1
8: 2 the grapes of E'phraim better than the vintage 4
11:25 are you any better than Balak the son of Zippor 4
14:18 What is sweeter than honey? What is stronger 4
18 sweeter than honey? What is stronger than a lion? 4
15: 2 sister fairer than she? Pray take her instead. 4
16:30 more than those whom he had slain during his life. 4
Rut 3:10 made this last kindness greater than the first 4
12 yet there is a kinsman nearer than I. 4
4:15 who loves you, who is more to you than seven sons 4
1Sm 1: 8 why do you . . ? Am I not more to you than ten sons? 4
9: 2 he was taller than any of the people. 4
10:23 he was taller than any of the people 4
15:22 to obey is better than sacrifice, and to hearken 4
22 is better . . to hearken than the fat of rams. 4
28 given it to a neighbor . . who is better than you. 4
27: 1 nothing better . . than that I should escape 2
2Sm 1:23 they were swifter than eagles 4
23 they were stronger than lions. 4
6:22 will make myself yet more contemptible than this 4
13:14 and being stronger than she, he forced her 4
15 the hatred . . was greater than the love 4
16 wrong in sending me . . is greater than the other 4
17:14 counsel of Hushai . . is better than the counsel 4
18: 8 forest devoured more people . . than the sword. 4
19: 7 and this will be worse for you than all the evil 4
43 words . . of Judah were fiercer than the words 4
1Kg 1:37 and make his throne greater than the throne of my 4
47 and make his throne greater than your throne.' 4
4:31 he was wiser than all other men, wiser than Ethan 4
31 wiser than Ethan the Ez'rahite, and Heman, Calcol 4
12:10 little finger is thicker than my father's loins. 4
16:33 Ahab did more . . than all the kings of Israel 4
19: 4 take . . my life; for I am no better than my fathers. 4
20:23 Their gods . . and so they were stronger than we; 4
23 surely we shall be stronger than they. 4
25 surely we shall be stronger than they. 4
2Kg 5:12 rivers of Damascus, better than all the waters 4
6:16 those . . with us are more than those..with them. 4
1Ch 24: 4 morechief men . . than among the sons of Ith'amar 4
2Ch 2: 5 for our God is greater than all gods. 4
10:10 little finger is thicker than my father's loins. 4
21:13 brothers . . who were better than yourself; 4
25: 9 The LORD is able to give you much more than this. 4
32: 7 for there is one greater with us than with him. 4
Ezr 9: 6 our iniquities have risen higher than our heads •
13 punished us less than our iniquities deserved 4
Est 1:19 give . . to another who is better than she. 4
6: 6 Whom would the king delight to honor more than me? 4
Job 6: 3 then it would be heavier than the sand of the sea; 4
7: 6 My days are swifter than a weaver's shuttle 4
9:25 My days are swifter than a runner; they flee away 4
11: 8 It is higher than heaven–what can you do? 4
8 Deeper than Sheol–what can you know? 4
9 Its measure is longer than the earth 4
9 longer than the earth, and broader than the sea. 4
17 your life will be brighter than the noonday; 4
15:10 aged are among us, older than your father. 4
30: 1 they make sport of me, men who are younger than I 4
32: 4 because they were older than he. 4
33:12 I will answer you. God is greater than man. 4
35: 3 How am I better off than if I had sinned? 4
5 behold the clouds, which are higher than you. 4
11 makes us wiser than the birds of the air? 4
Ps 8: 5 Yet thou hast made him little less than God 4
19:10 sweeter also than honey and drippings 4
37:16 Better . . than the abundance of many wicked. 4
40: 5 they would be more than can be numbered. 4
12 they are more than the hairs of my head; 4
51: 7 wash me, and I shall be whiter than snow. 4
55:21 His speech was smoother than butter 4
21 his words were softer than oil 4
61: 2 Lead thou me to the rock that is higher than I; 4
62: 9 they are together lighter than a breath. 4
63: 3 Because thy steadfast love is better than life 4
69: 4 More in number than the hairs of my head 4
84:10 thy courts is better than 1,000 elsewhere. 4
93: 4 Mightier than the thunders of many waters 4
4 mightier than the waves of the sea 4
105:24 LORD . . made them stronger than their foes. 4
118: 8 It is better to . . than to put confidence in man. 4
9 better to . . than to put confidence in princes. 4
119:72 better . . than thousands of gold and silver 4
98 Thy commandment makes me wiser than my enemies 4
103 words to my taste, sweeter than honey to my mouth! 4
123: 3 for we have had more than enough of contempt. •
130: 6 more than watchmen for the morning. •
139:18 If I would count them, they are more than the sand. 4
Prv 3:14 gain from it is better than gain from silver 4
14 its profit better than gold. 4
5: 3 her speech is smoother than oil; 4
8:11 for wisdom is better than jewels 4
19 My fruit is better than gold, even fine gold 4
19 my yield than choice silver. 4
12: 9 than one who plays the great man but lacks bread. 4
15:16 Better . . than great treasure and trouble with it. 4
17 Better is . . than a fatted ox and hatred with it. 4
16: 8 Better . . than great revenues with injustice. 4
16 To get wisdom is better than gold; 4
19 better . . than to divide the spoil with the proud. 4
32 He who is slow to anger is better than the mighty 4
32 he who rules his spirit than he who takes a city. 4
17: 1 quiet than a house full of feasting with strife. 4
10 than 100 blows into a fool. 4
18:24 friend who sticks closer than a brother. 4
19: 1 than a man who is perverse in speech, and is a fool. 4
22 poor man is better than a liar. 4
21: 9 than in a house shared with a contentious woman. 4
19 than with a contentious and fretful woman. 4
22: 1 favor is better than silver or gold. 4
24: 5 A wise man is mightier than a strong man •
5 man of knowledge than he who has strength; 4
25: 7 than to be put lower in the presence of the prince. 4
24 than in a house shared with a contentious woman. 4
26:16 than seven men who can answer discreetly. 4
27: 3 but a fool's provocation is heavier than both. 4
5 Better is open rebuke than hidden love. 4
10 neighbor . . near than a brother who is far away. 4
28: 6 than a rich man who is perverse in his ways. 4
Ecc 2: 7 and flocks, more than any who had been before me 4
24 nothing better . . than that he should eat 4
3:12 there is nothing better for them than to be happy 3
22 nothing better than that a man . . enjoy his work 4
4: 2 the dead . . more fortunate than the living 4
3 better than both is he who has not yet been 4
6 Better is . . than two hands full of toil 4
9 Two are better than one . . they have a good reward 4
13 Better is a . . youth than an old and foolish king 4
5: 1 is better than to offer the sacrifice of fools; 4
5 better . . not vow than that you should vow 4
6: 3 I say that an untimely birth is better off than he 4
9 Better is the sight . . than the wandering 4
10 not able to dispute with one stronger than he. 4
7: 1 A good name is better than precious ointment; 4
1 and the day of death, than the day of birth. 4
2 than to go to the house of feasting; 4
3 Sorrow is better than laughter 4
5 hear the rebuke . . than to hear the song of fools. 4
8 Better is the end of a thing than its beginning; 4
8 patient in spirit is better than the proud 4
10 Why were the former days better than these? 4
9: 4 for a living dog is better than a dead lion. 4
16 But I say that wisdom is better than might 4
17 wise heard in quiet are better than the shouting 4
18 Wisdom is better than weapons of war 4
Sng 1: 2 For your love is better than wine 4
4:10 how much better is your love than wine 4
10 and the fragrance of your oils than any spice! 4
Isa 10:10 images were greater than those of Jerusalem 4
13:12 fine gold, and mankind than the gold of Ophir. 4
55: 9 For as the heavens are higher than the earth 4
9 are my ways higher than your ways 4
9 your ways and my thoughts than your thoughts. 4
56: 5 a name better than sons and daughters; 4
Jer 3:11 shown herself less guilty than false Judah. 4
4:13 his horses are swifter than eagles 4
5: 3 They have made their faces harder than rock; 4
7:26 They did worse than their fathers. 4
15: 8 widows more in number than the sand of the seas; 4
16:12 because you have done worse than your fathers 4
20: 7 art stronger than I, and thou hast prevailed. •
46:23 because they are more numerous than locusts; 4
Lam 4: 6 chastisement . . has been greater than the punishment 4
7 princes were purer than snow, whiter than milk; 4
7 princes were purer than snow, whiter than milk; 4
7 their bodies were more ruddy than coral 4
8 Now their visage is blacker than soot 4
9 Happier . . than the victims of hunger 4
19 Our pursuers were swifter than the vultures 4
Ezk 3: 9 harder than flint have I made your forehead; 4
8:15 see still greater abominations than these. 4
16:51 you have committed more abominations than they 4
23:11 which was worse than that of her sister. 4
28: 3 you are indeed wiser than Daniel; 4
Dan 1:10 poorer condition than the youths . . of your own age. 4
15 better . . than all the youths who ate the king's 4
3:28 rather than serve and worship any god except •
7:20 horn . . which seemed greater than its fellows. 6
8: 3 one was higher than the other, and the higher one 4
11: 2 fourth shall be far richer than all of them; 4
5 but one of his princes shall be stronger than he 5
13 again raise a multitude, greater than the former; 4
Hos 2: 7 for it was better with me then than now.' 4
Ams 6: 2 Are they better than these kingdoms? 4
2 is their territory greater than your territory 4
Jon 4: 3 for it is better for me to die than to live. 4
8 It is better for me to die than to live. 4
11 city, in which there are more than 120,000 persons 4
Nah 3: 8 Are you better than Thebes that sat by the Nile 4
Hab 1: 8 Their horses are swifter than leopards 4
13 Thou who art of purer eyes than to behold evil 4
Hag 2: 9 of this house shall be greater than the former 4
Mat 3:11 he who is coming after me is mightier than I •
5:29 than that your whole body be thrown into hell. 10
30 members than that your whole body go into hell. 10
37 simply 'Yes' or 'No'; anything more than this comes •
47 what more are you doing than others? Do not even •
6:25 put on. Is not life more than food, and the body •
25 than food, and the body more than clothing? •
26 them. Are you not of more value than they? •
10:15 more tolerable . . than for that town. 8
31 you are of more value than many sparrows. •
11: 9 Yes, I tell you, and more than a prophet. •
11 has risen no one greater than John the Baptist •
11 least in the kingdom of heaven is greater than he. •
22 day of judgment for Tyre and Sidon than for you. 8
24 for the land of Sodom than for you. 8
12: 6 something greater than the temple is here. •
12 Of how much more value is a man than a sheep! •
41 behold, something greater than Jonah is here. •
42 behold, something greater than Solomon is here. •
45 seven other spirits more evil than himself •
45 worse than the first •
18: 8 than with two hands or two feet 8
9 than with two eyes to be thrown into the hell 8
13 rejoices over it more than over the 99 8
19:24 than for a rich man to enter the kingdom of God. 8
21:36 Again he sent other servants, more than the first; •
26:53 he will at once send me more than twelve legions •
27:64 the last fraud will be worse than the first. •
Mrk 1: 7 After me comes he who is mightier than I •
9:43 to enter life maimed than with two hands 8
45 to enter life lame than with two feet to be thrown 8
46 with one eye than with two eyes 8
10:25 than for a rich man to enter the kingdom of God. 8
12:31 no other commandment greater than these. •
33 much more than all whole burnt offerings •
43 this poor widow has put in more than all •
Lke 3:13 Collect no more than is appointed you. 12
16 he who is mightier than I is coming •
7:26 Yes, I tell you, and more than a prophet. •
28 none is greater than John •
28 who is least in the kingdom of God is greater than he. •
9:13 We have no more than five loaves and two fish 8
10:12 more tolerable . . for Sodom than for that town. 8
14 for Tyre and Sidon than for you. 8
11:22 when one stronger than he assails him •
26 seven other spirits more evil than himself •
26 the last state . . becomes worse than the first. •
31 behold, something greater than Solomon is here. •
32 behold, something greater than Jonah is here. •
12: 7 Fear not; you are of more value than many sparrows. •
23 life is more than food •
23 the body more than clothing. •
24 Of how much more value are you than the birds! •
13: 2 worse sinners than all the other Galileans 12
4 worse offenders than all the others 12
14: 8 lest a more eminent man than you be invited by him; •
15: 7 more joy . . over one . . than over 99 8
16: 8 more shrewd . . than the sons of light. 14
17 than for one dot of the law to become void. 8
17: 2 better . . than that he should cause . . to sin 8
18:25 easier for a camel . . than for a rich man 8
21: 3 this poor widow has put in more than all of them; •
Joh 1:50 You shall see greater things than these. •
3:19 and men loved darkness rather than light 8
4: 1 making and baptizing more disciples than John 8
12 Are you greater than our father Jacob •
5:20 greater works than these will he show him •

36 the testimony . . is greater than that of John •
7:31 will he do more signs than this man has done? •
8:53 Are you greater than our father Abraham, who died? •
10:29 My Father . . is greater than all •
12:43 more than the praise of God. 9
13:16 a servant is not greater than his master •
16 nor is he who is sent greater than he who sent him. •
14:12 greater works than these will he do •
28 the Father is greater than I. •
15:13 Greater love has no man than this •
20 'A servant is not greater than his master.' •
21:15 Simon, son of John, do you love me more than these? •
Act 4:19 to listen to you rather than to God 8
22 the man . . was more than 40 years old. •
5:29 We must obey God rather than men. 8
15:28 no greater burden than these necessary things 13
17:11 were more noble than those in Thessaloni'ca •
20:35 'It is more blessed to give than to receive.' 8
23:13 There were more than 40 who made this conspiracy. •
21 more than 40 of their men lie in ambush for him •
24:11 it is not more than twelve days since I went up •
25: 6 stayed among them not more than eight or ten days •
26:13 a light from heaven, brighter than the sun 14
27:11 more attention to the captain . . than . . Paul 8
Rom 13:11 nearer to us now than when we first believed; 8
1Co 1:25 For the foolishness of God is wiser than men •
25 the weakness of God is stronger than men. •
3:11 than that which is laid, which is Jesus Christ. 12
7: 9 it is better to marry than to be aflame with passion. 8
9:15 I would rather die than have any one deprive me 8
10:22 Are we stronger than he? •
14: 5 He who prophesies is greater than he who speaks 8
18 I speak in tongues more than you all; •
19 than 10,000 words in a tongue. 8
15:10 On the contrary, I worked harder than any of them •
2Co 11: 4 preaches another Jesus than the one we preached 11
12:13 less favored than the rest of the churches 14
Gal 4: 1 the heir . . is no better than a slave •
27 more than the children of her that is married. 8
5:10 you will take no other view than mine •
Eph 3:20 far more abundantly than all that we ask or think •
Php 2: 3 count others better than yourselves. •
1Ti 1: 4 rather than the divine training that is in faith; 8
5: 8 and is worse than an unbeliever. •
9 if she is not less than 60 years of age •
2Ti 3: 4 lovers of pleasure rather than lovers of God 8
Heb 1: 4 the name . . is more excellent than theirs. 12
2: 7 make him for a little while lower than the angels 12
9 for a little while was made lower than the angels 12
3: 3 counted worthy of . . much more glory than Moses 12
3 the builder of a house has more honor than the house. •
4:12 sharper than any two-edged sword 14
6:16 Men indeed swear by a greater than themselves •
8: 6 which is as much more excellent than the old as . . •
9:23 purified . . with better sacrifices than these. 12
11: 4 a more acceptable sacrifice than Cain 12
25 rather . . than to enjoy . . pleasures of sin. 8
26 greater wealth than the treasures of Egypt •
12:24 that speaks more graciously than the blood of Abel. 12
1Pe 1: 7 faith, more precious than gold •
3:17 suffer for doing right . . than for doing wrong. 8
2Pe 2:20 last state has become worse for them than the first. •
21 than after knowing it to turn back 8
1Jn 3:20 for God is greater than our hearts •
4: 4 greater than he who is in the world. 8
3Jn 1: 4 No greater joy can I have than this •
1Es 4:25 A man loves his wife more than his father 8
35 truth is great, and stronger than all things. 12
5:50 were stronger than they •
2Es 1:18 better . . than to die in this wilderness.' 16
2:43 of great stature, taller than any of the others •
43 but he was more exalted than they •
3:12 to be more ungodly than were their ancestors. 16
31 Are the deeds of Babylon better than those of Zion? 16
4:12 better for us not to be here than to come here 16
45 whether more time is to come than has passed 16
50 for as the rain is more than the drops 16
50 and the fire is greater than the smoke 16
5:13 you shall hear yet greater things than these. •
33 Or do you love him more than his Maker does? 17
54 are smaller . . than those who were before you 15
55 those who come after you will be smaller than you 16
6:31 declare to you greater things than these •
7:19 or wiser than the Most High! 17
56 and brass than silver, and iron than brass 17
56 and brass than silver, and iron than brass 17
56 and lead than iron, and clay than lead.' 17
56 and lead than iron, and clay than lead.' 17
66 For it is much better with them than with us 16
87 The seventh way, which is worse than all the ways •
98 The seventh order, which is greater than all •
125 but our faces shall be blacker than darkness? 17
8:30 those who are deemed worse than beasts •
9:15 are more who perish than those who will be saved 16
16 as a wave is greater than a drop of water. 17
10:23 And, what is more than all, the seal of Zion •
11: 4 the middle head was larger than the other heads •
27 this disappeared more quickly than the first. 16
29 for it was greater than the other two heads. •

12:13 shall be more terrifying than all the kingdoms •
15 for a longer time than any other of the 12. 15
45 For we are no better than those who died there. •
13:20 better . . than to pass from the world 16
24 are more blessed than those who have died. 17
14:16 evils worse than those which you have now seen •
Tob 3: 6 it is better for me to die than to live 8
12: 8 is better than much with wrongdoing 8
8 It is better to give alms than to treasure up gold. 8
Jdt 12:18 means more to me today than in all the days 12
Wis 4: 1 Better than this is childlessness with virtue •
7:24 For wisdom is more mobile than any motion; •
29 For she is more beautiful than the sun •
8: 5 what is richer than wisdom who effects all things? •
6 who more than she is fashioner of what exists? •
7 nothing . . is more profitable for men than these. •
10:12 godliness is more powerful than anything. •
13: 3 know how much better than these is their Lord •
14: 1 a piece of wood more fragile than •
15:10 His heart is ashes, his hope is cheaper than dirt •
10 his life is of less worth than clay •
17 he is better than the objects he worships •
18 which are worse than all others •
17: 6 worse than that unseen appearance. •
21 still heavier than darkness •
Sir 4:10 he will love you more than does your mother. 8
8:12 Do not lend to a man who is stronger than you •
10:24 greater than the man who fears the Lord. •
27 Better . . than one who goes about boasting 8
13: 2 a man mightier and richer than you •
14: 6 meaner than the man who is grudging to himself •
16: 3 one is better than 1,000 8
3 better than to have ungodly children. 8
5 has heard things more striking than these. •
17:31 What is brighter than the sun? •
18:16 So a word is better than a gift. 8
19:24 Better . . than the highly prudent man 8
20: 2 better it is to reprove than to stay angry! 8
18 better than a slip of the tongue 8
31 Better . . than the man who hides his wisdom. 8
22:11 the life of the fool is worse than death. 14
14 What is heavier than lead? 14
15 of iron are easier to bear than a stupid man. 8
23:19 10,000 times brighter than the sun •
27 nothing is better than the fear of the Lord •
27 nothing sweeter than to heed the commandments •
24:20 For the remembrance of me is sweeter than honey 14
20 and my inheritance sweeter than the honeycomb. 14
29 and her counsel deeper than the great abyss. 7
25:16 rather . . than dwell with an evil wife. 8
26: 5 all these are worse than death. 14
29:11 it will profit you more than gold. 8
22 Better . . than sumptuous food 8
30:14 Better off . . than a rich man 8
15 Health and soundness are better than all gold •
15 and a robust body than countless riches 8
16 There is no wealth better than health of body •
17 Death is better than a miserable life 14
17 and eternal rest than chronic sickness. 8
31:13 What has been created more greedy than the eye? •
33: 7 Why is any day better than another •
21 better . . than that you should look 8
34:11 I understand more than I can express. •
36:18 yet one food is better than another. •
21 one daughter is better than another. •
37:13 no one is more faithful to you than it is. •
14 keeps him better informed than seven watchmen 8
39:11 he will leave a name greater than 1,000 8
34 no one can say, "This is worse than that •
40:28 it is better to die than to beg. 8
41:12 longer than 1,000 great stores of gold. 8
15 Better . . than the man who hides his wisdom. 8
42:14 Better . . than a woman who does good 8
43:28 he is greater than all his works. 12
32 Many things greater than these lie hidden •
LJr 1:19 even more than they light for themselves 8
59 better . . than to be these false gods 8
59 better . . than these false gods. 8
59 better . . than these false gods. 8
68 The wild beasts are better than they are •
Aza 1:14 For we, O Lord, have become fewer than any nation 12
Man 1: 9 more in number than the sand of the sea •
1Mc 3:30 give more lavishly than preceding kings. 14
59 better . . to die . . than to see the misfortunes 8
6:43 It was taller than all the others •
12:24 with a larger force than before 14
13: 5 for I am not better than my brothers. •
2Mc 5: 5 Jason took no less than 1,000 men •
22 more barbarous than the man who appointed him; •
23 worse than the others did •
6:19 rather than life with pollution 8
7: 2 rather than transgress the laws of our fathers. 8
39 handled him worse than the others 12
8: 9 in command of no fewer than 20,000 Gentiles •
10:17 killing no fewer than 20,000. •
18 When no less than 9,000 took refuge •
23 he destroyed more than 20,000 •
12: 4 not less than 200. •
10 not less than 5,000 Arabs with 500 horsemen •

19 more than 10,000 men. •
13: 9 things far worse than those that had been done •
14:30 meeting him more rudely than had been his custom •
15:27 they laid low no less than 35,000 men •
3Mc 5:20 a savagery more worse than that of Phalaris •
7: 5 a cruelty more savage than that of Scythian custom •
4Mc 5:16 no compulsion more powerful than our obedience •
7:10 O aged man, more powerful than tortures •
10 O elder, fiercer than fire •
9: 4 to be more grievous than death itself. •
30 you are being tortured more than I •
11:14 I am younger in age than my brothers •
14: 2 O reason, more royal than kings •
2 more royal than kings and freer than the free! •
10 What could be more excruciatingly painful than this •
15: 1 more desirable to the mother than her children! •
4 have a deeper sympathy . . than do the fathers. •
6 more than any other mother, loved her children. •
30 O more noble than males in steadfastness •
30 more manly than men in endurance! •
16:14 you have proved more powerful than a man. •
24 die rather than violate God's commandment. 8

than even 1. ἤπερ

4Mc 15:16 more bitter pains than even the birth-pangs 1

than ever 1. πολύς

2Co 8:22 who is now more earnest than ever 1

thank 1. ידה 2. ἐξομολογέω 3. εὐχαριστέω 4. εὐχαριστία 5. χάριν ἀποδίδωμι 6. χάριν ἔχω 7. χάρις

1Ch 16: 4 to invoke, to thank, and to praise the LORD 1
23:30 every morning, thanking and praising the LORD 1
29:13 thank thee, our God, and praise thy glorious name 1
Ps 35:18 Then I will thank thee in the great congregation; 1
52: 9 I will thank thee for ever, because thou hast done 1
107: 8 Let them thank the LORD for his steadfast love 1
15 Let them thank the LORD for his steadfast love 1
21 Let them thank the LORD for his steadfast love 1
31 Let them thank the LORD for his steadfast love 1
118:21 I thank thee that thou hast answered me 1
Isa 38:18 For Sheol cannot thank thee, death cannot praise 1
19 the living, he thanks thee, as I do this day; 1
Mat 11:25 At that time Jesus declared, "I thank thee, Father 2
Lke 10:21 I thank thee, Father, Lord of heaven and earth 2
17: 9 Does he thank the servant 6
18:11 I thank thee that I am not like other men 3
Joh 11:41 Father, I thank thee that thou hast heard me. 3
Act 28:15 Paul thanked God and took courage. 3
Rom 1: 8 I thank my God through Jesus Christ for all of you 3
6:17 But thanks be to God 7
7:25 Thanks be to God through Jesus Christ our Lord! 7
1Co 14:18 I thank God that I speak in tongues 3
15:57 thanks be to God, who gives us the victory 7
2Co 2:14 thanks be to God 7
8:16 thanks be to God who puts the same earnest care 7
Php 1: 3 I thank my God in all my remembrance of you 3
Col 1: 3 We always thank God, the Father of our Lord Jesus 3
1Th 2:13 we also thank God constantly for this 3
1Ti 1:12 I thank him who has given me strength for this 6
2Ti 1: 3 I thank God whom I serve with a clear conscience 6
Phm 1: 4 I thank my God always 3
Rev 4: 9 creatures give glory and honor and thanks to him 4
Sir 12: 1 you will be thanked for your good deeds. 7
1Mc 14:25 How shall we thank Simon and his sons? 5
2Mc 1:11 we thank him greatly for taking our side 3
12:31 they thanked them 3

thank *See also* offering.

without being thanked 1. εἰς ἀχάριστα

Sir 29:25 provide drink without being thanked 1

thankful 1. εὐχαριστέω 2. εὐχάριστος

1Co 1:14 I am thankful that I baptized none of you 1
Php 1: 5 thankful for your partnership in the gospel •
Col 3:15 And be thankful. 2
Wis 18: 2 and were thankful 1

thankfulness 1. εὐχαριστία 2. χάρις

1Co 10:30 If I partake with thankfulness 2
Col 3:16 sing . . with thankfulness in your hearts to God. 2
AEs 16: 4 not only take away thankfulness from among men 1

thanks 1. ἀνθομολόγησις 2. ἐξομολογέω 3. ἐξομολόγησις 4. χάρις 5. gratia

2Co 9:15 Thanks be to God for his inexpressible gift! 4
2Es 2:37 be joyful, giving thanks to him 5
Sir 17:27 as do those who are alive and give thanks? 1
47: 8 In all that he did he gave thanks to the Holy One 3
2Mc 8:27 giving great praise and thanks to the Lord 2

thanks *See also* give.

thanksgiving 1. ידה 2. תּוֹדָה 3. ἐξομολογέω 4. ἐξομολόγησις 5. εὐχαριστία

Lev 7:12 If he offers it for a thanksgiving 2
13 his peace offerings for thanksgiving 2
15 offerings for thanksgiving shall be eaten 2

22:29 sacrifice of thanksgiving to the LORD 2
1Ch 16: 7 David first appointed that thanksgiving be sung 1
25: 3 in thanksgiving and praise to the LORD. 1
2Ch 5:13 in unison in praise and thanksgiving to the LORD 1
33:16 offered upon it sacrifices . . of thanksgiving; 2
Neh 11:17 leader to begin the thanksgiving in prayer 1
12:27 celebrate the dedication with . . thanksgivings 2
46 there were songs of praise and thanksgiving 1
Ps 50:14 Offer to God a sacrifice of thanksgiving 2
23 He who brings thanksgiving as his sacrifice 2
69:30 I will magnify him with thanksgiving. 2
95: 2 Let us come into his presence with thanksgiving; 2
100: 4 Enter his gates with thanksgiving, and his courts 2
107:22 let them offer sacrifices of thanksgiving 2
116:17 offer to thee the sacrifice of thanksgiving 2
147: 7 Sing to the LORD with thanksgiving; make melody 2
Isa 51: 3 found in her, thanksgiving and the voice of song. 2
Jer 30:19 Out of them shall come songs of thanksgiving 2
Ams 4: 5 offer a sacrifice of thanksgiving of that 2
Jon 2: 9 I with the voice of thanksgiving will sacrifice 2
1Co 14:16 say the "Amen" to your thanksgiving 5
2Co 4:15 increase thanksgiving, to the glory of God. 5
9:11 through us will produce thanksgiving to God; 5
12 also overflows in many thanksgivings to God. 5
Eph 5: 4 instead let there be thanksgiving. 5
Php 4: 6 by prayer and supplication with thanksgiving 5
Col 2: 7 abounding in thanksgiving. 5
4: 2 being watchful in it with thanksgiving; 5
1Th 3: 9 what thanksgiving can we render to God for you 5
1Ti 2: 1 prayers, intercessions, and thanksgiving 5
4: 3 to be received with thanksgiving 5
4 if it is received with thanksgiving; 5
Rev 7:12 Blessing and glory and wisdom and thanksgiving 5
Jdt 16: 1 Then Judith began this thanksgiving 4
Sir 17:28 thanksgiving has ceased 4
39:15 this you shall say in thanksgiving 3
51:11 will sing praise with thanksgiving 3
2Mc 10: 7 they offered hymns of thanksgiving to him •
38 with hymns and thanksgivings 4
3Mc 6:35 to the accompaniment of joyous thanksgiving 4
7:19 landed in peace with appropriate thanksgiving 4

thanksgiving *See also* song.

theater 1. θέατρον

Act 19:29 they rushed together into the theater 1
31 begged him not to venture into the theater. 1

theft 1. גְּנֵבָה 2. κλέμμα 3. κλοπή

Exd 22: 1 he shall be sold for his theft. 1
Mat 15:19 murder, adultery, fornication, theft 3
Mrk 7:21 fornication, theft, murder, adultery 3
Rev 9:21 nor did they repent of . . their thefts. 2
Wis 14:25 theft and deceit, corruption, faithlessness 3
Sir 41:19 of theft, in the place where you live 3

theme 1. דָּבָר

Ps 45: 1 My heart overflows with a goodly theme; 1

then 1. אַחַר 2. אַף 3. אֵפוֹ 4. גַּם 5. הַיּוֹם 6. הִנֵּה 7. וְעַתָּה לָכֵן 8. כִּי 9. לָכֵן 10. נָא 11. עַל כֵּן 12. עַתָּה 13. אֱדַיִן (A) 14. בֵּאדַיִן (A) 15. כָּל קֳבֵל דְּנָה (A) 16. לָקֳבֵל (A) 17. ἀλλά 18. ἄν 19. ἆρα 20. ἄρα 21. γάρ 22. γέ τοι 23. δέ 24. δὲ τοίνυν 25. δή 26. δὴ τοίνυν 27. διὰ τοῦτο 28. διό 29. εἴθε 30. εἰ μή γε 31. εἶτα 32. ἐνταῦθα 33. ἐπεί 34. ἔπειτα 35. εὐθέως 36. ἤδη 37. καὶ εἰμί 38. κἀκεῖθεν 39. λοιπός 40. μετὰ τοῦτο 41. νυνί 42. ὅθεν 43. οὗτος 44. οὕτως 45. πάλιν 46. ποτέ 47. τε 48. τίς 49. τοίνυν 50. ὕστερος 51. ὥστε 52. amodo 53. aut 54. enim 55. ergo 56. et 57. post 58. tunc

Gen 18:24 within the city; wilt thou then destroy the place 2
27:33 Who was it then that hunted game and brought it 3
37 What then can I do for you, my son? 3
30:15 Rachel said, "Then he may lie with you tonight 9
43:11 If it must be so, then do this: take some 3
Num22:29 sword in my hand, for then I would kill you. 12
Jdg 11:23 then the LORD, the God of Israel, dispossessed 12
12: 6 he said, "No," they said to him, "Then say Shibboleth 10
18: 1 for until then no inheritance among the tribes 5
1Kg 1:14 Then while you are still speaking with the king 6
2Kg 10:10 Know then that there shall fall to the earth 3
Ezr 4: 9 then wrote Rehum the commander, Shim'shai 13
16 you will then have no possession in the province 16
5: 2 Then Zerub'babel the son of She-al'ti-el and Jeshua 14
5 then answer be returned by letter concerning it. 13
9 Then we asked those elders and spoke to them thus 13
16 Then this Shesh-baz'zar came and laid 13
6: 1 Then Darius the king made a decree 14
13 Then, according to the word sent by Darius 13
7:17 With this money, then, you shall . . buy bulls 15
Job 3:13 For then I should have lain down and been quiet; 12
6: 3 then it would be heavier than the sand of the sea; 12
8: 6 surely then he will rouse himself for you 12
9:14 How then can I answer him, choosing my words 8
24 if it is not he, who then is it? 3
13:19 For then I would be silent and die. 12
14:16 For then thou wouldest number my steps 12
17:15 where then is my hope? Who will see my hope? 3
18: 2 Consider, and then we will speak. 1
19: 6 know then that God has put me in the wrong 3
Ps 50:22 Mark this, then, you who forget God 10
74: 6 then all its carved wood they broke down 12
Prv 6: 3 then do this, my son, and save yourself 3
Isa 7:13 he said, "Hear then, O house of David! 10
19:12 Where then are your wise men? Let them tell you 3
Jer 31:36 then shall the descendants of Israel cease 4
37 then I will cast off all the descendants 4
33:26 then I will reject the descendants of Jacob 4
42:15 then hear the word of the LORD, O remnant of Judah. 7
Ezk 44:26 count . . seven days, and then he shall be clean. ‡
Dan 2:14 Then Daniel replied with prudence 14
15 Then Ar'ioch made the matter known to Daniel. 13
17 Then Daniel went to his house and made the matter 13
19 Then the mystery was revealed to Daniel 13
19 Then Daniel blessed the God of heaven. 13
25 Then Ar'ioch brought in Daniel before the king 13
35 then the iron, the clay, the bronze, the silver 14
46 Then King Nebuchadnez'zar fell upon his face 14
48 Then the king gave Daniel high honors 13
3: 3 Then the satraps, the prefects, and the governors 14
13 Then Nebuchadnez'zar in furious rage commanded 14
13 Then they brought these men before the king. 14
19 Then Nebuchadnez'zar was full of fury 14
21 Then these men were bound in their mantles 14
24 Then King Nebuchadnez'zar was astonished 13
26 Then Nebuchadnez'zar came near to the door 14
26 Then Shadrach, Meshach, and Abed'nego came out 14
30 Then the king promoted Shadrach, Meshach 14
4: 7 Then the magicians, the enchanters 14
19 Then Daniel . . was dismayed for a moment 13
5: 3 Then they brought in the golden and silver 14
6 Then the king's color changed, 13
8 Then all the king's wise men came 13
9 Then King Belshaz'zar was greatly alarmed 13
13 Then Daniel was brought in before the king. 14
17 Then Daniel answered before the king, 14
24 Then from his presence the hand was sent 14
29 Then Belshaz'zar commanded, 14
6: 3 Then this Daniel became distinguished 13
4 Then the presidents and the satraps sought 13
5 Then these men said, "We shall not find any ground 13
6 Then these presidents and satraps came 13
11 Then these men came by agreement and found 13
12 Then they came near and said before the king 14
13 Then they answered before the king, 14
14 Then the king, when he heard these words, 13
15 Then these men came by agreement to the king 14
16 Then the king commanded, and Daniel was brought 14
18 Then the king went to his palace, 13
19 Then, at break of day, the king arose 14
21 Then Daniel said to the king, "O king, live for ever 13
23 Then the king was exceedingly glad 14
25 Then King Darius wrote to all the peoples 14
7: 1 Then he wrote down the dream, 14
11 looked then because of the sound 14
19 Then I desired to know the truth concerning 13
Hab 1:17 Is he then to keep on emptying his net 11
Mat 6: 1 for then you will have no reward 30
11: 8 Why then did you go out? 17
9 Why then did you go out? To see a prophet? 17
12:28 then the kingdom of God has come upon you. 20
14:22 Then he made the disciples get into the boat 35
17:26 Jesus said to him, "Then the sons are free. 20
19:25 Who then can be saved? 20
27 What then shall we have? 20
24:45 Who then is the faithful and wise servant 20
26:57 Then those who had seized Jesus 23
Mrk 4:17 then, when tribulation or persecution arises 31
28 then the ear, then the full grain in the ear. 31
28 then the ear, then the full grain in the ear. 31
41 Who then is this, that even wind and sea obey him? 20
7:18 Then are you also without understanding? 43
31 Then he returned from the region of Tyre 45
8:25 Then again he laid his hands upon his eyes 31
Lke 1:66 saying, "What then will this child be? 20
7:25 What then did you go out to see? 17
26 What then did you go out to see? A prophet? 17
8:12 then the devil comes and takes away the word 31
19 Then his mother and his brothers came to him 23
25 Who then is this 20
30 Jesus then asked him, "What is your name? 20
33 Then the demons came out of the man 23
35 Then people went out to see what had happened 23
10:34 then he set him on his own beast 23
11:20 then the kingdom of God has come upon you. 20
12:42 Who then is the faithful and wise steward 20
13:15 Then the Lord answered him, "You hypocrites! 23
16: 7 Then he said to another, 'And how much do you owe?' 34
17:15 Then one of them, when he saw that he was healed 23
17 Then said Jesus, "Were not ten cleansed? 23
20:13 Then the owner of the vineyard said 23
25 He said to them, "Then render to Caesar the things 49
22: 3 Then Satan entered into Judas called Iscariot 23
7 Then came the day of Unleavened Bread 23
52 Then Jesus said to the chief priests 23
54 Then they seized him and led him away 23
56 Then a maid, seeing him as he sat in the light 23
23:13 Pilate then called together the chief priests 23
56 then they returned 23
24:18 Then one of them, named Cle'opas, answered him 23
44 Then he said to them, "These are my words 23
50 Then he led them out as far as Bethany 23
Joh 11: 7 Then after this he said to the disciples 34
11 Thus he spoke, and then he said to them 40
13: 5 Then he poured water into a basin 31
19:27 Then he said to the disciple, "Behold, your mother! 31
20:27 Then he said to Thomas, "Put your finger here 31
Act 6: 9 Then some of those who belonged to the synagogue 23
8:35 Then Philip opened his mouth 23
9:41 Then calling the saints and widows 23
10:29 I ask then why you sent for me. 48
11:18 Then to the Gentiles also God has granted 20
13:21 Then they asked for a king; and God gave them Saul 38
16:34 Then he brought them up into his house 47
19:13 Then some of the itinerant Jewish exorcists 23
21:30 Then all the city was aroused 47
38 Are you not the Egyptian, then, who . . 20
23: 9 Then a great clamor arose 23
26:30 Then the king rose, and the governor and Berni'ce 47
27:17 then, fearing that they should run on the Syr'tis 47
36 Then they all were encouraged 23
Rom 3: 6 For then how could God judge the world? 33
7:17 So then it is no longer I that do it, but sin 41
10:20 Then Isaiah is so bold as to say, "I have been found 23
16:20 then the God of peace will soon crush Satan 23
1Co 4: 7 If then you received it, why do you boast 23
5:10 since then you would need to go out of the world. 20
11:33 So then, my brethren, when you come together to eat 51
12:28 then workers of miracles, then healers, helpers 34
28 then workers of miracles, then healers, helpers 34
15: 5 that he appeared to Cephas, then to the twelve. 31
6 Then he appeared to more than 500 brethren 34
7 Then he appeared to James 34
7 he appeared to James, then to all the apostles. 31
14 then our preaching is in vain 20
18 Then those also who have fallen asleep in Christ 20
23 then at his coming those who belong to Christ. 34
24 Then comes the end, when he delivers the kingdom 31
46 the physical, and then the spiritual. 34
2Co 6: 1 Working together with him, then 23
12:10 For the sake of Christ, then, I am content 28
Gal 1:18 Then after three years I went up to Jerusalem 34
21 Then I went into the regions of Syria 34
2: 1 Then after fourteen years I went up again 34
17 is Christ then an agent of sin? Certainly not! 19
21 then Christ died to no purpose. 20
3: 9 So then, those who are men of faith are blessed 51
21 then righteousness would indeed be by the law. 18
29 then you are Abraham's offspring 20
4:16 Have I then become your enemy 51
6:10 So then, as we have opportunity 20
Php 1:18 What then? Only that in every way 21
1Th 4:17 then we who are alive, who are left 34
5: 6 So then let us not sleep, as others do 20
1Ti 2:13 For Adam was formed first, then Eve; 31
3:10 then if they prove themselves blameless 31
Heb 4: 9 So then, there remains a sabbath rest 20
7: 2 then he is also king of Salem, that is, king of peace. 34
27 for his own sins and then for those of the people 34
9:26 for then he would have had to suffer repeatedly 33
10:13 then to wait 39
12: 8 then you are illegitimate children and not sons. 20
Jas 1:15 Then desire when it has conceived gives birth 31
3:17 wisdom from above is first pure, then peaceable 34
4:14 appears for a little time and then vanishes. 34
Rev 12:12 Rejoice then, O heaven and you that dwell therein! 27
1Es 4:13 Then the third . . began to speak 23
2Es 2:44 Then I asked an angel, "Who are these, my lord? 58
46 Then I said to the angel, "Who is that young man 56
48 Then the angel said to me, "Go, tell my people 56
3:28 Then I said in my heart 56
4: 1 Then the angel that had been sent to me 56
3 Then I said, "Yes, my lord. 56
11 how then can your mind comprehend the way 56
22 Then I answered and said, "I beseech you, my lord 56
33 Then I answered and said, "How long 56
38 Then I answered and said, "O sovereign Lord 56
43 Then the things that you desire to see 58
51 Then I prayed and said, "Do you think 56
5: 9 then shall reason hide itself 56
14 Then I awoke, and my body shuddered violently 56
19 Then I said to him, "Depart from me 56
19 and then you may come to me 58
22 Then my soul recovered . . understanding 56
35 Why then was I born? 53
37 and then I will explain to you the travail 58
43 Then I answered and said, "Couldst thou not 56
50 Then I inquired and said 56
6: 6 then I planned these things 58
39 then the Spirit was hovering 58
40 Then thou didst command 58
40 so that thy works might then appear. 58
49 Then thou didst keep in existence 58
7: 5 If any one, then, wishes to reach the sea 54
17 Then I answered and said, "O sovereign Lord, behold 56

36 Then the pit of torment shall appear 56
37 Then the Most High will say to the nations 56
45 O sovereign Lord, I said then and I say now 58
73 What, then, will they have to say in the judgment 56
97 being incorruptible from then on. 52
105 for then every one shall bear his own 58
106 I answered and said, "How then do we find 56
111 why will it not be so then as well? 58
115 no one will then be able to have mercy on him 58
8: 4 Then drink your fill of understanding, O my soul 55
14 If then thou wilt suddenly and quickly destroy 55
32 then thou wilt be called merciful. 58
62 Then I answered and said 56
9: 2 then you will know that it is the very time 58
4 then you will know that it was of these 58
9 Then those who have now abused my ways 58
18 and no one opposed me then, for no one existed; 58
25 then I will come and talk with you. 56
39 Then I dismissed the thoughts 56
10: 2 Then we all put out the lamps 56
5 Then I broke off the reflections 56
11 Who then ought to mourn the more 55
14 then I say to you, 'As you brought forth in sorrow 56
27 Then I was afraid, and cried with a loud voice 56
30 Then he grasped my right hand 56
46 then it was that the barren woman bore a son. 58
11:13 Then the next wing arose and reigned 56
18 Then the third wing raised itself up 56
36 Then I heard a voice saying to me, "Look before you 56
12: 3 Then I awoke in great perplexity of mind 56
18 nevertheless it shall not fall then 58
33 then he will destroy them. 58
39 Then he left me. 56
45 Then I answered them and said 56
13:13 Then many people came to him 56
13 Then in great fear I awoke 56
32 then my Son will be revealed, whom you saw as a man 58
46 Then they dwelt there until the last times 58
50 then he will show them very many wonders. 58
57 Then I arose and walked in the field 56
14: 3 Then he said to me, "I revealed myself in a bush 56
5 Then I commanded him, saying 56
19 Then I answered and said, "Let me speak 56
22 If then I have found favor before thee 54
27 Then I went as he commanded me 56
31 Then land was given to you for a possession 56
34 If you, then, will rule over your minds 55
35 then the names of the righteous 58
39 Then I opened my mouth, and behold, a full cup 56
15:31 then the dragons, remembering their origin 57
32 then these shall be disorganized and silenced 56
44 then the dust and smoke shall go up to heaven 56
16:21 then the calamities shall spring up on the earth 58
73 Then the tested quality of my elect 58
Tob 1:19 Then one of the men of Nineveh went and informed 23
2:14 Then she replied to me 23
6: 2 Then the young man went down to wash himself. 23
7: 8 Then Tobias said to Raphael, "Brother Azarias 23
8:18 Then he ordered his servants 23
14:12 Then Tobias returned with his wife 23
Jdt 5:21 then let my lord pass them by; 25
6:14 Then the men of Israel came down from their city 23
7: 7 and then returned to his army. *
9: 1 Then Judith fell upon her face 23
13:14 Then she said to them with a loud voice, "Praise God 23
Wis 1:11 Beware then of useless murmuring 49
14:16 Then the ungodly custom . . was kept as a law 31
18 Then the ambition of the craftsman impelled 23
Sir 1:23 then joy will burst forth for him. 50
4:18 Then she will come straight back to him 45
32: 1 take good care of them and then be seated; 43
LJr 1:46 how then can . . things . . made by them be gods? 25
Sus 1:34 Then the two elders stood up 23
42 Then Susanna cried out with a loud voice, and said 23
1Mc 4:36 Then said Judas and his brothers, "Behold 23
7:35 then if I return safely I will burn up this house. 37
11:69 Then the men in ambush emerged from their places 23
13:47 then entered it with hymns and praise. 44
2Mc 1:30 Then the priests sang the hymns. 23
3:24 then and there . . a manifestation 36
35 Then Heliodorus offered sacrifice to the Lord 23
4:22 Then he marched into Phoenicia. 29
5:13 Then there was killing of young and old 23
9:11 Then it was that, broken in spirit, he began . . 32
13 Then the abominable fellow made a vow to the Lord 23
10:33 Then Maccabeus and his men were glad 23
11: 7 Then they eagerly rushed off together. 23
12: 7 Then . . he withdrew 23
26 Then Judas marched against Carnaim 23
38 Then Judas assembled his army 23
40 Then . . they found sacred tokens of the idols 23
14:34 Then the priests stretched forth their hands 23
15:13 Then likewise a man appeared 29
29 Then there was shouting and tumult 23
3Mc 1: 9 Then, upon entering the place 25
16 Then the priests . . prostrated themselves 23
2:23 Then . . friends . . dragged him out 42
4: 1 In every place, then, where this decree arrived 23
5:13 Then the Jews . . praised their holy God 47
23 Then, as soon as the cock had crowed 23
35 Then the Jews, upon hearing what the king had said 47
6: 1 Then a certain Eleazar . . prayed as follows 23
30 Then the king . . summoned the official 31
37 Then they petitioned the king 23
40 Then they feasted 23
7:12 The king then . . granted them a general license 23
4Mc 1: 3 If, then, it is evident 20
12 then I shall turn to their story 44
31 Self-control, then, is dominance 26
4: 1 who then held the high priesthood for life 46
11 Then Apollonius fell down half dead 22
9:11 Then . . the guards brought forward the eldest 42
12:15 Then because he too was about to die, he said 42
13: 1 Since, then, the 7 brothers despised sufferings 24
16: 1 If, then, a woman . . endured seeing her children 49

then אָז

Gen 24:41; 49:4, Exd 4:26; 12:48; 15:1, Lev 26:34², 41, Num 21:17, Deu 4:41, Jos 1:8²; 8:30; 10:12; 14:11; 20:6; 22:1, Jdg 5:8, 11, 13, 19, 22; 8:3; 13:21, 1Sm 6:3; 20:12, 2Sm 5:24²; 19:6; 21:17, 18; 23:14, 1Kg 3:16; 8:1, 12; 9:24; 11:7; 16:21; 22:49, 2Kg 8:22; 13:19; 14:8; 16:5, 1Ch 11:16²; 14:15; 15:2; 16:7, 33; 20:4; 22:13, 2Ch 5:2; 6:1; 8:12, 17; 24:17, Job 3:13; 11:15; 13:20; 22:26; 28:27; 33:16; 38:21, Ps 2:5; 9:13; 0:7; 1:19²; 6:9; 6:12; 19:6; 24:3, 4, 5; 26:2, Prv 1:28; 2:5, 9; 3:23; 20:14, Ecc 2:15, Sng 8:10, Isa 33:23; 35:5, 6; 41:1; 58:8, 9, 14; 60:5, Jer 11:15, 18; 22:15, 16, 22; 31:13, Ezk 32:14, Hos 2:7, Mic 3:4, Hab 1:11, Zep 3:11, Mal 3:16

then *καί*

Mat 2:11; 23:32; 25:15; 27:36; 28:7, Mrk 3:19; 4:13; 5:22; 6:39; 10:26; 14:10, Lke 7:44, 49; 8:26, 37; 10:23; 14:4; 18:26; 19:20, 23; 23:1, 46, 53; 24:35, Joh 4:35, Act 7:58; 9:18, 40; 12:17, 19; 14:24; 21:6; 22:22; 23:23; 25:23; 26:20; 27:40, Rom 2:27; 8:17, 1Co 11:6, 2Co 6:17, Gal 4:7, Heb 6:6; 10:17, Jas 5:18, 1Jn 2:24, Rev 1:12; 5:5, 11; 6:11, 15; 7:2, 13; 8:2, 5, 13; 9:3, 13; 10:1, 8; 11:1, 12, 15, 19; 12:17; 13:11; 14:1, 6, 14, 18; 15:1; 16:1; 17:1; 18:4, 21; 19:6, 10, 11, 17; 20:1, 4, 11, 14; 21:1, 9; 22:1, 1Es 1:35; 2:8; 3:14, 17; 4:1, 41; 5:48; 8:54, 73, 92, 96; 9:1, 5, 7, 8, 10, 45, 49, Tob 1:13, 20, 21; 2:6, 11; 3:1; 5:1, 3, 7, 10, 13, 16; 6:4, 6, 17; 7:2, 6, 13, 15; 8:9, 11, 15; 9:1; 10:4; 11:2, 9, 14, 16; 12:1, 21; 13:1; 14:6, Jdt 1:7, 12, 16; 2:24, 27; 3:6, 9; 5:5, 9, 12, 13, 20; 6:10, 18, 20; 7:5, 8, 23, 29, 32; 8:28; 10:6, 9, 20; 11:1, 19; 12:1, 5, 16, 19; 13:4, 9, 10, 15; 14:1, 3², 8, 17; 15:8, 12; 16:1, AEs 11:10; 12:3; 13:8; 15:2, 8, 11, Wis 9:12; 13:15, Sir 3:17; 4:10; 6:29; 23:3, 14; 25:3; 38:17; 41:23; 42:8; 46:17; 48:1; 51:8, Bar 1:5, Aza 1:2, Sus 1:24, 37, 50, 56, 60, Bel 1:7, 8, 14², 19, 27, 36, 37, 1Mc 1:8, 33, 41; 2:15, 17, 18, 27, 35, 69; 3:1, 12, 25, 29, 37, 54, 57; 4:11, 13, 16, 23, 34, 39, 47, 50, 59; 5:6, 8, 17, 20, 23, 28², 33, 43, 45, 49, 51, 60, 65, 66; 6:5, 14, 32, 51, 55, 63; 7:5, 12, 18, 19, 20, 26, 36, 40, 47; 9:4, 11, 14, 19, 28, 40, 48, 50, 58, 62, 64, 67, 69, 72; 10:7, 12, 51, 59, 69, 82, 86; 11:1, 7, 13, 28, 45, 46, 57, 60, 62, 63, 66, 72; 12:30, 32, 39, 44, 49; 13:12, 24, 50; 15:15, 38; 16:6, 7, 18, 2Mc 4:34; 5:25, 26; 9:29; 10:3, 9, 3Mc 6:22; 7:20

then *οὖν*

Mat 5:19; 6:9, 23; 7:11, 24; 12:26; 13:18, 27, 28, 56; 17:10; 19:7; 21:25; 22:17, 43; 25:27; 26:54; 27:22, Mrk 11:31; 15:12; 16:19, Lke 3:10; 4:7; 7:31; 8:18; 10:40; 11:13, 36; 12:26; 16:11, 27; 20:15, 17; 22:70, Joh 1:21, 22, 25; 2:18, 20; 6:5, 11, 15, 21, 28, 30, 32, 41, 52, 62; 7:33, 45; 8:13, 22, 31, 57; 9:10, 19; 11:14, 32, 38; 12:19, 28; 13:14; 18:4, 10, 19, 24, 28; 19:1, 16, 21; 20:3, 6, 8, 10, 20, Act 5:41; 11:17; 17:29; 19:3, 36; 21:22; 25:11; 28:28, Rom 2:21; 3:1, 9, 27, 31; 4:1, 10; 5:18; 6:1, 15, 21; 7:7, 13, 25; 8:12, 31; 9:14, 18, 19, 30; 11:1, 7, 13, 22; 13:12; 14:8, 13, 19; 15:17, 1Co 3:5; 4:16; 6:4; 9:18; 10:19; 14:26; 15:11, Gal 3:19, 21, Eph 2:19; 5:15, Col 3:1, 12, 2Th 2:15, 1Ti 2:1, 8, 2Ti 1:8; 2:1, 21, Heb 4:14, 16; 13:15, Rev 2:5, 16; 3:3, 1Es 4:14, Wis 6:9, LJr 1:40, 44, 49, 52, 56, 65, Sus 1:54, 58, 1Mc 5:12; 6:58; 7:7; 11:43; 15:30, 2Mc 10:22; 15:37, 3Mc 2:1; 3:11; 6:29, 4Mc 2:24; 4:26; 6:31; 8:7; 13:5; 17:20

then *τότε*

Mat 2:7, 16, 17; 3:5, 13, 15; 4:1, 5, 10, 11; 5:24; 7:5, 23; 8:26; 9:6, 14, 15, 29, 37; 11:20; 12:13, 22, 29, 38, 44, 45; 13:26, 36, 43; 15:1, 12, 28; 16:12, 20, 24, 27; 17:13, 19; 18:21, 32; 19:13, 27; 20:20; 21:1; 22:8, 13, 15, 21; 23:1; 24:9, 10, 14, 16, 21, 23, 30², 40; 25:1, 7, 31, 34, 37, 41, 44, 45; 26:3, 14, 31, 36, 38, 45, 50, 56, 65, 67, 74; 27:9, 13, 16, 26, 27, 38, 58; 28:10, Mrk 2:20; 3:27; 13:14, 21, 26, 27, Lke 5:35; 6:42; 11:26; 13:26; 14:9, 10, 21; 16:16; 21:10, 20, 21, 27; 23:30; 24:45, Joh 7:10; 8:28; 12:16; 13:27, Act 1:12; 4:8; 5:26; 6:11; 7:4; 8:17; 10:46, 48; 13:3, 12; 15:22; 17:14; 21:13, 26, 33; 23:3; 25:12; 26:1; 27:21, 32; 28:1, 1Co 4:5; 13:12²; 15:28, 54, 2Co 12:10, Gal 6:4, Col 3:4, 1Th 5:3, 2Th 2:8, Heb 10:7, 9; 12:26, 2Pe 3:6, 1Es 2:25, 30; 3:4, 8; 4:33, 42, 43, 47; 6:2, 11, 20, 23; 7:1, Tob 6:13; 8:21; 12:6; 13:6, Jdt 6:6; 15:3; 16:11, Wis 5:1; 18:17, Sir 11:7; 24:8; 28:2; 48:19; 50:16, 17, 20, Aza 1:28, Sus 1:14, Bel 1:21, 1Mc 2:29, 42; 4:41; 14:32, 2Mc 2:8; 12:18, 3Mc 5:1, 44; 6:18, 4Mc 3:8; 8:2; 15:22

thence 1. ן 2. מִשָּׁם 3. שָׁם

Gen 12: 8 Thence he removed to the mountain on the east 2
Deu 5:15 LORD . . brought you out thence with a mighty 2
Jos 18:17 going on to En-she'mesh, and thence goes *
19:12 thence it goes to Dab'erath, then up to Japhi'a; 1
2Kg 2:25 Mount Carmel, and thence he returned to Sama'ria. 2
17:27 one of the priests whom you carried away thence; 2
Neh 1: 9 I will gather them thence and bring them 3
Job 39:29 Thence he spies out the prey; his eyes behold it 2
Isa 52:11 depart, go out thence, touch no unclean thing; 2
Ezk 47:19 thence along the Brook of Egypt to the Great Sea. *
48:28 thence along the Brook of Egypt to the Great Sea. *
Ams 6: 2 Calneh, and see; and thence go to Hamath the great; 2
Obd 1: 4 set among the stars, thence I will bring you down 2

thence *See also* go.

there 1. בָּה 2. בְּקֶרֶב 3. בְּתוֹךְ 4. הֵנָּה 5. הִנֵּה 6. זֶה 7. מִשָּׁם 8. עָלָיו 9. תַּחְתָּיו 10. תַּמָּה (A) 11. *αὐτόθι* 12. *αὐτοῦ* 13. *ἐκεῖθεν* 14. *ἐκεῖσε* 15. *ἔνθα* 16. *ἐνθάδε* 17. *ἐνταῦθα* 18. *ἐπ' αὐταῖς* 19. *ἐπί* 20. *ἰδού* 21. *κἀκεῖ* 22. *κἀκεῖθεν* 23. *κἀκεῖνος* 24. *κεῖμαι* 25. *ὅθεν* 26. *ὅπου* 27. *ὅς* 28. *οὗτος* 29. *πάρειμι* 30. *πρόκειμαι* 31. *ὧδε* 32. ibi 33. inde

Gen 15:13 a land that is not theirs, and will be slaves there *
24:54 ate and drank, and they spent the night there. *
30:42 the feebler of the flock he did not lay them there *
35:20 Rachel's tomb, which is there to this day. *
Exd 34: 2 present yourself there to me on the top *
Num 9:22 continued over the tabernacle, abiding there 8
Deu 2:10 Emim formerly lived there, a people great and many 1
20 Reph'aim formerly lived there, but the Ammonites 1
Jos 8:29 heap of stones, which stands there to this day. *
10:19 but do not stay there yourselves, pursue *
15: 9 and from there to the cities of Mount Ephron; *
18:15 and the boundary goes from there to Ephron *
21:43 having taken possession . . they settled there. 1
Jdg 3:25 and there lay their lord dead on the floor. 5
4:22 So he went in to her tent; and there lay Sis'era dead 5
18: 7 came to La'ish, and saw the people who were there 2
1Sm 5: 8 they brought the ark of the God of Israel there. *
9: 4 they passed through . . but they were not there. *
14:17 Jonathan and his armor-bearer were not there. *
20:29 and my brother has commanded me to be there. *
26: 7 there lay Saul sleeping within the encampment 5
1Kg 1:39 There Zadok . . took the horn of oil from the tent *
11:24 they went to Damascus and dwelt there 1
12:25 Jerobo'am built Shechem . . and dwelt there; 1
20:40 And your servant was busy here and there, 4
2Kg 6: 2 go to the Jordan and each of us get there a log 7
2Ch 5:10 the two tables which Moses put there at Horeb *
22: 7 when he came there he went out with Jeho'ram *
23:13 there was the king standing by his pillar 5
Ezr 2:62 not found there, and so they were excluded *
5:17 search . . the royal archives there in Babylon 10
6:12 May the God who has caused his name to dwell there 10
8:25 all Israel there present had offered; *
Neh 7:64 it was not found there, so they were excluded *
Est 6: 5 Haman is there, standing in the court. 5
Ps 59: 7 There they are, bellowing with their mouths 5
68:14 When the Almighty scattered kings there 1
137: 2 On the willows there we hung up our lyres 3
Sng 2: 9 Behold, there he stands behind our wall, gazing 6
Isa 33:24 the people who dwell there will be forgiven 1
Jer 18: 3 and there he was working at his wheel. 5
27:11 to till it and dwell there, says the LORD. *
31:24 Judah and all its cities shall dwell there 1
38: 9 he will die there of hunger, for there is no bread 9
Mat 4:21 going on from there he saw two other brothers 13
5:23 at the altar, and there remember 21
9:27 as Jesus passed on from there 13
11: 1 he went on from there to teach and preach 13
12: 9 And he went on from there, and entered 13
13: 2 so that he got into a boat and sat there *
53 he went away from there 13
15:29 Jesus went on from there 13
24:23 'Lo, here is the Christ!' or 'There he is!' 31
28:10 there they will see me. 21
Mrk 1:35 there he prayed 21
5:15 came to Jesus, and saw the demoniac sitting there *
6: 1 He went away from there 13
7:24 And from there he arose 13
9:30 They went on from there 22
10: 1 he left there and went to the region of Judea 13
Lke 6: 8 Come and stand here." And he rose and stood there. *
9: 4 stay there, and from there depart. 13
11:53 As he went away from there 22
16:26 none may cross from there to us.' 13
22:47 While he was still speaking, there came a crowd 20
Joh 2:12 and there they stayed for a few days. 12
3:22 there he remained with them and baptized. 12
5: 6 and knew that he had been lying there a long time *
11:54 but went from there to . . E'phraim 13
54 there he stayed with the disciples. 21
19:18 There they crucified him, and with him two others 26
29 A bowl full of vinegar stood there *
20: 5 he saw the linen cloths lying there *
21: 9 they saw a charcoal fire there 24
Act 7: 4 after his father died, God removed him from there 22
10:18 Simon who was called Peter was lodging there. 16
12:19 he went down . . and remained there. *
13: 4 from there they sailed to Cyprus. 13
14: 7 there they preached the gospel. 21
26 from there they sailed to Antioch 22
16:12 and from there to Philip'pi 22
17:21 the foreigners who lived there *
18: 7 he left there and went to the house of . . Titius 13
19 they came to Ephesus, and he left them there 23
23 After spending some time there he departed *
19: 1 There he found some disciples. *
20: 3 There he spent three months *
13 intending to take Paul aboard there 13
15 sailing from there we came . . opposite Chi'os 22
21: 1 the next day to Rhodes . . from there to Pat'ara 22
3 there the ship was to unload its cargo. 14
4 we stayed there for seven days. 12
5 when our days there were ended *

22: 5 to take those also who were there 14
10 there you will be told 21
12 well spoken of by all the Jews who lived there •
25: 4 he himself intended to go there shortly. •
20 be tried there regarding them. 21
27: 4 putting to sea from there 22
6 There the centurion found a ship of Alexandria 21
28:13 from there we made a circuit 25
14 There we found brethren 27
15 the brethren there, when they heard of us, came 22
2Co 2:13 because I did not find my brother Titus there •
8:12 For if the readiness is there, it is acceptable 30
Rev 4: 3 he who sat there appeared like jasper •
1Es 6:33 the Lord, whose name is there called upon, 12
8:41 we encamped there three days 11
62 When we had been there three days 11
9: 4 if any did not meet there within two or three days •
2Es 4:15 there also we may gain more territory 32
6:39 the sound of man's voice was not yet there. ‡
7:38 and there are fire and torments! 32
9:26 and there I sat among the flowers 32
10:30 behold, I lay there like a corpse •
12:45 For we are no better than those who died there. 32
13:42 there at least they might keep their statutes 32
46 Then they dwelt there until the last times 32
58 And I stayed there three days. 32
14:29 and they were delivered from there 33
37 we proceeded to the field, and remained there. 32
Jdt 2:22 From there Holofernes took his whole army 13
7:13 and camp there to keep watch 18
13: 6 and took down his sword that hung there. 12
Wis 13:15 and fastens it there with iron. •
Sir 38:32 men can neither sojourn nor live there. •
LJr 1: 3 I will bring you away from there in peace. 13
Bel 1:40 he looked in, and there sat Daniel. 20
1Mc 4: 5 he found no one there •
6:37 four armed men who fought from there 19
10:42 it belongs to the priests who minister there. •
11:61 From there he departed to Gaza 13
2Mc 3:24 then and there . . a manifestation 11
11: 8 there . . a horseman appeared at their head 11
12:10 When they had gone more than a mile from there 13
17 When they had gone 95 miles from there 13
27 great stores of war engines . . were there. 15
29 Setting out from there 13
38 they kept the sabbath there. 11
13: 6 There they all push to destruction any man 17
14:16 they set out from there immediately 13
3Mc 1:13 no one there had stopped him. 29
21 the supplications of those gathered there 28
4Mc 3:10 although springs were plentiful there •
6:25 There they burned him 15

there שָׁם

Gen 2:8, 10, 11, 12; 11:2, 7, 8, 9[2], 31; 12:8, 10; 13:4, 18; 18:16, 22, 31, 32; 19:22[2]; 20:1; 21:31, 33; 22:2, 9; 23:13; 24:6, 7, 8; 25:10; 26:8, 17[2], 19, 22, 23, 25[3]; 27:45; 28:2, 6, 11; 29:3; 31:46; 32:13, 29; 33:20; 35:1[2], 3, 7[2]; 38:2; 39:1, 11, 20, 22; 41:12; 42:2; 43:25, 30; 44:14; 45:11; 46:3; 48:7; 49:31[3]; 50:5, 10, Exd 8:22; 9:26; 10:26; 15:25[2], 27[2]; 17:3, 6; 19:2; 24:12; 25:22; 29:42, 43; 34:5, Lev 8:31; 16:23, Num 9:17; 11:16, 17, 34; 13:22, 23, 24, 28, 33; 14:35, 43; 19:18; 20:1[2], 26, 28; 21:12, 13, 16, 32; 22:41; 23:13, 27; 33:9, 14, 38; 35:11, 15, Deu 1:28, 37, 39; 4:28, 29, 42; 6:23; 10:5, 6[2], 7; 12:5, 7, 11, 14[2], 21; 13:12; 14:23, 24, 26; 16:2, 6, 11; 17:12; 18:7; 19:4, 12; 21:4; 24:18; 26:2, 5[2]; 27:5, 7; 28:36, 64, 65, 68; 30:4[2]; 31:26; 32:52; 33:19, 21; 34:4, 5, Jos 2:1, 16, 22; 3:1; 4:8, 9; 8:32; 14:12; 15:14, 15; 17:15; 18:1, 10, 13; 19:13, 34; 20:3, 9; 22:10; 24:26, Jdg 1:7, 11; 2:5; 5:11, 27; 6:24; 7:4; 8:8, 27; 9:21; 14:10; 16:1, 27; 17:7; 18:2, 13; 19:2, 4, 7, 15; 20:26, 27; 21:2, 4, 9, 24, Rut 1:2, 4, 17; 4:1, 1Sm 1:22, 28; 2:14; 4:4[2]; 5:11; 6:14[2]; 7:6, 17[3]; 9:6; 10:3[2], 5, 23; 11:14, 15[3]; 14:34; 19:23; 20:6; 21:6, 7; 22:1[2], 3, 22; 23:22, 29; 27:5; 31:12, 2Sm 1:21; 2:2, 4, 18, 23; 3:27; 4:3; 5:20, 21; 6:2, 7[2]; 10:18; 11:16; 13:38; 14:2, 30, 32; 15:21, 29, 35, 36; 16:14; 17:13; 18:7[2], 11; 20:1; 21:13; 23:9; 24:25, 1Kg 3:4; 5:9; 6:19; 8:8, 9, 16, 21, 29; 9:3[2], 28; 10:20; 11:16; 12:25; 13:17; 14:2, 21; 17:4, 9[2], 10; 18:40; 19:3, 9[2], 19, 2Kg 2:23, 25; 4:8, 10[2], 11[2]; 5:18; 6:2, 6, 9, 10, 14; 7:4, 5, 10; 9:2, 16, 27; 10:15; 11:16; 14:19; 15:20; 17:11, 25, 27[2]; 19:32; 23:16, 20, 27, 34, 1Ch 4:23, 40, 41[3], 43; 11:13; 12:39; 13:6, 10; 14:11, 12; 16:37; 21:26, 28, 2Ch 1:3, 5, 6; 5:9; 6:5, 6, 11; 7:7, 16[2]; 8:18; 9:19; 12:13; 20:26; 23:15; 25:27; 28:9, 18; 32:21, Ezr 8:15[2], 21, 32, Neh 1:3, 9; 2:11; 4:20; 5:16, Job 3:17[2], 19; 23:7; 35:12; 39:30, Ps 14:5; 6:12; 8:6; 3:5; 6:6; 8:27; 9:35; 6:3; 7:4, 6; 04:26; 07:36; 22:5; 32:17; 33:3; 37:1, 3; 39:8[2], 10, Prv 8:27; 9:18, Ecc 1:7; 3:16[2]; 11:3, Sng 7:12; 8:5, Isa 7:23, 24, 25; 13:20[2], 21[3]; 22:18[2]; 23:12; 27:10[2]; 28:10, 13; 33:21; 34:12, 14, 15[2]; 35:8, 9[2]; 37:33; 48:16; 52:4; 65:9, Jer 3:6; 7:2; 8:14, 22; 13:4, 6[2]; 16:13; 18:2; 19:2; 20:6[2]; 22:1, 12, 26, 27; 27:22; 29:6; 32:5; 36:12; 37:12, 13, 16, 20; 38:11, 26; 41:1, 3; 42:14, 15, 16[2], 17; 43:2, 12; 44:14; 49:16, 18, 33; 50:9, 40, Ezk 1:3; 3:15, 22[2], 23; 8:1, 4, 14; 11:18; 12:13; 17:20; 20:28[3], 35, 40[3], 43; 23:3; 29:14; 30:18; 32:22, 24, 26, 29, 30; 34:14; 35:10; 39:11, 16; 40:3[2]; 42:13, 14; 46:19; 47:9, 23; 48:35, Dan 10:13, Hos 2:15[2]; 6:7, 10; 9:15; 10:9; 12:4; 13:8, Jol 3:2, 11, 12, Ams 7:12[2]; 9:2[2], 3[2], 4, Jon 4:5, Mic 4:10, Nah 3:15, Hab 3:4, Zep 1:14, Hag 2:14, Zec 5:11

there ἐκεῖ

Mat 2:13, 15, 22; 5:24; 6:21; 8:12; 12:45; 13:42, 50, 58; 14:23; 15:29; 17:20; 18:20; 19:2; 21:17; 22:11, 13; 24:28, 51; 25:30; 27:36, 55, 61; 28:7, Mrk 1:38; 2:6; 3:1; 5:11; 6:5, 10, 33; 11:5; 13:21; 14:15; 16:7, Lke 2:6; 8:32; 9:4; 10:6; 11:26; 12:18, 34; 13:28; 15:13; 17:21, 23, 37; 22:12; 23:33, Joh 2:1, 6; 3:23[2]; 4:6, 40; 5:5; 6:3, 22, 24; 10:40, 42; 11:8, 15, 31; 12:2, 9, 26; 18:2, 3; 19:42, Act 9:33; 16:1; 17:14; 19:21; 25:9, 14, Rom 15:24, Tit 3:12, Heb 7:8, Jas 2:3; 3:16; 4:13, Rev 2:14; 21:25, 1Es 4:44; 8:42, 50; 9:2, Tob 6:1; 7:17; 10:7; 13:4, Jdt 1:16; 5:8, 9, 10[2]; 11:14, Wis 17:16, Sir 12:17; 32:12, Bar 3:26, LJr 1:3, Sus 1:16, Bel 1:31, 1Mc 1:34, 35; 2:7, 29; 4:61; 5:13; 6:2, 9, 16, 49, 50; 7:1; 8:3, 22; 10:1, 71; 11:6, 16, 40, 73; 12:34; 13:11, 23, 52; 14:33, 34; 15:41; 16:15, 2Mc 2:5; 3:38; 4:38; 9:4; 12:6, 30; 15:31, 3Mc 5:43; 7:18

thereafter 1. μετὰ ταῦτα

1Es 5:52 thereafter the continual offerings 1

thereby 1. בַּדָּבָר הַזֶּה 2. בָּהּ 3. בָּהֶם 4. בּוֹ 5. בָּזֶה 6. διὰ ταύτης 7. δι᾽ οὗ

Lev 6: 7 which one may do and thereby become guilty 2
15:32 an emission of semen, becoming unclean thereby 2
22: 9 lest they . . die thereby when they profane it 4
Deu 32:47 thereby you shall live long in the land 1
Job 22:21 be at peace; thereby good will come to you. 3
Mal 3:10 thereby put me to the test, says the LORD of hosts 5
Heb 13: 2 thereby some have entertained angels unawares. 6
4Mc 9:24 Thereby . . Providence . . may become merciful 7

therefore 1. אֲשֶׁר 2. גַּם 3. וְעַתָּה 4. כֵּן 5. לָהֵן 6. לָכֵן 7. נָא 8. עַל זֹאת 9. עַל כֵּן 10. עַתָּה 11. וְ (A) 12. כָּל קֳבֵל דְּנָה (A) 13. כְּעַן (A) 14. לָהֵן (A) 15. עַל דְּנָה (A) 16. ἀνθ᾽ οὗ 17. ἀνθ᾽ ὧν 18. ἀρά 19. δέ 20. δὴ τοίνυν 21. διὰ τοῦτο 22. διὰ τρόπον τοῦτον 23. δι᾽ ἣν αἰτίαν 24. διό 25. διόπερ 26. διότι 27. ἵνα 28. καί 29. καὶ νῦν 30. ὅθεν 31. οὗ χάριν 32. πρὸς ταῦτα 33. τοιγαροῦν 34. τοίνυν 35. ὥστε 36. ergo 37. ex hoc 38. ideo 39. ideoque 40. propter 41. propterea 42. quapropter 43. quoniam

Gen 2:24 Therefore a man leaves his father and his mother 9
10: 9 therefore it is said, "Like Nimrod a mighty hunter 9
11: 9 Therefore its name was called Ba'bel 9
16:14 Therefore the well was called Beer-la'hai-roi; 9
19:22 Therefore the name of the city was called Zo'ar. 9
20: 6 therefore I did not let you touch her. 9
21:23 now therefore swear to me here by God •
31 Therefore that place was called Beer-sheba; 9
25:30 Therefore his name was called Edom. 9
26:33 therefore the name of the city is Beer-sheba 9
27: 8 Now therefore, my son, obey my word as I command •
43 Now therefore, my son, obey my voice; •
29:15 you are my kinsman, should you therefore serve me •
34 therefore his name was called Levi. 9
35 therefore she called his name Judah; 9
30: 6 given me a son"; therefore she called his name Dan 9
31:48 Therefore he named it Galeed 9
32:32 Therefore to this day the Israelites do not eat 9
33:17 therefore the name of the place is called 9
38:29 Therefore his name was called Perez. •
41:33 Now therefore let Pharaoh select a man discreet •
42:21 therefore is this distress come upon us. 9
44:30 Now therefore, when I come to your servant •
33 Now therefore, let your servant, I pray you •
47:22 therefore they did not sell their land. 9
50: 5 Now therefore let me go up, I pray you, and bury my 10
11 Therefore the place was named A'bel-mizraim; 9
Exd 1:11 Therefore they set taskmasters over them •
4:12 Now therefore go, and I will be with your mouth •
5: 8 for they are idle; therefore they cry, "Let us go 9
17 you are idle; therefore you say, 'Let us go 9
6: 6 Say therefore to the people of Israel 6
9:19 therefore send, get your cattle and all that you •
10:17 Now therefore, forgive my sin, I pray you •
13:15 Therefore I sacrifice to the LORD all the males 9
15:23 it was bitter; therefore it was named Marah. 9
16:29 given you the sabbath, therefore on the sixth day 9
19: 5 Now therefore, if you will obey my voice and keep •
20:11 therefore the LORD blessed the sabbath day 9
22:31 You shall be men consecrated to me; therefore you •
31:16 Therefore the people of Israel shall keep •
32:10 now therefore let me alone, that my wrath may burn 10
Lev 17:12 Therefore I have said to the people of Israel 9
Num16:11 Therefore it is against the LORD that you and all 6
18:24 therefore I have said of them that 9
20:12 therefore you shall not bring this assembly 4
21:27 Therefore the ballad singers say, "Come 9
25:12 Therefore say, 'Behold, I give to him my covenant 6
Deu 5:15 therefore the LORD your God commanded you 9
10: 9 Therefore Levi has no portion or inheritance 9
15:11 poor will never cease . . therefore I command 9
15 therefore I command you this today. 9
19: 7 Therefore I command you, You shall set apart 9
24:18 therefore I command you to do this. 9
22 therefore I command you to do this. 9
Jos 7:26 Therefore to this day the name of that place is 9
22: 4 therefore turn and go to your home in the land 3
24:18 LORD drove out . . therefore we also will serve •
Jdg 9:16 Now therefore, if you acted in good faith •
10:13 served other gods; therefore I will deliver you 4
13: 4 Therefore beware, and drink no wine or strong 3
15:19 he revived. Therefore the name of it was called 9
18:14 Now therefore consider what you will do. •
Rut 1:13 would you therefore wait till they were grown? 5
13 Would you therefore refrain from marrying? 5
1Sm 2:30 Therefore the LORD the God of Israel declares 6
3:14 Therefore I swear to the house of Eli that 6
10:12 Therefore it became a proverb, "Is Saul also among 9
12:16 Now therefore stand . . and see this great thing 2
23:28 therefore that place was called the Rock of Escape 9
24:21 Swear to me therefore by the LORD that you will 3
27: 6 therefore Ziklag has belonged to . . Judah 6
28:18 therefore the LORD has done this thing to you 9
2Sm 5: 8 Therefore it is said, "The blind and the lame shall 9
20 Therefore the name of that place is called 9
7:22 Therefore thou art great, O LORD God; 9
27 therefore thy servant has found courage to pray 9
1Kg 9: 9 Because . . therefore the LORD has brought 9
14:10 therefore behold, I will bring evil 6
22:19 Therefore hear the word of the LORD: I saw the LORD 6
2Kg 1: 4 Now therefore thus says the LORD, 'You shall not 6
6 inquire of Ba'al-ze'bub . . Therefore you shall 6
16 Because you have sent . . therefore you shall not 6
19:32 Therefore thus says the LORD concerning 6
21:12 therefore thus says the LORD 6
22:20 Therefore, behold, I will gather you 6
1Ch 11: 7 therefore it was called the city of David. 9
14:11 Therefore the name of that place is called 9
17:25 therefore thy servant has found courage to pray 9
22: 5 I will therefore make preparation for it. 7
2Ch 7:22 therefore he has brought all this evil upon them' 9
18:18 Micai'ah said, "Therefore hear the word of the LORD 6
20:26 therefore the name of that place has been called 9
Ezr 4:14 therefore we send and inform the king 15
21 Therefore make a decree that these men . . cease 13
5:17 Therefore, if it seem good to the king, let search 13
6: 6 therefore, Tat'tenai, governor of the province •
9:12 Therefore give not your daughters to their sons 3
10: 3 Therefore let us make a covenant with our God 3
Est 9:19 Therefore the Jews of . . hold the fourteenth 9
26 Therefore they called these days Purim 9
26 And therefore, because of all that was written 9
Job 6: 3 therefore my words have been rash. 9
7:11 Therefore I will not restrain my mouth; 2
9:22 It is all one; therefore I say, he destroys both 9
17: 4 therefore thou wilt not let them triumph. 9
20: 2 Therefore my thoughts answer me 6
21 therefore his prosperity will not endure. 9
22:10 Therefore snares are round about you 9
23:15 Therefore I am terrified at his presence; 9
32: 6 therefore I was timid and afraid to declare 9
10 Therefore I say, 'Listen to me; 6
34:10 Therefore, hear me, you men of understanding 6
37:24 Therefore men fear him; 6
42: 3 Therefore I have uttered what I did not 6
6 therefore I despise myself, and repent 9
Ps 1: 5 Therefore the wicked will not stand 9
16: 9 Therefore my heart is glad, and my soul rejoices; 6
25: 8 therefore he instructs sinners in the way. 9
32: 6 Therefore let every one who is godly offer 8
42: 6 therefore I remember thee from the land 9
45: 2 therefore God has blessed you for ever. 9
7 Therefore God, your God, has anointed you 9
17 therefore the peoples will praise you for ever 9
46: 2 Therefore we will not fear 9
73: 6 Therefore pride is their necklace; 6
10 Therefore the people turn and praise them; 6
78:21 Therefore, when the LORD heard, he was full 6
95:11 Therefore I swore in my anger that they should 1
110: 7 therefore he will lift up his head. 9
119:104 therefore I hate every false way. 9
119 therefore I love thy testimonies. 6
127 Therefore I love thy commandments above gold 9
128 Therefore I direct my steps by all thy precepts; 9
129 are wonderful; therefore my soul keeps them. 9
Prv 6:15 therefore calamity will come upon him suddenly; 9
Ecc 5: 2 therefore let your words be few. 9
Sng 1: 3 your name is . . therefore the maidens love you. 9
Isa 1:24 Therefore the Lord says . . "Ah, I will vent my wrath 6
5:13 Therefore my people go into exile 6
14 Therefore Sheol has enlarged its appetite 6
24 Therefore, as the tongue of fire devours 6
25 Therefore the anger of the LORD was kindled 9
7:14 Therefore the Lord himself will give you a sign. 6
8: 7 therefore, behold, the Lord is bringing up 6
9:17 Therefore the Lord does not rejoice 9
10:16 Therefore the Lord . . will send wasting 6
24 Therefore thus says the Lord, the LORD of hosts 6
13: 7 Therefore all hands will be feeble 9
13 Therefore I will make the heavens tremble 9
15: 4 therefore the armed men of Moab cry aloud; 9
7 Therefore the abundance they have gained 9
16: 7 Therefore let Moab wail, let every one wail 6
9 Therefore I weep with the weeping of Jazer 9
11 Therefore my soul moans like a lyre for Moab 9
17:10 therefore, though you plant pleasant plants 9
21: 3 Therefore my loins are filled with anguish; 9
22: 4 Therefore I said: "Look away from me, let me weep 9
24: 6 Therefore a curse devours the earth 9
6 therefore the inhabitants of the earth 9
15 Therefore in the east give glory to the LORD; 9
25: 3 Therefore strong peoples will glorify thee; 9
27: 9 Therefore by this the guilt of Jacob will be 6
11 therefore he who made them will not have 9
28:14 Therefore hear the word of the LORD, you scoffers 6
16 therefore thus says the Lord GOD 6
29:14 therefore, behold, I will again do marvelous 6
22 Therefore thus says the LORD 6
30: 7 therefore I have called her "Rahab who sits still. 6

12 Therefore thus says the Holy One of Israel 6
13 therefore this iniquity shall be to you 6
16 upon horses," therefore you shall speed away; 9
16 therefore your pursuers shall be swift. 9
18 Therefore the LORD waits to be gracious to you; 6
18 therefore he exalts himself to show mercy 6
37:33 Therefore thus says the LORD 6
50: 7 helps me; therefore I have not been confounded; 9
7 therefore I have set my face like a flint 9
51:21 Therefore hear this, you who are afflicted 6
52: 6 Therefore my people shall know my name; 6
6 therefore in that day they shall know that it is I 6
53:12 Therefore I will divide him a portion 6
59: 9 Therefore justice is far from us 9
61: 7 therefore in your land you shall possess 6
65:13 Therefore thus says the Lord GOD: 6
Jer 2: 9 Therefore I still contend with you, says the LORD 6
5: 6 Therefore a lion from the forest shall slay them 9
14 Therefore thus says the LORD, the God of hosts 6
27 therefore they have become great and rich 9
6:15 Therefore they shall fall among those who fall; 6
18 Therefore hear, O nations, and know 6
21 Therefore thus says the LORD: 'Behold 6
7:20 Therefore thus says the Lord GOD: Behold, my anger 6
32 Therefore, behold, the days are coming 6
8:10 Therefore I will give their wives to others 6
12 Therefore they shall fall among the fallen; 6
9: 7 Therefore thus says the LORD of hosts: "Behold 6
15 Therefore thus says the LORD of hosts 6
10:21 therefore they have not prospered 9
11:11 Therefore, thus says the LORD, Behold 6
21 Therefore thus says the LORD 6
22 therefore thus says the LORD of hosts: "Behold 6
12: 8 her voice against me; therefore I hate her. 9
14:15 Therefore thus says the LORD 6
15:19 Therefore thus says the LORD: "If you return 6
16:14 Therefore, behold, the days are coming 6
21 Therefore, behold, I will make them know 6
18:13 Therefore thus says the LORD 6
21 Therefore deliver up their children to famine; 6
19: 6 therefore, behold, days are coming, says the LORD 6
20:11 therefore my persecutors will stumble 9
22:18 Therefore thus says the LORD concerning 6
23: 2 Therefore thus says the LORD, the God of Israel 6
7 Therefore, behold, the days are coming 6
12 Therefore their way shall be to them like 6
15 Therefore thus says the LORD of hosts 6
30 Therefore, behold, I am against the prophets 6
39 therefore, behold, I will surely lift you up 6
25: 8 Therefore thus says the LORD of hosts: 6
28:16 Therefore thus says the LORD 6
29:32 therefore thus says the LORD 6
30:16 Therefore all who devour you shall be devoured 6
31: 3 therefore I have continued my faithfulness 9
20 Therefore my heart yearns for him; 9
32:28 Therefore, thus says the LORD 6
36 Now therefore thus says the LORD 6
34:17 Therefore, thus says the LORD: You have not obeyed 6
35:17 Therefore, thus says the LORD, the God of hosts 6
19 therefore thus says the LORD of hosts 6
36:30 Therefore thus says the LORD 6
44:11 Therefore thus says the LORD of hosts 6
26 Therefore hear the word of the LORD 6
48:12 Therefore, behold, the days are coming 6
31 Therefore I wail for Moab; I cry out for all Moab; 9
36 Therefore my heart moans for Moab like a flute 9
36 therefore the riches they gained have perished. 9
49: 2 Therefore, behold, the days are coming 6
20 Therefore hear the plan which the LORD has made 6
26 Therefore her young men shall fall in her squares 6
50:18 Therefore, thus says the LORD of hosts 6
30 Therefore her young men shall fall 6
39 Therefore wild beasts shall dwell with hyenas 6
45 Therefore hear the plan which the LORD has made 6
51: 7 of her wine, therefore the nations went mad. 9
36 Therefore thus says the LORD: "Behold, I will plead 6
47 Therefore, behold, the days are coming 6
52 Therefore, behold, the days are coming 6
Lam 1: 8 sinned . . therefore she became filthy; 9
3:21 But this I call to mind, and therefore I have hope 9
24 LORD is my portion . . therefore I will hope 9
Ezk 5: 7 Therefore thus says the Lord GOD 6
8 therefore thus says the Lord GOD: Behold, I, even I 6
10 Therefore fathers shall eat their sons 6
11 therefore I will cut you down; 2
7:20 therefore I will make it an unclean thing to them. 9
8:18 Therefore I will deal in wrath; 2
11: 4 Therefore prophesy against them 6
7 Therefore thus says the Lord GOD 6
16 Therefore say, 'Thus says the Lord GOD 6
17 Therefore say, 'Thus says the Lord GOD: 6
12:23 Tell them therefore, 'Thus says the Lord GOD 6
28 Therefore say to them, Thus says the Lord GOD 6
13: 8 Therefore thus says the Lord God 6
8 therefore behold, I am against you, says the Lord 6
13 Therefore thus says the Lord GOD 6
23 therefore you shall no more see delusive 6
14: 4 Therefore speak to them, and say to them 6
6 Therefore say to the house of Israel 6
15: 6 Therefore thus says the Lord GOD 6
16:37 therefore, behold, I will gather all your lovers 6
43 therefore, behold, I will requite your deeds 2
17:19 Therefore thus says the Lord GOD: As I live, surely 6
18:30 Therefore I will judge you, O house of Israel 6
20:27 Therefore, son of man, speak to the house of Israel 6
21: 4 therefore my sword shall go out of its sheath 6
12 Smite therefore upon your thigh. 6
24 Therefore thus says the Lord GOD 6
22: 4 Therefore I have made you a reproach 9
19 Therefore thus says the Lord GOD 6
19 therefore, behold, I will gather you 6
23: 9 Therefore I delivered her into the hands of her 6
22 Therefore, O Oholi'bah, thus says the Lord GOD 6
35 Therefore thus says the Lord GOD 6
35 therefore bear the consequences •
24: 6 Therefore thus says the Lord GOD 6
9 Therefore thus says the Lord GOD 6
25: 4 therefore I am handing you over to the people 6
7 therefore, behold, I have stretched out my hand 6
9 therefore I will lay open the flank of Moab 6
13 therefore thus says the Lord GOD 6
16 therefore thus says the Lord GOD, Behold 6
26: 3 therefore thus says the Lord GOD 6
28: 6 therefore thus says the Lord GOD 6
7 therefore, behold, I will bring strangers upon 6
29: 8 therefore thus says the Lord GOD 6
10 therefore, behold, I am against you 6
19 Therefore thus says the Lord GOD: Behold 6
30:22 Therefore thus says the Lord GOD: Behold, I am 6
31:10 Therefore thus says the Lord GOD 6
33:25 Therefore say to them, Thus says the Lord GOD 6
34: 7 Therefore, you shepherds, hear the word 6
9 therefore, you shepherds, hear the word 6
20 Therefore, thus says the Lord GOD to them: Behold 6
35: 6 therefore, as I live, says the Lord GOD 6
11 therefore, as I live, says the Lord GOD, I will deal 6
36: 3 therefore prophesy, and say, Thus says the Lord 6
4 therefore, O mountains of Israel, hear the word 6
5 therefore thus says the Lord GOD 6
6 Therefore prophesy concerning the land 6
7 therefore thus says the Lord GOD: I swear 6
14 therefore you shall no longer devour men 6
22 Therefore say to the house of Israel 6
37:12 Therefore prophesy, and say to them 6
38:14 Therefore, son of man, prophesy, and say to Gog 6
39:25 Therefore thus says the Lord GOD 6
44: 9 Therefore thus says the Lord GOD: No foreigner •
12 therefore I have sworn concerning them 9
Dan 2: 6 Therefore show me the dream 14
9 Therefore tell me the dream, and I shall know 14
24 Therefore Daniel went in to Ar'ioch 12
3: 7 Therefore, as soon as all the peoples heard 12
8 Therefore at that time certain Chalde'ans came 12
29 Therefore I make a decree: Any people, nation 11
4: 6 Therefore I made a decree that all the wise men 11
27 Therefore, O king, let my counsel be acceptable 14
6: 9 Therefore King Darius signed the document 12
9:17 Now therefore, O our God, hearken to the prayer •
Hos 2: 6 Therefore I will hedge up her way with thorns; 6
9 Therefore I will take back my grain in its time 6
14 Therefore, behold, I will allure her, and bring her 6
4: 3 Therefore the land mourns, and all who dwell in it 9
13 Therefore your daughters play the harlot 9
6: 5 Therefore I have hewn them by the prophets 9
13: 3 Therefore they shall be like the morning mist 6
6 therefore they forgot me. 9
Ams 3: 2 therefore I will punish you for all 9
11 Therefore thus says the Lord GOD: "An adversary 6
4:12 Therefore thus I will do to you, O Israel; 6
5:11 Therefore because you trample upon the poor 6
13 Therefore he who is prudent will keep silent 6
16 Therefore thus says the LORD, the God of hosts 6
6: 7 Therefore they shall now be the first of those 6
7:17 Therefore thus says the LORD 6
Mic 1:14 Therefore you shall give parting gifts 6
2: 3 Therefore thus says the LORD 6
5 Therefore you will have none to cast the line 6
3: 6 Therefore it shall be night to you 6
12 Therefore because of you Zion shall be plowed 6
5: 3 Therefore he shall give them up 6
6:13 Therefore I have begun to smite you 2
Hab 1:16 Therefore he sacrifices to his net 9
Zep 2: 9 Therefore, as I live," says the LORD of hosts 6
3: 8 Therefore wait for me," says the LORD 6
Hag 1:10 Therefore the heavens above you have withheld 9
Zec 1:16 Therefore, thus says the LORD, I have returned 6
10: 2 Therefore the people wander like sheep; 9
Mat 6:25 Therefore I tell you, do not be anxious about 21
12:27 Therefore they shall be your judges. 21
31 Therefore I tell you, every sin and blasphemy 21
13:52 Therefore every scribe who has been trained 21
18:23 Therefore the kingdom of heaven may be compared 21
21:43 Therefore I tell you, the kingdom of God 21
23:34 Therefore I send you prophets and wise men 21
24:44 Therefore you also must be ready 21
27: 8 Therefore that field has been called the Field 24
Mrk 11:24 Therefore I tell you, whatever you ask in prayer 21
Lke 1:35 therefore the child . . will be called holy 24
7: 7 therefore I did not presume to come to you 24
47 Therefore I tell you, her sins, which are many 31
11:19 Therefore they shall be your judges. 21
49 Therefore also the Wisdom of God said, 'I will send 21
12: 3 Therefore whatever you have said in the dark 17
22 he said to his disciples, "Therefore I tell you 21
14:20 I have married a wife, and therefore I cannot come.' 21
Joh 9:23 Therefore his parents said, "He is of age, ask him. 21
12:39 Therefore they could not believe 21
15:19 therefore the world hates you. 21
16:15 therefore I said that he will take what is mine 21
19:11 therefore he . . has the greater sin. 21
Act 2:26 therefore my heart was glad 21
6: 3 Therefore, brethren, pick out . . seven men 19
13:35 Therefore he says also in another psalm 26
15:19 Therefore my judgment is 24
16:11 Setting sail therefore from Tro'as 19
20:26 Therefore I testify to you this day 26
31 Therefore be alert 24
25:26 Therefore I have brought him before you 24
26: 3 therefore I beg you to listen to me patiently. 24
27:34 Therefore I urge you to take some food 24
Rom 1:24 Therefore God gave them up in the lusts 24
2: 1 Therefore you have no excuse, O man 24
5:12 Therefore as sin came into the world through one 21
8: 1 There is therefore now no condemnation 18
13: 2 Therefore he who resists the authorities 35
5 Therefore one must be subject 24
15: 7 Welcome one another, therefore 24
9 Therefore I will praise thee among the Gentiles 21
1Co 1:31 therefore, as it is written, "Let him who boasts 27
4: 5 Therefore do not pronounce judgment 35
17 Therefore I sent to you Timothy 21
5: 8 Let us, therefore, celebrate the festival 35
8:13 Therefore, if food is a cause 25
10:12 Therefore let any one who thinks that he stands 35
14 Therefore, my beloved, shun the worship of idols. 25
11:27 Whoever, therefore, eats the bread 35
12: 3 Therefore I want you to understand 24
14:13 Therefore, he who speaks in a tongue should pray 24
15:58 Therefore, my beloved brethren, be steadfast 35
2Co 4: 1 Therefore, having this ministry 21
5:14 therefore all have died. 18
16 From now on, therefore, we regard 35
17 Therefore, if any one is in Christ 35
6:17 Therefore come out from them, and be separate 24
7:13 Therefore we are comforted 21
Eph 2:11 Therefore remember that . . 24
4: 8 Therefore it is said, "When he ascended on high 24
25 Therefore, putting away falsehood 24
5:14 Therefore it is said, "Awake, O sleeper 24
17 Therefore do not be foolish 21
6:13 Therefore take the whole armor of God 21
Php 2: 9 Therefore God has highly exalted him 24
12 Therefore, my beloved, as you have always obeyed 35
4: 1 Therefore, my brethren, whom I love and long 35
1Th 3: 1 Therefore when we could bear it no longer 24
4: 8 Therefore whoever disregards this 33
18 Therefore comfort one another 35
5:11 Therefore encourage one another 24
2Th 1: 4 Therefore we ourselves boast of you 35
2:11 Therefore God sends upon them a strong delusion 21
2Ti 1:12 therefore I suffer as I do 23
2:10 Therefore I endure everything 21
Tit 1:13 Therefore rebuke them sharply 23
Heb 1: 9 therefore God, thy God, has anointed thee 21
2: 1 Therefore we must pay the closer attention 21
17 Therefore he had to be made like his brethren 30
3: 1 Therefore, holy brethren . . consider Jesus 30
7 Therefore, as the Holy Spirit says 24
10 Therefore I was provoked with that generation 24
6: 1 Therefore let us leave the elementary doctrine 24
9:15 Therefore he is the mediator of a new covenant 21
11:12 Therefore from one man, and him as good as dead 24
16 Therefore God is not ashamed 24
12: 1 Therefore . . let us also lay aside every weight 33
12 Therefore lift your drooping hands 24
28 Therefore let us be grateful 24
13:13 Therefore let us go forth to him outside the camp 34
Jas 1:21 Therefore put away all filthiness 24
4: 6 But he gives more grace; therefore it says 24
1Pe 1:13 Therefore gird up your minds, be sober 24
4:19 Therefore let those who suffer 35
2Pe 1:10 Therefore, brethren, be the more zealous 24
12 Therefore I intend always to remind you 24
3:14 Therefore, beloved, since you wait for these 24
1Jn 2:18 therefore we know that it is the last hour. 30
4: 5 therefore what they say is of the world 21
Rev 3:18 Therefore I counsel you to buy from me gold •
7:15 Therefore are they before the throne of God 21
1Es 6:33 Therefore may the Lord . . destroy every king 21
8:84 Therefore do not give . . in marriage 29
2Es 2:34 Therefore I say to you, O nations 39
3:34 Now therefore weigh in a balance our iniquities 36
4:29 If therefore that which has been sown 36
5:18 Rise therefore and eat some bread 36
45 If therefore all creatures will live at one time •
46 Request it therefore to produce ten at one time. 36
54 Therefore you also should consider 36

6:31 If therefore you will pray again 36
33 Therefore he sent me to show you all these things 40
48 that therefore the nations might declare 37
7:14 Therefore unless the living pass through 36
18 The righteous therefore can endure 36
25 Therefore, Ezra, empty things are for the empty 40
57 Judge therefore which things are precious 36
64 and therefore we are tormented 40
72 For this reason, therefore, those who dwell 36
90 Therefore this is the teaching concerning them 40
100 Will time therefore be given to the souls 36
111 If therefore the righteous have prayed 36
112 therefore those who were strong prayed 40
115 Therefore no one will then be able to have mercy 36
131 Therefore there shall not be grief 43
8:17 Therefore I will pray before thee for myself 38
19 Therefore hear my voice, and understand my words 38
40 As I have spoken, therefore, so it shall be. 36
55 Therefore do not ask any more questions 36
61 Therefore my judgment is now drawing near; 42
9:13 Therefore, do not continue to be curious as to how 36
10:15 Now, therefore, keep your sorrow to yourself 36
17 Therefore go into the city to your husband. 36
24 Therefore shake off your great sadness 36
37 Now therefore I entreat you to give your servant 36
40 This therefore is the meaning of the vision. 36
51 Therefore I told you to remain in the field 41
53 Therefore I told you to go into the field 41
55 Therefore do not be afraid 36
11:45 Therefore you will surely disappear, you eagle 41
12: 6 Therefore I will now beseech the Most High 36
24 therefore they are called the heads of the eagle. 40
37 Therefore write all these things 36
44 Therefore if you forsake us, how much better 36
13:24 Understand therefore that those who are left 36
47 Therefore you saw the multitude 40
49 Therefore when he destroys the multitude 36
56 Therefore I have shown you this 40
14:13 Now therefore, set your house in order 36
15: 7 Therefore," says the Lord 41
26 therefore he will hand them over to death 41
48 therefore God says 41
55 therefore you shall receive your recompense. 41
16:51 Therefore do not be like her or her works. 41
Tob 12:18 Therefore praise him for ever. 30
Jdt 4: 2 they were therefore very greatly terrified 28
5:20 Now therefore, my master and lord 28
24 Therefore let us go up, Lord Holofernes 24
7:11 Therefore, my lord, do not fight against them 29
8:17 Therefore . . let us call upon him to help us 25
20 therefore we hope that he will not disdain us 30
24 Now therefore, brethren, let us set an example 28
11:10 Therefore . . do not disregard what he said 24
16 Therefore, when I, your servant, learned all this 30
17 therefore, my lord, I will remain with you 29
AEs 16:19 Therefore post a copy of this letter publicly 19
Wis 1: 8 therefore no one who utters unrighteous things 21
4:14 therefore he took him quickly 21
5:16 Therefore they will receive a glorious crown 21
6:25 Therefore be instructed by my words 35
7: 7 Therefore I prayed 21
25 therefore nothing defiled gains entrance 21
8: 9 Therefore I determined to take her to live 34
10:20 Therefore the righteous plundered the ungodly; 21
12: 2 Therefore thou dost correct little by little 24
23 Therefore . . thou didst torment 30
25 Therefore . . thou didst send thy judgment 21
27 Therefore the utmost condemnation 24
14: 5 therefore men trust their lives 21
11 Therefore there will be a visitation 21
14 therefore their speedy end has been planned. 21
16: 1 Therefore those men were deservedly punished 21
25 Therefore at that time also 21
17: 1 therefore unintructed souls have gone astray. 21
18: 3 Therefore thou didst provide a flaming pillar 16
Sir 2:13 Therefore it will not be sheltered. 21
10:13 Therefore the Lord brought upon them 21
18:11 Therefore the Lord is patient with them 21
12 therefore he grants them forgiveness 21
29: 7 Because of such wickedness, therefore *
31:13 Therefore it sheds tears from every face. 21
39:32 Therefore . . I have been convinced 21
41:16 Therefore show respect for my words 33
43:14 Therefore the storehouses are opened 21
44:17 therefore a remnant was left to the earth 21
21 Therefore the Lord assured him by an oath 21
45:24 Therefore a covenant of peace was established 21
51:12 Therefore I will give thanks to thee 21
20 therefore I will not be forsaken. 21
21 therefore I have gained a good possession. 21
LJr 1:16 Therefore they evidently are not gods 30
64 Therefore one must not think that they are gods 30
69 therefore do not fear them. 24
Bel 1:22 Therefore the king put them to death 28
1Mc 10:54 now therefore let us establish friendship 28
12:23 We therefore command *
2Mc 4:21 Therefore . . he proceeded to Jerusalem. 30
34 Therefore Menelaus . . urged him to kill Onias. 30
46 Therefore Ptolemy, taking the king aside 30
49 Therefore even the Tyrians . . provided 23
5: 4 Therefore all men prayed 24
17 therefore he was disregarding the holy place. 24
20 Therefore the place . . shared . . misfortunes 25
6:16 Therefore he never withdraws his mercy from us. 25
27 Therefore, by manfully giving up my life now 25
7: 8 Therefore he in turn underwent tortures 25
18 Therefore astounding things have happened. *
23 Therefore the Creator . . will . . give life 33
8:36 therefore the Jews were invulnerable 22
9: 2 Therefore the people rushed to the rescue 24
10: 7 Therefore . . they offered hymns 24
11:37 Therefore make haste and send some men 24
12:45 Therefore he made atonement for the dead 30
14: 7 Therefore I have laid aside my ancestral glory 30
19 Therefore he sent Posidonius and Theodotus 25
3Mc 3:24 Therefore . . we have taken precautions 24
25 Therefore we have given orders *
4Mc 1:34 Therefore . . we abstain 33
3:16 Therefore . . he poured out the drink 30
5:17 Therefore we consider that we should not 24
25 Therefore we do not eat defiling food 24
32 Therefore get your torture wheels ready 32
6:22 Therefore, O children of Abraham, die nobly 32
7:16 If, therefore, because of piety 20
9: 7 Therefore, tyrant, put us to the test 33
11:27 therefore, unconquered, we hold fast to reason. 21
13:16 Therefore let us put on the full armor 33
23 Therefore . . the brothers were . . 20
16:19 therefore you ought to endure any suffering 21
17: 4 Take courage, therefore, O holy-minded mother 33
18: 3 Therefore those . . were not only admired 17

therefore וְ

Gen 3:23, Exd 12:17; 13:10; 17:2; 33:6, 13, Lev 11:44, 45; 17:14; 18:5; 20:7, 22, 23, 25; 21:6; 22:9; 25:18, Num 11:18, 34; 14:16; 16:38; 18:30; 22:34; 24:11; 31:17, Deu 4:15, 39, 40; 5:25, 32; 6:3; 7:9, 11; 9:3, 6; 10:16, 19; 11:1, 8, 18; 23:14; 25:19; 26:16; 27:10; 28:48; 29:9, 27; 30:19; 31:19, Jos 1:2; 3:12; 4:17; 7:12, 14; 9:23; 13:7; 22:26; 23:6, 11; 24:10, 14, 27, Jdg 3:8; 6:32; 7:3; 9:32; 11:13, 27; 17:3; 20:13, 42, Rut 3:3, 1Sm 1:7, 13, 28; 3:9; 5:11; 10:19; 11:10; 12:7; 14:41; 15:1, 25; 16:19; 18:21; 19:2; 20:8, 31; 23:2, 23, 25; 24:15; 25:8, 17; 26:8, 19, 20; 27:12; 28:15, 22; 31:4, 2Sm 2:7, 16, 23; 7:8, 29; 12:10, 16; 13:13, 33; 14:32; 17:16; 18:3; 19:7, 10, 20, 27; 22:25; 23:17, 1Kg 1:2, 12; 2:6, 9, 24; 3:9; 5:6; 8:25, 26, 61; 9:13; 11:11, 40; 12:4; 13:26; 14:12; 16:16; 18:19; 20:28, 42; 22:23, 34, 2Kg 2:17; 4:31; 5:27; 7:9, 12; 9:26; 10:19; 12:7[2]; 13:5; 15:16; 17:4, 18, 25, 26; 19:4, 18; 22:17, 1Ch 10:4, 14; 11:19; 17:7, 27; 23:11; 28:8; 29:10, 2Ch 2:15; 6:16, 17; 10:4; 17:5; 18:22, 33; 25:15; 28:5; 29:8; 30:17; 32:15, 25; 33:11; 34:25; 36:17, Neh 9:27, 30, 32; 13:28, Job 5:17; 22:13; 34:33; 42:8, Ps 2:10; 8:24; 1:6; 06:23, 26; 16:2; 43:4, Prv 1:31; 20:19, Isa 28:13, 22; 30:3; 37:4, 19; 43:28; 47:8; 52:5; 63:10, Jer 3:3; 6:11; 7:14; 11:8, 14; 14:10; 16:13; 18:11; 25:30; 26:13; 32:23; 42:22; 44:6, 22, Lam 1:9, Ezk 12:3; 16:27, 34, 50; 21:6, 14; 22:13, 31; 23:31; 32:32; 35:6; 44:2, Dan 1:8, 19; 9:14, 23, 25, Hos 5:12; 10:14, Ams 5:27; 7:16, Jon 1:14; 4:3, Mic 1:6, Hag 1:5, Zec 1:3; 7:12; 8:19, Mal 3:6

therefore *οὖν*

Mat 3:10; 5:48; 6:31, 34; 9:38; 10:31; 19:6; 21:40; 22:9, 21, 28; 24:42; 25:13; 27:64; 28:19, Mrk 10:9; 13:35, Lke 3:7, 9; 10:2; 11:35; 13:18; 14:33; 19:12; 20:33; 21:14; 23:16, 22, Joh 2:22; 3:29; 4:48; 7:25; 8:19; 11:45, 54; 12:50; 19:10, Act 2:30, 33, 36; 3:19; 8:22; 10:32, 33; 13:38, 40; 15:10, 27; 16:36; 17:12, 20, 23; 19:38; 21:23; 23:15; 25:17; 28:20, Rom 5:1, 9; 6:4, 12; 12:1; 13:10; 15:28, 1Co 6:15; 14:23, 2Co 5:11, Gal 5:1, Eph 4:1; 5:1, 7; 6:14, Php 2:23, 28, Col 2:6, 16; 3:5, Heb 2:14; 4:1, 6, 11; 10:19, 35, Jas 4:4, 7; 5:7, 16, 1Pe 2:7; 4:1, 7; 5:6, 2Pe 3:17, 1Es 2:5, 24, 28; 4:46; 6:21; 8:11, Tob 11:8, AEs 13:6; 16:17, 22, Wis 2:6; 6:1, 11, 21, Sir 0:2, LJr 1:3, 73, Man 1:8, 1Mc 11:37; 12:9, 11, 16, 53; 15:5, 19, 21, 2Mc 2:16[2], 32; 4:37; 6:9; 9:26; 11:26, 30, 3Mc 4:15, 4Mc 5:19; 7:20; 8:10

therein 1. בָּהּ 2. בָּהֶם 3. בָּהֵנָּה 4. בָּם 5. עָלֶיהָ 6. *δι᾽ αὐτοῦ* 7. *ἐν αὐτοῖς*

Lev 6: 3 all the things which men do and sin therein 3
Num16:46 censer, and put fire therein from off the altar 5
Jos 24:13 cities . . you had not built, and you dwell therein; 2
Ps 24: 1 the world and those who dwell therein; 1
35: 8 let them fall therein to ruin! 1
69:34 the seas and everything that moves therein. 4
Isa 35: 8 not pass over it, and fools shall not err therein. *
Nah 1: 5 the world and all that dwell therein. 1
Hab 2: 8 to the earth, to cities and all who dwell therein. 1
17 to the earth, to cities and all who dwell therein. 1
Rev 5:13 every creature . . and all therein, saying 7
12:12 Rejoice then, O heaven and you that dwell therein! 7
2Mc 11:17 and have asked about the matters indicated therein. 6

thereof

Ps 24: 1 The earth is the LORD'S and the fulness thereof †

thereon 1. בָּהּ 2. בָּם 3. עַל 4. *ἐπάνω*

Exd 30: 9 You shall offer no unholy incense thereon 3
9 and you shall pour no libation thereon. 3
31: 7 the ark . . and the mercy seat that is thereon 3
Isa 8:15 many shall stumble thereon; they shall fall 2
Zec 9: 2 Hamath also, which borders thereon 1
Mat 21: 7 and he sat thereon. 4

thereupon 1. עַל זֹאת 2. *ἐνταῦθα*

Jer 31:26 Thereupon I awoke and looked 1
3Mc 2:21 Thereupon God . . scourged him 2

therewith 1. בּוֹ

Lev 8: 7 of the ephod, binding it to him therewith 1

thick 1. אֲפֵלָה 2. בָּצוּר 3. כָּבֵד 4. כֹּבֶד 5. עָב 6. עבה 7. רַב 8. רֹחַב 9. *παχύς* 10. *πλάτος* 11. *πολύς*

Exd 10:22 hand toward heaven, and there was thick darkness 1
19: 9 Lo, I am coming to you in a thick cloud 5
16 a thick cloud upon the mountain 3
1Kg 12:10 little finger is thicker than my father's loins. 6
2Ch 10:10 little finger is thicker than my father's loins. 6
Ps 18:11 his canopy thick clouds dark with water. 5
Isa 30:27 burning with his anger, and in thick rising smoke; 4
Ezk 19:11 it towered aloft among the thick boughs; 6
24:12 its thick rust does not go out of it by fire. 7
41: 5 measured the wall of the temple, six cubits thick; 2
12 the wall of the building was five cubits thick 8
Zec 11: 2 for the thick forest has been felled! 2
Jdt 1: 2 hewn stones three cubits thick 10
LJr 1:13 which is thick upon them. 11
2Mc 1:20 they had not found fire but thick liquid 9

thick *See also* branch, cloud, darkness, grove, grow, pall.

thick-bossed 1. עֲבִי גַבֵּי

Job 15:26 against him with a thick-bossed shield; 1

thicken 1. קפא

Zep 1:12 the men who are thickening upon their lees 1

thicket 1. יַעַר 2. סְבֹךְ 3. סְבַךְ 4. עָב 5. *δρυμός*

Gen 22:13 a ram, caught in a thicket by his horns; 3
Isa 9:18 it kindles the thickets of the forest 3
10:34 He will cut down the thickets of the forest 3
21:13 In the thickets in Arabia you will lodge 1
Jer 4: 7 A lion has gone up from his thicket 2
29 every city takes to flight; they enter thickets; 4
1Mc 4:38 they saw bushes sprung up as in a thicket 5
9:45 on this side and on that, with marsh and thicket; 5

thickness 1. עֳבִי 2. רֹחַב

1Kg 7:26 Its thickness was a handbreadth; and its brim 1
2Ch 4: 5 Its thickness was a handbreadth; and its brim was 1
Jer 52:21 its thickness was four fingers 1
Ezk 40: 5 so he measured the thickness of the wall, one reed; 2
41: 9 The thickness of the outer wall of the side 2

thief 1. גַּנָּב 2. *κλέπτης* 3. *κλέπτω*

Exd 22: 2 If a thief is found breaking in, and is struck 1
7 if the thief is found, he shall pay double. 1
8 If the thief is not found, the owner of the house 1
Deu 24: 7 then that thief shall die; 1
Job 24:14 in the night he is as a thief. 1
30: 5 they shout after them as after a thief. 1
Ps 50:18 If you see a thief, you are a friend of his; 1
Prv 6:30 Do not men despise a thief if he steals to satisfy 1
29:24 The partner of a thief hates his own life; 1
Isa 1:23 princes are rebels and companions of thieves. 1
Jer 2:26 As a thief is shamed when caught 1
48:27 Was he found among thieves 1
49: 9 If thieves came by night, would they not destroy 1
Hos 7: 1 for they deal falsely, the thief breaks 1
Jol 2: 9 they enter through the windows like a thief. 1
Obd 1: 5 If thieves came to you, if plunderers by night 1
Zec 5: 4 it shall enter the house of the thief 1
Mat 6:19 consume and where thieves break in and steal 3
20 where thieves do not break in and steal. 3
24:43 in what part of the night the thief was coming 2
Lke 12:33 where no thief approaches and no moth destroys. 2
39 at what hour the thief was coming 2
Joh 10: 1 that man is a thief and a robber; 2
8 All who came before me are thieves and robbers; 2
10 The thief comes only to steal and kill 2
12: 6 because he was a thief 2
1Co 6:10 nor thieves, nor the greedy, nor drunkards 3
Eph 4:28 Let the thief no longer steal 3
1Th 5: 2 the day of the Lord will come like a thief 2
4 for that day to surprise you like a thief. 2
1Pe 4:15 let none of you suffer as a murderer, or a thief 2
2Pe 3:10 But the day of the Lord will come like a thief 2
Rev 3: 3 If you will not awake, I will come like a thief 2
16:15 ("Lo, I am coming like a thief! 2
Sir 5:14 shame comes to the thief 2
20:25 A thief is preferable to a habitual liar 2
LJr 1:57 to save themselves from thieves and robbers. 2

thigh 1. יְסוֹד 2. יָרֵךְ 3. פַּחַד 4. שׁוֹק 5. יַרְכָה (A) 6. *μηρός* 7. femur

Gen 24: 2 servant . . "Put your hand under my thigh 2
9 servant put his hand under the thigh of Abraham 2
32:25 he touched the hollow of his thigh; 2
25 of his thigh; and Jacob's thigh was put out of joint 2
31 he passed Penu'el, limping because of his thigh. 2
32 the hip which is upon the hollow of the thigh 2
32 touched the hollow of Jacob's thigh on the sinew 2
47:29 put your hand under my thigh, and promise to deal 2
Exd 28:42 from the loins to the thighs they shall reach; 2
29:22 take . . the right thigh (for it is a ram 4
27 consecrate . . the thigh of the priests' portion 4
Lev 7:32 the right thigh you shall give to the priest 4

33 shall have the right thigh for a portion 4
34 For the breast that is waved and the thigh 4
8:25 he took . . the right thigh 4
26 placed them on the fat and on the right thigh 4
9:21 the breasts and the right thigh Aaron waved 4
10:14 the breast that is waved and the thigh 4
15 The thigh that is offered and the breast 4
Num 5:21 when the LORD makes your thigh fall away 2
22 make your body swell and your thigh fall away.' 2
27 body shall swell, and her thigh shall fall away 2
6:20 together with . . the thigh that is offered; 4
18:18 as the breast that is waved and as the right thigh 4
Jdg 3:16 girded it on his right thigh under his clothes. 2
21 his left hand, took the sword from his right thigh 2
15: 8 he smote them hip and thigh with great slaughter; 2
Job 40:17 the sinews of his thighs are knit together. 3
Ps 45: 3 Gird your sword upon your thigh, O mighty one 2
Sng 3: 8 each with his sword at his thigh, against alarms 2
7: 1 Your rounded thighs are like jewels 2
Jer 31:19 and after I was instructed, I smote upon my thigh; 2
Ezk 21:12 Smite therefore upon your thigh. 2
24: 4 all the good pieces, the thigh and the shoulder; 2
Dan 2:32 arms of silver, its belly and thighs of bronze 5
Hab 3:13 of the wicked, laying him bare from thigh to neck. 1
Rev 19:16 and on his thigh he has a name inscribed 6
2Es 15:36 a man's thigh and a camel's hock. 7
Jdt 9: 2 and uncovered her thigh to put her to shame 6
Sir 19:12 Like an arrow stuck in the flesh of the thigh 6

thin 1. דַּק 2. דַּק בָּשָׂר 3. רַק 4. רַקּוֹת בָּשָׂר
Gen 41: 3 behold, seven other cows, gaunt and thin, came up 2
4 the gaunt and thin cows ate up the seven sleek 1
6 seven ears, thin and blighted by the east wind. 1
7 the thin ears swallowed up the seven plump 1
19 cows . . poor and very gaunt and thin 4
20 the thin and gaunt cows ate up the first seven 3
23 seven ears, withered, thin, and blighted 1
24 the thin ears swallowed up the seven good ears. 1
Lev 13:30 if . . the hair in it is yellow and thin 1

thing 1. אֶל 2. אֵלֶּה 3. דָּבָר 4. כְּלִי 5. מַעֲלָה 6. מַעֲשֶׂה 7. מִלָּה (A) 8. εἰμί 9. ἔργον 10. λόγος 11. πρᾶγμα 12. ῥῆμα 13. σκεῦος 14. qui 15. sermo
Gen 15: 1 After these things the word of the LORD came 3
18:25 Far be it from thee to do such a thing 3
20: 8 Abim'elech . . told them all these things; 3
9 have done to me things that ought not to be done. 6
10 What were you thinking of, that you did this thing 3
21:11 the thing was very displeasing to Abraham 3
26 who has done this thing; you did not tell me 3
22: 1 After these things God tested Abraham 3
20 Now after these things it was told Abraham 3
24:28 told her mother's household about these things. 3
50 The thing comes from the LORD; we cannot speak 3
66 told Isaac all the things that he had done. 3
29:13 Jacob told Laban all these things 1
32:19 shall say the same thing to Esau when you meet him 3
34:14 They said to them, "We cannot do this thing 3
19 the young man did not delay to do the thing 3
38:23 Judah replied, "Let her keep the things as her own *
41:32 dream means that the thing is fixed by God 3
44: 7 Far be it . . that they should do such a thing! 3
Exd 2:14 Moses . . thought, "Surely the thing is known. 3
9: 5 the LORD will do this thing in the land. 3
6 on the morrow the LORD did this thing; 3
18:18 for the thing is too heavy for you; you are not able 3
29:33 They shall eat those things *
33:17 This very thing that you have spoken I will do; 3
35: 1 These are the things which the LORD has 3
4 This is the thing which the LORD has commanded. 3
38:21 This is the sum of the things for the tabernacle *
Lev 2: 8 cereal offering that is made of these things *
4:13 the thing is hidden from the eyes of the assembly 3
5: 2 Or if any one touches an unclean thing 3
13 committed in any one of these things *
6: 3 in any of all the things which men do and sin *
7 he shall be forgiven for any of the things *
8: 5 Moses said to the congregation, "This is the thing 3
36 all the things which the LORD commanded by Moses 3
9: 6 This is the thing which the LORD commanded you 3
10:19 yet such things as these have befallen me *
13:54 that they wash the thing in which is the disease *
14:11 shall set . . these things before the LORD *
15:10 he who carries such a thing shall wash *
27 whoever touches these things shall be unclean *
17: 2 This is the thing which the LORD has commanded 3
18:24 Do not defile yourselves by any of these things *
20:23 did all these things, and therefore I abhorred *
Num 4:15 things of the tent of meeting which the sons *
15:13 who are native shall do these things in this way *
16: 9 is it too small a thing for you that the God *
13 Is it a small thing that you have brought us up *
35:29 these things shall be for a statute and ordinance *
Deu 1:14 'The thing that you have spoken is good for us to do.' 3
18 commanded you . . all the things that you should do. 3
23 The thing seemed good to me, and I took twelve men 3
4: 9 forget the things which your eyes have seen 3
19 things which the LORD your God has allotted *
30 tribulation, and all these things come upon you 3
32 ask . . whether such a great thing as this 3
17: 5 bring . . man or woman who has done this evil thing 3
18:12 does these things is an abomination to the LORD; *
22: 5 whoever does these things is an abomination *
20 if the thing is true, that the tokens of virginity 3
23: 9 you shall keep yourself from every evil thing. 3
27:15 image . . a thing made by the hands of a craftsman 6
30: 1 when all these things come upon you, the blessing 3
Jos 9:24 we feared greatly . . and did this thing. 3
23:14 not one thing has failed of all the good things 3
14 of all the good things which the LORD . . promised 3
15 just as all the good things . . have been fulfilled 3
15 the LORD will bring upon you all the evil things 3
24:29 After these things Joshua the son of Nun . . died 3
Jdg 6:29 they said to one another, "Who has done this thing? 3
29 Gideon the son of Jo'ash has done this thing. 3
11:37 Let this thing be done for me; let me alone two 3
13:23 or shown us all these things, or now announced *
23 or now announced to us such things as these. *
19:24 but against this man do not do so vile a thing. 3
1Sm 2:23 Why do you do such things? For I hear of your evil 3
3:11 I am about to do a thing in Israel 3
8: 6 But the thing displeased Samuel when they said 3
12:16 see this great thing, which the LORD will do 3
14:12 Come up to us, and we will show you a thing. 3
17:22 And David left the things in charge of the keeper 4
18:20 and they told Saul, and the thing pleased him. 3
19: 7 and Jonathan showed him all these things. 3
24: 6 LORD forbid that I should do this thing to my lord 3
25:37 his wife told him these things, and his heart died 3
26:16 This thing that you have done is not good. 3
28:10 shall come upon you for this thing. 3
18 therefore the LORD has done this thing to you 3
2Sm 2: 6 do good to you because you have done this thing. 3
3:13 I will make a covenant . . but one thing I require 3
11:11 as your soul lives, I will not do this thing. 3
27 the thing . . David had done displeased the LORD. 3
12: 6 because he did this thing, and . . he had no pity. 3
12 but I will do this thing before all Israel 3
21 What is this thing that you have done? 3
13:21 When King David heard of all these things 3
24: 3 why does my lord the king delight in this thing? 3
1Kg 1:27 Has this thing been brought about by my lord 3
11:10 had commanded him concerning this thing 3
12:24 Return . . for this thing is from me.' 3
30 this thing became a sin, for the people went 3
13:33 After this thing Jerobo'am did not turn 3
34 this thing became sin to the house of Jerobo'am 3
18:36 and that I have done all these things at thy word. 3
20: 9 but this thing I cannot do.' 3
2Kg 1: 7 who came to meet you and told you these things? 3
5:13 prophet had commanded you to do some great thing 3
6:11 was greatly troubled because of this thing; 3
7: 2 If the LORD himself should . . could this thing be? 3
19 If the LORD himself . . could such a thing be? 3
8:13 What is . . that he should do this great thing? 3
11: 5 This is the thing that you shall do 3
17: 9 Israel did . . things that were not right. 3
11 they did wicked things, provoking the LORD 3
20: 9 the LORD will do the thing that he has promised 3
23:16 the man of God . . who had predicted these things. 3
17 man of God who came . . and predicted these things *
1Ch 11:19 These things did the three mighty men. *
24 These things did Benai'ah the son of Jehoi'ada *
13: 4 the thing was right in the eyes of all the people. 3
21: 7 God was displeased with this thing, and he smote 3
8 sinned greatly in that I have done this thing. 3
23:26 tabernacle or any of the things for its service 4
29:17 I have freely offered all these things *
2Ch 4:18 made all these things in great quantities 4
19 Solomon made all the things that were 4
11: 4 for this thing is from me.' 3
20:25 found cattle . . clothing, and precious things 4
23: 4 This is the thing that you shall do 3
29:36 for the thing came about suddenly. 3
32: 1 things and these acts of faithfulness 3
Ezr 7:27 such a thing as this into the heart of the king *
9: 1 After these things had been done, the officials *
Neh 2:19 What is this thing that you are doing? 3
4: 2 Will they restore things? Will they sacrifice? *
5: 9 I said, "The thing that you are doing is not good. 3
6: 8 No such things as you say have been done 3
14 according to these things that they did 6
13:17 What is this evil thing which you are doing 3
Est 2: 1 After these things . . he remembered Vashti 3
3: 1 After these things . . Ahasu-e'rus promoted Haman 3
8: 5 and if the thing seem right before the king 3
9:20 And Mor'decai recorded these things 3
Job 3:25 For the thing that I fear comes upon me †
8: 2 How long will you say these things *
10:13 Yet these things thou didst hide in thy heart; *
12: 3 Who does not know such things as these? *
16: 2 I have heard many such things; 2
23:14 many such things are in his mind. *
28:11 the thing that is hid he brings forth to light. *
33:29 God does all these things, twice, three times *
42: 3 I did not understand, things too wonderful for me *
Ps 15: 5 He who does these things shall never be moved. *
35:11 they ask me of things that I know not. *
41: 8 They say, "A deadly thing has fastened upon him; 3
42: 4 These things I remember, as I pour out my soul *
50:21 These things you have done and I have been silent; *
78: 3 things that we have heard and known *
107:43 Whoever is wise, let him give heed to these things; *
Prv 11:13 trustworthy in spirit keeps a thing hidden. 3
25: 2 It is the glory of God to conceal things 3
2 but the glory of kings is to search things out. 3
Ecc 1: 8 All things are full of weariness; 3
10 Is there a thing of which it is said, "See, this is new"? 3
7: 8 Better is the end of a thing than its beginning; 3
21 Do not give heed to all the things that men say 3
8: 1 And who knows the interpretation of a thing? 3
11: 9 for all these things God will bring *
Isa 38: 7 the LORD will do this thing that he has promised 3
16 O Lord, by these things men live *
42:16 These are the things I will do 3
44:21 Remember these things, O Jacob, and Israel *
45: 7 I am the LORD, who do all these things. *
46:10 from ancient times things not yet done, saying *
47: 7 that you did not lay these things to heart *
9 These two things shall come to you in a moment *
48:14 Who among them has declared these things? *
57: 6 Shall I be appeased for these things? *
64:12 thou restrain thyself at these things, O LORD? *
66: 2 All these things my hand has made *
2 all these things are mine, says the LORD. *
8 Who . . heard such a thing? Who has seen such things? 2
Jer 7:13 And now, because you have done all these things 6
10:16 for he is the one who formed all things *
13:22 Why have these things come upon me? *
14:22 our hope on thee, for thou doest all these things. *
20: 1 heard Jeremiah prophesying these things. 3
26:10 When the princes of Judah heard these things 3
30:15 I have done these things to you. *
40: 3 this thing has come upon you. 3
16 You shall not do this thing 3
42: 3 way we should go, and the thing that we should do. 3
44: 4 Oh, do not do this abominable thing that I hate! 3
48:44 I will bring these things upon Moab *
52: 3 things came to such a pass in Jerusalem and Judah *
20 bronze of all these things was beyond weight. 4
Lam 1:16 For these things I weep; my eyes flow with tears; *
5:17 for these things our eyes have grown dim *
Ezk 11: 5 I know the things that come into your mind. 5
25 all the things that the LORD had showed me. 3
16: 5 No eye pitied you, to do any of these things to you *
30 did all these things, the deeds of a brazen harlot; *
43 but have enraged me with all these things; *
17:12 Do you not know what these things mean? *
15 Can a man escape who does such things? *
18 he gave his hand and yet did all these things *
21:26 things shall not remain as they are; *
24:19 Will you not tell us what these things mean for us *
Dan 2:10 no . . king has asked such a thing of any magician 7
11 thing that the king asks is difficult 7
6:12 The thing stands fast, according to the law 7
7:16 known to me the interpretation of the things. 7
12: 7 all these things would be accomplished. *
8 O my lord, what shall be the issue of these things? *
Hos 10: 6 Yea, the thing itself shall be carried to Assyria *
13:15 strip his treasury of every precious thing. 4
14: 9 Whoever is wise, let him understand these things; *
Nah 2: 9 of treasure, or wealth of every precious thing. 4
Zec 8:12 this people to possess all these things. *
16 These are the things that you shall do 3
17 for all these things I hate, says the LORD. *
Mat 21:23 By what authority are you doing these things *
24 by what authority I do these things. *
27 by what authority I do these things. *
26:10 she has done a beautiful thing to me. 9
Mrk 7:15 the things which come out of a man are what defile *
12:17 Render to Caesar the things that are Caesar's *
17 and to God the things that are God's. *
14: 6 She has done a beautiful thing to me. 9
Lke 1: 1 a narrative of the things 11
4 the truth concerning the things 10
2:15 Let us go over to Bethlehem and see this thing 12
19 Mary kept all these things 12
51 his mother kept all these things in her heart. 12
12:20 the things you have prepared, whose will they be?' *
19:42 that . . you knew the things that make for peace *
20:25 render to Caesar the things that are Caesar's *
25 to God the things that are God's. *
24:18 who does not know the things that have happened *
27 the things concerning himself. *
Act 10:16 the thing was taken up at once to heaven. 13
13:42 begged that these things might be told them 12
18:25 and taught accurately the things concerning Jesus *
19:32 Now some cried one thing, some another *
21:19 he related one by one the things that God had done *
34 Some in the crowd shouted one thing, some another; *
26:16 the things in which you have seen me *
Rom 6:21 get from the things of which you are now ashamed? *
21 The end of those things is death. *
8: 5 who . . set their minds on the things of the flesh *
5 who . . set their minds on the things of the Spirit. *
13: 6 ministers of God, attending to this very thing. *

1Co 1:28 even things that are not •
28 to bring to nothing things that are •
2Co 11:30 I will boast of the things that show my weakness. •
12: 4 he heard things that cannot be told 12
Eph 1:10 things in heaven and things on earth. •
10 things in heaven and things on earth. •
Col 3: 1 seek the things that are above, where Christ is •
2 Set your minds on things that are above •
2 not on things that are on earth. •
2Th 3: 4 and will do the things which we command. •
1Ti 1: 7 the things about which they make assertions. •
Heb 6:18 through two unchangeable things 11
9: 5 Of these things we cannot now speak in detail. •
11: 1 faith is . . the conviction of things not seen. 11
3 was made out of things which do not appear. •
1Pe 1:12 the things which have now been announced to you •
12 things into which angels long to look. •
2Pe 1: 8 For if these things are yours and abound •
9 For whoever lacks these things is blind •
12 I intend always to remind you of these things •
15 you may be able at any time to recall these things. •
1Jn 2:15 Do not love the world or the things in the world. •
Jde 1:10 by those things that they know by instinct •
Rev 22:19 who testifies to these things says, "Surely I am •
1Es 1:17 the things that had to do with the sacrifices •
3: 5 Let each of us state what one thing is strongest; 10
4:18 gold and silver or any other beautiful thing 11
19 gold or silver or any other beautiful thing. 11
2Es 1:37 they will believe the things I have said. 14
4: 9 things through which you have passed •
7:101 the things of which you have been told 15
Tob 3:10 When she heard these things •
6:17 When Tobias heard these things, he fell in love •
7: 8 speak of those things which you talked about •
10: 8 they will inform him how things are with you. •
Jdt 7:28 the things which we have described! 12
8: 1 At that time Judith heard about these things •
32 I am about to do a thing 11
9: 5 thou hast designed the things that are now •
5 Yea, the things thou didst intend came to pass •
6 the things thou didst will •
10: 9 accomplish the things about which you spoke 10
11: 9 Now as for the things Achior said in your council 10
16 things that will astonish the whole world 11
12: 4 your servant will not use up the things I have with me 8
13: 3 she had said the same thing to Bagoas. 12
15:11 and piled the things on them. •
AEs 12: 4 The king made a permanent record of these things 10
Wis 11:24 none of the things which thou hast made •
12: 2 warn them of the things wherein they sin •
13:18 a thing that is utterly inexperienced; •
18 a thing that cannot take a step; •
19 a thing whose hands have no strength. •
14:31 not the power of the things by which men swear •
Sir 17: 2 authority over the things upon the earth. •
42: 6 where there are many hands, lock things up. •
1Mc 4:27 things had not happened . . as he had intended •
5:37 After these things 12
6: 8 because things had not turned out for him •
9:10 to do such a thing as to flee from them 11
37 After these things it was reported to Jonathan 10
44 today things are not as they were before. •
10:22 When Demetrius heard of these things 10
88 When Alexander the king heard of these things 10
14:25 When the people heard these things they said 10
36 in his days things prospered in his hands •
16: 2 things have prospered in our hands •
2Mc 6:20 to refuse things that it is not right to taste •
12:14 even blaspheming and saying unholy things. •
4Mc 5:25 we know that in the nature of things •

thing *See also* abominable, accursed, any, astonishing, astounding, attractive, bad, beautiful, bitter, brought, clean, commanded, consecrated, cowardly, crawling, created, creeping, cruel, dead, deadly, deceitful, dedicated, deep, delicious, detestable, devise, devoted, diseased, earthly, easy, empty, evil, fat, fearful, filthy, following, formed, former, full, future, glorious, good, great, green, hallowed, hard, harsh, heavenly, hidden, holy, hoped, horrible, last, later, lifeless, light, little, living, lost, loved, loyal, made, make, marvelous, moving, mysterious, necessary, needed, new, noble, one, other, perishable, perverse, possessed, precious, predicted, present, profane, revealed, rotten, sacred, same, secret, seen, shameful, sinful, slight, small, smooth, some, speechless, strange, such, swarming, sweet, terrible, unclean, unfit, ungodly, unrighteous, unsavory, unseen, vain, very, vile, weak, what, whatever, which, wicked, winged, wonderful, wondrous, wooden, worldly, worse, worthless.

things *See* all, few, four, many, other, six, sum, teem, three, two.

think 1. אמר 2. בְּעֵינַיִם 3. דבר 4. דמה 5. דמה בְּנֶפֶשׁ 6. זכר 7. חשב 8. פלל 9. ראה 10. סבר (A) 11. ἀκούω 12. διαλογίζομαι 13. διαλογισμός 14. διανοέω 15. διάνοια 16. δοκέω 17. ἐνθυμέομαι 18. ἡγέομαι 19. κρίνω 20. λογίζομαι 21. μιμνήσκω 22. μνημονεύω 23. νοέω 24. νομίζω 25. νομιστέον 26. οἴομαι 27. πίπτω βουλή 28. ὑπολαμβάνω 29. φρήν 30. φρονέω 31. φροντίζω 32. cogito 33. intellego 34. puto

Gen 20:10 What were you thinking of, that you did this thing 9
11 Abraham said, "I did it because I thought 1
26: 7 feared to say, "My wife," thinking •
9 Isaac said to him, "Because I thought 1
31:31 I was afraid, for I thought that you would take 1
32: 8 thinking, "If Esau comes to the one company 1
20 For he thought, "I may appease him with the present 1
38:15 When Judah saw her, he thought her to be a harlot 7
48:11 Israel said to Joseph, "I had not thought to see 8
Exd 2:14 Moses was afraid, and thought, "Surely the thing is 1
32:14 LORD repented of the evil which he thought to do 3
Num 33:56 I will do to you as I thought to do to them. 4
36: 6 Let them marry whom they think best; 2
Jos 22:28 And we thought, If this should be said to us 1
Jdg 3:24 they thought, "He is only relieving himself •
15: 2 I really thought that you utterly hated her; 1
Rut 4: 4 I thought I would tell you of it, and say, Buy it 1
1Sm 16: 6 When they came, he looked on Eli'ab and thought 1
18:11 and Saul cast the spear, for he thought, "I will pin 1
17 Saul thought, "Let not my hand be upon him 1
21 Saul thought, "Let me give her to him, 1
25 Now Saul thought to make David fall by the hand 7
20: 3 and he thinks, 'Let not Jonathan know this 1
26 Saul did not say anything . . for he thought 1
27:11 David saved neither . . thinking 1
12 And A'chish trusted David, thinking 1
2Sm 3:19 all that Israel and . . Benjamin thought good 2
4:10 told me . . and thought he was bringing good news 2
5: 6 who said . . thinking, "David cannot come in here. 1
10: 3 Do you think . . that he is honoring your father? 2
14:15 your handmaid thought, 'I will speak to the king; 1
17 And your handmaid thought, 'The word of my lord 1
18:27 I think the running of the foremost is like 9
21:16 And Ish'bi-be'nob . . thought to kill David. 1
2Kg 5:11 I thought that he would surely come out to me 1
7:12 they have gone out . . thinking, 'When they come out 1
18:20 Do you think that mere words are strategy 1
20:19 For he thought, "Why not, if there will be peace 1
1Ch 19: 3 Do you think, because David has sent comforters •
2Ch 13: 8 you think to withstand the kingdom of the LORD 1
32: 1 thinking to win them for himself. 1
Neh 6: 9 For they all wanted to frighten us, thinking 1
Est 4:13 Think not that in the king's palace you will 5
Job 4: 7 Think now, who that was innocent ever perished? 6
6:26 Do you think that you can reprove words 7
21: 6 When I think of it I am dismayed 6
29:18 Then I thought, ' shall die in my nest 1
35: 2 Do you think this to be just? 7
41: 8 think of the battle; you will not do it again! 6
32 one would think the deep to be hoary. 7
Ps 10: 6 He thinks in his heart, "I shall not be moved; 1
11 He thinks in his heart, "God has forgotten 1
48: 9 We have thought on thy steadfast love, O God 4
50:21 you thought that I was one like yourself. 4
59: 7 for "Who," they think, "will hear us? •
63: 6 I think of thee upon my bed, and meditate on thee 6
64: 5 laying snares secretly, thinking, "Who can see us? 1
73:16 when I thought how to understand this 7
77: 3 I think of God, and I moan; I meditate 6
94:18 When I thought, "My foot slips," thy steadfast love 1
119:52 When I think of thy ordinances from of old 6
59 When I think of thy ways, I turn my feet to thy 7
144: 3 LORD, what is . . son of man that thou dost think 7
Isa 10: 7 does not so intend, and his mind does not so think; 7
36: 5 Do you think that mere words are strategy 1
39: 8 For he thought, "There will be peace and security 1
Jer 3: 7 And I thought, 'After she has done all this 1
19 I thought how I would set you among my sons 1
19 And I thought you would call me, My Father 1
22:15 think you are a king because you compete in cedar? •
23:27 who think to make my people forget my name 7
40: 4 go wherever you think it good and right to go. 2
5 or go wherever you think it right to go. 2
Lam 3:20 My soul continually thinks of it and is bowed 6
Ezk 11: 5 Thus says the LORD: So you think, O house of Israel; 1
20: 8 Then I thought I would pour out my wrath upon them 1
13 Then I thought I would pour out my wrath upon them 1
21 Then I thought I would pour out my wrath upon them 1
Dan 7:25 shall think to change the times and the law; 10
Mal 1: 7 By thinking that the LORD'S table may be despised. 1
3:16 who feared the LORD and thought on his name. 7
Mat 5:17 Think not that I have come to abolish the law 24
6: 7 for they think that they will be heard for their 16
9: 4 Why do you think evil in your hearts? 17
10:34 Do not think that I have come to bring peace 24
17:25 What do you think, Simon? 16
18:12 What do you think? 16
20:10 they thought they would receive more 24
21:28 What do you think? A man had two sons 16
22:17 Tell us, then, what you think. 16
42 What do you think of the Christ? Whose son is he? 16
26:53 Do you think that I cannot appeal to my Father 16
Mrk 6:49 they thought it was a ghost, and cried out; 16
Lke 8:18 what he thinks that he has will be taken away. 16
10:36 Which of these three, do you think 16
12:17 he thought to himself, 'What shall I do 12
51 you think that I have come to give peace on earth? 16
13: 2 he answered them, "Do you think 16
4 do you think that they were worse offenders 16
Joh 5:39 because you think that . . you have eternal life; 16
45 Do not think that I shall accuse you to the Father 16
11:13 they thought that he meant taking rest in sleep. 16
56 What do you think? That he will not come to the feast 16
13:29 Some thought that . . Jesus was telling him 16
16: 2 will think he is offering service to God. 16
Act 8:20 you thought you could obtain the gift of God 24
12: 9 thought he was seeing a vision. 16
17:29 we ought not to think that the Deity is like gold 24
26: 2 I think myself fortunate that it is before you 18
8 Why is it thought incredible by any of you 19
28 In a short time you think to make me a Christian! •
Rom 1:21 but they became futile in their thinking 13
12: 3 more highly than he ought to think 30
3 but to think with sober judgment 30
14:14 it is unclean for any one who thinks it unclean. 20
1Co 3:18 If any one among you thinks that he is wise 16
4: 9 I think that God has exhibited us apostles 16
7:26 I think that in view of the present distress 24
36 If any one thinks that he is not behaving 24
40 I think that I have the Spirit of God. 16
10:12 Therefore let any one who thinks that he stands 16
12:23 those parts of the body which we think less honorable 16
13:11 I thought like a child, I reasoned like a child; 30
14:20 Brethren, do not be children in your thinking 29
20 be babes in evil, but in thinking be mature. 29
37 If any one thinks that he is a prophet, or spiritual 16
2Co 9: 5 So I thought it necessary to urge the brethren 18
11: 5 I think that I am not in the least inferior 20
16 I repeat, let no one think me foolish 16
12: 6 so that no one may think more of me than he sees 20
19 Have you been thinking all along 16
Gal 6: 3 if any one thinks he is something 16
Eph 3:20 far more abundantly than all that we ask or think 23
Php 1:17 not sincerely but thinking to afflict me 26
2:25 I have thought it necessary to send to you 18
3: 4 If any other man thinks he has reason 16
Heb 10:29 How much worse . . do you think will be deserved 16
11:15 If they had been thinking of that land 22
Jas 1:26 If any one thinks he is religious 16
2Pe 1:13 I think it right, as long as I am in this body 18
1Es 2:20 we think it best not to neglect such a matter 28
2Es 4: 2 do you think you can comprehend . . the Most High? 32
51 Do you think that I shall live until those days? 34
6:34 Do not be quick to think vain thoughts 32
7:59 Weigh within yourself what you have thought 32
8:28 Think not on those who have lived wickedly 32
51 think of your own case 33
16:63 and what you think in your hearts! 32
Jdt 8:14 nor find out what a man is thinking 15
AEs 16:14 He thought that in this way he would find us 26
Wis 1: 1 think of the Lord with uprightness 30
3: 2 their departure was thought to be an affliction 20
5: 4 We thought that his life was madness 20
8:17 and thought upon them in my mind 31
12:27 creatures which they had thought to be gods 16
14:30 because they thought wickedly of God 30
15:15 thought that all their heathen idols were gods 20
17: 3 thinking that . . they were unobserved 24
Sir 13:26 to devise proverbs requires painful thinking. 13
15: 8 liars will never think of her. 21
16:23 This is what one devoid of understanding thinks; 14
23 a senseless and misguided man thinks foolishly. 14
17: 6 he gave them ears and a mind for thinking. 14
18:24 Think of his wrath on the day of death 21
25 In the time of plenty think of the time of hunger; 21
25 in the days of wealth think of poverty and need. •
LJr 1:56 Why . . must any one admit or think that they are gods 25
Bel 1: 6 Do you not think that Bel is a living God? 16
1Mc 4:45 they thought it best to tear it down 27
5:61 thinking to do a brave deed 26
2Mc 1:18 we thought it necessary to notify you 18
4:32 thinking he had obtained a . . opportunity 24
5:21 thinking in his arrogance that . . 26
7:16 do not think that God has forsaken our people. 16
19 do not think that you will go unpunished 24
9: 8 he who had just been thinking that . . 16
10 the man who a little while before had thought 16
12 no mortal should think that he is equal to God. 30
12:12 Judas, thinking that they might really be useful 28
13: 3 thought that he would be established in office. 26
14:14 flocked to join Nicanor, thinking that . . 16
37 Razis . . was very well thought of 11
40 for he thought that . . he would do them an injury. 16
3Mc 5:22 insults for those they thought to be doomed. 16
49 thought that this was their last moment of life 16
4Mc 1:33 I for one think so. 26
5:16 think that there is no compulsion more powerful 24
6:17 May we . . never think so basely 30
9:30 Do you not think, you most savage tyrant 16
13:14 Let us not fear him who thinks he is killing us 16

think about 1. λογίζομαι

Php 4: 8 think about these things. 1

think good 1. ἄξιος 2. ἀξιόω

Act 15:38 Paul thought best not to take with them one 1
2Mc 4:19 Those . . thought best not to use it for sacrifice 2

think highly 1. ὑπερφρονέω
Rom 12: 3 not to think of himself more highly than he ought 1

think it easy 1. הוּן
Deu 1:41 thought it easy to go up into the hill country. 1

think more fortunate 1. שָׁבַח מִן
Ecc 4: 2 I thought the dead . . more fortunate 1

must think 1. νομιστέον
LJr 1:40 Why then must any one think that they are gods 1
44 Why then must any one think that they are gods 1
64 Therefore one must not think that they are gods 1

never think 1. ἀνυπονόητος
Sir 11: 5 one who was never thought of has worn a crown. 1

think out 1. תמם 2. διανοέω
Ps 64: 6 We have thought out a cunningly conceived plot. 1
Sir 39:32 have thought this out and left it in writing 2

think over 1. νοέω
2Ti 2: 7 Think over what I say 1

think upon 1. διανοέω
Sir 39:12 I have yet more to say, which I have thought upon 1

thinking *See* way.

third 1. שְׁלִישִׁי 2. שלש 3. שָׁלֹשׁ 4. שְׁלֹשׁ 5. תְּלִיתָי (A) 6. תְּלָת (A) 7. תַּלְתִּי (A) 8. τρίτος 9. tertius
Gen 1:13 evening and there was morning, a third day 1
2:14 the name of the third river is Tigris 1
6:16 make it with lower, second, and third decks. 1
22: 4 On the third day Abraham lifted up his eyes 1
31:22 told Laban on the third day that Jacob had fled 1
32:19 He likewise instructed the second and the third 1
34:25 On the third day, when they were sore 1
40:20 On the third day, which was Pharaoh's birthday 1
42:18 On the third day Joseph said to them 1
Exd 19: 1 On the third new moon after the people of Israel 1
11 be ready by the third day; 1
11 for on the third day the LORD will come down 1
15 he said to the people, "Be ready by the third day; 3
16 On the morning of the third day there were 1
20: 5 to the third and the fourth generation 4
28:19 the third row a jacinth, an agate, and an amethyst; 1
34: 7 to the third and the fourth generation. 4
39:12 the third row, a jacinth, an agate, and an amethyst; 1
Lev 7:17 the sacrifice on the third day shall be burned 1
18 peace offering is eaten on the third day 1
19: 6 anything left over until the third day 1
7 If it is eaten at all on the third day, 1
Num 2:24 They shall set out third on the march. 1
7:24 On the third day Eli'ab . . of the men of Zeb'ulun 1
14:18 upon the third and upon the fourth generation.' 4
19:12 cleanse himself . . on the third day 1
12 if he does not cleanse himself on the third day 1
19 sprinkle . . on the third day and on the seventh 1
29:20 On the third day eleven bulls, two rams, fourteen 1
31:19 purify . . on the third day and on the seventh day. 1
Deu 5: 9 children to the third and fourth generation 4
23: 8 children of the third generation that are born 1
26:12 paying . . tithe of your produce in the third year 1
Jos 9:17 and reached their cities on the third day. 1
17:11 Manas'seh had . . the third is Naphath. 3
19:10 The third lot came up for the tribe of Zeb'ulun 1
Jdg 20:30 Israel went up . . on the third day, and set 1
1Sm 3: 8 And the LORD called Samuel again the third time. 1
17:13 and next to him Abin'adab, and the third Shammah. 1
20:12 When . . about this time tomorrow, or the third day 1
19 And on the third day you will be greatly missed; 2
30: 1 David and his men came to Ziklag on the third day 1
2Sm 1: 2 on the third day, behold, a man came from Saul's 1
3: 3 and the third, Ab'salom the son of Ma'acah 1
1Kg 3:18 on the third day after I was delivered, this woman 1
6: 6 and the third was seven cubits broad; 1
8 by stairs . . from the middle story to the third. 1
12:12 Jerobo'am . . came to Rehobo'am the third day 1
12 as the king said, "Come to me again the third day. 1
15:28 Ba'asha killed him in the third year of Asa 3
33 In the third year of Asa king of Judah 3
18: 1 word of the LORD came . . in the third year, saying 1
22: 2 in the third year Jehosh'aphat . . came down 1
2Kg 1:13 Again the king sent the captain of a third 50 1
13 the third captain of 50 went up, and came 1
18: 1 In the third year of Hoshe'a son of Elah 3
19:29 in the third year sow, and reap, and plant 1
20: 5 I will heal you; on the third day you shall go up 1
8 I . . go up to the house of the LORD on the third day? 1
1Ch 2:13 Jesse was the father of . . Shim'ea the third 1
3: 2 the third Ab'salom, whose mother was Ma'acah 1
15 sons of Josi'ah . . the third Zedeki'ah 1
8: 1 Benjamin was the father of . . Ahar'ah the third 1
39 sons of Eshek . . and Eliph'elet the third. 1
12: 9 Ezer the chief, Obadi'ah second, Eli'ab third 1
23:19 sons of Hebron . . Jaha'ziel the third 1
24: 8 the third to Harim, the fourth to Se-o'rim 1
23 sons of Hebron . . Jaha'ziel the third, Jeka-me'am 1
25:10 the third to Zaccur, his sons and his brethren, 1
26: 2 Meshelemi'ah had sons . . Zebadi'ah the third 1
4 O'bed-e'dom had sons . . Jo'ah the third, Sachar 1
11 Tebali'ah the third, Zechari'ah the fourth 1
27: 5 The third commander . . was Benai'ah, 1
5 third commander, for the third month, was Benai'ah 1
2Ch 10:12 all the people came to Rehobo'am the third day 1
12 as the king said, "Come to me again the third day. 1
15:10 in the third month of the fifteenth year 1
17: 7 In the third year of his reign he sent his princes 3
27: 5 same amount in the second and the third years. 1
31: 7 In the third month they began to pile up the heaps 1
Ezr 6:15 finished on the third day of the month of Adar 6
Est 1: 3 in the third year of his reign he gave a banquet 3
5: 1 On the third day Esther put on her royal robes 1
8: 9 summoned at that time, in the third month, 1
Job 42:14 and the name of the third Ker'en-hap'puch. 1
Isa 19:24 Israel will be the third with Egypt and Assyria 1
37:30 then in the third year sow and reap 1
Jer 38:14 received him at the third entrance of the temple 1
Ezk 10:14 and the third the face of a lion 1
31: 1 In the eleventh year, in the third month 1
Dan 2:39 arise . . yet a third kingdom of bronze 5
5: 7 shall be the third ruler in the kingdom. 7
16 shall be the third ruler in the kingdom. 6
29 that he should be the third ruler in the kingdom. 6
8: 1 third year of the reign of King Belshaz'zar 3
10: 1 In the third year of Cyrus king of Persia 3
Hos 6: 2 on the third day he will raise us up 1
Zec 6: 3 the third white horses, and the fourth chariot 1
Mat 16:21 and be killed, and on the third day be raised. 8
17:23 he will be raised on the third day 8
20: 3 going out about the third hour he saw others 8
19 he will be raised on the third day. 8
22:26 So too the second and third, down to the seventh. 8
26:44 he went away and prayed for the third time 8
27:64 to be made secure until the third day 8
Mrk 12:21 the third likewise; 8
15:25 it was the third hour, when they crucified him. 8
Lke 9:22 be killed, and on the third day be raised. 8
12:38 If he comes in the second watch, or in the third 8
13:32 the third day I finish my course. 8
18:33 on the third day he will rise. 8
20:12 another servant . . he sent yet a third 8
31 the first took a wife . . and the third took her 8
24: 7 crucified, and on the third day rise. 8
21 it is now the third day since this happened. 8
46 on the third day rise from the dead 8
Joh 2: 1 On the third day there was a marriage at Cana 8
21:14 This was now the third time 8
17 He said to him the third time, "Simon, son of John 8
17 he said to him the third time, "Do you love me? 8
Act 2:15 since it is only the third hour of the day; 8
10:40 God raised him on the third day 8
23:23 At the third hour of the night get ready 8
27:19 the third day they cast out . . the tackle 8
1Co 12:28 first apostles, second prophets, third teachers 8
15: 4 that he was raised on the third day 8
2Co 12: 2 a man in Christ . . caught up to the third heaven 8
Rev 4: 7 the third living creature with the face of a man 8
6: 5 When he opened the third seal, I heard 8
5 I heard the third living creature say, "Come! 8
8:10 The third angel blew his trumpet, and a great star 8
11:14 behold, the third woe is soon to come. 8
14: 9 And another angel, a third, followed them, saying 8
16: 4 The third angel poured his bowl into the rivers 8
21:19 every jewel . . the third agate 8
1Es 3:12 The third wrote, "Women are strongest 8
5:11 Then the third . . began to speak 8
2Es 5: 4 thrown into confusion after the third period; 9
6:42 On the third day thou didst command the waters 9
44 These were made on the third day. 9
51 which had been dried up on the third day 9
7:83 The third way, they shall see the reward laid up 9
94 The third order, they see the witness 9
11:18 Then the third wing raised itself up 9
14: 1 On the third day, while I was sitting under an oak 9
Tob 1: 8 the third tenth I would give to those 8
AEs 15: 1 On the third day, when she ended her prayer 8
Sir 23:16 a third incurs wrath 8
23 third, she has committed adultery 8
26:28 because of a third anger comes over me 8
45:23 Phinehas the son of Eleazar is the third in glory 8
50:25 the third is no nation: 8
1Mc 14:27 which is the third year of Simon 8
2Mc 7:10 the third was the victim of their sport 8
4Mc 10: 1 the third was led 8
15:18 nor when the third expired; 8

third *See also* day, time.

thirst 1. נֶפֶשׁ 2. צמא 3. צָמָא 4. צָמֵא 5. צִמְאָה 6. δίψα 7. διψάω 8. δίψος 9. sitis
Exd 17: 3 the people thirsted there for water 2
3 our children and our cattle with thirst? 4
Deu 28:48 serve your enemies . . in hunger and thirst 4
Jdg 15:18 shall I now die of thirst, and fall into the hands 4
2Ch 32:11 may give you over to die by famine and by thirst 4
Neh 9:15 water for them from the rock for their thirst 2
20 gavest them water for their thirst. 2
Ps 42: 2 My soul thirsts for God, for the living God. 2
63: 1 my God, I seek thee, my soul thirsts for thee; 2
69:21 for my thirst they gave me vinegar to drink. 2
104:11 wild asses quench their thirst. 2
143: 6 my soul thirsts for thee like a parched land. •
Isa 5:13 their multitude is parched with thirst. 4
29: 8 awakes faint, with his thirst not quenched 1
41:17 and their tongue is parched with thirst 4
48:21 thirsted not when he led them through . . deserts; 2
49:10 they shall not hunger or thirst 2
50: 2 fish stink for lack of water, and die of thirst. 4
55: 1 Ho, every one who thirsts, come to the waters; 3
Jer 2:25 Keep . . your throat from thirst. 5
Lam 4: 4 The tongue of the nursling cleaves . . for thirst; 4
Hos 2: 3 like a parched land, and slay her with thirst. 4
Ams 8:11 not a famine of bread, nor a thirst for water 4
13 the young men shall faint for thirst. 4
Mat 5: 6 those who hunger and thirst for righteousness 7
Joh 4:13 Every one who drinks . . will thirst again 7
14 water that I shall give him will never thirst 7
15 Sir, give me this water, that I may not thirst 7
6:35 he who believes in me shall never thirst. 7
7:37 If any one thirst, let him come to me and drink. 7
19:28 Jesus . . said (to fulfil the scripture), "I thirst. 7
1Co 4:11 To the present hour we hunger and thirst 7
2Co 11:27 in hunger and thirst, often without food 8
Rev 7:16 shall hunger no more, neither thirst any more; 7
2Es 8:59 so the thirst and torment which are prepared 9
15:58 and drink their own blood in thirst for water. 9
Jdt 7:13 thirst will destroy them 6
22 the women and young men fainted from thirst 6
25 to strew us on the ground before them with thirst 6
Wis 11: 4 When they thirsted they called upon thee 7
4 slaking of thirst from hard stone. 6
8 showing by their thirst at that time 8
14 their thirst was not like that of the righteous. 7
Sir 12:16 his thirst for blood will be insatiable. •
24:21 those who drink me will thirst for more. 7
4Mc 3: 6 the story of King David's thirst. 6
10 he could not satisfy his thirst from them. 6
15 David, although he was burning with thirst 6

thirst *See also* suffer.

thirst for honor 1. φιλοδοξία
4Mc 1:26 thirst for honor, rivalry, and malice; 1

thirsty 1. עָיֵף 2. צמא 3. צָמָא 4. צָמֵא 5. שקק 6. διψάω 7. δίψος 8. sitio
Jdg 4:19 give me a little water to drink; for I am thirsty. 2
15:18 he was very thirsty, and he called on the LORD 2
Rut 2: 9 when you are thirsty, go to the vessels and drink 2
2Sm 17:29 The people are hungry and weary and thirsty 4
Job 5: 5 the thirsty pant after his wealth. 6
Ps 107: 5 hungry and thirsty, their soul fainted within 4
9 For he satisfies him who is thirsty 5
Prv 25:21 if he is thirsty, give him water to drink; 4
25 Like cold water to a thirsty soul, so is good news 1
Isa 21:14 To the thirsty bring water, meet the fugitive 4
32: 6 and to deprive the thirsty of drink. 4
44: 3 For I will pour water on the thirsty land 4
65:13 my servants shall drink, but you shall be thirsty; 2
Ezk 19:13 in the wilderness, in a dry and thirsty land. 3
Mat 25:35 I was thirsty and you gave me drink 6
37 when did we see thee . . thirsty and give thee drink? 6
42 I was thirsty and you gave me no drink 6
44 Lord, when did we see thee hungry or thirsty 6
Rom 12:20 if he is thirsty, give him drink; 6
Rev 21: 6 To the thirsty I will give from the fountain 6
22:17 And let him who is thirsty come 6
2Es 1:17 When you were hungry and thirsty 8
20 When you were thirsty 8
22 thirsty and blaspheming my name 8
Jdt 8:30 the people were very thirsty 6
Sir 26:12 As a thirsty wayfarer opens his mouth 7
51:24 why are your souls very thirsty? 6
4Mc 3:10 the king was extremely thirsty 7

thirsty *See also* ground.

ever thirsty 1. לֹא שׂבע
Prv 30:16 earth ever thirsty for water, and the fire 1

thirsty man 1. צָמֵא
Isa 29: 8 as when a thirsty man dreams he is drinking 1

thirteen 1. שְׁלֹשׁ עֶשְׂרֵה
Gen 17:25 Ish'mael his son was thirteen years old 1
Num 29:13 burnt offering . . thirteen young bulls 1
14 three tenths . . for each of the thirteen bulls 1
Jos 19: 6 thirteen cities with their villages; 1
21: 4 received by lot from . . thirteen cities. 1
6 Gersonites received by lot . . thirteen cities. 1
19 The cities . . were in all thirteen cities 1
33 in all thirteen cities with their pasture lands. 1
1Kg 7: 1 Solomon was building . . thirteen years 1
1Ch 6:60 All their cities . . were thirteen. 1
62 Gershomites . . were allotted thirteen cities 1

26:11 the sons and brethren of Hosah were thirteen. 1
Ezk 40:11 and the breadth of the gateway, thirteen cubits. 1

thirteenth 1. שְׁלֹשׁ עֶשְׂרֵה 2. τρισκαιδέκατος

Gen 14: 4 in the thirteenth year they rebelled. 1
1Ch 24:13 the thirteenth to Huppah, the fourteenth 1
25:20 thirteenth, Shu'ba-el, his sons and his brethren 1
Est 3:12 summoned on the thirteenth day of the first month 1
13 in one day, the thirteenth day of the twelfth month 1
8:12 on the thirteenth day of the twelfth month 1
9: 1 month of Adar, on the thirteenth day of the same 1
17 was on the thirteenth day of the month of Adar 1
18 on the thirteenth day and on the fourteenth 1
Jer 1: 2 Josi'ah . . in the thirteenth year of his reign. 1
25: 3 from the thirteenth year of Josi'ah the son of Amon 1
AEs 16:20 the thirteenth day of the twelfth month, Adar 2
1Mc 7:43 on the thirteenth day of the month of Adar 2
49 on the thirteenth day of Adar. 2
2Mc 15:36 the thirteenth day of the twelfth month 2

thirtyfold 1. τριάκοντα

Mrk 4: 8 thirtyfold and sixtyfold and a hundredfold. 1
20 thirtyfold and sixtyfold and a hundredfold. 1

this side and that 1. ἑκάτερος 2. ἔνθεν καὶ ἔνθεν

1Mc 9:45 the water of the Jordan is on this side and on that 2
2Mc 5: 3 and counterattacks made on this side and on that 1
3Mc 2:22 He shook him on this side and that 2

thistle 1. דַּרְדַּר 2. חוֹחַ 3. τρίβολος

Gen 3:18 thorns and thistles it shall bring forth to you; 1
2Kg 14: 9 A thistle on Lebanon sent to a cedar on Lebanon 2
9 a wild beast . . and trampled down the thistle. 2
2Ch 25:18 A thistle on Lebanon sent to a cedar on Lebanon 2
18 wild beast . . trampled down the thistle. 2
Isa 34:13 nettles and thistles in its fortresses. 2
Hos 10: 8 Thorn and thistle shall grow up on their altars; 1
Mat 7:16 gathered from thorns, or figs from thistles? 3
Heb 6: 8 if it bears thorns and thistles 3

thither 1. הֲלֹם 2. עָדֶיהָ 3. שָׁם 4. שָׁמָּה

Exd 26:33 bring the ark of the testimony in thither within 4
Deu 12: 5 thither you shall go 4
6 thither you shall bring your burnt offerings 4
11 thither you shall bring all that I command you 4
Jdg 5:14 From E'phraim they set out thither •
18:15 they turned aside thither, and came to the house 4
21:10 the congregation sent thither 12,000 3
1Sm 14:16 the multitude was surging hither and thither. 1
Neh 13: 9 brought back thither the vessels of the house 3
Job 6:20 they come thither and are confounded. 2
Isa 55:10 come down from heaven, and return not thither 4
57: 7 and thither you went up to offer sacrifice. 3

thong 1. אֲגֻדָּה 2. מוֹסֵר 3. שְׂרוֹךְ 4. ἱμάς

Gen 14:23 that I would not take a thread or a sandal-thong 3
Isa 5:27 is loose, not a sandal-thong broken; 3
58: 6 to undo the thongs of the yoke 1
Jer 27: 2 Make yourself thongs and yoke-bars 2
Mrk 1: 7 the thong of whose sandals 4
Lke 3:16 thong of whose sandals I am not worthy to untie 4
Joh 1:27 the thong of whose sandal I am not worthy to untie. 4
Act 22:25 when they had tied him up with the thongs 4
Sir 33:26 Yoke and thong will bow the neck 4
4Mc 9:11 bound his hands and arms with thongs on each side. 4

thorn 1. אָטָד 2. חֵדֶק 3. חוֹחַ 4. נַעֲצוּץ 5. סִיר 6. סַלּוֹן 7. צֵן 8. צְנִינִ 9. קוֹץ 10. קִמּוֹשׂ 11. שַׁיִת 12. שָׁמִיר 13. ἄκανθα 14. ἀκάνθινος 15. σκόλοψ 16. spina

Gen 3:18 thorns and thistles it shall bring forth to you; 9
Exd 22: 6 When fire breaks out and catches in thorns 9
Num33:55 be as pricks in your eyes and thorns in your sides 8
Jos 23:13 a scourge on your sides, and thorns in your eyes 8
Jdg 8: 7 will flail . . with the thorns of the wilderness 9
16 and he took thorns of the wilderness and briers 9
2Sm 23: 6 godless men . . like thorns that are thrown away; 9
Job 5: 5 the hungry eat, and he takes it even out of thorns; •
31:40 let thorns grow instead of wheat 3
Ps 58: 9 Sooner than your pots can feel the heat of thorns 1
118:12 they blazed like a fire of thorns; 9
Prv 15:19 The way of a sluggard is overgrown with thorns 2
22: 5 Thorns and snares are in the way of the perverse; 7
24:31 lo, it was all overgrown with thorns; 10
26: 9 Like a thorn that goes up into the hand 3
Ecc 7: 6 For as the crackling of thorns under a pot, 5
Isa 5: 6 not be . . hoed, and briers and thorns shall grow up; 11
7:23 every place . . will become briers and thorns. 11
24 for all the land will be briers and thorns; 11
25 not come there for fear of briers and thorns; 11
9:18 like a fire, it consumes briers and thorns; 11
10:17 burn and devour his thorns and briers in one day. 11
27: 4 Would that I had thorns and briers to battle! 12
32:13 soil of my people growing up in thorns and briers; 9
33:12 like thorns cut down, that are burned in the fire. 9
34:13 Thorns shall grow over its strongholds 5
55:13 Instead of the thorn shall come up the cypress; 4
Jer 4: 3 and sow not among thorns. 9
12:13 They have sown wheat and have reaped thorns 9
Ezk 2: 6 though briers and thorns are with you 6
28:24 no more a brier to prick or a thorn to hurt them 9
Hos 2: 6 Therefore I will hedge up her way with thorns; 5
9: 6 thorns shall be in their tents. 3
10: 8 Thorn and thistle shall grow up on their altars; 9
Nah 1:10 Like entangled thorns they are consumed 5
Mat 7:16 Are grapes gathered from thorns 13
13: 7 Other seeds fell upon thorns 13
7 and the thorns grew up and choked them. 13
22 As for what was sown among thorns 13
27:29 plaiting a crown of thorns they put it on his head 13
Mrk 4: 7 Other seed fell among thorns 13
7 the thorns grew up and choked it 13
18 others are the ones sown among thorns 13
15:17 plaiting a crown of thorns they put it on him. 14
Lke 6:44 figs are not gathered from thorns 13
8: 7 some fell among thorns 13
7 and the thorns grew with it and choked it. 13
14 as for what fell among the thorns 13
Joh 19: 2 the soldiers plaited a crown of thorns 13
5 Jesus came out, wearing the crown of thorns 14
2Co 12: 7 a thorn was given me in the flesh 15
Heb 6: 8 if it bears thorns and thistles 13
2Es 16:32 and all its paths shall bring forth thorns 16
77 and its path overwhelmed with thorns 16
Sir 28:24 See that you fence in your property with thorns 13
43:19 when it freezes, it becomes pointed thorns. 15

thorn *See also* bush, camel's, hedge.

thoroughfare 1. διέξοδος τῶν ὁδῶν

Mat 22: 9 Go therefore to the thoroughfares, and invite 1

thoroughly 1. רבה 2. δυνατός 3. πάντα τρόπον

Gen 11: 3 let us make bricks, and burn them thoroughly. †
Exd 21:19 and shall have him thoroughly healed. †
Ps 51: 2 Wash me thoroughly from my iniquity 1
Jer 6: 9 Glean thoroughly as a vine the remnant of Israel; †
Jdt 11: 8 you are . . thoroughly informed 2
4Mc 1:29 and ties up and waters and thoroughly irrigates 3

thoroughly *See also* glean, scourge.

though 1. אִם 2. אֲשֶׁר 3. בְּ 4. גַּם 5. גַּם כִּי 6. וְ 7. כְּ 8. כִּי 9. כִּי אִם 10. עוֹד 11. רַק 12. כָּל־קֳבֵל דִּי (A) 13. γάρ 14. δέ 15. ἐάν 16. εἰ 17. καθόσπερ 18. καί 19. καὶ ἄν 20. καίπερ 21. μέν 22. ὅτι 23. ὡς 24. ὡσανεί 25. ὥσπερ 26. quasi 27. si

Exd 7: 3 and though I multiply my signs and wonders •
Lev 5: 1 to testify, and though he is a witness •
17 though he does not know it, yet he is guilty 6
13:55 though the disease has not spread, it is unclean 6
26:37 they shall stumble . . though none pursues 6
Num 5:13 is undetected though she has defiled herself 6
14 jealous . . though she has not defiled herself; 6
20 though you are under your husband's authority •
29 when a wife, though under her husband's authority •
18:27 as though it were the grain of the threshing 7
22:18 Though Balak were to give me his house 1
35:23 so that he died, though he was not his enemy 6
Deu 15:22 eat it, as though it were a gazelle or a hart. •
19: 6 mortally, though the man did not deserve to die 6
21:18 though they chastise him, will not give heed •
22:24 she did not cry for help though she was in the city •
27 though the betrothed young woman cried for help •
29:19 though I walk in the stubbornness of my heart.' 8
Jos 5: 5 Though all the people who came out had been 8
17:18 though it is a forest, you shall clear it •
18 drive out . . though they have chariots of iron 8
18 though they have . . and though they are strong. 8
Rut 2:13 you have comforted me and . . though I am not one 6
1Sm 14:39 though it be in Jonathan my son, he shall . . die. 9
15:17 Though you are little in . . are you not the head 1
20:20 shoot three arrows . . as though I shot at a mark. •
24:11 I have not sinned . . though you hunt my life 6
2Sm 3:39 And I am this day weak, though anointed king; 6
2Kg 3: 2 He did what was evil . . though not like his father 11
25: 4 though the Chalde'ans were around the city. 6
1Ch 5: 2 though Judah became strong among his brothers 8
26:10 for though he was not the first-born •
2Ch 24:24 Though the army of the Syrians had come 8
Ezr 2:59 those who came up . . though they could not prove 6
3:12 wept . . though many shouted aloud for joy; 6
Neh 1: 9 though your dispersed be under the farthest 1
Est 4:16 I will go to the king, though it is against the law; 2
Job 8: 7 though your beginning was small •
9:15 Though I am innocent, I cannot answer him; 1
20 Though I am innocent, my own mouth would condemn 1
20 though I am blameless, he would prove me perverse. 1
10:19 and were as though I had not been 2
14: 8 Though its root grow old in the earth 1
20: 6 Though his height mount up to the heavens 1
12 Though wickedness is sweet in his mouth 1
12 in his mouth, though he hides it under his tongue •
13 though he is loath to let it go, and holds it •
27:16 Though he heap up silver like dust 1
33:14 though man does not perceive it. •
34: 6 incurable, though I am without transgression. •
39:16 though her labor be in vain, yet she has no fear; •
40:23 confident though Jordan rushes against his 8
41:26 Though the sword reaches him, it does not avail; •
Ps 23: 4 Even though I walk through the valley 8
27: 3 Though a host encamp against me 1
3 heart shall not fear; though war arise against me 1
35:14 as though I grieved for my friend or my brother; 7
37:10 though you look well at his place, he will not be 6
24 though he fall, he shall not be cast headlong 8
36 though I sought him, he could not be found. 6
44:17 though we have not forgotten thee, or been false 6
46: 2 we will not fear though the earth should change 3
2 though the mountains shake in the heart of the sea; 3
3 though its waters roar and foam •
3 though the mountains tremble with its tumult. •
49:11 though they named lands their own. •
18 Though, while he lives, he counts himself happy 8
18 though a man gets praise when he does well 8
68:13 though they stay among the sheepfolds– 1
92: 7 though the wicked sprout like grass 3
95: 9 put me to the proof, though they had seen my work. 4
119:61 Though the cords of the wicked ensnare me •
138: 6 For though the LORD is high, he regards the lowly; 8
7 Though I walk in the midst of trouble 1
Prv 6:35 nor be appeased though you multiply gifts. 8
26:26 though his hatred be covered with guile •
29:19 for though he understands, he will not give heed. •
Ecc 4:12 though a man might prevail against one 1
8:12 Though a sinner does evil . . yet I know that 2
17 even though a wise man claims to know 1
9:16 wisdom is better than might, though the poor man's 6
10:14 A fool multiplies words, though no man knows •
Isa 1:15 though you make many prayers, I will not listen; 8
18 though your sins are like scarlet 1
18 though they are red like crimson 1
6:13 though a tenth remain in it, it will be burned 10
10:22 For though your people Israel be as the sand 1
12: 1 O LORD, for though thou wast angry with me 8
17:10 therefore, though you plant pleasant plants •
11 though you make them grow on the day •
22: 3 were captured, though they had fled far away. •
30: 4 For though his officials are at Zo'an 8
20 though the Lord give you the bread of adversity 6
45: 4 I surname you, though you do not know me. 6
5 am the LORD . . I gird you, though you do not know me 6
63:16 art our Father, though Abraham does not know us 8
Jer 2:22 Though you wash yourself with lye 9
5: 2 Though they say, "As the LORD lives 1
22 though the waves toss, they cannot prevail 6
22 though they roar, they cannot pass over it. 6
11:11 though they cry to me, I will not listen to them. 6
12: 6 believe them not, though they speak fair words 8
14: 7 Though our iniquities testify against us 1
12 Though they fast, I will not hear their cry 8
12 and though they offer burnt offering 8
15: 1 Though Moses and Samuel stood before me 1
22:24 though Coni'ah the son of Jehoi'akim, king of Judah 9
26: 5 I send to you urgently, though you have not heeded 6
31:32 though I was their husband, says the LORD. 6
32: 5 though you fight against the Chalde'ans 8
25 though the city is given into the hands 6
33 and though I have taught them persistently 6
35 to Molech, though I did not command them 2
46:23 cut down her forest . . though it is impenetrable 8
49:16 Though you make your nest as high as the eagle's 8
50:11 Though you rejoice, though you exult 8
11 Though you rejoice, though you exult 8
11 though you are wanton as a heifer at grass 8
51:53 Though Babylon should mount up to heaven 8
53 and though she should fortify her strong height 8
Lam 3: 8 though I call and cry . . he shuts out my prayer; 5
32 though he cause grief, he will have compassion 1
Ezk 2: 6 though briers and thorns are with you 8
8:18 though they cry in my ears with a loud voice •
11:16 Though I removed them far off among the nations 8
16 and though I scattered them among the countries 8
12: 3 though they are a rebellious house. 8
14:18 though these three men were in it, as I live 6
15: 7 though they escape from the fire •
26:21 though you be sought for, you will never be found 6
28: 2 though you consider yourself as wise as a god 6
9 though you are but a man, and no god 6
33:13 Though I say to the righteous that he shall 3
14 though I say to the wicked, 'You shall surely die 3
Dan 5:22 not humbled your heart, though you knew all this 12
11:33 though they shall fall by sword and flame 6
Hos 3: 1 though they turn to other gods 6
4:15 Though you play the harlot, O Israel 1
8:10 Though they hire allies among the nations 5
9:16 Even though they bring forth, I will slay 8
13:15 Though he may flourish as the reed plant 8
Ams 5:22 Even though you offer me your burnt offerings 1
9: 2 Though they dig into Sheol 1
2 though they climb up to heaven 1
3 Though they hide themselves on the top of Carmel 1
3 though they hide from my sight at the bottom 1
4 And though they go into captivity 1
Obd 1: 4 Though you soar aloft like the eagle 1
4 though your nest is set among the stars 1
16 and shall be as though they had not been. 7
Nah 1:12 says the LORD, "Though they be strong and many 1

12 Though I have afflicted you, I will afflict you no 6
Hab 3:17 Though the fig tree do not blossom 8
Zep 1:13 Though they build houses, they shall not inhabit 6
13 though they plant vineyards, they shall not 6
Zec 9: 2 Tyre and Sidon, though they are very wise. 8
10: 6 they shall be as though I had not rejected them; 2
9 Though I scattered them among the nations 6
Mal 2:14 though she is your companion and your wife 6
Mat 14: 5 though he wanted to put him to death *
26:33 Though they all fall away because of you 16
60 though many false witnesses came forward *
Mrk 14:29 Even though they all fall away, I will not. 16
Lke 11: 8 though he will not get up and give him anything 16
18: 4 Though I neither fear God nor regard man 16
Joh 2: 9 though the servants who had drawn the water knew 14
9:25 one thing I know, that though I was blind, now I see. *
11:25 who believes in me, though he die, yet shall he live 19
12:37 Though he had done so many signs before them *
Act 3:12 as though . . we have made him walk? 23
7: 5 though he had no child. *
13:28 Though they could charge him with nothing *
17:25 as though he needed anything *
18:25 though he knew only the baptism of John. *
23:15 as though you were going to determine his case 23
20 as though they were going to inquire . . about him 23
28: 4 Though he has escaped from the sea *
17 though I had done nothing against the people *
19 though I had no charge to bring against my nation. 23
Rom 1:32 Though they know God's decree *
3: 4 Let God be true though every man be false 14
5: 7 though . . for a good man one will dare even to die 13
9: 6 But it is not as though the word of God had failed. 22
11 though they were not yet born *
27 Though the number of the sons of Israel be 15
12: 5 so we, though many, are one body in Christ *
1Co 3:15 though he himself will be saved 14
4:15 For though you have countless guides in Christ 15
18 Some are arrogant, as though I were not coming 23
5: 3 For though absent in body I am present in spirit *
7:29 who have wives live as though they had none 23
30 those who mourn as though they were not mourning 23
30 who rejoice as though they were not rejoicing 23
30 those who buy as though they had no goods 23
31 as though they had no dealings with it 23
9:19 For though I am free from all men *
20 though not being myself under the law *
12:12 all the members of the body, though many, are one *
15: 6 though some have fallen asleep. 14
10 though it was not I, but the grace of God 14
2Co 4:16 Though our outer nature is wasting away 16
5:16 even though we once regarded Christ 16
7: 8 I do not regret it (though I did regret it) 16
8 that letter grieved you, though only for a while. 16
8: 9 though he was rich *
10: 3 For though we live in the world *
14 as though we did not reach you 23
12: 6 Though if I wish to boast, I shall not be a fool 13
11 even though I am nothing. 16
13: 7 though we may seem to have failed. 14
Gal 2: 3 though he was a Greek. *
14 If you, though a Jew, live like a Gentile *
4: 1 though he is the owner of all the estate; *
14 though my condition was a trial to you *
Eph 3: 8 To me, though I am the very least of all the saints *
Php 2: 6 who, though he was in the form of God, did not count *
3: 4 Though I myself have reason for confidence 20
Col 2: 5 though I am absent in body 16
1Th 2: 2 though we had already suffered *
6 though we might have made demands *
1Ti 1:13 though I formerly blasphemed and persecuted *
Phm 1: 8 Accordingly, though I am bold enough in Christ *
Heb 5:12 For though by this time you ought to be teachers *
6: 9 Though we speak thus 16
7: 5 though these also are descended from Abraham. 20
11:39 all these, though well attested by their faith *
12:17 though he sought it with tears. 20
13: 3 as though in prison with them 23
Jas 3: 4 Look at the ships also; though they are so great *
1Pe 1: 6 though now for a . . while you may have to suffer 16
7 gold which though perishable is tested by fire 14
8 though you do not now see him you believe in him *
3: 1 though they do not obey the word 16
4: 6 that though judged in the flesh like men 21
12 as though something strange were happening 23
2Pe 1:12 though you know them and are established 20
2:11 angels, though greater in might and power *
2Jn 1: 5 I beg you, lady, not as though I were writing you 23
12 Though I have much to write to you *
Jde 1: 5 though you were once for all fully informed *
Rev 1:17 When I saw him, I fell at his feet as though dead. 23
5: 6 I saw a Lamb standing, as though it had been slain 23
1Es 1:48 though King Nebuchadnezzar had made him swear *
5:37 though they could not prove . . 18
53 though the temple of God was not yet built. 18
2Es 1:27 It is not as though you had forsaken me 26
37 though they do not see me with bodily eyes *
3:33 though they are unmindful of thy commandments. *
7:72 because though they had understanding *
72 and though they received the commandments *
72 and though they obtained the law *
118 For though it was you who sinned 27
8:58 though knowing full well that they must die. *
9:32 though our fathers received the law *
43 though I lived with my husband 30 years. *
13:20 come into these things, though incurring peril *
Tob 14: 5 though it will not be like the former one *
AEs 11:10 from their cry, as though from a tiny spring 24
Wis 2: 2 hereafter we shall be as though we had never been; 23
3: 4 For though in the sight of men they were punished 15
4: 7 though he die early 15
7:27 Though she is but one, she can do all things *
8:10 though I am young. *
11: 9 though they were being disciplined in mercy 20
14 though they had mockingly rejected him *
12: 9 though thou wast not unable *
10 though thou wast not unaware *
14:11 though part of what God created *
17 they might flatter the absent one as though present. 23
15:15 though these have neither the use of their eyes *
17:10 though it nowhere could be avoided. *
18: 2 thy holy ones, though previously wronged *
13 For though they had disbelieved everything *
19: 2 though they . . permitted thy people to depart *
Sir 40: 6 afterward in his sleep, as though he were on watch 23
42:10 though married, lest she be barren. *
43:27 Though we speak much we cannot reach the end *
44: 9 who have perished as though they had not lived; 23
9 they have become as though they had not been born 23
LJr 1:14 though unable to destroy any one who offends it. *
18 as though he were sentenced to death 23
19 though their gods can see none of them. *
41 as though Bel were able to understand. 23
Aza 1:16 as though it were with burnt offerings of rams 23
Sus 1:53 though the Lord said, 'Do not put to death *
1Mc 10:77 went to Azotus as though he were going farther 23
12: 9 Therefore, though we have no need of these things *
2Mc 2:21 though few in number *
6:16 Though he disciplines us with calamities *
30 though I might have been saved from death *
7:16 mortal though you are *
20 Though she saw her seven sons perish *
12: 3 as though there were no ill will to the Jews; 23
18 though in one place he had left a . . garrison. *
14:45 though his blood gushed forth *
3Mc 2: 9 though you have no need of anything *
24 though he had been punished *
3: 8 The Greeks in the city, though wronged in no way *
4:15 though uncompleted it stopped after 40 days. *
5:40 as though we are idiots 23
4Mc 4:25 though they had known beforehand *
5:22 as though living by it were irrational 25
6: 5 as though being tortured in a dream; 25
7 though he fell to the ground *
16 as though more bitterly tormented by this counsel 25
27 though I might have saved myself *
7: 2 though buffeted by the stormings of the tyrant *
12 though being consumed by the fire *
13 though he was an old man *
8:27 though about to be tortured *
9: 5 as though . . you learned nothing from Eleazar 25
14 though broken in every member *
22 as though transformed by fire into immortality 25
14: 5 as though running . . toward immortality 25
6 as though moved by . . devotion 23
19 as though with an iron dart sting 17
15:11 though so many factors influenced the mother 20
16: 5 though a mother 20
13 as though having a mind like adamant 25

though *See also* even.

thought 1. אמר 2. דָּבָר 3. הִגָּיוֹן 4. חֶשְׁבּוֹן 5. לֵב 6. מַדָּע 7. מְזִמָּה 8. מַחֲשָׁבָה 9. עַשְׁתּוּת 10. רוּחַ 11. רֵעַ 12. שִׂיחַ 13. שְׂעִפִּים 14. שַׂרְעַפִּים 15. רַעְיוֹן (A) 16. *διαλογισμός* 17. *διανόημα* 18. *διάνοια* 19. *ἐνθυμέομαι* 20. *ἐνθύμημα* 21. *ἐνθύμησις* 22. *ἐννόημα* 23. *ἔννοια* 24. *ἐπίνοια* 25. *καρδία* 26. *λέγω* 27. *λογισμός* 28. *μαρτυρία* 29. *μιμνήσκω* 30. *νόημα* 31. *ὑπονόημα* 32. cogitamentum 33. cogitatio 34. cogitatus 35. sensus

Gen 6: 5 and that every imagination of the thoughts 8
Deu 15: 9 be a base thought in your heart, and you say 2
1Ch 28: 9 LORD . . understands every plan and thought. 8
29:18 keep for ever such purposes and thoughts 8
Job 4:13 Amid thoughts from visions of the night 13
12: 5 In the thought of one who is at ease 9
20: 2 Therefore my thoughts answer me 13
21:27 Behold, I know your thoughts 8
Ps 10: 4 all his thoughts are, "There is no God. 7
33:11 the thoughts of his heart to all generations. 8
40: 5 LORD my God, thy wondrous deeds and thy thoughts 8
56: 5 all their thoughts are against me for evil. 8
92: 5 O LORD! Thy thoughts are very deep! 8
94:11 the LORD, knows the thoughts of man 8
139: 2 thou discernest my thoughts from afar. 11
17 How precious to me are thy thoughts, O God! 11
23 Try me and know my thoughts! 14
Prv 1:23 behold, I will pour out my thoughts to you; 10
12: 5 The thoughts of the righteous are just; 8
15:26 thoughts of the wicked are an abomination 8
Ecc 9:10 there is no work or thought or knowledge 4
10:20 Even in your thought, do not curse the king 6
Isa 55: 7 his way, and the unrighteous man his thoughts; 8
8 For my thoughts are not your thoughts 8
8 For my thoughts are not your thoughts 8
9 your ways and my thoughts than your thoughts. 8
9 your ways and my thoughts than your thoughts. 8
57:11 and did not remember me, did not give me a thought? 5
59: 7 their thoughts are thoughts of iniquity 8
7 their thoughts are thoughts of iniquity 8
66:18 For I know their works and their thoughts 8
Jer 4:14 How long shall your evil thoughts lodge within 8
Lam 3:62 lips and thoughts of my assailants are against 3
Ezk 20:32 the thought, 'Let us be like the nations 1
38:10 On that day thoughts will come into your mind 2
Dan 2:29 in bed came thoughts of what would be hereafter 15
30 that you may know the thoughts of your mind. 15
4:19 dismayed for a moment, and his thoughts alarmed 15
5: 6 color changed, and his thoughts alarmed 15
10 Let not your thoughts alarm you 15
7:28 As for me, Daniel, my thoughts greatly alarmed me 15
Ams 4:13 and declares to man what is his thought; 12
Mic 4:12 But they do not know the thoughts of the LORD 8
Mat 9: 4 Jesus, knowing their thoughts, said 21
12:25 Knowing their thoughts, he said to them 21
15:19 For out of the heart come evil thoughts, murder 16
Mrk 7:21 out of the heart of man, come evil thoughts 16
Lke 2:35 thoughts out of many hearts may be revealed. 16
6: 8 he knew their thoughts 16
9:47 Jesus perceived the thought of their hearts 16
11:17 he, knowing their thoughts, said to them 17
Rom 2:15 their conflicting thoughts accuse . . them 27
1Co 2:11 what person knows a man's thoughts *
11 So also no one comprehends the thoughts of God *
3:20 the thoughts of the wise are futile. 16
2Co 10: 5 take every thought captive to obey Christ 30
11: 3 your thoughts will be led astray 30
1Ti 3: 7 moreover he must be well thought of by outsiders 28
Heb 4:12 discerning the thoughts . . of the heart. 21
Jas 2: 4 and become judges with evil thoughts? 16
1Pe 4: 1 arm yourselves with the same thought 23
1Es 3:20 It turns every thought to feasting and mirth 18
4:21 with no thought of his father or his mother 29
2Es 3: 1 and my thoughts welled up in my heart 33
5:21 the thoughts of my heart were very grievous to me 33
6:34 Do not be quick to think vain thoughts *
7:22 they devised for themselves vain thoughts 32
92 to overcome the evil thought which was formed 32
9:39 the thoughts with which I had been engaged 34
10:31 your understanding and the thoughts of your mind 35
13:38 with their evil thoughts and the torments 32
14:14 put away from you mortal thoughts 33
15 the thoughts that are most grievous to you 32
16:54 their imaginations and their thoughts 33
Tob 8:10 with the thought, "Perhaps he too will die. 26
Jdt 8:14 and find out his mind or comprehend his thought 27
Wis 1: 3 For perverse thoughts separate men from God 27
5 and will rise and depart from foolish thoughts 27
2:14 He became to us a reproof of our thoughts; 23
6:16 meets them in every thought. 24
7:15 have thought worthy of what I have received 19
11:15 In return for their foolish and wicked thoughts 27
Sir 3:24 wrong opinion has caused their thoughts to slip. 18
8:19 Do not reveal your thoughts to every one 25
21:11 Whoever keeps the law controls his thoughts 22
22:17 A mind settled on an intelligent thought 18
23: 2 O that whips were set over my thoughts 17
24:29 for her thought is more abundant than the sea 17
25: 7 With nine thoughts I have gladdened my heart 31
27: 4 so a man's filth remains in his thoughts. 27
6 the expression of a thought 27
33: 5 and his thoughts like a turning axle. 16
40: 2 their anxious thought is the day of death 24
42:20 No thought escapes him 17
Bar 2: 8 from the thoughts of his wicked heart. 30
2Mc 2: 2 nor to be led astray in their thoughts 18
12:45 it was a holy and pious thought 24

thought *See also* fix, give, take.

no thought 1. שׁוּב
Mic 2: 8 who pass by trustingly with no thought of war. 1

thoughtful 1. *διανοέω* 2. *πολυφροντίς*
Wis 9:15 this earthy tent burdens the thoughtful mind. 2
Sir 31:15 in every matter be thoughtful. 1

thoughtful people 1. *διανοέω*
Sir 27:12 among thoughtful people stay on. 1

thoughtless 1. *ἀλόγιστος*
Wis 12:25 as to thoughtless children 1

thoughtless *See also* utterance.

thousand 1. אֶלֶף 2. שִׁנְאָן 3. אֲלַף (A) 4. μυριάς 5. χιλίας
Gen 24:60 be the mother of thousands of ten thousands; 1
Exd 18:21 place such men . . as rulers of thousands 1
25 Moses . . made them . . rulers of thousands 1
20: 6 showing steadfast love to thousands of those 1
34: 7 keeping steadfast love for thousands 1
Num31: 5 provided, out of the thousands of Israel 1
14 officers of the army, the commanders of thousands 1
48 officers who were over the thousands of the army 1
48 the officers . . the captains of thousands 1
52 offering . . from the commanders of thousands 1
54 received . . from the commanders of thousands 1
Deu 1:15 heads over you, commanders of thousands 1
5:10 steadfast love to thousands of those who love me 1
33:17 such are the thousands of Manas'seh. 1
1Sm 8:12 he will appoint . . commanders of thousands 1
10:19 present . . by your tribes and by your thousands. 1
18: 7 Saul has slain his thousands 1
8 and to me they have ascribed thousands; 1
21:11 Saul has slain his thousands 1
22: 7 will he make you all commanders of thousands 1
23:23 search him out among all the thousands of Judah. 1
29: 2 were passing on by hundreds and by thousands 1
5 'Saul has slain his thousands 1
2Sm 18: 1 and set over them commanders of thousands 1
4 army marched out by hundreds and by thousands. 1
1Ch 12:20 chiefs of thousands in Manas'seh 1
13: 1 commanders of thousands and of hundreds 1
15:25 David and . . and the commanders of thousands 1
26:26 officers of the thousands and the hundreds 1
27: 1 commanders of thousands and hundreds 1
28: 1 the commanders of thousands, the commanders 1
29: 6 the commanders of thousands and of hundreds 1
2Ch 1: 2 to the commanders of thousands and of hundreds 1
17:14 Of Judah, the commanders of thousands 1
25: 5 under commanders of thousands and of hundreds 1
Ps 68:17 twice 10,000, thousands upon thousands 1
17 twice 10,000, thousands upon thousands 2
119:72 better . . than thousands of gold and silver 1
Jer 32:18 who showest steadfast love to thousands 1
Dan 7:10 1,000 thousands served him, 3
Mic 6: 7 Will the LORD be pleased with thousands of rams 1
Lke 14:31 whether he is able with ten thousand to meet him 5
Act 21:20 how many thousands there are among the Jews 4
Rev 5:11 angels, numbering . . thousands of thousands 5
11 angels, numbering . . thousands of thousands 5
2Mc 11: 4 his thousands of cavalry, and his 80 elephants. 5

thousands *See* bring, captain, charge, ten, tens.

many thousands 1. μυριάς
Lke 12: 1 so many thousands of the multitude 1

thread 1. חוּט 2. פָּתִיל
Gen 14:23 that I would not take a thread or a sandal-thong 1
Exd 39: 3 gold leaf was hammered and cut into threads 2
Jdg 16:12 he snapped the ropes off his arms like a thread. 1
Sng 4: 3 Your lips are like a scarlet thread 1
Jer 51:13 your end has come, the thread of your life is cut. †

thread *See also* break.

scarlet thread 1. שָׁנִי
Gen 38:28 took and bound on his hand a scarlet thread 1
30 his brother came out with the scarlet thread 1

threat 1. אֶמְרָה 2. גְּעָרָה 3. ἀπειλέω 4. ἀπειλή
Isa 30:17 1,000 shall flee at the threat of one 2
17 at the threat of five you shall flee 2
Lam 2:17 The LORD has done . . has carried out his threat; 1
Act 4:29 now, Lord, look upon their threats 4
9: 1 Saul, still breathing threats and murder 4
Man 1: 5 wrath of thy threat to sinners is irresistible; 4
3Mc 2:24 but went away uttering bitter threats. 4
5:18 the king . . with sharp threats demanded to know why 4
43 suffered an unexpected and dangerous threat 4
4Mc 4: 8 uttering threats, Apollonius went 3
24 all his threats and punishments 4
8:19 consider the threats of torments 4
9:32 the threats that come from impiety 4
14: 9 yes, not only heard the direct word of threat 4

threaten 1. דבר 2. חשב 3. ἀπειλέω 4. ἀπειλή 5. διαπειλέω 6. λαλέω 7. στυγνάζω 8. comminor 9. horridus
Ps 73: 8 with malice; loftily they threaten oppression. 1
Jon 1: 4 the ship threatened to break up. 2
Mat 16: 3 for the sky is red and threatening 7
Eph 6: 9 forbear threatening 4
1Pe 2:23 when he suffered, he did not threaten; 3
2Es 15:34 and their appearance is very threatening 9
16:11 The Lord will threaten 8
Jdt 8:16 God is not like man, to be threatened 3
AEs 11: 9 they feared the evils that threatened them •
Sir 19:17 Question your neighbor before you threaten him; 3
Bar 2: 7 calamities with which the Lord threatened us 6
3Mc 4:19 After he had threatened them severely 3
5:30 with a threatening look he said 4
37 he said in a threatening tone 4
6:23 he wept and angrily threatened his friends 5
7: 6 we very severely threatened them for these acts 5
4Mc 9: 5 threatening us with death by torture 3
13: 6 towers . . hold back the threatening waves 4

threaten further 1. προσαπειλέω
Act 4:21 when they had further threatened them 1

threaten to destroy 1. ὀλεθροφόρος
4Mc 8:19 this arrogance that threatens to destroy us? 1

three 1. שְׁלִישִׁי 2. שלש 3. שָׁלֹשׁ 4. תְּלָת (A) 5. τρεῖς 6. τρίς 7. τρίτος 8. tres
Gen 6:10 Noah had three sons, Shem, Ham, and Japheth. 3
7:13 and Noah's wife and the three wives of his sons 3
9:19 These three were the sons of Noah; 3
18: 2 behold, three men stood in front of him. 3
6 Make ready quickly three measures of fine meal 3
29: 2 lo, three flocks of sheep lying beside it; 3
34 because I have borne him three sons"; 3
30:36 he set a distance of three days' journey 3
38:24 About three months later Judah was told 3
40:10 on the vine there were three branches; 3
12 This is its interpretation: the three branches 3
12 the three branches are three days; 3
13 within three days Pharaoh will lift up your head 3
16 there were three cake baskets on my head 3
18 the three baskets are three days; 3
18 the three baskets are three days; 3
19 within three days Pharaoh will lift up 3
42:17 put them all together in prison for three days. 3
Exd 2: 2 he was a goodly child, she hid him three months. 3
3:18 go a three days' journey into the wilderness 3
5: 3 let us go . . a three days' journey 3
8:27 We must go three days' journey 3
10:22 darkness in all the land of Egypt three days; 3
23 nor did any rise from his place for three days; 3
15:22 they went three days in the wilderness 3
23:14 Three times in the year you shall keep a feast 3
17 Three times in the year shall all your males 3
25:32 three branches of the lampstand out of one side 3
32 three branches of the lampstand out of one side 3
33 three cups made like almonds, each with capital 3
33 and three cups made like almonds 3
27: 1 the altar . . its height shall be three cubits. 3
14 with three pillars and three bases. 3
14 with three pillars and three bases. 3
15 with three pillars and three bases. 3
15 with three pillars and three bases. 3
34:23 Three times in the year shall all your males 3
24 before the LORD your God three times in the year. 3
37:18 three branches of the lampstand out of one side 3
18 three branches of the lampstand out of the other 3
19 three cups made like almonds, each with capital 3
19 three cups made like almonds, each with capital 3
38: 1 it was square, and three cubits was its height. 3
14 hangings . . three pillars and three bases. 3
14 hangings . . three pillars and three bases. 3
15 hangings . . three pillars and three bases. 3
15 hangings . . three pillars and three bases. 3
Lev 19:23 three years it shall be forbidden to you 3
25:21 that it will bring forth fruit for three years 3
27: 6 a female your valuation shall be three shekels 3
Num10:33 set out . . three days' journey; 3
33 ark . . went before them three days' journey 3
12: 4 Come out, you three, to the tent of meeting. 3
4 And the three of them came out. 3
22:28 that you have struck me these three times? 3
32 Why have you struck your ass these three times? 3
33 ass . . turned aside before me these three times. 3
24:10 behold, you have blessed them these three times. 3
33: 8 went a three days' journey in the wilderness of Etham 3
35:14 You shall give three cities beyond the Jordan 3
14 shall give . . three cities in the land of Canaan 3
Deu 4:41 Moses set apart three cities in the east 3
14:28 At the end of every three years you shall bring 3
16:16 Three times a year all your males shall appear 3
17: 6 On the evidence of two . . or of three witnesses 3
19: 2 set apart three cities for you in the land 3
7 command you, You shall set apart three cities. 3
9 you shall add three other cities to these three 3
9 you shall add three other cities to these three 3
15 evidence of two witnesses, or of three witnesses 3
Jos 1:11 within three days you are to pass over this 3
2:16 Go . . and hide yourselves there three days 3
22 into the hills, and remained there three days 3
3: 2 At the end of three days the officers went 3
9:16 At the end of three days after they had made 3
15:14 Caleb drove out from there the three sons of Anak 3
18: 4 Provide three men from each tribe, and I will send 3
21:32 Ham'moth-dor . . and Kartan . . three cities. 3
Jdg 1:20 and he drove out from it the three sons of Anak. 3
7:16 he divided the 300 men into three companies 3
20 the three companies blew the trumpets and broke 3
9:22 Abim'elech ruled over Israel three years. 3
43 his men and divided them into three companies 3
14:14 they could not in three days tell what the riddle 3
16:15 You have mocked me these three times, and you have 3
19: 4 made him stay, and he remained with him three days; 3
1Sm 1:24 she took him up . . along with a three-year-old bull 3
2:13 come . . with a three-pronged fork in his hand 3
21 and bore three sons and two daughters. 3
9:20 As for your asses that were lost three days ago 3
10: 3 three men going up to God at Bethel will meet you 3
3 three men . . one carrying three kids, another 3
3 another carrying three loaves of bread 3
11:11 Saul put the people in three companies; 3
13:17 And raiders came out . . in three companies; 3
17:13 The three eldest sons of Jesse had followed Saul 3
13 the names of his three sons who went to the battle 3
14 the three eldest followed Saul 3
20:20 And I will shoot three arrows to the side of it 3
41 David rose from beside . . and bowed three times; 3
30:12 or drunk water for three days and three nights. 3
12 or drunk water for three days and three nights. 3
13 left me . . because I fell sick three days ago. 3
31: 6 Saul died, and his three sons, and his armor-bearer 3
8 they found Saul and his three sons fallen 3
2Sm 2:18 And the three sons of Zeru'iah were there 3
6:11 the ark of the LORD remained . . three months; 3
13:38 and went to Geshur, and was there three years. 3
14:27 were born to Ab'salom three sons, and one daughter 3
18:14 he took three darts in his hand, and thrust them 3
20: 4 Call . . Judah together to me within three days 3
21: 1 a famine in the days of David for three years 3
23: 8 Josheb-basshe'beth . . he was chief of the three; 1
9 next . . among the three mighty men was Elea'zar 3
13 And three of the 30 chief men went down 3
16 Then the three mighty men broke through the camp 3
17 These things did the three mighty men. 3
18 and slew them, and won a name beside the three. 3
19 but he did not attain to the three. 3
22 and won a name beside the three mighty men. 3
23 but he did not attain to the three. 3
24:13 Shall three years of famine come . . in your land? 5
13 Or will you flee three months before your foes 3
13 there be three days' pestilence in your land? 3
1Kg 2:39 it happened at the end of three years that two 3
6:36 three courses of hewn stone and one course 3
7: 2 it was built upon three rows of cedar pillars 5
4 There were window frames in three rows 3
4 and window opposite window in three tiers. 3
5 and window was opposite window in three tiers. 3
12 The great court had three courses of hewn stone 3
25 twelve oxen, three facing north, three facing 3
25 twelve oxen . . three facing west, three facing 3
25 twelve oxen . . three facing south, and three 3
25 twelve oxen . . south, and three facing east; 3
27 long, four cubits wide, and three cubits high. 3
9:25 Three times a year Solomon used to offer up 3
10:17 three minas of gold went into each shield; 3
22 Once every three years the fleet . . used to come 3
12: 5 Depart for three days, then come again to me. 3
15: 2 He reigned for three years in Jerusalem. 3
17:21 he stretched himself upon the child three times 3
22: 1 For three years Syria and Israel continued 3
2Kg 2:17 for three days they sought him but did not find 3
3:10 The LORD has called these three kings to give 3
13 No; it is the LORD who has called these three kings 3
9:32 Two or three eunuchs looked out at him. 3
13:18 Strike . . "; and he struck three times, and stopped. 3
19 now you will strike down Syria only three times. 3
25 Three times Jo'ash defeated him and recovered 3
17: 5 to Sama'ria, and for three years he besieged it. 3
18:10 and at the end of three years he took it. 3
23:31 and he reigned three months in Jerusalem. 3
24: 1 and Jehoi'akim became his servant three years; 3
8 Jehoi'achin . . and he reigned three months 3
25:17 the height of the capital was three cubits; 3
18 took . . and the three keepers of the threshold; 3
1Ch 2: 3 these three Bath-shu'a the Canaanitess bore 3
16 Abi'shai, Jo'ab, and As'ahel, three. 3
3:23 Eli-o-e'nai, Hizki'ah, and Azri'kam, three. 3
7: 6 sons of Benjamin: Bela, Becher, and Jedi'a-el, three. 3
10: 6 he and his three sons and all his house died 3
11:11 Jasho'be-am, a Hach'monite, was chief of the three; •
12 next . . among the three mighty men was Elea'zar 3
15 Three of the 30 chief men went down to the rock 3
18 the three mighty men broke through the camp 3
19 These things did the three mighty men. 3
20 slew them, and won a name beside the three. 3
21 he did not attain to the three. 3
24 won a name beside the three mighty men. 3
25 but he did not attain to the three. 3
12:39 with David for three days, eating and drinking 3
13:14 in his house three months 3
21:12 either three years of famine; 3
12 or three months of devastation by your foes 3
12 or else three days of the sword of the LORD 3
23: 8 Jehi'el the chief, and Zetham, and Jo'el, three. 3
9 of Shim'e-i: Shelo'moth, Ha'zi-el, and Haran, three. 3
23 The sons of Mushi: Mahli, Eder, and Jer'emoth, three. 3
25: 5 had given Heman . . sons and three daughters. 3
2Ch 4: 4 It stood upon twelve oxen, three facing north 3
4 It stood upon twelve oxen . . three facing west 3
4 It stood upon twelve oxen . . three facing south 3

4 stood upon twelve oxen .. and three facing east; 3
6:13 bronze platform .. wide, and three cubits high 3
8:13 commandment .. for .. the three annual feasts- 3
9:21 once every three years the ships of Tarshish 3
10: 5 He said to them, "Come to me again in three days. 3
11:17 for three years they made Rehobo'am .. secure 3
17 walked for three years in the way of David 3
13: 2 He reigned for three years in Jerusalem. 3
20:25 three days in taking the spoil, it was so much. 3
31:16 males from three years old and upwards 3
36: 2 he reigned three months in Jerusalem. 3
9 reigned three months and ten days in Jerusalem. 3
Ezr 6: 4 with three courses of great stones 4
8:15 Aha'va, and there we encamped three days. 3
32 came to Jerusalem .. remained three days. 3
10: 8 that if any one did not come within three days 3
9 assembled at Jerusalem within the three days; 3
Neh 2:11 I came to Jerusalem and was there three days. 3
Est 4:16 a fast .. and neither eat nor drink for three days 3
Job 1: 2 were born to him seven sons and three daughters. 3
4 they would send and invite their three sisters 3
17 The Chalde'ans formed three companies 3
2:11 when Job's three friends heard of all this evil 3
32: 1 these three men ceased to answer Job 3
3 he was angry also at Job's three friends 3
5 was no answer in the mouth of these three men 3
42:13 He had also seven sons and three daughters. 3
Isa 16:14 In three years, like the years of a hireling 3
17: 6 three berries in the top of the highest bough 3
20: 3 naked and barefoot for three years as a sign 3
Jer 36:23 As Jehu'di read three or four columns 3
38:10 Take three men with you from here 3
52:24 priest, and the three keepers of the threshold; 3
Ezk 14:14 even if these three men, Noah, Daniel, and Job 3
16 even if these three men were in it 3
18 though these three men were in it, as I live 3
40:10 there were three side rooms on either side 3
10 the three were of the same size; 3
21 Its side rooms, three on either side, and its jambs 3
48 of the gate were three cubits on either side. 3
41: 6 the side chambers were in three stories 3
16 and round about all three had windows 3
22 an altar of wood, three cubits high 3
42: 3 was gallery against gallery in three stories. 1
6 For they were in three stories 2
48:31 three gates, the gate of Reuben, the gate of Judah 3
32 three gates, the gate of Joseph, the gate 3
33 three gates, the gate of Simeon, the gate 3
34 three gates, the gate of Gad, the gate of Asher 3
Dan 1: 5 educated for three years, and at the end 3
3:23 these three men, Shadrach, Meshach, and Abed'nego 4
24 Did we not cast three men bound into the fire? 4
6: 2 over them three presidents, 4
10 got down upon his knees three times a day 4
13 but makes his petition three times a day. 4
7: 5 had three ribs in its mouth between its teeth; 4
8 before which three of the first horns 4
20 other horn .. before which three of them fell 4
24 different .. and shall put down three kings. 4
10: 2 days I, Daniel, was mourning for three weeks. 3
3 ate no delicacies .. for the full three weeks. 3
11: 2 Behold, three more kings shall arise in Persia; 3
Ams 1: 3 For three transgressions of Damascus 3
6 For three transgressions of Gaza, and for four 3
9 For three transgressions of Tyre, and for four 3
11 For three transgressions of Edom, and for four 3
13 For three transgressions of the Ammonites 3
2: 1 For three transgressions of Moab, and for four 3
4 For three transgressions of Judah, and for four 3
6 For three transgressions of Israel, and for four 3
4: 4 every morning, your tithes every three days; 3
7 when there were yet three months to the harvest; 3
8 three cities wandered to one city to drink water 3
Jon 1:17 Jonah was in the belly of the fish three days 3
17 belly of the fish three days and three nights. 3
3: 3 great city, three days' journey in breadth. 3
Zec 11: 8 In one month I destroyed the three shepherds. 3
Mat 12:40 For as Jonah was three days and three nights 5
40 For as Jonah was three days and three nights 5
40 For as Jonah was three days and three nights 5
40 For as Jonah was three days and three nights 5
13:33 in three measures of flour 5
15:32 because they have been with me now three days 5
17: 4 if you wish, I will make three booths here 5
18:16 by the evidence of two or three witnesses. 5
20 For where two or three are gathered in my name 5
26:61 to build it in three days.' 5
27:40 destroy the temple and build it in three days 5
63 'After three days I will rise again.' 5
Mrk 8: 2 because they have been with me now three days 5
31 be killed, and after three days rise again. 5
9: 5 let us make three booths 5
31 when he is killed, after three days he will rise. 5
10:34 after three days he will rise. 5
14:58 in three days I will build another 5
15:29 destroy the temple and build it in three days 5
Lke 1:56 Mary remained with her about three months 5
2:46 After three days they found him in the temple 5
4:25 the heaven was shut up three years and six months 5
9:33 let us make three booths 5
10:36 Which of these three, do you think 5
11: 5 Friend, lend me three loaves; 5
12:52 three against two and two against three; 5
52 three against two and two against three; 5
13: 7 Lo, these three years I have come seeking fruit 5
21 took and hid in three measures of flour 5
Joh 2:19 this temple, and in three days I will raise it up. 5
20 and will you raise it up in three days? 5
Act 5: 7 After an interval of about three hours 5
7:20 brought up for three months in his father's house; 5
9: 9 for three days he was without sight 5
10:16 This happened three times 6
19 three men are looking for you. 5
11:10 This happened three times 6
11 three men arrived at the house in which we were 5
17: 2 for three weeks he argued with them 5
19: 8 and for three months spoke boldly 5
20: 3 There he spent three months 5
25: 1 after three days he went up to Jerusalem 5
28: 7 entertained us hospitably for three days. 5
11 After three months we set sail 5
12 we stayed there for three days. 5
17 After three days he called together .. leaders 5
1Co 13:13 So faith, hope, love abide, these three 5
14:27 let there be only two or at most three 5
29 Let two or three prophets speak 5
2Co 13: 1 by the evidence of two or three witnesses. 5
Gal 1:18 Then after three years I went up to Jerusalem 5
1Ti 5:19 except on the evidence of two or three witnesses. 5
Heb 10:28 at the testimony of two or three witnesses. 5
Jas 5:17 for three years and six months it did not rain 5
1Jn 5: 8 three witnesses, the Spirit, the water .. blood 5
8 and these three agree. 5
Rev 6: 6 and three quarts of barley for a denarius 5
8:13 trumpets which the three angels .. blow! 5
9:18 By .. three plagues a third of mankind was killed 5
11: 9 For three days and a half men from the peoples 5
11 after the three and a half days a breath of life 5
16:13 I saw .. three foul spirits like frogs; 5
19 The great city was split into three parts 5
21:13 on the east three gates, on the north three gates 5
13 on the east three gates, on the north three gates 5
13 on the south three gates 5
13 and on the west three gates. 5
1Es 1:35 he reigned three months in Judah and Jerusalem. 5
44 reigned three months and ten days in Jerusalem. 5
3: 4 the three young men of the bodyguard 5
9 the king and the three nobles of Persia 5
6:25 with three courses of hewn stone 5
8:41 we encamped there three days 5
62 When we had been there three days 7
9: 4 if any did not meet there within two or three days 5
5 assembled at Jerusalem within three days 5
2Es 4: 3 I have been sent to show you three ways 8
3 and to put before you three problems. 8
6:21 premature children at three and four months 8
24 so that for three hours they shall not flow. 8
35 in order to complete the three weeks 8
11: 1 had twelve feathered wings and three heads. 8
23 except the three heads that were at rest 8
12:22 As for your seeing three heads at rest 8
23 the Most High will raise up three kings 8
13:56 after three more days I will tell you 8
58 And I stayed there three days. 8
16:29 three or four olives may be left on every tree 8
31 in those days three or four shall be left by those 8
38 about her womb for two or three hours beforehand 8
Jdt 1: 2 hewn stones three cubits thick 5
2:21 They marched for three days from Nineveh 5
8: 4 three years and four months. 5
12: 7 she remained in the camp for three days 5
16:20 before the sanctuary for three months 5
Sir 25: 2 My soul hates three kinds of men 5
Aza 1:28 the three, as with one mouth, praised 5
1Mc 5:24 went three days' journey into the wilderness. 5
33 Then he came up behind them in three companies 5
10:30 the three districts added to it from Samaria 5
34 the three days before a feast 5
34 the three after a feast 5
38 three districts that have been added to Judea 5
11:18 But King Ptolemy died three days later 7
28 Judea and the three districts of Samaria 5
34 three districts of Aphairema and Lydda 5
2Mc 4:44 three men sent by the senate presented the case 5
5:14 Within the total of three days 5
7:27 nursed you for three years 5
13:12 lying prostrate for three days without ceasing 5
3Mc 6: 6 The three companions in Babylon 5
38 the three days 5
4Mc 13: 9 let us imitate the three youths in Assyria 5

three miles 1. *σταδίους εἴκοσι πέντε*

Joh 6:19 When they had rowed about three or four miles 1

three months 1. *τρίμηνος*

Heb 11:23 was hid for three months by his parents 1

three things 1. שָׁלֹשׁ 2. *τρεῖς*

Exd 21:11 if he does not do these three things for her 1
2Sm 24:12 Three things I offer you; choose one of them 1
1Ch 21:10 'Thus says the LORD, Three things I offer you; 1
Prv 30:15 Three things are never satisfied; 1
18 Three things are too wonderful for me; 1
21 Under three things the earth trembles; 1
29 Three things are stately in their tread; 1
Sir 25: 1 My soul takes pleasure in three things 2
26: 5 Of three things my heart is afraid 2

three times 1. שָׁלֹשׁ 2. *τρεῖς* 3. *τρίς*

Job 33:29 all these things, twice, three times, with a man 1
Mat 26:34 you will deny me three times. 3
75 you will deny me three times 3
Mrk 14:30 you will deny me three times. 3
72 you will deny me three times 3
Lke 22:34 until you three times deny that you know me. 3
61 you will deny me three times. 3
Joh 13:38 till you have denied me three times. 3
2Co 11:25 Three times I have been beaten with rods 3
25 Three times I have been shipwrecked 3
12: 8 Three times I besought the Lord about this 3
Sir 13: 7 until he has drained you two or three times 2
48: 3 also three times brought down fire. 2

three times as much 1. *τριπλασίος*

Sir 43: 4 the sun burns the mountains three times as much 1

three years 1. *τριετής* 2. *τριετία*

Act 20:31 for three years I did not cease night or day 2
2Mc 4:23 After a period of three years 1
14: 1 Three years later, word came to Judas and his men 1

three years old 1. שלשׁ

Gen 15: 9 He said to him, "Bring me a heifer three years old 1
9 a she-goat three years old, a ram three years old 1
9 a she-goat three years old, a ram three years old 1

three-year-old 1. *τριϊετίζω*

1Sm 1:24 she took him up .. along with a three-year-old bull 1

threefold 1. שלשׁ

Ecc 4:12 A threefold cord is not quickly broken. 1

threescore and ten 1. שִׁבְעִים

Ps 90:10 The years of our life are threescore and ten 1

thresh 1. דושׁ 2. דִּישׁ 3. מְדֻשָׁה

Lev 26: 5 your threshing shall last to the time of vintage 2
2Kg 13: 7 and made them like the dust at threshing. 1
1Ch 21:20 Now Ornan was threshing wheat; he turned and saw 1
Job 5:26 a shock of grain comes up to the threshing floor *
Isa 21:10 O my threshed and winnowed one, what I have heard 3
28:27 Dill is not threshed with a threshing sledge 1
28 No, he does not thresh it for ever; 1
41:15 you shall thresh the mountains and crush them 1
Hos 10:11 a trained heifer that loved to thresh 1
Ams 1: 3 punishment; because they have threshed Gilead 1
Mic 4:13 Arise and thresh, O daughter of Zion 1
1Co 9:10 the thresher thresh in hope of a share in the crop. *

thresh out 1. חבט

Isa 27:12 the LORD will thresh out the grain 1

thresher 1. *ἀλοάω*

1Co 9:10 the thresher thresh in hope of a share in the crop. 1

threshing *See* floor, sledge, time.

threshold 1. מִפְתָּן 2. סַף

Jdg 19:27 at the door .. with her hands on the threshold. 2
1Sm 5: 4 his hands were lying cut off upon the threshold; 1
5 do not tread on the threshold of Dagon in Ashdod 1
1Kg 14:17 as she came to the threshold of the house 2
2Kg 12: 9 the priests who guarded the threshold put in it 2
22: 4 the keepers of the threshold have collected 2
23: 4 the priests .. and the keepers of the threshold 2
25:18 took .. and the three keepers of the threshold; 2
1Ch 9:19 keepers of the thresholds of the tent 2
22 chosen as gatekeepers at the thresholds, were 212 2
2Ch 3: 7 lined the house with gold .. its thresholds 2
34: 9 money .. the Levites, the keepers of the threshold 2
Est 2:21 Bigthan and Teresh .. who guarded the threshold 2
6: 2 two .. eunuchs, who guarded the threshold 2
Isa 6: 4 the foundations of the thresholds shook 2
Jer 35: 4 the son of Shallum, keeper of the threshold. 2
52:24 priest, and the three keepers of the threshold; 2
Ezk 9: 3 had gone up .. to the threshold of the house; 1
10: 4 from the cherubim to the threshold of the house; 1
18 went forth from the threshold of the house 1
40: 6 and measured the threshold of the gate 2
7 and the threshold of the gate by the vestibule 2
41:16 Over against the threshold the temple was 2
43: 8 by setting their threshold by my threshold 2
8 by setting their threshold by my threshold 2
46: 2 he shall worship at the threshold of the gate. 1
47: 1 water was issuing from below the threshold 1
1 the south end of the threshold of the temple *

Ams 9: 1 Smite the capitals until the thresholds shake 2
Zep 1: 9 punish every one who leaps over the threshold 1
2:14 the raven croak on the threshold; 2

thrice 1. שְׁלִישִׁי
Ezk 21:14 let the sword come down twice, yea thrice 1

thrice accursed man 1. τρισαλιτήριος
AEs 16:15 to annihilation by this thrice accursed man 1

thrice-accursed 1. τρισαλιτήριος
2Mc 8:34 The thrice-accursed Nicanor 1
15: 3 the thrice-accursed wretch asked 1

thrill 1. המה 2. פחד
Sng 5: 4 and my heart was thrilled within me. 1
Isa 60: 5 be radiant, your heart shall thrill and rejoice; 2

thrive 1. צלח 2. רָטֹב 3. שׁלה
Job 8:16 He thrives before the sun, and his shoots spread 2
Jer 12: 1 Why do all who are treacherous thrive? 3
Ezk 17: 9 Say, Thus says the Lord GOD: Will it thrive? 1
10 Behold, when it is transplanted, will it thrive? 1

throat 1. גָּרוֹן 2. לֹעַ 3. λάρυγξ 4. πνίγω
Ps 5: 9 their throat is an open sepulchre 1
69: 3 I am weary with my crying; my throat is parched. 1
115: 7 they do not make a sound in their throat. 1
149: 6 Let the high praises of God be in their throats 1
Prv 23: 2 put a knife to your throat if you are a man 2
Jer 2:25 Keep . . your throat from thirst. 1
Mat 18:28 and seizing him by the throat he said 4
Rom 3:13 Their throat is an open grave 3

throb 1. סחר
Ps 38:10 My heart throbs, my strength fails me; 1

throne 1. כִּסֵּא 2. מלך 3. מַמְלָכָה 4. כָּרְסֵא (A) 5. ἀρχή 6. βῆμα 7. δίφρος 8. θρόνος 9. thronus
Gen 41:40 only as regards the throne will I be greater 1
Exd 11: 5 first-born of Pharaoh who sits upon his throne 1
12:29 first-born of Pharaoh who sat on his throne 1
Deu 17:18 when he sits on the throne of his kingdom, he shall 1
2Sm 3:10 and set up the throne of David over Israel 1
7:13 and I will establish the throne of his kingdom 1
16 your throne shall be established for ever. 1
14: 9 let the king and his throne be guiltless. 1
1Kg 1:13 reign after me, and he shall sit upon my throne"? Why 1
17 reign after me, and he shall sit upon my throne.' 1
20 who shall sit on the throne of my lord the king 1
24 reign after me, and he shall sit upon my throne'? 1
27 who should sit on the throne of my lord the king 1
30 reign after me, and he shall sit upon my throne 1
35 sit upon my throne; for he shall be king in my stead; 1
37 and make his throne greater than the throne of my 1
37 greater than the throne of my lord King David. 1
46 Solomon sits upon the royal throne. 1
47 and make his throne greater than your throne.' 1
47 and make his throne greater than your throne.' 1
48 granted one of my offspring to sit on my throne 1
2: 4 shall not fail you a man on the throne of Israel.' 1
12 Solomon sat upon the throne of David his father; 1
19 then he sat on his throne, and had a seat brought 1
24 me, and placed me on the throne of David my father 1
33 descendants, and to his house, and to his throne 1
45 the throne of David shall be established before 1
3: 6 hast given him a son to sit on his throne this day. 1
5: 5 whom I will set upon your throne in your place 1
7: 7 Hall of the Throne where he was to pronounce 1
8:20 I have risen . . and sit on the throne of Israel 1
25 a man before me to sit upon the throne of Israel 1
9: 5 I will establish your royal throne over Israel 1
5 not fail you a man upon the throne of Israel.' 1
10: 9 who has delighted in you and set you on the throne 1
18 The king also made a great ivory throne 1
19 The throne had six steps 1
19 at the back of the throne was a calf's head 1
16:11 as soon as he had seated himself on his throne 1
22:10 sitting on their thrones, arrayed in their robes 1
19 I saw the LORD sitting on his throne 1
2Kg 10: 3 the best . . and set him on his father's throne 1
30 your sons . . shall sit on the throne of Israel. 1
11:19 And he took his seat on the throne of the kings. 1
13:13 Jo'ash slept . . and Jerobo'am sat upon his throne; 1
15:12 Your sons shall sit upon the throne of Israel 1
1Ch 17:12 and I will establish his throne for ever. 1
14 and his throne shall be established for ever 1
22:10 I will establish his royal throne in Israel 1
28: 5 Solomon . . to sit upon the throne of the kingdom 1
29:23 Then Solomon sat on the throne of the LORD as king 1
2Ch 6:10 I have risen . . and sit on the throne of Israel 1
16 never fail you a man . . to sit upon the throne 1
7:18 then I will establish your royal throne 1
9: 8 LORD . . who has . . set you on his throne as king 1
17 The king also made a great ivory throne 1
18 The throne had six steps and a footstool of gold 1
18 which were attached to the throne 1
18: 9 sitting on their thrones, arrayed in their robes; 1
18 I saw the LORD sitting on his throne 1
21: 4 Jeho'ram had ascended the throne of his father 3
23:20 And they set the king upon the royal throne 1
Est 1: 2 when . . Ahasu-e'rus sat on his royal throne in Susa 1
5: 1 The king was sitting on his royal throne inside 1
Job 36: 7 with kings upon the throne he sets them for ever 1
Ps 9: 4 sat on the throne giving righteous judgment. 1
7 he has established his throne for judgment; 1
11: 4 in his holy temple, the LORD'S throne is in heaven; 1
45: 6 Your divine throne endures for ever and ever. 1
47: 8 God sits on his holy throne. 1
89: 4 build your throne for all generations.'" Selah 1
14 justice are the foundation of thy throne; 1
29 his throne as the days of the heavens. 1
36 his throne as long as the sun before me. 1
44 Thou hast . . cast his throne to the ground. 1
93: 2 thy throne is established from of old; 1
97: 2 justice are the foundation of his throne. 1
103:19 LORD has established his throne in the heavens 1
122: 5 There thrones for judgment were set 1
5 thrones of the house of David. 1
132:11 sons of your body I will set on your throne. 1
12 sons also for ever shall sit upon your throne. 1
Prv 16:12 throne is established by righteousness. 1
20: 8 A king who sits on the throne of judgment 1
28 throne is upheld by righteousness. 1
25: 5 throne will be established in righteousness. 1
29:14 his throne will be established for ever. 1
Ecc 4:14 even though he had gone from prison to the throne 2
Isa 6: 1 the Lord sitting upon a throne, high and lifted up; 1
9: 7 upon the throne of David, and over his kingdom 1
14: 9 it raises from their thrones all who were kings 1
13 above the stars of God I will set my throne on high; 1
16: 5 a throne will be established in steadfast love 1
22:23 become a throne of honor to his father's house. 1
47: 1 sit on the ground without a throne, O daughter 1
66: 1 Heaven is my throne and the earth is my footstool; 1
Jer 1:15 every one shall set his throne at the entrance 1
3:17 Jerusalem shall be called the throne of the LORD 1
13:13 the kings who sit on David's throne, the priests 1
14:21 do not dishonor thy glorious throne; 1
17:12 A glorious throne set on high from the beginning 1
25 kings who sit on the throne of David 1
22: 2 O King of Judah, who sit on the throne of David 1
4 kings who sit on the throne of David 1
30 shall succeed in sitting on the throne of David 1
29:16 the king who sits on the throne of David 1
33:17 David shall never lack a man to sit on the throne 1
21 that he shall not have a son to reign on his throne 1
36:30 He shall have none to sit upon the throne of David 1
43:10 he will set his throne above these stones 1
49:38 I will set my throne in Elam 1
Lam 5:19 thy throne endures to all generations. 1
Ezk 1:26 there was the likeness of a throne 1
26 and seated above the likeness of a throne 1
10: 1 like a sapphire, in form resembling a throne. 1
26:16 will step down from their thrones 1
43: 7 Son of man, this is the place of my throne 1
Dan 5:20 deposed from his kingly throne, 4
7: 9 As I looked, thrones were placed 4
9 throne was fiery flames, its wheels were burning 4
Jon 3: 6 he arose from his throne, removed his robe 1
Hag 2:22 to overthrow the throne of kingdoms; 1
Zec 6:13 and shall sit and rule upon his throne. 1
13 there shall be a priest by his throne 1
Mat 5:34 at all, either by heaven, for it is the throne of God 8
19:28 the Son of man shall sit on his glorious throne 8
28 will also sit on twelve thrones 8
23:22 swears by the throne of God 8
25:31 then he will sit on his glorious throne. 8
Lke 1:32 give to him the throne of his father David 8
52 he has put down the mighty from their thrones 8
22:30 sit on thrones judging the twelve tribes 8
Act 2:30 set one of his descendants upon his throne 8
7:49 'Heaven is my throne, and earth my footstool 8
12:21 took his seat upon the throne, and made an oration 6
Col 1:16 thrones or dominions or principalities 8
Heb 1: 8 Thy throne, O God, is for ever and ever 8
4:16 with confidence draw near to the throne of grace 8
8: 1 right hand of the throne of the Majesty in heaven 8
12: 2 seated at the right hand of the throne of God. 8
Rev 1: 4 from the seven spirits who are before his throne 8
2:13 'I know where you dwell, where Satan's throne is; 8
3:21 I will grant him to sit with me on my throne 8
21 and sat down with my Father on his throne. 8
4: 2 I was in the Spirit, and lo, a throne stood in heaven 8
2 in heaven, with one seated on the throne! 8
3 and round the throne was a rainbow 8
4 Round the throne were 24 thrones 8
4 Round the throne were 24 thrones 8
4 and seated on the thrones were 24 elders 8
5 From the throne issue flashes of lightning 8
5 before the throne burn seven torches of fire 8
6 before the throne there is as it were a sea 8
6 And round the throne, on each side of the throne 8
6 And round the throne, on each side of the throne 8
9 thanks to him who is seated on the throne 8
10 fall down before him who is seated on the throne 8
10 they cast their crowns before the throne, singing 8
5: 1 him who was seated on the throne 8
6 between the throne and the . . living creatures 8
7 right hand of him who was seated on the throne. 8
11 Then I looked, and I heard around the throne 8
13 To him who sits upon the throne and to the Lamb 8
6:16 hide us from . . him who is seated on the throne 8
7: 9 standing before the throne and before the Lamb 8
10 Salvation . . to our God who sits upon the throne 8
11 all the angels stood round the throne 8
11 they fell on their faces before the throne 8
15 Therefore are they before the throne of God 8
15 he who sits upon the throne will shelter them 8
17 For the Lamb in the midst of the throne will be 8
8: 3 upon the golden altar before the throne; 8
11:16 the 24 elders who sit on their thrones before God 8
12: 5 her child was caught up to God and to his throne 8
13: 2 to it the dragon gave his power and his throne 8
14: 3 and they sing a new song before the throne 8
16:10 angel poured his bowl on the throne of the beast 8
17 voice came . . from the throne, saying, "It is done! 8
19: 4 worshiped God who is seated on the throne, saying 8
5 And from the throne came a voice crying 8
20: 4 Then I saw thrones, and seated on them were those 8
11 I saw a great white throne and him who sat upon it; 8
12 dead, great and small, standing before the throne 8
21: 3 I heard a loud voice from the throne saying 8
5 And he who sat upon the throne said, "Behold 8
22: 1 flowing from the throne of God and of the Lamb 8
3 but the throne of God and of the Lamb shall be in it 8
2Es 8:21 whose throne is beyond measure 9
Jdt 1:12 swore by his throne and kingdom 8
9: 3 strike down . . princes on their thrones; 8
11:19 I will set your throne in the midst of it 7
AEs 15: 6 He was seated on his royal throne 8
8 in alarm he sprang from his throne 8
16:11 the person second to the royal throne. 8
Wis 5:23 evil-doing will overturn the thrones of rulers. 8
6:21 if you delight in thrones and scepters 8
7: 8 I preferred her to scepters and thrones 8
9: 4 give me the wisdom that sits by thy throne 8
10 from the throne of thy glory send her 8
12 shall be worthy of the throne of my father. 8
18:15 from heaven, from the royal throne 8
Sir 1: 8 greatly to be feared, sitting upon his throne. 8
10:14 The Lord has cast down the thrones of rulers 8
24: 4 my throne was in a pillar of cloud. 8
40: 3 the man who sits on a splendid throne 8
47:11 a throne of glory in Israel. 8
Bar 5: 6 carried in glory, as on a royal throne. 8
Aza 1:33 Blessed art thou upon the throne of thy kingdom 8
1Mc 2:57 inherited the throne of the kingdom for ever. 8
7: 4 took his seat upon the throne of his kingdom. 8
10:52 and have taken my seat on the throne of my fathers 8
53 we have taken our seat on the throne of his kingdom 8
55 and took your seat on the throne of their kingdom. 8
11:52 sat on the throne of his kingdom 8
4Mc 4:15 Antiochus Epiphanes succeeded to the throne 5
17:18 they now stand before the divine throne 8

throne *See also* sit.

throng 1. סָךְ 2. עַם 3. רַב 4. רִגְמָה 5. שָׁאוֹן 6. ὄχλος 7. πλῆθος 8. πληθύνω
Ps 35:18 in the mighty throng I will praise thee. 2
42: 4 how I went with the throng, and led them 1
68:27 princes of Judah in their throng, the princes 4
109:30 I will praise him in the midst of the throng. 3
Isa 5:14 go down, her throng and he who exults in her. 5
Mat 14:14 As he went ashore he saw a great throng 6
15:31 so that the throng wondered 6
Mrk 6:34 As he went ashore he saw a great throng 6
12:37 the great throng heard him gladly. 6
1Es 8:91 there gathered about him a very great throng 6
2Mc 3:19 Women . . thronged the streets 8
3Mc 6:14 The whole throng of infants and their parents 7

throng about 1. συνθλίβω
Mrk 5:24 a great crowd followed him and thronged about 1

through 1. אֶל 2. אֵת 3. בְּ 4. בְּיַד 5. בְּמוֹ 6. בְּעַד 7. בְּקֶרֶב 8. בְּתוֹךְ 9. דֶּרֶךְ 10. לְ 11. מִן 12. מִפְּנֵי 13. עַד 14. עַל 15. בְּ (A) 16. ἀνὰ μέσον 17. ἀπό 18. διά 19. διὰ χειρός 20. εἰς 21. ἐκ 22. ἐν 23. ἐνχειρί 24. ἐπί 25. ἔσω 26. κατά 27. μετά 28. ab 29. in 30. per
Gen 6:13 is filled with violence through them; 12
19:32 we may preserve offspring through our father. 11
34 we may preserve offspring through out father. 11
21:12 through Isaac shall your descendants be named. 3
30: 3 even I may have children through her. 11
41:36 that the land may not perish through the famine. 3
Exd 9:35 as the LORD had spoken through Moses. 4
10:15 through all the land of Egypt. 3
14:16 Israel may go on dry ground through the sea. 8
29 walked on dry ground through the sea 8
27: 7 the poles shall be put through the rings 3
29:35 through seven days shall you ordain them *
38: 7 he put the poles through the rings on the sides 3

Lev 6: 2 deposit or security, or through robbery 3
11:46 living creature that moves through the waters 3
22: 4 unclean through contact with the dead •
Num 4:49 commandment of the LORD through Moses 4
5: 2 unclean through contact with the dead; 10
9: 6 unclean through touching the dead body of a man 10
7 unclean through touching the dead body of a man; 10
10 unclean through touching a dead body 10
12: 2 Has the LORD indeed spoken only through Moses? 3
2 Has he not spoken through us also? 3
13:32 The land, through which we have gone, to spy it out 3
14: 7 The land, which we passed through to spy it out 3
16:40 as the LORD said to Elea'zar through Moses. 4
20:17 Now let us pass through your land. 3
17 We will not pass through field or vineyard 3
19 let me only pass through on foot, nothing more. 3
21 to give Israel passage through his territory; 3
21:22 Let me pass through your land; 3
23 not allow Israel to pass through his territory. 3
24: 8 pierce them through with his arrows. •
25: 8 pierced both of them . . through her body. 1
27:23 as the LORD directed through Moses. 4
31:23 everything . . you shall pass through the fire 3
23 whatever . . you shall pass through the water. 3
33: 8 passed through the midst of the sea 3
Deu 1:19 went through all that great and terrible 2
2: 4 You are about to pass through the territory 3
7 knows your going through this great wilderness; 2
27 'Let me pass through your land; I will go only 3
8:15 led you through the great and terrible wilderness 3
9:26 whom thou hast redeemed through thy greatness 3
15:17 awl, and thrust it through his ear into the door 3
29:16 how we came through the midst of the nations 3
31:29 him to anger through the work of your hands. 3
33:26 who rides through the heavens to your help •
26 who rides . . in his majesty through the skies. •
Jos 1:11 Pass through the camp, and command the people 7
2:15 she let them down by a rope through the window 6
18 in the window through which you let us down; 3
3: 2 the officers went through the camp 7
13:30 extended from Mahana'im, through all Bashan •
18:12 then up through the hill country westward; 3
20: 2 cities . . of which I spoke to you through Moses 4
21: 2 The LORD commanded through Moses that we be 4
8 as the LORD had commanded through Moses. 4
22: 9 by command of the LORD through Moses. 4
24: 3 and led him through all the land of Canaan 3
17 and among all the peoples through whom we passed; 7
Jdg 5:28 the mother of Sis'era gazed through the lattice 6
11:16 from Egypt, Israel went through the wilderness 3
17 Let us pass, we pray, through your land'; but the king 3
18 they journeyed through the wilderness, and went 3
19 Let us pass . . through your land to our country.' 3
20 not trust Israel to pass through his territory; 3
20:12 tribes of Israel sent men through all the tribe 3
1Sm 9: 4 they passed through the hill country of E'phraim 3
4 and passed through the land of Shal'ishah 3
4 they passed through the land of Sha'alim 3
4 Then they passed through the land of Benjamin 3
11: 3 send . . through all the territory of Israel. 3
19:12 So Michal let David down through the window; 6
2Sm 2:29 Abner . . went all that night through the Arabah; 3
20:14 Sheba passed through all the tribes of Israel 3
23:16 Then the three mighty men broke through the camp 3
24: 2 Go through all the tribes of Israel, from Dan 3
8 when they had gone through all the land, they came 3
1Kg 8:53 as thou didst declare through Moses, thy servant 4
10:29 so through the king's traders they were exported 4
18: 5 Go through the land to all the springs of water 3
22:36 about sunset a cry went through the army 3
2Kg 1: 2 Ahazi'ah fell through the lattice 6
3:11 no prophet . . through whom we may inquire 11
8: 8 inquire of the LORD through him, saying, 'Shall I 11
11:19 marching through the gate of the guards 9
1Ch 11:18 broke through the camp of the Philistines 3
2Ch 1:17 likewise through them these were exported 4
11:23 some of his sons through all the districts 10
17: 9 they went about through all the cities of Judah 3
22: 7 come about through his going to visit Joram. 10
23: 2 they went about through Judah 3
20 marching through the upper gate 8
29:25 from the LORD through his prophets. 4
30:10 through the country of E'phraim and Manas'seh 3
32: 4 the brook that flowed through the land 8
33: 8 all the law . . given through Moses. 4
34:14 book of the law of the LORD given through Moses. 4
Ezr 6:14 through the prophesying of Haggai the prophet 15
Neh 9:30 warn them by thy Spirit through thy prophets; 4
Est 6: 9 conduct the man . . through the open square 3
11 made him ride through the open square of the city 3
Job 15:20 through all the years that are laid up •
22:13 Can he judge through the deep darkness? 6
30 delivered through the cleanness of your hands. 3
29: 3 by his light I walked through darkness; •
30: 3 Through want and hard hunger they gnaw 3
14 As through a wide breach they come; •
Ps 5: 7 I through the abundance of thy steadfast love 3
19: 4 yet their voice goes out through all the earth 3
21: 5 His glory is great through thy help; 3
7 through the steadfast love of the Most High 3
23: 4 I walk through the valley of the shadow of death 3
32: 3 my body wasted away through my groaning all day 3
44: 5 Through thee we push down our foes; 3
5 through thy name we tread down our assailants. 3
66: 6 men passed through the river on foot. 3
12 we went through fire and through water; 3
12 we went through fire and through water; 3
68: 7 when thou didst march through the wilderness 3
69: 6 be put to shame through me, O Lord GOD of hosts; 3
6 brought to dishonor through me, O God of Israel. 3
73: 9 their tongue struts through the earth. 3
77:19 Thy way was through the sea 3
19 thy path through the great waters; 3
84: 6 As they go through the valley of Baca they make it 3
88: 9 my eye grows dim through sorrow. 11
105:32 lightning that flashed through their land. 3
41 flowed through the desert like a river. 3
106: 9 he led them through the deep as through a desert. 3
9 he led them through the deep as through a desert. •
43 were brought low through their iniquity. 3
107:17 Some were sick through their sinful ways 11
39 low through oppression, trouble, and sorrow 11
109:24 My knees are weak through fasting; 11
118:19 enter through them and give thanks to the LORD. 3
20 righteous shall enter through it. 3
119:104 Through thy precepts I get understanding; 11
136:14 made Israel pass through the midst of it 3
16 to him who led his people through the wilderness 3
Prv 7: 6 I have looked out through my lattice 6
13:23 but it is swept away through injustice. 3
14:32 The wicked is overthrown through his evil-doing 3
32 righteous finds refuge through his integrity. 3
Ecc 8:15 this will go with him . . through the days of life •
10:18 Through sloth the roof sinks in 3
18 and through indolence the house leaks. 3
12: 3 those that look through the windows are dimmed 3
Sng 2: 9 gazing in . . looking through the lattice. 11
Isa 9:19 Through the wrath of the LORD of hosts 3
30: 5 shame through a people that cannot profit them 14
6 Through a land of trouble and anguish 3
34:10 none shall pass through it for ever and ever. 3
43: 2 you pass through the waters I will be with you; 3
2 through the rivers, they shall not overwhelm you; 3
2 when you walk through fire you shall not be 5
48:21 thirsted not when he led them through . . deserts; 3
63:13 who led them through the depths? 3
Jer 4: 5 and say, "Blow the trumpet through the land; 3
5: 1 Run to and fro through the streets of Jerusalem 3
10 Go up through her vine-rows and destroy 3
14:18 and priest ply their trade through the land 1
37: 2 which he spoke through Jeremiah the prophet. 4
39: 4 garden through the gate between the two walls; 3
11 concerning Jeremiah through Nebu'zarad'an 4
51:43 and through which no son of man passes. 3
52 through all her land the wounded shall groan. 3
Lam 4:14 They wandered, blind, through the streets 3
Ezk 5:17 pestilence and blood shall pass through you; 3
6: 8 when you are scattered through the countries 3
9: 4 Go through the city, through Jerusalem 8
12: 5 Dig through the wall in their sight, and go out 3
5 Dig through the wall . . and go out through it. 3
7 I dug through the wall with my own hands; 3
12 and shall go forth; he shall dig through the wall 3
12 shall dig through the wall and go out through it; 3
15 when I . . scatter them through the countries. 3
14: 5 are all estranged from me through their idols. 3
15 If I cause wild beasts to pass through the land 3
16:14 it was perfect through the splendor 3
20:23 and disperse them through the countries 3
26 I defiled them through their very gifts 3
22:15 and disperse you through the countries 3
16 I shall be profaned through you 3
36:19 they were dispersed through the countries; 3
23 when through you I vindicate my holiness 3
38:16 when through you, O Gog, I vindicate my holiness 3
39:14 They will set apart men to pass through the land 3
15 when these pass through the land and any one sees 3
27 and through them have vindicated my holiness 3
41: 7 to the top story through the middle story. •
46:19 Then he brought me through the entrance 3
47: 3 and then led me through the water; 3
4 measured 1,000, and led me through the water; 3
4 measured 1,000, and led me through the water; •
Dan 8:12 host was given over . . through transgression; 3
10:20 when I am through with him, lo, the prince of Greece •
11: 2 when he has become strong through his riches •
20 exactor . . through the glory of the kingdom; •
Hos 1: 2 When the LORD first spoke through Hose'a 3
8: 4 They made kings, but not through me. 11
12:10 and through the prophets gave parables. 4
13: 1 but he incurred guilt through Ba'al and died. 3
Jol 2: 2 through the years of all generations. 13
8 they burst through the weapons 6
9 they enter through the windows like a thief. 6
Jon 3: 7 and published through Nin'eveh 3
Nah 2: 4 they rush to and fro through the squares; 3
Hab 1: 6 who march through the breadth of the earth 10
Zec 4:10 the eyes . . which range through the whole earth. 3
7:12 by his Spirit through the former prophets. 4
10:11 They shall pass through the sea of Egypt 3
12: 5 strength through the LORD of hosts, their God. 3
13: 3 mother who bore him shall pierce him through •
Mat 9:26 report of this went through all that district. 20
31 spread his fame through all that district. 22
10:20 the Spirit of your Father speaking through you. 22
12: 1 At that time Jesus went through the grainfields 18
19:24 for a camel to go through the eye of a needle 18
Mrk 2:23 he was going through the grainfields 18
7:13 through your tradition which you hand on. •
31 went through Sidon to the Sea of Galilee 18
31 through the region of the Decap'olis. 16
10:25 a camel to go through the eye of a needle 18
11:16 to carry anything through the temple. 18
Lke 1:65 through all the hill country of Judea; 22
78 through the tender mercy of our God 18
4:14 went out through all the surrounding country. 26
30 passing through the midst of them he went away. 18
5:19 and let him down with his bed through the tiles 18
6: 1 while he was going through the grainfields 18
7:17 through the whole of Judea 22
9: 6 they departed and went through the villages 26
13:22 He went on his way through towns and villages 26
18:25 to go through the eye of a needle 18
Joh 1: 3 all things were made through him 18
7 that all might believe through him. 18
10 and the world was made through him 18
17 For the law was given through Moses; 18
17 grace and truth came through Jesus Christ. 18
3:17 but that the world might be saved through him. 18
4: 4 He had to pass through Samar'ia. 18
17:20 those who believe in me through their word 18
Act 1: 2 had given commandment through the Holy Spirit 18
2:22 signs which God did through him in your midst 18
43 signs were done through the apostles. 18
3:16 the faith which is through Jesus 18
4:16 a notable sign has been performed through them 18
30 through the name of thy holy servant Jesus. 18
8:18 through the laying on of the apostles' hands 18
10:43 receives forgiveness of sins through his name. 18
12:10 they went out and passed on through one street; •
13:38 through this man forgiveness of sins 18
14:22 through many tribulations 18
15:11 saved through the grace of the Lord Jesus 18
12 what signs and wonders God had done through them 18
18:27 helped those who through grace had believed 18
20: 3 he determined to return through Macedo'nia. 18
19 which befell me through the plots of the Jews; 22
21: 4 Through the Spirit they told Paul not to go 18
19 done among the Gentiles through his ministry. 18
24: 2 Since through you we enjoy much peace 18
28:25 saying . . through Isaiah the prophet 18
Rom 1: 2 he promised beforehand through his prophets 18
5 through whom we have received grace 18
8 I thank my God through Jesus Christ for all of you 18
17 revealed through faith for faith; 21
17 He who through faith is righteous shall live. 21
3: 7 But if through my falsehood God's truthfulness 22
20 since through the law comes knowledge of sin. 18
22 the righteousness of God through faith in Jesus 18
24 through the redemption which is in Christ Jesus 18
30 and the uncircumcised through their faith. 18
4:13 The promise . . did not come through the law 18
13 but through the righteousness of faith. 18
5: 1 peace with God through our Lord Jesus Christ. 18
2 Through him we have obtained access 18
5 poured into our hearts through the Holy Spirit 18
11 rejoice in God through our Lord Jesus Christ 18
11 Jesus Christ, through whom we have now received 18
12 as sin came into the world through one man 18
12 sin came into the world . . death through sin 18
15 For if many died through one man's trespass •
17 death reigned through that one man 18
17 reign in life through the one man Jesus Christ. 18
21 grace also might reign through righteousness 18
21 to eternal life through Jesus Christ our Lord. 18
7: 4 have died to the law through the body of Christ 18
13 sin, working death in me through what is good 18
13 through the commandment might become sinful 18
25 Thanks be to God through Jesus Christ our Lord! 18
8:11 through his Spirit which dwells in you. 18
37 more than conquerors through him who loved us. 18
9: 7 Through Isaac shall your descendants be named. 22
30 attained it . . righteousness through faith; 21
32 Why? Because they did not pursue it through faith 21
11:11 through their trespass salvation has come •
20 but you stand fast only through faith. •
36 and through him and to him are all things. 18
15:18 except what Christ has wrought through me 18
16:26 through the prophetic writings is made known 18
27 be glory for evermore through Jesus Christ! 18
1Co 1:21 the world did not know God through wisdom 18
21 through the folly of what we preach to save 18
2:10 God has revealed to us through the Spirit 18
3: 5 Servants through whom you believed 18
15 but only as through fire. 18
4:15 your father in Christ Jesus through the gospel. 18

7: 5 tempt you through lack of self-control. 18
14 consecrated through his wife 22
14 consecrated through her husband 22
8: 6 through whom are all things 18
6 through whom we exist. 18
7 through being hitherto accustomed to idols *
10: 1 all passed through the sea 18
12: 8 To one is given through the Spirit the utterance 18
15:57 through our Lord Jesus Christ. 18
2Co 1: 5 so through Christ we share abundantly 18
20 That is why we utter the Amen through him 18
2:14 through us spreads the fragrance 18
3: 4 that we have through Christ toward God. 18
14 because only through Christ is it taken away. 22
5:18 who through Christ reconciled us to himself 18
20 God making his appeal through us 18
6: 4 through great endurance, in afflictions 22
7: 9 so that you suffered no loss through us. 21
9:11 which through us will produce thanksgiving 18
11:27 in toil . . through many a sleepless night 22
33 let down in a basket through a window in the wall 18
12:17 through any of those whom I sent to you? 18
Gal 1: 1 Paul an apostle–not from men nor through man 18
1 through Jesus Christ and God the Father 18
12 it came through a revelation of Jesus Christ. 18
15 called me through his grace 18
2:16 through faith in Jesus Christ 18
19 For I through the law died to the law 18
21 if justification were through the law 18
3:11 He who through faith is righteous shall live"; 21
14 receive the promise of the Spirit through faith 18
19 ordained by angels through an intermediary. 23
26 you are all sons of God, through faith. 18
4: 7 So through God you are no longer a slave but a son 18
23 the son of the free woman through promise. 18
5: 5 For through the Spirit, by faith, we wait *
6 faith working through love. 18
13 through love be servants of one another. 18
Eph 1: 5 to be his sons through Jesus Christ 18
7 In him we have redemption through his blood 18
2: 1 when you were dead through the trespasses *
5 even when we were dead through our trespasses *
8 For by grace you have been saved through faith; 18
16 reconcile us both . . through the cross 18
18 for through him we both have access in one Spirit 18
3: 6 partakers . . through the gospel. 18
10 through the church 18
12 confidence of access through our faith in him. 18
16 through his Spirit in the inner man 18
17 Christ may dwell in your hearts through faith; 18
4: 6 who is above all and through all and in all. 18
22 is corrupt through deceitful lusts 26
Php 1:11 which come through Jesus Christ 18
19 For I know that through your prayers 18
3: 9 that which is through faith in Christ 18
Col 1:16 all things were created through him 18
20 through him to reconcile to himself all things 18
2:12 through faith in the working of God 18
19 nourished and knit together through its joints 18
3:17 giving thanks to God the Father through him. 18
1Th 3: 7 comforted about you through your faith; 18
4: 2 we gave you through the Lord Jesus. 18
14 through Jesus, God will bring with him those who . . 18
5: 9 to obtain salvation through our Lord Jesus 18
2Th 2:13 through sanctification by the Spirit 22
14 To this he called you through our gospel 18
16 eternal comfort and good hope through grace 22
1Ti 2:15 woman will be saved through bearing children 18
4: 2 through the pretensions of liars 22
6:10 it is through this craving that . . *
2Ti 1: 6 within you through the laying on of my hands; 18
10 manifested through the appearing of our Savior 18
10 brought life . . to light through the gospel. 18
3:15 through faith in Christ Jesus. 18
Tit 1: 3 manifested in his word through the preaching 22
3: 6 through Jesus Christ our Savior 18
Phm 1: 7 the saints have been refreshed through you. 18
22 through your prayers to be granted to you. 18
Heb 1: 2 through whom also he created the world. 18
2:10 make . . perfect through suffering. 18
14 that through death he might destroy him 18
15 through fear of death 18
4: 7 saying through David so long afterward 22
5: 8 he learned obedience through what he suffered; 17
6:12 through faith and patience 18
18 through two unchangeable things 18
7: 9 Levi himself . . paid tithes through Abraham 18
11 attainable through the Levit'ical priesthood 18
19 through which we draw near to God. 18
25 to save those who draw near to God through him 18
9:11 then through the greater and more perfect tent 18
14 who through the eternal Spirit offered himself 18
10:10 sanctified through the offering of . . Jesus 18
20 through the curtain, that is, through his flesh 18
20 through the curtain, that is, through his flesh 18
11: 4 through which he received approval 18
4 through his faith he is still speaking. 18
18 Through Isaac shall your descendants be named. 22
33 who through faith conquered kingdoms 18

13:12 sanctify the people through his own blood. 18
15 Through him then let us continually offer up 18
21 through Jesus Christ; to whom be glory for ever 18
1Pe 1: 3 born anew . . through the resurrection of Jesus 18
5 who by God's power are guarded through faith 18
12 preached . . to you through the Holy Spirit 18
21 Through him you have confidence in God 18
23 through the living and abiding word of God; 18
2: 5 acceptable to God through Jesus Christ. 18
3:20 ark, in which a few . . were saved through water. 18
21 through the resurrection of Jesus Christ 18
4:11 God may be glorified through Jesus Christ. 18
2Pe 1: 3 through the knowledge of him who called us 18
4 promises, that through these you may escape 18
2:20 escaped . . through the knowledge of our Lord 22
3: 2 of the Lord and Savior through your apostles. *
6 through which the world . . perished 18
1Jn 4: 9 so that we might live through him. 18
Jde 1:25 God, our Savior through Jesus Christ our Lord 18
Rev 22: 2 through the middle of the street of the city; 22
2Es 1:13 Surely it was I who brought you through the sea 30
2: 1 I gave them commandments through my servants 30
4: 9 things through which you have passed 30
5:11 Has righteousness . . passed through you? 30
56 show thy servant through whom thou dost visit 30
6: 6 they were made through me 30
6 through me and not through another. 30
6 just as the end shall come through me 30
6 through me and not through another. 30
7:60 and through them my name has now been honored. 30
9:31 you shall be glorified through it for ever.' 29
11:39 the end of my times might come through them? 30
13:45 Through that region there was a long way to go 30
14:17 For the weaker the world becomes through old age 28
16:30 who search carefully through the vineyard *
Tob 4: 6 your ways will prosper through your deeds. 22
Jdt 8:32 a thing which will go down through all generations 20
10:11 The women went straight on through the valley; 22
11: 6 God will accomplish something through you 27
19 Then I will lead you through the middle of Judea 18
15: 2 across the plain and through the hill country. *
AEs 16: 7 through the pestilent behavior of those *
Wis 2:24 through the devil's envy death entered the world *
3: 7 will run like sparks through the stubble. 22
7:23 penetrating through all spirits 18
10:17 a starry flame through the night. *
18 and led them through deep waters; 18
11: 5 through the very things by which their enemies 18
13 through their own punishments 18
12:11 it was not through fear of any one *
19 Through such works thou has taught thy people 18
23 torment through their own abominations. 18
13: 3 through delight in the beauty of these things *
14: 3 a safe way through the waves 22
14 through the vanity of men they entered the world *
30 through contempt for holiness. *
16: 1 deservedly punished through such creatures 18
18: 4 through whom the . . law was to be given 18
Sir 0: 1 given to us through the law and the prophets 18
4:24 For wisdom is known through speech 22
24 education through the words of the tongue. 22
6: 2 not exalt yourself through your soul's counsel 22
7 When you gain a friend, gain him through testing 22
7:28 Remember . . through your parents you were born; 18
8:15 through his folly you will perish with him. *
10: 3 grow through the understanding of its rulers. 22
11:18 There is a man who is rich through his diligence 17
28 a man will be known through his children. 22
13:11 he will test you through much talk 21
14:23 He who peers through her windows 18
16: 4 through one man of understanding 17
4 through a tribe of lawless men *
20:13 makes himself beloved through his words 22
22 A man may lose his life through shame 18
23: 8 The sinner is overtaken through his lips 22
23 she has committed adultery through harlotry 22
26:28 a warrior in want through poverty 18
32:12 do not sin through proud speech. *
39: 4 travel through the lands of foreign nations 22
9 his name will live through all generations. 20
44:21 nations would be blessed through his posterity; 22
45: 4 He sanctified him through faithfulness 22
47:19 through your body 22
51:20 through purification I found her 22
Bar 1:20 the curse which the Lord declared through Moses *
3:28 no wisdom, they perished through their folly. 18
LJr 1:27 through them these gods are made to stand 18
Sus 1:57 and they were intimate with you through fear; *
Bel 1:13 through which they used to go in regularly 18
21 through which they were accustomed to enter 18
1Mc 5:46 they had to go through it. 18
48 Let us pass through your land to get to our land 18
51 Then he passed through the city over the slain. 18
62 those men through whom deliverance was given 19
6:31 They came through Idumea 18
11:47 and then spread out through the city 22
2Mc 2:18 as he promised through the law 18
4:11 secured through John the father of Eupolemus 18
5: 2 golden-clad horsemen charging through the air 18

6:25 through my pretense 18
7:30 was given to our fathers through Moses. 18
38 through me and my brothers 22
14: 8 through the folly of those whom I have mentioned *
43 the crowd was now rushing in through the doors 25
3Mc 5:18 to remain alive through the present day. *
6: 7 who through envious slanders was cast down *
36 had come to them through God. 18
7:23 through all times! Amen. 20
4Mc 1:11 their native land was purified through them. 18
2: 9 he is ruled by the law through his reason 18
14 when reason, through the law, can prevail 18
4:26 he himself, through torture, tried to compel everyone 18
6:14 you . . destroying yourself through these evil things? *
7: 9 through your glorious endurance 18
11 Aaron . . ran through the multitude of the people 18
14 in spirit through reason 18
22 to overcome the emotions through godliness? 18
8: 9 to destroy . . through tortures. 18
9: 4 our safety through transgression of the law 24
8 through this severe suffering and endurance 18
18 Through all these tortures I will convince you 18
11:12 through these noble sufferings 18
13:19 bequeathed through the fathers 18
20 growing . . through the same life 18
16:18 Remember that it is through God 18
17:18 and live through blessed eternity. *
22 through the blood of those devout ones 18
18:14 Even though you go through the fire 18

through *See also* bore, break, burn, carry, dig, feel, fly, go, journey, lead, march, night, pass, passage, pierce, run, sail, shine, strike, thrust, walk, way, work.

throughout 1. בְּ 2. בְּכֹל 3. כֹּל 4. לְ 5. לְכֹל 6. מִן 7. סָבִיב 8. עַל 9. בְּ (A) 10. *διά* 11. *εἰς* 12. *ἐν* 13. *ἐπί* 14. *καθ' ὅλην* 15. *κατά* 16. *κατὰ πᾶν* 17. *μέχρι* 18. *ὅλος* 19. *παρά* 20. in 21. super

Gen 17: 7 you and your descendants after you throughout 4
9 after you throughout their generations. 4
12 every male throughout your generations 4
23:17 field, throughout its whole area, was made over 7
41:29 years of great plenty throughout all the land 1
Exd 3:15 to be remembered throughout all generations. 4
5:12 scattered abroad throughout all the land 1
7:19 and there shall be blood throughout all the land 1
21 was blood throughout all the land of Egypt. 1
8:16 that it may become gnats throughout all the land 1
17 gnats throughout all the land of Egypt. 1
9: 9 throughout all the land of Egypt. 1
16 name may be declared throughout all the earth. 1
22 hail . . throughout the land of Egypt. 1
25 in the field throughout all the land of Egypt 1
11: 6 be a great cry throughout all the land of Egypt 1
12:14 throughout your generations you shall observe 4
17 observe this day, throughout your generations 4
42 Israel throughout their generations. 4
16:32 omer of it be kept throughout your generations 4
33 to be kept throughout your generations. 4
27:21 observed throughout their generations 4
29:42 burnt offering throughout your generations 4
30: 8 before the LORD throughout your generations. 4
10 once in the year throughout your generations; 4
21 descendants throughout their generations. 4
31 anointing oil throughout your generations. 4
31:13 between me and you throughout your generations 4
16 throughout their generations, as a perpetual 4
32:27 from gate to gate throughout the camp, and slay 1
34: 3 let no man be seen throughout all the mountain; 1
36: 6 word was proclaimed throughout the camp 1
40:15 priesthood throughout their generations. 4
36 Throughout all their journeys, whenever 1
38 For throughout all their journeys the cloud 1
Lev 3:17 statute throughout your generations 4
6:18 as decreed for ever throughout your generations 4
7:36 a perpetual due throughout their generations 4
10: 9 statute for ever throughout your generations 4
17: 7 statute . . throughout their generations 4
21:17 descendants throughout their generations 4
22: 3 your descendants throughout your generations 4
23:14 a statute for ever throughout your generations 4
21 it is a statute . . throughout your generations 4
31 statute for ever throughout your generations 4
41 a statute for ever throughout your generations 4
24: 3 a statute . . throughout your generations 4
25: 9 the trumpet throughout all your land 1
10 proclaim liberty throughout the land to all 1
30 to him who bought it, throughout his generations 4
Num10: 8 statute throughout your generations. 4
11:10 people weeping throughout their families 4
15:14 among you throughout your generations 4
15 statute throughout your generations; 4
21 offering throughout your generations. 4
23 from the day . . and onward throughout 4
38 make tassels . . throughout their generations 4
18:23 statute throughout your generations; 4
28:14 offering . . throughout the months of the year. 4
32:33 the cities of the land throughout the country. 7
35:29 throughout your generations 4

Deu 1:15 commanders . . and officers, throughout your tribes. 4
28:40 have olive trees throughout all your territory 1
52 walls . . come down throughout all your land; 1
52 all your towns throughout all your land 1
Jos 3:15 overflows . . throughout the time of harvest 3
Jdg 6:35 And he sent messengers throughout all Manas'seh; 1
7:24 Gideon sent messengers throughout all the hill 1
19:29 sent her throughout all the territory 1
20: 6 sent her throughout all the country . . of Israel 1
10 take ten men of a 100 throughout all the tribes 4
1Sm 5:11 was a deathly panic throughout the whole city. 1
11: 7 sent them throughout all the territory 1
13: 3 Saul blew the trumpet throughout all the land 1
19 no smith . . throughout all the land of Israel; 1
31: 9 sent . . throughout the land of the Philistines 1
2Sm 8:14 throughout all Edom he put garrisons 1
15:10 sent . . throughout all the tribes of Israel 1
19: 9 people were at strife throughout all the tribes 1
1Kg 1: 3 they sought . . throughout all the territory 1
2Kg 10:21 Jehu sent throughout all Israel; 1
32 defeated . . throughout the territory of Israel 2
1Ch 5:10 tents throughout all the region east of Gilead. 8
6:60 All their cities throughout their families 1
10: 9 throughout the land of the Philistines 1
21: 4 Jo'ab departed and went throughout all Israel 2
12 destroying throughout all . . Israel. 1
22: 5 of fame and glory throughout all lands; 4
27: 1 and went, month after month throughout the year 5
2Ch 16: 9 run to and fro throughout the whole earth 1
17:19 in the fortified cities throughout all Judah. 1
20: 3 proclaimed a fast throughout all Judah. 8
24: 9 proclamation was made throughout Judah 1
30: 5 to make a proclamation throughout all Israel 1
6 couriers went throughout all Israel and Judah 1
31: 1 throughout all Judah and Benjamin 6
20 Thus Hezeki'ah did throughout all Judah; 1
34: 7 throughout all the land of Israel. 1
36:22 made a proclamation throughout all his kingdom 1
Ezr 1: 1 made a proclamation throughout all his kingdom 1
10: 7 proclamation was made throughout Judah 1
Est 1:20 is proclaimed throughout all his kingdom 1
3: 6 all the Jews . . throughout the whole kingdom 1
8:12 to destroy . . throughout all the provinces 1
9: 2 in their cites throughout all the provinces 1
4 his fame spread throughout all the provinces; 1
28 days . . kept throughout every generation 1
Ps 10: 6 throughout all generations I shall not meet 4
72: 5 as long as the moon, throughout all generations! †
102:24 whose years endure throughout all generations! 1
105:31 flies, and gnats throughout their country. 2
135:13 thy renown, O LORD, throughout all ages. 4
145:13 dominion endures throughout all generations. 1
Jer 15:13 for all your sins, throughout all your territory. 1
17: 3 of your sin throughout all your territory. 1
Ezk 6:14 and waste, throughout all their habitations 1
30:23 and disperse them throughout the lands. 1
26 and disperse them throughout the countries. 1
45: 1 it shall be holy throughout its whole extent. 1
Dan 6: 1 120 satraps, to be throughout the whole kingdom; 9
Mat 4:24 So his fame spread throughout all Syria 18
24:14 preached throughout the whole world 12
Mrk 1:28 fame spread . . throughout all the surrounding region 11
39 he went throughout all Galilee 11
Lke 8:39 proclaiming throughout the whole city 15
23: 5 teaching throughout all Judea 15
Act 7:11 came a famine throughout all Egypt and Canaan 13
8: 1 scattered throughout the region of Judea and 15
9:31 the church throughout all Judea and Galilee and 15
42 it became known throughout all Joppa 15
10:37 word which was proclaimed throughout all Judea 15
13:49 spread throughout all the region. 10
19:26 almost throughout all Asia •
24: 5 among all the Jews throughout the world 15
26:20 throughout all the country of Judea •
Php 1:13 throughout the whole praetorian guard 12
1Pe 1:17 throughout the time of your exile. •
5: 9 your brotherhood throughout the world. 12
1Es 1:32 throughout the whole nation of Israel. 11
2: 2 made a proclamation throughout all his kingdom 12
8:23 throughout all Syria and Phoenicia 12
2Es 12:34 those who have been saved throughout my borders 21
15: 6 For iniquity has spread throughout every land 20
Tob 10: 7 throughout the nights she never stopped •
Jdt 2:11 throughout your whole region. 12
11: 8 it is reported throughout the whole world •
23 be renowned throughout the whole world. 19
16:21 throughout the whole country. 12
AEs 13: 2 open to travel throughout all its extent 17
Wis 4: 2 throughout all time it marches 12
17:14 throughout the night •
Sir 45:26 endure throughout their generations. 11
47:10 arranged their times throughout the year 17
Bel 1:14 they sifted them throughout the whole temple •
2Mc 2:22 the temple famous throughout the world 14
3:12 which is honored throughout the whole world. 15
14 no little distress throughout the whole city. 15
9:24 the people throughout the realm 15
14:14 the Gentiles throughout Judea 13
3Mc 6: 1 throughout his life 15
4Mc 3:13 went searching throughout the enemy camp 16
12:12 these throughout all time will never let you go. 11

throw 1. זרק 2. טול 3. ירה 4. נפל 5. פרש 6. צְנֵפָה
7. רמה 8. שׁלך 9. ἀνατρέπω 10. βάλλω 11. βολή
12. ἐκβάλλω 13. ἐμβάλλω 14. ἐντινάσσω
15. ἐπιβάλλω 16. ἐπιρίπτω 17. καταβάλλω
18. παραρρίπτω 19. πληρόω 20. ῥίπτω 21. mitto

Gen 37:20 let us kill him and throw him into one of the pits; 8
Exd 9: 8 ashes from the kiln, and let Moses throw them 1
10 and Moses threw them toward heaven, and it became 1
15: 1 the horse and his rider he has thrown into the sea. 7
21 his rider he has thrown into the sea. 7
25 a tree, and he threw it into the water, and the water 8
24: 6 and half of the blood he threw against the altar. 1
8 Moses took the blood and threw it upon the people 1
29:16 take its blood and throw it against the altar 1
20 throw the rest of the blood against the altar 1
32:19 Moses' anger burned hot, and he threw the tables 8
24 so they gave it to me, and I threw it into the fire 8
Lev 1: 5 present the blood, and throw the blood round 1
11 Aaron's sons the priests shall throw its blood 1
3: 2 Aaron's sons the priests shall throw the blood 1
8 shall throw its blood against the altar 1
13 the sons of Aaron shall throw its blood 1
7: 2 its blood shall be thrown on the altar round about 1
14 shall belong to the priest who throws the blood 1
8:19 threw the blood upon the altar round about 1
24 Moses threw the blood upon the altar round about 1
9:12 he threw it on the altar round about 1
18 blood, which he threw upon the altar round about 1
14:40 throw them into an unclean place outside the city 8
Num 19:13 water for impurity was not thrown upon him 1
20 water for impurity has not been thrown upon him 1
Deu 9:21 I threw the dust of it into the brook 8
Jos 10:27 took them down . . and threw them into the cave 8
Jdg 9:53 a certain woman threw an upper millstone 8
2Sm 18:17 they took Ab'salom, and threw him into a great pit 8
20:12 carried Ama'sa . . and threw a garment over him. 8
21 his head shall be thrown to you over the wall. 8
1Kg 13:24 his body was thrown in the road 8
25 and saw the body thrown in the road, and the lion 8
28 he went and found his body thrown in the road 8
2Kg 2:21 he went to the spring of water and threw salt in it 8
3:25 on every . . piece of land every man threw a stone 8
4:41 Then bring meal." And he threw it into the pot 8
6: 6 he cut off a stick, and threw it in there 8
16:13 and threw the blood of his peace offerings upon 1
15 throw upon it all the blood of the burnt offering 1
2Ch 29:22 blood and threw it against the altar; 1
22 their blood was thrown against the altar; 1
22 their blood was thrown against the altar. 1
30:14 they took away and threw into the Kidron valley. 8
33:15 he threw them outside of the city. 8
Neh 13: 8 threw all the household furniture of Tobi'ah 8
Prv 1:14 throw in your lot among us 4
26:18 madman who throws firebrands, arrows, and death 3
Isa 22:18 and throw you like a ball into a wide land; 6
Jer 36:23 and throw them into the fire in the brazier 8
Ezk 32: 3 Thus says the Lord GOD: I will throw my net over you 5
43:18 and for throwing blood against it 1
Jon 1: 5 they threw the wares that were in the ship 2
12 said to them, "Take me up and throw me into the sea; 2
15 they took up Jonah and threw him into the sea; 2
Nah 3: 6 I will throw filth at you 8
Mat 3:10 good fruit is cut down and thrown into the fire. 10
4: 6 If you are the Son of God, throw yourself down; 10
5:13 anything except to be thrown out and trodden 10
29 pluck it out and throw it away; it is better 10
29 than that your whole body be thrown into hell. 10
30 cut it off and throw it away; it is better 10
6:30 alive and tomorrow is thrown into the oven 10
7: 6 and do not throw your pearls before swine 10
19 tree . . is cut down and thrown into the fire. 10
8:12 while the sons of the kingdom will be thrown 12
13:42 throw them into the furnace of fire 10
47 like a net which was thrown into the sea 10
48 but threw away the bad. 10
50 throw them into the furnace of fire 10
15:26 and throw it to the dogs. 10
18: 8 or your foot . . cut it off and throw it away 10
8 to be thrown into the eternal fire. 10
9 pluck it out and throw it away 10
9 with two eyes to be thrown into the hell of fire 10
Mrk 7:27 throw it to the dogs. 10
9:42 he were thrown into the sea. 10
45 with two feet to be thrown into hell. 10
46 with two eyes to be thrown into hell 10
11: 7 and threw their garments on it 15
Lke 3: 9 every tree . . is cut down and thrown into the fire. 10
4: 9 throw yourself down from here; 10
12:28 tomorrow is thrown into the oven 10
14:35 men throw it away 10
19:35 throwing their garments on the colt 16
22:41 he withdrew from them about a stone's throw 11
23:19 a man who had been thrown into prison 10
25 the man who had been thrown into prison 10
Joh 8: 7 Let him . . be the first to throw a stone at her. 10
59 they took up stones to throw at him 10
15: 6 the branches are gathered, thrown into the fire 10
Act 16:23 they threw them into prison 10
37 have thrown us into prison 10
22:23 waved their garments and threw dust into the air 10
Rev 2:10 devil is about to throw some of you into prison 10
22 Behold, I will throw her on a sickbed 10
22 I will throw into great tribulation 10
8: 5 filled it with fire . . and threw it on the earth; 10
8 something like . . was thrown into the sea; 10
14:19 the angel . . threw it into the great wine press 10
18:19 And they threw dust on their heads, as they wept 10
21 took up a stone . . and threw it into the sea 10
19:20 These two were thrown alive into the lake of fire 10
20: 3 and threw him into the pit 10
10 the devil . . was thrown into the lake of fire 10
14 Death and Hades were thrown into the lake of fire 10
15 he was thrown into the lake of fire. 10
2Es 1:23 but threw a tree into the water 21
Tob 2: 3 strangled and thrown into the market place. 20
Sir 12:16 in his mind he will plan to throw you into a pit 9
22:20 One who throws a stone at birds scares them away 10
27:25 Whoever throws a stone straight up 10
25 throws it on his own head 10
Aza 1:23 the king's servants who threw them 13
1Mc 7:19 killed them and threw them into a great pit. •
2Mc 1:16 they threw stones and struck down the leader 10
16 threw them to the people outside. 18
4:41 and threw them in wild confusion at Lysimachus 14
10:30 they were thrown into disorder and cut to pieces. 19
4Mc 12: 1 When he also, thrown into the caldron, had died 17
16:21 Daniel the righteous was thrown to the lions 10
17: 1 she threw herself into the flames 20

throw against 1. προσάγω

1Mc 15:25 continually throwing his forces against it 1

throw away 1. נוד 2. שׁלך 3. ἀποβάλλω 4. ῥίπτω

Jdg 15:17 he threw away the jawbone out of his hand; 2
2Sm 23: 6 godless men . . like thorns that are thrown away; 1
2Kg 7:15 and equipment which the Syrians had thrown away 2
Ps 102:10 for thou hast taken me up and thrown me away. 2
Heb 10:35 Therefore do not throw away your confidence 3
1Mc 5:43 they threw away their arms 4

throw back 1. ἀντανακλάω

Wis 17:19 an echo thrown back from a hollow of the mountains 1

throw blame 1. ψογίζω

1Mc 11: 5 to throw blame on him 1
11 He threw blame on Alexander 1

throw down 1. הרס 2. נפל 3. שׁלך 4. שׁמט
5. βάλλω 6. κατακρημνίζω 7. καταλύω 8. ῥίπτω
9. ὑπερρίπτω 10. demolior

Jos 10:11 the LORD threw down great stones from heaven 3
2Sm 20:15 and they were battering the wall, to throw it down. 2
1Kg 18:30 he repaired the altar . . that had been thrown down; 1
19:10 forsaken thy covenant, thrown down thy altars 1
14 forsaken thy covenant, thrown down thy altars 1
2Kg 9:33 He said, "Throw her down." So they threw her down; 4
33 He said, "Throw her down." So they threw her down; 4
2Ch 25:12 threw them down from the top of the rock; 3
Job 18: 7 his own schemes throw him down. 3
Jer 50:15 bulwarks have fallen, her walls are thrown down. 1
Ezk 16:39 and they shall throw down your vaulted chamber 1
38:20 the mountains shall be thrown down 1
Jol 1: 7 it has stripped off their bark and thrown it down; 3
Mic 5:11 cut off . . and throw down all your strongholds; 1
Mat 24: 2 one stone . . that will not be thrown down. 7
27: 5 throwing down the pieces of silver in the temple 8
Mrk 13: 2 that will not be thrown down. 7
Lke 4:35 when the demon had thrown him down in the midst 8
21: 6 that will not be thrown down. 7
Rev 12: 9 And the great dragon was thrown down 5
9 the deceiver . . -he was thrown down to the earth 5
9 and his angels were thrown down with him. 5
10 the accuser of our brethren has been thrown down 5
13 dragon saw that he had been thrown down to earth 5
18:21 So shall Babylon the great city be thrown down 5
2Es 10:21 our altar thrown down, our temple destroyed; 10
Jdt 14:15 and found him thrown down on the platform dead 8
1Mc 7:44 they threw down their arms and fled. 8
11:51 they threw down their arms and made peace 8
2Mc 14:43 and manfully threw himself down into the crowd. 6
4Mc 6:25 they burned him . . threw him down 9

throw down headlong 1. κατακρημνίζω

Lke 4:29 that they might throw him down headlong. 1

throw fire 1. πυροβόλος

1Mc 6:51 engines of war to throw fire and stones 1

throw headlong from a height 1. κατακρημνίζω

4Mc 4:25 women . . were thrown headlong from heights 1

throw into 1. ἐμβάλλω
Bel 1:31 They threw Daniel into the lions' den 1
42 and threw into the den the men 1

throw into a panic 1. המם 2. חרד
Jos 10:10 the LORD threw them into a panic before Israel 1
Jdg 8:12 and he threw all the army into a panic. 2
2Sm 17: 2 I will come . . and throw him into a panic; 2

throw into confusion 1. הום 2. המם 3. turbo
Exd 23:27 will throw into confusion all the people 2
Deu 7:23 over to you, and throw them into great confusion 1
1Sm 7:10 LORD . . threw them into confusion; 2
2Es 5: 4 you shall see it thrown into confusion 3

throw off 1. ἀποβάλλω
Mrk 10:50 throwing off his mantle he sprang up 1

throw off restraint 1. עבר
Prv 14:16 but a fool throws off restraint and is careless. 1

throw out 1. שלך 2. ἐκβάλλω 3. ἐκρίπτω 4. ῥίπτω
2Sm 20:22 they cut off the head . . and threw it out to Jo'ab. 1
Act 27:38 throwing out the wheat into the sea. 2
Tob 1:17 dead and thrown out behind the wall of Nineveh 4
2Mc 9:15 but had planned to throw out with their children 3

throw overboard 1. ἀπορίπτω
Act 27:43 to throw themselves overboard first 1

throw overboard cargo 1. ἐκβολὴν ποιέω
Act 27:18 they began next day to throw the cargo overboard; 1

throw stone 1. סקל
2Sm 16: 6 he threw stones at David, and at all the servants 1
13 cursed . . and threw stones at him and flung dust. 1

throw up 1. שפך 2. ἀναβάλλω
Ezk 26: 8 and throw up a mound against you 1
Dan 11:15 king of the north shall . . throw up siegeworks 1
Tob 6: 3 seized the fish and threw it up on the land. 2

thrust 1. הדף 2. ינה 3. מַדְקֵרָה 4. נגח 5. נדח 6. נטה 7. נכה 8. נתן 9. תקע 10. ἀπωθέω
Deu 15:17 awl, and thrust it through his ear into the door 8
Jdg 3:21 took the sword . . and thrust it into his belly; 9
1Sm 2:14 he would thrust it into the pan, or kettle 7
2Sm 2:16 and thrust his sword in his opponent's side; •
18:14 and thrust them into the heart of Ab'salom 9
Job 18:18 He is thrust from light into darkness 1
24: 4 They thrust the poor off the road; 6
Prv 12:18 one whose rash words are like sword thrusts 3
Isa 8:22 they will be thrust into thick darkness. 5
22:19 I will thrust you from your office 1
Ezk 34:21 and thrust at all the weak with your horns 4
46:18 the people, thrusting them out of their property; 2
Act 13:46 Since you thrust it from you 10

thrust aside 1. נטה 2. ἀπωθέω
Mal 3: 5 against those who thrust aside the sojourner 1
Act 7:27 the man . . thrust him aside, saying 2
39 Our fathers . . thrust him aside 2

thrust away 1. הדף
2Kg 4:27 And Geha'zi came to thrust her away. 1

thrust back 1. שלך
Zec 5: 8 he thrust her back into the ephah 1

thrust down 1. דחה 2. הדף 3. ירד 4. נדח 5. שלך
Ps 36:12 the evildoers lie prostrate, they are thrust down 1
62: 4 They only plan to thrust him down 4
Jer 46:15 bull stand? Because the LORD thrust him down. 2
Ezk 26:20 I will thrust you down with those who descend 3
28: 8 They shall thrust you down into the Pit 3
Zec 5: 8 and thrust down the leaden weight upon its mouth. 5

thrust out 1. גרש 2. הדף 3. ἐκβάλλω 4. ἐξωθέω
Exd 12:39 because they were thrust out of Egypt and could 1
Deu 6:19 by thrusting out all your enemies from before you 2
9: 4 after the LORD . . has thrust them out before you 2
33:27 And he thrust out the enemy before you, and said 1
Jdg 11: 2 when . . sons grew up, they thrust Jephthah out 1
Lke 13:28 and you yourselves thrust out. 3
Act 7:45 the nations . . God thrust out before our fathers 4

thrust out quickly 1. בהל
2Ch 26:20 thrust him out quickly, and he himself hastened 1

thrust through 1. דקר 2. מחץ
Jdg 9:54 And his young man thrust him through, and he died. 1
1Sm 31: 4 Draw your sword, and thrust me through with it 1
4 these uncircumcised come and thrust me through 1
2Sm 22:39 I consumed them; I thrust them through 2
1Ch 10: 4 Draw your sword, and thrust me through with it 1
Ps 18:38 I thrust them through 2
Isa 13:15 Whoever is found will be thrust through 1

thumb 1. בֹּהֶן 2. בֹּהֶן יָד
Exd 29:20 upon the thumbs of their right hands 1
Lev 8:23 on the thumb of his right hand and on the great toe 1
24 blood . . on the thumbs of their right hands 1
14:14 on the thumb of his right hand, and on the great toe 1
17 the thumb of his right hand, and on the great toe 1
25 on the thumb of his right hand, and on the great toe 1
28 on the thumb of his right hand, and the great toe 1
Jdg 1: 6 and cut off his thumbs and his great toes. 2
7 kings with their thumbs and their great toes cut 2

thumbscrew 1. δακτυλήθρα
4Mc 8:13 braziers and thumbscrews and iron claws 1

thunder 1. המה 2. הָמוֹן 3. קוֹל 4. קֹלֹת אֱלֹהִים 5. רֹגֶז 6. רעם 7. רַעַם 8. βροντάω 9. βροντή 10. κεραυνός 11. tonitrus 12. tono
Exd 9:23 the LORD sent thunder and hail, and fire ran down 3
28 there has been enough of this thunder and hail 4
29 the thunder will cease, and there will be no more 3
33 the thunder and the hail ceased, and the rain 3
34 the rain and the hail and the thunder had ceased 3
19:16 third day there were thunders and lightnings 3
19 Moses spoke, and God answered him in thunder. 3
1Sm 2:10 against them he will thunder in heaven. 6
7:10 the LORD thundered with a mighty voice that day 6
12:17 call . . the LORD, that he may send thunder and rain; 3
18 and the LORD sent thunder and rain that day; 3
2Sm 22:14 The LORD thundered from heaven 6
Job 26:14 But the thunder of his power who can understand? 7
28:26 a way for the lightning of the thunder; 3
37: 2 Hearken to the thunder of his voice 5
4 he thunders with his majestic voice 6
5 God thunders wondrously with his voice; 6
39:25 the thunder of the captains, and the shouting. 7
40: 9 like God, and can you thunder with a voice like his? 6
Ps 18:13 The LORD also thundered in the heavens 6
29: 3 God of glory thunders, the LORD, upon many waters. 6
42: 7 calls to deep at the thunder of thy cataracts; 3
77:17 the skies gave forth thunder; thy arrows flashed 3
18 The crash of thy thunder was in the whirlwind; 7
81: 7 I answered you in the secret place of thunder; 7
93: 4 Mightier than the thunders of many waters 3
104: 7 at the sound of thy thunder they took to flight. 7
Isa 17:12 Ah, the thunder of many peoples 2
12 they thunder like the thundering of the sea! 1
12 they thunder like the thundering of the sea! 2
29: 6 be visited by the LORD of hosts with thunder 7
Ezk 1:24 many waters, like the thunder of the Almighty 3
Mrk 3:17 surnamed Bo-aner'ges, that is, sons of thunder; 9
Joh 12:29 heard it and said that it had thundered 9
Rev 6: 1 creatures say, as with a voice of thunder, "Come! 9
10: 3 when he called out, the seven thunders sounded. 9
4 when the seven thunders had sounded 9
4 Seal up what the seven thunders have said 9
14: 2 a voice . . like the sound of loud thunder; 9
2Es 6: 2 before the rumblings of thunder sounded 11
7:40 or cloud or thunder or lightning or wind or water 11
16:10 He will thunder, and who will not be terrified? 12
AEs 11: 5 thunders and earthquake, tumult upon the earth! 9
Wis 19:13 prior signs in the violence of thunder 10
Sir 32:10 Lightning speeds before the thunder 9
43:17 The voice of his thunder rebukes the earth 9
46:17 Then the Lord thundered from heaven 8

thunder *See also* clap, peal.

thunderbolt 1. חֲזִיז קוֹלוֹת 2. רֶשֶׁף 3. κεραυνός
Job 38:25 torrents of rain, and a way for the thunderbolt 1
Ps 78:48 to the hail, and their flocks to thunderbolts. 2
2Mc 10:30 they showered . . thunderbolts upon the enemy 3

thundering 1. קוֹל 2. תְּשֻׁאָה
Exd 20:18 when all the people perceived the thunderings 1
Job 36:29 of the clouds, the thunderings of his pavilion? 2

thunderous 1. הָמוֹן
Isa 33: 3 At the thunderous noise peoples flee 1

thunderpeal 1. βροντή
Rev 19: 6 like the sound of mighty thunderpeals, crying 1

thus 1. וְ 2. וְהָיָה וְ 3. זֶה 4. הַדָּבָר הַזֶּה 5. הַדְּבָרִים הָאֵלֶּה 6. כֹּה 7. כָּזֶה 8. כָּכָה 9. כְּמוֹ 10. כֵּן 11. לְ 12. לָכֵן 13. עַד 14. כִּדְנָה (A) 15. כֵּן (A) 16. כְּנֵמָא (A) 17. ἄρα 18. γάρ 19. γοῦν 20. δέ 21. δι' ἧς 22. εἰς 23. ἐν ᾧ 24. καθώς 25. καί 26. νῦν 27. ὅδε 28. οὖν 29. οὗτος 30. οὕτω 31. οὕτως 32. τοιοῦτος 33. ὥστε 34. et 35. hic
Gen 2: 1 Thus the heavens and the earth were finished 1
5: 5 Thus all the days that Adam lived were 930 years 1
8 Thus all the days of Seth were 912 years; 1
11 Thus all the days of Enosh were 905 years; 1
14 Thus all the days of Kenan were 910 years; 1
17 Thus all the days of Ma-hal'alel were 895 years; 1
20 Thus all the days of Jared were 962 years; 1
23 Thus all the days of Enoch were 365 years. 1
27 Thus all the days of Methu'selah were 969 years; 1
31 Thus all the days of Lamech were 777 years; 1
13:11 thus they separated from each other. 1
19:36 Thus both the daughters of Lot were with child 1
24:30 words of Rebekah his sister, "Thus the man spoke 6
61 thus the servant took Rebekah, and went his way. 1
25:22 and she said, "If it is thus, why do I live? 10
34 Thus Esau despised his birthright. 1
28: 5 Thus Isaac sent Jacob away; 1
30:43 Thus the man grew exceedingly rich 1
31: 9 Thus God has taken away the cattle of your father 1
40 Thus I was; by day the heat consumed me •
32: 4 instructing them, "Thus you shall say to my lord 6
4 Thus says your servant Jacob, 'I have sojourned 6
33:11 Thus he urged him, and he took it. 1
37:35 to my son, mourning." Thus his father wept for him 1
41:43 Thus he set him over all the land of Egypt. 1
42: 5 Thus the sons of Israel came to buy among 1
8 Thus Joseph knew his brothers 1
45: 9 to my father and say to him, 'Thus says your son 6
47:27 Thus Israel dwelt in the land of Egypt 1
48:20 and thus he put E'phraim before Manas'seh. •
50:12 Thus his sons did for him as he had commanded them; 10
21 Thus he reassured them and comforted them. 1
Exd 3:15 my name for ever, and thus I am to be remembered 3
22 thus you shall despoil the Egyptians. 1
4:22 you shall say to Pharaoh, 'Thus says the LORD 6
5: 1 went to Pharaoh and said, "Thus says the LORD 6
10 said to the people, "Thus says Pharaoh, 'I will not 6
15 Why do you deal thus with your servants? 6
6: 9 Moses spoke thus to the people of Israel; 10
7:17 Thus says the LORD, "By this you shall know 6
8: 1 say to him, 'Thus says the LORD, "Let my people go 6
20 say to him, 'Thus says the LORD, "Let my people go 6
23 Thus I will put a division between my people 1
9: 1 to Pharaoh, and say to him, 'Thus says the LORD 6
13 Thus says the LORD, the God of the Hebrews 6
10: 3 Thus says the LORD, the God of the Hebrews, 6
11: 4 Moses said, "Thus says the LORD: About midnight 6
12:36 Thus they despoiled the Egyptians. 1
50 Thus did all the people of Israel; 1
14:30 Thus the LORD saved Israel that day from the hand 1
19: 3 Thus you shall say to the house of Jacob, and tell 6
20:22 the LORD said to Moses, "Thus you shall say 6
26:24 thus shall it be with both of them; 10
28:30 thus Aaron shall bear the judgment of the people 1
29: 9 Thus you shall ordain Aaron and his sons. 1
35 Thus you shall do to Aaron and to his sons 1
32:27 he said to them, "Thus says the LORD God of Israel 6
33:11 Thus the LORD used to speak to Moses face to face 1
36:23 The frames for the tabernacle he made thus •
29 he made two of them thus, for the two corners. 10
39:18 thus they attached it in front •
32 Thus all the work of the tabernacle of the tent 1
40:16 Thus did Moses; according to all that the LORD •
Lev 4: 3 who sins, thus bringing guilt on the people 11
20 Thus shall he do with the bull 1
5:13 Thus the priest shall make atonement for him 1
14:20 Thus the priest shall make atonement for him 1
52 Thus he shall cleanse the house with the blood 1
15:31 Thus you shall keep the people of Israel 1
16: 3 thus shall Aaron come into the holy place 3
16 thus he shall make atonement for the holy place 1
23:44 Thus Moses declared to the people of Israel 1
24:23 Thus the people of Israel did as the LORD 1
Num 1:54 Thus did the people of Israel; they did according 10
2:34 Thus did the people of Israel. 1
4:19 deal thus with them, that they may live and not die 3
49 thus they were numbered by him 1
6:23 Thus you shall bless the people of Israel 6
8: 7 thus you shall do to them, to cleanse them 6
14 Thus you shall separate the Levites from among 1
20 Thus did Moses and Aaron . . to the Levites; 1
26 Thus shall you do to the Levites in assigning 8
11:15 If thou wilt deal thus with me, kill me at once 8
15:11 Thus it shall be done for each bull or ram 8
16:38 Thus they shall be a sign to the people of Israel. 1
17: 5 thus I will make to cease from me the murmurings 1
11 Thus did Moses; as the LORD commanded him 1
19:19 thus on the seventh day he shall cleanse him 1
20:14 Thus says your brother Israel: You know 6
21 Thus Edom refused to give Israel passage 1
21:31 Thus Israel dwelt in the land of the Amorites. 1
22:16 Thus says Balak the son of Zippor: 'Let nothing 6
23: 5 Return to Balak, and thus you shall speak. 6
16 Return to Balak, and thus shall you speak. 6
25: 8 Thus the plague was stayed from the people 1
32: 8 Thus did your fathers when I sent them 6
35:33 shall not thus pollute the land in which you live; •
Deu 7: 5 thus shall you deal with them 6
20:15 Thus you shall do to all the cities 10
29:24 'Why has the LORD done thus to this land? 8
32: 6 Do you thus requite the LORD, you foolish 3
33: 5 Thus the LORD became king in Jesh'urun 2
Jos 6: 3 Thus shall you do for six days. 6
7:10 Arise, why have you thus fallen upon your face? 3
13 Sanctify yourselves . . for thus says the LORD 6
10:25 thus the LORD will do to all your enemies 8
17: 5 Thus there fell to Manas'seh ten portions 1
21:43 Thus the LORD gave to Israel all the land 1

22:16 Thus says the whole congregation of the LORD 6
24: 2 Thus says the LORD, the God of Israel, 'Your fathers 6
Jdg 6: 8 Thus says the LORD, the God of Israel: I led you up 6
9:56 Thus God requited the crime of Abim'elech 1
11:15 Thus says Jephthah: Israel did not take away 6
18: 4 Thus and thus has Micah dealt with me: he has hired 7
4 Thus and thus has Micah dealt with me: he has hired 7
1Sm 2:17 Thus the sin of the young men was very great 1
27 Thus the LORD has said, 'I revealed myself 6
10:18 Thus says the LORD, the God of Israel, 'I brought up 6
11: 2 gouge out . . eyes, and thus put disgrace upon all *
9 Thus shall you say to the men of Ja'besh-gil'ead 6
15: 2 Thus says the LORD of hosts, 'I will punish 6
18:24 servants . . told him, "Thus and so did David speak. 5
25 Thus shall you say to David, 'The king desires no 6
19:17 Why have you deceived me thus, and let my enemy go 8
25: 6 And thus you shall salute him: 'Peace be to you 6
31: 6 Thus Saul died, and his three sons, 1
2Sm 7: 5 Thus says the LORD: Would you build me a house 6
8 therefore thus you shall say to my servant David 6
8 Thus says the LORD of hosts, I took you 6
11:25 David said . . "Thus shall you say to Jo'ab 6
12: 7 Thus says the LORD, the God of Israel, 'I anointed 6
11 Thus says the LORD, 'Behold, I will raise up evil 6
31 thus he did to all the cities of the Ammonites. 10
13:18 thus were the virgin daughters of the king clad 10
14: 3 and go to the king, and speak thus to him. 4
7 Thus they would quench my coal which is left 1
15: 6 Thus Ab'salom did to all . . who came to the king 4
17: 6 Ab'salom said to him, "Thus has Ahith'ophel spoken; 4
15 Thus and so did Ahith'ophel counsel Ab'salom 7
15 and thus and so have I counseled. 7
21 for thus and so has Ahith'ophel counseled 8
24:12 Thus says the LORD, Three things I offer you; 6
1Kg 1: 6 by asking, "Why have you done thus and so? 8
2:27 expelled Abi'athar . . thus fulfilling the word *
30 saying, "Thus said Jo'ab, and thus he answered me. 6
30 saying, "Thus said Jo'ab, and thus he answered me. 6
31 strike him down and bury him; and thus take away *
3:22 child is mine." Thus they spoke before the king. *
7:22 Thus the work of the pillars was finished. 1
51 Thus all the work . . was finished. 1
9: 8 Why has the LORD done thus to this land 8
10:23 Thus King Solomon excelled all the kings 1
11:31 Take . . ten pieces; for thus says the LORD 6
12:10 Thus shall you speak to this people 6
10 thus shall you say to them 6
24 'Thus says the LORD, You shall not go up or fight 6
13: 2 thus says the LORD: 'Behold, a son shall be born 6
21 Thus says the LORD, 'Because you have disobeyed 6
14: 5 Thus and thus shall you say to her. 7
5 Thus and thus shall you say to her. 7
7 Go, tell Jerobo'am, 'Thus says the LORD 6
16:12 Thus Zimri destroyed all the house of Ba'asha 1
17:14 For thus says the LORD the God of Israel 6
20: 2 Thus says Ben-ha'dad 6
5 Thus says Ben-ha'dad: 'I sent to you, saying 6
13 Thus says the LORD, Have you seen all this 6
14 Thus says the LORD, By the servants 6
28 Thus says the LORD, 'Because the Syrians have said 6
42 Thus says the LORD, 'Because you have let go 6
21:19 'Thus says the LORD, "Have you killed, and also taken 6
19 'Thus says the LORD: "In the place where dogs licked 6
22:11 Thus says the LORD, 'With these you shall push 6
27 'Thus says the king, "Put this fellow in prison 6
2Kg 1: 4 thus says the LORD, 'You shall not come down 10
6 Thus says the LORD, Is it because there is no God 6
16 Thus says the LORD, 'Because you have sent 6
2:21 Thus says the LORD, I have made this 6
3:16 Thus says the LORD, 'I will make this dry stream-bed 6
17 For thus says the LORD, 'You shall not see wind 6
4:43 that they may eat, for thus says the LORD 6
5: 4 Thus and so spoke the maiden from . . Israel. 7
6:10 Thus he used to warn him, so that he saved himself 1
7: 1 thus says the LORD, Tomorrow about this time 6
9: 3 'Thus says the LORD, I anoint you king over Israel.' 6
6 Thus says the LORD the God of Israel, I anoint you 6
12 And he said, "Thus and so he spoke to me, saying 7
12 Thus says the LORD, I anoint you king over Israel.' 6
14 Thus Jehu . . conspired against Joram. 1
18 and said, "Thus says the king, 'Is it peace?' 6
19 and said, "Thus the king has said, 'Is it peace?' 6
10:28 Thus Jehu wiped out Ba'al from Israel. 1
11: 2 Thus she hid him from Athali'ah, so that he was not 1
18:19 Say to Hezeki'ah, 'Thus says the great king 6
29 Thus says the king: 'Do not let Hezeki'ah deceive 6
31 thus says the king of Assyria: 'Make your peace 6
19: 3 Thus says Hezeki'ah, This day is a day of distress 6
6 Thus says the LORD: Do not be afraid 6
10 Thus shall you speak to Hezeki'ah king of Judah 6
20 Thus says the LORD, the God of Israel 6
32 thus says the LORD concerning the king 10
20: 1 Thus says the LORD, 'Set your house in order; 6
5 Thus says the LORD, the God of David your father 6
21:12 thus says the LORD, the God of Israel 6
22:15 Thus says the LORD, the God of Israel: 'Tell the man 6
16 Thus says the LORD, Behold, I will bring evil 6
18 as to the king of Judah . . thus shall you say to him 6
18 Thus says the LORD, the God of Israel 6
1Ch 10: 6 Thus Saul died; 1
17: 4 Thus says the LORD: You shall not build me a house 6
7 therefore thus shall you say to my servant David 6
7 Thus says the LORD of hosts 6
16 house, that thou hast brought me thus far? 13
20: 3 thus David did to all the cities 10
21:10 'Thus says the LORD, Three things I offer you; 6
11 Thus says the LORD, 'Take which you will 6
23:32 Thus they shall keep charge of the tent 1
29:14 that we should be able thus to offer willingly? 7
26 Thus David the son of Jesse reigned over all 1
2Ch 5: 1 Thus all the work that Solomon did for the house 1
7:11 Thus Solomon finished the house of the LORD 1
21 'Why has the LORD done thus to this land and to this 8
8:16 Thus was accomplished all the work of Solomon 1
9:22 Thus King Solomon excelled all the kings 1
10:10 Thus shall you speak to the people who said to you 6
10 thus shall you say to them 6
11: 4 Thus says the LORD, You shall not go up or fight 6
12: 5 Thus says the LORD, 'You abandoned me 6
13:13 thus his troops were in front of Judah 1
18 Thus the men of Israel were subdued at that time 1
18:10 Zedekiah . . said, "Thus says the LORD 6
26 say, 'Thus says the king, Put this fellow in prison 6
19: 9 Thus you shall do in the fear of the LORD 6
10 Thus you shall do, and you will not incur guilt. 6
20:15 Thus says the Lord to you, 'Fear not 6
31 Thus Jehosh'aphat reigned over Judah. 1
21:12 Thus says the LORD, the God of David your father 6
22:11 Thus Jeho-shab'e-ath . . hid him from Athali'ah 1
24:11 Thus they did day after day, and collected money 6
20 Thus says God, 'Why do you transgress 6
22 Thus Jo'ash the king did not remember 1
24 Thus they executed judgment on Jo'ash. 1
29:35 Thus the service of the house of the LORD 1
31:20 Thus Hezeki'ah did throughout all Judah; 1
32:10 Thus says Sennach'erib king of Assyria 6
34:23 Thus says the LORD, the God of Israel: 'Tell the man 6
24 Thus says the LORD, Behold, I will bring evil 6
26 to the king of Judah . . thus shall you say to him 6
26 Thus says the LORD . . Regarding the words 6
36:23 Thus says Cyrus king of Persia, 'The LORD, the God 6
Ezr 1: 2 Thus says Cyrus king of Persia: The LORD 6
5: 3 came to them and spoke to them thus, "Who gave you 15
9 Then we asked those elders and spoke to them thus 16
Neh 13:30 Thus I cleansed them from everything foreign 1
Est 6: 9 Thus shall it be done to the man whom the king 8
11 Thus shall it be done to the man whom the king 8
Job 1: 5 Thus Job did continually. 8
19:26 after my skin has been thus destroyed 3
34:25 Thus, knowing their works, he overturns them 12
Ps 73:15 If I had said, "I will speak thus 9
106:39 Thus they became unclean by their acts 1
128: 4 thus shall the man be blessed who fears the LORD. 10
147:20 He has not dealt thus with any other nation; 10
Sng 5: 9 What is your beloved . . that you thus adjure us? 8
Isa 7: 7 thus says the Lord GOD: It shall not stand 6
8:11 For the LORD spoke thus to me with his strong hand 6
10:24 Therefore thus says the Lord, the LORD of hosts 6
18: 4 For thus the LORD said to me: "I will quietly look 6
21: 6 For thus the Lord said to me: "Go, set a watchman 6
16 For thus the Lord said to me, "Within a year 6
22:15 Thus says the Lord GOD of hosts, "Come, go to this 6
24:13 For thus it shall be in the midst of the earth 6
28:16 thus says the Lord GOD, "Behold, I am laying in Zion 6
29:22 thus says the LORD, who redeemed Abraham 6
30:12 Therefore thus says the Holy One of Israel 6
15 For thus said the Lord GOD, the Holy One of Israel 6
31: 4 For thus the LORD said to me, As a lion 6
36: 4 Thus says the great king, the king of Assyria 6
14 Thus says the king: 'Do not let Hezeki'ah deceive 6
16 for thus says the king of Assyria 6
37: 3 Thus says Hezeki'ah, 'This day is a day of distress 6
6 Say to your master, 'Thus says the LORD 6
10 Thus shall you speak to Hezeki'ah king of Judah 6
21 Thus says the LORD, the God of Israel 6
33 thus says the LORD concerning the king 10
38: 1 Thus says the LORD: Set your house in order; 6
5 Thus says the LORD, the God of David your father 6
42: 5 Thus says God, the LORD, who created the heavens 6
43: 1 now thus says the LORD, he who created you 6
14 Thus says the LORD, your Redeemer 6
16 Thus says the LORD, who makes a way in the sea 6
44: 2 Thus says the LORD who made you, who formed you 6
6 Thus says the LORD, the King of Israel 6
24 Thus says the LORD, your Redeemer, who formed you 6
45: 1 Thus says the LORD to his anointed, to Cyrus 6
11 Thus says the LORD, the Holy One of Israel 6
14 Thus says the LORD: "The wealth of Egypt 6
18 For thus says the LORD, who created the heavens 6
48:17 Thus says the LORD, your Redeemer, the Holy One 6
49: 7 Thus says the LORD, the Redeemer of Israel 6
8 Thus says the LORD: "In a time of favor 6
22 Thus says the Lord GOD: "Behold, I will lift up my 6
25 Surely, thus says the LORD: "Even the captives 6
50: 1 Thus says the LORD: "Where is your mother's bill 6
51:22 thus says your Lord, the LORD, your God 6
52: 3 For thus says the LORD: "You were sold for nothing 6
4 For thus says the Lord GOD: My people went down 6
56: 1 Thus says the LORD: "Keep justice 6
4 For thus says the LORD: "To the eunuchs who keep 6
8 Thus says the Lord GOD, who gathers the outcasts *
57:15 For thus says the high and lofty One who inhabits 6
65: 8 Thus says the LORD: "As the wine is found 6
13 Therefore thus says the Lord GOD: 6
66: 1 Thus says the LORD: "Heaven is my throne 6
12 For thus says the LORD: "Behold, I will extend 6
Jer 2: 2 Thus says the LORD, I remember the devotion 6
5 Thus says the LORD 6
4: 3 For thus says the LORD to the men of Judah 6
27 For thus says the LORD 6
5:13 Thus shall it be done to them!' 6
14 Therefore thus says the LORD, the God of hosts 6
6: 6 For thus says the LORD of hosts: "Hew down her trees 6
9 Thus says the LORD of hosts 6
16 Thus says the LORD: "Stand by the roads, and look 6
21 Therefore thus says the LORD: 'Behold 6
22 Thus says the LORD: "Behold, a people is coming 6
7: 3 Thus says the LORD of hosts, the God of Israel 6
20 Therefore thus says the Lord GOD: Behold, my anger 6
21 Thus says the LORD of hosts, the God of Israel 6
8: 4 You shall say to them, Thus says the LORD 6
9: 7 Therefore thus says the LORD of hosts: "Behold 6
15 Therefore thus says the LORD of hosts 6
17 Thus says the LORD of hosts: "Consider, and call 6
22 Speak, "Thus says the LORD 6
23 Thus says the LORD: "Let not the wise man glory 6
10: 2 Thus says the LORD 6
11 Thus shall you say to them 14
18 For thus says the LORD 6
11: 3 You shall say to them, Thus says the LORD 6
11 Therefore, thus says the LORD, Behold 6
21 Therefore thus says the LORD 6
22 therefore thus says the LORD of hosts: "Behold 6
12:14 Thus says the LORD 6
13: 1 Thus said the LORD to me 6
9 Thus says the LORD: Even so will I spoil the pride 6
12 Thus says the LORD, the God of Israel 6
13 Then you shall say to them, 'Thus says the LORD 6
14:10 Thus says the LORD concerning this people 6
10 They have loved to wander thus 10
15 Therefore thus says the LORD 6
15: 2 you shall say to them, 'Thus says the LORD 6
19 Therefore thus says the LORD: "If you return 6
16: 3 For thus says the LORD concerning the sons 6
5 For thus says the LORD 6
9 For thus says the LORD of hosts, the God of Israel 6
17: 5 Thus says the LORD 6
19 Thus said the LORD to me 6
21 Thus says the LORD 6
18:11 Thus says the LORD, Behold, I am shaping evil 6
13 thus says the LORD: Ask among the nations 6
19: 1 Thus said the LORD, "Go, buy a potter's earthen flask 6
3 Thus says the LORD of hosts, the God of Israel 6
11 and shall say to them, 'Thus says the LORD of hosts 6
12 Thus will I do to this place, says the LORD 10
15 Thus says the LORD of hosts, the God of Israel 6
20: 4 thus says the LORD: Behold, I will make you a terror 6
21: 4 Thus you shall say to Zedeki'ah, 'Thus says the LORD 6
4 Thus you shall say to Zedeki'ah, 'Thus says the LORD 6
8 to this people you shall say: 'Thus says the LORD 6
12 O house of David! Thus says the LORD 6
22: 1 Thus says the LORD: "Go down to the house 6
3 Thus says the LORD: Do justice and righteousness 6
6 For thus says the LORD concerning the house 6
8 Why has the LORD dealt thus with this great city? 8
11 For thus says the LORD concerning Shallum 6
18 thus says the LORD concerning Jehoi'akim 6
30 Thus says the LORD: "Write this man down 6
23: 2 Therefore thus says the LORD, the God of Israel 6
15 Therefore thus says the LORD of hosts 6
16 Thus says the LORD of hosts 6
35 Thus shall you say, every one to his neighbor 6
37 Thus you shall say to the prophet 6
38 thus says the LORD, 'Because you have said these 6
24: 5 Thus says the LORD, the God of Israel 6
8 But thus says the LORD 6
25: 8 Therefore thus says the LORD of hosts: 6
15 Thus the LORD, the God of Israel, said to me 6
27 you shall say to them, 'Thus says the LORD of hosts 6
28 you shall say to them, 'Thus says the LORD of hosts 6
32 Thus says the LORD of hosts 6
26: 2 Thus says the LORD: Stand in the court of the LORD'S 6
4 You shall say to them, 'Thus says the LORD 6
18 Thus says the LORD of hosts, Zion shall be plowed 6
27: 2 Thus the LORD said to me: "Make yourself thongs 6
4 Thus says the LORD of hosts, the God of Israel 6
16 Thus says the LORD: Do not listen to the words 6
19 For thus says the LORD of hosts 6
21 thus says the LORD of hosts, the God of Israel 6
28: 2 Thus says the LORD of hosts, the God of Israel 6
11 Thus says the LORD: Even so will I break the yoke 6
13 Go, tell Hanani'ah, 'Thus says the LORD 6
14 For thus says the LORD of hosts, the God of Israel 6
16 Therefore thus says the LORD 6
29: 4 Thus says the LORD of hosts, the God of Israel 6
8 For thus says the LORD of hosts, the God of Israel 6
10 For thus says the LORD 6

16 Thus says the LORD concerning the king 6
17 Thus says the LORD of hosts, Behold 6
21 Thus says the LORD of hosts, the God of Israel 6
25 Thus says the LORD of hosts, the God of Israel 6
31 Send to all the exiles, saying, 'Thus says the LORD 6
32 thus says the LORD: Behold, I will punish Shemai'ah 6
30: 2 Thus says the LORD, the God of Israel 6
5 Thus says the LORD: We have heard a cry of panic 6
12 For thus says the LORD: Your hurt is incurable 6
18 Thus says the LORD: Behold, I will restore 6
31: 2 Thus says the LORD 6
7 For thus says the LORD: "Sing aloud with gladness 6
15 Thus says the LORD: "A voice is heard in Ramah 6
16 Thus says the LORD: "Keep your voice from weeping 6
23 Thus says the LORD of hosts, the God of Israel 6
35 Thus says the LORD, who gives the sun for light 6
37 Thus says the LORD 6
32: 3 Why do you prophesy and say, 'Thus says the LORD 6
14 Thus says the LORD of hosts, the God of Israel 6
15 For thus says the LORD of hosts, the God of Israel 6
28 Therefore, thus says the LORD 6
36 Now therefore thus says the LORD 6
42 For thus says the LORD 6
33: 2 Thus says the LORD who made the earth 6
4 For thus says the LORD, the God of Israel 6
10 Thus says the LORD: In this place of which you say 6
12 Thus says the LORD of hosts 6
17 For thus says the LORD 6
20 Thus says the LORD: If you can break my covenant 6
24 Thus they have despised my people 1
25 Thus says the LORD 6
34: 2 Thus says the LORD, the God of Israel: Go and speak 6
2 Thus says the LORD: Behold, I am giving this city 6
4 O Zedeki'ah . . ! Thus says the LORD concerning you 6
13 Thus says the LORD, the God of Israel 6
17 Therefore, thus says the LORD: You have not obeyed 6
35:13 Thus says the LORD of hosts, the God of Israel 6
17 Therefore, thus says the LORD, the God of hosts 6
18 Thus says the LORD of hosts, the God of Israel 6
19 therefore thus says the LORD of hosts 6
36:29 Thus says the LORD, You have burned this scroll 6
30 thus says the LORD concerning Jehoi'akim king 6
37: 7 Thus says the LORD, God of Israel 6
7 Thus shall you say to the king of Judah 6
9 Thus says the LORD, Do not deceive yourselves 6
38: 2 Thus says the LORD 6
3 Thus says the LORD, This city shall . . be given 6
17 Thus says the LORD, the God of hosts 6
39:16 Thus says the LORD of hosts, the God of Israel 6
42: 9 said to them, "Thus says the LORD, the God of Israel 6
15 Thus says the LORD of hosts, the God of Israel 6
18 For thus says the LORD of hosts, the God of Israel 6
43:10 Thus says the LORD of hosts, the God of Israel 6
44: 2 Thus says the LORD of hosts, the God of Israel 6
7 thus says the LORD God of hosts, the God of Israel 6
11 thus says the LORD of hosts, the God of Israel 6
25 Thus says the LORD of hosts, the God of Israel 6
30 Thus says the LORD 6
45: 2 Thus says the LORD, the God of Israel, to you 6
4 Thus shall you say to him, Thus says the LORD 6
4 Thus shall you say to him, Thus says the LORD 6
47: 2 Thus says the LORD: Behold, waters are rising 6
48: 1 Concerning Moab. Thus says the LORD of hosts 6
40 For thus says the LORD: "Behold, one shall fly 6
49: 1 Concerning the Ammonites. Thus says the LORD 6
7 Concerning Edom. Thus says the LORD of hosts 6
12 thus says the LORD: "If those who did not deserve 6
28 Thus says the LORD: "Rise up, advance against Kedar 6
35 Thus says the LORD of hosts: "Behold, I will break 6
50:18 Therefore, thus says the LORD of hosts 6
33 Thus says the LORD of hosts: The people of Israel 6
51: 1 Thus says the LORD: "Behold, I will stir up 6
33 For thus says the LORD of hosts, the God of Israel 6
36 Therefore thus says the LORD: "Behold, I will plead 6
58 Thus says the LORD of hosts 6
64 say, 'Thus shall Babylon sink, to rise no more 8
Lam 2:20 O LORD, and see! With whom hast thou dealt thus? 8
Ezk 1: 8 And the four had their faces and their wings thus •
2: 4 you shall say to them, 'Thus says the Lord GOD.' 6
3:11 say to them, 'Thus says the Lord GOD' 6
27 and you shall say to them, 'Thus says the Lord GOD' 6
4:13 Thus shall the people of Israel eat their bread 8
5: 5 Thus says the Lord GOD: This is Jerusalem; 6
7 Therefore thus says the Lord GOD 6
8 therefore thus says the Lord GOD: Behold, I, even I 6
13 Thus shall my anger spend itself 1
6: 3 Thus says the Lord GOD to the mountains 6
11 Thus says the Lord GOD: "Clap your hands 6
12 Thus I will spend my fury upon them. 1
7: 2 thus says the Lord GOD to the land of Israel: An end! 6
5 Thus says the Lord GOD: Disaster after disaster! 6
11: 5 and he said to me, "Say, Thus says the LORD 10
7 Therefore thus says the Lord GOD 6
16 Therefore say, 'Thus says the Lord GOD 10
17 Therefore say, 'Thus says the Lord 10
12:10 Say to them, 'Thus says the Lord GOD: This oracle 10
19 say of the people of the land, Thus says the Lord 6
23 Tell them therefore, 'Thus says the Lord GOD 10
28 Therefore say to them, Thus says the Lord GOD 10

13: 3 Thus says the Lord GOD, Woe to the foolish 6
8 Therefore thus says the Lord God 6
13 Therefore thus says the Lord GOD 6
15 Thus will I spend my wrath upon the wall •
18 and say, Thus says the Lord GOD 6
20 Wherefore thus says the Lord GOD 10
14: 4 and say to them, Thus says the Lord GOD 6
6 Thus says the Lord GOD: Repent and turn away 6
21 For thus says the Lord GOD 6
15: 6 Therefore thus says the Lord GOD 6
16: 3 and say, Thus says the Lord GOD to Jerusalem 6
13 Thus you were decked with gold and silver; 1
36 Thus says the Lord GOD, Because your shame was 6
59 Yea, thus says the Lord GOD: I will deal with you 6
17: 3 say, Thus says the Lord GOD 6
9 Say, Thus says the Lord GOD: Will it thrive? 6
19 Therefore thus says the Lord GOD: As I live, surely 6
22 Thus says the Lord GOD: "I myself will take a sprig 6
20: 3 and say to them, Thus says the Lord GOD 6
5 and say to them, Thus says the Lord GOD 6
27 and say to them, Thus says the Lord GOD 6
30 Thus says the Lord GOD: Will you defile 6
39 As for you, O house of Israel, thus says the Lord GOD 6
47 Hear the word of the LORD: Thus says the Lord GOD 6
21: 3 say to the land of Israel, Thus says the LORD 6
9 Son of man, prophesy and say, Thus says the Lord, 6
24 Therefore thus says the Lord GOD 10
26 thus says the Lord GOD: Remove the turban 6
28 son of man, prophesy, and say, Thus says the Lord 6
22: 3 You shall say, Thus says the Lord GOD 6
19 Therefore thus says the Lord GOD 6
28 divining lies for them, saying, 'Thus says the Lord 6
23:21 Thus you longed for the lewdness of your youth 1
22 Therefore, O Ohol'ibah, thus says the Lord GOD 10
27 Thus I will put an end to your lewdness 1
28 For thus says the Lord GOD: Behold, I will deliver 6
32 Thus says the Lord GOD: "You shall drink 6
35 Therefore thus says the Lord GOD 6
44 Thus they went in to Oho'lah and to Ohol'ibah 10
46 thus says the Lord GOD: "Bring up a host 6
48 Thus will I put an end to lewdness in the land 1
24: 3 say to them, Thus says the Lord GOD: Set on the pot 6
6 Therefore thus says the Lord GOD 10
9 Therefore thus says the Lord GOD 6
19 what these . . mean for us, that you are acting thus? •
21 Say to the house of Israel, Thus says the Lord GOD 6
24 Thus shall Ezekiel be to you a sign; 1
25: 3 Thus says the Lord GOD, Because you said, 'Aha!' 6
6 For thus says the Lord GOD 6
8 Thus says the Lord GOD: Because Moab said, Behold 6
12 Thus says the Lord GOD: Because Edom acted 6
13 therefore thus says the Lord GOD 6
15 Thus says the Lord GOD: Because the Philistines 6
16 therefore thus says the Lord GOD, Behold 6
26: 3 therefore thus says the Lord GOD 6
7 For thus says the Lord GOD: Behold, I will bring 6
15 Thus says the Lord GOD to Tyre 6
19 For thus says the Lord GOD: When I make you a city 6
27: 3 thus says the Lord GOD: "O Tyre, you have said 6
28: 2 to the prince of Tyre, Thus says the Lord GOD 6
6 therefore thus says the Lord GOD 6
12 king of Tyre, and say to him, Thus says the Lord GOD 6
22 Thus says the Lord GOD: "Behold, I am against you 6
25 Thus says the Lord GOD 6
29: 3 Thus says the Lord GOD: "Behold, I am against you 6
8 thus says the Lord GOD: Behold, I will bring a sword 6
13 thus says the Lord GOD: At the end of 40 years 6
19 thus says the Lord GOD: Behold, I will give the land 6
30: 2 Son of man, prophesy, and say, Thus says the Lord 6
6 Thus says the LORD: Those who support Egypt shall 6
10 Thus says the Lord GOD: I will put an end 6
13 Thus says the Lord GOD: I will destroy the idols 6
19 Thus I will execute acts of judgment upon Egypt. 1
22 Therefore thus says the Lord GOD: Behold, I am 6
31:10 Therefore thus says the Lord GOD 10
15 Thus says the Lord GOD: When it goes down to Sheol 6
18 Whom are you thus like in glory and in greatness 8
32: 3 Thus says the Lord GOD: I will throw my net over you 6
11 For thus says the Lord GOD: The sword of the king 6
33:10 say to the house of Israel, Thus have you said 10
25 Therefore say to them, Thus says the Lord GOD 10
27 Say this to them, Thus says the Lord GOD: As I live 6
34: 2 Thus says the Lord GOD: Ho, shepherds of Israel 6
10 Thus says the Lord GOD, Behold 6
11 For thus says the Lord GOD: Behold 6
17 As for you, my flock, thus says the Lord GOD: Behold 6
20 Therefore, thus says the Lord GOD to them: Behold 10
35: 3 and say to it, Thus says the Lord GOD: Behold 6
14 Thus says the Lord GOD: For the rejoicing 6
36: 2 Thus says the Lord GOD: Because the enemy said 6
3 therefore prophesy, and say, Thus says the Lord 10
4 Thus says the Lord GOD to the mountains 6
5 thus says the Lord GOD: I speak in my hot jealousy 6
6 Thus says the Lord GOD: Behold, I speak 6
7 thus says the Lord GOD: I swear that the nations 6
13 Thus says the Lord GOD: Because men say to you 6
22 Thus says the Lord GOD: It is not for your sake 6
33 Thus says the Lord GOD: On the day that I cleanse 6
37 Thus says the Lord GOD: This also I will let 6

37: 5 Thus says the Lord GOD to these bones 6
9 and say to the breath, Thus says the Lord GOD 6
12 prophesy, and say to them, Thus says the Lord GOD 10
19 say to them, Thus says the Lord GOD 6
21 then say to them, Thus says the Lord GOD 6
38: 3 Thus says the Lord GOD: Behold, I am against you 6
10 Thus says the Lord GOD: On that day thoughts will 6
14 Thus says the Lord GOD: On that day when my people 6
17 Thus says the Lord GOD: Are you he of whom I spoke 6
39: 1 Thus says the Lord GOD: Behold, I am against you 6
16 Thus shall they cleanse the land. 1
17 As for you, son of man, thus says the Lord GOD 6
25 Therefore thus says the Lord GOD 10
41: 7 thus one went up from the lowest story to the top 10
43:18 he said to me, "Son of man, thus says the Lord GOD 6
20 thus you shall cleanse the altar 1
44: 6 Thus says the Lord GOD: O house of Israel 6
9 Therefore thus says the Lord GOD: No foreigner 6
45: 9 Thus says the Lord GOD: Enough, O princes of Israel! 6
18 Thus says the Lord GOD: In the first month 6
46: 1 Thus says the Lord GOD: The gate of the inner court 6
15 Thus the lamb and the meal offering and the oil 1
16 Thus says the Lord GOD: If the prince makes a gift 6
47:13 Thus says the Lord GOD: "These are the boundaries 6
Dan 2:24 Daniel . . went and said thus to him 15
25 before the king in haste, and said thus to him 15
4:14 cried aloud and said thus, 'Hew down the tree 15
7:23 Thus he said: 'As for the fourth beast, there 15
Hos 10:15 Thus it shall be done to you, O house of Israel 8
Ams 1: 3 Thus says the LORD: "For three transgressions 6
6 Thus says the LORD: "For three transgressions 6
9 Thus says the LORD: "For three transgressions 6
11 Thus says the LORD: "For three transgressions 6
13 Thus says the LORD: "For three transgressions 6
2: 1 Thus says the LORD: "For three transgressions 6
4 Thus says the LORD: "For three transgressions 6
6 Thus says the LORD: "For three transgressions 6
3:11 thus says the Lord GOD: "An adversary shall 6
12 Thus says the LORD: "As the shepherd rescues 6
4:12 Therefore thus I will do to you, O Israel; 6
5: 3 For thus says the Lord GOD: "The city that went 6
4 thus says the LORD to the house of Israel 6
16 thus says the LORD, the God of hosts, the Lord 6
7: 1 Thus the Lord GOD showed me 6
4 Thus the Lord GOD showed me 6
11 For thus Amos has said, 'Jerobo'am shall die 6
17 thus says the LORD: 'Your wife shall be a harlot 6
8: 1 Thus the Lord GOD showed me 6
Obd 1: 1 Thus says the Lord GOD concerning Edom 6
Mic 2: 3 Therefore thus says the LORD 6
6 Do not preach"–thus they preach •
3: 5 Thus says the LORD concerning the prophets 6
7: 3 thus they weave it together. •
Nah 1:12 Thus says the LORD, "Though they be strong 6
Hag 1: 2 Thus says the LORD of hosts: This people say 6
5 Now therefore thus says the LORD of hosts 6
7 Thus says the LORD of hosts: Consider how you have 6
2: 6 For thus says the LORD of hosts 6
11 Thus says the LORD of hosts: Ask the priests 6
Zec 1: 3 Therefore say to them, Thus says the LORD of hosts 6
4 Thus says the LORD of hosts, Return from your evil 6
14 Thus says the LORD of hosts: I am exceedingly 6
16 Therefore, thus says the LORD, I have returned 6
17 Cry again, Thus says the LORD of hosts 6
2: 8 thus said the LORD of hosts, after his glory sent 6
3: 7 Thus says the LORD of hosts: If you will walk 6
6:12 say to him, 'Thus says the LORD of hosts 6
7: 9 Thus says the LORD of hosts, Render true 6
14 Thus the land they left was desolate 1
8: 2 Thus says the LORD of hosts: I am jealous for Zion 6
3 Thus says the LORD: I will return to Zion 6
4 Thus says the LORD of hosts: Old men and old women 6
6 Thus says the LORD of hosts: If it is marvelous 6
7 Thus says the LORD of hosts: Behold, I will save 6
9 Thus says the LORD of hosts: "Let your hands be 6
14 For thus says the LORD of hosts: "As I purposed to do 6
19 Thus says the LORD of hosts: The fast of the fourth 6
20 Thus says the LORD of hosts: Peoples shall yet 6
23 Thus says the LORD of hosts: In those days ten men 6
11: 4 Thus said the LORD my God: "Become shepherd 6
12: 1 Thus says the LORD, who stretched out the heavens •
Mat 3:15 thus it is fitting for us to fulfil all righteousness. 31
6: 2 Thus, when you give alms, sound no trumpet before 28
7:20 Thus you will know them by their fruits. 17
9:18 While he was thus speaking to them 29
22:45 If David thus calls him Lord, how is he his son? 28
23:31 Thus you witness against yourselves 33
Mrk 2: 7 Why does this man speak thus? It is blasphemy! 31
8 that they thus questioned within themselves 31
8 Why do you question thus in your hearts? 29
7:13 thus making void the word of God •
19 Thus he declared all foods clean.) •
14: 4 Why was the ointment thus wasted? 29
15:39 saw that he thus breathed his last 31
Lke 1:25 Thus the Lord has done to me 31
13: 2 because they suffered thus? 29
18:11 The Pharisee stood and prayed thus with himself 29
20:44 David thus calls him Lord; so how is he his son? 28
24:46 said to them, "Thus it is written 31

Joh 7:32 The Pharisees heard the crowd thus muttering 29
8:28 speak thus as the Father taught me. 29
30 As he spoke thus, many believed in him. 29
11:11 Thus he spoke, and then he said to them 29
48 If we let him go on thus 31
13:21 When Jesus had thus spoken 31
25 lying thus, close to the breast of Jesus, he said 31
Act 3:18 that his Christ should suffer, he thus fulfilled. 31
4:36 Thus Joseph who was surnamed by the apostles 20
20:36 when he had spoken thus, he knelt down and prayed 29
21:11 Thus says the Holy Spirit 27
24 Thus all will know 25
22:24 to find out why they shouted thus against him. 31
26:12 Thus I journeyed to Damascus 23
24 as he thus made his defense 29
Rom 4:11 who thus have righteousness reckoned to them 22
7: 2 Thus a married woman is bound by law 18
9:20 say to its molder, "Why have you made me thus? 31
11:14 to make . . jealous, and thus save some of them. *
15:20 thus making it my ambition to preach the gospel 31
1Co 8:12 Thus, sinning against your brethren 31
14:22 Thus, tongues are a sign not for believers 33
15:45 Thus it is written, "The first man Adam 31
2Co 5:16 we regard him thus no longer. 26
Gal 3: 6 Thus Abraham "believed God 24
Php 1: 7 It is right for me to feel thus about you all 24
3:15 Let those of us who are mature be thus minded; 29
4: 1 stand firm thus in the Lord, my beloved. 31
1Ti 6:19 thus laying up for themselves a good foundation *
Heb 6: 9 Though we speak thus 31
15 thus Abraham . . obtained the promise. 31
9: 6 These preparations having thus been made 31
12 thus securing an eternal redemption. *
23 Thus it was necessary . . 28
11:14 For people who speak thus make it clear 32
12:28 thus let us offer to God acceptable worship 21
2Pe 3:11 Since all these things are thus to be dissolved 31
1Jn 3: 3 every one who thus hopes in him purifies himself 29
Rev 3: 5 He who conquers shall be clad thus in white 31
11: 5 thus he is doomed to be killed. . 31
1Es 2: 3 Thus says Cyrus king of the Persians 27
2Es 1:12 speak to them and say, Thus says the Lord 35
15 Thus says the Lord Almighty 35
22 Thus says the Lord Almighty 35
28 Thus says the Lord Almighty 35
33 Thus says the Lord Almighty 35
2: 1 Thus says the Lord 35
10 Thus says the Lord to Ezra: "Tell my people 35
3:22 Thus the disease became permanent 34
7:38 Thus he will speak to them on the day of judgment- 35
15:21 Thus says the Lord God 35
Jdt 1:14 Thus he took possession of his cities 25
2: 5 Thus says the Great King 27
AEs 13: 1 The Great King, Artaxerxes . . writes thus 27
Wis 2:21 Thus they reasoned, but they were led astray 29
5:12 the air, thus divided, comes together at once *
9:18 thus the paths of those on earth were set right 31
17:16 and thus was kept shut up in a prison not made of iron 31
Sir 1:30 thus bring dishonor upon yourself *
7: 6 thus put a blot on your integrity. *
21: 4 thus the house of the proud will be laid waste. 31
33: 4 Prepare what to say, and thus you will be heard; 31
Bar 2:21 Thus says the Lord: Bend your shoulders and serve 31
Sus 1:62 Thus innocent blood was saved that day. 25
1Mc 2:26 Thus he burned with zeal for the law 25
3: 8 thus he turned away wrath from Israel. 25
4:25 Thus Israel had a great deliverance that day. 25
51 Thus they finished all the work 25
5:44 Thus Carnaim was conquered 25
61 Thus the people suffered a great rout 25
6:16 Thus Antiochus the king died there 25
8:29 Thus on these terms the Romans make a treaty 31
9:27 Thus there was great distress in Israel 25
41 Thus the wedding was turned into mourning 25
73 Thus the sword ceased from Israel 25
10:65 Thus the king honored him 25
11:13 Thus he put two crowns upon his head 25
2Mc 4:38 The Lord thus repaid him *
7:28 Thus also mankind comes into being. 30
8:36 Thus he . . proclaimed that . . 25
9: 8 Thus he . . was brought down to earth 20
11:22 The king's letter ran thus 31
34 sent them a letter, which read thus 31
15:15 as he gave it he addressed him thus 27
4Mc 1:11 thus their native land was purified 33
22 Thus desire precedes pleasure 28
2: 5 Thus the law says, "You shall not covet 19
8 Thus . . he is forced to act 19
20 he would not have spoken thus. 31
16: 2 Thus I have demonstrated 28

thus far 1. עַד הֲלֹם 2. עַד הֵנָּה 3. עַד פֹּה
4. ἄχρι τοῦ δεῦρο
2Sm 7:18 Who am I . . that thou hast brought me thus far? 1
Job 38:11 and said, 'Thus far shall you come, and no farther 3
Jer 48:47 Thus far is the judgment on Moab. 2
51:64 Thus far are the words of Jeremiah. 2
Rom 1:13 (but thus far have been prevented) 4

thwart 1. בצר 2. הדף 3. ἀθετέω
Job 42: 2 no purpose of thine can be thwarted. 1
Prv 10: 3 but he thwarts the craving of the wicked. 2
1Co 1:19 the cleverness of the clever I will thwart. 3

tiara 1. μίτρα
Jdt 10: 3 and combed her hair and put on a tiara 1
16: 8 fastened her hair with a tiara 1

tidings 1. בְּשֹׂרָה 2. דָּבָר 3. שְׁמוּעָה 4. שֵׁמַע
Gen 29:13 When Laban heard the tidings of Jacob 4
Exd 33: 4 people heard these evil tidings, they mourned; 2
1Sm 4:19 heard the tidings that the ark . . was captured 3
11: 5 they told him the tidings of the men of Jabesh. 2
27:11 neither man nor woman . . to bring tidings to Gath *
2Sm 13:30 While they were on the way, tidings came to David 3
18:25 If he is alone, there are tidings in his mouth. 1
27 He is a good man, and comes with good tidings. 1
1Kg 14: 6 I am charged with heavy tidings for you. *
Ps 112: 7 He is not afraid of evil tidings; his heart is firm 3
Jer 49:14 I have heard tidings from the LORD 3
23 confounded, for they have heard evil tidings; 3
Ezk 21: 7 you sigh?' you shall say, 'Because of the tidings 3
Dan 11:44 tidings from the east and the north shall alarm 3
Obd 1: 1 We have heard tidings from the LORD 3
Jon 3: 6 Then tidings reached the king of Nin'eveh 2

tidings *See also* bear, bring, carry, herald, reward.

good tidings 1. בשׂר
2Sm 18:31 Cushite said, "Good tidings for my lord the king! 1

tie 1. אסר 2. נתן 3. ענד 4. δέω
Exd 39:31 they tied to it a lace of blue, to fasten it 2
2Kg 7:10 nothing but the horses tied, and the asses tied 1
10 nothing but the horses tied, and the asses tied 1
Prv 6:21 tie them about your neck. 3
Mat 21: 2 immediately you will find an ass tied 4
Mrk 11: 2 you will find a colt tied 4
4 they went away, and found a colt tied at the door 4
Lke 19:30 where on entering you will find a colt tied 4
Act 27:40 loosening the ropes that tied the rudders *
4Mc 11:10 they tied him to it on his knees 4

tie one's arms 1. περιαγκωνίζω
4Mc 6: 3 after they had tied his arms on each side 1

tie up 1. צור 2. περιπλέκω 3. προτείνω
2Kg 5:23 and tied up two talents of silver in two bags 1
12:10 and they counted and tied up in bags the money 1
Act 22:25 when they had tied him up with the thongs 3
4Mc 1:29 and ties up and waters and thoroughly irrigates 2

tier 1. פַּעַם
1Kg 7: 4 and window opposite window in three tiers. 1
5 and window was opposite window in three tiers. 1

tight *See* make, stretch.

tighten further 1. προσεπικατατείνω
4Mc 9:19 they tightened the wheel further. 1

tile 1. κέραμος
Lke 5:19 and let him down with his bed through the tiles 1

till 1. וְ 2. לְ 3. לְמַעַן 4. לִפְנֵי 5. מִן 6. עַד 7. עַד אֲשֶׁר
8. עַד שֶׁ 9. עַד (A) 10. עַד דִּי (A) 11. ἄχρι 12. ἄχρις
13. εἰς 14. ἕως 15. ἕως ἄν 16. ἕως ὅτου 17. ἕως οὗ
18. καί 19. μετά 20. μέχρι
Gen 3:19 you shall eat bread till you return to the ground 6
19:22 I can do nothing till you arrive there. 6
38:11 your father's house, till Shelah my son grows 6
17 Will you give me a pledge, till you send it? 6
Exd 15:16 still as a stone, till thy people, O LORD, pass 6
16 till the people pass by whom thou hast 6
16:19 Let no man leave any of it till the morning. 6
20 some left part of it till the morning 6
23 left over lay by to be kept till the morning.' 6
24 So they laid it by till the morning, as Moses bade 6
35 ate the manna . . till they came to a habitable 6
35 they ate the manna, till they came to the border 6
18:13 stood about Moses from morning till evening. 6
14 stand about you from morning till evening? 6
40:37 then they did not go onward till the day 6
Lev 24:12 they put him in custody, till the will of the LORD 2
Num 12:15 till Miriam was brought in again. 6
23:24 it does not lie down till it devours the prey 6
Deu 28:45 curses . . overtake you, till you are destroyed 6
Jos 5: 6 Israel walked . . till all the nation..perished 6
8 remained . . in the camp till they were healed. 6
8: 6 they will come out . . till we have drawn them away 6
20: 9 not . . till he stood before the congregation. 6
23:13 they shall be a snare and a trap . . till you perish 6
Jdg 3:25 they waited till they were utterly at a loss; 6
4:21 into his temple, till it went down into the ground 1
6:18 And he said, "I will stay till you return. 6
16: 2 Let us wait till the light of the morning; 6
3 Samson lay till midnight, and at midnight he 6
19: 7 his father-in-law urged him, till he lodged there *
26 woman came and fell down . . till it was light. 6
21: 2 to Bethel, and sat there till evening before God 6
Rut 1:13 would you therefore wait till they were grown? 7
2:21 keep close by . . till they have finished all 6
1Sm 9:13 the people will not eat till he comes 6
16:11 for we will not sit down till he comes here. 6
20: 5 hide myself in the field till the third day 6
22: 3 let . . stay with you, till I know what God will do 7
2Sm 3:35 if I taste bread or . . till the sun goes down! 4
2Kg 2: 8 water was parted . . till the two of them could go 1
17 when they urged him till he was ashamed, he said 6
3:20 water came . . till the country was filled 1
24 attacked the Moabites, till they fled 1
25 they overthrew . . till only its stones were left 6
4:20 to his mother, the child sat on her lap till noon 6
7: 3 said to one another, "Why do we sit here till we die? 6
8:15 took . . and spread it over his face, till he died. 1
10:17 he slew all . . till he had wiped them out 6
20:17 which your fathers have stored up till this day 6
21:16 shed . . blood, till he had filled Jerusalem 7
25: 2 the city was besieged till the eleventh year 6
2Ch 26:15 he was marvelously helped, till he was strong. 6
36:16 till the wrath of the LORD rose against his people 6
16 till there was no remedy. 6
Ezr 5: 5 not stop them till a report should reach Darius 9
9:14 angry with us till thou wouldst consume us 6
10:14 till the fierce wrath of our God over this matter 6
Neh 4:11 not know or see till we come into the midst of them 6
21 from the break of dawn till the stars came out. 6
Est 3: 7 cast it month after month till the twelfth month 2
Job 7: 4 I am full of tossing till the dawn. 6
19 nor let me alone till I swallow my spittle? 6
14:12 till the heavens are no more he will not awake 6
14 I would wait, till my release should come. 6
27: 5 till I die I will not put away my integrity from me. 6
Ps 10:15 seek out his wickedness till thou find none. *
18:37 and did not turn back till they were consumed. 6
40:12 iniquities have overtaken me, till I cannot see; 1
57: 1 refuge, till the storms of destruction pass by. 6
59:13 in wrath, consume them till they are no more 1
71:18 till I proclaim thy might to all the generations 6
72: 7 and peace abound, till the moon be no more! 6
107: 7 straight way, till they reached a city to dwell 2
110: 1 till I make your enemies your footstool. 6
123: 2 look to the LORD our God, till he have mercy upon 8
Prv 7:18 Come, let us take our fill of love till morning; 6
23 till an arrow pierces its entrails; 6
Ecc 2: 3 lay hold on folly, till I might see what was good 7
Isa 5:11 who tarry late . . till wine inflames them! *
22:14 iniquity will not be forgiven you till you die. 6
30:17 you shall flee, till you are left like a flagstaff 6
39: 6 which your fathers have stored up till this day 6
42: 4 be discouraged till he has established justice 6
Jer 51:39 till they swoon away and sleep a perpetual sleep 3
52: 5 till the eleventh year of King Zedeki'ah. 6
11 and put him in prison till the day of his death. 6
Ezk 4: 8 till you have completed the days of your siege. 6
14 up till now I have never eaten what died of itself 6
24:13 till I have satisfied my fury upon you. 6
28:15 blameless . . till iniquity was found in you. 6
34:21 till you have scattered them abroad 6
39:15 till the buriers have buried it 6
19 And you shall eat fat till you are filled, 2
19 and drink blood till you are drunk 2
Dan 2: 9 lying . . words before me till the times change. 10
4:23 with the beasts . . till seven times pass over 9
25 till you know that the Most High rules 9
33 till his hair grew as long as eagles' feathers 9
6:14 labored till the sun went down to rescue him. 9
11:36 prosper till the indignation is accomplished; 6
12: 1 since there was a nation till that time; 6
6 How long shall it be till the end of these wonders? *
13 go your way till the end; and you shall rest 2
Hos 8: 5 How long will it be till they are pure *
9:12 I will bereave them till none is left. †
Jon 4: 5 till he should see what would become of the city. 6
Zep 2: 5 and I will destroy you till no inhabitant is left. 5
3: 3 wolves that leave nothing till the morning. 2
Zec 10:10 and to Lebanon, till there is no room for them. *
Mal 1: 4 till they are called the wicked country 1
3: 3 till they present right offerings to the LORD. *
Mat 2: 9 in the East went before them, till it came to rest 14
13 flee to Egypt, and remain there till I tell you; 14
5:18 For truly, I say to you, till heaven and earth pass 14
26 you will never get out till you have paid the last 14
12:20 till he brings justice to victory; 14
13:33 till it was all leavened. 14
18:30 put him in prison till he should pay the debt. 14
34 till he should pay all his debt. 14
22:44 till I put thy enemies under thy feet'? 15
24:34 not pass away till all these things take place. 14
Mrk 12:36 till I put thy enemies under thy feet.' 15
Lke 1:80 till the day of his manifestation to Israel. 14
2:37 and as a widow till she was 84 14
9:39 it convulses him till he foams, and shatters him 19
12:59 till you have paid the very last copper. 14
13: 8 till I dig about it and put on manure. 16
21 till it was all leavened. 17
17: 8 till I eat and drink 14

20:43 till I make thy enemies a stool for thy feet.' 15
21:32 till all has taken place. 15
Joh 13:38 till you have denied me three times. 17
Act 2:35 till I make thy enemies a stool for thy feet.' 15
7:18 till there arose over Egypt another king 11
8:40 till he came to Caesare'a. 14
21: 5 till we were outside the city 14
23:12 till they had killed Paul. 14
14 an oath to taste no food till we have killed Paul. 14
21 till they have killed him 14
28:23 from morning till evening 14
Gal 3:19 till the offspring should come 12
1Ti 4:13 Till I come, attend to the . . reading 14
Heb 1:13 till I make thy enemies a stool for thy feet"? 14
Rev 7: 3 till we have sealed the servants of our God 11
16:21 till men cursed God for the plague of the hail 18
20: 3 no more, till the 1,000 years were ended. 11
Jdt 2: 8 till their wounded shall fill their valleys 18
10 hold them for me till the day of their punishment. 13
11:19 till you come to Jerusalem 14
Sir 35:18 till he crushes the loins of the unmerciful 15
18 till he takes away the multitude of the insolent 14
19 till he repays the man according to his deeds 14
19 till he judges the case of his people 14
40: 1 till the day they return to the mother of all. 14
47:25 till vengeance came upon them. 14
48:15 till they were carried away captive 14
50:19 till the order of worship of the Lord was ended 14
1Mc 5:53 till he came to the land of Judah. 14
9:13 the battle raged from morning till evening. 14
10:80 men from early morning till late afternoon. 14
14:10 till his renown spread to the ends of the earth. 16
2Mc 8:35 till he reached Antioch *
3Mc 4:15 from the rising of the sun till its setting 20

till (2) 1. עבד 2. עֲבֹדָה 3. *γεωργέω* 4. operor

Gen 2: 5 and there was no man to till the ground; 1
15 put him in the garden of Eden to till it and keep it. 1
3:23 sent him forth . . to till the ground 1
4:12 When you till the ground, it shall no longer yield 1
2Sm 9:10 you and your sons . . shall till the land for him 1
1Ch 27:26 over those . . for tilling the soil was Ezri 2
Prv 12:11 He who tills his land will have plenty of bread 1
28:19 He who tills his land will have plenty of bread 1
Isa 30:24 the oxen and the asses that till the ground 1
Jer 27:11 to till it and dwell there, says the LORD. 1
Ezk 36: 9 you shall be tilled and sown; 1
34 the land that was desolate shall be tilled 1
48:19 all the tribes of Israel, shall till it. 1
1Es 4: 6 those who . . till the soil 3
2Es 15:13 Let the farmers that till the ground mourn 4
1Mc 14: 8 They tilled their land in peace 3

till *See* long.

tiller 1. אִישׁ עבד 2. עבד 3. *γεωργός*

Gen 4: 2 keeper of sheep, and Cain a tiller of the ground. 2
9:20 Noah was the first tiller of the soil. 3
Zec 13: 5 he will say, 'I am no prophet, I am a tiller of the soil; 1

tiller of the soil 1. אִכָּר

Jol 1:11 Be confounded, O tillers of the soil 1

tilt 1. צעה 2. שׁכב

Job 38:37 Or who can tilt the waterskins of the heavens 2
Jer 48:12 when I shall send to him tilters who will tilt him 1

tilter 1. צעה

Jer 48:12 when I shall send to him tilters who will tilt him 1

timber 1. עֵץ 2. אָע (A) 3. *ξύλινος* 4. *ξύλον*

Lev 14:45 its stones and timber and all the plaster 1
1Kg 5: 6 who knows how to cut timber like the Sido'nians. 1
8 in the matter of cedar and cypress timber. 1
10 the timber of cedar and cypress that he desired 1
18 and prepared the timber and the stone to build 1
6:10 it was joined to the house with timbers of cedar. 1
9:11 supplied . . cedar and cypress timber and gold 1
15:22 carried away the stones of Ramah and its timber 1
2Kg 12:12 as well as to buy timber and quarried stone 1
22: 6 for buying timber and quarried stone to repair 1
1Ch 22: 4 cedar timbers without number; 1
14 timber and stone too I have provided. 1
2Ch 2: 8 cedar, cypress, and algum timber from Lebanon 1
8 your servants know how to cut timber in Lebanon. 1
9 to prepare timber for me in abundance 1
10 give for your servants, the hewers who cut timber 1
16 will cut whatever timber you need from Lebanon 1
16: 6 carried away the stones of Ramah and its timber 1
34:11 to buy . . timber for binders and beams 1
Ezr 5: 8 huge stones, and timber is laid in the walls; 2
6: 4 courses of great stones and one course of timber; 2
Neh 2: 8 letter to Asaph . . that he may give me timber 1
Ezk 26:12 your stones and timber and soil they will cast 1
Zec 5: 4 his house and consume it, both timber and stones. 1
1Es 4:48 to bring cedar timber from Lebanon to Jerusalem 4
6: 9 with costly timber laid in the walls. 4
25 one course of new native timber 3

timbrel 1. תֹּף

Exd 15:20 Miriam . . took a timbrel in her hand; 1
20 went out after her with timbrels and dancing. 1
Jdg 11:34 out to meet him with timbrels and with dances; 1
1Sm 18: 6 to meet King Saul, with timbrels, with songs of joy 1
Ps 81: 2 sound the timbrel, the sweet lyre with the harp. 1
149: 3 making melody to him with timbrel and lyre! 1
150: 4 Praise him with timbrel and dance; 1
Isa 5:12 harp, timbrel and flute and wine at their feasts; 1
24: 8 The mirth of the timbrels is stilled 1
30:32 will be to the sound of timbrels and lyres; 1
Jer 31: 4 Again you shall adorn yourself with timbrels 1

timbrel *See also* play.

time 1. אָז 2. אַחֲרוֹן 3. אִשׁוֹן 4. דּוֹר 5. זְמָן 6. יוֹם 7. ילד 8. כָּ 9. כֵּן 10. מוֹעֵד 11. מוֹשָׁב 12. מִסְפַּר הַיָּמִים 13. עֵת 14. עַתָּה 15. רֶגַע 16. אֱדַיִן (A) 17. זְמָן (A) 18. זְמַן (A) 19. עִדָּן (A) 20. *αἰών* 21. *ἀποβαίνω* 22. *δέ* 23. *ἐπί* 24. *ἤδη* 25. *ἡμέρα* 26. *καί* 27. *καιρός* 28. *νῦν* 29. *πρόσκαιρος* 30. *τότε* 31. *χρόνος* 32. *ὥρα* 33. hora 34. saeculum 35. tempus

Gen 4: 3 In the course of time Cain brought to the LORD 6
26 At that time men began to call upon . . the LORD 1
12: 6 At that time the Canaanites were in the land. 1
13: 7 At that time the Canaanites and the Per'izzites 1
21: 2 in his old age at the time of which God had spoken 10
22 At that time Abim'elech and Phicol the commander 13
24:11 the well of water at the time of evening 13
11 evening, the time when women go out to draw water. 13
26: 8 When he had been there a long time 6
29: 7 it is not time for the animals to be gathered 13
21 may go in to her, for my time is completed. 6
38: 1 It happened at that time that Judah went down 13
12 In course of time the wife of Judah 6
27 When the time of her delivery came 13
39: 5 From the time that he made him overseer 1
7 after a time his master's wife cast her eyes upon *
40: 1 Some time after this, the butler of the king *
47:29 when the time drew near that Israel must die 6
Exd 9: 5 the LORD set a time, saying, "Tomorrow the LORD 10
18 Behold, tomorrow about this time I will cause 13
12:40 The time that the people of Israel dwelt in Egypt 11
13:14 when in time to come your son asks you, 'What does *
18:22 let them judge the people at all times; 13
26 they judged the people at all times; 13
Lev 12: 2 time of her menstruation, she shall be unclean 6
15:25 not at the time of her impurity 13
25 has a discharge beyond the time of her impurity *
16: 2 not to come at all times into the holy place 13
23:27 it shall be for you a time of holy convocation *
37 you shall proclaim as times of holy convocation *
25: 8 so that the time of the seven weeks of years shall 6
50 the time he was with his owner shall be rated *
50 shall be rated as the time of a hired servant 6
26: 5 your threshing shall last to the time of vintage *
5 the vintage shall last to the time for sowing *
Num 3: 1 at the time when the LORD spoke with Moses 6
6: 5 until the time is completed for which he 6
12 but the former time shall be void 6
13 time of his separation has been completed 6
13:20 time was the season of the first ripe grapes. 6
20:15 we dwelt in Egypt a long time; 6
22: 4 So Balak . . who was king of Moab at that time 13
35:26 manslayer shall at any time go beyond the bounds *
Deu 1: 9 At that time I said to you, 'I am not able 13
16 I charged your judges at that time, 'Hear the cases 13
18 I commanded you at that time all the things 13
2:14 the time from our leaving Ka'desh-bar'nea until 6
34 we captured all his cities at that time 13
3: 4 we took all his cities at that time . . 60 cities 13
8 took the land at that time out of the hand 13
12 When we took possession of this land at that time 13
18 I commanded you at that time, saying, 'The LORD 13
21 I commanded Joshua at that time, 'Your eyes 13
23 I besought the LORD at that time, saying 13
4:14 LORD commanded me at that time to teach you 13
5: 5 I stood between the LORD and you at that time 13
9:20 I prayed for Aaron also at the same time. 13
10: 1 At that time the LORD said to me, 'Hew two tables 13
8 At that time the LORD set apart the tribe of Levi 13
10 I stayed on the mountain, as at the first time 6
16: 6 passover . . at the time you came out of Egypt. 10
9 count . . from the time you first put the sickle *
20:19 When you besiege a city for a long time, making war 6
26: 3 go to the priest who is in office at that time 6
32:35 for the time when their foot shall slip; 13
Jos 3:15 overflows . . throughout the time of harvest 6
5: 2 At that time the LORD said to Joshua 13
6:26 Joshua laid an oath upon them at that time, saying 13
10:27 at the time of the going down of the sun 13
11: 6 tomorrow at this time I will give over all of them 13
10 Joshua turned back at that time, and took Hazor 13
18 Joshua made war a long time with all those kings. 6
21 Joshua came at that time, and wiped out the Anakim 13
14:10 since the time that the LORD spoke this word 1
20: 6 the death of him who is high priest at the time 6
23: 1 A long time afterward, when the LORD had given 6

Jdg 3:29 they killed at that time about 10,000 13
4: 4 Deb'orah . . was judging Israel at that time. 13
10:14 let them deliver you in the time of your distress 13
11: 4 After a time the Ammonites made war 6
26 why did you not recover them within that time? 13
12: 6 there fell at that time 42,000 of the E'phraimites 13
14: 4 At that time the Philistines had dominion over 13
15: 1 at the time of wheat harvest, Samson went to visit 6
21:14 Benjamin returned at that time; and they gave 13
24 Israel departed from there at that time 13
1Sm 3: 2 At that time Eli . . was lying down in his own place; 6
4:20 about the time of her death the women . . said 13
9:16 Tomorrow about this time I will send to you a man 13
11: 9 Tomorrow, by the time the sun is hot, you shall have 8
14:18 the ark of God went at that time with the people 6
18:19 at the time when Merab . . should have been given 13
26 Before the time had expired 6
20:12 When I . . about this time tomorrow, or the third 13
22: 4 they stayed with him all the time that David was 6
25: 7 missed nothing, all the time they were in Carmel. 6
2Sm 2:11 the time that David was king . . was seven years 12
7:11 from the time that I appointed judges 6
11: 1 In . . the time when kings go forth to battle 13
13: 1 after a time Amnon . . loved her. 9
24:15 from the morning until the appointed time; 13
1Kg 2: 1 When David's time to die drew near, he charged 6
5 avenging in time of peace blood which had been *
11 time that David reigned over Israel was 40 years; 6
26 I will not at this time put you to death 6
8:65 Solomon held the feast at that time 13
9: 3 my eyes and my heart will be there for all time. 6
11:29 at that time, when Jerobo'am went out of Jerusalem 13
42 the time that Solomon reigned in Jerusalem 6
14: 1 At that time Abi'jah . . fell sick. 13
20 the time that Jerobo'am reigned was 22 years; 6
18:29 until the time of the offering of the oblation *
36 at the time of the offering of the oblation *
19: 2 if I do not make . . by this time tomorrow. 13
20: 6 send my servants to you tomorrow about this time 13
2Kg 3: 6 King Jeho'ram marched out of Sama'ria at that time 6
20 about the time of offering the sacrifice, behold *
4:16 At this season, when the time comes round 13
17 bore a son about that time the following spring 10
5:26 Was it a time to accept money and garments 13
7: 1 Tomorrow about this time . . meal shall be sold 13
18 barley shall be sold . . about this time tomorrow 13
8:22 Then Libnah revolted at the same time. 13
10: 6 and come to me at Jezreel tomorrow at this time. 13
36 The time that Jehu reigned over Israel 6
16: 6 At that time the king of Edom recovered Elath 13
18:16 At that time Hezeki'ah stripped the gold 13
20:12 At that time Mero'dach-bal'adan . . sent envoys 13
24:10 At that time the servants . . came up to Jerusalem 13
1Ch 9:25 to come in every seven days, from time to time 13
25 to come in every seven days, from time to time 13
12:32 Is'sachar men who had understanding of the times 13
17:10 from the time that I appointed judges 6
20: 1 spring . . the time when kings go forth to battle 13
21:28 At that time, when David saw that the LORD had 13
29 were at that time in the high place at Gibeon; 13
29:27 time that he reigned over Israel was 40 years; 6
2Ch 7: 8 At that time Solomon held the feast 13
16 my eyes and my heart will be there for all time. 6
13:18 Thus the men of Israel were subdued at that time 13
15: 3 For a long time Israel was without the true God 6
5 In those times there was no peace 13
16: 7 At that time Hana'ni the seer came to Asa 13
10 upon some of the people at the same time. 13
21:10 At that time Libnah also revolted from his rule 13
25:27 From the time he turned away from the LORD 13
28:16 At that time King Ahaz sent to the king of Assyria 13
22 In the time of his distress 13
30: 3 could not keep it in its time because the priests 13
26 since the time of Solomon . . there had been 6
32:23 he was exalted . . from that time onward. 9
35:17 people . . kept the passover at that time 13
Ezr 5: 3 At the same time Tat'tenai the governor 18
16 from that time until now it has been in building 16
8:35 At that time those who had come from captivity 13
10:13 people are many, and it is a time of heavy rain; 13
14 taken foreign wives come at appointed times 13
Neh 2: 6 it pleased the king to send me; and I set him a time. 5
4:22 I also said to the people at that time, "Let every 13
5:14 Moreover from the time that I was appointed 6
6: 1 (although up to that time I had not set up the doors 13
9:27 in the time of their suffering they cried to thee 13
28 many times thou didst deliver them 13
32 since the time of the kings of Assyria until 6
10:34 at times appointed, year by year, to burn 13
13: 6 after some time I asked leave of the king 6
21 time on they did not come on the sabbath. 13
31 wood offering, at appointed times 13
Est 1:13 the king said to the wise men who knew the times- 13
4:14 For if you keep silence at such a time as this 13
14 have . . come to the kingdom for such a time as this? 13
8: 9 king's secretaries were summoned at that time 13
Job 6:17 In time of heat they disappear; 13
15:32 It will be paid in full before his time 6
22:16 They were snatched away before their time; 13

24: 1 are not times of judgment kept by the Almighty 13
27:10 Will he call upon God at all times? 13
34:23 For he has not appointed a time for any man to go •
38:23 which I have reserved for the time of trouble 13
39: 2 do you know the time when they bring forth 13
Ps 9: 9 The LORD is . . a stronghold in times of trouble. 13
10: 1 Why dost thou hide thyself in times of trouble? 13
5 His ways prosper at all times; 13
31:15 My times are in thy hand; 13
32: 6 at a time of distress, in the rush of great waters 13
34: 1 I will bless the LORD at all times; 13
37:19 they are not put to shame in evil times 13
39 he is their refuge in the time of trouble. 13
49: 5 Why should I fear in times of trouble 6
62: 8 Trust in him at all times, O people; 13
69:13 At an acceptable time, O God, in the abundance 13
71: 9 Do not cast me off in the time of old age; 13
77: 8 Are his promises at an end for all time? 4
102:13 time to favor her; the appointed time has come. 13
106: 3 Blessed . . who do righteousness at all times! 13
113: 2 LORD from this time forth and for evermore! 14
115:18 we will bless the LORD from this time forth 14
119:20 with longing for thy ordinances at all times. 13
126 It is time for the LORD to act 13
121: 8 from this time forth and for evermore. 14
125: 2 from this time forth and for evermore. 14
131: 3 hope . . from this time forth and for evermore. 14
Prv 5:19 her affection fill you at all times with delight 13
7: 9 at the time of night and darkness. 3
17:17 A friend loves at all times 13
25:13 Like the cold of snow in the time of harvest 6
19 Trust in a faithless man in time of trouble 6
31:25 she laughs at the time to come. 6
Ecc 3: 1 and a time for every matter under heaven 13
2 a time to be born, and a time to die; 13
2 a time to be born, and a time to die; 13
2 a time to plant, and a time to pluck up what is 13
2 to plant, and a time to pluck up what is planted; 13
3 a time to kill, and a time to heal; 13
3 a time to kill, and a time to heal; 13
3 a time to break down, and a time to build up; 13
3 a time to break down, and a time to build up; 13
4 a time to weep, and a time to laugh; 13
4 a time to weep, and a time to laugh; 13
4 a time to mourn, and a time to dance; 13
4 a time to mourn, and a time to dance; 13
5 a time to cast away stones, and a time to gather 13
5 cast away . . and a time to gather stones together; 13
5 a time to embrace, and a time to refrain 13
5 to embrace, and a time to refrain from embracing; 13
6 a time to seek, and a time to lose; 13
6 a time to seek, and a time to lose; 13
6 a time to keep, and a time to cast away; 13
6 a time to keep, and a time to cast away; 13
7 a time to rend, and a time to sew; 13
7 a time to rend, and a time to sew; 13
7 a time to keep silence, and a time to speak; 13
7 a time to keep silence, and a time to speak; 13
8 a time to love, and a time to hate; 13
8 a time to love, and a time to hate; 13
8 a time for war, and a time for peace. 13
8 a time for war, and a time for peace. 13
11 He has made everything beautiful in its time; 13
17 for he has appointed a time for every matter 13
7:17 why should you die before your time? 13
8: 5 the mind of a wise man will know the time and way. 13
6 For every matter has its time and way 13
9:11 but time and chance happen to them all. 13
12 For man does not know his time. 13
12 the sons of men are snared at an evil time 13
Sng 2:12 flowers appear . . the time of singing has come 13
Isa 9: 1 In the former time he brought into contempt 13
1 in the latter time he will make glorious the way •
7 with righteousness from this time forth 14
13:22 its time is close at hand and its days 13
17:14 At evening time, behold, terror! 13
18: 7 At that time gifts will be brought to the LORD 13
20: 2 at that time the LORD had spoken by Isaiah 13
26:17 cries out in her pangs, when she is near her time 7
30: 8 for the time to come as a witness for ever. 6
33: 2 Be . . our salvation in the time of trouble. 13
6 he will be the stability of your times 13
39: 1 At that time Mer'odach-bal'adan the son of Bal'adan 13
48: 6 From this time forth I make you hear new things 14
16 from the time it came to be I have been there. 13
49: 8 the LORD: "In a time of favor I have answered you 13
59:21 the LORD, from this time forth and for evermore. 14
60:22 I am the LORD; in its time I will hasten it. 13
Jer 2:27 But in the time of their trouble they say 13
28 if they can save you, in your time of trouble; 13
3:17 At that time Jerusalem shall be called 13
4:11 At that time it will be said to this people 13
6:15 at the time that I punish them 13
8: 1 At that time, says the LORD 13
7 Even the stork in the heavens knows her times; 10
7 swallow, and crane keep the time of their coming; 13
15 for a time of healing, but behold, terror. 13
10:15 at the time of their punishment 13
11:12 cannot save them in the time of their trouble. 13
14 when they call to me in the time of their trouble. 13
14: 8 thou hope of Israel, its savior in time of trouble 13
19 for a time of healing, but behold, terror. 13
15:11 in the time of trouble and in the time of distress! 13
11 in the time of trouble and in the time of distress! 13
18: 7 If at any time I declare concerning a nation 15
9 And if at any time I declare concerning a nation 15
23 deal with them in the time of thine anger. 13
27: 7 until the time of his own land comes; 13
30: 7 it is a time of distress for Jacob; 13
31: 1 At that time, says the LORD, I will be the God of all 13
33:15 at that time I will cause a righteous Branch 13
20 and night will not come at their appointed time 13
39:10 gave them vineyards and fields at the same time. 6
46:21 come upon them, the time of their punishment. 13
49: 8 calamity of Esau . . the time when I punish him. 13
50: 4 In those days and in that time, says the LORD 13
16 one who handles the sickle in time of harvest; 13
20 In those days and in that time, says the LORD 13
27 their day has come, the time of their punishment. 13
31 your day has come, the time when I will punish you. 13
51: 6 for this is the time of the LORD'S vengeance 13
18 the time of their punishment they shall perish. 13
33 threshing floor at the time when it is trodden; 13
33 and the time of her harvest will come. 13
Ezk 7: 7 the time has come, the day is near, a day of tumult 13
12 The time has come, the day draws near. 13
11: 3 who say, 'The time is not near to build houses; •
12:27 and he prophesies of times far off. 13
16:47 within a very little time you were more corrupt •
18: 6 or approach a woman in her time of impurity •
21:25 day has come, the time of your final punishment 13
29 day has come, the time of their final punishment. 13
22: 3 blood in the midst of her, that her time may come 13
30: 3 a day of clouds, a time of doom for the nations. 13
33:22 by the time the man came to me in the morning; •
35: 5 of the sword at the time of their calamity 13
5 at the time of their final punishment; 13
36:11 you to be inhabited as in your former times, •
Dan 1: 5 three years, and at the end of that time •
18 At the end of the time, when the king had commanded 6
2: 8 I know . . that you are trying to gain time 19
9 lying . . words before me till the times change. 19
16 Daniel . . besought the king to appoint him a time 18
21 He changes times and seasons; 19
3: 8 at that time certain Chalde'ans came forward 17
4:16 let seven times pass over him. 19
23 with the beasts . . till seven times pass over 19
25 seven times shall pass over you, 19
26 sure for you from the time that you know •
32 seven times shall pass over you, 19
36 At the same time my reason returned to me; 18
6:10 got down upon his knees three times a day 18
13 but makes his petition three times a day. 18
7:12 lives were prolonged for a season and a time. 19
22 time came when the saints received the kingdom. 18
25 shall think to change the times and the law; 18
25 into his hand for a time, two times, and half a time 19
25 for a time, two times, and half a time 19
25 into his hand for a time, two times, and half a time 19
8:17 Understand . . vision is for the time of the end. 13
9:21 came . . at the time of the evening sacrifice. 13
25 built again . . but in a troubled time. 13
11: 7 those times a branch from her roots shall arise 13
14 In those times many shall rise against the king 13
23 from the time that an alliance is made with him •
24 plans against strongholds, but only for a time. 13
29 it shall not be this time as it was before. 2
35 until the time of the end, for it is yet 13
40 time of the end the king of the south shall attack 13
12: 1 time shall arise Michael, the great prince 13
1 there shall be a time of trouble, 13
1 since there was a nation till that time; 13
1 but at that time your people shall be delivered 13
4 seal the book, until the time of the end. 13
7 would be for a time, two times, and half a time; 10
7 would be for a time, two times, and half a time; 10
7 would be for a time, two times, and half a time; •
9 shut up and sealed until the time of the end. 13
11 from the time that the continual burnt offering 13
Hos 2: 9 Therefore I will take back my grain in its time 13
15 at the time when she came out of the land of Egypt. 6
10:12 for it is the time to seek the LORD 13
Jol 3: 1 For behold, in those days and at that time 13
Ams 5:13 he who is prudent will keep silent in such a time; 13
13 keep silent . . for it is an evil time. 13
Mic 2: 3 not walk haughtily, for it will be an evil time. 13
3: 4 he will hide his face from them at that time 13
4: 7 reign . . from this time forth and for evermore. 14
5: 3 time when she who is in travail has brought forth; 13
Hab 2: 3 For still the vision awaits its time; 10
Zep 1:12 At that time I will search Jerusalem with lamps 13
3:19 Behold, at that time I will deal 13
20 At that time I will bring you home 13
20 at the time when I gather you together; 13
Hag 1: 2 the time has not yet come to rebuild the house 13
4 Is it a time for you yourselves to dwell 13
Zec 14: 7 for at evening time there shall be light. 13
Mat 1:11 at the time of the deportation to Babylon. 23
2: 7 ascertained from them what time the star 31
16 two years old or under, according to the time 31
4:17 From that time Jesus began to preach, saying 30
8:29 Have you come here to torment us before the time? 27
11:25 At that time Jesus declared, "I thank thee, Father 27
12: 1 At that time Jesus went through the grainfields 27
13:30 at harvest time I will tell the reapers 27
14: 1 At that time Herod the tetrarch heard 27
24 the boat by this time was many furlongs distant 24
16: 3 but you cannot interpret the signs of the times. 27
21 From that time Jesus began to show his disciples 30
18: 1 At that time the disciples came to Jesus, saying 32
25:19 Now after a long time 31
26:18 The Teacher says, My time is at hand 27
Mrk 1:15 saying, "The time is fulfilled 27
10:30 receive a hundredfold now in this time 27
12: 2 When the time came 27
13:33 for you do not know when the time will come. 27
Lke 1:20 which will be fulfilled in their time. 27
23 when his time of service was ended 25
57 Now the time came for Elizabeth to be delivered 31
2: 6 the time came for her to be delivered. 25
22 when the time came for their purification 25
4: 5 the kingdoms of the world in a moment of time 31
27 lepers in Israel in the time of the prophet Eli'sha 23
7:45 from the time I came in she has not ceased to kiss •
8:13 and in time of temptation fall away. 27
27 for a long time he had worn no clothes 31
29 For many a time it had seized him 31
12:56 do you not know how to interpret the present time? 27
13: 1 There were some present at that very time 27
14:17 at the time for the banquet he sent his servant 32
18:30 who will not receive manifold more in this time 27
19:44 you did not know the time of your visitation. 27
20:10 When the time came 27
21: 8 'The time is at hand!' Do not go after them. 27
13 This will be a time for you to bear testimony. 21
24 until the times of the Gentiles are fulfilled. 27
36 watch at all times 27
23: 7 who was himself in Jerusalem at that time. 25
Joh 5: 6 and knew that he had been lying there a long time 31
7: 6 Jesus said to them, "My time has not yet come 27
6 your time is always here. 27
8 my time has not yet fully come. 27
11:39 by this time there will be an odor 24
Act 1: 6 at this time restore the kingdom to Israel? 31
7 not for you to know times or seasons 31
21 during all the time that the Lord Jesus went 31
3:19 times of refreshing may come 27
21 until the time for establishing 31
7:17 as the time of the promise drew near 31
20 At this time Moses was born 27
8:11 for a long time he had amazed them with his magic. 31
12: 1 About that time 27
13:11 you shall be blind and unable to see the sun for a time 27
14: 3 So they remained for a long time 31
28 remained no little time with the disciples. 31
15:33 after they had spent some time 31
17:30 The times of ignorance God overlooked 31
18:23 After spending some time there he departed 31
19:23 About that time there arose no little stir 27
20:18 how I lived among you all the time 27
26:28 In a short time you think to make me a Christian! •
27: 9 As much time had been lost 31
Rom 3:26 prove at the present time that he . . is righteous 27
8:18 the sufferings of this present time are not worth 27
9: 9 the promise said, "About this time I will return 27
11: 5 So too at the present time there is a remnant 27
1Co 4: 5 do not pronounce judgment before the time 27
7:18 Was any one at the time of his call uncircumcised? •
18 Was any one at the time of his call uncircumcised? •
16: 7 I hope to spend some time with you 31
2Co 6: 2 At the acceptable time I have listened to you 27
2 Behold, now is the acceptable time 27
8:14 your abundance at the present time 27
Gal 4: 4 when the time had fully come 31
Eph 1:10 as a plan for the fulness of time 27
2:12 you were at that time separated from Christ 27
5:16 making the most of the time 27
6:18 Pray at all times in the Spirit 27
Col 4: 5 making the most of the time. 27
1Th 2:17 for a short time 27
5: 1 as to the times and the seasons, brethren 31
2Th 2: 6 so that he may be revealed in his time. 27
3:16 give you peace at all times in all ways •
1Ti 2: 6 testimony to which was borne at the proper time. 27
4: 1 in later times some will depart from the faith 27
6:15 this will be made manifest at the proper time 27
2Ti 3: 1 in the last days there will come times of stress. 27
4: 3 For the time is coming 27
6 the time of my departure has come. 27
Tit 1: 3 at the proper time manifested in his word 27
Heb 5:12 For though by this time you ought to be teachers 31
9:10 imposed until the time of reformation. 27
11:32 time would fail me to tell of Gideon, Barak, Samson 31
12:10 for a short time at their pleasure 25
1Pe 1: 5 salvation ready to be revealed in the last time. 27
11 they inquired what person or time was indicated 27
17 throughout the time of your exile. 31

20 He . . was made manifest at the end of the times 31
4: 2 so as to live for the rest of the time in the flesh 31
3 Let the time that is past suffice 31
17 For the time has come for judgment to begin 27
Jde 1:18 In the last time there will be scoffers 31
25 before all time and now and for ever. Amen. 20
Rev 1: 3 for the time is near. 27
2:21 I gave her time to repent, but she refuses 31
11:18 and the time for the dead to be judged 27
12:12 because he knows that his time is short! 27
14 be nourished for a time, and times, and half a time. 27
14 be nourished for a time, and times, and half a time. 27
14 be nourished for a time, and times, and half a time. 27
22:10 for the time is near. 27
1Es 1:19 people of Israel who were present at that time 27
20 since the times of Samuel the prophet; 31
58 keep sabbath all the time of its desolation 31
2:16 in the time of Artaxerxes king of the Persians 31
6: 3 At the same time Sisinnes . . came to them and said 31
20 in . . construction from that time until now •
8:64 the weight . . was recorded at that very time. 32
76 from the times of our fathers 31
79 to give us food in the time of our servitude. 27
9:12 come at the time appointed 31
2Es 3: 9 again, in its time thou didst bring the flood 35
14 to him only didst thou reveal the end of the times 35
18 and trouble the times. 34
23 the times passed and the years were completed 35
4:27 to bring . . in their appointed times 35
37 measured the times by measure 35
37 and numbered the times by number 35
45 whether more time is to come than has passed •
5:12 at that time men shall hope but not obtain 35
43 Couldst thou not have created at one time those •
44 neither can the world hold at one time those •
45 certainly give life at one time to thy creation? •
45 If therefore all creatures will live at one time •
45 to support all of them present at one time. •
46 Request it therefore to produce ten at one time. •
47 it cannot, but only each in its own time. 35
53 those born during the time of old age 35
6: 7 What will be the dividing of the times? 35
24 At that time friends shall make war on friends 35
34 vain thoughts concerning the former times 35
34 lest you be hasty concerning the last times.' 35
7:26 For behold, the time will come, when the signs 35
73 how will they answer in the last times? 35
74 For how long the time is 35
74 because of the times which he has foreordained! 35
75 we shall be kept in rest until those times come 35
77 it will not be shown to you until the last times. 35
87 they are to be judged in the last times. 35
89 During the time that they lived in it 35
100 Will time therefore be given to the souls 35
8: 5 for you have been given only a short time to live. •
11 may be nourished for a time 35
50 those who inhabit the world in the last times •
63 the signs which thou wilt do in the last times •
9: 2 then you will know that it is the very time 35
6 also are the times of the Most High 35
18 For there was a time in this age 35
10:34 do not forsake me, lest I die before my time. ‡
11:13 and it continued to reign a long time. 35
16 Hear me, you who have ruled the earth all this time; 35
39 the end of my times might come through them? 35
44 the Most High has looked upon his times 35
12: 9 worthy to be shown the end of the times 35
9 and the last events of the times. 35
15 for a longer time than any other of the 12. 35
18 In the midst of the time of that kingdom 35
20 whose times shall be short and their years swift; 35
21 when the middle of its time draws near 35
21 four shall be kept for the time 35
13:23 He who brings the peril at that time 35
46 Then they dwelt there until the last times 35
52 except in the time of his day. 35
58 because he governs the times 35
14: 5 and showed him the secrets of the times 35
5 and declared to him the end of the times 35
9 until the times are ended. 35
10 and the times begin to grow old. 35
15 and hasten to escape from these times. 35
16:38 when the time of her delivery draws near 33
Tob 10: 7 At that time Tobias said to Raguel, "Send me back 22
14: 4 in Media there will be peace for a time. 27
4 will be in ruins for a time. 31
5 until the times of the age are completed. 27
Jdt 4: 1 By this time the people of Israel . . heard 26
6 Joakim . . who was in Jerusalem at the time 25
5: 8 lived there for a long time. 25
16 lived there a long time. 25
7:30 by that time the Lord our God will restore . . •
8: 1 At that time Judith heard about these things 25
15 power to protect us within any time he pleases 25
13: 5 For now is the time to help thy inheritance 27
16:21 was honored in her time 27
25 for a long time after her death. 25
AEs 14:12 in this time of our affliction 27
16:20 who attack them at the time of their affliction. 27

24 most hateful for all time to beasts and birds. 31
Wis 2: 4 Our name will be forgotten in time 31
3: 7 In the time of their visitation 27
4:13 Being perfected in a short time •
7:18 the beginning and end and middle of times 31
8: 8 the outcome of seasons and times. 31
12:20 granting them time and opportunity 31
14:16 the ungodly custom, grown strong with time 31
15: 8 this man who was made of earth a short time before •
16: 3 after suffering want a short time •
25 Therefore at that time also 30
19:22 to help them at all times and in all places. 27
Sir 0: 3 using in that period of time great watchfulness 31
2: 2 do not be hasty in time of calamity. 27
11 he forgives sins and saves in time of affliction. 27
4:23 Do not refrain from speaking at the crucial time 27
5: 7 at the time of punishment you will perish. 27
6:37 meditate at all times on his commandments •
8: 9 learn how to give an answer in time of need. 27
10: 4 he will raise up the right man for the time. 27
26 glorify yourself at a time when you are in want. 27
11:19 he does not know how much time will pass 27
12:15 He will stay with you for a time 32
17: 2 He gave to men few days, a limited time 27
18:25 In the time of plenty think of the time of hunger; 27
25 In the time of plenty think of the time of hunger; 27
19: 9 when the time comes he will hate you. 27
22: 6 wisdom at all times. 27
23 stand by him in time of affliction 27
24:25 like the Tigris at the time of the first fruits. 25
26 like the Jordan at harvest time. 25
27 like the Gihon at the time of vintage. 25
26: 4 at all times his face is cheerful. 27
29: 2 Lend to your neighbor in the time of his need 27
5 at the time for repayment he will delay 27
5 will find fault with the time. 27
33:23 At the time when you end the days of your life 25
35:20 clouds of rain in the time of drought. 27
37: 4 in time of trouble are against him. 27
38:13 There is a time 27
39:16 whatever he commands will be done in his time. 27
17 in God's time all things will be sought after 27
28 in the time of consummation 27
31 when their times come 27
40:24 Brothers and help are for a time of trouble 27
43: 6 to mark the times and to be an everlasting sign. 27
44: 7 were the glory of their times. 25
17 in the time of wrath he was taken in exchange; 27
45:13 Before his time •
46:19 Before the time of his eternal sleep 27
47:10 arranged their times throughout the year 27
50: 1 in his time fortified the temple. 25
51:10 the time when there is no help against the proud. 27
30 in God's time he will give you your reward. 27
Bar 1: 2 at the time when the Chaldeans took Jerusalem 27
20 at the time when he brought our fathers out •
3:32 He who prepared the earth for all time filled it 31
4:35 for a long time she will be inhabited by demons. 31
LJr 1: 3 for a long time, up to seven generations 31
Aza 1:15 at this time there is no prince, or prophet 27
Sus 1:14 they arranged for a time when they could find her 27
1Mc 2:49 it is a time of ruin and furious anger. 27
53 Joseph in the time of his distress 27
4:60 At that time they fortified Mount Zion 27
7:35 delivered into my hands this time 28
9: 7 he had no time to assemble them. 27
10 If our time has come 27
27 since the time that prophets ceased to appear 25
31 Jonathan at that time accepted the leadership 27
55 at that time Alcimus was stricken 27
56 Alcimus died at that time in great agony. 27
10:30 from this day and for all time. 31
11:14 Alexander the king was in Cilicia at that time 27
36 from this time forth for ever. 28
12: 1 Jonathan saw that the time was favorable for him 27
10 considerable time has passed 27
13: 5 to spare my life in any time of distress 27
15: 8 canceled . . from henceforth and for all time. 31
33 which at one time had been unjustly taken 27
16:24 from the time that he became high priest •
2Mc 1: 5 may he not forsake you in time of evil. 27
19 the pious priests of that time took some of the fire 30
22 When this was done and some time had passed 31
3: 5 who at that time was governor of Coelesyria 27
5: 1 About this time 27
8:19 Moreover, he told them of the times when . . •
19 both the time of Sennacherib •
20 the time of the battle with the Galatians •
9: 1 About that time, as it happened 27
12:30 kind treatment of them in times of misfortune 27
36 men had been fighting for a long time and were weary •
39 by that time it had become necessary 31
13: 9 those that had been done in his father's time. 23
14: 3 defiled himself in the times of separation 31
38 in former times 31
15: 8 to keep in mind the former times •
22 thou didst send thy angel in the time of Hezekiah 23
37 from that time 27
3Mc 1:29 because indeed all at that time preferred death 30

3:26 for the remaining time 31
29 shall become useless for all time 31
4:17 the previously mentioned interval of time 31
5:18 After the party had been going on for some time •
25 at their last gasp, since the time had run out 31
6:28 from the time of our ancestors until now •
7:19 they decided . . during the time of their stay. 31
23 through all times! Amen. 31
4Mc 3:21 just at that time certain men attempted a revolution 30
5: 7 Although you have had them for so long a time 31
6:20 and during that time be a laughing stock to all 31
12: 4 be miserably tortured and die before your time 32
12 these throughout all time will never let you go. 20
13:20 the brothers dwelt the same length of time 31
20 and was shaped during the same period of time 31
21 they were born after an equal time of gestation 31
14:19 at the time for making honeycombs 27
15: 2 preserving her seven sons for a time 29
27 preserve the seven sons for a short time 31
18: 9 In the time of my maturity 31

time (2) 1. יָד 2. מֹנֶה 3. פַּעַם 4. רֶגֶל 5. חַד (A) 6. ἐκ 7. ἐν 8. ἐπί 9. ἕως

Gen 27:36 Jacob? For he has supplanted me these two times. 3
29:34 Now this time my husband will be joined to me 3
35 This time I will praise the LORD"; 3
31: 7 changed my wages ten times 2
41 flock, and you have changed my wages ten times. 2
33: 3 bowing himself to the ground seven times 3
43:34 but Benjamin's portion was five times as much 1
Exd 8:32 Pharaoh hardened his heart this time also 3
9:14 For this time I will send all my plagues upon 3
27 Pharaoh . . said to them, "I have sinned this time; 3
23:14 Three times in the year you shall keep a feast 4
17 Three times in the year shall all your males 3
34:23 Three times in the year shall all your males 3
24 before the LORD your God three times in the year. 3
Lev 4: 6 sprinkle part of the blood seven times 3
17 blood . . sprinkle it seven times before the LORD 3
8:11 he sprinkled some of it on the altar seven times 3
14: 7 he shall sprinkle it seven times upon him 3
16 with his finger seven times before the LORD 3
27 sprinkle . . seven times before the LORD 3
51 and sprinkle the house seven times 3
16:14 shall sprinkle the blood . . seven times 3
19 sprinkle . . with his finger seven times 3
25: 8 count . . weeks of years, seven times seven years 3
Num 14:22 yet have put me to the proof these ten times 3
19: 4 sprinkle some of her blood . . seven times. 3
22:28 that you have struck me these three times? 4
32 Why have you struck your ass these three times? 4
33 ass . . turned aside before me these three times. 4
24: 1 he did not go, as at other times, to look for omens 3
10 behold, you have blessed them these three times. 3
Deu 1:11 LORD . . make you a 1,000 times as many as you are 3
9:19 But the LORD hearkened to me that time also. 3
10:10 LORD hearkened to me that time also; 3
16:16 Three times a year all your males shall appear 3
Jos 6: 4 you shall march around the city seven times 3
15 and marched around the city . . seven times 3
15 they marched around the city seven times. 3
16 at the seventh time . . Joshua said to the people 3
10:42 took all these kings and their land at one time 3
Jdg 15: 3 said to them, "This time I shall be blameless 3
16:15 You have mocked me these three times, and you have 3
1Sm 3: 8 And the LORD called Samuel again the third time. •
18:21 Therefore Saul said to David a second time •
20:41 David rose from beside . . and bowed three times; 3
2Sm 14:29 And he sent a second time, but Jo'ab would not come. •
17: 7 This time the counsel . . is not good. 3
23: 8 against 800 whom he slew at one time. 3
24: 3 God add . . 100 times as many as they are 3
1Kg 9: 2 the LORD appeared to Solomon a second time •
25 Three times a year Solomon used to offer up 3
17:21 he stretched himself upon the child three times 3
18:43 He said, "Go again seven times. 3
44 at the seventh time he said, "Behold, a little cloud •
19: 7 the angel of the LORD came again a second time •
22:16 How many times shall I adjure you that you speak 3
2Kg 4:35 the child sneezed seven times 3
5:10 Go and wash in the Jordan seven times 3
14 and dipped himself seven times in the Jordan 3
13:18 Strike . . "; and he struck three times, and stopped. 3
19 and said, "You should have struck five or six times; 3
19 now you will strike down Syria only three times. 3
25 Three times Jo'ash defeated him and recovered 3
1Ch 11:11 his spear against 300 whom he slew at one time. 3
21: 3 May the LORD add to his people 100 times 3
2Ch 18:15 king said to him, "How many times shall I adjure you 3
Neh 4:12 When the Jews . . came they said to us ten times 3
6: 4 sent to me four times in this way and I answered 3
5 Sanbal'lat for the fifth time sent his servant 3
Job 19: 3 These ten times you have cast reproach upon me; 3
Ps 106:43 Many times he delivered them 3
Ecc 7:22 many times you have yourself cursed others. 3
8:12 Though a sinner does evil 100 times •
Jer 1:13 The word of the LORD came to me a second time •

10:18 I am slinging out the inhabitants . . at this time 3
13: 3 the word of the LORD came to me a second time *
33: 1 word of the LORD came to Jeremiah a second time *
Ezk 4: 6 you shall lie down a second time *
Dan 1:20 found them ten times better than all 1
3:19 ordered the furnace heated seven times more 5
7:10 10,000 times 10,000 stood before *
Jon 3: 1 word of the LORD came to Jonah the second time *
Hag 2:20 The word of the LORD came a second time to Haggai *
Zec 4:12 a second time I said to him, "What are these two *
Mat 18:22 not . . seven times, but 70 times seven. 9
26:42 Again, for the second time, he went away and prayed *
44 he went away and prayed for the third time *
Mrk 14:72 immediately the cock crowed a second time. 6
Joh 3: 4 Can he enter a second time into his mother's womb *
9:24 for the second time they called the man 6
21:14 This was now the third time *
16 A second time he said to him, "Simon, son of John *
17 He said to him the third time, "Simon, son of John *
17 he said to him the third time, "Do you love me? *
Act 7:12 he sent forth our fathers the first time. *
10:15 the voice came to him again a second time *
16 This happened three times 8
11: 9 the voice answered a second time from heaven *
10 This happened three times 8
Heb 9:28 will appear a second time, not to deal with sin 6
Rev 9:16 cavalry was twice 10,000 times 10,000 *
Jdt 8:29 Today is not the first time *
Wis 12:22 thou scourgest our enemies 10,000 times more 7
1Mc 9: 1 sent . . into the land of Judah a second time 6

time *See* course, due, end, know, length, loss, negotiate, pass, spend, stay, waste, when.

time ago 1. πρό
4Mc 9: 5 a short time ago 1

all time 1. αἰών 2. διηνεκής 3. παντελής
Heb 7:25 Consequently he is able for all time to save 3
10:12 offered for all time a single sacrifice for sins 2
14 perfected for all time those who are sanctified. 2
Wis 4: 2 throughout all time it marches 1

allotted time 1. καιρός
Wis 2: 5 For our allotted time is the passing of a shadow 1

ancient time 1. עוֹלָם
Jer 28: 8 preceded you and me from ancient times 1
8 preceded you and me from ancient times 1

another time 1. ποτέ
Wis 16:19 at another time . . it burned more intensely than fire 1

any time 1. מִיָּמִים 2. עוֹלָם 3. ἑκάστοτε
Lev 25:32 houses . . the Levites may redeem at any time 2
1Kg 1: 6 His father had never at any time displeased him 1
2Pe 1:15 you may be able at any time to recall these things. 3

appointed time 1. זְמָן 2. מוֹעֵד 3. καιρός 4. ὁρισμός
Gen 18:14 At the appointed time I will return to you 2
Exd 13:10 keep this ordinance at its appointed time 2
23:15 at the appointed time in the month of Abib 2
34:18 at the time appointed in the month Abib; 2
Lev 23: 4 you shall proclaim at the time appointed for them 2
Num 9: 2 Israel keep the passover at its appointed time. 2
3 you shall keep it at its appointed time; 2
7 kept from offering . . at its appointed time 2
13 offer the LORD'S offering at its appointed time; 2
1Sm 13: 8 waited seven days, the time appointed by Samuel; 2
2Sm 24:15 from the morning until the appointed time; 2
Est 9:27 they would . . at the time appointed every year 1
Ps 102:13 time to favor her; the appointed time has come. 2
Ezk 22: 4 the appointed time of your years has come. 3
4 the appointed time of your years has come. 3
Dan 8:19 for it pertains to the appointed time of the end. 2
11:27 for the end is yet to be at the time appointed. 2
29 At the time appointed he shall return and come 2
35 end, for it is yet for the time appointed. 2
1Co 7:29 the appointed time has grown very short 3
Sir 36: 8 Hasten the day, and remember the appointed time 4
48:10 ready at the appointed time, it is written 3
51:30 Do your work before the appointed time 3

before that time 1. כְּאֶתְמוֹל שִׁלְשֹׁם
1Sm 14:21 had been with the Philistines before that time 1

do a second time 1. שׁנה
1Kg 18:34 he said, "Do it a second time"; and they did 1

do a third time 1. שׁלשׁ
1Kg 18:34 he said, "Do it a third time"; and they did 1
34 Do it a third time"; and they did it a third time. 1

first time 1. בָּרִאשֹׁנָה 2. חלל 3. רִאשׁוֹן 4. תְּחִלָּה 5. πρώτως
Gen 43:18 which was replaced in our sacks the first time 4
20 my lord, we came down the first time to buy food; 4
Num10:13 for the first time at the command of the LORD 3
1Sm 22:15 Is today the first time that I have inquired 2
1Ch 15:13 Because you did not carry it the first time 1
Act 11:26 were for the first time called Christians. 5

time for setting 1. מָבוֹא
Ps 104:19 sun knows its time for setting. 1

former time 1. פָּנִים
Rut 4: 7 Now this was the custom in former times in Israel 1

full time 1. ὥρα
Rom 13:11 how it is full time now for you to wake from sleep. 1

good time 1. ὥρα
Sir 32:11 Leave in good time and do not be the last 1

harvest time 1. קָצִיר
2Sm 23:13 And three . . came about harvest time to David 1

little time 1. ὀλίγος
Jas 4:14 For you are a mist that appears for a little time 1

long time 1. יוֹם 2. יָמִים רַבִּים 3. עוֹלָם 4. ἄνωθεν 5. ἐπὶ πολύ
Num 9:22 Whether it was two days, or a month, or a longer time 1
Jos 24: 7 and you lived in the wilderness a long time. 2
1Sm 7: 2 From . . a long time passed, some twenty years 1
Isa 42:14 For a long time I have held my peace 3
57:11 Have I not held my peace, even for a long time 3
64: 5 in our sins we have been a long time, 3
Jer 32:14 in a . . vessel, that they may last for a long time. 2
Act 26: 5 They have known for a long time 4
28: 6 when they had waited a long time 5

time of bereavement 1. שִׁכֻּלִים
Isa 49:20 children born in the time of your bereavement 1

time of life 1. ἡλικία
2Mc 6:24 Such pretense is not worthy of our time of life 1

time of need 1. εὔκαιρος
Heb 4:16 find grace to help in time of need. 1

time of threshing 1. area
2Es 4:30 will produce until the time of threshing comes! 1
39 the time of threshing is delayed 1

old time 1. רִאשׁוֹן
2Sm 20:18 They were wont to say in old time, 'Let them but ask 1

one time 1. ἐφάπαξ 2. ποτέ 3. πρότερος
1Co 15: 6 appeared to more than 500 brethren at one time 1
Eph 2:11 at one time you Gentiles in the flesh 2
Jdt 5: 7 At one time they lived in Mesopotamia 3
Wis 16:18 At one time the flame was restrained 2

opportune time 1. καιρός
Lke 4:13 he departed from him until an opportune time. 1

time past 1. גַּם תְּמוֹל גַּם שִׁלְשׁוֹם 2. מֵאָז 3. מִתְּמוֹל שִׁלְשֹׁם 4. פָּנִים 5. תְּמוֹל 6. תְּמוֹל שִׁלְשׁוֹם 7. πρότερον
Deu 4:42 without being at enmity with him in time past 3
19: 4 without having been at enmity . . in time past; 3
6 not at enmity with his neighbor in time past. 3
Jos 20: 5 having had no enmity against him in times past. 5
2Sm 5: 2 In times past . . it was you that led 1
15:34 as I have been your father's servant in time past 2
1Ch 9:20 Phin'ehas . . was the ruler over them in time past; 4
11: 2 In times past, even when Saul was king, it was you 6
1Mc 12: 7 Already in time past a letter was sent to Onias 7

plowing time 1. חָרִישׁ
Exd 34:21 in plowing time and in harvest you shall rest. 1

proper time 1. עֵת 2. καιρός
Ecc 10:17 and your princes feast at the proper time 1
Mat 24:45 to give them their food at the proper time? 2
Lke 12:42 to give them . . food at the proper time? 2
1Es 5:50 they offered sacrifices at the proper times 2
Sir 20:20 for he does not tell it at its proper time. 2

right time 1. καιρός
Rom 5: 6 at the right time Christ died for the ungodly. 1
Sir 4:20 Observe the right time, and beware of evil 1

same time 1. ἅμα 2. ἐν 3. ἡνίκα 4. καί 5. ὁμοῦ 6. simul
Act 24:26 At the same time he hoped . . 1
27:40 at the same time loosening the ropes 1
Phm 1:22 At the same time, prepare a guest room for me 1
1Es 9:48 at the same time explaining what was read. 1
2Es 11: 8 Do not all watch at the same time 6
Bar 1: 8 At the same time, on the tenth day of Sivan, Baruch 2
3:14 you may at the same time discern where there is 1
1Mc 2:25 At the same time he killed the king's officer 4
10:77 At the same time he advanced into the plain 1
2Mc 8:14 and at the same time besought the Lord 5
15:10 at the same time pointing out the perfidy 1
4Mc 2:22 at the same time he enthroned the mind 3

second time 1. שֵׁנִי 2. תְּנְיָנוּת (A) 3. δευτερόω
Gen 22:15 called to Abraham a second time from heaven 1
41: 5 he fell asleep and dreamed a second time; 1
Lev 13:58 shall then be washed a second time, and be clean 1
Num10: 6 when you blow an alarm the second time, the camps 1
Jos 5: 2 and circumcise . . Israel again the second time. 1
1Ch 29:22 Solomon the son of David king the second time 1
Est 2:19 virgins were gathered together the second time 1
Isa 11:11 the Lord will extend his hand yet a second time 1
Dan 2: 7 answered a second time, "Let the king tell 2
Sir 50:21 they bowed down in worship a second time 3

set time 1. חֹק 2. מוֹעֵד 3. מעד
Deu 31:10 seven years, at the set time of the year of release 3
2Sm 20: 5 he delayed beyond the set time . . appointed him. 2
Job 14:13 that thou wouldest appoint me a set time 1
Ps 75: 2 At the set time which I appoint I will judge 2

some time 1. יוֹם
Gen 40: 4 and they continued for some time in custody. 1

some time past 1. גַּם תְּמוֹל גַּם שִׁלְשׁוֹם 2. ἄνωθεν
2Sm 3:17 For some time past you have been seeking David 1
Lke 1: 3 having followed all things closely for some time past 2

that time 1. אָז 2. τότε 3. tunc
2Kg 12:17 At that time Haz'ael . . went up and fought 1
15:16 At that time Men'ahem sacked Tappuah 1
Jer 32: 2 At that time the army of the king of Babylon 1
Zep 3: 9 Yea, at that time I will change the speech 1
Gal 4:29 as at that time he who was born 2
2Es 13:44 For at that time the Most High performed signs 3
Wis 11: 8 showing by their thirst at that time 2
1Mc 16: 9 At that time Judas . . was wounded 2

third time 1. שְׁלִישִׁי 2. τρίτος
1Sm 19:21 And Saul sent messengers again the third time 1
Mrk 14:41 he came the third time, and said to them 2
Lke 23:22 A third time he said to them, "Why 2
2Co 12:14 Here for the third time I am ready to come to you. 2
13: 1 This is the third time I am coming to you 2
3Mc 5:40 ordering now for a third time 2

time to come 1. אָחוֹר 2. מָחָר
Deu 6:20 When your son asks you in time to come, 'What is 2
Jos 4: 6 a sign . . when your children ask in time to come 2
21 your children ask their fathers in time to come 2
22:24 in time to come your children might say 2
27 your children say to our children in time to come 2
28 If this should be said to us . . in time to come 2
Isa 42:23 Who . . will attend and listen for the time to come? 1

time to time 1. per tempus
2Es 5:48 those who from time to time are sown in it. 1
13:57 his wonders, which he did from time to time 1

very time 1. ἄρτι
Jdt 9: 1 and at the very time when . . 1

time when 1. ἐπειδή
4Mc 3:20 At a time when our fathers were enjoying . . peace 1

wrong time 1. ἄκαιρος
Sir 20:19 like a story told at the wrong time 1
22: 6 a tale told at the wrong time 1

timely 1. ὡραῖος
Sir 20: 1 There is a reproof which is not timely 1

times *See* five, seven, three, two.

ancient times 1. קֶדֶם
Isa 46:10 from ancient times things not yet done, saying 1

how many times 1. ποσάκις
3Mc 5:37 How many times . . must I give you orders 1

many times 1. πλεονάκις 2. πολλάκις
1Mc 16: 2 so that we have delivered Israel many times. 1
4Mc 16: 6 O how wretched am I and many times unhappy! 2

many times over 1. πολυπλάσιος
2Mc 9:16 he would give back, all of them, many times over 1

other times 1. פַּעַם בְּפַעַם
Jdg 16:20 I will go out as at other times, and shake myself 1
20:30 in array against Gib'e-ah, as at other times. 1
31 as at other times they began to smite and kill 1
1Sm 3:10 the LORD came . . calling as at other times 1
20:25 The king sat upon his seat, as at other times 1

timid 1. זחל 2. δειλός 3. εὐλαβέομαι
Job 32: 6 I was timid and afraid to declare my opinion 1
Sir 2:12 Woe to timid hearts and to slack hands 2
22:18 so a timid heart with a fool's purpose 2
34:14 He who fears the Lord will not be timid 3

22:18 so a timid heart with a fool's purpose 2
34:14 He who fears the Lord will not be timid 3

timidity 1. δειλία
2Ti 1: 7 for God did not give us a spirit of timidity 1

tin 1. בְּדִיל 2. κασσίτερος
Num31:22 only . . the bronze, the iron, the tin, and the lead 1
Ezk 22:18 bronze and tin and iron and lead in the furnace 1
20 bronze and iron and lead and tin into a furnace 1
27:12 wealth of every kind; silver, iron, tin, and lead 1
Sir 47:18 you gathered gold like tin 2

tingle 1. צלל
1Sm 3:11 two ears of every one that hears it will tingle. 1
2Kg 21:12 the ears of every one who hears of it will tingle. 1
Jer 19: 3 the ears of every one who hears of it will tingle. 1

tinkle 1. עכס
Isa 3:16 mincing along . . tinkling with their feet; 1

tiny 1. μικρός
AEs 10: 6 The tiny spring which became a river 1
11:10 from their cry, as though from a tiny spring 1

tip 1. קָצָה 2. קָצֶה 3. תְּנוּךְ
Exd 29:20 blood and put it upon the tip of the right ear 3
20 upon the tips of the right ears of his sons 3
Lev 8:23 blood and put it on the tip of Aaron's right ear 3
24 the blood on the tips of their right ears 3
14:14 the priest shall put it on the tip of the right ear 3
17 priest shall put on the tip of the right ear 3
25 put it on the tip of the right ear of him who is to be 3
28 on the tip of the right ear of him 3
Jdg 6:21 angel of the LORD reached out the tip of the staff 2
1Sm 14:27 so he put forth the tip of the staff . . in his hand 2
43 I tasted a little honey with the tip of the staff 2
1Kg 6:24 ten cubits from the tip of one wing to the tip 1
24 from the tip of one wing to the tip of the other. 1

tip (2)
Wis 11:22 like a speck that tips the scales •

tip over 1. κλίνω
LJr 1:27 if it is tipped over, it cannot straighten itself; 1

tip the scale 1. ῥοπή
Sir 1:22 a man's anger tips the scale to his ruin. 1

tire out 1. חלה
Jer 12:13 they have tired themselves out 1
tired *See* grow.

tithe 1. מַעֲשֵׂר 2. עשׂר 3. ἀποδεκατόω 4. δέκατος
Lev 27:30 All the tithe of the land . . is the LORD'S 1
31 If a man wishes to redeem any of his tithe 1
32 all the tithe of herds and flocks 1
Num18:21 To the Levites I have given every tithe in Israel 1
24 For the tithe of the people of Israel 1
26 When you take from the people of Israel the tithe 1
26 you shall present . . a tithe of the tithe. 1
26 you shall present . . a tithe of the tithe. 1
28 present an offering . . from all your tithes 1
Deu 12: 6 thither you shall bring your . . tithes 1
11 bring . . your sacrifices, your tithes 1
17 not eat . . the tithe of your grain or of your wine 1
14:22 You shall tithe all the yield of your seed 2
23 you shall eat the tithe of your grain, of your wine 1
24 so that you are not able to bring the tithe •
28 bring forth all the tithe of your produce 1
26:12 finished paying all the tithe of your produce 1
12 third year, which is the year of tithing, giving it 1
14 I have not eaten of the tithe while I was mourning •
2Ch 31: 5 brought in abundantly the tithe of everything. 1
6 also brought in the tithe of cattle and sheep 1
12 brought in . . tithes and the dedicated things. 1
Neh 10:37 bring to the Levites the tithes from our ground 1
38 Levites shall bring up the tithe of the tithes 1
38 Levites shall bring up the tithe of the tithes 1
12:44 contributions, the first fruits, and the tithes 1
13: 5 previously put the . . tithes of grain, wine, and oil 1
12 Judah brought the tithe of the grain, wine, and oil 1
Ams 4: 4 every morning, your tithes every three days; 1
Mal 3: 8 we robbing thee?' In your tithes and offerings. 1
10 Bring the full tithes into the storehouse 1
Mat 23:23 you tithe mint and dill and cummin 3
Lke 11:42 you tithe mint and rue and every herb 3
Heb 7: 4 Abraham . . gave him a tithe of the spoils. 4
8 Here tithes are received by mortal men 4
9 Levi himself, who receives tithes, paid tithes 4
Tob 1: 6 Taking the first fruits and the tithes of my produce 4
5:13 offered . . the tithes of our produce 4
Jdt 11:13 the tithes of the wine and oil 4
Sir 35: 9 dedicate your tithe with gladness. 4
1Mc 3:49 the first fruits and the tithes 4
10:31 let . . her tithes and her revenues, be holy 4
11:35 the tithes, and the taxes due to us 4
tithe *See also* collect, give, pay, receive, take.

title 1. τίτλος
Joh 19:19 Pilate also wrote a title and put it on the cross; 1
20 Many of the Jews read this title 1

to and fro 1. הֵנָּה וְהֵנָּה 2. יצא וְשׁוּב
Gen 8: 7 it went to and fro until the waters were dried up 2
2Kg 4:35 he got up . . and walked once to and fro in the house 1
2Es 6:29 where I was standing began to rock to and fro ‡

today 1. בַּיּוֹם 2. בַּיּוֹם הַזֶּה 3. הַיּוֹם 4. הַיּוֹם הַזֶּה 5. יוֹם
6. ἡμέρα αὕτη 7. σήμερον
Gen 21:26 tell me, and I have not heard of it until today. 3
24:12 O LORD . . grant me success today, I pray thee 3
42 I came today to the spring, and said 3
30:32 let me pass through all your flock today 3
31:48 This heap is a witness between you and me today. 3
40: 7 Why are your faces downcast today? 3
41: 9 said to Pharaoh, "I remember my faults today. 3
50:20 people should be kept alive, as they are today. 4
Exd 2:18 How is it that you have come so soon today? 3
5:14 task of making bricks today, as hitherto? 3
14:13 LORD, which he will work for you today; 3
13 the Egyptians whom you see today, you shall never 3
16:25 Moses said, "Eat it today, for today is a sabbath 3
25 Eat it today, for today is a sabbath to the LORD; 3
25 today you will not find it in the field. 3
19:10 consecrate them today and tomorrow 3
32:29 Moses said, "Today you have ordained yourselves 3
Lev 8:34 As has been done today, the LORD has commanded 1
9: 4 for today the LORD will appear to you.' 3
10:19 Aaron said to Moses, "Behold, today they have 3
19 If I had eaten the sin offering today 3
Deu 15:15 therefore I command you this today. 3
31:27 today you have been rebellious against the LORD; 3
Jos 7:25 The LORD brings trouble on you today. 2
22:18 And if you rebel against the LORD today 5
22 If it was in rebellion . . spare us not today 4
31 Today we know that the LORD is in the midst of us 5
Jdg 21: 3 that there should be today one tribe lacking 3
Rut 2:19 Where did you glean today? 3
19 The man's name with whom I worked today is Bo'az. 3
3:18 will not rest, but will settle the matter today. 3
1Sm 4: 3 LORD put us to rout today before the Philistines? 5
16 I fled from the battle today. 3
9:12 people have a sacrifice today on the high place. 3
19 today you shall eat with me, and in the morning 3
10: 2 When you depart . . today you will meet two men 3
11:13 today the LORD has wrought deliverance 3
12:17 Is it not wheat harvest today? I will call upon 3
14:30 if the people had eaten freely today of the spoil 3
38 and know and see how this sin has arisen today. 3
20:27 not . . come to the meal, either yesterday or today? 3
21: 5 how much more today will their vessels be holy? 3
22:15 Is today the first time that I have inquired 3
24:10 the LORD gave you today into my hand in the cave; 3
26:23 the LORD gave you into my hand today 3
27:10 Against whom have you made a raid today? 3
2Sm 3: 8 and yet you charge me today with a fault 3
6:20 How the king of Israel honored himself today 3
20 How the king . . uncovering himself today 3
11:12 Remain here today also, and tomorrow I will let 3
14:22 Today your servant knows that I have found favor 3
15:20 and shall I today make you wander about with us 3
16: 3 Today the house of Israel will give me back 3
12 repay me with good for this cursing of me today. 3
18:20 Jo'ab said . . "You are not to carry tidings today; 4
20 but today you shall carry no tidings 4
19: 5 You have today covered with shame the faces 3
6 you have made it clear today that commanders 3
6 today I perceive that if Ab'salom were alive 3
6 if Ab'salom were alive and all of us . . dead today 3
1Kg 12: 7 be a servant to this people today and serve them 3
14:14 who shall cut off the house of Jerobo'am today. 3
18:15 I will surely show myself to him today. 3
2Kg 2: 3 today the LORD will take away your master 3
5 today the LORD will take away your master 3
4:23 he said, "Why will you go to him today? 3
6:28 Give your son, that we may eat him today 3
31 if the head . . remains on his shoulders today. 3
1Ch 28: 7 if he continues resolute . . as he is today. 4
29: 5 consecrating himself today to the LORD? 3
Neh 1:11 give success to thy servant today, and grant him 3
Job 23: 2 Today also my complaint is bitter 3
Ps 2: 7 You are my son, today I have begotten you. 3
95: 7 O that today you would hearken to his voice! 3
Prv 7:14 today I have paid my vows; 5
22:19 I have made them known to you today, even to you. 3
Isa 48: 7 before today you have never heard of them 5
Jer 36: 2 spoke to you, from the days of Josi'ah until today. 4
40: 4 Now, behold, I release you today from the chains 3
Zec 9:12 today I declare that I will restore to you double. 3
Mat 6:30 the grass of the field, which today is alive 7
16: 3 It will be stormy today, for the sky is red 7
21:28 'Son, go and work in the vineyard today.' 7
27:19 I have suffered much over him today in a dream. 7
Lke 4:21 Today this scripture has been fulfilled 7
5:26 saying, "We have seen strange things today. 7
12:28 the grass which is alive in the field today 7
13:32 perform cures today and tomorrow 7
33 today and tomorrow and the day following 7
19: 5 I must stay at your house today. 7
9 Today salvation has come to this house 7
22:61 Before the cock crows today, you will deny me 7
23:43 I say to you, today you will be with me in Paradise. 7
Act 4: 9 if we are being examined today 7
13:33 'Thou art my Son, today I have begotten thee.' 7
19:40 we are in danger of being charged with rioting today 7
26: 2 I am to make my defense today 7
27:33 Today is the fourteenth day 7
Heb 1: 5 Thou art my Son, today I have begotten thee"? 7
3: 7 Today, when you hear his voice 7
13 as long as it is called "today 7
15 while it is said, "Today, when you hear his voice 7
4: 7 again he sets a certain day, "Today 7
7 Today, when you hear his voice 7
5: 5 Thou art my Son, today I have begotten thee"; 7
13: 8 is the same yesterday and today and for ever. 7
Jas 4:13 Today or tomorrow we will go into . . a town 7
Tob 6:10 Brother, today we shall stay with Raguel 7
Jdt 6: 2 to prophesy among us as you have done today 7
8:29 Today is not the first time 7
12:18 because my life means more to me today 7
Sir 10:10 the king of today will die tomorrow. 7
20:15 today he lends and tomorrow he asks it back 7
38:22 yesterday it was mine, and today it is yours. 7
Bar 1:19 From the day when the Lord . . until today 6
2:26 house . . thou hast made as it is today 6
3: 8 Behold, we are today in our exile where thou hast 7
1Mc 2:63 Today he will be exalted 7
3:17 we are faint, for we have eaten nothing today. 7
4:10 crush this army before us today. 7
5:32 Fight today for your brethren! 7
6:26 today they have encamped against the citadel 7
7:42 So also crush this army before us today 7
9:30 So now we have chosen you today to take his place 7
44 today things are not as they were before. 7
10:20 we have appointed you today to be the high priest 7
3Mc 5:20 the Jews were benefited by today's sleep 7
6:13 cower today in fear of your invincible might 7

toe 1. אֶצְבַּע 2. אֶצְבַּע (A) 3. ποδὸς δάκτυλος
2Sm 21:20 who had six fingers . . and six toes on each foot 1
1Ch 20: 6 who had six fingers . . and six toes on each foot •
Dan 2:41 saw the feet and toes partly of potter's clay 2
42 toes of the feet were partly iron and partly clay 2
4Mc 15:15 their toes and fingers scattered on the ground 3

great toe 1. בֹּהֶן 2. בֹּהֶן רֶגֶל
Exd 29:20 upon the great toes of their right feet 1
Lev 8:23 right hand and on the great toe of his right foot 1
24 blood . . on the great toes of their right feet 1
14:14 on the great toe of his right foot 1
17 and on the great toe of his right foot 1
25 on the great toe of his right foot 1
28 the great toe of his right foot 1
Jdg 1: 6 and cut off his thumbs and his great toes. 2
7 with their thumbs and their great toes cut off 2

together 1. אֶחָד אֶל אֶחָד 2. אֲסֵפָה 3. אֵת 4. גַּם 5. וְ
6. יַחַד 7. יַחְדָּו 8. יַחְדָּיו 9. כְּאֶחָד 10. עַל 11. עִם
12. שְׁתֵּיהֶם 13. דָּא לְדָא (A) 14. דְּנָה עִם דְּנָה (A)
15. כַּחֲדָה (A) 16. ἅμα 17. ἑαυτοῦ 18. ἐπὶ τὸ αὐτό
19. καί 20. κατὰ τὸ αὐτό 21. κοινός 22. μετά
23. ὁμοθυμαδόν 24. ὁμοῦ 25. πρὸς ἑαυτούς 26. σύν
27. συνάγω 28. τε 29. χωρίς 30. ipse 31. simul
32. unus
Gen 11:31 and they went forth together from Ur 3
13: 6 support both of them dwelling together; 6
6 great that they could not dwell together 6
22: 6 they went both of them together. 6
8 So they went both of them together. 6
19 they arose and went together to Beer-sheba; 6
36: 7 were too great for them to dwell together; 6
46:15 to Jacob . . together with his daughter Dinah; 5
Exd 19: 8 all the people answered together and said 7
Num 6:20 together with the breast that is waved •
16: 3 assembled themselves together against Moses •
27 together with their wives, their sons, and their •
20: 2 assembled themselves together against Moses •
10 gathered the assembly together before the rock •
21:16 LORD said to Moses, "Gather the people together •
23 He gathered all his men together, and went out •
26:10 earth . . swallowed them up together with Korah •
27: 3 gathered themselves together against the LORD •
31: 6 together with Phin'ehas the son of Elea'zar 5
Deu 4:49 together with all the Arabah on the east side 5
22:10 You shall not plow with an ox and an ass together. 7
11 not wear a mingled stuff, wool and linen together. 7
25: 5 If brothers dwell together, and one of them dies 7
33: 5 gathered, all the tribes of Israel together. 6
Jos 9: 2 they gathered together with one accord to fight 7
11: 5 and encamped together at the waters of Merom 7
16: 9 together with the towns which were set apart 5
19: 8 together with all the villages round about 5
Jdg 6:33 all . . and the people of the East came together 7
19: 6 the two men sat and ate and drank together; 7

Rut 4:11 Rachel and Leah, who together built up . . Israel. 12
1Sm 11:11 scattered, so that no two . . were left together. 6
17:10 give me a man, that we may fight together. 6
28:23 his servants, together with the woman, urged him; 5
31: 6 Saul died . . on the same day together. 7
2Sm 2:16 And each caught . . so they fell down together. 7
8:11 these also . . together with the silver and gold 11
10:15 they gathered themselves together. 6
14:16 the man who would destroy me and my son together 6
21: 9 and the seven of them perished together. 6
15 and David went down together with his servants 5
1Kg 9:27 seamen . . together with the servants of Solomon; *
11:17 Hadad fled . . together with certain E'domites 3
2Kg 8: 6 all that was hers, together with all the produce 5
10: 5 he who was over the city, together with the elders 5
25:11 the deserters . . together with the rest 5
1Ch 10: 6 he . . and all his house died together. 7
11:10 together with all Israel, to make him king 11
18:11 dedicated . . together with the silver and gold 11
28: 1 together with the palace officials 11
2Ch 3:11 wings of the cherubim together extended twenty 7
8:18 went . . together with the servants of Solomon 11
21: 3 great gifts . . together with fortified cities 11
Ezr 2:64 whole assembly together was 42,360 9
3: 8 together with the rest of their brethren *
9 together took the oversight of the workmen 9
6:20 priests . . had purified themselves together; 9
Neh 4: 8 they all plotted together to come and fight 7
6: 2 Come and let us meet together in one 7
7 now come, and let us take counsel together. 7
7:66 The whole assembly together was 42,360 9
Est 5:12 I am invited by her together with the king. 11
Job 2:11 They made an appointment together to come 7
3:18 There the prisoners are at ease together; 6
9:32 that we should come to trial together. 7
16:10 they mass themselves together against me. 6
17:16 Shall we descend together into the dust? 6
19:12 His troops come on together; 6
31:38 its furrows have wept together; 6
34:15 all flesh would perish together 6
38: 7 when the morning stars sang together 6
38 into a mass and the clods cleave fast together? *
40:13 Hide them all in the dust together; 6
Ps 2: 2 the rulers take counsel together 6
31:13 as they scheme together against me, as they plot 6
34: 3 let us exalt his name together! 7
41: 7 All who hate me whisper together about me; 6
48: 4 lo, the kings assembled, they came on together. 7
49: 2 both low and high, rich and poor together! 6
55:14 We used to hold sweet converse together; 7
62: 9 they are together lighter than a breath. 6
65:13 they shout and sing together for joy. *
71:10 those who watch for my life consult together 7
88:17 they close in upon me together. 6
98: 8 let the hills sing for joy together 6
102:22 when peoples gather together, and kingdoms 7
122: 3 built as a city which is bound firmly together 7
141:10 Let the wicked together fall into their own nets 6
148:12 Young men and maidens together 4
Ecc 4:11 Again, if two lie together, they are warm; *
Isa 1:28 rebels and sinners shall be destroyed together 7
31 both . . shall burn together, with none to quench 7
9:21 and together they are against Judah. 7
11: 6 the calf and the lion and the fatling together 7
7 shall feed; their young shall lie down together; 7
14 together they shall plunder the . . east. 7
22: 3 All your rulers have fled together 6
24: 4 the heavens languish together with the earth. 11
22 They will be gathered together as prisoners 2
25:11 lay low his pride together with the skill of his 11
27: 4 against them, I would burn them up together. 6
31: 3 fall, and they will all perish together. 7
40: 5 be revealed, and all flesh shall see it together 7
41: 1 let us together draw near for judgment. 7
19 the cypress, the plane and the pine together; 7
20 men . . may consider and understand together 7
43: 9 Let all the nations gather together 7
26 Put me in remembrance, let us argue together; 6
44:11 terrified, they shall be put to shame together. 6
45:16 the makers of idols go in confusion together. 7
20 draw near together, you survivors of the nations! 7
21 let them take counsel together! 7
46: 2 They stoop, they bow down together 7
48:13 when I call to them, they stand forth together. 7
50: 8 will contend with me? Let us stand up together. 6
52: 8 lift up their voice, together they sing for joy; 7
9 Break forth together into singing 7
65: 7 their fathers' iniquities together, says 7
25 The wolf and the lamb shall feed together 9
66:17 shall come to an end together, says the LORD. 7
Jer 3:18 together they shall come from the land 7
6:12 turned over . . their fields and wives together; 7
21 they shall stumble; fathers and sons together 7
13:14 one against another, fathers and sons together 7
24: 1 king of Judah, together with the princes of Judah *
31: 8 with child and her who is in travail, together; 6
24 and all its cities shall dwell there together 7
41: 1 As they ate bread together there at Mizpah 7
46:12 they have both fallen together. 8
21 yea, they have turned and fled together 8
50: 4 and the people of Judah shall come together 7
51:38 They shall roar together like lions; 7
52:15 together with the rest of the artisans. *
Lam 2: 8 rampart and wall . . they languish together. 7
Ezk 22:13 I strike my hands together at the dishonest gain *
37:17 join them together into one stick 1
46: 5 together with a hin of oil to each ephah. *
7 together with a hin of oil to each ephah. *
11 together with a hin of oil to an ephah. *
48:20 together with the property of the city. *
Dan 2:35 iron . . gold, all together were broken in pieces 15
43 not hold together, just as iron does not mix 14
5: 6 limbs gave way, and his knees knocked together. 13
8:12 together with the continual burnt offering 10
Hos 1:11 Israel shall be gathered together 7
Ams 1:15 exile, he and his princes together," says the LORD. 7
3: 3 Do two walk together, unless they have made 7
Mic 2:12 I will set them together like sheep in a fold 6
Zec 10: 5 Together they shall be like mighty men in battle *
Lke 17:35 There will be two women grinding together 18
Joh 4:36 so that sower and reaper may rejoice together. 24
21: 2 two others of his disciples were together. 24
Act 1:14 together with the women *
2: 1 they were all together in one place. 24
44 all who believed were together 18
46 And day by day, attending the temple together 23
4:24 lifted their voices together to God and said 23
26 the rulers were gathered together 18
5:12 they were all together in Solomon's Portico. 23
7:57 stopped their ears and rushed together upon him. 23
14: 1 entered together into the Jewish synagogue 20
18: 8 Crispus . . together with all his household *
19:29 they rushed together into the theater 23
Rom 3:12 together they have gone wrong; 16
15: 6 together you may with one voice glorify the God 23
1Co 1: 2 together with all those who in every place 26
7: 5 then come together again, lest Satan tempt you 18
11:20 When you meet together, it is not the Lord's supper 18
16:19 together with the church in their house 26
Php 4: 3 together with Clement 19
1Th 4:17 we . . shall be caught up together with them 16
Heb 10:25 not neglecting to meet together 17
3Jn 1:14 and we will talk together face to face. *
Rev 17:12 receive authority . . together with the beast. *
1Es 5:56 together with their brethren 19
7:10 the Levites were purified together. 16
11 the Levites were all purified together 16
8:14 together with what is given by the nation 26
2Es 6:20 and all shall see it together. 31
11:28 planning between themselves to reign together 30
13:11 All these were mingled together 31
34 multitude shall be gathered together 32
Tob 5:13 when we went together to Jerusalem to worship 21
Jdt 2:14 and called together all the commanders, generals *
15 together with 12,000 archers on horseback 19
5: 2 he called together all the princes of Moab *
7: 2 together with the baggage 29
17 together with 5,000 Assyrians 22
13:10 Then the two of them went out together 16
AEs 16:13 together with their whole nation. 26
Wis 14:10 will be punished together with him who did it. 26
Sir 50:17 all the people together made haste 21
LJr 1:48 the priests consult together 25
Sus 1:14 And then together they arranged for a time 21
Bel 1:27 took pitch, fat, and hair, and boiled them together 18
1Mc 5:44 together with all who were in them 26
6:20 They gathered together and besieged the citadel 16
2Mc 1:14 together with his friends 28
11: 7 Then they eagerly rushed off together. 24
9 they all together praised the merciful God 24
3Mc 1:27 they turned, together with our people 26
3:25 together with their wives and children 26
27 together with his family. *
5: 3 returned to his feasting, together with . . his friends 27
6: 4 Pharaoh . . you destroyed together with his . . army 26
4Mc 3: 7 together with the soldiers of his nation 22
4: 9 the priests together with women and children 22
8:29 all with one voice together, as from one mind, said 24
13:13 all of them together looking at one another 24
15:12 each child singly and all together 24
16:15 when you and your sons were arrested together 22

together *See also* agree, assemble, band, bind, bring, burn, call, carouse, cleave, come, consult, couple, crowd, discuss, fasten, fight, fit, flock, fly, gather, glue, groan, grow, hold, huddle, join, knit, live, make, meet, reason, rejoice, run, sew, shake, sit, strike, strive, struggle, suffer, take, talk, weave, whisper, work.

all together 1. *ὁμοθυμαδόν* 2. *παμπληθεί*

Lke 23:18 they all cried out together, "Away with this man 2
Wis 18: 5 thou didst destroy them all together by a mighty flood 1
12 they all together . . had corpses 1
3Mc 4: 4 were they being sent off, all together, by the generals 1
6 all together raising a lament 1
6:39 and rescued them all together and unharmed. 1

toil 1. יְגִיעַ 2. יגע 3. יְד 4. עמל 5. עָמֵל 6. עָמָל 7. עֶצֶב 8. עִצָּבוֹן 9. פֹּעַל 10. *κακοπάθεια* 11. *κοπιάζω* 12. *κοπιάω* 13. *κόπος* 14. *μοχθέω* 15. *μόχθος* 16. *πόνος* 17. laboro

Gen 3:17 ground because of you; in toil you shall eat of it 8
5:29 from our work and from the toil of our hands. 8
Deu 26: 7 saw our affliction, our toil, and our oppression; 6
Job 24: 5 asses in the desert they go forth to their toil 9
Ps 90:10 yet their span is but toil and trouble; 6
105:44 took possession of the fruit of the peoples' toil 6
109:11 may strangers plunder the fruits of his toil! 1
Prv 14:23 In all toil there is profit 7
23: 4 Do not toil to acquire wealth; 2
Ecc 1: 3 What does man gain by all the toil 6
3 gain by . . the toil at which he toils under the sun? 4
2:10 for my heart found pleasure in all my toil 6
10 this was my reward for all my toil. 6
11 all . . my hands had done and the toil I had spent 6
18 I hated all my toil in which I had toiled 6
18 all my toil in which I had toiled under the sun 5
19 all for which I toiled and used my wisdom 4
20 gave my heart up . . over all the toil of my labors 6
21 a man who has toiled with wisdom and knowledge 6
21 all to be enjoyed by a man who did not toil for it. 4
22 What has a man from all the toil and strain 6
22 and strain with which he toils beneath the sun? 5
24 eat and drink, and find enjoyment in his toil. 6
3: 9 What gain has the worker from his toil? 5
13 eat and drink and take pleasure in all his toil. 6
4: 4 all toil and all skill in work come from . . envy 6
6 two hands full of toil and a striving after wind. 6
8 no end to all his toil . . so that he never asks 6
8 For whom am I toiling and depriving myself 5
9 because they have a good reward for their toil. 6
5:15 he shall go . . and shall take nothing for his toil 6
16 and what gain has he that he toiled for the wind 4
18 enjoyment in all the toil with which one toils 6
18 in all the toil with which one toils under the sun 4
19 to accept his lot and find enjoyment in his toil 6
6: 7 All the toil of man is for his mouth 6
8:15 enjoyment . . for this will go with him in his toil 6
17 However much man may toil in seeking 4
9: 9 portion in life and in your toil at which you toil 6
9 and in your toil at which you toil under the sun. 5
10:15 The toil of a fool wearies him 6
Jer 20:18 Why did I come forth from the womb to see toil 6
Hag 2:17 I smote you and all the products of your toil 3
Mat 6:28 how they grow; they neither toil nor spin; 12
Lke 5: 5 Master, we toiled all night and took nothing! 12
12:27 they neither toil nor spin 12
Act 20:35 by so toiling one must help the weak 12
2Co 11:27 in toil and hardship 13
Col 1:29 For this I toil 12
1Th 2: 9 For you remember our labor and toil, brethren 15
2Th 3: 8 with toil and labor we worked night and day 13
1Ti 4:10 For to this end we toil and strive 12
Rev 2: 2 I know your works, your toil and your patient 13
1Es 4:22 Do you not labor and toil 14
2Es 2:12 they shall neither toil nor become weary. 17
7:96 and besides they see the straits and toil ‡
Wis 9:10 be with me and toil 11
10:10 and increased the fruit of his toil. 16
15: 4 nor the fruitless toil of painters 16
17:17 a workman who toiled in the wilderness 15
Sir 6:19 in her service you will toil a little while 12
11:11 There is a man who works, and toils, and presses on 16
21 trust in the Lord and keep at your toil 16
14:15 what you acquired by toil to be divided by lot? 13
28:15 deprived them of the fruit of their toil. 16
31: 3 The rich man toils as his wealth accumulates 12
4 The poor man toils as his livelihood diminishes 12
34:23 what do they gain but toil? 13
2Mc 2:26 who have undertaken the toil of abbreviating 10

toil *See also* fruit.

anxious toil 1. עֶצֶב

Ps 127: 2 It is in vain . . eating the bread of anxious toil; 1

make toil 1. יגע

Jos 7: 3 do not make the whole people toil up there 1
2Sm 12:31 and made them toil at the brickkilns; *

misspent toil 1. *κακόμοχθος*

Wis 15: 8 With misspent toil, he forms a futile god 1

uncomfortable toil 1. *κακοπάθεια*

2Mc 2:27 we will gladly endure the uncomfortable toil 1

without toil 1. *ἀκοπιάστως*

Wis 16:20 without their toil thou didst supply them 1

toilsome 1. *ἐπίπονος* 2. laboriosus

2Es 7:12 were made narrow and sorrowful and toilsome; 2
Sir 7:15 Do not hate toilsome labor, or farm work 1

token 1. עֲרֻבָּה 2. *σύμβολον*

1Sm 17:18 See . . and bring some token from them. 1
Wis 16: 6 received a token of deliverance 2

token of virginity 1. בְּתוּלִים
Deu 22:14 I did not find in her the tokens of virginity,' 1
15 shall . . bring out the tokens of her virginity 1
17 I did not find . . the tokens of virginity. 1
17 these are the tokens of my daughter's virginity.' 1
20 true, that the tokens of virginity were not found 1

sacred token 1. ἱέρωμα
2Mc 12:40 they found sacred tokens of the idols of Jamnia 1

twice told 1. פַּעַם
Ecc 6: 6 though he . . live 1,000 years twice told 1

more tolerable 1. ἀνεκτός
Mat 10:15 it shall be more tolerable on the day of judgment 1
11:22 it shall be more tolerable on the day of judgment 1
24 it shall be more tolerable on the day of judgment 1
Lke 10:12 it shall be more tolerable on that day for Sodom 1
14 it shall be more tolerable in the judgment for Tyre 1

tolerate 1. נוח 2. ἀφίημι 3. ἔχω 4. sustineo
Est 3: 8 is not for the king's profit to tolerate them. 1
Rev 2:20 against you, that you tolerate the woman Jez'ebel 2
2Es 15: 8 neither will I tolerate their . . practices. 4
3Mc 1:22 would not tolerate the completion of his plans 3

toll 1. הֲלָךְ (A) 2. τέλος
Ezr 4:13 not pay tribute, custom, or toll 1
20 to whom tribute, custom, and toll were paid. 1
7:24 not be lawful to impose tribute, custom, or toll 1
Mat 17:25 From whom do kings of the earth take toll 2

tomb 1. בַּיִת 2. גָּדִישׁ 3. צְרִיחַ 4. קֶבֶר 5. קְבוּרָה
6. ἐπιτάφιον 7. μνῆμα 8. μνημεῖον 9. τάφος
10. monumentum
Gen 35:20 it is the pillar of Rachel's tomb 5
50: 5 I am about to die; in my tomb which I hewed out 4
Jdg 8:32 age, and was buried in the tomb of Jo'ash his father 4
16:31 buried him . . in the tomb of Mano'ah his father. 4
1Sm 10: 2 you will meet two men by Rachel's tomb 5
13: 6 hid themselves in . . and in tombs and in cisterns 3
2Sm 2:32 As'ahel, and buried him in the tomb of his father 4
4:12 took the head . . and buried it in the tomb of Abner 4
17:23 he died, and was buried in the tomb of his father. 4
21:14 And they buried . . in the tomb of Kish his father; 4
1Kg 13:22 body shall not come to the tomb of your fathers.' 4
2Kg 9:28 and buried him in his tomb with his fathers 5
21:26 And he was buried in his tomb in the garden of Uzza; 5
23:16 as Josi'ah turned, he saw the tombs . . on the mount; 4
16 and he sent and took the bones out of the tombs 4
17 It is the tomb of the man of God who came from Judah 4
30 his servants . . and buried him in his own tomb. 5
2Ch 16:14 They buried him in the tomb which he had hewn out 4
21:20 but not in the tombs of the kings. 4
24:25 they did not bury him in the tombs of the kings. 4
28:27 did not bring him into the tombs of the kings 4
32:33 the ascent of the tombs of the sons of David; 4
35:24 died, and was buried in the tombs of his fathers. 4
Job 21:32 watch is kept over his tomb. 2
Isa 14:18 kings . . lie in glory, each in his own tomb; 1
22:16 that you have hewn here a tomb for yourself 4
16 tomb for yourself, you who hew a tomb on the height 4
65: 4 who sit in tombs, and spend the night in secret 4
Jer 5:16 Their quiver is like an open tomb 4
8: 1 the bones . . shall be brought out of their tombs; 4
Mat 8:28 two demoniacs met him, coming out of the tombs 8
23:27 you are like whitewashed tombs 9
29 you build the tombs of the prophets 9
27:52 the tombs also were opened 8
53 coming out of the tombs after his resurrection 8
60 laid it in his own new tomb 8
60 rolled a great stone to the door of the tomb 8
28: 8 they departed quickly from the tomb with fear 8
Mrk 5: 2 there met him out of the tombs a man 8
3 who lived among the tombs 7
5 Night and day among the tombs 7
6:29 they came and took his body, and laid it in a tomb. 8
15:46 laid him in a tomb 8
46 he rolled a stone against the door of the tomb. 8
16: 2 they went to the tomb when the sun had risen. 8
3 the stone for us from the door of the tomb? 8
5 And entering the tomb, they saw a young man 8
8 And they went out and fled from the tomb; 8
Lke 8:27 he lived not in a house but among the tombs. 7
11:47 Woe to you! for you build the tombs of the prophets 8
48 they killed them, and you build their tombs. •
23:53 and laid him in a rock-hewn tomb 7
55 The women . . followed, and saw the tomb 8
24: 1 at early dawn, they went to the tomb 7
2 they found the stone rolled away from the tomb 8
9 returning from the tomb they told all this 8
22 They were at the tomb early in the morning 8
24 Some of those who were with us went to the tomb 8
Joh 5:28 all who are in the tombs will hear his voice. 8
11:17 Laz'arus had already been in the tomb four days. 8
31 supposing that she was going to the tomb to weep 8
38 Then Jesus, deeply moved again, came to the tomb 8
12:17 when he called Laz'arus out of the tomb 8
19:41 there was a garden, and in the garden a new tomb 8
42 as the tomb was close at hand 8
20: 1 Mary Mag'dalene came to the tomb early 8
1 the stone had been taken away from the tomb. 8
2 They have taken the Lord out of the tomb 8
3 they went toward the tomb. 8
4 outran Peter and reached the tomb first; 8
6 went into the tomb; he saw the linen cloths lying 8
8 the other disciple, who reached the tomb first 8
11 Mary stood weeping outside the tomb 8
11 as she wept she stooped to look into the tomb; 8
Act 2:29 his tomb is with us to this day. 7
7:16 tomb that Abraham had bought for a sum of silver 7
13:29 took him down from the tree, and laid him in a tomb. 8
Rev 11: 9 and refuse to let them be placed in a tomb 7
1Es 1:31 was buried in the tomb of his fathers. 9
2Es 2:16 and will bring them out from their tombs 10
1Mc 2:70 was buried in the tomb of his fathers at Modein. 9
9:19 buried him in the tomb of their fathers at Modein 9
13:27 the tomb of his father and his brothers 9
30 This is the tomb which he built in Modein 9
2Mc 5:10 he had . . no place in the tomb of his fathers. 9
4Mc 17: 8 to inscribe upon their tomb these words 6

tomorrow 1. יוֹם מָחָר 2. מָחָר 3. αὔριον 4. εἰς αὔριον
5. εἰς ἐπιτελοῦσαν ἡμέραν 6. crastinum
Exd 8:10 he said, "Tomorrow." Moses said, "Be it as you say 2
23 By tomorrow shall this sign be. 2
29 the swarms of flies may depart . . tomorrow; 2
9: 5 the LORD set a time, saying, "Tomorrow the LORD 2
18 Behold, tomorrow about this time I will cause 2
10: 4 behold, tomorrow I will bring locusts 2
16:23 Tomorrow is a day of solemn rest, a holy sabbath 2
17: 9 tomorrow I will stand on top of the hill 2
19:10 consecrate them today and tomorrow 2
32: 5 Tomorrow shall be a feast to the LORD. 2
Num11:18 Consecrate yourselves for tomorrow 2
14:25 turn tomorrow and set out for the wilderness 2
16: 7 put incense upon them before the LORD tomorrow 2
16 before the LORD, you and they, and Aaron, tomorrow; 2
Jos 3: 5 for tomorrow the LORD will do wonders among you. 2
7:13 and say, 'Sanctify yourselves for tomorrow; 2
11: 6 tomorrow at this time I will give over all of them 2
22:18 be angry with the whole . . of Israel tomorrow. 2
Jdg 19: 9 tomorrow you shall arise early in the morning 2
20:28 Go up; for tomorrow I will give them into your hand. 2
1Sm 9:16 Tomorrow about this time I will send to you a man 2
11: 9 Tomorrow, by the time the sun is hot, you shall have 2
10 Tomorrow we will give ourselves up to you 2
19:11 If you do not . . tomorrow you will be killed. 2
20: 5 tomorrow is the new moon, and I should not fail 2
12 When I . . about this time tomorrow, or the third 2
18 Tomorrow is the new moon; and you will be missed 2
28:19 and tomorrow you and your sons shall be with me; 2
2Sm 11:12 today also, and tomorrow I will let you depart. 2
1Kg 19: 2 if I do not make . . by this time tomorrow. 2
20: 6 send my servants to you tomorrow about this time 2
2Kg 6:28 your son . . today, and we will eat my son tomorrow.' 2
7: 1 Tomorrow . . a measure of fine meal shall be sold 2
18 about this time tomorrow in the gate of Sama'ria 2
10: 6 and come to me at Jezreel tomorrow at this time. 2
2Ch 20:16 Tomorrow go down against them; 2
17 tomorrow go out against them 2
Est 5: 8 and tomorrow I will do as the king has said. 2
12 And tomorrow also I am invited . . with the king. 2
9:13 let the Jews . . be allowed tomorrow also to do 2
Prv 3:28 Go, and come again, tomorrow I will give it"– 2
27: 1 Do not boast about tomorrow, for you do not know 1
Isa 22:13 Let us eat and drink, for tomorrow we die. 2
56:12 and tomorrow will be like this day 2
Mat 6:30 which today is alive and tomorrow is thrown 3
34 Therefore do not be anxious about tomorrow 3
34 for tomorrow will be anxious for itself. 3
Lke 12:28 tomorrow is thrown into the oven 3
13:32 perform cures today and tomorrow 3
33 today and tomorrow and the day following 3
Act 23:20 to bring Paul down to the council tomorrow 3
25:22 Tomorrow," said he, "you shall hear him. 3
1Co 15:32 Let us eat and drink, for tomorrow we die. 3
Jas 4:13 Today or tomorrow we will go into . . a town 3
14 whereas you do not know about tomorrow. 3
2Es 10:58 tomorrow night you shall remain here. 6
14:26 tomorrow at this hour you shall begin to write. 6
Sir 10:10 the king of today will die tomorrow. 3
20:15 today he lends and tomorrow he asks it back 3
1Mc 2:63 tomorrow he will not be found 3
5:27 to attack the strongholds tomorrow 4
3Mc 5:20 he added, "tomorrow . . prepare the elephants 5
38 the destruction of the Jews tomorrow! 3

tone 1. קוֹל (A) 2. ἦχος 3. φωνή
Dan 6:20 cried out in a tone of anguish and said to Daniel 1
Gal 4:20 to be present with you now and to change my tone 3
Sir 50:18 in sweet and full-toned melody. 2
2Mc 7:24 he was suspicious of her reproachful tone. 3
3Mc 5:37 he said in a threatening tone •

tong 1. מֶלְקָח
1Kg 7:49 the flowers, the lamps, and the tongs, of gold; 1
2Ch 4:21 flowers, the lamps, and the tongs, of purest gold; 1
Isa 6: 6 burning coal . . taken with tongs from the altar. 1

tongue 1. לָשׁוֹן 2. γλῶσσα 3. φωνή 4. lingua
Exd 4:10 but I am slow of speech and of tongue. 1
Jos 10:21 not a man moved his tongue against . . Israel. 1
Jdg 7: 5 that laps the water with his tongue, as a dog laps 1
2Sm 23: 2 Spirit . . speaks by me, his word is upon my tongue. 1
Job 5:21 You shall be hid from the scourge of the tongue 1
6:30 Is there any wrong on my tongue? 1
15: 5 you choose the tongue of the crafty. 1
20:12 in his mouth, though he hides it under his tongue 1
16 the tongue of a viper will kill him. 1
27: 4 my tongue will not utter deceit. 1
29:10 their tongue cleaved to the roof of their mouth. 1
33: 2 I open my mouth; the tongue in my mouth speaks. 1
41: 1 or press down his tongue with a cord? 1
Ps 5: 9 they flatter with their tongue. 1
10: 7 under his tongue are mischief and iniquity. 1
12: 3 cut off . . the tongue that makes great boasts 1
4 those who say, "With our tongue we will prevail 1
15: 3 who does not slander with his tongue 1
22:15 my tongue cleaves to my jaws; 1
31:20 under thy shelter from the strife of tongues. 1
34:13 Keep your tongue from evil, and your lips 1
35:28 Then my tongue shall tell of thy righteousness 1
37:30 utters wisdom, and his tongue speaks justice. 1
39: 1 guard my ways, that I may not sin with my tongue; 1
3 the fire burned; then I spoke with my tongue 1
45: 1 my tongue is like the pen of a ready scribe. 1
50:19 your tongue frames deceit. 1
51:14 my tongue will sing aloud of thy deliverance. 1
52: 2 Your tongue is like a sharp razor 1
4 love all words that devour, O deceitful tongue. 1
55: 9 O Lord, confuse their tongues; 1
57: 4 spears and arrows, their tongues sharp swords. 1
64: 3 who whet their tongues like swords 1
8 Because of their tongue he will bring them 1
66:17 he was extolled with my tongue. 1
68:23 tongues of your dogs may have their portion 1
71:24 my tongue will talk of thy righteous help 1
73: 9 their tongue struts through the earth. 1
78:36 they lied to him with their tongues. 1
109: 2 speaking against me with lying tongues. 1
119:172 My tongue will sing of thy word 1
120: 2 Deliver me, O LORD, from . . deceitful tongue. 1
3 what more . . be done to you, you deceitful tongue? 1
126: 2 our tongue with shouts of joy; 1
137: 6 Let my tongue cleave to the roof of my mouth, if I do 1
139: 4 Even before a word is on my tongue, lo, O LORD 1
140: 3 They make their tongue sharp as a serpent's 1
Prv 6:17 haughty eyes, a lying tongue 1
24 from the smooth tongue of the adventuress. 1
10:20 The tongue of the righteous is choice silver; 1
31 but the perverse tongue will be cut off. 1
12:18 but the tongue of the wise brings healing. 1
19 but a lying tongue is but for a moment. 1
15: 2 The tongue of the wise dispenses knowledge 1
4 A gentle tongue is a tree of life 1
16: 1 but the answer of the tongue is from the LORD. 1
17: 4 liar gives heed to a mischievous tongue. 1
20 one with a perverse tongue falls into calamity. 1
18:21 Death and life are in the power of the tongue 1
21: 6 The getting of treasures by a lying tongue 1
23 He who keeps his mouth and his tongue keeps 1
25:15 soft tongue will break a bone. 1
23 backbiting tongue, angry looks. 1
26:28 A lying tongue hates its victims 1
28:23 more favor than he who flatters with his tongue. 1
31:26 teaching of kindness is on her tongue. 1
Sng 4:11 honey and milk are under your tongue; 1
Isa 5:24 as the tongue of fire devours the stubble 1
11:15 utterly destroy the tongue of the sea of Egypt; 1
28:11 by men of strange lips and with an alien tongue 1
30:27 and his tongue is like a devouring fire; 1
32: 4 the tongue of the stammerers will speak readily 1
33:19 stammering in a tongue which you cannot 1
35: 6 and the tongue of the dumb sing for joy. 1
41:17 and their tongue is parched with thirst 1
45:23 every knee shall bow, every tongue shall swear. 1
50: 4 has given me the tongue of those who are taught 1
54:17 confute every tongue that rises against you 1
57: 4 you open your mouth wide and put out your tongue? 1
59: 3 spoken lies, your tongue mutters wickedness. 1
66:18 and I am coming to gather all nations and tongues; 1
Jer 9: 3 They bend their tongue like a bow; 1
5 they have taught their tongue to speak lies; 1
8 Their tongue is a deadly arrow; 1
18:18 Come, let us smite him with the tongue 1
23:31 who use their tongues and say, 'Says the LORD.' 1
Lam 4: 4 The tongue of the nursling cleaves . . for thirst; 1
Ezk 3:26 make your tongue cleave to the roof of your mouth 1
Hos 7:16 because of the insolence of their tongue. 1
Mic 6:12 and their tongue is deceitful in their mouth. 1
Zep 3:13 be found in their mouth a deceitful tongue. 1
Zec 8:23 the nations of every tongue shall take hold 1

14:12 their tongues shall rot in their mouths. 1
Mrk 7:33 he spat and touched his tongue; 2
35 his ears were opened, his tongue was released 2
16:17 they will speak in new tongues; 2
Lke 1:64 his mouth was opened and his tongue loosed 2
16:24 cool my tongue 2
Act 2: 3 there appeared to them tongues as of fire 2
4 began to speak in other tongues 2
11 we hear them telling in our own tongues 2
26 my heart was glad, and my tongue rejoiced; 2
10:46 For they heard them speaking in tongues 2
19: 6 they spoke with tongues and prophesied. 2
Rom 3:13 they use their tongues to deceive. 2
14:11 and every tongue shall give praise to God. 2
1Co 12:10 to another various kinds of tongues 2
10 to another the interpretation of tongues. 2
28 speakers in various kinds of tongues. 2
30 Do all speak with tongues? Do all interpret? 2
13: 1 If I speak in the tongues of men and of angels 2
8 as for tongues, they will cease 2
14: 2 who speaks in a tongue speaks not to men but to God; 2
4 He who speaks in a tongue edifies himself 2
5 Now I want you all to speak in tongues 2
5 he who speaks in tongues 2
6 Now, brethren, if I come to you speaking in tongues 2
9 if you in a tongue utter speech 2
13 who speaks in a tongue should pray for the power 2
14 For if I pray in a tongue, my spirit prays 2
18 I speak in tongues more than you all; 2
19 than 10,000 words in a tongue. 2
22 Thus, tongues are a sign not for believers 2
23 all speak in tongues 2
26 a hymn, a lesson, a revelation, a tongue 2
27 If any speak in a tongue 2
39 do not forbid speaking in tongues; 2
Php 2:11 every tongue confess that Jesus Christ is Lord 2
Jas 1:26 If any one . . does not bridle his tongue 2
3: 5 So the tongue is a little member and boasts 2
6 And the tongue is a fire. 2
6 The tongue is an unrighteous world 2
8 no human being can tame the tongue 2
1Pe 3:10 let him keep his tongue from evil 2
Rev 5: 9 ransom men for God from every tribe and tongue 2
7: 9 from all tribes and peoples and tongues 2
10:11 many peoples and nations and tongues and kings. 2
11: 9 the peoples and tribes and tongues and nations 2
13: 7 every tribe and people and tongue and nation 2
14: 6 to every nation and tribe and tongue and people; 2
16:10 men gnawed their tongues in anguish 2
17:15 peoples and multitudes and nations and tongues 2
2Es 13:10 from his tongue he shot forth a storm of sparks. 4
Jdt 3: 8 all their tongues and tribes 2
Wis 1: 6 a hearer of his tongue. 2
11 keep your tongue from slander 2
10:21 and made the tongues of babes speak clearly. 2
Sir 4:24 education through the words of the tongue. 2
5:13 a man's tongue is his downfall. 2
14 do not lie in ambush with your tongue 2
6: 5 a gracious tongue multiplies courtesies. 2
17: 6 He made for them tongue and eyes 2
19:16 Who has never sinned with his tongue? 2
20:18 better than a slip of the tongue 2
22:27 so that my tongue may not destroy me! 2
25: 7 a tenth I shall tell with my tongue 2
8 has not made a slip with his tongue 2
26: 6 a tongue-lashing makes it known to all. 2
28:17 a blow of the tongue crushes the bones. 2
18 not so many as have fallen because of the tongue. 2
26 Beware lest you err with your tongue •
37:18 it is the tongue that continually rules them. 2
51: 2 the snare of a slanderous tongue 2
5 from an unclean tongue and lying words– 2
6 slander of an unrighteous tongue to the king 2
22 The Lord gave me a tongue as my reward 2
LJr 1: 8 Their tongues are smoothed by the craftsman 2
2Mc 7:10 he quickly put out his tongue 2
27 she spoke in their native tongue as follows 3
15:33 he cut out the tongue of the ungodly Nicanor 2
3Mc 2:17 exult in the arrogance of their tongue, saying 2
6: 4 lawless insolence and boastful tongue 2
4Mc 10:17 Antiochus gave orders to cut out his tongue. 2
19 See, here is my tongue; cut it off 2
21 you are cutting out a tongue 2
18:21 and cut out their tongues 2

tongue *See also* cut, hold, man.

double tongued 1.δίγλωσσος 2.δίλογος

1Ti 3: 8 not double-tongued, not addicted to much wine 2
Sir 5: 9 the double-tongued sinner does that. 1
14 severe condemnation to the double-tongued. 1
6: 1 so fares the double-tongued sinner. 1

tonight 1.לַיְלָה 2.νύξ οὗτος

Gen 19: 5 Where are the men who came to you tonight? 1
34 father; let us make him drink wine tonight also; 1
30:15 Rachel said, "Then he may lie with you tonight 1
Jos 2: 2 certain men of Israel have come here tonight 1
4: 3 lay them . . in the place where you lodge tonight. 1
Rut 3: 2 See, he is winnowing barley tonight 1
1Sm 19:11 If you do not save your life tonight, tomorrow you 1
2Sm 17: 1 and I will set out and pursue David tonight. 1
16 Do not lodge tonight at the fords 1
Jdt 8:33 Stand at the city gate tonight 2

tonsure 1.קָרְחָה

Lev 21: 5 They shall not make tonsures upon their heads 1

tonsure *See also* make.

too 1.גַּם 2.וְ 3.מִן 4.αὐτός 5.δέ 6.καί 7.κἀκεῖ

Exd 33:13 Consider too that this nation is thy people. •
Jdg 3:31 with an oxgoad; and he too delivered Israel. 1
5:18 Naph'tali too, on the heights of the field. 2
6:35 Manas'seh; and they too were called out to follow 1
1Sm 14:22 they too followed hard after them in the battle. 1
19:24 And he too stripped off his clothes 1
24 stripped off his clothes, and he too prophesied 1
2Kg 6: 1 the place where we dwell . . is too small for us. 3
1Ch 22:14 timber and stone too I have provided. 2
Job 33: 6 I too was formed from a piece of clay. 1
Prv 23:15 if your heart is wise, my heart too will be glad. 1
Isa 14:10 say to you: 'You too have become as weak as we! 1
Jer 2:37 From it too you will come away 1
3: 8 but she too went and played the harlot. 1
48:26 in his vomit, and he too shall be held in derision. 1
Nah 3: 9 Ethiopia was her strength, Egypt too 2
Zec 9: 5 be afraid; Gaza too, and shall writhe in anguish; 2
7 it too shall be a remnant for our God; 1
Mat 20: 4 to them he said, 'You go into the vineyard too 6
7 He said to them, 'You go into the vineyard too.' 6
22:26 So too the second and third, down to the seventh. 6
Joh 4:45 for they too had gone to the feast. 6
7:52 They replied, "Are you from Galilee too? 6
9:27 Do you too want to become his disciples? 6
Act 10:26 Peter lifted him up, saying, "Stand up; I too am a man. 6
17:13 they came there too 7
Rom 6: 4 we too might walk in newness of life. 6
11: 5 So too at the present time there is a remnant 6
22 otherwise you too will be cut off. 6
2Co 1: 5 we share abundantly in comfort too. 6
4:13 we too believe, and so we speak 6
11:16 so that I too may boast a little. 6
18 I too will boast.) 6
Gal 6: 1 Look to yourself, lest you too be tempted. 6
3Jn 1:12 I testify to him too 6
Rev 14:17 another angel . . and he too had a sharp sickle. 6
Tob 8:10 with the thought, "Perhaps he too will die. 6
Sir 37: 1 Every friend will say, "I too am a friend 6
38:14 for they too will pray to the Lord 6
27 So too is every craftsman and master workman •
28 So too is the smith sitting by the anvil •
29 So too is the potter sitting at his work •
1Mc 10:42 this too is canceled 6
2Mc 7:13 When he too had died 6
15:37 So I too will here end my story. 4
3Mc 7:19 there too in like manner they decided to observe 7
4Mc 10: 1 When he too had endured a glorious death 6
11:13 After he too had died 6
12: 4 You too, if you do not obey, will be . . tortured 5
15 Then because he too was about to die, he said 6
16:22 You too must have the same faith in God 6

too (2) 1.מִן 2.ἐπί 3.πολύς 4.ὑπέρ 5.etiam valde

Gen 18:14 Is anything too hard for the LORD? •
36: 7 For their possessions were too great for them 1
Exd 1: 9 people of Israel are too many and too mighty 1
9 Israel are too many and too mighty for us. 1
12: 4 if the household is too small for a lamb, then a man 1
18:18 for the thing is too heavy for you; you are not able 1
Lev 27: 8 if a man is too poor to pay your valuation 1
Num11:14 burden is too heavy for me. 1
16: 3 You have gone too far! For all the congregation •
7 You have gone too far, sons of Levi! •
9 is it too small a thing for you that the God 1
22: 6 curse this people . . since they are too mighty 1
Deu 1:17 case that is too hard for you, you shall bring to me 1
2:36 there was not a city too high for us; the LORD 1
12:21 If the place . . is too far from you, then you may 1
14:24 if the way is too long for you, so that you 1
24 because the place is too far from you 1
17: 8 any case . . which is too difficult for you 1
30:11 this commandment . . is not too hard for you 1
Jos 17:15 the hill country of E'phraim is too narrow for you. •
19: 9 the portion of . . Judah was too large for them •
Jdg 6:27 but because he was too afraid of his family •
18:26 when Micah saw that they were too strong for him •
Rut 1:12 go your way, for I am too old to have a husband. 1
1Sm 30:10 stayed behind, who were too exhausted to cross 1
21 men, who had been too exhausted to follow David 1
2Sm 3:39 these men the sons of Zeru'iah are too hard for me. 1
10:11 And he said, "If the Syrians are too strong for me •
11 but if the Ammonites are too strong for you •
12: 8 if this were too little, I would add to you as much •
22:18 delivered me . . for they were too mighty for me. •
1Kg 8:64 the bronze altar . . was too small to receive •
19: 7 eat, else the journey will be too great for you. 1
1Ch 19:12 he said, "If the Syrians are too strong for me 1
12 if the Ammonites are too strong for you 1
Job 15:11 Are the consolations of God too small for you 1
42: 3 I did not understand, things too wonderful for me 1
Ps 18:17 for they were too mighty for me. 1
35:10 deliverest the weak from him who is too strong •
38: 4 they weigh like a burden too heavy for me. 1
131: 1 O LORD, my . . eyes are not raised too high; •
1 things too great and too marvelous for me. •
1 things too great and too marvelous for me. •
139: 6 Such knowledge is too wonderful for me; it is high •
142: 6 from my persecutors; for they are too strong •
Prv 24: 7 Wisdom is too high for a fool; •
30: 2 Surely I am too stupid to be a man. 1
18 Three things are too wonderful for me; 1
Isa 7:13 O house of David! Is it too little for you to weary men •
49: 6 is too light a thing that you should be my servant 1
19 you will be too narrow for your inhabitants •
20 say in your ears: 'The place is too narrow for me; •
Jer 9: 5 they commit iniquity and are too weary to repent. •
31:11 has redeemed him from hands too strong for him. •
32:17 Nothing is too hard for thee •
27 is anything too hard for me? •
Ezk 8:17 Is it too slight a thing for the house of Judah •
1Co 9:11 is it too much if we reap your material benefits? •
2Co 11:21 To my shame, I must say, we were too weak for that! •
1Es 9:11 we have sinned too much in these things. 2
2Es 10:25 so that I was too frightened to approach her 5
Sir 19: 4 One who trusts others too quickly •
20: 5 detested for being too talkative. 3
Sus 1:39 for he was too strong for us 4
1Mc 9: 9 we are too few. •

too *See* difficult, elated, few, full, great, hard, indulgent, long, much, soon.

tool 1.חֶרֶב 2.כְּלִי

Exd 20:25 for if you wield your tool upon it you profane it. 1
1Kg 6: 7 hammer nor axe nor any tool of iron was heard 2

tool *See also* graving.

iron tool 1.בַּרְזֶל

Deu 27: 5 you shall lift up no iron tool upon them. 1
Jos 8:31 stones, upon which no man has lifted an iron tool 1

tooth 1.מְתַלְּעוֹת 2.פֶּה 3.שֵׁן 4.שֵׁן (A) 5.ὀδούς 6.dens

Gen 49:12 and his teeth white with milk. 3
Exd 21:24 eye for eye, tooth for tooth, hand for hand 3
24 eye for eye, tooth for tooth, hand for hand 3
27 If he knocks out the tooth of his slave 3
27 shall let the slave go free for the tooth's sake. 3
Lev 24:20 eye for eye, tooth for tooth; as he has disfigured 3
20 eye for eye, tooth for tooth; as he has disfigured 3
Num11:33 While the meat was yet between their teeth 3
Deu 19:21 life for life, eye for eye, tooth for tooth 3
21 life for life, eye for eye, tooth for tooth 3
32:24 I will send the teeth of beasts against them 3
Job 4:10 the teeth of the young lions, are broken. 3
13:14 I will take my flesh in my teeth 3
16: 9 he has gnashed his teeth at me; 3
19:20 I have escaped by the skin of my teeth. 3
29:17 and made him drop his prey from his teeth. 3
41:14 Round about his teeth is terror. 3
Ps 3: 7 thou dost break the teeth of the wicked. 3
35:16 more and more, gnashing at me with their teeth. 3
37:12 The wicked . . gnashes his teeth at him; 3
57: 4 their teeth are spears and arrows 3
58: 6 O God, break the teeth in their mouths; 3
112:10 wicked man . . gnashes his teeth and melts away; 3
124: 6 LORD, who has not given us as prey to their teeth! 3
Prv 10:26 Like vinegar to the teeth, and smoke to the eyes 3
25:19 like a bad tooth or a foot that slips. 3
30:14 whose teeth are swords, whose teeth are knives 3
14 whose teeth are swords, whose teeth are knives 1
Sng 4: 2 Your teeth are like a flock of shorn ewes 3
6: 6 Your teeth are like a flock of ewes 3
7: 9 goes down smoothly, gliding over lips and teeth. 5
Isa 41:15 a threshing sledge, new, sharp, and having teeth; 2
Jer 31:29 and the children's teeth are set on edge. 3
30 eats sour grapes, his teeth shall be set on edge. 3
Lam 2:16 your enemies . . they hiss, they gnash their teeth 3
3:16 He has made my teeth grind on gravel 3
Ezk 18: 2 and the children's teeth are set on edge 3
Dan 7: 5 had three ribs in its mouth between its teeth; 4
7 great iron teeth; it devoured and broke in pieces 4
19 with its teeth of iron and claws of bronze; 4
Jol 1: 6 its teeth are lions' teeth 3
6 its teeth are lions' teeth 3
Ams 4: 6 I gave you cleanness of teeth in all your cities 3
Zec 9: 7 and its abominations from between its teeth; 3
Mat 5:38 An eye for an eye and a tooth for a tooth.' 5
38 An eye for an eye and a tooth for a tooth.' 5
8:12 there men will weep and gnash their teeth. 5
13:42 there men will weep and gnash their teeth. 5
50 there men will weep and gnash their teeth. 5
22:13 there men will weep and gnash their teeth.' 5
24:51 there men will weep and gnash their teeth. 5
25:30 there men will weep and gnash their teeth.' 5
Mrk 9:18 he foams and grinds his teeth and becomes rigid; 5
Lke 13:28 There you will weep and gnash your teeth 5

Act 7:54 they ground their teeth against him. 5
Rev 9: 8 and their teeth like lions' teeth; 5
8 and their teeth like lions' teeth; •
2Es 15:30 shall devastate a portion . . with their teeth. 6
Wis 16:10 even by the teeth of venomous serpents 5
Sir 21: 2 Its teeth are lion's teeth 5
2 Its teeth are lion's teeth 5
30:10 in the end you will gnash your teeth. 5
39:30 the teeth of wild beasts, and scorpions 5
4Mc 7: 6 you neither defiled your sacred teeth 5

tooth *See also* gnash.

top 1. גַּג 2. לְמַעְלָה 3. מַעְלָה 4. עֶלְיוֹן 5. צַמֶּרֶת 6. רֹאשׁ 7. רֹאשָׁה 8. רוּם (A) 9. ἄκρος 10. ἄνωθεν 11. κορυφή 12. cacumen 13. vertex

Gen 8: 5 of the month, the tops of the mountains were seen. 6
11: 4 a city, and a tower with its top in the heavens 6
28:12 and the top of it reached to heaven; 6
18 for a pillar and poured oil on the top of it. 6
Exd 17: 9 tomorrow I will stand on top of the hill 6
10 Aaron, and Hur went up to the top of the hill. 6
19:20 LORD came down . . to the top of the mountain; 6
20 the LORD called Moses to the top of the mountain 6
24:17 like a devouring fire on the top of the mountain 6
25:21 you shall put the mercy seat on the top of the ark; 2
26:24 be separate beneath, but joined at the top 6
30: 3 its top and its sides round about and its horns; 1
34: 2 present yourself . . on the top of the mountain. 6
36:29 they were separate beneath, but joined at the top 6
37:26 with pure gold, its top, and its sides round about 1
Num 4:25 covering of goatskin that is on top of it 3
20:28 Aaron died there on the top of the mountain. 6
21:20 in the region of Moab by the top of Pisgah 6
23: 9 For from the top of the mountains I see him 6
14 he took him to . . Zophim, to the top of Pisgah 6
28 Balak took Balaam to the top of Pe'or 6
Deu 3:27 Go up to the top of Pisgah, and lift up your eyes 6
34: 1 Mount Nebo, to the top of Pisgah . . opposite Jericho. 6
Jos 15: 8 and the boundary goes up to the top 6
9 boundary extends from the top of the mountain 6
Jdg 6:26 build an altar . . on the top of the stronghold 6
9: 7 he went and stood on the top of Mount Ger'izim 6
25 men in ambush against him on the mountain tops 6
36 Look, men are coming down from the mountain tops! 6
16: 3 shoulders and carried them to the top of the hill 6
1Sm 26:13 and stood afar off on the top of the mountain 6
2Sm 2:25 and took their stand on the top of a hill. 6
5:24 when you hear . . in the tops of the balsam trees 6
1Kg 7:16 capitals . . to set upon the tops of the pillars; 6
17 for the capitals upon the tops of the pillars; 6
18 the capital that was upon the top of the pillar; 6
19 capitals that were upon the tops of the pillars 6
22 upon the tops of the pillars was lily-work. 6
35 on the top of the stand there was a round band 6
35 on the top of the stand its stays and its panels 6
41 the capitals that were on the tops of the pillars; 6
41 the capitals that were on the tops of the pillars; 6
18:42 And Eli'jah went up to the top of Carmel; 6
2Kg 1: 9 to Eli'jah, who was sitting on the top of a hill 6
1Ch 14:15 sound of marching in the tops of the balsam trees 6
2Ch 3:15 with a capital of five cubits on the top of each. 6
16 chains . . and put them on the tops of the pillars; 6
4:12 the two capitals on the top of the pillars; 6
12 the capitals that were on the top of the pillars; 6
25:12 took them to the top of a rock and threw them down 6
12 threw them down from the top of the rock; 6
Est 5: 2 Esther . . and touched the top of the scepter. 6
Ps 72:16 on the tops of the mountains may it wave; 6
Prv 1:21 on the top of the walls she cries out; 6
23:34 like one who lies on the top of a mast. 6
Isa 17: 6 three berries in the top of the highest bough 6
30:17 left like a flagstaff on the top of a mountain 6
42:11 let them shout from the top of the mountains. 6
Ezk 6:13 on all the mountain tops, under every green tree 6
17: 3 came to Lebanon and took the top of the cedar; 5
22 will take a sprig from the lofty top of the cedar 5
31: 3 and of great height, its top among the clouds. 5
10 it towered high and set its top among the clouds 5
14 or set their tops among the clouds 5
41: 7 thus one went up from the lowest story to the top 4
43:12 upon the top of the mountain shall be most holy. 6
Dan 4:11 tree grew . . and its top reached to heaven 8
20 grew . . so that its top reached to heaven 8
Hos 4:13 They sacrifice on the tops of the mountains 6
Jol 2: 5 they leap on the tops of the mountains 6
Ams 1: 2 shepherds mourn, and the top of Carmel withers. 6
9: 3 Though they hide themselves on the top of Carmel 6
Zec 4: 2 lampstand all of gold, with a bowl on the top of it 6
2 on each of the lamps which are on the top of it. 6
7 he shall bring forward the top stone amid shouts 7
Mat 27:51 torn in two, from top to bottom 10
Mrk 15:38 torn in two, from top to bottom. 10
Joh 19:23 tunic was without seam, woven from top to bottom; 10
2Es 13:35 he shall stand on the top of Mount Zion. 12
16:60 and pools on the tops of the mountains 13
Jdt 6:12 ran out of the city to the top of the hill 11
7:10 not easy to reach the tops of their mountains. 11
13 We . . will go up to the tops of the nearby mountains 11
9:13 they have planned . . against the top of Zion 11
4Mc 14:16 building . . in holes and tops of trees 9

topaz 1. פִּטְדָה 2. τοπάζιον

Exd 28:17 A row of sardius, topaz, and carbuncle shall be 1
39:10 A row of sardius, topaz, and carbuncle 1
Job 28:19 The topaz of Ethiopia cannot compare with it 1
Ezk 28:13 carnelian, topaz, and jasper, chrysolite, beryl 1
Rev 21:20 the eighth beryl, the ninth topaz 2

topmost 1. רֹאשׁ

Ezk 17: 4 he broke off the topmost of its young twigs 1
22 break off from the topmost of its young twigs 1

torch 1. לַפִּיד 2. λαμπάς

Gen 15:17 pot and a flaming torch passed between these 1
Jdg 7:16 and empty jars, with torches inside the jars. 1
20 the jars, holding in their left hands the torches 1
15: 4 Samson . . caught 300 foxes, and took torches; 1
4 and put a torch between each pair of tails. 1
5 when he had set fire to the torches, he let 1
Isa 62: 1 and her salvation as a burning torch. 1
Ezk 1:13 like torches moving to and fro among the living 1
Dan 10: 6 his eyes like flaming torches, his arms and legs 1
Nah 2: 4 they gleam like torches 1
Zec 12: 6 Judah . . like a flaming torch among sheaves; 1
Joh 18: 3 went there with lanterns and torches 2
Rev 4: 5 before the throne burn seven torches of fire 2
8:10 great star fell from heaven, blazing like a torch 2
Sir 48: 1 his word burned like a torch. 2
1Mc 6:39 the hills . . gleamed like flaming torches. 2

flaming torch 1. לַפִּיד

Job 41:19 Out of his mouth go flaming torches; 1

torment 1. בעת 2. יגה 3. מַעֲצֵבָה 4. ענה 5. צרר 6. αἰκίζω 7. βασανίζω 8. βασανισμός 9. βάσανος 10. ἐπιτείνω 11. στρεβλόω 12. cruciamentum 13. cruciatus 14. crucio 15. tormento 16. tormentum 17. torqueo

Jdg 16:19 she began to torment him, and his strength left 4
1Sm 16:14 and an evil spirit from the LORD tormented him. 1
15 an evil spirit from God is tormenting you. 1
2Sm 13: 2 Amnon was so tormented that he made himself ill 5
Job 19: 2 How long will you torment me 2
Isa 50:11 have from my hand: you shall lie down in torment. 3
Mat 8:29 Have you come here to torment us before the time? 7
Mrk 5: 7 I adjure you by God, do not torment me. 7
Lke 8:28 I beseech you, do not torment me. 7
16:23 in Hades, being in torment, he lifted up his eyes 9
28 lest they also come into this place of torment.' 9
Rev 11:10 because these two prophets had been a torment 7
14:10 he shall be tormented with fire and sulphur 7
11 smoke of their torment goes up for ever and ever; 8
18: 7 give her a like measure of torment and mourning. 8
10 they will stand far off, in fear of her torment 8
15 in fear of her torment, weeping and mourning 8
20:10 they will be tormented day and night for ever 7
2Es 7:36 Then the pit of torment shall appear 16
38 and there are fire and torments! 16
47 bring delight to few, but torments to many. 16
64 and therefore we are tormented 17
66 nor do they know of any torment or salvation 12
67 we shall be preserved . . but cruelly tormented 15
72 those who dwell on earth shall be tormented 14
75 or whether we shall be tormented at once? 14
76 among those who are tormented. 14
80 shall immediately wander about in torments 12
84 they shall consider the torment laid up 12
86 how some of them will pass over into torments. 12
99 and the aforesaid are the ways of torment 13
8:59 so the thirst and torment which are prepared 13
9: 9 those . . shall dwell in torments. 12
12 these must in torment acknowledge it 12
13:38 the torments with which they are to be tortured 12
Wis 3: 1 no torment will ever touch them. 9
11: 9 they learned how the ungodly were tormented 7
12:23 torment through their own abominations. 7
16: 1 tormented by a multitude of animals. 7
4 how their enemies were being tormented. 7
17:13 prefers ignorance of what causes the torment. 9
19: 4 which their torments still lacked 9
Sir 4:17 will torment him by her discipline 9
3Mc 3:27 with the most hateful torments 9
4Mc 3:11 tormented and inflamed him 10
6:16 as though more bitterly tormented by this counsel 6
27 I am dying in burning torments 9
8:19 consider the threats of torments 9
9: 9 deservedly undergo . . eternal torment by fire 9
10:11 will undergo unceasing torments. 9
12: 3 they died in torments 11
13:15 the danger of eternal torment lying before those 9
15:18 nor when the second in torments looked at you 9
22 How great and how many torments 9

torment *See also* suffer.

tormentor 1. יגה 2. תּוֹלָל

Ps 137: 3 required of us songs, and our tormentors, mirth 2
Isa 51:23 I will put it into the hand of your tormentors 1

torn *See* flesh.

torn by beast 1. טרף 2. טְרֵפָה

Exd 22:13 it is torn by beasts, let him bring it as evidence; 1
31 you shall not eat any flesh that is torn by beasts 2
Lev 17:15 what dies of itself or what is torn by beasts 2
22: 8 That which dies of itself or is torn by beasts 2

torn by wild beast 1. טְרֵפָה

Gen 31:39 That which was torn by wild beasts I did not bring 1

torrent 1. נַחַל 2. סְפִיחַ 3. שֶׁטֶף 4. ποταμός

Jdg 5:21 The torrent Kishon swept them away 1
21 Kishon swept them away, the onrushing torrent 1
21 the onrushing torrent, the torrent Kishon. 1
2Sm 22: 5 the torrents of perdition assailed me; 1
Job 14:19 the torrents wash away the soil of the earth; 2
30: 6 In the gullies of the torrents they must dwell 1
38:25 Who has cleft a channel for the torrents of rain 3
Ps 18: 4 the torrents of perdition assailed me; 1
124: 4 torrent would have gone over us; 1
Jer 47: 2 and shall become an overflowing torrent; 1
Lam 2:18 tears stream down like a torrent day and night! 1
Sir 40:13 wealth of the unjust will dry up like a torrent 4

torrent *See also* bed.

torrential 1. שטף

Ezk 38:22 torrential rains and hailstones 1

tortuous *See* path.

torture 1. αἰκία 2. αἰκίζω 3. αἰκισμός 4. ἀποστρεβλόω 5. βασανίζω 6. βασανισμός 7. βάσανος 8. ἐπιτείνω 9. καταικίζω 10. στρεβλόω 11. τυμπανίζω 12. crucio

Heb 11:35 Some were tortured, refusing to accept release 11
Rev 9: 5 were allowed to torture them for five months 5
5 their torture was like the torture of a scorpion 6
5 their torture was like the torture of a scorpion 6
2Es 13:38 torments with which they are to be tortured 12
Wis 2:19 Let us test him with insult and torture 7
Sir 33:26 there are racks and tortures. 7
2Mc 7: 1 compelled . . under torture with whips and cords 2
8 Therefore he in turn underwent tortures 7
13 they maltreated and tortured the fourth 5
17 see how his mighty power will torture you 5
42 eating of sacrifices and the extreme tortures. 1
8:17 the torture of the derided city 3
28 those who had been tortured 2
30 giving to those who had been tortured 2
9: 5 with sharp internal tortures 7
6 he had tortured the bowels of others 5
7 to torture every limb of his body. 4
11 he was tortured with pain every moment. 8
3Mc 4:14 tortured with the outrages that he had ordered 10
4Mc 4:26 he himself, through torture, tried to compel everyone 7
5: 6 Before I begin to torture you, old man 7
6: 5 as though being tortured in a dream; 5
9 endured the tortures. 3
30 the holy man died nobly in his tortures 7
30 he resisted even to the very tortures of death 7
7: 2 and overwhelmed by the mighty waves of tortures 7
4 was consumed by tortures and racks 3
10 O aged man, more powerful than tortures 7
16 an aged man despised tortures even to death 7
8: 2 these should be tortured even more cruelly. 5
9 to destroy . . through tortures. 7
27 though about to be tortured 5
9: 5 threatening us with death by torture 7
6 the aged men . . lived piously while enduring torture 6
6 die despising your coercive tortures 7
7 do not suppose that you can injure us by torturing us. 5
16 you may be released from the tortures 7
18 Through all these tortures I will convince you 7
26 they bound him to the torture machine and catapult. •
27 Before torturing him, they inquired 5
30 you are being tortured more than I 5
10:16 Contrive tortures, tyrant, so that you may learn 7
11: 1 this one died also, after being cruelly tortured 9
2 to be tortured for the sake of virtue. 5
6 these deeds deserve honors, not tortures. 7
16 to torture me for not eating defiling foods 5
16 go on torturing! 5
20 While being tortured he said 5
23 you inventor of tortures 7
12: 4 be miserably tortured and die before your time 5
12 intense and eternal fire and tortures 7
13 to maltreat and torture them in this way? 5
13:27 maltreated and tortured to death. 5
14: 1 they encouraged them to face the torture 3
5 hastened to death by torture 7
8 youths . . encircled the sevenfold fear of tortures 7
11 over these men in their tortures 7
15:11 were the various tortures strong enough 7
14 who saw them tortured and burned one by one 10

19 in his tortures gazing boldly 7
20 many spectators of the torturings 7
21 the voices of the children in torture 7
22 her sons were tortured on the wheel 5
32 the torture of your sons 7
16: 1 endured seeing her children tortured to death 7
2 a woman has despised the fiercest tortures. 7
3 she saw her seven sons tortured in such varied ways. 5
15 you stood and watched Eleazar being tortured 5
17 to be terrified by tortures. 7
17: 3 against the earthquake of the tortures. 7
7 enduring their varied tortures to death 7
10 and enduring torture even to death. 7
23 their endurance under the tortures 7
18:20 to the catapult and back again to more tortures 7
21 and put them to death with various tortures. 7

torture *See also* examine, instrument, suffer, wheel.

torture on the wheel 1. στρεβλόω
4Mc 12:11 were you not ashamed to . . torture on the wheel 1

torture to death 1. ἀποτυμπανίζω
3Mc 3:27 whoever shelters any . . will be tortured to death 1

just tortured 1. προβασανίζω
4Mc 8: 5 the old man who has just been tortured 1
10:16 a brother to those who have just been tortured. 1

torturer 1. αἰκίζω 2. βασανίζω
4Mc 1:11 all people, even their torturers, marveled 1
6:10 the old man . . was victorious over his torturers; 2
11 in fact . . he amazed even his torturers 2

toss 1. געש 2. גרש 3. נְדוּד 4. נוֹד 5. ῥιπίζω
Job 7: 4 I am full of tossing till the dawn. 3
Ps 56: 8 Thou hast kept count of my tossings; 4
Isa 57:20 But the wicked are like the tossing sea; 2
Jer 5:22 though the waves toss, they cannot prevail 1
Jas 1: 6 wave of the sea . . driven and tossed by the wind. 5

toss about 1. גרש 2. מוג
Job 30:22 thou tossest me about in the roar of the storm. 2
Ams 8: 8 and be tossed about and sink again, like the Nile 1

toss to and fro 1. κλυδωνίζομαι
Eph 4:14 tossed to and fro and carried about 1

toss up 1. גרש
Isa 57:20 cannot rest, and its waters toss up mire and dirt. 1

total 1. מִסְפָּר 2. πάντοθεν 3. πᾶς
1Ch 23: 3 numbered, and the total was 38,000 men. 1
2Mc 3:11 totaled in all 400 talents of silver •
5:14 Within the total of three days 3
3Mc 4:10 with their eyes in total darkness 2

totter 1. דחה 2. מוג 3. מוט 4. σαλεύω
Ps 46: 6 The nations rage, the kingdoms totter; 3
60: 2 repair its breaches, for it totters. 3
62: 3 all of you, like a leaning wall, a tottering fence? 1
75: 3 When the earth totters, and all its inhabitants 2
Hab 3:16 my steps totter beneath me. •
Sir 13:21 When a rich man totters, he is steadied by friends 4

make totter 1. נוע
Ps 59:11 make them totter by thy power, and bring them down 1

touch 1. חבר 2. נגע 3. נגש 4. נשק 5. עלה עַל 6. פגע בְּ 7. ריח 8. ἅπτω 9. ἐπιτίθημι 10. θιγγάνω 11. παραβάλλω 12. προσψαύω 13. ψαύω 14. ψηλαφάω
Gen 3: 3 garden, neither shall you touch it, lest you die.' 2
20: 6 therefore I did not let you touch her. 2
26:11 Whoever touches this man or his wife shall be put 2
29 just as we have not touched you 2
32:25 he touched the hollow of his thigh; 2
32 because he touched the hollow of Jacob's thigh 2
Exd 4:25 her son's foreskin, and touched Moses' feet with it 2
12:22 and touch the lintel and the two doorposts 2
19:12 do not . . touch the border of it; 2
12 touches the mountain shall be put to death; 2
13 no hand shall touch him, but he shall be stoned 2
29:37 whatever touches the altar shall become holy. 2
30:29 whatever touches them will become holy. 2
Lev 5: 2 Or if any one touches an unclean thing 2
3 Or if he touches human uncleanness, of whatever 2
6:18 whoever touches them shall become holy 2
27 Whatever touches its flesh shall be holy 2
7:19 Flesh that touches any unclean thing shall not 2
21 if any one touches an unclean thing 2
11: 8 not eat, and their carcasses you shall not touch 2
24 whoever touches their carcass shall be unclean 2
26 every one who touches them shall be unclean 2
27 whoever touches their carcass shall be unclean 2
31 whoever touches them when they are dead shall be 2
36 whoever touches their carcass shall be unclean 2
39 he who touches its carcass shall be unclean 2
12: 4 she shall not touch any hallowed thing 2
15: 5 any one who touches his bed shall wash 2
10 whoever touches anything that was under him 2
11 Any one whom he that has the discharge touches 2
12 vessel which he . . touches shall be broken 2
19 whoever touches her shall be unclean 2
21 whoever touches her bed shall wash his clothes 2
22 whoever touches anything upon which she sits 2
23 when he touches it he shall be unclean 2
27 whoever touches these things shall be unclean 2
22: 4 Whoever touches anything that is unclean 2
5 whoever touches a creeping thing 2
6 the person who touches any such shall be unclean 2
Num 4:15 must not touch the holy things, lest they die. 2
9: 6 unclean through touching the dead body of a man •
7 unclean through touching the dead body of a man; •
10 unclean through touching a dead body •
16:26 Depart . . and touch nothing of theirs 2
19:11 He who touches the dead body of any person 2
13 Whoever touches a dead person . . and does not 2
16 Whoever . . touches one who is slain with a sword 2
18 sprinkle it . . upon him who touched the bone 2
21 he who touches the water for impurity shall be 2
22 unclean person touches shall be unclean; 2
22 any one who touches it shall be unclean 2
31:19 whoever has touched any slain 2
Deu 14: 8 flesh . . and their carcasses you shall not touch. 2
Jos 9:19 We have sworn . . and now we may not touch them. 2
16: 7 then it goes down . . and touches Jericho 6
19:11 boundary goes up . . and touches Dab'besheth 6
22 the boundary also touches Tabor, Shahazu'mah 6
26 on the west it touches Carmel and Shihor-lib'nath 6
27 and touches Zeb'ulun and the valley of Iph'tahel 6
34 goes . . to Hukkok, touching Zeb'ulun at the south 6
Jdg 6:21 angel . . touched the meat and the unleavened 2
16: 9 as a string of tow snaps when it touches the fire. 7
1Sm 1:11 to the LORD . . and no razor shall touch his head. 5
10:26 went men of valor whose hearts God had touched. 2
2Sm 14:10 bring him . . and he shall never touch you again. 2
23: 7 the man who touches them arms himself with iron 2
1Kg 6:27 a wing of one touched the one wall 2
27 a wing of the other cherub touched the other wall; 2
27 wings touched each other in the middle 2
19: 5 an angel touched him, and said to him, "Arise 2
7 the angel . . touched him, and said 2
2Kg 13:21 and as soon as the man touched the bones of Eli'sha 2
1Ch 16:22 Touch not my anointed ones, do my prophets no harm! 2
2Ch 3:11 one wing of . . touched the wall of the house 2
11 wing . . touched the wing of the other cherub; 2
12 one wing . . touched the wall of the house 2
Est 5: 2 Esther . . touched the top of the scepter. 2
Job 1:11 put forth thy hand now, and touch all that he has 2
2: 5 touch his bone and his flesh, and he will curse 2
4: 5 it touches you, and you are dismayed. 2
5:19 in seven there shall no evil touch you. 2
6: 7 My appetite refuses to touch them; 2
19:21 for the hand of God has touched me! 2
Ps 104:32 who touches the mountains and they smoke! 2
105:15 Touch not my anointed ones, do my prophets no harm! 2
144: 5 Touch the mountains that they smoke! 2
Prv 6:29 none who touches her will go unpunished. 2
Isa 6: 7 he touched my mouth, and said: "Behold 2
7 Behold, this has touched your lips; 2
52:11 depart, go out thence, touch no unclean thing; 2
Jer 1: 9 the LORD put forth his hand and touched my mouth; 2
12:14 all my evil neighbors who touch the heritage 2
Lam 4:14 defiled . . none could touch their garments. 2
15 men cried at them; "Away! Away! Touch not! 2
Ezk 1: 9 their wings touched one another; 1
11 wings, each of which touched the wing of another 1
3:13 sound of the wings . . as they touched one another 4
9: 6 but touch no one upon whom is the mark. 3
Dan 8: 5 he-goat came . . without touching the ground; 2
18 but he touched me and set me on my feet. 2
10:10 behold, a hand touched me and set me trembling 2
16 likeness of the sons of men touched my lips; 2
18 appearance of a man touched me and strengthened 2
Ams 9: 5 The Lord, GOD of hosts, he who touches the earth 2
Hag 2:12 and touches with his skirt bread, or pottage 2
13 contact with a dead body touches any of these 2
Zec 2: 8 he who touches you touches the apple of his eye. 2
8 he who touches you touches the apple of his eye. 2
14: 5 the valley of the mountains shall touch the side 2
Mat 8: 3 And he stretched out his hand and touched him 8
15 he touched her hand, and the fever left her 8
9:20 came up behind him and touched the fringe 8
21 she said to herself, "If I only touch his garment 8
29 Then he touched their eyes, saying 8
14:36 they might only touch the fringe of his garment 8
36 and as many as touched it were made well. 8
17: 7 Jesus came and touched them, saying 8
20:34 Jesus in pity touched their eyes 8
Mrk 1:41 stretched out his hand and touched him, and said 8
3:10 all who had diseases pressed upon him to touch him. 8
5:27 touched his garment. 8
28 If I touch even his garments, I shall be made well. 8
30 Who touched my garments? 8
31 yet you say, 'Who touched me?' 8
6:56 touch even the fringe of his garment 8
56 as many as touched it were made well. 8
7:33 he spat and touched his tongue; 8
8:22 begged him to touch him. 8
10:13 that he might touch them 8
Lke 5:13 he stretched out his hand, and touched him, saying 8
6:19 all the crowd sought to touch him 8
7:14 he came and touched the bier 8
39 what sort of woman this is who is touching him 8
8:44 touched the fringe of his garment 8
45 Jesus said, "Who was it that touched me? 8
46 Jesus said, "Some one touched me 8
47 before him declared . . why she had touched him 8
11:46 you yourselves do not touch the burdens 12
18:15 that he might touch them 8
22:51 he touched his ear and healed him. 8
Act 20:15 the next day we touched at Samos 11
1Co 7: 1 It is well for a man not to touch a woman. 8
2Co 6:17 touch nothing unclean; then I will welcome you 8
Col 2:21 Do not handle, Do not taste, Do not touch 10
Heb 11:28 the Destroyer . . might not touch them. 10
12:18 you have not come to what may be touched 14
20 If even a beast touches the mountain 10
1Jn 1: 1 we have looked upon and touched with our hands 14
5:18 and the evil one does not touch him. 8
1Es 4:28 Do not all lands fear to touch him? 8
Jdt 11:13 it is not lawful . . so much as to touch these things 8
AEs 15:11 and touched it to her neck; 9
Wis 3: 1 no torment will ever touch them. 8
18:16 and touched heaven while standing on the earth. 8
20 experience of death touched also the righteous 8
Sir 13: 1 Whoever touches pitch will be defiled 8
34:25 If a man washes after touching a dead body •
25 touches it again 8
LJr 1:29 touched by women in menstruation 8
Aza 1:27 the fire did not touch them at all . . or trouble them. 8
2Mc 9:10 he could touch the stars of heaven. 8
4Mc 17: 1 so that no one might touch her body. 13

whoever touches 1. נגע
Lev 15: 7 whoever touches the body of him 1

tow 1. נְעֹרֶת 2. στιππύον
Jdg 16: 9 as a string of tow snaps when it touches the fire. 1
Isa 1:31 the strong shall become tow, and his work a spark 1
Sir 21: 9 like tow gathered together 2
Aza 1:23 naphtha, pitch, tow, and brush. 2

toward 1. אֶל 2. אֶל דֶּרֶךְ 3. אֶל מוּל 4. אֵת 5. בְּ 6. דֶּרֶךְ 7. הֵנָּה 8. לְ 9. לִפְנֵי 10. לִקְרַאת 11. מִן 12. מֵעִם 13. עַד 14. עַל 15. עַל פְּנֵי 16. עַל פְּנֵי דֶרֶךְ 17. עִם 18. נֶגֶד (A) 19. עִם (A) 20. ἀπέναντι 21. ἀπό 22. εἰς 23. ἐν 24. ἐναντίον 25. ἐπί 26. κατά 27. ὁδός 28. πρός
Gen 12: 9 still going toward the Negeb. †
15: 5 Look toward heaven, and number the stars †
18:16 from there, and they looked toward Sodom; 15
22 the men turned from there, and went toward Sodom; †
19:28 he looked down toward Sodom and Gomor'rah 15
28 looked down . . toward all the land of the valley 14
20: 1 Abraham journeyed toward the territory †
24:27 love and his faithfulness toward my master. 12
28:10 Jacob left Beer-sheba, and went toward Haran. †
30:40 set the faces of the flocks toward the striped 1
31:21 set his face toward the hill country of Gilead. •
48:13 E'phraim in his right hand toward Israel's left 11
13 Manas'seh in his left hand toward Israel's right 11
Exd 9: 8 Take handfuls of ashes . . throw them toward heaven †
10 and Moses threw them toward heaven, and it became †
22 Moses, "Stretch forth your hand toward heaven 14
23 Moses stretched forth his rod toward heaven; 14
10:21 Stretch out your hand toward heaven that there 14
22 So Moses stretched out his hand toward heaven 14
13:18 the way of the wilderness toward the Red Sea. •
14: 5 mind . . was changed toward the people 1
16:10 they looked toward the wilderness, and behold 1
25:20 toward the mercy seat shall the faces . . be. 1
34: 8 made haste to bow his head toward the earth †
37: 9 toward the mercy seat were the faces 1
Lev 9:22 Then Aaron lifted up his hands toward the people 1
Num 2: 3 Those . . toward the sunrise shall be †
3:38 before the tent of meeting toward the sunrise †
12:10 Aaron turned towards Miriam, and behold 1
16:42 they turned toward the tent of meeting; 1
19: 4 toward the front of the tent of meeting 1
21:11 wilderness . . opposite Moab, toward the sunrise. 11
24: 1 Balaam . . set his face toward the wilderness. 1
34:15 at Jericho eastward, toward the sunrise. †
Deu 11:30 west of the road, toward the going down of the sun •
Jos 1: 4 to the Great Sea toward the going down of the sun 13
15 land . . beyond the Jordan toward the sunrise. •
3:16 and those flowing down toward the sea of Arabah 14
8:14 went out early to the descent toward the Arabah 9
18 Stretch out the javelin . . in your hand toward Ai; 1
18 stretched out the javelin . . toward the city. 1
9: 1 along the coast of the Great Sea toward Lebanon 3
11:17 lowland from Mount Halak, that rises toward Se'ir •
12: 1 land beyond the Jordan toward the sunrising †
7 Ba'al-gad . . to Mount Halak, that rises toward Se'ir †
13: 5 and all Lebanon, toward the sunrising •

15: 7 goes . . and so northward, turning toward Gilgal 1
21 in the extreme South, toward the boundary of Edom †
16: 6 the boundary turns round toward Ta'anath-shi'loh *
19:12 eastward toward the sunrise to the boundary *
13 it passes along on the east toward the sunrise †
13 and going on to Rimmon it bends toward Ne'ah; *
22:22 rebellion or in breach of faith toward the LORD 5
Jdg 7:22 army fled as far as Beth-shit'tah toward Zer'erah 13
13:20 the flame went up toward heaven from the altar †
19: 9 now the day has waned toward evening; pray tarry 8
20:45 they turned and fled toward the wilderness †
47 fled toward the wilderness to the rock of Rimmon †
1Sm 9:14 saw Samuel coming out toward them on his way up 10
13:17 one company turned toward Ophrah, to the land 2
18 another company turned toward Beth-hor'on 6
18 and another company turned toward the border 6
18 border that looks . . toward the wilderness. †
17:30 And he turned away from him toward another 1
48 David ran quickly toward the battle line to meet *
20:12 if he is well disposed toward David, shall I not 1
25:20 David and his men came down toward her; 10
2Sm 15:23 all the people passed on toward the wilderness. 16
24: 5 began from Aro'er . . toward Gad and on to Jazer. *
16 angel stretched . . his hand toward Jerusalem *
20 the king and his servants coming on toward him; 14
1Kg 3: 6 and in uprightness of heart toward thee; and thou 17
8:22 and spread forth his hands toward heaven; *
29 thy eyes may be open . . toward this house 1
29 which thy servant offers toward this place. 1
30 hearken . . when they pray toward this place; 1
35 if they pray toward this place, and acknowledge 1
38 and stretching out his hands toward this house; 1
42 when he comes and prays toward this house 1
44 pray . . toward the city which thou hast chosen 6
48 repent . . and pray to thee toward their land 6
54 knelt with hands outstretched toward heaven; *
18:43 he said . . "Go up now, look toward the sea. 6
2Kg 13:23 he turned toward them, because of his covenant 1
1Ch 18: 3 defeated Hadade'zer . . toward Hamath †
29:18 thy people, and direct their hearts toward thee. 1
2Ch 6:13 and spread forth his hands toward heaven; †
20 eyes may be open day and night toward this house 1
20 which thy servant offers toward this place. 1
21 hearken . . when they pray toward this place; 1
26 if they pray toward this place, and acknowledge 1
29 and stretching out his hands toward this house; 1
32 when he comes and prays toward this house 1
34 and they pray to thee toward this city which thou 6
38 if they repent . . and pray toward their land 6
16: 9 those whose heart is blameless toward him. 1
20:24 they looked toward the multitude; 1
24:16 done good in Israel, and toward God and his house. 17
Ezr 3:11 steadfast love endures for ever toward Israel. 14
Est 1:13 procedure toward all who were versed in law 9
Job 2:12 sprinkled dust upon their heads toward heaven. †
10:17 against me, and increase thy vexation toward me; 17
11:13 you will stretch out your hands toward him. 1
13: 8 Will you show partiality toward him *
24:18 no treader turns toward their vineyards. 6
32:21 or use flattery toward any man. 1
33: 6 Behold, I am toward God as you are; 8
39:26 soars, and spreads his wings toward the south? 8
Ps 5: 7 I will worship toward thy holy temple 1
25:15 My eyes are ever toward the LORD 1
28: 2 lift up my hands toward thy most holy sanctuary. 1
34:15 The eyes of the LORD are toward the righteous 1
15 the righteous, and his ears toward their cry. 1
40: 5 thy wondrous deeds and thy thoughts toward us; 1
73:22 I was like a beast toward thee. 17
78:37 Their heart was not steadfast toward him; 17
81:15 Those who hate the LORD would cringe toward him 8
85: 4 put away thy indignation toward us! 17
86:13 For great is thy steadfast love toward me; 14
103:11 so . . his steadfast love toward those who fear 14
117: 2 For great is his steadfast love toward us; 14
119:132 as is thy wont toward those who love thy name. 8
138: 2 I bow down toward thy holy temple and give thanks 1
141: 8 my eyes are toward thee, O LORD God; 1
Prv 3:34 Toward the scorners he is scornful *
17:24 understanding sets his face toward wisdom *
23: 5 flying like an eagle toward heaven. *
Ecc 10: 2 A wise man's heart inclines him toward the right 8
2 but a fool's heart toward the left. 8
Jer 4: 6 Raise a standard toward Zion, flee for safety †
11 A hot wind . . toward the daughter of my people 6
12: 3 thou seest me, and triest my mind toward thee. 4
15: 1 yet my heart would not turn toward this people. 1
39: 4 and they went toward the Arabah. 6
50: 5 the way to Zion, with faces turned toward it 7
Ezk 1:23 were stretched out straight, one toward another; 1
4: 3 set your face toward it 1
7 you shall set your face toward the siege 1
6: 2 set your face toward the mountains of Israel 1
8: 5 So I lifted up my eyes toward the north, and behold †
16 their faces toward the east, worshiping the sun †
16 men . . worshiping the sun toward the east. †
12:14 I will scatter toward every wind all who are 8
17: 6 vine, and its branches turned toward him 1
7 behold, this vine bent its roots toward him 14
7 and shot forth its branches toward him 8
20:46 Son of man, set your face toward the south 6
21: 2 Son of man, set your face toward Jerusalem 1
25: 2 Son of man, set your face toward the Ammonites 1
28:21 Son of man, set your face toward Sidon 1
38: 2 set your face toward Gog, of the land of Magog 1
40:20 there was a gate which faced toward the north 6
22 as those of the gate which faced toward the east; 6
24 he led me toward the south 6
27 he measured from gate to gate toward the south 6
41:11 one door toward the north, and another door 6
11 and another door toward the south; 8
19 face of a man toward the palm tree on the one side 1
19 the face of a young lion toward the palm tree 1
42: 1 led me out into the inner court, toward the north 6
7 parallel to the chambers, toward the outer court 6
47: 1 temple toward the east (for the temple faced east); †
2 to the outer gate, that faces toward the east 6
8 This water flows toward the eastern region 1
Dan 4: 2 signs . . Most High God has wrought toward me. 19
6:10 where he had windows . . open toward Jerusalem; 18
8: 8 four . . horns toward the four winds of heaven. 8
9 grew exceedingly great toward the south, 1
9 grew exceedingly great . . toward the east 1
9 exceedingly great . . toward the glorious land. 1
10:15 turned my face toward the ground and was dumb. †
11: 4 divided toward the four winds of heaven 8
19 face . . toward the fortresses of his own land; 8
12: 7 his right hand and his left hand toward heaven; 1
Zec 6: 6 the black horses goes toward the north country 1
6 the white ones go toward the west country 1
6 and the dappled ones go toward the south country. 1
8 Behold, those who go toward the north country 1
Mat 4:15 the land of Naph'tali, toward the sea 27
12:49 stretching out his hand toward his disciples 25
28: 1 toward the dawn of the first day of the week 22
Lke 7:44 Then turning toward the woman he said to Simon 28
9:53 because his face was set toward Jerusalem. 22
12:21 is not rich toward God. 22
13:22 teaching, and journeying toward Jerusalem. 22
24:29 it is toward evening and the day is now far spent 28
Joh 1:29 The next day he saw Jesus coming toward him 28
20: 3 they went toward the tomb. 22
Act 8:26 Rise and go toward the south 26
24:16 a clear conscience toward God and toward men. 28
16 a clear conscience toward God and toward men. *
Rom 11:22 severity toward those who have fallen 25
1Co 7:36 is not behaving properly toward his betrothed 25
9:21 not being without law toward God *
15:10 his grace toward me was not in vain 22
2Co 1:12 and still more toward you 28
3: 4 that we have through Christ toward God. 28
Eph 1:15 your love toward all the saints 22
2: 7 in kindness toward us in Christ Jesus. 25
Php 3:14 I press on toward the goal for the prize 26
Col 4: 5 Conduct yourselves wisely toward outsiders 28
Tit 3: 2 to show perfect courtesy toward all men. 28
Phm 1: 5 the faith which you have toward the Lord Jesus 28
Heb 6: 1 foundation . . of faith toward God 25
8:12 For I will be merciful toward their iniquities *
1Pe 5: 5 with humility toward one another *
2Pe 3: 9 The Lord . . is forbearing toward you 22
1Es 1:24 who sinned and acted wickedly toward the Lord 22
4:58 he lifted up his face to heaven toward Jerusalem 24
5:47 before the first gate toward the east. 28
2Es 7:134 he shows patience toward those who have sinned *
15:39 shall be driven violently toward the south *
Tob 3:12 I have turned my eyes and my face toward thee. 22
11:10 Tobit started toward the door, and stumbled 28
Jdt 2:25 fronting toward Arabia. *
7:18 they sent some of their men toward the south 28
18 toward the south and the east, toward Acraba 20
12: 9 until she ate her food toward evening. 28
Wis 16:21 manifested thy sweetness toward thy children; 28
Sir 6:13 be on guard toward your friends. 21
28: 4 Does he have no mercy toward a man like himself 25
33:29 Do not act immoderately toward anybody 25
48:20 spreading forth their hands toward him 28
Bar 4: 2 take her; walk toward the shining of her light. 28
36 Look toward the east, O Jerusalem 28
5: 5 stand upon the height and look toward the east 28
Sus 1:35 she, weeping, looked up toward heaven 28
1Mc 8: 1 were well-disposed toward all who made an alliance 23
11:33 because of the good will they show toward us. 28
14:35 which he had maintained toward his nation *
2Mc 3:15 called toward heaven upon him 22
5:23 In his malice toward the Jewish citizens 28
6: 8 should adopt the same policy toward the Jews 26
29 who . . had acted toward him with good will 28
9:26 good will . . toward me and my son. 22
11:19 will maintain your good will toward the government 22
14:33 toward the sanctuary 25
34 stretched forth their hands toward heaven 22
15:21 Maccabeus . . stretched out his hands toward heaven 22
30 his youthful good will toward his countrymen 22
3Mc 3: 1 but was . . hostile toward those in the countryside *
3 unswerving loyalty toward the dynasty; 28
18 the benevolence which we have toward all. 28
19 By maintaining their manifest ill-will toward us 22
21 our amnesty toward their compatriots here 28
23 who are sincerely disposed toward us 28
24 they are ill-disposed toward us in every way *
5: 3 who were especially hostile toward the Jews. 28
25 stretched their hands toward heaven 22
6:26 Who . . differed . . in their goodwill toward us 28
7: 4 ill-will . . toward all nations. 28
6 the clemency which we have toward all men 28
7 firm goodwill which they had toward us 28
11 never be favorably disposed toward . . government. *
4Mc 4:11 Apollonius . . stretched out his hands toward heaven 22
5:25 the Creator . . has shown sympathy toward us. *
9: 9 because of your bloodthirstiness toward us *
13:25 their goodwill and harmony toward one another 28
14: 5 running the course toward immortality 25
13 which draws everything toward an emotion 28
15: 4 have a deeper sympathy toward their offspring *
6 she had implanted in herself tender love toward them 28
9 she felt a greater tenderness toward them. 23

toward *See also* along, behave, turn, yearn.

toward the east 1. מִזְרָחָה

Jer 31:40 to the corner of the Horse Gate toward the east 1

toward the north 1. צָפוֹנָה

Jer 3:12 Go, and proclaim these words toward the north 1

towel 1. *λέντιον*

Joh 13: 4 girded himself with a towel. 1
5 to wipe them with the towel 1

tower 1. אַלְמָנָה 2. אַרְמוֹן 3. גבה 4. מִגְדָּל 5. מָצָב 6. מָצוֹר 7. *ἐπαίρω* 8. *πύργος* 9. *ὑψόω*

Gen 11: 4 a city, and a tower with its top in the heavens 4
5 the LORD came down to see the city and the tower 4
35:21 and pitched his tent beyond the tower of Eder. 4
Jdg 8: 9 I come again in peace, I will break down this tower. 4
17 he broke down the tower of Penu'el, and slew the men 4
9:46 the people of the Tower of Shechem heard of it 4
47 told that all the people of the Tower of Shechem 4
49 all the people of the Tower of Shechem also died 4
51 there was a strong tower within the city 4
51 and they went to the roof of the tower. 4
52 Abim'elech came to the tower, and fought 4
52 and drew near to the door of the tower to burn it 4
2Kg 9:17 watchman was standing on the tower in Jezreel 4
1Ch 27:25 in the cities, in the villages and in the towers 4
2Ch 14: 7 surround them with walls and towers 4
26: 9 Moreover Uzzi'ah built towers in Jerusalem 4
10 he built towers in the wilderness 4
15 engines . . to be on the towers and the corners 4
27: 4 built . . forts and towers on the wooded hills. 4
32: 5 built up all the wall . . and raised towers 4
Neh 3:25 repaired opposite the Angle and the tower 4
26 Water Gate on the east and the projecting tower. 4
27 section opposite the great projecting tower 4
Ps 37:35 towering like a cedar of Lebanon. 7
48:12 about Zion, go round about her, number her towers 4
61: 3 art my refuge, a strong tower against the enemy. 4
122: 7 Peace . . walls, and security within your towers! 2
Prv 12:12 The strong tower of the wicked comes to ruin *
18:10 The name of the LORD is a strong tower; 4
Sng 4: 4 Your neck is like the tower of David 4
7: 4 Your neck is like an ivory tower. 4
4 Your nose is like a tower of Lebanon 4
8:10 I was a wall, and my breasts were like towers; 4
Isa 2:15 against every high tower, and . . fortified wall; 4
13:22 Hyenas will cry in its towers 1
29: 3 and I will besiege you with towers 5
30:25 day of the great slaughter, when the towers fall. 4
33:18 Where is he who counted the towers? 4
Ezk 19:11 it towered aloft among the thick boughs; 3
26: 4 the walls of Tyre, and break down her towers; 4
9 with his axes he will break down your towers. 4
27:11 men of Gamad were in your towers; 4
31: 5 it towered high above all the trees of the forest; 3
10 thus says the Lord GOD: Because it towered high 3
Mic 4: 8 O tower of the flock, hill of the daughter of Zion 4
Hab 2: 1 stand to watch, and station myself on the tower 6
Zec 14:10 the Tower of Han'anel to the king's wine presses. 4
Mat 21:33 dug a wine press in it, and built a tower 8
Mrk 12: 1 built a tower, and let it out to tenants 8
Lke 13: 4 eighteen upon whom the tower in Silo'am fell 8
14:28 desiring to build a tower 8
1Es 1:55 burned their towers with fire 8
4: 4 they go, and conquer mountains, walls, and towers. 8
Tob 13:16 her towers and battlements with pure gold. 8
Jdt 1: 3 he built towers 100 cubits high 8
14 came to Ecbatana, captured its towers 8
7: 5 when they had kindled fires on their towers 8
32 the walls and towers of their city 8
Sir 50:10 like a cypress towering in the clouds. 9
1Mc 1:33 great strong wall and strong towers 8
4:60 with high walls and strong towers round about 8
5: 5 They were shut up by him in their towers 8
5 burned . . their towers and all who were in them. 8
65 and burned its towers round about. 8
6:37 upon the elephants were wooden towers 8

13:33 with high towers and great walls and gates 8
43 battered and captured one tower. 8
16:10 They also fled into the towers 8
2Mc 10:18 than 9,000 took refuge in two very strong towers 8
20 were bribed by some of those . . in the towers 8
22 immediately captured the two towers. 8
36 and set fire to the towers 8
13: 5 there is a tower in that place, 50 cubits high 8
14:41 When the troops were about to capture the tower 8
3Mc 2:27 he set up a stone on the tower in the courtyard 8
4Mc 13: 6 just as towers jutting out over harbors 8

siege tower 1. בַּחוּן 2. דָּיֵק 3. βελόστασις
Isa 23:13 Chalde'ans . . They erected their siege towers 1
Ezk 21:22 to cast up mounds, to build siege towers. 2
1Mc 6:20 he built siege towers and other engines of war. 3
51 He set up siege towers 3

town 1. בַּת 2. חַוָּה 3. עִיר 4. קִרְיָה 5. קֶרֶת 6. שַׁעַר 7. ἔπαυλις 8. κωμή 9. κωμόπολις 10. πόλις
Deu 12:12 the Levite that is within your towns 6
15 slaughter and eat flesh within any of your towns 6
17 You may not eat within your towns the tithe 6
18 eat . . you and . . the Levite who is within your towns; 6
21 may eat within your towns as much as you desire. 6
14:21 may give it to the alien who is within your towns 6
27 not forsake the Levite who is within your towns 6
28 all the tithe . . and lay it up within your towns; 6
29 fatherless, and the widow . . within your towns 6
15: 7 in any of your towns within your land 6
22 You shall eat it within your towns; 6
16: 5 not offer . . within any of your towns 6
11 Levite who is within your towns 6
14 fatherless, and the widow . . within your towns. 6
18 appoint judges and officers in all your towns 6
17: 2 found among you, within any of your towns 6
8 case within your towns which is too difficult 6
18: 6 Levite comes from any of your towns out of all Israel 6
23:16 place . . he shall choose within one of your towns 6
24:14 sojourners . . in your land within your towns; 6
26:12 that they may eat within your towns and be filled 6
28:52 They shall besiege you in all your towns, until 6
52 besiege you in all your towns throughout 6
55 your enemy shall distress you in all your towns. 6
57 your enemy shall distress you in your towns. 6
31:12 Assemble . . the sojourner within your towns 6
Jos 10:37 and smote it . . and its king and its towns 3
39 and he took it with its king and all its towns; 3
13:30 all Bashan . . and all the towns of Ja'ir 3
15:45 Ekron, with its towns and its villages; 1
47 Ashdod, its towns and its villages; 1
47 Gaza, its towns and its villages; 1
16: 9 together with the towns which were set apart 3
9 all those towns with their villages. 3
17: 8 but the town of Tap'puah . . belonged to the sons *
18: 9 a description of it by towns in seven divisions; 3
20: 6 the slayer may go again to his own town and . . home 3
6 to . . his own home, to the town from which he fled.' 3
24:33 buried him at Gib'e-ah, the town of Phin'ehas *
Jdg 6:27 too afraid of his family and the men of the town 3
28 When the men of the town rose early in the morning 3
30 the men of the town said to Jo'ash, "Bring out 3
14:19 to Ash'kelon and killed 30 men of the town *
17: 8 departed from the town of Bethlehem in Judah 3
20:48 all the towns which they found they set on fire. 3
21:23 went and returned . . and rebuilt the towns 3
Rut 1:19 the whole town was stirred because of them; 3
1Sm 23: 7 shut himself in by entering a town that has gates 3
27: 5 let a place be given me in one of the country towns 3
2Sm 2: 3 and they dwelt in the towns of Hebron. 3
2Kg 17: 9 They built . . high places at all their towns 3
1Ch 2:23 Kenath and its villages, 60 towns. 3
5:16 they dwelt in Gilead, in Bashan and in its towns 1
7:28 possessions and . . were Bethel and its towns 1
28 westward Gezer and its towns 1
28 westward Gezer . . Shechem and its towns 1
28 Gezer . . Shechem . . , and Ayyah and its towns; 1
29 Beth-she'an and its towns, Ta'anach and its towns 1
29 Beth-she'an and its towns, Ta'anach and its towns 1
29 Megid'do and its towns, Dor and its towns. 1
29 Megid'do and its towns, Dor and its towns. 1
8:12 Shemed, who built Ono and Lod with its towns. 1
Ezr 2: 1 returned to . . Judah, each to his own town. 3
70 temple servants lived in their towns 3
70 all Israel in their towns. 3
3: 1 When the . . sons of Israel were in the towns 3
Neh 7: 6 returned to Jerusalem and Judah, each to his town. 3
73 priests . . and all Israel, lived in their towns. 3
73 children of Israel were in their towns. 3
8:15 proclaim in all their towns and in Jerusalem, "Go 3
10:37 Levites . . collect the tithes in all our rural towns. 3
11: 1 while nine tenths remained in the other towns. 3
3 towns of Judah every one lived on his property 3
3 every one lived on his property in their towns 3
20 towns of Judah, every one in his inheritance. 3
12:44 gather . . according to the fields of the towns; 3
Est 9:19 Jews of the villages, who live in the open towns 3
Job 24:20 The squares of the town forget them; *
Prv 8: 3 beside the gates in front of the town 5
9: 3 to call from the highest places in the town 5
14 she takes a seat on the high places of the town 5
Isa 22: 2 you who are full of shoutings . . exultant town? 4
Jer 19:15 bringing upon this city and upon all its towns 3
Lam 5:11 ravished in Zion, virgins in the towns of Judah. 3
Hab 2:12 Woe to him who builds a town with blood 3
Mat 10: 5 and enter no town of the Samaritans 10
11 whatever town or village you enter 10
14 as you leave that house or town. 10
15 than for that town. 10
23 When they persecute you in one town 10
23 you will not have gone through all the towns 10
14:13 they followed him on foot from the towns. 10
23:34 persecute from town to town 10
34 persecute from town to town 10
Mrk 1:38 he said to them, "Let us go on to the next towns 9
45 so that Jesus could no longer openly enter a town 10
6:33 they ran there on foot from all the towns 10
Lke 9: 5 when you leave that town shake off the dust 10
10: 1 into every town and place 10
8 Whenever you enter a town and they receive you 10
10 whenever you enter a town 10
11 'Even the dust of your town that clings to our feet 10
12 more tolerable . . for Sodom than for that town. 10
13:22 He went on his way through towns and villages 10
23:50 from the Jewish town of Arimathe'a 10
Joh 11:54 but went . . to a town called E'phraim 10
Act 5:16 gathered from the towns around Jerusalem 10
8:40 he preached the gospel to all the towns 10
Tit 1: 5 appoint elders in every town as I directed you 10
Jas 4:13 tomorrow we will go into such and such a town 10
1Es 5: 8 each to his own town 10
46 the gatekeepers, and all Israel in their towns. 8
Jdt 1: 9 who were in Samaria and its surrounding towns 10
15: 7 the villages and towns in the hill country 7
1Mc 10:84 burned Azotus and the surrounding towns 10
2Mc 8: 6 he would set fire to towns and villages 10

town after town 1. κατὰ πόλιν
Lke 8: 4 people from town after town came to him 1

town clerk 1. γραμματεύς
Act 19:35 when the town clerk had quieted the crowd, he said 1

trace 1. ἐξιχνιάζω 2. ἴχνος
Ezk 21:27 ruin I will make it; there shall not be even a trace *
Dan 2:35 away, so that not a trace of them could be found. *
Wis 2: 4 like the traces of a cloud 2
5:10 when it has passed no trace can be found 2
Sir 18: 6 is it possible to trace the wonders of the Lord. 1

trace a course 1. ἐξιχνιάζω
Wis 6:22 I will trace her course 1

trace out 1. ἐξιχνιάζω
Wis 9:16 who has traced out what is in the heavens? 1

track 1. דֶּרֶךְ 2. מַעְגָּל 3. עָקֵב 4. עָקֵב 5. ἀτραπός 6. ἴχνος
Ps 65:11 the tracks of thy chariot drip with fatness. 2
Sng 1: 8 follow in the tracks of the flock 4
Jer 2:23 a restive young camel interlacing her tracks 1
Hos 6: 8 Gilead is a city . . tracked with blood. 3
Wis 5:10 nor track of its keel in the waves; 5
Sir 42:19 he reveals the tracks of hidden things. 6

track down 1. אָשַׁר
Ps 17:11 They track me down; now they surround me; 1

trackless 1. לֹא דֶרֶךְ 2. ἄβατος
Ps 107:40 makes them wander in trackless wastes; 1
Wis 5: 7 we journeyed through trackless deserts 2

trade 1. כְּנַעַן 2. נתן 3. סחר 4. רכל 5. רְכֻלָּה 6. תְּמוּרָה 7. ἐμπορεύομαι 8. ἐμπόριον 9. ἐργάζομαι 10. μέρος 11. πραγματεύομαι 12. τέχνη
Gen 34:10 the land shall be open to you; dwell and trade in it 3
21 let them dwell in the land and trade in it 3
42:34 and you shall trade in the land.' 3
Job 20:18 of his trading he will get no enjoyment. 6
Lam 1:11 they trade their treasures for food to revive 2
Ezk 16:29 harlotry also with the trading land of Chalde'a; 1
17: 4 its young twigs and carried it to a land of trade 1
27:13 Javan, Tubal, and Meshech traded with you; 4
15 The men of Rhodes traded with you; 4
17 Judah and the land of Israel traded with you; 4
20 Dedan traded with you in saddlecloths 4
22 The traders of Sheba and Ra'amah traded with you; 4
23 Canneh, Eden, Asshur, and Chilmad traded with you. 4
24 These traded with you in choice garments 4
24 in these they traded with you. *
28: 5 in trade you have increased your wealth 5
16 In the abundance of your trade you were filled 5
18 in the unrighteousness of your trade 5
Mat 25:16 went at once and traded with them 9
Lke 19:13 said to them, 'Trade with these till I come.' 11
Joh 2:16 not make my Father's house a house of trade. 8
Act 18: 3 by trade they were tentmakers. 12
19:27 this trade of ours may come into disrepute 10
Jas 4:13 and spend a year there and trade and get gain"; 7
Rev 18:17 sailors and all whose trade is on the sea 9
Sir 38:34 their prayer is in the practice of their trade. 12

trade *See also* ply.

same trade 1. ὁμότεχνος
Act 18: 3 because he was of the same trade 1

trader 1. אִישׁ הַתָּרִים 2. חַבָּר 3. כְּנַעַן 4. כְּנַעֲנִי 5. סחר 6. עַם כְּנַעַן 7. רכל 8. ἔμπορος
Gen 37:28 Then Mid'ianite traders passed by; 5
1Kg 10:15 which came from the traders and from the traffic 1
28 the king's traders received them . . at a price. 5
29 so through the king's traders they were exported *
2Ch 1:16 and the king's traders received them from Ku'e 5
9:14 that which the traders and merchants brought; 1
Job 41: 6 Will traders bargain over him? 2
Isa 23: 8 whose traders were the honored of the earth? 4
Ezk 27:22 The traders of Sheba and Ra'amah traded with you; 7
Hos 12: 7 A trader, in whose hands are false balances 3
Zep 1:11 For all the traders are no more; 6
Zec 14:21 no longer be a trader in the house of the LORD 4
1Mc 3:41 When the traders of the region heard 8

tradesman 1. κάπηλος
Sir 26:29 a tradesman will not be declared innocent of sin. 1

trading *See* gain.

tradition 1. δόγμα 2. θεσμός 3. παράδοσις 4. παραλαμβάνω
Mat 15: 2 Why do your disciples transgress the tradition 3
3 for the sake of your tradition? 3
6 for the sake of your tradition 3
Mrk 7: 3 observing the tradition of the elders; 3
4 many other traditions which they observe 4
5 according to the tradition of the elders 3
8 and hold fast the tradition of men. 3
9 in order to keep your tradition! 3
13 through your tradition which you hand on. 3
1Co 11: 2 maintain the traditions 3
Gal 1:14 for the traditions of my fathers. 3
Col 2: 8 according to human tradition 3
2Th 2:15 hold to the traditions which you were taught 3
3: 6 the tradition that you received from us. 3
3Mc 1: 3 apostatized from the ancestral traditions 1
4Mc 8: 7 the ancestral tradition of your national life. 2

traditional 1. παλαιός
3Mc 3:18 they were carried away by their traditional conceit 1

traffic 1. כְּנַעֲנִי 2. מִסְחָר 3. סחר
1Kg 10:15 which came . . from the traffic of the merchants 2
Isa 47:15 who have trafficked with you from your youth; 3
Ezk 27:12 Tarshish trafficked with you 3
16 trafficked with you because of your abundant 3
18 trafficked with you for your abundant goods 3
21 and goats; in these they trafficked with you. 3
Zec 11: 7 slain for those who trafficked in the sheep. 1

trafficker 1. כְּנַעֲנִי
Zec 11:11 traffickers in the sheep, who were watching me 1

train 1. ידע 2. יסר 3. למד 4. γυμνάζω 5. γυμνασία 6. διδακτός 7. ἐκμελετάω 8. ἐξασκέω 9. μαθητεύω 10. οἰκονομία 11. παιδεία 12. παιδευτής 13. παιδεύω 14. σωφρονίζω 15. paro
2Sm 22:35 He trains my hands for war, so that my arms can bend 3
1Ch 25: 7 brethren, who were trained in singing to the LORD 3
2Ch 2: 7 trained also in engraving, to be 1
14 He is trained to work in gold, silver, bronze, iron 1
Ps 18:34 He trains my hands for war 3
144: 1 LORD, my rock, who trains my hands for war 3
Hos 7:15 Although I trained and strengthened their arms 2
10:11 a trained heifer that loved to thresh 3
Mat 13:52 Therefore every scribe who has been trained 9
1Ti 1: 4 rather than the divine training that is in faith; 10
4: 7 Train yourself in godliness; 4
8 for while bodily training is of some value 5
2Ti 3:16 profitable . . for training in righteousness 11
Tit 2: 4 so train the young women to love their husbands 14
12 training us to renounce irreligion 13
Heb 5:14 their faculties trained by practice 4
12:11 those who have been trained by it. 4
2Pe 2:14 They have hearts trained in greed. 4
2Es 14:24 because they are trained to write rapidly; 15
Wis 2:12 and accuses us of sins against our training. 11
Sir 18:13 He rebukes and trains and teaches them 13
1Mc 4: 7 these men were trained in war. 6
2Mc 15:12 had been trained from childhood 7
4Mc 5:23 it also trains us in courage 8
34 I will not play false to you, O law that trained me 12
10:10 because of our godly training and virtue 11
13:24 trained in the same virtues 8

train (2) 1. אַחֲרֵי 2. מִצְעָד 3. שׁוּל 4. ἔνδυσις
Ps 45:14 virgin companions, her escort, in her train. 1
68:18 leading captives in thy train, and receiving •
Isa 6: 1 saw the Lord . . and his train filled the temple. 3
Dan 11:43 Libyans . . Ethiopians . . follow in his train. 2
AEs 15: 4 while the other followed carrying her train. 4

supply train 1. ἀπαρτία
Jdt 7:18 their tents and supply trains spread out 1

train up 1. חנך
Prv 22: 6 Train up a child in the way he should go 1

trained man 1. חָנִיךְ
Gen 14:14 he led forth his trained men, born in his house 1

traitor 1. ἀποστάτης 2. ἐπιβούλος 3. προδότης
Lke 6:16 Judas Iscariot, who became a traitor. 3
2Mc 5:15 a traitor both to the laws and to his country. 3
10:13 He heard himself called a traitor at every turn 3
22 he slew these men who had turned traitor 3
3Mc 3:24 traitors and barbarous enemies. 3
4:10 they should undergo treatment befitting traitors 2
6:12 deprived of life in the manner of traitors. 2
7: 3 to punish them . . as traitors; 1
5 as slaves, or rather as traitors 2

tramp 1. סאן
Isa 9: 5 For every boot of the tramping warrior in battle 1

trample 1. בוס 2. דושׁ 3. דרך 4. מְבוּסָה 5. מִרְמָס 6. רמס 7. καταπατέω 8. πατέω 9. πορεία
2Kg 9:33 and they trampled on her. 6
Job 9: 8 trampled the waves of the sea; 3
39:15 that the wild beast may trample them. 2
Ps 7: 5 let him trample my life to the ground 6
68:30 Trample under foot those who lust after tribute; •
Isa 1:12 who requires of you this trampling of my courts? 6
22: 5 a day of tumult and trampling and confusion 4
26: 6 The foot tramples it, the feet of the poor 6
41: 2 that he tramples kings under foot; •
25 he shall trample on rulers as on mortar •
63: 3 in my anger and trampled them in my wrath; 6
Ezk 26:11 With . . horses he will trample all your streets; 6
Dan 8:10 cast down to the ground, and trampled upon them. 6
13 sanctuary and host to be trampled under foot? 5
Ams 5:11 Therefore because you trample upon the poor 1
Hab 3:12 thou didst trample the nations in anger. 2
15 Thou didst trample the sea with thy horses 3
Zec 10: 5 mighty men in battle, trampling the foe in the mud 1
Mat 7: 6 lest they trample them under foot and turn 7
Rev 11: 2 they will trample over the holy city for 42 months. 8
3Mc 5:48 as well as by the trampling of the crowd 9
6:21 and began trampling and destroying them. 7

trample down 1. בוס 2. מִרְמָס 3. רמס 4. דושׁ (A) 5. καταπατέω
2Kg 14: 9 a wild beast . . and trampled down the thistle. 3
2Ch 25:18 wild beast . . passed by and trampled down 3
Isa 5: 5 break . . its wall, and it shall be trampled down. 2
Jer 12:10 they have trampled down my portion 1
Dan 7:23 devour the whole earth, and trample it down 4
1Mc 3:45 The sanctuary was trampled down 5
51 Thy sanctuary is trampled down and profaned 5
4:60 and trampling them down as they had done before. 5
3Mc 2:18 We have trampled down the house of the sanctuary 5
18 as offensive houses are trampled down.' 5

trample under foot 1. בוס 2. רמס
Num30: 6 married to a husband, while under her vows 2
1Ch 24: 4 organized them under sixteen heads 2
Job 38:14 It is changed like clay under the seal 2
Ps 91:13 lion . . serpent you will trample under foot. 2
Isa 14:25 and upon my mountains trample him under foot; 1
16: 4 he who tramples under foot has vanished 2
58: 5 and to spread sackcloth and ashes under him? 2
Jer 51:28 deputies, and every land under their dominion. 2
Dan 8:13 sanctuary and host to be trampled under foot? 2

trample upon 1. רמס 2. שׁאף 3. conculco
Ps 56: 1 Be gracious to me, O God, for men trample upon me; 2
2 my enemies trample upon me all day long 2
57: 3 he will put to shame those who trample upon me. 2
Dan 8: 7 cast him down to the ground and trampled upon him; 1
10 cast down to the ground, and trampled upon them. 1
Ams 8: 4 Hear this, you who trample upon the needy 2
2Es 8:57 they have even trampled upon his righteous ones 3

trance 1. ἔκστασις
Act 10:10 while they were preparing it, he fell into a trance 1
11: 5 in a trance I saw a vision, something descending 1
22:17 praying in the temple, I fell into a trance 1

tranquil 1. מַרְפֵּא
Prv 14:30 A tranquil mind gives life to the flesh 1

tranquillity 1. שְׁלֵוָה (A) 2. ἀκύματος 3. εὐστάθεια
Dan 4:27 perhaps be a lengthening of your tranquillity. 1
AEs 13: 2 to settle . . in lasting tranquillity 2
2Mc 14: 6 will not let the kingdom attain tranquillity. 3

transaction 1. דָּבָר
Rut 4: 7 to confirm a transaction, the one drew off his 1

transcendent 1. ὑπερβολή
2Co 4: 7 to show that the transcendent power belongs to God 1

transfer 1. סבב 2. עבר 3. μεθίστημι 4. μετάγω
Num36: 7 inheritance . . shall not be transferred 1
9 no inheritance shall be transferred from one 1
2Sm 3:10 to transfer the kingdom from the house of Saul 2
Col 1:13 transferred us to the kingdom of his beloved Son 3
AEs 16:14 would transfer the kingdom of the Persians 4

transfigure 1. μεταμορφόω
Mat 17: 2 he was transfigured before them 1
Mrk 9: 2 he was transfigured before them 1

transform 1. μεταβάλλω 2. μεταμορφόω 3. μετασχηματίζω
Rom 12: 2 but be transformed by the renewal of your mind 2
Wis 19:19 transformed into water creatures 1
4Mc 9:22 as though transformed by fire into immortality 3

transgress 1. מעל 2. עבר 3. פשׁע 4. פֶּשַׁע 5. παραβαίνω 6. παράβασις 7. παρανομέω 8. παραπίπτω 9. παρίημι 10. ὑπερβαίνω 11. delinquo 12. derelinquo 13. pecco 14. praetereo 15. transgredior
Num14:41 are you trangressing the command of the LORD 2
Deu 17: 2 who does what is evil . . in transgressing his covenant 2
26:13 I have not transgressed any of thy commandments 2
Jos 7:11 has sinned; they have transgressed my covenant 2
15 he has transgressed the covenant of the LORD 2
23:16 if you transgress the covenant of the LORD 2
Jdg 2:20 this people have transgressed my covenant 2
1Sm 15:24 I have transgressed the commandment of the LORD 2
2Kg 18:12 did not obey . . but transgressed his covenant 2
1Ch 2: 7 transgressed in the matter of the devoted thing 1
5:25 transgressed against the God of their fathers 1
2Ch 24:20 Why do you transgress the commandments 2
Ezr 10:13 we have greatly transgressed in this matter. 3
Est 3: 3 Why do you transgress the king's command? 2
Ps 17: 3 my mouth does not transgress. 2
Prv 8:29 waters might not transgress his command 2
28: 2 When a land transgresses it has many rulers; 4
Isa 24: 5 for they have transgressed the laws 2
43:27 and your mediators transgressed against me. 3
59:13 transgressing, and denying the LORD 3
Jer 2: 8 the rulers transgressed against me; 3
34:18 the men who transgressed my covenant 2
Lam 3:42 We have transgressed and rebelled 3
Ezk 2: 3 their fathers have transgressed against me 3
20:38 rebels . . and those who transgress against me; 3
33:12 shall not deliver him when he transgresses; 4
Dan 9:11 All Israel has transgressed thy law and turned 2
Hos 6: 7 But at Adam they transgressed the covenant; 2
8: 1 broken my covenant, and transgressed my law. 3
Ams 4: 4 Come to Bethel, and transgress; 3
Mat 15: 2 Why do your disciples transgress the tradition 5
3 And why do you transgress the commandment of God 5
1Th 4: 6 that no man transgress, and wrong his brother 10
1Es 1:48 transgressed the laws of the Lord 5
6:32 transgress . . any of the things herein written 5
8:24 all who transgress the law of your God 5
82 we have transgressed thy commandments 5
87 we turned back again to transgress thy law 5
2Es 3: 7 but he transgressed it 14
21 with an evil heart, transgressed and was 15
25 the inhabitants of the city transgressed 12
7:11 and when Adam transgressed my statutes 15
46 that has not transgressed thy covenant? 14
8:35 there is no one who has not transgressed. 11
14:30 which you also have transgressed after them. 15
15:26 the Lord knows all who transgress against him; 13
Tob 4: 5 to sin or to transgress his commandments 5
Jdt 2:13 to transgress any of your sovereign's commands 5
Wis 6: 9 that you may learn wisdom and not transgress. 8
Sir 10:19 Those who transgress the commandments. 5
19:24 highly prudent man who transgresses the law. 5
31:10 the power to transgress and did not transgress 5
10 the power to transgress and did not transgress 5
39:31 they will not transgress his word. 5
2Mc 7: 2 rather than transgress the laws of our fathers. 5
3Mc 7:10 who had willfully transgressed against the holy God 5
11 sake had transgressed the divine commandments 5
12 who had transgressed the law of God. 5
4Mc 5:17 we should not transgress it in any respect. 7
29 nor will I transgress the sacred oaths 9
8:14 when you transgress under compulsion. 7
9: 1 transgress our ancestral commandments; 5
13:15 who transgress the commandment of God. 6

transgress the law 1. παρανομέω
4Mc 5:20 to transgress the law in matters . . small or great 1
27 to compel us not only to transgress the law 1

transgression 1. פשׁע 2. פֶּשַׁע 3. ἀνομία 4. παράβασις 5. παρανομία 6. παράπτωμα 7. πλημμέλεια 8. delictum
Gen 50:17 Forgive, I pray you, the transgression 2
17 forgive the transgression of the servants 2
Exd 23:21 for he will not pardon your transgression; 2
34: 7 forgiving iniquity and transgression and sin 2
Lev 16:16 because of their transgressions, all their sins 2
21 confess . . all their transgressions 2
Num14:18 forgiving iniquity and transgression 2
Jos 24:19 not forgive your transgressions or your sins. 2
1Kg 8:50 forgive . . their transgressions which they 2
Job 7:21 Why dost thou not pardon my transgression 2
8: 4 into the power of their transgression. 2
13:23 Make me know my transgression and my sin. 2
14:17 my transgression would be sealed up in a bag 2
31:33 if I have concealed my transgressions from men 2
33: 9 You say, 'I am clean, without transgression; 2
34: 6 incurable, though I am without transgression. 2
35: 6 if your transgressions are multiplied 2
15 he does not greatly heed transgression 6
36: 9 to them their work and their transgressions 2
Ps 5:10 because of their many transgressions cast them out 2
19:13 and innocent of great transgression. 2
25: 7 the sins of my youth, or my transgressions; 2
32: 1 Blessed is he whose transgression is forgiven 2
5 I will confess my transgressions to the LORD"; 2
36: 1 Transgression speaks to the wicked 2
39: 8 Deliver me from all my transgressions. 2
51: 1 thy abundant mercy blot out my transgressions. 2
3 For I know my transgressions 2
59: 3 For no transgression or sin of mine, O LORD 2
65: 3 When our transgressions prevail over us 2
89:32 I will punish their transgression with the rod 2
103:12 far does he remove our transgressions from us. 2
Prv 10:19 words are many, transgression is not lacking 2
12:13 man is ensnared by the transgression of his lips 2
17:19 He who loves transgression loves strife; 2
28:13 conceals his transgressions will not prosper 2
24 robs . . and says, "That is no transgression 2
29: 6 An evil man is ensnared in his transgression 2
16 authority, transgression increases; 2
22 man given to anger causes much transgression. 2
Isa 24:20 earth . . its transgression lies heavy upon it 2
43:25 blots out your transgressions for my own sake 2
44:22 swept away your transgressions like a cloud 2
50: 1 for . . transgressions your mother was put away. 2
53: 5 But he was wounded for our transgressions 2
8 stricken for the transgression of my people? 2
57: 4 Are you not children of transgression 2
58: 1 declare to my people their transgression 2
59:12 our transgressions are multiplied before thee 2
12 for our transgressions are with us 2
20 to those in Jacob who turn from transgression 2
Jer 5: 6 because their transgressions are many 2
Lam 1: 5 suffer for the multitude of her transgressions; 2
14 My transgressions were bound into a yoke; 1
22 dealt with me because of all my transgressions; 2
Ezk 14:11 defile . . with all their transgressions 2
18:22 None of the transgressions which he has 2
28 and turned away from all the transgressions 2
30 Repent and turn from all your transgressions 2
31 Cast away from you all the transgressions 2
21:24 in that your transgressions are uncovered 2
33:10 Our transgressions and our sins are upon us 2
37:23 with any of their transgressions; but I will save 2
39:24 their uncleanness and their transgressions 2
Dan 8:12 host was given over . . through transgression; 2
13 transgression that makes desolate 2
9:24 finish the transgression, to put an end to sin 2
Ams 1: 3 For three transgressions of Damascus 2
6 For three transgressions of Gaza, and for four 2
9 For three transgressions of Tyre, and for four 2
11 For three transgressions of Edom, and for four 2
13 For three transgressions of the Ammonites 2
2: 1 For three transgressions of Moab, and for four 2
4 For three transgressions of Judah, and for four 2
6 For three transgressions of Israel, and for four 2
3:14 the day I punish Israel for his transgressions 2
4: 4 to Gilgal, and multiply transgression; 2
5:12 For I know how many are your transgressions 2
Mic 1: 5 All this is for the transgression of Jacob 2
5 What is the transgression of Jacob? 2
13 in you were found the transgressions of Israel. 2
3: 8 to declare to Jacob his transgression 2
6: 7 Shall I give my first-born for my transgression 2
7:18 and passing over transgression for the remnant 2
Rom 4:15 but where there is no law there is no transgression 4
5:14 sins . . not like the transgression of Adam 4
Gal 3:19 It was added because of transgressions 4
Heb 2: 2 every transgression or disobedience 4
9:15 the transgressions under the first covenant. 4
2Pe 2:16 was rebuked for his own transgression; 5
2Es 7:68 full of sins and burdened with transgressions. 8
Jdt 5:21 if there is no transgression in their nation 3
Wis 10: 1 she delivered him from his transgression 6
14:31 pursues the transgression of the unrighteous. 4
Sir 41:18 of a transgression, before a judge or magistrate; 7

Man 1: 9 my transgressions are multiplied, O Lord 3
12 I have sinned, and I know my transgressions. 3
13 Do not destroy me with my transgressions! 3
4Mc 5:13 any transgression that arises out of compulsion. 5

transgression of the law 1. παράνομος
4Mc 9: 4 our safety through transgression of the law 1

transgressor 1. פשע 2. ἄνομος 3. ἐν παραβάσει 4. παραβαίνω 5. παραβάτης 6. παράνομος
Ps 37:38 transgressors shall be altogether destroyed; 1
51:13 Then I will teach transgressors thy ways 1
Isa 46: 8 recall it to mind, you transgressors 1
53:12 and was numbered with the transgressors; 1
12 and made intercession for the transgressors. 1
Dan 8:23 transgressors have reached their full measure 1
Hos 14: 9 but transgressors stumble in them. 1
Lke 22:37 'And he was reckoned with transgressors' 2
Gal 2:18 then I prove myself a transgressor. 5
1Ti 2:14 was deceived and became a transgressor. 3
Jas 2: 9 are convicted by the law as transgressors. 5
11 you have become a transgressor of the law. 5
Sir 40:14 likewise transgressors will utterly fail. 4
3Mc 2:17 lest the transgressors boast in their wrath 6

transient 1. πρόσκαιρος
2Co 4:18 for the things that are seen are transient 1

translate 1. תרגם 2. ἑρμηνεία 3. ἑρμηνεύω 4. μετάγω
Ezr 4: 7 letter was written in Aramaic and translated. 1
AEs 11: 1 had been translated by Lysimachus 3
Sir 0: 2 despite our diligent labor in translating, 2
2 when translated into another language 4

translation 1. ἑρμηνεύω 2. μεθερμηνεύω
Heb 7: 2 by translation of his name 1
Sir 0: 3 to the translation of the following book, 2

transparent 1. διαυγής
Rev 21:21 street . . was pure gold, transparent as glass. 1

transplant 1. שתל
Ezk 17: 8 he transplanted it to good soil 1
10 Behold, when it is transplanted, will it thrive? 1
19:10 vine in a vineyard transplanted by the water 1
13 Now it is transplanted in the wilderness 1

transport 1. ἀπαρτία 2. ἐπαίρω
Jdt 2:17 camels and asses and mules for transport 1
2Mc 9: 4 Transported with rage 2

trap 1. לכד 2. מוֹקֵשׁ 3. מָזוֹר 4. מַלְכֹּדֶת 5. מַשְׁחִית 6. פַּח 7. פחת 8. θήρα 9. παγίς 10. σκάνδαλον
Jos 23:13 they shall be a snare and a trap for you, a scourge 2
Job 18: 9 A trap seizes him by the heel, a snare lays hold 6
10 for him in the ground, a trap for him in the path. 4
Ps 59:12 let them be trapped in their pride. 1
69:22 let their sacrificial feasts be a trap. 2
140: 5 Arrogant men have hidden a trap for me 6
141: 9 Keep me from the trap which they have laid for me 6
142: 3 path where I walk they have hidden a trap for me. 6
Isa 8:14 a trap and snare to the inhabitants 6
42:22 they are all of them trapped in holes and hidden 7
Jer 5:26 lying in wait. They set a trap; they catch men. 5
Ams 3: 5 Does a bird fall . . when there is no trap for it? 2
Obd 1: 7 your trusted friends have set a trap under you 3
Rom 11: 9 Let their table become a snare and a trap, a pitfall 8
Tob 14:10 Nadab fell into the trap and perished. 9
Wis 14:11 and became traps for the souls of men 10
1Mc 5: 4 who were a trap and a snare to the people 9

hidden trap 1. ἔνεδρον
Wis 14:21 this became a hidden trap for mankind 1

trappings 1. κόσμος
2Mc 5: 3 the flash of golden trappings 1

travail 1. חבל 2. חול 3. ילד 4. עָמָל 5. συνωδίνω 6. τίκτω 7. ὠδίν 8. ὠδίνω 9. labor 10. pario
Gen 35:16 Rachel travailed, and she had hard labor. 3
Sng 8: 5 There your mother was in travail with you 1
5 there she who bore you was in travail. 1
Isa 23: 4 I have neither travailed nor given birth 2
45:10 or to a woman, 'With what are you in travail?' 2
53:11 he shall see the fruit of the travail of his soul 4
54: 1 cry aloud, you who have not been in travail! 2
Jer 13:21 pangs . . like those of a woman in travail? 3
31: 8 the woman with child and her who is in travail 3
Mic 5: 3 time when she who is in travail has brought forth; 3
Joh 16:21 When a woman is in travail she has sorrow 6
Rom 8:22 creation has been groaning in travail together 5
Gal 4:19 little children, with whom I am again in travail 8
27 break forth and shout, you who are not in travail; 8
1Th 5: 3 as travail comes upon a woman with child 7
2Es 4:42 For just as a woman who is in travail makes haste 10
5:35 that I might not see the travail of Jacob 9
37 and then I will explain to you the travail 9
travail *See also* woman.

travel 1. הלך 2. עבר 3. שור 4. ἀποπλάνησις 5. διαπορεύομαι 6. διέρχομαι 7. ἐξοδεύω 8. πλανάω 9. πορευτός 10. πορεύω 11. συνέκδημος 12. συνοδεύω
Exd 13:21 that they might travel by day and by night; 1
Job 21:29 Have you not asked those who travel the roads 2
Ezk 27:25 The ships of Tarshish traveled for you 3
Act 9: 7 The men who were traveling with him 12
11:19 those . . traveled as far as Phoeni'cia and Cyprus 6
2Co 8:19 appointed by the churches to travel with us 11
1Es 4:23 goes out to travel and rob and steal 7
AEs 13: 2 open to travel throughout all its extent 9
Sir 8:15 Do not travel on the road with a foolhardy fellow 10
34:10 he that has traveled acquires much cleverness. 8
11 I have seen many things in my travels 4
39: 4 travel through the lands of foreign nations 6
Bar 4:26 My tender sons have traveled rough roads 10
1Mc 11:60 Then Jonathan . . traveled beyond the river 5
travel *See also* companion.

travel in company 1. συνοδεύω
Wis 6:23 neither will I travel in the company of . . envy 1

travel widely 1. pertranseo
2Es 3:33 I have traveled widely among the nations 1

traveler 1. הֲלִיכָה 2. הֵלֶךְ 3. הלך נְתִיבָה 4. עבר 5. רֶגֶל
Jdg 5: 6 ceased and travelers kept to the byways. 3
2Sm 12: 4 Now there came a traveler to the rich man 2
Job 6:19 of Tema look, the travelers of Sheba hope. 1
28: 4 they are forgotten by travelers 5
Ezk 39:11 the Valley of the Travelers east of the sea; 4
11 it will block the travelers 4
travels *See* go.

traverse 1. διοδεύω 2. περιάγω
Mat 23:15 you traverse sea and land 2
Wis 5:11 is traversed by the movement of its wings 1

tray 1. מַחְתָּה
Exd 25:38 Its snuffers and their trays shall be of pure 1
37:23 seven lamps and its snuffers and its trays 1
Num 4: 9 with its lamps, its snuffers, its trays 1

treacherous 1. בגד 2. מִרְמָה 3. רְמִיָּה 4. δόλιος 5. δόλος 6. μετὰ δόλου 7. προδότης
Job 6:15 My brethren are treacherous as a torrent-bed 1
Ps 25: 3 be ashamed who are wantonly treacherous. 1
Prv 2:22 treacherous will be rooted out of it. 1
11: 3 crookedness of the treacherous destroys them. 1
6 treacherous are taken captive by their lust. 1
12: 5 the counsels of the wicked are treacherous. 2
13: 2 desire of the treacherous is for violence. 1
Isa 24:16 For the treacherous deal treacherously 1
16 the treacherous deal very treacherously. 1
Jer 12: 1 Why do all who are treacherous thrive? 1
Hos 7:16 They turn to Ba'al; they are like a treacherous bow 3
Hab 2: 5 Moreover, wine is treacherous; 1
2Ti 3: 4 treacherous, reckless, swollen with conceit 7
Sir 22:22 disclosure of secrets, or a treacherous blow 4
27:25 a treacherous blow opens up wounds. 4
1Mc 7:10 with peaceable but treacherous words. 6
16:13 made treacherous plans against Simon and his sons 5
treacherous *See also* intent.

treacherous man 1. בגד
Jer 9: 2 all adulterers, a company of treacherous men. 1

treacherous one 1. בגד
Isa 33: 1 you treacherous one, with whom none has dealt 1

treacherously 1. מָעַל 2. עָרְמָה 3. שֶׁקֶר 4. δόλος 5. λόχος 6. μετὰ δόλου
Exd 21:14 attacks another to kill him treacherously 2
Num 31:16 caused . . Israel . . to act treacherously 1
2Sm 18:13 if I had dealt treacherously against his life 3
Ezk 20:27 blasphemed me, by dealing treacherously with me 1
Wis 14:24 they either treacherously kill one another 5
1Mc 7:27 treacherously sent . . this peaceable message 6
13:31 Trypho dealt treacherously with the young king 4
16:15 The son of Abubus received them treacherously 6
treacherously *See also* deal, plot.

act treacherously 1. בגד 2. מעל
Neh 13:27 evil and act treacherously against our God 2
Ps 78:57 but turned away and acted treacherously 1

treachery 1. כַּחַשׁ 2. מַעַל 3. מִרְמָה 4. קֶשֶׁר 5. רְמִיָּה 6. δόλος 7. ἐπιβουλή 8. κακία 9. κακουργία
Lev 26:40 their iniquity . . in their treachery 2
Jos 22:16 What is this treachery which you have committed 2
31 because you have not committed this treachery 2
2Kg 9:23 and fled, saying to Ahazi'ah, "Treachery, O Ahazi'ah! 3
17: 4 the king of Assyria found treachery in Hoshe'a; 4
Ps 38:12 meditate treachery all the day long. 3
52: 2 like a sharp razor, you worker of treachery. 5
55:23 men of blood and treachery shall not live 3
Jer 5:27 their houses are full of treachery; 3
Ezk 18:24 the treachery of which he is guilty and the sin 2
39:26 the treachery they have practiced against me 2
Dan 9: 7 treachery which they have committed against 2
Hos 7: 3 and the princes by their treachery. 1
1Mc 9:61 who were leaders in this treachery 8
2Mc 4:34 resorting to treachery 6
14:22 to prevent sudden treachery on the part of the enemy 9
4Mc 4:13 had been overcome by human treachery 7
treachery *See also* act, commit.

tread 1. בוא 2. דרך 3. מִדְרָךְ 4. מִרְמָס 5. צָעַד 6. רדה 7. רמס 8. ἐπιβαίνω 9. πατέω 10. adligo
Deu 1:36 I will give the land upon which he has trodden 2
2: 5 not so much as for the sole of the foot to tread 3
11:24 place . . sole of your foot treads shall be yours; 2
25 upon all the land that you shall tread 2
33:29 shall tread upon their high places. 2
Jos 1: 3 place that the sole of your foot will tread upon 2
14: 9 the land on which your foot has trodden shall be 2
Jdg 9:27 gathered the grapes . . and trod them, and held 2
1Sm 5: 5 priests . . do not tread on the threshold of Dagon 2
2Kg 7:17 and the people trod upon him in the gate 7
Neh 13:15 saw . . men treading wine presses on the sabbath 2
Job 22:15 you keep to the old way which wicked men have trod? 2
24:11 they tread the wine presses, but suffer thirst. 2
28: 8 The proud beasts have not trodden it; 2
Ps 91:13 You will tread on the lion and the adder 2
Prv 30:29 Three things are stately in their tread; 5
Isa 7:25 cattle are let loose and where sheep tread. 4
28: 3 of E'phraim will be trodden under foot; 7
41: 3 passes on safely, by paths his feet have not trod. 1
25 as on mortar, as the potter treads clay. 7
63: 2 garments like his that treads in the wine press? 2
3 I have trodden the wine press alone 2
3 I trod them in my anger and trampled them in my 2
Jer 25:30 and shout, like those who tread grapes 2
48:33 no one treads them with shouts of joy; 2
51:33 threshing floor at the time when it is trodden; 2
Lam 1:15 the Lord has trodden as in a wine press the virgin 2
Ezk 34:19 my sheep eat what you have trodden with your feet 4
Jol 3:13 Go in, tread, for the wine press is full. 6
Ams 4:13 and treads on the heights of the earth– the LORD 2
Mic 1: 3 and tread upon the high places of the earth. 2
5: 5 when the Assyrian . . treads upon our soil 2
6 into our land and treads within our border. 2
6:15 you shall tread olives, but not anoint 2
15 you shall tread grapes, but not drink wine. 2
Nah 3:14 go into the clay, tread the mortar 7
Lke 10:19 have given you authority to tread upon serpents 9
Rev 14:20 the wine press was trodden outside the city 9
19:15 will tread the wine press of the fury . . of God 9
2Es 16:26 The grapes shall ripen, and who will tread them? 10
Bar 4:13 nor tread the paths of discipline 8
25 you . . will tread upon their necks. 8

tread down 1. בוס 2. דוש 3. דרך 4. הדך 5. כבש 6. מִרְמָס 7. עסס 8. רמס 9. πατέω 10. conculco
Jdg 20:43 they pursued them and trod them down from Nohah 3
Job 40:12 tread down the wicked where they stand. 4
Ps 44: 5 through thy name we tread down our assailants. 1
58: 7 like grass let them be trodden down and wither. 3
60:12 it is he who will tread down our foes. 1
108:13 it is he who will tread down our foes. 1
Isa 10: 6 to tread them down like the mire of the streets. 6
6 to tread them down like the mire of the streets. 6
25:10 and Moab shall be trodden down in his place 2
10 as straw is trodden down in a dung-pit. 2
63: 6 I trod down the peoples in my anger 1
18 our adversaries have trodden it down. 1
Ezk 34:18 that you must tread down with your feet the rest 8
Mic 5: 8 it goes through, treads down and tears in pieces 8
7:10 now she will be trodden down like the mire 6
Zec 9:15 they shall devour and tread down the slingers; 5
Mal 4: 3 you shall tread down the wicked 7
Lke 21:24 Jerusalem will be trodden down by the Gentiles 9
2Es 5:29 have trodden down those who believed 10

make tread 1. דרך
Hab 3:19 he makes me tread upon my high places. 1

tread out 1. דוש 2. דרך
Deu 25: 4 not muzzle an ox when it treads out the grain. 1
Isa 16:10 no treader treads out wine in the presses; 2

tread out grain 1. ἀλοάω
1Co 9: 9 not muzzle an ox when it is treading out the grain. 1
1Ti 5:18 not muzzle an ox when it is treading out the grain 1

tread under foot 1. בוס 2. כבש 3. καταπατέω 4. conculcatio
Isa 14:19 to . . the Pit, like a dead body trodden under foot 1

Mic 7:19 he will tread our iniquities under foot. 2
Mat 5:13 thrown out and trodden under foot by men. 3
Lke 8: 5 some fell along the path, and was trodden under foot 3
2Es 16:69 and be trodden under foot. 4

tread upon 1. רמס 2. καταπατέω
2Kg 7:20 the people trod upon him in the gate and he died. 1
Lke 12: 1 they trod upon one another 2

treader 1. דרך
Job 24:18 no treader turns toward their vineyards. •
Isa 16:10 no treader treads out wine in the presses; 1
Ams 9:13 and the treader of grapes him who sows the seed; 1

treason 1. מַעַל 2. פֶּשַׁע 3. קֶשֶׁר
1Sm 24:11 see that there is no wrong or treason in my hands. 2
2Kg 11:14 And Athali'ah rent her clothes, and cried, "Treason! 3
14 rent her clothes, and cried, "Treason! Treason! 3
2Ch 23:13 Athali'ah . . cried, "Treason! Treason! 3
13 Athali'ah . . cried, "Treason! Treason! 3
Ezk 17:20 for the treason he has committed against me. 1
treason *See also* commit.

treasure 1. אוֹצָר 2. חֶמְדָּה 3. חֹסֶן 4. מַחְמָד 5. מַטְמוֹן 6. מִכְמָן 7. מַצְפּוּן 8. נְכֹת 9. סְגֻלָּה 10. עָתִיד 11. צפן 12. תְּכוּנָה 13. γάζα 14. θέμα 15. θησαυρός 16. χρῆμα 17. thesaurus
Gen 43:23 God . . must have put treasure in your sacks 5
Deu 33:19 they suck . . the hidden treasures of the sand. •
1Kg 14:26 took away the treasures of the house of the LORD 1
26 he took away . . the treasures of the king's house; 1
15:18 left in the treasures of the house of the LORD 1
18 left in . . and the treasures of the king's house 1
2Kg 16: 8 found . . and in the treasures of the king's house 1
20:13 and he showed them all his treasure house 8
24:13 and carried off all the treasures of the house 1
13 and the treasures of the king's house 1
1Ch 9:26 chambers and the treasures of the house of God. 1
29: 3 I have a treasure of my own of gold and silver 9
2Ch 12: 9 took away the treasures of the house of the LORD 1
9 he took away . . the treasures of the king's house; 1
16: 2 Then Asa took silver and gold from the treasures 1
36:18 treasures of the house of the LORD 1
18 treasures of the king and of his princes 1
Job 20:26 Utter darkness is laid up for his treasures; 11
23:12 I have treasured in my bosom the words of his 11
Prv 10: 2 Treasures gained by wickedness do not profit 1
15: 6 house of the righteous there is much treasure 3
16 Better . . than great treasure and trouble with it. 1
21: 6 The getting of treasures by a lying tongue 1
20 Precious treasure remains in a wise man's 1
Ecc 2: 8 and gold and the treasure of kings and provinces; 9
Isa 2: 7 filled . . and there is no end to their treasures; 1
10:13 removed . . and have plundered their treasures; 10
30: 6 and their treasures on the humps of camels 1
33: 6 the fear of the LORD is his treasure. 1
39: 2 he showed them his treasure house 8
45: 3 I will give you the treasures of darkness 1
Jer 15:13 wealth and your treasures I will give as spoil 1
17: 3 and all your treasures I will give for spoil 1
20: 5 and all the treasures of the kings of Judah 1
48: 7 trusted in your strongholds and your treasures 1
49: 4 daughter, who trusted in her treasures, saying 1
50:37 A sword upon all her treasures 1
51:13 O you who dwell by many waters, rich in treasures 1
Lam 1:11 they trade their treasures for food to revive 4
Ezk 22:25 they have taken treasure and precious things; 3
Dan 11:43 become ruler of the treasures of gold . . silver 6
Jol 3: 5 carried my rich treasures into your temples. 4
Obd 1: 6 Esau has been pillaged, his treasures sought out! 7
Mic 6:10 Can I forget the treasures of wickedness 1
Nah 2: 9 There is no end of treasure, or wealth 12
Hag 2: 7 that the treasures of all nations shall come 2
Mat 2:11 Then, opening their treasures, they offered him 15
6:19 Do not lay up for yourselves treasures on earth 15
20 lay up for yourselves treasures in heaven 15
21 For where your treasure is, there will your heart 15
12:35 out of his good treasure brings forth good 15
35 out of his evil treasure brings forth evil. 15
13:44 treasure hidden in a field 15
52 like a householder who brings out of his treasure 15
19:21 you will have treasure in heaven 15
Mrk 10:21 you will have treasure in heaven 15
Lke 6:45 The good man out of the good treasure of his heart 15
45 the evil man out of his evil treasure produces evil; •
12:33 with a treasure in the heavens that does not fail 15
34 where your treasure is, there will your heart be 15
18:22 you will have treasure in heaven 15
Act 8:27 a minister . . in charge of all her treasure 13
2Co 4: 7 we have this treasure in earthen vessels 15
Col 2: 3 all the treasures of wisdom and knowledge. 15
Heb 11:26 greater wealth than the treasures of Egypt 15
2Es 7:77 For you have a treasure of works laid up 17
8:54 the treasure of immortality is made manifest. 17
16:57 It is he who searches the deep and its treasures 17
Tob 4: 9 you will be laying up a good treasure 14
Wis 7:14 for it is an unfailing treasure for men 15
Sir 6:14 he that has found one has found a treasure. 15
20:30 Hidden wisdom and unseen treasure 15
29:11 Lay up your treasure 15
40:18 he who finds treasure is better off than both. 15
41:14 hidden wisdom and unseen treasure 15
1Mc 1:23 he took also the hidden treasures which he found. 15
2Mc 1:14 to secure most of its treasures as a dowry. 16
15 When the priests . . had set out the treasures •
4Mc 4: 4 to inform him of the rich treasure. 15
treasure *See also* lay, store.

treasure chest 1. κιβωτός
1Es 1:54 treasure chests of the Lord, and the royal stores 1

hid treasure 1. מַטְמוֹן
Job 3:21 and dig for it more than for hid treasures; 1

hidden treasure 1. מַטְמוֹן
Prv 2: 4 if you . . search for it as for hidden treasures; 1

treasure up 1. צפן 2. θησαυρίζω
Prv 2: 1 My son, if you . . treasure up my commandment 1
7: 1 My son . . treasure up my commandments with you; 1
Tob 12: 8 It is better to give alms than to treasure up gold. 2

treasurer 1. אוֹצָר 2. גְּדָבְרַיָּא (A) 3. גִּזְבָּר (A) 4. γαζοφύλαξ 5. οἰκονόμος
Ezr 1: 8 out in charge of Mith'redath the treasurer 1
7:21 make a decree to all the treasurers 3
Dan 3: 2 assemble the . . treasurers, the justices 2
3 counselors, the treasurers, the justices 2
Rom 16:23 Eras'tus, the city treasurer, and . . greet you. 5
1Es 2:11 he gave them to Mithridates his treasurer 4
4:47 wrote letters for him to all the treasurers 5
49 no officer or satrap or governor or treasurer 5
8:19 the treasurers of Syria and Phoenicia 4
46 the treasurers at that place 4
treasurer *See also* appoint.

treasury 1. אוֹצָר 2. גְּנָזִים 3. גַּנְזַךְ 4. בֵּית (A) 5. בֵּית גִּנְזַיָּא (A) 6. ἀργύριον 7. γαζοφυλάκιον 8. θησαυρός 9. κορβανᾶς 10. οἶκος 11. ταμιεῖον 12. thesaurus
Deu 28:12 will open to you his good treasury the heavens 1
32:34 laid up in store . . sealed up in my treasuries? 1
Jos 6:19 they shall go into the treasury of the LORD. 1
24 put into the treasury of the house of the LORD. 1
1Kg 7:51 stored them in the treasuries of the house 1
2Kg 12:18 found in the treasuries of the house of the LORD 1
14:14 and in the treasuries of the king's house 1
18:15 and in the treasuries of the king's house. 1
1Ch 26:20 had charge of the treasuries of the house of God 1
20 and the treasuries of the dedicated gifts. 1
22 in charge of the treasuries of the house 1
24 chief officer in charge of the treasuries. 1
26 all the treasuries of the dedicated gifts 1
27:25 Over the king's treasuries was Az'maveth the son 1
25 over the treasuries in the country, in the cities 1
28:11 the plan of . . and of its houses, its treasuries 3
12 treasuries of the house of God 1
12 and the treasuries for dedicated gifts; 1
29: 8 gave them to the treasury of the house of the LORD 1
2Ch 5: 1 stored . . in the treasuries of the house of God. 1
8:15 had commanded concerning . . the treasuries. 1
25:24 he seized also the treasuries of the king's house 1
32:27 made for himself treasuries for silver, for gold 1
Ezr 2:69 gave to the treasury of the work 61,000 darics 1
6: 4 let the cost be paid from the royal treasury. 4
7:20 may provide it out of the king's treasury. 5
Neh 7:70 governor gave to the treasury 1,000 darics of gold 1
71 heads . . gave into the treasury of the work 1
Est 3: 9 that they may put it into the king's treasuries. 2
4: 7 had promised to pay into the king's treasuries 2
Prv 8:21 those who love me, and filling their treasuries. 1
Ezk 28: 4 gathered gold and silver into your treasuries; 1
Hos 13:15 strip his treasury of every precious thing. 1
Zec 11:13 Then the LORD said to me, "Cast it into the treasury ‡
13 and cast them into the treasury in the house ‡
Mat 27: 6 It is not lawful to put them into the treasury 9
Mrk 12:41 he sat down opposite the treasury 7
41 the multitude putting money into the treasury. 7
43 all those who are contributing to the treasury. 7
Lke 21: 1 and saw the rich putting their gifts into the treasury; 7
Joh 8:20 These words he spoke in the treasury 7
1Es 5:45 would give to the sacred treasury for the work 7
6:25 the cost to be paid from the treasury of Cyrus 10
8:18 you may provide out of the royal treasury. 7
45 the leading man at the place of the treasury 7
2Es 6:40 be brought forth from thy treasuries 12
Sir 1:25 In the treasuries of wisdom are wise sayings 8
29:12 Store up almsgiving in your treasury 11
1Mc 3:29 saw that the money in the treasury was exhausted 8
14:49 to deposit copies of them in the treasury 7
15: 8 Every debt you owe to the royal treasury •
2Mc 3: 6 the treasury in Jerusalem 7
24 he arrived at the treasury with his bodyguard 7
28 had just entered the aforesaid treasury 7
40 Heliodorus and the protection of the treasury. 7
4:42 they killed close by the treasury. 7
5:18 whom Seleucus . . sent to inspect the treasury. 7
3Mc 3:28 2,000 drachmas from the royal treasury 6
4Mc 4: 3 in the Jerusalem treasuries 7
6 to seize the private funds in the treasury. 7
7 committed deposits to the sacred treasury 8

king's treasury 1. βασιλικός
2Mc 3:13 confiscated for the king's treasury. 1

royal treasury 1. βασιλικός
1Mc 13:15 the money that Jonathan . . owed the royal treasury 1

treat 1. נתן 2. עשה 3. שׂוּם 4. ἄγω 5. ἀναστρέφω 6. ἀπαντάω 7. ἔχω 8. παρέχω 9. ποιέω 10. προσφέρω 11. συμπεριφέρω 12. τύχη 13. χράομαι
Gen 34:31 they said, "Should he treat our sister as a harlot? 2
39:19 This is the way your servant treated me 2
Jer 24: 8 will I treat Zedeki'ah the king of Judah 1
Hos 11: 8 How can I treat you like Zeboi'im! 3
Lke 2:48 Son, why have you treated us so? 9
15:19 treat me as one of your hired servants."' 9
Act 27: 3 Julius treated Paul kindly 13
1Co 12:23 treated with greater modesty 7
2Co 6: 8 We are treated as impostors, and yet are true; •
Col 4: 1 Masters, treat your slaves justly and fairly 8
1Ti 5: 1 treat younger men like brothers •
Heb 10:33 sometimes being partners with those so treated. 5
12: 7 God is treating you as sons 10
Tob 8:16 thou hast treated us according to thy great mercy. 9
Jdt 10:16 he will treat you well. 9
11: 4 No one will hurt you, but all will treat you well 9
Sir 14:11 treat yourself well, according to your means 9
33:31 If you have a servant, treat him as a brother 4
1Mc 11:26 treated him as his predecessors had treated him; 9
26 treated him as his predecessors had treated him; 9
13:46 Do not treat us according to our wicked acts 13
2Mc 6:22 be saved from death, and be treated kindly 12
9:27 treat you with moderation and kindness. 11
3Mc 3:15 gladly treating them well. 9
20 since we treat all nations with benevolence. 6

treat as a first-born 1. בכר
Deu 21:16 not treat the son of the loved as the first-born 1

treat as a slave 1. עמר
Deu 21:14 not treat her as a slave, since you have humiliated 1
24: 7 if he treats him as a slave or sells him 1

treat as an equal 1. ἰσηγορέομαι
Sir 13:11 Do not try to treat him as an equal 1

treat as obsolete 1. παλαιόω
Heb 8:13 he treats the first as obsolete 1

treat contemptuously 1. καταφρονέω 2. σκυβαλίζω
Sir 26:28 men who are treated contemptuously 2
4Mc 4: 9 that was being treated so contemptuously 1

treat disgracefully 1. ἐπονείδιστος
3Mc 6:31 those disgracefully treated and near to death 1

treat harshly 1. רעע
Deu 26: 6 Egyptians treated us harshly, and afflicted us 1

treat ill 1. רעע
Gen 43: 6 Israel said, "Why did you treat me so ill 1

treat like a stranger 1. נכר
Gen 42: 7 but he treated them like strangers 1

treat outrageously 1. ὑβρίζω
3Mc 6: 9 who are being outrageously treated 1

treat shamefully 1. ἀτιμάζω 2. ὑβρίζω
Mat 22: 6 treated them shamefully, and killed them. 2
Mrk 12: 4 and treated him shamefully. 1
Lke 18:32 will be mocked and shamefully treated and spit upon; 2
20:11 him also they beat and treated shamefully 1
1Th 2: 2 we had . . been shamefully treated at Philip'pi 2

treat with contempt 1. נאץ 2. נבל 3. קלל 4. שׂוּט 5. ἐξουδενέω 6. ἐξουθενέω 7. καταφρονέω
1Sm 2:17 the men treated the offering . . with contempt. 1
Ezk 22: 7 and mother are treated with contempt in you; 3
28:24 neighbors who have treated them with contempt. 4
26 neighbors who have treated them with contempt. 4
Mic 7: 6 for the son treats the father with contempt 2
Nah 3: 6 throw filth at you and treat you with contempt 2
Mrk 9:12 suffer many things and be treated with contempt? 5
Lke 23:11 Herod . . treated him with contempt 6
2Mc 7:24 he was being treated with contempt 7

treatment 1. ἀγωγή 2. ἀπάντησις 3. πραγματεία
2Mc 2:31 to forego exhaustive treatment. 3
12:30 kind treatment of them in times of misfortune 2
3Mc 4:10 they should undergo treatment befitting traitors 1

harsh treatment 1. *σκυλμός*
3Mc 3:25 with insulting and harsh treatment 1
4: 6 were torn by the harsh treatment of the heathen. 1
7: 5 They . . led them out with harsh treatment as slaves 1

kind treatment 1. *εὐεργεσία*
4Mc 8:17 to accept kind treatment if we obey him 1

outrageous treatment 1. *αἰκία*
3Mc 6:26 Who . . has . . encompassed with outrageous treatment 1

treaty 1. בְּרִית 2. *συνθήκη*
1Sm 11: 1 Make a treaty with us, and we will serve you. 1
1Kg 5:12 and the two of them made a treaty. 1
2Mc 13:25 were indignant over the treaty 2

treaty *See also* make.

tree 1. עֵץ 2. אִילָן (A) 3. *δένδρον* 4. *ξύλινος* 5. *ξύλον* 6. *φυτόν* 7. arbor 8. lignum
Gen 1:11 earth put forth . . fruit trees bearing fruit 1
12 and trees bearing fruit in which is their seed 1
29 given . . every tree with seed in its fruit; 1
2: 9 God made to grow every tree that is pleasant 1
9 the tree of life also in the midst of the garden 1
9 and the tree of the knowledge of good and evil. 1
16 You may freely eat of every tree of the garden; 1
17 the tree of the knowledge of good and evil 1
3: 1 You shall not eat of any tree of the garden'? 1
2 may eat of the fruit of the trees of the garden; 1
3 God said, 'You shall not eat of the fruit of the tree 1
6 when the woman saw that the tree was good for food 1
6 the tree was to be desired to make one wise 1
8 hid themselves . . among the trees of the garden. 1
11 Have you eaten of the tree of which I commanded 1
12 The woman . . gave me fruit of the tree, and I ate. 1
17 and have eaten of the tree of which I commanded 1
22 take also of the tree of life, and eat, and live 1
24 sword . . to guard the way to the tree of life. 1
18: 4 feet, and rest yourselves under the tree 1
8 he stood by them under the tree while they ate. 1
23:17 all the trees that were in the field 1
40:19 your head-from you!-and hang you on a tree; 1
Exd 9:25 hail . . shattered every tree of the field. 1
10: 5 they shall eat every tree of yours which grows 1
15 they ate . . all the fruit of the trees 1
15 neither tree nor plant of the field, through all 1
15:25 cried to the LORD; and the LORD showed him a tree 1
Lev 19:23 When you . . plant all kinds of trees for food 1
23:40 you shall take . . fruit of goodly trees 1
40 take . . boughs of leafy trees, and willows 1
26: 4 the trees of the field shall yield their fruit 1
20 the trees of the land shall not yield their fruit 1
27:30 seed of the land or of the fruit of the trees 1
Deu 12: 2 upon the hills and under every green tree 1
16:21 not plant any tree as an Ashe'rah beside the altar 1
19: 5 his hand swings the axe to cut down a tree 1
20:19 not destroy its trees by wielding an axe 1
19 Are the trees in the field men that they should be 1
20 Only the trees which you know are not trees 1
20 trees which you know are not trees for food 1
21:22 if a man . . is put to death, and you hang him on a tree 1
23 his body shall not remain all night upon the tree 1
22: 6 come upon a bird's nest, in any tree or on the ground 1
28:42 All your trees and the fruit of your ground 1
Jos 8:29 he hanged the king of Ai on a tree until evening; 1
29 they took his body down from the tree 1
10:26 Joshua smote . . and he hung them on five trees. 1
26 And they hung upon the trees until evening; 1
27 they took them down from the trees, and threw them 1
Jdg 9: 8 The trees once went forth to anoint a king 1
9 leave my fatness . . and go to sway over the trees?' 1
10 the trees said to the fig tree, 'Come you, and reign 1
11 and my good fruit, and go to sway over the trees?' 1
12 the trees said to the vine, 'Come you, and reign over 1
13 cheers gods and men, and go to sway over the trees?' 1
14 all the trees said to the bramble, 'Come you 1
15 bramble said to the trees, 'If in good faith you are 1
2Sm 5:11 Hiram king of Tyre sent . . cedar trees 1
1Kg 4:33 He spoke of trees, from the cedar that is 1
14:23 on every high hill and under every green tree; 1
2Kg 3:19 and shall fell every good tree 1
25 and felled all the good trees; 1
6: 4 when they came to the Jordan, they cut down trees. 1
16: 4 and on the hills, and under every green tree. 1
17:10 Ashe'rim on every . . and under every green tree; 1
1Ch 14: 1 king of Tyre sent . . cedar trees, also masons 1
16:33 the trees of the wood sing for joy before the LORD 1
2Ch 28: 4 burned incense . . under every green tree. 1
Ezr 3: 7 to bring cedar trees from Lebanon to the sea 1
Neh 8:15 bring branches of . . palm, and other leafy trees 1
9:25 possession of . . orchards and fruit trees 1
10:35 bring . . first fruits of all fruit of every tree 1
37 bring . . fruit of every tree, the wine and the oil 1
Job 14: 7 For there is hope for a tree, if it be cut down 1
19:10 I am gone, and my hope has he pulled up like a tree. 1
24:20 wickedness is broken like a tree.' 1
Ps 1: 3 He is like a tree planted by streams of water 1
96:12 Then shall all the trees of the wood sing for joy 1
104:16 The trees of the LORD are watered abundantly 1
105:33 shattered the trees of their country. 1
148: 9 fruit trees and all cedars! 1
Prv 3:18 She is a tree of life to those who lay hold of her; 1
11:30 The fruit of the righteous is a tree of life 1
13:12 but a desire fulfilled is a tree of life. 1
15: 4 A gentle tongue is a tree of life 1
Ecc 2: 5 and planted in them all kinds of fruit trees. 1
6 pools . . to water the forest of growing trees. 1
11: 3 and if a tree falls to the south or to the north 1
3 the place where the tree falls, there it will lie. 1
Sng 2: 3 As an apple tree among the trees of the wood, so is 1
4:14 and cinnamon, with all trees of frankincense 1
Isa 7: 2 as the trees of the forest shake before the wind. 1
10:19 remnant of the trees of his forest will be so few 1
34 and Lebanon with its majestic trees will fall. •
44:14 lets it grow strong among the trees of the forest; 1
23 O mountains, O forest, and every tree in it! 1
55:12 the trees of the field shall clap their hands. 1
56: 3 let not the eunuch say, "Behold, I am a dry tree. 1
57: 5 lust among the oaks, under every green tree; 1
65:22 the days of a tree shall the days of my people be 1
Jer 2:20 and under every green tree you bowed down 1
27 who say to a tree, 'You are my father,' 1
3: 6 on every high hill and under every green tree 1
9 committing adultery with stone and tree. 1
13 favors among strangers under every green tree 1
6: 6 thus says the LORD of hosts: "Hew down her trees; 1
7:20 the trees of the field and the fruit of the ground; 1
10: 3 A tree from the forest is cut down 1
11:19 Let us destroy the tree with its fruit 1
17: 2 and their Ashe'rim, beside every green tree 1
8 He is like a tree planted by water 1
46:22 against her with axes, like those who fell trees. 1
Ezk 6:13 on all the mountain tops, under every green tree 1
15: 2 branch which is among the trees of the forest? 1
6 wood of the vine among the trees of the forest 1
17:24 the trees of the field shall know that I the LORD 1
24 shall know that I the LORD bring low the high tree 1
24 bring low the high tree, and make high the low tree 1
24 dry up the green tree, and make the dry tree 1
24 and make the dry tree flourish. 1
20:28 wherever they saw any high hill or any leafy tree 1
47 it shall devour every green tree in you 1
47 devour every green tree in you and every dry tree; 1
31: 4 its streams to all the trees of the forest. 1
5 it towered high above all the trees of the forest; 1
8 no tree in the garden of God was like it in beauty. 1
9 the trees of Eden envied it 1
14 in order that no trees by the waters may grow 1
14 no trees that drink water may reach up to them •
15 the trees of the field shall faint because of it. 1
16 the trees of Eden, the choice and best of Lebanon 1
18 in glory and in greatness among the trees of Eden? 1
18 You shall be brought down with the trees of Eden 1
34:27 the trees of the field shall yield their fruit 1
36:30 I will make the fruit of the tree and the increase 1
47: 7 I saw upon the bank of the river very many trees 1
12 there will grow all kinds of trees for food. 1
Dan 4:10 saw, and behold, a tree in the midst of the earth; 2
11 tree grew and became strong, and its top reached 2
14 'Hew down the tree and cut off its branches 2
20 tree you saw, which grew and became strong 2
23 'Hew down the tree and destroy it, 2
26 to leave the stump of the roots of the tree 2
Jol 1:12 all the trees of the field are withered; 1
19 and flame has burned all the trees of the field. 1
2:22 the tree bears its fruit 1
Hag 2:19 and the olive tree still yield nothing? 1
Zec 11: 2 for the glorious trees are ruined! •
Mat 3:10 Even now the axe is laid to the root of the trees; 3
10 every tree therefore that does not bear good 3
7:17 So, every sound tree bears good fruit 3
17 but the bad tree bears evil fruit. 3
18 A sound tree cannot bear evil fruit 3
18 nor can a bad tree bear good fruit. 3
19 Every tree that does not bear good fruit is cut 3
12:33 Either make the tree good, and its fruit good 3
33 or make the tree bad, and its fruit bad 3
33 for the tree is known by its fruit. 3
13:32 and becomes a tree 3
21: 8 others cut branches from the trees 3
Mrk 8:24 I see men; but they look like trees, walking. 3
Lke 3: 9 Even now the axe is laid to the root of the trees; 3
9 every tree . . that does not bear good fruit 3
6:43 For no good tree bears bad fruit 3
43 nor again does a bad tree bear good fruit; 3
44 for each tree is known by its own fruit 3
13:19 it grew and became a tree 3
21:29 Look at the fig tree, and all the trees; 3
Act 5:30 whom you killed by hanging him on a tree. 5
10:39 They put him to death by hanging him on a tree; 5
13:29 took him down from the tree, and laid him in a tomb. 5
Gal 3:13 Cursed be every one who hangs on a tree"- 5
1Pe 2:24 He himself bore our sins in his body on the tree 5
Jde 1:12 fruitless trees in late autumn, twice dead 3
Rev 2: 7 I will grant to eat of the tree of life 5
7: 1 blow on earth or sea or against any tree. 3
3 Do not harm the earth or the sea or the trees 3
8: 7 and a third of the trees were burnt up 3
9: 4 not to harm . . any green growth or any tree 3
22: 2 the tree of life with its twelve kinds of fruit 5
2 the leaves of the tree were for the healing 5
14 they may have the right to the tree of life 5
19 God will take away his share in the tree of life 5
2Es 1:20 I covered you with the leaves of trees. 7
23 but threw a tree into the water 8
2:12 The tree of life shall give them . . perfume 8
18 twelve trees loaded with various fruits 7
4:13 I went into a forest of trees of the plain 8
5:23 from all its trees thou hast chosen one vine 7
8:52 paradise is opened, the tree of life is planted 7
15:13 and their trees shall be ruined by blight 8
42 walls, mountains and hills, trees of the forests 8
62 all your forests and your fruitful trees. 8
16:25 The trees shall bear fruit, and who will gather it? 8
29 three or four olives may be left on every tree 7
Wis 13:11 may saw down a tree easy to handle 6
Sir 6: 3 will be left like a withered tree. 5
14:18 Like flourishing leaves on a spreading tree 3
27: 6 The fruit discloses the cultivation of a tree 5
38: 5 Was not water made sweet with a tree 5
Bar 5: 8 The woods and every fragrant tree have shaded 5
Sus 1:54 Under what tree did you see them being intimate 3
58 tell me: Under what tree did you catch them 3
1Mc 10:30 the half of the fruit of the trees 4
14: 8 the trees of the plains their fruit. 5
4Mc 14:16 building . . in holes and tops of trees 3
18:16 'There is a tree of life for those who do his will.' 5

tree *See also* almond, apple, balsam, broom, cedar, fig, fir, fruit, holm, lotus, mastic, myrtle, olive, palm, plane, pomegranate, sycamine, sycamore, tamarisk.

fruit tree 1. פרה 2. *ἥμερος φυτόν*
Isa 17: 6 four or five on the branches of a fruit tree 1
4Mc 2:14 The fruit trees of the enemy are not cut down 2

trellis 1. סְבָךְ
Ps 74: 5 they hacked the wooden trellis with axes. 1

tremble 1. גור 2. זוע 3. חול 4. חפז 5. חרד 6. חָרֵד 7. חֲרָדָה 8. ירע 9. נוע 10. סמר 11. פִּיק 12. פלץ 13. רגז 14. רַגָּז 15. רעד 16. רַעַד 17. רְעָדָה 18. רעש 19. רפף 20. רְתֵת 21. זוע (A) 22. *ἔντρομος* 23. *πτοέω* 24. *σαλεύω* 25. *σείω* 26. *τρέμω* 27. *τρόμος* 28. *φρικασμός* 29. *φρίσσω* 30. tremesco 31. tremo 32. tremor 33. trepido
Gen 27:33 Isaac trembled violently, and said, "Who was it 7
Exd 15:14 The peoples have heard, they tremble; 13
15 the leaders of Moab, trembling seizes them; 16
19:16 all the people who were in the camp trembled. 5
20:18 the people were afraid and trembled; 9
Deu 2:25 hear . . and shall tremble and be in anguish 13
20: 3 do not fear, or tremble, or be in dread of them; 4
28:65 LORD will give you there a trembling heart 14
Jdg 5: 4 the earth trembled, and the heavens dropped 18
7: 3 Whoever is fearful and trembling, let him return 6
1Sm 4:13 for his heart trembled for the ark of God. 6
13: 7 and all the people followed him trembling. 5
14:15 the garrison and even the raiders trembled; 5
28: 5 he was afraid, and his heart trembled greatly. 5
2Sm 22: 8 foundations of the heavens trembled and quaked 13
1Kg 1:49 guests . . trembled, and rose, and each went his own 5
1Ch 16:30 tremble before him, all the earth; 3
Ezr 9: 4 all who trembled at the words of the God of Israel 6
10: 3 those who tremble at the commandment of our God; 6
9 trembling because of this matter 15
Est 5: 9 Haman saw . . that he neither rose nor trembled 2
Job 4:14 trembling, which made all my bones shake. 17
9: 6 earth out of its place, and its pillars tremble; 12
26: 5 The shades below tremble 3
11 The pillars of heaven tremble, and are astounded 19
37: 1 At this also my heart trembles, and leaps out 5
Ps 2:11 Serve the LORD with fear, with trembling 17
18: 7 the foundations also of the mountains trembled 13
46: 3 though the mountains tremble with its tumult. 18
48: 6 trembling took hold of them there 17
55: 5 Fear and trembling come upon me 16
77:16 they were afraid, yea, the deep trembled. 13
18 the earth trembled and shook. 13
96: 9 tremble before him, all the earth! 3
97: 4 earth sees and trembles. 3
99: 1 The LORD reigns; let the peoples tremble! 13
104:32 who looks on the earth and it trembles 15
114: 7 Tremble, O earth, at the presence of the LORD 3
119:120 My flesh trembles for fear of thee, and I am afraid 10
Prv 30:21 Under three things the earth trembles; 13
Ecc 12: 3 the day when the keepers of the house tremble 2
Isa 10:29 Ramah trembles, Gib'e-ah of Saul has fled. 5
15: 4 of Moab cry aloud; his soul trembles. 8
19: 1 the idols of Egypt will tremble at his presence 9
16 tremble with fear before the hand which the LORD 5
21: 4 twilight . . turned for me into trembling. 7
24:18 and the foundations of the earth tremble. 18
32:11 Tremble, you women who are at ease 5

33:14 in Zion . . trembling has seized the godless 17
41: 5 the ends of the earth tremble; 5
64: 2 that the nations might tremble at thy presence! 13
66: 2 contrite in spirit, and trembles at my word. 6
5 the word of the LORD, you who tremble at his word 6
Jer 5:22 says the LORD; Do you not tremble before me? 3
33: 9 they shall fear and tremble 13
49:21 At . . their fall the earth shall tremble; 18
50:46 At . . capture of Babylon the earth shall tremble 18
51:29 The land trembles and writhes in pain 18
Ezk 12:18 and drink water with trembling 13
26:16 they will clothe themselves with trembling; 7
16 sit upon the ground and tremble every moment 5
18 Now the isles tremble on the day of your fall; 5
32:10 they shall tremble every moment 5
Dan 5:19 all . . trembled and feared before him; 21
6:26 all my royal dominion men tremble and fear 21
10: 7 but a great trembling fell upon them 7
11 speaking this word to me, I stood up trembling. 15
Hos 5: 8 Sound the alarm at Beth-a'ven; tremble, O Benjamin! *
10: 5 The inhabitants of Sama'ria tremble 1
13: 1 When E'phraim spoke, men trembled; 20
Jol 2: 1 Let all the inhabitants of the land tremble 13
10 earth quakes before them, the heavens tremble. 18
Ams 8: 8 Shall not the land tremble on this account 13
Nah 2:10 Hearts faint and knees tremble 11
Hab 3: 7 the curtains of the land of Mid'ian did tremble. 13
16 I hear, and my body trembles, my lips quiver 13
Mat 28: 4 for fear of him the guards trembled 25
Mrk 5:33 came in fear and trembling 26
16: 8 trembling and astonishment had come upon them 27
Lke 8:47 she came trembling 26
Act 7:32 Moses trembled and did not dare to look. 22
1Co 2: 3 in weakness and in much fear and trembling; 27
2Co 7:15 fear and trembling with which you received him. 27
Eph 6: 5 with fear and trembling, in singleness of heart 27
Php 2:12 your own salvation with fear and trembling; 27
Heb 12:21 Moses said, "I tremble with fear. 22
1Es 4:36 All God's works quake and tremble 26
2Es 3:18 move the world, and make the depths to tremble 31
6:16 They will tremble and be shaken 30
8:21 before whom the hosts of angels stand trembling 32
13: 3 everything under his gaze trembled 31
15:29 so that all who hear them fear and tremble. 33
33 fear and trembling shall come upon their army 32
37 be fear and great trembling upon the earth 32
37 they shall be seized with trembling 32
16:18 when all shall tremble 33
Jdt 15: 2 Fear and trembling came over them 27
16:10 The Persians trembled at her boldness 29
11 my weak people shouted and the enemy trembled; 23
Sir 16:18 will tremble at his visitation. 24
19 shake with trembling when he looks upon them. 27
48:12 all his days he did not tremble before any ruler 24
19 their hands trembled *
Man 1: 4 all things shudder, and tremble before thy power 26
1Mc 4:32 let them tremble in their destruction. 24
6:41 All who heard the noise . . trembled 24
13: 2 the people were trembling and fearful 22
2Mc 3:17 terror and bodily trembling 28
15:23 to carry terror and trembling before us. 27
4Mc 4:10 instilling in them great fear and trembling. 27

make tremble 1. זוע 2. מעד 3. רגז
Ps 69:23 make their loins tremble continually. 2
Isa 13:13 Therefore I will make the heavens tremble 3
14:16 Is this the man who made the earth tremble 3
Hab 2: 7 and those awake who will make you tremble? 1

tremble with fear 1. *ἔντρομος*
Act 16:29 and trembling with fear he fell down before Paul 1
trembling *See* fear, turn.

come trembling 1. חרג 2. חרד 3. רגז
1Sm 16: 4 The elders of the city came to meet him trembling 2
21: 1 Ahim'elech came to meet David trembling, and said 2
2Sm 22:46 and came trembling out of their fastnesses. *
Ps 18:45 came trembling out of their fastnesses. 1
Hos 11:10 and his sons shall come trembling from the west; 2
11 they shall come trembling like birds from Egypt 2
Mic 7:17 shall come trembling out of their strongholds 3

set trembling 1. נוע
Dan 10:10 hand . . set me trembling on my hands and knees. 1

tremendous 1. *παμπληθής*
2Mc 10:24 gathered a tremendous force of mercenaries 1

trench 1. תְּעָלָה
1Kg 18:32 And he made a trench about the altar 1
35 the water . . filled the trench also with water. 1
38 and licked up the water that was in the trench. 1

trespass 1. מעל 2. פֶּשַׁע 3. *παραπίπτω* 4. *παράπτωμα*
1Sm 25:28 Pray forgive the trespass of your handmaid; 2
Ezr 10:10 You have trespassed and married foreign women 1
Mat 6:14 For if you forgive men their trespasses 4
15 if you do not forgive men their trespasses *
15 will your Father forgive your trespasses. 4
Mrk 11:25 may forgive you your trespasses. 4
Rom 4:25 who was put to death for our trespasses 4
5:15 But the free gift is not like the trespass. 4
15 For if many died through one man's trespass 4
16 the free gift following many trespasses brings 4
17 If, because of one man's trespass, death reigned 4
18 one man's trespass led to condemnation for all 4
20 Law came in, to increase the trespass; 4
11:11 through their trespass salvation has come 4
12 Now if their trespass means riches for the world 4
2Co 5:19 not counting their trespasses against them 4
Gal 6: 1 Brethren, if a man is overtaken in any trespass 4
Eph 1: 7 the forgiveness of our trespasses 4
2: 1 you were dead through the trespasses and sins 4
5 even when we were dead through our trespasses 4
Col 2:13 were dead in trespasses 4
13 having forgiven us all our trespasses 4
Wis 12: 2 thou dost correct . . those who trespass 3

tress 1. רַהַט
Sng 7: 5 a king is held captive in the tresses. 1

trial 1. מַסָּה 2. מִשְׁפָּט 3. *κρίνω* 4. *πειρασμός*
Deu 4:34 by trials, by signs, by wonders, and by war 1
7:19 great trials which your eyes saw, the signs 1
29: 3 great trials which your eyes saw 1
Job 9:32 that we should come to trial together. 2
Ps 109: 6 let an accuser bring him to trial. †
Lke 22:28 those who have continued with me in my trials; 4
Act 20:19 with all humility and with tears and with trials 4
23: 6 with respect to . . the resurrection . . I am on trial. 3
24:21 I am on trial before you this day.' 3
26: 6 now I stand here on trial for hope in the promise 3
Gal 4:14 though my condition was a trial to you 4
Jas 1: 2 Count it all joy . . when you meet various trials 4
12 Blessed is the man who endures trial 4
1Pe 1: 6 you may have to suffer various trials 4
2Pe 2: 9 the Lord knows how to rescue the godly from trial 4
Rev 3:10 I will keep you from the hour of trial 4
Sir 33: 1 in trial he will deliver him again and again. 4
trial *See also* bring, make.

tribal 1. מַטֶּה 2. שֵׁבֶט
Jos 11:23 gave . . according to their tribal allotments. 2
22:14 ten chiefs, one from each of the tribal families 1
Ezk 45: 7 corresponding . . to one of the tribal portions *
48: 8 in length equal to one of the tribal portions *
21 the west border, parallel to the tribal portions *

tribe 1. אֶלֶף 2. אֻמָּה 3. בֵּן 4. מַטֶּה 5. מִשְׁפָּחָה 6. שֵׁבֶט 7. שֵׁבֶט (A) 8. *φυλή* 9. tribus
Gen 25:16 twelve princes according to their tribes. 2
49:16 judge his people as one of the tribes of Israel. 6
28 All these are the twelve tribes of Israel; 6
Exd 24: 4 twelve pillars, according to the twelve tribes 6
28:21 with its name, for the twelve tribes. 6
31: 2 Bez'alel and son . . of Hur, of the tribe of Judah 4
6 Oho'liab, the son of Ahis'amach, of the tribe of Dan; 4
35:30 the son of Uri, son of Hur, of the tribe of Judah; 4
34 Oho'liab the son of Ahis'amach of the tribe of Dan. 4
38:22 son of Uri, son of Hur, of the tribe of Judah 4
23 son of Ahis'amach, of the tribe of Dan, a craftsman 4
39:14 with its name, for the twelve tribes. 6
Lev 24:11 the daughter of Dibri, of the tribe of Dan 4
Num 1: 4 there shall be with you a man from each tribe 4
16 the leaders of their ancestral tribes 4
21 the number of the tribe of Reuben was 46,500 4
23 the number of the tribe of Simeon was 59,300 4
25 the number of the tribe of Gad was 45,650 4
27 the number of the tribe of Judah was 74,600 4
29 the number of the tribe of Is'sachar was 54,400 4
31 the number of the tribe of Zeb'ulun was 57,400 4
33 the number of the tribe of E'phraim was 40,500 4
35 the number of the tribe of Manas'seh was 32,200 4
37 the number of the tribe of Benjamin was 35,400 4
39 the number of the tribe of Dan was 62,700 4
41 the number of the tribe of Asher was 41,500 4
43 the number of the tribe of Naph'tali was 53,400 4
47 numbered by their ancestral tribe along 4
49 Only the tribe of Levi you shall not number 4
2: 5 the tribe of Is'sachar, the leader of the people 4
7 Then the tribe of Zeb'ulun, the leader 4
12 those to encamp next to him shall be the tribe 4
14 Then the tribe of Gad, the leader of the people 4
20 next to him shall be the tribe of Manas'seh 4
22 Then the tribe of Benjamin, the leader 4
27 next . . shall be the tribe of Asher 4
29 Then the tribe of Naph'tali 4
3: 6 Bring the tribe of Levi near, and set them before 4
4:18 tribe of the families of the Ko'hathites 6
7: 2 leaders of the tribes, who were over those 4
12 Nahshon . . of the tribe of Judah; 4
10: 4 leaders, the heads of the tribes of Israel 1
15 over the host of the tribe of the men of Is'sachar 4
16 over the host of the tribe of the men of Zeb'ulun 4
19 over the host of the tribe of the men of Simeon 4
20 over the host of the tribe of the men of Gad 4
23 over the host of the tribe of the men of Manas'seh 4
24 over the host of the tribe of the men of Benjamin 4
26 over the host of the tribe of the men of Asher 4
27 over the host of the tribe of the men of Naph'tali 4
13: 2 each tribe of their fathers shall you send a man 4
4 From the tribe of Reuben, ShSham'mu-a . . of Zaccur; 4
5 from the tribe of Simeon, Shaphat the son of Hori; 4
6 from the tribe of Judah, Caleb . . of Jephun'neh; 4
7 from the tribe of Is'sachar, Igal the son of Joseph; 4
8 from the tribe of E'phraim, Hoshe'a the son of Nun; 4
9 from the tribe of Benjamin, Palti the son of Raphu; 4
10 from the tribe of Zeb'ulun, Gad'diel the son of Sodi; 4
11 from the tribe of Joseph . . Gaddi the son of Susi; 4
11 Joseph (that is from the tribe of Manas'seh) 4
12 from the tribe of Dan, Am'miel the son of Gemal'li; 4
13 from the tribe of Asher, Sethur the son of Michael; 4
14 from the tribe of Naph'tali, Nahbi . . of Vophsi; 4
15 from the tribe of Gad, Geu'el the son of Machi. 4
18: 2 brethren also, the tribe of Levi 4
2 tribe of Levi, the tribe of your father 6
26:54 a large tribe you shall give a large inheritance *
54 every tribe shall be given its inheritance *
55 names of the tribes of their fathers 4
30: 1 Moses said to the heads of the tribes 4
31: 4 send 1,000 from each of the tribes of Israel to the war 4
5 Israel, 1,000 from each tribe, 12,000 armed for war 1
6 Moses sent them to the war, 1,000 from each tribe 4
32:28 heads of the fathers' houses of the tribes 4
33 to the half-tribe of Manas'seh the son of Joseph 6
33:54 a large tribe you shall give a large inheritance *
54 according to the tribes of your fathers 4
34:13 LORD has commanded to give to the nine tribes 4
13 to give to the nine tribes and to the half-tribe 4
14 tribe of the sons of Reuben by fathers' houses 4
14 tribe of the sons of Gad by their fathers' houses 4
14 also the half-tribe of Manas'seh; 4
15 two tribes and the half-tribe have received 4
15 two tribes and the half-tribe have received 4
18 You shall take one leader of every tribe 4
19 Of the tribe of Judah, Caleb the son of Jephun'neh. 4
20 Of the tribe of the sons of Simeon, Shemu'el 4
21 Of the tribe of Benjamin, Eli'dad 4
22 Of the tribe of the sons of Dan a leader, Bukki 4
23 of the tribe of the sons of Manas'seh a leader, 4
24 of the tribe of the sons of E'phraim a leader, Kemu'el 4
25 Of the tribe of the sons of Zeb'ulun a leader 4
26 Of the tribe of the sons of Is'sachar a leader 4
27 of the tribe of the sons of Asher a leader 4
28 Of the tribe of the sons of Naph'tali a leader 4
35: 8 from the larger tribes you shall take many *
36: 3 sons of the other tribes of the people of Israel 6
3 inheritance of the tribe to which they belong; 4
4 added to the inheritance of the tribe 4
4 inheritance of the tribe of our fathers. 4
5 The tribe of the sons of Joseph is right. 4
6 within the family of the tribe of their father. 4
7 not be transferred from one tribe to another; 4
7 cleave to the inheritance of the tribe 4
8 inheritance in any tribe of the people of Israel 4
8 wife to one . . family of the tribe of her father 4
9 no . . transferred from one tribe to another; 4
9 for each of the tribes of the people of Israel 4
12 inheritance remained in the tribe of the family 4
Deu 1:13 Choose . . men, according to your tribes 6
15 So I took the heads of your tribes 6
15 commanders . . and officers, throughout your tribes. 6
23 I took twelve men of you, one man for each tribe; 6
3:13 the rest . . I gave to the half-tribe of Manas'seh. 6
5:23 all the heads of your tribes, and your elders; 6
10: 8 LORD set apart the tribe of Levi to carry the ark 6
12: 5 LORD your God will choose out of all your tribes 6
14 place . . LORD will choose in one of your tribes 6
16:18 in all your towns . . according to your tribes; 6
18: 1 Levitical priests, that is, all the tribe of Levi 6
5 LORD . . has chosen him out of all your tribes 6
29: 8 inheritance to . . half-tribe of the Manas'sites. 6
10 heads of your tribes, your elders 6
18 lest there be . . a man or woman or family or tribe 6
21 single him out from all the tribes of Israel 6
31:28 Assemble to me all the elders of your tribes 6
33: 5 gathered, all the tribes of Israel together. 6
Jos 1:12 the Gadites, and the half-tribe of Manas'seh 6
3:12 Now . . take twelve men from the tribes of Israel 6
12 take twelve men . . from each tribe a man. 6
4: 2 Take twelve men . . from each tribe a man 6
4 whom he had appointed, a man from each tribe; 6
5 to the number of the tribes of the people of Israel 6
8 the number of the tribes of the people of Israel 6
12 and the sons of Gad and the half-tribe of Manas'seh 6
7: 1 Achan the son of Carmi . . of the tribe of Judah 4
14 you shall be brought near by your tribes; 6
14 the tribe which the LORD takes shall come near 6
16 and the tribe of Judah was taken; 6
18 and Achan . . of the tribe of Judah, was taken. 4
12: 6 and the Gadites and the half-tribe of Manas'seh. 6
7 and Joshua gave their land to the tribes 6
13: 7 divide this land . . to the nine tribes 6
7 the nine tribes and half the tribe of Manas'seh. 6

8 With the other half of the tribe of Manas'seh 8
14 To the tribe of Levi . . Moses gave no inheritance; 6
15 an inheritance to the tribe of the Reubenites 4
24 Moses gave . . also to the tribe of the Gadites 4
29 Moses gave . . to the half-tribe of Manas'seh; 6
29 was allotted to the half-tribe of the Manas'sites 4
33 to the tribe of Levi Moses gave no inheritance; 6
14: 1 houses of the tribes of the people of Israel 4
2 commanded . . for the nine and one-half tribes. 4
3 an inheritance to the two and one-half tribes 4
4 For the people of Joseph were two tribes 4
15: 1 The lot for the tribe of the people of Judah 4
20 inheritance of the tribe of the people of Judah 4
21 belonging to the tribe of the people of Judah 4
16: 8 the inheritance of the tribe of the E'phraimites 4
17: 1 Then allotment was made to the tribe of Manas'seh 4
2 were made to the rest of the tribe of Manas'seh 3
14 And the tribe of Joseph spoke to Joshua, saying 3
16 The tribe of Joseph said, "The hill country is not 3
18: 2 seven tribes whose inheritance had not yet been 6
4 Provide three men from each tribe, and I will send 6
7 and Gad and Reuben and half the tribe of Manas'seh 6
11 The lot of the tribe of Benjamin . . came up 4
11 fell between the tribe of Judah and . . of Joseph. 3
11 fell between . . Judah and the tribe of Joseph. 3
14 a city belonging to the tribe of Judah. 3
20 This is the inheritance of the tribe of Benjamin 3
21 Now the cities of the tribe of Benjamin 4
28 This is the inheritance of the tribe of Benjamin 3
19: 1 lot came out for Simeon, for the tribe of Simeon 4
1 midst of the inheritance of the tribe of Judah. 3
8 This was the inheritance of the tribe of Simeon 4
9 The inheritance of the tribe of Simeon formed 3
9 the portion of the tribe of Judah was too large 3
9 the tribe of Simeon obtained an inheritance 3
10 The third lot came up for the tribe of Zeb'ulun 3
16 This is the inheritance of the tribe of Zeb'ulun 3
17 fourth lot . . for the tribe of Is'sachar 3
23 This is the inheritance of the tribe of Is'sachar 3
24 The fifth lot came out for the tribe of Asher 4
31 This is the inheritance of the tribe of Asher 4
32 The sixth lot came out for the tribe of Naph'tali 3
32 sixth lot . . for the tribe of Naph'tali 3
39 This is the inheritance of the tribe of Naph'tali 4
40 The seventh lot came out for the tribe of Dan 4
48 This is the inheritance of the tribe of Dan 4
51 houses of the tribes of the people of Israel 4
20: 8 Bezer . . from the tribe of Reuben, and Ramoth 4
8 and Ramoth in Gilead, from the tribe of Gad 4
8 and Golan in Bashan, from the tribe of Manas'seh. 4
21: 1 fathers' houses of the tribes of the people 4
4 received . . from the tribes of Judah, Simeon 4
5 by lot from the families of the tribe of E'phraim 4
5 of the tribe of E'phraim, from the tribe of Dan 4
5 the tribe of Dan and the half-tribe of Manas'seh 4
6 by lot from the families of the tribe of Is'sachar 4
6 the tribe of Asher, from the tribe of Naph'tali 4
6 the tribe of Asher, from the tribe of Naph'tali 4
6 and from the half-tribe of Manas'seh in Bashan 4
7 Merar'ites . . received from the tribe of Reuben 4
7 Reuben, the tribe of Gad, and the tribe of Zeb'ulun 4
7 Reuben, the tribe of Gad, and the tribe of Zeb'ulun 4
9 Out of the tribe of Judah and . . Simeon they gave 4
9 Out of . . Judah and the tribe of Simeon they gave 4
16 nine cities out of these two tribes; 6
17 then out of the tribe of Benjamin, Gibeon 4
20 the cities . . were out of the tribe of E'phraim. 4
23 and out of the tribe of Dan, El'teke 4
25 and out of the half-tribe of Manas'seh, Ta'anach 4
27 were given out of the half-tribe of Manas'seh 4
28 and out of the tribe of Is'sachar, Ki'shion 4
30 and out of the tribe of Asher, Mishal with its 4
32 and out of the tribe of Naph'tali, Kedesh 4
34 the rest . . were given out of the tribe of Zeb'ulun 4
36 and out of the tribe of Reuben, Bezer with its 4
38 and out of the tribe of Gad, Ramoth in Gilead 4
22: 1 and the Gadites, and the half-tribe of Manas'seh 4
7 one half of the tribe of Manas'seh Moses had given 6
9 the Gadites and the half-tribe of Manas'seh 6
10 the Gadites and the half-tribe of Manas'seh built 6
11 and the half-tribe of Manas'seh have built 6
13 and the Gadites and the half-tribe of Manas'seh 6
15 to . . the Gadites, and the half-tribe of Manas'seh 6
21 the Gadites, and the half-tribe of Manas'seh said 6
23: 4 allotted . . as an inheritance for your tribes 6
24: 1 Then Joshua gathered all the tribes of Israel 6
Jdg 4: 6 men . . taking 10,000 from the tribe of Naph'tali 3
6 the tribe of Naph'tali and the tribe of Zeb'ulun. 3
13: 2 a certain man of Zorah, of the tribe of the Danites 5
18: 1 the tribe of the Danites was seeking for itself 6
1 no inheritance among the tribes of Israel had 6
2 sent . . men from the whole number of their tribe 5
11 600 men of the tribe of Dan, armed . . set forth 5
19 or to be priest to a tribe and family in Israel? 6
30 were priests to the tribe of the Danites until 6
20: 2 of all the people, of all the tribes of Israel 6
10 of a 100 throughout all the tribes of Israel 6
12 the tribes of Israel sent men through all 6
12 sent men through all the tribe of Benjamin 6

21: 3 there . . be today one tribe lacking in Israel? 6
5 Which of all the tribes of Israel did not come up 6
6 One tribe is cut off from Israel this day. 6
8 What one is there of the tribes of Israel that did 6
15 LORD had made a breach in the tribes of Israel. 6
17 that a tribe be not blotted out from Israel. 6
24 departed . . every man to his tribe and family 6
1Sm 2:28 chose him out of all the tribes of Israel to be my 6
9:21 Am I not . . from the least of the tribes of Israel? 6
21 of all the families of the tribe of Benjamin? 6
10:19 present yourselves . . by your tribes 6
20 Samuel brought all the tribes of Israel near 6
20 and the tribe of Benjamin was taken by lot. 6
21 He brought the tribe of Benjamin near 6
15:17 are you not the head of the tribes of Israel? 6
2Sm 5: 1 the tribes of Israel came to David at Hebron 6
15: 2 Your servant is of such and such a tribe in Israel 6
10 sent . . throughout all the tribes of Israel 6
19: 9 people were at strife throughout all the tribes 6
20:14 Sheba passed through all the tribes of Israel 6
24: 2 Go through all the tribes of Israel, from Dan 6
1Kg 7:14 He was the son of a widow of the tribe of Naph'tali 4
8: 1 the elders . . and all the heads of the tribes 4
16 I chose no city in all the tribes of Israel 6
11:13 I will give one tribe to your son 6
31 I am about to . . and will give you ten tribes 6
32 he shall have one tribe, for the sake of my servant 6
32 I have chosen out of all the tribes of Israel) 6
35 I will . . give it to you,ten tribes. 6
36 Yet to his son I will give one tribe 6
12:20 but the tribe of Judah only. 6
21 all the house of Judah, and the tribe of Benjamin 6
14:21 LORD had chosen out of all the tribes of Israel 6
18:31 the number of the tribes of the sons of Jacob 6
2Kg 17:18 none was left but the tribe of Judah only. 6
21: 7 I have chosen out of all the tribes of Israel 6
1Ch 5:18 the half-tribe of Manas'seh had valiant men 6
23 the half-tribe of Manas'seh dwelt in the land 6
26 them away . . and the half-tribe of Manas'seh 6
6:60 from the tribe of Benjamin, Geba 4
61 given by lot out of the family of the tribe 4
61 out of the half-tribe, the half of Manas'seh 4
62 out of the tribes of Is'sachar, Asher, Naph'tali 4
63 out of the tribes of Reuben, Gad, and Zeb'ulun. 4
65 out of the tribes of Judah, Simeon, and Benjamin 4
66 of their territory out of the tribe of E'phraim. 4
70 out of the half-tribe of Manas'seh, Aner 4
71 were given out of the half-tribe of Manas'seh 4
72 out of the tribe of Is'sachar: Kedesh . . Dab'erath 4
74 out of the tribe of Asher: Mashal . . Abdon 4
76 out of the tribe of Naph'tali: Kedesh 4
77 were allotted out of the tribe of Zeb'ulun 4
78 out of the tribe of Reuben: Bezer . . Jahzah 4
80 out of the tribe of Gad: Ramoth in Gilead 4
12:31 Of the half-tribe of Manas'seh 18,000 4
37 and Gadites and the half-tribe of Manas'seh 6
23:14 sons of Moses . . named among the tribe of Levi. 6
26:32 the Gadites, and the half-tribe of the Manas'sites 6
27:16 Over the tribes of Israel, for the Reubenites 6
20 for the half-tribe of Manas'seh, Jo'el the son 6
21 for the half-tribe of Manas'seh in Gilead, 6
22 These were the leaders of the tribes of Israel. 6
28: 1 officials of Israel, the officials of the tribes 6
29: 6 as did also the leaders of the tribes 6
2Ch 5: 2 assembled the . . and all the heads of the tribes 4
6: 5 I chose no city in all the tribes of Israel 6
11:16 came after them from all the tribes of Israel 6
12:13 out of all the tribes of Israel to put his name 6
33: 7 I have chosen out of all the tribes of Israel 6
Ezr 6:17 according to the number of the tribes of Israel. 7
Ps 74: 2 redeemed to be the tribe of thy heritage! 6
78:55 settled the tribes of Israel in their tents. 6
67 he did not choose the tribe of E'phraim; 6
68 he chose the tribe of Judah 6
105:37 there was none among his tribes who stumbled. 6
122: 4 to which the tribes go up, the tribes of the LORD 6
4 to which the tribes go up, the tribes of the LORD 6
Isa 19:13 cornerstones of her tribes . . led Egypt astray. 6
49: 6 be my servant to raise up the tribes of Jacob 6
63:17 of thy servants, the tribes of thy heritage. 6
Jer 1:15 all the tribes of the kingdoms of the north 5
10:16 and Israel is the tribe of his inheritance; 6
25: 9 behold, I will send for all the tribes of the north 5
51:19 and Israel is the tribe of his inheritance; 6
Ezk 20:32 like the tribes of the countries, and worship 5
37:19 and the tribes of Israel associated with him; 6
45: 8 Israel have the land according to their tribes. 6
47:13 inheritance among the twelve tribes of Israel. 6
21 among you according to the tribes of Israel. 6
22 an inheritance among the tribes of Israel. 6
23 In whatever tribe the alien resides 6
48: 1 These are the names of the tribes 6
19 workers of the city, from all the tribes of Israel 6
23 As for the rest of the tribes: from the east side 6
29 as an inheritance among the tribes of Israel 6
31 gates . . being named after the tribes of Israel. 6
Dan 1: 6 Daniel . . and Azari'ah of the tribe of Judah. 3
Hos 5: 9 among the tribes of Israel I declare what is sure. 6
Mic 6: 9 Hear, O tribe and assembly of the city! 4

Zec 9: 1 of Aram, even as all the tribes of Israel; 6
Mat 19:28 judging the twelve tribes of Israel. 8
24:30 then all the tribes of the earth will mourn 8
Lke 2:36 the tribe of Asher 8
22:30 judging the twelve tribes of Israel. 8
Act 13:21 Saul the son of Kish, a man of the tribe of Benjamin 8
Rom 11: 1 I myself am . . a member of the tribe of Benjamin. 8
Php 3: 5 of the people of Israel, of the tribe of Benjamin 8
Heb 7:13 belonged to another tribe 8
14 in connection with that tribe Moses said 8
Jas 1: 1 To the twelve tribes in the Dispersion 8
Rev 1: 7 tribes of the earth will wail on account of him. 8
5: 5 lo, the Lion of the tribe of Judah . . has conquered 8
9 ransom men for God from every tribe and tongue 8
7: 4 sealed, out of every tribe of the sons of Israel 8
5 12,000 sealed out of the tribe of Judah 8
5 12,000 of the tribe of Reuben 8
5 12,000 of the tribe of Gad 8
6 12,000 of the tribe of Asher 8
6 12,000 of the tribe of Naph'tali 8
6 12,000 of the tribe of Manas'seh 8
7 12,000 of the tribe of Simeon 8
7 12,000 of the tribe of Levi 8
7 12,000 of the tribe of Is'sachar 8
8 12,000 of the tribe of Zeb'ulun 8
8 12,000 of the tribe of Joseph 8
8 12,000 sealed out of the tribe of Benjamin. 8
9 multitude . . from every nation, from all tribes 8
11: 9 the peoples and tribes and tongues and nations 8
13: 7 authority was given it over every tribe 8
14: 6 to every nation and tribe and tongue and people; 8
21:12 names of the twelve tribes of the sons of Israel 8
1Es 2: 8 the heads of families of the tribes of Judah 8
5: 1 according to their tribes 8
4 according to their fathers' houses in the tribes 8
5 of the lineage of Phares, of the tribe of Judah. 8
66 the enemies of the tribe of Judah and Benjamin 8
9: 5 the men of the tribe of Judah and Benjamin 8
2Es 1: 3 son of Aaron, of the tribe of Levi 9
3: 7 From him there sprang nations and tribes 9
32 Or what tribes have so believed thy covenants 9
32 as these tribes of Jacob? 9
4:23 has been given over to godless tribes 9
13:40 these are the ten tribes 9
Tob 1: 1 the tribe of Naphtali 8
4 the whole tribe of Naphtali my forefather 8
4 chosen from among all the tribes of Israel 8
4 where all the tribes should sacrifice 8
5 All the tribes that joined in apostasy 8
4:12 a foreign woman, who is not of your father's tribe 8
5: 8 I may learn to what tribe he belongs 8
10 My brother, to what tribe and family do you belong? 8
11 Are you looking for a tribe and a family 8
13 because I tried to learn your tribe and family. 8
Jdt 3: 8 all their tongues and tribes 8
6:15 Uzziah the son of Micah, of the tribe of Simeon 8
8: 2 who belonged to her tribe and family 8
18 any tribe or family or people or city of ours 8
9:14 cause thy whole nation and every tribe to know 8
AEs 11: 2 Mordecai . . of the tribe of Benjamin 8
14: 5 I have heard in the tribe of my family 8
Sir 16: 4 through a tribe of lawless men 8
36:11 Gather all the tribes of Jacob 8
44:23 distributed them among twelve tribes. 8
45: 6 a holy man like him, of the tribe of Levi. 8
11 according to the number of the tribes of Israel; 8
25 David, the son of Jesse, of the tribe of Judah 8
48:10 to restore the tribes of Jacob. 8
2Mc 3: 4 a man named Simon, of the tribe of Benjamin 8

tribe *See also* entire, leader, twelve.

tribe by tribe 1. לְשְׁבָטִים

Num24: 2 Balaam . . saw Israel encamping tribe by tribe. 1
Jos 7:16 Joshua . . brought Israel near tribe by tribe 1

small tribe 1. מְעַט

Num26:54 small tribe you shall give a small inheritance; 1
33:54 a small tribe you shall give a small inheritance 1
35: 8 from the smaller tribes you shall take few; 1

mixed tribes 1. עֶרֶב

Jer 25:24 and all the kings of the mixed tribes 1

tribulation 1. צַר 2. צָרָה 3. תְּלָאָה 4. θλῖψις 5. στενοχωρία 6. pressura 7. tribulatio

Deu 4:30 When you are in tribulation, and all these things 1
1Sm 26:24 and may he deliver me out of all tribulation. 2
Lam 3: 5 enveloped me with bitterness and tribulation; 3
Mat 13:21 and when tribulation or persecution arises 4
24: 9 Then they will deliver you up to tribulation 4
21 For then there will be a great tribulation 4
29 Immediately after the tribulation 4
Mrk 4:17 then, when tribulation or persecution arises 4
13:19 such tribulation as has not been 4
24 in those days, after that tribulation 4
Joh 16:33 In the world you have tribulation 4
Act 14:22 through many tribulations 4
Rom 2: 9 There will be tribulation and distress 4

8:35 Shall tribulation, or distress, or persecution 4
12:12 Rejoice in your hope, be patient in tribulation 4
Rev 1: 9 share with you in Jesus the tribulation 4
2: 9 'I know your tribulation and your poverty 4
10 and for ten days you will have tribulation. 4
22 I will throw into great tribulation 4
7:14 they who have come out of the great tribulation; 4
2Es 2:27 when the day of tribulation and anguish comes 6
15:19 and because of great tribulation. 7
16:19 famine and plague, tribulation and anguish 7
67 and deliver you from all tribulation. 7
74 Behold, the days of tribulation are at hand 7
AEs 11: 8 tribulation and distress 4
3Mc 2:10 if . . tribulation should overtake us 5
4Mc 14: 9 as we hear of the tribulations of these young men; 4

tribunal 1. *βῆμα*
Act 18:12 brought him before the tribunal 1
16 he drove them from the tribunal. 1
17 and beat him in front of the tribunal 1
25: 6 the next day he took his seat on the tribunal 1
10 Paul said, "I am standing before Caesar's tribunal 1
17 but on the next day took my seat on the tribunal 1

tribune 1. *χιλίαρχος*
Act 21:31 word came to the tribune of the cohort 1
32 when they saw the tribune and the soldiers 1
33 Then the tribune came up and arrested him 1
37 brought into the barracks, he said to the tribune 1
22:24 the tribune commanded 1
26 he went to the tribune and said to him 1
27 So the tribune came and said to him 1
28 The tribune answered, "I bought this citizenship 1
29 the tribune also was afraid 1
23:10 the tribune . . commanded the soldiers to go down 1
15 give notice now to the tribune to bring him down 1
17 Take this young man to the tribune 1
18 took him and brought him to the tribune and said 1
19 The tribune took him by the hand 1
22 the tribune dismissed the young man 1
24:22 When Lys'ias the tribune comes down 1

military tribune 1. *χιλίαρχος*
Act 25:23 they entered . . with the military tribunes 1

tributary 1. *φόρος*
1Mc 1: 4 they became tributary to him. 1

tribute 1. כֶּסֶף 2. מֶכֶס 3. מִנְחָה 4. מַס 5. מִשָּׂה 6. מַשָּׂא 7. עֹנֶשׁ 8. מִנְדָּה (A) 9. *ἄφεμα* 10. *κῆνσος* 11. *φορά* 12. *φορολογία* 13. *φόρος*
Num31:28 levy for the LORD a tribute from the men of war 2
37 the LORD'S tribute of sheep was 675. 2
38 36,000, of which the LORD'S tribute was 72. 2
39 30,500, of which the LORD'S tribute was 61. 2
40 16,000, of which the LORD'S tribute was 32 2
41 Moses gave the tribute . . to Elea'zar the priest 2
Deu 16:10 keep . . with the tribute of a freewill offering 5
Jdg 3:15 The people of Israel sent tribute by him to Eglon 3
17 he presented the tribute to Eglon king of Moab. 3
18 when Ehud had finished presenting the tribute 3
18 sent away the people that carried the tribute. 3
2Sm 8: 2 the Moabites became . . and brought tribute. 3
6 the Syrians . . brought tribute. 3
1Kg 4:21 they brought tribute and served Solomon all 3
2Kg 17: 3 Hoshe'a became his vassal, and paid him tribute. 3
4 and offered no tribute to the king of Assyria 3
23:33 laid upon the land a tribute of 100 talents of silver 7
1Ch 18: 2 the Mo'abites . . brought tribute. 3
6 became servants to David, and brought tribute. 3
2Ch 17: 5 all Judah brought tribute to Jehosh'aphat; 3
11 Philistines brought . . silver for tribute; 3
26: 8 The Ammonites paid tribute to Uzzi'ah 3
28:21 Ahaz . . gave tribute to the king of Assyria; •
Ezr 4:13 not pay tribute, custom, or toll 8
20 to whom tribute, custom, and toll were paid. 8
6: 8 tribute of the province from Beyond the River. 8
7:24 not be lawful to impose tribute, custom, or toll 8
Est 10: 1 King Ahasu-e'rus laid tribute on the land 4
Ps 68:30 Trample under foot those who lust after tribute; 1
72:10 of Tarshish and of the isles render him tribute 3
Isa 33:18 where is he who weighed the tribute? •
Dan 11:20 one who shall send an exactor of tribute 6
Hos 10: 6 carried to Assyria, as tribute to the great king. 3
Mat 17:25 take toll or tribute 10
Lke 20:22 Is it lawful for us to give tribute to Caesar 13
23: 2 forbidding us to give tribute to Caesar 13
1Es 2:19 they will not only refuse to pay tribute 12
6:29 out of the tribute of Coelesyria and Phoenicia 12
8:22 no tribute or any other tax 12
1Mc 8: 4 the rest paid them tribute every year. 13
7 decreed that he . . should pay a heavy tribute 13
10:29 and exempt all the Jews from payment of tribute 11
13:37 to grant you release from tribute. 9
2Mc 8:10 to make up for the king the tribute due to the Romans 13
36 had undertaken to secure tribute for the Romans 13
tribute *See also* collector, exact, free, lay, levy, money, pay.

without tribute 1. *ἀφορολόγητος*
1Es 4:50 should be theirs without tribute 1

trick 1. *ἀθετέω* 2. *ἀπατάω* 3. *ἐμπαίζω*
Mat 2:16 Then Herod, when he saw that he had been tricked 3
Jdt 13:16 was my face that tricked him to his destruction 2
14:18 The slaves have tricked us! 1

trick out 1. exorno
2Es 15:54 Trick out the beauty of your face! 1

trickery 1. *δόλος* 2. *παραλογισμός*
AEs 16: 6 the false trickery of their evil natures 2
1Mc 11: 1 tried to get possession . . by trickery 1

trickle 1. בְּכִי
Job 28:11 binds up the streams so that they do not trickle 1

trifle 1. דָּבָר רֵיק 2. לֹא הוֹן 3. *διάφορος*
Deu 32:47 For it is no trifle for you, but it is your life 1
Ps 44:12 Thou hast sold thy people for a trifle 2
Sir 27: 1 Many have committed sin for a trifle 3

trigon 1. שַׂבְּכָא (A)
Dan 3: 5 hear the sound of the horn, pipe, lyre, trigon 1
7 heard the sound of the horn, pipe, lyre, trigon 1
10 hears the sound of the horn, pipe, lyre, trigon 1
15 hear the sound of the horn, pipe, lyre, trigon 1

trim 1. כסם 2. עשה 3. *κοσμέω*
2Sm 19:24 neither dressed his feet, nor trimmed his beard 2
Ezk 44:20 they shall only trim the hair of their heads. 1
Mat 25: 7 trimmed their lamps. 3

trip 1. *σκανδαλίζω* 2. *ὑποσχάζω*
Sir 12:17 he will trip you by the heel; 2
23: 8 the reviler and the arrogant are tripped by them. 1

trip up 1. דחה
Ps 140: 4 violent men, who have planned to trip up my feet. 1

trireme 1. *τριήρης*
2Mc 4:20 it was applied to the construction of triremes. 1

triumph 1. גאה 2. גַּאֲוָה 3. גדל 4. יְשׁוּעָה 5. עלץ 6. צדק 7. צְדָקָה 8. צלח 9. רום 10. רוע 11. *δοξάζω* 12. *εὐημερέω*
Exd 15: 1 to the LORD, for he has triumphed gloriously; 1
21 Sing to the LORD, for he has triumphed gloriously; 1
Deu 33:29 LORD, the shield . . and the sword of your triumph! 2
Jdg 5:11 there they repeat the triumphs of the LORD 7
11 LORD, the triumphs of his peasantry in Israel. 7
2Sm 22:51 Great triumphs he gives to his king 4
1Kg 22:12 Go up to Ramoth-gilead and triumph; 8
15 Go up and triumph; the LORD will give it 8
2Ch 18:11 Go up to Ramoth-gilead and triumph; 8
14 And he answered, "Go up and triumph; 8
Job 17: 4 therefore thou wilt not let them triumph. 9
Ps 18:50 Great triumphs he gives to his king 4
41:11 in that my enemy has not triumphed over me. 10
54: 7 my eye has looked in triumph on my enemies. •
59:10 my God will let me look in triumph on my enemies. •
118: 7 I shall look in triumph on those who hate me. •
Prv 28:12 When the righteous triumph, there is great glory; 5
Isa 45:25 the offspring of Israel shall triumph and glory. 6
Lam 1: 9 O LORD, behold . . for the enemy has triumphed! 3
2Th 3: 1 the word of the Lord may speed on and triumph 11
2Mc 13:16 withdrew in triumph. 12
triumph *See also* lead, march, shout.

triumph over 1. *θριαμβεύω* 2. *κατακαυχάομαι*
Col 2:15 triumphing over them in him. 1
Jas 2:13 yet mercy triumphs over judgment. 2

triumphant 1. צַדִּיק 2. רום
Deu 32:27 Our hand is triumphant, the LORD has not wrought 2
Zec 9: 9 triumphant and victorious is he 1

triumphantly 1. בְּיָד רָמָה
Num33: 3 Israel went out triumphantly in the sight of all 1

trivial 1. *ἐλαχύς*
1Co 6: 2 are you incompetent to try trivial cases? 1

troop 1. אֲגַף 2. גדד 3. גְּדוּד 4. הָמוֹן 5. מַחֲנֶה 6. עַם 7. צָבָא 8. *ἀνήρ* 9. *ἀνήρ πολεμιστής* 10. *δύναμις* 11. *ἴλη* 12. *ὄχλος* 13. *παρεμβολή* 14. *πλῆθος* 15. *στράτευμα* 16. *σύνταξις*
Jos 11: 4 they came out, with all their troops, a great host 5
Jdg 4: 7 river Kishon with his chariots and his troops; 4
1Sm 4: 3 when the troops came . . the elders of Israel said 6
13: 5 and troops like the sand on the seashore 6
2Sm 18:16 and the troops came back from pursuing Israel; 6
22:30 Yea, by thee I can crush a troop 3
1Kg 16:15 Now the troops were encamped against Gib'bethon 6
16 the troops who were encamped heard it said 6
1Ch 12:18 David . . made them officers of his troops. 3
24 bearing shield and spear were 6,800 armed troops 7
2Ch 13:13 thus his troops were in front of Judah •
Job 19:12 His troops come on together; 3
29:25 as chief, and I dwelt like a king among his troops 3
Ps 18:29 Yea, by thee I can crush a troop; 3
Jer 5: 7 and trooped to the houses of harlots. 2
Ezk 12:14 round about him, his helpers and all his troops; 1
17:21 all the pick of his troops shall fall by the sword 1
Dan 11:15 shall not stand, or even his picked troops 6
Nah 3:13 Behold, your troops are women in your midst. 6
Mat 22: 7 sent his troops and destroyed those murderers 15
Rev 9:16 The number of the troops of cavalry was twice 15
Jdt 1:16 a vast body of troops 9
2: 7 and will hand them over to be plundered by my troops •
15 mustered the picked troops by divisions 8
1Mc 2:31 the troops in Jerusalem the city of David 10
3:34 he turned over to Lysias half of his troops 10
37 the king took the remaining half of his troops 10
4:31 let them be ashamed of their troops 10
35 when Lysias saw the rout of his troops 16
6:33 his troops made ready for battle 10
40 some troops were on the plain •
9:52 in them he put troops and stores of food. 10
10: 6 Demetrius gave him authority to recruit troops 10
8 had given him authority to recruit troops. 10
21 he recruited troops 10
11:18 his troops in the strongholds were killed •
38 he dismissed all his troops 10
38 except the foreign troops 10
38 So all the troops . . hated him. 10
39 the troops were murmuring against Demetrius. 10
40 the hatred which the troops of Demetrius had 10
41 he remove the troops of the citadel from Jerusalem •
41 that he remove . . the troops in the strongholds •
43 all my troops have revolted. 10
55 All the troops that Demetrius had cast off 10
12:43 commanded his friends and his troops to obey him 10
45 the other strongholds and the remaining troops 10
46 he sent away the troops 10
49 Trypho sent troops and cavalry into Galilee 10
13:43 surrounded it with troops 13
15: 3 and have recruited a host of mercenary troops 10
10 All the troops rallied to him 10
12 his troops had deserted him. 10
38 gave him troops of infantry and cavalry. 10
41 stationed there horsemen and troops 10
16:18 asking him to send troops to aid him 10
2Mc 4:29 Crates, the commander of the Cyprian troops. •
5: 3 troops of horsemen drawn up 11
5 the troops upon the wall had been forced back •
14:41 When the troops were about to capture the tower 14
3Mc 1: 4 went to the troops with wailing and tears 10
2: 7 pursued them with chariots and a mass of troops 12

armed troop 1. צָבָא
1Ch 12:23 divisions of the armed troops, who came to David 1

foreign troop 1. עֵרֶב
Jer 50:37 and upon all the foreign troops in her midst 1

large troop 1. *πλῆθος*
1Mc 10:77 he had a large troop of cavalry 1

troop of infantry 1. *πεζός*
Jdt 2:19 horsemen and picked troops of infantry. 1

seasoned troop 1. יצא צָבָא
1Ch 12:33 Of Zeb'ulun 50,000 seasoned troops 1
36 Of Asher 40,000 seasoned troops ready for battle. 1

trophy of victory 1. *τρόπαιον*
2Mc 5: 6 he was setting up trophies of victory 1
troth *See* plight.

trouble 1. אָוֶן 2. בהל 3. בַּצָּרָה 4. דְּאָגָה 5. דלח 6. המם 7. זעף 8. חֲרָדָה 9. יַד צַר 10. כעס 11. מְהוּמָה 12. עכר 13. עָמָל 14. עַצֶּבֶת 15. פעם 16. צוק 17. צַר 18. צָרָה 19. צרר 20. רֹגֶז 21. רַע 22. רָעָה 23. רעע בְּעֵינַיִם 24. שִׂיחַ 25. *ἀδημονέω* 26. *ἐνοχλέω* 27. *ἐπιλυπέω* 28. *ἐπιταράσσω* 29. *θλῖψις* 30. *θορυβάζω* 31. *θορυβέω* 32. *κακία* 33. *κακός* 34. *κόπος* 35. *κόπους παρέχω* 36. *ὀχλέω* 37. *παρενοχλέω* 38. *πόνος* 39. *πρᾶγμα* 40. *σκύλλω* 41. *συγχέω* 42. *σύμπτωμα* 43. *ταράσσω* 44. *ταραχή* 45. casus 46. commoveo 47. conturbo 48. labor 49. laboro 50. turbo
Gen 21:17 said to her, "What troubles you, Hagar? Fear not; •
40: 6 in the morning and saw them, they were troubled. 7
41: 8 in the morning his spirit was troubled; 15
Num23:21 nor has he seen trouble in Israel. 13
33:55 shall trouble you in the land where you dwell. 19
Deu 31:17 many evils and troubles will come upon them 18
21 when many evils and troubles have come upon them 18
Jdg 11: 7 have you come to me now when you are in trouble? 17
1Sm 14:29 Jonathan said, "My father has troubled the land; 12
2Sm 11:25 Do not let this matter trouble you 23
14: 5 And the king said to her, "What is your trouble? •

20: 6 lest he get . . cities, and cause us trouble. ‡
1Kg 18:18 I have not troubled Israel; but you have 12
20: 7 Mark now, and see how this man is seeking trouble; 22
2Kg 4:13 See, you have taken all this trouble for us; 8
6:28 And the king asked her, "What is your trouble? *
33 This trouble is from the LORD! Why should I wait 22
14:10 why should you provoke trouble so that you fall 22
2Ch 15: 6 God troubled them with every sort of distress. 6
25:19 why should you provoke trouble so that you fall 22
Neh 1: 3 escaped exile are in great trouble and shame; 22
2:17 You see the trouble we are in, how Jerusalem lies 22
Job 3:10 nor hide trouble from my eyes. 13
17 There the wicked cease from troubling 20
26 I have no rest; but trouble comes. 20
4: 8 who plow iniquity and sow trouble reap the same. 13
5: 6 nor does trouble sprout from the ground; 1
7 man is born to trouble as the sparks fly upward. 13
19 He will deliver you from six troubles; 18
14: 1 born of a woman is of few days, and full of trouble. 20
27: 9 Will God hear his cry, when trouble comes upon him? 18
38:23 which I have reserved for the time of trouble 17
Ps 6: 2 O LORD, heal me, for my bones are troubled. 2
3 My soul also is sorely troubled. 2
10 my enemies shall be ashamed and sorely troubled; 2
9: 9 The LORD is . . a stronghold in times of trouble. 3
10: 1 Why dost thou hide thyself in times of trouble? 3
14 yea, thou dost note trouble and vexation 13
20: 1 The LORD answer you in the day of trouble! 18
22:11 Be not far from me, for trouble is near 18
25:17 Relieve the troubles of my heart 18
18 Consider my affliction and my trouble 13
22 Redeem Israel, O God, out of all his troubles. 18
27: 5 will hide me in his shelter in the day of trouble; 22
32: 7 thou preservest me from trouble; 17
34: 6 heard him, and saved him out of all his troubles. 18
17 and delivers them out of all their troubles. 18
37:39 he is their refuge in the time of trouble. 18
41: 1 The LORD delivers him in the day of trouble; 22
46: 1 God . . a very present help in trouble. 18
49: 5 Why should I fear in times of trouble 21
50:15 call upon me in the day of trouble; 18
54: 7 For thou hast delivered me from every trouble 18
55: 2 I am overcome by my trouble. I am distraught 24
3 they bring trouble upon me 1
10 mischief and trouble are within it 1
66:14 my mouth promised when I was in trouble. 17
71:20 Thou who hast made me see many sore troubles 18
73: 5 They are not in trouble as other men are; 13
77: 2 In the day of my trouble I seek the Lord; 18
4 I am so troubled that I cannot speak. 15
86: 7 In the day of my trouble I call on thee 18
88: 3 For my soul is full of troubles 22
90:10 yet their span is but toil and trouble; 1
91:15 I will be with him in trouble, I will rescue 18
94:13 to give him respite from days of trouble 21
107: 2 whom he has redeemed from trouble 9
6 Then they cried to the LORD in their trouble 17
13 Then they cried to the LORD in their trouble 17
19 Then they cried to the LORD in their trouble 17
28 Then they cried to the LORD in their trouble 17
39 low through oppression, trouble, and sorrow 22
119:143 Trouble and anguish have come upon me 17
138: 7 Though I walk in the midst of trouble 18
142: 2 complaint before him, I tell my trouble before 18
143:11 In thy righteousness bring me out of trouble! 18
Prv 10:10 He who winks the eye causes trouble 14
11: 8 The righteous is delivered from trouble 18
29 He who troubles his household will inherit wind 12
12:13 but the righteous escapes from trouble. 18
21 but the wicked are filled with trouble. 1
13:17 A bad messenger plunges men into trouble 21
15: 6 but trouble befalls the income of the wicked. 12
16 Better . . than great treasure and trouble with it. 11
16: 4 even the wicked for the day of trouble. 22
21:23 keeps his mouth . . keeps himself out of trouble. 18
25:19 Trust in a faithless man in time of trouble 18
27: 9 but the soul is torn by trouble. 42
Ecc 8: 6 although man's trouble lies heavy upon him. 22
Isa 30: 6 Through a land of trouble and anguish 18
33: 2 Be . . our salvation in the time of trouble. 18
46: 7 it does not answer or save him from his trouble. 18
65:16 because the former troubles are forgotten 18
Jer 2:27 But in the time of their trouble they say 22
28 if they can save you, in your time of trouble; 22
11:12 cannot save them in the time of their trouble. 22
14 when they call to me in the time of their trouble. 22
14: 8 thou hope of Israel, its savior in time of trouble 18
15:11 in the time of trouble and in the time of distress! 22
16:19 my stronghold, my refuge in the day of trouble 18
49:23 they melt in fear, they are troubled like the sea 4
51: 2 from every side on the day of trouble. 22
Lam 1:21 All my enemies have heard of my trouble; 22
Ezk 32: 2 trouble the waters with your feet 5
9 I will trouble the hearts of many peoples 10
13 no foot of man shall trouble them any more 5
13 nor shall the hoofs of beasts trouble them. 5
Dan 2: 1 spirit was troubled, and his sleep left him. 15
3 spirit is troubled to know the dream. 15
9:25 built again . . but in a troubled time. 16
12: 1 there shall be a time of trouble, 18
Nah 1: 7 LORD is good, a stronghold in the day of trouble; 18
Hab 1: 3 make me see wrongs and look upon trouble? 1
3:16 I will quietly wait for the day of trouble to come 18
Mat 2: 3 When Herod the king heard this, he was troubled 43
6:34 Let the day's own trouble be sufficient 32
26:10 Why do you trouble the woman? 35
37 he began to be sorrowful and troubled. 25
Mrk 5:35 Why trouble the Teacher any further? 40
14: 6 Jesus said, "Let her alone; why do you trouble her? 35
33 and began to be greatly distressed and troubled. 25
Lke 1:12 Zechari'ah was troubled when he saw him 43
6:18 those who were troubled with unclean spirits 26
7: 6 Lord, do not trouble yourself, for I am not worthy 40
8:49 do not trouble the Teacher any more. 40
10:41 you are anxious and troubled about many things; 30
24:38 he said to them, "Why are you troubled 43
Joh 5: 7 when the water is troubled 43
11:33 he was deeply moved in spirit and troubled; 43
12:27 Now is my soul troubled. And what shall I say? 43
13:21 he was troubled in spirit, and testified 43
14: 1 Let not your hearts be troubled; believe in God 43
27 Let not your hearts be troubled 43
Act 15:19 not trouble those of the Gentiles who turn to God 37
24 some persons from us have troubled you with words 43
1Co 7:28 Yet those who marry will have worldly troubles 29
Gal 1: 7 there are some who trouble you 43
5:10 he who is troubling you will bear his judgment 43
6:17 Henceforth let no man trouble me 35
Php 4:14 Yet it was kind of you to share my trouble. 29
1Pe 3:14 Have no fear of them, nor be troubled 43
1Es 2:22 troubling both kings and other cities 26
2Es 3: 1 I was troubled as I lay on my bed 47
18 and trouble the times. 47
5: 5 the peoples shall be troubled 46
14 and my soul was so troubled that it fainted. 49
6:36 my heart was troubled within me again 50
8:16 about the seed of Jacob, for whom I am troubled. 47
9:27 my heart was troubled again as it was before. 50
10:15 the troubles that have come upon you. 45
20 be persuaded because of the troubles of Zion 45
24 a relief from your troubles. 48
31 And why are you troubled? 47
31 And why are . . the thoughts of your mind troubled? 47
15: 3 do not be troubled by the unbelief of those 47
16:12 its waves and the fish also shall be troubled 50
Tob 6: 7 that person will never be troubled again. 36
AEs 11: 9 the whole righteous nation was troubled 43
Wis 10: 9 Wisdom rescued from troubles 38
16: 6 they were troubled for a little while as a warning 43
Sir 3:27 A stubborn mind will be burdened by troubles 38
4: 3 Do not add to the troubles of an angry mind *
6: 8 will not stand by you in your day of trouble. 29
10 will not stand by you in your day of trouble. 29
22:13 guard yourself from him to escape trouble 34
29: 4 cause trouble to those who help them. 34
30: 7 his feelings will be troubled at every cry. 43
37: 4 in time of trouble are against him. 29
40: 5 there is anger and envy and trouble and unrest 44
6 he is troubled by the visions of his mind 31
24 Brothers and help are for a time of trouble 29
Aza 1:27 did not touch them at all or hurt or trouble them. 37
1Mc 2:43 all who became fugitives to escape their troubles 33
3: 5 he burned those who troubled his people. 43
7:22 all who were troubling their people joined him. 43
10:15 the troubles that they had endured. 34
15:12 for he knew that troubles had converged upon him 33
2Mc 4:31 the king went hastily to settle the trouble 39
8:32 one who had greatly troubled the Jews. 27
9:24 the people . . would not be troubled 28
13: 4 this man was to blame for all the trouble 33
14:28 he was troubled and grieved 41
3Mc 1:27 to defend them in the present trouble *

trouble *See also* bring, cause, give, make, take.

cause trouble 1. *ἐνοχλέω*

Heb 12:15 root of bitterness" spring up and cause trouble 1

greatly trouble 1. סער 2. *διαταράσσω* 3. *ἐκταράσσω*

2Kg 6:11 the king . . was greatly troubled because of this 1
Lke 1:29 she was greatly troubled at the saying 2
Wis 18:17 at once apparitions . . greatly troubled them 3

out of trouble 1. *ἀμέριμνος*

Mat 28:14 we will satisfy him and keep you out of trouble. 1

sorely trouble 1. קָשַׁת רוּחַ

1Sm 1:15 No, my lord, I am a woman sorely troubled; 1

troubler 1. עכר

1Kg 18:17 Ahab said to him, "Is it you, you troubler of Israel? 1
1Ch 2: 7 The sons of Carmi: Achar, the troubler of Israel 1

trough 1. רַהַט 2. שֹׁקֶת

Gen 24:20 she quickly emptied her jar into the trough 2
Exd 2:16 drew water, and filled the troughs to water 1

kneading trough 1. מִשְׁאֶרֶת

Deu 28: 5 Blessed . . basket and your kneading-trough. 1
17 Cursed . . basket and your kneading-trough. 1

watering trough 1. שֹׁקֶת

Gen 30:38 the watering troughs, where the flocks came 1

true 1. אמן 2. אָמְנָם 3. אֱמֶת 4. יָשָׁר 5. כֵּן 6. נעם 7. צֶדֶק 8. שֶׁקֶר 9. יַצִּיב (A) 10. צְדָא (A) 11. *ἀγαθός* 12. *ἀλήθεια* 13. *ἀληθεύω* 14. *ἀληθής* 15. *ἀληθινός* 16. *ἀρά* 17. *γνήσιος* 18. *ἐμμένω* 19. *καλῶς* 20. verus

Deu 13:14 behold, if it be true and certain that 3
17: 4 if it is true and certain that such an abominable 3
22:20 if the thing is true, that the tokens of virginity 3
Jos 2: 4 True, men came to me, but I did not know where 5
Rut 3:12 And now it is true that I am a near kinsman 2
2Sm 7:28 O Lord GOD, thou art God, and thy words are true 3
20:21 That is not true. 5
1Kg 10: 6 The report was true which I heard in my own land 3
2Kg 9:12 they said, "That is not true; tell us now. 8
10:15 Is your heart true to my heart as mine is to yours? 4
2Ch 9: 5 The report was true which I heard in my own land 3
15: 3 For a long time Israel was without the true God 3
Neh 9:13 give them right ordinances and true laws 3
Job 5:27 Lo, this we have searched out; it is true. 5
19: 4 even if it be true that I have erred 2
Ps 19: 9 the ordinances of the LORD are true, and righteous 3
78:37 they were not true to his covenant. 1
119:142 righteous for ever, and thy law is true. 3
151 O LORD, and all thy commandments are true. 3
141: 6 then . . learn that the word of the LORD is true. 6
Prv 22:21 to show you what is right and true 3
21 that you may give a true answer to those who sent 3
Isa 43: 9 and let them hear and say, It is true. 3
Jer 10:10 the LORD is the true God; he is the living God 3
42: 5 May the LORD be a true and faithful witness 3
50: 7 sinned against the LORD, their true habitation 7
Ezk 18: 8 executes true justice between man and man 3
Dan 3:14 Is it true, O Shadrach, Meshach, and Abed'nego 10
24 counselors . . answered the king, "True, O king. 9
8:26 vision . . which has been told is true; 3
10: 1 word was true, and it was a great conflict. 3
Zec 7: 9 says the LORD of hosts, Render true judgments 3
8:16 judgments that are true and make for peace 3
Mal 2: 6 True instruction was in his mouth 3
Mat 22:16 Teacher, we know that you are true 14
Mrk 12:14 we know that you are true, and care for no man 14
Lke 16:11 who will entrust to you the true riches? 15
Joh 1: 9 The true light that enlightens every man 15
3:21 But he who does what is true comes to the light 12
33 sets his seal to this, that God is true. 14
4:23 true worshipers will worship the Father 15
37 For here the saying holds true, 'One sows 15
5:31 my testimony is not true; 14
32 the testimony which he bears to me is true. 14
6:32 my Father gives you the true bread from heaven. 15
7:18 he who seeks the glory of him who sent him is true 14
28 he who sent me is true, and him you do not know. 15
8:13 your testimony is not true. 14
14 my testimony is true, for I know whence I have come 14
16 Yet even if I do judge, my judgment is true 15
17 the testimony of two men is true; 14
26 he who sent me is true 14
10:41 everything . . John said about this man was true 14
15: 1 I am the true vine 15
17: 3 they know thee the only true God 15
19:35 his testimony is true 15
21:24 we know that his testimony is true. 14
Rom 2:28 nor is true circumcision something external *
3: 4 Let God be true though every man be false 14
11:20 That is true. They were broken off 19
1Co 15:15 whom he did not raise if it is true 16
2Co 6: 8 We are treated as impostors, and yet are true; 14
7:14 just as everything we said to you was true 12
14 so our boasting before Titus has proved true. 12
12:12 The signs of a true apostle were performed among you *
Eph 4:24 in true righteousness and holiness. 12
5: 9 found in all that is good and right and true 12
Php 3: 3 For we are the true circumcision *
4: 3 I ask you also, true yokefellow, help these women 17
8 Finally, brethren, whatever is true 14
1Th 1: 9 to serve a living and true God 15
1Ti 1: 2 To Timothy, my true child in the faith 17
Tit 1: 4 To Titus, my true child in a common faith 17
13 This testimony is true 14
2:10 nor to pilfer, but to show entire and true fidelity 11
Heb 8: 2 a minister in the sanctuary and the true tent 15
9:24 a copy of the true one 15
10:22 let us draw near with a true heart 15
1Pe 5:12 and declaring that this is the true grace of God; 14
2Pe 2:22 It has happened to them according to the true proverb 14
1Jn 2: 8 a new commandment, which is true in him and in you 14
8 and the true light is already shining. 15
27 anointing teaches . . and is true, and is no lie 14
5:20 given us understanding, to know him who is true; 15
20 we are in him who is true, in his Son Jesus Christ. 15
20 This is the true God and eternal life. 15
3Jn 1:12 and you know my testimony is true. 14

Rev 3:14 words of the Amen, the faithful and true witness 15
6:10 O Sovereign Lord, holy and true, how long before 15
15: 3 Just and true are thy ways, O King of the ages! 15
16: 7 Lord God . . true and just are thy judgments! 15
19: 2 for his judgments are true and just; 15
9 And he said to me, "These are true words of God. 15
11 He who sat upon it is called Faithful and True 15
21: 5 for these words are trustworthy and true. 15
22: 6 These words are trustworthy and true. 15
1Es 8:89 O Lord of Israel, thou art true 15
2Es 15: 2 for they are trustworthy and true. 20
Tob 3: 2 thou dost render true and righteous judgment for ever 15
5 are true in exacting penalty from me for my sins 15
4: 6 For if you do what is true 12
7:10 let me explain the true situation to you. 12
13: 6 to do what is true before him 12
Jdt 8:28 has been spoken out of a true heart 11
10:13 to give him a true report 12
11:10 keep it in your mind, for it is true 14
Wis 1: 6 a true observer of his heart 14
2:17 Let us see if his words are true 14
12:27 they saw and recognized as the true God 14
15: 1 thou, our God, art kind and true 14
Sir 28: 6 remember . . and be true to the commandments. 18
32:16 Those who fear the Lord will form true judgments •
34: 4 from something false what will be true? 13
Aza 1: 4 all thy works are true and thy ways right 15
5 Thou hast executed true judgments 12
8 thou hast done in true judgment. 15
3Mc 2:11 indeed you are faithful and true. 15
6:18 the most glorious, almighty, and true God 15
4Mc 6: 5 the courageous and noble man, as a true Eleazar 14
15: 4 Especially is this true of mothers •
17: 6 children were true descendants of father Abraham. •

true *See also* aim, come, form, hold, loyalty, prove.

true one 1. ἀληθινός

Rev 3: 7 the holy one, the true one, who has the key of David 1

wholly true 1. שָׁלֵם

1Kg 8:61 Let your heart . . be wholly true to the LORD 1
11: 4 his heart was not wholly true to the LORD his God 1
15: 3 his heart was not wholly true to the LORD his God 1
14 the heart of Asa was wholly true to the LORD 1

truly 1. אוּלָם 2. אַךְ 3. אָכֵן 4. אָמְנָם 5. אֱמֶת 6. אַף 7. בֶּאֱמֶת 8. כִּי 9. כִּי אִם 10. עַל כֵּן 11. מִן קְשֹׁט דִּי (A) 12. ἀληθής 13. ἀληθινός 14. ἀληθῶς 15. ἀμήν 16. ἐπ᾽ ἀληθείας 17. κατὰ ἀλήθειαν

Gen 4:24 truly Lamech seventy-sevenfold. •
24:49 if you will deal loyally and truly with my master 5
33:10 for truly to see your face is like seeing the face 10
47:29 and promise to deal loyally and truly with me. 5
Num14:21 truly, as I live, and as all the earth shall be 1
Jos 2:24 Truly the LORD has given all the land into our 8
1Sm 20: 3 But truly, as the LORD lives . . there is but a step 1
25:34 truly by morning there had not been left . . one 9
Job 9: 2 Truly I know that it is so: but how can a man be just 4
36: 4 For truly my words are not false; 4
Ps 49: 7 Truly no man can ransom himself †
66:19 But truly God has listened; he has given heed 3
73: 1 Truly God is good to the upright 2
18 Truly thou dost set them in slippery places; 2
Sng 1:16 you are beautiful, my beloved, truly lovely. 6
Isa 45:15 Truly, thou art a God who hidest thyself 3
Jer 3:23 Truly the hills are a delusion 3
23 Truly in the LORD our God is the salvation 3
7: 5 For if you truly amend your ways and your doings †
5 if you truly execute justice one with another †
10:19 But I said, "Truly this is an affliction 2
28: 9 then it will be known that the LORD has truly sent 7
Dan 2:47 Truly, your God is God of gods and Lord of kings 11
Mat 5:18 For truly, I say to you, till heaven and earth pass 15
26 truly, I say to you, you will never get out till you 15
6: 2 that they may be praised by men. Truly, I say to you 15
5 that they may be seen by men. Truly, I say to you 15
16 may be seen by men. Truly, I say to you, they have 15
8:10 Truly, I say to you, not even in Israel have I found 15
10:15 Truly, I say to you, it shall be more tolerable 15
23 for truly, I say to you, you will not have gone 15
42 truly, I say to you, he shall not lose his reward. 15
11:11 Truly, I say to you, among those born of women 15
13:17 Truly, I say to you 15
14:33 Truly you are the Son of God. 14
16:28 Truly, I say to you, there are some standing here 15
17:20 For truly I say to you, if you have faith as a grain 15
18: 3 said, "Truly, I say to you 15
13 if he finds it, truly, I say to you, he rejoices 15
18 Truly, I say to you, whatever you bind on earth 15
19:23 Jesus said to his disciples, "Truly, I say to you 15
28 Jesus said to them, "Truly, I say to you 15
21:21 Jesus answered them, "Truly, I say to you 15
31 Truly, I say to you 15
23:36 Truly, I say to you 15
24: 2 Truly, I say to you 15
34 Truly, I say to you 15
47 Truly, I say to you 15
25:12 he replied, 'Truly, I say to you, I do not know you.' 15
40 the King will answer them, 'Truly, I say to you 15
45 Then he will answer them, 'Truly, I say to you 15
26:13 Truly, I say to you 15
21 as they were eating, he said, "Truly, I say to you 15
34 Jesus said to him, "Truly, I say to you 15
27:54 Truly this was the Son of God! 14
Mrk 3:28 Truly, I say to you, all sins will be forgiven 15
8:12 Truly, I say to you, no sign shall be given 15
9: 1 he said to them, "Truly, I say to you 15
41 For truly, I say to you, whoever gives you a cup 15
10:15 Truly, I say to you, whoever does not receive 15
29 Jesus said, "Truly, I say to you, there is no one 15
11:23 Truly, I say to you, whoever says to this mountain 15
12:14 truly teach the way of God 16
32 you have truly said that he is one 16
43 said to them, "Truly, I say to you 15
13:30 Truly, I say to you, this generation will not pass 15
14: 9 truly, I say to you, wherever the gospel 15
18 Truly, I say to you, one of you will betray me 15
25 Truly, I say to you, I shall not drink again 15
30 Jesus said to him, "Truly, I say to you 15
15:39 he said, "Truly this man was the Son of God! 14
Lke 4:24 he said, "Truly, I say to you 15
9:27 I tell you truly, there are some standing here 14
12:37 truly, I say to you, he will gird himself 15
44 Truly, I say to you, he will set him over all 14
18:17 Truly, I say to you, whoever does not receive 15
29 he said to them, "Truly, I say to you, there is no man 15
20:21 truly teach the way of God. 16
21: 3 he said, "Truly I tell you 14
32 Truly, I say to you, this generation will not pass 15
23:43 he said to him, "Truly, I say to you 15
Joh 1:51 Truly, truly, I say to you, you will see heaven 15
51 truly, I say to you, you will see heaven opened 15
3: 3 Jesus answered him, "Truly, truly, I say to you 15
3 Jesus answered him, "Truly, truly, I say to you 15
5 Jesus answered, "Truly, truly, I say to you 15
5 Jesus answered, "Truly, truly, I say to you 15
11 Truly, truly, I say to you, we speak of what we know 15
11 Truly, truly, I say to you, we speak of what we know 15
4:18 this you said truly. 12
5:19 Jesus said to them, "Truly, truly, I say to you 15
19 Jesus said to them, "Truly, truly, I say to you 15
24 Truly, truly, I say to you 15
24 Truly, truly, I say to you 15
25 Truly, truly, I say to you, the hour is coming 15
25 Truly, truly, I say to you, the hour is coming 15
6:26 Jesus answered them, "Truly, truly, I say to you 15
26 Jesus answered them, "Truly, truly, I say to you 15
32 Jesus then said to them, "Truly, truly, I say to you 15
32 Jesus then said to them, "Truly, truly, I say to you 15
47 Truly, truly, I say to you 15
47 Truly, truly, I say to you 15
53 Jesus said to them, "Truly, truly, I say to you 15
53 Jesus said to them, "Truly, truly, I say to you 15
8:31 you are truly my disciples 14
34 Jesus answered them, "Truly, truly, I say to you 15
34 Jesus answered them, "Truly, truly, I say to you 15
51 Truly, truly, I say to you, if any one keeps my word 15
51 Truly, truly, I say to you, if any one keeps my word 15
58 Jesus said to them, "Truly, truly, I say to you 15
58 Jesus said to them, "Truly, truly, I say to you 15
10: 1 Truly, truly, I say to you 15
1 Truly, truly, I say to you 15
7 Jesus again said to them, "Truly, truly, I say to you 15
7 Jesus again said to them, "Truly, truly, I say to you 15
12:24 Truly, truly I say to you 15
24 Truly, truly I say to you 15
13:16 Truly, truly, I say to you, a servant is not greater 15
16 Truly, truly, I say to you, a servant is not greater 15
20 Truly, truly, I say to you, he who receives any one 15
20 Truly, truly, I say to you, he who receives any one 15
21 Truly, truly, I say to you, one of you will betray me. 15
21 Truly, truly, I say to you, one of you will betray me. 15
38 Truly, truly, I say to you, the cock will not crow 15
38 Truly, truly, I say to you, the cock will not crow 15
14:12 Truly, truly, I say to you 15
12 Truly, truly, I say to you 15
16:20 Truly, truly, I say to you 15
20 Truly, truly, I say to you 15
23 Truly, truly, I say to you 15
23 Truly, truly, I say to you 15
21:18 Truly, truly, I say to you 15
18 Truly, truly, I say to you 15
Act 4:27 truly in this city there were gathered together 16
10:34 Truly I perceive that God shows no partiality 16
1Jn 2: 5 in him truly love for God is perfected. 14
Sir 42: 8 Then you will be truly instructed 13
4Mc 5:18 Even if . . our law were not truly divine 17
11:23 enemy of those who are truly devout. 12
17:11 Truly the contest . . was divine 12

truly *See also* judge.

trumpet 1. חֲצֹצְרָה 2. יוֹבֵל 3. שׁוֹפָר 4. תָּקוֹעַ 5. תְּרוּעָה 6. σάλπιγξ 7. tuba

Exd 19:13 When the trumpet sounds a long blast 2
16 a very loud trumpet blast, so that all 3
19 as the sound of the trumpet grew louder 3
20:18 sound of the trumpet and the mountain smoking 3
Lev 25: 9 Then you shall send abroad the loud trumpet 3
9 send abroad the trumpet throughout all 3
Num10: 2 Make two silver trumpets; of hammered work 1
8 sons of Aaron . . shall blow the trumpets. 1
8 trumpets shall be to you for a perpetual statute •
9 then you shall sound an alarm with the trumpets 1
10 blow the trumpets over your burnt offerings 1
29: 1 It is a day for you to blow the trumpets 5
31: 6 with . . the trumpets for the alarm in his hand. 1
Jos 6: 4 And seven priests shall bear seven trumpets 3
4 march . . the priests blowing the trumpets. 3
5 as soon as you hear the sound of the trumpet 3
6 and let seven priests bear seven trumpets 3
8 priests bearing the seven trumpets of rams' 3
8 priests . . went forward, blowing the trumpets 3
9 went before the priests who blew the trumpets 3
9 while the trumpets blew continually. 3
13 bearing the seven trumpets of rams' horns 3
13 priests . . passed on, blowing the trumpets 3
13 while the trumpets blew continually. 3
16 when the priests had blown the trumpets 3
20 the people shouted, and the trumpets were blown. 3
20 soon as the people heard the sound of the trumpet 3
Jdg 3:27 he sounded the trumpet in the hill country 3
6:34 of Gideon; and he sounded the trumpet 3
7: 8 he took the jars . . and their trumpets; 3
16 and put trumpets into the hands of all of them 3
18 When I blow the trumpet, I and all who are with me 3
18 When I blow . . then blow the trumpets also 3
19 and they blew the trumpets and smashed the jars 3
20 the three companies blew the trumpets and broke 3
20 and in their right hands the trumpets to blow; 3
22 When they blew the 300 trumpets 3
1Sm 13: 3 Saul blew the trumpet throughout all the land 3
2Sm 2:28 Jo'ab blew the trumpet; and all the men stopped 3
15:10 As soon as you hear the sound of the trumpet 3
18:16 Jo'ab blew the trumpet, and the troops came back 3
20: 1 and he blew the trumpet, and said, "We have no 3
22 So he blew the trumpet, and they dispersed 3
1Kg 1:34 anoint him king . . then blow the trumpet, and say 3
39 anointed Solomon. Then they blew the trumpet; 3
41 when Jo'ab heard the sound of the trumpet, he said 3
2Kg 9:13 and they blew the trumpet, and proclaimed 3
11:14 the people . . rejoicing and blowing trumpets. 1
12:13 basins . . snuffers, bowls, trumpets, or any 1
1Ch 13: 8 making merry . . with . . cymbals and trumpets. 1
15:24 should blow the trumpets before the ark of God. 1
28 the sound of the horn, trumpets, and cymbals 1
16: 6 to blow trumpets continually, before the ark 1
42 had trumpets and cymbals for the music 1
2Ch 5:13 song was raised, with trumpets and cymbals 1
13:12 his priests with their battle trumpets 1
14 the priests blew the trumpets. 1
15:14 took oath to the LORD . . with trumpets 1
20:28 to Jerusalem with harps and lyres and trumpets 1
23:13 all the people of the land . . blowing trumpets 1
29:26 and the priests with the trumpets. 1
27 song to the LORD began also, and the trumpets 1
Ezr 3:10 priests . . came forward with trumpets 1
Neh 4:18 The man who sounded the trumpet was beside me. 3
20 place where you hear the sound of the trumpet 3
12:35 certain of the priests' sons with trumpets 1
41 priests Eli'akim . . and Hanani'ah, with trumpets; 1
Job 39:24 he cannot stand still at the sound of the trumpet. 3
25 When the trumpet sounds, he says 'Aha!' 3
Ps 47: 5 the LORD with the sound of a trumpet. 3
81: 3 Blow the trumpet at the new moon, at the full moon 3
98: 6 With trumpets and the sound of the horn 1
150: 3 Praise him with trumpet sound; 3
Isa 18: 3 a signal . . look! When a trumpet is blown, hear! 3
27:13 in that day a great trumpet will be blown 3
58: 1 spare not, lift up your voice like a trumpet; 3
Jer 4: 5 and say, "Blow the trumpet through the land; 3
19 I hear the sound of the trumpet, the alarm of war. 3
21 and hear the sound of the trumpet? 3
6: 1 Blow the trumpet in Teko'a, and raise a signal 3
17 saying, 'Give heed to the sound of the trumpet!' 3
42:14 shall not see war, or hear the sound of the trumpet 3
51:27 on the earth, blow the trumpet among the nations; 3
Ezk 7:14 They have blown the trumpet and made all ready; 4
33: 3 and blows the trumpet and warns the people; 3
4 then if any one who hears the sound of the trumpet 3
5 He heard the sound of the trumpet 3
6 sees the sword . . and does not blow the trumpet 3
Hos 5: 8 Blow the horn in Gib'e-ah, the trumpet in Ramah. 1
8: 1 Set the trumpet to your lips 3
Jol 2: 1 Blow the trumpet in Zion; 3
15 Blow the trumpet in Zion; sanctify a fast; 3
Ams 2: 2 amid shouting and the sound of the trumpet; 3

3: 6 Is a trumpet blown in a city, and the people are not 3
Zec 9:14 the Lord GOD will sound the trumpet, and march 3
1Co 15:52 at the last trumpet. For the trumpet will sound 6
Heb 12:19 the sound of a trumpet 6
Rev 1:10 and I heard behind me a loud voice like a trumpet 6
4: 1 which I had heard speaking to me like a trumpet 6
8: 2 and seven trumpets were given to them. 6
6 Now the seven angels who had the seven trumpets 6
13 woe . . at the blasts of the other trumpets 6
9:14 saying to the sixth angel who had the trumpet 6
1Es 5:59 with musical instruments and trumpets 6
64 while many came with trumpets and a joyful noise 6
65 that the people could not hear the trumpets 6
66 find out what the sound of the trumpets meant. 6
2Es 6:23 the trumpet shall sound aloud 7
Sir 50:16 they sounded the trumpets of hammered work 6
1Mc 3:54 they sounded the trumpets and gave a loud shout. 6
4:40 and sounded the signal on the trumpets 6
5:31 with trumpets and loud shouts 6
33 who sounded their trumpets 6
6:33 and sounded their trumpets. 6
7:45 Jews . . kept sounding the battle call on the trumpets. 6
9:12 phalanx advanced to the sound of the trumpets 6
12 the men with Judas also blew their trumpets. 6
16: 8 they sounded the trumpets 6
2Mc 15:25 his men advanced with trumpets and battle songs; 6

trumpet *See also* blast, blow, call, sound.

trumpet sound 1. σαλπίζω
1Co 15:52 at the last trumpet. For the trumpet will sound 1

trumpeter 1. חצצר 2. חֲצֹצְרָה 3. σαλπιστής
2Kg 11:14 the captains and the trumpeters beside the king 2
2Ch 5:12 120 priests who were trumpeters; 1
13 it was the duty of the trumpeters and singers 1
23:13 captains and the trumpeters beside the king 2
29:28 singers sang, and the trumpeters sounded; 2
Rev 18:22 the sound . . of flute players and trumpeters 3

trunk 1. ῥάχις 2. στέλεχος
1Sm 5: 4 only the trunk of Dagon was left to him. 1
Sir 50:12 they surrounded him like the trunks of palm trees 2

trust 1. אמן 2. בטח 3. בֶּטַח 4. בִּטְחָה 5. כֶּסֶל 6. מִבְטָח 7. שָׁלוֹם 8. אמן (A) 9. רחץ (A) 10. ἐλπίζω 11. ἐμπιστεύω 12. ἐπέχω 13. παραδίδωμι 14. πείθω 15. πιστεύω 16. πίστις 17. credo 18. fides
Deu 28:52 your . . walls, in which you trusted, come down 2
Jdg 11:20 Sihon did not trust Israel to pass through his 1
20:36 they trusted to the men in ambush whom they had 2
1Sm 27:12 And A'chish trusted David, thinking 1
2Kg 18: 5 He trusted in the LORD the God of Israel; 2
1Ch 5:20 because they trusted in him. 2
Job 8:14 his trust is a spider's web. 6
12:20 He deprives of speech those who are trusted 1
15:31 Let him not trust in emptiness 1
18:14 He is torn from the tent in which he trusted 6
31:24 If I have made gold my trust 5
Ps 13: 5 I have trusted in thy steadfast love; 2
21: 7 For the king trusts in the LORD; 2
22: 4 In thee our fathers trusted; 2
4 they trusted, and thou didst deliver them. 2
5 in thee they trusted, and were not disappointed. 2
25: 2 O my God, in thee I trust, let me not be put to shame; 2
26: 1 I have trusted in the LORD without wavering. 2
28: 7 in him my heart trusts; so I am helped 2
31: 6 pay regard to vain idols; but I trust in the LORD. 2
14 I trust in thee, O LORD, I say, "Thou art my God. 2
32:10 love surrounds him who trusts in the LORD. 2
33:21 glad in him, because we trust in his holy name. 2
37: 3 Trust in the LORD, and do good; 2
5 your way to the LORD; trust in him, and he will act. 2
40: 4 Blessed is the man who makes the LORD his trust 6
41: 9 Even my bosom friend in whom I trusted 2
44: 6 not in my bow do I trust, nor can my sword save me. 2
49: 6 men who trust in their wealth 2
52: 7 but trusted in the abundance of his riches 2
8 I trust in the steadfast love of God for ever 2
55:23 But I will trust in thee. 2
56: 4 whose word I praise, in God I trust without a fear. 2
11 in God I trust without fear. What can man do to me? 2
62: 8 Trust in him at all times, O people; 2
71: 5 thou . . art my hope, my trust, O LORD, from my youth. 6
78:22 and did not trust his saving power. 2
84:12 O LORD of hosts, blessed is the man who trusts 2
86: 2 save thy servant who trusts in thee. 2
91: 2 My refuge and my fortress; my God, in whom I trust. 2
112: 7 his heart is firm, trusting in the LORD. 2
115: 8 who make them are like them; so are all who trust 2
9 O Israel, trust in the LORD! 2
11 You who fear the LORD, trust in the LORD! 2
119:42 for those who taunt me, for I trust in thy word. 2
125: 1 Those who trust in the LORD are like Mount Zion 2
135:18 Like them . . yea, every one who trusts in them! 2
Prv 3: 5 Trust in the LORD with all your heart 2
11:28 He who trusts in his riches will wither 2
16:20 happy is he who trusts in the LORD. 2
21:22 brings down the stronghold in which they trust. 6
22:19 That your trust may be in the LORD 6
25:19 Trust in a faithless man in time of trouble 6
28:25 but he who trusts in the LORD will be enriched. 2
26 He who trusts in his own mind is a fool; 2
29:25 but he who trusts in the LORD is safe. 2
31:11 The heart of her husband trusts in her 2
Isa 12: 2 I will trust, and will not be afraid; 2
26: 3 in perfect peace . . because he trusts in thee. 2
4 Trust in the LORD for ever 2
30:12 trust in oppression and perverseness 2
15 and in trust shall be your strength. 4
31: 1 who trust in chariots because they are many 2
32:17 the result . . quietness and trust for ever. 3
42:17 utterly put to shame, who trust in graven images 2
50:10 has no light, yet trusts in the name of the LORD 2
Jer 2:37 for the LORD has rejected those in whom you trust 6
5:17 your fortified cities in which you trust 2
7: 4 Do not trust in these deceptive words 2
8 Behold, you trust in deceptive words to no avail. 2
14 which is called by my name, and in which you trust 2
13:25 you have forgotten me and trusted in lies. 2
17: 5 says the LORD: "Cursed is the man who trusts in man 2
7 Blessed is the man who trusts in the LORD 2
7 who trusts in the LORD, whose trust is the LORD. 6
46:25 upon Pharaoh and those who trust in him. 2
48: 7 because you trusted in your strongholds 2
49: 4 daughter, who trusted in her treasures, saying 2
11 and let your widows trust in me. 2
Ezk 16:15 you trusted in your beauty, and played the harlot 2
33:13 yet if he trusts in his righteousness 2
Dan 3:28 delivered his servants, who trusted in him 9
6:23 because he had trusted in his God. 8
Hos 10:13 Because you have trusted in your chariots 2
Obd 1: 7 your trusted friends have set a trap under you 7
Hab 2:18 For the workman trusts in his own creation 2
Zep 3: 2 She does not trust in the LORD 2
Mat 27:43 He trusts in God; let God deliver him now 14
Lke 11:22 he takes away his armor in which he trusted 14
18: 9 to some who trusted in themselves 14
Joh 2:24 but Jesus did not trust himself to them 15
Rom 4: 5 but trusts him who justifies the ungodly 15
Php 2:24 I trust in the Lord 14
Heb 2:13 again, "I will put my trust in him. 14
1Pe 2:23 but he trusted to him who judges justly. 13
2Es 7:83 who have trusted the covenants of the Most High. 17
94 they kept the law which was given them in trust. 18
Jdt 9: 7 they trust in shield and spear, in bow and sling 10
Wis 3: 9 Those who trust in him will understand truth 14
13: 7 they trust in what they see 14
14: 5 therefore men trust their lives 15
29 for because they trust in lifeless idols 14
16:24 relaxes on behalf of those who trust in thee. 14
26 thy word preserves those who trust in thee. 15
18: 6 the oaths in which they trusted. 15
Sir 1:15 among their descendants she will be trusted. 11
2: 6 Trust in him, and he will help you 15
8 You who fear the Lord, trust in him 15
10 who ever trusted in the Lord and was put to shame? 11
13 Woe to the faint heart, for it has no trust! 15
4:17 will torment him . . until she trusts him 11
6: 7 do not trust him hastily. 11
7:26 do not trust yourself to one whom you detest. 11
11:21 trust in the Lord and keep at your toil 15
12:10 Never trust your enemy 15
13:11 nor trust his abundance of words 15
16: 3 Do not trust in their survival 11
19: 4 One who trusts others too quickly 11
22:23 Gain the trust of your neighbor in his poverty 16
32:24 he who trusts the Lord will not suffer loss. 15
33: 3 A man of understanding will trust in the law 11
35:12 do not trust to an unrighteous sacrifice; 12
36:26 who will trust a nimble robber 15
26 So who will trust a man that has no home •
Bar 3:17 who hoard up silver and gold, in which men trust 14
Aza 1:17 will be no shame for those who trust in thee. 14
Sus 1:35 for her heart trusted in the Lord. 14
1Mc 7: 7 Now then send a man whom you trust 15
16 So they trusted him 11
8:16 They trust one man each year to rule over them 15
10:37 be put in positions of trust in the kingdom 16
12:46 Jonathan trusted him and did as he said 11
2Mc 3:12 had trusted in the holiness of the place 15
8:18 For they trust to arms and acts of daring," he said 14
18 we trust in the Almighty God 14
15: 7 did not cease to trust with all confidence 14
3Mc 2: 4 who trusted in their strength and boldness 14
4Mc 7:21 trusts in God 15
8: 7 Trust me 15

trust *See also* breach, leave, office.

make trust 1. בטח
Jer 28:15 and you have made this people trust in a lie. 1
29:31 I did not send him, and has made you trust in a lie 1

trusted *See* friend.

trustee 1. οἰκονόμος
Gal 4: 2 he is under guardians and trustees 1

trustingly 1. בֶּטַח 2. לָבֶטַח
Prv 3:29 neighbor who dwells trustingly beside you. 2
Mic 2: 8 who pass by trustingly with no thought of war. 1

trustworthy 1. אמן 2. אֱמֶת 3. πιστός 4. fidelis
Exd 18:21 choose . . men who are trustworthy 2
Ps 111: 7 all his precepts are trustworthy 1
Prv 11:13 trustworthy in spirit keeps a thing hidden. 1
1Co 4: 2 that they be found trustworthy. 3
7:25 one who by the Lord's mercy is trustworthy. 3
Rev 21: 5 for these words are trustworthy and true. 3
22: 6 These words are trustworthy and true. 3
2Es 15: 2 for they are trustworthy and true. 4
Sir 31:23 testimony to his excellence is trustworthy. 3
37:22 may be trustworthy on his lips. 3
23 will be trustworthy. 3
46:15 he became known as a trustworthy seer. 3
1Mc 14:41 until a trustworthy prophet should arise 3

trustworthy *See also* find.

truth 1. אֲבָל 2. אֱמוּנָה 3. אָמֵן 4. אָמְנָה 5. אֱמֶת 6. הַאִם 7. כון 8. כִּי אִם 9. מנם 10. צֶדֶק 11. תָּמִים 12. יַצִּיב (A) 13. ἀλήθεια 14. ἀληθής 15. ἀληθινῶς 16. ἀληθῶς 17. ἀσφάλεια 18. καλός 19. πίστις 20. veritas 21. verum
Gen 42:16 words may be tested, whether there is truth in you 5
21 In truth we are guilty concerning our brother 1
Jos 7:20 Of a truth I have sinned against the LORD 4
1Sm 21: 5 Of a truth women have been kept from us as always 8
1Kg 17:24 the word of the LORD in your mouth is truth. 5
22:16 that you speak . . the truth in the name of the LORD? 5
2Kg 19:17 Of a truth, O LORD, the kings . . have laid waste 9
2Ch 18:15 speak to me nothing but the truth 5
Est 9:30 Letters were sent . . in words of peace and truth 5
Job 6:13 In truth I have no help in me 6
34:12 Of a truth, God will not do wickedly 9
Ps 5: 9 For there is no truth in their mouth; 7
15: 2 what is right, and speaks truth from his heart; 5
25: 5 Lead me in thy truth, and teach me 5
43: 3 Oh send out thy light and thy truth; 5
45: 4 ride forth victoriously for the cause of truth 5
51: 6 Behold, thou desirest truth in the inward being; 5
52: 3 lying more than speaking the truth. Selah 10
86:11 Teach me . . O LORD, that I may walk in thy truth; 5
96:13 He will judge . . the peoples with his truth. 2
119:43 take not the word of truth utterly out of my mouth 5
160 The sum of thy word is truth; 5
145:18 LORD is near to . . all who call upon him in truth. 5
Prv 8: 7 for my mouth will utter truth; 5
12:17 He who speaks the truth gives honest evidence 2
23:23 Buy truth, and do not sell it; 5
Ecc 12:10 and uprightly he wrote words of truth. 5
Isa 10:20 lean upon . . the Holy One of Israel, in truth. 5
37:18 Of a truth, O LORD, the kings of Assyria have 9
45:19 I the LORD speak the truth 10
48: 1 and confess . . but not in truth or right. 5
59:14 for truth has fallen in the public squares 5
15 Truth is lacking, and he who departs from evil 5
65:16 shall bless himself by the God of truth 3
16 in the land shall swear by the God of truth; 3
Jer 4: 2 if you swear, 'As the LORD lives,' in truth, in justice 5
5: 1 find a man, one who does justice and seeks truth; 2
3 O LORD, do not thy eyes look for truth? 2
7:28 truth has perished; it is cut off from their lips. 2
9: 3 falsehood and not truth has grown strong 19
5 and no one speaks the truth; 5
26:15 for in truth the LORD sent me to you to speak 5
Dan 7:16 asked him the truth concerning all this. 12
8:12 truth was cast down to the ground 5
9:13 our iniquities and giving heed to thy truth. 5
10:21 tell you what is inscribed in the book of truth 5
11: 2 now I will show you the truth. 5
Ams 5:10 and they abhor him who speaks the truth. 11
Zec 8:16 that you shall do: Speak the truth to one another 5
19 therefore love truth and peace. 5
Mrk 5:33 told him the whole truth. 13
Lke 1: 4 that you may know the truth 17
4:25 in truth, I tell you, there were many widows 13
Joh 1:14 Word . . dwelt among us, full of grace and truth; 13
17 grace and truth came through Jesus Christ. 13
4:23 will worship the Father in spirit and truth 13
24 must worship in spirit and truth. 13
5:33 and he has borne witness to the truth. 13
8:32 you will know the truth 13
32 the truth will make you free. 13
40 has told you the truth which I heard from God 13
44 and has nothing to do with the truth 13
44 because there is no truth in him 13
45 because I tell the truth, you do not believe me. 13
46 If I tell the truth, why do you not believe me? 13
14: 6 I am the way, and the truth, and the life 13
17 even the Spirit of truth 13
15:26 even the Spirit of truth 13
16: 7 Nevertheless I tell you the truth 13
13 When the Spirit of truth comes 13
13 he will guide you into all the truth 13
17: 8 and know in truth that I came from thee 16

17 Sanctify them in the truth; thy word is truth. 13
17 Sanctify them in the truth; thy word is truth. 13
19 that they also may be consecrated in truth. 13
18:37 I was born . . to bear witness to the truth 13
37 Every one who is of the truth hears my voice. 13
38 Pilate said to him, "What is truth? 13
19:35 he knows that he tells the truth 14
Act 26:25 I am speaking the sober truth. 13
Rom 1:18 men who by their wickedness suppress the truth. 13
25 they exchanged the truth about God for a lie 13
2: 8 those who are factious and do not obey the truth 13
20 in the law the embodiment of knowledge and truth- 13
9: 1 I am speaking the truth in Christ, I am not lying; 13
1Co 5: 8 the unleavened bread of sincerity and truth. 13
2Co 4: 2 by the open statement of the truth 13
11:10 As the truth of Christ is in me 13
12: 6 for I shall be speaking the truth 13
13: 8 For we cannot do anything against the truth 13
8 but only for the truth. 13
Gal 2: 5 the truth of the gospel might be preserved 13
14 straightforward about the truth of the gospel 13
5: 7 who hindered you from obeying the truth? 13
Eph 1:13 you also, who have heard the word of truth 13
4:21 as the truth is in Jesus. 13
25 let every one speak the truth with his neighbor 13
6:14 having girded your loins with truth 13
Php 1:18 whether in pretense or in truth 13
Col 1: 5 you have heard before in the word of the truth 13
6 heard and understood the grace of God in truth 13
2Th 2:10 refused to love the truth and so be saved. 13
12 may be condemned who did not believe the truth 13
13 belief in the truth. 13
1Ti 2: 4 to come to the knowledge of the truth. 13
7 (I am telling the truth, I am not lying) 13
7 a teacher of the Gentiles in faith and truth. 13
3:15 the pillar and bulwark of the truth. 13
4: 3 those who believe and know the truth. 13
6: 5 who are depraved in mind and bereft of the truth 13
2Ti 1:14 guard the truth that has been entrusted to you 18
2:15 rightly handling the word of truth. 13
18 swerved from the truth 13
25 they will repent and come to know the truth 13
3: 7 can never arrive at a knowledge of the truth. 13
8 these men also oppose the truth 13
4: 4 will turn away from listening to the truth 13
Tit 1: 1 knowledge of the truth 13
14 commands of men who reject the truth. 13
Heb 10:26 after receiving the knowledge of the truth 13
Jas 1:18 he brought us forth by the word of truth 13
3:14 do not boast and be false to the truth. 13
5:19 if any one among you wanders from the truth 13
1Pe 1:22 your obedience to the truth for a sincere love 13
2Pe 1:12 you know them and are established in the truth 13
2: 2 because of them the way of truth will be reviled. 13
1Jn 1: 6 we lie and do not live according to the truth; 13
8 we deceive ourselves, and the truth is not in us. 13
2: 4 is a liar, and the truth is not in him; 13
21 not because you do not know the truth 13
21 and know that no lie is of the truth. 13
3:18 let us not love in word . . but in deed and in truth 13
19 By this we shall know that we are of the truth 13
4: 6 the spirit of truth and the spirit of error 13
5: 7 because the Spirit is the truth. 13
2Jn 1: 1 lady and her children, whom I love in the truth 13
1 and not only I but also all who know the truth 13
2 because of the truth which abides in us 13
3 from Jesus Christ . . in truth and love. 13
4 to find some of your children following the truth 13
3Jn 1: 1 to the beloved Ga'ius, whom I love in truth. 13
3 brethren . . testified to the truth of your life 13
3 as indeed you do follow the truth. 13
4 to hear that my children follow the truth. 13
8 that we may be fellow workers in the truth. 13
12 testimony . . from the truth itself 13
1Es 3:12 truth is victor over all things. 13
4:13 Zerubbabel, who had spoken of women and truth 13
33 he began to speak about truth 13
35 truth is great, and stronger than all things. 13
36 The whole earth calls upon truth 13
37 There is no truth in them 13
38 truth endures and is strong for ever 13
40 Blessed be the God of truth! 13
41 Great is truth, and strongest of all! 13
2Es 5: 1 and the way of truth shall be hidden 20
6:28 the truth, which has been so long without fruit 20
7:34 only judgment shall remain, truth shall stand 20
104and displays to all the seal of truth 20
114and truth has appeared. 20
8:23 and whose truth is established for ever- 20
26 at those who have served thee in truth. 20
35 For in truth there is no one among those 20
11:41 you have judged the earth, but not with truth; 20
42 you have hated those who tell the truth 21
14:18 For truth shall go farther away 20
Tob 1: 3 in the ways of truth and righteousness 13
3: 2 all thy deeds and all thy ways are mercy and truth 13
5 we did not walk in truth before thee. 13
14: 6 the Gentiles will turn to fear the Lord God in truth 15
7 who love the Lord God in truth and righteousness 13

Jdt 5: 5 I will tell you the truth about this people 13
Wis 3: 9 Those who trust in him will understand truth 13
5: 6 it was we who strayed from the way of truth 13
6:22 I will not pass by the truth; 13
Sir 4:25 Never speak against the truth 13
28 Strive even to death for the truth 13
12:12 at last you will realize the truth of my words •
27: 9 truth returns to those who practice it. 13
37:15 he may direct your way in truth. 13
41:19 Be ashamed before the truth of God 13
Aza 1: 4 all thy judgments are truth. 13
5 in truth and justice thou hast brought all this 13
1Mc 7:18 they said, "There is no truth or justice in them 13
2Mc 7: 6 in truth has compassion on us 13
3Mc 4:16 with a mind alienated from truth 13
7:12 approving the truth of what they said 14
4Mc 5:10 by holding a vain opinion concerning the truth 14
11 the truth of what is beneficial 13
6:18 who have lived in accordance with truth to old age 13

truth *See also* know, speak, tell.

spiritual truth 1. *πνευματικός*
1Co 2:13 interpreting spiritual truths to those 1

truthful 1. אֱמֶת 2. *ἀλήθεια* 3. *πιστός*
Prv 12:19 Truthful lips endure for ever 1
14:25 A truthful witness saves lives 1
2Co 6: 7 truthful speech, and the power of God 2
Sir 34: 8 wisdom is made perfect in truthful lips. 3

truthfulness 1. *ἀλήθεια*
Rom 3: 7 if . . God's truthfulness abounds to his glory 1
15: 8 to the circumcised to show God's truthfulness 1

try 1. עשׂה 2. *ἐκζητέω* 3. *ἐπέχω* 4. *ἐπιχειρέω* 5. *ζητέω* 6. *πειράζω* 7. *πειράομαι* 8. *πειράω* 9. quaero
Exd 8:18 The magicians tried by their secret arts 1
Dan 2: 8 I know . . that you are trying to gain time •
Mat 21:46 But when they tried to arrest him, they feared 5
Mrk 12:12 they tried to arrest him 5
Lke 20:19 tried to lay hands on him at that very hour 5
Joh 10:39 Again they tried to arrest him 5
Act 21:31 as they were trying to kill him 5
24: 6 He even tried to profane the temple 6
26:11 and tried to make them blaspheme •
21 Jews seized me in the temple and tried to kill me. 7
28:23 trying to convince them about Jesus •
1Co 4:13 when slandered, we try to conciliate •
10:33 just as I try to please all men in everything I do •
Gal 1:10 Or am I trying to please men? 5
13 and tried to destroy it; •
23 now preaching the faith he once tried to destroy •
1Es 1:28 tried to fight with him 4
2Es 13: 7 I tried to see the region or place 9
Tob 5:13 because I tried to learn your tribe and family. 5
Jdt 8:16 Do not try to bind the purposes of the Lord our God; •
34 Only, do not try to find out what I plan •
Sir 4:26 do not try to stop the current of a river. •
12:12 lest he try to take your seat of honor 5
13:11 Do not try to treat him as an equal 3
1Mc 6: 3 So he came and tried to take the city 5
18 They were trying in every way to harm them 5
56 he was trying to seize control of the government. 5
9: 9 they tried to dissuade him, saying •
32 he tried to kill him. 5
71 he would not try to harm him as long as he lived. 2
11: 1 he tried to get possession of Alexander's kingdom 5
10 he has tried to kill me. 5
12:53 nations round about them tried to destroy them 5
2Mc 7:19 for having tried to fight against God! 4
3Mc 1:25 the king tried in various ways to change his . . mind 8
3: 8 They did try to console them •
7: 5 they tried . . to put them to death. 4
4Mc 4:26 he himself, through torture, tried to compel everyone •
9: 5 You are trying to terrify us by threatening us •
12: 2 tried to console him, saying 8

try (2) 1. בחן 2. חקר 3. נסה 4. צרף 5. *διαπειράζω* 6. *δοκιμάζω* 7. *πειράζω*
1Ch 29:17 I know, my God, that thou triest the heart 1
2Ch 32:31 in order to try him and to know 3
Job 12:11 Does not the ear try words as the palate tastes 1
23:10 when he has tried me, I shall come forth as gold. 1
34:36 Would that Job were tried to the end 1
Ps 7: 9 thou who triest the minds and hearts 1
17: 3 If thou triest my heart, if thou visitest me 1
26: 2 Prove me, O LORD, and try me; test my heart 3
66:10 thou hast tried us as silver is tried. 4
10 thou hast tried us as silver is tried. 4
119:140Thy promise is well tried 4
139:23 Try me and know my thoughts! 2
Prv 17: 3 furnace is for gold, and the LORD tries hearts. 1
23:30 those who go to try mixed wine. 2
Isa 48:10 I have tried you in the furnace of affliction. 1
Jer 11:20 who triest the heart and the mind 1
12: 3 thou seest me, and triest my mind toward thee. 1
17:10 I the LORD search the mind and try the heart 1
20:12 O LORD of hosts, who triest the righteous 1
Rev 3:10 to try those who dwell upon the earth. 7
Wis 3: 6 like gold in the furnace he tried them 6
11: 9 For when they were tried 7
3Mc 5:40 O king, how long will you try us 5
4Mc 15:16 O mother, tried now by more bitter pains 7

try (3) 1. שׁפט 2. *κρίνω*
Ps 109: 7 When he is tried, let him come forth guilty; 1
Act 25: 9 and there be tried on these charges before me? 2
10 Caesar's tribunal, where I ought to be tried 2
20 be tried there regarding them. 2
1Co 6: 2 are you incompetent to try trivial cases? •

try attacking 1. *καταπειράζω*
2Mc 13:18 The king . . tried strategy in attacking their positions. 1

try in vain 1. יאל
1Sm 17:39 David girded his . . and he tried in vain to go 1

try to enter 1. *προσβαίνω*
Jdt 4: 7 it was easy to stop any who tried to enter 1

try to find 1. *ζητέω*
Wis 19:17 each tried to find the way through his own door. 1

try to learn 1. *δοκιμάζω*
Eph 5:10 try to learn what is pleasing to the Lord. 1

try with fire 1. *πυρόω*
Jdt 8:27 For he has not tried us with fire, as he did them 1

tube 1. אָפִיק
Job 40:18 His bones are tubes of bronze 1

tumble 1. הפך 2. נפל 3. *ἀποκυλίζω*
Jdg 7:13 lo, a cake of barley bread tumbled into the camp 1
Ezk 38:20 every wall shall tumble to the ground. 2
Jdt 13: 9 Then she tumbled his body off the bed 3

tumor 1. טְחוֹר
1Sm 5: 6 and he terrified and afflicted them with tumors 1
9 so that tumors broke out upon them. 1
12 the men who did not die were stricken with tumors 1
6: 4 Five golden tumors and five golden mice 1
5 make images of your tumors and . . of your mice 1
11 box with . . mice and the images of their tumors. 1
17 These are the golden tumors . . one for Ashdod 1

tumult 1. גַּאֲוָה 2. המה 3. הָמוֹן 4. הֲמֻלָּה 5. חמר 6. מְהוּמָה 7. נְהָמָה 8. שָׁאוֹן 9. *ἀκαταστασία* 10. *θόρυβος* 11. *κίνημα* 12. *ὀχλέω* 13. *ταραχή* 14. *τάραχος* 15. tumultus 16. turbatio
1Sm 14:19 the tumult in the camp . . increased more and more; 3
2Sm 18:29 When Jo'ab sent your servant, I saw a great tumult 3
Job 39: 7 He scorns the tumult of the city; 3
Ps 38: 8 I groan because of the tumult of my heart. 7
46: 3 though the mountains tremble with its tumult. 1
65: 7 roaring of their waves, the tumult of the peoples; 3
83: 2 For lo, thy enemies are in tumult; 2
Isa 13: 4 a tumult on the mountains as of a great multitude! 3
22: 5 a day of tumult and trampling and confusion 6
Jer 10:13 When he utters his voice there is a tumult 3
48:45 forehead of Moab, the crown of the sons of tumult. 8
51:16 there is a tumult of waters in the heavens 3
Lam 1:20 Behold . . for I am in distress, my soul is in tumult 5
2:11 My eyes are spent . . my soul is in tumult; 5
Ezk 1:24 a sound of tumult like the sound of a host; 4
7: 7 the time has come, the day is near, a day of tumult 6
22: 5 will mock you, you infamous one, full of tumult. 6
Ams 3: 9 of Sama'ria, and see the great tumults within her 6
Mat 26: 5 lest there be a tumult among the people. 10
Mrk 5:38 he saw a tumult 10
14: 2 lest there be a tumult of the people. 10
Lke 21: 9 when you hear of wars and tumults 9
Act 24:18 without any crowd or tumult. 10
2Co 6: 5 beatings, imprisonments, tumults, labors 9
2Es 9: 3 tumult of peoples, intrigues of nations 16
12: 2 and their reign was brief and full of tumult. 15
30 the reign which was brief and full of tumult 16
AEs 11: 5 thunders and earthquake, tumult upon the earth! 14
8 affliction and great tumult upon the earth! 14
Wis 14:25 deceit, corruption, faithlessness, tumult 14
1Mc 13:44 a great tumult arose in the city. 11
2Mc 15:29 Then there was shouting and tumult 13
3Mc 3: 8 saw an unexpected tumult around these people 13
5:41 As a result the city is in a tumult 12

tumult *See also* make.

battle tumult 1. רַעַשׁ
Isa 9: 5 boot of the tramping warrior in battle tumult 1

tumult of war 1. שָׁאוֹן
Hos 10:14 the tumult of war shall arise among your people 1

tumultuous 1. המה 2. הָמוֹן
Isa 22: 2 you who are full of shoutings, tumultuous city 1

Jer 51:42 she is covered with its tumultuous waves. 2
tumultuous *See also* noise, procession.

tune 1. *μέλος*
Sir 44: 5 those who composed musical tunes 1

tunic 1. כְּתֹנֶת 2. פַּסִּים (A) 3. *χιτών*
Job 30:18 it binds me about like the collar of my tunic. 1
Dan 3:21 bound in their mantles, their tunics, their hats 2
Mat 10:10 no bag for your journey, nor two tunics 3
Mrk 6: 9 to wear sandals and not put on two tunics. 3
Lke 9: 3 do not have two tunics. 3
Joh 19:23 also his tunic 3
23 the tunic was without seam 3
Act 9:39 showing tunics and other garments 3
Jdt 14:19 rent their tunics and were greatly dismayed 3
2Mc 12:40 under the tunic of every one of the dead 3
4Mc 9:11 having torn off his tunic 3

tunnel 1. *ὀρύσσω*
Sir 48:17 he tunneled the sheer rock with iron 1

turban 1. טְבוּל 2. מִצְנֶפֶת 3. פְּאֵר 4. צָנִיף 5. *κίδαρις*
Exd 28: 4 a coat of checker work, a turban, and a girdle; 2
37 you shall fasten it on the turban by a lace of blue; 2
37 it shall be on the front of the turban. 2
39 you shall make a turban of fine linen 2
29: 6 you shall set the turban on his head 2
6 put the holy crown upon the turban. 2
39:28 the turban of fine linen, and the caps 2
31 a lace of blue, to fasten it on the turban above; 2
Lev 8: 9 he set the turban upon his head, and on the turban 2
9 on the turban, in front, he set the golden plate 2
16: 4 and wear the linen turban 2
Job 29:14 my justice was like a robe and a turban. 4
Isa 3:23 the linen garments, the turbans, and the veils. 4
Ezk 21:26 Remove the turban, and take off the crown; 2
23:15 with flowing turbans on their heads, all of them 1
24:17 Bind on your turban, and put . . shoes on your feet; 3
23 Your turbans shall be on your heads 3
44:18 They shall have linen turbans upon their heads 3
Zec 3: 5 I said, "Let them put a clean turban on his head. 4
5 they put a clean turban on his head 4
1Es 3: 6 a turban of fine linen 5
Jdt 4:15 With ashes upon their turbans 5
Sir 45:12 with a gold crown upon his turban 5

turbulent 1. המן 2. עשק 3. *βίαιος*
Job 40:23 if the river is turbulent he is not frightened; 2
Ezk 5: 7 Because you are more turbulent than the nations 1
Wis 13: 2 the circle of the stars, or turbulent water 3

turmoil 1. המה 2. רֹגֶז 3. רתח
Job 30:27 My heart is in turmoil, and is never still; 3
Ps 39: 6 Surely for nought are they in turmoil; 1
Isa 14: 3 from your pain and turmoil and the hard service 2

turn 1. הפך 2. חמק 3. יטה 4. יסר 5. נטה 6. נקע 7. נתן 8. סבב 9. סָבִיב 10. סוג 11. סור 12. עבר 13. עטף 14. פנה 15. פְּנוֹת אַחֲרֵי 16. שׂוּם 17. שׁוּב 18. *ἀποστρέφω* 19. *δίδωμι* 20. *εἰμί* 21. *ἐκκλίνω* 22. *ἐναντίον* 23. *ἐναπερείδω* 24. *ἐντρέπω* 25. *ἐπιπέμπω* 26. *ἐπιστρέφω* 27. *μεταστρέφω* 28. *μετατίθημι* 29. *στρέφω* 30. *στροφή* 31. *συντρέφω* 32. *τρέπω* 33. averto 34. converto 35. converto pedes 36. momentum 37. transfero
Gen 18:22 the men turned from there, and went toward Sodom; 14
24:49 tell me; that I may turn to the right hand 14
30:30 and the LORD has blessed you wherever I turned. †
38: 1 Judah . . turned in to a certain Adullamite 3
Exd 7:23 Pharaoh turned and went into his house 14
10: 6 Then he turned and went out from Pharaoh. 14
19 the LORD turned a very strong west wind 1
32:12 Turn from thy fierce wrath, and repent of this 17
15 Moses turned, and went down from the mountain 14
Lev 19: 4 Do not turn to idols or make for yourselves 14
31 Do not turn to mediums or wizards; do not seek them 14
20: 6 If a person turns to mediums and wizards 14
26:23 if by this discipline you are not turned to me 4
Num 12:10 Aaron turned towards Miriam, and behold 14
14:25 turn tomorrow and set out for the wilderness 14
16:42 they turned toward the tent of meeting; 14
21:33 Then they turned and went up by the way to Bashan; 14
22:23 Balaam struck the ass, to turn her into the road. 5
26 in a narrow place, where there was no way to turn 5
34: 4 boundary shall turn south of the ascent of Akrab'bim 8
5 boundary shall turn from Azmon to the Brook 8
Deu 1: 7 turn and take your journey, and go to the hill 14
24 they turned and went up into the hill country 14
40 as for you, turn, and journey into the wilderness 14
2: 1 we turned, and journeyed into the wilderness 14
3 going about . . long enough; turn northward. 14
8 And we turned and went in the direction 14
3: 1 Then we turned and went up the way to Bashan; 14
9:15 I turned and came down from the mountain 14
10: 5 Then I turned and came down from the mountain 14
13:17 LORD may turn from the fierceness of his anger 17
14:25 then you shall turn it into money, and bind up 7
16: 7 morning you shall turn and go to your tents. 14
30:10 if you turn to the LORD . . with all your heart 17
31:18 evil . . because they have turned to other gods. 14
20 they will turn to other gods and serve them 14
Jos 1: 7 all the law . . turn not from it to the right hand 11
7: 8 what can I say, when Israel has turned their backs 1
12 they turn their backs before their enemies 14
26 then the LORD turned from his burning anger. 17
15: 7 goes . . and so northward, turning toward Gilgal 14
18:14 boundary goes . . turning on the western side 8
19:27 then it turns eastward, it goes to Beth-dagon 17
29 then the boundary turns to Ramah, reaching 17
29 the boundary turns to Hosah, and it ends at the sea; 17
34 the boundary turns westward to Az'noth-tabor 17
22: 4 therefore turn and go to your home in the land 14
24:20 then he will turn and do you harm, and consume you 17
Jdg 6:14 the LORD turned to him and said, "Go in this might 14
7:13 struck it . . and turned it upside down 1
8:33 Israel turned again and played the harlot after 17
11: 8 That is why we have turned to you now, that you may 17
15: 4 he turned them tail to tail, and put a torch 14
18:21 they turned and departed, putting the little 14
26 when Micah saw . . he turned and went back to his 14
20:39 the men of Israel should turn in battle. 1
41 the men of Israel turned, and the men of Benjamin 1
42 they turned their backs before the men of Israel 14
45 they turned and fled toward the wilderness 14
47 600 men turned and fled toward the wilderness 14
1Sm 6:12 they turned neither to the right nor to the left 11
10: 9 When he turned his back to leave Samuel 14
13:17 one company turned toward Ophrah, to the land 14
18 another company turned toward Beth-hor'on 14
18 and another company turned toward the border 14
14:21 even they also turned to be with the Israelites 9
47 wherever he turned he put them to the worse. 14
15:12 set up a monument . . and turned, and passed on 8
27 As Samuel turned to go away, Saul laid hold upon 8
17:30 And he turned away from him toward another 8
22:17 king said . . "Turn and kill the priests of the LORD; 8
18 king said . . "You turn and fall upon the priests. 8
18 And Do'eg . . turned and fell upon the priests 8
28:16 LORD has turned from you and become your enemy? 11
2Sm 1:22 the bow of Jonathan turned not back, and the sword 10
2:19 he turned neither to the right . . nor to the left 5
26 people turn from the pursuit of their brethren? 17
1Kg 2: 3 prosper in all that you do and wherever you turn; 14
8:35 acknowledge thy name, and turn from their sin 17
10:13 she turned and went back to her own land 14
13:33 Jerobo'am did not turn from his evil way 17
17: 3 Depart from here and turn eastward 14
18:37 and that thou hast turned their hearts back. 8
20:39 a soldier turned and brought a man to me, 11
22:32 It is surely the king of Israel." So they turned 11
34 Turn about, and carry me out of the battle 1
2Kg 2:24 he turned around, and when he saw them, he cursed 14
4: 8 whenever . . he would turn in there to eat food. 11
11 he turned into the chamber and rested there. 11
5:12 So he turned and went away in a rage. 14
26 when the man turned from his chariot to meet you? 1
10:31 he did not turn from the sins of Jerobo'am 11
13:23 he turned toward them, because of his covenant 14
17:13 Turn from your evil ways and keep my . . statutes 17
20: 2 Hezeki'ah turned his face to the wall, and prayed 8
21:13 wiping it and turning it upside down. 1
23:16 as Josi'ah turned, he saw the tombs . . on the mount; 14
25 who turned to the LORD with all his heart 17
26 the LORD did not turn from . . his great wrath 17
24: 1 then he turned and rebelled against him. 17
1Ch 21:20 Ornan . . he turned and saw the angel 17
2Ch 6:26 and acknowledge thy name, and turn from their sin 17
7:14 if my people . . and turn from their wicked ways 17
9:12 So she turned and went back to her own land 1
12:12 the wrath of the LORD turned from him 17
15: 4 when in their distress they turned to the LORD 17
18:31 So they turned to fight against him; 8
29: 6 turned their backs. 7
36:13 hardened his heart against turning to the LORD 17
Ezr 6:22 LORD . . turned the heart of the king of Assyria 8
Neh 9:28 turned and cried to thee thou didst hear 17
29 turned a stubborn shoulder and stiffened 7
35 they did not turn from their wicked works. 17
Job 5: 1 To which of the holy ones will you turn? 14
6:29 Turn, I pray, let no wrong be done. 17
29 Turn now, my vindication is at stake. 17
15:13 that you turn your spirit against God 17
19:19 those whom I loved have turned against me. 1
20:14 yet his food is turned in his stomach; 1
23: 9 I turn to the right hand, but I cannot see him. 13
13 But he is unchangeable and who can turn him? 17
24:18 no treader turns toward their vineyards. 14
30:15 Terrors are turned upon me; 1
36:21 Take heed, do not turn to iniquity 14
37:12 They turn round and round by his guidance 1
Ps 6: 4 Turn, O LORD, save my life; deliver me 17
9: 3 When my enemies turned back, they stumbled 17
22:27 of the earth shall remember and turn to the LORD; 17
25:16 Turn thou to me, and be gracious to me; 14
35: 4 Let them be turned back and confounded 10
40: 4 the man . . who does not turn to the proud 14
14 let them be turned back and brought to dishonor 10
44:18 Our heart has not turned back 10
56: 9 Then my enemies will be turned back in the day 17
69:16 according to thy abundant mercy, turn to me. 14
70: 2 Let them be turned back and brought to dishonor 10
73:10 Therefore the people turn and praise them; 17
81:14 turn my hand against their foes. 17
85: 3 thou didst turn from thy hot anger. 17
8 saints, to those who turn to him in their hearts. 26
86:16 Turn to me and take pity on me; 14
105:25 He turned their hearts to hate his people 1
114: 3 The sea looked and fled, Jordan turned back. 8
5 What ails you . . O Jordan, that you turn back? 8
119:37 Turn my eyes from looking at vanities; 12
59 I turn my feet to thy testimonies; 17
79 Let those who fear thee turn to me 17
132 Turn to me and be gracious to me, as is thy wont 14
129: 5 who hate Zion be put to shame and turned backward! 10
Prv 9: 4 Whoever is simple, let him turn in here! 11
16 Whoever is simple, let him turn in here! 11
17: 8 wherever he turns he prospers. 14
21: 1 he turns it wherever he will. 5
26:14 As a door turns on its hinges, so does a sluggard 8
Ecc 2:12 turned to consider wisdom and madness and folly; 14
7:25 I turned my mind to know and to search out 8
Sng 2:17 turn, my beloved, be like a gazelle 8
5: 6 I opened . . but my beloved had turned and gone. 2
6: 1 Whither has your beloved turned 14
Isa 1:25 I will turn my hand against you 17
6:10 lest they see . . and turn and be healed. 17
8:21 curse . . their God, and turn their faces upward; 14
9:13 The people did not turn to him who smote them 17
13:14 every man will turn to his own people 14
31: 6 Turn to him from whom you have deeply revolted 17
38: 2 Then Hezeki'ah turned his face to the wall 8
44:25 who turns wise men back 17
45:22 Turn to me and be saved, all the ends of the earth! 14
50: 5 I was not rebellious, I turned not backward. 10
53: 6 astray; we have turned every one to his own way; 14
56:11 they have all turned to their own way 14
59:14 Justice is turned back, 10
20 to those in Jacob who turn from transgression 17
60: 5 the abundance of the sea shall be turned to you 1
Jer 2:27 For they have turned their back to me 14
35 I am innocent; surely his anger has turned from me.' 17
3:19 and would not turn from following me. 17
8: 6 Every one turns to his own course 17
15: 1 yet my heart would not turn toward this people. •
7 my people; they did not turn from their ways. 17
19 shall turn to you, but you shall not turn to them. 17
19 shall turn to you, but you shall not turn to them. 17
18: 8 turns from its evil, I will repent of the evil 17
23:14 so that no one turns from his wickedness; 17
22 they would have turned them from their evil way 17
25: 5 saying, 'Turn now, every one of you, 17
26: 3 will listen, and every one turn from his evil way 17
31:39 to the hill Gareb, and shall then turn to Go'ah. 8
32:33 have turned to me their back and not their face; 14
40 that I will not turn away from doing good to them; 17
40 me in their hearts, that they may not turn from me. 11
35:15 Turn now every one of you from his evil way 17
36: 3 so that every one may turn from his evil way 17
7 and that every one will turn from his evil way 17
38:22 sunk in the mire, they turn away from you. 10
44: 5 incline their ear, to turn from their wickedness 17
46: 5 They are dismayed and have turned backward. 10
21 yea, they have turned and fled together 14
48:39 they wail! How Moab has turned his back in shame! 14
49:24 she turned to flee, and panic seized her; 14
50: 5 the way to Zion, with faces turned toward it •
16 every one shall turn to his own people 14
Lam 1: 8 yea, she herself groans, and turns her face away. 17
3: 3 against me he turns his hand again and again 1
Ezk 1: 9 straight forward, without turning as they went. 8
12 they went, without turning as they went. 8
17 four directions without turning as they went. 8
3:19 and he does not turn from his wickedness 17
20 if a righteous man turns from his righteousness 17
4: 8 so that you cannot turn from one side to the other 1
7:22 I will turn my face from them 8
10:11 four directions without turning as they went 8
11 followed without turning as they went. 8
16 the wheels did not turn from beside them. 8
13:22 that he should not turn from his wicked way 17
17: 6 vine, and its branches turned toward him 14
18:23 rather that he should turn from his way and live? 17
30 Repent and turn from all your transgressions 17
32 says the Lord GOD; so turn, and live. 17
23:18 as I had turned from her sister. 6
29:16 their iniquity, when they turn to them for aid. 15
33: 8 not speak to warn the wicked to turn from his way •
9 if you warn the wicked to turn from his way 17
9 and he does not turn from his way; he shall die 17
11 but that the wicked turn from his way and live; 17
12 not fall by it when he turns from his wickedness; 17
14 if he turns from his sin and does what is lawful 17
18 the righteous turns from his righteousness 17
19 when the wicked turns from his wickedness 17

36: 9 For, behold, I am for you, and I will turn to you 14
42:17 Then he turned and measured the north side 26
18 Then he turned and measured the south side 26
19 Then he turned to the west side and measured 8
Dan 9: 3 Then I turned my face to the Lord God, seeking him 7
13 turning from our iniquities and giving heed 17
10:15 turned my face toward the ground and was dumb. 7
11:18 shall turn his face to the coastlands 16
Hos 3: 1 they turn to other gods and love cakes of raisins. 14
7: 8 E'phraim is a cake not turned. 1
16 They turn to Ba'al; they are like a treacherous bow 17
14: 4 for my anger has turned from them. 17
Jol 2:14 Who knows whether he will not turn and repent 17
Ams 1: 8 I will turn my hand against Ekron; 17
Jon 3: 8 yea, let every one turn from his evil way 17
9 God may yet repent and turn from his fierce anger 17
10 what they did, how they turned from their evil way 17
Zec 7:11 to hearken, and turned a stubborn shoulder 7
13: 7 I will turn my hand against the little ones. 17
Mal 2: 6 he turned many from iniquity. 17
4: 6 he will turn the hearts of fathers 17
Mat 5:39 on the right cheek, turn to him the other also; 29
7: 6 and turn to attack you. 29
9:22 Jesus turned, and seeing her he said, "Take heart 29
13:15 and turn for me to heal them.' 26
16:23 he turned and said to Peter, "Get behind me, Satan! 29
18: 3 unless you turn and become like children 29
24:18 let him who is in the field not turn back 26
Mrk 8:33 turning and seeing his disciples 26
13:16 not turn back to take his mantle. 26
Lke 1:16 he will turn many of the sons of Israel to the Lord 26
17 to turn the hearts of the fathers to the children 26
7: 9 turned and said to the multitude that followed 29
44 Then turning toward the woman he said to Simon 29
9:55 he turned and rebuked them. 29
10:23 Then turning to the disciples he said privately 29
14:25 he turned and said to them 29
17: 4 turns to you seven times, and says, 'I repent,' 26
31 likewise let him who is in the field not turn back. 26
22:32 when you have turned again 26
61 the Lord turned and looked at Peter 29
23:28 Jesus turning to them said 29
Joh 1:38 Jesus turned, and saw them following, and said 29
12:40 turn for me to heal them. 29
20:16 She turned and said to him in Hebrew, "Rab-bo'ni! 29
21:20 Peter turned 26
Act 3:26 in turning every one of you from your wickedness 18
7:39 in their hearts they turned to Egypt 29
42 God turned and gave them over 29
9:35 they turned to the Lord. 26
40 then turning to the body he said, "Tabitha, rise. 26
11:21 a great number that believed turned to the Lord. 26
13:46 behold, we turn to the Gentiles. 29
14:15 turn from these vain things to a living God 26
15:19 not trouble those of the Gentiles who turn to God 26
16:18 turned and said to the spirit 26
26:18 they may turn from darkness to light 26
20 they should repent and turn to God 26
28:27 turn for me to heal them.' 26
2Co 2: 7 so you should rather turn to forgive and comfort 22
3:16 when a man turns to the Lord the veil is removed. 26
7: 5 we were afflicted at every turn •
Gal 1: 6 turning to a different gospel- •
1Th 1: 9 how you turned to God from idols 26
Rev 1:12 I turned to see the voice that was speaking to me 26
12 and on turning I saw seven golden lampstands 26
1Es 3:20 It turns every thought to feasting and mirth 27
2Es 1:24 I will turn to other nations 37
31 When you offer oblations to me, I will turn my face 33
3:34 which way the turn of the scale will incline. 36
9:39 I dismissed the thoughts . . and turned to her 34
11:31 the head turned with those that were with it 34
13: 3 wherever he turned his face to look 34
15:20 to turn and repay what they have given them. 34
31 combine in great power and turn to pursue 34
32 and shall turn and flee. 35
16:20 they will not turn from their iniquities 33
Tob 3:12 I have turned my eyes and my face toward thee. 19
13: 6 If you turn to him with all your heart 26
6 he will turn to you and will not hide his face 26
14: 6 all the Gentiles will turn to fear the Lord God 26
Jdt 8:11 unless the Lord turns and helps us 26
AEs 14:11 turn their plan against themselves 29
13 turn his heart to hate 28
Wis 8: 8 she understands turns of speech 30
Sir 5: 7 Do not delay to turn to the Lord 26
6:12 if you are brought low he will turn against you 20
17:25 Turn to the Lord and forsake your sins 26
29 those who turn to him! 26
33: 5 and his thoughts like a turning axle. 29
37: 2 when a companion and friend turns to enmity? 32
38:29 turning the wheel with his feet 31
48:10 to turn the heart of the father to the son 26
Bar 2:29 multitude will surely turn into a small number 18
33 turn from their stubbornness and their wicked 18
4: 2 Turn, O Jacob, and take her 26
Sus 1:47 All the people turned to him, and said 26
1Mc 1:18 Ptolemy turned and fled before him 24
9:16 they turned and followed close behind Judas 26
45 there is no place to turn. 21
72 then he turned and departed to his own land 18
2Mc 7:24 if he would turn from the ways of his fathers 28
9: 4 turning upon the Jews the injury 23
12:42 they turned to prayer 32
3Mc 1:27 they turned . . to call upon him who has all power 32
6: 6 turning the flame against all their enemies. 25
15 and have not turned your face from us 18
4Mc 1:12 then I shall turn to their story 32
7: 3 in no way did he turn the rudder of religion 32

turn (2) 1. תּוֹר 2. ἀνὰ μέρος 3. δὴ τοίνυν 4. ἑξῆς 5. καί 6. μέρος 7. πάλιν 8. successio 9. tempus

Est 2:12 Now when the turn came for each maiden to go 1
15 When the turn came for Esther . . to go 1
Act 7:45 Our fathers in turn brought it in with Joshua 5
1Co 14:27 speak in a tongue . . and each in turn; 2
2Es 11: 8 and watch in his turn; 9
14:42 and by turns they wrote what was dictated 8
Sir 29: 2 in turn, repay your neighbor promptly. 7
37:18 four turns of fortune appear 6
2Mc 7: 8 Therefore he in turn underwent tortures 4
4Mc 1:17 This, in turn, is education in the law 3

turn (3) 1. היה 2. הפך 3. נתן 4. סבב 5. שׂום 6. שׁאה 7. שׁוב 8. ἀποβαίνω 9. γίνομαι 10. εἰς 11. μεταστρέφω 12. μετατρέπω 13. περιτρέπω 14. στρέφω 15. τίθημι 16. τρέπω

Exd 7:15 take . . the rod which was turned into a serpent. 2
17 the water . . and it shall be turned to blood 2
20 all the water . . in the Nile turned to blood. 2
Lev 13: 2 a spot, and it turns into a leprous disease 1
3 if the hair in the diseased spot has turned white 2
4 if . . the hair in it has not turned white 2
10 swelling . . which has turned the hair white 2
13 it has all turned white, and he is clean 2
17 if the disease has turned white, then the priest 2
20 if . . its hair has turned white, then the priest 2
25 if the hair in the spot has turned white 2
Deu 23: 5 LORD your God turned the curse into a blessing 2
1Sm 10: 6 prophesy . . and be turned into another man. 2
2Sm 19: 2 So the victory that day was turned into mourning 1
2Kg 19:25 you . . turn fortified cities into heaps of ruins 6
Neh 13: 2 yet our God turned the curse into a blessing. 2
Est 9:22 and as the month that had been turned for them 2
Job 10: 9 wilt thou turn me to dust again? 7
30:21 Thou hast turned cruel to me; 2
31 My lyre is turned to mourning 1
41:28 for him slingstones are turned to stubble. 2
Ps 30:11 Thou hast turned for me my mourning into dancing; 2
66: 6 He turned the sea into dry land; 2
78:44 He turned their rivers to blood 2
105:29 He turned their waters into blood 2
107:33 He turns rivers into a desert 5
35 He turns a desert into pools of water 5
114: 8 who turns the rock into a pool of water 2
Isa 21: 4 twilight . . has been turned for me 5
29:17 Lebanon shall be turned into a fruitful field 7
30: 3 the protection of Pharaoh turn to your shame 1
34: 9 the streams of Edom shall be turned into pitch 2
42:15 I will turn the rivers into islands 5
16 I will turn the darkness before them into light 5
43:14 the shouting . . will be turned to lamentations. •
63:10 therefore he turned to be their enemy 2
Jer 2:21 How then have you turned degenerate 2
13:16 while you look for light he turns it into gloom 5
30: 6 Why has every face turned pale? 2
31:13 I will turn their mourning into joy 2
Lam 5:15 our dancing has been turned to mourning. 2
Ezk 28:18 I turned you to ashes upon the earth 3
Jol 2:31 The sun shall be turned to darkness 2
Ams 5: 7 O you who turn justice to wormwood 2
8 and turns deep darkness into the morning 2
6:12 But you have turned justice into poison 2
8:10 I will turn your feasts into mourning 2
Zec 14:10 The whole land shall be turned into a plain 4
Joh 16:20 your sorrow will turn into joy. 9
Act 2:20 the sun shall be turned into darkness 11
26:24 your great learning is turning you mad. 13
Jas 4: 9 Let your laughter be turned to mourning 12
Rev 11: 6 power over the waters to turn them into blood 14
Tob 2: 6 Your feasts shall be turned into mourning 14
Jdt 1:14 turned its beauty into shame. 15
8:23 the Lord our God will turn it to dishonor. 15
AEs 13:17 turn our mourning into feasting 14
Wis 2: 3 the body will turn to ashes 8
Sir 11:31 for he lies in wait, turning good into evil 11
39:23 just as he turns fresh water into salt. 11
27 just as they turn into evils for sinners. 16
Bar 4:34 her insolence will be turned to grief. 10
1Mc 1:39 her feasts were turned into mourning 14
40 her exaltation was turned into mourning. 14
9:41 Thus the wedding was turned into mourning 11
2Mc 8: 5 the wrath of the Lord had turned to mercy. 16
10:22 he slew these men who had turned traitor 9
3Mc 6:22 Then the king's anger was turned to pity and tears 11

turn (4) 1. סבב 2. ἀποδίδωμι

1Ch 12:23 to turn the kingdom of Saul over to him 1
Lke 16: 2 Turn in the account of your stewardship 2

turn about 1. הפך יָד 2. סבב 3. שׁוב 4. ἐπιστρέφω

Jos 15: 3 along by Hezron, up to Addar, turns about to Karka 2
19:14 the boundary turns about to Han'nathon 2
1Kg 2:15 the kingdom has turned about and become my 2
2Ch 18:33 Turn about, and carry me out of the battle 1
Job 10: 8 now thou dost turn about and destroy me. •
Ecc 2:20 I turned about and gave my heart up to despair 2
Jer 41:14 all the people . . turned about and came back 2
Ezk 38: 4 I will turn you about, and put hooks into your jaws 3
39: 2 I will turn you about and drive you forward 3
Mrk 5:30 immediately turned about in the crowd, and said 4

turn again 1. שׁוב 2. ἐπιστρέφω

Exd 5:22 Then Moses turned again to the LORD and said 1
33:11 When Moses turned again into the camp 1
Lev 13:16 if the raw flesh turns again and is changed 1
1Kg 8:33 When thy people . . if they turn again to thee 1
12:27 this people will turn again to their lord 1
2Ch 6:24 when they turn again and acknowledge thy name 1
30: 6 that he may turn again to the remnant of you 1
Ps 80:14 Turn again, O God of hosts! Look down from heaven 1
Ecc 3:20 all are from the dust, and all turn to dust again. 1
Mrk 4:12 lest they should turn again, and be forgiven. 2
Act 3:19 Repent therefore, and turn again 2

turn and flee 1. ἐντρέπω

1Mc 6: 6 but had turned and fled before the Jews 1

turn around 1. שׁוב

Jer 34:11 But afterward they turned around and took back 1
16 but then you turned around and profaned my name 1

turn aside 1. לפת 2. נטה 3. סבב 4. סור 5. שׂטה 6. שׁוב 7. ἀποκλίνω 8. ἐκκλίνω 9. μετατρέπω 10. παραβαίνω 11. παρέρχομαι

Gen 19: 2 said, "My lords, turn aside, I pray you 4
3 they turned aside to him and entered his house; 4
Exd 3: 3 I will turn aside and see this great sight 4
4 When the LORD saw that he turned aside to see 4
23: 2 in a suit, turning aside after a multitude 2
32: 8 they have turned aside quickly out of the way 4
Num 5:19 if you have not turned aside to uncleanness 5
20:17 not turn aside to the right hand or to the left 2
21:22 we will not turn aside into field or vineyard; 2
22:23 the ass turned aside out of the road 2
33 ass saw me, and turned aside before me these three 2
33 If she had not turned aside from me, surely 2
Deu 2:27 turn aside neither to the right nor to the left. 4
5:32 not turn aside to the right hand or to the left. 4
9:12 they have turned aside quickly out of the way 4
16 you had turned aside quickly from the way 4
11:16 deceived, and you turn aside and serve other gods 4
28 not obey . . but turn aside from the way 4
17:11 you shall not turn aside from the verdict 4
20 not turn aside from the commandment, either 4
28:14 if you do not turn aside from any of the words 4
31:29 surely act corruptly, and turn aside from the way 4
Jos 23: 6 keep and do all . . turning aside from it neither 4
Jdg 2:17 they soon turned aside from the way 4
4:18 said to him, "Turn aside, my lord, turn aside to me; 4
18 said to him, "Turn aside, my lord, turn aside to me; 4
18 So he turned aside to her into the tent 4
14: 8 he turned aside to see the carcass of the lion 4
18: 3 they turned aside and said to him, "Who brought you 4
15 they turned aside thither, and came to the house 4
19:11 let us turn aside to this city . . and spend the night 4
12 We will not turn aside into the city 4
15 they turned aside there, to go 4
Rut 4: 1 Bo'az said, "Turn aside, friend; sit down here"; 4
1 and he turned aside and sat down. 4
1Sm 8: 3 not walk in his ways, but turned aside after gain; 2
12:20 do not turn aside from following the LORD 4
21 and do not turn aside after vain things 4
2Sm 2:21 Turn aside to your right hand or to your left 2
21 As'ahel would not turn aside from following him. 4
22 Turn aside from following me; why should I smite 4
23 But he refused to turn aside; 4
18:30 And the king said, "Turn aside, and stand here. 3
30 So he turned aside, and stood still. 3
22:23 and from his statutes I did not turn aside. 4
1Kg 9: 6 if you turn aside from following me 6
15: 5 David . . did not turn aside from anything 4
22:43 in all the way of Asa . . he did not turn aside from it 4
2Kg 10:29 Jehu did not turn aside from the sins of Jerobo'am 4
22: 2 did not turn aside to the right hand or to the left. 4
2Ch 7:19 if you turn aside and forsake my statutes and my 6
8:15 they did not turn aside from what the king 4
20:32 did not turn aside from it; 4
34: 2 he did not turn aside to the right or to the left. 4
Job 6:18 The caravans turn aside from their course; 1
23:11 I have kept his way and have not turned aside. 2
31: 7 if my step has turned aside from the way 2
33:17 that he may turn man aside from his deed 4
34:27 because they turned aside from following him 4

36:18 the greatness of the ransom turn you aside. 2
Ps 119:102 I do not turn aside from thy ordinances 4
Prv 7:25 Let not your heart turn aside to her ways 5
16:17 The highway of the upright turns aside from evil; 4
Isa 10: 2 to turn aside the needy from justice and to rob 2
29:21 with an empty plea turn aside him . . in the right. 2
30:11 leave the way, turn aside from the path 2
Jer 5:23 they have turned aside and gone away. 4
14: 8 a wayfarer who turns aside to tarry for a night? 2
15: 5 Who will turn aside to ask about your welfare? 4
Lam 3:35 to turn aside the right of a man 2
Dan 9: 5 turning aside from thy commandments 4
11 Israel has transgressed . . and turned aside 4
Ams 5:12 take a bribe, and turn aside the needy in the gate. 2
Mal 2: 8 you have turned aside from the way; 4
3: 7 you have turned aside from my statutes 4
Act 1:25 the place . . from which Judas turned aside 10
Rom 3:12 All have turned aside 8
Sir 2: 7 turn not aside, lest you fall. 8
9: 9 lest your heart turn aside to her 8
1Mc 2:22 by turning aside from our religion 11
5:35 Next he turned aside to Alema 7
68 Judas turned aside to Azotus 8
12:31 So Jonathan turned aside against the Arabs 8
33 He turned aside to Joppa and took it by surprise 8
4Mc 15:18 it did not turn you aside 9

turn aside upon 1. נטה
Ps 125: 5 those who turn aside upon their crooked ways 1

turn away 1. אֲחֹרַנִּית 2. הפך לְדֶרֶךְ 3. חדל 4. מְשׁוּבָה 5. נטה 6. סבב 7. סוג 8. סור 9. עבר 10. פנה 11. שׂטה 12. שׁוב 13. ἀποστρέφω 14. ἀποστροφή 15. διαστρέφω 16. ἐκκλίνω 17. μεθίστημι 18. τροπή
Gen 9:23 their faces were turned away, and they did not see 1
27:44 with him . . until your brother's fury turns away 12
45 until your brother's anger turns away 12
42:24 Then he turned away from them and wept; 6
Num 20:21 so Israel turned away from him. 5
25: 4 anger of the LORD may turn away from Israel. 12
32:15 For if you turn away from following him 12
Deu 7: 4 they would turn away your sons from following me 8
17:17 not multiply wives . . lest his heart turn away; 8
23:14 see anything indecent among you, and turn away 12
29:18 heart turns away this day from the LORD our God 10
30:17 if your heart turns away, and you will not hear 10
Jos 22:16 in turning away this day from following the LORD 12
18 that you must turn away this day from . . the LORD? 12
23 an altar to turn away from following the LORD; 12
29 and turn away this day from following the LORD 12
1Sm 6: 3 why his hand does not turn away from you. 8
25:12 David's young men turned away, and came back 2
28:15 God has turned away from me and answers me no 8
1Kg 11: 2 they will turn away your heart after their gods"; 5
3 and his wives turned away his heart. 5
4 his wives turned away his heart after other gods; 5
9 his heart had turned away from the LORD 5
21: 4 he lay down on his bed, and turned away his face 6
2Kg 15:24 he did not turn away from the sins of Jerobo'am 8
2Ch 6:42 do not turn away the face of thy anointed one! 12
25:27 From the time he turned away from the LORD 8
29: 6 turned away their faces from the habitation 6
10 that his fierce anger may turn away from us. 12
30: 8 that his fierce anger may turn away from you. 12
9 will not turn away his face from you, if you return 8
34:33 they did not turn away from following the LORD 8
35:22 Nevertheless Josi'ah would not turn away 6
Job 1: 1 one who feared God, and turned away from evil. 8
8 man, who fears God and turns away from evil? 8
2: 3 man, who fears God and turns away from evil? 8
Ps 27: 9 Turn not thy servant away in anger 5
78:57 but turned away and acted treacherously 7
106:23 to turn away his wrath from destroying them. 12
119:39 Turn away the reproach which I dread; 9
51 I do not turn away from thy law. 5
132:10 do not turn away the face of thy anointed one. 12
Prv 1:32 For the simple are killed by their turning away 4
3: 7 fear the LORD, and turn away from evil. 8
4: 5 do not turn away from the words of my mouth. 5
15 turn away from it and pass on. 11
27 turn your foot away from evil. 8
12:26 A righteous man turns away from evil •
13:19 turn away from evil is an abomination to fools. 8
14:16 A wise man is cautious and turns away from evil 8
15: 1 A soft answer turns away wrath 12
24:18 LORD . . be displeased, and turn away his anger 12
28: 9 If one turns away his ear from hearing the law 8
29: 8 but wise men turn away wrath. 12
Sng 6: 5 Turn away your eyes from me, for they disturb me- 6
Isa 2:22 Turn away from man in whose nostrils is breath 3
5:25 For all this his anger is not turned away 12
9:12 For all this his anger is not turned away 12
17 For all this his anger is not turned away 12
21 For all this his anger is not turned away 12
10: 4 For all this his anger is not turned away 12
12: 1 thy anger turned away, and thou didst comfort me. 12
59:13 the LORD, and turning away from following our God 7
Jer 5:25 Your iniquities have turned these away 5
8: 4 If one turns away, does he not return? 12
5 Why then has this people turned away 12
17: 5 whose heart turns away from the LORD. 8
13 those who turn away from thee shall be written 8
18:20 good for them, to turn away thy wrath from them. 12
31:19 For after I had turned away I repented; 12
50: 6 astray, turning them away on the mountains; 12
Ezk 14: 6 Repent and turn away from your idols; 12
6 turn away your faces from all your abominations. 12
18:21 But if a wicked man turns away from all his sins 12
24 man turns away from his righteousness 12
26 man turns away from his righteousness 12
27 when a wicked man turns away from the wickedness 12
28 and turned away from all the transgressions 12
Dan 9:16 anger . . wrath turn away from thy city Jerusalem 12
Hos 11: 7 My people are bent on turning away from me; 4
Act 13: 8 to turn away the proconsul from the faith. 15
19:26 and turned away a considerable company of people 17
2Ti 1:15 all who are in Asia turned away from me 13
4: 4 will turn away from listening to the truth 13
1Pe 3:11 let him turn away from evil and do right; 16
Tob 3: 6 do not turn thy face away from me. 13
4: 7 Do not turn your face away from any poor man 13
7 the face of God will not be turned away from you. 13
Sir 4: 4 nor turn your face away from the poor. 13
7: 2 it will turn away from you. 16
8: 5 Do not reproach a man who is turning away from sin; 13
9: 8 Turn away your eyes from a shapely woman 13
17:26 turn away from iniquity 13
18:24 moment of vengeance when he turns away his face. 14
45:23 stood fast, when the people turned away 18
46:11 who did not turn away from the Lord 13
Bar 1:13 his wrath have not turned away from us. 13
2: 8 by turning away, each of us, from the thoughts 13
13 Let thy anger turn away from us, for we are left 13
4:12 because they turned away from the law of God. 16
Sus 1: 9 and turned away their eyes from looking to Heaven 16
1Mc 3: 8 thus he turned away wrath from Israel. 13

turn away in flight 1. ἐκκλίνω
1Mc 6:47 they turned away in flight. 1

turn back 1. הפך 2. סבב 3. סוג 4. פנה 5. שׁוב 6. ἀνακάμπτω 7. ἀναστρέφω 8. ἀνατρέπω 9. ἀποστρέφω 10. δείκνυμι ἐπιστροφήν 11. ἐπανάγω 12. ἐπιστρέφω 13. τροπόω 14. ὑποστρέφω 15. averto 16. converto 17. recutio
Gen 14: 7 then they turned back and came to Enmish'pat 5
Exd 14: 2 Tell the people of Israel to turn back and encamp 5
Num 14:43 you have turned back from following the LORD 5
25:11 Phin'ehas . . has turned back my wrath 5
33: 7 from Etham, and turned back to Pi-hahi'roth 5
Deu 23:13 turn back and cover up your excrement. 5
Jos 8:20 the people . . turned back upon the pursuers. 1
21 then they turned back and smote the men of Ai. 5
10:38 Then Joshua, with all Israel, turned back to Debir 5
11:10 Joshua turned back at that time, and took Hazor 5
23:12 For if you turn back, and join the remnant of these 5
Jdg 2:19 whenever the judge died, they turned back 5
3:19 he himself turned back at the sculptured stones 5
20:48 the men of Israel turned back against 5
Rut 1:11 Turn back, my daughters, why will you go with me? 5
12 Turn back, my daughters, go your way, 5
1Sm 15:11 he has turned back from following me 5
31 Samuel turned back after Saul; 5
2Sm 22:38 I pursued . . and did not turn back 5
1Kg 12:26 the kingdom will turn back to the house of David; 5
22:33 they turned back from pursuing him. 5
2Kg 15:20 the king of Assyria turned back, and did not stay 5
19:28 I will turn you back on the way by which you came. 5
20: 5 Turn back, and say to Hezeki'ah the prince 5
2Ch 18:32 they turned back from pursuing him. 5
Neh 2:15 I turned back and entered by the Valley Gate 5
4: 4 turn back their taunt upon their own heads 5
9:26 warned them in order to turn them back to thee 5
29 warn them in order to turn them back to thy law. 5
Job 9:13 God will not turn back his anger; 5
39:22 he does not turn back from the sword. 5
Ps 6:10 they shall turn back, and be put to shame 5
18:37 and did not turn back till they were consumed. 5
78: 9 E'phraimites . . turned back on the day of battle. 1
80:18 Then we will never turn back from thee; 3
89:43 Yea, thou hast turned back the edge of his sword 5
90: 3 Thou turnest man back to the dust, and sayest 5
3 Thou . . sayest, "Turn back, O children of men! 5
132:11 sure oath from which he will not turn back 5
Prv 30:30 lion, which . . does not turn back before any; 5
Isa 14:27 His hand is stretched out, and who will turn it back? 5
28: 6 strength to those who turn back the battle 5
37:29 I will turn you back on the way by which you came. 5
38: 8 the sun turned back on the dial the ten steps 5
42:17 They shall be turned back 3
58:13 If you turn back your foot from the sabbath 5
Jer 4: 8 the fierce anger of the LORD has not turned back 5
28 I have not relented nor will I turn back. 5
11:10 They have turned back to the iniquities 5
21: 4 Behold, I will turn back the weapons of war 2
23:20 The anger of the LORD will not turn back 5
30:24 The fierce anger of the LORD will not turn back 5
49: 8 Flee, turn back, dwell in the depths, O inhabitants 4
Lam 1:13 he spread a net for my feet; he turned me back; 5
Ezk 7:13 wrath . . it shall not turn back; 5
33:11 turn back, turn back from your evil ways; 5
11 turn back, turn back from your evil ways; 5
Dan 11:18 indeed he shall turn his insolence back upon him. 5
19 shall turn his face back toward the fortresses 5
30 shall be afraid and withdraw, and shall turn back 5
30 turn back and give heed to those who forsake 5
Hos 12:14 and will turn back upon him his reproaches. 5
Nah 2: 8 Halt! Halt!" they cry; but none turns back. 4
Zep 1: 6 who have turned back from following the LORD 3
Lke 17:15 one of them . . turned back 14
Gal 4: 9 how can you turn back again to the weak 12
2Pe 2:21 to turn back from the holy commandment 14
22 The dog turns back to his own vomit 12
1Es 1:28 Josiah did not turn back to his chariot 9
8:87 we turned back again to transgress thy law 6
2Es 7:30 the world shall be turned back to . . silence 16
16: 3 and who is there to turn it back? 15
7 Can one turn back an arrow shot by a strong archer? 17
Tob 13: 6 Turn back, you sinners, and do right before him 12
Jdt 16:11 the enemy were turned back. 8
Wis 2: 5 because it is sealed up and no one turns back. 7
Sir 17: 1 turned him back to it again. 9
18:13 turns them back, as a shepherd his flock. 12
21 when you are on the point of sinning, turn back. 10
26:28 a man who turns back from righteousness to sin 11
40:11 turn back to the earth 7
Sus 1:14 But turning back, they met again; 6
1Mc 4:16 Then Judas and his force turned back 9
5:28 Judas . . turned back by the wilderness road to Bozrah 9
11:72 he turned back to the battle against the enemy 14
12:51 they turned back. 12
13:24 Trypho turned back and departed to his own land. 12
2Mc 5:18 and turned back from his rash act 8
13:19 He advanced against Beth-zur . . was turned back 13
3Mc 6:21 The beasts turned back upon the armed forces 9
4Mc 13: 5 who were not turned back by fiery agonies? 12

turn black 1. שׁחר
Job 30:30 My skin turns black and falls from me 1

every turn 1. παρ' ἕκαστα
2Mc 10:13 He heard himself called a traitor at every turn 1
14 and at every turn kept on warring against the Jews. 1

turn every way 1. הפך
Gen 3:24 a flaming sword which turned every way 1

turn in disgust 1. יקע 2. יקע נֶפֶשׁ 3. נקע נֶפֶשׁ
Ezk 23:17 she turned from them in disgust. 2
18 I turned in disgust from her, as I had turned 1
22 your lovers from whom you turned in disgust 3
28 hands of those from whom you turned in disgust; 3

turn in dread 1. פחד
Mic 7:17 they shall turn in dread to the LORD our God 1

turn in fear 1. פחד
Jer 36:16 they turned one to another in fear; 1

turn in repentance 1. conversionem facio
2Es 7:133 who turn in repentance to his law; 1

turn into 1. εἰς
1Mc 2:62 his splendor will turn into dung and worms. 1

turn into foolishness 1. סכל
2Sm 15:31 turn the counsel of Ahith'ophel into foolishness. 1

turn left 1. שׂמאל
Isa 30:21 turn to the right or when you turn to the left. 1

make turn 1. נתן 2. שׁוב
Exd 23:27 I will make all your enemies turn their backs 1
2Sm 22:41 Thou didst make my enemies turn their backs to me 1
Ps 18:40 Thou didst make my enemies turn their backs to me †
44:10 Thou hast made us turn back from the foe; 2

make turn back 1. שׁוב
Isa 38: 8 make the shadow . . turn back ten steps. 1

turn of affairs 1. נְסִבָּה 2. סִבָּה
1Kg 12:15 it was a turn of affairs brought about by the LORD 2
2Ch 10:15 for it was a turn of affairs brought about by God 1

turn of fortune 1. μέρος
Sir 37:18 four turns of fortune appear 1

turn one to righteousness 1. צדק
Dan 12: 3 who turn many to righteousness, like the stars 1

turn out 1. נפל 2. ἀναστρέφω 3. ἀποβαίνω 4. γίνομαι 5. ἐκβαίνω 6. ἐρρωμένος 7. ἔσχατος

8. συμβαίνω 9. χωρέω
Rut 3:18 Wait .. until you learn how the matter turns out 1
Php 1:19 this will turn out for my deliverance 3
Sir 30: 1 he may rejoice at the way he turns out. 7
8 A horse that is untamed turns out to be stubborn 5
8 a son unrestrained turns out to be wilful. 5
33:12 he turned them out of their place. 2
1Mc 4:27 nor had they turned out as the king had commanded 5
6: 8 because things had not turned out for him 4
2Mc 13:26 how the king's attack and withdrawal turned out. 9
15:37 This .. is how matters turned out with Nicanor. 9
3Mc 1: 3 so it turned out that this man incurred the vengeance 8
4 matters were turning out rather in favor of Antiochus 6

turn over 1. הפך 2. לפת 3. סבב 4. παραδίδωμι
Rut 3: 8 At midnight the man was startled, and turned over 2
1Ch 10:14 the LORD .. turned the kingdom over to David 3
Jer 6:12 Their houses shall be turned over to others 3
Lam 5: 2 inheritance has been turned over to strangers 1
1Mc 3:34 he turned over to Lysias half of his troops 4
16:18 to turn over to him the cities and the country. 4

turn pale 1. μεταβάλλω χρῶμα
AEs 15: 7 the queen faltered, and turned pale and faint 1

turn round 1. סבב 2. סבב פָּנִים 3. ἐπιστρέφω 4. στρέφω
Jos 16: 6 the boundary turns round toward Ta'anath-shi'loh 1
Jdg 18:23 shouted to the Danites, who turned round and said 2
2Kg 9:18 Turn round and ride behind me. 1
19 Turn round and ride behind me. 1
Joh 20:14 Saying this, she turned round 4
1Mc 12:45 and will turn round and go home 3

turn to ashes 1. τεφρόω
2Pe 2: 6 if by turning the cities .. to ashes 1

turn to the left 1. שמאל
2Sm 14:19 one cannot turn to the right hand or to the left 1

turn to the right 1. ימן
Isa 30:21 when you turn to the right 1

turn to the right hand 1. ימן
2Sm 14:19 one cannot turn to the right hand or to the left 1

turn toward 1. ἐπιστρέφω
Wis 16: 7 For he who turned toward it was saved 1

turn trembling 1. חרד
Gen 42:28 they turned trembling to one another 1

turn up 1. הפך
Job 28: 5 but underneath it is turned up as by fire. 1

turn upside down 1. הָפַךְ 2. ἀναστατόω
Isa 29:16 You turn things upside down! 1
Act 17: 6 These men who have turned the world upside down 2

turn wantonly 1. זנה
Ezk 6: 9 eyes which turn wantonly after their idols 1

turtledove 1. תֹּר 2. τρυγών
Gen 15: 9 a ram .. a turtledove, and a young pigeon. 1
Lev 1:14 then he shall bring his offering of turtledoves 1
5: 7 bring .. two turtledoves or two young pigeons 1
11 afford two turtledoves or two young pigeons 1
12: 6 a young pigeon or a turtledove for a sin offering 1
8 take two turtledoves or two young pigeons 1
14:22 also two turtledoves or two young pigeons 1
30 offer, of the turtledoves or young pigeons 1
15:14 on the eighth day he shall take two turtledoves 1
29 two turtledoves or two young pigeons 1
Num 6:10 bring two turtledoves or two young pigeons 1
Sng 2:12 the voice of the turtledove is heard in our land. 1
Jer 8: 7 turtledove, swallow, and crane keep the time 1
Lke 2:24 a pair of turtledoves, or two young pigeons. 2

tusk 1. קֶרֶן
Ezk 27:15 brought you in payment ivory tusks and ebony. 1

twelfth 1. שְׁנֵים עָשָׂר 2. δωδέκατος
Num 7:78 On the twelfth day Ahi'ra .. of Naph'tali 1
1Kg 19:19 twelve yoke .. and he was with the twelfth. 1
2Kg 8:25 In the twelfth year of Joram the son of Ahab 1
17: 1 In the twelfth year of Ahaz king of Judah 1
25:27 in the 37th year .. in the twelfth month 1
1Ch 24:12 the eleventh to Eli'ashib, the twelfth to Jakim 1
25:19 twelfth to Hashabi'ah, his sons and his brethren 1
27:15 Twelfth .. was Heldai the Netoph'athite 1
15 Twelfth, for the twelfth month, was Heldai 1
2Ch 34: 3 twelfth year he began to purge Judah 1
Ezr 8:31 departed from the river Aha'va on the twelfth day 1
Est 3: 7 of Nisan, in the twelfth year of King Ahasu-e'rus 1
7 cast it month after month till the twelfth month 1
13 in one day, the thirteenth day of the twelfth month 1
8:12 on the thirteenth day of the twelfth month 1
9: 1 in the twelfth month, which is the month of Adar 1
Jer 52:31 in the twelfth month, on the 25th day 1
Ezk 29: 1 the tenth month, on the twelfth day of the month 1
32: 1 In the twelfth year, in the twelfth month 1
1 In the twelfth year, in the twelfth month 1
17 In the twelfth year, in the first month 1
33:21 In the twelfth year of our exile 1
Rev 21:20 the eleventh jacinth, the twelfth amethyst. 2
1Es 8:61 on the twelfth day of the first month 2
Jdt 1: 1 the twelfth year of the reign of Nebuchadnezzar 2
AEs 13: 6 on the fourteenth day of the twelfth month 2
16:20 the thirteenth day of the twelfth month, Adar 2
2Mc 15:36 the thirteenth day of the twelfth month 2

twelve 1. שְׁנֵים עָשָׂר 2. תְּרֵי עֲשַׂר (A) 3. δέκα δύο 4. δώδεκα 5. duodecim
Gen 14: 4 Twelve years they had served Ched-or-lao'mer 1
17:20 he shall be the father of twelve princes 1
25:16 twelve princes according to their tribes. 1
35:22 Now the sons of Jacob were twelve. 1
42:13 said, "We, your servants, are twelve brothers 1
32 we are twelve brothers, sons of our father; 1
49:28 All these are the twelve tribes of Israel; 1
Exd 15:27 Elim, where there were twelve springs of water 1
24: 4 built .. twelve pillars, according 1
4 twelve pillars, according to the twelve tribes 1
28:21 There shall be twelve stones with their names 1
21 with its name, for the twelve tribes. 1
39:14 There were twelve stones with their names 1
14 with its name, for the twelve tribes. 1
Lev 24: 5 you shall take fine flour, and bake twelve cakes 1
Num 1:44 twelve men, each representing his fathers' house. 1
7: 3 offering .. six covered wagons and twelve oxen 1
84 dedication offering .. twelve silver plates 1
84 dedication offering .. twelve silver basins 1
84 dedication offering .. twelve golden dishes 1
86 the twelve golden dishes, full of incense 1
87 cattle for the burnt offering twelve bulls 1
87 burnt offering .. twelve rams 1
87 burnt offering .. twelve male lambs a year old 1
87 twelve male goats for a sin offering; 1
17: 2 get from them .. twelve rods. 1
6 according to their fathers' houses, twelve rods; 1
29:17 On the second day twelve young bulls, two rams 1
33: 9 at Elim there were twelve springs of water 1
Deu 1:23 I took twelve men of you, one man for each tribe; 1
Jos 3:12 Now .. take twelve men from the tribes of Israel 1
4: 2 Take twelve men from the people, from each .. a man 1
3 Take twelve stones from here out of the .. Jordan 1
4 Joshua called the twelve men from the people 1
8 and took up twelve stones out of the midst 1
9 And Joshua set up twelve stones in the .. Jordan 1
20 those twelve stones .. Joshua set up in Gilgal. 1
18:24 twelve cities with their villages 1
19:15 twelve cities with their villages. 1
21: 7 received from .. Zeb'ulun, twelve cities. 1
40 those allotted .. were in all twelve cities. 1
Jdg 19:29 he divided her, limb by limb, into twelve pieces 1
2Sm 2:15 passed over by number, twelve for Benjamin 1
15 by number .. and twelve of the servants of David. 1
1Kg 4: 7 Solomon had twelve officers over all Israel, who 1
7:15 twelve cubits measured its circumference; 1
25 It stood upon twelve oxen, three facing north 1
44 one sea, and the twelve oxen underneath the sea. 1
10:20 twelve lions stood there, one on each end of a step 1
11:30 laid hold .. and tore it into twelve pieces. 1
16:23 Omri .. reigned for twelve years; 1
18:31 Eli'jah took twelve stones 1
19:19 Eli'sha .. was plowing, with twelve yoke of oxen 1
2Kg 3: 1 and he reigned twelve years. 1
21: 1 Manas'seh was twelve years old when he began 1
1Ch 6:63 twelve cities out of the tribes of Reuben, Gad 1
25: 9 Gedali'ah .. his brethren and his sons, twelve; 1
10 third to Zaccur, his sons and his brethren, twelve; 1
11 fourth to Izri, his sons and his brethren, twelve; 1
12 to Nethani'ah, his sons and his brethren, twelve; 1
13 Bukki'ah, his sons and his brethren, twelve; 1
14 to Jeshare'lah, his sons and his brethren, twelve; 1
15 to Jeshai'ah, his sons and his brethren, twelve; 1
16 to Mattani'ah, his sons and his brethren, twelve; 1
17 tenth to Shim'e-i, his sons and his brethren, twelve; 1
18 to Az'arel, his sons and his brethren, twelve; 1
19 to Hashabi'ah, his sons and his brethren, twelve; 1
20 Shu'ba-el, his sons and his brethren, twelve; 1
21 Mattithi'ah, his sons and his brethren, twelve; 1
22 to Jer'emoth, his sons and his brethren, twelve; 1
23 to Hanani'ah, his sons and his brethren, twelve; 1
24 Joshbekash'ah, his sons and his brethren, twelve; 1
25 to Hana'ni, his sons and his brethren, twelve; 1
26 to Mallo'thi, his sons and his brethren, twelve; 1
27 to Eli'athah, his sons and his brethren, twelve; 1
28 to Hothir, his sons and his brethren, twelve; 1
29 to Giddal'ti, his sons and his brethren, twelve; 1
30 to Maha'zi-oth, his sons and his brethren, twelve; 1
31 Romam'ti-e'zer, his sons and his brethren, twelve. 1
2Ch 4: 4 It stood upon twelve oxen, three facing north 1
15 the one sea, and the twelve oxen underneath it. 1
9:19 while twelve lions stood there, one on each end 1
33: 1 Manas'seh was twelve .. when he began to reign 1
Ezr 6:17 sin offering for all Israel twelve he-goats 2
8:24 Then I set apart twelve of the leading priests 1
35 twelve bulls for all Israel, 96 rams 1
35 as a sin offering twelve he-goats; 1
Neh 5:14 twelve years, neither I nor my brethren 1
Est 2:12 being twelve months under the regulations 1
Jer 52:20 the twelve bronze bulls which were under the sea 1
21 its circumference was twelve cubits 1
Ezk 40:49 was twenty cubits, and the breadth twelve cubits; 4
43:16 be square, twelve cubits long by twelve broad. 1
16 be square, twelve cubits long by twelve broad. 1
47:13 inheritance among the twelve tribes of Israel. 1
Dan 4:29 end of twelve months he was walking on the roof 2
Mat 9:20 a hemorrhage for twelve years 4
10: 1 he called to him his twelve disciples 4
2 The names of the twelve apostles are these 4
5 These twelve Jesus sent out, charging them 4
11: 1 instructing his twelve disciples 4
14:20 they took up twelve baskets 4
19:28 will also sit on twelve thrones 4
28 judging the twelve tribes of Israel. 4
20:17 he took the twelve disciples aside 4
26:14 one of the twelve, who was called Judas Iscariot 4
20 he sat at table with the twelve disciples; 4
47 Judas came, one of the twelve 4
53 send me more than twelve legions of angels? 4
Mrk 3:14 he appointed twelve, to be with him 4
4:10 those who were about him with the twelve 4
5:25 woman who had had a flow of blood for twelve years 4
42 she was twelve years of age 4
6: 7 he called to him the twelve 4
43 they took up twelve baskets 4
8:19 They said to him, "Twelve. 4
9:35 he sat down and called the twelve; and he said 4
10:32 taking the twelve again, he began to tell them 4
11:11 he went out to Bethany with the twelve. 4
14:10 Then Judas Iscariot, who was one of the twelve 4
17 when it was evening he came with the twelve. 4
20 He said to them, "It is one of the twelve 4
43 Judas came, one of the twelve 4
Lke 2:42 when he was twelve years old 4
6:13 called his disciples, and chose from them twelve 4
8: 1 the twelve were with him 4
42 he had an only daughter, about twelve years of age 4
43 woman who had had a flow of blood for twelve years 4
9: 1 And he called the twelve together 4
12 the twelve came and said to him 4
17 twelve baskets of broken pieces. 4
18:31 taking the twelve, he said to them, "Behold 4
22: 3 who was of the number of the twelve; 4
30 judging the twelve tribes of Israel. 4
47 the man called Judas, one of the twelve, was leading 4
Joh 6:13 filled twelve baskets with fragments 4
67 Jesus said to the twelve 4
70 Did I not choose you, the twelve 4
71 he, one of the twelve, was to betray him. 4
11: 9 Are there not twelve hours in the day? 4
20:24 Now Thomas, one of the twelve, called the Twin 4
Act 6: 2 the twelve summoned the body of the disciples 4
7: 8 Jacob of the twelve patriarchs. 4
19: 7 There were about twelve of them in all. 4
24:11 it is not more than twelve days since I went up 4
1Co 15: 5 that he appeared to Cephas, then to the twelve. 4
Jas 1: 1 To the twelve tribes in the Dispersion 4
Rev 12: 1 and on her head a crown of twelve stars; 4
21:12 It had a great, high wall, with twelve gates 4
12 and at the gates twelve angels 4
12 names of the twelve tribes of the sons of Israel 4
14 And the wall of the city had twelve foundations 4
14 twelve names of the twelve apostles of the Lamb. 4
14 twelve names of the twelve apostles of the Lamb. 4
21 And the twelve gates were twelve pearls 4
21 And the twelve gates were twelve pearls 4
22: 2 the tree of life with its twelve kinds of fruit 4
1Es 7: 8 twelve he-goats for the sin of all Israel 4
8 the twelve leaders of the tribes of Israel; 4
8:54 I set apart twelve of the leaders of the priests 3
57 twelve bronze vessels of fine bronze 4
65 offered sacrifices .. twelve bulls for all Israel 4
66 72 lambs, and as a thank offering twelve he-goats 3
2Es 2:18 twelve trees loaded with various fruits 5
11: 1 an eagle that had twelve feathered wings 5
22 the twelve wings and the two little wings 5
12:14 twelve kings shall reign in it 5
15 longer time than any other of the twelve. 5
16 the interpretation of the twelve wings 5
14:11 For the age is divided into twelve parts 5
Sir 44:23 distributed them among twelve tribes. 3
49:10 May the bones of the twelve prophets revive 4
Bel 1: 3 they spent on it twelve bushels of fine flour 4
1Mc 1: 7 after Alexander had reigned twelve years 4

twelve tribes 1. δωδεκάφυλον
Act 26: 7 to which our twelve tribes hope to attain 1

twelve years 1. δωδεκαετής
1Es 5:41 All those of Israel, twelve or more years of age 1

twentieth 1. עֶשְׂרִים 2. *εἰκάς*

Num10:11 second month, on the twentieth day of the month 1
1Kg 15: 9 In the twentieth year of Jerobo'am king of Israel 1
2Kg 15:30 the twentieth year of Jotham the son of Uzzi'ah. 1
1Ch 24:16 to Pethahi'ah, the twentieth to Jehez'kel 1
25:27 twentieth, to Eli'athah, his sons and his brethren 1
Ezr 10: 9 ninth month, on the twentieth day of the month. 1
Neh 1: 1 month of Chislev, in the twentieth year 1
2: 1 Nisan, in the twentieth year of King Ar-ta-xerx'es 1
5:14 from the twentieth year to the 32nd 1
1Es 9: 5 on the twentieth day of the month. 2

twenty 1. עֶשְׂרִים 2. *εἰκοσαετής* 3. *εἴκοσι*

Gen 18:31 Suppose twenty are found there. 1
31 He answered, "For the sake of twenty I will not 1
31:38 These twenty years I have been with you; 1
41 These twenty years I have been in your house; 1
32:14 200 she-goats and twenty he-goats 1
14 200 ewes and twenty rams 1
15 bulls, twenty she-asses and ten he-asses. 1
37:28 sold him to the Ish'maelites for twenty shekels 1
Exd 26:18 twenty frames for the south side; 1
19 bases . . you shall make under the twenty frames 1
20 the tabernacle, on the north side twenty frames 1
27:10 pillars shall be twenty and their bases twenty 1
10 pillars shall be twenty and their bases twenty 1
11 hangings . . their pillars twenty and their 1
11 pillars twenty and their bases twenty, of bronze 1
16 there shall be a screen twenty cubits long 1
30:13 (the shekel is twenty gerahs) 1
14 from twenty years old and upward, shall give 1
36:23 made thus: twenty frames for the south side; 1
24 he made 40 bases of silver under the twenty frames 1
25 on the north side, he made twenty frames 1
38:10 their pillars were twenty and their bases 1
10 were twenty and their bases twenty, of bronze 1
11 their pillars twenty, their bases twenty 1
11 their pillars twenty, their bases twenty 1
18 it was twenty cubits long and five cubits high 1
26 from twenty years old and upward, 603,550 men. 1
Lev 27: 3 then your valuation of a male from twenty years 1
5 is from five years old up to twenty years old 1
5 your valuation shall be for a male twenty shekels 1
25 twenty gerahs shall make a shekel 1
Num 1: 3 from twenty years old and upward, all in Israel 1
18 names from twenty years old and upward 1
20 every male from twenty years old and upward 1
22 every male from twenty years old and upward 1
24 from twenty years old and upward 1
26 from twenty years old and upward, every man able 1
28 from twenty years old and upward, every man able 1
30 from twenty years old and upward, every man able 1
32 number of names, from twenty years old and upward 1
34 from twenty years old and upward, every man able 1
36 from twenty years old and upward, every man able 1
38 from twenty years old and upward, every man able 1
40 according to the number of names, from twenty 1
42 from twenty years old and upward, every man able 1
45 from twenty years old and upward, every man able 1
3:47 of the sanctuary, the shekel of twenty gerahs 1
11:19 You shall not eat . . ten days, or twenty days 1
14:29 numbered from twenty years old and upward, who 1
18:16 shekel of the sanctuary, which is twenty gerahs. 1
26: 2 from twenty years old and upward 1
4 people, from twenty years old and upward 1
32:11 none . . from twenty years old and upward 1
Jdg 4: 3 oppressed . . Israel cruelly for twenty years. 1
11:33 the neighborhood of Minnith, twenty cities 1
15:20 he judged Israel . . twenty years. 1
16:31 He had judged Israel twenty years. 1
1Sm 7: 2 From . . a long time passed, some twenty years 1
14:14 that first slaughter . . was of about twenty men 1
2Sm 3:20 Abner came with twenty men to David at Hebron 1
9:10 Now Ziba had fifteen sons and twenty servants. 1
19:17 fifteen sons and his twenty servants, rushed 1
24: 8 at the end of nine months and twenty days. 1
1Kg 4:23 fat oxen, and twenty pasture-fed cattle 1
6: 2 The house . . was 60 cubits long, twenty cubits wide 1
3 The vestibule . . was twenty cubits long 1
16 He built twenty cubits of the rear of the house 1
20 The inner sanctuary was twenty cubits long 1
20 was twenty cubits long, twenty cubits wide 1
20 long, twenty cubits wide, and twenty cubits high; 1
9:10 At the end of twenty years . . Solomon had built 1
11 Solomon gave to Hiram twenty cities in the land 1
2Kg 4:42 bringing . . twenty loaves of barley 1
15:27 began to reign . . and reigned twenty years. 1
16: 2 Ahaz was twenty years old when he began to reign 1
1Ch 23:24 from twenty years old and upward 1
27 number of the Levites from twenty years old 1
27:23 did not number those below twenty years of age 1
2Ch 3: 3 60 cubits, and the breadth twenty cubits. 1
4 The vestibule . . was twenty cubits long 1
8 most holy place; its length . . was twenty cubits; 1
8 most holy place . . breadth was twenty cubits; 1
11 The wings . . together extended twenty cubits 1
13 wings of these cherubim extended twenty cubits; 1
4: 1 He made an altar of bronze, twenty cubits long 1
1 an altar of bronze . . and twenty cubits wide 1
8: 1 At the end of twenty years, in which Solomon had 1
25: 5 He mustered those twenty years old and upward 1
28: 1 Ahaz was twenty years old when he began to reign 1
31:17 Levites from twenty years old and upwards 1
Ezr 3: 8 Levites, from twenty years old and upward 1
8:19 Hashabi'ah . . his kinsmen and their sons, twenty; 1
27 twenty bowls of gold worth 1,000 darics 1
Ezk 4:10 food . . shall be by weight, twenty shekels a day; 1
40:14 He measured also the vestibule, twenty cubits; •
49 The length of the vestibule was twenty cubits 1
41: 2 40 cubits, and its breadth, twenty cubits. 1
4 he measured the length of the room, twenty cubits 1
4 and its breadth, twenty cubits, beyond the nave. 1
10 court was a breadth of twenty cubits round about 1
42: 3 Adjoining the twenty cubits which belonged 1
45:12 The shekel shall be twenty gerahs; 1
Hag 2:16 When one came to a heap of twenty measures 1
16 to draw 50 measures, there were but twenty 1
Zec 5: 2 a flying scroll; its length is twenty cubits 1
Act 27:28 So they sounded and found twenty fathoms 3
1Es 4:51 that twenty talents a year should be given 3
5:58 the Levites who were twenty or more years of age 2
8:48 and their sons, twenty men; 3
57 twenty golden bowls, and twelve bronze vessels 3
2Mc 10:35 twenty young men in the army of Maccabeus 3

twenty gallons 1. *μετρητάς δύο*

Joh 2: 6 jars . . each holding twenty or 30 gallons 1

twice 1. כפל 2. מִשְׁנֶה 3. פַּעַם 4. שׁנה 5. שְׁנַיִם 6. *δεύτερος* 7. *δίς*

Gen 43:10 not delayed, we would now have returned twice. 3
Exd 16: 5 it will be twice as much as they gather daily. 2
22 the sixth day they gathered twice as much bread 2
Num20:11 Moses . . struck the rock with his rod twice; 3
1Sm 18:11 But David evaded him twice. 3
26: 8 let me . . and I will not strike him twice. 4
1Kg 11: 9 the LORD . . who had appeared to him twice 3
2Kg 6:10 he saved himself there more than once or twice. 5
Neh 13:20 lodged outside Jerusalem once or twice. 5
Job 33:29 God does all these things, twice, three times 3
40: 5 twice, but I will proceed no further. 5
42:10 the LORD gave Job twice as much as he had before. 2
Ps 62:11 Once God has spoken; twice have I heard this 5
Ezk 21:14 clap your hands and let the sword come down twice 1
Nah 1: 9 he will not take vengeance twice on his foes. 3
Mrk 14:30 this very night, before the cock crows twice 7
72 Before the cock crows twice 7
Lke 18:12 I fast twice a week, I give tithes of all that I get.' 7
Tit 3:10 after admonishing him once or twice 6
Jde 1:12 trees in late autumn, twice dead, uprooted; 7
Jdt 13: 8 she struck his neck twice with all her might 7
Sir 7: 8 Do not commit a sin twice 7
32: 7 no more than twice, and only if asked. 7
45:14 shall be wholly burned twice every day 7
1Mc 10:72 fathers were twice put to flight in their own land. 7

twice *See also* 10,000, told.

twice as much 1. *διπλάσιος* 2. *διπλοῦς*

Mat 23:15 you make him twice as much a child of hell 2
Sir 12: 5 you will receive twice as much evil 1

twig

Ezk 17: 5 He set it like a willow twig •

young twig 1. יוֹנֶקֶת 2. יְנִיקָה

Ezk 17: 4 he broke off the topmost of its young twigs 2
22 break off from the topmost of its young twigs 1

twilight 1. נֶשֶׁף 2. עֶרֶב

Exd 16:12 say to them, 'At twilight you shall eat flesh 2
1Sm 30:17 David smote them from twilight until the evening 1
2Kg 7: 5 So they arose at twilight to go to the . . Syrians; 1
7 So they fled away in the twilight 1
Job 24:15 the adulterer also waits for the twilight 1
Prv 7: 9 in the twilight, in the evening 1
Isa 21: 4 the twilight I longed for has been turned 1
59:10 we stumble at noon as in the twilight 1
Jer 13:16 your feet stumble on the twilight mountains 1

twin 1. תּוֹאָם

Gen 25:24 behold, there were twins in her womb. 1
38:27 delivery came, there were twins in her womb. 1
Sng 4: 5 breasts are like two fawns, twins of a gazelle 1
7: 3 breasts are like two fawns, twins of a gazelle. 1

twine 1. סבב 2. שׁזר

Exd 26: 1 with ten curtains of fine twined linen and blue 2
31 scarlet stuff and fine twined linen; 2
36 scarlet stuff and fine twined linen 2
27: 9 court shall have hangings of fine twined linen 2
16 a screen . . of . . fine twined linen 2
18 with hangings of fine twined linen and bases 2
28: 5 purple and scarlet stuff, and fine twined linen. •
6 of fine twined linen, skilfully worked. 2
8 purple and scarlet stuff, and fine twined linen. 2
15 of . . fine twined linen shall you make it. 2
36: 8 they were made of fine twined linen and blue 2
35 purple and scarlet stuff and fine twined linen; 2
37 scarlet stuff and fine twined linen 2
38: 9 hangings of the court were of fine twined linen 2
16 hangings . . were of fine twined linen. 2
18 purple and scarlet stuff and fine twined linen; 2
39: 2 purple and scarlet stuff, and fine twined linen. 2
5 purple and scarlet stuff, and fine twined linen; 2
8 purple and scarlet stuff, and fine twined linen. 2
24 scarlet stuff and fine twined linen. 2
28 and the linen breeches of fine twined linen 2
29 the girdle of fine twined linen and of blue 2
Job 8:17 His roots twine about the stoneheap; 1

twined *See* linen.

twinkle 1. *ῥιπή*

1Co 15:52 in a moment, in the twinkling of an eye 1

twins *See* bear.

twist 1. גַּבְלֻת 2. הפך 3. עֲבֹת 4. עוה 5. עֲקַלָּתוֹן 6. פתל 7. *διαστρέφω* 8. *κατακάμπτω* 9. *κλώθω* 10. *στρεβλόω*

Exd 28:14 two chains of pure gold, twisted like cords; 3
22 shall make for the breastpiece twisted chains 1
39:15 they made on the breastpiece twisted chains 1
Ps 78:57 they twisted like a deceitful bow. 2
Prv 8: 8 there is nothing twisted or crooked in them. 6
Isa 24: 1 waste the earth . . and he will twist its surface 4
27: 1 Leviathan the twisting serpent 5
2Pe 3:16 which the ignorant and unstable twist 10
Sir 27:23 later he will twist his speech 7
45:11 with twisted scarlet, the work of a craftsman; 9
4Mc 9:17 Cut my limbs, burn my flesh, and twist my joints. 10
11:10 twisted his back around the wedge on the wheel 8

two 1. צֶמֶד 2. שְׁנַיִם 3. *ἀμφότεροι* 4. *ἄμφω* 5. *δύο* 6. *ἑκάτερος* 7. *μέσος* 8. duo

Gen 1:16 God made the two great lights 2
4:19 Lamech took two wives; the name of the one 2
6:19 you shall bring two of every sort into the ark 2
20 two of every sort shall come in to you 2
7: 9 two and two, male and female, went into the ark 2
9 two and two, male and female, went into the ark 2
15 two and two of all flesh in which there 2
15 two and two of all flesh in which there 2
9:22 of his father, and told his two brothers outside. 2
10:25 To Eber were born two sons 2
11:10 father of Arpach'shad two years after the flood; †
19: 1 The two angels came to Sodom in the evening; 2
8 Behold, I have two daughters who have not known 2
15 take your wife and your two daughters 2
16 seized . . his wife and his two daughters 2
30 Lot . . dwelt in the hills with his two daughters 2
30 he dwelt in a cave with his two daughters. 2
22: 3 took two of his young men with him, and his son 2
24:22 took . . two bracelets for her arms 2
25:23 the LORD said to her, "Two nations are in your womb 2
23 and two peoples, born of you, shall be divided; 2
27: 9 Go to the flock, and fetch me two good kids 2
36 Jacob? For he has supplanted me these two times. †
29:16 Now Laban had two daughters; 2
31:33 into the tent of the two maidservants 2
37 kinsmen, that they may decide between us two. 2
41 fourteen years for your two daughters 2
32: 7 flocks and herds and camels, into two companies 2
10 and now I have become two companies. 2
22 The same night he arose and took his two wives 2
22 took . . his two maids, and his eleven children 2
33: 1 among Leah and Rachel and the two maids. 2
34:25 when they were sore, two of the sons of Jacob 2
40: 2 Pharaoh was angry with his two officers 2
41: 1 After two whole years, Pharaoh dreamed †
50 Joseph had two sons, whom As'enath 2
42:37 Slay my two sons if I do not bring him back to you; 2
45: 6 the famine has been in the land these two years; †
46:27 who were born to him in Egypt, were two; 2
48: 1 with him his two sons, Manas'seh and E'phraim. 2
5 now your two sons, who were born to you in the land 2
Exd 2:13 behold, two Hebrews were struggling together; 2
4: 9 If they will not believe even these two signs 2
12: 7 the blood, and put it on the two doorposts 2
22 touch . . the two doorposts with the blood 2
23 the blood on the lintel and on the two doorposts 2
16:22 gathered twice as much bread, two omers apiece; 2
29 on the sixth day he gives you bread for two days; †
18: 3 her two sons, of whom the name of the one was 2
6 with your wife and her two sons with her 2
21:21 if the slave survives a day or two, he is not to be †
25:10 two cubits and a half shall be its length †
12 two rings on the one side of it, and two rings 2
12 and two rings on the other side of it. 2
17 two cubits and a half shall be its length †
18 you shall make two cherubim of gold; 2
18 cherubim . . on the two ends of the mercy seat. 2
19 shall you make the cherubim on its two ends. 2
22 the two cherubim that are upon the ark 2
23 two cubits shall †
26:17 There shall be two tenons in each frame 2

19 two bases under one frame for its two tenons 2
19 two bases under one frame for its two tenons 2
19 two bases under another frame for its two tenons; 2
19 two bases under another frame for its two tenons; 2
21 forty bases of silver, two bases under one frame 2
21 and two bases under another frame; 2
23 you shall make two frames for corners 2
24 they shall form the two corners. 2
25 two bases under one frame, and two bases 2
25 and two bases under another frame. 2
27: 7 the poles shall be upon the two sides of the altar 2
28: 7 It shall have two shoulder-pieces attached 2
7 two shoulder-pieces attached to its two edges 2
9 you shall take two onyx stones, and engrave 2
11 shall you engrave the two stones with the names 2
12 set the two stones upon the shoulder-pieces 2
12 upon his two shoulders for remembrance. 2
14 two chains of pure gold, twisted like cords; 2
23 shall make for the breastpiece two rings of gold 2
23 two rings on the two edges of the breastpiece. 2
23 two rings on the two edges of the breastpiece. 2
24 the two cords of gold in the two rings at the edges 2
24 the two cords of gold in the two rings at the edges 2
25 the two ends of the two cords you shall attach 2
25 the two ends of the two cords you shall attach 2
25 two cords you shall attach to the two settings 2
26 you shall make two rings of gold, and put them 2
26 put them at the two ends of the breastpiece 2
27 you shall make two rings of gold, and attach them 2
27 to the lower part of the two shoulder-pieces 2
29: 1 Take one young bull and two rams without blemish 2
3 and bring the bull and the two rams. 2
13 take . . the two kidneys with the fat 2
22 take . . the two kidneys with the fat 2
38 two lambs a year old day by day continually. 2
38 two lambs a year old day by day continually. †
30: 2 and two cubits shall be its height; †
4 two golden rings shall you make for it; 2
4 under its molding on two opposite sides of it 2
31:18 gave to Moses . . two tables of the testimony 2
32:15 went down from the mountain with the two tables 2
34: 1 The LORD said to Moses, "Cut two tables of stone 2
4 Moses cut two tables of stone like the first; 2
4 and took in his hand two tables of stone. 2
29 with the two tables of the testimony in his hand 2
36:22 Each frame had two tenons, for fitting together; 2
24 two bases under one frame for its two tenons 2
24 two bases under one frame for its two tenons 2
24 two bases under another frame for its two 2
24 bases under another frame for its two tenons. 2
26 their forty bases of silver, two bases under one 2
26 and two bases under another frame. 2
28 he made two frames for corners 2
29 he made two of them thus, for the two corners. 2
29 he made two of them thus, for the two corners. 2
30 sixteen bases, under every frame two bases. 2
37: 1 two cubits and a half was its length †
3 two rings on its one side and two rings on its 2
3 its one side and two rings on its other side. 2
6 two cubits and a half was its length †
7 he made two cherubim of hammered gold; 2
7 on the two ends of the mercy seat he made them 2
8 mercy seat he made the cherubim on its two ends. 2
10 two cubits was its length, a cubit its breadth †
25 it was square, and two cubits was its height; †
27 made two rings of gold on it under its molding 2
27 under its molding, on two opposite sides of it 2
39: 4 shoulder-pieces, joined to it at its two edges. 2
16 they made two settings of gold filigree 2
16 they made . . two gold rings, and put the two rings 2
16 put the two rings on the two edges 2
16 two rings on the two edges of the breastpiece; 2
17 they put the two cords of gold in the two rings 2
17 two cords of gold in the two rings at the edges 2
18 Two ends of the two cords they had attached 2
18 Two ends of the two cords they had attached 2
18 had attached to the two settings of filigree; 2
19 Then they made two rings of gold 2
19 and put them at the two ends of the breastpiece 2
20 they made two rings of gold, and attached them 2
20 to the lower part of the two shoulder-pieces 2
Lev 3: 4 the two kidneys with the fat that is on them 2
10 the two kidneys with the fat that is on them 2
15 the two kidneys with the fat that is on them 2
4: 9 the two kidneys with the fat that is on them 2
5: 7 bring . . two turtledoves or two young pigeons 2
7 bring . . two turtledoves or two young pigeons 2
11 afford two turtledoves or two young pigeons 2
11 afford two turtledoves or two young pigeons 2
7: 4 the two kidneys with the fat that is on them 2
8: 2 Take . . the two rams, and the basket 2
16 he took . . the two kidneys with their fat 2
25 he took . . the two kidneys with their fat 2
12: 5 then she shall be unclean two weeks †
8 take two turtledoves or two young pigeons 2
8 take two turtledoves or two young pigeons 2
14: 4 take . . two living birds and cedarwood 2
10 on the eighth day he shall take two male lambs 2
22 also two turtledoves or two young pigeons 2
22 also two turtledoves or two young pigeons 2
49 he shall take two small birds 2
15:14 on the eighth day he shall take two turtledoves 2
14 take two turtledoves or two young pigeons 2
29 two turtledoves or two young pigeons 2
29 two turtledoves or two young pigeons 2
16: 1 after the death of the two sons of Aaron 2
5 two male goats for a sin offering 2
7 take the two goats, and set them before the LORD 2
8 Aaron shall cast lots upon the two goats 2
12 and two handfuls of sweet incense beaten small †
23:17 You shall bring from your dwellings two loaves 2
18 present . . one young bull, and two rams 2
19 offer . . two male lambs a year old as a sacrifice 2
20 wave offering before the LORD, with the two lambs 2
24: 6 you shall set them in two rows, six in a row 2
Num 6:10 bring two turtledoves or two young pigeons 2
10 bring two turtledoves or two young pigeons 2
7: 3 wagon for every two of the leaders 2
7 Two wagons and four oxen he gave to . . Gershon 2
17 for the sacrifice of peace offerings, two oxen 2
23 for the sacrifice of peace offerings, two oxen 2
29 for the sacrifice of peace offerings, two oxen 2
35 for the sacrifice of peace offerings, two oxen 2
41 for the sacrifice of peace offerings, two oxen 2
47 for the sacrifice of peace offerings, two oxen 2
53 for the sacrifice of peace offerings, two oxen 2
59 for the sacrifice of peace offerings, two oxen 2
65 for the sacrifice of peace offerings, two oxen 2
71 for the sacrifice of peace offerings, two oxen 2
77 for the sacrifice of peace offerings, two oxen 2
83 for the sacrifice of peace offerings, two oxen 2
89 voice . . from between the two cherubim; 2
9:22 Whether it was two days, or a month, or a longer time †
10: 2 Make two silver trumpets; of hammered work 2
11:19 You shall not eat one day, or two days, or five days †
26 Now two men remained in the camp, one named Eldad 2
31 about two cubits above the face of the earth. †
13:23 they carried it on a pole between two of them; 2
22:22 his two servants were with him. 2
28: 3 two male lambs a year old without blemish 2
9 two male lambs a year old without blemish 2
11 burnt offering . . two young bulls, one ram 2
19 burnt offering . . two young bulls, one ram 2
27 burnt offering . . two young bulls, one ram 2
29:13 burnt offering . . two rams, fourteen male lambs 2
17 On the second day twelve young bulls, two rams 2
20 On the third day eleven bulls, two rams, fourteen 2
23 On the fourth day ten bulls, two rams, fourteen 2
26 On the fifth day nine bulls, two rams, fourteen 2
29 On the sixth day eight bulls, two rams, fourteen 2
32 On the seventh day seven bulls, two rams, fourteen 2
34:15 two tribes and the half-tribe have received 2
Deu 3: 8 out of the hand of the two kings of the Amorites 2
21 that the LORD your God has done to these two kings; 2
4:13 wrote them upon two tables of stone. 2
47 two kings of the Amorites, who lived to the east 2
5:22 wrote them upon two tables of stone, and gave them 2
9:10 LORD gave me the two tables of stone written 2
11 at the end . . LORD gave me the two tables of stone 2
15 two tables of the covenant were in my two hands. 2
15 two tables of the covenant were in my two hands. 2
17 I took hold of the two tables, and cast them out 2
17 two tables, and cast them out of my two hands 2
10: 1 Hew two tables of stone like the first, and come up 2
3 I made an ark . . and hewed two tables of stone 2
3 up the mountain with the two tables in my hand. 2
14: 6 Every animal that . . has the hoof cloven in two 2
17: 6 On the evidence of two witnesses or of three 2
18: 3 give to the priest . . the two cheeks †
19:15 only on the evidence of two witnesses, or of three 2
21:15 If a man has two wives, the one loved and the other 2
25:13 not . . two kinds of weights, a large and a small. †
14 not . . two kinds of measures, a large and a small. †
32:30 How should . . two put 10,000 to flight 2
Jos 2: 1 And Joshua . . sent two men secretly from Shittim 2
4 the woman had taken the two men and hidden them; 2
10 and what you did to the two kings of the Amorites 2
23 Then the two men came down again from the hills 2
6:22 said to the two men who had spied out the land 2
9:10 all that he did to the two kings of the Amorites 2
14: 3 an inheritance to the two and one-half tribes 2
4 For the people of Joseph were two tribes 2
15:60 two cities with their villages. 2
21:16 nine cities out of these two tribes; 2
25 Ta'anach . . and Gath-rim'mon . . two cities. 2
27 Golan . . and Beesh'terah . . two cities; 2
24:12 drove them out . . the two kings of the Amorites; 2
Jdg 3:16 himself a sword with two edges, a cubit in length; 2
5:30 dividing the spoil?-A maiden or two for every man; †
30 two pieces . . embroidered for my neck †
7:25 they took the two princes of Mid'ian, Oreb and Zeeb; 2
8:12 took the two kings of Mid'ian, Zebah and Zalmun'na 2
9:44 while the two companies rushed upon all who were 2
11:37 for me; let me alone two months, that I may go 2
38 And he sent her away for two months; 2
39 at the end of two months, she returned to her 2
15:13 they bound him with two new ropes, and brought him 2
16: 3 took hold of the doors . . and the two posts 2
28 that I may be avenged . . for one of my two eyes. 2
29 Samson grasped the two middle pillars 2
19: 6 the two men sat and ate and drank together; 2
Rut 1: 1 a certain man . . he and his wife and his two sons. 2
2 the names of his two sons were Mahlon and Chil'ion; 2
3 and she was left with her two sons. 2
5 woman was bereft of her two sons and her husband. 2
7 she set out from . . with her two daughters-in-law 2
8 But Na'omi said to her two daughters-in-law 2
19 the two of them went on until they came 2
1Sm 1: 2 He had two wives; the name of the one was Hannah 2
3 two sons of Eli, Hophni and Phin'ehas, were priests 2
2:21 and bore three sons and two daughters. 2
34 shall befall your two sons, Hophni and Phin'ehas 2
3:11 two ears of every one that hears it will tingle. 2
4: 4 the two sons of Eli . . were there with the ark 2
11 and the two sons of Eli . . were slain. 2
17 your two sons also, Hophni and Phin'ehas, are dead 2
6: 7 take and prepare a new cart and two milch cows 2
10 and took two milch cows and yoked them to the cart 2
10: 2 you will meet two men by Rachel's tomb 2
4 will greet you and give you two loaves of bread 2
11:11 scattered, so that no two . . were left together. 2
13: 1 and he reigned . . and two years over Israel. 2
14:49 and the names of his two daughters were these 2
23:18 the two of them made a covenant before the LORD; 2
25:18 and took 200 loaves, and two skins of wine 2
27: 3 David with his two wives, Ahin'o-am . . and Ab'igail 2
28: 8 Saul . . went, he and two men with him; 2
30: 5 David's two wives also had been taken captive 2
12 a piece of a cake . . and two clusters of raisins. 2
18 and David rescued his two wives. 2
2Sm 1: 1 David remained two days in Ziklag; 2
2: 2 David went up there, and his two wives also 2
10 Ish-bo'sheth . . and he reigned two years. 2
4: 2 Now Saul's son had two men who were captains 2
8: 2 two lines he measured to be put to death 2
12: 1 There were two men in a certain city 2
13:23 After two full years Ab'salom had sheepshearers †
14: 6 your handmaid had two sons, and they quarreled 2
28 Ab'salom dwelt two full years in Jerusalem †
15:27 go back . . you and Abi'athar, with your two sons 2
36 Behold, their two sons are with them there 2
18:24 Now David was sitting between the two gates; 2
21: 8 took the two sons of Rizpah the daughter of Ai'ah 2
23:20 a doer of great deeds; he smote two ariels of Moab. 2
1Kg 2: 5 dealt with the two commanders of the armies 2
32 slew with the sword two men more righteous 2
39 two of Shim'e-i's slaves ran away to Achish, son 2
3:16 two harlots came to the king, and stood before 2
18 no one else . . only we two were in the house. 2
25 Divide the living child in two, and give half 2
5:12 and the two of them made a treaty. 2
14 be a month in Lebanon and two months at home; 2
6:23 he made two cherubim of olivewood 2
32 He covered the two doors of olivewood 2
34 and two doors of cypress wood; 2
34 the two leaves of the one door were folding 2
34 the two leaves of the other door were folding. 2
7:15 He cast two pillars of bronze. 2
16 He also made two capitals of molten bronze 2
17 two nets of checker work with wreaths of chain 5
18 in two rows round about upon the one network 2
20 The capitals were upon the two pillars and also 2
20 200 pomegranates, in two rows round about; 2
24 the gourds were in two rows, cast with it 2
41 the two pillars, the two bowls 2
41 the two bowls of the capitals that were 2
41 the two networks to cover the two bowls 2
41 networks to cover the two bowls of the capitals 2
42 400 pomegranates for the two networks 2
42 two rows of pomegranates for each network 2
42 cover the two bowls of the capitals that were 2
8: 9 the two tables of stone which Moses put there 2
9:10 years, in which Solomon had built the two houses 2
10:19 and two lions standing beside the arm rests 2
11:29 the two of them were alone in the open country. 2
12:28 king took counsel, and made two calves of gold. 2
15:25 Nadab . . and he reigned over Israel two years. †
16: 8 Elah . . began to reign . . and reigned two years. †
24 He bought the hill . . for two talents of silver; †
18:21 How long will you go limping with two . . opinions? 2
23 Let two bulls be given to us; 2
32 as great as would contain two measures of seed. †
20:27 encamped before them like two little flocks 2
21:10 set two base fellows opposite him 2
13 the two base fellows came in and sat opposite him; 2
22:51 and he reigned two years over Israel. †
2Kg 1:14 fire . . consumed the two former captains 2
2: 6 So the two of them went on. 2
8 the two of them could go over on dry ground. 2
11 and horses of fire separated the two of them. 2
12 his own clothes and rent them in two pieces. 2
24 And two she-bears came out of the woods 2
4: 1 the creditor has come to take my two children 2
33 he went in and shut the door upon the two of them 2
5:17 let there be given . . two mules' burden of earth; 1
22 There have just now come to me . . two young men 2
22 give them . . silver and two festal garments.' 2

23 Na'aman said, "Be pleased to accept two talents. †
23 and tied up two talents of silver in two bags †
23 and tied up two talents of silver in two bags 2
23 talents of silver . . with two festal garments 2
23 and laid them upon two of his servants; 2
7: 1 and two measures of barley for a shekel †
14 they took two mounted men, and the king sent them 2
16 and two measures of barley for a shekel †
18 Two measures of barley shall be sold for a shekel †
9:32 Two or three eunuchs looked out at him. 2
10: 4 the two kings could not stand before him; 2
8 Lay them in two heaps at the entrance of the gate 2
11: 7 the two divisions of you, which come on duty 2
15:23 Pekahi'ah . . and he reigned two years. †
17:16 made for themselves molten images of two calves; 2
21: 5 built altars . . in the two courts of the house 2
19 Amon . . and he reigned two years in Jerusalem. 2
23:12 had made in the two courts of the house of the LORD 2
25: 4 by the way of the gate between the two walls †
16 As for the two pillars, the one sea, and the stands 2
1Ch 1:19 To Eber were born two sons: the name of the one was 2
4: 5 Asshur . . had two wives, Helah and Na'arah; 2
11:22 doer of great deeds; he smote two ariels of Moab. 2
26:17 as well as two and two at the storehouse; 2
17 as well as two and two at the storehouse; 2
18 were four at the road and two at the parbar. 2
2Ch 3:10 most holy place he made two cherubim of wood 2
15 he made two pillars 35 cubits high 2
4: 3 gourds were in two rows, cast with it when it was 2
12 the two pillars, the bowls, and the two capitals 2
12 the two pillars, the bowls, and the two capitals 2
12 the two networks to cover the two bowls 2
12 networks to cover the two bowls of the capitals 2
13 400 pomegranates for the two networks 2
13 two rows of pomegranates for each network 2
13 to cover the two bowls of the capitals that were 2
5:10 except the two tables which Moses put there 2
9:18 two lions standing beside the arm rests 2
21:19 at the end of two years, his bowels came out 2
24: 3 Jehoi'ada got for him two wives, and he had sons 2
33: 5 built altars . . in the two courts of the house 2
21 Amon . . reigned two years in Jerusalem. 2
Ezr 8:27 two vessels of fine bright bronze as precious 2
10:13 Nor is this a work for one day or for two; 2
Neh 12:31 appointed two great companies which gave 2
Est 2:21 Bigthan and Teresh, two of the king's eunuchs 2
6: 2 Bigthana and Teresh, two of the king's eunuchs 2
9:27 that without fail they would keep these two days 2
Job 33:14 For God speaks in one way, and in two 2
42: 7 against you and against your two friends; 2
Prv 30:15 The leech has two daughters; "Give, give," they cry. 2
Ecc 4: 6 two hands full of toil and a striving after wind. †
9 Two are better than one . . they have a good reward 2
11 Again, if two lie together, they are warm; 2
12 against one who is alone, two will withstand him. 2
Sng 4: 5 Your two breasts are like two fawns 2
5 Your two breasts are like two fawns 2
6:13 look upon the . . as upon a dance before two armies? †
7: 3 Your two breasts are like two fawns 2
3 breasts are like two fawns, twins of a gazelle. 2
Isa 6: 2 each had six wings: with two he covered his face 2
2 each had six wings . . with two he covered his feet 2
2 each had six wings . . and with two he flew. 2
7: 4 faint because of these two smoldering stumps 2
16 the land before whose two kings you are in dread 2
21 a man will keep alive a young cow and two sheep; 2
17: 6 two . . berries in the top of the highest bough 2
22:11 You made a reservoir between the two walls †
47: 9 These two things shall come to you in a moment 2
51:19 These two things have befallen you– 2
Jer 2:13 for my people have committed two evils 2
3:14 will take you, one from a city and two from a family 2
24: 1 showed me this vision: Behold, two baskets of figs 2
28: 3 Within two years I will bring back to this place †
11 break the yoke of . . the nations within two years. †
33:24 The LORD has rejected the two families 2
34:18 I will make like the calf which they cut in two 2
39: 4 garden through the gate between the two walls; †
52: 7 a gate between the two walls, by the king's garden †
20 As for the two pillars, the one sea 2
Ezk 1:11 each creature had two wings 2
11 wing of another, while two covered their bodies. 2
23 each creature had two wings covering its body. 2
21:19 Son of man, mark two ways for the sword of the king 2
21 at the head of the two ways, to use divination; 2
23: 2 there were two women, the daughters of one mother; 2
35:10 These two nations and these two countries shall 2
10 These two nations and these two countries shall 2
37:22 they shall be no longer two nations 2
22 and no longer divided into two kingdoms. 2
40: 9 and its jambs, two cubits; 2
39 And in the vestibule of the gate were two tables 2
40 the entrance of the north gate were two tables; 2
40 of the vestibule of the gate were two tables. 2
44 there were two chambers in the inner court 5
41: 3 measured the jambs of the entrance, two cubits; 2
18 Every cherub had two faces 2
22 cubits high, two cubits long, and two cubits broad; 2
22 cubits high, two cubits long, and two cubits broad; 5

24 The doors had two leaves apiece 2
24 two swinging leaves for each door. 2
43:14 base on the ground to the lower ledge, two cubits 2
47:13 Joseph shall have two portions. •
Dan 7: 4 made to stand upon two feet like a man; †
25 into his hand for a time, two times, and half a time †
8: 3 It had two horns; and both horns were high, †
6 He came to the ram with the two horns †
7 struck the ram and broke his two horns; 2
20 As for the ram which you saw with the two horns †
11:27 two kings, their minds shall be bent on mischief; 2
12: 5 Then I Daniel looked, and behold, two others stood 2
7 would be for a time, two times, and half a time; †
Hos 6: 2 After two days he will revive us; †
Ams 1: 1 he saw . . two years before the earthquake. †
3: 3 Do two walk together, unless they have made 2
12 from the mouth of the lion two legs, or a piece 2
4: 8 two or three cities wandered to one city to drink 2
Zec 4: 3 there are two olive trees by it 2
11 What are these two olive trees on the right 2
12 What are these two branches of the olive trees 2
12 trees, which are beside the two golden pipes 2
14 These are the two anointed who stand by the Lord 2
5: 9 and saw, and behold, two women coming forward! 2
6: 1 chariots came out from between two mountains; 2
11: 7 I took two staffs; one I named Grace 2
Mat 4:18 he saw two brothers, Simon who is called Peter 5
21 going on from there he saw two other brothers 5
5:41 forces you to go one mile, go with him two miles. 5
6:24 No one can serve two masters; for either he will 5
8:28 country of the Gadarenes, two demoniacs met him 5
9:27 two blind men followed him, crying aloud 5
10:10 no bag for your journey, nor two tunics 5
29 Are not two sparrows sold for a penny? 5
14:17 We have only five loaves here and two fish. 5
19 and taking the five loaves and the two fish 5
18: 8 than with two hands or two feet 5
8 than with two hands or two feet 5
9 with two eyes to be thrown into the hell of fire 5
16 if he does not listen, take one or two others along 5
16 by the evidence of two or three witnesses. 5
19 Again I say to you, if two of you agree on earth 5
20 For where two or three are gathered in my name 5
19: 5 and the two shall become one flesh'? 5
6 So they are no longer two but one flesh 5
20:21 Command that these two sons of mine may sit 5
24 they were indignant at the two brothers. 5
30 behold, two blind men sitting by the roadside 5
21: 1 then Jesus sent two disciples 5
28 What do you think? A man had two sons 5
31 Which of the two did the will of his father? 5
22:40 On these two commandments depend all the law 5
24:40 Then two men will be in the field 5
41 Two women will be grinding at the mill 5
25:15 to one he gave five talents, to another two 5
17 he who had the two talents made two talents more. 5
17 he who had the two talents made two talents more. 5
22 he also who had the two talents came forward 5
22 Master, you delivered to me two talents 5
22 here I have made two talents more.' 5
26: 2 after two days the Passover is coming 5
37 taking with him Peter and the two sons of Zeb'edee 5
60 At last two came forward 5
27:21 Which of the two do you want me to release for you? 5
38 Then two robbers were crucified with him 5
51 behold, the curtain of the temple was torn in two 5
Mrk 6: 7 began to send them out two by two 5
7 began to send them out two by two 5
9 to wear sandals and not put on two tunics. 5
38 they said, "Five, and two fish. 5
41 taking the five loaves and the two fish 5
41 he divided the two fish among them all. 5
9:43 with two hands to go to hell 5
45 with two feet to be thrown into hell. 5
46 with two eyes to be thrown into hell 5
10: 8 the two shall become one flesh 5
8 So they are no longer two but one flesh. 5
11: 1 he sent two of his disciples 5
12:42 a poor widow came, and put in two copper coins 5
14: 1 It was now two days before the Passover 5
13 he sent two of his disciples, and said to them, "Go 5
15:27 with him they crucified two robbers 5
38 the curtain of the temple was torn in two 5
16:12 After this he appeared in another form to two 5
Lke 2:24 a pair of turtledoves, or two young pigeons. 5
3:11 He who has two coats, let him share 5
5: 2 he saw two boats by the lake 5
7:19 John, calling to him two of his disciples 5
41 A certain creditor had two debtors 5
9: 3 do not have two tunics. 5
13 We have no more than five loaves and two fish 5
16 taking the five loaves and the two fish 5
30 behold, two men talked with him, Moses and Eli'jah 5
32 his glory and the two men who stood with him. 5
10: 1 sent them on ahead of him, two by two 5
1 sent them on ahead of him, two by two 5
35 the next day he took out two denarii 5
12: 6 Are not five sparrows sold for two pennies? 5
52 three against two and two against three; 5

52 three against two and two against three; 5
15:11 he said, "There was a man who had two sons; 5
16:13 No servant can serve two masters 5
17:34 in that night there will be two in one bed 5
35 There will be two women grinding together 5
18:10 Two men went up into the temple to pray 5
19:29 he sent two of the disciples 5
21: 2 he saw a poor widow put in two copper coins. 5
22:38 they said, "Look, Lord, here are two swords. 5
23:32 Two others also, who were criminals, were led away 5
45 the curtain of the temple was torn in two. 7
24: 4 behold, two men stood by them in dazzling apparel; 5
13 two of them were going to a village named Emma'us 5
Joh 1:35 John was standing with two of his disciples; 5
37 The two disciples heard him say this 5
40 One of the two who heard John speak . . was Andrew 5
4:40 and he stayed there two days. 5
43 After the two days he departed to Galilee. 5
6: 9 a lad here who has five barley loaves and two fish; 5
8:17 the testimony of two men is true; 5
11: 6 he stayed two days longer in the place where he was. 5
19:18 There they crucified him, and with him two others 5
20:12 she saw two angels in white 5
21: 2 two others of his disciples were together. 5
Act 1:10 behold, two men stood by them in white robes 5
23 they put forward two, Joseph called Barsab'bas 5
24 show which one of these two thou hast chosen 5
7:29 Mid'ian, where he became the father of two sons. 5
9:38 the disciples . . sent two men to him entreating 5
10: 7 called two of his servants and a devout soldier 5
12: 6 Peter was sleeping between two soldiers 5
6 bound with two chains 5
19:10 This continued for two years 5
22 having sent into Macedo'nia two of his helpers 5
34 for about two hours they all . . cried out 5
21:33 ordered him to be bound with two chains 5
23:23 Then he called two of the centurions and said 5
1Co 6:16 as it is written, "The two shall become one flesh. 5
14:27 let there be only two or at most three 5
29 Let two or three prophets speak 5
2Co 13: 1 by the evidence of two or three witnesses. 5
Gal 4:22 For it is written that Abraham had two sons 5
24 these women are two covenants 5
Eph 2:15 create . . one new man in place of the two 5
5:31 the two shall become one flesh. 5
Php 1:23 I am hard pressed between the two. 5
1Ti 5:19 except on the evidence of two or three witnesses. 5
2Ti 3: 9 as was that of those two men. •
Heb 6:18 through two unchangeable things 5
10:28 at the testimony of two or three witnesses. 5
Rev 9:12 behold, two woes are still to come. 5
11: 3 I will grant my two witnesses power to prophesy 5
4 two olive trees . . which stand before the Lord 5
4 two lampstands which stand before the Lord 5
10 because these two prophets had been a torment 5
12:14 woman was given the two wings of the great eagle 5
13:11 it had two horns like a lamb 5
19:20 These two were thrown alive into the lake of fire 5
1Es 5:73 they were kept from building for two years 5
9: 4 if any did not meet there within two or three days 5
11 This is not a work we can do in one day or two 5
2Es 1:11 the people of two provinces, Tyre and Sidon 8
6:49 didst keep in existence two living creatures; 8
7:50 the Most High has made not one world but two. 8
11:22 wings and the two little wings disappeared; 8
24 behold, two little wings separated from the six 8
28 the two that remained were planning 8
29 for it was greater than the other two heads. 8
30 I saw how it allied the two heads with itself 8
31 it devoured the two little wings 8
34 the two heads remained 8
12: 2 And the two wings that had gone over to it arose 8
21 two of them shall perish 8
21 but two shall be kept until the end. 8
27 as for the two who remained 8
29 two little wings passing over to the head 8
14:12 so two of its parts remain 8
16:28 out of the field, two who have hidden themselves 8
38 about her womb for two or three hours beforehand 8
Tob 1:21 before two of Sennacherib's sons killed him 5
3:17 Raphael was sent to heal the two of them 5
8: 4 When the door was shut and the two were alone 4
17 thou hast had compassion on two only children. 5
9: 2 Brother Azarias, take a servant and two camels 5
12: 5 Take half of all that you two have brought back. •
6 the angel called the two of them privately 5
Jdt 1:12 as far as the coasts of the two seas. 5
4: 7 only wide enough for two men at the most. 5
13:10 Then the two of them went out together 5
AEs 10: 7 The two dragons are Haman and myself. 5
10 For this purpose he made two lots 5
11 these two lots came to the hour and moment and day 5
11: 6 behold, two great dragons came forward 5
12: 1 Gabatha and Tharra, the two eunuchs of the king 5
3 Then the king examined the two eunuchs 5
6 because of the two eunuchs of the king. 5
15: 2 Then . . she took her two maids with her 5
Wis 14:30 just penalties will overtake them on two counts 3
Sir 2:12 Woe . . to the sinner who walks along two ways! 5

23:16 Two sorts of men multiply sins 5
38:17 for one day, or two, to avoid criticism 5
46: 4 did not one day become as long as two? 5
8 these two alone were preserved 5
50:25 With two nations my soul is vexed 5
LJr 1:55 the gods will be burnt in two like beams. 7
Sus 1: 5 two elders . . were appointed as judges. 5
8 The two elders used to see her every day 5
15 she went in as before with only two maids 5
16 And no one was there except the two elders 5
19 the two elders rose and ran to her, and said 5
24 and the two elders shouted against her. 5
28 the two elders came, full of their wicked plot 5
34 the two elders stood up in the midst of the people 5
36 this woman came in with two maids 5
59 is waiting with his sword to saw you in two 7
61 And they rose against the two elders 5
Bel 1:32 they had been given two human bodies and two sheep 5
32 they had been given two human bodies and two sheep 5
1Mc 1:29 Two years later the king sent to the cities 5
6:38 on the two flanks of the army 5
9:11 The cavalry was divided into two companies 5
12 Flanked by the two companies 5
57 the land of Judah had rest for two years. 5
10:49 The two kings met in battle, and the army 5
60 went with pomp to Ptolemais and met the two kings; 5
11:13 Thus he put two crowns upon his head 5
13:16 two of his sons as hostages 5
16: 2 Simon called in his two older sons Judas and John 5
16 they killed him and his two sons 5
2Mc 3:26 Two young men also appeared to him 5
4:28 the two of them were summoned by the king 5
6:10 For example, two women were brought in 5
10:18 than 9,000 took refuge in two very strong towers 5
22 immediately captured the two towers. 5
23 more than 20,000 in the two strongholds. 5
28 the two armies joined battle 6
3Mc 1: 4 promising to give them each two minas of gold 5
6:18 two glorious angels of fearful aspect 5
4Mc 1:20 The two most comprehensive types 5
28 two plants growing from the body and the soul 5
3:12 two staunch young soldiers 5
15: 2 Two courses were open to this mother 5
26 this mother held two ballots 5
two *See also* cut, saw, split.

two kinds 1. כִּלְאַיִם
Lev 19:19 you shall not sow your field with two kinds of seed 1
19 a garment of cloth made of two kinds of stuff 1
Deu 22: 9 not sow your vineyard with two kinds of seed 1

two men 1. שְׁנַיִם
Gen 21:27 to Abim'elech, and the two men made a covenant. 1

two miles 1. σταδίων δεκαπέντε
Joh 11:18 Bethany was near Jerusalem, about two miles off 1

two parts 1. חָצִי
1Kg 16:21 the people of Israel were divided into two parts; 1

two sons 1. שְׁנַיִם
Gen 44:27 said to us, 'You know that my wife bore me two sons; 1

two things 1. שְׁנַיִם 2. δύο
1Sm 26:25 You will do many things and will succeed in them. 1
2Sm 23:22 These things did Benai'ah the son of Jehoi'ada 1
2Kg 2:10 he said, "You have asked a hard thing; 1
7: 8 another tent, and carried off things from it 1
21:11 Manas'seh . . has done things more wicked 1
Job 13:20 Only grant two things to me, then I will not hide 1
Prv 30: 7 Two things I ask of thee; deny them not to me 1
Isa 29:16 You turn things upside down! 1
44: 9 and the things they delight in do not profit; 1
51:19 These two things have befallen you– 1
55:11 and prosper in the thing for which I sent it. 1
56: 4 who choose the things that please me 1
Jer 2: 8 and went after things that do not profit. 1
5: 9 Shall I not punish them for these things? 1
19 Why has . . our God done all these things to us?' 1
29 Shall I not punish them for these things? 1
9: 9 Shall I not punish them for these things? 1
24 for in these things I delight, says the LORD. 1
Sir 26:28 At two things my heart is grieved 2

two times 1. δίς
Sir 13: 7 until he has drained you two or three times 1

two years 1. διετής 2. διετία
Mat 2:16 in all that region who were two years old or under 1
Act 24:27 when two years had elapsed 2
28:30 he lived there two whole years at his own expense 2
2Mc 10: 3 they offered sacrifices, after a lapse of two years 1

two-edged 1. פִּיוֹת 2. δίστομος
Ps 149: 6 Let . . two-edged swords in their hands 1
Prv 5: 4 she is . . sharp as a two-edged sword. 1
Heb 4:12 sharper than any two-edged sword 2
Rev 1:16 from his mouth issued a sharp two-edged sword 2
2:12 The words of him who has the sharp two-edged sword. 2
Sir 21: 3 All lawlessness is like a two-edged sword 2

twofold 1. διπλοῦς 2. δισσός
Wis 11:12 for a twofold grief possessed them 1
Sir 42:24 All things are twofold, one opposite the other 2

type 1. τύπος 2. φύσις
Rom 5:14 Adam, who was a type of the one who was to come. 1
4Mc 1:20 The two most comprehensive types 2

tyrannical 1. τυραννικός
4Mc 5:27 It would be tyrannical for you to compel us 1

tyrannize 1. τυραννέω
4Mc 5:38 You may tyrannize the ungodly 1

tyranny 1. τυραννίς
4Mc 1:11 the downfall of tyranny over their nation 1
8:15 their right reasoning nullified his tyranny. 1
9:30 the arrogant design of your tyranny 1
11:24 We six boys have paralyzed your tyranny! 1

under tyranny 1. τυραννικός
3Mc 3: 8 they lived under tyranny 1

tyrant 1. עָרִיץ 2. τύραννος
Isa 49:24 or the captives of a tyrant be rescued? 1
25 be taken, and the prey of the tyrant be rescued 1
2Mc 4:25 having the hot temper of a cruel tyrant 2
7:27 deriding the cruel tyrant 2
3Mc 6:24 surpassing tyrants in cruelty 2
4Mc 1:11 By their endurance they conquered the tyrant 2
5: 1 The tyrant Antiochus, sitting in state 2
4 and known to many in the tyrant's court 2
14 When the tyrant urged him in this fashion 2
6: 1 the exhortations of the tyrant 2
21 if we should be despised by the tyrant as unmanly 2
23 you, guards of the tyrant, why do you delay? 2
7: 2 though buffeted by the stormings of the tyrant 2
8: 2 when the tyrant was conspicuously defeated 2
3 When the tyrant had given these orders 2
4 When the tyrant saw them 2
13 the tyrant resumed speaking 2
15 also opposed the tyrant with their own philosophy 2
29 as soon as the tyrant had ceased counseling them 2
9: 1 Why do you delay, O tyrant? 2
3 Tyrant and counselor of lawlessness 2
7 Therefore, tyrant, put us to the test 2
10 the tyrant not only was angry 2
15 Most abominable tyrant 2
24 and take vengeance on the accursed tyrant. 2
30 To the tyrant he said 2
30 Do you not think, you most savage tyrant 2
32 You will not escape, most abominable tyrant 2
10:10 We, most abominable tyrant, are suffering 2
15 by the eternal destruction of the tyrant 2
16 Contrive tortures, tyrant, so that you may learn 2
11: 2 I will not refuse, tyrant 2
12 he said, "Tyrant, they are splendid favors 2
13 When the tyrant inquired . . he said 2
21 religious knowledge, O tyrant, is invincible. 2
27 it is not the guards of the tyrant 2
12: 2 the tyrant had been fearfully reproached 2
11 profane tyrant, most impious of all the wicked 2
15: 1 reason of the children, tyrant over the emotions! 2
2 as the tyrant had promised. 2
16:14 you have conquered even a tyrant 2
17: 2 nullified the violence of the tyrant 2
9 because of the violence of the tyrant 2
14 The tyrant was the antagonist 2
17 The tyrant himself and all his council marveled 2
21 the tyrant was punished 2
23 the tyrant Antiochus . . proclaimed them 2
18: 5 The tyrant Antiochus was both punished on earth 2
20 that bitter tyrant of the Greeks 2
22 justice . . will pursue the accursed tyrant. 2

U

ugly 1. πονηρός
Sir 20:24 A lie is an ugly blot on a man 1

ulcer 1. טְחוֹר
Deu 28:27 smite you . . with the ulcers and the scurvy 1

umpire 1. יכח
Job 9:33 There is no umpire between us 1

unable 1. לֹא יכל 2. ἀδυνατέω 3. μή 4. μὴ δύναμαι 5. μήτε 6. οὐ 7. οὐ δύναμαι 8. οὐκ ἰσχύω 9. non possum
1Kg 9:21 whom the people of Israel were unable to destroy 1
Ps 36:12 they are thrust down, unable to rise. 1
76: 5 all the men of war were unable to use their hands. •
Ezk 3:26 you shall be dumb and unable to reprove them; •
Lke 1:20 behold, you will be silent and unable to speak 4
Act 13:11 you shall be blind and unable to see the sun for a time 3
Heb 3:19 we see that they were unable to enter 7
4:15 is unable to sympathize with our weaknesses 4
2Es 10:32 I saw, and still see, what I am unable to explain. 9
AEs 16:12 unable to restrain his arrogance 6
Wis 12: 9 though thou wast not unable 2
13: 1 they were unable . . to know him who exists 8
Sir 7: 6 lest you be unable to remove iniquity 8
LJr 1:14 though unable to destroy any one who offends it. 6
1Mc 9:60 they were unable to do it 7
2Mc 10:13 Unable to command the respect due his office 5
4Mc 4: 1 unable to injure Onias in the eyes of the nation 8
8: 2 being unable to compel an aged man 4

unable even 1. μηδὲ δύναμαι
3Mc 2:22 he . . was unable even to speak 1

unable to help 1. ἀβοήθητος
2Mc 3:28 but was now unable to help himself 1

unanswered *See* go.

unapproachable 1. ἄβατος 2. ἀνέφικτος 3. ἀπρόσιτος
1Ti 6:16 dwells in unapproachable light 3
3Mc 2:15 your dwelling . . is unapproachable by man. 2
3:29 to be made unapproachable and burned with fire 1

unaware 1. ἀγνοέω
Wis 12:10 though thou wast not unaware 1

unawares 1. בֶּטַח 2. לֹא ידע 3. λανθάνω
Gen 34:25 came upon the city unawares, and killed all 1
Ps 35: 8 Let ruin come upon them unawares! 2
Heb 13: 2 thereby some have entertained angels unawares. 3

unbearably 1. ὑπὲρ δύναμιν
2Co 1: 8 we were so utterly, unbearably crushed 1

unbecoming 1. ἀπρεπής
4Mc 6:17 out of cowardice we feign a role unbecoming to us! 1

unbelief 1. ἀπιστία 2. incredulitas
Mat 13:58 because of their unbelief. 1
Mrk 6: 6 he marveled because of their unbelief 1
9:24 cried out and said, "I believe; help my unbelief! 1
16:14 he upbraided them for their unbelief 1
Rom 11:20 They were broken off because of their unbelief 1
23 if they do not persist in their unbelief 1
1Ti 1:13 because I had acted ignorantly in unbelief 1
Heb 3:19 they were unable to enter because of unbelief. 1
2Es 7:114 unbelief has been cut off 2
15: 3 the unbelief of those who oppose you. 2
4 For every unbeliever shall die in his unbelief. 2

unbelievable 1. παραδοκέω
Jdt 13:13 it was unbelievable that she had returned 1

unbeliever 1. ἀπειθέω 2. ἄπιστος 3. incredulus
Rom 15:31 I may be delivered from the unbelievers in Judea 1
1Co 6: 6 that before unbelievers? 2
7:12 if any brother has a wife who is an unbeliever 2
13 If any woman has a husband who is an unbeliever 2
10:27 If one of the unbelievers invites you to dinner 2
14:22 a sign not for believers but for unbelievers 2
22 while prophecy is not for unbelievers 2
23 outsiders or unbelievers enter 2
24 an unbeliever or outsider enters 2
2Co 4: 4 blinded the minds of the unbelievers 2
6:14 Do not be mismated with unbelievers 2
15 what has a believer in common with an unbeliever? 2
1Ti 5: 8 and is worse than an unbeliever. 2
2Es 15: 4 For every unbeliever shall die in his unbelief. 3

unbelieving 1. ἀπειθέω 2. ἀπιστέω 3. ἀπιστία 4. ἄπιστος
Act 14: 2 the unbelieving Jews stirred up the Gentiles 1
1Co 7:14 For the unbelieving husband is consecrated 4
14 the unbelieving wife is consecrated 4
15 if the unbelieving partner desires to separate 4
Tit 1:15 to the corrupt and unbelieving nothing is pure; 4
Heb 3:12 an evil, unbelieving heart 3
Wis 10: 7 standing as a monument to an unbelieving soul. 2

unbind 1. λύω
Joh 11:44 Jesus said to them, "Unbind him, and let him go. 1
Act 22:30 he unbound him 1

unbind the hair 1. פרע
Num 5:18 priest . . unbind the hair of the woman's head 1

unblamable 1. ἄμεμπτος
1Th 3:13 so that he may establish your hearts unblamable 1

yet unborn 1. ברא 2. ילד
Ps 22:31 proclaim his deliverance to a people yet unborn 2
78: 6 might know them, the children yet unborn 2
102:18 so that a people yet unborn may praise the LORD 1

unbreakable 1. ἄρρηκτος
3Mc 4: 9 had their feet secured by unbreakable fetters 1

unbroken 1. πᾶς
2Mc 3: 1 the holy city was inhabited in unbroken peace 1

unburied 1. ἄταφος
2Mc 5:10 He who had cast out many to lie unburied 1

unceasing 1. בִּלְתִּי סָרָה 2. נֵצַח 3. תָּמִיד 4. ἀδιάλειπτος 5. ἀκατάλυτος
Isa 14: 6 that smote . . in wrath with unceasing blows 1
Jer 15:18 Why is my pain unceasing, my wound incurable 2
Nah 3:19 For upon whom has not come your unceasing evil? 3
Rom 9: 2 great sorrow and unceasing anguish in my heart. 4
4Mc 10:11 will undergo unceasing torments. 5

unceasingly 1. ἀδιαλείπτως
3Mc 6:33 king . . gave thanks to heaven unceasingly 1

uncertain 1. ἄδηλος 2. ἀδηλότης 3. ἀπορέω
Joh 13:22 uncertain of whom he spoke. 3
1Ti 6:17 nor to set their hopes on uncertain riches 2
2Mc 7:34 and puffed up by uncertain hopes 1

uncertainty 1. ἄδηλος καταστροφή
3Mc 4: 4 some . . reflected upon the uncertainty of life 1

without uncertainty 1. ἀδιάκριτος
Jas 3:17 wisdom . . is . . without uncertainty 1

unchangeable 1. בְּאֶחָד 2. ἀμετάθετος
Job 23:13 But he is unchangeable and who can turn him? 1
Heb 6:17 the unchangeable character of his purpose 2
18 through two unchangeable things 2

unchanging 1. ἀπαραλλάκτως
AEs 13: 3 is distinguished for his unchanging good will 1

unchastity 1. πορνεία
Mat 5:32 his wife, except on the ground of unchastity 1
19: 9 except for unchastity 1
Act 15:20 from unchastity and from what is strangled 1
29 from what is strangled and from unchastity 1
21:25 from what is strangled and from unchastity. 1
1Th 4: 3 you abstain from unchastity; 1

uncircumcised 1. עָרֵל 2. עָרְלָה 3. ἀκροβυστία 4. ἀπερίτμητος
Gen 17:14 Any uncircumcised male who is not circumcised 1
34:14 to give our sister to one who is uncircumcised 2
Exd 6:12 to me, who am a man of uncircumcised lips? 1
30 Moses said . . "Behold, I am of uncircumcised lips; 1
Lev 26:41 if then their uncircumcised heart is humbled 1
Jos 5: 7 they were uncircumcised, because they had not 1
Jdg 14: 3 take a wife from the uncircumcised Philistines? 1
15:18 and fall into the hands of the uncircumcised? 1
1Sm 14: 6 go over to the garrison of these uncircumcised; 1
17:26 For who is this uncircumcised Philistine 1
36 this uncircumcised Philistine shall be like 1
31: 4 lest these uncircumcised come and thrust me 1
2Sm 1:20 lest the daughters of the uncircumcised exult. 1
1Ch 10: 4 these uncircumcised come and make sport of me. 1
Isa 52: 1 shall no more come into you the uncircumcised 1
Jer 9:25 who are circumcised but yet uncircumcised- 2
26 for all these nations are uncircumcised 1
26 the house of Israel is uncircumcised in heart. 1
Ezk 28:10 You shall die the death of the uncircumcised 1
31:18 you shall lie among the uncircumcised 1
32:19 Go down, and be laid with the uncircumcised. 1
21 lie still, the uncircumcised, slain by the sword 1
24 went down uncircumcised into the nether world 1
25 all of them uncircumcised, slain by the sword; 1
26 all of them uncircumcised, slain by the sword; 1
28 shall be broken and lie among the uncircumcised 1
29 they lie with the uncircumcised 1
30 they lie uncircumcised with those who are slain 1
32 he shall be laid among the uncircumcised 1
44: 7 foreigners, uncircumcised in heart and flesh 1
9 No foreigner, uncircumcised in heart and flesh 1
Act 7:51 uncircumcised in heart and ears 4
11: 3 saying, "Why did you go to uncircumcised men 3
Rom 2:26 if a man who is uncircumcised keeps the . . law 3
27 Then those who are physically uncircumcised 3
3:30 and the uncircumcised through their faith. 3
4: 9 only . . or also upon the uncircumcised? 3
11 had by faith while he was still uncircumcised. 3
1Co 7:18 Was any one at the time of his call uncircumcised? 3
Gal 2: 7 entrusted with the gospel to the uncircumcised 3
Col 3:11 circumcised and uncircumcised, barbarian 3
AEs 14:15 abhor the bed of the uncircumcised 4
1Mc 1:48 to leave their sons uncircumcised 4
2:46 circumcised all the uncircumcised boys 4

uncircumcised person 1. עָרֵל
Exd 12:48 But no uncircumcised person shall eat of it. 1

uncircumcision 1. ἀκροβυστία
Rom 2:25 your circumcision becomes uncircumcision. 1
26 uncircumcision be regarded as circumcision? 1
1Co 7:19 nor uncircumcision 1
Gal 5: 6 neither circumcision nor uncircumcision 1
6:15 nor uncircumcision, but a new creation. 1
Eph 2:11 called the uncircumcision 1
Col 2:13 the uncircumcision of your flesh 1

uncle 1. דּוֹד
Lev 10: 4 sons of Uz'ziel the uncle of Aaron, and said to them 1
20:20 he has uncovered his uncle's nakedness 1
25:49 or his uncle, or his cousin may redeem him 1
1Sm 10:14 Saul's uncle said to him . . "Where did you go? 1
15 Saul's uncle said, "Pray, tell me what Samuel said 1
16 Saul said to his uncle, "He told us plainly that 1
14:50 commander . . was Abner the son of Ner, Saul's uncle; 1
2Kg 24:17 king . . made Mattani'ah, Jehoi'achin's uncle, king 1
1Ch 27:32 Jonathan, David's uncle, was a counselor 1
Est 2: 7 brought up . . Esther, the daughter of his uncle 1
15 the daughter of Ab'ihail the uncle of Mor'decai 1
Jer 32: 7 Behold, Han'amel the son of Shallum your uncle 1
uncle *See also* wife.

unclean 1. טמא 2. טָמֵא 3. טֻמְאָה 4. נִדָּה
5. ἀκαθαρσία 6. ἀκάθαρτος 7. κοινός
Lev 5: 2 Or if any one touches an unclean thing 2
2 whether the carcass of an unclean beast 2
2 or a carcass of unclean cattle or a carcass 2
2 or a carcass of unclean swarming things 2
7:21 or an unclean beast or any unclean abomination 2
21 if any one touches . . any unclean abomination 2
10:10 between the unclean and the clean 2
11: 4 does not part the hoof, is unclean to you 2
5 does not part the hoof, is unclean to you 2
6 does not part the hoof, is unclean to you 2
7 does not chew the cud, is unclean to you 2
8 shall not touch; they are unclean to you 2
24 whoever touches their carcass shall be unclean 1
25 shall wash his clothes and be unclean 2
26 or does not chew the cud is unclean to you 2
26 every one who touches them shall be unclean 1
27 all that go . . are unclean to you 2
27 whoever touches their carcass shall be unclean 1
28 shall wash his clothes and be unclean 2
28 they are unclean to you 2
29 unclean to you among the swarming things 2
31 These are unclean to you among all that swarm 2
31 whoever touches them . . shall be unclean until 1
32 anything . . when they are dead shall be unclean 1
32 it shall be unclean until the evening 2
33 all that is in it shall be unclean 1
34 Any food in it . . shall be unclean; and all drink 1
34 drink . . from every such vessel shall be unclean 1
35 everything . . shall be unclean; whether oven 1
35 they are unclean, and shall be unclean to you 2
35 they are unclean, and shall be unclean to you 2
36 whatever touches their carcass shall be unclean 1
38 if . . carcass falls on it, it is unclean to you 2
39 he who touches its carcass shall be unclean 1
40 he . . shall . . be unclean until the evening 1
40 he . . shall wash his clothes and be unclean 1
47 distinction between the unclean and the clean 2
12: 2 then she shall be unclean seven days 1
2 time of her menstruation, she shall be unclean 1
5 then she shall be unclean two weeks 1
13:11 he shall not shut him up, for he is unclean 2
14 when raw flesh appears . . he shall be unclean 1
15 raw flesh is unclean, for it is leprosy 2
36 if the itch has spread . . he is unclean 2
44 he is a leprous man, he is unclean 2
45 cover his upper lip and cry, 'Unclean, unclean.' 2
45 cover his upper lip and cry, 'Unclean, unclean.' 2
46 he is unclean; he shall dwell alone 2
51 the disease is a malignant leprosy; it is unclean 2
55 though the disease has not spread, it is unclean 2
59 to decide whether it is clean or unclean 1
14:40 throw them into an unclean place outside the city 2
41 shall pour into an unclean place outside the city 2
44 leprosy in the house; it is unclean 2
45 out of the city to an unclean place 2
46 he . . shall be unclean until the evening 1
57 to show when it is unclean and when it is clean 2
15: 2 from his body, his discharge is unclean 2
4 he who has the discharge lies shall be unclean 1
4 everything on which he sits shall be unclean 1
5 in water, and be unclean until the evening 1
6 bathe . . and be unclean until the evening 1
7 bathe . . and be unclean until the evening 1
8 bathe . . and be unclean until the evening 1
9 who has the discharge rides shall be unclean 1
10 touches . . shall be unclean until the evening 1
10 bathe . . and be unclean until the evening 1
11 bathe . . and be unclean until the evening 1
16 shall bathe . . and be unclean until the evening 1
17 be washed . . and be unclean until the evening 1
18 bathe . . and be unclean until the evening 1
19 touches her shall be unclean until the evening 1
20 during her impurity shall be unclean 1
20 upon which she sits shall be unclean 1
21 bathe . . and be unclean until the evening 1
22 bathe . . and be unclean until the evening 1
23 touches it he shall be unclean until the evening 1
24 impurity is on him, he shall be unclean seven days 1
24 every bed on which he lies shall be unclean 1
25 the days of her impurity, she shall be unclean 2
26 everything on which she sits shall be unclean 2
27 whoever touches these things shall be unclean 1
27 bathe . . and be unclean until the evening 1
30 atonement for her . . for her unclean discharge 3
33 the man who lies with a woman who is unclean 2
17:15 bathe . . and be unclean until the evening 1
20:25 between the clean beast and the unclean 2
25 and between the unclean bird and the clean 2
22: 4 Whoever touches anything that is unclean 1
6 the person who touches any such shall be unclean 1
27:11 if it is an unclean animal such as is not offered 2
27 if it is an unclean animal, then he shall buy it 2
Num 5: 2 put out of the camp . . every one that is unclean 2
9: 6 unclean through touching the dead body of a man 2
7 unclean through touching the dead body of a man; 2
10 unclean through touching a dead body 2
18:15 firstling of unclean beasts you shall redeem. 2
19: 7 priest shall be unclean until evening. 1
8 shall be unclean until evening 1
10 he who gathers . . be unclean until evening. 1
11 He who touches . . shall be unclean seven days; 1
13 unclean; his uncleanness is still on him. 2
14 every one . . shall be unclean seven days. 1
15 every open vessel . . is unclean. 2
16 shall be unclean seven days. 1
17 For the unclean they shall take some ashes 2
19 clean person shall sprinkle upon the unclean 2
20 man who is unclean and does not cleanse himself 2
20 has not been thrown upon him, he is unclean. 2
21 touches . . shall be unclean until evening. 1
22 unclean person touches shall be unclean; 2
22 touches it shall be unclean until evening. 1
Deu 12:15 unclean and the clean may eat of it 2
22 unclean and the clean alike may eat of it. 2
14: 7 chew the cud but do not part the hoof, are unclean 2
8 parts the hoof but does not chew . . is unclean 2
10 you shall not eat; it is unclean for you. 2
19 all winged insects are unclean for you; 2
15:22 unclean and the clean alike may eat it, as though 2
26:14 have not . . removed any of it while I was unclean 2
Jos 22:19 if your land is unclean, pass over into the LORD's 2
Jdg 13: 4 drink no wine . . and eat nothing unclean 2
7 drink no wine . . and eat nothing unclean 3
2Ch 23:19 no one should enter who was in any way unclean. 2
Ezr 9:11 land unclean with the pollutions of the peoples 4
Job 14: 4 Who can bring a clean thing out of an unclean? 2
Ecc 9: 2 the good and the evil, to the clean and the unclean 2
Isa 6: 5 For I am lost; for I am a man of unclean lips 2
5 I dwell in the midst of a people of unclean lips; 2
35: 8 the Holy Way; the unclean shall not pass over it 2
52: 1 there shall no more come into you . . the unclean. 2
64: 6 We have all become like one who is unclean 2
Lam 4:15 Away! Unclean!" men cried at them; 2
Ezk 4:13 the people of Israel eat their bread unclean 2
22:10 women who are unclean in their impurity. 2
26 difference between the unclean and the clean 2
44:23 distinguish between the unclean and the clean. 2
Hos 9: 3 and they shall eat unclean food in Assyria. 2
Ams 7:17 you yourself shall die in an unclean land 2
Hag 2:13 If one who is unclean by contact with a dead body 1
14 what they offer there is unclean. 2
Zec 13: 2 the land the prophets and the unclean spirit. 3
Mat 10: 1 and gave them authority over unclean spirits 6
12:43 When the unclean spirit has gone out of a man 6
Mrk 1:23 in their synagogue a man with an unclean spirit; 6
26 the unclean spirit, convulsing him and crying 6
27 he commands even the unclean spirits 6
3:11 whenever the unclean spirits beheld him 6
30 for they had said, "He has an unclean spirit. 6
5: 2 a man with an unclean spirit 6
8 Come out of the man, you unclean spirit! 6
13 unclean spirits came out, and entered the swine; 6
6: 7 and gave them authority over the unclean spirits. 6
7:25 possessed by an unclean spirit 6
9:25 he rebuked the unclean spirit, saying to it 6
Lke 4:33 a man who had the spirit of an unclean demon 6
36 he commands the unclean spirits, and they come out. 6
6:18 those who were troubled with unclean spirits 6
8:29 he had commanded the unclean spirit to come out 6
9:42 But Jesus rebuked the unclean spirit 6
11:24 When the unclean spirit has gone out of a man 6
Act 5:16 those afflicted with unclean spirits 6
8: 7 unclean spirits came out of many 6
10:14 never eaten anything that is common or unclean. 6
28 I should not call any man common or unclean. 6
11: 8 nothing . . unclean has ever entered my mouth.' 6
Rom 14:14 persuaded . . that nothing is unclean in itself; 7
14 it is unclean for any one who thinks it unclean. 7
14 it is unclean for any one who thinks it unclean. 7
1Co 7:14 Otherwise, your children would be unclean 6
2Co 6:17 touch nothing unclean; then I will welcome you 6
Rev 21:27 But nothing unclean shall enter it 7
Wis 2:16 he avoids our ways as unclean 5
Sir 51: 5 from an unclean tongue and lying words– 6
1Mc 1:47 to sacrifice swine and unclean animals 7
48 abominable by everything unclean and profane 6
4:43 removed the defiled stones to an unclean place. 6
unclean *See also* declare, exclude, food, hold, make, pronounce.

become unclean 1. טמא
Lev 5: 2 it is hidden from him, and he has become unclean 1
3 with which one becomes unclean, and it is hidden 1
11:24 by these you shall become unclean 1
43 shall not defile . . lest you become unclean 1
15:32 an emission of semen, becoming unclean thereby 1
Ps 106:39 Thus they became unclean by their acts 1
Hag 2:13 touches any of these, does it become unclean? 1
13 The priests answered, "It does become unclean. 1

unclean deed 1. ἀκαθαρσία
1Es 1:49 beyond all the unclean deeds of all the nations 1

unclean person 1. טָמֵא
Num 19:22 whatever the unclean person touches shall be 1

remain unclean 1. טמא
Lev 13:46 He shall remain unclean as long as he has 1

unclean thing 1. דָּוֶה 2. טָמֵא 3. טֻמְאָה 4. נִדָּה
5. ἀκάθαρτος
Lev 7:19 Flesh that touches any unclean thing shall not 2
21 if any one touches an unclean thing 2
Jdg 13:14 let her drink wine . . or eat any unclean thing; 3
Isa 30:22 You will scatter them as unclean things; 1
52:11 depart, go out thence, touch no unclean thing; 2
Ezk 7:19 and their gold is like an unclean thing; 4
20 therefore I will make it an unclean thing to them. 4
Sir 34: 4 From an unclean thing what will be made clean? 5

uncleanness 1. טֻמְאָה 2. טֻמְאָה 3. נִדָּה 4. ἀκαθαρσία
Lev 5: 3 Or if he touches human uncleanness, of whatever 2
3 whatever sort the uncleanness may be 2
7:20 eats . . peace offerings while an uncleanness 2
21 an unclean thing, whether the uncleanness of man 2
14:19 him who is to be cleansed from his uncleanness 2
15: 3 this is the law of his uncleanness 2
3 from discharge, it is uncleanness in him 2
25 she shall continue in uncleanness 2
26 be unclean, as in the uncleanness of her impurity 2
31 keep . . Israel separate from their uncleanness 2
31 lest they die in their uncleanness by defiling 2
16:16 because of the uncleannesses of the people 2
16 with them in the midst of their uncleannesses 2
19 from the uncleannesses of the people of Israel 2
18:19 while she is in her menstrual uncleanness 2
22: 3 approaches . . while he has an uncleanness 2
5 may take uncleanness, whatever his uncleanness– 2
Num 5:19 if you have not turned aside to uncleanness 2
19:13 unclean; his uncleanness is still on him. 2
2Sm 11: 4 was purifying herself from her uncleanness. 2
2Ch 29:16 brought out all the uncleanness that they found 2
Ezr 9:11 filled it from end to end with their uncleanness. 2
Lam 1: 9 Her uncleanness was in her skirts; 2
Ezk 36:17 like the uncleanness of a woman in her impurity. 2
25 you shall be clean from all your uncleannesses 2
29 I will deliver you from all your uncleannesses; 2
39:24 I dealt with them according to their uncleanness 2
Mic 2:10 because of uncleanness that destroys 1
Zec 13: 1 to cleanse them from sin and uncleanness. 3
Mat 23:27 dead men's bones and all uncleanness. 4
Eph 4:19 greedy to practice every kind of uncleanness. 4
1Th 2: 3 does not spring from error or uncleanness 4
4: 7 God has not called us for uncleanness 4
1Es 1:42 about . . his uncleanness and impiety 4
8:83 they have filled it with their uncleanness. 4
87 the uncleanness of the peoples of the land. 4
1Mc 13:48 He cast out of it all uncleanness 4
14: 7 he removed its uncleanness from it 4
uncleanness *See also* take.

unclothed 1. ἐκδύω
2Co 5: 4 not that we would be unclothed 1
uncomfortable *See* toil.

uncompleted 1. ἀνήνυτος
3Mc 4:15 though uncompleted it stopped after 40 days. 1

unconcern 1. ἀκηδία
Sir 29: 5 will pay in words of unconcern 1

unconcerned 1. καταφρονέω
Bel 1:13 They were unconcerned 1

uncondemned 1. ἀκατάγνωστος 2. ἀκατάκριτος
Act 16:37 beaten us publicly, uncondemned 2
22:25 a man who is a Roman citizen, and uncondemned? 2
2Mc 4:47 who would have been freed uncondemned 1

unconquered 1. ἀνίκητος
4Mc 11:27 therefore, unconquered, we hold fast to reason. 1

uncontrollable 1. ἀκατάσχετος
3Mc 6:17 and brought an uncontrollable terror upon the army. 1

uncounted 1. ἀναρίθμητος
Wis 7:11 in her hands uncounted wealth. 1
3Mc 2:26 his uncounted licentious deeds 1

uncover 1. גלה 2. חשׂף 3. ערה 4. *ἀκάλυπτος* 5. *ἀκατακάλυπτος* 6. *ἀνακαλύπτω* 7. *γυμνόω*

Lev 18: 6 approach any one . . to uncover nakedness 1
7 You shall not uncover the nakedness 1
7 your mother, you shall not uncover her nakedness 1
8 not uncover the nakedness of your father's wife 1
9 You shall not uncover the nakedness 1
10 You shall not uncover the nakedness of your son's 1
11 You shall not uncover the nakedness of your 1
12 You shall not uncover the nakedness 1
13 not uncover the nakedness of your mother's sister 1
14 You shall not uncover the nakedness 1
15 uncover the nakedness of your daughter-in-law 1
15 son's wife, you shall not uncover her nakedness 1
16 You shall not uncover the nakedness 1
17 You shall not uncover the nakedness of a woman 1
17 her daughter's daughter to uncover her nakedness 1
18 uncovering her nakedness while her sister is 1
19 not approach a woman to uncover her nakedness 1
20:11 The man . . has uncovered his father's nakedness 1
17 he has uncovered his sister's nakedness 1
18 If a man . . uncovers her nakedness 1
18 and she has uncovered the fountain of her blood 1
19 You shall not uncover the nakedness 1
20 he has uncovered his uncle's nakedness 1
21 it is impurity; he has uncovered his brother's 1
Num24: 4 falling down, but having his eyes uncovered 1
16 falling down, but having his eyes uncovered 1
Deu 22:30 nor shall he uncover her who is his father's. 1
27:20 because he has uncovered her who is his father's.' 1
Rut 3: 4 then, go and uncover his feet and lie down; 1
7 she came . . and uncovered his feet, and lay down. 1
2Sm 6:20 How the king . . uncovering himself today 1
20 one of the vulgar fellows . . uncovers himself! 1
Job 12:22 He uncovers the deeps out of darkness 1
Isa 20: 4 naked and barefoot, with buttocks uncovered 2
22: 6 bore the quiver . . and Kir uncovered the shield. 3
47: 2 uncover your legs, pass through the rivers. 1
3 Your nakedness shall be uncovered 1
57: 8 for, deserting me, you have uncovered your bed 1
Jer 49:10 I have uncovered his hiding places 1
Lam 4:22 he will punish, he will uncover your sins. 1
Ezk 16:36 your nakedness uncovered in your harlotries 1
37 and will uncover your nakedness to them 1
57 before your wickedness was uncovered? 1
21:24 in that your transgressions are uncovered 1
22:10 In you men uncover their fathers' nakedness; 1
23:10 These uncovered her nakedness; they seized her 1
29 nakedness of your harlotry shall be uncovered. 1
Hos 2:10 Now I will uncover her lewdness 1
Mic 1: 6 down her stones . . and uncover her foundations. 1
1Co 11:13 for a woman to pray to God with her head uncovered? 5
1Es 8:79 to uncover a light for us in the house of the Lord 6
Tob 2: 9 my face was uncovered. 4
Jdt 9: 1 uncovered the sackcloth she was wearing 7
2 and uncovered her thigh to put her to shame 7
LJr 1:31 their heads uncovered. 4

uncovered *See* lie.

undaunted 1. *θαρσαλέος*

4Mc 13:13 looking at one another, cheerful and undaunted 1

undefended 1. *ἔρημος*

AEs 16:14 he would find us undefended 1

undefiled 1. *ἀμίαντος*

Heb 13: 4 let the marriage bed be undefiled 1
Jas 1:27 Religion that is pure and undefiled before God 1
1Pe 1: 4 an inheritance which is . . undefiled 1
Wis 3:13 blessed is the barren woman who is undefiled 1
4: 2 in the contest for prizes that a: e undefiled. 1
8:20 rather, being good, I entered an undefiled body. 1
2Mc 14:36 keep undefiled for ever this house 1
15:34 he who has kept his own place undefiled. 1

under 1. אֶל 2. בְּ 3. כְּ 4. לְ 5. לִפְנֵי 6. מִן 7. מִתַּחַת 8. עַל 9. תַּחַת 10. תְּחוֹת (A) 11. *διά* 12. *ἐκ* 13. *ἐν* 14. *ἐπί* 15. *ἔχω* 16. *καθύπερθε* 17. *κατά* 18. *κατωτέρω* 19. *μετά* 20. *περί* 21. *ὑπό* 22. *ὑποκάτω* 23. *ὑποτάσσω* 24. sub

Gen 1: 7 the waters which were under the firmament 9
9 God said, "Let the waters under the heavens 9
6:17 from under heaven; everything that is 9
7:19 all the high mountains under the whole heaven 9
18: 4 feet, and rest yourselves under the tree 9
8 he stood by them under the tree while they ate. 9
19: 8 for they have come under the shelter of my roof. 2
21:15 she cast the child under one of the bushes. 9
24: 2 servant . . "Put your hand under my thigh 9
9 servant put his hand under the thigh of Abraham 9
35: 4 and Jacob hid them under the oak which was near 9
8 died, and she was buried under an oak below Bethel; 9
41:35 lay up grain under the authority of Pharaoh 9
47:29 put your hand under my thigh, and promise to deal 9
Exd 2:23 people of Israel groaned under their bondage 6
23 and their cry under bondage came up to God. 6
6: 6 I will bring you out from under the burdens 9
7 God, who has brought you out from under 9
17:12 so they took a stone and put it under him, and he sat 9
14 remembrance of Am'alek from under heaven. 9
18:11 people from under the hand of the Egyptians 9
20: 4 anything . . that is in the water under the earth; 9
21:20 the slave dies under his hand, he shall be 9
23: 5 see the ass . . lying under its burden 9
24:10 there was under his feet as it were a pavement 9
25:35 a capital . . under each pair of the six branches 9
26:19 bases . . you shall make under the twenty frames 9
19 two bases under one frame for its two tenons 9
19 two bases under another frame for its two tenons; 9
21 forty bases of silver, two bases under one frame 9
21 and two bases under another frame; 9
25 two bases under one frame, and two bases 9
25 and two bases under another frame. 9
27: 5 you shall set it under the ledge of the altar 9
30: 4 under its molding on two opposite sides of it 9
36:24 he made 40 bases of silver under the twenty frames 9
24 two bases under one frame for its two tenons 9
24 bases under another frame for its two tenons. 9
26 bases of silver, two bases under one frame 9
26 and two bases under another frame. 9
30 sixteen bases, under every frame two bases. 9
37:21 a capital of one piece with it under each pair 9
27 made two rings of gold on it under its molding 9
38: 4 made . . a network of bronze, under its ledge 9
21 the Levites under the direction of Ith'amar 2
Lev 15:10 whoever touches anything that was under him 9
27:32 all that pass under the herdsman's staff 9
Num 4:28 work is to be under the oversight of Ith'amar 2
33 under the hand of Ith'amar the son of Aaron 2
5:19 while you were under your husband's authority 9
20 though you are under your husband's authority 9
29 when a wife, though under her husband's authority 9
6:18 under the sacrifice of the peace offering. 9
7: 8 under the direction of Ith'amar the son of Aaron 2
16:31 the ground under them split asunder; 9
22:27 ass saw the angel . . she lay down under Balaam; 9
31:49 counted the men of war who are under our command 2
Deu 2:25 peoples that are under the whole of heaven 9
3:17 Salt Sea, under the slopes of Pisgah on the east. 9
4:18 any fish that is in the water under the earth. 9
19 all the peoples under the whole heaven. 9
49 Sea of the Arabah, under the slopes of Pisgah. 9
5: 8 anything . . that is in the water under the earth; 9
7:24 shall make their name perish from under heaven; 9
9:14 I may . . blot out their name from under heaven; 9
12: 2 upon the hills and under every green tree 9
25:19 remembrance of Am'alek from under heaven; 9
28:23 earth under you shall be iron. 9
29:20 LORD would blot out his name from under heaven. 9
Jos 11: 3 the Hivites under Hermon in the land of Mizpah. 9
24:26 and set it up there under the oak in the sanctuary 9
Jdg 1: 7 kings . . used to pick up scraps under my table; 9
3:16 girded it on his right thigh under his clothes. 9
30 was subdued that day under the hand of Israel. 9
4: 5 She used to sit under the palm of Deb'orah between 9
6:11 the angel . . came and sat under the oak at Ophrah 9
19 brought them to him under the oak and presented 9
9:29 Would that this people were under my hand! 2
Rut 2:12 the LORD . . under whose wings you have come 9
1Sm 3: 1 Samuel was ministering to the LORD under Eli. 5
14: 2 Saul was staying . . under the pomegranate tree 9
22: 6 at Gib'e-ah, under the tamarisk tree on the height 9
25:20 and came down under cover of the mountain 2
31:13 buried them under the tamarisk tree in Jabesh 9
2Sm 18: 2 the army, one third under the command of Jo'ab 2
2 one third under the command of Abi'shai the son 2
2 and one third under the command of It'tai 2
9 the mule went under the . . branches of a great oak 9
9 while the mule that was under him went on. 9
22:10 and came down; thick darkness was under his feet. 9
37 Thou didst give a wide place for my steps under me 9
39 so that they did not rise; they fell under my feet. 9
40 thou didst make my assailants sink under me. 9
48 God who . . brought down peoples under me 9
1Kg 4:25 every man under his vine and under his fig tree 9
25 every man under his vine and under his fig tree 9
5: 3 the LORD put them under the soles of his feet. 9
7:24 Under its brim were gourds, for 30 cubits 9
13:14 and found him sitting under an oak; 9
14:23 on every high hill and under every green tree; 9
19: 4 and came and sat down under a broom tree; 9
5 he lay down and slept under a broom tree; 9
2Kg 6: 1 where we dwell under your charge is too small 4
9:13 every man . . took his garment, and put it under him 9
14:27 blot out the name of Israel from under heaven 9
16: 4 and on the hills, and under every green tree. 9
17 sea from off the bronze oxen that were under it 9
17: 7 out of . . Egypt from under the hand of Pharaoh 9
10 Ashe'rim on every . . and under every green tree; 9
1Ch 10:12 they buried their bones under the oak in Jabesh 9
12:32 and all their kinsmen under their command. 8
17: 1 ark of the covenant of the LORD is under a tent. 9
25: 2 sons of Asaph, under the direction of Asaph 8
2 who prophesied under the direction of the king. 8
3 under the direction of their father Jedu'thun 8
6 all under the direction of their father 8
6 and Heman were under the order of the king. 8
2Ch 4: 3 Under it were figures of gourds 9
14: 5 And the kingdom had rest under him. 5
23:18 under the direction of the Levitical priests 2
25: 5 under commanders of thousands and of hundreds 4
26:11 under the direction of Hanani'ah 8
13 Under their command was an army of 307,500 8
28: 4 burned incense . . under every green tree. 9
Neh 1: 9 your dispersed be under the farthest skies 2
2:14 no place for the beast that was under me to pass. 9
3: 7 who were under the jurisdiction of the governor 4
Est 2: 3 harem . . under custody of Hegai the king's eunuch 1
12 being . . under the regulations for the women 3
Job 20:12 in his mouth, though he hides it under his tongue 9
26: 8 the cloud is not rent under them. 9
28:24 and sees everything under the heavens. 9
30: 7 under the nettles they huddle together. 9
37: 3 Under the whole heaven he lets it go 9
40:21 Under the lotus plants he lies 9
41:11 Whatever is under the whole heaven is mine. 9
Ps 8: 6 thou hast put all things under his feet 9
10: 7 under his tongue are mischief and iniquity. 9
18: 9 thick darkness was under his feet. 9
36 Thou didst give a wide place for my steps under me 9
38 were not able to rise; they fell under my feet. 9
39 thou didst make my assailants sink under me. 9
47 gave me vengeance and subdued peoples under me; 9
27: 5 he will conceal me under the cover of his tent 2
31:20 thou holdest them safe under thy shelter 2
45: 5 the peoples fall under you. 9
47: 3 He subdued peoples under us, and nations 9
3 peoples under us, and nations under our feet. 9
61: 4 Oh to be safe under the shelter of thy wings! Selah 2
68:30 Trample under foot those who lust after tribute; •
90: 9 For all our days pass away under thy wrath 2
91: 4 under his wings you will find refuge; 9
106:42 brought into subjection under their power. 9
140: 3 under their lips is the poison of vipers. Selah 9
144: 2 who subdues the peoples under him. 9
Prv 22:27 why should your bed be taken from under you? 9
30:21 Under three things the earth trembles; 9
21 three things . . under four it cannot bear up 9
Ecc 1: 3 gain by . . the toil at which he toils under the sun? 9
9 and there is nothing new under the sun. 9
13 to seek . . by wisdom all that is done under heaven; 9
14 I have seen everything that is done under the sun; 9
2: 3 for . . men to do under heaven during the few days 9
11 and there was nothing to be gained under the sun. 9
17 what is done under the sun was grievous to me; 9
18 all my toil in which I had toiled under the sun 9
19 which I toiled and used my wisdom under the sun. 9
20 all the toil of my labors under the sun 9
3: 1 and a time for every matter under heaven 9
16 I saw under the sun that in the place of justice 9
4: 1 oppressions that are practiced under the sun. 9
3 the evil deeds that are done under the sun. 9
7 Again, I saw vanity under the sun 9
15 I saw all the living who move about under the sun 9
5:13 a grievous evil which I have seen under the sun 9
18 one toils under the sun the few days of his life 9
6: 1 There is an evil which I have seen under the sun 9
12 tell man what will be after him under the sun? 9
7: 6 For as the crackling of thorns under a pot, 9
8: 9 applying my mind to all that is done under the sun 9
15 no good thing under the sun but to eat and drink 9
15 days of life which God gives him under the sun. 9
17 find out the work that is done under the sun. 9
9: 3 This is an evil in all that is done under the sun 9
6 have no . . share in all that is done under the sun. 9
9 vain life which he has given you under the sun 9
9 and in your toil at which you toil under the sun. 9
11 saw that under the sun the race is not to the swift 9
13 also seen this example of wisdom under the sun 9
10: 5 There is an evil which I have seen under the sun 9
Sng 2: 6 O that his left hand were under my head 9
4:11 honey and milk are under your tongue; 9
8: 3 O that his left hand were under my head 9
5 Under the apple tree I awakened you. 9
Isa 3: 6 this heap of ruins shall be under your rule"; 9
10:16 and under his glory a burning will be kindled 9
24: 5 The earth lies polluted under its inhabitants; 9
28: 3 of E'phraim will be trodden under foot; 2
57: 5 lust among the oaks, under every green tree; 9
5 valleys, and under the clefts of the rocks? 9
Jer 2:20 and under every green tree you bowed down 9
3: 6 on every high hill and under every green tree 9
13 favors among strangers under every green tree 9
10:11 from the earth and from under the heavens. 9
17 O you who dwell under siege! 2
27: 8 and put its neck under the yoke of the king 2
11 nation which will bring its neck under the yoke 2
12 Bring your necks under the yoke of the king 2
33:13 flocks shall again pass under the hands 8
52:20 the twelve bronze bulls which were under the sea 9
Lam 3: 1 has seen affliction under the rod of his wrath; 2
34 To crush under foot all the prisoners 9
66 and destroy them from under thy heavens, O LORD. 9
4:20 Under his shadow we shall live among . . nations. 2
5:13 and boys stagger under loads of wood. 2

Ezk 1: 8 Under their wings on their four sides 7
23 under the firmament their wings were stretched 9
4:17 and waste away under their punishment. 2
6:13 on all the mountain tops, under every green tree 9
13 under every leafy oak, wherever they offered 9
10: 8 have the form of a human hand under their wings. 9
17:13 made a covenant with him, putting him under oath. 2
23 cedar; and under it will dwell all kinds of beasts; 9
20:37 I will make you pass under the rod 9
24: 5 pile the logs under it; boil its pieces 9
31: 6 under its branches all the beasts of the field 9
6 under its shadow dwelt all great nations. 2
17 yea, those who dwelt under its shadow 2
32:27 whose swords were laid under their heads 9
Dan 4:12 beasts of the field found shade under it 10
14 let the beasts flee from under it 10
21 under which beasts of the field found shade 10
7:27 kingdoms under the whole heaven shall be given 10
8:25 cunning . . make deceit prosper under his hand 2
9:12 under the whole heaven there has not been done 9
Hos 4:13 make offerings upon the hills, under oak, poplar 9
Jol 1:17 The seed shrivels under the clods 9
Obd 1: 7 your trusted friends have set a trap under you 9
Jon 4: 5 He sat under it in the shade 9
Mic 1: 4 And the mountains will melt under him 9
4: 4 but they shall sit every man under his vine 9
4 every man under his vine and under his fig tree 9
Zec 3:10 of you will invite his neighbor under his vine 9
10 under his vine and under his fig tree. 9
Mal 4: 3 they will be ashes under the soles of your feet 9
Mat 2:16 in all that region who were two years old or under 18
5:15 lamp and put it under a bushel, but on a stand 21
7: 6 lest they trample them under foot and turn 13
8: 8 Lord, I am not worthy to have you come under my roof 21
9 I am a man under authority, with soldiers under me; 21
9 I am a man under authority, with soldiers under me; 21
22:44 till I put thy enemies under thy feet'? 22
23:37 as a hen gathers her brood under her wings 21
Mrk 4:21 brought in to be put under a bushel, or under a bed 21
21 under a bushel, or under a bed, and not on a stand? 21
5:26 who had suffered much under many physicians 21
7:28 Yes, Lord; yet even the dogs under the table eat 22
12:36 till I put thy enemies under thy feet.' 22
Lke 7: 6 for I am not worthy to have you come under my roof; 21
8 I am a man set under authority 21
8 man set under authority, with soldiers under me 21
8:16 puts it under a bed 22
11:33 puts it in a cellar or under a bushel, but on a stand 21
13:34 as a hen gathers her brood under her wings 21
23:40 you are under the same sentence of condemnation? 13
Joh 1:48 when you were under the fig tree, I saw you. 21
50 Because I said to you, I saw you under the fig tree 22
Act 2: 5 devout men from every nation under heaven. 21
4:12 no other name under heaven given among men 21
21:23 We have four men who are under a vow; 14
Rom 2:12 and all who have sinned under the law 13
3: 9 both Jews and Greeks, are under the power of sin 21
13 The venom of asps is under their lips. 21
19 the law . . speaks to those who are under the law 13
6:14 since you are not under law but under grace. 21
14 since you are not under law but under grace. 21
15 Are we to sin because we are not under law 21
15 because we are not under law but under grace? 21
7: 6 so that we serve not under the old written code •
14 but I am carnal, sold under sin. 21
16:20 God . . will soon crush Satan under your feet. 21
1Co 7:37 firmly established . . being under no necessity 15
37 having his desire under control •
9:20 to those under the law I became as one under the law 21
20 to those under the law I became as one under the law 21
20 though not being myself under the law 21
20 that I might win those under the law. 21
10: 1 our fathers were all under the cloud 21
15:25 until he has put all his enemies under his feet. 21
27 all things in subjection under his feet. 21
27 All things are put in subjection under him 23
27 he is excepted who put all things under him. 23
2Co 9: 7 not reluctantly or under compulsion 12
13 Under the test of this service 11
11:32 the governor under King Ar'etas guarded the city •
Gal 3:10 all who rely on works of the law are under a curse; 21
23 we were confined under the law 21
25 we are no longer under a custodian; 21
4: 2 he is under guardians and trustees 21
4 born of woman, born under the law 21
5 to redeem those who were under the law 21
21 Tell me, you who desire to be under law 21
5:18 led by the Spirit you are not under the law. 21
Eph 1:22 he has put all things under his feet 21
Php 3: 6 as to righteousness under the law blameless. 13
Col 1:23 been preached to every creature under heaven 21
1Ti 6: 1 all who are under the yoke of slavery 21
Heb 2: 8 everything in subjection under his feet 22
7:11 (for under it the people received the law) 14
9:15 the transgressions under the first covenant. 14
22 under the law 17
Jas 2:12 those . . to be judged under the law of liberty. 11
5:12 that you may not fall under condemnation. 21
1Pe 4:16 but under that name let him glorify God. 13
5: 6 under the mighty hand of God 21
Rev 5: 3 no one in heaven or on earth or under the earth 22
13 every creature . . under the earth and in the sea 22
6: 9 I saw under the altar the souls of those 22
12: 1 clothed with the sun, with the moon under her feet 22
1Es 3: 1 for all that were under him 21
2 all the . . governors that were under him 21
8 put them under the pillow of Darius the king 21
5:36 under the leadership of Cherub, Addan, and Immer •
2Es 1:30 as a hen gathers her brood under her wings 24
11: 6 I saw how all things under heaven were subjected 24
24 and remained under the head 24
13: 3 everything under his gaze trembled 24
14: 1 On the third day, while I was sitting under an oak 24
Tob 1:15 under him the highways were unsafe •
Jdt 6:13 However, they got under the shelter of the hill 22
10:21 under a canopy which was woven with purple 13
11: 7 will live by your power under Nebuchadnezzar 14
AEs 13: 1 to the governors under them 23
10 earth and every wonderful thing under heaven 21
16:19 permit the Jews to live under their own laws. •
Wis 17: 2 shut in under their roofs •
Sir 6:25 do not fret under her bonds. •
14:26 he will place his children under her shelter 13
26 will camp under her boughs; 21
29:10 do not let it rust under a stone and be lost. 21
22 a poor man under the shelter of his roof 21
33: 6 he neighs under every one who sits on him. 22
51:26 Put your neck under the yoke 21
Bar 1:12 we shall live under the protection 21
12 under the protection of Belshazzar his son 21
2: 2 Under the whole heaven there has not been done 22
5: 3 show your splendor everywhere under heaven. 21
Sus 1:54 Under what tree did you see them being intimate 21
54 He answered, "Under a mastic tree. 21
58 tell me: Under what tree did you catch them 21
58 He answered, "Under an evergreen oak. 21
Bel 1:30 under compulsion he handed Daniel over to them. •
1Mc 6:46 He got under the elephant 21
9:38 and went up and hid under cover of the mountain. 21
53 put them under guard in the citadel at Jerusalem. 13
10:38 they are considered to be under one ruler 21
13:12 Jonathan was with him under guard. 13
14: 3 took him to Arsaces, who put him under guard. 13
12 Each man sat under his vine and his fig tree 21
2Mc 2:18 and will gather us from everywhere under heaven 21
3: 6 to fall under the control of the king. 21
19 girded with sackcloth under their breasts 21
4:12 he founded a gymnasium right under the citadel 21
6: 7 the Jews were taken, under bitter constraint 19
30 When he was about to die under the blows •
30 I am enduring terrible sufferings . . under this beating •
7: 1 compelled . . under torture with whips and cords •
36 drunk of everflowing life under God's covenant; 21
9:11 to come to his senses under the scourge of God •
12:19 who were captains under Maccabeus 20
40 under the tunic of every one of the dead 21
3Mc 4: 9 driven under the constraint of iron bonds •
10 they were confined under a solid deck 16
4Mc 8:14 when you transgress under compulsion. 11
22 for fearing the king when we are under compulsion. 11
17:19 All who are consecrated are under your hands. 21
23 their endurance under the tortures 14

under *See also* bear, dominion, foot, guard, leadership, obligation, pretense, pretext, punishment, spread, take, tyranny.

underbrush 1. silva
2Es 16:77 as a field is choked with underbrush 1

undergird 1. *ὑποζώννυμι*
Act 27:17 they took measures to undergird the ship 1

undergo 1. *καρτερέω* 2. *λαμβάνω* 3. *ὑπέχω*
Jde 1: 7 serve as an example by undergoing a punishment 3
2Mc 7: 8 Therefore he in turn underwent tortures 2
3Mc 4:10 they should undergo treatment befitting traitors 2
4Mc 9: 9 will deservedly undergo . . eternal torment 1
10:11 will undergo unceasing torments. 1

underhanded way 1. *κρυπτός*
2Co 4: 2 renounced disgraceful, underhanded ways 1

undermine 1. *ἐκκόπτω*
2Co 11:12 to do, in order to undermine the claim 1

underneath 1. מִתַּחַת 2. תַּחַת
Deu 33:27 underneath are the everlasting arms. 1
Jos 7:21 hidden . . with the silver underneath. 2
22 hidden in his tent with the silver underneath. 2
1Kg 7:32 the four wheels were underneath the panels; 1
44 one sea, and the twelve oxen underneath the sea. 2
8: 6 underneath the wings of the cherubim. 2
2Ch 4:15 the one sea, and the twelve oxen underneath it. 2
5: 7 place, underneath the wings of the cherubim. 2
Job 28: 5 but underneath it is turned up as by fire. 2
Ezk 10: 2 the whirling wheels underneath the cherubim; 2
20 living creatures that I saw underneath the God 2
21 and each four wings, and underneath their wings 2

underneath *See also* roast.

underpart 1. תַּחַת
Job 41:30 His underparts are like sharp potsherds; 1

understand 1. בין 2. בִּינָה 3. ידע 4. נכר 5. ראה 6. שכל 7. שֵׂכֶל 8. שמע 9. תְּבוּנָה 10. בִּינָה (A) 11. *ἀγνοέω* 12. *αἰσθάνομαι* 13. *ἀκούω* 14. *γινώσκω* 15. *διαλαμβάνω* 16. *διανοέω* 17. *ἐπιγινώσκω* 18. *ἐπίσταμαι* 19. *ἵσταμαι* 20. *κατανοέω* 21. *λογίζομαι* 22. *νοέω* 23. *οἶδα* 24. *οὐ ἀγνοέω* 25. *σύνεσις* 26. *συνετός* 27. *συνίημι* 28. apprehendo 29. cognosco 30. intellego 31. scio 32. video
Gen 11: 7 they may not understand one another's speech. 8
42:23 They did not know that Joseph understood them 8
Exd 10: 7 do you not yet understand that Egypt is ruined? 3
Deu 1:13 Choose wise, understanding, and experienced men 1
4: 6 that will be your wisdom and your understanding 2
6 great nation is a wise and understanding people.' 1
28:49 nation whose language you do not understand 8
29: 4 LORD has not given you a mind to understand 3
32:29 If they were wise, they would understand this 6
1Sm 25: 3 woman was of good understanding and beautiful 7
28: 1 Understand that you . . are to go out with me 3
2Sm 3:37 and all Israel understood . . that it had not 3
1Kg 3: 9 Give thy servant . . an understanding mind 8
11 asked . . understanding to discern what is right 1
2Kg 18:26 speak . . in the Aramaic.., for we understand it; 8
1Ch 15:22 should direct the music, for he understood it. 1
22:12 LORD grant you discretion and understanding 2
27:32 being a man of understanding and a scribe; 1
28: 9 LORD . . understands every plan and thought. 1
2Ch 2:12 son, endued with discretion and understanding 2
13 a skilled man, endued with understanding 2
Neh 6:12 I understood, and saw that God had not sent him 4
8: 2 men . . and all who could hear with understanding 1
3 men and the women and those who could understand; 1
7 helped the people to understand the law 1
8 so that the people understood the reading. 1
12 understood the words that were declared to them. 1
Job 13: 1 my ear has heard and understood it. 1
15: 9 What do you understand that is not clear to us? 1
17: 4 thou hast closed their minds to understanding 7
20: 3 out of my understanding a spirit answers me. 2
23: 5 and understand what he would say to me. 1
26:12 by his understanding he smote Rahab. 9
14 But the thunder of his power who can understand? 1
28:12 And where is the place of understanding? 2
20 where is the place of understanding? 2
23 God understands the way to it 1
28 and to depart from evil is understanding.' 2
32: 9 nor the aged that understand what is right. 1
34:16 If you have understanding, hear this; 2
36:29 any one understand the spreading of the clouds 1
38: 4 Tell me, if you have understanding. 2
36 or given understanding to the mists? 2
39:17 and given her no share in understanding. 2
42: 3 I have uttered what I did not understand 1
Ps 32: 9 like a horse or a mule, without understanding 1
49: 3 meditation of my heart shall be understanding. 9
73:16 when I thought how to understand this 3
92: 6 the stupid cannot understand this 1
94: 8 Understand, O dullest of the people! 1
119:100 I understand more than the aged 1
147: 5 his understanding is beyond measure. 9
Prv 1: 2 That men may . . understand words of insight 1
6 to understand a proverb and a figure 1
2: 5 then you will understand the fear of the LORD 1
9 Then you will understand righteousness 1
5: 1 incline your ear to my understanding; 9
8: 9 They are all straight to him who understands 1
11:12 but a man of understanding remains silent. 9
16:16 to get understanding is to be chosen 2
20:24 how then can man understand his way? 1
21:16 A man who wanders from the way of understanding 6
23:23 buy wisdom, instruction, and understanding. 2
28: 2 but with men of understanding and knowledge 1
5 Evil men do not understand justice 1
5 who seek the LORD understand it completely. 1
16 A ruler who lacks understanding is a cruel 9
29: 7 wicked man does not understand such knowledge. 1
19 for though he understands, he will not give heed. 1
30: 2 I have not the understanding of a man. 2
18 Three things . . four I do not understand 3
Isa 1: 3 does not know, my people does not understand. 1
6: 9 Hear and hear, but do not understand; 1
10 lest they . . understand with their hearts 1
11: 2 the spirit of wisdom and understanding 2
28:19 be sheer terror to understand the message. 1
29:24 who err in spirit will come to understanding 2
33:19 in a tongue which you cannot understand. 2
36:11 speak . . in Aramaic, for we understand it; 8
40:14 and showed him the way of understanding? 9
21 Have you not understood from the foundations 1
28 his understanding is unsearchable. 9
41:20 men . . may consider and understand together 6

42:25 him on fire round about, but he did not understand; 3
43:10 that you may know and believe me and understand 1
44:18 and their minds, so that they cannot understand. 6
52:15 they have not heard they shall understand. 1
57: 1 men are taken away, while no one understands. 1
Jer 5:15 nor can you understand what they say. 8
9:12 Who is the man so wise that he can understand this? 1
24 glory in this, that he understands and knows me 6
10:12 his understanding stretched out the heavens. 9
17: 9 heart is deceitful . . who can understand it? 3
23:20 In the latter days you will understand it 1
30:24 In the latter days you will understand this. 1
51:15 by his understanding stretched out the heavens. 9
Ezk 3: 6 language, whose words you cannot understand. 8
12: 3 Perhaps they will understand 5
28: 4 by . . your understanding you have gotten wealth 9
Dan 1:20 every matter of wisdom and understanding 2
2:21 knowledge to those who have understanding; 10
8:15 seen the vision, I sought to understand it; 2
17 said to me, "Understand, O son of man, 1
23 king . . one who understands riddles 1
27 appalled by the vision and did not understand it. 1
9:22 come out to give you wisdom and understanding. 2
23 therefore consider . . understand the vision. 1
25 Know therefore and understand that 6
10: 1 understood the word and had understanding 1
1 word and had understanding of the vision. 2
12 first day that you set your mind to understand 1
12: 8 I heard, but I did not understand. 1
10 none of the wicked shall understand; 1
10 those who are wise shall understand. 1
Hos 4:14 people without understanding . . come to ruin. 1
14: 9 Whoever is wise, let him understand these things; 1
Mic 4:12 of the LORD, they do not understand his plan 1
Mat 13:13 hearing they do not hear, nor do they understand. 27
14 You shall indeed hear but never understand 27
15 and understand with their heart 27
19 and does not understand it 27
23 hears the word and understands it 27
51 Have you understood all this? 27
15:10 Hear and understand 27
16:12 Then they understood 27
17:13 Then the disciples understood 27
24:15 (let the reader understand) 22
Mrk 4:12 and may indeed hear but not understand 27
13 Do you not understand this parable? 23
13 How then will you understand all the parables? 14
6:52 for they did not understand about the loaves 27
7:14 Hear me, all of you, and understand 27
8:17 Do you not yet perceive or understand? 27
21 he said to them, "Do you not yet understand? 27
9:32 they did not understand the saying 11
13:14 let the reader understand 22
14:68 I neither know nor understand what you mean. 18
Lke 2:50 they did not understand the saying 27
8:10 hearing they may not understand. 27
9:45 they did not understand this saying 11
18:34 they understood none of these things 27
24:45 to understand the scriptures 27
Joh 3:10 a teacher . . and yet you do not understand this? 14
8:27 They did not understand 14
43 Why do you not understand what I say? 14
10: 6 they did not understand what he was saying 14
38 that you may know and understand 14
11:50 you do not understand that it is expedient 21
12:16 His disciples did not understand this at first; 14
13: 7 afterward you will understand. 14
Act 7:25 He supposed that his brethren understood 27
25 they did not understand. 27
8:30 asked, "Do you understand what you are reading? 14
13:27 nor understand the utterances of the prophets *
28:26 You shall indeed hear but never understand 27
27 understand with their heart 27
Rom 3:11 no one understands, no one seeks for God. 27
7:15 I do not understand my own actions. 14
10:19 Again I ask, did Israel not understand? 14
11:25 I want you to understand this mystery, brethren 24
15:21 shall understand who have never heard of him. 27
1Co 2: 8 None of the rulers of this age understood this; 14
12 understand the gifts bestowed on us by God. 23
14 he is not able to understand them 14
11: 3 I want you to understand 23
13: 2 and understand all mysteries and all knowledge 23
14: 2 no one understands him, but he utters mysteries 13
2Co 1:13 nothing but what you can read and understand 17
13 I hope you will understand fully 17
14 as you have understood in part 17
10:11 Let such people understand 21
Eph 5:17 but understand what the will of the Lord is. 27
Col 1: 6 heard and understood the grace of God in truth 17
2Ti 3: 1 understand this 14
Heb 11: 3 By faith we understand . . 22
13:23 You should understand . . 14
2Pe 1:20 First of all you must understand this 14
3: 3 First of all you must understand this 14
Jde 1:10 men revile whatever they do not understand 23
2Es 2:34 I say to you, O nations that hear and understand 30
4:10 he said to me, "You cannot understand the things 29
11 how can one . . understand incorruption? 30
12 and to suffer and not understand why. 30
21 can understand only what is on the earth 30
21 can understand what is above . . the heavens. *
22 been endowed with the power of understanding? 30
5:34 I strive to understand the way of the Most High 28
37 the travail that you ask to understand. 32
6:15 and the foundations of the earth will understand 30
7:37 Look now, and understand whom you have denied 30
71 now understand from your own words 30
95 they understand the rest which they now enjoy 30
8:19 Therefore hear my voice, and understand my words 30
9:11 and did not understand but despised it 30
10:35 and I have heard what I do not understand. 31
13:18 because they understand what is reserved 30
24 Understand therefore that those who are left 31
16:35 and understand them, O servants of the Lord. 29
Jdt 9:14 to know and understand that thou art God 23
AEs 11:12 sought all day to understand it in every detail. 17
13: 5 We understand that this people . . 15
Wis 3: 9 Those who trust in him will understand truth 27
4:15 Yet the peoples saw and did not understand 22
17 not understand what the Lord purposed for him 22
6: 1 Listen therefore, O kings, and understand 27
8: 8 she understands turns of speech 19
9: 9 who understand what is pleasing in thy sight 18
11 For she knows and understands all things 27
Sir 18:29 Those who understand sayings become skilled 26
34:11 I understand more than I can express. 25
38:33 nor do they understand the sentence of judgment; 16
Bar 3:20 the way to knowledge, nor understood her paths 27
LJr 1:41 as though Bel were able to understand. 12
2Mc 9:25 I understand how the princes . . keep watching 20

understand *See also* hard, want.

understand fully 1. ἐπιγινώσκω

1Co 13:12 Now I know in part; then I shall understand fully 1
12 even as I have been fully understood. 1

make understand 1. בין

Job 6:24 make me understand how I have erred. 1
32: 8 the Almighty, that makes him understand. 1
Ps 119:27 Make me understand the way of thy precepts 1
Dan 8:16 Gabriel, make this man understand the vision. 1
10:14 came to make you understand what is to befall 1
11:33 people who are wise shall make many understand 1

understanding 1. בין 2. חֵקֶר 3. ידע 4. לֵב 5. לֵבָב 6. עֵצָה 7. שכל 8. שֵׂכֶל 9. תְּבוּנָה 10. תּוּשִׁיָּה 11. שָׂכְלְתָנוּ (A) 12. βουλή 13. διανόημα 14. διάνοια 15. ἐπιστήμων 16. καρδία 17. νοέω 18. νοῦς 19. οἶδα 20. σύνεσις 21. συνετός 22. συνίημι 23. φρόνησις 24. cor 25. intellectus 26. sapio 27. sensus

Deu 32:28 there is no understanding in them. 9
1Kg 4:29 gave Solomon wisdom and understanding beyond 9
7:14 he was full of wisdom, understanding, and skill 9
Neh 10:28 all who have knowledge and understanding 1
Job 8:10 and utter words out of their understanding? 4
9:10 who does great things beyond understanding 2
11: 6 For he is manifold in understanding. 10
12: 3 I have understanding as well as you; 5
12 and understanding in length of days. 9
13 he has counsel and understanding. 9
24 He takes away understanding from the chiefs 4
34:10 Therefore, hear me, you men of understanding 5
34 Men of understanding will say to me 5
36: 5 he is mighty in strength of understanding. 4
Ps 53: 4 Have those who work evil no understanding 3
82: 5 They have neither knowledge nor understanding 1
111:10 good understanding have all those who practice 8
119:32 when thou enlargest my understanding! 4
99 I have more understanding than all my teachers 7
136: 5 to him who by understanding made the heavens 9
Prv 2: 2 inclining your heart to understanding; 9
3 if you . . raise your voice for understanding 9
6 from his mouth come knowledge and understanding; 9
11 understanding will guard you; 9
3:13 Happy is . . the man who gets understanding 9
19 by understanding he established the heavens; 9
8: 1 does not understanding raise her voice? 9
10:13 lips of him who has understanding wisdom is found 1
23 wise . . is pleasure to a man of understanding. 9
14:29 He who is slow to anger has great understanding 9
15:14 mind . . who has understanding seeks knowledge 1
21 but a man of understanding walks aright. 9
32 he who heeds admonition gains understanding. 4
17:27 who has a cool spirit is a man of understanding. 9
18: 2 A fool takes no pleasure in understanding 9
19: 8 he who keeps understanding will prosper. 9
20: 5 but a man of understanding will draw it out. 9
21:30 No wisdom, no understanding, no counsel, can avail 9
24: 3 house . . by understanding it is established; 9
28:11 man who has understanding will find him out. 1
Isa 10:13 and by my wisdom, for I have understanding; 1
29:16 say of him who formed it, "He has no understanding"? 1
56:11 The shepherds also have no understanding; 1
Jer 3:15 feed you with knowledge and understanding. 7
4:22 stupid children, they have no understanding. 1
Dan 1:17 Daniel had understanding in all visions 1
5:11 light and understanding and wisdom 11
12 excellent spirit, knowledge, and understanding 11
14 light and understanding and excellent wisdom 11
Hos 4:11 Wine and new wine take away the understanding. 4
Obd 1: 7 trap under you–there is no understanding of it. 9
8 out of Edom, and understanding out of Mount Esau? 9
Zec 6:13 peaceful understanding shall be between them 6
Mat 11:25 these things from the wise and understanding 21
Mrk 12:33 with all the understanding 20
Lke 2:47 who heard him were amazed at his understanding 20
10:21 hidden . . from the wise and understanding 21
2Co 10:12 they are without understanding. 22
Eph 4:18 they are darkened in their understanding 14
Php 4: 7 the peace of God, which passes all understanding 18
Col 1: 9 in all spiritual wisdom and understanding 20
2: 2 to have all the riches of assured understanding 20
1Ti 1: 7 without understanding 17
9 understanding this 19
2Ti 2: 7 the Lord will grant you understanding 20
Jas 3:13 Who is wise and understanding among you? 15
1Jn 5:20 the Son of God . . has given us understanding 14
Rev 13:18 let him who has understanding reckon the number 18
1Es 1:33 his splendor, and his understanding of the law 20
2Es 4: 2 Your understanding has utterly failed 24
5:22 my soul recovered the spirit of understanding 25
7:72 because though they had understanding 27
8: 4 Then drink your fill of understanding, O my soul 27
6 and cultivation of our understanding 27
25 as long as I have understanding I will answer. 26
10:30 and I was deprived of my understanding 25
31 your understanding and the thoughts of your mind 25
13:55 and called understanding your mother. 27
14:25 light in your heart the lamp of understanding 25
40 my heart poured forth understanding 25
42 the Most High gave understanding to the five men 25
47 in them is the spring of understanding 25
16:61 and gave him breath and life and understanding 25
Tob 4:19 none of the nations has understanding 12
Jdt 8:29 the people have recognized your understanding 20
Wis 3:15 the root of understanding does not fail. 23
4: 9 understanding is gray hair for men 23
11 lest evil change his understanding 20
6:15 perfect understanding 23
7: 7 understanding was given me 23
16 as are all understanding and skill in crafts. 23
8: 6 if understanding is effective 23
18 in the experience of her company, understanding 23
9: 5 with little understanding of judgment and laws; 20
Sir 0: 1 the readers . . should acquire understanding 15
1: 4 prudent understanding from eternity. 20
3:13 even if he is lacking in understanding 20
23 matters too great for human understanding 20
5:10 Be steadfast in your understanding 20
12 If you have understanding, answer your neighbor; 20
7:25 give her to a man of understanding. 21
8: 9 because from them you will gain understanding 20
10: 3 grow through the understanding of its rulers. 20
25 a man of understanding will not grumble. 15
15: 3 will feed him with the bread of understanding 20
16: 4 through one man of understanding 21
23 This is what one devoid of understanding thinks; 16
17: 7 filled them with knowledge and understanding 20
21:15 When a man of understanding hears a wise saying 15
24:26 It makes them full of understanding 20
25: 5 understanding and counsel in honorable men! 13
33: 3 A man of understanding will trust in the law 21
34: 9 will speak with understanding. 20
37:22 the fruits of his understanding 20
23 the fruits of his understanding 20
39: 6 will be filled with the spirit of understanding; 20
9 Many will praise his understanding 20
44: 3 giving counsel by their understanding 20
4 in understanding of learning for the people 20
47:14 You overflowed like a river with understanding. 20
23 ample in folly and lacking in understanding 20
50:27 Instruction in understanding and knowledge 20
51:20 I gained understanding with her from the first 16
Bar 3:14 Learn . . where there is understanding 20
23 sons . . who seek for understanding on the earth 20
23 seekers for understanding, have not learned 20
32 he found her by his understanding. 20

understanding *See also* get, give, impart, man.

understanding man 1. συνετός

Sir 10: 1 the rule of an understanding man 1

no understanding 1. ἀσύνετος

Sir 34: 1 A man of no understanding has vain and false hopes 1

without understanding 1. ἀσύνετος

Mat 15:16 Are you also still without understanding? 1
Mrk 7:18 Then are you also without understanding? 1

undertake 1. חלל 2. יאל 3. מִשְׁלַח יָד 4. קבל 5. ἀναδέχομαι 6. ἐν ταῖς χερσίν 7. ἐπιδέχομαι 8. ἐπιτηδεύω 9. ἐπιχειρέω 10. πειράω 11. ποιέω 12. incipio

Deu 1: 5 Moses undertook to explain this law, saying 2

12: 7 rejoice . . in all that you undertake 3
18 rejoice . . in all that you undertake. 3
15:10 LORD . . bless you . . in all that you undertake. 3
23:20 LORD . . may bless you in all that you undertake 3
28: 8 blessing . . in all that you undertake; 3
20 in all that you undertake to do 3
2Ch 31:21 every work that he undertook in the service 1
Est 9:23 the Jews undertook to do as they had begun 4
Lke 1: 1 many have undertaken to compile a narrative 9
Act 19:13 undertook to pronounce the name of the Lord 9
1Es 9:14 undertook the matter on these terms 7
2Es 4:18 which would you undertake to justify 12
AEs 16: 3 they even undertake to scheme 9
12 he undertook to deprive us of our kingdom 8
1Mc 4:51 they finished all the work they had undertaken. 11
12:10 undertaken to send to renew our brotherhood 10
2Mc 2:26 who have undertaken the toil of abbreviating 7
29 one who undertakes its painting and decoration 9
7:26 she undertook to persuade her son. 7
8:36 had undertaken to secure tribute for the Romans 5
10:23 success at arms in everything he undertook 6
3Mc 2:14 undertakes to violate the holy place 8

undertaking 1. דֶּרֶךְ 2. ἐπιτήδευμα 3. ἔργον 4. πρᾶξις
1Sm 18:14 And David had success in all his undertakings; 1
Act 5:38 if this plan or this undertaking is of men 3
Jdt 13: 5 to carry out my undertaking 2
Sir 37:16 counsel precedes every undertaking. 4

undetected 1. סתר
Num 5:13 is undetected though she has defiled herself 1

undisciplined 1. ἀπαίδευτος
Sir 10: 3 An undisciplined king will ruin his people 1
22: 3 the father of an undisciplined son 1

undisturbed 1. ἀτάραχος
2Mc 11:23 be undisturbed in caring for their own affairs. 1

undivided *See* devotion.

undo 1. אבד 2. מַשְׁחִית 3. נתר 4. שׁבר 5. λύω 6. παραλύω
Num17:12 Behold, we perish, we are undone, we are all undone. 1
12 Behold, we perish, we are undone, we are all undone. 1
21:29 O Moab! You are undone, O people of Chemosh! 1
2Ch 22: 4 they were his counselors, to his undoing. 2
Isa 58: 6 to undo the thongs of the yoke 3
Jer 48:46 Woe to you, O Moab! The people of Chemosh is undone 1
Dan 11:26 who eat his rich food shall be his undoing; 4
Jdt 16: 7 Judith the daughter of Merari undid him 6
4Mc 3:11 undid and consumed him. 5

undone 1. דמה
Isa 15: 1 Because Ar is laid waste in a night Moab is undone; 1
1 Kir is laid waste in a night Moab is undone. 1

undone *See also* leave.

undressed *See* vine.

undying 1. ἀφθαρσία
Eph 6:24 love our Lord Jesus Christ with love undying. 1

uneducated 1. ἀγράμματος
Act 4:13 perceived that they were uneducated, common men 1

unerring 1. ἀψευδής
Wis 7:17 he who gave me unerring knowledge of what exists 1

uneven *See* ground.

unexamined 1. ἀδιεξέταστος
Sir 21:18 knowledge of the ignorant is unexamined talk. 1

unexpected 1. ἀδόκητος 2. ἀπροσδόκητος 3. οὐ δοκέω 4. παραδοκέω 5. παράδοξος
Lke 12:40 the Son of man is coming at an unexpected hour. 3
Wis 5: 2 will be amazed at his unexpected salvation. 5
17:15 sudden and unexpected fear overwhelmed them. 2
18:17 unexpected fears assailed them; 1
2Mc 9:24 if anything unexpected happened 4
3Mc 3: 8 when they saw an unexpected tumult 2
4: 2 groaned because of the unexpected destruction 2
5:33 suffered an unexpected and dangerous threat 2

unexpectedly 1. ἀνελπίστως
Wis 11: 7 thou gavest them abundant water unexpectedly 1

unfading 1. ἀμαράντινος 2. ἀμάραντος
1Pe 1: 4 an inheritance which is . . unfading 2
5: 4 you will obtain the unfading crown of glory. 1
Wis 6:12 Wisdom is radiant and unfading 2

unfailing 1. ἀνεκλιπής 2. ἐκτενής 3. πᾶς 4. indeficiens
2Ti 4: 2 be unfailing in patience and in teaching. 3
1Pe 4: 8 hold unfailing your love for one another 2
2Es 9:19 which is supplied both with an unfailing table 4
Wis 7:14 for it is an unfailing treasure for men 1
8:18 in the labors of her hands, unfailing wealth 1

unfaithful 1. מעל 2. ἀπιστέω 3. ἄπιστος 4. παραβαίνω 5. fidem non habeo
1Ch 10:13 Saul . . was unfaithful to the LORD 1
2Ch 12: 2 because they had been unfaithful to the LORD 1
29: 6 For our fathers have been unfaithful 1
36:14 likewise were exceedingly unfaithful 1
Neh 1: 8 'If you are unfaithful, I will scatter you among 1
Lke 12:46 will punish him, and put him with the unfaithful. 3
Rom 3: 3 What if some were unfaithful? 2
2Es 7:24 they have been unfaithful to his statutes 5
Sir 42:10 having a husband, lest she prove unfaithful 4

unfaithful *See also* creature.

unfaithfully 1. מַעַל
Num 5:12 If any man's wife . . acts unfaithfully against 1
27 if she has . . acted unfaithfully 1

unfaithfully *See also* deal.

act unfaithfully 1. מעל
Num 5:27 if she has . . acted unfaithfully 1

unfaithfulness 1. מַעַל
1Ch 9: 1 exile . . because of their unfaithfulness. 1
10:13 Saul died for his unfaithfulness; 1

unfaithfulness *See also* lead.

unfasten 1. ἀνίημι
Act 16:26 every one's fetters were unfastened. 1

unfit 1. ἀδόκιμος 2. οὐχ ἱκανός
1Co 15: 9 unfit to be called an apostle 2
Tit 1:16 detestable, disobedient, unfit for any good deed. 1

unfit thing 1. μὴ καθήκω
2Mc 6: 4 things for sacrifice that were unfit. 1

unfold 1. פֶּתַח
Ps 119:130 The unfolding of thy words gives light; 1

unforgotten 1. לֹא שׁכח
Deu 31:21 (for it will live unforgotten in the mouths 1

unformed *See* substance.

unfortunate man 1. ταλαίπωρος
2Mc 4:47 while he sentenced to death those unfortunate men 1

unfruitful 1. שׁכל 2. ἄκαρπος 3. infructuosus
2Kg 2:19 but the water is bad, and the land is unfruitful. 1
Mat 13:22 and it proves unfruitful. 2
Mrk 4:19 it proves unfruitful. 2
1Co 14:14 my spirit prays but my mind is unfruitful. 2
Eph 5:11 Take no part in the unfruitful works of darkness 2
Tit 3:14 not to be unfruitful. 2
2Pe 1: 8 keep you from being ineffective or unfruitful 2
2Es 9:29 the untrodden and unfruitful wilderness; 3

ungird 1. פתח
Gen 24:32 Laban ungirded the camels, and gave him straw 1
Isa 45: 1 ungird the loins of kings, to open doors 1

ungodliness 1. חָנֵף 2. חֲנֻפָּה 3. ἀσέβεια 4. impietas
Isa 32: 6 to practice ungodliness, to utter error 1
Jer 23:15 ungodliness has gone forth into all the land. 2
Rom 1:18 against all ungodliness and wickedness of men 3
11:26 he will banish ungodliness from Jacob"; 3
2Ti 2:16 it will lead people into more and more ungodliness 3
Jde 1:15 to convict . . of all their deeds of ungodliness 3
2Es 4:12 to come here and live in ungodliness 4
30 how much ungodliness it has produced until now 4
31 how much fruit of ungodliness 4
38 all of us also are full of ungodliness. 4
12:32 he will denounce them for their ungodliness 4
13:37 he . . will reprove . . for their ungodliness 4
Wis 14: 9 the ungodly man and his ungodliness 3

ungodly 1. חָנֵף 2. לֹא חָסִיד 3. עֲוִיל 4. עַוָּל 5. ἀσέβεια 6. ἀσεβέω 7. ἀσεβής 8. δυσσέβημα 9. δυσσεβής 10. impietas 11. impius
Job 16:11 God gives me up to the ungodly 3
18:21 Surely such are the dwellings of the ungodly 4
Ps 43: 1 defend my cause against an ungodly people; 2
53: 5 For God will scatter the bones of the ungodly; •
Jer 23:11 Both prophet and priest are ungodly; 1
Rom 4: 5 but trusts him who justifies the ungodly 7
5: 6 at the right time Christ died for the ungodly. 7
1Ti 1: 9 for the ungodly and sinners 7
2Pe 2: 5 he brought a flood upon the world of the ungodly; 7
6 an example to those who were to be ungodly; 7
3: 7 judgment and destruction of ungodly men. 7
Jde 1: 4 ungodly persons who pervert the grace of our God 7
15 to convict all the ungodly of all their deeds 7
15 harsh things which ungodly sinners have spoken 7
18 scoffers, following their own ungodly passions 5
1Es 1:52 his anger . . because of their ungodly acts 8
2Es 3:12 to be more ungodly than were their ancestors. 10
7:17 but that the ungodly shall perish. 11
51 while the ungodly abound 11
93 in which the souls of the ungodly wander 11
102 will be able to intercede for the ungodly 11
111 the righteous have prayed for the ungodly now 11
9:13 be curious as to how the ungodly will be punished; 11
14:35 the deeds of the ungodly will be disclosed. 11
Wis 3:10 the ungodly will be punished 7
4: 3 the prolific brood of the ungodly 7
16 will condemn the ungodly who are living 7
10: 6 when the ungodly were perishing 7
20 Therefore the righteous plundered the ungodly; 7
11: 9 they learned how the ungodly were tormented 7
10 thou didst examine the ungodly •
12: 9 give the ungodly into the hands of the righteous 7
14:16 the ungodly custom, grown strong with time 7
16:16 the ungodly, refusing to know thee 7
18 consume the creatures sent against the ungodly 7
19: 1 the ungodly were assailed to the end 7
Sir 7:17 the punishment of the ungodly is fire and worms. 7
9:12 Do not delight in what pleases the ungodly; 7
12: 5 do not give to the ungodly 7
6 will inflict punishment on the ungodly. 7
13:24 poverty is evil in the opinion of the ungodly. 7
15:20 He has not commanded any one to be ungodly 6
16: 1 nor rejoice in ungodly sons. 7
3 better than to have ungodly children. 7
34:19 not pleased with the offerings of the ungodly; 7
39:30 the sword that punishes the ungodly 7
40:15 The children of the ungodly 7
41: 5 they frequent the haunts of the ungodly. 7
7 Children will blame an ungodly father 7
8 Woe to you, ungodly men, who have forsaken the law 7
10 so the ungodly go from curse to destruction. 7
42: 2 of rendering judgment to acquit the ungodly; 7
Bar 2:12 sinned, we have been ungodly, we have done wrong 6
1Mc 3: 8 he destroyed the ungodly out of the land; 7
6:21 some of the ungodly Israelites joined them. 7
7: 5 the lawless and ungodly men of Israel 7
9 he sent him, and with him the ungodly Alcimus 7
9:25 Bacchides chose the ungodly 7
73 he destroyed the ungodly out of Israel. 7
2Mc 4:13 who was ungodly and no high priest 7
8: 2 which had been profaned by ungodly men 7
14 who had been sold by the ungodly Nicanor 9
15:33 he cut out the tongue of the ungodly Nicanor 9
4Mc 5:38 You may tyrannize the ungodly 7

ungodly deed 1. δυσσέβημα 2. impietas
2Es 3:29 I saw ungodly deeds without number 2
15: 8 be silent . . concerning their ungodly deeds 2
2Mc 12: 3 some men of Joppa did so ungodly a deed as this 1

ungodly man 1. ἀσεβέω 2. ἀσεβής 3. δυσσεβής
Wis 1: 9 the counsels of an ungodly man 2
16 But ungodly men . . summoned death 2
5:14 Because the hope of the ungodly man is like chaff 2
14: 9 the ungodly man and his ungodliness 1
Sir 21:27 When an ungodly man curses his adversary 2
22:12 for a fool or an ungodly man it lasts all his life. 2
1Mc 3:15 again a strong army of ungodly men went up 2
2Mc 9: 9 so the ungodly man's body swarmed with worms 3
10:10 who was the son of that ungodly man 2

ungodly thing 1. impius
2Es 3: 8 and did ungodly things before thee 1

ungracious 1. ἄχαρις 2. ἀχάριστος
Sir 18:18 A fool is ungracious and abusive 2
20:19 An ungracious man is like a story 1

ungrateful 1. ἀχάριστος 2. ingratus
Lke 6:35 he is kind to the ungrateful and the selfish. 1
2Ti 3: 2 disobedient to their parents, ungrateful, unholy 1
2Es 8:60 and have been ungrateful to him 2
4Mc 9:10 also was enraged, as at those who are ungrateful. 1

ungrateful man 1. ἀχάριστος
Wis 16:29 the hope of an ungrateful man 1

ungrudgingly 1. ἄνευ γογγυσμοῦ
1Pe 4: 9 Practice hospitality ungrudgingly 1

unhallowed 1. חָלָל
Ezk 21:25 you, O unhallowed wicked one, prince of Israel 1
29 to be laid on the necks of the unhallowed wicked 1

unhappy 1. רַע 2. τρισάθλιος 3. miser
Ecc 1:13 it is an unhappy business that God has given 1
4: 8 This also is vanity and an unhappy business. 1
2Es 15:59 Unhappy above all others 3
4Mc 16: 6 O how wretched am I and many times unhappy! 2

unharmed 1. ἀβλαβής 2. ἀπήμαντος 3. ἄπταιστος 4. ἀσινής
Wis 19: 6 thy children might be kept unharmed. 1
2Mc 12:25 his solemn promise to restore them unharmed 2

3Mc 6: 6 you rescued unharmed, even to a hair 2
7 Daniel . . you brought up to the light unharmed. 4
8 restored unharmed to all his family. 2
39 and rescued them all together and unharmed. 3
7:20 they departed unharmed, free, and overjoyed 4

unhealthy 1. ἀκάθαρτος
Sir 40:15 they are unhealthy roots upon sheer rock. 1

unheard *See* go.

unhewn 1. שָׁלֵם 2. ὁλόκληρος
Deu 27: 6 altar to the LORD your God of unhewn stones; 1
Jos 8:31 as it is written . . an altar of unhewn stones 1
1Mc 4:47 Then they took unhewn stones, as the law directs 2

unhindered 1. ἀκωλύτως 2. ἀνεμπόδιστος
Act 28:31 teaching . . quite openly and unhindered. 1
Wis 17:20 was engaged in unhindered work 2
19: 7 an unhindered way out of the Red Sea 2

unholy 1. זוּר 2. ἀνόσιος 3. μὴ θέμις
Exd 30: 9 You shall offer no unholy incense thereon 1
Lev 10: 1 and offered unholy fire before the LORD 1
Num 3: 4 they offered unholy fire before the LORD 1
26:61 when they offered unholy fire before the LORD. 1
1Ti 1: 9 for the unholy and profane 2
2Ti 3: 2 disobedient to their parents, ungrateful, unholy 2
Wis 12: 4 their works of sorcery and unholy rites 2
2Mc 7:34 you, unholy wretch, you most defiled of all men 2
12:14 even blaspheming and saying unholy things. 3

most unholy 1. ἀνόσιος
2Mc 8:32 a most unholy man 1

uniform 1. ἐσθής
2Mc 8:35 took off his splendid uniform 1

unifying of the kingdom 1. συναρχία
AEs 13: 4 the unifying of the kingdom which we . . intend 1

unimpeded 1. ἀπαραπόδιστος
3Mc 6:28 has granted an unimpeded and notable stability 1

uninformed 1. ἀγνοέω
1Co 12: 1 I do not want you to be uninformed. 1

uninhabited 1. לֹא יָשַׁב 2. ἀοίκητος 3. ἔρημος
Jer 6: 8 lest I make you a desolation, an uninhabited land. 1
17: 6 of the wilderness, in an uninhabited salt land. 1
22: 6 make you a desert, an uninhabited city. 1
Ezk 29:11 it shall be uninhabited 40 years. 1
Zec 9: 5 perish from Gaza; Ash'kelon shall be uninhabited; 1
Jdt 5:19 because it was uninhabited. 3
Wis 11: 2 They journeyed through an uninhabited wilderness 2
1Mc 3:45 Jerusalem was uninhabited like a wilderness; 2

uninstructed 1. ἀπαίδευτος
Wis 17: 1 therefore uninstructed souls have gone astray. 1
Sir 6:20 She seems very harsh to the uninstructed 1

unintelligent man 1. ἀσύνετος
Sir 22:13 do not visit an unintelligent man 1

unintentionally 1. בִּבְלִי דַעַת
Deu 4:42 who kills his neighbor unintentionally 1
19: 4 If any one kills his neighbor unintentionally 1

union 1. חֶבֶל 2. κοίτη 3. ὕπνος
Zec 11: 7 staffs; one I named Grace, the other I named Union. 1
14 Then I broke my second staff Union 1
Wis 3:13 who has not entered into a sinful union 2
16 the offspring of an unlawful union will perish. 2
4: 6 children born of unlawful unions 3

wedded union 1. ἀπάντησις
3Mc 1:19 bridal chambers prepared for wedded union 1

unique 1. μονογενής
Wis 7:22 a spirit that is intelligent, holy, unique 1

unison 1. קוֹל אֶחָד 2. ὁμοθυμαδόν
2Ch 5:13 to make themselves heard in unison in praise 1
Jdt 4:12 and cried out in unison 2

unit 1. גְּדוּד
1Ch 7: 4 were units of the army for war, 36,000 1

unite 1. חָבַר 2. יחד 3. ἀνακεφαλαιόω 4. καταρτίζω 5. κολλάω 6. ὁμοθυμαδόν 7. σύμφυτος 8. συνάγω
Jdg 20:11 gathered against the city, united as one man. 1
Ps 86:11 unite my heart to fear thy name. 2
Act 18:12 the Jews made a united attack upon Paul 6
Rom 6: 5 if we have been united with him in a death 7
5 be united with him in a resurrection like his. •
1Co 1:10 that you be united in the same mind 4
6:17 he who is united to the Lord becomes one spirit 5
Eph 1:10 to unite all things in him 3
1Mc 2:42 there united with them a company of Hasideans 8

unity 1. יַחַד 2. ἑνότης
Ps 133: 1 how good . . it is when brothers dwell in unity! 1
Eph 4: 3 eager to maintain the unity of the Spirit 2
13 until we all attain to the unity of the faith 2

unity of spirit 1. ὁμόφρων
1Pe 3: 8 Finally, all of you, have unity of spirit, sympathy 1

universal 1. κοσμοπληθής
4Mc 15:31 carrying the world in the universal flood 1

universe 1. κόσμος 2. ὁ πᾶς
Gal 4: 3 slaves to the elemental spirits of the universe. 1
Col 2: 8 the elemental spirits of the universe 1
20 died to the elemental spirits of the universe 1
Heb 1: 3 upholding the universe by his word of power 2
AEs 13: 9 the universe is in thy power 2
Wis 16:17 the universe defends the righteous. 1
Sir 18: 1 who lives for ever created the whole universe; 2
23:20 Before the universe was created 2
42:17 the universe may stand firm in his glory. 2
2Mc 7: 9 the King of the universe will raise us up 1

unjust 1. עוֹל 2. עַוָּל 3. עָוֶל 4. עַוְלָה 5. ἄδικος
Ps 43: 1 from deceitful and unjust men deliver me! 4
71: 4 from the grasp of the unjust and cruel man. 1
Prv 29:27 An unjust man is an abomination to the righteous 3
Zep 3: 5 but the unjust knows no shame. 2
Mat 5:45 and sends rain on the just and on the unjust. 5
Lke 18:11 extortioners, unjust, adulterers 5
Act 24:15 a resurrection of both the just and the unjust. 5
Rom 3: 5 That God is unjust to inflict wrath on us? 5
Heb 6:10 For God is not so unjust as to overlook your work 5
Sir 19:25 is a cleverness which is scrupulous but unjust 5
40:13 wealth of the unjust will dry up like a torrent 5
Aza 1: 9 an unjust king, the most wicked in all the world. 5
Sus 1:53 pronouncing unjust judgments 5
2Mc 4:35 displeased at the unjust murder of the man. 5
40 launched an unjust attack 5
48 quickly suffered the unjust penalty. 5
3Mc 6:27 Loose and untie their unjust bonds! 5

unjust *See also* dealing, gain.

unjustly 1. עָוֶל 2. ἀδίκως 3. ἀκρίτως
Ps 82: 2 How long will you judge unjustly 1
1Pe 2:19 he endures pain while suffering unjustly. 2
Wis 12:13 prove that thou hast not judged unjustly; 2
1Mc 2:37 you are killing us unjustly. 3
15:33 unjustly taken by our enemies. 3

unkindly 1. φαῦλος
Sir 20:16 those who eat my bread speak unkindly. 1

unknown 1. לֹא יָדַע 2. ἀγνοέω 3. ἄγνωστος
Gen 41:31 the plenty will be unknown in the land by reason 1
Act 17:23 'To an unknown god.' 3
23 What therefore you worship as unknown 2
2Co 6: 9 as unknown, and yet well known 2
Wis 11:18 or newly created unknown beasts full of rage 3
18: 3 a guide for thy people's unknown journey 3
2Mc 1:19 the place was unknown to any one. 3
2: 7 The place shall be unknown 3

unlawful 1. ἀθέμιτος 2. ἄνομος 3. παράνομος
Act 10:28 You yourselves know how unlawful it is for a Jew 1
Wis 3:16 the offspring of an unlawful union will perish. 3
4: 6 children born of unlawful unions 2
2Mc 4:14 to take part in the unlawful proceedings 3
6:21 who were in charge of that unlawful sacrifice 3
7: 1 to partake of unlawful swine's flesh. 1
3Mc 1:27 not to overlook this unlawful and haughty deed. 2

unlawfully 1. ἔκθεσμος
4Mc 5:14 urged him . . to eat meat unlawfully 1

unleavened 1. מַצָּה 2. ἄζυμος
Exd 12:39 they baked unleavened cakes of the dough 1
29: 2 unleavened bread, unleavened cakes mixed 1
2 unleavened cakes mixed with oil, and unleavened 1
2 and unleavened wafers spread with oil. 1
Lev 2: 4 it shall be unleavened cakes of fine flour 1
4 unleavened wafers spread with oil 1
5 shall be of fine flour unleavened, mixed with oil 1
6:16 it shall be eaten unleavened in a holy place 1
7:12 offer with the thank offering unleavened cakes 1
12 unleavened wafers spread with oil, and cakes 1
8:26 he took one unleavened cake, and one cake of bread 1
10:12 eat it unleavened beside the altar 1
Num 6:15 unleavened wafers spread with oil 1
19 take . . one unleavened cake out of the basket 1
19 priest shall take . . one unleavened wafer 1
1Co 5: 7 as you really are unleavened 2

unleavened *See also* bread, cake.

unless 1. אִם לֹא 2. בִּלְתִּי 3. בִּלְתִּי אִם 4. וְאֵין 5. כִּי אִם 6. כִּי לוּלֵי 7. לֹא 8. לָהֵן (A) 9. ἐὰν μή 10. εἰ μή 11. εἰ μήτι 12. ἐκτός εἰ μή 13. si non
Gen 32:26 I will not let you go, unless you bless me. 5
42:15 go from this place unless your youngest brother 5
43: 3 You shall not see my face, unless your brother is 2
5 You shall not see my face, unless your brother is 2
44:23 Unless your youngest brother comes down 1
26 cannot see . . unless our youngest brother is 4
Exd 3:19 not let you go unless compelled by a mighty hand. 9
Lev 22: 6 shall not eat . . unless he has bathed his body 5
Deu 32:30 unless their Rock had sold them 1
Jos 7:12 I will be with you no more, unless you destroy 1
1Sm 25:34 unless you had made haste . . truly by morning 6
2Sm 3:13 you shall not see my face, unless you first bring 5
2Kg 4:24 do not slacken the pace for me unless I tell you. 5
Est 2:14 she did not go . . again, unless the king delighted 5
Ps 127: 1 Unless the LORD builds the house, those who build 1
1 Unless the LORD watches over the city 1
Prv 4:16 cannot sleep unless they have done wrong; 1
16 unless they have made some one stumble. 1
Lam 3:37 it came to pass, unless the Lord has ordained it? 7
Dan 6: 5 unless we find it in connection with the law 8
Ams 3: 3 together, unless they have made an appointment? 3
6 Does evil befall a city, unless the LORD has done it? 1
Mat 5:20 For I tell you, unless your righteousness 9
12:29 unless he first binds the strong man 9
18: 3 unless you turn and become like children 9
26:42 My Father, if this cannot pass unless I drink it 9
Mrk 3:27 unless he first binds the strong man 9
7: 3 do not eat unless they wash their hands 9
4 they do not eat unless they purify themselves 9
Lke 9:13 unless we are to go and buy food 11
13: 3 unless you repent you will all likewise perish. 9
5 unless you repent you will all likewise perish. 9
Joh 3: 2 no one can do these signs . . unless God is with him. 9
3 unless one is born anew, he cannot see the kingdom 9
5 unless one is born of water and the Spirit 9
4:48 Unless you see signs and wonders 9
6:44 unless the Father who sent me draws him 9
53 unless you eat the flesh of the Son of man 9
65 unless it is granted him by the Father. 9
8:24 unless you believe that I am he. 9
12:24 unless a grain of wheat falls into the earth 9
15: 4 unless it abides in the vine 9
4 neither can you, unless you abide in me. 9
19:11 unless it had been given you from above 10
20:25 Unless I see in his hands the print of the nails 9
Act 8:31 he said, "How can I, unless some one guides me? 9
15: 1 Unless you are circumcised 9
27:31 Unless these men stay in the ship 9
Rom 10:15 And how can men preach unless they are sent? 9
1Co 14: 5 unless some one interprets 12
6 unless I bring you some revelation or knowledge 9
15: 2 unless you believed in vain. 12
36 What you sow does not come to life unless it dies. 9
2Th 2: 3 unless the rebellion comes first 9
2Ti 2: 5 unless he competes according to the rules. 9
Rev 2: 5 and remove your lampstand . . unless you repent 9
22 unless they repent of her doings; 9
13:17 that no one can buy or sell unless he has the mark 10
2Es 7: 5 unless he passes through the narrow part? 13
9 unless he passes through the danger 13
14 Therefore unless the living pass through 13
Jdt 8:11 unless the Lord turns and helps us 9
11:10 unless they sin against their God. 9
Wis 8:21 would not possess wisdom unless God gave her 9
9:17 unless thou hast given wisdom 10
Sir 16: 2 unless the fear of the Lord is in them. 10
19: 8 unless it would be a sin for you, do not disclose it; 10
34: 6 Unless they are sent from the Most High 9
LJr 1:24 will not shine unless some one wipes off the rust; 9
1Mc 6:27 unless you quickly prevent them 9
7:35 Unless Judas and his army are delivered 9
4Mc 2: 7 unless reason is clearly lord of the emotions? 10
9: 2 unless we should practice ready obedience 10

unless indeed 1. εἰ μήτι
2Co 13: 5 unless indeed you fail to meet the test! 1

unlifted 1. ἀνακαλύπτω
2Co 3:14 that same veil remains unlifted 1

unlike 1. ἀνόμοιος
Wis 2:15 his manner of life is unlike that of others 1

unload 1. ἀποφορτίζομαι
Act 21: 3 there the ship was to unload its cargo. 1

unloved woman 1. שׂנא
Prv 30:23 an unloved woman when she gets a husband 1

unmanly 1. ἄνανδρος
4Mc 6:21 if we should be despised by the tyrant as unmanly 1
8:16 if some of them had been cowardly and unmanly 1

unmarried 1. לֹא הָיָה לְאִישׁ 2. ἄγαμος 3. παρθένος
Ezk 44:25 for brother or unmarried sister they may defile 1

Act 21: 9 four unmarried daughters, who prophesied. 3
1Co 7: 8 To the unmarried and the widows I say 2
25 Now concerning the unmarried, I have no command 3
34 the unmarried woman or girl is anxious 2
4Mc 16: 9 some unmarried, others married 2

unmarried man 1. ἄγαμος
1Co 7:32 The unmarried man is anxious about the affairs 1

unmerciful 1. ἀνελεήμων
Sir 35:18 till he crushes the loins of the unmerciful 1

unmindful 1. נשה 2. ἀμνημονέω 3. non memoro
Deu 32:18 You were unmindful of the Rock that begot you 1
2Es 3:33 though they are unmindful of thy commandments. 3
Sir 37: 6 be not unmindful of him in your wealth. 2

unmixed 1. ἄκρατος
Rev 14:10 poured unmixed into the cup of his anger 1

unmoved 1. אֵיתָן 2. οὐδὲν μετατρέπω 3. οὐ μετατρέπω
Gen 49:24 yet his bow remained unmoved 1
4Mc 6: 5 as a true Eleazar, was unmoved 2
7:12 Eleazar . . remained unmoved in his reason. 3

unnatural 1. ἕτερος 2. παρὰ φύσιν
Rom 1:26 exchanged natural relations for unnatural 2
Jde 1: 7 acted immorally and indulged in unnatural lust 1
unnoticed *See* go.

unobserved 1. ἀπαρασήμαντος 2. λανθάνω
Wis 17: 3 in their secret sins they were unobserved 2
2Mc 15:36 never to let this day go unobserved 1

unpleasant 1. רַע
Ecc 8: 3 go . . do not delay when the matter is unpleasant 1

unpolluted 1. ἀμόλυντος
Wis 7:22 manifold, subtle, mobile, clear, unpolluted 1

unpresentable part 1. ἀσχήμων
1Co 12:23 unpresentable parts are treated with . . modesty 1

unprofitable 1. לֹא סכן 2. ἀνόνητος 3. ἀνωφελής 4. ἄχρηστος
Job 15: 3 Should he argue in unprofitable talk 1
Tit 3: 9 they are unprofitable and futile. 3
Wis 3:11 their labors are unprofitable 2
Sir 37:19 yet be unprofitable to himself. 4

unpunished 1. ἄδεια
Wis 12:11 didst leave them unpunished for their sins. 1
unpunished *See also* go, leave.

unquenchable 1. ἄσβεστος
Mat 3:12 the chaff he will burn with unquenchable fire. 1
Mrk 9:43 to go to hell, to the unquenchable fire. 1
Lke 3:17 the chaff he will burn with unquenchable fire. 1

unreasonable 1. ἀλόγιστος 2. ἄλογος 3. παρὰ λόγον
Act 25:27 it seems to me unreasonable 2
2Mc 4:36 with regard to the unreasonable murder of Onias 3
4Mc 16:23 It is unreasonable . . not to withstand pain. 1

unreasoning 1. ἄλογος
4Mc 14:14 Even unreasoning animals, like mankind 1
18 by the example of unreasoning animals 1

unrelenting 1. בְּלִי חשׂך
Isa 14: 6 in anger with unrelenting persecution. 1

unresponsive 1. ἀπερίσπαστος
Wis 16:11 become unresponsive to thy kindness. 1

unrest 1. רגז 2. σάλος 3. constabilitio
Jer 50:34 but unrest to the inhabitants of Babylon. 1
2Es 15:16 For there shall be unrest among men 3
Sir 40: 5 there is anger and envy and trouble and unrest 2

unrestrained 1. ἀνίημι
Sir 30: 8 a son unrestrained turns out to be wilful. 1

unrestraint 1. incontinentia
2Es 5:10 and unrestraint shall increase on earth. 1

unrighteous 1. אָוֶן 2. עַוָּל 3. ἀδικία 4. ἄδικος 5. iniquus 6. iniustus
Job 27: 7 that rises up against me be as the unrighteous. 2
29:17 I broke the fangs of the unrighteous 2
31: 3 Does not calamity befall the unrighteous 2
Isa 55: 7 his way, and the unrighteous man his thoughts; 1
Lke 16: 9 make friends . . by means of unrighteous mammon 3
11 not been faithful in the unrighteous mammon 4
18: 6 Hear what the unrighteous judge says. 3
1Co 6: 1 does he dare go to law before the unrighteous 4
9 unrighteous will not inherit the kingdom of God? 4
Jas 3: 6 The tongue is an unrighteous world 3
1Pe 3:18 the righteous for the unrighteous 4
2Pe 2: 9 and to keep the unrighteous under punishment 4
1Es 4:36 with him there is nothing unrighteous. 4
37 Wine is unrighteous, the king is unrighteous 4
37 Wine is unrighteous, the king is unrighteous 4
37 the king is unrighteous, women are unrighteous 4
37 all the sons of men are unrighteous 4
37 all their works are unrighteous 4
39 instead of anything that is unrighteous 4
40 there is nothing unrighteous in her judgment. 4
2Es 2: 8 who conceal the unrighteous in your midst 5
8:47 often compared yourself to the unrighteous 6
Wis 3:19 the end of an unrighteous generation 4
12:12 to plead as an advocate for unrighteous men? 4
14:31 pursues the transgression of the unrighteous. 4
16:19 to destroy the crops of the unrighteous land. 4
24 exerts itself to punish the unrighteous 4
Sir 1:22 Unrighteous anger cannot be justified 4
35:12 do not trust to an unrighteous sacrifice; 4
18 breaks the scepters of the unrighteous; 4
51: 6 slander of an unrighteous tongue to the king 4

unrighteous deed 1. iniustitia
2Es 7:35 and unrighteous deeds shall not sleep. 1

unrighteous man 1. ἄδικος
Wis 4:16 the prolonged old age of the unrighteous man. 1
10: 3 when an unrighteous man departed from her 1

unrighteous thing 1. ἄδικος
Wis 1: 8 therefore no one who utters unrighteous things 1

unrighteously 1. ἀδίκως
Wis 12:23 those who in folly of life lived unrighteously 1
14:28 prophesy lies, or live unrighteously 1

unrighteousness 1. לֹא צֶדֶק 2. עָוֶל 3. עַוְלָה 4. ἀδικία 5. ἄδικος 6. iniustitia
Job 22:23 you remove unrighteousness far from your tents 3
Ps 92:15 my rock, and there is no unrighteousness in him. 3
Jer 22:13 to him who builds his house by unrighteousness 1
Ezk 28:18 in the unrighteousness of your trade 2
2Th 2:12 had pleasure in unrighteousness. 4
1Jn 1: 9 and cleanse us from all unrighteousness. 4
1Es 4:37 in their unrighteousness they will perish. 4
2Es 5: 2 unrighteousness shall be increased 6
10 unrighteousness and unrestraint 6
7:105 his own righteousness and unrighteousness. 6
111 and unrighteousness has multiplied 6
12:31 and reproving him for his unrighteousness 6
Wis 1: 5 ashamed at the approach of unrighteousness. 4
Sir 17:14 he said to them, "Beware of all unrighteousness. 5
35: 3 to forsake unrighteousness is atonement. 4
unripe *See* grape.

unsafe 1. ἀκαταστατέω
Tob 1:15 under him the highways were unsafe 1
unsatisfied *See* leave.

unsavory thing 1. תִּפְלָה
Jer 23:13 I saw an unsavory thing: they prophesied by Ba'al 1

unsearchable 1. אֵין חֵקֶר 2. לֹא חֵקֶר 3. ἀνεξεραύνητος 4. ἀνεξιχνίαστος
Job 5: 9 who does great things and unsearchable 1
36:26 the number of his years is unsearchable. 2
Ps 145: 3 his greatness is unsearchable. 1
Prv 25: 3 so the mind of kings is unsearchable. 1
Isa 40:28 his understanding is unsearchable. 1
Rom 11:33 How unsearchable are his judgments 3
Eph 3: 8 the unsearchable riches of Christ 4
Man 1: 6 yet . . unsearchable is thy promised mercy 4

unseemly 1. ἀπόρρητος 2. ingratus
2Es 7:124 because we have lived in unseemly places? 2
Sir 13:22 he speaks unseemly words, and they justify him 1

unseen 1. לֹא ידע 2. ἀθεώρητος 3. ἀόρατος 4. ἀφανής 5. μηδέπω βλέπω 6. μὴ θεωρέω
Ps 77:19 yet thy footprints were unseen. 1
Heb 11: 7 being warned by God concerning events as yet unseen 5
Wis 17: 6 worse than that unseen appearance. 6
19 the unseen running of leaping animals 2
Sir 20:30 Hidden wisdom and unseen treasure 4
41:14 hidden wisdom and unseen treasure 4
2Mc 9: 5 struck him an incurable and unseen blow 3

unseen thing 1. μὴ βλέπω
2Co 4:18 but to the things that are unseen 1
18 the things that are unseen are eternal. 1

unsettle 1. ἀνασκευάζω 2. ἀναστατόω
Act 15:24 unsettling your minds 1
Gal 5:12 who unsettle you would mutilate themselves! 2

unshaken 1. βέβαιος
2Co 1: 7 Our hope for you is unshaken 1

unsheathe 1. ריק
Lev 26:33 I will unsheathe the sword after you 1
Ezk 5: 2 and I will unsheathe the sword after them. 1
12 and will unsheathe the sword after them. 1
12:14 I will unsheathe the sword after them. 1

unshod 1. יָחֵף
Jer 2:25 Keep your feet from going unshod 1

unshrunk 1. ἄγναφος
Mat 9:16 no one puts a piece of unshrunk cloth 1
Mrk 2:21 sews a piece of unshrunk cloth on an old garment; 1

unskilled 1. ἄπειρος 2. ἰδιώτης
2Co 11: 6 Even if I am unskilled in speaking 2
Heb 5:13 is unskilled in the word of righteousness 1

unsold
Act 5: 4 While it remained unsold •

unsoundly 1. οὐκ ὀρθῶς
Wis 2: 1 they reasoned unsoundly, saying to themselves 1

unsown 1. לֹא זרע 2. non semino
Deu 29:23 burnt-out waste, unsown, and growing nothing 1
2Es 6:22 Sown places shall suddenly appear unsown 2

unsparing 1. לֹא חמל
Job 6:10 I would even exult in pain unsparing; 1

unspiritual 1. ψυχικός
1Co 2:14 The unspiritual man does not receive the gifts 1
Jas 3:15 wisdom . . is earthly, unspiritual, devilish. 1

unspoiled 1. incorruptus
2Es 7:123 whose fruit remains unspoiled 1

unstable 1. פַּחַז 2. ἀκατάστατος 3. ἀστήρικτος
Gen 49: 4 Unstable as water, you shall not have 1
Jas 1: 7 a double-minded man, unstable in all his ways 2
2Pe 3:16 which the ignorant and unstable twist 3

unstained 1. ἀμίαντος 2. ἄσπιλος
1Ti 6:14 I charge you to keep the commandment unstained 2
Heb 7:26 such a high priest, holy, blameless, unstained 1
Jas 1:27 to keep oneself unstained from the world. 2

unsteady 1. ἀστήρικτος
2Pe 2:14 They entice unsteady souls. 1

unstop 1. פתח
Isa 35: 5 be opened, and the ears of the deaf unstopped; 1

unsuspecting 1. בטח 2. בֶּטַח
Jdg 18: 7 manner of the Sido'nians, quiet and unsuspecting 1
10 you will come to an unsuspecting people. 1
27 came to La'ish, to a people quiet and unsuspecting 1
Ezk 30: 9 from me to terrify the unsuspecting Ethiopians; 2

unswerving 1. ἀδιάστροφος 2. ἀκλινής
3Mc 3: 3 to maintain good will and unswerving loyalty 1
4Mc 6: 7 he kept his reason upright and unswerving. 2
17: 3 you held firm and unswerving 2

untamed 1. ἀδάμαστος
Sir 30: 8 A horse that is untamed turns out to be stubborn 1

untaught 1. ἀπαίδευτος
Sir 51:23 Draw near to me, you who are untaught 1

untie 1. ἐκλύω 2. λύω
Mat 21: 2 untie them and bring them to me. 2
Mrk 1: 7 I am not worthy to stoop down and untie. 2
11: 2 untie it and bring it. 2
4 they untied it. 2
5 What are you doing, untying the colt? 2
Lke 3:16 thong of whose sandals I am not worthy to untie 2
13:15 Does not each of you on the sabbath untie his ox 2
19:30 untie it and bring it here. 2
31 If any one asks you, 'Why are you untying it?' 2
33 as they were untying the colt, its owners said 2
33 Why are you untying the colt? 2
Joh 1:27 the thong of whose sandal I am not worthy to untie. 2
Act 13:25 the sandals of whose feet I am not worthy to untie.' 2
Jdt 6:14 they untied him and brought him into Bethulia 2
3Mc 6:27 Loose and untie their unjust bonds! 1

until 1. בִּלְתִּי 2. וְ 3. לְ 4. עַד 5. עַד אֲשֶׁר 6. עַד שֶׁ 7. עַל 8. עַד (A) 9. ἄχρι 10. ἐὰν μή 11. εἰ μὴ ὅταν 12. εἰς 13. εἰς μέλλω 14. ἕως 15. ἕως ἄν 16. καί 17. μέχρι 18. μέχρι ἄν 19. donec 20. in 21. quoadusque 22. usque 23. usque dum 24. usquequo
Gen 8: 5 to abate until the tenth month; 4
7 it went to and fro until the waters were dried up 4
21:26 tell me, and I have not heard of it until today. 1
24:19 camels also, until they have done drinking. 4
33 but he said, "I will not eat until I have told 4
26:13 more and more until he became very wealthy. 4

27:44 with him . . until your brother's fury turns away 4
45 until your brother's anger turns away 4
28:15 for I will not leave you until I have done that 4
29: 8 they said, "We cannot until all the flocks are 4
32: 4 I have sojourned with Laban, and stayed until now 4
24 wrestled with him until the breaking of the day. 4
33: 3 seven times, until he came near to his brother. 4
14 lead on slowly . . until I come to my lord in Se'ir. 4
34: 5 so Jacob held his peace until they came. 4
39:16 his garment by her until his master came home 4
41:49 stored up grain . . until he ceased to measure it 4
46:34 keepers of cattle from our youth even until now 4
49:10 shall not depart . . until he comes to whom it 4
Exd 9:18 in Egypt from the day it was founded until now. 4
10:26 must serve the LORD until we arrive there. 4
12: 6 you shall keep it until the fourteenth day 4
10 you shall let none of it remain until the morning 4
10 anything that remains until the morning 4
15 from the first day until the seventh day 4
18 so until the twenty-first day of the month 4
22 go out of the door of his house until the morning. 4
17:12 so his hands were steady until the going down 4
23:18 fat of my feast remain until the morning. 4
30 before you, until you are increased and possess 4
24:14 Tarry here for us, until we come to you again; 4
29:34 if any . . of the bread, remain until the morning 4
33: 8 looked after Moses, until he had gone 4
22 I will cover you . . until I have passed by; 4
34:25 of the passover be left until the morning. 3
34 he took the veil off, until he came out; 4
35 until he went in to speak with him. 4
Lev 6: 9 upon the altar all night until the morning 4
7:15 he shall not leave any of it until the morning 4
8:33 for seven days, until the days of your ordination 4
11:24 touches . . shall be unclean until the evening 4
25 shall . . be unclean until the evening 4
27 shall be unclean until the evening 4
28 shall . . be unclean until the evening 4
31 shall be unclean until the evening 4
32 it shall be unclean until the evening 4
39 he . . shall be unclean until the evening 4
40 he . . shall . . be unclean until the evening 4
40 he . . shall . . be unclean until the evening 4
12: 4 until the days of her purifying are completed 4
14:46 he . . shall be unclean until the evening 4
15: 5 in water, and be unclean until the evening 4
6 bathe . . and be unclean until the evening 4
7 bathe . . and be unclean until the evening 4
8 bathe . . and be unclean until the evening 4
10 touches . . shall be unclean until the evening 4
10 bathe . . and be unclean until the evening 4
11 bathe . . and be unclean until the evening 4
16 shall bathe . . and be unclean until the evening 4
17 be washed . . and be unclean until the evening 4
18 bathe . . and be unclean until the evening 4
19 touches her shall be unclean until the evening 4
21 bathe . . and be unclean until the evening 4
22 bathe . . and be unclean until the evening 4
23 touches it he shall be unclean until the evening 4
27 bathe . . and be unclean until the evening 4
16:17 until he comes out and has made atonement 4
17:15 bathe . . and be unclean until the evening 4
19: 6 anything left over until the third day 4
13 not remain with you all night until the morning 4
22: 4 may eat of the holy things until he is clean 4
6 any such shall be unclean until the evening 4
30 you shall leave none of it until the morning 4
23:14 you shall eat neither . . until this same day 4
14 eat . . until you have brought the offering 4
25:22 until the ninth year, when its produce comes 4
28 remain . . until the year of jubilee 4
40 He shall serve with you until the year 4
50 when he sold himself until the year of jubilee 4
52 but a few years until the year of jubilee 4
27:18 the years that remain until the year of jubilee 4
Num 6: 5 until the time is completed for which he 4
9:12 They shall leave none of it until the morning 4
15 like the appearance of fire until morning. 4
21 cloud remained from evening until morning; 4
11:20 a whole month, until it comes out at your nostrils 4
14:19 forgiven this people, from Egypt even until now. 4
33 until the last of your dead bodies lies 4
19: 7 priest shall be unclean until evening. 4
8 shall be unclean until evening 4
10 he who gathers . . be unclean until evening. 4
21 touches . . shall be unclean until evening. 4
22 touches it shall be unclean until evening. 4
20:17 until we have passed through your territory. 4
21:22 until we have passed through your territory. 4
30 we laid waste until fire spread to Med'eba. 4
35 until there was not one survivor left to him; 4
32:13 40 years, until all the generation that had done evil 4
17 until we have brought them to their place; 4
18 until the people of Israel have inherited 4
21 until he has driven out his enemies from before 4
35:12 not die until he stands before the congregation 4
25 live in it until the death of the high priest 4
28 city of refuge until the death of the high priest; 4
Deu 1:31 way that you went until you came to this place.' 4
2:14 Ka'desh-bar'nea until we crossed the brook Zered 4
14 until the entire generation . . had perished 4
15 to destroy them . . until they had perished. 4
29 until I go over the Jordan into the land 4
3: 3 smote him until no survivor was left to him. 4
20 until the LORD gives rest to your brethren 4
7:20 until those who are left and hide themselves 4
23 into great confusion, until they are destroyed. 4
24 until you have destroyed them. 4
9: 7 from . . until you came to this place 4
21 grinding it . . until it was as fine as dust; 4
11: 5 did to you . . until you came to this place; 4
16: 4 nor shall any . . remain all night until morning. 3
20:20 siegeworks against the city . . until it falls. 4
22: 2 shall be with you until your brother seeks it; 4
28:20 until you are destroyed and perish quickly 4
21 until he has consumed you off the land which you 4
22 they shall pursue you until you perish. 4
24 come down upon you until you are destroyed. 4
48 yoke of iron . . until he has destroyed you. 4
51 shall eat . . until you are destroyed; 4
51 until they have caused you to perish. 4
52 besiege . . until your high and fortified walls 4
61 LORD will bring upon you, until you are destroyed. 4
31:30 Moses spoke . . this song until they were finished 4
Jos 1:15 you shall help them, until the LORD gives rest 4
2:16 and hide . . until the pursuers have returned; 4
22 there three days, until the pursuers returned; 4
3:17 stood . . until all the nation finished passing 4
4:10 in the . . Jordan, until everything was finished 4
23 God dried up the waters . . until you passed over 4
23 Red Sea, which he dried up . . until we passed over 4
5: 1 dried up the waters . . until they had crossed over 4
6:10 shall not shout . . until the day I bid you shout; 4
7: 6 upon his face before the ark . . until the evening 4
13 you cannot stand . . until you take away 4
8:22 and Israel smote them, until there was left none 4
26 not draw back . . until he had utterly destroyed 4
29 he hanged the king of Ai on a tree until evening; 4
10:13 the moon stayed, until the nation took vengeance 4
20 a very great slaughter, until they were wiped out 4
26 And they hung upon the trees until evening; 4
33 Joshua smote . . until he left none remaining. 4
11: 8 they smote them, until they left none remaining. 4
14 they smote . . until they had destroyed them 4
20: 6 he shall remain . . until he has stood before 4
6 remain . . until the death of him who is high priest 4
23:15 bring . . evil things, until he have destroyed you 4
Jdg 4:24 until they destroyed Jabin king of Canaan. 4
5: 7 The peasantry . . they ceased until you arose 4
6:18 Do not depart from here . . until I come to thee 4
16:13 Until now you have mocked me, and told me lies; 4
18: 1 for until then no inheritance among the tribes 4
30 were priests . . until the day of the captivity 4
19: 8 and tarry until the day declines." So they ate 4
25 and abused her all night until the morning. 4
30 been seen from the day . . until this day; 4
20:23 and wept before the LORD until the evening; 4
26 the LORD, and fasted that day until evening 4
Rut 1:19 the two . . went on until they came to Bethlehem. 4
2: 7 she has continued from early morning until now 4
14 and she ate until she was satisfied 2
17 she gleaned in the field until evening; 4
23 gleaning until the end of the barley and wheat 4
3: 3 not make yourself known . . until he has finished 4
13 Lie down until the morning. 4
14 she lay at his feet until the morning 4
18 Wait . . until you learn how the matter turns out 4
1Sm 1:23 wait until you have weaned him; 4
23 woman . . nursed her son, until she weaned him. 4
3:15 Samuel lay until morning; 4
9:24 it was kept for you until the hour appointed 3
10: 8 Seven days you shall wait, until I come to you 4
11:11 cut down the Ammonites until the heat of the day; 4
12: 2 walked before you from my youth until this day. 4
14: 9 If they say to us, 'Wait until we come to you,' 4
24 Cursed be the man who eats food until . . evening 4
36 and despoil them until the morning light; 4
15:18 and fight against them until they are consumed. 4
35 did not see Saul again until the day of his death 4
19:23 he prophesied, until he came to Nai'oth in Ramah. 4
20:41 and wept . . until David recovered himself. 4
25:36 she told him nothing . . until the morning light. 4
29: 8 from the day I entered your service until now 4
30: 4 and wept, until they had no more strength to weep. 5
17 from twilight until the evening of the next day; 4
2Sm 1:12 they mourned and wept and fasted until evening 4
10: 5 Remain at Jericho until your beards have grown 4
13:27 Ab'salom pressed him until he let Amnon . . go 2
15:24 set down the ark . . until the people had 4
28 I will wait . . until word comes from you to inform 4
17:13 drag it . . until not even a pebble is to be found 4
19: 7 evil . . come upon you from your youth until now. 4
24 from the day the king departed until the day he 4
20: 3 they were shut up until the day of their death 4
21:10 from the beginning of harvest until rain fell 4
22:38 and did not turn back until they were consumed. 4
23:10 struck . . Philistines until his hand was weary 4
24:15 from the morning until the appointed time; 4
1Kg 3: 1 brought her . . until he had finished building 4
5: 3 until the LORD put them under the soles 4
6:22 he overlaid . . until all the house was finished. 4
10: 7 I did not believe the reports until I came 4
11:16 remained there six months, until he had cut off 4
40 and was in Egypt until the death of Solomon. 4
14:10 as a man burns up dung until it is all gone. 4
15:29 killed all the house . . until he had destroyed it 4
17:14 oil shall not fail, until the day . . the LORD sends 4
18:26 called on . . Ba'al from morning until noon, saying 4
28 cut themselves . . until the blood gushed out 4
29 they raved on until the time of the . . oblation 4
22:11 push the Syrians until they are destroyed.' 4
27 feed him with scant fare . . until I come in peace."' 4
35 king was propped up . . until at evening he died; 2
2Kg 3:25 every man threw a stone, until it was covered; 2
6:25 a great famine . . until an ass's head was sold 4
7: 9 if we are silent and wait until the morning light 4
8: 6 from the day that she left the land until now. 4
11 and stared at him, until he was ashamed. 4
10: 8 Lay them in two heaps . . until the morning. 4
11 Jehu slew all . . until he left him none 4
13:17 fight the Syrians . . until you have made an end 4
19 struck down Syria until you had made an end of it 4
23 nor has he cast them from his presence until now. 4
17:20 the LORD rejected . . until he had cast them out 4
23 until the LORD removed Israel 4
23 Israel was exiled . . to Assyria until this day. 4
18: 4 until those days the people . . burned incense 4
32 until I come and take you away 4
1Ch 4:31 These were their cities until David reigned. 4
5:22 And they dwelt in their place until the exile. 4
6:32 until Solomon had built the house of the LORD 4
12:22 until there was a great army, like an army of God. 4
19: 5 Remain at Jericho until your beards have grown 4
28:20 until all the work for the service of the house 4
2Ch 8:16 from the day . . was laid until it was finished. 4
9: 6 I did not believe the reports until I came 4
14:13 the Ethiopians fell until none remained alive; 4
15:19 there was no more war until the 35th year 4
18:10 push the Syrians until they are destroyed.' 4
26 fellow in prison . . until I return in peace.' 4
34 in his chariot facing the Syrians until evening; 4
20:25 took for themselves until they could carry no 3
21:15 until your bowels come out 4
24:10 into the chest until they had finished. 4
29:28 all this continued until the burnt offering 4
34 until other priests had sanctified themselves 4
34 Levites helped them, until the work was finished 4
31: 1 until they had destroyed them all. 4
35:14 busied in offering . . the fat parts until night; 4
36:20 until the establishment of the kingdom 4
21 until the land had enjoyed its sabbaths. 4
Ezr 2:63 until there should be a priest to consult 4
4: 5 even until the reign of Darius king of Persia. 4
21 city be not rebuilt, until a decree is made by me. 4
24 it ceased until the second year . . of Darius 8
5:16 from that time until now it has been in building 8
8:29 Guard them and keep them until you weigh them 4
9: 4 sat appalled until the evening sacrifice. 4
Neh 2: 7 let me pass through until I come to Judah; 4
7: 3 not the gates . . be opened until the sun is hot; 4
65 until a priest with Urim and Thummim 4
8: 3 read . . from early morning until midday 4
9:32 time of the kings of Assyria until this day. 4
12:22 priests until the reign of Darius the Persian. 7
23 Book of the Chronicles until the days of Joha'nan 4
13:19 should not be opened until after the sabbath. 4
Job 14:13 thou wouldest conceal me until thy wrath be past 4
Ps 73:17 until I went into the sanctuary of God; 4
94:13 until a pit is dug for the wicked. 4
104:23 to his work and to his labor until the evening. 4
105:19 until what he had said came to pass 4
112: 8 until he sees his desire on his adversaries. 4
132: 5 until I find a place for the LORD, a dwelling place 4
Prv 4:18 shines brighter and brighter until full day. 4
18:17 until the other comes and examines him. 2
28:17 let him be a fugitive until death; let no one help 4
Sng 2: 7 you stir not up nor awaken love until it please. 6
17 Until the day breathes and the shadows flee 4
3: 4 and would not let him go until I had brought him 4
5 stir not up nor awaken love until it please. 6
4: 6 Until the day breathes and the shadows flee 4
8: 4 stir not up nor awaken love until it please. 4
Isa 5: 8 who add field to field, until there is no more room 4
6:11 How long, O Lord?" And he said: "Until cities lie waste 4
26:20 for a little while until the wrath is past. 4
29:17 Is it not yet a very little while until Lebanon 2
32:15 until the Spirit is poured upon us from on high 4
36:17 until I come and take you away to a land 4
38:13 I cry for help until morning; 4
62: 1 until her vindication goes forth as brightness 4
7 give him no rest until he establishes Jerusalem 4
Jer 1: 3 until the end of the eleventh year of Zedeki'ah 4
3 until the captivity of Jerusalem in the fifth 4
9:16 the sword after them, until I have consumed them. 4
23:20 until he has executed and accomplished 4
24:10 until they shall be utterly destroyed 4
27: 7 until the time of his own land comes; 4

8 until I have consumed it by his hand. 4
22 until the day when I give attention to them 4
30:24 will not turn back until he has executed 4
32: 5 and there he shall remain until I visit him 4
36: 2 spoke to you, from the days of Josi'ah until today. 4
23 until the entire scroll was consumed in the fire 4
37:21 until all the bread of the city was gone. 4
38:28 until the day that Jerusalem was taken. 4
44:27 sword and by famine, until there is an end of them. 4
49:37 the sword after them, until I have consumed them; 4
52:34 his daily need, until the day of his death 4
Lam 3:50 until the LORD from heaven looks down and sees; 4
Ezk 21:27 until he comes whose right it is; 4
46: 2 but the gate shall not be shut until evening. 4
Dan 1:21 Daniel continued until the first year of King 4
4:32 until you have learned that the Most High rules 8
5:21 until he knew that the Most High God rules 8
7:22 until the Ancient of Days came, and judgment 8
9:27 until the decreed end is poured out 4
11:35 until the time of the end, for it is yet 4
12: 4 seal the book, until the time of the end. 4
9 shut up and sealed until the time of the end. 4
Hos 5:15 until they acknowledge their guilt 4
7: 4 the kneading of the dough until it is leavened. 4
Ams 9: 1 Smite the capitals until the thresholds shake 2
Mic 5: 3 until the time when she who is in travail 4
7: 9 until he pleads my cause and executes judgment 4
Mat 1:25 knew her not until she had borne a son; 14
2:15 remained there until the death of Herod. 14
5:18 pass from the law until all is accomplished. 14
10:11 and stay with him until you depart. 14
11:12 From the days of John the Baptist until now 14
13 the prophets and the law prophesied until John; 14
23 it would have remained until this day. 17
13:30 Let both grow together until the harvest 14
17: 9 until the Son of man is raised from the dead. 14
23:39 I tell you, you will not see me again, until you say 15
24:21 from the beginning of the world until now 14
38 until the day when Noah entered the ark 9
39 they did not know until the flood came 14
26:29 until that day when I drink it new with you 14
27:45 over all the land until the ninth hour. 14
64 to be made secure until the third day 14
Mrk 6:10 stay there until you leave the place. 15
9: 9 until the Son of man should have risen 11
13:19 the creation which God created until now 14
14:25 until that day when I drink it new in the kingdom 14
15:33 over the whole land until the ninth hour. 14
Lke 1:20 unable to speak until the day 9
4:13 he departed from him until an opportune time. 9
12:50 how I am constrained until it is accomplished! 14
13:35 I tell you, you will not see me until you say 14
15: 4 go after the one which is lost, until he finds it? 14
8 seek diligently until she finds it? 14
16:16 The law and the prophets were until John 17
17:27 until the day when Noah entered the ark 9
21:24 until the times of the Gentiles are fulfilled. 9
22:16 I shall not eat it until it is fulfilled 14
18 until the kingdom of God comes. 14
34 until you three times deny that you know me. 14
23:44 darkness over the whole land until the ninth hour 14
24:49 stay in the city, until you are clothed with power 14
Joh 2:10 but you have kept the good wine until now. 14
9:18 until they called the parents of the man 14
21:22 If it is my will that he remain until I come 14
23 If it is my will that he remain until I come 14
Act 1: 2 until the day when he was taken up 9
22 until the day when he was taken up from us 14
3:21 until the time for establishing 9
4: 3 put them in custody until the morrow 12
7:45 So it was until the days of David 14
13:20 he gave them judges until Samuel the prophet. 14
20: 7 he prolonged his speech until midnight. 17
11 conversed with them a long while, until daybreak 9
25:21 until I could send him to Caesar. 14
Rom 8:22 whole creation has been groaning . . until now; 9
11:25 until the full number of the Gentiles come in 9
1Co 11:26 you proclaim the Lord's death until he comes. 9
15:25 until he has put all his enemies under his feet. 9
16: 8 I will stay in Ephesus until Pentecost 14
Gal 3:23 until faith should be revealed. 13
24 the law was our custodian until Christ came 12
4: 2 until the date set by the father. 9
19 until Christ be formed in you! 17
Eph 1:14 until we acquire possession of it 12
4:13 until we all attain to the unity of the faith 17
Php 1: 5 from the first day until now. 9
1Th 4:15 who are left until the coming of the Lord 12
2Th 2: 7 only he . . will do so until he is out of the way. 14
1Ti 6:14 until the appearing of our Lord Jesus Christ; 17
2Ti 1:12 I am sure that he is able to guard until that Day 12
Heb 6:11 the full assurance of hope until the end 9
9:10 imposed until the time of reformation. 17
10:13 until his enemies should be made a stool 14
Jas 5: 7 Be patient . . until the coming of the Lord. 14
7 until it receives the early and the late rain 14
2Pe 1:19 until the day dawns and the morning star rises 14
2: 4 into hell . . to be kept until the judgment; 12
9 under punishment until the day of judgment 12

3: 7 kept until the day of judgment and destruction 12
Jde 1: 6 kept . . until the judgment of the great day; 12
Rev 2:25 only hold fast what you have, until I come. 9
26 He . . who keeps my works until the end 9
6:11 until the number of their fellow servants 14
15: 8 until the seven plagues . . were ended 9
17:17 until the words of God shall be fulfilled. 9
20: 5 until the 1,000 years were ended. 9
1Es 1:14 the priests were offering the fat until night 14
52 until . . he gave command 14
57 until the Persians began to reign 17
58 Until the land has enjoyed its sabbaths 14
58 until the completion of 70 years. 12
2:30 until the second year of the reign of Darius 17
4:51 until it was completed 17
55 until the day when the temple should be finished 14
5:40 until a high priest should appear 14
73 until the reign of Darius. 14
6: 6 until word could be sent to Darius 17
20 in . . construction from that time until now 17
28 until the house of the Lord is finished; 17
8:59 Be watchful and on guard until you deliver them 14
72 I sat . . until the evening sacrifice. 14
77 in shame until this day. 17
9:13 until we are freed from the wrath of the Lord 14
41 from early morning until midday 14
2Es 2:32 Embrace your children until I come 23
4:30 how much ungodliness it has produced until now 22
30 will produce until the time of threshing comes! 22
37 or arouse them until that measure is fulfilled.' 22
51 Do you think that I shall live until those days? 22
7:75 we shall be kept in rest until those times come 19
77 it will not be shown to you until the last times. 22
10: 2 I remained quiet until evening of the second day 22
4 but without ceasing mourn and fast until I die. 22
12:21 but two shall be kept until the end. 20
32 whom the Most High has kept until the end of days 20
34 he will make them joyful until the end comes 21
13:44 until they had passed over. 24
46 Then they dwelt there until the last times 22
14: 9 until the times are ended. 24
25 until what you are about to write is finished. 21
15:21 Just as they have done to my elect until this day 22
16:14 shall not return until they come over the earth. 19
15 until it consumes the foundations of the earth. 19
Tob 2: 4 to a place of shelter until sunset. 14
10 took care of me until he went to Elymais. 14
6: 5 until they came near to Ecbatana. 14
7:11 until you make a binding agreement with me. 14
8:20 until the fourteen days . . were ended 10
10: 7 until the fourteen days . . had expired 14
11: 1 until they came near to Nineveh. 17
14: 5 until the times of the age are completed. 14
Jdt 6: 5 until I take revenge on this race 14
8 will not die until you perish along with them. 14
7:20 until all the vessels of water . . were empty; 16
8:34 for I will not tell you until I have finished 14
10:10 watched her until she had gone down the mountain 14
12: 5 she slept until midnight 17
9 until she ate her food toward evening. 17
14 it will be a joy to me until the day of my death! 14
14: 8 until the moment of her speaking to them. 14
16:23 until she was 105 years old •
AEs 14:18 since the day that I was brought here until now 17
15: 8 took her in his arms until she came to herself 17
Wis 10:14 until she brought him the scepter of a kingdom 14
Sir 1:23 A patient man will endure until the right moment 14
24 He will hide his words until the right moment 14
4:17 will torment him . . until she trusts him 14
6:18 until you are old you will keep finding wisdom. 14
11:19 until he leaves them to others and dies. 16
13: 7 until he has drained you two or three times 14
18:22 do not wait until death to be released from it. 14
20: 7 A wise man will be silent until the right moment 14
23:16 will not be quenched until it is consumed 14
16 will never cease until the fire burns him up. 14
17 he will never cease until he dies. 14
29: 5 will kiss another's hands until he gets a loan 14
35:17 he will not be consoled until it reaches the Lord; 14
17 he will not desist until the Most High visits him 14
Bar 1:19 From the day when the Lord . . until today 14
1Mc 3:33 until he returned. 14
4:41 until he had cleansed the sanctuary. 14
46 until there should come a prophet 17
5:19 do not engage in battle . . until we return. 14
8: 4 until they crushed them 14
9: 6 until no more than 800 of them were left. •
10:50 He pressed the battle strongly until the sun set 14
12:29 his men did not know it until morning 14
14:41 until a trustworthy prophet should arise 14
16: 2 the wars of Israel from our youth until this day 14
9 John pursued them until Cendebeus reached Kedron 14
2Mc 2: 7 until God gathers his people together again 14
5:25 waited until the holy sabbath day 14
6:14 until . . the full measure of their sins 17
9: 4 until he completed the journey •
3Mc 5:10 until they had been filled •
6:28 from the time of our ancestors until now 17
40 until the fourteenth day 17

7: 4 until this was accomplished 18
4Mc 7: 3 until he sailed into the haven of . . victory. 14

untimely 1. *ἄωρος*
Isa 14:19 cast out . . like a loathed untimely birth •
Wis 14:15 consumed with grief at an untimely bereavement 1
untimely *See also* bear, birth.

unto 1. אֶל 2. עַד 3. *ἄχρι* 4. *εἰς* 5. *μέχρι* 6. *πρός*
Job 31:12 that would be a fire which consumes unto Abaddon 2
Jol 1:19 Unto thee, O LORD, I cry. 1
Joh 11: 4 This illness is not unto death 6
Act 11:18 God has granted repentance unto life. 4
Php 2: 8 became obedient unto death, even death on a cross 5
Jde 1:21 the mercy of our Lord . . unto eternal life. 4
Rev 2:10 Be faithful unto death 3
unto *See also* even.

untold 1. *ἀμύθητος*
2Mc 3: 6 the treasury . . was full of untold sums of money 1
untold *See also* number.

untrained 1. לֹא לֻמָּד
Jer 31:18 I was chastened, like an untrained calf; 1

untrodden 1. *ἄβατος* 2. non calco
2Es 5: 3 the land . . shall be waste and untrodden ‡
9:29 the untrodden and unfruitful wilderness; 2
Wis 11: 2 and pitched their tents in untrodden places. 1

untroubled 1. *ἀτάραχος*
AEs 13: 7 completely secure and untroubled hereafter. 1

untrue 1. בגד
Ps 73:15 I would have been untrue to the generation of thy 1

unusual 1. *ἔξαλλος* 2. *ξένος* 3. *οὐ τυγχάνω*
4. *παράνομος*
Act 28: 2 the natives showed us unusual kindness 3
Wis 16:16 unusual rains and hail and relentless storms 2
3Mc 4: 4 at the sight of their unusual punishments 1
5:27 being struck by the unusual invitation to come out 4

unutterable 1. *ἀνεκλάλητος*
1Pe 1: 8 rejoice with unutterable and exalted joy. 1

unveiled 1. *ἀκαλύπτως* 2. *ἀκατακάλυπτος*
3. *ἀνακαλύπτω* 4. *ἀποκαλύπτω*
1Co 11: 5 who prays or prophesies with her head unveiled 2
2Co 3:18 we all, with unveiled face 3
Sus 1:32 the wicked men ordered her to be unveiled 4
3Mc 4: 6 and were carried away unveiled 1

unwalled 1. פְּרָזִי
Deu 3: 5 besides very many unwalled villages. 1
1Sm 6:18 both fortified cities and unwalled villages. 1
unwalled *See also* village.

unwashed 1. *ἄνιπτος*
Mat 15:20 to eat with unwashed hands does not defile a man. 1
Mrk 7: 2 ate with hands defiled, that is, unwashed. 1

unweighed
1Kg 7:47 Solomon left all the vessels unweighed •

unwelcome 1. *δυσχερής*
2Mc 9:24 if . . any unwelcome news came 1

unwilling 1. חמל 2. לֹא אבה 3. רַע בְּעַיִן
4. *οὐ βούλομαι* 5. *οὐδὲν βούλομαι* 6. *οὐ θέλω*
Deu 10:10 LORD was unwilling to destroy you. 2
Jos 24:15 And if you be unwilling to serve the LORD 3
2Sm 12: 4 and he was unwilling to take one of his own flock 1
Mat 1:19 Joseph, being a just man and unwilling to put her 6
15:32 I am unwilling to send them away hungry 6
1Mc 12:14 We were unwilling to annoy you 4
3Mc 3:19 and are unwilling to regard any action as sincere. 5

unwise 1. לֹא חָכָם
Hos 13:13 but he is an unwise son; 1

unwise man 1. *ἄσοφος*
Eph 5:15 not as unwise men but as wise 1

unwisely 1. *ἀβουλεύτως*
1Mc 5:67 they went out to battle unwisely. 1
unwitting *See* error, offense.

unwittingly 1. בִּבְלִי דַעַת 2. בִּשְׁגָגָה 3. לִשְׁגָגָה
Lev 4: 2 If any one sins unwittingly in any of the things 2
22 sins, doing unwittingly any one of all the things 2
27 If any one of the common people sins unwittingly 2
5:15 If any one . . sins unwittingly in any of the holy 2
22:14 if a man eats of a holy thing unwittingly 2
Num15:24 then if it was done unwittingly 3
27 If one person sins unwittingly, he shall offer 2
28 when he sins unwittingly, to make atonement 2

29 one law for him who does anything unwittingly 2
Jos 20: 3 who kills . . without intent or unwittingly 1
5 he killed his neighbor unwittingly 1

unwittingly *See also* commit.

unworthily 1. ἀνάξιος

AEs 16: 7 those who exercise authority unworthily 1

unworthy 1. ἀνάξιος 2. ἀναξίως 3. ἀχρεῖος 4. οὐκ ἄξιος 5. indignus

Lke 17:10 say, 'We are unworthy servants 3
Act 13:46 judge yourselves unworthy of eternal life 4
2Es 14:45 and let the worthy and the unworthy read them; 5
Man 1: 9 I am unworthy to look up and see the height 4
14 unworthy as I am, thou wilt save me 1
2Mc 14:42 and suffer outrages unworthy of his noble birth. 2

unworthy *See also* manner.

unworthy of honor 1. ἄτιμος

Sir 10:19 What race is unworthy of honor? The human race. 1
19 What race is unworthy of honor? The human race. 1

up 1. בְּ 2. זרח 3. מֵעַל 4. עַד 5. עַל 6. עלה 7. קום 8. עַד (A) 9. ἄνω 10. ἄχρι 11. εἰς ὕψος 12. ἐπάνω 13. ἕως 14. μέγας 15. μέχρι 16. πόρρω

Gen 19:14 Up, get out of this place; 7
44: 4 Joseph said to his steward, "Up, follow after 7
Exd 9:32 for they are late in coming up.) *
32: 1 said to him, "Up, make us gods, who shall go before us; 7
Lev 19:16 You shall not go up and down as a slanderer *
27: 3 a male from twenty years old up to 60 years old 4
5 is from five years old up to twenty years old 4
6 If the person is from a month old up to five years 4
23 the valuation for it up to the year of jubilee 4
Num 4: 3 from 30 years old up to 50 years old 6
23 from 30 years old up to 50 years old 6
30 from 30 years old up to 50 years old 6
35 from 30 years old up to 50 years old 6
39 from 30 years old up to 50 years old 6
43 from 30 years old up to 50 years old 6
47 from 30 years old up to 50 years old 6
Deu 1:28 the cities are great and fortified up to heaven; 1
9: 1 cities great and fortified up to heaven 1
Jos 7:13 Up, sanctify the people, and say 7
15: 3 goes up . . along by Hezron, up to Addar, turns about 6
18:12 then up through the hill country westward; 6
19:12 thence it goes to Dab'erath, then up to Japhi'a; 6
Jdg 4:14 Deb'orah said to Barak, "Up! For this is the day 7
9:33 in the morning, as soon as the sun is up, rise early 2
40 many fell wounded, up to the entrance of the gate. 4
1Sm 9:26 Up, that I may send you on your way. 7
2Sm 18:24 and the watchman went up to the roof of the gate *
2Ch 13: 4 Then Abi'jah stood up on Mount Zemara'im 3
28: 9 in a rage which has reached up to heaven. 4
Ezr 7:22 up to 100 talents of silver 8
9: 6 our guilt has mounted up to the heavens. 4
Neh 6: 1 (although up to that time I had not set up the doors 4
Ps 69: 1 O God! For the waters have come up to my neck. 4
88:15 Afflicted and close to death from my youth up *
118:27 up to the horns of the altar! 4
Isa 30:28 overflowing stream that reaches up to the neck; 4
Jer 6: 4 war against her; up, and let us attack at noon! 7
5 Up, and let us attack by night, and destroy her 7
Ezk 4:14 up till now I have never eaten what died of itself *
41:16 round about, from the floor up to the windows 4
47: 4 through the water; and it was up to the loins. *
Dan 8:11 magnified . . even up to the Prince of the host; 4
Hos 11: 3 taught E'phraim to walk, I took them up in my arms; 5
Mat 20: 8 beginning with the last, up to the first.' 13
Joh 2: 7 And they filled them up to the brim. 13
Act 22:22 Up to this word they listened to him 10
23: 1 I have lived . . in all good conscience up to this day. 10
Heb 11:24 Moses, when he was grown up 14
12:15 root of bitterness" spring up and cause trouble 9
1Es 8:20 up to 100 talents of silver 13
20 likewise up to 100 cors of wheat 13
9:47 they lifted up their hands, and fell to the ground 9
Sir 6:18 My son, from your youth up choose instruction *
27:25 Whoever throws a stone straight up 11
31:21 get up in the middle of the meal 16
37: 5 in the face of battle take up the shield. *
Bar 2: 5 They were brought low and not raised up 12
LJr 1: 3 for a long time, up to seven generations 13
4Mc 9:28 flayed all his flesh up to his chin 15

up *See also* bear, bind, blaze, block, break, bring, build, burn, carry, cast, catch, chop, churn, climb, close, come, count, cover, cut, deliver, dip, divide, draw, drawn, drink, dry, eat, fill, finish, gather, get, gird, give, go, grow, halfway, hang, haul, heap, hedge, help, hitch, hoard, hoist, hold, lay, lead, leap, lick, lift, light, line, lock, look, make, march, mount, offer, open, pass, pick, pile, pluck, prop, puff, pull, raise, reach, receive, reckon, rip, rise, roll, root, round, rouse, run, seal, send, set, shoot, shrivel, shut, sit, split, spring, stand, stir, stop, store, suck, sum, swallow, swell, take, throw, tie, toss, train, treasure, trip, turn, use, vomit, wake, wall, way, well, wrap, yield.

up there 1. שָׁם

Jos 7: 3 do not make the whole people toil up there 1

up upon 1. super

2Es 13: 6 a great mountain, and flew up upon it. 1

upbraid 1. רִיב 2. ὀνειδίζω

Gen 31:36 Then Jacob became angry, and upbraided Laban; 1
Jdg 8: 1 with Mid'ian?" And they upbraided him violently. 1
Mat 11:20 Then he began to upbraid the cities 2
Mrk 16:14 he upbraided them for their unbelief 2
Sir 20:15 He gives little and upbraids much 2
41:22 do not upbraid after making a gift; 2

upbringing 1. ἀνατροφή

4Mc 16: 8 the more grievous anxieties of your upbringing. 1

upbuild 1. οἰκοδομή

Rom 14:19 makes for peace and for mutual upbuilding. 1
1Co 14: 3 upbuilding and encouragement 1
2Co 12:19 all for your upbuilding, beloved. 1
Eph 4:16 makes bodily growth and upbuilds itself in love. 1

uphold 1. דין 2. סמך 3. סעד 4. עוד 5. קום 6. תמך 7. ἀντιλαμβάνω 8. ἵστημι 9. φέρω

Job 4: 4 Your words have upheld him who was stumbling 5
Ps 37:17 the LORD upholds the righteous. 2
41:12 But thou hast upheld me because of my integrity 6
51:12 uphold me with a willing spirit. 2
63: 8 My soul clings to thee; thy right hand upholds me. 6
119:116 Uphold me according to thy promise 2
145:14 The LORD upholds all who are falling 2
146: 9 LORD . . upholds the widow and the fatherless; 4
Prv 20:28 throne is upheld by righteousness. 3
Isa 9: 7 establish it, and to uphold it with justice 3
41:10 I will uphold you with my victorious right hand. 6
42: 1 Behold my servant, whom I uphold 6
59:16 and his righteousness upheld him. 2
63: 5 I was appalled, but there was no one to uphold; 2
5 arm brought me victory, and my wrath upheld me. 2
Jer 30:13 There is none to uphold your cause 1
Rom 3:31 By no means! On the contrary, we uphold the law. 8
14: 4 And he will be upheld 8
Heb 1: 3 upholding the universe by his word of power 9
2Mc 14:15 always upholds his own heritage 7

upholder 1. ἀντιλήμπτωρ

Ps 54: 4 the Lord is the upholder of my life. 1
Jdt 9:11 helper of the oppressed, upholder of the weak 1

uplift 1. רום 2. ὑψηλός 3. excello

Job 38:15 their uplifted arm is broken. 1
Act 13:17 with uplifted arm he led them out of it. 2
'Es 15:11 with a mighty hand and with an uplifted arm 3

upon 1. אֶל 2. אֵת 3. בְּ 4. בַּעַד 5. לְ 6. לִפְנֵי 7. מִמַּעַל 8. מִן 9. מֵעַל 10. מִפְּנֵי 11. עַל פְּנֵי 12. עִם 13. בְּ (A) 14. מִן (A) 15. עַל (A) 16. ἀντί 17. ἀπό 18. εἰς 19. ἐκ 20. ἐν 21. ἐπάνω 22. καί 23. κατά 24. μετά 25. περί 26. πρός 27. ad 28. in 29. super

Gen 1:25 and everything that creeps upon the ground *
4:26 time men began to call upon the name of the LORD. 3
9: 2 upon everything that creeps on the ground 3
21:16 for she said, "Let me not look upon the death 3
22: 9 laid him on the altar, upon the wood. 7
26:25 and called upon the name of the LORD 3
31:35 before you, for the way of women is upon me. 5
32:31 The sun rose upon him as he passed Penu'el 5
37:22 in the wilderness, but lay no hand upon him 3
34 put sackcloth upon his loins, and mourned for his 3
39: 5 the blessing of the LORD was upon all that he had 3
7 his master's wife cast her eyes upon Joseph 1
Exd 4: 9 from the Nile and pour it upon the dry ground; *
9 water . . will become blood upon the dry ground. 3
7: 4 then I will lay my hand upon Egypt and bring forth 3
9: 3 very severe plague upon your cattle which are 3
11 for the boils were upon the magicians and upon 3
11 boils were upon the magicians and upon all 3
14 send all my plagues upon your heart 1
14 plagues . . upon your servants and your people 3
33 the rain no longer poured upon the earth. †
10:13 brought an east wind upon the land all that day 3
14:24 looked down upon the host of the Egyptians 1
15:26 diseases upon you which I put upon the Egyptians; 3
19:22 lest the LORD break out upon them. 3
28:41 put them upon Aaron your brother, and upon his sons *
29:13 you shall . . burn them upon the altar. †
18 burn the whole ram upon the altar; †
30: 1 You shall make an altar to burn incense upon; *
31:18 made an end of speaking with him upon Mount Sinai 3
Lev 2: 2 as its memorial portion upon the altar *
4:19 shall take from it and burn upon the altar *
31 the priest shall burn it upon the altar *
9:10 from the sin offering he burned upon the altar *
20 the breasts, and he burned the fat upon the altar *
16:25 the sin offering he shall burn upon the altar *
19:28 or tattoo any marks upon you: I am the LORD 3
20: 9 cursed his father . . his blood is upon him 3
11 be put to death, their blood is upon them 3
12 have committed incest, their blood is upon them 3
13 they shall be put to death, their blood is upon them 3
16 they shall be put to death, their blood is upon them 3
27 their blood shall be upon them 3
21: 5 They shall not make tonsures upon their heads 3
25:21 I will command my blessing upon you in the sixth 5
Num 5:26 burn it upon the altar *
30 the priest shall execute upon her all this law. 5
6:25 The LORD make his face to shine upon you 1
26 The LORD lift up his countenance upon you 1
15:31 utterly cut off; his iniquity shall be upon him. 3
23: 4 I have offered upon each altar a bull and a ram. 3
33: 4 upon their gods also the LORD executed 3
Deu 1:36 I will give the land upon which he has trodden 3
4: 7 as the LORD . . is to us, whenever we call upon him? 1
7: 7 that the LORD set his love upon you and chose you 3
15 none of the evil diseases . . will he inflict upon you 3
15 he will lay them upon all who hate you. 3
10:15 LORD set his heart in love upon your fathers 3
11:12 eyes of the LORD your God are always upon it 3
20 write them . . upon your gates 3
22: 6 If you chance to come upon a bird's nest, in any tree 6
8 may not bring the guilt of blood upon your house 3
24:15 (for he is poor, and sets his heart upon it); 1
28: 8 command the blessing upon you in your barns 2
20 LORD will send upon you curses, confusion 3
46 They shall be upon you as a sign and a wonder 3
46 upon you . . and upon your descendants for ever. 3
60 bring upon you again all the diseases of Egypt 3
63 LORD will take delight in bringing ruin upon you 2
29: 5 your clothes have not worn out upon you 9
20 curses written in this book would settle upon 3
32:23 evils upon them; I will spend my arrows upon them; 3
46 all the words . . I enjoin upon you this day 3
33: 2 came from Sinai, and dawned from Se'ir upon us; 5
16 Let these come upon the head of Joseph 5
16 these come . . upon the crown of the head of him 5
Jos 1: 3 place that the sole of your foot will tread upon 3
2:19 If any one goes . . his blood shall be upon his head 3
19 but if a hand is laid upon any one who is with you 3
6:18 lest when you . . and bring trouble upon it. 2
8:20 the people . . turned back upon the pursuers. 1
9: 4 and took worn-out sacks upon their asses 5
10: 9 Joshua came upon them suddenly 1
11: 7 Joshua came suddenly . . and fell upon them. 3
22:17 came a plague upon the congregation of the LORD 3
Jdg 1:35 the hand of . . Joseph rested heavily upon them *
3:23 of the roof chamber upon him, and locked them. 4
8:21 Rise yourself, and fall upon us; for as the man is 3
9:57 the wickedness . . fall back upon their heads 3
57 and upon them came the curse of Jotham the son 1
15: 7 is what you do, I swear I will be avenged upon you 3
12 Swear to me that you will not fall upon me 3
16 With the jawbone of an ass, heaps upon heaps *
16:28 be avenged upon the Philistines for one of my two 8
18:25 lest angry fellows fall upon you, and you lose 3
20:37 men in ambush made haste and rushed upon Gib'e-ah 1
Rut 1:21 and the Almighty has brought calamity upon me? 5
2: 9 your eyes be upon the field . . they are reaping 3
1Sm 2:29 by fattening yourselves upon the choicest 8
5: 4 his hands were lying cut off upon the threshold; 1
6 the LORD was heavy upon the people of Ashdod 1
9 so that tumors broke out upon them. 5
6: 4 same plague was upon all of you and . . your lords. 5
4 same plague was upon . . you and upon your lords. 5
15 took down the . . and set them upon the great stone; 1
9:26 Samuel called to Saul upon the roof *
12:17 I will call upon the LORD, that he may send thunder 1
18 Samuel called upon the LORD, and the LORD sent 1
13:12 the Philistines will come down upon me at Gilgal 1
14:32 the people flew upon the spoil, and took sheep 1
15:27 Saul laid hold upon the skirt of his robe 3
16:13 the Spirit of the LORD came mightily upon David 1
23 whenever the evil spirit from God was upon Saul 1
18:10 an evil spirit from God rushed upon Saul 1
17 Let not my hand be upon him, but . . the Philistines 3
17 but let the hand of the Philistines be upon him. 3
19: 9 Then an evil spirit from the LORD came upon Saul 1
20:25 king sat upon his seat . . upon the seat by the wall; 1
22:17 put forth their hand to fall upon the priests 3
18 king said . . "You turn and fall upon the priests. 3
18 And Do'eg . . turned and fell upon the priests 3
23:26 Saul and . . were closing in upon David and his men 1
24: 7 Saul rose up and left . . and went upon his way. 3
12 may the LORD avenge me upon you; 8
25:39 returned the evil . . of Nabal upon his own head. 3
27: 8 and made raids upon the Gesh'urites, and Gir'zites 1
28:20 Saul fell at once full length upon the ground †
23 he arose from the earth, and sat upon the bed. 1
30: 1 had made a raid upon the Negeb and upon Ziklag. 1
1 had made a raid upon the Negeb and upon Ziklag. 1
31: 3 The battle pressed hard upon Saul 1
2Sm 1:15 David called . . and said, "Go, fall upon him. 3
2:32 all night, and the day broke upon them at Hebron. 5
3:29 fall upon . . Jo'ab, and upon all his father's house; 1
5:23 and come upon them opposite the balsam trees. 5
6: 3 And they carried the ark of God upon a new cart 1
9: 8 What . . that you should look upon a dead dog 1
11:25 strengthen your attack upon the city 1
12:16 and went in and lay all night upon the ground. †

16:12 may be that the LORD will look upon my affliction 3
17:12 So we shall come upon him in some place 1
14 so that the LORD might bring evil upon Ab'salom. 1
24:15 the LORD sent a pestilence upon Israel 3
1Kg 2: 5 putting innocent blood upon the girdle about my 3
5 about my loins, and upon the sandals on my feet. 3
33 blood come back upon the head of Jo'ab and upon 3
33 head of Jo'ab and upon the head of his descendants 3
37 shall die; your blood shall be upon your own head. 3
44 will bring back your evil upon your own head. 3
8:32 by bringing his conduct upon his own head 3
13:29 took up the body . . and laid it upon the ass 1
14:10 I will bring evil upon the house of Jerobo'am 1
18: 1 Go . . to Ahab; and I will send rain upon the earth. 11
42 he bowed himself down upon the earth †
19:11 stand upon the mount before the LORD. 3
19 Eli'jah passed . . and cast his mantle upon him. 1
20:31 sackcloth on our loins and ropes upon our heads 3
21:21 Behold, I will bring evil upon you; 1
22:17 I saw all Israel scattered upon the mountains 1
2Kg 2:16 cast him upon some mountain or into some valley. 3
4: 4 and shut the door upon yourself and your sons 4
5 and shut the door upon herself and her sons; 4
21 laid him on the bed . . and shut the door upon him 4
33 he went in and shut the door upon the two of them 4
5:23 and laid them upon two of his servants; 1
8: 1 called for a famine, and it will come upon the land 1
24: 3 this came upon Judah at the command of the LORD 3
25: 6 king of Babylon . . who passed sentence upon him. 2
1Ch 5:19 made war upon the Hagrites, Jetur, Naphish 12
13:11 because the LORD had broken forth upon Uzzah; 3
14:14 and come upon them opposite the balsam trees. 5
15:13 LORD our God broke forth upon us 3
15 ark of God upon their shoulders with the poles 3
21: 3 Why should he bring guilt upon Israel? 5
12 sword of the LORD, pestilence upon the land 3
14 the LORD sent a pestilence upon Israel; 3
17 but let not the plague be upon thy people. 3
26 called upon the LORD, and he answered him 1
22: 8 have shed so much blood before me upon the earth. †
2Ch 6:23 guilty by bringing his conduct upon his own head 3
12: 7 my wrath shall not be poured out upon Jerusalem 3
20:12 our God, wilt thou not execute judgment upon them? 3
33 people had not yet set their hearts upon the God 5
22: 8 executing judgment upon the house of Ahab 12
25:13 fell upon the cities of Judah 3
30:12 The hand of God was also upon Judah to give them 3
34:25 my wrath will be poured out upon this place 3
35: 3 you need no longer carry it upon your shoulders. 3
36: 3 king of Egypt . . laid upon the land a tribute 2
Ezr 5: 5 But the eye of their God was upon the elders 15
6:11 he shall be impaled upon it, and his house 15
7:17 you shall offer them upon the altar 15
24 to impose . . toll upon any one of the priests 15
26 let judgment be strictly executed upon him 14
Neh 4: 4 turn back their taunt upon their own heads 1
5: 4 king's tax upon our fields and our vineyards. •
9:32 come upon . . our kings, our princes, our priests 5
12:31 I brought up the princes of Judah upon the wall 9
Est 1:17 to look with contempt upon their husbands †
6: 2 who had sought to lay hands upon King Ahasu-e'rus. 3
8:12 to destroy . . upon one day throughout all 3
13 to avenge themselves upon their enemies. 8
Job 1:12 only upon himself do not put forth your hand. 1
20 fell upon the ground, and worshiped. †
7: 8 while thy eyes are upon me, I shall be gone. 3
17 that thou dost set thy mind upon him 1
12: 4 I, who called upon God and he answered me 5
16:10 they have struck me insolently upon the cheek •
14 He breaks me with breach upon breach; 11
20:17 He will not look upon the rivers 3
36: 7 with kings upon the throne he sets them for ever 5
Ps 7:16 His mischief returns upon his own head 3
21: 3 thou dost set a crown of fine gold upon his head. 5
27: 5 he will set me high upon a rock. 3
41: 8 They say, "A deadly thing has fastened upon him; 3
45: 2 grace is poured upon your lips; 3
55: 5 Fear and trembling come upon me 3
16 I call upon God; and the LORD will save me. 1
67: 1 and bless us and make his face to shine upon us 2
2 that thy way may be known upon earth 3
4 with equity and guide the nations upon earth. 3
68: 4 lift up a song to him who rides upon the clouds; 3
17 twice 10,000, thousands upon thousands •
73:25 there is nothing upon earth that I desire 3
110: 3 day you lead your host upon the holy mountains. 3
113: 6 who looks far down upon the heavens and the earth? 3
119:135 Make thy face shine upon thy servant, and teach me 3
148 awake . . that I may meditate upon thy promise. 3
129: 8 do not say, "The blessing of the LORD be upon you! 1
132:12 sons also for ever shall sit upon your throne. 5
133: 2 down upon the beard, upon the beard of Aaron •
144: 9 upon a ten-stringed harp I will play to thee 3
147: 7 make melody to our God upon the lyre! 3
8 he makes grass grow upon the hills. •
Prv 23: 5 When your eyes light upon it, it is gone; 3
26:27 come back upon him who starts it rolling. 1
29:16 but the righteous will look upon their downfall. 3
Ecc 11: 1 Cast your bread upon the waters, 11

Sng 6:13 return, return, that we may look upon you. 3
13 Why should you look upon the Shu'lammite 3
13 Why should you look upon the Shu'lammite 3
Isa 3: 9 For they have brought evil upon themselves. 5
26 mourn; ravaged, she shall sit upon the ground. 5
9: 8 a word . . and it will light upon Israel; 3
11:14 they shall swoop down upon the . . Philistines 3
12: 4 Give thanks to the LORD, call upon his name; 3
26:16 a prayer when thy chastening was upon them. 5
28:10 For it is precept upon precept 5
10 is precept upon precept, precept upon precept 5
10 precept upon precept, line upon line 5
10 line upon line, here a little, there a little. 5
13 will be to them precept upon precept 5
13 precept upon precept, precept upon precept 5
13 precept upon precept, line upon line 5
13 line upon line, line upon line 5
33: 4 as locusts leap, men leap upon it. 3
15 who . . shuts his eyes from looking upon evil 3
40: 7 fades, when the breath of the LORD blows upon it; 3
24 when he blows upon them, and they wither 3
43:22 Yet you did not call upon me, O Jacob; 2
50:10 trusts in the . . LORD and relies upon his God? 3
59:17 and a helmet of salvation upon his head; 3
64: 7 There is no one that calls upon thy name 3
66: 4 and bring their fears upon them; 5
7 before her pain came upon her she was delivered 5
16 execute judgment, and by his sword, upon all flesh; 2
20 offering to the LORD, upon horses, and in chariots 3
20 in litters, and upon mules, and upon dromedaries 3
Jer 2: 3 evil came upon them, says the LORD. 1
17 Have you not brought this upon yourself 5
4:12 Now it is I who speak in judgment upon them. 2
18 ways and your doings have brought this upon you. 5
6:19 behold, I am bringing evil upon this people 1
9: 6 Heaping oppression upon oppression 3
6 deceit upon deceit, they refuse to know me 3
11:11 I am bringing evil upon them 1
20 let me see thy vengeance upon them 8
23 For I will bring evil upon the men of An'athoth 1
15:17 I sat alone, because thy hand was upon me 10
19:15 Behold, I am bringing upon this city 1
20:12 let me see thy vengeance upon them 8
22:23 how you will groan when pangs come upon you 5
24:10 I will send sword . . and pestilence upon them 3
26:15 blood . . upon this city and its inhabitants 1
31: 5 plant vineyards upon the mountains of Sama'ria; 3
32:42 brought all this great evil upon this people 1
36:31 and upon the men of Judah, all the evil 1
39: 5 and he passed sentence upon him. 2
40: 3 this thing has come upon you. 5
46:20 but a gadfly from the north has come upon her. 3
25 I am bringing punishment upon Amon of Thebes 1
47: 5 Baldness has come upon Gaza 1
48: 8 The destroyer shall come upon every city 1
21 Judgment has come upon the tableland, upon Holon 1
21 Judgment has come upon the tableland, upon Holon 1
44 I will bring these things upon Moab 1
49:36 I will bring upon Elam the four winds 1
50:35 A sword . . upon the inhabitants of Babylon 1
35 and upon her princes and her wise men! 1
36 A sword upon the diviners, that they may become 1
36 upon her warriors, that they may be destroyed! 1
37 A sword upon her horses and upon her chariots 1
37 A sword upon her horses and upon her chariots 1
37 and upon all the foreign troops in her midst 1
37 A sword upon all her treasures 1
38 A drought upon her waters, that they may be dried 1
51:35 My blood be upon the inhabitants of Chalde'a 1
53 yet destroyers would come from me upon her 5
60 all the evil that should come upon Babylon 1
52: 9 and he passed sentence upon him. 2
Lam 1:12 sorrow like my sorrow which was brought upon me 5
3:47 panic and pitfall have come upon us 5
Ezk 1:15 I saw a wheel upon the earth 3
2: 6 thorns are with you and you sit upon scorpions; 1
5:13 I will vent my fury upon them and satisfy myself; 3
13 in my jealousy, when I spend my fury upon them. 3
6:12 Thus I will spend my fury upon them. 3
13 round about their altars, upon every high hill 1
7: 3 I will let loose my anger upon you 3
12 for wrath is upon all their multitude. 1
13 For wrath is upon all their multitude; 1
14 for my wrath is upon all their multitude. 1
18 horror covers them; shame is upon all faces 1
9:10 but I will requite their deeds upon their heads. 3
11: 9 and execute judgments upon you. 3
21 I will requite their deeds upon their own heads 3
12:12 lift his baggage upon his shoulder in the dark 1
13:15 Thus will I spend my wrath upon the wall 3
15 and upon those who have daubed it with whitewash; 3
14:13 break its staff of bread and send famine upon it 3
21 I send upon Jerusalem my four sore acts 1
16:12 I put . . a beautiful crown upon your head. 3
41 burn your houses and execute judgments upon you 3
43 behold, I will requite your deeds upon your head 3
17:19 which he broke, I will requite upon his head. 3
18: 6 if he does not eat upon the mountains 1
11 but eats upon the mountains 1

13 surely die; his blood shall be upon himself. 3
19: 9 no more be heard upon the mountains of Israel. 1
21:12 Smite therefore upon your thigh. 1
22: 9 and men in you who eat upon the mountains; 1
31 their way have I requited upon their heads 3
23:10 when judgment had been executed upon her. 3
12 She doted upon the Assyrians 1
30 have brought this upon you 5
37 and blood is upon their hands; 3
42 they put bracelets upon the hands of the women 1
45 are adulteresses, and blood is upon their hands. 3
24:13 till I have satisfied my fury upon you. 3
25:11 I will execute judgments upon Moab. 3
12 offended in taking vengeance upon them 3
14 I will lay my vengeance upon Edom 3
17 I will execute great vengeance upon them 3
17 I am the LORD, when I lay my vengeance upon them. 3
26: 7 bring upon Tyre from the north Nebuchadrez'zar 1
28:26 execute judgments upon all their neighbors 3
30: 4 A sword shall come upon Egypt 3
9 and anguish shall come upon them 3
14 and will execute acts of judgment upon Thebes. 3
19 Thus I will execute acts of judgment upon Egypt. 3
31:13 upon its branches will be all the beasts 1
33: 4 his blood shall be upon his own head. 3
5 his blood shall be upon himself. 3
22 Now the hand of the LORD had been upon me 1
34:14 upon the mountain heights of Israel 3
37: 9 breathe upon these slain, that they may live. 3
22 nation in the land, upon the mountains of Israel; 3
40: 2 and set me down upon a very high mountain 1
4 and set your mind upon all that I shall show you 5
43: 3 I fell upon my face. 1
20 corners of the ledge, and upon the rim round about; 1
44: 4 I fell upon my face. 1
47: 7 I saw upon the bank of the river very many trees 1
Dan 2:46 Then King Nebuchadnez'zar fell upon his face 15
3:27 no smell of fire had come upon them. 13
4:24 a decree . . which has come upon my lord the king 15
28 All this came upon King Nebuchadnez'zar. 15
33 the word was fulfilled upon Nebuchadnez'zar. 15
6:10 he got down upon his knees three times a day 15
17 a stone was . . laid upon the mouth of the den 15
23 no kind of hurt was found upon him 13
7: 4 made to stand upon two feet like a man 15
11:18 indeed he shall turn his insolence back upon him. 5
Hos 2: 4 Upon her children also I will have no pity 2
8 and who lavished upon her silver and gold 5
7: 7 and none of them calls upon me. 1
9 gray hairs are sprinkled upon him 3
8:14 but I will send a fire upon his cities 3
10:12 that he may come and rain salvation upon you. 5
12:14 and will turn back upon him his reproaches. 5
Jol 2: 9 They leap upon the city, they run upon the walls; 3
9 They leap upon the city, they run upon the walls; 3
32 that all who call upon the name of the LORD 3
3: 4 will requite your deed upon your own head 3
7 and I will requite your deed upon your own head. 3
Ams 1: 4 I will send a fire upon the house of Haz'ael 3
7 I will send a fire upon the wall of Gaza 3
10 I will send a fire upon the wall of Tyre 3
12 I will send a fire upon Teman 3
2: 2 I will send a fire upon Moab, and it shall devour 3
5 I will send a fire upon Judah 3
6:12 Do horses run upon rocks? Does one plow the sea 3
8: 2 The end has come upon my people Israel; 1
9: 8 eyes of the Lord GOD are upon the sinful kingdom 3
Jon 1: 4 the LORD hurled a great wind upon the sea 1
6 Arise, call upon your god! 1
7 know on whose account this evil has come upon us. 5
8 on whose account this evil has come upon us? 5
2: 4 how shall I again look upon thy holy temple? 1
6 I went down to the land whose bars closed upon me 4
10 it vomited out Jonah upon the dry land. 1
Mic 1:15 I will again bring a conqueror upon you 5
4:11 and let our eyes gaze upon Zion. 3
5:15 vengeance upon the nations that did not obey. 2
Hag 2:15 Before a stone was placed upon a stone 1
Zec 5: 8 and thrust down the leaden weight upon its mouth. 1
6:11 make a crown, and set it upon the head of Joshua 3
Mal 1:10 that you might not kindle fire upon my altar •
2: 2 then I will send the curse upon you 3
Mat 23:22 by him who sits upon it. 21
27:30 they spat upon him, and took the reed and struck 18
28: 2 came and rolled back the stone, and sat upon it. 21
Mrk 1:10 the Spirit descending upon him like a dove; 18
Lke 10:19 have given you authority to tread upon serpents 21
16:24 'Father Abraham, have mercy upon me •
21:23 and wrath upon this people; •
Joh 1:16 have we all received, grace upon grace. 16
7:22 you circumcise a man upon the sabbath. 20
19:12 Upon this Pilate sought to release him 19
Act 2:43 fear came upon every soul •
24:24 and heard him speak upon faith in Christ Jesus. 25
Rom 2: 1 in passing judgment upon him you condemn •
4: 6 So also David pronounces a blessing upon the man •
9:16 So it depends not upon man's will or exertion •
16 it depends . . upon God's mercy. •
10:12 and bestows his riches upon all who call 18

11:25 a hardening has come upon part of Israel 17
32 that he may have mercy upon all. *
1Co 7:35 not to lay any restraint upon you *
9:12 If others share this rightful claim upon you *
10:11 upon whom the end of the ages has come. 18
11:29 eats and drinks judgment upon himself. *
2Co 11:28 there is the daily pressure upon me *
Gal 3:14 Abraham might come upon the Gentiles 18
Eph 1: 8 which he lavished upon us. 18
1Th 5: 3 as travail comes upon a woman with child *
2Th 1: 8 inflicting vengeance upon those *
8 inflicting vengeance . . upon those *
2:11 Therefore God sends upon them a strong delusion *
Heb 5: 4 one does not take the honor upon himself *
1Pe 4:12 fiery ordeal which comes upon you to prove you 20
2Pe 2:11 do not pronounce a reviling judgment upon them 23
3:10 and the works that are upon it will be burned up. 20
Rev 5: 3 able to open the scroll or to look upon it *
4 no one was found worthy . . to look upon it. *
11: 7 the beast . . will make war upon them and conquer 24
21:23 the city has no need of sun or moon to shine upon it *
1Es 4:36 The whole earth calls upon truth *
5:61 his glory are for ever upon all Israel. *
8:21 wrath may not come upon the kingdom of the king 18
2Es 1: 8 and hurl all evils upon them 29
23 I did not send fire upon you for your blasphemies *
2: 6 that you may bring confusion upon them *
35 eternal light will shine upon you for evermore. *
3: 9 thou didst bring the flood upon the inhabitants 29
10 as death came upon Adam, so the flood upon them. *
10 as death came upon Adam, so the flood upon them. *
4:21 also those who dwell upon earth 29
7: 8 so that only one man can walk upon that path. *
33 shall be revealed upon the seat of judgment 29
8:41 the farmer sows many seeds upon the ground 29
10: 9 so many who have come into being upon her. 29
11: 2 and all the winds of heaven blew upon him 27
7 and behold, the eagle rose upon his talons 29
44 the Most High has looked upon his times 29
15: 5 Behold," says the Lord, "I bring evils upon the world 29
19 A man shall have no pity upon his neighbors *
19 but shall make an assault upon their houses 28
27 now calamities have come upon the whole earth 29
33 fear and trembling shall come upon their army 28
33 and indecision upon their kings. 28
35 shall pour out a heavy tempest upon the earth 29
37 be fear and great trembling upon the earth 29
40 shall pour out upon every high and lofty place 29
44 and all its wrath upon her 29
50 when the heat rises that is sent upon you. 29
16:16 the calamities that are sent upon the earth 28
21 Behold, provision will be so cheap upon earth 29
39 will not delay in coming forth upon the earth 29
59 and founded it upon the waters; 29
Tob 2: 2 Upon seeing the abundance of food I said to my son 22
3:15 command that . . pity be taken upon me *
13:14 will rejoice for you upon seeing all your glory *
Jdt 4:15 to look with favor upon the whole house of Israel. *
8:22 he will bring upon our heads among the Gentiles 18
24 their lives depend upon us 19
27 nor has he taken revenge upon us *
35 to take revenge upon our enemies. *
9: 9 send thy wrath upon their heads 18
11 nor thy might upon men of strength 20
11:22 to bring destruction upon those . . 20
14:18 brought disgrace upon . . King Nebuchadnezzar! 18
AEs 13:15 the eyes of our foes are upon us to annihilate us *
17 have mercy upon thy inheritance *
Wis 3: 9 because grace and mercy are upon his elect *
5: 6 the sun did not rise upon us. *
8:17 and thought upon them in my mind *
12:22 we may meditate upon thy goodness when we judge *
14:11 a visitation also upon the heathen idols 20
18:20 a plague came upon the multitude in the desert *
24 thy majesty on the diadem upon his head. *
19:15 punishment of some sort will come upon the former *
Sir 10: 5 confers his honor upon the person of the scribe. *
17:11 He bestowed knowledge upon them *
27:27 If a man does evil, it will roll back upon him 18
33:22 bring no stain upon your honor. 20
36: 1 Have mercy upon us, O Lord, the God of all *
12 Have mercy, O Lord, upon the people *
12 Have mercy . . upon Israel *
37:24 A wise man will have praise heaped upon him *
38:31 All these rely upon their hands 18
43:11 Look upon the rainbow, and praise him who made it *
45:12 with a gold crown upon his turban 21
47: 6 when the glorious diadem was bestowed upon him. *
20 You put stain upon your honor 20
49: 3 He set his heart upon the Lord 26
Bar 2:20 For thou hast sent thy anger and thy wrath upon us 18
LJr 1:10 spend it upon themselves 18
18 just as the gates are shut on every side upon a man *
1Mc 4:45 lest it bring reproach upon them *
6:43 he supposed that the king was upon it. 20
46 it fell to the ground upon him and he died. 21
7: 7 brought upon us and upon the land of the king *
18 fear and dread of them fell upon all the people 18
8: 4 inflicted great disaster upon them 20
11:13 Thus he put two crowns upon his head 25
14:27 and put it upon pillars on Mount Zion 20
48 to inscribe this decree upon bronze tablets 20
15: 9 we will bestow great honor upon you *
2Mc 2: 2 upon seeing the gold and silver statues *
4:14 no longer intent upon their service at the altar 25
15 the highest value upon Greek forms of prestige. *
21 upon arriving at Joppa *
9: 4 turning upon the Jews the injury 18
10:30 they showered . . thunderbolts upon the enemy 18
14:15 they sprinkled dust upon their heads *
15:18 Their concern for wives . . lay upon them less heavily *
3Mc 1: 9 Then, upon entering the place *
2:16 bestowed your glory upon your people Israel 20
4: 4 some . . reflected upon the uncertainty of life *
5:11 the Lord sent upon the king a portion of sleep 18
27 upon receiving the report *
35 Then the Jews, upon hearing what the king had said *
6: 4 manifesting . . your mercy upon the nation of Israel. *
17 and brought an uncontrollable terror upon the army. *
7:10 Upon receiving this letter the Jews *
4Mc 8:18 and venture upon a disobedience that brings death? *
10: 8 his vertebrae were being dislocated upon it 25
15: 4 We impress upon the character of a small child 18

upon עַל

Gen 1:2, 11, 15, 17, 26, 28, 29; 2:5, 21; 3:14; 6:12, 17; 7:3, 4, 6, 10, 12, 17, 18, 19, 21^2, 23, 24; 8:4, 17, 19; 9:2^2, 16, 17, 23; 11:4; 15:11, 12; 22:2; 24:15, 18, 61; 26:10; 27:12, 13, 16^2; 29:3; 30:3; 31:10, 12, 34; 32:32; 34:25, 27; 35:5, 20; 37:27; 38:30; 42:21, 36; 43:18; 44:21; 45:14^2, 15; 47:20, 31; 48:14^2, 17, 18; 50:23, Exd 1:16; 3:12; 5:8, 9, 21; 7:5; 8:5, 7; 9:19, 22, 23; 10:12; 11:1^2, 5; 12:13; 14:26^3, 30; 15:16, 19, 26; 17:12, 16; 19:11, 16, 18, 20; 20:5, 25; 21:22, 30; 22:3; 24:8; 25:11, 22, 37; 26:32^2, 34; 27:4, 7; 28:8, 12^2, 28, 29, 30^2, 35, 38^2, 43^2; 29:6, 10, 12, 15, 19, 20^4, 21^2, 38; 30:10, 32; 32:16, 20, 21, 29, 34, 35; 33:16, 21; 34:1, 7, 28, 35; 37:16; 39:5, 21, 25, 26, 30; 40:27, 29, 35, 38, Lev 1:4, 7, 8^2, 12^2, 17; 2:1, 15; 3:2, 5^2, 8, 13; 4:10, 15, 24, 33, 35; 5:11, 12^2; 6:9, 10, 12, 13; 8:7, 9, 14, 19, 24, 30^2; 9:13, 17, 18, 20, 24; 10:6, 7; 11:20, 29, 32, 34, 35, 37, 41, 42, 44, 46; 14:7, 17; 15:20^2, 22, 23; 16:2^2, 8, 13, 15, 19, 21^2, 22; 17:11; 21:10, 12; 22:22; 24:4, 6, 14; 26:21, 25, 30, 35, Num 1:53; 4:7, 10, 14; 5:14^2, 15, 30; 6:5, 7, 19, 27; 7:89; 8:7, 10, 12; 11:9, 11, 17^2, 25^3, 26, 29; 14:18^3; 15:38; 16:7, 17, 18; 17:2, 3; 18:5, 17; 19:2, 13, 15, 18^4, 19, 20; 21:20; 22:30; 24:2; 27:18, 23; 30:14; 35:23, Deu 2:25; 4:10, 13, 26, 32; 5:9, 22; 6:6, 8; 8:4; 11:18, 20, 25; 12:1, 2^2, 16, 24; 19:10; 21:23; 22:6^2, 14, 19; 26:6; 27:3, 5, 8, 12, 13; 28:2, 15, 24, 45, 48, 56, 61; 29:27; 30:1, 7; 32:2^2, 23; 33:10, 29; 34:9, Jos 2:9; 4:5; 7:6^2, 10; 8:31, 32; 9:20; 10:11, 24, 26; 11:4, 7; 18:13; 22:20; 23:15; 24:7, Jdg 3:10; 6:28; 7:12; 9:5, 24^2, 33, 44, 53; 11:29, 38; 13:5, 19; 14:6, 19; 15:14; 16:9, 12, 14, 17, 19, 20, 29^2, 30^2; 18:19; 19:28; 20:34, 41, Rut 3:15, 1Sm 4:12, 13, 19; 5:7^2; 6:7; 9:25; 10:6, 10; 11:2, 6, 7; 13:18; 16:16; 17:6; 18:4; 19:20, 23; 20:9, 25, 31; 23:27; 25:24; 26:12; 30:14^3; 31:4, 5, 2Sm 1:2, 6, 16, 19, 21, 24, 25; 3:29; 4:11; 6:8; 11:2, 21; 14:7; 15:14, 32; 16:8, 22; 17:2, 12, 19; 18:9; 19:7, 26; 20:8; 21:10^2; 22:11, 28; 23:2, 1Kg 1:13, 17, 20, 24, 30, 35, 46, 47; 2:12, 32; 3:4; 5:5; 6:32^2, 35; 7:2^2, 3, 16, 17, 18^2, 19, 20, 22, 25^2, 29, 42, 43; 8:25, 36; 9:5, 9, 25; 12:4, 9, 11, 32; 13:2^3, 3; 17:14, 19, 20, 21; 18:28; 20:30; 21:27, 29, 2Kg 3:15, 22, 27^2; 4:29, 31, 34^5, 35; 6:26, 30^2; 7:6, 17; 9:37; 11:12; 12:12; 13:13, 16; 14:20; 15:12; 16:13, 15^2, 17; 18:23; 21:12; 22:16, 20; 23:6, 16, 20^2, 33; 25:17, 1Ch 6:49^2; 9:27; 10:3, 4, 5; 12:8; 13:7; 14:17; 16:40; 21:16, 26; 27:24; 28:5; 29:25, 30, 2Ch 1:6; 4:4^2, 13, 14; 6:13^2, 16, 27; 7:3, 22; 8:12; 10:4, 9, 11; 13:18; 14:14; 15:1; 16:10; 17:10; 18:16; 19:7, 10; 20:9, 12, 14; 23:11, 20; 24:9, 18; 25:28; 28:11, 13; 29:23; 32:5, 12, 18, 25, 26; 33:11, 16; 34:24^2, 28, Ezr 3:2, 3^2; 7:6, 9, 28; 8:18, 22, 31; 9:5, 13, Neh 2:8, 18; 5:15, 18; 9:1, 4, 13, 33; 10:32, 34; 12:31, 38; 13:18, Est 5:14; 8:17; 9:2, 3, 25, 27, 31, Job 1:17, 19; 2:11, 12; 3:4, 5; 5:10^2; 7:1; 9:33; 13:11; 14:3; 15:27; 16:14, 15; 18:15; 19:8, 25; 20:4, 23, 25; 21:5, 9, 17; 24:18, 23; 25:3; 26:7, 10; 27:9; 29:3, 4, 13, 22; 30:15; 31:1, 10; 33:7, 15, 19; 34:21; 36:28; 37:15; 38:5, 24; 39:23; 41:23, 33; 42:11, Ps 3:8; :6; 4:2; 6:4; 8:10; 1:5; 2:9, 10; 4:2^2; 9:3^2; 2:4, 8; 3:22; 7:29; 0:2; 5:3; 3:2; 5:3, 4, 15; 0:8; 2:3; 3:6; 9:24, 27; 1:6; 8:24, 27; 0:17; 8:7, 17; 9:19; 0:17^2; 03:17; 05:38; 07:40; 08:9; 25:3; 28:6; 29:3; 32:18; 33:2^2; 36:6; 39:5; 40:10, Prv 1:27; 6:15, 21, 28; 19:12; 24:25, Ecc 5:2; 6:1; 8:6; 9:12, Sng 2:8, 17; 3:1; 5:5, 15; 8:5, 6^2, 9, 14, Isa 5:6; 6:1; 7:17^3; 8:1; 9:6, 7; 10:20^2; 11:2; 14:25; 15:9; 16:9, 12; 18:2, 6^2; 19:8; 21:8; 22:25; 23:17; 24:17, 20; 28:22; 29:10; 30:16^2, 25, 32; 31:4^2; 32:11, 12, 15; 34:5^2; 35:10; 36:8; 42:1, 5, 25; 44:3; 45:12; 46:7; 47:9, 11^2; 51:11; 52:7; 53:5; 57:7; 58:14; 59:21; 60:1, 2^2; 61:1; 62:6; 63:3; 65:3, 7^2; 66:12^2, 20, Jer 1:14; 2:20, 37; 5:12, 15; 6:11^2, 23, 26; 7:20^2; 9:22; 10:25^2; 11:8; 12:12; 13:4; 14:16; 15:8; 16:17; 17:18; 18:22; 19:3, 13, 15; 23:12, 17, 19, 40; 24:6; 25:5, 13; 26:15, 19; 28:14; 30:18, 23; 31:19, 33; 32:42; 36:4, 30, 31^2; 42:17; 44:2^2; 45:5; 46:21, 25; 48:32, 37; 49:5, 8, 37; 50:35, 42; 51:35, 52, 56^2, 64; 52:22^2, 23, Lam 1:14; 4:8, Ezk 1:3, 28; 2:1, 2; 3:14, 22, 24, 25; 4:1, 4^3, 8, 9; 5:16, 17; 6:3; 7:2, 3, 8, 26; 8:1, 10; 9:4, 6, 8^2; 11:5, 8, 13, 23; 12:6, 7; 13:18; 14:17, 19, 22^2; 16:14; 17:22; 18:15, 20^2; 20:8, 13, 21; 21:31^2; 22:20, 21, 22, 31; 23:7, 8, 9, 14, 16, 20, 41, 42, 49; 24:7, 11; 26:16; 27:11^2; 28:7, 18; 29:5, 7, 8; 30:15; 31:13; 32:5, 8, 27; 33:2, 3, 10; 36:10, 11, 12, 18, 25, 29; 37:1, 2, 6^2, 8, 10, 16; 38:8, 20, 22; 39:4, 14, 17, 29; 40:1; 43:12, 18, 24, 27; 44:18, Dan 8:17; 9:11, 12, 13, 14, 17, 27; 10:7, 16; 11:40, Hos 4:13; 5:1, 10; 7:14; 9:1; 10:8; 12:14; 14:3, Jol 2:2, 29, Ams 2:8; 3:9; 4:2, 7^2; 5:8, 9, 11; 6:4^2; 8:10; 9:4, 6^2, 15, Obd 1:15, 16, Jon 1:7, 12; 4:8, Mic 1:3; 2:1; 3:6, 11^2; 5:1, 7; 7:3, Nah 3:19, Hab 2:2, 16; 3:8, 19, Zep 1:12; 2:2^2; 3:7, 8, Hag 1:11, Zec 1:8; 3:9; 6:13; 12:4; 14:17, 18, Mal 1:7; 2:3

upon ἐπί

Mic 5:5, Mat 7:24, 26; 10:13, 27; 11:29; 12:18, 28; 13:7; 23:35, 36; 24:2, Mrk 4:16, 20, 26, 31; 6:39; 8:25; 10:16; 11:7; 13:2, Lke 1:12, 35; 2:25, 40; 3:22; 4:18; 5:36; 6:48; 9:38; 10:6; 11:20; 12:3, 49; 13:4; 19:43, 44; 21:6, 23, 25, 34, 35^2; 24:49, Joh 1:51; 3:36; 11:38; 12:14, Act 1:8; 2:17, 30; 4:29, 33; 5:5, 11^2, 28; 7:57; 8:24; 10:11; 12:21; 13:11^2; 15:10; 18:6; 19:17; 26:16, Rom 2:2; 4:9^2; 9:28; 12:20, 2Co 12:9, Gal 6:16, Eph 2:20; 5:6, Php 2:17, 27, 1Th 2:16, Tit 3:6, Heb 6:7, Jas 2:21, 1Pe 1:13; 3:12; 4:14, Rev 1:17; 2:24; 3:3, 10; 4:4; 5:13; 6:10; 7:3, 10, 15; 8:3; 9:4; 12:3; 13:1^2; 14:15, 16; 16:2; 17:1; 19:11, 19, 21; 20:11; 21:5, 1Es 1:4; 5:49; 6:32; 8:15, 61, Tob 3:3; 11:11; 12:16, Jdt 2:28; 4:15; 6:19; 8:24; 9:1; 11:11; 14:1; 15:3, 5, AEs 11:5, 8; 14:16; 15:7, Wis 7:3; 11:22; 12:27; 18:24, Sir 1:8, 9; 3:27; 4:17; 17:2, 8, 19; 18:11; 22:27; 30:18^2; 31:12, 19; 34:16; 36:2; 38:8; 40:1, 5, 8, 15; 43:19, 20; 44:23; 46:6; 47:20, 25; 48:2; 50:7, 17, Bar 1:10; 2:7, 9; 3:20, 37; 4:25; 5:5, LJr 1:13, 48, 72, Aza 1:5, 33, Sus 1:34, 1Mc 1:30, 54, 59, 64; 2:23, 24, 30; 3:25; 4:2; 6:7, 37^3, 39; 7:4; 8:31; 9:40; 12:26; 13:29, 32; 15:12, 2Mc 5:5^2; 9:18; 10:17, 26, 28; 14:45, 3Mc 2:27; 6:3^2, 21, 4Mc 9:12; 11:18; 15:20^3; 16:20; 17:8

upon *See also* attendance, bear, beat, bestow, blow, bring, build, call, cast, chance, close, come, compassion, confer, converge, dawn, depend, enter, enthrone, fall, feed, fix, gird, hang, impose, inflict, intent, lay, look, mercy, place, pour, press, presume, prevail, prey, pronounce, put, rain, reflect, rely, rest, rush, send, set, sit, spit, sprinkle, take, think, trample, tread, turn, up, wait.

upon this 1. ὅθεν

3Mc 5:42 Upon this the king . . firmly swore an . . oath 1

upper 1. עִלִּי 2. עֶלְיוֹן 3. רֶכֶב 4. ἄνω 5. ἀνωτερικός 6. ἐπάνω 7. supernus

Jos 15:19 gave . . the upper springs and the lower springs. 1
16: 5 was At'aroth-ad'dar as far as Upper Beth-hor'on 2
Jdg 1:15 Caleb gave her the upper springs and the lower 1
9:53 woman threw an upper millstone upon Abim'elech's 3
1Sm 9:24 the cook took up the leg and the upper portion *
2Sm 11:21 Did not a woman cast an upper millstone upon him 3
2Kg 15:35 He built the upper gate of the house of the LORD. 2
18:17 came and stood by the conduit of the upper pool 2
1Ch 7:24 who built both Lower and Upper Beth-hor'on 2
2Ch 8: 5 He also built Upper Beth-Hor'on and Lower 2
23:20 marching through the upper gate 2
27: 3 He built the upper gate of the house of the LORD 2
32:30 closed the upper outlet of the waters of Gihon 2
Neh 3:25 projecting from the upper house of the king 2
Ps 74: 5 At the upper entrance they hacked the wooden *
Isa 7: 3 the conduit of the upper pool on the highway 2
36: 2 the upper pool on the highway to the Fuller's 2
Jer 20: 2 the upper Benjamin Gate of the house of the LORD. 2
36:10 which was in the upper court, at the entry 2
Ezk 9: 2 six men came from the direction of the upper gate 2
42: 5 Now the upper chambers were narrower 2
6 the upper chambers were set back from the ground *
Act 19: 1 Paul passed through the upper country 5
2Es 8:20 and whose upper chambers are in the air 7
Jdt 1: 8 Upper Galilee and the great Plain of Esdraelon 4
2:21 mountain which is to the north of Upper Cilicia. 4
1Mc 3:37 and went through the upper provinces. 6
6: 1 Antiochus was going through the upper provinces 6
2Mc 9:23 made expeditions into the upper country 4
25 when I hastened off to the upper provinces 6

upper *See also* chamber, hand, lip, millstone, room.

uppermost 1. עֶלְיוֹן

Gen 40:17 in the uppermost basket there were all sorts 1

upright 1. טוֹב 2. ישׁר 3. יָשָׁר 4. יֹשֶׁר 5. עַל עֹמֶד 6. עמד 7. צַדִּיק 8. תֹּם 9. δίκαιος 10. δικαίως 11. ὀρθός 12. ὀρθόω

Exd 26:15 you shall make upright frames 6
36:20 he made the upright frames for the tabernacle 6
2Ch 19:11 may the LORD be with the upright! 1
29:34 for the Levites were more upright in heart 3
Job 1: 1 was Job; and that man was blameless and upright 3
8 a blameless and upright man, who fears God 3
2: 3 a blameless and upright man, who fears God 3
4: 7 Or where were the upright cut off? 3
8: 6 if you are pure and upright 3
Ps 7:10 with God, who saves the upright in heart. 3
11: 2 to shoot in the dark at the upright in heart; 3
7 the upright shall behold his face. 3
25: 8 Good and upright is the LORD; 3
32:11 shout for joy, all you upright in heart! 3
33: 1 O you righteous! Praise befits the upright. 3
4 For the word of the LORD is upright; 3
36:10 thy salvation to the upright of heart! 3
37:37 Mark the blameless man, and behold the upright 3
64:10 Let all the upright in heart glory! 3
73: 1 Truly God is good to the upright *
78:72 With upright heart he tended them 8
92:15 to show that the LORD is upright; 3
94:15 all the upright in heart will follow it. 3
97:11 Light dawns . . and joy for the upright in heart. 3
107:42 The upright see it and are glad; 3
111: 1 company of the upright, in the congregation. 3
112: 2 generation of the upright will be blessed. 3
4 Light rises in the darkness for the upright; 3
119: 7 I will praise thee with an upright heart 4
125: 4 to those who are upright in their hearts! 3
140:13 upright shall dwell in thy presence. 3
Prv 2: 7 he stores up sound wisdom for the upright; 3
21 For the upright will inhabit the land 3
3:32 but the upright are in his confidence. 3
10:29 LORD is a stronghold to him whose way is upright 8
11: 3 The integrity of the upright guides them 3
6 The righteousness of the upright delivers them 3
11 By the blessing of the upright a city is exalted 3
12: 6 but the mouth of the upright delivers men. 3
13: 6 Righteousness guards him whose way is upright 8
14: 9 scorns the wicked, but the upright enjoy his favor. 3
11 but the tent of the upright will flourish. 3

15: 8 but the prayer of the upright is his delight. 3
19 but the path of the upright is a level highway. 3
16:17 The highway of the upright turns aside from evil; 3
21:18 faithless for the upright. 3
28:10 misleads the upright into an evil way will fall 3
Ecc 7:29 God made man upright, but they have sought out 3
Dan 10:11 stand upright, for now I have been sent to you. 5
Hos 14: 9 and the upright walk in them 7
Mic 7: 2 and there is none upright among men; 3
4 the most upright of them a thorn hedge. 3
Hab 2: 4 he whose soul is not upright in him shall fail 2
Act 10:22 a centurion, an upright and God-fearing man 9
Tit 1: 8 lover of goodness, master of himself, upright 9
2:12 to live sober, upright, and godly lives in this world 10
1Es 1:23 the deeds of Josiah were upright 12
LJr 1:27 If any one sets one of them upright 11
3Mc 3: 5 the good deeds of upright people 9
4Mc 6: 7 he kept his reason upright and unswerving. 11

upright *See also* stand.

upright man 1. יָשָׁר

Job 17: 8 Upright men are appalled at this 1
23: 7 There an upright man could reason with him 1
Prv 21:29 but an upright man considers his ways. 1

uprightly 1. יָשָׁר 2. יֹשֶׁר 3. מֵישָׁר 4. תָּמִים 5. δικαιοσύνη

Ps 37:14 to slay those who walk uprightly; 1
58: 1 you gods? Do you judge the sons of men uprightly? 3
84:11 LORD withhold from those who walk uprightly. 4
Ecc 12:10 and uprightly he wrote words of truth. 2
Isa 33:15 He who walks righteously and speaks uprightly 3
Mic 2: 7 Do not my words do good to him who walks uprightly? 1
Tob 4: 5 Live uprightly all the days of your life 5
7 Give alms . . to all who live uprightly 5

uprightness 1. יָשָׁר 2. יֹשֶׁר 3. יְשָׁרָה 4. מִישׁוֹר 5. מֵישָׁר 6. נְכֹחַ 7. צְדָקָה 8. ἀγαθότης 9. εὐθύτης 10. directio

Deu 9: 5 Not because of . . the uprightness of your heart 2
1Kg 3: 6 and in uprightness of heart toward thee; and thou 3
9: 4 walk . . with integrity of heart and uprightness 2
1Ch 29:17 that thou . . hast pleasure in uprightness; 5
17 in the uprightness of my heart I have freely 2
Job 33: 3 My words declare the uprightness of my heart 2
Ps 25:21 May integrity and uprightness preserve me 2
111: 8 performed with faithfulness and uprightness. 1
Prv 2:13 who forsake the paths of uprightness 2
4:11 I have led you in the paths of uprightness. 2
14: 2 He who walks in uprightness fears the LORD 1
Isa 26:10 in the land of uprightness he deals perversely 6
57: 2 rest in their beds who walk in their uprightness. 6
59:14 for truth . . and uprightness cannot enter. 6
Jer 4: 2 in truth, in justice, and in uprightness 7
Mal 2: 6 He walked with me in peace and uprightness 4
2Es 6:32 for the Mighty One has seen your uprightness 10
Wis 1: 1 think of the Lord with uprightness 8
9: 3 and pronounce judgment in uprightness of soul 9

uprising 1. ἐπισύστασις

1Es 5:73 by plots and demagoguery and uprisings 1

uproar 1. הום 2. המה 3. הָמוֹן 4. שָׁאוֹן 5. βοή 6. θόρυβος

1Sm 4:14 When Eli heard . . he said, "What is this uproar? 3
1Kg 1:41 he said, "What does this uproar in the city mean? 2
45 there rejoicing, so that the city is in an uproar. 1
Ps 74:23 the uproar of thy adversaries which goes up 4
Isa 13: 4 Hark, an uproar of kingdoms, of nations gathering 4
66: 6 an uproar from the city! A voice from the temple! 4
Ams 2: 2 and Moab shall die amid uproar, amid shouting 4
Act 20: 1 After the uproar ceased 6
21:34 because of the uproar 6
3Mc 1:28 cry of the crowds resulted in an immense uproar; 5

set in an uproar 1. θορυβέω

Act 17: 5 they gathered a crowd, set the city in an uproar 1

uproot 1. נתשׁ 2. עקר 3. שׁרשׁ 4. ἐκριζόω 5. ἐκριζωτής

Deu 29:28 LORD uprooted them from their land in anger 1
Ps 52: 5 he will uproot you from the land of the living. 3
Jer 24: 6 I will plant them, and not uproot them. 1
31:40 It shall not be uprooted or overthrown any more 1
Zep 2: 4 and Ekron shall be uprooted. 2
Jde 1:12 trees in late autumn, twice dead, uprooted; 4
Wis 4: 4 they will be uprooted. 4
Sir 3: 9 a mother's curse uproots their foundations. 4
4Mc 3: 5 For reason does not uproot the emotions 5

upset 1. ἀνατρέπω 2. διαστρέφω

2Ti 2:18 They are upsetting the faith of some. 1
Tit 1:11 since they are upsetting whole families 1
Sir 11:34 he will upset you with commotion 2

upside down 1. לְמַעְלָה 2. עַל פְּנֵי

Jdg 7:13 struck it . . and turned it upside down 1
2Kg 21:13 wiping it and turning it upside down. 2

upsurge

2Sm 1:21 be no dew or rain . . nor upsurging of the deep! •

upward 1. גבה 2. לְמַעְלָה 3. מַעַל 4. מַעְלָה 5. מַעְלָה 6. מָרוֹם 7. ἄνω 8. sursum

Exd 30:14 from twenty years old and upward, shall give 5
38:26 from twenty years old and upward, 603,550 men. 5
Lev 27: 7 if the person is 60 years old and upward 3
Num 1: 3 from twenty years old and upward, all in Israel 3
18 twenty years old and upward, head by head 3
20 every male from twenty years old and upward 3
22 every male from twenty years old and upward 3
24 from twenty years old and upward 3
26 from twenty years old and upward, every man able 5
28 from twenty years old and upward, every man able 3
30 from twenty years old and upward, every man able 3
32 number of names, from twenty years old and upward 3
34 from twenty years old and upward, every man able 3
36 from twenty years old and upward, every man able 3
38 from twenty years old and upward, every man able 3
40 from twenty years old and upward, every man able 3
42 from twenty years old and upward, every man able 3
45 from twenty years old and upward, every man able 3
3:15 every male from a month old and upward you shall 3
22 all the males from a month old and upward was 7,500 5
28 from a month old and upward, there were 8,600 5
34 males from a month old and upward was 6,200. 5
39 all the males from a month old and upward 3
40 from a month old and upward 5
43 first-born males . . from a month old and upward 3
8:24 from 25 years old and upward they shall go 3
14:29 numbered from twenty years old and upward, who 5
26: 2 from twenty years old and upward 3
4 people, from twenty years old and upward 5
62 23,000, every male from a month old and upward; 5
32:11 none . . from twenty years old and upward 5
Deu 28:13 you shall tend upward only, and not downward; 2
Jdg 1:36 the ascent of Akrab'bim, from Sela and upward. 3
1Sm 9: 2 from his shoulders upward he was taller than any 4
10:23 he was taller than . . from his shoulders upward. 3
2Kg 19:30 again take root downward, and bear fruit upward; 2
1Ch 23: 3 The Levites, 30 years old and upward, were numbered 5
24 from twenty years old and upward 5
27 of the Levites from twenty years old and upward 5
2Ch 25: 5 He mustered those twenty years old and upward 3
31:16 males from three years old and upwards 2
17 Levites from twenty years old and upwards 2
Ezr 3: 8 Levites, from twenty years old and upward 5
Job 5: 7 man is born to trouble as the sparks fly upward. 1
Prv 15:24 The wise man's path leads upward to life, that he 2
Isa 8:21 curse . . their God, and turn their faces upward; 2
37:31 take root downward, and bear fruit upward; 2
38:14 My eyes are weary with looking upward. 6
Ezk 1:27 upward from what had the appearance of his loins 2
41: 7 on the side of the temple a stairway led upward 2
43:15 from the altar hearth projecting upward 2
Php 3:14 the prize of the upward call of God in Christ 7
2Es 6:41 that one part might move upward 8

upward *See also* go, project, roll.

urge 1. אוץ 2. אכף 3. אלץ 4. דחף 5. חזק בְּ 6. נהג וְהלך 7. סות 8. פגע 9. פצר 10. פרץ 11. ἐπισπεύδω 12. ἐποτρύνω 13. κατασπεύδω 14. ὀτρύνω 15. παραινέω 16. παρακαλέω 17. παράκειμαι 18. πείθω 19. προτρέπω

Gen 19: 3 he urged them strongly; 9
15 When morning dawned, the angels urged Lot 1
33:11 Thus he urged him, and he took it. 9
Jos 15:18 she urged him to ask her father for a field; 7
Jdg 1:14 to him, she urged him to ask her father for a field; 7
16:16 pressed him hard . . and urged him, his soul was 3
19: 7 his father-in-law urged him, till he lodged there 9
1Sm 28:23 his servants, together with the woman, urged him; 9
2Kg 2:17 when they urged him till he was ashamed, he said 9
4: 8 a wealthy woman . . who urged him to eat some food. 5
24 Urge the beast on; do not slacken the pace for me 6
5:16 And he urged him to take it, but he refused. 9
23 he urged him, and tied up two talents of silver 10
Est 8:14 rode out in haste, urged by the king's command; 4
Prv 16:26 worker's . . mouth urges him on. 2
Jer 36:25 Gemari'ah urged the king not to burn the scroll 8
Act 13:43 urged them to continue in the grace of God. 18
25: 2 they urged him 16
27:33 Paul urged them all to take some food, saying 16
34 Therefore I urge you to take some food 16
1Co 4:16 I urge you, then, be imitators of me. 16
16:12 I strongly urged him to visit you 16
16 I urge you to be subject to such men 16
2Co 8: 6 Accordingly we have urged Titus 16
9: 5 So I thought it necessary to urge the brethren 16
12:18 I urged Titus to go, and sent the brother with him. 16
1Ti 1: 3 As I urged you when I was going to Macedonia 16
2: 1 First of all, then, I urge that . . 16
6: 2 Teach and urge these duties. 16
Tit 2: 6 Likewise urge the younger men 16
Heb 13:19 I urge you the more earnestly to do this 16
1Es 1:27 The Lord is with me, urging me on! 11
Jdt 15: 4 to urge all to rush out upon their enemies •
Sir 0: 2 You are urged therefore to read with good will 16
1Mc 13:21 urging him to come to them 13
2Mc 4:34 Therefore Menelaus . . urged him to kill Onias. 16
6:12 Now I urge those who read this book 16
21 urged him to bring meat of his own providing 16
7:25 urged her to advise the youth to save himself. 15
26 After much urging on his part 15
9:26 I therefore urge and beseech you 16
11: 7 he urged the others to risk their lives with him 19
15 Maccabeus . . agreed to all that Lysias urged. 16
13: 3 and with utter hypocrisy urged Antiochus on 16
14:25 he urged him to marry and have children; 16
3Mc 5:17 he urged them to give themselves over to revelry 15
36 king . . urged the guests to return to their celebrating. 16
46 and urged the king on to the matter at hand. 14
7: 3 frequently urging us with malicious intent 17
4Mc 5:14 When the tyrant urged him in this fashion 12
10: 1 many repeatedly urged him to save himself 16
15:12 Instead, the mother urged them on 19
16:13 she implored them and urged them on to death 19

frenzied urge 1. οἰστρηλασία

4Mc 2: 4 to rule over the frenzied urge of sexual desire 1

insistently urge 1. προσεδρεύω

1Mc 11:40 and insistently urged him to hand Antiochus over 1

urgent 1. אוץ 2. חזק 3. ἀναγκαῖος 4. ἐπίκειμαι 5. ἐπισχύω 6. ἐφίστημι 7. κατασπεύδω

Exd 5:13 The taskmasters were urgent, saying, "Complete 1
12:33 the Egyptians were urgent with the people 2
Lke 23: 5 they were urgent, saying, "He stirs up the people 5
23 they were urgent, demanding with loud cries 4
2Ti 4: 2 be urgent in season and out of season, convince 6
Tit 3:14 so as to help cases of urgent need 3
Sir 28:11 urgent strife sheds blood. 7

urgently 1. שכם

Jer 26: 5 the prophets whom I send to you urgently 1

urgently *See also* need.

urine 1. שַׁיִן

2Kg 18:27 to eat their own dung and to drink their own urine? 1
Isa 36:12 to eat their own dung and drink their own urine? 1

urn 1. στάμνος

Heb 9: 4 which contained a golden urn holding the manna 1

use 1. אמר 2. דבר 3. היה 4. לקח 5. מְלָאכָה 6. מַעֲשֶׂה 7. מצא 8. משׁל 9. עשׂה 10. עשׂה מְלָאכָה 11. שׂוּם 12. שׁרת 13. ἀναλίσκομαι 14. ἀπόχρησις 15. γίνομαι 16. δαπανάω 17. διά 18. δίαιτα 19. εἶπον 20. εἰς 21. ἐν 22. ἔργον 23. ἔχω 24. ἵνα 25. κατά 26. καταχράομαι 27. ποιέω 28. προσφέρω 29. συμφέρω 30. τίθημι 31. χράομαι 32. χρεία 33. χρησιμεύω 34. χρῆσις

Exd 35:21 offering to be used for the tent of meeting 5
24 found acacia wood of any use in the work 5
38:24 All the gold that was used for the work 9
Lev 7:24 The fat . . may be put to any other use 5
11:32 any vessel that is used for any purpose 9
13:51 whatever be the use of the skin 9
Num 4:12 the vessels . . which are used in the sanctuary 12
14 utensils . . which are used for the service 12
7: 5 that they may be used in doing the service 3
10: 2 shall use them for summoning the congregation •
35:23 or used a stone, by which a man may die •
Jdg 16:11 bind me with new ropes that have not been used 10
2Kg 25:14 vessels of bronze used in the temple service 12
1Ch 28:15 the use of each lampstand in the service •
2Ch 4: 6 to rinse off what was used for the burnt offering 6
24: 7 used all the dedicated things . . for the Ba'als. 9
Ps 76: 5 all the men of war were unable to use their hands. 7
Prv 18:23 poor use entreaties . . rich answer roughly. 2
Ecc 2: 2 I said . . of pleasure, "What use is it? 9
Jer 2:22 you wash yourself with lye and use much soap •
23:31 who use their tongues and say, 'Says the LORD.' 4
29:22 Because of them this curse shall be used by all 4
31:23 they shall use these words in the land of Judah 1
46:11 In vain you have used many medicines; •
52:18 the vessels of bronze used in the temple service; 12
Ezk 5: 1 take a sharp sword; use it as a barber's razor 4
7:20 beautiful ornament they used for vainglory 11
12:23 they shall no more use it as a proverb in Israel. •
15: 5 Behold, when it was whole, it was used for nothing; 9
5 it is charred, can it ever be used for anything! 9
18: 3 proverb shall no more be used by you in Israel. 8
48:15 in length, shall be for ordinary use for the city •
Hos 2: 8 silver and gold which they used for Ba'al. 9
Mrk 4:30 what parable shall we use for it? 30
Joh 10: 6 This figure Jesus used with them 19
Act 14: 8 there was a man sitting, who could not use his feet; •
Rom 3:13 they use their tongues to deceive. •
12: 6 Having gifts . . let us use them •
2Co 13:10 not have to be severe in my use of the authority 25
Gal 5:13 only do not use your freedom as an opportunity •

Col 2:22 things which all perish as they are used 14
1Th 2: 5 never used either words of flattery, as you know 15
1Ti 1: 8 if any one uses it lawfully 31
5:23 No longer drink only water, but use a little wine 31
2Ti 2:20 some for noble use, some for ignoble. 20
21 he will be a vessel for noble use 20
Heb 9:21 both the tent and all the vessels used in worship. *
1Pe 2:16 without using your freedom as a pretext for evil; 23
2Jn 1:12 I would rather not use paper and ink 17
1Es 6:30 for daily use as the priests . . may indicate 13
8:17 given you for the use of the temple of your God 32
Tob 6: 6 of what use is the liver and heart and gall *
Jdt 11:12 determined to use all that God . . has forbidden 16
12:15 received . . for her daily use 18
Wis 4: 3 will be of no use 33
15: 7 both the vessels that serve clean uses 22
7 those for contrary uses *
7 which shall be the use of each of these 34
15 these have neither the use of their eyes to see 34
Sir 0: 3 using . . great watchfulness and skill 28
13: 4 A rich man will exploit you if you can be of use 33
14: 3 man; and of what use is property to an envious man? 24
18: 8 What is man, and of what use is he? 34
23:15 A man accustomed to use insulting words *
26:10 when she finds liberty, she use it to her hurt. 31
30:19 Of what use to an idol is an offering of fruit? 29
38:33 they are not found using proverbs. 21
39:21 everything has been created for its use. 32
LJr 1:28 The priests . . use the money 26
1Mc 1:58 They kept using violence against Israel 27
11:20 he built many engines of war to use against it. *
2Mc 4:19 Those . . thought best not to use it for sacrifice 31
6:21 of his own providing, proper for him to use 31
3Mc 4:20 the paper and the pens they used for writing 31
4Mc 8:16 what arguments might have been used 31
13:13 let us use our bodies as a bulwark for the law. 31

use *See also* make.

use a name for a curse 1. שׁבע בְּ
Ps 102: 8 those who deride me use my name for a curse. 1

use a proverb 1. משׁל
Ezk 16:44 one who uses proverbs will use this proverb 1

use as perfume 1. ריח
Exd 30:38 Whoever makes any like it to use as perfume 1

use divination 1. קסם
Ezk 21:21 at the head of the two ways, to use divination; 1

use flattery 1. כנה
Job 32:21 show partiality to any person or use flattery 1

use in battle 1. *πόλεμος*
1Mc 3:12 and used it in battle the rest of his life. 1

use in the king's service 1. אֲחַשְׁתְּרָן
Est 8:10 horses that were used in the king's service 1
14 horses . . used in the king's service 1

menial use 1. *ἀτιμία*
Rom 9:21 one vessel for beauty and another for menial use? 1

no use 1. *ἀργός*
Wis 15:15 their feet are of no use for walking. 1

use the fruit 1. חלל
Deu 28:30 plant a vineyard, and you shall not use the fruit 1

use too many 1. *πλεονάζω*
Sir 20: 8 Whoever uses too many words will be loathed 1

use up 1. אכל 2. *δαπανάω* 3. *καταργέω*
Gen 31:15 he has been using up the money given for us. 1
Lke 13: 7 Cut it down; why should it use up the ground?' 3
Jdt 12: 4 your servant will not use up the things I have with me 2

what use 1. לָמָּה
Gen 25:32 I am about to die; of what use is a birthright to me? 1

use wisdom 1. חכם
Ecc 2:19 all for which I toiled and used my wisdom 1

used 1. היה 2. לָמַד 3. נסה
Exd 33: 7 Now Moses used to take the tent and pitch it *
11 Thus the LORD used to speak to Moses face to face *
Jdg 1: 7 kings . . used to pick up scraps under my table; 1
4: 5 She used to sit under the palm of Deb'orah between *
14:10 made a feast there; for so the young men used to do. *
1Sm 1: 3 Now this man used to go up year by year *
6 her rival used to provoke her sorely, to irritate *
7 as often as she went up . . she used to provoke her. *
2:19 his mother used to make for him a little robe *
17:34 Your servant used to keep sheep for his father; *
39 he tried in vain to go, for he was not used to them. 3
39 I cannot go with these; for I am not used to them. 3
2Sm 12: 3 it used to eat of his morsel, and drink from his cup *
14:26 for at the end of every year he used to cut it; *
15: 2 Ab'salom used to rise early and stand beside *
17:17 a maidservant used to go and tell them *
1Kg 3: 4 Solomon used to offer . . burnt offerings *
9:25 Solomon used to offer up burnt offerings *
10:22 the fleet . . used to come bringing gold, silver *
2Kg 6:10 Thus he used to warn him, so that he saved himself *
13:20 bands of Moabites used to invade . . in the spring *
2Ch 9:21 ships of Tarshish used to come bringing gold *
Job 1: 4 His sons used to go and hold a feast in the house *
18:19 no survivor where he used to live. *
Ps 55:14 We used to hold sweet converse together; *
Ecc 8:10 they used to go in and out of the holy place *
Isa 7:23 every place where there used to be 1,000 vines *
Jer 2:24 a wild ass used to the wilderness 2
Mrk 15: 6 he used to release for them one prisoner *
Joh 9: 8 Is not this the man who used to sit and beg? *
12: 6 he used to take what was put into it. *
1Pe 3: 5 the holy women . . used to adorn themselves *
Tob 1: 5 All the tribes . . used to sacrifice to the calf Baal *
14 I used to go into Media *
2:12 She used to send the product to the owners *
5:13 I used to know Ananias and Jathan *
Jdt 10: 3 which she used to wear *
Sus 1: 4 and the Jews used to come to him *
8 The two elders used to see her every day *
Bel 1:13 through which they used to go in regularly *
1Mc 3:30 the gifts which he used to give *
14:36 a citadel from which they used to sally forth *

where it used 1. מִשְׁפָּט
Jer 30:18 the palace shall stand where it used to be. 1

useful 1. צלח 2. *εὔθετος* 3. *εὔχρηστος* 4. *χρήσιμος*
Ezk 15: 4 it is charred, is it useful for anything? 1
2Ti 2:21 consecrated and useful to the master of the house 3
Phm 1:11 now he is indeed useful to you and to me.) 3
Heb 6: 7 useful to those for whose sake it is cultivated 2
Tob 4:18 do not despise any useful counsel. 4
Wis 13:11 with pleasing workmanship make a useful vessel 4
13 useful for nothing 3
2Mc 12:12 they might really be useful in many ways 4

very useful 1. *εὔχρηστος*
2Ti 4:11 he is very useful in serving me. 1

usefulness 1. *χρεία*
3Mc 5:32 our nurture in common and your usefulness. 1

useless 1. אֵין חֵפֶץ 2. *ἀνωφελής* 3. *ἀχρεῖος* 4. *ἄχρηστος*
Hos 8: 8 they are among the nations as a useless vessel. 1
Phm 1:11 (Formerly he was useless to you 4
Wis 1:11 Beware then of useless murmuring 2
2:11 what is weak proves itself to be useless. 4
3:11 their works are useless. 4
4: 5 their fruit will be useless, not ripe enough to eat 4
13:10 likenesses of animals, or a useless stone 4
Sir 16: 1 Do not desire a multitude of useless children 4
LJr 1:17 For just as one's dish is useless when it is broken 3
3Mc 3:29 shall become useless for all time 4

useless *See also* hang.

uselessness 1. *ἀνωφελής*
Heb 7:18 because of its weakness and uselessness 1

usher 1. *εἰσδέχομαι*
2Mc 4:22 and ushered in with a blaze of torches 1

usurp the right 1. *ἐνεξουσιάζομαι*
Sir 20: 8 whoever usurps the right to speak will be hated. 1

utensil 1. כְּלִי 2. *σκεῦος*
Exd 25:39 shall it be made, with all these utensils. 1
27: 3 all its utensils you shall make of bronze. 1
19 All the utensils of the tabernacle for every use 1
30:27 the table and all its utensils, and the lampstand 1
27 its utensils, and the lampstand and its utensils 1
28 altar of burnt offering with all its utensils 1
31: 8 table and its utensils, and the pure lampstand 1
8 pure lampstand with all its utensils 1
9 altar of burnt offering with all its utensils 1
35:13 the table with its poles and all its utensils 1
14 with its utensils and its lamps, and the oil 1
16 with . . its poles, and all its utensils, the laver 1
37:24 He made it and all its utensils of a talent 1
38: 3 he made all the utensils of the altar, the pots 1
3 all its utensils he made of bronze. 1
30 he made . . all the utensils of the altar 1
39:33 the tent and all its utensils, its hooks 1
36 the table with all its utensils, and the bread 1
37 its lamps with the lamps set and all its utensils 1
39 grating of bronze, its poles, and all its utensils; 1
40 the utensils for the service of the tabernacle 1
40:10 altar of burnt offering and all its utensils 1
Lev 8:11 anointed the altar and all its utensils 1
Num 4:10 shall put it with all its utensils in a covering 1
14 they shall put on it all the utensils of the altar 1
14 basins, all the utensils of the altar; 1
7: 1 consecrated the altar with all its utensils 1
1Ch 9:28 Some . . had charge of the utensils of service 1
29 were appointed . . over all the holy utensils 1
2Ch 24:14 made utensils for the house of the LORD 1
29:18 the altar of burnt offering and all its utensils 1
18 the table for the showbread and all its utensils. 1
19 utensils which King Ahaz discarded in his reign 1
LJr 1:59 a household utensil that serves its owner's need 2
1Mc 1:21 lampstand for the light, and all its utensils. 2

utmost 1. *τέρμα*
Wis 12:27 the utmost condemnation came upon them. 1

utmost *See also* vigor.

utter 1. אמר 2. דבר 3. הגה 4. יצא 5. כזב 6. מלל 7. משׁל 8. נבע 9. נגד 10. נשׂא 11. נתן 12. ספר 13. פֶּה 14. פוח 15. פצה 16. שׁמע 17. *ἀφίημι* 18. *βλασφημέω* 19. *δίδωμι* 20. *εἶπον* 21. *ἐργάζομαι* 22. *ἐρεύγομαι* 23. *λαλέω* 24. *μετά* 25. *προεῖπον* 26. *τίθημι* 27. *φημί* 28. *φθέγγομαι* 29. do 30. emitto
Exd 23: 1 You shall not utter a false report. 10
Jdg 5:12 awake, Deb'orah! Awake, awake, utter a song! 2
2Sm 22:14 and the Most High uttered his voice. 11
1Kg 4:32 He also uttered 3,000 proverbs; 2
8:56 promise, which he uttered by Moses his servant. 2
2Kg 9:25 the LORD uttered this oracle against him 10
1Ch 16:12 the wonders he wrought, the judgments he uttered 13
Job 8:10 and utter words out of their understanding? 4
26: 4 With whose help have you uttered words 9
27: 4 my tongue will not utter deceit. 3
42: 3 I have uttered what I did not understand 9
Ps 12: 2 Every one utters lies to his neighbor; 2
18:13 the Most High uttered his voice 11
27: 2 assail me, uttering slanders against me †
37:30 The mouth of the righteous utters wisdom 3
41: 6 when one comes to see me, he utters empty words 2
46: 6 he utters his voice, the earth melts. 11
59:12 For the cursing and lies which they utter 12
66:14 that which my lips uttered and my mouth promised 15
76: 8 From the heavens thou didst utter judgment; 16
78: 2 I will utter dark sayings from of old 8
105: 5 Remember . . the judgments he uttered 13
106: 2 Who can utter the mighty doings of the LORD 6
Prv 8: 7 for my mouth will utter truth; 3
10:18 he who utters slander is a fool. 4
14:25 but one who utters lies is a betrayer. 14
19: 5 he who utters lies will not escape. 14
9 he who utters lies will perish. 14
23:33 your mind utter perverse things. 2
Ecc 1: 8 All . . are full of weariness; a man cannot utter it; 2
5: 2 let your heart be hasty to utter a word before God 4
Isa 32: 6 to utter error concerning the LORD 2
59:13 and uttering from the heart lying words. 3
Jer 1:16 And I will utter my judgments against them 2
10:13 When he utters his voice there is a tumult 11
15:19 If you utter what is precious 4
25:13 all the words which I have uttered against it 2
30 and from his holy habitation utter his voice; 11
28:16 you have uttered rebellion against the LORD. 2
48:34 as far as Jahaz they utter their voice 11
51:16 When he utters his voice there is a tumult 11
Ezk 13: 7 and uttered a lying divination 1
8 you have uttered delusions and seen lies 2
24: 3 utter an allegory to the rebellious house 7
35:12 have heard all the revilings which you uttered 1
Hos 10: 4 They utter mere words; 2
Jol 2:11 The LORD utters his voice before his army 11
3:16 and utters his voice from Jerusalem 11
Ams 1: 2 from Zion, and utters his voice from Jerusalem; 11
Mic 2:11 If a man should go about and utter wind and lies 5
7: 3 the great man utters the evil desire of his soul; 2
Zep 3:13 they shall do no wrong and utter no lies 2
Zec 10: 2 For the teraphim utter nonsense 2
Mat 5:11 and persecute you and utter all kinds of evil 20
10:27 What I tell you in the dark, utter in the light 20
12:36 for every careless word they utter; 23
13:35 I will utter what has been hidden 22
Mrk 3:28 whatever blasphemies they utter; 18
15:37 Jesus uttered a loud cry, and breathed his last. 17
Joh 3:34 For he whom God has sent utters the words of God 23
1Co 14: 2 he utters mysteries in the Spirit. 23
9 if you in a tongue utter speech 19
2Co 1:20 That is why we utter the Amen through him *
12: 4 which man may not utter. 23
1Pe 4:11 whoever speaks, as one who utters oracles of God; *
2Pe 2:18 For, uttering loud boasts of folly, they entice 28
Rev 13: 5 a mouth uttering haughty and blasphemous words 23
6 it opened its mouth to utter blasphemies *
2Es 5: 5 and the stone shall utter its voice 29
10:26 she suddenly uttered a loud and fearful cry 30
11: 7 and uttered a cry to his wings, saying 30
37 how he uttered a man's voice to the eagle 30
Wis 1: 8 therefore no one who utters unrighteous things 28
Sir 15:10 For a hymn of praise should be uttered in wisdom 20
51: 2 lips that utter lies 21
2Mc 6:29 the words he had uttered 25
9:12 he uttered these words 27
3Mc 2:24 but went away uttering bitter threats. 26

4:16 uttering improper words 23
4Mc 4: 8 uttering threats, Apollonius went 24

utter (2) 1. אִישׁוֹן 2. כֹּל 3. נֶפֶשׁ 4. פָּנִים 5. μέγας 6. ὅλος 7. πᾶς 8. πολύς

Ezr 9: 7 been given . . to plundering, and to utter shame 4
Job 20:26 Utter darkness is laid up for his treasures; 2
Prv 5:14 point of utter ruin in the assembled congregation. 2
20:20 his lamp will be put out in utter darkness. 1
Jer 50:13 but shall be an utter desolation; 2
Ezk 29:10 I will make the land of Egypt an utter waste †
36: 5 with wholehearted joy and utter contempt 3
Joh 9:34 You were born in utter sin, 6
Jdt 7:25 thirst and utter destruction. 5
2Mc 13: 3 and with utter hypocrisy urged Antiochus 8
15: 6 in his utter boastfulness and arrogance 7

utter *See* destruction.

utter a complaint 1. שִׂיחַ

Ps 55:17 at noon I utter my complaint and moan 1

utter a curse 1. אלה

Jdg 17: 2 you uttered a curse, and also spoke it in my ears 1

utter a lament 1. קִנֵּן

2Ch 35:25 Jeremiah also uttered a lament for Josi'ah; 1

utter a lie 1. ψεύδω

Sir 7:13 Refuse to utter any lie 1

utter an oath 1. שבע

Lev 5: 4 Or if any one utters with his lips a rash oath 1

utter blasphemy 1. βλασφημέω

Mat 26:65 He has uttered blasphemy 1

utter deceit 1. רמה

Prv 12:17 but a false witness utters deceit. 1

utter the name 1. ὀνομάζω 2. ὀνομασία

Sir 23: 9 do not habitually utter the name of the Holy One; 2
10 the man who always swears and utters the Name 1

utterance 1. ἀποφθέγγομαι 2. λέξις 3. λόγος 4. στόμα 5. φωνή 6. dictum

Prv 6: 2 if you are snared in the utterance of your lips *
Act 2: 4 as the Spirit gave them utterance. 1
13:27 nor understand the utterances of the prophets 5
1Co 12: 8 through the Spirit the utterance of wisdom 3
8 to another the utterance of knowledge 3
2Co 8: 7 in faith, in utterance, in knowledge 3
Eph 6:19 that utterance may be given me 3
2Es 8:22 and whose utterances are certain 6
Sir 21:17 The utterance of a sensible man will be sought 4
23:12 is an utterance which is comparable to death 2

utterance *See also* give.

prophetic utterance 1. προφητεία

1Ti 1:18 the prophetic utterances which pointed to you 1
4:14 which was given you by prophetic utterance 1

thoughtless utterance 1. מִבְטָא

Num30: 6 her vows or any thoughtless utterance of her lips 1
8 void . . the thoughtless utterance of her lips 1

utterly 1. אַךְ 2. יַחַד 3. כֹּל 4. כָּלִיל 5. מְאֹד 6. עַד מְאֹד 7. תמם 8. εἰς συντέλειαν 9. εἰς τέλος 10. ἐπὶ πολὺ σφόδρα 11. ἕως ἐσχάτου 12. καθ' ὑπερβολήν 13. λίαν ἐκ περισσοῦ 14. ὅλος 15. παντελῶς 16. συντελέω 17. σφόδρα

Exd 17:14 I will utterly blot out the remembrance †
22:17 If her father utterly refuses to give her to him †
23:24 but you shall utterly overthrow them and break †
Num15:31 that person shall be utterly cut off; †
Deu 4:26 that you will soon utterly perish from the land †
26 not live long . . but will be utterly destroyed. †
7: 2 then you must utterly destroy them; †
26 you shall utterly detest and abhor it; †
20:17 utterly destroy . . Hittites and the Amorites †
Jos 17:13 and did not utterly drive them out. †
Jdg 1:28 forced labor, but did not utterly drive them out. †
15: 2 I really thought that you utterly hated her; †
1Sm 27:12 has made himself utterly abhorred by . . Israel; †
2Sm 12:14 by this deed you have utterly scorned the LORD †
17:10 the valiant man . . will utterly melt with fear; †
23: 7 and they are utterly consumed with fire. †
2Ch 20:23 rose against . . destroying them utterly †
Ps 38: 6 I am utterly bowed down and prostrate; 6
8 I am utterly spent and crushed; 6
73:19 swept away utterly by terrors! 7
74: 8 said to themselves, "We will utterly subdue them"; 2
78:59 full of wrath, and he utterly rejected Israel. 5
119: 8 O forsake me not utterly! 6
43 take not the word of truth utterly out of my mouth 6
51 Godless men utterly deride me, but I do not turn 6
Sng 8: 7 If a man offered . . it would be utterly scorned. †
Isa 1: 4 they are utterly estranged. †
2:18 the idols shall utterly pass away. 4
6:11 without men, and the land is utterly desolate †
16: 7 Mourn, utterly stricken, for the raisin-cakes 1
19:11 The princes of Zo'an are utterly foolish; 1
24: 3 The earth shall be utterly laid waste †
3 The earth shall be . . utterly despoiled; †
19 The earth is utterly broken, the earth is rent †
32:19 the forest will utterly go down †
19 and the city will be utterly laid low. †
42:17 be turned back and utterly put to shame †
60:12 those nations shall be utterly laid waste. †
Jer 2:12 be shocked, be utterly desolate, says the LORD 5
4:10 Ah, Lord GOD, surely thou hast utterly deceived †
5:11 Israel and . . Judah have been utterly faithless to me †
9:19 How we are ruined! We are utterly shamed 5
12:17 then I will utterly pluck it up and destroy it †
14:19 Hast thou utterly rejected Judah? †
50:12 your mother shall be utterly shamed 5
Lam 5:22 Or hast thou utterly rejected us? †
Ezk 17:10 Will it not utterly wither when the east wind †
Dan 11:22 Armies shall be utterly swept away before him †
Hos 10:15 the king of Israel shall be utterly cut off. †
Obd 1: 2 among . . nations, you shall be utterly despised. 5
Mic 2: 4 We are utterly ruined; he changes the portion †
Nah 1:15 he is utterly cut off. 3
Zep 1: 2 I will utterly sweep away everything †
Zec 11:17 wholly withered, his right eye utterly blinded! †
Mrk 6:51 they were utterly astounded 13
2Co 1: 8 we were so utterly, unbearably crushed 12
1Es 1:56 utterly destroyed all its glorious things. 16
Jdt 5:18 they were utterly defeated in many battles 10
7:30 he will not forsake us utterly. 9
AEs 14: 2 she utterly humbled her body 17
Wis 4:19 they will be left utterly dry and barren 11
Sir 10:13 destroyed them utterly. 9
40:14 likewise transgressors will utterly fail. 8
Aza 1:11 For thy name's sake do not give us up utterly 9
2Mc 3:12 he said that it was utterly impossible 15
6: 3 Harsh and utterly grievous 14
7: 5 When he was utterly helpless 14

utterly *See also* abominable, consume, destroy, fail, inexperienced, shatter, sweep.

uttermost part 1. אַחֲרִית 2. יַרְכָה 3. קָצָה 4. ἔσχατος

Deu 30: 4 outcasts are in the uttermost parts of heaven 3
Ps 139: 9 dwell in the uttermost parts of the sea 1
Ezk 32:23 graves are set in the uttermost parts of the Pit 2
38: 6 from the uttermost parts of the north 2
15 place out of the uttermost parts of the north 2
39: 2 from the uttermost parts of the north, and lead you 2
Act 13:47 to the uttermost parts of the earth.' 4

utters *See* man.

V

vagabond 1. הלך
Prv 6:11 poverty will come upon you like a vagabond 1

vain 1. אַיִן 2. הֶבֶל 3. חִנָּם 4. יאשׁ 5. רִיק 6. שָׁוְא 7. שֶׁקֶר 8. תֹּהוּ 9. κενός 10. κενῶς 11. μάταιος 12. ματαιόω 13. μάτην 14. sine causa 15. vanitas 16. vanum 17. vanus
Exd 20: 7 take the name of the LORD your God in vain; 6
7 hold him guiltless who takes his name in vain. 6
Lev 26:16 And you shall sow your seed in vain, 5
20 your strength shall be spent in vain 5
Deu 5:11 not take the name of the LORD your God in vain 6
11 not hold him guiltless who takes his name in vain. 6
1Sm 12:21 do not turn aside after . . for they are vain. 8
25:21 Surely in vain have I guarded all that 7
Job 9:29 I shall be condemned; why then do I labor in vain? 2
39:16 though her labor be in vain, yet she has no fear; 5
Ps 2: 1 nations conspire, and the peoples plot in vain? 5
31: 6 Thou hatest those who pay regard to vain idols; 6
60:11 help against the foe, for vain is the help of man! 6
73:13 All in vain have I kept my heart clean 5
108:12 grant us help . . for vain is the help of man! 6
119:118 yea, their cunning is in vain. 7
127: 1 those who build it labor in vain. 6
1 watchman stays awake in vain. 6
2 in vain that you rise up early and go late to rest 6
Prv 1:17 For in vain is a net spread in the sight of any bird; 3
14: 6 A scoffer seeks wisdom in vain 1
31:30 Charm is deceitful, and beauty is vain 2
Ecc 6:12 while he lives the few days of his vain life 2
7:15 In my vain life I have seen everything; 2
9: 9 all the days of your vain life which he has given 2
Isa 1:13 Bring no more vain offerings; 6
49: 4 But I said, "I have labored in vain 5
65:23 They shall not labor in vain, or bear children 5
Jer 2:30 In vain have I smitten your children 6
4:30 In vain you beautify yourself. 6
6:29 in vain the refining goes 6
18:12 That is in vain! We will follow our own plans 4
46:11 In vain you have used many medicines; 6
Ezk 6:10 I have not said in vain that I would do this evil 3
24:12 In vain I have wearied myself; *
Jon 2: 8 Those who pay regard to vain idols 6
Mal 1:10 you might not kindle fire upon my altar in vain! 3
3:14 You have said 'It is vain to serve God. 6
Mat 15: 9 in vain do they worship me, teaching as doctrines 13
Mrk 7: 7 in vain do they worship me 13
1Co 15:10 his grace toward me was not in vain 9
14 then our preaching is in vain 9
14 and your faith is in vain. 9
58 in the Lord your labor is not in vain. 9
2Co 6: 1 not to accept the grace of God in vain. 9
Gal 2: 2 somehow I should be running or had run in vain. 9
Php 2:16 I did not run in vain or labor in vain. 9
16 I did not run in vain or labor in vain. 9
1Th 2: 1 our visit to you was not in vain; 9
3: 5 our labor would be in vain. 9
Jas 1:26 this man's religion is vain. 11
4: 5 you suppose it is in vain that the scripture says 10
2Es 4:16 the plan of the forest was in vain 16
6:34 Do not be quick to think vain thoughts 17
7:14 the difficult and vain experiences 17
22 they devised for themselves vain thoughts 15
9:22 the multitude . . which has been born in vain 14
16:45 Because those who labor, labor in vain; 14
Jdt 6: 4 he has spoken; none of his words shall be in vain. 12
AEs 14:10 the praise of vain idols 11
Wis 3:11 Their hope is vain 9
Sir 34: 1 A man of no understanding has vain and false hopes 9
1Mc 9:68 his plan and his expedition had been in vain. 9
2Mc 7:18 Do not deceive yourself in vain 13
34 do not be elated in vain 13
4Mc 8:18 why do we take pleasure in vain resolves 9
16: 8 In vain, my sons, I endured many birth-pangs for you 13
vain *See also* all, discussion, hope, opinion, prove, try, word.

become vain 1. הבל
Job 27:12 why then have you become altogether vain? 1

vain thing 1. תֹּהוּ 2. κενός 3. μάταιος
1Sm 12:21 and do not turn aside after vain things 1
Act 4:25 the peoples imagine vain things? 2
14:15 turn from these vain things to a living God 3
3Mc 6: 6 as not to serve vain things 2

vain-minded 1. ματαιόφρων
3Mc 6:11 Let not the vain-minded praise their vanities 1

vainglory 1. גָּאוֹן 2. κενοδοξία
Ezk 7:20 beautiful ornament they used for vainglory 1
4Mc 2:15 lust for power, vainglory, boasting, arrogance 2

vainly 1. הֶבֶל
Lam 4:17 Our eyes failed, ever watching vainly for help; 1

vale 1. עֵמֶק
Ps 60: 6 and portion out the Vale of Succoth. 1
108: 7 I will . . portion out the Vale of Succoth. 1

valiant 1. בֶּן חַיִל 2. חַיִל 3. ἀνδρίζω 4. πολεμικός 5. υἱὸς δυνατός
1Sm 14:52 when Saul saw any strong man, or any valiant man 1
18:17 only be valiant for me and fight . . battles. 1
31:12 valiant men arose, and went all night 2
2Sm 2: 7 Now . . let your hands be strong, and be valiant; 1
11:16 Uri'ah to . . where he knew there were valiant men. 2
13:28 Be courageous and be valiant. 1
23:20 Benai'ah . . was a valiant man of Kabzeel, a doer 2
24: 9 in Israel there were 800,000 valiant men 2
1Ch 10:12 all the valiant men arose 2
11:22 Benai'ah . . was a valiant man of Kabzeel 2
2Ch 13: 3 having an army of valiant men of war 2
Neh 11: 6 All the sons of Perez . . were 468 valiant men. 2
Isa 5:22 valiant men in mixing strong drink 2
Jdt 14: 2 let every valiant man take his weapons and go out 4
Sir 31:25 Do not aim to be valiant over wine 3
1Mc 3:58 Judas said, "Gird yourselves and be valiant 5

valiant man 1. בֶּן חַיִל
2Sm 17:10 the valiant man . . will utterly melt with fear; 1
10 those who are with him are valiant men. 1
1Ch 5:18 valiant men, who carried shield and sword 1

valiant one 1. אֶרְאֵל
Isa 33: 7 Behold, the valiant ones cry without; 1

valiantly 1. חַיִל 2. fortiter
Num24:18 be dispossessed, while Israel does valiantly. 1
1Sm 14:48 And he did valiantly, and smote the Amal'ekites 1
Ps 60:12 With God we shall do valiantly; 1
108:13 With God we shall do valiantly; 1
118:15 The right hand of the LORD does valiantly 1
16 the right hand of the LORD does valiantly! 1
2Es 2:47 who had stood valiantly for the name of the Lord. 2

valid 1. βέβαιος 2. κύριος
Heb 2: 2 For if the message declared by angels was valid 1
1Mc 8:30 any addition or deletion . . shall be valid. 2

remain valid 1. ἵστημι
1Mc 13:38 the grants that we have made to you remain valid 1

valley 1. בִּקְעָה 2. גַּיְא 3. כִּכָּר 4. נַחַל 5. עֵמֶק 6. αὐλών 7. κοιλάς 8. φάραγξ 9. χειμάρρος
Gen 13:10 the Jordan valley was well watered everywhere 3
11 Lot chose for himself all the Jordan valley 3
12 while Lot dwelt among the cities of the valley 3
14: 3 all these joined forces in the valley of Siddim 5
8 they joined battle in the Valley of Siddim 5
10 Now the Valley of Siddim was full of bitumen pits; 5
17 meet him at the Valley of Shaveh 5
17 of Shaveh (that is, the King's Valley). 5
19:17 do not look back or stop anywhere in the valley; 3
25 he overthrew those cities, and all the valley 3
28 looked down . . toward all the land of the valley 3
29 when God destroyed the cities of the valley 3
26:17 Isaac . . encamped in the valley of Gerar 4
19 when Isaac's servants dug in the valley 4
37:14 he sent him from the valley of Hebron 5
Num13:23 they came to the Valley of Eshcol, and cut down 4
24 That place was called the Valley of Eshcol 4
14:25 Canaanites dwell in the valleys 5
21:12 set out, and encamped in the Valley of Zered. 4
14 Waheb in Suphah, and the valleys of the Arnon 4
15 slope of the valleys that extends to the seat 4
20 Bamoth to the valley lying in the region of Moab 2
24: 6 Like valleys that stretch afar 4
32: 9 For when they went up to the Valley of Eshcol 4
Deu 1:24 came to the Valley of Eshcol and spied it out. 4
2:24 'Rise up . . and go over the valley of the Arnon; 4
36 Aro'er . . on the edge of the valley of the Arnon 4
36 from the city . . in the valley, as far as Gilead 4
3: 8 from the valley of the Arnon to Mount Hermon 4
12 Aro'er, which is on the edge of the valley of the Arnon 4
16 from Gilead as far as the valley of the Arnon 4
16 with the middle of the valley as a boundary 4
29 we remained in the valley opposite Beth-pe'or. 2
4:46 in the valley opposite Beth-pe'or, in the land 2
48 Aro'er . . on the edge of the valley of the Arnon 4
8: 7 a land . . flowing forth in valleys and hills 1
11:11 land of hills and valleys, which drinks water 1
21: 4 bring the heifer . . to a valley with running water 4
4 break the heifer's neck there in the valley. 4
6 heifer whose neck was broken in the valley; 4
34: 3 valley of Jericho the city of palm trees 1
6 buried him in the valley in the land of Moab 2
Jos 7:24 and they brought them up to the Valley of Achor. 5
26 name of that place is called the Valley of Achor. 5
8:13 But Joshua spent that night in the valley. 5
10:12 stand . . and thou Moon in the valley of Ai'jalon. 5
11: 8 and eastward as far as the valley of Mizpeh; 1
17 as far as Ba'al-gad in the valley of Lebanon 1
12: 1 from the valley of the Arnon to Mount Hermon 4
2 Aro'er . . on the edge of the valley of the Arnon 4
2 from the middle of the valley as far as the river 4
7 from Ba'al-gad in the valley of Lebanon 1
13: 9 Aro'er . . on the edge of the valley of the Arnon 4
9 and the city that is in the middle of the valley 4
16 Aro'er . . on the edge of the valley of the Arnon 4
16 and the city that is in the middle of the valley 4
19 and Zer'eth-sha'har on the hill of the valley 5
27 in the valley of Beth-ha'ram, Beth-nim'rah, Succoth 5
15: 7 goes up to Debir from the Valley of Achor 5
7 Adum'mim, which is on the south side of the valley; 4
8 goes up by the valley of the son of Hinnom 2
8 over against the valley of Hinnom, on the west 2
8 at the northern end of the valley of Reph'aim; 5
17:16 those in . . and those in the Valley of Jezreel. 5
18:16 of the mountain that overlooks the valley 2
16 which is at the north end of the valley of Reph'aim; 5
16 and it then goes down the valley of Hinnom 2
19:14 boundary . . and it ends at the valley of Iph'tahel; 2
27 and touches Zeb'ulun and the valley of Iph'tahel 2
Jdg 5:14 From E'phraim they set out . . into the valley 7
15 into the valley they rushed forth at his heels. 5
6:33 Jordan they encamped in the Valley of Jezreel. 5
7: 1 camp . . was . . by the hill of Moreh, in the valley. 5
8 the camp of Mid'ian was below him in the valley. 5
12 Mid'ianites . . lay along the valley 5
16: 4 he loved a woman in the valley of Sorek, whose name 4
18:28 It was in the valley which belongs to Beth-rehob. 5
1Sm 6:13 were reaping their wheat harvest in the valley; 5

13:18 border that looks down upon the valley of Zebo’im 2
15: 5 Saul came . . and lay in wait in the valley. 4
17: 2 were gathered, and encamped in the valley of Elah 5
3 on the other side, with a valley between them. 2
19 all . . Israel, were in the valley of Elah 5
21: 9 Goliath . . whom you killed in the valley of Elah 5
31: 7 men of Israel . . on the other side of the valley 5
2Sm 5:18 had come and spread out in the valley of Reph’aim. 5
22 spread out in the valley of Reph’aim. 5
8:13 he slew . . E’domites in the Valley of Salt. 2
17:13 and we shall drag it into the valley 4
18:18 set up . . the pillar which is in the King’s Valley 5
23:13 a band . . was encamped in the valley of Reph’aim. 5
24: 5 from the city that is in the middle of the valley 4
1Kg 18: 5 to all the springs of water and to all the valleys; 4
20:28 The LORD is . . not a god of the valleys 5
2Kg 2:16 cast him upon some mountain or into some valley. 2
10:33 from Aro’er, which is by the valley of the Arnon 4
14: 7 He killed . . E’domites in the Valley of Salt 2
23:10 which is in the valley of the sons of Hinnom 2
1Ch 4:39 They journeyed . . to the east side of the valley 2
10: 7 when all the men of Israel who were in the valley 5
11:15 was encamped in the valley of Reph’aim. 5
12:15 and put to flight all those in the valleys 5
14: 9 had come and made a raid in the valley of Reph’aim. 5
13 Philistines yet again made a raid in the valley. 5
18:12 slew 18,000 E’domites in the Valley of Salt. 2
27:29 over the herds in the valleys was Shaphat the son 5
2Ch 14:10 battle in the valley of Zeph’athah at Mare’shah. 2
20:16 you will find them at the end of the valley 4
26 they assembled in the Valley of Bera’cah 5
26 been called the Valley of Bera’cah to this day. 5
25:11 went to the Valley of Salt and smote 10,000 men 2
26: 9 built towers in Jerusalem . . at the Valley Gate 2
28: 3 burned incense in the valley of the son of Hinnom 2
30:14 they took away and threw into the Kidron valley. 4
33: 6 as an offering in the valley of the son of Hinnom 2
14 outer wall for the city of David . . in the valley 4
Neh 2:15 went up . . by the valley and inspected the wall; 4
11:30 from Beer-sheba to the valley of Hinnom. 2
35 Lod, and Ono, the valley of craftsmen. 2
Job 21:33 The clods of the valley are sweet to him; 4
28: 4 open shafts in a valley away from where men live; 4
39:10 or will he harrow the valleys after you? 5
21 He paws in the valley, and exults in his strength; 5
Ps 23: 4 I walk through the valley of the shadow of death 2
60: 0 12,000 of Edom in the Valley of Salt. 2
65:13 the valleys deck themselves with grain 5
84: 6 As they go through the valley of Baca they make it 5
104: 8 The mountains rose, the valleys sank down 1
10 Thou makest springs gush forth in the valleys; 4
Prv 30:17 picked out by the ravens of the valley and eaten 4
Sng 2: 1 I am a rose of Sharon, a lily of the valleys. 5
6:11 went down . . to look at the blossoms of the valley 4
Isa 17: 5 the ears of grain in the Valley of Reph’aim. 5
22: 1 The oracle concerning the valley of vision. 2
5 day of . . confusion in the valley of vision 2
7 Your choicest valleys were full of chariots 5
28: 1 the rich valley of those overcome with wine! 2
4 beauty, which is on the head of the rich valley 2
21 he will be wroth as in the valley of Gibeon; 5
40: 4 Every valley shall be lifted up 2
41:18 and fountains in the midst of the valleys; 1
57: 5 who slay your children in the valleys 4
6 Among the smooth . . of the valley is your portion 4
63:14 Like cattle that go down into the valley 1
65:10 the Valley of Achor a place for herds to lie down 5
Jer 2:23 Look at your way in the valley; 2
7:31 which is in the valley of the son of Hinnom 2
32 called Topheth, or the valley of the son of Hinnom 2
32 but the valley of Slaughter: for they will bury 2
19: 2 and go out to the valley of the son of Hinnom 2
6 called Topheth, or the valley of the son of Hinnom 2
6 valley of . . Hinnom, but the valley of Slaughter. 2
21:13 I am against you, O inhabitant of the valley 5
31:40 The whole valley of the dead bodies and the ashes 5
32:35 They built the high places of Ba’al in the valley 2
48: 8 the valley shall perish 5
49: 4 Why do you boast of your valleys 5
Ezk 6: 3 says the Lord . . to the ravines and the valleys; 2
7:16 like doves of the valleys, all of them moaning 2
31:12 in all the valleys its branches will fall 2
32: 5 and fill the valleys with your carcass. 2
35: 8 hills and in your valleys and in all your ravines 2
36: 4 and the hills, the ravines and the valleys, 2
6 to the ravines and valleys, Thus says the Lord GOD 2
37: 1 and set me down in the midst of the valley; 1
2 behold, there were very many upon the valley; 1
39:11 the Valley of the Travelers east of the sea; 2
11 it will be called the Valley of Hamon-gog. 2
15 have buried it in the Valley of Hamon-gog. 2
Hos 1: 5 break the bow of Israel in the valley of Jezreel. 5
2:15 and make the Valley of Achor a door of hope. 5
Jol 3: 2 and bring them down to the valley of Jehosh’aphat 5
12 and come up to the valley of Jehosh’aphat; 5
14 multitudes, in the valley of decision! 5
14 day of the LORD is near in the valley of decision. 5
18 and water the valley of Shittim. 4
Ams 1: 5 cut off the inhabitants from the Valley of Aven 1
Mic 1: 4 valleys will be cleft, like wax before the fire 5
6 and I will pour down her stones into the valley 2
Zec 14: 4 in two from east to west by a very wide valley; 2
5 the valley of my mountains shall be stopped up 2
5 the valley of the mountains shall touch the side 2
Lke 3: 5 Every valley shall be filled 8
Joh 18: 1 he went forth . . across the Kidron valley 9
Jdt 2: 8 till their wounded shall fill their valleys 8
4: 4 Choba and Aesora and the valley of Salem 6
7: 3 They encamped in the valley near Bethulia 6
4 neither the high mountains nor the valleys 8
17 they encamped in the valley 6
10:10 and passed through the valley 6
11 The women went straight on through the valley; 6
11:17 your servant will go out into the valley 8
12: 7 and went out each night to the valley of Bethulia 8
13:10 and circled around the valley 8
16: 4 their multitude blocked up the valleys 9
Bar 5: 7 the valleys filled up, to make level ground 8
1Mc 12:37 part of the wall on the valley to the east 9
3Mc 6:17 even the nearby valleys resounded with them 6

valor 1. חַיִל 2. ἀνδραγαθία 3. ἀρετή 4. εὐανδρία

Deu 3:18 all your men of valor shall pass over armed 1
Jos 1:14 but all the men of valor among you shall pass over 1
6: 2 Jericho, with its king and mighty men of valor. 1
8: 3 and Joshua chose 30,000 mighty men of valor 1
10: 7 Joshua went up . . and all the mighty men of valor. 1
Jdg 6:12 him, "The LORD is with you, you mighty man of valor. 1
20:44 men of Benjamin fell, all of them men of valor. 1
46 men that drew the sword, all of them men of valor. 1
1Sm 10:26 Saul also went . . and with him went men of valor 1
16:18 who is skilful in playing, a man of valor 1
2Kg 5: 1 He was a mighty man of valor, but he was a leper. 1
24:14 all the princes, and all the mighty men of valor 1
16 brought captive to Babylon all the men of valor 1
1Ch 12:21 were all mighty men of valor, and were commanders 1
25 the Simeonites, mighty men of valor for war, 7,100 1
28 Zadok, a young man mighty in valor 1
30 Of the E’phraimites 20,800, mighty men of valor 1
2Ch 14: 8 all these were mighty men of valor. 1
17:13 He had . . mighty men of valor, in Jerusalem. 1
14 Adnah . . with 300,000 mighty men of valor 1
16 Amasi’ah . . with 200,000 mighty men of valor. 1
17 Of Benjamin: Eli’ada, a mighty man of valor 1
25: 6 hired . . 100,000 mighty men of valor from Israel 1
26:12 heads of fathers’ houses of mighty men of valor 1
17 80 priests of the LORD who were men of valor; 1
28: 6 Pekah . . slew 120,000 . . , all of them men of valor 1
Neh 11:14 their brethren, mighty men of valor, 128; 1
2Mc 8: 7 talk of his valor spread everywhere. 4
10:28 not only . . valor but their reliance upon the Lord 3
14:18 hearing of the valor of Judas and his men 2
15:17 so noble and so effective in arousing valor 3

valuable *See* possession.

valuation 1. עֵרֶךְ

Lev 27: 2 vow of persons to the LORD at your valuation 1
3 then your valuation of a male from twenty years 1
4 your valuation shall be 30 shekels 1
5 your valuation shall be for a male twenty shekels 1
6 your valuation shall be for a male five shekels 1
6 a female your valuation shall be three shekels 1
7 then your valuation for a male shall be fifteen 1
8 if a man is too poor to pay your valuation 1
13 he shall add a fifth to the valuation 1
15 he shall add a fifth of the valuation in money 1
16 then your valuation shall be according 1
17 it shall stand at your full valuation 1
18 a deduction shall be made from your valuation 1
19 he shall add a fifth of the valuation in money 1
23 then the priest shall compute the valuation 1
23 the man shall give the amount of the valuation 1
25 Every valuation shall be according 1
27 then he shall buy it back at your valuation 1
27 it shall be sold at your valuation 1

value 1. מְחִיר 2. סלה 3. ערך 4. עֵרֶךְ 5. διαφέρω 6. τιμή 7. τίμιος 8. ὠφέλεια 9. ὠφελέω 10. ὠφέλιμος

Lev 5:15 a ram . . valued by you in shekels of silver 4
18 valued by you at the price for a guilt offering 4
6: 6 a ram . . valued by you at the price for a guilt 4
22:14 he shall add the fifth of its value to it •
27: 8 before the priest, and the priest shall value him 3
8 him who vowed the priest shall value him 3
12 the priest shall value it as either good or bad 3
12 as you, the priest, value it, so it shall be 4
14 the priest shall value it as either good or bad 3
14 as the priest values it, so it shall stand 3
16 a sowing of a homer of barley shall be valued •
1Kg 21: 2 I will give you its value in money. 1
Job 28:16 It cannot be valued in the gold of Ophir 2
19 nor can it be valued in pure gold. 2
Mat 6:26 them. Are you not of more value than they? 5
Lke 12:24 Of how much more value are you than the birds! 5
Act 19:19 they counted the value of them 6
20:24 I do not account my life of any value 7
Rom 2:25 Circumcision . . is of value if you obey the law; 9
3: 1 Or what is the value of circumcision? 8
Col 2:23 they are of no value 6
1Ti 4: 8 for while bodily training is of some value 10
8 godliness is of value in every way 10

value *See also* weigh.

great value 1. πολύτιμος

Mat 13:46 on finding one pearl of great value 1

high value 1. καλός

2Mc 4:15 and putting the highest value upon . . 1

more value 1. διαφέρω

Mat 10:31 you are of more value than many sparrows. 1
12:12 Of how much more value is a man than a sheep! 1
Lke 12: 7 Fear not; you are of more value than many sparrows. 1

most valued 1. ἔντιμος

Wis 18:12 their most valued children had been destroyed. 1

vanish 1. אבד 2. דעך 3. הלך 4. כלה 5. מאס 6. מלח 7. סרח 8. פסס 9. תמם 10. ἀποχωρίζω 11. ἀφανὴς γίνομαι 12. ἀφανίζω 13. ἄφαντος 14. παρέρχομαι

Jdg 6:21 the angel of the LORD vanished from his sight. 3
Job 6:17 when it is hot, they vanish from their place. 2
7: 9 As the cloud fades and vanishes 3
Ps 9: 6 The enemy have vanished in everlasting ruins; 9
12: 1 for the faithful have vanished 8
37:20 like the glory of the pastures, they vanish- 4
58: 7 Let them vanish like water that runs away; 5
Isa 16: 4 he who tramples . . has vanished from the land 9
51: 6 for the heavens will vanish like smoke 6
Jer 49: 7 from the prudent? Has their wisdom vanished? 7
Ezk 26:17 and say to you, ‘How you have vanished from the seas 1
Lke 24:31 he vanished out of their sight. 13
Jas 4:14 appears for a little time and then vanishes. 12
Rev 6:14 the sky vanished like a scroll that is rolled up 10
Wis 5: 9 All those things have vanished like a shadow 14
Sir 21:18 Like a house that has vanished 12
45:26 so that their prosperity may not vanish 12
Bar 3:19 They have vanished and gone down to Hades 12
2Mc 3:34 Having said this they vanished. 11

vanish away 1. כלה 2. ἀφανισμός

Ps 37:20 they vanish-like smoke they vanish away. 1
Heb 8:13 is ready to vanish away. 2

make vanish 1. כלה

Ps 78:33 he made their days vanish like a breath 1

vanity 1. הֶבֶל 2. שָׁוְא 3. κενοδοξία 4. μάταιος 5. ματαιότης

Ps 89:47 for what vanity thou hast created all . . men! 2
119:37 Turn my eyes from looking at vanities; 2
Ecc 1: 2 Vanity of vanities, says the Preacher 1
2 Vanity of vanities, says the Preacher 1
2 vanities, says the Preacher, vanity of vanities! 1
2 vanities, says the Preacher, vanity of vanities! 1
2 vanity of vanities! All is vanity. 1
14 behold, all is vanity and a striving after wind. 1
2: 1 But behold, this also was vanity. 1
11 all was vanity and a striving after wind 1
15 And I said to myself that this also is vanity. 1
17 for all is vanity and a striving after wind. 1
19 This also is vanity. 1
21 This also is vanity and a great evil. 1
23 This also is vanity. 1
26 This also is vanity and a striving after wind. 1
3:19 man has no advantage . . for all is vanity. 1
4: 4 This also is vanity and a striving after wind. 1
7 Again, I saw vanity under the sun 1
8 This also is vanity and an unhappy business. 1
16 this also is vanity and a striving after wind. 1
5:10 this also is vanity. 1
6: 2 this is vanity; it is a sore affliction. 1
4 For it comes into vanity and goes into darkness 1
9 this also is vanity and a striving after wind. 1
11 The more words, the more vanity 1
7: 6 so is the laughter of . . this also is vanity. 1
8:10 This also is vanity. 1
14 There is a vanity which takes place on earth 1
14 I said that this also is vanity. 1
9: 1 Everything before them is vanity 5
11: 8 All that comes is vanity. 1
10 for youth and the dawn of life are vanity. 1
12: 8 Vanity of vanities, says the Preacher; 1
8 Vanity of vanities, says the Preacher; 1
8 Vanity . . says the Preacher; all is vanity. 1
Isa 49: 4 I have spent my strength for nothing and vanity; 1
Hos 5:11 because he was determined to go after vanity. 4
Wis 14:14 through the vanity of men they entered the world 3
3Mc 6:11 Let not the vain-minded praise their vanities 4

vanquish 1. נדף

Job 32:13 have found wisdom; God may vanquish him, not man. 1

vapor 1. הֶבֶל 2. ἀτμίς
Prv 21: 6 fleeting vapor and a snare of death. 1
Act 2:19 blood, and fire, and vapor of smoke; 2
Sir 22:24 vapor and smoke of the furnace precede the fire; 2
43: 4 it breathes out fiery vapors 2

variance 1. διαφέρω
Wis 18: 2 pardon for having been at variance with them. 1

variation 1. παραλλαγή
Jas 1:17 Father of lights with whom there is no variation 1

varied ways 1. ποικίλος
4Mc 16: 3 she saw her seven sons tortured in such varied ways. 1

variety 1. διαίρεσις 2. διαφορά
1Co 12: 4 there are varieties of gifts, but the same Spirit; 1
5 there are varieties of service, but the same Lord; 1
6 there are varieties of working 1
Wis 7:20 the varieties of plants and the virtues of roots; 2
variety *See also* make.

great variety 1. ποικιλία
Sir 38:27 each is diligent in making a great variety 1

various 1. ἀλλαχόθεν 2. διάφορος 3. ἑαυτοῦ 4. κατά 5. παμποίκιλος 6. ποικιλία 7. ποικίλος 8. varius
Mat 4:24 the sick, those afflicted with various diseases 7
24: 7 famines and earthquakes in various places 4
Mrk 1:34 healed many who were sick with various diseases 7
13: 8 there will be earthquakes in various places 4
Lke 4:40 any that were sick with various diseases 7
21:11 in various places famines and pestilences 4
1Co 12:10 to another various kinds of tongues •
28 speakers in various kinds of tongues. •
2Ti 3: 6 swayed by various impulses 7
Tit 3: 3 slaves to various passions and pleasures 7
Heb 2: 4 signs and wonders and various miracles 7
9:10 food and drink and various ablutions 2
Jas 1: 2 Count it all joy . . when you meet various trials 7
1Pe 1: 6 you may have to suffer various trials 7
2Es 2:18 twelve trees loaded with various fruits 8
Jdt 7:32 he dismissed the people to their various posts 3
2Mc 12: 2 some of the governors in various places 4
3Mc 1:21 Various were the supplications 7
2:26 he framed evil reports in the various localities; •
4Mc 1: 7 prove to you from many and various examples 1
15:11 were the various tortures strong enough 5
24 the ingenious and various rackings 6
18:21 and put them to death with various tortures. 7
various *See also* many.

various kinds 1. זַן
2Ch 16:14 filled with various kinds of spices prepared 1

various ways 1. πολλαχῶς 2. πολυτρόπως
Heb 1: 1 In many and various ways God spoke 2
3Mc 1:25 the king tried in various ways to change his . . mind 1

vary 1. διαλλάσσω 2. ποικίλος 3. multiformis
1Pe 4:10 as good stewards of God's varied grace 2
2Es 6:44 and of varied appeal to the taste 3
Wis 15: 4 a figure stained with varied colors 1
19:18 on a harp the notes vary the nature of the rhythm 1
2Mc 15:21 the varied supply of arms 2
3Mc 2: 6 inflicting many and varied punishments 2
4Mc 17: 7 enduring their varied tortures to death 2

vassal 1. מַס 2. עֶבֶד
2Kg 17: 3 Hoshe'a became his vassal, and paid him tribute. 2
Lam 1: 1 She that was a princess . . has become a vassal. 1

vast 1. גָּדוֹל 2. עצם 3. רַב 4. ἐπιμήκης 5. μέγας 6. πᾶς 7. πολὺ σφόδρα 8. inmensus
Est 1:20 throughout all his kingdom, vast as it is 3
Ps 139:17 thy thoughts, O God! How vast is the sum of them! 2
Lam 2:13 For vast as the sea is your ruin; who can restore you? 1
1Es 4:34 The earth is vast, and heaven is high 5
2Es 7: 3 so that it is broad and vast 8
Jdt 1:16 a vast body of troops 7
2:17 He collected a vast number of camels and asses 7
5:24 they will be devoured by your vast army. 6
7:18 they formed a vast multitude. 7
15: 7 there was a vast quantity of it. 7
Bar 3:24 And how vast the territory that he possesses! 4
vast *See also* number.

vastness 1. magnitudo
2Es 10:55 see the splendor and vastness of the building 1

vat 1. יֶקֶב
Prv 3:10 your vats will be bursting with wine. 1
Jol 2:24 the vats shall overflow with wine and oil. 1
3:13 The vats overflow, for their wickedness is great. 1
vat *See also* wine.

vault 1. אֲגֻדָּה 2. חוּג 3. γῦρος
Job 22:14 he walks on the vault of heaven.' 2
Ams 9: 6 and founds his vault upon the earth 1
Sir 24: 5 I have made the circuit of the vault of heaven 3
vaulted *See* chamber.

vaunt 1. פאר
Jdg 7: 2 hand, lest Israel vaunt themselves against me 1
Isa 10:15 the axe vaunt itself over him who hews with it 1

vegetable 1. זֵרֹעַ 2. זֵרְעֹן 3. יָרָק 4. λάχανον
Deu 11:10 like a garden of vegetables; 3
1Kg 21: 2 Give . . that I may have it for a vegetable garden 3
Dan 1:12 us be given vegetables to eat and water to drink. 1
16 steward took away . . and gave them vegetables. 2
Rom 14: 2 while the weak man eats only vegetables. 4

vegetation 1. דֶּשֶׁא 2. עֵשֶׂב 3. βοτάνη
Gen 1:11 God said, "Let the earth put forth vegetation 1
12 The earth brought forth vegetation 1
Ps 105:35 which devoured all the vegetation in their land 2
Zec 10: 1 to every one the vegetation in the field. 2
Heb 6: 7 For land which . . brings forth vegetation 3

vehement 1. ἐμπονέω
3Mc 1:28 The continuous, vehement, and concerted cry 1
vehement *See also* flame.

vehemently 1. ἐκπερισσῶς 2. εὐτόνως
Mrk 14:31 he said vehemently, "If I must die with you 1
Lke 23:10 the scribes stood by, vehemently accusing him. 2

more vehemently 1. σφοδρός
4Mc 5:32 fan the fire more vehemently! 1

veil 1. חֶבְיוֹן 2. מַסְוֶה 3. מַסֵּכָה 4. מִסְפָּחָה 5. פָּרֹכֶת 6. צַמָּה 7. צָעִיף 8. רְדִיד 9. κάλυμμα 10. κάλυμνα 11. καλύπτω 12. κατακαλύπτω
Gen 24:65 she took her veil and covered herself 7
38:14 she put off her widow's garments, and put on a veil 7
19 taking off her veil she put on the garments 7
Exd 26:31 you shall make a veil of blue and purple 5
33 you shall hang the veil from the clasps, and bring 5
33 ark of the testimony in thither within the veil; 5
33 ark of the testimony in thither within the veil; 5
35 you shall set the table outside the veil 5
27:21 In the tent of meeting, outside the veil 5
30: 6 you shall put it before the veil that is by the ark 5
34:33 speaking with them, he put a veil on his face; 2
34 he took the veil off, until he came out; 2
35 and Moses would put the veil upon his face again 2
35:12 the mercy seat, and the veil of the screen; 5
36:35 he made the veil of blue and purple and scarlet 5
38:27 bases of the sanctuary, and the bases of the veil; 5
39:34 goatskins, and the veil of the screen; 5
40: 3 and you shall screen the ark with the veil. 5
21 the tabernacle, and set up the veil of the screen 5
22 north side of the tabernacle, outside the veil 5
26 in the tent of meeting before the veil 5
Lev 4: 6 in front of the veil of the sanctuary 5
17 before the LORD in front of the veil 5
16: 2 come . . into the holy place within the veil 5
12 and he shall bring it within the veil 5
15 and bring its blood within the veil 5
21:23 he shall not come near the veil or approach 5
24: 3 Outside the veil of the testimony, in the tent 5
Num 4: 5 go in and take down the veil of the screen 5
18: 7 for all . . that is within the veil; 5
2Ch 3:14 he made the veil of blue and purple and crimson 5
Sng 4: 1 Your eyes are doves behind your veil. 6
3 halves of a pomegranate behind your veil. 6
6: 7 like halves of a pomegranate behind your veil. 6
Isa 3:23 the linen garments, the turbans, and the veils. 8
25: 7 the veil that is spread over all nations. 3
47: 2 grind meal, put off your veil, strip off your robe 6
Ezk 13:18 and make veils for the heads of persons 4
21 Your veils also I will tear off 4
Hab 3: 4 from his hand; and there he veiled his power. 1
1Co 11: 6 For if a woman will not veil herself 12
10 That is why a woman ought to have a veil on her head 10
2Co 3:13 not like Moses, who put a veil over his face 9
14 that same veil remains unlifted 9
15 a veil lies over their minds; 9
16 when a man turns to the Lord the veil is removed. 9
4: 3 even if our gospel is veiled 11
3 it is veiled only to those who are perishing. 11
Sus 1:32 As she was veiled, the wicked men ordered her 12
veil *See also* wear.

venerable 1. σεμνός
4Mc 7:15 O man of blessed age and of venerable gray hair 1

vengeance 1. נָקָם 2. נְקָמָה 3. ἐκδίκησις 4. κόλασις
Lev 26:25 that shall execute vengeance for the covenant 1
Num 31: 3 to execute the LORD'S vengeance on Mid'ian. 2
Deu 32:35 Vengeance is mine, and recompense 1
41 I will take vengeance on my adversaries 1
43 for he . . takes vengeance on his adversaries 1
2Sm 22:48 who gave me vengeance and brought down peoples 2
Ps 18:47 the God who gave me vengeance 2
58:10 will rejoice when he sees the vengeance; 1
94: 1 O LORD, thou God of vengeance 2
1 thou God of vengeance, shine forth! 2
149: 7 to wreak vengeance on the nations 2
Isa 34: 8 For the LORD has a day of vengeance 1
35: 4 Behold, your God will come with vengeance 1
47: 3 I will take vengeance, and I will spare no man. 1
59:17 he put on garments of vengeance for clothing 1
61: 2 and the day of vengeance of our God; 1
63: 4 For the day of vengeance was in my heart 1
Jer 11:20 let me see thy vengeance upon them 2
20:12 let me see thy vengeance upon them 2
46:10 a day of vengeance, to avenge himself on his foes. 2
50:15 For this is the vengeance of the LORD 2
28 to declare in Zion the vengeance of the LORD 2
28 vengeance of . . God, vengeance for his temple. 2
51: 6 for this is the time of the LORD'S vengeance 2
11 for that is the vengeance of the LORD 2
11 of the LORD, the vengeance for his temple. 2
36 plead your cause and take vengeance for you. 2
Lam 3:60 Thou hast seen all their vengeance 2
Ezk 24: 8 To rouse my wrath, to take vengeance 1
25:14 I will lay my vengeance upon Edom 2
14 they shall know my vengeance, says the Lord GOD. 2
17 I will execute great vengeance upon them 2
17 I am the LORD, when I lay my vengeance upon them. 2
Mic 5:15 And in anger and wrath I will execute vengeance 1
Lke 21:22 these are days of vengeance 3
Rom 12:19 Vengeance is mine, I will repay, says the Lord. 3
2Th 1: 8 inflicting vengeance upon those 3
Heb 10:30 Vengeance is mine, I will repay. 3
Sir 18:24 moment of vengeance when he turns away his face. 3
25:14 any vengeance, but not the vengeance of enemies! 3
14 any vengeance, but not the vengeance of enemies! 3
27:28 vengeance lies in wait for him like a lion. 3
28: 1 He that takes vengeance will suffer vengeance 3
35:18 repays vengeance on the nations 3
39:28 winds that have been created for vengeance 3
29 all these have been created for vengeance; 3
47:25 till vengeance came upon them. 3
48: 7 heard . . judgments of vengeance at Horeb; 3
1Mc 3:15 to take vengeance on the sons of Israel. 3
7:24 took vengeance on the men who had deserted 3
38 Take vengeance on this man and on his army 3
3Mc 1: 3 incurred the vengeance meant for the king. 4
vengeance *See also* avert, execute, take.

venom 1. חֵמָה 2. רֹאשׁ 3. ἰός
Deu 32:24 with venom of crawling things of the dust. 1
33 their wine is . . the cruel venom of asps. 2
Ps 58: 4 They have venom like the venom of a serpent 1
4 They have venom like the venom of a serpent 1
Rom 3:13 The venom of asps is under their lips. 3
Sir 25:15 There is no venom worse than a snake's venom •
15 There is no venom worse than a snake's venom •

venomous 1. ἰοβόλος
Wis 16:10 even by the teeth of venomous serpents 1

vent 1. נוח 2. פתח
Job 32:19 Behold, my heart is like wine that has no vent; 2
Ezk 5:13 I will vent my fury upon them and satisfy myself; 1
vent *See also* give.

vent wrath 1. נחם 2. עבר
Ps 78:62 and vented his wrath on his heritage. 2
Isa 1:24 I will vent my wrath on my enemies, and avenge 1

venture 1. נסה 2. עִנְיָן 3. תֹּם 4. δίδωμι ἑαυτόν 5. τολμάω
Deu 28:56 who would not venture to set the sole of her foot 1
1Kg 22:34 a certain man drew his bow at a venture 3
2Ch 18:33 a certain man drew his bow at a venture 3
Job 4: 2 If one ventures a word with you 1
Ecc 5:14 and those riches were lost in a bad venture; 2
Act 19:31 begged him not to venture into the theater. 4
Rom 15:18 For I will not venture to speak of anything 5
2Co 10:12 venture to class or compare ourselves with some 5
3Mc 3:21 and we ventured to make a change 5
4Mc 8:18 and venture upon a disobedience that brings death? 5

verdict 1. דָּבָר 2. κρίμα
Deu 17:11 you shall not turn aside from the verdict 1
Sir 19:25 people who distort kindness to gain a verdict. 2

verdure 1. יָרָק
Isa 15: 6 the new growth fails, the verdure is no more. 1

verify 1. אמן
Gen 42:20 your words will be verified, and you shall not 1

vermilion 1. שָׁשַׁר
Jer 22:14 and painting it with vermilion. 1
Ezk 23:14 images of the Chalde'ans portrayed in vermilion 1

vermin
Jer 43:12 as a shepherd cleans his cloak of vermin; •

verse 1. מַעֲשֶׂה 2. ἔπος
Ps 45: 1 I address my verses to the king; 1
Sir 44: 5 set forth verses in writing; 2

versed 1. ידע
Est 1:13 toward all who were versed in law and judgment 1

well versed 1. δυνατός
Act 18:24 an eloquent man, well versed in the scriptures. 1

vertebra 1. σπόνδυλος
4Mc 10: 8 his vertebrae were being dislocated upon it 1

very 1. גָּדוֹל 2. יטב 3. יתר 4. לְמַעְלָה 5. מְאֹד 6. עַד מְאֹד 7. קָט 8. רַב 9. יַתִּיר (A) 10. שַׂגִּיא (A) 11. ἐπὶ πλεῖον 12. εὖ μάλα 13. κατά 14. λίαν 15. μάλα 16. μεγάλως 17. μέγας 18. παντελῶς 19. πάνυ 20. πᾶς 21. πολύς 22. σφόδρα 23. σφοδρός 24. valde
Gen 1:31 behold, it was very good. And there was evening 5
4: 5 Cain was very angry, and his countenance fell. 5
12:14 saw that the woman was very beautiful. 5
13: 2 Now Abram was very rich in cattle 5
15: 1 I am your shield; your reward shall be very great. 5
18:20 is great and their sin is very grave 5
20: 8 and the men were very much afraid. 5
21:11 the thing was very displeasing to Abraham 5
24:16 The maiden was very fair to look upon 5
26:13 more and more until he became very wealthy. 5
34: 7 the men were indignant and very angry, because he 5
41:19 cows . . poor and very gaunt and thin 5
31 will follow, for it will be very grievous. 5
47:13 for the famine was very severe, so that the land 5
50: 9 horsemen; it was a very great company. 5
10 lamented there with a very great and sorrowful 5
Exd 1:20 the people multiplied and grew very strong. 5
8:28 only you shall not go very far away. •
9: 3 will fall with a very severe plague upon 5
18 I will cause very heavy hail to fall, such as never 5
24 there was . . very heavy hail, such as had never 5
10:19 the LORD turned a very strong west wind 5
11: 3 Moreover, the man Moses was very great in the land 5
12:38 and very many cattle, both flocks and herds. 5
19:16 a very loud trumpet blast, so that all 5
Num 6: 9 if any man dies very suddenly beside him †
11:33 LORD smote the people with a very great plague. 5
12: 3 the man Moses was very meek, more than all men 5
13:28 cities are fortified and very large; and besides 5
16:15 Moses was very angry, and said to the LORD 5
32: 1 sons of Gad had a very great multitude of cattle; 5
Deu 3: 5 besides very many unwalled villages. 5
9:21 burned . . and crushed it, grinding it very small 2
20:15 do to all the cities which are very far from you 5
24: 8 Take heed . . to be very careful to do according 5
27: 8 write upon the stones . . all this law very plainly. 2
30:14 word is very near you; it is in your mouth 5
Jos 1: 7 Only be strong and very courageous 5
8: 4 do not go very far from the city 5
9: 9 From a very far country your servants have come 5
13 shoes . . are worn out from the very long journey. 5
22 Why . . deceive us, saying, 'We are very far from you 5
10:20 slaying them with a very great slaughter 5
11: 4 they came . . with very many horses and chariots. 5
13: 1 there remains yet very much land to be possessed. 5
22: 8 Go . . with much wealth, and with very many cattle 5
23: 6 Therefore be very steadfast to keep and do all 5
Jdg 3:17 Eglon king of Moab. Now Eglon was a very fat man. 5
6: 6 Israel was brought very low because of Mid'ian; 5
11:33 he smote them . . with a very great slaughter. 5
35 you have brought me very low, and you have become †
13: 6 countenance of the angel of God, very terrible; 5
15:18 he was very thirsty, and he called on the LORD 5
18: 9 have seen the land, and behold, it is very fertile. 5
Rut 1:20 the Almighty has dealt very bitterly with me. 5
1Sm 2: 3 Talk no more so very proudly †
17 the sin . . was very great in the sight of the LORD; 5
22 Now Eli was very old, and he heard all that his sons 5
4:10 and there was a very great slaughter 5
5: 9 LORD was against . . causing a very great panic 5
11 The hand of God was very heavy there; 5
14:20 and there was very great confusion. 5
31 And the people were very faint; 5
18: 8 Saul was very angry, and this saying displeased 5
23:22 it is told me that he is very cunning. †
25: 2 The man was very rich; he had 3,000 sheep 5
15 men were very good to us, and we suffered no harm 5
36 Nabal's heart was merry . . for he was very drunk; 6
2Sm 1:26 my . . Jonathan; very pleasant have you been to me; 5
2:17 And the battle was very fierce that day; 6
3: 8 Then Abner was very angry over the words 5
8: 8 And from . . King David took very much bronze. 5
11: 2 he saw . . and the woman was very beautiful. 5
12: 2 The rich man had very many flocks and herds; 5
30 brought forth the spoil . . a very great amount. 5
13: 3 and Jon'adab was a very crafty man. 5
15 Then Amnon hated her with very great hatred; 5
21 When King David heard . . he was very angry. 5
36 king . . and all his servants wept very bitterly. 5
18:17 raised over him a very great heap of stones; 5
19:32 Barzil'lai was a very aged man, 80 years old; 5
32 he had provided . . for he was a very wealthy man. 5
24:10 for I have done very foolishly. 5
1Kg 1: 4 The maiden was very beautiful; and she became 5
6 He was also a very handsome man; and he was born 5
15 now the king was very old, and Ab'ishag 5
2:18 said, "Very well; I will speak for you to the king. •
10: 2 She came to Jerusalem with a very great retinue 5
2 with camels bearing spices, and very much gold 5
10 gold, and a very great quantity of spices 5
11 brought from Ophir a very great amount of almug 5
19:10 I have been very jealous for the LORD †
14 I have been very jealous for the LORD †
21:26 He did very abominably in going after idols 5
2Kg 14:26 the affliction of Israel was very bitter 5
17:18 Therefore the LORD was very angry with Israel 5
21:16 Manas'seh shed very much innocent blood 5
1Ch 4:40 land was very broad, quiet, and peaceful; †
9:13 very able men for . . the service of the house •
18: 8 and from Cun . . David took very much bronze; 5
20: 2 the spoil of the city, a very great amount. 5
21: 8 for I have done very foolishly. 5
13 the hand of the LORD, for his mercy is very great; 5
17 It is I who have sinned and done very wickedly. •
23:17 but the sons of Rehabi'ah were very many. 4
2Ch 7: 8 all Israel with him, a very great congregation 5
9: 1 having a very great retinue and camels 5
1 camels bearing spices and very much gold 5
9 she gave . . a very great quantity of spices 5
11:12 in all the cities, and made them very strong. 5
14:13 The men of Judah carried away very much booty. 5
16:14 they made a very great fire in his honor. 5
20:19 to praise the LORD . . with a very loud voice. 4
24:24 LORD delivered into their hand a very great army 5
25:10 And they became very angry with Judah 5
26: 8 his fame spread . . for he became very strong. 4
30:13 many people came . . a very great assembly. 5
32:27 Hezeki'ah had very great riches and honor; 5
29 God had given him very great possessions. 5
33:14 round Ophel, and raised it to a very great height; 5
Ezr 10: 1 very great assembly of men, women, and children 5
Neh 1: 7 We have acted very corruptly against thee †
2: 2 Then I was very much afraid. 5
4: 7 heard . . they were very angry; 5
5: 6 I was very angry when I heard their outcry 5
8:17 And there was very great rejoicing. 5
13: 8 very angry, and I threw all the . . furniture 5
Job 1: 3 500 she-asses, and very many servants; 5
2:13 for they saw that his suffering was very great. 5
8: 7 your latter days will be very great. 5
Ps 46: 1 God . . a very present help in trouble. 5
79: 8 for we are brought very low. 5
92: 5 O LORD! Thy thoughts are very deep! 5
93: 5 Thy decrees are very sure; 5
104: 1 O LORD my God, thou art very great! 5
105:24 LORD made his people very fruitful 5
142: 6 Give heed to my cry; for I am brought very low! 5
Ecc 2:15 why then have I been so very wise? 3
7:24 That which is, is far off, and deep, very deep; •
Sng 1: 5 I am very dark, but comely, O daughters •
Isa 21: 7 let him listen diligently, very diligently. 8
24:16 the treacherous deal very treacherously. †
31: 1 and in horsemen because they are very strong 5
48: 8 I knew that you would deal very treacherously †
52:13 exalted and lifted up, and shall be very high. 5
Jer 14:17 with a great wound, with a very grievous blow. 5
18:13 virgin Israel has done a very horrible thing. 5
24: 2 One basket had very good figs, like first-ripe 5
2 but the other basket had very bad figs 5
3 the good figs very good, and the bad figs very bad 5
3 the good figs very good, and the bad figs very bad 5
48:29 have heard of the pride of Moab–he is very proud 5
Lam 1:20 I am in . . because I have been very rebellious. †
Ezk 16:47 within a very little time you were 7
37: 2 behold, there were very many upon the valley; 5
2 and lo, they were very dry. 5
40: 2 and set me down upon a very high mountain 5
47: 7 I saw upon the bank of the river very many trees 5
9 there will be very many fish; 5
10 its fish will be of very many kinds 5
Dan 2:12 the king was angry and very furious, 10
3:22 order was strict and the furnace very hot 9
Jol 2:11 For the day of the LORD is great and very terrible; 5
Zec 1: 2 The LORD was very angry with your fathers. 17
15 I am very angry with the nations 1
9: 2 Tyre and Sidon, though they are very wise. 5
14: 4 in two from east to west by a very wide valley; 5
Mat 4: 8 the devil took him to a very high mountain 14
26:22 they were very sorrowful, and began to say to him 22
Mrk 16: 2 very early on the first day of the week 14
4 the stone was rolled back; –it was very large. 22
Lke 18:23 he became sad, for he was very rich. 22
23: 8 When Herod saw Jesus, he was very glad 22
2Co 3:12 Since we have such a hope, we are very bold 21
2Ti 3: 9 they will not get very far 11
Jde 1: 3 Beloved, being very eager to write to you 20
1Es 1:30 Take me away from the battle, for I am very weak. 14
8:91 there gathered about him a very great throng 22
2Es 5:21 the thoughts of my heart were very grievous 24
7:140 there would probably be left only very few 24
12: 5 still weary in mind and very weak in my spirit 24
15:34 and their appearance is very threatening 24
Tob 14: 3 When he had grown very old 16
Jdt 1:12 Then Nebuchadnezzar was very angry 22
4: 2 they were therefore very greatly terrified 22
5: 2 he was very angry 22
9 much gold and silver and very many cattle. 22
7: 2 a very great multitude. 22
8: 7 had a very lovely face 22
30 the people were very thirsty 22
10: 4 and made herself very beautiful 22
Sir 6:20 She seems very harsh to the uninstructed 22
13:13 Keep words to yourself and be very watchful 23
39:16 they are very good 22
43:29 Terrible is the Lord and very great 22
51:24 why are your souls very thirsty? 22
Bar 2:29 this very great multitude will surely turn 21
Sus 1: 2 Susanna . . a very beautiful woman 22
4 Joakim was very rich, and had a spacious garden 22
Bel 1:28 they were very indignant 14
1Mc 1: 4 He gathered a very strong army 22
64 very great wrath came upon Israel. 22
3:27 a very strong army. 22
4:54 At the very season and on the very day 13
54 At the very season and on the very day 13
58 There was very great gladness among the people 22
5: 1 they became very angry 22
38 it is a very large force. 22
45 a very large company 22
46 This was a large and very strong city 22
6: 2 Its temple was very rich 22
41 the army was very large and strong. 22
8: 6 cavalry and chariots and a very large army. 22
19 They went to Rome, a very long journey 22
9:22 have not been recorded, for they were very many. 22
24 In those days a very great famine occurred 22
10: 2 he assembled a very large army 22
13:22 that night a very heavy snow fell 22
49 So they were very hungry 22
16: 7 the cavalry of the enemy were very numerous. 22
2Mc 3:11 a man of very prominent position 22
33 Be very grateful to Onias the high priest 21
9: 6 and that very justly, for he had tortured 19
10:18 9,000 took refuge in two very strong towers 12
11: 1 Very soon after this 18
12:18 he had left a very strong garrison. 15
43 In doing this he acted very well and honorably 19
14:37 and was very well thought 22
3Mc 5:51 and cried out in a very loud voice 22

very (2) 1. בְּעֶצֶם 2. גַּם 3. עוֹד 4. עֶצֶם 5. רַב 6. αὐτός 7. ἐκεῖνος 8. καί 9. μέχρι 10. οὗτος 11. σήμερον 12. ipse
Gen 17:23 of their foreskins that very day, as God had said 4
26 That very day Abraham and his son Ish'mael 4
Exd 12:17 for on this very day I brought your hosts out 4
41 at the end . . on that very day 4
51 on that very day the LORD brought the people 4
24:10 like the very heaven for clearness. 4
33:17 the LORD said to Moses, "This very thing 2
Lev 19: 9 you shall not reap your field to its very border •
23:22 you shall not reap your field to its very border •
Deu 32:48 LORD said to Moses that very day 1
Jos 4: 3 from the very place where the priests' feet stood •
5:11 on the morrow after the passover, on that very day 4
10:27 great stones . . which remain to this very day. 4
Neh 5:11 Return to them this very day their fields •
Est 1:18 This very day the ladies . . will be telling it •
9: 1 on the very day when the enemies of the Jews hoped •
11 That very day the number of those slain in Susa •
Ps 9: 6 the very memory of them has perished. •
146: 4 on that very day his plans perish. •
Prv 6:26 but an adulteress stalks a man's very life. •
Sng 8:12 My vineyard, my very own, is for myself; •
Isa 1: 7 in your very presence aliens devour your land; •
10:32 This very day he will halt at Nob 3
Jer 4:10 whereas the sword has reached their very life. •
18 it is bitter; it has reached your very heart. •
28:16 This very year you shall die •
51:24 I will requite . . Chalde'a before your very eyes •
Ezk 2: 3 have transgressed against me to this very day. 4
10:22 the very faces whose appearance I had seen •
20:26 I defiled them through their very gifts •
24: 2 write down the name of this day, this very day. 4
2 has laid siege to Jerusalem this very day. 4
40: 1 on that very day, the hand of the LORD was upon me •
Dan 5:30 That very night Belshaz'zar the Chalde'an king •
Zec 8: 4 each with staff in hand for very age. 5
Mat 8:13 And the servant was healed at that very moment. •
21:42 The very stone which the builders rejected •
24:33 you know that he is near, at the very gates. •
26:34 this very night, before the cock crows •
Mrk 12:10 The very stone which the builders rejected 10

13:29 you know that he is near, at the very gates. •
14:30 this very night, before the cock crows twice 11
Lke 2:38 coming up at that very hour she gave thanks to God 6
12:12 the Holy Spirit will teach you in that very hour 6
59 till you have paid the very last copper. 8
13: 1 There were some present at that very time 6
31 At that very hour some Pharisees came, and said 6
19:40 the very stones would cry out. •
20:17 The very stone which the builders rejected 10
19 tried to lay hands on him at that very hour 6
23:12 became friends with each other that very day 6
24:13 That very day two of them were going to a village 6
Joh 5:36 these very works which I am doing 6
Act 12: 6 The very night when Herod was about 7
16:18 it came out that very hour. 6
22:13 in that very hour I received my sight and saw him. 6
27:23 this very night there stood by me an angel •
Rom 2: 1 you, the judge, are doing the very same things. •
7:10 the very commandment which promised life 10
15 but I do the very thing I hate. •
9:17 for the very purpose of showing my power in you 6
26 And in the very place where it was said to them •
11: 8 ears that should not hear, down to this very day. †
13: 6 ministers of God, attending to this very thing. 6
2Co 5: 5 He who has prepared us for this very thing is God 6
Gal 2:10 which very thing I was eager to do. 6
Eph 6:22 I have sent him to you for this very purpose 6
Col 4: 8 I have sent him to you for this very purpose 6
Tit 1:15 their very minds and consciences are corrupted. •
1Pe 2: 7 The very stone which the builders rejected •
2Pe 1: 5 For this very reason make every effort 6
1Es 4:16 brought up the very men who plant the vineyards 6
8:64 the weight . . was recorded at that very time. 6
2Es 9: 2 then you will know that it is the very time 12
13:19 and for that very reason! •
Tob 3:17 At that very moment Tobit returned 6
6:15 this very night she will be given to you •
Jdt 11:15 on that very day they will be handed over 7
13:14 but has destroyed our enemies . . this very night! •
AEs 16:20 on that very day they may defend themselves 6
Wis 2:15 the very sight of him is a burden to us 8
2Mc 4:38 led him about the whole city to that very place 6
4Mc 4:20 at the very citadel of our native land 6
5: 8 should you abhor eating the very excellent meat •
6:26 When he was now burned to his very bones 9
30 he resisted even to the very tortures of death •

very *See* able, aged, boldly, costly, dear, earnest, end, expensive, fertile, few, fragrant, great, heart, heavy, highly, hot, large, last, least, little, long, many, merciful, midst, moment, much, near, numerous, old, precious, reckless, religious, same, severely, small, sorrowful, stamp, strong, time, useful, warmly, well, young.

very thing

Wis 11: 5 through the very things by which their enemies •
16 punished by the very things by which he sins. •

vessel 1. כְּלִי 2. נֵבֶל 3. מָאן (A) 4. ἀγγεῖον 5. ἄγγος 6. κατασκευάζω 7. ναῦς 8. σκεῦος

Exd 37:16 he made the vessels of pure gold which were to be 1
Lev 6:28 the earthen vessel in which it is boiled 1
28 if it is boiled in a bronze vessel 1
11:32 any vessel that is used for any purpose 1
33 if any of them falls into any earthen vessel 1
34 drink which may be drunk from every such vessel 1
14: 5 kill one of the birds in an earthen vessel 1
50 shall kill one of the birds in an earthen vessel 1
15:12 the earthen vessel which he . . touches 1
12 every vessel of wood shall be rinsed in water 1
Num 3:31 vessels of the sanctuary with which the priests 1
4: 9 with its lamps . . and all the vessels for oil 1
12 they shall take all the vessels of the service 1
16 oversight . . of the sanctuary and its vessels. 1
5:17 shall take holy water in an earthen vessel 1
7:85 all the silver of the vessels 2,400 shekels 1
18: 3 not come near to the vessels of the sanctuary 1
19:15 every open vessel . . is unclean. 1
17 running water shall be added in a vessel; 1
31: 6 sent them . . with the vessels of the sanctuary 1
Deu 23:24 you shall not put any in your vessel. 1
Jos 6:19 silver and gold, and vessels of bronze and iron 1
24 and gold, and the vessels of bronze and of iron 1
Rut 2: 9 when you are thirsty, go to the vessels and drink 1
1Sm 21: 5 the vessels of the young men are holy 1
5 how much more today will their vessels be holy? 1
2Sm 17:28 brought beds, basins, and earthen vessels, wheat 1
1Kg 7:45 all these vessels in the house of the LORD 1
47 Solomon left all the vessels unweighed 1
48 made all the vessels . . in the house of the LORD 1
51 silver, the gold, and the vessels, and stored them 1
8: 4 and all the holy vessels that were in the tent; 1
10:21 All King Solomon's drinking vessels were of gold 1
21 all the vessels of the House . . were of pure gold; 1
15:15 his . . votive gifts, silver, and gold, and vessels. 1
17:10 Bring me a little water in a vessel 1
2Kg 4: 3 Go outside, borrow vessels of all your neighbors 1
3 borrow . . empty vessels and not too few. 1
4 shut the door . . and pour into all these vessels; 1
5 as she poured they brought the vessels to her. •
6 When the vessels were full, she said to her son 1
6 she said to her son, "Bring me another vessel. 1
12:13 trumpets, or any vessels of gold, or of silver 1
14:14 and all the vessels that were found in the house 1
23: 4 to bring out . . all the vessels made for Ba'al 1
24:13 and cut in pieces all the vessels of gold 1
25:14 and all the vessels of bronze used in the temple 1
16 bronze of all these vessels was beyond weight. 1
1Ch 18: 8 Solomon made . . the pillars and the vessels 1
22:19 so that the ark . . and the holy vessels of God 1
28:13 for all the vessels for the service in the house 1
14 for all golden vessels for each service 1
14 weight of silver vessels for each service 1
2Ch 5: 1 stored the silver, the gold, and all the vessels 1
5 brought up . . and all the holy vessels that were 1
9:20 All King Solomon's drinking vessels were of gold 1
20 all the vessels of the House . . were of pure gold; 1
15:18 votive gifts, silver, and gold, and vessels. 1
24:14 vessels of gold and silver. 1
25:24 seized . . all the vessels that were found 1
28:24 Ahaz gathered together the vessels of the house 1
24 cut in pieces the vessels of the house of God 1
32:27 treasuries . . for all kinds of costly vessels; 1
36: 7 carried part of the vessels of the . . LORD 1
10 precious vessels of the house of the LORD 1
18 vessels of the house of God, great and small 1
19 destroyed all its precious vessels. 1
Ezr 1: 6 aided them with vessels of silver, with gold 1
7 Cyrus . . brought out the vessels of the house 1
10 bowls of silver, and 1,000 other vessels; 1
11 all the vessels of gold and of silver were 5,469. 1
5:14 gold and silver vessels of the house of God 3
15 Take these vessels, go and put them in the temple 3
6: 5 gold and silver vessels of the house of God 3
7:19 vessels that have been given you for the service 3
8:25 weighed out . . silver and the gold and the vessels 1
26 silver vessels worth 100 talents 1
27 two vessels of fine bright bronze as precious 1
28 You are holy to the LORD, and the vessels are holy; 1
30 took over the weight of . . gold and the vessels 1
33 silver and the gold and the vessels were weighed 1
Neh 10:39 chambers, where are the vessels of the sanctuary 1
13: 5 previously put the . . vessels, and the tithes 1
9 brought back . . the vessels of the house of God 1
Ps 2: 9 dash them in pieces like a potter's vessel. 1
31:12 I have become like a broken vessel. 1
Prv 25: 4 dross . . and the smith has material for a vessel; 1
Isa 18: 2 by the Nile, in vessels of papyrus upon the waters 1
22:24 every . . vessel, from the cups to all the flagons. 1
30:14 its breaking is like that of a potter's vessel 2
52:11 purify . . you who bear the vessels of the LORD. 1
65: 4 broth of abominable things is in their vessels; 1
66:20 in a clean vessel to the house of the LORD. 1
Jer 14: 3 no water, they return with their vessels empty; 1
18: 4 And the vessel he was making of clay was spoiled 1
4 and he reworked it into another vessel 1
19:11 this city, as one breaks a potter's vessel 1
22:28 a despised, broken pot, a vessel no one cares for? 1
27:16 saying, 'Behold, the vessels of the LORD'S house 1
18 that the vessels which are left in the house 1
19 and the rest of the vessels which are left 1
21 vessels which are left in the house of the LORD 1
28: 3 to this place all the vessels of the LORD'S house 1
6 from Babylon the vessels of the house of the LORD 1
32:14 and put them in an earthenware vessel 1
40:10 fruits and oil, and store them in your vessels 1
48:11 he has not been emptied from vessel to vessel 1
11 he has not been emptied from vessel to vessel 1
12 tilters who will tilt him, and empty his vessels 1
38 for I have broken Moab like a vessel 1
51:34 has made me an empty vessel, he has swallowed me 1
52:18 dishes for incense, and all the vessels of bronze 1
Ezk 4: 9 and put them into a single vessel, and make bread 1
15: 3 Do men take a peg from it to hang any vessel on? 1
27:13 and vessels of bronze for your merchandise. 1
Dan 5: 2 commanded that the vessels of gold and of silver 3
3 brought in the golden and silver vessels 3
23 vessels of his house have been brought in before 3
11: 8 molten images and with their precious vessels 1
Hos 8: 8 they are among the nations as a useless vessel. 1
Mat 13:48 sat down and sorted the good into vessels 5
Lke 8:16 covers it with a vessel 8
Act 27:41 striking a shoal they ran the vessel aground 7
Rom 9:21 to make out of the same lump one vessel for beauty 8
22 endured with much patience the vessels of wrath 8
23 the riches of his glory for the vessels of mercy 8
2Co 4: 7 we have this treasure in earthen vessels 8
2Ti 2:20 there are not only vessels of gold and silver 8
21 he will be a vessel for noble use 8
Heb 9:21 both the tent and all the vessels used in worship. 8
1Es 1:41 also took some holy vessels of the Lord 8
45 the holy vessels of the Lord 8
54 all the holy vessels of the Lord, great and small 8
2:10 also brought out the holy vessels of the Lord 8
13 2,410 silver bowls, and 1,000 other vessels. 8
14 All the vessels were handed over, gold and silver 8
4:44 to send back all the vessels that were taken 8
57 he sent back from Babylon all the vessels 8
6:18 the holy vessels of gold and of silver 8
19 he should take all these vessels back 8
26 the holy vessels of the house of the Lord 8
8:17 deliver the holy vessels of the Lord 8
55 the holy vessels of the house of our Lord 8
56 silver vessels worth a 100 talents 8
57 twelve bronze vessels of fine bronze 8
58 the vessels are holy 8
60 the vessels which had been in Jerusalem 8
Jdt 4: 3 the sacred vessels and the altar and the temple 8
7:20 until all the vessels of water . . were empty; 4
10: 5 she wrapped up all her vessels 4
16:19 all the vessels of Holofernes 8
Wis 13:11 with pleasing workmanship make a useful vessel 6
14: 2 it was desire for gain that planned that vessel •
15: 7 and laboriously molds each vessel for our service •
7 both the vessels that serve clean uses 8
13 he makes from earthy matter fragile vessels 8
Sir 27: 5 The kiln tests the potter's vessels 8
50: 9 like a vessel of hammered gold 8
Bar 1: 8 Baruch took the vessels of the house of the Lord 8
8 silver vessels which Zedekiah . . had made 8
1Mc 1:23 the silver and the gold, and the costly vessels 8
2: 9 her glorious vessels 8
4:49 They made new holy vessels 8
6:12 I seized all her vessels of silver and gold 8
14:15 added to the vessels of the sanctuary. 8
2Mc 4:32 other vessels, as it happened, he had sold to Tyre •
48 the city and the villages and the holy vessels 8
5:16 He took the holy vessels with his polluted hands 8
9:16 the holy vessels he would give back 8

earthen vessel 1. חֶרֶשׂ

Prv 26:23 Like the glaze covering an earthen vessel 1
Isa 45: 9 with his Maker, an earthen vessel with the potter! 1

gold vessel 1. χρύσωμα

2Mc 4:32 Menelaus . . stole some of the gold vessels of the temple 1
39 many of the gold vessels had already been stolen. 1

vessel of bronze 1. χαλκίον

Mrk 7: 4 washing of cups and pots and vessels of bronze.) 1

vessel of stone 1. אֶבֶן

Exd 7:19 both in vessels of wood and in vessels of stone.' 1

vessel of wood 1. עֵץ

Exd 7:19 both in vessels of wood and in vessels of stone.' 1

vestibule 1. אוּלָם 2. אֵילָם 3. מִסְדְּרוֹן 4. αἰλαμμών

Jdg 3:23 Ehud went out into the vestibule, and closed 3
1Kg 6: 3 The vestibule in front of the nave of the house 1
7:12 inner court . . and the vestibule of the house. 1
19 capitals . . in the vestibule were of lily-work 1
21 set up the pillars at the vestibule of the temple; 1
1Ch 28:11 the plan of the vestibule of the temple 1
2Ch 3: 4 The vestibule . . was twenty cubits long 1
8:12 which he had built before the vestibule 1
15: 8 altar . . in front of the vestibule of the house 1
29: 7 They also shut the doors of the vestibule 1
17 they came to the vestibule of the LORD; 1
Ezk 40: 7 and the threshold of the gate by the vestibule 1
8 Then he measured the vestibule of the gateway 1
9 the vestibule of the gate was at the inner end. 1
14 He measured also the vestibule, twenty cubits; •
14 and round about the vestibule of the gateway was •
15 to the end of the inner vestibule of the gate 1
16 the vestibule had windows round about inside 2
21 its jambs and its vestibule were of the same size 2
22 its windows, its vestibule, and its palm trees 2
22 its vestibule was on the inside. 2
24 he measured its jambs and its vestibule; 2
25 in its vestibule, like the windows of the others; 2
26 its vestibule was on the inside; 2
29 Its side rooms, its jambs, and its vestibule were 2
29 windows round about in it and in its vestibule; 2
30 there were vestibules round about 2
31 Its vestibule faced the outer court 2
33 Its side rooms, its jambs, and its vestibule were 2
33 windows round about in it and in its vestibule; 2
34 Its vestibule faced the outer court 2
36 Its side rooms, its jambs, and its vestibule were 2
37 Its vestibule faced the outer court 4
38 was a chamber with its door in the vestibule •
39 And in the vestibule of the gate were two tables 1
40 on the outside of the vestibule at the entrance •
40 on the other side of the vestibule of the gate 1
48 Then he brought me to the vestibule of the temple 1
48 and measured the jambs of the vestibule 1
49 The length of the vestibule was twenty cubits 1
41:15 and the inner room and the outer vestibule 1
25 of wood in front of the vestibule outside. 1
26 either side, on the sidewalls of the vestibule. 1
44: 3 he shall enter by way of the vestibule of the gate 1
46: 2 prince shall enter by the vestibule of the gate 1
8 he shall go in by the vestibule of the gate 1
Jol 2:17 Between the vestibule and the altar 1

vestment 1.לְבוּשׁ 2.לבשׁ 3.מַלְבּוּשׁ 4.ἐσθής
2Kg 10:22 Bring out the vestments for all the worshipers 1
22 So he brought out the vestments for them. 3
Ezr 3:10 priests in their vestments came forward 2
3Mc 1:16 the priests in all their vestments 4

splendid vestment 1.εὐκοσμία
Sir 45: 7 He blessed him with splendid vestments 1

vesture 1.סוּת
Gen 49:11 he washes . . his vesture in the blood of grapes; 1

vex 1.סַר 2.קצר 3.βαρέως φέρω 4.βασανίζω 5.προσοχθίζω
Jdg 16:16 and urged him, his soul was vexed to death. 2
1Kg 21: 4 Ahab went into his house vexed and sullen 1
5 Why is your spirit so vexed that you eat no food? 1
2Pe 2: 8 he was vexed in his righteous soul day after day 4
Sir 50:25 With two nations my soul is vexed 5
2Mc 11: 1 being vexed at what had happened 3

vexation 1.כעס 2.כַּעַס 3.כַּעַשׂ
1Sm 1:16 speaking out of my great anxiety and vexation. 2
Job 5: 2 Surely vexation kills the fool 3
6: 2 O that my vexation were weighed 3
10:17 against me, and increase thy vexation toward me; 3
Ps 10:14 yea, thou dost note trouble and vexation 2
Prv 12:16 The vexation of a fool is known at once 2
Ecc 1:18 For in much wisdom is much vexation 2
2:23 days are full of pain, and his work is a vexation; 2
5:17 all his days . . in much vexation and sickness 1
11:10 Remove vexation from your mind, and put away pain 2

vial 1.פַּךְ
1Sm 10: 1 Samuel took a vial of oil and poured it on his head 1

vice 1.κακία
3Mc 2: 5 who were notorious for their vices 1

vicinity 1.χώρα
Ezr 2:70 some . . lived in Jerusalem and its vicinity; 1
1Es 5:46 settled in Jerusalem and its vicinity 1

vicious 1.πονηρός
Act 18:14 a matter of wrongdoing or vicious crime 1

victim 1.דַּךְ 2.חָלָל
2Ch 35:11 while the Levites flayed the victims. *
Prv 7:26 for many a victim has she laid low; 2
26:28 A lying tongue hates its victims 1
Jer 14:16 victims of famine and sword, with none to bury *
Lam 4: 9 Happier were the victims of the sword 2
9 Happier . . than the victims of hunger 2

victim of sport 1.ἐμπαίζω
2Mc 7:10 the third was the victim of their sport 1

victor 1.νικάω
1Es 3:12 truth is victor over all things. 1
Wis 4: 2 victor in the contest for prizes 1
4Mc 17:15 Reverence for God was victor 1

victorious 1.בשׁלום 2.ישׁע 3.צֶדֶק 4.ἀθλοφόρος 5.μετὰ νίκης 6.νικάω 7.vinco
Jdg 11:31 when I return victorious from the Ammonites 1
Isa 41:10 I will uphold you with my victorious right hand. 3
Zec 9: 9 triumphant and victorious is he 2
2Es 7:115or to harm him who is victorious. 7
128if he is victorious he shall receive 7
3Mc 3:20 when we arrived in Egypt victorious 5
4Mc 6:10 the old man . . was victorious over his torturers; 6
18:23 with their victorious mother are gathered 4

victoriously 1.צלח
Ps 45: 4 In your majesty ride forth victoriously 1

victory 1.גבורה 2.יְשׁוּעָה 3.יֵשַׁע 4.צֶדֶק 5.תְּשׁוּעָה 6.ἐπινίκιος 7.νίκη 8.νῖκος
Exd 32:18 It is not the sound of shouting for victory 1
1Sm 14:45 who has wrought this great victory in Israel? 2
19: 5 the LORD wrought a great victory for all Israel. 5
2Sm 19: 2 So the victory that day was turned into mourning 5
23:10 and the LORD wrought a great victory that day; 5
12 and the LORD wrought a great victory. 5
2Kg 5: 1 by him the LORD had given victory to Syria. 5
13:17 The LORD's arrow of victory, the arrow of victory 5
17 LORD's arrow . . the arrow of victory over Syria! 5
1Ch 11:14 and the LORD saved them by a great victory. 5
29:11 Thine, O LORD, is . . the glory, and the victory 7
2Ch 20:17 see the victory of the LORD on your behalf, O Judah 2
Ps 20: 5 May we shout for joy over your victory 2
6 with mighty victories by his right hand. 3
33:17 The war horse is a vain hope for victory 5
44: 4 my God, who ordainest victories for Jacob. 2
48:10 Thy right hand is filled with victory; 4
98: 2 The LORD has made known his victory 2
3 ends of the earth have seen the victory of our God. 2
118:15 Hark, glad songs of victory in the tents 2
144:10 who givest victory to kings, who rescuest David 5
149: 4 pleasure . . adorns the humble with victory. 2
Prv 21:31 but the victory belongs to the LORD. 5
24: 6 abundance of counselors there is victory. 5
Isa 41: 2 from the east whom victory meets at every step? 4
Hab 3: 8 ride upon thy horses, upon thy chariot of victory? 2
Mat 12:20 till he brings justice to victory; 8
1Co 15:54 Death is swallowed up in victory. 8
55 O death, where is thy victory? 8
57 thanks be to God, who gives us the victory 8
1Jn 5: 4 this is the victory that overcomes the world 7
1Es 3: 9 the victory shall be given 8
4:59 From thee is the victory; from thee is wisdom 7
1Mc 3:19 victory in battle depends 7
2Mc 8:33 While they were celebrating the victory 6
10:28 the one having as pledge of success and victory 7
38 gives them the victory. 8
13:15 He gave his men the watchword, "God's victory 7
15: 8 now to look for the victory 7
21 he gains the victory for those who deserve it. 7
4Mc 7: 3 he sailed into the haven of immortal victory. 7

victory *See also* bring, get, give, honor, monument, shout, trophy, win.

victual 1.אֹכֶל
Deu 23:19 interest on money, interest on victuals 1

view 1.לִפְנֵי 2.ראה 3.διά 4.κατά 5.σκοπός 6.φρονέω
Deu 32:49 view the land of Canaan, which I give to . . Israel 2
Jos 2: 1 saying, "Go, view the land, especially Jericho. 2
18: 4 writing . . it with a view to their inheritances 1
2Kg 16:12 when the king came . . the king viewed the altar. 2
Act 28:22 we desire to hear from you what your views are 6
1Co 7:26 I think that in view of the present distress 3
1Mc 14:38 In view of these things 4
2Mc 4: 5 having in view the welfare . . of all the people. 5
6:11 in view of their regard for that most holy day. 4

view *See also* point, take.

full view 1.πρόσωπον
Jdt 7: 6 in full view of the Israelites in Bethulia 1

public view 1.δημόσιος
3Mc 4: 7 In bonds and in public view 1

vigilance 1.מִשְׁמָר
Prv 4:23 Keep your heart with all vigilance; 1

vigilant 1.ἀγρυπνέω
Wis 6:15 he who is vigilant on her account 1

vigor 1.כֶּלַח 2.ἰσχύω
Job 30: 2 could I gain from . . men whose vigor is gone? 1
Sir 41: 1 still has the vigor to enjoy his food! 2

full vigor 1.אַשְׁמַנִּים
Isa 59:10 among those in full vigor we are like dead men. 1

utmost vigor 1.εὔτονος
2Mc 12:23 Judas pressed the pursuit with the utmost vigor 1

youthful vigor 1.עֲלוּמִים
Job 20:11 His bones are full of youthful vigor 1
33:25 let him return to the days of his youthful vigor 1

vigorous 1.חָיֶה 2.εὐρώστως
Exd 1:19 for they are vigorous and are delivered before 1
2Mc 12:27 and made a vigorous defense 2

vigorously 1.εὐρώστως
2Mc 10:17 Attacking them vigorously 1

vile 1.נְבָלָה 2.קלל 3.רַע 4.שֹׁעָר 5.μιαρός 6.φαῦλος
Jdg 19:24 but against this man do not do so vile a thing. 1
Jer 3: 2 have polluted the land with your vile harlotry. 3
29:17 I will make them like vile figs which are so bad 4
Ezk 8: 9 he said to me, "Go in, and see the vile abominations 3
Nah 1:14 I will make your grave, for you are vile. 2
Jas 3:16 there will be disorder and every vile practice. 6
2Mc 4:19 the vile Jason sent envoys 5
15:32 He showed them the vile Nicanor's head 5

vile deed 1.מְזִמָּה
Jer 11:15 when she has done vile deeds? 1

vile thing 1.נְבָלָה
Jdg 19:23 seeing that . . do not do this vile thing. 1

vileness 1.זֻלּוּת
Ps 12: 8 as vileness is exalted among the sons of men. 1

village 1.בַּת 2.חַוָּה 3.חָצֵר 4.כְּפִירִים 5.כָּפָר 6.כֹּפֶר 7.עִיר 8.פְּרָזִי 9.δῆμος 10.θυγάτηρ 11.κώμη
Gen 25:16 these are their names, by their villages 3
Lev 25:31 the houses of the villages which have no wall 3
Num21:25 settled in . . Heshbon, and in all its villages. 1
32 sent to spy out Jazer; and they took its villages 1
32:41 Ja'ir . . of Manas'seh went and took their villages 2
42 Nobah went and took Kenath and its villages 1
Deu 2:23 for the Avvim, who lived in villages as far as Gaza 3
3: 5 besides very many unwalled villages. 7
14 Ja'ir . . called the villages after his own name *
Jos 13:23 their families with their cities and villages. 3
28 their families, with their cities and villages. 3
15:32 in all, 29 cities, with their villages. 3
36 fourteen cities with their villages. 3
41 sixteen cities with their villages. 3
44 nine cities with their villages. 3
45 Ekron, with its towns and its villages; 3
46 by the side of Ashdod, with their villages. 3
47 Ashdod, its towns and its villages; 3
47 Gaza, its towns and its villages; 3
51 eleven cities with their villages. 3
54 nine cities with their villages. 3
57 ten cities with their villages. 3
59 six cities with their villages. 3
60 two cities with their villages. 3
62 six cities with their villages. 3
16: 9 all those towns with their villages. 3
17:11 Manas'seh had Beth-she'an and its villages 1
11 Manas'seh had . . and Ibleam and its villages 1
11 and the inhabitants of Dor and its villages 1
11 and the inhabitants of En-dor and its villages 1
11 and the inhabitants of Ta'anach and its villages 1
11 and the inhabitants of Megid'do and its villages; 1
16 those in Beth-she'an and its villages and those 1
18:24 twelve cities with their villages 3
28 fourteen cities with their villages. 3
19: 6 thirteen cities with their villages; 3
7 four cities with their villages; 3
8 with all the villages round about these cities 3
15 twelve cities with their villages. 3
16 these cities with their villages. 3
22 sixteen cities with their villages. 3
23 the cities with their villages. 3
30 22 cities with their villages. 3
31 these cities with their villages. 3
38 nineteen cities with their villages. 3
39 the cities with their villages. 3
48 these cities with their villages. 3
21:12 the fields of the city and its villages had been 3
Jdg 1:27 the inhabitants of Beth-she'an and its villages 1
27 did not drive out . . or Ta'anach and its villages 1
27 or the inhabitants of Dor and its villages 1
27 or the inhabitants of Ibleam and its villages 1
27 or the inhabitants of Megid'do and its villages; 1
11:26 While Israel dwelt in Heshbon and its villages 1
26 in Aro'er and its villages, and in all the cities 1
1Sm 6:18 both fortified cities and unwalled villages. 6
1Kg 4:13 Ben-geber . . (he had the villages of Ja'ir the son 2
1Ch 2:23 Kenath and its villages, 60 towns. 1
4:32 villages were Etam, A'in, Rimmon, Tochen, 3
33 villages which were round about these cities 3
6:56 fields of the city and its villages 3
9:16 who dwelt in the villages of the Netoph'athites. 3
22 enrolled by genealogies in their villages. 3
25 their kinsmen who were in their villages 3
18: 1 he took Gath and its villages out of the hand 1
27:25 in the cities, in the villages and in the towers 6
2Ch 13:19 took cities from him, Bethel with its villages 1
19 took cities . . Jesha'nah with its villages 1
19 took cities . . Ephron with its villages. 1
28:18 had taken . . Soco with its villages, Timnah 1
18 had taken . . Timnah with its villages, and Gimzo 1
18 had taken . . and Gimzo with its villages; 1
Neh 6: 2 meet . . in one of the villages in the plain of Ono. 4
11:25 as for the villages, with their fields 3
25 some . . lived in Kir'iath-ar'ba and its villages 1
25 some . . lived . . in Dibon and its villages 1
25 some . . lived . . in Jekab'zeel and its villages 3
27 in Ha'zar-shu'al, in Beer-sheba and its villages 1
28 in Ziklag, in Meco'nah and its villages 1
30 Zano'ah, Adullam, and their villages 3
30 Aze'kah and its villages. 1
31 Michmash, Ai'ja, Bethel and its villages 1
12:28 from the villages of the Netoph'athites; 3
29 built . . villages around Jerusalem. 3
Est 9:19 Jews of the villages . . hold the fourteenth day 8
Ps 10: 8 He sits in ambush in the villages; 3
Sng 7:11 go . . into the fields, and lodge in the villages; 6
Isa 42:11 the villages that Kedar inhabits; 3
Jer 49: 2 and its villages shall be burned with fire; 1
Ezk 38:13 Tarshish and all its villages will say to you 5
Mat 9:35 Jesus went about all the cities and villages 11
10:11 whatever town or village you enter 11
14:15 send the crowds away to go into the villages 11
21: 2 saying to them, "Go into the village opposite you 11
Mrk 6: 6 he went about among the villages teaching. 11
36 to go into the country and villages round about 11
56 wherever he came, in villages, cities, or country 11
8:23 led him out of the village 11
26 Do not even enter the village. 11
27 to the villages of Caesare'a Philip'pi 11
11: 2 said to them, "Go into the village opposite you 11
Lke 5:17 had come from every village of Galilee and Judea 11

8: 1 he went on through cities and villages 11
9: 6 they departed and went through the villages 11
12 to go into the villages and country round about 11
52 who went and entered a village of the Samaritans 11
56 And they went on to another village. 11
10:38 Now as they went on their way, he entered a village; 11
13:22 He went on his way through towns and villages 11
17:12 as he entered a village, he was met by ten lepers 11
19:30 saying, "Go into the village opposite 11
24:13 two of them were going to a village named Emma'us 11
28 drew near to the village to which they were going 11
Joh 7:42 comes from Bethlehem, the village where David was? 11
11: 1 the village of Mary and her sister Martha. 11
30 Now Jesus had not yet come to the village 11
Act 8:25 many villages of the Samaritans. 11
1Es 4:50 should give up the villages of the Jews 11
Jdt 4: 5 fortified the villages on them 11
15: 7 the villages and towns in the hill country 11
1Mc 5: 8 He also took Jazer and its villages 10
65 He struck Hebron and its villages 10
7:46 men came out of all the villages of Judea round about 11
2Mc 4:48 the city and the villages and the holy vessels 9
8: 1 secretly entered the villages 11
6 he would set fire to towns and villages 11
14:16 at a village called Dessau. 11

unwalled village 1. פְּרָזָה
Ezk 38:11 go up against the land of unwalled villages; 1

village without a wall 1. פְּרָזָה
Zec 2: 4 shall be inhabited as villages without walls 1

villainy 1. בְּלִיַּעַל 2. זִמָּה
Hos 6: 9 on the way to Shechem, yea, they commit villainy. 2
Nah 1:11 evil against the LORD, and counseled villainy? 1

vindicate 1. דין 2. צדק 3. קדשׁ 4. שׁפט 5. *δικαιόω* 6. *ἐκδικέω* 7. *ποιέω ἐκδίκησιν*
Deu 32:36 For the LORD will vindicate his people 1
1Kg 8:32 and vindicating the righteous by rewarding him 2
2Ch 6:23 vindicating the righteous by rewarding him 2
Job 11: 2 a man full of talk be vindicated? 2
13:18 I know that I shall be vindicated. 2
Ps 26: 1 Vindicate me, O LORD 4
35:24 Vindicate me, O LORD, my God 4
43: 1 Vindicate me, O God, and defend my cause 4
54: 1 O God, by thy name, and vindicate me by thy might. 1
135:14 For the LORD will vindicate his people 1
Isa 50: 8 he who vindicates me is near. 2
Ezk 36:23 when through you I vindicate my holiness 3
Lke 18: 3 saying, 'Vindicate me against my adversary.' 6
5 I will vindicate her 6
7 will not God vindicate his elect 7
8 I tell you, he will vindicate them speedily. 7
1Ti 3:16 vindicated in the Spirit, seen by angels 5
AEs 10:12 God . . vindicated his inheritance. 5
4Mc 17:10 They vindicated their nation 6

vindicate holiness 1. קדשׁ
Ezk 36:23 I will vindicate the holiness of my great name 1
23 when through you I vindicate my holiness 1
38:16 when through you, O Gog, I vindicate my holiness 1
39:27 and through them have vindicated my holiness 1

vindication 1. יְשׁוּעָה 2. כְּסוּת 3. מִשְׁפָּט 4. צֶדֶק 5. צְדָקָה
Gen 20:16 silver; it is your vindication in the eyes 2
Job 6:29 Turn now, my vindication is at stake. 4
Ps 17: 2 From thee let my vindication come! 3
24: 5 and vindication from the God of his salvation. 5
35:27 those who desire my vindication shout for joy 4
37: 6 will bring forth your vindication as the light 4
98: 2 revealed his vindication in the sight 5
103: 6 LORD works vindication and justice for all 5
Isa 54:17 and their vindication from me, says the LORD. 5
62: 1 until her vindication goes forth as brightness 4
2 The nations shall see your vindication 4
63: 1 It is I, announcing vindication, mighty to save. 5
Jer 51:10 The LORD has brought forth our vindication; 5
Jol 2:23 he has given the early rain for your vindication 5

vindicator 1. *ἔκδικος*
4Mc 15:29 O mother of the nation, vindicator of the law 1

vine 1. גֶּפֶן 2. גֶּפֶן יַיִן 3. *ἄμπελος* 4. vinea
Gen 40: 9 said to him, "In my dream there was a vine before me 1
10 on the vine there were three branches; 1
49:11 Binding his foal to the vine 1
Num20: 5 It is no place for . . or vines, or pomegranates; 1
Deu 8: 8 a land of . . vines and fig trees and pomegranates 1
32:32 For their vine comes from the vine of Sodom 1
32 For their vine comes from the vine of Sodom 1
Jdg 9:12 trees said to the vine, 'Come you, and reign over us.' 1
13 the vine said to them, 'Shall I leave my wine 1
13:14 may not eat of anything that comes from the vine 2
1Kg 4:25 every man under his vine and under his fig tree 1
2Kg 4:39 went out . . found a wild vine and gathered from it 1
18:31 then every one of you will eat of his own vine 1
Job 15:33 He will shake off his unripe grape, like the vine 1
Ps 78:47 He destroyed their vines with hail 1
80: 8 Thou didst bring a vine out of Egypt; 1
14 from heaven, and see; have regard for this vine 1
105:33 He smote their vines and fig trees 1
128: 3 wife . . like a fruitful vine within your house; 1
Sng 2:13 The fig tree . . and the vines are in blossom; 1
6:11 to . . see whether the vines had budded 1
7: 8 Oh, may your breasts be like clusters of the vine 1
12 let us go . . and see whether the vines have budded 1
Isa 7:23 every place where there used to be 1,000 vines 1
16: 8 fields . . languish, and the vine of Sibmah; 1
9 with the weeping of Jazer for the vine of Sibmah; 1
24: 7 The wine mourns, the vine languishes 1
32:12 for the pleasant fields, for the fruitful vine 1
34: 4 host shall fall, as leaves fall from the vine 1
36:16 then every one of you will eat of his own vine 1
Jer 2:21 have . . turned degenerate and become a wild vine? 1
5:17 they shall eat up your vines and your fig trees; 1
6: 9 Glean thoroughly as a vine the remnant of Israel; 1
8:13 there are no grapes on the vine 1
48:32 More than for Jazer I weep for you, O vine of Sibmah! 1
Ezk 15: 2 how does the wood of the vine surpass any wood 1
6 Like the wood of the vine among the trees 1
17: 6 it sprouted and became a low spreading vine 1
6 So it became a vine, and brought forth branches 1
7 behold, this vine bent its roots toward him 1
8 and bear fruit, and become a noble vine. 1
19:10 Your mother was like a vine in a vineyard 1
12 But the vine was plucked up in fury •
Hos 2:12 And I will lay waste her vines and her fig trees 1
10: 1 a luxuriant vine that yields its fruit. 1
14: 7 they shall blossom as the vine 1
Jol 1: 7 It has laid waste my vines 1
12 The vine withers, the fig tree languishes. 1
2:22 and fig tree and vine give their full yield. 1
Mic 4: 4 but they shall sit every man under his vine 1
Hab 3:17 fig tree do not blossom, nor fruit be on the vines 1
Hag 2:19 Do the vine, the fig tree, the pomegranate 1
Zec 3:10 of you will invite his neighbor under his vine 1
8:12 sowing of peace; the vine shall yield its fruit 1
Mal 3:11 your vine in the field shall not fail to bear 1
Mat 26:29 I shall not drink again of this fruit of the vine 3
Mrk 14:25 I shall not drink again of the fruit of the vine 3
Lke 22:18 I shall not drink of the fruit of the vine 3
Joh 15: 1 I am the true vine 3
4 unless it abides in the vine 3
5 I am the vine, you are the branches. 3
Rev 14:18 and gather the clusters of the vine of the earth 3
2Es 5:23 from all its trees thou hast chosen one vine 4
16:43 also him that prunes the vines 4
Sir 24:17 Like a vine I caused loveliness to bud 3
1Mc 14:12 Each man sat under his vine and his fig tree 3

vine *See also* branch.

choice vine 1. שֹׂרֵק 2. שֹׂרֵקָה
Gen 49:11 Binding . . his ass's colt to the choice vine 2
Isa 5: 2 cleared it . . and planted it with choice vines; 1
Jer 2:21 I planted you a choice vine, wholly of pure seed. 1

undressed vine 1. נָזִיר
Lev 25: 5 grapes of your undressed vine you shall not 1
11 nor gather the grapes from the undressed vines 1

vine-row 1. שׁוּרָה
Jer 5:10 Go up through her vine-rows and destroy 1

vinedresser 1. כרם 2. *ἀμπελουργός* 3. *γεωργός*
2Kg 25:12 the poorest . . to be vinedressers and plowmen. 1
2Ch 26:10 he had farmers and vinedressers in the hills 1
Isa 61: 5 foreigners shall be your . . vinedressers; 1
Jer 52:16 the poorest of the land to be vinedressers 1
Jol 1:11 wail, O vinedressers, for the wheat and the barley; 1
Lke 13: 7 he said to the vinedresser, 'Lo, these three years 2
Joh 15: 1 my Father is the vinedresser. 3

vinegar 1. חֹמֶץ 2. *ὄξος*
Num 6: 3 he shall drink no vinegar made from wine 1
Ps 69:21 for my thirst they gave me vinegar to drink. 1
Prv 10:26 Like vinegar to the teeth, and smoke to the eyes 1
25:20 like vinegar on a wound. 1
Mat 27:48 ran and took a sponge, filled it with vinegar 2
Mrk 15:36 filling a sponge full of vinegar, put it on a reed 2
Lke 23:36 coming up and offering him vinegar 2
Joh 19:29 A bowl full of vinegar stood there 2
29 they put a sponge full of the vinegar on hyssop 2
30 When Jesus had received the vinegar, he said 2

vineyard 1. כֶּרֶם 2. *ἀμπελών* 3. vindemia 4. vinea
Gen 9:20 tiller of the soil. He planted a vineyard; 1
Exd 22: 5 When a man causes a field or vineyard to be grazed 1
5 best in his own field and in his own vineyard. 1
23:11 You shall do likewise with your vineyard 1
Lev 19:10 you shall not strip your vineyard bare 1
10 gather the fallen grapes of your vineyard 1
25: 3 six years you shall prune your vineyard 1
4 shall not sow your field or prune your vineyard 1
Num16:14 given us inheritance of fields and vineyards. 1
20:17 We will not pass through field or vineyard 1
21:22 we will not turn aside into field or vineyard; 1
22:24 stood in a narrow path between the vineyards 1
Deu 6:11 vineyards and olive trees, which you did not plant 1
20: 6 what man is there that has planted a vineyard 1
22: 9 not sow your vineyard with two kinds of seed 1
9 crop . . sown and the yield of the vineyard. 1
23:24 When you go into your neighbor's vineyard 1
24:21 When you gather the grapes of your vineyard 1
28:30 plant a vineyard, and you shall not use the fruit 1
39 You shall plant vineyards and dress them 1
Jos 24:13 you eat the fruit of vineyards and oliveyards 1
Jdg 9:27 and gathered the grapes from their vineyards 1
14: 5 to Timnah, and he came to the vineyards of Timnah. 1
21:20 Go and lie in wait in the vineyards 1
21 come out of the vineyards and seize each man 1
1Sm 8:14 the best of your fields and vineyards and olive 1
15 take the tenth of your grain and . . vineyards 1
22: 7 give every one of you fields and vineyards 1
1Kg 21: 1 Naboth the Jezreelite had a vineyard in Jezreel 1
2 Give me your vineyard, that I may have it 1
2 Give me . . and I will give you a better vineyard 1
6 Give me your vineyard for money; 1
6 or else . . I will give you another vineyard for it'; 1
6 and he answered, 'I will not give you my vineyard.' 1
7 I will give you the vineyard of Naboth 1
15 Arise, take possession of the vineyard of Naboth 1
16 Ahab arose to go down to the vineyard of Naboth 1
18 Ahab . . is in the vineyard of Naboth 1
2Kg 5:26 and garments, olive orchards and vineyards 1
18:32 of grain and wine, a land of bread and vineyards 1
19:29 sow, and reap, and plant vineyards, and eat 1
1Ch 27:27 over the vineyards was Shim'e-i the Ra'mathite; 1
27 over the produce of the vineyards for the wine 1
Neh 5: 3 We are mortgaging our fields, our vineyards 1
4 king's tax upon our fields and our vineyards. 1
5 for other men have our fields and our vineyards. 1
11 Return . . their fields, their vineyards 1
9:25 possession of . . cisterns hewn out, vineyards 1
Job 24: 6 they glean the vineyard of the wicked man. 1
18 no treader turns toward their vineyards. 1
Ps 107:37 sow fields, and plant vineyards 1
Prv 24:30 I passed by . . the vineyard of a man without sense; 1
31:16 fruit of her hands she plants a vineyard. 1
Ecc 2: 4 I built houses and planted vineyards for myself; 1
Sng 1: 6 they made me keeper of the vineyards; 1
6 but, my own vineyard I have not kept! 1
14 cluster of henna . . in the vineyards of En-ge'di 1
2:15 foxes, the little foxes, that spoil the vineyards 1
15 for our vineyards are in blossom. 1
7:12 let us go out early to the vineyards 1
8:11 Solomon had a vineyard at Ba'al-ha'mon; 1
11 he let out the vineyard to keepers; 1
12 My vineyard, my very own, is for myself; 1
Isa 1: 8 Zion is left like a booth in a vineyard 1
3:14 It is you who have devoured the vineyard 1
5: 1 my beloved a love song concerning his vineyard 1
1 My beloved had a vineyard on a very fertile hill. 1
3 judge, I pray you, between me and my vineyard. 1
4 What more was there to do for my vineyard 1
5 now I will tell you what I will do to my vineyard. 1
7 the vineyard of the LORD . . is the house of Israel 1
10 ten acres of vineyard shall yield but one bath 1
16:10 and in the vineyards no songs are sung 1
27: 2 In that day: "A pleasant vineyard, sing of it! 1
36:17 of grain and wine, a land of bread and vineyards. 1
37:30 and plant vineyards, and eat their fruit. 1
65:21 shall plant vineyards and eat their fruit. 1
Jer 12:10 Many shepherds have destroyed my vineyard 1
31: 5 Again you shall plant vineyards 1
32:15 vineyards shall again be bought in this land. 1
35: 7 you shall not plant or have a vineyard; 1
9 We have no vineyard or field or seed; 1
39:10 gave them vineyards and fields at the same time. 1
Ezk 19:10 Your mother was like a vine in a vineyard •
28:26 they shall build houses and plant vineyards. 1
Hos 2:15 And there I will give her her vineyards 1
Ams 4: 9 I laid waste your gardens and your vineyards; 1
5:11 you have planted pleasant vineyards 1
17 and in all vineyards there shall be wailing 1
9:14 they shall plant vineyards and drink their wine 1
Mic 1: 6 Sama'ria a heap . . a place for planting vineyards; 1
Zep 1:13 though they plant vineyards, they shall not 1
Mat 20: 1 to hire laborers for his vineyard. 2
2 he sent them into his vineyard. 2
4 to them he said, 'You go into the vineyard too 2
7 He said to them, 'You go into the vineyard too.' 2
8 the owner of the vineyard said to his steward 2
21:28 'Son, go and work in the vineyard today.' 2
33 There was a householder who planted a vineyard 2
39 they took him and cast him out of the vineyard 2
40 When therefore the owner of the vineyard comes 2
41 and let out the vineyard to other tenants 2
Mrk 12: 1 A man planted a vineyard 2
2 some of the fruit of the vineyard. 2
8 and cast him out of the vineyard. 2
9 What will the owner of the vineyard do? 2
9 give the vineyard to others. 2
Lke 13: 6 A man had a fig tree planted in his vineyard 2

20: 9 A man planted a vineyard, and let it out to tenants 2
10 give him some of the fruit of the vineyard 2
13 the owner of the vineyard said, 'What shall I do? 2
15 they cast him out of the vineyard and killed him. 2
15 What then will the owner of the vineyard do to them? 2
16 give the vineyard to others 2
1Co 9: 7 Who plants a vineyard without eating 2
1Es 4:16 brought up the very men who plant the vineyards 2
2Es 16:30 or as when a vineyard is gathered 4
30 who search carefully through the vineyard 3
1Mc 3:56 were betrothed, or were planting vineyards 2
4Mc 2: 9 nor gathers the last grapes from the vineyard 2

vintage 1. בָּצִיר 2. ἄμπελος 3. τρύγητος 4. vindemia

Lev 26: 5 your threshing shall last to the time of vintage 1
5 the vintage shall last to the time for sowing 1
Jdg 8: 2 of E'phraim better than the vintage of Abi-e'zer? 1
Isa 24:13 as at the gleaning when the vintage is done. 1
32:10 the vintage will fail, the fruit harvest will not 1
Jer 48:32 upon your summer fruits and your vintage 1
Mic 7: 1 as when the vintage has been gleaned 1
Rev 14:19 the angel . . gathered the vintage of the earth 2
2Es 12:42 like a cluster of grapes from the vintage 4
Sir 24:27 like the Gihon at the time of vintage. 3

vintage *See also* shout.

violate 1. חלל 2. חלף 3. ענה 4. רשע 5. ἀθετέω 6. ἀποπαρθενόω 7. καθυβρίζω 8. παραβαίνω

Deu 22:24 man because he violated his neighbor's wife; 3
29 shall be his wife, because he has violated her; 3
Job 37:23 abundant righteousness he will not violate. 3
Ps 55:20 against his friends, he violated his covenant. 1
89:31 if they violate my statutes 1
34 I will not violate my covenant 1
Isa 24: 5 transgressed the laws, violated the statutes 2
Dan 11:32 seduce . . those who violate the covenant; 4
1Ti 5:12 having violated their first pledge. 5
Heb 10:28 A man who has violated the law of Moses dies 5
Sir 20: 4 Like a eunuch's desire to violate a maiden 6
1Mc 7:18 they have violated the agreement 8
3Mc 2:14 undertakes to violate the holy place 7
4Mc 16:24 die rather than violate God's commandment. 8

violation 1. παράβασις

2Mc 15:10 pointing out . . their violation of oaths. 1

violation of the law 1. παρανομία

4Mc 4:19 in complete violation of the law 1

violence 1. חָמָס 2. יָד 3. מְרוּצָה 4. פָּרִיץ 5. רַב כֹּחַ 6. שֹׁד 7. ἀνάγκη 8. βία 9. βίαιος 10. βιαίως 11. ἰσχύς 12. ὁρμή 13. ὅρμημα 14. ὕβρις 15. vis

Gen 6:11 the earth was filled with violence. 1
13 for the earth is filled with violence 1
49: 5 weapons of violence are their swords. 1
Jdg 9:24 the violence done to the 70 sons of Jerubba'al 1
2Sm 22: 3 my God . . my savior; thou savest me from violence. 1
49 thou didst deliver me from men of violence. 1
Job 16:17 although there is no violence in my hands 1
19: 7 Behold, I cry out, 'Violence!' but I am not answered; 1
30:18 With violence it seizes my garment; 5
Ps 7:16 on his own pate his violence descends. 1
11: 5 his soul hates him that loves violence. 1
18:48 thou didst deliver me from men of violence. 1
27:12 risen against me, and they breathe out violence. 1
55: 9 for I see violence and strife in the city. 1
58: 2 your hands deal out violence on earth. 1
72:14 From oppression and violence he redeems 1
73: 6 violence covers them as a garment. 1
74:20 are full of the habitations of violence. 1
Prv 3:31 Do not envy a man of violence 1
4:17 drink the wine of violence. 1
10: 6 but the mouth of the wicked conceals violence. 1
11 but the mouth of the wicked conceals violence. 1
13: 2 desire of the treacherous is for violence. 1
16:29 A man of violence entices his neighbor 1
21: 7 The violence of the wicked will sweep them away 6
24: 2 for their minds devise violence 6
26: 6 cuts off his own feet and drinks violence. 1
Isa 28: 2 he will cast down to the earth with violence. 2
53: 9 in his death, although he had done no violence 1
59: 6 and deeds of violence are in their hands. 1
60:18 Violence shall no more be heard in your land 1
Jer 6: 7 violence and destruction are heard within her; 1
20: 8 I cry out, I shout, "Violence and destruction! 1
22:17 for practicing oppression and violence. 3
51:35 The violence done to me and to my kinsmen 1
46 violence is in the land 1
Ezk 7:11 Violence has grown up into a rod of wickedness; 1
23 the city is full of violence 1
8:17 that they should fill the land with violence 1
12:19 of the violence of all those who dwell in it. 1
28:16 you were filled with violence, and you sinned; 1
45: 9 Israel! Put away violence and oppression 1
Dan 11:14 men of violence among your own people 4
Hos 12: 1 they multiply falsehood and violence; 6
Jol 3:19 for the violence done to the people of Judah 1
Ams 3:10 those who store up violence and robbery in their 1
6: 3 and bring near the seat of violence? 1
Obd 1:10 For the violence done to your brother Jacob 1
Jon 3: 8 from the violence which is in his hands. 1
Mic 6:12 Your rich men are full of violence; 1
Hab 1: 2 Or cry to thee "Violence!" and thou wilt not save? 1
3 Destruction and violence are before me; 1
9 They all come for violence; 1
2: 8 for the blood of men and violence to the earth 1
17 The violence done to Lebanon will overwhelm you; 1
17 for the blood of men and violence to the earth 1
Zep 1: 9 who fill their master's house with violence 1
Mal 2:16 covering one's garment with violence 1
Act 5:26 brought them, but without violence 8
21:35 because of the violence of the crowd; 8
Rev 18:21 So shall Babylon . . be thrown down with violence 13
2Es 11:46 that the whole earth, freed from your violence 15
AEs 13: 7 may in one day go down in violence to Hades 10
Wis 4: 4 by the violence of the winds 8
19:13 prior signs in the violence of thunder 8
Sir 20: 4 a man who executes judgments by violence. 8
21: 4 Terror and violence will lay waste riches 14
1Mc 1:58 They kept using violence against Israel 11
3Mc 1:16 to avert the violence of this evil design 12
4: 5 the violence with which they were driven 9
4Mc 5:37 as one who does not fear your violence 7
11:26 and your violence powerless. 8
17: 2 nullified the violence of the tyrant 8
9 because of the violence of the tyrant 8

violence *See also* gain, man, rob, suffer, take.

do violence 1. חמס 2. שדד

Prv 19:26 who does violence to his father and chases away 2
24:15 do not violence to his home; 2
Jer 22: 3 And do no wrong or violence to the alien 1
Ezk 22:26 Her priests have done violence to my law 1
Zep 3: 4 they do violence to the law. 1

violent 1. חָמָס 2. עַוְלָה 3. פָּרִיץ 4. κακόω 5. καρτερός 6. πλήκτης 7. πολύς 8. σφόδρα 9. impetus

1Ch 17: 9 violent men shall waste them no more, as formerly 2
Ps 17: 4 I have avoided the ways of the violent. 3
25:19 foes, and with what violent hatred they hate me. 1
140: 1 preserve me from violent men 1
4 preserve me from violent men, who have planned 1
11 let evil hunt down the violent man speedily! 1
Act 12: 1 Herod the king laid violent hands upon some 4
23:10 when the dissension became violent 7
1Ti 3: 3 no drunkard, not violent but gentle 6
Tit 1: 7 a drunkard or violent or greedy for gain 6
2Es 4:49 and poured down a heavy and violent rain 9
4Mc 8: 2 then in violent rage he commanded 8
15:32 the flood of your emotions and the violent winds 5

violent man 1. בֶּן עַוְלָה 2. עָרִיץ

2Sm 7:10 and violent men shall afflict them no more 1
Prv 11:16 violent men get riches. 2

more violent 1. βίαιος

4Mc 2:15 reason rules even the more violent emotions 1

violently 1. בְּחָזְקָה 2. גָּדוֹל עַד מְאֹד 3. טַלְטֵלָה 4. βία 5. καθ' ὑπερβολήν 6. μετὰ βίας 7. πικρός 8. σφοδρῶς 9. valde

Gen 27:33 Isaac trembled violently, and said, "Who was it 2
Jdg 8: 1 with Mid'ian?" And they upbraided him violently. 1
Isa 22:17 will hurl you away violently, O you strong man. 3
24:19 is rent asunder, the earth is violently shaken. †
Act 27:18 As we were violently storm-tossed 8
Gal 1:13 how I persecuted the church of God violently 5
2Es 5:14 Then I awoke, and my body shuddered violently 9
Wis 17:18 the rhythm of violently rushing water 4
3Mc 4: 7 they were violently dragged along 6
4Mc 6: 1 dragged him violently 7

violently *See also* deal, drive, enter, take.

violet 1. תְּכֵלֶת

Jer 10: 9 their clothing is violet and purple; 1

viper 1. אֶפְעֶה 2. עַכְשׁוּב 3. שְׁפִיפֹן 4. ἔχιδνα 5. ἔχις

Gen 49:17 Dan shall be . . a viper by the path 3
Job 20:16 the tongue of a viper will kill him. 1
Ps 140: 3 under their lips is the poison of vipers. Selah 2
Isa 30: 6 the lion, the viper and the flying serpent 1
59: 5 and from one which is crushed a viper is hatched. 1
Mat 3: 7 he said to them, "You brood of vipers! 4
12:34 You brood of vipers! how can you speak good 4
23:33 You serpents, you brood of vipers 4
Lke 3: 7 You brood of vipers! 4
Act 28: 3 when a viper came out because of the heat 4
Sir 39:30 scorpions and vipers 5

virgin 1. בְּתוּלָה 2. בְּתוּלִים 3. נַעֲרָה בְתוּלָה 4. παρθενία 5. παρθένος 6. virgo

Gen 24:16 fair to look upon, a virgin, whom no man had known. 1
Exd 22:16 If a man seduces a virgin who is not betrothed 1
17 pay . . the marriage present for virgins. 1
Lev 21: 3 or his virgin sister (who is near to him 1
14 he shall take to wife a virgin of his own people 1
Deu 22:19 brought an evil name upon a virgin of Israel; 1
23 If there is a betrothed virgin, and a man meets her 3
28 If a man meets a virgin who is not betrothed 1
32:25 destroying both young man and virgin 1
Jdg 19:24 here are my virgin daughter and his concubine; 1
21:12 found . . 400 young virgins who had not known man 1
2Sm 13: 2 ill because of his sister . . for she was a virgin 1
18 thus were the virgin daughters of the king clad 1
2Kg 19:21 she scorns you–the virgin daughter of Zion; 1
2Ch 36:17 had no compassion on young man or virgin 1
Est 2: 2 Let beautiful young virgins be sought out 1
3 to gather all the beautiful young virgins 1
17 found grace and . . more than all the virgins 1
19 the virgins were gathered together the second 1
Job 31: 1 how then could I look upon a virgin? 1
Ps 45:14 she is led to the king, with her virgin companions 1
Isa 23: 4 reared young men nor brought up virgins. 1
12 O oppressed virgin daughter of Sidon; 1
37:22 she scorns you–the virgin daughter of Zion; 1
47: 1 and sit in the dust, O virgin daughter of Babylon; 1
62: 5 as a young man marries a virgin, so shall your sons 1
Jer 14:17 for the virgin daughter of my people is smitten 1
18:13 virgin Israel has done a very horrible thing. 1
31: 4 and you shall be built, O virgin Israel! 1
21 Return, O virgin Israel 1
46:11 and take balm, O virgin daughter of Egypt! 1
Lam 1:15 as in a . . press the virgin daughter of Judah. 1
2:13 that I may comfort you, O virgin daughter of Zion? 1
5:11 ravished in Zion, virgins in the towns of Judah. 1
Ezk 23: 3 and their virgin bosoms handled. 2
8 had lain with her and handled her virgin bosom 2
44:22 a virgin of the stock of the house of Israel 1
Jol 1: 8 Lament like a virgin girded with sackcloth 1
Ams 5: 2 Fallen, no more to rise, is the virgin Israel; 1
8:13 the fair virgins and the young men shall faint 1
Mat 1:23 Behold, a virgin shall conceive and bear a son 5
Lke 1:27 a virgin betrothed to a man whose name was Joseph 5
27 and the virgin's name was Mary. 5
1Es 1:53 did not spare young man or virgin 5
2Es 10:22 our virgins have been defiled 6
16:33 Virgins shall mourn 6
Jdt 9: 2 had loosed the girdle of a virgin to defile her 5
16: 5 and take my virgins as booty. 5
Sir 9: 5 Do not look intently at a virgin 5
42:10 while a virgin, lest she be defiled 4
2Mc 5:13 slaughter of virgins and infants. 5
3Mc 1:18 virgins who had been enclosed in their chambers 5
4Mc 18: 7 I was a pure virgin 5

virginity 1. בְּתוּלִים 2. παρθενία

Lev 21:13 he shall take a wife in her virginity 1
Jdg 11:37 I may go and wander . . and bewail my virginity 1
38 and she departed . . and bewailed her virginity 1
Lke 2:36 seven years from her virginity 2
4Mc 18: 8 defile the purity of my virginity. 2

virginity *See also* token.

virtually 1. σχεδόν

3Mc 5:45 had been brought virtually to a state of madness 1

virtue 1. ἀρετή 2. διά 3. δύναμις 4. κατά

2Ti 1: 9 not in virtue of our works 4
9 called us . . in virtue of his own purpose 4
Tit 3: 5 in virtue of his own mercy 4
2Pe 1: 5 to supplement your faith with virtue 1
5 to supplement . . virtue with knowledge 1
Wis 4: 1 Better than this is childlessness with virtue 1
1 in the memory of virtue is immortality *
5:13 we had no sign of virtue to show 1
7:20 the powers of spirits . . and the virtues of roots; 3
8: 7 her labors are virtues 1
3Mc 6: 1 had been adorned with every virtue 1
4Mc 1: 2 it includes the praise of the highest virtue 1
8 those who died for the sake of virtue 1
10 it is fitting for me to praise for their virtues 1
30 For reason is the guide of the virtues 1
30 by virtue of . . self-control. 2
2:10 virtue is not abandoned for their sakes. 1
7:22 to endure any suffering for the sake of virtue 1
9: 8 shall have the prize of virtue 1
18 where virtue is concerned. 1
31 the joys that come from virtue 1
10:10 because of our godly training and virtue 1
11: 2 to be tortured for the sake of virtue. 1
12:14 having slain . . the contestants for virtue. 1
13:24 trained in the same virtues 1
17:12 on that day virtue gave the awards 1
23 when he saw the courage of their virtue 1

virtue *See also* hater.

virtuous 1. ἀρετή 2. ἐνάρετος 3. bonus

2Es 16:49 a . . virtuous woman abhors a harlot 3
4Mc 11: 5 and live according to his virtuous law? 2
13:27 nature and companionship and virtuous habits 1

visage 1. תֹּאַר
Lam 4: 8 Now their visage is blacker than soot 1

visible 1. חֲזוֹת (A) 2. *ἐμφανής* 3. *ὁρατός* 4. *φαιδρός* 5. compareo
Dan 4:11 tree . . visible to the end of the whole earth. 1
20 visible to the end of the whole earth; 1
Col 1:16 in heaven and on earth, visible and invisible 3
2Es 10:27 behold, the woman was no longer visible to me 5
Wis 14:17 made a visible image of the king 2
3Mc 6:18 visible to all but the Jews. 4

become visible 1. *φανερόω*
Eph 5:13 exposed by the light it becomes visible 1
13 for anything that becomes visible is light. 1

vision 1. דָּבָר 2. חָזוֹן 3. חָזוּת 4. חָזוֹת 5. חִזָּיוֹן 6. מַחֲזֶה 7. מַרְאֶה 8. מַרְאָה 9. רֹאֶה 10. חֵזוּ (A) 11. *ἆ ὁράω* 12. *ὀπτασία* 13. *ὅραμα* 14. *ὅρασις* 15. *ὕπαρ* 16. visio 17. visus
Gen 15: 1 the word of the LORD came to Abram in a vision 6
46: 2 God spoke to Israel in visions of the night 8
Num12: 6 I the LORD make myself known to him in a vision 8
24: 4 oracle of . . who sees the vision of the Almighty 6
16 who sees the vision of the Almighty 6
1Sm 3: 1 was rare . . there was no frequent vision. 2
15 And Samuel was afraid to tell the vision to Eli. 8
2Sm 7:17 in accordance with all this vision, Nathan spoke 5
1Ch 17:15 and in accordance with all this vision 2
2Ch 9:29 and in the visions of Iddo the seer 4
32:32 written in the vision of Isaiah the prophet 2
Job 4:13 Amid thoughts from visions of the night 5
7:14 scare me with dreams and terrify me with visions 5
20: 8 he will be chased away like a vision of the night. 5
33:15 In a dream, in a vision of the night, 5
Ps 89:19 thou didst speak in a vision to thy faithful one 2
Isa 1: 1 The vision of Isaiah the son of Amoz, which he saw 2
21: 2 A stern vision is told to me; 3
22: 1 The oracle concerning the valley of vision. 5
5 day of . . confusion in the valley of vision 5
28: 7 with strong drink; they err in vision 9
29: 7 shall be like a dream, a vision of the night. 2
11 the vision of all this has become to you 3
Jer 14:14 They are prophesying to you a lying vision 2
23:16 they speak visions of their own minds 2
24: 1 the LORD showed me this vision *
38:21 this is the vision which the LORD has shown to me 1
Lam 2: 9 and her prophets obtain no vision from the LORD. 2
Ezk 1: 1 the heavens were opened, and I saw visions of God. 8
7:26 they seek a vision from the prophet 2
8: 3 and brought me in visions of God to Jerusalem 8
4 like the vision that I saw in the plain. 7
11:24 and brought me in the vision by the Spirit of God 7
24 Then the vision that I had seen went up from me. 7
12:22 days grow long, and every vision comes to nought 2
23 are at hand, and the fulfilment of every vision. 2
24 For there shall be no more any false vision 2
27 The vision that he sees is for many days hence 2
13: 7 Have you not seen a delusive vision 6
16 and saw visions of peace for her 2
21:29 while they see for you false visions *
40: 2 and brought me in the visions of God into the land 8
43: 3 vision I saw was like the vision which I had seen 7
3 vision I saw was like the vision which I had seen 7
3 the vision which I had seen by the river Chebar; 7
Dan 1:17 understanding in all visions and dreams. 2
2:19 mystery was revealed . . in a vision of the night. 10
28 Your dream and the visions of your head as you lay 10
4: 5 fancies and the visions of my head alarmed me. 10
10 visions of my head as I lay in bed were these 10
13 I saw in the visions of my head as I lay in bed 10
7: 1 Daniel had a dream and visions of his head 10
2 Daniel said, "I saw in my vision by night, 10
7 After this I saw in the night visions, 10
13 I saw in the night visions, and behold 10
15 visions of my head alarmed me. 10
8: 1 third year . . vision appeared to me, Daniel 2
2 I saw in the vision; and when I saw, I was in Susa 2
2 saw in the vision, and I was at the river U'lai. 2
13 For how long is the vision concerning 2
15 Daniel, had seen the vision, I sought 2
16 Gabriel, make this man understand the vision. 7
17 Understand . . vision is for the time of the end. 2
26 vision of the evenings and the mornings 7
26 seal up the vision, for it pertains to many days 2
27 appalled by the vision and did not understand it. 7
9:21 Gabriel, whom I had seen in the vision at the first 2
23 therefore consider . . understand the vision. 7
24 seal both vision and prophet, 2
10: 1 word and had understanding of the vision. 7
7 I, Daniel, alone saw the vision, 8
7 men who were with me did not see the vision 8
8 I was left alone and saw this great vision 8
14 For the vision is for days yet to come. 2
16 by reason of the vision pains have come upon me 8
11:14 lift themselves up in order to fulfil the vision; 2
Hos 12:10 it was I who multiplied visions 2
Jol 2:28 and your young men shall see visions. 5
Obd 1: 1 The vision of Obadi'ah. 2
Mic 3: 6 it shall be night to you, without vision 2
Nah 1: 1 The book of the vision of Nahum of Elkosh. 2
Hab 2: 2 Write the vision; make it plain upon tablets 2
3 For still the vision awaits its time; 2
Zec 13: 4 every prophet will be ashamed of his vision 5
Mat 17: 9 Tell no one the vision 13
Lke 1:22 perceived that he had seen a vision in the temple; 12
24:23 saying that they had even seen a vision of angels 12
Act 2:17 your young men shall see visions 14
9:10 The Lord said to him in a vision, "Anani'as. 13
10: 3 he saw clearly in a vision an angel of God 13
17 perplexed as to what the vision . . might mean 13
19 while Peter was pondering the vision 13
11: 5 in a trance I saw a vision, something descending 13
12: 9 thought he was seeing a vision. 13
16: 9 a vision appeared to Paul in the night 13
10 when he had seen the vision 13
18: 9 the Lord said to Paul one night in a vision 13
26:19 I was not disobedient to the heavenly vision 12
2Co 12: 1 go on to visions and revelations of the Lord. 12
Col 2:18 taking his stand on visions 11
Rev 9:17 this was how I saw the horses in my vision 14
2Es 2:21 let the blind man have a vision of my splendor. 16
10:37 an explanation of this bewildering vision. *
40 This therefore is the meaning of the vision. 16
59 will show you in those dream visions 16
12: 8 and meaning of this terrifying vision 17
10 interpretation of this vision which you 16
11 appeared in a vision to your brother Daniel. 17
13:21 I will tell you the interpretation of the vision 16
25 This is the interpretation of the vision 16
14:18 the eagle which you saw in the vision 16
Tob 12:19 you were seeing a vision. 14
Sir 34: 3 The vision of dreams is this against that 14
40: 6 he is troubled by the visions of his mind 14
48:22 who was great and faithful in his vision. 14
49: 8 It was Ezekiel who saw the vision of glory 14
2Mc 15:11 a sort of vision, which was worthy of belief. 15

delusive vision 1. שָׁוְא
Ezk 13: 9 against the prophets who see delusive visions 1
23 you shall no more see delusive visions 1

visit 1. פקד 2. ראה 3. שָׁלוֹם 4. *γίνομαι* 5. *διέρχομαι* 6. *εἰσέρχομαι πρός* 7. *εἴσοδος* 8. *ἐπέρχομαι* 9. *ἐπισκέπτομαι* 10. *ἔρχομαι πρός* 11. *ἐφοδεύω* 12. *ἱστορέω* 13. *μετέρχομαι* 14. *παραγίνομαι* 15. *πορεύω πρός* 16. *πρός* 17. *προσέρχομαι* 18. visito
Gen 21: 1 The LORD visited Sarah as he had said 1
34: 1 Dinah . . went out to visit the women of the land; 2
50:24 but God will visit you, and bring you up out of this 1
25 God will visit you, and you shall carry up 1
Exd 4:31 that the LORD had visited the people of Israel 1
13:19 solemnly sworn . . saying, "God will visit you; 1
20: 5 visiting the iniquity of the fathers upon 1
32:34 Nevertheless, in the day when I visit, I will visit 1
34 I visit, I will visit their sin upon them. 1
34: 7 visiting the iniquity of the fathers upon 1
Num14:18 visiting the iniquity of fathers upon children 1
16:29 or if they are visited by the fate of all men 1
Deu 5: 9 visiting the iniquity of the fathers 1
Jdg 15: 1 harvest, Samson went to visit his wife with a kid; 1
Rut 1: 6 LORD had visited his people and given them food. 1
1Sm 2:21 And the LORD visited Hannah, and she conceived 1
2Kg 9:16 And Ahazi'ah . . had come down to visit Joram. 2
10:13 and we came down to visit the royal princes 3
2Ch 22: 7 come about through his going to visit Joram. *
Job 7:18 dost visit him every morning 1
Ps 17: 3 if thou visitest me by night, if thou testest me 1
65: 9 Thou visitest the earth and waterest it 1
Prv 19:23 he will not be visited by harm. 1
Isa 23:17 the end of 70 years, the LORD will visit Tyre 1
26:14 thou hast visited them with destruction 1
29: 6 you will be visited by the LORD of hosts 1
Jer 15:15 O LORD, thou knowest; remember me and visit me 1
29:10 I will visit you 1
32: 5 and there he shall remain until I visit him 1
Mat 25:36 I was sick and you visited me 9
39 did we see thee sick or in prison and visit thee?' 10
43 sick and in prison and you did not visit me.' 9
Lke 1:68 he has visited and redeemed his people 9
7:16 God has visited his people! 9
Act 7:13 at the second visit *
23 it came into his heart to visit his brethren 9
10:28 to associate with or to visit any one 17
15:14 how God first visited the Gentiles 9
36 let us return and visit the brethren 9
16:40 So they went out of the prison, and visited Lydia; 6
28: 8 Paul visited him and prayed 6
1Co 16: 5 I will visit you 10
2Co 1:16 I wanted to visit you on my way to Macedo'nia 5
13: 2 as I did when present on my second visit *
Gal 1:18 I went up to Jerusalem to visit Cephas 12
1Th 2: 1 our visit to you was not in vain; 7
Jas 1:27 to visit orphans and widows in their affliction 9
2Es 5:56 through whom thou dost visit thy creation. 18
6:18 I draw near to visit the inhabitants 18
9: 2 when the Most High is about to visit the world 18
Jdt 7: 7 visited the springs that supplied their water 11
13:20 may he visit you with blessings 9
Sir 6:36 If you see an intelligent man, visit him early 16
7:35 Do not shrink from visiting a sick man 9
22:13 do not visit an unintelligent man 15
35:17 he will not desist until the Most High visits him 9
1Mc 16:14 Now Simon was visiting the cities of the country 11
2Mc 9:17 would visit every inhabited place 8
12: 5 the cruelty visited on his countrymen 4
3Mc 1: 6 decided to visit the neighboring cities 8
8 he was all the more eager to visit them 14
4Mc 10:21 God will visit you swiftly 13

visit *See also* make.

visitation 1. *ἐπισκοπή*
Lke 19:44 you did not know the time of your visitation. 1
1Pe 2:12 and glorify God on the day of visitation. 1
Wis 3: 7 In the time of their visitation 1
14:11 Therefore there will be a visitation 1
Sir 16:18 will tremble at his visitation. 1
18:20 in the hour of visitation 1
34: 6 sent from the Most High as a visitation 1

visitor 1. *ἐπιδημέω* 2. *παροικέω*
Lke 24:18 the only visitor to Jerusalem who does not know 2
Act 2:10 visitors from Rome, both Jews and proselytes 1

voice 1. קוֹל 2. שָׂפָה 3. קוֹל (A) 4. *βοή* 5. *γλῶσσα* 6. *ἠχώ* 7. *λάρυγξ* 8. *στόμα* 9. *φθόγγος* 10. *φωνέω* 11. *φωνή* 12. vox
Gen 3:17 you have listened to the voice of your wife 1
4:10 The voice of your brother's blood is crying to me 1
23 wives: "Adah and Zillah, hear my voice; 1
16: 2 And Abram hearkened to the voice of Sar'ai. 1
21:16 the child lifted up his voice and wept. 1
17 God heard the voice of the lad; 1
17 Fear not; for God has heard the voice of the lad 1
22:18 because you have obeyed my voice. 1
26: 5 Abraham obeyed my voice and kept my charge 1
27:22 who felt him and said, "The voice is Jacob's voice 1
22 who felt him and said, "The voice is Jacob's voice 1
38 And Esau lifted up his voice and wept. 1
43 Now therefore, my son, obey my voice; 1
30: 6 God . . has also heard my voice and given me a son"; 1
39:14 with me, and I cried out with a loud voice; 1
15 when he heard that I lifted up my voice and cried 1
18 as soon as I lifted up my voice and cried, he left 1
Exd 3:18 they will hearken to your voice; and you 1
4: 1 they will not believe me or listen to my voice 1
9 will not . . heed your voice, you shall take some 1
5: 2 Who is the LORD, that I should heed his voice 1
15:26 hearken to the voice of the LORD your God 1
18:19 Listen now to my voice; I will give you counsel 1
24 Moses gave heed to the voice of his father-in-law 1
19: 5 if you will obey my voice and keep my covenant 1
23:21 Give heed to him and hearken to his voice 1
22 if you hearken attentively to his voice and do 1
24: 3 all the people answered with one voice, and said 1
Num 7:89 Moses . . heard the voice speaking to him 1
14:22 have not hearkened to my voice 1
20:16 when we cried to the LORD, he heard our voice 1
21: 3 LORD hearkened to the voice of Israel, and gave 1
Deu 1:45 LORD did not hearken to your voice or give ear 1
4:12 words, but saw no form; there was only a voice. 1
30 return to the LORD your God and obey his voice 1
33 Did any people ever hear the voice of a god 1
36 Out of heaven he let you hear his voice 1
5:22 spoke to all your assembly . . with a loud voice; 1
23 heard the voice out of the midst of the darkness 1
24 heard his voice out of the midst of the fire; 1
25 if we hear the voice of the LORD our God any more 1
26 heard the voice of the living God speaking 1
8:20 you would not obey the voice of the LORD your God. 1
9:23 did not believe him or obey his voice. 1
13: 4 keep his commandments and obey his voice 1
18 if you obey the voice of the LORD your God, keeping 1
15: 5 if only you will obey the voice of the LORD 1
18:16 'Let me not hear again the voice of the LORD my God 1
21:18 son, who will not obey the voice of his father 1
18 son, who will not obey . . the voice of his mother 1
20 This our son . . will not obey our voice; 1
26: 7 LORD heard our voice, and saw our affliction 1
14 I have obeyed the voice of the LORD my God 1
17 walk in his ways . . and will obey his voice; 1
27:10 therefore obey the voice of the LORD your God 1
14 Levites shall declare . . with a loud voice 1
28: 1 if you obey the voice of the LORD your God 1
2 if you obey the voice of the LORD your God. 1
15 if you will not obey the voice of the LORD your God 1
45 you did not obey the voice of the LORD your God 1
62 you did not obey the voice of the LORD your God. 1
30: 2 obey his voice in all that I command you this day 1
8 again obey the voice of the LORD, and keep all 1
10 if you obey the voice of the LORD your God, to keep 1
20 loving . . obeying his voice, and cleaving to him; 1
33: 7 Hear, O LORD, the voice of Judah, and bring him 1

Jos 5: 6 they did not hearken to the voice of the LORD; 1
6:10 You shall not shout or let your voice be heard 1
10:14 when the LORD hearkened to the voice of a man; 1
22: 2 have obeyed my voice in all that I have commanded 1
24:24 LORD . . we will serve, and his voice we will obey. 1
Jdg 2: 4 the people lifted up their voices and wept. 1
20 and have not obeyed my voice 1
6:10 But you have not given heed to my voice. 1
13: 9 God listened to the voice of Mano'ah, and the angel 1
18: 3 they recognized the voice of the young Levite; 1
25 Do not let your voice be heard among us, lest angry 1
20:13 would not listen to the voice of their brethren 1
21: 2 they lifted up their voices and wept bitterly. 1
Rut 1: 9 and they lifted up their voices and wept. 1
14 Then they lifted up their voices and wept again; 1
1Sm 1:13 only her lips moved, and her voice was not heard; 1
2:25 would not listen to the voice of their father; 1
7:10 the LORD thundered with a mighty voice that day 1
8: 7 Hearken to the voice of the people in all 1
9 hearken to their voice; only, you shall . . warn 1
19 people refused to listen to the voice of Samuel; 1
22 Hearken to their voice, and make them a king. 1
12: 1 I have hearkened to your voice 1
14 fear . . and serve him and hearken to his voice 1
15 if you will not hearken to the voice of the LORD 1
15:19 Why then did you not obey the voice of the LORD? 1
20 I have obeyed the voice of the LORD, I have gone 1
22 as in obeying the voice of the LORD? 1
24 I feared the people and obeyed their voice. 1
19: 6 And Saul hearkened to the voice of Jonathan; 1
24:16 Saul said, "Is this your voice, my son David? 1
16 And Saul lifted up his voice and wept. 1
25:35 I have hearkened to your voice 1
26:17 Saul recognized David's voice, and said 1
17 Saul . . said, "Is it your voice, my son David? 1
17 And David said, "It is my voice, my lord, O king. 1
28:12 When the woman . . she cried out with a loud voice; 1
18 Because you did not obey the voice of the LORD 1
30: 4 and the people . . raised their voices and wept 1
2Sm 3:32 the king lifted up his voice and wept at the grave 1
13:36 sons came, and lifted up their voice and wept; 1
19: 4 the king cried with a loud voice, "O my son Ab'salom 1
35 listen to the voice of singing men and . . women? 1
22: 7 From his temple he heard my voice, and my cry came 1
14 and the Most High uttered his voice. 1
1Kg 8:55 and blessed all the assembly . . with a loud voice 1
17:22 the LORD hearkened to the voice of Eli'jah; 1
18:26 O Ba'al, answer us!" But there was no voice 1
29 they raved on . . but there was no voice; 1
19:12 and after the fire a still small voice. 1
13 And behold, there came a voice to him, and said 1
20:25 And he hearkened to their voice, and did so. 1
36 Because you have not obeyed the voice of the LORD 1
2Kg 18:12 they did not obey the voice of the LORD their God 1
28 Rab'shakeh stood and called out in a loud voice 1
19:22 Against whom have you raised your voice 1
2Ch 15:14 They took oath to the LORD with a loud voice 1
20:19 to praise the LORD . . with a very loud voice. 1
30:27 their voice was heard 1
32:18 they shouted it with a loud voice in the language 1
Ezr 3:12 wept with a loud voice when they saw 1
10:12 Then all the assembly answered with a loud voice 1
Neh 9: 4 cried with a loud voice to the LORD their God. 1
Job 2:12 they raised their voices and wept; 1
3:18 they hear not the voice of the taskmaster. 1
4:10 The roar of the lion, the voice of the fierce lion 1
16 there was silence, then I heard a voice 1
9:16 not believe that he was listening to my voice. 1
29:10 the voice of the nobles was hushed 1
30:31 and my pipe to the voice of those who weep. 1
37: 2 Hearken to the thunder of his voice 1
4 After it his voice roars; 1
4 he thunders with his majestic voice 1
4 the lightnings when his voice is heard. 1
5 God thunders wondrously with his voice; 1
38:34 Can you lift up your voice to the clouds 1
40: 9 like God, and can you thunder with a voice like his? 1
Ps 5: 3 O LORD, in the morning thou dost hear my voice; 1
18: 6 From his temple he heard my voice, and my cry to him 1
13 the Most High uttered his voice 1
19: 3 nor are there words; their voice is not heard; 1
4 yet their voice goes out through all the earth 9
28: 2 Hear the voice of my supplication, as I cry to thee 1
6 for he has heard the voice of my supplications. 1
29: 3 The voice of the LORD is upon the waters; 1
4 The voice of the LORD is powerful 1
4 voice of the LORD is full of majesty. 1
5 The voice of the LORD breaks the cedars 1
7 voice of the LORD flashes forth flames of fire. 1
8 The voice of the LORD shakes the wilderness 1
9 voice of the LORD makes the oaks to whirl 1
46: 6 he utters his voice, the earth melts. 1
55:17 my complaint and moan, and he will hear my voice. 1
58: 5 so that it does not hear the voice of charmers 1
64: 1 Hear my voice, O God, in my complaint; 1
66:19 he has given heed to the voice of my prayer. 1
68:33 lo, he sends forth his voice, his mighty voice. 1
33 lo, he sends forth his voice, his mighty voice. 1
81: 5 I hear a voice I had not known 2
11 my people did not listen to my voice; 1
93: 3 O LORD, the floods have lifted up their voice 1
95: 7 O that today you would hearken to his voice! 1
103:20 do his word, hearkening to the voice of his word! 1
106:25 murmured . . did not obey the voice of the LORD. 1
116: 1 has heard my voice and my supplications. 1
119:149 Hear my voice in thy steadfast love; 1
130: 2 Lord, hear my voice! Let thy ears be attentive 1
2 attentive to the voice of my supplications! 1
140: 6 give ear to the voice of my supplications, O LORD! 1
141: 1 Give ear to my voice, when I call to thee! 1
142: 1 I cry with my voice to the LORD 1
1 with my voice I make supplication to the LORD 1
Prv 1:20 in the markets she raises her voice; 1
2: 3 if you . . raise your voice for understanding 1
5:13 I did not listen to the voice of my teachers 1
8: 1 does not understanding raise her voice? 1
27:14 He who blesses his neighbor with a loud voice 1
Ecc 5: 3 dream comes . . and a fool's voice with many words. 1
6 why should God be angry at your voice, and destroy 1
10:20 a bird of the air will carry your voice 1
12: 4 and one rises up at the voice of a bird 1
Sng 2: 8 The voice of my beloved! Behold, he comes 1
12 the voice of the turtledove is heard in our land. 1
14 let me see your face, let me hear your voice 1
14 your voice is sweet, and your face is comely. 1
8:13 my companions are listening for your voice; 1
Isa 6: 4 thresholds shook at the voice of him who called 1
8 I heard the voice of the Lord saying, "Whom shall I 1
15: 4 cry out, their voice is heard as far as Jahaz; 1
24:14 They lift up their voices, they sing for joy; 1
28:23 Give ear, and hear my voice; 1
29: 4 your voice shall come from the ground 1
4 come from the ground like the voice of a ghost 1
30:30 the LORD will cause his majestic voice to be heard 1
31 will be terror-stricken at the voice of the LORD 1
32: 9 Rise up, you women who are at ease, hear my voice; 1
36:13 in a loud voice in the language of Judah 1
37:23 Against whom have you raised your voice 1
40: 3 A voice cries: "In the wilderness prepare the way 1
6 A voice says, "Cry!" And I said, "What shall I cry? 1
9 lift up your voice with strength, O Jerusalem 1
42: 2 He will not cry or lift up his voice 1
11 Let the desert and its cities lift up their voice •
50:10 fears the LORD and obeys the voice of his servant 1
51: 3 found in her, thanksgiving and the voice of song. 1
52: 8 Hark, your watchmen lift up their voice 1
58: 1 spare not, lift up your voice like a trumpet; 1
4 will not make your voice to be heard on high. 1
66: 6 an uproar from the city! A voice from the temple! 1
6 voice from the temple! The voice of the LORD 1
Jer 3:13 that you have not obeyed my voice, says the LORD. 1
21 A voice on the bare heights is heard 1
25 we have not obeyed the voice of the LORD our God.". 1
4:15 For a voice declares from Dan and proclaims evil 1
7:23 But this command I gave them, 'Obey my voice 1
28 the nation that did not obey the voice of the LORD 1
34 from the streets of Jerusalem the voice of mirth 1
34 the voice of mirth and the voice of gladness 1
34 voice of the bridegroom and . . voice of the bride; 1
34 voice of the bridegroom and . . voice of the bride; 1
9:13 have not obeyed my voice, or walked in accord 1
10:13 When he utters his voice there is a tumult 1
11: 4 Listen to my voice, and do all that I command you. 1
7 even to this day, saying, Obey my voice. 1
12: 8 she has lifted up her voice against me; 1
16: 9 the voice of mirth and the voice of gladness 1
9 the voice of mirth and the voice of gladness 1
9 voice of gladness, the voice of the bridegroom 1
9 of the bridegroom and the voice of the bride. 1
18:10 does evil in my sight, not listening to my voice 1
22:20 cry out, and lift up your voice in Bashan; 1
21 that you have not obeyed my voice. 1
25:10 I will banish from them the voice of mirth 1
10 the voice of mirth and the voice of gladness 1
10 voice of gladness, the voice of the bridegroom 1
10 of the bridegroom and the voice of the bride 1
30 and from his holy habitation utter his voice; 1
26:13 and obey the voice of the LORD your God 1
30:19 and the voices of those who make merry. 1
31:15 Thus says the LORD: "A voice is heard in Ramah 1
16 Thus says the LORD: "Keep your voice from weeping 1
32:23 But they did not obey thy voice or walk in thy law; 1
33:11 the voice of mirth and the voice of gladness 1
11 the voice of mirth and the voice of gladness 1
11 voice of . . bridegroom and the voice of the bride 1
11 voice of . . bridegroom and the voice of the bride 1
11 voice of the bride, the voices of those who sing 1
35: 8 We have obeyed the voice of Jon'adab 1
38:20 Obey now the voice of the LORD in what I say to you 1
40: 3 Because you sinned . . and did not obey his voice 1
42: 6 we will obey the voice of the LORD our God 1
6 when we obey the voice of the LORD our God. 1
13 disobeying the voice of the LORD your God 1
21 you have not obeyed the voice of the LORD your God 1
43: 4 the people did not obey the voice of the LORD 1
7 for they did not obey the voice of the LORD. 1
44:23 and did not obey the voice of the LORD 1
48:34 as far as Jahaz they utter their voice 1
51:16 When he utters his voice there is a tumult 1
55 laying . . waste, and stilling her mighty voice. 1
55 the noise of their voice is raised; 1
Ezk 1:25 there came a voice from above the firmament 1
28 and I heard the voice of one speaking. 1
8:18 though they cry in my ears with a loud voice 1
9: 1 Then he cried in my ears with a loud voice, saying 1
10: 5 like the voice of God Almighty when he speaks. 1
11:13 fell down upon my face, and cried with a loud voice 1
19: 9 that his voice should no more be heard 1
21:22 with a cry, to lift up the voice with shouting 1
33:32 one who sings love songs with a beautiful voice 1
Dan 4:31 there fell a voice from heaven, "O King 3
8:16 I heard a man's voice between the banks of the U'lai 1
9:10 not obeyed the voice of the LORD our God 1
11 turned aside, refusing to obey thy voice. 1
14 we have not obeyed his voice. 1
Jol 2:11 The LORD utters his voice before his army 1
3:16 and utters his voice from Jerusalem 1
Ams 1: 2 from Zion, and utters his voice from Jerusalem; 1
Jon 2: 2 of Sheol I cried, and thou didst hear my voice. 1
9 I with the voice of thanksgiving will sacrifice 1
Mic 6: 1 and let the hills hear your voice. 1
9 The voice of the LORD cries to the city 1
Nah 2:13 voice of your messengers shall no more be heard. 1
Hab 3:10 the deep gave forth its voice, it lifted its hands 1
Zep 3: 2 She listens to no voice 1
Hag 1:12 the people, obeyed the voice of the LORD their God 1
Zec 6:15 if you will diligently obey the voice of the LORD 1
Mat 2:18 A voice was heard in Ramah, wailing and loud 11
3: 3 prophet Isaiah when he said, "The voice of one 11
17 a voice from heaven, saying, "This is my beloved Son 11
12:19 nor will any one hear his voice in the streets; 11
17: 5 and a voice from the cloud said 11
27:46 Jesus cried with a loud voice 11
50 Jesus cried again with a loud voice 11
Mrk 1: 3 the voice of one crying in the wilderness 11
11 a voice came from heaven, "Thou art my beloved Son; 11
26 convulsing him and crying with a loud voice 11
5: 7 crying out with a loud voice, he said 11
9: 7 a voice came out of the cloud 11
15:34 at the ninth hour Jesus cried with a loud voice 11
Lke 1:44 when the voice of your greeting came to my ears 11
3: 4 The voice of one crying in the wilderness 11
22 a voice came from heaven 11
4:33 and he cried out with a loud voice 11
8:28 fell down before him, and said with a loud voice 11
9:35 a voice came out of the cloud, saying, "This is my Son 11
36 when the voice had spoken, Jesus was found alone. 11
11:27 a woman in the crowd raised her voice and said 11
17:13 lifted up their voices and said, "Jesus, Master 11
15 turned back, praising God with a loud voice; 11
19:37 began to rejoice and praise God with a loud voice 11
23:23 their voices prevailed. 11
46 Then Jesus, crying with a loud voice, said, "Father 11
Joh 1:23 I am the voice of one crying in the wilderness 11
3:29 friend . . rejoices greatly at the bridegroom's voice; 11
5:25 when the dead will hear the voice of the Son of God 11
28 all who are in the tombs will hear his voice. 11
37 His voice you have never heard 11
10: 3 the sheep hear his voice 11
4 the sheep follow him, for they know his voice. 11
5 for they do not know the voice of strangers. 11
16 they will heed my voice 11
27 My sheep hear my voice, and I know them 11
11:43 When he had said this, he cried with a loud voice 11
12:28 Then a voice came from heaven 11
30 Jesus answered, "This voice has come for your sake 11
18:37 Every one who is of the truth hears my voice. 11
Act 2:14 Peter . . lifted up his voice and addressed them 11
4:24 lifted their voices together to God and said 11
7:31 as he drew near to look, the voice of the Lord came 11
57 they cried out with a loud voice 11
60 he knelt down and cried with a loud voice 11
8: 7 unclean spirits . . crying with a loud voice 11
9: 4 he fell to the ground and heard a voice saying 11
7 hearing the voice but seeing no one. 11
10:13 there came a voice to him, "Rise, Peter; kill and eat. 11
15 the voice came to him again a second time 11
11: 7 I heard a voice saying to me, 'Rise, Peter 11
9 the voice answered a second time from heaven 11
12:14 Recognizing Peter's voice 11
22 people shouted, "The voice of a god, and not of man! 11
14:10 said in a loud voice, "Stand upright on your feet. 11
11 they lifted up their voices, saying in Lycao'nian 11
16:28 Paul cried with a loud voice, "Do not harm yourself 11
19:34 they all with one voice cried out 11
22: 7 I fell to the ground and heard a voice saying to me 11
9 did not hear the voice of the one who was speaking 11
14 to see the Just One and to hear a voice from his mouth 11
22 then they lifted up their voices and said 11
26:14 heard a voice saying to me in the Hebrew language 11
24 Festus said with a loud voice, "Paul, you are mad 11
Rom 10:18 Their voice has gone out to all the earth 9
15: 6 together you may with one voice glorify the God 8
Heb 3: 7 Today, when you hear his voice 11
15 while it is said, "Today, when you hear his voice 11
4: 7 Today, when you hear his voice 11
12:19 a voice whose words made the hearers entreat 11

26 His voice then shook the earth 11
2Pe 1:17 the voice was borne to him by the Majestic Glory 11
18 we heard this voice borne from heaven 11
2:16 a dumb ass spoke with human voice 11
Rev 1:10 and I heard behind me a loud voice like a trumpet 11
12 I turned to see the voice that was speaking to me 11
15 and his voice was like the sound of many waters; 11
3:20 if any one hears my voice and opens the door 11
4: 1 the first voice, which I had heard speaking to me 11
5 issue . . voices and peals of thunder 11
5: 2 a strong angel proclaiming with a loud voice 11
11 I heard . . the voice of many angels 11
12 saying with a loud voice, "Worthy is the Lamb 11
6: 1 creatures say, as with a voice of thunder, "Come! 11
6 I heard what seemed to be a voice in the midst 11
7 I heard the voice of the fourth living creature 11
10 they cried out with a loud voice, "O Sovereign Lord 11
7: 2 he called with a loud voice to the four angels 11
10 crying out with a loud voice, "Salvation 11
8: 5 there were peals of thunder, voices, flashes 11
13 I heard an eagle crying with a loud voice 11
9:13 I heard a voice from the four horns of the . . altar 11
10: 3 called out with a loud voice, like a lion roaring; 11
4 but I heard a voice from heaven saying 11
8 voice which I had heard from heaven spoke to me 11
11:12 Then they heard a loud voice from heaven saying 11
15 and there were loud voices in heaven, saying 11
19 flashes of lightning, voices, peals of thunder 11
12:10 And I heard a loud voice in heaven, saying 11
14: 2 I heard a voice from heaven 11
2 the voice I heard was like the sound of harpers 11
7 and he said with a loud voice, "Fear God 11
9 another angel . . saying with a loud voice 11
13 And I heard a voice from heaven saying, "Write this 11
15 another angel . . calling with a loud voice 11
18 another angel . . called with a loud voice 10
16: 1 Then I heard a loud voice from the temple 11
17 and a loud voice came out of the temple 11
18 flashes of lightning, voices, peals of thunder 11
18: 2 And he called out with a mighty voice 11
4 Then I heard another voice from heaven saying 11
23 the voice of bridegroom and bride shall be heard 11
19: 1 After this I heard what seemed to be a loud voice 11
5 And from the throne came a voice crying 11
6 what seemed to be the voice of a great multitude 11
17 and with a loud voice he called to all the birds 11
21: 3 I heard a loud voice from the throne saying 11
1Es 9:10 the multitude shouted and said with a loud voice 11
2Es 5: 5 and the stone shall utter its voice 12
7 one . . shall make his voice heard by night 12
7 and all shall hear his voice. 12
37 or show me the picture of a voice 12
6:13 and you will hear a full, resounding voice. 12
15 while the voice is speaking, do not be terrified; *
17 and behold, a voice was speaking 12
21 Infants a year old shall speak with their voices 12
32 because your voice has surely been heard 12
39 the sound of man's voice was not yet there. 12
8:19 Therefore hear my voice, and understand my words 12
9:38 she was mourning and weeping with a loud voice 12
10:27 I was afraid, and cried with a loud voice and said 12
11:10 and behold, the voice did not come from his heads 12
15 behold, a voice sounded, saying to it. 12
36 Then I heard a voice saying to me, "Look before you 12
37 he uttered a man's voice to the eagle, and spoke 12
12:17 As for your hearing a voice that spoke 12
45 And they wept with a loud voice 12
13: 4 whenever his voice issued from his mouth 12
4 all who heard his voice melted as wax melts 12
33 when all the nations hear his voice 12
14: 1 behold, a voice came out of a bush opposite me 12
38 on the next day, behold, a voice called me, saying 12
16:27 to see another, or even to hear his voice. 12
Tob 13: 6 give thanks to him with your full voice 8
Jdt 7:23 and cried out with a loud voice 11
29 they cried out to the Lord God with a loud voice. 11
8:17 he will hear our voice, if it pleases him. 11
9: 1 Judith cried out to the Lord with a loud voice 11
13:12 When the men of her city heard her voice 11
14 Then she said to them with a loud voice, "Praise God 11
14:16 cried out with a loud voice and wept and groaned 11
16:11 they lifted up their voices 11
14 there is none that can resist thy voice. 11
AEs 14:19 hear the voice of the despairing 11
Wis 18: 1 Their enemies heard their voices 11
Sir 6: 5 A pleasant voice multiplies friends 7
17:13 their ears heard the glory of his voice. 11
21:20 A fool raises his voice when he laughs 11
29: 5 will lower his voice 11
34:24 to whose voice will the Lord listen? 11
39:35 now sing praise with all your heart and voice 8
40:21 a pleasant voice is better than both. 5
43:17 The voice of his thunder rebukes the earth 11
45: 5 He made him hear his voice 11
46:17 made his voice heard with a mighty sound; 11
20 lifted up his voice out of the earth in prophecy 11
47: 9 to make sweet melody with their voices. 6
50:18 the singers praised him with their voices 11
Bar 1:18 have not heeded the voice of the Lord our God 11
19 we have been negligent, in not heeding his voice. 11
21 We did not heed the voice of the Lord our God 11
2: 5 we sinned . . in not heeding his voice. 11
10 Yet we have not obeyed his voice, to walk 11
22 But if you will not obey the voice of the Lord 11
23 the voice of mirth and the voice of gladness 11
23 the voice of mirth and the voice of gladness 11
23 voice of the bridegroom and the voice 11
23 of the bridegroom and the voice of the bride 11
24 we did not obey thy voice, to serve the king 11
29 If you will not obey my voice, this very great 11
3: 4 who did not heed the voice of the Lord their God 11
Sus 1:24 Then Susanna cried out with a loud voice 11
42 Then Susanna cried out with a loud voice, and said 11
46 he cried with a loud voice, "I am innocent 11
Bel 1:18 looked at the table, and shouted in a loud voice 11
41 the king shouted with a loud voice 11
1Mc 2:19 Mattathias answered and said in a loud voice 11
27 cried out in the city with a loud voice, saying 11
9:41 the voice of their musicians into a funeral dirge. 11
13: 8 they answered in a loud voice, "You are our leader 11
45 they cried out with a loud voice 11
3Mc 5: 7 with tears and a voice hard to silence 4
51 and cried out in a very loud voice 11
4Mc 8:29 all with one voice together, as from one mind, said 11
15:21 the voices of the children in torture 11

void 1. אבד 2. בֹּהוּ 3. נפל 4. תֹּהוּ 5. *καταργέω*
6. irritus

Gen 1: 2 The earth was without form and void 2
Num 6:12 but the former time shall be void 3
Deu 32:28 For they are a nation void of counsel 1
Job 26: 7 He stretches out the north over the void 4
Jer 4:23 I looked on the earth, and lo, it was waste and void; 2
Rom 4:14 If . . faith is null and the promise is void. 5
2Es 2: 1 and made my counsels void. 6

void *See also* make.

become void 1. *πίπτω*

Lke 16:17 than for one dot of the law to become void. 1

volume 1. *βιβλίον*

2Mc 2:23 has been set forth by Jason of Cyrene in five volumes 1

voluntarily 1. נְדָבָה 2. *αὐθαίρετος*

Deu 23:23 voluntarily vowed to the LORD your God 1
3Mc 6: 6 had voluntarily surrendered their lives to the flames 2

volunteer 1. נדב

2Ch 17:16 a volunteer for the service of the LORD 1

vomit 1. קֵא 2. קוה 3. קיא 4. קִיא 5. *ἐξέραμα*

Prv 25:16 only . . lest you be sated with it and vomit 3
26:11 Like a dog that returns to his vomit is a fool 1
Isa 19:14 Egypt . . as a drunken man staggers in his vomit. 4
28: 8 For all tables are full of vomit 4
Jer 25:27 Drink, be drunk and vomit, fall and rise no more 2
48:26 so that Moab shall wallow in his vomit 4
2Pe 2:22 The dog turns back to his own vomit 5

vomit out 1. קיא

Lev 18:25 the land vomited out its inhabitants 1
28 lest the land vomit you out, when you defile it 1
28 as it vomited out the nation that was before you 1
20:22 that the land . . may not vomit you out 1
Jon 2:10 it vomited out Jonah upon the dry land. 1

vomit up 1. קיא

Job 20:15 He swallows down riches and vomits them up again; 1
Prv 23: 8 will vomit up the morsels which you have eaten 1

vote 1. *ψήφισμα* 2. *ψῆφος*

Act 26:10 I cast my vote against them. 2
2Mc 10: 8 They decreed by public ordinance and vote 1
12: 4 this was done by public vote of the city 1
15:36 they all decreed by public vote 1

votive *See* gift, offering.

vouch 1. שָׂהֵד

Job 16:19 in heaven, and he that vouches for me is on high. 1

vow 1. יצא מִפֶּה 2. נדר 3. נֶדֶר 4. *εὐχή* 5. *εὔχομαι*
6. *ὄμνυμι*

Gen 28:20 Jacob made a vow, saying, "If God will be with me 3
31:13 you anointed a pillar and made a vow to me. 3
Lev 22:21 of peace offerings to the LORD, to fulfil a vow 3
27: 2 When a man makes a special vow of persons 3
8 according to the ability of him who vowed 2
Num 6: 2 When either a man or a woman makes a special vow 2
2 makes a special vow, the vow of a Nazirite 3
5 All the days of his vow of separation no razor 3
21 in accordance with the vow which he takes 3
15: 3 to fulfil a vow or as a freewill offering 3
8 prepare a bull for . . a sacrifice, to fulfil a vow 3
21: 2 Israel vowed a vow to the LORD, and said 2
2 Israel vowed a vow to the LORD, and said 3
30: 2 a man vows a vow to the LORD, or swears an oath 2
2 a man vows a vow to the LORD, or swears an oath 3
3 Or when a woman vows a vow to the LORD 2
3 Or when a woman vows a vow to the LORD 3
4 her father hears of her vow and of her pledge 3
4 then all her vows shall stand 3
5 no vow of hers, no pledge . . shall stand; 3
6 married to a husband, while under her vows 3
7 then her vows shall stand, and her pledges 3
8 then he shall make void her vow which was on her 3
9 any vow of a widow or of a divorced woman 3
10 if she vowed in her husband's house 2
11 did not oppose her; then all her vows shall stand 3
12 proceeds out of her lips concerning her vows 3
13 Any vow and any binding oath to afflict herself 3
14 then he establishes all her vows 3
Deu 12:11 votive offerings which you vow to the LORD. 2
17 any of your votive offerings which you vow 2
23:18 not bring . . in payment for any vow 3
21 When you make a vow to the LORD your God 3
22 if you refrain from vowing, it . . no sin in you. 2
23 voluntarily vowed to the LORD your God 2
Jdg 11:30 Jephthah made a vow to the LORD, and said, "If thou 3
35 to the LORD, and I cannot take back my vow. *
39 did . . according to his vow which he had made. 3
1Sm 1:11 And she vowed a vow and said, "O LORD of hosts, 2
11 And she vowed a vow and said, "O LORD of hosts, 3
21 offer . . the yearly sacrifice, and to pay his vow. 3
2Sm 15: 7 let me . . pay my vow, which I have vowed to the LORD 3
7 let me . . pay my vow, which I have vowed to the LORD 2
8 your servant vowed a vow while I dwelt at Geshur 2
8 your servant vowed a vow while I dwelt at Geshur 3
Job 22:27 he will hear you; and you will pay your vows. 3
Ps 22:25 my vows I will pay before those who fear him. 3
50:14 pay your vows to the Most High; 3
56:12 My vows to thee I must perform, O God; 3
61: 5 For thou, O God, hast heard my vows 3
8 praises to thy name, as I pay my vows day after day. 3
65: 1 to thee shall vows be performed 3
66:13 with burnt offerings; I will pay thee my vows 3
116:14 I will pay my vows to the LORD in the presence 3
18 I will pay my vows to the LORD in the presence 3
132: 2 to the LORD and vowed to the Mighty One of Jacob 2
Prv 7:14 today I have paid my vows; 3
20:25 snare . . to reflect only after making his vows. 3
31: 2 What, son of my womb? What, son of my vows? 3
Ecc 5: 4 When you vow a vow to God, do not delay paying it; 2
4 When you vow a vow to God, do not delay paying it; 3
4 Pay what you vow. 2
5 It is better that you should not vow than that you 2
5 better . . than that you should vow and not pay. 2
Isa 19:21 they will make vows to the LORD and perform them. 3
Jer 11:15 Can vows and sacrificial flesh avert your doom? 4
44:17 But we will do everything that we have vowed 1
25 will surely perform our vows that we have made 3
25 Then confirm your vows and perform your vows! 3
25 Then confirm your vows and perform your vows! 3
Jon 1:16 offered a sacrifice to the LORD and made vows. 3
2: 9 sacrifice to thee; what I have vowed I will pay. 2
Nah 1:15 Keep your feasts, O Judah, fulfil your vows 3
Mal 1:14 the cheat who has a male in his flock, and vows it 2
Mrk 6:23 he vowed to her, "Whatever you ask me, I will give 6
Act 18:18 At Cen'chre-ae he cut his hair, for he had a vow. 4
21:23 We have four men who are under a vow; 4
1Es 4:43 Remember the vow which you made 4
44 vowed to send them back there. 5
45 You also vowed to build the temple 5
46 I pray therefore that you fulfil the vow 4
46 the vow whose fulfilment you vowed 5
5:44 vowed that they would erect the house on its site 5
53 all who had made any vow to God 4
8:13 gifts . . which I and my friends have vowed 5
58 the silver and the gold are vowed to the Lord 4
Jdt 4:14 the vows and freewill offerings of the people. 4
Sir 18:22 nothing hinder you from paying a vow promptly 4
LJr 1:35 if one makes a vow to them and does not keep it 4
2Mc 3:35 and made very great vows to the Savior of his life 4

vow *See also* make, payment, take.

vow complete destruction 1. *ἀναθεματίζω*

1Mc 5: 5 vowed their complete destruction 1

marriage vow 1. *κλίνη*

Sir 23:18 A man who breaks his marriage vows says 1

vow willingly 1. נדב (A)

Ezr 7:16 vowed willingly for the house of their God 1

voyage 1. *παράπλους* 2. *πλόος*

Act 21: 7 When we had finished the voyage from Tyre 2
27: 9 the voyage was already dangerous 2
10 I perceive that the voyage will be with injury 2
3Mc 4:11 the voyage was concluded as the king had decreed 1

voyage *See also* make.

voyage over 1. *διοδεύω*

Wis 14: 1 and about to voyage over raging waves 1

vulgar fellow 1. רֵיק

2Sm 6:20 one of the vulgar fellows . . uncovers himself! 1

vulgarity 1. ἀπαιδευσία

Sir 23:13 Do not accustom your mouth to lewd vulgarity 1

vulture 1. בֶּן נֶשֶׁר 2. נֶשֶׁר 3. פֶּרֶס 4. קָאַת

Lev 11:13 an abomination: the eagle, the vulture, the osprey 3
Deu 14:12 shall not eat: the eagle, the vulture, the osprey 3
Ps 102: 6 I am like a vulture of the wilderness, like an owl 4
Prv 30:17 ravens of the valley and eaten by the vultures. 1
Lam 4:19 were swifter than the vultures in the heavens; 2
Hos 8: 1 for a vulture is over the house of the LORD 2
Zep 2:14 the vulture and the hedgehog shall lodge in her 4

carrion vulture 1. רָחָם

Lev 11:18 the water hen, the pelican, the carrion vulture 1

W

wafer 1. צְפִיחִת 2. רָקִיק
Exd 16:31 taste of it was like wafers made with honey. 1
29: 2 and unleavened wafers spread with oil. 2
23 one cake of bread with oil, and one wafer 2
Lev 2: 4 unleavened wafers spread with oil 2
7:12 unleavened wafers spread with oil, and cakes 2
8:26 took . . one cake of bread with oil, and one wafer 2
Num 6:15 unleavened wafers spread with oil 2
19 priest shall take . . one unleavened wafer 2
1Ch 23:29 cereal offering, the wafers of unleavened bread 2

waft 1. נזל
Sng 4:16 my garden, let its fragrance be wafted abroad. 1

wag 1. נוד 2. נוע 3. κινέω
2Kg 19:21 she wags her head behind you-the daughter 2
Ps 22: 7 they make mouths at me, they wag their heads; 2
64: 8 all who see them will wag their heads. 1
109:25 my accusers; when they see me, they wag their heads. 2
Isa 37:22 she wags her head behind you- 2
Jer 48:27 whenever you spoke of him you wagged your head? 1
Lam 2:15 they hiss and wag their heads at the daughter 2
Mat 27:39 passed by derided him, wagging their heads 3
Mrk 15:29 wagging their heads, and saying, "Aha! 3

wage 1. גרה 2. עשה 3. ἐπάγω 4. συνίστημι
1Ch 22: 8 have shed much blood and have waged great wars; 2
Ps 55:18 my soul in safety from the battle that I wage •
Prv 20:18 by wise guidance wage war. 2
24: 6 for by wise guidance you can wage your war 2
Dan 11:25 king of the south shall wage war 1
Sir 46: 3 he waged the wars of the Lord. 3
1Mc 3: 3 he girded on his armor of war and waged battles 4

wage (2) 1. מְחִיר 2. מַשְׂכֹּרֶת 3. פֹּעַל 4. פְּעֻלָּה 5. שָׂכָר 6. μισθός 7. ὀψώνιον
Gen 29:15 Tell me, what shall your wages be? 2
30:28 name your wages, and I will give it. 5
32 among the goats; and such shall be my wages. 5
33 when you come to look into my wages with you. 5
31: 7 your father has cheated me and changed my wages 2
8 If he said, 'The spotted shall be your wages,' 5
8 and if he said, 'The striped shall be your wages,' 5
41 flock, and you have changed my wages ten times. 2
Exd 2: 9 nurse him for me, and I will give you your wages. 5
Lev 19:13 The wages of a hired servant shall not remain 4
Deu 23:18 bring the hire of a harlot, or the wages of a dog 1
1Kg 5: 6 I will pay you for your servants such wages 5
Job 7: 2 like a hireling who looks for his wages 3
Prv 10:16 The wage of the righteous leads to life 4
11:18 A wicked man earns deceptive wages 4
Jer 22:13 for nothing, and does not give him his wages; 3
Ezk 29:19 it shall be the wages for his army. 5
Zec 8:10 For before those days there was no wage for man 5
10 there was no wage for man or any wage for beast 5
11:12 If it seems right to you, give me my wages; 5
12 they weighed out as my wages 30 shekels 5
Mal 3: 5 those who oppress the hireling in his wages 5
Mat 20: 8 Call the laborers and pay them their wages 6
Lke 3:14 be content with your wages. 7
10: 7 the laborer deserves his wages 6
Joh 4:36 He who reaps receives wages 6
Rom 4: 4 his wages are not reckoned as a gift but as his due. 6
6:23 For the wages of sin is death 7
1Co 3: 8 each shall receive his wages 6
1Ti 5:18 The laborer deserves his wages. 6
Jas 5: 4 the wages of the laborers who mowed your fields 6
1Es 4:56 He wrote that land and wages should be provided 7
Tob 2:12 Once when they paid her wages 6
14 It was given to me as a gift in addition to my wages 6
4:14 the wages of any man who works for you 6
5: 3 I will pay him wages as long as I live 6
14 tell me, what wages am I to pay you-a drachma a day 6
15 besides, I will add to your wages 6
12: 1 see to the wages of the man who went with you; 6
Wis 2:22 nor hope for the wages of holiness 6
Sir 34:22 to deprive an employee of his wages 6
1Mc 14:32 paid them wages. 7

wage *See* earn.

wage a contest 1. certo
2Es 7:127 the contest which every man . . shall wage 1

wage war 1. גרה 2. מִלְחָמָה 3. צבא 4. πολεμέω 5. στρατεύω 6. expugno
2Kg 16: 5 came up to wage war on Jerusalem 2
Isa 7: 1 Rezin . . came up to Jerusalem to wage war against 2
Dan 11:10 His sons shall wage war and assemble a multitude 1
Zec 14:12 the peoples that wage war against Jerusalem 3
Jas 4: 2 you . . cannot obtain; so you fight and wage war. 4
1Pe 2:11 passions . . that wage war against your soul. 5
2Es 13: 8 against him, to wage war with him 6
1Mc 12:13 the kings round about us have waged war against us. 4
24 to wage war against him. 4

wage warfare 1. στρατεύω
1Ti 1:18 inspired by them you may wage the good warfare 1

wager *See* make.

wagon 1. גַּלְגַּל 2. עֲגָלָה
Gen 45:19 Do this: take wagons from the land of Egypt 2
21 and Joseph gave them wagons 2
27 and when he saw the wagons which Joseph had sent 2
46: 5 carried . . in the wagons which Pharaoh had sent 2
Num 7: 3 offering . . six covered wagons and twelve oxen 2
3 wagon for every two of the leaders 2
6 Moses took the wagons and the oxen, and gave them 2
7 Two wagons and four oxen he gave to . . Gershon 2
8 four wagons and eight oxen he gave 2
Ezk 23:24 with chariots and wagons and a host of peoples; 1
26:10 noise of the horsemen and wagons and chariots 1

wail 1. זעק 2. ילל 3. יְלָלָה 4. מִסְפֵּד 5. נהה 6. נְהִי 7. נְי 8. שמע 9. ἀλαλάζω 10. γόος 11. θρηνέω 12. κλαυθμός 13. κοπετός 14. κόπτω 15. κωκυτός 16. οἶκτος 17. οἰμώζω 18. ὀλοφύρομαι 19. lugeo 20. plango
Est 4: 1 went out . . wailing with a loud and bitter cry; 1
Isa 13: 6 Wail, for the day of the LORD is near; 2
14:31 Wail, O gate; cry, O city; melt in fear 2
15: 2 over Nebo and over Med'eba Moab wails. 2
3 in . . squares every one wails and melts in tears. 2
8 the wailing reaches to Egla'im 3
8 to Egla'im, the wailing reaches to Beer-e'lim. 3
16: 7 Therefore let Moab wail, let every one wail 2
7 let Moab wail, let every one wail for Moab. 2
23: 1 Wail, O ships of Tarshish, for Tyre is laid waste 2
6 to Tarshish, wail, O inhabitants of the coast! 2
14 Wail, O ships of Tarshish 2
52: 5 Their rulers wail, says the LORD 2
65:14 cry out . . and shall wail for anguish of spirit. 2
Jer 4: 8 For this gird you with sackcloth, lament and wail; 2
9:10 Take up weeping and wailing for the mountains 6
18 let them make haste and raise a wailing over us 6
19 For a sound of wailing is heard from Zion 6
25:34 Wail, you shepherds, and cry, and roll in ashes 2
36 the cry of the shepherds, and the wail of the lords 3
47: 2 and every inhabitant of the land shall wail. 2
48:20 Moab is put to shame, for it is broken; wail and cry! 2
31 Therefore I wail for Moab; I cry out for all Moab; 2
39 How it is broken! How they wail! How Moab has 2
49: 3 Wail, O Heshbon, for Ai is laid waste! 2
51: 8 wail for her! Take balm for her pain; 2
Ezk 21:12 Cry and wail, son of man, for it is against my people; 2
27:30 and wail aloud over you, and cry bitterly. 8
32 In their wailing they raise a lamentation 7
30: 2 Thus says the Lord GOD: "Wail, 'Alas for the day! 2
32:18 Son of man, wail over the multitude of Egypt 5
Hos 7:14 but they wail upon their beds; 2
10: 5 and its idolatrous priests shall wail over it •
Jol 1: 5 and wail, all you drinkers of wine 2
11 wail, O vinedressers, for the wheat and the barley; 2
13 lament, O priests, wail, O ministers of the altar. 2
Ams 5:16 In all the squares there shall be wailing 4
16 and to wailing those who are skilled 4
17 and in all vineyards there shall be wailing 4
Mic 1: 8 For this I will lament and wail; 2
11 the wailing of Beth-e'zel shall take away from you 4
2: 4 and wail with bitter lamentation, and say 5
Zep 1:10 a wail from the Second Quarter 3
11 Wail, O inhabitants of the Mortar! 2
Zec 11: 2 Wail, O cypress, for the cedar has fallen 2
2 Wail, oaks of Bashan 2
3 Hark, the wail of the shepherds, for their glory 3
Mat 2:18 A voice was heard in Ramah, wailing and loud 12
11:17 we wailed, and you did not mourn.' 11
Mrk 5:38 people weeping and wailing loudly. 9
Lke 7:32 we wailed, and you did not weep.' 11
Rev 1: 7 tribes of the earth will wail on account of him. 14
18: 9 the kings . . will weep and wail over her 14
2Es 15:44 all who are about her shall wail over her. 19
16: 2 and wail for your children, and lament for them 20
Sir 38:17 your wailing fervent 13
3Mc 1: 4 went to the troops with wailing and tears 16
4: 3 filled with mourning and wailing for them? 10
6 young women . . exchanged joy for wailing 10
6:32 Putting an end to all mourning and wailing 15
4Mc 12:14 you will wail bitterly 17
16:12 did not wail with such a lament for any of them 18

become wailings 1. ילל
Ams 8: 3 The songs of the temple shall become wailings 1

waist 1. מָתְנַיִם 2. ὀσφῦς
Isa 11: 5 Righteousness shall be the girdle of his waist 1
Mat 3: 4 leather girdle around his waist; and his food was 2
Mrk 1: 6 a leather girdle around his waist 2

waistcloth 1. אֵזוֹר
Job 12:18 binds a waistcloth on their loins. 1
Isa 5:27 not a waistcloth is loose, not a sandal-thong 1
Jer 13: 1 Go and buy a linen waistcloth 1
2 I bought a waistcloth according to the word 1
4 Take the waistcloth which you have bought 1
6 and take from there the waistcloth 1
7 and dug, and I took the waistcloth from the place 1
7 And behold, the waistcloth was spoiled; 1
10 shall be like this waistcloth 1
11 For as the waistcloth clings to the loins of a man 1

wait 1. אָרַב 2. דמם 3. היה 4. חול 5. חכה 6. יָחִיל 7. יחל 8. יצב 9. ישב 10. מהה 11. נוח 12. נצב 13. נצב לִקְרָאת 14. עמד 15. קוה 16. שבר 17. שמר 18. ἀναμένω 19. ἀπεκδέχομαι 20. ἀφίημι 21. ἐκδέχομαι 22. ἐπέχω 23. ἐπιτηρέω 24. ἵστημι 25. μέλλω 26. μένω 27. περιμένω 28. προσδέχομαι 29. προσδοκάω 30. προσμένω 31. τηρέω 32. ὑπομένω 33. sustineo
Gen 8:10 He waited another seven days 7
12 Then he waited another seven days 7
49:18 I wait for thy salvation, O LORD. 15
Exd 5:20 met Moses and Aaron, who were waiting for them 12
7:15 Go to Pharaoh . . wait for him by the river's brink 13
8:20 Rise up early in the morning and wait for Pharaoh 8
24:12 Come up to me on the mountain, and wait there; 3
Num 9: 8 Wait, that I may hear what the LORD will command 14
Jdg 3:25 they waited till they were utterly at a loss; 6
16: 2 Let us wait till the light of the morning; •
Rut 1:13 would you therefore wait till they were grown? 16
3:18 Wait, my daughter, until you learn how the matter 9
1Sm 1:23 Do what seems best . . wait until you have weaned 9
10: 8 Seven days you shall wait, until I come to you 7

13: 8 He waited seven days, the time appointed 7
14: 9 If they say to us, 'Wait until we come to you,' 2
25: 9 said all this to Nabal . . and then they waited. 11
2Sm 15:28 See, I will wait at the fords of the wilderness 10
17:17 Jonathan and Ahim'a-az were waiting at En-ro'gel; 14
1Kg 20:38 the prophet departed, and waited for the king 14
2Kg 6:33 Why should I wait for the LORD any longer? 7
7: 9 if we are silent and wait until the morning light 5
Job 6:11 What is my strength, that I should wait? 7
14:14 All the days of my service I would wait 7
24:15 the adulterer also waits for the twilight 17
29:21 Men listened to me, and waited, and kept silence 7
23 They waited for me as for the rain; 7
30:26 when I waited for light, darkness came. 7
32: 4 Now Eli'hu had waited to speak to Job 5
11 Behold, I waited for your words 7
16 And shall I wait, because they do not speak 7
35:14 the case is before him, and you are waiting for him! 4
38:40 in their dens, or lie in wait in their covert? 1
Ps 25: 3 Yea, let none that wait for thee be put to shame; 15
5 for thee I wait all the day long. 15
21 May integrity . . preserve me, for I wait for thee. 15
27:14 Wait for the LORD; be strong 15
14 let your heart take courage; yea, wait for the LORD! 15
31:24 take courage, all you who wait for the LORD! 7
33:20 Our soul waits for the LORD; he is our help 5
37: 9 who wait for the LORD shall possess the land. 15
34 Wait for the LORD, and keep to his way 15
38:15 But for thee, O LORD, do I wait; it is thou, O LORD 7
39: 7 now, Lord, for what do I wait? My hope is in thee. 15
40: 1 I waited patiently for the LORD; 15
56: 6 As they have waited for my life 15
62: 1 For God alone my soul waits in silence; •
69: 3 My eyes grow dim with waiting for my God. 7
106:13 they did not wait for his counsel. 5
130: 5 I wait for the LORD, my soul waits 15
5 for the LORD, my soul waits, and in his word I hope; 15
6 my soul waits for the LORD more than watchmen •
Prv 8:34 watching daily . . waiting beside my doors. 17
20:22 wait for the LORD, and he will help you. 15
Isa 8:17 I will wait for the LORD, who is hiding his face 5
25: 9 God; we have waited for him, that he might save us. 15
9 This is the LORD; we have waited for him; 15
26: 8 In the path of thy judgments . . we wait for thee; 15
30:18 Therefore the LORD waits to be gracious to you; 5
18 blessed are all those who wait for him. 5
33: 2 O LORD, be gracious to us; we wait for thee. 15
40:31 who wait for the LORD shall renew their strength 15
42: 4 and the coastlands wait for his law. 7
49:23 those who wait for me shall not be put to shame. 15
51: 5 the coastlands wait for me, and for my arm they 15
60: 9 For the coastlands shall wait for me 15
64: 4 God . . who works for those who wait for him. 5
Lam 3:25 The LORD is good to those who wait for him 15
26 wait quietly for the salvation of the LORD. 6
Dan 12:12 Blessed is he who waits and comes 5
Hos 12: 6 and wait continually for your God. 15
Mic 5: 7 which tarry not . . nor wait for the sons of men. 7
7: 7 I will wait for the God of my salvation; 7
Hab 2: 3 If it seem slow, wait for it; it will surely come 5
Zep 3: 8 Therefore wait for me," says the LORD 5
Mat 27:49 Wait, let us see whether Eli'jah will come to save 20
Mrk 15:36 gave it to him to drink, saying, "Wait 20
Lke 1:21 the people were waiting for Zechari'ah 29
8:40 they were all waiting for him. 29
12:36 be like men who are waiting for their master 28
Act 1: 4 to wait for the promise of the Father 27
17:16 Now while Paul was waiting for them at Athens 21
20: 5 These went on and were waiting for us at Tro'as 26
22:16 now why do you wait? Rise and be baptized 25
23:21 they are ready, waiting for the promise from you. 28
28: 6 They waited, expecting him to swell up 29
6 when they had waited a long time 29
Rom 8:19 For the creation waits with eager longing 19
23 groan inwardly as we wait for adoption as sons 19
25 if we hope . . we wait for it with patience. 19
1Co 1: 7 as you wait for the revealing of our Lord Jesus 19
11:33 wait for one another- 21
Gal 5: 5 we wait for the hope of righteousness. 19
1Th 1:10 to wait for his Son from heaven 18
Heb 10:13 then to wait 21
Jas 5: 7 farmer waits for the precious fruit of the earth 21
1Pe 3:20 when God's patience waited in the days of Noah 19
2Pe 3:12 waiting for . . the coming of the day of God 29
13 we wait for new heavens and a new earth 29
14 since you wait for these, be zealous 29
Jde 1:21 wait for the mercy of our Lord Jesus Christ 28
2Es 12:39 wait here seven days more, so that you may be shown 33
Tob 2: 2 and I will wait for you. 26
5: 7 Wait for me, and I shall tell my father. 32
Jdt 8:17 while we wait for his deliverance 18
10:18 she waited outside the tent of Holofernes 24
12:16 he had been waiting for an opportunity to deceive her 31
13: 3 to wait for her to come out 23
15: 2 they did not wait for one another 26
Wis 8:12 When I am silent they will wait for me 27
Sir 2: 7 You who fear the Lord, wait for his mercy 18
6:19 wait for her good harvest 18
18:22 do not wait until death to be released from it. 26
36:16 Reward those who wait for thee 32
51: 8 thou dost deliver those who wait for thee 32
Sus 1:59 angel . . waiting with his sword to saw you in two 26
2Mc 5:25 waited until the holy sabbath day 22
6:14 the Lord waits patiently to punish them 18
7:30 What are you waiting for? 26
3Mc 5:24 they were eagerly waiting for daybreak. 29
7:17 the fleet waited for them . . for seven days. 30

wait (2) 1. היה לִפְנֵי 2. שרת 3. *παρίστημι* 4. *προσκαρτερέω*

Gen 40: 4 charged Joseph with them, and he waited on them; 2
2Kg 5: 2 a little maid . . and she waited on Na'aman's wife. 1
Act 10: 7 from among those that waited on him 4
Jdt 6:10 his slaves, who waited on him in his tent 3

wait *See* lay, lie.

wait anxiously 1. חול

Mic 1:12 inhabitants of Maroth wait anxiously for good 1

eagerly wait 1. *ἀπεκδέχομαι*

Heb 9:28 to save those who are eagerly waiting for him. 1

wait in silence 1. דמם

Ps 62: 5 For God alone my soul waits in silence 1

make wait 1. *παρέλκω*

Sir 29: 8 do not make him wait for your alms. 1

wait patiently 1. חול

Ps 37: 7 still before the LORD, and wait patiently for him; 1

wait quietly 1. נוח

Hab 3:16 I will quietly wait for the day of trouble to come 1

wait to see 1. *προσδοκάω*

2Mc 9:25 and waiting to see what will happen. 1

wait upon 1. עָמְדָה לִפְנֵי

1Kg 1: 2 and let her wait upon the king, and be his nurse; let 1

keep waiting 1. *παρέλκω*

Sir 4: 1 do not keep needy eyes waiting. 1

wake 1. עור 2. קיץ 3. *γρηγορέω* 4. *διεγείρω* 5. *ἐγείρω* 6. *ἔξυπνος*

Ps 3: 5 I wake again, for the LORD sustains me. 2
Jer 51:39 sleep a perpetual sleep and not wake 2
57 they shall sleep a perpetual sleep and not wake 2
Zec 4: 1 angel who talked with me came again, and waked me 1
Mat 1:24 When Joseph woke from sleep, he did as the angel 5
8:25 they went and woke him, saying, "Save, Lord 5
Mrk 4:38 they woke him and said to him 5
Lke 8:24 they went and woke him, saying, "Master, Master 4
Act 12: 7 he struck Peter on the side and woke him, saying 5
16:27 When the jailer woke 6
Rom 13:11 how it is full time now for you to wake from sleep. 5
1Th 5:10 so that whether we wake or sleep we might live 3
1Es 3: 9 said, "When the king wakes 5

wake (2) 1. נָתִיב

Job 41:32 Behind him he leaves a shining wake; 1

wake up 1. *ἐγείρω* 2. *ἐξεγείρω*

Jdt 14:13 Wake up our lord 1
Sir 40: 7 at the moment of his rescue he wakes up 2

wakeful 1. *ἀγρυπνία*

Sir 31: 2 Wakeful anxiety prevents slumber 1
42: 9 A daughter keeps her father secretly wakeful 1

wakefulness 1. *ἀγρυπνία*

Sir 31: 1 Wakefulness over wealth wastes away one's flesh 1

waken 1. עור 2. *διαγρηγορέω*

Isa 50: 4 Morning by morning he wakens, he wakens my ear 1
4 he wakens my ear to hear as those who are taught. 1
Zec 4: 1 like a man that is wakened out of his sleep. 1
Lke 9:32 when they wakened they saw his glory 2

walk 1. אשר 2. דֶּרֶךְ 3. הלך 4. עבר 5. צעד 6. הלך (A) 7. *βαδίζω* 8. *βῆμα* 9. *διαβαίνω* 10. *διοδεύω* 11. *ἐπίβασις* 12. *περιπατέω* 13. *πορευτός* 14. *πορεύω* 15. *στοιχέω* 16. ambulo 17. capit vestigium 18. transeo

Gen 3: 8 they heard the sound of the LORD God walking 3
5:22 Enoch walked with God after the birth 3
24 Enoch walked with God; 3
6: 9 in his generation; Noah walked with God. 3
9:23 both their shoulders, and walked backward 3
13:17 Arise, walk through the length and the breadth 3
17: 1 I am God Almighty; walk before me, and be blameless. 3
24:40 he said to me, 'The LORD, before whom I walk 3
65 Who is . . walking in the field to meet us? 3
48:15 my fathers Abraham and Isaac walked, the God 3
Exd 2: 5 and her maidens walked beside the river; 3
14:29 the people of Israel walked on dry ground 3
15:19 the people of Israel walked on dry ground 3
16: 4 I may prove them, whether they will walk in my law 3
18:20 make them know the way in which they must walk 3
Lev 18: 3 You shall not walk in their statutes 3
4 keep my statutes and walk in them 3
20:23 you shall not walk in the customs of the nation 3
26: 3 walk in my statutes and observe my commandments 3
12 I will walk among you, and will be your God 3
21 Then if you walk contrary to me 3
23 And if . . you . . walk contrary to me 3
24 then I also will walk contrary to you 3
27 And if . . you . . walk contrary to me 3
28 then I will walk contrary to you in fury 3
40 iniquity . . also in walking contrary to me 3
41 so that I walked contrary to them 3
Deu 5:33 walk in all the way which the LORD your God 3
6: 7 shall talk of them when . . you walk by the way 3
8: 6 by walking in his ways and by fearing him. 3
10:12 require . . but . . to walk in all his ways, to love 3
11:19 talking of them . . when you are walking by the way 3
22 commandment . . walking in all his ways 3
13: 4 shall walk after the LORD your God and fear him 3
5 way in which the LORD . . commanded you to walk. 3
19: 9 loving the LORD . . by walking ever in his ways- 3
23:14 LORD your God walks in the midst of your camp 3
26:17 walk in his ways, and keep his statutes 3
28: 9 keep the commandments . . and walk in his ways. 3
29:19 though I walk in the stubbornness of my heart.' 3
30:16 obey . . by walking in his ways 3
Jos 5: 6 the people of Israel walked 40 years 3
14:10 since . . while Israel walked in the wilderness; 3
22: 5 to love the LORD . . and to walk in all his ways 3
Jdg 2:17 from the way in which their fathers had walked 3
22 take care to walk in the way of the LORD as their 3
5:10 Tell of it . . you who walk by the way. 3
1Sm 8: 3 his sons did not walk in his ways, but turned aside 3
5 you are old and your sons do not walk in your ways; 3
12: 2 And now, behold, the king walks before you; 3
2 I have walked before you from my youth until this 3
2Sm 11: 2 when David arose . . and was walking upon the roof 3
1Kg 2: 3 walking in his ways and keeping his statutes, his 3
4 their way, to walk before me in faithfulness 3
3: 3 Solomon loved the LORD, walking in the statutes 3
6 because he walked before thee in faithfulness 3
14 if you will walk in my ways, keeping my statutes 3
14 walk in my ways . . as your father David walked 3
6:12 walk in my statutes and obey my ordinances 3
12 and keep all my commandments and walk in them 3
8:23 who . . walk before thee with all their heart; 3
25 sons take heed . . to walk before me as you have 3
25 to walk before me as you have walked before me.' 3
36 teach them the good way in which they should walk; 3
58 walk in all his ways, and to keep his commandments 3
61 true to the LORD . . walking in his statutes 3
9: 4 you . . walk before me, as David your father walked 3
4 you . . walk before me, as David your father walked 3
11:33 he has forsaken me . . and has not walked in my ways 3
38 if you will hearken . . and will walk in my ways 3
15: 3 he walked in all the sins which his father did 3
26 and walked in the way of his father, and in his sin 3
34 and walked in the way of Jerobo'am and in his sin 3
16: 2 and you have walked in the way of Jerobo'am 3
19 his sins . . walking in the way of Jerobo'am 3
26 For he walked in all the way of Jerobo'am 3
31 to walk in the sins of Jerobo'am the son of Nebat 3
22:43 He walked in all the way of Asa his father; 3
52 walked in the way of his father, and . . his mother 3
2Kg 4:35 he got up . . and walked once to and fro in the house 3
8:18 he walked in the way of the kings of Israel 3
27 He also walked in the way of the house of Ahab 3
10:31 Jehu was not careful to walk in the law of the LORD 3
13: 6 did not depart from the sins . . but walked in them; 3
11 depart from all the sins . . but he walked in them. 3
16: 3 but he walked in the way of the kings of Israel. 3
17: 8 and walked in the customs of the nations 3
19 Judah also . . walked in the customs which Israel 3
22 Israel walked in all the sins which Jerobo'am did; 3
20: 3 I have walked before thee in faithfulness 3
21:21 He walked in all the way . . his father walked 3
21 He walked in all the way . . his father walked 3
22 and did not walk in the way of the LORD. 3
22: 2 and walked in all the way of David his father 3
23: 3 a covenant . . to walk after the LORD and to keep 3
2Ch 6:14 who walk before thee with all their heart; 3
16 heed to their way, to walk in my law as you have 3
16 to walk in my law as you have walked before me. 3
27 teach them the good way in which they should walk; 3
31 that they may fear thee and walk in thy ways 3
7:17 if you walk before me, as David your father walked 3
17 if you walk before me, as David your father walked 3
11:17 walked for three years in the way of David 3
17: 3 he walked in the earlier ways of his father; 3
4 God of his father and walked in his commandments 3
20:32 He walked in the way of Asa his father 3
21: 6 he walked in the way of the kings of Israel 3
12 not walked in the ways of Jehosh'aphat 3
13 have walked in the way of the kings of Israel 3
22: 3 He also walked in the ways of the house of Ahab 3
28: 2 walked in the ways of the kings of Israel. 3

34: 2 walked in the ways of David his father; 3
31 made a covenant . . to walk after the LORD 3
Neh 5: 9 Ought you not to walk in the fear of our God 3
10:29 enter into a curse and an oath to walk in God's law 3
Est 2:11 Mor'decai walked in front of the court 3
Job 18: 8 a net by his own feet, and walks on a pitfall. 3
22:14 he walks on the vault of heaven.' 3
29: 3 by his light I walked through darkness; 3
31: 5 If I have walked with falsehood 3
34: 8 with evildoers and walks with wicked men? 3
38:16 or walked in the recesses of the deep? 3
Ps 1: 1 Blessed is the man who walks not in the counsel 3
15: 2 He who walks blamelessly, and does what is right 3
23: 4 I walk through the valley of the shadow of death 3
26: 1 I have walked in my integrity, and I have trusted 3
3 I walk in faithfulness to thee. 3
11 But as for me, I walk in my integrity; 3
37:14 to slay those who walk uprightly; 2
55:14 within God's house we walked in fellowship. 3
56:13 that I may walk before God in the light of life. 3
68:21 hairy crown of him who walks in his guilty ways. 3
78:10 but refused to walk according to his law. 3
81:13 O that . . Israel would walk in my ways! 3
84:11 LORD withhold from those who walk uprightly. 3
86:11 Teach me . . O LORD, that I may walk in thy truth; 3
89:15 who walk, O LORD, in the light of thy countenance 3
30 If . . do not walk according to my ordinances 3
101: 2 walk with integrity of heart within my house; 3
6 he who walks in the way that is blameless 3
115: 7 have hands, but do not feel; feet, but do not walk; 3
116: 9 I walk before the LORD in the land of the living. 3
119: 1 Blessed are those . . who walk in the law of the LORD! 3
3 who also do no wrong, but walk in his ways! 3
45 I shall walk at liberty 3
128: 1 Blessed . . fears the LORD, who walks in his ways! 3
138: 7 Though I walk in the midst of trouble 3
142: 3 path where I walk they have hidden a trap for me. 3
Prv 1:15 my son, do not walk in the way with them 3
2: 7 he is a shield to those who walk in integrity 3
13 to walk in the ways of darkness 3
20 you will walk in the way of good men 3
3:23 Then you will walk on your way securely 3
4:12 When you walk, your step will not be hampered; 3
14 do not walk in the way of evil men. 1
6:22 When you walk, they will lead you; 3
28 can one walk upon hot coals and his feet 3
8:20 I walk in the way of righteousness 3
9: 6 walk in the way of insight. 1
10: 9 He who walks in integrity walks securely 3
9 He who walks in integrity walks securely 3
13:20 He who walks with wise men becomes wise 3
14: 2 He who walks in uprightness fears the LORD 3
15:21 but a man of understanding walks aright. 3
19: 1 Better is a poor man who walks in his integrity 3
20: 7 A righteous man who walks in his integrity– 3
28: 6 Better is a poor man who walks in his integrity 3
18 He who walks in integrity will be delivered 3
26 but he who walks in wisdom will be delivered. 3
Ecc 2:14 but the fool walks in darkness; 3
10: 3 when the fool walks on the road, he lacks sense 3
7 and princes walking on foot like slaves. 3
11: 9 walk in the ways of your heart and . . of your eyes. 3
Isa 2: 3 us his ways and that we may walk in his paths. 3
5 come, let us walk in the light of the LORD. 3
3:16 haughty and walk with outstretched necks 3
8:11 warned me not to walk in the way of this people 3
9: 2 The people who walked in darkness have seen 3
20: 2 and he had done so, walking naked and barefoot– 3
3 my servant Isaiah has walked naked and barefoot 3
30:21 behind you, saying, "This is the way, walk in it 3
33:15 He who walks righteously and speaks uprightly 3
35: 9 but the redeemed shall walk there. 3
38: 3 how I have walked before thee in faithfulness 3
40:31 not be weary, they shall walk and not faint. 3
42: 5 who gives . . spirit to those who walk in it 3
24 the LORD . . in whose ways they would not walk 3
43: 2 when you walk through fire you shall not be 3
50:10 servant, who walks in darkness and has no light 3
11 Walk by the light of your fire 3
57: 2 rest in their beds who walk in their uprightness. 3
59: 9 and for brightness, but we walk in gloom. 3
65: 2 people, who walk in a way that is not good 3
Jer 6:16 and walk in it, and find rest for your souls. 3
16 But they said, 'We will not walk in it.' 3
25 Go not forth into the field, nor walk on the road; 3
7:23 and walk in all the way that I command you 3
24 but walked in their own counsels 3
9:13 not obeyed my voice, or walked in accord with it 3
10: 5 they have to be carried, for they cannot walk. 5
23 it is not in man who walks to direct his steps. 3
11: 8 walked in the stubbornness of his evil heart. 3
23:14 they commit adultery and walk in lies; 3
26: 4 If you will not listen to me, to walk in my law 3
32:23 But they did not obey thy voice or walk in thy law; 3
44:10 nor have they feared, nor walked in my law 3
23 or walk in his law and in his statutes 3
Lam 4:18 we could not walk in our streets; our end drew near; 3
Ezk 5: 6 and not walking in my statutes. 3
7 and have not walked in my statutes 3

11:12 for you have not walked in my statutes 3
20 that they may walk in my statutes 3
16:47 Yet you were not content to walk in their ways 3
18: 9 walks in my statutes 3
17 observes my ordinances, and walks in my statutes; 3
20:13 they did not walk in my statutes 3
16 my ordinances and did not walk in my statutes 3
18 Do not walk in the statutes of your fathers 3
19 I the LORD am your God; walk in my statutes 3
21 they did not walk in my statutes 3
28:14 in the midst of the stones of fire you walked. 3
33:15 and walks in the statutes of life 3
36:12 Yea, I will let men walk upon you, even my people 3
27 and cause you to walk in my statutes 3
Dan 3:25 four men loose, walking in the midst of the fire 6
4:29 walking on the roof of the royal palace of Babylon 6
37 those who walk in pride he is able to abase. 6
Hos 14: 9 and the upright walk in them 3
Ams 2: 4 lies . . after which their fathers walked. 3
3: 3 Do two walk together, unless they have made 3
Mic 2: 3 and you shall not walk haughtily 3
7 Do not my words do good to him who walks uprightly? 3
4: 2 may teach us his ways and we may walk in his paths. 3
5 all the peoples walk each in the name of its god 3
5 but we will walk in the name of the LORD our God 3
6: 8 to love kindness, and to walk humbly with your God? 3
16 and you have walked in their counsels; 3
Zep 1:17 that they shall walk like the blind 3
3: 6 waste their streets so that none walks in them; 4
Zec 3: 7 If you will walk in my ways and keep my charge 3
Mal 2: 6 He walked with me in peace and uprightness 3
3:14 walking as in mourning before the LORD of hosts? 3
Mat 4:18 As he walked by the Sea of Galilee, he saw two 12
9: 5 or to say, 'Rise and walk'? 12
11: 5 the blind receive their sight and the lame walk 12
14:25 he came to them, walking on the sea 12
26 when the disciples saw him walking on the sea 12
29 walked on the water and came to Jesus; 12
15:31 the maimed whole, the lame walking 12
Mrk 2: 9 or to say, 'Rise, take up your pallet and walk'? 12
5:42 immediately the girl got up and walked 12
6:48 he came to them, walking on the sea 12
49 when they saw him walking on the sea 12
8:24 I see men; but they look like trees, walking. 12
11:27 as he was walking in the temple 12
16:12 as they were walking into the country. 14
Lke 1: 6 walking in all the commandments and ordinances 14
5:23 or to say, 'Rise and walk'? 12
7:22 the blind receive their sight, the lame walk 12
11:44 men walk over them without knowing it. 12
24:17 which you are holding with each other as you walk? 12
Joh 1:36 and he looked at Jesus as he walked, and said 12
5: 8 Rise, take up your pallet, and walk. 12
9 he took up his pallet and walked. 12
11 'Take up your pallet, and walk.' 12
12 'Take up your pallet, and walk'? 12
6:19 they saw Jesus walking on the sea 12
8:12 he who follows me will not walk in darkness 12
10:23 it was winter, and Jesus was walking in the temple 12
11: 9 If any one walks in the day, he does not stumble 12
10 if any one walks in the night, he stumbles 12
12:35 Walk while you have the light 12
35 he who walks in the darkness 12
21:18 you girded yourself and walked where you would; 12
Act 3: 6 in the name of Jesus Christ of Nazareth, walk. 12
8 stood and walked and entered the temple 12
8 walking and leaping and praising God. 12
9 all the people saw him walking and praising God 12
12 as though . . we have made him walk? 12
9:31 walking in the fear of the Lord 14
14: 8 he was a cripple from birth, who had never walked. 12
10 he sprang up and walked. 12
16 allowed all the nations to walk in their own ways; 14
Rom 6: 4 we too might walk in newness of life. 12
8: 4 in us, who walk not according to the flesh 12
14:15 you are no longer walking in love. 12
2Co 5: 7 for we walk by faith, not by sight. 12
Gal 5:16 I say, walk by the Spirit 12
25 let us also walk by the Spirit. 15
6:16 Peace and mercy be upon all who walk by this rule 15
Eph 2: 2 in which you once walked 12
10 that we should walk in them. 12
5: 2 walk in love, as Christ loved us 12
8 walk as children of light 12
15 Look carefully then how you walk 12
Col 3: 7 In these you once walked, when you lived in them. 12
1Jn 1: 6 while we walk in darkness 12
7 if we walk in the light, as he is in the light 12
2: 6 ought to walk in the same way in which he walked. 12
6 ought to walk in the same way in which he walked. 12
11 is in the darkness and walks in the darkness 12
Jde 1:11 Woe to them! For they walk in the way of Cain 14
Rev 2: 1 who walks among the seven golden lampstands. 12
3: 4 they . . walk with me in white, for they are worthy 12
9:20 idols . . which cannot either see or hear or walk; 12
21:24 By its light shall the nations walk; 12
1Es 4:24 he faces lions, and he walks in darkness 7
2Es 3: 8 every nation walked after its own will 16
7: 8 so that only one man can walk upon that path. 17

122 but we have walked in the most wicked ways? 16
8:50 because they have walked in great pride. 16
13:57 Then I arose and walked in the field 18
Tob 1: 3 I, Tobit, walked in the ways of truth 14
3: 5 we did not walk in truth before thee. 14
4: 5 do not walk in the ways of wrongdoing. 14
Jdt 13:20 walking in the straight path before our God 14
Wis 6: 4 nor walk according to the purpose of God 14
15:15 their feet are of no use for walking. 11
Sir 4:17 at first she will walk with him on tortuous paths 14
5: 2 walking according to the desires of your heart. 14
9:13 Know that you are walking in the midst of snares 9
21: 6 walks in the steps of the sinner *
24: 5 have walked in the depths of the abyss. 12
45: 9 to send forth a sound as he walked 8
Bar 1:18 to walk in the statutes of the Lord which he set 14
2:10 to walk in the statutes of the Lord which he set 14
3:13 If you had walked in the way of God, you would be 14
4: 2 take her; walk toward the shining of her light. 10
13 walk in the ways of God's commandments 14
5: 7 so that Israel may walk safely in the glory of God 7
Sus 1: 7 would go into her husband's garden to walk. 12
36 As we were walking in the garden alone 12
2Mc 5:21 he could sail on the land and walk on the sea 13

walk *See also* teach.

walk about 1. הלך 2. סבב 3. *περιπατέω*

Ps 48:12 Walk about Zion, go round about her 2
82: 5 nor understanding, they walk about in darkness; 1
Sir 13:13 you are walking about with your own downfall. 3
Aza 1: 1 they walked about in the midst of the flames 3
Sus 1: 8 two . . used to see her . . going in and walking about 3

walk abroad 1. הלך

Exd 21:19 rises again and walks abroad with his staff 1

walk ahead 1. *προάγω*

Mrk 10:32 Jesus was walking ahead of them 1

walk along 1. *ἐπιβαίνω*

Sir 2:12 Woe . . to the sinner who walks along two ways! 1

walk among 1. *ἐμπεριπατέω*

Wis 19:21 perishable creatures that walked among them 1

walk in procession 1. *πομπεύω*

2Mc 6: 7 they were compelled to walk in the procession 1

make walk 1. הלך

Lev 26:13 I have . . made you walk erect 1
Jer 31: 9 I will make them walk by brooks of water 1

walk through 1. הלך

Gen 13:17 Arise, walk through the length and the breadth 1

walk up and down 1. הלך

Job 1: 7 from walking up and down on it. 1
2: 2 on the earth, and from walking up and down on it. 1

walking *See* manner.

wall 1. בִּנְיָן 2. גְּבוּל 3. גדר 4. גָּדֵר 5. גְּדֵרָה 6. חוֹמָה 7. חַיִץ 8. חֵל 9. כֹּתֶל 10. קִיר 11. שׁוּר 12. כְּתַל (A) 13. שׁוּר (A) 14. *περίβολος* 15. *τεῖχος* 16. *τοῖχος* 17. *φραγμός* 18. murus

Gen 49:22 his branches run over the wall. 11
Exd 14:22 on dry ground, the waters being a wall to them 6
29 through the sea, the waters being a wall to them 6
Lev 14:37 if the disease is in the walls of the house 10
39 if the disease has spread in the walls 10
25:29 If a man sells a dwelling house in a walled city 6
30 then the house that is in the walled city 6
31 the villages which have no wall around them 6
Num22:24 narrow path . . with a wall on either side. 4
25 ass . . pushed against the wall 10
25 ass . . pressed Balaam's foot against the wall; 10
35: 4 shall reach from the wall of the city outward 10
Deu 3: 5 cities fortified with high walls, gates, and bars 6
28:52 besiege . . until your high and fortified walls 6
Jos 2:15 house was built . . so that she dwelt in the wall. 6
6: 5 and the wall of the city will fall down flat 6
20 people raised a . . shout, and the wall fell down 6
1Sm 18:11 he thought, "I will pin David to the wall. 10
19:10 sought to pin David to the wall with the spear; 10
10 so that he struck the spear into the wall. 10
20:25 king sat upon his seat . . upon the seat by the wall; 10
25:16 they were a wall to us both by night and by day 6
31:10 they fastened his body to the wall of Beth-shan. 6
12 took the body of Saul . . from the wall of Beth-shan; 6
2Sm 11:20 Did you not know . . they would shoot from the wall? 6
21 a woman cast . . millstone upon him from the wall 6
21 Why did you go so near the wall? 6
24 the archers shot at your servants from the wall; 6
18:24 went up to the roof of the gate by the wall 6
20:15 and they were battering the wall, to throw it down. 6
21 his head shall be thrown to you over the wall. 6
22:30 Yea, by thee . . and by my God I can leap over a wall. 11
1Kg 3: 1 house of the LORD and the wall around Jerusalem. 6
4:13 60 great cities with walls and bronze bars); 6

33 cedar . . to the hyssop that grows out of the wall; 10
6: 5 built a structure against the wall of the house 10
5 running round the walls of the house 10
6 outside of the house he made offsets on the wall *
6 beams should not be inserted into the walls 10
15 He lined the walls of the house on the inside 10
27 a wing of one touched the one wall 10
27 a wing of the other cherub touched the other wall; 10
29 He carved all the walls of the house round about 10
9:15 build . . the Millo and the wall of Jerusalem 6
20:30 the wall fell upon 27,000 men that were left. 6
2Kg 3:27 offered him for a burnt offering upon the wall. 6
4:10 Let us make a small roof chamber with walls 10
6:26 as the king of Israel was passing by upon the wall 6
30 clothes–now he was passing by upon the wall–and 6
9:33 her blood spattered on the wall and on the horses 10
14:13 broke down the wall of Jerusalem for 400 cubits 6
18:26 the hearing of the people who are on the wall. 6
27 men sitting on the wall, who are doomed with you 6
20: 2 Hezeki'ah turned his face to the wall, and prayed 10
25: 4 by the way of the gate between the two walls 6
10 all . . broke down the walls around Jerusalem. 6
1Ch 29: 4 for overlaying the walls of the house 10
2Ch 3: 7 lined the house with gold . . its walls 10
7 and he carved cherubim on the walls. 10
11 one wing of . . touched the wall of the house 10
12 one wing . . touched the wall of the house 10
8: 5 fortified cities with walls, gates, and bars 6
14: 7 surround them with walls and towers 6
25:23 broke down the wall of Jerusalem for 400 cubits 6
26: 6 broke down the wall of Gath and the wall of Jabneh 6
6 broke down the wall of Gath and the wall of Jabneh 6
6 broke down the wall of Gath . . the wall of Ashdod; 6
27: 3 did much building on the wall of Ophel. 6
32: 5 built up all the wall that was broken down 6
5 outside it he built another wall; 6
18 the people of Jerusalem who were upon the wall 6
33:14 built an outer wall for the city of David 6
36:19 broke down the wall of Jerusalem, and burned all 6
Ezr 4:12 finishing the walls and repairing 13
13 if this city is rebuilt and the walls finished 13
16 if this city is rebuilt and its walls finished 13
5: 8 huge stones, and timber is laid in the walls; 12
Neh 1: 3 wall of Jerusalem is broken down, and its gates 6
2: 8 to make beams for . . the wall of the city 6
13 I inspected the walls of Jerusalem 6
15 went up . . by the valley and inspected the wall; 6
17 Come, let us build the wall of Jerusalem 6
3: 8 restored Jerusalem as far as the Broad Wall. 6
13 repaired 1,000 cubits of the wall 6
15 built the wall of the Pool of Shelah of the king's 6
27 another section . . as far as the wall of Ophel. 6
4: 1 Sanbal'lat heard that we were building the wall 6
3 fox goes up . . he will break down their stone wall! 6
6 built the wall; and all the wall was joined 6
6 wall was joined together to half its height. 6
7 repairing of the walls of Jerusalem was going 6
10 we are not able to work on the wall. 6
13 in the lowest parts of the space behind the wall 6
15 we all returned to the wall, each to his work. 6
17 who were building on the wall. 6
19 we are separated on the wall, far from one another. 6
5:16 I also held to the work on this wall 6
6: 1 when it was reported . . that I had built the wall 6
6 that is why you are building the wall; 6
15 wall was finished . . in 52 days. 6
7: 1 wall had been built and I had set up the doors 6
12:27 dedication of the wall of Jerusalem they sought 6
30 purified the people and the gates and the wall. 6
31 I brought up the princes of Judah upon the wall 6
31 One went to the right upon the wall to the Dung Gate; 6
37 stairs of the city . . at the ascent of the wall 6
38 upon the wall, above the Tower of the Ovens 6
38 I followed them . . to the Broad Wall 6
13:21 Why do you lodge before the wall? If you do so again 6
Ps 18:29 by my God I can leap over a wall. 11
51:18 rebuild the walls of Jerusalem 6
55:10 Day and night they go around it on its walls; 6
62: 3 all of you, like a leaning wall, a tottering fence? 10
80:12 Why then hast thou broken down its walls 4
89:40 Thou hast breached all his walls; 5
122: 7 Peace be within your walls, and security within 8
Prv 1:21 on the top of the walls she cries out; *
18:11 like a high wall protecting him. 6
24:31 its stone wall was broken down. 4
25:28 like a city broken into and left without walls. 6
Ecc 10: 8 serpent will bite him who breaks through a wall. 4
Sng 2: 9 Behold, there he stands behind our wall, gazing 9
5: 7 they beat me . . those watchmen of the walls. 6
8: 9 If she is a wall, we will build upon her 6
10 I was a wall, and my breasts were like towers; 6
Isa 2:15 high tower, and against every fortified wall; 6
5: 5 break down its wall, and it shall be trampled 4
22: 5 day of . . a battering down of walls 10
10 you broke down the houses to fortify the wall. 6
11 You made a reservoir between the two walls 6
25: 4 the ruthless is like a storm against a wall 10
12 fortifications of his walls he will bring down 6
26: 1 he sets up salvation as walls and bulwarks. 6
30:13 iniquity . . like a break in a high wall 6
36:11 within the hearing of the people . . on the wall. 6
12 to you, and not to the men sitting on the wall 6
38: 2 Then Hezeki'ah turned his face to the wall 10
49:16 Behold . . your walls are continually before me. 6
54:12 and all your wall of precious stones. 2
56: 5 give in my house and within my walls a monument 6
59:10 We grope for the wall like the blind 10
60:10 Foreigners shall build up your walls 6
18 you shall call your walls Salvation 6
62: 6 Upon your walls, O Jerusalem, I have set watchmen; 6
Jer 1:15 against all its walls round about 6
18 a fortified city, an iron pillar, and bronze walls 6
4:19 the walls of my heart! My heart is beating wildly; 10
15:20 I will make you . . a fortified wall of bronze; 6
21: 4 Chalde'ans . . besieging you outside the walls; 6
39: 4 garden through the gate between the two walls; 6
8 and broke down the walls of Jerusalem. 6
49:27 And I will kindle a fire in the wall of Damascus 6
50:15 bulwarks have fallen, her walls are thrown down. 6
51:12 Set up a standard against the walls of Babylon; 6
44 the wall of Babylon has fallen. 6
58 The broad wall of Babylon shall be leveled 6
52: 7 a gate between the two walls, by the king's garden 6
14 broke down all the walls round about Jerusalem. 6
Lam 2: 7 he has delivered . . the walls of her palaces; 6
8 to lay in ruins the wall of the daughter of Zion; 6
8 he caused rampart and wall to lament 6
3: 7 He has walled me about so that I cannot escape; 3
Ezk 4: 3 place it as an iron wall between you and the city; 10
8: 7 when I looked, behold, there was a hole in the wall. 10
8 Then said he to me, "Son of man, dig in the wall"; 10
8 and when I dug in the wall, lo, there was a door. 10
10 and there, portrayed upon the wall round about 10
12: 5 Dig through the wall in their sight, and go out 10
7 I dug through the wall with my own hands; 10
12 and shall go forth; he shall dig through the wall 10
13: 5 or built up a wall for the house of Israel 4
10 the people build a wall, these prophets daub it 7
12 when the wall falls, will it not be said to you 10
14 I will break down the wall that you have daubed 10
15 Thus will I spend my wrath upon the wall 10
15 The wall is no more, nor those who daubed it 10
22:30 for a man among them who should build up the wall 4
23:14 she saw men portrayed upon the wall, the images 10
26: 4 They shall destroy the walls of Tyre 6
9 shock of his battering rams against your walls 6
10 your walls will shake at the noise 6
12 they will break down your walls 6
27:11 The men of Arvad and Helech were upon your walls 6
11 they hung their shields upon your walls 6
30:16 Thebes shall be breached, and its walls broken *
33:30 people who talk together about you by the walls 10
38:11 all of them dwelling without walls 6
20 every wall shall tumble to the ground. 6
40: 5 a wall all around the outside of the temple area 6
5 so he measured the thickness of the wall, one reed; 1
41: 5 Then he measured the wall of the temple 10
6 offsets all around the wall of the temple 10
6 so that they should not be supported by the wall 10
9 The thickness of the outer wall of the side 10
12 the wall of the building was five cubits thick 10
13 the yard and the building with its walls 10
15 and its walls on either side, 100 cubits. *
17 on all the walls round about in the inner room 10
20 cherubim and palm trees were carved on the wall. 10
22 its corners, its base, and its walls were of wood. 10
25 palm trees, such as were carved on the walls; 10
42: 7 was a wall outside parallel to the chambers 4
10 where the outside wall begins. 4
12 and opposite them was a dividing wall. 5
20 It had a wall around it, 500 cubits long 6
43: 8 with only a wall between me and them. 10
Dan 5: 5 appeared and wrote on the plaster of the wall 12
Hos 2: 6 and I will build a wall against her 4
Jol 2: 7 they charge, like soldiers they scale the wall. 6
9 They leap upon the city, they run upon the walls; 6
Ams 1: 7 I will send a fire upon the wall of Gaza 6
10 I will send a fire upon the wall of Tyre 6
14 I will kindle a fire in the wall of Rabbah 6
5:19 and leaned with his hand against the wall 10
7: 7 standing beside a wall built with a plumb line 6
Mic 5: 1 Now you are walled about with a wall; *
1 Now you are walled about with a wall; *
7:11 A day for the building of your walls! 4
Nah 2: 5 they hasten to the wall, the mantelet is set up. 6
3: 8 Thebes . . her rampart a sea, and water her wall? 6
Hab 2:11 For the stone will cry out from the wall 10
Zec 2: 5 For I will be to her a wall of fire round about 6
Act 9:25 and let him down over the wall 15
23: 3 God shall strike you, you whitewashed wall! 16
2Co 11:33 let down in a basket through a window in the wall 15
Eph 2:14 has broken down the dividing wall of hostility 17
Heb 11:30 By faith the walls of Jericho fell down 15
Rev 21:12 It had a great, high wall, with twelve gates 15
14 And the wall of the city had twelve foundations 15
15 to measure the city and its gates and walls. 15
17 He also measured its wall 15
18 The wall was built of jasper 15
19 The foundations of the wall of the city 15
1Es 1:55 broke down the walls of Jerusalem 15
2:18 repairing its market places and walls 15
19 Now if this city is built and the walls finished 15
24 if this city is built and its walls finished 15
4: 4 they go, and conquer mountains, walls, and towers. 15
6: 9 with costly timber laid in the walls. 16
2Es 2:22 Protect the old and the young within your walls; 18
11:42 and have laid low the walls of those 18
15:42 they shall destroy cities and walls, mountains 18
Tob 1:17 dead and thrown out behind the wall of Nineveh 15
2: 9 I slept by the wall of the courtyard 16
10 there were sparrows on the wall 16
13:16 her walls with precious stones 15
Jdt 1: 2 he is the king who built walls about Ecbatana 15
2 he made the walls 70 cubits high 15
7:32 they went up on the walls 15
14: 1 hang it upon the parapet of your wall. 15
11 they hung the head of Holofernes on the wall 15
Wis 13:15 sets it in the wall 16
Sir 14:24 will also fasten his tent peg to her walls; 16
22:17 the stucco decoration on the wall of a colonnade. 16
23:18 Darkness surrounds me, and the walls hide me 16
49:13 he raised for us the walls that had fallen 15
50: 2 laid the foundations for the high double walls *
2 high retaining walls for the temple enclosure. *
1Mc 1:31 and tore down its houses and its surrounding walls. 15
33 fortified . . with a great strong wall 15
4:60 they fortified Mount Zion with high walls 15
6: 7 had surrounded the sanctuary with high walls 15
62 and gave orders to tear down the wall all around. 15
9:50 with high walls and gates and bars. 15
54 the wall of the inner court of the sanctuary 15
10:11 to build the walls . . for better fortification 15
45 the cost of rebuilding the walls of Jerusalem 15
45 the cost of rebuilding the walls in Judea 15
12:36 to build the walls of Jerusalem still higher 15
37 part of the wall on the valley to the east 15
13:10 hastened to complete the walls of Jerusalem 15
33 high towers and great walls and gates and bolts 15
45 went up on the wall with their clothes rent 15
14:37 and built the walls of Jerusalem higher. 15
16:23 the building of the walls which he built 15
2Mc 1:15 inside the wall of the sacred precinct 14
3:19 Some . . ran together . . to the walls 15
5: 5 the troops upon the wall had been forced back 15
6:10 then hurled them down headlong from the wall. 15
10:17 and beat off all who fought upon the wall 15
35 bravely stormed the wall 15
11: 9 the wildest beasts or walls of iron. 15
12:13 strongly fortified with earthworks and walls 15
14 relying on the strength of the walls 15
15 his men . . rushed furiously upon the walls. 15
27 young men took their stand before the walls 15
14:43 He bravely ran up on the wall 15
3Mc 1:29 the walls and the whole earth around echoed 15
4:11 had been built with a monstrous perimeter wall *

wall *See also* village.

wall all around 1. περιτειχίζω
1Mc 13:33 and walled them all around 1

city wall 1. קִיר הַחוֹמָה
Jos 2:15 her house was built into the city wall 1

siege wall 1. דָּיֵק
Ezk 4: 2 and build a siege wall against it 1
17:17 cast up and siege walls built to cut off many lives 1
26: 8 he will set up a siege wall against you 1

wall up 1. גדר
Job 19: 8 He has walled up my way, so that I cannot pass 1

wallet 1. יַלְקוּט
1Sm 17:40 and put them in his shepherd's bag or wallet; 1

wallow 1. ספק 2. פלש 3. ἐγκυλίω 4. κυλισμός
Jer 48:26 so that Moab shall wallow in his vomit 1
Ezk 27:30 They cast dust on their heads and wallow in ashes; 2
2Pe 2:22 and the sow is washed only to wallow in the mire. 4
Sir 23:12 they will not wallow in sins. 3

wallowing *See* lie.

wander 1. אבד 2. הלך 3. נדד 4. נוע 5. נסע 6. שגה 7. תעה 8. ἐκτρέπω 9. νέμομαι 10. ξενιτεία 11. πλανάω 12. πλανήτης 13. ῥέμβομαι 14. vagor
Gen 21:14 And she departed, and wandered in the wilderness 7
37:15 a man found him wandering in the fields; 7
Deu 26: 5 wandering Aramean was my father; 1
Jdg 11:37 that I may go and wander on the mountains *
1Ch 16:20 wandering from nation to nation 2
Ps 55: 7 yea, I would wander afar 3
105:13 wandering from nation to nation 2
107: 4 Some wandered in desert wastes, finding no way 7
119:10 let me not wander from thy commandments! 6
21 accursed ones, who wander from thy commandments; 6
Prv 5: 6 her ways wander, and she does not know it. 4
21:16 A man who wanders from the way of understanding 7

Ecc 6: 9 Better is . . than the wandering of desire; 2
Sng 1: 7 like one who wanders beside the flocks 13
Jer 14:10 They have loved to wander thus 4
31:24 farmers and those who wander with their flocks. *
Lam 4:14 They wandered, blind, through the streets 4
Ezk 34: 6 scattered, they wandered over all the mountains 6
Hos 8: 9 gone up to Assyria, a wild ass wandering alone; *
Ams 4: 8 three cities wandered to one city to drink water 4
8:12 They shall wander from sea to sea 4
Zec 10: 2 Therefore the people wander like sheep; 5
11:16 not care for the perishing, or seek the wandering ‡
2Ti 4: 4 will turn away . . and wander into myths. 8
Heb 11:38 wandering over deserts and mountains 11
Jas 5:19 if any one among you wanders from the truth 11
Jde 1:13 wandering stars for whom the nether gloom 12
2Es 7:93 in which the souls of the ungodly wander 14
Wis 18: 3 a harmless sun for their glorious wandering. 10
Sir 29:18 they have wandered among foreign nations. 11
2Mc 10: 6 wandering in the mountains and caves 9

wander about 1. הלך 2. נוע 3. תעה 4. πλανάω 5. vagor

2Sm 15:20 and shall I today make you wander about with us 1
Job 38:41 cry to God, and wander about for lack of food? 3
Ps 109:10 May his children wander about and beg; 2
Isa 47:15 they wander about each in his own direction; 3
2Es 7:80 shall immediately wander about in torments 5
Sir 9: 7 nor wander about in its deserted sections. 4
36:25 a man will wander about and sigh. 4

wander abroad 1. נדד

Job 15:23 He wanders abroad for bread, saying, 'Where is it?' 1

wander away 1. נוד 2. ἀποπλανάω 3. ἐκτρέπω

Jer 49:30 Flee, wander far away, dwell in the depths 1
1Ti 1: 6 have wandered away into vain discussion 3
6:10 some have wandered away from the faith 2

cause to wander 1. נוד 2. תעה

Gen 20:13 God caused me to wander from my father's house 2
2Kg 21: 8 I will not cause the feet of Israel to wander 1

make wander 1. נוע 2. תעה

Num32:13 he made them wander in the wilderness 40 years 1
2Sm 15:20 and shall I today make you wander about with us 1
Job 12:24 and makes them wander in a pathless waste. 2
Ps 107:40 makes them wander in trackless wastes; 2

wanderer 1. נדד 2. נוד

Gen 4:12 you shall be a fugitive and a wanderer 2
14 I shall be a fugitive and a wanderer on the earth 2
Hos 9:17 they shall be wanderers among the nations. 1

become a wanderer 1. נוע

Lam 4:15 they became fugitives and wanderers; 1

wane 1. רפה 2. μειόω

Jdg 19: 9 now the day has waned toward evening; pray tarry 1
Sir 43: 7 a light that wanes when it has reached the full. 2

want 1. βούλομαι 2. ἐθέλω 3. volo

Neh 6: 9 For they all wanted to frighten us, thinking *
14 prophets who wanted to make me afraid. *
Lam 4: 9 stricken by want of the fruits of the field. *
Mat 13:28 Then do you want us to go and gather them? 2
14: 5 though he wanted to put him to death 2
20:21 he said to her, "What do you want?" She said to him 2
32 What do you want me to do for you? 2
27:15 for the crowd any one prisoner whom they wanted. 2
17 Whom do you want me to release for you 2
21 Which of the two do you want me to release for you? 2
Mrk 6:19 wanted to kill him. But she could not 2
25 I want you to give me at once the head of John 2
26 he did not want to break his word to her. 2
10:35 we want you to do for us whatever we ask of you. 2
36 he said to them, "What do you want me to do for you? 2
51 Jesus said . . "What do you want me to do for you? 2
15: 9 you want me to release for you the King of the Jews? 2
Lke 9:54 do you want us to bid fire come down from heaven 2
13:31 Get away from here, for Herod wants to kill you. 2
18:41 What do you want me to do for you? 2
19:14 'We do not want this man to reign over us.' 2
27 who did not want me to reign over them 2
Joh 5: 6 he said to him, "Do you want to be healed? 2
6:11 so also the fish, as much as they wanted. 2
7:44 Some of them wanted to arrest him 2
9:27 Why do you want to hear it again? 2
27 Do you too want to become his disciples? 2
16:19 Jesus knew that they wanted to ask him 2
Act 5:33 they were enraged and wanted to kill them. 1
7:28 Do you want to kill me as you killed the Egyptian 2
14:13 and wanted to offer sacrifice with the people. 2
15:37 Barnabas wanted to take with them John 1
16: 3 Paul wanted Timothy to accompany him 2
Rom 1:13 I want you to know, brethren 2
7:15 I do not do what I want 2
16 Now if I do what I do not want, I agree that the law is 2
19 For I do not do the good I want, but the evil I do not 2
19 but the evil I do not want is what I do. 2
20 Now if I do what I do not want, it is no longer I 2
21 when I want to do right, evil lies close at hand. 2
11:25 I want you to understand this mystery, brethren 2
1Co 7:32 I want you to be free from anxieties 2
10: 1 I want you to know, brethren 2
20 I do not want you to be partners with demons. 2
11: 3 I want you to understand 2
12: 1 I do not want you to be uninformed. 2
14: 5 Now I want you all to speak in tongues 2
16: 7 For I do not want to see you now just in passing 2
2Co 1: 8 For we do not want you to be ignorant, brethren 2
15 I wanted to come to you first 1
16 I wanted to visit you on my way to Macedo'nia *
17 Was I vacillating when I wanted to do this? 1
Gal 1: 7 want to pervert the gospel of Christ. 2
4: 9 whose slaves you want to be once more? 2
17 want to shut you out, that you may make much 2
6:12 those who want to make a good showing in the flesh 2
Php 1:12 I want you to know, brethren 1
Col 2: 1 For I want you to know how greatly I strive for you 2
1Th 2:18 because we wanted to come to you 2
Phm 1:20 Yes, brother, I want some benefit from you *
Jas 2:20 Do you want to be shown, you shallow man 2
3Jn 1:10 and also stops those who want to welcome them 1
2Es 16:63 Woe to those who sin and want to hide their sins! 3
1Mc 3:34 and gave him orders about all that he wanted done 1
7: 5 were led by Alcimus, who wanted to be high priest. 1
11:45 they wanted to kill the king. 1
2Mc 13:25 so angry that they wanted to annul its terms. 2

want (2) 1. אַיִן 2. בְּלִי 3. חסר 4. חָסֵר 5. חֹסֶר 6. מַחְסוֹר 7. חַסִּר (A) 8. ἀπορία 9. ἔνδεια 10. στενοχωρία 11. ὑστερέω 12. ὑστέρημα 13. ὑστέρησις 14. ὕστερος

Deu 28:48 serve your enemies . . in want of all things; 5
57 she will eat them secretly, for want of all things 5
Jdg 19:20 I will care for all your wants; only, do not spend 6
Job 24: 8 and cling to the rock for want of shelter. 2
30: 3 Through want and hard hunger they gnaw 4
Ps 23: 1 The LORD is my shepherd, I shall not want; 3
34: 9 for those who fear him have no want! 6
Prv 6:11 want like an armed man. 6
14:23 but mere talk tends only to want. 6
21: 5 but every one who is hasty comes only to want. 6
24:34 poverty will come . . and want like an armed man. 6
28:22 does not know that want will come upon him. 4
27 He who gives to the poor will not want 6
Isa 5:13 my people go into exile for want of knowledge; 2
Dan 5:27 weighed in the balances and found wanting; 7
Zec 10: 2 they are afflicted for want of a shepherd. 1
Lke 15:14 he began to be in want. 11
2Co 8:14 supply their want 12
14 so that their abundance may supply your want 12
9:12 not only supplies the wants of the saints 12
11: 9 when I was with you and was in want 11
Php 4:11 Not that I complain of want 13
12 facing plenty and hunger, abundance and want. 11
Tob 4:13 in shiftlessness there is loss and great want 9
Wis 16: 4 inexorable want should come 9
Sir 4: 2 nor anger a man in want. 8
10:26 glorify yourself at a time when you are in want. 10
11:11 is so much the more in want. 11
26:28 a warrior in want through poverty 14

want *See* come, suffer.

want one to know 1. γνωρίζω

2Co 8: 1 We want you to know, brethren, about the grace 1

want to understand 1. γνωρίζω

1Co 12: 3 Therefore I want you to understand 1

wanton 1. זנה 2. פוש 3. פחז 4. στρηνιάω

Prv 9:13 A foolish woman . . is wanton and knows no shame. *
Jer 50:11 though you are wanton as a heifer at grass 2
Ezk 6: 9 when I have broken their wanton heart 1
Zep 3: 4 Her prophets are wanton, faithless men; 3
Rev 18: 9 committed fornication and were wanton 4

wanton *See also* craving, crime, folly, fool, play.

wantonly 1. חִנָּם 2. רֵיקָם

Ps 25: 3 be ashamed who are wantonly treacherous. 2
Prv 1:11 let us wantonly ambush the innocent; 1

wantonly *See also* deal, glance, go, turn.

wantonness 1. נְבָלָה 2. רָצוֹן 3. στρῆνος

Gen 49: 6 and in their wantonness they hamstring oxen. 2
Jdg 20: 6 have committed abomination and wantonness 1
Rev 18: 3 grown rich with the wealth of her wantonness. 3

war 1. אִישׁ מִלְחָמָה 2. חַיִל 3. חֶרֶב 4. לחם 5. לָחֶם 6. מִלְחָמָה 7. צבא 8. צָבָא 9. קְרָב 10. קְרָב (A) 11. ἀντιστρατεύομαι 12. πολεμέω 13. πολεμικός 14. πολεμιστής 15. πόλεμος 16. πολεμοτροφέω 17. στρατεύω 18. bellicosus 19. bellum

Gen 14: 2 these kings made war with Bera king of Sodom 6
Exd 1:10 if war befall us, they join our enemies and fight 6
13:17 Lest the people repent when they see war 6
15: 3 The LORD is a man of war; the LORD is his name. 6
17:16 The LORD will have war with Am'alek 6
32:17 There is a noise of war in the camp. 6
Num 1: 3 all in Israel who are able to go forth to war 8
20 old and upward, all who were able to go forth to war 8
22 all who were able to go forth to war 8
24 people . . all who were able to go forth to war 8
26 every man able to go forth to war 8
28 every man able to go forth to war 8
30 every man able to go forth to war 8
32 every man able to go forth to war 8
34 every man able to go forth to war 8
36 every man able to go forth to war 8
38 every man able to go forth to war 8
40 every man able to go forth to war 8
42 every man able to go forth to war 8
45 every man able to go forth to war in Israel- 8
10: 9 go to war in your land against the adversary 6
26: 2 all in Israel who are able to go forth to war. 8
31: 3 Arm men from among you for the war, 8
4 send 1,000 from each of the tribes of Israel to the war 8
5 there were provided . . 12,000 armed for war. 8
6 Moses sent them to the war, 1,000 from each tribe 8
7 warred against Mid'ian, as the LORD commanded 7
14 officers . . who had come from service in the war. 6
21 Elea'zar the priest said to the men of war 8
28 levy for the LORD a tribute from the men of war 6
32 remaining of the spoil that the men of war took 8
36 half, the portion of those who had gone out to war 8
49 Your servants have counted the men of war 6
53 men of war had taken booty, every man for himself.) 8
32: 6 your brethren go to the war while you sit here? 6
20 take up arms to go before the LORD for war 6
27 every man . . armed for war, before the LORD to battle 8
Deu 1:41 And every man of you girded on his weapons of war 6
2:14 entire generation, that is, the men of war 6
16 when all the men of war had perished and were dead 6
4:34 by trials, by signs, by wonders, and by war 6
20: 1 When you go forth to war against your enemies 6
12 if it makes no peace . . but makes war against you 6
20 siegeworks against the city that makes war 6
21:10 When you go forth to war against your enemies 6
Jos 4:13 about 40,000 ready armed for war passed over 8
5: 4 all the males of . . all the men of war, had died 6
6 all the nation, the men of war that came forth 6
6: 3 march . . all the men of war going around the city 6
10: 7 Joshua . . he and all the people of war with him 6
24 Joshua . . and said to the chiefs of the men of war 6
11: 7 Joshua came . . with all his people of war 6
18 Joshua made war a long time with all those kings. 6
23 And the land had rest from war. 6
14:11 my strength . . for war, and for going and coming. 6
15 And the land had rest from war. 6
17: 1 were allotted . . because he was a man of war. 6
22:33 Israel . . spoke no more of making war against 8
Jdg 3: 1 Israel who had no experience of any war in Canaan; 6
2 Israel might know war, that he might teach war *
2 that he might teach war to such at least as had not 6
10 judged Israel; he went out to war, and the LORD 6
5: 8 new gods were chosen, then war was in the gates. 5
18:11 600 men . . armed with weapons of war, set forth 6
16 men . . armed with their weapons of war, stood 6
17 with the 600 men armed with weapons of war 6
20:17 men that drew sword; all these were men of war. 6
1Sm 8:12 to make his implements of war and the equipment 6
16:18 skilful in playing, a man of valor, a man of war 6
17:33 and he has been a man of war from his youth. 6
18: 5 David . . so that Saul set him over the men of war. 6
19: 8 there was war again; and David went out and fought 6
23: 8 And Saul summoned all the people to war 6
28: 1 the Philistines gathered their forces for war 8
15 the Philistines are warring against me 4
2Sm 1:27 How are . . and the weapons of war perished! 6
3: 1 There was a long war between the house of Saul 6
6 there was war between the house of Saul 6
8:10 Hadade'zer had often been at war with To'i. 1
11: 7 how the people fared, and how the war prospered. 6
21:15 The Philistines had war again with Israel 6
18 there was again war with the Philistines at Gob; 6
19 there was again war with the Philistines at Gob; 6
20 And there was again war at Gath 6
22:35 He trains my hands for war, so that my arms can bend 6
1Kg 2: 5 in time of peace blood which had been shed in war 6
14:19 acts of Jerobo'am, how he warred and how he reigned 4
30 there was war between Rehobo'am and Jerobo'am 6
15: 6 there was war between Rehobo'am and Jerobo'am 6
7 there was war between Abi'jam and Jerobo'am. 6
16 there was war between Asa and Ba'asha 6
32 there was war between Asa and Ba'asha 6
20:18 if they have come out for war, take them alive. 6
22: 1 Syria and Israel continued without war. 6
45 acts of Jehosh'aphat . . and how he warred 4
2Kg 6: 8 the king of Syria was warring against Israel 4
8:28 He went with Joram . . to make war against Haz'ael 6
13:25 he had taken from Jeho'ahaz his father in war. 6
18:20 that mere words are strategy and power for war? 6
24:16 all of them strong and fit for war. 6
25: 4 the king with all the men of war fled by night 6

19 officer who had been in command of the men of war 6
1Ch 5:10 in the days of Saul they made war on the Hagrites 6
18 valiant men, who . . drew the bow, expert in war 6
19 made war upon the Hagrites, Jetur, Naphish 6
22 For many fell slain, because the war was of God. 6
7: 4 were units of the army for war, 36,000 6
11 mighty warriors, 17,200, ready for service in war. 6
40 Their number . . for service in war, was 26,000 men. 6
12: 1 were among the mighty men who helped him in war. 6
25 the Simeonites, mighty men of valor for war, 7,100 8
33 equipped for battle with all the weapons of war 6
37 120,000 men armed with all the weapons of war. 6
38 All these, men of war, arrayed in battle order 6
18:10 for Hadade'zer had often been at war with To'u. 6
20: 4 there arose war with the Philistines at Gezer; 6
5 there was again war with the Philistines; 6
6 there was again war at Gath 6
22: 8 have shed much blood and have waged great wars; 6
2Ch 12:15 continual wars between Rehobo'am and Jerobo'am. 6
13: 2 Now there was war between Abi'jah and Jerobo'am. 6
3 army of valiant men of war, 400,000 picked men; 6
14: 6 no war in those years, for the LORD gave him peace. 6
15:19 there was no more war until the 35th year 6
16: 9 for from now on you will have wars. 6
17:18 Jeho'zabad with a 180,000 armed for war. 8
18: 3 We will be with you in the war. 6
22: 5 went with Jeho'ram . . to make war against Haz'ael 6
25: 5 300,000 picked men, fit for war 8
8 if you suppose that . . you will be strong for war 6
26:11 Uzzi'ah had an army of soldiers, fit for war 6
13 307,500, who could make war with mighty power 6
27: 7 Now the rest of the acts of Jotham, and all his wars 6
28:12 stood up against those . . coming from the war 8
35:21 against the house with which I am at war; 6
Job 5:20 from death, and in war from the power of the sword. 6
38:23 the time of trouble, for the day of battle and war? 6
Ps 18:34 He trains my hands for war 6
27: 3 heart shall not fear; though war arise against me 6
33:17 The war horse is a vain hope for victory •
46: 9 He makes wars cease to the end of the earth; 6
55:21 was smoother than butter, yet war was in his heart; 9
68:30 scatter the peoples who delight in war. 9
76: 3 the shield, the sword, and the weapons of war. 6
5 all the men of war were unable to use their hands. 2
120: 7 I am for peace; but when I speak, they are for war! 6
140: 2 stir up wars continually. 6
144: 1 LORD, my rock, who trains my hands for war 9
Prv 20:18 by wise guidance wage war. 6
24: 6 for by wise guidance you can wage your war 6
Ecc 3: 8 a time for war, and a time for peace. 6
8: 8 there is no discharge from war 6
9:18 Wisdom is better than weapons of war 9
Sng 3: 8 all girt with swords and expert in war 6
Isa 2: 4 neither shall they learn war any more. 6
36: 5 that mere words are strategy and power for war? 6
42:13 like a man of war he stirs up his fury; 6
Jer 4:19 I hear the sound of the trumpet, the alarm of war. 6
6: 4 Prepare war against her; up, and let us attack 6
21: 4 Behold, I will turn back the weapons of war 6
28: 8 from ancient times prophesied war, 6
42:14 go to the land of Egypt, where we shall not see war 6
48:14 'We are heroes and mighty men of war'? 6
51:20 You are my hammer and weapon of war 6
27 prepare the nations for war against her •
28 Prepare the nations for war against her •
52: 7 the men of war fled and went out from the city 6
25 officer who had been in command of the men of war 6
Ezk 17:17 will not help him in war, when mounds are cast up 6
27:10 Lud and Put were in your army as your men of war; 6
27 men of war who are in you, with all your company 6
32:27 who went down to Sheol with their weapons of war 6
38: 8 go against the land that is restored from war 3
Dan 7:21 horn made war with the saints, and prevailed over 10
9:26 flood and to the end there shall be war; 6
11:25 king of the south shall wage war 6
Hos 1: 7 nor by war, nor by horses, nor by horsemen. 6
2:18 and I will abolish the bow, the sword, and war 6
10: 9 Shall not war overtake them in Gib'e-ah? 6
Jol 3: 9 Prepare war, stir up the mighty men. 6
9 Let all the men of war draw near, let them come up. 6
Mic 2: 8 who pass by trustingly with no thought of war. 6
3: 5 declare war against him who puts nothing 6
4: 3 neither shall they learn war any more; 6
Zec 9:10 from E'phraim and the war horse from Jerusalem; •
Mat 24: 6 you will hear of wars and rumors of wars 15
6 you will hear of wars and rumors of wars 15
Mrk 13: 7 when you hear of wars and rumors of wars 15
7 when you hear of wars and rumors of wars 15
Lke 14:31 what king, going to encounter another king in war 15
21: 9 when you hear of wars and tumults 15
Rom 7:23 another law at war with the law of my mind 11
Heb 11:34 became mighty in war 15
Jas 4: 1 What causes wars, and what causes fightings 15
1 Is it not your passions . . at war in your members? 17
Rev 2:16 and war against them with the sword of my mouth. 12
11: 7 the beast . . will make war upon them and conquer 15
12: 7 Now war arose in heaven, Michael and his angels 15
17 went off to make war on the rest of her offspring 15
13: 7 Also it was allowed to make war on the saints 15
19:11 and in righteousness he judges and makes war. 12
19 kings . . with their armies gathered to make war 15
1Es 1:25 went to make war at Carchemish on the Euphrates 15
27 my war is at the Euphrates 15
2:27 that the men in it were given to rebellion and war 15
4: 4 If he tells them to make war on one another 15
2Es 4:14 Come, let us go and make war against the sea 19
13: 9 hand nor held a spear or any weapon of war; 18
28 as for his not holding a spear or weapon of war 18
16:18 the beginning of wars 19
34 Their bridegrooms shall be killed in war 19
Jdt 1: 5 Nebuchadnezzar made war against King Arphaxad 15
11 refused to join him in the war 15
4: 5 and stored up food in preparation for war 15
5: 1 the people of Israel had prepared for war 15
7: 1 make war on the Israelites. 15
2 their force of men of war was 170,000 infantry 14
9: 7 the Lord who crushest wars 15
16: 3 For God is the Lord who crushes wars 15
AEs 11: 7 at their roaring every nation prepared for war 15
Wis 8:15 show myself capable, and courageous in war. 15
Sir 37:11 with a coward about war 15
46: 1 Joshua the son of Nun was mighty in war 15
3 he waged the wars of the Lord. 15
6 He hurled down war upon that nation 15
47: 5 to slay a man mighty in war 15
Bar 3:26 giants . . great in stature, expert in war. 15
LJr 1:15 it cannot save itself from war and robbers. 15
48 For when war or calamity comes upon them 15
49 they cannot save themselves from war or calamity? 15
1Mc 3: 3 he girded on his armor of war and waged battles 13
4: 7 these men were trained in war. 15
5:56 the heroic war they had fought. 15
6:30 32 elephants accustomed to war. 15
8: 2 Men told him of their wars and of the brave deeds 15
24 If war comes first to Rome 15
27 if war comes first to the nation of the Jews 15
9:22 his wars and the brave deeds that he did 15
67 and set fire to the machines of war. •
11: 4 those whom Jonathan had burned in the war 15
12:13 many wars have encircled us 15
14 to annoy you . . with these wars 15
44 when we are not at war? 15
13: 3 you know also the wars and the difficulties 15
14: 9 youths donned the glories and garments of war. 15
29 Since wars often occurred in the country 15
15:19 or make alliance with those who war against them. 12
16: 2 have fought the wars of Israel from our youth 15
23 The rest of the acts of John and his wars 15
2Mc 2:14 on account of the war which had come upon us 15
20 further the wars against Antiochus Epiphanes 15
10:10 the principal calamities of the wars. 15
14 and at every turn kept on warring against the Jews. 16
3Mc 1: 2 to kill him and thereby end the war. 15
4Mc 4:22 For when he was warring against Ptolemy in Egypt 15

war *See also* carry, club, cry, engine, expert, go, horse, keep, machine, make, prize, tumult, wage.

war against 1. מִלְחָמָה
Isa 41:12 who war against you shall be as nothing at all. 1

ward off 1. סור 2. κωλύω
2Sm 5: 6 but the blind and the lame will ward you off 1
4Mc 14:16 the others . . ward off the intruder. 2

wardrobe 1. בֶּגֶד 2. מֶלְתָּחָה
2Kg 10:22 He said to him who was in charge of the wardrobe 2
22:14 of Tikvah, son of Harhas, keeper of the wardrobe 1
2Ch 34:22 Tokhath, son of Hasrah, keeper of the wardrobe 1
Jer 38:11 and went to the house of the king, to a wardrobe •

ware 1. כְּלִי 2. מֶכֶר 3. מִמְכָּר 4. מַעֲרָב 5. מַקָּחָה 6. עִזָּבוֹן
Neh 10:31 if the peoples . . bring in wares or any grain 5
13:16 brought in fish and all kinds of wares and sold 2
20 merchants and sellers of all kinds of wares 3
Ezk 27: 9 mariners were in you, to barter for your wares. 4
12 iron, tin, and lead they exchanged for your wares. 6
14 Beth-togar'mah exchanged for your wares horses 6
16 they exchanged for your wares emeralds, purple 6
19 wine from Uzal they exchanged for your wares; 6
22 exchanged for your wares the best of all kinds 6
27 Your riches, your wares, your merchandise 6
33 When your wares came from the seas 6
Jon 1: 5 they threw the wares that were in the ship 1
Rev 18:15 The merchants of these wares, who gained wealth •

costly ware 1. מִגְדָּנָה
Ezr 1: 6 aided them . . with costly wares, besides 1

warfare 1. מִלְחָמָה 2. צָבָא 3. στρατεία 4. bellum
1Kg 5: 3 warfare with which his enemies surrounded him 1
Isa 40: 2 and cry to her that her warfare is ended 2
2Co 10: 4 for the weapons of our warfare are not worldly 3
1Ti 1:18 inspired by them you may wage the good warfare 3
2Es 13:33 the warfare that they have against one another; 4

warfare *See also* wage.

warm 1. חֹם 2. חמם 3. θερμαίνω
Jos 9:12 it was still warm when we took it from our houses 2
1Kg 1: 2 in your bosom, that my lord the king may be warm. 2
Job 30: 4 to warm themselves the roots of the broom. 2
31:20 if he was not warmed with the fleece of my sheep; 2
39:14 her eggs . . and lets them be warmed on the ground 2
Ecc 4:11 Again, if two lie together, they are warm; 2
11 they are warm; but how can one be warm alone? 2
Isa 44:15 fuel . . he takes a part of it and warms himself 2
16 also he warms himself and says, "Aha, I am warm 2
16 and says, "Aha, I am warm, I have seen the fire! 2
47:14 No coal for warming oneself is this 2
Hag 1: 6 you clothe yourselves, but no one is warm; 1
Mrk 14:54 warming himself at the fire. 3
67 seeing Peter warming himself, she looked at him 3
Joh 18:18 they were standing and warming themselves 3
18 standing and warming himself. 3
25 Simon Peter was standing and warming himself. 3
Jas 2:16 Go in peace, be warmed and filled 3
Wis 16:27 when simply warmed by a fleeting ray of the sun 3

warm *See also* get.

become warm 1. חמם
2Kg 4:34 the flesh of the child became warm. 1

warmly 1. ψυχικῶς
2Mc 14:24 he was warmly attached to the man. 1

very warmly 1. προθύμως
Tob 7: 8 They received them very warmly 1

warn 1. דבר 2. זהר 3. זכר 4. יסר 5. מוּסָר 6. עוד 7. צוה 8. ἀνακαλέω 9. ἀπειλέω 10. διαμαρτύρομαι 11. μαρτυρέω 12. νουθετέω 13. προεῖπον 14. προλέγω 15. ὑποδείκνυμι 16. χρηματίζω 17. commoneo
Gen 26:11 Abim'elech warned all the people, saying 7
43: 3 Judah said to him, "The man solemnly warned us 6
Exd 19:21 LORD said to Moses, "Go down and warn the people 6
21:29 its owner has been warned but has not kept it 6
Deu 8:19 I solemnly warn you this day 6
Jdg 2:15 as the LORD had warned, and as the LORD had sworn 1
1Sm 8: 9 you shall solemnly warn them, and show them 6
2Kg 6:10 Thus he used to warn him, so that he saved himself 2
17:13 Yet the LORD warned Israel and Judah 6
Neh 9:26 prophets, who had warned them in order to turn 6
29 warn them in order to turn them back to thy law. 6
30 Many years thou . . didst warn them by thy Spirit 6
13:15 warned them on the day when they sold food. 6
21 I warned them and said to them, "Why do you lodge 6
Job 33:16 and terrifies them with warnings 5
Ps 2:10 O kings, be wise; be warned, O rulers of the earth. 4
19:11 Moreover by them is thy servant warned; 2
Isa 8:11 the LORD spoke thus . . and warned me 4
Jer 4:16 Warn the nations that he is coming; 3
6: 8 Be warned, O Jerusalem 4
11: 7 For I solemnly warned your fathers 6
7 warning them persistently, even to this day 6
42:19 Know for a certainty that I have warned you 6
Ezk 3:18 nor speak to warn the wicked from his wicked way 2
19 But if you warn the wicked, and he does not turn 2
20 because you have not warned him, he shall die 2
21 if you warn the righteous man not to sin 2
33: 3 and blows the trumpet and warns the people; 2
6 so that the people are not warned 2
8 and you do not speak to warn the wicked to turn 2
9 if you warn the wicked to turn from his way 2
Mat 2:12 being warned in a dream not to return to Herod 16
22 go there, and being warned in a dream he withdrew 16
3: 7 You brood of vipers! Who warned you to flee 15
Lke 3: 7 Who warned you to flee from the wrath to come? 15
12: 5 I will warn you whom to fear 15
16:28 for I have five brothers, so that he may warn them 10
Act 4:17 let us warn them to speak no more to any one 9
2Co 13: 2 I warned those who sinned before 13
2 I warn them now while absent 14
Gal 5:21 I warn you, as I warned you before 14
21 I warn you, as I warned you before 13
Col 1:28 warning every man and teaching every man 12
2Th 3:15 warn him as a brother. 12
Heb 11: 7 being warned by God concerning events as yet unseen 16
12:25 they refused him who warned them on earth 16
25 if we reject him who warns from heaven. •
Rev 22:18 I warn every one who hears the words 11
2Es 14:20 who will warn those who will be born hereafter? 17
Wis 11:10 thou didst test them as a father does in warning 12
12: 2 dost remind and warn them 12
4Mc 14:17 warning them with their own calls. 8

warning 1. מוּסָר 2. נֵס 3. עֵדוּת 4. νουθεσία 5. τύπος
Num26:10 together with Korah . . they became a warning. 2
2Kg 17:15 covenant . . and the warnings which he gave them. 3
Neh 9:34 not . . heeded . . warnings which thou didst give 3
Ezk 5:15 a warning and a horror, to the nations round about 1
1Co 10: 6 Now these things are warnings for us 5

11 Now these things happened to them as a warning 4
Wis 16: 6 they were troubled for a little while as a warning 4

warning *See also* give, heed, take.

without warning 1. בְּשַׁלְוָה 2. ἀπροσδοκήτως

Dan 8:25 Without warning he shall destroy many; 1
11:21 come in without warning and obtain the kingdom 1
24 Without warning he shall come into the richest 1
2Mc 8: 6 Coming without warning 2

warp 1. שְׁתִי

Lev 13:48 in warp or woof of linen or wool, or in a skin 1
49 whether in warp or woof or in skin or in anything 1
51 If the disease has spread in the garment, in warp 1
52 garment, whether diseased in warp or woof 1
53 the disease has not spread in the garment in warp 1
56 the garment or the skin or the warp or woof 1
57 then if it appears again in the garment, in warp 1
58 the garment, warp or woof, or anything of skin 1
59 disease . . either in warp or woof, or in anything 1

warrior 1. אִישׁ מִלְחָמָה 2. גִּבּוֹר 3. עִזּוּז 4. עֹשֵׂה מִלְחָמָה 5. קְרוֹב 6. תֹּפֵשׂ מִלְחָמָה 7. ἀνήρ 8. ἀνὴρ δυνατός 9. ἀνὴρ πολεμιστής 10. δύναμις 11. δυνατός 12. ἰσχυρός 13. πολεμιστής 14. bellator

Num31:27 between the warriors who went out to battle 6
Jdg 11: 1 Now Jephthah the Gileadite was a mighty warrior 2
1Kg 12:21 he assembled . . 180,000 chosen warriors 4
1Ch 5:24 mighty warriors, famous men 2
7: 2 mighty warriors of their generations 2
5 of Is'sachar were in all 87,000 mighty warriors 2
7 heads of fathers' houses, mighty warriors; 2
9 heads of their fathers' houses, mighty warriors 2
11 sons of Jedi'a-el . . mighty warriors 2
40 men of Asher . . approved, mighty warriors 2
8:40 sons of Ulam were men who were mighty warriors 2
12: 8 mighty and experienced warriors 2
28: 1 the mighty men, and all the seasoned warriors. 2
3 for you are a warrior and have shed blood. 1
2Ch 13: 3 with 800,000 picked mighty warriors. 2
32:21 cut off all the mighty warriors and commanders 2
Job 16:14 he runs upon me like a warrior. 2
Ps 33:16 a warrior is not delivered by his great strength. 2
120: 4 A warrior's sharp arrows, with glowing coals 2
127: 4 Like arrows in the hand of a warrior are the sons 2
Sng 4: 4 bucklers, all of them shields of warriors. 2
Isa 9: 5 boot of the tramping warrior in battle tumult *
43:17 brings forth chariot and horse, army and warrior 3
Jer 20:11 But the LORD is with me as a dread warrior; 2
26:21 And when King Jehoi'akim, with all his warriors 2
46: 5 Their warriors are beaten down, and have fled 2
6 The swift cannot flee . . nor the warrior escape; 2
9 Let the warriors go forth: men of Ethiopia and Put 2
12 for warrior has stumbled against warrior; 2
12 for warrior has stumbled against warrior; 2
48:41 The heart of the warriors of Moab 2
49:22 heart of the warriors of Edom shall be in that day 2
50: 9 Their arrows are like a skilled warrior 2
36 upon her warriors, that they may be destroyed! 2
51:30 The warriors of Babylon have ceased fighting 2
56 her warriors are taken, their bows are broken 2
57 her governors, her commanders, and her warriors; 2
Ezk 23: 6 warriors clothed in purple, governors 5
12 warriors clothed in full armor, horsemen riding 5
23 commanders all of them, officers and warriors *
39:20 men and all kinds of warriors,' says the Lord GOD. 1
Hos 10:13 trusted . . in the multitude of your warriors 2
Jol 2: 7 Like warriors they charge 2
3:10 let the weak say, "I am a warrior. 2
11 Bring down thy warriors, O LORD. 2
Hab 3:14 pierce with thy shafts the head of his warriors 14
Zep 3:17 God . . a warrior who gives victory; 2
Zec 9:13 O Greece, and wield you like a warrior's sword. 2
Jdt 7: 2 all their warriors moved their camp that day; 8
16: 4 he came with myriads of his warriors 10
Wis 18:15 thy all-powerful word . . a stern warrior 13
Sir 26:28 a warrior in want through poverty 9
1Mc 2:42 Hasideans, mighty warriors of Israel 12
66 has been a mighty warrior from his youth 12
9:11 as did all the chief warriors. 11
10:19 a mighty warrior and worthy to be our friend. 11
13:10 So he assembled all the warriors 7
15:13 with him were 120,000 warriors and 8,000 cavalry. 9
16: 4 20,000 warriors and horsemen 9

chief warrior 1. πρωταγωνιστής

1Mc 9:11 as did all the chief warriors. 1

chosen warrior 1. בחר

2Ch 11: 1 180,000 chosen warriors, to fight against Israel 1

experienced warrior 1. אִישׁ צָבָא לַמִּלְחָמָה

1Ch 12: 8 mighty and experienced warriors 1

mighty warrior 1. גִּבּוֹר 2. δυνατός

Zec 10: 7 Then E'phraim shall become like a mighty warrior 1
1Mc 4:30 who didst crush the attack of the mighty warrior 2

stout warrior 1. מִשְׁמָן

Isa 10:16 send wasting sickness among his stout warriors 1

warship 1. πλοῖον πολεμικόν

1Mc 15: 3 have equipped warships 1

wary 1. φυλάσσω

Sir 37: 8 Be wary of a counselor 1

wash 1. דּוּחַ 2. כָּבַס 3. רָחַץ 4. רַחְצָה 5. שָׁטַף 6. ἀπολούω 7. ἀπονίπτω 8. βαπτίζω 9. βαπτισμός 10. λουτρόν 11. λούω 12. νίπτω 13. περικλύζω 14. πλύνω

Gen 18: 4 Let a little water be brought, and wash your feet 3
19: 2 spend the night, and wash your feet; 3
24:32 gave . . water to wash his feet 3
43:24 when . . they had washed their feet 3
31 Then he washed his face and came out; 3
49:11 he washes his garments in wine 2
Exd 19:10 and let them wash their garments 2
14 the people; and they washed their garments. 2
29: 4 bring . . his sons . . and wash them with water. 3
17 and wash its entrails and its legs, and put them 3
30:18 a laver of bronze . . for washing. 3
19 his sons wash their hands and their feet. 3
20 they shall wash with water, lest they die. 3
21 They shall wash their hands and their feet 3
40:12 bring Aaron . . and shall wash them with water 3
30 the laver . . and put water in it for washing 3
31 Aaron and his sons washed their hands 3
32 when they approached the altar, they washed; 3
Lev 1: 9 its entrails and its legs he shall wash with water 3
13 the entrails and the legs he shall wash with water 3
6:27 shall wash that on which it was sprinkled 2
8: 6 Aaron and his sons, and washed them with water 3
21 entrails and the legs were washed with water 3
9:14 he washed the entrails and the legs, and burned 3
11:25 whoever carries . . their carcass shall wash 2
28 he who carries their carcass shall wash 2
40 he who eats of its carcass shall wash his clothes 2
40 he . . shall wash his clothes and be unclean 2
13: 6 and he shall wash his clothes, and be clean 2
34 he shall wash his clothes, and be clean 2
54 that they wash the thing in which is the disease 2
55 examine . . after it has been washed 2
56 and the disease is dim after it is washed 2
58 which the disease departs when you have washed it 2
58 shall then be washed a second time, and be clean 2
14: 8 he who is to be cleansed shall wash his clothes 2
9 Then he shall wash his clothes, and bathe his body 2
47 lies down in the house shall wash his clothes 2
47 he who eats in the house shall wash his clothes 2
15: 5 one who touches his bed shall wash his clothes 2
6 shall wash his clothes, and bathe himself 2
7 shall wash his clothes, and bathe himself 2
8 then he shall wash his clothes, and bathe himself 2
10 he . . shall wash his clothes, and bathe himself 2
11 shall wash his clothes, and bathe himself in water 2
13 and wash his clothes; and he shall bathe his body 2
17 which the semen comes shall be washed with water 2
21 whoever touches her bed shall wash his clothes 2
22 shall wash his clothes, and bathe himself in water 2
27 shall wash his clothes, and bathe himself in water 2
16:26 he . . shall wash his clothes and bathe his body 2
28 he who burns them shall wash his clothes 2
17:15 shall wash his clothes, and bathe himself in water 2
16 if he does not wash them or bathe his flesh 2
Num 8: 7 wash their clothes and cleanse themselves. 2
21 purified themselves . . washed their clothes; 2
19: 7 priest shall wash his clothes and bathe his body 2
8 burns the heifer shall wash his clothes in water 2
10 he who gathers . . shall wash his clothes 2
19 he shall wash his clothes and bathe himself 2
21 water for impurity shall wash his clothes; 2
31:24 You must wash your clothes on the seventh day 2
Deu 21: 6 elders . . wash their hands over the heifer 3
Jdg 19:21 and they washed their feet, and ate and drank. 3
Rut 3: 3 Wash therefore and anoint yourself 3
1Sm 25:41 to wash the feet of the servants of my lord. 3
2Sm 11: 8 Go down to your house, and wash your feet. 3
12:20 David arose . . and washed, and anointed himself 3
19:24 nor trimmed his beard, nor washed his clothes 2
1Kg 22:38 they washed the chariot by the pool of Sama'ria 5
38 and the harlots washed themselves in it 3
2Kg 5:10 Go and wash in the Jordan seven times 3
12 Could I not wash in them, and be clean? 3
13 when he says to you, 'Wash, and be clean'? 3
2Ch 4: 6 He also made ten lavers in which to wash 3
6 and the sea was for the priests to wash in. 3
Job 9:30 If I wash myself with snow, and cleanse my hands 3
29: 6 when my steps were washed with milk 3
Ps 26: 6 I wash my hands in innocence 3
51: 2 Wash me thoroughly from my iniquity 2
7 wash me, and I shall be whiter than snow. 2
73:13 my heart clean and washed my hands in innocence. 3
Sng 4: 2 shorn ewes that have come up from the washing 4
6: 6 flock of ewes, that have come up from the washing 4
Isa 1:16 Wash yourselves; make yourselves clean; 3
Jer 2:22 Though you wash yourself with lye 2
4:14 O Jerusalem, wash your heart from wickedness 2
Ezk 16: 4 nor were you washed with water to cleanse you 3
40:38 gate, where the burnt offering was to be washed. 1
Mat 6:17 when you fast, anoint your head and wash your face 12
15: 2 For they do not wash their hands when they eat. 12
27:24 took water and washed his hands before the crowd 7
Mrk 7: 3 do not eat unless they wash their hands 12
4 washing of cups and pots and vessels of bronze.) 9
Lke 5: 2 were washing their nets. 14
11:38 he did not first wash before dinner. 8
Joh 9: 7 saying to him, "Go, wash in the pool of Silo'am 12
7 So he went and washed and came back seeing. 12
11 'Go to Silo'am and wash'; so I went and washed 12
11 so I went and washed and received my sight. 12
15 I washed, and I see. 12
13: 5 began to wash the disciples' feet 12
6 Peter said to him, "Lord, do you wash my feet? 12
8 Peter said to him, "You shall never wash my feet. 12
8 If I do not wash you, you have no part in me. 12
10 does not need to wash, except for his feet 12
12 When he had washed their feet 12
14 I . . your Lord and Teacher, have washed your feet 12
14 you also ought to wash one another's feet. 12
Act 9:37 when they had washed her 11
16:33 washed their wounds 11
1Co 6:11 you were washed, you were sanctified 6
Eph 5:26 cleansed her by the washing of water with the word 10
1Ti 5:10 washed the feet of the saints 12
Tit 3: 5 by the washing of regeneration 10
Heb 10:22 our bodies washed with pure water. 11
2Pe 2:22 and the sow is washed only to wallow in the mire. 11
Rev 7:14 they have washed their robes and made them white 14
22:14 Blessed are those who wash their robes 14
Tob 2: 5 when I returned I washed myself 11
6: 2 Then the young man went down to wash himself. 13
Sir 34:25 If a man washes after touching a dead body 8
25 what has he gained by his washing? 10

wash away 1. יצף 2. רחץ 3. שטף 4. ἀπολούω

Job 14:19 the torrents wash away the soil of the earth; 3
22:16 their foundation was washed away. 1
Isa 4: 4 when the Lord shall have washed away the filth 2
Act 22:16 and wash away your sins, calling on his name.' 4

wash off 1. מחה 2. שטף

Num 5:23 wash them off into the water of bitterness; 1
Ezk 16: 9 with water and washed off your blood from you 2

washbasin 1. סִיר רַחַץ

Ps 60: 8 Moab is my washbasin; upon Edom I cast my shoe; 1
108: 9 Moab is my washbasin; upon Edom I cast my shoe; 1

wasp 1. σφήξ

Wis 12: 8 didst send wasps as forerunners of thy army 1

waste 1. בלה 2. בער 3. בָּתָה 4. חרב 5. חָרֵב 6. חֹרֶב 7. חָרְבָּה 8. כלה 9. מָזֶה 10. מְשַׁמָּה 11. עשש 12. שדד 13. שׁוֹאָה 14. שחת 15. שַׁמָּה 16. שְׁמָמָה 17. תֹּהוּ 18. inconpositus

Lev 26:16 consumption, and fever that waste the eyes 8
31 And I will lay your cities waste, 7
33 a desolation, and your cities shall be a waste 7
Num24:22 nevertheless Kain shall be wasted. 2
Deu 32:10 found him . . in the howling waste of the wilderness; 17
24 they shall be wasted with hunger, and devoured 9
Jdg 6: 5 so that they wasted the land as they came in. 14
1Ch 17: 9 violent men shall waste them no more, as formerly 1
Job 6:18 they go up into the waste, and perish. 17
12:24 and makes them wander in a pathless waste. 17
38:27 to satisfy the waste and desolate land 13
Ps 31: 9 my eye is wasted from grief 11
91: 6 nor the destruction that wastes at noonday. 12
107:40 makes them wander in trackless wastes; 17
Prv 23: 8 vomit . . and waste your pleasant words. 14
Isa 5: 6 will make it a waste; it shall not be pruned or hoed 3
49:19 Surely your waste and your desolate places 7
Jer 2:15 They have made his land a waste; 15
4: 7 forth from his place to make your land a waste; 15
23 I looked on the earth, and lo, it was waste and void; 17
7:34 for the land shall become a waste. 7
25:11 This whole land shall become a ruin and a waste 15
12 making the land an everlasting waste. 16
18 a desolation and a waste, a hissing and a curse 15
38 for their land has become a waste 15
33:10 which you say, 'It is a waste without man or beast 5
12 In this place which is waste, without man or beast 5
44: 6 they became a waste and a desolation 7
22 and a waste and a curse, without inhabitant 15
46:19 For Memphis shall become a waste, a ruin 15
49:13 shall become a horror, a taunt, a waste, and a curse; 6
13 and all her cities shall be perpetual wastes. 7
33 become a haunt of jackals, an everlasting waste; 16
51:26 you shall be a perpetual waste, says the LORD. 16
Ezk 6: 6 Wherever you dwell your cities shall be waste 4
6 so that your altars will be waste and ruined 4
14 and make the land desolate and waste 10
29: 9 land of Egypt shall be a desolation and a waste. 7

10 I will make the land of Egypt an utter waste 7
33:28 I will make the land a desolation and a waste; 10
29 when I have made the land a desolation and a waste 10
35: 3 I will make you a desolation and a waste. 10
4 I will lay your cities waste 7
7 I will make Mount Se'ir a waste and a desolation; 16
36: 4 the desolate wastes and the deserted cities 7
35 the waste and desolate and ruined cities 5
38 the waste cities be filled with flocks of men. 5
38: 8 Israel, which had been a continual waste; 7
Jol 1: 7 It has laid waste my vines 15
Mic 1: 7 and all her idols I will lay waste; 16
Nah 3: 7 Wasted is Nin'eveh; who will bemoan her? 12
Zep 2: 9 possessed by nettles . . and a waste for ever. 16
Mal 1: 3 I have laid waste his hill country 16
2Es 5: 3 the land . . shall be waste and untrodden 18

waste (2) 1. ἀπώλεια 2. ἄχρηστος 3. διασκορπίζω 4. ἐκχέω

Mat 26: 8 they were indignant, saying, "Why this waste? 1
Mrk 14: 4 Why was the ointment thus wasted? 1
Lke 16: 1 this man was wasting his goods. 3
Wis 16:29 and flow away like waste water. 2
Sir 20:13 the courtesies of fools are wasted. 4

waste *See* lay, lie.

waste away 1. כלה 2. חרב 3. כלה 4. מסס 5. מקק 6. עשש 7. διαμάχομαι 8. διαφθείρω 9. ἐκτήκω 10. τήκω

Job 13:28 Man wastes away like a rotten thing 1
14:11 a river wastes away and dries up 2
33:21 His flesh is so wasted away that it cannot be seen; 3
Ps 6: 7 My eye wastes away because of grief, it grows weak 6
31:10 because of my misery, and my bones waste away. 6
32: 3 When I declared not my sin, my body wasted away 1
49:14 they descend, and their form shall waste away; 1
Isa 10:18 it will be as when a sick man wastes away. 4
Ezk 4:17 and waste away under their punishment. 5
33:10 sins are upon us, and we waste away because of them; 5
2Co 4:16 Though our outer nature is wasting away 8
Jdt 7:14 their wives and children will waste away with famine 10
Sir 31: 1 Wakefulness over wealth wastes away one's flesh 9
38:28 he wastes away in the heat of the furnace; 7
3Mc 6: 8 wasting away in . . a huge, sea-born monster 10

burnt-out waste 1. שְׂרֵפָה

Deu 29:23 burnt-out waste, unsown, and growing nothing 1

desert waste 1. מִדְבָּר

Ps 107: 4 Some wandered in desert wastes, finding no way 1

dry waste 1. צִיָּה

Zep 2:13 a desolation, a dry waste like the desert. 1

make waste away 1. כלה

Lam 3: 4 He has made my flesh and my skin waste away 1

waste place 1. חָרְבָּה

Ps 102: 6 like a vulture . . like an owl of the waste places; 1
Isa 51: 3 Zion; he will comfort all her waste places 1
52: 9 into singing, you waste places of Jerusalem; 1
Ezk 33:24 of these waste places in the land of Israel 1
27 those who are in the waste places shall fall 1
36:10 shall be inhabited and the waste places rebuilt; 1
33 and the waste places shall be rebuilt 1
38:12 and carry off plunder; to assail the waste places 1

salty waste 1. מְלֵחָה

Ps 107:34 a fruitful land into a salty waste 1

waste time 1. יחל

2Sm 18:14 I will not waste time like this with you. 1

utterly waste away 1. detabesco

2Es 7:87 because they shall utterly waste away 1

wasteland 1. χέρσος

Wis 10: 7 a continually smoking wasteland 1

wasting *See* disease, sickness.

watch 1. אַשְׁמוּרָה 2. מִשְׁמָר 3. מִשְׁמֶרֶת 4. צפה 5. צְפִיָּה 6. ראה 7. שמר 8. שָׁמֻר 9. שקד 10. ἀγρυπνέω 11. ἀγρυπνία 12. ἀποσκοπεύω 13. γρηγορέω 14. ἐκζητέω 15. ἐπισκοπή 16. ἐφίστημι 17. θεωρέω 18. ὁράω 19. παρατηρέω 20. προσέχω 21. σκοπεύω 22. σκοπιά 23. συντηρέω 24. τηρέω 25. φυλακή 26. φυλάσσω 27. vigilo

Gen 31:49 The LORD watch between you and me 4
Exd 12:42 It was a night of watching by the LORD, to bring 8
42 is a night of watching kept to the LORD by all 8
14:24 And in the morning watch the LORD 1
Jdg 7:19 came . . at the beginning of the middle watch 1
19 came . . when they had just set the watch; 7
21:21 Go and lie in wait . . and watch; if the daughters 6
1Sm 4:13 Eli was sitting upon his seat . . watching 4
6: 9 And watch; if . . then it is he who has done 6
11:11 they came into . . the camp in the morning watch 1
19:11 sent messengers to David's house to watch him 7
1Ch 26:16 Watch corresponded to watch. 2
16 Watch corresponded to watch. 2
Neh 12:24 watch corresponding to watch. 2
24 watch corresponding to watch. 2
Job 13:27 my feet in the stocks, and watchest all my paths; 7
33:11 my feet in the stocks, and watches all my paths. 7
Ps 5: 3 I prepare a sacrifice for thee, and watch. 4
37:32 The wicked watches the righteous 4
56: 6 together, they lurk, they watch my steps. 7
59: 0 of David, when Saul sent men to watch his house 7
71:10 those who watch for my life consult together 7
90: 4 yesterday . . is past, or as a watch in the night. 1
119:82 My eyes fail with watching for thy promise; •
123 My eyes fail with watching for thy salvation •
148 My eyes are awake before the watches of the night 1
142: 4 I look to the right and watch, but there is none 6
Prv 2:11 discretion will watch over you; 7
5:21 he watches all his paths. 21
6:22 when you lie down, they will watch over you; 7
8:34 who listens to me, watching daily at my gates 9
Ecc 5: 8 for the high official is watched by a higher 7
Isa 29:20 all who watch to do evil shall be cut off 9
Jer 1:12 for I am watching over my word to perform it. 9
5: 6 A leopard is watching against their cities 9
20:10 all my familiar friends, watching for my fall. 7
31:28 come to pass that as I have watched over them 9
28 so I will watch over them to build and to plant 9
44:27 I am watching over them for evil and not for good; 9
48:19 Stand by the way and watch, O inhabitant of Aro'er! 4
51:12 make the watch strong; set up watchmen; 2
Lam 2:19 Arise, cry out . . at the beginning of the watches! 1
4:17 Our eyes failed, ever watching vainly for help; •
17 in our watching we watched for a nation 5
17 we watched for a nation which could not save. 4
Nah 2: 1 Man the ramparts; watch the road; gird your loins; 4
Hab 2: 1 I will take my stand to watch 3
Zec 11:11 traffickers in the sheep, who were watching me 7
Mat 14:25 in the fourth watch of the night he came to them 25
24:42 Watch therefore, for you do not know 13
43 he would have watched 13
25:13 Watch therefore, for you know neither the day 13
26:38 remain here, and watch with me. 13
40 So, could you not watch with me one hour? 13
41 Watch and pray that you may not enter 13
Mrk 3: 2 they watched him, to see whether he would heal him 19
6:48 about the fourth watch of the night he came 25
12:41 watched the multitude 17
13:33 Take heed, watch; for you do not know 10
34 commands the doorkeeper to be on watch. 13
35 Watch therefore-for you do not know 13
37 what I say to you I say to all: Watch. 13
14:34 remain here, and watch. 13
37 Simon, are you asleep? Could you not watch one hour? 13
38 Watch and pray that you may not enter 13
Lke 2: 8 keeping watch over their flock by night. 25
6: 7 the scribes and the Pharisees watched him 19
12:38 If he comes in the second watch, or in the third 25
14: 1 they were watching him. 19
20:20 So they watched him, and sent spies 19
21:36 watch at all times 10
23:35 the people stood by, watching 17
Act 9:24 were watching the gates day and night, to kill him; 19
2Co 6: 5 imprisonments, tumults, labors, watching, hunger; 11
2Es 2:13 The kingdom is already prepared for you; watch! 27
11: 8 Do not all watch at the same time 27
8 and watch in his turn; 27
Tob 4:14 Watch yourself, my son, in everything you do 20
Jdt 10:10 the men of the city watched her 12
12: 5 Along toward the morning watch she arose 25
Wis 3: 9 he watches over his holy ones. •
4:15 he watches over his holy ones. 15
Sir 12:11 watch yourself, and be on your guard against him; 16
19: 9 for some one has heard you and watched you 26
26:10 Keep strict watch over a headstrong daughter 25
27:12 Among stupid people watch for a chance to leave 23
33:16 I was the last on watch 10
40: 6 afterward in his sleep, as though he were on watch 22
42:11 Keep strict watch over a headstrong daughter 25
43:10 they never relax in their watches. 25
Bar 3:34 the stars shone in their watches, and were glad; 25
LJr 1: 7 and he is watching your lives. 14
Sus 1:12 they watched eagerly, day after day, to see her. 19
15 while they were watching for an opportune day 19
16 who had hid themselves and were watching her. 19
2Mc 14:29 he watched for an opportunity 24
4Mc 13:27 watching their brothers being maltreated 18
15:15 She watched the flesh of her children consumed 18
16:15 you stood and watched Eleazar being tortured 18

watch *See also* duty, keep.

watch for an omen 1. נחש

1Kg 20:33 the men were watching for an omen 1

watch of the night 1. אַשְׁמוּרָה

Ps 63: 6 meditate on thee in the watches of the night; 1

watch over 1. נצר 2. שמר 3. ἀφοράω 4. ἐπεῖδον 5. ἐπισκέπτομαι 6. ἐπόπτης 7. ἐποπτικός 8. ἐφοράω 9. φυλάσσω

Job 29: 2 as in the days when God watched over me; 2
Ps 61: 7 steadfast love and faithfulness watch over him! 1
127: 1 Unless the LORD watches over the city 2
146: 9 The LORD watches over the sojourners 2
Ezk 34:16 the fat and the strong I will watch over; 9
Sir 46:14 the Lord watched over Jacob. 5
2Mc 3:39 he . . watches over that place himself 6
7: 6 The Lord God is watching over us 8
3Mc 6: 8 Jonah . . you, Father, watched over 3
12 watch over us now and have mercy upon us 4
4Mc 5:13 if there is some power watching over this religion 7

stealthily watch 1. צפן

Ps 10: 8 His eyes stealthily watch for the hapless 1

watcher 1. נצר 2. עִיר (A)

Job 7:20 If I sin, what do I do to thee, thou watcher of men? 1
Dan 4:13 a watcher, a holy one, came down from heaven. 2
17 The sentence is by the decree of the watchers 2
23 king saw a watcher, a holy one, coming down 2

watchful 1. ἀγρυπνέω 2. γρηγορέω 3. προσέχω

1Co 16:13 Be watchful, stand firm in your faith 2
Col 4: 2 being watchful in it with thanksgiving; 2
1Pe 5: 8 Be sober, be watchful. Your adversary the devil 2
1Es 8:59 Be watchful and on guard until you deliver them 1
Sir 13:13 Keep words to yourself and be very watchful 3

watchfulness 1. ἀγρυπνία

Sir 0: 3 using . . great watchfulness and skill 1

keep watching 1. ἐπέχω

2Mc 9:25 how the princes . . keep watching for opportunities 1

watchman 1. נצר 2. פְּקִדָּה 3. צפה 4. שמר 5. σκοπός 6. φυλάσσω

1Sm 14:16 the watchmen of Saul in Gib'e-ah . . looked; 3
2Sm 18:24 and the watchman went up to the roof of the gate 3
25 And the watchman called out and told the king. 3
26 And the watchman saw another man running; 3
26 and the watchman called to the gate and said 3
27 And the watchman said, "I think the running 3
2Kg 9:17 Now the watchman was standing on the tower 3
18 And the watchman reported, saying 3
20 Again the watchman reported, "He reached them 3
11:18 And the priest posted watchmen over the house 2
2Ch 23:18 posted watchmen for the house of the LORD 2
Job 27:18 like a booth which a watchman makes. 1
Ps 127: 1 watchman stays awake in vain. 4
130: 6 more than watchmen for the morning, 4
6 more than watchmen for the morning. 4
Sng 3: 3 The watchmen found me, as they went about 4
5: 7 The watchmen found me, as they went about the city; 4
7 they beat me . . those watchmen of the walls. 4
Isa 21: 6 Go, set a watchman, let him announce what he sees. 3
11 calling . . Watchman, what of the night? 4
11 what of the night? Watchman, what of the night? 4
12 The watchman says: "Morning comes 4
52: 8 Hark, your watchmen lift up their voice 3
56:10 His watchmen are blind, they are all without 3
62: 6 Upon your walls, O Jerusalem, I have set watchmen; 4
Jer 6:17 I set watchmen over you, saying, 'Give heed 3
31: 6 For there shall be a day when watchmen will call 1
51:12 make the watch strong; set up watchmen; 4
Ezk 3:17 I have made you a watchman for the house of Israel; 3
33: 2 from among them, and make him their watchman; 3
6 if the watchman sees the sword coming 3
6 his blood I will require at the watchman's hand. 3
7 I have made a watchman for the house of Israel; 3
Hos 9: 8 The prophet is the watchman of E'phraim 3
Mic 7: 4 The day of their watchmen, of their punishment 3
Jdt 13:11 called out . . to the watchmen at the gates 6
Sir 37:14 seven watchmen sitting high on a watchtower. 5

watchtower 1. בַּחַן 2. מִגְדָּל 3. מִגְדַּל נצר 4. מִצְפָּה 5. σκοπή

2Kg 17: 9 their towns, from watchtower to fortified city; 3
18: 8 He smote . . from watchtower to fortified city. 3
2Ch 20:24 Judah came to the watchtower of the wilderness 4
Isa 5: 2 he built a watchtower in the midst of it 2
21: 8 who saw cried: "Upon a watchtower I stand, O Lord 4
32:14 hill and the watchtower . . become dens for ever 1
Sir 37:14 seven watchmen sitting high on a watchtower. 5

watchword 1. σύνθημα

2Mc 8:23 gave the watchword, "God's help 1
13:15 He gave his men the watchword, "God's victory 1

water 1. זרף 2. ירא 3. ירה 4. מַי 5. נָהָר 6. רוה 7. רָוֶה 8. שׁוֹק 9. שקה 10. ἔνυδρος 11. ἐπάρδω 12. ποτίζω 13. ὑγρός 14. ὕδωρ 15. aqua 16. poto

Gen 1: 2 Spirit . . was moving over the face of the waters 4
6 a firmament in the midst of the waters 4
6 let it separate the waters from the waters 4

6 let it separate the waters from the waters 4
7 the waters which were under the firmament 4
7 from the waters which were above the firmament 4
9 God said, "Let the waters under the heavens 4
10 and the waters that were gathered together 4
20 God said, "Let the waters bring forth swarms 4
21 creature that moves, with which the waters swarm 4
22 and multiply and fill the waters in the seas 4
2: 6 from the earth and watered the whole face 9
10 A river flowed out of Eden to water the garden 9
6:17 I will bring a flood of waters upon the earth 4
7: 6 when the flood of waters came upon the earth. 4
7 into the ark, to escape the waters of the flood. 4
10 after seven days the waters of the flood came 4
17 and the waters increased, and bore up the ark 4
18 The waters prevailed and increased greatly 4
18 the ark floated on the face of the waters. 4
19 the waters prevailed so mightily upon the earth 4
20 the waters prevailed above the mountains 4
24 the waters prevailed upon the earth 150 days. 4
8: 1 wind blow over the earth, and the waters subsided; 4
3 the waters receded from the earth continually. 4
3 At the end of 150 days the waters had abated; 4
5 the waters continued to abate 4
7 it went to and fro until the waters were dried up 4
8 to see if the waters had subsided from the face 4
9 the waters were still on the face 4
11 Noah knew that the waters had subsided 4
13 the waters were dried from off the earth; 4
9:11 all flesh be cut off by the waters of a flood 4
15 all flesh; and the waters shall never again 4
13:10 the Jordan valley was well watered everywhere 9
16: 7 found her by a spring of water in the wilderness 4
18: 4 Let a little water be brought, and wash your feet 4
21:14 Abraham . . took bread and a skin of water 4
15 When the water in the skin was gone 4
19 opened her eyes, and she saw a well of water; 4
19 she went, and filled the skin with water 4
25 to Abim'elech about a well of water 4
24:11 kneel down outside the city by the well of water 4
13 Behold, I am standing by the spring of water 4
13 daughters . . are coming out to draw water. 4
14 maiden . . who shall say, 'Drink, and I will water 9
17 give me a little water to drink from your jar. 4
32 gave . . water to wash his feet 4
43 behold, I am standing by the spring of water; 4
43 Pray give me a little water from your jar to drink 4
26:18 Isaac dug again the wells of water 4
19 found there a well of springing water 4
20 quarreled . . saying, "The water is ours. 4
32 they had dug, and said to him, "We have found water 4
29: 2 for out of that well the flocks were watered. 9
3 shepherds would . . water the sheep 9
7 water the sheep, and go, pasture them. 9
8 mouth of the well; then we water the sheep. 9
10 Jacob . . watered the flock of Laban his mother's 9
37:24 The pit was empty, there was no water in it. 4
43:24 the men into Joseph's house, and given them water 4
49: 4 Unstable as water, you shall not have 4
Exd 2:10 she said, "Because I drew him out of the water. 4
16 drew water . . to water their father's flock. 9
17 Moses . . helped them, and watered their flock. 9
19 drew water for us and watered the flock. 9
4: 9 you shall take some water from the Nile and pour 4
9 and the water which you shall take from the Nile 4
7:15 Go to Pharaoh . . as he is going out to the water; 4
17 I will strike the water that is in the Nile 4
18 will loathe to drink water from the Nile. 4
19 stretch out your hand over the waters of Egypt 4
19 over . . all their pools of water, that they may 4
20 he . . struck the water that was in the Nile 4
20 all the water . . in the Nile turned to blood. 4
21 Egyptians could not drink water from the Nile; 4
24 the Egyptians dug . . for water to drink 4
24 for they could not drink the water of the Nile. 4
8: 6 stretched out his hand over the waters of Egypt; 4
20 wait for Pharaoh, as he goes out to the waters 4
12: 9 Do not eat any of it raw or boiled with water 4
14:21 the sea dry land, and the waters were divided. 4
22 on dry ground, the waters being a wall to them 4
26 the water may come back upon the Egyptians 4
28 The waters returned and covered the chariots 4
29 through the sea, the waters being a wall to them 4
15: 8 At the blast of thy nostrils the waters piled up 4
10 they sank as lead in the mighty waters. 4
19 the LORD brought back the waters of the sea upon 4
22 went . . in the wilderness and found no water. 4
23 not drink the water of Marah because it was 4
25 a tree, and he threw it into the water, and the water 4
25 and the water became sweet. There the LORD made 4
27 12 springs of water and 70 palm trees; 4
27 and they encamped there by the water. 4
17: 1 there was no water for the people to drink. 4
2 the people . . said, "Give us water to drink. 4
3 the people thirsted there for water 4
6 strike the rock, and water shall come out of it 4
20: 4 anything . . that is in the water under the earth; 4
23:25 and I will bless your bread and your water; 4
29: 4 bring . . his sons . . and wash them with water. 4
30:18 a laver . . and you shall put water in it 4
20 they shall wash with water, lest they die. 4
32:20 scattered it upon the water, and made the people 4
34:28 he neither ate bread nor drank water. 4
40: 7 place the laver . . and put water in it. 4
12 bring Aaron . . and shall wash them with water 4
30 the laver . . and put water in it for washing 4
Lev 1: 9 its entrails and its legs he shall wash with water 4
13 the entrails and the legs he shall wash with water 4
6:28 that shall be scoured, and rinsed in water 4
8: 6 Aaron and his sons, and washed them with water 4
21 entrails and the legs were washed with water 4
11: 9 These you may eat, of all that are in the waters 4
9 Everything in the waters that has fins and scales 4
10 the swarming creatures in the waters 4
10 of the living creatures that are in the waters 4
12 Everything in the waters that has not fins 4
32 it must be put into water, and it shall be unclean 4
34 Any food . . upon which water may come 4
36 a cistern holding water shall be clean 4
38 if water is put on the seed 4
46 living creature that moves through the waters 4
14: 5 kill . . one of the birds . . over running water 4
6 the bird that was killed over the running water 4
8 shave off all his hair, and bathe himself in water 4
9 and bathe his body in water, and he shall be clean 4
50 in an earthen vessel over running water 4
51 dip them in the blood . . and in the running water 4
52 cleanse the house . . with the running water 4
15: 5 wash his clothes, and bathe himself in water 4
6 shall . . bathe himself in water, and be unclean 4
7 shall . . bathe himself in water, and be unclean 4
8 and bathe himself in water, and be unclean 4
10 wash his clothes, and bathe himself in water 4
11 touches without having rinsed his hands in water 4
11 shall wash his clothes, and bathe himself in water 4
12 every vessel of wood shall be rinsed in water 4
13 he shall bathe his body in running water 4
16 he shall bathe his whole body in water 4
17 which the semen comes shall be washed with water 4
18 both of them shall bathe themselves in water 4
21 shall wash his clothes, and bathe himself in water 4
22 shall wash his clothes, and bathe himself in water 4
27 shall wash his clothes, and bathe himself in water 4
16: 4 He shall bathe his body in water 4
24 he shall bathe his body in water in a holy place 4
26 shall wash his clothes and bathe his body in water 4
28 wash his clothes and bathe his body in water 4
17:15 shall wash his clothes, and bathe himself in water 4
22: 6 unless he has bathed his body in water 4
Num 5:17 shall take holy water in an earthen vessel 4
17 some of the dust . . and put it into the water. 4
18 priest shall have the water of bitterness 4
19 be free from this water of bitterness 4
22 may this water that brings the curse pass 4
23 wash them off into the water of bitterness; 4
24 make the woman drink the water of bitterness 4
24 water that brings the curse shall enter into her 4
26 afterward shall make the woman drink the water. 4
27 when he has made her drink the water, 4
27 water that brings the curse shall enter into her 4
8: 7 sprinkle the water of expiation upon them 4
19: 7 priest shall wash . . and bathe his body in water 4
8 burns the heifer shall wash his clothes in water 4
8 wash his clothes . . and bathe his body in water 4
9 they shall be kept . . for the water for impurity 4
12 shall cleanse himself with the water *
13 water for impurity was not thrown upon him 4
17 running water shall be added in a vessel; 4
18 shall take hyssop, and dip it in the water 4
19 wash his clothes and bathe himself in water 4
20 water for impurity has not been thrown upon him 4
21 He who sprinkles the water for impurity 4
21 he who touches the water for impurity shall be 4
20: 2 Now there was no water for the congregation; 4
5 evil place . . and there is no water to drink. 4
8 rock before their eyes to yield its water; 4
8 so you shall bring water out of the rock for them; 4
10 shall we bring forth water for you out of this rock? 4
11 water came forth abundantly 4
13 These are the waters of Mer'ibah, where the people 4
17 neither will we drink water from a well; 4
19 if we drink of your water . . then I will pay for it; 4
24 against my command at the waters of Mer'ibah. 4
21: 5 For there is no food and no water, and we loathe 4
16 Gather the people . . and I will give them water. 4
22 we will not drink the water of a well; 4
24: 6 like cedar trees beside the waters. 4
7 Water shall flow from his buckets 4
7 his seed shall be in many waters 4
27:14 to sanctify me at the waters before their eyes. 4
14 (These are the waters of Mer'ibah of Kadesh 4
31:23 also be purified with the water of impurity; 4
23 whatever . . you shall pass through the water. 4
33: 9 at Elim there were twelve springs of water 4
14 Reph'idim, where there was no water for the people 4
Deu 2: 6 buy water of them for money, that you may drink. 4
28 shall . . give me water for money, that I may drink; 4
4:18 likeness of any fish that is in the water 4
5: 8 anything . . that is in the water under the earth; 4
8: 7 good land, a land of brooks of water 4
15 thirsty ground where there was no water 4
15 who brought you water out of the flinty rock 4
9: 9 I neither ate bread nor drank water. 4
18 I neither ate bread nor drank water 4
10: 7 Jot'bathah, a land with brooks of water. 4
11: 4 how he made the water of the Red Sea overflow them 4
10 sowed your seed and watered it with your feet 9
11 land . . which drinks water by the rain 4
12:16 blood . . pour it out upon the earth like water. 4
24 you shall pour it out upon the earth like water. 4
14: 9 Of all that are in the waters you may eat these 4
15:23 blood . . pour it out on the ground like water. 4
23: 4 not meet you with bread and with water on the way 4
11 evening comes on, he shall bathe himself in water 4
29:11 both he who hews . . and he who draws your water 4
32:51 broke faith . . at the waters of Mer'i-bath-ka'desh 4
33: 8 whom thou didst strive at the waters of Mer'ibah; 4
Jos 2:10 LORD dried up the water of the Red Sea before you 4
3: 8 you come to the brink of the waters of the Jordan 4
13 soles . . shall rest in the waters of the Jordan 4
13 the waters of the Jordan shall be stopped 4
13 the waters coming down from above shall stand 4
15 the feet . . were dipped in the brink of the water 4
16 waters coming down from above stood and rose up 4
4: 7 that the waters of the Jordan were cut off 4
7 the waters of the Jordan were cut off. 4
18 the waters of the Jordan returned to their place 4
23 LORD . . dried up the waters of the Jordan for you 4
5: 1 the LORD had dried up the waters of the Jordan 4
7: 5 hearts of the people melted, and became as water. 4
9:21 they became hewers of wood and drawers of water 4
23 be slaves, hewers of wood and drawers of water 4
27 made them . . hewers of wood and drawers of water 4
11: 5 and encamped together at the waters of Merom 4
7 Joshua came suddenly . . by the waters of Merom 4
15: 7 boundary passes . . to the waters of En-she'mesh 4
9 from . . to the spring of the Waters of Nephto'ah 4
19 since you have . . give me also springs of water. 4
16: 1 allotment . . went . . east of the waters of Jericho 4
18:15 to Ephron, to the spring of the Waters of Nephto'ah; 4
Jdg 1:15 me in the . . Negeb, give me also springs of water. 4
4:19 give me a little water to drink; for I am thirsty. 4
5: 4 heavens dropped, yea, the clouds dropped water. 4
19 fought . . at Ta'anach, by the waters of Megid'do 4
25 He asked water and she gave him milk 4
6:38 dew from the fleece to fill a bowl with water. 4
7: 4 take them down to the water and I will test them 4
5 he brought the people down to the water; 4
5 Every one that laps the water with his tongue 4
6 the rest of the people knelt down to drink water. 4
24 Mid'ianites and seize the waters against them 4
24 and they seized the waters as far as Beth-bar'ah 4
15:19 the hollow place . . and there came water from it; 4
1Sm 7: 6 and drew water and poured it out before the LORD 4
9:11 they met young maidens coming out to draw water 4
25:11 Shall I take my bread and my water 4
26:11 take now the spear . . and the jar of water 4
12 David took the spear and the jar of water 4
16 see where the king's spear is, and the jar of water 4
30:11 and he ate, they gave him water to drink 4
12 had not eaten bread or drunk water for three days 4
2Sm 12:27 moreover, I have taken the city of waters. 4
14:14 we are like water spilt on the ground 4
17:20 They have gone over the brook of water. 4
21 Arise, and go quickly over the water; 4
22:12 He made . . thick clouds, a gathering of water. 4
17 he took me, he drew me out of many waters. 4
23:15 O that some one would give me water to drink 4
16 and drew water out of the well of Bethlehem 4
1Kg 13: 8 I will not eat bread or drink water in this place; 4
9 neither eat bread, nor drink water, nor return 4
16 neither will I eat bread nor drink water with you 4
17 You shall neither eat bread nor drink water 4
18 that he may eat bread and drink water.' 4
19 ate bread in his house, and drank water. 4
22 and have eaten bread and drunk water in the place 4
22 he said to you, "Eat no bread, and drink no water"; 4
14:15 will smite Israel, as a reed is shaken in the water 4
17:10 Bring me a little water . . that I may drink. 4
18: 4 hid them . . and fed them with bread and water.) 4
5 Go through the land to all the springs of water 4
13 and fed them with bread and water? 4
33 Fill four jars with water, and pour it 4
35 the water ran round about the altar 4
35 the water . . filled the trench also with water. 4
38 and licked up the water that was in the trench. 4
19: 6 a cake baked on hot stones and a jar of water. 4
22:27 and feed him with scant fare of bread and water 4
2Kg 2: 8 Eli'jah took his mantle . . and struck the water 4
8 struck the water, and the water was parted 4
14 took the mantle . . and struck the water, saying 4
14 when he had struck the water, the water was parted 4
14 when he had struck the water, the water was parted *
19 but the water is bad, and the land is unfruitful. 4
21 he went to the spring of water and threw salt in it 4
21 Thus says . . I have made this water wholesome; 4
22 So the water has been wholesome to this day 4

3: 9 there was no water for the army or for the beasts 4
11 Eli'sha . . poured water on the hands of Eli'jah. 4
17 that stream-bed shall be filled with water 4
19 and stop up all springs of water 4
20 water came from the direction of Edom 4
20 till the country was filled with water. 4
22 they rose . . and the sun shone upon the water 4
22 the Moabites saw the water . . as red as blood. 4
25 they stopped every spring of water 4
5:12 Are not . . better than all the waters of Israel? 4
6: 5 felling a log, his axe head fell into the water; 4
22 Set bread and water before them, that they may eat 4
8:15 the coverlet and dipped it in water and spread it 4
18:31 every . . will drink the water of his own cistern; 4
19:24 I dug wells and drank foreign waters 4
20:20 how he made . . and brought water into the city 4
1Ch 11:17 O that some one would give me water to drink 4
18 drew water out of the well of Bethlehem 4
2Ch 18:26 feed him with scant fare of bread and water 4
32: 3 planned . . to stop the water of the springs 4
4 kings of Assyria come and find much water? 4
30 closed the upper outlet of the waters of Gihon 4
Ezr 10: 6 neither eating bread nor drinking water; 4
Neh 9:11 into the depths, as a stone into mighty waters. 4
15 bring forth water for them from the rock 4
20 gavest them water for their thirst. 4
13: 2 not meet . . Israel with bread and water 4
Job 3:24 my groanings are poured out like water. 4
5:10 upon the earth and sends waters upon the fields; 4
8:11 Can reeds flourish where there is no water? 4
11:16 you will remember it as waters that have passed 4
12:15 If he withholds the waters, they dry up; 4
14: 9 yet at the scent of water it will bud 4
11 As waters fail from a lake, and a river wastes away 4
19 the waters wear away the stones; 4
15:16 corrupt, a man who drinks iniquity like water! 4
22: 7 You have given no water to the weary to drink 4
11 you cannot see, and a flood of water covers you. 4
24:18 swiftly carried away upon the face of the waters; 4
19 Drought and heat snatch away the snow waters; 4
26: 5 tremble, the waters and their inhabitants. 4
8 He binds up the waters in his thick clouds 4
10 described a circle upon the face of the waters 4
28:25 and meted out the waters by measure; 4
29:19 my roots spread out to the waters 4
34: 7 man is like Job, who drinks up scoffing like water 4
36:27 For he draws up the drops of water 4
37:10 the broad waters are frozen fast. 4
38:30 The waters become hard like stone 4
34 to the clouds, that a flood of waters may cover you? 4
Ps 1: 3 He is like a tree planted by streams of water 4
18:11 his canopy thick clouds dark with water. 4
16 he took me, he drew me out of many waters. 4
22:14 I am poured out like water 4
23: 2 He leads me beside still waters; 4
29: 3 The voice of the LORD is upon the waters; 4
3 God of glory thunders, the LORD, upon many waters. 4
32: 6 rush of great waters, they shall not reach him. 4
33: 7 He gathered the waters of the sea as in a bottle; 4
46: 3 though its waters roar and foam 4
58: 7 Let them vanish like water that runs away; 4
63: 1 as in a dry and weary land where no water is. 4
65: 9 Thou visitest the earth and waterest it 8
9 the river of God is full of water; 4
66:12 we went through fire and through water; 4
69: 1 O God! For the waters have come up to my neck. 4
2 there is no foothold; I have come into deep waters 4
14 let me be delivered . . from the deep waters. 4
72: 6 like rain . . like showers that water the earth! 1
74:13 break the heads of the dragons on the waters. 4
77:16 When the waters saw thee, O God 4
16 O God, when the waters saw thee, they were afraid 4
17 The clouds poured out water; the skies gave forth 4
19 thy path through the great waters; 4
78:13 and made the waters stand like a heap. 4
16 caused waters to flow down like rivers. 4
20 He smote the rock so that water gushed out 4
79: 3 blood like water round about Jerusalem 4
81: 7 I tested you at the waters of Mer'ibah. Selah 4
93: 4 Mightier than the thunders of many waters 4
104: 3 hast laid the beams of thy chambers on the waters 4
6 waters stood above the mountains. 4
13 From thy lofty abode . . waterest the mountains; 9
105:29 He turned their waters into blood 4
41 He opened the rock, and water gushed forth; 4
106:11 waters covered their adversaries; 4
32 They angered him at the waters of Mer'ibah 4
107:23 doing business on the great waters; 4
33 turns . . springs of water into thirsty ground 4
35 He turns a desert into pools of water 4
35 turns . . a parched land into springs of water. 4
109:18 may it soak into his body like water 4
114: 8 who turns the rock into a pool of water 4
8 who turns the . . flint into a spring of water. 4
124: 5 then over us would have gone the raging waters. 4
136: 6 to him who spread out the earth upon the waters 4
137: 1 waters of Babylon, there we sat down and wept 5
144: 7 rescue me and deliver me from the many waters 4
147:18 he makes his wind blow, and the waters flow. 4
148: 4 Praise him, you . . waters above the heavens! 4
Prv 5:15 Drink water from your own cistern 4
16 streams of water in the streets? 4
8:24 when . . no springs abounding with water. 4
29 waters might not transgress his command 4
9:17 Stolen water is sweet 4
11:25 one who waters will himself be watered. 6
25 one who waters will himself be watered. 2
17:14 beginning of strife is like letting out water; 4
18: 4 The words of a man's mouth are deep waters; 4
20: 5 The purpose in a man's mind is like deep water 4
21: 1 heart is a stream of water in the hand of the LORD; 4
25:21 if he is thirsty, give him water to drink; 4
25 Like cold water to a thirsty soul, so is good news 4
27:19 As in water face answers to face, so the mind of man 4
30: 4 Who has wrapped up the waters in a garment? 4
16 earth ever thirsty for water, and the fire 4
Ecc 2: 6 pools . . to water the forest of growing trees. 9
11: 1 Cast your bread upon the waters, 4
Sng 4:15 a garden fountain, a well of living water 4
5:12 His eyes are like doves beside springs of water 4
8: 7 Many waters cannot quench love 4
Isa 1:22 Your silver . . dross, your wine mixed with water. 4
30 like an oak . . and like a garden without water. 4
3: 1 whole stay of bread, and the whole stay of water; 4
8: 6 this people have refused the waters of Shilo'ah 4
7 bringing up against them the waters of the River 4
11: 9 of the knowledge . . as the waters cover the sea. 4
12: 3 you will draw water from the wells of salvation. 4
14:23 a possession of the hedgehog, and pools of water 4
15: 6 the waters of Nimrim are a desolation; 4
9 For the waters of Dibon are full of blood; 4
17:12 they roar like the roaring of mighty waters! 4
13 The nations roar like the roaring of many waters 4
18: 2 by the Nile, in vessels of papyrus upon the waters 4
19: 5 the waters of the Nile will be dried up 4
8 they . . languish who spread nets upon the water. 4
21:14 To the thirsty bring water, meet the fugitive 4
22: 9 you collected the waters of the lower pool 4
11 reservoir between the two walls for the water 4
23: 3 were on many waters; your revenue was the grain 4
27: 3 I, the LORD, am its keeper; every moment I water it 9
28: 2 like a storm of mighty, overflowing waters 4
17 and waters will overwhelm the shelter. 4
30:14 or to dip up water out of the cistern. 4
20 bread of adversity and the water of affliction 4
25 there will be brooks running with water 4
32: 2 like streams of water in a dry place 4
20 Happy are you who sow beside all waters 4
33:16 his bread will be given him, his water will be sure. 4
35: 6 For waters shall break forth in the wilderness 4
7 a pool, and the thirsty ground springs of water; 4
36:16 one . . will drink the water of his own cistern; 4
37:25 I dug wells and drank waters 4
40:12 has measured the waters in the hollow of his hand 4
41:17 the poor and needy seek water, and there is none 4
18 I will make the wilderness a pool of water 4
18 a pool of water, and the dry land springs of water. 4
43: 2 you pass through the waters I will be with you; 4
16 a way in the sea, a path in the mighty waters 4
20 for I give water in the wilderness 4
44: 3 For I will pour water on the thirsty land 4
4 They shall spring up like grass amid waters 14
12 strength fails, he drinks no water and is faint. 4
48:21 he made water flow for them from the rock; 4
21 he cleft the rock and the water gushed out. 4
49:10 and by springs of water will guide them. 4
50: 2 fish stink for lack of water, and die of thirst. 4
51:10 didst dry up the sea, the waters of the great deep; 4
54: 9 I swore that the waters of Noah should no more go 4
55: 1 Ho, every one who thirsts, come to the waters; 4
10 and return not thither but water the earth 6
57:20 cannot rest, and its waters toss up mire and dirt. 4
58:11 you shall be like a watered garden, like a spring 7
11 like a watered garden, like a spring of water 4
11 like a spring of water, whose waters fail not. 4
63:12 who divided the waters before them 4
64: 2 and the fire causes water to boil- 4
Jer 2:13 have forsaken me, the fountain of living waters 4
13 broken cisterns, that can hold no water. 4
18 by going to Egypt, to drink the waters of the Nile? 4
18 to Assyria, to drink the waters of the Euphra'tes? 4
6: 7 As a well keeps its water fresh 4
8:14 and has given us poisoned water to drink 4
9: 1 O that my head were waters, and my eyes a fountain 4
15 and give them poisonous water to drink. 4
18 with tears, and our eyelids gush with water. 4
10:13 there is a tumult of waters in the heavens 4
13: 1 put it on your loins, and do not dip it in water. 4
14: 3 Her nobles send their servants for water; 4
3 they come to the cisterns, they find no water 4
15:18 like a deceitful brook, like waters that fail? 4
17: 8 He is like a tree planted by water 4
13 forsaken the LORD, the fountain of living water. 4
18:14 Do the mountain waters run dry 4
23:15 wormwood, and give them poisoned water to drink; 4
31: 9 I will make them walk by brooks of water 4
12 their life shall be like a watered garden 7
38: 6 there was no water in the cistern, but only mire 4
46: 7 like the Nile, like rivers whose waters surge? 4
8 like the Nile, like rivers whose waters surge. 4
47: 2 Behold, waters are rising out of the north 4
48:34 the waters of Nimrim also have become desolate. 4
50:38 A drought upon her waters, that they may be dried 4
51:13 O you who dwell by many waters, rich in treasures 4
16 there is a tumult of waters in the heavens 4
55 Their waves roar like many waters 4
Lam 2:19 Pour out your heart like water before 4
3:54 water closed over my head; I said, 'I am lost.' 4
5: 4 We must pay for the water we drink 4
Ezk 1:24 their wings like the sound of many waters 4
4:11 And water you shall drink by measure 4
16 they shall drink water by measure and in dismay. 4
17 I will do this that they may lack bread and water 4
7:17 All hands are feeble, and all knees weak as water. 4
12:18 and drink water with trembling 4
19 with fearfulness, and drink water in dismay 4
16: 4 nor were you washed with water to cleanse you 4
9 Then I bathed you with water 4
17: 5 he placed it beside abundant waters. 4
7 its branches toward him that he might water it. 9
8 transplanted it to good soil by abundant waters 4
19:10 vine in a vineyard transplanted by the water 4
10 full of branches by reason of abundant water. 4
21: 7 all knees will be weak as water. 4
24: 3 Set on the pot, set it on, pour in water also; 4
26:12 soil they will cast into the midst of the waters. 4
19 the deep over you, and the great waters cover you 4
27:34 wrecked by the seas, in the depths of the waters; 4
31: 4 The waters nourished it, the deep made it grow 4
5 long, from abundant water in its shoots. 4
7 for its roots went down to abundant waters. 4
14 in order that no trees by the waters may grow 4
14 no trees that drink water may reach up to them 4
15 many waters shall be stopped; 4
16 choice and best of Lebanon, all that drink water 4
32: 2 trouble the waters with your feet 4
13 all its beasts from beside many waters; 4
14 Then I will make their waters clear 4
34:18 to drink of clear water, that you must foul 4
36:25 I will sprinkle clean water upon you 4
43: 2 his coming was like the sound of many waters; 4
47: 1 water was issuing from below the threshold 4
1 water was flowing down from below the south end 4
2 the water was coming out on the south side. 4
3 and then led me through the water; 4
4 measured 1,000, and led me through the water; 4
4 measured 1,000, and led me through the water; 4
5 I could not pass through, for the water had risen; 4
8 This water flows toward the eastern region 4
8 when it enters the stagnant waters of the sea •
8 the water will become fresh. 4
9 for this water goes there 4
9 that the waters of the sea may become fresh; •
12 the water for them flows from the sanctuary. 4
19 it shall run from Tamar as far as the waters 4
48:28 from Tamar to the waters of Meribath-ka'desh 4
Dan 1:12 us be given vegetables to eat and water to drink. 4
12: 6 man . . who was above the waters of the stream 4
7 man . . who was above the waters of the stream 4
Hos 2: 5 my lovers, who give me my bread and my water 4
5:10 upon them I will pour out my wrath like water. 4
6: 3 as the spring rains that water the earth. 3
10: 7 perish, like a chip on the face of the waters. 4
Jol 1:20 cry to thee because the water brooks are dried up 4
3:18 the stream beds of Judah shall flow with water; 4
18 and water the valley of Shittim. 9
Ams 4: 8 three cities wandered to one city to drink water 4
5: 8 who calls for the waters of the sea, and pours them 4
24 But let justice roll down like waters 4
8:11 not a famine of bread, nor a thirst for water 4
9: 6 who calls for the waters of the sea, and pours them 4
Jon 2: 5 The waters closed in over me 4
3: 7 let them not feed, or drink water 4
Mic 1: 4 like waters poured down a steep place. 4
Nah 2: 8 Nin'eveh is like a pool whose waters run away. 4
3: 8 Thebes that sat by the Nile, with water around her 4
8 Thebes . . her rampart a sea, and water her wall? 4
14 Draw water for the siege, strengthen your forts; 4
Hab 2:14 will be filled . . as the waters cover the sea. 4
3:10 the raging waters swept on; 4
15 trample the sea . . the surging of mighty waters. 4
Zec 14: 8 living waters shall flow out from Jerusalem 4
Mat 3:11 I baptize you with water for repentance, but he 14
16 he went up immediately from the water, and behold 14
8:32 into the sea, and perished in the waters. 14
10:42 a cup of cold water because he is a disciple •
14:28 Lord, if it is you, bid me come to you on the water. 14
29 walked on the water and came to Jesus; 14
17:15 and often into the water. 14
27:24 took water and washed his hands before the crowd 14
Mrk 1: 8 I have baptized you with water 14
10 when he came up out of the water 14
9:22 often cast him into the fire and into the water 14
41 whoever gives you a cup of water to drink 14
14:13 a man carrying a jar of water will meet you 14
Lke 3:16 John answered them all, "I baptize you with water; 14
7:44 you gave me no water for my feet 14

8:23 they were filling with water, and were in danger. •
25 he commands even wind and water, and they obey 14
13:15 and lead it away to water it? 12
16:24 send Laz'arus to dip the end of his finger in water 14
22:10 a man carrying a jar of water will meet you 14
Joh 1:26 John answered them, "I baptize with water; 14
31 but for this I came baptizing with water 14
33 but he who sent me to baptize with water said to me 14
2: 7 Jesus said to them, "Fill the jars with water. 14
9 the steward . . tasted the water now become wine 14
9 though the servants who had drawn the water knew 14
3: 5 unless one is born of water and the Spirit 14
23 near Salim, because there was much water there; 14
4: 7 There came a woman of Samar'ia to draw water. 14
10 and he would have given you living water. 14
11 where do you get that living water? 14
13 who drinks of this water will thirst again 14
14 whoever drinks of the water that I shall give him 14
14 the water that I shall give him will become in him 14
14 a spring of water welling up to eternal life. 14
15 Sir, give me this water, that I may not thirst 14
46 Cana in Galilee, where he had made the water wine. 14
5: 7 when the water is troubled 14
7:38 shall flow rivers of living water.' 14
13: 5 Then he poured water into a basin 14
19:34 at once there came out blood and water. 14
Act 1: 5 for John baptized with water 14
8:36 they came to some water 14
36 the eunuch said, "See, here is water! 14
38 both went down into the water 14
39 when they came up out of the water 14
10:47 Can any one forbid water for baptizing 14
11:16 John baptized with water 14
1Co 3: 6 I planted, Apol'los watered 12
7 neither he who plants nor he who waters is 12
8 He who plants and he who waters are equal 12
Eph 5:26 cleansed her by the washing of water with the word 14
Heb 9:19 with water and scarlet wool and hyssop 14
10:22 our bodies washed with pure water. 14
Jas 3:11 from the same opening fresh water and brackish? •
12 No more can salt water yield fresh. 14
1Pe 3:20 ark, in which a few . . were saved through water. 14
2Pe 3: 5 an earth formed out of water and by means of water 14
5 an earth formed out of water and by means of water 14
6 world . . was deluged with water and perished 14
1Jn 5: 6 This is he who came by water and blood, Jesus 14
6 he who came . . not with the water only 14
6 but with the water and the blood. 14
8 three witnesses, the Spirit, the water . . blood 14
Rev 1:15 and his voice was like the sound of many waters; 14
7:17 and he will guide them to springs of living water; 14
8:10 it fell . . on the fountains of water. 14
11 A third of the waters became wormwood 14
11 men died of the water, because it was made bitter. 14
11: 6 power over the waters to turn them into blood 14
12:15 The serpent poured water . . out of his mouth 14
14: 2 a voice from heaven like the sound of many waters 14
7 who made . . the sea and the fountains of water 14
16: 4 into the rivers and the fountains of water 14
5 And I heard the angel of water say 14
12 the river Euphra'tes, and its water was dried up 14
17: 1 the great harlot who is seated upon many waters 14
15 The waters that you saw, where the harlot is 14
19: 6 like the sound of many waters 14
21: 6 I will give from the fountain of the water of life 14
22: 1 Then he showed me the river of the water of life 14
17 let him who desires take the water of life 14
1Es 9: 2 he did not eat bread or drink water 14
2Es 1:20 so that waters flowed in abundance 15
23 but threw a tree into the water 15
4:49 after this a cloud full of water passed before me 15
5: 9 salt waters shall be found in the sweet 15
6:17 its sound was like the sound of many waters. 15
41 command him to divide and separate the waters 15
42 On the third day thou didst command the waters 15
47 where the water had been gathered together 15
48 The dumb and lifeless water 15
50 where the water had been gathered together 15
7: 7 and deep water on the left; 15
8 that is, between the fire and the water 15
40 or cloud or thunder or lightning or wind or water 15
8: 8 is preserved in fire and water 15
14:39 it was full of something like water 15
15:41 hail and flying swords and floods of water 15
41 be filled with the abundance of those waters. 15
58 and drink their own blood in thirst for water. 15
16:58 has enclosed the sea in the midst of the waters 15
58 has suspended the earth over the water; 15
59 and founded it upon the waters; 15
60 who has put springs of water in the desert 15
60 to send rivers from the heights to water the earth; 16
Jdt 2: 7 Tell them to prepare earth and water 14
7: 7 visited the springs that supplied their water 14
12 only . . take possession of the spring of water 14
20 until all the vessels of water . . were empty; 14
21 did not have enough water to drink their fill 14
8: 9 because they were faint for lack of water 14
9:12 Lord of heaven and earth, Creator of the waters 14
10: 3 bathed her body with water 14
11:12 their water has almost given out 14
16:15 be shaken to their foundations with the waters; 14
AEs 10: 6 there was light and the sun and abundant water 14
11:10 there came a great river, with abundant water; 14
Wis 5:10 like a ship that sails through the billowy water 14
22 the water of the sea will rage against them 14
10:18 and led them through deep waters; 14
11: 4 water was given them out of flinty rock 14
7 thou gavest them abundant water unexpectedly 14
13: 2 the circle of the stars, or turbulent water 14
16:17 in the water, which quenches all things 14
19 even in the midst of water 14
29 and flow away like waste water. 14
17:18 the rhythm of violently rushing water 14
19: 7 and dry land emerging where water had stood before 14
19 transformed into water creatures 10
20 Fire even in water retained its normal power 14
20 water forgot its fire-quenching nature. 14
Sir 3:30 Water extinguishes a blazing fire 14
15: 3 give him the water of wisdom to drink. 14
16 He has placed before you fire and water 14
18:10 Like a drop of water from the sea 14
24:31 I will water my orchard and drench my garden plot 12
25:25 Allow no outlet to water 14
26:12 drinks from any water near him 14
29:21 The essentials for life are water and bread 14
31:26 Fire and water prove the temper of steel •
38: 5 Was not water made sweet with a tree 14
39:13 bud like a rose growing by a stream of water; 13
17 At his word the waters stood in a heap 14
17 reservoirs of water 14
26 water and fire and iron and salt and wheat flour 14
40:11 what is from the waters returns to the sea. 14
16 The reeds by any water or river bank 14
43:20 ice freezes over the water 14
20 it rests upon every pool of water 14
20 the water puts it on like a breastplate. 14
48:17 brought water into the midst of it 14
17 built pools for water. 14
50: 3 In his days a cistern for water was quarried out 14
8 like lilies by a spring of water 14
Aza 1:38 Bless the Lord, all waters above the heaven 14
57 whales and all creatures that move in the waters 14
1Mc 5:40 his army drew near to the stream of water 14
42 When Judas approached the stream of water 14
9:33 camped by the water of the pool of Asphar. 14
45 the water of the Jordan is on this side and on that 14
11:67 his army encamped by the waters of Gennesaret. 14
2Mc 15:39 again, to drink water alone 14
39 wine mixed with water is sweet and delicious 14
4Mc 1:29 and ties up and waters and thoroughly irrigates 11
3:11 the water in the enemy's territory 14

water *See also* channel, draw, drink, drop, get, hold, jar, shaft, supply.

water abundantly 1. רוה 2. שׂבע
Ps 65:10 Thou waterest its furrows abundantly 1
104:16 The trees of the LORD are watered abundantly 2

flowing water 1. נזל
Prv 5:15 flowing water from your own well. 1

fresh water 1. ὕδωρ
Sir 39:23 just as he turns fresh water into salt. 1

water hen 1. תִּנְשֶׁמֶת
Lev 11:18 the water hen, the pelican, the carrion vulture 1
Deu 14:16 the little owl and the great owl, the water hen 1

running water 1. אֵיתָן
Deu 21: 4 bring the heifer . . to a valley with running water 1

watercourse 1. אָפִיק
Ps 126: 4 fortunes . . like the watercourses in the Negeb! 1
Ezk 31:12 lie broken in all the watercourses of the land; 1
32: 6 the watercourses will be full of you. 1

watering *See* trough.

watering place 1. מַשְׁאָב
Jdg 5:11 To the sound of musicians at the watering places 1

waterless 1. אֵין מַיִם 2. ἄνυδρος
Zec 9:11 set your captives free from the waterless pit. 1
Mat 12:43 he passes through waterless places 2
Lke 11:24 he passes through waterless places seeking rest; 2
2Pe 2:17 These are waterless springs and mists 2
Jde 1:12 waterless clouds, carried along by the winds; 2

waterskin 1. נֵבֶל
Job 38:37 Or who can tilt the waterskins of the heavens 1

watery 1. humidus
2Es 6:52 didst give the seventh part, the watery part 1

wave 1. בָּמָה 2. גַּל 3. מִשְׁבָּר 4. κλύδων 5. κῦμα 6. σάλος 7. ὕδωρ 8. fluctus
2Sm 22: 5 For the waves of death encompassed me 3
Job 9: 8 trampled the waves of the sea; 1
38:11 here shall your proud waves be stayed 2
Ps 42: 7 thy waves and thy billows have gone over me. 3
65: 7 roaring of the seas, the roaring of their waves 2
88: 7 thou dost overwhelm me with all thy waves. Selah 3
89: 9 when its waves rise, thou stillest them. 2
93: 4 mightier than the waves of the sea 3
107:25 stormy wind, which lifted up the waves of the sea. 2
29 waves of the sea were hushed. 2
Isa 48:18 and your righteousness like the waves of the sea; 2
51:15 God, who stirs up the sea so that its waves roar 2
Jer 5:22 though the waves toss, they cannot prevail •
31:35 who stirs up the sea so that its waves roar 2
51:42 she is covered with its tumultuous waves. 2
55 Their waves roar like many waters 2
Ezk 26: 3 against you, as the sea brings up its waves. 2
Jon 2: 3 all thy waves and thy billows passed over me. 3
Zec 10:11 the waves of the sea shall be smitten 2
Mat 8:24 so that the boat was being swamped by the waves; 5
14:24 distant from the land, beaten by the waves 5
Mrk 4:37 the waves beat into the boat 5
Lke 8:24 awoke and rebuked the wind and the raging waves 7
21:25 at the roaring of the sea and the waves 6
Jas 1: 6 he who doubts is like a wave of the sea 4
Jde 1:13 wild waves of the sea, casting up the foam 5
2Es 4:15 the waves of the sea also made a plan and said, 'Come 8
17 likewise also the plan of the waves of the sea 8
19 to the sea is assigned a place to carry its waves. 8
21 and the sea to its waves 8
9:16 as a wave is greater than a drop of water. 8
13: 2 and stirred up all its waves. 8
16:12 its waves and the fish also shall be troubled 8
Wis 5:10 nor track of its keel in the waves; 5
14: 1 and about to voyage over raging waves 5
3 a safe way through the waves 5
19: 7 a grassy plain out of the raging waves 4
Sir 24: 6 In the waves of the sea, in the whole earth 5
29:18 has shaken them like a wave of the sea 5
2Mc 9: 8 he could command the waves of the sea 5
4Mc 7: 5 broke the maddening waves of the emotion. 4
13: 6 towers . . hold back the threatening waves 5
15:31 stoutly endured the waves 4

wave (2) 1. נוף 2. רעשׁ 3. תְּנוּפָה 4. ῥίπτω
Exd 29:24 wave them for a wave offering before the LORD. 1
26 take the breast . . and wave it for a wave offering 1
27 portion, which is waved, and which is offered 1
Lev 7:30 that the breast may be waved as a wave offering 1
34 For the breast that is waved and the thigh 3
8:27 waved them as a wave offering before the LORD 1
29 Moses took the breast, and waved it for a wave 1
9:21 the right thigh Aaron waved for a wave offering 1
10:14 the breast that is waved and the thigh 3
15 the breast that is waved they shall bring 3
15 to wave for a wave offering before the LORD 1
14:12 shall . . wave them for a wave offering 1
21 male lamb for a guilt offering to be waved 3
24 the priest shall wave them for a wave offering 1
23:11 he shall wave the sheaf before the LORD 1
11 after the sabbath the priest shall wave it 1
12 on the day when you wave the sheaf, you shall offer 1
17 bring . . two loaves of bread to be waved 3
20 the priest shall wave them with the bread 1
Num 5:25 shall wave the cereal offering before the LORD 1
6:20 the priest shall wave them for a wave offering 1
20 together with the breast that is waved 3
18:18 as the breast that is waved and as the right thigh 3
2Kg 5:11 wave his hand over the place, and cure the leper. 1
Ps 72:16 on the tops of the mountains may it wave; 2
Isa 11:15 wave his hand over the River with his scorching 1
13: 2 wave . . for them to enter the gates of the nobles. 1
Act 22:23 as they cried out and waved their garments 4

wave *See* offering.

mighty wave 1. τρικυμία
4Mc 7: 2 and overwhelmed by the mighty waves of tortures 1

wave proudly 1. עלס
Job 39:13 The wings of the ostrich wave proudly; 1

waver 1. חמק 2. מעד 3. נוד 4. συστέλλω 5. inconstantia
Ps 26: 1 I have trusted in the LORD without wavering. 2
Jer 4: 1 abominations from my presence, and do not waver 3
31:22 How long will you waver, O faithless daughter? 1
2Es 9: 3 wavering of leaders, confusion of princes 5
3Mc 5:33 his eyes wavered and his face fell. 4

make waver 1. διακρίνω
Rom 4:20 No distrust made him waver 1

without wavering 1. ἀκλινής
Heb 10:23 Let us hold fast . . without wavering 1

wavy 1. תַּלְתַּלִּים
Sng 5:11 his locks are wavy, black as a raven. 1

wax 1. דּוֹנַג 2. κηρός 3. cera
Ps 22:14 all my bones are out of joint; my heart is like wax 1
68: 2 as wax melts before fire, the wicked perish 1

97: 5 The mountains melt like wax before the LORD 1
Mic 1: 4 valleys will be cleft, like wax before the fire 1
2Es 13: 4 all who heard his voice melted as wax melts 3
Jdt 16:15 at thy presence the rocks shall melt like wax 2

wax fat 1. שׁמן

Deu 32:15 Jesh'urun waxed fat, and kicked; 1
15 waxed fat, you grew thick, you became sleek; 1

way 1. אֹרַח 2. בוא 3. דָּבָר 4. דֶּרֶךְ 5. הֲלִיכָה 6. הלך 7. הֵנָּה 8. כֹּה 9. כָּכָה 10. מַעְגָּל 11. מַעְגָּלָה 12. מַעֲשֶׂה 13. מִשְׁפָּט 14. נְתִיבָה 15. עַל 16. פָּנִים 17. אֹרַח (A) 18. ἀναστροφή 19. διά 20. εἰς 21. εἴσοδος 22. ἐν 23. ἔρχομαι 24. κατά 25. μέσος 26. ὁδός 27. οὗτος 28. οὕτως 29. ποῖος 30. πορεύομαι 31. προσάγω 32. πῶς 33. τρίβος 34. τρόπος 35. ὡς 36. circa 37. iter 38. mos 39. semita 40. ubi 41. via

Gen 3:24 sword . . to guard the way to the tree of life. 4
6:12 flesh had corrupted their way upon the earth. 4
12:20 and they set him on the way, with his wife •
14:11 all their provisions, and went their way; •
16: 7 in the wilderness, the spring on the way to Shur. 4
18:19 household after him to keep the way of the LORD 4
33 the LORD went his way, when he had finished •
19: 2 then you may rise up early and go on your way. 4
24:27 the LORD has led me in the way to the house 4
40 angel with you and prosper your way; 4
42 if now thou wilt prosper the way which I go 4
48 the LORD . . who had led me by the right way to take 4
56 since the LORD has prospered my way; let me go 4
61 thus the servant took Rebekah, and went his way. •
25:34 and he ate and drank, and rose and went his way. •
28:20 will keep me in this way that I go, and will give me 4
31:35 before you, for the way of women is upon me. 4
32: 1 Jacob went on his way and the angels of God met him; 4
33:12 Let us journey on our way, and I will go before you. •
16 Esau returned that day on his way to Se'ir. 4
18 in the land of Canaan, on his way from Paddan-aram 2
35:19 she was buried on the way to Ephrath 4
37:25 Ish'maelites . . on their way to carry it down 6
39:19 This is the way your servant treated me 3
42:33 take grain . . and go your way. •
45:24 he said to them, "Do not quarrel on the way. 4
48: 7 Rachel . . died in the land of Canaan on the way 4
7 and I buried her there on the way to Ephrath 4
49:17 Dan shall be a serpent in the way 4
Exd 2:12 He looked this way and that, and seeing no one •
4:24 At a lodging place on the way the LORD met him 4
13:17 lead them by way of the land of the Philistines 4
18 the way of the wilderness toward the Red Sea. 4
21 pillar of cloud to lead them along the way 4
18: 8 hardship that had come upon them in the way 4
20 make them know the way in which they must walk 4
27 and he went his way to his own country. •
23:20 angel before you, to guard you on the way 4
32: 8 quickly out of the way which I commanded them; 4
33: 3 go up among you, lest I consume you in the way 4
13 show me now thy ways, that I may know thee 4
Lev 26:22 so that your ways shall become desolate 4
Num14:25 out for the wilderness by the way to the Red Sea. 4
15:13 who are native shall do these things in this way 9
21: 1 that Israel was coming by the way of Atharim 4
4 Mount Hor they set out by the way to the Red Sea 4
4 the people became impatient on the way. 4
33 Then they turned and went up by the way to Bashan; 4
22:22 took his stand in the way as his adversary. 4
26 in a narrow place, where there was no way to turn 4
31 he saw the angel of the LORD standing in the way 4
32 because your way is perverse before me; 4
24:25 Balak also went his way. 4
Deu 1: 2 from Horeb by the way of Mount Se'ir 4
19 on the way to the hill country of the Amorites 4
22 bring us word again of the way by which we must go 4
31 LORD . . bore you, . . , in all the way that you went 4
33 went before you in the way to seek you out a place 4
33 went . . to show you by what way you should go 4
3: 1 Then we turned and went up the way to Bashan; 4
5:33 walk in all the way which the LORD your God 4
6: 7 shall talk of them when . . you walk by the way 4
8: 2 you shall remember all the way which the LORD 4
6 by walking in his ways and by fearing him. 4
9:12 they have turned aside quickly out of the way 4
16 from the way which the LORD had commanded you. 4
10:12 require . . but . . to walk in all his ways, to love 4
11:19 talking of them . . when you are walking by the way 4
22 commandment . . walking in all his ways 4
28 not obey . . but turn aside from the way 4
13: 5 to make you leave the way in which the LORD 4
14:24 if the way is too long for you, so that you 4
17:16 You shall never return that way again.' 4
19: 6 overtake him, because the way is long 4
9 loving the LORD . . by walking ever in his ways- 4
22: 4 brother's ass or his ox fallen down by the way 4
23: 4 not meet you with bread and with water on the way 4
24: 9 LORD . . did to Miriam on the way as you came forth 4
25:17 Am'alek did to you on the way as you came out 4
18 how he attacked you on the way, when you were faint 4
26:17 walk in his ways, and keep his statutes 4
28: 7 come out against you one way, and flee before you 4
7 one way, and flee before you seven ways. 4
9 keep the commandments . . and walk in his ways. 4
25 go out one way against them, and flee seven ways 4
25 go out one way . . and flee seven ways before them; 4
29 not prosper in your ways; and you shall be only 4
30:16 obey . . by walking in his ways 4
31:29 surely act corruptly, and turn aside from the way 4
32: 4 his work is perfect; for all his ways are justice. 4
Jos 1: 8 for then you shall make your way prosperous 4
2: 7 pursued . . them on the way to the Jordan as far 4
16 then afterward you may go your way. 4
22 for the pursuers had made search all along the way 4
3: 4 follow it, that you may know the way you shall go 4
4 for you have not passed this way before. 4
5: 4 the males . . had died on the way in the wilderness 4
5 people . . born on the way in the wilderness 4
7 they had not been circumcised on the way. 4
8:20 and they had no power to flee this way or that 7
10:10 chased them by the way of the ascent of Beth-hor'on 4
22: 5 to love the LORD . . and to walk in all his ways 4
23:14 And now I am about to go the way of all the earth 4
24:17 and preserved us in all the way that we went 4
Jdg 2:17 from the way in which their fathers had walked 4
19 their practices or their stubborn ways. 4
22 to walk in the way of the LORD as their fathers did 4
5:10 Tell of it . . you who walk by the way. 4
9:25 they robbed all who passed by them along that way; 4
18:26 the Danites went their way; and when Micah saw 4
19:14 So they passed on and went their way; and the sun •
27 when he . . went out to go on his way, behold, there 4
Rut 1: 7 and they went on the way to return to . . Judah. 4
12 Turn back, my daughters, go your way, •
1Sm 1:18 she said . . " Then the woman went her way and ate 4
6: 8 Then send it off, and let it go its way. •
9 if it goes up on the way to its own land 4
8: 3 his sons did not walk in his ways, but turned aside 4
5 you are old and your sons do not walk in your ways; 4
9 and show them the ways of the king who shall reign 13
11 These will be the ways of the king who will reign 13
9: 8 I will give it to the man of God, to tell us our way. 4
21 Why then have you spoken to me in this way? 3
26 Up, that I may send you on your way. •
12:23 I will instruct you in the good and the right way. 4
15: 2 what Am'alek did . . in opposing them on the way 4
17:27 And the people answered him in the same way 3
30 he turned . . and spoke in the same way; 3
52 the wounded . . fell on the way from Sha-ara'im 4
24: 3 And he came to the sheepfolds by the way 4
7 Saul rose up and left . . and went upon his way. 4
26:25 David went his way, and Saul returned to his place. 4
28:22 you may have strength when you go on your way. 4
30: 2 but carried them off, and went their way. 4
2Sm 2:24 lies . . on the way to the wilderness of Gibeon. 4
4: 7 and went by the way of the Arabah all night 4
13:30 While they were on the way, tidings came to David 4
15: 2 rise early and stand beside the way of the gate; 4
18:23 Then Ahi'ma-az ran by the way of the plain 4
19:36 Your servant will go a little way over the Jordan •
22:22 For I have kept the ways of the LORD, and have not 4
31 This God–his way is perfect; 4
33 God is my strong refuge, and has made my way safe. 4
1Kg 1:49 all the guests . . rose, and each went his own way. 4
2: 2 I am about to go the way of all the earth. Be strong 4
3 walking in his ways and keeping his statutes, his 4
4 take heed to their way, to walk before me 4
3:14 walk in my ways, keeping my statutes and my 4
8:25 your sons take heed to their way, to walk before me 4
36 teach them the good way in which they should walk; 4
39 and render to each . . according to all his ways 4
44 go out to battle . . by whatever way thou 4
58 walk in all his ways, and to keep his commandments 4
11:33 he has forsaken me . . and has not walked in my ways 4
38 if you will hearken . . and will walk in my ways 4
13: 9 drink water, nor return by the way that you came.' 4
10 he went another way, and did not return by the way 4
10 did not return by the way that he came to Bethel. 4
12 their father said to them, "Which way did he go? 4
12 his sons showed him the way which the man of God 4
17 nor return by the way that you came.' 4
26 the prophet who had brought him back from the way 4
33 Jerobo'am did not turn from his evil way 4
15:26 and walked in the way of his father, and in his sin 4
34 and walked in the way of Jerobo'am and in his sin 4
16: 2 and you have walked in the way of Jerobo'am 4
19 his sins . . walking in the way of Jerobo'am 4
26 For he walked in all the way of Jerobo'am 4
18: 7 as Obadi'ah was on the way, behold, Eli'jah met him; 4
19:15 return on your way to the wilderness of Damascus; 4
20:38 departed, and waited for the king by the way 4
22:43 He walked in all the way of Asa his father; 4
52 walked in the way of his father, and . . his mother 4
52 walked in . . and in the way of his mother 4
52 walked . . in the way of Jerobo'am the son of Nebat 4
53 provoked the LORD . . to anger in every way •
2Kg 2: 1 Eli'jah and Eli'sha were on their way from Gilgal. 6
23 while he was going up on the way, some . . boys came 4
3: 8 Then he said, "By which way shall we march? 4
8 answered, "By the way of the wilderness of Edom. 4
4: 8 So whenever he passed that way, he would turn •
9 man of God, who is continually passing our way. 15
6:19 This is not the way, and this is not the city; 4
7:15 and, lo, all the way was littered with garments 4
8:18 he walked in the way of the kings of Israel 4
27 He also walked in the way of the house of Ahab 4
10:12 to Sama'ria. On the way, when he was at Beth-eked 4
12:20 house of Millo, on the way that goes down to Silla. •
16: 3 but he walked in the way of the kings of Israel. 4
17:13 Turn from your evil ways and keep my . . statutes 4
19:28 I will turn you back on the way by which you came. 4
33 By the way that he came, by the same he shall return 4
21:21 He walked in all the way . . his father walked 4
22 and did not walk in the way of the LORD. 4
22: 2 and walked in all the way of David his father 4
25: 4 fled . . by the way of the gate between the two 4
2Ch 6:16 if only your sons take heed to their way, to walk 4
27 when thou dost teach them the good way 4
30 render to each . . according to all his ways 4
31 that they may fear thee and walk in thy ways 4
34 go out . . by whatever way thou shalt send them 4
7:14 if my people . . and turn from their wicked ways 4
11:17 they walked . . in the way of David and Solomon. 4
13:22 the acts of Abi'jah, his ways and his sayings 4
17: 3 he walked in the earlier ways of his father; 4
4 walked . . not according to the ways of Israel. 12
6 His heart was courageous in the ways of the LORD; 4
18:23 Which way did the Spirit of the LORD go 4
20:32 He walked in the way of Asa his father 4
21: 6 he walked in the way of the kings of Israel 4
12 not walked in the ways of Jehosh'aphat 4
12 not walked . . in the ways of Asa king of Judah 4
13 have walked in the way of the kings of Israel 4
22: 3 He also walked in the ways of the house of Ahab 4
23:19 no one should enter who was in any way unclean. 3
25: 8 if you suppose that in this way you will be strong •
27: 6 ordered his ways before the LORD his God. 4
7 rest of the acts of Jotham . . and his ways 4
28: 2 walked in the ways of the kings of Israel. 4
26 his acts and all his ways, from first to last 4
34: 2 walked in the ways of David his father; 4
Ezr 8:21 to seek from him a straight way for ourselves 4
22 protect us against the enemy on our way; 4
31 hand of the enemy and from ambushes by the way. 4
Neh 4:17 carried burdens were laden in such a way •
6: 4 sent to me four times in this way and I answered 3
5 In the same way Sanbal'lat for the fifth time sent •
13 that I should be afraid and act in this way and sin •
8:10 Go your way, eat the fat and drink sweet wine •
12 all the people went their way to eat and drink •
9:12 pillar of fire . . to light for them the way 4
19 pillar of cloud which led them in the way did not 4
19 pillar of fire . . which lighted for them the way 4
13:18 Did not your fathers act in this way 8
Est 2:13 when the maiden went in to the king in this way •
Job 3:23 Why is light given to a man whose way is hid 4
4: 6 and the integrity of your ways your hope? 4
8:19 Behold, this is the joy of his way; 4
13:15 yet I will defend my ways to his face. 4
16:22 I shall go the way whence I shall not return. 1
17: 9 Yet the righteous holds to his way 4
19: 8 He has walled up my way, so that I cannot pass 1
21:14 We do not desire the knowledge of thy ways. 4
31 Who declares his way to his face 4
22: 3 is it gain to him if you make your ways blameless? 4
15 you keep to the old way which wicked men have trod? 1
28 light will shine on your ways. 4
23:10 But he knows the way that I take; 4
11 I have kept his way and have not turned aside. 4
24:13 who are not acquainted with its ways 4
23 his eyes are upon their ways. 4
26:14 Lo, these are but the outskirts of his ways; 4
28:13 Man does not know the way to it 26
23 God understands the way to it 4
26 a way for the lightning of the thunder; 4
29:25 I chose their way, and sat as chief 4
30:12 cast up against me their ways of destruction. 1
31: 4 Does not he see my ways, and number all my steps? 4
7 if my step has turned aside from the way 4
34:11 according to his ways he will make it befall him. 1
21 For his eyes are upon the ways of a man 4
27 had no regard for any of his ways 4
36:23 Who has prescribed for him his way, 4
38:19 Where is the way to the dwelling of light 4
24 What is the way to the place where the light is 4
25 torrents of rain, and a way for the thunderbolt 4
Ps 1: 1 nor stands in the way of sinners 4
6 for the LORD knows the way of the righteous 4
6 but the way of the wicked will perish. 4
2:12 lest he be angry, and you perish in the way; 4
5: 8 make thy way straight before me. 4
10: 5 His ways prosper at all times; 4
17: 4 I have avoided the ways of the violent. 1
18:21 For I have kept the ways of the LORD 4
30 This God–his way is perfect; 4
32 girded me with strength, and made my way safe. 4
25: 4 Make me to know thy ways, O LORD; teach me 4
8 therefore he instructs sinners in the way. 4
9 in what is right, and teaches the humble his way. 4

12 instruct in the way that he should choose. 4
27:11 Teach me thy way, O LORD; and lead me 4
32: 8 instruct you and teach you the way you should go; 4
35: 6 Let their way be dark and slippery 4
36: 4 he sets himself in a way that is not good; 4
37: 5 Commit your way to the LORD; trust in him 4
7 fret not . . over him who prospers in his way 4
23 he establishes him in whose way he delights; 4
34 Wait for the LORD, and keep to his way 4
39: 1 I said, "I will guard my ways, that I may not sin 4
44:18 nor have our steps departed from thy way 1
50:23 to him who orders his way aright I will show 4
51:13 Then I will teach transgressors thy ways 4
57: 6 They dug a pit in my way, but they have fallen 16
67: 2 that thy way may be known upon earth 4
77:13 Thy way, O God, is holy. 4
19 Thy way was through the sea 4
80:12 so that all who pass along the way pluck its fruit? 4
81:13 O that . . Israel would walk in my ways! 4
85:13 make his footsteps a way. 4
86:11 Teach me thy way, O LORD, that I may walk 4
91:11 charge of you to guard you in all your ways. 4
95:10 err in heart, and they do not regard my ways. 4
101: 2 I will give heed to the way that is blameless. 4
6 he who walks in the way that is blameless 4
103: 7 He made known his ways to Moses 4
107: 4 finding no way to a city to dwell in; 4
7 he led them by a straight way, till they reached 4
17 Some were sick through their sinful ways 4
110: 7 He will drink from the brook by the way; 4
119: 1 Blessed are those whose way is blameless 4
3 who also do no wrong, but walk in his ways! 4
5 O that my ways may be steadfast 4
9 How can a young man keep his way pure? 1
14 In the way of thy testimonies I delight 4
15 on thy precepts, and fix my eyes on thy ways. 1
26 When I told of my ways, thou didst answer me; 4
27 Make me understand the way of thy precepts 4
29 Put false ways far from me; 4
30 I have chosen the way of faithfulness 4
32 I will run in the way of thy commandments 4
33 Teach me, O LORD, the way of thy statutes; 4
37 give me life in thy ways. 4
59 When I think of thy ways, I turn my feet to thy 4
101I hold back my feet from every evil way 1
104therefore I hate every false way. 1
128I hate every false way. 1
168for all my ways are before thee. 4
128: 1 Blessed . . fears the LORD, who walks in his ways! 4
138: 5 they shall sing of the ways of the LORD 4
139: 3 Thou . . art acquainted with all my ways. 4
24 see if there be any wicked way in me 4
24 lead me in the way everlasting! 4
142: 3 When my spirit is faint, thou knowest my way! 14
143: 8 Teach me the way I should go, for to thee I lift up 4
145:17 LORD is just in all his ways, and kind in all 4
146: 9 but the way of the wicked he brings to ruin. 4
Prv 1:15 my son, do not walk in the way with them 4
19 Such are the ways of all who get gain by violence; 1
31 therefore they shall eat the fruit of their way 4
2: 8 preserving the way of his saints. 4
12 delivering you from the way of evil 4
13 to walk in the ways of darkness 4
15 men . . who are devious in their ways. 11
20 you will walk in the way of good men 4
3: 6 In all your ways acknowledge him 4
17 Her ways are ways of pleasantness 4
17 Her ways are ways of pleasantness 4
23 Then you will walk on your way securely 4
31 do not choose any of his ways; 4
4:11 I have taught you the way of wisdom; 4
14 do not walk in the way of evil men. 4
19 The way of the wicked is like deep darkness; 4
26 then all your ways will be sure. 4
5: 6 her ways wander, and she does not know it. 10
8 Keep your way far from her 4
21 For a man's ways are before the eyes of the LORD 4
6: 6 consider her ways, and be wise. 4
23 reproofs of discipline are the way of life 4
7:25 Let not your heart turn aside to her ways 4
27 Her house is the way to Sheol 4
8: 2 On the heights beside the way 4
13 way of evil and perverted speech I hate. 4
20 I walk in the way of righteousness 1
32 happy are those who keep my ways. 4
9: 6 walk in the way of insight. 4
15 who are going straight on their way 1
10: 9 but he who perverts his ways will be found out. 4
29 LORD is a stronghold to him whose way is upright 4
11: 5 righteousness . . keeps his way straight 4
20 but those of blameless ways are his delight. 4
12:15 The way of a fool is right in his own eyes 4
26 but the way of the wicked leads them astray. 4
28 but the way of error leads to death. 4
13: 6 Righteousness guards him whose way is upright 4
15 but the way of the faithless is their ruin. 4
14: 2 but he who is devious in his ways despises him. 4
8 The wisdom of a prudent man is to discern his way 4
12 There is a way which seems right to a man 4
12 but its end is the way to death. 4
14 perverse man . . filled with the fruit of his ways 4
15: 9 way of the wicked is an abomination to the LORD 4
10 severe discipline for him who forsakes the way; 1
19 The way of a sluggard is overgrown with thorns 4
16: 2 All the ways of a man are pure in his own eyes 4
7 When a man's ways please the LORD 4
9 A man's mind plans his way 4
17 he who guards his way preserves his life. 4
25 There is a way which seems right to a man 4
25 but its end is the way to death. 4
29 leads him in a way that is not good. 4
17:23 accepts a bribe . . to pervert the ways of justice. 1
19: 3 When a man's folly brings his way to ruin 4
20:24 how then can man understand his way? 4
21: 2 Every way of a man is right in his own eyes 4
8 The way of the guilty is crooked 4
16 A man who wanders from the way of understanding 4
29 but an upright man considers his ways. 4
22: 5 Thorns and snares are in the way of the perverse; 4
6 Train up a child in the way he should go 4
25 learn his ways and entangle yourself in a snare. 1
23:19 my son, and be wise, and direct your mind in the way. 4
26 My son . . let your eyes observe my ways. 4
28: 6 than a rich man who is perverse in his ways. 4
10 misleads the upright into an evil way will fall 4
18 who is perverse in his ways will fall into a pit. 4
29:27 way is straight is an abomination to the wicked. 4
30:19 the way of an eagle in the sky, the way of a serpent 4
19 way of a serpent on a rock, the way of a ship 4
19 way of a ship on the high seas, and the way of a man 4
19 way of a man with a maiden. 4
20 This is the way of an adulteress: she eats 4
31: 3 Give not your . . ways to those who destroy kings. 4
27 She looks well to the ways of her household 5
Ecc 8: 5 the mind of a wise man will know the time and way. 13
6 For every matter has its time and way 13
10:15 that he does not know the way to the city. 6
11: 9 walk in the ways of your heart and . . of your eyes. 4
12: 5 afraid also of what . . and terrors are in the way; 4
Isa 2: 3 that he may teach us his ways and that we may walk 4
8:11 warned me not to walk in the way of this people 4
9: 1 he will make glorious the way of the sea 4
16: 1 sent lambs . . from Sela, by way of the desert †
26: 7 The way of the righteous is level; 1
30:11 leave the way, turn aside from the path 4
21 behind you, saying, "This is the way, walk in it 4
35: 8 a highway . . and it shall be called the Holy Way; 4
37:29 I will turn you back on the way by which you came. 4
34 By the way that he came, by the same he shall return 4
40: 3 In the wilderness prepare the way of the LORD 4
14 and showed him the way of understanding? 4
27 My way is hid from the LORD 4
42:16 I will lead the blind in a way that they know not 4
24 the LORD . . in whose ways they would not walk 4
43:16 Thus says the LORD, who makes a way in the sea 4
19 I will make a way in the wilderness 4
45:13 and I will make straight all his ways; 4
48:15 I have brought him, and he will prosper in his way. 4
17 your God . . who leads you in the way you should go. 4
49: 9 They shall feed along the ways, on all bare 4
11 And I will make all my mountains a way 4
51:10 of the sea a way for the redeemed to pass over? 4
53: 6 astray; we have turned every one to his own way; 4
55: 7 let the wicked forsake his way 4
8 neither are your ways my ways, says the LORD. 4
8 neither are your ways my ways, says the LORD. 4
9 are my ways higher than your ways 4
9 are my ways higher than your ways 4
56:11 they have all turned to their own way 4
57:10 You were wearied with the length of your way 4
14 shall be said, "Build up, build up, prepare the way 4
14 remove every obstruction from my people's way. 4
17 went on backsliding in the way of his own heart. 4
18 I have seen his ways, but I will heal him; 4
58: 2 Yet they seek me daily and delight to know my ways 4
13 if you honor it, not going your own ways 4
59: 8 The way of peace they know not 4
62:10 through the gates, prepare the way for the people; 4
63:17 O LORD, why dost thou make us err from thy ways 4
64: 5 those that remember thee in thy ways. 4
65: 2 people, who walk in a way that is not good 4
66: 3 These have chosen their own ways 4
Jer 2:17 the LORD your God, when he led you in the way? 4
23 Look at your way in the valley; 4
33 even to wicked women you have taught your ways. 4
36 How lightly you gad about, changing your way! 4
3:21 because they have perverted their way 4
4:18 Your ways and your doings have brought this upon 4
5: 4 for they do not know the way of the LORD 4
5 for they know the way of the LORD 4
6:16 ask for the ancient paths, where the good way is; 4
27 that you may know and assay their ways. 4
7: 3 Amend your ways and your doings 4
5 For if you truly amend your ways and your doings 4
23 and walk in all the way that I command you 4
10: 2 Learn not the way of the nations, nor be dismayed 4
23 I know, O LORD, that the way of man is not in himself 4
12: 1 Why does the way of the wicked prosper? 4
16 will diligently learn the ways of my people 4
15: 7 my people; they did not turn from their ways. 4
16:17 For my eyes are upon all their ways; 4
17:10 to give to every man according to his ways 4
18:11 Return, every one from his evil way 4
11 and amend your ways and your doings. 4
15 have stumbled in their ways, in the ancient roads 4
21: 8 Behold, I set before you the way of life 4
8 before you the way of life and the way of death. 4
22:21 This has been your way from your youth 4
23:12 their way shall be to them like slippery paths 4
22 they would have turned them from their evil way 4
25: 5 turn . . from his evil way and wrong doings 4
26: 3 will listen, and every one turn from his evil way 4
13 Now therefore amend your ways and your doings 4
28:11 But Jeremiah the prophet went his way. 4
32:19 whose eyes are open to all the ways of men 4
19 rewarding every man according to his ways 4
39 I will give them one heart and one way 4
35:15 Turn now every one of you from his evil way 4
36: 3 so that every one may turn from his evil way 4
7 and that every one will turn from his evil way 4
39: 4 by way of the king's garden through the gate 4
42: 3 that the LORD your God may show us the way 4
48:19 Stand by the way and watch, O inhabitant of Aro'er! 4
50: 5 They shall ask the way to Zion 4
52: 7 went out from the city by night by the way of a gate 4
Lam 2:15 All who pass along the way clap their hands at you; 4
3: 9 he has blocked my ways with hewn stones 4
11 he led me off my way and tore me to pieces; 4
40 Let us test and examine our ways, and return 4
Ezk 3:18 nor speak to warn the wicked from his wicked way 4
19 turn from his wickedness, or from his wicked way 4
7: 3 and will judge you according to your ways; 4
4 but I will punish you for your ways 4
8 and judge you according to your ways; 4
9 I will punish you according to your ways 4
27 According to their way I will do to them 4
13:22 not turn from his wicked way to save his life; 4
14:22 and you see their ways and their doings 4
23 They will console you, when you see their ways 4
16:47 Yet you were not content to walk in their ways 4
47 you were more corrupt than they in all your ways. 4
61 Then you will remember your ways, and be ashamed 4
18:23 rather that he should turn from his way and live? 4
25 Yet you say, 'The way of the Lord is not just.' 4
25 Hear now, O house of Israel: Is my way not just? 4
25 Is it not your ways that are not just? 4
29 Israel says, 'The way of the Lord is not just. 4
29 O house of Israel, are my ways not just? 4
29 Is it not your ways that are not just? 4
30 O house of Israel, every one according to his ways 4
20:43 there you shall remember your ways 4
44 not according to your evil ways, nor according 4
21:19 Son of man, mark two ways for the sword of the king 4
19 a signpost, make it at the head of the way to a city; 4
20 mark a way for the sword to come to Rabbah 4
21 king of Babylon stands at the parting of the way 4
21 at the head of the two ways, to use divination; 4
22:31 their way have I requited upon their heads 4
23:13 that she was defiled; they both took the same way. 4
31 You have gone the way of your sister; 4
24:14 according to your ways . . I will judge you 4
28:15 You were blameless in your ways 4
33: 8 not speak to warn the wicked to turn from his way 4
9 if you warn the wicked to turn from his way 4
9 and he does not turn from his way; he shall die 4
11 but that the wicked turn from his way and live; 4
11 turn back, turn back from your evil ways; 4
17 Yet your people say, 'The way of the Lord is not just 4
17 when it is their own way that is not just. 4
20 Yet you say, 'The way of the Lord is not just.' 4
20 I will judge each of you according to his ways. 4
36:17 they defiled it by their ways and their doings; 4
31 Then you will remember your evil ways 4
32 Be ashamed and confounded for your ways 4
44: 3 he shall enter by way of the vestibule of the gate 4
3 and shall go out by the same way. 4
4 he brought me by way of the north gate to the front 4
46: 8 he shall go out by the same way. 4
9 no one shall return by way of the gate by which he 4
47: 2 Then he brought me out by way of the north gate 4
15 by way of Hethlon to the entrance of Hamath 4
48: 1 from the sea by way of Hethlon to the entrance 4
Dan 3:29 no other god who is able to deliver in this way. *
4:37 for all his works are right and his ways are just; 17
5:23 whose are all your ways, you have not honored. 17
12: 9 Go your way, Daniel, for the words are shut up *
13 go your way till the end; and you shall rest *
Hos 2: 6 Therefore I will hedge up her way with thorns; 4
4: 9 I will punish them for their ways 4
6: 9 they murder on the way to Shechem 4
9: 8 yet a fowler's snare is on all his ways 4
12: 2 and will punish Jacob according to his ways 4
13: 7 like a leopard I will lurk beside the way. 4
14: 9 for the ways of the LORD are right 4
Jol 2: 7 They march each on his way, they do not swerve 4
Ams 8:14 O Dan,' and, 'As the way of Beer-sheba lives,' 4
Jon 3: 8 yea, let every one turn from his evil way 4

10 what they did, how they turned from their evil way 4
Mic 1:11 Pass on your way, inhabitants of Shaphir *
4: 2 that he may teach us his ways 4
Nah 1: 3 His way is in whirlwind and storm 4
Hab 3: 6 His ways were as of old. 5
Zec 1: 4 Return from your evil ways and from your evil 4
6 for our ways and deeds, so has he dealt with us. 4
3: 7 If you will walk in my ways and keep my charge 4
Mal 2: 8 you have turned aside from the way; 4
9 inasmuch as you have not kept my ways 4
3: 1 I send my messenger to prepare the way before me 4
Mat 1:18 the birth of Jesus Christ took place in this way. *
2: 9 When they had heard the king they went their way; *
12 departed to their own country by another way. 26
3: 3 Prepare the way of the Lord, make his paths 26
7:13 for the gate is wide and the way is easy 26
14 For the gate is narrow and the way is hard 26
8:28 so fierce that no one could pass that way. 26
11:10 who shall prepare thy way before thee.' 26
15:32 lest they faint on the way. 26
20:17 and on the way he said to them 26
21:32 For John came to you in the way of righteousness 26
22:16 you are true, and teach the way of God truthfully 26
27:44 the robbers . . also reviled him in the same way. *
Mrk 1: 2 who shall prepare thy way; 26
3 Prepare the way of the Lord 26
2:23 as they made their way 26
8: 3 they will faint on the way 26
27 on the way he asked his disciples 26
9:33 What were you discussing on the way? 26
34 on the way they had discussed with one another 26
10:52 Go your way; your faith has made you well *
52 received his sight and followed him on the way. 26
11:18 scribes heard it and sought a way to destroy him; 32
12:14 truly teach the way of God 26
Lke 1:76 you will go before the Lord to prepare his ways 26
79 to guide our feet into the way of peace. 26
3: 4 Prepare the way of the Lord 26
5:19 no way to bring him in, because of the crowd 29
7:27 who shall prepare thy way before thee.' 26
8:14 as they go on their way *
10: 3 Go your way; behold, I send you out as lambs *
12:58 make an effort to settle with him on the way 26
17:11 On the way to Jerusalem 30
19: 4 he was to pass that way. *
20:21 truly teach the way of God. 26
Joh 1:23 'Make straight the way of the Lord,' 26
14: 4 you know the way where I am going. 26
5 how can we know the way? 26
6 I am the way, and the truth, and the life 26
21: 1 and he revealed himself in this way. *
Act 1:11 Jesus . . will come in the same way as you saw him go 34
2:28 Thou hast made known to me the ways of life 26
8:39 went on his way rejoicing. 26
9: 2 if he found any belonging to the Way, men or women 26
13:34 he spoke in this way *
14:16 allowed all the nations to walk in their own ways; 26
16: 4 As they went on their way through the cities *
17 who proclaim to you the way of salvation. 26
17:14 the brethren . . sent Paul off on his way to the sea 30
18:25 He had been instructed in the way of the Lord; 26
26 expounded to him the way of God more accurately. 26
19: 9 speaking evil of the Way before the congregation 26
23 there arose no little stir concerning the Way. 26
22: 4 I persecuted this Way to the death 26
24:14 according to the Way, which they call a sect 26
22 having a rather accurate knowledge of the Way 26
25: 3 planning an ambush to kill him on the way. 26
26:13 I saw on the way a light from heaven 26
Rom 3: 2 Much in every way. 34
17 the way of peace they do not know. 26
11:33 and how inscrutable his ways! 26
15:15 written to you very boldly by way of reminder 35
28 I shall go on by way of you to Spain; 19
1Co 1: 5 that in every way you were enriched in him *
4:17 to remind you of my ways in Christ 26
7: 6 I say this by way of concession, not of command. 24
9:12 an obstacle in the way of the gospel of Christ. *
12:31 I will show you a still more excellent way. 26
13: 5 Love does not insist on its own way *
11 when I became a man, I gave up childish ways. *
2Co 1:16 I wanted to visit you on my way to Macedo'nia 20
16 and have you send me on my way to Judea. 20
4: 8 We are afflicted in every way *
6: 4 we commend ourselves in every way *
9:11 You will be enriched in every way for great generosity *
11: 6 in every way we have made this plain to you *
9 and will refrain from burdening you in any way. *
Eph 4:15 we are to grow up in every way into him *
6: 6 not in the way of eye-service, as men-pleasers 24
Php 1:18 What then? Only that in every way 34
1Th 3:11 our Lord Jesus, direct our way to you; 26
2Th 2: 3 Let no one deceive you in any way 34
7 only he . . will do so until he is out of the way. 25
3:16 give you peace at all times in all ways 34
17 it is the way I write. 27
1Ti 2: 2 godly and respectful in every way. *
3: 4 submissive and respectful in every way; *
4: 8 godliness is of value in every way *
5:10 and devoted herself to doing good in every way. *
Heb 3:10 they have not known my ways.' 26
4: 4 For he has . . spoken of the seventh day in this way *
9: 8 the way into the sanctuary is not yet opened 26
10:20 by the new and living way which he opened for us 26
Jas 1: 7 a double-minded man, unstable in all his ways 26
2:25 when she . . sent them out another way? 26
5:20 brings back a sinner from the error of his way 26
1Pe 1:18 you were ransomed from the futile ways 18
2Pe 1:13 to arouse you by way of reminder 22
2: 2 because of them the way of truth will be reviled. 26
15 Forsaking the right way they have gone astray; 26
15 they have followed the way of Balaam 26
21 to have known the way of righteousness 26
3: 1 aroused your sincere mind by way of reminder; 22
Jde 1:11 Woe to them! For they walk in the way of Cain 26
Rev 15: 3 Just and true are thy ways, O King of the ages! 26
16:12 to prepare the way for the kings of the east. 26
1Es 8:61 he delivered us from every enemy on the way 21
2Es 3:31 shown to any one how thy way may be comprehended. 41
34 which way the turn of the scale will incline. 40
4: 2 you can comprehend the way of the Most High? 41
3 I have been sent to show you three ways 41
4 I also will show you the way you desire to see 41
11 can your mind comprehend the way of the Most High? 41
23 For I did not wish to inquire about the ways above 41
5: 1 and the way of truth shall be hidden 41
12 shall labor but their ways shall not prosper. 41
34 I strive to understand the way of the Most High 39
7:23 and they ignored his ways! 41
48 into corruption and the ways of death 37
79 and have not kept the way of the Most High 41
80 ever grieving and sad, in seven ways. 41
81 The first way, because they have scorned the law 41
82 The second way, because they cannot now make 41
83 The third way, they shall see the reward laid up 41
84 The fourth way, they shall consider the torment 41
85 The fifth way, they shall see how the habitations 41
86 The sixth way, they shall see how some of them 41
87 The seventh way, which is worse than all the ways 41
87 worse than all the ways that have been mentioned 41
88 who have kept the ways of the Most High 41
99 and the aforesaid are the ways of torment 41
122 but we have walked in the most wicked ways? 41
129 For this is the way of which Moses . . spoke 41
8:29 who have had the ways of cattle 38
31 have passed our lives in ways that bring death 38
56 and forsook his ways. 41
9: 9 those who have now abused my ways shall be amazed 41
19 those . . have become corrupt in their ways. 38
10:13 with the earth according to the way of the earth 41
12: 4 because you search out the ways of the Most High. 41
13:45 Through that region there was a long way to go 41
54 because you have forsaken your own ways 36
14:31 the ways which the Most High commanded you. 41
Tob 1: 3 I, Tobit, walked in the ways of truth 26
3: 2 all thy deeds and all thy ways are mercy and truth 26
4: 5 do not walk in the ways of wrongdoing. 26
15 let drunkenness go with you on your way. 26
19 ask him that your ways may be made straight 26
5: 6 I am familiar with the way 26
16 God who dwells in heaven will prosper your way 26
6: 1 Now as they proceeded on their way 26
Jdt 5: 8 For they had left the ways of their ancestors 26
14 he led them by the way of Sinai and Kadesh-barnea 26
18 departed from the way which he had appointed 26
9: 6 all thy ways are prepared in advance 26
10:13 I am on my way to the presence of Holofernes 23
13 I will show him a way by which he can go 26
12: 8 prayed the Lord God of Israel to direct her way 26
13:16 who has protected me in the way I went 26
AEs 16:14 He thought that in this way he would find us 34
Wis 2:15 his ways are strange. 33
16 he avoids our ways as unclean 26
5: 6 it was we who strayed from the way of truth 26
7 the way of the Lord we have not known. 26
10:17 she guided them along a marvelous way 26
14: 3 a safe way through the waves 33
18:23 and cut off its way to the living. 26
19: 7 an unhindered way out of the Red Sea 26
Sir 2: 6 make your ways straight, and hope in him. 26
12 Woe . . to the sinner who walks along two ways! 33
15 those who love him will keep his ways 26
6:26 keep her ways with all your might. 26
14:21 He who reflects in his mind on her ways 26
16:20 Who will ponder his ways? 26
17:15 Their ways are always before him 26
19 his eyes are continually upon their ways. 26
21:10 The way of sinners is smoothly paved with stones 26
23:19 they look upon all the ways of men 26
30: 1 he may rejoice at the way he turns out. *
32:21 Do not be overconfident on a smooth way 26
33:11 appointed their different ways; 26
13 all his ways are as he pleases 26
31 which way will you go to seek him? 26
37: 9 tell you, "Your way is good," and then stand aloof 26
15 he may direct your way in truth. 26
39:24 To the holy his ways are straight 26
47:23 gave Ephraim a sinful way. 26
48:22 he held strongly to the ways of David his father 26
49: 9 did good to those who directed their ways aright. 26
Bar 2:33 for they will remember the ways of their fathers 26
3:13 If you had walked in the way of God, you would be 26
20 they have not learned the way to knowledge 26
21 Their sons have strayed far from her way. 26
23 have not learned the way to wisdom, nor given 26
27 God did not . . nor give them the way to knowledge; 26
31 No one knows the way to her, or is concerned about 26
36 He found the whole way to knowledge, and gave her 26
4:13 walk in the ways of God's commandments 26
LJr 1:71 In the same way, their gods of wood 34
Aza 1: 4 all thy works are true and thy ways right 26
1Mc 5:53 encouraging the people all the way 26
8:27 In the same way, if war comes first 24
13:20 he circled around by the way to Adora 26
21 to come to them by way of the wilderness 19
14: 5 opened a way to the isles of the sea. 21
35 He sought in every way to exalt his people. 34
2Mc 1:17 Blessed in every way be our God 24
2: 6 Some . . came up to mark the way 26
6:14 he does not deal in this way with us 28
31 in this way he died 34
7: 7 After the first brother had died in this way 34
8:35 and made his way alone like a runaway slave 34
11:31 none of them shall be molested in any way 34
36 we are on our way to Antioch. 31
12: 8 meant in the same way to wipe out the Jews 34
11 to help his people in all other ways. *
12 they might really be useful in many ways *
22 and were swept on, this way and that †
41 they all blessed the ways of the Lord *
14: 3 realized that there was no way for him to be safe 34
3Mc 3:24 they are ill-disposed toward us in every way 34
5:20 prepare the elephants in the same way 24
7:14 on their way they punished . . any whom they met 26
4Mc 2: 8 he is forced to act contrary to his natural ways 34
3: 2 reason can provide a way for us not to be enslaved *
4:24 When . . he had not been able in any way 34
5:27 to eat in such a way that you may deride us *
7: 3 in no way did he turn the rudder of religion 34
8: 3 modest, noble, and accomplished in every way *
10: 7 they were not able in any way to break his spirit 34
11: 4 destroying us in this way? 34
12:13 to maltreat and torture them in this way? 34
18: 1 obey this law and exercise piety in every way 34

way *See also* adoption, all, bring, commit, continue, crooked, eat, every, find, fine, give, go, guilty, hindrance, human, learn, leave, light, make, mend, miss, obstacle, one, parting, put, rough, same, send, set, speed, stand, start, turn, underhanded, varied, various.

another way 1. ἀλλαχόθεν
Joh 10: 1 but climbs in by another way 1

any way 1. οὐδαμῶς 2. σύνολον 3. ὡς
Gen 43: 7 could we in any way know that he would say †
Jdt 3: 4 deal with them in any way that seems good to you. 3
2Mc 9: 7 Yet he did not in any way stop his insolence 1
18 when his sufferings did not in any way abate 1
3Mc 4:11 nor in any way claim 2

way back 1. ἐπανάγω
2Mc 9:21 On my way back from the region of Persia 1

covered way 1. מוּסָךְ
2Kg 16:18 the covered way for the sabbath . . he removed 1

every way 1. πᾶς
1Es 8:52 will support them in every way. 1
Sir 50:22 who in every way does great things 1

good way 1. רחק
Jdg 18:22 When they were a good way from the home of Micah 1

good way off 1. רחק
Gen 21:16 sat down over against him a good way off 1

great way off 1. πόρρω
Lke 14:32 while the other is yet a great way off 1

way into 1. מָבוֹא
Jdg 1:24 Pray, show us the way into the city, and we will deal 1
25 he showed them the way into the city; 1

long way 1. μακρόθεν
Mrk 8: 3 some of them have come a long way. 1

no way 1. μηδείς 2. οὐδείς
Act 4:21 they let them go, finding no way to punish them 1
3Mc 3: 8 The Greeks in the city, though wronged in no way 2

no way whatever 1. οὐδὲν οὐδαμῶς
4Mc 18: 5 Since in no way whatever was he able 1

way of escape 1. מָנוֹס 2. διαφεύγω 3. ἔκβασις
Job 11:20 all way of escape will be lost to them 1
1Co 10:13 will also provide the way of escape 3
Jdt 7:19 there was no way of escape from them. 2

way of life 1. βίος 2. ἐμβίωσις 3. πολιτεία 4. χαρακτήρ
2Mc 4:10 he at once shifted . . over to the Greek way of life. 4
8:17 the overthrow of their ancestral way of life. 3
3Mc 3:23 in accordance with their infamous way of life 2
4Mc 8: 8 by adopting the Greek way of life 1
17: 9 wished to destroy the way of life of the Hebrews. 3

way of living 1. ἀγωγή 2. πολιτεία
2Mc 4:11 he destroyed the lawful ways of living 2
16 those whose ways of living they admired 1
11:24 but prefer their own way of living 1

way of thinking 1. λογισμός
Wis 12:10 their way of thinking would never change. 1

out of the way 1. ἄτοπος
2Mc 14:23 and did nothing out of the way 1

way that is ordained 1. מִשְׁפָּט
1Ch 15:13 we did not care for it in the way that is ordained. 1

way through 1. δίοδος
Wis 19:17 each tried to find the way through his own door. 1

way up 1. עלה
1Sm 9:14 Samuel coming . . on his way up to the high place. 1

wayfarer 1. אִישׁ אֹרֵחַ 2. ארח 3. אֹרֵחַ 4. ὁδοιπόρος
Jdg 19:17 saw the wayfarer in the open square of the city; 1
2Sm 12: 4 take one of his own . . to prepare for the wayfarer 2
Job 31:32 I have opened my doors to the wayfarer 3
Jer 9: 2 O that I had in the desert a wayfarers' lodging 2
14: 8 a wayfarer who turns aside to tarry for a night? 2
Sir 26:12 As a thirsty wayfarer opens his mouth 4

wayfaring man 1. עֹבֵר אֹרַח
Isa 33: 8 highways lie waste, the wayfaring man ceases. 1

waymark 1. צִיּוּן
Jer 31:21 Set up waymarks for yourself 1

many ways 1. πολυμερῶς
Heb 1: 1 In many and various ways God spoke 1

ways of fathers 1. πάτριος
2Mc 7:24 if he would turn from the ways of his fathers 1

ways prosper 1. εὐοδία
Tob 4: 6 your ways will prosper through your deeds. 1

wayside 1. דֶּרֶךְ 2. יַד מַעְגָּל 3. ὁδός
Gen 38:21 harlot who was at Enaim by the wayside? 1
Ps 140: 5 by the wayside they have set snares for me. Selah 2
Jer 3: 2 By the waysides you have sat awaiting lovers 1
Mat 21:19 seeing a fig tree by the wayside he went to it 3

wayward 1. סרר 2. עַוְלָה 3. πλανάω
Prv 7:11 She is loud and wayward 1
Hos 10:10 I will come against the wayward people 2
Heb 5: 2 He can deal gently with the ignorant and wayward 3

weak 1. אֵין כֹּחַ 2. דַּל 3. חלה 4. חַלָּשׁ 5. כשל 6. עָנִי 7. רַךְ 8. רפה 9. רָפֶה 10. ἀδύνατος 11. ἀσθενέω 12. ἀσθενής 13. ἐκλείπω 14. ἥσσων 15. μικρός 16. παραλύω 17. debilis 18. infirmus 19. invalidus
Gen 29:17 Leah's eyes were weak, but Rachel was beautiful 7
Num13:18 people who dwell in it are strong or weak 9
Jdg 6:15 Behold, my clan is the weakest in Manas'seh 2
16:13 If you weave . . then I shall become weak, and be *
2Sm 3: 1 the house of Saul became weaker and weaker. 2
1 the house of Saul became weaker and weaker. †
39 And I am this day weak, though anointed king; 7
2Ch 14:11 between the mighty and the weak. 1
15: 7 But you, take courage! Do not let your hands be weak 8
Job 4: 3 you have strengthened the weak hands. 8
Ps 35:10 who is like thee, thou who deliverest the weak 6
10 the weak and needy from him who despoils him? 6
72:13 He has pity on the weak and the needy 2
82: 3 Give justice to the weak and the fatherless; 2
4 Rescue the weak and the needy; 2
109:24 My knees are weak through fasting; 5
Isa 35: 3 Strengthen the weak hands 8
Ezk 7:17 All hands are feeble, and all knees weak as water. *
21: 7 all knees will be weak as water. *
34: 4 The weak you have not strengthened 3
16 and I will strengthen the weak 3
21 and thrust at all the weak with your horns 13
Jol 3:10 let the weak say, "I am a warrior. 4
Mat 26:41 the flesh is weak. 12
Mrk 14:38 the flesh is weak. 12
Act 20:35 by so toiling one must help the weak 11
Rom 5: 6 While we were still weak . . Christ died 12
14: 1 As for the man who is weak in faith, welcome him 11
2 while the weak man eats only vegetables. 11
15: 1 ought to bear with the failings of the weak 10
1Co 1:27 God chose what is weak in the world 12
4:10 We are weak, but you are strong. 12
8: 7 their conscience, being weak, is defiled. 12
9 somehow become a stumbling block to the weak. 12
10 if his conscience is weak 12
12 wounding their conscience when it is weak 11
9:22 To the weak I became weak 12
22 To the weak I became weak 12
22 that I might win the weak 12
11:30 many of you are weak and ill, and some have died 12
12:22 which seem to be weaker are indispensable 12
2Co 10:10 his bodily presence is weak 12
11:21 To my shame, I must say, we were too weak for that! 11
29 Who is weak, and I am not weak? 11
29 Who is weak, and I am not weak? 11
12:10 when I am weak, then I am strong. 11
13: 3 He is not weak in dealing with you 11
4 we are weak in him 11
9 we are glad when we are weak and you are strong. 11
Gal 4: 9 weak and beggarly elemental spirits 12
1Th 5:14 encourage the fainthearted, help the weak 12
Heb 12:12 and strengthen your weak knees 16
1Pe 3: 7 bestowing honor on the woman as the weaker sex 12
1Es 1:30 Take me away from the battle, for I am very weak. 11
2Es 2:21 care for the injured and the weak 17
7:112 those who were strong prayed for the weak. 19
12: 5 am still weary in mind and very weak in my spirit 19
14:14 and divest yourself now of your weak nature 18
17 For the weaker the world becomes through old age 19
Jdt 9:11 helper of the oppressed, upholder of the weak 11
16:11 my weak people shouted and the enemy trembled; 11
Wis 2:11 what is weak proves itself to be useless. 12
9: 5 a man who is weak and short-lived 12
17:13 the inner expectation of help, being weak 14
Sir 25:23 Drooping hands and weak knees 16
LJr 1:36 rescue the weak from the strong. 15
weak *See also* grow.

become weak 1. חלה
Jdg 16: 7 If they bind me . . then I shall become weak 1
11 If they bind me . . then I shall become weak, and be 1
17 my strength will leave me, and I shall become weak 1
Isa 14:10 say to you: 'You too have become as weak as we! 1

weak man 1. ἀσθενέω
1Co 8:11 so by your knowledge this weak man is destroyed 1

weak thing 1. ἀσθενής
Wis 13:18 For health he appeals to a thing that is weak 1

weak woman 1. γυναικάριον
2Ti 3: 6 capture weak women, burdened with sins 1

weaken 1. רפא 2. ἀσθενέω 3. infirmo
Jer 38: 4 for he is weakening the hands of the soldiers 1
Rom 4:19 He did not weaken in faith 2
8: 3 what the law, weakened by the flesh, could not do 2
2Es 15:51 You shall be weakened like a wretched woman 3
weaker *See* sex.

weakling 1. ἀκάρδιος
Sir 6:20 a weakling will not remain with her. 1

weakness 1. עֶרְוָה 2. ἀσθένεια 3. ἀσθενής
Gen 42: 9 you have come to see the weakness of the land. 1
12 He said to them, "No, it is the weakness of the land 1
Rom 8:26 Likewise the Spirit helps us in our weakness; 2
1Co 1:25 the weakness of God is stronger than men. 3
2: 3 And I was with you in weakness 2
15:43 It is sown in weakness, it is raised in power. 2
2Co 11:30 I will boast of the things that show my weakness. 2
12: 5 I will not boast, except of my weaknesses. 2
9 for my power is made perfect in weakness 2
9 I will all the more gladly boast of my weaknesses 2
10 I am content with weaknesses, insults, hardships 2
13: 4 For he was crucified in weakness 2
Heb 4:15 is unable to sympathize with our weaknesses 2
5: 2 since he himself is beset with weakness. 2
7:18 because of its weakness and uselessness 3
28 appoints men in their weakness as high priests 2
11:34 won strength out of weakness 2
Sir 11:30 like a spy he observes your weakness; 1
4Mc 7:20 because of the weakness of their reason. 3

weal 1. שָׁלוֹם
Isa 45: 7 I make weal and create woe 1

wealth 1. און 2. הון 3. הָמוֹן 4. חַיִל 5. חֹסֶן 6. יְגִיעַ 7. יֵשׁ 8. כבד 9. כָּבוֹד 10. כֹּחַ 11. נֶכֶס 12. עֹצֶר 13. עֹשֶׁר 14. δύναμις 15. εὐπορία 16. πλοῦτος 17. τιμιότης 18. ὑπάρχω 19. χρῆμα 20. abundantia 21. honestas
Gen 31: 1 was our father's he has gained all this wealth. 9
34:29 all their wealth, all their little ones 4
Deu 8:17 power and . . my hand have gotten me this wealth.' 4
18 LORD . . who gives you power to get wealth; 4
Jos 22: 8 Go back to your homes with much wealth 11
Jdg 18: 7 lacking nothing . . and possessing wealth 12
Rut 2: 1 a kinsman of her husband's, a man of wealth 4
1Sm 9: 1 name was Kish . . a Benjaminite, a man of wealth; 4
2Ch 1:11 you have not asked possessions, wealth, honor 11
Job 5: 5 the thirsty pant after his wealth. 4
6:22 Or, 'From your wealth offer a bribe for me'? 10
15:29 he will not be rich, and his wealth will not endure 4
20:10 his hands will give back his wealth. 1
27:19 he opens his eyes, and his wealth is gone. *
31:25 if I have rejoiced because my wealth was great 4
Ps 45:13 with all kinds of wealth. 8
49: 6 men who trust in their wealth 4
10 must perish and leave their wealth to others. 4
52: 7 of his riches, and sought refuge in his wealth! ‡
112: 3 Wealth and riches are in his house; 2
Prv 8:18 with me, enduring wealth and prosperity. 2
21 endowing with wealth those who love me 7
10:15 A rich man's wealth is his strong city; 2
12:27 but the diligent man will get precious wealth. 2
13: 7 another pretends to be poor, yet has great wealth. 2
8 The ransom of a man's life is his wealth 13
11 Wealth hastily gotten will dwindle 2
22 sinner's wealth is laid up for the righteous. 4
18:11 A rich man's wealth is his strong city 2
19: 4 Wealth brings many new friends 2
14 House and wealth are inherited from fathers 2
22:16 oppresses the poor to increase his own wealth *
28: 8 augments his wealth by interest and increase 2
22 A miserly man hastens after wealth 2
Ecc 5:10 nor he who loves wealth, with gain 3
19 given wealth and possessions and power to enjoy 13
6: 2 to whom God gives wealth, possessions, and honor 13
Sng 8: 7 a man offered for love all the wealth of his house 2
Isa 8: 4 the wealth of Damascus and the spoil of Sama'ria 4
10: 3 and where will you leave your wealth? 9
14 found like a nest the wealth of the peoples; 4
45:14 wealth of Egypt and the merchandise of Ethiopia 6
60: 5 the wealth of the nations shall come to you. 4
11 men may bring to you the wealth of the nations 4
61: 6 you shall eat the wealth of the nations 4
66:12 the wealth of the nations like an overflowing 9
Jer 15:13 wealth and your treasures I will give as spoil 4
17: 3 Your wealth and all your treasures I will give 4
20: 5 Moreover, I will give all the wealth of the city 5
Ezk 7:11 remain, nor their abundance, nor their wealth; *
27:12 because of your great wealth of every kind; 2
18 goods, because of your great wealth of every kind; 2
33 with your abundant wealth and merchandise 2
28: 4 by . . your understanding you have gotten wealth 4
5 in trade you have increased your wealth 4
5 your heart has become proud in your wealth 4
29:19 he shall carry off its wealth and despoil it 3
30: 4 her wealth is carried away 3
10 I will put an end to the wealth of Egypt 3
Hos 12: 8 Ah, but I am rich, I have gained wealth for myself": 1
Obd 1:11 on the day that strangers carried off his wealth 4
Mic 4:13 their wealth to the Lord of the whole earth. 4
Nah 2: 9 of treasure, or wealth of every precious thing. 9
Zec 9: 4 her possessions and hurl her wealth into the sea 4
14:14 the wealth of all the nations round about 4
Act 19:25 Men . . from this business we have our wealth. 15
2Co 8: 2 overflowed in a wealth of liberality 16
Heb 11:26 greater wealth than the treasures of Egypt 16
Rev 5:12 to receive power and wealth and wisdom and might 16
18: 3 grown rich with the wealth of her wantonness. 14
17 In one hour all this wealth has been laid waste. 16
19 all who had ships at sea grew rich by her wealth! 17
2Es 3: 2 and the wealth of those who lived in Babylon. 20
33 and have seen that they abound in wealth *
15:63 and shall plunder your wealth 21
Tob 4:21 You have great wealth if you fear God 18
Wis 5: 8 what good has our boasted wealth brought us? 16
7: 8 I accounted wealth as nothing 16
11 in her hands uncounted wealth. 16
13 I do not hide her wealth 16
8:18 in the labors of her hands, unfailing wealth 16
Sir 5: 1 Do not set your heart on your wealth 19
8 Do not depend on dishonest wealth 19
10: 8 injustice and insolence and wealth. 19
30 while a rich man is honored for his wealth. 16
31 A man honored in poverty, how much more in wealth! 16
31 a man dishonored in wealth 16
11:14 poverty and wealth, come from the Lord. 16
18:25 in the days of wealth think of poverty and need. 16
28:10 in proportion to his wealth 16
30:16 There is no wealth better than health of body 16
31: 1 Wakefulness over wealth wastes away one's [illegible] 16
3 The rich man toils as his wealth accumulates 19
37: 6 be not unmindful of him in your wealth. 19
40:13 wealth of the unjust will dry up like a torrent 19
LJr 1:35 they are not able to give either wealth or money; 16
1Mc 6: 1 a city famed for its wealth in silver and gold. 16
wealth *See also* acquire, gain.

wealthy 1. גָּדוֹל 2. חַיִל
2Sm 19:32 he had provided . . for he was a very wealthy man. 1
2Kg 4: 8 went on to Shunem, where a wealthy woman lived 1
15:20 from Israel, that is, from all the wealthy men 2

become wealthy 1. גדל
Gen 26:13 more and more until he became very wealthy. 1

wean 1. גמל
Gen 21: 8 the child grew, and was weaned; 1
8 great feast on the day that Isaac was weaned. 1
1Sm 1:22 As soon as the child is weaned, I will bring him 1
23 wait until you have weaned him; 1
23 woman . . nursed her son, until she weaned him. 1
24 when she had weaned him, she took him up with her 1
1Kg 11:20 his son, whom Tah'penes weaned in Pharaoh's house; 1
Isa 28: 9 Those who are weaned from the milk 1
Hos 1: 8 When she had weaned Not pitied, she conceived 1

weaned *See* child.

weapon 1. אֲזֵן 2. כְּלִי 3. נֶשֶׁק 4. שֶׁלַח 5. ὅπλον 6. πανοπλία 7. σκεῦος πολεμικόν 8. vas
Gen 27: 3 take your weapons, your quiver and your bow 2
49: 5 weapons of violence are their swords. 2
Num35:18 struck him down with a weapon of wood in the hand 2
Deu 1:41 And every man of you girded on his weapons of war 2
23:13 you shall have a stick with your weapons; 1
Jdg 18:11 600 men . . armed with weapons of war, set forth 2
16 men . . armed with their weapons of war, stood 2
17 with the 600 men armed with weapons of war 2
1Sm 20:40 And Jonathan gave his weapons to his lad, and said 2
21: 8 I have brought neither my sword nor my weapons 2
2Sm 1:27 How are . . and the weapons of war perished! 2
2Kg 10: 2 and horses, fortified cities also, and weapons 3
11: 8 surround . . each with his weapons in his hand; 2
11 every man with his weapons in his hand 2
1Ch 12:33 equipped for battle with all the weapons of war 2
37 120,000 men armed with all the weapons of war. 2
2Ch 23: 7 each with his weapons in his hand; 2
10 every man with his weapon in his hand 4
32: 5 He also made weapons and shields in abundance. 4
Neh 4:17 one hand . . and with the other held his weapon. 4
23 each kept his weapon in his hand. 4
Job 20:24 He will flee from an iron weapon; 3
39:21 in his strength; he goes out to meet the weapons. 3
Ps 7:13 he has prepared his deadly weapons 2
76: 3 the shield, the sword, and the weapons of war. •
Ecc 9:18 Wisdom is better than weapons of war 2
Isa 13: 5 the LORD and the weapons of his indignation 2
22: 8 looked to the weapons of the House of the Forest 3
54:16 of coals, and produces a weapon for its purpose. 2
17 no weapon that is fashioned against you shall 2
Jer 21: 4 Behold, I will turn back the weapons of war 2
22: 7 destroyers against you, each with his weapons; 2
50:25 and brought out the weapons of his wrath 2
51:20 You are my hammer and weapon of war 2
Ezk 9: 1 each with his destroying weapon in his hand. 2
2 man with his weapon for slaughter in his hand 2
32:27 who went down to Sheol with their weapons of war 2
39: 9 and make fires of the weapons and burn them 3
10 for they will make their fires of the weapons; 3
Jol 2: 8 they burst through the weapons 4
Joh 18: 3 lanterns and torches and weapons. 5
2Co 6: 7 with the weapons of righteousness 5
10: 4 for the weapons of our warfare are not worldly 5
2Es 13: 9 hand nor held a spear or any weapon of war; 8
28 as for his not holding a spear or weapon of war 8
Jdt 6:12 they caught up their weapons and ran out of the city 5
7: 5 Then each man took up his weapons 7
14: 2 let every valiant man take his weapons and go out 7
11 every man took his weapons 5
1Mc 6: 2 golden shields, breastplates, and weapons 5
9:39 tambourines and musicians and many weapons. 5
14:42 the country and the weapons and the strongholds 5
15: 7 All the weapons which you have prepared 5
16:16 Ptolemy and his men rose up, took their weapons 5
2Mc 11: 8 brandishing weapons of gold. 6
4Mc 4:10 with lightning flashing from their weapons 5

weapon *See also* armor.

wear 1. חגר 2. לבש 3. נשא 4. עַל 5. צנף 6. εἰμὶ ἐπί 7. ἔνδυσις 8. ἐνδύω 9. ἔχω 10. μετά 11. μέχρι 12. περιβάλλω 13. περιβολή 14. περίκειμαι 15. περιτίθημι 16. στολίζω 17. ὑπό 18. ὑποδέω 19. φορέω
Gen 28:20 give me bread to eat and clothing to wear 2
37:23 the long robe with sleeves that he wore; 4
Exd 29:30 The son . . shall wear them seven days 2
Lev 13:45 The leper . . shall wear torn clothes •
16: 4 and wear the linen turban 5
32 make atonement, wearing the holy linen garments 2
21:10 who has been consecrated to wear his garments 2
Deu 22: 5 woman . . not wear anything that pertains to a man •
11 not wear a mingled stuff, wool and linen together. 2
Jdg 8:26 the purple garments worn by the kings of Mid'ian •
Rut 3:15 Bring the mantle you are wearing and hold it out. •
1Sm 2:28 go up to my altar, to burn incense, to wear an ephod 3
14: 3 and Ahi'jah the son of Ahi'tub . . wearing an ephod. 3
22:18 he killed . . persons who wore the linen ephod. 3
2Sm 13:18 Now she was wearing a long robe with sleeves; 4
19 put ashes . . and rent the long robe which she wore; 4
20: 8 Now Jo'ab was wearing a soldier's garment 1
1Kg 22:30 I will disguise . . but you wear your robes. 2
2Kg 1: 8 They answered him, "He wore a garment of haircloth •
1Ch 15:27 and David wore a linen ephod. •
2Ch 18:29 but you will wear your robes. 2
Est 6: 8 royal robes . . which the king has worn 2
Job 27:17 he may pile it up, but the just will wear it 2
Ps 35:13 But I, when they were sick–I wore sackcloth 2
Isa 4: 1 We will eat our own bread and wear our own clothes 2
Ezk 44:17 they shall wear linen garments; 2
Mat 3: 4 Now John wore a garment of camel's hair 9
6:31 shall we drink?' or 'What shall we wear?' 12
11: 8 those who wear soft raiment are in kings' houses. 19
Mrk 6: 9 to wear sandals and not put on two tunics. 18
Lke 8:27 for a long time he had worn no clothes 8
Joh 19: 5 Jesus came out, wearing the crown of thorns 19
2Ti 2: 9 for which I am suffering and wearing fetters 11
Jas 2: 3 to the one who wears the fine clothing 19
1Pe 3: 3 adorning . . and wearing of fine clothing 7
Rev 9:17 the riders wore breastplates the color of fire 9
1Es 5:40 a high priest . . wearing Urim and Thummim. 8
Jdt 8: 5 wore the garments of her widowhood. 6
9: 1 uncovered the sackcloth she was wearing 8
10: 3 the sackcloth which she had been wearing 8
3 which she used to wear 16
15:13 bearing their arms and wearing garlands 10
AEs 14:16 I do not wear it on the days when I am at leisure. 19
Wis 5:18 wear impartial justice as a helmet; 15
Sir 6:31 You will wear her like a glorious robe 8
11: 4 Do not boast about wearing fine clothes 13
5 one who was never thought of has worn a crown. 19
27: 8 will attain it and wear it as a glorious robe. 8
40: 4 the man who wears purple and a crown 19
LJr 1:24 As for the gold which they wear for beauty 14
58 the robes they wear 14
1Mc 8:14 or worn purple as a mark of pride 12
11:58 dress in purple and wear a gold buckle. 9
2Mc 4:12 he induced . . the young men to wear the Greek hat. 17
6: 7 wearing wreaths of ivy. 9
12:40 which the law forbids the Jews to wear •

wear a veil 1. κατακαλύπτω
1Co 11: 6 let her wear a veil. 1

wear away 1. שחק 2. κλίνω
Job 14:19 the waters wear away the stones; 1
Lke 9:12 Now the day began to wear away 2

wear gold 1. χρυσοφορέω
1Mc 14:43 he should be clothed in purple and wear gold. 1

wear long hair 1. κομάω
1Co 11:14 for a man to wear long hair is degrading to him 1

wear off 1. בלה
Deu 29: 5 your sandals have not worn off your feet; 1

wear out 1. בלה 2. לאה 3. נבל 4. בלא (A) 5. ἐκτρίβω 6. κοπιάω 7. ὑπωπιάζω
Exd 18:18 You and the people . . will wear yourselves out 3
Deu 8: 4 Your clothing did not wear out upon you 1
29: 5 your clothes have not worn out upon you 1
Jos 9:13 shoes . . are worn out from the very long journey. 1
Neh 9:21 their clothes did not wear out and their feet 1
Job 16: 7 Surely now God has worn me out; 2
Ps 102:26 they will all wear out like a garment. 1
Prv 26:15 wears him out to bring it back to his mouth. 2
Isa 50: 9 Behold, all of them will wear out like a garment; 1
51: 6 like smoke, the earth will wear out like a garment 1
Dan 7:25 shall wear out the saints of the Most High 4
Lke 18: 5 she will wear me out by her continual coming.' 7
2Es 4:11 one who is already worn out by the corrupt world •
Sir 6:36 let your foot wear out his doorstep. 5
4Mc 9:12 When they had worn themselves out beating him 6

weariness 1. יְגִיעָה 2. יעף 3. תְּלָאָה
Jdg 4:21 he was lying fast asleep from weariness. 2
Ecc 12:12 and much study is a weariness of the flesh. 1
Mal 1:13 What a weariness this is,' you say 3

weariness *See also* full.

wearisome *See* task.

weary 1. דלל 2. יְגִיעַ כֹּחַ 3. יגע 4. יָגֵעַ 5. יעף 6. לאה 7. עָיֵף 8. פוג 9. קוץ 10. ἀκηδία 11. ἀκηδιάω 12. ἐγκακέω 13. κατάκοπος 14. κοπιάω 15. κοπόω 16. κόπτω 17. fatigo
Gen 19:11 so that they wearied themselves groping 6
27:46 Rebekah said to Isaac, "I am weary of my life 9
Deu 25:18 attacked you . . when you were faint and weary 4
2Sm 16:14 And the king, and all the people . . arrived weary 7
17: 2 I will come . . while he is weary and discouraged 4
29 The people are hungry and weary and thirsty 7
23:10 struck . . Philistines until his hand was weary 3
Job 3:17 there the weary are at rest. 2
22: 7 You have given no water to the weary to drink 7
Ps 6: 6 I am weary with my moaning; 3
63: 1 my flesh faints for thee, as in a dry and weary land 7
69: 3 I am weary with my crying; my throat is parched. 3
77: 2 my hand is stretched out without wearying; 8
Prv 3:11 My son, do not . . be weary of his reproof 9
Ecc 10:15 The toil of a fool wearies him 3
Isa 1:14 become a burden to me, I am weary of bearing them. 6
5:27 None is weary, none stumbles, none slumbers 7
7:13 for you to weary men, that you weary my God also? 6
13 for you to weary men, that you weary my God also? 6
16:12 when he wearies himself upon the high place 6
28:12 This is rest; give rest to the weary; 7
32: 2 like the shade of a great rock in a weary land. 7
38:14 My eyes are weary with looking upward. 1
40:30 Even youths shall faint and be weary 3
31 they shall run and not be weary 3
43:22 but you have been weary of me, O Israel! 3
23 or wearied you with frankincense. 3
24 you have wearied me with your iniquities. 3
46: 1 are loaded as burdens on weary beasts. 7
47:13 You are wearied with your many counsels; 6
50: 4 know how to sustain with a word him that is weary. 5
57:10 You were wearied with the length of your way 3
Jer 2:24 None who seek her need weary themselves; 5
6:11 the wrath of the LORD; I am weary of holding it in. 6
9: 5 they commit iniquity and are too weary to repent. 6
12: 5 raced with men on foot, and they have wearied you 6
15: 6 and destroyed you;–I am weary of relenting. 6
20: 9 and I am weary with holding it in, and I cannot. 6
31:25 For I will satisfy the weary soul 7
45: 3 I am weary with my groaning, and I find no rest. 3
51:58 the nations weary themselves only for fire. 5
Lam 5: 5 we are . . driven; we are weary, we are given no rest. 3
Ezk 24:12 In vain I have wearied myself; •
Mic 6: 3 In what have I wearied you? Answer me! 6
Hab 2:13 and nations weary themselves for nought? 5
Mal 2:17 You have wearied the LORD with your words. 3
17 Yet you say, "How have we wearied him? 3
Joh 4: 6 Jesus, wearied as he was with his journey, sat down 14
2Th 3:13 Brethren, do not be weary in well-doing. 12
2Es 12: 5 Behold, I am still weary in mind 17
Jdt 13: 1 they went to bed, for they all were weary 16
Sir 22:13 you will never be wearied by his madness. 11
Bar 3: 1 soul in anguish and the wearied spirit cry out 10
1Mc 12:44 Why have you wearied all these people 15
2Mc 12:36 men had been fighting for a long time and were weary 13

weary *See also* grow.

become weary 1. שבע 2. fatigo
Prv 25:17 lest he become weary of you and hate you. 1
2Es 2:12 they shall neither toil nor become weary. 2

weasel 1. חֹלֶד
Lev 11:29 the weasel, the mouse, the great lizard 1

bad weather 1. χειμών
1Es 9: 6 shivering because of the bad weather 1

fair weather 1. εὐδία
Mat 16: 2 When it is evening, you say, 'It will be fair weather; 1
Sir 3:15 as frost in fair weather, your sins will melt away. 1

weave 1. ארג 2. מִשְׁבְּצוֹת 3. καθυφαίνω 4. ὑφαντός
Exd 28:32 with a woven binding around the opening 1
39:22 the robe of the ephod woven all of blue; 1
27 They also made the coats, woven of fine linen 1
Jdg 16:13 If you weave the seven locks of my head 1
14 seven locks . . and wove them into the web. •
2Kg 23: 7 where the women wove hangings for the Ashe'rah. 1
Ps 45:13 decked in her chamber with gold-woven robes; 2
Isa 59: 5 watch adders' eggs, they weave the spider's web; 1
Joh 19:23 tunic was without seam, woven from top to bottom; 4
Jdt 10:21 under a canopy which was woven with purple 3

weave in checker work 1. שבץ
Exd 28:39 you shall weave the coat in checker work of fine 1

weave together 1. עבת
Mic 7: 3 thus they weave it together. 1

weaver 1. ארג
Exd 35:35 by a weaver–by any sort of workman or skilled 1
1Sm 17: 7 And the shaft of his spear was like a weaver's beam 1
2Sm 21:19 the shaft of whose spear was like a weaver's beam. 1
1Ch 11:23 a spear like a weaver's beam; 1
20: 5 the shaft of whose spear was like a weaver's beam. 1
Isa 19: 9 be in despair, and the weavers of white cotton. 1
38:12 like a weaver I have rolled up my life; 1

weaver *See also* shuttle.

web 1. בַּיִת 2. מַסֶּכֶת 3. קוּר
Jdg 16:13 weave the seven locks of my head with the web 2
14 seven locks . . and wove them into the web. •
14 and pulled away the pin, the loom, and the web. 2
Job 8:14 his trust is a spider's web. 1
27:18 The house which he builds is like a spider's web •
Isa 59: 5 watch adders' eggs, they weave the spider's web; 3
6 Their webs will not serve as clothing; 3

wedded *See* union.

wedding 1. חֲתֻנָּה 2. γάμος 3. νυμφών
Sng 3:11 his mother crowned him on the day of his wedding 1
Mat 9:15 Jesus said to them, "Can the wedding guests mourn 3
22: 8 Then he said to his servants, 'The wedding is ready 2
11 he saw there a man who had no wedding garment; 2

12 how did you get in here without a wedding garment?' 2
Mrk 2:19 Jesus said to them, "Can the wedding guests fast 3
Lke 5:34 Can you make wedding guests fast 3
1Mc 9:37 sons of Jambri are celebrating a great wedding 2
41 Thus the wedding was turned into mourning 2
10:58 celebrated her wedding at Ptolemais 2
wedding *See also* chamber, feast, hall, song.

wedge 1. *συντρίβω* 2. *σφήν*
Sir 27: 2 sin is wedged in between selling and buying. 1
4Mc 8:13 iron claws and wedges and bellows 2
11:10 twisted his back around the wedge on the wheel 2
wedlock *See* break.

weed 1. סוּף 2. *ζιζάνιον* 3. *περικαθαίρω*
Jon 2: 5 round about me; weeds were wrapped about my head 1
Mat 13:25 his enemy came and sowed weeds among the wheat 2
26 then the weeds appeared also. 2
27 How then has it weeds? 2
29 lest in gathering the weeds you root up the wheat 2
30 Gather the weeds first and bind them in bundles 2
36 the parable of the weeds of the field. 2
38 the weeds are the sons of the evil one 2
40 Just as the weeds are gathered 2
4Mc 1:29 the master cultivator, reason, weeds and prunes 3

foul weed 1. בָּאְשָׁה
Job 31:40 thorns . . and foul weeds instead of barley. 1

poisonous weed 1. רֹאשׁ
Hos 10: 4 so judgment springs up like poisonous weeds 1

week 1. שָׁבוּעַ 2. שָׁבְעִים יָמִים 3. שַׁבָּת 4. *ἑβδομάς*
5. *σάββατον* 6. ebdomada
Gen 29:27 Complete the week of this one, and we will give 1
28 Jacob did so, and completed her week; 1
Exd 34:22 you shall observe the feast of weeks 1
Lev 12: 5 then she shall be unclean two weeks 1
23:15 seven full weeks shall they be 3
25: 8 you shall count seven weeks of years, seven times 3
8 so that the time of the seven weeks of years shall 3
Deu 16: 9 count seven weeks; begin to count the seven weeks 1
9 begin to count the seven weeks from the time 1
10 Then you shall keep the feast of weeks to the LORD 1
16 appear . . at . . the feast of weeks 1
2Ch 8:13 three annual feasts- . . the feast of weeks 1
Jer 5:24 keeps . . the weeks appointed for the harvest.' 1
Dan 9:24 70 weeks of years are decreed concerning 1
25 there shall be seven weeks. 1
25 Then for 62 weeks it shall be built again 1
26 after the 62 weeks, an anointed one 1
27 make a strong covenant with many for one week; 1
27 for half of the week he shall cause sacrifice 1
10: 2 days I, Daniel, was mourning for three weeks. 2
3 ate no delicacies . . for the full three weeks. 2
Mat 28: 1 toward the dawn of the first day of the week 5
Mrk 16: 2 very early on the first day of the week 5
9 Now when he rose early on the first day of the week 5
Lke 18:12 I fast twice a week, I give tithes of all that I get.' 5
24: 1 on the first day of the week, at early dawn 5
Joh 20: 1 Now on the first day of the week 5
19 the first day of the week 5
Act 17: 2 for three weeks he argued with them 5
20: 7 On the first day of the week 5
1Co 16: 2 On the first day of every week 5
2Es 6:35 in order to complete the three weeks 6
7:43 For it will last for about a week of years. 6
Tob 2: 1 which is the sacred festival of the seven weeks 4
2Mc 12:31 the feast of weeks was close at hand. 4
week *See also* feast.

weep 1. בִּבְכִי 2. בכה 3. בְּכִי 4. בְּכִית 5. דמע
6. דִּמְעָה 7. מרר 8. *δακρύω* 9. *κλαίω* 10. *κλαυθμός*
11. defleo 12. fleo 13. ploro
Gen 21:16 the child lifted up his voice and wept. 2
23: 2 and Abraham went in to mourn for Sarah and to weep 2
27:38 And Esau lifted up his voice and wept. 2
29:11 Then Jacob kissed Rachel, and wept aloud. 2
33: 4 on his neck and kissed him, and they wept. 2
37:35 to my son, mourning." Thus his father wept for him 2
42:24 Then he turned away from them and wept; 2
43:30 and he sought a place to weep. 2
30 And he entered his chamber and wept there. 2
45: 2 he wept aloud, so that the Egyptians heard it 3
14 he fell upon his brother Benjamin's neck and wept 2
14 and Benjamin wept upon his neck. 2
15 he kissed all his brothers and wept upon them; 2
46:29 and wept on his neck a good while. 2
50: 1 Joseph fell on his father's face, and wept over him 2
3 And the Egyptians wept for him 70 days. 2
4 when the days of weeping for him were past 4
17 Joseph wept when they spoke to him. 2
Num11: 4 people of Israel also wept again 2
10 Moses heard the people weeping throughout 2
13 For they weep before me and say, 'Give us meat 2
18 you have wept in the hearing of the LORD, saying 2
20 rejected the LORD . . and have wept before him 2
14: 1 raised a loud cry; and the people wept that night. 2
20:29 all the house of Israel wept for Aaron 30 days 2
25: 6 while they were weeping at the door of the tent 2
Deu 1:45 returned and wept before the LORD; 2
34: 8 Israel wept for Moses in the plains of Moab 2
8 then the days of weeping and mourning for Moses 3
Jdg 2: 4 the people lifted up their voices and wept. 2
14:16 Samson's wife wept before him, and said, "You only 2
17 She wept before him the seven days 2
20:23 people of Israel went up and wept before the LORD 2
26 the whole army, went up and came to Bethel and wept 2
21: 2 they lifted up their voices and wept bitterly. 2
Rut 1: 9 and they lifted up their voices and wept. 2
14 Then they lifted up their voices and wept again; 2
1Sm 1: 7 Therefore Hannah wept and would not eat. 2
8 Hannah, why do you weep? And why do you not eat? 2
10 She . . and prayed to the LORD, and wept bitterly. 2
11: 4 they reported . . and all the people wept aloud. 2
5 What ails the people, that they are weeping? 2
20:41 kissed one another, and wept with one another 2
24:16 And Saul lifted up his voice and wept. 2
30: 4 and the people . . raised their voices and wept 2
4 and wept, until they had no more strength to weep. 2
2Sm 1:12 they mourned and wept and fasted until evening 2
24 Ye daughters of Israel, weep over Saul 2
3:16 her husband went . . weeping after her all the way 2
32 the king lifted up his voice and wept at the grave 2
32 They buried Abner . . and all the people wept. 2
34 And all the people wept again over him. 2
12:21 You fasted and wept for the child while it was 2
22 While the child was still alive, I fasted and wept; 2
13:36 sons came, and lifted up their voice and wept; 2
36 king . . and all his servants wept very bitterly. 2
15:23 all the country wept aloud as . . people passed by 2
30 David went up . . weeping as he went, barefoot 2
30 and they went up, weeping as they went. 2
18:33 and went up to the chamber over the gate, and wept; 2
19: 1 the king is weeping and mourning for Ab'salom. 2
2Kg 8:11 And the man of God wept. 2
12 Haz'ael said, "Why does my lord weep? 2
13:14 Jo'ash . . went down to him, and wept before him 2
20: 3 And Hezeki'ah wept bitterly. 2
22:19 and you have rent your clothes and wept before me 2
2Ch 34:27 have rent your clothes and wept before me 2
Ezr 3:12 wept with a loud voice when they saw 2
13 from the sound of the people's weeping 3
10: 1 weeping and casting himself down before 2
1 for the people wept very bitterly. 2
Neh 1: 4 When I heard these words I sat down and wept 2
8: 9 This day is holy . . do not mourn or weep. 2
9 For all the people wept when they heard the words 2
Est 4: 3 great mourning . . with fasting and weeping 3
Job 2:12 they raised their voices and wept; 2
30:25 Did not I weep for him whose day was hard? 2
31 and my pipe to the voice of those who weep. 2
31:38 its furrows have wept together; 2
Ps 6: 6 I drench my couch with my weeping. 6
8 for the LORD has heard the sound of my weeping. 3
30: 5 Weeping may tarry for the night 3
126: 6 He that goes forth weeping, bearing the seed 2
137: 1 waters of Babylon, there we sat down and wept 2
Ecc 3: 4 a time to weep, and a time to laugh; 2
Isa 15: 2 Dibon has gone up to the high places to weep; 3
5 Luhith they go up weeping; on the road to Horona'im 1
16: 9 Therefore I weep with the weeping of Jazer 3
9 Therefore I weep with the weeping of Jazer 3
22:12 Lord GOD of hosts called to weeping and mourning 3
30:19 who dwell at Jerusalem; you shall weep no more. 2
33: 7 the envoys of peace weep bitterly. 2
38: 3 And Hezeki'ah wept bitterly. 2
65:19 no more shall be heard in it the sound of weeping 3
Jer 3:21 the weeping and pleading of Israel's sons 3
9: 1 that I might weep day and night for the slain 2
10 Take up weeping and wailing for the mountains 3
13:17 if you will not listen, my soul will weep in secret 2
17 my eyes will weep bitterly 5
22:10 Weep not for him who is dead, nor bemoan him; 2
31: 9 With weeping they shall come 3
15 heard in Ramah, lamentation and bitter weeping. 3
15 Rachel is weeping for her children; 2
16 Thus says the LORD: "Keep your voice from weeping 3
41: 6 out from Mizpah to meet them, weeping as he came. 2
48: 5 For at the ascent of Luhith they go up weeping; 3
32 More than for Jazer I weep for you, O vine of Sibmah! 2
50: 4 Judah shall come together, weeping as they come; 2
Lam 1: 2 She weeps bitterly in the night 2
16 For these things I weep; my eyes flow with tears; 2
2:11 My eyes are spent with weeping; 6
Ezk 8:14 and behold, there sat women weeping for Tammuz. 2
24:16 yet you shall not mourn or weep 2
23 you shall not mourn or weep, but you shall pine 2
27:31 they weep over you in bitterness of soul 2
Hos 12: 4 he wept and sought his favor. 2
Jol 1: 5 Awake, you drunkards, and weep; 2
2:12 with all your heart, with fasting, with weeping 3
17 let the priests, the ministers of the LORD, weep 2
Mic 1:10 Tell it not in Gath, weep not at all; 2
Zec 12:10 over him, as one weeps over a first-born. 7
Mal 2:13 with tears, with weeping and groaning because he 3
Mat 2:18 wailing and loud lamentation, Rachel weeping 9
8:12 the outer darkness; there men will weep and gnash 10
13:42 there men will weep and gnash their teeth. 10
50 there men will weep and gnash their teeth. 10
22:13 there men will weep and gnash their teeth.' 10
24:51 there men will weep and gnash their teeth. 10
25:30 there men will weep and gnash their teeth.' 10
26:75 he went out and wept bitterly. 9
Mrk 5:38 people weeping and wailing loudly. 9
39 Why do you make a tumult and weep? 9
14:72 he broke down and wept. 9
16:10 as they mourned and wept. 9
Lke 6:21 Blessed are you that weep now, for you shall laugh. 9
25 you shall mourn and weep. 9
7:13 compassion on her and said to her, "Do not weep. 9
32 we wailed, and you did not weep.' 9
38 standing behind him at his feet, weeping 9
8:52 all were weeping and bewailing her 9
52 Do not weep; for she is not dead but sleeping. 9
13:28 There you will weep and gnash your teeth 10
19:41 when he drew near and saw the city he wept over it 9
22:62 he went out and wept bitterly. 9
23:28 Daughters of Jerusalem, do not weep for me 9
28 weep for yourselves and for your children. 9
Joh 11:31 she was going to the tomb to weep there. 9
33 When Jesus saw her weeping 9
33 and the Jews who came with her also weeping 9
16:20 you will weep and lament 9
20:11 Mary stood weeping outside the tomb 9
11 as she wept she stooped to look into the tomb; 9
13 They said to her, "Woman, why are you weeping? 9
15 Woman, why are you weeping? Whom do you seek? 9
Act 9:39 All the widows stood beside him weeping 9
20:37 they all wept and embraced Paul and kissed him. 10
21:13 What are you doing, weeping and breaking my heart? 9
Rom 12:15 weep with those who weep. 9
15 weep with those who weep. 9
Jas 4: 9 Be wretched and mourn and weep. 9
5: 1 weep and howl for the miseries that are coming 9
Rev 5: 4 I wept much that no one was found worthy to open 9
5 Then one of the elders said to me, "Weep not; 9
18: 9 the kings . . will weep and wail over her 9
11 the merchants of the earth weep and mourn for her 9
15 fear of her torment, weeping and mourning aloud 9
19 as they wept and mourned, crying out, "Alas, alas 9
1Es 5:63 came . . with outcries and loud weeping 10
65 because of the weeping of the people 10
8:91 weeping and lying upon the ground 9
91 there was great weeping among the multitude. 10
9:50 now they were all weeping as they heard the law- 9
2Es 2:27 others shall weep and be sorrowful 13
5:13 and if you pray again, and weep as you do now 13
20 I fasted seven days, mourning and weeping 13
6:35 Now after this I wept again and fasted seven days 12
9:38 she was mourning and weeping with a loud voice 13
40 said to her, "Why are you weeping 12
41 that I may weep for myself and continue to mourn 11
12:45 And they wept with a loud voice 13
Tob 2: 6 And I wept. 9
3: 1 in my grief I wept, and I prayed in anguish, saying 9
5:17 Anna, his mother, began to weep, and said to Tobit 9
21 So she stopped weeping. 9
7: 6 Then Raguel sprang up and kissed him and wept. 9
7 he was stricken with grief and wept. 9
8 his wife Edna and his daughter Sarah wept 9
17 the girl began to weep 9
11: 9 now I am ready to die." And they both wept. 9
14 he wept and said, "Blessed art thou, O God 9
Jdt 14:16 cried out with a loud voice and wept and groaned 10
16:17 they shall weep in pain for ever. 9
Sir 7:34 Do not fail those who weep 9
12:16 an enemy will weep with his eyes 8
22:11 Weep for the dead, for he lacks the light 9
11 weep for the fool, for he lacks intelligence 9
11 weep less bitterly for the dead 9
38:17 Let your weeping be bitter 10
Bar 1: 5 they wept, and fasted, and prayed before the Lord; 9
4:11 I sent them away with weeping and sorrow. 10
23 For I sent you out with sorrow and weeping 10
Sus 1:33 her family and friends and all who saw her wept. 9
35 she, weeping, looked up toward heaven 9
1Mc 7:36 they wept and said 9
9:20 wept for him 9
2Mc 4:37 wept because of the moderation and good conduct 8
13:12 besought the merciful Lord with weeping 10
3Mc 6:23 he wept and angrily threatened his friends 8
4Mc 15:19 nor did you weep 9

weep bitterly 1. בכה 2. מרר
Jer 22:10 but weep bitterly for him who goes away 1
Zec 12:10 weep bitterly over him, as . . over a first-born. 2

weep out 1. כלה
1Sm 2:33 spared to weep out his eyes and grieve his heart; 1

weep tears 1. בַּבְּכִי
Isa 22: 4 Look away from me, let me weep bitter tears; 1
weeping *See* red.

weigh 1. אזן 2. כבד 3. מִשְׁקָל 4. שקל 5. תכן 6. תְּקַל(A) 7. αἴρω 8. ἀπό 9. διακρίνω 10. ἵστημι 11. ὁλκή 12. pondero
Gen 24:22 the man took a gold ring weighing a half shekel 3
22 two bracelets for her arms weighing ten gold 3
Num 7:85 each silver plate weighing 130 shekels •
86 golden dishes . . weighing ten shekels apiece •
Jos 7:21 I saw . . and a bar of gold weighing 50 shekels 3
1Sm 2: 3 the LORD is . . and by him actions are weighed. 5
17: 7 and his spear's head weighed 600 shekels of iron; •
2Sm 14:26 he weighed the hair of his head, 200 shekels 4
21:16 whose spear weighed 300 shekels of bronze 3
1Ch 20: 2 he found that it weighed a talent of gold 3
22: 3 as well as bronze in quantities beyond weighing 3
14 silver, and bronze and iron beyond weighing 3
Ezr 8:29 Guard them and keep them until you weigh them 4
33 silver and the gold and the vessels were weighed 4
34 whole was counted and weighed, and the weight 3
Job 6: 2 O that my vexation were weighed 4
28:15 silver cannot be weighed as its price. 4
31: 6 Let me be weighed in a just balance 4
Ps 38: 4 they weigh like a burden too heavy for me. 2
Prv 16: 2 but the LORD weighs the spirit. 5
21: 2 but the LORD weighs the heart. 5
24:12 does not he who weighs the heart perceive it? 5
Ecc 12: 9 weighing and studying and arranging proverbs 1
Isa 33:18 where is he who weighed the tribute? 4
40:12 weighed the mountains in scales 4
Jer 32:10 got witnesses, and weighed the money on scales. 4
Ezk 5: 1 take balances for weighing, and divide the hair. 3
Dan 5:27 TEKEL, you have been weighed in the balances 6
Act 27:13 they weighed anchor and sailed along Crete 7
1Co 14:29 let the others weigh what is said. 9
1Es 8:56 I weighed and gave to them 650 talents of silver 10
62 the silver and the gold were weighed 10
64 The whole was counted and weighed 11
2Es 3:34 Now therefore weigh in a balance our iniquities 12
4: 5 he said to me, "Go, weigh for me the weight of fire 12
36 for he has weighed the age in the balance 12
7:59 Weigh within yourself what you have thought 12
Sir 21:25 will be weighed in the balance. 10
1Mc 14:24 a large gold shield weighing 1,000 minas 11
15:18 have brought a gold shield weighing 1,000 minas. 8
2Mc 9: 8 he could weigh the high mountains in a balance 10

weigh down 1. שחה 2. βαρέω 3. βαρύνω 4. εἰμὶ ἐπί 5. κατά
Prv 12:25 Anxiety in a man's heart weighs him down 1
Lke 21:34 lest your hearts be weighed down 2
Wis 9:15 for a perishable body weighs down the soul 2
Sir 6:21 will weigh him down like a heavy testing stone 4
38:19 the life of the poor man weighs down his heart. 5

weigh out 1. נְטִיל 2. שקל 3. תכן 4. ἵστημι
Gen 23:16 Abraham weighed out for Ephron the silver 2
2Kg 12:11 they would give the money that was weighed out 3
Ezr 8:25 And I weighed out to them the silver and the gold 2
26 I weighed out into their hand 650 talents 2
Isa 46: 6 from the purse, and weigh out silver in the scales 2
Jer 32: 9 I bought . . and weighed out the money to him 2
Zep 1:11 all who weigh out silver are cut off. 1
Zec 11:12 they weighed out as my wages 30 shekels 2
1Es 8:55 I weighed out to them the silver and the gold 4

weigh the value 1. ἄξιος
Sir 26:15 no balance can weigh the value of a chaste soul. 1

weight 1. אֶבֶן 2. טֹרַח 3. כָּבוֹד 4. מִשְׁקוֹל 5. מִשְׁקָל 6. βάρος 7. ὄγκος 8. ὁλκή 9. σταθμίον 10. σταθμός 11. pondus
Gen 23:16 according to the weights current •
Lev 19:35 in measures of length or weight or quantity 5
36 You shall have just balances, just weights 1
26:26 and shall deliver your bread again by weight 5
Num 7:13 one silver plate whose weight was 130 shekels 5
19 one silver plate, whose weight was 130 shekels 5
25 one silver plate, whose weight was 130 shekels 5
31 one silver plate whose weight was 130 shekels 5
37 one silver plate, whose weight was 130 shekels 5
43 one silver plate, whose weight was 130 shekels 5
49 one silver plate, whose weight was 130 shekels 5
55 one silver plate, whose weight was 130 shekels 5
61 one silver plate, whose weight was 130 shekels 5
67 one silver plate, whose weight was 130 shekels 5
73 one silver plate, whose weight was 130 shekels 5
79 one silver plate, whose weight was 130 shekels 5
Deu 1:12 How can I bear alone the weight and burden of you 2
25:13 not . . two kinds of weights, a large and a small. 1
15 full and just weight . . a full and just measure 1
Jdg 8:26 the weight of the golden earrings that he 5
1Sm 17: 5 the weight of the coat was 5,000 shekels 5
2Sm 12:30 he took the crown . . the weight of it was a talent 5
14:26 200 shekels by the king's weight. 1
1Kg 7:47 the weight of the bronze was not found out. 5
10:14 the weight of gold that came to Solomon 5
2Kg 25:16 bronze of all these vessels was beyond weight. 5
1Ch 21:25 David paid Ornan 600 shekels of gold by weight 5
28:14 the weight of gold for all golden vessels 5
14 weight of silver vessels for each service 5
15 weight of the golden lampstands and their lamps 5
15 weight of gold for each lampstand and its lamps 5
15 weight of silver for a lampstand and its lamps 5
16 weight of gold for each table for the showbread 5
17 for the golden bowls and the weight of each; 5
17 for the silver bowls and the weight of each. 5
18 for the altar of incense . . and its weight; 5
2Ch 3: 9 The weight of the nails was one shekel to 50 5
4:18 weight of the bronze was not ascertained. 5
9:13 weight of gold that came to Solomon in one year 5
Ezr 8:30 took over the weight of the silver and the gold 5
34 weight of everything was recorded. 5
Job 28:25 When he gave to the wind its weight 5
Prv 11: 1 but a just weight is his delight. 1
16:11 all the weights in the bag are his work. 1
20:10 Diverse weights and diverse measures are both 1
23 Diverse weights are an abomination to the LORD 1
Isa 22:24 hang on him the whole weight of his father's house 3
Jer 52:20 bronze of all these things was beyond weight. 5
Ezk 4:10 the food which you eat shall be by weight 4
16 they shall eat bread by weight 5
Mic 6:11 acquit the man . . with a bag of deceitful weights? 1
Zec 5: 8 and thrust down the leaden weight upon its mouth. 1
Joh 19:39 about 100 pounds' weight. •
2Co 4:17 preparing for us an eternal weight of glory 6
Heb 12: 1 Therefore . . let us also lay aside every weight 7
1Es 8:64 the weight of everything was recorded 8
2Es 4: 5 he said to me, "Go, weigh for me the weight of fire 11
Jdt 7: 4 the hills will bear their weight. 6
Wis 11:20 measure and number and weight. 10
Sir 13: 2 Do not lift a weight beyond your strength 6
16:25 I will impart instruction by weight 10
42: 4 of accuracy with scales and weights 9
7 let it be by number and weight 10
weight *See also* feel, worth.

weight down 1. κατακάμπτω
Man 1:10 I am weighted down with many an iron fetter 1

full weight 1. מִשְׁקָל
Gen 43:21 in the mouth of his sack, our money in full weight; 1

lean weight 1. סמך
Jdg 16:29 and he leaned his weight upon them 1

weighty 1. נָטֵל 2. βαρύς 3. gravis
Prv 27: 3 A stone is heavy, and sand is weighty 1
2Co 10:10 For they say, "His letters are weighty and strong 2
2Es 13:56 and explain weighty and wondrous matters to you. 3
weighty *See also* matter.

welcome 1. שמח 2. שמח עַל 3. ἀναδέχομαι 4. ἀποδέχομαι 5. ἀσπάζομαι 6. δέχομαι 7. εἰσδέχομαι 8. εἴσοδος 9. ἐπιδέχομαι 10. καλός 11. παραδέχομαι 12. προσδέχομαι 13. προσλαμβάνω 14. συνάγω 15. ὑγιαίνω ἔρχομαι 16. ὑποδέχομαι 17. ὡραῖος
2Kg 20:13 Hezeki'ah welcomed them, and he showed them all 2
Isa 39: 2 Hezeki'ah welcomed them; 1
Mat 25:35 I was a stranger and you welcomed me 14
38 when did we see thee a stranger and welcome thee 14
43 I was a stranger and you did not welcome me 14
Lke 8:40 Now when Jesus returned, the crowd welcomed him 4
9:11 he welcomed them and spoke to them of the kingdom 4
Joh 4:45 he came to Galilee, the Galileans welcomed him 6
Act 15: 4 were welcomed by the church and the apostles 11
25:13 Agrippa . . arrived at Caesare'a to welcome Festus. 5
28: 2 they kindled a fire and welcomed us all 13
30 welcomed all who came to him 4
Rom 14: 1 As for the man who is weak in faith, welcome him 13
3 for God has welcomed him. 13
15: 7 Welcome one another, therefore 13
7 therefore, as Christ has welcomed you 13
2Co 6:17 touch nothing unclean; then I will welcome you 7
1Th 1: 9 report concerning us what a welcome we had 8
3Jn 1:10 he refuses himself to welcome the brethren 9
10 and also stops those who want to welcome them 9
Tob 5:13 Tobit said to him, "You are welcome, my brother 15
11:17 he blessed her, saying, "Welcome, daughter! 15
Jdt 3: 7 welcomed him with garlands and dances 6
Sir 15: 2 like the wife of his youth she will welcome him. 12
35:20 Mercy is as welcome when he afflicts them 17
41: 2 O death, how welcome is your sentence 10
1Mc 10: 1 They welcomed him, and there he began to reign. 9
12: 8 Onias welcomed the envoy with honor 9
2Mc 3: 9 he . . had been kindly welcomed by the high priest 4
4:22 He was welcomed magnificently by Jason 4
6:19 welcoming death with honor 3
4Mc 13:17 Abraham and Isaac and Jacob will welcome us 16
welcome *See also* gift, give.

welfare 1. טוֹב 2. שָׁלוֹם 3. ἀγαθός 4. εἰρήνη 5. σύμφορος 6. σωτηρία
Gen 43:27 he inquired about their welfare, and said 2
Exd 18: 7 and they asked each other of their welfare 2
Jdg 18:15 young Levite . . and asked him of his welfare. 2
Neh 2:10 seek the welfare of the children of Israel. 1
Est 10: 3 he sought the welfare of his people 1
Ps 35:27 LORD, who delights in the welfare of his servant! 2
Prv 3: 2 abundant welfare will they give you. 2
Isa 38:17 Lo, it was for my welfare 2
Jer 14:11 Do not pray for the welfare of this people. 1
15: 5 Who will turn aside to ask about your welfare? 2
29: 7 seek the welfare of the city where I have sent you 2
7 for in its welfare you will find your welfare. 2
7 for in its welfare you will find your welfare. 2
11 says the LORD, plans for welfare and not for evil 2
38: 4 this man is not seeking . . welfare of this people 2
Php 2:20 who will be genuinely anxious for your welfare. •
1Mc 12:22 please write us concerning your welfare; 4
2Mc 4: 5 having in view the welfare . . of all the people. 5
11:19 to help promote your welfare. 3
13: 3 not for the sake of his country's welfare 6

well 1. אֲבָל 2. טוֹב 3. יטב 4. לָכֵן 5. מְאֹד 6. שָׁלוֹם 7. ἀγαθός 8. ἀκριβῶς 9. βελτίων 10. εὖ 11. εὐοδόω 12. καλός 13. καλῶς 14. ὀρθῶς 15. πᾶς 16. τοίνυν 17. χρηστῶς 18. sic
Gen 13:10 the Jordan valley was well watered everywhere •
29: 6 He said to them, "Is it well with him? 6
6 They said, "It is well; and see, Rachel 6
37:14 Go now, see if it is well with your brothers 6
40:14 remember me, when it is well with you 3
Exd 4:14 Aaron . . the Levite? I know that he can speak well; †
Num 11:18 For it was well with us in Egypt. 2
13:30 occupy it; for we are well able to overcome it. •
Deu 15:16 since he fares well with you 2
19:13 so that it may be well with you. 2
Jos 23: 1 and Joshua was old and well advanced in years •
2 I am now old and well advanced in years; •
Jdg 8: 7 Gideon said, "Well then, when the LORD has given 4
9:16 if you have dealt well with Jerubba'al and his 2
Rut 2:22 It is well . . that you go out with his maidens 2
3: 1 seek a home for you, that it may be well with you? 3
13 if he will do the part of the next of kin . . well; 2
1Sm 9:10 Saul said to his servant, "Well said; come, let us go. 2
12:14 If you will fear the LORD and . . it will be well; •
16:17 Provide for me a man who can play well, and bring 3
19: 4 Jonathan spoke well of David to Saul his father 2
20: 3 Your father knows well that I have found favor †
7 If he says, 'Good!' it will be well with your servant; 6
24:18 you have dealt well with me 2
2Sm 18:28 Then Ahi'ma-az cried out to the king, "All is well. 6
29 Is it well with the young man Ab'salom? 6
32 king said . . "Is it well with the young man Ab'salom? 6
20: 9 Jo'ab said to Ama'sa, "Is it well with you, my brother? 6
1Kg 2:18 said, "Very well; I will speak for you to the king. 2
18:24 And all the people answered, "It is well spoken. 2
2Kg 4:14 Well, she has no son, and her husband is old. 1
23 She said, "It will be well. 6
26 Is it well with you? Is it well with your husband? 6
26 Is it well with you? Is it well with your husband? 6
26 Is it well with you? . . Is it well with the child? 6
26 And she answered, "It is well. 6
5:21 he alighted . . to meet him, and said, "Is all well? 6
22 he said, "All is well. My master has sent me to say 6
9:11 Is all well? Why did this mad fellow come to you? 6
25:24 serve the king . . and it shall be well with you. 3
Job 13: 9 Will it be well with you when he searches you out? 2
Ps 75: 8 there is a cup, with foaming wine, well mixed; †
78:29 they ate and were well filled 5
112: 5 well with the man who deals generously and lends 2
119:65 Thou hast dealt well with thy servant, O LORD 2
140 Thy promise is well tried 5
128: 2 you shall be happy, and it shall be well with you. 2
Prv 27:23 Know well the condition of your flocks †
31:27 She looks well to the ways of her household •
Ecc 8:12 I know that it will be well with those who fear God 2
13 but it will not be well with the wicked 2
Isa 3:10 it shall be well with them, for they shall eat 2
25: 6 feast . . of wine on the lees well refined. •
Jer 1:12 Then the LORD said to me, "You have seen well 3
4:10 saying, 'It shall be well with you'; 6
7:23 that I command you, that it may be well with you. 3
22:15 righteousness? Then it was well with him. 2
16 the cause of the poor and needy; then it was well. 2
23:17 who despise . . the LORD, 'It shall be well with you'; 6
38:20 in what I say to you, and it shall be well with you 3
39:12 Take him, look after him well and do him no harm •
40: 4 to Babylon, come, and I will look after you well; •
9 serve . . Babylon, and it shall be well with you. 3
42: 6 that it may be well with us when we obey 3
Ezk 24:10 kindle the fire, boil well the flesh •
33:32 and plays well on an instrument, for they hear 3
44: 5 And the LORD said to me, "Son of man, mark well †
5 mark well those who may be admitted to the temple †
Dan 3:15 fall down and worship the image . . well and good; •
Mat 15: 7 You hypocrites! Well did Isaiah prophesy of you 13
17: 4 Lord, it is well that we are here 12
Mrk 7: 6 Well did Isaiah prophesy of you hypocrites 13
37 He had done all things well 13
9: 5 Master, it is well that we are here 12
12:28 seeing that he answered them well, asked him 13
Lke 6:26 Woe to you, when all men speak well of you 13

48 because it had been well built. 13
9:33 Master, it is well that we are here 12
13: 9 if it bears fruit next year, well and good *
20:39 Teacher, you have spoken well. 13
Act 15:29 you will do well. Farewell 10
Rom 2: 7 who by patience in well-doing seek for glory 7
1Co 7: 1 It is well for a man not to touch a woman. 12
8 it is well for them to remain single as I do. 12
26 it is well for a person to remain as he is. 12
37 to keep her as his betrothed, he will do well. 13
38 So that he who marries his betrothed does well; 13
38 he who refrains from marriage will do better. 7
9:26 Well, I do not run aimlessly 16
14:17 For you may give thanks well enough 13
Gal 5: 7 You were running well 13
6: 9 let us not grow weary in well-doing 12
Eph 6: 3 that it may be well with you 10
1Th 5: 2 you yourselves know well that the day of the Lord 8
1Ti 3: 4 He must manage his own household well 13
7 moreover he must be well thought of by outsiders 12
12 let them manage . . their households well; 13
13 those who serve well as deacons 13
5:10 she must be well attested for her good deeds *
17 the elders who rule well 13
2Ti 1:18 you well know all the service he rendered 9
Heb 11:39 all these, though well attested by their faith *
13: 9 is well that the heart be strengthened by grace 12
Jas 2: 8 If you really fulfill the . . law . . you do well. 13
19 You believe that God is one; you do well. 13
2Pe 1:19 You will do well to pay attention to this 13
3Jn 1: 2 I know that it is well with your soul. 11
6 You will do well to send them on their journey 13
2Es 3:35 what nation has kept thy commandments so well? 18
Tob 14: 9 so that it may be well with you. 13
Jdt 10:16 he will treat you well. 10
11: 4 No one will hurt you, but all will treat you well 10
22 God has done well to send you before the people 10
AEs 16:17 You will therefore do well 13
Wis 8: 1 she orders all things well. 17
Sir 10: 1 the rule . . will be well ordered. 6
14:11 treat yourself well, according to your means 10
Aza 1: 7 that it might go well with us. 10
1Mc 8:23 May all go well with the Romans 13
11:43 you will do well to send me men who will help me 14
2Mc 10:18 well equipped to withstand a siege 15
32 especially well garrisoned 10
11:26 You will do well, therefore, to send word to them 10
12:43 In doing this he acted very well and honorably 13
14:37 and was very well thought 13
15:38 If it is well told and to the point 13
3Mc 3:15 gladly treating them well. 10

well (2) 1. גַּם 2. וְ 3. וְעַד 4. כְּ 5. כְּמוֹ 6. לְעֻמַּת 7. עִם 8. *αὐτός* 9. *ἔτι* 10. *καθώς* 11. *καθώς καί* 12. *καί* 13. *προστίθημι* 14. *τε* 15. *ὡς* 16. et

Gen 50: 8 as well as all the household of Joseph 2
Lev 7:10 all the sons of Aaron, one as well as another *
24:16 the sojourner as well as the native 4
Deu 5:14 that your manservant . . may rest as well as you. 4
29:15 as well as with him who stands here with us 2
Jos 1:15 LORD gives rest to your brethren as well as to you 4
8:33 And all Israel, sojourner as well as homeborn 4
Jdg 15: 5 standing grain, as well as the olive orchards. 3
2Kg 12:12 as well as to buy timber and quarried stone 2
22: 6 as well as for buying timber and quarried stone 2
1Ch 22: 3 as well as bronze in quantities beyond weighing 2
26:17 as well as two and two at the storehouse; *
Job 12: 3 I have understanding as well as you; 5
Ecc 4:15 living . . as well as that youth, who was to stand 7
7:14 God has made the one as well as the other 6
Sng 7:13 over . . are all choice fruits, new as well as old 1
Ezk 18: 4 soul of the father as well as the soul of the son *
Mat 5:40 your coat, let him have your cloak as well; 12
6:33 all these things shall be yours as well. 13
Lke 12:31 these things shall be yours as well. 13
Act 17:12 a few Greek women of high standing as well as men. 12
Rom 1:13 as well as among the rest of the Gentiles 11
16: 2 a helper of many and of myself as well. 8
1Co 16:18 for they refreshed my spirit as well as yours. 12
Heb 5: 3 as well as for those of the people. 10
7:12 necessarily a change in the law as well. 12
1Pe 5: 1 as well as a partaker in the glory that is to be 12
2Es 7:11 why will it not be so then as well? 16
9:36 as well as our heart which received it; 16
14:12 as well as half of the tenth part 16
Sir 38:27 labors by night as well as by day 15
1Mc 12:45 as well as the other strongholds 12
2Mc 12: 2 as well as Hieronymus and Demophon 9
3Mc 5:48 as well as by the trampling of the crowd 14

well (3) 1. טוֹב 2. שָׁלוֹם 3. *ἰσχύω* 4. *ῥώννυμι* 5. *σῴζω* 6. *ὑγιαίνω* 7. *ὑγιής*

Gen 43:27 Is your father well, the old man of whom you spoke? 2
28 They said, "Your servant our father is well 2
1Sm 16:16 when . . he will play it, and you will be well. 1
23 so Saul was refreshed, and was well 1
Mat 9:12 Those who are well have no need of a physician 3
Mrk 2:17 Those who are well have no need of a physician 3
Lke 5:31 Those who are well have no need of a physician 6
7:10 they found the slave well. 6
8:50 Do not fear; only believe, and she shall be well. 5
Joh 5:14 See, you are well! 7
7:23 on the sabbath I made a man's whole body well? 7
Act 4:10 by him this man is standing before you well. 7
Tob 10: 6 Be still and stop worrying; he is well. 6
Sir 17:28 he who is alive and well sings the Lord's praises. 7
30:14 Better off is a poor man who is well and strong 7
2Mc 9:20 If you and your children are well 4
11:28 If you are well, it is as we desire 4

well (4) 1. בְּאֵר 2. בֹּאר 3. בּוֹר 4. מַעְיָן 5. עַיִן 6. *πηγή* 7. *φρέαρ*

Gen 16:14 Therefore the well was called Beer-la'hai-roi; 1
21:19 opened her eyes, and she saw a well of water; 1
25 to Abim'elech about a well of water 1
30 you may be a witness for me that I dug this well. 1
24:11 kneel down outside the city by the well of water 1
20 she . . ran again to the well to draw 1
26:15 filled with earth all the wells 1
18 Isaac dug again the wells of water 1
19 found there a well of springing water 1
20 he called the name of the well Esek 1
21 Then they dug another well, and they quarreled 1
22 he moved from there and dug another well 1
25 And there Isaac's servants dug a well. 1
32 came and told him about the well which they had dug 1
29: 2 As he looked, he saw a well in the field 1
2 for out of that well the flocks were watered. 1
2 The stone on the well's mouth was large 1
3 would roll the stone from the mouth of the well 1
3 back in its place upon the mouth of the well. 1
8 the stone is rolled from the mouth of the well; 1
10 Jacob . . rolled the stone from the well's mouth 1
Exd 2:15 Moses fled . . and he sat down by a well. 1
Num20:17 neither will we drink water from a well; 1
21:16 Beer . . the well of which the LORD said to Moses 1
17 Israel sang this song: "Spring up, O well!-Sing to it!- 1
18 the well which the princes dug, which the nobles 1
22 we will not drink the water of a well; 1
1Sm 19:22 went to Ramah, and came to the great well . . in Secu; 3
2Sm 17:18 a man at Bahu'rim, who had a well in his courtyard; 1
19 took and spread a covering over the well's mouth 1
21 After they had gone, the men came up out of the well 1
23:15 some one would give me water to drink from the well 2
16 and drew water out of the well of Bethlehem 2
2Kg 19:24 I dug wells and drank foreign waters *
1Ch 11:17 from the well of Bethlehem which is by the gate! 3
18 drew water out of the well of Bethlehem 3
Neh 2:13 went . . to the Jackal's Well and to the Dung Gate 5
Prv 5:15 flowing water from your own well. 1
23:27 an adventuress is a narrow well. 1
Sng 4:15 a garden fountain, a well of living water 1
Isa 12: 3 you will draw water from the wells of salvation. 4
37:25 I dug wells and drank waters *
Jer 6: 7 As a well keeps its water fresh 3
Lke 14: 5 a son or an ox that has fallen into a well 7
Joh 4: 6 Jacob's well was there, and so Jesus . . sat down 6
6 Jesus . . sat down beside the well. 6
11 you have nothing to draw with, and the well is deep; 7
12 Jacob, who gave us the well, and drank from it 7

well *See* advanced, consider, deal, direct, disciplined, disposed, done, drawn, fare, fed, fortified, go, govern, instruct, keep, known, look, make, mixed, nigh, ordered, please, pleased, speak, versed.

do well 1. טוֹב 2. יטב 3. *εὖγε*

Gen 4: 7 If you do well, will you not be accepted? 2
7 if you do not do well, sin is couching at the door; 2
1Kg 8:18 Whereas . . you did well that it was in your heart; 1
2Kg 10:30 you have done well in carrying out what is right 1
2Ch 6: 8 you did well that it was in your heart; 1
Ps 49:18 a man gets praise when he does well for himself 2
Jon 4: 4 the LORD said, "Do you do well to be angry? 2
9 to Jonah, "Do you do well to be angry for the plant? 2
9 he said, "I do well to be angry, angry enough to die. 2
Lke 19:17 he said to him, 'Well done, good servant! 3

full well 1. quidem

2Es 8:58 though knowing full well that they must die. 1

well off 1. טוֹב 2. יעל 3. *ἀγαθός* 4. *περισσεύω*

Job 35: 3 How am I better off than if I had sinned? 2
Ecc 6: 3 I say that an untimely birth is better off than he 1
1Co 8: 8 and no better off if we do. 4
Sir 30:14 Better off is a poor man who is well and strong 3

right well 1. מְאֹד

Ps 139:14 Thou knowest me right well; 1

well up 1. *ἅλλομαι* 2. ascendo

Joh 4:14 a spring of water welling up to eternal life. 1
2Es 3: 1 and my thoughts welled up in my heart 2

very well 1. לָכֵן 2. *καλός* 3. *καλῶς* 4. *ὀρθῶς*

1Sm 28: 2 Very well, you shall know what your servant can 1
2 Very well, I will make you my bodyguard for life. 1
Act 25:10 I have done no wrong, as you know very well. 3
Sus 1:55 Very well! You have lied against your own head 4
59 Daniel said to him, "Very well! You also have lied 4
2Mc 3: 1 the laws were very well observed 2

well-doing 1. *καλοποιέω*

2Th 3:13 Brethren, do not be weary in well-doing. 1

well-fed 1. זוּן

Jer 5: 8 They were well-fed lusty stallions 1

well-set *See* hair.

welt 1. *μώλωψ*

Sir 28:17 The blow of a whip raises a welt 1

welter 1. בוס

Ezk 16: 6 passed by you, and saw you weltering in your blood 1
22 you were naked and bare, weltering in your blood. 1

west 1. אָחוֹר 2. אַחֲרוֹן 3. אַחֲרֵי 4. יָם 5. מְבוֹא הַשֶּׁמֶשׁ 6. מַעֲרָב 7. עֵבֶר 8. *δυσμή* 9. *ἐπὶ δυσμάς* 10. occidens

Gen 12: 8 with Bethel on the west and Ai on the east; 4
28:14 you shall spread abroad to the west 4
Exd 10:19 the LORD turned a very strong west wind 4
27:12 for the breadth of the court on the west side 4
38:12 for the west side were hangings of 50 cubits 4
Num 3:23 encamp behind the tabernacle on the west 4
35: 5 shall measure . . for the west side 2,000 cubits 4
Deu 11:30 beyond the Jordan, west of the road, toward 3
Jos 5: 1 Amorites that were beyond the Jordan to the west 4
8: 9 and lay between Bethel and Ai, to the west of Ai; 4
12 between Bethel and Ai, to the west of the city 4
13 and its rear guard west of the city. 4
11: 2 in the lowland, and in Naphoth-dor on the west 4
3 sent . . to the Canaanites in the east and the west 4
12: 7 Joshua . . defeated on the west side of the Jordan 4
15: 8 that lies over against the valley . . on the west 4
10 the boundary circles west of Ba'alah to . . Se'ir 4
12 And the west boundary was the Great Sea with its 4
19:26 on the west it touches Carmel and Shihor-lib'nath 4
34 touching . . Asher on the west, and Judah 4
22: 7 a possession . . in the land west of the Jordan. 4
23: 4 from the Jordan to the Great Sea in the west. 5
Jdg 18:12 to this day; behold, it is west of Kir'iath-je'arim. 3
20:33 in ambush rushed out of their place west of Geba. 8
1Kg 4:24 all the region west of the Euphra'tes 7
24 over all the kings west of the Euphra'tes; 7
7:25 twelve oxen . . three facing west, three facing 4
1Ch 9:24 on the four sides, east, west, north and south; 4
12:15 put to flight . . to the east and to the west. 6
26:16 For Shuppim and Hosah it came out for the west 6
18 for the parbar on the west there were four 6
2Ch 4: 4 It stood upon twelve oxen . . three facing west 4
33:14 outer wall for the city of David west of Gihon 6
Job 18:20 They of the west are appalled at his day 2
Ps 75: 6 For not from the east or from the west 6
103:12 as far as the east is from the west 6
107: 3 gathered in from . . the east and from the west 6
Isa 9:12 the Philistines on the west devour Israel 1
11:14 upon the shoulder of the Philistines in the west 4
24:14 the majesty of the LORD they shout from the west. 4
43: 5 from the east, and from the west I will gather you; 6
45: 6 from the rising of the sun and from the west 6
49:12 and lo, these from the north and from the west 4
59:19 they shall fear the name of the LORD from the west 6
Ezk 41:12 that was facing the temple yard on the west side 4
15 building facing the yard which was at the west 3
42:19 Then he turned to the west side and measured 4
45: 7 the city, on the west and on the east 4
47:20 On the west side, the Great Sea 4
20 This shall be the west side. 4
48: 1 and extending from the east side to the west, 4
2 territory of Dan, from the east side to the west 4
3 territory of Asher, from the east side to the west 4
4 from the east side to the west, Manas'seh 4
5 of Manas'seh, from the east side to the west 4
6 from the east side to the west, Reuben, one portion. 4
7 from the east side to the west, Judah, one portion. 4
8 territory of Judah, from the east side to the west 4
8 tribal portions, from the east side to the west 4
16 the east side 4,500, and the west side 4,500. 4
17 on the east 250, and on the west 250. 4
18 10,000 cubits to the east, and 10,000 to the west 4
21 from the 25,000 cubits to the west border 4
23 tribes: from the east side to the west, Benjamin 4
24 from the east side to the west, Simeon, one portion 4
25 from the east side to the west, Is'sachar 4
26 the east side to the west, Zeb'ulun, one portion. 4
27 from the east side to the west, Gad, one portion. 4
34 On the west side, which is to be 4,500 cubits 4
Dan 8: 5 he-goat came from the west across the . . earth 6
Hos 11:10 and his sons shall come trembling from the west; 4
Zec 6: 6 the white ones go toward the west country *
8: 7 from the east country and from the west country; 5
14: 4 split in two from east to west 4
Mat 8:11 I tell you, many will come from east and west 8
24:27 lightning . . shines as far as the west 8
Lke 12:54 When you see a cloud rising in the west 8
13:29 come from east and west, and from north and south 8

Rev 21:13 and on the west three gates. 8
2Es 15:38 from the north, and another part from the west. 10
39 driven violently toward the south and west. 10
Jdt 1: 7 all who lived in the west 8
2: 6 Go and attack the whole west country 9
19 cover the whole face of the earth to the west 8
5: 4 they alone, of all who live in the west 8
Bar 4:37 they are coming, gathered from east and west 8
5: 5 see your children gathered from west and east 8

west *See also* side.

western 1. אַחֲרוֹן 2. יָם 3. יָמָּה
Num34: 6 western boundary, you shall have the Great Sea 2
6 Sea and its coast . . your western boundary. 2
Deu 11:24 from the . . river Euphra'tes, to the western sea. 1
34: 2 all the land of Judah as far as the Western Sea 1
Jos 18:14 goes . . turning on the western side southward 2
14 boundary goes . . This forms the western side. 2
Ezk 45: 7 extending from the western to the eastern 2
46:19 I saw a place at the extreme western end of them. 3
48:10 10,000 cubits in breadth on the western side 2
Jol 2:20 the eastern sea, and his rear into the western sea; 1
Zec 14: 8 eastern sea and half of them to the western sea; 1

westward 1. יָם 2. יָמָּה 3. לְיָמָּה 4. לְמַעֲרָב 5. מַעֲרָבָה
Gen 13:14 southward and eastward and westward; 2
Exd 26:22 for the rear of the tabernacle westward 1
27 the side of the tabernacle at the rear westward. 1
36:27 for the rear of the tabernacle westward he made 1
32 frames of the tabernacle at the rear westward. 2
Deu 3:27 lift up your eyes westward and northward 2
Jos 16: 3 then it goes down westward to the territory 1
8 the boundary goes westward to the brook Kanah 1
18:12 then up through the hill country westward; 1
19:11 its boundary goes up westward, and on to Mar'eal 3
34 the boundary turns westward to Az'noth-tabor 1
1Ch 7:28 westward Gezer and its towns 4
26:30 the oversight of Israel westward of the Jordan 5
Ezk 48:21 westward from the 25,000 cubits to the west 2
Dan 8: 4 charging westward and northward and southward; 2

wet 1. מלא 2. רטב 3. צבע (A) 4. βρέχω
Job 24: 8 They are wet with the rain of the mountains 2
Sng 5: 2 my head is wet with dew, my locks with the drops 1
Dan 4:15 Let him be wet with the dew of heaven; 3
23 let him be wet with the dew of heaven; 3
25 wet with the dew of heaven, 3
33 body was wet with the dew of heaven 3
5:21 body was wet with the dew of heaven 3
Lke 7:38 she began to wet his feet with her tears 4
44 she has wet my feet with her tears 4

whale 1. κῆτος
Mat 12:40 three nights in the belly of the whale 1
Aza 1:57 whales and all creatures that move in the waters 1

what 1. אִי 2. אֵי זֶה 3. אֵיךְ 4. אֵיכָה 5. דָּבָר 6. דְּבַר אֲשֶׁר 7. הַמַּעֲשֶׂה אֲשֶׁר 8. הִנֵּה 9. זֶה 10. כַּאֲשֶׁר 11. כָּזֶה 12. כַּמָּה 13. לָמָּה 14. מַדּוּעַ 15. מִי 16. מִי זֶה 17. מִלָּה 18. מִן 19. מַעֲשֶׂה 20. דִּי (A) 21. מָה (A) 22. מָה דִי (A) 23. מָן (A) 24. ἀλλά 25. γάρ 26. ἐάν 27. εἶπον 28. εἴ τι 29. ἔργον 30. ἤ 31. καθ' ὅ 32. καθώς 33. κατά 34. λόγος 35. μέλος 36. ὁ 37. οἷος 38. ὁποῖος 39. ὅς 40. ὅσος 41. ὅ τι 42. οὗτος 43. πόθεν 44. ποῖος 45. πόσος 46. ποταπός 47. ποῦ 48. πῶς 49. τις 50. ὡς 51. qui 52. quis 53. ut
Gen 33: 8 Esau said, "What do you mean by all his company 15
15 What need is there? Let me find favor in the sight 13
Exd 13: 8 It is because of what the LORD did for me 9
18:17 Moses' father-in-law said to him, "What you are doing 5
20 make them know . . what they must do. 19
29: 1 this is what you shall do to them to consecrate 5
Num22:20 but only what I bid you, that shall you do. 5
30: 1 This is what the LORD has commanded. 5
Deu 3:24 what god is there in heaven or on earth who can do 15
17:10 Then . . do according to what they declare to you 6
20: 8 What man is there that is fearful 15
Jos 7:20 I have sinned . . and this is what I did 11
14: 6 You know what the LORD said to Moses 6
Jdg 13:17 What is your name, so that, when your words come 15
21: 8 What one is there of the tribes of Israel that did 15
1Sm 28:21 I . . have hearkened to what you have said to me. 6
2Sm 7:18 Who am I . . and what is my house, that thou hast 15
23 What other nation on earth is like thy people 15
15: 2 Ab'salom would call . . "From what city are you? 9
26 here I am, let him do to me what seems good to him. 10
18:11 What, you saw him! Why then did you not strike him 8
1Kg 1:41 he said, "What does this uproar in the city mean? 14
21: 4 sullen because of what Naboth . . had said to him; 6
2Kg 6:15 the servant said, "Alas, my master! What shall we do? 4
1Ch 17:16 said, "Who am I, O LORD God, and what is my house 15
21 What other nation on earth is like thy people 15
29:14 But who am I, and what is my people 15
Ezr 5: 4 What are the names of the men who are building 23
6: 8 regarding what you shall do for these elders 22
8:17 telling them what to say to Iddo and his brethren 5
Neh 6:11 what man such as I could go into the temple 15
Job 15:17 what I have seen I will declare 9
23: 5 I would learn what he would answer me 17
34: 7 What man is like Job, who drinks up scoffing 15
38:24 What is the way to the place where the light is 2
Ps 34:12 What man is there who desires life 15
77:13 What god is great like our God? 15
89:48 What man can live and never see death? 15
Ecc 1: 9 and what has been done is what will be done; 18
2:17 what is done under the sun was grievous to me; 18
3:11 he cannot find out what God has done 7
Sng 3: 6 What is that coming up from the wilderness 15
Isa 66: 1 is the house . . and what is the place of my rest? 2
Jer 49:19 What shepherd can stand before me? 16
50:44 What shepherd can stand before me? 16
Dan 2:22 he knows what is in the darkness, 21
23 hast now made known to me what we asked of thee 20
28 made known . . what will be in the latter days. 22
29 in bed came thoughts of what would be hereafter 22
29 who reveals mysteries made known to you what is 22
45 made known to the king what shall be hereafter. 22
4:35 none can . . say to him, "What doest thou? 21
Jon 1: 8 What is your country? And of what people are you? 1
Mic 1: 5 What is the transgression of Jacob? 15
5 And what is the sin of the house of Judah? 15
Zep 2:15 What a desolation she has become 3
Zec 2: 2 To measure Jerusalem, to see what is its breadth 12
2 what is its breadth and what is its length. 12
4: 7 What are you, O great mountain? 15
Mal 1:13 What a weariness this is,' you say 18
Mat 1:22 took place to fulfil what the Lord had spoken 36
2: 7 ascertained from them what time the star 36
15 This was to fulfil what the Lord had spoken 36
17 Then was fulfilled what was spoken 36
23 Nazareth, that what was spoken by the prophets 36
4:14 that what was spoken by the prophet Isaiah 36
6: 8 for your Father knows what you need before you 39
8:17 This was to fulfil what was spoken by the prophet 36
33 they told everything, and what had happened 36
10:27 What I tell you in the dark, utter in the light 39
27 what you hear whispered, proclaim 39
11: 4 Go and tell John what you hear and see 39
12: 2 your disciples are doing what is not lawful to do 39
17 This was to fulfil what was spoken by the prophet 36
13:12 even what he has will be taken away. 39
17 men longed to see what you see, and did not see it 39
17 and to hear what you hear, and did not hear it. 39
19 and snatches away what is sown in his heart 36
19 this is what was sown along the path. 36
20 As for what was sown on rocky ground 36
22 As for what was sown among thorns 36
23 As for what was sown on good soil 36
35 This was to fulfil what was spoken by the prophet 36
15: 5 What you would have gained from me is given to God 39
11 not what goes into the mouth defiles a man 36
11 what comes out of the mouth, this defiles a man. 36
18 what comes out of the mouth 36
20 These are what defile a man 36
16:27 then he will repay every man for what he has done. 33
18:28 'Pay what you owe.' 28
31 his fellow servants saw what had taken place 36
19: 6 What therefore God has joined together 39
17 said to him, "Why do you ask me about what is good? 36
21 If you would be perfect, go, sell what you possess 36
20:14 Take what belongs to you, and go 36
15 to do what I choose with what belongs to me 36
15 to do what I choose with what belongs to me 36
21: 4 to fulfil what was spoken by the prophet, saying 36
21 not only do what has been done to the fig tree 36
23 By what authority are you doing these things 44
24 by what authority I do these things. 44
27 by what authority I do these things. 44
22:31 have you not read what was said to you by God 36
23: 3 but not what they do 33
24:17 to take what is in his house; 36
42 you do not know on what day your Lord is coming. 44
43 in what part of the night the thief was coming 44
25:25 Here you have what is yours.' 36
27 what was my own with interest. 36
29 even what he has will be taken away. 39
26:13 what she has done will be told in memory of her. 39
27: 9 what had been spoken by the prophet Jeremiah 36
54 saw the earthquake and what took place 36
Mrk 1:44 and offer for your cleansing what Moses commanded 39
2:24 Look, why are they doing what is not lawful 39
4:25 from him who has not, even what he has will be taken 39
30 With what can we compare the kingdom of God 48
5:16 those who had seen it told what had happened 48
33 the woman, knowing what had been done to her, came 39
36 But ignoring what they said 34
7:11 What you would have gained from me is Corban' 39
9: 9 he charged them to tell no one what they had seen 39
10: 9 What therefore God has joined together 39
21 go, sell what you have, and give to the poor 40
11: 6 they told them what Jesus had said 32
23 believes that what he says will come to pass 39
28 By what authority are you doing these things 44
29 tell you by what authority I do these things. 44
33 by what authority I do these things. 44
13:37 what I say to you I say to all: Watch. 39
14: 8 She has done what she could 39
9 what she has done will be told in memory of her. 39
Lke 4:23 what we have heard you did at Caper'na-um, do here 40
6: 2 Why are you doing what is not lawful to do 39
3 Jesus answered, "Have you not read what David did 39
32 If you love those who love you, what credit is that 44
33 what credit is that to you 44
34 what credit is that to you 44
46 Why do you call me 'Lord, Lord,' and not do what I tell 39
7:40 he answered, "What is it, Teacher? 27
8:18 what he thinks that he has will be taken away. 39
35 Then people went out to see what had happened 36
9:10 the apostles told him what they had done 40
33 not knowing what he said. 39
36 told no one . . anything of what they had seen. 39
10:23 Blessed are the eyes which see what you see! 39
24 kings desired to see what you see, and did not see 39
24 and to hear what you hear, and did not hear it. 39
12: 3 what you have whispered in private rooms 39
12 what you ought to say. 39
39 at what hour the thief was coming 44
14:22 Sir, what you commanded has been done 39
17:10 we have only done what was our duty.' 39
19:21 you take up what you did not lay down 39
21 reap what you did not sow.' 39
22 a severe man, taking up what I did not lay down 39
22 reaping what I did not sow? 39
26 even what he has will be taken away. 39
20: 2 Tell us by what authority you do these things 44
8 by what authority I do these things. 44
22:60 Peter said, "Man, I do not know what you are saying. 39
Joh 3:11 Truly, truly, I say to you, we speak of what we know 39
11 and bear witness to what we have seen; 39
32 He bears witness to what he has seen and heard 39
4:22 You worship what you do not know; 39
22 we worship what we know 39
8:25 Even what I have told you from the beginning. 41
26 I declare to the world what I have heard from him. 39
38 I speak of what I have seen with my Father 39
38 you do what you have heard from your father. 39
11:46 told them what Jesus had done. 39
12:33 He said this to show by what death he was to die. 44
50 What I say, therefore 39
13: 7 Jesus answered . . "What I am doing you do not know 39
27 What you are going to do, do quickly. 39
29 Buy what we need for the feast 39
15:14 You are my friends if you do what I command you. 39
18:21 what I said to them; they know what I said. 39
32 to show by what death he was to die. 44
19:22 What I have written I have written. 39
21:19 to show by what death he was to glorify God 44
Act 3: 6 I have no silver and gold, but I give you what I have; 39
18 what God foretold 39
4: 7 By what power or by what name did you do this? 44
7 By what power or by what name did you do this? 44
20 cannot but speak of what we have seen and heard. 39
23 reported what the chief priests . . had said 40
7:49 What house will you build for me, says the Lord 44
8:24 nothing of what you have said may come upon me. 39
30 asked, "Do you understand what you are reading? 39
9: 6 you will be told what you are to do. 39
10:15 What God has cleansed, you must not call common. 39
11: 9 'What God has cleansed you must not call common.' 39
14:11 when the crowds saw what Paul had done 39
15:12 what signs and wonders God had done through them 40
17:23 What therefore you worship as unknown 39
21:23 Do therefore what we tell you 39
24 is nothing in what they have been told about you 39
22:15 a witness . . of what you have seen and heard. 39
23:34 he asked to what province he belonged 44
24:13 prove to you what they now bring up against me. 39
26:22 saying nothing but what the prophets . . said 39
28:22 we desire to hear from you what your views are 39
Rom 2:14 Gentiles . . do by nature what the law requires 36
3:27 On what principle? On the principle of works? 44
4:21 that God was able to do what he had promised. 39
7:16 Now if I do what I do not want, I agree that the law is 39
19 but the evil I do not want is what I do. 42
20 Now if I do what I do not want, it is no longer I 39
8:24 For who hopes for what he sees? 39
25 if we hope for what we do not see, we wait for it 39
14:22 no reason to judge himself for what he approves. 39
15:18 except what Christ has wrought through me 39
1Co 1:12 What I mean is that each one of you says 42
2: 9 What no eye has seen, nor ear heard 39
9 what God has prepared for those who love him 39
4: 6 learn by us not to go beyond what is written 39
10:15 judge for yourselves what I say. 39
20 No, I imply that what pagans sacrifice 39
11:22 What! Do you not have houses to eat and drink in? 25
23 what I also delivered to you 39
14:36 What! Did the word of God originate with you 30
37 acknowledge that what I am writing to you 39
15:10 by the grace of God I am what I am 39
36 What you sow does not come to life unless it dies. 39
37 what you sow is not the body which is to be 39
2Co 1:13 For we write you nothing but what you can read 39
2:10 What I have forgiven, if I have forgiven anything 39
5:10 according to what he has done in the body. 39

7:11 what earnestness this godly grief has produced 45
11 what eagerness to clear yourselves 24
11 what indignation, what alarm, what longing 24
11 what indignation, what alarm, what longing 24
11 what indignation, what alarm, what longing 24
11 what longing, what zeal, what punishment 24
11 what longing, what zeal, what punishment 24
8:12 it is acceptable according to what a man has 26
12 not according to what he has not. 36
10:11 what we say by letter when absent 37
11:12 what I do I will continue to do 39
17 (What I am saying 39
12:20 I may come and find you not what I wish 37
20 you may find me not what you wish 37
13: 9 What we pray for is your improvement. 42
Gal 1:20 In what I am writing to you, before God, I do not lie! 39
2: 6 what they were makes no difference to me 38
4:15 What has become of the satisfaction you felt? 47
5:17 to prevent you from doing what you would. 39
Php 1:10 so that you may approve what is excellent 36
3:16 Only let us hold true to what we have attained. 39
4: 9 What you have learned and received and heard 39
Col 3: 5 Put to death therefore what is earthly in you 35
1Th 1: 5 You know what kind of men we proved to be 37
9 report concerning us what a welcome we had 38
1Ti 1: 7 either what they are saying or . . 39
2Ti 2: 2 what you have heard from me 39
7 Think over what I say 39
3:11 what befell me at Antioch, at Ico'nium 37
11 what persecutions I endured 37
14 as for you, continue in what you have learned 39
Tit 1:11 by teaching . . what they have no right to teach. 39
2: 1 as for you, teach what befits sound doctrine. 39
Heb 5: 8 he learned obedience through what he suffered; 39
Jas 1:24 and at once forgets what he was like. 38
4:14 What is your life? 44
1Pe 2:20 For what credit is it, if when you do wrong 44
1Jn 2:24 Let what you heard from the beginning abide 39
24 what you heard from the beginning abides in you 39
3: 1 See what love the Father has given us 46
2Jn 1: 8 that you may not lose what you have worked for 39
3Jn 1:10 So if I come, I will bring up what he is doing 29
Rev 1: 1 show to his servants what must soon take place; 39
11 saying, "Write what you see in a book and send it 39
19 Now write what you see 39
19 what is and what is to take place hereafter. 39
19 what is and what is to take place hereafter. 39
2: 5 Remember then from what you have fallen 43
10 Do not fear what you are about to suffer. 39
24 learned what some call the deep things of Satan 50
25 only hold fast what you have, until I come. 39
3: 3 Remember then what you received and heard; 48
3 you will not know at what hour I will come upon you 44
11 I am coming soon; hold fast what you have 39
4: 1 I will show you what must take place after this. 39
10: 4 Seal up what the seven thunders have said 39
22: 6 to show his servants what must soon take place. 39
1Es 3: 5 Let each of us state what one thing is strongest; 39
23 they do not remember what they have done. 39
4:42 the king said to him, "Ask what you wish 39
46 now, O lord the king, this is what I ask and request 39
2Es 1:21 What more can I do for you? says the Lord. 52
24 What shall I do to you, O Jacob? 52
30 But now, what shall I do to you? 52
34 and have done what is evil in my sight. 51
35 Those . . will do what I have commanded. 51
35 Those . . will do what I have commanded. 51
2: 3 and have done what is evil in my sight. 51
4 now what can I do for you? 52
8 O wicked nation, remember what I did to Sodom 52
3:22 but what was good departed 51
32 Or what tribes have so believed thy covenants 51
35 what nation has kept thy commandments so well? 51
4:21 can understand only what is on the earth 51
21 can understand what is above . . the heavens. 51
25 what will he do for his name, by which we are called? 52
46 For I know what has gone by 51
46 but I do not know what is to come. 52
5: 2 shall be increased beyond what you yourself see 51
2 and beyond what you heard of formerly. 51
19 He heard what I said and left me. 53
41 what will those do who were before us 52
6: 7 What will be the dividing of the times? 51
7:11 what had been made was judged. 51
16 considered in your mind what is to come 51
16 rather than what is now present? 51
21 what they should do to live 52
21 what they should observe to avoid punishment. 52
42 by which all shall see what has been determined 51
58 what is plentiful is of less worth 51
58 for what is more rare is more precious. 51
59 Weigh within yourself what you have thought 51
59 for he who has what is hard to get 51
62 O earth, what have you brought forth 52
67 For what does it profit us 52
72 dealt unfaithfully with what they received. 51
73 What, then, will they have to say in the judgment 52
100 to see what you have described to me? 51
117 For what good is it to all that they live in sorrow 52
118 O Adam, what have you done? 52
119 For what good is it to us 52
126 we did not consider what we should suffer 52
128 he shall suffer what you have said 51
128 he shall receive what I have said. 51
8: 9 womb gives up again what has been created in it 51
11 that what has been fashioned may be nourished 51
14 to what purpose was he made? 52
34 what is man, that thou art angry with him 52
9:33 they did not keep what had been sown in them. 51
42 I said to her, "What has happened to you? Tell me. 52
10: 6 do you not see our mourning, and what has happened 51
23 And, what is more than all, the seal of Zion 51
25 While I was wondering what this meant 52
31 What is the matter with you? 52
32 I saw, and still see, what I am unable to explain. 51
35 For I have seen what I did not know 51
35 and I have heard what I do not understand. 51
49 you began to console her for what had happened. 51
59 what the Most High will do to those 51
11:36 Look before you and consider what you see. 51
12:41 and what harm have we done you 52
13:18 what is reserved for the last days 51
20 and not to see what shall happen in the last days. 51
52 explore or know what is in the depths of the sea 52
14:25 until what you are about to write is finished. 51
32 in due time he took from you what he had given. 51
38 and drink what I give you to drink. 51
42 and by turns they wrote what was dictated 51
15:20 to turn and repay what they have given them. 51
16:18 What shall they do in these circumstances 52
36 do not disbelieve what the Lord says. 51
63 and what you think in your hearts! 51
66 What will you do? Or how will you hide your sins 52
Tob 4:15 what you hate, do not do to any one 39
5: 8 I may learn to what tribe he belongs 44
10 My brother, to what tribe and family do you belong? 44
14 tell me, what wages am I to pay you–a drachma a day 49
6: 6 of what use is the liver and heart and gall 49
12: 2 to give him half of what I have brought back. 39
6 for what he has done for you. 39
13: 6 see what he will do with you 39
14: 4 I fully believe what Jonah the prophet said 40
8 what the prophet Jonah said will surely happen. 39
10 See, my son, what Nadab did to Ahikar 49
10 with what he repaid him 40
11 consider what almsgiving accomplishes 49
Jdt 7:31 I will do what you say. 33
8:11 What you have said to the people today 34
14 nor find out what a man is thinking 34
26 Remember what he did with Abraham 40
26 what happened to Jacob in Mesopotamia in Syria 40
30 to do for them what we have promised 33
34 until I have finished what I am about to do. 39
9: 9 give to me, a widow, the strength to do what I plan. 39
12: 4 carries out . . what he has determined to do. 39
19 drank before him what her maid had prepared. 39
14: 8 Now tell me what you have done during these days. 40
Wis 7:21 both what is secret and what is manifest 40
21 both what is secret and what is manifest 40
12:21 with what strictness thou hast judged thy sons 45
Sir 2:14 What will you do when the Lord punishes you? 49
3:22 Reflect upon what has been assigned to you 39
5: 4 Do not say, "I sinned, and what happened to me? 49
7:28 what can you give back to them 49
8:18 for you do not know what he will divulge. 49
9:11 for you do not know what his end will be. 49
10:19 What race is worthy of honor? The human race 44
19 What race is worthy of honor? The human race 44
19 What race is unworthy of honor? The human race. 44
19 What race is unworthy of honor? The human race. 44
11:23 Do not say, "What do I need 49
23 what prosperity could be mine in the future? 49
24 what calamity could happen to me in the future? 49
13:17 What fellowship has a wolf with a lamb? 49
18 What peace is there between a hyena and a dog? 49
18 what peace between a rich man and a poor man? 49
14: 3 man; and of what use is property to an envious man? 49
15:11 for he will not do what he hates. 39
16:17 what is my soul in the boundless creation? 49
17:31 What is brighter than the sun? 49
18: 8 What is man, and of what use is he? 49
8 What is man, and of what use is he? 49
8 What is his good and what is his evil? 49
8 What is his good and what is his evil? 49
20:30 what advantage is there in either of them? 49
22: 8 at the end he will say, "What is it? 49
14 What is heavier than lead? 49
14 what is its name except "Fool"? 49
25: 4 What an attractive thing 50
30:19 Of what use to an idol is an offering of fruit? 49
31:13 What has been created more greedy than the eye? 49
27 What is life to a man who is without wine? 49
34: 4 From an unclean thing what will be made clean? 49
4 from something false what will be true? 49
23 what do they gain but toil? 49
25 what has he gained by his washing? 49
26 what has he gained by humbling himself? 49
37: 8 learn first what is his interest 49
27 see what is bad for it and do not give it that. 49
39:17 No one can say, "What is this?" "Why is that? 49
21 No one can say, "What is this?" "Why is that? 49
42:15 will declare what I have seen 39
LJr 1:45 they can be nothing but what the craftsmen wish 39
Sus 1:54 Under what tree did you see them being intimate 49
58 tell me: Under what tree did you catch them 49
1Mc 2:10 What nation has not inherited her palaces 44
3:52 thou knowest what they plot against us. 39
8: 3 what they had done in the land of Spain 40
10:27 repay you with good for what you do for us. 39
11: 5 They also told the king what Jonathan had done 39
40 He also reported to Imalkue what Demetrius had done 40
16: 1 reported . . what Cendebeus had done. 39
2Mc 7:16 you do what you please 39
11:18 he has agreed to what was possible. 39
35 With regard to what Lysias . . has granted you 39
3Mc 1: 9 and did what was fitting for the holy place 49
4: 3 What district or city 49
3 or what habitable place at all 49
3 what streets were not filled with mourning 49
5:27 inquired what the matter was 49
4Mc 1:14 We shall decide just what reason is 49
14 what reason is and what emotion is 49
8:16 what arguments might have been used 44
11: 4 for what act of ours are you destroying us 49
14:10 What could be more excruciatingly painful than this 49
17 they do what they can to help their young 31
15: 4 In what manner might I express 49

what אֲשֶׁר

Gen 9:24; 14:24; 18:17, 19; 27:45; 31:1, 43; 33:9; 38:10, 18; 41:25, 28, 55; 49:1, 28, Exd 4:12, 15; 6:1; 10:2; 12:16; 14:12; 16:5, 16, 23[3], 32; 19:4; 23:16; 29:38; 34:11, 34, Lev 5:16; 6:4; 9:5; 10:3; 17:15, Num 6:21; 8:24; 14:28; 18:12; 23:12; 24:13, 14; 31:50; 36:6, Deu 1:33; 4:3, 7, 8; 7:18; 8:2; 9:18; 11:4, 5, 6; 15:2; 17:2; 20:5, 6, 7; 23:10, 23; 24:9; 25:17, Jos 2:10; 9:3; 24:5, 7, Jdg 9:48; 11:24, 36; 14:6; 18:27; 20:9; 21:11, Rut 2:9, 17, 18[2]; 3:4, 1Sm 2:35; 6:4; 10:8; 12:24; 13:14; 15:2, 16; 16:3, 4; 24:19; 25:35; 28:2, 9; 30:23; 31:11, 2Sm 3:9; 18:21; 19:35[2]; 21:11; 24:10, 1Kg 2:5, 9; 3:13; 8:24, 25; 10:13; 11:10; 15:5; 16:5; 18:13; 20:22; 21:25; 22:14, 2Kg 5:20; 7:12; 10:10; 19:11; 25:15, 1Ch 4:10; 21:24, 2Ch 6:4, 15, 16; 9:12; 18:13, Neh 4:3; 7:72, Est 2:1[2], 15, Job 3:25; 15:18; 27:11, Ps 24:4; 6:16; 9:4, Prv 23:1; 25:7, Ecc 2:3, 12; 5:4, 18; 6:10; 7:13; 10:14, Isa 2:8, 22; 5:5; 17:8; 20:6; 21:6, 10; 33:13; 37:11; 41:22; 44:7; 47:13; 65:12; 66:1, Jer 3:6; 6:18; 7:12; 15:4; 23:25; 32:24; 38:20; 45:4[2]; 51:12; 52:19, Lam 2:17, Ezk 2:8[2]; 3:1; 5:9; 8:12; 18:18, 27, Dan 1:13; 8:19; 9:12; 10:14; 11:24, Jon 2:9; 4:5, Mic 6:1, 14, Hag 1:11; 2:14

what מָה

Gen 2:19; 3:13; 4:10; 12:18; 15:2; 20:9, 10; 21:17, 29; 23:15; 26:10; 27:37; 29:15, 25; 30:31; 31:26, 32, 36[2], 37; 32:27; 37:10, 15, 20, 26; 38:16, 29; 42:28; 44:15, 16[2]; 46:33; 47:3, Exd 2:4; 3:13[2]; 4:2; 10:26; 12:26; 13:14; 14:5, 11; 15:24; 16:7, 8, 15[2]; 17:4; 18:14; 22:27; 32:1, 21, 23; 33:5, Lev 25:20, Num 9:8; 13:18; 15:34; 16:11; 22:19, 28; 23:11, 17, 23, Deu 6:20; 10:12; 29:24; 32:20, Jos 4:6, 21; 5:14; 7:8, 9, 19; 15:18; 22:16, 24, Jdg 1:14; 2:2; 7:11; 8:1, 2, 3; 11:12; 13:8, 12[2]; 14:18[2]; 15:11; 16:5; 18:3[2], 8, 14, 18, 23, 24[2]; 20:12; 21:7, 16, 1Sm 3:17; 4:6, 14; 5:8; 6:2[2]; 9:7[2]; 10:2, 11, 15; 11:5; 13:11; 14:43; 15:14; 17:26, 29; 20:1[3], 32; 21:3; 22:3; 25:17; 26:18[2]; 28:13, 14, 15; 29:3, 8, 2Sm 3:24; 7:20; 9:8; 12:21; 14:5; 16:10, 20; 17:5; 18:22, 23, 29; 19:22, 28; 21:3, 4; 24:13, 17, 1Kg 1:16; 3:5; 9:13; 11:22; 12:9, 16; 14:3; 17:18; 19:9, 13, 20; 22:22, 2Kg 1:7; 2:9; 3:13; 4:2[2], 13, 14; 6:28; 8:13, 14; 9:18, 19, 22; 18:19; 20:8, 14, 15; 23:17, 1Ch 12:32; 17:18; 21:12, 17, 2Ch 1:7; 10:9, 16; 18:20; 19:6; 20:12; 25:9; 32:10, 13; 35:21, Ezr 9:10, Neh 2:4, 12, 16, 19; 4:2; 13:17, Est 1:15; 4:5; 5:3[2], 6[2]; 6:3, 6; 7:2[2]; 8:1; 9:12[3], 26, Job 6:11[2], 25; 7:17, 20; 9:12; 11:8[2]; 13:13; 15:9, 14; 16:3; 21:15[2], 21; 22:13, 17; 23:5; 27:8; 30:2; 31:2, 14[2]; 34:4, 33; 35:3, 6[2], 7[2]; 37:19; 38:6; 40:4, Ps 8:4; 1:3; 0:9; 8:4, 7; 0:16; 6:4, 11; 5:8; 9:47[2]; 14:5; 16:12; 18:6; 20:3[2]; 44:3, Prv 4:19; 25:8; 27:1; 30:4[2]; 31:2, Ecc 1:3, 9[3]; 2:2, 12, 22; 3:9, 22; 5:11, 16; 6:8[2], 11, 12[2]; 8:4, 7; 10:14; 11:2, Sng 5:9[2]; 8:8, Isa 1:11; 3:15; 5:4; 10:3; 14:32; 19:12; 21:11[2]; 22:1, 16; 36:4; 38:15, 22; 39:3, 4; 40:6, 18; 41:22; 45:9, 10[2]; 52:5, Jer 1:11, 13; 2:5, 18[2], 23; 4:30; 5:15, 31; 6:20; 7:17; 8:6, 9; 11:15; 13:21; 16:10[2]; 23:28, 33, 35[2], 37[2]; 24:3; 33:24; 37:18; 38:25[2]; 48:19, Lam 2:13[3]; 5:1, Ezk 8:6; 12:9, 22; 17:12; 18:2; 19:2; 20:29; 21:13; 24:19; 33:30; 37:18, Dan 12:8, Hos 6:4[2]; 9:5, 14; 10:3; 14:8, Jol 3:4, Ams 4:13; 8:2, Jon 1:6, 8[2], 10, 11, Mic 6:3[2], 5[2], 6, 8, Nah 1:9, Hab 2:1[2], 18, Zec 1:9[2], 19, 21; 4:2, 4, 5, 11, 12, 13; 5:2, 5, 6; 6:4; 13:6, Mal 2:15; 3:14

what *τίς*

Mat 5:46, 47; 6:3, 25[3], 31[3]; 7:9; 8:29; 9:13; 10:19[2]; 11:7, 16; 12:3, 7, 11; 16:26[2]; 17:25; 18:12; 19:16, 20, 27; 20:21, 22, 32; 21:16, 28, 40; 22:17, 42; 24:3; 26:15, 62, 66, 70; 27:4, 22, 23, Mrk 1:24, 27; 2:25; 4:24, 30; 5:7, 9, 14; 6:2[2], 24; 8:36, 37; 9:6, 10, 16, 33; 10:3, 17, 36, 38, 51; 11:5; 12:9; 13:4, 11; 14:36[2], 40, 60, 64, 68; 15:12, 14, 24, Lke 1:62, 66; 3:10, 12, 14; 4:34, 36; 6:11, 47; 7:24, 25, 26, 31[2]; 8:9, 28, 30; 9:25; 10:25, 26; 11:11; 12:11[2], 17, 22[2], 29[2]; 13:18[2], 20; 14:31; 15:4, 8, 26; 16:2, 3, 4; 18:6, 18, 36, 41; 19:15; 20:13, 15, 17; 21:7; 22:71; 23:22, 31, 34; 24:17, Joh 1:21, 22, 38; 2:4, 18, 25; 4:27; 5:19; 6:6, 9, 28, 30[2]; 7:36, 51; 8:5; 9:17, 26; 10:6; 11:47, 56; 12:27, 49[2]; 13:12; 15:15; 16:17, 18[2]; 18:21, 29, 35, 38; 21:22, 23, Act 2:12, 37; 4:9, 16; 5:24, 35; 7:40, 49; 8:36; 10:4, 17, 21; 12:18; 13:25; 16:30; 17:18, 19, 20; 19:3, 35; 21:13, 22, 33; 22:10, 26; 23:19; 24:20, Rom 3:1[2], 3, 5, 9; 4:1, 3; 6:1, 15, 21; 7:7; 8:31; 9:14, 30; 10:8; 11:2, 4, 7, 15; 12:2, 1Co 2:11; 3:5[2]; 4:7, 21; 5:12; 9:18; 10:19; 11:22; 14:15, 16, 26; 15:29, 32, 2Co 6:14[2], 15[2], 16; 12:13, Gal 4:30, Eph 1:18[2], 19; 3:9, 18; 4:9; 5:10, 17; 6:21, Php 1:18, 1Th 2:19; 3:9; 4:2, Heb 1:5, 13; 2:6; 7:11; 11:32; 12:7; 13:6, Jas 2:14, 16, 1Pe 4:17, 1Jn 3:2, Rev 2:7, 11, 17, 29; 3:6, 13, 22; 18:18, 1Es 1:26; 5:66; 8:82, Jdt 5:3[3]; 10:12, AEs 11:12; 15:9, Wis 4:17[2]; 5:8[2]; 6:22; 8:5; 9:9[2], 10, 13[2]; 12:12, Sir 13:6; 41:14, Sus 1:47, 1Mc 3:50; 4:44; 5:16; 6:11; 10:23, 2Mc 7:2, 30

what *See also* use.

what about 1. τίς
Joh 21:21 he said to Jesus, "Lord, what about this man? 1

what person 1. τίς
1Pe 1:11 they inquired what person or time was indicated 1
4Mc 7:21 What person who lives as a philosopher 1

what sort 1. ὁποῖος 2. ποῖος 3. ποταπός
Mat 8:27 the men marveled, saying, "What sort of man is this 3
Lke 1:29 considered . . what sort of greeting this might be. 3
7:39 known who and what sort of woman this is 3
1Co 3:13 test what sort of work each one has done. 1
2Mc 3:37 what sort of person would be suitable 2

what sort of person 1. ποταπός
2Pe 3:11 what sort of persons ought you to be 1

what thing 1. ποῖος
Lke 24:19 he said to him, "What things? 1

whatever 1. אֲשֶׁר 2. דְּבַר מָה 3. הוּא 4. כְּכֹל 5. כֹּל 6. כֹּל אֲשֶׁר 7. כֹּל הַדָּבָר 8. מָה 9. מָה שֶׁ 10. כֹּל דִּי (A) 11. מָה (A) 12. מָה דִּי (A) 13. ἐάν τις 14. εἴ τις 15. καθὸ ἄν 16. καθώς 17. ὅς 18. ὃς ἄν 19. ὃς ἐάν 20. ὅσος 21. ὅσος ἄν 22. ὅσος ἐάν 23. ὅστις 24. ὅς τις ἄν 25. ὅς τις ἐάν 26. ὁστισοῦν 27. πᾶς 28. πᾶς ὁ 29. πᾶς ὅς 30. πᾶς ὃς ἐάν 31. πᾶς ὅσος 32. πᾶς ὅσος ἄν 33. πᾶς ὅς τις ἐάν 34. τίς 35. quisquis
Gen 2:19 whatever the man called every living creature 6
21:12 whatever Sarah says to you, do as she tells you 6
31:16 now then, whatever God has said to you, do. 6
34:11 and whatever you say to me I will give. 1
28 took . . their asses, and whatever was in the city 1
39:22 and whatever was done there, he was the doer of it; 6
23 and whatever he did, the LORD made it prosper. 1
Exd 13: 2 whatever is the first to open the womb 5
21:30 he shall give . . whatever is laid upon him. 6
29:37 whatever touches the altar shall become holy. 5
30:29 whatever touches them will become holy. 5
Lev 5: 3 touches human uncleanness, of whatever sort 5
6:27 Whatever touches its flesh shall be holy 6
7:26 Moreover you shall eat no blood whatever *
11: 3 Whatever parts the hoof and is cloven-footed 5
36 whatever touches their carcass shall be unclean *
42 Whatever goes on its belly 5
42 whatever goes on all fours 5
42 whatever has many feet, all the swarming things 5
13:51 whatever be the use of the skin 5
22: 5 may take uncleanness, whatever his uncleanness- 5
Num 3:38 whatever had to be done for the people of Israel; *
5:10 whatever any man gives to the priest shall be his. 1
10:32 whatever good the LORD will do to us 3
18: 8 have given you whatever is kept of the offerings *
19:22 whatever the unclean person touches shall be 5
22:17 whatever you say to me I will do; 6
23: 3 whatever he shows me I will tell you. 2
30:12 then whatever proceeds out of her lips 5
31:23 whatever cannot stand the fire, you shall pass 6
Deu 12: 8 every man doing whatever is right in his own eyes; 5
14: 9 whatever has fins and scales you may eat. 1
10 whatever does not have fins and scales 6
26 spend the money for whatever you desire, oxen 6
26 you desire . . whatever your appetite craves; 6
15: 3 but whatever of yours is with your brother 1
8 lend him sufficient for his need, whatever it may be. 1
21 blind, or has any serious blemish whatever *
17: 1 ox . . in which is a blemish, any defect whatever; *
Jos 1:18 disobeys your words, whatever you command him 6
Jdg 10:15 have sinned; do to us whatever seems good to thee; 5
1Sm 10: 7 do whatever your hand finds to do, for God is 1
11:10 and you may do to us whatever seems good to you. 4
14:36 And they said, "Do whatever seems good to you. 5
20: 4 Whatever you say, I will do for you. 8
21: 3 Give me five loaves of bread, or whatever is here. *
25: 8 give whatever you have at hand to your servants 1
2Sm 15:15 ready to do whatever my lord the king decides. 4
35 whatever you hear . . tell it to Zadok 7
18: 4 king said . . "Whatever seems best to you I will do. 1
19:37 and do for him whatever seems good to you. 1
38 and I will do for him whatever seems good to you; 1
1Kg 8:37 whatever plague, whatever sickness there is; 5
37 whatever plague, whatever sickness there is; 5
38 whatever prayer, whatever supplication is made 5
38 whatever prayer, whatever supplication is made 5
44 go out to battle . . by whatever way thou *
9:19 to build . . whatever Solomon desired to build 1
10:13 all that she desired, whatever she asked 1
20: 6 and lay hands on whatever pleases them 5
2Kg 10: 5 do whatever is good in your eyes. *
18:14 whatever you impose on me I will bear. 1
1Ch 26:31 of whatever genealogy or fathers' houses. *
2Ch 2:16 will cut whatever timber you need from Lebanon *
6:28 whatever plague, whatever sickness there is; 5
28 whatever plague, whatever sickness there is; 5
29 whatever prayer, whatever supplication is made 5
29 whatever prayer, whatever supplication is made 5
34 go out . . by whatever way thou shalt send them 1
8: 6 whatever Solomon desired to build in Jerusalem 5
9:12 gave . . all that she desired, whatever she asked 1
Ezr 1: 4 let each survivor, in whatever place he sojourns 5
6: 9 whatever is needed- . . -let that be given to them 11
7:18 Whatever seems good to you and your brethren 12
21 Whatever Ezra the priest . . requires of you 10
23 Whatever is commanded by the God of heaven 10
Est 2:13 she was given whatever she desired to take 6
Job 41:11 Whatever is under the whole heaven is mine. 3
Ps 8: 8 whatever passes along the paths of the sea. *
115: 3 Our God . . does whatever he pleases. 6
135: 6 Whatever the LORD pleases he does 6
Prv 4: 7 Get wisdom, and whatever you get, get insight. 5
Ecc 2:10 whatever my eyes desired I did not keep from them; 6
3:14 I know that whatever God does endures for ever; 6
6:10 Whatever has come to be has already been named 9
8: 3 do not delay . . for he does whatever he pleases. 6
9:10 Whatever your hand finds to do, do it 6
Jer 1: 7 and whatever I command you you shall speak. 6
42: 4 and whatever the LORD answers you I will tell you; 7
20 whatever the LORD our God says declare to us 6
Ezk 10:11 but in whatever direction the front wheel faced *
47:23 In whatever tribe the alien resides 1
Zec 14:15 asses, and whatever beasts may be in those camps. 5
Mat 7:12 So whatever you wish that men would do to you, do 22
10:11 whatever town or village you enter 18
14: 7 to give her whatever she might ask. 19
15:17 Do you not see that whatever goes into the mouth 28
16:19 whatever you bind on earth shall be bound 19
19 whatever you loose on earth 19
17:12 but did to him whatever they pleased. 20
18:18 Truly, I say to you, whatever you bind on earth 22
18 whatever you loose on earth 22
20: 4 and whatever is right I will give you 19
21:22 whatever you ask in prayer, you will receive 21
23: 3 so practice and observe whatever they tell you 22
Mrk 3:28 whatever blasphemies they utter; 22
6:22 Ask me for whatever you wish, and I will grant it. 19
23 he vowed . . "Whatever you ask me, I will give you 25
7:18 whatever goes into a man from outside 27
9:13 they did to him whatever they pleased 20
10:35 we want you to do for us whatever we ask of you. 19
11:24 Therefore I tell you, whatever you ask in prayer 31
13:11 say whatever is given you in that hour 19
Lke 9: 4 whatever house you enter, stay there 18
10: 5 Whatever house you enter, first say, 'Peace 18
35 whatever more you spend, I will repay you 24
11: 8 he will rise and give him whatever he needs. 20
12: 3 whatever you have said in the dark shall be heard 20
Joh 2: 5 said to the servants, "Do whatever he tells you. 24
5:19 whatever he does, that the Son does likewise. 18
11:22 whatever you ask from God, God will give you. 21
14:13 Whatever you ask in my name, I will do it 24
15: 7 ask whatever you will, and it shall be done for you. 19
16 whatever you ask the Father in my name 24
16:13 whatever he hears he will speak 20
Act 3:22 You shall listen to him in whatever he tells you. 32
4:28 to do whatever thy hand . . had predestined 20
28:10 they put on board whatever we needed. *
Rom 3:19 Now we know that whatever the law says 20
14:23 for whatever does not proceed from faith is sin. 29
15: 4 For whatever was written in former days 20
16: 2 and help her in whatever she may require from you 17
1Co 7:24 So, brethren, in whatever state each was called 17
10:25 Eat whatever is sold in the meat market 27
27 eat whatever is set before you 27
31 So, whether you eat or drink, or whatever you do 34
Gal 6: 7 whatever a man sows, that he will also reap. 19
Eph 6: 8 knowing that whatever good any one does 13
Php 3: 7 whatever gain I had 23
4: 8 Finally, brethren, whatever is true 20
8 whatever is honorable, whatever is just 20
8 whatever is honorable, whatever is just 20
8 whatever is pure, whatever is lovely 20
8 whatever is pure, whatever is lovely 20
8 whatever is gracious, if there is any excellence 20
11 I have learned, in whatever state I am, to be content. *
Col 3:17 whatever you do, in word or deed 33
23 Whatever your task, work heartily 19
1Ti 1:10 whatever else is contrary to sound doctrine 14
2Pe 2:19 whatever overcomes a man, to that he is enslaved. 17
1Jn 3:22 we receive from him whatever we ask 19
5: 4 For whatever is born of God overcomes the world; 27
15 if we know that he hears us in whatever we ask 19
Jde 1:10 men revile whatever they do not understand 20
1Es 4: 3 whatever he says to them they obey. 30
5 whatever spoil they take and everything else. 22
8:16 whatever you and your brethren are minded to do 32
18 whatever else occurs to you as necessary 21
19 whatever Ezra the priest . . sends 21
2Es 12:39 whatever it pleases the Most High to show you. 35
Tob 2: 2 bring whatever poor man . . you may find 19
Jdt 3: 2 Do with us whatever you will. 16
3 do with them whatever you please. 15
12:14 Surely whatever pleases him I will do at once 29
Sir 2: 4 Accept whatever is brought upon you 29
39:16 whatever he commands will be done in his time. 27
18 At his command whatever pleases him is done 27
41:10 Whatever is from the dust returns to dust 31
42: 7 Whatever you deal out 19
LJr 1:44 Whatever is done for them is false 27
69 we have no evidence whatever that they are gods; †
1Mc 13:39 whatever other tax has been collected 14
14:34 whatever was necessary for their restoration. 20
2Mc 13:20 Judas sent in to the garrison whatever was necessary. *
3Mc 6:10 destroy us, Lord, by whatever fate you choose. 17
7: 7 every charge of whatever kind. 26
4Mc 8:14 whatever justice you revere will be merciful 17
whatever *See also* any, no, way.

whatever else 1. שְׁאָר (A)
Ezr 7:20 whatever else is required for the house 1

whatever thing 1. qui
2Es 13:58 whatever things come to pass in their seasons. 1

wheat 1. בַּר 2. חִטָּה 3. חִנְטָה (A) 4. πυρός 5. σῖτος
Gen 30:14 In the days of wheat harvest Reuben went 2
Exd 9:32 the wheat and the spelt were not ruined 2
29: 2 You shall make them of fine wheat flour. 2
34:22 observe . . the first fruits of wheat harvest 2
Deu 8: 8 a land of wheat and barley, of vines and fig trees 2
32:14 with the finest of the wheat-and of the blood 2
Jdg 6:11 Gideon was beating out wheat in the wine press 2
15: 1 at the time of wheat harvest, Samson went to visit 2
Rut 2:23 until the end of the barley and wheat harvests; 2
1Sm 6:13 Beth-she'mesh were reaping their wheat harvest 2
12:17 Is it not wheat harvest today? I will call upon 2
2Sm 4: 6 the doorkeeper . . had been cleaning wheat 4
17:28 brought . . wheat, barley, meal, parched grain 2
1Kg 5:11 gave Hiram . . wheat as food for his household 2
1Ch 21:20 Now Ornan was threshing wheat; he turned and saw 2
23 I give . . the wheat for a cereal offering. 2
2Ch 2:10 20,000 cors of crushed wheat 2
15 Now therefore the wheat and barley, oil and wine 2
27: 5 gave him that year . . and 10,000 cors of wheat 2
Ezr 6: 9 wheat, salt, wine, or oil, as the priests at Jerusalem 3
7:22 up to . . 100 cors of wheat 3
Job 31:40 let thorns grow instead of wheat 2
Ps 81:16 I would feed you with the finest of the wheat 2
147:14 he fills you with the finest of the wheat. 2
Sng 7: 2 belly is a heap of wheat, encircled with lilies. 2
Isa 28:25 put in wheat in rows and barley in its proper 2
Jer 12:13 They have sown wheat and have reaped thorns 2
23:28 What has straw in common with wheat? 1
41: 8 we have stores of wheat, barley, oil, and honey 2
Ezk 4: 9 you, take wheat and barley, beans and lentils 2
27:17 they exchanged for your merchandise wheat 2
45:13 one sixth of an ephah from each homer of wheat 2
Jol 1:11 wail, O vinedressers, for the wheat and the barley; 2
Ams 5:11 the poor and take from him exactions of wheat 1
8: 5 And the sabbath, that we may offer wheat for sale 1
6 buy the poor . . and sell the refuse of the wheat? 1
Mat 3:12 clear his threshing floor and gather his wheat 5
13:25 sowed weeds among the wheat, and went away. 5
29 lest in gathering the weeds you root up the wheat 5
30 but gather the wheat into my barn. 5
Lke 3:17 to gather the wheat into his granary 5
16: 7 He said, 'A 100 measures of wheat.' 5
22:31 he might sift you like wheat 5
Joh 12:24 unless a grain of wheat falls into the earth 5
Act 27:38 throwing out the wheat into the sea. 5
1Co 15:37 perhaps of wheat or of some other grain. 5
Rev 6: 6 A quart of wheat for a denarius 5
18:13 wine, oil, fine flour and wheat, cattle and sheep 5
1Es 6:30 likewise wheat and salt and wine and oil 4
8:20 likewise up to 100 cors of wheat 4
Jdt 2:27 he went down . . during the wheat harvest 4
3: 3 all our wheat fields, and our flocks and herds 4
Sir 39:26 iron and salt and wheat flour and milk and honey 4

wheel 1. אֹבֶן 2. אוֹפַן 3. גַּלְגַּל 4. גִּלְגָּל 5. גַּלְגַּל (A) 6. τροχιαῖος 7. τροχός
Exd 14:25 clogging their chariot wheels 2
1Kg 7:30 stand had four bronze wheels and axles of bronze; 2
32 the four wheels were underneath the panels; 2
32 the axles of the wheels were of one piece 2
32 and the height of a wheel was a cubit and a half. 2
33 The wheels were made like a chariot wheel; 2
33 The wheels were made like a chariot wheel; 2
Prv 20:26 A wise king . . drives the wheel over them. 2
Ecc 12: 6 or the wheel broken at the cistern 3
Isa 5:28 like flint, and their wheels like the whirlwind. 3
28:27 nor is a cart wheel rolled over cummin; 2
28 he drives his cart wheel over it with his horses 4
Jer 18: 3 and there he was working at his wheel. 1
47: 3 at the rumbling of their wheels the fathers look 3
Ezk 1:15 I saw a wheel upon the earth 2
16 As for the appearance of the wheels 2
16 being as it were a wheel within a wheel. 2
16 being as it were a wheel within a wheel. 2
18 The four wheels had rims and they had spokes; *
19 creatures went, the wheels went beside them; 2
19 creatures rose from the earth, the wheels rose. 2
20 they went, and the wheels rose along with them; 2
20 the spirit of the . . creatures was in the wheels. 2
21 when those rose from the earth, the wheels rose 2

21 the spirit of the . . creatures was in the wheels. 2
3:13 and the sound of the wheels beside them 2
10: 6 he went in and stood beside a wheel. 2
9 I looked, and behold, there were four wheels 2
9 the appearance of the wheels was like sparkling 2
10 likeness, as if a wheel were within a wheel. 2
10 likeness, as if a wheel were within a wheel. 2
11 but in whatever direction the front wheel faced •
12 And their rims, and their spokes, and the wheels 2
12 the wheels that the four of them had. 2
13 As for the wheels, they were called in my hearing 2
16 the cherubim went, the wheels went beside them; 2
16 the wheels did not turn from beside them. 2
19 as they went forth, with the wheels beside them; 2
11:22 their wings, with the wheels beside them; 2
Dan 7: 9 throne . . flames, its wheels were burning fire. 5
Nah 3: 2 The crack of whip, and rumble of wheel 2
Sir 33: 5 The heart of a fool is like a cart wheel 7
38:29 turning the wheel with his feet 7
4Mc 8:13 wheels and joint-dislocators 7
9:12 they placed him upon the wheel. 7
17 your wheel is not so powerful 7
19 they tightened the wheel further. 7
20 The wheel was completely smeared with blood 7
10: 8 They immediately brought him to the wheel 7
11:10 twisted his back around the wedge on the wheel 6
17 When he had said this, they led him to the wheel. 7
15:22 her sons were tortured on the wheel 7

wheel *See also* break.

wheel around 1. *περισπασμός*

2Mc 10:36 Others . . wheeled around against the defenders 1

torture wheel 1. *τροχός*

4Mc 5:32 Therefore get your torture wheels ready 1

whirling wheel 1. גַּלְגַּל

Ezk 10: 2 Go in among the whirling wheels 1
6 Take fire from between the whirling wheels 1
13 were called in my hearing the whirling wheels. 1

whelp 1. בֵּן 2. גּוּר 3. גּוֹר

Gen 49: 9 Judah is a lion's whelp; 2
Deu 33:22 Dan is a lion's whelp, that leaps forth from Bashan. 2
Job 4:11 the whelps of the lioness are scattered. 1
Jer 51:38 they shall growl like lions' whelps. 3
Ezk 19: 2 in the midst of young lions, rearing her whelps. 2
3 she brought up one of her whelps; 2
5 she took another of her whelps 2
Nah 2:12 The lion tore enough for his whelps 3

when 1. אַחֲרֵי 2. אַךְ 3. אִם 4. אֲשֶׁר 5. בְּיוֹם 6. בַּעַד 7. בְּעֵת 8. גַּם 9. הֵן 10. הִנֵּה 11. יוֹם 12. כְּ 13. כַּאֲשֶׁר 14. כָּעֵת 15. כְּשֶׁ 16. לְ 17. לְעֵת 18. מִן 19. מָתַי 20. עַד 21. עַד שֶׁ 22. עִם 23. עֵת 24. בְּעִדָּן (A) 25. כְּ (A) 26. כְּדִי (A) 27. *ἅμα* 28. *ἀπό* 29. *γάρ* 30. *δέ* 31. *διά* 32. *ἐάν* 33. *ἐγένετο ὡς* 34. *εἰ* 35. *ἐν* 36. *ἐν αἷς* 37. *ἐν ἡμέραις* 38. *ἐπάν* 39. *ἐπεί* 40. *ἐπειδή* 41. *ἐπί* 42. *ἕως* 43. *ἤδη* 44. *ἡνίκα* 45. *ἡνίκα ἐάν* 46. *ἰδού* 47. *ἵνα* 48. *καθώς* 49. *καί* 50. *καιρός* 51. *κατά* 52. *μετά* 53. *ὁπηνίκα* 54. *ὁπηνίκα ἄν* 55. *ὁπότε* 56. *ὅπου* 57. *ὅς* 58. *ὃς ἐάν* 59. *οὖν* 60. *πότε* 61. *τότε* 62. *ὡς* 63. *ὡς ἄν* 64. cum 65. et 66. in 67. in quibus 68. in quo 69. quando 70. quo tempore 71. ubi 72. ut

Gen 6: 4 afterward, when the sons of God came 4
12:11 When he was about to enter Egypt, he said to Sar'ai 13
18:33 when he had finished speaking to Abraham; 13
19:17 when they had brought them forth, they said 12
20:13 when God caused me to wander 13
24:11 evening, the time when women go out to draw water. 17
22 When the camels had done drinking 13
30 When he saw the ring, and the bracelets 12
30 when he heard the words of Rebekah his sister 12
36 a son to my master when she was old; 1
52 When Abraham's servant heard their words 13
27:34 When Esau heard the words of his father, he cried 12
40 but when you break loose you shall break his yoke 13
29:10 Now when Jacob saw Rachel the daughter of Laban 13
13 When Laban heard the tidings of Jacob 12
30:25 When Rachel had borne Joseph, Jacob said to Laban 13
30 But now when shall I provide for my own household 19
32: 2 when Jacob saw them he said, "This is God's army! 13
34: 7 came in from the field when they heard of it; 12
37:23 when Joseph came to his brothers 13
38: 9 when he went in to his brother's wife he spilled 3
39:11 one day, when he went into the house to do his work 12
13 when she saw that he had left his garment 12
15 when he heard that I lifted up my voice and cried 12
19 When his master heard the words which his wife 12
40:13 his hand as formerly, when you were his butler. 4
14 remember me, when it is well with you 13
43: 2 when they had eaten the grain which they had 13
44:30 Now therefore, when I come to your servant 12
31 when he sees that the lad is not with us, he will die 12
Exd 8: 9 Be pleased to command me when I am to entreat 19
11: 1 when he lets you go, he will drive you away 12
14:27 sea returned . . when the morning appeared; 16
28:35 it shall be upon Aaron when he ministers 16
29:30 when he comes into the tent of meeting 4
30:15 when you give the LORD'S offering 16
31:18 when he had made an end of speaking with him 12
33: 9 When Moses entered the tent, the pillar of cloud 12
Lev 4:22 When a ruler sins, doing unwittingly 4
6:20 offer to the LORD on the day when he is anointed 5
13:58 which the disease departs when you have washed it 4
25:22 until the ninth year, when its produce comes 20
Num 5:29 when a wife . . goes astray and defiles herself 4
11:25 when the spirit rested upon them, they prophesied. 12
24:23 Alas, who shall live when God does this? 18
33: 1 stages . . of Israel, when they went forth out 4
36: 4 when the jubilee of the people of Israel comes 3
Deu 2:16 when all the men of war had perished and were dead 13
5:23 when you heard the voice out of the midst 12
17:18 when he sits on the throne of his kingdom, he shall 12
19: 5 when a man goes into the forest with his neighbor 4
20: 2 when you draw near to the battle, the priest shall 12
9 when the officers have made an end of speaking 12
23:11 when evening comes on, he shall bathe himself 16
11 when the sun is down, he may come within the camp. 12
24:13 when the sun goes down, you shall restore to him 12
31: 4 as he did to Sihon and Og . . when he destroyed 4
14 Behold, the days approach when you must die; 16
24 When Moses had finished writing the words 12
Jos 3: 3 When you see the ark . . then you shall set out 12
8 When you come to the . . Jordan, you shall stand 12
13 And when the soles of the feet of the priests 12
15 when those who bore the ark had come to the Jordan 12
4: 1 When all the nation had . . the LORD said to Joshua 13
11 when all the people had finished passing over 13
21 When your children ask their fathers in time 4
5: 1 When all the kings . . their heart melted 12
8 When the circumcising . . was done, they remained 13
7: 8 what can I say, when Israel has turned their backs 4
8: 8 when you have . . you shall set the city on fire 12
14 when the king of Ai saw this he . . made haste 12
24 When Israel had finished . . all Israel returned 12
9: 1 When all the kings . . heard of this 12
10: 1 When Ado'ni-ze'dek king of Jerusalem heard 12
20 When Joshua and the men of Israel had finished 12
24 when they brought . . Joshua summoned all the men 12
11: 1 When Jabin king of Hazor heard of this, he sent 12
Jdg 3:18 when Ehud had finished presenting the tribute 13
25 but when he still did not open the doors 10
7:15 When Gideon heard the telling of the dream 12
17 when I come to the outskirts of the camp, do as I do. 10
19 came . . when they had just set the watch; 2
11: 5 when the Ammonites made war against Israel 13
7 Why . . come to me now when you are in trouble? 13
35 when he saw her, he rent his clothes, and said, "Alas 12
14:11 And when the people saw him, they brought 30 12
15:17 When he had finished speaking, he threw away 12
18:10 When you go, you will come to an unsuspecting 12
20:10 that when they come they may requite Gib'e-ah 16
Rut 1:19 And when they came . . the whole town was stirred 12
1Sm 1:24 when she had weaned him, she took him up with her 13
4: 5 When the ark . . all Israel gave a mighty shout 12
18 When he mentioned the ark of God, Eli fell over 12
5:10 when the ark of God came to Ekron 12
8: 1 When Samuel became old, he made his sons judges 13
6 But the thing displeased Samuel when they said 13
10: 9 When he turned . . God gave him another heart; 12
11: 6 spirit . . came mightily upon Saul when he heard 12
12: 8 When Jacob went into Egypt . . then your fathers 13
17:55 When Saul saw David go forth . . he said to Abner 12
18: 1 When he had finished . . the soul of Jonathan was 12
19 when Merab . . should have been given to David 7
20:19 where you hid . . when the matter was in hand 5
24: 1 When Saul returned . . he was told 13
16 When David had finished speaking . . Saul said 12
2Sm 5:24 when you hear the sound . . then bestir yourself; 12
11:19 When you have finished telling all the news 12
12:21 but when the child died, you arose and ate food. 13
13:28 Mark when Amnon's heart is merry with wine 12
16:16 And when Hushai . . came to Ab'salom, Hushai said 13
17:27 When David came to Mahana'im, Shobi 12
18:29 When Jo'ab sent your servant, I saw a great tumult 16
20:13 When he was taken out . . all the people went 13
1Kg 1:21 come to pass, when my lord the king sleeps with his 12
5: 7 When Hiram heard the words . . he rejoiced 12
8:30 hearken . . when they pray toward this place; 4
9: 1 When Solomon had finished building the house 12
11: 4 when Solomon was old his wives turned away 17
12: 2 when Jerobo'am the son of Nebat heard of it 12
13: 4 when the king heard the saying of the man of God 12
14: 5 When she came, she pretended to be another woman. 12
6 when Ahi'jah heard the sound of her feet 12
15:21 when Ba'asha heard of it, he stopped building 12
16:18 when Zimri saw that the city was taken, he went 12
18:17 When Ahab saw Eli'jah, Ahab said to him, "Is it you 12
19:13 when Eli'jah heard it, he wrapped his face in his 12
20:12 When Ben-ha'dad heard this message . . he said 12
21:27 when Ahab heard those words, he rent his clothes 12
22:25 on that day when you go into an inner chamber 4
32 when the captains . . saw Jehosh'aphat, they said 12
33 when the captains . . saw that it was not the king 12
2Kg 2: 9 When they had crossed, Eli'jah said to Eli'sha, "Ask 12
3: 5 when Ahab died, the king of Moab rebelled 12
15 when the minstrel played, the power of the LORD 12
4: 6 When the vessels were full, she said to her son 12
16 At this season, when the time comes round 12
25 When the man of God saw her coming, he said 12
5: 6 When this letter reaches you, know that I have 12
7 when the king of Israel read the letter 12
8 when Eli'sha the man of God heard . . he sent 12
26 when the man turned from his chariot to meet you? 13
6:21 When the king of Israel saw them he said to Eli'sha 12
30 When the king heard . . he rent his clothes 12
32 Look, when the messenger comes, shut the door 12
7:18 when the man of God had said to the king 12
9:22 when Joram saw Jehu, he said, "Is it peace, Jehu? 12
10: 7 when the letter came . . they took the king's sons 12
19: 1 When King Hezeki'ah heard it, he rent his clothes 12
22:11 when the king heard the words . . he rent his 12
23:29 Neco slew him at Megid'do, when he saw him. 12
1Ch 14:15 when you hear the sound of marching 12
17: 1 Now when David dwelt in his house 13
21:15 when he was about to destroy it, the LORD saw 12
2Ch 5:13 when the song was raised . . in praise to the LORD 12
6:21 hearken . . when they pray toward this place; 4
7: 1 When Solomon had ended his prayer, fire came down 12
13 When I shut up the heavens so that there is no rain 9
10: 2 when Jerobo'am the son of Nebat heard of it 12
12: 1 When the rule of Rehobo'am was established 12
15: 8 When Asa heard these words . . he took courage 12
16: 5 when Ba'asha heard of it 12
18:24 see on that day when you go into an inner chamber 4
31 when the captains . . saw Jehosh'aphat, they said 12
32 for when the captains of the chariots saw 12
20:23 when they had made an end of the inhabitants 12
22: 8 when Jehu was executing judgment 12
24:14 when they had finished, they brought 12
22 when he was dying, he said, "May the LORD see 12
26:16 when he was strong he grew proud 12
29:29 When the offering was finished, the king 12
31: 1 Now when all this was finished, all Israel 12
33:12 when he was in distress he entreated the favor 12
34: 8 when he had purged the land and the house 16
19 When the king heard the words of the law 12
35:20 when Josi'ah had prepared the temple 4
Ezr 1:11 when the exiles were brought up from Babylonia 22
9: 3 When I heard this, I rent my garments and my mantle 12
Neh 1: 4 When I heard these words I sat down and wept 12
2: 3 when the city, the place of my fathers' sepulchres 4
6 long will you be gone, and when will you return? 19
4: 1 Now when Sanbal'lat heard that we were building 12
7 when Sanbal'lat and Tobi'ah and the Arabs 13
12 When the Jews who lived by them came they said 13
15 When our enemies heard that it was known to us 13
5: 6 I was very angry when I heard their outcry 13
6: 1 Now when it was reported to Sanbal'lat and Tobi'ah 13
16 when all our enemies heard of it, all the nations 13
7: 1 Now when the wall had been built and I had set up 13
8: 5 when he opened it all the people stood. 12
9 people wept when they heard the words of the law. 12
13: 3 When the people heard the law, they separated 12
19 When it began to be dark at the gates of Jerusalem 13
Est 1: 2 in those days when King Ahasu-e'rus sat . . in Susa 12
10 when the heart of the king was merry with wine 12
2: 1 when the anger of King Ahasu-e'rus had abated 12
3: 4 when they spoke to him . . they told Haman 12
5: 2 when the king saw . . she found favor in his sight 12
9 But when Haman saw . . he was filled with wrath 12
9: 1 when the king's command and edict were about 4
1 on the very day when the enemies of the Jews hoped 4
1 a day when the Jews should get the mastery over 4
Job 7: 4 When I lie down I say, 'When shall I arise?' 3
4 When I lie down I say, 'When shall I arise?' 19
9: 5 when he overturns them in his anger; 4
23 When disaster brings sudden death, he mocks 3
21: 6 When I think of it I am dismayed 3
28:25 When he gave to the wind its weight 16
36:20 night, when peoples are cut off in their place. 16
39: 1 Do you know when the mountain goats bring forth? 23
18 When she rouses herself to flee, she laughs 14
41:25 When he raises himself up the mighty are afraid; 18
Ps 20: 9 O LORD; answer us when we call. 5
21: 9 make them as a blazing oven when you appear. 17
41: 5 When will he die, and his name perish? 19
6 when one comes to see me, he utters empty words 3
42: 2 When shall I come and behold the face of God? 19
56: 3 When I am afraid, I put my trust in thee. 11
63: 6 when I think of thee upon my bed 3
71: 9 forsake me not when my strength is spent. 12
73:20 They are like a dream when one awakes 18
78:34 When he slew them, they sought for him; 3
42 or the day when he redeemed them from the foe; 4
43 when he wrought his signs in Egypt 4
94: 8 Fools, when will you be wise? 19
18 When I thought, "My foot slips," thy steadfast love 3
95: 9 when your fathers tested me, and put me 4
101: 2 Oh when wilt thou come to me? 19
119:82 I ask, "When wilt thou comfort me? 19
84 When wilt thou judge those who persecute me? 19
139:15 not hidden . . when I was being made in secret 4
Prv 3:30 Do not contend . . when he has done you no harm. 3

6: 9 When will you arise from your sleep? 19
10:25 When the tempest passes, the wicked is no more 12
20:16 when he gives surety for foreigners. 6
23:35 When shall I awake? I will seek another drink? 19
27:13 when he gives surety for foreigners. 6
Ecc 4:10 but woe to him who is alone when he falls 18
5: 1 Guard your steps when you go to the house of God; 13
4 When you vow a vow to God, do not delay paying it; 13
8:16 When I applied my mind to know wisdom 13
9:12 at an evil time, when it suddenly falls upon them. 15
10:16 Woe to you, O land, when your king is a child 18
17 Happy . . when your king is the son of free men 18
12: 1 and the years draw nigh, when you will say 4
3 the day when the keepers of the house tremble 18
Sng 3: 4 Scarcely had I passed them, when I found him 21
Isa 4: 4 when the Lord shall have washed away the filth 3
7:15 when he knows how to refuse the evil 16
10:18 it will be as when a sick man wastes away. 12
13:19 Sodom and Gomor'rah when God overthrew them. 12
17: 5 it shall be as when the reaper gathers 12
5 as when one gleans the ears of grain in the Valley 12
18: 3 when a signal is raised on the mountains, look! 12
3 a signal . . look! When a trumpet is blown, hear! 12
5 For before the harvest, when the blossom is over 12
23: 5 When the report comes to Egypt 13
24:13 as when an olive tree is beaten 12
13 as at the gleaning when the vintage is done. 3
26: 9 For when thy judgments are in the earth 13
28: 4 when a man sees it, he eats it up 4
25 When he has leveled its surface 3
29: 8 As when a hungry man dreams he is eating 13
8 as when a thirsty man dreams he is drinking 13
11 When men give it to one who can read, saying 4
30:19 of your cry; when he hears it, he will answer you. 12
29 gladness of heart, as when one sets out 12
31: 4 when a band of shepherds is called forth 4
33: 1 When you have ceased to destroy, 0 12
1 when you have made an end of dealing 12
37: 1 When King Hezeki'ah heard it, he rent his clothes 12
40:24 when he blows upon them, and they wither 8
51:13 the oppressor, when he sets himself to destroy? 12
53:10 when he makes himself an offering for sin 3
64: 2 as when fire kindles brushwood 12
Jer 2:17 when he led you in the way 7
5:31 but what will you do when the end comes? 16
8:12 when I punish them, they shall be overthrown 7
10:13 When he utters his voice there is a tumult 16
11: 4 when I brought them out of the land of Egypt 5
7 when I brought them up out of the land of Egypt 5
26: 8 And when Jeremiah had finished speaking 12
31:32 when I took them by the hand to bring them out 5
34:13 when I brought them out of the land of Egypt 5
36:16 When they heard all the words, they turned 12
39: 3 When Jerusalem was taken 13
4 When Zedeki'ah king of Judah and all the soldiers 13
41: 7 When they came into the city, Ish'mael . . slew them 12
13 when all the people who were with Ish'mael saw 12
43: 1 When Jeremiah finished speaking 12
49:18 As when Sodom and Gomor'rah . . were overthrown 12
50:40 As when God overthrew Sodom and Gomor'rah 12
51:61 said to Serai'ah: "When you come to Babylon 12
63 When you finish reading this book 12
Ezk 2: 2 And when he spoke to me, the Spirit entered 13
5: 2 when the days of the siege are completed; 12
6: 9 when I have broken their wanton heart 4
16:50 therefore I removed them, when I saw it. 13
17:10 utterly wither when the east wind strikes it 12
23:16 When she saw them she doted upon them 16
19 days of her youth, when she played the harlot 4
31:15 says the Lord GOD: When it goes down to Sheol 5
33:12 shall not deliver him when he transgresses; 5
12 when he turns from his wickedness; 5
12 to live by his righteousness when he sins. 5
34:12 when some of his sheep have been scattered 5
35:11 make myself known among you, when I judge you. 13
37:18 when your people say to you, 'Will you not show us 13
39:29 when I pour out my Spirit upon the house of Israel 4
Dan 1:18 At the end of the time, when the king had commanded 4
3: 5 when you hear the sound of the horn, 24
15 when you hear the sound of the horn, 24
5:20 when his heart was lifted up 26
6:10 When Daniel knew that the document had been 26
14 Then the king, when he heard these words, 26
20 When he came near to the den where Daniel was 25
8: 8 when he was strong, the great horn was broken 12
23 when the transgressors have reached 12
10: 9 when I heard the sound of his words, I fell 12
19 when he spoke to me, I was strengthened and said 12
11: 2 when he has become strong through his riches 12
4 when he has arisen, his kingdom shall be broken 12
12: 7 when the shattering of the power of the holy 12
Hos 2:13 days of the Ba'als when she burned incense to them 4
7: 1 when I would heal Israel 12
13: 1 When E'phraim spoke, men trembled; 12
Jol 3: 1 when I restore the fortunes of Judah 4
Ams 7: 2 When they had finished eating the grass 3
8: 5 When will the new moon be over, that we may sell 19
Jon 4: 2 is not this what I said when I was yet in my country? 20
8 When the sun rose, God appointed a sultry east 12
Mic 5: 8 which, when it goes through, treads down 3
Nah 2: 3 The chariots flash . . when mustered in array; 5
Hab 2:18 in his own creation when he makes dumb idols! 16
Zec 14: 3 as when he fights on a day of battle. 11
Mal 3:17 my special possession on the day when I act 4
4: 3 on the day when I act, says the LORD of hosts. 4
Mat 2: 8 for the child, and when you have found him bring me 38
7: 4 when there is the log in your own eye? 46
24: 1 when his disciples came to point out to him 49
3 when will this be, and what will be the sign 60
38 until the day when Noah entered the ark 57
25:37 'Lord, when did we see thee hungry and feed thee 60
38 And when did we see thee a stranger 60
39 And when did we see thee sick or in prison 60
44 'Lord, when did we see thee hungry or thirsty 60
27:12 when he was accused by the chief priests 35
Mrk 2:26 when Abi'athar was high priest 41
5:38 When they came to the house 49
6:35 when it grew late, his disciples came to him 43
7: 1 Now when the Pharisees gathered together to him 49
13: 4 when will this be, and what will be the sign 60
33 you do not know when the time will come. 60
35 you do not know when the master of the house 60
15:25 it was the third hour, when they crucified him. 49
Lke 1: 8 when his division was on duty 35
23 when his time of service was ended 33
25 done to me in the days when he looked on me 57
41 when Elizabeth heard the greeting of Mary 33
44 when the voice of your greeting came to my ears 62
78 when the day shall dawn upon us from on high 35
2:15 When the angels went away from them into heaven 62
27 when the parents brought in the child Jesus 35
39 when they had performed everything 62
3:21 Now when all the people were baptized 35
4:25 when there came a great famine over all the land; 62
5: 4 when he had ceased speaking, he said to Simon 62
8:40 Now when Jesus returned, the crowd welcomed him 35
9:36 when the voice had spoken, Jesus was found alone. 35
51 When the days drew near for him to be received up 35
10:35 I will repay you when I come back.' 35
11: 1 when he ceased, one of his disciples said to him 62
22 when one stronger than he assails him 38
34 when it is not sound, your body is full of darkness. 38
14: 1 when he went to dine at the house of a ruler 35
17:20 asked . . when the kingdom of God was coming 60
19: 5 when Jesus came to the place, he looked up and said 62
15 When he returned, having received the kingdom 35
29 When he drew near to Beth'phage and Bethany 62
41 when he drew near and saw the city he wept over it 62
43 when your enemies will cast up a bank about you 49
21: 6 the days will come when there shall not be left 36
7 will be the sign when this is about to take place? 60
22:66 When day came 62
23:29 For behold, the days are coming when they will say 36
31 if they do this when the wood is green 35
31 what will happen when it is dry? 35
24:30 When he was at table with them, he took the bread 35
Joh 2: 9 When the steward of the feast tasted the water 62
23 when he was in Jerusalem at the Passover feast 62
4: 1 when the Lord knew that the Pharisees had heard 62
40 So when the Samaritans came to him, they asked him 62
6:12 when they had eaten their fill 62
16 When evening came 62
25 Rabbi, when did you come here? 60
11: 6 when he heard that he was ill 62
20 When Martha heard that Jesus was coming 62
29 when she heard it, she rose quickly and went 62
32 Mary, when she came where Jesus was and saw him 62
33 When Jesus saw her weeping 62
12: 9 When the great crowd of the Jews learned 59
32 when I am lifted up from the earth 32
13:26 I shall give this morsel when I have dipped it 49
14: 3 when I go and prepare a place for you 32
16: 2 when whoever kills you will think . . 47
32 when you will be scattered, every man to his home 47
17: 1 When Jesus had spoken these words 49
18: 6 When he said to them, "I am he 62
21: 9 When they got out on land, they saw a charcoal fire 62
Act 1:22 until the day when he was taken up from us 57
2: 1 When the day of Pentecost had come 35
5:24 when . . the chief priests heard these words 62
7:23 When he was 40 years old 62
45 when they dispossessed the nations 35
8: 6 when they heard him and saw the signs which he did. 35
9:23 When many days had passed 62
10: 7 When the angel who spoke to him had departed 62
25 When Peter entered, Cornelius met him 62
13:29 when they had fulfilled all that was written 62
14: 5 When an attempt was made by . . Gentiles and Jews 62
16:10 when he had seen the vision 62
15 when she was baptized, with her household 62
17:13 when the Jews of Thessaloni'ca learned 62
18: 5 When Silas and Timothy arrived from Macedo'nia 62
19: 9 when some were stubborn and disbelieved 62
20:14 when he met us at Assos, we took him on board 62
18 when they came to him, he said to them 62
21: 1 when we had parted from them and set sail 62
12 When we heard this 62
26 to give notice when . . purification would be fulfilled 42
27 When the seven days were almost completed 62
22:11 when I could not see 62
25 when they had tied him up with the thongs 62
27: 1 when it was decided that we should sail for Italy 62
27 When the fourteenth night had come 62
28: 4 When the natives saw the creature 62
Rom 3: 4 and prevail when thou art judged. 35
7: 9 but when the commandment came, sin revived 60
1Co 11:34 I will give directions when I come. 63
14:16 when he does not know what you are saying? 40
16:10 When Timothy comes, see that you put him at ease 32
2Co 1: 6 which you experience when you patiently endure 35
3:14 for to this day, when they read the old covenant 41
16 when a man turns to the Lord the veil is removed. 45
Gal 4:18 not only when I am present with you. 35
Eph 4:16 when each part is working properly 51
2Th 1: 7 when the Lord Jesus is revealed from heaven 35
1Ti 4:14 when the . . elders laid their hands upon you. 52
6:12 you were called when you made the good confession 49
2Ti 1: 3 when I remember you constantly in my prayers. 62
Heb 3: 7 Today, when you hear his voice 32
15 while it is said, "Today, when you hear his voice 32
4: 7 Today, when you hear his voice 32
7:15 when another priest arises 34
8: 8 when I will establish a new covenant 49
10:32 when . . you endured a hard struggle 36
1Pe 4:13 and be glad when his glory is revealed. 35
1Jn 2:28 so that when he appears we may have confidence 32
3: 2 we know that when he appears we shall be like him 32
3Jn 1: 5 when you render any service to the brethren 58
1Es 4:43 in the day when you became king 57
5:44 when they came to the temple of God 35
6:15 when our fathers sinned against the Lord 39
9:37 when the sons . . were in their settlements 49
46 when he opened the law, they all stood erect 35
2Es 1:17 When you were hungry and thirsty 64
20 When you were thirsty 64
22 When you were in the wilderness 64
26 When you call upon me, I will not listen to you 69
31 When you offer oblations to me, I will turn my face 64
2:23 When you find any who are dead 71
27 when the day of tribulation and anguish comes 64
33 When I came to them they rejected me 64
3: 4 when thou didst form the earth 69
12 When those who dwelt on earth began to multiply 64
13 when they were committing iniquity before thee 64
17 when thou didst lead his descendants out 64
29 when I came here 64
35 When have the inhabitants . . not sinned 69
4:11 When I heard this, I fell on my face 64
32 When heads of grain without number are sown 69
33 How long and when will these things be? 69
35 And when will come the harvest of our reward? 69
36 When the number of those like yourselves 69
40 when her nine months have been completed 69
48 and when the flame had gone by I looked, and behold 64
49 and when the rainstorm had passed 64
5: 1 when those who dwell on earth shall be seized 65
31 When I had spoken these words 64
6: 7 when will be the end of the first age 69
17 When I heard this, I rose to my feet and listened 64
18 when I draw near to visit the inhabitants 69
19 when I require from the doers of iniquity 69
19 and when the humiliation of Zion is complete 69
20 when the seal is placed upon the age 64
23 when all hear it 64
52 by whom thou wilt, and when thou wilt. 69
7: 1 When I had finished speaking these words 64
11 and when Adam transgressed my statutes 69
21 those who came into the world, when they came 69
26 when the signs which I have foretold to you 69
70 When the Most High made the world 69
75 when thou wilt renew the creation 67
78 When the decisive decree has gone forth 69
88 when they shall be separated 69
97 The sixth order, when it is shown to them 69
111 when corruption has increased 69
116 or else, when it had produced him 64
8: 9 when the womb gives up again 69
36 when thou art merciful to those who have no store 64
63 thou hast not shown me when thou wilt do them. 70
9: 1 when you see that a certain part . . are past 64
2 when the Most High is about to visit the world 68
3 when there shall appear in the world 69
18 when I was preparing for those who now exist 64
29 when they came out from Egypt 69
29 when they came into the . . wilderness; 69
34 when it happens that what was sown . . 64
38 When I said these things in my heart 64
47 when he grew up and I came to take a wife for him 64
10: 1 when my son entered his wedding chamber 64
3 when they all had stopped consoling me 64
12:13 the days are coming when a kingdom shall arise 65
21 the time when its end approaches 64
33 and when he has reproved them 64
40 When all the people heard that the seven days 64
13: 4 as wax melts when it feels the fire. 69
9 behold, when he saw the onrush 72
11 When I saw it, I was amazed. 65

29 when the Most High will deliver those 69
32 when these things come to pass 64
33 when all the nations hear his voice 69
49 Therefore when he destroys the multitude 69
14: 3 when my people were in bondage in Egypt; 69
26 when you have finished 64
35 the judgment will come, when we shall live again; 69
40 I took it and drank; and when I had drunk it 64
45 when the 40 days were ended 64
15:50 when the heat rises that is sent upon you. 64
53 and talking about their death when you were drunk? 64
16: 6 when once it has begun to burn? 64
13 and will not miss when they begin to be shot 64
18 when there shall be much lamentation 65
18 the beginning of famine, when many shall perish; 65
18 when the powers shall be terrified 65
18 when all shall tremble 65
18 when the calamities come? 64
38 when the time of her delivery draws near 66
50 when she decks herself out 64
50 when he comes who will defend him 64
65 when your sins come out before men 64
Tob 1:18 When the bodies were sought by the king 49
4: 3 My son, when I die, bury me 32
7 begrudge the gift when you make it 35
16 let your eye begrudge the gift when you made it. 35
5: 2 when I do not know the man? 49
13 when we went together to Jerusalem to worship 62
6: 9 When they approached Ecbatana 62
16 When you enter the bridal chamber 32
17 When Tobias heard these things, he fell in love 62
7: 1 When they reached Ecbatana 49
11 when each came to her he died in the night. 55
8: 4 When the door was shut and the two were alone 62
10: 1 when the days for the journey had expired 62
11:12 when his eyes began to smart he rubbed them 62
17 When Tobit came near to Sarah his daughter-in-law 62
14: 3 When he had grown very old 30
Jdt 2: 4 When he had finished setting forth his plan 62
5 When you leave my presence 46
5: 1 When Holofernes . . heard 49
10 When a famine spread over Canaan 29
22 When Achior had finished saying this 62
6: 1 When the disturbance . . died down 62
12 When the men of the city saw them 62
7: 4 When the Israelites saw their vast numbers 62
8: 9 When Judith heard the wicked words 49
10: 1 When Judith had ceased crying out 62
7 When they saw her 62
10 When they had done this, Judith went out 49
14 When the men heard her words 62
16 when you stand before him 32
22 When they told him of her 49
23 when Judith came 62
11:11 when they do what is wrong. 54
15 When the word reaches them 63
17 tell me when they have committed their sins. 60
12: 8 When she came up from the spring 62
13: 1 When evening came, his slaves quickly withdrew 62
12 When the men of her city heard her voice 62
20 when our nation was brought low 31
14: 6 when he came and saw the head of Holofernes 62
7 when they raised him up he fell at Judith's feet 62
9 when she had finished 62
12 when the Assyrians saw them 62
15 when no one answered 62
19 When the leaders of the Assyrian army heard this 62
15: 1 When the men in the tents heard it 62
5 when the Israelites heard it 62
9 when they met her they all blessed her 62
16:18 When they arrived at Jerusalem 62
AEs 15: 1 On the third day, when she ended her prayer 62
Wis 2: 1 there is no remedy when a man comes to his end 35
3:13 she will have fruit when God examines souls. 35
4: 6 when God examines them. 35
20 come with dread when their sins are reckoned up 35
10: 5 when the nations . . had been confounded 35
11 When his oppressors were covetous 35
14 when he was in prison she did not leave him 35
18:13 yet, when their first-born were destroyed 41
Sir 6: 7 When you gain a friend, gain him through testing 34
7: 9 when I make an offering to the Most High God 35
8: 6 Do not disdain a man when he is old 35
9:10 when it has aged you will drink it with pleasure. 32
10:11 when a man is dead 35
11: 9 nor sit with sinners when they judge a case. 35
19 when he says, "I have found rest 35
12: 9 A man's enemies are grieved when he prospers 35
16:19 shake with trembling when he looks upon them. 35
26 when he made them, he determined their divisions. 28
18:15 cause grief . . when you present a gift. 35
21 when you are on the point of sinning, turn back. 35
24 moment of vengeance when he turns away his face. 35
33 when you have nothing in your purse. 49
19: 9 when the time comes he will hate you. 35
28 he will do evil when he finds an opportunity. 32
29 is known by his face, when you meet him. 28
20: 6 keeps silent because he knows when to speak. 50
21 when he rests he feels no remorse. 35
21: 7 the sensible man, when he slips, is aware of it. 35
15 When a man of understanding hears a wise saying 32
20 A fool raises his voice when he laughs 35
27 When an ungodly man curses his adversary 35
22:13 you will not be soiled when he shakes himself off; 35
23:14 when you sit among great men 29
25:22 when a wife supports her husband. 32
27: 4 When a sieve is shaken, the refuse remains 35
30: 5 when he died he was not grieved; 35
31: 3 when he rests he fills himself with his dainties. 35
4 when he rests he becomes needy. 35
32:19 when you have acted, do not regret it. 35
33: 7 when all the daylight in the year is from the sun? 49
35:14 nor the widow when she pours out her story. 32
38: 9 My son, when you are sick do not be negligent 35
23 When the dead is at rest 35
23 be comforted for him when his spirit is departed. 35
39:31 when their times come 35
41: 9 When you are born, you are born to a curse 32
9 when you die, a curse is your lot. 32
42: 9 when she is young, lest she do not marry 35
43: 2 The sun, when it appears, making proclamation 35
7 a light that wanes when it has reached the full. 41
44:20 when he was tested he was found faithful. 35
45:23 stood fast, when the people turned away 35
46: 2 How glorious he was when he lifted his hands 35
5 when enemies pressed him on every side 35
16 when his enemies pressed him on every side 35
47: 4 when he lifted his hand with a stone in the sling 35
6 when the glorious diadem was bestowed upon him. 35
48:13 when he was dead his body prophesied. 35
50: 5 when the people gathered round him 35
6 like the moon when it is full; 37
11 When he put on his glorious robe 35
12 when he received the portions 35
51:29 may you not be put to shame when you praise him. 35
Bar 1: 2 at the time when the Chaldeans took Jerusalem 57
19 From the day when the Lord brought our fathers 57
20 at the time when he brought our fathers out 57
Sus 1: 7 When the people departed at noon 44
19 When the maids had gone out, the two elders rose 62
26 When the household servants heard the shouting 62
27 And when the elders told their tale 44
28 when the people gathered at the house 62
52 When they were separated from each other 62
Bel 1: 1 When King Astyages was laid with his fathers 49
14 When they had gone out 62
28 When the Babylonians heard it 62
40 When he came to the den he looked in 49
1Mc 1:16 When Antiochus saw 49
2: 7 to dwell there when it was given over to the enemy 35
23 When he had finished speaking these words 62
24 When Mattathias saw it, be burned with zeal 49
39 When Mattathias and his friends learned of it 49
52 Was not Abraham found faithful when tested 35
3:11 When Judas learned of it, he went out to meet him 49
13 Now when Seron . . heard 49
16 When he approached the ascent of Beth-horon 49
17 when they saw the army coming to meet them 62
23 When he finished speaking 62
27 When king Antiochus heard these reports 62
40 when they arrived they encamped near Emmaus 49
41 When the traders of the region heard 49
4: 5 When Gorgias entered the camp of Judas by night 49
12 When the foreigners looked up 49
30 When he saw that the army was strong, he prayed 49
5:16 When Judas and the people heard these messages 62
34 when the army of Timothy realized 49
42 When Judas approached the stream of water 62
6: 1 when he heard 49
8 When the king heard this news, he was astounded 62
17 when Lysias learned that the king was dead 49
39 When the sun shone upon the shields of gold 62
47 when the Jews saw the royal might 49
62 when the king entered Mount Zion 49
7: 3 when this act became known to him, he said 49
25 When Alcimus saw that Judas . . had grown strong 62
31 When Nicanor learned 49
44 When his army saw that Nicanor had fallen 62
9: 1 When Demetrius heard 49
6 When they saw the huge number of the enemy forces 49
7 When Judas saw that his army had slipped away 49
16 When those on the left wing saw 49
32 When Bacchides learned of this 49
42 when they had fully avenged . . their brother 49
43 When Bacchides heard of this 49
57 When Bacchides saw that Alcimus was dead 49
63 When Bacchides learned of this 49
70 When Jonathan learned of this 49
10: 2 When Demetrius the king heard of it 49
22 When Demetrius heard of these things 49
46 When Jonathan and the people heard these words 62
64 when his accusers saw the honor that was paid him 62
68 When Alexander the king heard of it 49
74 When Jonathan heard the words of Apollonius 62
77 When Apollonius heard of it 49
88 When Alexander the king heard of these things 62
11: 3 when Ptolemy entered the cities 62
4 When he approached Azotus 62
23 When Jonathan heard this 62
38 Now when Demetrius the king saw 49
44 when they came to the king 49
49 When the men of the city saw 49
60 When he came to Askalon 49
73 When his men who were fleeing saw this 49
12: 1 Now when Jonathan saw 49
27 So when the sun set 62
28 When the enemy heard 49
35 When Jonathan returned he convened the elders 49
42 When Trypho saw that he had come 49
48 when Jonathan entered Ptolemais 62
51 When their pursuers saw that they would fight 49
13: 7 when they heard these words 27
23 When he approached Baskama, he killed Jonathan 62
14: 2 When Arsaces the king of Persia and Media heard 49
17 When they heard 62
25 When the people heard these things they said 62
15: 9 When we gain control of our kingdom 62
16: 6 when his men saw him, they crossed over after him. 49
2Mc 1:20 when they reported to us 62
21 when the materials . . were presented 62
22 When this was done and some time had passed 62
31 when the materials . . were consumed 48
32 When this was done, a flame blazed up 62
33 When this matter became known 62
2: 7 When Jeremiah learned of it 62
5:20 when the great Lord became reconciled. 35
8:19 when 185,000 perished 62
20 when 8,000 in all went into the affair 62
9:23 on the occasions when he made expeditions 57
11: 6 When Maccabeus and his men got word 62
3Mc 4:12 when this had happened 62
5:48 when the Jews saw the dust 62
7:13 When they had applauded him in fitting manner 61
4Mc 2:11 one rebukes her when she breaks the law. 31
13 one rebukes friends when they act wickedly. 31
14 when reason, through the law, can prevail 56
21 Now when God fashioned man 53
4: 1 When . . he was unable to injure Onias 40
22 For when he was warring against Ptolemy in Egypt 40
24 When . . he had not been able in any way 39
26 when, then, his decrees were despised 39
6:34 when it masters even external agonies 56
8: 2 when the tyrant was conspicuously defeated 40
13 when the guards had placed before them wheels 62
9:12 When they had worn themselves out beating him 62
11: 1 When this one died also 62
12: 1 When he also, thrown into the caldron, had died 62
17: 1 when she also was about to be seized 62

when כִּי

Gen 4:12; 6:1; 12:12; 24:41; 26:8; 27:1; 31:49; 32:17; 43:21; 44:24; 46:33, Exd 3:21; 7:9; 12:25, 26, 48; 13:5, 11, 14, 15; 18:16; 21:2, 7, 18, 20, 22, 26, 28, 33[2], 35; 22:5, 6; 23:23; 30:12, Lev 1:2; 2:1, 4; 5:5; 6:4; 13:29, 38, 47; 14:34; 15:2, 13, 19; 19:5, 23, 33; 22:21, 27, 29; 23:10; 24:19; 25:2; 27:2, 14, Num 5:6; 6:2; 15:2, 8; 18:26; 30:2, 3; 33:51; 34:2; 35:10, Deu 4:25; 6:10, 20; 7:1; 11:29; 12:20, 25, 28, 29; 14:24; 15:13; 17:14; 18:9; 19:1; 20:1, 10, 19; 21:9, 10; 22:8; 23:9, 21; 24:1, 5, 20, 21; 25:11; 26:1, 12; 30:1; 31:21; 32:36, Jos 4:6; 8:5; 17:13; 22:7, Jdg 1:28; 6:7; 8:1; 12:5; 13:17; 15:3; 16:16, 25; 21:22, 1Sm 10:7; 13:11; 17:48; 20:12; 22:22; 25:30; 28:22, 2Sm 4:10, 11; 6:13; 7:1, 12; 14:26; 19:25, 1Kg 5:1; 8:35, 36, 2Kg 5:13; 7:12; 17:21; 18:32, 1Ch 17:11, 2Ch 6:26, 27, Neh 9:18, Job 1:5; 3:22; 5:21; 7:13; 13:9; 27:8[2], 9; 29:11; 30:26; 31:14[2], 26, 29; 36:13; 37:4; 38:40, 41, Ps 8:3; 2:3; 9:16[2], 18; 8:10; 1:23; 3:21; 02:0; 16:10; 19:32; 20:7; 27:5, Prv 3:25; 4:3; 6:30; 20:16; 22:6; 23:1, 22, 31[2]; 26:25; 27:13; 30:22[2], 23, Isa 1:12; 8:19; 10:12; 16:4, 12[2]; 19:20; 28:15, 18; 30:21[2]; 40:7; 43:2[2]; 54:6; 58:7, Jer 2:26; 3:16; 5:19; 6:15; 8:12; 12:1; 13:21; 15:2; 16:10; 17:8; 18:22; 23:33; 29:13; 37:16; 42:6; 44:19; 51:2, Lam 3:28, Ezk 14:13, 23; 21:7[2]; 25:3[3]; 46:12, Hos 4:14[2]; 11:1, Mic 5:6; 7:8, Hab 2:18; 3:8, Zec 7:5, 6, Mal 1:8

when ὅταν

Mat 5:11; 6:2, 5, 6, 16; 9:15; 10:19; 12:43; 15:2; 19:28; 21:40; 23:15; 24:15, 33; 25:31; 26:29, Mrk 2:20; 4:15, 16, 29, 31, 32; 8:38; 11:19; 12:25; 13:4, 7, 11, 14, 29; 14:25, Lke 5:35; 6:22[2], 26; 8:13; 9:26; 11:2, 21, 24, 34, 36; 12:11, 54, 55; 14:8, 10[2], 12, 13; 16:4, 9; 17:10; 21:7, 9, 20, 31; 23:42, Joh 2:10; 4:25; 5:7; 7:27, 31; 8:28, 44; 10:4; 13:19; 14:29; 15:26; 16:4, 13, 21[2]; 21:18, Act 23:35; 24:22, Rom 2:14; 11:27, 1Co 3:4; 13:10; 14:26; 15:24, 27, 28, 54; 16:2, 3, 12, 2Co 10:6; 12:10; 13:9, Col 3:4; 4:16, 1Th 5:3, 2Th 1:10, 1Ti 5:11, Tit 3:12, Heb 1:6, Jas 1:2, 1Jn 5:2, Rev 8:1; 9:5; 11:7; 12:4; 17:10; 18:9; 20:7, 1Es 3:9, 22, 23; 4:24, Tob 4:4; 6:17; 8:21, Jdt 6:6, Sir 0:2; 2:14; 18:7, LJr 1:41, 43, 48, 55, 61, 62

when ὅτε

Mat 7:28; 9:25; 11:1; 12:3; 13:26, 48, 53; 19:1; 21:1, 34; 26:1; 27:31, Mrk 2:25; 4:6, 10; 6:21; 7:17; 8:19; 11:1; 14:12; 15:20, 41, Lke 2:21, 22, 42; 4:25; 6:3, 13; 15:30; 17:22; 22:14, 35; 23:33, Joh 1:19; 2:22; 4:21, 23, 45; 5:25; 6:24; 9:4; 12:16, 17; 13:12, 31; 16:25; 19:6, 8, 23, 30; 20:24; 21:15, 18, Act 1:13; 8:12, 39; 12:6; 21:5, 35; 22:20; 27:39; 28:16, Rom 6:20; 13:11, 1Co 12:2; 13:11, Gal 1:15; 2:11, 12, 14; 4:3, 4, Php 4:15, Col 3:7, 1Th 3:4, 2Th 3:10, 2Ti 4:3, Tit 3:4, Heb 7:10, 1Pe 3:20, Jde 1:9, Rev 1:17; 5:8; 6:1, 3, 5, 7, 9, 12; 10:3, 4, 10; 12:13; 22:8, 1Es 1:39, 43; 3:13; 4:44, 45, 58, Tob 1:4, 9, 10, 15; 2:1, 7, 13; 8:1, 3; 12:12[2], 13; 14:2, 12, Jdt 5:18, Wis 9:9; 11:9, 13; 16:5; 19:11, 17, Sir 38:13; 44:17, LJr 1:24, Sus 1:14, 1Mc 4:9; 5:1; 6:28; 10:8; 16:16, 2Mc 1:18, 19, 20, 4Mc 16:15; 18:20

when it is time 1. ἐν

Sir 4:31 withdrawn when it is time to repay. 1

when once 1. מֵאָז
Ps 76: 7 stand before thee when once thy anger is roused? 1

whence 1. אֵי מִזֶּה 2. אֵיפֹה 3. מֵאַיִן 4. מִשָּׁם 5. ὅθεν 6. πόθεν
Gen 10:14 Caslu'him (whence came the Philistines) 4
Jdg 13: 6 I did not ask him whence he was, and he did not tell 1
19:17 said, "Where are you going? and whence do you come? 3
2Kg 6:27 the LORD will not help you, whence shall I help you? 3
20:14 did these men say? And whence did they come to you? 3
1Ch 1:12 Caslu'him (whence came the Philis'tines) 4
Job 1: 7 The LORD said to Satan, "Whence have you come? 3
2: 2 the LORD said to Satan, "Whence have you come? 1
10:21 before I go whence I shall not return 5
16:22 I shall go the way whence I shall not return. •
28:20 Whence then comes wisdom? 3
Isa 39: 3 did these men say? And whence did they come to you? 3
49:21 I was left alone; whence then have these come?' 2
Jon 1: 8 What is your occupation? And whence do you come? 3
Nah 3: 7 whence shall I seek comforters for her? 3
Mat 21:25 The baptism of John, whence was it? 6
Lke 20: 7 they did not know whence it was. 6
Joh 3: 8 you do not know whence it comes or whither it goes; 6
8:14 I know whence I have come and whither I am going 6
14 do not know whence I come or whither I am going. 6
Rev 7:13 Who are these . . and whence have they come? 6
4Mc 13:12 reminded them, "Remember whence you came 6

from whence 1. מֵאַיִן
Ps 121: 1 From whence does my help come? 1

whenever 1. אִם 2. בְּ 3. בְּכֹל 4. בְּכֹל אֲשֶׁר 5. בְּעֵת 6. וְ 7. כְּ 8. כַּאֲשֶׁר 9. כִּי 10. כֹּל 11. לְ 12. לְפִי 13. מִדֵּי 14. ἡνίκα ἄν 15. ὃς ἄν 16. ὅταν 17. ὅτι ἐάν 18. ubicumque
Gen 30:41 Whenever the stronger of the flock were breeding 3
Exd 17:11 Whenever Moses held up his hand, Israel 8
11 and whenever he lowered his hand, Am'alek 8
33: 8 Whenever Moses went out to the tent 7
34:34 whenever Moses went in before the LORD to speak 2
40:36 whenever the cloud was taken up 2
Num 9:17 whenever the cloud was taken up from over 12
10: 6 alarm is to be blown whenever they are to set out. 11
34 whenever they set out from the camp. 2
35 whenever the ark set out, Moses said, "Arise, O LORD 2
Deu 4: 7 as the LORD . . is to us, whenever we call upon him? 3
Jdg 2:15 Whenever they marched out, the hand of the LORD 4
18 Whenever the LORD raised up judges for them 9
19 whenever the judge died, they turned back 2
6: 3 For whenever the Israelites put in seed 1
1Sm 16:23 whenever the evil spirit . . David took the lyre 2
2Sm 15: 5 whenever a man came . . he would put out his hand 2
1Kg 8:52 giving ear to them whenever they call to thee. 3
2Kg 4: 8 So whenever he passed that way, he would turn 13
10 so that whenever he comes to us, he can go in there. 2
12:10 whenever they saw that there was much money 7
1Ch 23:31 whenever burnt offerings are offered 10
2Ch 7: 6 whenever David offered praises by their 2
19:10 whenever a case comes to you from your brethren •
24:11 whenever the chest was brought to the king's 5
Jer 20: 8 For whenever I speak, I cry out, I shout 13
48:27 whenever you spoke of him you wagged your head? 13
Ezk 3:17 whenever you hear a word from my mouth 6
13: 7 a lying divination, whenever you have said 6
33: 7 whenever you hear a word from my mouth 6
Mrk 3:11 whenever the unclean spirits beheld him 16
11:25 whenever you stand praying, forgive 16
14: 7 whenever you will, you can do good to them; 16
Lke 10: 8 Whenever you enter a town and they receive you 15
10 whenever you enter a town 15
2Co 3:15 Yes, to this day whenever Moses is read 14
1Jn 3:20 whenever our hearts condemn us; 17
Rev 4: 9 whenever the living creatures give glory 16
1Es 4: 6 whenever they sow, reap the harvest 16
2Es 13: 4 whenever his voice issued from his mouth 18
Wis 12:18 hast power to act whenever thou dost choose. 16

where 1. אַי 2. אַיֵּה 3. אַיֵּה אֵפוֹא 4. אֵי זֶה 5. אֵיכָה 6. אַיִן 7. אֵיפֹה 8. אֶל אֲשֶׁר 9. אָן 10. אֲשֶׁר 11. אֲשֶׁר בְּ 12. אֲשֶׁר עַל 13. אֲשֶׁר שָׁם 14. אֲשֶׁר שָׁמָּה 15. בְּ 16. כַּאֲשֶׁר 17. וְ 18. וְשָׁם 19. זֶה 20. זוּ 21. מֵאַיִן 22. מִן 23. עָלֵימוֹ 24. עַל כֵּן 25. שָׁם 26. שֶׁ שָׁם 27. תַּחַת 28. דִּי (A) 29. ἐκ 30. ἐκεῖ 31. ἐκεῖθεν 32. ἐν 33. ἐν οἷς 34. ἐπί 35. καί 36. κατά 37. ὅθεν 38. ὅπου 39. ὅς 40. οὗ 41. οὗπερ 42. οὗτος 43. πόθεν 44. ποῦ 45. τόπος 46. ὡς 47. et 48. quo 49. ubi
Gen 2:11 the whole land of Havilah, where there is gold; 13
3: 9 to the man, and said to him, "Where are you? 1
4: 9 the LORD said to Cain, "Where is Abel your brother? 1
13: 3 Bethel, to the place where his tent had been 25
4 to the place where he had made an altar 25
14 look from the place where you are 25
16: 8 he said "Hagar, maid of Sar'ai, where have you 1
8 have you come from and where are you going? 9
18: 9 They said to him, "Where is Sarah your wife? 2
19: 5 they called to Lot, "Where are the men who came 2
27 to the place where he had stood before the LORD; 10
20:15 land is before you; dwell where it pleases you. •
21:17 God has heard the voice of the lad where he is. 13
23 and with the land where you have sojourned. 10
22: 7 but where is the lamb for a burnt offering? 2
29: 4 My brothers, where do you come from? 6
30:38 the watering troughs, where the flocks came 10
31: 4 Leah into the field where his flock was •
13 I am the God of Bethel, where you anointed a pillar 10
32:17 'To whom do you belong? Where are you going? 9
35:13 went up from him in the place where he had spoken 10
14 a pillar in the place where he had spoken with him 10
15 name of the place where God had spoken with him 10
27 (that is, Hebron), where Abraham and Isaac 10
37:16 tell me . . where they are pasturing the flock. 7
30 The lad is gone; and I, where shall I go? 9
38:21 Where is the harlot who was at Enaim 2
39:20 the prison, the place where the king's prisoners 10
40: 3 in the prison where Joseph was confined. 10
42: 7 spoke roughly to them. "Where do you come from? 6
Exd 2:20 He said to his daughters, "And where is he? 1
8:22 the land of Goshen, where my people dwell 10
9:26 the land of Goshen, where the people of Israel 13
10:23 people of Israel had light where they dwelt. •
12:13 a sign . . upon the houses where you are; 25
30 for there was not a house where one was not dead. 13
15:27 Elim, where there were twelve springs of water 25
18: 5 the wilderness where he was encamped 13
20:21 drew near to the thick darkness where God was. 13
24 place where I cause my name to be remembered 10
29:42 tent of meeting . . where I will meet with you 13
30: 6 over the testimony, where I will meet with you. 13
36 the tent of meeting where I shall meet with you; 13
33:21 there is a place by me where you shall stand upon •
Lev 4:12 a clean place, where the ashes are poured out •
12 where the ashes are poured out it shall be burned •
24 in the place where they kill the burnt offering 10
33 the place where they kill the burnt offering 10
6:25 In the place where the burnt offering is killed 10
7: 2 in the place where they kill the burnt offering 10
14:13 in the place where they kill the sin offering 10
28 the place where the blood of the guilt offering •
18: 3 in the land of Egypt, where you dwelt 10
20:22 that the land where I am bringing you to dwell 13
Num 9:17 in the place where the cloud settled down 10
11:13 Where am I to get meat to give to all this people? 21
14:30 land where I swore that I would make you dwell 13
17: 4 before the testimony, where I meet with you. 10
20:13 Mer'ibah, where the people of Israel contended 10
21:14 Where it is said in the Book of the Wars of the LORD 24
22:26 in a narrow place, where there was no way to turn 10
33:14 encamped at Reph'idim, where there was no water 17
55 shall trouble you in the land where you dwell. 10
35: 6 where you shall permit the manslayer to flee 10
Deu 1:31 wilderness, where you have seen how the LORD 10
4:27 among the nations where the LORD will drive you. 10
8:15 thirsty ground where there was no water 10
11:10 Egypt . . where you sowed your seed and watered 10
12: 2 places where the nations . . served their gods 10
18: 6 comes from any of your towns . . where he lives– 10
21:14 let her go where she will •
19 city at the gate of the place where he lives •
23:16 where it pleases him best; you shall not oppress •
28:37 among . . peoples where the LORD will lead you away. 14
29:23 growing nothing, where no grass can sprout 17
30: 1 nations where the LORD your God has driven you 14
3 peoples where the LORD your God has scattered 14
31:16 land, where they go to be among them 14
32:37 'Where are their gods, the rock in which they took 1
Jos 2: 4 men came . . but I did not know where they came from; 6
5 where the men went I do not know; 9
4: 3 from the very place where the priests' feet stood •
3 lay them . . in the place where you lodge tonight. 11
5:15 Put off . . for the place where you stand is holy. 12
8:24 in the open wilderness where they pursued them 11
9: 8 Who are you? And where do you come from? 6
10:27 into the cave where they had hidden themselves 13
22: 4 your home in the land where your possession lies •
19 LORD's land where the LORD's tabernacle stands 13
33 to destroy the land where the Reubenites 11
Jdg 5:27 at her feet . . where he sank, there he fell dead. 16
6:13 And where are all his wonderful deeds 2
8:18 Where are the men whom you slew at Tabor? 7
9:38 Where is your mouth now, you who said, 'Who is 3
17: 8 departed . . to live where he could find a place; 16
9 Micah said to him, "From where do you come? 6
9 and I am going to sojourn where I may find a place. 16
18:10 God has given . . a place where there is no lack 13
19:17 Where are you going? and whence do you come? 9
26 at the door of the man's house where her master was 13
20:22 the same place where they had formed it 13
Rut 1: 7 she set out from the place where she was 14
16 where you go I will go, and where you lodge I will 8
16 and where you lodge I will lodge; 16
17 where you die I will die, and there . . be buried. 16
2:19 Where did you glean today? 7
3: 4 when he lies down, observe the place where he lies; 13
1Sm 1: 3 Shiloh, where the two sons of Eli . . were priests 25
3: 3 the temple of the LORD, where the ark of God was. 13
9:10 they went to the city where the man of God was. 13
18 and said, "Tell me where is the house of the seer? 1
10: 5 Gib'e-ath-elo'him, where there is a garrison 13
14 Saul's uncle said . . "Where did you go? 9
14:11 coming out of the holes where they have hid 13
19: 3 stand beside my father in the field where you are 13
22 he asked,"Where are Samuel and David? 7
20:19 then go to the place where you hid yourself 13
23:22 know and see the place where his haunt is 10
23 note . . all the lurking places where he hides 13
24: 3 came to the sheepfolds . . where there was a cave; 25
25:11 give it to men who come from I do not know where? 1
26: 5 and came to the place where Saul had encamped; 13
5 and David saw the place where Saul lay, with Abner 13
16 see where the king's spear is, and the jar of water 1
30: 9 Besor, where those stayed who were left behind. •
13 To whom do you belong? And where are you from? 19
31 the places where David and his men had roamed. 13
2Sm 1: 3 David said to him, "Where do you come from? 19
13 And David said . . "Where do you come from? 19
2:23 and he fell there, and died where he was. 27
23 to the place where As'ahel had fallen and died 13
7: 7 In all places where I have moved with . . Israel 10
9: 4 The king said to him, "Where is he? 7
11:16 the place where he knew there were valiant men. 13
13: 8 went to . . Amnon's house, where he was lying down. •
13 As for me, where could I carry my shame? 9
15:20 make you wander . . seeing I go I know not where? 10
32 David came to the summit, where God was worshiped 13
16: 3 And the king said, "And where is your master's son? 2
17:12 come upon him in some place where he is to be found 13
20 they said, "Where are Ahim'a-az and Jonathan? 2
21:12 Beth-shan . . where the Philistines had hanged 13
23:11 at Lehi, where there was a plot . . full of lentils; 25
1Kg 4:28 they brought to the place where it was required 13
7: 7 Hall of the Throne where he was to pronounce 13
8 His own house where he was to dwell . . was of like 13
8: 9 Horeb, where the LORD made a covenant 10
54 altar of the LORD, where he had knelt 22
11:36 the city where I have chosen to put my name. 13
13:25 told it in the city where the old prophet dwelt. 11
17:19 into the upper chamber, where he lodged 13
21:18 in the vineyard . . where he has gone 13
19 In the place where dogs licked up the blood 10
2Kg 2:14 saying, "Where is the LORD, the God of Eli'jah? 2
4: 8 went on to Shunem, where a wealthy woman lived 25
5:25 Eli'sha said to him, "Where have you been, Geha'zi? 21
6: 1 the place where we dwell . . is too small for us. 13
6 the man of God said, "Where did it fall? 9
13 Go and see where he is, that I may send and seize 5
8:28 to make war . . where the Syrians wounded Joram. •
14: 6 what is written . . where the LORD commanded 10
16: 6 and the E'domites came to Elath, where they dwell 18
18:34 Where are the gods of Hamath and Arpad? 2
34 Where are the gods of Sepharva'im, Hena, and Ivvah? 2
19:13 Where is the king of Hamath, the king of Arpad 1
23: 7 house of the LORD, where the women wove hangings 13
8 places where the priests had burned incense 14
1Ch 3: 4 born to him in Hebron, where he reigned •
4:40 where they found rich, good pasture •
11: 4 Jebus, where the Jeb'usites were 25
17: 6 In all places where I have moved with Israel 10
20: 6 at Gath, where there was a man of great stature •
2Ch 3: 1 Mori'ah, where the LORD had appeared to David 10
5:10 Horeb, where the LORD made a covenant 10
6:20 place where thou hast promised to set thy name 10
25: 4 in the book of Moses, where the LORD commanded 10
Ezr 6: 1 house of the archives where the documents 28
3 place where sacrifices are offered 28
10: 6 where he spent the night, neither eating bread 25
Neh 2:16 And the officials did not know where I had gone 9
4: 4 plundered in a land where they are captives. •
12 From all the places where they live 10
20 place where you hear the sound of the trumpet 10
10:39 chambers, where are the vessels of the sanctuary 25
13: 5 chamber where they had previously put 25
Est 7: 5 Who is he, and where is he, that would . . do this? 4
8 to the place where they were drinking wine •
8 Haman was falling on the couch where Esther was; 12
Job 4: 7 Or where were the upright cut off? 7
6:16 dark with ice, and where the snow hides itself. 23
8:11 Can papyrus grow where there is no marsh? •
11 Can reeds flourish where there is no water? •
10:22 gloom and chaos, where light is as darkness. •
14:10 man breathes his last, and where is he? 1
15:23 He wanders abroad for bread, saying, 'Where is it? 2
17:15 where then is my hope? Who will see my hope? 2
18:19 no survivor where he used to live. •
20: 7 those who have seen him will say, 'Where is he?' 1
21:28 Where is the house of the prince? 2
28 Where is the tent in which the wicked dwelt? 2
23: 3 Oh, that I knew where I might find him •
28: 4 open shafts in a valley away from where men live; •
12 But where shall wisdom be found? 21
12 And where is the place of understanding? 1
20 where is the place of understanding? 1
34:22 deep darkness where evildoers may hide 25
35:10 But none says, 'Where is God my Maker 2
36:16 into a broad place where there was no cramping •
38: 4 Where were you when I laid the foundation 7

19 Where is the way to the dwelling of light 1
19 where is the place of darkness 1
24 way to the place where the light is distributed *
24 where the east wind is scattered upon the earth? *
26 to bring rain on a land where no man is *
39:30 suck up blood; and where the slain are, there is he. 16
40:20 food for him where all the wild beasts play. 25
Ps 26: 8 thy house, and the place where thy glory dwells. *
33:14 from where he sits enthroned he looks forth *
41: 8 he will not rise again from where he lies. 10
42: 3 men say to me continually, "Where is your God? 2
10 they say to me continually, "Where is your God? 2
63: 1 as in a dry and weary land where no water is. *
68:16 yea, where the LORD will dwell for ever! *
69: 2 I sink in deep mire, where there is no foothold; *
74: 2 Remember Mount Zion, where thou hast dwelt. *
78:60 at Shiloh, the tent where he dwelt among men *
79:10 Why should the nations say, "Where is their God? 2
84: 3 where she may lay her young, at thy altars 10
89:49 Lord, where is thy steadfast love of old 2
115: 2 Why should the nations say, "Where is their God? 2
142: 3 path where I walk they have hidden a trap for me. 20
Prv 11:14 Where there is no guidance, a people falls; 15
14: 4 Where there are no oxen, there is no grain; 15
15 but the prudent looks where he is going. *
15:17 Better is a dinner of herbs where love is 25
26:20 where there is no whisperer, quarreling ceases. 15
29:18 Where there is no prophecy the people cast off 15
Ecc 1: 5 and hastens to the place where it rises. 25
7 to the place where the streams flow 26
8:10 in the city where they had done such things. 10
11: 3 in the place where the tree falls, there it . . lie. 26
Sng 1: 7 Tell me . . where you pasture your flock 5
7 Tell me . . where you make it lie down at noon; 5
Isa 7:23 every place where there used to be 1,000 vines 10
25 will become a place where cattle are let loose *
25 cattle are let loose and where sheep tread. *
10: 3 and where will you leave your wealth? 9
19:12 Where then are your wise men? Let them tell you 1
29: 1 Ho Ariel, Ariel, the city where David encamped! *
30: 6 from where come the lioness and the lion *
33:18 Where is he who counted, 2
18 where is he who weighed the tribute? 2
18 Where is he who counted the towers? 2
21 a place . . where no galley with oars can go *
36:19 Where are the gods of Hamath and Arpad? 2
19 Where are the gods of Sepharva'im? 2
37:13 Where is the king of Hamath, the king of Arpad 2
50: 1 Where is your mother's bill of divorce 1
51:13 And where is the fury of the oppressor? 2
63:11 Where is he who brought up out of the sea 2
11 Where is he who put in the midst of them 2
15 Where are thy zeal and thy might? 2
64:11 Our holy . . house, where our fathers praised thee 10
Jer 2: 6 They did not say, 'Where is the LORD 2
6 that none passes through, where no man dwells?' 25
8 The priests did not say, 'Where is the LORD? 2
28 But where are your gods that you made 2
3: 2 Where have you not been lain with? 7
6:16 ask for the ancient paths, where the good way is; 1
7:12 in Shiloh, where I made my name dwell at first 13
8: 3 in all the places where I have driven them 13
13: 7 waistcloth from the place where I had hidden it. 14
20 Where is the flock that was given you 2
15: 2 And when they ask you, 'Where shall we go?' 9
16:15 out of . . the countries where he had driven them. 14
17:15 Where is the word of the LORD? 2
19:14 Topheth, where the LORD had sent him to prophesy 13
22:12 in the place where they have carried him captive 13
26 into another country, where you were not born 13
23: 3 out of all the countries where I have driven them 13
8 out of . . the countries where he had driven them. 13
24: 9 in all the places where I shall drive them. 13
29: 7 seek the welfare of the city where I have sent you 13
14 and all the places where I have driven you 13
18 among all the nations where I have driven them 13
35: 7 may live many days in the land where you sojourn. 13
36:19 and let no one know where you are. 7
37:19 Where are your prophets who prophesied to you 2
42:14 go to the land of Egypt, where we shall not see war 10
22 in the place where you desire to go to live. 13
44: 8 in the land of Egypt where you have come to live 13
Lam 2:12 They cry . . Where is bread and wine? 2
Ezk 6: 9 the nations where they are carried captive 13
8: 3 where was the seat of the image of jealousy 13
11:16 in the countries where they have gone. 13
17 the countries where you have been scattered 10
12:16 abominations among the nations where they go 13
13:12 Where is the daubing with which you daubed it? 2
17: 6 its roots remained where it stood. *
7 From the bed where it was planted *
10 wither away on the bed where it grew? *
16 the place where the king dwells who made him king *
20:34 you out of the countries where you are scattered 11
38 bring them out of the land where they sojourn *
41 the countries where you have been scattered; 11
21:16 Cut . . to right and left where your edge is directed. 9
30 In the place where you were created 10
34:12 from all places where they have been scattered 13

37:25 shall dwell in the land where your fathers dwelt *
38: 8 the land where people were gathered *
40:38 gate, where the burnt offering was to be washed. 25
42:10 where the outside wall begins. *
12 on the east side, where one enters the passage *
13 holy chambers, where the priests who approach 13
43: 7 where I will dwell in the midst of the people 13
46:20 This is the place where the priests shall boil 13
20 where they shall bake the cereal offering 10
24 These are the kitchens where those who minister 13
47: 9 everything will live where the river goes. 13
Dan 6:10 house where he had windows in his upper chamber *
20 When he came near to the den where Daniel was *
8:17 came near where I stood; and when he came *
Hos 1:10 and in the place where it was said to them 10
13:10 Where now is your king, to save you; 44
10 where are all your princes, to defend you- *
14 O Death, where are your plagues? 44
14 O Sheol, where is your destruction? 44
Jol 2:17 Why should they say . . Where is their God? 2
Mic 7:10 her who said to me, "Where is the LORD your God? 1
Nah 2:11 Where is the lions' den, the cave of the young 2
11 where the lion brought his prey 13
11 where his cubs were, with none to disturb? *
3:17 they fly away; no one knows where they are. 1
Zec 1: 5 Your fathers, where are they? 2
2: 2 Then I said, "Where are you going?" 9
5:10 Then I said . . Where are they taking the Ephah? 9
Mal 1: 6 If then I am a father, where is my honor? 2
6 And if I am a master, where is my fear? 2
2:17 Or by asking, "Where is the God of justice?" 2
Mat 2: 2 Where is he who has been born king of the Jews? 44
4 inquired of them where the Christ was to be born 44
9 came to rest over the place where the child was. 40
6:19 on earth, where moth and rust consume and where 38
19 where moth and rust consume and where thieves 38
20 in heaven, where neither moth nor rust consumes 38
20 where thieves do not break in and steal. 38
21 For where your treasure is, there will your heart 38
11:20 where most of his mighty works had been done 32
13: 5 where they had not much soil 38
54 Where did this man get this wisdom 43
56 Where then did this man get all this? 43
15:33 Where are we to get bread enough in the desert 43
18:20 in my name, there am I in the midst of them. 40
25:24 reaping where you did not sow 38
24 gathering where you did not winnow; 37
26 You knew that I reap where I have not sowed 38
26 gather where I have not winnowed? 37
26:17 Where will you have us prepare for you 44
57 where the scribes and the elders had gathered. 38
28: 6 Come, see the place where he lay. 38
Mrk 4: 5 where it had not much soil 38
15 the ones along the path, where the word is sown; 38
5:40 and went in where the child was. 38
6: 2 Where did this man get all this? 43
10 he said to them, "Where you enter a house, stay there 38
55 to any place where they heard he was. 38
9:47 where their worm does not die 38
13:14 set up where it ought not to be 38
14:12 Where will you have us go 44
14 'The Teacher says, Where is my guest room 44
14 where I am to eat the passover with my disciples?' 38
15:47 Mary the mother of Joses saw where he was laid. 44
16: 6 he is not here; see the place where they laid him. 38
Lke 4:16 to Nazareth, where he had been brought up; 39
17 book and found the place where it was written 40
8:25 He said to them, "Where is your faith? 44
10: 1 place where he himself was about to come. 39
33 a Samaritan, as he journeyed, came to where he was; 36
12:33 where no thief approaches and no moth destroys. 38
34 where your treasure is, there will your heart be 38
13:25 'I do not know where you come from.' 43
27 I do not know where you come from; depart from me 43
17:17 Were not ten cleansed? Where are the nine? 44
37 they said to him, "Where, Lord? 44
37 Where the body is, there the eagles will be 38
20:37 where he calls the Lord the God of Abraham 46
22: 9 They said to him, "Where will you have us prepare it? 44
11 Where is the guest room 44
11 where I am to eat the passover with my disciples?' 38
23:53 tomb, where no one had ever yet been laid. 39
Joh 1:28 beyond the Jordan, where John was baptizing. 38
38 said to him, "Rabbi . . where are you staying? 44
39 They came and saw where he was staying; 44
2: 9 and did not know where it came 43
3: 8 The wind blows where it wills 38
4:11 where do you get that living water? 43
20 Jerusalem is . . where men ought to worship. 38
46 Cana in Galilee, where he had made the water wine. 38
6:23 the place where they ate the bread 38
62 the Son of man ascending where he was before? 38
7:11 The Jews were . . saying, "Where is he? 44
27 Yet we know where this man comes from; 43
27 no one will know where he comes from. 43
28 You know me, and you know where I come from? 43
34 where I am you cannot come. 38
35 Where does this man intend to go 42
36 'Where I am you cannot come'? 38

42 comes from Bethlehem, the village where David was? 38
8:10 Jesus . . said to her, "Woman, where are they? 44
19 They said to him therefore, "Where is your Father? 44
21 where I am going, you cannot come. 38
22 since he says, 'Where I am going, you cannot come'? 38
9:12 They said . . "Where is he?" He said, "I do not know 44
29 we do not know where he comes from. 43
30 You do not know where he comes 43
10:40 to the place where John at first baptized 38
11:30 still in the place where Martha had met him. 38
32 Mary, when she came where Jesus was and saw him 38
34 he said, "Where have you laid him? 44
57 orders that if any one knew where he was 44
12: 1 Jesus came to Bethany, where Laz'arus was 38
26 where I am, there shall my servant be also 38
35 walks in the darkness does not know where he goes. 44
13:33 'Where I am going you cannot come.' 38
36 Simon Peter said . . Lord, where are you going? 44
36 Where I am going you cannot follow me now 44
14: 3 that where I am you may be also. 38
4 you know the way where I am going. 38
5 Lord, we do not know where you are going 44
16: 5 yet none of you asks me, 'Where are you going?' 44
17:24 may be with me where I am 38
18: 1 where there was a garden 38
20 where all Jews come together 38
19: 9 he . . said to Jesus, "Where are you from? 43
20 the place where Jesus was crucified 38
41 Now in the place where he was crucified 38
20: 2 we do not know where they have laid him. 44
12 sitting where the body of Jesus had lain 38
13 I do not know where they have laid him. 44
15 tell me where you have laid him, and I will take him 44
19 the doors being shut where the disciples were 38
21:18 you girded yourself and walked where you would; 38
18 carry you where you do not wish to go. 38
Act 1:13 to the upper room, where they were staying 39
2: 2 it filled all the house where they were sitting. 39
7:29 Mid'ian, where he became the father of two sons. 39
12:12 the house of Mary . . where many were gathered 39
14:26 where they had been commended to the grace of God 37
16:13 the riverside, where we supposed there was 39
17: 1 where there was a synagogue of the Jews. 38
20: 6 at Tro'as, where we stayed for seven days.T 38
8 the upper chamber where we were gathered 39
25:10 Caesar's tribunal, where I ought to be tried; 39
Rom 4:15 where there is no law there is no transgression. 40
5:13 but sin is not counted where there is no law. *
20 but where sin increased, grace abounded 39
9:26 in the very place where it was said to them 39
15:20 not where Christ has already been named, 42
1Co 1:20 Where is the wise man? 44
20 Where is the scribe? 44
20 Where is the debater of this age? 44
12:17 whole body . . an eye, where would be the hearing? 44
17 whole . . an ear, where would be the sense of smell? 44
19 all were a single organ, where would the body be? 44
15:55 O death, where is thy victory? 44
55 O death, where is thy sting? 44
2Co 3:17 and where the Spirit of the Lord is, 39
Col 3: 1 where Christ is, seated at the right hand of God. 40
Heb 3: 9 where your fathers put me to the test 39
6:20 where Jesus has gone as a forerunner 38
9:16 For where a will is involved 38
10:18 Where there is forgiveness of these 38
11: 8 he went out, not knowing where he was to go. 44
Jas 3:16 For where jealousy and selfish ambition exist 38
1Pe 4:18 where will the impious and sinner appear? 44
2Pe 3: 4 and saying, "Where is the promise of his coming? 44
1Jn 2:11 the darkness, and does not know where he is going 44
Rev 2:13 I know where you dwell, where Satan's throne is 44
13 'I know where you dwell, where Satan's throne is; 38
13 who was killed among you, where Satan dwells. 38
11: 8 great city . . where their Lord was crucified. 38
12: 6 wilderness, where she has a place prepared by God 38
14 to the place where she is to be nourished 38
17:15 The waters . . where the harlot is seated 39
20:10 lake . . where the beast and the false prophet 38
1Es 6:24 in Jerusalem, where they sacrifice with . . fire 38
26 to be placed where they had been. 40
2Es 1:17 Where are the benefits which I bestowed on you? 49
4:29 if the place where the evil has been sown 49
29 the field where the good has been sown 49
5:16 Where have you been? And why is your face sad? 49
6:14 if the place where you are standing is . . shaken 48
29 the place where I was standing began to rock ‡
47 where the water had been gathered together 49
50 where the water had been gathered together 49
51 where to live in it, where there are 1,000 mountains; 49
9:24 a field of flowers where no house has been built 49
10:28 Where is the angel Uriel, who came to me at first? 49
51 remain in the field where no house had been built 49
53 where there was no foundation of any building 49
54 a place where the city . . was to be revealed. 49
13:41 where mankind had never lived 49
14: 4 Mount Sinai, where I kept him with me many days; 47
Tob 1: 4 where all the tribes should sacrifice *
4 where the temple . . was consecrated *
2:13 So I said to her, "Where did you get the kid? 43

14 Where are your charities 44
7: 3 Raguel asked them, "Where are you from, brethren? 43
Jdt 1: 6 the plain where Arioch ruled the Elymaeans. *
5:19 occupied Jerusalem, where their sanctuary is 40
7:10 the height of the mountains where they live 33
13 where . . the people . . get their water 31
9: 8 the tabernacle where thy glorious name rests *
10: 2 she rose from where she lay prostrate *
12 where are you coming 43
12 you coming from, and where are you going? 44
12: 1 bring her in where his silver dishes were kept 40
3 where can we get more like it for you? 43
14:17 he went to the tent where Judith had stayed 40
Wis 19: 7 and dry land emerging where water had stood before 29
8 where those protected by thy hand passed 39
Sir 0: 2 in cases where, despite our diligent labor 39
8:16 where no help is at hand, he will strike you down. 38
19:22 nor is there prudence where sinners take 38
27 where no one notices, he will forestall you 38
23:21 where he least suspects it, he will be seized. 39
27:27 he will not know where it came from. 43
29:24 where you are a stranger you may not open 39
32: 4 Where there is entertainment, do not pour 38
36:25 Where there is no fence, the property 39
25 where there is no wife, a man will wander 39
41:19 and of theft, in the place where you live 39
42: 6 Where there is an evil wife, a seal is a good thing; 34
6 Where there is an evil wife, a seal 38
43:28 Where shall we find strength to praise him? 44
46:12 May their bones revive from where they lie 45
49:10 May the bones . . revive from where they lie 45
Bar 2: 4 peoples, where the Lord has scattered them. 39
13 among the nations where thou hast scattered us. 39
29 among the nations where I will scatter them. 39
3: 8 our exile where thou has scattered us 39
14 Learn where there is wisdom, 44
14 Learn . . where there is strength, 44
14 Learn . . where there is understanding, 44
14 discern where there is length of days and life, 44
14 where there is light for the eyes and peace. 44
16 Where are the princes of the nations 44
LJr 1:48 consult . . as to where they can hide themselves 44
1Mc 1:57 Where the book of the covenant was found 38
3:50 Where shall we take them? 44
5: 6 where he found a strong band and many people 35
10:73 where there is no stone or pebble, or place to flee. 38
14:33 Judea, where formerly the arms of the enemy 39
2Mc 1:33 in the place where the exiled priests 39
2: 4 to the mountain where Moses had gone up 39
4:38 very place where he had committed the outrage 41
10:19 for places where he was more urgently needed. *
32 where Chaereas was commander. 30
14:32 that they did not know where the man was 44
3Mc 1: 1 Raphia, where Antiochus's supporters were 38
4: 1 In every place, then, where this decree arrived 38

where אָנָה
Rut 2:19

whereas 1. וְ 2. יַעַן אֲשֶׁר 3. תַּחַת 4. תַּחַת אֲשֶׁר 5. דִּי (A) 6. *δέ* 7. *ἐπεί* 8. *ὅπου* 9. *ὅστις* 10. *πάλιν* 11. quia
Deu 9: 4 whereas it is because of the wickedness 1
28:62 Whereas you were as the stars of heaven 4
1Sm 24:17 good, whereas I have repaid you evil. 1
1Kg 8:18 Whereas it was in your heart to build a house 2
12:11 now, whereas my father laid upon you a heavy yoke *
2Ch 6: 8 'Whereas it was in your heart to build a house 2
10:11 now, whereas my father laid upon you a heavy yoke *
Isa 60:15 Whereas you have been forsaken and hated 3
Jer 4:10 whereas the sword has reached their very life. 1
Dan 4:23 whereas the king saw a watcher, a holy one 5
1Ti 1: 5 whereas the aim of our charge is love 6
5: 6 whereas she who is self-indulgent is dead 6
Jas 4:14 whereas you do not know about tomorrow. 9
2Pe 2:11 whereas angels, though greater in might 8
2Es 7:51 For whereas you have said that the righteous 11
Wis 16:23 whereas the fire . . forgot its native power. 10
Sir 0: 1 Whereas many great teachings have been given *
1Mc 15: 3 Whereas . . pestilent men have gained control 7

whereever 1. אֲשֶׁר שָׁם
Ezk 36:20 whereever they came, they profaned my holy name 1

wherefore 1. לָכֵן 2. *ὅθεν*
Ezk 5:11 Wherefore, as I live, says the Lord GOD 1
13:20 Wherefore thus says the Lord GOD 1
16:35 Wherefore, O harlot, hear the word of the LORD 1
20:30 Wherefore say to the house of Israel 1
Act 26:19 Wherefore, O King Agrippa, I was not disobedient 2

wherein 1. בּוֹ 2. בַּמָּה 3. מָה
Jdg 16: 5 see wherein his great strength lies 2
6 Please tell me wherein your great strength lies 2
15 not told me wherein your great strength lies. 2
1Kg 18: 9 he said, "Wherein have I sinned 3
Job 3: 3 Let the day perish wherein I was born 1

whereon 1. עַל
Sng 4: 4 for an arsenal, whereon hang 1,000 bucklers 1

wherever 1. אֶל כָּל אֲשֶׁר 2. אֶל כָּל אֲשֶׁר שָׁם 3. אֲשֶׁר שָׁם 4. אֲשֶׁר שָׁמָּה 5. בַּאֲשֶׁר 6. בְּכֹל 7. בְּכֹל אֲשֶׁר 8. בִּמְקוֹם אֲשֶׁר שָׁם 9. דֶּרֶךְ אֲשֶׁר 10. כֹּל 11. כֹּל אֲשֶׁר 12. כֹּל אֲשֶׁר שָׁם 13. לְכֹל אֲשֶׁר 14. מֵאֲשֶׁר 15. מְקוֹם אֲשֶׁר 16. מְקוֹם אֲשֶׁר שָׁם 17. שָׁם 18. שָׁמָּה 19. כֹּל דִּי (A) 20. *κατὰ τόπον* 21. *ὅπου* 22. *ὅπου ἄν* 23. *ὅπου ἐάν* 24. *ὅς* 25. *ὅσος ἄν* 26. *οὗ ἄν* 27. *οὗ ἐάν* 28. ubi
Gen 28:15 I am with you and will keep you wherever you go 7
30:30 and the LORD has blessed you wherever I turned. †
35: 3 God who . . has been with me wherever I have gone. 9
Exd 5:11 get your straw wherever you can find it; 14
Num33:54 wherever the lot falls to any man, that shall be his 17
Deu 2:37 wherever the LORD our God forbade us. 11
Jos 1: 7 that you may have good success wherever you go. 7
9 for the LORD your God is with you wherever you go. 7
16 and wherever you send us we will go. 1
1Sm 14:47 wherever he turned he put them to the worse. 7
18: 5 David . . was successful wherever Saul sent him; 6
23:13 and they went wherever they could go. 5
2Sm 7: 9 and I have been with you wherever you went 7
8: 6 the LORD gave victory to David wherever he went. 7
14 the LORD gave victory to David wherever he went. 7
15:21 wherever my lord the king shall be . . there also 8
1Kg 2: 3 prosper in all that you do and wherever you turn; 12
2Kg 8: 1 Arise, and depart . . and sojourn wherever you can; 5
12: 5 repair the house wherever any need of repairs is 13
18: 7 wherever he went forth, he prospered. 7
1Ch 17: 8 I have been with you wherever you went 7
18: 6 LORD gave victory to David wherever he went. 11
13 the LORD gave victory to David wherever he went. 11
Est 4: 3 wherever the king's command and his decree came 15
8:17 wherever the king's command and his edict came 15
Prv 17: 8 wherever he turns he prospers. 11
21: 1 he turns it wherever he will. 11
Jer 40: 4 go wherever you think it good and right to go. 18
5 or go wherever you think it right to go. 10
Ezk 1:12 wherever the spirit would go, they went 4
20 Wherever the spirit would go, they went 3
6: 6 Wherever you dwell your cities shall be waste 6
13 wherever they offered pleasing odor 16
20:28 wherever they saw any high hill or any leafy tree *
47: 9 wherever the river goes every living creature 2
Dan 2:38 into whose hand he has given, wherever they dwell 19
Mat 8:19 Teacher, I will follow you wherever you go. 23
24:28 Wherever the body is, there the eagles will be 23
26:13 wherever this gospel is preached 23
Mrk 6:56 wherever he came, in villages, cities, or country 22
9:18 wherever it seizes him, it dashes him down 23
14: 9 wherever the gospel is preached 21
14 wherever he enters, say to the householder 23
Lke 9: 5 wherever they do not receive you 25
57 I will follow you wherever you go. 23
1Co 16: 6 may speed me on my journey, wherever I go. 27
Jas 3: 4 wherever the will of the pilot directs. 21
Rev 14: 4 it is these who follow the Lamb wherever he goes; 22
1Es 2: 6 let each man, wherever he may live, be helped 20
2Es 13: 3 wherever he turned his face to look 28
Jdt 8:22 wherever we serve as slaves 27
Sir 36:26 has no home, and lodges wherever night finds him? 27
1Mc 5:63 wherever their name was heard. 24
6:36 took their position . . wherever the beast was 26
36 wherever it went they went with it 27

wherewith 1. אֲשֶׁר
1Kg 8:59 words . . wherewith I have made supplication 1

whet 1. לטשׁ 2. קלל 3. שׁנן
Deu 32:41 if I whet my glittering sword, and my hand 3
Ps 7:12 If a man does not repent, God will whet his sword; 1
64: 3 who whet their tongues like swords 3
Ecc 10:10 If the iron is blunt, and one does not whet the edge 2

whether 1. אוֹ 2. אִם 3. בְּ 4. בֵּין 5. כְּמוֹ 6. מִן 7. עַד 8. עַל 9. הֵן (A) 10. *δέ* 11. *ἐάν* 12. *ἐάν τε καί* 13. *εἰ* 14. *εἰμί* 15. *ἤ* 16. *καί* 17. *οὔτε* 18. *πότερος* 19. si
Gen 17:12 your generations, whether born in your house *
18:21 I will go down to see whether they have done *
24:21 gazed at her in silence to learn whether the LORD *
27:21 know whether you are really my son Esau or not. 2
31:39 whether stolen by day or stolen by night. *
37:32 we have found; see now whether it is your son's robe 2
42:16 words may be tested, whether there is truth in you *
Exd 4:18 Let me . . see whether they are still alive. *
12:19 cut off . . whether he is a sojourner or a native 3
16: 4 I may prove them, whether they will walk in my law *
19:13 whether beast or man, he shall not live.' 2
21:16 Whoever steals a man, whether he sells him or is *
22: 4 whether it is an ox or an ass or a sheep 6
8 to show whether or not he has put his hand to his 2
9 whether it is for ox, for ass, for sheep *
11 between them both to see whether he has not put 2
Lev 5: 1 whether he has seen or come to know the matter 1
2 whether the carcass of an unclean beast 1
7:21 an unclean thing, whether the uncleanness of man *
26 eat no blood . . whether of fowl or of animal *
11: 9 whether in the seas or in the rivers *
32 whether it is an article of wood or a garment *
35 everything . . shall be unclean; whether oven *
12: 6 days of her purifying . . whether for a son *
13:47 disease . . whether a woolen or a linen garment *
49 whether in warp or woof or in skin or in anything 1
52 he shall burn the garment, whether diseased 1
55 burn . . whether the leprous spot is on the back *
59 to decide whether it is clean or unclean *
15: 3 whether his body runs with his discharge *
23 whether it is the bed or anything 2
17:15 whether he is a native or a sojourner *
18: 9 whether born at home or born abroad 2
22:18 presents his offering, whether in payment *
28 whether the mother is a cow or a ewe *
27:26 whether ox or sheep, it is the LORD'S 2
28 no devoted thing . . whether of man or beast 6
30 tithe of the land, whether of the seed of the land 6
33 A man shall not inquire whether it is good or bad 4
Num 9:22 Whether it was two days, or a month, or a longer time 1
11:23 see whether my word will come true for you or not. *
13:18 whether the people who dwell in it are strong *
18 whether they are few or many *
19 whether the land that they dwell in is good or bad *
19 whether the cities that they dwell in are camps *
20 whether the land is rich or poor *
20 whether there is wood in it or not. *
15:30 high hand, whether he is native or a sojourner *
18:15 opens the womb of all flesh, whether man or beast *
Deu 4:32 ask . . whether such a great thing as this *
8: 2 whether you would keep his commandments, or not. *
13: 3 to know whether you love the LORD your God *
7 whether near you or far off from you *
18: 3 offering a sacrifice, whether it be ox or sheep 2
24:14 not oppress . . whether he is one of your brethren *
27:22 sister, whether the daughter of his father *
Jos 24:15 choose . . whether the gods your fathers served 2
Jdg 2:22 test Israel, whether they will take care to walk *
3: 4 to know whether Israel would obey *
18: 5 may know whether the journey . . will succeed. *
Rut 3:10 not gone after young men, whether poor or rich. 2
1Sm 30:19 Nothing was missing, whether small or great 7
2Sm 12:22 Who knows whether the LORD will be gracious to me *
15:21 wherever my lord . . whether for death or for life 2
2Kg 1: 2 inquire of Ba'al-ze'bub . . whether I shall recover 2
2Ch 15:13 put to death, whether young or old, man or woman. *
Ezr 2:59 not prove . . whether they belonged to Israel 2
5:17 see whether a decree was issued by Cyrus the king 9
7:26 whether for death or for banishment 9
Neh 7:61 their descent, whether they belonged to Israel 2
Est 3: 4 to see whether Mor'decai's words would avail; *
4:14 whether you have not come to the kingdom 2
Job 34:29 who can behold him, whether it be a nation or a man? 8
37:13 Whether for correction, or for his land 2
Ps 58: 9 feel the heat of thorns, whether green or ablaze 5
Prv 20:11 whether what he does is pure and right. 2
Ecc 2:19 who knows whether he will be a wise man or a fool? *
3:21 Who knows whether the spirit of man goes upward *
5:12 sleep of a laborer, whether he eats little or much 2
9: 1 whether it is love or hate man does not know. *
11: 6 do not know . . or whether both alike will be good. 2
12:14 with every secret thing, whether good or evil. 2
Sng 6:11 to . . see whether the vines had budded *
11 see . . whether the pomegranates were in bloom. *
7:12 let us go . . and see whether the vines have budded 2
12 see . . whether the grape blossoms have opened 2
Jer 42: 6 Whether it is good or evil, we will obey the voice 2
Ezk 2: 5 whether they hear or refuse to hear 2
7 speak . . whether they hear or refuse to hear; 2
3:11 whether they hear or refuse to hear. 2
44:31 shall not eat of anything, whether bird or beast 6
Jol 2:14 Who knows whether he will not turn and repent *
Mat 27:49 let us see whether Eli'jah will come to save him. 13
Mrk 3: 2 they watched him, to see whether he would heal him 13
15:36 let us see whether Eli'jah will come 13
44 he asked him whether he was already dead. 13
Lke 6: 7 to see whether he would heal on the sabbath 13
14:28 whether he has enough to complete it? 13
31 whether he is able with ten thousand to meet him 13
23: 6 he asked whether the man was a Galilean. 13
Joh 7:17 he shall know whether the teaching is from God 18
17 whether I am speaking on my own authority. 13
9:25 He answered, "Whether he is a sinner, I do not know; 13
Act 4:19 Whether it is right in the sight of God 13
5: 8 Tell me whether you sold the land for so much. 13
10:18 ask whether Simon . . was lodging there. 13
25:20 I asked whether he wished to go to Jerusalem 13
26:29 Paul said, "Whether short or long, I would to God 16
Rom 14: 8 whether we live or whether we die, we are the Lord's. 11
8 whether we live or whether we die, we are the Lord's. 11
1Co 1:16 I do not know whether I baptized any one else.) 13
3:22 whether Paul or Apol'los or Cephas or the world 13
7:16 whether you will save your husband 13
16 how do you know whether you will save your wife? 13
10:31 So, whether you eat or drink, or whatever you do 13
15:11 Whether then it was I or they 13
2Co 2: 9 know whether you are obedient in everything. 13

5: 9 So whether we are at home or away 13
12: 2 whether in the body or out of the body 13
3 whether in the body or out of the body 13
13: 5 to see whether you are holding to your faith. 13
Eph 6: 8 whether he is a slave or free. 13
Php 1:18 whether in pretense or in truth 13
20 whether by life or by death. 13
27 so that whether I come and see you or am absent 13
Col 1:16 whether thrones or dominions 13
20 all things, whether on earth or in heaven 13
1Th 2: 6 whether from you or from others 17
5:10 so that whether we wake or sleep we might live 13
1Pe 2:13 whether it be to the emperor as supreme 13
1Jn 4: 1 test the spirits to see whether they are of God; 13
1Es 8:24 whether by death or some other punishment 12
2Es 4:45 whether more time is to come than has passed 19
45 whether for us the greater part has gone by. *
7:75 whether after death . . we shall be kept in rest 19
75 or whether we shall be tormented at once? *
102 whether on the day of judgment the righteous 19
Tob 5: 8 and whether he is a reliable man to go with you. 13
8:12 Send one of the maids to see whether he is alive 13
Wis 11:11 Whether absent or present 16
14:23 whether they kill children 15
17:17 whether he was a farmer or a shepherd or a workman 13
18 Whether there came a whistling wind 13
Sir 26: 4 Whether rich or poor, his heart is glad 10
41: 4 Whether life is for ten or 100 . . years 14
LJr 1:34 Whether one does evil to them or good 17
1Mc 4:10 to see whether he will favor us 13
2Mc 3: 9 inquired whether this really was the situation. 13
6:26 yet whether I live or die 17
3Mc 1:15 whether they wish it or not? *
4Mc 1: 1 whether devout reason is sovereign 13
13 whether reason is sovereign over the emotions. 13
14 whether reason rules over all these. 13
11:13 whether he was willing to eat and be released 13

whether perhaps 1. *μήποτε*
Lke 3:15 questioned . . whether perhaps he were the Christ 1

whichever 1. *ὃς ἐάν*
Sir 15:16 stretch out your hand for whichever you wish. 1
17 whichever he chooses will be given to him. 1

while 1. אֲשֶׁר 2. בַּעֲבוּר 3. בְּעוֹד 4. הִנֵּה 5. יוֹם
6. יָמִים אֲחָדִים 7. כְּ 8. כַּאֲשֶׁר 9. כִּי 10. כָּל יָמִים
11. מְעַט 12. עַד 13. עַד שֶׁ 14. עוֹד 15. עִם 16. רֶגַע
17. תַּחַת 18. *βραχύς* 19. *δέ* 20. *ἐν*
21. *ἐν ταῖς ἡμέραις ἐν αἷς* 22. *ἐν ταῖς ἡμέραις* 23. *ἐπί*
24. *ἐπὶ χρόνον* 25. *ἕως* 26. *ἕως ὅτου* 27. *ἕως οὗ* 28. *καί*
29. *καιρός* 30. *μέν* 31. *ὀλίγος* 32. *ὅπου* 33. *ὅτε*
34. *πρόσκαιρος* 35. *χρόνος* 36. *ὥρα* 37. *ὡς* 38. cum
39. dum 40. et
Gen 8:22 While the earth remains, seedtime and harvest 14
24:55 Let the maiden remain with us a while, at least ten 5
25: 6 and while he was still living he sent them away 3
27:44 stay with him a while, until your brother's fury 6
29: 9 While he was still speaking with them 14
Lev 14:46 he who enters the house while it is shut up 10
Jos 14:10 since . . while Israel walked in the wilderness; 1
Jdg 3:26 Ehud escaped while they delayed, and passed 12
14: 8 And after a while he returned to take her; 5
15: 1 After a while, at the time of wheat harvest, Samson 5
16:14 while he slept, Deli'lah took the seven locks *
1Sm 2:13 servant would come, while the meat was boiling 7
9:27 when he has passed . . stop here yourself for a while 5
14:19 while Saul was talking to the priest 12
25:16 they were a wall . . all the while we were with them 5
27:11 all the while he dwelt in the country 5
2Sm 12:21 fasted and wept for the child while it was alive; 2
1Kg 1:14 while you are still speaking with the king, I also 4
3:17 I gave birth to a child while she was in the house. 15
17: 7 after a while the brook dried up 5
2Kg 4:40 But while they were eating . . they cried out 7
1Ch 12: 1 while he could not move about freely 14
Ezr 10: 1 While Ezra prayed and made confesssion 7
Neh 6: 3 work stop while I leave it and come down to you? 8
7: 3 while they are still standing guard let them 12
Job 32:11 while you searched out what to say. 12
Ps 141:10 wicked . . into their own nets, while I escape. 12
Prv 19:18 Discipline your son while there is hope; 9
Ecc 8: 9 all that is done . . while man lords it over man 1
Sng 1:12 While the king was on his couch, my nard gave forth 13
Isa 10:25 in a very little while my indignation will come 11
26:20 hide yourselves for a little while 16
65:24 while they are yet speaking I will hear. 14
Jer 17: 2 while their children remember their altars 7
Lam 1:19 my . . perished in the city, while they sought food 9
Ezk 7:13 not return to what he has sold, while they live. 14
9: 8 And while they were smiting, and I was left alone 7
11:13 And it came to pass, while I was prophesying 7
16 yet I have been a sanctuary to them for a while 11
23: 5 Oho'lah played the harlot while she was mine; 17
42: 8 while those opposite the temple were 100 4
Dan 9:20 While I was speaking and praying, confessing 14
21 while I was speaking in prayer, the man Gabriel 14
Mat 5:25 quickly with your accuser, while you are going 26
8:12 while the sons . . will be thrown into the . . darkness 19
13:21 but endures for a while 34
25 while men were sleeping, his enemy came and sowed 20
14:22 while he dismissed the crowds. 25
22: 6 while the rest seized his servants 19
26:36 Sit here, while I go yonder and pray. 27
73 After a little while the bystanders came up *
Mrk 4:17 endure for a while 34
6:31 rest a while 31
45 while he dismissed the crowd. 25
14:32 he said to his disciples, "Sit here, while I pray. 25
Lke 1: 8 Now while he was serving as priest before God 20
2: 6 while they were there 20
5: 1 While the people pressed upon him 20
12 While he was in one of the cities 20
34 while the bridegroom is with them? 20
6: 1 while he was going through the grainfields 20
8:13 they believe for a while 29
11:16 while others, to test him, sought from him a sign 19
37 While he was speaking 20
18: 4 For a while he refused 24
20: 9 went into another country for a long while. 35
24: 4 While they were perplexed about this 20
15 While they were talking and dicussing together 20
32 while he talked to us on the road 37
32 while he opened to us the scriptures? 37
51 While he blessed them, he parted from them 20
Joh 5:35 willing to rejoice for a while in his light. 36
7:12 While some said, "He is a good man 30
9: 4 work the works of him who sent me, while it is day; 25
11:20 she went and met him, while Mary sat in the house. 19
12:35 Walk while you have the light 37
36 While you have the light, believe in the light 37
13:33 Little children, yet a little while I am with you. *
14:19 Yet a little while *
16:16 A little while, and you will see me no more *
16 again a little while, and you will see me. *
17 A little while, and you will not see me *
17 again a little while, and you will see me *
18 They said, "What does he mean by 'a little while'? *
19 what I meant by saying, 'A little while . . *
19 again a little while, and you will see me'? *
17:12 While I was with them, I kept them in thy name 33
18:16 while Peter stood outside at the door 19
Act 1:10 while they were gazing into heaven as he went 37
4:30 while thou stretchest out thy hand to heal 20
5:34 ordered the men to be put outside for a while. 18
10:17 Now while Peter was inwardly perplexed 37
19: 1 While Apol'los was at Corinth 20
22 he himself stayed in Asia for a while. 35
20:11 he conversed with them a long while 23
Rom 4:11 had by faith while he was still uncircumcised. 20
7: 5 While we were living in the flesh 33
14: 2 while the weak man eats only vegetables. 19
5 while another man esteems all days alike. 19
6 while he who abstains, abstains in honor 28
1Co 3: 3 For while there is jealousy and strife among you 32
14:22 while prophecy is not for unbelievers 19
2Co 7: 8 that letter grieved you, though only for a while. 36
1Ti 4: 8 for while bodily training is of some value 19
2Ti 3:13 while evil men . . will go on from bad to worse 19
Phm 1:15 was parted from you for a while 36
Heb 3:15 while it is said, "Today, when you hear his voice 20
10:37 yet a little while, and the coming one shall come *
Jas 2: 3 while you say to the poor man, "Stand there 28
1Jn 1: 6 while we walk in darkness 28
Rev 17:10 when he comes he must remain only a little while. *
20: 3 After that he must be loosed for a little while. 35
21:18 while the city was pure gold, clear as glass. 28
1Es 5:64 while many came with trumpets and a joyful noise 28
8:91 While Ezra was praying 33
2Es 6:15 while the voice is speaking, do not be terrified; 38
29 While he spoke to me, behold, little by little 38
7:129 of which Moses, while he was alive, spoke 38
9:11 scorned my law while they still had freedom 38
11 while an opportunity of repentance was . . open 38
10:25 While I was talking to her, behold, her face 38
25 While I was wondering what this meant ‡
11:13 while it was reigning it came to its end 38
14 while it was reigning its end came also 38
29 while they were planning, behold, one of the heads 38
12: 1 While the lion was saying these words 39
14: 1 On the third day, while I was sitting under an oak 40
Jdt 10: 3 while her husband Manasseh was living. 22
18 she waited . . while they told him about her. 25
15:13 while all the men of Israel followed 28
Wis 4: 4 For even if they put forth boughs for a while 29
15: 8 after a little while goes to the earth *
16: 4 while to these it was merely shown 19
6 they were troubled for a little while as a warning *
17:21 while . . heavy night was spread 19
18:16 and touched heaven while standing on the earth. 19
Sir 10:30 while a rich man is honored for his wealth. 28
13:11 while he smiles he will be examining you. 37
20: 5 while another is detested 28
6 while another keeps silent 28
30: 5 while alive he saw and rejoiced 20
12 beat his sides while he is young 37
33:20 While you are still alive and have breath in you 25
37:27 My son, test your soul while you live 20
42:10 while a virgin, lest she be defiled 20
47:10 while they praised God's holy name 20
Sus 1:15 while they were watching for an opportune day 20
1Mc 4: 4 while the division was still absent 25
5:55 Now while Judas and Jonathan were in Gilead 21
6:38 while being themselves protected by the phalanxes 28
9:65 while he went out into the country 28
2Mc 2:32 while cutting short the history itself. 19
3:19 while others peered out of the windows. 19
22 While they were calling upon the Almighty Lord 30
29 While he lay prostrate 28
30 which a little while before was full of fear *
4:29 while Sostratus left Crates 19
47 while he sentenced to death those unfortunate men 19
6:25 while I defile and disgrace my old age. 28
10:28 while the other made rage their leader 19
3Mc 1:25 while the elders . . tried . . to change 19
2:24 After a while he recovered 35
4Mc 6:20 if we should survive for a little while 35
13:11 While one said, "Courage, brother 30
16:17 while an aged man endures such agonies 30

while before 1. *πρότερον*
2Mc 9:10 the man who a little while before had thought 1

while before day 1. *ἔννυχος*
Mrk 1:35 in the morning, a great while before day, he rose 1

good while 1. עוֹד
Gen 46:29 and wept on his neck a good while. 1

great while 1. רָחֹק
1Ch 17:17 thy servant's house for a great while to come 1

great while to come 1. מֵרָחוֹק
2Sm 7:19 spoken also of . . for a great while to come 1

little while 1. מְעַט 2. מִצְעָר 3. עַד כֹּה וְעַד כֹּה
4. *βραχέως* 5. *βραχύς* 6. *μικρός* 7. *ὀλίγος* 8. paululus
9. pusillus
1Kg 18:45 in a little while the heavens grew black 3
Job 24:24 They are exalted a little while, and then are gone; 1
Ps 37:10 Yet a little while, and the wicked will be no more; 1
Isa 29:17 Is it not yet a very little while until Lebanon 1
63:18 possessed thy sanctuary a little while; 2
Jer 51:33 a little while and the time of . . harvest will come. 1
Hos 1: 4 Call his name Jezreel; for yet a little while 1
8:10 cease for a little while from anointing king 1
Hag 2: 6 again, in a little while, I will shake the heavens 1
Mrk 14:70 after a little while again the bystanders said 6
Heb 2: 7 make him for a little while lower than the angels 5
9 for a little while was made lower than the angels 5
1Pe 1: 6 now for a little while you may have to suffer 7
5:10 after you have suffered a little while 7
2Es 10:41 The woman who appeared to you a little while ago 8
16:52 For behold, just a little while 9
Sir 6:19 in her service you will toil a little while 7
2Mc 5:17 the Lord was angered for a little while 4
7:33 if our living Lord is angry for a little while 4

while yet 1. בְּעוֹד
Jer 15: 9 her sun went down while it was yet day; 1

whip 1. יסר 2. נכא 3. שׁוֹט 4. *μάστιξ* 5. *φραγέλλιον*
Deu 22:18 elders of that city shall take the man and whip 1
1Kg 12:11 My father chastised you with whips, but I will 3
14 my father chastised you with whips, but I will 3
2Ch 10:11 My father chastised you with whips 3
14 my father chastised you with whips 3
Job 30: 8 they have been whipped out of the land. 2
Prv 26: 3 A whip for the horse, a bridle for the ass, and a rod 3
Nah 3: 2 The crack of whip, and rumble of wheel 3
Joh 2:15 And making a whip of cords, he drove them all 5
Sir 23: 2 O that whips were set over my thoughts 4
28:17 The blow of a whip raises a welt 4
30: 1 He who loves his son will whip him often 4
2Mc 7: 1 being compelled . . under torture with whips and cords 4

whip severely
Sir 42: 5 of whipping a wicked servant severely. †

whir 1. צְלָצַל
Isa 18: 1 Ah, land of whirring wings . . beyond the rivers 1

whirl 1. גרר 2. חול
Jer 23:19 Wrath has gone forth, a whirling tempest; 2
30:23 Wrath has gone forth, a whirling tempest; 1

make whirl 1. חול
Ps 29: 9 voice of the LORD makes the oaks to whirl 1

whirl round and round 1. צנף
Isa 22:18 whirl you round and round and throw you 1

whirling *See* dust, wheel.

whirlwind 1. גַּלְגַּל 2. סוּפָה 3. סְעָרָה 4. λαῖλαψ
5. συστροφὴ πνεύματος
2Kg 2: 1 about to take Eli'jah up to heaven by a whirlwind 3
11 And Eli'jah went up by a whirlwind into heaven. 3
Job 27:20 in the night a whirlwind carries him off. 2
37: 9 From its chamber comes the whirlwind 2
38: 1 Then the LORD answered Job out of the whirlwind 3
40: 6 Then the LORD answered Job out of the whirlwind 3
Ps 77:18 The crash of thy thunder was in the whirlwind; 1
Prv 1:27 when . . your calamity comes like a whirlwind 2
Isa 5:28 like flint, and their wheels like the whirlwind. 2
21: 1 As whirlwinds in the Negeb sweep on 2
29: 6 with whirlwind and tempest, and the flame 2
Jer 4:13 his chariots like the whirlwind; 2
Hos 8: 7 and they shall reap the whirlwind. 2
Ams 1:14 with a tempest in the day of the whirlwind; 2
Nah 1: 3 His way is in whirlwind and storm 2
Zec 9:14 and march forth in the whirlwinds of the south. 3
Sir 43:17 the tempest from the north and the whirlwind 5
48: 9 You who were taken up by a whirlwind of fire 4
12 It was Elijah who was covered by the whirlwind 4

whirlwind *See also* come, rush, scatter.

whisper 1. דִּבָּה 2. דָּבָר 3. לחשׁ 4. צפף 5. שֶׁמֶץ
6. διαψιθυρίζω 7. εἰς τὸ οὖς 8. πρὸς τὸ οὖς λαλέω
Job 4:12 stealthily, my ear received the whisper of it. 5
26:14 how small a whisper do we hear of him! 2
Ps 31:13 Yea, I hear the whispering of many– 1
41: 7 All who hate me whisper together about me; 3
Isa 29: 4 and your speech shall whisper out of the dust. 4
Jer 20:10 I hear many whispering. Terror is on every side! 1
Mat 10:27 what you hear whispered, proclaim 7
Lke 12: 3 what you have whispered in private rooms 8
Sir 12:18 whisper much, and change his expression. 6

whisper together 1. לחשׁ
2Sm 12:19 saw that his servants were whispering together 1

whisperer 1. רגן 2. ψιθυρίζω 3. ψίθυρος
Prv 16:28 whisperer separates close friends. 1
18: 8 words of a whisperer are like delicious morsels; 1
26:20 where there is no whisperer, quarreling ceases. 1
22 words of a whisperer are like delicious morsels; 1
Sir 21:28 A whisperer defiles his own soul 2
28:13 Curse the whisperer and deceiver 3

whistle 1. שׁרק 2. διασυρίζω 3. συρίζω
Isa 5:26 and whistle for it from the ends of the earth; 1
7:18 In that day the LORD will whistle for the fly 1
Wis 17:18 Whether there came a whistling wind 3
Aza 1:27 the furnace like a moist whistling wind 2

white 1. חור 2. לבן 3. לָבָן 4. צחח 5. צַחַר
6. חִוָּר (A) 7. λευκός
Gen 30:35 every one that had white on it 3
37 fresh rods . . and peeled white streaks in them 3
37 in them, exposing the white of the rods. 3
49:12 and his teeth white with milk. 3
Exd 4: 6 behold, his hand was leprous, as white as snow. *
16:31 was like coriander seed, white, and the taste of it 3
Lev 13: 3 if the hair in the diseased spot has turned white 3
4 if the spot is white in the skin of his body 3
4 if . . the hair in it has not turned white 3
10 if there is a white swelling in the skin 3
10 swelling . . which has turned the hair white 3
13 it has all turned white, and he is clean 3
16 if the raw flesh . . is changed to white 3
17 if the disease has turned white, then the priest 3
19 there comes a white swelling or a reddish-white 3
19 there comes . . a reddish-white spot 3
20 if . . its hair has turned white, then the priest 3
21 if . . the hair on it is not white 3
24 flesh . . becomes . . reddish-white or white 3
24 flesh . . becomes . . reddish-white or white 3
25 if the hair in the spot has turned white 3
26 if . . the hair in the spot is not white 3
38 has spots on the skin of the body, white spots 3
39 spots on the skin of the body are of a dull white 3
42 if there is . . a reddish-white diseased spot 3
43 if the diseased swelling is reddish-white 3
Num12:10 behold, Miriam was leprous, as white as snow. *
2Kg 5:27 So he went out . . a leper, as white as snow. *
Est 8:15 Mor'decai went . . in royal robes of blue and white 1
Ps 51: 7 wash me, and I shall be whiter than snow. 2
Ecc 9: 8 Let your garments be always white; 3
Isa 1:18 sins are like scarlet, they shall be white as snow; 2
Lam 4: 7 princes were purer than snow, whiter than milk; 4
Ezk 27:18 great wealth . . wine of Helbon, and white wool 5
Dan 7: 9 raiment was white as snow, and the hair of his head 6
Zec 1: 8 behind him were red, sorrel, and white horses. 3
6: 3 the third white horses, and the fourth chariot 3
6 the white ones go toward the west country 3
Mat 5:36 head, for you cannot make one hair white or black. 7
17: 2 and his garments became white as light. 7
28: 3 his raiment white as snow. 7
Mrk 9: 3 garments became glistening, intensely white 7
16: 5 they saw a young man . . dressed in a white robe; 7
Lke 9:29 his raiment became dazzling white. 7
Joh 4:35 see how the fields are already white for harvest 7
20:12 she saw two angels in white 7
Act 1:10 behold, two men stood by them in white robes 7
Rev 1:14 his head and his hair were white as white wool 7
14 his head and his hair were white as white wool 7
14 his head and his hair were . . white as snow; 7
2:17 and I will give him a white stone 7
3: 4 they . . walk with me in white, for they are worthy 7
5 He who conquers shall be clad thus in white 7
18 and white garments to clothe you 7
4: 4 elders, clad in white garments, with golden 7
6: 2 I saw . . a white horse, and its rider had a bow; 7
11 Then they were each given a white robe and told 7
7: 9 clothed in white robes, with palm branches 7
13 Who are these, clothed in white robes 7
14:14 Then I looked, and lo, a white cloud 7
19:11 Then I saw heaven opened, and behold, a white horse! 7
14 arrayed in fine linen, white and pure 7
14 armies of heaven . . followed him on white horses 7
20:11 I saw a great white throne and him who sat upon it; 7
2Mc 11: 8 clothed in white 7

white *See also* cotton, curtain, film, make, people.

whiteness 1. λευκότης
Sir 43:18 The eye marvels at the beauty of its whiteness 1

whitewash 1. טפל 2. תָּפֵל 3. κονιάω
Job 13: 4 As for you, you whitewash with lies; 1
Ezk 13:10 a wall, these prophets daub it with whitewash; 2
11 say to those who daub it with whitewash 2
14 the wall that you have daubed with whitewash 2
15 and upon those who have daubed it with whitewash; 2
22:28 prophets have daubed for them with whitewash 2
Mat 23:27 you are like whitewashed tombs 3
Act 23: 3 God shall strike you, you whitewashed wall! 3

whither 1. אָן 2. אָנָה 3. אֲשֶׁר 4. אֲשֶׁר עַל 5. אֲשֶׁר שָׁם
6. עַל אֲשֶׁר 7. ποῦ
Exd 34:12 inhabitants of the land whither you go 4
Deu 1:28 Whither are we going up? 1
1Kg 12: 2 he was still in Egypt, whither he had fled 3
18:10 no nation or kingdom whither my lord has not sent 5
12 the Spirit . . will carry you whither I know not; 6
2Ch 10: 2 in Egypt, whither he had fled from King Solomon) 3
Ps 139: 7 Whither shall I go from thy Spirit? 2
7 Or whither shall I flee from thy presence? 2
Sng 6: 1 Whither has your beloved gone, O fairest 2
1 Whither has your beloved turned 2
Ezk 4:13 among the nations whither I will drive them. 5
Joh 3: 8 you do not know whence it comes or whither it goes; 7
8:14 I know whence I have come and whither I am going 7
14 do not know whence I come or whither I am going. 7

whoever 1. אִישׁ אֲשֶׁר 2. אֲשֶׁר 3. כֹּל 4. כֹּל אִישׁ
5. כֹּל אֲשֶׁר 6. כֹּל נֶפֶשׁ 7. מִי 8. מִי אֲשֶׁר 9. כֹּל אֱנָשׁ (A)
10. כֹּל דִּי (A) 11. מַן דִּי (A) 12. εἴ τις 13. ὁ 14. ὅς
15. ὃς ἄν 16. ὃς δ' ἄν 17. ὃς δή ποτέ 18. ὃς ἐάν
19. ὅσος ἐάν 20. ὅστις 21. ὅστις ἐάν 22. πᾶς 23. πᾶς ὁ
24. πᾶς ὅς 25. τίς 26. omnis qui
Gen 4:14 on the earth, and whoever finds me will slay me. 3
9: 6 Whoever sheds the blood of man *
26:11 Whoever touches this man or his wife shall be put *
44: 9 With whomever of your servants it be found 2
Exd 19:12 whoever touches the mountain shall be put 3
21:12 Whoever strikes a man so that he dies shall be put *
15 Whoever strikes his father or his mother shall *
16 Whoever steals a man, whether he sells him or is *
17 Whoever curses his father or his mother shall be *
22:19 Whoever lies with a beast shall be put to death. 3
20 Whoever sacrifices to any god, save to the LORD *
24:14 whoever has a cause, let him go to them. 7
30:33 Whoever compounds any like it or whoever puts 1
33 whoever puts any of it on an outsider shall be cut 2
38 Whoever makes any like it to use as perfume 1
31:14 whoever does any work on it 3
15 whoever does any work on the sabbath day shall be 3
32:33 the LORD said to Moses, "Whoever has sinned 8
35: 2 whoever does any work on it shall be put to death; 3
5 whoever is of a generous heart, let him bring 3
Lev 6:18 whoever touches them shall become holy 3
7:27 Whoever eats of any blood, that person shall be 6
11:24 whoever touches their carcass shall be unclean 3
25 whoever carries any part of their carcass 3
27 whoever touches their carcass shall be unclean 3
31 whoever touches them when they are dead shall be 3
15:10 whoever touches anything that was under him 3
19 whoever touches her shall be unclean 3
21 whoever touches her bed shall wash his clothes 3
22 whoever touches anything upon which she sits 3
27 whoever touches these things shall be unclean 3
17:14 whoever eats it shall be cut off 3
18:29 For whoever shall do any of these abominations 3
22: 4 Whoever touches anything that is unclean *
5 whoever touches a creeping thing 1
23:29 For whoever is not afflicted on this same day 6
30 whoever does any work on this same day 6
24:15 Whoever curses his God shall bear his sin *
Num19:13 Whoever touches a dead person . . and does not 3
16 Whoever in the open field touches one who is 3
31:19 whoever of you has killed any person 3
19 whoever has touched any slain 3
Deu 18:12 For whoever does these things is an abomination 3
19 whoever will not give heed to my words which he 1
22: 5 whoever does these things is an abomination 3
Jos 1:18 Whoever rebels against . . shall be put to death. 4
15:16 Whoever smites . . to him will I give Achsah 2
Jdg 6:31 Whoever contends for him shall be put to death 2
7: 3 Whoever is fearful and trembling, let him return 7
11:31 whoever comes forth from the doors of my house 2
1Sm 11: 7 Whoever does not come . . so shall it be done to his 2
28: 8 and bring up for me whomever I shall name to you. 2
2Sm 5: 8 Whoever would smite the Jeb'usites, let him get up 3
17: 9 when some . . fall.., whoever hears it will say *
20:11 Whoever favors Jo'ab . . let him follow Jo'ab. 8
11 and whoever is for David, let him follow Jo'ab. 8
2Kg 10:19 whoever is missing shall not live. 5
11: 8 and whoever approaches the ranks is to be slain. *
1Ch 11: 6 David said, "Whoever shall smite the Jeb'usites 3
29: 8 whoever had precious stones gave them *
2Ch 13: 9 Whoever comes to consecrate himself 3
15:13 whoever would not seek the LORD, the God of Israel 5
23: 7 whoever enters the house shall be slain. *
36:23 Whoever is among you of all his people 7
Ezr 1: 3 Whoever is among you of all his people, may his God 7
7:26 Whoever will not obey the law of your God 10
Ps 107:43 Whoever is wise, let him give heed to these things; 7
Prv 9: 4 Whoever is simple, let him turn in here! 7
16 Whoever is simple, let him turn in here! 7
12: 1 Whoever loves discipline loves knowledge *
20: 1 whoever is led astray by it is not wise. 3
Isa 13:15 Whoever is found will be thrust through 3
15 and whoever is caught will fall by the sword. 3
54:15 whoever stirs up strife with you shall fall 7
Jer 27: 5 and I give it to whomever it seems right to me. 2
49:19 and I will appoint over her whomever I choose. 7
50:44 I will appoint over her whomever I choose. 7
Dan 3: 6 whoever does not fall down and worship shall 11
11 whoever does not fall down and worship 11
5: 7 Whoever reads this writing, and shows me its 9
6: 7 whoever makes petition to any god or man 10
Hos 14: 9 Whoever is wise, let him understand these things; 7
9 whoever is discerning, let him know them; *
Zec 4:10 For whoever has despised the day of small things 7
Mat 5:19 Whoever then relaxes one of the least of these 18
21 shall not kill; and whoever kills shall be liable 15
22 to judgment; whoever insults his brother shall 15
22 whoever says, 'You fool!' shall be liable to the hell 15
31 It was also said, 'Whoever divorces his wife 15
32 adultress; and whoever marries a divorced woman 18
10:33 whoever denies me before men, I also will deny 20
42 whoever gives to one of these little ones 18
12:32 whoever says a word against the Son of man 15
32 but whoever speaks against the Holy Spirit 15
50 For whoever does the will of my Father in heaven 20
16:25 For whoever would save his life will lose it 18
25 whoever loses his life for my sake will find it. 15
18: 4 Whoever humbles himself like this child 20
5 Whoever receives one such child in my name 18
6 whoever causes one of these little ones . . to sin 15
19: 9 I say to you: whoever divorces his wife 15
20:26 whoever would be great among you 18
27 whoever would be first among you 15
23:12 whoever exalts himself will be humbled 20
12 whoever humbles himself will be exalted. 20
Mrk 3:29 whoever blasphemes against the Holy Spirit 15
35 Whoever does the will of God is my brother 15
8:35 For whoever would save his life will lose it; 18
35 whoever loses his life for my sake 15
38 whoever is ashamed of me and of my words 18
9:37 Whoever receives one such child in my name 15
37 whoever receives me, receives not me 15
41 whoever gives you a cup of water to drink 15
42 Whoever causes one of these little ones 15
10:11 Whoever divorces his wife and marries another 15
15 whoever does not receive the kingdom of God 15
43 whoever would be great among you 15
44 whoever would be first among you 15
11:23 Truly, I say to you, whoever says to this mountain 15
Lke 9:24 For whoever would save his life will lose it; 15
24 whoever loses his life for my sake, he will save it. 15
26 For whoever is ashamed of me and of my words 15
48 Whoever receives this child in my name 15
48 whoever receives me receives him who sent me 15
14:27 Whoever does not bear his own cross 20
33 whoever of you does not renounce all that he has 24
17:33 Whoever seeks to gain his life will lose it 18
33 whoever loses his life will preserve it. 15
18:17 whoever does not receive the kingdom of God 15
Joh 3:15 whoever believes in him may have eternal life. 22
16 that whoever believes in him should not perish 22
4:14 whoever drinks of the water that I shall give him 16
11:26 whoever lives and believes in me 22
12:46 whoever believes in me 22
16: 2 when whoever kills you will think . . 22
Act 2:21 whoever calls on the name of the Lord 18
Rom 2: 1 you have no excuse, O man, whoever you are 22

9:18 So then he has mercy upon whomever he wills 14
18 and he hardens the heart of whomever he wills. 14
1Co 7:37 whoever is firmly established in his heart 14
11:27 Whoever, therefore, eats the bread 15
Gal 5:10 whoever he is. 21
1Th 4: 8 Therefore whoever disregards this •
Heb 4:10 whoever enters God's rest 13
11: 6 whoever would draw near to God •
Jas 2:10 For whoever keeps the whole law 20
4: 4 whoever wishes to be a friend of the world 14
17 Whoever knows what is right to do •
5:20 whoever brings back a sinner from the error •
1Pe 4: 1 whoever has suffered in the flesh •
11 whoever speaks, as one who utters oracles of God; 25
11 whoever renders service, as one who renders it 25
2Pe 1: 9 For whoever lacks these things is blind 14
1Jn 2: 5 but whoever keeps his word 14
3:10 whoever does not do right is not of God 22
4: 6 We are of God. Whoever knows God listens to us •
15 Whoever confesses that Jesus is the Son of God 18
Rev 14:11 and whoever receives the mark of its name. 12
2Es 6:25 whoever remains after all that I have foretold 26
Tob 4:19 he humbles whomever he wishes. 18
Wis 3:11 whoever despises wisdom and instruction •
17:16 whoever was there fell down 17
Sir 3: 3 Whoever honors his father atones for sins 13
4 whoever glorifies his mother 13
5 Whoever honors his father will be gladdened 13
6 Whoever glorifies his father will have 13
6 whoever obeys the Lord will refresh his mother; 13
16 Whoever forsakes his father is like a blasphemer 13
16 whoever angers his mother is cursed by the Lord. 13
26 whoever loves danger will perish by it. 13
31 Whoever requites favors 13
4:12 Whoever loves her loves life 13
13 Whoever holds her fast will obtain glory 13
15 whoever gives heed to her will dwell secure. 13
6:17 Whoever fears the Lord directs his friendship 13
13: 1 Whoever touches pitch will be defiled 13
1 whoever associates with a proud man 13
14: 4 Whoever accumulates by depriving himself 13
20: 8 Whoever uses too many words will be loathed 13
8 whoever usurps the right to speak will be hated. 13
28 Whoever cultivates the soil 13
28 whoever pleases great men 13
21: 6 Whoever hates reproof •
11 Whoever keeps the law controls his thoughts 13
22:26 whoever hears of it will beware of him. 23
24:22 Whoever obeys me will not be put to shame 13
27: 1 whoever seeks to get rich will avert his eyes. 13
16 Whoever betrays secrets destroys confidence 13
21 whoever has betrayed secrets is without hope. 13
22 Whoever winks his eye plans evil deeds •
25 Whoever throws a stone straight up 13
28:16 Whoever pays heed to slander will not find rest 13
34:21 whoever deprives them of it is a man of blood. 13
1Mc 1:50 whoever does not obey the command of the king 15
10:43 whoever takes refuge at the temple in Jerusalem 19
14:45 Whoever acts contrary to these decisions 15
3Mc 3:27 whoever shelters any of the Jews 15
5:11 who grants it to whomever he wishes. 15

whoever *See also* sits, touches.

whole 1. יוֹם 2. כֹּל 3. כָּלִיל 4. פָּנִים 5. שָׁלוֹם 6. שָׁלֵם 7. תָּמִים 8. תמם 9. כל (A) 10. *ἅπας* 11. *κοινός* 12. *ὁλκή* 13. *ὅλος* 14. *ὁμοῦ* 15. *παμμιγής* 16. *παντελῶς* 17. *πᾶς* 18. *σύμπας* 19. *ὑγιής* 20. omnis 21. orbis

Gen 2: 6 and watered the whole face of the ground- 2
11 which flows around the whole land of Havilah 2
13 which flows around the whole land of Cush. 2
7:19 all the high mountains under the whole heaven 2
8: 9 were still on the face of the whole earth. 2
9:19 from these the whole earth was peopled. 2
11: 1 the whole earth had one language and few words. 2
4 abroad upon the face of the whole earth. 2
13: 9 Is not the whole land before you? 2
18:26 I will spare the whole place for their sake. 2
28 Wilt thou destroy the whole city for lack of five? 2
23:17 field, throughout its whole area, was made over 2
41: 1 After two whole years, Pharaoh dreamed 1
Exd 10:14 settled on the whole country of Egypt 2
15 For they covered the face of the whole land 2
12: 6 when the whole assembly of the congregation 2
16: 2 the whole congregation of the people of Israel 2
3 brought us out . . to kill this whole assembly 2
9 Say to the whole congregation of the people 2
10 as Aaron spoke to the whole congregation 2
19:18 and the whole mountain quaked greatly. 2
25:36 the whole of it one piece of hammered work of pure 2
26: 6 that the tabernacle may be one whole. •
11 the tent together that it may be one whole. •
29:18 burn the whole ram upon the altar; 2
36:13 so the tabernacle was one whole. •
18 tent together that it might be one whole. •
37:22 the whole of it was one piece of hammered work 2
Lev 1: 9 the priest shall burn the whole on the altar 2
13 the priest shall offer the whole, and burn it 2
4:12 the whole bull he shall carry forth outside 2
13 If the whole congregation of Israel commits a sin 2
6:22 the whole of it shall be burned 3
8:21 Moses burned the whole ram on the altar 2
10: 6 but your brethren, the whole house of Israel 2
15:16 he shall bathe his whole body in water 2
25:29 redeem it within a whole year after its sale 8
Num 1:18 they assembled the whole congregation 2
45 So the whole number of the people of Israel 2
46 their whole number was 603,550. 2
2: 9 The whole number of the camp of Judah 2
16 The whole number of the camp of Reuben 2
24 The whole number of the camp of E'phraim 2
31 The whole number of the camp of Dan is 157,600 2
3: 7 duties . . for the whole congregation 2
4:31 whole of their service in the tent of meeting 2
33 whole of their service in the tent of meeting 2
8: 9 assemble the whole congregation of . . Israel. 2
11:20 a whole month, until it comes out at your nostrils 1
21 give them meat, that they may eat a whole month!' 1
14: 2 whole congregation said to them, "Would that we 2
15:26 whole population was involved in the error. 2
20: 1 people of Israel, the whole congregation, came 2
22 Israel, the whole congregation, came to Mount 2
25: 6 sight of the whole congregation of the people 2
27:21 all . . Israel with him, the whole congregation. 2
22 before Elea'zar . . and the whole congregation 2
Deu 2:25 peoples that are under the whole of heaven 2
3: 4 we took . . 60 cities, the whole region of Argob 2
13 whole of that Bashan is called the land of Reph'aim. 2
4:19 all the peoples under the whole heaven. 2
29:23 whole land brimstone and salt, and a burnt-out 2
Jos 7: 3 do not make the whole people toil up there 2
10:13 did not hasten to go down for about a whole day. 7
40 Joshua defeated the whole land 2
11:23 Joshua took the whole land 2
13:30 all Bashan, the whole kingdom of Og king of Bashan 2
18: 1 the whole congregation of . . Israel assembled 2
22:12 the whole assembly of . . Israel gathered 2
16 Thus says the whole congregation of the LORD 2
18 he will be angry with the whole congregation 2
Jdg 9: 1 them and to the whole clan of his mother's family 2
20:26 all the people of Israel, the whole army, went up 2
40 the whole of the city went up in smoke to heaven. 3
21:13 the whole congregation sent word 2
Rut 1:19 the whole town was stirred because of them; 2
1Sm 5:11 was a deathly panic throughout the whole city. 2
7: 9 lamb and offered it as a whole burnt offering 3
2Sm 2:29 and marching the whole forenoon they came 2
3:19 Israel and the whole house of Benjamin thought 2
6:19 all the people, the whole multitude of Israel 2
8: 9 David had defeated the whole army of Hadade'zer 2
14: 7 And now the whole family has risen against 2
1Kg 6:10 He built the structure against the whole house 2
22 he overlaid the whole house with gold 2
22 Also the whole altar . . he overlaid with gold. 2
10:24 the whole earth sought the presence of Solomon 2
11:34 I will not take the whole kingdom out of his hand; 2
2Kg 7:13 will fare like the whole multitude of Israel 2
9: 8 For the whole house of Ahab shall perish; 2
20: 3 walked . . in faithfulness and with a whole heart 6
1Ch 18: 9 David had defeated the whole army of Hadade'zer 2
28: 9 serve him with a whole heart 6
29: 9 with a whole heart they had offered freely 6
19 Grant to Solomon my son that with a whole heart 6
2Ch 15:15 had sought him with their whole desire 2
16: 9 run to and fro throughout the whole earth 2
19: 9 in faithfulness, and with your whole heart 6
26:12 The whole number of the heads of fathers' houses 2
29:28 whole assembly worshiped, and the singers sang 2
30:23 the whole assembly agreed together to keep 2
25 whole assembly of Judah, and the priests 2
25 whole assembly that came out of Israel 2
31:18 enrolled with . . the whole multitude; 2
Ezr 2:64 whole assembly together was 42,360 2
4:20 ruled over the whole province Beyond the River 2
7:16 find in the whole province of Babylonia 9
8:34 whole was counted and weighed, and the weight 2
10:14 Let our officials stand for the whole assembly; 2
Neh 7:66 The whole assembly together was 42,360 2
Est 3: 6 throughout the whole kingdom of Ahasu-e'rus. 2
Job 34:13 who laid on him the whole world? 2
37: 3 Under the whole heaven he lets it go 2
41:11 Whatever is under the whole heaven is mine. 2
Ps 9: 1 I will give thanks to the LORD with my whole heart; 2
72:19 may his glory fill the whole earth! Amen and Amen! 2
86:12 I give thanks to thee . . with my whole heart 2
111: 1 I will give thanks to the LORD with my whole heart 2
119: 2 Blessed . . who seek him with their whole heart 2
10 With my whole heart I seek thee; let me not wander 2
34 keep thy law and observe it with my whole heart. 2
69 with my whole heart I keep thy precepts; 2
145 With my whole heart I cry; answer me, O LORD! 2
138: 1 I give thee thanks, O LORD, with my whole heart; 2
Prv 1:12 like Sheol let us swallow them alive and whole 7
Ecc 12:13 Fear God . . for this is the whole duty of man. 2
Isa 1: 5 The whole head is sick, and the whole heart faint. 2
5 The whole head is sick, and the whole heart faint. 2
3: 1 whole stay of bread, and the whole stay of water; 2
1 whole stay of bread, and the whole stay of water; 2
4: 5 create over the whole site of Mount Zion 2
6: 3 the whole earth is full of his glory. 2
13: 5 his indignation, to destroy the whole earth. 2
14: 7 The whole earth is at rest and quiet; 2
26 purpose . . purposed concerning the whole earth; 2
21: 8 by day, and at my post I am stationed whole nights. 2
22:24 hang on him the whole weight of his father's house 2
27: 6 fill the whole world with fruit. 4
28:22 decree of destruction . . upon the whole land. 2
38: 3 in faithfulness and with a whole heart 6
39: 2 his whole armory, all that was found 2
53: 5 upon him was the chastisement that made us whole 5
54: 5 Redeemer, the God of the whole earth he is called. 2
Jer 1:18 against the whole land, against the kings 2
3:10 Judah did not return to me with her whole heart 2
4:20 the whole land is laid waste. 2
27 The whole land shall be a desolation; 2
8:16 at . . their stallions the whole land quakes. 2
12:11 The whole land is made desolate 2
13:11 I made the whole house of Israel . . cling to me 2
11 I made . . the whole house of Judah cling to me 2
15:10 a man of strife and contention to the whole land! 2
24: 7 they shall return to me with their whole heart. 2
25:11 This whole land shall become a ruin and a waste 2
31:40 The whole valley of the dead bodies and the ashes 2
35: 3 his sons, and the whole house of the Re'chabites. 2
37:10 For even if you should defeat the whole army 2
40: 4 See, the whole land is before you; 2
45: 4 I am plucking up-that is, the whole land. 2
50:23 How the hammer of the whole earth is cut down 2
51:25 mountain . . which destroys the whole earth; 2
41 Babylon . . the praise of the whole earth seized! 2
47 her whole land shall be put to shame 2
Lam 3: 3 surely against me he turns . . the whole day long. 2
Ezk 11:15 your fellow exiles, the whole house of Israel 2
15: 5 Behold, when it was whole, it was used for nothing; 7
32: 4 gorge the beasts of the whole earth with you. 2
35:14 For the rejoicing of the whole earth 2
36:10 men upon you, the whole house of Israel, all of it; 2
37:11 these bones are the whole house of Israel. 2
39:25 and have mercy upon the whole house of Israel; 2
41:19 They were carved on the whole temple round about; 2
43:11 its exits and its entrances, and its whole form; 2
12 the whole territory round about upon the top 2
45: 1 it shall be holy throughout its whole extent. 2
6 it shall belong to the whole house of Israel. 2
48:13 The whole length shall be 25,000 cubits 2
20 The whole portion which you shall set apart 2
Dan 2:35 great mountain and filled the whole earth. 9
48 ruler over the whole province of Babylon 9
4:11 tree . . visible to the end of the whole earth. 9
20 visible to the end of the whole earth; 9
6: 1 120 satraps, to be throughout the whole kingdom; 9
3 king planned to set him over the whole kingdom. 9
7:23 kingdom . . shall devour the whole earth 9
27 kingdoms under the whole heaven shall be given 9
8: 5 he-goat came . . across the face of the whole earth 2
9:12 under the whole heaven there has not been done 2
11:17 come with the strength of his whole kingdom 2
Ams 1: 6 carried into exile a whole people to deliver 6
9 because they delivered up a whole people to Edom 6
3: 1 against the whole family which I brought up out 2
Mic 4:13 their wealth to the Lord of the whole earth. 2
Zec 4:10 the eyes . . which range through the whole earth. 2
14 who stand by the Lord of the whole earth. 2
5: 3 that goes out over the face of the whole land; 2
13: 8 In the whole land, says the LORD 2
14:10 The whole land shall be turned into a plain 2
Mal 3: 9 you are robbing me; the whole nation of you. 2
Mat 5:29 than that your whole body be thrown into hell. 13
30 members than that your whole body go into hell. 13
6:22 eye is sound, your whole body will be full of light; 13
23 your eye is not sound, your whole body will be full 13
8:32 behold, the whole herd rushed down the steep bank 17
12:13 and it was restored, whole like the other. 19
13: 2 and the whole crowd stood on the beach. 17
15:31 the dumb speaking, the maimed whole 19
16:26 if he gains the whole world and forfeits his life? 13
24:14 preached throughout the whole world 13
26:13 this gospel is preached in the whole world 13
59 the chief priests and the whole council sought 13
27:27 they gathered the whole battalion before him. 13
Mrk 1:33 the whole city was gathered together 13
4: 1 the whole crowd was beside the sea on the land. 17
5:33 told him the whole truth. 17
6:55 and ran about the whole neighborhood 13
8:36 what does it profit a man, to gain the whole world 13
12:44 put in everything she had, her whole living. 13
14: 9 the gospel is preached in the whole world 13
55 Now the chief priests and the whole council 13
15: 1 the whole council held a consultation 13
16 they called together the whole battalion 13
33 there was darkness over the whole land 13
16:15 preach the gospel to the whole creation. 17
Lke 1:10 the whole multitude of the people were praying 17
7:17 through the whole of Judea 13
8:39 proclaiming throughout the whole city 13
9:25 what does it profit a man if he gains the whole world 13

11:34 your whole body is full of light 13
36 whole body is full of light, having no part dark 13
19:37 the whole multitude of the disciples 10
21:35 all who dwell upon the face of the whole earth; 17
23: 1 Then the whole company of them arose 10
44 darkness over the whole land until the ninth hour 13
Joh 7:23 on the sabbath I made a man's whole body well? 13
11:50 the whole nation should not perish. 13
Act 5:11 great fear came upon the whole church 13
6: 5 what they said pleased the whole multitude 17
10:22 who is well spoken of by the whole Jewish nation 13
11:26 For a whole year they met with the church 13
13: 6 had gone through the whole island as far as Paphos 13
44 almost the whole city gathered together 17
15:22 apostles and the elders, with the whole church 13
20:27 declaring to you the whole counsel of God. 17
22: 5 the high priest and the whole council of elders 13
25:24 about whom the whole Jewish people petitioned 10
28:30 he lived there two whole years at his own expense 13
Rom 3:19 the whole world may be held accountable to God. 17
8:22 the whole creation has been groaning in travail 17
11:16 If the dough . . is holy, so is the whole lump; •
16:23 Ga'ius, who is host to me and to the whole church 13
1Co 5: 6 a little leaven leavens the whole lump? 13
12:17 If the whole body were an eye 13
17 If the whole body were an ear 13
14:23 If, therefore, the whole church assembles 13
2Co 1: 1 with all the saints who are in the whole of Acha'ia 13
Gal 5: 3 he is bound to keep the whole law. 13
9 A little leaven leavens the whole lump. 13
14 For the whole law is fulfilled in one word 17
Eph 2:21 in whom the whole structure is joined together 17
4:16 the whole body, joined and knit together 17
Php 1:13 throughout the whole praetorian guard 13
Col 1: 6 as indeed in the whole world it is bearing fruit 17
2: 9 in him the whole fulness of deity dwells bodily 17
19 the whole body, nourished and knit together 17
Tit 1:11 since they are upsetting whole families 13
Jas 2:10 For whoever keeps the whole law 13
3: 2 a perfect man, able to bridle the whole body also. 13
3 we guide their whole bodies. 13
6 staining the whole body 13
1Jn 2: 2 but also for the sins of the whole world. 13
5:19 the whole world is in the power of the evil one. 13
Rev 3:10 hour of trial which is coming on the whole world 13
12: 9 deceiver of the whole world–he was thrown down 13
13: 3 the whole earth followed the beast with wonder. 13
16:14 who go abroad to the kings of the whole world 13
1Es 1:32 throughout the whole nation of Israel. 10
4:36 The whole earth calls upon truth 17
8:64 The whole was counted and weighed 12
9:38 the whole multitude gathered with one accord 17
2Es 10: 8 but we, the whole world, for our mother. ‡
11:32 this head gained control of the whole earth 20
45 and your whole worthless body 20
46 that the whole earth, freed from your violence 20
12: 3 and the whole body of the eagle was burned 20
15:27 now calamities have come upon the whole earth 21
Tob 1: 4 the whole tribe of Naphtali my forefather 17
Jdt 1: 9 Raamses and the whole land of Goshen 17
11 all who lived in the whole region 17
12 very angry with this whole region 17
12 take revenge on the whole territory of Cilicia 17
13 overthrew the whole army of Arphaxad 17
2: 1 carrying out his revenge on the whole region 17
5 the Great King, the lord of the whole earth 17
6 Go and attack the whole west country 17
7 will cover the whole face of the earth 17
9 to the ends of the whole earth. 17
11 throughout your whole region. 17
19 he set out with his whole army 17
19 cover the whole face of the earth to the west 17
22 From there Holofernes took his whole army 17
4: 8 the senate of the whole people of Israel 17
15 to look with favor upon the whole house of Israel. 17
5:12 he afflicted the whole land of Egypt 17
21 we shall be put to shame before the whole world. 17
6: 4 Nebuchadnezzar, the lord of the whole earth 17
7: 1 The next day Holofernes ordered his whole army 17
4 These men will now lick up the face of the whole land 17
18 covered the whole face of the land 17
20 The whole Assyrian army, their infantry 17
26 Now call them in and surrender the whole city 17
9:14 cause thy whole nation and every tribe to know 17
10:18 There was great excitement in the whole camp 17
19 they will be able to ensnare the whole world! 17
11: 7 Nebuchadnezzar the king of the whole earth 17
8 it is reported throughout the whole world 17
8 you are the one good man in the whole kingdom 17
16 things that will astonish the whole world 17
18 then you shall go out with your whole army 17
23 be renowned throughout the whole world. 17
16:21 throughout the whole country. 17
AEs 11: 9 the whole righteous nation was troubled 17
13: 2 master of the whole world 17
16:13 together with their whole nation. 17
Wis 5:23 Lawlessness will lay waste the whole earth 17
8:21 with my whole heart I said 13
11:22 Because the whole world before thee 13
17:20 the whole world was illumined 13
18:24 upon his long robe the whole world was depicted 13
19: 6 the whole creation in its nature 13
Sir 1:17 fills their whole house with desirable goods 17
18: 1 He who lives for ever created the whole universe; 11
24: 6 In the waves of the sea, in the whole earth 17
50:13 before the whole congregation of Israel. 17
20 lifted up his hands over the whole congregation 17
Bar 2: 2 Under the whole heaven there has not been done 17
23 the whole land will be a desolation without 17
3:36 He found the whole way to knowledge, and gave her 17
LJr 1:62 God commands the clouds to go over the whole world 13
Aza 1:22 the only God, glorious over the whole world. 13
Bel 1:14 they sifted them throughout the whole temple 13
1Mc 1:41 Then the king wrote to his whole kingdom 17
51 In such words he wrote to his whole kingdom 17
5:43 the whole army followed him 17
8: 4 how they had gained control of the whole region 17
2Mc 2:21 they seized the whole land 17
29 must be concerned with the whole construction 13
3:12 which is honored throughout the whole world. 18
14 no little distress throughout the whole city. 13
21 the prostration of the whole populace 15
4:38 led him about the whole city to that very place 13
7:38 which has justly fallen on our whole nation. 18
40 putting his whole trust in the Lord. 16
8: 9 to wipe out the whole race of Judea 18
18 to strike down . . even the whole world. 13
9: 9 the whole army felt revulsion at his decay. 17
10: 8 the whole nation of the Jews 17
12: 7 and root out the whole community of Joppa. 18
14: 8 our whole nation is now in no small misfortune. 18
15:12 praying . . for the whole body of the Jews. 17
3Mc 1:29 the walls and the whole earth around echoed 17
2: 7 the Ruler over the whole creation. 10
4:10 during the whole voyage 17
5: 5 the whole nation would experience 14
30 because . . his whole mind had been deranged 17
6: 5 had already gained control of the whole world 17
14 The whole throng of infants and their parents 17
36 in their whole community 17
7:13 their priests and the whole multitude 17
4Mc 3: 8 around which the whole army . . had encamped. 17
7:18 as many as attend to religion with a whole heart 13
21 the whole rule of philosophy 13
16:13 the whole number of her sons •

whole *See also* armor, month, number, yield.

wholehearted 1. כֹּל לֵב
Ezk 36: 5 with wholehearted joy and utter contempt 1

wholesome 1. חַיִּים 2. רפא 3. *σωτήριος*
2Kg 2:22 So the water has been wholesome to this day 2
Prv 15:31 He whose ear heeds wholesome admonition 1
Wis 1:14 the generative forces of the world are wholesome 3

wholesome *See also* make.

wholly 1. אַךְ 2. כֹּל 3. כָּלִיל 4. לְכֹל 5. מלא 6. שָׁלוֹם 7. תמם 8. *εἰς τέλος* 9. *ἐκτελέω* 10. *ὅλος* 11. *ὁλοτελής* 12. *τελείως*
Lev 6:23 offering of a priest shall be wholly burned 3
Num 3: 9 they are wholly given to him from among †
8:16 wholly given to me from among the people †
32:11 because they have not wholly followed me; 5
12 they have wholly followed the LORD.' 5
Deu 1:36 because he has wholly followed the LORD!' 5
Jos 3:16 those flowing down toward . . were wholly cut off; 7
14: 8 yet I wholly followed the LORD my God. 5
9 you have wholly followed the LORD my God. 5
14 he wholly followed the LORD, the God of Israel. 5
1Kg 11: 6 Solomon . . did not wholly follow the LORD 5
1Ch 28:21 all the people will be wholly at your command. 4
Job 19:13 my acquaintances are wholly estranged from me. 1
21:23 full prosperity, being wholly at ease and secure 2
Prv 16:33 but the decision is wholly from the LORD. 2
Jer 2:21 I planted you a choice vine, wholly of pure seed. 2
13:19 is taken into exile, wholly taken into exile. 6
Zec 11:17 Let his arm be wholly withered †
Lke 11:36 it will be wholly bright 10
1Th 5:23 May the God of peace himself sanctify you wholly; 11
Aza 1:17 may we wholly follow thee 9
2Mc 8:29 to be wholly reconciled with his servants. 8
12:42 that the sin . . might be wholly blotted out 12

wholly *See also* burn, follow, true.

why 1. אֲשֶׁר 2. בַּמָּה 3. יַעַן מָה 4. לָכֵן 5. לָמָּה 6. לָמָּה זֶּה 7. מַדּוּעַ 8. מָה 9. מָה זֶּה 10. עַל כֵּן 11. עַל מָה 12. תַּחַת מָה 13. עַל מָה (A) 14. *αἰτία* 15. *ἀλλά* 16. *γάρ* 17. *διά* 18. *δι' αἰτίαν* 19. *διὰ τί* 20. *διά τινα αἰτίαν* 21. *διὰ τοῦτο* 22. *δι' ἣν αἰτίαν* 23. *δι' ὅ* 24. *διό* 25. *εἰς* 26. *εἰς τί* 27. *εἰς τοῦτο* 28. *ἐφ' ὅ* 29. *ἵνα τί* 30. *ὅτι* 31. *πόθεν* 32. *πρὸς τί* 33. *πῶς* 34. *τίνος ἕνεκα* 35. *τίνος ἕνεκεν* 36. *τίνος ἕνεκεν αἰτίας* 37. *τις* 38. *τίς* 39. *χάριν τίνος* 40. *χάρις* 41. ad quis 42. de qua res 43. propter 44. propter quod 45. quare 46. quid 47. quis 48. ut quis
Gen 4: 6 The LORD said to Cain, "Why are you angry 5
6 Why are you angry, and why has your countenance 5
12:18 Why did you not tell me that she was your wife? 5
19 Why did you say, 'She is my sister,' 5
18:13 LORD said to Abraham, "Why did Sarah laugh, 5
24:31 blessed of the LORD; why do you stand outside? 5
25:22 and she said, "If it is thus, why do I live? 5
26:27 Isaac said to them, "Why have you come to me 7
27:45 Why should I be bereft of you both in one day? 5
29:25 Why then have you deceived me? 5
31:27 Why did you flee secretly, and cheat me 5
28 why did you not permit me to kiss my sons •
30 father's house, but why did you steal my gods? 5
32:29 But he said, "Why is it that you ask my name? 5
40: 7 Why are your faces downcast today? 7
42: 1 he said to his sons, "Why do you look at one another 5
43: 6 Israel said, "Why did you treat me so ill 5
44: 4 say to them, 'Why have you returned evil for good? 5
4 Why have you stolen my silver cup? 38
7 said to him, "Why does my lord speak such words 5
47:15 Give us food; why should we die before your eyes? 5
19 Why should we die before your eyes 5
Exd 1:18 Why have you done this, and let the male children 7
2:13 Why do you strike your fellow? 5
20 where is he? Why have you left the man? 9
3: 3 see this great sight, why the bush is not burnt. 7
5: 4 Moses and Aaron, why do you take the people away 5
14 foremen . . were asked, "Why have you not done all 7
15 cried to Pharaoh, "Why do you deal thus 5
22 Moses . . said, "O LORD, why hast thou done evil 5
22 O LORD . . Why didst thou ever send me? 5
14:15 The LORD said to Moses, "Why do you cry to me? 8
17: 2 And Moses said to them, "Why do you find fault 8
2 Why do you put the LORD to the proof? 8
3 murmured against Moses, and said, "Why did you 5
18:14 Why do you sit alone, and all the people stand 7
32:11 and said, "O LORD, why does thy wrath burn hot 5
12 Why should the Egyptians say, 'With evil intent 5
Lev 10:17 Why have you not eaten the sin offering 7
Num 9: 7 why are we kept from offering the LORD'S offering 5
11:11 Why has thou dealt ill with thy servant? 5
11 why have I not found favor in thy sight 5
20 Why did we come forth out of Egypt?"' 5
12: 8 Why then were you not afraid to speak against 7
14: 3 Why does the LORD bring us into this land, to fall 5
41 Why now are you trangressing the command 5
16: 3 why then do you exalt yourselves above 7
20: 4 Why have you brought the assembly of the LORD 5
5 why have you made us come up out of Egypt 5
21: 5 Why have you brought us up out of Egypt to die 5
22:32 Why have you struck your ass these three times? 11
37 Why did you not come to me? Am I not able to honor 5
27: 4 Why should the name of our father be taken away 5
32: 7 Why will you discourage the heart of . . Israel 5
Deu 5:25 Now therefore why should we die? 5
29:24 'Why has the LORD done thus to this land? 11
Jos 5: 4 this is the reason why Joshua circumcised them 1
7: 7 why hast thou brought this people over the Jordan 5
10 Arise, why have you thus fallen upon your face? 5
25 And Joshua said, "Why did you bring trouble on us? 8
9:22 Why did you deceive us . . when you dwell among us? 5
17:14 Why have you given me but one lot and one portion 7
Jdg 5:16 Why did you tarry among the sheepfolds, to hear 5
17 and Dan, why did he abide with the ships? Asher sat 5
28 Why is his chariot so long in coming? Why tarry 7
28 Why tarry the hoofbeats of his chariots?' 7
6:13 LORD is with us, why then has all this befallen us? 5
9:28 father of Shechem? Why then should we serve him? 7
11: 7 Why have you come to me now . . in trouble? 7
8 That is why we have turned to you now, that you may 4
26 why did you not recover them within that time? 7
12: 1 Why did you cross over to fight against 7
3 why then have you come up to me this day, to fight 5
13:18 Why do you ask my name, seeing it is wonderful? 5
15:10 men of Judah said, "Why have you come up against us 5
21: 3 O LORD, the God of Israel, why has this come to pass 5
Rut 1:11 Turn back, my daughters, why will you go with me? 5
21 Why call me Na'omi, when the LORD has afflicted me 5
2:10 Why have I found favor in your eyes 7
1Sm 1: 8 Hannah, why do you weep? And why do you not eat? 5
8 Hannah, why do you weep? And why do you not eat? 5
8 And why do you not eat? And why is your heart sad? 5
2:23 Why do you do such things? For I hear of your evil 5
29 Why then look with greedy eye at my sacrifices 5
4: 3 Why has the LORD put us to rout today 5
5: 5 This is why the priests . . do not tread 10
6: 3 why his hand does not turn away from you. 5
6 Why should you harden your hearts 5
9:21 Am I . . ? Why then have you spoken to me in this way? 5
14:41 O LORD . . why hast thou not answered thy servant 46
15:19 Why then did you not obey the voice of the LORD? 5
19 Why did you swoop on the spoil, and do what was evil •
17: 8 Why have you come out to draw up for battle? 5
28 Why have you come down? And with whom 5
19: 5 why then will you sin against innocent blood 5
17 Why have you deceived me thus, and let my enemy go 5

17 He said to me, 'Let me go; why should I kill you?' 5
20: 2 and why should my father hide this from me? 7
8 why should you bring me to your father? 5
27 Why has not the son of Jesse come to the meal 7
32 Why should he be put to death? What has he done? 5
21: 1 Why are you alone, and no one with you? 7
14 man is mad; why then have you brought him to me? 5
22:13 Saul said . . "Why have you conspired against me 5
24: 9 Why do you listen to the words of men 5
26:15 Who is like you . . ? Why then have you not kept watch 5
18 he said, "Why does my lord pursue after his servant? 5
27: 5 why should your servant dwell in the royal city 5
28: 9 Why then are you laying a snare for my life 5
12 Why have you deceived me? You are Saul. 5
15 Why have you disturbed me by bringing me up? 5
16 Why then do you ask me, since the LORD has turned 5
2Sm 2:22 Turn aside . . why should I smite you to the ground? 5
3: 7 Why have you gone in to my father's concubine? 7
24 Abner came . . why is it that you have sent him away 5
7: 7 saying, "Why have you not built me a house of cedar? 5
11:10 Why did you not go down to your house? 7
20 he says . . 'Why did you go so near the city to fight? 7
21 Why did you go so near the wall? 5
12: 9 Why have you despised the word of the LORD 7
23 he is dead; why should I fast? Can I bring him back 5
13: 4 why are you so haggard morning after morning? 7
26 the king said to him, "Why should he go with you? 5
14:13 Why then have you planned . . against the people 5
31 Why have your servants set my field on fire? 5
32 Why have I come from Geshur? It would be better 5
15:19 Why do you also go with us? Go . . stay with the king; 5
16: 2 the king said to Ziba, "Why have you brought these? 8
9 Why should this dead dog curse my lord the king? 5
10 who then shall say, 'Why have you done so?' 7
17 Why did you not go with your friend? 5
18:11 Why then did you not strike him . . to the ground? 7
22 And Jo'ab said, "Why will you run, my son 5
19:10 why do you say nothing about bringing the king 5
11 Why should you be the last to bring the king back 5
12 why then should you be the last to bring back 5
25 Why did you not go with me, Mephib'osheth? 5
29 Why speak any more of your affairs? I have decided 5
35 Why then should your servant be an added burden 5
36 Why should the king recompense me with such 5
41 Why have . . the men of Judah stolen you away 7
42 Why then are you angry over this matter? 5
43 we have more than you. Why then did you despise us? 7
20:19 why will you swallow up the heritage of the LORD? 5
24: 3 why does my lord the king delight in this thing? 5
21 Why has my lord the king come to his servant? 7
1Kg 1: 6 by asking, "Why have you done thus and so? 7
13 sit upon my throne"? Why then is Adoni'jah king?' 7
2:22 And why do you ask Ab'ishag . . for Adoni'jah? Ask 5
43 Why then have you not kept your oath to the LORD 7
9: 8 Why has the LORD done thus to this land 11
11:27 this was the reason why he lifted up his hand 1
14: 6 wife of Jerobo'am; why do you pretend to be another? 5
21: 5 Why is your spirit so vexed that you eat no food? 9
2Kg 1: 5 he said to them, "Why have you returned? 9
4:23 he said, "Why will you go to him today? 7
5: 8 Why have you rent your clothes? 5
6:33 Why should I wait for the LORD any longer? 8
7: 3 said to one another, "Why do we sit here till we die? 8
8:12 Haz'ael said, "Why does my lord weep? 7
9:11 Is all well? Why did this mad fellow come to you? 7
12: 7 Why are you not repairing the house? 7
14:10 why should you provoke trouble so that you fall 5
20:19 Why not, if there will be peace . . in my days? *
1Ch 17: 6 saying, "Why have you not built me a house of cedar? 5
21: 3 Why then should my lord require this? 5
3 Why should he bring guilt upon Israel? 5
2Ch 7:21 'Why has the LORD done thus to this land and to this 2
24: 6 Why have you not required the Levites to bring 7
20 Why do you transgress the commandments 5
25:15 Why have you resorted to the gods of a people 5
16 Stop! Why should you be put to death? 5
19 why should you provoke trouble so that you fall 5
32: 4 Why should the kings of Assyria come and find 5
Ezr 4:15 That was why this city was laid waste. *
22 why should damage grow to the hurt of the king? 5
Neh 2: 2 Why is your face sad, seeing you are not sick? 7
3 Why should not my face be sad, when the city 7
6: 3 Why should the work stop while I leave it 5
6 that is why you are building the wall; 10
13:11 Why is the house of God forsaken? 7
21 Why do you lodge before the wall? If you do so again 7
Est 3: 3 Why do you transgress the king's command? 7
4: 5 to go . . to learn what this was and why it was. 11
Job 3:11 Why did I not die at birth 5
12 Why did the knees receive me? 7
12 Or why the breasts, that I should suck? 8
16 Or why was I not as a hidden untimely birth *
20 Why is light given to him that is in misery 5
23 Why is light given to a man whose way is hid *
7:20 watcher of men? Why hast thou made me thy mark? 5
20 Why have I become a burden to thee? *
21 Why dost thou not pardon my transgression 8
9:29 I shall be condemned; why then do I labor in vain? 5
10: 2 let me know why thou dost contend against me. 11

18 Why didst thou bring me forth from the womb? 5
13:24 Why dost thou hide thy face 5
15:12 Why does your heart carry you away 8
12 why do your eyes flash 8
18: 3 Why are we counted as cattle? 7
3 Why are we stupid in your sight? *
19:22 Why do you, like God, pursue me? 5
22 Why are you not satisfied with my flesh? *
21: 4 Why should I not be impatient? 7
7 Why do the wicked live, reach old age 7
24: 1 Why are not times of judgment kept 7
1 why do those who know him never see his days? *
27:12 why then have you become altogether vain? 5
33:13 Why do you contend against him, saying 7
Ps 2: 1 Why do the nations conspire, and the peoples plot 5
10: 1 Why dost thou stand afar off, O LORD? 5
1 Why dost thou hide thyself in times of trouble? *
13 Why does the wicked renounce God 11
22: 1 My God, my God, why hast thou forsaken me? 5
1 Why art thou so far from helping me *
42: 5 Why are you cast down, O my soul 8
5 O my soul, and why are you disquieted within me? *
9 I say to God, my rock: "Why hast thou forgotten me? 5
9 Why go I mourning because of the oppression 5
11 Why are you cast down, O my soul 8
11 O my soul, and why are you disquieted within me? 8
43: 2 why hast thou cast me off? Why go I mourning 5
2 why hast thou cast me off? Why go I mourning 5
5 Why are you cast down, O my soul 8
5 O my soul, and why are you disquieted within me? 8
44:23 Rouse thyself! Why sleepest thou, O Lord? Awake! 5
24 Why dost thou hide thy face? 5
24 Why dost thou forget our affliction *
49: 5 Why should I fear in times of trouble 5
52: 1 Why do you boast, O mighty man, of mischief done 8
68:16 Why look you with envy, O many-peaked mountain 5
74: 1 O God, why dost thou cast us off for ever? 5
1 Why does thy anger smoke against the sheep *
11 Why dost thou hold back thy hand 5
11 why dost thou keep thy right hand in thy bosom? *
79:10 Why should the nations say, "Where is their God? 5
80:12 Why then hast thou broken down its walls 5
88:14 O LORD, why dost thou cast me off? 5
14 Why dost thou hide thy face from me? *
115: 2 Why should the nations say, "Where is their God? 5
Prv 5:20 Why should you be infatuated, my son 5
17:16 Why should a fool have a price in his hand 5
22:27 why should your bed be taken from under you? 5
Ecc 2:15 why then have I been so very wise? 5
5: 6 why should God be angry at your voice, and destroy 5
7:10 Why were the former days better than these? 8
16 why should you destroy yourself? 5
17 why should you die before your time? 5
Sng 1: 7 why should I be like one who wanders beside 5
6:13 Why should you look upon the Shu'lammite 8
Isa 1: 5 Why will you still be smitten, that you continue 11
5: 4 to yield grapes, why did it yield wild grapes? 7
40:27 Why do you say, O Jacob, and speak, O Israel 5
50: 2 Why, when I came, was there no man? 7
55: 2 Why do you spend your money for that which is not 5
58: 3 'Why have we fasted, and thou seest it not? 5
3 Why have we humbled ourselves, and thou takest no 5
63: 2 Why is thy apparel red, and thy garments 7
17 O LORD, why dost thou make us err from thy ways 5
Jer 2:14 Why then has he become a prey? 7
29 Why do you complain against me? 5
31 Why then do my people say, 'We are free 7
5:19 Why has the LORD . . done all these things to us?' 12
8: 5 Why then has this people turned away 7
14 Why do we sit still? Gather together 11
19 Why have they provoked me to anger 7
22 Why then has the health . . not been restored? 7
9:12 Why is the land ruined and laid waste 11
12: 1 Why does the way of the wicked prosper? 7
1 Why do all who are treacherous thrive? *
13:22 Why have these things come upon me? 7
14: 8 why shouldst thou be like a stranger in the land 5
9 Why shouldst thou be like a man confused 5
19 Why hast thou smitten us so . . there is no healing 7
15:18 Why is my pain unceasing, my wound incurable 5
16:10 Why has the LORD pronounced all this great evil 11
20:18 Why did I come forth from the womb to see toil 5
22: 8 Why has the LORD dealt thus with this great city? 11
28 Why are he and his children hurled and cast 7
26: 9 Why have you prophesied in the name of the LORD 7
27:13 Why will you and your people die by the sword 5
17 Why should this city become a desolation? 5
29:27 Now why have you not rebuked Jeremiah 5
30: 6 Why then do I see every man with his hands 7
6 Why has every face turned pale? *
15 Why do you cry out over your hurt? 8
32: 3 Why do you prophesy and say, 'Thus says the LORD 7
36:29 burned this scroll, saying "Why have you written 7
40:15 Why should he take your life 5
44: 7 Why do you commit this great evil 5
8 why do you provoke me to anger *
46: 5 Why have I seen it? They are dismayed 7
15 Why has Apis fled? Why did not your bull stand? 7
15 Why has Apis fled? Why did not your bull stand? *

49: 1 Why then has Milcom dispossessed Gad 7
4 Why do you boast of your valleys 8
Lam 3:39 Why should a living man complain 8
5:20 Why dost thou forget us for ever 5
20 why dost thou so long forsake us? 5
Ezk 18:19 Why should not the son suffer for the iniquity 7
31 Why will you die, O house of Israel? 5
21: 7 when they say to you, 'Why do you sigh?' 11
33:11 for why will you die, O house of Israel? 5
Dan 2:15 Why is the decree of the king so severe? 13
10:20 Then he said, "Do you know why I have come to you? 5
Jol 2:17 Why should they say among the peoples 5
Ams 5:18 Why would you have the day of the LORD? 6
Jon 4: 2 That is why I made haste to flee to Tarshish; 10
Mic 4: 9 Now why do you cry aloud? Is there no king in you? 5
Hab 1: 3 Why dost thou make me see wrongs 5
13 why dost thou look on faithless men 5
Hag 1: 9 Why? says the LORD of hosts. Because of my house 3
Mal 2:10 Why then are we faithless to one another 7
17 You ask, "Why does he not? 11
Mat 6:28 And why are you anxious about clothing? Consider 38
7: 3 Why do you see the speck 38
8:26 he said to them, "Why are you afraid 38
9: 4 Why do you think evil in your hearts? 29
11 Why does your teacher eat with tax collectors 19
14 Why do we and the Pharisees fast 19
11: 8 Why then did you go out? 38
9 Why then did you go out? To see a prophet? 38
13:10 Why do you speak to them in parables? 19
13 This is why I speak to them in parables 21
14: 2 that is why these powers are at work in him. 21
31 O man of little faith, why did you doubt? 26
15: 2 Why do your disciples transgress the tradition 19
3 And why do you transgress the commandment of God 19
16: 8 why do you discuss among yourselves the fact 38
17:10 Then why do the scribes say 38
19 Why could we not cast it out? 19
19: 7 Why then did Moses command 38
17 said to him, "Why do you ask me about what is good? 38
20: 6 he said to them, 'Why do you stand here idle all day? 38
21:25 'Why then did you not believe him?' 19
22:18 Why put me to the test, you hypocrites? 38
26: 8 they were indignant, saying, "Why this waste? 26
10 Why do you trouble the woman? 38
50 Jesus said to him, "Friend, why are you here? 28
65 Why do we still need witnesses? 38
27:23 he said, "Why, what evil has he done? *
46 My God, my God, why hast thou forsaken me? 29
Mrk 1:38 for that is why I came out. 27
2: 7 Why does this man speak thus? It is blasphemy! 38
8 Why do you question thus in your hearts? 38
16 Why does he eat with tax collectors and sinners? 30
18 Why do John's disciples . . fast 19
24 Look, why are they doing what is not lawful 38
4:40 Why are you afraid? Have you no faith? 38
5:35 Why trouble the Teacher any further? 38
39 Why do you make a tumult and weep? 38
6:14 that is why these powers are at work in him. 21
7: 5 Why do your disciples not live 19
8:12 Why does this generation seek a sign? 38
17 Why do you discuss the fact that you have no bread? 38
9:11 they asked him, "Why do the scribes say 30
28 Why could we not cast it out? 30
10:18 Why do you call me good? No one is good but God 38
11: 3 If any one says to you, 'Why are you doing this?' 38
31 he will say, 'Why then did you not believe him? 19
12:15 Why put me to the test? 38
24 Jesus said to them, "Is not this why you are wrong 21
14: 4 Why was the ointment thus wasted? 26
6 Jesus said, "Let her alone; why do you trouble her? 38
63 Why do we still need witnesses? 38
15:14 Pilate said to them, "Why, what evil has he done? *
34 My God, my God, why hast thou forsaken me? 26
Lke 1:43 why is this granted me 31
2:48 Son, why have you treated us so? 38
5:22 Why do you question in your hearts? 38
30 Why do you eat and drink with tax collectors 19
6: 2 Why are you doing what is not lawful to do 38
41 Why do you see the speck 38
46 Why do you call me 'Lord, Lord,' and not do what I tell 38
8:47 before him declared . . why she had touched him 22
12: 7 Why, even the hairs of your head are all numbered. 15
26 why are you anxious about the rest? 38
56 why do you not know how to interpret the present 33
57 why do you not judge for yourselves what is right? 38
13: 7 Cut it down; why should it use up the ground?' 29
18:19 Why do you call me good? No one is good but God 38
19:23 Why then did you not put my money into the bank 19
31 If any one asks you, 'Why are you untying it?' 19
33 Why are you untying the colt? 38
20: 5 he will say, 'Why did you not believe him?' 19
22:46 he said to them, "Why do you sleep? 38
23:22 Why, what evil has he done? *
24: 5 Why do you seek the living among the dead? 38
38 he said to them, "Why are you troubled 38
38 why do questionings rise in your hearts? 19
Joh 1:25 They asked him, "Then why are you baptizing 38
4:27 do you wish?" or, "Why are you talking with her? 38
5:16 this was why the Jews persecuted Jesus 17

18 This was why the Jews sought . . to kill him 17
6:65 he said, "This is why I told you 17
7:19 Why do you seek to kill me? 38
45 who said to them, "Why did you not bring him? 19
8:43 Why do you not understand what I say? 19
46 If I tell the truth, why do you not believe me? 19
9:27 Why do you want to hear it again? 38
30 The man answered, "Why, this is a marvel! 16
10:20 he is mad; why listen to him? 38
12: 5 Why was this ointment not sold for 300 denarii 19
13:11 that was why he said, "You are not all clean. 17
28 no one at the table knew why he said this to him. 32
37 Peter said . . "Lord, why cannot I follow you now? 19
18:21 Why do you ask me? Ask those who have heard me 38
23 if I have spoken rightly, why do you strike me? 38
20:13 They said to her, "Woman, why are you weeping? 38
15 Jesus said to her, "Woman, why are you weeping? 38
Act 1:11 why do you stand looking into heaven? 38
3:12 Men of Israel, why do you wonder at this 38
12 why do you stare at us 38
4:25 Why did the Gentiles rage 29
5: 3 why has Satan filled your heart to lie 19
7:26 you are brethren, why do you wrong each other?' 29
9: 4 Saul, Saul, why do you persecute me? 38
11: 3 saying, "Why did you go to uncircumcised men *
14:15 Men, why are you doing this? 38
15:10 Now therefore why do you make trial of God 38
19:32 most . . did not know why they had come together. 34
22: 7 'Saul, Saul, why do you persecute me?' 38
16 now why do you wait? Rise and be baptized 38
24 to find out why they shouted thus against him. 22
30 to know the real reason why the Jews accused him 38
26: 8 Why is it thought incredible by any of you 38
14 Saul, Saul, why do you persecute me? 38
Rom 3: 7 why am I still being condemned as a sinner? 38
8 And why not do evil that good may come? *
4:16 That is why it depends on faith 21
22 That is why his faith was "reckoned to him 24
5: 7 Why, one will hardly die for a righteous man 16
9:19 Why does he still find fault? 38
20 say to its molder, "Why have you made me thus? 38
32 Why? Because they did not pursue it through faith 19
14:10 Why do you pass judgment on your brother? 38
10 Or you, why do you despise your brother? 38
1Co 4: 7 why do you boast as if it were not a gift? 38
6: 4 why do you lay them before those *
7 Why not rather suffer wrong? 19
7 Why not rather be defrauded? 19
10:29 why should my liberty be determined by another 29
30 why am I denounced 38
11:10 That is why a woman ought to have a veil on her head 21
30 why many of you are weak and ill, and some have died 21
15:29 why are people baptized on their behalf? 38
30 Why am I in peril every hour? 38
2Co 1: 9 Why, we felt that we had received 15
20 That is why we utter the Amen through him 24
2: 9 For this is why I wrote, that I might test you 27
11:11 why? Because I do not love you? God knows I do! 19
Gal 3:19 Why then the law? 38
5:11 why am I still persecuted 38
Col 2:20 why do you live as if you still belonged 38
20 Why do you submit to regulations *
Tit 1: 5 This is why I left you in Crete 40
Phm 1:15 Perhaps this is why he was parted from you 21
Heb 2:11 why he is not ashamed to call them brethren 14
1Pe 4: 6 For this is why the gospel was preached 25
1Jn 3:12 And why did he murder him? 39
Rev 17: 7 But the angel said to me, "Why marvel? I will tell you 19
1Es 2:23 That is why this city was laid waste. 18
4:12 Gentlemen, why is not the king the strongest 33
32 Gentlemen, why are not women strong 33
2Es 1:18 saying, 'Why hast thou led us into this wilderness 48
3:28 Is that why she has gained dominion over Zion? 43
4: 4 and will teach you why the heart is evil. 45
12 and to suffer and not understand why. 42
20 but why have you not judged so in your own case? 45
22 why have I been endowed with . . understanding? ‡
23 why Israel has been given over to the Gentiles 43
23 why the people whom you loved has been given over *
24 why we pass from the world like locusts *
33 Why are our years few and evil? 45
5:16 Where have you been? And why is your face sad? 45
28 now, O Lord, why hast thou given over the one 48
35 "You cannot." And I said, "Why not, my lord? 45
35 Why then was I born? 41
35 Or why did not my mother's womb become my grave 45
46 If you bear ten children, why one after another?' 45
52 Why are those whom you have borne recently 45
6:59 why do we not possess our world as an inheritance? 45
7:15 now why are you disturbed 45
15 why are you moved, seeing that you are mortal? 47
16 why have you not considered in your mind 45
111 why will it not be so then as well? 45
9:40 said to her, "Why are you weeping 47
40 and why are you grieved at heart? 47
10:31 And why are you troubled? 45
31 And why are . . the thoughts of your mind troubled? 47
13:51 Why did I see the man coming up from . . the sea? 44
Tob 3: 9 Why do you beat us? If they are dead, go with them! 37
15 Why should I live? 29
4: 2 Why do I not call my son Tobias 37
5:17 Why have you sent our child away? 37
Jdt 5: 4 why have they . . refused to come out and meet me? 19
8:19 why our fathers were handed over to the sword 40
11: 3 now tell me why you have fled from them 35
Wis 5: 5 Why has he been numbered among the sons of God? 33
5 why is his lot among the saints? *
18:18 one here . . made known why they were dying; 14
19 not perish without knowing why they suffered. 23
Sir 23:18 no one sees me. Why should I fear? 37
33: 7 Why is any day better than another 19
37: 3 why were you formed to cover the land with deceit? 31
39:17 No one can say, "What is this?" "Why is that? 26
21 No one can say, "What is this?" "Why is that? 26
51:24 Why do you say you are lacking in these things 37
24 why are your souls very thirsty? *
Bar 3:10 Why is it, O Israel, why is it that you are in the land 38
10 why is it that you are in the land of your enemies 38
LJr 1:30 For why should they be called gods? 31
40 Why then must any one think that they are gods 33
44 Why then must any one think that they are gods 33
56 Why then must any one admit . . 33
Sus 1:21 and this was why you sent your maids away. 21
Bel 1: 5 the king said to him, "Why do you not worship Bel? 19
1Mc 2: 7 said, "Alas! Why was I born to see this 37
13 Why should we live any longer? 29
8:31 Why have you made your yoke heavy 19
10:70 Why do you assume authority against us 19
12:44 Why have you wearied all these people 29
45 For that is why I am here. 40
2Mc 3: 9 stated why he had come 35
12:40 this was why these men had fallen. 14
3Mc 1:13 he inquired why 19
15 why should not I at least enter 20
5:18 why the Jews had been allowed to remain alive 36
4Mc 1: 5 why is it not sovereign over forgetfulness 33
2: 1 why is it amazing 37
19 Why else did Jacob, our most wise father, censure 17
5: 8 Why, when nature has granted it to us 19
6:14 Eleazar, why are you . . destroying yourself 38
23 you, guards of the tyrant, why do you delay? 37
8: 1 For this is why even the very young . . prevailed 17
18 why do we take pleasure in vain resolves 37
23 Why do we banish ourselves 37
26 Why does such contentiousness excite us 31
9: 1 Why do you delay, O tyrant? 37
14:18 why is it necessary to demonstrate sympathy 37

why *See also* reason.

wick 1. פְּשְׁתָּה 2. λίνον

Isa 42: 3 and a dimly burning wick he will not quench; 1
43:17 they are extinguished, quenched like a wick 1
Mat 12:20 or quench a smoldering wick 2

wicked 1. אָוֶן 2. בְּלִיַּעַל 3. בֶּן עַוְלָה 4. הַוָּה 5. עֹצֶב
6. רַע 7. רעע 8. רשע 9. רֶשַׁע 10. רָשָׁע 11. רִשְׁעָה
12. בְּאִישׁ (A) 13. ἀδικία 14. ἀθέμιτος 15. ἄθεσμος
16. ἀλιτήριος 17. ἁμαρτωλός 18. ἄνομος 19. ἀσεβής
20. ἄτοπος 21. κακία 22. κακός 23. κακοῦργος
24. κακῶς 25. πονηρία 26. πονηρός 27. delinquo
28. inique 29. malus

Gen 13:13 Now the men of Sodom were wicked, great sinners 6
18:23 indeed destroy the righteous with the wicked? 10
25 to slay the righteous with the wicked 10
25 wicked, so that the righteous fare as the wicked! 10
38: 7 Er . . was wicked in the sight of the LORD; 6
Exd 23: 7 for I will not acquit the wicked. 10
Num14:27 How long shall this wicked congregation murmur 6
35 this will I do to all this wicked congregation 6
16:26 Depart . . from the tents of these wicked men 10
1Sm 2: 9 but the wicked shall be cut off in darkness; 10
24:13 'Out of the wicked comes forth wickedness'; 10
30:22 all the wicked and base fellows among the men who 6
2Sm 3:34 as one falls before the wicked you have fallen. 3
4:11 when wicked men have slain a righteous man 10
2Kg 17:11 they did wicked things, provoking the LORD 6
1Ch 2: 3 Er . . was wicked in the sight of the LORD 6
2Ch 7:14 if my people . . and turn from their wicked ways 6
19: 2 Should you help the wicked 10
Ezr 4:12 rebuilding that rebellious and wicked city; 12
Neh 9:35 they did not turn from their wicked works. 6
Est 7: 6 Esther said, "A foe and enemy! This wicked Haman! 6
9:25 his wicked plot . . should come upon his own head 6
Job 3:17 There the wicked cease from troubling 10
8:22 the tent of the wicked will be no more. 10
9:22 he destroys both the blameless and the wicked. 10
24 The earth is given into the hand of the wicked; 10
10: 3 favor the designs of the wicked? 10
15 If I am wicked, woe to me! 8
11:20 But the eyes of the wicked will fail; 10
16:11 casts me into the hands of the wicked. 10
18: 5 Yea, the light of the wicked is put out 10
20: 5 that the exulting of the wicked is short 10
29 This is the wicked man's portion from God 10
21: 7 Why do the wicked live, reach old age 10
16 The counsel of the wicked is far from me. 10
17 often is it that the lamp of the wicked is put out? 10
28 Where is the tent in which the wicked dwelt?' 10
22:15 you keep to the old way which wicked men have trod? 1
18 but the counsel of the wicked is far from me. 10
24:11 among the olive rows of the wicked they make oil; *
27: 7 Let my enemy be as the wicked 10
13 This is the portion of a wicked man with God 10
34: 8 with evildoers and walks with wicked men? 9
36 because he answers like wicked men. 1
36: 6 He does not keep the wicked alive 10
17 you are full of the judgment on the wicked; 10
38:13 the wicked be shaken out of it? 10
15 From the wicked their light is withheld 10
40:12 tread down the wicked where they stand. 10
Ps 1: 1 the man who walks not in the counsel of the wicked 10
4 The wicked are not so, but are like chaff 10
5 the wicked will not stand in the judgment 10
6 but the way of the wicked will perish. 10
3: 7 thou dost break the teeth of the wicked. 10
7: 9 O let the evil of the wicked come to an end 10
9: 5 thou hast destroyed the wicked; 10
16 wicked are snared in the work of their own hands. 10
17 The wicked shall depart to Sheol 10
10: 2 In arrogance the wicked hotly pursue the poor; 10
3 For the wicked boasts of the desires of his heart 10
4 the wicked does not seek him; 10
13 Why does the wicked renounce God 10
15 Break thou the arm of the wicked and evildoer; 10
11: 2 for lo, the wicked bend the bow 10
5 The LORD tests the righteous and the wicked 10
6 On the wicked he will rain coals of fire 10
12: 8 On every side the wicked prowl 10
17: 9 from the wicked who despoil me, my deadly enemies 10
13 Deliver my life from the wicked by thy sword 10
26: 5 I will not sit with the wicked. 10
28: 3 Take me not off with the wicked 10
31:17 let the wicked be put to shame 10
32:10 Many are the pangs of the wicked; 10
34:21 Evil shall slay the wicked; 10
36: 1 Transgression speaks to the wicked 10
11 nor the hand of the wicked drive me away. 10
37: 1 Fret not yourself because of the wicked 7
9 For the wicked shall be cut off; 7
10 Yet a little while, and the wicked will be no more; 10
12 The wicked plots against the righteous 10
13 the LORD laughs at the wicked *
14 The wicked draw the sword and bend their bows 10
16 Better . . than the abundance of many wicked. 10
17 For the arms of the wicked shall be broken; 10
20 But the wicked perish; the enemies of the LORD 10
21 The wicked borrows, and cannot pay back 10
28 but the children of the wicked shall be cut off. 10
32 The wicked watches the righteous 10
34 you will look on the destruction of the wicked. 10
38 the posterity of the wicked shall be cut off. 10
40 he delivers them from the wicked, and saves them 10
39: 1 so long as the wicked are in my presence. 10
50:16 But to the wicked God says: "What right have you 10
55: 3 because of the oppression of the wicked. 10
58: 3 The wicked go astray from the womb 10
10 he will bathe his feet in the blood of the wicked. 10
64: 2 hide me from the secret plots of the wicked 7
68: 2 as wax melts . . let the wicked perish before God! 10
71: 4 Rescue me, O my God, from the hand of the wicked 10
73: 3 when I saw the prosperity of the wicked. 10
12 Behold, these are the wicked; always at ease 10
75: 4 and to the wicked, "Do not lift up your horn; 10
8 all the wicked of the earth shall drain it down 10
10 All the horns of the wicked he will cut off 10
82: 2 How long . . show partiality to the wicked? Selah 10
4 deliver them from the hand of the wicked. 10
89:22 the wicked shall not humble him. 3
91: 8 look . . and see the recompense of the wicked. 10
92: 7 though the wicked sprout like grass 10
94: 3 O LORD, how long shall the wicked 10
3 O LORD . . how long shall the wicked exult? 10
13 until a pit is dug for the wicked. 10
16 Who rises up for me against the wicked? 7
20 Can wicked rulers be allied with thee 4
97:10 delivers them from the hand of the wicked. 10
101: 8 morning I will destroy all the wicked in the land 10
104:35 let the wicked be no more! 10
106:18 flame burned up the wicked. 10
109: 2 wicked and deceitful mouths are opened against 10
119:53 Hot indignation seizes me because of the wicked 10
61 Though the cords of the wicked ensnare me 10
95 The wicked lie in wait to destroy me; 10
110 The wicked have laid a snare for me 10
119 the wicked of the earth thou dost count as dross; 10
155 Salvation is far from the wicked 10
129: 4 righteous; he has cut the cords of the wicked. 10
139:19 O that thou wouldst slay the wicked, O God 10
24 see if there be any wicked way in me 5
140: 4 Guard me, O LORD, from the hands of the wicked; 10
8 Grant not, O LORD, the desires of the wicked; 10
141: 4 busy myself with wicked deeds in company 9
5 but let the oil of the wicked never anoint my head; 17
10 Let the wicked together fall into their own nets 10
145:20 but all the wicked he will destroy. 10

146: 9 but the way of the wicked he brings to ruin. 10
147: 6 LORD . . casts the wicked to the ground. 10
Prv 2:22 but the wicked will be cut off from the land 10
3:25 Do not be afraid . . of the ruin of the wicked 10
33 LORD'S curse is on the house of the wicked 10
4:14 Do not enter the path of the wicked 10
19 The way of the wicked is like deep darkness; 10
5:22 The iniquities of the wicked ensnare him 10
6:12 A worthless person, a wicked man 1
18 a heart that devises wicked plans 1
10: 3 but he thwarts the craving of the wicked. 10
6 but the mouth of the wicked conceals violence. 10
7 but the name of the wicked will rot. 10
11 but the mouth of the wicked conceals violence. 10
16 leads to life, the gain of the wicked to sin. 10
20 the mind of the wicked is of little worth. 10
24 What the wicked dreads will come upon him 10
25 When the tempest passes, the wicked is no more 10
27 but the years of the wicked will be short. 10
28 expectation of the wicked comes to nought. 10
30 but the wicked will not dwell in the land. 10
32 but the mouth of the wicked, what is perverse. 10
11: 5 but the wicked falls by his own wickedness. 10
7 When the wicked dies, his hope perishes 10
8 trouble, and the wicked gets into it instead. 10
10 wicked perish there are shouts of gladness. 10
11 but it is overthrown by the mouth of the wicked. 10
23 the expectation of the wicked in wrath. 10
31 how much more the wicked and the sinner! 10
12: 5 the counsels of the wicked are treacherous. 10
6 The words of the wicked lie in wait for blood 10
7 The wicked are overthrown and are no more 10
10 but the mercy of the wicked is cruel. 10
12 The strong tower of the wicked comes to ruin 10
21 but the wicked are filled with trouble. 10
26 but the way of the wicked leads them astray. 10
13: 6 but sin overthrows the wicked. 11
9 but the lamp of the wicked will be put out. 10
25 but the belly of the wicked suffers want. 10
14: 9 God scorns the wicked, but the upright enjoy •
11 The house of the wicked will be destroyed 10
19 the wicked at the gates of the righteous. 10
32 The wicked is overthrown through his evil-doing 10
15: 6 but trouble befalls the income of the wicked. 10
8 sacrifice of the wicked is an abomination 10
9 way of the wicked is an abomination to the LORD 10
26 thoughts of the wicked are an abomination 6
28 mouth of the wicked pours out evil things. 10
29 The LORD is far from the wicked 10
16: 4 even the wicked for the day of trouble. 10
17: 4 An evildoer listens to wicked lips; 1
15 He who justifies the wicked and he who condemns 10
19:28 mouth of the wicked devours iniquity. 10
20:26 A wise king winnows the wicked 10
21: 4 eyes and a proud heart, the lamp of the wicked 10
7 The violence of the wicked will sweep them away 10
10 The soul of the wicked desires evil; 10
12 The righteous observes the house of the wicked; 10
12 wicked are cast down to ruin. 10
18 The wicked is a ransom for the righteous 10
26 All day long the wicked covets 19
27 The sacrifice of the wicked is an abomination; 10
24:16 but the wicked are overthrown by calamity. 10
19 be not envious of the wicked; 10
20 lamp of the wicked will be put out. 10
24 He who says to the wicked, "You are innocent 10
25 those who rebuke the wicked have delight •
25: 5 away the wicked from the presence of the king 10
26 righteous man who gives way before the wicked. 10
28: 1 The wicked flee when no one pursues 10
4 Those who forsake the law praise the wicked 10
12 but when the wicked rise, men hide themselves. 10
15 bear is a wicked ruler over a poor people. 10
28 When the wicked rise, men hide themselves 10
29: 2 but when the wicked rule, the people groan. 10
10 who is blameless, and the wicked seek his life. •
12 falsehood, all his officials will be wicked. 10
16 When the wicked are in authority, transgression 10
27 way is straight is an abomination to the wicked. 10
Ecc 3:17 God will judge the righteous and the wicked 10
7:17 Be not wicked overmuch, neither be a fool; 8
8:10 Then I saw the wicked buried; 10
13 but it will not be well with the wicked 10
14 it happens according to the deeds of the wicked 10
9: 2 one fate . . to all, to the righteous and the wicked 10
10:13 and the end of his talk is wicked madness. 6
Isa 3:11 Woe to the wicked! It shall be ill with him 10
11: 4 with the breath of his lips . . slay the wicked. 10
13:11 I will punish . . the wicked for their iniquity; 10
14: 5 The LORD has broken the staff of the wicked 10
26:10 If favor is shown to the wicked, he does not learn 10
48:22 There is no peace," says the LORD, "for the wicked. 10
53: 9 they made his grave with the wicked 10
55: 7 let the wicked forsake his way 10
57:20 But the wicked are like the tossing sea; 10
21 There is no peace, says my God, for the wicked. 10
58: 4 and to fight and to hit with wicked fist. 9
Jer 6:29 for the wicked are not removed. 6
12: 1 Why does the way of the wicked prosper? 10

15:21 I will deliver you out of the hand of the wicked 6
23:19 it will burst upon the head of the wicked. 10
25:31 the wicked he will put to the sword, says the LORD. 10
30:23 it will burst upon the head of the wicked. 10
Ezk 3:18 If I say to the wicked, 'You shall surely die,' 10
18 nor speak to warn the wicked from his wicked way 10
18 nor speak to warn the wicked from his wicked way 10
19 But if you warn the wicked, and he does not turn 10
19 turn from his wickedness, or from his wicked way 10
7:21 a prey, and to the wicked of the earth for a spoil; 10
11: 2 who devise iniquity and who give wicked counsel 6
13:22 and you have encouraged the wicked 10
22 not turn from his wicked way to save his life; 6
18:20 wickedness of the wicked shall be upon himself. 10
23 Have I any pleasure in the death of the wicked 10
21: 3 will cut off from you both righteous and wicked. 10
4 I will cut off from you both righteous and wicked 10
25 you, O unhallowed wicked one, prince of Israel 10
29 to be laid on the necks of the unhallowed wicked 10
33: 8 If I say to the wicked, O wicked man 10
8 and you do not speak to warn the wicked to turn 10
9 if you warn the wicked to turn from his way 10
11 I have no pleasure in the death of the wicked 10
11 but that the wicked turn from his way and live; 10
12 as for the wickedness of the wicked, he shall not 10
14 though I say to the wicked, 'You shall surely die 10
15 if the wicked restores the pledge 10
19 when the wicked turns from his wickedness 10
Dan 12:10 but the wicked shall do wickedly; 10
10 none of the wicked shall understand; 10
Hos 7:12 I will chastise them for their wicked deeds. •
Mic 6:10 of wickedness in the house of the wicked 10
11 Shall I acquit the man with wicked scales 9
Nah 1:15 never again shall the wicked come against you 2
Hab 1: 4 the wicked surround the righteous 10
13 the wicked swallows up the man more righteous 10
3:13 Thou didst crush the head of the wicked 10
Zep 1: 3 I will overthrow the wicked; 10
Mal 1: 4 till they are called the wicked country 11
3:18 between the righteous and the wicked 10
4: 3 you shall tread down the wicked 10
Mat 18:32 'You wicked servant! I forgave you all that debt 26
24:48 if that wicked servant says to himself 22
25:26 You wicked and slothful servant! 26
Lke 19:22 I will condemn you . . you wicked servant! 26
Act 17: 5 taking some wicked fellows of the rabble 26
2Th 2:10 with all wicked deception 13
3: 2 that we may be delivered from wicked and evil men; 20
2Pe 2: 7 distressed by the licentiousness of the wicked 15
2Jn 1:11 for he who greets him shares his wicked work. 26
1Es 2:18 are building that rebellious and wicked city 26
29 that such wicked proceedings go no further 21
4:39 anything that is unrighteous or wicked 26
2Es 2: 8 O wicked nation, remember what I did to Sodom 29
7:23 proposed to themselves wicked frauds 27
15: 8 will I tolerate their wicked practices 28
Jdt 8: 9 When Judith heard the wicked words 26
AEs 14:15 I hate the splendor of the wicked 18
Wis 10: 5 the nations in wicked agreement 25
11:15 In return for their foolish and wicked thoughts 13
14:29 they swear wicked oaths 24
19:13 they justly suffered because of their wicked acts; 25
Sir 20:18 the downfall of the wicked will occur speedily. 22
21: 9 An assembly of the wicked 18
33:26 for a wicked servant there are racks 23
39:24 just as they are obstacles to the wicked. 18
40:10 All these were created for the wicked 18
42: 5 of whipping a wicked servant severely. 26
46: 7 stilled their wicked murmuring. 25
Bar 1:21 each followed the intent of his own wicked heart 26
2: 8 from the thoughts of his wicked heart. 26
33 from their stubbornness and their wicked deeds; 26
Sus 1:28 the two elders came, full of their wicked plot 18
52 You old relic of wicked days 22
1Mc 7:25 and brought wicked charges against them. 26
2Mc 10:34 and hurled out wicked words. 14
3Mc 3:16 to honor the temple of those wicked people 16
4Mc 12:11 profane tyrant, most impious of all the wicked 26

wicked *See also* device.

wicked act 1. *πονηρία*

1Mc 13:46 Do not treat us according to our wicked acts 1

wicked deed 1. רַע 2. רָעָה

Ps 141: 5 my prayer is . . against their wicked deeds. 1
Hos 7: 1 corruption . . and the wicked deeds of Sama'ria; 2

do a wicked thing 1. רעע

2Kg 21:11 Manas'seh . . has done things more wicked 1

wicked man 1. רַע 2. רָשָׁע 3. *ἄνομος* 4. *παράνομος* 5. *πονηρός*

Exd 23: 1 You shall not join hands with a wicked man 2
Job 15:20 The wicked man writhes in pain all his days 2
21:30 the wicked man is spared in the day of calamity 1
24: 6 they glean the vineyard of the wicked man. 2
34:18 'Worthless one,' and to nobles, 'Wicked man'; 2
Ps 7:14 Behold, the wicked man conceives evil •
37:35 I have seen a wicked man overbearing 2
109: 6 Appoint a wicked man against him; 2
112:10 wicked man sees it and is angry; 2
10 desire of the wicked man comes to nought. 2
Prv 9: 7 he who reproves a wicked man incurs injury. 2
11:18 A wicked man earns deceptive wages 2
13: 5 wicked man acts shamefully and disgracefully. 2
17:23 A wicked man accepts a bribe from the bosom 2
18: 5 It is not good to be partial to a wicked man 2
21:29 A wicked man puts on a bold face 2
24:15 Lie not in wait as a wicked man against 2
29: 7 wicked man does not understand such knowledge. 2
Ecc 7:15 and there is a wicked man who prolongs his life 2
8:14 and there are wicked men to whom it happens 2
Jer 5:26 For wicked men are found among my people; 2
Ezk 3:18 that wicked man shall die in his iniquity; 2
18:21 But if a wicked man turns away from all his sins 2
24 abominable things that the wicked man does 2
27 when a wicked man turns away from the wickedness 2
33: 8 to the wicked, O wicked man, you shall surely die 2
8 that wicked man shall die in his iniquity 2
Sir 49: 3 in the days of wicked men 3
Sus 1:32 the wicked men ordered her to be unveiled 4
1Mc 14:14 and did away with every lawless and wicked man. 5

most wicked 1. *πονηρός* 2. malus

2Es 7:122 but we have walked in the most wicked ways? 2
Aza 1: 9 an unjust king, the most wicked in all the world. 1

wicked person 1. *πονηρός*

1Co 5:13 Drive out the wicked person from among you. 1

wicked thing 1. *πονηρός*

Wis 3:14 who has not devised wicked things against the Lord; 1

wicked woman 1. מִרְשַׁעַת 2. רָעָה

2Ch 24: 7 Athali'ah, that wicked woman 1
Jer 2:33 even to wicked women you have taught your ways. 2

wickedly 1. רשע 2. רִשְׁעָה 3. *ἀδίκως* 4. *ἀνοσίως* 5. *κακῶς* 6. false 7. impie 8. male

2Sm 22:22 and have not wickedly departed from my God. 1
2Ch 20:35 Ahazi'ah king of Israel, who did wickedly. 1
Ps 18:21 and have not wickedly departed from my God. 1
Ezk 5: 6 she has wickedly rebelled 2
2Es 3:30 and hast spared those who act wickedly 7
7:18 those who have done wickedly 7
121 but we have lived wickedly? 8
8:27 not the endeavors of those who act wickedly 7
28 those who have lived wickedly in thy sight 6
35 no one . . who has not acted wickedly 7
AEs 16: 7 What has been wickedly accomplished 4
Wis 14:30 because they thought wickedly of God 5
1Mc 7:42 Nicanor has spoken wickedly 5
2Mc 8:16 who were wickedly coming against them 3

wickedly *See also* invent, plan.

act wickedly 1. רשע 2. רשע 3. *ἀσεβέω* 4. *πονηρία*

Gen 19: 7 do not act so wickedly. 1
Jdg 19:23 No, my brethren, do not act so wickedly; 1
1Kg 8:47 'We have . . and have acted perversely and wickedly'; 2
2Ch 6:37 'We have sinned, and have acted . . wickedly' 2
Neh 9:33 dealt faithfully and we have acted wickedly; 2
Dan 9: 5 done wrong and acted wickedly and rebelled 2
1Es 1:24 who sinned and acted wickedly toward the Lord 3
4Mc 2:13 one rebukes friends when they act wickedly. 4

do wickedly 1. עוה 2. רעע 3. רשע

1Sm 12:25 if you still do wickedly, you shall be swept away 2
2Sm 24:17 Lo, I have sinned, and I have done wickedly; 1
1Ch 21:17 It is I who have sinned and done very wickedly. 2
2Ch 22: 3 his mother was his counselor in doing wickedly. 3
Job 34:12 Of a truth, God will not do wickedly 3
Ps 106: 6 have committed iniquity, we have done wickedly. 3
Dan 9:15 we have sinned, we have done wickedly. 3
12:10 but the wicked shall do wickedly; 3

wickedness 1. אָוֶן 2. זִמָּה 3. עַוְלָה 4. רַע 5. רֹעַ 6. רָעָה 7. רֶשַׁע 8. רָשָׁע 9. רִשְׁעָה 10. *ἀδικία* 11. *ἀναγνεία* 12. *ἀνομία* 13. *κακία* 14. *πονηρία* 15. *φαυλότης* 16. impietas 17. iniustitia

Gen 6: 5 The LORD saw that the wickedness of man was great 6
39: 9 I do this great wickedness, and sin against God? 6
Lev 18:17 they are your near kinswomen; it is wickedness 2
19:29 and the land become full of wickedness 2
20:14 takes a wife and her mother also, it is wickedness 2
14 that there may be no wickedness among you 2
Deu 9: 4 it is because of the wickedness of these nations 9
5 because of the wickedness of these nations 9
27 do not regard . . their wickedness, or their sin 7
13:11 never again do any such wickedness as this among 4
Jdg 9:57 all the wickedness of the men of Shechem 6
20: 3 Tell us, how was this wickedness brought to pass? 6
12 What wickedness is this that has taken place 6
1Sm 12:17 shall know and see that your wickedness is great 6
24:13 'Out of the wicked comes forth wickedness'; 7
2Sm 3:39 The LORD requite . . according to his wickedness! 6
1Kg 1:52 but if wickedness is found in him, he shall die. 6

Job 11:14 let not wickedness dwell in your tents. 3
20:12 Though wickedness is sweet in his mouth 6
22: 5 Is not your wickedness great? 6
24:20 wickedness is broken like a tree.' 3
34:10 far be it from God that he should do wickedness 7
26 He strikes them for their wickedness 7
35: 8 Your wickedness concerns a man like yourself 7
Ps 5: 4 thou art not a God who delights in wickedness; 7
10:15 seek out his wickedness till thou find none. 7
17: 3 testest me, thou wilt find no wickedness in me; 10
45: 7 you love righteousness and hate wickedness. 7
84:10 than dwell in the tents of wickedness. 7
94:23 wipe them out for their wickedness; 6
107:34 because of the wickedness of its inhabitants. 6
42 all wickedness stops its mouth. 3
125: 3 scepter of wickedness shall not rest upon 7
Prv 4:17 For they eat the bread of wickedness 7
8: 7 wickedness is an abomination to my lips. 7
10: 2 Treasures gained by wickedness do not profit 7
11: 5 but the wicked falls by his own wickedness. 9
12: 3 A man is not established by wickedness 7
18: 3 When wickedness comes, contempt comes also; 8
26:26 his wickedness will be exposed in the assembly. 6
Ecc 3:16 the place of justice, even there was wickedness 7
16 of righteousness, even there was wickedness. 7
7:25 and to know the wickedness of folly 7
8: 8 will wickedness deliver those . . given to it. 7
Isa 9:18 For wickedness burns like a fire, it consumes 9
47:10 You felt secure in your wickedness 6
58: 6 that I choose: to loose the bonds of wickedness 7
9 of the finger, and speaking wickedness 1
59: 3 spoken lies, your tongue mutters wickedness. 3
Jer 1:16 for all their wickedness in forsaking me; 6
2:19 Your wickedness will chasten you 6
4:14 O Jerusalem, wash your heart from wickedness 6
5:28 They know no bounds in deeds of wickedness; 4
6: 7 she keeps fresh her wickedness; 6
7:12 did to it for the wickedness of my people Israel. 6
8: 6 no man repents of his wickedness 6
12: 4 For the wickedness of those who dwell in it 6
14:16 For I will pour out their wickedness upon them. 6
20 We acknowledge our wickedness, O LORD 7
22:22 and confounded because of all your wickedness. 6
23:11 even in my house I have found their wickedness 6
14 so that no one turns from his wickedness; 6
33: 5 from this city because of all their wickedness. 6
44: 3 because of the wickedness which they committed 6
5 incline their ear, to turn from their wickedness 6
9 Have you forgotten the wickedness 6
9 the wickedness of the kings of Judah 6
9 forgotten . . the wickedness of their wives 6
9 Have you forgotten . . your own wickedness 6
9 wickedness of your wives, which they committed 6
Ezk 3:19 and he does not turn from his wickedness 7
7:11 Violence has grown up into a rod of wickedness; 7
16:23 And after all your wickedness (woe, woe to you! 6
57 before your wickedness was uncovered? 6
18:20 wickedness of the wicked shall be upon himself. 9
27 when a wicked man turns away from the wickedness 9
31:11 surely deal with it as its wickedness deserves. 7
33:12 as for the wickedness of the wicked, he shall not 9
12 not fall by it when he turns from his wickedness; 7
19 when the wicked turns from his wickedness 9
Hos 7: 3 By their wickedness they make the king glad 6
9:15 Because of the wickedness of their deeds 5
10:15 done to you . . because of your great wickedness. 6
Jol 3:13 The vats overflow, for their wickedness is great. 6
Jon 1: 2 for their wickedness has come up before me. 6
Mic 2: 1 Woe to those who devise wickedness and work evil 1
6:10 Can I forget the treasures of wickedness 7
Zec 5: 8 he said, "This is Wickedness. 9
Mat 24:12 because wickedness is multiplied 12
Mrk 7:22 coveting, wickedness, deceit, licentiousness 14
Lke 11:39 inside you are full of extortion and wickedness. 14
Act 1:18 bought a field with the reward of his wickedness; 10
3:26 in turning every one of you from your wickedness 14
8:22 Repent therefore of this wickedness of yours 13
Rom 1:18 against all ungodliness and wickedness of men 10
18 men who by their wickedness suppress the truth. 10
29 all . . wickedness, evil, covetousness, malice. 10
2: 8 and do not obey the truth, but obey wickedness 10
3: 5 our wickedness serves to show the justice of God 10
6:13 your members . . as instruments of wickedness 10
Eph 6:12 against the spiritual hosts of wickedness 14
Jas 1:21 all filthiness and rank growth of wickedness 13
2Es 12:25 they who shall sum up his wickedness 16
32 for their ungodliness and for their wickedness 17
Jdt 2: 2 all the wickedness of the region; 13
Wis 2:21 their wickedness blinded them 13
4:12 the fascination of wickedness obscures what is good 15
14 took him quickly from the midst of wickedness. 14
5:13 were consumed in our wickedness. 13
10: 7 Evidence of their wickedness still remains 13
12: 2 that they may be freed from wickedness 13
10 evil and their wickedness inborn 13
20 opportunity to give up their wickedness 13
16:14 A man in his wickedness kills another 13
17:11 For wickedness is a cowardly thing 14
Sir 3:28 a plant of wickedness has taken root in him. 14
12:10 like the rusting of copper, so is his wickedness. 14
19: 5 One who rejoices in wickedness 14
22 the knowledge of wickedness is not wisdom 14
25:13 Any wickedness, but not the wickedness of a wife! 14
13 Any wickedness, but not the wickedness of a wife! 14
17 The wickedness of a wife changes her appearance 14
29: 7 Because of such wickedness, therefore 14
35: 3 To keep from wickedness is pleasing to the Lord 14
42:13 from a woman comes woman's wickedness. 14
14 Better is the wickedness of a man 14
46:20 to blot out the wickedness of the people. 12
47:25 For they sought out every sort of wickedness 14
Bar 2:26 wickedness of the house of Israel and the house 14
Sus 1:38 and when we saw this wickedness we ran to them. 12
57 would not endure your wickedness. 12
1Mc 5: 4 remembered the wickedness of the sons of Baean 13
7:42 judge him according to this wickedness. 13
2Mc 4:13 because of the surpassing wickedness of Jason 11
50 remained in office, growing in wickedness 13

wickedness *See also* great, hatred.

wide 1. גָּדוֹל 2. רַב 3. רחב 4. רָחָב 5. רֹחַב
6. רַחֲבַת יָדַיִם 7. μέγας 8. πλατεῖα 9. πλάτος
10. πλατύνω 11. spatiosus

Exd 25:25 shall make around it a frame a handbreadth wide *
37:12 he made around it a frame a handbreadth wide *
Deu 15:11 You shall open wide your hand to your brother †
1Kg 6: 2 The house . . was 60 cubits long, twenty cubits wide 5
20 was twenty cubits long, twenty cubits wide 5
7:27 each stand was four cubits long, four cubits wide 5
2Ch 4: 1 an altar of bronze . . and twenty cubits wide 5
6:13 bronze platform five . . long, five cubits wide 5
Neh 7: 4 city was wide and large, but the people within it 6
Job 30:14 As through a wide breach they come; 4
Ps 104:25 Yonder is the sea, great and wide, which teems 5
110: 6 he will shatter chiefs over the wide earth. 2
Isa 22:18 and throw you like a ball into a wide land; 4
Ezk 42: 4 was a passage inward, ten cubits wide 5
Hab 2: 5 His greed is as wide as Sheol; 3
Zec 14: 4 in two from east to west by a very wide valley; 1
Mat 7:13 for the gate is wide and the way is easy 8
1Co 16: 9 for a wide door for effective work has opened 7
2Co 6:11 our heart is wide. 10
2Es 7: 3 There is a sea set in a wide expanse 11
Jdt 1: 2 70 cubits high and 50 cubits wide; 9
3 100 cubits high and 60 cubits wide 9
4 70 cubits high and 40 cubits wide 9
2Mc 12:16 the adjoining lake, a quarter of a mile wide 9

wide *See also* experience, far, make, open.

only wide enough 1. ἐπί

Jdt 4: 7 only wide enough for two men at the most. 1

wide-spreading 1. ἀμφιλαφής

Wis 17:18 birds in wide-spreading branches 1

widely 1. ἐφ' ἱκανόν

2Mc 7: 5 The smoke from the pan spread widely 1

widely *See also* seen, spread, travel.

widen 1. πλατύνω

2Co 6:13 widen your hearts also. 1

widow 1. אַלְמָנָה 2. אַלְמָנוּת 3. אִשָּׁה 4. אִשָּׁה אַלְמָנָה
5. γυνή 6. χήρα 7. χήρευσις 8. χηρεύω 9. vidua
10. viduus

Gen 38:11 Remain a widow in your father's house 1
14 she put off her widow's garments, and put on a veil 2
Exd 22:22 You shall not afflict any widow or orphan. 1
24 your wives shall become widows 1
Lev 21:14 A widow, or one divorced, or a woman who has been 1
22:13 if a priest's daughter is a widow or divorced 1
Num30: 9 any vow of a widow or of a divorced woman 1
Deu 10:18 executes justice for . . the widow 1
14:29 Levite . . the fatherless, and the widow 1
16:11 rejoice . . you and . . the fatherless, and the widow 1
14 rejoice . . you and . . the widow who are within 1
24:17 not . . take a widow's garment in pledge; 1
19 for the sojourner, the fatherless, and the widow; 1
20 for the sojourner, the fatherless, and the widow. 1
21 for the sojourner, the fatherless, and the widow. 1
26:12 giving it to the . . fatherless, and the widow 1
13 given it to the . . fatherless, and the widow 1
27:19 who perverts the justice due to . . the widow.' 1
Rut 4: 5 buying Ruth the Moabitess, the widow of the dead 3
10 Also Ruth the Moabitess, the widow of Mahlon 3
1Sm 27: 3 Ahin'o-am . . and Ab'igail of Carmel, Nabal's widow. 3
30: 5 Ab'igail the widow of Nabal of Carmel. 3
2Sm 2: 2 Ab'igail the widow of Nabal of Carmel. 3
3: 3 Chil'e-ab, of Ab'igail the widow of Nabal of Carmel; 3
14: 5 answered, "Alas, I am a widow; my husband is dead. 4
1Kg 7:14 He was the son of a widow of the tribe of Naph'tali 4
11:26 whose mother's name was Zeru'ah, a widow 4
17: 9 I have commanded a widow there to feed you. 4
10 a widow was there gathering sticks; 4
20 hast thou brought calamity even upon the widow 1
Job 22: 9 You have sent widows away empty 1
24: 3 they take the widow's ox for a pledge. 1
21 and do no good to the widow. 1
27:15 buries, and their widows make no lamentation. 1
29:13 I caused the widow's heart to sing for joy. 1
31:16 or have caused the eyes of the widow to fail 1
Ps 68: 5 of the fatherless and protector of widows 1
78:64 their widows made no lamentation. 1
94: 6 They slay the widow and the sojourner 1
109: 9 his children be fatherless, and his wife a widow! 1
146: 9 LORD . . upholds the widow and the fatherless; 1
Prv 15:25 but maintains the widow's boundaries. 1
Isa 1:17 defend the fatherless, plead for the widow. 1
23 the widow's cause does not come to them. 1
9:17 no compassion on their fatherless and widows; 1
10: 2 rob the poor . . that widows may be their spoil 1
47: 8 I shall not sit as a widow or know the loss 1
Jer 7: 6 oppress the alien, the fatherless or the widow 1
15: 8 I have made their widows more in number 1
18:21 let their wives become childless and widowed. 1
22: 3 to the alien, the fatherless, and the widow 1
49:11 and let your widows trust in me. 1
Lam 1: 1 How like a widow has she become, she that was great 1
5: 3 our mothers are like widows. 1
Ezk 22: 7 the fatherless and the widow are wronged in you. 1
25 they have made many widows in the midst of her. 1
44:22 They shall not marry a widow, or a divorced woman 1
22 or a widow who is the widow of a priest. 1
22 or a widow who is the widow of a priest. 1
Zec 7:10 do not oppress the widow, the fatherless 1
Mal 3: 5 hireling in his wages, the widow and the orphan 1
Mat 22:24 his brother must marry the widow 5
Mrk 12:40 who devour widows' houses 6
42 a poor widow came, and put in two copper coins 6
43 this poor widow has put in more than all 6
Lke 2:37 and as a widow till she was 84 6
4:25 were many widows in Israel in the days of Eli'jah 6
26 to a woman who was a widow. 6
7:12 the only son of his mother, and she was a widow 6
18: 3 a widow in that city who kept coming to him 6
5 yet because this widow bothers me 6
20:47 who devour widows' houses 6
21: 2 he saw a poor widow put in two copper coins. 6
3 this poor widow has put in more than all of them; 6
Act 6: 1 because their widows were neglected 6
9:39 All the widows stood beside him weeping 6
41 Then calling the saints and widows 6
1Co 7: 8 To the unmarried and the widows I say 6
1Ti 5: 3 Honor widows who are real widows. 6
3 Honor widows who are real widows. 6
4 If a widow has children or grandchildren 6
5 She who is a real widow, and is left all alone 6
9 Let a widow be enrolled 6
11 refuse to enrol younger widows 6
14 I would have younger widows marry, bear children *
16 If any believing woman has relatives who are widows 6
16 it may assist those who are real widows. 6
Jas 1:27 to visit orphans and widows in their affliction 6
Rev 18: 7 I am no widow, mourning I shall never see,' 6
2Es 2: 2 'Go, my children, because I am a widow and forsaken. 9
4 For I am a widow and forsaken 9
20 Guard the rights of the widow 9
16:44 that do not marry, like those who are widowed. 10
Jdt 8: 4 Judith had lived at home as a widow 8
9: 4 O God, my God, hear me also, a widow. 6
9 give to me, a widow, the strength to do what I plan. 6
10: 3 and took off her widow's garments 7
16: 8 For she took off her widow's mourning 7
Wis 2:10 let us not spare the widow 6
Sir 35:14 nor the widow when she pours out her story. 6
15 Do not the tears of the widow run down her cheek 6
Bar 4:12 a widow and bereaved of many; I was left desolate 6
16 They led away the widow's beloved sons 6
LJr 1:38 They cannot take pity on a widow 6
2Mc 3:10 some deposits belonging to widows and orphans 6
8:28 the widows and orphans 6
30 to the orphans and widows, and also to the aged 6
4Mc 16:10 a widow and alone, with many sorrows. 6

remain a widow 1. οὐ γινώσκω ἀνήρ

Jdt 16:22 she remained a widow all the days of her life 1

widowhood 1. אַלְמֹן 2. אַלְמָנוּת 3. χήρευσις
4. viduitas

Gen 38:19 she put on the garments of her widowhood. 2
2Sm 20: 3 they were shut up . . living as if in widowhood. 2
Isa 47: 9 the loss of children and widowhood shall come 1
54: 4 of your youth, and the reproach of your widowhood 2
2Es 15:49 I will send evils upon you, widowhood, poverty 4
Jdt 8: 5 wore the garments of her widowhood. 3
6 She fasted all the days of her widowhood 3

width 1. רֹחַב

1Kg 6: 3 twenty cubits . . equal to the width of the house 1
2Ch 3: 4 twenty cubits . . equal to the width of the house; 1

wield 1. נדח 2. נוף 3. עור 4. שׂום 5. תפשׂ
6. καταφέρω 7. gero

Exd 20:25 for if you wield your tool upon it you profane it. 2
Deu 20:19 not destroy its trees by wielding an axe 1
2Sm 23: 8 he wielded his spear against 800 whom he slew *
18 he wielded his spear against 300 men 3
1Ch 11:11 he wielded his spear against 300 whom he slew 3
20 he wielded his spear against 300 men and slew them 3
Isa 10:15 the saw magnify itself against him who wields it? 2
15 As if a rod should wield him who lifts it 2
26 the LORD . . will wield against them a scourge 3
Ezk 30:21 that it may become strong to wield the sword. 5
38: 4 with buckler and shield, wielding swords; 5
Zec 9:13 O Greece, and wield you like a warrior's sword. 4
2Es 11:19 they wielded power one after another 7
4Mc 16:20 when Isaac saw his father's hand wielding a sword 6

wife 1.אִשָּׁה 2.בַּעַל 3.אִשָּׁה(A) 4.שֵׁגָל(A) 5.γαμετή 6.γυνή 7.ἔχω 8.σκεῦος 9.mulier 10.uxor

Gen 2:24 leaves . . his mother and cleaves to his wife 1
25 the man and his wife were both naked 1
3: 8 and the man and his wife hid themselves 1
17 you have listened to the voice of your wife 1
20 The man called his wife's name Eve 1
21 made for Adam and for his wife garments of skins 1
4: 1 Adam knew Eve his wife, and she conceived 1
17 Cain knew his wife, and she conceived 1
19 Lamech took two wives; the name of the one 1
23 Lamech said to his wives: "Adah and Zillah 1
23 hear my voice; you wives of Lamech 1
25 Adam knew his wife again, and she bore a son 1
6: 2 and they took to wife such of them 1
18 you, your sons, your wife, and your sons' wives 1
18 you, your sons, your wife, and your sons' wives 1
7: 7 Noah and his sons and his wife and his sons' wives 1
7 wife and his sons' wives with him went into the ark 1
13 and Noah's wife and the three wives of his sons 1
13 and Noah's wife and the three wives of his sons 1
8:16 Go forth from the ark, you and your wife 1
16 your sons and your sons' wives with you. 1
18 went forth, and his sons and his wife and his sons' 1
18 his wife and his sons' wives with him. 1
11:29 Abram and Nahor took wives; 1
29 the name of Abram's wife was Sar'ai 1
29 and the name of Nahor's wife, Milcah 1
31 Sar'ai . . his son Abram's wife 1
12: 5 Abram took Sar'ai his wife, and Lot 1
11 he said to Sar'ai his wife 1
12 will say, 'This is his wife'; then they will kill me 1
17 plagues because of Sar'ai, Abram's wife. 1
18 Why did you not tell me that she was your wife? 1
19 so that I took her for my wife? 1
19 Now then, here is your wife, take her, and be gone. 1
20 and they set him on the way, with his wife 1
13: 1 he and his wife, and all that he had 1
16: 1 Now Sar'ai, Abram's wife, bore him no children. 1
3 Sar'ai, Abram's wife, took Hagar the Egyptian 1
3 gave her to Abram her husband as a wife. 1
17:15 God said to Abraham, "As for Sar'ai your wife 1
19 God said, "No, but Sarah your wife shall bear 1
18: 9 They said to him, "Where is Sarah your wife? 1
10 and Sarah your wife shall have a son. 1
19:15 take your wife and your two daughters 1
16 he lingered; so the men seized him and his wife 1
26 Lot's wife behind him looked back 1
20: 2 Abraham said of Sarah his wife, "She is my sister. 1
3 woman whom you have taken; for she is a man's wife. 2
7 Now then restore the man's wife; 1
11 and they will kill me because of my wife. 1
12 of my mother; and she became my wife. 1
14 to Abraham, and restored Sarah his wife to him. 1
17 God healed Abim'elech, and also healed his wife 1
18 of Abim'elech because of Sarah, Abraham's wife. 1
21:21 and his mother took a wife for him from the land 1
23:19 After this, Abraham buried Sarah his wife 1
24: 3 you will not take a wife for my son 1
4 to my kindred, and take a wife for my son Isaac. 1
7 you shall take a wife for my son from there. 1
15 Bethu'el the son of Milcah, the wife of Nahor 1
36 Sarah my master's wife bore a son to my master 1
37 You shall not take a wife for my son 1
38 to my kindred, and take a wife for my son.' 1
40 and you shall take a wife for my son 1
51 let her be the wife of your master's son 1
67 Rebekah, and she became his wife; and he loved her. 1
25: 1 Abraham took another wife, whose name was 1
10 There Abraham was buried, with Sarah his wife. 1
20 Isaac was 40 years old when he took to wife Rebekah 1
21 Isaac prayed to the LORD for his wife 1
21 his prayer, and Rebekah his wife conceived. 1
26: 7 When the men of the place asked him about his wife 1
7 She is my sister"; for he feared to say, "My wife 1
8 window and saw Isaac fondling Rebekah his wife. 1
9 Behold, she is your wife; how then could you say 1
10 the people might easily have lain with your wife 1
11 this man or his wife shall be put to death. 1
34 When Esau was 40 years old, he took to wife Judith 1
28: 2 take as wife from there one of the daughters 1
6 away to Paddan-aram to take a wife from there 1
9 Esau . . took to wife, besides the wives he had 1
9 Esau . . took to wife, besides the wives he had 1
29:21 Then Jacob said to Laban, "Give me my wife 1
28 then Laban gave him his daughter Rachel to wife. 1
30: 4 she gave him her maid Bilhah as a wife; 1
9 maid Zilpah and gave her to Jacob as a wife. 1
26 Give me my wives and my children for whom I have 1
31:17 arose, and set his sons and his wives on camels; 1
50 or if you take wives besides my daughters 1
32:22 The same night he arose and took his two wives 1
34: 4 Get me this maiden for my wife. 1
12 only give me the maiden to be my wife. 1
29 little ones and their wives, all that was 1
36: 2 Esau took his wives from the Canaanites 1
6 Then Esau took his wives, his sons, his daughters 1
10 El'iphaz the son of Adah the wife of Esau 1
10 Reu'el the son of Bas'emath the wife of Esau. 1
12 These are the sons of Adah, Esau's wife. 1
13 These are the sons of Bas'emath, Esau's wife. 1
14 daughter of Anah the son of Zib'eon, Esau's wife 1
17 Edom; they are the sons of Bas'emath, Esau's wife 1
18 These are the sons of Oholiba'mah, Esau's wife 1
18 the daughter of Anah, Esau's wife. 1
39 his wife's name was Mehet'abel 1
37: 2 sons of Bilhah and Zilpah, his father's wives; 1
38: 6 Judah took a wife for Er his first-born 1
8 Judah said to Onan, "Go in to your brother's wife 1
9 went in to his brother's wife he spilled the semen 1
12 of time the wife of Judah, Shua's daughter, died; 1
39: 7 after a time his master's wife cast her eyes upon 1
8 his master's wife, "Lo, having me my master has no 1
9 from me except yourself, because you are his wife 1
19 his master heard the words which his wife spoke 1
44:27 said to us, 'You know that my wife bore me two sons; 1
45:19 wagons . . for your little ones and for your wives 1
46: 5 carried . . their little ones, and their wives 1
19 of Rachel, Jacob's wife: Joseph and Benjamin. 1
26 own offspring, not including Jacob's sons' wives 1
49:31 There they buried Abraham and Sarah his wife; 1
31 there they buried Isaac and Rebekah his wife; 1
Exd 4:20 So Moses took his wife and his sons and set them 1
6:20 Amram took to wife Joch'ebed his father's sister 1
23 Aaron took to wife Eli'sheba, the daughter 1
25 Elea'zar . . took to wife one of the daughters 1
18: 2 Jethro . . had taken Zippo'rah, Moses' wife 1
5 Jethro . . came with his sons and his wife 1
6 is coming to you with your wife and her two sons 1
20:17 you shall not covet your neighbor's wife 1
21: 3 if . . married, then his wife shall go out with him. 1
4 If his master gives him a wife and she bears him 1
4 the wife and her children shall be her master's 1
5 I love my master, my wife, and my children; 1
10 If he takes another wife to himself, he shall not *
22:16 he shall . . make her his wife. 1
24 your wives shall become widows 1
32: 2 rings of gold which are in the ears of your wives 1
Lev 18: 8 not uncover the nakedness of your father's wife 1
11 the nakedness of your father's wife's daughter 1
14 you shall not approach his wife; she is your aunt 1
15 your daughter-in-law; she is your son's wife 1
16 not uncover the nakedness of your brother's wife 1
20 shall not lie carnally with your neighbor's wife 1
20:10 commits adultery with the wife of his neighbor 1
11 The man who lies with his father's wife 1
14 If a man takes a wife and her mother also 1
21 If a man takes his brother's wife, it is impurity 1
21:13 he shall take a wife in her virginity 1
14 he shall take to wife a virgin of his own people 1
Num 5:12 If any man's wife goes astray and acts 1
14 he is jealous of his wife who has defiled herself; 1
14 jealous of his wife, though she has not defiled 1
15 then the man shall bring his wife to the priest 1
29 when a wife . . goes astray and defiles herself 1
30 when . . he is jealous of his wife; 1
14: 3 Our wives and our little ones will become a prey; 1
16:27 together with their wives, their sons, and their 1
26:59 name of Amram's wife was Joch'ebed the daughter 1
30:16 statutes . . as between a man and his wife 1
32:26 Our little ones, our wives, our flocks, and all our 1
36: 8 shall be wife to one of the family of the tribe 1
Deu 3:19 your wives, your little ones, and your cattle 1
5:21 'Neither shall you covet your neighbor's wife; 1
13: 6 If . . the wife of your bosom, . . , entices you 1
17:17 not multiply wives for himself, lest his heart 1
20: 7 what man is there that has betrothed a wife 1
21:11 desire for her and would take her . . as wife 1
13 be her husband, and she shall be your wife. 1
15 If a man has two wives, the one loved and the other 1
22:13 If a man takes a wife, and goes in to her 1
16 I gave my daughter to this man to wife 1
19 she shall be his wife; he may not put her away 1
22 man is found lying with the wife of another man 1
24 man because he violated his neighbor's wife; 1
29 shekels of silver, and she shall be his wife 1
30 A man shall not take his father's wife 1
24: 1 When a man takes a wife and marries her 1
2 if she goes and becomes another man's wife *
3 the latter husband dies, who took her to be his wife 1
4 husband . . may not take her again to be his wife 1
5 year, to be happy with his wife whom he has taken. 1
25: 5 wife of the dead shall not be married outside 1
5 husband's brother shall . . take her as his wife 1
11 wife of the one draws near to rescue her husband 1
27:20 'Cursed be he who lies with his father's wife 1
28:30 betroth a wife, and another man shall lie with her; 1
54 man . . grudge food to . . the wife of his bosom 1
29:11 your little ones, your wives, and the sojourner 1
Jos 1:14 Your wives, your little ones, and your cattle 1
15:16 to him will I give Achsah my daughter as wife. 1
17 and he gave him Achsah his daughter as wife. 1
Jdg 1:12 I will give him Achsah my daughter as wife. 1
13 and he gave him Achsah his daughter as wife. 1
3: 6 they took their daughters to themselves for wives 1
4: 4 Now Deb'orah, a prophetess, the wife of Lapp'idoth 1
17 to the tent of Ja'el, the wife of Heber the Ken'ite; 1
21 Ja'el the wife of Heber took a tent peg 1
5:24 blessed . . be Ja'el, the wife of Heber the Ken'ite 1
8:30 Gideon had 70 sons . . for he had many wives. 1
11: 2 Gilead's wife also bore him sons; 1
2 when his wife's sons grew up, they thrust Jephthah 1
13: 2 Mano'ah . . his wife was barren and had no children 1
11 Mano'ah arose and went after his wife, and came 1
20 ascended . . while Mano'ah and his wife looked on; 1
21 angel . . appeared no more to Mano'ah and to his wife. 1
22 Mano'ah said to his wife, "We shall surely die 1
23 his wife said to him, "If the LORD had meant to kill 1
14: 2 at Timnah; now get her for me as my wife. 1
3 you must go to take a wife from the uncircumcised 1
15 they said to Samson's wife, "Entice your husband 1
16 Samson's wife wept before him, and said, "You only 1
20 Samson's wife was given to his companion 1
15: 1 harvest, Samson went to visit his wife with a kid; 1
1 and he said, "I will go in to my wife in the chamber. 1
6 taken his wife and given her to his companion. 1
21: 7 What shall we do for wives for those who are left 1
7 will not give them any of our daughters for wives? 1
16 What shall we do for wives for those who are left 1
18 Yet we cannot give them wives of our daughters. 1
18 sworn, "Cursed be he who gives a wife to Benjamin. 1
21 and seize each man his wife from the daughters 1
22 we did not take for each man . . his wife in battle 1
23 and took their wives, according to their number 1
Rut 1: 1 a certain man . . he and his wife and his two sons. 1
2 man was Elim'elech and the name of his wife Na'omi 1
4 These took Moabite wives; 1
4:10 Also Ruth . . I have bought to be my wife 1
13 Bo'az took Ruth and she became his wife; 1
1Sm 1: 2 He had two wives; the name of the one was Hannah 1
4 portions to Penin'nah his wife and to all her sons 1
19 And Elka'nah knew Hannah his wife, and the LORD 1
2:20 Then Eli would bless Elka'nah and his wife, and say 1
4:19 Now his daughter-in-law, the wife of Phin'ehas 1
14:50 and the name of Saul's wife was Ahin'o-am 1
18:17 Here is . . Merab; I will give her to you for a wife; 1
19 was given to A'driel the Meho'lathite for a wife. 1
27 And Saul gave him his daughter Michal for a wife. 1
19:11 But Michal, David's wife, told him, "If you do not save 1
25: 3 man was Nabal, and the name of his wife Ab'igail. 1
14 But one of the young men told Ab'igail, Nabal's wife 1
37 his wife told him these things, and his heart died 1
39 Then David . . wooed Ab'igail, to make her his wife. 1
40 David has sent us . . to take you to him as his wife. 1
42 she went after . . David, and became his wife. 1
43 and both of them became his wives. 1
44 Saul had given Michal . . David's wife, to Palti 1
27: 3 David with his two wives, Ahin'o-am . . and Ab'igail 1
30: 3 wives and sons and daughters taken captive. 1
5 David's two wives also had been taken captive 1
18 and David rescued his two wives. 1
22 may lead away his wife and children, and depart. 1
2Sm 2: 2 David went up there, and his two wives also 1
3: 5 and the sixth, Ith're-am, of Eglah, David's wife. 1
14 Give me my wife Michal, whom I betrothed 1
5:13 David took more concubines and wives 1
11: 3 Bathshe'ba . . the wife of Uri'ah the Hittite? 1
11 go . . to eat and to drink, and to lie with my wife? 1
26 the wife of Uri'ah heard . . her husband was dead 1
27 David sent and brought . . and she became his wife 1
12: 8 I gave . . and your master's wives into your bosom 1
9 You have smitten Uri'ah . . and have taken his wife 1
9 and have taken his wife to be your wife 1
10 have taken the wife of Uri'ah . . to be your wife. 1
10 have taken the wife of Uri'ah . . to be your wife. 1
11 and I will take your wives before your eyes 1
11 and he shall lie with your wives in the sight 1
15 the LORD struck the child that Uri'ah's wife bore 1
24 Then David comforted his wife, Bathshe'ba 1
19: 5 and the lives of your wives and your concubines 1
1Kg 2:17 to give me Ab'ishag the Shu'nammite as my wife. 1
21 Ab'ishag . . be given to Adoni'jah . . as his wife. 1
4:11 Ben-abin'adab . . (he had Taphath . . as his wife); 1
15 Ahi'ma-az . . (he had taken Bas'emath . . as his wife) 1
9:16 given it as dowry to his daughter, Solomon's wife; 1
10: 8 Happy are your wives! 6
11: 3 He had 700 wives, princesses 1
3 and his wives turned away his heart. 1
4 his wives turned away his heart after other gods; 1
8 so he did for all his foreign wives 1

19 he gave him in marriage the sister of his own wife 1
14: 2 Jerobo'am said to his wife, "Arise 1
2 it be not known that you are the wife of Jerobo'am 1
4 Jerobo'am's wife did so; she arose, and went 1
5 the wife of Jerobo'am is coming to inquire of you 1
6 Come in, wife of Jerobo'am; why do you pretend 1
17 Jerobo'am's wife arose, and departed 1
16:31 he took for wife Jez'ebel the daughter of Ethba'al 1
20: 3 your fairest wives and children also are mine.' 1
5 Deliver to me . . your wives and your children"; 1
7 he sent to me for my wives and my children 1
21: 5 Jez'ebel his wife came to him, and said to him 1
7 Jez'ebel his wife said to him, "Do you now govern 1
25 like Ahab, whom Jez'ebel his wife incited. 1
2Kg 4: 1 the wife of one of the sons of the prophets cried 1
5: 2 a little maid . . and she waited on Na'aman's wife. 1
8:18 for the daughter of Ahab was his wife. 1
14: 9 saying, 'Give your daughter to my son for a wife'; 1
22:14 Huldah the prophetess, the wife of Shallum 1
24:15 the king's mother, the king's wives, his officials 1
1Ch 1:50 his wife's name Mehet'abel the daughter of Matred 1
2:18 Caleb . . had children by his wife Azu'bah 1
24 Eph'rathah, the wife of Hezron his father 1
26 Jerah'meel also had another wife, whose name was 1
29 Abi'shur's wife was Ab'ihail, and she bore him Ahban 1
3: 3 the sixth Ith'ream, by his wife Eglah; 1
4: 5 Asshur . . had two wives, Helah and Na'arah; 1
18 his Jewish wife bore Jered the father of Gedor 1
19 The sons of the wife of Hodi'ah, the sister of Naham 1
7: 4 36,000, for they had many wives and sons. 1
15 Machir took a wife for Huppim and for Shuppim. 1
16 Ma'acah the wife of Machir bore a son 1
23 E'phraim went in to his wife, and she conceived 1
8: 8 he had sent away Hushim and Ba'ara his wives. 1
9 by Hodesh his wife: Jobab, Zib'i-a, Mesha, Malcam 1
29 Je-i'el . . the name of his wife was Ma'acah. 1
9:35 Je-i'el, and the name of his wife was Ma'acah 1
14: 3 David took more wives in Jerusalem 1
2Ch 8:11 My wife shall not live in the house of David 1
9: 7 Happy are your wives! 6
11:18 Rehobo'am took as wife Ma'halath 1
21 above all his wives and concubines 1
21 (he took eighteen wives and 60 concubines 1
23 procured wives for them. 1
13:21 took fourteen wives, and had 22 sons 1
20:13 little ones, their wives, and their children. 1
21: 6 for the daughter of Ahab was his wife. 1
14 LORD will bring a great plague on . . your wives 1
17 carried away . . also his sons and his wives 1
22:11 Jeho-shab'e-ath . . wife of Jehoi'ada the priest 1
24: 3 Jehoi'ada got for him two wives, and he had sons 1
25:18 Give your daughter to my son for a wife 1
29: 9 our sons and our . . wives are in captivity 1
31:18 little children, their wives, their sons 1
34:22 Huldah the . . wife of Shallum the son of Tokhath 1
Ezr 2:61 sons of Barzil'lai (who had taken a wife 1
9: 2 taken some of their daughters to be wives •
10: 3 to put away all these wives and their children 1
11 separate yourselves . . from the foreign wives. 1
14 all in our cities who have taken foreign wives 1
19 pledged themselves to put away their wives 1
Neh 4:14 fight for your . . daughters, your wives 1
5: 1 great outcry of the people and of their wives 1
6:18 taken the daughter of Meshul'lam . . as his wife. •
7:63 Barzil'lai (who had taken a wife of the daughters 1
10:28 wives, their sons, their daughters, all who have 1
Est 5:10 he . . fetched his friends and his wife Zeresh. 1
14 his wife Zeresh and all his friends said to him 1
6:13 Haman told his wife Zeresh and all his friends 1
13 Then his wise men and his wife Zeresh said to him 1
Job 2: 9 Then his wife said to him, "Do you still hold fast 1
19:17 I am repulsive to my wife 1
31:10 then let my wife grind for another 1
Ps 109: 9 his children be fatherless, and his wife a widow! 1
128: 3 wife . . like a fruitful vine within your house; 1
Prv 5:18 rejoice in the wife of your youth 1
6:29 So is he who goes in to his neighbor's wife; 1
12: 4 A good wife is the crown of her husband 1
18:22 He who finds a wife finds a good thing 1
19:13 wife's quarreling is a continual dripping 1
14 but a prudent wife is from the LORD. 1
31:10 A good wife who can find? She is far more precious 1
Ecc 9: 9 Enjoy life with the wife whom you love 1
Isa 13:16 houses . . plundered and their wives ravished. 1
54: 6 For the LORD has called you like a wife forsaken 1
6 like a wife of youth when she is cast off 1
Jer 3: 1 If a man divorces his wife and she goes from him 1
1 she goes from him and becomes another man's wife •
20 Surely, as a faithless wife leaves her husband 1
5: 8 each neighing for his neighbor's wife. 1
6:11 both husband and wife shall be taken 1
12 turned over to others, their fields and wives 1
8:10 Therefore I will give their wives to others 1
14:16 their wives, their sons, and their daughters. 1
16: 2 You shall not take a wife, nor shall you have sons 1
18:21 let their wives become childless and widowed. 1
29: 6 Take wives and have sons and daughters; 1
6 have sons and daughters; take wives for your sons 1
23 committed adultery with their neighbors' wives 1
35: 8 ourselves, our wives, our sons, or our daughters 1
38:23 All your wives and your sons shall be led out 1
44: 9 forgotten . . the wickedness of their wives 1
9 wickedness of your wives, which they committed 1
15 their wives had offered incense to other gods 1
25 and your wives have declared with your mouths 1
Ezk 16:32 Adulterous wife, who receives strangers 1
18: 6 does not defile his neighbor's wife 1
11 upon the mountains, defiles his neighbor's wife 1
15 does not defile his neighbor's wife 1
22:11 commits abomination with his neighbor's wife; 1
24:18 in the morning, and at evening my wife died. 1
33:26 each of you defiles his neighbor's wife; 1
Dan 5: 2 king and his lords, his wives, and his concubines 4
3 king and his lords, his wives, and his concubines 4
23 lords, your wives, and your concubines have drunk 4
6:24 den of lions–they, their children, and their wives; 3
Hos 1: 2 Go, take to yourself a wife of harlotry 1
2: 2 for she is not my wife, and I am not her husband– 1
12:12 land of Aram, there Israel did service for a wife 1
12 and for a wife he herded sheep.) 1
Ams 7:17 Your wife shall be a harlot in the city 1
Zec 12:12 David by itself, and their wives by themselves; 1
12 Nathan by itself, and their wives by themselves; 1
13 Levi by itself, and their wives by themselves; 1
13 Levi by itself, and their wives by themselves; 1
14 each by itself, and their wives by themselves. 1
Mal 2:14 covenant between you and the wife of your youth 1
14 though she is your companion and your wife 1
15 let none be faithless to the wife of his youth. 1
Mat 1: 6 David . . the father of Solomon by the wife of Uri'ah •
20 do not fear to take Mary your wife, for that 6
24 of the Lord commanded him; he took his wife 6
5:31 It was also said, 'Whoever divorces his wife 6
32 I say to you that every one who divorces his wife 6
14: 3 Hero'di-as, his brother Philip's wife; 6
18:25 with his wife and children and all that he had 6
19: 3 Is it lawful to divorce one's wife for any cause? 6
5 and be joined to his wife 6
8 Moses allowed you to divorce your wives 6
9 I say to you: whoever divorces his wife 6
10 If such is the case of a man with his wife 6
22:25 having no children left his wife to his brother. 6
28 to which of the seven will she be wife 6
27:19 his wife sent word to him 6
Mrk 6:17 Hero'di-as, his brother Philip's wife 6
18 is not lawful for you to have your brother's wife. 6
10: 2 Is it lawful for a man to divorce his wife? 6
7 be joined to his wife 6
11 Whoever divorces his wife and marries another 6
12:19 if a man's brother dies and leaves a wife 6
19 the man must take the wife, and raise up children 6
20 There were seven brothers; the first took a wife 6
23 In the resurrection whose wife will she be? 6
23 the seven had her as wife. 6
Lke 1: 5 he had a wife of the daughters of Aaron 6
13 your wife Elizabeth will bear you a son 6
18 I am an old man, and my wife is advanced in years. 6
24 After these days his wife Elizabeth conceived 6
3:19 Hero'di-as, his brother's wife 6
8: 3 Joan'na, the wife of Chuza, Herod's steward 6
14:20 I have married a wife, and therefore I cannot come.' 6
26 his own father and mother and wife and children 6
16:18 Every one who divorces his wife 6
17:32 Remember Lot's wife. 6
18:29 there is no man who has left house or wife 6
20:28 if a man's brother dies, having a wife but no children 6
28 the man must take the wife and raise up children 6
29 the first took a wife, and died without children; 6
33 whose wife will the woman be 6
33 the seven had her as wife. 6
Joh 19:25 his mother's sister, Mary the wife of Clopas •
Act 5: 1 a man named Anani'as with his wife Sapphi'ra 6
2 and with his wife's knowledge 6
7 his wife came in, not knowing what had happened. 6
18: 2 lately come from Italy with his wife Priscilla 6
21: 5 they all, with wives and children 6
24:24 Felix came with his wife Drusil'la 6
1Co 5: 1 a man is living with his father's wife. 6
7: 2 each man should have his own wife 6
3 should give to his wife her conjugal rights 6
3 likewise the wife to her husband. 6
4 For the wife does not rule over her own body 6
4 but the wife does. 6
10 the wife should not separate from her husband 6
11 the husband should not divorce his wife. 6
12 if any brother has a wife who is an unbeliever 6
14 consecrated through his wife 6
14 the unbelieving wife is consecrated 6
16 Wife, how do you know 6
16 how do you know whether you will save your wife? 6
27 Are you bound to a wife? Do not seek to be free. 6
27 Are you free from a wife? Do not seek marriage. 6
29 who have wives live as though they had none 6
33 how to please his wife 6
39 A wife is bound to her husband as long as he lives. 6
9: 5 we not have the right to be accompanied by a wife 6
Eph 5:22 Wives, be subject to your husbands, as to the Lord. 6
23 For the husband is the head of the wife as Christ 6
24 let wives also be subject in everything 6
25 Husbands, love your wives 6
28 Even so husbands should love their wives 6
28 He who loves his wife loves himself 6
31 be joined to his wife 6
33 let each one of you love his wife as himself 6
33 let the wife see that she respects her husband. 6
Col 3:18 Wives, be subject to your husbands 6
19 Husbands, love your wives 6
1Th 4: 4 each one of you know how to take a wife for himself 8
1Ti 3: 2 the husband of one wife, temperate, sensible 6
12 Let deacons be the husband of one wife 6
5: 9 having been the wife of one husband; 6
Tit 1: 6 if any man is blameless, the husband of one wife 6
1Pe 3: 1 wives, be submissive to your husbands 6
1 won without a word by the behavior of their wives 6
7 husbands, live considerately with your wives •
Rev 21: 9 Come, I will show you the Bride, the wife of the Lamb. 6
1Es 4:20 A man leaves . . and cleaves to his wife. 6
21 With his wife he ends his days 6
25 A man loves his wife more than his father 6
5: 1 with their wives and sons and daughters 6
8:93 we will put away all our foreign wives 6
9: 9 separate . . from your foreign wives. 6
12 those in our settlements who have foreign wives 6
17 the cases of the men who had foreign wives 6
18 were brought in and found to have foreign wives 6
20 pledged themselves to put away their wives 6
2Es 9:47 when he grew up and I came to take a wife for him 10
10:22 and our wives have been ravished 9
Tob 1:20 nothing was left to me except my wife Anna 6
2: 1 my wife Anna and my son Tobias were restored to me 6
11 Then my wife Anna earned money at women's work. 6
3: 8 before he had been with her as his wife 6
15 for whom I should keep myself as wife. 6
4:12 First of all take a wife 6
12 all took wives from among their brethren 6
13 by refusing to take a wife for yourself 6
6:15 to take a wife from among your own people 6
15 she will become your wife 6
7: 2 Then Raguel said to his wife Edna 6
8 his wife Edna and his daughter Sarah wept 6
13 he gave her to Tobias to be his wife, saying 6
14 Next he called his wife Edna 6
16 Raguel called his wife Edna and said to her 6
8: 6 gavest him Eve his wife as a helper and support. 6
12 said to his wife Edna, "Send one of the maids 6
21 the rest would be his "when my wife and I die. 6
9: 6 Gabael blessed Tobias and his wife. 6
10: 4 his wife said to him, "The lad has perished 6
10 Raguel arose and gave him his wife Sarah 6
11: 1 he blessed Raguel and his wife Edna 6
3 Let us run ahead of your wife 6
12: 3 he has led me back to you safely, he cured my wife 6
14:12 Then Tobias returned with his wife 6
Jdt 4:10 their wives and their children and their cattle 6
12 not to give up . . their wives as booty 6
7:14 their wives and children will waste away with famine 6
27 or see our wives . . draw their last breath. 6
9: 4 thou gavest their wives for a prey 6
AEs 13: 6 all, with their wives and children 6
Wis 3:12 Their wives are foolish, and their children evil; 6
Sir 7:19 Do not deprive yourself of a wise and good wife 6
26 If you have a wife who pleases you 6
9: 1 Do not be jealous of the wife of your bosom 6
9 Never dine with another man's wife 6
15: 2 like the wife of his youth she will welcome him. 6
25: 1 a wife and a husband who live in harmony. 6
8 happy is he who lives with an intelligent wife 6
13 Any wickedness, but not the wickedness of a wife! 6
16 rather . . than dwell with an evil wife. 6
17 The wickedness of a wife changes her appearance 6
19 insignificant compared to a wife's iniquity 6
20 such is a garrulous wife for a quiet husband. 6
22 when a wife supports her husband. 6
23 a wounded heart are caused by an evil wife. 6
23 the wife who does not make her husband happy. •
25 Allow . . no boldness of speech in an evil wife. 6
26: 1 Happy is the husband of a good wife 6
2 A loyal wife rejoices her husband 6
3 A good wife is a great blessing 6
6 when a wife is envious of a rival 6
7 An evil wife is an ox yoke which chafes 6
8 There is great anger when a wife is drunken 6
9 A wife's harlotry shows in her lustful eyes 6
13 A wife's charm delights her husband 6
14 A silent wife is a gift of the Lord 6
15 A modest wife adds charm to charm 6
16 beauty of a good wife in her well-ordered home. 6
33:19 To son or wife, to brother or friend 6
36:24 He who acquires a wife gets his best possession 6
25 where there is no wife 6
40:19 a blameless wife is accounted better than both. 6
23 a wife with her husband is better than both. 6
41:21 gazing at another man's wife; 6
42: 6 Where there is an evil wife, a seal is a good thing; 6
LJr 1:28 likewise their wives preserve some with salt 6
33 to clothe their wives and children. 6
Sus 1: 2 And he took a wife named Susanna 6

29 Send for Susanna . . who is the wife of Joakim. 6
63 Hilkiah and his wife praised God 6
Bel 1:10 besides their wives and children 6
15 the priests came with their wives and children 6
21 seized the priests and their wives and children; 6
1Mc 2:30 they, their sons, their wives, and their cattle 6
38 they died, with their wives and children 6
3:20 to destroy us and our wives and our children 6
5:13 the enemy have captured their wives 6
23 with their wives and children 6
45 with their wives and children and goods 6
8:10 the Romans took captive their wives and children; 6
10:54 give me now your daughter as my wife 6
11: 9 my daughter who was Alexander's wife 7
13: 6 the sanctuary and your wives and children 6
45 The men in the city, with their wives and children 6
2Mc 12: 3 to embark, with their wives and children, on boats 6
15:18 Their concern for wives and children 6
3Mc 1: 4 defend . . their children and wives bravely 6
3:25 together with their wives and children 6
4Mc 2: 5 You shall not covet your neighbor's wife 6
11 It is superior to love for one's wife 5

wife *See also* take.

brother's wife 1. יְבֵמֶת
Deu 25: 7 if the man does not wish to take his brother's wife 1
7 then his brother's wife shall go up to the gate 1
9 then his brother's wife shall go up to him 1

rival wife 1. צָרָה
Lev 18:18 not take a woman as a rival wife to her sister 1

uncle's wife 1. דֹּדָה
Lev 20:20 If a man lies with his uncle's wife 1

wild 1. אֲשֶׁר בַּשָּׂדֶה 2. נָכְרִי 3. רָעָה 4. שָׂדֶה 5. ἄγριος 6. ἀνάχυσις 7. χορτώδης 8. agrestis
Gen 37:20 we shall say that a wild beast has devoured him 3
33 a wild beast has devoured him; Joseph is without 3
Exd 23:11 what they leave the wild beasts may eat. 4
29 lest . . the wild beasts multiply against you. 4
Lev 26:22 I will let loose the wild beasts among you 4
Deu 7:22 lest the wild beasts grow too numerous for you. 4
2Sm 2:18 Now As'ahel was as swift of foot as a wild gazelle; 1
2Kg 4:39 went out . . found a wild vine and gathered from it 4
39 and gathered from it his lap full of wild gourds 4
14: 9 a wild beast of Lebanon passed by and trampled 4
2Ch 25:18 wild beast of Lebanon passed by and trampled 4
Jer 2:21 have . . turned degenerate and become a wild vine? 2
48: 6 Save yourselves! Be like a wild ass in the desert! 5
Ezk 5:17 I will send famine and wild beasts against you 3
14:15 If I cause wild beasts to pass through the land 3
34: 5 they became food for all the wild beasts. 4
8 my sheep have become food for all the wild beasts 4
25 and banish wild beasts from the land 3
39: 4 and to the wild beasts to be devoured. 4
Mat 3: 4 waist; and his food was locusts and wild honey. 5
Mrk 1: 6 ate locusts and wild honey. 5
1Pe 4: 4 do not now join them in the same wild profligacy 6
Jde 1:13 wild waves of the sea, casting up the foam 5
2Es 5: 8 the wild beasts shall roam beyond their haunts 8
2Mc 5:27 they continued to live on what grew wild 7
11: 9 the wildest beasts or walls of iron. 5

wild *See also* animal, beast, confusion, creature, grape, olive.

wild ass 1. פֶּרֶא 2. עֲרָד (A) 3. ὄναγρος 4. ὄνος
Gen 16:12 He shall be a wild ass of a man 1
Job 6: 5 Does the wild ass bray when he has grass 1
11:12 when a wild ass's colt is born a man. 1
24: 5 like wild asses in the desert they go forth 1
39: 5 Who has let the wild ass go free? 1
Ps 104:11 wild asses quench their thirst. 1
Isa 32:14 dens for ever, a joy of wild asses 1
Jer 2:24 a wild ass used to the wilderness 1
14: 6 The wild asses stand on the bare heights 1
48: 6 Save yourselves! Be like a wild ass in the desert! 4
Dan 5:21 dwelling was with the wild asses; he was fed grass 2
Hos 8: 9 gone up to Assyria, a wild ass wandering alone; 1
Sir 13:19 Wild asses . . are the prey of lions 3

wild boar 1. aper
2Es 15:30 shall go forth like wild boars of the forest 1

wild goat 1. אַקּוֹ 2. יָעֵל
Deu 14: 5 the hart, the gazelle, the roebuck, the wild goat 1
Ps 104:18 The high mountains are for the wild goats; 2

wild ox 1. רְאֵם
Num23:22 they have as it were the horns of the wild ox. 1
24: 8 he has as it were the horns of the wild ox 1
Deu 33:17 his horns are the horns of a wild ox; 1
Job 39: 9 Is the wild ox willing to serve you? 1
Ps 22:21 my afflicted soul from the horns of the wild oxen! 1
92:10 thou hast exalted my horn like that of the wild ox; 1
Isa 34: 7 Wild oxen shall fall with them 1

young wild ox 1. בֶּן רְאֵמִים
Ps 29: 6 skip like a calf, and Si'rion like a young wild ox. 1

wilderness 1. יְשִׁימוֹן 2. מִדְבָּר 3. עֲרָבָה 4. ἐρημία 5. ἔρημος 6. desertum
Gen 14: 6 far as El-paran on the border of the wilderness; 2
16: 7 found her by a spring of water in the wilderness 2
21:14 wandered in the wilderness of Beer-sheba. 2
20 the lad . . lived in the wilderness 2
21 He lived in the wilderness of Paran; 2
36:24 who found the hot springs in the wilderness 2
37:22 cast him into this pit here in the wilderness 2
Exd 3: 1 flock to the west side of the wilderness 2
18 days' journey into the wilderness, that we may 2
4:27 Aaron, "Go into the wilderness to meet Moses. 2
5: 1 may hold a feast to me in the wilderness.' 2
3 a three days' journey into the wilderness 2
7:16 that they may serve me in the wilderness; 2
8:27 go three days' journey into the wilderness 2
28 sacrifice to the LORD your God in the wilderness; 2
13:18 the way of the wilderness toward the Red Sea. 2
20 encamped at Etham, on the edge of the wilderness. 2
14: 3 in the land; the wilderness has shut them in.' 2
11 you have taken us away to die in the wilderness? 2
12 the Egyptians than to die in the wilderness. 2
15:22 they went into the wilderness of Shur; 2
22 they went three days in the wilderness 2
16: 1 people of Israel came to the wilderness of Sin 2
2 murmured against Moses and . . in the wilderness 2
3 you have brought us out into this wilderness 2
10 they looked toward the wilderness, and behold 2
14 there was on the face of the wilderness 2
32 bread with which I fed you in the wilderness 2
17: 1 Israel moved on from the wilderness of Sin 2
18: 5 Jethro . . came . . to Moses in the wilderness 2
19: 1 that day they came into the wilderness of Sinai. 2
2 came into the wilderness of Sinai 2
2 they encamped in the wilderness; 2
23:31 from the wilderness to the Euphra'tes; 2
Lev 7:38 to the LORD, in the wilderness of Sinai 2
16:10 be sent away into the wilderness of Aza'zel 2
21 the goat, and send him away into the wilderness 2
22 he shall let the goat go in the wilderness 2
Num 1: 1 The LORD spoke to Moses in the wilderness 2
19 So he numbered them in the wilderness of Sinai. 2
3: 4 before the LORD in the wilderness of Sinai; 2
14 the LORD said to Moses in the wilderness of Sinai 2
9: 1 LORD spoke to Moses in the wilderness of Sinai 2
5 kept the passover . . in the wilderness of Sinai; 2
10:12 set out by stages from the wilderness of Sinai; 2
12 cloud settled down in the wilderness of Paran. 2
31 you know how we are to encamp in the wilderness 2
12:16 people . . encamped in the wilderness of Paran. 2
13: 3 Moses sent them from the wilderness of Paran 2
21 land from the wilderness of Zin to Rehob 2
26 in the wilderness of Paran, at Kadesh; 2
14: 2 Or would that we had died in the wilderness! 2
16 therefore he has slain them in the wilderness.' 2
22 my signs which I wrought . . in the wilderness 2
25 out for the wilderness by the way to the Red Sea. 2
29 your dead bodies shall fall in this wilderness; 2
32 your dead bodies shall fall in this wilderness. 2
33 shall be shepherds in the wilderness 40 years 2
33 last of your dead bodies lies in the wilderness. 2
35 in this wilderness they shall come to a full end 2
15:32 people of Israel were in the wilderness 2
16:13 brought us up . . to kill us in the wilderness 2
20: 1 Israel . . came into the wilderness of Zin 2
4 assembly of the LORD into this wilderness 2
21: 5 up out of Egypt to die in the wilderness? 2
11 in the wilderness which is opposite Moab 2
13 Arnon, which is in the wilderness 2
18 from the wilderness they went on to Mat'tanah 2
23 went out against Israel to the wilderness 2
24: 1 Balaam . . set his face toward the wilderness. 2
26:64 numbered . . Israel in the wilderness of Sinai. 2
65 They shall die in the wilderness. 2
27: 3 Our father died in the wilderness; 2
14 rebelled . . in the wilderness of Zin 2
14 Mer'ibah of Kadesh in the wilderness of Zin.) 2
32:13 he made them wander in the wilderness 40 years 2
15 he will again abandon them in the wilderness; 2
33: 6 Etham, which is on the edge of the wilderness 2
8 through the midst of the sea into the wilderness 2
8 went a three days' journey in the wilderness of Etham 2
11 encamped in the wilderness of Sin. 2
12 set out from the wilderness of Sin, and encamped 2
15 encamped in the wilderness of Sinai. 2
16 they set out from the wilderness of Sinai 2
36 set out . . and encamped in the wilderness of Zin 2
34: 3 south side shall be from the wilderness of Zin 2
Deu 1: 1 all Israel beyond the Jordan in the wilderness 2
19 through all that great and terrible wilderness 2
31 wilderness, where you have seen how the LORD 2
40 journey into the wilderness in the direction 2
2: 1 journeyed into the wilderness in the direction 2
7 knows your going through this great wilderness; 2
8 went in the direction of the wilderness of Moab. 2
26 messengers from the wilderness of Ked'emoth 2
4:43 Bezer in the wilderness on the tableland 2
8: 2 God has led you these 40 years in the wilderness 2
15 led you through the great and terrible wilderness 2
16 who fed you in the wilderness with manna 2
9: 7 provoked the LORD . . to wrath in the wilderness; 2
28 brought them out to slay them in the wilderness. 2
11: 5 what he did to you in the wilderness, until 2
24 from the wilderness and Lebanon 2
29: 5 I have led you 40 years in the wilderness; 2
32:10 found him . . in the howling waste of the wilderness; 1
51 Mer'i-bath-ka'desh, in the wilderness of Zin; 2
Jos 1: 4 From the wilderness and this Lebanon as far 2
5: 4 the males . . had died on the way in the wilderness 2
5 people . . born on the way in the wilderness 2
6 Israel walked 40 years in the wilderness 2
8:15 and fled in the direction of the wilderness. 2
20 people that fled to the wilderness turned back 2
24 slaughtering all . . of Ai in the open wilderness 2
12: 8 in the Arabah, in the slopes, in the wilderness 2
14:10 since . . while Israel walked in the wilderness; 2
15: 1 to the boundary of Edom, to the wilderness of Zin 2
61 In the wilderness, Beth-arabah, Middin, Seca'cah 2
16: 1 went from the Jordan . . into the wilderness 2
18:12 and it ends at the wilderness of Beth-a'ven. 2
20: 8 Bezer in the wilderness on the tableland 2
24: 7 and you lived in the wilderness a long time. 2
Jdg 1:16 the city of palms into the wilderness of Judah 2
8: 7 will flail . . with the thorns of the wilderness 2
16 and he took thorns of the wilderness and briers 2
11:16 Israel went through the wilderness to the Red 2
18 they journeyed through the wilderness, and went 2
22 Jabbok and from the wilderness to the Jordan. 2
20:42 turned . . in the direction of the wilderness; 2
45 fled toward the wilderness to the rock of Rimmon; 2
47 fled toward the wilderness to the rock of Rimmon 2
1Sm 4: 8 who smote the Egyptians . . in the wilderness. 2
13:18 border that looks . . toward the wilderness. 2
17:28 left those few sheep in the wilderness? I know 2
23:14 remained in the strongholds in the wilderness 2
14 in the hill country of the Wilderness of Ziph. 2
15 David was in the Wilderness of Ziph at Horesh. 2
24 David and his men were in the wilderness of Ma'on 2
25 to the rock which is in the wilderness of Ma'on. 2
25 pursued after David in the wilderness of Ma'on. 2
24: 1 Behold, David is in the wilderness of En-ge'di. 2
25: 1 David . . went down to the wilderness of Paran. 2
4 David heard in the wilderness 2
14 David sent messengers out of the wilderness 2
21 all that this fellow has in the wilderness 2
26: 2 Saul . . went down to the wilderness of Ziph 2
2 went . . to seek David in the wilderness of Ziph. 2
3 But David remained in the wilderness; 2
3 saw that Saul came after him into the wilderness 2
2Sm 2:24 lies . . on the way to the wilderness of Gibeon. 2
15:23 all the people passed on toward the wilderness. 2
28 See, I will wait at the fords of the wilderness 2
16: 2 the wine for those who faint in the wilderness 2
17:16 Do not lodge . . at the fords of the wilderness 2
29 hungry and weary and thirsty in the wilderness. 2
1Kg 2:34 he was buried in his own house in the wilderness. 2
9:18 Ba'alath and Tamar in the wilderness 2
19: 4 he . . went a day's journey into the wilderness 2
15 return on your way to the wilderness of Damascus; 2
2Kg 3: 8 answered, "By the way of the wilderness of Edom. 2
1Ch 12: 8 to David at the stronghold in the wilderness 2
21:29 which Moses had made in the wilderness 2
2Ch 1: 3 the LORD had made in the wilderness, was there 2
8: 4 He built Tadmor in the wilderness 2
20:16 the valley, east of the wilderness of Jeru'el. 2
20 went out into the wilderness of Teko'a; 2
24 Judah came to the watchtower of the wilderness 2
24: 9 tax . . laid upon Israel in the wilderness. 2
26:10 he built towers in the wilderness 2
Neh 9:19 mercies didst not forsake them in the wilderness; 2
21 40 years . . sustain them in the wilderness 2
Job 1:19 behold, a great wind came across the wilderness 2
24: 5 seeking prey in the wilderness as food 3
Ps 29: 8 The voice of the LORD shakes the wilderness 2
8 LORD shakes the wilderness of Kadesh. 2
55: 7 I would lodge in the wilderness, Selah 2
63: 0 of David, when he was in the Wilderness of Judah. 2
65:12 The pastures of the wilderness drip 2
68: 7 when thou didst march through the wilderness 1
75: 6 not from the wilderness comes lifting up; 2
78:15 He cleft rocks in the wilderness 2
19 Can God spread a table in the wilderness? 2
40 they rebelled against him in the wilderness 2
52 guided them in the wilderness like a flock. 2
95: 8 Mer'ibah, as on the day of Massah in the wilderness 2
102: 6 I am like a vulture of the wilderness, like an owl 2
106:14 they had a wanton craving in the wilderness 2
26 swore . . would make them fall in the wilderness 2
136:16 to him who led his people through the wilderness 2
Sng 3: 6 What is that coming up from the wilderness 2
8: 5 Who is that coming up from the wilderness 2
Isa 21: 1 oracle concerning the wilderness of the sea. 2
27:10 forsaken, like the wilderness; 2
32:15 and the wilderness becomes a fruitful field 2
16 Then justice will dwell in the wilderness 2
35: 1 The wilderness and the dry land shall be glad 2
6 For waters shall break forth in the wilderness 2

40: 3 In the wilderness prepare the way of the LORD 2
41:18 I will make the wilderness a pool of water 2
19 I will put in the wilderness the cedar 2
43:19 I will make a way in the wilderness 2
20 for I give water in the wilderness 2
51: 3 and will make her wilderness like Eden 2
64:10 Thy holy cities have become a wilderness 2
10 Zion has become a wilderness, 2
Jer 2: 2 how you followed me in the wilderness 2
6 who led us in the wilderness, in a land of deserts 2
24 a wild ass used to the wilderness 2
31 Have I been a wilderness to Israel 2
3: 2 awaiting lovers like an Arab in the wilderness. 2
9:10 lamentation for the pastures of the wilderness 2
12 land ruined and laid waste like a wilderness 2
12:10 my pleasant portion a desolate wilderness. 2
17: 6 dwell in the parched places of the wilderness 2
23:10 and the pastures of the wilderness are dried up. 2
31: 2 who survived . . found grace in the wilderness; 2
50:12 last of the nations, a wilderness dry and desert. 2
Lam 4: 3 cruel, like the ostriches in the wilderness. 2
19 they lay in wait for us in the wilderness. 2
5: 9 because of the sword in the wilderness. 2
Ezk 6:14 desolate . . from the wilderness to Riblah. 2
19:13 Now it is transplanted in the wilderness 2
20:10 and brought them into the wilderness. 2
13 Israel rebelled against me in the wilderness; 2
13 in the wilderness, to make a full end of them. 2
15 Moreover I swore to them in the wilderness 2
17 or make a full end of them in the wilderness. 2
18 I said to their children in the wilderness 2
21 spend my anger against them in the wilderness. 2
23 Moreover I swore to them in the wilderness 2
35 bring you into the wilderness of the peoples 2
36 judgment with your fathers in the wilderness 2
23:42 drunkards were brought from the wilderness; 2
29: 5 I will cast you forth into the wilderness 2
34:25 that they may dwell securely in the wilderness 2
Hos 2: 3 and make her like a wilderness 2
14 allure her, and bring her into the wilderness 2
9:10 Like grapes in the wilderness, I found Israel. 2
13: 5 It was I who knew you in the wilderness 2
15 the LORD, shall come, rising from the wilderness; 2
Jol 1:19 devoured the pastures of the wilderness 2
20 has devoured the pastures of the wilderness. 2
2: 3 but after them a desolate wilderness 2
22 for the pastures of the wilderness are green; 2
3:19 and Edom a desolate wilderness, 2
Ams 2:10 and led you 40 years in the wilderness 2
5:25 and offerings the 40 years in the wilderness 2
Mat 3: 1 Baptist, preaching in the wilderness of Judea 5
3 voice of one crying in the wilderness: Prepare 5
4: 1 led up by the Spirit into the wilderness 5
11: 7 What did you go out into the wilderness to behold? 5
24:26 So, if they say to you, 'Lo, he is in the wilderness,' 5
Mrk 1: 3 the voice of one crying in the wilderness 5
4 John the baptizer appeared in the wilderness 5
12 immediately drove him out into the wilderness. 5
13 he was in the wilderness 40 days, tempted by Satan 5
Lke 1:80 he was in the wilderness 5
3: 2 John the son of Zechari'ah in the wilderness; 5
4 The voice of one crying in the wilderness 5
4: 2 for 40 days in the wilderness *
5:16 he withdrew to the wilderness and prayed. 5
7:24 What did you go out into the wilderness to behold? 5
15: 4 does not leave the 99 in the wilderness 5
Joh 1:23 I am the voice of one crying in the wilderness 5
3:14 as Moses lifted up the serpent in the wilderness 5
6:31 Our fathers ate the manna in the wilderness 5
49 Your fathers ate the manna in the wilderness 5
11:54 from there to the country near the wilderness 5
Act 7:30 an angel appeared to him in the wilderness 5
36 and in the wilderness for 40 years. 5
38 he who was in the congregation in the wilderness 5
42 40 years in the wilderness, O house of Israel? 5
44 the tent of witness in the wilderness 5
13:18 he bore with them in the wilderness. 5
21:38 led . . out into the wilderness? 5
1Co 10: 5 for they were overthrown in the wilderness. 5
2Co 11:26 danger in the city, danger in the wilderness 4
Heb 3: 8 on the day of testing in the wilderness 5
17 who sinned, whose bodies fell in the wilderness 5
Rev 12: 6 and the woman fled into the wilderness 5
14 might fly from the serpent into the wilderness 5
17: 3 And he carried me away . . into a wilderness 5
2Es 1:17 When you were . . thirsty in the wilderness 6
18 led us into this wilderness to kill us? 6
18 better . . than to die in this wilderness.' 6
22 When you were in the wilderness 6
9:29 to our fathers in the wilderness 6
29 the untrodden and unfruitful wilderness; 6
Jdt 5:14 and drove out all the people of the wilderness. 5
Wis 11: 2 They journeyed through an uninhabited wilderness 5
17:17 a workman who toiled in the wilderness 4
Sir 8:16 do not cross the wilderness with him 5
13:19 Wild asses in the wilderness 5
43:21 burns up the wilderness 5
45:18 envied him in the wilderness 5
1Mc 2:29 many . . went down to the wilderness to dwell there 5
31 had gone down to the hiding places in the wilderness. 5
3:45 Jerusalem was uninhabited like a wilderness; 5
5:24 went three days' journey into the wilderness. 5
28 Judas . . turned back by the wilderness road to Bozrah 5
9:33 they fled into the wilderness of Tekoa 5
62 withdrew to Bethbasi in the wilderness 5
13:21 to come to them by way of the wilderness 5
2Mc 5:27 Judas . . got away to the wilderness 5

wilderness *See also* creature.

wildly *See* beat.

wile 1. נֵכֶל 2. *ἔνεδρον* 3. *μεθοδεία*

Num25:18 for they have harassed you with their wiles 1
Eph 4:14 by their craftiness in deceitful wiles. 3
6:11 able to stand against the wiles of the devil. 3
Sir 11:29 many are the wiles of the crafty. 2

wilful 1. *αὐθάδης* 2. *προαλής*

2Pe 2:10 Bold and wilful, they are not afraid to revile 1
Sir 30: 8 a son unrestrained turns out to be wilful. 2

wilfully 1. *ἑκουσίως*

2Mc 14: 3 had wilfully defiled himself 1

will 1. אבה 2. חפץ 3. חֵפֶץ 4. חָפֵץ 5. נֶפֶשׁ 6. רָצוֹן 7. צבא (A) 8. רְעוּ (A) 9. *ἄκων* 10. *βουλεύω* 11. *βουλή* 12. *βούλημα* 13. *βούλομαι* 14. *ἐθέλω* 15. *ἑκών* 16. *εὔχομαι* 17. *θέλημα* 18. *θέλησις* 19. *θέλω* 20. *ὁρμή* 21. volo 22. voluntas

1Sm 2:25 for it was the will of the LORD to slay them. 2
31: 4 But his armor-bearer would not; for he feared 1
2Sm 3:37 it had not been the king's will to slay Abner *
12:17 to raise him . . but he would not, nor did he eat food 1
1Kg 13:33 any who would, he consecrated to be priests 4
1Ch 10: 4 armor-bearer would not; for he feared greatly. 1
11:18 But David would not drink of it; 1
13: 2 good to you, and if it is the will of the LORD our God *
Ezr 7:18 you may do, according to the will of your God. 8
10:11 make confession to the LORD . . and do his will; 6
Neh 9:24 that they might do with them as they would. 6
Ps 27:12 Give me not up to the will of my adversaries; 5
40: 8 I delight to do thy will, O my God; 6
41: 2 dost not give him up to the will of his enemies. 5
Prv 31:13 She . . works with willing hands. 3
Isa 30:15 trust shall be your strength." And you would not, 1
Dan 5:19 whom he would he slew, and . . kept alive; 7
19 he slew, and whom he would he kept alive; 7
19 whom he would he raised up, and . . put down. 7
19 he raised up, and whom he would he put down. 7
Mat 6:10 Thy will be done, On earth as it is in heaven. 17
7:21 who does the will of my Father who is in heaven. 17
8: 2 saying, "Lord, if you will, you can make me clean. 19
3 saying, "I will; be clean. 19
10:29 fall to the ground without your Father's will. *
12:50 For whoever does the will of my Father in heaven 17
18:14 it is not the will of my Father who is in heaven 17
21:31 Which of the two did the will of his father? 17
23:37 and you would not! 14
26:39 nevertheless, not as I will, but as thou wilt. 19
39 nevertheless, not as I will, but as thou wilt. *
42 thy will be done. 17
Mrk 1:40 If you will, you can make me clean. 19
41 I will; be clean. 19
3:35 Whoever does the will of God is my brother 17
14: 7 whenever you will, you can do good to them; 19
36 yet not what I will, but what thou wilt. 19
36 yet not what I will, but what thou wilt. *
Lke 4: 6 I give it to whom I will. 19
5:12 Lord, if you will, you can make me clean. 19
13 I will; be clean. 19
12:47 did not make ready or act according to his will 17
47 did not make ready or act according to his will 17
22:42 nevertheless not my will, but thine, be done. 17
23:25 Jesus he delivered up to their will. 17
Joh 1:13 born, not of blood nor of the will of the flesh 17
13 born, not of blood . . nor of the will of man 17
3: 8 The wind blows where it wills 19
4:34 My food is to do the will of him who sent me 17
5:21 so also the Son gives life to whom he will. 19
30 because I seek not my own will 17
30 but the will of him who sent me. 17
6:38 not . . own will, but the will of him who sent me; 17
38 not . . own will, but the will of him who sent me; 17
39 this is the will of him who sent me 17
40 this is the will of my Father 17
7:17 if any man's will is to do his will 19
8:44 your will is to do your father's desires 19
9:31 if any one is a worshiper of God and does his will 17
15: 7 ask whatever you will, and it shall be done for you. 19
18:39 will you have me release for you the King 13
21:18 you girded yourself and walked where you would; 14
22 If it is my will that he remain until I come 19
23 If it is my will that he remain until I come 19
Act 13:22 a man after my heart, who will do all my will.' 17
18:21 I will return to you if God wills 19
21:14 The will of the Lord be done. 17
22:14 God of our fathers appointed you to know his will 17
26:29 Paul said, "Whether short or long, I would to God 16
Rom 1:10 by God's will I may now at last succeed in coming 17
2:18 know his will and approve what is excellent 17
7:18 I can will what is right, but I cannot do it. 19
8:20 not of its own will but by the will of him 15
20 by the will of him who subjected it in hope; *
27 the Spirit intercedes . . according to the will of God. *
9:16 So it depends not upon man's will or exertion 19
18 So then he has mercy upon whomever he wills 19
18 and he hardens the heart of whomever he wills. 19
19 For who can resist his will? 12
12: 2 that you may prove what is the will of God 17
15:32 that by God's will I may come to you with joy 17
1Co 4:19 I will come to you soon, if the Lord wills 19
9:17 For if I do this of my own will, I have a reward 15
17 if not of my own will 9
12:11 to each one individually as he wills. 13
Gal 5:17 to prevent you from doing what you would. 14
Eph 1: 1 Paul, an apostle of Christ Jesus by the will of God 17
5 according to the purpose of his will. 17
9 has made known . . the mystery of his will 17
11 according to the counsel of his will 17
5:17 but understand what the will of the Lord is. 17
6: 6 doing the will of God from the heart 17
Col 1: 1 by the will of God, and Timothy our brother 17
9 you may be filled with the knowledge of his will 17
4:12 fully assured in all the will of God. 17
1Th 4: 3 For this is the will of God, your sanctification 17
5:18 for this is the will of God in Christ Jesus 17
1Ti 5:14 I would have younger widows marry, bear children 13
2Ti 1: 1 Paul, an apostle of Christ Jesus by the will of God 17
2:26 after being captured by him to do his will. 17
Heb 2: 4 distributed according to his own will. 18
10: 7 I said, 'Lo, I have come to do thy will, O God,' 17
9 he added, "Lo, I have come to do thy will. 17
10 by that will we have been sanctified through 17
36 you may do the will of God 17
13:21 you may do his will 17
Jas 3: 4 wherever the will of the pilot directs. 20
4:15 If the Lord wills, we shall live 19
2Jn 1:12 I would rather not use paper and ink 13
1Es 7:15 had changed the will of the king of the Assyrians 11
8:16 perform it in accordance with the will of your God; 17
9: 9 do his will 17
2Es 3: 8 every nation walked after its own will 22
6:52 thou hast kept them to be eaten by whom thou wilt 21
52 by whom thou wilt, and when thou wilt. 21
8: 5 not of your own will did you come into the world ‡
29 it not be thy will to destroy those 21
Tob 4:19 according to his will he humbles whomever he wishes 13
12:18 by the will of our God 19
Jdt 9: 6 the things thou didst will 10
AEs 13: 9 if it is thy will to save Israel. 14
Wis 9:13 who can discern what the Lord wills? 19
11:25 if thou hadst not willed it 19
2Mc 1: 3 to do his will with a strong heart 17
12:16 They took the city by the will of God 19
3Mc 2:26 many of his friends . . followed his will. 19

will (2) 1. *διαθήκη*

Heb 9:16 For where a will is involved 1
17 a will takes effect only at death 1

against the will 1. *ἄκων* 2. nolo

2Es 8: 5 and against your will you depart 2
4Mc 11:12 that you grant us against your will 1

free will 1. *αὐθαίρετος* 2. *ἑκούσιος*

2Co 8: 3 beyond their means, of their own free will 1
Phm 1:14 not . . by compulsion but of your own free will. 2

good will 1. *εὐγνωμοσύνη* 2. *εὐδοκία* 3. *εὐμένεια* 4. *εὐμενής* 5. *εὔνοια* 6. *προθυμία* 7. *φιλανθρωπία*

2Co 8:19 for the glory of the Lord and to show our good will. 6
Eph 6: 7 rendering service with a good will 5
Php 1:15 but others from good will. 2
AEs 13: 3 is distinguished for his unchanging good will 5
16: 6 the sincere good will of their sovereigns. 1
11 the good will that we have for every nation 7
Sir 0: 2 urged . . to read with good will and attention, 5
1Mc 11:33 because of the good will they show toward us. 5
2Mc 6:29 who . . had acted toward him with good will 3
9:21 I remember . . your esteem and good will 5
26 to maintain your present good will, each of you 5
11:19 will maintain your good will toward the government 5
12:30 the Jews . . bore witness to the good will 5
13:26 Lysias . . gained their good will 4
14:26 Alcimus noticed their good will for one another 5
37 for his good will was called father of the Jews. 5
15:30 his youthful good will toward his countrymen 5
3Mc 3: 3 to maintain good will and unswerving loyalty 5

gracious will 1. *εὐδοκία*

Mat 11:26 yea, Father, for such was thy gracious will. 1
Lke 10:21 yea, Father, for such was thy gracious will. 1

willfully 1. *αὐθαίρετος*

3Mc 7:10 who had willfully transgressed against the holy God 1

willfully *See also* attack.

willing 1. אבה 2. חפץ 3. חָפֵץ 4. יֵשׁ אֶת נַפְשְׁ 5. נָדִיב 6. βούλομαι 7. ἐθέλω 8. εὐδοκέω 9. θέλω 10. πρόθυμος

Gen 23: 8 If you are willing that I should bury my dead 4
24: 5 Perhaps the woman may not be willing to follow me 1
8 if the woman is not willing to follow you 1
Exd 35:22 all who were of a willing heart brought brooches 5
Rut 3:13 he is not willing to do the part of the next of kin 2
2Sm 6:10 David was not willing to take the ark of the LORD 1
1Kg 22:49 but Jehosh'aphat was not willing. 1
1Ch 19:19 Syrians were not willing to help the Ammonites 1
28: 9 serve him with . . and with a willing mind; 3
2Ch 29:31 of a willing heart brought burnt offerings. 5
Job 39: 9 Is the wild ox willing to serve you? 1
Ps 51:12 uphold me with a willing spirit. 5
Isa 1:19 If you are willing and obedient, you shall eat 1
Ezk 3: 7 for they are not willing to listen to me; 1
Mat 11:14 if you are willing to accept it, he is Eli'jah 9
26:41 the spirit indeed is willing 10
Mrk 14:38 the spirit indeed is willing 10
Lke 22:42 if thou art willing, remove this cup from me; 6
Joh 5:35 you were willing to rejoice for a while 9
Act 26: 5 if they are willing to testify 9
1Th 3: 1 we were willing to be left behind at Athens alone 8
AEs 13:13 willing to kiss the soles of his feet 8
Sir 6:32 If you are willing, my son, you will be taught 7
39: 6 If the great Lord is willing 9
2Mc 1: 3 a strong heart and a willing spirit. 6
3Mc 3:28 Any one willing to give information 6
4Mc 5: 3 If any were not willing to eat defiling food 7
9:27 they inquired if he were willing to eat 6
11:13 whether he was willing to eat and be released 6

willing *See also* gift, make.

willing man 1. נָדִיב

1Ch 28:21 with you in all the work will be every willing man 1

willingly 1. לְנָדְבָה 2. מִלֵּב 3. ἑκουσίως 4. ἐκ ψυχῆς 5. προθύμως 6. voluntas

Jdg 8:25 And they answered, "We will willingly give them. †
2Ch 35: 8 princes contributed willingly to the people 1
Lam 3:33 he does not willingly afflict or grieve . . men. 2
1Pe 5: 2 Tend . . not by constraint but willingly 3
2Es 8:28 those who have willingly acknowledged 6
1Mc 8:27 the Romans shall willingly act as their allies 4
2Mc 6:28 die a good death willingly and nobly 5
4Mc 5:23 we endure any suffering willingly; 3

willingly *See also* accept, give, offer, vow.

willow 1. עֲרָבָה 2. צַפְצָפָה

Lev 23:40 take . . trees, and willows of the brook 1
Job 40:22 the willows of the brook surround him. 1
Ps 137: 2 On the willows there we hung up our lyres 1
Isa 15: 7 they carry away over the Brook of the Willows. 1
44: 4 like grass . . like willows by flowing streams. 1
Ezk 17: 5 He set it like a willow twig 2

wily 1. נצר 2. פתל

Job 5:13 the schemes of the wily are brought to a quick end. 2
Prv 7:10 dressed as a harlot, wily of heart. 1

win 1. בקע 2. ירש 3. נשא לִפְנֵי 4. נתן 5. עשה 6. קנה 7. ἀπολαμβάνω 8. ἐκτελέω 9. εὑρίσκω 10. κερδαίνω 11. νικάω 12. περιποιέω 13. ποιέω

2Sm 8:13 And David won a name for himself. 5
23:18 and slew them, and won a name beside the three. •
22 These things did Benai'ah . . and won a name beside •
1Ch 11:20 slew them, and won a name beside the three. •
24 won a name beside the three mighty men. •
26:27 From spoil won in battles they dedicated gifts •
2Ch 32: 1 thinking to win them for himself. 1
Est 2: 9 And the maiden pleased him and won his favor; 3
Ps 44: 3 for not by their own sword did they win the land 2
78:54 the mountain which his right hand had won. 6
Prv 13:15 Good sense wins favor 4
Ecc 10:12 The words of a wise man's mouth win him favor •
Rom 15:18 to win obedience from the Gentiles •
1Co 9:19 a slave to all, that I might win the more. 10
20 To the Jews I became as a Jew, in order to win Jews 10
20 that I might win those under the law. 10
21 that I might win those outside the law. 10
22 that I might win the weak 10
1Pe 3: 1 so that some . . may be won without a word 10
2Jn 1: 8 that you may not lose . . but may win a full reward 7
1Mc 6:44 to win for himself an everlasting name. 12
11:24 he went to the king . . And he won his favor. 9
14:35 glory which he had resolved to win for his nation 13
2Mc 15: 9 reminding them . . of the struggles they had won 8
3Mc 1: 4 two minas of gold if they won the battle. 11

win a victory 1. εὐημερέω

2Mc 12:11 Judas and his men won the victory 1

win honor 1. δοξάζομαι

1Mc 3:14 and win honor in the kingdom 1

win over 1. πείθω

2Mc 4:45 to win over the king. 1

win over by pleading 1. διαιτέω

Jdt 8:16 nor like a human being, to be won over by pleading. 1

win strength 1. δυναμόω

Heb 11:34 won strength out of weakness 1

win victory 1. νικάω

1Es 4: 5 if they win the victory 1

wind 1. רוּחַ 2. רוּחַ (A) 3. ἄνεμος 4. πνεῦμα 5. πνέω 6. πνοή 7. flatus 8. spiritus 9. ventus

Gen 8: 1 God made a wind blow over the earth, and the waters 1
Exd 10:13 the LORD brought an east wind upon the land 1
13 and when it was morning the east wind had brought 1
19 the LORD turned a very strong west wind 1
14:21 the sea back by a strong east wind all night 1
15:10 Thou didst blow with thy wind, the sea covered 1
Num 11:31 there went forth a wind from the LORD 1
2Sm 22:11 he was seen upon the wings of the wind. 1
1Kg 18:45 the heavens grew black with clouds and wind 1
19:11 a great and strong wind rent the mountains 1
11 but the LORD was not in the wind; 1
11 and after the wind an earthquake 1
2Kg 3:17 You shall not see wind or rain, but that stream-bed 1
Job 1:19 behold, a great wind came across the wilderness 1
6:26 when the speech of a despairing man is wind? 1
8: 2 and the words of your mouth be a great wind? 1
15:30 his blossom will be swept away by the wind. 1
21:18 That they are like straw before the wind 1
26:13 By his wind the heavens were made fair; 1
28:25 When he gave to the wind its weight 1
30:15 my honor is pursued as by the wind 1
22 Thou liftest me up on the wind, 1
37:21 skies, when the wind has passed and cleared them. 1
Ps 1: 4 but are like chaff which the wind drives away. 1
11: 6 scorching wind shall be the portion of their 1
18:10 he came swiftly upon the wings of the wind. 1
42 I beat them fine as dust before the wind; 1
35: 5 Let them be like chaff before the wind 1
48: 7 By the east wind thou didst shatter the ships 1
55: 8 a shelter from the raging wind and tempest. 1
78:39 but flesh, a wind that passes and comes not again. 1
83:13 like whirling dust, like chaff before the wind. 1
103:16 for the wind passes over it, and it is gone 1
104: 3 who ridest on the wings of the wind 1
4 who makest the winds thy messengers 1
107:25 For he commanded, and raised the stormy wind 1
135: 7 brings forth the wind from his storehouses. 1
147:18 he makes his wind blow, and the waters flow. 1
148: 8 stormy wind fulfilling his command! 1
Prv 11:29 He who troubles his household will inherit wind 1
25:14 Like clouds and wind without rain is a man 1
23 The north wind brings forth rain; 1
27:16 to restrain her is to restrain the wind 1
30: 4 Who has gathered the wind in his fists? 1
Ecc 1: 6 The wind blows to the south, and goes round •
6 round and round goes the wind, and on its circuits 1
6 and on its circuits the wind returns. 1
14 behold, all is vanity and a striving after wind. 1
17 this also is but a striving after wind. 1
2:11 all was vanity and a striving after wind 1
17 for all is vanity and a striving after wind. 1
26 This also is vanity and a striving after wind. 1
4: 4 This also is vanity and a striving after wind. 1
6 two hands full of toil and a striving after wind. 1
16 this also is vanity and a striving after wind. 1
5:16 and what gain has he that he toiled for the wind 1
6: 9 this also is vanity and a striving after wind. 1
11: 4 He who observes the wind will not sow; 1
Isa 7: 2 as the trees of the forest shake before the wind. 1
11:15 hand over the River with his scorching wind 1
17:13 like chaff on the mountains before the wind 1
26:18 we writhed, we have as it were brought forth wind. 1
32: 2 Each will be like a hiding place from the wind 1
41:16 winnow them and the wind shall carry them away 1
29 their molten images are empty wind. 1
57:13 idols deliver you! The wind will carry them off 1
59:19 stream, which the wind of the LORD drives. 1
64: 6 and our iniquities, like the wind, take us away. 1
Jer 2:24 a wild ass . . in her heat sniffing the wind! 1
4:11 A hot wind from the bare heights in the desert 1
12 a wind too full for this comes for me. 1
5:13 The prophets will become wind; 1
10:13 he brings forth the wind from his storehouses. 1
13:24 I will scatter you like chaff driven by the wind 1
18:17 Like the east wind I will scatter them 1
22:22 The wind shall shepherd all your shepherds 1
49:32 I will scatter to every wind those who cut 1
36 I will bring upon Elam the four winds 1
36 and I will scatter them to all those winds 1
51:16 he brings forth the wind from his storehouses. 1
Ezk 1: 4 behold, a stormy wind came out of the north 1
5: 2 and a third part you shall scatter to the wind 1
10 you who survive I will scatter to all the winds. 1
12 and a third part I will scatter to all the winds 1
12:14 toward every wind all who are round about him 1
13:11 hailstones will fall, and a stormy wind break out; 1
13 I will make a stormy wind break out in my wrath; 1
17:10 utterly wither when the east wind strikes it 1
21 the survivors shall be scattered to every wind; 1
19:12 cast down to the ground; the east wind dried it up; 1
27:26 wind has wrecked you in the heart of the seas. 1
37: 9 Come from the four winds, O breath 1
Dan 2:35 wind carried them away, so that not a trace of them 2
7: 2 four winds of heaven were stirring up the great 2
8: 8 four . . horns toward the four winds of heaven. 1
11: 4 divided toward the four winds of heaven 1
Hos 4:19 A wind has wrapped them in its wings 1
8: 7 For they sow the wind 1
12: 1 E'phraim herds the wind, and pursues the east wind 1
13:15 the east wind, the wind of the LORD, shall come 1
Ams 4:13 he who forms the mountains, and creates the wind 1
Jon 1: 4 the LORD hurled a great wind upon the sea 1
4: 8 the sun rose, God appointed a sultry east wind 1
Mic 2:11 If a man should go about and utter wind and lies 1
Hab 1:11 they sweep by like the wind and go on, guilty men 1
Zec 2: 6 I have spread you abroad as the four winds 1
5: 9 women coming forward! The wind was in their wings; 1
6: 5 These are going forth to the four winds of heaven 1
Mat 7:25 rain fell, and the floods came, and the winds blew 3
27 rain fell, and the floods came, and the winds blew 3
8:26 Then he rose and rebuked the winds and the sea 3
27 that even winds and sea obey him? 3
11: 7 A reed shaken by the wind? 3
14:24 for the wind was against them. 3
30 when he saw the wind, he was afraid 3
32 when they got into the boat, the wind ceased. 3
24:31 they will gather his elect from the four winds 3
Mrk 4:37 a great storm of wind arose 3
39 he awoke and rebuked the wind, and said to the sea 3
39 said to the sea, "Peace! Be still!" And the wind ceased 3
41 Who then is this, that even wind and sea obey him? 3
6:48 the wind was against them 3
51 got into the boat with them and the wind ceased. 3
13:27 gather his elect from the four winds 3
Lke 7:24 A reed shaken by the wind? 3
8:23 a storm of wind came down on the lake 3
24 awoke and rebuked the wind and the raging waves 3
25 he commands even wind and water, and they obey 3
Joh 3: 8 The wind blows where it wills 4
6:18 The sea rose because a strong wind was blowing. 3
Act 2: 2 a sound . . like the rush of a mighty wind 6
27: 4 because the winds were against us. 3
7 and as the wind did not allow us to go on 3
14 soon a tempestuous wind, called the northeaster 3
15 the ship was caught and could not face the wind 3
40 then hoisting the foresail to the wind 5
Eph 4:14 carried about with every wind of doctrine 3
Heb 1: 7 Of the angels he says, "Who makes his angels winds 4
Jas 3: 4 though they . . are driven by strong winds 3
Jde 1:12 waterless clouds, carried along by the winds; 3
Rev 7: 1 angels . . holding back the four winds 3
1 that no wind might blow on earth or sea 3
2Es 1:33 I will drive you out as the wind drives straw; 9
3:19 of fire and earthquake and wind and ice 8
4: 5 or measure for me a measure of wind 9
9 asked you only about fire and wind and the day 9
5:37 bring forth for me the winds shut up in them 7
6: 1 and before the assembled winds blew 9
7:40 or cloud or thunder or lightning or wind or water 9
8:22 they are changed to wind and fire ‡
11: 2 and all the winds of heaven blew upon him 9
13: 2 behold, a wind arose from the sea 9
3 this wind made something like the figure of a man ‡
5 gathered together from the four winds of heaven 9
27 as for your seeing wind and fire and a storm 8
15:39 the winds from the east shall prevail 9
39 by the east wind shall be driven violently 9
Wis 4: 4 they will be shaken by the wind 3
4 by the violence of the winds 3
5:14 like chaff carried by the wind 3
14 it is dispersed like smoke before the wind 3
23 a mighty wind will rise against them 4
13: 2 either fire or wind or swift air 4
17:18 Whether there came a whistling wind 4
Sir 5: 9 Do not winnow with every wind 3
22:18 a high place will not stand firm against the wind; 3
34: 2 catches at a shadow and pursues the wind 3
39:28 winds that have been created for vengeance 4
43:20 The cold north wind blows 3
LJr 1:61 the wind likewise blows in every land. 4
Aza 1:27 like a moist whistling wind 4
43 Bless the Lord, all winds 4
Bel 1:36 with the rushing sound of the wind itself. 4
3Mc 2:22 as a reed is shaken by the wind 3
4Mc 15:32 the flood of your emotions and the violent winds 3

wind *See also* driven.

east wind 1. קָדִים

Gen 41: 6 seven ears, thin and blighted by the east wind. 1
23 ears, withered . . and blighted by the east wind 1
27 blighted by the east wind are also seven years 1
Job 15: 2 fill himself with the east wind? 1

27:21 The east wind lifts him up and he is gone; 1
38:24 where the east wind is scattered upon the earth? 1
Ps 78:26 He caused the east wind to blow in the heavens 1
Isa 27: 8 with his fierce blast in the day of the east wind. 1
Hos 12: 1 and pursues the east wind all day long; 1
13:15 the east wind, the wind of the LORD, shall come 1

hot wind 1. καύσωνος
Sir 34:16 a shelter from the hot wind 1

north wind 1. צָפוֹן
Sng 4:16 Awake, O north wind, and come, O south wind! 1

scattering wind 1. זרה
Job 37: 9 cold from the scattering winds. 1

scorching wind 1. שָׁרָב
Isa 49:10 neither scorching wind nor sun shall smite them 1

south wind 1. דָּרוֹם 2. תֵּימָן 3. νότος
Job 37:17 when the earth is still because of the south wind? 1
Ps 78:26 by his power he led out the south wind; 2
Sng 4:16 Awake, O north wind, and come, O south wind! 2
Lke 12:55 when you see the south wind blowing, you say 3
Act 27:13 when the south wind blew gently 3
28:13 after one day a south wind sprang up 3
Sir 43:16 at his will the south wind blows. 3

windfall 1. εὕρεμα
Sir 20: 9 a windfall may result in a loss. 1
29: 4 Many persons regard a loan as a windfall 1
6 will regard that as a windfall 1

window 1. אֲרֻבָּה 2. חַלּוֹן 3. מֶחֱזָה 4. כַּוָּה (A) 5. θυρίς 6. χώρα
Gen 7:11 and the windows of the heavens were opened. 1
8: 2 and the windows of the heavens were closed 1
6 Noah opened the window of the ark 2
26: 8 looked out of a window and saw Isaac 2
Jos 2:15 she let them down by a rope through the window 2
18 you shall bind this scarlet cord in the window 2
21 and she bound the scarlet cord in the window. 2
Jdg 5:28 Out of the window she peered, the mother of Sis'era 2
1Sm 19:12 So Michal let David down through the window; 2
2Sm 6:16 Michal . . looked out of the window, and saw 2
1Kg 6: 4 he made for the house windows with recessed 2
7: 4 and window opposite window in three tiers. 3
4 and window opposite window in three tiers. 3
5 All the doorways and windows had square frames 6
5 and window was opposite window in three tiers. 3
5 and window was opposite window in three tiers. 3
2Kg 7: 2 If the LORD . . should make windows in heaven 1
19 If the LORD . . should make windows in heaven 1
9:30 adorned her head, and looked out of the window. 2
32 he lifted up his face to the window, and said 2
13:17 said, "Open the window eastward": and he opened it. 2
1Ch 15:29 Michal . . looked out of the window 2
Prv 7: 6 For at the window of my house I have looked out 2
Ecc 12: 3 those that look through the windows are dimmed 1
Sng 2: 9 there he stands . . gazing in at the windows 2
Isa 24:18 For the windows of heaven are opened 1
60: 8 like a cloud, and like doves to their windows? 1
Jer 9:21 For death has come up into our windows 2
22:14 and cuts out windows for it, paneling it with cedar 2
Ezk 40:16 the gateway had windows round about 2
16 the vestibule had windows round about inside 2
22 its windows, its vestibule, and its palm trees 2
25 there were windows round about in it 2
25 in its vestibule, like the windows of the others; 2
29 there were windows round about in it 2
33 there were windows round about in it 2
36 as the others; and it had windows round about; 2
41:16 and round about all three had windows 2
16 round about, from the floor up to the windows 2
16 (now the windows were covered) 2
26 there were recessed windows and palm trees 2
Dan 6:10 house where he had windows in his upper chamber 4
Hos 13: 3 they shall be . . like smoke from a window. 1
Jol 2: 9 they enter through the windows like a thief. 2
Zep 2:14 the owl shall hoot in the window 2
Mal 3:10 if I will not open the windows of heaven for you 1
Act 20: 9 Eu'tychus was sitting in the window 5
2Co 11:33 let down in a basket through a window in the wall 5
Tob 3:11 she prayed by her window and said 5
Sir 14:23 He who peers through her windows 5
2Mc 3:19 while others peered out of the windows. 5

window *See also* frame.

windy 1. רוּחַ
Job 15: 2 Should a wise man answer with windy knowledge 1
16: 3 Shall windy words have an end? 1

wine 1. חֹמֶץ 2. חֶמֶר 3. יַיִן 4. סֹבֶא 5. עָסִיס 6. תִּירוֹשׁ 7. חֲמַר (A) 8. οἶνος 9. vinum
Gen 9:21 he drank of the wine, and became drunk 3
24 When Noah awoke from his wine 3
14:18 king of Salem brought out bread and wine; 3
19:32 Come, let us make our father drink wine 3
33 they made their father drink wine that night; 3
34 father; let us make him drink wine tonight also; 3
35 they made their father drink wine that night 3
27:25 and he brought him wine, and he drank. 3
28 of the earth, and plenty of grain and wine. 6
37 and with grain and wine I have sustained him. 6
49:11 he washes his garments in wine 3
12 his eyes shall be red with wine 3
Exd 29:40 a fourth of a hin of wine for a libation. 3
Lev 10: 9 Drink no wine nor strong drink, you nor your sons 3
23:13 the drink offering with it shall be of wine 3
Num 6: 3 separate himself from wine and strong drink; 3
3 he shall drink no vinegar made from wine 3
20 after that the Nazirite may drink wine. 3
15: 5 wine for the drink offering, a fourth of a hin 3
7 drink . . you shall offer a third of a hin of wine 3
10 offer for the drink offering half a hin of wine 3
18:12 All the best of the oil, and all the best of the wine 6
28:14 offerings shall be half a hin of wine for a bull 3
Deu 7:13 also bless . . grain and your wine and your oil 6
11:14 gather in your grain and your wine and your oil. 6
12:17 not eat . . the tithe of your grain or of your wine 6
14:23 you shall eat the tithe of your grain, of your wine 6
26 whatever you desire . . wine or strong drink 3
18: 4 first fruits of . . your wine and of your oil 6
28:39 but you shall neither drink of the wine nor 3
51 who also shall not leave you grain, wine, or oil 6
29: 6 have not drunk wine or strong drink; 3
32:14 of the blood of the grape you drank wine. 2
33 their wine is the poison of serpents 3
38 who . . drank the wine of their drink offering? 3
33:28 Israel dwelt . . in a land of grain and wine; 6
Jdg 9:13 Shall I leave my wine which cheers gods and men 6
13: 4 beware, and drink no wine or strong drink, and eat 3
7 drink no wine or strong drink, and eat nothing 3
14 neither let her drink wine or strong drink 3
19:19 with bread and wine for me and your maidservant 3
Rut 2:14 eat some bread, and dip your morsel in the wine. 1
1Sm 1:14 How long will you . . Put away your wine from you. 3
15 I have drunk neither wine nor strong drink 3
24 a . . bull, an ephah of flour, and a skin of wine; 3
10: 3 and another carrying a skin of wine. 3
16:20 Jesse took an ass . . and a skin of wine and a kid 3
25:18 and took 200 loaves, and two skins of wine 3
37 in the morning, when the wine had gone out of Nabal 3
2Sm 13:28 Mark when Amnon's heart is merry with wine 3
16: 1 100 of summer fruits, and a skin of wine. 3
2 and the wine for those who faint . . to drink. 3
2Kg 18:32 a land like your own land, a land of grain and wine 6
1Ch 9:29 over the fine flour, the wine, the oil, the incense 3
12:40 and wine and oil, oxen and sheep 3
27:27 produce of the vineyards for the wine cellars 3
2Ch 2:10 20,000 cors of barley, 20,000 baths of wine 3
15 Now therefore the wheat and barley, oil and wine 3
11:11 and put . . in them, stores of food, oil, and wine. 3
31: 5 gave in abundance the first fruits of grain, wine 6
32:28 storehouses also for the yield of grain, wine 6
Ezr 6: 9 wheat, salt, wine, or oil, as the priests at Jerusalem 7
7:22 up to . . 100 baths of wine 7
Neh 2: 1 when wine was before him, I took up the wine 3
1 I took up the wine and gave it to the king. 3
5:11 Return . . 100th of money, grain, wine, and oil 6
15 took from them food and wine 3
18 every ten days skins of wine in abundance; 3
10:37 bring . . fruit of every tree, the wine and the oil 6
39 bring the contribution of grain, wine, and oil 6
13: 5 previously put the . . tithes of grain, wine, and oil 6
12 Judah brought the tithe of the grain, wine, and oil 6
15 also wine, grapes, figs, and all kinds of burdens 3
Est 1: 7 and the royal wine was lavished 3
10 when the heart of the king was merry with wine 3
5: 6 And as they were drinking wine, the king said 3
7: 2 And on the second day, as they were drinking wine 3
8 to the place where they were drinking wine 3
Job 1:13 daughters were eating and drinking wine 3
18 Your . . daughters were eating and drinking wine 3
32:19 Behold, my heart is like wine that has no vent; 3
Ps 4: 7 than they have when their grain and wine abound. 6
60: 3 thou hast given us wine to drink that made us reel. 3
75: 8 there is a cup, with foaming wine, well mixed; 3
78:65 like a strong man shouting because of wine. 3
104:15 wine to gladden the heart of man 3
Prv 3:10 your vats will be bursting with wine. 6
4:17 drink the wine of violence. 3
9: 2 slaughtered her beasts, she has mixed her wine 3
5 eat of my bread and drink of the wine I have mixed. 3
20: 1 Wine is a mocker, strong drink a brawler; 3
21:17 he who loves wine and oil will not be rich. 3
23:30 Those who tarry long over wine 3
31 Do not look at wine when it is red 3
31: 4 not for kings to drink wine, or for rulers 3
6 Give . . wine to those in bitter distress; 3
Ecc 2: 3 I searched . . how to cheer my body with wine 3
9: 7 Go, eat . . and drink your wine with a merry heart; 3
10:19 Bread is . . for laughter, and wine gladdens life 3
Sng 1: 2 For your love is better than wine 3
4 we will extol your love more than wine; 3
4:10 how much better is your love than wine 3
5: 1 I drink my wine with my milk. 3
7: 9 and your kisses like the best wine that goes down 3
8: 2 I would give you spiced wine to drink 3
Isa 1:22 Your silver . . dross, your wine mixed with water. 4
5:11 who tarry late . . till wine inflames them! 3
12 harp, timbrel and flute and wine at their feasts; 3
22 Woe to those who are heroes at drinking wine 3
16:10 no treader treads out wine in the presses; 3
22:13 behold . . eating flesh and drinking wine. 3
24: 7 The wine mourns, the vine languishes 6
9 No more do they drink wine with singing; 3
11 There is an outcry in the streets for lack of wine; 3
28: 1 the rich valley of those overcome with wine! 3
7 These also reel with wine and stagger 3
7 they are confused with wine, they stagger 3
29: 9 Be drunk, but not with wine; 3
36:17 like your own land, a land of grain and wine 6
49:26 shall be drunk with their own blood as with wine. 5
51:21 who are afflicted, who are drunk, but not with wine 3
55: 1 Come, buy wine and milk without money 3
56:12 Come," they say, "let us get wine 3
62: 8 and foreigners shall not drink your wine 6
65: 8 As the wine is found in the cluster 6
Jer 13:12 Every jar shall be filled with wine. 3
12 know that every jar will be filled with wine? 3
23: 9 like a drunken man, like a man overcome by wine 3
25:15 Take from my hand this cup of the wine of wrath 3
31:12 over the grain, the wine, and the oil 6
35: 2 then offer them wine to drink. 3
5 set before the Re'chabites pitchers full of wine 3
5 wine, and cups; and I said to them, "Drink wine. 3
6 But they answered, "We will drink no wine 3
6 our father, commanded us, 'You shall not drink wine 3
8 that he commanded us, to drink no wine all our days 3
14 gave to his sons, to drink no wine, has been kept; 3
40:10 as for you, gather wine and summer fruits and oil 3
12 they gathered wine and summer fruits 3
48:33 I have made the wine cease from the wine presses; 3
51: 7 the nations drank of her wine 3
Lam 2:12 They cry to their mothers, "Where is bread and wine? 3
Ezk 27:18 great wealth . . wine of Helbon, and white wool 3
19 wine from Uzal they exchanged for your wares; 8
44:21 No priest shall drink wine, when he enters 3
Dan 1: 5 rich food . . and of the wine which he drank. 3
8 not defile . . with the wine which he drank; 3
16 steward took away their rich food and the wine 3
5: 1 drank wine in front of the 1,000. 7
2 Belshaz'zar, when he tasted the wine, 7
4 drank wine, and praised the gods of gold 7
23 you . . and your concubines have drunk wine 7
10: 3 no delicacies, no meat or wine entered my mouth 3
Hos 2: 8 I who gave her the grain, the wine, and the oil 6
9 I will take back . . my wine in its season; 6
22 and the earth shall answer the grain, the wine 6
4:11 Wine and new wine take away the understanding. 3
7: 5 the princes became sick with the heat of wine; 3
14 for grain and wine they gash themselves 6
9: 4 They shall not pour libations of wine to the LORD; 3
14: 7 fragrance shall be like the wine of Lebanon. 3
Jol 1: 5 and wail, all you drinkers of wine 3
10 because the grain is destroyed, the wine fails 6
2:19 Behold, I am sending to you grain, wine, and oil 6
24 the vats shall overflow with wine and oil. 6
3: 3 and have sold a girl for wine, and have drunk it. 3
Ams 2: 8 they drink the wine of those who have been fined. 3
12 But you made the Nazirites drink wine 3
5:11 vineyards, but you shall not drink their wine. 3
6: 6 who drink wine in bowls, and anoint themselves 3
9:14 they shall plant vineyards and drink their wine 3
Mic 2:11 I will preach to you of wine and strong drink 3
6:15 you shall tread grapes, but not drink wine. 3
Hab 2: 5 Moreover, wine is treacherous; 3
Zep 1:13 they shall not drink wine from them. 3
Hag 2:12 or pottage, or wine, or oil, or any kind of food 3
Zec 9:15 they shall drink their blood like wine 3
10: 7 their hearts shall be glad as with wine. 3
Mat 9:17 Neither is new wine put into old wineskins 8
17 if it is, the skins burst, and the wine is spilled 8
17 but new wine is put into fresh wineskins 8
27:34 they offered him wine to drink, mingled with gall; 8
Mrk 2:22 no one puts new wine into old wineskins 8
22 if he does, the wine will burst the skins 8
22 the wine is lost, and so are the skins 8
22 new wine is for fresh skins. 8
15:23 they offered him wine mingled with myrrh 8
Lke 1:15 he shall drink no wine nor strong drink 8
5:37 no one puts new wine into old wineskins 8
37 if he does, the new wine will burst the skins 8
38 new wine must be put into fresh wineskins. 8
39 no one after drinking old wine desires new •
7:33 has come eating no bread and drinking no wine 8
10:34 bound up his wounds, pouring on oil and wine 8
Joh 2: 3 When the wine failed, the mother of Jesus said 8
3 the mother of Jesus said to him, "They have no wine. 8
9 the steward . . tasted the water now become wine 8
10 said to him, "Every man serves the good wine first; 8
10 and when men have drunk freely, then the poor wine; •
10 but you have kept the good wine until now. 8
4:46 Cana in Galilee, where he had made the water wine. 8
Rom 14:21 it is right not to eat meat or drink wine 8

Eph 5:18 do not get drunk with wine, for that is debauchery; 8
1Ti 3: 8 not double-tongued, not addicted to much wine 8
5:23 use a little wine for the sake of your stomach 8
Rev 6: 6 but do not harm oil and wine! 8
14: 8 drink the wine of her impure passion. 8
10 he also shall drink the wine of God's wrath 8
17: 2 and with the wine of whose fornication 8
18: 3 all nations have drunk the wine of her . . passion 8
13 wine, oil, fine flour and wheat, cattle and sheep 8
19:15 will tread the wine press of the fury . . of God 8
1Es 3:10 The first wrote, "Wine is strongest. 8
17 the first, who had spoken of the strength of wine 8
18 Gentlemen, how is wine the strongest? 8
23 when they recover from the wine 8
24 Gentlemen, is not wine the strongest 8
4:14 is not wine strong? 8
16 the vineyards from which comes wine. 8
37 Wine is unrighteous, the king is unrighteous 8
6:30 likewise wheat and salt and wine and oil 8
8:20 100 baths of wine, and salt in abundance. 8
2Es 9:24 and taste no meat and drink no wine 9
Tob 4:15 Do not drink wine to excess 8
Jdt 10: 5 gave her maid a bottle of wine and a flask of oil 8
11:13 the tithes of the wine and oil 8
12: 1 to serve her with his own wine. 8
13 drink wine and be merry with us 8
20 drank a great quantity of wine 8
13: 2 he was overcome with wine. 8
AEs 14:17 I have not . . drunk the wine of the libations. 8
Wis 2: 7 Let us take our fill of costly wine and perfumes 8
Sir 9: 9 nor revel with her at wine 8
10 A new friend is like new wine 8
19: 2 Wine and women lead intelligent men astray 8
31:25 Do not aim to be valiant over wine 8
25 wine has destroyed many. 8
26 so wine tests hearts in the strife of the proud. 8
27 Wine is like life to men 8
27 What is life to a man who is without wine? 8
28 Wine drunk in season and temperately 8
29 Wine drunk to excess is bitterness of soul 8
31 Do not reprove your neighbor at a banquet of wine 8
32: 5 a concert of music at a banquet of wine. 8
6 the melody of music with good wine. 8
40:20 Wine and music gladden the heart 8
49: 1 like music at a banquet of wine. 8
Bel 1: 3 40 sheep and 50 gallons of wine. 8
11 set forth the food and mix and place the wine 8
2Mc 15:39 For just as it is harmful to drink wine alone 8
39 wine mixed with water is sweet and delicious 8
3Mc 5: 2 plenty of unmixed wine 8
10 been filled with a great abundance of wine 8
45 the very fragrant draughts of wine 8
6:30 both wines and everything else 8

mixed wine 1. מֶזֶג 2. מִמְסָךְ
Prv 23:30 those who go to try mixed wine. 2
Sng 7: 2 navel is a . . bowl that never lacks mixed wine. 1
Isa 65:11 and fill cups of mixed wine for Destiny; 2

new wine 1. תִּירוֹשׁ 2. γλεῦκος
Hos 4:11 Wine and new wine take away the understanding. 1
9: 2 and the new wine shall fail them. 1
Hag 1:11 upon the grain, the new wine, the oil 1
Zec 9:17 young men flourish, and new wine the maidens. 1
Act 2:13 They are filled with new wine. 2

wine on the lees 1. שֶׁמֶר
Isa 25: 6 a feast of wine on the lees, of fat things full 1
6 feast . . of wine on the lees well refined. 1

wine press 1. גַּת 2. יֶקֶב 3. פּוּרָה 4. ληνός
Num18:27 reckoned . . as the fulness of the wine press. 2
30 reckoned . . as produce of the wine press; 2
Deu 15:14 furnish him liberally . . out of your wine press; 2
16:13 make your ingathering from . . your wine press; 2
Jdg 6:11 Gideon was beating out wheat in the wine press 1
7:25 and Zeeb they killed at the wine press of Zeeb 2
2Kg 6:27 From the threshing floor, or from the wine press? 2
Neh 13:15 saw . . men treading wine presses on the sabbath 1
Job 24:11 they tread the wine presses, but suffer thirst. 2
Isa 63: 2 garments like his that treads in the wine press? 1
3 I have trodden the wine press alone 3
Jer 48:33 I have made the wine cease from the wine presses; 2
Lam 1:15 the Lord has trodden as in a wine press the virgin 1
Jol 3:13 Go in, tread, for the wine press is full. 1
Zec 14:10 the Tower of Han'anel to the king's wine presses. 2
Mat 21:33 dug a wine press in it, and built a tower 4
Rev 14:19 into the great wine press of the wrath of God; 4
20 the wine press was trodden outside the city 4
20 and blood flowed from the wine press 4
19:15 will tread the wine press of the fury . . of God 4
Sir 33:16 like a grape-gatherer I filled my wine press. 4

sweet wine 1. מַמְתַקִּים 2. עָסִיס
Neh 8:10 Go your way, eat the fat and drink sweet wine 1
Jol 1: 5 because of the sweet wine, for it is cut off 2
3:18 in that day the mountains shall drip sweet wine 2
Ams 9:13 the mountains shall drip sweet wine 2

wine vat 1. יֶקֶב
Isa 5: 2 planted it . . and hewed out a wine vat in it; 1

winebibber 1. סבא יַיִן
Prv 23:20 Be not among winebibbers, or among gluttonous 1

wineskin 1. אוֹב 2. נֹאד 3. נֹאד יַיִן 4. ἀσκός
Jos 9: 4 took . . wineskins, worn-out and torn and mended 3
13 these wineskins were new when we filled them 2
Job 32:19 like new wineskins, it is ready to burst. 1
Ps 119:83 For I have become like a wineskin in the smoke 2
Mat 9:17 Neither is new wine put into old wineskins 4
17 but new wine is put into fresh wineskins 4
Mrk 2:22 no one puts new wine into old wineskins 4
Lke 5:37 no one puts new wine into old wineskins 4
38 new wine must be put into fresh wineskins. 4

winevat 1. יֶקֶב
Hos 9: 2 Threshing floor and winevat shall not feed them 1
Hag 2:16 when one came to the winevat to draw 50 measures 1

wing 1. אֵבֶר 2. כָּנָף 3. צִיץ 4. גַּף (A) 5. κέρας 6. μέρος 7. πτέρυξ 8. ala 9. pinna 10. pinnaculum
Exd 19: 4 You have seen . . how I bore you on eagles' wings 2
25:20 The cherubim shall spread out their wings 2
20 overshadowing the mercy seat with their wings 2
37: 9 The cherubim spread out their wings above 2
9 overshadowing the mercy seat with their wings 2
Lev 1:17 he shall tear it by its wings, but shall not divide 2
Deu 32:11 spreading out its wings, catching them 2
Rut 2:12 under whose wings you have come to take refuge! 2
2Sm 22:11 he was seen upon the wings of the wind. 2
1Kg 6:24 Five cubits was . . one wing of the cherub 2
24 and five cubits . . the other wing of the cherub; 2
24 from the tip of one wing to the tip of the other. 2
27 the wings of the cherubim were spread out 2
27 a wing of one touched the one wall 2
27 a wing of the other cherub touched the other wall; 2
27 their other wings touched . . in the middle 2
8: 6 underneath the wings of the cherubim. 2
7 cherubim spread out their wings over the place 2
1Ch 28:18 of the cherubim that spread their wings •
2Ch 3:11 wings of the cherubim together extended twenty 2
11 one wing of the one, of five cubits, touched 2
11 its other wing, of five cubits, touched the wing 2
11 wing . . touched the wing of the other cherub; 2
12 one wing . . touched the wall of the house 2
12 the other wing . . was joined to the wing 2
12 other wing . . was joined to the wing of the first 2
13 wings of these cherubim extended twenty cubits; 2
5: 7 place, underneath the wings of the cherubim. 2
8 cherubim spread out their wings over the . . ark 2
Job 39:13 The wings of the ostrich wave proudly; 2
26 soars, and spreads his wings toward the south? 2
Ps 17: 8 hide me in the shadow of thy wings 2
18:10 he came swiftly upon the wings of the wind. 2
36: 7 men take refuge in the shadow of thy wings. 2
55: 6 I say, "O that I had wings like a dove! I would fly away 1
57: 1 in the shadow of thy wings I will take refuge 2
61: 4 Oh to be safe under the shelter of thy wings! Selah 2
63: 7 in the shadow of thy wings I sing for joy. 2
68:13 wings of a dove covered with silver, its pinions 2
91: 4 under his wings you will find refuge; 2
104: 3 who ridest on the wings of the wind 2
139: 9 If I take the wings of the morning and dwell 2
Prv 23: 5 for suddenly it takes to itself wings 2
Isa 6: 2 Above him stood the seraphim; each had six wings 2
8: 8 outspread wings . . fill the breadth of your land 2
10:14 and there was none that moved a wing 2
18: 1 Ah, land of whirring wings . . beyond the rivers 2
40:31 they shall mount up with wings like eagles 1
Jer 48: 9 Give wings to Moab, for she would fly away; 3
40 like an eagle, and spread his wings against Moab; 2
49:22 an eagle, and spread his wings against Bozrah 2
Ezk 1: 6 had four faces, and each of them had four wings. 2
8 Under their wings on their four sides 2
8 And the four had their faces and their wings thus 2
9 their wings touched one another; 2
11 And their wings were spread out above; •
11 each creature had two wings 2
11 wings, each of which touched the wing of another •
23 their wings were stretched out straight 2
23 each creature had two wings covering its body. 2
24 when they went, I heard the sound of their wings 2
24 when they stood still, they let down their wings. 2
25 when they stood still, they let down their wings. 2
3:13 the sound of the wings of the living creatures 2
10: 5 the sound of the wings of the cherubim was heard 2
8 have the form of a human hand under their wings. 2
16 the cherubim lifted up their wings to mount up 2
19 cherubim lifted up their wings and mounted up 2
21 Each had four faces, and each four wings 2
21 and each four wings, and underneath their wings 2
11:22 Then the cherubim lifted up their wings 2
17: 3 A great eagle with great wings and long pinions 2
7 there was another great eagle with great wings 2
Dan 7: 4 The first was like a lion and had eagles' wings. 4
4 Then as I looked its wings were plucked off 4
6 leopard, with four wings of a bird on its back; 4
9:27 upon the wing of abominations shall come one 2
Hos 4:19 A wind has wrapped them in its wings 2
Nah 3:16 The locust spreads its wings and flies away. •
Zec 5: 9 women coming forward! The wind was in their wings; 2
9 they had wings like the wings of a stork 2
9 they had wings like the wings of a stork 2
Mal 4: 2 sun of . . shall rise, with healing in its wings. 2
Mat 23:37 as a hen gathers her brood under her wings 7
Lke 13:34 as a hen gathers her brood under her wings 7
Rev 4: 8 four living creatures, each . . with six wings 7
9: 9 the noise of their wings was like the noise 7
12:14 woman was given the two wings of the great eagle 7
2Es 1:30 as a hen gathers her brood under her wings 8
11: 1 an eagle that had twelve feathered wings 8
2 and behold, he spread his wings over all the earth 8
3 out of his wings there grew opposing wings 9
3 out of his wings there grew opposing wings 9
3 wings; but they became little, puny wings. 10
5 I looked, and behold, the eagle flew with his wings 9
7 and uttered a cry to his wings, saying 9
11 I counted his opposing wings, and behold 9
12 behold, on the right side one wing arose 9
13 Then the next wing arose and reigned •
18 Then the third wing raised itself up •
19 so it went with all the wings 8
20 the wings that followed also rose up 9
22 the twelve wings and the two little wings 9
25 I looked, and behold, these little wings planned ‡
32 all the wings that had gone before. 8
33 just as the wings had done. 8
45 and your terrifying wings 8
12: 2 And the two wings that had gone over to it arose 8
16 the interpretation of the 12 wings which you saw. 8
19 eight little wings clinging to his wings 8
Wis 5:11 is traversed by the movement of its wings 7
1Mc 9: 1 and with them the right wing of the army. 5
12 Bacchides was on the right wing 5
15 they crushed the right wing 6
16 When those on the left wing saw 5
16 the right wing was crushed 5

little wing 1. pinnaculum
2Es 11:22 wings and the two little wings disappeared; 1
23 the three heads . . and six little wings. 1
24 behold, two little wings separated from the six 1
31 it devoured the two little wings ‡
45 and your most evil little wings 1
12:19 eight little wings clinging to his wings ‡
29 two little wings passing over to the head ‡

winged 1. כָּנָף 2. עוֹף
Gen 1:21 every winged bird according to its kind 1
Lev 11:20 All winged insects that go upon all fours are 2
21 Yet among the winged insects that go on all fours 2
23 all other winged insects which have four feet 2
Deu 4:17 likeness of any winged bird that flies in the air 1
14:19 all winged insects are unclean for you; 2
Ps 78:27 like dust, winged birds like the sand of the seas; 1

winged *See also* creature.

winged thing 1. עוֹף
Deu 14:20 All clean winged things you may eat. 1

wings *See* give.

wink 1. עצה 2. קרץ 3. διανεύω
Ps 35:19 those wink the eye who hate me without cause. 2
Prv 6:13 winks with his eyes, scrapes with his feet 2
10:10 He who winks the eye causes trouble 2
16:30 He who winks his eyes plans perverse things 1
Sir 27:22 Whoever winks his eye plans evil deeds 3

winnow 1. זרה 2. διασκορπίζω 3. λικμάω
Rut 3: 2 See, he is winnowing barley tonight 1
Prv 20: 8 throne of judgment winnows all evil with his eyes. 1
26 A wise king winnows the wicked 1
Isa 30:24 provender, which has been winnowed with shovel 1
41:16 You shall winnow them and the wind shall carry 1
Jer 4:11 toward . . my people, not to winnow or cleanse 1
15: 7 I have winnowed them with a winnowing fork 1
51: 2 to Babylon winnowers, and they shall winnow her 1
Mat 25:24 gathering where you did not winnow; 2
26 gather where I have not winnowed? 2
Sir 5: 9 Do not winnow with every wind 3

winnow away 1. ἐκλικμάω
Wis 5:23 like a tempest it will winnow them away. 1

winnowed one 1. בֶּן גֹּרֶן
Isa 21:10 O my threshed and winnowed one, what I have heard 1

winnower 1. זרה
Jer 51: 2 I will send to Babylon winnowers 1

winnowing *See* fork.

winter 1. חרף 2. חֹרֶף 3. סְתָו 4. παραχειμάζω 5. παραχειμασία 6. χειμερινός 7. χειμών 8. hiems
Gen 8:22 cold and heat, summer and winter, day and night 2

Ps 74:17 thou hast made summer and winter. 2
Sng 2:11 lo, the winter is past, the rain is over and gone. 3
Isa 18: 6 the beasts of the earth will winter upon them. 1
Jer 36:22 the king was sitting in the winter house 2
Ams 3:15 I will smite the winter house 2
Zec 14: 8 it shall continue in summer as in winter. 2
Mat 24:20 in winter or on a sabbath. 7
Mrk 13:18 Pray that it may not happen in winter. 7
Joh 10:23 it was winter, and Jesus was walking in the temple 7
Act 27:12 because the harbor was not suitable to winter in 5
12 they could reach Phoenix . . and winter there. 4
28:11 in a ship which had wintered in the island 4
2Ti 4:21 Do your best to come before winter 7
1Es 9:11 the multitude is great and it is winter 6
2Es 7:41 or summer or spring or heat or winter or frost 8

winter *See also* cold, fruit, spend.

wintry 1. *χειμέριος*

Wis 16:29 will melt like wintry frost 1

wintry *See also* storm.

wipe 1. מחה 2. *ἐκμάσσω*

2Kg 21:13 I will wipe Jerusalem as one wipes a dish 1
13 I will wipe Jerusalem as one wipes a dish 1
13 as one wipes a dish, wiping it and turning it 1
Prv 30:20 adulteress: she eats, and wipes her mouth, and says 1
Lke 7:38 wiped them with the hair of her head 2
44 wiped them with her hair. 2
Joh 11: 2 wiped his feet with her hair 2
12: 3 wiped his feet with her hair 2
13: 5 to wipe them with the towel 2
LJr 1:13 their faces are wiped 2

wipe away 1. מחה 2. *ἀπαλείφω* 3. *ἐξαλείφω*

Prv 6:33 his disgrace will not be wiped away. 1
Isa 25: 8 the Lord GOD will wipe away tears from all faces 1
Rev 7:17 and God will wipe away every tear from their eyes. 3
21: 4 he will wipe away every tear from their eyes 3
3Mc 2:19 Wipe away our sins and disperse our errors 2

wipe off 1. *ἀπομάσσω* 2. *ἐκμάσσω*

Lke 10:11 'Even the dust . . we wipe off against you 1
LJr 1:24 will not shine unless some one wipes off the rust; 2

wipe out 1. אבד 2. כחד 3. כרת 4. מחה 5. צמת 6. שמד 7. תמם 8. *ἐκτρίβω* 9. *ἐξαίρω* 10. *ἐπιτελέω* 11. contero

Jos 10:20 a very great slaughter, until they were wiped out 7
11:21 Joshua came at that time, and wiped out the Anakim 3
2Kg 10:17 he slew all . . till he had wiped them out 6
28 Thus Jehu wiped out Ba'al from Israel. 6
Neh 13:14 wipe not out my good deeds that I have done 4
Ps 83: 4 They say, "Come, let us wipe them out as a nation; 2
94:23 wipe them out for their wickedness; 5
23 LORD our God will wipe them out. 5
Isa 26:14 and wiped out all remembrance of them. 1
Ezk 6: 6 altars cut down, and your works wiped out. 4
2Es 15:57 and your cities shall be wiped out 11
Sir 36: 7 destroy the adversary and wipe out the enemy. 8
46:18 he wiped out the leaders of the people of Tyre 8
47: 7 For he wiped out his enemies on every side 8
48:21 his angel wiped them out. 8
1Mc 3:35 to wipe out and destroy the strength of Israel 8
2Mc 8: 9 to wipe out the whole race of Judea 9
12: 8 meant in the same way to wipe out the Jews 10

wisdom 1. בִּינָה 2. חָכָם 3. חָכְמָה 4. לֵב 5. שֵׂכֶל 6. תּוּשִׁיָּה 7. חָכְמָה (A) 8. *σοφία* 9. *σύνεσις* 10. *φρόνησις* 11. intellectus 12. sapientia

Deu 4: 6 that will be your wisdom and your understanding 3
34: 9 Joshua . . was full of the spirit of wisdom 3
2Sm 14:20 But my lord has wisdom like . . the angel of God 2
20 lord has wisdom like the wisdom of the angel of God 3
20:22 the woman went to all the people in her wisdom. 3
1Kg 2: 6 Act . . according to your wisdom, but do not let 3
3:28 they perceived that the wisdom of God was in him 3
4:29 gave Solomon wisdom and understanding beyond 3
30 Solomon's wisdom surpassed the wisdom of all 3
30 Solomon's wisdom surpassed the wisdom of all 3
30 the wisdom of all . . and all the wisdom of Egypt. 3
34 men came . . to hear the wisdom of Solomon 3
34 kings of the earth, who had heard of his wisdom. 3
5:12 the LORD gave Solomon wisdom, as he promised him; 3
7:14 he was full of wisdom, understanding, and skill 3
10: 4 queen of Sheba had seen all the wisdom of Solomon 3
6 The report . . of your affairs and of your wisdom 3
7 your wisdom and prosperity surpass the report 3
8 who . . stand before you and hear your wisdom! 3
23 Solomon excelled all . . in riches and in wisdom. 3
24 whole earth sought . . Solomon to hear his wisdom 3
11:41 acts of Solomon, and all that he did, and his wisdom 3
2Ch 1:10 Give me now wisdom and knowledge to go out 3
11 have asked wisdom and knowledge for yourself 3
12 wisdom and knowledge are granted to you. 3
9: 3 queen of Sheba had seen the wisdom of Solomon 3
5 The report was true . . and of your wisdom 3
6 half the greatness of your wisdom was not told me; 3
7 servants, who continually . . hear your wisdom! 3
22 Solomon excelled . . in riches and in wisdom. 3
23 sought . . Solomon to hear his wisdom 3
Ezr 7:25 you, Ezra, according to the wisdom of your God 7
Job 4:21 do they not die, and that without wisdom?' 3
11: 6 and that he would tell you the secrets of wisdom! 3
12: 2 you are the people, and wisdom will die with you. 3
12 Wisdom is with the aged 3
13 With God are wisdom and might; 3
16 With him are strength and wisdom; 6
13: 5 keep silent, and it would be your wisdom! 3
15: 8 do you limit wisdom to yourself? 3
26: 3 How you have counseled him who has no wisdom 3
28:12 But where shall wisdom be found? 3
18 the price of wisdom is above pearls. 3
20 Whence then comes wisdom? 3
28 Behold, the fear of the Lord, that is wisdom; 3
32: 7 Let days speak, and many years teach wisdom. 3
13 Beware lest you say, 'We have found wisdom; 3
33:33 be silent, and I will teach you wisdom. 3
38:36 Who has put wisdom in the clouds 3
37 Who can number the clouds by wisdom? 3
39:17 because God has made her forget wisdom 3
26 Is it by your wisdom that the hawk soars 1
Ps 37:30 The mouth of the righteous utters wisdom 3
49: 3 My mouth shall speak wisdom; 3
51: 6 therefore teach me wisdom in my secret heart. 3
90:12 number our days that we may get a heart of wisdom. 3
104:24 In wisdom hast thou made them all; 3
111:10 The fear of the LORD is the beginning of wisdom; 3
Prv 1: 2 That men may know wisdom and instruction 3
7 fools despise wisdom and instruction. 3
20 Wisdom cries aloud in the street; 3
2: 2 making your ear attentive to wisdom 3
6 For the LORD gives wisdom; 3
10 for wisdom will come into your heart 3
3:13 Happy is the man who finds wisdom 3
19 LORD by wisdom founded the earth; 3
4: 5 Get wisdom; get insight. 3
7 The beginning of wisdom is this: Get wisdom 3
7 The beginning of wisdom is this: Get wisdom 3
11 I have taught you the way of wisdom; 3
5: 1 My son, be attentive to my wisdom 3
7: 4 Say to wisdom, "You are my sister 3
8: 1 Does not wisdom call 3
11 for wisdom is better than jewels 3
12 I, wisdom, dwell in prudence 3
9: 1 Wisdom has built her house 3
10 The fear of the LORD is the beginning of wisdom 3
10:13 lips of him who has understanding wisdom is found 3
31 The mouth of the righteous brings forth wisdom 3
11: 2 but with the humble is wisdom. 3
13:10 but with those who take advice is wisdom. 3
14: 1 Wisdom builds her house 3
6 A scoffer seeks wisdom in vain 3
8 The wisdom of a prudent man is to discern his way 3
24 The crown of the wise is their wisdom •
33 Wisdom abides in the mind of . . understanding 3
15:33 The fear of the LORD is instruction in wisdom 3
16:16 To get wisdom is better than gold; 3
22 Wisdom is a fountain of life to him who has it 5
17:16 fool have a price in his hand to buy wisdom 3
24 understanding sets his face toward wisdom 3
18: 4 fountain of wisdom is a gushing stream. 3
19: 8 He who gets wisdom loves himself; 4
21:30 No wisdom, no understanding, no counsel, can avail 3
23: 9 for he will despise the wisdom of your words. 5
23 buy wisdom, instruction, and understanding. 3
24: 3 By wisdom a house is built 3
7 Wisdom is too high for a fool; 3
14 Know that wisdom is such to your soul; 3
28:26 but he who walks in wisdom will be delivered. 3
29: 3 He who loves wisdom makes his father glad 3
15 The rod and reproof give wisdom 3
30: 3 I have not learned wisdom, nor have I knowledge 3
31:26 She opens her mouth with wisdom 3
Ecc 1:13 to seek and to search out by wisdom all that is 3
16 I have acquired great wisdom, surpassing all 3
16 had great experience of wisdom and knowledge. 3
17 to know wisdom and to know madness and folly. 3
18 For in much wisdom is much vexation 3
2: 3 my mind still guiding me with wisdom 3
9 became great . . also my wisdom remained with me. 3
12 turned to consider wisdom and madness and folly; 3
13 wisdom excels folly as light excels darkness. 3
21 a man who has toiled with wisdom and knowledge 3
26 God gives wisdom and knowledge and joy; 3
7:10 For it is not from wisdom that you ask this. 3
11 Wisdom is good with an inheritance, an advantage 3
12 For the protection of wisdom is like . . of money; 3
12 that wisdom preserves the life of him who has it. 3
19 Wisdom gives strength . . more than ten rulers 3
23 All this I have tested by wisdom; 3
25 to know . . and to seek wisdom and the sum of things 3
8: 1 A man's wisdom makes his face shine 3
16 When I applied my mind to know wisdom 3
9:10 work or thought or knowledge or wisdom in Sheol 3
13 also seen this example of wisdom under the sun 3
15 wise man, and he by his wisdom delivered the city. 3
16 But I say that wisdom is better than might 3
16 though the poor man's wisdom is despised 3
18 Wisdom is better than weapons of war 3
10: 1 so a little folly outweighs wisdom and honor. 3
10 but wisdom helps one to succeed. 3
Isa 10:13 and by my wisdom, for I have understanding; 3
11: 2 the spirit of wisdom and understanding 3
28:29 wonderful in counsel, and excellent in wisdom. 6
29:14 the wisdom of their wise men shall perish 3
33: 6 abundance of salvation, wisdom, and knowledge; 3
47:10 your wisdom and your knowledge led you astray 3
Jer 8: 9 and what wisdom is in them? 3
9:23 Let not the wise man glory in his wisdom 3
10:12 who established the world by his wisdom 3
49: 7 Is wisdom no more in Teman? Has counsel perished 3
7 from the prudent? Has their wisdom vanished? 3
51:15 who established the world by his wisdom 3
Ezk 28: 4 by your wisdom . . you have gotten wealth 3
5 by your great wisdom in trade you have increased 3
7 their swords against the beauty of your wisdom 3
12 You were the signet of perfection, full of wisdom 3
17 you corrupted your wisdom 3
Dan 1:17 learning and skill in all letters and wisdom; 3
20 every matter of wisdom and understanding 3
2:20 name of God . . to whom belong wisdom and might. 7
21 he gives wisdom to the wise and knowledge 7
23 for thou hast given me wisdom and strength 7
30 as for me, not because of any wisdom that I have 7
5:11 light and understanding and wisdom 7
11 light . . and wisdom, like the wisdom of the gods 7
14 light and understanding and excellent wisdom 7
Mat 11:19 Yet wisdom is justified by her deeds. 8
12:42 to hear the wisdom of Solomon 8
13:54 Where did this man get this wisdom 8
Mrk 6: 2 What is the wisdom given to him? 8
Lke 1:17 the disobedient to the wisdom of the just 10
2:40 grew and became strong, filled with wisdom; 8
52 Jesus increased in wisdom and in stature 8
7:35 Yet wisdom is justified by all her children. 8
11:31 to hear the wisdom of Solomon 8
49 Therefore also the Wisdom of God said, 'I will send 8
21:15 for I will give you a mouth and wisdom 8
Act 6: 3 full of the Spirit and of wisdom 8
10 could not withstand the wisdom and the Spirit 8
7:10 favor and wisdom before Pharaoh, king of Egypt 8
22 instructed in all the wisdom of the Egyptians 8
Rom 11:33 the riches and wisdom and knowledge of God! 8
1Co 1:17 to preach . . and not with eloquent wisdom 8
19 I will destroy the wisdom of the wise 8
20 Has not God made foolish the wisdom of the world? 8
21 since, in the wisdom of God, the world did not know 8
21 the world did not know God through wisdom 8
22 For Jews demand signs and Greeks seek wisdom 8
24 Christ the power of God and the wisdom of God. 8
30 whom God made our wisdom, our righteousness 8
2: 1 the testimony of God in lofty words or wisdom. 8
4 not in plausible words of wisdom 8
5 your faith might not rest in the wisdom of men 8
6 Yet among the mature we do impart wisdom 8
6 although it is not a wisdom of this age 8
7 we impart a secret and hidden wisdom of God 8
13 in words not taught by human wisdom 8
3:19 For the wisdom of this world is folly with God. 8
12: 8 through the Spirit the utterance of wisdom 8
2Co 1:12 not by earthly wisdom but by the grace of God. 8
Eph 1: 9 he has made known to us in all wisdom and insight 8
17 may give you a spirit of wisdom and of revelation 8
3:10 the manifold wisdom of God 8
Col 1: 9 in all spiritual wisdom and understanding 8
28 teaching every man in all wisdom 8
2: 3 all the treasures of wisdom and knowledge. 8
23 These have indeed an appearance of wisdom 8
3:16 teach and admonish one another in all wisdom 8
Jas 1: 5 If any of you lacks wisdom, let him ask God 8
3:13 let him show his works in the meekness of wisdom. 8
15 This wisdom is not such as comes down from above 8
17 wisdom from above is first pure, then peaceable 8
2Pe 3:15 Paul wrote . . according to the wisdom given him 8
Rev 5:12 to receive power and wealth and wisdom and might 8
7:12 Blessing and glory and wisdom and thanksgiving 8
13:18 This calls for wisdom 8
17: 9 This calls for a mind with wisdom 8
1Es 3: 7 because of his wisdom he shall sit next to Darius 8
4:59 From thee is the victory; from thee is wisdom 8
60 Blessed art thou, who hast given me wisdom 8
8:23 according to the wisdom of God 8
2Es 5: 9 and wisdom shall withdraw into its chamber 11
8: 4 and drink wisdom, O my heart! ‡
12 and reproved him in thy wisdom. 11
52 and wisdom perfected beforehand. 12
13:55 for you have devoted your life to wisdom 12
14:40 and wisdom increased in my breast 12
47 the fountain of wisdom 12
Jdt 8:29 not the first time your wisdom has been shown 8
11: 8 For we have heard of your wisdom and skill 8
20 they marveled at her wisdom and said 8
21 either for beauty of face or wisdom of speech! 9
Wis 1: 4 because wisdom will not enter a deceitful soul 8
6 For wisdom is a kindly spirit 8
3:11 whoever despises wisdom and instruction 8

6: 9 that you may learn wisdom and not transgress. 8
12 Wisdom is radiant and unfading 8
17 The beginning of wisdom *
20 the desire for wisdom leads to a kingdom. 8
21 honor wisdom, that you may reign for ever. 8
22 will tell you what wisdom is and how she came to be 8
23 for envy does not associate with wisdom. 8
7: 7 the spirit of wisdom came to me. 8
12 I rejoiced in them all, because wisdom leads them; 8
15 the guide even of wisdom 8
22 wisdom, the fashioner of all things, taught me 8
24 For wisdom is more mobile than any motion; 8
28 nothing so much as the man who lives with wisdom. 8
30 against wisdom evil does not prevail. 8
8: 5 what is richer than wisdom who effects all things? 8
17 in kinship with wisdom there is immortality 8
9: 2 by thy wisdom hast formed man, to have dominion 8
4 give me the wisdom that sits by thy throne 8
6 yet without the wisdom that comes from thee 8
9 With thee is wisdom, who knows thy works 8
17 unless thou hast given wisdom 8
18 were saved by wisdom. 8
10: 1 Wisdom protected the first-formed father *
4 wisdom again saved it 8
5 Wisdom also . . recognized the righteous man *
6 Wisdom rescued a righteous man *
8 For because they passed wisdom by 8
9 Wisdom rescued from troubles 8
13 wisdom did not desert him *
15 wisdom delivered from a nation of oppressors. *
21 because wisdom opened the mouth of the dumb 8
11: 1 Wisdom prospered their works *
14: 2 wisdom was the craftsman who built it; 8
5 works of thy wisdom should not be without effect; 8
17: 7 their boasted wisdom was scornfully rebuked. 10
Sir 0: 1 should praise Israel for instruction and wisdom; 8
1 write something pertaining to . . wisdom 8
1: 1 All wisdom comes from the Lord 8
3 the abyss, and wisdom-who can search them out? 8
4 Wisdom was created before all things 8
6 The root of wisdom-to whom has it been revealed? 8
9 The Lord himself created wisdom; *
14 To fear the Lord is the beginning of wisdom 8
16 To fear the Lord is wisdom's full measure 8
18 The fear of the Lord is the crown of wisdom 8
20 To fear the Lord is the root of wisdom 8
25 In the treasuries of wisdom are wise sayings 8
26 If you desire wisdom, keep the commandments 8
27 the fear of the Lord is wisdom and instruction 8
4:11 Wisdom exalts her sons and gives help 8
23 do not hide your wisdom. *
24 For wisdom is known through speech 8
6:18 until you are old you will keep finding wisdom. 8
22 wisdom is like her name 8
37 your desire for wisdom will be granted. 8
11: 1 The wisdom of a humble man will lift up his head 8
14:20 Blessed is the man who meditates on wisdom 8
22 Pursue wisdom like a hunter *
15: 1 he who holds to the law will obtain wisdom. *
3 give him the water of wisdom to drink. 8
10 For a hymn of praise should be uttered in wisdom 8
18 For great is the wisdom of the Lord 8
18:28 Every intelligent man knows wisdom 8
19:20 All wisdom is the fear of the Lord 8
20 in all wisdom there is the fulfilment of the law. 8
22 the knowledge of wickedness is not wisdom 8
23 there is a fool who merely lacks wisdom. 8
20:30 Hidden wisdom and unseen treasure 8
31 Better . . than the man who hides his wisdom. 8
21:11 wisdom is the fulfilment of the fear of the Lord. 8
18 so is wisdom to a fool 8
22: 6 wisdom at all times. 8
23: 2 the discipline of wisdom over my mind! 8
24: 1 Wisdom will praise herself 8
25 It fills men with wisdom, like the Pishon 8
25: 5 How attractive is wisdom in the aged 8
10 How great is he who has gained wisdom! 8
34: 8 wisdom is made perfect in truthful lips. 8
37:21 since he is lacking in all wisdom. 8
38:24 The wisdom of the scribe 8
39: 1 will seek out the wisdom of all the ancients 8
6 he will pour forth words of wisdom 8
10 Nations will declare his wisdom 8
40:20 the love of wisdom is better than both. 8
41:14 hidden wisdom and unseen treasure 8
15 Better . . than the man who hides his wisdom. 8
42:21 He has ordained the splendors of his wisdom 8
43:33 to the godly he has granted wisdom. 8
44:15 Peoples will declare their wisdom 8
45:26 May the Lord grant you wisdom in your heart 8
50:27 who out of his heart poured forth wisdom. 8
51:13 I sought wisdom openly in my prayer. 8
17 to him who gives wisdom I will give glory. 8
18 For I resolved to live according to wisdom *
19 My soul grappled with wisdom *
Bar 3: 9 life, O Israel; give ear, and learn wisdom! 10
12 You have forsaken the fountain of wisdom. 8
14 Learn where there is wisdom, where there is 10
23 have not learned the way to wisdom, nor given 8

28 so they perished because they had no wisdom 10
2Mc 2: 9 being possessed of wisdom 8
4Mc 1:15 with sound logic prefers the life of wisdom. 8
16 Wisdom, next, is the knowledge of . . 8
18 Now the kinds of wisdom are rational judgment 8

wisdom *See also* display, gain, give, make, possess, teach, use.

sound wisdom 1. תּוּשִׁיָּה
Prv 2: 7 he stores up sound wisdom for the upright; 1
3:21 My son, keep sound wisdom and discretion; 1
8:14 I have counsel and sound wisdom 1
Mic 6: 9 and it is sound wisdom to fear thy name 1

without wisdom 1. insipiens
2Es 5:39 I am without wisdom 1

wise 1. בין 2. בִּינָה 3. חכם 4. חָכָם 5. חֲכַם לֵב 6. לֵב 7. שׂכל 8. חַכִּים (A) 9. ἀγαθός 10. ἄσοφος 11. ἐπιστήμη 12. ἐπιστήμων 13. σοφία 14. σοφός 15. σύνεσις 16. φρόνιμος 17. intellego 18. sapio
Gen 41:33 let Pharaoh select a man discreet and wise 4
39 there is none so discreet and wise as you are; 4
Deu 1:13 Choose wise, understanding, and experienced men 4
15 heads of your tribes, wise and experienced men 4
4: 6 great nation is a wise and understanding people.' 4
16:19 bribe blinds the eyes of the wise and subverts 4
32:29 If they were wise, they would understand this 3
Jdg 5:29 Her wisest ladies make answer, nay, she gives 4
2Sm 14: 2 sent to Teko'a, and fetched from there a wise woman 4
20:16 Then a wise woman called from the city, "Hear! Hear! 4
1Kg 2: 9 hold him not guiltless, for you are a wise man; you 4
3:12 I give you a wise and discerning mind, so that none 4
4:31 he was wiser than all other men, wiser than Ethan 3
31 wiser than Ethan the Ez'rahite, and Heman, Calcol 3
5: 7 the LORD . . who has given to David a wise son 4
2Ch 2:12 who has given King David a wise son 4
Job 5:13 He takes the wise in their own craftiness; 4
9: 4 He is wise in heart, and mighty in strength 4
22: 2 Surely he who is wise is profitable to himself. 7
32: 9 It is not the old that are wise 3
34:34 the wise man who hears me will say 4
37:24 not regard any who are wise in their own conceit. 4
Ps 2:10 Now therefore, O kings, be wise; be warned, O rulers 7
49:10 Yea, he shall see that even the wise die 4
53: 2 to see if there are any that are wise 7
94: 8 Fools, when will you be wise? 7
107:43 Whoever is wise, let him give heed to these things; 4
Prv 1: 6 understand . . words of the wise and their riddles. 4
3: 7 Be not wise in your own eyes; 4
35 wise will inherit honor, but fools get disgrace. 4
6: 6 consider her ways, and be wise. 3
8:33 Hear instruction and be wise, and do not neglect 3
9: 9 instruction to a wise man . . will be still wiser; 3
12 If you are wise, you are wise for yourself; 3
12 If you are wise, you are wise for yourself; 3
10: 1 A wise son makes a glad father 4
8 The wise of heart will heed commandments 4
11:29 fool will be servant to the wise. 5
12:18 but the tongue of the wise brings healing. 4
13: 1 A wise son hears his father's instruction 4
14 The teaching of the wise is a fountain of life 4
14: 3 but the lips of the wise will preserve them. 4
24 The crown of the wise is their wisdom 4
15: 2 The tongue of the wise dispenses knowledge 4
7 The lips of the wise spread knowledge; 4
12 A scoffer . . will not go to the wise. 4
20 A wise son makes a glad father 4
31 He whose ear heeds . . will abide among the wise. 4
16:14 wise man will appease it. 4
21 The wise of heart is called a man of discernment 4
23 The mind of the wise makes his speech judicious 4
17:28 Even a fool who keeps silent is considered wise; 4
18:15 the ear of the wise seeks knowledge. 4
20: 1 whoever is led astray by it is not wise. 3
26 A wise king winnows the wicked 4
22:17 Incline your ear, and hear the words of the wise 4
23: 4 not . . acquire wealth; be wise enough to desist. 2
15 if your heart is wise, my heart too will be glad. 3
19 Hear, my son, and be wise, and direct your mind 3
24: 5 A wise man is mightier than a strong man 4
23 These also are sayings of the wise. 4
25:12 wise reprover to a listening ear. 4
26: 5 lest he be wise in his own eyes. 4
12 Do you see a man who is wise in his own eyes? 4
16 sluggard is wiser in his own eyes than seven men 4
27:11 Be wise, my son, and make my heart glad 4
28: 7 He who keeps the law is a wise son 1
11 A rich man is wise in his own eyes, but a poor man 4
29: 9 If a wise man has an argument with a fool, the fool 4
30:24 Four things . . are exceedingly wise 4
Ecc 2:15 why then have I been so very wise? 3
4:13 Better is a poor and wise youth than an old 4
7: 4 The heart of the wise is in the house of mourning; 4
5 better for a man to hear the rebuke of the wise 4
23 I said, "I will be wise"; but it was far from me. 3
9: 1 the righteous and the wise . . are in the hand 4
11 nor the battle to the strong, nor bread to the wise 4
15 But there was found in it a poor wise man 4

17 The words of the wise . . in quiet are better 4
12: 9 Besides being wise, the Preacher also taught 4
11 The sayings of the wise are like goads 4
Isa 5:21 Woe to those who are wise in their own eyes 4
19:11 the wise counselors of Pharaoh give stupid 4
11 I am a son of the wise, a son of ancient kings"? 4
31: 2 yet he is wise and brings disaster 4
Jer 8: 8 How can you say, 'We are wise 4
9:12 Who is the man so wise that he can understand this? 4
18:18 perish from the priest, nor counsel from the wise 4
Ezk 28: 2 though you consider yourself as wise as a god 6
3 you are indeed wiser than Daniel; 4
6 Because you consider yourself as wise as a god 6
Dan 2:21 he gives wisdom to the wise and knowledge 8
11:33 people who are wise shall make many understand 7
35 some of those who are wise shall fall 7
12: 3 those who are wise shall shine like 7
10 those who are wise shall understand. 7
Hos 14: 9 Whoever is wise, let him understand these things; 4
Zec 9: 2 Tyre and Sidon, though they are very wise. 3
Mat 7:24 will be like a wise man who built his house 16
10:16 so be wise as serpents and innocent as doves. 16
11:25 these things from the wise and understanding 14
24:45 Who then is the faithful and wise servant 16
25: 2 Five of them were foolish, and five were wise. 16
4 the wise took flasks of oil with their lamps. 16
8 the foolish said to the wise 16
9 the wise replied 16
Lke 10:21 hidden . . from the wise and understanding 14
12:42 Who then is the faithful and wise steward 16
Rom 1:14 both to the wise and to the foolish 14
22 Claiming to be wise, they became fools 14
11:25 Lest you be wise in your own conceits 16
16:19 I would have you wise as to what is good 14
27 to the only wise God be glory for evermore 14
1Co 1:19 I will destroy the wisdom of the wise 14
25 For the foolishness of God is wiser than men 14
26 not many of you were wise 14
27 to shame the wise 14
3:18 If any one among you thinks that he is wise 14
18 let him become a fool that he may become wise. 14
19 He catches the wise in their craftiness 14
20 the thoughts of the wise are futile. 14
4:10 you are wise in Christ 16
6: 5 there is no man among you wise enough to decide 14
2Co 11:19 For you gladly bear with fools, being wise 16
Eph 5:15 not as unwise men but as wise 10
Jas 3:13 Who is wise and understanding among you? 14
1Es 3: 5 to him whose statement seems wisest 14
9 the three nobles of Persia judge to be wisest 14
4:42 for you have been found to be the wisest 14
5: 6 who spoke wise words before Darius 14
2Es 7:19 or wiser than the Most High! 17
12:38 shall teach them to the wise among your people 18
14:13 and instruct those that are wise ‡
26 and some you shall deliver in secret to the wise 18
46 to give them to the wise among your people. 18
Jdt 11:23 beautiful in appearance, but wise in speech 9
Wis 7:15 the corrector of the wise. 14
Sir 1: 8 There is One who is wise, greatly to be feared 14
25 In the treasuries of wisdom are wise sayings 11
6:33 if you incline your ear you will become wise. 14
34 Who is wise? Cleave to him. 14
35 do not let wise proverbs escape you. 15
7:19 Do not deprive yourself of a wise and good wife 14
9:14 consult with the wise. 14
17 so a people's leader is proved wise by his words. 14
10: 1 A wise magistrate will educate his people 14
25 Free men will be at the service of a wise servant 14
18:27 A wise man is cautious in everything 14
20: 1 there is a man who keeps silent but is wise. 16
5 There is one who by keeping silent is found wise 14
7 A wise man will be silent until the right moment 14
29 Presents and gifts blind the eyes of the wise; 14
21:15 When a man of understanding hears a wise saying 14
27:11 The talk of the godly man is always wise 13
33: 2 A wise man will not hate the law 14
37:22 A man may be wise to his own advantage 14
23 A wise man will instruct his own people 14
24 A wise man will have praise heaped upon him 14
26 He who is wise among his people 14
44: 4 wise in their words of instruction; 14
47:12 After him rose up a wise son who fared amply 12
4Mc 7:23 only the wise and courageous man 14

wise *See also* conduct, dealing, guidance, make, saying, son.

all wise 1. πάνσοφος
4Mc 1:12 giving glory to the all-wise God. 1
13:19 the divine and all-wise Providence 1

become wise 1. חכם 2. σοφίζω
Prv 13:20 He who walks with wise men becomes wise 1
21:11 scoffer is punished, the simple becomes wise; 1
Sir 38:24 he who has little business may become wise. 2
25 How can he become wise who handles the plow 2
47:14 How wise you became in your youth! 2
50:28 he who lays them to heart will become wise. 2

wise in counsel 1. ἀνὴρ βουλῆς
1Mc 2:65 Simeon your brother is wise in counsel 1

wise man 1. חָכָם 2. שׂכל 3. חַכִּים (A) 4. μάγος 5. σοφός 6. φρόνιμος
Gen 41: 8 all the magicians of Egypt and all its wise men; 1
Exd 7:11 Pharaoh summoned the wise men and the sorcerers; 1
Est 1:13 the king said to the wise men who knew the times– 1
6:13 Then his wise men and his wife Zeresh said to him 1
Job 15: 2 Should a wise man answer with windy knowledge 1
18 what wise men have told 1
17:10 I shall not find a wise man among you. 1
34: 2 Hear my words, you wise men 1
Prv 1: 5 wise man also may hear and increase in learning 1
9: 8 reprove a wise man, and he will love you. 1
9 Give instruction to a wise man, and he will be 1
10:14 Wise men lay up knowledge 1
12:15 but a wise man listens to advice. 1
13:20 He who walks with wise men becomes wise 1
14:16 A wise man is cautious and turns away from evil 1
15:24 The wise man's path leads upward to life, that he 2
21:11 wise man is instructed, he gains knowledge. 1
20 treasure remains in a wise man's dwelling 1
22 A wise man scales the city of the mighty 1
29: 8 but wise men turn away wrath. 1
11 but a wise man quietly holds it back. 1
Ecc 2:14 The wise man has his eyes in his head 1
16 of the wise man as of the fool there is no enduring 1
16 How the wise man dies just like the fool! 1
19 who knows whether he will be a wise man or a fool? 1
6: 8 For what advantage has the wise man over the fool 1
7: 7 Surely oppression makes the wise man foolish 1
19 gives strength to the wise man more 1
8: 1 Who is like the wise man? 1
5 the mind of a wise man will know the time and way. 1
17 even though a wise man claims to know 1
10: 2 A wise man's heart inclines him toward the right 1
12 The words of a wise man's mouth win him favor 1
Isa 19:12 Where then are your wise men? Let them tell you 1
29:14 the wisdom of their wise men shall perish 1
44:25 who turns wise men back 1
Jer 8: 9 The wise men shall be put to shame 1
9:23 Let not the wise man glory in his wisdom 1
50:35 and upon her princes and her wise men! 1
51:57 I will make drunk her princes and her wise men 1
Dan 2:12 all the wise men of Babylon be destroyed. 3
13 decree went forth . . wise men were to be slain 3
14 who had gone out to slay the wise men of Babylon; 3
18 might not perish with the rest of the wise men 3
24 appointed to destroy the wise men of Babylon; 3
24 Do not destroy the wise men of Babylon; 3
27 No wise men, enchanters, magicians 3
48 chief prefect over all the wise men of Babylon. 3
4: 6 all the wise men of Babylon should be brought 3
18 because all the wise men of my kingdom 3
5: 7 king said to the wise men of Babylon, 3
8 Then all the king's wise men came 3
15 wise men, the enchanters, have been brought 3
Obd 1: 8 Will I not on that day . . destroy the wise men 1
Mat 2: 1 behold, wise men from the East came 4
7 Then Herod summoned the wise men secretly 4
16 he saw that he had been tricked by the wise men 4
16 time which he had ascertained from the wise men. 4
23:34 I send you prophets and wise men and scribes 5
1Co 1:20 Where is the wise man? Where is the scribe? 5
Tob 4:18 Seek advice from every wise man 6
Wis 4:17 For they will see the end of the wise man 5
6:24 A multitude of wise men 5
Sir 3:29 an attentive ear is the wise man's desire. 5
20:13 The wise man makes himself beloved 5
21:13 The knowledge of a wise man will increase 5
26 the mouth of wise men is in their mind. 5

most wise 1. πάνσοφος
4Mc 2:19 Why else did Jacob, our most wise father, censure 1

wise one 1. חָכָם
Jer 10: 7 for among all the wise ones of the nations 1

seem wise 1. κρίνω
1Es 6:21 Now therefore, if it seems wise, O king 1

wisely 1. νουνεχῶς 2. σοφός 3. σωφρόνως
Mrk 12:34 when Jesus saw that he answered wisely 1
Wis 9:11 she will guide me wisely in my actions 3
Sir 20:27 He who speaks wisely will advance himself 2
wisely *See also* deal.

act wisely 1. שׂכל
Ps 14: 2 to see if there are any that act wisely 1
36: 3 he has ceased to act wisely and do good. 1

wish 1. אוה 2. אמר 3. חָפֵץ 4. חפק 5. לוּ 6. נֶפֶשׁ 7. βούλομαι 8. γνώμη 9. ἐθέλω 10. ἐπιθυμέω 11. εὔχομαι 12. ζητέω 13. ὄφελον 14. volo
Lev 27:13 if he wishes to redeem it, he shall add a fifth •
15 if he who dedicates it wishes to redeem his house •
19 if he who dedicates the field wishes to redeem it •
20 if he does not wish to redeem the field •
31 If a man wishes to redeem any of his tithe •
Num15:14 wishes to offer an offering by fire, a pleasing •
22:29 I wish I had a sword in my hand, 5
Deu 23:24 eat your fill of grapes, as many as you wish 6
25: 7 if the man does not wish to take his brother's wife 3
8 if he persists, saying, 'I do not wish to take her,' 3
Jos 15:18 Caleb said to her, "What do you wish? •
Jdg 1:14 and Caleb said to her, "What do you wish? †
1Sm 2:16 burn the fat . . and then take as much as you wish 1
1Kg 5: 9 you shall meet my wishes by providing food 4
Neh 6: 6 wish to become their king •
Job 9: 3 If one wished to contend with him, one could not 3
37:20 Did a man ever wish that he would be swallowed up? 2
Mat 7:12 So whatever you wish that men would do to you, do 9
12:38 Teacher, we wish to see a sign from you. 9
17: 4 if you wish, I will make three booths here 9
18:23 a king who wished to settle accounts 9
Mrk 6:22 Ask me for whatever you wish, and I will grant it. 9
15:15 So Pilate, wishing to satisfy the crowd 7
Lke 6:31 as you wish that men would do to you, do so to them. 9
Joh 4:27 What do you wish?" or, "Why are you talking 12
6:67 Do you also wish to go away? 9
12:21 Sir, we wish to see Jesus. 9
21:18 carry you where you do not wish to go. 9
Act 17:20 wish to know therefore what these things mean 7
18:27 when he wished to cross to Acha'ia 7
19:30 Paul wished to go in among the crowd 7
33 wishing to make a defense to the people. 9
25: 9 Festus, wishing to do the Jews a favor, said to Paul 9
9 Do you wish to go up to Jerusalem 9
20 I asked whether he wished to go to Jerusalem 7
27:43 the centurion, wishing to save Paul 7
28:18 they wished to set me at liberty 7
Rom 9: 3 For I could wish that I myself were accursed 11
1Co 4:21 What do you wish? Shall I come to you with a rod 9
7: 7 I wish that all were as I myself am 9
36 let him do as he wishes: let them marry–it is no sin. 9
39 married to whom she wishes, only in the Lord. 9
2Co 11: 1 I wish you would bear with me 13
12: 6 Though if I wish to boast, I shall not be a fool 9
20 I may come and find you not what I wish 9
20 you may find me not what you wish 9
Gal 4:20 I could wish to be present with you now 9
5:12 I wish those who unsettle you 13
Jas 4: 4 whoever wishes to be a friend of the world 7
2Pe 3: 9 not wishing that any should perish 7
1Es 4:42 the king said to him, "Ask what you wish 9
2Es 4:23 For I did not wish to inquire about the ways above 14
7: 5 If any one, then, wishes to reach the sea 14
14:22 those who wish to live in the last days may live. 14
Tob 4:19 he humbles whomever he wishes. 9
Wis 14:19 For he, perhaps wishing to please his ruler 7
Sir 0: 3 those living abroad who wished to gain learning, 7
15:16 stretch out your hand for whichever you wish. 9
23:14 then you will wish that you had never been born 9
LJr 1:45 nothing but what the craftsmen wish them to be. 7
Sus 1:15 she went in . . and wished to bathe in the garden 10
1Mc 5:67 some priests, who wished to do a brave deed, fell 7
8:13 Those whom they wish to help and to make kings 7
13 those whom they wish they depose 7
2Mc 2:24 who wish to enter upon the narratives of history 9
25 we have aimed to please those who wish to read 7
4:16 wished to imitate completely 9
9:20 If . . your affairs are as you wish 8
11:29 you wish to return home 7
12: 4 because they wished to live peaceably 9
35 wishing to take the accursed man alive 7
14:39 wishing to exhibit the enmity which he had 7
3Mc 1:15 whether they wish it or not? 9
5:11 who grants it to whomever he wishes. 9
47 wishing to witness, with invulnerable heart 7
4Mc 17: 9 wished to destroy the way of life of the Hebrews. 9

good wish for health 1. ὑγιαίνω
2Mc 9:19 and good wishes for their health and prosperity. 1

good wish for prosperity 1. εὖ πράσσω
2Mc 9:19 and good wishes for their health and prosperity. 1

wit 1. חָכְמָה
Ps 107:27 reeled and staggered . . were at their wits' end. 1
witchcraft *See* practice.

withdraw 1. אסף 2. גרע 3. הלך מן 4. חבא 5. חלק 6. מוש 7. נסע 8. עלה 9. עלה מן 10. קום 11. שוב 12. שוב אחור 13. ἀναλύω 14. ἀναχωρέω 15. ἄπειμι 16. ἀποσπάω 17. ἀποχωρέω 18. ἀφίστημι 19. ἐκλύω 20. ἐκνεύω 21. ἐκχωρέω 22. συστέλλω 23. ὑποχωρέω 24. excedo 25. separo
Num 8:25 they shall withdraw from the work of the service 11
1Sm 14:19 and Saul said to the priest, "Withdraw your hand. 1
2Sm 17:13 If he withdraws into a city . . we shall drag it 1
20: 2 the men of Israel withdrew from David 9
21 MIN#give up him alone, and I will withdraw 3
23: 9 and the men of Israel withdrew. 8
1Kg 15:19 that he may withdraw from me. 8
2Kg 3:27 they withdrew from him and returned 7
18:14 I have done wrong; withdraw from me; 11
2Ch 16: 3 that he may withdraw from me. 8
Ezr 10: 6 Then Ezra withdrew from before the house of God 10
Job 29: 8 the young men saw me and withdrew 4
36: 7 He does not withdraw his eyes from the righteous 2
Ps 85: 3 Thou didst withdraw all thy wrath; 1
Isa 60:20 no more go down, nor your moon withdraw itself; 1
Jer 34:21 king of Babylon which has withdrawn from you. 8
37: 5 they withdrew from Jerusalem. 8
11 the Chalde'an army had withdrawn from Jerusalem 8
Lam 2: 3 he has withdrawn from them his right hand 12
Dan 11:30 shall be afraid and withdraw, and shall turn back •
Hos 5: 6 will not find him; he has withdrawn from them. 5
Jol 2:10 and the stars withdraw their shining. 1
3:15 and the stars withdraw their shining. 1
Zec 14: 4 one half of the Mount shall withdraw northward 6
Mat 2:22 go there, and being warned in a dream he withdrew 14
4:12 had been arrested, he withdrew into Galilee; 14
12:15 Jesus, aware of this, withdrew from there 14
14:13 when Jesus heard this, he withdrew from there 14
15:21 and withdrew to the district of Tyre and Sidon. 14
Mrk 3: 7 Jesus withdrew with his disciples to the sea 14
Lke 5:16 he withdrew to the wilderness and prayed. 23
9:10 he took them and withdrew apart to a city 23
22:41 he withdrew from them about a stone's throw 16
Joh 5:13 Jesus had withdrawn 20
6:15 Jesus withdrew again to the mountain by himself. 14
Act 15:38 one who had withdrawn from them in Pamphyl'ia 18
19: 9 he withdrew from them 18
22:29 withdrew from him instantly 18
26:31 when they had withdrawn, they said to one another 14
2Es 5: 9 and wisdom shall withdraw into its chamber 25
7:33 and patience shall be withdrawn; ‡
12:48 neither forsaken you nor withdrawn from you 24
Jdt 13: 1 When evening came, his slaves quickly withdrew 13
14 has not withdrawn his mercy 18
Sir 4:31 withdrawn when it is time to repay. 22
Aza 1:12 do not withdraw thy mercy from us 18
1Mc 9:62 withdrew to Bethbasi in the wilderness 21
12:28 they kindled fires in their camp and withdrew. •
2Mc 4:33 having first withdrawn to a place of sanctuary 17
6:16 Therefore he never withdraws his mercy from us. 18
12: 7 because the city's gates were closed, he withdrew 13
13:16 withdrew in triumph. 19
22 gave pledges, received theirs, withdrew 15

withdraw far 1. רחק
Job 13:21 withdraw thy hand far from me 1

make withdraw 1. עלה
Jer 21: 2 and will make him withdraw from us. 1

withdrawal 1. ἀναζυγή
2Mc 13:26 how the king's attack and withdrawal turned out. 1

wither 1. אמל 2. יבש 3. מכך 4. מלל 5. נבל 6. נפל 7. צנם 8. ἀναξηραίνω 9. ἀποσβέννυμι 10. μαραίνω 11. ξηραίνω 12. ξηρός 13. aridus 14. marcesco 15. sicco
Gen 41:23 seven ears, withered, thin, and blighted 7
Job 8:12 not cut down, they wither before any other plant. 2
14: 2 He comes forth like a flower, and withers; 4
18:16 roots dry up . . and his branches wither above. 4
24:24 they wither and fade like the mallow; 3
Ps 1: 3 fruit in its season, and its leaf does not wither. 5
37: 2 like the grass, and wither like the green herb. 5
58: 7 like grass let them be trodden down and wither. •
90: 6 in the evening it fades and withers. 2
102: 4 My heart is smitten like grass, and withered; 2
129: 6 like the grass . . which withers before it grows up 2
137: 5 forget you, O Jerusalem, let my right hand wither! •
Prv 11:28 He who trusts in his riches will wither 6
Isa 1:30 For you shall be like an oak whose leaf withers 5
15: 6 the grass is withered, the new growth fails 2
24: 4 The earth mourns and withers 5
4 the world languishes and withers; 5
40: 7 The grass withers, the flower fades 2
8 The grass withers, the flower fades; 2
24 when he blows upon them, and they wither 2
Jer 8:13 even the leaves are withered 5
12: 4 and the grass of every field wither? 2
Ezk 17: 9 so that all its fresh sprouting leaves wither? 2
10 Will it not utterly wither when the east wind 2
19:12 its strong stem was withered; the fire consumed 2
47:12 Their leaves will not wither nor their fruit 5
Jol 1:12 The vine withers, the fig tree languishes. 2
12 all the trees of the field are withered; 2
Ams 1: 2 shepherds mourn, and the top of Carmel withers. 2
4: 7 and the field on which it did not rain withered; 2
Jon 4: 7 attacked the plant, so that it withered. 2
Nah 1: 4 Bashan and Carmel wither 1
Zec 11:17 Let his arm be wholly withered 2
Mat 12:10 behold, there was a man with a withered hand 12
21:19 And the fig tree withered at once. 11
20 How did the fig tree wither at once? 11
Mrk 3: 1 a man was there who had a withered hand. 11
3 he said to the man who had the withered hand 12
11:21 The fig tree which you cursed has withered. 11

Lke 6: 6 a man was there whose right hand was withered. 12
8 he said to the man who had the withered hand 12
Joh 15: 6 he is cast forth as a branch and withers 11
Jas 1:11 the sun rises . . and withers the grass 11
1Pe 1:24 The grass withers, and the flower falls 11
2Es 5:36 and make the withered flowers bloom again for me; 13
7:87 and shall wither with fear at seeing the glory 14
15:50 the glory . . shall wither like a flower 15
Wis 2: 8 before they wither. 10
Sir 6: 3 will be left like a withered tree. 12
14: 9 mean injustice withers the soul. 8
43:21 withers the tender grass like fire. 9

wither away 1. יבשׁ 2. קמל 3. *ξηραίνω*

Ps 102:11 I wither away like grass. 1
Isa 33: 9 Lebanon is confounded and withers away; 2
Ezk 17:10 wither away on the bed where it grew? 1
Mat 13: 6 since they had no root they withered away. 3
Mrk 4: 6 since it had no root it withered away. 3
11:20 they saw the fig tree withered away to its roots. 3
Lke 8: 6 as it grew up, it withered away 3

withhold 1. אפק 2. חשׂך 3. כלא 4. כלה 5. מנע 6. נוח 7. עצר 8. שׁוב 9. *ἀποκωλύω* 10. *κωλύω* 11. *στερέω*

Gen 22:12 you fear God, seeing you have not withheld 2
16 you . . have not withheld your son, your only son 2
23: 6 none of us will withhold from you his sepulchre 4
30: 2 God, who has withheld from you the fruit 5
2Sm 13:13 for he will not withhold me from you. 5
Neh 9:20 didst not withhold thy manna from their mouth 5
Job 6:14 He who withholds kindness from a friend ‡
12:15 If he withholds the waters, they dry up; 7
22: 7 you have withheld bread from the hungry. 5
31:16 If I have withheld anything that the poor 5
38:15 From the wicked their light is withheld 5
Ps 21: 2 and hast not withheld the request of his lips. 5
40:11 Do not thou, O LORD, withhold thy mercy from me 3
84:11 No good thing does the LORD withhold 5
Prv 3:27 Do not withhold good from those to whom it is due 5
11:24 another withholds what he should give 2
23:13 Do not withhold discipline from a child; 5
Ecc 7:18 hold of this, and from that withhold not your hand; 6
11: 6 sow . . and at evening withhold not your hand; 6
Isa 43: 6 north, Give up, and to the south, Do not withhold; 3
63:15 heart and thy compassion are withheld from me. 1
Jer 3: 3 Therefore the showers have been withheld 5
Ezk 18: 8 withholds his hand from iniquity 8
17 withholds his hand from iniquity 8
20:22 But I withheld my hand 8
Jol 1:13 are withheld from the house of your God. 5
Ams 4: 7 I also withheld the rain from you when there were 5
Hag 1:10 the heavens above you have withheld the dew 3
10 the earth has withheld its produce. 3
Lke 6:29 do not withhold even your shirt. 10
Sir 7:21 do not withhold from him his freedom. 11
33 withhold not kindness from the dead. 9

withhold help 1. עלם

Deu 22: 1 ox or his sheep go astray, and withhold your help 1
3 you may not withhold your help. 1
4 fallen down . . and withhold your help from them; 1

within 1. אֶל 2. אֶל מִבַּיִת 3. אֶל תּוֹךְ 4. בָּ 5. בְּבֶטֶן 6. בַּבַּיִת 7. בְּחֵיק 8. בֶּטֶן 9. בַּיְתָה 10. בְּעוֹד 11. בְּקֶרֶב 12. בְּתוֹךְ 13. כָּ 14. לָ 15. לְמִבַּיִת 16. מִבַּיִת 17. עַד 18. עַל 19. פְּנִימָה 20. קֶרֶב 21. תָּוֶךְ 22. בְּגוֹא (A) 23. עַד (A) 24. *εἰς μέσον* 25. *ἐν* 26. *ἔνδοθεν* 27. *ἔνδον* 28. *ἔνειμι* 29. *ἔσωθεν* 30. *ὑπὸ καιρόν* 31. in 32. intra

Gen 18:24 Suppose there are 50 righteous within the city; 12
25:22 The children struggled together within her; 11
40:13 within three days Pharaoh will lift up your head 10
19 within three days Pharaoh will lift up 10
Exd 8:25 Go, sacrifice to your God within the land. 4
20:10 the sojourner who is within your gates; 4
25:11 within and without shall you overlay it 16
26:33 ark of the testimony in thither within the veil; 16
37: 2 he overlaid it with pure gold within and without 16
Lev 16: 2 come . . into the holy place within the veil 16
12 and he shall bring it within the veil 14
15 and bring its blood within the veil 2
22:24 you shall not . . sacrifice within your land 4
25:29 he may redeem it within a whole year 17
30 If it is not redeemed within a full year 17
26:25 if you gather within your cities I will send 1
Num 3:38 having charge of the rites within the sanctuary •
18: 7 for all . . that is within the veil; 15
30: 3 vows a vow . . while within her father's house 4
16 while in her youth, within her father's house. •
36: 6 marry within the family of the tribe 14
Deu 5:14 or the sojourner who is within your gates 4
12:12 the Levite that is within your towns 4
15 slaughter and eat flesh within any of your towns 4
17 You may not eat within your towns the tithe 4
18 eat . . you and . . the Levite who is within your towns; 4
21 may eat within your towns as much as you desire. 4
14:21 may give it to the alien who is within your towns 4
27 not forsake the Levite who is within your towns 4
28 all the tithe . . and lay it up within your towns; 4
29 fatherless, and the widow . . within your towns 4
15: 7 towns within your land which the LORD . . gives 4
22 You shall eat it within your towns; 4
16: 5 not offer . . within any of your towns 4
11 Levite who is within your towns 4
14 fatherless, and the widow . . within your towns. 4
17: 2 found among you, within any of your towns 4
8 case within your towns which is too difficult 4
23:10 outside the camp . . not come within the camp; 3
11 when the sun is down, he may come within the camp. 3
16 place . . he shall choose within one of your towns 4
24:14 sojourners . . in your land within your towns; 4
26:12 that they may eat within your towns and be filled 4
28:11 abound . . within the land which the LORD swore 18
31:12 Assemble . . the sojourner within your towns 4
Jos 1:11 within three days you are to pass over this 10
6: 1 Jericho was shut up from within and from without •
17 all that is within it shall be devoted to the LORD 4
24 they burned the city with fire, and all within it; 4
16: 9 set apart for . . within the inheritance 12
Jdg 2: 9 buried him within the bounds of his inheritance 4
9:51 there was a strong tower within the city 12
11:26 why did you not recover them within that time? 4
14:12 tell me . . within the seven days of the feast •
1Sm 3: 3 Samuel was lying . . within the temple of the LORD 4
13:11 you did not come within the days appointed 14
14:14 twenty men within . . half a furrow's length 4
18:10 and he raved within his house 12
25:36 And Nabal's heart was merry within him 18
37 his wife told him . . and his heart died within him 11
26: 5 Saul was lying within the encampment 4
7 there lay Saul sleeping within the encampment 4
27: 1 of seeking me . . within the borders of Israel 4
2Sm 20: 4 Call . . Judah together to me within three days •
1Kg 6:16 he built this within as an inner sanctuary 16
18 The cedar within the house was carved in the form 1
7:31 Its opening was within a crown which projected 16
21:23 The dogs shall eat Jez'ebel within the bounds 4
2Kg 7:11 and it was told within the king's household. 19
18:26 do not speak . . within the hearing of the people 4
1Ch 6:54 their settlements within their borders 4
Ezr 8:29 within the chambers of the house of the LORD. •
33 On the fourth day, within the house of our God 4
9: 8 to give us a secure hold within his holy place 4
10: 8 that if any one did not come within three days 14
9 assembled at Jerusalem within the three days; 14
Neh 4:22 every man . . pass the night within Jerusalem 12
6:10 together in the house of God, within the temple 3
7: 4 city . . large, but the people within it were few 12
Est 1:12 the king . . and his anger burned within him. 4
Job 4:21 If their tent-cord is plucked up within them 4
19:27 not another. My heart faints within me! 7
20: 2 answer me, because of my haste within me. 4
14 in his stomach; it is the gall of asps within him. 11
30:16 now my soul is poured out within me; 18
32:18 the spirit within me constrains me. 8
Ps 22:14 my heart is like wax, it is melted within my breast; 12
39: 3 my heart became hot within me. 11
40: 8 O my God; thy law is within my heart. 12
10 I have not hid thy saving help within my heart 12
42: 5 O my soul, and why are you disquieted within me? 18
6 My soul is cast down within me 18
11 O my soul, and why are you disquieted within me? 18
43: 5 O my soul, and why are you disquieted within me? 18
48: 3 Within her citadels God has shown himself a sure 4
51:10 O God, and put a new and right spirit within me. 11
55: 4 My heart is in anguish within me 11
10 mischief and trouble are within it 11
14 within God's house we walked in fellowship. 4
101: 2 walk with integrity of heart within my house; 11
103: 1 all that is within me, bless his holy name! 20
107: 5 hungry and thirsty, their soul fainted within 4
109:22 poor and needy, and my heart is stricken within 11
122: 2 feet . . standing within your gates, O Jerusalem! 4
7 Peace be within your walls, and security within 4
7 Peace . . walls, and security within your towers! 4
8 I will say, "Peace be within you! 4
128: 3 wife . . like a fruitful vine within your house; 4
143: 4 Therefore my spirit faints within me; 21
4 my heart within me is appalled. 12
147:13 For he . . blesses your sons within you. 11
Prv 4:21 keep them within your heart. 12
22:18 for it will be pleasant if you keep them within 5
Sng 3:10 it was lovingly wrought within by the daughters 21
5: 4 and my heart was thrilled within me. 18
Isa 7: 8 Within 65 years E'phraim will be broken 10
19: 1 heart of the Egyptians will melt within them. 11
3 spirit of the Egyptians within them will be 11
14 LORD . . mingled within her a spirit of confusion; 11
21:16 Within a year, according to the years 10
26: 9 my spirit within me earnestly seeks thee. 11
36:11 within the hearing of the people . . on the wall. 4
56: 5 give in my house and within my walls a monument 4
60:18 or destruction within your borders; 4
Jer 4:14 How long shall your evil thoughts lodge within 11
6: 6 there is nothing but oppression within her. 11
7 violence and destruction are heard within her; 4
8:18 beyond healing, my heart is sick within me. 18
23: 9 My heart is broken within me, all my bones shake; 11
28: 3 Within two years I will bring back to this place 10
11 of all the nations within two years. 10
31:33 says the LORD: I will put my law within them 11
Lam 1:20 my soul is in tumult, my heart is wrung within me 11
3:20 soul . . thinks of it and is bowed down within me. 18
Ezk 1:16 being as it were a wheel within a wheel. 12
3:24 said to me, "Go, shut yourself within your house. 12
7:15 pestilence and famine are within; 16
10:10 likeness, as if a wheel were within a wheel. 12
11:19 and put a new spirit within them; 11
12:24 no . . divination within the house of Israel. 12
16:47 within a very little time you were more corrupt 13
25: 6 and rejoiced with all the malice within you 4
30: 6 to Syene they shall fall within her by the sword 4
36:26 and a new spirit I will put within you; 11
27 I will put my spirit within you 11
37:14 I will put my Spirit within you, and you shall live 4
40:43 hooks . . were fastened round about within. 6
44:17 at the gates of the inner court, and within. 9
Dan 6:12 god or man within 30 days except to you, O king 23
7:15 As for me, Daniel, my spirit within me was anxious 22
11:20 within a few days he shall be broken 4
Hos 5: 4 For the spirit of harlotry is within them 11
11: 8 My heart recoils within me, my compassion grows 18
Ams 3: 9 of Sama'ria, and see the great tumults within her 12
Jon 2: 7 my soul fainted within me, I remembered the LORD; 18
Mic 5: 6 into our land and treads within our border. 4
Zep 3: 3 Her officials within her are roaring lions; 11
5 The LORD within her is righteous, he does no wrong; 11
Zec 2: 5 says the LORD, and I will be the glory within her. 12
12: 1 and formed the spirit of man within him 11
Mat 23:27 within they are full of dead men's bones 29
28 within you are full of hypocrisy and iniquity. 29
Mrk 2: 8 that they thus questioned within themselves 25
7:21 from within, out of the heart of man 29
23 All these evil things come from within 29
Lke 11: 7 he will answer from within, 'Do not bother me 29
41 give for alms those things which are within; 28
19:44 you and your children within you 25
24:32 Did not our hearts burn within us 25
Joh 5:42 you have not the love of God within you. 25
Act 17:16 his spirit was provoked within him 25
Rom 7:17 no longer I . . but sin which dwells within me 25
18 For I know that nothing good dwells within me 25
20 no longer I . . but sin which dwells within me. 25
1Co 6:19 a temple of the Holy Spirit within you 25
2Co 7: 5 fighting without and fear within. 29
Eph 3:20 the power at work within us 25
Col 1:29 the energy which he mightily inspires within me. 25
2Ti 1: 6 rekindle the gift of God that is within you 25
14 the Holy Spirit who dwells within us. 25
1Pe 1:11 indicated by the Spirit of Christ within them 25
Rev 4: 8 creatures . . full of eyes all around and within 29
5: 1 I saw . . a scroll written within and on the back 29
7:15 and serve him day and night within his temple; 25
11:19 ark of his covenant was seen within his temple; 25
1Es 9: 4 if any did not meet there within two or three days 25
5 assembled at Jerusalem within three days 25
2Es 2:22 Protect the old and the young within your walls; 32
4:40 her womb can keep the child within her any longer. 31
6:36 my heart was troubled within me again 31
7:59 Weigh within yourself what you have thought 31
9: 8 in my land and within my borders 31
13:48 who are found within my holy borders 31
Tob 3: 6 great is the sorrow within me 25
13:10 May he cheer those within you who are captives 25
10 love those within you who are distressed 25
Jdt 8:11 the Lord turns and helps us within so many days. 25
15 choose to help us within these five days 25
15 power to protect us within any time he pleases 25
33 within the days after which you have promised 25
14: 4 you and all who live within the borders of Israel •
Wis 7: 2 within the period of ten months •
1Mc 2:46 that they found within the borders of Israel. 25
5:30 and attacking the Jews within. •
11:45 the men of the city assembled within the city 24
2Mc 5:14 Within the total of three days 25
6: 4 within the sacred precincts 25
7:20 she saw her seven sons perish within a single day 30
22 who set in order the elements within each of you. •
10:34 The men within . . blasphemed terribly 27
12:14 those who were within 27
28 25,000 of those who were within it. 27
3Mc 5:42 changes of mind which had come about within him 25
4Mc 18: 2 reason is master . . not only of sufferings from within 26

within *See also* dwell.

without 1. אַיִן 2. אֶפֶס 3. בְּאַיִן 4. בְּאֶפֶס 5. בְּלֹא 6. בְּלִי 7. בִּלְעֲדֵי 8. וְלֹא 9. חָסֵר 10. כִּי אִם 11. כרת מִן 12. לֹא 13. לֹא בָּ 14. לְלֹא 15. מֵאַיִן 16. מִבְּלִי 17. מִבַּלְעַד 18. מִבַּלְעֲדֵי 19. מִן 20. סור 21. עַד אַיִן 22. פקד 23. דִּי לָא (A) 24. לָא (A) 25. *ἄνευ* 26. *ἄπειμι* 27. *ἀπό* 28. *ἄτερ* 29. *ἐὰν μή* 30. *ἐλαττόω* 31. *ἔρημος* 32. *ἤ* 33. *καὶ μή* 34. *καὶ οὐ* 35. *μή* 36. *μηδείς* 37. *μὴ ἔχω* 38. *οὐ* 39. *οὐδέ* 40. *οὐκ ἀπό* 41. *οὐκ ἔχω* 42. *οὐ μετά* 43. *χωρίς* 44. non 45. non sum 46. sine

Gen 41:44 to Joseph, "I am Pharaoh, and without your consent 7
Exd 14:20 night passed without one coming near the other 12
21:11 go out for nothing, without payment of money. 1
22:10 or is driven away, without any one seeing it 1
Lev 15:11 touches without having rinsed his hands in water 12
26:43 while it lies desolate without them 19
Num15:24 done unwittingly without the knowledge 19
35:22 But if he stabbed him suddenly without enmity 5
22 if he . . hurled anything on him without lying in wait 5
23 stone . . and without seeing him cast it upon him 5
Deu 4:42 without being at enmity with him in time past 12
8: 9 in which you will eat bread without scarcity 12
19: 4 kills . . without having been at enmity with him 6
32: 4 God of faithfulness and without iniquity, just 1
Jdg 7:12 and their camels were without number, as the sand 1
Rut 2: 7 she has . . without resting even for a moment. 38
1Sm 20: 2 does nothing . . without disclosing it to me; 8
2Sm 3:29 never be without one who has a discharge 11
14:28 Ab'salom dwelt . . without coming into the king's 8
20:10 and shed his . . without striking a second blow; 8
1Kg 2:32 without the knowledge of my father David 12
22: 1 Syria and Israel continued without war. 1
2Kg 18:25 is it without the LORD that I have come up 18
1Ch 22: 4 cedar timbers without number; 1
15 and all kinds of craftsmen without number 1
2Ch 5:11 without regard to their divisions; 1
12: 3 people were without number who came with him 1
15: 3 For a long time Israel was without the true God 14
3 Israel was . . and without a teaching priest 14
3 For a long time Israel was . . without law; 14
Ezr 6: 8 cost is to be paid . . in full and without delay 23
9 let that be given to them day by day without fail 23
7:22 oil, and salt without prescribing how much. 24
Est 4:11 goes to the king . . without being called 12
9:27 that without fail they would keep these two days 12
Job 4:20 they perish for ever without any regarding it. 6
21 do they not die, and that without wisdom?' 13
5: 9 marvelous things without number 21
6: 6 that which is tasteless be eaten without salt 6
7: 6 and come to their end without hope. 4
9:10 and marvelous things without number. 21
35 Then I would speak without fear of him 8
11:15 then you will lift up your face without blemish; 19
12:25 They grope in the dark without light; 8
21:10 Their bull breeds without fail; their cow calves 8
24: 7 They lie all night naked, without clothing 6
10 They go about naked, without clothing; hungry 6
31:19 lack of clothing, or a poor man without covering; 1
39 if I have eaten its yield without payment 6
33: 9 You say, 'I am clean, without transgression; 6
34: 6 incurable, though I am without transgression. 6
24 He shatters the mighty without investigation 12
35 Job speaks without knowledge 13
35 his words are without insight. 13
35:16 he multiplies words without knowledge. 6
36:12 perish by the sword, and die without knowledge. 6
38: 2 darkens counsel by words without knowledge? 6
41:33 there is not his like, a creature without fear. 6
42: 3 this that hides counsel without knowledge? 6
Ps 26: 1 I have trusted in the LORD without wavering. 12
32: 9 like a horse or a mule, without understanding 1
35:15 whom I knew not slandered me without ceasing; 12
40:12 For evils have encompassed me without number; 21
56: 4 whose word I praise, in God I trust without a fear. 12
11 in God I trust without fear. What can man do to me? 12
64: 4 shooting at him suddenly and without fear. 12
77: 2 my hand is stretched out without wearying; 12
105:34 locusts came, and young locusts without number; 1
Prv 1:33 will be at ease, without dread of evil. 19
6: 7 Without having any chief, officer or ruler 1
7: 7 I have seen . . a young man without sense 9
9: 4 To him who is without sense she says 9
16 to him who is without sense she says 9
11:22 is a beautiful woman without discretion. 20
14:28 but without people a prince is ruined. 2
15:22 Without counsel plans go wrong 3
17:18 A man without sense gives a pledge, and becomes 9
19: 2 It is not good for a man to be without knowledge 5
24:30 I passed by . . the vineyard of a man without sense; 9
25:14 Like clouds and wind without rain is a man 1
28 A man without self-control is like a city broken 1
28 like a city broken into and left without walls. 1
Sng 6: 8 80 concubines, and maidens without number. 1
Isa 1:30 like an oak . . and like a garden without water. 1
5: 9 beautiful houses, without inhabitant. 15
6:11 said: "Until cities lie waste without inhabitant 15
11 cities . . and houses without men 15
22: 3 rulers . . without the bow they were captured. 19
23: 1 for Tyre is laid waste, without house or haven! 19
27:11 For this is a people without discernment; 12
28: 8 full of vomit, no place is without filthiness. 6
30: 2 to go down to Egypt, without asking for my counsel 12
34:16 none shall be without her mate. 22
36:10 Moreover, is it without the LORD that I have come 18
47: 1 sit on the ground without a throne, O daughter 1
52: 3 and you shall be redeemed without money. 13
55: 1 Come, buy wine and milk without money 5
1 wine and milk without money and without price. 5
56:10 are blind, they are all without knowledge; 12
Jer 2:15 his cities are in ruins, without inhabitant. 16
32 people have forgotten me days without number. 1
4: 7 your cities will be ruins without inhabitant. 15
9:11 Judah a desolation, without inhabitant. 16
10:14 Every man is stupid and without knowledge; 19
15:13 treasures I will give as spoil, without price 13
20:16 cities which the LORD overthrew without pity; 12
26: 9 this city shall be desolate, without inhabitant'? 15
32:43 It is a desolation, without man or beast; 15
33:10 which you say, 'It is a waste without man or beast 15
10 desolate, without man or inhabitant or beast 15
12 In this place which is waste, without man or beast 15
34:22 Judah a desolation without inhabitant. 15
44:19 was it without our husbands' approval 17
22 and a waste and a curse, without inhabitant 15
46:19 become a waste, a ruin, without inhabitant. 15
23 numerous than locusts; they are without number. 1
48:45 fugitives stop without strength; 19
51:17 Every man is stupid and without knowledge; 19
29 Babylon a desolation, without inhabitant. 15
37 a horror and a hissing, without inhabitant. 15
Lam 1: 6 they fled without strength before the pursuer. 5
2: 2 Lord has destroyed without mercy all . . Jacob; 8
17 as he ordained . . he has demolished without pity; 8
21 hast slain them, slaughtering without mercy. 12
3: 2 and brought me into darkness without any light; 8
43 Thou hast . . and pursued us, slaying without pity; 12
49 My eyes will flow without ceasing 8
49 eyes will flow without ceasing, without respite 15
Ezk 1: 9 straight forward, without turning as they went. 12
12 they went, without turning as they went. 12
17 four directions without turning as they went. 12
10:11 four directions without turning as they went 12
11 followed without turning as they went. 12
22:29 extorted from the sojourner without redress. 5
24: 6 piece after piece, without making any choice. †
38:11 all of them dwelling without walls 3
42:14 outer court without laying there the garments †
Dan 8: 5 he-goat came . . without touching the ground; 1
Hos 3: 4 shall dwell many days without king or prince 1
4 dwell many days . . without sacrifice or pillar 1
4 dwell many days . . without ephod or teraphim. 1
4:14 people without understanding . . come to ruin. 12
7:11 E'phraim is like a dove, silly and without sense 1
8: 4 They set up princes, but without my knowledge. 12
Jol 1: 6 against my land, powerful and without number; 1
Ams 3: 7 GOD does nothing, without revealing his secret 10
Mic 3: 6 it shall be night to you, without vision 19
6 and darkness to you, without divination. 19
Nah 3: 3 heaps of corpses, dead bodies without end– 1
9 was her strength . . and that without limit; 1
Zep 3: 6 cities have been made desolate, without a man 6
6 desolate, without a man, without an inhabitant. 6
Mat 9:36 like sheep without a shepherd. 41
10:29 fall to the ground without your Father's will. 25
13:34 he said nothing to them without a parable. 43
22:12 how did you get in here without a wedding garment?' 37
23:23 without neglecting the others. 35
Mrk 4:34 he did not speak to them without a parable 43
6:34 because they were like sheep without a shepherd; 41
Lke 6:49 a house on the ground without a foundation; 43
11:42 without neglecting the others. 33
44 men walk over them without knowing it. 38
Joh 1: 3 without him was not anything made that was made. 43
7:51 judge a man without first giving him a hearing 29
Act 5:26 brought them, but without violence 42
9: 9 for three days he was without sight 35
38 Please come to us without delay. 35
10:20 go down, and accompany them without hesitation; 36
24:18 without any crowd or tumult. 42
Rom 10:14 And how are they to hear without a preacher? 43
1Co 4: 8 Without us you have become kings! 43
9: 7 without eating any of its fruit 38
7 without getting some of the milk? 38
10:25 without raising any question *
27 eat . . without raising any question *
11:29 who eats and drinks without discerning the body 35
2Co 10:12 they are without understanding. 38
16 without boasting of work already done 38
Eph 5:27 without spot or wrinkle or any such thing 37
Php 2:14 Do all things without grumbling or questioning 43
1Ti 1: 7 without understanding 35
2: 8 lifting holy hands without anger or quarreling; 43
5:21 I charge you to keep these rules without favor 43
Phm 1:14 I preferred to do nothing without your consent 43
Heb 4:15 who . . has been tempted as we are, yet without sin. 43
7:20 it was not without an oath. 43
21 took their office without an oath 43
9: 7 not without taking blood 43
18 was not ratified without blood. 43
22 without the shedding of blood 43
10:28 dies without mercy 43
11: 6 without faith it is impossible to please him. 43
12: 8 If you are left without discipline 43
14 holiness without which no one will see the Lord. 43
Jas 1: 5 God, who gives to all . . without reproaching 35
2:16 without giving them the things needed 35
1Pe 1: 8 Without having seen him you love him; 38
2:16 without using your freedom as a pretext for evil; 35
3: 1 won without a word by the behavior of their wives 25
1Es 4:17 men cannot exist without women. 43
8:88 to destroy us without leaving a root or seed 35
2Es 1:35 who without having heard me will believe 44
3: 7 peoples and clans without number. 45
29 I saw ungodly deeds without number 45
4: 9 and without which you cannot exist 46
32 When heads of grain without number are sown 45
6:28 the truth, which has been so long without fruit 46
7:98 and shall be confident without confusion 44
98 and shall be glad without fear 44
10: 4 but without ceasing mourn and fast until I die. 46
13:36 the mountain carved out without hands. 46
38 and will destroy them without effort by the law 46
14:20 and its inhabitants are without light. 46
Tob 6:12 without incurring the penalty of death 32
8:12 let us bury him without any one knowing about it. †
Jdt 10:13 without losing one of his men, captured or slain. 34
12:12 let such a woman go without enjoying her company 38
AEs 13: 6 destroyed . . without pity or mercy 25
Wis 9: 6 yet without the wisdom that comes from thee 26
16:22 Snow and ice withstood fire without melting 34
19:13 not come upon the sinners without prior signs 25
Sir 19:16 A person may make a slip without intending it. 40
31:27 What is life to a man who is without wine? 30
32:19 Do nothing without deliberation 25
33:29 do nothing without discretion. 25
34: 8 Without such deceptions 25
38:32 Without them a city cannot be established 25
51:25 Get these things for yourselves without money. 25
Bar 2:23 land will be a desolation without inhabitants. 27
Sus 1:48 condemned . . without examination 38
48 condemned . . without learning the facts? 39
Bel 1:26 I will slay the dragon without sword or club. 25
1Mc 8:26 without receiving any return. *
28 do so without deceit. 42
14:44 to convene an assembly . . without his permission 25
2Mc 4: 6 without the king's attention 25
12:15 without battering-rams or engines of war 28
3Mc 5: 6 the Jews were left without any aid 31
7: 5 without any inquiry or examination 25
12 freely and without royal authority 25
4Mc 2: 8 to lend without interest to the needy 43

without (2) 1. בַּחוּץ 2. חוּץ 3. חוּצָה 4. מִחוּץ
5. ἔξωθεν

Exd 25:11 within and without shall you overlay it 4
37: 2 he overlaid it with pure gold within and without 4
Jos 6: 1 Jericho was shut up from within and from without †
Isa 33: 7 Behold, the valiant ones cry without; 2
Ezk 7:15 The sword is without 1
40:44 he brought me from without into the inner court 3
46: 2 enter by the vestibule of the gate from without 2
Hos 7: 1 thief breaks in, and the bandits raid without. 1
2Co 7: 5 fighting without and fear within. 5
4Mc 18: 2 but also of those from without. 5

without *See* God, anything, blemish, cause, ceasing, child, cost, defect, delay, distraction, doubt, effect, exception, excuse, fail, father, fear, food, form, genealogy, grudging, guile, help, honor, hope, insincerity, intelligence, intent, knowing, law, leave, meaning, mercy, mother, number, objection, offspring, pay, paying, payment, pity, price, quibbling, reproach, result, seam, sin, spot, stopping, toil, tribute, uncertainty, understanding, village, warning, wavering, wisdom, witness.

without even 1. μηδέ

2Mc 13: 7 without even burial in the earth. 1

withstand 1. חזק 2. יצב 3. עמד בְּפָנִים 4. עמד לְנֶגֶד
5. עמד לִפְנֵי 6. עמד נֶגֶד 7. עמד עַל 8. קום 9. שָׂטָן
10. ἀνθίστημι 11. ἀνυπόστατος 12. ἐν 13. κωλύω
14. πρός 15. ὑπομένω 16. ὑφίστημι 17. sustineo

Num22:32 Behold, I have come forth to withstand you 9
Jos 21:44 not one of all their enemies had withstood them 3
23: 9 no man has been able to withstand you to this day. 3
Jdg 2:14 they could no longer withstand their enemies. 5
2Ch 13: 7 when Rehobo'am . . could not withstand them. 1
8 you think to withstand the kingdom of the LORD 1
20: 6 so that none is able to withstand thee. 2
26:18 they withstood King Uzzi'ah, and said to him 7
Ecc 4:12 against one who is alone, two will withstand him. 6
Lam 1:14 into the hands of those whom I cannot withstand. 8
Dan 10:13 prince . . Persia withstood me 21 days; 4
Lke 21:15 will be able to withstand or contradict. 10
Act 6:10 could not withstand the wisdom and the Spirit 10
11:17 who was I that I could withstand God? 13
13: 8 El'ymas the magician . . withstood them 10
Eph 6:13 that you may be able to withstand in the evil day 10
2Es 7:89 and withstood danger every hour 17
Jdt 6: 4 They cannot withstand us 10
11:18 not one of them will withstand you. 10
Wis 10:16 withstood dread kings with wonders and signs. 10
11: 3 They withstood their enemies 10
21 who can withstand the might of thy arm? 10
16:22 Snow and ice withstood fire without melting 15
18:21 he withstood the anger 10
Sir 43: 3 who can withstand its burning heat? 16
46: 7 they withstood the congregation 10

50: 4 fortified the city to withstand a seige. 12
1Mc 3:53 How will we be able to withstand them 16
6: 4 they withstood him in battle 10
7:25 realized that he could not withstand them 16
10:73 now you will not be able to withstand my cavalry 16
2Mc 8: 5 the Gentiles could not withstand him 11
10:18 well equipped to withstand a siege 14
4Mc 15:32 endured nobly and withstood the wintry storms 15
16:23 It is unreasonable . . not to withstand pain. 10

withstand a siege 1. *συγκλείω*

1Mc 6:49 they had no provisions there to withstand a siege 1

witness 1. עֵד 2. עֵדָה 3. עוּד 4. ענה 5. שׂמע
6. *διαμαρτυρία* 7. *μαρτυρέω* 8. *μαρτυρία*
9. *μαρτύριον* 10. *μάρτυς* 11. *οἶδα* 12. testimonium
13. testis

Gen 21:30 you may be a witness for me that I dug this well. 2
31:44 and let it be a witness between you and me. 1
48 This heap is a witness between you and me today. 1
50 remember, God is witness between you and me. 1
52 This heap is a witness, and the pillar is a witness 1
52 This heap is a witness, and the pillar is a witness 2
Exd 20:16 You shall not bear false witness against 1
23: 1 with a wicked man, to be a malicious witness. 1
Lev 5: 1 to testify, and though he is a witness 1
Num 5:13 there is no witness against her 1
35:30 put to death on the evidence of witnesses; 1
30 no . . put to death on the testimony of one witness. 1
Deu 5:20 'Neither shall you bear false witness 1
17: 6 On the evidence of two witnesses or of three 1
6 On the evidence of two . . or of three witnesses 1
6 not be put to death on the evidence of one witness. 1
7 hand of the witnesses shall be first against him 1
19:15 A single witness shall not prevail against a man 1
15 only on the evidence of two witnesses, or of three 1
15 evidence of two witnesses, or of three witnesses 1
16 If a malicious witness rises against any man 1
18 if the witness is a false witness and has accused 1
18 if the witness is a false witness and has accused 1
31:19 that this song may be a witness for me against 1
21 this song shall confront them as a witness 1
26 that it may be there for a witness against you. 1
Jos 22:27 but to be a witness between us and you 1
28 but to be a witness between us and you.' 1
34 The Reubenites and . . called the altar Witness; 1
34 it is a witness between us that the LORD is God. 1
24:22 You are witnesses against yourselves 1
22 And they said, "We are witnesses. 1
27 this stone shall be a witness against us; 2
27 therefore it shall be a witness against you 2
Jdg 11:10 The LORD will be witness between us; we will 5
Rut 4: 9 You are witnesses this day that I have bought 1
10 you are witnesses this day. 1
11 people . . and the elders, said, "We are witnesses. 1
1Sm 6:18 The great stone . . is a witness to this day 1
12: 5 The LORD is witness against you, and his anointed 1
5 The LORD . . and his anointed is witness this day 1
5 And they said, "He is witness. 1
6 The LORD is witness, who appointed Moses 10
20:12 The LORD, the God of Israel, be witness! 11
Job 10:17 thou dost renew thy witnesses against me 1
16: 8 has shriveled me up, which is a witness against me; 1
19 Even now, behold, my witness is in heaven 1
Ps 27:12 for false witnesses have risen against me 1
35:11 Malicious witnesses rise up; 1
Prv 6:19 a false witness who breathes out lies 1
12:17 but a false witness utters deceit. 1
14: 5 A faithful witness does not lie 1
5 but a false witness breathes out lies. 1
25 A truthful witness saves lives 1
19: 5 A false witness will not go unpunished 1
9 A false witness will not go unpunished 1
28 A worthless witness mocks at justice 1
21:28 A false witness will perish 1
24:28 not a witness against your neighbor without cause 1
25:18 who bears false witness against his neighbor 1
Isa 3: 9 Their partiality witnesses against them; 4
8: 2 I got reliable witnesses, Uri'ah the priest 1
19:20 It will be a sign and a witness to the LORD of hosts 1
30: 8 for the time to come as a witness for ever. 1
33: 8 Covenants are broken, witnesses are despised 1
43: 9 Let them bring their witnesses to justify them 1
10 You are my witnesses," says the LORD 1
12 and you are my witnesses," says the LORD. 1
44: 8 you are my witnesses! Is there a God besides me? 1
9 their witnesses neither see nor know 1
55: 4 Behold, I made him a witness to the peoples 1
Jer 29:23 I am the one who knows, and I am witness 1
32:10 I signed the deed, sealed it, got witnesses 1
12 in the presence of the witnesses who signed 1
25 Buy the field for money and get witnesses 1
44 deeds shall be signed and sealed and witnessed 3
42: 5 May the LORD be a true and faithful witness 1
Hos 7:10 The pride of Israel witnesses against him; 4
Mic 1: 2 and let the Lord GOD be a witness against you 1
Zep 3: 8 for the day when I arise as a witness. 1
Mal 2:12 any to witness or answer, or to bring an offering *
14 Because the LORD was witness to the covenant 3
3: 5 I will be a swift witness against the sorcerers 1
Mat 18:16 by the evidence of two or three witnesses. 10
23:31 Thus you witness against yourselves 7
26:65 Why do we still need witnesses? 10
Mrk 14:56 their witness did not agree. 8
63 Why do we still need witnesses? 10
Lke 11:48 So you are witnesses 10
24:48 You are witnesses of these things. 10
Joh 15:27 you also are witnesses 7
Act 1: 8 you shall be my witnesses in Jerusalem 10
22 become with us a witness to his resurrection. 10
2:32 of that we all are witnesses. 10
3:15 To this we are witnesses. 10
5:32 we are witnesses to these things 10
6:13 and set up false witnesses who said 10
7:44 the tent of witness in the wilderness 9
58 the witnesses laid down their garments 10
10:39 we are witnesses to all that he did 10
41 to us who were chosen by God as witnesses 10
13:31 who are now his witnesses to the people. 10
22:15 you will be a witness for him to all men 10
20 when the blood of Stephen thy witness was shed 10
Rom 1: 9 For God is my witness, whom I serve with my spirit 10
2Co 1:23 I call God to witness against me 10
13: 1 by the evidence of two or three witnesses. 10
Php 1: 8 For God is my witness 10
1Th 2: 5 or a cloak for greed, as God is witness; 10
10 You are witnesses, and God also 10
1Ti 5:19 except on the evidence of two or three witnesses. 10
6:12 in the presence of many witnesses. 10
2Ti 2: 2 have heard from me before many witnesses 10
Heb 7:17 For it is witnessed of him 7
10:28 at the testimony of two or three witnesses. 10
12: 1 surrounded by so great a cloud of witnesses 10
1Pe 5: 1 elder and witness of the sufferings of Christ 10
1Jn 5: 7 the Spirit is the witness 7
8 three witnesses, the Spirit, the water . . blood 7
Rev 1: 5 and from Jesus Christ the faithful witness 10
2:13 the days of An'tipas my witness, my faithful one 10
3:14 words of the Amen, the faithful and true witness 10
6: 9 slain for the word of God and for the witness 8
11: 3 I will grant my two witnesses power to prophesy 10
15: 5 temple of the tent of witness in heaven was opened 9
2Es 2: 5 I call upon you, father, as a witness 13
7:94 they see the witness which he who formed them 12
Wis 1: 6 because God is witness of his inmost feelings 10
4: 6 witnesses of evil against their parents 10
Sir 36:15 Bear witness to those 9
4Mc 16:16 you are called to bear witness for the nation. 6

witness (2) 1. חזה (A) 2. *θεάομαι* 3. *ὁράω*

Ezr 4:14 not fitting for us to witness the king's dishonor 1
Jdt 7:27 we shall not witness the death of our babes 3
15: 8 came to witness the good things 2
3Mc 5:47 wishing to witness, with invulnerable heart 2
4Mc 15:24 witnessed the destruction of seven children 3

witness *See* bear, call.

false witness 1. *ψευδομαρτυρία* 2. *ψευδόμαρτυς*

Mat 15:19 fornication, theft, false witness, slander. 1
26:60 though many false witnesses came forward 2

without witness 1. *ἀμάρτυρος*

Act 14:17 yet he did not leave himself without witness 1

wizard 1. יִדְּעֹנִי

Lev 19:31 Do not turn to mediums or wizards; do not seek them 1
20: 6 If a person turns to mediums and wizards 1
27 A man or a woman who is a medium or a wizard 1
Deu 18:11 charmer, or a medium, or a wizard, or a necromancer. 1
1Sm 28: 3 And Saul had put the mediums and the wizards out 1
9 cut off the mediums and . . wizards from the land. 1
2Kg 21: 6 and dealt with mediums and with wizards. 1
23:24 Josi'ah put away the mediums and the wizards 1
2Ch 33: 6 dealt with mediums and with wizards. 1
Isa 8:19 the mediums and the wizards who chirp and mutter 1
19: 3 the sorcerers, and the mediums and the wizards; 1

woe 1. אוֹי 2. אוֹיָה 3. אִי 4. אַלְלַי 5. הוֹי 6. הִי 7. רַע
8. *οὐαί* 9. vae

Num21:29 Woe to you, O Moab! You are undone, O people 1
1Sm 4: 7 Woe to us! For nothing like this has happened 1
8 Woe to us! Who can deliver us from the power 1
Job 10:15 If I am wicked, woe to me! 4
Ps 120: 5 Woe is me, that I sojourn in Meshech 2
Prv 23:29 Who has woe? Who has sorrow? Who has strife? 1
Ecc 4:10 but woe to him who is alone when he falls 8
10:16 Woe to you, O land, when your king is a child 3
Isa 3: 9 Woe to them! For they have brought evil 1
11 Woe to the wicked! It shall be ill with him 1
5: 8 Woe to those who join house to house 5
11 Woe to those who rise early in the morning 5
18 Woe to those who draw iniquity with . . falsehood 5
20 Woe to those who call evil good and good evil 5
21 Woe to those who are wise in their own eyes 5
22 Woe to those who are heroes at drinking wine 5
6: 5 Woe is me! For I am lost; for I am a man of unclean 1
10: 1 Woe to those who decree iniquitous decrees 5
24:16 But I say, "I pine away, I pine away. Woe is me! 1
28: 1 Woe to the proud crown of the drunkards 5
29:15 Woe to those who hide deep from the LORD their 5
30: 1 Woe to the rebellious children," says the LORD 5
31: 1 Woe to those who go down to Egypt for help 5
33: 1 Woe to you, destroyer, who yourself have not 5
45: 7 I make weal and create woe 7
9 Woe to him who strives with his Maker 5
10 Woe to him who says to a father, 'What are you 5
Jer 4:13 woe to us, for we are ruined! 1
31 Woe is me! I am fainting before murderers. 1
6: 4 attack at noon!" "Woe to us, for the day declines 1
10:19 Woe is me because of my hurt! My wound is grievous. 1
13:27 Woe to you, O Jerusalem! 1
15:10 Woe is me, my mother, that you bore me, a man 1
22:13 Woe to him who builds his house 5
23: 1 Woe to the shepherds who destroy and scatter 5
45: 3 Woe is me! for the LORD has added sorrow to my pain; 1
48: 1 Woe to Nebo, for it is laid waste! 5
46 Woe to you, O Moab! The people of Chemosh is undone 1
50:27 Woe to them, for their day has come 5
Lam 5:16 crown has fallen . . woe to us, for we have sinned! 1
Ezk 2:10 on it words of lamentation and mourning and woe. 6
13: 3 says the Lord GOD, Woe to the foolish prophets 5
18 Woe to the women who sew magic bands 5
16:23 woe, woe to you! says the Lord GOD 1
23 woe, woe to you! says the Lord GOD 1
24: 6 Woe to the bloody city 1
9 thus says the Lord GOD: Woe to the bloody city! 1
Hos 7:13 Woe to them, for they have strayed from me! 1
9:12 Woe to them when I depart from them! 1
Ams 5:18 Woe to you who desire the day of the LORD! 5
6: 1 Woe to those who are at ease in Zion 5
Mic 2: 1 Woe to those who devise wickedness and work evil 5
7: 1 Woe is me! For I have become as when the summer 4
Nah 3: 1 Woe to the bloody city, all full of lies and booty 5
Hab 2: 6 say, "Woe to him who heaps up what is not his own 5
9 Woe to him who gets evil gain for his house 5
12 Woe to him who builds a town with blood 5
15 Woe to him who makes his neighbors drink 5
19 Woe to him who says to a wooden thing, Awake; 5
Zep 2: 5 Woe to you inhabitants of the seacoast 5
3: 1 Woe to her that is rebellious and defiled 5
Zec 11:17 Woe to my worthless shepherd 5
Mat 11:21 Woe to you, Chora'zin! woe to you, Beth-sa'ida! 8
21 Woe to you, Chora'zin! woe to you, Beth-sa'ida! 8
18: 7 Woe to the world for temptations to sin! 8
7 woe to the man by whom the temptation comes! 8
23:13 woe to you, scribes and Pharisees, hypocrites! 8
15 Woe to you, scribes and Pharisees, hypocrites! 8
16 Woe to you, blind guides, who say 8
23 Woe to you, scribes and Pharisees, hypocrites! 8
25 Woe to you, scribes and Pharisees, hypocrites! 8
27 Woe to you, scribes and Pharisees, hypocrites! 8
29 Woe to you, scribes and Pharisees, hypocrites! 8
26:24 woe to that man by whom the Son of man is betrayed! 8
Mrk 14:21 woe to that man by whom the Son of man is betrayed! 8
Lke 6:24 woe to you that are rich 8
25 Woe to you that are full now, for you shall hunger. 8
25 Woe to you that laugh now, for you shall mourn 8
26 Woe to you, when all men speak well of you 8
10:13 Woe to you, Chora'zin! woe to you, Beth-sa'ida! 8
13 Woe to you, Chora'zin! woe to you, Beth-sa'ida! 8
11:42 woe to you Pharisees! 8
43 Woe to you Pharisees! 8
44 Woe to you! for you are like graves 8
46 he said, "Woe to you lawyers also! 8
47 Woe to you! for you build the tombs of the prophets 8
52 Woe to you lawyers! 8
17: 1 woe to him by whom they come! 8
22:22 woe to that man by whom he is betrayed! 8
1Co 9:16 Woe to me if I do not preach the gospel! 8
Jde 1:11 Woe to them! For they walk in the way of Cain 8
Rev 8:13 Woe, woe, woe to those who dwell on the earth 8
13 Woe, woe, woe to those who dwell on the earth 8
13 Woe, woe, woe to those who dwell on the earth 8
9:12 The first woe has passed; 8
12 behold, two woes are still to come. 8
11:14 The second woe has passed; behold, the third woe 8
14 behold, the third woe is soon to come. 8
12:12 woe to you, O earth and sea, for the devil has come 8
2Es 2: 8 Woe to you, Assyria, who conceal the unrighteous 9
15:24 Woe to those who sin 9
47 woe to you, miserable wretch! 9
16: 1 Woe to you, Babylon and Asia! 9
1 Woe to you, Egypt and Syria! 9
63 Woe to those who sin and want to hide their sins! 9
77 Woe to those who are choked by their sins 9
Jdt 16:17 Woe to the nations that rise up against my people! 8
Sir 2:12 Woe to timid hearts and to slack hands 8
13 Woe to the faint heart, for it has no trust! 8
14 Woe to you who have lost your endurance! 8
41: 8 Woe to you, ungodly men, who have forsaken the law 8

wolf 1. זְאֵב 2. *λύκος* 3. lupus

Gen 49:27 Benjamin is a ravenous wolf 1
Isa 11: 6 The wolf shall dwell with the lamb 1
65:25 The wolf and the lamb shall feed together 1

Jer 5: 6 a wolf from the desert shall destroy them. 1
Ezk 22:27 Her princes in the midst of her are like wolves 1
Hab 1: 8 horses . . more fierce than the evening wolves; 1
Zep 3: 3 her judges are evening wolves 1
Mat 7:15 but inwardly are ravenous wolves. 2
10:16 I send you out as sheep in the midst of wolves 2
Lke 10: 3 I send you out as lambs in the midst of wolves. 2
Joh 10:12 sees the wolf coming and leaves the sheep 2
12 the wolf snatches them and scatters them. 2
Act 20:29 fierce wolves will come in among you 2
2Es 5:18 his flock in the power of cruel wolves. 3
Sir 13:17 What fellowship has a wolf with a lamb? 2

woman 1. אִשָּׁה 2. בַּת 3. נָוֶה 4. נְקֵבָה 5. γυναικεῖος 6. γυνή 7. θῆλυς 8. mulier

Gen 2:22 the rib . . he made into a woman 1
23 flesh of my flesh; she shall be called Woman 1
3: 1 He said to the woman, "Did God say, 'You shall not eat 1
2 the woman said to the serpent, "We may eat 1
4 the serpent said to the woman, "You will not die. 1
6 when the woman saw that the tree was good for food 1
12 The woman whom thou gavest to be with me 1
13 God said to the woman, "What is this that you have 1
13 The woman said, "The serpent beguiled me, and I ate. 1
15 I will put enmity between you and the woman 1
16 To the woman he said, "I will greatly multiply 1
12:11 I know that you are a woman beautiful to behold; 1
14 saw that the woman was very beautiful. 1
15 And the woman was taken into Pharaoh's house. 1
14:16 his goods, and the women and the people. 1
18:11 to be with Sarah after the manner of women. 1
20: 3 Behold, you are a dead man, because of the woman 1
24: 5 Perhaps the woman may not be willing to follow me 1
8 if the woman is not willing to follow you 1
11 evening, the time when women go out to draw water. •
39 'Perhaps the woman will not follow me.' 1
44 let her be the woman whom the LORD has appointed 1
27:46 weary of my life because of the Hittite women. 2
46 If Jacob marries one of the Hittite women 2
46 marries . . one of the women of the land 2
28: 1 You shall not marry one of the Canaanite women. 2
6 You shall not marry one of the Canaanite women 2
8 Canaanite women did not please Isaac his father 2
30:13 Happy am I! For the women will call me happy"; 2
31:35 before you, for the way of women is upon me. 1
33: 5 raised his eyes and saw the women and children 1
34: 1 Dinah . . went out to visit the women of the land; 2
38:20 to receive the pledge from the woman's hand 1
Exd 1:19 the Hebrew women are not like the Egyptian women; 1
2: 2 The woman conceived and bore a son; 1
9 So the woman took the child and nursed him. 1
11: 2 that they ask . . every woman of her neighbor 1
12:37 besides women and children. •
15:20 and all the women went out after her 1
19:15 Be ready . . do not go near a woman. 1
21:22 men strive together, and hurt a woman with child 1
22 according as the woman's husband shall lay upon 1
28 When an ox gores a man or a woman to death 1
29 if . . it kills a man or a woman 1
35:22 So they came, both men and women; 1
25 all women who had ability spun with their hands 1
26 all the women whose hearts were moved 1
29 All the men and women, the people of Israel 1
36: 6 Let neither man nor woman do anything more 1
Lev 12: 2 Say to the people of Israel, If a woman conceives 1
13:29 When a man or woman has a disease on the head 1
38 When a man or a woman has spots on the skin 1
15:18 If a man lies with a woman and has an emission 1
19 When a woman has a discharge of blood 1
25 If a woman has a discharge of blood for many days 1
33 the man who lies with a woman who is unclean •
18:17 You shall not uncover the nakedness of a woman 1
18 not take a woman as a rival wife to her sister 1
19 not approach a woman to uncover her nakedness 1
22 You shall not lie with a male as with a woman 1
23 neither shall any woman give herself to a beast 1
19:20 If a man lies carnally with a woman who is a slave 1
20:13 If a man lies with a male as with a woman 1
16 If a woman approaches any beast and lies with it 1
16 you shall kill the woman and the beast 1
18 If a man lies with a woman having her sickness 1
27 A man or a woman who is a medium or a wizard 1
21: 7 shall not marry . . a woman who has been defiled 1
7 marry a woman divorced from her husband 1
14 a woman who has been defiled, or a harlot •
24:10 Now an Israelite woman's son, whose father was 1
11 the Israelite woman's son blasphemed the Name 1
26:26 ten women shall bake your bread in one oven 1
Num 5: 6 When a man or woman commits any of the sins 1
18 the priest shall set the woman before the LORD 1
18 priest . . unbind the hair of the woman's head 1
21 priest make the woman take the oath of the curse 1
21 (let the priest . . say to the woman) 1
22 And the woman shall say, 'Amen, Amen.' 1
24 make the woman drink the water of bitterness 1
25 offering of jealousy out of the woman's hand 1
26 afterward shall make the woman drink the water. 1
27 woman shall become an execration among 1
28 if the woman has not defiled herself and is clean 1
30 then he shall set the woman before the LORD 1
31 but the woman shall bear her iniquity. 1
6: 2 When either a man or a woman makes a special vow 1
12: 1 because of the Cushite woman whom he had married 1
1 for he had married a Cushite woman; 1
25: 8 both of them, the man of Israel and the woman 1
15 name of the Mid'ianite woman who was slain 1
30: 3 Or when a woman vows a vow to the LORD 1
31: 9 Israel took captive the women of Mid'ian 1
15 Moses said to them, "Have you let all the women live? 4
17 kill every woman who has known man by lying 1
35 women who had not known man by lying with him. 1
Deu 2:34 destroyed every city, men, women, and children; 1
3: 6 destroying every city, men, women, and children. 1
4:16 form of any figure, the likeness of male or female 4
17: 2 a man or woman who does what is evil 1
5 bring . . man or woman who has done this evil thing 1
5 stone that man or woman to death with stones. 1
20:14 women and the little ones the cattle 1
21:11 see among the captives a beautiful woman 1
22: 5 woman . . not wear anything that pertains to a man 1
5 nor shall a man put on a woman's garment; 1
14 I took this woman, and when I came near her 1
22 both . . shall die, the man who lay with the woman 1
22 both . . shall die, the man . . , and the woman; 1
29:18 lest there be . . a man or woman or family or tribe 1
31:12 Assemble the people, men, women, and little ones 1
Jos 2: 4 the woman had taken the two men and hidden them; 1
6:21 all in the city, both men and women, young and old 1
22 bring out . . the woman, and all who belong to her 1
8:25 both men and women, were 12,000 1
35 before all the assembly of Israel, and the women 1
23:12 so that you marry their women and they yours •
Jdg 4: 9 LORD will sell Sis'era into the hand of a woman. 1
5:24 Most blessed of women be Ja'el, the wife of Heber 1
24 be Ja'el . . of tent-dwelling women most blessed. 1
9:49 of Shechem also died, about 1,000 men and women. 1
51 people of the city fled to it, all the men and women 1
53 a certain woman threw an upper millstone 1
54 kill me, lest men say of me, 'A woman killed him.' 1
11: 2 for you are the son of another woman. 1
13: 3 angel of the LORD appeared to the woman and said 1
6 Then the woman came and told her husband 1
9 the angel of God came again to the woman as she sat 1
10 the woman ran in haste and told her husband 1
11 Are you the man who spoke to this woman? 1
13 Of all that I said to the woman let her beware. 1
24 the woman bore a son, and called his name Samson; 1
14: 3 Is there not a woman among the daughters 1
7 he went down and talked with the woman; 1
10 his father went down to the woman, and Samson 1
16: 4 he loved a woman in the valley of Sorek, whose name 1
27 the house was full of men and women; all the lords 1
27 on the roof there were about 3,000 men and women 1
19:26 the woman came and fell down at the door 1
20: 4 the husband of the woman who was murdered 1
21:10 Go and smite . . also the women and the little ones. 1
11 male and every woman that has lain with a male 1
14 they gave them the women whom they had saved 1
14 had saved alive of the women of Ja'besh-gil'ead; 1
16 since the women are destroyed out of Benjamin? 1
Rut 1: 5 the woman was bereft of her two sons 1
19 and the women said, "Is this Na'omi? •
3: 8 and turned over, and behold, a woman lay at his feet! 1
11 my . . townsmen know that you are a woman of worth. 1
14 that the woman came to the threshing floor. 1
4:11 May the LORD make the woman . . like Rachel 1
14 the women said to Na'omi, "Blessed be the LORD 1
1Sm 1:15 No, my lord, I am a woman sorely troubled; 1
18 she said . . " Then the woman went her way and ate 1
23 the woman remained and nursed her son 1
26 I am the woman who was standing here 1
2:20 The LORD give you children by this woman 1
22 he heard . . how they lay with the women who served 1
15: 3 do not spare them, but kill both man and woman 1
33 As your sword has made women childless 1
33 so shall your mother be childless among women. 1
18: 6 the women came out of all the cities of Israel 1
7 the women sang to one another as they made merry 1
21: 4 if . . young men have kept themselves from women. 1
5 women have been kept from us as always when I go 1
22:19 both men and women, children and sucklings, oxen 1
25: 3 woman was of good understanding and beautiful 1
27: 9 David . . left neither man nor woman alive 1
11 And David saved neither man nor woman alive 1
28: 7 Seek out for me a woman who is a medium, 1
8 and they came to the woman by night. 1
9 The woman said to him, "Surely you know what Saul 1
11 Then the woman said, "Whom shall I bring up for you 1
12 When the woman saw Samuel, she cried out 1
12 the woman said to Saul, "Why have you deceived me? 1
13 the woman said to Saul, "I see a god coming up 1
21 the woman came to Saul, and when she saw . . she said 1
23 his servants, together with the woman, urged him; 1
24 Now the woman had a fatted calf in the house 1
30: 2 and taken captive the women and all who were in it 1
2Sm 1:26 your love to me was . . passing the love of women. 1
3: 8 you charge me . . with a fault concerning a woman. 1
6:19 the whole multitude of Israel, both men and women 1
11: 2 he saw from the roof a woman bathing; 1
2 he saw . . and the woman was very beautiful. 1
3 And David sent and inquired about the woman. 1
5 And the woman conceived; and she sent and told 1
21 Did not a woman cast an upper millstone upon him 1
13:17 Put this woman out of my presence, and bolt •
14: 2 sent to Teko'a, and fetched from there a wise woman 1
2 behave like a woman who has been mourning 1
4 When the woman of Teko'a came to the king 1
8 Then the king said to the woman, "Go to your house 1
9 And the woman of Teko'a said to the king 1
12 Then the woman said, "Pray let your handmaid speak 1
13 woman said, "Why then have you planned 1
18 the king answered the woman, "Do not hide from me 1
18 And the woman said, "Let my lord the king speak. 1
19 The woman answered and said, "As surely as you live 1
27 whose name was Tamar; she was a beautiful woman. 1
17:19 And the woman took and spread a covering 1
20 Ab'salom's servants came to the woman at the house 1
20 And the woman said to them, "They have gone over 1
20:16 Then a wise woman called from the city, "Hear! Hear! 1
17 came near her; and the woman said, "Are you Jo'ab? 1
21 the woman said to Jo'ab, "Behold, his head shall be 1
22 the woman went to all the people in her wisdom. 1
1Kg 3:17 The one woman said, "Oh, my lord, this woman and I 1
17 my lord, this woman and I dwell in the same house; 1
18 after I was delivered, this woman also gave birth; 1
19 this woman's son died in the night, because she lay 1
22 the other woman said, "No, the living child is mine 1
26 the woman whose son was alive said to the king 1
27 Give the living child to the first woman, and by no •
11: 1 Now King Solomon loved many foreign women 1
1 Ammonite, E'domite, Sido'nian, and Hittite women •
14: 5 When she came, she pretended to be another woman. •
17:17 After this the son of the woman . . became ill; 1
24 the woman said to Eli'jah, "Now I know 1
2Kg 4: 8 went on to Shunem, where a wealthy woman lived 1
17 the woman conceived, and she bore a son 1
6:26 a woman cried out to him, saying, "Help, my lord, 1
28 She answered, "This woman said to me, 'Give your son 1
30 When the king heard the words of the woman 1
8: 1 Now Eli'sha had said to the woman . . "Arise 1
2 So the woman arose, and did according to the word 1
3 when the woman returned . . she went forth 1
5 the woman whose son he had restored . . appealed 1
5 O king, here is the woman, and here is her son 1
6 And when the king asked the woman, she told him. 1
23: 7 where the women wove hangings for the Ashe'rah. 1
1Ch 16: 3 distributed to all Israel, both men and women 1
2Ch 2:14 the son of a woman of the daughters of Dan 1
15:13 put to death, whether young or old, man or woman. 1
28: 8 took captive 200,000 of their kinsfolk, women, sons 1
Ezr 10: 1 very great assembly of men, women, and children 1
2 married foreign women from the peoples 1
10 You have trespassed and married foreign women 1
17 end of all the men who had married foreign women. 1
18 sons . . who had married foreign women 1
44 All these had married foreign women 1
Neh 8: 2 assembly, both men and women and all who could 1
3 read . . in the presence of the men and the women 1
12:43 women and children also rejoiced. 1
13:23 married women of Ashdod, Ammon, and Moab; 1
26 Did not Solomon . . sin on account of such women? •
26 nevertheless foreign women made even him to sin. 1
27 against our God by marrying foreign women? 1
Est 1: 9 also gave a banquet for the women in the palace 1
17 this deed . . will be made known to all women 1
20 all women will give honor to their husbands 1
2: 3 the king's eunuch who is in charge of the women; 1
8 in custody of Hegai who had charge of the women. 1
12 being . . under the regulations for the women 1
12 six months with spices and ointments for women– 1
15 Hegai the . . eunuch, who had charge of the women 1
17 the king loved Esther more than all the women 1
3:13 slay . . all Jews, young and old, women and children 1
4:11 if any man or woman goes . . there is but one law; 1
8:11 annihilate any . . with their children and women 1
Job 14: 1 Man that is born of a woman is of few days 1
15:14 he that is born of a woman, that he can be righteous? 1
25: 4 How can he who is born of woman be clean? 1
31: 9 If my heart has been enticed to a woman 1
42:15 there were no women so fair as Job's daughters; 1
Ps 68:12 women at home divide the spoil 3
Prv 2:16 You will be saved from the loose woman 1
6:24 to preserve you from the evil woman 1
7: 5 to preserve you from the loose woman 1
10 lo, a woman meets him, dressed as a harlot 1
9:13 A foolish woman is noisy; 1
11:16 A gracious woman gets honor 1
22 snout is a beautiful woman without discretion. 1
21: 9 than in a house shared with a contentious woman. 1
19 than with a contentious and fretful woman. 1
25:24 than in a house shared with a contentious woman. 1
27:15 continual dripping . . contentious woman are alike; 1
31: 3 Give not your strength to women 1
29 Many women have done excellently 2
30 but a woman who fears the LORD is to be praised. 1
Ecc 7:26 more bitter . . the woman whose heart is snares 1

28 but a woman among all these I have not found. 1
Sng 1: 8 If you do not know, O fairest among women 1
5: 9 What is your beloved . . O fairest among women? 1
6: 1 has your beloved gone, O fairest among women? 1
Isa 3:12 are their oppressors, and women rule over them. 1
4: 1 seven women shall take hold of one man in that day 1
19:16 In that day the Egyptians will be like women 1
27:11 women come and make a fire of them. 1
32: 9 Rise up, you women who are at ease, hear my voice; 1
11 Tremble, you women who are at ease *
45:10 or to a woman, 'With what are you in travail?' 1
49:15 Can a woman forget her sucking child 1
Jer 7:18 and the women knead dough, to make cakes 1
9:20 Hear, O women, the word of the LORD 1
13:21 pangs . . like those of a woman in travail? 1
31:22 a new thing on the earth: a woman protects a man. 4
38:22 Behold, all the women left in the house of the king 1
40: 7 and had committed to him men, women, and children 1
41:16 soldiers, women, children, and eunuchs 1
43: 6 the men, the women, the children, the princesses 1
44: 7 to cut off from you man and woman, infant and child 1
15 and all the women who stood by, a great assembly 1
19 And the women said, "When we burned incense *
20 Jeremiah said to all the people, men and women 1
24 Jeremiah said to all the people and all the women 1
48:41 like the heart of a woman in her pangs; 1
49:22 like the heart of a woman in her pangs. 1
50:37 troops in her midst, that they may become women! 1
51:22 with you I break in pieces man and woman; 1
30 strength has failed, they have become women; 1
Lam 2:20 Should women eat their offspring 1
4:10 The hands of compassionate women have boiled 1
5:11 Women are ravished in Zion, virgins in . . Judah. 1
Ezk 8:14 and behold, there sat women weeping for Tammuz. 1
9: 6 young men and maidens, little children and women 1
13:18 Woe to the women who sew magic bands *
16:34 different from other women in your harlotries; 1
41 judgments upon you in the sight of many women; 1
18: 6 or approach a woman in her time of impurity 1
22:10 women who are unclean in their impurity. *
23: 2 there were two women, the daughters of one mother; 1
10 she became a byword among women 1
42 they put bracelets upon the hands of the women *
45 and with the sentence of women that shed blood; †
48 that all women may take warning 1
30:17 and the women shall go into captivity. *
36:17 like the uncleanness of a woman in her impurity. *
Dan 11:17 give him the daughter of women to destroy 1
37 give no heed . . to the one beloved by women; 1
Hos 3: 1 Go again, love a woman who is beloved of a paramour 1
Mic 2: 9 The women of my people you drive out 1
Nah 3:13 Behold, your troops are women in your midst. 1
Zec 5: 7 there was a woman sitting in the ephah! 1
9 and saw, and behold, two women coming forward! 1
14: 2 the houses plundered and the women ravished; 1
Mat 5:28 who looks at a woman lustfully has already 6
9:20 behold, a woman who had suffered 6
22 well." And instantly the woman was made well. 6
11:11 Truly, I say to you, among those born of women 6
13:33 leaven which a woman took and hid 6
14:21 about 5,000 men, besides women and children. 6
15:22 behold, a Canaanite woman from that region 6
28 Jesus answered her, "O woman, great is your faith! 6
38 4,000 men, besides women and children. 6
22:27 After them all, the woman died. 6
24:41 Two women will be grinding at the mill *
26: 7 a woman came up to him 6
10 Why do you trouble the woman? 6
27:55 There were also many women there 6
28: 5 the angel said to the women, "Do not be afraid 6
Mrk 5:25 woman who had had a flow of blood for twelve years 6
33 the woman, knowing what had been done to her, came 6
7:25 a woman, whose little daughter was possessed 6
26 the woman was a Greek, a Syrophoeni'cian by birth. 6
12:22 Last of all the woman also died. 6
14: 3 a woman came with an alabaster flask of ointment 6
15:40 There were also women looking on from afar 6
41 also many other women who came up with him *
Lke 1:42 Blessed are you among women 6
4:26 to a woman who was a widow. 6
7:28 among those born of women none is greater 6
37 behold, a woman of the city, who was a sinner 6
39 what sort of woman this is who is touching him 6
44 Then turning toward the woman he said to Simon 6
44 Do you see this woman? 6
50 he said to the woman, "Your faith has saved you 6
8: 2 also some women who had been healed 6
43 woman who had had a flow of blood for twelve years 6
47 when the woman saw that she was not hidden 6
10:38 a woman named Martha received him 6
11:27 a woman in the crowd raised her voice and said 6
13:11 a woman who had had a spirit of infirmity 6
12 Woman, you are freed from your infirmity. 6
21 It is like leaven which a woman took and hid 6
15: 8 what woman, having ten silver coins 6
16:18 he who marries a woman divorced from her husband *
17:35 There will be two women grinding together *
20:32 Afterward the woman also died. 6
33 whose wife will the woman be 6

22:57 he denied it, saying, "Woman, I do not know him. 6
23:27 women who bewailed and lamented him. 6
49 the women who had followed him from Galilee 6
55 The women who had come with him from Galilee 6
24:22 Moreover, some women of our company amazed us. 6
24 and found it just as the women had said 6
Joh 2: 4 O woman, what have you to do with me? 6
4: 7 There came a woman of Samar'ia to draw water. 6
9 The Samaritan woman said to him, "How is it that you 6
9 you, a Jew, ask a drink of me, a woman of Samar'ia? 6
11 woman said to him, "Sir, you have nothing to draw 6
15 The woman said to him, "Sir, give me this water 6
17 The woman answered him, "I have no husband. 6
19 The woman said to him, "Sir, I perceive 6
21 Woman, believe me, the hour is coming 6
25 The woman said to him, "I know that Messiah 6
27 They marveled that he was talking with a woman 6
28 the woman left her water jar, and went away 6
39 believed in him because of the woman's testimony 6
42 They said to the woman, "It is no longer 6
8: 3 The scribes and the Pharisees brought a woman 6
4 this woman has been caught in the act of adultery 6
9 left alone with the woman standing before him. 6
10 Woman, where are they? Has no one condemned you? 6
16:21 When a woman is in travail she has sorrow 6
19:26 he said to his mother, "Woman, behold, your son! 6
20:13 They said to her, "Woman, why are you weeping? 6
15 Jesus said to her, "Woman, why are you weeping? 6
Act 1:14 with the women and Mary the mother of Jesus 6
5:14 multitudes both of men and women 6
8: 3 he dragged off men and women 6
12 they were baptized, both men and women. 6
9: 2 if he found any belonging to the Way, men or women 6
13:50 the Jews incited the devout women of high standing 6
16: 1 the son of a Jewish woman who was a believer 6
13 and spoke to the women who had come together. 6
14 One who heard us was a woman named Lydia 6
17: 4 not a few of the leading women. 6
12 with not a few Greek women of high standing 6
34 a woman named Dam'aris and others with them. 6
22: 4 delivering to prison both men and women 6
Rom 1:26 Their women exchanged natural relations 7
27 the men . . gave up natural relations with women 7
7: 2 a married woman is bound by law to her husband 6
1Co 7: 1 It is well for a man not to touch a woman. 6
13 If any woman has a husband who is an unbeliever 6
34 the unmarried woman or girl is anxious 6
11: 3 the head of a woman is her husband 6
5 any woman who prays or prophesies with her head 6
6 For if a woman will not veil herself 6
6 is disgraceful for a woman to be shorn or shaven 6
7 woman is the glory of man. 6
8 man was not made from woman, but woman from man 6
8 man was not made from woman, but woman from man 6
9 was man created for woman, but woman for man.) 6
9 was man created for woman, but woman for man.) 6
10 That is why a woman ought to have a veil on her head 6
11 woman is not independent of man nor man of woman; 6
11 woman is not independent of man nor man of woman; 6
12 as woman was made from man 6
12 so man is now born of woman 6
13 for a woman to pray to God with her head uncovered? 6
15 if a woman has long hair, it is her pride 6
14:34 the women should keep silence in the churches. 6
35 it is shameful for a woman to speak in church. 6
Gal 4: 4 born of woman, born under the law 6
1Th 5: 3 as travail comes upon a woman with child *
1Ti 2: 9 women should adorn themselves modestly 6
10 as befits women who profess religion. 6
11 Let a woman learn in silence 6
12 I permit no woman to teach 6
14 Adam was not deceived, but the woman was deceived 6
15 woman will be saved through bearing children *
3:11 The women likewise must be serious 6
Heb 11:35 Women received their dead by resurrection. 6
1Pe 3: 5 women who hoped in God used to adorn themselves 6
7 bestowing honor on the woman as the weaker sex 5
Rev 2:20 against you, that you tolerate the woman Jez'ebel 6
9: 8 their hair like women's hair, and their teeth like 6
12: 1 a woman clothed with the sun 6
4 And the dragon stood before the woman 6
6 and the woman fled into the wilderness 6
13 he pursued the woman who had borne the male child. 6
14 woman was given the two wings of the great eagle 6
15 The serpent poured water . . after the woman 6
16 But the earth came to the help of the woman 6
17 Then the dragon was angry with the woman 6
14: 4 who have not defiled themselves with women 6
17: 3 and I saw a woman sitting on a scarlet beast 6
4 The woman was arrayed in purple and scarlet 6
6 I saw the woman, drunk with the blood of the saints 6
7 I will tell you the mystery of the woman 6
9 are seven mountains on which the woman is seated; 6
18 And the woman that you saw is the great city 6
1Es 1:32 the principal men, with the women 6
3:12 The third wrote, "Women are strongest 6
4:13 Zerubbabel, who had spoken of women and truth 6
14 Is it not women? 6
15 Women gave birth to the king and to every people 6

16 From women they came *
16 women brought up . . men who plant the vineyards *
17 Women make men's clothes; they bring men glory *
17 men cannot exist without women. 6
18 then see a woman lovely in appearance and beauty 6
22 Hence you must realize that women rule over you! 6
22 bring everything and give it to women? 6
24 he brings it back to the woman he loves. *
26 Many men have lost their minds because of women 6
27 stumbled, or sinned, because of women. 6
32 Gentlemen, why are not women strong 6
34 Gentlemen, are not women strong? 6
37 the king is unrighteous, women are unrighteous 6
8:91 a very great throng . . , men and women and youths 6
92 have married foreign women 6
9: 7 broken the law and married foreign women 6
36 All these had married foreign women 6
40 all the multitude, men and women 6
41 in the presence of both men and women 6
2Es 4:42 For just as a woman who is in travail makes haste *
5: 8 menstruous women shall bring forth monsters. 8
46 He said to me, "Ask a woman's womb, and say to it 8
49 a woman who has become old does not bring forth *
51 He replied to me, "Ask a woman who bears children *
9:38 I lifted up my eyes and saw a woman on my right 8
10: 6 You most foolish of women 8
16 and will be praised among women. 8
27 behold, the woman was no longer visible to me 8
41 The woman who appeared to you a little while ago 8
42 you do not now see the form of a woman 8
44 This woman whom you saw, whom you now behold 8
16:33 women shall mourn 8
49 a respectable and virtuous woman abhors a harlot 8
Tob 2:11 Then my wife Anna earned money at women's work. 6
4:12 do not marry a foreign woman 6
6: 7 make a smoke from these before the man or woman 6
Jdt 4:11 the men and women of Israel, and their children 6
6:16 their young men and their women ran to the assembly 6
7:22 the women and young men fainted from thirst 6
23 all the people, the young men, the women 6
32 The women and children he sent home 6
8:31 pray for us, since you are a devout woman 6
9:10 crush their arrogance by the hand of a woman. 7
10:11 The women went straight on through the valley; *
19 who have women like this among them 6
11: 1 Then Holofernes said to her, "Take courage, woman 6
21 There is not such a woman . . 6
12:11 Go now and persuade the Hebrew woman 6
12 it will be a disgrace if we let such a woman go 6
15 arrayed herself in all her woman's finery 5
13:15 Lord has struck him down by the hand of a woman. 7
18 blessed . . above all women on earth 6
14:18 One Hebrew woman has brought disgrace 6
15:12 Then all the women of Israel gathered to see her 6
12 gave them to the women who were with her; 6
13 leading all the women 6
16: 6 has foiled them by the hand of a woman. 7
Sir 9: 2 Do not give yourself to a woman 6
3 Do not go to meet a loose woman 6
8 Turn away your eyes from a shapely woman 6
8 many have been misled by a woman's beauty 6
10:18 nor fierce anger for those born of women. 6
19: 2 Wine and women lead intelligent men astray 6
23:22 it is with a woman who leaves her husband 6
25:21 Do not be ensnared by a woman's beauty 6
21 do not desire a woman for her possessions. 6
24 From a woman sin had its beginning 6
28:15 Slander has driven away courageous women 6
36:21 A woman will accept any man 6
22 A woman's beauty gladdens the countenance 6
37:11 Do not consult with a woman about her rival 6
41:20 looking at a woman who is a harlot 6
42:12 do not sit in the midst of women; 6
13 from a woman comes woman's wickedness. 6
13 from a woman comes woman's wickedness. 6
14 Better . . than a woman who does good 6
14 it is a woman who brings shame and disgrace. 6
47:19 you laid your loins beside women 6
LJr 1:30 Women serve meals for gods of silver and gold 6
43 the women, with cords about them 6
Bel 1:20 the footsteps of men and women and children. 6
1Mc 1:26 the beauty of women faded. 6
32 they took captive the women and children 6
60 the women who had their children circumcised 6
2Mc 3:19 Women, girded with sackcloth 6
5:13 destruction of boys, women, and children 6
24 to sell the women and boys as slaves. 6
6: 4 had intercourse with women 6
10 For example, two women were brought in 6
7:21 fired her woman's reasoning with a man's courage 7
12:21 he sent off the women and the children 6
3Mc 1:19 Those women . . abandoned the bridal chambers *
4Mc 4: 9 the priests together with women and children 6
25 women . . were thrown headlong from heights 6
14:11 since the mind of woman despised . . agonies 6
15:17 O woman, who alone gave birth 6
16: 1 a woman, advanced in years and mother of seven 6
2 a woman has despised the fiercest tortures. 6
5 If this woman . . had been fainthearted 6

14 O mother . . elder and woman! 6
17: 9 aged priest and an aged woman and seven sons 6
18: 7 I guarded the rib from which woman was made. •

woman *See also* attending, barren, base, beautiful, believing, bred, complacent, cursed, desolate, divorced, drunken, each, foolish, free, lonely, loose, married, ministering, mourning, old, other, pregnant, rebellious, singer, singing, skilful, slave, tender, unloved, weak, wicked, wretched, young.

woman in travail 1. חול 2. ילד 3. τίκτω 4. ὠδίνω

Ps 48: 6 trembling . . anguish as of a woman in travail. 2
Isa 13: 8 they will be in anguish like a woman in travail. 2
21: 3 pangs . . like the pangs of a woman in travail; 2
42:14 now I will cry out like a woman in travail 2
Jer 4:31 For I heard a cry as of a woman in travail 1
6:24 taken hold of us, pain as of a woman in travail. 2
22:23 pangs come upon you, pain as of a woman in travail! 2
49:24 taken hold of her, as of a woman in travail. 2
50:43 anguish seized him, pain as of a woman in travail. 2
Mic 4: 9 that pangs have seized you like a woman in travail? 2
10 groan, O daughter of Zion, like a woman in travail; 2
Sir 34: 5 like a woman in travail the mind has fancies. 4
48:19 they were in anguish, like women in travail. 3

woman next 1. πλησίον

LJr 1:43 she derides the woman next to her 1

womb 1. בֶּטֶן 2. מֵעֶה 3. רֶחֶם 4. γαστήρ 5. κοιλία 6. μήτρα 7. matrix 8. venter

Gen 20:18 For the LORD had closed all the wombs of the house 3
25:23 the LORD said to her, "Two nations are in your womb 1
24 behold, there were twins in her womb. 1
29:31 LORD saw that Leah was hated, he opened her womb; 3
30: 2 withheld from you the fruit of the womb? 1
22 God hearkened to her and opened her womb. 3
38:27 delivery came, there were twins in her womb. 1
49:25 blessings of the breasts and of the womb. 3
Exd 13: 2 first to open the womb among the people of Israel 3
12 to the LORD all that first opens the womb. 3
15 all the males that first open the womb; 3
34:19 All that opens the womb is mine, all your male 3
Num 3:12 instead of every first-born that opens the womb 3
8:16 instead of all that open the womb, the first-born 3
12:12 consumed when he comes out of his mother's womb. 3
18:15 Everything that opens the womb of all flesh 3
Jdg 16:17 have been a Nazirite to God from my mother's womb. 1
Rut 1:11 Have I yet sons in my womb that they may become 2
1Sm 1: 5 only one . . because the LORD had closed her womb. 3
6 because the LORD had closed her womb. 3
Job 1:21 he said, "Naked I came from my mother's womb 1
3:10 it did not shut the doors of my mother's womb 1
11 die at birth, come forth from the womb and expire? 1
10:18 Why didst thou bring me forth from the womb? 3
19 carried from the womb to the grave. 1
31:15 Did not he who made me in the womb make him? 1
15 And did not one fashion us in the womb? 3
18 from his mother's womb I guided him 1
38: 8 when it burst forth from the womb; 3
29 From whose womb did the ice come forth 1
Ps 22: 9 Yet thou art he who took me from the womb; 1
58: 3 The wicked go astray from the womb 3
71: 6 thou art he who took me from my mother's womb. 2
110: 3 From the womb of the morning like dew your youth 3
127: 3 fruit of the womb a reward. 1
139:13 thou didst knit me together in my mother's womb. 1
Prv 30:16 Sheol, the barren womb, the earth ever thirsty 3
31: 2 What, son of my womb? What, son of my vows? 1
Ecc 5:15 As he came from his mother's womb he shall go again 1
11: 5 how the spirit comes to the bones in the womb 1
Isa 13:18 they will have no mercy on the fruit of the womb; 1
44: 2 LORD who made you, who formed you from the womb 1
24 your Redeemer, who formed you from the womb 1
46: 3 borne by me from your birth, carried from the womb; 3
49: 1 The LORD called me from the womb 1
5 who formed me from the womb to be his servant 1
15 have no compassion on the son of her womb? 1
66: 9 shall I, who cause to bring forth, shut the womb? •
Jer 1: 5 Before I formed you in the womb I knew you 1
20:17 because he did not kill me in the womb; 3
17 and her womb for ever great. 3
18 Why did I come forth from the womb to see toil 3
Hos 9:14 Give them a miscarrying womb and dry breasts. 3
12: 3 In the womb he took his brother by the heel 1
Lke 1:15 with the Holy Spirit, even from his mother's womb. 5
31 you will conceive in your womb and bear a son 4
41 the babe leaped in her womb 5
42 blessed is the fruit of your womb! 5
44 the babe in my womb leaped for joy. 5
2:21 before he was conceived in the womb. 5
23 Every male that opens the womb shall be called holy 6
11:27 Blessed is the womb that bore you 5
23:29 the wombs that never bore 5
Joh 3: 4 Can he enter a second time into his mother's womb 5
Rom 4:19 he considered the barrenness of Sarah's womb. 6
2Es 4:40 her womb can keep the child within her any longer. 7
41 the chambers of the souls are like the womb. 7
5:35 Or why did not my mother's womb become my grave 7
46 He said to me, "Ask a woman's womb, and say to it 7
48 Even so have I given the womb of the earth to those 7
53 the time of old age, when the womb is failing.' 7
8: 8 the body which is now fashioned in the womb 7
8 the womb which thou has formed endures •
9 when the womb gives up again 7
10:12 for I have lost the fruit of my womb 8
16:38 Just as a woman . . has great pains about her womb 8
38 and when the child comes forth from the womb 8
Jdt 9: 2 polluted her womb to disgrace her 6
Wis 7: 1 in the womb of a mother I was molded into flesh 5
Sir 1:14 she is created with the faithful in the womb. 6
40: 1 the day they come forth from their mother's womb 4
49: 7 he had been consecrated in the womb as prophet 6
2Mc 7:22 I do not know how you came into being in my womb 5
27 I carried you nine months in my womb 4
4Mc 13:19 which was implanted in the mother's womb. 4

womb *See also* mouth.

wonder 1. מוֹפֵת 2. פלא 3. פֶּלֶא 4. שׁמם 5. תמה 6. תְּמַהּ (A) 7. תְּמַה (A) 8. ἀποθαυμάζω 9. θάμβος 10. θαῦμα 11. θαυμάζω 12. θαυμάσιος 13. θαυμαστός 14. τέρας 15. cogito 16. mirabilis 17. portentum 18. prodigium

Exd 3:20 smite Egypt with all the wonders which I will do 2
7: 3 multiply my . . wonders in the land of Egypt 1
11: 9 that my wonders may be multiplied in the land 1
10 Moses . . did all these wonders before Pharaoh; 1
15:11 terrible in glorious deeds, doing wonders? 3
Deu 4:34 by trials, by signs, by wonders, and by war 1
6:22 showed signs and wonders, great and grievous 1
7:19 eyes saw, the signs, the wonders, the mighty hand 1
13: 1 prophet arises . . gives you a sign or a wonder 1
2 sign or wonder which he tells you comes to pass 1
26: 8 with great terror, with signs and wonders; 1
28:46 They shall be upon you as a sign and a wonder 1
29: 3 your eyes saw, the signs, and those great wonders; 1
34:11 none like him for all the signs and the wonders 1
Jos 3: 5 for tomorrow the LORD will do wonders among you. 2
Jdg 13:19 offered . . to the LORD, to him who works wonders. 13
1Ch 16:12 the wonders he wrought, the judgments he uttered 1
Neh 9:10 perform signs and wonders against Pharaoh 1
17 not mindful of the wonders which thou didst 2
Ps 77:11 yea, I will remember thy wonders of old. 3
14 Thou art the God who workest wonders 3
78: 4 his might, and the wonders which he has wrought. 2
32 despite his wonders they did not believe. 2
88:10 Dost thou work wonders for the dead? 3
12 Are thy wonders known in the darkness 3
89: 5 Let the heavens praise thy wonders, O LORD 3
135: 9 sent signs and wonders against Pharaoh 1
136: 4 to him who alone does great wonders 2
Isa 59:16 wondered that there was no one to intervene; 4
Jer 32:20 hast shown signs and wonders in the land of Egypt 1
21 out of the land of Egypt with signs and wonders 1
Dan 4: 2 show the signs and wonders that the Most High God 6
3 How great are his signs, how mighty his wonders! 7
6:27 works signs and wonders in heaven and on earth 7
12: 6 How long shall it be till the end of these wonders? 3
Hab 1: 5 wonder and be astounded. For I am doing a work 5
Mat 15:31 so that the throng wondered 11
24:24 show great signs and wonders, so as to lead astray 14
27:14 so that the governor wondered greatly. 11
Mrk 13:22 show signs and wonders 14
15: 5 so that Pilate wondered. 11
44 Pilate wondered if he were already dead; 11
Lke 1:21 they wondered at his delay in the temple. 11
2:18 wondered at what the shepherds told them. 11
4:22 wondered at the gracious words 11
24:41 they still disbelieved for joy, and wondered 11
Joh 4:48 Unless you see signs and wonders 14
Act 2: 7 they were amazed and wondered, saying 11
19 I will show wonders in the heaven above 14
22 with mighty works and wonders and signs 14
43 many wonders and signs were done 14
3:10 they were filled with wonder and amazement 9
12 Men of Israel, why do you wonder at this 11
4:13 they wondered 11
30 signs and wonders are performed 14
5:12 Now many signs and wonders were done 14
24 wondering what this would come to. •
6: 8 did great wonders and signs among the people. 14
7:31 When Moses saw it he wondered at the sight 11
36 having performed wonders and signs in Egypt 14
13:41 'Behold, you scoffers, and wonder, and perish 11
14: 3 granting . . wonders to be done by their hands. 14
15:12 what signs and wonders God had done through them 14
Rom 15:19 by the power of signs and wonders 14
2Co 11:14 no wonder, for even Satan disguises himself 10
12:12 with signs and wonders and mighty works. 14
2Th 2: 9 with pretended signs and wonders 14
Heb 2: 4 while God also bore witness by signs and wonders 14
1Jn 3:13 Do not wonder, brethren, that the world hates you. 11
Rev 13: 3 the whole earth followed the beast with wonder. 11
2Es 1:14 and did great wonders among you 16
2:48 how great and many are the wonders of the Lord God 16
7:27 every one . . shall see my wonders. 16
9: 6 the beginnings are manifest in wonders 18
10:25 While I was wondering what this meant 15
13:14 thou hast shown thy servant these wonders 16
50 then he will show them very many wonders. 17
57 because of his wonders, which he did 16
AEs 10: 9 God has done great signs and wonders 14
Wis 8: 8 she has foreknowledge of signs and wonders 14
10:16 withstood dread kings with wonders and signs. 14
19: 8 after gazing on marvelous wonders. 14
Sir 11:21 Do not wonder at the works of a sinner 11
16:11 it will be a wonder if he remains unpunished 13
18: 6 is it possible to trace the wonders of the Lord. 12
26:11 do not wonder if she sins against you. 11
36: 6 Show signs anew, and work further wonders 12
40: 7 wonders that his fear came to nothing. 8
45:19 he wrought wonders against them 14
48:14 As in his life he did wonders 14
Bar 2:11 with signs and wonders and with great power 14
3Mc 5:39 wondering at his instability of mind 11

wonder *See also* work, worker.

wonderful 1. פלא 2. פֶּלֶא 3. פִּלְאִי 4. θαυμαστός 5. ποταπός

Jdg 13:18 Why do you ask my name, seeing it is wonderful? 3
2Sm 1:26 your love to me was wonderful, passing the love 1
2Ch 2: 9 house I am to build will be great and wonderful. 1
Job 42: 3 I did not understand, things too wonderful for me 1
Ps 119:129 Thy testimonies are wonderful; 2
139: 6 Such knowledge is too wonderful for me; it is high 3
14 praise thee, for thou art fearful and wonderful. •
14 fearful and wonderful. Wonderful are thy works! 1
Prv 30:18 Three things are too wonderful for me; 1
Isa 9: 6 and his name will be called "Wonderful Counselor 2
28:29 the LORD of hosts; he is wonderful in counsel 1
29:14 with this people, wonderful and marvelous; 1
Mrk 13: 1 Look, Teacher, what wonderful stones 5
1 and what wonderful buildings! 5
Rev 15: 1 another portent in heaven, great and wonderful 4
3 Great and wonderful are thy deeds, O Lord God 4
Tob 12:22 confessed the great and wonderful works of God 4
Jdt 16:13 wonderful in strength, invincible. 4
AEs 15:14 For you are wonderful, my lord 4
Sir 11: 4 the works of the Lord are wonderful 4

wonderful *See also* work.

wonderful deed 1. פלא 2. ἀρετή

Jdg 6:13 And where are all his wonderful deeds 1
Ps 9: 1 I will tell of all thy wonderful deeds. 1
Jer 21: 2 according to all his wonderful deeds 1
1Pe 2: 9 you may declare the wonderful deeds of him 2

wonderful thing 1. פֶּלֶא 2. θαυμάζω 3. θαυμάσιος

Isa 25: 1 for thou hast done wonderful things 1
Mat 21:15 the wonderful things that he did 3
AEs 13:10 earth and every wonderful thing under heaven 2
Sir 31: 9 he has done wonderful things among his people. 3

wondrous 1. מִפְלָאָה 2. פלא 3. θαυμάσιος 4. mirabilis

Job 37:14 stop and consider the wondrous works of God. 2
16 the wondrous works of him who is perfect 1
Ps 145: 5 on thy wondrous works, I will meditate. 2
2Es 13:56 and explain weighty and wondrous matters to you. 4
4Mc 15: 4 a wondrous likeness both of mind and of form. 3

wondrous *See also* work.

wondrous deed 1. פלא 2. θαυμάσιος

Ps 26: 7 and telling all thy wondrous deeds. 1
40: 5 LORD my God, thy wondrous deeds and thy thoughts 1
71:17 I still proclaim thy wondrous deeds. 1
75: 1 call on thy name and recount thy wondrous deeds. 1
Sir 48: 4 in your wondrous deeds 2

wondrous thing 1. פלא 2. mirabilis

Ps 72:18 God of Israel, who alone does wondrous things. 1
86:10 For thou art great and doest wondrous things 1
119:18 that I may behold wondrous things out of thy law. 1
2Es 14: 5 I told him many wondrous things 2

wondrous work 1. mirabilis

2Es 6:48 the nations might declare thy wondrous works. 1

wondrously 1. פלא

Job 37: 5 God thunders wondrously with his voice; 1
Jol 2:26 your God, who has dealt wondrously with you. 1

wondrously *See also* show.

wont 1. מִשְׁפָּט 2. חוה (A)

2Sm 20:18 They were wont to say in old time, 'Let them but ask •
Ps 119:132 Turn to me and be gracious to me, as is thy wont 1
Dan 3:19 seven times more than it was wont to be heated. 2
Mrk 15: 8 to ask Pilate to do as he was wont to do for them. •

wonted *See* flow.

woo 1. דבר

1Sm 25:39 David sent and wooed Ab'igail, to make her his wife. 1

wood 1. יַעַר 2. עֵץ 3. אָע (A) 4. *δρυμός* 5. *ξύλινος* 6. *ξύλον* 7. lignum

Gen 6:14 Make yourself an ark of gopher wood; 2
22: 3 and he cut the wood for the burnt offering 2
6 Abraham took the wood of the burnt offering 2
7 He said, "Behold, the fire and the wood; 2
9 Abraham . . laid the wood in order 2
9 laid him on the altar, upon the wood. 2
Exd 25: 5 tanned rams' skins, goatskins, acacia wood 2
10 They shall make an ark of acacia wood; 2
13 You shall make poles of acacia wood, and overlay 2
23 you shall make a table of acacia wood; 2
28 You shall make the poles of acacia wood 2
26:15 frames for the tabernacle of acacia wood. 2
26 you shall make bars of acacia wood 2
27: 1 You shall make the altar of acacia wood 2
6 make . . poles of acacia wood, and overlay them 2
30: 1 of acacia wood shall you make it. 2
5 You shall make the poles of acacia wood 2
31: 5 in carving wood, for work in every craft. 2
35: 7 tanned rams' skins, and goatskins; acacia wood 2
24 man with whom was found acacia wood of any use 2
33 cutting stones for setting, and in carving wood 2
36:20 frames for the tabernacle of acacia wood. 2
31 he made bars of acacia wood, five for the frames 2
37: 1 Bez'alel made the ark of acacia wood; 2
4 And he made poles of acacia wood 2
10 He also made the table of acacia wood; 2
15 the poles of acacia wood to carry the table 2
25 He made the altar of incense of acacia wood; 2
28 he made the poles of acacia wood, and overlaid 2
38: 1 altar of burnt offering also of acacia wood; 2
6 he made the poles of acacia wood, and overlaid 2
Lev 1: 7 and lay wood in order upon the fire 2
8 lay . . in order upon the wood that is on the fire 2
12 in order upon the wood that is on the fire 2
17 burn it . . upon the wood that is on the fire 2
3: 5 burnt offering, which is upon the wood on the fire 2
4:12 and shall burn it on a fire of wood 2
6:12 the priest shall burn wood on it every morning 2
11:32 whether it is an article of wood or a garment 2
15:12 every vessel of wood shall be rinsed in water 2
Num13:20 whether there is wood in it or not. 2
31:20 purify . . every article of wood. 2
35:18 struck him down with a weapon of wood in the hand 2
Deu 4:28 there you will serve gods of wood and stone 2
10: 1 come up to me . . and make an ark of wood. 2
3 I made an ark of acacia wood, and hewed two tables 2
19: 5 into the forest with his neighbor to cut wood 2
28:36 shall serve other gods, of wood and stone. 2
64 there . . serve other gods, of wood and stone 2
29:11 both he who hews your wood and he who draws 2
17 their idols of wood and stone, of silver and gold 2
Jos 9:21 they became hewers of wood and drawers of water 2
23 be slaves, hewers of wood and drawers of water 2
27 made them . . hewers of wood and drawers of water 2
Jdg 6:26 as a burnt offering with the wood of the Ashe'rah 2
1Sm 6:14 they split up the wood of the cart 2
2Sm 24:22 sledges and the yokes of the oxen for the wood. 2
1Kg 6:15 he covered them on the inside with wood; 2
34 and two doors of cypress wood; 2
10.11 from Ophir a very great amount of almug wood 2
12 the king made of the almug wood supports 2
12 no such almug wood has come or been seen, 2
18:23 cut it in pieces and lay it on the wood 2
23 prepare the other bull and lay it on the wood 2
33 he put the wood in order, and cut the bull in pieces 2
33 and cut the bull in pieces and laid it on the wood. 2
33 pour it on the burnt offering, and on the wood. 2
38 consumed the burnt offering, and the wood 2
2Kg 2:24 And two shebears came out of the woods 1
19:18 no gods, but the work of men's hands, wood and stone; 2
1Ch 16:33 the trees of the wood sing for joy before the LORD 1
21:23 I give . . the threshing sledges for the wood 2
29: 2 and wood for the things of wood 2
2Ch 2:14 trained to work in gold, silver . . stone, and wood 2
3:10 most holy place he made two cherubim of wood 6
9:10 brought algum wood and precious stones. 2
11 king made of the algum wood steps for the house 2
Neh 10:34 cast lots . . for the wood offering, to bring it 2
13:31 provided for the wood offering, at appointed 2
Job 41:27 counts iron as straw, and bronze as rotten wood. 2
Ps 96:12 Then shall all the trees of the wood sing for joy 1
Prv 26:20 For lack of wood the fire goes out; 2
21 As charcoal to hot embers and wood to fire, so is 2
Sng 2: 3 As an apple tree among the trees of the wood, so is 1
3: 9 made . . a palanquin from the wood of Lebanon. 2
Isa 10:15 or as if a staff should lift him who is not wood! 2
30:33 deep and wide, with fire and wood in abundance; 2
37:19 but the work of men's hands, wood and stone; 2
40:20 chooses for an offering wood that will not rot; 2
44:19 Shall I fall down before a block of wood? 2
60:17 instead of wood, bronze, instead of stones, iron. 2
Jer 5:14 this people wood, and the fire shall devour them. 2
7:18 children gather wood, the fathers kindle fire 2
10: 8 the instruction of idols is but wood! 2
Lam 4: 8 their skin has . . become as dry as wood. 2
5: 4 We must pay for . . the wood we get must be bought. 2
13 and boys stagger under loads of wood. 2
Ezk 15: 2 how does the wood of the vine surpass any wood 2
2 how does the wood of the vine surpass any wood 2
3 Is wood taken from it to make anything? 2
6 Like the wood of the vine among the trees 2
20:32 and worship wood and stone. 2
21:10 despised the rod, my son, with everything of wood. 2
34:25 in the wilderness and sleep in the woods. 1
39:10 they will not need to take wood out of the field 2
41:16 the temple was paneled with wood round about 2
22 an altar of wood, three cubits high 2
22 its corners, its base, and its walls were of wood. 2
25 there was a canopy of wood in front 2
Dan 5: 4 praised the gods of . . wood, and stone. 3
23 gods of . . bronze, iron, wood, and stone 3
Hag 1: 8 to the hills and bring wood and build the house 2
Zec 12: 6 Judah like a blazing pot in the midst of wood 2
Lke 23:31 if they do this when the wood is green 6
1Co 3:12 with gold, silver, precious stones, wood, hay, straw- 6
2Ti 2:20 also of wood and earthenware 5
Rev 9:20 idols of . . silver and bronze and stone and wood 5
18:12 all kinds of scented wood, all articles of ivory 6
12 articles of costly wood, bronze, iron and marble 6
2Es 5: 5 Blood shall drip from wood 7
Wis 10: 4 steering . . by a paltry piece of wood. 6
14: 1 one . . calls upon a piece of wood 6
5 even to the smallest piece of wood 6
7 the wood by which righteousness comes. 6
21 men . . bestowed on objects of stone or wood the name 6
Sir 8: 3 nor heap wood on his fire. 6
Bar 5: 8 The woods and every fragrant tree have shaded 4
LJr 1: 4 you will see gods made of silver and gold and wood 5
11 these gods of silver and gold and wood 5
30 serve meals for gods of silver and gold and wood; 5
50 Since they are made of wood 5
63 sent from above to consume mountains and woods 4
70 gods of wood, overlaid with gold and silver. 5
71 their gods of wood, overlaid with gold and silver 5
2Mc 1:21 to sprinkle the liquid on the wood 6
4:41 some picked up stones, some blocks of wood 6

wood *See also* make, vessel.

carved wood 1. פִּתּוּחַ

Ps 74: 6 then all its carved wood they broke down 1

thing of wood 1. עֵץ

1Ch 29: 2 and wood for the things of wood 1
Hos 4:12 My people inquire of a thing of wood 1

woodcutter 1. *ὑλοτόμος*

Wis 13:11 A skilled woodcutter may saw down a tree 1

wooded 1. יַעַר

Jer 26:18 and the mountain of the house a wooded height. 1
Mic 3:12 and the mountain of the house a wooded height. 1

wooded *See also* hill.

wooden 1. עֵץ 2. *ξύλινος*

Neh 8: 4 Ezra the scribe stood on a wooden pulpit 1
Ps 74: 5 they hacked the wooden trellis with axes. 1
Isa 45:20 no knowledge who carry about their wooden idols 1
Jer 28:13 Thus says the LORD: You have broken wooden bars 1
1Es 9:42 stood on the wooden platform 2
Sir 22:16 A wooden beam firmly bonded into a building 2
LJr 1:55 When fire breaks out in a temple of wooden gods 2
59 better also a wooden pillar in a palace 2
1Mc 6:37 upon the elephants were wooden towers 2

wooden thing 1. עֵץ

Hab 2:19 Woe to him who says to a wooden thing, Awake; 1

woodwork 1. עֵץ

Hab 2:11 and the beam from the woodwork respond. 1

woof 1. עֵרֶב

Lev 13:48 in warp or woof of linen or wool, or in a skin 1
49 whether in warp or woof or in skin or in anything 1
51 in the garment, in warp or woof, or in the skin 1
52 garment, whether diseased in warp or woof 1
53 garment in warp or woof or in anything of skin 1
56 the garment or the skin or the warp or woof 1
57 garment, in warp or woof, or in anything of skin 1
58 the garment, warp or woof, or anything of skin 1
59 disease . . either in warp or woof, or in anything 1

wool 1. צֶמֶר 2. צְמַר (A) 3. *ἔριον*

Lev 13:48 disease . . whether a woolen or a linen garment 1
59 leprous disease in a garment of wool or linen 1
Deu 22:11 not wear a mingled stuff, wool and linen together. 1
Jdg 6:37 I am laying a fleece of wool on the threshing 1
2Kg 3: 4 had to deliver . . and the wool of 100,000 rams. 1
Ps 147:16 He gives snow like wool; he scatters hoarfrost 1
Prv 31:13 She seeks wool and flax, and works 1
Isa 1:18 red like crimson, they shall become like wool. 1
51: 8 and the worm will eat them like wool; 1
Ezk 27:18 great wealth . . wine of Helbon, and white wool 1
34: 3 you clothe yourselves with the wool 1
44:17 they shall have nothing of wool on them 1
Dan 7: 9 as snow, and the hair of his head like pure wool; 2
Hos 2: 5 give me . . my wool and my flax, my oil and my drink 1
9 and I will take away my wool and my flax 1
Heb 9:19 with water and scarlet wool and hyssop 3
Rev 1:14 his head and his hair were white as white wool 3

woolen 1. צֶמֶר

Lev 13:47 disease . . whether a woolen or a linen garment 1
52 woolen or linen, or anything of skin 1

word 1. אֵמֶר 2. אֹמֶר 3. אִמְרָה 4. דבר 5. דָּבָר 6. דְּבַר שְׂפָתַיִם 7. מִלָּה 8. פֶּה 9. פִּי אִישׁ 10. קוֹל 11. שָׂפָה 12. מֵאמַר (A) 13. מִלָּה (A) 14. *ἀκούω* 15. *εἶπον* 16. *λαλιά* 17. *λέγω* 18. *λόγιον* 19. *λογισμός* 20. *λόγος* 21. *ῥῆμα* 22. *στόμα* 23. *τρόπος* 24. *φάσις* 25. *φθέγμα* 26. *χεῖλος* 27. *χείρ* 28. sermo 29. verbum

Gen 11: 1 the whole earth had one language and few words. 5
15: 1 After these things the word of the LORD came 5
4 behold, the word of the LORD came to him 5
24:30 when he heard the words of Rebekah his sister 5
52 When Abraham's servant heard their words 5
27: 8 my son, obey my word as I command you. 10
13 only obey my word, and go, fetch them to me. 10
34 When Esau heard the words of his father, he cried 5
42 words of Esau her older son were told to Rebekah; 5
34:18 Their words pleased Hamor and Hamor's son 5
37: 8 yet more for his dreams and for his words. 5
14 Go now . . and bring me word again. 5
39:19 his master heard the words which his wife spoke 5
42:16 that your words may be tested 5
20 your words will be verified, and you shall not 5
44: 6 he overtook them, he spoke to them these words. 5
7 Why does my lord speak such words as these? 5
18 I pray you, speak a word in my lord's ears 5
24 we told him the words of my lord. 5
45:27 when they told him all the words of Joseph 5
Exd 4:15 speak to him and put the words in his mouth; 5
28 Moses told Aaron all the words of the LORD 5
30 Aaron spoke all the words which the LORD had 5
5: 9 that they may . . pay no regard to lying words. 5
8:13 the LORD did according to the word of Moses; 5
9:20 Then he who feared the word of the LORD among 5
21 he who did not regard the word of the LORD 5
19: 6 These are the words which you shall speak 5
7 these words which the LORD had commanded him. 5
8 And Moses reported the words of the people 5
9 Moses told the words of the people to the LORD. 5
20: 1 God spoke all these words, saying 5
24: 3 told the people all the words of the LORD 5
3 and said, "All the words which the LORD has spoken 5
4 Moses wrote all the words of the LORD. 5
8 in accordance with all these words. 5
32:28 the sons of Levi did according to the word of Moses; 5
34: 1 write upon the tables the words that were 5
27 the LORD said to Moses, "Write these words; 5
27 in accordance with these words I have made 5
28 wrote upon the tables the words of the covenant 5
36: 6 So Moses gave command, and word was proclaimed 10
Lev 10: 7 And they did according to the word of Moses 5
Num 3:16 numbered them according to the word of the LORD 8
51 according to the word of the LORD, as the LORD 8
11:23 see whether my word will come true for you or not. 5
24 Moses . . told the people the words of the LORD; 5
12: 6 said, "Hear my words: If there is a prophet among you 5
13:26 they brought back word to them and to all 5
14:20 LORD said, "I have pardoned, according to your word; 5
39 Moses told these words to all . . Israel 5
15:31 Because he has despised the word of the LORD 5
16:31 as he finished speaking all these words 5
22: 8 Lodge here this night, and I will bring back word 5
35 only the word which I bid you, that shall you 5
38 word that God puts in my mouth, that must I speak. 5
23: 5 the LORD put a word in Balaam's mouth, and said 5
16 LORD met Balaam, and put a word in his mouth 5
24: 4 oracle of him who hears the words of God 1
13 I would not be able to go beyond the word of the LORD 8
16 the oracle of him who hears the words of God 1
27:14 rebelled against my word in the wilderness 8
21 at his word they shall go out, and . . come 8
21 go out, and at his word they shall come 8
30: 2 he shall not break his word; he shall do 5
36: 5 Israel according to the word of the LORD, saying 8
Deu 1: 1 words that Moses spoke to all Israel 5
22 bring us word again of the way by which we must go 5
25 brought us word again, and said, 'It is a good land 5
32 Yet in spite of this word you did not believe 5
34 LORD heard your words, and was angered, 5
2:26 sent . . to Sihon . . , with words of peace, saying 5
4: 2 You shall not add to the word which I command you 5
10 that I may let them hear my words, so that they 5
12 you heard the sound of words, but saw no form; 5
36 you heard his words out of the midst of the fire. 5
5: 5 I stood . . to declare to you the word of the LORD; 5
22 These words the LORD spoke to all your assembly 5
28 LORD heard your words, when you spoke to me; 5
28 'I have heard the words of this people 5
6: 6 these words which I command you this day 5

9: 5 that he may confirm the word which the LORD swore 5
10 all the words which the LORD had spoken with you 5
10: 2 I will write on the tables the words 5
11:18 lay up these words of mine in your heart 5
12:28 heed all these words which I command you 5
13: 3 you shall not listen to the words of that prophet 5
17:19 fear the LORD . . keeping all the words of this law 5
18:18 I will put my words in his mouth, and he shall speak 5
19 whoever will not give heed to my words which he 5
20 prophet who presumes to speak a word in my name 5
21 we know the word which the LORD has not spoken?' 5
22 if the word does not come to pass or come true 5
22 that is a word which the LORD has not spoken; 5
21: 5 by their word every dispute . . shall be settled. 8
27: 3 shall write upon them all the words of this law 5
8 write upon the stones all the words of this law 5
26 not confirm the words of this law by doing them.' 5
28:14 if you do not turn aside from any of the words 5
58 If . . not careful to do all the words of this law 5
29: 1 These are the words of the covenant 5
9 be careful to do the words of this covenant 5
19 when he hears the words of this sworn covenant 5
29 that we may do all the words of this law. 5
30:14 word is very near you; it is in your mouth 5
31: 1 continued to speak these words to all Israel. 5
12 may . . be careful to do all the words of this law 5
24 finished writing the words of this law in a book 5
28 that I may speak these words in their ears 5
30 Then Moses spoke the words of this song 5
32: 1 let the earth hear the words of my mouth. 1
44 Moses came and recited all the words of this song 5
45 finished speaking all these words to all Israel 5
46 Lay to heart all the words which I enjoin upon you 5
46 may be careful to do all the words of this law. 5
33: 9 they observed thy word, and kept they covenant. 3
34: 5 died there . . according to the word of the LORD 8
Jos 1:13 Remember the word which Moses . . commanded you 5
18 rebels against . . and disobeys your words 5
2:21 And she said, "According to your words, so be it. 5
3: 9 Come . . and hear the words of the LORD your God. 5
6:10 neither shall any word go out of your mouth 5
8:27 Israel took . . according to the word of the LORD 5
34 all the words of the law, the blessing and . . curse 5
35 There was not a word . . which Joshua did not read 5
14: 7 and I brought him word again as it was in my heart. 5
10 the time that the LORD spoke this word to Moses 5
22:30 heard the words that the Reubenites . . spoke 5
32 returned . . and brought back word to them. 5
24:26 Joshua wrote these words in the book of the law 5
27 it has heard all the words of the LORD 1
Jdg 2: 4 spoke these words to all the people of Israel 5
9: 3 kinsmen spoke all these words on his behalf 5
30 When Zebul . . heard the words of Ga'al the son 5
11:11 Jephthah spoke all his words before the LORD 5
13:12 when your words come true, what is to be the boy's 5
17 when your words come true, we may honor you? 5
16:16 she pressed him hard with her words day after day 5
21:13 the whole congregation sent word 4
1Sm 1:23 wait . . only, may the LORD establish his word. 5
3: 1 And the word of the LORD was rare in those days; 5
7 the word of the LORD had not yet been revealed 5
19 and let none of his words fall to the ground. 5
21 LORD revealed himself . . by the word of the LORD. 5
4: 1 And the word of Samuel came to all Israel. 5
8:10 Samuel told all the words of the LORD 5
21 when Samuel had heard all the words of the people 5
9:27 that I may make known to you the word of God. 5
11: 6 came . . upon Saul when he heard these words 5
15: 1 now therefore hearken to the words of the LORD. 5
10 The word of the LORD came to Samuel 5
23 Because you have rejected the word of the LORD 5
24 transgressed the commandment . . and your words 5
26 for you have rejected the word of the LORD 5
17:11 all Israel heard these words of the Philistine 5
23 came up . . and spoke the same words as before. 5
29 What have I done now? Was it not but a word? 5
31 When the words which David spoke were heard 5
18:23 servants spoke those words in the ears of David. 5
26 And when his servants told David these words 5
21:12 And David took these words to heart 5
24: 7 David persuaded his men with these words 5
9 Why do you listen to the words of men 5
16 David had finished speaking these words to Saul 5
25:24 and hear the words of your handmaid. 5
26:19 let my lord . . hear the words of his servant. 5
28:20 filled with fear because of the words of Samuel; 5
23 urged him; and he hearkened to their words. 10
2Sm 3: 8 Abner was . . angry over the words of Ish-bo'sheth 5
11 Ish-bo'sheth could not answer Abner another word 5
7: 4 that . . night the word of the LORD came to Nathan 5
7 did I speak a word with any of the judges of Israel 5
17 In accordance with all these words 5
25 confirm for ever the word which thou hast spoken 5
28 O Lord GOD, thou art God, and thy words are true 5
12: 9 you despised the word of the LORD, to do . . evil 5
14: 3 speak thus . . " So Jo'ab put the words in her mouth. 5
12 Pray let your handmaid speak a word to my lord 5
17 The word of my lord the king will set me at rest'; 5
19 it was he who put all these words in the mouth 5
32 I sent word to you, 'Come here, that I may send you •
15:28 I will wait . . until word comes from you to inform 5
19:11 when the word of all Israel has come to the king? 5
43 But the words of the men of Judah were fiercer 5
43 were fiercer than the words of the men of Israel. 5
20:17 Listen to the words of your maidservant. 5
22: 1 And David spoke to the LORD the words of this song 5
23: 1 Now these are the last words of David 5
2 Spirit . . speaks by me, his word is upon my tongue. 7
24: 4 But the king's word prevailed against Jo'ab 5
11 the word of the LORD came to the prophet Gad 5
19 David went up at Gad's word, as . . commanded. 5
1Kg 1:14 I also will come in . . and confirm your words. 5
2: 4 the LORD may establish his word which he spoke 5
23 if this word does not cost Adoni'jah his life! 5
27 thus fulfilling the word of the LORD which he had 5
30 Benai'ah brought the king word again, saying, "Thus 5
3:12 I now do according to your word. Behold, I give you 5
5: 2 Solomon sent word to Hiram •
7 When Hiram heard the words of Solomon 5
6:11 Now the word of the LORD came to Solomon 5
12 I will establish my word with you, which I spoke 5
8:26 let thy word be confirmed, which thou hast spoken 5
56 not one word has failed of all his good promise 5
59 Let these words of mine . . be near to the LORD 5
12: 7 serve them, and speak good words to them 5
15 brought about . . that he might fulfil his word 5
22 the word of God came to Shemai'ah the man of God 5
24 they hearkened to the word of the LORD 5
24 went home . . according to the word of the LORD. 5
13: 1 man of God came out of Judah by the word 5
2 cried against the altar by the word of the LORD 5
5 which the man . . had given by the word of the LORD. 5
9 so was it commanded me by the word of the LORD 5
11 the words also which he had spoken to the king 5
17 it was said to me by the word of the LORD 5
18 an angel spoke to me by the word of the LORD, saying 5
20 the word of the LORD came to the prophet 5
21 Because you have disobeyed the word of the LORD 8
26 the man of God, who disobeyed the word of the LORD; 8
26 the word which the LORD spoke to him. 5
32 the saying which he cried by the word of the LORD 5
14:18 mourned for him, according to the word of the LORD 5
15:29 destroyed it, according to the word of the LORD 5
16: 1 the word of the LORD came to Jehu the son 5
7 the word of the LORD came by the prophet Jehu 5
12 Thus Zimri . . according to the word of the LORD 5
34 according to the word of the LORD, which he spoke 5
17: 1 neither dew nor rain . . except by my word. 5
2 And the word of the LORD came to him 5
5 he went and did according to the word of the LORD; 5
8 Then the word of the LORD came to him 5
16 according to the word of the LORD which he spoke 5
24 the word of the LORD in your mouth is truth. 5
18: 1 the word of the LORD came to Eli'jah . . saying, "Go 5
21 And the people did not answer him a word. 5
31 Jacob, to whom the word of the LORD came, saying 5
36 and that I have done all these things at thy word. 5
19: 9 the word of the LORD came to him, and he said to him 5
20: 9 the messengers departed and brought him word 5
21:11 the men of his city . . did as Jez'ebel had sent word •
17 the word of the LORD came to Eli'jah the Tishbite 5
27 when Ahab heard those words, he rent his clothes 5
28 the word of the LORD came to Eli'jah the Tishbite 5
22: 5 Inquire first for the word of the LORD. 5
13 the words of the prophets . . are favorable 5
13 let your word be like the word of one of them 5
13 let your word be like the word of one of them 5
19 Therefore hear the word of the LORD: I saw the LORD 5
38 dogs licked . . according to the word of the LORD 5
2Kg 1:16 there is no God in Israel to inquire of his word? 5
17 So he died according to the word of the LORD 5
2:22 according to the word which Eli'sha spoke. 5
3: 7 he went and sent word to Jehosh'aphat •
12 said, "The word of the LORD is with him. 5
4:13 Would you have a word spoken on your behalf •
44 had some left, according to the word of the LORD. 5
5: 7 this man sends word to me to cure a man •
14 dipped . . according to the word of the man of God; 5
6: 9 the man of God sent word to the king of Israel •
12 tells the king of Israel the words that you speak 5
30 When the king heard the words . . he rent his clothes 5
7: 1 Hear the word of the LORD: thus says the LORD 5
16 for a shekel, according to the word of the LORD. 5
8: 2 and did according to the word of the man of God; 5
9:26 in accordance with the word of the LORD. 5
36 This is the word of the LORD, which he spoke 5
10:10 shall fall . . nothing of the word of the LORD 5
17 he slew all . . according to the word of the LORD 5
14: 9 Jeho'ash king of Israel sent word to Amazi'ah •
25 according to the word of the LORD, the God 5
18:20 Do you think that mere words are strategy 6
27 to speak these words to your master and to you 5
28 Hear the word of the great king 5
36 people were silent and answered him not a word 5
37 came . . and told him the words of the Rab'shakeh. 5
19: 4 the LORD . . heard all the words of the Rab'shakeh 5
4 will rebuke the words which the LORD . . has heard; 5
6 be afraid because of the words . . you have heard 5
16 hear the words of Sennach'erib, which he has sent 5
21 This is the word that the LORD has spoken 5
20: 4 the word of the LORD came to him 5
16 Isaiah said to Hezeki'ah, "Hear the word of the LORD 5
19 The word of the LORD which you have spoken is good. 5
22:11 the king heard the words of the book of the law 5
13 Go, inquire . . concerning the words of this book 5
13 fathers have not obeyed the words of this book 5
16 I will bring evil . . all the words of the book 5
18 Regarding the words which you have heard 5
20 And they brought back word to the king. 5
23: 2 all the words of the book of the covenant 5
3 to perform the words of this covenant 5
16 and defiled it, according to the word of the LORD 5
24 that he might establish the words of the law 5
24: 2 to destroy it, according to the word of the LORD 5
1Ch 11: 3 according to the word of the LORD by Samuel. 5
10 to make him king, according to the word of the LORD 5
12:23 according to the word of the LORD. 8
15:15 commanded according to the word of the LORD. 5
16:15 mindful . . of the word that he commanded 5
17: 3 same night the word of the LORD came to Nathan 5
6 did I speak a word with any of the judges of Israel 5
15 In accordance with all these words 5
23 now, O LORD, let the word which thou hast spoken 5
21: 4 the king's word prevailed against Jo'ab. 5
19 David went up at Gad's word, which he had spoken 5
22: 8 the word of the LORD came to me, saying 5
23:27 for by the last words of David these were 5
2Ch 2: 3 Solomon sent word to Huram the king of Tyre •
6:17 O LORD, God of Israel, let thy word be confirmed 5
10: 7 If you will . . speak good words to them 5
15 that the LORD might fulfil his word 5
11: 2 word of the LORD came to Shemai'ah the man of God 5
4 So they hearkened to the word of the LORD 5
12: 7 word of the LORD came to Shemai'ah 5
15: 8 When Asa heard these words . . he took courage 5
18: 4 Inquire first for the word of the LORD. 5
12 Behold, the words of the prophets with one accord 5
12 let your word be like the word of one of them 5
12 let your word be like the word of one of them •
18 Micai'ah said, "Therefore hear the word of the LORD 5
25:18 Jo'ash the king of Israel sent word to Amazi'ah •
29:15 the king had commanded, by the words of the LORD 5
30 praises . . with the words of David and of Asaph 5
30:12 commanded by the word of the LORD. 5
32: 8 took confidence from the words of Hezeki'ah 5
33:18 words of the seers who spoke to him 5
34:19 When the king heard the words of the law 5
21 inquire . . concerning the words of the book 5
21 our fathers have not kept the word of the LORD 5
26 Regarding the words which you have heard 5
27 humbled yourself . . when you heard his words 5
28 they brought back word to the king. 5
30 read in their hearing all the words of the book 5
31 to perform the words of the covenant 5
35: 6 to do according to the word of the LORD by Moses. 5
22 did not listen to the words of Neco from . . God 5
36:16 despising his words, and scoffing at his 5
21 to fulfil the word of the LORD by . . Jeremiah 5
22 that the word of the LORD by the mouth of Jeremiah 5
Ezr 1: 1 that the word of the LORD by the mouth of Jeremiah 5
6:13 according to the word sent by Darius the king •
9: 4 all who trembled at the words of the God of Israel 5
Neh 1: 1 The words of Nehemi'ah the son of Hacali'ah. 5
4 When I heard these words I sat down and wept 5
8 Remember the word which thou didst command 5
2:18 also of the words which the king had spoken to me. 5
5: 6 I was very angry when I heard . . these words. 5
8 They were silent, and could not find a word to say. 5
6: 7 reported to the king according to these words. 5
19 Also they . . reported my words to him. 5
8: 9 people wept when they heard the words of the law. 5
12 understood the words that were declared to them. 5
13 came . . in order to study the words of the law. 5
Est 3: 4 to see whether Mor'decai's words would avail; 5
7: 8 As the words left the mouth of the king 5
9 prepared for Mor'decai, whose word saved the king 4
9:30 Letters were sent . . in words of peace and truth 5
Job 2:13 no one spoke a word to him 5
4: 2 If one ventures a word with you 5
4 Your words have upheld him who was stumbling 7
12 Now a word was brought to me stealthily 5
6: 3 therefore my words have been rash. 5
10 for I have not denied the words of the Holy One. 1
25 How forceful are honest words! 1
26 Do you think that you can reprove words 7
8: 2 and the words of your mouth be a great wind? 1
10 and utter words out of their understanding? 7
9:14 can I answer him, choosing my words with him? 5
11: 2 Should a multitude of words go unanswered 5
12:11 the ear try words as the palate tastes food? 7
13:17 Listen carefully to my words 7
15: 3 or in words with which he can do no good? 7
11 or the word that deals gently with you? 5
13 and let such words go out of your mouth? 7
16: 3 Shall windy words have an end? 5
4 I could join words together against you 7
18: 2 How long will you hunt for words? 7

19: 2 you torment me, and break me in pieces with words? 7
23 Oh that my words were written! 7
21: 2 Listen carefully to my words 7
22:22 lay up his words in your heart. 1
23:12 treasured in my bosom the words of his mouth. 1
26: 4 With whose help have you uttered words 7
29:22 not speak again, and my word dropped upon them. 7
31:40 The words of Job are ended. 5
32:11 Behold, I waited for your words 5
12 that confuted Job, or that answered his words 1
14 He has not directed his words against me 7
15 they answer no more; they have not a word to say. 7
18 For I am full of words 7
33: 1 hear my speech, O Job, and listen to all my words. 5
3 My words declare the uprightness of my heart 1
5 set your words in order before me; take your stand. *
8 I have heard the sound of your words. 7
13 He will answer none of my words'? 5
34: 2 Hear my words, you wise men 7
3 the ear tests words as the palate tastes food. 7
35 his words are without insight. 5
37 among us, and multiplies his words against God. 1
35:16 he multiplies words without knowledge. 7
36: 4 For truly my words are not false; 7
38: 2 darkens counsel by words without knowledge? 7
42: 7 After the LORD had spoken these words to Job 5
Ps 5: 1 Give ear to my words, O LORD; 2
17: 4 by the word of thy lips I have avoided the ways 5
6 O God; incline thy ear to me, hear my words. 3
18: 0 David . . who addressed the words of this song 5
19: 3 There is no speech, nor are there words; 5
4 and their words to the end of the world. 7
14 Let the words of my mouth . . be acceptable 1
22: 1 far from helping me, from the words of my groaning? 5
33: 4 For the word of the LORD is upright; 5
6 By the word of the LORD the heavens were made 5
35:20 in the land they conceive words of deceit. 5
36: 3 The words of his mouth are mischief and deceit; 5
44:16 at the words of the taunters and revilers 10
50:17 you cast my words behind you. 5
52: 4 You love all words that devour 5
54: 2 O God; give ear to the words of my mouth. 1
55:21 his words were softer than oil 5
56: 4 In God, whose word I praise, in God I trust 5
10 In God, whose word I praise 5
10 in the LORD, whose word I praise 5
59:12 the sin of their mouths, the words of their lips 5
64: 3 who aim bitter words like arrows 5
78: 1 incline your ears to the words of my mouth! 1
94: 4 They pour out their arrogant words, they boast 4
103:20 O you his angels, you mighty ones who do his word 5
20 do his word, hearkening to the voice of his word! 5
105: 8 He is mindful of . . the word that he commanded 5
19 until . . came to pass the word of the LORD tested 3
28 they rebelled against his words. 5
106:12 Then they believed his words; 5
107:11 for they had rebelled against the words of God 1
20 he sent forth his word, and healed them 5
109: 3 They beset me with words of hate 5
119: 9 way pure? By guarding it according to thy word. 5
11 I have laid up thy word in my heart 3
16 I will not forget thy word. 5
17 that I may live and observe thy word. 5
25 revive me according to thy word! 5
28 strengthen me according to thy word! 5
42 for those who taunt me, for I trust in thy word. 5
43 take not the word of truth utterly out of my mouth 5
49 Remember thy word to thy servant 5
57 LORD is my portion; I promise to keep thy words. 5
65 with thy servant, O LORD, according to thy word. 5
67 I went astray; but now I keep thy word. 3
74 rejoice, because I have hoped in thy word. 5
81 I hope in thy word. 5
89 O LORD, thy word is firmly fixed in the heavens. 5
101 from every evil way, in order to keep thy word. 5
103 How sweet are thy words to my taste 3
105 Thy word is a lamp to my feet and a light to my path. 5
107 give me life, O LORD, according to thy word! 5
114 I hope in thy word. 5
130 The unfolding of thy words gives light; 5
139 consumes me, because my foes forget thy words. 5
147 I . . cry for help; I hope in thy words. 5
160 The sum of thy word is truth; 5
161 my heart stands in awe of thy words. 5
162 I rejoice at thy word like one who finds 3
169 give me understanding according to thy word! 5
170 deliver me according to thy word. 3
172 My tongue will sing of thy word 3
130: 5 for the LORD, my soul waits, and in his word I hope; 5
138: 2 exalted above everything thy name and thy word. 3
4 for they have heard the words of thy mouth; 1
139: 4 Even before a word is on my tongue, lo, O LORD 7
141: 6 then . . learn that the word of the LORD is true. 1
145:13 The LORD is faithful in all his words 5
147:15 command to the earth; his word runs swiftly. 5
18 He sends forth his word, and melts them; 5
19 He declares his word to Jacob 5
Prv 1: 2 That men may . . understand words of insight 1
6 understand . . words of the wise and their riddles. 5

23 I will make my words known to you. 5
2: 1 My son, if you receive my words 1
16 saved from . . adventuress with her smooth words 1
4: 4 Let your heart hold fast my words; 5
5 do not turn away from the words of my mouth. 1
10 Hear, my son, and accept my words 1
20 My son, be attentive to my words; 5
5: 7 do not depart from the words of my mouth. 1
6: 2 if you are . . caught in the words of your mouth; 1
7: 1 My son, keep my words 1
5 from the adventuress with her smooth words. 1
24 O sons . . be attentive to the words of my mouth. 1
8: 8 All the words of my mouth are righteous; 1
10:19 words are many, transgression is not lacking 5
12: 6 The words of the wicked lie in wait for blood 5
14 fruit of his words a man is satisfied with good 9
25 but a good word makes him glad. 5
13:13 despises the word brings destruction on himself 5
14: 7 for there you do not meet words of knowledge. 11
15: 1 but a harsh word stirs up anger. 5
23 word in season, how good it is! 5
26 words of the pure are pleasing to him. 1
16:20 He who gives heed to the word will prosper 5
24 Pleasant words are like a honeycomb 1
17:27 He who restrains his words has knowledge 1
18: 4 The words of a man's mouth are deep waters; 5
8 words of a whisperer are like delicious morsels; 5
19: 7 He pursues them with words, but does not have them. 1
16 he who despises the word will die. *
27 only to stray from the words of knowledge. 1
21:28 but the word of a man who hears will endure. 4
22:12 but he overthrows the words of the faithless. 5
17 Incline your ear, and hear the words of the wise 5
23: 8 vomit . . and waste your pleasant words. 5
9 for he will despise the wisdom of your words. 7
12 Apply . . your ear to words of knowledge. 1
25:11 A word fitly spoken is like apples of gold 5
27 so be sparing of complimentary words. 20
26:22 words of a whisperer are like delicious morsels; 5
29:19 By mere words a servant is not disciplined 5
20 Do you see a man who is hasty in his words? 5
30: 1 The words of Agur son of Jakeh of Massa. 5
5 Every word of God proves true; 3
6 Do not add to his words, lest he rebuke you 5
31: 1 The words of Lemuel, king of Massa 5
Ecc 1: 1 The words of the Preacher, the son of David 5
5: 2 let your heart be hasty to utter a word before God 5
2 therefore let your words be few. 5
3 dream comes . . and a fool's voice with many words. 5
7 For when dreams increase, empty words grow many 5
6:11 The more words, the more vanity 5
8: 4 For the word of the king is supreme, and who may say 5
9:16 poor man's wisdom . . and his words are not heeded. 5
17 The words of the wise . . in quiet are better 5
10:12 The words of a wise man's mouth win him favor 5
13 The beginning of the words of his mouth is 5
14 A fool multiplies words, though no man knows 5
12:10 The Preacher sought to find pleasing words 5
10 and uprightly he wrote words of truth. 5
Isa 1:10 Hear the word of the LORD, you rulers of Sodom! 5
2: 1 The word which Isaiah the son of Amoz saw 5
3 the law, and the word of the LORD from Jerusalem. 5
5:24 have despised the word of the Holy One of Israel. 3
8:10 come to nought; speak a word, but it will not stand 5
20 for this word which they speak there is no dawn. 5
9: 8 The Lord has sent a word against Jacob 5
16:13 This is the word which the LORD spoke concerning 5
24: 3 for the LORD has spoken this word. 5
28:13 Therefore the word of the LORD will be to them 5
14 Therefore hear the word of the LORD, you scoffers 5
29: 4 from low in the dust your words shall come; 3
11 this has become to you like the words of a book 5
18 In that day the deaf shall hear the words of a book 5
21 who by a word make a man out to be an offender 5
30:12 Because you despise this word 5
21 your ears shall hear a word behind you 5
31: 2 he does not call back his words 5
32: 7 wicked devices to ruin the poor with lying words 1
36: 5 you think . . mere words are strategy and power 6
12 Has my master sent me to speak these words 5
13 Hear the words of the great king 5
21 they were silent and answered him not a word 5
22 and told him the words of the Rab'shakeh. 5
37: 4 may be . . God heard the words of the Rab'shakeh 5
4 rebuke the words which the LORD . . has heard; 5
6 afraid because of the words that you have heard 5
17 hear all the words of Sennach'erib 5
22 this is the word that the LORD has spoken 5
38: 4 Then the word of the LORD came to Isaiah 5
39: 5 Isaiah said to Hezeki'ah, "Hear the word of the LORD 5
8 word of the LORD which you have spoken is good. 5
40: 8 fades; but the word of our God will stand for ever. 5
41:26 none who proclaimed, none who heard your words. 1
44:26 who confirms the word of his servant 5
45:23 gone forth . . a word that shall not return 5
50: 4 know how to sustain with a word him that is weary. 5
51:16 I have put my words in your mouth, and hid you 5
55:11 shall my word be that goes forth from my mouth; 5
59:13 and uttering from the heart lying words. 5

21 and my words which I have put in your mouth 5
66: 2 contrite in spirit, and trembles at my word. 5
5 Hear the word of the LORD, 5
5 the word of the LORD, you who tremble at his word 5
Jer 1: 1 The words of Jeremiah, the son of Hilki'ah 5
2 to whom the word of the LORD came 5
4 Now the word of the LORD came to me saying 5
9 Behold, I have put my words in your mouth. 5
11 the word of the LORD came to me, saying, "Jeremiah 5
12 for I am watching over my word to perform it. 5
13 The word of the LORD came to me a second time 5
2: 1 The word of the LORD came to me, saying 5
4 Hear the word of the LORD, O house of Jacob 5
31 And you, O generation, heed the word of the LORD. 5
3:12 Go, and proclaim these words toward the north 5
5:13 prophets . . become wind; the word is not in them. 4
14 Because they have spoken this word 5
14 behold, I am making my words in your mouth a fire 5
6:10 the word of the LORD is to them an object of scorn 5
19 because they have not given heed to my words; 5
7: 1 The word that came to Jeremiah from the LORD 5
2 and proclaim there this word, and say 5
2 and say, Hear the word of the LORD 5
4 Do not trust in these deceptive words 5
8 Behold, you trust in deceptive words to no avail. 5
27 you shall speak all these words to them 5
8: 9 lo, they have rejected the word of the LORD 5
9:20 Hear, O women, the word of the LORD 5
20 and let your ear receive the word of his mouth; 5
10: 1 Hear the word which the LORD speaks to you 5
11: 1 The word that came to Jeremiah from the LORD 5
2 Hear the words of this covenant 5
3 who does not heed the words of this covenant 5
6 Proclaim all these words in the cities of Judah 5
6 Hear the words of this covenant and do them. 5
8 brought upon them all the words of this covenant 5
10 their forefathers, who refused to hear my words; 5
13: 2 a waistcloth according to the word of the LORD 5
3 the word of the LORD came to me a second time 5
8 Then the word of the LORD came to me 5
10 This evil people, who refuse to hear my words 5
12 You shall speak to them this word 5
14: 1 The word of the LORD which came to Jeremiah 5
17 You shall say to them this word 5
15:16 Thy words were found, and I ate them 5
16 thy words became to me a joy 5
16: 1 The word of the LORD came to me 5
10 And when you tell this people all these words 5
17:15 they say to me, "Where is the word of the LORD? 5
20 say: 'Hear the word of the LORD, you kings of Judah 5
18: 1 The word that came to Jeremiah from the LORD 5
2 and there I will let you hear my words. 5
5 Then the word of the LORD came to me 5
18 from the wise, nor the word from the prophet. 5
18 let us not heed any of his words. 5
19: 2 and proclaim there the words that I tell you. 5
3 You shall say, 'Hear the word of the LORD 5
15 stiffened their neck, refusing to hear my words. 5
20: 8 the word of the LORD has become for me a reproach 5
21: 1 the word which came to Jeremiah from the LORD 5
11 to . . Judah say, 'Hear the word of the LORD 5
22: 1 and speak there this word 5
2 and say, 'Hear the word of the LORD, O King of Judah 5
4 For if you will indeed obey this word 5
5 if you will not heed these words, I swear by myself 5
29 O land, land, land, hear the word of the LORD! 5
23: 9 because of the LORD and because of his holy words. 5
16 Do not listen to the words of the prophets 5
17 to those who despise the word of the LORD 4
18 of the LORD to perceive and to hear his word 5
18 or who has given heed to his word and listened? 5
22 then they would have proclaimed my words 5
28 let him who has my word speak my word faithfully. 5
28 let him who has my word speak my word faithfully. 5
29 Is not my word like fire, says the LORD 5
30 prophets . . who steal my words from one another. 5
36 for the burden is every man's own word 5
36 and you pervert the words of the living God 5
38 you have said these words, "The burden of the LORD 5
24: 4 Then the word of the LORD came to me 5
25: 1 The word that came to Jeremiah 5
3 to this day, the word of the LORD has come to me 5
8 Because you have not obeyed my words 5
13 all the words which I have uttered against it 5
30 shall prophesy against them all these words 5
26: 1 this word came from the LORD 5
2 all the words that I command you to speak to them; 5
2 to speak to them; do not hold back a word. 5
5 to heed the words of my servants the prophets 5
7 the people heard Jeremiah speaking these words 5
12 to prophesy . . all the words you have heard. 5
15 me to you to speak all these words in your ears. 5
20 prophesied . . in words like those of Jeremiah. 5
21 his warriors and all the princes, heard his words 5
27: 1 this word came to Jeremiah from the LORD. 5
3 Send word to the king of Edom, the king of Moab *
14 Do not listen to the words of the prophets 5
16 Do not listen to the words of your prophets 5
18 and if the word of the LORD is with them 5

28: 6 make the words . . you have prophesied come true 5
7 Yet hear now this word which I speak 5
9 when the word of that prophet comes to pass 5
12 the word of the LORD came to Jeremiah 5
29: 1 These are the words of the letter which Jeremiah 5
19 because they did not heed my words, says the LORD 5
20 Hear the word of the LORD, all you exiles 5
23 and they have spoken in my name lying words 5
30 Then the word of the LORD came to Jeremiah 5
30: 1 The word that came to Jeremiah from the LORD 5
2 Write in a book all the words that I have spoken 5
4 These are the words which the LORD spoke 5
31:10 Hear the word of the LORD, O nations, and declare it 5
23 they shall use these words in the land of Judah 5
32: 1 The word that came to Jeremiah from the LORD 5
6 Jeremiah said, "The word of the LORD came to me 5
8 came . . in accordance with the word of the LORD 5
8 Then I knew that this was the word of the LORD. 5
26 The word of the LORD came to Jeremiah 5
33: 1 word of the LORD came to Jeremiah a second time 5
19 The word of the LORD came to Jeremiah 5
23 The word of the LORD came to Jeremiah 5
34: 1 The word which came to Jeremiah from the LORD 5
4 Yet hear the word of the LORD, O Zedeki'ah 5
5 For I have spoken the word, says the LORD. 5
6 Then Jeremiah the prophet spoke all these words 5
8 The word which came to Jeremiah from the LORD 5
12 word of the LORD came to Jeremiah from the LORD 5
35: 1 The word which came to Jeremiah from the LORD 5
12 Then the word of the LORD came to Jeremiah 5
13 and listen to my words? says the LORD. 5
36: 1 this word came to Jeremiah from the LORD 5
2 write on it all the words that I have spoken to you 5
4 the words of the LORD which he had spoken to him. 5
6 you shall read the words of the LORD 5
8 reading from the scroll the words of the LORD 5
10 read the words of Jeremiah from the scroll 5
11 heard all the words of the LORD from the scroll 5
13 Micai'ah told them all the words that he had heard 5
16 When they heard all the words, they turned 5
16 We must report all these words to the king. 5
17 Tell us, how did you write all these words? 5
18 He dictated all these words to me 5
20 and they reported all the words to the king. 5
24 nor any of his servants who heard all these words 5
27 the scroll with the words which Baruch wrote 5
27 the word of the LORD came to Jeremiah 5
28 scroll and write on it all the former words 5
32 who wrote on it . . all the words of the scroll 5
32 and many similar words were added to them. 5
37: 2 nor the people of the land listened to the words 5
6 the word of the LORD came to Jeremiah the prophet 5
17 and said, "Is there any word from the LORD? 5
38: 1 and Pashhur the son of Malchi'ah heard the words 5
4 weakening the hands . . by speaking such words 5
24 said to Jeremiah, "Let no one know of these words 5
39:15 The word of the LORD came to Jeremiah 5
16 Behold, I will fulfil my words against this city 5
40: 1 The word that came to Jeremiah from the LORD 5
42: 5 if we do not act according to all the word 5
7 the word of the LORD came to Jeremiah. 5
15 then hear the word of the LORD, O remnant of Judah. 5
43: 1 speaking . . all these words of the LORD their God 5
8 Then the word of the LORD came to Jeremiah 5
44: 1 The word that came to Jeremiah 5
16 As for the word which you have spoken to us 5
24 Hear the word of the LORD, all you of Judah 5
26 Therefore hear the word of the LORD 5
28 shall know whose word will stand, mine or theirs. 5
29 that you may know that my words will surely stand 5
45: 1 The word that Jeremiah the prophet spoke 5
1 when he wrote these words in a book 5
46: 1 The word of the LORD which came to Jeremiah 5
13 The word which the LORD spoke to Jeremiah 5
47: 1 The word of the LORD that came to Jeremiah 5
49:34 The word of the LORD that came to Jeremiah 5
50: 1 word which the LORD spoke concerning Babylon 5
51:59 The word which Jeremiah the prophet commanded 5
60 upon Babylon, all these words that are written 5
61 see that you read all these words 5
64 Thus far are the words of Jeremiah. 5
Lam 1:18 in the right, for I have rebelled against his word; 8
Ezk 1: 3 the word of the LORD came to Ezekiel the priest 5
2: 6 not afraid of them, nor be afraid of their words 5
6 be not afraid of their words 5
7 you shall speak my words to them 5
10 there were written on it words of lamentation •
3: 4 and speak with my words to them. 5
6 language, whose words you cannot understand. 5
10 Son of man, all my words that I shall speak to you 5
16 the word of the LORD came to me 5
17 whenever you hear a word from my mouth 5
6: 1 The word of the LORD came to me 5
3 mountains of Israel, hear the word of the Lord GOD! 5
7: 1 The word of the LORD came to me 5
9:11 brought back word, saying, "I have done 5
11:14 the word of the LORD came to me 5
12: 1 The word of the LORD came to me 5
8 In the morning the word of the LORD came to me 5
17 Moreover the word of the LORD came to me 5
21 the word of the LORD came to me 5
25 I the LORD will speak the word which I will speak 5
25 I will speak the word and perform it, says the Lord 5
26 Again the word of the LORD came to me 5
28 None of my words will be delayed any longer 5
28 but the word which I speak will be performed 5
13: 1 The word of the LORD came to me 5
2 prophesy and say . . 'Hear the word of the LORD!' 5
6 yet they expect him to fulfil their word. 5
14: 2 the word of the LORD came to me 5
9 if the prophet be deceived and speak a word 5
12 the word of the LORD came to me 5
15: 1 the word of the LORD came to me 5
16: 1 Again the word of the LORD came to me 5
35 Wherefore, O harlot, hear the word of the LORD 5
17: 1 The word of the LORD came to me 5
11 Then the word of the LORD came to me 5
18: 1 The word of the LORD came to me again 5
20: 2 the word of the LORD came to me 5
45 the word of the LORD came to me 5
47 Hear the word of the LORD: Thus says the Lord GOD 5
21: 1 The word of the LORD came to me 5
8 the word of the LORD came to me 5
18 The word of the LORD came to me again 5
22: 1 Moreover the word of the LORD came to me, saying 5
17 the word of the LORD came to me 5
23 the word of the LORD came to me 5
23: 1 The word of the LORD came to me 5
24: 1 the word of the LORD came to me 5
15 Also the word of the LORD came to me 5
20 I said to them, "The word of the LORD came to me 5
25: 1 The word of the LORD came to me 5
3 Say to the Ammonites, Hear the word of the Lord GOD 5
26: 1 the word of the LORD came to me 5
27: 1 The word of the LORD came to me 5
28: 1 The word of the LORD came to me 5
11 Moreover the word of the LORD came to me 5
20 The word of the LORD came to me 5
29: 1 the word of the LORD came to me 5
17 the word of the LORD came to me 5
30: 1 The word of the LORD came to me 5
20 the word of the LORD came to me 5
31: 1 the word of the LORD came to me 5
32: 1 the word of the LORD came to me 5
17 the word of the LORD came to me 5
33: 1 The word of the LORD came to me 5
7 whenever you hear a word from my mouth 5
23 The word of the LORD came to me 5
30 Come, and hear what the word is that comes forth 5
34: 1 The word of the LORD came to me 5
7 you shepherds, hear the word of the LORD 5
9 you shepherds, hear the word of the LORD 5
35: 1 The word of the LORD came to me 5
13 and multiplied your words against me; I heard it. 5
36: 1 O mountains of Israel, hear the word of the LORD. 5
4 O mountains of Israel, hear the word of the Lord 5
16 The word of the LORD came to me 5
37: 4 say to them, O dry bones, hear the word of the LORD. 5
15 The word of the LORD came to me 5
38: 1 The word of the LORD came to me 5
Dan 2: 5 The word from me is sure: if you do not make known 13
8 because you see that the word from me is sure 13
9 agreed to speak lying and corrupt words 13
4:17 decision by the word of the holy ones 12
31 While the words were still in the king's mouth 13
33 word was fulfilled upon Nebuchadnez'zar. 13
5:10 because of the words of the king and his lords 13
6:14 Then the king, when he heard these words, 13
7:11 looked . . because of the sound of the great words 13
25 He shall speak words against the Most High 13
9: 2 according to the word of the LORD to Jeremiah 5
12 confirmed his words, which he spoke against us 5
23 At the beginning . . a word went forth 5
23 therefore consider the word and understand 5
25 going forth of the word to restore and build 5
10: 1 third year . . a word was revealed to Daniel 5
1 word was true, and it was a great conflict. 5
1 understood the word and had understanding 5
6 sound of his words like the noise of a multitude. 5
9 Then I heard the sound of his words; 5
9 when I heard the sound of his words, I fell 5
11 Daniel . . give heed to the words that I speak 5
11 While he was speaking this word to me, I stood up 5
12 from the first day . . your words have been heard 5
12 I have come because of your words. 5
15 When he had spoken to me according to these words 5
12: 4 Daniel, shut up the words, and seal the book 5
9 words are shut up and sealed until the . . end. 5
Hos 1: 1 The word of the LORD that came to Hose'a 5
4: 1 Hear the word of the LORD, O people of Israel; 5
6: 5 I have slain them by the words of my mouth 1
10: 4 They utter mere words; 5
14: 2 Take with you words and return to the LORD; 5
Jol 1: 1 The word of the LORD that came to Joel 5
2:11 he that executes his word is powerful. 5
Ams 1: 1 The words of Amos, who was among the shepherds 5
3: 1 Hear this word that the LORD has spoken against 5
4: 1 Hear this word, you cows of Bashan 5
5: 1 Hear this word which I take up over you 5
7:10 the land is not able to bear all his words. 5
16 Now therefore hear the word of the LORD. 5
8:11 but of hearing the words of the LORD. 5
12 run to and fro, to seek the word of the LORD 5
Jon 1: 1 Now the word of the LORD came to Jonah 5
3: 1 Then the word of the LORD came to Jonah 5
3 to Nin'eveh, according to the word of the LORD. 5
Mic 1: 1 The word of the LORD that came to Micah 5
2: 7 Do not my words do good to him who walks uprightly? 5
4: 2 the law, and the word of the LORD from Jerusalem. 5
Zep 1: 1 The word of the LORD which came to Zephani'ah 5
2: 5 The word of the LORD is against you, O Canaan 5
Hag 1: 1 the word of the LORD came by Haggai the prophet 5
3 the word of the LORD came by Haggai the prophet 5
12 the LORD their God, and the words of Haggai 5
2: 1 the word of the LORD came by Haggai the prophet 5
10 the word of the LORD came by Haggai the prophet 5
20 The word of the LORD came a second time to Haggai 5
Zec 1: 1 the word of the LORD came to Zechari'ah 5
6 But my words and my statutes, which I commanded 5
7 the word of the LORD came to Zechari'ah 5
13 gracious and comforting words to the angel 5
4: 6 This is the word of the LORD to Zerub'babel 5
8 Moreover the word of the LORD came to me, saying 5
6: 9 the word of the LORD came to me 5
7: 1 the word of the LORD came to Zechari'ah 5
4 Then the word of the LORD of hosts came to me; 5
7 were not these the words which the LORD 5
8 the word of the LORD came to Zechari'ah, saying 5
12 lest they should hear the law and the words 5
8: 1 the word of the LORD of hosts came to me, saying 5
9 these words from the mouth of the prophets 5
18 the word of the LORD of hosts came to me, saying 5
9: 1 word of the LORD is against the land of Hadrach 5
11:11 watching me, knew that it was the word of the LORD. 5
12: 1 An Oracle The word of the LORD concerning Israel 5
Mal 1: 1 the word of the LORD to Israel by Mal'achi. 5
2:17 You have wearied the LORD with your words. 5
3:13 Your words have been stout against me 5
Mat 4: 4 by bread alone, but by every word that proceeds 21
7:24 Every one then who hears these words of mine 20
26 And every one who hears these words of mine 20
8: 8 but only say the word 20
16 and he cast out the spirits with a word 20
10:14 or listen to your words 20
11: 2 he sent word by his disciples •
12:32 whoever says a word against the Son of man 20
36 will render account for every careless word 21
37 for by your words you will be justified 20
37 and by your words you will be condemned. 20
13:19 When any one hears the word of the kingdom 20
20 this is he who hears the word 20
21 persecution arises on account of the word 20
22 this is he who hears the word 20
22 and the delight in riches choke the word 20
23 this is he who hears the word 20
15: 6 you have made void the word of God. 20
23 he did not answer her a word 20
18:16 that every word may be confirmed 21
22:46 no one was able to answer him a word 20
24:35 but my words will not pass away. 20
26:44 for the third time, saying the same words. 20
27:19 his wife sent word to him 17
Mrk 2: 2 he was preaching the word to them. 20
4:14 The sower sows the word. 20
15 the ones along the path, where the word is sown; 20
15 takes away the word which is sown in them. 20
16 who, when they hear the word, immediately receive 20
17 persecution arises on account of the word 20
18 they are those who hear the word 20
19 enter in and choke the word 20
20 the ones who hear the word and accept it 20
33 With many such parables he spoke the word to them 20
6:26 he did not want to break his word to her. •
7:13 thus making void the word of God 20
8:38 whoever is ashamed of me and of my words 20
10:24 the disciples were amazed at his words 20
13:31 my words will not pass away. 20
14:39 went away and prayed, saying the same words. 20
Lke 1: 2 eyewitnesses and ministers of the word 20
20 because you did not believe my words 20
38 let it be to me according to your word 21
2:29 according to thy word; 21
3: 2 the word of God came to John the son of Zechari'ah 21
4 the book of the words of Isaiah the prophet 20
4:22 wondered at the gracious words 20
32 his word was with authority. 20
36 What is this word? 20
5: 1 people pressed upon him to hear the word of God 20
5 But at your word I will let down the nets. 21
6:47 who comes to me and hears my words and does them 20
7: 7 But say the word, and let my servant be healed. 20
8:11 the parable is this: The seed is the word of God. 20
12 takes away the word from their hearts 20
13 who, when they hear the word, receive it with joy 20
15 they are those who, hearing the word, hold it fast 20
21 those who hear the word of God and do it. 20
9:26 For whoever is ashamed of me and of my words 20

44 Let these words sink into your ears 20
11:28 Blessed rather are those who hear the word of God 20
12:10 every one who speaks a word against the Son of man 20
19:48 all the people hung upon his words. 14
21:33 my words will not pass away. 20
22:61 Peter remembered the word of the Lord 21
65 they spoke many other words against him •
24: 8 they remembered his words 21
11 these words seemed to them an idle tale 21
19 a prophet mighty in deed and word before God 20
44 These are my words which I spoke to you 20
Joh 1: 1 and the Word was with God, and the Word was God. 20
1 In the beginning was the Word 20
1 and the Word was with God, and the Word was God. 20
14 And the Word became flesh and dwelt among us 20
2:22 believed . . the word which Jesus had spoken. 20
3:34 For he whom God has sent utters the words of God 21
4:41 And many more believed because of his word. 20
42 no longer because of your words that we believe 16
50 The man believed the word that Jesus spoke to him 20
5:24 he who hears my word and believes him who sent me 20
38 do not have his word abiding in you 20
47 how will you believe my words? 21
6:63 the words that I have spoken to you 21
68 You have the words of eternal life; 21
7:40 When they heard these words 20
8:20 These words he spoke in the treasury 21
31 If you continue in my word 20
37 because my word finds no place in you. 20
43 It is because you cannot bear to hear my word. 20
47 He who is of God hears the words of God 21
51 if any one keeps my word, he will never see death. 20
52 and you say, 'If any one keeps my word 20
55 I do know him and I keep his word. 20
10:19 a division . . because of these words. 20
35 If he called them gods to whom the word of God came 20
12:38 the word spoken by the prophet Isaiah 20
48 the word that I have spoken will be his judge 20
14:10 The words that I say to you 21
23 If a man loves me, he will keep my word 20
24 He who does not love me does not keep my words 20
24 the word which you hear is not mine 20
15: 3 made clean by the word which I have spoken to you. 20
7 If you abide in me, and my words abide in you 21
20 Remember the word that I said to you 20
20 if they kept my word, they will keep yours also. 20
25 to fulfil the word that is written in their law 20
17: 1 When Jesus had spoken these words •
6 thou gavest them to me, and they have kept thy word. 20
8 I have given them the words which thou gavest me 21
14 I have given them thy word 20
17 Sanctify them in the truth; thy word is truth. 20
20 those who believe in me through their word 20
18: 1 When Jesus had spoken these words •
9 This was to fulfil the word which he had spoken 20
32 to fulfil the word which Jesus had spoken 20
19: 8 When Pilate heard these words 20
13 When Pilate heard these words 20
Act 2:14 let this be known to you, and give ear to my words. 21
22 Men of Israel, hear these words 20
40 he testified with many other words and exhorted 20
41 So those who received his word were baptized 20
4: 4 many of those who heard the word believed 20
29 grant to thy servants to speak thy word 20
31 spoke the word of God with boldness. 20
5: 5 When Anani'as heard these words 20
20 speak to the people all the words of this Life. 21
24 when . . the chief priests heard these words 20
6: 2 give up preaching the word of God to serve tables. 20
4 to prayer and to the ministry of the word. 20
7 the word of God increased 20
11 blasphemous words against Moses and God. 21
13 to speak words against this holy place and the law; 21
7:22 he was mighty in his words and deeds. 20
8: 4 those . . went about preaching the word. 20
14 Sama'ria had received the word of God 20
25 had testified and spoken the word of the Lord 20
10:36 You know the word which he sent to Israel 20
37 word which was proclaimed throughout all Judea 21
44 the Holy Spirit fell on all who heard the word. 20
11: 1 the Gentiles also had received the word of God. 20
16 I remembered the word of the Lord, how he said 21
19 speaking the word to none except Jews. 20
12:24 the word of God grew and multiplied. 20
13: 5 proclaimed the word of God in the synagogues 20
7 sought to hear the word of God. 20
15 Brethren, if you have any word of exhortation 20
44 gathered together to hear the word of God. 20
46 the word of God should be spoken first to you. 20
48 they were glad and glorified the word of God; 20
49 the word of the Lord spread 20
14: 3 who bore witness to the word of his grace 20
18 With these words they scarcely restrained •
25 when they had spoken the word in Perga 20
15: 7 the Gentiles should hear the word of the gospel 20
15 the words of the prophets agree, as it is written 20
24 some persons from us have troubled you with words 20
27 who . . will tell you the same things by word of mouth. 20
32 exhorted the brethren with many words 20
35 teaching and preaching the word of the Lord 20
36 in every city where we proclaimed the word 20
16: 6 forbidden . . to speak the word in Asia. 20
32 they spoke the word of the Lord to him 20
36 the jailer reported the words to Paul, saying 20
38 police reported these words to the magistrates 21
17:11 they received the word with all eagerness 20
13 the word of God was proclaimed by Paul at Beroe'a 20
18:11 teaching the word of God among them. 20
15 a matter of questions about words and names 20
19:10 the residents of Asia heard the word of the Lord 20
20 the word of the Lord grew and prevailed 20
20:32 I commend you . . to the word of his grace 20
35 remembering the words of the Lord Jesus 20
38 sorrowing . . because of the word he had spoken 20
21:31 word came to the tribune of the cohort 24
22:22 Up to this word they listened to him 20
Rom 3: 4 That thou mayest be justified in thy words 20
4:23 the words . . were written not for his sake alone •
9: 6 But it is not as though the word of God had failed. 20
10: 8 The word is near you, on your lips and in your heart 21
8 (that is, the word of faith which we preach); 21
18 and their words to the ends of the world. 21
15:18 obedience from the Gentiles, by word and deed 20
1Co 1:18 For the word of the cross is folly 20
2: 1 the testimony of God in lofty words or wisdom. 20
4 not in plausible words of wisdom 20
13 in words not taught by human wisdom 20
14:19 I would rather speak five words with my mind . . than 20
19 than 10,000 words in a tongue. 20
36 What! Did the word of God originate with you 20
2Co 1:18 our word to you has not been Yes and No. 20
2:17 For we are not, like so many, peddlers of God's word; 20
4: 2 practice cunning or to tamper with God's word 20
Gal 5:14 For the whole law is fulfilled in one word 20
6: 6 Let him who is taught the word 20
Eph 1:13 you also, who have heard the word of truth 20
5: 6 Let no one deceive you with empty words 20
26 cleansed her by the washing of water with the word 21
6:17 the sword of the Spirit, which is the word of God. 21
Php 1:14 bold to speak the word of God without fear. 20
2:16 holding fast the word of life 20
Col 1: 5 you have heard before in the word of the truth 20
25 to make the word of God fully known 20
3:16 Let the word of Christ dwell in you richly 20
17 whatever you do, in word or deed 20
4: 3 God may open to us a door for the word 20
1Th 1: 5 for our gospel came to you not only in word 20
6 received the word in much affliction 20
8 not only has the word of the Lord sounded forth 20
2: 5 never used either words of flattery, as you know 20
13 when you received the word of God 20
13 you accepted it not as the word of men 20
13 but as what it really is, the word of God 20
4:15 For this we declare to you by the word of the Lord 20
18 comfort one another with these words. 20
2Th 2: 2 either by spirit or by word, or by letter 20
15 taught . . either by word of mouth or by letter. 20
17 establish them in every good work and word. 20
3: 1 the word of the Lord may speed on and triumph 20
1Ti 4: 5 is consecrated by the word of God and prayer. 20
6 nourished on the words of the faith 20
6: 3 does not agree with the sound words of our Lord 20
2Ti 1:13 the sound words which you have heard from me 20
2: 9 the word of God is not fettered. 20
15 rightly handling the word of truth. 20
4: 2 preach the word 20
Tit 1: 3 at the proper time manifested in his word 20
9 he must hold firm to the sure word as taught 20
2: 5 the word of God may not be discredited. 20
Heb 1: 3 upholding the universe by his word of power 21
4:12 For the word of God is living and active 20
5:12 teach you . . the first principles of God's word. 18
13 is unskilled in the word of righteousness 20
6: 5 have tasted the goodness of the word of God 21
7:28 the word of the oath, which came later than the law 20
11: 3 the world was created by the word of God 21
12:19 a voice whose words made the hearers entreat 21
13: 7 those who spoke to you the word of God 20
22 bear with my word of exhortation 20
Jas 1:18 he brought us forth by the word of truth 20
21 receive with meekness the implanted word 20
22 But be doers of the word, and not hearers only 20
23 For if any one is a hearer of the word and not a doer 20
1Pe 1:23 through the living and abiding word of God; 20
25 but the word of the Lord abides for ever. 21
25 That word is the good news which was preached 21
2: 8 they stumble because they disobey the word 20
3: 1 though they do not obey the word 20
1 won without a word by the behavior of their wives 20
2Pe 1:19 we have the prophetic word made more sure. 20
2: 3 they will exploit you with false words 20
3: 5 by the word of God heavens existed long ago 20
7 But by the same word the heavens and earth 20
1Jn 1: 1 concerning the word of life- 20
10 we make him a liar, and his word is not in us. 20
2: 5 but whoever keeps his word 20
7 old commandment is the word which you have heard 20
• 14 and the word of God abides in you 20
3:18 let us not love in word or speech but in deed 20
3Jn 1:10 he is . . prating against me with evil words. 20
Rev 1: 2 who bore witness to the word of God 20
3 he who reads aloud the words of the prophecy 20
9 on account of the word of God 20
2: 1 The words of him who holds the seven stars 17
8 The words of the first and the last 17
12 The words of him who has the sharp two-edged sword. 17
18 words of the Son of God, who has eyes like a flame 17
3: 1 The words of him who has the seven spirits of God 17
7 'The words of the holy one, the true one 17
8 you have kept my word and have not denied my name 20
10 you have kept my word of patient endurance 20
14 words of the Amen, the faithful and true witness 17
6: 9 slain for the word of God and for the witness 20
12:11 conquered him . . by the word of their testimony 20
17:17 until the words of God shall be fulfilled. 20
19: 9 And he said to me, "These are true words of God. 20
13 the name by which he is called is The Word of God. 20
20: 4 for . . testimony to Jesus and for the word of God 20
21: 5 for these words are trustworthy and true. 20
22: 6 These words are trustworthy and true. 20
7 Blessed is he who keeps the words of the prophecy 20
9 with those who keep the words of this book. 20
10 Do not seal up the words of the prophecy 20
18 I warn every one who hears the words 20
19 if any one takes away from the words of the book 20
1Es 1:24 the words of the Lord rose up against Israel. 20
28 did not heed the words of Jeremiah the prophet 21
47 the words that were spoken by Jeremiah 20
57 in fulfilment of the word of the Lord 21
2: 1 the word of the Lord by the mouth of Jeremiah 21
5: 6 who spoke wise words before Darius 20
8:43 I sent word to Eliezar, Iduel, Maasmas •
72 all who were ever moved at the word of the Lord 21
9:55 because they were inspired by the words 21
2Es 1: 4 The word of the Lord came to me, saying 29
3: 3 I began to speak anxious words to the Most High 29
5:22 and I began once more to speak words 28
31 When I had spoken these words 28
6:15 because the word concerns the end 29
38 and thy word accomplished the work. 29
43 For thy word went forth 29
7: 1 When I had finished speaking these words 29
2 he said to me, "Rise, Ezra, and listen to the words 28
71 now understand from your own words 28
116I answered and said, "This is my first and last word 28
139those who were created by his word 29
8:19 Therefore hear my voice, and understand my words 28
19 The beginning of the words of Ezra's prayer 29
22 whose word is sure 29
24 the petition of thy creature; attend to my words. 29
37 it will come to pass according to your words. 28
9:30 and give heed to my words, O descendants of Jacob. 28
10:29 As I was speaking these words, behold, the angel •
12: 1 While the lion was saying these words 29
31 and as for all his words that you have heard 28
14: 6 'These words you shall publish openly 29
28 Hear these words, O Israel 29
15: 1 speak . . the words of the prophecy 28
16:36 Behold the word of the Lord, receive it 29
40 Hear my words, O my people; prepare for battle 29
56 At his word the stars were fixed 29
58 by his word has suspended the earth 29
Tob 6:15 Do you not remember the words 20
8: 2 As he went he remembered the words of Raphael 20
Jdt 5: 5 Let my lord now hear a word 20
6: 4 he has spoken; none of his words shall be in vain. 21
5 said these words on the day of your iniquity 20
9 I have spoken and none of my words shall fail. 21
7: 9 Let our lord hear a word 20
16 These words pleased Holofernes 20
8: 9 When Judith heard the wicked words 21
28 there is no one who can deny your words. 20
9:13 Make my deceitful words to be their wound 20
10: 1 had ended all these words 21
14 When the men heard her words 21
11: 5 Accept the words of your servant 21
6 if you follow out the words of your maidservant 20
9 we have heard his words 21
20 Her words pleased Holofernes 20
AEs 15: 8 he comforted her with soothing words, and said 20
Wis 1: 6 will not free a blasphemer from the guilt of his words; 26
9 a report of his words will come to the Lord 20
11 because no secret word is without result 25
16 men by their words and deeds summoned death 20
2:17 Let us see if his words are true 20
6: 9 To you then, O monarchs, my words are directed 20
11 Therefore set your desire on my words 20
25 Therefore be instructed by my words 21
7:16 For both we and our words are in his hand 20
8:18 renown in sharing her words 20
9: 1 who hast made all things by thy word 20
12: 9 dread wild beasts or thy stern word. 20
16:12 it was thy word, O Lord, which heals all men. 20
26 thy word preserves those who trust in thee. 21
18:15 thy all-powerful word leaped from heaven 20
22 by his word he subdued the punisher 20
Sir 1:24 He will hide his words until the right moment 20

2:15 who fear the Lord will not disobey his words 21
3: 8 Honor your father by word and deed 20
4:24 education through the words of the tongue. 21
8:11 lest he lie in ambush against your words. 22
9:17 so a people's leader is proved wise by his words. 20
11: 8 nor interrupt a speaker in the midst of his words. 20
12:12 at last you will realize the truth of my words 20
13:11 nor trust his abundance of words 20
12 Cruel is he who does not keep words to himself 20
13 Keep words to yourself and be very watchful •
22 he speaks unseemly words, and they justify him •
16:24 pay close attention to my words. 20
28 they will never disobey his word. 21
18:15 nor cause grief by your words 20
16 So a word is better than a gift. 20
17 Indeed, does not a word surpass a good gift? 20
19:10 Have you heard a word? Let it die with you. 20
11 With such a word a fool will suffer pangs 20
12 so is a word inside a fool. 20
20: 8 Whoever uses too many words will be loathed 20
13 makes himself beloved through his words 20
21:17 they will ponder his words in their minds. 20
25 the words of the prudent 20
23:15 A man accustomed to use insulting words 20
27:23 with your own words he will give offense. 20
23 he admires your words 20
28:25 make balances and scales for your words 20
29: 3 Confirm your word and keep faith with him 20
5 will pay in words of unconcern 20
25 besides this you will hear bitter words •
31:22 in the end you will appreciate my words 20
31 speak no word of reproach to him 20
32: 8 Speak concisely, say much in few words •
36:19 so an intelligent mind detects false words. 20
37:20 A man skilled in words may be hated 20
39: 6 he will pour forth words of wisdom 21
17 At his word the waters stood in a heap 20
17 at the word of his mouth. 21
31 they will not transgress his word. 20
41:16 Therefore show respect for my words 21
42:15 By the words of the Lord his works are done. 20
20 not one word is hidden from him. 20
43:26 by his word all things hold together. 20
27 the sum of our words is: "He is the all. 20
44: 4 wise in their words of instruction; 20
45: 3 By his words he caused signs to cease 20
46:15 by his words 21
48: 1 his word burned like a torch. 20
3 By the word of the Lord he shut up the heavens 20
5 by the word of the Most High; 20
49: 6 according to the word of Jeremiah. 27
51: 5 from an unclean tongue and lying words- 20
Bar 1: 1 These are the words of the book which Baruch 20
3 Baruch read the words of this book in the hearing 20
21 in all the words of the prophets whom he sent to us 20
2: 1 'So the Lord confirmed his word, which he spoke 20
24 thou hast confirmed thy words, which thou didst 20
4:37 they are coming . . , at the word of the Holy One 21
5: 5 gathered . . at the word of the Holy One 21
Man 1: 3 who hast shackled the sea by thy word of command 20
1Mc 1:30 Deceitfully he spoke peaceable words to them 20
51 In such words he wrote to his whole kingdom 20
2:22 We will not obey the king's words 20
23 When he had finished speaking these words 20
62 Do not fear the words of a sinner 20
7:10 with peaceable but treacherous words. 20
11 they paid no attention to their words 20
15 he spoke peaceable words . . and swore this oath 20
16 in accordance with the word which was written 20
9:55 so that he could no longer say a word 20
10: 3 sent Jonathan a letter in peaceable words 20
17 sent it to him, in the following words 20
24 I also will write them words of encouragement 20
25 he sent a message to them in the following words 20
46 When Jonathan and the people heard these words 20
47 he had been the first to speak peaceable words 20
74 When Jonathan heard the words of Apollonius 20
11: 2 He set out for Syria with peaceable words 20
13: 7 when they heard these words 20
14:23 put a copy of their words in the public archives 20
15:32 He reported to him the words of the king 20
35 Athenobius did not answer him a word 20
36 reported to him these words 20
2Mc 2: 3 with other similar words he exhorted them 17
6:29 the words he had uttered 20
7:24 Antiochus not only appealed to him in words 20
8:12 Word came to Judas •
21 With these words •
9:12 he uttered these words •
10:34 and hurled out wicked words. 20
12:25 with many words he had confirmed his . . promise •
14:34 in these words 17
15:11 the inspiration of brave words 20
17 Encouraged by the words of Judas 20
22 he called upon him in these words 23
24 With these words he ended his prayer. •
3Mc 3:17 They accepted our presence by word 20
4:16 uttering improper words •
5:30 But at these words he was filled with . . wrath 15
6: 5 speaking grievous words with boasting •
4Mc 4: 7 The people indignantly protested his words 20
13 Moved by these words 20
5:14 Eleazar asked to have a word. 20
38 dominate . . either by word or by deed. 19
7: 9 you made your words of divine philosophy credible. 20
14: 9 yes, not only heard the direct word of threat 20
16:14 in word and deed you have proved more powerful 20
24 By these words the mother . . encouraged 20
17: 8 to inscribe upon their tomb these words 17

word *See also* break, bring, deep, dispute, get, say, send.

abusive word 1. *ὀνειδισμός*
Sir 41:22 abusive words, before friends 1

word already quoted 1. *προεῖπον*
Heb 4: 7 in the words already quoted 1

blasphemous word 1. *βλασφημία*
Rev 13: 5 a mouth uttering haughty and blasphemous words 1

word come 1. *προσαγγέλλω* 2. *προσπίπτω*
2Mc 10:21 When word of what had happened came to Maccabeus 1
13: 1 word came to Judas and his men 2
14: 1 Three years later, word came to Judas and his men 2

empty word 1. שָׁוְא
Ps 41: 6 when one comes to see me, he utters empty words 1

fair word 1. טוֹב 2. *χρηστολογία*
Jer 12: 6 believe them not, though they speak fair words 1
Rom 16:18 and by fair and flattering words they deceive 2

flattering word 1. *εὐλογία*
Rom 16:18 and by fair and flattering words they deceive 1

word of praise 1. *αἶνος* 2. *ἐξομολογέω*
Tob 14: 1 Here Tobit ended his words of praise. 2
3Mc 7:16 giving thanks . . in words of praise 1

rash word 1. בטה
Prv 12:18 one whose rash words are like sword thrusts 1

word reach 1. *ἀναγγέλλω*
Jdt 11:15 When the word reaches them 1

soft word 1. רַךְ
Job 41: 3 Will he speak to you soft words? 1

word that goes forth 1. מוֹצָא
Ps 89:34 alter the word that went forth from my lips. 1

vain word 1. רִיק
Ps 4: 2 How long will you love vain words 1

many words 1. *πολυλογία*
Mat 6: 7 that they will be heard for their many words. 1

work 1. בנה 2. גְּמוּל 3. דָּבָר 4. דֶּרֶךְ 5. יְגִיעַ 6. יָד
7. מְלָאכָה 8. מַעְבָּד 9. מַעֲלָל 10. מַעֲשֶׂה 11. מִפְלָאָה
12. מִפְעָל 13. מִשְׁמֶרֶת 14. נתן 15. עבד 16. עֶבֶד
17. עֲבֹדָה 18. עלה 19. עמל 20. עִנְיָן 21. עשה
22. עשה מְלָאכָה 23. עֶשֶׁת 24. פעל 25. פֹּעַל 26. פְּעֻלָּה
27. צָבָא 28. מַעֲבַד (A) 29. עבד (A) 30. עֲבִידָה (A)
31. *ἀργέω* 32. *ἐνέργεια* 33. *ἐνεργέω* 34. *ἐνέργημα*
35. *ἐργάζομαι* 36. *ἐργασία* 37. *ἔργον* 38. *ἔχω πόνον*
39. *κατεργάζομαι* 40. *κοπιάω* 41. *λόγος* 42. *ποιέω*
43. *συνεργέω* 44. *συνεργός* 45. *σύνταξις* 46. factum
47. opus 48. plasmatio

Gen 2: 2 on the seventh day God finished his work 7
2 rested . . from all his work which he had done. 7
3 God rested from all his work which he had done 7
5:29 this one shall bring us relief from our work 10
39:11 went into the house to do his work 7
Exd 1:14 bitter . . in all kinds of work in the field; 17
14 all their work they made them serve with rigor. 17
5: 4 why do you take the people away from their work? 10
9 Let heavier work be laid upon the men 17
11 but your work will not be lessened in the least.' 17
13 Complete your work, your daily task 10
18 Go now, and work; for no straw shall be given you 15
7: 9 'Prove yourselves by working a miracle,' 14
12:16 no work shall be done on those days; 7
14:13 see the salvation . . which he will work for you 21
31 Israel saw the great work which the LORD did 6
20: 9 Six days you shall labor, and do all your work; 7
10 in it you shall not do any work, you, or your son 7
23:12 Six days you shall do your work, but on the seventh 10
24 nor serve them, nor do according to their works 10
26: 1 cherubim skilfully worked shall you make them. 10
31 in skilled work shall it be made, with cherubim. 10
28: 6 of fine twined linen, skilfully worked. 10
15 breastpiece of judgment, in skilled work; 10
15 like the work of the ephod you shall make it; 10
31: 4 to work in gold, silver, and bronze 21
5 in carving wood, for work in every craft. 7
14 whoever does any work on it 7
15 Six days shall work be done, but the seventh day 7
15 whoever does any work on the sabbath day shall be 7
32:16 the tables were the work of God, and the writing 10
34:10 all the people . . shall see the work of the LORD; 10
21 Six days you shall work, but on the seventh day 15
35: 2 Six days shall work be done, but on the seventh day 7
2 whoever does any work on it shall be put to death; 7
24 wood of any use in the work, brought it. 7
29 heart moved them to bring anything for the work 7
32 to devise artistic designs, to work in gold 21
33 in carving wood, for work in every skilled craft. 7
35 work done by a craftsman or by a designer 7
36: 1 to know how to do any work in the construction 7
1 work in accordance with all that the LORD has 7
2 heart stirred him up to come to do the work; 7
3 had brought for doing the work on the sanctuary. 7
5 much more than enough for doing the work 7
7 was sufficient to do all the work, and more. 7
8 were made . . with cherubim skilfully worked. 10
35 with cherubim skilfully worked he made it. 10
38:21 for the work of the Levites under the direction 17
24 All the gold that was used for the work 7
39: 3 cut into threads to work into the blue and purple 21
8 He made the breastpiece, in skilled work 10
8 breastpiece . . like the work of the ephod 10
32 Thus all the work of the tabernacle of the tent 17
42 so the people of Israel had done all the work. 17
43 Moses saw all the work, and behold, they had done it; 7
40:33 So Moses finished the work. 7
Lev 16:29 shall afflict yourselves, and shall do no work 7
23: 3 Six days shall work be done; but on the seventh day 7
3 you shall do no work; it is a sabbath to the LORD 7
7 convocation; you shall do no laborious work 7
8 convocation; you shall do no laborious work 7
21 you shall do no laborious work: it is a statute 7
25 You shall do no laborious work 7
28 you shall do no work on this same day; for it is a day 7
30 whoever does any work on this same day 7
31 You shall do no work: it is a statute for ever 7
35 convocation; you shall do no laborious work 7
36 solemn assembly; you shall do no laborious work 7
Num 4: 3 to do the work in the tent of meeting. 7
23 for service, to do the work in the tent of meeting. 17
28 work is to be under the oversight of Ith'amar 13
30 service, to do the work of the tent of meeting. 17
35 enter the service, for work in the tent of meeting; 17
39 enter the service for work in the tent of meeting- 17
43 enter the service, for work in the tent of meeting- 17
47 could enter to do the work of service 17
47 could enter to do . . the work of bearing burdens 17
8:24 shall go in to perform the work in the service 27
25 they shall withdraw from the work of the service 27
16:28 LORD has sent me to do all these works 10
29: 7 afflict yourselves; you shall do no work 7
35 solemn assembly: you shall do no laborious work. 7
31:20 purify . . all work of goats' hair 10
Deu 2: 7 LORD . . blessed you in all the work of your hands; 10
3:24 what god . . can do such works and mighty acts 10
4:28 gods of wood and stone, the work of men's hands 10
5:13 Six days you shall labor, and do all your work; 7
14 not do any work, you, or your son, or your daughter 7
11: 7 all the great work of the LORD which he did. 10
14:29 LORD . . may bless you in all the work 10
15:10 LORD . . bless you in all your work 10
16: 8 seventh day . . you shall do no work on it. 7
15 LORD . . will bless . . all the work of your hands 10
21: 3 heifer which has never been worked 15
24:19 LORD . . bless you in all the work of your hands. 10
28:12 to bless all the work of your hands; 10
30: 9 make . . prosperous in all the work of your hand 10
31:29 him to anger through the work of your hands. 10
32: 4 The Rock, his work is perfect; for all his ways 25
33:11 Bless, O LORD . . and accept the work of his hands; 25
Jos 24:31 and had known all the work which the LORD did 10
Jdg 2: 7 all the great work which the LORD had done 10
10 the LORD or the work which he had done for Israel. 10
13:19 offered . . to the LORD, to him who works wonders. 42
19:16 an old man was coming from his work in the field 10
Rut 2:19 Where did you glean . . ? And where have you worked? 21
19 told her mother-in-law with whom she had worked 21
19 The man's name with whom I worked today is Bo'az. 21
1Sm 8:16 He will take your . . and put them to his work. 7
14: 6 it may be that the LORD will work for us; 21
1Kg 5:16 officers who were over the work, who had charge 7
16 had charge of the people who carried on the work. 7
7:14 full of wisdom . . for making any work in bronze. 7
14 He came to King Solomon, and did all his work. 7
17 nets of checker work with wreaths of chain work 10
17 nets of checker work with wreaths of chain work 10
19 the capitals . . were of lily-work, four cubits. 10
22 upon the tops of the pillars was lily-work. 7
22 Thus the work of the pillars was finished. 7
29 Upon the frames . . were wreaths of beveled work. 10
40 Hiram finished all the work that he did 7
51 all the work that King Solomon did on the house 7
9:23 the chief officers who were over Solomon's work 7
23 had charge of the people who carried on the work. 7
16: 7 provoking him to anger with the work of his hands 10
2Kg 12:11 builders who worked upon the house of the LORD 21

19:18 they were no gods, but the work of men's hands, wood 10
22:17 provoke me . . with all the work of their hands 10
1Ch 4:23 they dwelt there with the king for his work. 7
6:49 for all the work of the most holy place 7
9:13 for the work of the service of the house of God. 7
19 were in charge of the work of the service 7
22:15 craftsmen without number, skilled in working 7
23: 4 have charge of the work in the house of the LORD 7
24 who were to do the work for the service 7
28 and any work for the service of the house of God; 10
25: 1 list of those who did the work and of their duties 7
26:30 for all the work of the LORD and for the service 7
27:26 over those who did the work of the field 7
28:13 the work of the service in the house of the LORD; 7
19 all the work to be done according to the plan. 7
20 all the work for the service . . is finished. 7
21 with you in all the work will be every willing man 7
29: 1 young and inexperienced, and the work is great; 7
5 for all the work to be done by craftsmen 7
6 and the officers over the king's work. 7
2Ch 2: 7 now send me a man skilled to work in gold, silver 21
14 He is trained to work in gold, silver, bronze, iron 21
3:14 he made the veil . . and worked cherubim on it. 18
4:11 Huram finished the work that he did for King 7
5: 1 work that Solomon did for the house of the LORD 7
8: 9 of . . Israel Solomon made no slaves for his work; 7
16 Thus was accomplished all the work of Solomon 7
15: 7 for your work shall be rewarded. 26
16: 5 stopped building Ramah, and let his work cease. 7
24:12 charge of the work of the house of the LORD 17
13 those who were engaged in the work labored 7
29:34 Levites helped them, until the work was finished 7
31:21 every work that he undertook in the service 10
32:19 gods . . which are the work of men's hands. 10
30 Hezeki'ah prospered in all his works. 10
34:10 workmen who were working in the house of the LORD 21
12 the men did the work faithfully. 7
13 directed all who did work in every kind 7
25 provoke me . . with all the works of their hands 10
Ezr 2:69 gave to the treasury of the work 61,000 darics 7
3: 8 Levites . . to have the oversight of the work 7
4:24 the work on the house of God which is in Jerusalem 30
5: 8 this work goes on diligently and prospers 30
6: 7 let the work on this house of God alone; 30
22 aided them in the work of the house of God 7
10:13 Nor is this a work for one day or for two; 7
Neh 2:16 officials, and the rest that were to do the work. 7
18 strengthened their hands for the good work. •
3: 5 did not put their necks to the work of their Lord. 17
4: 6 For the people had a mind to work. 21
10 we are not able to work on the wall. 1
11 till we come . . and kill them and stop the work. 7
15 we all returned to the wall, each to his work. 7
16 half of my servants worked on construction 21
17 each with one hand labored on the work 7
19 The work is great and widely spread 7
21 we labored at the work, and half of them held 7
5:16 I also held to the work on this wall 7
16 my servants were gathered there for the work. 7
6: 3 I am doing a great work and I cannot come down. 7
3 Why should the work stop while I leave it 7
9 Their hands will drop from the work 7
16 perceived that this work had been accomplished 7
7:70 heads of fathers' houses gave to the work. 7
71 heads . . gave into the treasury of the work 7
9:35 they did not turn from their wicked works. 9
10:33 for all the work of the house of our God. 7
11:12 their brethren who did the work of the house, 822; 7
16 who were over the outside work of the house of God; 7
22 singers, over the work of the house of God. 7
13:10 Levites and the singers, who did the work, 7
30 established the duties . . each in his work; 7
Job 1:10 Thou hast blessed the work of his hands 10
10: 3 to oppress, to despise the work of thy hands 5
14:15 thou wouldest long for the work of thy hands. 10
34:11 according to the work of a man he will requite him 25
19 for they are all the work of his hands? 10
25 Thus, knowing their works, he overturns them 8
36: 9 then he declares to them their work 25
24 to extol his work, of which men have sung. 25
37: 7 every man, that all men may know his work. 10
16 works of him who is perfect in knowledge 11
40:19 He is the first of the works of God; 4
Ps 8: 3 When I look at thy heavens, the work of thy fingers 10
6 given him dominion over the works of thy hands; 10
9:16 wicked are snared in the work of their own hands. 25
17: 4 With regard to the works of men, by the word 26
28: 4 Requite them according to their work 25
4 requite . . according to the work of their hands; 10
5 they do not regard the works of the LORD 26
5 the works of the LORD, or the work of his hands 10
33: 4 all his work is done in faithfulness. 10
46: 8 Come, behold the works of the LORD 12
53: 4 Have those who work evil no understanding 24
59: 2 deliver me from those who work evil, and save me 24
62:12 For thou dost requite a man according to his work. 10
73:28 GOD my refuge, that I may tell of all thy works. 7
74:12 working salvation in the midst of the earth. 24
77:12 I will meditate on all thy work 25
14 Thou art the God who workest wonders 21
78: 7 hope in God, and not forget the works of God 9
86: 8 nor are there any works like thine. 10
88:10 Dost thou work wonders for the dead? 21
90:16 Let thy work be manifest to thy servants 25
17 establish thou the work of our hands upon us 10
17 yea, the work of our hands establish thou it. 10
92: 4 For thou, O LORD, hast made me glad by thy work; 25
4 at the works of thy hands I sing for joy. 10
5 How great are thy works, O LORD! 10
95: 9 put me to the proof, though they had seen my work. 25
101: 3 I hate the work of those who fall away; 21
102:25 heavens are the work of thy hands. 10
103: 6 LORD works vindication and justice for all 21
22 Bless the LORD, all his works, in all places 10
104:13 earth is satisfied with the fruit of thy work. 10
23 to his work and to his labor until the evening. 25
24 O LORD, how manifold are thy works! 10
31 may the LORD rejoice in his works 10
106:13 they soon forgot his works; 10
111: 2 Great are the works of the LORD 10
3 Full of honor and majesty is his work 25
6 He has shown his people the power of his works 10
7 The works of his hands are faithful and just; 10
115: 4 idols are silver and gold, the work of men's hands. 10
135:15 idols . . silver and gold, the work of men's hands. 10
138: 8 Do not forsake the work of thy hands. 10
139:14 fearful and wonderful. Wonderful are thy works! 10
141: 4 wicked . . in company with men who work iniquity; 24
145: 4 One generation shall laud thy works to another 10
5 on thy wondrous works, I will meditate. 3
10 All thy works shall give thanks to thee, O LORD 10
Prv 8:22 The LORD created me at the beginning of his work 4
12: 9 man of humble standing who works for himself 16
14 and the work of a man's hand comes back to him. 2
16: 3 Commit your work to the LORD 10
11 all the weights in the bag are his work. 10
26 A worker's appetite works for him; 19
18: 9 slack in his work is a brother to him who destroys. 7
22:29 Do you see a man skilful in his work? 7
24:12 will he not requite man according to his work? 25
27 Prepare your work outside, get everything ready 7
26:28 flattering mouth works ruin. 21
31:13 She . . works with willing hands. 21
31 let her works praise her in the gates. 10
Ecc 2: 4 I made great works; I built houses and planted 10
23 days are full of pain, and his work is a vexation; 20
26 to the sinner he gives the work of gathering 20
3:17 a time for every matter, and for every work. 10
22 a man should enjoy his work, for that is his lot; 10
4: 4 all toil and all skill in work come from . . envy 10
5: 6 why should God . . destroy the work of your hands? 10
7:13 Consider the work of God; 10
8:17 then I saw all the work of God, that man cannot find 10
17 find out the work that is done under the sun. 10
9:10 there is no work or thought or knowledge 10
11: 5 do not know the work of God who makes everything. 10
Sng 5:14 His body is ivory work 23
7: 1 thighs are like jewels, the work of a master hand. 10
Isa 1:31 the strong shall become tow, and his work a spark 25
2: 8 the work of their hands, to what their own fingers 10
5:12 the deeds of the LORD, or see the work of his hands. 10
19 who say: "Let him make haste, let him speed his work 10
10:12 the Lord has finished all his work on Mount Zion 10
17: 8 regard for the altars, the work of their hands 10
19:10 and all who work for hire will be grieved. 21
25 Blessed be . . and Assyria the work of my hands 10
26:12 O LORD . . thou hast wrought for us all our works. 10
28:21 and to work his work-alien is his work! 15
21 and to work his work-alien is his work! 17
21 and to work his work-alien is his work! 17
29:23 For when he sees his children, the work of my hands 10
31: 2 against the helpers of those who work iniquity. 24
37:19 they were no gods, but the work of men's hands 10
41:24 Behold, you are nothing, and your work is nought; 25
29 they are all a delusion; their works are nothing; 10
43:13 I am God . . I work and who can hinder it? 24
44:12 fashions it and works it over the coals; 24
45: 9 Does the clay say . . 'Your work has no handles'? 25
11 or command me concerning the work of my hands? 25
59: 6 Their works are works of iniquity 10
6 Their works are works of iniquity 10
60:21 the shoot of my planting, the work of my hands 10
64: 4 God . . who works for those who wait for him. 21
5 meetest him that joyfully works righteousness 21
8 art our potter; we are all the work of thy hand. 10
65:22 chosen shall long enjoy the work of their hands. 10
66:18 For I know their works and their thoughts 10
Jer 1:16 and worshiped the works of their own hands. 10
10: 3 and worked with an axe by the hands of a craftsman. 10
9 They are the work of the craftsman 10
9 they are all the work of skilled men. 10
15 They are worthless, a work of delusion; 10
17:22 out of your houses on the sabbath or do any work 7
24 but keep the sabbath day holy and do no work on it 7
18: 3 and there he was working at his wheel. 21
25: 6 provoke me to anger with the work of your hands. 10
7 provoke me to anger with the work of your hands 10
14 their deeds and the work of their hands. 10
31:16 for your work shall be rewarded, says the LORD 26
32:30 to anger by the work of their hands, says the LORD. 10
44: 8 provoke me to anger with the works of your hands 10
48:10 he who does the work of the LORD with slackness; 7
50:25 for the Lord GOD of hosts has a work to do 7
51:10 let us declare in Zion the work of the LORD our God. 10
18 They are worthless, a work of delusion; 10
Lam 3:64 requite . . according to the work of their hands. 10
4: 2 reckoned as . . pots, the work of a potter's hands! 10
Ezk 6: 6 altars cut down, and your works wiped out. 10
29:20 because they worked for me, says the Lord GOD. 21
46: 1 The gate . . shall be shut on the six working days; 10
Dan 4:37 for all his works are right and his ways are just; 28
6:27 works signs and wonders in heaven and on earth 29
9:14 righteous in all the works which he has done 10
11:28 shall work his will, and return to his own land. 21
Hos 13: 2 idols . . all of them the work of craftsmen. 10
14: 3 will say no more, 'Our God,' to the work of our hands. 10
Mic 2: 1 devise wickedness and work evil upon their beds! 24
5:13 shall bow down no more to the work of your hands; 10
6:16 have kept . . all the works of the house of Ahab; 10
Hab 1: 5 For I am doing a work in your days 25
3: 2 the report of thee, and thy work, O LORD, do I fear. 25
Hag 1:14 they came and worked on the house of the LORD 22
2: 4 work, for I am with you, says the LORD of hosts 21
14 and so with every work of their hands; 10
Mat 5:16 that they may see your good works and give glory 37
14: 2 that is why these powers are at work in him. 33
20:12 saying, 'These last worked only one hour 42
21:28 'Son, go and work in the vineyard today.' 35
Mrk 6:14 that is why these powers are at work in him. 33
13:34 puts his servants in charge, each with his work 37
16:20 while the Lord worked with them 43
Joh 4:34 and to accomplish his work. 37
5:17 Jesus answered them, "My Father is working still 35
17 My Father is working still, and I am working. 35
20 greater works than these will he show him 37
36 the works which the Father has granted me 37
36 these very works which I am doing 37
6:28 What must we do, to be doing the works of God? 35
29 Jesus answered them, "This is the work of God 37
7: 3 your disciples may see the works you are doing. 37
4 For no man works in secret 42
7 because I testify of it that its works are evil. 37
9: 3 that the works of God might be made manifest in him. 37
4 We must work the works of him who sent me 35
4 We must work the works of him who sent me 37
4 night comes, when no one can work. 35
10:25 The works that I do in my Father's name 37
32 I have shown you many good works from the Father; 37
33 It is not for a good work that we stone you 37
37 If I am not doing the works of my Father 37
38 believe the works 37
14:10 the Father who dwells in me does his works. 37
11 believe me for the sake of the works themselves. 37
12 who believes in me will also do the works that I do; 37
12 greater works than these will he do •
15:24 done among them the works which no one else did 37
17: 4 having accomplished the work 37
21: 7 he put on his clothes, for he was stripped for work •
Act 2:11 the mighty works of God •
7:41 rejoiced in the works of their hands. 37
9:36 She was full of good works and acts of charity. 37
13: 2 the work to which I have called them. 37
14:26 the work which they had fulfilled. 37
15:38 and had not gone with them to the work. 37
18: 3 he stayed with them, and they worked 35
Rom 2: 6 will render to every man according to his works 37
3:20 justified in his sight by works of the law 37
27 On what principle? On the principle of works? 37
28 man is justified by faith apart from works of law. 37
4: 2 For if Abraham was justified by works 37
4 Now to one who works, his wages are not reckoned 35
5 to one who does not work but trusts him 35
6 God reckons righteousness apart from works 37
7: 5 sinful passions . . were at work in our members 33
13 sin, working death in me through what is good 39
8:28 God works for good with those who love him 43
9:11 not because of works but because of his call 37
32 but as if it were based on works. 37
11: 6 it is no longer on the basis of works; 37
13:12 Let us then cast off the works of darkness 37
14:20 Do not, for the sake of food, destroy the work 37
15:17 I have reason to be proud of my work for God. •
16: 6 Greet Mary, who has worked hard among you. 40
12 beloved Persis, who has worked hard in the Lord. 40
1Co 3:13 each man's work will become manifest 37
13 test what sort of work each one has done. 37
14 If the work which any man has built 37
15 If any man's work is burned up, he will suffer loss 37
4:12 we labor, working with our own hands 35
9: 6 have no right to refrain from working for a living? 35
12: 6 there are varieties of working 34
10 to another the working of miracles 34
29 Are all teachers? Do all work miracles? •
15:10 On the contrary, I worked harder than any of them 40
58 always abounding in the work of the Lord 37
16:10 he is doing the work of the Lord, as I am. 37
2Co 1:24 we work with you for your joy 44

4:12 death is at work in us, but life in you. 33
9: 8 provide in abundance for every good work. 37
11:12 they work on the same terms as we do. *
Gal 2:16 a man is not justified by works of the law 37
16 not by works of the law 37
16 by works of the law shall no one be justified. 37
3: 2 Did you receive the Spirit by works of the law 37
5 works miracles among you 33
5 by works of the law, or by hearing with faith? 37
10 all who rely on works of the law are under a curse; 37
5: 6 faith working through love. 33
19 Now the works of the flesh are plain 37
6: 4 let each one test his own work 37
Eph 1:19 according to the working of his great might 32
2: 2 is now at work in the sons of disobedience. 33
9 not because of works, lest any man should boast. 37
10 created in Christ Jesus for good works 37
3: 7 which was given me by the working of his power. 32
20 the power at work within us 33
4:12 to equip the saints for the work of ministry 37
16 when each part is working properly 32
5:11 Take no part in the unfruitful works of darkness 37
Php 1: 6 I am sure that he who began a good work in you 37
2:13 for God is at work in you, both to will and to work 33
13 both to will and to work for his good pleasure. 33
30 for he nearly died for the work of Christ 37
Col 1:10 bearing fruit in every good work 37
2:12 through faith in the working of God 32
3:23 Whatever your task, work heartily 35
4:13 I bear him witness that he has worked hard for you 38
1Th 1: 3 work of faith and labor of love 37
2: 9 worked night and day, that we might not burden any 35
13 the word of God, which is at work in you believers. 33
4:11 to work with your hands, as we charged you; 35
5:13 because of their work 37
2Th 1:11 may fulfil every . . work of faith by his power 37
2: 7 the mystery of lawlessness is already at work; 33
17 establish them in every good work and word. 37
3: 8 with toil and labor we worked night and day 35
10 If any one will not work, let him not eat. 35
2Ti 1: 9 not in virtue of our works 37
2:21 ready for any good work. 37
3:17 equipped for every good work. 37
4: 5 do the work of an evangelist 37
Tit 3: 1 to be obedient, to be ready for any honest work 37
Heb 1:10 the heavens are the work of thy hands; 37
3: 9 and saw my works for 40 years. 37
4: 3 although his works were finished 37
4 God rested on the seventh day from all his works. 37
6: 1 foundation of repentance from dead works 37
10 For God is not so unjust as to overlook your work 37
9:14 purify your conscience from dead works 37
10:24 to stir up one another to love and good works 37
13:21 working . . that which is pleasing in his sight 42
Jas 1:20 anger of man does not work the righteousness of God. 35
2:14 if a man says he has faith but has not works? 37
17 So faith by itself, if it has no works, is dead. 37
18 some one will say, "You have faith and I have works. 37
18 Show me your faith apart from your works 37
18 and I by my works will show you my faith. 37
20 that faith apart from works is barren? 37
21 Was not Abraham our father justified by works 37
22 faith was active along with his works 37
22 and faith was completed by works 37
24 You see that a man is justified by works 37
25 was not also Rahab the harlot justified by works 37
26 so faith apart from works is dead. 37
3:13 let him show his works in the meekness of wisdom. 37
2Pe 3:10 and the works that are upon it will be burned up. 37
1Jn 3: 8 to destroy the works of the devil. 37
2Jn 1: 8 that you may not lose what you have worked for 35
11 for he who greets him shares his wicked work. 37
Rev 2: 2 I know your works, your toil and your patient 37
5 repent and do the works you did at first. 37
6 you hate the works of the Nicola'itans 37
19 'I know your works, your love and faith and service 37
19 and that your latter works exceed the first. 37
23 I will give to each of you as your works deserve. 37
26 He who conquers and who keeps my works 37
3: 1 I know your works; you have the name of being alive 37
2 not found your works perfect in the sight of God. 37
8 'I know your works. 37
15 'I know your works: you are neither cold nor hot. 37
9:20 did not repent of the works of their hands 37
13:13 It works great signs, even making fire come down 42
14 and by the signs which it is allowed to work 42
19:20 worked the signs by which he deceived 42
1Es 4:36 All God's works quake and tremble 37
37 all their works are unrighteous 37
5:45 would give to the sacred treasury for the work 37
58 to have charge of the work of the Lord 37
58 the Levites, as one man pressing forward the work 37
58 the Levites, as one man pressing forward the work †
6:10 the work is prospering in their hands 37
7: 2 supervised the holy work with very great care 37
3 the holy work prospered 37
9:11 This is not a work we can do in one day or two 37
2Es 6:38 and thy word accomplished the work. 47
40 so that thy works might then appear. 47
43 and at once the work was done. 47
54 as ruler over all the works which thou hadst made; 46
7:24 and have not performed his works. 47
77 For you have a treasure of works laid up 47
134since they are his own works; 47
8: 7 we are a work of thy hands, as thou hast declared. 48
13 thou wilt make him live, for he is thy work. 47
32 who have no works of righteousness 47
33 who have many works laid up with thee 47
36 to those who have no store of good works. 47
9: 7 and will be able to escape on account of his works 47
17 as is the work, so is the product 47
10:54 for no work of man's building could endure 47
13:23 who have works and have faith in the Almighty. 47
16:51 Therefore do not be like her or her works. 47
54 Behold, the Lord knows all the works of men 47
64 the Lord will strictly examine all their works 47
Tob 2:11 Then my wife Anna earned money at women's work. *
3:11 May all thy works praise thee for ever. 37
4:14 the wages of any man who works for you 35
12: 6 worthily declaring the works of God 37
7 gloriously to reveal the works of God 37
11 gloriously to reveal the works of God.' 37
22 confessed the great and wonderful works of God 37
Jdt 13: 4 look in this hour upon the work of my hands 37
AEs 13: 8 calling to remembrance all the works of the Lord 37
Wis 1:12 nor bring on destruction by the works of your hands; 37
2: 4 no one will remember our works 37
3:11 their works are useless. 37
6: 3 who will search out your works 37
7:26 a spotless mirror of the working of God 32
8: 4 an associate in his works. 37
9: 9 With thee is wisdom, who knows thy works 37
12 Then my works will be acceptable 37
11: 1 Wisdom prospered their works 37
12: 4 their works of sorcery and unholy rites 37
19 Through such works thou has taught thy people 37
13: 1 while paying heed to his works 37
4 if men were amazed at their power and working 32
7 as they live among his works they keep searching 37
10 who give the name "gods" to the works of men's hands 37
10 a useless stone, the work of an ancient hand. 37
12 and burn the castoff pieces of his work 36
19 money-making and work and success with his hands 36
14: 5 works of thy wisdom should not be without effect; 37
20 the multitude, attracted by the charm of his work 36
17:20 was engaged in unhindered work 37
Sir 0: 2 Not only this work, but even the law itself, *
1: 9 he poured her out upon all his works. 37
9:17 work will be praised 37
10:26 when you do your work 37
27 Better is a man who works 35
11: 4 the works of the Lord are wonderful 37
4 his works are concealed from men. 37
11 There is a man who works, and toils, and presses on 40
20 grow old in your work. 37
21 Do not wonder at the works of a sinner 37
16:21 so most of his works are concealed. 37
26 works of the Lord have existed 37
27 He arranged his works in an eternal order 37
17: 8 to show them the majesty of his works. 37
10 to proclaim the grandeur of his works. 37
19 All their works are as the sun before him 37
18: 4 To none has he given power to proclaim his works; 37
24:22 those who work with my help will not sin. 35
31:22 In all your work be industrious 37
33:15 Look upon all the works of the Most High 37
24 bread and discipline and work for a servant. 37
27 Put him to work, that he may not be idle 36
28 Set him to work, as is fitting for him 37
35:19 repays . . works of men 37
37:11 with an idler about any work 37
11 about completing his work *
16 Reason is the beginning of every work 37
38: 6 he might be glorified in his marvelous works. *
8 His works will never be finished 37
25 who drives oxen and is occupied with their work 37
27 he is careful to finish his work. 37
29 So too is the potter sitting at his work 37
29 he is always deeply concerned over his work 37
31 each is skilful in his own work. 37
39:14 bless the Lord for all his works; 37
16 All things are the works of the Lord 37
19 The works of all flesh are before him 37
33 The works of the Lord are all good 37
42:15 I will now call to mind the works of the Lord 37
15 By the words of the Lord his works are done. 37
16 the work of the Lord is full of his glory. 37
22 How greatly to be desired are all his works 37
43: 2 a marvelous instrument, the work of the Most High. 37
4 A man tending a furnace works in burning heat 37
25 for in it are strange and marvelous works 37
28 he is greater than all his works. 37
32 we have seen but few of his works. 37
45:10 the work of an embroiderer 37
11 with twisted scarlet, the work of a craftsman; 37
11 in a setting of gold, the work of a jeweler 37
12 a distinction to be prized, the work of an expert 37
47:22 nor cause any of his works to perish 41
51: 8 thy work from of old 36
30 Do your work before the appointed time 35
Bar 2: 9 for the Lord is righteous in all his works 37
LJr 1:51 they are not gods but the work of men's hands 37
51 there is no work of God in them. 37
Aza 1: 4 all thy works are true and thy ways right 37
20 Deliver us in accordance with thy marvelous works *
35 Bless the Lord, all works of the Lord 37
1Mc 2:47 the work prospered in their hands. 37
4:51 they finished all the work they had undertaken. 37
9:54 He tore down the work of the prophets! 37
55 and his work was hindered 37
10:11 He directed those who were doing the work 37
2Mc 5:25 then, finding the Jews not at work 31
15:39 the ears of those who read the work 45
3Mc 2: 8 when they had seen works of your hands 37

work *See also* checker, effective, perform, press, room, weave.

work a wonder 1. τερατοποιός
2Mc 15:21 and called upon the Lord who works wonders 1

work already done 1. ἕτοιμος
2Co 10:16 work already done in another's field. 1

carved work 1. חקה
1Kg 6:35 with gold evenly applied upon the carved work. 1

cedar work 1. אַרְזָה
Zep 2:14 for her cedar work will be laid bare. 1

work destruction 1. שחת
2Sm 24:16 said to the angel who was working destruction 1

do work 1. עבד 2. ἐργάζομαι
Deu 15:19 shall do no work with the firstling of your herd 1
Lke 13:14 There are six days on which work ought to be done; 2
Eph 4:28 let him labor, doing honest work with his hands 2
2Th 3:11 mere busybodies, not doing any work. 2
12 to do their work in quietness 2
Wis 14: 8 because he did the work 2

dyed work 1. צֶבַע
Jdg 5:30 two pieces of dyed work embroidered for my neck 1

embroidered work 1. רִקְמָה
Ezk 27:16 embroidered work, fine linen, coral, and agate. 1
24 in clothes of blue and embroidered work 1

work evil 1. רעע
Jer 25:29 For behold, I begin to work evil at the city 1

evil work 1. רָעָה
Hos 7: 2 that I remember all their evil works. 1

farm work 1. γεωργία
Sir 7:15 Do not hate toilsome labor, or farm work 1

work finely 1. שְׂרָד
Exd 31:10 finely worked garments, the holy garments 1
39:41 the finely worked garments for ministering 1

work further 1. ἀλλοιόω
Sir 36: 6 Show signs anew, and work further wonders 1

gracious work 1. χάρις
2Co 8: 6 also complete among you this gracious work. 1
7 see that you excel in this gracious work also. 1
19 to travel with us in this gracious work 1

hammered work 1. מִקְשָׁה 2. ἐλατός
Exd 25:18 of hammered work shall you make them 1
31 the lampstand shall be made of hammered work; 1
36 one piece of hammered work of pure gold. 1
37:17 the lampstand were made of hammered work; 1
22 was one piece of hammered work of pure gold. 1
Num 8: 4 lampstand, hammered work of gold; from its base 1
4 from its base to its flowers, it was hammered work; 1
10: 2 trumpets; of hammered work you shall make them; 1
Sir 50:16 they sounded the trumpets of hammered work 2

laborious work 1. מְלֶאכֶת עֲבֹדָה
Num28:18 a holy convocation: you shall do no laborious work 1
25 holy convocation; you shall do no laborious work 1
26 holy convocation; you shall do no laborious work 1
29: 1 holy convocation; you shall do no laborious work 1
12 holy convocation; you shall do no laborious work 1

make work 1. עבד
2Ch 2:18 as overseers to make the people work. 1

marvelous work 1. פלא 2. θαυμάσιος
1Ch 16:24 his marvelous works among all the peoples! 1
Ps 96: 3 his marvelous works among all the peoples! 1
Sir 42:17 to recount all his marvelous works 2

mighty work 1. δύναμις 2. virtus
Mat 7:22 and do many mighty works in your name?' 1
11:20 where most of his mighty works had been done 1

21 for if the mighty works done in you had been done 1
23 For if the mighty works done in you had been done 1
13:54 this wisdom and these mighty works? 1
58 he did not do many mighty works there 1
Mrk 6: 2 What mighty works are wrought by his hands! 1
5 he could do no mighty work there 1
9:39 no one who does a mighty work in my name 1
Lke 10:13 if the mighty works done in you 1
19:37 for all the mighty works that they had seen 1
Act 2:22 a man attested . . with mighty works and wonders 1
2Co 12:12 with signs and wonders and mighty works. 1
2Es 9: 6 in wonders and mighty works 2

work out 1. κατεργάζομαι
Php 2:12 work out your own salvation with fear 1

set to work 1. קוּם 2. ἐργάζομαι
2Ch 30:14 set to work and removed the altars that were 1
Sir 33:25 Set your slave to work, and you will find rest; 2

set to work resolutely 1. חזק
2Ch 32: 5 He set to work resolutely and built up 1

work through 1. ἐνεργέω
Gal 2: 8 for he who worked through Peter 1
8 worked through me also for the Gentiles) 1

work together 1. συνεργέω
2Co 6: 1 Working together with him, then 1

wonderful work 1. פלא
1Ch 16: 9 Sing to him . . tell of all his wonderful works! 1
12 Remember the wonderful works that he has done 1
Ps 105: 2 tell of all his wonderful works! 1
5 Remember the wonderful works that he has done 1
106: 7 fathers . . not consider thy wonderful works; 1
107: 8 for his wonderful works to the sons of men! 1
15 for his wonderful works to the sons of men! 1
21 for his wonderful works to the sons of men! 1
31 for his wonderful works to the sons of men! 1
111: 4 caused his wonderful works to be remembered; 1

work wonders 1. פלא
Job 10:16 like a lion, and again work wonders against me; 1

wondrous work 1. פלא
Job 37:14 stop and consider the wondrous works of God. 1
Ps 106:22 wondrous works in the land of Ham 1
107:24 saw . . his wondrous works in the deep. 1
119:27 I will meditate on thy wondrous works. 1

worker 1. חרשׁ 2. חָרָשׁ 3. עבד 4. עֲבֹדָה 5. עָמֵל 6. עָצֵב 7. עשׂה 8. פעל 9. ἐργάζομαι 10. ἐργάτης 11. κοπιάω
1Kg 7:14 his father was a man of Tyre, a worker in bronze; 1
1Ch 4:21 the house of linen workers at Beth-ashbe'a; 4
2Ch 24:12 workers in iron and bronze to repair 2
Job 31: 3 and disaster the workers of iniquity? 8
Ps 6: 8 Depart from me, all you workers of evil; 8
28: 3 the wicked, with those who are workers of evil 8
52: 2 like a sharp razor, you worker of treachery. 7
Prv 16:26 A worker's appetite works for him; 5
Ecc 3: 9 What gain has the worker from his toil? 7
Isa 19: 9 The workers in combed flax will be in despair 3
58: 3 your own pleasure, and oppress all your workers. 6
Ezk 48:18 shall be food for the workers of the city. 3
19 workers of the city, from all the tribes of Israel 3
Lke 13:27 depart from me, all you workers of iniquity!' 10
Rom 16:12 Greet those workers in the Lord 11
Php 3: 2 look out for the evil-workers 10
Sir 27:10 so does sin for the workers of iniquity. 9
40:18 Life is sweet for the self-reliant and the worker 10

fellow worker 1. συνεργέω 2. συνεργός
Rom 16: 3 my fellow workers in Christ Jesus 2
9 Greet Urba'nus, our fellow worker in Christ 2
21 Timothy, my fellow worker, greets you; 2
1Co 3: 9 For we are God's fellow workers; you are God's field 2
16:16 to every fellow worker and laborer. 1
2Co 8:23 my partner and fellow worker in your service; 2
Php 2:25 my brother and fellow worker and fellow soldier 2
4: 3 with Clement and the rest of my fellow workers 2
Col 4:11 men of the circumcision among my fellow workers 2
Phm 1: 1 To Phile'mon our beloved fellow worker 2
24 Aristar'chus, Demas, and Luke, my fellow workers. 2
3Jn 1: 8 that we may be fellow workers in the truth. 2

worker in clay 1. πηλουργός
Wis 15: 7 the worker in clay decides. 1

worker in copper 1. χαλκοπλάστης
Wis 15: 9 and imitates workers in copper 1

worker in gold 1. χρυσουργός
Wis 15: 9 he competes with workers in gold and silver 1

worker of miracles 1. δύναμις
1Co 12:28 then workers of miracles, then healers, helpers •1

worker of wonders 1. τερατοποιός
3Mc 6:32 God, their Savior and worker of wonders 1

skilled worker 1. חָכָם
2Ch 2: 7 to be with the skilled workers who are with me 1

workman 1. חָרָשׁ 2. יצר חָרָשׁ 3. עָמֵל 4. עשׂה 5. עשׂה מְלָאכָה 6. ἐργάτης
Exd 35:35 by any sort of workman or skilled designer. 5
36: 8 able men among the workmen made the tabernacle 4
Jdg 5:26 She put . . her right hand to the workmen's mallet; 3
2Kg 12:11 give the money . . into the hands of the workmen 5
14 that was given to the workmen who were repairing 5
15 pay out to the workmen, for they dealt honestly. 5
22: 5 let it be given into the hand of the workmen 5
5 give it to the workmen . . at the house of the LORD 5
9 have delivered it into the hand of the workmen 5
1Ch 22:15 You have an abundance of workmen 5
2Ch 34:10 delivered it to the workmen 5
10 workmen who were working in the house of the LORD 5
17 delivered it into the hand of . . the workmen. 5
Ezr 3: 9 together took the oversight of the workmen 5
Isa 40:19 The idol! a workman casts it 1
Hos 8: 6 in Israel? A workman made it; it is not God. 1
Hab 2:18 For the workman trusts in his own creation 2
Act 19:25 with the workmen of like occupation 6
2Co 11:13 such men are false apostles, deceitful workmen 6
2Ti 2:15 a workman who has no need to be ashamed 6
Wis 17:17 whether he was a farmer or a shepherd or a workman 6
Sir 19: 1 A workman who is a drunkard will not become rich; 6

master workman 1. אָמוֹן 2. ἀρχιτέκτων
Prv 8:30 then I was beside him, like a master workman; 1
Sir 38:27 So too is every craftsman and master workman 2

workmanship 1. מַעֲשֶׂה 2. ἔργον 3. ποίημα 4. τεχνάομαι 5. figmentum
Exd 28: 8 shall be of the same workmanship and materials 1
39: 5 was of the same materials and workmanship 1
Num 8: 4 workmanship of the lampstand, hammered work 1
1Kg 7: 8 His own house . . was of like workmanship. 1
1Co 9: 1 Are not you my workmanship in the Lord? 2
Eph 2:10 we are his workmanship, created in Christ Jesus 3
2Es 3: 5 Yet he was the workmanship of thy hands 5
Wis 13:11 with pleasing workmanship make a useful vessel 4

world 1. אֶרֶץ 2. חֶלֶד 3. תֵּבֵל 4. αἰών 5. γῆ 6. κόσμος 7. οἰκουμένη 8. σάρξ 9. mundus 10. orbis 11. saeculum 12. terra
1Sm 2: 8 the pillars . . and on them he has set the world. 3
2Sm 22:16 the foundations of the world were laid bare 3
1Ch 16:30 yea, the world stands firm, never to be moved. 3
Job 18:18 into darkness, and driven out of the world. 3
34:13 who laid on him the whole world? 3
Ps 9: 8 he judges the world with righteousness 3
17:14 from men whose portion in life is of the world. 2
18:15 the foundations of the world were laid bare 3
19: 4 and their words to the end of the world. 3
24: 1 the world and those who dwell therein; 3
33: 8 the inhabitants of the world stand in awe of him! 3
49: 1 Give ear, all inhabitants of the world 2
50:12 for the world and all that is in it is mine. 3
77:18 thy lightnings lighted up the world; 3
89:11 world and all that is in it, thou hast founded them. 3
90: 2 ever thou hadst formed the earth and the world 3
93: 1 world is established; it shall never be moved; 3
96:10 world is established, it shall never be moved; 3
13 He will judge the world with righteousness 3
97: 4 His lightnings lighten the world; 3
98: 7 world and those who dwell in it! 3
9 will judge the world with righteousness 3
Prv 8:26 first of the dust of the world. 3
31 rejoicing in his inhabited world 1
Isa 13:11 I will punish the world for its evil 3
14:17 who made the world like a desert 3
21 and fill the face of the world with cities. 3
18: 3 All you inhabitants of the world, you who dwell 3
23:17 with all the kingdoms of the world upon the face 1
24: 4 the world languishes and withers; 3
26: 9 the inhabitants of the world learn 3
18 and the inhabitants of the world have not fallen. 3
27: 6 fill the whole world with fruit. 3
34: 1 the world, and all that comes from it. 3
38:11 man no more among the inhabitants of the world. 2
Jer 10:12 who established the world by his wisdom 3
25:26 and all the kingdoms of the world 1
51:15 who established the world by his wisdom 3
Lam 4:12 kings . . or any of the inhabitants of the world 3
Ezk 26:20 I will make you to dwell in the nether world 1
31:14 to death, to the nether world among mortal men 1
16 will be comforted in the nether world. 1
18 down with the trees of Eden to the nether world; 1
32:18 to the nether world, to those who have gone down 1
24 went down uncircumcised into the nether world 1
Nah 1: 5 the world and all that dwell therein. 3
Mat 4: 8 the kingdoms of the world and the glory of them; 6
5:14 You are the light of the world. A city set on a hill 6
13:22 but the cares of the world . . choke the word 4
35 hidden since the foundation of the world. 6
38 the field is the world 6
16:26 if he gains the whole world and forfeits his life? 6
18: 7 Woe to the world for temptations to sin! 6
24:14 preached throughout the whole world 7
21 from the beginning of the world until now 6
25:34 from the foundation of the world; 6
26:13 this gospel is preached in the whole world 6
Mrk 4:19 the cares of the world, and the delight in riches 4
8:36 to gain the whole world and forfeit his life? 6
14: 9 the gospel is preached in the whole world 6
16:15 Go into all the world and preach the gospel 6
Lke 2: 1 all the world should be enrolled. 7
4: 5 the kingdoms of the world in a moment of time 7
9:25 what does it profit a man if he gains the whole world 6
11:50 blood . . shed from the foundation of the world 6
12:30 all the nations of the world seek these things; 6
16: 8 the sons of this world are more shrewd 4
21:26 foreboding of what is coming on the world 7
Joh 1: 9 The true light . . was coming into the world. 6
10 He was in the world 6
10 and the world was made through him 6
10 yet the world knew him not. 6
29 who takes away the sin of the world! 6
3:16 God so loved the world that he gave his only Son 6
17 For God sent the Son into the world 6
17 God sent the Son . . not to condemn the world 6
17 but that the world might be saved through him. 6
19 that the light has come into the world 6
4:42 this is indeed the Savior of the world. 6
6:14 the prophet who is to come into the world! 6
33 gives life to the world. 6
51 bread which I shall give for the life of the world 6
7: 4 If you do these things, show yourself to the world. 6
7 The world cannot hate you, but it hates me 6
8:12 I am the light of the world 6
23 you are of this world, I am not of this world. 6
23 you are of this world, I am not of this world. 6
26 I declare to the world what I have heard from him. 6
9: 5 As long as I am in the world 6
5 I am the light of the world. 6
32 Never since the world began has it been heard 4
39 Jesus said, "For judgment I came into this world 6
10:36 the Father consecrated and sent into the world 6
11: 9 because he sees the light of this world. 6
27 the Son of God, he who is coming into the world. 6
12:19 look, the world has gone after him. 6
25 he who hates his life in this world will keep it 6
31 Now is the judgment of this world 6
31 now shall the ruler of this world be cast out; 6
46 I have come as light into the world 6
47 not . . to judge the world but to save the world. 6
47 not . . to judge the world but to save the world. 6
13: 1 to depart out of this world to the Father 6
1 having loved his own who were in the world 6
14:17 whom the world cannot receive 6
19 the world will see me no more 6
22 manifest yourself to us, and not to the world? 6
27 not as the world gives do I give to you 6
30 the ruler of this world is coming 6
31 so that the world may know that I love the Father. 6
15:18 If the world hates you, know that it has hated me 6
19 If you were of the world 6
19 the world would love its own 6
19 because you are not of the world 6
19 I chose you out of the world 6
19 therefore the world hates you. 6
16: 8 when he comes, he will convince the world 6
11 because the ruler of this world is judged. 6
20 the world will rejoice 6
21 for joy that a child is born into the world. 6
28 have come into the world 6
28 I am leaving the world and going to the Father. 6
33 In the world you have tribulation 6
33 be of good cheer, I have overcome the world. 6
17: 5 glory which I had . . before the world was made. 6
6 the men whom thou gavest me out of the world 6
9 I am not praying for the world 6
11 now I am no more in the world 6
11 they are in the world, and I am coming to thee 6
13 these things I speak in the world 6
14 the world has hated them 6
14 they are not of the world, even as I am not 6
14 are not of the world, even as I am not of the world. 6
15 that thou shouldst take them out of the world 6
16 They are not of the world, even as I am not 6
16 are not of the world, even as I am not of the world. 6
18 As thou didst send me into the world 6
18 so I have sent them into the world. 6
21 the world may believe that thou hast sent me. 6
23 so that the world may know that thou hast sent me 6
24 given me . . before the foundation of the world. 6
25 O righteous Father, the world has not known thee 6
18:20 I have spoken openly to the world 6
36 Jesus answered, "My kingship is not of this world; 6
36 if my kingship were of this world 6
36 my kingship is not from the world. •
37 for this I have come into the world 6
21:25 the world itself could not contain the books 6

Act 11:28 there would be a great famine over all the world; 7
17: 6 These men who have turned the world upside down 7
24 The God who made the world and everything in it 6
31 he has fixed a day on which he will judge the world 7
19:27 she whom all Asia and the world worship. 7
24: 5 among all the Jews throughout the world 7
Rom 1: 8 your faith is proclaimed in all the world. 6
20 Ever since the creation of the world 6
3: 6 By no means! For then how could God judge the world 6
19 the whole world may be held accountable to God. 6
4:13 promise . . that they should inherit the world 6
5:12 as sin came into the world through one man 6
13 sin indeed was in the world before the law 6
10:18 and their words to the ends of the world. 7
11:12 Now if their trespass means riches for the world 6
15 means the reconciliation of the world 6
12: 2 Do not be conformed to this world 4
1Co 1:20 Has not God made foolish the wisdom of the world? 6
21 the world did not know God through wisdom 6
27 God chose what is foolish in the world 6
27 God chose what is weak in the world 6
28 God chose what is low and despised in the world 6
2:12 Now we have received not the spirit of the world 6
3:19 For the wisdom of this world is folly with God. 6
22 the world or life or death or the present 6
4: 9 a spectacle to the world, to angels and to men. 6
13 as the refuse of the world 6
5:10 not at all meaning the immoral of this world 6
10 since then you would need to go out of the world. 6
6: 2 know that the saints will judge the world 6
2 if the world is to be judged by you 6
7:31 those who deal with the world 6
31 the form of this world is passing away. 6
11:32 may not be condemned along with the world. 6
14:10 many different languages in the world 6
2Co 1:12 we have behaved in the world 6
4: 4 the god of this world has blinded the minds 4
5:19 in Christ God was reconciling the world 6
10: 3 For though we live in the world 8
Gal 6:14 by which the world has been crucified to me 6
14 I to the world. 6
Eph 1: 4 chose us in him before the foundation of the world 6
2: 2 following the course of this world 6
12 having no hope and without God in the world. 6
Php 2:15 among whom you shine as lights in the world 6
Col 1: 6 as indeed in the whole world it is bearing fruit 6
2:20 you live as if you still belonged to the world 6
1Ti 1:15 Jesus came into the world to save sinners 6
3:16 believed on in the world, taken up in glory. 6
6: 7 for we brought nothing into the world 6
7 we cannot take anything out of the world; •
17 As for the rich in this world 4
2Ti 4:10 Demas, in love with this present world 4
Tit 2:12 to live sober, upright, and godly lives in this world 4
Heb 1: 2 through whom also he created the world. 4
6 when he brings the first-born into the world 6
2: 5 God subjected the world to come 7
4: 3 were finished from the foundation of the world. 6
9:26 since the foundation of the world 6
10: 5 when Christ came into the world, he said 6
11: 3 the world was created by the word of God 4
7 by this he condemned the world 6
38 of whom the world was not worthy 6
Jas 1:27 to keep oneself unstained from the world. 6
2: 5 Has not God chosen those who are poor in the world 6
3: 6 The tongue is an unrighteous world 6
4: 4 friendship with the world is enmity with God? 6
4 whoever wishes to be a friend of the world 6
1Pe 1:20 destined before the foundation of the world 6
5: 9 your brotherhood throughout the world. 6
2Pe 1: 4 escape from the corruption that is in the world 6
2: 5 if he did not spare the ancient world 6
5 he brought a flood upon the world of the ungodly; 6
20 they have escaped the defilements of the world 6
3: 6 the world that then existed was deluged with water 6
1Jn 2: 2 but also for the sins of the whole world. 6
15 Do not love the world or the things in the world. 6
15 Do not love the world or the things in the world. 6
15 If any one loves the world 6
16 For all that is in the world, the lust of the flesh 6
16 is not of the Father but is of the world. 6
17 the world passes away, and the lust of it; 6
3: 1 The reason why the world does not know us 6
13 Do not wonder, brethren, that the world hates you. 6
17 if any one has the world's goods 6
4: 1 many false prophets have gone out into the world 6
3 antichrist . . and now it is in the world 6
4 greater than he who is in the world. 6
5 They are of the world 6
5 therefore what they say is of the world 6
5 and the world listens to them. 6
9 that God sent his only Son into the world 6
14 Father has sent his Son as the Savior of the world 6
17 because as he is so are we in this world. 6
5: 4 For whatever is born of God overcomes the world; 6
4 this is the victory that overcomes the world 6
5 Who is it that overcomes the world 6
19 the whole world is in the power of the evil one. 6
2Jn 1: 7 For many deceivers have gone out into the world 6

Rev 3:10 hour of trial which is coming on the whole world 7
11:15 The kingdom of the world has become the kingdom 6
12: 9 deceiver of the whole world–he was thrown down 7
13: 8 written before the foundation of the world 6
16:14 who go abroad to the kings of the whole world 7
17: 8 from the foundation of the world 6
1Es 2: 3 the Lord Most High, has made me king of the world 7
2Es 2:47 whom they confessed in the world 11
3: 9 the flood upon the inhabitants of the world 11
18 shake the earth, and move the world 10
34 those of the inhabitants of the world 11
4: 2 Your understanding . . regarding this world 11
11 one who is already worn out by the corrupt world 11
24 why we pass from the world like locusts 11
5:24 from all the lands of the world thou hast chosen 10
24 from all the flowers of the world 10
44 neither can the world hold at one time those 11
49 so have I organized the world which I created. 11
6: 1 before the portals of the world were in place 11
25 shall see my salvation and the end of my world. 11
55 for us that thou didst create this world. 11
59 If the world has indeed been created for us 11
59 why do we not possess our world as an inheritance? 11
7:11 For I made the world for their sake 11
12 so the entrances of this world were made narrow 11
13 the entrances of the greater world are broad 11
21 those who came into the world, when they came •
30 the world shall be turned back to . . silence 11
31 after seven days the world, which is not yet awake 11
47 that the world to come will bring delight to few 11
50 the Most High has made not one world but two. 11
70 When the Most High made the world 11
74 those who inhabit the world 11
112This present world is not the end 11
132those who have not yet come into the world; 11
137the world with those who inhabit it 11
8: 1 The Most High made this world for the sake of many 11
1 but the world to come for the sake of few. •
2 so is the course of the present world. 11
5 not of your own will did you come into the world ‡
41 those who have been sown in the world 11
50 those who inhabit the world in the last times 11
9: 2 when the Most High is about to visit the world 11
3 there shall appear in the world earthquakes 11
5 everything that has occurred in the world 11
18 before the world was made for them to dwell 11
19 now those who have been created in this world 9
20 I considered my world, and behold, it was lost 11
10: 8 but we, the whole world, for our mother. ‡
45 it is because there were 3,000 years in the world 11
11:32 and it had greater power over the world than all 10
39 which I had made to reign in my world 11
40 have held sway over the world with much terror 11
13:20 to pass from the world like a cloud 11
14:17 For the weaker the world becomes through old age 11
20 For the world lies in darkness 11
22 write everything that has happened in the world 11
15: 5 Behold," says the Lord, "I bring evils upon the world 10
14 Alas for the world and for those who live in it! 11
16:13 they begin to be shot to the ends of the world. 12
39 and the world will groan, and pains will seize it 11
Jdt 5:21 we shall be put to shame before the whole world. 5
10:19 they will be able to ensnare the whole world! 5
11: 8 it is reported throughout the whole world 5
16 things that will astonish the whole world 5
23 be renowned throughout the whole world. 5
AEs 13: 2 master of the whole world 7
4 among all the nations in the world 7
Wis 1: 7 the Spirit of the Lord has filled the world 7
14 the generative forces of the world are wholesome 6
2:24 through the devil's envy death entered the world 6
6:24 the salvation of the world 6
7:17 to know the structure of the world 6
9: 3 rule the world in holiness and righteousness 6
9 was present when thou didst make the world 6
10: 1 protected the first-formed father of the world 6
11:17 which created the world out of formless matter 6
22 Because the whole world before thee 6
13: 2 the gods that rule the world. 6
9 they could investigate the world 4
14: 6 the hope of the world took refuge on a raft 6
6 left to the world the seed of a new generation. 4
14 through the vanity of men they entered the world 6
17:20 the whole world was illumined 6
18: 4 to be given to the world. 4
24 upon his long robe the whole world was depicted 6
Sir 38:34 they keep stable the fabric of the world 4
LJr 1:62 God commands the clouds to go over the whole world 7
Aza 1: 9 an unjust king, the most wicked in all the world. 5
14 and are brought low this day in all the world 5
22 the only God, glorious over the whole world. 7
2Mc 2:22 the temple famous throughout the world 7
3:12 which is honored throughout the whole world. 6
5:15 to enter the most holy temple in all the world 5
7:23 the Creator of the world 6
8:18 to strike down . . even the whole world. 6
12:15 calling upon the great Sovereign of the world 6
13:14 the Creator of the world 6
3Mc 6: 5 gained control of the whole world by the spear 5

4Mc 5:25 the Creator of the world . . has shown sympathy 6
8:23 deprive ourselves of this delightful world? 6
16:18 you have had a share in the world and have enjoyed 6
17:14 the world and the human race were the spectators. 6

world *See also* carry, habitable, ruler.

world below 1. טמן
Job 40:13 bind their faces in the world below. 1

new world 1. *παλιγγενεσία*
Mat 19:28 in the new world, when the Son of man shall sit 1

worldly 1. *κατὰ σάρκα* 2. *κοσμικός* 3. *κόσμος* 4. *σαρκικός* 5. *σάρξ*
1Co 7:28 Yet those who marry will have worldly troubles 5
33 the married man is anxious about worldly affairs 3
34 the married woman is anxious about worldly affairs 3
2Co 7:10 worldly grief produces death. 3
10: 3 we are not carrying on a worldly war 1
4 for the weapons of our warfare are not worldly 4
Tit 2:12 to renounce irreligion and worldly passions 2

worldly *See also* fashion, standard.

worldly man 1. *σάρξ*
2Co 1:17 Do I make my plans like a worldly man 1

worldly people 1. *ψυχικός*
Jde 1:19 worldly people, devoid of the Spirit. 1

worldly thing 1. *σάρξ*
2Co 11:18 since many boast of worldly things 1

worm 1. סָס 2. רִמָּה 3. תּוֹלָע 4. תּוֹלֵעָה 5. *ἑρπετόν* 6. *σκώληξ*
Exd 16:20 the morning, and it bred worms and became foul; 3
24 become foul, and there were no worms in it. 2
Deu 28:39 for the worm shall eat them. 4
Job 7: 5 My flesh is clothed with worms and dirt; 2
17:14 if I say . . to the worm, 'My mother,' or 'My sister,' 2
21:26 alike in the dust, and the worms cover them. 2
25: 6 and the son of man, who is a worm! 4
Ps 22: 6 I am a worm, and no man; scorned by men, 4
Isa 14:11 maggots . . and worms are your covering. 4
41:14 Fear not, you worm Jacob, you men of Israel! 4
51: 8 and the worm will eat them like wool; 1
66:24 for their worm shall not die, 4
Jon 4: 7 God appointed a worm which attacked the plant 4
Mrk 9:47 where their worm does not die 6
Jdt 16:17 fire and worms he will give to their flesh 6
Sir 7:17 the punishment of the ungodly is fire and worms. 6
10:11 creeping things, and wild beasts, and worms. 6
19: 3 Decay and worms will inherit him 6
LJr 1:20 when worms from the earth devour them 5
1Mc 2:62 his splendor will turn into dung and worms. 6
2Mc 9: 9 so the ungodly man's body swarmed with worms 6

worm *See also* eaten.

wormwood 1. לַעֲנָה 2. *ἄψινθος*
Prv 5: 4 in the end she is bitter as wormwood 1
Jer 9:15 Behold, I will feed this people with wormwood 1
23:15 Behold, I will feed them with wormwood 1
Lam 3:15 he has sated me with wormwood. 1
19 Remember my . . the wormwood and the gall! 1
Ams 5: 7 O you who turn justice to wormwood 1
6:12 and the fruit of righteousness into wormwood 1
Rev 8:11 The name of the star is Wormwood. 2
11 A third of the waters became wormwood 2

worn-out 1. בָּלֶה
Jos 9: 4 and took worn-out sacks upon their asses 1
4 took . . wineskins, worn-out and torn and mended 1
5 with worn-out, patched sandals on their feet 1
5 patched sandals . . and worn-out clothes; 1

worn-out *See also* clothes.

worry 1. *εὐλαβέομαι* 2. *λόγον ἔχω* 3. *μέριμνα* 4. *ὑποπτεύω*
Tob 5:20 Tobit said to her, "Do not worry, my sister 2
6:15 do not worry about the demon 2
10: 6 Be still and stop worrying; he is well. 2
Sir 9:13 you will not be worried by the fear of death 4
22:22 do not worry, for reconciliation is possible 1
42: 9 worry over her robs him of sleep 3
1Mc 6:10 I am downhearted with worry. 3

worse *See* grow.

far worse thing 1. *χείρων*
2Mc 13: 9 things far worse than those that had been done 1

worse than 1. *ὑπέρ*
Sir 25:15 There is no venom worse than a snake's venom 1
15 no wrath worse than an enemy's wrath. 1

worship 1. דרשׁ 2. ירא 3. עבד 4. שׁחה 5. שׁרת 6. סגד (A) 7. *εὐσεβέω* 8. *θεραπεία* 9. *θρησκεία* 10. *θρησκεύω* 11. *λατρεία* 12. *λατρεύω* 13. *λειτουργέω* 14. *λειτουργία* 15. *προσκυνέω*

16. προσκύνησις 17. σεβάζομαι 18. σέβασμα
19. σέβω
Gen 22: 5 I and the lad will go yonder and worship 4
24:26 The man bowed his head and worshiped the LORD 4
48 Then I bowed my head and worshiped the LORD 4
Exd 4:31 they bowed their heads and worshiped. 4
12:27 the people bowed their heads and worshiped. 4
24: 1 Come up to the LORD . . and worship afar off. 4
32: 8 have worshiped it and sacrificed to it 4
33:10 all the people would rise up and worship 4
34: 8 bow his head toward the earth, and worshiped. 4
14 for you shall worship no other god, for the LORD 4
Deu 4:19 you be drawn away and worship them and serve them 4
8:19 after other gods and serve them and worship them 4
11:16 turn aside and serve other gods and worship 4
17: 3 gone and served other gods and worshipped them 4
26:10 set it down . . worship before the LORD your God; 4
29:26 went and served other gods and worshiped them 4
30:17 but are drawn away to worship other gods 4
Jos 5:14 Joshua fell on his face . . and worshiped, and said 4
22:25 make our children cease to worship the LORD. 2
Jdg 7:15 When Gideon heard . . he worshiped; 4
1Sm 1: 3 go up . . from his city to worship and to sacrifice 4
19 rose early . . and worshiped before the LORD; 4
28 And they worshiped the LORD there. 4
15:25 and return with me, that I may worship the LORD. 4
30 return . . that I may worship the LORD your God. 4
31 and Saul worshiped the LORD. 4
2Sm 12:20 he went into the house of the LORD, and worshiped; 4
15:32 David came to the summit, where God was worshiped 4
1Kg 9: 6 if you . . go and serve other gods and worship them 4
9 laid hold on other gods, and worshiped them 4
11:33 he has forsaken me, and worshiped Ash'toreth 4
16:31 and went and served Ba'al, and worshiped him. 4
22:53 He served Ba'al and worshiped him 4
2Kg 5:18 goes into the house of Rimmon to worship there 4
17:16 and worshiped all the host of heaven, and served 4
18:22 You shall worship before this altar 4
19:37 he was worshiping in the house of Nisroch his god 4
21: 3 and worshiped all the host of heaven, and served 4
21 and served the idols . . and worshiped them; 4
1Ch 16:29 Worship the LORD in holy array; 4
29:20 bowed their heads, and worshipped the LORD 4
2Ch 7: 3 bowed down . . and worshiped and gave thanks 4
19 turn aside . . serve other gods and worship them 4
22 laid hold on other gods, and worshiped them 4
20:18 fell down before the LORD, worshiping the LORD. 4
25:14 worshiped them, making offerings to them. 4
29:28 whole assembly worshiped, and the singers sang 4
29 all . . bowed themselves and worshiped. 4
30 sang praises . . bowed down and worshiped. 4
32:12 Before one altar you shall worship 4
33: 3 worshiped all the host of heaven, and served them. 4
Ezr 4: 2 for we worship your God as you do, and we have been 1
6:21 separated . . to worship the LORD, the God of Israel. 1
Neh 8: 6 bowed their heads and worshiped the LORD 4
9: 3 for another fourth . . worshiped the LORD their God. 4
6 host of heaven worships thee. 4
Job 1:20 fell upon the ground, and worshiped. 4
Ps 5: 7 I will worship toward thy holy temple 4
22:27 the nations shall worship before him. 4
29: 2 worship the LORD in holy array. 4
66: 4 earth worships thee; they sing praises to thee 4
95: 6 O come, let us worship and bow down, let us kneel 4
96: 9 Worship the LORD in holy array; 4
99: 5 LORD our God; worship at his footstool! Holy is he! 4
9 LORD our God, and worship at his holy mountain; 4
102:22 peoples . . and kingdoms, to worship the LORD. 3
106:19 calf in Horeb and worshiped a molten image. 4
132: 7 Let us go . . let us worship at his footstool! 4
Isa 2:20 which they made for themselves to worship 4
19:21 Egyptians will . . worship with sacrifice 3
23 the Egyptians will worship with the Assyrians. 3
27:13 come and worship the LORD on the holy mountain 4
36: 7 You shall worship before this altar"? 4
37:38 he was worshiping in the house of Nisroch his god 4
44:15 also he makes a god and worships it 4
17 his idol; and falls down to it and worships it; 4
46: 6 makes . . a god; then they fall down and worship! 4
66:23 all flesh shall come to worship before me 4
Jer 1:16 and worshiped the works of their own hands. 4
7: 2 who enter these gates to worship the LORD. 4
8: 2 and which they have sought and worshiped; 4
13:10 after other gods to serve them and worship them 4
16:11 other gods and have served and worshiped them 4
22: 9 and worshiped other gods and served them. 4
25: 6 do not go after other gods to serve and worship 4
26: 2 the cities of Judah which come to worship 4
Ezk 8:16 their faces toward the east, worshiping the sun 4
20:32 and worship wood and stone. 5
46: 2 he shall worship at the threshold of the gate. 4
3 people of the land shall worship at the entrance 4
9 he who enters by the north gate to worship 4
Dan 3: 5 fall down and worship the golden image 6
6 whoever does not fall down and worship shall 6
7 all . . fell down and worshiped the golden image 6
10 fall down and worship the golden image; 6
11 not fall down and worship shall be cast 6
12 not serve your gods or worship the golden image 6
14 not serve my gods or worship the golden image 6
15 fall down and worship the image which I have made 6
15 if you do not worship, you shall immediately 6
18 not serve your gods or worship the golden image 6
28 serve and worship any god except their own God. 6
Zec 14:16 shall go up year after year to worship the King 4
17 to Jerusalem to worship the King, the LORD 4
Mat 2: 2 in the East, and have come to worship him. 15
8 bring me word, that I too may come and worship him. 15
11 his mother, and they fell down and worshiped him. 15
4: 9 you, if you will fall down and worship me. 15
10 is written, 'You shall worship the Lord your God 15
14:33 those in the boat worshiped him, saying 15
15: 9 in vain do they worship me, teaching as doctrines 19
28: 9 took hold of his feet and worshiped him. 15
17 when they saw him they worshiped him 15
Mrk 5: 6 when he saw Jesus from afar, he ran and worshiped 15
7: 7 in vain do they worship me 19
Lke 2:37 worshiping with fasting and prayer 12
4: 7 If you, then, will worship me, it shall all be yours. 15
8 It is written, 'You shall worship the Lord your God 15
Joh 4:20 Our fathers worshiped on this mountain; 15
20 Jerusalem is . . where men ought to worship. 15
21 nor in Jerusalem will you worship the Father. 15
22 You worship what you do not know; 15
22 we worship what we know 15
23 will worship the Father in spirit and truth 15
23 for such the Father seeks to worship him. 15
24 those who worship him must worship in spirit 15
24 must worship in spirit and truth. 15
9:38 He said, "Lord, I believe"; and he worshiped him. 15
12:20 among those who went up to worship at the feast 15
Act 7: 7 they shall come out and worship me in this place.' 12
42 God . . gave them over to worship the host of heaven 12
43 the figures which you made to worship 15
8:27 had come to Jerusalem to worship 15
10:25 and fell down at his feet and worshiped him. 15
13: 2 While they were worshiping the Lord and fasting 13
17:23 What therefore you worship as unknown 7
18:13 worship God contrary to the law. 19
19:27 she whom all Asia and the world worship. 19
24:11 since I went up to worship at Jerusalem; 15
14 I admit to you . . I worship the God of our fathers 12
26: 7 as they earnestly worship night and day 12
27:23 the God to whom I belong and whom I worship 12
Rom 1:25 worshiped and served the creature rather 17
9: 4 giving of the law, the worship, and the promises; 11
12: 1 which is your spiritual worship. 11
1Co 14:25 and so, falling on his face, he will worship God 15
Php 3: 3 who worship God in spirit, and glory in Christ 12
Col 2:18 self-abasement and worship of angels 9
Heb 1: 6 he says, "Let all God's angels worship him. 15
9: 1 the first covenant had regulations for worship 11
21 both the tent and all the vessels used in worship. 14
Rev 4:10 worship him who lives for ever and ever; 15
5:14 and the elders fell down and worshiped. 15
7:11 they fell on their faces . . and worshiped God 15
9:20 nor give up worshiping demons and idols of gold 15
11: 1 the temple of God . . and those who worship there 15
16 elders . . fell on their faces and worshiped God 15
13: 4 Men worshiped the dragon 15
4 and they worshiped the beast, saying 15
8 and all who dwell on earth will worship it 15
12 makes . . inhabitants worship the first beast 15
15 and to cause those who would not worship 15
14: 7 and worship him who made heaven and earth 15
9 If any one worships the beast and its image 15
15: 4 All nations shall come and worship thee 15
16: 2 the mark of the beast and worshiped its image. 15
19: 4 living creatures fell down and worshiped God 15
10 Then I fell down at his feet to worship him 15
10 Worship God. 15
20 and those who worshiped its image. 15
20: 4 and who had not worshiped the beast or its image 15
22: 3 and his servants shall worship him; 12
8 I fell down to worship at the feet of the angel 15
9 who keep the words of this book. Worship God. 15
1Es 1: 4 worship the Lord your God and serve his people 12
9:47 fell to the ground and worshiped the Lord. 15
Tob 5:13 when we went together to Jerusalem to worship 15
Jdt 3: 8 all nations should worship Nebuchadnezzar 12
5: 8 they worshiped the God of heaven 15
6:18 Then the people fell down and worshiped God 15
8:18 which worshiped gods made with hands 15
10: 8 she worshiped God. 15
13:17 All the people . . bowed down and worshiped God 15
16:18 they worshiped God 15
AEs 15: 1 took off the garments in which she had worshiped 8
Wis 11:15 led them astray to worship irrational serpents 10
14:16 graven images were worshiped. 10
18 to intensify their worship. 9
27 the worship of idols not to be named 9
15: 6 who either make or desire or worship them. 19
18 worship even the most hateful animals 19
Sir 50:17 to worship their Lord, the Almighty, God Most High. 15
19 till the order of worship of the Lord was ended *
LJr 1: 5 the multitude . . worshiping them. 15
6 It is thou, O Lord, whom we must worship. 15
Aza 1:68 Bless him, all who worship the Lord, the God of gods 19
Bel 1: 4 revered it and went every day to worship it 15
4 Daniel worshiped his own God. 15
5 the king said to him, "Why do you not worship Bel? 15
24 this is a living god; so worship him. 15
25 Daniel said, "I will worship the Lord my God 15
27 Daniel said, "See what you have been worshiping! 18
1Mc 4:55 worshiped and blessed Heaven 15
2Mc 1: 3 May he give you all a heart to worship him 19
3Mc 3: 4 because they worshiped God 19
7 they gossiped about the differences in worship 16
4Mc 5:24 we worship the only real God. 19

worship *See also* bow, object, offer.

worship of an idol 1. εἰδωλολατρία
1Co 10:14 Therefore, my beloved, shun the worship of idols. 1

worshiper 1. עבד 2. λατρεύω 3. προσκυνέω
4. προσκυνητής 5. σέβω
2Kg 10:19 of Ba'al, all his worshipers and all his priests; 1
19 in order to destroy the worshipers of Ba'al. 1
21 Jehu sent . . all the worshipers of Ba'al came 1
22 vestments for all the worshipers of Ba'al. 1
23 Jehu went . . and he said to the worshipers of Ba'al 1
23 no . . among you, but only the worshipers of Ba'al. 1
Ps 97: 7 All worshipers of images are put to shame 1
Joh 4:23 true worshipers will worship the Father 4
Act 16:14 who was a worshiper of God 5
18: 7 Titius Justus, a worshiper of God 5
Heb 9: 9 cannot perfect the conscience of the worshiper 2
10: 2 If the worshipers had once been cleansed 2
Rev 14:11 these worshipers of the beast and its image 3
Wis 14:28 For their worshipers either rave in exultation *
Aza 1:10 thy servants and worshipers. 5

worshiper of God 1. θεοσεβής
Joh 9:31 if any one is a worshiper of God and does his will 1

worships *See* object.

worth 1. בְּ 2. חַיִל 3. ἀξία 4. ἄξιος 5. ἀξιόω
6. δοκιμή
Gen 23:15 a piece of land worth 400 shekels of silver *
Rut 3:11 my . . townsmen know that you are a woman of worth. 2
2Sm 18: 3 But you are worth 10,000 of us; *
Ezr 8:26 silver vessels worth 100 talents *
27 twenty bowls of gold worth 1,000 darics *
Prv 10:20 the mind of the wicked is of little worth. *
Isa 7:23 vines, worth 1,000 shekels of silver 1
Mrk 6:37 we go and buy 200 denarii worth of bread *
Rom 8:18 the sufferings . . are not worth comparing 4
Php 2:22 Timothy's worth you know 6
1Es 8:56 silver vessels worth a 100 talents *
Sir 10:28 honor according to your worth. 3
2Mc 9:15 whom he had not considered worth burying 5

less worth 1. ἄτιμος 2. vilis
2Es 7:58 what is plentiful is of less worth 2
Wis 15:10 his life is of less worth than clay 1

worth more than 1. ὑπέρ
Sir 7:19 her charm is worth more than gold. 1

surpassing worth 1. ὑπερέχω
Php 3: 8 the surpassing worth of knowing Christ Jesus 1

worth weight 1. סלא
Lam 4: 2 sons of Zion, worth their weight in fine gold 1

worthily 1. ἀγαθός 2. ἐντίμως
Tob 12: 6 worthily declaring the works of God 2
13:10 Give thanks worthily to the Lord 1

worthless 1. אֱוִלִי 2. אֱלִיל 3. בְּלִיַּעַל 4. הֶבֶל 5. זלל
6. קְלֹקֵל 7. רֵיק 8. שָׁוְא 9. ἀδόκιμος 10. ἀχρεῖος
11. δειλός 12. ἐξουδενόω 13. εὐτελής 14. vanus
Num 21: 5 no food and . . we loathe this worthless food. 6
Jdg 9: 4 hired worthless and reckless fellows 7
11: 3 worthless fellows collected round Jephthah 7
1Sm 15: 9 all that was despised and worthless 12
2Sm 16: 7 Begone . . you man of blood, you worthless fellow! 3
20: 1 there happened to be there a worthless fellow 3
2Ch 13: 7 certain worthless scoundrels gathered about 7
Job 11:11 For he knows worthless men; when he sees iniquity 8
13: 4 worthless physicians are you all. 2
Prv 6:12 A worthless person, a wicked man 3
16:27 A worthless man plots evil 3
19:28 A worthless witness mocks at justice 3
Isa 30: 7 For Egypt's help is worthless and empty 4
Jer 10:15 They are worthless, a work of delusion; 4
14:14 are prophesying to you . . worthless divination 2
15:19 utter what is precious, and not what is worthless 5
51:18 They are worthless, a work of delusion; 4
Zec 11:15 Take . . the implements of a worthless shepherd. 1
17 Woe to my worthless shepherd 2
Mat 25:30 cast the worthless servant 10
Heb 6: 8 it is worthless and near to being cursed 9
2Es 11:45 and your whole worthless body 14
Wis 9:14 For the reasoning of mortals is worthless 11

11:15 irrational serpents and worthless animals 13
13:14 or makes it like some worthless animal 13
worthless *See also* idol, pursuit.

become worthless 1. הבל
Jer 2: 5 went after worthlessness, and became worthless? 1

worthless fellow 1. בֶּן בְּלִיַּעַל
1Sm 10:27 worthless fellows said, "How can this man save 1

worthless man 1. בֶּן בְּלִיַּעַל
1Sm 2:12 Now the sons of Eli were worthless men; 1

worthless one 1. בְּלִיַּעַל
Job 34:18 who says to a king, 'Worthless one,' 1

worthless thing 1. הֶבֶל
Jer 16:19 worthless things in which there is no profit. 1

worthlessness 1. הֶבֶל 2. ἀτιμία
Jer 2: 5 went far from me, and went after worthlessness 1
LJr 1:26 revealing to mankind their worthlessness. 2

worthy 1. חַיִל 2. αἱρετός 3. ἀξία 4. ἄξιος 5. ἀξίως 6. ἐπιτήδειος 7. ἱκανός 8. χρηστός 9. dignus 10. idoneus
1Kg 1:42 for you are a worthy man and bring good news. 1
52 If he prove to be a worthy man, not one of his hairs 1
Ps 18: 3 I call upon the LORD, who is worthy to be praised *
Mat 3:11 whose sandals I am not worthy to carry; he will 7
8: 8 Lord, I am not worthy to have you come under my roof 7
10:11 find out who is worthy in it 4
13 if the house is worthy, let your peace come upon it; 3
13 if it is not worthy, let your peace return to you. 3
37 is not worthy of me; 4
37 is not worthy of me; 4
38 is not worthy of me. 4
22: 8 but those invited were not worthy. 4
Mrk 1: 7 I am not worthy to stoop down and untie. 7
Lke 3:16 thong of whose sandals I am not worthy to untie 7
7: 4 He is worthy to have you do this for him 4
6 for I am not worthy to have you come under my roof; 7
15:19 I am no longer worthy to be called your son 4
21 I am no longer worthy to be called your son.' 4
Joh 1:27 the thong of whose sandal I am not worthy to untie. 4
Act 13:25 the sandals of whose feet I am not worthy to untie.' 4
26:20 and perform deeds worthy of their repentance 4
Eph 4: 1 to lead a life worthy of the calling 5
Php 1:27 manner of life be worthy of the gospel of Christ 5
Col 1:10 to lead a life worthy of the Lord 5
1Th 2:12 to lead a life worthy of God 5
1Ti 1:15 The saying is sure and worthy of full acceptance 4
4: 9 is sure and worthy of full acceptance. 4
6: 1 regard their masters as worthy of all honor 4
Heb 11:38 of whom the world was not worthy 4
Rev 3: 4 they . . walk with me in white, for they are worthy 4
4:11 Worthy art thou, our Lord and God, to receive glory 4
5: 2 Who is worthy to open the scroll and break 4
4 that no one was found worthy to open the scroll 4
9 Worthy art thou to take the scroll and to open 4
12 Worthy is the Lamb who was slain, to receive power 4
2Es 4:24 and we are not worthy to obtain mercy. 9
44 and if it is possible, and if I am worthy 10
12: 9 For thou hast judged me worthy to be shown the end 9
36 you alone were worthy to learn this secret 9
13:14 and hast deemed me worthy to have my prayer heard 9
14:45 and let the worthy and the unworthy read them; 9
Wis 3: 5 God tested them and found them worthy of himself; 4
6:16 she goes about seeking those worthy of her 4
7:15 have thought worthy of what I have received 5
9:12 shall be worthy of the throne of my father. 4
12: 7 receive a worthy colony of the servants of God. 3
Sir 11:31 to worthy actions he will attach blame. 2
14:11 present worthy offerings to the Lord. 4
1Mc 10:19 a mighty warrior and worthy to be our friend. 6
2Mc 6:23 worthy of his years and the dignity of his old age 4
24 Such pretense is not worthy of our time of life 4
27 I will show myself worthy of my old age 4
7:20 admirable and worthy of honorable memory 3
29 prove worthy of your brother 4
9:19 To his worthy Jewish citizens 8
4Mc 7: 6 O priest, worthy of the priesthood 4
9:21 the courageous youth, worthy of Abraham †
worthy *See also* account, consider, count, deem, make.

worthy of belief 1. ἀξιόπιστος
2Mc 15:11 a sort of vision, which was worthy of belief. 1

worthy of honor 1. ἔντιμος
Sir 10:19 What race is worthy of honor? The human race 1
19 What race is worthy of honor? The human race 1
20 Among brothers their leader is worthy of honor 1
20 worthy of honor in his eyes. *

worthy of praise 1. αἰνετός 2. ἔπαινος
Php 4: 8 if there is anything worthy of praise 2
Aza 1: 3 Blessed art thou . . and worthy of praise 1

worthy of the least 1. קטן
Gen 32:10 I am not worthy of the least of all the steadfast 1

worthy to be praised 1. הלל
2Sm 22: 4 I call upon the LORD, who is worthy to be praised 1

would
Deu 28:67 morning you shall say, 'Would it were evening!' *
67 at evening you shall say, 'Would it were morning!' *

would that 1. אַחֲלַי 2. בּיי 3. לוּ 4. מִי נתן 5. ἐθέλω 6. εἰ 7. ὄφελον
Exd 16: 3 said to them, "Would that we had died by the hand 4
Num20: 3 Would that we had died when our brethren died 3
Jos 7: 7 Would that we had been content to dwell beyond 3
Jdg 9:29 Would that this people were under my hand! 4
2Kg 5: 3 Would that my lord were with the prophet 1
Job 34:36 Would that Job were tried to the end 2
Isa 27: 4 Would that I had thorns and briers to battle! †
Lke 12:49 would that it were already kindled! 5
19:42 Would that . . you knew the things that make for peace 6
1Co 4: 8 would that you did reign, so that we might share 7
Rev 3:15 Would that you were cold or hot! 7

wound 1. דקר 2. חַבּוּרָה 3. חול 4. חלה 5. חלל 6. חָלָל 7. חֵץ 8. כאב 9. מָזוֹר 10. מַחֲלוּי 11. מחץ 12. מַחַץ 13. מַכְאוֹב 14. מַכָּה 15. נֶגַע 16. נכה 17. עַצֶּבֶת 18. פצע 19. פֶּצַע 20. שבר 21. שֶׁבֶר 22. ἀδικέω 23. ἄτρωτος 24. ἕλκος 25. ἔχω πληγήν 26. μώλωψ 27. πληγή 28. σφάζω 29. τιτρώσκω 30. τραῦμα 31. τραυματίας 32. τραυματίας ποιέω 33. τραυματίζω 34. τύπτω 35. mastigo a vulneribus
Gen 4:23 I have slain a man for wounding me 19
Exd 21:25 burn for burn, wound for wound, stripe for stripe. 19
25 burn for burn, wound for wound, stripe for stripe. 19
Deu 19: 6 overtake him . . and wound him mortally 16
11 attacks . . wounds him mortally so that he dies 16
32:39 I kill and I make alive; I wound and I heal; 11
Jdg 9:40 many fell wounded, up to the entrance of the gate. 6
1Sm 17:52 the wounded Philistines fell on the way 6
31: 3 and he was badly wounded by the archers. 3
2Sm 10:18 David slew . . and wounded Shobach the commander 16
1Kg 20:37 And the man struck him, smiting and wounding him. 18
22:34 carry me out of the battle, for I am wounded. 4
35 the blood of the wound flowed into the bottom 14
2Kg 8:28 to make war . . where the Syrians wounded Joram. 16
29 Joram returned to be healed . . of the wounds 14
9:15 Joram had returned to be healed . . of the wounds 14
1Ch 10: 3 Saul . . was wounded by the archers. 3
2Ch 18:33 carry me out of the battle, for I am wounded. 4
22: 5 And the Syrians wounded Joram 16
6 healed . . of the wounds which he had received 14
24:25 departed from him, leaving him severely wounded 10
35:23 king said . . Take me away, for I am badly wounded. 4
Job 5:18 For he wounds, but he binds up; 8
9:17 and multiplies my wounds without cause; 19
24:12 the soul of the wounded cries for help; 6
34: 6 I am counted a liar; my wound is incurable 7
Ps 38: 5 My wounds grow foul and fester 2
64: 7 his arrow at them; they will be wounded suddenly. 14
69:26 him whom thou hast wounded, they afflict still 13
147: 3 brokenhearted, and binds up their wounds. 17
Prv 6:33 Wounds and dishonor will he get 15
20:30 Blows that wound cleanse away evil; 19
23:29 has wounds without cause? Who has redness of eyes? 19
25:20 like vinegar on a wound. 24
26:10 Like an archer who wounds everybody is he who 5
27: 6 Faithful are the wounds of a friend; 19
Sng 5: 7 they beat me, they wounded me, they took away my 18
Isa 1: 6 but bruises and sores and bleeding wounds; 14
30:26 and heals the wounds inflicted by his blow. 12
53: 5 But he was wounded for our transgressions 5
Jer 6: 7 sickness and wounds are ever before me. 14
14 They have healed the wound of my people lightly 21
8:11 They have healed the wound of my people lightly 21
21 For the wound of the daughter of my people 21
21 For the wound of . . my people is my heart wounded 20
10:19 Woe is me because of my hurt! My wound is grievous. 14
14:17 my people is smitten with a great wound 21
15:18 Why is my pain unceasing, my wound incurable 14
30:12 hurt is incurable, and your wound is grievous. 14
13 no medicine for your wound, no healing for you. 9
17 and your wounds I will heal, says the LORD 14
50:13 be appalled, and hiss because of all her wounds. 14
51: 4 fall down slain . . and wounded in her streets. 1
52 through all her land the wounded shall groan. 6
Ezk 26:15 at the sound of your fall, when the wounded groan 6
28: 9 and no god, in the hands of those who wound you? 5
30:24 groan before him like a man mortally wounded. 6
Hos 5:13 E'phraim saw his sickness, and Judah his wound 9
13 But he is not able to cure you or heal your wound. 9
Mic 1: 9 For her wound is incurable; 27
Nah 3:19 no assuaging your hurt, your wound is grievous. 14
Zec 13: 6 if one asks him, 'What are these wounds on your back 14
Lke 10:34 and went to him and bound up his wounds 30
20:12 this one they wounded and cast out. 33
Act 16:33 washed their wounds 27
19:16 they fled out of that house naked and wounded. 33
1Co 8:12 wounding their conscience when it is weak 34
1Pe 2:24 By his wounds you have been healed. 26
Rev 9:19 their tails . . and by means of them they wound. 22
13: 3 One of its heads seemed to have a mortal wound 28
3 but its mortal wound was healed 27
12 the first beast, whose mortal wound was healed. 27
14 the beast which was wounded by the sword 25
2Es 15:51 a wretched woman who is beaten and wounded 35
Jdt 2: 8 till their wounded shall fill their valleys 31
6: 6 shall fall among their wounded, when I return. 31
9:13 Make my deceitful words to be their wound 30
16:12 were wounded like the children of fugitives 29
Sir 21: 3 there is no healing for its wound. 27
25:13 Any wound, but not a wound of the heart! 27
13 Any wound, but not a wound of the heart! 27
23 A dejected mind, a gloomy face, and a wounded heart 27
27:21 a wound may be bandaged 30
25 a treacherous blow opens up wounds. 30
30: 7 He who spoils his son will bind up his wounds 30
31:30 reducing his strength and adding wounds. 30
1Mc 1:18 many were wounded and fell. 31
3:11 Many were wounded and fell, and the rest fled. 31
8:10 Many of them were wounded and fell 31
9:17 many on both sides were wounded and fell. 31
40 Many were wounded and fell 31
16: 8 many of them were wounded and fell 31
9 Judas the brother of John was wounded 33
2Mc 3:16 to be wounded at heart 29
4:42 As a result, they wounded many of them 32
8:24 wounded and disabled most of Nicanor's army 32
10:30 they kept him from being wounded 23
11:12 Most of them got away stripped and wounded 31
14:45 his wounds were severe 30
wound *See also* receive.

deadly wound 1. רֶצַח
Ps 42:10 As with a deadly wound in my body 1

wound in the head 1. κεφαλαιόω
Mrk 12: 4 another servant, and they wounded him in the head 1

wounded man 1. דקר 2. חָלָל
Jer 37:10 and there remained of them only wounded men 1
Lam 2:12 faint like wounded men in the streets of the city 2

wrangle 1. διαπαρατριβή 2. ἐρίζω
Mat 12:19 He will not wrangle or cry aloud 2
1Ti 6: 5 wrangling among men who are depraved in mind 1

wrap 1. חבש 2. כנס 3. לבש 4. לוט 5. סכך 6. עטה 7. צרר 8. ἐνειλέω 9. ἐντυλίσσω 10. περιβάλλω 11. περιδέω
Deu 4:11 mountain . . wrapped in darkness, cloud, and gloom. *
1Sm 21: 9 sword of Goliath . . is here wrapped in a cloth 4
28:14 An old man is coming up; and he is wrapped in a robe. 6
1Kg 19:13 Eli'jah . . wrapped his face in his mantle 4
Ps 109:29 they be wrapped in their own shame as in a mantle! 6
Isa 28:20 the covering too narrow to wrap oneself in it. 2
59:17 and wrapped himself in fury as a mantle. 6
Lam 3:43 hast wrapped thyself with anger and pursued us 5
44 thou hast wrapped thyself with a cloud 5
Ezk 7:27 The king mourns, the prince is wrapped in despair 3
Hos 4:19 A wind has wrapped them in its wings 7
Jon 2: 5 round about me; weeds were wrapped about my head 1
Mat 27:59 and wrapped it in a clean linen shroud 9
Mrk 15:46 taking him down, wrapped him in the linen shroud 8
Lke 23:53 he took it down and wrapped it in a linen shroud 9
Joh 11:44 his face wrapped with a cloth 11
Rev 10: 1 coming down from heaven, wrapped in a cloud 10

wrap around 1. περιβάλλω
Act 12: 8 Wrap your mantle around you and follow me. 1

wrap in smoke 1. עשן
Exd 19:18 Mount Sinai was wrapped in smoke 1

wrap in swaddling cloths 1. σπαργανόω
Lke 2: 7 and wrapped him in swaddling cloths 1
12 you will find a babe wrapped in swaddling cloths 1

wrap round 1. עטה
Ps 109:19 May it be like a garment which he wraps round him 1

wrap up 1. עלף 2. צרר 3. περιδιπλόω 4. συστέλλω
Gen 38:14 garments, and put on a veil, wrapping herself up 1
Prv 30: 4 Who has wrapped up the waters in a garment? 2
Act 5: 6 The young men rose and wrapped him up 4
Jdt 10: 5 she wrapped up all her vessels 3

wrath 1. אַף 2. זַעַם 3. זַעַף 4. חֵמָה 5. חרה 6. חָרוֹן 7. עֶבְרָה 8. קֶצֶף 9. רֹגֶז 10. קְצַף (A) 11. θυμός 12. μῆνις 13. ὀργή 14. χόλος 15. ira 16. iracundia
Gen 49: 7 Cursed . . their wrath, for it is cruel! 7
Exd 22:24 my wrath will burn, and I will kill you 1
32:10 now therefore let me alone, that my wrath may burn 1
11 why does thy wrath burn hot against thy people 1

12 Turn from thy fierce wrath, and repent of this 1
Num 1:53 that there may be no wrath upon the congregation 8
16:46 for wrath has gone forth from the LORD, the plague 8
18: 5 there be wrath no more upon the people of Israel. 8
25:11 Phin'ehas . . has turned back my wrath 4
Deu 29:23 which the LORD overthrew in his anger and wrath- 4
28 uprooted . . in anger and fury and great wrath 8
Jos 9:20 lest wrath be upon us, because of the oath 8
22:20 and wrath fell upon all the congregation 8
1Sm 28:18 carry out his fierce wrath against Am'alek 1
2Kg 3:27 And there came great wrath upon Israel; 8
22:13 great is the wrath of the LORD that is kindled 4
17 my wrath will be kindled against this place 4
23:26 turn from the fierceness of his great wrath 1
1Ch 27:24 yet wrath came upon Israel for this 8
2Ch 12: 7 my wrath shall not be poured out upon Jerusalem 4
12 when he humbled himself the wrath of the LORD 1
19: 2 Because of this, wrath has gone out against you 8
10 wrath may not come upon you and your brethren. 8
24:18 wrath came upon Judah and Jerusalem for this 8
29: 8 the wrath of the LORD came on Judah and Jerusalem 8
32:25 wrath came upon him and Judah and Jerusalem. 8
26 wrath of the LORD did not come upon them 8
34:21 great is the wrath of the LORD that is poured out 4
25 my wrath will be poured out upon this place 4
36:16 till the wrath of the LORD rose against his people 4
Ezr 7:23 lest his wrath be against the realm of the king 10
8:22 power of his wrath is against all that forsake 1
10:14 till the fierce wrath of our God over this matter 1
Neh 13:18 Yet you bring more wrath upon Israel 6
Est 1:18 and there will be contempt and wrath in plenty. 8
5: 9 he was filled with wrath against Mor'decai. 4
7: 7 And the king rose from the feast in wrath 4
Job 14:13 thou wouldest conceal me until thy wrath be past 1
16: 9 He has torn me in his wrath, and hated me; 1
19:11 He has kindled his wrath against me 1
29 for wrath brings the punishment of the sword 4
20:28 dragged off in the day of God's wrath. 1
21:20 let them drink of the wrath of the Almighty. 4
30 that he is rescued in the day of wrath? 7
36:18 Beware lest wrath entice you into scoffing; 4
42: 7 My wrath is kindled against you 1
Ps 2: 5 Then he will speak to them in his wrath 1
12 for his wrath is quickly kindled. 1
6: 1 not in thy anger, nor chasten me in thy wrath. 4
21: 9 The LORD will swallow them up in his wrath; 1
37: 8 Refrain from anger, and forsake wrath! 4
38: 1 not in thy anger, nor chasten me in thy wrath! 4
56: 7 in wrath cast down the peoples, O God! 1
59:13 consume them in wrath, consume them till they are 4
76:10 Surely the wrath of men shall praise thee; 4
10 the residue of wrath thou wilt gird upon thee. 4
78:38 did not stir up all his wrath. 4
49 He let loose on them his fierce anger, wrath 7
85: 3 Thou didst withdraw all thy wrath; 7
88: 7 Thy wrath lies heavy upon me 4
16 Thy wrath has swept over me; 6
89:46 How long will thy wrath burn like fire? 4
90: 7 by thy wrath we are overwhelmed. 4
9 For all our days pass away under thy wrath 7
11 thy wrath according to the fear of thee? 7
106:23 to turn away his wrath from destroying them. 4
110: 5 shatter kings on the day of his wrath. 1
138: 7 out thy hand against the wrath of my enemies 1
Prv 11: 4 Riches do not profit in the day of wrath 7
23 the expectation of the wicked in wrath. 7
14:35 but his wrath falls on one who acts shamefully. 7
15: 1 A soft answer turns away wrath 4
16:14 A king's wrath is a messenger of death 4
19:12 A king's wrath is like the growling of a lion 3
19 A man of great wrath will pay the penalty; 4
21:14 bribe in the bosom, strong wrath. 4
27: 4 Wrath is cruel, anger is overwhelming; 4
29: 8 but wise men turn away wrath. 1
22 A man of wrath stirs up strife 1
Isa 9:19 Through the wrath of the LORD of hosts 7
10: 6 and against the people of my wrath I command him 7
13: 9 the LORD comes . . with wrath and fierce anger 7
13 tremble . . at the wrath of the LORD of hosts 7
14: 6 that smote the peoples in wrath 7
26:20 for a little while until the wrath is past. 2
27: 4 I have no wrath. 4
51:17 drunk at the hand of the LORD the cup of his wrath 4
20 they are full of the wrath of the LORD 4
22 the bowl of my wrath you shall drink no more; 4
54: 8 In overflowing wrath for a moment I hid my face 8
59:18 wrath to his adversaries, requital to his 4
60:10 for in my wrath I smote you 8
63: 3 in my anger and trampled them in my wrath; 4
5 arm brought me victory, and my wrath upheld me. 4
6 in my anger, I made them drunk in my wrath 4
Jer 4: 4 lest my wrath go forth like fire, and burn 4
6:11 Therefore I am full of the wrath of the LORD; 4
7:20 and my wrath will be poured out on this place 4
29 and forsaken the generation of his wrath. 7
10:10 At his wrath the earth quakes 8
25 Pour out thy wrath upon the nations 4
18:20 good for them, to turn away thy wrath from them. 4
21: 5 in anger, and in fury, and in great wrath. 8
12 lest my wrath go forth like fire 4
23:19 Wrath has gone forth, a whirling tempest; 4
25:15 Take from my hand this cup of the wine of wrath 4
30:23 Behold the storm of the LORD! Wrath has gone forth 4
32:31 This city has aroused my anger and wrath 4
37 in my anger and my wrath and in great indignation; 4
33: 5 men whom I shall smite in my anger and my wrath 4
36: 7 the anger and wrath that the LORD has pronounced 4
42:18 As my anger and my wrath were poured out 4
18 so my wrath will be poured out on you when you go 4
44: 6 my wrath and my anger were poured forth 4
50:13 Because of the wrath of the LORD she shall not be 8
25 and brought out the weapons of his wrath 2
Lam 2: 2 in his wrath he has broken down the strongholds 7
3: 1 has seen affliction under the rod of his wrath; 7
4:11 The LORD gave full vent to his wrath 4
Ezk 7: 8 Now I will soon pour out my wrath upon you 4
12 for wrath is upon all their multitude. 6
13 For wrath is upon all their multitude; •
14 for my wrath is upon all their multitude. 6
19 to deliver them in the day of the wrath of the LORD; 7
8:18 I will deal in wrath; my eye will not spare 4
9: 8 in the outpouring of thy wrath upon Jerusalem? 4
13:13 I will make a stormy wind break out in my wrath; 4
13 and great hailstones in wrath to destroy it. 4
15 Thus will I spend my wrath upon the wall 4
14:19 and pour out my wrath upon it with blood 4
16:38 bring upon you the blood of wrath and jealousy. 4
20: 8 Then I thought I would pour out my wrath upon them 4
13 Then I thought I would pour out my wrath upon them 4
21 Then I thought I would pour out my wrath upon them 4
33 and with wrath poured out, I will be king over you. 4
34 an outstretched arm, and with wrath poured out; 4
21:31 I will blow upon you with the fire of my wrath; 7
22:20 so I will gather you in my anger and in my wrath 4
21 and blow upon you with the fire of my wrath 7
22 I the LORD have poured out my wrath upon you. 4
31 I have consumed them with the fire of my wrath; 7
24: 8 To rouse my wrath, to take vengeance 4
25:14 according to my anger and according to my wrath; 4
30:15 I will pour my wrath upon Pelusium 4
36: 6 Behold, I speak in my jealous wrath 4
18 I poured out my wrath upon them for the blood 4
38:18 says the Lord GOD, my wrath will be roused. 4
19 in my jealousy and in my blazing wrath I declare 7
Dan 8: 6 ran at him in his mighty wrath. 4
9:16 anger and thy wrath turn away from thy city 4
Hos 5:10 upon them I will pour out my wrath like water. 7
13:11 and I have taken them away in my wrath. 7
Ams 1:11 tore perpetually, and he kept his wrath for ever. 7
Mic 5:15 And in anger and wrath I will execute vengeance 4
Nah 1: 2 the LORD . . keeps wrath for his enemies. •
6 His wrath is poured out like fire 4
Hab 2:15 makes his neighbors drink of the cup of his wrath 4
3: 2 in wrath remember mercy. 9
8 Was thy wrath against the rivers, O LORD? 5
Zep 1:15 A day of wrath is that day, a day of distress 7
18 deliver them on the day of the wrath of the LORD. 7
2: 2 comes upon you the day of the wrath of the LORD. 1
3 may be hidden on the day of the wrath of the LORD. 1
Zec 7:12 great wrath came from the LORD of hosts. 8
8: 2 I am jealous for her with great wrath. 4
Mat 3: 7 Who warned you to flee from the wrath to come? 13
Lke 3: 7 Who warned you to flee from the wrath to come? 13
4:28 all in the synagogue were filled with wrath. 11
21:23 and wrath upon this people; 13
Joh 3:36 but the wrath of God rests upon him. 13
Rom 1:18 For the wrath of God is revealed from heaven 13
2: 5 storing up wrath for yourself on the day of wrath 13
5 storing up wrath for yourself on the day of wrath 13
8 for those . . there will be wrath and fury. 13
3: 5 That God is unjust to inflict wrath on us? 13
4:15 For the law brings wrath 13
5: 9 shall we be saved by him from the wrath of God. 13
9:22 What if God, desiring to show his wrath 13
22 endured with much patience the vessels of wrath 13
12:19 but leave it to the wrath of God; 13
13: 4 to execute his wrath on the wrongdoer. 13
5 one must be subject, not only to avoid God's wrath 13
Eph 2: 3 we were by nature children of wrath 13
4:31 wrath and anger and clamor and slander 11
5: 6 the wrath of God comes 13
Col 3: 6 On account of these the wrath of God is coming. 13
8 wrath, malice, slander, and foul talk 11
1Th 1:10 Jesus who delivers us from the wrath to come. 13
2:16 God's wrath has come upon them at last! 13
5: 9 For God has not destined us for wrath 13
Heb 3:11 As I swore in my wrath 13
4: 3 as he has said, "As I swore in my wrath . . 13
Rev 6:16 hide us . . from the wrath of the Lamb; 13
17 for the great day of their wrath has come 13
11:18 The nations raged, but thy wrath came 13
12:12 for the devil has come down to you in great wrath 11
14:10 he also shall drink the wine of God's wrath 11
19 into the great wine press of the wrath of God; 11
15: 1 for with them the wrath of God is ended. 11
7 seven golden bowls full of the wrath of God 11
16: 1 pour out . . the seven bowls of the wrath of God. 11
19 to make her drain the cup of the fury of his wrath. 13
19:15 of the fury of the wrath of God the Almighty. 13
1Es 8:21 wrath may not come upon the kingdom of the king 13
9:13 until we are freed from the wrath of the Lord 13
2Es 15:23 a fire will go forth from his wrath 15
30 the Carmonians, raging in wrath, shall go forth 15
34 very threatening, full of wrath and storm. 15
37 who see that wrath shall be horror-stricken 15
39 the cloud that was raised in wrath 15
40 full of wrath and tempest 15
44 they shall pour out the tempest and all its wrath 15
16: 9 Fire will go forth from his wrath 16
Jdt 9: 9 send thy wrath upon their heads 13
AEs 16:24 shall be destroyed in wrath with spear and fire. 13
Wis 5:20 sharpen stern wrath for a sword 13
22 hailstones full of wrath will be hurled 11
10:10 fled from his brother's wrath 13
11: 9 when judged in wrath. 13
16: 5 thy wrath did not continue to the end; 13
18:20 the wrath did not long continue. 13
22 He conquered the wrath not by strength of body 14
23 he intervened and held back the wrath 13
25 merely to test the wrath was enough. 13
Sir 5: 6 both mercy and wrath are with him 13
7 suddenly the wrath of the Lord will go forth 13
7:16 remember that wrath does not delay. 13
16: 6 in a disobedient nation wrath was kindled. 13
11 mercy and wrath are with the Lord 13
11 he is mighty to forgive, and he pours out wrath. 13
18:24 Think of his wrath on the day of death 11
23:16 a third incurs wrath 13
25:15 no wrath worse than an enemy's wrath. 11
15 no wrath worse than an enemy's wrath. 11
22 There is wrath and impudence and great disgrace 13
27:30 Anger and wrath, these also are abominations 13
28: 5 If he himself, being flesh, maintains wrath 12
10 he will heighten his wrath. 13
36: 7 Rouse thy anger and pour out thy wrath 13
9 be consumed in the fiery wrath 13
39:23 The nations will incur his wrath 13
44:17 in the time of wrath he was taken in exchange; 13
45:18 in wrath and anger. 13
19 in the wrath of his anger they were destroyed 11
47:20 you brought wrath upon your children 13
48:10 calm the wrath of God before it breaks out in fury 13
Bar 1:13 the anger of the Lord and his wrath have not 13
2:20 For thou hast sent thy anger and thy wrath upon us 13
4: 9 For she saw the wrath that came upon you from God 13
25 the wrath that has come upon you from God 13
Man 1: 5 wrath of thy threat to sinners is irresistible; 13
10 I have provoked thy wrath 11
1Mc 1:64 very great wrath came upon Israel. 13
2:44 struck down . . lawless men in their wrath 11
3: 8 thus he turned away wrath from Israel. 13
15:36 returned in wrath to the king and reported to him 11
2Mc 5:20 what was forsaken in the wrath of the Almighty 13
7:38 to bring to an end the wrath of the Almighty 13
8: 5 the wrath of the Lord had turned to mercy. 13
3Mc 2:17 lest the transgressors boast in their wrath 11
5: 1 king . . was filled with overpowering anger and wrath 13
30 he was filled with an overpowering wrath 14
4Mc 4:11 and propitiate the wrath of the heavenly army. •
9:32 the judgments of the divine wrath. 13

wrath *See also* full, provoke, vent.

burning wrath 1. ardor
2Es 16:68 behold, the burning wrath of a great multitude 1

wrath come 1. קצף
Lev 10: 6 lest wrath come upon all the congregation 1

dread wrath 1. אֵימָה
Prv 20: 2 dread wrath of a king is like the growling of a lion; 1

fierce wrath 1. חֲרוֹן אַף
2Ch 28:11 for the fierce wrath of the LORD is upon you. 1
13 there is fierce wrath against Israel. 1

jealous wrath 1. קִנְאָה
Ps 79: 5 Will thy jealous wrath burn like fire? 1
Zep 1:18 In the fire of his jealous wrath 1
3: 8 for in the fire of my jealous wrath 1

wrathful 1. בַּעַל חֵמָה 2. חֵמָה
Prv 22:24 nor go with a wrathful man 2
Ezk 25:17 upon them with wrathful chastisements. 2
Nah 1: 2 the LORD is avenging and wrathful; 1

wrathful man 1. *θυμώδης*
Sir 8:16 Do not fight with a wrathful man 1

wreak 1. עשה
Ps 149: 7 to wreak vengeance on the nations 1

wreath 1. גְּדִלִים 2. לֹיָה 3. *στέφανος*
1Kg 7:17 nets of checker work with wreaths of chain work 1
29 Upon the frames . . were wreaths of beveled work. 2
30 The supports were cast, with wreaths at the side 2
36 he carved . . with wreaths round about. 2

1Co 9:25 They do it to receive a perishable wreath 3
Sir 32: 2 receive a wreath for your excellent leadership. 3

wreath of ivy 1. *κισσός*
2Mc 6: 7 wearing wreaths of ivy. 1

olive wreath 1. *ἐλαία*
Jdt 15:13 they crowned themselves with olive wreaths 1

ivy wreathed 1. *θύρσος*
2Mc 10: 7 bearing ivy-wreathed wands 1

wreck 1. שבר 2. adlido
1Kg 22:48 the ships were wrecked at E'zion-ge'ber. 1
2Ch 20:37 the ships were wrecked and were not able to go 1
Ezk 27:26 wind has wrecked you in the heart of the seas. 1
34 Now you are wrecked by the seas, in the depths 1
2Es 15:60 as they pass they shall wreck the hateful city 2

wrench apart 1. *διασπάω*
Mrk 5: 4 but the chains he wrenched apart 1

wrestle 1. אבק 2. פתל
Gen 30: 8 With mighty wrestlings I have wrestled with my 2
8 With mighty wrestlings I have wrestled with my 2
32:24 Jacob was left alone; and a man wrestled with him 1
25 put out of joint as he wrestled with him. 1

wrestling *See* arena.

wretch 1. *κακός* 2. *τάλας*
Mat 21:41 put those wretches to a miserable death 1
2Es 15:47 woe to you, miserable wretch! *
2Mc 7:34 you, unholy wretch, you most defiled of all men *
15: 3 the thrice-accursed wretch asked *
4Mc 8:17 O wretches that we are and so senseless! 2

accursed wretch 1. *ἀλάστωρ*
2Mc 7: 9 he said, "You accursed wretch 1

poor wretch 1. *ἄθλιος*
3Mc 5:37 How many times, you poor wretch 1

wretched 1. *δείλαιος* 2. *μέλεος* 3. *ταλαιπωρέω* 4. *ταλαίπωρος*
Rom 7:24 Wretched man that I am! Who will deliver me 4
Jas 4: 9 Be wretched and mourn and weep. 3
Rev 3:17 not knowing that you are wretched, pitiable, poor 4
Bar 4:31 Wretched will be those who afflicted you 1
32 Wretched will be the cities 1
32 wretched will be the city 1
3Mc 5: 5 and bound the hands of the wretched people 3
4Mc 16: 6 O how wretched am I and many times unhappy! 2
7 fruitless nurturings and wretched nursings! 4

wretched woman 1. paupera
2Es 15:51 You shall be weakened like a wretched woman 1

wretchedness 1. רָעָה
Num11:15 kill me . . that I may not see my wretchedness. 1

wring 1. הפך 2. מלק 3. מצה
Lev 5: 8 he shall wring its head from its neck 2
Jdg 6:38 he wrung enough dew from the fleece to fill a bowl 3
Lam 1:20 my soul is in tumult, my heart is wrung within me 1

wring off 1. מלק
Lev 1:15 shall bring it to the altar and wring off its head 1

wrinkle 1. *ῥυτίς*
Eph 5:27 without spot or wrinkle or any such thing 1

wrist 1. אַצִּיל
Ezk 13:18 women who sew magic bands upon all wrists 1

write 1. דָּבָר 2. כתב 3. כְּתָב 4. מִכְתָּב 5. סֵפֶר 6. כתב (A) 7. *ἀναγράφω* 8. *γραπτός* 9. *γραφή* 10. *γραφικός* 11. *γράφω* 12. *ἐγγράφω* 13. *ἐπιγράφω* 14. *ἐπιστέλλω* 15. *καταγράφω* 16. *προγράφω* 17. *συγγράφω* 18. *φημί* 19. *χαράσσω* 20. scribo
Exd 17:14 the LORD said to Moses, "Write this as a memorial 2
24: 4 Moses wrote all the words of the LORD. 2
12 which I have written for their instruction. 2
31:18 tables of stone, written with the finger of God. 2
32:15 tables that were written on both sides; 2
15 on the one side and on the other were they written. 2
32 out of thy book which thou hast written. 2
34: 1 I will write upon the tables the words 2
27 the LORD said to Moses, "Write these words; 2
28 he wrote upon the tables the words 2
39:30 made the plate . . and wrote upon it an inscription 2
Num 5:23 the priest shall write these curses in a book 2
17: 2 Write each man's name upon his rod 2
3 write Aaron's name upon the rod of Levi. 2
Deu 4:13 wrote them upon two tables of stone. 2
5:22 wrote them upon two tables of stone, and gave them 2
6: 9 shall write them on the doorposts of your house 2
9:10 tables of stone written with the finger of God; 2
10: 2 I will write on the tables the words 2
4 he wrote on the tables . . the ten commandments 2
4 wrote on the tables, as at the first writing 4
11:20 you shall write them upon the doorposts 2
17:18 write for himself in a book a copy of this law 2
24: 1 writes her a bill of divorce and puts it 2
3 latter husband . . writes her a bill of divorce 2
27: 3 shall write upon them all the words of this law 2
8 write upon the stones all the words of this law 2
28:58 do all the words . . which are written in this book 2
29:20 curses written in this book would settle upon 2
21 curses of the covenant written in this . . law. 2
27 bringing . . all the curses written in this book; 2
30:10 keep . . which are written in this book of the law 2
31: 9 Moses wrote this law, and gave it to the priests 2
19 Now therefore write this song, and teach it 2
22 Moses wrote this song the same day, and taught it 2
24 finished writing the words of this law in a book 2
Jos 1: 8 to do according to all that is written in it; 2
8:31 as it is written in the book of the law of Moses 2
32 he wrote upon the stones a copy of the law of Moses 2
32 a copy of the law of Moses, which he had written. 2
34 to all that is written in the book of the law. 2
10:13 Is this not written in the Book of Jashar? 2
18: 4 go up and down the land, writing a description 2
8 who went to write the description of the land 2
8 Go up and down and write a description of the land 2
23: 6 all that is written in the book of the law of Moses 2
24:26 Joshua wrote these words in the book of the law 2
1Sm 10:25 he wrote them in a book and laid it up 2
2Sm 1:18 it is written in the Book of Jashar. He said 2
11:14 In the morning David wrote a letter to Jo'ab 2
15 In the letter he wrote, "Set Uri'ah in the forefront 2
1Kg 2: 3 the charge . . as it is written in the law of Moses 2
11:41 are they not written in the book of the acts 2
14:19 the acts of Jerobo'am . . are written in the Book 2
29 the acts of . . are they not written in the Book 2
15: 7 acts of Abi'jam . . are they not written in the Book 2
23 acts of Asa . . are they not written in the Book 2
31 acts of Nadab . . are they not written in the Book 2
16: 5 acts of Ba'asha . . are they not written in the Book 2
14 acts of Elah . . are they not written in the Book 2
20 acts of Zimri . . are they not written in the Book 2
27 acts of Omri . . are they not written in the Book 2
21: 8 she wrote letters in Ahab's name and sealed them 2
9 she wrote in the letters, "Proclaim a fast 2
11 As it was written in the letters 2
22:39 acts of Ahab . . are they not written in the Book 2
45 written in the Book of the Chronicles 2
2Kg 1:18 the acts of . . are they not written in the Book 2
8:23 acts of Joram . . are they not written in the Book 2
10: 1 Jehu wrote letters, and sent them to Sama'ria 2
6 he wrote to them a second letter, saying, "If you are 2
34 acts of Jehu . . are they not written in the Book 2
12:19 acts of Jo'ash . . are they not written in the Book 2
13: 8 acts of Jeho'ahaz . . are they not written 2
12 acts of Jo'ash . . are they not written in the Book 2
14: 6 what is written in the book of the law of Moses 2
15 the acts of . . are they not written in the Book 2
18 deeds of Amazi'ah, are they not written in the Book 2
28 the acts of . . are they not written in the Book 2
15: 6 the acts of . . are they not written in the Book 2
11 the deeds of Zechari'ah . . are written in the Book 2
15 the deeds of Shallum . . are written in the Book 2
21 the deeds of . . are they not written in the Book 2
26 the deeds of . . they are written in the Book 2
31 acts of Pekah . . they are written in the Book 2
36 acts of Jotham . . are they not written in the Book 2
16:19 acts of Ahaz . . are they not written in the Book 2
17:37 law and the commandment which he wrote for you 2
20:20 the deeds of . . are they not written in the Book 2
21:17 the acts of . . are they not written in the Book 2
25 acts of Amon . . are they not written in the Book 2
22:13 according to all that is written concerning us. 2
23: 3 words of this covenant . . written in this book; 2
21 Keep the passover . . as it is written in this book 2
24 words of the law which were written in the book 2
28 acts of Josi'ah . . are they not written in the Book 2
24: 5 the deeds of . . are they not written in the Book 2
1Ch 9: 1 written in the Book of the Kings of Israel. 2
16:40 all that is written in the law of the LORD 2
29:29 are written in the Chronicles of Samuel the seer 2
2Ch 9:29 are they not written in the history of Nathan 2
12:15 written in the chronicles of Shemai'ah 2
13:22 written in the story of the prophet Iddo. 2
16:11 written in the Book of the Kings 2
20:34 written in the chronicles of Jehu 2
23:18 as it is written in the law of Moses 2
24:27 Accounts . . written in the Commentary 2
25: 4 according to what is written in the law 2
26 are they not written in the Book of the Kings 2
26:22 Isaiah the prophet the son of Amoz wrote. 2
27: 7 behold, they are written in the Book of the Kings 2
28:26 behold, they are written in the Book of the Kings 2
30: 1 Hezeki'ah . . wrote letters also to E'phraim 2
31: 3 as it is written in the law of the LORD. 2
32:17 he wrote letters to cast contempt on the LORD 2
32 written in the vision of Isaiah the prophet 2
33:19 written in the Chronicles of the Seers. 2
34:21 do according to all that is written in this book. 2
24 all the curses that are written in the book 2
31 the covenant that were written in this book. 2
35:12 as it is written in the book of Moses. 2
25 behold, they are written in the Laments. 2
26 his good deeds according to what is written 2
27 behold, they are written in the Book of the Kings 2
36: 8 behold, they are written in the Book of the Kings 2
Ezr 3: 2 as it is written in the law of Moses the man of God. 2
4 kept the feast of booths, as it is written 2
4: 6 wrote an accusation against the inhabitants 2
7 rest of their associates wrote to Ar-ta-xerx'es 2
7 letter was written in Aramaic and translated. 2
8 wrote a letter against Jerusalem to Ar-ta-xerx'es 2
9 then wrote Rehum the commander, Shim'shai *
5: 7 sent him a report, in which was written as follows 6
6: 2 scroll . . on which this was written: "A record. 6
18 as it is written in the book of Moses. 6
Neh 6: 6 In it was written, "It is reported 2
7: 5 I found the book . . and I found written in it 2
8:14 found it written in the law that the LORD 2
15 branches . . to make booths, as it is written. 2
9:38 make a firm covenant and write it 2
10:34 burn upon the altar . . as it is written in the law. 2
36 first-born . . as it is written in the law 2
12:23 Levi . . written in the Book of the Chronicles 2
13: 1 found written that no Ammonite or Moabite 2
Est 1:19 let it be written among the laws of the Persians 2
3:12 an edict . . was written to the king's satraps 2
12 it was written in the name of King Ahasu-e'rus 2
4: 8 Mor'decai . . gave him a copy of the written decree 2
6: 2 it was found written how Mor'decai had told about 2
8: 5 let an order be written to revoke the letters 2
5 letters . . which he wrote to destroy the Jews 2
8 may write as you please with regard to the Jews 2
8 an edict written in the name of the king 2
9 an edict was written . . concerning the Jews 2
13 A copy of what was written was to be issued 3
9:23 to do as . . and as Mor'decai had written to them. 2
26 because of all that was written in this letter 1
27 keep these . . days according to what was written 2
10: 2 all the acts . . are they not written in the Book 2
Job 13:26 For thou writest bitter things against me 2
19:23 Oh that my words were written! 2
31:35 I had the indictment written by my adversary! 2
Ps 40: 7 Lo, I come; in the roll of the book it is written of me; 2
139:16 thy book were written, every one of them, the days 2
149: 9 to execute on them the judgment written! 2
Prv 3: 3 write them on the tablet of your heart. 2
7: 3 write them on the tablet of your heart. 2
22:20 Have I not written for you 30 sayings 2
Ecc 12:10 and uprightly he wrote words of truth. 2
Isa 8: 1 Take a large tablet and write upon it 2
10: 1 the writers who keep writing oppression 2
30: 8 now, go, write it before them on a tablet 2
44: 5 and another will write on his hand, 'The LORD'S,' 2
65: 6 it is written before me: "I will not keep silent 2
Jer 17: 1 The sin of Judah is written with a pen of iron; 2
13 turn away from thee shall be written in the earth 2
25:13 against it, everything written in this book 2
30: 2 Write in a book all the words that I have spoken 2
31:33 and I will write it upon their hearts; 2
36: 2 write on it all the words that I have spoken to you 2
4 Baruch wrote upon a scroll 2
6 from the scroll which you have written 2
17 Tell us, how did you write all these words? 2
18 while I wrote them with ink on the scroll. 2
27 the scroll with the words which Baruch wrote 2
28 scroll and write on it all the former words 2
29 burned this scroll, saying "Why have you written 2
32 who wrote on it at the dictation of Jeremiah 2
45: 1 when he wrote these words in a book 2
51:60 Jeremiah wrote in a book all the evil 2
60 upon Babylon, all these words that are written 2
Ezk 2: 9 a hand . . and, lo, a written scroll was in it; 5
10 there were written on it words of lamentation 2
37:16 Son of man, take a stick and write on it, 'For Judah 2
16 take another stick and write upon it, 'For Joseph 2
20 When the sticks on which you write 2
Dan 5: 5 appeared and wrote on the plaster of the wall 6
5 king saw the hand as it wrote. 6
6:25 Then King Darius wrote to all the peoples 6
9:11 which are written in the law of Moses the servant 2
13 As it is written in the law of Moses 2
12: 1 every one whose name . . found written in the book. 2
Hos 8:12 Were I to write for him my laws by ten thousands 2
Hab 2: 2 Write the vision; make it plain upon tablets 2
Mal 3:16 a book of remembrance was written before him 2
Mat 2: 5 Judea; for so it is written by the prophet 11
4: 4 But he answered, "It is written, 'Man shall not live 11
6 for it is written, 'He will give his angels charge 11
7 Jesus said to him, "Again it is written, 'You shall 11
10 Jesus said to him, "Begone, Satan! for it is written 11
11:10 This is he of whom it is written 11
21:13 He said to them, "It is written 11
26:24 The Son of man goes as it is written of him 11
31 it is written, 'I will strike the shepherd 11
Mrk 1: 2 As it is written in Isaiah the prophet 11
7: 6 as it is written, 'This people honors me 11
9:12 how is it written of the Son of man 11

13 as it is written of him. 11
10: 4 allowed a man to write a certificate of divorce 11
5 he wrote you this commandment. 11
11:17 he taught, and said to them, "Is it not written 11
12:19 Teacher, Moses wrote for us 11
14:21 For the Son of man goes as it is written of him 11
27 it is written, 'I will strike the shepherd 11
Lke 1: 3 to write an orderly account for you 11
63 for a writing tablet, and wrote, "His name is John. 11
2:23 as it is written in the law of the Lord 11
3: 4 As it is written in the book of the words of Isaiah 11
4: 4 It is written, 'Man shall not live by bread alone.' 11
8 It is written, 'You shall worship the Lord your God 11
10 it is written, 'He will give his angels charge 11
17 found the place where it was written 11
7:27 This is he of whom it is written 11
10:20 rejoice that your names are written in heaven. 11
26 What is written in the law? How do you read? 11
16: 6 and sit down quickly and write 50' 11
7 He said to him, 'Take your bill, and write 80.' 11
18:31 everything that is written of the Son of man 11
19:46 saying to them, "It is written 11
20:17 What then is this that is written 11
28 Moses wrote for us that if a man's brother dies 11
21:22 to fulfil all that is written. 11
22:37 what is written about me has its fulfilment. •
24:44 everything written about me in the law of Moses 11
46 said to them, "Thus it is written 11
Joh 1:45 Moses in the law and also the prophets wrote 11
2:17 His disciples remembered that it was written 11
5:46 you would believe me, for he wrote of me. 11
6:31 as it is written, 'He gave them bread from heaven 11
45 It is written in the prophets 11
8: 6 Jesus . . wrote with his finger on the ground. 15
8 and wrote with his finger on the ground. 11
17 In your law it is written 11
10:34 Jesus answered them, "Is it not written in your law 11
12:14 as it is written 11
16 had been written of him and had been done to him. 11
15:25 to fulfil the word that is written in their law 11
19:19 Pilate also wrote a title and put it on the cross; 11
20 it was written in Hebrew, in Latin, and in Greek. 11
21 Do not write, 'The King of the Jews,' 11
22 What I have written I have written. 11
22 What I have written I have written. 11
20:30 which are not written in this book; 11
31 these are written that you may believe 11
21:24 who has written these things 11
25 were every one of them to be written 11
25 the books that would be written. 11
Act 1:20 it is written in the book of Psalms 11
7:42 as it is written in the book of the prophets 11
13:29 when they had fulfilled all that was written 11
33 as also it is written in the second psalm 11
15:15 the words of the prophets agree, as it is written 11
20 write to them to abstain from . . idols 14
18:27 wrote to the disciples to receive him 11
23: 5 it is written, 'You shall not speak evil of a ruler 11
25 he wrote a letter to this effect 11
24:14 written in the prophets 11
25:26 nothing definite to write to my lord about him 11
26 I may have something to write. 11
Rom 1:17 as it is written 11
2:15 what the law requires is written on their hearts 8
24 For, as it is written, "The name of God is blasphemed 11
3: 4 Let God be true . . as it is written 11
10 as it is written: "None is righteous, no, not one; 11
4:17 as it is written, "I have made you the father 11
23 the words . . were written not for his sake alone 11
8:36 As it is written, "For thy sake we are being killed 11
9:13 As it is written, "Jacob I loved, but Esau I hated. 11
33 as it is written, "Behold, I am laying in Zion 11
10: 5 Moses writes that the man who practices 11
15 As it is written, "How beautiful are the feet 11
11: 8 as it is written, "God gave them a spirit of stupor 11
26 so all Israel will be saved; as it is written 11
12:19 for it is written, "Vengeance is mine, I will repay 11
14:11 for it is written, "As I live, says the Lord 11
15: 3 but, as it is written, "The reproaches of those 11
4 was written for our instruction 11
9 As it is written, "Therefore I will praise thee 11
15 written to you very boldly by way of reminder 11
21 as it is written, "They shall see who have never 11
1Co 1:19 it is written, "I will destroy the wisdom 11
31 therefore, as it is written, "Let him who boasts 11
2: 9 But, as it is written, "What no eye has seen 11
3:19 it is written, "He catches the wise 11
4: 6 learn by us not to go beyond what is written 11
14 I do not write this to make you ashamed 11
5: 9 I wrote to you in my letter 11
11 rather I wrote to you 11
6:16 as it is written, "The two shall become one flesh. 18
7: 1 concerning the matters about which you wrote. 11
9: 9 For it is written in the law of Moses 11
10 It was written for our sake 11
15 nor am I writing this 11
10: 7 as it is written, "The people sat down to eat 11
14:21 In the law it is written, "By men of strange tongues 11
37 acknowledge that what I am writing to you 11
15:45 Thus it is written, "The first man Adam 11
54 then shall come to pass the saying that is written 11
16:21 I, Paul, write this greeting with my own hand. •
2Co 1:13 For we write you nothing but what you can read 11
2: 3 I wrote as I did, so that when I came 11
4 For I wrote you out of much affliction 11
9 For this is why I wrote, that I might test you 11
3: 2 written on your hearts, to be known and read by all 12
3 written not with ink but with the Spirit 12
4:13 as he had who wrote, "I believed, and so I spoke 11
7:12 So although I wrote to you 11
8:15 As it is written, "He who gathered much had nothing 11
9: 1 Now it is superfluous for me to write to you 11
9 As it is written, "He scatters abroad 11
13:10 I write this while I am away from you 11
Gal 1:20 In what I am writing to you, before God, I do not lie!) 11
3:10 it is written, "Cursed be every one 11
10 abide by all things written in the book of the law 11
13 having become a curse for us-for it is written 11
4:22 For it is written that Abraham had two sons 11
27 For it is written, "Rejoice, O barren one 11
6:11 See with what large letters I am writing to you 11
Eph 3: 3 as I have written briefly. 16
Php 3: 1 To write the same things to you is not irksome 11
Col 4:18 I, Paul, write this greeting with my own hand. •
1Th 4: 9 you have no need to have any one write to you 11
5: 1 you have no need to have anything written to you. 11
2Th 3:17 I, Paul, write this greeting with my own hand •
17 it is the way I write. 11
1Ti 3:14 I am writing these instructions to you 11
Phm 1:19 I, Paul, write this with my own hand, I will repay 11
21 Confident of your obedience, I write to you 11
Heb 8:10 write them on their hearts 13
10: 7 as it is written of me in the roll of the book. 11
16 and write them on their minds 13
13:22 I have written to you briefly. 14
1Pe 1:16 since it is written, "You shall be holy, for I am 11
5:12 By Silva'nus . . I have written briefly to you 11
2Pe 3: 1 This is now the second letter that I have written 11
15 So also our beloved brother Paul wrote to you 11
1Jn 1: 4 we are writing this that our joy may be complete. 11
2: 1 I am writing this to you so that you may not sin 11
7 Beloved, I am writing you no new commandment 11
8 Yet I am writing you a new commandment 11
12 I am writing to you, little children 11
13 I am writing to you, fathers, because you know him 11
13 I am writing to you, young men 11
13 I write to you, children 11
14 I write to you, fathers, because you know him 11
14 I write to you, young men, because you are strong 11
21 I write to you, not because you do not know 11
26 I write this to you about those who would deceive 11
5:13 I write this to you who believe in the name 11
2Jn 1: 5 as though I were writing you a new commandment 11
12 Though I have much to write to you 11
3Jn 1: 9 I have written something to the church; 11
13 I had much to write to you 11
13 but I would rather not write with pen and ink; 11
Jde 1: 3 eager to write to you of our common salvation 11
3 I found it necessary to write appealing to you 11
Rev 1: 3 who hear, and who keep what is written therein; 11
11 saying, "Write what you see in a book and send it 11
19 Now write what you see 11
2: 1 To the angel of the church in Ephesus write 11
8 And to the angel of the church in Smyrna write 11
12 And to the angel of the church in Per'gamum write 11
17 with a new name written on the stone 11
18 And to the angel of the church in Thyati'ra write 11
3: 1 And to the angel of the church in Sardis write 11
7 to the angel of the church in Philadelphia write 11
12 and I will write on him the name of my God 11
14 And to the angel of the church in La-odice'a write 11
5: 1 I saw . . a scroll written within and on the back 11
10: 4 I was about to write, but I heard a voice 11
4 and do not write it down. 11
13: 8 name has not been written . . in the book of life 11
14: 1 his Father's name written on their foreheads. 11
13 And I heard a voice from heaven saying, "Write this 11
17: 5 on her forehead was written a name of mystery 11
8 names have not been written in the book of life 11
19: 9 And the angel said to me, "Write this 11
20:12 dead were judged by what was written in the books 11
15 name was not found written in the book of life 11
21: 5 Write this, for these words are trustworthy 11
27 only those . . written in the Lamb's book of life 11
1Es 1:11 as it is written in the book of Moses 11
33 written in the book of the histories of the kings 7
42 written in the chronicles of the kings. 7
2:16 wrote him the following letter 15
22 will find . . what has been written about them 11
3: 8 each wrote his own statement 11
9 shall be given according to what is written. 11
10 The first wrote, "Wine is strongest. 11
11 The second wrote, "The king is strongest. 11
12 The third wrote, "Women are strongest 11
17 Explain to us what you have written 11
4:42 Ask what you wish, even beyond what is written 11
47 wrote letters for him to all the treasurers 11
48 he wrote letters to all the governors 11
49 he wrote for all the Jews who were going up 11
54 He wrote also concerning their support 11
55 He wrote that . . 11
56 He wrote that land and wages should be provided 11
6: 7 wrote and sent to Darius 11
17 Cyrus wrote that this house should be rebuilt. 11
7: 6 according to what was written in the book •
8: 8 written commission from Artaxerxes the king 11
2Es 4:23 and the written covenants no longer exist; 20
12:37 write all these things that you have seen 20
14:22 I will write everything that has happened 20
22 the things which were written in thy law 20
24 because they are trained to write rapidly; 20
25 until what you are about to write is finished. 20
26 tomorrow at this hour you shall begin to write. 20
42 and by turns they wrote what was dictated 20
42 They sat 40 days, and wrote during the daytime 20
44 during the 40 days 94 books were written. 20
45 Make public the 24 books that you wrote first 20
46 but keep the 70 that were written last •
15: 2 cause them to be written on paper 20
Tob 12:20 Write in a book everything that has happened. 11
13: 1 Then Tobit wrote a prayer of rejoicing, and said 11
Jdt 4: 6 wrote to the people of Bethulia 11
AEs 12: 4 Mordecai wrote an account of them. 11
13: 1 The Great King, Artaxerxes . . writes thus 11
Sir 0: 1 write something pertaining to instruction 17
48:10 ready at the appointed time, it is written 15
50:27 I have written in this book 19
Bar 1: 1 the words . . which Baruch . . wrote in Babylon 11
2: 2 what is written in the law of Moses 11
28 thou didst command him to write thy law 11
1Mc 1:41 Then the king wrote to his whole kingdom 11
51 In such words he wrote to his whole kingdom 11
7:16 in accordance with the word which was written 11
8:31 we have written to him as follows 11
10:17 he wrote a letter and sent it to him 11
24 I also will write them words of encouragement 11
56 now I will do for you as you wrote 11
59 Then Alexander the king wrote to Jonathan 11
11:22 he wrote Jonathan not to continue the siege 11
29 The king consented, and wrote a letter to Jonathan 11
31 the letter which we wrote concerning you 11
31 we have written to you also 11
57 the young Antiochus wrote to Jonathan, saying 11
12: 5 the letter which Jonathan wrote to the Spartans 11
22 please write us concerning your welfare; 11
13:35 and wrote him a letter as follows 11
37 to write to our officials to grant you release 11
42 the people began to write in their documents 11
14:18 they wrote to him on bronze tablets 11
27 This is a copy of what they wrote 9
43 contracts . . should be written in his name 11
15:15 letters . . in which the following was written 11
19 We therefore have decided to write to the kings 11
22 The consul wrote the same thing to Demetrius 11
16:18 Then Ptolemy wrote a report about these things 11
24 behold, they are written in the chronicles 11
2Mc 1: 7 we Jews wrote to you . . in those years 11
2:16 we write to you 11
8: 8 he wrote to Ptolemy, the governor of Coelesyria 11
9:18 wrote to the Jews the following letter 11
25 I have written to him what is written here. 11
11:16 The letter written to the Jews by Lysias 11
14:27 The king . . wrote to Nicanor 11
3Mc 3:11 wrote this letter against them 11
30 The letter was written in the above form. 11
4:20 both the paper and the pens they used for writing 10
6:41 wrote the following letter for them 11

write down 1. כתב 2. כתב (A) 3. γράφω

Num33: 2 Moses wrote down their starting places 1
Jdg 8:14 and he wrote down for him the officials 1
Ezr 5:10 write down the names of the men at their head. 2
Isa 10:19 trees . . so few that a child can write them down. 1
Jer 22:30 says the LORD: "Write this man down as childless 1
Ezk 24: 2 write down the name of this day, this very day. 1
43:11 write it down in their sight 1
Dan 7: 1 Then he wrote down the dream, 2
1Co 10:11 they were written down for our instruction 3

write here 1. ὑπογράφω

2Mc 9:25 I have written to him what is written here. 1

write in former days 1. προγράφω

Rom 15: 4 For whatever was written in former days 1

write in reply 1. ἀντιγράφω

1Es 2:25 the king, in reply to Rehum . . wrote as follows 1
1Mc 8:22 a copy of the letter which they wrote in reply 1

write on one's part 1. ἀντιγράφω

1Mc 12:23 we on our part write to you 1

write out 1. γράφω

Tob 7:14 and took a scroll and wrote out the contract 1

writer 1. כתב 2. γράφω

Isa 10: 1 the writers who keep writing oppression 1
Rom 16:22 I Tertius, the writer of this letter, greet you 2

writhe 1. חול 2. σκολιός

Isa 26:17 who writhes and cries out in her pangs 1
18 we were with child, we writhed 1
Mic 4:10 Writhe and groan, O daughter of Zion 1
Hab 3:10 The mountains saw thee, and writhed; 1
Zec 9: 5 be afraid; Gaza too, and shall writhe in anguish; 1
Wis 16: 5 destroyed by the bites of writhing serpents 2

writhe in pain 1. חול

Job 15:20 The wicked man writhes in pain all his days 1
Jer 4:19 My anguish, my anguish! I writhe in pain! 1
51:29 The land trembles and writhes in pain 1

writing 1. כתב 2. מִכְתָּב 3. סֵפֶר 4. כתב (A) 5. כְּתָב (A) 6. γράμμα 7. γραπτός 8. γραφή 9. γράφω

Exd 32:16 and the writing was the writing of God 2
16 and the writing was the writing of God 2
1Ch 28:19 clear by the writing from the hand of the LORD 1
2Ch 36:22 proclamation . . and also put it in writing 2
Est 8:10 The writing was in the name of King Ahasu-e'rus 1
9:25 he gave orders in writing that his wicked plot 3
32 Esther fixed . . and it was recorded in writing. 3
Isa 38: 9 A writing of Hezeki'ah king of Judah 2
Ezk 2:10 and it had writing on the front and on the back 1
Dan 5: 7 Whoever reads this writing, and shows me its 5
8 could not read the writing or make known 4
15 brought in before me to read this writing 4
16 Now if you can read the writing and make known 4
17 nevertheless I will read the writing to the king 4
24 hand was sent, and this writing was inscribed. 4
25 writing that was inscribed: MENE, MENE, TEKEL 4
Joh 5:47 if you do not believe his writings 6
Rom 16:26 through the prophetic writings is made known 8
2Ti 3:15 have been acquainted with the sacred writings 6
1Es 2: 2 also put it in writing 7
3: 9 they will give him the writing 6
13 they took the writing and gave it to him 6
15 the writing was read in their presence. 6
5:55 the decree which they had in writing from Cyrus 9
6:12 in order that we might inform you in writing 9
Sir 0: 1 help the outsiders by both speaking and writing, 9
39:32 have thought this out and left it in writing 8
44: 5 set forth verses in writing; 8
1Mc 12:21 found in writing concerning the Spartans 8
2Mc 2: 4 was also in the writing 8
13 the writings of David, and letters of kings •
11:15 which Maccabeus delivered to Lysias in writing. 7

writing *See also* case, put, tablet.

written *See* code, give.

thing herein written 1. πρερῶ προσγράφω

1Es 6:32 nullify any of the things herein written 1

wrong 1. אָוֶן 2. אשׁם 3. אַשְׁמָה 4. הכר 5. זִמָּה 6. חַטָּאת 7. חמס 8. חָמָס 9. ינה 10. עָוֶל 11. עַוְלָה 12. עַוְּתָה 13. עַל יָשָׁר 14. עָמָל 15. רַע 16. רֹעַ 17. רָעָה 18. רֶשַׁע 19. תִּפְלָה 20. חֲבוּלָא (A) 21. ἀδικέω 22. ἀδίκημα 23. ἀδικία 24. ἄδικος 25. ἀτοπία 26. ἄτοπος 27. ἐκδίκησις 28. κακία 29. κακός 30. κακῶς 31. πλανάω 32. πλεονεκτέω 33. πονηρός

Gen 16: 5 May the wrong done to me be on you! I gave my maid 8
Exd 2:13 he said to the man that did the wrong, "Why do you 18
9:27 I and my people are in the wrong. 18
22:21 You shall not wrong a stranger or oppress him 9
Lev 19:35 You shall do no wrong in judgment 10
25:14 you shall not wrong one another 9
17 You shall not wrong one another, but you shall 9
Num 5: 7 he shall make full restitution for his wrong 2
Deu 19:15 for any wrong in connection with any offense 6
Jdg 11:27 and you do me wrong by making war on me; 17
1Sm 24:11 see that there is no wrong or treason in my hands. 17
29: 6 I have found nothing wrong in you 17
2Sm 13:16 this wrong in sending me away is greater 17
1Ch 12:17 although there is no wrong in my hands 8
Job 1:22 Job did not sin or charge God with wrong. 19
6:29 Turn, I pray, let no wrong be done. 11
30 Is there any wrong on my tongue? 11
19: 3 are you not ashamed to wrong me? 4
21:27 know your thoughts, and your schemes to wrong me. 7
36:23 or who can say, 'Thou hast done wrong'? 11
Ps 7: 3 if I have done this, if there is wrong in my hands 10
58: 2 Nay, in your hearts you devise wrongs; 11
69: 5 the wrongs I have done are not hidden from thee. 3
119: 3 who also do no wrong, but walk in his ways! 11
Prv 10:23 It is like sport to a fool to do wrong 5
17:26 to flog noble men is wrong. 13
30:20 adulteress . . says, "I have done no wrong. 1
Isa 61: 8 I the LORD love justice, I hate robbery and wrong; 11
Jer 2: 5 What wrong did your fathers find in me 10
25: 5 turn . . from his evil way and wrong doings 16
40: 4 if it seems wrong to you to come with me to Babylon 15
Lam 3:59 Thou hast seen the wrong done to me, O LORD; 12
Ezk 18:16 does not wrong any one, exacts no pledge 9
22: 7 the fatherless and the widow are wronged in you. 9
Dan 6:22 also before you, O king, I have done no wrong. 20
Mic 3:10 build Zion with blood and Jerusalem with wrong. 11
Hab 1: 3 Why dost thou make me see wrongs 1
13 than to behold evil and canst not look on wrong 14
Zep 3: 5 The LORD within her is righteous, he does no wrong; 11
13 they shall do no wrong and utter no lies 11
Mal 2: 6 no wrong was found on his lips. 11
Mat 22:29 Jesus answered them, "You are wrong 31
Mrk 12:24 Jesus said to them, "Is not this why you are wrong 31
27 you are quite wrong. 31
Lke 23:41 this man has done nothing wrong. 26
Joh 18:23 bear witness to the wrong 29
Act 7:24 seeing one of them being wronged 21
26 you are brethren, why do you wrong each other?' 21
27 the man who was wronging his neighbor 21
23: 9 We find nothing wrong in this man. 29
25: 5 if there is anything wrong about the man 26
Rom 13: 4 But if you do wrong, be afraid 29
10 Love does no wrong to a neighbor; 29
14:20 but it is wrong for any one to make others fall 29
1Co 6: 8 you yourselves wrong and defraud 21
13: 6 it does not rejoice at wrong 23
2Co 7: 2 we have wronged no one, we have corrupted no one 21
12:13 Forgive me this wrong! 23
13: 7 we pray God that you may not do wrong 29
1Th 4: 6 that no man transgress, and wrong his brother 32
Phm 1:18 If he has wronged you at all, or owes you anything 21
Jdt 11:11 when they do what is wrong. 25
Sir 3:24 wrong opinion has caused their thoughts to slip. 33
4: 9 Deliver him who is wronged 21
7: 2 Stay away from wrong 24
28: 2 Forgive your neighbor the wrong he has done 22
35:13 will listen to the prayer of one who is wronged. 21
LJr 1:54 or deliver one who is wronged 21
1Mc 2:67 avenge the wrong done to your people. 27
8:31 the wrongs which King Demetrius is doing 29
10: 5 for he will remember all the wrongs which we did 29
46 because they remembered the great wrongs 28
2Mc 10:12 because of the wrong that had been done to them 23
3Mc 1:14 it was wrong to take this as a sign in itself. 30
3: 8 The Greeks in the city, though wronged in no way 21
4Mc 5: 9 wrong to spurn the gifts of nature. 24

wrong *See also* declare, go, put, restitution, suffer, time.

do wrong 1. אשׁם 2. חטא 3. ינה 4. מעל 5. עוה 6. עָוֶל 7. עַוְלָה 8. פשׁע 9. רשׁע 10. ἀδικέω 11. ἁμαρτάνω 12. κακοποιέω 13. πλημμελέω

Gen 44: 5 You have done wrong in so doing.' 9
Lev 19:33 a stranger . . you shall not do him wrong 3
Num 5: 7 giving it to him whom he did the wrong. 1
1Sm 26:21 Saul said, "I have done wrong; return, my son David 2
2Sm 19:19 your servant did wrong on the day . . the king left 5
2Kg 18:14 I have done wrong; withdraw from me; 2
2Ch 26:18 Go out of the sanctuary; for you have done wrong 4
Est 1:16 Not only to the king has Queen Vashti done wrong 5
Job 34:10 from the Almighty that he should do wrong. 6
Ps 125: 3 righteous put forth their hands to do wrong. 7
Prv 4:16 cannot sleep unless they have done wrong; 9
28:21 but for a piece of bread a man will do wrong. 8
Jer 22: 3 And do no wrong or violence to the alien 3
37:18 What wrong have I done to you or your servants 2
Dan 9: 5 sinned and done wrong and acted wickedly 5
Mat 20:13 Friend, I am doing you no wrong 10
Act 25:10 to the Jews I have done no wrong 10
2Co 7:12 not on account of the one who did the wrong 10
Gal 4:12 You did me no wrong; 10
Col 3:25 will be paid back for the wrong he has done 10
1Pe 2:14 sent by him to punish those who do wrong 12
20 if when you do wrong and are beaten for it 11
3:17 suffer for doing right . . than for doing wrong. 12
Sir 13: 3 A rich man does wrong, and he even adds reproaches; 10
19: 4 one who sins does wrong to himself. 13
Bar 2:12 we have been ungodly, we have done wrong, O Lord 10
2Mc 3:12 it was utterly impossible that wrong should be done 10
14:28 when the man had done no wrong. 10

wrongdoer 1. עשׂה עַוְלָה 2. ἀδικέω 3. κακοποιέω 4. κακοποιός 5. κακός

Ps 37: 1 be not envious of wrongdoers! 1
Act 25:11 If then I am a wrongdoer 2
Rom 13: 4 to execute his wrath on the wrongdoer. 5
Col 3:25 For the wrongdoer will be paid back 2
1Pe 2:12 in case they speak against you as wrongdoers 3
4:15 let none of you suffer as . . a wrongdoer 4
Sir 4: 9 Deliver . . from the hand of the wrongdoer 2

wrongdoing 1. סרה 2. עֲלִילָה 3. ἀδίκημα 4. ἀδικία 5. πλημμέλεια

Deu 19:16 malicious witness . . accuse him of wrongdoing 1
Ps 99: 8 but an avenger of their wrongdoings. 2
Act 18:14 a matter of wrongdoing or vicious crime 3
24:20 say what wrongdoing they found 3
2Pe 2:13 suffering wrong for their wrongdoing. 4
15 Balaam . . who loved gain from wrongdoing 4
1Jn 5:17 All wrongdoing is sin 4
Tob 4: 5 do not walk in the ways of wrongdoing. 4
12: 8 is better than much with wrongdoing 4
Sir 18:27 in days of sin he guards against wrongdoing. 5
26:29 A merchant can hardly keep from wrongdoing 5

previously wronged 1. προαδικέω

Wis 18: 2 thy holy ones, though previously wronged 1

wrongfully 1. שֶׁקֶר

Ps 35:19 those rejoice over me who are wrongfully my foes 1
38:19 many are those who hate me wrongfully. 1

wrongfully *See also* obtain.

wrongly 1. ἄλλως 2. κακῶς

Joh 18:23 Jesus answered him, "If I have spoken wrongly 2
Jas 4: 3 You . . do not receive, because you ask wrongly 2
4Mc 5:18 Even if . . we had wrongly held it to be divine 1

wroth 1. רגז

Isa 28:21 he will be wroth as in the valley of Gibeon; 1

wrought 1. ברא 2. מְלָאכָה 3. מַעֲשֶׂה 4. עשׂה 5. עֲשׂוֹת 6. פעל 7. פֹּעַל 8. רצף 9. שׂום 10. שׂוּם דָּבָר 11. עבר (A) 12. γίνομαι 13. ἐργάζομαι 14. κατεργάζομαι 15. ποιέω

Gen 34: 7 because he had wrought folly in Israel by lying 4
Exd 34:10 marvels, such as have not been wrought in all 1
Num 14:11 all the signs which I have wrought among them? 4
22 seen . . my signs which I wrought in Egypt 4
23:23 be said of Jacob and Israel, 'What has God wrought!' 6
31:51 received . . the gold, all wrought articles. 3
Deu 22:21 wrought folly in Israel by playing the harlot 4
32:27 LORD has not wrought all this. 6
34:12 which Moses wrought in the sight of all Israel. 4
1Sm 11:13 the LORD has wrought deliverance in Israel. 4
14:45 who has wrought this great victory in Israel? 4
45 for he has wrought with God this day. 4
19: 5 the LORD wrought a great victory for all Israel. 4
2Sm 7:21 thou hast wrought all this greatness 4
23:10 and the LORD wrought a great victory that day; 4
12 and the LORD wrought a great victory. 4
1Ch 16:12 the wonders he wrought, the judgments he uttered •
17:19 thou hast wrought all this greatness 4
Ps 22:31 to a people yet unborn, that he has wrought it. 4
31:19 and wrought for those who take refuge in thee 6
46: 8 how he has wrought desolations in the earth. 9
64: 9 men will fear; they will tell what God has wrought 7
68:28 O God, thou who hast wrought for us. 6
78: 4 his might, and the wonders which he has wrought. 4
12 In the sight of their fathers he wrought marvels 4
43 when he wrought his signs in Egypt 9
105:27 They wrought his signs among them, and miracles 10
143: 5 I muse on what thy hands have wrought. 3
Sng 3:10 it was lovingly wrought within by the daughters 8
Isa 26:12 O LORD . . thou hast wrought for us all our works. 6
18 We have wrought no deliverance in the earth 4
Ezk 27:19 wrought iron, cassia, and calamus were bartered 5
28:13 and wrought in gold were your settings 2
Dan 4: 2 signs . . Most High God has wrought toward me. 11
Mrk 6: 2 What mighty works are wrought by his hands! 12
Joh 3:21 seen that his deeds have been wrought in God. 13
Rom 7: 8 sin . . wrought in me all kinds of covetousness. 14
15:18 except what Christ has wrought through me 14
Sir 45:19 he wrought wonders against them 15

finely wrought 1. שְׂרָד

Exd 35:19 the finely wrought garments for ministering 1
39: 1 they made finely wrought garments 1

intricately wrought 1. רקם

Ps 139:15 intricately wrought in the depths of the earth. 1

Y

yard 1. גִּזְרָה
Ezk 41:13 the yard and the building with its walls 1
14 the temple and the yard, 100 cubits. 1
15 the length of the building facing the yard 1
42:10 On the south also, opposite the yard 1
13 opposite the yard are the holy chambers 1

temple yard 1. גִּזְרָה
Ezk 42: 1 chambers which were opposite the temple yard 1
41:12 The building that was facing the temple yard 1

yawn 1. ἀχανής
Wis 19:17 surrounded by yawning darkness 1

yea 1. אַךְ 2. אַף 3. גַּם 4. הִנֵּה 5. וְ 6. כִּי 7. γε 8. ναί
Exd 6: 1 yea, with a strong hand he will drive them out 5
Deu 29:24 yea, all the nations would say, 'Why has the LORD *
33: 3 Yea, he loved his people; all those consecrated 2
28 yea, his heavens drop down dew. 2
Jdg 5: 4 heavens dropped, yea, the clouds dropped water. 3
18:10 land is broad; yea, God has given it into your hands 6
2Sm 22:29 Yea, thou art my lamp, O LORD 6
30 Yea, by thee I can crush a troop 6
23: 5 Yea, does not my house stand so with God? 6
1Kg 8:24 yea, thou didst speak with thy mouth 5
30 hearken . . yea, hear thou in heaven thy dwelling 5
1Ch 16:30 yea, the world stands firm, never to be moved. 2
2Ch 6:15 yea, thou didst speak with thy mouth 5
21 yea, hear thou from heaven thy dwelling place; 5
Neh 1: 6 Yea, I and my father's house have sinned. 5
Job 3: 7 Yea, let that night be barren; 4
18: 5 Yea, the light of the wicked is put out 3
30:23 Yea, I know that thou wilt bring me to death 6
Ps 10:14 Thou dost see; yea, thou dost note trouble 6
16: 6 in pleasant places; yea, I have a goodly heritage. 2
18:28 Yea, thou dost light my lamp; 6
29 Yea, by thee I can crush a troop; 6
48 yea, thou didst exalt me above my adversaries; 2
21: 6 Yea, thou dost make him most blessed for ever; 6
22:16 Yea, dogs are round about me; 6
29 Yea, to him shall all the proud of the earth bow *
25: 3 Yea, let none that wait for thee be put to shame; 3
27:14 let your heart take courage; yea, wait for the LORD! 5
31: 3 Yea, thou art my rock and my fortress; 6
13 Yea, I hear the whispering of many– 6
33:21 Yea, our heart is glad in him, because we trust 6
38:14 Yea, I am like a man who does not hear 5
49:10 Yea, he shall see that even the wise die 6
55: 7 yea, I would wander afar 4
56:13 my soul from death, yea, my feet from falling *
68:16 yea, where the LORD will dwell for ever! 2
77:11 yea, I will remember thy wonders of old. 6
16 they were afraid, yea, the deep trembled. 2
83: 5 Yea, they conspire with one accord; 6
84: 2 soul longs, yea, faints for the courts of the LORD; 3
85:12 Yea, the LORD will give what is good 3
89:43 Yea, thou hast turned back the edge of his sword 2
90:17 yea, the work of our hands establish thou it. 5
93: 1 Yea, the world is established; 2
96:10 Yea, the world is established, it shall never 2
119:111 testimonies . . yea, they are the joy of my heart. 6
118 yea, their cunning is in vain. 6
135:18 Like them . . yea, every one who trusts in them! *
Prv 7:26 yea, all her slain are a mighty host. 5
Isa 30:19 Yea, O people in Zion who dwell at Jerusalem; 6
33 yea, for the king it is made ready 3
32:13 yea, for all the joyous houses in the joyful city. 6
34:14 yea, there shall the night hag alight 1
15 yea, there shall the kites be gathered 1
65: 6 I will repay, yea, I will repay into their bosom 5
Jer 2:20 Yea, upon every high hill . . you bowed down 6
46:21 yea, they have turned and fled together 6
Lam 1: 8 yea, she herself groans, and turns her face away. 3
10 yea, she has seen the nations invade her 6
Ezk 13:10 Because, yea, because they have misled my people *
16: 8 yea, I plighted my troth to you 5
28 yea, you played the harlot with them 5
59 Yea, thus says the Lord GOD: I will deal with you 6
21:14 let the sword come down twice, yea thrice *
26:18 yea, the isles that are in the sea are dismayed 5
31:17 yea, those who dwelt under its shadow *
36: 3 Because, yea, because they made you desolate, *
12 Yea, I will let men walk upon you, even my people 5
Hos 6: 9 on the way to Shechem, yea, they commit villainy. 6
10: 6 Yea, the thing itself shall be carried to Assyria 3
11:10 yea, he will roar, and his sons shall come 6
Jon 3: 8 yea, let every one turn from his evil way 5
Hab 1: 8 Yea, their horsemen come from afar; *
Zep 1:18 for a full, yea, sudden end he will make 1
2:11 yea, he will famish all the gods of the earth 6
3: 9 Yea, at that time I will change the speech 6
20 yea, I will make you renowned and praised 6
Zec 9:17 Yea, how good and how fair it shall be! 6
Mat 11:26 yea, Father, for such was thy gracious will. 8
Lke 10:21 yea, Father, for such was thy gracious will. 8
Act 2:18 yea, and on my menservants and my maidservants 7

year 1. יוֹם 2. שָׁנָה 3. שְׁנָה (A) 4. ἐνιαυτός 5. ἔτος 6. ἐφέτειος 7. ἡλικία 8. ἡμέρα 9. χρόνος 10. annus
Gen 1:14 let them be . . for seasons and for days and years 2
5: 3 When Adam had lived 130 years 2
4 The days of Adam . . were 800 years; 2
5 days . . Adam lived were 930 years; and he died. 2
6 When Seth had lived 105 years 2
7 Seth lived after the birth of Enosh 807 years 2
8 Thus all the days of Seth were 912 years; 2
9 When Enosh had lived 90 years 2
10 Enosh lived after the birth of Kenan 815 years 2
11 Thus all the days of Enosh were 905 years; 2
12 When Kenan had lived 70 years 2
13 lived after the birth of Ma-hal'alel 840 years 2
14 Thus all the days of Kenan were 910 years; 2
15 When Ma-hal'alel had lived 65 years 2
16 Ma-hal'alel lived after the birth . . 830 years 2
17 Thus all the days of Ma-hal'alel were 895 years; 2
18 When Jared had lived 162 years 2
19 Jared lived after the birth of Enoch 800 years 2
20 Thus all the days of Jared were 962 years; 2
21 When Enoch had lived 65 years 2
22 after the birth of Methu'selah 300 years 2
23 Thus all the days of Enoch were 365 years. 2
25 When Methu'selah had lived 187 years 2
26 Methu'selah lived after the birth . . 782 years 2
27 Thus all the days of Methu'selah were 969 years; 2
28 When Lamech had lived 182 years 2
30 Lamech lived after the birth of Noah 595 years 2
31 Thus all the days of Lamech were 777 years; 2
32 After Noah was 500 years old 2
6: 3 he is flesh, but his days shall be 120 years. 2
7: 6 Noah was 600 years old when the flood . . came 2
11 In the 600th year of Noah's life 2
8:13 In the 601st year, in the first month 2
9:28 After the flood Noah lived 350 years; 2
29 All the days of Noah were 950 years; 2
11:10 When Shem was 100 years old 2
10 father of Arpach'shad two years after the flood; 2
11 Shem lived after the birth . . 500 years 2
12 When Arpach'shad had lived 35 years 2
13 Arpach'shad lived after the birth . . 403 years 2
14 When Shelah had lived 30 years 2
15 Shelah lived after the birth of Eber 403 years 2
16 When Eber had lived 34 years 2
17 Eber lived after the birth of Peleg 430 years 2
18 When Peleg had lived 30 years 2
19 Peleg lived after the birth of Re'u 209 years 2
20 When Re'u had lived 32 years 2
21 Re'u lived after the birth of Serug 207 years 2
22 When Serug had lived 30 years 2
23 Serug lived after the birth of Nahor 200 years 2
24 When Nahor had lived 29 years 2
25 Nahor lived after the birth of Terah 119 years 2
26 When Terah had lived 70 years 2
32 The days of Terah were 205 years; 2
12: 4 Abram was 75 years old when he departed 2
14: 4 Twelve years they had served Ched-or-lao'mer 2
4 in the thirteenth year they rebelled. 2
5 In the fourteenth year Ched-or-lao'mer 2
15:13 they will be oppressed for 400 years; 2
16: 3 after Abram had dwelt ten years in the land 2
16 Abram was 86 years old when Hagar bore Ish'mael 2
17: 1 When Abram was 99 years old the LORD appeared 2
17 Shall a child be born to a man who is 100 years old? 2
17 Shall Sarah, who is 90 years old, bear a child? 2
21 bear to you at this season next year. 2
24 Abraham was 99 years old 2
25 Ish'mael his son was thirteen years old 2
21: 5 Abraham was 100 years old when . . Isaac was born 2
23: 1 Sarah lived 127 years; 2
1 these were the years of the life of Sarah. 2
24: 1 Abraham was old, well advanced in years; 1
25: 7 These are the days of the years of Abraham's life 2
7 days of the years of Abraham's life, 175 years. 2
8 an old man and full of years, and was gathered 8
17 These are the years of the life of Ish'mael 2
17 years of the life of Ish'mael, 137 years; 2
20 Isaac was 40 years old when he took to wife Rebekah 2
26 Isaac was 60 years old when she bore them. 2
26:12 Isaac . . reaped in the same year a hundredfold. 2
34 When Esau was 40 years old, he took to wife Judith 2
29:18 he said, "I will serve you seven years 2
20 Jacob served seven years for Rachel 2
27 in return for serving me another seven years. 2
30 and served Laban for another seven years. 2
31:38 These twenty years I have been with you; 2
41 These twenty years I have been in your house; 2
41 I served you fourteen years for your two 2
41 served you . . six years for your flock 2
35:28 Now the days of Isaac were 180 years. 2
37: 2 Joseph, being seventeen years old 2
41: 1 After two whole years, Pharaoh dreamed 2
26 good cows are seven years, and the seven good ears 2
26 and the seven good ears are seven years; 2
27 cows that came up after them are seven years 2
27 east wind are also seven years of famine. 2
29 There will come seven years of great plenty 2
30 there will arise seven years of famine 2
34 of Egypt during the seven plenteous years. 2
35 the food of these good years that are coming 2
36 a reserve . . against the seven years of famine 2
46 Joseph was 30 years old when he entered 2
47 During the seven plenteous years the earth 2
48 food of the seven years when there was plenty 2
50 Before the year of famine came 2
53 The seven years of plenty that prevailed 2
54 the seven years of famine began to come 2
45: 6 the famine has been in the land these two years; 2
6 there are yet five years in which there will be 2
11 for there are yet five years of famine to come; 2
47: 8 How many are the days of the years of your life? 2
9 The days of the years of my sojourning are 2
9 The days . . of my sojourning are 130 years; 2
9 evil have been the days of the years of my life 2
9 to the days of the years of the life of my fathers 2
17 food in exchange for all their cattle that year. 2
18 when that year was ended, they came to him 2
18 they came to him the following year, and said 2
28 Jacob lived in the land of Egypt seventeen years; 2
28 Jacob, the years of his life, were 147 years. 2
28 Jacob, the years of his life, were 147 years. 2
50:22 and Joseph lived 110 years. 2
25 Joseph died, being 110 years old; 2
Exd 6:16 the years of the life of Levi being 137 years. 2
16 the years of the life of Levi being 137 years. 2
18 the years of the life of Kohath being 133 years. 2
18 the years of the life of Kohath being 133 years. 2

20 the years of the life of Amram being 137 years. 2
20 the years of the life of Amram being 137 years. 2
7: 7 Now Moses was 80 years old 2
7 Moses was 80 . . and Aaron 83 years old 2
12: 2 it shall be the first month of the year for you. 2
5 lamb . . without blemish, a male a year old; 2
40 time that the people . . dwelt in Egypt was 430 years. 2
41 at the end of 430 years, on that very day 2
13:10 keep this ordinance . . from year to year. 1
10 keep this ordinance . . from year to year. 1
16:35 the people of Israel ate the manna forty years 2
21: 2 you buy a Hebrew slave, he shall serve six years 2
23:10 For six years you shall sow your land 2
11 the seventh year you shall let it rest and lie *
14 Three times in the year you shall keep a feast 2
16 the feast of ingathering at the end of the year 2
17 Three times in the year shall all your males 2
29 not drive them out from before you in one year 2
29:38 two lambs a year old day by day continually. 2
30:10 make atonement upon its horns once a year; 2
10 he shall make atonement for it once in the year 2
14 from twenty years old and upward, shall give 2
34:22 the feast of ingathering at the year's end. 2
23 Three times in the year shall all your males 2
24 before the LORD your God three times in the year. 2
38:26 from twenty years old and upward, 603,550 men. 2
40:17 first month in the second year, on the first day 2
Lev 9: 3 calf and a lamb, both a year old without blemish 2
12: 6 bring . . a lamb a year old for a burnt offering 2
14:10 and one ewe lamb a year old without blemish 2
16:34 for the people of Israel once in the year 2
19:23 three years it shall be forbidden to you 2
24 in the fourth year all their fruit shall be holy 2
25 But in the fifth year you may eat of their fruit 2
23:12 you shall offer a male lamb a year old 2
18 present . . seven lambs a year old 2
19 offer . . two male lambs a year old as a sacrifice 2
41 as a feast . . seven days in the year 2
25: 3 Six years you shall sow your field 2
3 six years you shall prune your vineyard 2
4 in the seventh year there shall be a sabbath 2
5 it shall be a year of solemn rest for the land 2
8 you shall count seven weeks of years, seven times 2
8 weeks . . seven times seven years 2
8 so that the time of the seven weeks of years shall 2
8 seven weeks of years shall be to you 49 years 2
10 you shall hallow the 50th year, and proclaim 2
11 A jubilee shall that 50th year be to you 2
13 In this year of jubilee each of you shall return 2
15 According to the number of years after 2
15 and according to the number of years for crops 2
16 If the years are many you shall increase the price 2
16 if the years are few you shall diminish the price 2
20 if you say, 'What shall we eat in the seventh year 2
21 command my blessing upon you in the sixth year 2
21 that it will bring forth fruit for three years 2
22 When you sow in the eighth year, you will be eating 2
22 until the ninth year, when its produce comes 2
27 let him reckon the years since he sold it and pay 2
28 remain . . until the year of jubilee 2
29 redeem it within a whole year after its sale 2
30 If it is not redeemed within a full year 2
40 serve with you until the year of the jubilee 2
50 reckon . . from the year when he sold himself 2
50 when he sold himself until the year of jubilee 2
50 according to the number of his release of years 2
51 If there are still many years, according to them 2
52 If there remain but a few years until the year 2
52 but a few years until the year of jubilee 2
52 according to the years of service due from him 2
53 As a servant hired year by year shall he be 2
53 a servant hired year by year shall he be with him 2
54 then he shall be released in the year of jubilee 2
27: 3 a male from twenty years old up to 60 years old 2
3 a male from twenty years old up to 60 years old 2
5 If the person is from five years old up to twenty 2
5 is from five years old up to twenty years old 2
6 If the person is from a month old up to five years 2
7 if the person is 60 years old and upward 2
17 If he dedicates his field from the year 2
18 the money-value for it according to the years 2
18 the money-value for it according to the years 2
23 shall compute . . up to the year of jubilee 2
24 In the year of jubilee the field shall return 2
Num 1: 1 in the second year after they had come out 2
3 from twenty years old and upward, all in Israel 2
18 names from twenty years old and upward 2
20 every male from twenty years old and upward 2
22 every male from twenty years old and upward 2
24 from twenty years old and upward 2
26 from twenty years old and upward, every man able 2
28 from twenty years old and upward, every man able 2
30 from twenty years old and upward, every man able 2
32 number of names, from twenty years old and upward 2
34 from twenty years old and upward, every man able 2
36 from twenty years old and upward, every man able 2
38 from twenty years old and upward, every man able 2
40 from twenty years old and upward, every man able 2
42 from twenty years old and upward, every man able 2
45 from twenty years old and upward, every man able 2
4: 3 from 30 years old up to 50 years old 2
3 from 30 years old up to 50 years old 2
23 from 30 years old up to 50 years old 2
23 from 30 years old up to 50 years old 2
30 from 30 years old up to 50 years old 2
30 from 30 years old up to 50 years old 2
35 from 30 years old up to 50 years old 2
35 from 30 years old up to 50 years old 2
39 from 30 years old up to 50 years old 2
39 from 30 years old up to 50 years old 2
43 from 30 years old up to 50 years old 2
43 from 30 years old up to 50 years old 2
47 from 30 years old up to 50 years old 2
47 from 30 years old up to 50 years old 2
6:12 bring a male lamb a year old for a guilt offering; 2
14 one male lamb a year old . . for a burnt offering 2
14 one ewe lamb a year old . . as a sin offering 2
7:15 ram, one male lamb a year old, for a burnt offering; 2
17 peace offerings . . five male lambs a year old. 2
21 ram, one male lamb a year old, for a burnt offering; 2
23 peace offerings . . five male lambs a year old. 2
27 ram, one male lamb a year old, for a burnt offering; 2
29 peace offerings . . five male lambs a year old. 2
33 ram, one male lamb a year old, for a burnt offering; 2
35 peace offerings . . five male lambs a year old. 2
39 ram, one male lamb a year old, for a burnt offering; 2
41 peace offerings . . five male lambs a year old. 2
45 ram, one male lamb a year old, for a burnt offering; 2
47 peace offerings . . five male lambs a year old. 2
51 ram, one male lamb a year old, for a burnt offering; 2
53 peace offerings . . five male lambs a year old. 2
57 ram, one male lamb a year old, for a burnt offering; 2
59 peace offerings . . five male lambs a year old. 2
63 ram, one male lamb a year old, for a burnt offering; 2
65 peace offerings . . five male lambs a year old. 2
69 ram, one male lamb a year old, for a burnt offering; 2
71 peace offerings . . five male lambs a year old. 2
75 ram, one male lamb a year old, for a burnt offering; 2
77 peace offerings . . five male lambs a year old. 2
81 ram, one male lamb a year old, for a burnt offering; 2
83 peace offerings . . five male lambs a year old. 2
87 burnt offering . . twelve male lambs a year old 2
88 peace offerings . . male lambs a year old 60 2
8:24 from 25 years old and upward they shall go 2
25 from the age of 50 years they shall withdraw 2
9: 1 in the first month of the second year after 2
10:11 In the second year, in the second month 2
13:22 (Hebron was built seven years before Zo'an 2
14:29 numbered from twenty years old and upward, who 2
33 shall be shepherds in the wilderness 40 years 2
34 for every day a year, you shall bear your iniquity 2
34 you shall bear your iniquity, 40 years 2
15:27 offer a female goat a year old for a sin offering. 2
26: 2 from twenty years old and upward 2
4 people, from twenty years old and upward 2
28: 3 two male lambs a year old without blemish 2
9 two male lambs a year old without blemish 2
11 seven male lambs a year old without blemish; 2
14 offering . . throughout the months of the year. 2
19 a burnt offering . . seven male lambs a year old; 2
27 a burnt offering . . seven male lambs a year old; 2
29: 2 seven male lambs a year old without blemish; 2
8 a burnt offering . . seven male lambs a year old; 2
13 bulls, two rams, fourteen male lambs a year old; 2
17 second day . . fourteen male lambs a year old 2
20 third day . . fourteen male lambs a year old 2
23 fourth day . . fourteen male lambs a year old 2
26 fifth day . . fourteen male lambs a year old 2
29 sixth day . . fourteen male lambs a year old 2
32 seventh day . . fourteen male lambs a year old 2
36 burnt offering . . seven male lambs a year old 2
32:11 none . . from twenty years old and upward 2
13 he made them wander in the wilderness 40 years 2
33:38 in the 40th year after the people of Israel 2
39 Aaron was 123 years old when he died on Mount Hor. 2
Deu 1: 3 in the 40th year, on the first day 2
2: 7 these 40 years the LORD your God has been with you 2
14 38 years, until the entire generation 2
8: 2 the LORD your God has led you these 40 years 2
4 your foot did not swell, these 40 years. 2
11:12 from the beginning of the year to the end 2
12 from the beginning . . to the end of the year. 2
14:22 comes forth from the field year by year. 2
22 comes forth from the field year by year. 2
28 At the end of every three years you shall bring 2
28 all the tithe of your produce in the same year 2
15: 1 end of every seven years you shall grant a release. 2
9 The seventh year, the year of release is near,' 2
9 The seventh year, the year of release is near,' 2
12 brother . . shall serve you six years 2
12 in the seventh year you shall let him go free 2
18 at half the cost . . he has served you six years. 2
20 eat it . . before the LORD your God year by year 2
20 eat it . . before the LORD your God year by year 2
16:16 Three times a year all your males shall appear 2
24: 5 newly married . . shall be free at home one year 2
26:12 paying . . tithe of your produce in the third year 2
12 third year, which is the year of tithing, giving it 2
29: 5 I have led you 40 years in the wilderness; 2
31: 2 said to them, "I am 120 years old this day; 2
10 At the end of every seven years, at the set time 2
10 seven years, at the set time of the year of release 2
32: 7 of old, consider the years of many generations; 2
34: 7 Moses was 120 years old when he died; 2
Jos 5: 6 the people of Israel walked 40 years 2
12 ate of the fruit of the land of Canaan that year. 2
13: 1 Now Joshua was old and advanced in years; 1
1 You are old and advanced in years 1
14: 7 I was 40 years old when Moses . . sent me 2
10 LORD has kept me alive . . these 45 years 2
10 and now, lo, I am this day 85 years old. 2
23: 1 and Joshua was old and well advanced in years 1
2 I am now old and well advanced in years; 1
24:29 Joshua . . died, being 110 years old. 2
Jdg 2: 8 Joshua . . died at the age of 110 years. 2
3: 8 Israel served Cu'shan-rishatha'im eight years. 2
11 the land had rest 40 years. Then Oth'ni-el the son 2
14 served Eglon the king of Moab eighteen years. 2
30 And the land had rest for 80 years. 2
4: 3 oppressed . . Israel cruelly for twenty years. 2
5:31 And the land had rest for 40 years. 2
6: 1 gave them into the hand of Mid'ian seven years. 2
25 father's bull, the second bull seven years old 2
8:28 the land had rest 40 years in the days of Gideon 2
9:22 Abim'elech ruled over Israel three years. 2
10: 2 And he judged Israel 23 years. Then he died 2
3 Ja'ir the Gileadite, who judged Israel 22 years. 2
8 crushed and oppressed . . Israel that year. 2
8 For eighteen years they oppressed . . Israel 2
11:26 While Israel dwelt . . 300 years, why did you not 2
40 daughters of Israel went year by year to lament 1
40 daughters of Israel went year by year to lament 1
40 went . . to lament . . four days in the year. 2
12: 7 Jephthah judged Israel six years. 2
9 And he judged Israel seven years. 2
11 Elon . . and he judged Israel ten years. 2
14 rode on 70 asses; and he judged Israel eight years. 2
13: 1 the hand of the Philistines for 40 years. 2
15:20 he judged Israel . . twenty years. 2
16:31 He had judged Israel twenty years. 2
17:10 and I will give you ten pieces of silver a year 1
Rut 1: 4 They lived there about ten years; 2
1Sm 1: 3 this man used to go up year by year . . to worship 1
3 this man used to go up year by year . . to worship 1
7 it went on year by year; as often as . . she used 2
7 it went on year by year; as often as . . she used 2
4:15 Now Eli was 98 years old and his eyes were set 2
18 Eli fell . . He had judged Israel 40 years. 2
7: 2 From . . a long time passed, some twenty years 2
16 he went . . year by year to Bethel, Gilgal 2
16 he went . . year by year to Bethel, Gilgal 2
13: 1 Saul was . . years old when he began to reign; 2
1 and he reigned . . and two years over Israel. 2
17:12 the man was already old and advanced in years. 5
27: 7 number of the days . . was a year and four months. 1
29: 3 who has been with me now for days and years 2
2Sm 2:10 Ish-bo'shet . . was 40 years old when he began to reign 2
10 Ish-bo'sheth . . and he reigned two years. 2
11 the time that . . was seven years and six months. 2
4: 4 He was five years old when the news . . came 2
5: 4 David was 30 years old when he began to reign 2
4 David was 30 years old . . and he reigned 40 years. 2
5 he reigned over Judah seven years and six months 2
5 at Jerusalem he reigned . . 33 years. 2
11: 1 In the spring of the year . . David sent Jo'ab 2
13:23 After two full years Ab'salom had sheepshearers 2
38 and went to Geshur, and was there three years. 2
14:28 Ab'salom dwelt two full years in Jerusalem 2
15: 7 at the end of four years Ab'salom said to the king 2
19:32 Barzil'lai was a very aged man, 80 years old; 2
34 How many years have I still to live 2
35 I am this day 80 years old; can I discern 2
21: 1 a famine in the days of David for three years 2
1 was a famine . . for three years, year after year; 2
1 was a famine . . for three years, year after year; 2
24:13 Shall three years of famine come . . in your land? 2
1Kg 1: 1 King David was old and advanced in years; 1
2:11 the time that David reigned . . was 40 years; 2
11 he reigned seven years in Hebron 2
11 David . . reigned . . 33 years in Jerusalem. 2
39 it happened at the end of three years that two 2
4: 7 had to make provision for one month in the year. 2
5:11 Solomon gave this to Hiram year by year. 2
11 Solomon gave this to Hiram year by year. 2
6: 1 the 480th year after . . Israel came out of . . Egypt 2
1 in the fourth year of Solomon's reign over Israel 2
37 In the fourth year the foundation . . was laid 2
38 in the eleventh year . . the house was finished 2
38 He was seven years in building it. 2
7: 1 Solomon was building . . thirteen years 2
9:10 At the end of twenty years . . Solomon had built 2
25 Three times a year Solomon used to offer up 2
10:14 gold that came to Solomon in one year was 666 2
22 Once every three years the fleet . . used to come 2
25 Every one of them brought . . so much year by year. 2
25 Every one of them brought . . so much year by year. 2
11:42 time that Solomon reigned . . was 40 years. 2

14:20 the time that Jerobo'am reigned was 22 years; 2
21 Rehobo'am was 41 years old when he began to reign 2
21 and he reigned seventeen years in Jerusalem 2
25 In the fifth year of King Rehobo'am 2
15: 1 Now in the eighteenth year of King Jerobo'am 2
2 He reigned for three years in Jerusalem. 2
9 In the twentieth year of Jerobo'am king of Israel 2
10 he reigned 41 years in Jerusalem. 2
25 to reign over Israel in the second year of Asa 2
25 Nadab . . and he reigned over Israel two years. 2
28 Ba'asha killed him in the third year of Asa 2
33 In the third year of Asa king of Judah 2
33 Ba'asha . . reigned 24 years. 2
16: 8 In the 26th year of Asa king of Judah 2
8 Elah . . began to reign . . and reigned two years. 2
10 killed him, in the 27th year of Asa 2
15 In the 27th year of Asa king of Judah 2
23 In the 31st year of Asa king of Judah 2
23 Omri . . reigned for twelve years; 2
23 Omri . . reigned . . six years he reigned in Tirzah. 2
29 In the 38th year of Asa king of Judah 2
29 Ahab . . reigned over Israel in Sama'ria 22 years. 2
17: 1 there shall be neither dew nor rain these years 2
18: 1 word of the LORD came . . in the third year, saying 2
22: 1 For three years Syria and Israel continued 2
2 in the third year Jehosh'aphat . . came down 2
41 began to reign . . in the fourth year of Ahab 2
42 Jehosh'aphat was 35 years old when he began 2
42 and he reigned 25 years in Jerusalem. 2
51 in the seventeenth year of Jehosh'aphat 2
51 and he reigned two years over Israel. 2
2Kg 1:17 became king . . in the second year of Jeho'ram 2
3: 1 In the eighteenth year of Jehosh'aphat 2
1 and he reigned twelve years. 2
8: 1 and it will come upon the land for seven years. 2
2 in the land of the Philistines seven years. 2
3 at the end of the seven years . . she went forth 2
16 In the fifth year of Joram the son of Ahab 2
17 He was 32 years old when became king 2
17 and he reigned eight years in Jerusalem. 2
25 In the twelfth year of Joram the son of Ahab 2
26 Ahazi'ah was 22 years old when he began to reign 2
26 and he reigned one year in Jerusalem. 2
9:29 In the eleventh year of Joram . . Ahazi'ah began 2
10:36 time that Jehu reigned . . in Sama'ria was 28 years. 2
11: 3 he remained with her six years, hid in the house 2
4 in the seventh year Jehoi'ada sent and brought 2
21 Jeho'ash was seven years old when he began 2
12: 1 In the seventh year of Jehu Jeho'ash began 2
1 Jeho'ash . . reigned 40 years in Jerusalem. 2
6 But by the 23rd year of King Jeho'ash 2
13: 1 In the 23rd year of Jo'ash the son of Ahazi'ah 2
1 Jeho'ahaz . . and he reigned seventeen years. 2
10 In the 37th year of Jo'ash king of Judah 2
10 Jeho'ahaz began . . and he reigned sixteen years. 2
20 used to invade the land in the spring of the year. 2
14: 1 In the second year of Jo'ash the son of Jo'ahaz 2
2 He was 25 years old when he began to reign 2
2 and he reigned 29 years in Jerusalem. 2
17 Amazi'ah . . lived fifteen years after the death 2
21 people . . took Azari'ah, who was sixteen years old 2
23 In the fifteenth year of Amazi'ah the son of Jo'ash 2
23 began to reign in Sama'ria, and he reigned 41 years. 2
15: 1 In the 27th year of Jerobo'am king of Israel 2
2 He was sixteen years old when he began to reign 2
2 and he reigned 52 years in Jerusalem. 2
8 In the 38th year of Azari'ah king of Judah 2
13 Shallum . . began to reign in the 39th year 2
17 In the 39th year of Azari'ah the king of Judah 2
17 Men'ahem . . and he reigned ten years in Sama'ria. 2
23 In the 50th year of Azari'ah king of Judah 2
23 Pekahi'ah . . and he reigned two years. 2
27 In the 52nd year of Azari'ah king of Judah 2
27 began to reign . . and reigned twenty years. 2
30 the twentieth year of Jotham the son of Uzzi'ah. 2
32 In the second year of Pekah the son of Remali'ah 2
33 He was 25 years old when he began to reign 2
33 and he reigned sixteen years in Jerusalem. 2
16: 1 In the seventeenth year of Pekah the son 2
2 Ahaz was twenty years old when he began to reign 2
2 and he reigned sixteen years in Jerusalem. 2
17: 1 In the twelfth year of Ahaz king of Judah 2
1 Hoshe'a . . and he reigned nine years. 2
4 offered no tribute . . as he had done year by year; 2
4 offered no tribute . . as he had done year by year; 2
5 to Sama'ria, and for three years he besieged it. 2
6 In the ninth year of Hoshe'a 2
18: 1 In the third year of Hoshe'a son of Elah 2
2 He was 25 years old when he began to reign 2
2 and he reigned 29 years in Jerusalem. 2
9 In the fourth year of King Hezeki'ah 2
9 which was the seventh year of Hoshe'a son of Elah 2
10 and at the end of three years he took it. 2
10 In the sixth year of Hezeki'ah . . Sama'ria was 2
10 which was the ninth year of Hoshe'a king of Israel 2
13 In the fourteenth year of King Hezeki'ah 2
19:29 this year you shall eat what grows of itself 2
29 and in the second year what springs of the same; 2
29 in the third year sow, and reap, and plant 2

20: 6 And I will add fifteen years to your life. 2
21: 1 Manas'seh was twelve years old when he began 2
1 and he reigned 55 years in Jerusalem. 2
19 Amon was 22 years old when he began to reign 2
19 Amon . . and he reigned two years in Jerusalem. 2
22: 1 Josi'ah was eight years old when he began to reign 2
1 and he reigned 31 years in Jerusalem. 2
3 In the eighteenth year of King Josi'ah 2
23:23 but in the eighteenth year of King Josi'ah 2
31 Jeho'ahaz was 23 years old when he began to reign 2
36 Jehoi'akim was 25 years old when he began to reign 2
36 and he reigned eleven years in Jerusalem. 2
24: 1 and Jehoi'akim became his servant three years; 2
8 Jehoi'achin was eighteen years old 2
12 took him prisoner in the eighth year of his reign 2
18 Zedeki'ah was 21 years old when he became king 2
18 Zedeki'ah was . . and he reigned eleven years 2
25: 1 in the ninth year of his reign, in the tenth month 2
2 besieged till the eleventh year of . . Zedeki'ah. 2
8 was the nineteenth year of King Nebuchadnez'zar 2
27 And in the 37th year of the exile of Jehoi'achin 2
27 in the year that he began to reign 2
1Ch 2:21 whom he married when he was 60 years old; 2
3: 4 where he reigned for seven years and six months. 2
4 And he reigned 33 years in Jerusalem. 2
20: 1 In the spring of the year . . Jo'ab led out the army 2
21:12 either three years of famine; 2
23: 3 The Levites, 30 years old and upward, were numbered 2
24 from twenty years old and upward 2
27 number of the Levites from twenty years old 2
26:31 In the 40th year of David's reign search was made 2
27: 1 and went, month after month throughout the year 2
23 did not number those below twenty years of age 2
29:27 time that he reigned over Israel was 40 years; 2
27 reigned seven years in Hebron, and 33 in Jerusalem 2
2Ch 3: 2 the second month of the fourth year of his reign. 2
8: 1 At the end of twenty years, in which Solomon had 2
9:13 weight of gold that came to Solomon in one year 2
21 once every three years the ships of Tarshish 2
24 brought his present . . so much year by year. 2
24 brought his present . . so much year by year. 2
30 reigned . . over all Israel 40 years. 2
11:17 for three years they made Rehobo'am . . secure 2
17 walked for three years in the way of David 2
12: 2 In the fifth year of King Rehobo'am 2
13 41 years old when he began to reign 2
13 he reigned seventeen years in Jerusalem 2
13: 1 In the eighteenth year of King Jerobo'am 2
2 He reigned for three years in Jerusalem. 2
14: 1 In his days the land had rest for ten years. 2
6 no war in those years, for the LORD gave him peace. 2
15:10 in the third month of the fifteenth year 2
19 there was no more war until the 35th year 2
16: 1 In the 36th year of the reign of Asa 2
12 In the 39th year of his reign Asa 2
13 dying in the 41st year of his reign. 2
17: 7 In the third year of his reign he sent his princes 2
18: 2 After some years he went down to Ahab in Sama'ria. 2
20:31 35 years old when he began to reign 2
31 he reigned 25 years in Jerusalem. 2
21: 5 was 32 years old when he became king 2
5 Jeho'ram . . reigned eight years in Jerusalem. 2
19 at the end of two years, his bowels came out •
20 He was 32 years old when he began to reign •
20 he reigned eight years in Jerusalem; 2
22: 2 was 42 years old when he began to reign 2
2 Ahazi'ah . . reigned one year in Jerusalem. 2
12 he remained with them six years 2
23: 1 in the seventh year Jehoi'ada took courage 2
24: 1 Jo'ash was seven years old when he began to reign 2
1 Jo'ash . . reigned 40 years in Jerusalem; 2
5 to repair the house of your God from year to year; 2
5 to repair the house of your God from year to year; 2
15 Jehoi'ada . . was 130 years old at his death. 2
23 At the end of the year the army of the Syrians 2
25: 1 Amazi'ah was 25 years old when he began 2
1 he reigned 29 years in Jerusalem. 2
5 He mustered those twenty years old and upward 2
25 Amazi'ah . . lived fifteen years after the death 2
26: 1 Judah took Uzzi'ah, who was sixteen years old 2
3 Uzzi'ah was sixteen years old when he began 2
3 reigned 52 years in Jerusalem. 2
27: 1 Jotham was 25 years old when he began 2
1 Jotham . . reigned sixteen years in Jerusalem. 2
5 Ammonites gave him that year 100 talents 2
5 same amount in the second and the third years. 2
8 was 25 years old when he began to reign 2
8 he reigned sixteen years in Jerusalem. 2
28: 1 Ahaz was twenty years old when he began to reign 2
1 Ahaz . . reigned sixteen years in Jerusalem. 2
29: 1 began to reign when he was 25 years old 2
1 Hezeki'ah . . reigned 29 years 2
3 In the first year of his reign, in the first month 2
31:16 males from three years old and upwards 2
17 Levites from twenty years old and upwards 2
33: 1 Manas'seh was twelve years old when he began 2
1 he reigned 55 years in Jerusalem. 2
21 Amon was 22 years old when he began to reign 2
21 Amon . . reigned two years in Jerusalem. 2

34: 1 Josi'ah was eight years old when he began to reign 2
1 Josi'ah . . reigned 31 years 2
3 eighth year of his reign, while he was yet a boy 2
3 twelfth year he began to purge Judah 2
8 Now in the eighteenth year of his reign 2
35:19 In the eighteenth year of the reign of Josi'ah 2
36: 2 Jeho'ahaz was 23 years old when he 2
5 25 years old when he began to reign 2
5 he reigned eleven years in Jerusalem. 2
9 Jehoi'achin was eight years old when he began 2
10 In the spring of the year King Nebuchadnez'zar 2
11 21 years old when he began to reign 2
11 he reigned eleven years in Jerusalem. 2
21 it kept sabbath, to fulfil 70 years. 2
22 Now in the first year of Cyrus king of Persia 2
Ezr 1: 1 In the first year of Cyrus king of Persia 2
3: 8 second year of their coming to the house of God 2
8 Levites, from twenty years old and upward 2
4:24 second year of the reign of Darius king of Persia 3
5:11 rebuilding the house . . built many years ago 3
13 first year of Cyrus king of Babylon 3
6: 3 In the first year of Cyrus the king 3
15 in the sixth year of the reign of Darius the king. 3
7: 7 went up . . in the seventh year of Ar-ta-xerx'es 2
8 which was in the seventh year of the king 2
Neh 1: 1 month of Chislev, in the twentieth year 2
2: 1 Nisan, in the twentieth year of King Ar-ta-xerx'es 2
5:14 from the 20th year to the 32nd 2
14 20th year to the 32nd year 2
14 twelve years, neither I nor my brethren 2
9:21 40 years . . sustain them in the wilderness 2
30 Many years thou didst bear with them 2
10:31 forego the crops of the seventh year 2
34 at times appointed, year by year, to burn 2
34 at times appointed, year by year, to burn 2
35 first fruits . . year by year, to the house of the LORD; 2
35 first fruits . . year by year, to the house of the LORD; 2
13: 6 32nd year of Ar-ta-xerx'es king 2
Est 1: 3 in the third year of his reign he gave a banquet 2
2:16 month of Tebeth, in the seventh year of his reign 2
3: 7 of Nisan, in the twelfth year of King Ahasu-e'rus 2
9:21 that they should keep . . year by year 2
21 that they should keep . . year by year 2
27 they would . . at the time appointed every year 2
Job 3: 6 let it not rejoice among the days of the year 2
10: 5 thy days as the days of man, or thy years as man's 2
5 as the days of man, or thy years as man's years 1
15:20 all the years that are laid up for the ruthless. 2
16:22 For when a few years have come I shall go 2
32: 6 I am young in years, and you are aged; 1
7 Let days speak, and many years teach wisdom. 2
36:11 in prosperity, and their years in pleasantness. 2
26 the number of his years is unsearchable. 2
42:16 after this Job lived 140 years 2
Ps 31:10 is spent with sorrow, and my years with sighing; 2
61: 6 the king; may his years endure to all generations! 2
65:11 Thou crownest the year with thy bounty; 2
77: 5 the days of old, I remember the years long ago. 2
78:33 vanish like a breath, and their years in terror. 2
90: 4 1,000 years in thy sight are but as yesterday 2
9 our years come to an end like a sigh. 2
15 as many years as we have seen evil. 2
95:10 40 years I loathed that generation and said 2
102:24 whose years endure throughout all generations! 2
27 thou art the same, and thy years have no end. 2
Prv 3: 2 length of days and years of life 2
4:10 Hear . . that the years of your life may be many. 2
5: 9 lest you give . . your years to the merciless; 2
9:11 For by me . . years will be added to your life. 2
10:27 but the years of the wicked will be short. 2
Ecc 6: 3 and lives many years, so that the days . . are many 2
3 many years, so that the days of his years are many 2
11: 8 if a man lives many years, let him rejoice in them 2
12: 1 before the evil days come, and the years draw nigh 2
Isa 6: 1 In the year that King Uzzi'ah died I saw the Lord 2
7: 8 Within 65 years E'phraim will be broken 2
14:28 In the year that King Ahaz died came this oracle 2
16:14 In three years, like the years of a hireling 2
14 In three years, like the years of a hireling 2
20: 1 In the year that the commander in chief 2
3 barefoot for three years as a sign and a portent 2
21:16 Within a year, according to the years 2
16 a year, according to the years of a hireling 2
23:15 Tyre will be forgotten for 70 years 2
15 At the end of 70 years, it will happen to Tyre 2
17 the end of 70 years, the LORD will visit Tyre 2
29: 1 Add year to year; let the feasts run their round. 2
1 Add year to year; let the feasts run their round. 2
32:10 In little more than a year you will shudder 2
34: 8 a year of recompense for the cause of Zion. 2
36: 1 In the fourteenth year of King Hezeki'ah 2
37:30 this year eat what grows of itself 2
30 in the second year what springs of the same; 2
30 then in the third year sow and reap 2
38: 5 behold, I will add fifteen years to your life. 2
10 consigned to . . Sheol for the rest of my years. 2
61: 2 to proclaim the year of the LORD'S favor 2
63: 4 and my year of redemption has come. 2
65:20 for the child shall die 100 years old 2

20 sinner 100 years old shall be accursed. 2
Jer 1: 2 Josi'ah . . in the thirteenth year of his reign. 2
3 until the end of the eleventh year of Zedeki'ah 2
11:23 bring evil . . the year of their punishment. 2
17: 8 and is not anxious in the year of drought 2
23:12 evil upon them in the year of their punishment 2
25: 1 in the fourth year of Jehoi'akim the son of Josi'ah 2
1 the first year of Nebuchadrez'zar king of Babylon 2
3 For 23 years, from the thirteenth year of Josi'ah 2
3 from the thirteenth year of Josi'ah the son of Amon 2
11 nations shall serve the king of Babylon 70 years. 2
12 Then after 70 years are completed 2
28: 1 In that same year, at the beginning of the reign 2
1 in the fifth month of the fourth year, Hanani'ah 2
3 Within two years I will bring back to this place 2
11 break the yoke of . . the nations within two years. 2
16 This very year you shall die 2
17 In that same year, in the seventh month 2
29:10 When 70 years are completed for Babylon 2
32: 1 in the tenth year of Zedeki'ah king of Judah 2
1 was the eighteenth year of Nebuchadrez'zar. 2
34:14 At the end of six years each of you must set free 2
14 has been sold to you and has served you six years; 2
36: 1 In the fourth year of Jehoi'akim the son of Josi'ah 2
9 In the fifth year of Jehoi'akim the son of Josi'ah 2
39: 1 In the ninth year of Zedeki'ah king of Judah 2
2 in the eleventh year of Zedeki'ah 2
45: 1 in the fourth year of Jehoi'akim the son of Josi'ah 2
46: 2 defeated in the fourth year of Jehoi'akim 2
48:44 in the year of their punishment, says the LORD. 2
51:46 when a report comes in one year 2
46 one year and afterward a report in another year 2
59 to Babylon, in the fourth year of his reign. 2
52: 1 Zedeki'ah 21 years old when he became king; 2
1 and he reigned eleven years in Jerusalem. 2
4 in the ninth year of his reign, in the tenth month 2
5 till the eleventh year of King Zedeki'ah. 2
12 which was the nineteenth year of King 2
28 carried away captive: in the seventh year 2
29 in the eighteenth year of Nebuchadrez'zar 2
30 in the 23rd year of Nebuchadrez'zar 2
31 in the 37th year of the captivity 2
31 king of Babylon, in the year that he became king 2
Ezk 1: 1 In the 30th year, in the fourth month 2
2 the fifth year of the exile of King Jehoi'achin 2
4: 5 the number of the years of their punishment; 2
6 40 days I assign you, a day for each year. 2
8: 1 In the sixth year, in the sixth month 2
20: 1 In the seventh year, in the fifth month 2
22: 4 the appointed time of your years has come. 2
24: 1 In the ninth year, in the tenth month, on the tenth 2
26: 1 In the eleventh year, on the first day of the month 2
29: 1 In the tenth year, in the tenth month 2
11 it shall be uninhabited 40 years. 2
12 her cities shall be a desolation 40 years 2
13 thus says the Lord GOD: At the end of 40 years 2
17 In the 27th year, in the first 2
30:20 In the eleventh year, in the first month 2
31: 1 In the eleventh year, in the third month 2
32: 1 In the twelfth year, in the twelfth month 2
17 In the twelfth year, in the first month 2
33:21 In the twelfth year of our exile 2
38: 8 in the latter years you will go against the land 2
17 who in those days prophesied for years 2
39: 9 they will make fires of them for seven years; 2
40: 1 In the 25th year of our exile 2
1 at the beginning of the year, on the tenth day 2
1 fourteenth year after the city was conquered 2
46:13 He shall provide a lamb a year old 2
17 it shall be his to the year of liberty; 2
Dan 1: 5 educated for three years, and at the end 2
21 Daniel . . until the first year of King Cyrus. 2
2: 1 second year of the reign of Nebuchadnez'zar 2
5:31 Darius . . being about 62 years old. 3
7: 1 In the first year of Belshaz'zar king of Babylon 3
8: 1 third year of the reign of King Belshaz'zar 2
9: 1 In the first year of Darius the son of Ahasu-e'rus 2
2 first year of his reign, I, Daniel, perceived 2
2 perceived in the books the number of years 2
2 number of years . . namely, 70 years. 2
24 70 weeks of years are decreed concerning •
10: 1 In the third year of Cyrus king of Persia 2
11: 1 as for me, in the first year of Darius the Mede 2
6 After some years they shall make an alliance 2
8 for some years he shall refrain from attacking 2
13 after some years he shall come on with a great 2
Jol 2: 2 through the years of all generations. 2
25 I will restore to you the years 2
Ams 1: 1 he saw . . two years before the earthquake. 2
2:10 and led you 40 years in the wilderness 2
5:25 and offerings the 40 years in the wilderness 2
Mic 6: 6 with burnt offerings, with calves a year old? 2
Hab 3: 2 In the midst of the years renew it; 2
2 in the midst of the years make it known; 2
Hag 1: 1 In the second year of Darius the king 2
15 In the second year of Darius the king 2
2:10 the ninth month, in the second year of Darius 2
Zec 1: 1 In the eighth month, in the second year of Darius 2
7 the month of Shebat, in the second year of Darius 2
12 thou hast had indignation these 70 years? 2
7: 1 In the fourth year of King Darius 2
3 in the fifth month, as I have done for so many years? 2
5 for these 70 years, was it for me that you fasted? 2
14:16 shall go up year after year to worship the King 2
16 shall go up year after year to worship the King 2
Mal 3: 4 as in the days of old and as in former years. 2
Mat 9:20 a hemorrhage for twelve years 5
Mrk 5:25 woman who had had a flow of blood for twelve years 5
42 she was twelve years of age 5
Lke 1: 7 both were advanced in years. 8
18 I am an old man, and my wife is advanced in years. 8
2:36 seven years from her virginity 5
41 Now his parents went to Jerusalem every year 5
42 when he was twelve years old 5
3: 1 In the fifteenth year of the reign of Tiber'ius 5
23 Jesus . . was about 30 years of age 5
4:19 to proclaim the acceptable year of the Lord. 4
25 the heaven was shut up three years and six months 5
8:42 he had an only daughter, about twelve years of age 5
43 woman who had had a flow of blood for twelve years 5
12:19 Soul, you have ample goods laid up for many years; 5
13: 7 Lo, these three years I have come seeking fruit 5
8 he answered him, 'Let it alone, sir, this year also 5
11 had had a spirit of infirmity for eighteen years; 5
16 whom Satan bound for eighteen years 5
15:29 Lo, these many years I have served you 5
Joh 2:20 It has taken 46 years to build this temple 5
5: 5 One man was there, who had been ill for 38 years. 5
8:57 You are not yet 50 years old 5
11:49 Ca'iaphas, who was high priest that year, said 4
51 being high priest that year he prophesied 4
18:13 Ca'iaphas, who was high priest that year. 4
Act 4:22 the man . . was more than 40 years old. 5
7: 6 and ill-treat them 400 years. 5
30 Now when 40 years had passed 5
36 and in the wilderness for 40 years. 5
42 40 years in the wilderness, O house of Israel? 5
9:33 Aene'as, who had been bedridden for eight years 5
11:26 For a whole year they met with the church 4
13:19 for about 450 years 5
21 God gave them Saul . . for 40 years. 5
18:11 he stayed a year and six months 4
19:10 This continued for two years 5
24:10 many years you have been judge over this nation 5
17 after some years I came to bring to my nation alms 5
Rom 15:23 since I have longed for many years to come to you 5
2Co 12: 2 who fourteen years ago was caught up 5
Gal 1:18 Then after three years I went up to Jerusalem 5
2: 1 Then after fourteen years I went up again 5
3:17 the law, which came 430 years afterward 5
4:10 days, and months, and seasons, and years! 4
1Ti 5: 9 if she is not less than 60 years of age 5
Heb 1:12 thou art the same, and thy years will never end. 5
3: 9 and saw my works for 40 years. 5
17 And with whom was he provoked 40 years? 5
9: 7 and he but once a year 4
Jas 4:13 and spend a year there and trade and get gain"; 4
5:17 for three years and six months it did not rain 4
2Pe 3: 8 with the Lord one day is as a 1,000 years 5
8 and a 1,000 years as one day. 5
Rev 9:15 ready for the hour, the day, the month, and the year 4
20: 2 seized the dragon . . and bound him for a 1,000 years 5
3 no more, till the 1,000 years were ended. 5
4 and reigned with Christ a 1,000 years. 5
5 until the 1,000 years were ended. 5
6 and they shall reign with him a 1,000 years. 5
7 And when the 1,000 years are ended 5
1Es 1:22 In the eighteenth year of the reign of Josiah 5
34 who was 23 years old 5
39 Jehoiakim was 25 years old 5
43 when he was made king he was eighteen years old 5
45 after a year 4
46 Zedekiah was 21 years old 5
46 he reigned eleven years. 5
58 until the completion of 70 years. 5
2: 1 In the first year of Cyrus as king of the Persians 5
30 until the second year of the reign of Darius 5
4:51 that twenty talents a year should be given 4
52 an additional ten talents a year 4
5: 6 in the second year of his reign 5
56 In the second year 5
57 new moon of the second month in the second year 5
73 they were kept from building for two years 5
6: 1 Now in the second year of the reign of Darius 5
14 the house was built many years ago 5
17 in the first year that Cyrus reigned 5
24 In the first year of the reign of Cyrus 5
30 regularly every year, without quibbling 4
7: 5 in the sixth year of King Darius 5
8: 6 in the seventh year of the reign of Artaxerxes 5
6 the fifth month (this was the king's seventh year); 4
2Es 3: 1 the 30th year after the destruction of our city 10
23 the times passed and the years were completed 10
25 This was done for many years 10
29 has seen many sinners during these 30 years ‡
4:33 Why are our years few and evil? 10
6: 5 before the present years were reckoned 10
7:28 and those who remain shall rejoice 400 years. 10
29 after these years my son the Messiah shall die 10
43 For it will last for about a week of years. 10
9:43 though I lived with my husband 30 years. 10
44 every hour and every day during those 30 years 10
45 after 30 years God heard your handmaid 10
10:45 that she was barren for 30 years 10
45 it is because there were 3,000 years in the world 10
46 after 3,000 years Solomon built the city 10
12:20 whose times shall be short and their years swift; 10
13:45 a long way to go, a journey of a year and a half 10
Tob 1: 7 and spend the proceeds each year at Jerusalem; 4
14: 2 He was 58 years old when he lost his sight 5
2 after eight years he regained it 5
11 He was 158 years old 5
14 at the age of a 127 years. 5
Jdt 1: 1 the twelfth year of the reign of Nebuchadnezzar 5
13 In the seventeenth year 5
2: 1 In the eighteenth year 5
8: 4 three years and four months. 5
16:23 until she was 105 years old 5
AEs 11: 1 In the fourth year of the reign of Ptolemy 5
2 In the second year of the reign of Artaxerxes 5
13: 6 of the twelfth month, Adar, of this present year 5
Wis 4: 8 nor measured by number of years; 5
13 he fulfilled long years; 9
7:19 the cycles of the year 4
Sir 0: 3 in the 38th year of the reign of Euergetes 5
18: 9 is great if he reaches 100 years. 5
10 so are a few years in the day of eternity. 5
26: 2 he will complete his years in peace. 5
33: 7 when all the daylight in the year is from the sun? 4
37:11 with a man hired for a year 6
41: 4 for ten or 100 or 1,000 years 5
47:10 arranged their times throughout the year •
Bar 1: 2 in the fifth year, on the seventh day of the month 5
LJr 1: 3 you will remain there for many years 5
Sus 1: 5 In that year two elders . . were appointed 4
1Mc 1: 7 after Alexander had reigned twelve years 5
9 so did their sons after them for many years; 5
10 He began to reign in the 137th year 5
20 Antiochus returned in the 143rd year 5
29 Two years later the king sent to the cities 5
54 fifteenth day of Chislev, in the 145th year 5
2:70 He died in the 146th year 5
3:28 and gave a year's pay to his forces 4
37 from Antioch his capital in the 147th year 5
4:28 the next year 4
52 the month of Chislev, in the 148th year 5
6:16 Antiochus the king died there in the 149th year. 5
20 besieged the citadel in the 150th year 5
53 because it was the seventh year 5
7: 1 In the 151st year Demetrius the son of Seleucus 5
9: 3 In the first month of the 152nd year 5
54 In the 153rd year, in the second month 5
57 the land of Judah had rest for two years. 5
10: 1 In the 160th year 5
21 the 160th year 5
41 have not paid as they did in the first years 5
57 in the 162nd year. 5
67 In the 165th year 5
11:19 So Demetrius became king in the 167th year. 5
13:41 In the 170th year 5
42 In the first year of Simon the great high priest 5
51 the 23rd day of the second month, in the 171st year 5
14: 1 In the 172nd year Demetrius the king 5
27 On the eighteenth day of Elul, in the 172nd year 5
27 which is the third year of Simon 5
15:10 In the 174th year Antiochus set out and invaded 5
16: 3 you by His mercy are mature in years 5
14 his sons, in the 177th year, in the eleventh month 5
2Mc 1: 7 In the reign of Demetrius, in the 169th year 5
7 we Jews wrote to you . . in those years 5
9 in the month of Chislev, in the 188th year. 5
20 after many years had passed 5
4:40 a man advanced in years 7
6:23 worthy of his years and the dignity of his old age 7
7:27 nursed you for three years 5
10: 8 should observe these days every year. 4
11: 3 to put up the high priesthood for sale every year. 5
21 Farewell. The 148th year, Dioscorinthius 24th. 5
33 Farewell. The 148th year, Xanthicus fifteenth. 5
38 Farewell. The 148th year, Xanthicus fifteenth. 5
13: 1 In the 149th year 5
14: 4 went to King Demetrius in about the 151st year 5
3Mc 1:11 he only once a year 4
4Mc 2: 8 to cancel the debt when the seventh year arrives. •
5:11 adopt a mind appropriate to your years 7

year *See also* advanced, three, two, twelve.

year after year 1. κατ' ἐνιαυτόν

Heb 10: 1 are continually offered year after year 1
3 there is a reminder of sin year after year. 1

year ago 1. ἀπὸ πέρυσι

2Co 8:10 what a year ago you began not only to do 1

each year 1. מִיָּמִים יָמִימָה 2. κατ' ἐνιαυτόν

1Sm 2:19 make . . a little robe and take it to him each year 1

1Mc 7:49 this day should be celebrated each year 2
8:16 They trust one man each year to rule over them 2
11:34 the king formerly received from them each year 2

every year 1. יָמִים לְיָמִים 2. ἐνιαυτὸν κατ᾽ ἐνιαυτόν 3. κατ᾽ ἐνιαυτόν
2Sm 14:26 for at the end of every year he used to cut it; 1
1Mc 4:59 every year at that season 2
8: 4 the rest paid them tribute every year. 3
10:42 which my officials have received every year 3
13:52 that every year they should celebrate this day 3

full year 1. יוֹם
Lev 25:29 for a full year he shall have the right 1

last year 1. πέρυσι
2Co 9: 2 Acha'ia has been ready since last year 1

next year 1. μέλλω
Lke 13: 9 if it bears fruit next year, well and good 1

year old 1. anniculus
2Es 6:21 Infants a year old shall speak with their voices 1

sabbatical year 1. σάββατον
1Mc 6:49 since it was a sabbatical year for the land. 1

yearly 1. בְּשָׁנָה 2. יוֹם 3. מִיָּמִים יָמִימָה 4. κατ᾽ ἐνιαυτόν
Jdg 21:19 there is the yearly feast of the LORD at Shiloh 3
1Sm 1:21 went up to offer to the LORD the yearly sacrifice 2
2:19 she went up . . to offer the yearly sacrifice. 2
20: 6 there is a yearly sacrifice there for all 2
Neh 10:32 charge ourselves yearly with the third part 1
Heb 9:25 as the high priest enters the Holy Place yearly 4
1Mc 10:40 15,000 shekels of silver yearly 4

yearn 1. אוה 2. המה 3. הָמוֹן 4. כמר 5. ἐπιποθέω 6. κολλάω 7. ὄρεξις
Gen 43:30 made haste, for his heart yearned for his brother 4
1Kg 3:26 to the king, because her heart yearned for her son 4
Isa 26: 9 My soul yearns for thee in the night 1
63:15 The yearning of thy heart and thy compassion 3
Jer 31:20 Therefore my heart yearns for him; 2
Php 1: 8 how I yearn for you all 5
Tob 6:17 fell in love with her and yearned deeply for her. 6
Wis 15: 5 whose appearance arouses yearning in fools 7

yearn over 1. ἐπιποθέω
Jas 4: 5 He yearns jealously over the spirit 1

yearn toward 1. φιλόστοργος
4Mc 15:13 yearning of parents toward offspring 1

years of life 1. יְמֵי שְׁנוֹת
Ps 90:10 The years of our life are threescore and ten 1

yellow 1. צָהֹב
Lev 13:30 if . . the hair in it is yellow and thin 1
32 if . . there is in it no yellow hair 1
36 the priest need not seek for the yellow hair 1

yes 1. גַּם 2. כִּי 3. ἀλλά 4. ἀλλά γε 5. μᾶλλον δέ 6. ναί 7. τε 8. ita
Gen 20: 6 Yes, I know that you have done this 1
27:33 have blessed him?–yes, and he shall be blessed. 1
1Kg 20:33 took it up . . and said, "Yes, your brother Ben-ha'dad. *
2Kg 2: 3 And he said, "Yes, I know it; hold your peace. 1
5 he answered, "Yes, I know it; hold your peace. 1
Neh 4: 3 Yes, what they are building–if a fox goes up on it 1
Prv 2: 3 yes, if you cry out for insight 2
Mat 5:37 Let what you say be simply 'Yes' or 'No'; 6
9:28 They said to him, "Yes, Lord. 6
11: 9 Yes, I tell you, and more than a prophet. 6
13:51 They said to him, "Yes. 6
15:27 She said, "Yes, Lord, yet even the dogs eat the crumbs 6
17:25 He said "Yes. 6
21:16 Jesus said to them, "Yes 6
Mrk 7:28 Yes, Lord; yet even the dogs under the table eat *
Lke 7:26 Yes, I tell you, and more than a prophet. 6
11:51 Yes, I tell you, it shall be required 6
12: 5 yes, I tell you, fear him! 6
14:26 yes, and even his own life 7
24:21 Yes, and besides all this, it is now the third day 4
Joh 11:27 She said to him, "Yes, Lord; I believe 6
21:15 He said to him, "Yes, Lord; you know that I love you. 6
16 He said to him, "Yes, Lord; you know that I love you. 6
Act 5: 8 she said, "Yes, for so much. 6
22:27 Tell me, are you a Roman citizen?" And he said, "Yes. 6
Rom 3:29 God of Gentiles also? Yes, of Gentiles also 6
8:34 Jesus, who died, yes, who was raised from the dead 5
2Co 1:17 like a worldly man, ready to say Yes and No at once? 6
18 our word to you has not been Yes and No. 6
19 was not Yes and No; but in him it is always Yes. 6
19 was not Yes and No; but in him it is always Yes. 6
20 For all the promises of God find their Yes in him. 6
3:15 Yes, to this day whenever Moses is read 3
Php 1:19 Yes, and I shall rejoice. 3
Phm 1:20 Yes, brother, I want some benefit from you 6
Jas 5:12 let your yes be yes and your no be no 6
12 let your yes be yes and your no be no 6
2Es 4: 3 Then I said, "Yes, my lord. 8
Tob 7: 4 they said, "Yes, we do. *
4Mc 14: 9 yes, not only heard the direct word of threat 3

yesterday 1. אֶמֶשׁ 2. יוֹם אֶתְמוֹל 3. תְּמוֹל 4. ἐχθές
1Sm 20:27 not . . come to the meal, either yesterday or today? 3
2Sm 15:20 You came only yesterday, and shall I today 3
2Kg 9:26 As surely as I saw yesterday the blood 1
Job 8: 9 for we are but of yesterday, and know nothing 3
Ps 90: 4 1,000 years in thy sight are but as yesterday 2
Joh 4:52 Yesterday at the seventh hour the fever left him. 4
Act 7:28 kill me as you killed the Egyptian yesterday?' 4
Heb 13: 8 Jesus Christ is the same yesterday and today 4
Sir 38:22 yesterday it was mine, and today it is yours. 4

yet 1. אוּלַי 2. אָז 3. אַךְ 4. אִם 5. אַף 6. אֶפֶס 7. בְּזֶה 8. גַּם 9. וְ 10. וְגַם 11. וְעַתָּה 12. טֶרֶם 13. יסף 14. כִּי 15. כִּי גַּם 16. לָכֵן 17. מִבְּלִי 18. מִן 19. נָא 20. עַד 21. עַד הַיָּמִים הָהֵם 22. עַד הֵן 23. עַד כֹּה 24. עַד כֵּן 25. עֲדֶנָה 26. עַד עַתָּה 27. עוֹד 28. רַק 29. אָחֳרָן (A) 30. ἀλλά 31. ἅμα 32. γάρ 33. γε 34. δέ 35. ἔτι 36. καί 37. καίτοι 38. μέντοι 39. μηδέπω 40. μήπω 41. ὅμως 42. οὐδέπω 43. οὔπω 44. πάλιν 45. πλήν 46. προστίθημι 47. τε 48. ὡς 49. adhuc 50. attamen 51. autem 52. enim 53. et 54. faceo 55. iterato 56. nam 57. necdum 58. nondum 59. sed 60. sed tamen 61. si enim 62. tamen
Gen 3:16 yet your desire shall be for your husband 9
15:16 iniquity of the Amorites is not yet complete. 22
21: 7 Yet I have borne him a son in his old age. 14
31: 7 yet your father has cheated me 9
32:30 seen God . . and yet my life is preserved. *
37: 8 they hated him yet more for his dreams 27
38: 5 Yet again she bore a son 27
40:23 Yet the chief butler did not remember Joseph 9
45: 6 there are yet five years in which there will be 27
11 for there are yet five years of famine to come; 27
49:24 yet his bow remained unmoved 9
Exd 3: 2 the bush was burning, yet it was not consumed. 9
5:16 No straw is given to your servants, yet they say 9
18 no straw . . yet you shall deliver the same 9
7:16 and behold, you have not yet obeyed. 23
9:30 I know that you do not yet fear the LORD God. 12
34 he sinned yet again, and hardened his heart *
10: 7 do you not yet understand that Egypt is ruined? 12
11: 1 The LORD said to Moses, "Yet one plague more I will 27
21:22 a miscarriage, and yet no harm follows 9
33:12 Yet thou hast said, 'I know you by name 9
Lev 5: 1 yet does not speak, he shall bear his iniquity 4
17 though he does not know it, yet he is guilty 9
10:19 yet such things as these have befallen me *
11:21 Yet among the winged insects that go on all fours 3
18:18 while her sister is yet alive *
19:20 betrothed to another man and not yet ransomed *
22:13 yet no outsider shall eat of it 9
26:44 Yet for all that, when they are in the land 5
Num 9:13 yet refrains from keeping the passover 9
11:33 While the meat was yet between their teeth 27
13:28 Yet the people who dwell in the land are strong 6
14:22 yet have put me to the proof these ten times *
Deu 1:26 Yet you would not go up, but rebelled 9
32 Yet in spite of this word you did not believe 9
10:15 yet the LORD set his heart in love upon 28
12: 9 not as yet come to the rest and to the inheritance 26
14: 7 Yet of those . . you shall not eat these 3
22:17 yet these are the tokens of . . virginity *
31:27 behold, while I am yet alive with you, today 27
Jos 3: 4 Yet there shall be a space between you and it 3
5: 5 yet all the people that were born on the way 9
13: 1 there remains yet very much land *
2 This is the land that yet remains: *
13 Yet . . Israel did not drive out the Gesh'urites 9
14: 8 my brethren . . yet I wholly followed the LORD 9
17:12 Yet . . Manas'seh could not take possession 9
16 yet all the Canaanites . . have chariots of iron 9
18: 2 inheritance had not yet been apportioned. *
Jdg 2:17 yet they did not listen to their judges; 8
8: 4 300 men who were with him, faint yet pursuing. 9
10:13 Yet you have forsaken me and served other gods; 9
20:28 Shall we yet again go out to battle against our 27
21:18 Yet we cannot give them wives of our daughters. 9
Rut 1:11 Have I yet sons in my womb that they may become 27
3:12 I am a near kinsman, yet there is a kinsman nearer 8
1Sm 3: 3 the lamp of God had not yet gone out 12
7 Now Samuel did not yet know the LORD 12
7 word of the LORD had not yet been revealed to him. 12
8: 3 Yet his sons did not walk in his ways 9
12:20 you have done all this . . yet do not turn aside 3
15:30 I have sinned; yet honor me now before the elders 19
16:11 And he said, "There remains yet the youngest 27
20:26 Yet Saul did not say anything that day; 9
25:15 Yet the men were very good to us 9
2Sm 1: 9 anguish has seized me, and yet my life . . lingers.' 27
3: 8 I keep showing loyalty . . and yet you charge me *
35 persuade David to eat bread while it was yet day; 27
5:22 the Philistines came up yet again 27
7:19 yet this was a small thing in thy eyes, O Lord GOD; 27
12:18 while the child was yet alive, we spoke *
1Kg 3: 2 because no house had yet been built for the name 21
8:28 Yet have regard to the prayer of thy servant 9
47 yet if they lay it to heart 9
11:12 Yet for the sake of David your father I will not 3
17 Hadad fled . . Hadad being yet a little child. *
36 Yet to his son I will give one tribe 9
12: 6 his father while he was yet alive *
14: 8 and yet you have not been like my servant David *
19:18 Yet I will leave 7,000 in Israel 9
22: 8 There is yet one man by whom we may inquire 27
43 yet the high places were not taken away 3
2Kg 2:10 You have asked a hard thing; yet, if you see me *
8:19 Yet the LORD would not destroy Judah 9
14: 3 And he did . . yet not like David his father; 28
17: 2 did what was evil . . yet not as the kings of Israel 28
13 Yet the LORD warned Israel and Judah 9
1Ch 5: 2 yet the birthright belonged to Joseph 9
12:19 Yet he did not help them, for the rulers 9
14:13 Philistines yet again made a raid in the valley. 27
27:24 yet wrath came upon Israel for this 9
28: 4 Yet the LORD God of Israel chose me from all 9
2Ch 6:19 Yet have regard to the prayer of thy servant 9
37 yet if they lay it to heart in the land 9
10: 6 before Solomon his father while he was yet alive *
13: 6 Yet Jerobo'am . . rose up and rebelled against 9
16: 8 Yet because you relied on the LORD 9
12 yet even in his disease he did not seek the LORD 9
18: 7 yet one man by whom we may inquire of the LORD 27
20:33 people had not yet set their hearts upon the God 27
21: 7 Yet the LORD would not destroy the house of David 9
24:19 Yet he sent prophets among them 9
25: 2 yet not with a blameless heart. 28
30:18 yet they ate the passover 14
34: 3 eighth year of his reign, while he was yet a boy 27
Ezr 3: 6 foundation of the temple . . was not yet laid. *
5:16 been in building, and it is not yet finished.' *
9: 9 yet our God has not forsaken us in our bondage 9
Neh 2:16 I had not yet told the Jews, the priests, the nobles 24
5: 5 yet we are forcing our sons and our daughters *
18 yet with all this I did not demand the food 9
9:28 yet when they turned and cried to thee 9
29 Yet they acted presumptuously and did not obey 9
30 thy prophets; yet they would not give ear. 9
33 Yet thou hast been just in all that has come upon 9
13: 2 yet our God turned the curse into a blessing. 9
18 Yet you bring more wrath upon Israel 9
Est 5:13 Yet all this does me no good, so long as I see 9
6:14 While they were yet talking with him, 27
Job 1:16 While he was yet speaking, there came another 27
17 While he was yet speaking, there came another, 27
18 While he was yet speaking, there came another 27
4: 2 Yet who can keep from speaking? 9
8:12 While yet in flower and not cut down, they wither 27
21 He will yet fill your mouth with laughter 20
9:31 yet thou wilt plunge me into a pit 2
10:13 Yet these things thou didst hide in thy heart; 9
13:15 yet I will defend my ways to his face. 3
14: 9 yet at the scent of water it will bud 18
17: 9 Yet the righteous holds to his way 9
20:14 yet his food is turned in his stomach; *
22:18 Yet he filled their houses with good things– 9
24:12 yet God pays no attention to their prayer. 9
22 Yet God prolongs the life of the mighty 9
29: 5 when the Almighty was yet with me 27
30:24 Yet does not one in a heap of ruins stretch out 3
36: 2 for I have yet something to say on God's behalf. 27
39:16 though her labor be in vain, yet she has no fear; *
Ps 8: 5 Yet thou hast made him little less than God 9
19: 4 yet their voice goes out through all the earth *
22: 3 Yet thou art holy, enthroned on the praises 9
9 Yet thou art he who took me from the womb; 14
27: 3 war arise against me, yet I will be confident. 7
37:10 Yet a little while, and the wicked will be no more; 27
25 yet I have not seen the righteous forsaken 9
44: 9 Yet thou hast cast us off and abased us 5
55:21 was smoother than butter, yet war was in his heart; 9
21 were softer than oil, yet they were drawn swords. 9
66:12 yet hou hast brought us forth to a spacious place. 9
71:14 and will praise thee yet more and more. *
74:12 Yet God my King is from of old, working salvation 9
77:19 yet thy footprints were unseen. 9
78:17 Yet they sinned still more against him 27
23 Yet he commanded the skies above 9
38 Yet he, being compassionate, forgave 9
56 Yet they tested and rebelled 9
90:10 yet their span is but toil and trouble; 9
106: 8 Yet he saved them for his name's sake 9
119:83 yet I have not forgotten thy statutes. *
141 yet I do not forget thy precepts. *
129: 2 yet they have not prevailed against me. 8
139:16 when as yet there was none of them. *
Prv 11:24 One man gives freely, yet grows all the richer; 27
13: 7 One man pretends to be rich, yet has nothing; 9
7 another pretends to be poor, yet has great wealth. 9
27:22 yet his folly will not depart from him. *

29: 1 He who is often reproved, yet stiffens his neck •
30:25 yet they provide their food in the summer; 9
26 yet they make their homes in the rocks; 9
27 locusts have no king, yet all of them march in rank; 9
28 yet it is in kings' palaces. 9
31:15 She rises while it is yet night and provides food 27
Ecc 1:11 any remembrance of later things yet to happen •
2:14 yet I perceived that one fate comes to all of them. 8
19 Yet he will be master of all for which I toiled 9
3:11 yet so that he cannot find out what God has done 17
4: 3 better than both is he who has not yet been 25
8 has no one . . yet there is no end to all his toil 9
16 Yet those who come later will not rejoice in him. 8
5: 8 and there are yet higher ones over them. •
6: 2 God gives . . yet God does not give him power 9
5 yet it finds rest rather than he. •
6 Even though he should live . . yet enjoy no good 9
7 the toil . . yet his appetite is not satisfied. 10
8:12 Though a sinner does evil . . yet I know that 15
9:15 Yet no one remembered that poor man. 9
Isa 11:11 the Lord will extend his hand yet a second time 13
15: 9 yet I will bring upon Dibon even more 14
17:11 yet the harvest will flee away in a day of grief •
28:12 and this is repose"; yet they would not hear. 9
29: 2 Yet I will distress Ariel 9
17 Is it not yet a very little while until Lebanon 27
30:20 yet your Teacher will not hide himself any more 9
31: 2 yet he is wise and brings disaster 8
43: 8 the people who are blind, yet have eyes 9
8 blind, yet have eyes, who are deaf, yet have ears! 9
22 Yet you did not call upon me, O Jacob; 9
46:10 from ancient times things not yet done, saying •
49: 4 yet surely my right is with the LORD •
15 Even these may forget, yet I will not forget you. 9
20 The children . . of your bereavement will yet say 27
50:10 has no light, yet trusts in the name of the LORD •
53: 4 yet we esteemed him stricken, smitten by God 9
7 and he was afflicted, yet he opened not his mouth; 9
10 Yet it was the will of the LORD to bruise him; 9
12 yet he bore the sin of many, and made intercession 9
56: 8 I will gather yet others to him 27
58: 2 Yet they seek me daily and delight to know my ways 9
64: 8 Yet, O LORD, thou art our Father; we are the clay 11
65:24 while they are yet speaking I will hear. 27
Jer 2:21 Yet I planted you a choice vine 9
32 Yet my people have forgotten me 9
34 Yet in spite of all these things 14
3: 3 yet you have a harlot's brow 9
8 yet her false sister Judah did not fear 9
10 Yet . . her false sister Judah did not return to me 9
4:27 yet I will not make a full end. 9
5: 2 As the LORD lives," yet they swear falsely. 16
7:26 yet they did not listen to me, or incline their ear 9
9:25 who are circumcised but yet uncircumcised– •
11: 8 Yet they did not obey or incline their ear 9
12: 1 yet I would plead my case before thee. 3
14: 9 Yet thou, O LORD, art in the midst of us 9
15: 1 yet my heart would not turn toward this people. •
10 nor have I borrowed, yet all of them curse me. •
17:23 Yet they did not listen or incline their ear 9
18:20 Yet they have dug a pit for my life. 14
23 Yet, thou, O LORD, knowest all their plotting 9
22: 6 yet surely I will make you a desert •
24 ring on my right hand, yet I would tear you off 14
23:21 I did not send the prophets, yet they ran; 9
21 I did not speak to them, yet they prophesied. 9
25: 7 Yet you have not listened to me, says the LORD 9
28: 7 Yet hear now this word which I speak 3
30: 7 yet he shall be saved out of it. 9
32:25 Yet thou, O Lord GOD, hast said to me, "Buy the field 9
34: 4 Yet hear the word of the LORD, O Zedeki'ah 3
36:24 Yet neither the king, nor any of his servants 9
37: 4 for he had not yet been put in prison. •
44: 4 Yet I persistently sent to you all my servants 9
48:47 Yet I will restore the fortunes of Moab 9
51:33 yet a little while and the time of her harvest 27
53 yet destroyers would come from me upon her •
Lam 3:29 his mouth in the dust–there may yet be hope; 1
Ezk 5: 9 I will do with you what I have never yet done •
6: 8 Yet I will leave some of you alive. 9
11:16 yet I have been a sanctuary to them for a while 9
12:13 yet he shall not see it; and he shall die there. 9
13: 6 yet they expect him to fulfil their word. •
14: 4 yet comes to the prophet, I the LORD will answer •
7 yet comes to a prophet to inquire for himself •
22 Yet, if there should be left in it any survivors 9
15: 7 from the fire, the fire shall yet consume them; •
16: 7 your hair had grown; yet you were naked and bare. 9
31 Yet you were not like a harlot 9
47 Yet you were not content to walk in their ways 9
60 yet I will remember my covenant with you 9
17:15 Can he break the covenant and yet escape? •
18 he gave his hand and yet did all these things •
18:19 Yet you say, 'Why should not the son suffer 9
25 Yet you say, 'The way of the Lord is not just.' 9
29 Yet the house of Israel says, 'The way of the Lord is 9
23:11 yet she was more corrupt than she in her doting 9
19 Yet she increased her harlotry 9
24:16 yet you shall not mourn or weep 9

28: 2 yet you are but a man, and no god 9
29:18 yet neither he nor his army got anything 9
33:13 yet if he trusts in his righteousness 9
14 You shall surely die,' yet if he turns from his sin 9
17 Yet your people say, 'The way of the Lord is not just 9
20 Yet you say, 'The way of the Lord is not just.' 9
24 was only one man, yet he got possession of the land; 9
36:20 yet they had to go out of his land. •
44:14 Yet I will appoint them to keep charge 9
Dan 2:39 arise . . yet a third kingdom of bronze 29
9:13 yet we have not entreated the favor of the LORD 9
10:14 For the vision is for days yet to come. 27
11:27 for the end is yet to be at the time appointed. 27
35 end, for it is yet for the time appointed. 27
45 yet he shall come to his end, with none to help him. 9
Hos 1: 4 for yet a little while, and I will punish the house 27
10 Yet the number of the people of Israel shall be 9
4: 4 Yet let no one contend, and let none accuse 3
7:10 yet they do not return to the LORD their God 9
15 yet they devise evil against me. 9
9: 8 yet a fowler's snare is on all his ways •
11: 3 Yet it was I who taught E'phraim to walk 9
Jol 2:12 Yet even now," says the LORD, "return to me 9
Ams 2: 9 Yet I destroyed the Amorite before them 9
4: 6 yet you did not return to me," says the LORD. 9
7 when there were yet three months to the harvest; 27
8 yet you did not return to me," says the LORD. 9
9 yet you did not return to me," says the LORD. 9
10 yet you did not return to me," says the LORD. 9
11 yet you did not return to me," says the LORD. 9
Jon 2: 6 yet thou didst bring up my life from the Pit, O LORD 9
3: 4 Yet 40 days, and Nin'eveh shall be overthrown! 27
9 God may yet repent and turn from his fierce anger •
4: 2 is not this what I said when I was yet in my country? 20
Mic 3:11 yet they lean upon the LORD and say 9
Nah 3:10 Yet she was carried away, she went into captivity; 8
Hab 3:18 yet I will rejoice in the LORD 9
Zep 1: 5 and swear to the LORD and yet swear by Milcom; •
Hag 1: 2 the time has not yet come to rebuild the house •
2: 4 Yet now take courage, O Zerub'babel, says the LORD; 9
17 yet you did not return to me, says the LORD. 9
19 Is the seed yet in the barn? 27
Zec 8:20 says the LORD of hosts: Peoples shall yet come 27
10: 9 yet in far countries they shall remember me 9
Mal 1: 2 Yet I have loved Jacob 9
14 and yet sacrifices to the LORD what is blemished; •
2:17 Yet you say, "How have we wearied him? 9
3: 8 Will man rob God? Yet you are robbing me. 14
13 Yet you say, 'How have we spoken against thee?' 9
Mat 6:26 barns, and yet your heavenly Father feeds them. •
29 yet I tell you, even Solomon in all his glory was not 34
11:11 yet he who is least in the kingdom of heaven 34
19 Yet wisdom is justified by her deeds. 36
13:21 yet he has no root in himself 34
15:27 She said, "Yes, Lord, yet even the dogs eat the crumbs 32
16: 9 Do you not yet perceive? 43
24: 6 this must take place, but the end is not yet. 43
Mrk 4:32 yet when it is sown it grows up 36
5:31 yet you say, 'Who touched me?' •
6:20 yet he heard him gladly. •
7:24 yet he could not be hid. 36
28 Yes, Lord; yet even the dogs under the table eat •
8:17 Do you not yet perceive or understand? 43
21 he said to them, "Do you not yet understand? 43
13: 7 this must take place, but the end is not yet. 43
14:36 yet not what I will, but what thou wilt. 30
59 Yet not even so did their testimony agree. 36
Lke 7:28 yet he who is least in the kingdom of God 34
35 Yet wisdom is justified by all her children. 36
11: 8 yet because of his importunity he will rise 33
12:24 yet God feeds them •
27 yet I tell you, even Solomon in all his glory 34
14:32 while the other is yet a great way off 35
15:20 while he was yet at a distance 35
29 yet you never gave me a kid, that I might make merry 36
18: 5 yet because this widow bothers me 33
20:12 he sent yet a third 46
Joh 1:10 yet the world knew him not. 36
2: 4 Jesus said to her . . My hour has not yet come. 43
3:10 a teacher . . and yet you do not understand this? •
24 For John had not yet been put in prison. 43
32 yet no one receives his testimony; 36
4:35 'There are yet four months, then comes the harvest'? 35
5:40 yet you refuse to come to me 36
6:17 and Jesus had not yet come to them. 43
36 you have seen me and yet do not believe. •
7: 6 Jesus said to them, "My time has not yet come 43
8 my time has not yet fully come. 43
13 Yet for fear of the Jews no one spoke openly 38
19 Yet none of you keeps the law. 36
27 Yet we know where this man comes from; 30
30 because his hour had not yet come. 43
31 Yet many of the people believed in him; they said 34
39 as yet the Spirit had not been given 43
39 because Jesus was not yet glorified. 42
8:16 Yet even if I do judge, my judgment is true 36
20 because his hour had not yet come. 43
37 yet you seek to kill me 30
50 Yet I do not seek my own glory 34

57 You are not yet fifty years old 43
9:30 and yet he opened my eyes. •
11:25 who believes in me, though he die, yet shall he live •
30 Now Jesus had not yet come to the village 43
12:37 yet they did not believe in him; 34
13:33 Little children, yet a little while I am with you. 35
14: 9 yet you do not know me, Philip? •
19 Yet a little while 35
16: 5 yet none of you asks me, 'Where are you going?' 36
12 I have yet many things to say to you 35
32 yet I am not alone, for the Father is with me. 36
20: 9 for as yet they did not know the scripture 42
17 for I have not yet ascended to the Father 43
29 those who have not seen and yet believe. •
21: 4 yet the disciples did not know that it was Jesus. 38
23 yet Jesus did not say to him that he was not to die 34
Act 5:28 yet here you have filled Jerusalem 36
7: 5 yet he gave him no inheritance in it 36
48 Yet the Most High does not dwell in houses 30
8:16 for it had not yet fallen on any of them 42
13:28 yet they asked Pilate to have him killed. •
14:17 yet he did not leave himself without witness 37
17:27 Yet he is not far from each one of us 33
23: 3 yet contrary to the law you order me to be struck? •
28:17 yet I was delivered prisoner from Jerusalem •
Rom 2: 3 and yet do them yourself 36
5: 8 while we were yet sinners Christ died for us. 35
14 Yet death reigned from Adam to Moses 30
7: 7 Yet, if it had not been for the law 30
9:11 though they were not yet born 40
1Co 2: 6 Yet among the mature we do impart wisdom 34
3: 2 even yet you are not ready 35
7:28 Yet those who marry will have worldly troubles 34
8: 2 he does not yet know as he ought to know. 43
6 yet for us there is one God, the Father 30
12:20 As it is, there are many parts, yet one body. 34
2Co 6: 8 We are treated as impostors, and yet are true; •
9 as unknown, and yet well known •
9 as punished, and yet not killed; •
10 as sorrowful, yet always rejoicing 34
10 as poor, yet making many rich 34
10 as having nothing, and yet possessing •
8: 9 yet for your sake he became poor •
Gal 2:16 yet who know that a man is not justified by works 34
Php 1:22 Yet which I shall choose I cannot tell. 36
4:14 Yet it was kind of you to share my trouble. 45
Col 2: 5 yet I am with you in spirit 30
1Ti 2:15 Yet woman will be saved 34
2Ti 3:11 yet from them all the Lord rescued me. 36
Phm 1: 9 yet for love's sake I prefer to appeal to you–I, Paul •
Heb 2: 8 do not yet see everything in subjection to him. 43
3: 3 Yet Jesus has been counted worthy of . . glory 32
16 Who were they that heard and yet were rebellious? •
4:15 who . . has been tempted as we are, yet without sin. •
6: 9 yet in your case, beloved 34
9: 8 the way into the sanctuary is not yet opened 40
10:37 yet a little while, and the coming one shall come 35
11: 7 being warned by God concerning events as yet unseen 39
12: 4 not yet resisted to the point of . . blood 43
26 Yet once more I will shake not only the earth 35
27 This phrase, "Yet once more," indicates . . 35
Jas 2:13 yet mercy triumphs over judgement. •
1Pe 2:16 Live as free men, yet without using your freedom 36
3:15 yet do it with gentleness and reverence; 30
4:16 yet if one suffers as a Christian 34
1Jn 2: 8 Yet I am writing you a new commandment 44
3: 2 it does not yet appear what we shall be 43
17 sees . . in need, yet closes his heart against him 36
Jde 1: 8 Yet in like manner these men . . defile the flesh 36
Rev 2: 6 Yet this you have, you hate . . the Nicola'itans 30
3: 4 Yet you have still a few names in Sardis 30
8 yet you have kept my word and . . not denied my name •
13:14 which was wounded by the sword and yet lived; •
17:10 seven kings . . one is, the other has not yet come 43
12 ten kings who have not yet received royal power 43
1Es 4: 7 yet he is only one man! •
29 Yet I have seen him with Apame •
5:53 though the temple of God was not yet built. 43
6: 5 Yet the elders of the Jews were dealt with kindly 36
20 it has not yet reached completion.' •
2Es 1:14 Yet you have forgotten me, says the Lord. 51
36 yet will recall their former state. 53
37 yet with the spirit they will believe the things 59
3: 5 Yet he was the workmanship of thy hands 59
20 Yet thou didst not take away from them 53
33 Yet their reward has not appeared •
4: 8 nor as yet into hell 49
28 sown, but the harvest of it has not yet come. 57
5:13 you shall hear yet greater things than these. 55
36 Count up for me those who have not yet come 57
41 I said, "Yet behold, O Lord 59
6:39 the sound of man's voice was not yet there. 58
7:31 after seven days the world, which is not yet awake 58
132those who have not yet come into the world; 58
8:41 and yet not all that have been sown will come up 59
9:32 yet the fruit of the law did not perish 54
33 Yet those who received it perished 56
35 yet with us it has not been so. 61
11:20 some . . that ruled, yet disappeared suddenly; 60

13: 8 all . . were much afraid, yet dared to fight. 62
20 Yet it is better to come into these things 50
28 yet destroying the onrushing multitude 52
16:20 Yet for all this they will not turn 53
Jdt 9: 2 'It shall not be done'-yet they did it. 36
13:16 yet he committed no act of sin with me *
Wis 4:15 Yet the peoples saw and did not understand 34
9: 6 yet without the wisdom that comes from thee *
13: 6 Yet these men are little to be blamed 41
8 Yet again, not even they are to be excused; 34
17: 9 yet, scared by the passing of beasts *
18:13 yet, when their first-born were destroyed *
Sir 17:24 Yet to those who repent he grants a return 45
31 Yet its light fails 30
28: 3 yet seek for healing from the Lord? *
4 yet pray for his own sins? *
30: 4 The father may die, and yet he is not dead 48
32: 8 be as one who knows and yet holds his tongue. 31
36:18 yet one food is better than another. 34
37:19 yet be unprofitable to himself. *
38:33 Yet they are not sought out 30
49: 7 yet he had been consecrated in the womb 36
Bar 2: 8 Yet we have not entreated the favor of the Lord 36
10 Yet we have not obeyed his voice, to walk 36
27 'Yet thou hast dealt with us, O Lord our God 36
LJr 1:42 Yet they themselves cannot perceive this 36
Aza 1:16 Yet with a contrite heart . . may we be accepted 30
Sus 1:43 Yet I have done none of the things *
Man 1: 6 yet immeasurable . . is thy promised mercy 47
1Mc 2:20 yet I and my sons and my brothers will live *
8:14 Yet for all this not one of them has put on a crown 36
2Mc 6:26 yet whether I live or die 30
7:35 You have not yet escaped the judgment 43
8:15 yet for the sake of the covenants 30
9: 7 Yet he did not in any way stop his insolence 34
3Mc 5:26 The rays of the sun were not yet shed abroad 43
4Mc 6: 6 yet while the old man's eyes were raised to heaven 30
15: 8 yet because of the fear of God *
16:12 Yet the sacred . . mother did not wail 30
18:20 O bitter was that day-and yet not bitter- *

yet *See also* again, even, ever, more, no, unborn, while.

yet to be 1. בוא
Isa 44: 7 Let them tell us what is yet to be. 1

yield 1. אבה 2. גדל 3. גֶּרֶשׁ 4. זרע 5. כֹּחַ 6. נשא 7. נשא 8. נתן 9. נתן יָד 10. עשה 11. שוה 12. תְּבוּאָה 13. ἀποδίδωμι 14. δίδωμι 15. εἴκω 16. ἐκδίδωμι 17. παρίστημι 18. πείθω 19. ποιέω 20. συνείκω 21. ὑπείκω 22. ὑποτάσσω 23. φέρω
Gen 1:11 put forth vegetation, plants yielding seed 4
29 I have given . . every plant yielding seed 4
4:12 the ground . . shall no longer yield to you 8
49:20 be rich, and he shall yield royal dainties. 8
Exd 23:10 shall sow your land and gather in its yield; 12
Lev 19:25 that they may yield more richly for you 12
25: 7 in your land all its yield shall be for food 12
12 you shall eat what it yields out of the field 12
19 The land will yield its fruit, and you will eat 8
26: 4 the land shall yield its increase 8
4 the trees of the field shall yield their fruit 8
20 your land shall not yield its increase 8
20 the trees of the land shall not yield their fruit 8
Num20: 8 rock before their eyes to yield its water; 8
Deu 11:17 no rain, and the land yield no fruit, and you perish 8
13: 8 you shall not yield to him or listen to him 1
14:22 You shall tithe all the yield of your seed 12
22: 9 crop . . sown and the yield of the vineyard. 12
33:14 with the . . rich yield of the months 3
2Ch 30: 8 but yield yourselves to the LORD, and come 9
32:28 storehouses also for the yield of grain, wine 12
Neh 9:37 rich yield goes to the kings whom thou hast set 12
Job 31:39 if I have eaten its yield without payment 5
40:20 For the mountains yield food for him 6
Ps 1: 3 a tree . . that yields its fruit in its season 8
67: 6 The earth has yielded its increase; 8
85:12 our land will yield its increase. 8
107:37 sow . . plant . . , and get a fruitful yield. 12
Prv 8:19 my yield than choice silver. 12
13:23 The fallow ground of the poor yields much food *
18:20 man . . is satisfied by the yield of his lips. 12
Sng 5:13 like beds of spices, yielding fragrance. 2
Isa 5: 2 he looked for it to yield grapes 10
2 to yield grapes, but it yielded wild grapes. 10
4 When I looked for it to yield grapes 10
4 to yield grapes, why did it yield wild grapes? 10
10 ten acres of vineyard shall yield but one bath 10
10 a homer of seed shall yield but an ephah. 10
Ezk 34:27 the trees of the field shall yield their fruit 8
27 and the earth shall yield its increase 8
36: 8 and yield your fruit to my people Israel; 7
Hos 8: 7 grain has no heads, it shall yield no meal; 10
7 if it were to yield, aliens would devour it. 10
10: 1 a luxuriant vine that yields its fruit. 11
Hab 3:17 the olive fail and the fields yield no food 10
Hag 2:19 and the olive tree still yield nothing? 6
Zec 8:12 sowing of peace; the vine shall yield its fruit 8
Mat 13:23 he indeed bears fruit, and yields 19
Mrk 4: 7 it yielded no grain. 14
8 growing up and increasing and yielding 23
Lke 8: 8 some . . grew, and yielded a hundredfold 19
Act 23:21 do not yield to them 18
Rom 6:13 Do not yield your members to sin 17
13 but yield yourselves to God 17
16 if you yield . . to any one as obedient slaves 17
19 as you once yielded your members to impurity 17
19 so now yield your members to righteousness 17
Gal 2: 5 we did not yield submission even for a moment 15
Heb 12:11 later it yields the . . fruit of righteousness 13
Jas 3:12 Can a fig tree, my brethren, yield olives 19
12 No more can salt water yield fresh. 19
Rev 22: 2 tree of life . . yielding its fruit each month; 13
Jdt 2:10 They will yield themselves to you 16
Wis 18:25 To these the destroyer yielded, these he feared; 15
2Mc 13:23 yielded and swore to observe all their rights 22
4Mc 6:35 and in no respect yields to them. 21
8: 5 I also exhort you to yield to me 20

full yield 1. חַיִל
Jol 2:22 and fig tree and vine give their full yield. 1

really yield 1. facio
2Es 7:13 and really yield the fruit of immortality. 1

yield seed 1. זרע
Gen 1:12 brought forth vegetation, plants yielding seed 1

yield to persuasion 1. πείθω
4Mc 12: 5 if you yield to persuasion you will be my friend 1

yield up 1. יהב (A) 2. ἀφίημι 3. reddo
Dan 3:28 yielded up their bodies rather than serve 1
Mat 27:50 Jesus cried . . and yielded up his spirit. 2
2Es 7:75 as soon as every one of us yields up his soul 3

whole yield 1. מְלֵאָה
Deu 22: 9 lest the whole yield be forfeited 1

yoke 1. אסר 2. כְּלִי 3. מוט 4. מוֹטָה 5. על 6. צמד 7. צֶמֶד 8. ζεῦγος 9. ζυγός
Gen 27:40 but when you break loose you shall break his yoke 5
Lev 26:13 I have broken the bars of your yoke 5
Num19: 2 red heifer . . upon which a yoke has never come. 5
25: 3 Israel yoked himself to Ba'al of Pe'or. 6
5 men who have yoked themselves to Ba'al of Pe'or. 6
Deu 21: 3 heifer . . which has not pulled in the yoke. 5
28:48 he will put a yoke of iron upon your neck, until 5
1Sm 6: 7 two . . cows upon which there has never come a yoke 5
7 yoke the cows to the cart, but take their calves 1
10 and took two milch cows and yoked them to the cart 1
11: 7 He took a yoke of oxen, and cut them in pieces 7
2Sm 24:22 the threshing sledges and the yokes of the oxen 2
1Kg 12: 4 Your father made our yoke heavy. 5
4 lighten . . his heavy yoke upon us 5
9 'Lighten the yoke that your father put upon us'? 5
10 'Your father made our yoke heavy 5
11 my father laid upon you a heavy yoke, I will add 5
11 laid upon you a heavy yoke, I will add to your yoke. 5
14 My father made your yoke heavy, but I will add 5
14 made your yoke heavy, but I will add to your yoke; 5
19:21 and took the yoke of oxen, and slew them, and boiled 7
21 and boiled their flesh with the yokes of the oxen 2
2Ch 10: 4 Your father made our yoke heavy. 5
4 lighten the hard service . . and his heavy yoke 5
9 'Lighten the yoke that your father put upon us'? 5
10 'Your father made our yoke heavy 5
11 now, whereas my father laid upon you a heavy yoke 5
11 laid . . a heavy yoke, I will add to your yoke. 5
14 My father made your yoke heavy, but I will add to it; 5
Job 1: 3 3,000 camels, 500 yoke of oxen 7
42:12 had 14,000 sheep, 6,000 camels, 1,000 yoke of oxen 7
Isa 9: 4 the yoke of his burden, and the staff for his 5
10:27 his yoke will be destroyed from your neck. 5
14:25 and his yoke shall depart from them 5
47: 6 on the aged you made your yoke exceedingly heavy. 5
58: 6 to undo the thongs of the yoke 4
6 the oppressed go free, and to break every yoke? 4
9 If you take away from the midst of you the yoke 4
Jer 2:20 For long ago you broke your yoke 5
5: 5 But they all alike had broken the yoke 5
27: 8 and put its neck under the yoke of the king 5
11 nation which will bring its neck under the yoke 5
12 Bring your necks under the yoke of the king 5
28: 2 I have broken the yoke of the king of Babylon. 5
4 for I will break the yoke of the king of Babylon. 5
11 Even so will I break the yoke of Nebuchadnez'zar 5
14 upon the neck of all these nations an iron yoke 5
30: 8 that I will break the yoke from off their neck 5
Lam 1:14 My transgressions were bound into a yoke; 5
3:27 good . . that he bear the yoke in his youth. 5
5: 5 With a yoke on our necks we are hard driven; 9
Ezk 34:27 when I break the bars of their yoke, and deliver 5
Hos 11: 4 as one, who eases the yoke on their jaws 5
7 so they are appointed to the yoke 5
Nah 1:13 And now I will break his yoke from off you 3
Mat 11:29 Take my yoke upon you, and learn from me 9
30 For my yoke is easy, and my burden is light. 9
Lke 14:19 another said, 'I have bought five yoke of oxen 8
Act 15:10 by putting a yoke upon the neck of the disciples 9
Gal 5: 1 do not submit again to a yoke of slavery. 9
1Ti 6: 1 all who are under the yoke of slavery 9
Sir 6:30 Her yoke is a golden ornament 5
28:19 who has not borne its yoke 9
20 for its yoke is a yoke of iron 9
20 for its yoke is a yoke of iron 9
33:26 Yoke and thong will bow the neck 9
40: 1 a heavy yoke is upon the sons of Adam 9
51:26 Put your neck under the yoke 9
1Mc 8:18 to free themselves from the yoke 9
31 Why have you made your yoke heavy 9
13:41 the yoke of the Gentiles was removed from Israel 9

yoke of oxen 1. צֶמֶד
1Kg 19:19 Eli'sha . . was plowing, with 12 yoke of oxen 1

ox yoke 1. βοοζύγιον
Sir 26: 7 An evil wife is an ox yoke which chafes 1

yoke-bar 1. מוֹטָה
Jer 27: 2 Make yourself thongs and yoke-bars 1
28:10 Then the prophet Hanani'ah took the yoke-bars 1
12 the prophet Hanani'ah had broken the yoke-bars 1

yokefellow 1. σύζυγος
Php 4: 3 I ask you also, true yokefellow, help these women 1

yon 1. זֶה
Jdg 5: 5 mountains quaked . . yon Sinai before the LORD 1
Ps 68: 8 yon Sinai quaked at the presence of God 1

yonder 1. הַלָּז 2. הַלָּזֶה 3. זֶה 4. כֹּה 5. עַד כֹּה 6. ἐκεῖ 7. ἐκεῖνος
Gen 19:20 Behold, yonder city is near enough to flee to 3
22: 5 I and the lad will go yonder and worship 5
24:65 said to the servant, "Who is the man yonder 2
Num13:17 Go up into the Negeb yonder, and go up into the hill 3
23:15 Stand here . . while I meet the LORD yonder. 4
1Sm 14: 1 go . . to the Philistine garrison on yonder side. 1
20:19 go to . . and remain beside yonder stone heap. 7
2Kg 4:25 he said . . "Look, yonder is the Shu'nammite; 1
23:17 Then he said, "What is yonder monument that I see? 1
Ps 104:25 Yonder is the sea, great and wide, which teems 3
Mat 26:36 Sit here, while I go yonder and pray. 6

young 1. אֶפְרֹחַ 2. בֵּן 3. בֶּן בָּקָר 4. גּוֹזָל 5. גור 6. חֵבֶל 7. טַף 8. יֶלֶד 9. נְעוּרִים 10. נַעַר 11. נַעֲרָה 12. עול 13. עַשְׁתְּרוֹת 14. צָעִיר 15. צָעִיר לְיָמִים 16. קָטֹן 17. קָטָן 18. בֵּן (A) 19. βλάστημα 20. ἐλάσσων 21. μικρός 22. νεάζω 23. νεανίσκος 24. νέος 25. νεότης 26. νεοττός 27. νεόφυτος 28. νήπιος 29. νοσσός 30. ὀξέως 31. τέκνον 32. iuvenis
Gen 9:24 knew what his youngest son had done to him 17
19: 4 the men of Sodom, both young and old 10
31 the first-born said to the younger 14
34 on the next day, the first-born said to the younger 14
35 and the younger arose, and lay with him; 14
38 The younger also bore a son, and called his name 14
25:23 the elder shall serve the younger. 14
27:15 and put them on Jacob her younger son; 17
42 she sent and called Jacob her younger son 17
29:16 was Leah, and the name of the younger was Rachel. 17
18 seven years for your younger daughter Rachel. 17
26 to give the younger before the first-born. 14
41:12 A young Hebrew was there with us, a servant 10
42:13 and behold, the youngest is this day with our 16
15 go from this place unless your youngest brother 16
20 bring your youngest brother to me; 16
32 the youngest is this day with our father 16
34 Bring your youngest brother to me; 16
43:29 Is this your youngest brother, of whom you spoke 16
33 and the youngest according to his youth; 14
44: 2 my cup . . in the mouth of the sack of the youngest 16
12 he searched . . ending with the youngest; 16
20 We have a father, an old man, and a young brother 17
23 Unless your youngest brother comes down 16
26 If our youngest brother goes with us, then we will 16
26 cannot . . unless our youngest brother is 16
48:14 the head of E'phraim, who was the younger 14
19 nevertheless his younger brother shall be 16
Exd 10: 9 Moses said, "We will go with our young and our old; 10
29: 1 Take one young bull and two rams without blemish 3
Lev 1:14 offering of turtledoves or of young pigeons 2
5: 7 bring . . two turtledoves or two young pigeons 2
11 afford two turtledoves or two young pigeons 2
12: 6 a young pigeon or a turtledove for a sin offering 2
8 take two turtledoves or two young pigeons 2
14:22 also two turtledoves or two young pigeons 2
30 offer . . young pigeons such as he can afford 2
15:14 take two turtledoves or two young pigeons 2
29 two turtledoves or two young pigeons 2
16: 3 with a young bull for a sin offering and a ram 3
22:28 you shall not kill both her and her young 2
23:18 present . . one young bull, and two rams 3
Num 6:10 bring two turtledoves or two young pigeons 2

28:11 burnt offering . . two young bulls, one ram 3
19 burnt offering . . two young bulls, one ram 3
27 burnt offering . . two young bulls, one ram 3
29:13 burnt offering . . thirteen young bulls 3
17 On the second day twelve young bulls, two rams 3
31:18 all the young girls who have not known man 7
Deu 7:13 bless . . the young of your flock 13
22: 6 mother sitting upon the young or upon the eggs 1
6 you shall not take the mother with the young; 2
7 let the mother go, but the young you may take 2
28: 4 Blessed shall be . . the young of your flock. 13
18 Cursed shall be . . the young of your flock. 13
50 who shall not . . show favor to the young 10
51 not leave you . . the young of your flock 13
32:11 Like an eagle that . . flutters over its young 4
Jos 6:21 all in the city, both men and women, young and old 10
Jdg 1:13 Oth'ni-el the son of Kenaz, Caleb's younger brother 16
3: 9 the son of Kenaz, Caleb's younger brother. 16
9: 5 Jotham the youngest son of Jerubba'al was left 16
15: 2 Is not her younger sister fairer than she? 17
18: 3 they recognized the voice of the young Levite; 10
15 and came to the house of the young Levite 10
21:12 found . . 400 young virgins who had not known man 11
1Sm 1:24 she took him up . . and the child was young. 10
5: 9 afflicted the men of the city, both young and old 16
14:49 and the name of the younger Michal; 17
16:11 And he said, "There remains yet the youngest 17
17:14 David was the youngest; 17
2Sm 9:12 Mephib'osheth had a young son, whose name was 17
1Kg 1: 2 Let a young maiden be sought for my lord the king 11
2Kg 3:21 who were able . . from the youngest to the oldest †
1Ch 22: 5 Solomon my son is young and inexperienced 10
24:31 head . . and his younger brother alike, cast lots 17
29: 1 Solomon my son . . is young and inexperienced 10
2Ch 13: 7 when Rehobo'am was young and irresolute 10
9 comes to consecrate himself with a young bull 3
15:13 put to death, whether young or old, man or woman. 16
21:17 left to him except Jeho'ahaz, his youngest son. 16
22: 1 made Ahazi'ah his youngest son king in his stead; 16
31:15 portions to their brethren, old and young alike 17
Ezr 6: 9 young bulls, rams, or sheep for burnt offerings 18
Est 2: 2 Let beautiful young virgins be sought out 11
3 to gather all the beautiful young virgins 11
3:13 annihilate all Jews, young and old, women 10
Job 14: 9 bud and put forth branches like a young plant. 27
30: 1 they make sport of me, men who are younger than I 15
32: 6 I am young in years, and you are aged; 14
39: 3 offspring, and are delivered of their young? 6
16 She deals cruelly with her young 2
Ps 37:25 I have been young, and now am old; 10
84: 3 where she may lay her young, at thy altars 1
144:14 may our cattle be heavy with young •
147: 9 food, and to the young ravens which cry. 2
Isa 11: 7 shall feed; their young shall lie down together; 8
20: 4 both the young and the old, naked and barefoot 10
34:15 lay and hatch and gather her young in her shadow; •
40:11 and gently lead those that are with young. 12
Jer 31:12 and over the young of the flock and the herd; 2
Lam 2:21 In the dust of . . streets lie the young and the old; 10
4: 3 jackals give the breast and suckle their young 5
Ezk 16:46 your younger sister, who lived to the south of you 16
61 your sisters, both your elder and your younger 16
23:21 your bosom and pressed your young breasts. 9
45:18 you shall take a young bull without blemish, 2
Mrk 15:40 Mary the mother of James the younger and of Joses 21
Lke 2:24 a pair of turtledoves, or two young pigeons. 29
15:12 the younger of them said to his father, 'Father 24
13 the younger son gathered all he had 24
22:26 the greatest among you become as the youngest 24
Joh 21:18 when you were young, you girded yourself 24
Rom 9:12 she was told, "The elder will serve the younger. 20
1Ti 5:11 refuse to enrol younger widows 24
14 I would have younger widows marry, bear children 24
1Pe 5: 5 you that are younger be subject to the elders. 24
2Es 2:22 Protect the old and the young within your walls; 32
5:50 Is our mother . . still young? 32
Wis 3:18 If they die young, they will have no hope 30
8:10 though I am young. 24
Sir 30:12 beat his sides while he is young 28
42: 8 the aged man who quarrels with the young 24
9 when she is young, lest she do not marry 25
50:12 like a young cedar on Lebanon 19
51:13 While I was still young 24
Sus 1:45 the holy spirit of a young lad named Daniel; 24
1Mc 11:54 the young boy Antiochus who began to reign 24
57 the young Antiochus wrote to Jonathan, saying 24
13:31 Trypho dealt treacherously with the young king 24
2Mc 5:13 Then there was killing of young and old 24
6:24 he said, "lest many of the young should suppose 24
28 leave to the young a noble example 24
31 not only to the young 24
7:24 The youngest brother being still alive 24
15:17 and awaking manliness in the souls of the young 24
4Mc 2: 3 when he was young 24
3:12 two staunch young soldiers 23
5:31 to be young in reason on behalf of piety. 22
6:19 become a pattern of impiety to the young 24
11:14 I am younger in age than my brothers 24
12: 1 the seventh and youngest of all came forward. 24
14:15 the ones that are tame protect their young 26
17 they do what they can to help their young 31
151 1: 1 and youngest in my father's house; 24

young *See also* ass, bring, bull, camel, cast, child, cow, ewe, goat, lion, locust, maiden, pigeon, plant, son, stag, steer, twig.

become young again 1. *ἀνανεάζω*

4Mc 7:13 Most amazing . . he became young again 1

young fellow 1. *μειράκιον*

4Mc 8:14 Be afraid, young fellows 1

young man 1. בָּחוּר 2. בֵּן 3. יֶלֶד 4. נַעַר 5. *ἐφήβος* 6. *νεανίας* 7. *νεανίσκος* 8. *νέος* 9. *παιδάριον* 10. iuvenis

Gen 4:23 I have slain . . a young man for striking me. 3
14:24 take nothing but what the young men have eaten 4
22: 3 took two of his young men with him, and his son 4
5 Then Abraham said to his young men, "Stay here 4
19 Abraham returned to his young men 4
34:19 the young man did not delay to do the thing 4
Exd 24: 5 he sent young men of the people of Israel 4
33:11 his servant Joshua the son of Nun, a young man 4
Num11:27 And a young man ran and told Moses 4
Deu 32:25 destroying both young man and virgin 1
Jos 6:23 the young men who had been spies went 4
Jdg 8:14 he caught a young man of Succoth, and questioned 4
9:54 called hastily to the young man his armor-bearer 4
54 And his young man thrust him through, and he died. 4
14:10 made a feast there; for so the young men used to do. 1
17: 7 there was a young man of Bethlehem in Judah 4
11 the young man became to him like one of his sons. 4
12 and the young man became his priest 4
19:19 and the young man with your servants; 4
Rut 2: 9 Have I not charged the young men not to molest you? 4
9 go . . and drink what the young men have drawn. 4
15 Bo'az instructed his young men, saying 4
3:10 you have not gone after young men . . poor or rich. 1
1Sm 2:17 Thus the sin of the young men was very great 4
9: 2 a son whose name was Saul, a handsome young man. 1
14: 1 Jonathan . . said to the young man who bore his armor 4
6 Jonathan said to the young man who bore his armor 4
16:18 One of the young men answered, "Behold, I have seen 4
17:58 Saul said to him, "Whose son are you, young man? 4
21: 2 I have made an appointment with the young men 4
4 if only the young men have kept . . from women. 4
5 the vessels of the young men are holy 4
25: 5 David sent ten young men; 4
5 and David said to the young men, "Go up to Carmel 4
8 Ask your young men, and they will tell you. 4
8 Therefore let my young men find favor 4
9 When David's young men came, they said all this 4
12 David's young men turned away, and came back 4
14 But one of the young men told Ab'igail, Nabal's wife 4
19 And she said to her young men, "Go on before me; 4
25 your handmaid did not see the young men of my lord 4
27 now let this present . . be given to the young men 4
26:22 Let one of the young men come over and fetch it. 4
30:13 I am a young man of Egypt, servant to an Amal'ekite; 4
17 not a man of them escaped, except 400 young men 4
2Sm 1: 5 Then David said to the young man who told him 4
6 And the young man who told him said, "By chance I 4
13 And David said to the young man who told him 4
15 Then David called one of the young men and said, "Go 4
2:14 Let the young men arise and play before us. 4
21 Turn aside . . and seize one of the young men 4
4:12 David commanded his young men, and they killed 4
13:17 He called the young man who served him and said 4
32 have killed all the young men the king's sons 4
34 young man who kept the watch lifted up his eyes 4
14:21 I grant this; go, bring back the young man Ab'salom. 4
16: 2 bread and summer fruit for the young men to eat 4
18: 5 Deal gently for my sake with the young man 4
12 'For my sake protect the young man Ab'salom.' 4
15 ten young men . . surrounded Ab'salom and struck 4
29 Is it well with the young man Ab'salom? 4
32 king said . . "Is it well with the young man Ab'salom? 4
32 May the enemies of . . be like that young man. 4
1Kg 11:28 Solomon saw that the young man was industrious 4
12: 8 took counsel with the young men who had grown up 3
10 the young men who had grown up with him said 3
14 according to the counsel of the young men, saying 3
2Kg 5:22 There have just now come to me . . two young men 4
6:17 LORD opened the eyes of the young man, and he saw; 4
8:12 you will slay their young men with the sword 1
9: 4 the young man, the prophet, went to Ramoth-gilead. 4
6 and the young man poured the oil on his head •
1Ch 12:28 Zadok, a young man mighty in valor 4
2Ch 10: 8 took counsel with the young men 3
10 the young men who had grown up with him said 3
14 according to the counsel of the young men, saying 3
36:17 slew their young men with the sword in the house 1
17 had no compassion on young man or virgin 1
Job 29: 8 the young men saw me and withdrew 4
Ps 78:63 Fire devoured their young men, and their maidens 1
119: 9 How can a young man keep his way pure? 4
148:12 Young men and maidens together 1
Prv 7: 7 I have seen . . a young man without sense 4
20:29 The glory of young men is their strength 1
Ecc 11: 9 Rejoice, O young man, in your youth 1
Sng 2: 3 an apple tree . . so is my beloved among young men. 2
Isa 9:17 the Lord does not rejoice over their young men 1
13:18 Their bows will slaughter the young men; 4
23: 4 I have neither reared young men nor brought up 1
31: 8 and his young men shall be put to forced labor. 1
40:30 and young men shall fall exhausted; 1
62: 5 as a young man marries a virgin, so shall your sons 1
Jer 6:11 and upon the gatherings of young men, also; 1
9:21 and the young men from the squares. 1
11:22 the young men shall die by the sword; 1
15: 8 against the mothers of young men a destroyer 1
31:13 and the young men and the old shall be merry. 1
48:15 and the choicest of his young men have gone down 1
49:26 Therefore her young men shall fall in her squares 1
50:30 her young men shall fall in her squares 1
51: 3 Spare not her young men; 1
22 I break in pieces the young man and the maiden; 1
Lam 1:15 he summoned an assembly . . to crush my young men; 1
18 and my young men have gone into captivity. 1
2:21 my maidens and my young men have fallen 1
5:13 Young men are compelled to grind at the mill; 1
14 old men have quit . . the young men their music. 1
Ezk 9: 6 slay old men outright, young men and maidens 1
23: 6 desirable young men, horsemen riding on horses. 1
12 on horses, all of them desirable young men. 1
23 the Assyrians with them, desirable young men 1
30:17 The young men of On and of Pibe'seth 1
Jol 2:28 and your young men shall see visions. 1
Ams 2:11 and some of your young men for Nazirites. 1
4:10 I slew your young men with the sword; 1
8:13 the fair virgins and the young men shall faint 1
Zec 2: 4 and said to him, "Run, say to that young man 4
9:17 Grain shall make the young men flourish 1
Mat 19:20 The young man said to him 7
22 When the young man heard this he went away 7
Mrk 14:51 a young man followed him 7
16: 5 And entering the tomb, they saw a young man 7
Lke 7:14 he said, "Young man, I say to you, arise. 7
Act 2:17 your young men shall see visions 7
5: 6 The young men rose and wrapped him up 8
10 When the young men came in they found her dead 7
7:58 at the feet of a young man named Saul. 6
20: 9 a young man named Eu'tychus 6
23:17 Take this young man to the tribune 6
18 Paul . . asked me to bring this young man to you 7
22 the tribune dismissed the young man 7
1Ti 5: 1 treat younger men like brothers 8
Tit 2: 6 urge the younger men to control themselves. 8
1Jn 2:13 I am writing to you, young men 7
14 I write to you, young men, because you are strong 7
1Es 1:53 These slew their young men with the sword 7
53 did not spare young man or virgin 7
3: 4 the three young men of the bodyguard 7
16 he said, "Call the young men 7
4:58 When the young man went out 7
8:50 There I proclaimed a fast for the young men 7
2Es 2:43 In their midst was a young man of great stature 10
46 Who is that young man who places crowns on them 10
10:22 our young men have been enslaved 10
Tob 1: 4 in the land of Israel, while I was still a young man 8
5:16 the young man's dog was with them. 9
6: 2 Then the young man went down to wash himself. 9
2 A fish . . would have swallowed the young man; 9
3 the young man seized the fish 9
5 the young man did as the angel told him 9
6 the young man said to the angel, "Brother Azarias 9
10 the angel said to the young man 9
13 the young man said to the angel, "Brother Azarias 9
7: 2 How much the young man resembles my cousin Tobit! 7
Jdt 2:27 and put to death all their young men 7
6:16 their young men and their women ran to the assembly 7
7:22 the women and young men fainted from thirst 7
23 all the people, the young men, the women 7
10: 9 they ordered the young men to open the gate 7
16: 5 and kill my young men with the sword 7
7 did not fall by the hands of the young men 7
Sir 32: 7 Speak, young man, if there is need of you 7
Bar 3:20 Young men have seen the light of day, and have 8
Sus 1:21 that a young man was with you 7
37 Then a young man, who had been hidden, came to her 7
40 and asked her who the young man was 7
1Mc 1:26 maidens and young men became faint 7
2Mc 3:26 Two young men also appeared to him 6
33 the same young men appeared again 6
4:12 the noblest of the young men 5
7:12 those . . were astonished at the young man's spirit 7
25 Since the young man would not listen to him at all 6
30 While she was still speaking, the young man said 6
10:35 twenty young men in the army of Maccabeus 6
12:27 Stalwart young men took their stand 6
13:15 with a picked force of the bravest young men 7
4Mc 8: 5 Young men, I admire each and every one of you 6
9: 6 that we young men should die 8
14: 9 as we hear of the tribulations of these young men; 6
12 the mother of the seven young men 7
20 did not sway the mother of the young men 7
16:17 if . . you young men were to be terrified 7

young one 1. אֶפְרֹחַ 2. בֵּן 3. יֶלֶד

Deu 22: 6 nest . . with young ones or eggs and the mother 1
Job 38:41 the raven its prey, when its young ones cry to God 3
39: 4 Their young ones become strong, they grow up 2
30 His young ones suck up blood; 1

young people 1. נַעַר

Job 1:19 it fell upon the young people, and they are dead; 1

very young 1. *μειρακίσκος*

4Mc 8: 1 even the very young . . have prevailed 1

young woman 1. נַעֲרָה 2. עַלְמָה 3. *νεᾶνις* 4. *νέος*

Gen 24:43 let the young woman who comes out to draw 2
Deu 22:15 then the father of the young woman and her mother 1
16 father of the young woman shall say to the elders 1
19 give them to the father of the young woman 1
20 tokens . . were not found in the young woman 1
21 bring out the young woman to the door 1
24 young woman because she did not cry for help 1
25 a man meets a young woman who is betrothed 1
26 But to the young woman you shall do nothing; 1
26 in the young woman there is no offense 1
27 though the betrothed young woman cried for help 1
29 give to the father of the young woman 1
Rut 4:12 that the LORD will give you by this young woman. 1
Isa 7:14 a young woman shall conceive and bear a son 2
1Ti 5: 2 younger women like sisters, in all purity. 4
Tit 2: 4 so train the young women to love their husbands 4
3Mc 4: 6 young women . . exchanged joy for wailing 3

youth 1. בָּחוּר 2. בְּחוּרִים 3. בֵּן 4. יֶלֶד 5. יַלְדוּת 6. נְעוּרוֹת 7. נְעוּרִים 8. נַעַר 9. נֹעַר 10. עַוִר 11. עֲלוּמִים 12. עֶלֶם 13. צְעִירָה 14. *ἡλικία* 15. *μειράκιον* 16. *μεῖραξ* 17. *νεανίας* 18. *νεανικὴ ἡλικία* 19. *νεανίσκος* 20. *νεότης* 21. *παρθενία* 22. iuventus

Gen 8:21 man's heart is evil from his youth; 7
43:33 and the youngest according to his youth; 13
46:34 keepers of cattle from our youth even until now 7
Lev 22:13 returns to her father's house, as in her youth 7
Num30: 3 within her father's house, in her youth 7
16 father and his daughter, while in her youth 7
Jdg 8:20 slay them." But the youth did not draw his sword; 8
20 for he was afraid, because he was still a youth. 8
1Sm 12: 2 walked before you from my youth until this day. 7
17:33 you are but a youth, and he has been a man of war 8
33 and he has been a man of war from his youth. 7
42 for he was but a youth, ruddy and comely 8
55 he said . . "Abner, whose son is this youth? 8
20:22 if I say to the youth, 'Look, the arrows are beyond 12
2Sm 19: 7 evil . . come upon you from your youth until now. 7
1Kg 18:12 I . . have revered the LORD from my youth. 7
Job 13:26 and makest me inherit the iniquities of my youth. 7
31:18 for from his youth I reared him as a father 7
33:25 let his flesh become fresh with youth; 9
36:14 They die in youth, and their life ends in shame. 9
Ps 25: 7 Remember not the sins of my youth 7
71: 5 thou . . art my hope, my trust, O LORD, from my youth. 7
17 O God, from my youth thou hast taught me 7
88:15 Afflicted and close to death from my youth up 9
89:45 Thou hast cut short the days of his youth; 11
103: 5 so that your youth is renewed like the eagle's. 7
110: 3 like dew your youth will come to you. 5
127: 4 Like arrows . . are the sons of one's youth. 7
129: 1 Sorely have they afflicted me from my youth 7
2 Sorely have they afflicted me from my youth 7
144:12 our sons in their youth be like plants full grown 7
Prv 1: 4 knowledge and discretion to the youth– 8
2:17 who forsakes the companion of her youth 7
5:18 rejoice in the wife of your youth 7
7: 7 I have perceived among the youths 3
Ecc 4:13 Better is a poor and wise youth than an old 4
15 living . . as well as that youth, who was to stand 4
11: 9 Rejoice, O young man, in your youth 5
9 let your heart cheer you in the days of your youth; 2
10 for youth and the dawn of life are vanity. 5
12: 1 Remember also . . in the days of your youth 2
Isa 3: 5 the youth will be insolent to the elder 8
40:30 Even youths shall faint and be weary 8
47:12 with which you have labored from your youth; 7
15 who have trafficked with you from your youth; 7
54: 4 for you will forget the shame of your youth 11
6 like a wife of youth when she is cast off 7
Jer 1: 6 I do not know how to speak, for I am only a youth. 8
7 the LORD said to me, "Do not say, 'I am only a youth' 8
2: 2 I remember the devotion of your youth 7
3: 4 My father, thou art the friend of my youth 10
24 from our youth the shameful thing has devoured 7
25 we and our fathers, from our youth even to this day; 7
18:21 their youths be slain by the sword in battle. 1
22:21 This has been your way from your youth 7
31:19 because I bore the disgrace of my youth. 7
32:30 nothing but evil in my sight from their youth; 6
48:11 Moab has been at ease from his youth 7
51:22 I break in pieces the old man and the youth; 8
Lam 3:27 good . . that he bear the yoke in his youth. 7
Ezk 4:14 from my youth . . I have never eaten what died 7
16:22 you did not remember the days of your youth 7
43 you have not remembered the days of your youth 7
60 my covenant with you in the days of your youth 7
23: 3 they played the harlot in their youth; 7
8 in her youth men had lain with her and handled her 7
19 her harlotry, remembering the days of her youth 7
21 Thus you longed for the lewdness of your youth 7
Dan 1:10 poorer condition than the youths . . of your own age. 4
13 our appearance and the appearance of the youths 4
15 better . . than all the youths who ate the king's 4
17 As for these four youths, God gave them learning 4
Hos 2:15 there she shall answer as in the days of her youth 7
Jol 1: 8 Lament . . for the bridegroom of her youth. 7
Zec 13: 5 the land has been my possession since my youth. 7
Mal 2:14 covenant between you and the wife of your youth 7
15 let none be faithless to the wife of his youth. 7
Mrk 10:20 Teacher, all these I have observed from my youth. 20
Lke 18:21 he said, "All these I have observed from my youth. 20
Act 26: 4 My manner of life from my youth . . is known 20
1Ti 4:12 Let no one despise your youth 20
1Es 8:91 a very great throng . . , men and women and youths 17
2Es 5:53 Those born in the strength of youth 22
55 is aging and passing the strength of youth. 22
6:32 which you have maintained from your youth. 22
14:10 For the age has lost its youth 22
Wis 2: 6 and make use of the creation to the full as in youth. 20
4:16 youth that is quickly perfected 20
8: 2 I loved her and sought her from my youth 20
Sir 6:18 My son, from your youth up choose instruction 20
7:23 make them obedient from their youth. 20
15: 2 like the wife of his youth she will welcome him. 21
25: 3 You have gathered nothing in your youth 20
30:11 Give him no authority in his youth 20
12 Bow down his neck in his youth •
47: 4 In his youth did he not kill a giant 20
14 How wise you became in your youth! 20
51:15 from my youth I followed her steps. 20
1Mc 1: 6 who had been brought up with him from youth 20
2: 9 her youths by the sword of the foe. 19
66 has been a mighty warrior from his youth 20
14: 9 youths donned the glories and garments of war. 19
16: 2 have fought the wars of Israel from our youth 20
2Mc 7:25 urged her to advise the youth to save himself. 15
3Mc 4: 8 in the prime of youth 18
4Mc 8: 8 enjoy your youth 20
10 Even I, your enemy, have compassion for your youth 14
20 Let us take pity on our youth 14
27 the youths . . neither said any of these things 17
9:13 the noble youth was stretched out around this 17
21 the courageous youth, worthy of Abraham 17
25 the saintly youth broke the thread of life. 17
13: 7 the seven-towered right reason of the youths 19
9 let us imitate the three youths in Assyria 19
14: 4 None of the seven youths proved coward 15
6 those holy youths . . agreed to go to death for its sake. 16
8 these youths . . encircled the sevenfold fear of tortures 16

youth *See also* body.

youthful 1. *ἡλικία* 2. *νεωτερικός*

2Ti 2:22 shun youthful passions 2
2Mc 15:30 his youthful good will toward his countrymen 1
3Mc 4: 8 instead of good cheer and youthful revelry 2

youthful *See also* vigor.

Z

zeal 1. קנא 2. קִנְאָה 3. ἐκτένεια 4. ζῆλος 5. ζηλόω 6. ζηλωτής 7. σπουδή

2Sm 21: 2 to slay them in his zeal for the people of Israel 1
2Kg 10:16 "Come with me, and see my zeal for the LORD. 2
19:31 The zeal of the LORD will do this. 2
Ps 69: 9 For zeal for thy house has consumed me 2
119:139 My zeal consumes me, because my foes forget 2
Isa 9: 7 The zeal of the LORD of hosts will do this. 2
26:11 them see thy zeal for thy people, and be ashamed. 2
37:32 zeal of the LORD of hosts will accomplish this. 2
63:15 Where are thy zeal and thy might? 2
Joh 2:17 "Zeal for thy house will consume me. 4
Rom 10: 2 I bear them witness that they have a zeal for God 4
12: 8 he who gives aid, with zeal; 7
11 Never flag in zeal, be aglow with the Spirit 7
2Co 7: 7 your zeal for me 4
11 what longing, what zeal, what punishment 4
12 in order that your zeal for us might be revealed 7
9: 2 your zeal has stirred up most of them. 4
Php 3: 6 as to zeal a persecutor of the church 4
Wis 5:17 The Lord will take his zeal as his whole armor 4
14:17 by their zeal they might flatter the absent one 7
Sir 48: 2 by his zeal he made them few in number. 4
Bar 4:28 return with tenfold zeal to seek him. •
1Mc 2:58 Elijah because of great zeal for the law 5
2Mc 14:38 he had with all zeal risked body and life. 3
4Mc 18:12 He told you of the zeal of Phineas 6

zeal *See also* burn.

common zeal 1. ὁμοζηλία

4Mc 13:25 A common zeal for nobility 1

show zeal 1. ζηλόω

1Mc 2:50 Now, my children, show zeal for the law 1

zealot 1. ζηλωτής

2Mc 4: 2 a zealot for the laws. 1

zealous 1. ζηλεύω 2. ζηλόω 3. ζηλωτής 4. κατὰ σπουδήν 5. σπεύδω 6. σπουδάζω 7. φιλότιμος

Act 21:20 they are all zealous for the law 3
22: 3 being zealous for God as you all are this day. 3
Gal 1:14 so extremely zealous was I for the traditions 3
Tit 2:14 who are zealous for good deeds. 3
1Pe 3:13 if you are zealous for what is right? 3
2Pe 1:10 more zealous to confirm your call and election 6
3:14 be zealous to be found by him without spot 6
Rev 3:19 I reprove and chasten; so be zealous and repent. 1
2Es 6:58 thy first-born, only begotten, zealous for thee •
Jdt 9: 4 thy beloved sons, who were zealous for thee 2
Sir 27: 3 If a man is not steadfast and zealous 4
45:23 he was zealous in the fear of the Lord 2
51:18 I was zealous for the good 2
1Mc 2:27 Let every one who is zealous for the law 2
3Mc 4:15 bitter haste and zealous intentness 7
4Mc 16:20 Abraham was zealous to sacrifice his son Isaac 5

deeply zealous 1. ζηλόω ζῆλον

1Mc 2:54 Phinehas . . because he was deeply zealous 1

zealously 1. μετὰ σπουδῆς 2. περισσότερος 3. πρόθυμος 4. φιλοτίμως

Mrk 7:36 the more zealously they proclaimed it. 2
2Mc 2:21 those who strove zealously on behalf of Judaism 4
3Mc 5:27 this had been so zealously completed for him. 1
4Mc 16:16 Fight zealously for our ancestral law. 3

Names

Aaron 1. אַהֲרֹן 2. ᾿Ααρών 3. Ααρωνιδης 4. Aaron

Exd 4:14 Is there not Aaron, your brother, the Levite? 1
27 The LORD said to Aaron, "Go into the wilderness 1
28 Moses told Aaron all the words of the LORD 1
29 Then Moses and Aaron went and gathered together 1
30 Aaron spoke all the words which the LORD had 1
5: 1 Afterward Moses and Aaron went to Pharaoh 1
4 Moses and Aaron, why do you take the people away 1
20 They met Moses and Aaron, who were waiting 1
6:13 the LORD spoke to Moses and Aaron, and gave them 1
20 and she bore him Aaron and Moses 1
23 Aaron took to wife Eli'sheba, the daughter 1
25 Elea'zar, Aaron's son, took to wife one 1
26 These are the Aaron and Moses to whom the LORD 1
27 they who spoke . . this Moses and this Aaron. 1
7: 1 and Aaron your brother shall be your prophet. 1
2 and Aaron your brother shall tell Pharaoh to let 1
6 Moses and Aaron did so; 1
7 Moses was 80 . . and Aaron 83 years old 1
8 the LORD said to Moses and Aaron 1
9 you shall say to Aaron, 'Take your rod and cast it 1
10 So Moses and Aaron went to Pharaoh and did 1
10 Aaron cast down his rod before Pharaoh 1
12 But Aaron's rod swallowed up their rods. 1
19 And the LORD said to Moses, "Say to Aaron, 1
20 Moses and Aaron did as the LORD commanded; 1
8: 5 the LORD said to Moses, "Say to Aaron, 'Stretch out 1
6 So Aaron stretched out his hand over the waters 1
8 Then Pharaoh called Moses and Aaron, and said 1
12 So Moses and Aaron went out from Pharaoh; 1
16 Then the LORD said to Moses, "Say to Aaron, 'Stretch 1
17 they did so; Aaron stretched out his hand 1
25 Then Pharaoh called Moses and Aaron, and said, "Go 1
9: 8 the LORD said to Moses and Aaron, "Take handfuls 1
27 Then Pharaoh sent, and called Moses and Aaron 1
10: 3 Moses and Aaron went in to Pharaoh, and said 1
8 So Moses and Aaron were brought back to Pharaoh; 1
16 Then Pharaoh called Moses and Aaron in haste 1
11:10 Moses and Aaron did all these wonders before 1
12: 1 The LORD said to Moses and Aaron in the land 1
28 as the LORD had commanded Moses and Aaron 1
31 he summoned Moses and Aaron by night, and said 1
43 the LORD said to Moses and Aaron, "This is 1
50 as the LORD commanded Moses and Aaron, 1
15:20 Then Miriam, the prophetess, the sister of Aaron 1
16: 2 Israel murmured against Moses and Aaron 1
6 So Moses and Aaron said to all the people 1
9 Moses said to Aaron, "Say to the whole 1
10 as Aaron spoke to the whole congregation 1
33 Moses said to Aaron, "Take a jar, and put an omer 1
34 so Aaron placed it before the testimony 1
17:10 and Moses, Aaron, and Hur went up to the top 1
12 Aaron and Hur held up his hands, one on one side 1
18:12 and Aaron came with all the elders of Israel 1
19:24 Go down, and come up bringing Aaron with you; 1
24: 1 Come up . . you and Aaron, Nadab, and Abi'hu 1
9 Then Moses and Aaron, Nadab, and . . went up. 1
14 and, behold, Aaron and Hur are with you; 1
27:21 Aaron and his sons shall tend it from evening 1
28: 1 Then bring near to you Aaron your brother 1
1 to serve me as priests-Aaron and Aaron's sons 1
1 to serve me as priests-Aaron and Aaron's sons 1
2 make holy garments for Aaron your brother 1
3 that they make Aaron's garments to consecrate 1
4 make holy garments for Aaron your brother 1
12 Aaron shall bear their names before the LORD 1
29 Aaron shall bear all the names of . . Israel 1
30 they shall be upon Aaron's heart, when he goes 1
30 thus Aaron shall bear the judgment of the people 1
35 it shall be upon Aaron when he ministers 1
38 It shall be upon Aaron's forehead, and Aaron shall 1
38 Aaron shall take upon himself any guilt 1
40 for Aaron's sons you shall make coats and girdles 1
41 you shall put them upon Aaron your brother 1
43 they shall be upon Aaron, and upon his sons 1
29: 4 You shall bring Aaron and his sons to the door 1
5 put on Aaron the coat and the robe of the ephod 1
9 Thus you shall ordain Aaron and his sons. 1
10 Aaron and his sons shall lay their hands upon 1
15 Aaron and his sons shall lay their hands upon 1
19 Aaron and his sons shall lay their hands upon 1
20 tip of the right ear of Aaron and upon the tips 1
21 sprinkle it upon Aaron and his garments 1
24 you shall put all these in the hands of Aaron 1
26 the ram of Aaron's ordination and wave it 1
27 since it is for Aaron and for his sons. 1
28 It shall be for Aaron and his sons as a perpetual 1
29 The holy garments of Aaron shall be for his sons 1
32 Aaron and his sons shall eat the flesh of the ram 1
35 Thus you shall do to Aaron and to his sons 1
44 Aaron also and his sons I will consecrate 1
30: 7 Aaron shall burn fragrant incense on it; 1
8 when Aaron sets up the lamps in the evening 1
10 Aaron shall make atonement upon its horns 1
19 with which Aaron and his sons wash 1
30 you shall anoint Aaron and his sons 1
31:10 holy garments for Aaron the priest 1
32: 1 gathered themselves together to Aaron, and said 1
2 Aaron said to them, "Take off the rings of gold 1
3 rings of gold . . and brought them to Aaron. 1
5 When Aaron saw this, he built an altar before it; 1
5 and Aaron made proclamation and said, "Tomorrow 1
21 Moses said to Aaron, "What did this people do 1
22 Aaron said, "Let not the anger of my lord burn hot; 1
25 (for Aaron had let them break loose, to their shame 1
35 because they made the calf which Aaron made. 1
34:30 when Aaron and all the people of Israel saw Moses 1
31 Moses called to them; and Aaron and all 1
35:19 the holy garments for Aaron the priest 1
38:21 under the direction of Ith'amar the son of Aaron 1
39: 1 they made the holy garments for Aaron; 1
27 coats, woven of fine linen, for Aaron and his sons 1
41 the holy garments for Aaron the priest 1
40:12 you shall bring Aaron and his sons to the door 1
13 put upon Aaron the holy garments 1
31 with which Moses and Aaron and his sons washed 1
Lev 1: 5 Aaron's sons the priests shall present the blood 1
7 the sons of Aaron the priest shall put fire 1
8 Aaron's sons the priests shall lay the pieces 1
11 Aaron's sons the priests shall throw its blood 1
2: 2 bring it to Aaron's sons the priests 1
3 cereal offering shall be for Aaron and his sons 1
10 cereal offering shall be for Aaron and his sons 1
3: 2 Aaron's sons the priests shall throw the blood 1
5 Then Aaron's sons shall burn it on the altar 1
8 Aaron's sons shall throw its blood 1
13 the sons of Aaron shall throw its blood 1
6: 9 Command Aaron and his sons, saying, This is 1
14 The sons of Aaron shall offer it before the LORD 1
16 the rest of it Aaron and his sons shall eat 1
18 Every male among the children of Aaron may eat 1
20 This is the offering which Aaron and his sons 1
22 The priest from among Aaron's sons •
25 Say to Aaron and his sons, This is the law 1
7:10 all the sons of Aaron, one as well as another 1
31 but the breast shall be for Aaron and his sons 1
33 he among the sons of Aaron who offers the blood 1
34 I . . have given them to Aaron the priest 1
35 This is the portion of Aaron and of his sons 1
8: 2 Take Aaron and his sons with him, 1
6 Moses brought Aaron and his sons, and washed them 1
12 poured some of the anointing oil on Aaron's head 1
13 Moses brought Aaron's sons, and clothed them 1
14 Aaron and his sons laid their hands upon the head 1
18 Aaron and his sons laid their hands on the head 1
22 Aaron and his sons laid their hands on the head 1
23 blood and put it on the tip of Aaron's right ear 1
24 Aaron's sons were brought, and Moses put some 1
27 he put all these in the hands of Aaron 1
30 sprinkled it upon Aaron and his garments 1
30 so he consecrated Aaron and his garments 1
31 Moses said to Aaron and his sons, "Boil the flesh 1
31 saying, 'Aaron and his sons shall eat it' 1
36 Aaron and his sons did all the things 1
9: 1 On the eighth day Moses called Aaron and his sons 1
2 he said to Aaron, "Take a bull calf 1
7 Then Moses said to Aaron, "Draw near to the altar 1
8 So Aaron drew near to the altar, and killed 1
9 the sons of Aaron presented the blood to him 1
12 Aaron's sons delivered to him the blood 1
18 Aaron's sons delivered to him the blood 1
21 the breasts and the right thigh Aaron waved 1
22 Then Aaron lifted up his hands toward the people 1
23 Moses and Aaron went into the tent of meeting 1
10: 1 Now Nadab and Abi'hu, the sons of Aaron 1
3 Then Moses said to Aaron, "This is what the LORD 1
3 And Aaron held his peace 1
4 the sons of Uz'ziel the uncle of Aaron, 1
6 Moses said to Aaron and to Elea'zar and Ith'amar 1
8 the LORD spoke to Aaron, saying 1
12 Moses said to Aaron and to Elea'zar and Ith'amar 1
16 Ithamar, the sons of Aaron who were left 1
19 Aaron said to Moses, "Behold, today they have 1
11: 1 the LORD said to Moses and Aaron 1
13: 1 The LORD said to Moses and Aaron 1
2 then he shall be brought to Aaron the priest 1
14:33 The LORD said to Moses and Aaron 1
15: 1 The LORD said to Moses and Aaron 1
16: 1 after the death of the two sons of Aaron 1
2 Tell Aaron your brother not to come at all times 1
3 thus shall Aaron come into the holy place 1
6 Aaron shall offer the bull as a sin offering 1
8 Aaron shall cast lots upon the two goats 1
9 Aaron shall present the goat on which the lot fell 1
11 Aaron shall present the bull as a sin offering 1
21 Aaron shall lay both his hands upon the head 1
23 Then Aaron shall come into the tent of meeting 1
17: 2 Say to Aaron and his sons, and to all the people 1
21: 1 Speak to the priests, the sons of Aaron, and say 1
17 Say to Aaron, None of your descendants 1
21 no man of the descendants of Aaron the priest 1
24 So Moses spoke to Aaron and to his sons 1
22: 2 Tell Aaron and his sons to keep away 1
4 None of the line of Aaron who is a leper 1
18 Say to Aaron and to his sons and all the people 1
24: 3 Aaron shall keep it in order from evening 1
8 Every sabbath day Aaron shall set it in order •
9 it shall be for Aaron and his sons 1
Num 1: 3 you and Aaron shall number them 1
17 Moses and Aaron took these men who have been 1
44 whom Moses and Aaron numbered with the help 1
2: 1 The LORD said to Moses and Aaron 1
3: 1 These are the generations of Aaron and Moses 1
2 These are the names of the sons of Aaron 1
3 these are the names of the sons of Aaron 1
4 served . . in the lifetime of Aaron 1
6 set them before Aaron the priest, that they may 1
9 you shall give the Levites to Aaron and his sons; 1
10 you shall appoint Aaron and his sons 1
32 Elea'zar the son of Aaron . . was to be chief 1
38 Moses and Aaron and his sons, having charge 1
39 Levites, whom Moses and Aaron numbered 1
48 give the money . . to Aaron and his sons. 1
51 gave the redemption money to Aaron and his sons 1
4: 1 The LORD said to Moses and Aaron 1
5 Aaron and his sons shall go in and take down 1
15 when Aaron and his sons have finished covering 1
16 Elea'zar the son of Aaron the priest 1
17 The LORD said to Moses and Aaron 1
19 Aaron and his sons shall go in and appoint them 1
27 service . . at the command of Aaron and his sons 1
28 Ith'amar the son of Aaron the priest. 1
33 Ith'amar the son of Aaron the priest. 1
34 Moses and Aaron and the leaders 1
37 Ko'hathites . . Moses and Aaron numbered 1

41 whom Moses and Aaron numbered according 1
45 Merar'i, whom Moses and Aaron numbered 1
46 whom Moses and Aaron and the leaders of Israel 1
6:23 Say to Aaron and his sons, Thus you shall bless 1
7: 8 Ith'amar the son of Aaron the priest. 1
8: 2 Say to Aaron, When you set up the lamps 1
3 Aaron did so; he set up its lamps to give light 1
11 Aaron shall offer the Levites before the LORD 1
13 cause the Levites to attend Aaron and his sons 1
19 given the Levites as a gift to Aaron and his sons 1
20 Thus did Moses and Aaron . . to the Levites; 1
21 Aaron offered them as a wave offering 1
21 Aaron made atonement for them to cleanse them. 1
22 in attendance upon Aaron and his sons; 1
9: 6 they came before Moses and Aaron on that day; 1
10: 8 sons of Aaron . . shall blow the trumpets. 1
12: 1 Miriam and Aaron spoke against Moses 1
4 LORD said to Moses and to Aaron and Miriam 1
5 LORD came down . . and called Aaron and Miriam; 1
10 Aaron turned towards Miriam, and behold 1
11 Aaron said to Moses, "Oh, my lord, do not punish us 1
13:26 they came to Moses and Aaron and to all 1
14: 2 people . . murmured against Moses and Aaron; 1
5 Then Moses and Aaron fell on their faces 1
26 the LORD said to Moses and to Aaron 1
15:33 who found him . . brought him to Moses and Aaron 1
16: 3 assembled . . against Moses and against Aaron 1
11 what is Aaron that you murmur against him? 1
16 before the LORD, you and they, and Aaron, tomorrow; 1
17 you also, and Aaron, each his censer. 1
18 at . . the tent of meeting with Moses and Aaron. 1
20 the LORD said to Moses and to Aaron 1
37 Elea'zar the son of Aaron the priest to take up 1
40 no one who . . is not of the descendants of Aaron 1
41 murmured against Moses and against Aaron, saying 1
42 assembled against Moses and against Aaron 1
43 Moses and Aaron came to the front of the tent 1
46 Moses said to Aaron, "Take your censer, 1
47 Aaron took it as Moses said, and ran into the midst 1
50 Aaron returned to Moses at the entrance 1
17: 3 write Aaron's name upon the rod of Levi. 1
6 the rod of Aaron was among their rods. 1
8 rod of Aaron . . had sprouted and put forth buds 1
10 Put back the rod of Aaron before the testimony 1
18: 1 LORD said to Aaron, "You and your sons 1
8 Then the LORD said to Aaron, "And behold 1
20 LORD said to Aaron, "You shall have no inheritance 1
28 give the LORD'S offering to Aaron the priest. 1
19: 1 Now the LORD said to Moses and to Aaron 1
20: 2 assembled themselves . . against . . Aaron. 1
6 Then Moses and Aaron went from the presence 1
8 assemble the congregation, you and Aaron 1
10 Moses and Aaron gathered the assembly together 1
12 LORD said to Moses and Aaron, "Because you did not 1
23 the LORD said to Moses and Aaron at Mount Hor 1
24 Aaron shall be gathered to his people; 1
25 Take Aaron and Elea'zar his son, and bring them up 1
26 strip Aaron of his garments, and put them upon 1
26 Aaron shall be gathered to his people 1
28 Moses stripped Aaron of his garments 1
28 Aaron died there on the top of the mountain. 1
29 all the congregation saw that Aaron was dead 1
29 all the house of Israel wept for Aaron 30 days 1
25: 7 Phin'ehas . . of Elea'zar, son of Aaron the priest 1
11 Phin'ehas . . of Elea'zar, son of Aaron the priest 1
26: 1 Elea'zar the son of Aaron, the priest 1
9 who contended against Moses and Aaron 1
59 she bore to Amram Aaron and Moses and Miriam 1
60 And to Aaron were born Nadab, Abi'hu, Elea'zar 1
64 of those numbered by Moses and Aaron the priest 1
27:13 as your brother Aaron was gathered 1
33: 1 went . . under the leadership of Moses and Aaron. 1
38 Aaron the priest went up Mount Hor at the command 1
39 Aaron was 123 years old when he died on Mount Hor. 1
Deu 9:20 LORD was so angry with Aaron that he was ready 1
20 I prayed for Aaron also at the same time. 1
10: 6 Mose'rah. There Aaron died, and . . was buried; 1
32:50 as Aaron your brother died in Mount Hor 1
Jos 21: 4 who were descendants of Aaron the priest 1
10 cities . . which went to the descendants of Aaron 1
13 to the descendants of Aaron . . they gave Hebron 1
19 cities of the descendants of Aaron, the priests 1
24: 5 And I sent Moses and Aaron, and I plagued Egypt 1
33 Elea'zar the son of Aaron died; and they buried him 1
Jdg 20:28 Phin'ehas the son of Elea'zar, son of Aaron 1
1Sm 12: 6 The LORD . . who appointed Moses and Aaron 1
8 the LORD sent Moses and Aaron, who brought forth 1
1Ch 6: 3 The children of Amram: Aaron, Moses, and Miriam. 1
3 The sons of Aaron: Nadab, Abi'hu, Elea'zar 1
49 Aaron and his sons made offerings upon the altar 1
50 sons of Aaron: Elea'zar his son, Phin'ehas his son 1
54 sons of Aaron of the families of Ko'hathites 1
57 To the sons of Aaron they gave the cities 1
15: 4 together the sons of Aaron and the Levites 1
23:13 The sons of Amram: Aaron and Moses. 1
13 Aaron was set apart to consecrate 1
28 their duty shall be to assist the sons of Aaron 1
32 shall attend the sons of Aaron, their brethren 1
24: 1 The divisions of the sons of Aaron were these. 1
1 sons of Aaron: Nadab, Abi'hu, Elea'zar, 1
19 established for them by Aaron their father 1
31 lots, just as their brethren the sons of Aaron 1
27:17 for Levi, Hashabi'ah . . for Aaron, Zadok; 1
2Ch 13: 9 the priests . . the sons of Aaron, and the Levites 1
10 We have priests . . who are sons of Aaron 1
26:18 but for the priests the sons of Aaron 1
29:21 commanded the priests the sons of Aaron to offer 1
31:19 sons of Aaron . . who were in the fields of common 1
35:14 priests the sons of Aaron . . busied in offering 1
14 for the priests the sons of Aaron. 1
Ezr 7: 5 son of Elea'zar, son of Aaron the chief priest– 1
Neh 10:38 priest, the son of Aaron, shall be with the Levites 1
12:47 set apart that which was for the sons of Aaron. 1
Ps 77:20 like a flock by the hand of Moses and Aaron. 1
99: 6 Moses and Aaron were among his priests 1
105:26 sent Moses . . and Aaron whom he had chosen. 1
106:16 men in the camp were jealous of Moses and Aaron 1
115:10 O house of Aaron, put your trust in the LORD! 1
12 house of Israel; he will bless the house of Aaron; 1
118: 3 house of Aaron say, "His steadfast love endures 1
133: 2 down upon the beard, upon the beard of Aaron 1
135:19 Israel . . O house of Aaron, bless the LORD! 1
Mic 6: 4 and I sent before you Moses, Aaron, and Miriam. 1
Lke 1: 5 he had a wife of the daughters of Aaron 2
Act 7:40 saying to Aaron, 'Make for us gods to go before us 2
Heb 5: 4 he is called by God, just as Aaron was. 2
7:11 rather than one named after the order of Aaron? 2
9: 4 Aaron's rod that budded 2
1Es 1:13 their brethren the priests, the sons of Aaron 2
14 their brethren the priests, the sons of Aaron. 2
5: 5 the priests, the sons of Phinehas, son of Aaron; 2
8: 2 son of Eleazar, son of Aaron the chief priest. 2
2Es 1: 3 son of Aaron, of the tribe of Levi 4
13 I gave you Moses as leader and Aaron as priest; 4
Tob 1: 6 the priests, the sons of Aaron 2
Sir 36:17 according to the blessing of Aaron 2
45: 6 He exalted Aaron, the brother of Moses 2
20 He added glory to Aaron and gave him a heritage 2
25 so the heritage of Aaron is for his descendants. 2
50:13 all the sons of Aaron in their splendor 2
16 the sons of Aaron shouted 2
1Mc 7:14 A priest of the line of Aaron has come with the army 2
4Mc 7:11 our father Aaron, armed with the censer 2
12 the descendant of Aaron, Eleazar 3

house of Aaron 1. אַהֲרֹן
1Ch 12:27 prince Jehoi'ada, of the house of Aaron 1

Abaddon 1. אֲבַדּוֹן 2. Ἀβαδδών
Job 26: 6 naked before God, and Abaddon has no covering. 1
28:22 Abaddon and Death say, 'We have heard a rumor 1
31:12 that would be a fire which consumes unto Abaddon 1
Ps 88:11 or thy faithfulness in Abaddon? 1
Prv 15:11 Sheol and Abaddon lie open before the LORD 1
27:20 Sheol and Abaddon are never satisfied 1
Rev 9:11 his name in Hebrew is Abad'don 2

Abagtha 1. אֲבַגְתָא
Est 1:10 Mehu'man, Biztha, Harbo'na, Bigtha and Abag'tha 1

Abana 1. אֲבָנָה
2Kg 5:12 Are not Aba'na and Pharpar, the rivers of Damascus 1

Abarim 1. עֲבָרִים
Num27:12 Go up into this mountain to Ab'arim, and see 1
33:47 encamped in the mountains of Ab'arim, before Nebo. 1
48 set out from the mountains of Ab'arim 1
Deu 32:49 Ascend this mountain of the Ab'arim, Mount Nebo 1
Jer 22:20 cry from Ab'arim, for all your lovers 1

Abda 1. עַבְדָּא
1Kg 4: 6 Adoni'ram the son of Abda was in charge 1
Neh 11:17 Abda the son of Sham'mua, son of Galal 1

Abdeel 1. עַבְדְּאֵל
Jer 36:26 and Shelemi'ah the son of Abdeel to seize Baruch 1

Abdi 1. עַבְדִּי 2. Ωβαδιος
1Ch 6:44 Ethan the son of Kishi, son of Abdi, son of Malluch 1
2Ch 29:12 Levites arose . . Kish the son of Abdi 1
Ezr 10:26 of Elam: Mattani'ah, Zechari'ah, Jehi'el, Abdi 1
1Es 9:27 Jehiel and Abdi, and Jeremoth and Elijah. 2

Abdiel 1. עַבְדִּיאֵל
1Ch 5:15 Ahi the son of Ab'di-el, son of Guni 1

Abdon 1. עַבְדּוֹן
Jos 21:30 Mishal with its . . Abdon with its pasture lands 1
Jdg 12:13 Abdon the son of Hillel the Pira'thonite judged 1
15 Abdon the son of Hillel the Pira'thonite died 1
1Ch 6:74 out of . . Asher . . Abdon with its pasture lands 1
8:23 Abdon, Zichri, Hanan 1
30 His first-born son: Abdon, then Zur, Kish, Ba'al 1
9:36 first-born son Abdon, then Zur, Kish, Ba'al, Ner 1
2Ch 34:20 king commanded . . Abdon the son of Micah 1

Abed-nego 1. עֲבֵד נְגוֹ 2. עֲבֵד נְגוֹ (A)
Dan 1: 7 Azari'ah he called Abed'nego. 1
2:49 appointed Shadrach, Meshach, and Abed'nego 2
3:12 Shadrach, Meshach, and Abed'nego. These men 2
13 commanded that Shadrach, Meshach, and Abed'nego 2
14 Is it true, O Shadrach, Meshach, and Abed'nego 2
16 Shadrach, Meshach, and Abed'nego answered 2
19 against Shadrach, Meshach, and Abed'nego. 2
20 bind Shadrach, Meshach, and Abed'nego, and to cast 2
22 men who took up Shadrach, Meshach, and Abed'nego. 2
23 these three men, Shadrach, Meshach, and Abed'nego 2
26 Shadrach, Meshach, and Abed'nego, servants 2
26 Then Shadrach, Meshach, and Abed'nego came out 2
28 Blessed be the God of Shadrach . . and Abed'nego 2
29 God of Shadrach, Meshach, and Abed'nego 2
30 king promoted Shadrach, Meshach, and Abed'nego 2

Abel 1. אָבֵל 2. הֶבֶל 3. Ἄβελ
Gen 4: 2 again, she bore his brother Abel. 2
2 Abel was a keeper of sheep, and Cain a tiller 2
4 Abel brought of the firstlings of his flock 2
4 And the LORD had regard for Abel and his offering 2
8 Cain said to Abel his brother, "Let us go out 2
8 Cain rose up against his brother Abel 2
9 the LORD said to Cain, "Where is Abel your brother? 2
25 another child instead of Abel, for Cain slew him. 2
2Sm 20:14 Sheba passed through . . to Abel of Bethma'acah; 1
15 Jo'ab came and besieged him in Abel of Bethma'acah; 1
18 in old time, 'Let them but ask counsel at Abel'; 1
Mat 23:35 from the blood of innocent Abel 3
Lke 11:51 from the blood of Abel to the blood of Zechari'ah 3
Heb 11: 4 Abel offered to God a more acceptable sacrifice 3
12:24 that speaks more graciously than the blood of Abel. 3
4Mc 18:11 He read to you about Abel slain by Cain 3

Abel-beth-maacah 1. אָבֵל בֵּית מַעֲכָה
1Kg 15:20 conquered I'jon, Dan, A'bel-beth-ma'acah 1
2Kg 15:29 captured I'jon, A'bel-beth-ma'acah, Jan-o'ah, Kedesh 1

Abel-keramim 1. אָבֵל כְּרָמִים
Jdg 11:33 and as far as Abel-keramim, with a very great 1

Abel-maim 1. אָבֵל מַיִם
2Ch 16: 4 conquered I'jon, Dan, A'bel-ma'im 1

Abel-meholah 1. אָבֵל מְחוֹלָה
Jdg 7:22 as far as the border of A'bel-meho'lah, by Tabbath. 1
1Kg 4:12 from Beth-she'an to A'bel-meho'lah, as far 1
19:16 Eli'sha the son of Shaphat of A'bel-meho'lah 1

Abel-mizraim 1. אָבֵל מִצְרַיִם
Gen 50:11 Therefore the place was named A'bel-mizraim; 1

Abel-shittim 1. אָבֵל הַשִּׁטִּים
Num33:49 from Beth-jes'himoth as far as Abel-shittim 1

Abi 1. אֲבִיָּהוּ
2Kg 18: 2 mother's name was Abi the daughter of Zechari'ah. 1

Abi-albon 1. אֲבִי עַלְבוֹן
2Sm 23:31 Abi-al'bon the Ar'bathite, Az'maveth of Bahu'rim 1

Abiasaph 1. אֲבִיאָסָף
Exd 6:24 The sons of Korah: Assir, Elka'nah, and Abi'asaph; 1

Abiathar 1. אֶבְיָתָר 2. Ἀβιαθάρ
1Sm 22:20 one of the sons . . named Abi'athar, escaped 1
21 Abi'athar told David that Saul had killed 1
22 And David said to Abi'athar, "I knew on that day 1
23: 6 When Abi'athar the son of Ahim'elech fled to David 1
9 he said to Abi'athar the priest, "Bring the ephod 1
30: 7 said to Abi'athar the priest, the son of Ahim'elech 1
7 Abi'athar brought the ephod to David. 1
2Sm 8:17 Ahim'elech the son of Abi'athar were priests; 1
15:24 And Abi'athar came up, and lo, Zadok came also 1
27 go back to the city in peace, you and Abi'athar •
27 Ahim'a-az . . and Jonathan the son of Abi'athar. 1
29 So Zadok and Abi'athar carried the ark of God back 1
35 Are not Zadok and Abi'athar the priests with you 1
35 tell it to Zadok and Abi'athar the priests. 1
36 their two sons . . and Jonathan, Abi'athar's son; 1
17:15 Hushai said to Zadok and Abi'athar the priests 1
19:11 David sent . . to Zadok and Abi'athar the priests 1
20:25 and Zadok and Abi'athar were priests; 1
1Kg 1: 7 He conferred . . and with Abi'athar the priest; 1
19 the sons of the king, Abi'athar the priest, 1
25 the king's sons, Jo'ab . . and Abi'athar the priest; 1
42 Jonathan the son of Abi'athar the priest came; 1
2:22 on his side are Abi'athar the priest and Jo'ab 1
26 to Abi'athar the priest the king said, "Go 1
27 Solomon expelled Abi'athar from being priest 1
35 king put Zadok . . in the place of Abi'athar. 1
4: 4 of the army; Zadok and Abi'athar were priests; 1
1Ch 15:11 David summoned the priests Zadok and Abi'athar 1
18:16 Ahim'elech the son of Abi'athar 1
24: 6 Zadok . . and Ahim'elech the son of Abi'athar 1
27:34 was succeeded by Jehoi'ada . . and Abi'athar. 1
Mrk 2:26 when Abi'athar was high priest 2

Abib 1. אָבִיב
Exd 13: 4 This day you are to go forth, in the month of Abib. 1

23:15 at the appointed time in the month of Abib 1
34:18 at the time appointed in the month Abib; 1
18 for in the month Abib you came out from Egypt. 1
Deu 16: 1 Observe the month of Abib, and keep the passover 1
1 in the month of Abib the LORD your God brought you 1

Abida 1. אֲבִידָע
Gen 25: 4 Hanoch, Abi'da, and Elda'ah. All these were 1
1Ch 1:33 Mid'ian: Ephah, Epher, Hanoch, Abida, and Elda'ah. 1

Abidan 1. אֲבִידָן
Num 1:11 from Benjamin, Abi'dan the son of Gideo'ni; 1
2:22 leader of the people of Benjamin being Abi'dan 1
7:60 Abi'dan the . . leader of the men of Benjamin 1
65 was the offering of Abi'dan the son of Gideo'ni. 1
10:24 over the host . . was Abi'dan the son of Gideo'ni. 1

Abiel 1. אֲבִיאֵל
1Sm 9: 1 whose name was Kish, the son of Abi'el, son of Zeror 1
14:51 and Ner the father of Abner was the son of Abi'el. 1
1Ch 11:32 Abi'el the Ar'bathite. 1

Abiezer 1. אֲבִיעֶזֶר 2. בְּנֵי אֲבִיעֶזֶר
Jos 17: 2 their families Abi-e'zer, Helek, As'ri-el 2
Jdg 8: 2 of E'phraim better than the vintage of Abi-e'zer? 1
2Sm 23:27 Abi-e'zer, of An'athoth, Mebun'nai the Hu'shathite 1
1Ch 7:18 Hammo'lecheth bore . . Abi-e'zer, and Mahlah. 1
11:28 Ira the son of Ikkesh of Teko'a, Abi-e'zer of An'athoth 1
27:12 Ninth . . was Abi-e'zer of An'athoth, a Benjaminite; 1

Abiezrite 1. אֲבִי הָעֶזְרִי 2. אֲבִיעֶזֶר
Jdg 6:11 at Ophrah, which belonged to Jo'ash the Abiez'rite 1
24 at Ophrah, which belongs to the Abiez'rites. 1
34 and the Abiez'rites were called out to follow 2
8:32 tomb of Jo'ash . . at Ophrah of the Abiez'rites. 1

Abigail 1. אֲבִיגַיִל 2. אֲבִיגָל
1Sm 25: 3 man was Nabal, and the name of his wife Ab'igail. 1
14 But one of the young men told Ab'igail, Nabal's wife 1
18 Ab'igail made haste, and took 200 loaves 1
23 When Ab'igail saw David, she made haste 1
32 David said to Ab'igail, "Blessed be the LORD 2
36 And Ab'igail came to Nabal; 1
39 Then David . . wooed Ab'igail, to make her his wife. 1
40 the servants of David came to Ab'igail at Carmel 1
42 Ab'igail made haste and rose and mounted on an ass 1
27: 3 Ahin'o-am . . and Ab'igail of Carmel, Nabal's widow. 1
30: 5 Ahin'o-am . . and Ab'igail the widow of Nabal 1
2Sm 2: 2 his two wives also, Ahin'o-am . . and Ab'igail 1
3: 3 Chil'e-ab, of Ab'igail the widow of Nabal of Carmel; 1
1Ch 2:16 their sisters were Zeru'iah and Ab'igail. 1
17 Ab'igail bore Ama'sa, and the father of Ama'sa was 1
3: 1 the second Daniel, by Ab'igail the Car'melitess 1

Abigal 1. אֲבִיגַל
2Sm 17:25 a man named Ithra . . who had married Ab'igal 1

Abihail 1. אֲבִיחַיִל
Num 3:35 head . . was Zu'riel the son of Ab'ihail; 1
1Ch 2:29 Abi'shur's wife was Ab'ihail, and she bore him Ahban 1
5:14 the sons of Ab'ihail the son of Huri, son of Jaro'ah 1
2Ch 11:18 Ma'Halath the daughter . . of Ab'ihail 1
Est 2:15 Esther the daughter of Ab'ihail the uncle 1
9:29 Queen Esther, the daughter of Ab'ihail 1

Abihu 1. אֲבִיהוּא
Exd 6:23 she bore him Nadab, Abi'hu, Elea'zar, and Ith'amar. 1
24: 1 Come up . . you and Aaron, Nadab, and Abi'hu 1
9 Then Moses and Aaron, Nadab, and Abi'hu, 1
28: 1 Nadab and Abi'hu, Elea'zar and Ith'amar. 1
Lev 10: 1 Now Nadab and Abi'hu, the sons of Aaron 1
Num 3: 2 Nadab the first-born, and Abi'hu, Elea'zar 1
4 Nadab and Abi'hu died before the LORD 1
26:60 And to Aaron were born Nadab, Abi'hu, Elea'zar 1
61 Nadab and Abi'hu died when they offered unholy 1
1Ch 6: 3 The sons of Aaron: Nadab, Abi'hu, Elea'zar 1
24: 1 sons of Aaron: Nadab, Abi'hu, Elea'zar, 1
2 Nadab and Abi'hu died before their father 1

Abihud 1. אֲבִיהוּד
1Ch 8: 3 Bela had sons: Addar, Gera, Abi'hud 1

Abijah 1. אֲבִיָּהוּ 2. Ἀβιά
1Sm 8: 2 first-born . . and the name of his second, Abi'jah; 1
1Kg 14: 1 Abi'jah the son of Jerobo'am fell sick. 1
1Ch 3:10 descendants of Solomon: Rehobo'am, Abi'jah his son 1
6:28 sons of Samuel: Jo'el . . the second Abi'jah. 1
7: 8 sons of Becher . . Abi'jah, An'athoth, and Al'emeth. 1
24:10 the seventh to Hakkoz, the eighth to Abi'jah 1
2Ch 11:20 Ma'acah . . bore him Abi'jah, Attai, Ziza 1
22 Rehobo'am appointed Abi'jah . . as chief prince 1
12:16 Abi'jah his son reigned in his stead. 1
13: 1 Jerobo'am Abi'jah began to reign over Judah. 1
2 Now there was war between Abi'jah and Jerobo'am. 1
3 Abi'jah went out to battle having an army 1
4 Then Abi'jah stood up on Mount Zemara'im 1
15 defeated Jerobo'am . . before Abi'jah and Judah. 1
17 Abi'jah and his people slew them 1
19 Abi'jah pursued Jerobo'am, and took cities 1
20 did not recover his power in the days of Abi'jah; 1
21 Abi'jah grew mighty. And he took fourteen wives 1
22 The rest of the acts of Abi'jah 1
14: 1 Abi'jah slept with his fathers 1
29: 1 His mother's name was Abi'jah 1
Neh 10: 7 Meshul'lam, Abi'jah, Mi'jamin 1
12: 4 Iddo, Gin'nethoi, Abi'jah 1
17 of Abi'jah, Zichri; of Mini'amin, of Moadi'ah, Pil'tai; 1
Mat 1: 7 and Rehoboam the father of Abi'jah 2
7 and Abi'jah the father of Asa 2
Lke 1: 5 Zechari'ah, of the division of Abi'jah 2

Abijam 1. אֲבִיָּם
1Kg 14:31 And Abi'jam his son reigned in his stead. 1
15: 1 Abi'jam began to reign over Judah. 1
7 The rest of the acts of Abi'jam, and all that he did 1
7 there was war between Abi'jam and Jerobo'am. 1
8 Abi'jam slept with his fathers; 1

Abilene 1. Ἀβιληνή
Lke 3: 1 Lysa'nias tetrarch of Abile'ne 1

Abimael 1. אֲבִימָאֵל
Gen 10:28 Obal, Abim'a-el, Sheba 1
1Ch 1:22 Ebal, Abim'a-el, Sheba 1

Abimelech 1. אֲבִימֶלֶךְ
Gen 20: 2 And Abim'elech king of Gerar sent and took Sarah. 1
3 God came to Abim'elech in a dream by night 1
4 Now Abim'elech had not approached her, so he said 1
8 Abim'elech rose early in the morning 1
9 Then Abim'elech called Abraham, and said to him 1
10 Abim'elech said to Abraham, "What were you 1
14 Then Abim'elech took sheep and oxen 1
15 Abim'elech said, "Behold, my land is before you; 1
17 Abraham prayed to God; and God healed Abim'elech 1
18 the wombs of the house of Abim'elech 1
21:22 At that time Abim'elech and Phicol the commander 1
25 Abraham complained to Abim'elech about a well 1
25 water which Abim'elech's servants had seized 1
26 Abim'elech said, "I do not know who has done this 1
27 took sheep and oxen and gave them to Abim'elech 1
29 Abim'elech said to Abraham, "What is the meaning 1
32 Then Abim'elech and Phicol the commander 1
26: 1 And Isaac went to Gerar, to Abim'elech 1
8 Abim'elech king of the Philistines looked out 1
9 Abim'elech called Isaac, and said 1
10 Abim'elech said, "What is this you have done to us 1
11 Abim'elech warned all the people, saying 1
16 Abim'elech said to Isaac, "Go away from us; 1
26 Then Abim'elech went to him from Gerar 1
Jdg 8:31 bore him a son, and he called his name Abim'elech. 1
9: 1 Abim'elech the son of Jerubba'al went to Shechem 1
3 and their hearts inclined to follow Abim'elech 1
4 Abim'elech hired worthless and reckless 1
6 they went and made Abim'elech king, by the oak 1
16 faith and honor when you made Abim'elech king 1
18 and have made Abim'elech . . king over . . Shechem 1
19 then rejoice in Abim'elech, and let him also 1
20 let fire come out from Abim'elech, and devour 1
20 let fire come out . . and devour Abim'elech. 1
21 fled . . for fear of Abim'elech his brother. 1
22 Abim'elech ruled over Israel three years. 1
23 God sent an evil spirit between Abim'elech 1
23 Shechem dealt treacherously with Abim'elech; 1
24 blood be laid upon Abim'elech their brother 1
25 by them along that way; and it was told Abim'elech. 1
27 god, and ate and drank and reviled Abim'elech. 1
28 Who is Abim'elech, and who are we of Shechem 1
29 under my hand! then I would remove Abim'elech 1
29 would remove Abim'elech, I would say to Abim'elech 1
31 he sent messengers to Abim'elech at Aru'mah 1
34 Abim'elech and all . . with him rose up by night 1
35 and Abim'elech and the men that were with him rose 1
38 said, 'Who is Abim'elech, that we should serve him?' 1
39 Ga'al went out . . and fought with Abim'elech. 1
40 Abim'elech chased him, and he fled before him; 1
41 Abim'elech dwelt at Aru'mah; and Zebul drove out 1
42 men went out . . And Abim'elech was told. 1
44 Abim'elech and the company . . with him rushed 1
45 Abim'elech fought against the city all that day; 1
47 Abim'elech was told that all the people 1
48 Abim'elech went up to Mount Zalmon 1
48 Abim'elech took an axe in his hand, and cut down 1
49 and following Abim'elech put it against 1
50 Then Abim'elech went to Thebez, and encamped 1
52 Abim'elech came to the tower, and fought 1
53 threw an upper millstone upon Abim'elech's head 1
55 the men of Israel saw that Abim'elech was dead 1
56 Thus God requited the crime of Abim'elech 1
10: 1 After Abim'elech there arose to deliver Israel 1
2Sm 11:21 Who killed Abim'elech the son of Jerub'besheth? 1
Ps 34: 0 when he feigned madness before Abimelech 1

Abinadab 1. אֲבִינָדָב
1Sm 7: 1 brought it to the house of Abin'adab on the hill; 1
16: 8 Jesse called Abin'adab, and made him pass before 1
17:13 and next to him Abin'adab, and the third Shammah. 1
31: 2 the Philistines slew Jonathan and Abin'adab 1
2Sm 6: 3 and brought it out of the house of Abin'adab 1
3 Uzzah and Ahi'o, the sons of Abin'adab, were driving 1
1Ch 2:13 Jesse was the father of . . Abin'adab the second 1
8:33 Saul of . . Mal'chishu'a, Abin'adab, and Eshba'al; 1
9:39 Saul of Jonathan . . Abin'adab, and Eshba'al; 1
10: 2 Philistines slew Jonathan and Abin'adab 1
13: 7 upon a new cart, from the house of Abin'adab 1

Abinoam 1. אֲבִינֹעַם
Jdg 4: 6 Barak the son of Abin'o-am from Kedesh in Naph'tali 1
12 told that Barak the son of Abin'o-am had gone up 1
5: 1 Then sang Deb'orah and Barak the son of Abin'o-am 1
12 lead away your captives, O son of Abin'o-am. 1

Abiram 1. אֲבִירָם 2. Αβιρων
Num16: 1 Dathan and Abi'ram the sons of Eli'ab, and On 1
12 Moses sent to call Dathan and Abi'ram 1
24 about the dwelling of Korah, Dathan, and Abi'ram. 1
25 Then Moses rose and went to Dathan and Abi'ram; 1
27 got away from about the dwelling of . . Abi'ram 1
27 Dathan and Abi'ram came out and stood at the door 1
26: 9 The sons of Eli'ab: Nem'uel, Dathan, and Abi'ram. 1
9 These are the Dathan and Abi'ram . . who contended 1
Deu 11: 6 what he did to Dathan and Abi'ram the sons of Eli'ab 1
1Kg 16:34 he laid its foundation at the cost of Abi'ram 1
Ps 106:17 earth opened . . covered the company of Abi'ram. 1
Sir 45:18 Dathan and Abiram and their men 2
4Mc 2:17 When Moses was angry with Dathan and Abiram 2

Abishag 1. אֲבִישַׁג
1Kg 1: 3 they sought . . and found Ab'ishag the Shu'nammite 1
15 Ab'ishag the Shu'nammite was ministering 1
2:17 to give me Ab'ishag the Shu'nammite as my wife. 1
21 Let Ab'ishag the Shu'nammite be given to Adoni'jah 1
22 why do you ask Ab'ishag the Shu'nammite 1

Abishai 1. אֲבִישַׁי
1Sm 26: 6 David said . . to Jo'ab's brother Abi'shai 1
6 And Abi'shai said, "I will go down with you. 1
7 David and Abi'shai went to the army by night; 1
8 Then said Abi'shai to David, "God has given 1
9 But David said to Abi'shai, "Do not destroy him; 1
2Sm 2:18 sons of Zeru'iah . . Jo'ab, Abi'shai, and As'ahel. 1
24 But Jo'ab and Abi'shai pursued Abner; 1
3:30 Jo'ab and Abi'shai his brother slew Abner 1
10:10 he put in the charge of Abi'shai his brother 1
14 they likewise fled before Abi'shai 1
16: 9 Then Abi'shai the son of Zeru'iah said to the king 1
11 David said to Abi'shai and to all his servants 1
18: 2 under the command of Abi'shai the son of Zeru'iah 1
5 And the king ordered Jo'ab and Abi'shai and It'tai 1
12 the king commanded you and Abi'shai and It'tai 1
19:21 Abi'shai the son of Zeru'iah answered 1
20: 6 And David said to Abi'shai, "Now Sheba . . will do 1
7 And there went out after Abi'shai, Jo'ab •
10 Then Jo'ab and Abi'shai his brother pursued Sheba 1
21:17 But Abi'shai the son of Zeru'iah came to his aid 1
23:18 Now Abi'shai . . was chief of the 30. 1
1Ch 2:16 The sons of Zeru'iah: Abi'shai, Jo'ab, and As'ahel 1
11:20 Abi'shai, the brother of Jo'ab, was chief of the 30 1
18:12 Abi'shai, the son of Zeru'iah, slew 18,000 E'domites 1
19:11 the rest of his men he put in the charge of Abi'shai 1
15 likewise fled before Abi'shai, Jo'ab's brother 1

Abishalom 1. אֲבִישָׁלוֹם
1Kg 15: 2 name was Ma'acah the daughter of Abish'alom. 1
10 name was Ma'acah the daughter of Abish'alom. 1

Abishua 1. אֲבִישׁוּעַ 2. Αβισουε 3. Abissei
1Ch 6: 4 the father of Phin'ehas, Phin'ehas of Abishu'a 1
5 Abishu'a of Bukki, Bukki of Uzzi 1
50 sons of Aaron . . Phin'ehas . . Abishu'a his son 1
8: 4 Abishu'a, Na'aman, Aho'ah 1
Ezr 7: 5 son of Abi'shu-a, son of Phin'ehas 1
1Es 8: 2 son of Uzzi, son of Bukki, son of Abishua 2
2Es 1: 2 son of Borith, son of Abishua, son of Phinehas 3

Abishur 1. אֲבִישׁוּר
1Ch 2:28 The sons of Sham'mai: Nadab and Abi'shur. 1
29 The name of Abi'shur's wife was Ab'ihail 1

Abital 1. אֲבִיטַל
2Sm 3: 4 and the fifth, Shephati'ah the son of Abi'tal; 1
1Ch 3: 3 the fifth Shephati'ah, by Abi'tal; 1

Abitub 1. אֲבִיטוּב
1Ch 8:11 He also had sons by Hushim: Abi'tub and Elpa'al. 1

Abiud 1. Ἀβιούδ
Mat 1:13 Zerub'babel the father of Abi'ud 1
13 and Abi'ud the father of Eli'akim 1

Abner 1. אֲבִינֵר
1Sm 14:50 the name of the commander of his army was Abner 1
51 and Ner the father of Abner was the son of Abi'el. 1
17:55 he said to Abner, the commander of the army 1
55 he said . . "Abner, whose son is this youth? 1
55 Abner said, "As your soul lives . . I cannot tell. 1
57 as David returned . . Abner took him, and brought 1

20:25 The king sat . . and Abner sat by Saul's side 1
26: 5 the place where Saul lay, with Abner the son of Ner 1
7 lay Saul . . and Abner and the army lay around him. 1
14 David called . . to Abner the son of Ner 1
14 Will you not answer, Abner?" Then Abner answered 1
14 Abner answered, "Who are you that calls to the king? 1
15 And David said to Abner, "Are you not a man? 1
2Sm 2: 8 Now Abner the son of Ner . . had taken Ish-bo'sheth 1
12 Abner the son of Ner . . went out from Mahana'im 1
14 Abner said to Jo'ab, "Let the young men arise 1
17 Abner and the men of Israel were beaten before 1
19 As'ahel pursued Abner, and . . turned neither 1
19 he turned . . from following Abner. 1
20 Abner looked behind him and said, "Is it you, As'ahel? 1
21 Abner said to him, "Turn aside . . and seize one 1
22 And Abner said again to As'ahel, "Turn aside 1
23 Abner smote him in the belly with . . his spear 1
24 But Jo'ab and Abi'shai pursued Abner; 1
25 And the Benjaminites gathered . . behind Abner 1
26 Abner called to Jo'ab, "Shall the sword devour 1
29 Abner and his men went . . through the Arabah; 1
30 Jo'ab returned from the pursuit of Abner; 1
31 servants . . had slain of Benjamin 360 of Abner's men. 1
3: 6 Abner was making himself strong in the house 1
7 and Ish-bo'sheth said to Abner, "Why have you gone 1
8 Then Abner was very angry over the words 1
9 God do so to Abner, and more also, if I do not 1
11 Ish-bo'sheth could not answer Abner another word 1
12 Abner sent messengers to David at Hebron, saying 1
16 Then Abner said to him, "Go, return"; 1
17 Abner conferred with the elders of Israel 1
19 Abner also spoke to Benjamin; and then Abner went 1
19 then Abner went to tell David at Hebron 1
20 Abner came with twenty men to David at Hebron 1
20 David made a feast for Abner and the men 1
21 And Abner said to David, "I will arise and go 1
21 David sent Abner away; and he went in peace. 1
22 But Abner was not with David at Hebron 1
23 Abner the son of Ner came to the king 1
24 Abner came to you; why is it that you have sent him 1
25 You know that Abner the son of Ner came to deceive 1
26 When Jo'ab came . . he sent messengers after Abner 1
27 when Abner returned . . Jo'ab took him aside 1
28 guiltless before the LORD for the blood of Abner 1
30 Jo'ab and Abi'shai his brother slew Abner 1
31 and gird on sackcloth, and mourn before Abner. 1
32 They buried Abner at Hebron; 1
32 and the king . . wept at the grave of Abner; 1
33 And the king lamented for Abner, saying 1
33 Should Abner die as a fool dies? 1
37 it had not been the king's will to slay Abner 1
4: 1 Saul's son . . heard that Abner had died at Hebron 1
12 took the head . . and buried it in the tomb of Abner 1
1Kg 2: 5 commanders . . Abner the son of Ner, and Ama'sa 1
32 slew . . Abner the son of Ner, commander of the army 1
1Ch 26:28 Abner the son of Ner, and Jo'ab the son of Zeru'iah 1
27:21 for Benjamin, Ja-a'si-el the son of Abner; 1

Abraham 1. אַבְרָהָם 2. ᾿Αβραάμ 3. Αβρααμειτις
4. Αβραμιαιος 5. Abraham

Gen 17: 5 be Abram, but your name shall be Abraham; 1
9 God said to Abraham, "As for you 1
15 God said to Abraham, "As for Sar'ai your wife 1
17 Then Abraham fell on his face and laughed 1
18 Abraham said to God, "O that Ish'mael might live 1
22 talking with him, God went up from Abraham. 1
23 Then Abraham took Ish'mael his son 1
23 every male among the men of Abraham's house 1
24 Abraham was 99 years old 1
26 That very day Abraham and his son Ish'mael 1
18: 6 Abraham hastened into the tent to Sarah, and said 1
7 Abraham ran to the herd, and took a calf 1
11 Now Abraham and Sarah were old, advanced in age; 1
13 The LORD said to Abraham, "Why did Sarah laugh 1
16 looked toward Sodom; and Abraham went with them 1
17 Shall I hide from Abraham what I am about to do 1
18 seeing that Abraham shall become a great 1
19 bring to Abraham what he has promised him. 1
22 Sodom; but Abraham still stood before the LORD. 1
23 Then Abraham drew near, and said 1
27 Abraham answered, "Behold, I have taken 1
33 when he had finished speaking to Abraham; 1
33 to Abraham; and Abraham returned to his place. 1
19:27 Abraham went early in the morning to the place 1
29 God remembered Abraham, and sent Lot out 1
20: 1 From there Abraham journeyed 1
2 Abraham said of Sarah his wife, "She is my sister. 1
9 Then Abim'elech called Abraham, and said to him 1
10 Abim'elech said to Abraham, "What were you 1
11 Abraham said, "I did it because I thought 1
14 male and female slaves, and gave them to Abraham 1
17 Abraham prayed to God; and God healed Abim'elech 1
18 of Abim'elech because of Sarah, Abraham's wife. 1
21: 2 Sarah conceived, and bore Abraham a son 1
3 Abraham called the name of his son who was born 1
4 Abraham circumcised his son Isaac 1
5 Abraham was 100 years old when . . Isaac was born 1
7 she said, "Who would have said to Abraham 1
8 and Abraham made a great feast 1
9 the Egyptian, whom she had borne to Abraham 1
10 she said to Abraham, "Cast out this slave woman 1
11 the thing was very displeasing to Abraham 1
12 God said to Abraham, "Be not displeased 1
14 Abraham rose early in the morning 1
22 commander of his army said to Abraham 1
24 And Abraham said, "I will swear. 1
25 Abraham complained to Abim'elech about a well 1
27 Abraham took sheep and oxen and gave them 1
28 Abraham set seven ewe lambs of the flock apart. 1
29 Abim'elech said to Abraham, "What is the meaning 1
33 Abraham planted a tamarisk tree in Beer-sheba 2
34 Abraham sojourned many days in the land 1
22: 1 After these things God tested Abraham 1
1 God tested Abraham, and said to him, "Abraham! 1
3 Abraham rose early in the morning 1
4 On the third day Abraham lifted up his eyes 1
5 Then Abraham said to his young men, "Stay here 1
6 Abraham took the wood of the burnt offering 1
7 Isaac said to his father Abraham, "My father! 1
8 Abraham said, "God will provide himself the lamb 1
9 Abraham built an altar there 1
10 Then Abraham put forth his hand 1
11 called to him from heaven, and said, "Abraham 1
11 Abraham, Abraham!" And he said, "Here am I. 1
13 Abraham lifted up his eyes and looked 1
13 and Abraham went and took the ram 1
14 Abraham called the name of that place 1
15 the angel of the LORD called to Abraham 1
19 Abraham returned to his young men 1
19 and Abraham dwelt at Beer-sheba. 1
20 Now after these things it was told Abraham 1
23 Milcah bore to Nahor, Abraham's brother. 1
23: 2 and Abraham went in to mourn for Sarah and to weep 1
3 Abraham rose up from before his dead 1
5 The Hittites answered Abraham 1
7 Abraham rose and bowed to the Hittites 1
10 Ephron the Hittite answered Abraham 1
12 Then Abraham bowed down before the people 1
14 Ephron answered Abraham 1
16 Abraham agreed with Ephron; 1
16 Abraham weighed out for Ephron the silver 1
18 to Abraham as a possession in the presence 1
19 After this, Abraham buried Sarah his wife 1
20 were made over to Abraham as a possession 1
24: 1 Abraham was old, well advanced in years; 1
1 the LORD had blessed Abraham in all things. 1
2 Abraham said to his servant 1
6 Abraham said to him, "See to it that you do not take 1
9 servant put his hand under the thigh of Abraham 1
12 he said, "O LORD, God of my master Abraham 1
12 show steadfast love to my master Abraham. 1
15 the wife of Nahor, Abraham's brother, came out 1
27 Blessed be the LORD, the God of my master Abraham 1
34 he said, "I am Abraham's servant. 1
42 and said, 'O LORD, the God of my master Abraham 1
48 blessed the LORD, the God of my master Abraham 1
52 When Abraham's servant heard their words 1
59 sent away . . Abraham's servant and his men. 1
25: 1 Abraham took another wife, whose name was 1
5 Abraham gave all he had to Isaac. 1
6 to the sons of his concubines Abraham gave gifts 1
7 These are the days of the years of Abraham's life 1
8 Abraham breathed his last and died 1
10 the field which Abraham purchased 1
10 There Abraham was buried, with Sarah his wife. 1
11 After the death of Abraham God blessed Isaac 1
12 the descendants of Ish'mael, Abraham's son 1
12 the Egyptian, Sarah's maid, bore to Abraham. 1
19 the descendants of Isaac, Abraham's son 1
19 Abraham was the father of Isaac 1
26: 1 former famine that was in the days of Abraham. 1
3 oath which I swore to Abraham your father. 1
5 Abraham obeyed my voice and kept my charge 1
15 had dug in the days of Abraham his father. 1
18 which had been dug in the days of Abraham 1
18 stopped them after the death of Abraham; 1
24 I am the God of Abraham your father; fear not 1
24 your descendants for my servant Abraham's sake. 1
28: 4 May he give the blessing of Abraham to you 1
4 of your sojournings which God gave to Abraham! 1
9 the daughter of Ish'mael Abraham's son 1
13 I am the LORD, the God of Abraham your father 1
31:42 If the God of my father, the God of Abraham 1
53 The God of Abraham and the God of Nahor 1
32: 9 God of my father Abraham and God of my father 1
35:12 The land which I gave to Abraham and Isaac I will 1
27 (that is, Hebron), where Abraham and Isaac 1
48:15 God before whom my fathers Abraham and Isaac 1
16 the name of my fathers Abraham and Isaac; 1
49:30 in the cave . . which Abraham bought 1
31 There they buried Abraham and Sarah his wife; 1
50:13 the cave . . which Abraham bought with the field 1
24 to the land which he swore to Abraham, 1
Exd 2:24 his covenant with Abraham, with Isaac 1
3: 6 I am the God of your father, the God of Abraham 1
15 God of Abraham, the God of Isaac, and the God 1
16 God of Abraham, of Isaac, and of Jacob, has appeared 1
4: 5 LORD . . the God of Abraham, the God of Isaac 1
6: 3 I appeared to Abraham, to Isaac, and to Jacob, as God 1
8 swore to give to Abraham, to Isaac, and to Jacob; 1
32:13 Remember Abraham, Isaac, and Israel, thy servants 1
33: 1 go up . . to the land of which I swore to Abraham 1
Lev 26:42 I will remember . . my covenant with Abraham 1
Num32:11 I swore to give to Abraham, to Isaac, and to Jacob 1
Deu 1: 8 to your fathers, to Abraham, to Isaac, and to Jacob 1
6:10 to your fathers, to Abraham, to Isaac, and to Jacob 1
9: 5 to your fathers, to Abraham, to Isaac, and to Jacob. 1
27 Remember thy servants, Abraham, Isaac, and Jacob; 1
29:13 as he swore to . . Abraham, to Isaac, and to Jacob. 1
30:20 to your fathers, to Abraham, to Isaac, and to Jacob 1
34: 4 land . . I swore to Abraham, to Isaac, and to Jacob 1
Jos 24: 2 Your fathers . . Terah, the father of Abraham 1
3 I took your father Abraham from beyond the River 1
1Kg 18:36 O LORD, God of Abraham, Isaac, and Israel, 1
2Kg 13:23 his covenant with Abraham, Isaac, and Jacob 1
1Ch 1:27 Abram, that is, Abraham. 1
28 The sons of Abraham: Isaac and Ish'mael. 1
32 The sons of Ketu'rah, Abraham's concubine 1
34 Abraham was the father of Isaac. 1
16:13 O offspring of Abraham his servant 1
16 the covenant which he made with Abraham 1
29:18 O LORD, the God of Abraham, Isaac, and Israel 1
2Ch 20: 7 give it for ever to the descendants of Abraham 1
30: 6 the LORD, the God of Abraham, Isaac, and Israel 1
Neh 9: 7 the God who didst . . give him the name Abraham; 1
Ps 47: 9 gather as the people of the God of Abraham. 1
105: 6 O offspring of Abraham, his servant 1
9 covenant which he made with Abraham 1
42 For he remembered . . Abraham his servant. 1
Isa 29:22 thus says the LORD, who redeemed Abraham 1
41: 8 Israel . . the offspring of Abraham, my friend; 1
51: 2 Look to Abraham your father and to Sarah 1
63:16 art our Father, though Abraham does not know us 1
Jer 33:26 to rule over the seed of Abraham, Isaac, and Jacob. 1
Ezk 33:24 Abraham was only one man, yet he got possession 1
Mic 7:20 Thou wilt show . . steadfast love to Abraham 1
Mat 1: 1 Jesus Christ, the son of David, the son of Abraham. 2
2 Abraham was the father of Isaac 2
17 So all the generations from Abraham to David 2
3: 9 say to yourselves, 'We have Abraham as our father'; 2
9 from these stones to raise up children to Abraham. 2
8:11 sit at table with Abraham, Isaac, and Jacob 2
22:32 'I am the God of Abraham, and the God of Isaac 2
Mrk 12:26 I am the God of Abraham, and the God of Isaac 2
Lke 1:55 to Abraham and to his posterity for ever. 2
73 the oath which he swore to our father Abraham 2
3: 8 'We have Abraham as our father' 2
8 these stones to raise up children to Abraham. 2
34 son of Isaac, the son of Abraham, the son of Terah 2
13:16 a daughter of Abraham whom Satan bound 2
28 when you see Abraham and Isaac and Jacob 2
16:22 and was carried by the angels to Abraham's bosom 2
23 he lifted up his eyes, and saw Abraham far off 2
24 he called out, 'Father Abraham, have mercy 2
25 Abraham said, 'Son, remember 2
29 Abraham said, 'They have Moses and the prophets; 2
30 he said, 'No, father Abraham 2
19: 9 since he also is a son of Abraham. 2
20:37 where he calls the Lord the God of Abraham 2
Joh 8:33 answered him, "We are descendants of Abraham 2
37 I know that you are descendants of Abraham 2
39 They answered him, "Abraham is our father. 2
39 Jesus said to them, "If you were Abraham's children 2
39 you would do what Abraham did 2
40 this is not what Abraham did. 2
52 Abraham died, as did the prophets 2
53 Are you greater than our father Abraham, who died? 2
56 Abraham rejoiced that he was to see my day 2
57 and have you seen Abraham? 2
58 before Abraham was, I am. 2
Act 3:13 The God of Abraham and of Isaac and of Jacob 2
25 saying to Abraham, 'And in your posterity 2
7: 2 The God of glory appeared to our father Abraham 2
8 so Abraham became the father of Isaac •
16 tomb that Abraham had bought for a sum of silver 2
17 which God had granted to Abraham 2
32 the God of Abraham and of Isaac and of Jacob 2
13:26 Brethren, sons of the family of Abraham 2
Rom 4: 1 What then shall we say about Abraham 2
2 For if Abraham was justified by works 2
3 Abraham believed God, and it was reckoned to him 2
9 faith was reckoned to Abraham as righteousness. 2
12 the faith which our father Abraham had 2
13 The promise to Abraham and his descendants 2
16 but also to those who share the faith of Abraham 2
9: 7 and not all are children of Abraham 2
11: 1 I myself am an Israelite, a descendant of Abraham 2
2Co 11:22 Are they descendants of Abraham? So am I. 2
Gal 3: 6 Thus Abraham "believed God 2
7 it is men of faith who are the sons of Abraham. 2
8 preached the gospel beforehand to Abraham 2
9 blessed with Abraham who had faith. 2
14 that in Christ Jesus the blessing of Abraham 2
16 Now the promises were made to Abraham 2
18 God gave it to Abraham by a promise. 2
29 then you are Abraham's offspring 2

4:22 For it is written that Abraham had two sons 2
Heb 2:16 concerned . . with the descendants of Abraham. 2
6:13 For when God made a promise to Abraham 2
15 thus Abraham . . obtained the promise. •
7: 1 met Abraham returning from the slaughter 2
2 to him Abraham apportioned a tenth part 2
4 Abraham . . gave him a tithe of the spoils. 2
5 though these also are descended from Abraham. 2
6 received tithes from Abraham 2
9 Levi himself . . paid tithes through Abraham 2
11: 8 By faith Abraham obeyed 2
17 By faith Abraham . . offered up Isaac 2
Jas 2:21 Was not Abraham our father justified by works 2
23 Abraham believed God 2
1Pe 3: 6 as Sarah obeyed Abraham, calling him lord. 2
2Es 1:39 to them I will give as leaders Abraham, Isaac 5
3:13 one of them, whose name was Abraham; 5
6: 8 He said to me, "From Abraham to Isaac 5
7:106 first Abraham prayed for the people of Sodom 5
Tob 4:12 Noah, Abraham, Isaac, and Jacob, our fathers 2
Jdt 8:26 Remember what he did with Abraham 2
AEs 13:15 now, O Lord God and King, God of Abraham 2
14:18 except in thee, O Lord God of Abraham. 2
Sir 44:19 Abraham was the great father of . . nations 2
22 for the sake of Abraham his father. 2
Bar 2:34 fathers, to Abraham and to Isaac and to Jacob 2
Aza 1:12 for the sake of Abraham thy beloved 2
Man 1: 1 God . . of Abraham and Isaac and Jacob 2
8 repentance . . for Abraham and Isaac and Jacob 2
1Mc 2:52 Was not Abraham found faithful when tested 2
12:21 are brethren and are of the family of Abraham. 2
2Mc 1: 2 remember his covenant with Abraham and Isaac 2
3Mc 6: 3 look upon the descendants of Abraham, O Father 2
4Mc 6:17 May we, the children of Abraham, never think 2
22 Therefore, O children of Abraham, die nobly 2
7:19 like our patriarchs Abraham and Isaac and Jacob 2
9:21 the courageous youth, worthy of Abraham 4
13:17 Abraham and Isaac and Jacob will welcome us 2
14:20 she was of the same mind as Abraham. 2
15:28 as the daughter of God-fearing Abraham 2
16:20 our father Abraham was zealous to sacrifice 2
25 as do Abraham and Isaac and Jacob 2
17: 6 were true descendants of father Abraham. 2
18: 1 offspring of the seed of Abraham 4
20 those seven sons of the daughter of Abraham 3
23 the sons of Abraham with their . . mother 4

Abram 1. אַבְרָם

Gen 11:26 Terah . . the father of Abram, Nahor, and Haran. 1
27 Terah was the father of Abram, Nahor, and Haran; 1
29 Abram and Nahor took wives; 1
29 the name of Abram's wife was Sar'ai 1
31 Terah took Abram his son and Lot the son of Haran 1
31 Sar'ai . . his son Abram's wife 1
12: 1 Now the LORD said to Abram, "Go from your country 1
4 Abram went, as the LORD had told him; 1
4 Abram was 75 years old when he departed 1
5 Abram took Sar'ai his wife, and Lot 1
6 Abram passed through the land to the place 1
7 Then the LORD appeared to Abram, and said 1
9 Abram journeyed on 1
10 So Abram went down to Egypt to sojourn there 1
14 When Abram entered Egypt the Egyptians saw that 1
16 for her sake he dealt well with Abram; 1
17 plagues because of Sar'ai, Abram's wife. 1
18 Pharaoh called Abram, and said, "What is this 1
13: 1 Abram went up from Egypt, he and his wife 1
2 Now Abram was very rich in cattle 1
4 there Abram called on the name of the LORD. 1
5 Lot, who went with Abram, also had flocks 1
7 strife between the herdsmen of Abram's cattle 1
8 Then Abram said to Lot, "Let there be no strife 1
12 Abram dwelt in the land of Canaan 1
14 The LORD said to Abram, after Lot had separated 1
18 Abram moved his tent, and came and dwelt 1
14:12 they also took Lot, the son of Abram's brother 1
13 one . . came, and told Abram the Hebrew 1
13 Eshcol and of Aner; these were allies of Abram. 1
14 When Abram heard that his kinsman had been taken 1
19 he blessed him and said, "Blessed be Abram by God 1
20 And Abram gave him a tenth of everything. •
21 the king of Sodom said to Abram 1
22 Abram said to the king of Sodom 1
23 lest you should say, 'I have made Abram rich.' 1
15: 1 the word of the LORD came to Abram in a vision 1
1 Fear not, Abram, I am your shield; 1
2 Abram said, "O Lord GOD, what wilt thou give me 1
3 Abram said, "Behold, thou hast given me 1
11 upon the carcasses, Abram drove them away. 1
12 a deep sleep fell on Abram; 1
13 Then the LORD said to Abram, "Know of a surety 1
18 On that day the LORD made a covenant with Abram 1
16: 1 Now Sar'ai, Abram's wife, bore him no children. 1
2 Sar'ai said to Abram, "Behold now, the LORD has 1
2 And Abram hearkened to the voice of Sar'ai. 1
3 after Abram had dwelt ten years in the land 1
3 Sar'ai, Abram's wife, took Hagar the Egyptian 1
3 Sar'ai . . gave her to Abram her husband 1
5 Sar'ai said to Abram, "May the wrong done to me be 1
6 Abram said to Sar'ai 1
15 Hagar bore Abram a son; and Abram called the name 1
15 Hagar bore Abram a son; and Abram called the name 1
16 Abram was 86 years old when Hagar bore Ish'mael 1
16 when Hagar bore Ish'mael to Abram. 1
17: 1 When Abram was 99 years old the LORD appeared 1
1 the LORD appeared to Abram, and said to him 1
3 Then Abram fell on his face; and God said to him 1
5 No longer shall your name be Abram 1
1Ch 1:27 Abram, that is, Abraham. 1
Neh 9: 7 God who didst choose Abram and bring him forth 1

Abron 1. Αβρωνα

Jdt 2:24 all the hilltop cities along the brook Abron 1

Abronah 1. עַבְרֹנָה

Num33:34 set out from Jot'bathah, and encamped at Abro'nah. 1
35 they set out from Abro'nah, and encamped 1

Absalom 1. אֲבִישָׁלוֹם 2. Αβεσσαλωμ 3. Αψαλωμος

2Sm 3: 3 and the third, Ab'salom the son of Ma'acah 1
13: 1 Now Ab'salom, David's son, had a beautiful sister 1
4 I love Tamar, my brother Ab'salom's sister. 1
20 And her brother Ab'salom said to her 1
20 Tamar dwelt . . in her brother Ab'salom's house. 1
22 But Ab'salom spoke to Amnon neither good nor bad; 1
22 Ab'salom hated Amnon, because he had forced 1
23 Ab'salom had sheepshearers at Ba'al-ha'zor 1
23 and Ab'salom invited all the king's sons. 1
24 And Ab'salom came to the king, and said, "Behold 1
25 But the king said to Ab'salom, "No, my son 1
26 Then Ab'salom said, "If not, pray let . . Amnon go 1
27 Ab'salom pressed him until he let Amnon . . go 1
28 Then Ab'salom commanded his servants 1
29 So the servants of Ab'salom did to Amnon 1
29 did to Amnon as Ab'salom had commanded. 1
30 Ab'salom has slain all the king's sons 1
32 by . . Ab'salom this has been determined 1
34 But Ab'salom fled. 1
37 But Ab'salom fled, and went to Talmai 1
38 So Ab'salom fled, and went to Geshur 1
39 spirit of the king longed to go forth to Ab'salom; 1
14: 1 that the king's heart went out to Ab'salom. 1
21 I grant this; go, bring back the young man Ab'salom. 1
23 Jo'ab arose . . and brought Ab'salom to Jerusalem. 1
24 Ab'salom dwelt apart in his own house 1
25 no one . . to be praised for his beauty as Ab'salom; 1
27 were born to Ab'salom three sons, and one daughter 1
28 Ab'salom dwelt two full years in Jerusalem 1
29 Then Ab'salom sent for Jo'ab, to send him to the king; 1
30 Ab'salom's servants set the field on fire. 1
31 Then Jo'ab arose and went to Ab'salom at his house 1
32 Ab'salom answered Jo'ab, "Behold, I sent word to you 1
33 Then Jo'ab . . told him; and he summoned Ab'salom. 1
33 and the king kissed Ab'salom. 1
15: 1 Ab'salom got himself a chariot and horses 1
2 Ab'salom used to rise early and stand beside 1
2 Ab'salom would call to him, and say, "From what city 1
3 Ab'salom would say to him, "See, your claims are good 1
4 Ab'salom said moreover, "Oh that I were judge 1
6 Thus Ab'salom did to all . . who came to the king 1
6 so Ab'salom stole the hearts of the men of Israel. 1
7 Ab'salom said to the king, "Pray let me go 1
10 Ab'salom sent secret messengers throughout all 1
10 As soon as . . then say, 'Ab'salom is king at Hebron!' 1
11 With Ab'salom went 200 men from Jerusalem 1
12 And while Ab'salom was offering the sacrifices 1
12 and the people with Ab'salom kept increasing. 1
13 The . . men of Israel have gone after Ab'salom. 1
14 else there will be no escape for us from Ab'salom; 1
31 is among the conspirators with Ab'salom. 1
34 But if you return to the city, and say to Ab'salom 1
37 just as Ab'salom was entering Jerusalem. 1
16: 8 the kingdom into the hand of your son Ab'salom. 1
15 Ab'salom and all the people . . came to Jerusalem 1
16 And when Hushai . . came to Ab'salom, Hushai said 1
16 Hushai said to Ab'salom, "Long live the king! 1
17 And Ab'salom said to Hushai, "Is this your loyalty 1
18 And Hushai said to Ab'salom, "No; 1
20 Ab'salom said to Ahith'ophel, "Give your counsel; 1
21 Ahith'ophel said to Ab'salom, "Go in to your father's 1
22 So they pitched a tent for Ab'salom upon the roof; 1
22 and Ab'salom went in to his father's concubines 1
23 so was . . esteemed, both by David and by Ab'salom. 1
17: 1 Moreover Ahith'ophel said to Ab'salom 1
4 the advice pleased Ab'salom and all the elders 1
5 Then Ab'salom said, "Call Hushai the Archite also 1
6 And when Hushai came to Ab'salom, Ab'salom said 1
6 when Hushai came to Ab'salom, Ab'salom said to him 1
7 Then Hushai said to Ab'salom 1
9 slaughter among the people who follow Ab'salom.' 1
14 And Ab'salom and all the men of Israel said 1
14 so that the LORD might bring evil upon Ab'salom. 1
15 counsel Ab'salom and the elders of Israel; 1
18 But a lad saw them, and told Ab'salom; 1
20 Ab'salom's servants came to the woman at the house 1
24 Ab'salom crossed the Jordan with all . . Israel. 1
25 Ab'salom had set Ama'sa over the army instead 1
26 And Israel and Ab'salom encamped in the land 1
18: 5 Deal gently . . with the young man Ab'salom. 1
5 the king gave orders to all . . about Ab'salom. 1
9 Ab'salom chanced to meet the servants of David. 1
9 Ab'salom was riding upon his mule 1
10 Behold, I saw Ab'salom hanging in an oak. 1
12 'For my sake protect the young man Ab'salom.' 1
14 and thrust them into the heart of Ab'salom 1
15 ten young men . . surrounded Ab'salom and struck 1
17 they took Ab'salom, and threw him into a great pit 1
18 Ab'salom . . set up for himself the pillar 1
18 and it is called Ab'salom's monument to this day. 1
29 Is it well with the young man Ab'salom? 1
32 king said . . "Is it well with the young man Ab'salom? 1
33 said, "O my son Ab'salom, my son, my son Ab'salom! 1
33 said, "O my son Ab'salom, my son, my son Ab'salom! 1
33 Would I had died instead of you, O Ab'salom, my son 1
19: 1 the king is weeping and mourning for Ab'salom. 1
4 O my son Ab'salom, O Ab'salom, my son, my son! 1
4 O my son Ab'salom, O Ab'salom, my son, my son! 1
6 if Ab'salom were alive and all of us . . dead today 1
9 and now he has fled out of the land from Ab'salom. 1
10 But Ab'salom, whom we anointed over us, is dead 1
20: 6 Now Sheba . . will do us more harm than Ab'salom; 1
1Kg 1: 6 handsome man; and he was born next after Ab'salom. 1
2: 7 met me when I fled from Ab'salom your brother. 1
28 Adoni'jah although he had not supported Ab'salom- 1
1Ch 3: 2 the third Ab'salom, whose mother was Ma'acah 1
2Ch 11:20 After her he took Ma'acah the daughter of Ab'salom 1
21 Rehobo'am loved Ma'acah the daughter of Ab'salom 1
Ps 3: 0 David, when he fled from Absalom his son. 1
1Mc 11:70 Mattathias the son of Absalom 3
13:11 He sent Jonathan the son of Absalom to Joppa 3
2Mc 11:17 John and Absalom, who were sent by you 2

Abubus 1. Αβουβος

1Mc 16:11 Ptolemy the son of Abubus 1
15 The son of Abubus received them treacherously 1

Accad 1. אַכַּד

Gen 10:10 his kingdom was Ba'bel, Erech, and Accad 1

Acco 1. עַכּוֹ

Jdg 1:31 Asher did not drive out the inhabitants of Acco 1

Accos 1. Ακκως

1Mc 8:17 Eupolemus the son of John, son of Accos 1

Achaia 1. 'Αχαΐα

Act 18:12 when Gallio was proconsul of Acha'ia 1
27 when he wished to cross to Acha'ia 1
19:21 to pass through Macedo'nia and Acha'ia 1
Rom 15:26 For Macedo'nia and Acha'ia have been pleased 1
1Co 16:15 were the first converts in Acha'ia 1
2Co 1: 1 with all the saints who are in the whole of Acha'ia 1
9: 2 Acha'ia has been ready since last year 1
11:10 shall not be silenced in the regions of Acha'ia. 1
1Th 1: 7 all the believers in Macedo'nia and in Acha'ia. 1
8 sounded forth from you in Macedo'nia and Acha'ia 1

Achaicus 1. 'Αχαϊκός

1Co 16:17 Steph'anas and Fortuna'tus and Acha'icus 1

Achan 1. עָכָן 2. Achar

Jos 7: 1 Achan . . of Judah, took some of the devoted things; 1
18 and Achan the son of Carmi . . of Judah, was taken. 1
19 Joshua said to Achan, "My son, give glory to the LORD 1
20 Achan answered Joshua, "Of a truth I have sinned 1
24 Joshua . . took Achan the son of Zerah 1
22:20 Did not Achan . . break faith in the matter 1
2Es 7:107 Joshua after him for Israel in the days of Achan 2

Achar 1. עָכָר

1Ch 2: 7 The sons of Carmi: Achar, the troubler of Israel 1

Achbor 1. עַכְבּוֹר

Gen 36:38 Ba'al-ha'nan the son of Achbor reigned in his 1
39 Ba'al-ha'nan the son of Achbor died 1
2Kg 22:12 Ahi'kam the son of . . and Achbor the son of Micai'ah 1
14 and Ahi'kam, and Achbor, and Shaphan, and Asai'ah 1
1Ch 1:49 Ba'al-ha'nan, the son of Achbor, reigned in his stead 1
Jer 26:22 Elna'than the son of Achbor and others with him 1
36:12 Elna'than the son of Achbor 1

Achim 1. 'Αχίμ

Mat 1:14 and Zadok the father of Achim 1
14 and Achim the father of Eli'ud 1

Achior 1. Αχιωρ

Jdt 5: 5 Then Achior, the leader of all the Ammonites, said 1
22 When Achior had finished saying this 1
6: 1 Holofernes . . said to Achior 1
2 who are you, Achior, and you hirelings of Ephraim 1
5 you, Achior, you Ammonite hireling 1
10 to seize Achior and take him to Bethulia 1
13 they bound Achior 1
16 they set Achior in the midst of all their people 1
20 they consoled Achior, and praised him greatly. 1
11: 9 Now as for the things Achior said in your council 1
14: 5 bring Achior the Ammonite to me 1

6 they summoned Achior from the house of Uzziah. 1
10 Achior saw all that the God of Israel had done 1

Achish 1. אָכִישׁ

1Sm 21:10 David rose . . and went to A'chish the king of Gath. 1
11 And the servants of A'chish said to him 1
12 and was much afraid of A'chish the king of Gath. 1
14 said A'chish to his servants, "Lo . . the man is mad; 1
27: 2 arose and went over . . to A'chish the son of Ma'och 1
3 David dwelt with A'chish at Gath, he and his men 1
5 Then David said to A'chish, "If I have found favor 1
6 that day A'chish gave him Ziklag; 1
9 but took away . . and came back to A'chish. 1
10 A'chish asked, "Against whom have you made a raid 1
12 And A'chish trusted David, thinking 1
28: 1 And A'chish said to David 1
2 David said to A'chish, "Very well, you shall know 1
2 And A'chish said to David, "Very well 1
29: 2 David and his men were . . in the rear with A'chish 1
3 And A'chish said to the commanders 1
6 Then A'chish called David and said to him 1
8 And David said to A'chish, "But what have I done? 1
9 And A'chish made answer to David, "I know 1
1Kg 2:39 ran away to Achish, son of Ma'acah, king of Gath. 1
40 Shim'e-i arose . . and went to Gath to Achish 1

Achor 1. עָכוֹר

Jos 7:24 and they brought them up to the Valley of Achor. 1
26 name of that place is called the Valley of Achor. 1
15: 7 goes up to Debir from the Valley of Achor 1
Isa 65:10 the Valley of Achor a place for herds to lie down 1
Hos 2:15 and make the Valley of Achor a door of hope. 1

Achsah 1. עַכְסָה

Jos 15:16 to him will I give Achsah my daughter as wife. 1
17 and he gave him Achsah his daughter as wife. 1
Jdg 1:12 I will give him Achsah my daughter as wife. 1
13 and he gave him Achsah his daughter as wife. 1
1Ch 2:49 and the daughter of Caleb was Achsah. 1

Achshaph 1. אַכְשָׁף

Jos 11: 1 he sent to . . the king of Ach'shaph 1
12:20 the king of Ach'shaph, one; 1
19:25 included Helkath, Hali, Beten, Ach'shaph 1

Achzib 1. אַכְזִיב

Jos 15:44 Kei'lah, Achzib, and Mare'shah 1
19:29 and it ends at the sea; Mahalab, Achzib 1
Jdg 1:31 inhabitants of Sidon, or of Ahlab, or of Achzib 1
Mic 1:14 the houses of Achzib shall be a deceitful thing 1

Acraba 1. Εγρεβηλ

Jdt 7:18 toward the south and the east, toward Acraba 1

Adadah 1. עַדְעָדָה

Jos 15:22 Kinah, Dimo'nah, Ada'dah 1

Adah 1. עָדָה

Gen 4:19 took two wives; the name of the one was Adah 1
20 Adah bore Jabal; he was the father 1
23 Lamech said to his wives: "Adah and Zillah 1
36: 2 the Canaanites: Adah the daughter of Elon 1
4 Adah bore to Esau, El'iphaz; 1
10 Esau's sons: El'iphaz the son of Adah the wife 1
12 These are the sons of Adah, Esau's wife. 1
16 the land of Edom; they are the sons of Adah. 1

Adaiah 1. עֲדָיָהוּ 2. Ιεδαιος

2Kg 22: 1 mother's name was Jedi'dah the daughter of Adai'ah 1
1Ch 6:41 son of Ethni, son of Zerah, son of Adai'ah 1
8:21 Adai'ah, Berai'ah, and Shimrath . . sons of Shim'e-i. 1
9:12 Adai'ah the son of Jero'ham, son of Pashhur 1
2Ch 23: 1 commanders . . Ma-asei'ah the son of Adai'ah 1
Ezr 10:29 of Bani were Meshul'lam, Malluch, Adai'ah, Jashub 1
39 Shelemi'ah, Nathan, Adai'ah 1
Neh 11: 5 Hazai'ah, son of Adai'ah, son of Joi'arib 1
12 Adai'ah the son of Jero'ham, son of Pelali'ah 1
1Es 9:30 Of the sons of Bani: Meshullam, Malluch, Adaiah 2

Adalia 1. אֲדַלְיָא

Est 9: 8 and Pora'tha and Ada'lia and Arida'tha 1

Adam 1. אָדָם 2. Ἀδάμ 3. Adam

Gen 3:17 to Adam he said, "Because you have listened 1
21 made for Adam and for his wife garments of skins 1
4: 1 Adam knew Eve his wife, and she conceived 1
25 Adam knew his wife again, and she bore a son 1
5: 1 This is the book of the generations of Adam. 1
3 When Adam had lived 130 years 1
4 The days of Adam after he became the father 1
5 Thus all the days that Adam lived were 930 years 1
Jos 3:16 stood . . in a heap far off, at Adam, the city that is 1
1Ch 1: 1 Adam, Seth, Enosh; 1
Hos 6: 7 But at Adam they transgressed the covenant; 1
Lke 3:38 son of Seth, the son of Adam, the son of God. 2
Rom 5:14 Yet death reigned from Adam to Moses 2
14 sins . . not like the transgression of Adam 2
1Co 15:22 For as in Adam all die 2
45 The first man Adam became a living being 2
45 the last Adam became a life-giving spirit. 2
1Ti 2:13 For Adam was formed first, then Eve; 2
14 Adam was not deceived, but the woman was deceived 2
Jde 1:14 Enoch in the seventh generation from Adam 2
2Es 3: 5 it gave thee Adam, a lifeless body 3
10 as death came upon Adam, so the flood upon them. 3
21 For the first Adam, burdened with an evil heart 3
26 in everything doing as Adam . . had done 3
4:30 For a grain of evil seed was sown in Adam's heart 3
6:54 over these thou didst place Adam 3
56 other nations which have descended from Adam 3
7:11 and when Adam transgressed my statutes 3
70 the world and Adam and all who have come from him 3
116 better if the earth had not produced Adam, or else 3
118 O Adam, what have you done? 3
Tob 8: 6 Thou madest Adam and gavest him Eve his wife 2
Sir 33:10 Adam was created of the dust. 2
40: 1 a heavy yoke is upon the sons of Adam 2
49:16 Adam above every living being in the creation. 2

Adamah 1. אֲדָמָה

Jos 19:36 Ad'amah, Ramah, Hazor 1

Adami-nekeb 1. אֲדָמִי הַנֶּקֶב

Jos 19:33 from the oak in Za-anan'nim, and Ad'ami-nekeb 1

Adar 1. אֲדָר 2. אֲדָר (A) 3. Αδαρ

Ezr 6:15 finished on the third day of the month of Adar 2
Est 3: 7 the twelfth month, which is the month of Adar. 1
13 of the twelfth month, which is the month of Adar 1
8:12 of the twelfth month, which is the month of Adar. 1
9: 1 in the twelfth month, which is the month of Adar 1
15 also on the fourteenth day of the month of Adar 1
17 was on the thirteenth day of the month of Adar 1
19 hold the fourteenth day of the month of Adar 1
21 keep the fourteenth day of the month Adar 1
1Es 7: 5 the 23rd day of the month of Adar 3
AEs 10:13 observe these days in the month of Adar 3
13: 6 of the twelfth month, Adar, of this present year 3
16:20 the thirteenth day of the twelfth month, Adar 3
1Mc 7:43 on the thirteenth day of the month of Adar 3
49 on the thirteenth day of Adar. 3
2Mc 15:36 which is called Adar in the Syrian language 3

Adasa 1. Αδασα

1Mc 7:40 Judas encamped in Adasa with 3,000 men 1
45 from Adasa as far as Gazara 1

Adbeel 1. אַדְבְּאֵל

Gen 25:13 first-born of Ish'mael; and Kedar, Adbeel, Mibsam 1
1Ch 1:29 Ish'mael, Neba'ioth; and Kedar, Adbeel, Mibsam 1

Addan 1. אַדָּן 2. Αδαν

Ezr 2:59 those who came up from . . Cherub, Addan, and Immer 1
1Es 5:36 under the leadership of Cherub, Addan, and Immer 2

Addar 1. אַדָּר

Jos 15: 3 goes up . . along by Hezron, up to Addar, turns about 1
1Ch 8: 3 Bela had sons: Addar, Gera, Abi'hud 1

Addi 1. Ἀδδί

Lke 3:28 the son of Melchi, the son of Addi, the son of Cosam 1
1Es 9:31 Of the sons of Addi: Naathus and Moossias 1

Addon 1. אַדּוֹן

Neh 7:61 came up from . . Cherub, Addon, and Immer 1

Addus 1. Αδδους

1Es 5:34 the sons of Gas, the sons of Addus, the sons of Subas 1

Adida 1. Αδιδα

1Mc 12:38 Simon built Adida in the Shephelah 1
13:13 Simon encamped in Adida, facing the plain. 1

Adiel 1. עֲדִיאֵל

1Ch 4:36 Asai'ah, Ad'i-el, Jesim'iel, Benai'ah 1
9:12 Ma'asai the son of Ad'i-el, son of Jah'zerah 1
27:25 Az'maveth the son of Ad'i-el; 1

Adin 1. עָדִין 2. Αδιν

Ezr 2:15 sons of Adin, 454. 1
8: 6 Of the sons of Adin, Ebed the son of Jonathan 1
Neh 7:20 sons of Adin, 655. 1
10:16 Adoni'jah, Bigva'i, Adin 1
1Es 5:14 The sons of Bigvai, 2,066. The sons of Adin, 454 2
8:32 Of the sons of Adin, Obed the son of Jonathan 2

Adina 1. עֲדִינָא

1Ch 11:42 Ad'ina the son of Shiza the Reubenite 1

Adithaim 1. עֲדִיתַיִם

Jos 15:36 Shaara'im, Aditha'im, Gede'rah, Gederotha'im 1

Adlai 1. עַדְלָי

1Ch 27:29 in the valleys was Shaphat the son of Adlai. 1

Admah 1. אַדְמָה

Gen 10:19 direction of Sodom . . Admah, and Zeboi'im 1
14: 2 Shinab king of Admah, Sheme'ber king of Zeboi'im 1
8 the king of Admah, the king of Zeboi'im 1
Deu 29:23 an overthrow like that of . . Admah and Zeboi'im 1
Hos 11: 8 How can I make you like Admah! 1

Admatha 1. אַדְמָתָא

Est 1:14 Carshe'na, Shethar, Adma'tha, Tarshish, Meres 1

Admin 1. Ἀδμίν

Lke 3:33 the son of Ammin'adab, the son of Admin 1

Adna 1. עַדְנָא

Ezr 10:30 of Pa'hath-mo'ab: Adna, Chelal, Benai'ah, Ma-asei'ah 1
Neh 12:15 of Harim, Adna; of Merai'oth, Hel'kai; 1

Adnah 1. עַדְנָא 2. עַדְנָה

1Ch 12:20 men of Manas'seh . . Adnah, Joz'abad, Jedi'a-el 2
2Ch 17:14 Adnah the commander, with 300,000 mighty men 1

Adoni-bezek 1. אֲדֹנִי בֶזֶק

Jdg 1: 5 They came upon Ado'ni-be'zek at Bezek, and fought 1
6 Ado'ni-be'zek fled; but they pursued him, and caught 1
7 Ado'ni-be'zek said, "70 kings with their thumbs 1

Adoni-zedek 1. אֲדֹנִי צֶדֶק

Jos 10: 1 When Ado'ni-ze'dek king of Jerusalem heard 1
3 Ado'ni-ze'dek king of Jerusalem sent to Hoham 1

Adonijah 1. אֲדֹנִיָּהוּ

2Sm 3: 4 and the fourth, Adoni'jah the son of Haggith; 1
1Kg 1: 5 Adoni'jah the son of Haggith exalted himself 1
7 and they followed Adoni'jah and helped him. 1
8 and David's mighty men were not with Adoni'jah. 1
9 Adoni'jah sacrificed sheep, oxen, and fatlings 1
11 that Adoni'jah the son of Haggith has become king 1
13 sit upon my throne"? Why then is Adoni'jah king?' 1
18 behold, Adoni'jah is king, although you, my lord 1
24 Adoni'jah shall reign after me, and he shall sit 1
25 before him, and saying, 'Long live King Adoni'jah!' 1
41 Adoni'jah and all . . with him heard it as they 1
42 Adoni'jah said, "Come in, for you are a worthy man 1
43 Jonathan answered Adoni'jah, "No, for our lord King 1
49 guests of Adoni'jah trembled, and rose, and each 1
50 Adoni'jah feared Solomon; and he arose, and went 1
51 Adoni'jah fears King Solomon; for, lo, he has laid 1
2:13 Adoni'jah the son of Haggith came to Bathshe'ba 1
19 Solomon, to speak to him on behalf of Adoni'jah. 1
21 Let Ab'ishag . . be given to Adoni'jah your brother 1
22 And why do you ask Ab'ishag . . for Adoni'jah? Ask 1
23 if this word does not cost Adoni'jah his life! 1
24 Adoni'jah shall be put to death this day. 1
28 Jo'ab had supported Adoni'jah 1
1Ch 3: 2 the fourth Adoni'jah, whose mother was Haggith; 1
2Ch 17: 8 the Levites . . Jehon'athan, Adoni'jah, Tobi'jah 1
Neh 10:16 Adoni'jah, Bigva'i, Adin 1

Adonikam 1. אֲדֹנִיקָם 2. Αδωνικαμ

Ezr 2:13 sons of Adoni'kam, 666. 1
8:13 Of the sons of Adoni'kam, those who came later 1
Neh 7:18 sons of Adoni'kam, 667. 1
1Es 5:14 The sons of Adonikam, 667. 2
8:39 Of the sons of Adonikam, the last ones 2

Adoniram 1. אֲדֹנִירָם

1Kg 4: 6 Adoni'ram the son of Abda was in charge 1
5:14 Adoni'ram was in charge of the levy. 1

Adora 1. Αδωρα

1Mc 13:20 he circled around by the way to Adora 1

Adoraim 1. אֲדוֹרַיִם

2Ch 11: 9 Adora'im, Lachish, Aze'kan 1

Adoram 1. אֲדֹרָם

2Sm 20:24 and Ador'am was in charge of the forced labor; 1
1Kg 12:18 Then King Rehobo'am sent Ador'am 1

Adrammelech 1. אַדְרַמֶּלֶךְ

2Kg 17:31 burned their children . . to Adram'melech 1
19:37 Adram'melech and Share'zer, his sons, slew him 1
Isa 37:38 Adram'melech and Share'zer, his sons, slew him 1

Adramyttium 1. Ἀδραμυττηνός

Act 27: 2 embarking in a ship of Adramyt'tium 1

Adria 1. Ἀδρίας

Act 27:27 as we were drifting across the sea of A'dria 1

Adriel 1. עַדְרִיאֵל

1Sm 18:19 was given to A'driel the Meho'lathite for a wife. 1
2Sm 21: 8 the five sons of Merab . . whom she bore to A'driel 1

Aduel 1. Αδουηλ

Tob 1: 1 son of Ananiel, son of Aduel, son of Gabael 1

Adullam 1. עֲדֻלָּם 2. Οδολλαμ

Jos 12:15 the king of Libnah, one; the king of Adullam, one; 1
15:35 Jarmuth, Adullam, Socoh, Aze'kah 1
1Sm 22: 1 David . . and escaped to the cave of Adullam; 1
2Sm 23:13 and came . . to David at the cave of Adullam 1

1Ch 11:15 to the rock to David at the cave of Adullam 1
2Ch 11: 7 Beth-zur, Soco, Adullam 1
Neh 11:30 Zano'ah, Adullam, and their villages 1
Mic 1:15 the glory of Israel shall come to Adullam. 1
2Mc 12:38 went to the city of Adullam 2

Adullamite 1. עֲדֻלָּמִי
Gen 38: 1 Judah . . turned in to a certain Adullamite 1
12 he and his friend Hirah the Adullamite. 1
20 Judah sent the kid by his friend the Adullamite 1

Adummim 1. אֲדֻמִּים
Jos 15: 7 Gilgal, which is opposite the ascent of Adum'mim 1
18:17 Geli'loth, which is opposite the ascent of Adum'mim; 1

Aeneas 1. Αἰνέας
Act 9:33 There he found a man named Aene'as 1
34 Peter said to him, "Aene'as, Jesus Christ heals you; 1

Aenon 1. Αἰνών
Joh 3:23 John also was baptizing at Ae'non near Salim 1

Aesora 1. Αισωρα
Jdt 4: 4 Choba and Aesora and the valley of Salem 1

Agabus 1. Ἅγαβος
Act 11:28 one of them named Ag'abus stood up 1
21:10 a prophet named Ag'abus came down from Judea. 1

Agag 1. אֲגַג
Num24: 7 his king shall be higher than Agag 1
1Sm 15: 8 And he took Agag the king of the Amal'ekites alive 1
9 But Saul and the people spared Agag, and the best 1
20 I have brought Agag the king of Am'alek 1
32 Bring here to me Agag the king of the Amal'ekites. 1
32 And Agag came to him cheerfully. 1
32 Agag said, "Surely the bitterness . . is past. 1
33 And Samuel hewed Agag in pieces before the LORD 1

Agagite 1. אֲגָגִי
Est 3: 1 King Ahasu-e'rus promoted Haman the Ag'agite 1
10 signet ring . . and gave it to Haman the Ag'agite 1
8: 3 to avert the evil design of Haman the Ag'agite 1
5 by Haman the Ag'agite, the son of Hammeda'tha 1
9:24 For Haman the Ag'agite, the son of Hammeda'tha 1

Agee 1. אָגֵא
2Sm 23:11 next . . was Shammah, the son of Agee the Har'arite. 1

Agia 1. Αυγια
1Es 5:38 Agia, one of the daughters of Barzillai 1

Agrippa 1. Ἀγρίππας
Act 25:13 Agrippa the king and Berni'ce 1
22 Agrippa said to Festus, "I should like to hear 1
23 So on the morrow Agrippa and Berni'ce came 1
24 King Agrippa and all who are present with us 1
26 especially before you, King Agrippa 1
26: 1 Agrippa said to Paul, "You have permission 1
2 it is before you, King Agrippa 1
19 Wherefore, O King Agrippa, I was not disobedient 1
27 King Agrippa, do you believe the prophets? 1
28 Agrippa said to Paul 1
32 Agrippa said to Festus 1

Agur 1. אָגוּר
Prv 30: 1 The words of Agur son of Jakeh of Massa. 1

Ahab 1. אַחְאָב
1Kg 16:28 and Ahab his son reigned in his stead. 1
29 Ahab the son of Omri began to reign over Israel 1
29 Ahab . . reigned over Israel in Sama'ria 22 years. 1
30 Ahab . . did evil in the sight of the LORD 1
33 Ahab made an Ashe'rah. 1
33 Ahab did more to provoke the LORD . . to anger 1
17: 1 Now Eli'jah the Tishbite . . said to Ahab 1
18: 1 Go, show yourself to Ahab; and I will send rain 1
2 So Eli'jah went to show himself to Ahab. 1
3 Ahab called Obadi'ah, who was over the household. 1
5 Ahab said to Obadi'ah, "Go through the land 1
6 Ahab went in one direction by himself 1
9 you would give your servant into the hand of Ahab 1
12 when I come and tell Ahab . . he will kill me 1
16 Obadi'ah went to meet Ahab, and told him; 1
16 Obadi'ah . . told him; and Ahab went to meet Eli'jah. 1
17 When Ahab saw Eli'jah, Ahab said to him, "Is it you 1
17 Ahab said to him, "Is it you, you troubler of Israel? 1
20 So Ahab sent to all the people of Israel 1
41 Eli'jah said to Ahab, "Go up, eat and drink; 1
42 So Ahab went up to eat and to drink. 1
44 Go up, say to Ahab, 'Prepare your chariot and go down 1
45 And Ahab rode and went to Jezreel. 1
46 Eli'jah . . girded up his loins and ran before Ahab 1
19: 1 Ahab told Jez'ebel all that Eli'jah had done 1
20: 2 he sent messengers . . to Ahab king of Israel 1
13 a prophet came near to Ahab . . and said, "Thus says 1
14 Ahab said, "By whom?" He said, "Thus says the LORD 1
34 And Ahab said, "I will let you go on these terms. •
21: 1 a vineyard in Jezreel, beside the palace of Ahab 1
2 Ahab said to Naboth, "Give me your vineyard 1
3 Naboth said to Ahab, "The LORD forbid that I should 1
4 Ahab went into his house vexed and sullen 1
8 she wrote letters in Ahab's name and sealed them 1
15 Jez'ebel said to Ahab, "Arise, take possession 1
16 as soon as Ahab heard . . Ahab arose to go down 1
16 Ahab arose to go down to the vineyard of Naboth 1
18 Arise, go down to meet Ahab . . who is in Sama'ria; 1
20 Ahab said to Eli'jah, "Have you found me, 1
21 I . . will cut off from Ahab every male, bond or free 1
24 Any one belonging to Ahab who dies in the city 1
25 There was none who sold himself . . like Ahab 1
27 when Ahab heard those words, he rent his clothes 1
29 Have you seen how Ahab has humbled himself 1
22:20 'Who will entice Ahab, that he may go up and fall 1
39 the rest of the acts of Ahab, and all that he did 1
40 So Ahab slept with his fathers; 1
41 began to reign . . in the fourth year of Ahab 1
49 Ahazi'ah the son of Ahab said to Jehosh'aphat, "Let 1
51 Ahazi'ah the son of Ahab began to reign 1
2Kg 1: 1 After the death of Ahab, Moab rebelled 1
3: 1 Jeho'ram the son of Ahab became king over Israel 1
5 when Ahab died, the king of Moab rebelled 1
8:16 In the fifth year of Joram the son of Ahab 1
18 he walked . . as the house of Ahab had done 1
18 for the daughter of Ahab was his wife. 1
25 In the twelfth year of Joram the son of Ahab 1
27 He also walked in the way of the house of Ahab 1
27 did what was evil . . as the house of Ahab had done 1
27 for he was son-in-law to the house of Ahab. 1
28 went with Joram the son of Ahab to make war 1
29 Ahazi'ah . . went down to see Joram the son of Ahab 1
9: 7 strike down the house of Ahab your master 1
8 For the whole house of Ahab shall perish; 1
8 I will cut off from Ahab every male . . in Israel. 1
9 I will make the house of Ahab like . . of Jerobo'am 1
25 you and I rode side by side behind Ahab his father 1
29 In the eleventh year of Joram the son of Ahab 1
10: 1 Now Ahab had 70 sons in Sama'ria. 1
1 sent . . and to the guardians of the sons of Ahab 1
10 the LORD spoke concerning the house of Ahab; 1
11 Jehu slew all that remained of the house of Ahab 1
17 he slew all that remained to Ahab in Sama'ria 1
18 Ahab served Ba'al a little; 1
30 and have done to the house of Ahab according 1
21: 3 made an Ashe'rah, as Ahab king of Israel had done 1
13 and the plummet of the house of Ahab; 1
2Ch 18: 1 he made a marriage alliance with Ahab. 1
2 After some years he went down to Ahab in Sama'ria. 1
2 Ahab killed an abundance of sheep and oxen 1
3 Ahab king of Israel said to Jehosh'aphat 1
19 LORD said, 'Who will entice Ahab the king of Israel 1
21: 6 he walked . . as the house of Ahab had done; 1
6 for the daughter of Ahab was his wife. 1
13 house of Ahab led Israel into unfaithfulness 1
22: 3 He also walked in the ways of the house of Ahab 1
4 did what was evil . . as the house of Ahab had done; 1
5 went with Jeho'ram the son of Ahab king of Israel 1
6 Ahazi'ah . . went down to see Joram the son of Ahab 1
7 LORD had anointed to destroy the house of Ahab. 1
8 executing judgment upon the house of Ahab 1
Jer 29:21 concerning Ahab the son of Kola'iah and Zedeki'ah 1
22 The LORD make you like Zedeki'ah and Ahab 1
Mic 6:16 have kept . . all the works of the house of Ahab; 1

Aharah 1. אַחְרַח
1Ch 8: 1 Benjamin was the father of . . Ahar'ah the third 1

Aharhel 1. אֲחַרְחֵל
1Ch 4: 8 the families of Ahar'hel the son of Harum. 1

Ahasbai 1. אֲחַסְבַּי
2Sm 23:34 Eliph'elet the son of Ahas'bai of Ma'acah 1

Ahasuerus 1. אֲחַשְׁוֵרוֹשׁ 2. Ασυερος
Ezr 4: 6 reign of Ahasu-e'rus, in the beginning of his reign 1
Est 1: 1 In the days of Ahasu-e'rus . . who reigned 1
1 Ahasu-e'rus who reigned from India to Ethiopia 1
2 when King Ahasu-e'rus sat on his . . throne in Susa 1
9 in the palace which belonged to King Ahasu-e'rus. 1
10 the seven eunuchs who served King Ahasu-e'rus 1
15 performed the command of King Ahasu-e'rus 1
16 who are in all the provinces of King Ahasu-e'rus. 1
17 Ahasu-e'rus commanded Queen Vashti to be brought 1
19 Vashti is to come no more before King Ahasu-e'rus 1
2: 1 when the anger of King Ahasu-e'rus had abated 1
12 came for each maiden to go in to King Ahasu-e'rus 1
16 And when Esther was taken to King Ahasu-e'rus 1
21 angry and sought to lay hands on King Ahasu-e'rus. 1
3: 1 King Ahasu-e'rus promoted Haman the Ag'agite 1
6 throughout the whole kingdom of Ahasu-e'rus. 1
7 of Nisan, in the twelfth year of King Ahasu-e'rus 1
8 Then Haman said to King Ahasu-e'rus 1
12 it was written in the name of King Ahasu-e'rus 1
6: 2 who had sought to lay hands upon King Ahasu-e'rus. 1
7: 5 King Ahasu-e'rus said to Queen Esther, "Who is he 1
8: 1 King Ahasu-e'rus gave . . Esther the house of Haman 1
7 Ahasu-e'rus said to Queen Esther and to Mor'decai 1
10 The writing was in the name of King Ahasu-e'rus 1
12 throughout all the provinces of King Ahasu-e'rus 1
9: 2 throughout all the provinces of King Ahasu-e'rus 1
20 provinces of King Ahasu-e'rus, both near and far 1
30 to the 127 provinces of the kingdom of Ahasu-e'rus 1
10: 1 King Ahasu-e'rus laid tribute on the land 1
3 Mor'decai . . was next in rank to King Ahasu-e'rus 1
Dan 9: 1 In the first year of Darius the son of Ahasu-e'rus 1
Tob 14:15 Nebuchadnezzar and Ahasuerus had captured. 2

Ahava 1. אַהֲוָא
Ezr 8:15 I gathered them to the river that runs to Aha'va 1
21 Then I proclaimed a fast there, at the river Aha'va 1
31 departed from the river Aha'va on the twelfth day 1

Ahaz 1. אָחָז 2. Ἀχάζ
2Kg 15:38 Jotham slept . . and Ahaz his son reigned 1
16: 1 Ahaz the son of Jotham . . began to reign. 1
2 Ahaz was twenty years old when he began to reign 1
5 they besieged Ahaz but could not conquer him. 1
7 So Ahaz sent messengers to Tig'lath-pile'ser 1
8 Ahaz also took the silver and gold . . and sent 1
10 When King Ahaz went to Damascus to meet 1
10 King Ahaz sent to Uri'ah . . a model of the altar 1
11 in accordance with all that King Ahaz had sent 1
11 Uri'ah . . made it, before King Ahaz arrived 1
15 King Ahaz commanded Uri'ah the priest, saying 1
16 Uri'ah the priest did . . as King Ahaz commanded. 1
17 King Ahaz cut off the frames of the stands 1
19 Now the rest of the acts of Ahaz which he did 1
20 And Ahaz slept with his fathers, and was buried 1
17: 1 In the twelfth year of Ahaz king of Judah 1
18: 1 Hezeki'ah the son of Ahaz . . began to reign. 1
20:11 by which the sun had declined on the dial of Ahaz. 1
23:12 altars on the roof of the upper chamber of Ahaz 1
1Ch 3:13 Ahaz his son, Hezeki'ah his son, Manas'seh his son 1
8:35 The sons of Micah: Pithon, Melech, Tare'a, and Ahaz. 1
36 Ahaz was the father of Jeho'addah; 1
9:41 sons of Micah: Pithon, Melech, Tahr'e-a, and Ahaz •
42 Ahaz was the father of Jarah 1
2Ch 27: 9 Ahaz his son reigned in his stead. 1
28: 1 Ahaz was twenty years old when he began to reign 1
16 King Ahaz sent to the king of Assyria for help. 1
19 For the LORD brought Judah low because of Ahaz 1
21 For Ahaz took from the house of the LORD 1
22 more faithless to the LORD–this same King Ahaz. 1
24 Ahaz gathered together the vessels of the house 1
27 Ahaz slept with his fathers, and they buried him 1
29:19 utensils which King Ahaz discarded in his reign 1
Isa 1: 1 in the days of Uzzi'ah, Jotham, Ahaz, and Hezeki'ah 1
7: 1 In the days of Ahaz the son of Jotham, son of Uzzi'ah 1
3 the LORD said to Isaiah, "Go forth to meet Ahaz 1
10 Again the LORD spoke to Ahaz 1
12 Ahaz said, "I will not ask 1
14:28 In the year that King Ahaz died came this oracle 1
38: 8 shadow cast by the declining sun on the dial of Ahaz 1
Hos 1: 1 in the days of Uzzi'ah, Jotham, Ahaz, and Hezeki'ah 1
Mic 1: 1 Jotham, Ahaz, and Hezeki'ah, kings of Judah 1
Mat 1: 9 and Jotham the father of Ahaz 2
9 and Ahaz the father of Hezeki'ah 2

Ahaziah 1. אֲחַזְיָהוּ
1Kg 22:40 Ahab slept . . and Ahazi'ah his son reigned 1
49 Ahazi'ah the son of Ahab said to Jehosh'aphat, "Let 1
51 Ahazi'ah . . began to reign over Israel in Sama'ria 1
2Kg 1: 2 Ahazi'ah fell through the lattice 1
17 became king . . because Ahazi'ah had no son. •
18 Now the rest of the acts of Ahazi'ah which he did 1
8:24 and Ahazi'ah his son reigned in his stead. 1
25 Ahazi'ah the son of Jeho'ram . . began to reign. 1
26 Ahazi'ah was 22 years old when he began to reign 1
29 Ahazi'ah . . went down to see Joram the son of Ahab 1
9:16 And Ahazi'ah . . had come down to visit Joram. 1
21 Then Joram . . and Ahazi'ah king of Judah set out 1
23 Joram reined about and fled, saying to Ahazi'ah 1
23 and fled, saying to Ahazi'ah, "Treachery, O Ahazi'ah! 1
27 When Ahazi'ah the king of Judah saw this, he fled 1
29 In the eleventh year of . . Ahazi'ah began to reign 1
10:13 Jehu met the kinsmen of Ahazi'ah king of Judah 1
13 We are the kinsmen of Ahazi'ah, and we came down 1
11: 1 Athali'ah the mother of Ahazi'ah saw that her son 1
2 Jehosh'eba . . sister of Ahazi'ah, took Jo'ash 1
2 Jehosh'eba . . took Jo'ash the son of Ahazi'ah 1
12:18 gifts that Jehosh'aphat and Jeho'ram and Ahazi'ah 1
13: 1 In the 23rd year of Jo'ash the son of Ahazi'ah 1
14:13 Amazi'ah . . the son of Jeho'ash, son of Ahazi'ah 1
1Ch 3:11 Joram his son, Ahazi'ah his son, Jo'ash his son 1
2Ch 20:35 After this Jehosh'aphat . . joined with Ahazi'ah 1
37 Because you have joined with Ahazi'ah 1
22: 1 inhabitants of Jerusalem made Ahazi'ah . . king 1
1 Ahazi'ah the son of Jeho'ram . . reigned. 1
2 Ahazi'ah was 42 . . when he began to reign 1
6 Ahazi'ah . . went down to see Joram the son of Ahab 1
7 ordained by God that the downfall of Ahazi'ah 1
8 Jehu . . met . . the sons of Ahazi'ah's brothers 1
8 Ahazi'ah's brothers, who attended Ahazi'ah 1
9 He searched for Ahazi'ah, and he was captured 1
9 house of Ahazi'ah had no one able to rule 1
10 Athali'ah the mother of Ahazi'ah saw that her son 1
11 Jeho-shab'e-ath . . took Jo'ash the son of Ahazi'ah 1

11 because she was a sister of Ahazi'ah, hid him 1
25:23 Amazi'ah . . son of Jo'ash, son of Ahazi'ah 1

Ahban 1. אַחְבָּן
1Ch 2:29 Ab'ihail, and she bore him Ahban and Molid. 1

Aher 1. אַחֵר
1Ch 7:12 Hushim the sons of Aher. 1

Ahi 1. אֲחִיָהוּ
1Ch 5:15 Ahi . . was chief in their fathers' houses; 1

Ahiah 1. אֲחִיָּהוּ
Neh 10:26 Ahi'ah, Hanan, Anan 1

Ahiam 1. אֲחִיאָם
2Sm 23:33 Shammah . . Ahi'am the son of Sharar the Har'arite 1
1Ch 11:35 Ahi'am the son of Sachar the Har'arite 1

Ahian 1. אַחְיָן
1Ch 7:19 sons of Shemi'da were Ahi'an, Shechem, Likhi 1

Ahiezer 1. אֲחִיעֶזֶר
Num 1:12 from Dan, Ahi-e'zer the son of Ammishad'dai; 1
2:25 the leader . . Ahi-e'zer the son of Ammishad'dai 1
7:66 Ahie'zer the . . leader of the men of Dan 1
71 offering of Ahie'zer the son of Ammishad'dai. 1
10:25 over their host was Ahie'zer . . of Ammishad'dai. 1
1Ch 12: 3 The chief was Ahi-e'zer, then Jo'ash, both sons 1

Ahihud 1. אֲחִיהוּד 2. אֲחִיחוּד
Num34:27 of Asher a leader, Ahi'hud the son of Shelo'mi. 1
1Ch 8: 7 Gera, that is, Heglam . . father of Uzza and Ahi'hud. 2

Ahijah 1. אֲחִיָּהוּ 2. Achia
1Sm 14: 3 Ahi'jah the son of Ahi'tub, Ich'abod's brother 1
18 Saul said to Ahi'jah, "Bring hither the ark of God. 1
1Kg 4: 3 Elihor'eph and Ahi'jah the sons of Shisha were 1
11:29 the prophet Ahi'jah the Shi'lonite found him 1
29 Now Ahi'jah had clad himself with a new garment; *
30 Ahi'jah laid hold of the new garment 1
12:15 LORD spoke by Ahi'jah the Shi'lonite to Jerobo'am 1
14: 2 go to Shiloh; behold, Ahi'jah the prophet is there 1
4 went to Shiloh, and came to the house of Ahi'jah. 1
4 Ahi'jah could not see, for his eyes were dim 1
5 the LORD said to Ahi'jah, "Behold 1
6 when Ahi'jah heard the sound of her feet 1
18 he spoke by his servant Ahi'jah the prophet. 1
15:27 Ba'asha the son of Ahi'jah, of the house of Is'sachar 1
29 he spoke by his servant Ahi'jah the Shi'lonite; 1
33 Ba'asha the son of Ahi'jah began to reign 1
21:22 and like the house of Ba'asha the son of Ahi'jah 1
2Kg 9: 9 and like the house of Ba'asha the son of Ahi'jah. 1
1Ch 2:25 The sons of Jerah'meel . . Oren, Ozem, and Ahi'jah. 1
8: 7 Na'aman, Ahi'jah, and Gera, that is, Heglam 1
11:36 Hepher the Meche'rathite, Ahi'jah the Pel'onite 1
26:20 of the Levites, Ahi'jah had charge 1
2Ch 9:29 and in the prophecy of Ahi'jah the Shi'lonite 1
10:15 which he spoke by Ahi'jah the Shi'lonite 1
2Es 1: 2 son of Ahijah, son of Phinehas, son of Eli 2

Ahikam 1. אֲחִיקָם
2Kg 22:12 Hilki'ah the priest, and Ahi'kam the son of Shaphan 1
14 and Ahi'kam, and Achbor, and Shaphan, and Asai'ah 1
25:22 the son of Ahi'kam, son of Shaphan, governor. 1
2Ch 34:20 king commanded . . Ahi'kam the son of Shaphan 1
Jer 26:24 the hand of Ahi'kam the son of Shaphan 1
39:14 They entrusted him to Gedali'ah the son of Ahi'kam 1
40: 5 then return to Gedali'ah the son of Ahi'kam 1
6 Then Jeremiah went to Gedali'ah the son of Ahi'kam 1
7 had appointed Gedali'ah the son of Ahi'kam 1
9 Gedali'ah the son of Ahi'kam, son of Shaphan, swore 1
11 and had appointed Gedali'ah the son of Ahi'kam 1
14 But Gedali'ah the son of Ahi'kam would not believe 1
16 But Gedali'ah the son of Ahi'kam said to Joha'nan 1
41: 1 came . . to Gedali'ah the son of Ahi'kam, at Mizpah. 1
2 Gedali'ah the son of Ahi'kam, son of Shaphan 1
6 Come in to Gedali'ah the son of Ahi'kam. 1
10 had committed to Gedali'ah the son of Ahi'kam. 1
16 after he had slain Gedali'ah the son of Ahi'kam 1
18 Ish'mael . . had slain Gedali'ah the son of Ahi'kam 1
43: 6 guard had left with Gedali'ah the son of Ahi'kam 1

Ahikar 1. Αχιαχαρος
Tob 1:21 appointed Ahikar, the son of my brother Anael 1
22 Ahikar interceded for me 1
22 Now Ahikar was cupbearer, keeper of the signet 1
2:10 Ahikar, however, took care of me 1
11:18 Ahikar and his nephew Nadab came 1
14:10 what Nadab did to Ahikar who had reared him 1
10 Ahikar was saved 1
10 Ahikar gave alms and escaped the deathtrap 1

Ahilud 1. אֲחִילוּד
2Sm 8:16 Jehosh'aphat the son of Ahi'lud was recorder; 1
20:24 Jehosh'aphat the son of Ahi'lud was the recorder; 1
1Kg 4: 3 Jehosh'aphat the son of Ahi'lud was the recorder; 1
12 Ba'ana the son of Ahi'lud, in Ta'anach, Megid'do 1
1Ch 18:15 Jehosh'aphat the son of Ahi'lud was recorder; 1

Ahimaaz 1. אֲחִימַעַץ
1Sm 14:50 Saul's wife was Ahin'o-am the daughter of Ahim'aaz. 1
2Sm 15:27 your two sons, Ahim'a-az your son, and Jonathan 1
36 their two sons . . Ahim'a-az, Zadok's son, and Jonathan 1
17:17 Jonathan and Ahim'a-az were waiting at En-ro'gel; 1
20 they said, "Where are Ahim'a-az and Jonathan? 1
18:19 Then said Ahi'ma-az the son of Zadok, "Let me run 1
22 Then Ahi'ma-az the son of Zadok said again to Jo'ab 1
23 Then Ahi'ma-az ran by the way of the plain 1
27 is like the running of Ahi'ma-az the son of Zadok. 1
28 Then Ahi'ma-az cried out to the king, "All is well. 1
29 Ahi'ma-az answered, "When Jo'ab sent your servant 1
1Kg 4:15 Ahi'ma-az, in Naph'tali (he had taken Bas'emath 1
1Ch 6: 8 Ahi'tub of Zadok, Zadok of Ahim'a-az 1
9 Ahim'a-az of Azari'ah, Azari'ah of Joha'nan 1
53 Zadok his son, Ahim'a-az his son. 1

Ahiman 1. אֲחִימַן
Num13:22 came to Hebron; and Ahi'man, She'shai, and Talmai 1
Jos 15:14 three sons of Anak, She'shai and Ahi'man and Talmai 1
Jdg 1:10 they defeated She'shai and Ahi'man and Talmai. 1
1Ch 9:17 gatekeepers were . . Ahi'man, and their kinsmen 1

Ahimelech 1. אֲחִימֶלֶךְ
1Sm 21: 1 Then came David to Nob to Ahim'elech the priest; 1
1 Ahim'elech came to meet David trembling, and said 1
2 And David said to Ahim'elech the priest 1
8 David said to Ahim'elech, "And have you . . a spear 1
22: 9 coming to Nob, to Ahim'elech the son of Ahi'tub 1
11 the king sent to summon Ahim'elech the priest 1
14 Then Ahim'elech answered the king 1
16 You shall surely die, Ahim'elech, you and all 1
20 one of the sons of Ahim'elech the son of Ahi'tub 1
23: 6 When Abi'athar the son of Ahim'elech fled to David 1
26: 6 Then David said to Ahim'elech the Hittite 1
30: 7 said to Abi'athar the priest, the son of Ahim'elech 1
2Sm 8:17 Ahim'elech the son of Abi'athar were priests; 1
1Ch 18:16 Zadok . . and Ahim'elech . . were priests; 1
24: 3 help of . . Ahim'elech of the sons of Ith'amar 1
6 Zadok . . and Ahim'elech the son of Abi'athar 1
31 in the presence of King David, Zadok, Ahim'elech 1
Ps 52: 0 David has come to the house of Ahimelech. 1

Ahimoth 1. אֲחִימוֹת
1Ch 6:25 The sons of Elka'nah: Ama'sai and Ahi'moth 1

Ahinadab 1. אֲחִינָדָב
1Kg 4:14 Ahin'adab the son of Iddo, in Mahana'im; 1

Ahinoam 1. אֲחִינֹעַם
1Sm 14:50 Saul's wife was Ahin'o-am the daughter of Ahim'aaz. 1
25:43 David also took Ahin'o-am of Jezreel; 1
27: 3 his two wives, Ahin'o-am of Jezreel, and Ab'igail 1
30: 5 David's two wives . . Ahin'o-am of Jezreel 1
2Sm 2: 2 his two wives . . Ahin'o-am of Jezreel, and Ab'igail 1
3: 2 his first-born was Amnon, of Ahin'o-am of Jezreel; 1
1Ch 3: 1 first-born Amnon, by Ahin'o-am the Jezreelitess; 1

Ahio 1. אַחְיוֹ
2Sm 6: 3 and Uzzah and Ahi'o . . were driving the new cart 1
4 with the ark of God; and Ahi'o went before the ark. 1
1Ch 8:14 Ahi'o, Shashak, and Jer'emoth. 1
31 Gedor, Ahi'o, Zecher 1
9:37 Gedor, Ahi'o, Zechari'ah and Mikloth; 1
13: 7 and Uzzah and Ahi'o were driving the cart. 1

Ahira 1. אֲחִירַע
Num 1:15 from Naph'tali, Ahi'ra the son of Enan. 1
2:29 the leader . . being Ahi'ra the son of Enan 1
7:78 Ahi'ra the . . leader of the men of Naph'tali 1
83 This was the offering of Ahi'ra the son of Enan. 1
10:27 over the host . . was Ahi'ra the son of Enan. 1

Ahiram 1. אֲחִירָם
Num26:38 of Ahi'ram, the family of the Ahi'ramites; 1

Ahiramite 1. אֲחִירָמִי
Num26:38 of Ahi'ram, the family of the Ahi'ramites; 1

Ahisamach 1. אֲחִיסָמָךְ
Exd 31: 6 appointed with him Oho'liab, the son of Ahis'amach 1
35:34 Oho'liab the son of Ahis'amach of the tribe of Dan. 1
38:23 with him was Oho'liab the son of Ahis'amach 1

Ahishahar 1. אֲחִישָׁחַר
1Ch 7:10 sons of Bilhan . . Tarshish, and Ahish'ahar. 1

Ahishar 1. אֲחִישָׁר
1Kg 4: 6 Ahi'shar was in charge of the palace; and Adoni'ram 1

Ahithophel 1. אֲחִיתֹפֶל
2Sm 15:12 he sent for Ahith'opel the Gi'lonite 1
31 Ahith'ophel is among the conspirators 1
31 turn the counsel of Ahith'ophel into foolishness. 1
34 you will defeat for me the counsel of Ahith'ophel. 1
16:15 came to Jerusalem, and Ahith'ophel with him. 1
20 Ab'salom said to Ahith'ophel, "Give your counsel; 1
21 Ahith'ophel said to Ab'salom, "Go in to your father's 1
23 the counsel which Ahith'ophel gave was 1
23 so was all the counsel of Ahith'ophel esteemed 1
17: 1 Moreover Ahith'ophel said to Ab'salom 1
6 Ab'salom said to him, "Thus has Ahith'ophel spoken; 1
7 the counsel . . Ahith'ophel has given is not good. 1
14 is better than the counsel of Ahith'ophel. 1
14 to defeat the good counsel of Ahith'ophel 1
15 Thus and so did Ahith'ophel counsel Ab'salom 1
21 thus . . has Ahith'ophel counseled against you. 1
23 Ahith'ophel saw that the counsel was not followed 1
23:34 Eli'am the son of Ahith'ophel of Gilo 1
1Ch 27:33 Ahith'ophel was the king's counselor 1
34 Ahith'ophel was succeeded by Jehoi'ada 1

Ahitub 1. אֲחִיטוּב 2. Αχιτωβ 3. Acitob
1Sm 14: 3 Ahi'jah the son of Ahi'tub, Ich'abod's brother 1
22: 9 coming to Nob, to Ahim'elech the son of Ahi'tub 1
11 summon Ahim'elech the priest, the son of Ahi'tub 1
12 Saul said, "Hear now, son of Ahi'tub." 1
20 one of the sons of Ahim'elech the son of Ahi'tub 1
2Sm 8:17 Zadok the son of Ahi'tub . . were priests; 1
1Ch 6: 7 Merai'oth of Amari'ah, Amari'ah of Ahi'tub 1
8 Ahi'tub of Zadok, Zadok of Ahim'a-az 1
11 Azari'ah . . father of Amari'ah, Amari'ah of Ahi'tub 1
12 Ahi'tub of Zadok, Zadok of Shallum 1
52 Merai'oth his son, Amari'ah his son, Ahi'tub his son 1
9:11 Ahi'tub . . chief officer of the house of God; 1
18:16 Zadok the son of Ahi'tub 1
Ezr 7: 2 son of Shallum, son of Za-dok, son of Ahi'tub 1
Neh 11:11 Merai'oth, son of Ahi'tub, ruler of the house of God 1
1Es 8: 2 son of Zadok, son of Ahitub, son of Amariah 2
2Es 1: 1 son of Shallum, son of Zadok, son of Ahitub 3
Jdt 8: 1 son of Gideon, son of Raphaim, son of Ahitub 2

Ahlab 1. אַחְלָב
Jdg 1:31 inhabitants of Sidon, or of Ahlab, or of Achzib 1

Ahlai 1. אַחְלָי
1Ch 2:31 The sons of Sheshan: Ahlai. 1
11:41 Uri'ah the Hittite, Zabad the son of Ahlai 1

Ahoah 1. אֲחוֹחַ
1Ch 8: 4 Abishu'a, Na'aman, Aho'ah 1

Ahohi 1. אֲחוֹחִי
2Sm 23: 9 next . . was Elea'zar the son of Dodo, son of Aho'hi. 1

Ahohite 1. אֲחוֹחִי
2Sm 23:28 Zalmon the Aho'hite, Ma'harai of Netoph'ah 1
1Ch 11:12 Elea'zar the son of Dodo, the Aho'hite. 1
29 Sib'becai the Hu'shathite, I'lai the Aho'hite 1
27: 4 Dodai the Aho'hite was in charge of the division 1

Ahumai 1. אֲחוּמַי
1Ch 4: 2 and Jahath was the father of Ahu'mai and Lahad. 1

Ahuzzam 1. אֲחֻזָּם
1Ch 4: 6 Na'arah bore him Ahuz'zam, Hepher, Te'meni 1

Ahuzzath 1. אֲחֻזַּת
Gen 26:26 to him from Gerar with Ahuz'zath his adviser 1

Ahzai 1. אַחְזָיְהוּ
Neh 11:13 Amash'sai, the son of Az'arel, son of Ah'zai 1

Ai 1. עַי
Gen 12: 8 with Bethel on the west and Ai on the east; 1
13: 3 had been at the beginning, between Bethel and Ai 1
Jos 7: 2 Joshua sent men from Jericho to Ai . . and said 1
2 And the men went up and spied out Ai. 1
3 about 2,000 or 3,000 men go up and attack Ai; 1
4 and they fled before the men of Ai 1
5 the men of Ai killed about 36 men of them 1
8: 1 take all the fighting men . . and arise, go up to Ai; 1
1 given into your hand the king of Ai, and his people 1
2 and you shall do to Ai and its king as you did 1
3 Joshua arose, and . . the fighting men, to go up to Ai; 1
9 went to the place . . and lay between Bethel and Ai 1
9 and lay between Bethel and Ai, to the west of Ai; 1
10 and went up . . before the people to Ai. 1
11 drew near . . and encamped on the north side of Ai 1
11 encamped on . . with a ravine between them and Ai. 1
12 and set them in ambush between Bethel and Ai 1
14 when the king of Ai saw this he . . made haste 1
17 not a man left in Ai or Bethel, who did not go out 1
18 Stretch out the javelin . . in your hand toward Ai; 1
20 when the men of Ai looked back, behold, the smoke 1
21 then they turned back and smote the men of Ai. 1
23 But the king of Ai they took alive, and brought him 1
24 finished slaughtering all the inhabitants of Ai 1
24 all Israel returned to Ai, and smote it 1
25 all who fell . . were 12,000, all the people of Ai. 1
26 he had . . destroyed all the inhabitants of Ai. 1
28 Joshua burned Ai, and made it . . a heap of ruins 1
29 he hanged the king of Ai on a tree until evening; 1
9: 3 heard what Joshua had done to Jericho and to Ai 1
10: 1 When Ado'ni-ze'dek . . heard how Joshua had taken Ai 1
1 doing to Ai and its king as he had done to Jericho 1

2 it was greater than Ai, and all its men were mighty. 1
12: 9 the king of Ai, which is beside Bethel, one; 1
Ezr 2:28 men of Bethel and Ai, 223. 1
Neh 7:32 men of Bethel and Ai, 123. 1
Jer 49: 3 Wail, O Heshbon, for Ai is laid waste! 1

Aiah 1. אַיָּה
Gen 36:24 These are the sons of Zib'eon: A'iah and Anah; 1
2Sm 3: 7 whose name was Rizpah, the daughter of Ai'ah; 1
21: 8 took the two sons of Rizpah the daughter of Ai'ah 1
10 Then Rizpah the daughter of Ai'ah took sackcloth 1
11 Rizpah the daughter of Ai'ah, the concubine 1
1Ch 1:40 The sons of Zib'eon: Ai'ah and Anah. 1

Aiath 1. עַיָּת
Isa 10:28 he has come to Ai'ath; he has passed through Migron 1

Aija 1. עַיָּה
Neh 11:31 Michmash, Ai'ja, Bethel and its villages 1

Aijalon 1. אַיָּלוֹן
Jos 10:12 stand . . and thou Moon in the valley of Ai'jalon. 1
19:42 Sha-alab'bin, Ai'jalon, Ithlah 1
21:24 Ai'jalon with its pasture lands, Gath-rim'mon 1
Jdg 1:35 dwelling in Har-heres, in Ai'jalon, and in Sha-al'bim 1
12:12 and was buried at Ai'jalon in the land of Zeb'ulun. 1
1Sm 14:31 They struck down . . from Michmash to Ai'jalon. 1
1Ch 6:69 Ai'jalon with its pasture lands 1
8:13 fathers' houses of the inhabitants of Ai'jalon 1
2Ch 11:10 Zorah, Ai'jalon, and Hebron, fortified cities 1
28:18 had taken Beth-she'mesh, Ai'jalon, Gede'roth 1

Ain 1. עַיִן
Num34:11 from Shepham to Riblah on the east side of A'in; 1
Jos 15:32 Leba'oth, Shilhim, A'in, and Rimmon 1
21:16 A'in with its pasture lands, Juttah with its 1
1Ch 4:32 villages were Etam, A'in, Rimmon, Tochen, 1

Akan 1. עֲקָן
Gen 36:27 the sons of Ezer: Bilhan, Za'avan, and Akan. 1

Akeldama 1. Ἀκελδαμάχ
Act 1:19 the field was called in their language Akel'dama 1

Akkub 1. עַקּוּב 2. Ακκουβ 3. Ακουβ
1Ch 3:24 sons of Eli-o-e'nai . . Pelai'ah, Akkub, Joha'nan 1
9:17 gatekeepers . . Shallum, Akkub, Talmon, Ahi'man 1
Ezr 2:42 sons of the gatekeepers: the . . sons of Akkub 1
45 the sons of Hag'abah, the sons of Akkub 1
Neh 7:45 gatekeepers . . sons of Talmon, the sons of Akkub 1
8: 7 Also . . Akkub, Shab'bethai, Hodi'ah, Ma-asei'ah 1
11:19 gatekeepers, Akkub, Talmon and their brethren 1
12:25 Obadi'ah, Meshul'lam, Talmon, and Akkub 1
1Es 5:28 the sons of Akkub, the sons of Hatita 3
30 the sons of Akkub, the sons of Uthai 2
9:48 Jeshua and Anniuth and Sherebiah, Jamin, Akkub 2

Akrabattene 1. Ακραβαττηνη
1Mc 5: 3 Judas made war . . at Akrabattene 1

Akrabbim 1. עַקְרַבִּים
Num34: 4 boundary shall turn south of the ascent of Akrab'bim 1
Jos 15: 3 it goes out southward of the ascent of Akrab'bim 1
Jdg 1:36 the ascent of Akrab'bim, from Sela and upward. 1

Alamoth 1. עֲלָמוֹת
1Ch 15:20 were to play harps according to Al'amoth; 1
Ps 46: 0 A Psalm . . According to Alamoth. A Song. 1

Alcimus 1. Αλκιμος
1Mc 7: 5 were led by Alcimus, who wanted to be high priest. 1
9 he sent him, and with him the ungodly Alcimus 1
12 appeared in a body before Alcimus and Bacchides 1
20 He placed Alcimus in charge of the country 1
21 Alcimus strove for the high priesthood 1
23 the evil that Alcimus and those with him had done 1
25 When Alcimus saw that Judas . . had grown strong 1
9: 1 he sent Bacchides and Alcimus 1
54 Alcimus gave orders to tear down the wall 1
55 at that time Alcimus was stricken 1
56 Alcimus died at that time in great agony. 1
57 When Bacchides saw that Alcimus was dead 1
2Mc 14: 3 a certain Alcimus . . formerly been high priest 1
13 to set up Alcimus as high priest 1
26 Alcimus noticed their good will for one another 1

Alema 1. Αλεμα 2. Αλεμοι
1Mc 5:26 in Alema and Chaspho, Maked and Carnaim 2
35 Next he turned aside to Alema 1

Alemeth 1. עָלֶמֶת
1Ch 6:60 Geba . . Al'emeth with its pasture lands 1
7: 8 sons of Becher . . Abi'jah, An'athoth, and Al'emeth. 1
8:36 Jeho'addah . . father of Al'emeth, Az'maveth 1
9:42 and Jarah of Al'emeth, Az'maveth, and Zimri; 1

Alexander 1. Ἀλέξανδρος
Mrk 15:21 the father of Alexander and Rufus 1
Act 4: 6 Ca'iaphas and John and Alexander 1
19:33 Some of the crowd prompted Alexander 1
33 Alexander motioned with his hand 1
1Ti 1:20 among them Hymenae'us and Alexander 1
2Ti 4:14 Alexander the coppersmith did me great harm 1
1Mc 1: 1 After Alexander son of Philip, the Macedonian 1
7 after Alexander had reigned twelve years 1
6: 2 weapons left there by Alexander 1
10: 1 Alexander Epiphanes, the son of Antiochus 1
4 before he makes peace with Alexander against us 1
15 Now Alexander the king heard of all the promises 1
18 King Alexander to his brother Jonathan, greeting 1
23 Alexander has gotten ahead of us 1
47 They favored Alexander 1
48 Now Alexander the king assembled large forces 1
49 Alexander pursued him and defeated them. 1
51 Then Alexander sent ambassadors to Ptolemy 1
58 Alexander the king met him 1
59 Then Alexander the king wrote to Jonathan 1
88 When Alexander the king heard of it 1
88 When Alexander the king heard of these things 1
11: 1 he tried to get possession of Alexander's kingdom 1
2 Alexander the king had commanded them to meet him 1
2 since he was Alexander's father-in-law. •
8 he kept devising evil designs against Alexander. 1
9 my daughter who was Alexander's wife 1
11 He threw blame on Alexander •
12 He was estranged from Alexander 1
14 Alexander the king was in Cilicia at that time 1
15 Alexander heard of it 1
16 Alexander fled into Arabia to find protection there 1
17 Zabdiel the Arab cut off the head of Alexander 1
39 formerly . . one of Alexander's supporters 1
39 Antiochus, the young son of Alexander 1

Alexandria 1. Ἀλεξάνδρεια 2. Ἀλεξανδρεύς 3. Ἀλεξανδρῖνος
Act 18:24 Now a Jew named Apol'los, a native of Alexandria 2
27: 6 There the centurion found a ship of Alexandria 3
28:11 a ship of Alexandria 3
3Mc 3: 1 those Jews who lived in Alexandria 1

Alexandrian 1. Ἀλεξάνδρειος 2. Ἀλεξανδρεύς
Act 6: 9 of the Cyre'nians, and of the Alexandrians 2
3Mc 2:30 shall have equal citizenship with the Alexandrians. 2
3:21 to deem them worthy of Alexandrian citizenship 1

Aliah 1. עַלְיָה
1Ch 1:51 chiefs of Edom were: chiefs Timna, Al'iah, Jetheth 1

Alian 1. עַלְיָן
1Ch 1:40 The sons of Shobal: Al'ian, Man'ahath, Ebal, Shephi 1

Allammelech 1. אַלַּמֶּלֶךְ
Jos 19:26 Allam'melech, Amad, and Mishal; on the west it 1

Allon 1. אַלּוֹן
1Ch 4:37 Ziza the son of Shiphi, son of Allon, son of Jedai'ah 1

Allon-bacuth 1. אַלּוֹן בָּכוּת
Gen 35: 8 so the name of it was called Al'lon-bacuth. 1

Almodad 1. אַלְמוֹדָד
Gen 10:26 Joktan became the father of Almo'dad, Sheleph 1
1Ch 1:20 the father of Almo'dad, Sheleph, Hazarma'veth 1

Almon 1. עַלְמוֹן
Jos 21:18 An'athoth . . and Almon with its pasture lands 1

Almon-diblathaim 1. עַלְמֹן דִּבְלָתָיְמָה
Num33:46 Dibon-gad, and encamped at Al'mon-diblatha'im. 1
47 set out from Al'mon-diblatha'im, and encamped 1

Alphaeus 1. Ἁλφαῖος
Mat 10: 3 James the son of Alphaeus, and Thaddaeus; 1
Mrk 2:14 as he passed on, he saw Levi the son of Alphaeus 1
3:18 Matthew, and Thomas, and James the son of Alphaeus 1
Lke 6:15 Matthew, and Thomas, and James the son of Alphaeus 1
Act 1:13 James the son of Alphaeus and Simon the Zealot 1

Alush 1. אָלוּשׁ
Num33:13 they set out from Dophkah, and encamped at Alush. 1
14 they set out from Alush, and encamped at Reph'idim 1

Alvah 1. עַלְוָה
Gen 36:40 by their names: the chiefs Timna, Alvah, Jetheth 1

Alvan 1. עַלְוָן
Gen 36:23 the sons of Shobal: Alvan, Man'ahath, Ebal 1

Amad 1. עַמְעָד
Jos 19:26 Allam'melech, Amad, and Mishal; on the west it 1

Amal 1. עָמָל
1Ch 7:35 sons of Helem . . Zophah, Imna, Shelesh, and Amal. 1

Amalek 1. עֲמָלֵק
Gen 36:12 (Timna . . bore Am'alek to El'iphaz.) 1
16 Korah, Gatam, and Am'alek; these are the chiefs 1
Exd 17: 8 came Am'alek and fought with Israel at Reph'idim. 1
9 Choose for us men, and go out, fight with Am'alek; 1
10 So Joshua . . fought with Am'alek; 1
11 whenever he lowered his hand, Am'alek prevailed. 1
13 Joshua mowed down Am'alek and his people 1
14 I will . . blot out the remembrance of Am'alek 1
16 The LORD will have war with Am'alek 1
Num24:20 he looked on Am'alek, and took up his discourse 1
20 Am'alek was the first of the nations, but in the end 1
Deu 25:17 Remember what Am'alek did to you on the way 1
19 blot out the remembrance of Am'alek from under 1
1Sm 15: 2 I will punish what Am'alek did to Israel 1
3 Now go and smite Am'alek, and utterly destroy all 1
5 the city of Am'alek, and lay in wait in the valley. 1
20 I have brought Agag the king of Am'alek 1
28:18 carry out his fierce wrath against Am'alek 1
2Sm 8:12 Edom, Moab, the Ammonites, the Philistines, Am'alek 1
1Ch 1:36 Zephi, Gatam, Kenaz, Timna, and Am'alek. 1
18:11 Moab, the Ammonites, the Philistines, and Am'alek. 1
Ps 83: 7 Gebal and Ammon and Am'alek 1

Amalekite 1. עֲמָלֵקִי 2. אִישׁ עֲמָלֵקִי 3. בֶּן עֲמָלֵק 4. עֲמָלֵקִי
Gen 14: 7 and subdued all the country of the Amal'ekites 4
Num13:29 Amal'ekites dwell in the land of the Negeb; 3
14:25 since the Amal'ekites and the Canaanites dwell 4
43 Amal'ekites and the Canaanites are before you 4
45 Amal'ekites and the Canaanites who dwelt 4
Jdg 3:13 to himself the Ammonites and the Amal'ekites 2
6: 3 Mid'ianites and the Amal'ekites and the people 3
33 Mid'ianites and the Amal'ekites and the people 3
7:12 the Mid'ianites and the Amal'ekites and all 3
10:12 The Sido'nians also, and the Amal'ekites 3
12:15 E'phraim, in the hill country of the Amal'ekites. 4
1Sm 14:48 And he did valiantly, and smote the Amal'ekites 3
15: 6 Go, depart, go down from among the Amal'ekites 4
6 Ken'ites departed from among the Amal'ekites. 3
7 Saul defeated the Amal'ekites 3
8 And he took Agag the king of the Amal'ekites alive 3
15 They have brought them from the Amal'ekites 4
18 Go, utterly destroy the sinners, the Amal'ekites 3
20 and I have utterly destroyed the Amal'ekites. 3
32 Bring here to me Agag the king of the Amal'ekites. 3
27: 8 the Gesh'urites, and Gir'zites, and the Amal'ekites; 4
30: 1 the Amal'ekites had made a raid upon the Negeb 4
13 I am a young man of Egypt, servant to an Amal'ekite; 1
18 David recovered all . . the Amal'ekites had taken; 3
2Sm 1: 1 returned from the slaughter of the Amal'ekites 3
8 'Who are you?' I answered him, 'I am an Amal'ekite.' 4
13 I am the son of a sojourner, an Amal'ekite. 4
1Ch 4:43 the remnant of the Amal'ekites that had escaped 3

Amam 1. אֲמָם
Jos 15:26 Amam, Shema, Mola'dah 1

Amana 1. אֲמָנָה
Sng 4: 8 Depart from the peak of Ama'na, from . . Senir 1

Amariah 1. אֲמַרְיָהוּ 2. Αμαριας 3. Ζαμβρις 4. Ameria
1Ch 6: 7 Merai'oth of Amari'ah, Amari'ah of Ahi'tub 1
7 Merai'oth of Amari'ah, Amari'ah of Ahi'tub 1
11 Azari'ah . . father of Amari'ah, Amari'ah of Ahi'tub 1
11 Azari'ah . . father of Amari'ah, Amari'ah of Ahi'tub 1
52 Merai'oth his son, Amari'ah his son, Ahi'tub his son 1
23:19 sons of Hebron: Jeri'ah . . Amari'ah the second 1
24:23 sons of Hebron . . Amari'ah the second, Jaha'ziel 1
2Ch 19:11 Amari'ah the chief priest is over you 1
31:15 Jeshua, Shemai'ah, Amari'ah, and Shecani'ah 1
Ezr 7: 3 son of Amari'ah, son of Azari'ah, son of Merai'oth 1
10:42 Shallum, Amari'ah, and Joseph. 1
Neh 10: 3 Pashhur, Amari'ah, Malchi'jah 1
11: 4 Zechari'ah, son of Amari'ah, son of Shephati'ah 1
12: 2 Amari'ah, Malluch, Hattush 1
13 of Ezra, Meshul'lam; of Amari'ah, Jehoha'nan; 1
Zep 1: 1 son of Gedali'ah, son of Amari'ah, son of Hezeki'ah 1
1Es 8: 2 son of Zadok, son of Ahitub, son of Amariah 2
9:34 Shashai, Azarel, Azael, Shemaiah, Amariah, Joseph. 3
2Es 1: 2 son of Eli, son of Amariah, son of Azariah 4

Amasa 1. עֲמָשָׂא
2Sm 17:25 Ab'salom had set Ama'sa over the army instead 1
25 Ama'sa was the son of a man named Ithra 1
19:13 say to Ama'sa, 'Are you not my bone and my flesh? 1
20: 4 Then the king said to Ama'sa, "Call the men of Judah 1
5 Ama'sa went to summon Judah; but he delayed 1
8 When they were at . . Ama'sa came to meet them. 1
9 Jo'ab said to Ama'sa, "Is it well with you, my brother? 1
9 Jo'ab took Ama'sa by the beard with his right hand 1
10 But Ama'sa did not observe the sword which was 1
11 And one of Jo'ab's men took his stand by Ama'sa •
12 Ama'sa lay wallowing in his blood in the highway. 1
12 he carried Ama'sa out of the highway 1
1Kg 2: 5 Abner the son of Ner, and Ama'sa the son of Jether 1
32 Ama'sa the son of Jether, commander of the army 1
1Ch 2:17 Ab'igail bore Ama'sa, and the father of Ama'sa was 1
17 the father of Ama'sa was Jether the Ish'maelite. 1
2Ch 28:12 chiefs . . and Ama'sa the son of Had-lai 1

Amasai 1. עֲמָשַׂי

1Ch 6:25 The sons of Elka'nah: Ama'sai and Ahi'moth 1
35 son of Elka'nah, son of Mahath, son of Ama'sai 1
12:18 Then the Spirit came upon Ama'sai, chief of the 30 1
15:24 Shebani'ah, Josh'aphat, Nethan'el, Ama'sai 1
2Ch 29:12 Then the Levites arose, Mahath the son of Ama'sai 1

Amashsai 1. עֲמַשְׁסַי

Neh 11:13 Amash'sai, the son of Az'arel, son of Ah'zai 1

Amasiah 1. עֲמַסְיָה

2Ch 17:16 next to him Amasi'ah the son of Zichri 1

Amaw 1. בְּנֵי עַמּוֹ

Num22: 5 near the River, in the land of Amaw to call him 1

Amaziah 1. אֲמַצְיָהוּ

2Kg 12:21 and Amazi'ah his son reigned in his stead. 1
13:12 the might with which he fought against Amazi'ah 1
14: 1 Amazi'ah the son of Jo'ash, king of Judah, began 1
8 Then Amazi'ah sent messengers to Jeho'ash 1
9 Jeho'ash . . sent word to Amazi'ah king of Judah 1
11 Amazi'ah would not listen. 1
11 he and Amazi'ah king of Judah faced one another 1
13 Jeho'ash . . captured Amazi'ah king of Judah 1
15 acts of Jeho'ash . . and how he fought with Amazi'ah 1
17 Amazi'ah . . lived fifteen years after the death 1
18 Now the rest of the deeds of Amazi'ah 1
21 and made him king instead of his father Amazi'ah. 1
23 In the fifteenth year of Amazi'ah the son of Jo'ash 1
15: 1 Azari'ah the son of Amazi'ah . . began to reign. 1
3 to all that his father Amazi'ah had done. 1
1Ch 3:12 Amazi'ah his son, Azari'ah his son, Jotham his son 1
4:34 Mesho'bab, Jamlech, Joshah the son of Amazi'ah 1
6:45 son of Hashabi'ah, son of Amazi'ah, son of Hilki'ah 1
2Ch 24:27 And Amazi'ah his son reigned in his stead. 1
25: 1 Amazi'ah was 25 years old when he began 1
5 Then Amazi'ah assembled the men of Judah 1
9 Amazi'ah said to the man of God 1
10 Amazi'ah discharged the army that had come to him 1
11 Amazi'ah took courage, and led out his people 1
13 the men of the army whom Amazi'ah sent back 1
14 Amazi'ah came from the slaughter of the E'domites 1
15 Therefore the LORD was angry with Amazi'ah 1
17 Amazi'ah . . took counsel and sent to Jo'ash 1
18 Jo'ash . . sent word to Amazi'ah king of Judah 1
20 Amazi'ah would not listen; for it was of God 1
21 he and Amazi'ah king of Judah faced one another 1
23 Jo'ash . . captured Amazi'ah king of Judah 1
25 Amazi'ah . . lived fifteen years after the death 1
26 rest of the deeds of Amazi'ah, from first to last 1
26: 1 made him king instead of his father Amazi'ah. 1
4 all that his father Amazi'ah had done. 1
Ams 7:10 Amazi'ah the priest of Bethel sent to Jerobo'am 1
12 Amazi'ah said to Amos, "O seer, go, flee away 1
14 Then Amos answered Amazi'ah, "I am no prophet 1

Ami 1. אָמִי 2. Αλλων

Ezr 2:57 of Po'chereth-hazzeba'im, and the sons of Ami. 1
1Es 5:34 the sons of Shaphat, the sons of Ami. 2

Amittai 1. אֲמִתַּי

2Kg 14:25 he spoke by his servant Jonah the son of Amit'tai 1
Jon 1: 1 the LORD came to Jonah the son of Amit'tai, saying 1

Ammah 1. אַמָּה

2Sm 2:24 as the sun was . . they came to the hill of Ammah 1

Ammidian 1. Αμμιδαιοι

1Es 5:20 The Chadiasans and Ammidians, 422. 1

Ammiel 1. עַמִּיאֵל

Num13:12 from the tribe of Dan, Am'miel the son of Gemal'li; 1
2Sm 9: 4 He is in the house of Machir the son of Am'miel 1
5 from the house of Machir the son of Am'miel 1
17:27 and Machir the son of Am'miel from Lo'debar 1
1Ch 3: 5 Bath-shu'a, the daughter of Am'mi-el; 1
26: 5 Am'mi-el the sixth, Is'sachar the seventh 1

Ammihud 1. עַמִּיהוּד

Num 1:10 from E'phraim, Eli'shama the son of Ammi'hud 1
2:18 the leader . . Eli'shama the son of Ammi'hud 1
7:48 Eli'shama the son of Ammi'hud, the leader of the men 1
53 was the offering of Eli'shama the son of Ammi'hud. 1
10:22 over their host was Eli'shama the son of Ammi'hud. 1
34:20 tribe . . of Simeon, Shemu'el the son of Ammi'hud. 1
28 of Naph'tali a leader, Pedah'el the son of Ammi'hud. 1
2Sm 13:37 went to Talmai the son of Ammi'hud, king of Geshur. 1
1Ch 7:26 Ladan his son, Ammi'hud his son, Eli'shama his son 1
9: 4 Uthai the son of Ammi'hud, son of Omri, son of Imri 1

Amminadab 1. עַמִּינָדָב 2. 'Αμιναδάβ

Exd 6:23 took . . Eli'sheba, the daughter of Ammin'adab 1
Num 1: 7 from Judah, Nahshon the son of Ammin'adab; 1
2: 3 leader . . being Nahshon the son of Ammin'adab 1
7:12 Nahshon the son of Ammin'adab, of . . Judah; 1
17 was the offering of Nahshon the son of Ammin'adab 1
10:14 Nahshon the son of Ammin'adab. 1
Rut 4:19 Hezron of Ram, Ram of Ammin'adab 1
20 Ammin'adab of Nahshon, Nahshon of Salmon 1
1Ch 2:10 Ram was the father of Ammin'adab 1
10 Ammin'adab was the father of Nahshon, prince 1
6:22 of Kohath: Ammin'adab his son, Korah . . Assir 1
15:10 of the sons of Uz'ziel, Ammin'adab the chief 1
11 Levites . . Jo'el, Shemai'ah, Eli'el, and Ammin'adab 1
Mat 1: 4 Ram the father of Ammin'adab 2
4 Ammin'adab the father of Nahshon 2
Lke 3:33 the son of Ammin'adab, the son of Admin 2

Ammishaddai 1. עַמִּישַׁדָּי

Num 1:12 from Dan, Ahi-e'zer the son of Ammishad'dai; 1
2:25 the leader . . Ahi-e'zer the son of Ammishad'dai 1
7:66 Ahie'zer the son of Ammishad'dai, the leader 1
71 offering of Ahie'zer the son of Ammishad'dai. 1
10:25 Ahie'zer the son of Ammishad'dai. 1

Ammizabad 1. עַמִּיזָבָד

1Ch 27: 6 Ammiz'abad his son was in charge of his division. 1

Ammon 1. עַמּוֹן 2. עַמּוֹנִי 3. Αμμωνιτης 4. 'Αμών

Deu 2:19 when you approach the frontier of the sons of Ammon 1
19 not give you any of the land of the sons of Ammon 1
37 land of the sons of Ammon you did not draw near 1
Jdg 11:27 the people of Israel and the people of Ammon. 1
2Ch 20:10 behold, the men of Ammon and Moab and Mount Se'ir 1
22 LORD set an ambush against the men of Ammon, 1
23 For the men of Ammon and Moab rose against 1
Neh 13:23 Jews . . married women of Ashdod, Ammon, and Moab; 2
Ps 83: 7 Gebal and Ammon and Am'alek 1
Jer 9:26 Egypt, Judah, Edom, the sons of Ammon, Moab 1
25:21 Edom, Moab, and the sons of Ammon; 1
27: 3 the king of the sons of Ammon, the king of Tyre 1
Jdt 1:12 the people of Ammon, and all Judea 4
5: 2 the commanders of Ammon 4
7:18 the sons of Esau and the sons of Ammon went up 4
2Mc 4:26 was driven . . into the land of Ammon. 3

Ammonite 1. עַמּוֹן 2. בֶּן עַמּוֹן 3. עַמּוֹנִי 4. Αμμανιτις 5. Αμμωνιτης 6. 'Αμών 7. υἱὸς Αμμων

Gen 19:38 Ben-ammi; he is the father of the Ammonites 2
Num21:24 to the Jabbok, as far as to the Ammonites; 1
24 for Jazer was the boundary of the Ammonites. 1
Deu 2:20 but the Ammonites call them Zamzum'mim 2
3:11 bedstead . . is it not in Rabbah of the Ammonites? 2
16 river Jabbok, the boundary of the Ammonites; 1
23: 3 No Ammonite or Moabite shall enter the assembly 3
Jos 12: 2 the river Jabbok, the boundary of the Ammonites 1
13:10 cities . . as far as the boundary of the Ammonites; 2
25 and half the land of the Ammonites, to Aro'er 1
Jdg 3:13 He gathered to himself the Ammonites 1
10: 6 the gods of the Ammonites, and the gods 1
7 sold them . . and into the hand of the Ammonites 1
9 the Ammonites crossed the Jordan to fight also 1
11 from the Amorites, from the Ammonites 1
17 Then the Ammonites were called to arms 1
18 Who . . will begin to fight against the Ammonites? 1
11: 4 a time the Ammonites made war against Israel. 1
5 when the Ammonites made war against Israel 1
6 our leader, that we may fight with the Ammonites. 1
8 you may go with us and fight with the Ammonites 1
9 bring me home again to fight with the Ammonites 1
12 sent messengers to the king of the Ammonites 1
13 the king of the Ammonites answered 1
14 sent messengers . . to the king of the Ammonites 1
15 Israel did not take . . the land of the Ammonites 1
28 the king of the Ammonites did not heed 1
29 from Mizpah . . he passed on to the Ammonites. 1
30 If thou wilt give the Ammonites into my hand 1
31 when I return victorious from the Ammonites 1
32 Jephthah crossed over to the Ammonites to fight 1
33 the Ammonites were subdued before the people 1
36 avenged you on your enemies, on the Ammonites. 1
12: 1 you cross over to fight against the Ammonites 1
2 and my people had a great feud with the Ammonites; 1
3 I took . . and crossed over against the Ammonites 1
1Sm 11: 1 Then Nahash the Ammonite went up and besieged 3
2 But Nahash the Ammonite said to them 3
11 cut down the Ammonites until the heat of the day; 2
12:12 saw that Nahash the king of the Ammonites came 1
14:47 he fought . . against Moab, against the Ammonites 1
2Sm 8:12 from Edom, Moab, the Ammonites, the Philistines 1
10: 1 After this the king of the Ammonites died 1
2 servants came into the land of the Ammonites. 1
3 But the princes of the Ammonites said to Hanun 1
6 the Ammonites saw that they had become odious 1
6 the Ammonites sent and hired the Syrians 1
8 And the Ammonites came out and drew up in battle 1
10 and he arrayed them against the Ammonites. 1
11 but if the Ammonites are too strong for you 1
14 when the Ammonites saw that the Syrians fled 1
14 Jo'ab returned from fighting . . the Ammonites 1
19 Syrians feared to help the Ammonites any more. 1
11: 1 and they ravaged the Ammonites, and besieged 1
12: 9 have slain him with the sword of the Ammonites. 1
26 Now Jo'ab fought against Rabbah of the Ammonites 1
31 thus he did to all the cities of the Ammonites. 1
17:27 the son of Nahash from Rabbah of the Ammonites 1
23:37 Zelek the Ammonite, Na'harai of Be-er'oth 3
1Kg 11: 1 and Moabite, Ammonite, E'domite, Sido'nian 3
5 after Milcom the abomination of the Ammonites. 3
7 for Molech the abomination of the Ammonites 1
33 Chemosh . . and Milcom the god of the Ammonites 1
2Kg 23:13 for Milcom the abomination of the Ammonites. 1
24: 2 bands of the Moabites, and bands of the Ammonites 1
1Ch 11:39 Zelek the Ammonite, Na'harai of Be-er'oth 3
18:11 all the nations, from Edom, Moab, the Ammonites 2
19: 1 after this Nahash the king of the Ammonites died 1
2 came to Hanun in the land of the Ammonites 1
3 the princes of the Ammonites said to Hanun 1
6 Ammonites saw that they had made themselves 1
6 Hanun and the Ammonites sent 1,000 talents 1
7 Ammonites were mustered from their cities 1
9 Ammonites came out and drew up in battle array 1
11 and they were arrayed against the Ammonites. 1
12 if the Ammonites are too strong for you 1
15 when the Ammonites saw that the Syrians fled 1
19 Syrians were not willing to help the Ammonites 1
20: 1 and ravaged the country of the Ammonites 1
3 David did to all the cities of the Ammonites. 1
2Ch 20: 1 After this the Moabites and Ammonites 1
26: 8 The Ammonites paid tribute to Uzzi'ah 3
27: 5 He fought with the king of the Ammonites 1
5 Ammonites gave him that year 100 talents 1
5 Ammonites paid him the same amount 1
Ezr 9: 1 Per'izzites, the Jeb'usites, the Ammonites 3
Neh 2:10 Tobi'ah the servant, the Ammonite 3
19 Tobi'ah the servant, the Ammonite, and Geshem 3
4: 3 Tobi'ah the Ammonite was by him, and he said 3
7 when . . the Ammonites and the Ash'dodites heard 3
13: 1 no Ammonite or Moabite should ever enter 3
Isa 11:14 Edom and Moab, and the Ammonites shall obey them. 1
Jer 40:11 in Moab and among the Ammonites and in Edom 1
14 Do you know that Ba'alis the king of the Ammonites 1
41:10 and set out to cross over to the Ammonites. 1
15 escaped . . and went to the Ammonites. 1
49: 1 Concerning the Ammonites. Thus says the LORD 1
2 cry to be heard against Rabbah of the Ammonites; 1
6 I will restore the fortunes of the Ammonites 1
Ezk 21:20 the sword to come to Rabbah of the Ammonites 1
28 Thus says the Lord GOD concerning the Ammonites 1
25: 2 Son of man, set your face toward the Ammonites 1
3 Say to the Ammonites, Hear the word of the Lord GOD 1
5 the cities of the Ammonites a fold for flocks. 1
10 I will give it along with the Ammonites 1
Dan 11:41 Edom and Moab and the main part of the Ammonites. 1
Ams 1:13 For three transgressions of the Ammonites 1
Zep 2: 8 I have heard . . the revilings of the Ammonites 1
9 and the Ammonites like Gomor'rah 1
Jdt 5: 5 Then Achior, the leader of all the Ammonites, said 7
6: 5 you, Achior, you Ammonite hireling 6
7:17 the army of the Ammonites moved forward 7
14: 5 bring Achior the Ammonite to me 5
1Mc 5: 6 Then he crossed over to attack the Ammonites 7
2Mc 5: 7 and fled again into the country of the Ammonites. 4

Ammonitess 1. עַמּוֹנִי

1Kg 14:21 His mother's name was Na'amah the Ammonitess. 1
31 His mother's name was Na'amah the Ammonitess. 1
2Ch 12:13 His mother's name was Na'amah the Ammonitess. 1
24:26 Zabad the son of Shim'e-ath the Ammonitess 1

Amnon 1. אַמְנוֹן

2Sm 3: 2 sons were born . . his first-born was Amnon 1
13: 1 after a time Amnon, David's son, loved her. 1
2 Amnon was so tormented that he made himself ill 1
2 it seemed impossible to Amnon to do anything 1
3 But Amnon had a friend, whose name was Jon'adab 1
4 Amnon said to him, "I love Tamar 1
6 Amnon lay down, and pretended to be ill; 1
6 when the king came to see him, Amnon said 1
7 Go to your brother Amnon's house, and prepare food 1
8 Tamar went to her brother Amnon's house 1
9 Amnon said, "Send out every one from me. 1
10 Then Amnon said to Tamar, "Bring the food 1
10 and brought them . . to Amnon her brother. 1
15 Then Amnon hated her with very great hatred; 1
15 And Amnon said to her, "Arise, be gone. 1
20 Has Amnon your brother been with you? 1
22 But Ab'salom spoke to Amnon neither good nor bad; 1
22 Ab'salom hated Amnon, because he had forced 1
26 If not, pray let my brother Amnon go with us. 1
27 he let Amnon and all the king's sons go with him. 1
28 Mark when Amnon's heart is merry with wine 1
28 and when I say to you, 'Strike Amnon,' then kill him. 1
29 did to Amnon as Ab'salom had commanded. 1
32 Amnon alone is dead, for by the command of Ab'salom 1
33 for Amnon alone is dead. 1
39 he was comforted about Amnon, seeing he was dead. 1
1Ch 3: 1 sons of David . . the first-born Amnon, by Ahin'o-am 1
4:20 sons of Shimon: Amnon, Rinnah, Ben-ha'nan, 1

Amok 1. עָמוֹק

Neh 12: 7 Sallu, Amok, Hilki'ah, Jedai'ah. 1
20 of Sal'lai, Kal'lai; of Amok, Eber; 1

Amon 1. אָמוֹן
1Kg 22:26 take him back to Amon the governor of the city 1
2Kg 21:18 Manas'seh slept . . and Amon his son reigned 1
19 Amon was 22 years old when he began to reign 1
23 And the servants of Amon conspired against him 1
24 all those who had conspired against King Amon 1
25 Now the rest of the acts of Amon which he did 1
1Ch 3:14 Amon his son, Josi'ah his son. 1
2Ch 18:25 take him back to Amon the governor of the city 1
33:20 Amon his son reigned in his stead. 1
21 Amon was 22 years old when he began to reign 1
22 Amon sacrificed to all the images that Manas'seh 1
23 but this Amon incurred guilt more and more. 1
25 slew all . . who had conspired against King Amon; 1
Neh 7:59 sons of Po'chereth-hazzeba'im, the sons of Amon. 1
Jer 1: 2 in the days of Josi'ah the son of Amon, king of Judah 1
25: 3 from the thirteenth year of Josi'ah the son of Amon 1
46:25 I am bringing punishment upon Amon of Thebes 1
Zep 1: 1 Hezeki'ah, in the days of Josi'ah the son of Amon 1

Amorite 1. אֱמֹרִי 2. Αμορραιος
Gen 10:16 the Jeb'usites, the Amorites, the Gir'gashites 1
14: 7 also the Amorites who dwelt in Haz'azon-ta'mar. 1
13 the oaks of Mamre the Amorite, brother of Eshcol 1
15:16 for the iniquity of the Amorites is not yet 1
21 the Amorites, the Canaanites, the Gir'gashites 1
48:22 which I took from the hand of the Amorites 1
Exd 3: 8 of the Canaanites, the Hittites, the Amorites 1
17 to the land of . . the Hittites, the Amorites 1
13: 5 the Amorites, the Hivites, and the Jeb'usites 1
23:23 brings you in to the Amorites, and the Hittites 1
33: 2 I will drive out the Canaanites, the Amorites 1
34:11 drive out . . the Amorites, the Canaanites 1
Num13:29 Hittites, the Jeb'usites, and the Amorites dwell 1
21:13 extends from the boundary of the Amorites; 1
13 boundary of Moab, between Moab and the Amorites. 1
21 sent messengers to Sihon king of the Amorites 1
25 Israel settled in all the cities of the Amorites 1
26 city of Sihon the king of the Amorites 1
29 his sons fugitives . . to an Amorite king, Sihon. 1
31 Thus Israel dwelt in the land of the Amorites. 1
32 dispossessed the Amorites that were there. 1
34 do to him as you did to Sihon king of the Amorites 1
22: 2 all that Israel had done to the Amorites. 1
32:33 gave . . the kingdom of Sihon king of the Amorites 1
39 dispossessed the Amorites who were in it. 1
Deu 1: 4 defeated Sihon the king of the Amorites 1
7 go to the hill country of the Amorites, and to all 1
19 on the way to the hill country of the Amorites 1
20 'You have come to the hill country of the Amorites 1
27 give us into the hand of the Amorites, to destroy us. 1
44 Then the Amorites . . came out against you 1
2:24 I have given into your hand Sihon the Amorite 1
3: 2 as you did to Sihon the king of the Amorites 1
8 out of the hand of the two kings of the Amorites 1
9 Si'rion, while the Amorites call it Senir) 1
4:46 in the land of Sihon the king of the Amorites, who 1
47 two kings of the Amorites, who lived to the east 1
7: 1 Hittites, the Gir'gashites, the Amorites 1
20:17 utterly destroy . . Hittites and the Amorites 1
31: 4 Sihon and Og, the kings of the Amorites 1
Jos 2:10 and what you did to the two kings of the Amorites 1
3:10 Gir'gashites, the Amorites, and the Jeb'usites. 1
5: 1 all the kings of the Amorites that were beyond 1
7: 7 to give us into the hands of the Amorites 1
9: 1 When all . . the Hittites, the Amorites 1
10 all that he did to the two kings of the Amorites 1
10: 5 Then the five kings of the Amorites . . gathered 1
6 the kings of the Amorites . . in the hill country 1
12 when the LORD gave the Amorites over to . . Israel; 1
11: 3 the Amorites, the Hittites, the Per'izzites 1
12: 2 these are the kings . . Sihon king of the Amorites 1
8 the land of the Hittites, the Amorites 1
13: 4 to Aphek, to the boundary of the Amorites 1
10 all the cities of Sihon king of the Amorites 1
21 and all the kingdom of Sihon king of the Amorites 1
24: 8 Then I brought you to the land of the Amorites 1
11 the Amorites, the Per'izzites, the Canaanites 1
12 drove them out . . the two kings of the Amorites; 1
15 the gods of the Amorites in whose land you dwell; 1
18 the peoples, the Amorites who lived in the land; 1
Jdg 1:34 The Amorites pressed the Danites back 1
35 the Amorites persisted in dwelling in Har-heres 1
36 the border of the Amorites ran from the ascent 1
3: 5 among the Canaanites, the Hittites, the Amorites 1
6:10 the gods of the Amorites, in whose land you dwell 1
10: 8 beyond the Jordan in the land of the Amorites 1
11 Did I not deliver you . . from the Amorites 1
11:19 sent messengers to Sihon king of the Amorites 1
21 took possession of all the land of the Amorites 1
22 possession of all the territory of the Amorites 1
23 the LORD . . dispossessed the Amorites 1
1Sm 7:14 was peace also between Israel and the Amorites. 1
2Sm 21: 2 the Gib'eonites . . of the remnant of the Amorites; 1
1Kg 4:19 Gilead, the country of Sihon king of the Amorites 1
9:20 All . . who were left of the Amorites, the Hittites 1
21:26 going after idols, as the Amorites had done 1
2Kg 21:11 more wicked than all that the Amorites did 1
1Ch 1:14 the Jeb'usites, the Am'orites, the Gir'gashites 1
2Ch 8: 7 All the people who were left of . . the Amorites 1
Ezr 9: 1 Moabites, the Egyptians, and the Amorites. 1
Neh 9: 8 land of the Canaanite, the Hittite, the Amorite 1
Ps 135:11 Sihon, king of the Amorites, and Og, king of Bashan 1
136:19 Sihon, king of the Amorites 1
Isa 17: 9 deserted places of the Hivites and the Amorites 2
Ezk 16: 3 your father was an Amorite 1
45 mother was a Hittite and your father an Amorite. 1
Ams 2: 9 Yet I destroyed the Amorite before them 1
10 and led you . . to possess the land of the Amorite. 1
Jdt 5:15 they lived in the land of the Amorites 2

Amos 1. עָמוֹס 2. Ἀμώς 3. Amos
Ams 1: 1 of Amos, who was among the shepherds of Teko'a 1
7:10 saying, "Amos has conspired against you 1
11 Amos has said, 'Jerobo'am shall die by the sword 1
12 Amazi'ah said to Amos, "O seer, go, flee away 1
14 Then Amos answered Amazi'ah, "I am no prophet 1
8: 2 he said, "Amos, what do you see? 1
Mat 1:10 and Manas'seh the father of Amos 2
10 and Amos the father of Josi'ah 2
Lke 3:25 the son of Mattathi'as, the son of Amos 2
2Es 1:39 Jacob and Hosea and Amos and Micah and Joel 3
Tob 2: 6 Then I remembered the prophecy of Amos 2

Amoz 1. אָמוֹץ
2Kg 19: 2 he sent . . to the prophet Isaiah the son of Amoz. 1
20 Isaiah the son of Amoz sent to Hezeki'ah, saying 1
20: 1 Isaiah . . the son of Amoz came to him, and said 1
2Ch 26:22 Isaiah the prophet the son of Amoz wrote. 1
32:20 Isaiah the prophet, the son of Amoz 1
32 written in the vision of Isaiah . . son of Amoz 1
Isa 1: 1 The vision of Isaiah the son of Amoz, which he saw 1
2: 1 The word which Isaiah the son of Amoz saw 1
13: 1 oracle . . which Isaiah the son of Amoz saw. 1
20: 2 the LORD had spoken by Isaiah the son of Amoz 1
37: 2 he sent . . to the prophet Isaiah the son of Amoz. 1
21 Isaiah the son of Amoz sent to Hezeki'ah, saying 1
38: 1 Isaiah the prophet the son of Amoz came to him 1

Amphipolis 1. Ἀμφίπολις
Act 17: 1 Now when they had passed through Amphip'olis 1

Ampliatus 1. Ἀμπλιᾶτος
Rom16: 8 Greet Amplia'tus, my beloved in the Lord. 1

Amram 1. עַמְרָם 2. Μαηρος
Exd 6:18 sons of Kohath: Amram, Izhar, Hebron, and Uz'ziel 1
20 Amram took to wife Joch'ebed his father's sister 1
20 the years of the life of Amram being 137 years. 1
Num 3:19 sons of Kohath . . Amram, Izhar, Hebron 1
26:58 Kohath was the father of Amram. 1
59 name of Amram's wife was Joch'ebed the daughter 1
59 she bore to Amram Aaron and Moses and Miriam 1
1Ch 6: 2 sons of Kohath: Amram, Izhar, Hebron, and Uz'ziel. 1
3 The children of Amram: Aaron, Moses, and Miriam. 1
18 sons of Kohath: Amram, Izhar, Hebron, and Uz'ziel. 1
23:12 sons of Kohath: Amram, Izhar, Hebron, and Uz'ziel 1
13 The sons of Amram: Aaron and Moses. 1
24:20 sons of Levi: of the sons of Amram, Shu'ba-el; 1
Ezr 10:34 Of the sons of Bani: Ma-ada'i, Amram, Uel 1
1Es 9:34 Of the sons of Bani: Jeremai, Maadai, Amram, Joel 2

Amramite 1. עַמְרָמִי
Num 3:27 Of Kohath were the family of the Amramites 1
1Ch 26:23 Of the Am'ramites, the Iz'harites, the He'bronites 1

Amraphel 1. אַמְרָפֶל
Gen 14: 1 In the days of Am'raphel king of Shinar 1
9 Tidal king of Goi'im, Am'raphel king of Shinar 1

Amzi 1. אַמְצִי
1Ch 6:46 son of Amzi, son of Bani, son of Shemer 1
Neh 11:12 Pelali'ah, son of Amzi, son of Zechari'ah 1

Anab 1. עֲנָב
Jos 11:21 hill country, from Hebron, from Debir, from Anab 1
15:50 Anab, Esh'temoh, Anim 1

Anael 1. Αναηλ
Tob 1:21 appointed Ahikar, the son of my brother Anael 1

Anah 1. עֲנָה
Gen 36: 2 Oholiba'mah the daughter of Anah 1
14 sons of Oholiba'mah the daughter of Anah 1
18 born of Oholiba'mah the daughter of Anah 1
20 of the land: Lotan, Shobal, Zib'eon, Anah 1
24 These are the sons of Zib'eon: A'iah and Anah; 1
24 Anah; he is the Anah who found the hot springs 1
25 These are the children of Anah 1
25 Dishon and Oholiba'mah the daughter of Anah. 1
29 Horites: the chiefs Lotan, Shobal, Zib'eon, Anah 1
1Ch 1:38 The sons of Se'ir: Lotan, Shobal, Zib'eon, Anah 1
40 The sons of Zib'eon: Ai'ah and Anah. 1
41 The sons of Anah: Dishon. The sons of Dishon 1

Anaharath 1. אֲנָחֲרַת
Jos 19:19 Haph'ara-im, Shion, Ana'harath 1

Anaiah 1. עֲנָיָה 2. Ἁνανίας
Neh 8: 4 beside him stood Mattithi'ah, Shema, Anai'ah, Uri'ah 1
10:22 Pelati'ah, Hanan, Anai'ah 1
1Es 9:43 beside him stood Mattathiah, Shema, Anaiah 2

Anak 1. עֲנָק
Num13:22 Ahi'man . . and Talmai, the descendants of Anak 1
28 besides, we saw the descendants of Anak there. 1
33 (the sons of Anak, who come from the Nephilim); 1
Deu 9: 2 said, 'Who can stand before the sons of Anak?' 1
Jos 15:13 Kir'iath-ar'ba . . (Arba was the father of Anak). 1
14 Caleb drove out from there the three sons of Anak 1
14 Caleb drove out . . the descendants of Anak. 1
21:11 Kir'iath-ar'ba (Arba being the father of Anak) 1
Jdg 1:20 and he drove out from it the three sons of Anak. 1

Anakim 1. עֲנָק 2. Ενακιμ
Deu 1:28 moreover we have seen the sons of the Anakim there. 1
2:10 Emim . . great and many, and tall as the Anakim; 1
11 like the Anakim they were also known as Reph'idim 1
21 a people great and many, and tall as the Anakim; 1
9: 2 people great and tall, the sons of the Anakim 1
Jos 11:21 Joshua came at that time, and wiped out the Anakim 1
22 There was none of the Anakim left in the land 1
14:12 you heard on that day how the Anakim were there 1
15 this Arba was the greatest man among the Anakim. 1
Jer 47: 5 O remnant of the Anakim, how long will you gash 2

Anamim 1. עֲנָמִים
Gen 10:13 Egypt became the father of Ludim, An'amim 1
1Ch 1:11 father of Ludim, An'amim, Le'habim, Naph-tu'him 1

Anammelech 1. עֲנַמֶּלֶךְ
2Kg 17:31 in the fire to Adram'melech and Anam'melech 1

Anan 1. עָנָן
Neh 10:26 Ahi'ah, Hanan, Anan 1

Anani 1. עֲנָנִי
1Ch 3:24 sons of Eli-o-e'nai . . Joha'nan, Delai'ah, and Ana'ni 1

Ananiah 1. עֲנַנְיָה
Neh 3:23 Azari'ah the son of Ma-asei'ah, son of Anani'ah 1
11:32 An'athoth, Nob, Anani'ah 1

Ananias 1. Ἁνανίας
Act 5: 1 a man named Anani'as with his wife Sapphi'ra 1
3 Peter said, "Anani'as 1
5 When Anani'as heard these words 1
9:10 there was a disciple at Damascus named Anani'as. 1
10 The Lord said to him in a vision, "Anani'as." 1
12 he has seen a man named Anani'as come 1
13 Anani'as answered, "Lord 1
17 So Anani'as departed and entered the house. 1
22:12 one Anani'as, a devout man according to the law 1
23: 2 the high priest Anani'as commanded . . to strike him 1
24: 1 the high priest Anani'as came down with some elders 1
Tob 5:12 I am Azarias the son of the great Ananias 1
13 I used to know Ananias and Jathan 1
Jdt 8: 1 son of Elkiah, son of Ananias, son of Gideon 1

Ananiel 1. Ανανιηλ
Tob 1: 1 son of Ananiel, son of Aduel, son of Gabael 1

Anasib 1. Ανασιβ
1Es 5:24 of the sons of Anasib, 972 1

Anath 1. עֲנָת
Jdg 3:31 Shamgar the son of Anath, who killed 600 1
5: 6 In the days of Shamgar, son of Anath, in the days 1

Anathoth 1. עֲנָתוֹת 2. עַנְּתֹתִי 3. Αναθωθ
Jos 21:18 An'athoth with its pasture lands, and Almon 1
2Sm 23:27 Abi-e'zer, of An'athoth, Mebun'nai the Hu'shathite 2
1Kg 2:26 Go to An'athoth, to your estate; for you deserve 1
1Ch 6:60 Al'emeth . . and An'athoth with its pasture lands. 1
7: 8 sons of Becher . . Abi'jah, An'athoth, and Al'emeth. 1
11:28 the son of Ikkesh of Teko'a, Abi-e'zer of An'athoth 2
12: 3 Ber'acah, Jehu of An'athoth 2
27:12 Ninth . . was Abi-e'zer of An'athoth, a Benjaminite; 2
Ezr 2:23 men of An'athoth, 128. 1
Neh 7:27 men of An'athoth, 128. 1
10:19 Hariph, An'athoth, Ne'bai 1
11:32 An'athoth, Nob, Anani'ah 1
Isa 10:30 Hearken, O La'ishah! Answer her, O An'athoth! 1
Jer 1: 1 Jeremiah . . of the priests who were in An'athoth 1
11:21 says the LORD concerning the men of An'athoth 1
23 For I will bring evil upon the men of An'athoth 1
29:27 why have you not rebuked Jeremiah of An'athoth 2
32: 7 Buy my field which is at An'athoth 1
8 and said to me, 'Buy my field which is at An'athoth 1
9 And I bought the field at An'athoth from Han'amel 1
1Es 5:18 The men of Netophah, 55. The men of Anathoth, 158. 3

Andrew 1. Ἀνδρέας
Mat 4:18 Simon who is called Peter and Andrew his brother 1
10: 2 and Andrew his brother 1
Mrk 1:16 he saw Simon and Andrew the brother of Simon 1

29 entered the house of Simon and Andrew 1
3:18 Andrew, and Philip, and Bartholomew, and Matthew 1
13: 3 James and John and Andrew asked him privately 1
Lke 6:14 whom he named Peter, and Andrew his brother 1
Joh 1:40 Andrew, Simon Peter's brother. 1
44 from Beth-sa'ida, the city of Andrew and Peter. 1
6: 8 Andrew, Simon Peter's brother, said to him 1
12:22 Philip went and told Andrew 1
22 Andrew went with Philip and they told Jesus. 1
Act 1:13 Peter and John and James and Andrew 1

Andronicus 1. 'Ανδρόνικος
Rom 16: 7 Greet Androni'cus and Ju'nias, my kinsmen 1
2Mc 4:31 leaving Andronicus . . to act as his deputy. 1
32 gave them to Andronicus 1
34 Menelaus, taking Andronicus aside 1
34 Andronicus came to Onias •
38 stripped off the purple robe from Andronicus 1
5:23 at Gerizim, Andronicus 1

Anem 1. עָנֵם
1Ch 6:73 Ramoth . . and Anem with its pasture lands; 1

Aner 1. עָנֵר
Gen 14:13 of Eshcol and of Aner; these were allies of Abram. 1
24 let Aner, Eshcol, and Mamre take their share. 1
1Ch 6:70 Aner with its pasture lands, and Bil'e-am 1

Angle 1. מִקְצֹעַ
2Ch 26: 9 built towers in Jerusalem . . at the Angle 1
Neh 3:19 opposite the ascent to the armory at the Angle. 1
20 section from the Angle to the door of the house 1
24 section, from the house of Azari'ah to the Angle 1
25 repaired opposite the Angle and the tower 1

Aniam 1. אֲנִיעָם
1Ch 7:19 sons of Shemi'da were . . Likhi, and Ani'am. 1

Anim 1. עָנִים
Jos 15:50 Anab, Esh'temoh, Anim 1

Anna 1. "Αννα
Lke 2:36 a prophetess, Anna, the daughter of Phan'uel 1
Tob 1: 9 I married Anna, a member of our family 1
20 nothing was left to me except my wife Anna 1
2: 1 my wife Anna and my son Tobias were restored to me 1
11 Then my wife Anna earned money at women's work. 1
5:17 Anna, his mother, began to weep, and said to Tobit 1
11: 5 Now Anna sat looking intently down the road 1
9 Then Anna ran to meet them, and embraced her son 1
14:12 when Anna died he buried her with his father. 1

Annan 1. Ανναν
1Es 9:32 Of the sons of Annan, Elionas and Asaias 1

Annas 1. "Αννας
Lke 3: 2 in the high-priesthood of Annas and Ca'iaphas 1
Joh 18:13 First they led him to Annas 1
24 Annas then sent him bound to Ca'iaphas 1
Act 4: 6 Annas the high priest and Ca'iaphas and John 1

Annias 1. Αννιας
1Es 5:16 The sons of Annias,101. The sons of Arom. 1

Anniuth 1. Αννιουθ
1Es 9:48 Jeshua and Anniuth and Sherebiah, Jamin, Akkub 1

Annunus 1. Αννουνος
1Es 8:48 also Hashabiah and Annunus and Jeshaiah 1

Anthothijah 1. עַנְתֹתִיָּה
1Ch 8:24 Hanani'ah, Elam, Anthothi'jah 1

Antilebanon 1. Αντιλιβανος
Jdt 1: 7 Damascus and Lebanon and Antilebanon 1

Antioch 1. 'Αντιόχεια 2. 'Αντιοχεύς
Act 6: 5 Par'menas, and Nicola'us, a proselyte of Antioch. 2
11:19 as far as Phoeni'cia and Cyprus and Antioch 1
20 who on coming to Antioch spoke to the Greeks also 1
22 they sent Barnabas to Antioch. 1
26 when he had found him, he brought him to Antioch. 1
26 in Antioch the disciples were . . Christians 1
27 prophets came down from Jerusalem to Antioch. 1
13: 1 Now in the church at Antioch there were prophets 1
14 and came to Antioch of Pisid'ia 1
14:19 Jews came there from Antioch and Ico'nium; 1
21 returned to Lystra and to Ico'nium and to Antioch 1
26 from there they sailed to Antioch 1
15:22 send them to Antioch with Paul and Barnabas 1
23 the brethren who are of the Gentiles in Antioch 1
30 when they were sent off, they went down to Antioch; 1
35 Paul and Barnabas remained in Antioch 1
18:22 and then went down to Antioch. 1
Gal 2:11 when Cephas came to Antioch 1
2Ti 3:11 what befell me at Antioch, at Ico'nium 1
1Mc 3:37 departed from Antioch his capital 1
4:35 he departed to Antioch and enlisted mercenaries 1
6:63 he departed with haste and returned to Antioch. 1
10:68 he was greatly grieved and returned to Antioch. 1
11:13 Then Ptolemy entered Antioch 1
44 sent . . men to him at Antioch 1
56 Trypho . . gained control of Antioch. 1
2Mc 4: 9 the men of Jerusalem as citizens of Antioch. 2
33 a place of sanctuary at Daphne near Antioch. 1
5:21 hurried away to Antioch 1
8:35 till he reached Antioch 1
11:36 we are on our way to Antioch. 1
13:23 Philip . . had revolted in Antioch 1
26 and set out for Antioch 1
14:27 to send Maccabeus to Antioch as a prisoner 1

Antiochian citizen 1. 'Αντιοχεύς
2Mc 4:19 chosen as being Antiochian citizens 1

Antiochis 1. Αντιοχις
2Mc 4:30 Antiochis, the king's concubine. 1

Antiochus 1. Αντιοχος
1Mc 1:10 a sinful root, Antiochus Epiphanes 1
10 Antiochus Epiphanes, son of Antiochus the king; 1
16 Antiochus saw that his kingdom was established 1
20 Antiochus returned in the 143rd year 1
3:27 When king Antiochus heard these reports 1
33 Lysias was also to take care of Antiochus his son 1
6: 1 Antiochus was going through the . . provinces 1
15 that he might guide Antiochus his son 1
16 Thus Antiochus the king died there 1
17 he set up Antiochus the king's son to reign 1
55 King Antiochus while still living 1
55 had appointed to bring up Antiochus his son 1
7: 2 the army seized Antiochus and Lysias 1
8: 6 They also defeated Antiochus the Great, king of Asia 1
10: 1 Alexander Epiphanes, the son of Antiochus 1
11:39 Imalkue the Arab, who was bringing up Antiochus 1
40 and insistently urged him to hand Antiochus over •
54 the young boy Antiochus who began to reign 1
57 the young Antiochus wrote to Jonathan, saying 1
12:16 We . . have chosen Numenius the son of Antiochus 1
39 to raise his hand against Antiochus the king. 1
13:31 the young king Antiochus 1
14:22 Numenius the son of Antiochus 1
15: 1 Antiochus, the son of Demetrius the king 1
2 King Antiochus to Simon the high priest 1
10 In the 174th year Antiochus set out and invaded 1
11 Antiochus pursued him 1
13 So Antiochus encamped against Dor 1
25 Antiochus the king besieged Dor anew 1
26 Simon sent to Antiochus 2,000 picked men •
2Mc 1:14 Antiochus came to the place 1
15 Antiochus had come with a few men 1
2:20 further the wars against Antiochus Epiphanes 1
4: 7 Antiochus who was called Epiphanes 1
21 Antiochus learned that . . 1
37 Therefore Antiochus was grieved at heart 1
5: 1 Antiochus made his second invasion of Egypt. 1
5 When a false rumor arose that Antiochus was dead 1
15 Antiochus dared to enter the most holy temple •
17 Antiochus was elated in spirit 1
21 Antiochus carried off 1,800 talents 1
24 Antiochus sent Apollonius •
7:24 Antiochus felt that . . 1
24 Antiochus not only appealed to him in words •
9: 1 Antiochus had retreated in disorder 1
2 Antiochus and his men were defeated •
2 Antiochus was put to flight by the inhabitants 1
19 Antiochus their king and general 1
25 I have appointed my son Antiochus to be king 1
29 fearing the son of Antiochus 1
10: 9 Such then was the end of Antiochus 1
10 tell what took place under Antiochus Eupator 1
13 and had gone over to Antiochus Epiphanes. 1
11:22 King Antiochus to his brother Lysias, greeting. 1
27 King Antiochus to the senate of the Jews 1
13: 1 Antiochus Eupator was coming with a great army 1
3 and with utter hypocrisy urged Antiochus 1
4 the King of kings aroused the anger of Antiochus 1
14: 2 having made away with Antiochus 1
3Mc 1: 1 the regions . . had been seized by Antiochus 1
1 where Antiochus's supporters were encamped. 1
4 matters were turning out rather in favor of Antiochus 1
4Mc 4:15 Antiochus Epiphanes succeeded to the throne 1
21 and caused Antiochus himself to make war on them. 1
5: 1 The tyrant Antiochus, sitting in state 1
5 When Antiochus saw him he said 1
16 We, O Antiochus, who have been persuaded 1
10:17 murderous, and utterly abominable Antiochus 1
17:23 the tyrant Antiochus . . proclaimed them 1
18: 5 The tyrant Antiochus was both punished on earth 1

Antipas 1. 'Αντιπᾶς
Rev 2:13 you did not deny . . even in the days of An'tipas 1

Antipater 1. Αντιπατρος
1Mc 12:16 Antipater the son of Jason 1
14:22 Antipater the son of Jason 1

Antipatris 1. 'Αντιπατρίς
Act 23:31 the soldiers . . brought him by night to Antip'atris. 1

Anub 1. עָנוּב
1Ch 4: 8 Koz was the father of Anub, Zobe'bah 1

Apame 1. Απαμη
1Es 4:29 Yet I have seen him with Apame 1

Apelles 1. 'Απελλῆς
Rom 16:10 Greet Apel'les, who is approved in Christ. 1

Aphairema 1. Αφαιρεμα
1Mc 11:34 Aphairema and Lydda and Rathamin 1

Aphek 1. אֲפֵק
Jos 12:18 the king of Aphek, one; the king of Lashar'on, one; 1
13: 4 to Aphek, to the boundary of the Amorites 1
19:30 Mahalab, Achzib, Ummah, Aphek and Rehob 1
1Sm 4: 1 and the Philistines encamped at Aphek. 1
29: 1 Philistines gathered all their forces at Aphek; 1
1Kg 20:26 Ben-ha'dad mustered . . and went up to Aphek 1
30 the rest fled into the city of Aphek; 1
2Kg 13:17 For you shall fight the Syrians in Aphek until 1

Aphekah 1. אֲפֵקָה
Jos 15:53 Janim, Beth-tap'puah, Aphe'kah 1

Apherra 1. Αφερρα
1Es 5:34 the sons of Apherra, the sons of Barodis 1

Aphiah 1. אֲפִיחַ
1Sm 9: 1 son of Zeror, son of Beco'rath, son of Aphi'ah 1

Aphik 1. אֲפִיק
Jdg 1:31 inhabitants . . of Helbah, or of Aphik, or of Rehob; 1

Apis 1. Απις
Jer 46:15 Why has Apis fled? Why did not your bull stand? 1

Apollonia 1. 'Απολλωνία
Act 17: 1 when they had passed through . . Apollo'nia 1

Apollonius 1. 'Απολλώνιος
1Mc 3:10 Apollonius gathered together Gentiles 1
12 Judas took the sword of Apollonius 1
10:69 Apollonius the governor of Coelesyria 1
74 When Jonathan heard the words of Apollonius 1
75 Apollonius had a garrison in Joppa. 1
77 When Apollonius heard of it 1
79 Now Apollonius had . . left 1,000 cavalry 1
2Mc 3: 5 he went to Apollonius of Tarsus 1
7 When Apollonius met the king 1
4: 4 Apollonius, the son of Menestheus 1
21 Apollonius the son of Menestheus 1
5:24 Antiochus sent Apollonius 1
12: 2 Timothy and Apollonius the son of Gennaeus 1
4Mc 4: 2 he came to Apollonius, governor of Syria 1
4 When Apollonius learned the details 1
8 Apollonius went on to the temple. 1
10 while Apollonius was going up 1
11 Then Apollonius fell down half dead 1
13 Apollonius had been overcome 1
14 Apollonius . . went away to report to the king •

Apollophanes 1. Απολλοφανης
2Mc 10:37 his brother Chaereas, and Apollophanes. 1

Apollos 1. 'Απολλῶς
Act 18:24 Now a Jew named Apol'los, a native of Alexandria 1
19: 1 While Apol'los was at Corinth 1
1Co 1:12 I belong to Paul," or "I belong to Apol'los 1
3: 4 and another, "I belong to Apol'los 1
5 What then is Apol'los? What is Paul? 1
6 I planted, Apol'los watered 1
22 whether Paul or Apol'los or Cephas or the world 1
4: 6 I have applied all this to myself and Apol'los 1
16:12 As for our brother Apol'los 1
Tit 3:13 speed Zenas the lawyer and Apol'los on their way 1

Apollyon 1. 'Απολλύων
Rev 9:11 and in Greek he is called Apol'lyon. 1

Appaim 1. אַפַּיִם
1Ch 2:30 sons of Nadab: Seled and Ap'pa-im; and Seled died 1
31 The sons of Ap'pa-im: Ishi. 1

Apphia 1. 'Απφία
Phm 1: 2 Ap'phia our sister and Archip'pus our fellow soldier 1

Apphus 1. Απφους
1Mc 2: 5 Jonathan called Apphus. 1

Appius 1. 'Αππίος
Act 28:15 as far as the Forum of Ap'pius and Three Taverns 1

Aquila 1. 'Ακύλας
Act 18: 2 he found a Jew named Aq'uila, a native of Pontus 1

18 and with him Priscilla and Aq'uila 1
26 when Priscilla and Aq'uila heard him 1
Rom16: 3 Greet Prisca and Aq'uila, my fellow workers 1
1Co 16:19 Aq'uila and Prisca, together with the church 1
2Ti 4:19 Greet Prisca and Aq'uila 1

Ar 1. עָר
Num21:15 slope .. valleys that extends to the seat of Ar 1
28 It devoured Ar of Moab, the lords of the heights 1
Deu 2: 9 have given Ar to the sons of Lot for a possession.' 1
18 day you are to pass over the boundary of Moab at Ar; 1
29 as .. the Moabites who live in Ar did for me 1
Isa 15: 1 Because Ar is laid waste in a night Moab is undone; 1

Ara 1. אֲרָא
1Ch 7:38 The sons of Jether: Jephun'neh, Pispa, and Ara. 1

Arab 1. עֲרָב 2. עֲרָב 3. עַרְבִי 4. Αραψ
Jos 15:52 Arab, Dumah, Eshan 1
2Ch 17:11 Arabs also brought him 7,700 rams 3
21:16 against Jeho'ram the anger .. of the Arabs 3
22: 1 band of men that came with the Arabs .. had slain 3
26: 7 against the Arabs that dwelt in Gurba'al 3
Neh 2:19 Sanbal'lat .. Tobi'ah .., and Geshem the Arab 3
4: 7 when Sanbal'lat and Tobi'ah and the Arabs 2
6: 1 to Geshem the Arab and to the rest of our enemies 3
Isa 13:20 no Arab will pitch his tent there 3
Jer 3: 2 awaiting lovers like an Arab in the wilderness. 3
1Mc 5:39 They also have hired Arabs to help them 4
11:17 Zabdiel the Arab cut off the head of Alexander 4
39 So he went to Imalkue the Arab 4
12:31 the Arabs who are called Zabadeans 4
2Mc 5: 8 Accused before Aretas the ruler of the Arabs 4
12:10 not less than 5,000 Arabs with 500 horsemen 4

Arabah 1. עֲרָבָה
Deu 1: 1 the wilderness, in the Arabah over against Suph 1
7 go to .. all their neighbors in the Arabah 1
2: 8 from the Arabah road from Elath and E'zi-on-ge'ber. 1
3:17 the Arabah also, with the Jordan as the boundary 1
17 from Chin'nereth as far as the sea of the Arabah 1
4:49 together with all the Arabah on the east side 1
49 as far as the Sea of the Arabah, under the slopes 1
11:30 land of the Canaanites who live in the Arabah 1
Jos 3:16 and those flowing down toward the sea of Arabah 1
8:14 went out early to the descent toward the Arabah 1
11: 2 to the kings who were in .. the Arabah south 1
16 land of Goshen and the lowland and the Arabah 1
12: 1 their land .. with all the Arabah eastward 1
3 and the Arabah to the Sea of Chin'neroth eastward 1
3 to the sea of the Arabah, the Salt Sea, southward 1
8 in the hill country, in the lowland, in the Arabah 1
18:18 and passing on .. it goes down to the Arabah; 1
1Sm 23:24 of Ma'on, in the Arabah to the south of Jeshi'mon. 1
2Sm 2:29 Abner .. went all that night through the Arabah; 1
4: 7 and went by the way of the Arabah all night 1
2Kg 14:25 from the .. as far as the Sea of the Arabah 1
25: 4 And they went in the direction of the Arabah. 1
Jer 39: 4 and they went toward the Arabah. 1
52: 7 And they went in the direction of the Arabah. 1
Ezk 47: 8 the eastern region and goes down into the Arabah; 1
Ams 6:14 entrance of Hamath to the Brook of the Arabah. 1

Arabia 1. עֲרָב 2. ᾿Αραβία 3. Arabus
1Kg 10:15 which came .. from all the kings of Arabia 1
2Ch 9:14 kings of Arabia and the governors of the land 1
Isa 21:13 The oracle concerning Arabia. 1
13 In the thickets in Arabia you will lodge 1
Jer 25:24 all the kings of Arabia 1
Ezk 27:21 Arabia and all the princes of Kedar were 1
30: 5 Ethiopia, and Put, and Lud, and all Arabia, and Libya 1
Gal 1:17 I went away into Arabia 2
4:25 Now Hagar is Mount Sinai in Arabia 2
2Es 15:29 The nations of the dragons of Arabia 3
Jdt 2:25 fronting toward Arabia. 2
1Mc 11:16 Alexander fled into Arabia to find protection there 2

Arabian 1. ῎Αραψ
Act 2:11 Cretans and Arabians 1

Arad 1. עֲרָד
Num21: 1 Canaanite, the king of Arad, who dwelt in the Negeb 1
33:40 Canaanite, the king of Arad, who dwelt in the Negeb 1
Jos 12:14 the king of Hormah, one; the king of Arad, one; 1
Jdg 1:16 of Judah, which lies in the Negeb near Arad; 1
1Ch 8:15 Zebadi'ah, Arad, Eder 1

Aradus 1. Αραδος
1Mc 15:23 to Aradus and Gortyna and Cnidus and Cyprus 1

Arah 1. אָרַח 2. Αρες
1Ch 7:39 The sons of Ulla: Arah, Han'niel, and Rizi'a. 1
Ezr 2: 5 sons of Arah, 775. 1
Neh 6:18 son-in-law of Shecani'ah the son of Arah 1
7:10 sons of Arah, 652. 1
1Es 5:10 The sons of Arah, 756 2

Aram 1. אֲרָם
Gen 10:22 of Shem: Elam, Asshur, Arpach'shad, Lud, and Aram. 1
23 The sons of Aram: Uz, Hul, Gether, and Mash. 1
22:21 Buz his brother, Kemu'el the father of Aram 1
Num23: 7 From Aram Balak has brought me 1
2Sm 8: 6 Then David put garrisons in Aram of Damascus; 1
15: 8 vowed a vow while I dwelt at Geshur in Aram, saying 1
1Ch 1:17 The sons of Shem .. Lud, Aram, Uz, Hul, Gether 1
2:23 Geshur and Aram took .. Havvoth-ja'ir, Kenath 1
7:34 sons of Shemer .. Rohgah, Jehub'bah, and Aram. 1
Hos 12:12 (Jacob fled to the land of Aram 1
Zec 9: 1 For to the LORD belong the cities of Aram •

Aram-maacah 1. אֲרַם מַעֲכָה
1Ch 19: 6 from Aram-ma'acah, and from Zobah 1

Aram-naharaim 1. אֲרַם נַהֲרַיִם
Ps 60: 0 he strove with Aram-naharaim and with Aram-zobah 1

Aram-zobah 1. אֲרַם צוֹבָה
Ps 60: 0 he strove with Aram-naharaim and with Aram-zobah 1

Aramaic 1. אֲרָמִי 2. אֲרָמִית
2Kg 18:26 speak to your servants in the Aramaic language 1
Ezr 4: 7 letter was written in Aramaic and translated. 2
Isa 36:11 Pray, speak to your servants in Aramaic 2

Aramean 1. אֲרַמִּי
Gen 25:20 Rebekah, the daughter of Bethu'el the Aramean 1
20 Rebekah .. the sister of Laban the Aramean. 1
28: 5 Bethu'el the Aramean, the brother of Rebekah 1
31:20 Jacob outwitted Laban the Aramean, in that he did 1
24 God came to Laban the Aramean in a dream by night 1
Deu 26: 5 wandering Aramean was my father; 1
1Ch 7:14 As'ri-el, whom his Aramean concubine bore; 1

Aran 1. אֲרָן
Gen 36:28 These are the sons of Dishan: Uz and Aran. 1
1Ch 1:42 The sons of Dishan: Uz and Aran. 1

Ararat 1. אֲרָרָט 2. Αραρατ
Gen 8: 4 ark came to rest upon the mountains of Ar'arat. 1
2Kg 19:37 slew him .. and escaped into the land of Ar'arat. 1
Isa 37:38 slew him .. and escaped into the land of Ar'arat. 1
Jer 51:27 the kingdoms, Ar'arat, Minni, and Ash'kenaz; 1
Tob 1:21 they fled to the mountains of Ararat 2

Araunah 1. אֲרַוְנָה
2Sm 24:16 by the threshing floor of Arau'nah the Jeb'usite. 1
18 on the threshing floor of Arau'nah the Jeb'usite. 1
20 when Arau'nah looked down, he saw the king 1
20 Arau'nah went forth, and did obeisance to the king 1
21 And Arau'nah said, "Why has my lord the king come 1
22 Arau'nah said to David, "Let my lord the king take 1
23 All this, O king, Arau'nah gives to the king. 1
23 And Arau'nah said to the king, "The LORD your God 1
24 But the king said to Arau'nah, "No, but I will buy it 1

Arba
Jos 14:15 this Arba was the greatest man among the Anakim. •
15:13 Kir'iath-ar'ba .. (Arba was the father of Anak). •
21:11 Kir'iath-ar'ba (Arba being the father of Anak) •

Arbathite 1. עַרְבָתִי
2Sm 23:31 Abi-al'bon the Ar'bathite, Az'maveth of Bahu'rim 1
1Ch 11:32 Abi'el the Ar'bathite. 1

Arbatta 1. Αρβαττα
1Mc 5:23 Then he took the Jews of Galilee and Arbatta 1

Arbela 1. Αρβηλα
1Mc 9: 2 encamped against Mesaloth in Arbela 1

Arbite 1. אַרְבִּי
2Sm 23:35 Hezro of Carmel, Pa'arai the Arbite 1

Archelaus 1. ᾿Αρχέλαος
Mat 2:22 he heard that Archela'us reigned over Judea 1

Archippus 1. ῎Αρχιππος
Col 4:17 say to Archip'pus 1
Phm 1: 2 Ap'phia our sister and Archip'pus our fellow soldier 1

Archite 1. אַרְכִּי
Jos 16: 2 along to At'aroth, the territory of the Archites; 1
2Sm 15:32 Hushai the Archite came to meet him 1
16:16 And when Hushai the Archite, David's friend, came 1
17: 5 Call Hushai the Archite also, and let us hear 1
14 The counsel of Hushai the Archite is better 1
1Ch 27:33 and Hushai the Archite was the king's friend. 1

Ard 1. אַרְדְּ
Gen 46:21 Gera, Na'aman, Ehi, Rosh, Muppim, Huppim, and Ard 1
Num26:40 the sons of Bela were Ard and Na'aman 1
40 of Ard, the family of the Ard'ites; •

Ardat 1. Ardat
2Es 9:26 I went .. into the field which is called Ardat 1

Ardite 1. אַרְדִּי
Num26:40 of Ard, the family of the Ard'ites; 1

Ardon 1. אַרְדּוֹן
1Ch 2:18 these were her sons: Jesher, Shobab, and Ardon. 1

Areli 1. אַרְאֵלִי
Gen 46:16 sons of Gad: Ziph'ion .. Eri, Aro'di, and Are'li 1
Num26:17 of Are'li, the family of the Are'lites. 1

Arelite 1. אַרְאֵלִי
Num26:17 of Are'li, the family of the Are'lites. 1

Areopagite 1. ᾿Αρεοπαγίτης
Act 17:34 believed, among them Dionys'ius the Are-op'agite 1

Areopagus 1. ῎Αρειος πάγος
Act 17:19 and brought him to the Are-op'agus 1
22 Paul, standing in the middle of the Are-op'agus 1

Aretas 1. ῾Αρέτας
2Co 11:32 the governor under King Ar'etas guarded the city 1
2Mc 5: 8 Accused before Aretas the ruler of the Arabs 1

Argob 1. אַרְגֹּב
Deu 3: 4 whole region of Argob, the kingdom of Og in Bashan 1
13 kingdom of Og, that is, all the region of Argob 1
14 Ja'ir the Manas'site took all the region of Argob 1
1Kg 4:13 he had the region of Argob, which is in Bashan 1

Ariarathes 1. Αριαραθης
1Mc 15:22 Attalus and Ariarathes and Arsaces 1

Aridai 1. אֲרִידַי
Est 9: 9 Parmash'ta and Ar'isai and Ar'idai and Vaiza'tha 1

Aridatha 1. אֲרִידָתָא
Est 9: 8 and Pora'tha and Ada'lia and Arida'tha 1

Ariel 1. אֲרִיאֵל
Ezr 8:16 Then I sent for Elie'zer, Ar'i-el, Shemai'ah, 1
Isa 29: 1 Ho Ariel, Ariel, the city where David encamped! 1
1 Ho Ariel, Ariel, the city where David encamped! 1
2 Yet I will distress Ariel 1
2 she shall be to me like an Ariel. 1
7 all the nations that fight against Ariel 1

Arimathea 1. ῾Αριμαθαία
Mat 27:57 a rich man from Arimathe'a, named Joseph 1
Mrk 15:43 Joseph of Arimathe'a, a respected member of the council 1
Lke 23:50 from the Jewish town of Arimathe'a 1
Joh 19:38 Joseph of Arimathe'a, who was a disciple of Jesus 1

Arioch 1. אַרְיוֹךְ 2. אַרְיוֹךְ (A) 3. Αριωχ
Gen 14: 1 Am'raphel king of Shinar, Ar'ioch king of Ella'sar 1
9 Ar'ioch king of Ella'sar, four kings against five. 1
Dan 2:14 replied with prudence and discretion to Ar'ioch 2
15 said to Ar'ioch, the king's captain 2
15 Then Ar'ioch made the matter known to Daniel. 2
24 Therefore Daniel went in to Ar'ioch 2
25 Then Ar'ioch brought in Daniel before the king 2
Jdt 1: 6 the plain where Arioch ruled the Elymaeans. 3

Arisai 1. אֲרִיסַי
Est 9: 9 Parmash'ta and Ar'isai and Ar'idai and Vaiza'tha 1

Aristarchus 1. ᾿Αρίσταρχος
Act 19:29 dragging with them Ga'ius and Aristar'chus 1
20: 4 of the Thessalo'nians, Aristar'chus and Secun'dus; 1
27: 2 we put to sea, accompanied by Aristar'chus 1
Col 4:10 Aristar'chus my fellow prisoner greets you 1
Phm 1:24 so do Mark, Aristar'chus, Demas, and Luke 1

Aristobulus 1. ᾿Αριστόβουλος
Rom16:10 those who belong to the family of Aristobu'lus. 1
2Mc 1:10 Aristobulus .. of the anointed priests 1

Arius 1. ῎Αρειος
1Mc 12: 7 to Onias the high priest from Arius 1
20 Arius, king of the Spartans 1

Arkite 1. עַרְקִי
Gen 10:17 the Hivites, the Arkites, the Sinites 1
1Ch 1:15 the Hivites, the Arkites, the Sinites 1

Armageddon 1. ῾Αρμαγεδών
Rev 16:16 the place which is called in Hebrew Armaged'don. 1

Armoni 1. אַרְמֹנִי
2Sm 21: 8 two sons of Rizpah .. Armo'ni and Mephib'osheth; 1

Arna 1. Arna
2Es 1: 2 son of Meraioth, son of Arna, son of Uzzi 1

Arnan 1. אַרְנָן
1Ch 3:21 sons of Hanani'ah .. Arnan, his son Obadi'ah 1

Arni 1. ᾿Αρνί
Lke 3:33 the son of Arni, the son of Hezron, the son of Perez 1

Arnon 1. אַרְנוֹן

Num21:13 encamped on the other side of the Arnon 1
13 Arnon is the boundary of Moab 1
14 Waheb in Suphah, and the valleys of the Arnon 1
24 took . . his land from the Arnon to the Jabbok 1
26 all his land out of his hand, as far as the Arnon. 1
28 Ar of Moab, the lords of the heights of the Arnon. 1
22:36 city of Moab, on the boundary formed by the Arnon 1
Deu 2:24 'Rise up . . and go over the valley of the Arnon; 1
36 Aro'er . . on the edge of the valley of the Arnon 1
3: 8 from the valley of the Arnon to Mount Hermon 1
12 Aro'er, which is on the edge of the valley of the Arnon 1
16 from Gilead as far as the valley of the Arnon 1
4:48 Aro'er . . on the edge of the valley of the Arnon 1
Jos 12: 1 from the valley of the Arnon to Mount Hermon 1
2 Aro'er . . on the edge of the valley of the Arnon 1
13: 9 Aro'er . . on the edge of the valley of the Arnon 1
16 Aro'er . . on the edge of the valley of the Arnon 1
Jdg 11:13 my land, from the Arnon to the Jabbok 1
18 and camped on the other side of the Arnon; 1
18 for the Arnon was the boundary of Moab 1
22 territory . . from the Arnon to the Jabbok 1
26 all the cities that are on the banks of the Arnon 1
2Kg 10:33 from Aro'er, which is by the valley of the Arnon 1
Isa 16: 2 the daughters of Moab at the fords of the Arnon. 1
Jer 48:20 Tell it by the Arnon, that Moab is laid waste. 1

Arod 1. אֲרוֹד

Num26:17 of Ar'od, the family of the Ar'odites; 1

Arodi 1. אֲרוֹדִי

Gen 46:16 sons of Gad: Ziph'ion . . Eri, Aro'di, and Are'li 1

Arodite 1. אֲרוֹדִי

Num26:17 of Ar'od, the family of the Ar'odites; 1

Aroer 1. עֲרֹעֵר

Num32:34 the sons of Gad built Dibon, At'aroth, Aro'er 1
Deu 2:36 From Aro'er . . as far as Gilead, there was not 1
3:12 I gave . . the territory beginning at Aro'er 1
4:48 from Aro'er, which is on the edge of the valley 1
Jos 12: 2 who dwelt at Heshbon, and ruled from Aro'er 1
13: 9 Aro'er . . on the edge of the valley of the Arnon 1
16 their territory was from Aro'er . . and the city 1
25 to Aro'er, which is east of Rabbah 1
Jdg 11:26 in Aro'er and its villages, and in all the cities 1
33 he smote them from Aro'er to the neighborhood 1
1Sm 30:28 for those . . in Aro'er, in Siphmoth, in Eshtemo'a 1
2Sm 24: 5 They crossed the Jordan, and began from Aro'er 1
2Kg 10:33 from Aro'er, which is by the valley of the Arnon 1
1Ch 5: 8 who dwelt in Aro'er, as far as Nebo and Ba'al-me'on. 1
Jer 48:19 Stand by the way and watch, O inhabitant of Aro'er! 1

Aroerite 1. עֲרֹעֵרִי

1Ch 11:44 Shama and Je-i'el the sons of Hotham the Aro'erite 1

Arom 1. Αρομ

1Es 5:16 The sons of Annias,101. The sons of Arom. 1

Arpachshad 1. אַרְפַּכְשַׁד

Gen 10:22 of Shem: Elam, Asshur, Arpach'shad, Lud, and Aram. 1
24 Arpach'shad became the father of Shelah; 1
11:10 he became the father of Arpach'shad 1
11 Shem lived after the birth of Arpach'shad 1
12 When Arpach'shad had lived 35 years 1
13 Arpach'shad lived after the birth of Shelah 1
1Ch 1:17 of Shem: Elam, Asshur, Arpach'shad, Lud, Aram, Uz 1
18 Arpach'shad was the father of Shelah; 1
24 Shem, Arpach'shad, Shelah; 1

Arpad 1. אַרְפָּד

2Kg 18:34 Where are the gods of Hamath and Arpad? 1
19:13 Where is the king of Hamath, the king of Arpad 1
Isa 10: 9 Is not Hamath like Arpad? 1
36:19 Where are the gods of Hamath and Arpad? 1
37:13 Where is the king of Hamath, the king of Arpad 1
Jer 49:23 Hamath and Arpad are confounded 1

Arphaxad 1. Ἀρφαξάδ

Lke 3:36 the son of Ca-i'nan, the son of Arphax'ad 1
Jdt 1: 1 in the days of Arphaxad 1
5 Nebuchadnezzar made war against King Arphaxad 1
13 he led his forces against King Arphaxad 1
13 overthrew the whole army of Arphaxad 1
15 He captured Arphaxad in the mountains of Ragae 1

Arsaces 1. Αρσακης

1Mc 14: 2 When Arsaces the king of Persia and Media heard 1
3 seized him and took him to Arsaces 1
15:22 Attalus and Ariarathes and Arsaces 1

Arsinoe 1. Αρσινοη

3Mc 1: 1 he . . took with him his sister Arsinoe 1
4 Arsinoe went to the troops 1

Artaxerxes 1. אַרְתַּחְשַׁסְתְּא 2. אַרְתַּחְשַׁשְׂתְּא 3. אַרְתַּחְשַׁסְתָּא (A) 4. אַרְתַּחְשַׁשְׂתָּא (A) 5. Ἀρταξέρξης 6. Artaxerses

Ezr 4: 7 in the days of Ar-ta-xerx'es, Bishlam 2
7 rest of their associates wrote to Ar-ta-xerx'es 2
8 wrote a letter against Jerusalem to Ar-ta-xerx'es 2
11 To Ar-ta-xerx'es the king: Your servants 2
23 the copy of King Ar-ta-xerx'es' letter was read 2
6:14 by decree of Cyrus and Darius and Ar-ta-xerx'es 4
7: 1 in the reign of Ar-ta-xerx'es king of Persia 1
7 in the seventh year of Ar-ta-xerx'es the king 1
11 copy of the letter which King Ar-ta-xerx'es gave 1
12 Ar-ta-xerx'es, king of kings, to Ezra the priest 3
21 I, Ar-ta-xerx'es the king, make a decree 3
8: 1 Babylonia, in the reign of Ar-ta-xerx'es the king 1
Neh 2: 1 Nisan, in the twentieth year of King Ar-ta-xerx'es 1
5:14 to the 32nd year of Ar-ta-xerx'es the king 2
13: 6 year of Ar-ta-xerx'es king of Babylon 2
1Es 2:16 in the time of Artaxerxes king of the Persians 5
17 To King Artaxerxes our lord 5
30 when the letter from King Artaxerxes was read 5
7: 4 consent of Cyrus and Darius and Artaxerxes 5
8: 1 Artaxerxes the king of the Persians 5
6 in the seventh year of the reign of Artaxerxes 5
8 written commission from Artaxerxes the king 5
9 King Artaxerxes to Ezra the priest 5
19 I, Artaxerxes the king, have commanded 5
28 in the reign of Artaxerxes the king 5
2Es 1: 3 in the reign of Artaxerxes, king of the Persians. 6
AEs 11: 2 the reign of Artaxerxes the Great 5
12: 2 preparing to lay hands upon Artaxerxes the king; 5
13: 1 The Great King, Artaxerxes . . writes thus 5
16: 1 The Great King, Artaxerxes 5

Artemas 1. Ἀρτεμᾶς

Tit 3:12 When I send Artemas or Tych'icus to you 1

Artemis 1. Ἄρτεμις

Act 19:24 a silversmith, who made silver shrines of Ar'temis 1
27 the temple of the great goddess Ar'temis 1
28 Great is Ar'temis of the Ephesians! 1
34 Great is Ar'temis of the Ephesians! 1
35 the city . . is temple keeper of the great Ar'temis 1

Arubboth 1. אֲרֻבּוֹת

1Kg 4:10 Ben-hesed, in Arub'both 1

Arumah 1. ארוּמָה

Jdg 9:31 he sent messengers to Abim'elech at Aru'mah •
41 Abim'elech dwelt at Aru'mah; and Zebul drove out 1

Arvad 1. אַרְוַד

Ezk 27: 8 inhabitants of Sidon and Arvad were your rowers; 1
11 The men of Arvad and Helech were upon your walls 1

Arvadite 1. אַרְוָדִי

Gen 10:18 the Ar'vadites, the Zem'arites 1
1Ch 1:16 the Ar'vadites, the Zem'arites 1

Arza 1. אַרְצָא

1Kg 16: 9 drinking himself drunk in the house of Arza 1

Arzareth 1. Arzar

2Es 13:45 and that country is called Arzareth. 1

Asa 1. אָסָא

1Kg 15: 8 And Asa his son reigned in his stead. 1
9 Asa began to reign over Judah 1
11 Asa did what was right in the eyes of the LORD 1
13 Asa cut down her image and burned it at . . Kidron. 1
14 the heart of Asa was wholly true to the LORD 1
16 there was war between Asa and Ba'asha 1
17 no one to go out or come in to Asa king of Judah. 1
18 Asa took all the silver and the gold 1
18 Asa sent them to Ben-ha'dad the son of Tabrim'mon 1
20 Ben-ha'dad hearkened to King Asa 1
22 King Asa made a proclamation to all Judah 1
22 King Asa built Geba of Benjamin and Mizpah. 1
23 the rest of all the acts of Asa, all his might 1
24 Asa slept with his fathers, and was buried 1
25 to reign over Israel in the second year of Asa 1
28 killed him in the third year of Asa king of Judah 1
32 there was war between Asa and Ba'asha 1
33 In the third year of Asa king of Judah 1
16: 8 In the 26th year of Asa king of Judah 1
10 in the 27th year of Asa king of Judah 1
15 In the 27th year of Asa king of Judah 1
23 In the 31st year of Asa king of Judah 1
29 In the 38th year of Asa king of Judah 1
22:41 Jehosh'aphat the son of Asa began to reign 1
43 He walked in all the way of Asa his father; 1
46 who remained in the days of his father Asa 1
1Ch 3:10 descendants of Solomon . . Asa his son 1
9:16 Berechi'ah the son of Asa, son of Elka'nah 1
2Ch 14: 1 Asa his son reigned in his stead. 1
2 Asa did what was good and right 1
8 Asa had an army of 300,000 from Judah 1
10 Asa went out to meet him 1
11 Asa cried to the LORD his God 1
12 the LORD defeated the Ethiopians before Asa 1
13 Asa and the people . . pursued them as far 1
15: 2 he went out to meet Asa, and said to him, "Hear me, 1
2 Hear me, Asa, and all Judah and Benjamin 1
8 When Asa heard these words . . he took courage 1
10 month of the fifteenth year of the reign of Asa. 1
16 King Asa removed from being queen mother 1
16 Asa cut down her image, crushed it, and burned it 1
17 the heart of Asa was blameless all his days. 1
19 until the 35th year of the reign of Asa. 1
16: 1 In the 36th year of the reign of Asa 1
1 no one to go out or come in to Asa king of Judah. 1
2 Then Asa took silver and gold from the treasures 1
4 Ben-ha'dad hearkened to King Asa 1
6 Then King Asa took all Judah 1
7 Hana'ni the seer came to Asa king of Judah 1
10 Then Asa was angry with the seer 1
10 Asa inflicted cruelties upon some of the people 1
11 The acts of Asa, from first to last, are written 1
12 Asa was diseased in his feet 1
13 Asa slept with his fathers 1
17: 2 cities . . which Asa his father had taken. 1
20:32 He walked in the way of Asa his father 1
21:12 not walked . . in the ways of Asa king of Judah 1
Jer 41: 9 was the large cistern which King Asa had made 1
Mat 1: 7 and Abi'jah the father of Asa •
8 Asa the father of Jehosh'aphat •

Asahel 1. עֲשָׂהאֵל 2. Ἀσαηλος

2Sm 2:18 sons of Zeru'iah . . Jo'ab, Abi'shai, and As'ahel. 1
18 Now As'ahel was as swift of foot as a wild gazelle; 1
19 As'ahel pursued Abner, and . . turned neither 1
20 Abner looked behind him and said, "Is it you, As'ahel? 1
21 But As'ahel would not turn . . from following him. 1
22 And Abner said again to As'ahel, "Turn aside 1
23 to the place where As'ahel had fallen and died 1
30 were missing . . nineteen men besides As'ahel. 1
32 And they took up As'ahel, and buried him in the tomb 1
3:27 he died, for the blood of As'ahel his brother. 1
30 he had killed their brother As'ahel in the battle 1
23:24 As'ahel the brother of Jo'ab was one of the 30; 1
1Ch 2:16 The sons of Zeru'iah: Abi'shai, Jo'ab, and As'ahel 1
11:26 mighty men . . were As'ahel the brother of Jo'ab 1
27: 7 As'ahel the brother of Jo'ab was fourth 1
2Ch 17: 8 with them the Levites . . Zebadi'ah, As'ahel 1
31:13 As'ahel, Jer'imoth, Jo'zabad . . were overseers 1
Ezr 10:15 Only Jonathan the son of As'ahel and Jahzei'ah 1
1Es 9:14 Jonathan the son of Asahel and Jahzeiah 2

Asaiah 1. עֲשָׂיָה

2Kg 22:12 and Shaphan . . and Asai'ah the king's servant 1
14 and Ahi'kam, and Achbor, and Shaphan, and Asai'ah 1
1Ch 4:36 Asai'ah, Ad'i-el, Jesim'iel, Benai'ah 1
6:30 Shim'e-a . . Haggi'ah his son, and Asai'ah his son. 1
9: 5 of the Shi'lonites: Asai'ah the first-born 1
15: 6 of the sons of Merar'i, Asai'ah the chief 1
11 Levites Uri'el, Asai'ah, Jo'el, Shemai'ah, Eli'el 1
2Ch 34:20 king commanded . . Asai'ah the king's servant 1

Asaias 1. Ασαιας

1Es 9:32 Of the sons of Annan, Elionas and Asaias 1

Asaph 1. אָסָף 2. Ἀσάφ

2Kg 18:18 and Jo'ah the son of Asaph, the recorder. 1
37 Eli'akim . . and Shebna.., and Jo'ah the son of Asaph 1
1Ch 6:39 his brother Asaph, who stood on his right hand 1
39 namely, Asaph the son of Berechi'ah, son of Shim'e-a 1
9:15 the son of Mica, son of Zichri, son of Asaph; 1
15:17 of his brethren Asaph the son of Berechi'ah 1
19 The singers, Heman, Asaph, and Ethan 1
16: 5 Asaph was the chief, and second to him were 1
5 Asaph was to sound the cymbals 1
7 sung to the LORD by Asaph and his brethren. 1
37 David left Asaph and his brethren there 1
25: 1 set apart for the service . . of the sons of Asaph 1
2 sons of Asaph: Zaccur, Joseph, Nethani'ah 1
2 Zaccur . . and Ashare'lah, sons of Asaph 1
2 sons of Asaph, under the direction of Asaph 1
6 Asaph, Jedu'thun, and Heman were under the order 1
9 The first lot fell for Asaph to Joseph; 1
26: 1 the son of Ko're, of the sons of Asaph. 1
2Ch 5:12 Levitical singers, Asaph, Heman, and Jedu'thun 1
20:14 Mattani'ah, a Levite of the sons of Asaph 1
29:13 of the sons of Asaph, Zechari'ah and Mattani'ah; 1
30 praises . . with the words of . . Asaph the seer. 1
35:15 singers, the sons of Asaph, were in their place 1
15 command of David, and Asaph, and Heman 1
Ezr 2:41 singers: the sons of Asaph, 128. 1
3:10 Levites, the sons of Asaph, with cymbals 1
Neh 2: 8 letter to Asaph, the keeper of the king's forest 1
7:44 singers: the sons of Asaph, 148. 1
11:17 Mattani'ah . . of Mica, son of Zabdi, son of Asaph 1
22 son of Mattani'ah, son of Mica, of the sons of Asaph 1
12:35 son of Micai'ah, son of Zaccur, son of Asaph; 1
46 For in the days of David and Asaph of old there was 1
Ps 50: 0 A Psalm of Asaph. 1
73: 0 A Psalm of Asaph. 1
74: 0 A Maskil of Asaph. 1
75: 0 Do Not Destroy. A Psalm of Asaph. A Song. 1
76: 0 A Psalm of Asaph. A Song. 1
77: 0 according to Jeduthun. A Psalm of Asaph. 1
78: 0 A Maskil of Asaph. 1

79: 0 A Psalm of Asaph. 1
80: 0 A Testimony of Asaph. A Psalm. 1
81: 0 A Psalm of Asaph. 1
82: 0 A Psalm of Asaph. 1
83: 0 A Song. A Psalm of Asaph. 1
Isa 36: 3 and Jo'ah the son of Asaph, the recorder. 1
22 Jo'ah the son of Asaph, the recorder 1
1Es 1:15 the temple singers, the sons of Asaph 2
15 Asaph, Zechariah, and Eddinus 2
5:27 The temple singers: the sons of Asaph, 128. 2
59 the Levites, the sons of Asaph, with cymbals 2

Asaramel
1Mc 14:28 in Asaramel, in the great assembly of the priests •

Asarel 1. אֲשַׂרְאֵל
1Ch 4:16 sons of Jehal'lelel . . Ziphah, Tir'i-a, and As'arel. 1

Ascalon 1. Ασκαλων
Jdt 2:28 Those who lived in Azotus and Ascalon 1

Asenath 1. אָסְנַת
Gen 41:45 in marriage As'enath, the daughter of Poti'phera 1
50 As'enath, the daughter of Poti'phera priest of On 1
46:20 Manas'seh and E'phraim, whom As'enath, 1

Ashan 1. עָשָׁן
Jos 15:42 Libnah, Ether, Ashan 1
19: 7 En-rimmon, Ether, and Ashan 1
1Ch 4:32 villages were Etam, A'in, Rimmon . . and Ashan 1
6:59 Ashan with its pasture lands 1

Asharelah 1. אֲשַׂרְאֵלָה
1Ch 25: 2 sons of Asaph . . Nethani'ah, and Ashare'lah 1

Ashbel 1. אַשְׁבֵּל
Gen 46:21 the sons of Benjamin: Bela, Becher, Ashbel, Gera 1
Num26:38 of Ashbel, the family of the Ash'belites; 1
1Ch 8: 1 Benjamin was the father of . . Ashbel the second 1

Ashbelite 1. אַשְׁבֵּלִי
Num26:38 of Ashbel, the family of the Ash'belites; 1

Ashdod 1. אַשְׁדּוֹד 2. אַשְׁדּוֹדִי 3. אַשְׁדּוֹדִית
Jos 11:22 in Gaza, in Gath, and in Ashdod, did some remain. 1
13: 3 there are five . . those of Gaza, Ashdod, Ash'kelon 2
15:46 from Ekron . . all that were by the side of Ashdod 1
47 Ashdod, its towns and its villages; 1
1Sm 5: 1 they carried it from Ebene'zer to Ashdod; 1
5 do not tread on the threshold of Dagon in Ashdod 1
6 and afflicted . . both Ashdod and its territory. 1
7 the men of Ashdod saw how things were, they said 1
6:17 the golden tumors . . one for Ashdod, one for Gaza 1
2Ch 26: 6 broke down the wall of Gath . . the wall of Ashdod; 1
Neh 13:23 married women of Ashdod, Ammon, and Moab; 2
24 half . . spoke the language of Ashdod 3
Isa 20: 1 came to Ashdod and fought against it and took it,- 1
Jer 25:20 Gaza, Ekron, and the remnant of Ashdod); 1
Ams 1: 8 I will cut off the inhabitants from Ashdod 1
Zep 2: 4 Ashdod's people shall be driven out at noon 1
Zec 9: 6 a mongrel people shall dwell in Ashdod; 1

people of Ashdod 1. אַשְׁדּוֹדִי
1Sm 5: 3 when the people of Ashdod rose early the next day 1
6 the LORD was heavy upon the people of Ashdod 1

territory of Ashdod 1. אַשְׁדּוֹד
2Ch 26: 6 built cities in the territory of Ashdod 1

Ashdodite 1. אַשְׁדּוֹדִי
Neh 4: 7 when . . the Ammonites and the Ash'dodites heard 1

Asher 1. אָשֵׁר 2. בְּנֵי אָשֵׁר 3. Ἀσήρ
Gen 30:13 will call me happy"; so she called his name Asher. 1
35:26 The sons of Zilpah, Leah's maid: Gad and Asher. 1
46:17 The sons of Asher: Imnah, Ishvah, Ishvi, Beri'ah 1
49:20 Asher's food shall be rich 1
Exd 1: 4 Dan and Naph'tali, Gad and Asher. 1
Num 1:13 from Asher, Pa'giel the son of Ochran; 1
40 Of the people of Asher, their generations 1
41 the number of the tribe of Asher was 41,500 1
2:27 next . . shall be the tribe of Asher 1
27 leader of the people of Asher being Pa'giel 1
7:72 Pa'giel the . . leader of the men of Asher 1
10:26 over the host of the tribe of the men of Asher 1
13:13 from the tribe of Asher, Sethur the son of Michael; 1
26:44 The sons of Asher according to their families 1
46 the name of the daughter of Asher was Serah. 1
47 These are the families of the sons of Asher 1
34:27 of the tribe of the sons of Asher a leader 1
Deu 27:13 stand upon Mount Ebal . . Reuben, Gad, Asher 1
33:24 of Asher he said, "Blessed above sons be Asher; 1
24 of Asher he said, "Blessed above sons be Asher; 1
Jos 17: 7 Manas'seh reached from Asher to Mich-me'thath 1
10 on the north Asher is reached, and on the east 1
11 in Is'sachar and in Asher Manas'seh had Beth-she'an 1
19:24 The fifth lot came out for the tribe of Asher 2
31 This is the inheritance of the tribe of Asher 2
34 touching . . Asher on the west, and Judah 1
21: 6 the tribe of Asher, from the tribe of Naph'tali 1
30 and out of the tribe of Asher, Mishal with its 1
Jdg 1:31 Asher did not drive out the inhabitants of Acco 1
5:17 Asher sat still at the coast of the sea 1
6:35 sent messengers to Asher, Zeb'ulun, and Naph'tali; 1
7:23 Naph'tali and from Asher and from all Manas'seh 1
1Kg 4:16 Ba'ana the son of Hushai, in Asher and Bealoth; 1
1Ch 2: 2 Dan, Joseph, Benjamin, Naph'tali, Gad, and Asher. 1
6:62 out of the tribes of Is'sachar, Asher, Naph'tali 1
74 out of the tribe of Asher: Mashal . . Abdon 1
7:30 The sons of Asher: Imnah, Ishvah, Ishvi, Beri'ah 1
40 men of Asher, heads of fathers' houses, approved 1
12:36 Of Asher 40,000 seasoned troops ready for battle. 1
2Ch 30:11 a few men of Asher, of Manas'seh, and of Zeb'ulun 1
Ezk 48: 2 from the east side to the west, Asher, one portion. 1
3 Adjoining the territory of Asher, from the east 1
34 of Gad, the gate of Asher, and the gate of Naph'tali. 1
Lke 2:36 the tribe of Asher 3
Rev 7: 6 12,000 of the tribe of Asher 3
Tob 1: 2 in Galilee above Asher. 3

Asherah 1. אֲשֵׁרָה
Deu 16:21 not plant any tree as an Ashe'rah beside the altar 1
Jdg 6:25 pull down the altar . . and cut down the Ashe'rah 1
26 the wood of the Ashe'rah which you shall cut down. 1
28 and the Ashe'rah beside it was cut down 1
30 altar of Ba'al and cut down the Ashe'rah beside it. 1
1Kg 15:13 she had an abominable image made for Ashe'rah; 1
16:33 Ahab made an Ashe'rah. 1
18:19 gather . . and the 400 prophets of Ashe'rah 1
2Kg 13: 6 and the Ashe'rah also remained in Sama'ria.) 1
17:16 they made an Ashe'rah, and worshiped all the host 1
18: 4 and broke the pillars, and cut down the Ashe'rah. 1
21: 3 he erected altars for Ba'al, and made an Ashe'rah 1
7 the graven image of Ashe'rah . . he set in the house 1
23: 4 the vessels made for Ba'al, for Ashe'rah, and for all 1
6 he brought out the Ashe'rah from the house 1
7 where the women wove hangings for the Ashe'rah. 1
15 crushing them . . also he burned the Ashe'rah. 1
2Ch 15:16 she had made an abominable image for Ashe'rah. 1
19: 3 for you destroyed the Ashe'rahs out of the land 1
33: 3 erected altars to the Ba'als, and made Ashe'rahs 1

Asherim 1. אֲשֵׁרָה
Exd 34:13 You shall . . cut down their Ashe'rim 1
Deu 7: 5 you shall . . hew down their Ashe'rim 1
12: 3 and burn their Ashe'rim with fire; 1
1Kg 14:15 they have made their Ashe'rim, provoking the LORD 1
23 built . . high places, and pillars, and Ashe'rim 1
2Kg 17:10 they set up for themselves pillars and Ashe'rim 1
23:14 broke . . the pillars, and cut down the Ashe'rim 1
2Ch 14: 3 hewed down the Ashe'rim 1
17: 6 high places and the Ashe'rim out of Judah. 1
24:18 served the Ashe'rim and the idols. 1
31: 1 all Israel . . hewed down the Ashe'rim 1
33:19 sites on which he . . set up the Ashe'rim 1
34: 3 purge Judah and Jerusalem of the . . Ashe'rim 1
4 he broke in pieces the Ashe'rim and the graven 1
7 beat the Ashe'rim and the images into powder 1
Isa 17: 8 their own fingers have made, either the Ashe'rim 1
27: 9 no Ashe'rim or incense altars will remain 1
Jer 17: 2 remember their altars and their Ashe'rim 1
Mic 5:14 I will root out your Ashe'rim from among you 1

Asherite 1. אָשֵׁרִי
Jdg 1:32 the Asherites dwelt among the Canaanites 1

Asheroth 1. אֲשֵׁרָה
Jdg 3: 7 God, and serving the Ba'als and the Ashe'roth. 1

Ashhur 1. אַשְׁחוּר
1Ch 2:24 she bore him Ashhur, the father of Teko'a. 1
4: 5 Ashhur, the father of Teko'a, had two wives 1

Ashima 1. אֲשִׁימָא
2Kg 17:30 Cuth made Nergal, the men of Hamath made Ashi'ma 1

Ashimah 1. אַשְׁמָה
Ams 8:14 Those who swear by Ash'imah of Sama'ria, and say 1

Ashkelon 1. אַשְׁקְלוֹן 2. אֶשְׁקְלוֹנִי
Jos 13: 3 there are five . . those of Gaza, Ashdod, Ash'kelon 2
Jdg 1:18 its territory, and Ash'kelon with its territory 1
14:19 he went down to Ash'kelon and killed 30 men 1
1Sm 6:17 Ashdod, one for Gaza, one for Ash'kelon, one for Gath 1
2Sm 1:20 in Gath, publish it not in the streets of Ash'kelon; 1
Jer 25:20 the Philistines (Ash'kelon, Gaza, Ekron 1
47: 5 Ash'kelon has perished. 1
7 Against Ash'kelon and against the seashore 1
Ams 1: 8 and him that holds the scepter from Ash'kelon; 1
Zep 2: 4 and Ash'kelon shall become a desolation; 1
7 and in the houses of Ash'kelon they shall lie down 1
Zec 9: 5 Ash'kelon shall see it, and be afraid; 1
5 perish from Gaza; Ash'kelon shall be uninhabited; 1

Ashkenaz 1. אַשְׁכְּנַז
Gen 10: 3 The sons of Gomer: Ash'kenaz, Riphath 1
1Ch 1: 6 sons of Gomer: Ash'kenaz, Diphath, and To-gar'mah. 1
Jer 51:27 the kingdoms, Ar'arat, Minni, and Ash'kenaz; 1

Ashnah 1. אַשְׁנָה
Jos 15:33 And in the lowland, Eshta'ol, Zorah, Ashnah 1
43 Iphtah, Ashnah, Nezib 1

Ashtaroth 1. עַשְׁתָּרוֹת 2. עַשְׁתֹּרֶת
Deu 1: 4 king of Bashan, who lived in Ash'taroth 1
Jos 9:10 and Og king of Bashan, who dwelt in Ash'taroth. 1
12: 4 and Og . . who dwelt in Ash'taroth and at Ed're-i 1
13:12 of Og . . who reigned in Ash'taroth and in Ed're-i 1
31 and half Gilead, and Ash'taroth, and Ed're-i 1
Jdg 2:13 served the Ba'als and the Ash'taroth. 2
10: 6 evil . . and served the Ba'als and the Ash'taroth 2
1Sm 7: 3 put away the foreign gods and the Ash'taroth 2
4 So Israel put away the Ba'als and the Ash'taroth 2
12:10 and have served the Ba'als and the Ash'taroth; 2
31:10 They put his armor in the temple of Ash'taroth; 2
1Ch 6:71 were given . . Ash'taroth with its pasture lands; 1

Ashterathite 1. עַשְׁתְּרָתִי
1Ch 11:44 Uzzi'a the Ash'terathite, Shama and Je-i'el 1

Ashteroth-karnaim 1. עַשְׁתְּרֹת קַרְנַיִם
Gen 14: 5 subdued the Reph'aim in Ash'teroth-karna'im 1

Ashtoreth 1. עַשְׁתֹּרֶת
1Kg 11: 5 Solomon went after Ash'toreth the goddess 1
33 worshiped Ash'toreth the goddess 1
2Kg 23:13 which Solomon . . had built for Ash'toreth 1

Ashurite 1. אַשּׁוּרִי
2Sm 2: 9 he made him king over Gilead and the Ash'urites 1

Ashvath 1. עַשְׁוָת
1Ch 7:33 The sons of Japhlet: Pasach, Bimhal, and Ashvath. 1

Asia 1. Ἀσία 2. Asia
Act 2: 9 Judea and Cappado'cia, Pontus and Asia 1
6: 9 of those from Cili'cia and Asia 1
16: 6 forbidden . . to speak the word in Asia. 1
19:10 the residents of Asia heard the word of the Lord 1
22 he himself stayed in Asia for a while. 1
26 almost throughout all Asia 1
27 she whom all Asia and the world worship. 1
20:16 so that he might not have to spend time in Asia 1
18 from the first day that I set foot in Asia 1
21:27 the Jews from Asia . . stirred up all the crowd 1
24:18 some Jews from Asia- 1
27: 2 about to sail to the ports along the coast of Asia 1
Rom16: 5 Epae'netus, who was the first convert in Asia 1
1Co 16:19 The churches of Asia send greetings 1
2Co 1: 8 the affliction we experienced in Asia 1
2Ti 1:15 all who are in Asia turned away from me 1
1Pe 1: 1 the Dispersion in . . Asia, and Bithyn'ia 1
Rev 1: 4 John to the seven churches that are in Asia 1
2Es 15:46 you, Asia, who share in the glamour of Babylon 2
16: 1 Woe to you, Babylon and Asia! 2
1Mc 8: 6 They also defeated Antiochus the Great, king of Asia 1
11:13 entered Antioch and put on the crown of Asia. 1
13 the crown of Egypt and that of Asia. 1
12:39 Then Trypho attempted to become king in Asia 1
13:32 putting on the crown of Asia 1
2Mc 3: 3 even Seleucus, the king of Asia 1
10:24 collected the cavalry from Asia 1
3Mc 3:14 When our expedition took place in Asia 1
4Mc 3:20 even Seleucus Nicanor, king of Asia 1

Asian 1. Ἀσιανός
Act 20: 4 and the Asians, Tych'icus and Troph'imus. 1

Asiarch 1. Ἀσιάρχης
Act 19:31 some of the A'si-archs also, who were friends of his 1

Asibias 1. Ασιβιας
1Es 9:26 Mijamin, and Eleazar, and Asibias, and Benaiah 1

Asiel 1. עֲשִׂיאֵל 2. Ἀσιηλ 3. Asihel
1Ch 4:35 the son of Joshibi'ah, son of Serai'ah, son of As'i-el 1
2Es 14:24 with you Sarea, Dabria, Selemia, Ethanus, and Asiel- 3
Tob 1: 1 of the descendants of Asiel 2

Askalon 1. Ασκαλων
1Mc 10:86 encamped against Askalon 1
11:60 When he came to Askalon 1
12:33 and marched through the country as far as Askalon 1

Asmodeus 1. Ασμοδαιος
Tob 3: 8 the evil demon Asmodeus had slain each of them 1
17 to bind Asmodeus the evil demon 1

Asnah 1. אַסְנָה 2. Ασανα
Ezr 2:50 sons of Asnah, the sons of Me-u'nim 1
1Es 5:31 the sons of Besai, the sons of Asnah 2

Aspatha 1. אַסְפָּתָא
Est 9: 7 also slew Par-shan-da'tha and Dalphon and Aspa'tha 1

Asphar 1. Ασφαρ
1Mc 9:33 camped by the water of the pool of Asphar. 1

Asriel 1. אַשְׂרִיאֵל 2. בְּנֵי אַשְׂרִיאֵל
Num26:31 of As'riel, the family of the As'rielites; 1
Jos 17: 2 their families Abi-e'zer, Helek, As'ri-el 2
1Ch 7:14 As'ri-el, whom his Aramean concubine bore; 1

Asrielite 1. אַשְׂרְאֵלִי
Num26:31 of As'riel, the family of the As'rielites; 1

Asshur 1. אַשּׁוּר
Gen 10:22 The sons of Shem: Elam, Asshur, Arpach'shad 1
Num24:22 How long shall Asshur take you away captive? 1
24 ships . . shall afflict Asshur and Eber; 1
1Ch 1:17 of Shem: Elam, Asshur, Arpach'shad, Lud, Aram, Uz 1
Ezk 27:23 Canneh, Eden, Asshur, and Chilmad traded with you. 1

Asshurim 1. אַשּׁוּרִם
Gen 25: 3 The sons of Dedan were Asshu'rim, Letu'shim 1

Assir 1. אַסִּיר
Exd 6:24 The sons of Korah: Assir, Elka'nah, and Abi'asaph; 1
1Ch 6:22 of Kohath: Aminn'adab . . Korah . . Assir his son 1
23 Elka'nah his son, Ebi'asaph his son, Assir his son 1
37 son of Assir, son of Ebi'asaph, son of Korah 1

Assos 1. *Ασσος
Act 20:13 But going ahead to the ship, we set sail for Assos 1
14 when he met us at Assos, we took him on board 1

Assyria 1. אַשּׁוּר 2. Ασσυριος 3. Assur
Gen 2:14 river is Tigris, which flows east of Assyria. 1
10:11 From that land he went into Assyria 1
25:18 is opposite Egypt in the direction of Assyria; 1
2Kg 15:19 Pul the king of Assyria came against the land; 1
20 exacted . . to give to the king of Assyria. 1
20 the king of Assyria turned back, and did not stay 1
29 Tig'lath-pile'ser king of Assyria came 1
29 and he carried the people captive to Assyria. 1
16: 7 Ahaz sent . . to Tig'lath-pile'ser king of Assyria 1
8 and sent a present to the king of Assyria. 1
9 And the king of Assyria hearkened to him; 1
9 the king of Assyria marched up against Damascus 1
10 to meet Tig'lath-pile'ser king of Assyria 1
18 he removed . . because of the king of Assyria. 1
17: 3 Against him came up Shalmane'ser king of Assyria; 1
4 the king of Assyria found treachery in Hoshe'a; 1
4 and offered no tribute to the king of Assyria 1
4 the king of Assyria shut him up, and bound him 1
5 Then the king of Assyria invaded all the land 1
6 the king of Assyria captured Sama'ria 1
6 and he carried the Israelites away to Assyria 1
23 Israel was exiled from their own land to Assyria 1
24 the king of Assyria brought people from Babylon 1
26 So the king of Assyria was told 1
27 Then the king of Assyria commanded, "Send 1
18: 7 He rebelled against the king of Assyria 1
9 Shalmane'ser king of Assyria came up against 1
11 The king of Assyria carried the Israelites away 1
11 king . . carried the Israelites away to Assyria 1
13 Sennach'erib king of Assyria came up against all 1
14 Hezeki'ah . . sent to the king of Assyria 1
14 And the king of Assyria required of Hezeki'ah 1
16 and gave it to the king of Assyria. 1
17 the king of Assyria sent the Tartan, the Rab'saris 1
19 Thus says the great king, the king of Assyria 1
23 make a wager with my master the king of Assyria 1
28 the word of the great king, the king of Assyria! 1
30 not be given into the hand of the king of Assyria.' 1
31 thus says the king of Assyria: 'Make your peace 1
33 his land out of the hand of the king of Assyria? 1
19: 4 his master the king of Assyria has sent to mock 1
6 the servants of the king of Assyria have reviled 1
8 found the king of Assyria fighting against 1
10 not be given into the hand of the king of Assyria. 1
11 what the kings of Assyria have done to all lands 1
17 the kings of Assyria have laid waste the nations 1
20 prayer to me about Sennach'erib king of Assyria 1
32 says the LORD concerning the king of Assyria 1
36 Sennach'erib king of Assyria departed, and went 1
20: 6 deliver . . out of the hand of the king of Assyria 1
23:29 Pharaoh Neco . . went up to the king of Assyria 1
1Ch 5: 6 Til'gath-pilne'ser king of Assyria 1
26 stirred up the spirit of Pul king of Assyria 1
26 the spirit of Til'gath-pilne'ser king of Assyria 1
2Ch 28:16 King Ahaz sent to the king of Assyria for help. 1
20 Til'gath-pilne'ser king of Assyria came against 1
21 Ahaz . . gave tribute to the king of Assyria; 1
30: 6 escaped from the hand of the kings of Assyria. 1
32: 1 Sennach'erib king of Assyria came and invaded 1
4 Why should the kings of Assyria come and find 1
7 Do not be . . dismayed before the king of Assyria 1
9 After this Sennach'erib king of Assyria 1
10 Thus says Sennach'erib king of Assyria 1
11 deliver us from the hand of the king of Assyria"? 1
21 in the camp of the king of Assyria. 1
22 from the hand of Sennach'erib king of Assyria 1
33:11 commanders of the army of the king of Assyria 1
Ezr 4: 2 since the days of E'sar-had'don king of Assyria 1
6:22 LORD . . turned the heart of the king of Assyria 1
Neh 9:32 since the time of the kings of Assyria until 1
Ps 83: 8 Assyria also has joined them; 1
Isa 7:17 departed from Judah–the king of Assyria. 1
18 for the bee which is in the land of Assyria. 1
20 shave with a razor . . –with the king of Assyria 1
8: 4 carried away before the king of Assyria. 1
7 the king of Assyria and all his glory; 1
10: 5 Ah, Assyria, the rod of my anger, the staff of my fury! 1
12 the arrogant boasting of the king of Assyria 1
11:11 remnant . . of his people, from Assyria, from Egypt 1
16 a highway from Assyria for the remnant 1
19:23 there will be a highway from Egypt to Assyria 1
23 Egypt, and the Egyptian into Assyria 1
24 Israel will be the third with Egypt and Assyria 1
25 Blessed be . . and Assyria the work of my hands 1
20: 1 commander . . sent by Sargon the king of Assyria 1
4 so shall . . Assyria lead away the Egyptians 1
6 for help to be delivered from the king of Assyria! 1
23:13 Chalde'ans! This is the people; it was not Assyria. 1
27:13 those who were lost in the land of Assyria 1
36: 1 Sennach'erib king of Assyria came up against all 1
2 the king of Assyria sent the Rab'shakeh 1
4 Thus says the great king, the king of Assyria 1
8 make a wager with my master the king of Assyria 1
13 the words of the great king, the king of Assyria! 1
15 not be given into the hand of the king of Assyria. 1
16 for thus says the king of Assyria 1
18 his land out of the hand of the king of Assyria? 1
37: 4 Rab'shakeh, whom his master the king of Assyria 1
6 servants of the king of Assyria have reviled me. 1
8 Rab'shakeh . . found the king of Assyria fighting 1
10 not be given into the hand of the king of Assyria. 1
11 what the kings of Assyria have done to all lands 1
18 kings of Assyria have laid waste all the nations 1
21 concerning Sennach'erib king of Assyria 1
33 says the LORD concerning the king of Assyria 1
37 Then Sennach'erib king of Assyria departed 1
38: 6 this city out of the hand of the king of Assyria 1
Jer 2:18 Or what do you gain by going to Assyria 1
36 by Egypt as you were put to shame by Assyria. 1
50:17 First the king of Assyria devoured him 1
18 as I punished the king of Assyria. 1
Lam 5: 6 We have given the hand to Egypt, and to Assyria 1
Ezk 23: 7 upon them, the choicest men of Assyria all of them; 1
32:22 Assyria is there, and all her company 1
Hos 5:13 then E'phraim went to Assyria 1
7:11 calling to Egypt, going to Assyria. 1
8: 9 For they have gone up to Assyria 1
9: 3 and they shall eat unclean food in Assyria. 1
6 For behold, they are going to Assyria; •
10: 6 Yea, the thing itself shall be carried to Assyria 1
11: 5 and Assyria shall be their king 1
11 trembling . . like doves from the land of Assyria; 1
12: 1 they make a bargain with Assyria 1
14: 3 Assyria shall not save us 1
Ams 3: 9 Proclaim to the strongholds in Assyria 2
Mic 5: 6 shall rule the land of Assyria with the sword 1
7:12 they will come to you, from Assyria to Egypt 1
Nah 3:18 Your shepherds are asleep, O king of Assyria; 1
Zep 2:13 his hand against the north, and destroy Assyria; 1
Zec 10:10 and gather them from Assyria; 1
11 The pride of Assyria shall be laid low 1
2Es 2: 8 Woe to you, Assyria, who conceal the unrighteous 3
4Mc 13: 9 let us imitate the three youths in Assyria 2

Assyrian 1. אַשּׁוּר 2. בֶּן אַשּׁוּר 3. Ασσουρ 4. Ασσυριος 5. υἱὸς Ασσουρ 6. Assyrius
2Kg 19:35 slew 185,000 in the camp of the Assyrians; 1
Isa 10:24 be not afraid of the Assyrians when they smite 1
14:25 that I will break the Assyrian in my land 1
19:23 the Assyrian will come into Egypt 1
23 the Egyptians will worship with the Assyrians. 1
30:31 The Assyrians will be terror-stricken 1
31: 8 the Assyrian shall fall by a sword, not of man; 1
37:36 slew . . in the camp of the Assyrians; 1
52: 4 and the Assyrian oppressed them for nothing. 1
Ezk 16:28 You played the harlot also with the Assyrians 2
23: 5 and she doted on her lovers the Assyrians 1
9 the hands of the Assyrians, upon whom she doted. 2
12 She doted upon the Assyrians 2
23 and Sho'a and Ko'a, and all the Assyrians with them 2
Mic 5: 5 when the Assyrian comes into our land 1
6 and they shall deliver us from the Assyrian 1
1Es 5:69 the days of Esarhaddon king of the Assyrians 4
7:15 had changed the will of the king of the Assyrians 4
2Es 13:40 Shalmaneser the king of the Assyrians 6
15:30 a portion of the land of the Assyrians 6
33 from the land of the Assyrians an enemy in ambush 6
Tob 1: 2 in the days of Shalmaneser, king of the Assyrians 4
3 who went with me into the land of the Assyrians 4
Jdt 1: 1 who ruled over the Assyrians 4
7 Then Nebuchadnezzar king of the Assyrians sent 4
11 Nebuchadnezzar king of the Assyrians 4
2: 1 Nebuchadnezzar king of the Assyrians 4
4 Nebuchadnezzar king of the Assyrians 4
14 generals, and officers of the Assyrian army 3
4: 1 Nebuchadnezzar the king of the Assyrians 4
5: 1 Holofernes, the general of the Assyrian army 3
6: 1 Holofernes, the commander of the Assyrian army 3
17 had said in the presence of the Assyrian leaders 5
7:17 together with 5,000 Assyrians 5
18 The rest of the Assyrian army 4
20 The whole Assyrian army, their infantry 3
24 not making peace with the Assyrians. 5
8: 9 to surrender the city to the Assyrians 4
9: 7 the Assyrians are increased in their might 4
10:11 an Assyrian patrol met her 4
12:13 one of the daughters of the Assyrians 5
13:15 Holofernes, the commander of the Assyrian army 3
14: 2 going down . . against the Assyrian outpost 3
3 rouse the officers of the Assyrian army 3
12 when the Assyrians saw them 5
19 When the leaders of the Assyrian army heard this 3
15: 6 The rest . . fell upon the Assyrian camp 3
16: 4 The Assyrian came down from the mountains 3
Sir 48:21 The Lord smote the camp of the Assyrians 4
1Mc 7:41 thy angel . . struck down 185,000 of the Assyrians. •
3Mc 6: 5 oppressive king of the Assyrians 4

Astyages 1. Αστυαγης
Bel 1: 1 When King Astyages was laid with his fathers 1

Asur 1. Ασουρ
1Es 5:31 the sons of Asur, the sons of Pharakim 1

Asyncritus 1. ᾿Ασύγκριτος
Rom16:14 Greet Asyn'critus, Phlegon, Hermes, Pat'robas 1

Atad 1. אָטָד
Gen 50:10 When they came to the threshing floor of Atad 1
11 saw the mourning on the threshing floor of Atad 1

Atarah 1. עֲטָרָה
1Ch 2:26 wife . . At'arah; she was the mother of Onam. 1

Atargatis 1. Ατεργατιον
2Mc 12:26 Judas marched against . . the temple of Atargatis 1

Ataroth 1. עֲטָרוֹת
Num32: 3 At'aroth, Dibon, Jazer, Nimrah, Heshbon, Elea'leh 1
34 the sons of Gad built Dibon, At'aroth, Aro'er 1
Jos 16: 2 from Bethel to Luz, it passes along to At'aroth 1
7 goes down from Jan-o'ah to At'aroth and to Na'arah 1

Ataroth-addar 1. עַטְרוֹת אַדָּר
Jos 16: 5 the boundary . . was At'aroth-ad'dar as far 1
18:13 then the boundary goes down to At'aroth-ad'dar 1

Ater 1. אָטֵר 2. Αταρ 3. Ατηρ
Ezr 2:16 sons of Ater, namely of Hezeki'ah, 98. 1
42 sons of the gatekeepers: the . . sons of Ater 1
Neh 7:21 sons of Ater, namely of Hezeki'ah, 98. 1
45 gatekeepers: the sons of Shallum, the sons of Ater 1
10:17 Ater, Hezeki'ah, Azzur 1
1Es 5:15 The sons of Ater, namely of Hezekiah, 92. 3
28 the sons of Ater, the sons of Talmon 2

Athach 1. עֲתָךְ
1Sm 30:30 for those . . in Hormah, in Borash'an, in A'thach 1

Athaiah 1. עֲתָיָה
Neh 11: 4 Of the sons of Judah: Athai'ah the son of Uzzi'ah 1

Athaliah 1. עֲתַלְיָהוּ
2Kg 8:26 His mother's name was Athali'ah; 1
11: 1 Now when Athali'ah . . saw that her son was dead 1
2 she hid him from Athali'ah, so that he was not slain; 1
3 while Athali'ah reigned over the land. 1
13 When Athali'ah heard the noise . . she went 1
14 And Athali'ah rent her clothes, and cried, "Treason! 1
20 the city was quiet after Athali'ah had been slain 1
1Ch 8:26 Sham'sherai, Shehari'ah, Athali'ah 1
2Ch 22: 2 His mother's name was Athali'ah 1
10 Now when Athali'ah . . saw that her son was dead 1
11 Jeho-shab'e-ath . . hid him from Athali'ah 1
12 while Athali'ah reigned over the land. 1
23:12 When Athali'ah heard the noise of the people 1
13 Athali'ah rent her clothes, and cried, "Treason! 1
21 after Athali'ah had been slain with the sword. 1
24: 7 sons of Athali'ah . . had broken 1
Ezr 8: 7 Of the sons of Elam, Jeshai'ah the son of Athali'ah 1

Atharim 1. אֲתָרִים
Num21: 1 that Israel was coming by the way of Atharim 1

Athenian 1. ᾿Αθηναῖος
Act 17:21 Now all the Athenians and the foreigners 1
2Mc 6: 1 the king sent an Athenian senator 1

Athenobius 1. Αθηνοβιος
1Mc 15:28 He sent to him Athenobius, one of his friends 1
32 So Athenobius the friend of the king came 1
35 Athenobius did not answer him a word •

Athens 1. ᾿Αθῆναι 2. ᾿Αθηναῖος
Act 17:15 who conducted Paul brought him as far as Athens; 1
16 Now while Paul was waiting for them at Athens 1
22 Paul . . said: "Men of Athens 2
18: 1 After this he left Athens and went to Corinth. 1
1Th 3: 1 we were willing to be left behind at Athens alone 1
2Mc 9:15 make, all of them, equal to citizens of Athens; 2

Athlai 1. עַתְלָי
Ezr 10:28 of Be'bai were . . Hanani'ah, Zab'bai, and Ath'lai. 1

Atroth-beth-joab 1. עַטְרוֹת בֵּית יוֹאָב
1Ch 2:54 sons of Salma . . At'roth-beth-jo'ab 1

Atroth-shophan 1. עַטְרֹת שׁוֹפָן
Num32:35 At'roth-sho'phan, Jazer, Jog'behah 1

Attai 1. עַתַּי
1Ch 2:35 gave his daughter . . and she bore him Attai. 1
36 Attai . . father of Nathan and Nathan of Zabad. 1
12:11 Attai sixth, Eli'el seventh 1
2Ch 11:20 Ma'acah . . bore him Abi'jah, Attai, Ziza 1

Attalia 1. ᾿Αττάλεια
Act 14:25 they went down to Attali'a; 1

Attalus 1. ῎Ατταλος
1Mc 15:22 Attalus and Ariarathes and Arsaces 1

Attharates 1. Ατταρατης
1Es 9:49 Then Attharates said to Ezra the chief priest 1

Attharias 1. Ατθαριας
1Es 5:40 Nehemiah and Attharias told them . . 1

Augustan 1. Σεβαστός
Act 27: 1 a centurion of the Augustan Cohort, named Julius. 1

Augustus 1. Αὔγουστος
Lke 2: 1 a decree went out from Caesar Augustus 1

Auranus 1. Αυρανος
2Mc 4:40 under the leadership of a certain Auranus 1

Avaran 1. Αυαραν
1Mc 2: 5 Eleazar called Avaran 1
6:43 Eleazar, called Avaran, saw 1

Aven 1. אָוֶן
Hos 10: 8 The high places of Aven, the sin of Israel 1
Ams 1: 5 cut off the inhabitants from the Valley of Aven 1

Avith 1. עֲוִית
Gen 36:35 in his stead, the name of his city being Avith. 1
1Ch 1:46 and the name of his city was Avith. 1

Avva 1. עַוָּה
2Kg 17:24 brought people from Babylon, Cuthah, Avva, Hamath 1

Avvim 1. עַוִּים
Deu 2:23 for the Avvim, who lived in villages as far as Gaza 1
Jos 13: 3 all the regions of . . and those of the Avvim 1
18:23 Avvim, Parah, Ophrah 1

Avvite 1. עַוִּי
2Kg 17:31 and the Av'vites made Nibhaz and Tartak; 1

Ayyah 1. עַיָּה
1Ch 7:28 Gezer . . Shechem . . , and Ayyah and its towns; 1

Azael 1. Αζαηλος
1Es 9:34 Shashai, Azarel, Azael, Shemaiah, Amariah, Joseph. 1

Azaliah 1. אֲצַלְיָהוּ
2Kg 22: 3 king sent Shaphan the son of Azali'ah, son 1
2Ch 34: 8 sent Shaphan the son of Azali'ah, and Ma-asei'ah 1

Azaniah 1. אֲזַנְיָהוּ
Neh 10: 9 Levites: Jeshua the son of Azani'ah, Bin'nui 1

Azarel 1. עֲזַרְאֵל 2. Εζριλ
1Ch 12: 6 Az'arel, Jo-e'zer, and Jasho'be-am, the Ko'rahites; 1
25:18 eleventh to Az'arel, his sons and his brethren 1
27:22 for Dan, Az'arel the son of Jero'ham. 1
Ezr 10:41 Az'arel, Shelemi'ah, Shemari'ah 1
Neh 11:13 Amash'sai, the son of Az'arel, son of Ah'zai 1
12:36 kinsmen, Shemai'ah, Az'arel, Mil'alai, Gil'alai, Ma'ai 1
1Es 9:34 Of the sons of Ezora: Shashai, Azarel, Azael 2

Azariah 1. עֲזַרְיָהוּ 2. עֲזַרְיָה (A) 3. ᾿Αζαρίας 4. Azarei 5. Aziei
1Kg 4: 2 Azari'ah the son of Zadok was the priest; 1
5 Azari'ah the son of Nathan was over the officers; 1
2Kg 14:21 the people . . took Azari'ah, who was sixteen 1
15: 1 Azari'ah the son of Amazi'ah . . began to reign. 1
6 the rest of the acts of Azari'ah, and all that he did 1
7 And Azari'ah slept with his fathers 1
8 In the 38th year of Azari'ah king of Judah 1
17 In the 39th year of Azari'ah the king of Judah 1
23 In the 50th year of Azari'ah king of Judah 1
27 In the 52nd year of Azari'ah king of Judah 1
1Ch 2: 8 Ethan's son was Azari'ah. 1
38 Obed was the father of Jehu, and Jehu of Azari'ah. 1
39 Azari'ah was the father of Helez 1
3:12 Amazi'ah his son, Azari'ah his son, Jotham his son 1
6: 9 Ahim'a-az of Azari'ah, Azari'ah of Joha'nan 1
9 Ahim'a-az of Azari'ah, Azari'ah of Joha'nan 1
10 Joha'nan of Azari'ah (it was he who served as priest 1
11 Azari'ah . . father of Amari'ah, Amari'ah of Ahi'tub 1
13 Shallum of Hilki'ah, Hilki'ah of Azari'ah 1
14 Azari'ah of Serai'ah, Serai'ah of Jehoz'adak; 1
36 son of Jo'el, son of Azari'ah, son of Zephani'ah 1
9:11 Azari'ah the son of Hilki'ah, son of Meshul'lam 1
2Ch 15: 1 Spirit of God came upon Azari'ah the son of Oded 1
8 the prophecy of Azari'ah the son of Oded •
21: 2 sons of Jehosh'aphat: Azari'ah, Jehi'el, Zechari'ah 1
2 sons of Jehosh'aphat . . Azari'ah, Michael 1
23: 1 commanders . . Azari'ah the son of Jero'ham 1
1 commanders . . Azari'ah the son of Obed, Ma-asei'ah 1
26:17 Azari'ah the priest went in after him 1
20 Azari'ah the chief priest, and all the priests 1
28:12 chiefs . . Azari'ah the son of Joha'nan, Berechi'ah 1
29:12 Levites arose . . Jo'el the son of Azari'ah 1
12 Levites arose . . Azari'ah the son of Jehal'lelel; 1
31:10 Azari'ah the chief priest . . answered him 1
13 by the appointment of Hezeki'ah . . and Azari'ah 1
Ezr 7: 1 son of Serai'ah, son of Azari'ah, son of Hilki'ah 1
3 son of Amari'ah, son of Azari'ah, son of Merai'oth 1
Neh 3:23 Azari'ah the son of Ma-asei'ah, son of Anani'ah 1
24 section, from the house of Azari'ah to the Angle 1
7: 7 came with . . Azari'ah, Raami'ah, Naham'ani, 1
8: 7 Also . . Keli'ta, Azari'ah, Jo'zabad, Hanan 1
10: 2 Serai'ah, Azari'ah, Jeremiah 1
12:33 Azari'ah, Ezra, Meshul'lam 1
Jer 42: 1 Azari'ah the son of Hoshai'ah, and all the people 3
43: 2 Azari'ah the son of Hoshai'ah 1
Dan 1: 6 Daniel, Hanani'ah, Mish'a-el, and Azari'ah 1
7 Azari'ah he called Abed'nego. 1
11 over Daniel, Hanani'ah, Mish'a-el, and Azari'ah; 1
19 like Daniel, Hanani'ah, Mish'a-el, and Azari'ah; 1
2:17 matter known to Hanani'ah, Mish'a-el, and Azari'ah 2
1Es 8: 1 the son of Seraiah, son of Azariah, son of Hilkiah 3
9:21 Maaseiah and Shemaiah and Jehiel and Azariah. 3
43 Azariah, Uriah, Hezekiah 3
48 Maaseiah and Kelita, Azariah and Jozabad 3
2Es 1: 1 the son of Seraiah, son of Azariah, son of Hilkiah 4
2 son of Eli, son of Amariah, son of Azariah 5
Aza 1: 2 Then Azariah stood and offered this prayer 3
26 came down into the furnace to be with Azariah 3
66 Bless the Lord, Hananiah, Azariah, and Mishael 3
1Mc 2:59 Hannaniah, Azariah, and Mishael believed 3
5:18 Azariah, a leader of the people 3
56 Azariah, the commanders of the forces 3
60 Then Joseph and Azariah were routed 3
4Mc 16:21 Hananiah, Azariah, and Mishael 3
18:12 he taught you about Hananiah, Azariah, and Mishael 3

Azarias 1. ᾿Αζαρίας
Tob 5:12 I am Azarias the son of the great Ananias 1
6: 6 the young man said to the angel, "Brother Azarias 1
13 the young man said to the angel, "Brother Azarias 1
7: 8 Then Tobias said to Raphael, "Brother Azarias 1
9: 2 Brother Azarias, take a servant and two camels 1

Azaru 1. Αζαρου
1Es 5:15 The sons of Azaru, 432 1

Azaz 1. עָזָז
1Ch 5: 8 Bela the son of Azaz, son of Shema, son of Jo'el 1

Azazel 1. עֲזָאזֵל
Lev 16: 8 one lot for the LORD and the other lot for Aza'zel 1
10 the goat on which the lot fell for Aza'zel 1
10 be sent away into the wilderness of Aza'zel 1
26 he who lets the goat go to Aza'zel shall wash 1

Azaziah 1. עֲזַזְיָהוּ
1Ch 15:21 Miknei'ah, O'bed-e'dom, Je-i'el, and Azazi'ah 1
27:20 for the E'phraimites, Hoshe'a the son of Azazi'ah; 1
2Ch 31:13 while Jehi'el, Azazi'ah, Nahath . . were overseers 1

Azbuk 1. עַזְבּוּק
Neh 3:16 After him Nehemi'ah the son of Azbuk, ruler of half 1

Azekah 1. עֲזֵקָה
Jos 10:10 and smote them as far as Aze'kah and Makke'dah. 1
11 LORD threw down great stones . . as far as Aze'kah 1
15:35 Jarmuth, Adullam, Socoh, Aze'kah 1
1Sm 17: 1 and encamped between Socoh and Aze'kah 1
2Ch 11: 9 Adora'im, Lachish, Aze'kan 1
Neh 11:30 Aze'kah and its villages. 1
Jer 34: 7 the cities . . that were left, Lachish and Aze'kah; 1

Azel 1. אָצֵל
1Ch 8:37 Raphah was his son, Ele-a'sah his son, Azel his son. 1
38 Azel had six sons, and these are their names 1
38 All these were the sons of Azel. 1
9:43 Rephai'ah . . Ele-a'sah his son, Azel his son. 1
44 Azel had six sons and these are their names 1
44 these were the sons of Azel. 1

Azetas 1. Αζηταs
1Es 5:15 The sons of Kilan and Azetas, 67. 1

Azgad 1. עַזְגָּד 2. Ασγαδ
Ezr 2:12 sons of Azgad, 1,222. 1
8:12 Of the sons of Azgad, Joha'nan the son of Hak'katan 1
Neh 7:17 sons of Azgad, 2,322. 1
10:15 Bunni, Azgad, Be'bai 1
1Es 5:13 The sons of Bebai, 623 The sons of Azgad, 1,322 2
8:38 Of the sons of Azgad, Johanan the son of Hakkatan 2

Aziel 1. עֲזִיאֵל
1Ch 15:20 Zechari'ah, A'zi-el, Shemi'ramoth, Jehi'el, Unni 1

Aziza 1. עֲזִיזָא
Ezr 10:27 of Zattu . . Jer'emoth, Zabad, and Azi'za. 1

Azmaveth 1. עַזְמָוֶת
2Sm 23:31 Abi-al'bon the Ar'bathite, Az'maveth of Bahu'rim 1
1Ch 8:36 Jeho'addah . . father of Al'emeth, Az'maveth 1
9:42 and Jarah of Al'emeth, Az'maveth, and Zimri; 1
11:33 Az'maveth of Baha'rum, Eli'ahba of Sha-al'bon 1
12: 3 also Je'zi-el and Pelet the sons of Az'maveth; 1
27:25 Over the king's treasuries was Az'maveth the son 1
Ezr 2:24 sons of Az'maveth, 42. 1
Neh 12:29 from the region of Geba and Az'maveth; 1

Azmon 1. עַצְמוֹן
Num34: 4 go on to Ha'zar-ad'dar, and pass along to Azmon; 1
5 boundary . . turn from Azmon to the Brook of Egypt 1
Jos 15: 4 passes along to Azmon, goes out by the Brook 1

Aznoth-tabor 1. אַזְנוֹת תָּבוֹר
Jos 19:34 the boundary turns westward to Az'noth-tabor 1

Azor 1. ᾿Αζώρ
Mat 1:13 and Eli'akim the father of Azor 1
14 Azor the father of Zadok 1

Azotus 1. ῎Αζωτος
Act 8:40 Philip was found at Azo'tus 1
Jdt 2:28 Those who lived in Azotus and Ascalon 1
1Mc 4:15 to the plains of Idumea, and to Azotus and Jamnia; 1
5:68 Judas turned aside to Azotus 1
9:15 he pursued them as far as Mount Azotus. 1
10:77 went to Azotus as though he were going farther 1
78 Jonathan pursued him to Azotus 1
83 They fled to Azotus and entered Beth-dagon 1
84 Jonathan burned Azotus 1
11: 4 When he approached Azotus 1
4 Azotus and its suburbs destroyed 1
14:34 Gazara, which is on the borders of Azotus 1
16:10 the towers that were in the fields of Azotus 1

Azriel 1. עַזְרִיאֵל
1Ch 5:24 heads of their fathers' houses . . Az'ri-el 1
27:19 for Naph'tali, Jer'emoth the son of Az'riel; 1
Jer 36:26 the king commanded . . Serai'ah the son of Az'ri-el 1

Azrikam 1. עַזְרִיקָם
1Ch 3:23 sons of Neari'ah: Eli-o-e'nai, Hizki'ah, and Azri'kam 1
8:38 Azel had six sons . . Azri'kam, Bo'cheru, Ish'mael 1
9:14 Hasshub, son of Azri'kam, son of Hashabi'ah 1
44 Azel had six sons . . Azri'kam, Bo'cheru, Ish'mael 1
2Ch 28: 7 slew . . Azri'kam the commander of the palace 1
Neh 11:15 Shemai'ah the son of Hasshub, son of Azri'kam 1

Azubah 1. עֲזוּבָה
1Kg 22:42 mother's name was Azu'bah the daughter of Shilhi. 1
1Ch 2:18 Caleb . . had children by his wife Azu'bah 1
19 When Azu'bah died, Caleb married Ephrath 1
2Ch 20:31 His mother's name was Azu'bah 1

Azzan 1. עַזָּן
Num34:26 of Is'sachar a leader, Pal'tiel the son of Azzan. 1

Azzur 1. עַזּוּר
Neh 10:17 Ater, Hezeki'ah, Azzur 1
Jer 28: 1 Hanani'ah the son of Azzur 1
Ezk 11: 1 I saw among them Ja-azani'ah the son of Azzur 1

Baal 1. בַּעַל 2. Βάαλ
Deu 4: 3 destroyed . . men who followed the Ba'al of Pe'or; 1
Jdg 2:11 evil in the sight of the LORD and served the Ba'als; 1
13 served the Ba'als and the Ash'taroth. 1
3: 7 God, and serving the Ba'als and the Ashe'roth. 1
6:25 father's bull . . and pull down the altar of Ba'al 1
28 the altar of Ba'al was broken down, and the Ashe'rah 1
30 he has pulled down the altar of Ba'al and cut down 1
31 Will you contend for Ba'al? Or will you defend 1
32 that is to say, "Let Ba'al contend against him 1
8:33 turned . . and played the harlot after the Ba'als 1
10: 6 evil . . and served the Ba'als and the Ash'taroth 1
10 have forsaken our God and have served the Ba'als. 1
1Sm 7: 4 So Israel put away the Ba'als and the Ash'taroth 1

12:10 and have served the Ba'als and the Ash'taroth; 1
1Kg 16:31 took for wife Jez'ebel . . and went and served Ba'al 1
32 He erected an altar for Ba'al in the house of Ba'al 1
32 He erected an altar for Ba'al in the house of Ba'al 1
18:18 forsaken . . the LORD and followed the Ba'als. 1
19 send and gather . . and the 450 prophets of Ba'al 1
21 If the LORD . . but if Ba'al, then follow him. 1
22 Ba'al's prophets are 450 men. 1
25 Then Eli'jah said to the prophets of Ba'al, "Choose 1
26 they prepared it, and called on the name of Ba'al 1
26 called on the name of Ba'al . . "O Ba'al, answer us! 1
40 Eli'jah said to them, "Seize the prophets of Ba'al; 1
19:18 leave . . all the knees that have not bowed to Ba'al 1
22:53 He served Ba'al and worshiped him 1
2Kg 3: 2 the pillar of Ba'al which his father had made. 1
10:18 Ahab served Ba'al a little; 1
19 all the prophets of Ba'al, all his worshipers 1
19 I have a great sacrifice to offer to Ba'al; 1
19 in order to destroy the worshipers of Ba'al. 1
20 Sanctify a solemn assembly for Ba'al. 1
21 Jehu sent . . all the worshipers of Ba'al came 1
21 And they entered the house of Ba'al 1
21 they entered . . and the house of Ba'al was filled 1
22 vestments for all the worshipers of Ba'al. 1
23 Jehu went into the house of Ba'al with Jehon'adab 1
23 Jehu went . . and he said to the worshipers of Ba'al 1
23 no . . among you, but only the worshipers of Ba'al. 1
25 and went into the inner room of the house of Ba'al 1
26 the pillar that was in the house of Ba'al 1
27 they demolished the pillar of Ba'al 1
27 they . . demolished the house of Ba'al 1
28 Thus Jehu wiped out Ba'al from Israel. 1
11:18 the people of the land went to the house of Ba'al 1
18 and they slew Mattan the priest of Ba'al 1
17:16 and worshiped all the host . . and served Ba'al. 1
21: 3 he erected altars for Ba'al, and made an Ashe'rah 1
23: 4 the vessels made for Ba'al, for Ashe'rah, and for all 1
5 burned incense to Ba'al, to the sun, and the moon 1
1Ch 4:33 were round about these cities as far as Ba'al. 1
5: 5 Micah his son, Re-ai'ah his son, Ba'al his son 1
8:30 His first-born son: Abdon, then Zur, Kish, Ba'al, 1
9:36 and his first-born son Abdon, then Zur, Kish, Ba'al, 1
2Ch 17: 3 he did not seek the Ba'als 1
23:17 people went to the house of Ba'al, and tore it down; 1
17 slew Mattan the priest of Ba'al before the altars. 1
24: 7 used all the dedicated things . . for the Ba'als. 1
28: 2 He even made molten images for the Ba'als; 1
33: 3 erected altars to the Ba'als, and made Ashe'rahs 1
34: 4 broke down the altars of the Ba'als 1
Jer 2: 8 the prophets prophesied by Ba'al 1
23 am not defiled, I have not gone after the Ba'als'? 1
7: 9 burn incense to Ba'al, and go after other gods 1
9:14 after the Ba'als, as their fathers taught them. 1
11:13 set up to shame, altars to burn incense to Ba'al. 1
17 to anger by burning incense to Ba'al. 1
12:16 even as they taught my people to swear by Ba'al 1
19: 5 and have built the high places of Ba'al 1
5 burnt offerings to Ba'al, which I did not command 1
23:13 I saw an unsavory thing: they prophesied by Ba'al 1
27 even as their fathers forgot my name for Ba'al? 1
32:29 incense has been offered to Ba'al 1
35 They built the high places of Ba'al in the valley 1
Hos 2: 8 silver and gold which they used for Ba'al. 1
13 I will punish her for the feast days of the Ba'als 1
16 and no longer will you call me, 'My Ba'al.' 1
17 will remove the names of the Ba'als from her mouth 1
7:16 They turn to Ba'al; they are like a treacherous bow •
9:10 and consecrated themselves to Ba'al •
11: 2 they kept sacrificing to the Ba'als 1
13: 1 but he incurred guilt through Ba'al and died. 1
Zep 1: 4 I will cut off from this place the remnant of Ba'al 1
Rom 11: 4 7,000 men who have not bowed the knee to Ba'al". 2
Tob 1: 5 All the tribes . . used to sacrifice to the calf Baal 2

Baal of Peor 1. בַּעַל פְּעוֹר
Num25: 3 Israel yoked himself to Ba'al of Pe'or. 1
5 men who have yoked themselves to Ba'al of Pe'or. 1
Ps 106:28 attached themselves to the Ba'al of Pe'or 1

Baal-berith 1. בַּעַל בְּרִית
Jdg 8:33 turned again . . and made Ba'al-be'rith their god. 1
9: 4 pieces of silver out of the house of Ba'al-be'rith 1

Baal-gad 1. בַּעַל גָּד
Jos 11:17 as far as Ba'al-gad in the valley of Lebanon 1
12: 7 from Ba'al-gad in the valley of Lebanon 1
13: 5 from Ba'al-gad below Mount Hermon to the entrance 1

Baal-hamon 1. בַּעַל הָמוֹן
Sng 8:11 Solomon had a vineyard at Ba'al-ha'mon; 1

Baal-hanan 1. בַּעַל חָנָן
Gen 36:38 Shaul died, and Ba'al-ha'nan the son of Achbor 1
39 Ba'al-ha'nan the son of Achbor died 1
1Ch 1:49 When Sha'ul died, Ba'al-ha'nan . . reigned 1
50 When Ba'al-ha'nan died, Hadad reigned in his stead; 1
27:28 Over the . . was Ba'al-ha'nan the Gede'rite; 1

Baal-hazor 1. בַּעַל חָצוֹר
2Sm 13:23 Ab'salom had sheepshearers at Ba'al-ha'zor 1

Baal-hermon 1. בַּעַל חֶרְמוֹן
Jdg 3: 3 Lebanon, from Mount Ba'al-her'mon as far 1
1Ch 5:23 were very numerous from Bashan to Ba'al-her'mon 1

Baal-meon 1. בַּעַל מְעוֹן
Num32:38 Nebo, and Ba'al-me'on (their names to be changed) 1
1Ch 5: 8 who dwelt in Aro'er, as far as Nebo and Ba'al-me'on. 1
Ezk 25: 9 Beth-jesh'imoth, Ba'al-me'on, and Kiriatha'im. 1

Baal-peor 1. בַּעַל פְּעוֹר
Deu 4: 3 eyes have seen what the LORD did at Ba'al-pe'or; 1
Hos 9:10 But they came to Ba'al-pe'or 1

Baal-perazim 1. בַּעַל פְּרָצִים
2Sm 5:20 David came to Ba'al-pera'zim, and . . defeated them 1
20 the name of that place is called Ba'al-pera'zim. 1
1Ch 14:11 went up to Ba'al-pera'zim, and David defeated them 1
11 the name of that place is called Ba'al-pera'zim. 1

Baal-shalishah 1. בַּעַל שָׁלִשָׁה
2Kg 4:42 A man came from Ba'al-shal'ishah, bringing 1

Baal-tamar 1. בַּעַל תָּמָר
Jdg 20:33 and set themselves in array at Ba'al-ta'mar; 1

Baal-zebub 1. בַּעַל זְבוּב
2Kg 1: 2 inquire of Ba'al-ze'bub . . whether I shall recover 1
3 that you are going to inquire of Ba'al-ze'bub 1
6 that you are sending to inquire of Ba'al-ze'bub 1
16 sent messengers to inquire of Ba'al-ze'bub 1

Baal-zephon 1. בַּעַל צְפוֹן
Exd 14: 2 encamp . . in front of Ba'al-ze'phon; 1
9 at the sea, by Pi-ha-hi'roth, in front of Ba'al-ze'phon. 1
Num33: 7 Pi-hahi'roth, which is east of Ba'al-ze'phon; 1

Baalah 1. בַּעֲלָה
Jos 15: 9 then the boundary bends round to Ba'alah 1
10 boundary circles west of Ba'alah to Mount Se'ir 1
11 to Shik'keron, and passes along to Mount Ba'alah 1
29 Ba'alah, I'im, Ezem 1
1Ch 13: 6 David and all Israel went up to Ba'alah 1

Baalath 1. בַּעֲלָת
Jos 19:44 El'tekeh, Gib'bethon, Ba'alath 1
1Kg 9:18 Ba'alath and Tamar in the wilderness 1
2Ch 8: 6 Ba'alath, and all the store-cities . . Solomon had 1

Baalath-beer 1. בַּעֲלַת בְּאֵר
Jos 19: 8 as far as Ba'alath-beer, Ramah of the Negeb. 1

Baale-judah 1. בַּעֲלֵי יְהוּדָה
2Sm 6: 2 David arose and went . . from Ba'ale-judah 1

Baalis 1. בַּעֲלִיס
Jer 40:14 Do you know that Ba'alis the king of the Ammonites 1

Baalsamus 1. Βααλσαμος
1Es 9:43 Baalsamus on his right hand 1

Baana 1. בַּעֲנָא
1Kg 4:12 Ba'ana the son of Ahi'lud, in Ta'anach, Megid'do 1
16 Ba'ana the son of Hushai, in Asher and Bealoth; 1
Neh 3: 4 next to them Zadok the son of Ba'ana repaired. 1

Baanah 1. בַּעֲנָה 2. Βαανα
2Sm 4: 2 the name of the one was Ba'anah 1
5 sons of Rimmon . . Rechab and Ba'anah, set out 1
6 so Rechab and Ba'anah his brother slipped in. 1
9 David answered Rechab and Ba'anah his brother 1
23:29 Heleb the son of Ba'anah of Netoph'ah 1
1Ch 11:30 Heled the son of Ba'anah of Netoph'ah 1
Ezr 2: 2 came with . . Mispar, Bigva'i, Rehum, and Ba'anah. 1
Neh 7: 7 came with . . Bigva'i, Nehum, Ba'anah. 1
10:27 Malluch, Harim, Ba'anah. 1
1Es 5: 8 Mispar, Reeliah, Rehum, and Baanah, their leaders 2

Baara 1. בַּעֲרָא
1Ch 8: 8 he had sent away Hushim and Ba'ara his wives. 1

Baaseiah 1. בַּעֲשֵׂיָה
1Ch 6:40 son of Michael, son of Ba-ase'iah, son of Malchi'jah 1

Baasha 1. בַּעְשָׁא
1Kg 15:16 was war between Asa and Ba'asha king of Israel 1
17 Ba'asha king of Israel went up against Judah 1
19 go, break your league with Ba'asha king of Israel 1
21 when Ba'asha heard of it, he stopped building 1
22 its timber, with which Ba'asha had been building; 1
27 Ba'asha . . conspired against him; 1
27 Ba'asha struck him down at Gib'bethon 1
28 Ba'asha killed him in the third year of Asa 1
32 war between Asa and Ba'asha king of Israel 1
33 Ba'asha the son of Ahi'jah began to reign 1
16: 1 word of the LORD came to Jehu . . against Ba'asha 1
3 I will utterly sweep away Ba'asha and his house 1
4 Any one belonging to Ba'asha who dies in the city 1
5 the acts of Ba'asha, and what he did, and his might 1
6 Ba'asha slept with his fathers, and was buried 1
7 came . . against Ba'asha and his house 1
8 Elah the son of Ba'asha began to reign over Israel 1
11 he killed all the house of Ba'asha; 1
12 Thus Zimri destroyed all the house of Ba'asha 1
12 word of the LORD, which he spoke against Ba'asha 1
13 for all the sins of Ba'asha and the sins of Elah 1
21:22 I will make your house . . like the house of Ba'asha 1
2Kg 9: 9 and like the house of Ba'asha the son of Ahi'jah. 1
2Ch 16: 1 Ba'asha king of Israel went up against Judah 1
3 go, break your league with Ba'asha king of Israel 1
5 when Ba'asha heard of it 1
6 with which Ba'asha had been building 1
Jer 41: 9 made for defense against Ba'asha king of Israel; 1

Babel 1. בָּבֶל
Gen 10:10 The beginning of his kingdom was Ba'bel, Erech 1
11: 9 Therefore its name was called Ba'bel 1

Babylon 1. בָּבֶל 2. שֵׁשַׁךְ 3. בָּבֶל (A) 4. Βαβυλών 5. Babylon 6. Babylonia
2Kg 17:24 the king of Assyria brought people from Babylon 1
30 the men of Babylon made Suc'coth-be'noth 1
20:12 Mero'dach-bal'adan the son of . . king of Babylon 1
14 They have come from a far country, from Babylon. 1
17 all that is in . . shall be carried to Babylon; 1
18 be eunuchs in the palace of the king of Babylon. 1
24: 1 Nebuchadnez'zar king of Babylon came up 1
7 the king of Babylon had taken all that belonged 1
10 the servants of Nebuchadnez'zar king of Babylon 1
11 Nebuchadnez'zar king of Babylon came to the city 1
12 the king . . gave himself up to the king of Babylon 1
12 The king of Babylon took him prisoner 1
15 And he carried away Jehoi'achin to Babylon; 1
15 took into captivity from Jerusalem to Babylon. 1
16 the king of Babylon brought captive to Babylon 1
16 the king of Babylon brought captive to Babylon 1
17 the king of Babylon made Mattani'ah . . king 1
20 Zedeki'ah rebelled against the king of Babylon. 1
25: 1 Nebuchadnez'zar king of Babylon came with all 1
6 and brought him up to the king of Babylon 1
7 and bound him in fetters, and took him to Babylon. 1
8 year of . . Nebuchadnez'zar, king of Babylon 1
8 Nebu'zarad'an . . a servant of the king of Babylon 1
11 who had deserted to the king of Babylon 1
13 and carried the bronze to Babylon. 1
20 took them, and brought them to the king of Babylon 1
21 the king of Babylon smote . . and put them to death 1
22 whom Nebuchadnez'zar king of Babylon had left 1
23 the king of Babylon had appointed Gedali'ah 1
24 dwell in the land, and serve the king of Babylon 1
27 Evil-mero'dach king of Babylon . . freed 1
28 of the kings who were with him in Babylon. 1
1Ch 9: 1 And Judah was taken into exile in Babylon 1
2Ch 32:31 matter of the envoys of the princes of Babylon 1
33:11 bound . . and brought him to Babylon. 1
36: 6 came up Nebuchadnez'zar king of Babylon 1
6 bound him in fetters to take him to Babylon. 1
7 carried part of the vessels . . to Babylon 1
7 to Babylon and put them in his palace in Babylon. 1
10 Nebuchadnez'zar sent and brought him to Babylon 1
18 all these he brought to Babylon. 1
20 took into exile in Babylon those who had escaped 1
Ezr 2: 1 exiles whom Nebuchadnez'zar the king of Babylon 1
5:12 into the hand of Nebuchadnez'zar king of Babylon 3
13 first year of Cyrus king of Babylon 3
14 taken . . and brought into the temple of Babylon 3
14 Cyrus the king took out of the temple of Babylon 3
17 search . . the royal archives there in Babylon 3
6: 5 took . . and brought to Babylon 3
Neh 7: 6 exiles whom Nebuchadnez'zar the king of Babylon 1
13: 6 year of Ar-ta-xerx'es king of Babylon 1
Est 2: 6 Nebuchadnez'zar king of Babylon had carried 1
Ps 87: 4 know me I mention Rahab and Babylon; 1
137: 1 waters of Babylon, there we sat down and wept 1
8 O daughter of Babylon, you devastator! 1
Isa 13: 1 The oracle concerning Babylon which Isaiah 1
19 Babylon, the glory of kingdoms, the splendor 1
14: 4 take up this taunt against the king of Babylon 1
22 and will cut off from Babylon name and remnant 1
21: 9 And he answered, "Fallen, fallen is Babylon; 1
39: 1 the son of Bal'adan, king of Babylon, sent envoys 1
3 have come to me from a far country, from Babylon. 1
6 be carried to Babylon; nothing shall be left 1
7 be eunuchs in the palace of the king of Babylon. 1
43:14 I will send to Babylon and break down all the bars 1
47: 1 and sit in the dust, O virgin daughter of Babylon; 1
48:14 he shall perform his purpose on Babylon 1
20 Go forth from Babylon, flee from Chalde'a 1
Jer 20: 4 all Judah into the hand of the king of Babylon; 1
4 he shall carry them captive to Babylon 1
5 and seize them, and carry them to Babylon. 1
6 shall go into captivity; to Babylon you shall go; 1
21: 2 Nebuchadrez'zar king of Babylon is making war 1
4 you are fighting against the king of Babylon 1

7 into the hand of Nebuchadrez'zar king of Babylon 1
10 be given into the hand of the king of Babylon 1
22:25 into the hand of Nebuchadrez'zar king of Babylon 1
24: 1 After Nebuchadrez'zar king of Babylon had taken 1
1 and had brought them to Babylon 1
25: 1 the first year of Nebuchadrez'zar king of Babylon 1
9 and for Nebuchadrez'zar the king of Babylon 1
11 nations shall serve the king of Babylon 70 years. 1
12 I will punish the king of Babylon and that nation 1
26 And after them the king of Babylon shall drink. 2
27: 6 Nebuchadnez'zar, the king of Babylon, my servant 1
8 not serve this Nebuchadnez'zar king of Babylon 1
8 put its neck under the yoke of the king of Babylon 1
9 You shall not serve the king of Babylon. 1
11 under the yoke of the king of Babylon and serve 1
12 under the yoke of the king of Babylon, 1
13 nation which will not serve the king of Babylon? 1
14 You shall not serve the king of Babylon, 1
16 will now shortly be brought back from Babylon, 1
17 Do not listen to them; serve the king of Babylon 1
18 and in Jerusalem may not go to Babylon. 1
20 Nebuchadnez'zar king of Babylon did not take 1
20 took into exile from Jerusalem to Babylon 1
22 They shall be carried to Babylon 1
28: 2 I have broken the yoke of the king of Babylon. 1
3 which Nebuchadnez'zar king of Babylon took away 1
3 away from this place and carried to Babylon. 1
4 and all the exiles from Judah who went to Babylon 1
4 for I will break the yoke of the king of Babylon. 1
6 and bring back to this place from Babylon 1
11 the yoke of Nebuchadnez'zar king of Babylon 1
14 servitude to Nebuchadnez'zar king of Babylon 1
29: 1 had taken into exile from Jerusalem to Babylon. 1
3 whom Zedeki'ah king of Judah sent to Babylon 1
3 to Babylon to Nebuchadnez'zar king of Babylon. 1
4 I have sent into exile from Jerusalem to Babylon 1
10 When 70 years are completed for Babylon 1
15 The LORD has raised up prophets for us in Babylon, 1
20 whom I sent away from Jerusalem to Babylon 1
21 into the hand of Nebuchadrez'zar king of Babylon 1
22 be used by all the exiles from Judah in Babylon 1
22 Ahab, whom the king of Babylon roasted in the fire 1
28 For he has sent to us in Babylon, saying 1
32: 2 the king of Babylon was besieging Jerusalem 1
3 this city into the hand of the king of Babylon 1
4 be given into the hand of the king of Babylon 1
5 and he shall take Zedeki'ah to Babylon 1
28 into the hand of Nebuchadrez'zar king of Babylon 1
36 It is given into the hand of the king of Babylon 1
34: 1 when Nebuchadrez'zar king of Babylon 1
2 this city into the hand of the king of Babylon 1
3 you shall see the king of Babylon eye to eye 1
3 and you shall go to Babylon. 1
7 when the army of the king of Babylon was fighting 1
21 into the hand of the army of the king of Babylon 1
35:11 when Nebuchadrez'zar king of Babylon came up 1
36:29 the king of Babylon will certainly come 1
37: 1 whom Nebuchadrez'zar king of Babylon made king 1
17 delivered into the hand of the king of Babylon. 1
19 The king of Babylon will not come against you 1
38: 3 of the army of the king of Babylon and be taken. 1
17 surrender to the princes of the king of Babylon 1
18 surrender to the princes of the king of Babylon 1
22 led out to the princes of the king of Babylon 1
23 but shall be seized by the king of Babylon; 1
39: 1 Nebuchadrez'zar king of Babylon and all his army 1
3 the princes of the king of Babylon came and sat 1
3 the rest of the officers of the king of Babylon. 1
5 up to Nebuchadrez'zar king of Babylon, at Riblah 1
6 The king of Babylon slew the sons of Zedeki'ah 1
6 the king of Babylon slew all the nobles of Judah. 1
7 and bound him in fetters to take him to Babylon. 1
9 the guard, carried into exile to Babylon the rest 1
11 Nebuchadrez'zar king of Babylon gave command 1
13 all the chief officers of the king of Babylon 1
40: 1 and Judah who were being exiled to Babylon. 1
4 If it seems good to you to come with me to Babylon 1
4 if it seems wrong to you to come with me to Babylon 1
5 whom the king of Babylon appointed governor 1
7 men heard that the king of Babylon had appointed 1
7 who had not been taken into exile to Babylon 1
9 Dwell in the land, and serve the king of Babylon 1
11 heard that the king of Babylon had left a remnant 1
41: 2 whom the king of Babylon had appointed governor 1
18 whom the king of Babylon had made governor 1
42:11 Do not fear the king of Babylon 1
43: 3 they may kill us or take us into exile in Babylon. 1
10 and take Nebuchadrez'zar the king of Babylon 1
44:30 into the hand of Nebuchadrez'zar king of Babylon 1
46: 2 which Nebuchadrez'zar king of Babylon defeated 1
13 the coming of Nebuchadrez'zar king of Babylon 1
26 into the hand of Nebuchadrez'zar king of Babylon 1
49:28 which Nebuchadrez'zar king of Babylon smote. 1
30 Nebuchadrez'zar king of Babylon has made a plan 1
50: 1 word which the LORD spoke concerning Babylon 1
2 proclaim, conceal it not, and say: 'Babylon is taken 1
8 Flee from the midst of Babylon 1
9 I am stirring up and bringing against Babylon 1
13 one who passes by Babylon shall be appalled 1
14 Set yourselves in array against Babylon 1
16 Cut off from Babylon the sower 1
17 now at last Nebuchadrez'zar king of Babylon 1
18 I am bringing punishment on the king of Babylon 1
23 How Babylon has become a horror among the nations! 1
24 I set a snare for you and you were taken, O Babylon 1
28 they flee and escape from the land of Babylon 1
29 Summon archers against Babylon 1
34 but unrest to the inhabitants of Babylon. 1
35 A sword . . upon the inhabitants of Babylon 1
39 wild beasts shall dwell with hyenas in Babylon •
42 for battle against you, O daughter of Babylon! 1
43 The king of Babylon heard the report of them 1
45 hear the plan . . the LORD has made against Babylon 1
46 At the sound of the capture of Babylon 1
51: 1 the spirit of a destroyer against Babylon 1
2 I will send to Babylon winnowers 1
6 Flee from the midst of Babylon 1
7 Babylon was a golden cup in the LORD'S hand 1
8 Suddenly Babylon has fallen and been broken; 1
9 We would have healed Babylon 1
11 his purpose concerning Babylon is to destroy it 1
12 Set up a standard against the walls of Babylon; 1
12 spoke concerning the inhabitants of Babylon. 1
24 I will requite Babylon 1
29 for the LORD'S purposes against Babylon stand 1
29 to make the land of Babylon a desolation 1
30 The warriors of Babylon have ceased fighting 1
31 to tell the king of Babylon that his city is taken 1
33 daughter of Babylon is like a threshing floor 1
34 the king of Babylon has devoured me 1
35 The violence done to me . . be upon Babylon 1
37 Babylon shall become a heap of ruins 1
41 How Babylon is taken •
41 How Babylon has become a horror among the nations! 1
42 The sea has come up on Babylon; 1
44 I will punish Bel in Babylon 1
44 the wall of Babylon has fallen. 1
47 when I will punish the images of Babylon; 1
48 the earth . . shall sing for joy over Babylon; 1
49 Babylon must fall for the slain of Israel 1
49 as for Babylon have fallen the slain of all 1
53 Though Babylon should mount up to heaven 1
54 Hark! a cry from Babylon! 1
55 For the LORD is laying Babylon waste 1
56 for a destroyer has come upon her, upon Babylon; 1
58 The broad wall of Babylon shall be leveled 1
59 he went with Zedeki'ah king of Judah to Babylon 1
60 all the evil that should come upon Babylon 1
60 words that are written concerning Babylon. 1
61 said to Serai'ah: "When you come to Babylon 1
64 say, 'Thus shall Babylon sink, to rise no more 1
52: 3 Zedeki'ah rebelled against the king of Babylon. 1
4 king of Babylon came with all his army 1
9 and brought him up to the king of Babylon 1
10 The king of Babylon slew the sons of Zedeki'ah 1
11 and the king of Babylon took him to Babylon 1
11 and the king of Babylon took him to Babylon 1
12 Nebuchadrez'zar, king of Babylon-Nebu'zarad'an 1
12 the bodyguard who served the king of Babylon 1
15 who had deserted to the king of Babylon 1
17 in pieces, and carried all the bronze to Babylon. 1
26 and brought them to the king of Babylon at Riblah. 1
27 And the king of Babylon smote them 1
31 king of Babylon, in the year that he became king 1
32 of the kings who were with him in Babylon. 1
Ezk 12:13 I will bring him to Babylon 1
17:12 Behold, the king of Babylon came to Jerusalem 1
12 her princes and brought them to him to Babylon. 1
16 in Babylon he shall die. 1
20 in my snare, and I will bring him to Babylon 1
19: 9 in a cage, and brought him to the king of Babylon; 1
21:19 ways for the sword of the king of Babylon to come; 1
21 king of Babylon stands at the parting of the way 1
24: 2 The king of Babylon has laid siege to Jerusalem 1
26: 7 Nebuchadrez'zar king of Babylon, king of kings 1
29:18 Nebuchadrez'zar king of Babylon made his army 1
19 give . . Egypt to Nebuchadrez'zar king of Babylon; 1
30:10 by the hand of Nebuchadrez'zar king of Babylon. 1
24 I will strengthen the arms of the king of Babylon 1
25 strengthen the arms of the king of Babylon, 1
25 I put my sword into the hand of the king of Babylon 1
32:11 sword of the king of Babylon shall come upon you. 1
Dan 2:12 all the wise men of Babylon be destroyed. 3
14 who had gone out to slay the wise men of Babylon; 3
18 perish with the rest of the wise men of Babylon. 3
24 appointed to destroy the wise men of Babylon; 3
24 Do not destroy the wise men of Babylon; 3
48 ruler over the whole province of Babylon 3
48 chief prefect over all the wise men of Babylon. 3
49 over the affairs of the province of Babylon; 3
3: 1 plain of Dura, in the province of Babylon. 3
12 over the affairs of the province of Babylon 3
30 king promoted . . in the province of Babylon. 3
4: 6 all the wise men of Babylon should be brought 3
29 walking on the roof of the royal palace of Babylon 3
30 great Babylon, which I have built by my mighty 3
5: 7 king said to the wise men of Babylon, 3
7: 1 In the first year of Belshaz'zar king of Babylon 3
Mic 4:10 you shall go to Babylon. 1
Zec 2: 7 you who dwell with the daughter of Babylon. 1
6:10 and Jedai'ah, who have arrived from Babylon; and go 1
Mat 1:11 at the time of the deportation to Babylon. 4
12 after the deportation to Babylon: Jechon'iah was 4
17 and from David to the deportation to Babylon 4
17 from the deportation to Babylon to the Christ 4
Act 7:43 I will remove you beyond Babylon.' 4
1Pe 5:13 She who is at Babylon, who is likewise chosen 4
Rev 14: 8 Fallen, fallen is Babylon the great 4
16:19 and God remembered great Babylon 4
17: 5 Babylon the great, mother of harlots 4
18: 2 Fallen, fallen is Babylon the great! 4
10 alas! thou great city, thou mighty city, Babylon! 4
21 So shall Babylon the great city be thrown down 4
1Es 1:40 Nebuchadnezzar king of Babylon 4
40 took him away to Babylon. 4
41 stored them in his temple in Babylon. 4
45 Nebuchadnezzar sent and removed him to Babylon 4
54 they took and carried away to Babylon. 4
56 he led away to Babylon with the sword 4
2:15 the returning exiles from Babylon to Jerusalem. 4
4:44 set apart when he began to destroy Babylon 4
57 he sent back from Babylon all the vessels 4
61 he took the letters, and went to Babylon 4
5: 7 Nebuchadnezzar king of Babylon 4
7 had carried away to Babylon 4
6:15 the hands of Nebuchadnezzar king of Babylon 4
16 carried the people away captive to Babylon 4
18 took out again from the temple in Babylon 4
21 the royal archives . . that are in Babylon; 4
23 royal archives that were deposited in Babylon. 4
26 house in Jerusalem and carried away to Babylon 4
8: 3 This Ezra came up from Babylon as a scribe 4
6 left Babylon on the new moon of the first month 4
28 their groups, who went up with me from Babylon 4
2Es 3: 1 I Salathiel . . was in Babylon 5
2 and the wealth of those who lived in Babylon. 5
28 the deeds of those who inhabit Babylon 5
31 Are the deeds of Babylon better than those of Zion? 5
15:43 they shall go on steadily to Babylon 5
46 you, Asia, who share in the glamour of Babylon 5
60 as they return from devastated Babylon. 6
16: 1 Woe to you, Babylon and Asia! 5
AEs 11: 4 Nebuchadnezzar king of Babylon 4
Bar 1: 1 the words . . which Baruch . . wrote in Babylon 4
4 all who dwelt in Babylon by the river Sud. 4
9 after Nebuchadnezzar king of Babylon had 4
9 and brought them to Babylon. 4
11 Nebuchadnezzar king of Babylon 4
12 Nebuchadnezzar king of Babylon 4
2:21 serve the king of Babylon, and you will remain 4
22 if you . . will not serve the king of Babylon 4
24 not obey thy voice, to serve the king of Babylon; 4
LJr 1: 1 those who were to be taken to Babylon as captives 4
2 you will be taken to Babylon as captives 4
3 when you have come to Babylon 4
4 Now in Babylon you will see gods made of silver 4
Sus 1: 1 a man living in Babylon whose name was Joakim. 4
5 Iniquity came forth from Babylon 4
Bel 1:34 Take the dinner which you have to Babylon 4
35 Habakkuk said, "Sir, I have never seen Babylon 4
36 lifted him by his hair and set him down in Babylon 4
1Mc 6: 4 departed from there to return to Babylon. 4
3Mc 6: 6 The three companions in Babylon 4

Babylonia 1. בָּבֶל 2. בָּבֶל (A) 3. Βαβυλωνια

Ezr 1:11 brought up from Babylonia to Jerusalem. 1
2: 1 carried captive to Babylonia; 1
5:12 carried away the people to Babylonia. 2
6: 1 made a decree, and search was made in Babylonia 2
7: 6 this Ezra went up from Babylonia. He was a scribe 1
9 go up from Babylonia, and on the first day 1
16 find in the whole province of Babylonia 2
8: 1 those who went up with me from Babylonia 1
1Es 4:53 all who came from Babylonia to build the city 3
6:17 Cyrus reigned over the country of Babylonia 3
8:13 may be found in the country of Babylonia 3
2Mc 8:20 that took place in Babylonia 3

Babylonian 1. בֶּן בָּבֶל 2. בַּבְלִי (A) 3. Βαβυλωνιος

Ezr 4: 9 men of Erech, the Babylonians, the men of Susa 2
Ezk 23:15 looking like officers, a picture of Babylonians 1
17 the Babylonians came to her into the bed of love 1
23 the Babylonians and all the Chalde'ans 1
LJr 1: 1 the king of the Babylonians 3
2 Nebuchadnezzar, king of the Babylonians. 3
Bel 1: 3 Now the Babylonians had an idol called Bel 3
23 a great dragon, which the Babylonians revered. 3
28 When the Babylonians heard it 3

Baca 1. בָּכָא

Ps 84: 6 As they go through the valley of Baca they make it 1

Bacchides 1. Βακχιδης

1Mc 7: 8 So the king chose Bacchides 1
12 appeared in a body before Alcimus and Bacchides 1
19 Then Bacchides departed from Jerusalem 1
20 then Bacchides went back to the king. 1

9: 1 he sent Bacchides and Alcimus 1
11 the army of Bacchides marched out from the camp •
12 Bacchides was on the right wing 1
14 Bacchides and the strength of his army 1
25 Bacchides chose the ungodly 1
26 brought them to Bacchides 1
29 like him to go against our enemies and Bacchides 1
32 When Bacchides learned of this 1
34 Bacchides found this out on the sabbath day 1
43 When Bacchides heard of this 1
47 Jonathan stretched out his hand to strike Bacchides 1
49 about 1,000 of Bacchides' men fell that day. 1
50 Bacchides then returned to Jerusalem •
57 When Bacchides saw that Alcimus was dead 1
58 So now let us bring Bacchides back 1
63 When Bacchides learned of this 1
68 They fought with Bacchides 1
10:12 the strongholds that Bacchides had built 1
2Mc 8:30 the forces of Timothy and Bacchides 1

Bacenor 1. Βακηνωρ
2Mc 12:35 a certain Dositheus, one of Bacenor's men 1

Baean 1. Βαιαν
1Mc 5: 4 remembered the wickedness of the sons of Baean 1

Bagoas 1. Βαγωας
Jdt 12:11 he said to Bagoas 1
13 Bagoas went out from the presence of Holofernes 1
15 the soft fleeces which she had received from Bagoas 1
13: 1 Bagoas closed the tent from outside 1
3 she had said the same thing to Bagoas. 1
14:14 Bagoas went in and knocked at the door of the tent 1

Baharum 1. בַּחֲרוּמִי
1Ch 11:33 Az'maveth of Baha'rum, Eli'ahba of Sha-al'bon 1

Bahurim 1. בַּחֻרִים
2Sm 3:16 went . . weeping after her all the way to Bahu'rim. 1
16: 5 When King David came to Bahu'rim, there came out 1
17:18 went . . and came to the house of a man at Bahu'rim 1
19:16 Shim'e-i . . the Benjaminite, from Bahu'rim 1
23:31 Abi-al'bon the Ar'bathite, Az'maveth of Bahu'rim •
1Kg 2: 8 Shim'e-i . . the Benjaminite from Bahu'rim, who 1

Baiterus 1. Βαιτηρους
1Es 5:17 The sons of Baiterus, 3,005. 1

Bakbakkar 1. בַּקְבַּקַּר
1Ch 9:15 Bakbak'kar, Heresh, Galal, and Mattani'ah 1

Bakbuk 1. בַּקְבּוּק 2. Βακβουκ
Ezr 2:51 sons of Bakbuk, the sons of Haku'pha 1
Neh 7:53 sons of Bakbuk, the sons of Haku'pha 1
1Es 5:31 the sons of Bakbuk, the sons of Hakupha 2

Bakbukiah 1. בַּקְבֻּקְיָה
Neh 11:17 Bakbuki'ah, the second among his brethren; 1
12: 9 Bakbuki'ah and Unno their brethren 1
25 Mattani'ah, Bakbuki'ah, Obadi'ah, Meshul'lam, 1

Balaam 1. בִּלְעָם 2. Βαλαάμ
Num22: 5 sent messengers to Balaam the son of Be'or 1
7 elders . . came to Balaam, and gave him 1
8 so the princes of Moab stayed with Balaam. 1
9 God came to Balaam and said, "Who are these men 1
10 Balaam said to God, "Balak the son of Zippor 1
12 God said to Balaam, "You shall not go with them; 1
13 Balaam rose in the morning, and said 1
14 to Balak, and said, "Balaam refuses to come with us. 1
16 came to Balaam and said to him, "Thus says Balak 1
18 Balaam answered and said to the servants 1
20 God came to Balaam at night and said to him 1
21 Balaam rose in the morning, and saddled his ass 1
23 Balaam struck the ass, to turn her into the road. 1
25 ass . . pressed Balaam's foot against the wall; 1
27 ass saw the angel . . she lay down under Balaam; 1
27 Balaam's anger was kindled, and he struck the ass 1
28 opened the mouth of the ass, and she said to Balaam 1
29 Balaam said to the ass, "Because you have 1
30 ass said to Balaam, "Am I not your ass 1
31 the LORD opened the eyes of Balaam, and he saw 1
34 Balaam said to the angel of the LORD, "I have sinned 1
35 angel of the LORD said to Balaam, "Go with the men; 1
35 So Balaam went on with the princes of Balak. 1
36 When Balak heard that Balaam had come, he went 1
37 Balak said to Balaam, "Did I not send to you to call 1
38 Balaam said to Balak, "Lo, I have come to you! 1
39 Then Balaam went with Balak, and they came 1
40 Balak . . sent to Balaam and to the princes 1
41 on the morrow Balak took Balaam and brought him 1
23: 1 Balaam said to Balak, "Build for me here 1
2 Balak did as Balaam had said; and Balak and Balaam 1
2 Balak and Balaam offered . . a bull and a ram. 1
3 Balaam said to Balak 1
4 God met Balaam; and Balaam said to him 1
4 God met Balaam; and Balaam said to him •
5 the LORD put a word in Balaam's mouth, and said 1
7 Balaam took up his discourse, and said •
11 Balak said to Balaam, "What have you done to me? 1
15 Balaam said to Balak, "Stand here •
16 LORD met Balaam, and put a word in his mouth 1
18 Balaam took up his discourse, and said, "Rise, Balak •
25 Balak said to Balaam, "Neither curse them at all 1
26 Balaam answered Balak, "Did I not tell you 1
27 Balak said to Balaam, "Come now, I will take you 1
28 Balak took Balaam to the top of Pe'or 1
29 Balaam said to Balak, "Build for me here 1
30 Balak did as Balaam had said, and offered 1
24: 1 Balaam saw that it pleased the LORD to bless 1
2 Balaam lifted up his eyes, and saw Israel 1
3 oracle of Balaam the sons of Be'or 1
10 Balak's anger was kindled against Balaam 1
10 Balak said to Balaam, "I called you 1
12 Balaam said to Balak, "Did I not tell 1
15 The oracle of Balaam the son of Be'or 1
25 Then Balaam rose, and went back to his place; 1
31: 8 also slew Balaam the son of Be'or with the sword. 1
16 caused . . Israel, by the counsel of Balaam 1
Deu 23: 4 hired . . Balaam the son of Be'or from Pethor 1
5 LORD your God would not hearken to Balaam; 1
Jos 13:22 Balaam also . . the people of Israel killed 1
24: 9 and invited Balaam the son of Be'or to curse you 1
10 but I would not listen to Balaam; 1
Neh 13: 2 hired Balaam against them to curse them 1
Mic 6: 5 and what Balaam the son of Be'or answered him 1
2Pe 2:15 they have followed the way of Balaam 2
Jde 1:11 and abandon themselves . . to Balaam's error 2
Rev 2:14 some there who hold the teaching of Balaam 2

Baladan 1. בַּלְאֲדָן
2Kg 20:12 Mero'dach-bal'adan the son of Bal'adan, king 1
Isa 39: 1 the son of Bal'adan, king of Babylon, sent envoys 1

Balah 1. בָּלָה
Jos 19: 3 Hazar-shu'al, Balah, Ezem 1

Balak 1. בָּלָק 2. Βαλάκ
Num22: 2 Balak . . saw all that Israel had done 1
4 So Balak the son of Zippor, who was king of Moab 1
7 came to Balaam, and gave him Balak's message. 1
10 Balak the son of Zippor, king of Moab, has sent to me 1
13 Balaam . . said to the princes of Balak 1
14 princes of Moab rose and went to Balak, and said 1
15 Once again Balak sent princes, more in number 1
16 Thus says Balak the son of Zippor: 'Let nothing 1
18 Balaam . . said to the servants of Balak 1
18 Though Balak were to give me his house 1
35 So Balaam went on with the princes of Balak. 1
36 When Balak heard that Balaam had come, he went 1
37 Balak said to Balaam, "Did I not send to you to call 1
38 Balaam said to Balak, "Lo, I have come to you! 1
39 Then Balaam went with Balak, and they came 1
40 Balak sacrificed oxen and sheep, and sent 1
41 on the morrow Balak took Balaam and brought him 1
23: 1 Balaam said to Balak, "Build for me here 1
2 Balak did as Balaam had said; and Balak and Balaam 1
2 Balak and Balaam offered . . a bull and a ram. 1
3 Balaam said to Balak 1
5 Return to Balak, and thus you shall speak. 1
7 From Aram Balak has brought me 1
11 Balak said to Balaam, "What have you done to me? 1
13 Balak said to him, "Come with me to another place 1
15 Balaam said to Balak, "Stand here 1
16 Return to Balak, and thus shall you speak. 1
17 Balak said to him, "What has the LORD spoken? 1
18 Rise, Balak, and hear; hearken to me, O son of Zippor 1
25 Balak said to Balaam, "Neither curse them at all 1
26 Balaam answered Balak, "Did I not tell you 1
27 Balak said to Balaam, "Come now, I will take you 1
28 Balak took Balaam to the top of Pe'or 1
29 Balaam said to Balak, "Build for me here 1
30 Balak did as Balaam had said, and offered 1
24:10 Balak's anger was kindled against Balaam 1
10 Balak said to Balaam, "I called you 1
12 Balaam said to Balak, "Did I not tell 1
13 'If Balak should give me his house full of silver 1
25 Balak also went his way. 1
Jos 24: 9 Balak the son of Zippor, king of Moab, arose 1
Jdg 11:25 are you any better than Balak the son of Zippor 1
Mic 6: 5 remember what Balak king of Moab devised 1
Rev 2:14 Balaam, who taught Balak to put a stumbling block 2

Balamon 1. Βαλαμων
Jdt 8: 3 the field between Dothan and Balamon. 1

Balbaim 1. Βελβαιμ
Jdt 7: 3 spread out . . over Dothan as far as Balbaim 1

Bamah 1. בָּמָה
Ezk 20:29 its name is called Bamah to this day 1

Bamoth 1. בָּמוֹת
Num21:19 to Nahal'iel, and from Nahal'iel to Bamoth 1
20 Bamoth to the valley lying in the region of Moab 1

Bamoth-baal 1. בָּמוֹת בַּעַל
Num22:41 took Balaam and brought him up to Bamoth-ba'al; 1
Jos 13:17 Dibon, and Ba'moth-ba'al, and Beth-ba'al-me'on 1

Bani 1. בָּנִי 2. Βαανι 3. Βανι 4. Μανι
2Sm 23:36 Igal the son of Nathan of Zobah, Bani the Gadite 1
1Ch 6:46 son of Amzi, son of Bani, son of Shemer 1
9: 4 son of Ammi'hud, son of Omri, son of Imri, son of Bani 1
Ezr 2:10 sons of Bani, 642. 1
8:10 Of the sons of Bani, Shelo'mith the son 3
10:29 Of the sons of Bani were Meshul'lam, Malluch 1
34 Of the sons of Bani: Ma-ada'i, Amram, Uel 1
Neh 3:17 Levites repaired: Rehum the son of Bani; 1
8: 7 Also Jesh'ua, Bani, Sherebi'ah, Jamin, Akkub 1
9: 4 stood Jeshua, Bani, Kad'mi-el, Shebani'ah, Bunni 1
4 stood . . Bunni, Sherebi'ah, Bani, and Chena'ni; 1
5 Levites, Jeshua, Kad'mi-el, Bani, Hashabnei'ah 1
10:13 Hodi'ah, Bani, Beni'nu. 1
14 chiefs . . Parosh, Pa'hath-mo'ab, Elam, Zattu, Bani 1
11:22 overseer . . Uzzi the son of Bani 1
1Es 5:12 The sons of Chorbe, 705. The sons of Bani, 648. 3
8:36 Of the sons of Bani, Shelomith 3
9:30 Of the sons of Bani: Meshullam, Malluch, Adaiah 4
34 Of the sons of Bani: Jeremai, Maadai, Amram, Joel 2

Bannas 1. Βαννας
1Es 5:26 sons of Jeshua and Kadmiel and Bannas and Sudias 1

Baptist 1. βαπτιστής
Mat 3: 1 In those days came John the Baptist, preaching 1
11:11 has risen no one greater than John the Baptist 1
12 From the days of John the Baptist until now 1
14: 2 he said to this servants, "This is John the Baptist 1
8 she said, "Give me the head of John the Baptist 1
16:14 Some say John the Baptist, others say Eli'jah 1
17:13 he was speaking to them of John the Baptist. 1
Mrk 6:25 at once the head of John the Baptist on a platter. 1
8:28 they told him, "John the Baptist 1
Lke 7:20 John the Baptist has sent us to you, saying 1
33 For John the Baptist has come eating no bread 1
9:19 they answered, "John the Baptist 1

Bar-Jesus 1. Βαριησοῦς
Act 13: 6 a Jewish false prophet, named Bar-Jesus. 1

Bar-Jona 1. Βαριωνᾶ
Mat 16:17 Blessed are you, Simon Bar-Jona! 1

Barabbas 1. Βαραββᾶς
Mat 27:16 a notorious prisoner, called Barab'bas. 1
17 Barab'bas or Jesus who is called Christ? 1
20 elders persuaded the people to ask for Barab'bas 1
21 they said, "Barab'bas. 1
26 Then he released for them Barab'bas 1
Mrk 15: 7 there was a man called Barab'bas. 1
11 to have him release for them Barab'bas instead. 1
15 to satisfy the crowd, released for them Barab'bas; 1
Lke 23:18 release to us Barab'bas"– 1
Joh 18:40 They cried out again, "Not this man, but Barab'bas! 1
40 Now Barab'bas was a robber. 1

Barachel 1. בַּרַכְאֵל
Job 32: 2 Then Eli'hu the son of Bar'achel the Buzite 1
6 Eli'hu the son of Bar'achel the Buzite answered 1

Barachiah 1. Βαραχίας
Mat 23:35 to the blood of Zechari'ah the son of Barachi'ah 1

Barak 1. בָּרָק 2. Βαράκ
Jdg 4: 6 She sent and summoned Barak the son of Abin'o-am 1
8 Barak said to her, "If you will go with me, I will go; 1
9 Deb'orah arose, and went with Barak to Kedesh. 1
10 Barak summoned Zeb'ulun and Naph'tali to Kedesh; 1
12 Sis'era was told that Barak the son of Abin'o-am 1
14 Deb'orah said to Barak, "Up! For this is the day 1
14 So Barak went down from Mount Tabor with 10,000 1
15 all his army before Barak at the edge of the sword; 1
16 Barak pursued the chariots and the army 1
22 behold, as Barak pursued Sis'era, Ja'el went out 1
5: 1 Then sang Deb'orah and Barak the son of Abin'o-am 1
12 Arise, Barak, lead away your captives, O son 1
15 with Deb'orah, and Is'sachar faithful to Barak; 1
1Sm 12:11 the LORD sent Jerubba'al and Barak, and Jephthah 2
Heb 11:32 to tell of Gideon, Barak, Samson, Jephthah, of David 2

Bariah 1. בָּרִיחַ
1Ch 3:22 And the sons of Shemai'ah: Hattush, Igal, Bari'ah 1

Barkos 1. בַּרְקוֹס 2. Βαρχους
Ezr 2:53 sons of Barkos, the sons of Sis'era 1
Neh 7:55 sons of Barkos, the sons of Sis'era 1
1Es 5:32 the sons of Charea, the sons of Barkos 2

Barnabas 1. Βαρναβᾶς
Act 4:36 who was surnamed by the apostles Barnabas 1
9:27 Barnabas took him 1
11:22 they sent Barnabas to Antioch. 1
25 Barnabas went to Tarsus to look for Saul; •

30 by the hand of Barnabas and Saul. 1
12:25 Barnabas and Saul returned from Jerusalem 1
13: 1 Barnabas, Simeon who was called Niger 1
2 Set apart for me Barnabas and Saul 1
7 who summoned Barnabas and Saul 1
43 many Jews . . followed Paul and Barnabas 1
46 Paul and Barnabas spoke out boldly, saying 1
50 persecution against Paul and Barnabas 1
14:12 Barnabas they called Zeus 1
14 when the apostles Barnabas and Paul heard of it 1
20 on the next day he went on with Barnabas to Derbe. 1
15: 2 when Paul and Barnabas had no small dissension 1
2 Paul and Barnabas and some of the others 1
12 they listened to Barnabas and Paul 1
22 send them to Antioch with Paul and Barnabas 1
25 with our beloved Barnabas and Paul 1
35 Paul and Barnabas remained in Antioch 1
36 after some days Paul said to Barnabas, "Come 1
37 Barnabas wanted to take with them John 1
39 Barnabas took Mark with him 1
1Co 9: 6 Or is it only Barnabas and I who have no right 1
Gal 2: 1 I went up again to Jerusalem with Barnabas 1
9 gave to me and Barnabas the right hand 1
13 so that even Barnabas was carried away 1
Col 4:10 Mark the cousin of Barnabas 1

Barodis 1. Βαρωδις
1Es 5:34 the sons of Apherra, the sons of Barodis 1

Barsabbas 1. Βαρσαββᾶς
Act 1:23 Joseph called Barsab'bas, who was surnamed Justus 1
15:22 They sent Judas called Barsab'bas, and Silas 1

Bartacus 1. Βαρτακος
1Es 4:29 the daughter of the illustrious Bartacus 1

Bartholomew 1. Βαρθολομαῖος
Mat 10: 3 Philip and Bartholomew; Thomas and Matthew 1
Mrk 3:18 Andrew, and Philip, and Bartholomew, and Matthew 1
Lke 6:14 James and John, and Philip, and Bartholomew 1
Act 1:13 Philip and Thomas, Bartholomew and Matthew 1

Bartimaeus 1. Βαρτιμαῖος
Mrk 10:46 Bartimae'us, a blind beggar, the son of Timae'us 1

Baruch 1. בָּרוּךְ 2. Βαρουχ
Neh 3:20 After him Baruch the son of Zab'bai repaired 1
10: 6 Daniel, Gin'nethon, Baruch 1
11: 5 Ma-asei'ah the son of Baruch, son of Col-ho'zeh 1
Jer 32:12 and I gave the deed of purchase to Baruch 1
13 I charged Baruch in their presence, saying 1
16 After I had given the deed of purchase to Baruch 1
36: 4 Then Jeremiah called Baruch the son of Neri'ah 1
4 Baruch wrote upon a scroll 1
5 And Jeremiah ordered Baruch, saying 1
8 Baruch the son of Neri'ah did all that 1
10 Then, in the hearing of all the people, Baruch read 1
13 that he had heard, when Baruch read the scroll 1
14 to say to Baruch, "Take in your hand the scroll 1
14 Baruch the son of Neri'ah took the scroll 1
15 Baruch read it to them. 1
16 they said to Baruch, "We must report all these 1
17 Then they asked Baruch, "Tell us, how did you write 1
18 Baruch answered them, "He dictated 1
19 Then the princes said to Baruch, "Go and hide 1
26 and Shelemi'ah the son of Abdeel to seize Baruch 1
27 the scroll with the words which Baruch wrote 1
32 another scroll and gave it to Baruch the scribe 1
43: 3 Baruch the son of Neri'ah has set you against us 1
6 also Jeremiah . . and Baruch the son of Neri'ah. 1
45: 1 the prophet spoke to Baruch the son of Neri'ah 1
2 Thus says the LORD . . to you, O Baruch 1
Bar 1: 1 Baruch the son of Neraiah, son of Mahseiah 2
3 Baruch read the words of this book in the hearing 2
8 Baruch took the vessels of the house of the Lord 1

Barzillai 1. בַּרְזִלַּי 2. Βερζελλει
2Sm 17:27 and Barzil'lai the Gileadite from Ro'gelim 1
19:31 Now Barzil'lai the Gileadite had come down 1
32 Barzil'lai was a very aged man, 80 years old; 1
33 the king said to Barzil'lai, "Come over with me 1
34 But Barzil'lai said to the king, "How many years 1
39 and the king kissed Barzil'lai and blessed him 1
21: 8 to A'driel the son of Barzil'lai the Meho'lathite; 1
1Kg 2: 7 with the sons of Barzil'lai the Gileadite, and let 1
Ezr 2:61 of the sons of the priests . . sons of Barzil'lai 1
61 wife from the daughters of Barzil'lai 1
Neh 7:63 priests . . sons of Hakkoz, the sons of Barzil'lai 1
63 daughters of Barzil'lai the Gileadite 1
1Es 5:38 Agia, one of the daughters of Barzillai 2

Basemath 1. בָּשְׂמַת
Gen 26:34 Esau . . took . . Bas'emath the daughter of Elon 1
36: 3 Bas'emath, Ish'mael's daughter, the sister 1
4 Bas'emath bore Reu'el; 1
10 Reu'el the son of Bas'emath the wife of Esau. 1
13 These are the sons of Bas'emath, Esau's wife. 1
17 Edom; they are the sons of Bas'emath, Esau's wife 1
1Kg 4:15 he had taken Bas'emath the daughter of Solomon 1

Bashan 1. בָּשָׁן
Num21:33 Then they turned and went up by the way to Bashan; 1
33 Og the king of Bashan came out against them 1
32:33 Moses gave . . the kingdom of Og king of Bashan 1
Deu 1: 4 defeated . . Og the king of Bashan, who lived 1
3: 1 Then we turned and went up the way to Bashan; 1
1 Og the king of Bashan came out against us 1
3 gave into our hand Og also, the king of Bashan 1
4 region of Argob, the kingdom of Og in Bashan. 1
10 tableland and all Gilead and all Bashan, as far 1
10 cities of the kingdom of Og in Bashan. 1
11 For only Og the king of Bashan was left 1
13 rest of Gilead, and all Bashan, the kingdom of Og 1
13 whole of that Bashan is called the land of Reph'aim. 1
14 all the region of Argob, that is, Bashan 1
4:43 Gadites, and Golan in Bashan for the Manas'sites. 1
47 possession of . . the land of Og the king of Bashan 1
29: 7 Sihon . . of Heshbon and Og the king of Bashan 1
32:14 fat of lambs and rams, herds of Bashan and goats 1
33:22 Dan is a lion's whelp, that leaps forth from Bashan. 1
Jos 9:10 Sihon the king of Heshbon, and Og king of Bashan 1
12: 4 and Og king of Bashan, one of the . . Reph'aim 1
5 and all Bashan to the boundary of the Gesh'urites 1
13:11 and all Mount Hermon, and all Bashan to Sal'ecah; 1
12 all the kingdom of Og in Bashan 1
30 extended from Mahana'im, through all Bashan 1
30 all Bashan, the whole kingdom of Og king of Bashan 1
30 all Bashan . . and all the towns of Ja'ir 1
31 the cities of the kingdom of Og in Bashan; 1
17: 1 To Machir . . were allotted Gilead and Bashan 1
5 ten . . besides the land of Gilead and Bashan 1
20: 8 appointed . . and Golan in Bashan, from the tribe 1
21: 6 and from the half-tribe of Manas'seh in Bashan 1
27 given . . Golan in Bashan with its pasture lands 1
22: 7 Moses had given a possession in Bashan; 1
1Kg 4:13 he had the region of Argob, which is in Bashan 1
19 Gilead, the country . . and of Og king of Bashan. 1
2Kg 10:33 from Aro'er . . that is, Gilead and Bashan. 1
1Ch 5:11 in the land of Bashan as far as Sal'ecah 1
12 Jo'el . . Shapham . . Ja'nai, and Shaphat in Bashan. 1
16 they dwelt in Gilead, in Bashan and in its towns 1
23 were very numerous from Bashan to Ba'al-her'mon 1
6:62 tribes of . . Naph'tali, and Manas'seh in Bashan. 1
71 given . . Golan in Bashan with its pasture lands 1
Neh 9:22 possession of . . the land of Og king of Bashan. 1
Ps 22:12 strong bulls of Bashan surround me; 1
68:15 O mighty mountain, mountain of Bashan; 1
15 O many-peaked mountain, mountain of Bashan! 1
22 The Lord said, "I will bring them back from Bashan 1
135:11 Sihon, king of the Amorites, and Og, king of Bashan 1
136:20 Og, king of Bashan, for his steadfast love endures 1
Isa 2:13 cedars . . and against all the oaks of Bashan; 1
33: 9 and Bashan and Carmel shake off their leaves. 1
Jer 22:20 cry out, and lift up your voice in Bashan; 1
50:19 and he shall feed on Carmel and in Bashan 1
Ezk 27: 6 Of oaks of Bashan they made your oars; 1
39:18 of bulls, all of them fatlings of Bashan. 1
Ams 4: 1 Hear this word, you cows of Bashan 1
Mic 7:14 let them feed in Bashan and Gilead 1
Nah 1: 4 Bashan and Carmel wither 1
Zec 11: 2 Wail, oaks of Bashan 1

Baskama 1. Βασκαμα
1Mc 13:23 When he approached Baskama, he killed Jonathan 1

Bath-rabbim 1. בַּת רַבִּים
Sng 7: 4 eyes are pools . . by the gate of Bath-rab'bim. 1

Bath-shua 1. בַּת שׁוּעַ
1Ch 2: 3 these three Bath-shu'a the Canaanitess bore 1
3: 5 Bath-shu'a, the daughter of Am'mi-el; 1

Bathsheba 1. בַּת שֶׁבַע
2Sm 11: 3 Is not this Bathshe'ba, the daughter of Eli'am 1
12:24 Then David comforted his wife, Bathshe'ba 1
1Kg 1:11 Nathan said to Bathshe'ba the mother of Solomon 1
15 So Bathshe'ba went to the king into his chamber 1
16 Bathshe'ba bowed and did obeisance to the king 1
28 King David answered, "Call Bathshe'ba to me." So she 1
31 Bathshe'ba bowed . . and did obeisance 1
2:13 came to Bathshe'ba the mother of Solomon. 1
18 Bathshe'ba said, "Very well; I will speak for you 1
19 Bathshe'ba went to King Solomon, to speak to him 1
Ps 51: 0 came to him, after he had gone in to Bathsheba. 1

Bavvai 1. בַּוַּי
Neh 3:18 brethren repaired: Bav'vai the son of Hen'adad 1

Bazlith 1. בַּצְלִית
Neh 7:54 sons of Bazlith, the sons of Mehi'da 1

Bazluth 1. בַּצְלוּת 2. Βασαλωθ
Ezr 2:52 sons of Bazluth, the sons of Mehi'da 1
1Es 5:31 the sons of Pharakim, the sons of Bazluth 2

Bealiah 1. בְּעַלְיָה
1Ch 12: 5 Beali'ah, Shemari'ah, Shephati'ah the Har'uphite; 1

Bealoth 1. בְּעָלוֹת
Jos 15:24 Ziph, Telem, Be-a'loth 1
1Kg 4:16 Ba'ana the son of Hushai, in Asher and Bealoth; 1

Bear 1. עַיִשׁ
Job 9: 9 who made the Bear and Orion, the Plei'ades 1
38:32 or can you guide the Bear with its children? 1

Bebai 1. בֵּבַי 2. Βηβαι
Ezr 2:11 sons of Be'bai, 623. 1
8:11 Of the sons of Be'bai, Zechari'ah, the son of Be'bai 1
11 Of the sons of Be'bai, Zechari'ah, the son of Be'bai 1
10:28 Of the sons of Be'bai were Jehoha'nan, Hanani'ah 1
Neh 7:16 sons of Be'bai, 628. 1
10:15 Bunni, Azgad, Be'bai 1
1Es 5:13 The sons of Bebai, 623 The sons of Azgad, 1,322 2
8:37 Of the sons of Bebai, Zechariah the son of Bebai 2
37 Of the sons of Bebai, Zechariah the son of Bebai 2
9:29 Of the sons of Bebai: Jehohanan and Hananiah 2
Jdt 15: 4 Betomasthaim and Bebai and Choba and Kola 2

Becher 1. בֶּכֶר
Gen 46:21 the sons of Benjamin: Bela, Becher, Ashbel, Gera 1
Num26:35 of Becher, the family of the Bech'erites; 1
1Ch 7: 6 sons of Benjamin: Bela, Becher, and Jedi'a-el, three. 1
8 The sons of Becher: Zemi'rah, Jo'ash, Elie'zer 1
8 All these were the sons of Becher; 1

Becherite 1. בַּכְרִי
Num26:35 of Becher, the family of the Bech'erites; 1

Becorath 1. בְּכוֹרַת
1Sm 9: 1 son of Zeror, son of Beco'rath, son of Aphi'ah 1

Bectileth 1. Βεκτιλεθ
Jdt 2:21 from Nineveh to the plain of Bectileth 1
21 camped opposite Bectileth 1

Bedad 1. בְּדַד
Gen 36:35 Hadad the son of Bedad, who defeated Mid'ian 1
1Ch 1:46 When Husham died, Hadad the son of Bedad 1

Bedan 1. בְּדָן
1Ch 7:17 The sons of Ulam: Bedan. 1

Bedeiah 1. בֵּדְיָה 2. Πεδιας
Ezr 10:35 Benai'ah, Bedei'ah, Chel'uhi 1
1Es 9:34 Mamdai and Bedeiah and Vaniah 2

Beeliada 1. בְּעֶלְיָדָע
1Ch 14: 7 Eli'shama, Beeli'ada, and Eliph'elet. 1

Beelzebul 1. Βεελζεβούλ
Mat 10:25 called the master of the house Be-el'zebul 1
12:24 It is only by Be-el'zebul, the prince of demons 1
27 if I cast out demons by Be-el'zebul 1
Mrk 3:22 He is possessed by Be-el'zebul 1
Lke 11:15 He casts out demons by Be-el'zebul 1
18 you say that I cast out demons by Be-el'zebul. 1
19 if I cast out demons by Be-el'zebul 1

Beer 1. בְּאֵר
Num21:16 from there they continued to Beer; 1
Jdg 9:21 Jotham . . fled, and went to Beer and dwelt there 1

Beer-elim 1. בְּאֵר אֵילִים
Isa 15: 8 to Egla'im, the wailing reaches to Beer-e'lim. 1

Beer-lahai-roi 1. בְּאֵר לַחַי רֹאִי
Gen 16:14 Therefore the well was called Beer-la'hai-roi; 1
24:62 Now Isaac had come from Beer-la'hai-roi 1
25:11 And Isaac dwelt at Beer-la'hai-roi. 1

Beer-sheba 1. בְּאֵר שֶׁבַע
Gen 21:14 wandered in the wilderness of Beer-sheba. 1
31 Therefore that place was called Beer-sheba; 1
32 they made a covenant at Beer-sheba, 1
33 Abraham planted a tamarisk tree in Beer-sheba 1
22:19 they arose and went together to Beer-sheba; 1
19 and Abraham dwelt at Beer-sheba. 1
26:23 From there he went up to Beer-sheba. 1
33 name of the city is Beer-sheba to this day. 1
28:10 Jacob left Beer-sheba, and went toward Haran. 1
46: 1 Israel . . came to Beer-sheba, and offered 1
5 Then Jacob set out from Beer-sheba; 1
Jos 15:28 Hazar-shu'al, Beer-sheba, Biziothi'ah 1
19: 2 And it had for its inheritance Beer-sheba 1
Jdg 20: 1 people of Israel came out, from Dan to Beer-sheba 1
1Sm 3:20 And all Israel from Dan to Beer-sheba knew that 1
8: 2 Jo'el . . Abi'jah; they were judges in Beer-sheba. 1
2Sm 3:10 over Israel and . . Judah, from Dan to Beer-sheba. 1
17:11 all Israel be gathered . . from Dan to Beer-sheba 1
24: 2 all the tribes of Israel, from Dan to Beer-sheba 1
7 they went out to the Negeb of Judah at Beer-sheba. 1
15 died . . from Dan to Beer-sheba 70,000 men. 1
1Kg 4:25 Judah and Israel . . from Dan even to Beer-sheba 1
19: 3 and he arose and went . . and came to Beer-sheba 1
2Kg 12: 1 His mother's name was Zib'iah of Beer-sheba. 1

23: 8 the high places . . from Geba to Beer-sheba; 1
1Ch 4:28 They dwelt in Beer-sheba, Mola'dah, Ha'zar-shu'al 1
21: 2 Go, number Israel, from Beer-sheba to Dan 1
2Ch 19: 4 from Beer-sheba to the hill country of E'phraim 1
24: 1 his mother's name was Zib'iah of Beer-sheba. 1
30: 5 throughout all Israel, from Beer-sheba to Dan 1
Neh 11:27 in Ha'zar-shu'al, in Beer-sheba and its villages 1
30 from Beer-sheba to the valley of Hinnom. 1
Ams 5: 5 not enter into Gilgal or cross over to Beer-sheba; 1
8:14 O Dan,' and, 'As the way of Beer-sheba lives,' 1

Beera 1. בְּאֵרָא

1Ch 7:37 Bezer, Hod, Shamma, Shilshah, Ithran, and Be-e'ra. 1

Beerah 1. בְּאֵרָה

1Ch 5: 6 Be-er'ah his son . . chieftain of the Reubenites. 1

Beeri 1. בְּאֵרִי

Gen 26:34 Judith the daughter of Be-e'ri the Hittite 1
Hos 1: 1 The word . . that came to Hose'a the son of Be-e'ri 1

Beeroth 1. בְּאֵרוֹת 2. בְּאֵרֹתִי 3. Βηρωτ

Jos 9:17 Chephi'rah, Be-er'oth, and Kir'iath-je'arim. 1
18:25 Gibeon, Ramah, Be-er'oth 1
2Sm 4: 2 sons of Rimmon a man of Benjamin from Be-er'oth 2
2 for Be-er'oth also is reckoned to Benjamin; 1
23:37 Na'harai of Be-er'oth, the armor-bearer of Jo'ab 2
1Ch 11:39 Na'harai of Be-er'oth, the armor-bearer of Jo'ab 2
Ezr 2:25 sons of Kir'iathar'im . . and Be-er'oth, 743. 1
Neh 7:29 men of . . Chephi'rah, and Be-er'oth, 743 1
1Es 5:19 The men of Chephirah and Beeroth, 743 3

Beeroth Bene-jaakan 1. בְּאֵרֹת בְּנֵי־יַעֲקָן

Deu 10: 6 Israel journeyed from Be-er'oth Bene-ja'akan 1

Beerothite 1. בְּאֵרֹתִי

2Sm 4: 3 the Be-er'othites fled to Gitta'im 1
5 sons of Rimmon the Be-er'othite, Rechab and Ba'anah 1
9 answered . . the sons of Rimmon the Be-er'othite 1

Beeshterah 1. בְּעֶשְׁתְּרָה

Jos 21:27 Golan . . and Beesh'terah with its pasture 1

Behemoth 1. בְּהֵמוֹת 2. Enoch

Job 40:15 Behold, Be'hemoth, which I made as I made you; 1
2Es 6:49 the name of one thou didst call Behemoth 2
51 thou didst give Behemoth one of the parts 2

Bel 1. בֵּל 2. Βηλ

Isa 46: 1 Bel bows down, Nebo stoops 1
Jer 50: 2 and say: 'Babylon is taken, Bel is put to shame 1
51:44 I will punish Bel in Babylon 1
LJr 1:41 they bring him and pray Bel that the man may speak 2
41 as though Bel were able to understand. •
Bel 1: 3 Now the Babylonians had an idol called Bel 2
5 the king said to him, "Why do you not worship Bel? 2
6 Do you not think that Bel is a living God? 2
9 if you prove that Bel is eating them 2
9 because he blasphemed against Bel 2
10 Now there were 70 priests of Bel 2
10 the king went with Daniel into the temple of Bel. 2
11 the priests of Bel said, "Behold 2
12 if you do not find that Bel has eaten it all 2
14 the king set forth the food for Bel 2
18 You are great, O Bel; and with you there is no deceit 2
22 and gave Bel over to Daniel 2
28 he has destroyed Bel, and slain the dragon 2

Bela 1. בֶּלַע

Gen 14: 2 of Zeboi'im, and the king of Bela (that is, Zo'ar). 1
8 of Zeboi'im, and the king of Bela (that is, Zo'ar) 1
36:32 Bela the son of Be'or reigned in Edom 1
33 Bela died, and Jobab the son of Zerah of Bozrah 1
46:21 the sons of Benjamin: Bela, Becher, Ashbel, Gera 1
Num26:38 of Bela, the family of the Be'la-ites; 1
40 the sons of Bela were Ard and Na'aman 1
1Ch 1:43 Bela the son of Be'or . . whose city was Din'habah 1
44 When Bela died, Jobab the son of Zerah of Bozrah 1
5: 8 Bela the son of Azaz, son of Shema, son of Jo'el 1
7: 6 sons of Benjamin: Bela, Becher, and Jedi'a-el, three. 1
7 sons of Bela: Ezbon, Uzzi, Uz'ziel, Jer'imoth, and Iri 1
8: 1 Benjamin was the father of Bela his first-born 1
3 Bela had sons: Addar, Gera, Abi'hud 1

Belaite 1. בַּלְעִי

Num26:38 of Bela, the family of the Be'la-ites; 1

Belial 1. Βελιάλ

2Co 6:15 What accord has Christ with Be'lial? 1

Belmain 1. Βαιλμαιν

Jdt 4: 4 Kona and Beth-horon and Belmain and Jericho 1

Belnuus 1. Βαλνουος

1Es 9:31 Bescaspasmys and Sesthel, and Belnuus 1

Belshazzar 1. בֵּלְאשַׁצַּר 2. בֵּלְשַׁאצַּר (A) 3. Βαλτασαρ

Dan 5: 1 King Belshaz'zar made a great feast 2
2 Belshaz'zar, when he tasted the wine, 2
9 Then King Belshaz'zar was greatly alarmed 2
22 his son, Belshaz'zar, have not humbled your heart 2
29 Belshaz'zar commanded, and Daniel was clothed 2
30 night Belshaz'zar the Chalde'an king was slain. 2
7: 1 In the first year of Belshaz'zar king of Babylon 2
8: 1 third year of the reign of King Belshaz'zar 1
Bar 1:11 pray . . for the life of Belshazzar his son 3
12 under the protection of Belshazzar his son 3

Belteshazzar 1. בֵּלְטְשַׁאצַּר 2. בֵּלְטְשַׁאצַּר (A)

Dan 1: 7 Daniel he called Belteshaz'zar 1
2:26 king said to Daniel, whose name was Belteshaz'zar 2
4: 8 Daniel . . named Belteshaz'zar after the name 2
9 O Belteshaz'zar, chief of the magicians 2
18 you, O Belteshaz'zar, declare the interpretation 2
19 Daniel, whose name was Belteshaz'zar 2
19 king said, "Belteshaz'zar, let not the dream 2
19 Belteshaz'zar answered, "My lord, may the dream 2
5:12 this Daniel, whom the king named Belteshaz'zar. 2
10: 1 revealed to Daniel, who was named Belteshaz'zar. 1

Beltethmus 1. Βεελτεθμος

1Es 2:16 Bishlam, Mithridates, Tabeel, Rehum, Beltethmus 1
25 Rehum the recorder and Beltethmus and Shimshai 1

Ben-abinadab 1. בֶּן אֲבִינָדָב

1Kg 4:11 Ben-abin'adab, in all Naphath-dor (he had Taphath 1

Ben-ammi 1. בֶּן עַמִּי

Gen 19:38 bore a son, and called his name Ben-ammi; 1

Ben-deker 1. בֶּן דֶּקֶר

1Kg 4: 9 Ben-deker, in Makaz, Shaal'bim, Beth-she'mesh 1

Ben-geber 1. בֶּן גֶּבֶר

1Kg 4:13 Ben-geber, in Ra'moth-gil'ead (he had the villages 1

Ben-hadad 1. בֶּן הֲדַד

1Kg 15:18 Asa sent them to Ben-ha'dad the son of Tabrim'mon 1
20 Ben-ha'dad hearkened to King Asa 1
20: 1 Ben-ha'dad the king of Syria gathered . . his army 1
2 Thus says Ben-ha'dad 1
5 Thus says Ben-ha'dad: 'I sent to you, saying 1
9 So he said to the messengers of Ben-ha'dad 1
10 Ben-ha'dad sent to him and said 1
12 When Ben-ha'dad heard this message . . he said •
16 Ben-ha'dad was drinking himself drunk 1
17 Ben-ha'dad sent out scouts, and they reported 1
20 Ben-ha'dad . . escaped on a horse with horsemen. 1
26 Ben-ha'dad mustered the Syrians, and went up 1
30 Ben-ha'dad also fled, and entered an inner chamber 1
32 Your servant Ben-ha'dad says, 'Pray, let me live.' 1
33 took it up . . and said, "Yes, your brother Ben-ha'dad. 1
33 and bring him." Then Ben-ha'dad came forth to him; 1
34 And Ben-ha'dad said to him, "The cities •
2Kg 6:24 Ben-ha'dad king of Syria mustered his entire army 1
8: 7 Ben-ha'dad the king of Syria was sick; 1
9 Your son Ben-ha'dad king of Syria has sent me to you 1
13: 3 gave them continually . . into the hand of Ben-ha'dad 1
24 When Haz'ael . . died, Ben-ha'dad his son became king 1
25 Jeho'ash . . took again from Ben-ha'dad the son 1
2Ch 16: 2 sent them to Ben-ha'dad king of Syria 1
4 Ben-ha'dad hearkened to King Asa 1
Jer 49:27 it shall devour the strongholds of Ben-ha'dad. 1
Ams 1: 4 it shall devour the strongholds of Ben-ha'dad. 1

Ben-hail 1. בֶּן חַיִל

2Ch 17: 7 he sent his princes, Ben-hail, Obadi'ah, Zechari'ah 1

Ben-hanan 1. בֶּן חָנָן

1Ch 4:20 sons of Shimon: Amnon, Rinnah, Ben-ha'nan, 1

Ben-hesed 1. בֶּן חֶסֶד

1Kg 4:10 Ben-hesed, in Arub'both 1

Ben-hur 1. בֶּן חוּר

1Kg 4: 8 names: Ben-hur, in the hill country of E'phraim; 1

Ben-oni 1. בֶּן אוֹנִי

Gen 35:18 she called his name Ben-o'ni; 1

Ben-zoheth 1. בֶּן זוֹחֵת

1Ch 4:20 The sons of Ishi: Zoheth and Ben-zo'heth. 1

Benaiah 1. בְּנָיָהוּ 2. Βαναιας

2Sm 8:18 Benai'ah the son of Jehoi'ada was over 1
20:23 Benai'ah . . was in command of the Cher'ethites 1
23:20 Benai'ah the son of Jehoi'ada was a valiant man 1
21 but Benai'ah went down to him with a staff •
22 These things did Benai'ah the son of Jehoi'ada 1
30 Benai'ah of Pira'thon, Hid'dai of the brooks 1
1Kg 1: 8 Zadok the priest, and Benai'ah the son of Jehoi'ada 1
10 but he did not invite Nathan . . or Benai'ah 1
26 Zadok the priest, and Benai'ah the son of Jehoi'ada 1
32 the prophet, and Benai'ah the son of Jehoi'ada." So 1
36 Benai'ah the son of Jehoi'ada answered the king 1
38 and Benai'ah the son of Jehoi'ada 1
44 Nathan . . and Benai'ah the son of Jehoi'ada 1
2:25 So King Solomon sent Benai'ah the son of Jehoi'ada; 1
29 Solomon sent Benai'ah the son of Jehoi'ada, saying 1
30 Benai'ah came to the tent of the LORD, and said 1
30 Benai'ah brought the king word again, saying, "Thus 1
34 Benai'ah the son of Jehoi'ada went up, and struck 1
35 king put Benai'ah the son of Jehoi'ada over 1
46 the king commanded Benai'ah the son of Jehoi'ada; 1
4: 4 Benai'ah the son of Jehoi'ada was in command 1
1Ch 4:36 Asai'ah, Ad'i-el, Jesim'iel, Benai'ah 1
11:22 Benai'ah . . was a valiant man of Kabzeel 1
23 but Benai'ah went down to him with a staff •
24 These things did Benai'ah the son of Jehoi'ada 1
31 Benai'ah of Pira'thon 1
15:18 Eli'ab, Benai'ah, Ma-asei'ah, Mattithi'ah, 1
20 Jehi'el, Unni, Eli'ab, Ma-asei'ah, and Benai'ah 1
24 Ama'sai, Zechari'ah, Benai'ah, and Elie'zer 1
16: 5 second to him . . Benai'ah, O'bed-e'dom, and Je-i'el 1
6 Benai'ah and Jaha'ziel the priests were to blow 1
18:17 Benai'ah . . was over the Cher'ethites 1
27: 5 The third commander . . was Benai'ah, 1
6 Benai'ah who was a mighty man of the 30 1
14 Eleventh . . was Benai'ah of Pira'thon 1
34 was succeeded by Jehoi'ada the son of Benai'ah 1
2Ch 20:14 Jaha'ziel the son of Zechari'ah, son of Benai'ah 1
31:13 Ismachi'ah, Mahath, and Benai'ah were overseers 1
Ezr 10:25 of Parosh . . Elea'zar, Hashabi'ah, and Benai'ah. 1
30 of Pa'hath-mo'ab: Adna, Chelal, Benai'ah, Ma-asei'ah 1
35 Benai'ah, Bedei'ah, Chel'uhi 1
43 of Nebo . . Zebi'na, Jaddai, Jo'el, and Benai'ah. 1
Ezk 11: 1 the son of Azzur, and Pelati'ah the son of Benai'ah 1
13 Pelati'ah the son of Benai'ah died. 1
1Es 9:26 Mijamin, and Eleazar, and Asibias, and Benaiah 2
35 Mattithiah, Zabad, Iddo, Joel, Benaiah. 2

Bene-berak 1. בְּנֵי בְרַק

Jos 19:45 Jehud, Bene-be'rak, Gath-rim'mon 1

Bene-jaakan 1. בְּנֵי יַעֲקָן

Num33:31 from Mose'roth, and encamped at Bene-ja'akan. 1
32 set out from Bene-ja'akan, and encamped 1

Beninu 1. בְּנִינוּ

Neh 10:13 Hodi'ah, Bani, Beni'nu. 1

Benjamin 1. בִּנְיָמִן בְּנֵי בִנְיָמִן 2. בִּנְיָמִין 3. יְמִינִי 4. Βενιαμίν

Gen 35:18 Ben-o'ni; but his father called his name Benjamin 2
24 The sons of Rachel: Joseph and Benjamin. 2
42: 4 Jacob did not send Benjamin, Joseph's brother 2
36 is no more, and now you would take Benjamin; 2
43:14 may send back your other brother and Benjamin. 2
15 took double the money with them, and Benjamin; 2
16 When Joseph saw Benjamin with them, he said 2
29 and saw his brother Benjamin, his mother's son 2
34 but Benjamin's portion was five times as much 2
44:12 and the cup was found in Benjamin's sack. 2
45:12 eyes of my brother Benjamin see, that it is my 2
14 he fell upon his brother Benjamin's neck and wept 2
14 and Benjamin wept upon his neck. 2
22 but to Benjamin he gave 300 shekels of silver 2
46:19 of Rachel, Jacob's wife: Joseph and Benjamin. 2
21 the sons of Benjamin: Bela, Becher, Ashbel, Gera 2
49:27 Benjamin is a ravenous wolf 2
Exd 1: 3 Is'sachar, Zeb'ulun, and Benjamin 2
Num 1:11 from Benjamin, Abi'dan the son of Gideo'ni; 2
36 Of the people of Benjamin, their generations 2
37 the number of the tribe of Benjamin was 35,400 2
2:22 Then the tribe of Benjamin, the leader 2
22 leader of the people of Benjamin being Abi'dan 2
7:60 Abi'dan the . . leader of the men of Benjamin 2
10:24 over the host of the tribe of the men of Benjamin 2
13: 9 from the tribe of Benjamin, Palti the son of Raphu; 2
26:38 sons of Benjamin according to their families 2
41 sons of Benjamin according to their families; 2
34:21 Of the tribe of Benjamin, Eli'dad 2
Deu 27:12 stand upon Mount Ger'izim . . Joseph, and Benjamin. 2
33:12 Of Benjamin he said, "The beloved of the LORD 2
Jos 18:11 The lot of the tribe of Benjamin . . came up 2
20 This is the inheritance of the tribe of Benjamin 2
21 Now the cities of the tribe of Benjamin 1
28 This is the inheritance of the tribe of Benjamin 2
21: 4 from the tribes of Judah, Simeon, and Benjamin 2
17 then out of the tribe of Benjamin, Gibeon 2
Jdg 1:21 the people of Benjamin did not drive out 2
21 have dwelt with the people of Benjamin 2
5:14 following you, Benjamin, with your kinsmen; 2
10: 9 to fight . . against Judah and against Benjamin 2
19:14 on them near Gib'e-ah, which belongs to Benjamin 2
20: 4 I came to Gib'e-ah that belongs to Benjamin 2
10 that . . they may requite Gib'e-ah of Benjamin 2
12 sent men through all the tribe of Benjamin 2
17 the men of Israel, apart from Benjamin, mustered 2
20 Israel went out to battle against Benjamin; 2
25 Benjamin went against them out of Gib'e-ah 2
35 the LORD defeated Benjamin before Israel; 2
35 Israel destroyed 25,100 men of Benjamin that day 2
36 The men of Israel gave ground to Benjamin 2
39 Benjamin had begun to smite and kill about 2
41 the men of Benjamin were dismayed, for they saw 2

44 18,000 men of Benjamin fell, all of them men 2
46 all who fell that day of Benjamin were 25,000 men 2
21: 1 give his daughter in marriage to Benjamin. 2
6 had compassion for Benjamin their brother 2
14 Benjamin returned at that time; and they gave 2
15 the people had compassion on Benjamin 2
16 since the women are destroyed out of Benjamin? 2
17 an inheritance for the survivors of Benjamin 2
18 sworn, "Cursed be he who gives a wife to Benjamin. 2
21 and go to the land of Benjamin. 2
1Sm 4:12 A man of Benjamin ran from the battle line 2
9: 1 There was a man of Benjamin whose name was Kish 2
4 Then they passed through the land of Benjamin 3
16 I will send to you a man from the land of Benjamin 2
21 of all the families of the tribe of Benjamin? 2
10: 2 tomb in the territory of Benjamin at Zelzah 2
20 and the tribe of Benjamin was taken by lot. 2
21 He brought the tribe of Benjamin near 2
13: 2 1,000 were . . in Gib'e-ah of Benjamin; 2
15 and went up from Gilgal to Gib'e-ah of Benjamin. 2
16 Saul, and Jonathan . . stayed in Geba of Benjamin; 2
14:16 watchmen of Saul in Gib'e-ah of Benjamin looked; 2
2Sm 2: 9 Jezreel and E'phraim and Benjamin and . . Israel. 2
15 twelve for Benjamin and Ish-bo'sheth 2
31 servants . . had slain of Benjamin 360 of Abner's men. 2
3:19 Abner also spoke to Benjamin; and then Abner went 2
19 Israel and the whole house of Benjamin thought 2
4: 2 sons of Rimmon a man of Benjamin from Be-er'oth 2
2 for Be-er'oth also is reckoned to Benjamin; 2
19:17 and with him were 1,000 men from Benjamin. 2
21:14 they buried the bones . . in the land of Benjamin 2
1Kg 4:18 Shim'e-i the son of Ela, in Benjamin; 2
12:21 all the house of Judah, and the tribe of Benjamin 2
23 Say to . . all the house of Judah and Benjamin 2
15:22 King Asa built Geba of Benjamin and Mizpah. 2
1Ch 2: 2 Dan, Joseph, Benjamin, Naph'tali, Gad, and Asher. 2
6:60 from the tribe of Benjamin, Geba 2
65 out of the tribes of Judah, Simeon, and Benjamin 2
7: 6 sons of Benjamin: Bela, Becher, and Jedi'a-el, three. 2
10 sons of Bilhan: Je'ush, Benjamin, Ehud, Chena'anah 2
8: 1 Benjamin was the father of Bela his first-born 2
9: 3 some of the people of Judah, Benjamin, E'phraim 2
12:16 some of the men of Benjamin and Judah 2
21: 6 not include Levi and Benjamin in the numbering 2
27:21 for Benjamin, Ja-a'si-el the son of Abner; 2
2Ch 11: 1 he assembled the house of Judah, and Benjamin 2
3 Say . . to all Israel in Judah and Benjamin 2
10 cities which are in Judah and in Benjamin. 2
12 strong. So he held Judah and Benjamin. 2
23 through all the districts of Judah and Benjamin 2
14: 8 280,000 men from Benjamin,that carried shields 2
15: 2 Hear me, Asa, and all Judah and Benjamin 2
8 from all the land of Judah and Benjamin 2
9 he gathered all Judah and Benjamin 2
17:17 Of Benjamin: Eli'ada, a mighty man of valor 2
25: 5 under commanders . . for all Judah and Benjamin. 2
31: 1 throughout all Judah and Benjamin 2
34: 9 collected . . from all Judah and Benjamin 2
32 all . . present in Jerusalem and in Benjamin 2
Ezr 1: 5 heads of the fathers' houses of . . Benjamin 2
4: 1 Now when the adversaries of Judah and Benjamin 2
10: 9 Then all the men of Judah and Benjamin assembled 2
32 Benjamin, Malluch, and Shemari'ah. 2
Neh 3:23 Benjamin . . repaired opposite their house. 2
11: 4 Jerusalem lived certain . . of the sons of Benjamin. 2
7 these are the sons of Benjamin: Sallu the son 2
31 people of Benjamin also lived from Geba onward 2
36 Levites in Judah were joined to Benjamin. 2
12:34 Judah, Benjamin, Shemai'ah, and Jeremiah 2
Ps 68:27 There is Benjamin, the least of them, in the lead 2
80: 2 before E'phraim and Benjamin and Manas'seh! 2
Jer 1: 1 who were in An'athoth in the land of Benjamin 2
6: 1 Flee for safety, O people of Benjamin 2
17:26 from the land of Benjamin, from the Shephe'lah 2
32: 8 which is at An'athoth in the land of Benjamin 2
44 and sealed and witnessed, in the land of Benjamin 2
33:13 the cities of the Negeb, in the land of Benjamin 2
37:12 from Jerusalem to go to the land of Benjamin 2
Ezk 48:22 of Judah and the territory of Benjamin. 2
23 the east side to the west, Benjamin, one portion. 2
24 Adjoining the territory of Benjamin 2
32 the gate of Benjamin, and the gate of Dan. 2
Hos 5: 8 Sound the alarm at Beth-a'ven; tremble, O Benjamin! 2
Obd 1:19 and Benjamin shall possess Gilead. 2
Act 13:21 Saul the son of Kish, a man of the tribe of Benjamin 4
Rom11: 1 I myself am . . a member of the tribe of Benjamin. 4
Php 3: 5 of the people of Israel, of the tribe of Benjamin 4
Rev 7: 8 12,000 sealed out of the tribe of Benjamin. 4
1Es 2: 8 the tribes of Judah and Benjamin 4
5:66 the enemies of the tribe of Judah and Benjamin 4
9: 5 the men of the tribe of Judah and Benjamin 4
AEs 11: 2 Mordecai . . of the tribe of Benjamin 4
2Mc 3: 4 a man named Simon, of the tribe of Benjamin 4

Benjamin Gate 1. שַׁעַר בִּנְיָמִן
Jer 17:19 Go and stand in the Benjamin Gate •
20: 2 the upper Benjamin Gate of the house of the LORD. 1
37:13 When he was at the Benjamin Gate 1
38: 7 the king was sitting in the Benjamin Gate 1

Gate of Benjamin 1. שַׁעַר בִּנְיָמִן
Zec 14:10 aloft upon its site from the Gate of Benjamin 1

Benjaminite 1. אִישׁ יְמִינִי 2. בֶּן אִישׁ יְמִינִי 3. בֶּן בִּנְיָמִן 4. בִּנְיָמִן 5. בֶּן יְמִינִי
Jdg 3:15 a deliverer, Ehud, the son of Gera, the Benjaminite 5
19:16 Gib'e-ah; the men of the place were Benjaminites 5
20: 3 Now the Benjaminites heard that the people 3
13 the Benjaminites would not listen to the voice 3
14 the Benjaminites came together . . to go out 3
15 the Benjaminites mustered out of their cities 3
18 go up first to battle against the Benjaminites? 3
21 The Benjaminites came out of Gib'e-ah 3
23 battle against our brethren the Benjaminites? 3
24 Israel came near against the Benjaminites 3
28 battle against our brethren the Benjaminites 3
30 Israel went up against the Benjaminites 3
31 the Benjaminites went out against the people 3
32 the Benjaminites said, "They are routed before us 3
34 the Benjaminites did not know that disaster was •
36 the Benjaminites saw that they were defeated. 3
40 the Benjaminites looked behind them; and behold 4
43 Cutting down the Benjaminites, they pursued 4
48 Israel turned back against the Benjaminites 3
21:13 congregation sent word to the Benjaminites 3
20 they commanded the Benjaminites, saying, "Go 3
23 the Benjaminites did so, and took their wives 3
1Sm 9: 1 name was Kish . . a Benjaminite, a man of wealth; 2
21 Am I not a Benjaminite . . ? Why then have you spoken 5
22: 7 Saul said . . "Hear now, you Benjaminites; 5
2Sm 2:25 And the Benjaminites gathered . . behind Abner 3
16:11 how much more now may this Benjaminite! 5
19:16 Shim'e-i the son of Gera, the Benjaminite 5
20: 1 name was Sheba, the son of Bichri, a Benjaminite; 1
23:29 the son of Ri'bai of Gib'e-ah of the Benjaminites. 3
1Kg 2: 8 Shim'e-i . . the Benjaminite from Bahu'rim, who 5
1Ch 8:40 All these were Benjaminites. 4
9: 7 Of the Benjaminites: Sallu the son of Meshul'lam 4
11:31 son of Ribai of Gib'e-ah of the Benjaminites 4
12: 2 they were Benjaminites, Saul's kinsmen. 4
29 Of the Benjaminites, the kinsmen of Saul, 3,000 4
27:12 Ninth . . was Abi-e'zer of An'athoth, a Benjaminite; 5
Est 2: 5 Mor'decai . . son of Kish, a Benjaminite 1
Ps 7: 0 sang to the LORD concerning Cush a Benjaminite. 5

Beno 1. בְּנוֹ
1Ch 24:26 The sons of Ja-azi'ah: Beno. 1
27 of Ja-azi'ah, Beno, Shoham, Zaccur, and Ibri. 1

Beon 1. בְּעֹן
Num32: 3 Nimrah, Heshbon, Elea'leh, Sebam, Nebo, and Be'on 1

Beor 1. בְּעוֹר 2. Βεώρ
Gen 36:32 Bela the son of Be'or reigned in Edom 1
Num22: 5 sent messengers to Balaam the son of Be'or 1
24: 3 oracle of Balaam the sons of Be'or 1
15 The oracle of Balaam the son of Be'or 1
31: 8 also slew Balaam the son of Be'or with the sword. 1
Deu 23: 4 hired . . Balaam the son of Be'or from Pethor 1
Jos 13:22 Balaam also, the son of Be'or, the soothsayer 1
24: 9 and invited Balaam the son of Be'or to curse you 1
1Ch 1:43 son of Be'or, the name of whose city was Din'habah 1
Mic 6: 5 and what Balaam the son of Be'or answered him 1
2Pe 2:15 the way of Balaam, the son of Be'or 2

Bera 1. בֶּרַע
Gen 14: 2 these kings made war with Bera king of Sodom 1

Beracah 1. בְּרָכָה
1Ch 12: 3 Ber'acah, Jehu of An'athoth 1
2Ch 20:26 they assembled in the Valley of Bera'cah 1
26 been called the Valley of Bera'cah to this day. 1

Beraiah 1. בְּרָאיָה
1Ch 8:21 Adai'ah, Berai'ah, and Shimrath . . sons of Shim'e-i. 1

Berea 1. Βερεα
1Mc 9: 4 then they marched off and went to Berea 1

Berechiah 1. בֶּרֶכְיָהוּ
1Ch 3:20 Berechi'ah, Hasadi'ah, and Ju'shab-he'sed, five. 1
6:39 namely, Asaph the son of Berechi'ah, son of Shim'e-a 1
9:16 Berechi'ah the son of Asa, son of Elka'nah 1
15:17 of his brethren Asaph the son of Berechi'ah 1
23 Berechi'ah . . to be gatekeepers for the ark. 1
2Ch 28:12 chiefs . . Berechi'ah the son of Meshil'lemoth 1
Neh 3: 4 next to them Meshul'lam the son of Berechi'ah 1
30 Meshul'lam the son of Berechi'ah repaired 1
6:18 daughter of Meshul'lam the son of Berechi'ah 1
Zec 1: 1 to Zechari'ah the son of Berechi'ah, son of Iddo 1
7 the son of Berechi'ah, son of Iddo, the prophet; 1

Bered 1. בֶּרֶד
Gen 16:14 Beer-la'hai-roi; it lies between Kadesh and Bered. 1
1Ch 7:20 Shuthe'lah, and Bered his son, Tahath his son 1

Beri 1. בֵּרִי
1Ch 7:36 sons of Zophah: Su'ah, Har'nepher, Shu'al, Beri, 1

Beriah 1. בְּרִיעָה
Gen 46:17 The sons of Asher: Imnah, Ishvah, Ishvi, Beri'ah 1
17 And the sons of Beri'ah: Heber and Mal'chi-el 1
Num26:44 of Beri'ah, the family of the Beri'ites. 1
45 Of the sons of Beri'ah: of Heber . . of Mal'chi-el 1
1Ch 7:23 E'phraim . . called his name Beri'ah 1
30 sons of Asher . . Beri'ah, and their sister Serah. 1
31 The sons of Beri'ah: Heber and Mal'chi-el 1
8:13 Beri'ah and Shema . . heads of fathers' houses 1
16 Michael, Ishpah, and Joha were sons of Beri'ah. 1
23:10 sons of Shim'e-i . . Zina, and Je'ush, and Beri'ah 1
11 but Je'ush and Beri'ah had not many sons 1

Beriite 1. בְּרִיעִי
Num26:44 of Beri'ah, the family of the Beri'ites. 1

Bernice 1. Βερνίκη
Act 25:13 Agrippa the king and Berni'ce 1
23 So on the morrow Agrippa and Berni'ce came 1
26:30 Then the king rose, and the governor and Berni'ce 1

Beroea 1. Βέροια 2. Βεροιαῖος
Act 17:10 sent . . Silas away by night to Beroe'a 1
13 the word of God was proclaimed by Paul at Beroe'a 1
20: 4 Sop'ater of Beroe'a, the son of Pyrrhus 2
2Mc 13: 4 he ordered them to take him to Beroea 1

Berothah 1. בֵּרוֹתָה
Ezk 47:16 Bero'thah, Sib'raim (which lies on the border 1

Berothai 1. בֵּרֹתַי
2Sm 8: 8 from Betah and from Bero'thai . . King David took 1

Besai 1. בֵּסַי 2. Βασθαι
Ezr 2:49 sons of Uzza, the sons of Pase'ah, the sons of Besai 1
Neh 7:52 sons of Besai, the sons of Me-u'nim 1
1Es 5:31 the sons of Besai, the sons of Asnah 2

Bescaspasmys 1. Βεσκασπασμυς
1Es 9:31 Bescaspasmys and Sesthel, and Belnuus 1

Besodeiah 1. בְּסוֹדְיָה
Neh 3: 6 Joi'ada . . and Meshul'lam the son of Besodei'ah 1

Besor 1. בְּשׂוֹר
1Sm 30: 9 and they came to the brook Besor 1
10 who were too exhausted to cross the brook Besor. 1
21 men . . who had been left at the brook Besor; 1

Betah 1. בֶּטַח
2Sm 8: 8 from Betah and from Bero'thai . . King David took 1

Beten 1. בֶּטֶן
Jos 19:25 Its territory included Helkath, Hali, Beten 1

Beth-anath 1. בֵּית עֲנָת
Jos 19:38 Mig'dal-el, Horem, Beth-anath, and Beth-she'mesh 1
Jdg 1:33 drive out . . or the inhabitants of Beth-anath 1
33 inhabitants of Beth-she'mesh and of Beth-anath 1

Beth-anoth 1. בֵּית עֲנוֹת
Jos 15:59 Ma'arath, Beth-anoth, and El'tekon 1

Beth-arabah 1. בֵּית הָעֲרָבָה 2. Βαιθαραβα
Jos 15: 6 boundary . . passes along north of Beth-arabah; 1
61 In the wilderness, Beth-arabah, Middin, Seca'cah 1
18:18 to the north of the shoulder of Beth-arabah 2
22 Beth-arabah, Zemara'im, Bethel 1

Beth-arbel 1. בֵּית אַרְבֵאל
Hos 10:14 as Shalman destroyed Beth-ar'bel 1

Beth-ashbea 1. בֵּית אַשְׁבֵּעַ
1Ch 4:21 the house of linen workers at Beth-ashbe'a; 1

Beth-aven 1. בֵּית אָוֶן
Jos 7: 2 from Jericho to Ai, which is near Beth-a'ven 1
18:12 and it ends at the wilderness of Beth-a'ven. 1
1Sm 13: 5 encamped in Michmash, to the east of Beth-a'ven. 1
14:23 and the battle passed beyond Beth-a'ven. 1
Hos 4:15 Enter not into Gilgal, nor go up to Beth-a'ven 1
5: 8 Sound the alarm at Beth-a'ven; tremble, O Benjamin! 1
10: 5 tremble for the calf of Beth-a'ven. 1

Beth-azmaveth 1. בֵּית עַזְמָוֶת
Neh 7:28 men of Beth-az'maveth, 42. 1

Beth-baal-meon 1. בֵּית בַּעַל מְעוֹן
Jos 13:17 Dibon, and Ba'moth-ba'al, and Beth-ba'al-me'on 1

Beth-barah 1. בֵּית בָּרָה
Jdg 7:24 seize the waters . . as far as Beth-bar'ah 1
24 waters as far as Beth-bar'ah, and also the Jordan. 1

Beth-biri 1. בֵּית בִּרְאִי
1Ch 4:31 Ha'zar-su'sim, Beth-biri, and Sha-ara'im. 1

Beth-car 1. בֵּית כָּר
1Sm 7:11 and smote them, as far as below Beth-car. 1

Beth-dagon 1. בֵּית דָּגוֹן 2. Βηθδαγων
Jos 15:41 Gede'roth, Beth-da'gon, Na'amah, and Makke'dah 1
19:27 it goes to Beth-dagon, and touches Zeb'ulun 1
1Mc 10:83 They fled to Azotus and entered Beth-dagon 2

Beth-diblathaim 1. בֵּית דִּבְלָתָיִם
Jer 48:22 and Dibon, and Nebo, and Beth-diblatha'im 1

Beth-eden 1. בֵּית עֶדֶן
Ams 1: 5 and him that holds the scepter from Beth-eden; 1

Beth-eked 1. בֵּית עֵקֶד
2Kg 10:12 when he was at Beth-eked of the Shepherds 1
14 took them . . and slew them at the pit of Beth-eked 1

Beth-emek 1. בֵּית הָעֵמֶק
Jos 19:27 touches . . northward to Beth-emek and Nei'el; 1

Beth-ezel 1. בֵּית הָאֵצֶל
Mic 1:11 the wailing of Beth-e'zel shall take away from you 1

Beth-gader 1. בֵּית גָּדֵר
1Ch 2:51 and Hareph the father of Beth-gader. 1

Beth-gamul 1. בֵּית גָּמוּל
Jer 48:23 and Kiriatha'im, and Beth-ga'mul, and Beth-me'on 1

Beth-gilgal 1. בֵּית גִּלְגָּל
Neh 12:29 also from Beth-gilgal and from the region of Geba 1

Beth-haccherem 1. בֵּית הַכֶּרֶם
Neh 3:14 ruler of the district of Beth-hacche'rem 1
Jer 6: 1 and raise a signal on Beth-hacche'rem; 1

Beth-haggan 1. בֵּית הַגָּן
2Kg 9:27 Ahazi'ah . . fled in the direction of Beth-haggan. 1

Beth-haram 1. בֵּית הָרָם
Jos 13:27 in the valley of Beth-ha'ram, Beth-nim'rah, Succoth 1

Beth-haran 1. בֵּית הָרָן
Num32:36 Beth-nim'rah and Beth-har'an, fortified cities 1

Beth-hoglah 1. בֵּית חָגְלָה
Jos 15: 6 the boundary goes up to Beth-hoglah, and passes 1
18:19 passes . . north of the shoulder of Beth-hoglah; 1
21 cities . . were Jericho, Beth-hoglah, Emek-ke'ziz 1

Beth-horon 1. בֵּית חוֹרוֹן 2. Βαιθωρων
Jos 10:10 chased them by the way of the ascent of Beth-hor'on 1
11 they were going down the ascent of Beth-hor'on 1
16: 3 as far as the territory of Lower Beth-hor'on 1
5 was At'aroth-ad'dar as far as Upper Beth-hor'on 1
18:13 mountain that lies south of Lower Beth-hor'on. 1
14 that lies to the south, opposite Beth-hor'on 1
21:22 Beth-hor'on with its pasture lands 1
1Sm 13:18 another company turned toward Beth-hor'on 1
1Kg 9:17 rebuilt Gezer) and Lower Beth-hor'on 1
1Ch 6:68 Beth-hor'on with its pasture lands 1
7:24 who built both Lower and Upper Beth-hor'on 1
2Ch 8: 5 He also built Upper Beth-Hor'on and Lower 1
5 He also built Upper . . and Lower Beth-Ho'ron 1
25:13 cities of Judah, from Sama'ria to Beth-hor'on 1
Jdt 4: 4 Kona and Beth-horon and Belmain and Jericho 2
Sir 46: 6 at the descent of Beth-horon *
1Mc 3:16 When he approached the ascent of Beth-horon 2
24 They pursued them down the descent of Beth-horon 2
7:39 Nicanor . . encamped in Beth-horon 2
9:50 Emmaus, and Beth-horon, and Bethel, and Timnath 2

Beth-jeshimoth 1. בֵּית יְשִׁימוֹת
Num33:49 from Beth-jes'himoth as far as Abel-shittim 1
Jos 12: 3 and in the direction of Beth-jesh'imoth, to the sea 1
13:20 and the slopes of Pisgah, and Beth-jesh'imoth 1
Ezk 25: 9 the country, Beth-jesh'imoth, Ba'al-me'on 1

Beth-leaphrah 1. בֵּית לְעַפְרָה
Mic 1:10 in Beth-le-aph'rah roll yourselves in the dust. 1

Beth-lebaoth 1. בֵּית לְבָאוֹת
Jos 19: 6 Beth-leba'oth, and Sharu'hen 1

Beth-maacah 1. בֵּית מַעֲכָה
2Sm 20:14 Sheba passed through . . to Abel of Bethma'acah; 1
15 Jo'ab came and besieged him in Abel of Bethma'acah; 1

Beth-marcaboth 1. בֵּית מַרְכָּבוֹת
Jos 19: 5 Ziklag, Beth-mar'caboth, Ha'zar-su'sah 1
1Ch 4:31 Beth-mar'caboth, Ha'zar-su'sim, Beth-biri 1

Beth-meon 1. בֵּית מְעוֹן
Jer 48:23 and Kiriatha'im, and Beth-ga'mul, and Beth-me'on 1

Beth-millo 1. בֵּית מִלּוֹא
Jdg 9: 6 of Shechem came together, and all Beth-millo 1
20 devour the citizens of Shechem, and Beth-millo; 1
20 from the citizens of Shechem, and from Beth-millo 1

Beth-nimrah 1. בֵּית נִמְרָה
Num32:36 Beth-nim'rah and Beth-har'an, fortified cities 1
Jos 13:27 in the valley of Beth-ha'ram, Beth-nim'rah, Succoth 1

Beth-pazzez 1. בֵּית פַּצֵּץ
Jos 19:21 Remeth, En-gan'nim, En-had'dah, Beth-paz'zez; 1

Beth-pelet 1. בֵּית פֶּלֶט
Jos 15:27 Ha'zar-gad'dah, Heshmon, Beth-pel'et 1
Neh 11:26 in Jeshua and in Mola'dah and Beth-pelet 1

Beth-peor 1. בֵּית פְּעוֹר
Deu 3:29 we remained in the valley opposite Beth-pe'or. 1
4:46 in the valley opposite Beth-pe'or, in the land 1
34: 6 buried . . in the land of Moab opposite Beth-pe'or; 1
Jos 13:20 and Beth-pe'or, and the slopes of Pisgah 1

Beth-rapha 1. בֵּית רָפָא
1Ch 4:12 Eshton was the father of Bethra'pha, Pase'ah 1

Beth-rehob 1. בֵּית רְחוֹב
Jdg 18:28 It was in the valley which belongs to Beth-rehob. 1
2Sm 10: 6 Ammonites . . hired the Syrians of Beth-re'hob 1

Beth-saida 1. Βηθσαϊδά
Mat 11:21 Woe to you, Chora'zin! woe to you, Beth-sa'ida! 1
Mrk 6:45 go before him to the other side, to Beth-sa'ida 1
8:22 they came to Beth-sa'ida 1
Lke 9:10 withdrew apart to a city called Beth-sa'ida. 1
10:13 Woe to you, Chora'zin! woe to you, Beth-sa'ida! 1
Joh 1:44 Now Philip was from Beth-sa'ida, the city of Andrew 1
12:21 Philip . . from Beth-sa'ida in Galilee 1

Beth-shan 1. בֵּית שָׁן 2. Βαιθσαν
1Sm 31:10 they fastened his body to the wall of Beth-shan. 1
12 took the body of Saul . . from the wall of Beth-shan; 1
2Sm 21:12 stolen them from the public square of Beth-shan 1
1Mc 5:52 into the large plain before Beth-shan. 2
12:40 he marched forth and came to Beth-shan. 2
41 he came to Beth-shan. 2

Beth-shean 1. בֵּית שְׁאָן
Jos 17:11 Manas'seh had Beth-she'an and its villages 1
16 those in Beth-she'an and its villages and those 1
Jdg 1:27 the inhabitants of Beth-she'an and its villages 1
1Kg 4:12 all Beth-she'an which is beside Zarethan below 1
12 from Beth-she'an to A'bel-meho'lah, as far 1
1Ch 7:29 Beth-she'an and its towns, Ta'anach and its towns 1

Beth-shemesh 1. בֵּית הַשִּׁמְשִׁי 2. בֵּית שֶׁמֶשׁ
Jos 15:10 and goes down to Beth-she'mesh, and passes along 2
19:22 also touches Tabor, Shahazu'mah, and Beth-she'mesh 2
38 Mig'dal-el, Horem, Beth-anath, and Beth-she'mesh 2
21:16 A'in with . . Beth-she'mesh with its pasture lands 2
Jdg 1:33 not drive out the inhabitants of Beth-she'mesh 2
33 inhabitants of Beth-she'mesh and of Beth-anath 2
1Sm 6: 9 goes up on the way to its own land, to Beth-she'mesh 2
12 cows went . . in the direction of Beth-she'mesh 2
12 went after them as far as the border of Beth-she'mesh 2
13 Now the people of Beth-she'mesh were reaping 2
14 came into the field of Joshua of Beth-she'mesh 1
15 the men of Beth-she'mesh offered burnt offerings 2
18 this day in the field of Joshua of Beth-she'mesh. 1
19 And he slew some of the men of Beth-she'mesh 2
20 the men of Beth-she'mesh said, "Who is able to stand 2
1Kg 4: 9 Shaal'bim, Beth-she'mesh, and E'lonbeth-ha'nan; 2
2Kg 14:11 faced one another in battle at Beth-she'mesh 2
13 Jeho'ash . . captured Amazi'ah.., at Beth-she'mesh 2
1Ch 6:59 Beth-she'mesh with its pasture lands; 2
2Ch 25:21 faced one another in battle at Beth-she'mesh 2
23 Jo'ash . . captured Amazi'ah . . at Beth-she'mesh 2
28:18 had taken Beth-she'mesh, Ai'jalon, Gede'roth 2

Beth-shittah 1. בֵּית הַשִּׁטָּה
Jdg 7:22 army fled as far as Beth-shit'tah toward Zer'erah 1

Beth-tappuah 1. בֵּית תַּפּוּחַ
Jos 15:53 Janim, Beth-tap'puah, Aphe'kah 1

Beth-togarmah 1. בֵּית תּוֹגַרְמָה
Ezk 27:14 Beth-togar'mah exchanged for your wares horses 1
38: 6 Beth-togar'mah from the uttermost parts 1

Beth-zaith 1. Βηθζαιθ
1Mc 7:19 Then Bacchides . . encamped in Beth-zaith 1

Beth-zatha 1. Βηθζαθά
Joh 5: 2 a pool, in Hebrew called Beth-za'tha 1

Beth-zechariah 1. Βαιθζαχαρια
1Mc 6:32 and encamped at Beth-zechariah 1
33 along the road to Beth-zechariah 1

Beth-zur 1. בֵּית צוּר 2. Βαιθσουρα
Jos 15:58 Halhul, Beth-zur, Gedor 1
1Ch 2:45 and Ma'on was the father of Bethzur. 1
2Ch 11: 7 Beth-zur, Soco, Adullam 1
Neh 3:16 ruler of half the district of Beth-zur 1
1Mc 4:29 They came into Idumea and encamped at Beth-zur 2
61 He also fortified Beth-zur 2
6: 7 also Beth-zur, his city. 2
26 have fortified both the sanctuary and Beth-zur; 2
31 encamped against Beth-zur 2
49 He made peace with the men of Beth-zur 2
50 So the king took Beth-zur 2
9:52 He also fortified the city of Beth-zur, and Gazara 2
10:14 Only in Beth-zur did some remain 2
11:65 Simon encamped before Beth-zur 2
14: 7 he ruled over Gazara and Beth-zur and the citadel 2
33 He fortified the cities of Judea, and Beth-zur 2
2Mc 11: 5 Invading Judea, he approached Beth-zur 2
13:19 He advanced against Beth-zur . . was turned back 2
22 the people in Beth-zur 2

Bethany 1. Βατανη 2. Βηθανία
Mat 21:17 went out of the city to Bethany and lodged there. 2
26: 6 when Jesus was at Bethany in the house of Simon 2
Mrk 11: 1 drew near to Jerusalem, to Beth'phage and Bethany 2
11 he went out to Bethany with the twelve. 2
12 On the following day, when they came from Bethany 2
14: 3 at Bethany in the house of Simon the leper 2
Lke 19:29 When he drew near to Beth'phage and Bethany 2
24:50 Then he led them out as far as Bethany 2
Joh 1:28 This took place in Bethany beyond the Jordan 2
11: 1 Now a certain man was ill, Laz'arus of Bethany 2
18 Bethany was near Jerusalem, about two miles off 2
12: 1 Jesus came to Bethany, where Laz'arus was 2
Jdt 1: 9 as far as Jerusalem and Bethany and Chelous 1

Bethasmoth 1. Βαιτασμωθ
1Es 5:18 The men of Bethasmoth, 42. 1

Bethbasi 1. Βαιθβασι
1Mc 9:62 withdrew to Bethbasi in the wilderness 1
64 Then he came and encamped against Bethbasi 1

Bethel 1. בֵּית־אֵל 2. Βαιθηλ
Gen 12: 8 removed to the mountain on the east of Bethel 1
8 with Bethel on the west and Ai on the east; 1
13: 3 he journeyed on from the Negeb as far as Bethel 1
3 had been at the beginning, between Bethel and Ai 1
28:19 He called the name of that place Bethel; 1
31:13 I am the God of Bethel, where you anointed a pillar 1
35: 1 God said to Jacob, "Arise, go up to Bethel 1
3 then let us arise and go up to Bethel 1
6 Jacob came to Luz (that is, Bethel) 1
8 died, and she was buried under an oak below Bethel; 1
15 where God had spoken with him, Bethel. 1
16 Then they journeyed from Bethel; 1
Jos 7: 2 to Ai, which is near Beth-a'ven, east of Bethel 1
8: 9 went to the place . . and lay between Bethel and Ai 1
12 and set them in ambush between Bethel and Ai 1
17 not a man left in Ai or Bethel, who did not go out 1
12: 9 the king of Ai, which is beside Bethel, one; 1
16 the king of Makke'dah, one; the king of Bethel, one; 1
16: 1 up from Jericho into the hill country to Bethel; 1
2 from Bethel to Luz, it passes along to At'aroth 1
18:13 to the shoulder of Luz (the same is Bethel) 1
22 Beth-arabah, Zemara'im, Bethel 1
Jdg 1:22 The house of Joseph also went up against Bethel; 1
23 And the house of Joseph sent to spy out Bethel. 1
4: 5 of Deb'orah between Ramah and Bethel in the hill 1
20:18 Israel . . went up to Bethel, and inquired of God 1
26 the whole army, went up and came to Bethel and wept 1
31 in the highways, one of which goes up to Bethel 1
21: 2 the people came to Bethel, and sat there till 1
19 Shiloh, which is north of Bethel, on the east 1
19 the highway that goes up from Bethel to Shechem 1
1Sm 7:16 went on a circuit . . to Bethel, Gilgal, and Mizpah; 1
10: 3 three men going up to God at Bethel will meet you 1
13: 2 in Michmash and the hill country of Bethel 1
30:27 it was for those in Bethel, in Ramoth of the Negeb 1
1Kg 12:29 he set one in Bethel, and the other he put in Dan. 1
30 the people went to the one at Bethel 2
32 so he did in Bethel, sacrificing to the calves 1
32 he placed in Bethel the priests . . he had made. 1
33 He went up to the altar which he had made in Bethel 1
13: 1 a man of God came out of Judah . . to Bethel. 1
4 which he cried against the altar at Bethel 1
10 did not return by the way that he came to Bethel. 1
11 there dwelt an old prophet in Bethel. 1
11 all that the man of God had done that day in Bethel; 1
32 the saying . . against the altar in Bethel 1
16:34 In his days Hi'el of Bethel built Jericho; 1
2Kg 2: 2 the LORD has sent me as far as Bethel. 1
2 So they went down to Bethel. 1
3 sons of the prophets who were in Bethel came out 1
23 He went up from there to Bethel; 1
10:29 the golden calves that were in Bethel, and in Dan. 1
17:28 one of the priests . . came and dwelt in Bethel 1
23: 4 he burned them . . and carried their ashes to Bethel. 1
15 the altar at Bethel . . he pulled down and he broke 1
17 which you have done against the altar at Bethel. 1
19 according to all that he had done at Bethel. 1
1Ch 7:28 possessions and . . were Bethel and its towns 1

2Ch 13:19 took cities from him, Bethel with its villages 1
Ezr 2:28 men of Bethel and Ai, 223. 1
Neh 7:32 men of Bethel and Ai, 123. 1
11:31 Michmash, Ai'ja, Bethel and its villages 1
Jer 48:13 as the house of Israel was ashamed of Bethel 1
Hos 12: 4 He met God at Bethel, and there God spoke with him- 1
Ams 3:14 I will punish the altars of Bethel 1
4: 4 Come to Bethel, and transgress; 1
5: 5 do not seek Bethel, and do not enter into Gilgal 1
5 go into exile, and Bethel shall come to nought. 1
6 and it devour, with none to quench it for Bethel 1
7:10 Amazi'ah the priest of Bethel sent to Jerobo'am 1
13 but never again prophesy at Bethel 1
Zec 7: 2 Now the people of Bethel had sent Share'zer 1
1Es 5:21 The men of Bethel, 52. The sons of Magbish, 156. 2
1Mc 9:50 Emmaus, and Beth-horon, and Bethel, and Timnath 2

Bethlehem 1. בֵּית לֶחֶם 2. Βηθλέεμ 3. Βιθλεεμ
Gen 35:19 on the way to Ephrath (that is, Bethlehem) 1
48: 7 on the way to Ephrath (that is, Bethlehem). 1
Jos 19:15 Kattath, Nahal'al, Shimron, I'dalah, and Bethlehem 1
Jdg 12: 8 After him Ibzan of Bethlehem judged Israel. 1
10 Then Ibzan died, and was buried at Bethlehem. 1
17: 7 there was a young man of Bethlehem in Judah 1
8 departed from the town of Bethlehem in Judah 1
9 I am a Levite of Bethlehem in Judah, and I am going 1
19: 1 took . . a concubine from Bethlehem in Judah. 1
2 to her father's house at Bethlehem in Judah 1
18 passing from Bethlehem in Judah to the remote 1
18 I went to Bethlehem in Judah; and I am going to my 1
Rut 1: 1 a certain man of Bethlehem in Judah went 1
2 they were Eph'rathites from Bethlehem in Judah. 1
19 the two . . went on until they came to Bethlehem. 1
19 And when they came to Bethlehem, the whole town 1
22 And they came to Bethlehem at . . barley harvest. 1
2: 4 And behold, Bo'az came from Bethlehem; 1
4:11 and be renowned in Bethlehem; 1
1Sm 16: 4 Samuel did . . and came to Bethlehem. 1
17:12 an Eph'rathite of Bethlehem in Judah, named Jesse 1
15 went . . to feed his father's sheep at Bethlehem. 1
20: 6 David . . asked leave of me to run to Bethlehem 1
28 David . . asked leave of me to go to Bethlehem; 1
2Sm 2:32 in the tomb of his father, which was at Bethlehem. 1
23:14 and the garrison . . was then at Bethlehem. 1
15 give me water to drink from the well of Bethlehem 1
16 out of the well of Bethlehem which was by the gate 1
24 As'ahel . . Elha'nan the son of Dodo of Bethlehem 1
1Ch 2:51 Salma, the father of Bethlehem 1
54 sons of Salma: Bethlehem, the Netoph'athites 1
4: 4 Eph'rathah, the father of Bethlehem. 1
11:16 of the Philistines was then at Bethlehem. 1
17 from the well of Bethlehem which is by the gate! 1
18 drew water out of the well of Bethlehem 1
26 Elha'nan the son of Dodo of Bethlehem 1
2Ch 11: 6 He built Bethlehem, Etam, Teko'a 1
Ezr 2:21 sons of Bethlehem, 123. 1
Neh 7:26 men of Bethlehem and Neto'phah, 188. 1
Jer 41:17 and stayed at Geruth Chimham near Bethlehem 1
Mic 5: 2 But you, O Bethlehem Eph'rathah, who are little 1
Mat 2: 1 Now when Jesus was born in Bethlehem of Judea 2
5 They told him, "In Bethlehem of Judea; 2
6 you, O Bethlehem, in the land of Judah, are by no 2
8 he sent them to Bethlehem, saying, "Go and search 2
16 killed all the male children in Bethlehem 2
Lke 2: 4 to the city of David, which is called Bethlehem 2
15 Let us go over to Bethlehem and see this thing 2
Joh 7:42 comes from Bethlehem, the village where David was? 2
1Es 5:17 The sons of Bethlehem, 123. 3

Bethlehemite 1. בֵּית לַחְמִי
1Sm 16: 1 and go; I will send you to Jesse the Bethlehemite 1
18 I have seen a son of Jesse the Bethlehemite 1
17:58 I am the son of . . Jesse the Bethlehemite. 1
2Sm 21:19 Elha'nan . . son of Ja'areor'egim, the Bethlehemite 1

Bethphage 1. Βηθφαγή
Mat 21: 1 and came to Beth'phage, to the Mount of Olives 1
Mrk 11: 1 drew near to Jerusalem, to Beth'phage and Bethany 1
Lke 19:29 When he drew near to Beth'phage and Bethany 1

Bethuel 1. בְּתוּאֵל
Gen 22:22 Chesed, Hazo, Pildash, Jidlaph, and Bethu'el. 1
23 Bethu'el became the father of Rebekah. 1
24:15 behold, Rebekah, who was born to Bethu'el 1
24 She said to him, "I am the daughter of Bethu'el 1
47 She said, The daughter of Bethu'el, Nahor's son 1
50 Laban and Bethu'el answered, "The thing comes 1
25:20 Rebekah, the daughter of Bethu'el the Aramean 1
28: 2 Arise, go to Paddan-aram to the house of Bethu'el 1
5 went to Paddan-aram to Laban, the son of Bethu'el 1
1Ch 4:30 Bethu'el, Hormah, Ziklag 1

Bethul 1. בְּתוּל
Jos 19: 4 Elto'lad, Bethul, Hormah 1

Bethulia 1. Βαιτυλουα
Jdt 4: 6 the people of Bethulia and Betomesthaim 1
6:10 to seize Achior and take him to Bethulia 1
11 came to the springs below Bethulia. 1
14 they untied him and brought him into Bethulia 1
7: 1 to break camp and move against Bethulia 1
3 They encamped in the valley near Bethulia 1
3 spread out . . in length from Bethulia to Cyamon 1
6 in full view of the Israelites in Bethulia 1
13 where all the people of Bethulia get their water 1
20 belonging to every inhabitant of Bethulia 1
8: 3 took to his bed and died in Bethulia his city 1
11 Listen to me, rulers of the people of Bethulia! 1
10: 6 Then they went out to the city gate of Bethulia 1
11: 9 the men of Bethulia spared him 1
12: 7 and went out each night to the valley of Bethulia 1
13:10 and went up the mountain to Bethulia 1
15: 3 had camped in the hills around Bethulia 1
6 The rest of the people of Bethulia 1
16:21 Judith went to Bethulia 1
23 She died in Bethulia 1

Betomasthaim 1. Βαιτομασθαιμ
Jdt 15: 4 Uzziah sent men to Betomasthaim and Bebai 1

Betomesthaim 1. Βαιτομεσθαιμ
Jdt 4: 6 the people of Bethulia and Betomesthaim 1

Betonim 1. בְּטֹנִים
Jos 13:26 and from Heshbon to Ra'math-miz'peh and Bet'onim 1

Bezai 1. בֵּצָי 2. Βασσαι
Ezr 2:17 sons of Be'zai, 323. 1
Neh 7:23 sons of Be'zai, 324. 1
10:18 Hodi'ah, Hashum, Be'zai 1
1Es 5:16 The sons of Bezai, 323. The sons of Jorah, 112. 2

Bezalel 1. בְּצַלְאֵל
Exd 31: 2 called by name Bez'alel and son of Uri, son of Hur 1
35:30 has called by name Bez'alel the son of Uri 1
36: 1 Bez'alel and Oho'liab and every able man in whom 1
2 Moses called Bez'alel and Oho'liab and every able 1
37: 1 Bez'alel made the ark of acacia wood; 1
38:22 Bez'alel the son of Uri, son of Hur, of the tribe 1
1Ch 2:20 and Uri was the father of Bez'alel. 1
2Ch 1: 5 bronze altar that Bez'alel . . had made 1
Ezr 10:30 of Pa'hath-mo'ab . . Mattani'ah, Bez'alel, Bin'nui 1

Bezek 1. בֶּזֶק
Jdg 1: 4 and they defeated 10,000 of them at Bezek. 1
5 They came upon Ado'ni-be'zek at Bezek, and fought 1
1Sm 11: 8 When he mustered them at Bezek, the men of Israel 1

Bezer 1. בֶּצֶר
Deu 4:43 Bezer in the wilderness on the tableland 1
Jos 20: 8 they appointed Bezer in the wilderness 1
21:36 out of . . Reuben, Bezer with its pasture lands 1
1Ch 6:78 Bezer in the steppe with its pasture lands 1
7:37 Bezer, Hod, Shamma, Shilshah, Ithran, and Be-e'ra. 1

Bichri 1. בִּכְרִי
2Sm 20: 1 a . . fellow, whose name was Sheba, the son of Bichri 1
2 men of Israel . . followed Sheba the son of Bichri; 1
6 Sheba the son of Bichri will do us more harm 1
7 they went out . . to pursue Sheba the son of Bichri. 1
10 Then Jo'ab and . . pursued Sheba the son of Bichri. 1
13 went on . . to pursue Sheba the son of Bichri. 1
21 a man of . . E'phraim, called Sheba the son of Bichri 1
22 they cut off the head of Sheba the son of Bichri 1

Bichrite
2Sm 20:14 and all the Bichrites assembled, and followed •

Bidkar 1. בִּדְקַר
2Kg 9:25 Jehu said to Bidkar his aide, "Take him up 1

Bigtha 1. בִּגְתָא
Est 1:10 Mehu'man, Biztha, Harbo'na, Bigtha and Abag'tha 1

Bigthan 1. בִּגְתָן
Est 2:21 Bigthan and Teresh . . became angry and sought 1

Bigthana 1. בִּגְתָנָא
Est 6: 2 how Mor'decai had told about Bigthana and Teresh 1

Bigvai 1. בִּגְוַי 2. Βαγο 3. Βαγουαι 4. Ενηνιος
Ezr 2: 2 came with . . Bilshan, Mispar, Bigva'i, Rehum 1
14 sons of Bigva'i, 2,056. 1
8:14 Of the sons of Bigva'i, Uthai and Zaccur 1
Neh 7: 7 came with . . Bigva'i, Nehum, Ba'anah. 1
19 sons of Bigva'i, 2,067. 1
10:16 Adoni'jah, Bigva'i, Adin 1
1Es 5: 8 Nehemiah, Seraiah, Resaiah, Bigvai, Mordecai 4
14 The sons of Bigvai, 2,066. The sons of Adin, 454 3
8:40 Of the sons of Bigvai, Uthai the son of Istalcurus 2

Bildad 1. בִּלְדַּד
Job 2:11 Eli'phaz the Te'manite, Bildad the Shuhite 1
8: 1 Then Bildad the Shuhite answered 1
18: 1 Then Bildad the Shuhite answered 1
25: 1 Then Bildad the Shuhite answered 1
42: 9 Bildad the Shuhite and Zophar the Na'amathite 1

Bileam 1. בִּלְעָם
1Ch 6:70 Aner . . and Bil'e-am with its pasture lands 1

Bilgah 1. בִּלְגָּה
1Ch 24:14 the fifteenth to Bilgah, the sixteenth to Immer 1
Neh 12: 5 Mi'jamin, Ma-adi'ah, Bilgah 1
18 of Bilgah, Sham'mu-a; of Shemai'ah, Jehon'athan; 1

Bilgai 1. בִּלְגַּי
Neh 10: 8 Ma-azi'ah, Bil'gai, Shemai'ah; these are the priests. 1

Bilhah 1. בִּלְהָה
Gen 29:29 Laban gave his maid Bilhah to his daughter 1
30: 3 Then she said, "Here is my maid Bilhah; go in to her 1
4 she gave him her maid Bilhah as a wife; 1
5 Bilhah conceived and bore Jacob a son. 1
7 Rachel's maid Bilhah conceived again 1
35:22 Bilhah his father's concubine; and Israel heard 1
25 The sons of Bilhah, Rachel's maid: Dan 1
37: 2 he was a lad with the sons of Bilhah and Zilpah 1
46:25 these are the sons of Bilhah, whom Laban gave 1
1Ch 4:29 Bilhah, Ezem, Tolad 1
7:13 Jah'zi-el, Guni . . the offspring of Bilhah. 1

Bilhan 1. בִּלְהָן
Gen 36:27 the sons of Ezer: Bilhan, Za'avan, and Akan. 1
1Ch 1:42 The sons of Ezer: Bilhan, Za'avan, and Ja'akan. 1
7:10 The sons of Jedi'a-el: Bilhan. 1
10 sons of Bilhan: Je'ush, Benjamin, Ehud, Chena'anah 1

Bilshan 1. בִּלְשָׁן 2. Βεελσαρος
Ezr 2: 2 came with . . Bilshan, Mispar, Bigva'i, Rehum 1
Neh 7: 7 came with . . Mor'decai, Bilshan, Mis'pereth, Bigva'i 1
1Es 5: 8 Resaiah, Bigvai, Mordecai, Bilshan, Mispar 2

Bimhal 1. בִּמְהָל
1Ch 7:33 The sons of Japhlet: Pasach, Bimhal, and Ashvath. 1

Binea 1. בִּנְעָא
1Ch 8:37 Moza was the father of Bin'e-a; Raphah was his son 1
9:43 Moza . . father of Bin'e-a; and Rephai'ah was his son 1

Binnui 1. בִּנּוּי 2. Βαννους 3. Σαβαννος
Ezr 8:33 Levites . . No-adi'ah the son of Bin'nui. 1
10:30 of Pa'hath-mo'ab . . Bin'nui, and Manas'seh. 1
38 Of the sons of Bin'nui: Shim'e-i 1
Neh 3:24 After him Bin'nui the son of Hen'adad repaired 1
7:15 sons of Bin'nui, 648. 1
10: 9 Levites: Jeshua . . Bin'nui of the sons of Hen'adad 1
12: 8 Levites: Jeshua, Bin'nui, Kad'mi-el 1
1Es 8:63 Jozabad . . and Moeth the son of Binnui 3
9:34 Eliashib and Machnadebai, Eliasis, Binnui 2

Birsha 1. בִּרְשַׁע
Gen 14: 2 Bera king of Sodom, Birsha king of Gomor'rah 1

Birzaith 1. בִּרְזָיִת
1Ch 7:31 Mal'chi-el, who was the father of Bir'zaith. 1

Bishlam 1. בִּשְׁלָם 2. Βεσλεμος
Ezr 4: 7 Bishlam and Mith'redath and Tab'eel and the rest 1
1Es 2:16 Bishlam, Mithridates, Tabeel, Rehum, Beltethmus 2

Bithiah 1. בִּתְיָה
1Ch 4:17 Bith'i-ah, the daughter of Pharaoh 1

Bithynia 1. Βιθυνία
Act 16: 7 they attempted to go into Bithyn'ia 1
1Pe 1: 1 the Dispersion in . . Asia, and Bithyn'ia 1

Biziothiah 1. בִּזְיוֹתְיָה
Jos 15:28 Hazar-shu'al, Beer-sheba, Biziothi'ah 1

Biztha 1. בִּזְּתָא
Est 1:10 he commanded Mehu'man, Biztha, Harbo'na, Bigtha 1

Blastus 1. Βλάστος
Act 12:20 persuaded Blastus, the king's chamberlain 1

Boanerges 1. Βοανηργές
Mrk 3:17 whom he surnamed Bo-aner'ges 1

Boaz 1. בֹּעַז 2. Βόες 3. Βόος
Rut 2: 1 Now Na'omi had a kinsman . . whose name was Bo'az. 1
3 to come to the part of the field belonging to Bo'az 1
4 And behold, Bo'az came from Bethlehem; 1
5 Bo'az said to his servant who was in charge 1
8 Then Bo'az said to Ruth, "Now, listen, my daughter 1
11 Bo'az answered her, "All that you have done 1
14 And at mealtime Bo'az said to her, "Come here 1
15 Bo'az instructed his young men, saying 1
19 The man's name with whom I worked today is Bo'az. 1
23 she kept close to the maidens of Bo'az 1
3: 2 Now is not Bo'az our kinsman 1
7 Bo'az had eaten and drunk, and his heart was merry 1
4: 1 And Bo'az went up to the gate and sat down there; 1
1 the next of kin, of whom Bo'az had spoken, came by. 1
1 Bo'az said, "Turn aside, friend; sit down here"; •

5 Bo'az said, "The day you buy the field from . . Na'omi 1
8 the next of kin said to Bo'az, "Buy it for yourself 1
9 Then Bo'az said to the elders and all the people 1
13 Bo'az took Ruth and she became his wife; 1
21 Salmon of Bo'az, Bo'az of Obed 1
21 Salmon of Bo'az, Bo'az of Obed 1
1Kg 7:21 the pillar on the north and called its name Bo'az. 1
1Ch 2:11 Nahshon was the father of Salma, Salma of Bo'az 1
12 Bo'az of Obed, Obed of Jesse. 1
2Ch 3:17 pillars . . Jachin, and that on the north Bo'az. 1
Mat 1: 5 Salmon the father of Bo'az by Rahab 2
5 Bo'az the father of Obed by Ruth 2
Lke 3:32 the son of Jesse, the son of Obed, the son of Bo'az 3

Bocheru 1. בֹּכְרוּ
1Ch 8:38 Azel had six sons . . Azri'kam, Bo'cheru, Ish'mael 1
9:44 Azel had six sons . . Azri'kam, Bo'cheru, Ish'mael 1

Bochim 1. בֹּכִים
Jdg 2: 1 angel of the LORD went up from Gilgal to Bochim 1
5 name of that place Bochim; and they sacrificed 1

Bohan 1. בֹּהַן
Jos 15: 6 goes up to the stone of Bohan the son of Reuben; 1
18:17 it goes down to the Stone of Bohan the son of Reuben; 1

Book of the Wars of the LORD
1. סֵפֶר מִלְחֲמֹת יְהוָה
Num21:14 Where it is said in the Book of the Wars of the LORD 1

Bor-ashan 1. בּוֹר עָשָׁן
1Sm 30:30 for those . . in Hormah, in Borash'an, in A'thach 1

Borith 1. Borith
2Es 1: 2 son of Borith, son of Abishua, son of Phinehas 1

Bosor 1. Βοσορ
1Mc 5:26 Many of them have been shut up in Bozrah and Bosor 1
36 marched on and took Chaspho, Maked, and Bosor 1

Bougaean 1. Βουγαῖος
AEs 12: 6 Haman, the son of Hammedatha, a Bougaean 1

Bozez 1. בּוֹצֵץ
1Sm 14: 4 name of the one was Bozez, and the . . other Seneh. 1

Bozkath 1. בָּצְקַת
Jos 15:39 Lachish, Bozkath, Eglon 1
2Kg 22: 1 was Jedi'dah the daughter of Adai'ah of Bozkath. 1

Bozrah 1. בָּצְרָה 2. Βοσορρα
Gen 36:33 son of Zerah of Bozrah reigned in his stead. 1
1Ch 1:44 When Bela died, Jobab the son of Zerah of Bozrah 1
Isa 34: 6 For the LORD has a sacrifice in Bozrah 1
63: 1 that comes . . in crimsoned garments from Bozrah 1
Jer 48:24 Ker'i-oth, and Bozrah, and all the cities of the land 1
49:13 says the LORD, that Bozrah shall become a horror 1
22 an eagle, and spread his wings against Bozrah 1
Ams 1:12 it shall devour the strongholds of Bozrah. 1
1Mc 5:26 Many of them have been shut up in Bozrah and Bosor 2
28 Judas . . turned back by the wilderness road to Bozrah 2

Bukki 1. בֻּקִּי 2. Βοκκα
Num34:22 tribe . . of Dan a leader, Bukki the son of Jogli. 1
1Ch 6: 5 Abishu'a of Bukki, Bukki of Uzzi 1
5 Abishu'a of Bukki, Bukki of Uzzi 1
51 Bukki his son, Uzzi his son, Zerahi'ah his son 1
Ezr 7: 4 son of Zerahi'ah, son of Uzzi, son of Bukki 1
1Es 8: 2 son of Uzzi, son of Bukki, son of Abishua 2

Bukkiah 1. בֻּקִּיָּהוּ
1Ch 25: 4 sons of Heman: Bukki'ah, Mattani'ah, Uz'ziel, 1
13 sixth to Bukki'ah, his sons and his brethren 1

Bul 1. בּוּל
1Kg 6:38 in the month of Bul, which is the eighth month 1

Bunah 1. בּוּנָה
1Ch 2:25 The sons of Jerah'meel . . Bunah, Oren, Ozem 1

Bunni 1. בֻּנִּי
Neh 9: 4 stood . . Bunni, Sherebi'ah, Bani, and Chena'ni; 1
10:15 Bunni, Azgad, Be'bai 1
11:15 son of Azri'kam, son of Hashabi'ah, son of Bunni; 1

Buz 1. בּוּז
Gen 22:21 Uz the first-born, Buz his brother 1
1Ch 5:14 sons of Ab'ihail . . son of Jahdo, son of Buz; 1
Jer 25:23 Buz, and all who cut the corners of their hair; 1

Buzi 1. בּוּזִי
Ezk 1: 3 came to Ezekiel the priest, the son of Buzi 1

Buzite 1. בּוּזִי
Job 32: 2 Then Eli'hu the son of Bar'achel the Buzite 1
6 Eli'hu the son of Bar'achel the Buzite answered 1

Cabbon 1. כַּבּוֹן
Jos 15:40 Cabbon, Lahmam, Chitlish 1

Cabul 1. כָּבוּל
Jos 19:27 then it continues in the north to Cabul 1
1Kg 9:13 So they are called the land of Cabul to this day. 1

Caesar 1. Καῖσαρ
Mat 22:17 Is it lawful to pay taxes to Caesar, or not? 1
21 They said, "Caesar's." Then he said to them 1
21 Render therefore to Caesar 1
21 the things that are Caesar's 1
Mrk 12:14 Is it lawful to pay taxes to Caesar, or not? 1
16 They said to him, "Caesar's. 1
17 Render to Caesar the things that are Caesar's 1
17 Render to Caesar the things that are Caesar's 1
Lke 2: 1 a decree went out from Caesar Augustus 1
3: 1 fifteenth year of the reign of Tiber'ius Caesar 1
20:22 Is it lawful for us to give tribute to Caesar 1
24 They said, "Caesar's. 1
25 render to Caesar the things that are Caesar's 1
25 render to Caesar the things that are Caesar's 1
23: 2 forbidding us to give tribute to Caesar 1
Joh 19:12 you are not Caesar's friend 1
12 every one . . sets himself against Caesar. 1
15 We have no king but Caesar. 1
Act 17: 7 are all acting against the decrees of Caesar 1
25: 8 nor against the temple, nor against Caesar 1
10 Paul said, "I am standing before Caesar's tribunal 1
11 I appeal to Caesar. 1
12 You have appealed to Caesar 1
12 to Caesar you shall go. 1
21 until I could send him to Caesar. 1
26:32 if he had not appealed to Caesar. 1
27:24 you must stand before Caesar 1
28:19 I was compelled to appeal to Caesar 1
Php 4:22 especially those of Caesar's household. 1

Caesarea 1. Καισάρεια
Mat 16:13 into the district of Caesare'a Philip'pi 1
Mrk 8:27 to the villages of Caesare'a Philip'pi 1
Act 8:40 till he came to Caesare'a. 1
9:30 they brought him down to Caesare'a 1
10: 1 At Caesare'a there was a man named Cornelius 1
24 on the following day they entered Caesare'a. 1
11:11 three men arrived . . sent to me from Caesare'a. 1
12:19 Then he went down from Judea to Caesare'a 1
18:22 When he had landed at Caesare'a, he went up 1
21: 8 On the morrow we departed and came to Caesare'a; 1
16 some of the disciples from Caesare'a went with us 1
23:23 get ready . . to go as far as Caesare'a. 1
33 When they came to Caesare'a 1
25: 1 he went up to Jerusalem from Caesare'a. 1
4 Paul was being kept at Caesare'a 1
6 he went down to Caesare'a 1
13 Agrippa . . arrived at Caesare'a to welcome Festus. 1

Caiaphas 1. Καϊάφας
Mat 26: 3 the high priest, who was called Ca'iaphas 1
57 led him to Ca'iaphas the high priest 1
Lke 3: 2 in the high-priesthood of Annas and Ca'iaphas 1
Joh 11:49 Ca'iaphas, who was high priest that year, said 1
18:13 he was the father-in-law of Ca'iaphas 1
14 It was Ca'iaphas who had given counsel to the Jews 1
24 Annas then sent him bound to Ca'iaphas 1
28 they led Jesus from the house of Ca'iaphas 1
Act 4: 6 Annas the high priest and Ca'iaphas and John 1

Cain 1. קַיִן 2. Κάϊν
Gen 4: 1 she conceived and bore Cain, saying, "I have gotten 1
2 keeper of sheep, and Cain a tiller of the ground. 1
3 In the course of time Cain brought to the LORD 1
5 for Cain and his offering he had no regard. 1
5 Cain was very angry, and his countenance fell. 1
6 The LORD said to Cain, "Why are you angry 1
8 Cain said to Abel his brother, "Let us go out 1
8 Cain rose up against his brother Abel 1
9 the LORD said to Cain, "Where is Abel your brother? 1
13 Cain said to the LORD, "My punishment is greater 1
15 If any one slays Cain, vengeance shall be taken 1
15 And the LORD put a mark on Cain 1
16 Cain went away from the presence of the LORD 1
17 Cain knew his wife, and she conceived 1
24 If Cain is avenged sevenfold 1
25 another child instead of Abel, for Cain slew him. 1
Heb 11: 4 a more acceptable sacrifice than Cain 2
1Jn 3:12 and not be like Cain who was of the evil one 2
Jde 1:11 Woe to them! For they walk in the way of Cain 2
4Mc 18:11 He read to you about Abel slain by Cain 2

Cainan 1. Καϊνάμ
Lke 3:36 the son of Ca-i'nan, the son of Arphax'ad 1
37 the son of Maha'lele-el, the son of Ca-i'nan 1

Calah 1. כֶּלַח
Gen 10:11 and built Nin'eveh, Reho'both-Ir, Calah 1
12 Resen between Nin'eveh and Calah; 1

Calcol 1. כַּלְכֹּל
1Kg 4:31 wiser than Ethan . . and Heman, Calcol, and Darda 1
1Ch 2: 6 sons of Zerah: Zimri, Ethan, Heman, Calcol, and Dara 1

Caleb 1. כָּלֵב 2. Χαλεβ
Num13: 6 from the tribe of Judah, Caleb . . of Jephun'neh; 1
30 Caleb quieted the people before Moses, and said 1
14: 6 Joshua . . of Nun and Caleb the son of Jephun'neh 1
24 my servant Caleb . . I will bring into the land 1
30 except Caleb the son of Jephun'neh and Joshua 1
38 Joshua . . and Caleb . . remained alive 1
26:65 not left a man . . except Caleb . . and Joshua 1
32:12 except Caleb the son of Jephun'neh the Ken'izzite 1
34:19 Of the tribe of Judah, Caleb the son of Jephun'neh. 1
Deu 1:36 except Caleb the son of Jephun'neh; he shall see it 1
Jos 14: 6 and Caleb the son of Jephun'neh the Ken'izzite 1
13 Joshua blessed him; and he gave Hebron to Caleb 1
14 Hebron became the inheritance of Caleb 1
15:13 he gave to Caleb the son of Jephun'neh a portion 1
14 Caleb drove out from there the three sons of Anak 1
16 And Caleb said, "Whoever smites Kir'iath-se'pher 1
17 Oth'ni-el the son of Kenaz, the brother of Caleb 1
18 she alighted from her ass, and Caleb said to her 1
19 Caleb gave her the upper springs and the lower •
21:12 But the fields . . had been given to Caleb 1
Jdg 1:12 Caleb said, "He who attacks Kir'iath-se'pher 1
13 Oth'ni-el the son of Kenaz, Caleb's younger brother 1
14 and Caleb said to her, "What do you wish? 1
15 Caleb gave her the upper springs and the lower 1
20 Hebron was given to Caleb, as Moses had said; 1
3: 9 the son of Kenaz, Caleb's younger brother. 1
1Sm 30:14 made a raid . . and upon the Negeb of Caleb; 1
1Ch 2:18 Caleb the son of Hezron had children by his wife 1
19 Caleb married Ephrath, who bore him Hur. 1
24 Caleb went in to Eph'rathah, the wife of Hezron 1
42 The sons of Caleb the brother of Jerah'meel 1
46 Ephah also, Caleb's concubine, bore Haran, Moza 1
48 Ma'acah, Caleb's concubine, bore Sheber 1
49 and the daughter of Caleb was Achsah. 1
50 These were the descendants of Caleb. 1
4:15 Caleb the son of Jephun'neh 1
6:56 they gave to Caleb the son of Jephun'neh. 1
Sir 46: 7 he and Caleb the son of Jephunneh 2
9 the Lord gave Caleb strength 2
1Mc 2:56 Caleb . . received an inheritance in the land. 2

Calebite 1. כָּלִבִּי
1Sm 25: 3 was churlish and ill-behaved; he was a Calebite. 1

Callisthenes 1. Καλλισθένης
2Mc 8:33 Callisthenes and some others 1

Calneh 1. כַּלְנֵה
Ams 6: 2 Pass over to Calneh, and see; 1

Calno 1. כַּלְנוֹ
Isa 10: 9 Is not Calno like Car'chemish? 1

Cana 1. Κανά
Joh 2: 1 there was a marriage at Cana in Galilee 1
11 first of his signs, Jesus did at Cana in Galilee 1
4:46 So he came again to Cana in Galilee 1
21: 2 Nathan'a-el of Cana in Galilee, the sons of Zeb'edee 1

Canaan 1. כְּנַעַן 2. Χανάαν
Gen 9:18 Ham was the father of Canaan. 1
22 Ham, the father of Canaan, saw the nakedness 1
25 he said, "Cursed be Canaan; 1
26 and let Canaan be his slave. 1
27 tents of Shem; and let Canaan be his slave. 1
10: 6 The sons of Ham: Cush, Egypt, Put, and Canaan. 1
15 Canaan became the father of Sidon 1
11:31 of the Chalde'ans to go into the land of Canaan; 1
12: 5 and they set forth to go to the land of Canaan. 1
5 When they had come to the land of Canaan 1
13:12 Abram dwelt in the land of Canaan 1
16: 3 had dwelt ten years in the land of Canaan 1
17: 8 land of your sojournings, all the land of Canaan 1
23: 2 Sarah died . . in the land of Canaan; 1
19 of Mamre (that is, Hebron) in the land of Canaan. 1
31:18 to go to the land of Canaan to his father Isaac. 1
33:18 the city of Shechem, which is in the land of Canaan 1
35: 6 Luz . . which is in the land of Canaan 1
36: 5 who were born to him in the land of Canaan. 1
6 which he had acquired in the land of Canaan; 1
37: 1 his father's sojournings, in the land of Canaan. 1
42: 5 for the famine was in the land of Canaan. 1
7 They said, "From the land of Canaan, to buy food. 1
13 the sons of one man in the land of Canaan; 1
29 came to Jacob their father in the land of Canaan 1
32 this day with our father in the land of Canaan.' 1
44: 8 we brought back to you from the land of Canaan; 1
45:17 load your beasts and go back to the land of Canaan; 1
25 and came to the land of Canaan to their father 1
46: 6 goods, which they had gained in the land of Canaan 1
12 but Er and Onan died in the land of Canaan 1
31 My brothers . . who were in the land of Canaan 1
47: 1 my brothers . . have come from the land of Canaan; 1

4 for the famine is severe in the land of Canaan; 1
13 land of Egypt and the land of Canaan languished 1
14 money . . in the land of Canaan, for the grain 1
15 in the land of Egypt and in the land of Canaan 1
48: 3 God . . appeared to me . . in the land of Canaan 1
7 Rachel to my sorrow died in the land of Canaan 1
49:30 to the east of Mamre, in the land of Canaan 1
50: 5 in my tomb . . in the land of Canaan, 1
13 for his sons carried him to the land of Canaan 1
Exd 6: 4 covenant . . to give them the land of Canaan 1
15:15 all the inhabitants of Canaan have melted away. 1
16:35 they came to the border of the land of Canaan. 1
Lev 14:34 When you come into the land of Canaan, which I give 1
18: 3 not . . as they do in the land of Canaan 1
25:38 to give you the land of Canaan, and to be your God 1
Num13: 2 Send men to spy out the land of Canaan 1
17 Moses sent them to spy out the land of Canaan 1
26:19 Er and Onan died in the land of Canaan. 1
32:30 possessions among you in the land of Canaan. 1
32 pass over armed . . into the land of Canaan 1
33:40 king . . dwelt in the Negeb in the land of Canaan 1
51 pass over the Jordan into the land of Canaan 1
34: 2 When you enter the land of Canaan (this is the land 1
2 inheritance, the land of Canaan in its full extent) 1
29 divide the inheritance . . in the land of Canaan. 1
35:10 When you cross the Jordan into the land of Canaan 1
14 shall give . . three cities in the land of Canaan 1
Deu 32:49 view the land of Canaan, which I give to . . Israel 1
Jos 5:12 Israel . . ate of the fruit of the land of Canaan 1
14: 1 which . . Israel received in the land of Canaan 1
21: 2 they said to them at Shiloh in the land of Canaan 1
22: 9 at Shiloh, which is in the land of Canaan 1
10 to the region . . that lies in the land of Canaan 1
11 an altar at the frontier of the land of Canaan 1
32 returned from . . Gilead to the land of Canaan 1
24: 3 and led him through all the land of Canaan 1
Jdg 3: 1 Israel who had no experience of any war in Canaan; 1
4: 2 hand of Jabin king of Canaan, who reigned in Hazor; 1
23 God subdued Jabin the king of Canaan before 1
24 harder and harder on Jabin the king of Canaan 1
24 until they destroyed Jabin king of Canaan. 1
5:19 then fought the kings of Canaan, at Ta'anach 1
21:12 the camp at Shiloh, which is in the land of Canaan. 1
1Ch 1: 8 The sons of Ham: Cush, Egypt, Put, and Canaan. 1
13 Canaan was the father of Sidon his first-born 1
16:18 saying, "To you I will give the land of Canaan 1
Ps 105:11 saying, "To you I will give the land of Canaan 1
106:38 whom they sacrificed to the idols of Canaan; 1
135:11 Sihon . . Og, . . , and all the kingdoms of Canaan 1
Isa 19:18 cities . . which speak the language of Canaan 1
23:11 the LORD has given command concerning Canaan 1
Zep 2: 5 The word of the LORD is against you, O Canaan 1
Act 7:11 came a famine throughout all Egypt and Canaan 2
13:19 destroyed seven nations in the land of Canaan 2
Jdt 5: 9 go to the land of Canaan 2
10 When a famine spread over Canaan 2
Bar 3:22 She has not been heard of in Canaan, nor seen 2
Sus 1:56 You offspring of Canaan and not of Judah 2
1Mc 9:37 a daughter of one of the great nobles of Canaan 2

Canaanite 1. כְּנַעַן 2. כְּנַעֲנִי 3. υἱὸς Χαναάν 4. Χαναναῖος 5. Chananeus

Gen 10:18 Afterward the families of the Canaanites 2
19 the territory of the Canaanites extended 2
12: 6 At that time the Canaanites were in the land. 2
13: 7 At that time the Canaanites and the Per'izzites 2
15:21 the Amorites, the Canaanites, the Gir'gashites 2
24: 3 a wife . . from the daughters of the Canaanites 2
37 my son from the daughters of the Canaanites 2
28: 1 You shall not marry one of the Canaanite women. 1
6 You shall not marry one of the Canaanite women 1
8 Canaanite women did not please Isaac his father 1
34:30 of the land, the Canaanites and the Per'izzites; 2
36: 2 Esau took his wives from the Canaanites 1
38: 2 Judah saw the daughter of a certain Canaanite 2
50:11 When the inhabitants of the land, the Canaanites 2
Exd 3: 8 to the place of the Canaanites, the Hittites 2
17 bring you . . to the land of the Canaanites 2
13: 5 brings you into the land of the Canaanites 2
11 brings you into the land of the Canaanites 2
23:23 the Per'izzites, and the Canaanites, the Hivites 2
28 shall drive out Hivite, Canaanite, and Hittite 2
33: 2 I will drive out the Canaanites, the Amorites 2
34:11 the Canaanites, the Hittites, the Per'izzites 2
Num13:29 Canaanites dwell by the sea, and along the Jordan. 2
14:25 since the Amal'ekites and the Canaanites dwell 2
43 Amal'ekites and the Canaanites are before you 2
45 Amal'ekites and the Canaanites who dwelt 2
21: 1 When the Canaanite, the king of Arad, who dwelt 2
3 the LORD . . gave over the Canaanites; 2
33:40 Canaanite, the king of Arad, who dwelt in the Negeb 2
Deu 1: 7 by the seacoast, the land of the Canaanites 2
7: 1 Amorites, the Canaanites, the Per'izzites 2
11:30 land of the Canaanites who live in the Arabah 2
20:17 destroy . . Canaanites and the Per'izzites 2
Jos 3:10 drive out . . the Canaanites, the Hittites 2
5: 1 and all the kings of the Canaanites . . by the sea 2
7: 9 For the Canaanites and all . . will hear of it 2
9: 1 Hittites, the Amorites, the Canaanites 2
11: 3 sent . . to the Canaanites in the east and the west 2
12: 8 the Amorites, the Canaanites, the Per'izzites 2
13: 3 from . . it is reckoned as Canaanite; 2
4 in the south, all the land of the Canaanites 2
16:10 However they did not drive out the Canaanites 2
10 the Canaanites have dwelt in the midst 2
17:12 Canaanites persisted in dwelling in that land. 2
13 they put the Canaanites to forced labor 2
16 yet all the Canaanites . . have chariots of iron 2
18 you shall drive out the Canaanites 2
24:11 the Amorites, the Per'izzites, the Canaanites 2
Jdg 1: 1 go up . . against the Canaanites, to fight 2
3 that we may fight against the Canaanites; 2
4 LORD gave the Canaanites and the Per'izzites 2
5 defeated the Canaanites and the Per'izzites. 2
9 went down to fight against the Canaanites who 2
10 Judah went against the Canaanites who dwelt 2
17 defeated the Canaanites who inhabited Zephath 2
27 Canaanites persisted in dwelling in that land. 2
28 they put the Canaanites to forced labor, but did 2
29 E'phraim did not drive out the Canaanites who 2
29 but the Canaanites dwelt in Gezer among them. 2
30 Canaanites dwelt among them, and became subject 2
32 among the Canaanites, the inhabitants 2
33 dwelt among the Canaanites, the inhabitants 2
3: 3 the Philistines, and all the Canaanites 2
5 among the Canaanites, the Hittites, the Amorites 2
2Sm 24: 7 to all the cities of the Hivites and Canaanites; 2
1Kg 9:16 had slain the Canaanites who dwelt in the city 2
Ezr 9: 1 from the Canaanites, the Hittites 2
Neh 9: 8 to his descendants the land of the Canaanite 2
24 inhabitants of the land, the Canaanites 2
Ezk 16: 3 and your birth are of the land of the Canaanites; 2
Mat 15:22 behold, a Canaanite woman from that region 4
1Es 8:69 the Canaanites, the Hittites, the Perizzites 4
2Es 1:21 I drove out the Canaanites, the Perizzites 5
Jdt 5: 3 said to them, "Tell me, you Canaanites 3
16 they drove out before them the Canaanites 4

Canaanite woman 1. כְּנַעֲנִי

Exd 6:15 Zohar, and Shaul, the son of a Canaanite woman; 1

Canaanitess 1. כְּנַעֲנִי

1Ch 2: 3 these three Bath-shu'a the Canaanitess bore 1

Canaanitish woman 1. כְּנַעֲנִי

Gen 46:10 and Shaul, the son of a Canaanitish woman. 1

Cananaean 1. Καναναῖος

Mat 10: 4 Simon the Cananaean, and Judas Iscariot 1
Mrk 3:18 Thaddaeus, and Simon the Cananaean 1

Candace 1. Κανδάκη

Act 8:27 minister of the Can'dace, queen of the Ethiopians 1

Canneh 1. כַּנֵּה

Ezk 27:23 Canneh, Eden, Asshur, and Chilmad traded with you. 1

Capernaum 1. Καφαρναούμ

Mat 4:13 leaving Nazareth he went and dwelt in Caper'na-um 1
8: 5 As he entered Caper'na-um, a centurion came 1
11:23 you, Caper'na-um, will you be exalted to heaven? 1
17:24 When they came to Caper'na-um 1
Mrk 1:21 And they went into Caper'na-um 1
2: 1 when he returned to Caper'na-um after some days 1
9:33 they came to Caper'na-um 1
Lke 4:23 what we have heard you did at Caper'na-um, do here 1
31 he went down to Caper'na-um, a city of Galilee. 1
7: 1 he entered Caper'na-um. 1
10:15 you, Caper'na-um, will you be exalted to heaven? 1
Joh 2:12 After this he went down to Caper'na-um 1
4:46 And at Caper'na-um there was an official whose son 1
6:17 started across the sea to Caper'na-um 1
24 they . . got into the boats and went to Capernaum 1
59 as he taught at Caper'na-um. 1

Caphar-salama 1. Χαφαρσαλαμα

1Mc 7:31 to meet Judas in battle near Caphar-salama. 1

Caphtor 1. כַּפְתּוֹר

Deu 2:23 Caph'torim, who came from Caphtor, destroyed them 1
Jer 47: 4 the remnant of the coastland of Caphtor. 1
Ams 9: 7 bring up . . and the Philistines from Caphtor 1

Caphtorim 1. כַּפְתֹּרִי

Gen 10:14 came the Philistines), and Caph'torim. 1
Deu 2:23 Caph'torim, who came from Caphtor, destroyed them 1
1Ch 1:12 (whence came the Philis'tines), and Caph'torim 1

Cappadocia 1. Καππαδοκία

Act 2: 9 residents of Mesopota'mia, Judea and Cappado'cia 1
1Pe 1: 1 the Dispersion in Pontus, Galatia, Cappado'cia 1

Carabasion 1. Καραβασιων

1Es 9:34 Carabasion and Eliashib and Machnadebai 1

Carchemish 1. כַּרְכְּמִישׁ 2. Χαρκαμυς

2Ch 35:20 to fight at Car'chemish on the Euphra'tes 1
Isa 10: 9 Is not Calno like Car'chemish? 1
Jer 46: 2 which was by the river Euphra'tes at Car'chemish 1
1Es 1:25 went to make war at Carchemish on the Euphrates 2

Caria 1. Καρια

1Mc 15:23 to Myndos, and to Sicyon, and to Caria, and to Samos 1

Carite 1. כָּרִי

2Kg 11: 4 the captains of the Carites and of the guards 1
19 he took the captains, the Carites, the guards 1

Carkas 1. כַּרְכַּס

Est 1:10 Harbo'na, Bigtha and Abag'tha, Zethar and Carkas 1

Carmel 1. כַּרְמֶל 2. כַּרְמְלִי 3. Καρμηλος

Jos 12:22 of Kedesh, one; the king of Jok'ne-am in Carmel, one; 1
15:55 Ma'on, Carmel, Ziph, Juttah 1
19:26 on the west it touches Carmel and Shihor-lib'nath 1
1Sm 15:12 Saul came to Carmel, and . . he set up a monument 1
25: 2 a man in Ma'on, whose business was in Carmel. 1
2 He was shearing his sheep in Carmel. 1
5 Go up to Carmel, and go to Nabal, and greet him 1
7 missed nothing, all the time they were in Carmel. 1
40 the servants of David came to Ab'igail at Carmel 1
27: 3 Ahin'o-am . . and Ab'igail of Carmel, Nabal's widow. 2
30: 5 Ab'igail the widow of Nabal of Carmel. 2
2Sm 2: 2 Ab'igail the widow of Nabal of Carmel. 2
3: 3 Chil'e-ab, of Ab'igail the widow of Nabal of Carmel; 2
23:35 Hezro of Carmel, Pa'arai the Arbite 2
1Kg 18:19 send and gather all Israel to me at Mount Carmel 1
20 and gathered the prophets . . at Mount Carmel. 1
42 And Eli'jah went up to the top of Carmel; 1
2Kg 2:25 From there he went on to Mount Carmel 1
4:25 So she . . came to the man of God at Mount Carmel. 1
1Ch 11:37 Hezro of Carmel, Na'arai the son of Ezbai 2
Sng 7: 5 Your head crowns you like Carmel 1
Isa 33: 9 and Bashan and Carmel shake off their leaves. 1
35: 2 the majesty of Carmel and Sharon. 1
Jer 46:18 and like Carmel by the sea, shall one come. 1
50:19 and he shall feed on Carmel and in Bashan 1
Ams 1: 2 shepherds mourn, and the top of Carmel withers. 1
9: 3 Though they hide themselves on the top of Carmel 1
Nah 1: 4 Bashan and Carmel wither 1
Jdt 1: 8 those among the nations of Carmel and Gilead 3

Carmelitess 1. כַּרְמְלִי

1Ch 3: 1 the second Daniel, by Ab'igail the Car'melitess 1

Carmi 1. כַּרְמִי

Gen 46: 9 sons of Reuben: Hanoch, Pallu, Hezron, and Carmi 1
Exd 6:14 Hanoch, Pallu, Hezron, and Carmi; these are 1
Num26: 6 of Carmi, the family of the Carmites. 1
Jos 7: 1 Achan the son of Carmi, son of Zabdi, son of Zerah 1
18 Achan the son of Carmi, son of Zabdi, son of Zerah 1
1Ch 2: 7 The sons of Carmi: Achar, the troubler of Israel 1
4: 1 sons of Judah: Perez, Hezron, Carmi, Hur, and Shobal. 1
5: 3 sons of Reuben . . Pallu, Hezron, and Carmi. 1

Carmite 1. כַּרְמִי

Num26: 6 of Carmi, the family of the Carmites. 1

Carmonian 1. Carmonius

2Es 15:30 the Carmonians, raging in wrath, shall go forth 1

Carnaim 1. Καρναιν 2. Καρνιον

1Mc 5:26 in Alema and Chaspho, Maked and Carnaim 1
43 and fled into the sacred precincts at Carnaim. 1
44 Thus Carnaim was conquered 1
2Mc 12:21 a place called Carnaim 2
26 Then Judas marched against Carnaim 2

Carpus 1. Κάρπος

2Ti 4:13 bring the cloak that I left with Carpus at Tro'as 1

Carshena 1. כַּרְשְׁנָא

Est 1:14 the men next to him being Carshe'na, Shethar 1

Casiphia 1. כָּסִפְיָא

Ezr 8:17 Iddo, the leading man at the place Casiphi'a 1
17 temple servants at the place Casiphi'a 1

Casluhim 1. כַּסְלֻחִים

Gen 10:14 Pathru'sim, Caslu'him (whence came 1
1Ch 1:12 Pathru'sim, Caslu'him (whence came the Philis'tines 1

Caspin 1. Κασπιν

2Mc 12:13 Its name was Caspin. 1

Cathua 1. Καθουα

1Es 5:30 sons of Hana, the sons of Cathua, the sons of Gahar 1

Cauda 1. Καῦδα

Act 27:16 a small island called Cauda 1

Cenchreae 1. Κεγχρεαί

Act 18:18 At Cen'chre-ae he cut his hair, for he had a vow. 1
Rom16: 1 Phoebe, a deaconess of the church at Cen'chre-ae 1

Cendebeus 1. Κενδεβαιος
1Mc 15:38 Then the king made Cendebeus commander-in-chief 1
40 So Cendebeus came to Jamnia 1
16: 1 reported . . what Cendebeus had done. 1
4 they marched against Cendebeus 1
8 Cendebeus and his army were put to flight 1
9 John pursued them until Cendebeus reached Kedron •

Cephas 1. Κηφᾶς
Joh 1:42 You shall be called Cephas" (which means Peter). 1
1Co 1:12 I belong to Cephas," or "I belong to Christ. 1
3:22 whether Paul or Apol'los or Cephas or the world 1
9: 5 the brothers of the Lord and Cephas? 1
15: 5 that he appeared to Cephas, then to the twelve. 1
Gal 1:18 I went up to Jerusalem to visit Cephas 1
2: 9 James and Cephas and John 1
11 when Cephas came to Antioch 1
14 I said to Cephas before them all 1

Chabris 1. Χαβρις
Jdt 6:15 Chabris the son of Gothoniel 1
8:10 to summon Chabris and Charmis 1
10: 6 the elders of the city, Chabris and Charmis. 1

Chadiasan 1. Χαδιασαι
1Es 5:20 The Chadiasans and Ammidians, 422. 1

Chaereas 1. Χαιρεας
2Mc 10:32 where Chaereas was commander. 1
37 his brother Chaereas, and Apollophanes. 1

Chaldea 1. כַּשְׂדִּים 2. לֵב קָמָי 3. Χαλδαῖος
Isa 48:20 Go forth from Babylon, flee from Chalde'a 1
Jer 50:10 Chalde'a shall be plundered; 1
51: 1 against the inhabitants of Chalde'a 2
24 Babylon and all the inhabitants of Chalde'a 1
35 My blood be upon the inhabitants of Chalde'a 1
Ezk 11:24 by the Spirit of God into Chalde'a, to the exiles. 1
16:29 harlotry also with the trading land of Chalde'a; 1
23:15 of Babylonians whose native land was Chalde'a. 1
16 and sent messengers to them in Chalde'a. 1
Jdt 5: 7 the gods of their fathers who were in Chaldea. 3

Chaldean 1. כַּשְׂדִּים 2. כַּשְׂדָּי (A) 3. כַּשְׂדָּי (A) 4. υἱὸς Χελεουδ 5. Χαλδαῖος
Gen 11:28 land of his birth, in Ur of the Chalde'ans. 1
31 went forth together from Ur of the Chalde'ans 1
15: 7 from Ur of the Chalde'ans, to give you this land 1
2Kg 24: 2 the LORD sent against him bands of the Chalde'ans 1
25: 4 though the Chalde'ans were around the city. 1
5 But the army of the Chalde'ans pursued the king 1
10 the army of the Chalde'ans . . broke down the walls 1
13 the pillars . . the Chalde'ans broke in pieces 1
24 not be afraid because of the Chalde'an officials; 1
25 Gedali'ah . . and the Chalde'ans who were with him 1
26 for they were afraid of the Chalde'ans. 1
2Ch 36:17 he brought up . . the king of the Chalde'ans 1
Ezr 5:12 Nebuchadnez'zar king of Babylon, the Chalde'an 2
Neh 9: 7 bring him forth out of Ur of the Chalde'ans 1
Job 1:17 The Chalde'ans formed three companies 1
Isa 13:19 Babylon . . splendor and pride of the Chalde'ans 1
23:13 Behold the land of the Chalde'ans! 1
43:14 the shouting of the Chalde'ans will be turned 1
47: 1 without a throne, O daughter of the Chalde'ans! 1
5 go into darkness, O daughter of the Chalde'ans 1
48:14 and his arm shall be against the Chalde'ans. 1
Jer 21: 4 and against the Chalde'ans who are besieging you 1
9 he who goes out and surrenders to the Chalde'ans 1
22:25 and into the hand of the Chalde'ans. 1
24: 5 from this place to the land of the Chalde'ans. 1
25:12 and that nation, the land of the Chalde'ans 1
32: 4 shall not escape out of the hand of the Chalde'ans 1
5 though you fight against the Chalde'ans 1
24 the city is given into the hands of the Chalde'ans 1
25 the city is given into the hands of the Chalde'ans 1
28 giving this city into the hands of the Chalde'ans 1
29 Chalde'ans who are fighting against this city 1
43 it is given into the hands of the Chalde'ans. 1
33: 5 The Chalde'ans are coming in to fight 1
35:11 for fear of the army of the Chalde'ans 1
37: 5 the Chalde'ans who were besieging Jerusalem 1
8 And the Chalde'ans shall come back and fight 1
9 The Chalde'ans will surely stay away from us 1
10 army of Chalde'ans who are fighting against you 1
11 Now when the Chalde'an army had withdrawn 1
13 saying, "You are deserting to the Chalde'ans. 1
14 It is false; I am not deserting to the Chalde'ans. 1
38: 2 but he who goes out to the Chalde'ans shall live; 1
18 shall be given into the hand of the Chalde'ans 1
19 the Jews who have deserted to the Chalde'ans 1
23 and your sons shall be led out to the Chalde'ans 1
39: 5 But the army of the Chalde'ans pursued them 1
8 The Chalde'ans burned the king's house 1
40: 9 saying, "Do not be afraid to serve the Chalde'ans. 1
10 at Mizpah, to stand for you before the Chalde'ans 1
41: 3 the Chalde'an soldiers who happened to be there. 1
18 because of the Chalde'ans; for they were afraid 1
43: 3 to deliver us into the hand of the Chalde'ans 1
50: 1 concerning the land of the Chalde'ans 1
8 and go out of the land of the Chalde'ans 1
25 has a work to do in the land of the Chalde'ans. 1
35 A sword upon the Chalde'ans, says the LORD 1
45 purposes . . against the land of the Chalde'ans 1
51: 4 fall down slain in the land of the Chalde'ans 1
5 the land of the Chalde'ans is full of guilt •
54 destruction from the land of the Chalde'ans! 1
52: 7 while the Chalde'ans were round about the city. 1
8 But the army of the Chalde'ans pursued the king 1
14 And all the army of the Chalde'ans 1
17 the Chalde'ans broke in pieces, and carried all 1
Ezk 1: 3 in the land of the Chalde'ans by the river Chebar; 1
12:13 bring him to Babylon in the land of the Chalde'ans 1
23:14 images of the Chalde'ans portrayed in vermilion 1
23 the Babylonians and all the Chalde'ans 1
Dan 2: 2 commanded that the . . Chalde'ans be summoned 1
4 Then the Chalde'ans said to the king, "O king 1
5 king answered the Chalde'ans, "The word from me 3
10 Chalde'ans answered the king, "There is not a man 3
10 such a thing of any magician . . or Chalde'an. 3
3: 8 at that time certain Chalde'ans came forward 3
4: 7 magicians, the enchanters, the Chalde'ans 3
5: 7 enchanters, the Chalde'ans, and the astrologers. 3
11 chief of the . . Chalde'ans, and astrologers 3
30 night Belshaz'zar the Chalde'an king was slain. 3
9: 1 became king over the realm of the Chalde'ans– 1
Hab 1: 6 For lo, I am rousing the Chalde'ans 1
Act 7: 4 Then he departed from the land of the Chalde'ans 5
1Es 1:52 bring against them the kings of the Chaldeans. 5
4:45 when Judea was laid waste by the Chaldeans. 5
6:15 king of Babylon, king of the Chaldeans; 5
Jdt 1: 6 Many nations joined the forces of the Chaldeans. 4
5: 6 This people is descended from the Chaldeans. 5
Bar 1: 2 at the time when the Chaldeans took Jerusalem 5
LJr 1:40 Besides, even the Chaldeans . . dishonor them; 5
Aza 1:25 it broke through and burned those of the Chaldeans 5

Chalphi 1. Χαλφι
1Mc 11:70 Judas the son of Chalphi 1

Chaphenatha 1. Χαφεναθα
1Mc 12:37 he repaired the section called Chaphenatha. 1

Charax 1. Χαραξ
2Mc 12:17 they came to Charax 1

Charea 1. Χαρεα
1Es 5:32 the sons of Charea, the sons of Barkos 1

Charmis 1. Χαρμις
Jdt 6:15 Charmis the son of Melchiel. 1
8:10 to summon Chabris and Charmis 1
10: 6 the elders of the city, Chabris and Charmis. 1

Chaspho 1. Χασφω
1Mc 5:26 in Alema and Chaspho, Maked and Carnaim 1
36 marched on and took Chaspho, Maked, and Bosor 1

Chebar 1. כְּבָר
Ezk 1: 1 as I was among the exiles by the river Chebar 1
3 in the land of the Chalde'ans by the river Chebar; 1
3:15 exiles at Tel-abib, who dwelt by the river Chebar. 1
23 the glory which I had seen by the river Chebar; 1
10:15 living creatures that I saw by the river Chebar. 1
20 underneath the God of Israel by the river Chebar; 1
22 whose appearance I had seen by the river Chebar. 1
43: 3 the vision which I had seen by the river Chebar; 1

Chedor-laomer 1. כְּדָר לָעֹמֶר
Gen 14:17 return from the defeat of Ched-or-lao'mer 1

Chedorlaomer 1. כְּדָרְלָעֹמֶר
Gen 14: 1 king of Ella'sar, Ched-or-lao'mer king of Elam 1
4 Twelve years they had served Ched-or-lao'mer 1
5 In the fourteenth year Ched-or-lao'mer 1
9 with Ched-or-lao'mer king of Elam 1

Chelal 1. כְּלָל
Ezr 10:30 of Pa'hath-mo'ab: Adna, Chelal, Benai'ah, Ma-asei'ah 1

Chellean 1. Χελεοι
Jdt 2:23 south of the country of the Chelleans. 1

Chelous 1. Χελους
Jdt 1: 9 Jerusalem and Bethany and Chelous and Kadesh 1

Chelub 1. כְּלוּב
1Ch 4:11 Chelub . . brother of Shuhah, . . father of Mehir 1
27:26 over those who . . was Ezri the son of Chelub; 1

Chelubai 1. כְּלוּבָי
1Ch 2: 9 sons of Hezron . . Jerah'meel, Ram, and Chelu'bai. 1

Cheluhi 1. כְּלֻהִי
Ezr 10:35 Benai'ah, Bedei'ah, Chel'uhi 1

Chemosh 1. כְּמוֹשׁ
Num21:29 O Moab! You are undone, O people of Chemosh! 1
Jdg 11:24 Will you not possess what Chemosh your god gives 1
1Kg 11: 7 Solomon built a high place for Chemosh 1
33 Ash'toreth . . Chemosh the god of Moab, and Milcom 1
2Kg 23:13 for . . and for Chemosh the abomination of Moab 1
Jer 48: 7 and Chemosh shall go forth into exile 1
13 Then Moab shall be ashamed of Chemosh 1
46 Woe to you, O Moab! The people of Chemosh is undone; 1

Chenaanah 1. כְּנַעֲנָה
1Kg 22:11 Zedeki'ah the son of Chena'anah made . . horns 1
24 Zedeki'ah the son of Chena'anah came near 1
1Ch 7:10 sons of Bilhan: Je'ush, Benjamin, Ehud, Chena'anah 1
2Ch 18:10 Zedeki'ah the son of Chena'anah 1
23 Zedeki'ah the son of Chena'anah came near 1

Chenani 1. כְּנָנִי
Neh 9: 4 stood . . Bunni, Sherebi'ah, Bani, and Chena'ni; 1

Chenaniah 1. כְּנַנְיָהוּ
1Ch 15:22 Chenani'ah, leader of the Levites in music 1
27 singers, and Chenani'ah the leader of the music 1
26:29 Chenani'ah and his sons were appointed 1

Chephar-ammoni 1. כְּפַר הָעַמּוֹנִי
Jos 18:24 Che'phar-am'moni, Ophni, Geba 1

Chephirah 1. כְּפִירָה 2. Καπιρας
Jos 9:17 Now their cities were Gibeon, Chephi'rah 1
18:26 Mizpeh, Chephi'rah, Mozah 1
Ezr 2:25 sons of Kir'iathar'im, Chephi'rah, 1
Neh 7:29 men of Kir'iath-je'arim, Chephi'rah 1
1Es 5:19 The men of Chephirah and Beeroth, 743 2

Cheran 1. כְּרָן
Gen 36:26 sons of Dishon . . Eshban, Ithran, and Cheran. 1
1Ch 1:41 sons of Dishon: Hamran, Eshban, Ithran, and Cheran. 1

Cherethite 1. כְּרֵתִי
1Sm 30:14 made a raid upon the Negeb of the Cher'ethites 1
2Sm 8:18 was over the Cher'ethites and the Pel'ethites; 1
15:18 all the Cher'ethites, and all the Pel'ethites 1
20: 7 there went out . . Jo'ab and the Cher'ethites 1
23 command of the Cher'ethites and the Pel'ethites; 1
1Kg 1:38 the Cher'ethites and the Pel'ethites, went down 1
44 and the Cher'ethites and the Pel'ethites; 1
1Ch 18:17 Benai'ah . . was over the Cher'ethites 1
Ezk 25:16 I will cut off the Cher'ethites 1
Zep 2: 5 Woe to you . . you nation of the Cher'ethites! 1

Cherith 1. כְּרִית
1Kg 17: 3 Depart . . and hide yourself by the brook Cherith 1
5 he went and dwelt by the brook Cherith 1

Cherub 1. כְּרוּב 2. Χαρααθ
Ezr 2:59 those who came up from . . Cherub, Addan, and Immer 1
Neh 7:61 came up from . . Cherub, Addon, and Immer 1
1Es 5:36 under the leadership of Cherub, Addan, and Immer 2

Chesalon 1. כְּסָלוֹן
Jos 15:10 shoulder of Mount Je'arim (that is, Ches'alon) 1

Chesed 1. כֶּשֶׂד
Gen 22:22 Chesed, Hazo, Pildash, Jidlaph, and Bethu'el. 1

Chesil 1. כְּסִיל
Jos 15:30 Elto'lad, Chesil, Hormah 1

Chesulloth 1. כְּסוּלוֹת
Jos 19:18 territory included Jezreel, Chesul'loth, Shunem 1

Chezib 1. כְּזִיב 2. Χασεβα
Gen 38: 5 name Shelah. She was in Chezib when she bore him. 1
1Es 5:31 the sons of Nekoda, the sons of Chezib 2

Chidon 1. כִּידֹן
1Ch 13: 9 when they came to the threshing floor of Chidon 1

Chileab 1. כִּלְאָב
2Sm 3: 3 Chil'e-ab, of Ab'igail the widow of Nabal of Carmel; 1

Chilion 1. כִּלְיוֹן
Rut 1: 2 the names of his two sons were Mahlon and Chil'ion; 1
5 and both Mahlon and Chil'ion died 1
4: 9 and all that belonged to Chil'ion and to Mahlon. 1

Chilmad 1. כִּלְמַד
Ezk 27:23 Canneh, Eden, Asshur, and Chilmad traded with you. 1

Chimham 1. כִּמְהָם
2Sm 19:37 But here is your servant Chimham; let him go over 1
38 the king answered, "Chimham shall go over with me 1
40 The king went on . . and Chimham went on with him; 1
Jer 41:17 and stayed at Geruth Chimham near Bethlehem 1

Chinnereth 1. כִּנֶּרֶת
Num34:11 reach to the shoulder of the sea of Chin'nereth 1
Deu 3:17 from Chin'nereth as far as the sea of the Arabah 1
Jos 13:27 to the lower end of the Sea of Chin'nereth 1
19:35 are Ziddim, Zer, Hammath, Rakkath, Chin'nereth 1

Chinneroth 1. כִּנֶּרֶת
Jos 11: 2 and in the Arabah south of Chin'neroth 1
12: 3 and the Arabah to the Sea of Chin'neroth eastward 1
1Kg 15:20 and conquered Ijon, Dan . . and all Chin'neroth 1

Chios 1. Χίος
Act 20:15 we came the following day opposite Chi'os 1

Chislev 1. כִּסְלֵו 2. Χασελευ
Neh 1: 1 Now it happened in the month of Chislev 1
Zec 7: 1 fourth day of the ninth month, which is Chislev. 1
1Mc 1:54 Now on the fifteenth day of Chislev 2
4:52 the ninth month, which is the month of Chislev 2
59 the 25th day of the month of Chislev. 2
2Mc 1: 9 in the month of Chislev, in the 188th year. 2
18 on the 25th day of Chislev 2
10: 5 the same month, which was Chislev. 2

Chislon 1. כִּסְלוֹן
Num34:21 tribe of Benjamin, Eli'dad the son of Chislon. 1

Chisloth-tabor 1. כִּסְלֹת תָּבוֹר
Jos 19:12 eastward . . to the boundary of Chis'loth-ta'bor; 1

Chitlish 1. כִּתְלִישׁ
Jos 15:40 Cabbon, Lahmam, Chitlish 1

Chloe 1. Χλόη
1Co 1:11 For it has been reported to me by Chlo'e's people 1

Choba 1. Χωβα
Jdt 4: 4 Choba and Aesora and the valley of Salem 1
15: 4 Betomasthaim and Bebai and Choba and Kola 1
5 and cut them down as far as Choba 1

Chorazin 1. Χοραζίν
Mat 11:21 Woe to you, Chora'zin! woe to you, Beth-sa'ida! 1
Lke 10:13 Woe to you, Chora'zin! woe to you, Beth-sa'ida! 1

Chorbe 1. Χορβε
1Es 5:12 The sons of Chorbe, 705. The sons of Bani, 648. 1

Chosamaeus 1. Χοσαμαιος
1Es 9:32 Melchias and Sabbaias and Simon Chosamaeus. 1

Christ 1. Χριστός
Mat 1: 1 The book of the genealogy of Jesus Christ 1
16 Jesus was born, who is called Christ. 1
17 to Babylon to the Christ fourteen generations. 1
18 the birth of Jesus Christ took place in this way. 1
2: 4 of them where the Christ was to be born. 1
11: 2 about the deeds of the Christ 1
16:16 You are the Christ, the Son of the living God. 1
20 to tell no one that he was the Christ. 1
22:42 What do you think of the Christ? Whose son is he? 1
23:10 you have one master, the Christ. 1
24: 5 'I am the Christ,' and they will lead many astray. 1
23 Then if any one says to you, 'Lo, here is the Christ!' 1
26:63 tell us if you are the Christ, the Son of God. 1
68 saying, "Prophesy to us, you Christ! 1
27:17 Barab'bas or Jesus who is called Christ? 1
22 what shall I do with Jesus who is called Christ? 1
Mrk 1: 1 The beginning of the Gospel of Jesus Christ 1
8:29 Peter answered him, "You are the Christ. 1
9:41 because you bear the name of Christ 1
12:35 scribes say that the Christ is the son of David? 1
13:21 then if any one says to you, 'Look, here is the Christ!' 1
14:61 Are you the Christ, the Son of the Blessed? 1
15:32 Let the Christ, the King of Israel, come down now 1
Lke 2:11 a Savior, who is Christ the Lord. 1
26 before he had seen the Lord's Christ. 1
3:15 questioned . . whether perhaps he were the Christ 1
4:41 because they knew that he was the Christ. 1
9:20 Peter answered, "The Christ of God. 1
20:41 How can they say that the Christ is David's son? 1
22:67 If you are the Christ, tell us. 1
23: 2 saying that he himself is Christ a king. 1
35 if he is the Christ of God, his Chosen One! 1
39 saying, "Are you not the Christ? Save yourself and us! 1
24:26 necessary that the Christ should suffer 1
46 the Christ should suffer 1
Joh 1:17 grace and truth came through Jesus Christ. 1
20 He confessed . . "I am not the Christ. 1
25 if you are neither the Christ, nor Elijah 1
41 We have found the Messiah" (which means Christ). 1
3:28 I am not the Christ, but I have been sent before him. 1
4:25 Messiah is coming (he who is called Christ); 1
29 Can this be the Christ? 1
7:26 this is the Christ? 1
27 when the Christ appears 1
31 When the Christ appears 1
41 Others said, "This is the Christ. 1
41 But some said, "Is the Christ to come from Galilee? 1
42 the Christ is descended from David 1
9:22 if any one should confess him to be Christ 1
10:24 If you are the Christ, tell us plainly. 1
11:27 I believe that you are the Christ, the Son of God 1
12:34 the Christ remains for ever 1
17: 3 Jesus Christ whom thou hast sent. 1
20:31 Jesus is the Christ, the Son of God 1
Act 2:31 spoke of the resurrection of the Christ 1
36 God has made him both Lord and Christ 1
38 in the name of Jesus Christ 1
3: 6 in the name of Jesus Christ of Nazareth, walk. 1
18 that his Christ should suffer, he thus fulfilled. 1
20 he may send the Christ appointed for you, Jesus 1
4:10 by the name of Jesus Christ of Nazareth 1
5:42 preaching Jesus as the Christ. 1
8: 5 proclaimed to them the Christ. 1
12 the name of Jesus Christ 1
9:22 by proving that Jesus was the Christ. 1
34 Peter said to him, "Aene'as, Jesus Christ heals you; 1
10:36 preaching good news of peace by Jesus Christ 1
48 baptized in the name of Jesus Christ 1
11:17 when we believed in the Lord Jesus Christ 1
15:26 for the sake of our Lord Jesus Christ. 1
16:18 I charge you in the name of Jesus Christ 1
17: 3 necessary for the Christ to suffer and to rise 1
3 This Jesus, whom I proclaim to you, is the Christ. 1
18: 5 testifying to the Jews that the Christ was Jesus. 1
28 showing . . that the Christ was Jesus. 1
20:21 faith in our Lord Jesus Christ. •
24:24 and heard him speak upon faith in Christ Jesus. 1
26:23 that the Christ must suffer 1
28:31 teaching about the Lord Jesus Christ 1
Rom 1: 1 Paul, a servant of Jesus Christ 1
4 Jesus Christ our Lord 1
6 who are called to belong to Jesus Christ 1
7 from God our Father and the Lord Jesus Christ. 1
8 I thank my God through Jesus Christ for all of you 1
2:16 God judges the secrets of men by Christ Jesus. 1
3:22 through faith in Jesus Christ for all 1
24 through the redemption which is in Christ Jesus 1
5: 1 peace with God through our Lord Jesus Christ. 1
6 at the right time Christ died for the ungodly. 1
8 while we were yet sinners Christ died for us. 1
11 rejoice in God through our Lord Jesus Christ 1
15 in the grace of that one man Jesus Christ 1
17 reign in life through the one man Jesus Christ. 1
21 to eternal life through Jesus Christ our Lord. 1
6: 3 all of us who have been baptized into Christ 1
4 so that as Christ was raised from the dead 1
8 But if we have died with Christ, we believe . . 1
9 For we know that Christ . . will never die again; 1
11 dead to sin and alive to God in Christ Jesus. 1
23 is eternal life in Christ Jesus our Lord. 1
7: 4 have died to the law through the body of Christ 1
25 Thanks be to God through Jesus Christ our Lord! 1
8: 1 for those who are in Christ Jesus. 1
2 For the law of the Spirit of life in Christ Jesus 1
9 Any one who does not have the Spirit of Christ 1
10 if Christ is in you . . your spirits are alive 1
11 he who raised Christ Jesus from the dead 1
17 heirs of God and fellow heirs with Christ 1
34 who is to condemn? Is it Christ Jesus, who died, yes 1
35 Who shall separate us from the love of Christ? 1
39 from the love of God in Christ Jesus our Lord. 1
9: 1 I am speaking the truth in Christ, I am not lying; 1
3 that I myself were accursed and cut off from Christ 1
5 of their race . . is the Christ. 1
10: 4 For Christ is the end of the law 1
6 (that is, to bring Christ down) 1
7 (that is, to bring Christ up from the dead). 1
17 what is heard comes by the preaching of Christ. 1
12: 5 so we, though many, are one body in Christ 1
13:14 But put on the Lord Jesus Christ 1
14: 9 For to this end Christ died and lived again 1
15 cause the ruin of one for whom Christ died. 1
18 he who thus serves Christ is acceptable to God 1
15: 3 For Christ did not please himself; 1
5 in such harmony . . in accord with Christ Jesus 1
6 the God and Father of our Lord Jesus Christ. 1
7 therefore, as Christ has welcomed you 1
8 Christ became a servant to the circumcised 1
16 to be a minister of Christ Jesus to the Gentiles 1
17 In Christ Jesus, then, I have reason to be proud 1
18 except what Christ has wrought through me 1
19 I have fully preached the gospel of Christ 1
20 not where Christ has already been named 1
29 come in the fulness of the blessing of Christ. 1
30 I appeal to you, brethren, by our Lord Jesus Christ 1
16: 3 my fellow workers in Christ Jesus 1
5 Epae'netus . . first convert in Asia for Christ. 1
7 and they were in Christ before me. 1
9 Greet Urba'nus, our fellow worker in Christ 1
10 Greet Apel'les, who is approved in Christ. 1
16 All the churches of Christ greet you. 1
18 For such persons do not serve our Lord Christ 1
20 The grace of our Lord Jesus Christ be with you. •
25 my gospel and the preaching of Jesus Christ 1
27 be glory for evermore through Jesus Christ! 1
1Co 1: 1 by the will of God to be an apostle of Christ Jesus 1
2 to those sanctified in Christ Jesus 1
2 call on the name of our Lord Jesus Christ 1
3 God our Father and the Lord Jesus Christ. 1
4 given you in Christ Jesus 1
6 even as the testimony to Christ was confirmed 1
7 for the revealing of our Lord Jesus Christ; 1
8 guiltless in the day of our Lord Jesus Christ. 1
9 the fellowship of his Son, Jesus Christ our Lord. 1
10 by the name of our Lord Jesus Christ 1
12 I belong to Cephas," or "I belong to Christ. 1
13 Is Christ divided? Was Paul crucified for you? 1
17 For Christ did not send me to baptize 1
17 lest the cross of Christ be emptied of its power. 1
23 we preach Christ crucified 1
24 Christ the power of God and the wisdom of God. 1
30 He is the source of your life in Christ Jesus 1
2: 2 except Jesus Christ and him crucified. 1
16 we have the mind of Christ. 1
3: 1 as men of the flesh, as babes in Christ. 1
11 than that which is laid, which is Jesus Christ. 1
23 you are Christ's; and Christ is God's. 1
23 you are Christ's; and Christ is God's. 1
4: 1 as servants of Christ 1
10 We are fools for Christ's sake, but you are wise 1
10 you are wise in Christ 1
15 For though you have countless guides in Christ 1
15 I became your father in Christ Jesus 1
17 to remind you of my ways in Christ 1
5: 7 Christ, our paschal lamb, has been sacrificed. 1
6:11 justified in the name of the Lord Jesus Christ 1
15 know that your bodies are members of Christ 1
15 Shall I therefore take the members of Christ 1
7:22 who was free when called is a slave of Christ. 1
8: 6 one Lord, Jesus Christ 1
11 the brother for whom Christ died. 1
12 you sin against Christ. 1
9:12 an obstacle in the way of the gospel of Christ. 1
21 but under the law of Christ 1
10: 4 the Rock was Christ. 1
16 is it not a participation in the blood of Christ? 1
16 is it not a participation in the body of Christ? 1
11: 1 Be imitators of me, as I am of Christ. 1
3 the head of every man is Christ 1
3 the head of Christ is God. 1
12:12 so it is with Christ. 1
27 you are the body of Christ 1
15: 3 Christ died for our sins 1
12 Now if Christ is preached as raised from the dead 1
13 then Christ has not been raised; 1
14 if Christ has not been raised 1
15 we testified of God that he raised Christ 1
16 then Christ has not been raised. 1
17 If Christ has not been raised 1
18 who have fallen asleep in Christ have perished. 1
19 If for this life only we have hoped in Christ 1
20 in fact Christ has been raised from the dead 1
22 so also in Christ shall all be made alive. 1
23 each in his own order: Christ the first fruits 1
23 then at his coming those who belong to Christ. 1
31 which I have in Christ Jesus our Lord 1
57 through our Lord Jesus Christ. 1
16:24 My love be with you all in Christ Jesus. Amen. 1
2Co 1: 1 Paul, an apostle of Christ Jesus by the will of God 1
2 God our Father and the Lord Jesus Christ. 1
3 Father of our Lord Jesus Christ 1
5 as we share abundantly in Christ's sufferings 1
5 so through Christ we share abundantly 1
19 For the Son of God, Jesus Christ, whom we preached 1
21 it is God who establishes us with you in Christ 1
2:10 has been for your sake in the presence of Christ. 1
12 to preach the gospel of Christ 1
14 who in Christ always leads us in triumph 1
15 For we are the aroma of Christ to God 1
17 in the sight of God we speak in Christ. 1
3: 3 that you are a letter from Christ delivered by us 1
4 that we have through Christ toward God. 1
14 because only through Christ is it taken away. 1
4: 4 the light of the gospel of the glory of Christ 1
5 Jesus Christ as Lord 1
6 the glory of God in the face of Christ. 1
5:10 appear before the judgment seat of Christ 1
14 For the love of Christ controls us 1
16 even though we once regarded Christ 1
17 if any one is in Christ, he is a new creation 1
18 who through Christ reconciled us to himself 1
19 in Christ God was reconciling the world 1
20 So we are ambassadors for Christ 1
20 We beseech you on behalf of Christ 1
6:15 What accord has Christ with Be'lial? 1
8: 9 For you know the grace of our Lord Jesus Christ 1
23 messengers of the churches, the glory of Christ. 1
9:13 acknowledging the gospel of Christ 1
10: 1 by the meekness and gentleness of Christ 1
5 take every thought captive to obey Christ 1
7 If any one is confident that he is Christ's 1
7 as he is Christ's, so are we. 1
14 all the way to you with the gospel of Christ. 1
11: 2 I betrothed you to Christ 1
3 from a sincere and pure devotion to Christ. 1
10 As the truth of Christ is in me 1
13 disguising themselves as apostles of Christ. 1
23 Are they servants of Christ? I am a better one 1
12: 2 I know a man in Christ 1
9 that the power of Christ may rest upon me. 1

10 For the sake of Christ, then, I am content 1
19 speaking in Christ, and all for your upbuilding 1
13: 3 you desire proof that Christ is speaking in me. 1
5 realize that Jesus Christ is in you 1
14 The grace of the Lord Jesus Christ 1
Gal 1: 1 through Jesus Christ and God the Father 1
3 God the Father and our Lord Jesus Christ 1
6 who called you in the grace of Christ 1
7 want to pervert the gospel of Christ. 1
10 I should not be a servant of Christ. 1
12 it came through a revelation of Jesus Christ. 1
22 the churches of Christ in Judea; 1
2: 4 spy out our freedom which we have in Christ Jesus 1
16 through faith in Jesus Christ 1
16 even we have believed in Christ Jesus 1
16 in order to be justified by faith in Christ 1
17 if, in our endeavor to be justified in Christ 1
17 is Christ then an agent of sin? Certainly not! 1
20 I have been crucified with Christ 1
20 Christ who lives in me 1
21 then Christ died to no purpose. 1
3: 1 Jesus Christ was publicly portrayed 1
13 Christ redeemed us from the curse of the law 1
14 that in Christ Jesus the blessing of Abraham 1
16 And to your offspring," which is Christ. 1
22 what was promised to faith in Jesus Christ 1
24 the law was our custodian until Christ came 1
26 for in Christ Jesus you are all sons of God 1
27 For as many of you as were baptized into Christ 1
27 baptized into Christ have put on Christ. 1
28 for you are all one in Christ Jesus. 1
29 if you are Christ's, then you are Abraham's 1
4:14 as an angel of God, as Christ Jesus. 1
19 until Christ be formed in you! 1
5: 1 For freedom Christ has set us free 1
2 Christ will be of no advantage to you. 1
4 You are severed from Christ 1
6 in Christ Jesus neither circumcision 1
24 those who belong to Christ Jesus 1
6: 2 and so fulfil the law of Christ. 1
12 not be persecuted for the cross of Christ. 1
14 except in the cross of our Lord Jesus Christ 1
18 The grace of our Lord Jesus Christ 1
Eph 1: 1 Paul, an apostle of Christ Jesus by the will of God 1
1 the saints who are also faithful in Christ Jesus 1
2 God our Father and the Lord Jesus Christ. 1
3 the God and Father of our Lord Jesus Christ 1
3 who has blessed us in Christ 1
5 to be his sons through Jesus Christ 1
9 his purpose which he set forth in Christ •
12 we who first hoped in Christ 1
17 God of our Lord Jesus Christ, the Father of glory 1
20 which he accomplished in Christ 1
2: 5 made us alive together with Christ 1
6 in the heavenly places in Christ Jesus 1
7 in kindness toward us in Christ Jesus. 1
10 we are his workmanship, created in Christ Jesus 1
12 you were at that time separated from Christ 1
13 in Christ Jesus you . . have been brought near 1
13 have been brought near in the blood of Christ. 1
20 Christ Jesus himself being the cornerstone 1
3: 1 Paul, a prisoner for Christ Jesus on behalf of you 1
4 perceive my insight into the mystery of Christ 1
6 partakers of the promise in Christ Jesus 1
8 the unsearchable riches of Christ 1
11 which he has realized in Christ Jesus our Lord 1
17 Christ may dwell in your hearts through faith; 1
19 to know the love of Christ 1
21 to him be glory in the church and in Christ Jesus 1
4: 7 us according to the measure of Christ's gift. 1
12 for building up the body of Christ 1
13 measure of the stature of the fulness of Christ; 1
15 into him who is the head, into Christ 1
20 You did not so learn Christ!- 1
32 forgiving one another, as God in Christ forgave 1
5: 2 walk in love, as Christ loved us 1
5 has any inheritance in the kingdom of Christ 1
14 Christ shall give you light. 1
20 in the name of our Lord Jesus Christ 1
21 out of reverence for Christ. 1
23 as Christ is the head of the church 1
24 As the church is subject to Christ 1
25 Christ loved the church 1
29 cherishes it, as Christ does the church 1
32 am saying that it refers to Christ and the church; 1
6: 5 in singleness of heart, as to Christ; 1
6 as servants of Christ, doing the will of God 1
23 God the Father and the Lord Jesus Christ. 1
24 Grace be with all who love our Lord Jesus Christ 1
Php 1: 1 Paul and Timothy, servants of Christ Jesus 1
1 To all the saints in Christ Jesus 1
2 God our Father and the Lord Jesus Chris.. 1
6 at the day of Jesus Christ. 1
8 with the affection of Christ Jesus. 1
10 pure and blameless for the day of Christ 1
11 which come through Jesus Christ 1
13 my imprisonment is for Christ; 1
15 Some indeed preach Christ from envy and rivalry 1
17 the former proclaim Christ out of partisanship 1
18 Christ is proclaimed; and in that I rejoice 1
19 the help of the Spirit of Jesus Christ 1
20 Christ will be honored in my body 1
21 For to me to live is Christ, and to die is gain. 1
23 My desire is to depart and be with Christ 1
26 ample cause to glory in Christ Jesus 1
27 manner of life be worthy of the gospel of Christ 1
29 granted to you that for the sake of Christ 1
2: 1 So if there is any encouragement in Christ 1
5 which is yours in Christ Jesus 1
11 every tongue confess that Jesus Christ is Lord 1
16 so that in the day of Christ I may be proud 1
21 not those of Jesus Christ. 1
30 for he nearly died for the work of Christ 1
3: 3 worship God in spirit, and glory in Christ Jesus 1
7 I counted as loss for the sake of Christ. 1
8 the surpassing worth of knowing Christ Jesus 1
8 in order that I may gain Christ 1
9 that which is through faith in Christ 1
12 because Christ Jesus has made me his own. 1
14 prize of the upward call of God in Christ Jesus. 1
18 live as enemies of the cross of Christ. 1
20 from it we await a Savior, the Lord Jesus Christ 1
4: 7 keep your hearts and your minds in Christ Jesus. 1
19 his riches in glory in Christ Jesus. 1
21 Greet every saint in Christ Jesus 1
23 grace of the Lord Jesus Christ 1
Col 1: 1 Paul, an apostle of Christ Jesus by the will of God 1
2 faithful brethren in Christ at Colos'sae 1
3 God, the Father of our Lord Jesus Christ 1
4 we have heard of your faith in Christ Jesus 1
7 He is a faithful minister of Christ on our behalf 1
24 what is lacking in Christ's afflictions 1
27 which is Christ in you, the hope of glory. 1
28 that we may present every man mature in Christ. 1
2: 2 the knowledge of God's mystery, of Christ 1
5 the firmness of your faith in Christ. 1
6 As therefore you received Christ Jesus the Lord 1
8 not according to Christ. 1
11 in the circumcision of Christ; 1
17 the substance belongs to Christ. 1
20 If with Christ you died to the elemental spirits 1
3: 1 If then you have been raised with Christ 1
1 seek the things that are above, where Christ is 1
3 your life is hid with Christ in God. 1
4 When Christ who is our life appears 1
11 Christ is all, and in all. 1
15 let the peace of Christ rule in your hearts 1
16 Let the word of Christ dwell in you richly 1
24 you are serving the Lord Christ. 1
4: 3 to declare the mystery of Christ 1
12 Ep'aphras . . a servant of Christ Jesus 1
1Th 1: 1 in God the Father and the Lord Jesus Christ 1
3 steadfastness of hope in our Lord Jesus Christ. 1
2: 6 might have made demands as apostles of Christ. 1
14 became imitators of the churches of God in Christ 1
3: 2 brother and God's servant in the gospel of Christ 1
4:16 the dead in Christ will rise first; 1
5: 9 salvation through our Lord Jesus Christ 1
18 is the will of God in Christ Jesus for you. 1
23 at the coming of our Lord Jesus Christ. 1
28 The grace of our Lord Jesus Christ be with you. 1
2Th 1: 1 God our Father and the Lord Jesus Christ 1
2 God the Father and the Lord Jesus Christ. 1
12 the grace of our God and the Lord Jesus Christ. 1
2: 1 concerning the coming of our Lord Jesus Christ 1
14 may obtain the glory of our Lord Jesus Christ. 1
16 Now may our Lord Jesus Christ himself 1
3: 5 to the steadfastness of Christ. 1
6 in the name of our Lord Jesus Christ 1
12 exhort in the Lord Jesus Christ to do their work 1
18 The grace of our Lord Jesus Christ be with you 1
1Ti 1: 1 Paul, an apostle of Christ Jesus by command of God 1
1 God our Savior and of Christ Jesus our hope 1
2 God the Father and Christ Jesus our Lord. 1
12 Christ Jesus our Lord 1
14 the faith and love that are in Christ Jesus. 1
15 Christ Jesus came into the world to save 1
16 Jesus Christ might display . . 1
2: 5 the man Christ Jesus 1
3:13 the faith which is in Christ Jesus. 1
4: 6 you will be a good minister of Christ Jesus 1
5:11 when they grow wanton against Christ 1
21 In the presence of God and of Christ Jesus 1
6: 3 sound words of our Lord Jesus Christ 1
13 In the presence of . . of Christ Jesus 1
14 until the appearing of our Lord Jesus Christ; 1
2Ti 1: 1 Paul, an apostle of Christ Jesus by the will of God 1
1 the promise of the life which is in Christ Jesus. 1
2 God the Father and Christ Jesus our Lord. 1
9 the grace which he gave us in Christ Jesus ages ago 1
10 the appearing of our Savior Christ Jesus 1
13 in the faith and love which are in Christ Jesus; 1
2: 1 be strong in the grace that is in Christ Jesus 1
3 as a good soldier of Christ Jesus. 1
8 Remember Jesus Christ, risen from the dead 1
10 they also may obtain salvation in Christ Jesus 1
3:12 all who desire to live a godly life in Christ 1
15 through faith in Christ Jesus. 1
4: 1 in the presence of God and of Christ Jesus 1
Tit 1: 1 a servant of God and an apostle of Jesus Christ 1
4 God the Father and Christ Jesus our Savior. 1
2:13 glory of our great God and Savior Jesus Christ 1
3: 6 through Jesus Christ our Savior 1
Phm 1: 1 Paul, a prisoner for Christ Jesus 1
3 God our Father and the Lord Jesus Christ. 1
6 knowledge of all the good that is ours in Christ. 1
8 though I am bold enough in Christ to command you 1
9 now a prisoner also for Christ Jesus- 1
20 Refresh my heart in Christ. 1
23 Ep'aphras, my fellow prisoner in Christ Jesus 1
25 The grace of the Lord Jesus Christ 1
Heb 3: 6 Christ was faithful over God's house as a son 1
14 we share in Christ 1
5: 5 Christ did not exalt himself 1
6: 1 let us leave the elementary doctrine of Christ 1
8: 6 Christ has obtained a ministry •
9:11 when Christ appeared as a high priest 1
14 how much more shall the blood of Christ 1
24 For Christ has entered 1
28 Christ . . offered once to bear the sins of many 1
10: 5 when Christ came into the world, he said •
10 the offering of the body of Jesus Christ 1
12 when Christ had offered . . a single sacrifice •
11:26 He considered abuse suffered for the Christ 1
13: 8 Jesus Christ is the same yesterday and today 1
21 through Jesus Christ; to whom be glory for ever 1
Jas 1: 1 servant of God and of the Lord Jesus Christ 1
2: 1 as you hold the faith of our Lord Jesus Christ 1
1Pe 1: 1 Peter, an apostle of Jesus Christ 1
2 sanctified . . for obedience to Jesus Christ 1
3 the God and Father of our Lord Jesus Christ 1
3 the resurrection of Jesus Christ from the dead 1
7 and honor at the revelation of Jesus Christ. 1
11 indicated by the Spirit of Christ within them 1
11 sufferings of Christ and the subsequent glory. 1
13 coming to you at the revelation of Jesus Christ. 1
19 with the precious blood of Christ 1
2: 5 acceptable to God through Jesus Christ. 1
21 because Christ also suffered for you 1
3:15 in your hearts reverence Christ as Lord. 1
16 those who revile your good behavior in Christ 1
18 For Christ also died for sins once for all 1
21 through the resurrection of Jesus Christ 1
4: 1 Since therefore Christ suffered in the flesh 1
11 God may be glorified through Jesus Christ. 1
13 in so far as you share Christ's sufferings 1
14 If you are reproached for the name of Christ 1
5: 1 elder and witness of the sufferings of Christ 1
10 who has called you to his eternal glory in Christ 1
14 Peace to all of you that are in Christ. 1
2Pe 1: 1 Peter, a servant and apostle of Jesus Christ 1
1 righteousness of our . . Savior Jesus Christ 1
8 in the knowledge of our Lord Jesus Christ. 1
11 kingdom of our Lord and Savior Jesus Christ. 1
14 will be soon, as our Lord Jesus Christ showed me. 1
16 the power and coming of our Lord Jesus Christ 1
2:20 knowledge of our Lord and Savior Jesus Christ 1
3:18 knowledge of our Lord and Savior Jesus Christ. 1
1Jn 1: 3 with the Father and with his Son Jesus Christ. 1
2: 1 an advocate . . Jesus Christ the righteous; 1
22 he who denies that Jesus is the Christ 1
3:23 believe in the name of his Son Jesus Christ 1
4: 2 every spirit which confesses that Jesus Christ 1
5: 1 Every one who believes that Jesus is the Christ 1
6 he who came by water and blood, Jesus Christ 1
20 we are in him who is true, in his Son Jesus Christ. 1
2Jn 1: 3 and from Jesus Christ the Father's Son 1
7 the coming of Jesus Christ in the flesh; 1
9 and does not abide in the doctrine of Christ 1
Jde 1: 1 Jude, a servant of Jesus Christ 1
1 To those who are . . and kept for Jesus Christ 1
4 and deny our only Master and Lord, Jesus Christ. 1
17 of the apostles of our Lord Jesus Christ; 1
21 wait for the mercy of our Lord Jesus Christ 1
25 God, our Savior through Jesus Christ our Lord 1
Rev 1: 1 The revelation of Jesus Christ, which God gave 1
2 bore witness . . to the testimony of Jesus Christ 1
5 and from Jesus Christ the faithful witness 1
11:15 become the kingdom of our Lord and of his Christ 1
12:10 and the authority of his Christ have come 1
20: 4 and reigned with Christ a 1,000 years. 1
6 but they shall be priests of God and of Christ 1

false Christ 1. ψευδόχριστος

Mat 24:24 For false Christs and false prophets will arise 1
Mrk 13:22 False Christs and false prophets will arise 1

Christian 1. Χριστιανός

Act 11:26 were for the first time called Christians. 1
26:28 In a short time you think to make me a Christian! 1
1Pe 4:16 yet if one suffers as a Christian 1

Chusi 1. Χουσι

Jdt 7:18 which is near Chusi beside the brook Mochmur. 1

Chuza 1. Χουζᾶς

Lke 8: 3 Joan'na, the wife of Chuza, Herod's steward 1

Cilicia 1. Κιλικία
Act 6: 9 of those from Cili'cia and Asia 1
15:23 the brethren . . in Antioch and Syria, and Cili'cia 1
41 he went through Syria and Cili'cia 1
21:39 Paul replied, "I am a Jew, from Tarsus in Cili'cia 1
22: 3 I am a Jew, born at Tarsus in Cili'cia 1
23:34 When he learned that he was from Cili'cia 1
27: 5 the sea which is off Cili'cia and Pamphyl'ia 1
Gal 1:21 I went into the regions of Syria and Cili'cia. 1
Jdt 1: 7 those who lived in Cilicia and Damascus 1
12 take revenge on the whole territory of Cilicia 1
2:21 mountain which is to the north of Upper Cilicia. 1
25 He also seized the territory of Cilicia 1
1Mc 11:14 Alexander the king was in Cilicia at that time 1
2Mc 4:36 the king returned from the region of Cilicia 1
4Mc 4: 2 governor of Syria, Phoenicia, and Cilicia 1

Claudia 1. Κλαυδία
2Ti 4:21 as do Pudens and Linus and Claudia 1

Claudius 1. Κλαύδιος
Act 11:28 this took place in the days of Claudius. 1
18: 2 Claudius had commanded all the Jews to leave 1
23:26 Claudius Lys'ias to his Excellency the governor 1

Clement 1. Κλήμης
Php 4: 3 together with Clement 1

Cleopas 1. Κλεοπᾶς
Lke 24:18 Then one of them, named Cle'opas, answered him 1

Cleopatra 1. Κλεοπατρα
AEs 11: 1 the reign of Ptolemy and Cleopatra 1
1Mc 10:57 he and Cleopatra his daughter 1
58 Ptolemy gave him Cleopatra . . in marriage 1

Clopas 1. Κλωπᾶς
Joh 19:25 his mother's sister, Mary the wife of Clopas 1

Cnidus 1. Κνίδος
Act 27: 7 arrived with difficulty off Cni'dus 1
1Mc 15:23 to Aradus and Gortyna and Cnidus and Cyprus 1

Coele-Syria 1. Κοιλη Συρια
3Mc 3:15 nations inhabiting Coele-Syria and Phoenicia 1

Coelesyria 1. Κοιλη Συρια
1Es 2:17 their council in Coelesyria and Phoenicia 1
24 no longer have access to Coelesyria 1
27 exacted tribute from Coelesyria and Phoenicia. 1
4:48 all the governors in Coelesyria and Phoenicia 1
6:29 out of the tribute of Coelesyria and Phoenicia 1
7: 1 Sisinnes the governor of Coelesyria 1
8:67 the governors of Coelesyria and Phoenicia 1
1Mc 10:69 Apollonius the governor of Coelesyria 1
2Mc 3: 5 was governor of Coelesyria and Phoenicia. 1
8 the cities of Coelesyria and Phoenicia 1
4: 4 governor of Coelesyria and Phoenicia 1
8: 8 he wrote to Ptolemy, the governor of Coelesyria 1
10:11 to be chief governor of Coelesyria and Phoenicia. 1

Col-hozeh 1. כָּל חֹזֶה
Neh 3:15 Shallum the son of Colho'zeh, ruler 1
11: 5 Ma-asei'ah the son of Baruch, son of Col-ho'zeh 1

Colossae 1. Κολοσσαί
Col 1: 2 faithful brethren in Christ at Colos'sae 1

Conaniah 1. כּוֹנַנְיָהוּ
2Ch 31:12 chief officer . . was Conani'ah the Levite 1
13 overseers assisting Conani'ah and Shim'e-i 1
35: 9 Conani'ah also, and Shemai'ah and Nethan'el 1

Coniah 1. כָּנְיָהוּ
Jer 22:24 though Coni'ah the son of Jehoi'akim, king of Judah 1
28 Is this man Coni'ah a despised, broken pot 1
37: 1 reigned instead of Coni'ah the son of Jehoi'akim. 1

Corinth 1. Κόρινθος
Act 18: 1 After this he left Athens and went to Corinth. 1
19: 1 While Apol'los was at Corinth 1
1Co 1: 2 To the church of God which is at Corinth 1
2Co 1: 1 To the church of God which is at Corinth 1
23 I refrained from coming to Corinth. 1
2Ti 4:20 Eras'tus remained at Corinth 1

Corinthian 1. Κορίνθιος
Act 18: 8 many of the Corinthians hearing Paul believed 1
2Co 6:11 Our mouth is open to you, Corinthians 1

Cornelius 1. Κορνήλιος
Act 10: 1 At Caesare'a there was a man named Cornelius 1
3 an angel . . saying to him, "Cornelius. 1
17 behold, the men that were sent by Cornelius 1
22 they said, "Cornelius, a centurion 1
24 Cornelius was expecting them 1
25 When Peter entered, Cornelius met him 1
30 Cornelius said, "Four days ago, about this hour 1
31 saying, 'Cornelius, your prayer has been heard 1

Corner Gate 1. שַׁעַר הַפִּנָּה
Jer 31:38 from the tower of Han'anel to the Corner Gate. 1

Cos 1. Κῶ
Act 21: 1 we came by a straight course to Cos 1
1Mc 15:23 to Rhodes, and to Phaselis, and to Cos, and to Side 1

Cosam 1. Κωσάμ
Lke 3:28 the son of Melchi, the son of Addi, the son of Cosam 1

Cozbi 1. כָּזְבִּי
Num25:15 name of the Mid'ianite woman . . was Cozbi 1
18 in the matter of Cozbi, the daughter of the prince 1

Cozeba 1. כֹּזֵבָא
1Ch 4:22 and the men of Co-ze'ba, and Jo'ash, and Saraph 1

Crates 1. Κρατης
2Mc 4:29 Crates, the commander of the Cyprian troops. 1

Crescens 1. Κρήσκης
2Ti 4:10 Crescens has gone to Galatia, Titus to Dalmatia. 1

Cretan 1. Κρής
Act 2:11 Cretans and Arabians 1
Tit 1:12 Cretans are always liars, evil beasts 1

Crete 1. Κρήτη
Act 27: 7 sailed under the lee of Crete off Salmo'ne. 1
12 they could reach Phoenix, a harbor of Crete 1
13 sailed along Crete, close inshore. 1
21 should not have set sail from Crete 1
Tit 1: 5 This is why I left you in Crete 1
1Mc 10:67 Demetrius the son of Demetrius came from Crete 1

Crispus 1. Κρίσπος
Act 18: 8 Crispus, the ruler of the synagogue 1
1Co 1:14 baptized none of you except Crispus and Ga'ius; 1

Cun 1. כּוּן
1Ch 18: 8 And from Tibhath and from Cun, cities of Hadade'zer 1

Cush 1. כּוּשׁ
Gen 2:13 which flows around the whole land of Cush. 1
10: 6 The sons of Ham: Cush, Egypt, Put, and Canaan. 1
7 sons of Cush: Seba, Hav'ilah, Sabtah, Ra'amah 1
8 Cush became the father of Nimrod; 1
1Ch 1: 8 The sons of Ham: Cush, Egypt, Put, and Canaan. 1
9 sons of Cush: Seba, Hav'ilah, Sabta, Ra'ama 1
10 Cush was the father of Nimrod; 1
Ps 7: 0 sang to the LORD concerning Cush a Benjaminite. 1
Ezk 38: 5 Persia, Cush, an Put are with them, all of them 1

Cushan 1. כּוּשָׁן
Hab 3: 7 I saw the tents of Cushan in affliction; 1

Cushan-rishathaim 1. כּוּשַׁן רִשְׁעָתַיִם
Jdg 3: 8 Cu'shan-rishatha'im king of Mesopotamia 1
8 Israel served Cu'shan-rishatha'im eight years. 1
10 Cu'shan-rishatha'im king of Mesopota'mia into his 1
10 and his hand prevailed over Cu'shan-rishatha'im. 1

Cushi 1. כּוּשִׁי
Jer 36:14 son of Nethani'ah, son of Shelemi'ah, son of Cushi 1
Zep 1: 1 Zephani'ah the son of Cushi, son of Gedali'ah 1

Cushite 1. כּוּשִׁי
Num12: 1 because of the Cushite woman whom he had married 1
1 for he had married a Cushite woman; 1
2Sm 18:21 Then Jo'ab said to the Cushite, "Go, tell the king 1
21 The Cushite bowed before Jo'ab, and ran. 1
22 Come what may, let me also run after the Cushite. 1
23 Then Ahi'ma-az ran . . and outran the Cushite. 1
31 And behold, the Cushite came; and the Cushite said 1
31 and the Cushite said, "Good tidings for my lord 1
32 The king said to the Cushite, "Is it well 1
32 the Cushite answered, "May the enemies of my lord 1

Cuth 1. כּוּתָה
2Kg 17:30 the men of Cuth made Nergal, the men of Hamath 1

Cutha 1. Κουθα
1Es 5:32 the sons of Mehida, the sons of Cutha 1

Cuthah 1. כּוּתָה
2Kg 17:24 brought people from Babylon, Cuthah, Avva, Hamath 1

Cyamon 1. Κυαμων
Jdt 7: 3 spread out . . in length from Bethulia to Cyamon 1

Cyprian 1. Κύπριος
2Mc 4:29 Crates, the commander of the Cyprian troops. 1

Cyprus 1. כִּתִּי 2. Κυπριαρχης 3. Κύπριος 4. Κύπρος
Isa 23: 1 From the land of Cyprus it is revealed to them. 1
12 daughter of Sidon; arise, pass over to Cyprus 1
Jer 2:10 For cross to the coasts of Cyprus and see 1
Ezk 27: 6 made your deck of pines from the coasts of Cyprus 1
Act 4:36 a Levite, a native of Cyprus 3
11:19 those . . traveled as far as Phoeni'cia and Cyprus 4
20 there were some of them, men of Cyprus and Cyre'ne 3
13: 4 from there they sailed to Cyprus. 4
15:39 took Mark with him and sailed away to Cyprus 4
21: 3 When we had come in sight of Cyprus 4
16 bringing us to the house of Mnason of Cyprus 3
27: 4 we sailed under the lee of Cyprus 4
1Mc 15:23 Gortyna and Cnidus and Cyprus and Cyrene. 4
2Mc 10:13 because he had abandoned Cyprus 4
12: 2 these Nicanor the governor of Cyprus 2

Cyrene 1. Κυρηναῖος 2. Κυρήνη
Mat 27:32 they came upon a man of Cyre'ne, Simon by name 1
Mrk 15:21 they compelled a passer-by, Simon of Cyre'ne 1
Lke 23:26 they seized one Simon of Cyre'ne 1
Act 2:10 Egypt and the parts of Libya belonging to Cyre'ne 2
11:20 there were some of them, men of Cyprus and Cyre'ne 1
13: 1 Lucius of Cyre'ne 1
1Mc 15:23 Gortyna and Cnidus and Cyprus and Cyrene. 2
2Mc 2:23 has been set forth by Jason of Cyrene in five volumes 1

Cyrenian 1. Κυρηναῖος
Act 6: 9 the synagogue . . of the Cyre'nians 1

Cyrus 1. כּוֹרֶשׁ 2. כּוֹרֶשׁ(A) 3. Κυρος
2Ch 36:22 Now in the first year of Cyrus king of Persia 1
22 LORD stirred up the spirit of Cyrus king 1
23 Thus says Cyrus king of Persia, 'The LORD, the God 1
Ezr 1: 1 In the first year of Cyrus king of Persia 1
1 LORD stirred up the spirit of Cyrus king of Persia 1
2 Thus says Cyrus king of Persia: The LORD 1
7 Cyrus the king also brought out the vessels 1
8 Cyrus king of Persia brought these out in charge 1
3: 7 according to the grant which they had from Cyrus 1
4: 3 as King Cyrus the king of Persia has commanded us. 1
5 days of Cyrus king of Persia, even until the reign 1
5:13 first year of Cyrus king of Babylon 2
13 Cyrus the king made a decree that this house 2
14 Cyrus the king took out of the temple of Babylon 2
17 see whether a decree was issued by Cyrus the king 2
6: 3 In the first year of Cyrus the king 2
3 Cyrus the king issued a decree: Concerning 2
14 by decree of Cyrus and Darius and Ar-ta-xerx'es 2
Isa 44:28 who says of Cyrus, 'He is my shepherd 1
45: 1 Thus says the LORD to his anointed, to Cyrus 1
Dan 1:21 Daniel . . until the first year of King Cyrus. 1
6:28 during the . . reign of Cyrus the Persian. 2
10: 1 In the third year of Cyrus king of Persia 1
1Es 2: 1 In the first year of Cyrus as king of the Persians 3
2 the Lord stirred up the spirit of Cyrus 3
3 Thus says Cyrus king of the Persians 3
10 Cyrus the king also brought out the holy vessels 3
11 When Cyrus king of the Perians brought these out 3
4:44 which Cyrus set apart 3
57 all the vessels which Cyrus had set apart 3
57 everything that Cyrus had ordered to be done 3
5:55 the decree . . from Cyrus king of the Persians. 3
71 as Cyrus the king of the Persians has commanded 3
73 as long as King Cyrus lived 3
6:17 Cyrus reigned over the country of Babylonia 3
17 Cyrus wrote that this house should be rebuilt. 3
18 these Cyrus the king took out again 3
22 was done with the consent of King Cyrus 3
24 In the first year of the reign of Cyrus 3
24 King Cyrus ordered the building of the house 3
25 the cost to be paid from the treasury of Cyrus 3
7: 4 with the consent of Cyrus and Darius 3
Bel 1: 1 Cyrus the Persian received his kingdom. 3

Dabbesheth 1. דַּבֶּשֶׁת
Jos 19:11 boundary goes up . . and touches Dab'besheth 1

Daberath 1. דָּבְרַת
Jos 19:12 thence it goes to Dab'erath, then up to Japhi'a; 1
21:28 Ki'shion with . . Dab'erath with its pasture lands 1
1Ch 6:72 of Is'sachar . . Dab'erath with its pasture lands 1

Dabria 1. Dabria
2Es 14:24 and take with you Sarea, Dabria, Selemia, Ethanus 1

Dagon 1. דָּגוֹן 2. Δαγων
Jdg 16:23 to offer a great sacrifice to Dagon their god 1
1Sm 5: 2 the ark . . and brought it into the house of Dagon 1
2 took the ark of God . . and set it up beside Dagon. 1
3 Dagon had fallen face downward . . before the ark 1
3 So they took Dagon and put him back in his place. 1
4 Dagon had fallen face downward . . before the ark 1
4 head of Dagon and . . his hands were lying cut off 1
4 only the trunk of Dagon was left to him. 1
5 the priests of Dagon . . do not tread 1
5 priests . . and all who enter the house of Dagon 1
5 do not tread on the threshold of Dagon in Ashdod 1
7 his hand is heavy upon us and upon Dagon our god. 1
1Ch 10:10 and fastened his head in the temple of Dagon. 1
1Mc 10:84 the temple of Dagon 2
11: 4 they showed him the temple of Dagon burned down 2

Dalmanutha 1. Δαλμανουθά
Mrk 8:10 went to the district of Dalmanu'tha. 1

Dalmatia 1. Δαλματία
2Ti 4:10 Crescens has gone to Galatia, Titus to Dalmatia. 1

Dalphon 1. דַּלְפוֹן
Est 9: 7 also slew Par-shan-da'tha and Dalphon and Aspa'tha 1

Damaris 1. Δάμαρις
Act 17:34 a woman named Dam'aris and others with them. 1

Damascus 1. דַּמֶּשֶׂק 2. Δαμασκηνός 3. Δαμασκός
Gen 14:15 pursued them to Hobah, north of Damascus. 1
15: 2 heir of my house is Elie'zer of Damascus? 1
2Sm 8: 5 the Syrians of Damascus came to help Hadade'zer 1
6 Then David put garrisons in Aram of Damascus; 1
1Kg 11:24 they went to Damascus and dwelt there 1
24 they went . . and made him king in Damascus. 1
15:18 sent them to Ben-ha'dad . . who dwelt in Damascus 1
19:15 return on your way to the wilderness of Damascus; 1
20:34 establish bazaars for yourself in Damascus 1
2Kg 5:12 Are not Aba'na and Pharpar, the rivers of Damascus 1
8: 7 Eli'sha came to Damascus. Ben-ha'dad . . was sick; 1
9 took a present . . all kinds of goods of Damascus 1
14:28 how he recovered for Israel Damascus and Hamath 1
16: 9 the king of Assyria marched up against Damascus 1
10 When King Ahaz went to Damascus to meet 1
10 Ahaz . . he saw the altar that was at Damascus. 1
11 all that King Ahaz had sent from Damascus 1
11 before King Ahaz arrived from Damascus. 1
12 And when the king came from Damascus 1
1Ch 18: 5 Syrians of Damascus came to help Hadade'zer 1
6 Then David put garrisons in Syria of Damascus; 1
2Ch 16: 2 Ben-ha'dad king of Syria, who dwelt in Damascus 1
24:23 sent all their spoil to the king of Damascus. 1
28: 5 brought them to Damascus. 1
23 For he sacrificed to the gods of Damascus 1
Sng 7: 4 a tower of Lebanon, overlooking Damascus. 1
Isa 7: 8 For the head of Syria is Damascus 1
8 the head of Damascus is Rezin. 1
8: 4 the wealth of Damascus and the spoil of Sama'ria 1
10: 9 Is not Sama'ria like Damascus? 1
17: 1 An oracle concerning Damascus. 1
1 Behold, Damascus will cease to be a city 1
3 from E'phraim, and the kingdom from Damascus; 1
Jer 49:23 Concerning Damascus. 1
24 Damascus has become feeble, she turned to flee 1
27 And I will kindle a fire in the wall of Damascus 1
Ezk 27:18 Damascus trafficked with you for your abundant 1
47:16 lies on the border between Damascus and Hamath) 1
17 which is on the northern border of Damascus 1
18 from Hazar-e'non between Hauran and Damascus; 1
48: 1 border of Damascus over against Hamath), 1
Ams 1: 3 For three transgressions of Damascus 1
5 I will break the bar of Damascus, and cut off 1
5:27 I will take you into exile beyond Damascus 1
Zec 9: 1 The word of the LORD . . will rest upon Damascus. 1
Act 9: 2 letters to the synagogues at Damascus 3
3 Now as he journeyed he approached Damascus 3
8 brought him into Damascus. 3
10 there was a disciple at Damascus named Anani'as. 3
19 he was with the disciples at Damascus. 3
22 confounded the Jews who lived in Damascus 3
27 how at Damascus he had preached boldly 3
22: 5 I journeyed to Damascus 3
6 As I made my journey and drew near to Damascus 3
10 the Lord said to me, 'Rise, and go into Damascus 3
11 came into Damascus. 3
26:12 Thus I journeyed to Damascus 3
20 declared first to those at Damascus 3
2Co 11:32 At Damascus, the governor under King Ar'etas 3
32 guarded the city of Damascus in order to seize me 2
Gal 1:17 again I returned to Damascus. 3
Jdt 1: 7 those who lived in Cilicia and Damascus 3
12 Cilicia and Damascus and Syria 3
2:27 Then he went down into the plain of Damascus 3
15: 5 even beyond Damascus and its borders. 3
1Mc 11:62 he passed through the country as far as Damascus. 3
12:32 Then he broke camp and went to Damascus 3

Dan 1. בְּנֵי דָן 2. דָּן 3. דָּנִי
Gen 14:14 of them, and went in pursuit as far as Dan. 2
30: 6 given me a son"; therefore she called his name Dan 2
35:25 sons of Bilhah, Rachel's maid: Dan and Naph'tali 2
46:23 The sons of Dan: Hushim. 2
49:16 Dan shall judge his people as one of the tribes 2
17 Dan shall be a serpent in the way 2
Exd 1: 4 Dan and Naph'tali, Gad and Asher. 2
31: 6 Oho'liab, the son of Ahis'amach, of the tribe of Dan; 2
35:34 Oho'liab the son of Ahis'amach of the tribe of Dan. 2
38:23 son of Ahis'amach, of the tribe of Dan, a craftsman 2
Lev 24:11 the daughter of Dibri, of the tribe of Dan 2
Num 1:12 from Dan, Ahi-e'zer the son of Ammishad'dai; 2
38 Of the people of Dan, their generations 2
39 the number of the tribe of Dan was 62,700 2
2:25 the camp of Dan by their companies 2
25 leader of the people of Dan being Ahi-e'zer 2
31 The whole number of the camp of Dan is 157,600 2
7:66 Ahie'zer the . . leader of the men of Dan 2
10:25 Then the standard of the camp of the men of Dan 2
13:12 from the tribe of Dan, Am'miel the son of Gemal'li; 2
26:42 sons of Dan according to their families 2
42 families of Dan according to their families. 2
34:22 Of the tribe of the sons of Dan a leader, Bukki 2
Deu 27:13 stand upon Mount Ebal . . Zeb'ulun, Dan 2
33:22 of Dan he said, "Dan is a lion's whelp 2
22 Dan is a lion's whelp, that leaps forth from Bashan. 2
34: 1 LORD showed him all the land. Gilead as far as Dan 2
Jos 19:40 The seventh lot came out for the tribe of Dan 1
47 settled . . calling Leshem, Dan, after the name 2
47 after the name of Dan their ancestor. 2
48 This is the inheritance of the tribe of Dan 1
21: 5 of the tribe of E'phraim, from the tribe of Dan 2
23 and out of the tribe of Dan, El'teke 2
Jdg 5:17 and Dan, why did he abide with the ships? Asher sat 2
18:11 men of the tribe of Dan, armed with weapons of war 3
29 they named the city Dan, after the name of Dan 2
29 after the name of Dan their ancestor, who was born 2
20: 1 people of Israel came out, from Dan to Beer-sheba 2
1Sm 3:20 And all Israel from Dan to Beer-sheba knew that 2
2Sm 3:10 over Israel and . . Judah, from Dan to Beer-sheba. 2
17:11 all Israel be gathered . . from Dan to Beer-sheba 2
24: 2 all the tribes of Israel, from Dan to Beer-sheba 2
6 they came to Dan, and from Dan they went . . to Sidon 2
6 came to Dan, and from Dan they went around to Sidon •
15 died . . from Dan to Beer-sheba 70,000 men. 2
1Kg 4:25 Judah and Israel . . from Dan even to Beer-sheba 2
12:29 he set one in Bethel, and the other he put in Dan. 2
30 people went . . and to the other as far as Dan. 2
15:20 Ben-ha'dad . . conquered Ijon, Dan, 2
2Kg 10:29 the golden calves that were in Bethel, and in Dan. 2
1Ch 2: 2 Dan, Joseph, Benjamin, Naph'tali, Gad, and Asher. 2
21: 2 Go, number Israel, from Beer-sheba to Dan 2
27:22 for Dan, Az'arel the son of Jero'ham. 2
2Ch 2:14 the son of a woman of the daughters of Dan 2
16: 4 conquered I'jon, Dan, A'bel-ma'im 2
30: 5 throughout all Israel, from Beer-sheba to Dan 2
Jer 4:15 For a voice declares from Dan and proclaims evil 2
8:16 The snorting of their horses is heard from Dan; 2
Ezk 48: 1 from the east side to the west, Dan, one portion. 2
2 Adjoining the territory of Dan, from the east 2
32 the gate of Benjamin, and the gate of Dan. 2
Ams 8:14 who swear . . and say, 'As thy god lives, O Dan,' 2

Daniel 1. דָּנִאֵל 2. דָּנִיֵּאל (A) 3. Δανιήλ 4. Danihel
1Ch 3: 1 sons of David . . the second Daniel 1
Ezr 8: 2 Of the sons of Ith'amar, Daniel. 1
Neh 10: 6 Daniel, Gin'nethon, Baruch 1
Ezk 14:14 even if these three men, Noah, Daniel, and Job 1
20 even if Noah, Daniel, and Job were in it, as I live 1
28: 3 you are indeed wiser than Daniel; 1
Dan 1: 6 Daniel, Hanani'ah, Mish'a-el, and Azari'ah 1
7 Daniel he called Belteshaz'zar 1
8 Daniel resolved that he would not defile 1
9 God gave Daniel favor and compassion 1
10 chief of the eunuchs said to Daniel, "I fear lest my 1
11 Then Daniel said to the steward whom the chief 1
11 over Daniel, Hanani'ah, Mish'a-el, and Azari'ah; 1
17 Daniel had understanding in all visions 1
19 like Daniel, Hanani'ah, Mish'a-el, and Azari'ah; 1
21 Daniel continued until the first year of King 1
2:13 sought Daniel and his companions, to slay them. 2
14 Daniel replied with prudence and discretion 2
15 Then Ar'ioch made the matter known to Daniel. 2
16 Daniel went in and besought the king to appoint 2
17 Then Daniel went to his house and made the matter 2
18 Daniel and his companions might not perish 2
19 mystery was revealed to Daniel in a vision 2
19 Then Daniel blessed the God of heaven. 2
20 Daniel said: "Blessed be the name of God for ever 2
24 Therefore Daniel went in to Ar'ioch 2
25 Then Ar'ioch brought in Daniel before the king 2
26 king said to Daniel, whose name was Belteshaz'zar 2
27 Daniel answered the king, "No wise men, enchanters 2
46 fell upon his face, and did homage to Daniel 2
47 king said to Daniel, "Truly, your God is God of gods 2
48 Then the king gave Daniel high honors 2
49 Daniel made request of the king, and he appointed 2
49 but Daniel remained at the king's court. 2
4: 8 At last Daniel came in before me–he who was named 2
19 Then Daniel . . was dismayed for a moment 2
5:12 excellent spirit . . were found in this Daniel 2
12 Now let Daniel be called, 2
13 Then Daniel was brought in before the king. 2
13 king said to Daniel, "You are that Daniel 2
13 You are that Daniel, one of the exiles of Judah 2
17 Daniel answered before the king, "Let your gifts 2
29 Daniel was clothed with purple, a chain of gold 2
6: 2 three presidents, of whom Daniel was one 2
3 Daniel became distinguished above all 2
4 against Daniel with regard to the kingdom; 2
5 not find any . . complaint against this Daniel 2
10 Daniel knew that the document had been signed 2
11 found Daniel making petition and supplication 2
13 That Daniel, who is one of the exiles from Judah 2
14 distressed, and set his mind to deliver Daniel; 2
16 Daniel was brought and cast into the den 2
16 king said to Daniel, "May your God, 2
17 nothing might be changed concerning Daniel. 2
20 When he came near to the den where Daniel was 2
20 cried out in a tone of anguish and said to Daniel 2
20 O Daniel, servant of the living God, 2
21 Then Daniel said to the king, "O king, live for ever 2
23 commanded that Daniel be taken up out of the den. 2
23 Daniel was taken up out of the den, 2
24 men who had accused Daniel were brought and cast 2
26 men tremble and fear before the God of Daniel 2
27 who has saved Daniel from the power of the lions 2
28 Daniel prospered during the reign of Darius 2
7: 1 Daniel had a dream and visions of his head 2
2 Daniel said, "I saw in my vision by night, 2
15 As for me, Daniel, my spirit within me was anxious 2
28 As for me, Daniel, my thoughts greatly alarmed me 2
8: 1 vision appeared to me, Daniel, after that 1
15 Daniel, had seen the vision, I sought 1
27 I, Daniel, was overcome and lay sick for some days; 1
9: 2 first year of his reign, I, Daniel, perceived 1
22 O Daniel, I have now come out to give you wisdom 1
10: 1 third year . . a word was revealed to Daniel 1
2 days I, Daniel, was mourning for three weeks. 1
7 I, Daniel, alone saw the vision, 1
11 said to me, "O Daniel, man greatly beloved, give heed 1
12 Fear not, Daniel, for from the first day 1
12: 4 Daniel, shut up the words, and seal the book 1
5 Then I Daniel looked, and behold, two others stood 1
9 Go your way, Daniel, for the words are shut up 1
Mat 24:15 sacrilege spoken of by the prophet Daniel 3
2Es 12:11 appeared in a vision to your brother Daniel. 4
Sus 1:45 the holy spirit of a young lad named Daniel; 3
51 Daniel said to them, "Separate them 3
55 Daniel said, "Very well! You have lied 3
59 Daniel said to him, "Very well! You also have lied 3
61 Daniel had convicted them of bearing false witness 3
64 Daniel had a great reputation among the people. 3
Bel 1: 2 Daniel was a companion of the king 3
4 Daniel worshiped his own God. 3
7 Then Daniel laughed, and said, "Do not be deceived 3
9 Daniel shall die 3
9 Daniel said to the king 3
10 the king went with Daniel into the temple of Bel. 3
12 we will die; or else Daniel will 3
14 Then Daniel ordered his servants to bring ashes 3
16 the king rose and came, and Daniel with him. 3
17 the king said, "Are the seals unbroken, Daniel? 3
19 Then Daniel laughed 3
22 and gave Bel over to Daniel 3
24 the king said to Daniel 3
25 Daniel said, "I will worship the Lord my God 3
27 Then Daniel took pitch, fat, and hair 3
27 Daniel said, "See what you have been worshiping! •
29 Going to the king, they said, "Hand Daniel over to us 3
30 under compulsion he handed Daniel over to them. 3
31 They threw Daniel into the lions' den •
32 so that they might devour Daniel. 3
34 to Babylon, to Daniel, in the lions' den. 3
37 Then Habakkuk shouted, "Daniel, Daniel! 3
37 Then Habakkuk shouted, "Daniel, Daniel! 3
38 Daniel said, "Thou hast remembered me, O God 3
39 Daniel arose and ate 3
40 the king came to mourn for Daniel 3
40 he looked in, and there sat Daniel. 3
41 Thou art great, O Lord God of Daniel 3
42 he pulled Daniel out •
1Mc 2:60 Daniel because of his innocence 3
3Mc 6: 7 Daniel . . you brought up to the light unharmed. 3
4Mc 16: 3 The lions surrounding Daniel were not so savage 3
21 Daniel the righteous was thrown to the lions 3
18:13 He praised Daniel in the den of the lions 3

Danite 1. בֶּן דָּן 2. דָּנִי
Jos 19:47 the territory of the Danites was lost to them 1
47 the Danites went up and fought against Leshem 1
Jdg 1:34 Amorites pressed the Danites back into the hill 1
13: 2 a certain man of Zorah, of the tribe of the Danites 2
18: 1 the tribe of the Danites was seeking for itself 2
2 the Danites sent five able men from the whole 1
16 600 men of the Danites, armed with their weapons 1
22 were called out, and they overtook the Danites. 1
23 they shouted to the Danites, who turned round 1
25 the Danites said to him, "Do not let your voice be 1
26 the Danites went their way; and when Micah saw 1
27 the Danites came to La'ish, to a people quiet •
30 the Danites set up the graven image 1
30 were priests to the tribe of the Danites until 2
1Ch 12:35 Of the Danites 28,600 men equipped for battle. 2

Dannah 1. דִּנָּה
Jos 15:49 Dannah, Kir'iath-san'nah (that is, Debir) 1

Daphne 1. Δαφνη
2Mc 4:33 a place of sanctuary at Daphne near Antioch. 1

Dara 1. דָּרַע
1Ch 2: 6 sons of Zerah: Zimri, Ethan, Heman, Calcol, and Dara 1

Darda 1. דַּרְדַּע
1Kg 4:31 wiser than Ethan . . and Heman, Calcol, and Darda 1

Darius 1. דָּרְיָוֶשׁ 2. דָּרְיָוֶשׁ(A) 3. Δαρειος
Ezr 4: 5 even until the reign of Darius king of Persia. 1
24 second year of the reign of Darius king of Persia 2
5: 5 not stop them till a report should reach Darius 2
6 copy of the letter . . sent to Darius the king; 2
7 written as follows: "To Darius the king, all peace. 2
6: 1 Darius the king made a decree, and search was made 2
12 I Darius make a decree; let it be done 2
13 according to the word sent by Darius the king 2
13 did . . what Darius the king had ordered. *
14 by decree of Cyrus and Darius and Ar-ta-xerx'es 2
15 in the sixth year of the reign of Darius the king. 2
Neh 12:22 priests until the reign of Darius the Persian. 1
Dan 5:31 Darius the Mede received the kingdom, 2
6: 1 pleased Darius to set over the kingdom 120 2
6 said to him, "O King Darius, live for ever! 2
9 King Darius signed the document and interdict. 2
25 Then King Darius wrote to all the peoples 2
28 Daniel prospered during the reign of Darius 2
9: 1 In the first year of Darius the son of Ahasu-e'rus 1
11: 1 as for me, in the first year of Darius the Mede 1
Hag 1: 1 In the second year of Darius the king 1
15 In the second year of Darius the king 1
2:10 the ninth month, in the second year of Darius 1
Zec 1: 1 In the eighth month, in the second year of Darius 1
7 the month of Shebat, in the second year of Darius 1
7: 1 In the fourth year of King Darius 1
1Es 2:30 until the second year of the reign of Darius 3
3: 1 Now King Darius gave a great banquet 3
3 Darius the king went to his bedroom 3
5 Darius the king will give rich gifts 3
7 because of his wisdom he shall sit next to Darius 3
7 shall be called kinsman of Darius. 3
8 put them under the pillow of Darius the king 3
4:47 Darius the king rose, and kissed him 3
5: 2 Darius sent with them 1,000 horsemen 3
6 who spoke wise words before Darius 3
73 until the reign of Darius. 3
6: 1 Now in the second year of the reign of Darius 3
6 word could be sent to Darius concerning them 3
7 wrote and sent to Darius 3
8 To King Darius, greeting 3
23 Darius commanded that search be made 3
27 Darius commanded Sisinnes the governor of Syria *
34 I, King Darius, have decreed that it be done 3
7: 1 following the orders of King Darius 3
4 consent of Cyrus and Darius and Artaxerxes 3
5 in the sixth year of King Darius 3
1Mc 1: 1 Darius, king of the Persians and the Medes 3

Darkon 1. דַּרְקוֹן
Ezr 2:56 sons of Ja'alah, the sons of Darkon 1
Neh 7:58 sons of Ja'ala, the sons of Darkon 1

Dathan 1. דָּתָן 2. Δαθαν
Num16: 1 Dathan and Abi'ram the sons of Eli'ab, and On 1
12 Moses sent to call Dathan and Abi'ram 1
24 Get away from about the dwelling of Korah, Dathan 1
25 Then Moses rose and went to Dathan and Abi'ram; 1
27 got away from about the dwelling of Korah, Dathan 1
27 Dathan and Abi'ram came out and stood at the door 1
26: 9 The sons of Eli'ab: Nem'uel, Dathan, and Abi'ram. 1
9 These are the Dathan and Abi'ram . . who contended 1
Deu 11: 6 what he did to Dathan and Abi'ram the sons of Eli'ab 1
Ps 106:17 earth opened and swallowed up Dathan 1
Sir 45:18 Dathan and Abiram and their men 2
4Mc 2:17 When Moses was angry with Dathan and Abiram 2

Dathema 1. Δαθεμα
1Mc 5: 9 they fled to the stronghold of Dathema 1
29 they went all the way to the stronghold of Dathema. *

David 1. דָּוִד 2. Δαυιδ 3. David
Rut 4:17 he was the father of Jesse, the father of David. 1
22 Obed of Jesse, and Jesse of David. 1
1Sm 16:13 the Spirit of the LORD came mightily upon David 1
19 Send me David your son, who is with the sheep. 1
20 and sent them by David his son to Saul. 1
21 And David came to Saul, and entered his service. 1
22 Let David remain in my service, for he has found 1
23 David took the lyre and played it with his hand; 1
17:12 David was the son of an Eph'rathite of Bethlehem 1
14 David was the youngest; 1
15 but David went back and forth from Saul 1
17 And Jesse said to David his son, "Take 1
20 David rose early in the morning 1
22 And David left the things in charge of the keeper 1
23 spoke the same words . . And David heard him. 1
26 And David said to the men who stood by him 1
28 and Eli'ab's anger was kindled against David 1
29 And David said, "What have I done now? 1
31 When the words which David spoke were heard 1
32 David said to Saul, "Let no man's heart fail 1
33 And Saul said to David, "You are not able to go 1
34 But David said to Saul, "Your servant used to keep 1
37 David said, "The LORD who . . will deliver me 1
37 Saul said to David, "Go, and the LORD be with you! 1
38 Then Saul clothed David with his armor; 1
39 And David girded his sword over his armor 1
39 Then David said to Saul, "I cannot go with these; 1
39 I am not used to them." And David put them off. 1
41 the Philistine came on and drew near to David 1
42 And when the Philistine looked, and saw David 1
43 And the Philistine said to David, "Am I a dog 1
43 And the Philistine cursed David by his gods. 1
44 The Philistine said to David, "Come to me 1
45 Then David said to the Philistine 1
48 Philistine . . came and drew near to meet David 1
48 David ran quickly toward the battle line to meet 1
49 David put his hand in his bag and took out a stone 1
50 David prevailed . . with a sling and with a stone 1
50 there was no sword in the hand of David. 1
51 Then David ran and stood over the Philistine 1
54 David took the head of the Philistine 1
55 Saul saw David go forth against the Philistine 1
57 as David returned from the slaughter 1
58 David answered, "I am the son of your servant Jesse 1
18: 1 the soul of Jonathan was knit to the soul of David 1
3 Then Jonathan made a covenant with David 1
4 of the robe . . and gave it to David, and his armor 1
5 And David went out and was successful 1
6 David returned from slaying the Philistine 1
7 Saul has slain . . and David his ten thousands. 1
8 They have ascribed to David ten thousands 1
9 Saul eyed David from that day on. 1
10 and he raved . . while David was playing the lyre 1
11 he thought, "I will pin David to the wall. 1
11 But David evaded him twice. 1
12 Saul was afraid of David 1
14 And David had success in all his undertakings; 1
16 But all Israel and Judah loved David; 1
17 Saul said to David, "Here is my elder daughter Merab; 1
18 David said to Saul, "Who am I, and who are 1
19 when Merab . . should have been given to David 1
20 Michal loved David; and they told Saul 1
21 Therefore Saul said to David a second time 1
22 Speak to David in private and say, 'Behold, the king 1
23 servants spoke those words in the ears of David. 1
23 And David said, "Does it seem to you a little thing 1
24 servants . . told him, "Thus and so did David speak. 1
25 Thus shall you say to David, 'The king desires no 1
25 Now Saul thought to make David fall by the hand 1
26 And when his servants told David these words 1
26 it pleased David well to be the king's son-in-law. 1
27 David arose and went . . and killed 200 1
27 and David brought their foreskins 1
28 Saul saw and knew that the LORD was with David 1
29 Saul was still more afraid of David. 1
29 Saul was David's enemy continually. 1
30 David had more success than all the servants 1
19: 1 Saul spoke to . . that they should kill David. 1
1 But Jonathan, Saul's son, delighted much in David. 1
2 Jonathan told David, "Saul . . seeks to kill you; 1
4 Jonathan spoke well of David to Saul his father 1
4 Let not the king sin against his servant David; 1
5 sin against innocent blood by killing David 1
7 Jonathan called David, and . . showed him all 1
7 And Jonathan brought David to Saul, and he was 1
8 David went out and fought with the Philistines 1
9 as he sat in . . and David was playing the lyre. 1
10 Saul sought to pin David to the wall 1
10 he eluded Saul . . And David fled, and escaped. 1
11 Saul sent messengers to David's house to watch 1
11 But Michal, David's wife, told him, "If you do not save 1
12 So Michal let David down through the window; 1
14 when Saul sent messengers to take David, she said 1
15 Saul sent the messengers to see David, saying 1
18 Now David fled and escaped, and he came to Samuel 1
19 Behold, David is at Nai'oth in Ramah. 1
20 Then Saul sent messengers to take David; 1
22 and he asked, "Where are Samuel and David? 1
20: 1 Then David fled from Nai'oth in Ramah 1
3 David replied, "Your father knows well that I have 1
4 Then said Jonathan to David, "Whatever . . I will do 1
5 David said to Jonathan, "Behold, tomorrow is 1
6 David earnestly asked . . to run to Bethlehem 1
10 Then said David to Jonathan, "Who will tell me 1
11 Jonathan said to David, "Come, let us go out 1
12 Jonathan said to David, "The LORD . . be witness! 1
12 if he is well disposed toward David, shall I not 1
15 LORD cuts off every one of the enemies of David 1
16 of Jonathan be cut off from the house of David. 1
16 may the LORD take vengeance on David's enemies. 1
17 Jonathan made David swear . . by his love for him; 1
24 David hid himself in the field; 1
25 Abner sat by Saul . . but David's place was empty. 1
27 But on the second day . . David's place was empty. 1
28 David . . asked leave of me to go to Bethlehem; 1
33 his father was determined to put David to death. 1
34 and ate no food . . for he was grieved for David 1
35 Jonathan went . . to the appointment with David 1
39 only Jonathan and David knew the matter. 1
41 David rose from beside the stone heap 1
41 and wept . . until David recovered himself. 1
42 Then Jonathan said to David, "Go in peace 1
21: 1 Then came David to Nob to Ahim'elech the priest; 1
1 Ahim'elech came to meet David trembling, and said 1
2 And David said to Ahim'elech the priest 1
4 the priest answered David, "I have no common bread 1
5 And David answered the priest, "Of a truth 1
8 David said to Ahim'elech, "And have you . . a spear 1
9 David said, "There is none like that; give it to me. 1
10 And David rose and fled that day from Saul 1
11 Is not this David the king of the land? 1
11 'Saul has slain his . . and David his ten thousands'? 1
12 And David took these words to heart 1
22: 1 David departed from there and escaped 1
3 And David went from there to Mizpeh of Moab; 1
4 all the time that David was in the stronghold. 1
5 Then the prophet Gad said to David, "Do not remain 1
5 David departed, and went into the forest 1
6 Now Saul heard that David was discovered 1
14 And who among all . . is so faithful as David 1
17 their hand also is with David, and they knew 1
20 Abi'athar, escaped and fled after David. 1
21 Abi'athar told David that Saul had killed 1
22 And David said to Abi'athar, "I knew on that day 1
23: 1 Now they told David, "Behold, the Philistines are 1
2 David inquired of the LORD, "Shall I go and attack 1
2 And the LORD said to David, "Go and attack 1
3 David's men said to him, "Behold, we are afraid here 1
4 Then David inquired of the LORD again. 1
5 And David and his men went to Kei'lah, and fought 1
5 David delivered the inhabitants of Kei'lah. 1
6 When Abi'athar . . fled to David to Kei'lah 1
7 it was told Saul that David had come to Kei'lah. 1
8 go down to Kei'lah, to besiege David and his men. 1
9 David knew that Saul was plotting . . against him; 1
10 Then said David, "O LORD, the God of Israel 1
12 Then said David, "Will the men . . surrender me 1
13 Then David and his men . . arose and departed 1
13 Saul was told that David had escaped from Kei'lah 1
14 And David remained in the strongholds 1
15 David was afraid because Saul had come out 1
15 David was in the Wilderness of Ziph at Horesh. 1
16 Jonathan . . rose, and went to David at Horesh 1
18 David remained at Horesh, and Jonathan went home. 1
19 Does not David hide among us in the strongholds 1
24 David and his men were in the wilderness of Ma'on 1
25 David was told; therefore he went down to the rock 1
25 And when Saul heard that, he pursued after David 1
26 Saul went . . David and his men on the other side 1
26 and David was making haste to get away from Saul 1
26 Saul and . . were closing in upon David and his men 1
28 Saul returned from pursuing after David 1
29 David went up from there 1
24: 1 Behold, David is in the wilderness of En-ge'di. 1
2 Saul took . . and went to seek David and his men 1
3 David and his men were sitting in the . . cave. 1
4 And the men of David said to him, "Here is the day 1
4 David arose and . . cut off the skirt of Saul's robe 1
5 David's heart smote him, because he had cut off 1
7 David persuaded his men with these words 1
8 David also arose, and went out of the cave 1
8 David bowed with his face to the earth 1
9 David said to Saul, "Why do you listen 1
9 men who say, 'Behold, David seeks your hurt'? 1
16 David had finished speaking these words to Saul 1
16 Saul said, "Is this your voice, my son David? 1
17 He said to David, "You are more righteous than I; 1
22 And David swore this to Saul. Then Saul went home; 1
22 but David and his men went up to the stronghold. 1
25: 1 Then David rose and went down to the wilderness 1
4 David heard . . Nabal was shearing his sheep. 1
5 David sent ten young men; 1
5 and David said to the young men, "Go up to Carmel 1
8 give . . to your servants and to your son David. 1
9 When David's young men came, they said all this 1
9 they said all this to Nabal in the name of David; 1
10 Nabal answered David's servants, "Who is David? 1
10 Who is David? Who is the son of Jesse? 1
12 David's young men turned away, and came back 1
13 David said to his men, "Every man gird on his sword! 1
13 David also girded on his sword; 1
13 and about 400 men went up after David 1
14 David sent messengers . . to salute our master; 1
20 David and his men came down . . and she met them. 1
21 Now David had said, "Surely in vain have I guarded 1
22 God do so to David and more also 2
23 When Ab'igail saw David, she made haste 1
23 and fell before David on her face, and bowed 1
32 David said to Ab'igail, "Blessed be the LORD 1
35 Then David received . . what she had brought him; 1
39 When David heard that Nabal was dead, he said 1
39 David sent and wooed Ab'igail, to make her his wife. 1
40 the servants of David came to Ab'igail at Carmel 1
40 David has sent us . . to take you to him as his wife. 1
42 she went after the messengers of David 1
43 David also took Ahin'o-am of Jezreel; 1
44 Saul had given Michal . . David's wife, to Palti 1
26: 1 Is not David hiding . . on the hill of Hachi'lah 1
2 Saul arose and went . . to seek David 1
3 But David remained in the wilderness; 1

4 David sent out spies, and learned of a certainty 1
5 David rose and came to . . where Saul had encamped; 1
5 and David saw the place where Saul lay, with Abner 1
6 Then David said to Ahim'elech the Hittite 1
7 David and Abi'shai went to the army by night; 1
8 Then said Abi'shai to David, "God has given 1
9 But David said to Abi'shai, "Do not destroy him; 1
10 David said, "As the LORD lives, the LORD will smite 1
12 David took the spear and the jar of water 1
13 Then David went over to the other side 1
14 David called to the army, and to Abner . . saying 1
15 And David said to Abner, "Are you not a man? 1
17 Saul recognized David's voice, and said 1
17 Saul . . said, "Is it your voice, my son David? 1
17 And David said, "It is my voice, my lord, O king. 1
21 Saul said, "I have done wrong; return, my son David 1
22 And David made answer, "Here is the spear, O king! 1
25 Saul said to David, "Blessed be you, my son David! 1
25 Saul said to David, "Blessed be you, my son David! 1
25 David went his way, and Saul returned to his place. 1
27: 1 David said in his heart, "I shall now perish one day 1
2 David arose and went over, he and the 600 men 1
3 David dwelt with A'chish at Gath, he and his men 1
3 David with his two wives, Ahin'o-am . . and Ab'igail 1
4 ·hen it was told Saul that David had fled to Gath 1
5 Then David said to A'chish, "If I have found favor 1
7 David dwelt in the country of the Philistines 1
8 Now David and his men went up, and made raids 1
9 David smote the land 1
10 David would say, "Against the Negeb of Judah 1
11 And David saved neither man nor woman alive 1
11 Lest they should . . and say, 'So David has done.' 1
12 And A'chish trusted David, thinking 1
28: 1 And A'chish said to David 1
2 David said to A'chish, "Very well, you shall know 1
2 And A'chish said to David, "Very well 1
17 and given it to your neighbor, David. 1
29: 2 and David and his men were passing on in the rear 1
3 Is not this David, the servant of Saul 1
5 Is not this David, of whom they sing to one another 1
5 'Saul has slain . . and David his ten thousands'? 1
6 Then A'chish called David and said to him 1
8 And David said to A'chish, "But what have I done? 1
9 And A'chish made answer to David, "I know 1
11 David set out with his men early in the morning 1
30: 1 David and his men came to Ziklag on the third day 1
3 when David and his men came to the city, they found 1
4 David and the people . . raised their voices 1
5 David's two wives also had been taken captive 1
6 And David was greatly distressed; 1
6 David strengthened himself in the LORD his God. 1
7 David said to Abi'athar . . "Bring me the ephod. 1
7 Abi'athar brought the ephod to David. 1
8 And David inquired of the LORD, "Shall I pursue 1
9 David set out, and the 600 men who were with him 1
10 But David went on with the pursuit 1
11 found an Egyptian . . and brought him to David; 1
13 And David said to him, "To whom do you belong? 1
15 David said to him, "Will you take me down to this 1
17 David smote them from twilight until the evening 1
18 David recovered all . . the Amal'ekites had taken; 1
18 and David rescued his two wives. 1
19 Nothing was missing . . David brought back all. 1
20 David also captured all the flocks and herds; 1
20 and said, "This is David's spoil. 1
21 Then David came to the 200 men 1
21 men, who had been too exhausted to follow David 1
21 they went out to meet David and to meet the people 1
21 when David drew near to the people he saluted 1
22 fellows among the men who had gone with David 1
23 But David said, "You shall not do so, my brothers 1
26 When David came to Ziklag, he sent . . the spoil 1
31 the places where David and his men had roamed. 1
2Sm 1: 1 when David had returned from the slaughter 1
1 David remained two days in Ziklag; 1
2 And when he came to David, he fell to the ground 1
3 David said to him, "Where do you come from? 1
4 David said to him, "How did it go? Tell me. 1
5 Then David said to the young man who told him 1
11 Then David took hold of his clothes, and rent them; 1
13 And David said to the young man who told him 1
14 David said to him, "How is it you were not afraid 1
15 Then David called one of the young men and said, "Go 1
16 David said to him, "Your blood be upon your head; 1
17 David lamented with this lamentation over Saul 1
2: 1 David inquired of the LORD, "Shall I go up into any 1
1 Go up." David said, "To which shall I go up? 1
2 David went up there, and his two wives also 1
3 And David brought up his men who were with him 1
4 there they anointed David king over . . Judah. 1
4 they told David, "It was the men of Ja'besh-gil'ead 1
5 David sent messengers to . . Ja'besh-gil'ead 1
10 But the house of Judah followed David. 1
11 David was king in Hebron . . seven years 1
13 Jo'ab . . and the servants of David, went out and met 1
15 by number . . and twelve of the servants of David. 1
17 were beaten before the servants of David. 1
30 there were missing of David's servants nineteen 1
31 the servants of David had slain . . 360 . . men. 1

3: 1 between the house of Saul and the house of David; 1
1 and David grew stronger and stronger 1
2 And sons were born to David at Hebron 1
5 and the sixth, Ith're-am, of Eglah, David's wife. 1
5 These were born to David in Hebron. 1
6 between the house of Saul and the house of David 1
8 I . . have not given you into the hand of David; 1
9 accomplish for David what the LORD has sworn 1
10 and set up the throne of David over Israel 1
12 Abner sent messengers to David at Hebron, saying 1
14 David sent messengers to Ish-bo'sheth Saul's son 1
17 you have been seeking David as king over you. 1
18 the LORD has promised David, saying, 'By the hand 1
18 By the hand of my servant David I will save my 1
19 then Abner went to tell David at Hebron 1
20 Abner came with twenty men to David at Hebron 1
20 David made a feast for Abner and the men 1
21 And Abner said to David, "I will arise and go 1
21 David sent Abner away; and he went in peace. 1
22 the servants of David arrived . . from a raid 1
22 But Abner was not with David at Hebron 1
26 When Jo'ab came out from David's presence 1
26 they brought him back . . but David did not know 1
28 Afterward, when David heard of it, he said 1
31 Then David said to Jo'ab and to all the people 1
31 And King David followed the bier. 1
35 the people came to persuade David to eat bread 1
35 but David swore, saying, "God do so to me and more 1
4: 8 and brought the head of Ish-bo'sheth to David 1
9 David answered Rechab and Ba'anah his brother 1
12 David commanded his young men, and they killed 1
5: 1 the tribes of Israel came to David at Hebron 1
3 King David made a covenant with them at Hebron 1
3 and they anointed David king over Israel. 1
4 David was 30 years old when he began to reign 1
6 Jeb'usites . . who said to David, "You will not come 1
6 who said . . thinking, "David cannot come in here. 1
7 Nevertheless David took the stronghold of Zion 1
7 the stronghold of Zion, that is, the city of David. 1
8 David said on that day, "Whoever would smite 1
8 lame and the blind, who are hated by David's soul. 1
9 And David dwelt in the stronghold 1
9 the stronghold, and called it the city of David. 1
9 David built the city round about from the Millo 1
10 And David became greater and greater 1
11 And Hiram king of Tyre sent messengers to David 1
11 carpenters and masons who built David a house. 1
12 David perceived . . the LORD had established him 1
13 David took more concubines and wives 1
13 and more sons and daughters were born to David. 1
17 that David had been anointed king over Israel 1
17 all the Philistines went up in search of David; 1
17 David heard . . and went down to the stronghold. 1
19 And David inquired of the LORD, "Shall I go up 1
19 And the LORD said to David, "Go up; for I will 1
20 David came to Ba'al-pera'zim, and . . defeated them 1
20 to Ba'al-pera'zim, and David defeated them there; 1
21 and David and his men carried them away. 1
23 And when David inquired of the LORD, he said 1
25 And David did as the LORD commanded him 1
6: 1 David again gathered all the chosen . . of Israel 1
2 David arose and went . . from Ba'ale-judah 1
5 David and all the house of Israel were . . merry 1
8 David was angry because the LORD had broken 1
9 And David was afraid of the LORD that day; 1
10 David was not willing to take the ark of the LORD 1
10 to take the ark of the LORD into the city of David; 1
10 but David took it aside into the house 1
12 And it was told King David, "The LORD has blessed 1
12 David went and brought up the ark of God 1
12 and brought up the ark . . to the city of David 1
14 David danced before the LORD with all his might; 1
14 and David was girded with a linen ephod. 1
15 David and all . . Israel brought up the ark 1
16 As the ark of the LORD came into the city of David 1
16 Michal . . saw King David leaping and dancing 1
17 inside the tent which David had pitched for it; 1
17 and David offered burnt . . and peace offerings 1
18 when David had finished offering the burnt 1
20 David returned to bless his household. 1
20 But Michal . . came out to meet David, and said 1
21 And David said to Michal, "It was before the LORD 1
7: 5 Go and tell my servant David, 'Thus says the LORD 1
8 therefore thus you shall say to my servant David 1
17 in accordance with all . . Nathan spoke to David. 1
18 Then King David went in and sat before the LORD 1
20 And what more can David say to thee? 1
26 house of thy servant David will be established 1
8: 1 David defeated the Philistines and subdued 1
1 David took Meth'eg-am'mah out of the hand 1
2 And the Moabites became servants to David 1
3 David also defeated Hadade'zer the son of Rehob 1
4 David took from him 1,700 horsemen 1
4 and David hamstrung all the chariot horses 1
5 David slew 22,000 men of the Syrians. 1
6 Then David put garrisons in Aram of Damascus; 1
6 the Syrians became servants to David 1
6 the LORD gave victory to David wherever he went. 1
7 David took the shields . . and brought them 1

8 And from . . King David took very much bronze. 1
9 David had defeated the whole army of Hadade'zer 1
10 To'i sent his son Joram to King David, to greet him 1
11 these also King David dedicated to the LORD 1
13 And David won a name for himself. 1
14 and all the E'domites became David's servants. 1
14 the LORD gave victory to David wherever he went. 1
15 David reigned over all Israel; 1
15 David administered justice and equity to all 1
18 and David's sons were priests. 1
9: 1 And David said, "Is there still any one left 1
2 whose name was Ziba, and they called him to David; 1
5 Then King David sent and brought him 1
6 Mephib'osheth . . came to David, and fell on his 1
6 And David said, "Mephib'osheth! 1
7 David said to him, "Do not fear; 1
11 Mephib'osheth ate at David's table 2
10: 2 And David said, "I will deal loyally with Hanun 1
2 David sent by his servants to console him 1
2 David's servants came into the land 1
3 Do you think, because David has sent comforters 1
3 Has not David sent his servants to you to search 1
4 Hanun took David's servants, and shaved off half 1
5 When it was told David, he sent to meet them 1
6 Ammonites saw . . they had become odious to David 1
7 when David heard of it, he sent Jo'ab 1
17 when it was told David, he gathered all Israel 1
17 the Syrians arrayed themselves against David 1
18 David slew of the Syrians the men of 700 chariots 1
11: 1 David sent Jo'ab, and his servants with him 1
1 But David remained at Jerusalem. 1
2 when David arose from his couch and was walking 1
3 And David sent and inquired about the woman. 1
4 David sent messengers, and took her; 1
5 and she sent and told David, "I am with child. 1
6 David sent word to Jo'ab, "Send me Uri'ah 1
6 Send me Uri'ah . . And Jo'ab sent Uri'ah to David. 1
7 David asked how Jo'ab was doing, and how the people 1
8 Then David said to Uri'ah, "Go down to your house 1
10 When they told David . . David said to Uri'ah 1
10 David said to Uri'ah, "Have you not come 1
11 Uri'ah said to David, "The ark and Israel and Judah 1
12 Then David said to Uri'ah, "Remain here today also 1
13 And David invited him, and he ate . . and drank 1
14 In the morning David wrote a letter to Jo'ab 1
17 and some of the servants of David . . fell. 1
18 Jo'ab sent and told David . . about the fighting; 1
22 messenger . . told David all that Jo'ab had sent 1
23 The messenger said to David, "The men gained 1
25 David said to the messenger, "Thus shall you say 1
27 David sent and brought her to his house 1
27 the thing . . David had done displeased the LORD. 1
12: 1 And the LORD sent Nathan to David. 1
5 David's anger was . . kindled against the man; 1
7 Nathan said to David, "You are the man. 1
13 David said to Nathan, "I have sinned 1
13 Nathan said to David, "The LORD . . put away 1
15 struck the child that Uri'ah's wife bore to David 1
16 David therefore besought God for the child; 1
16 and David fasted, and went in and lay all night 1
18 And the servants of David feared to tell him 1
19 David saw that his servants were whispering 1
19 David perceived that the child was dead; 1
19 and David said to his servants, "Is the child dead? 1
20 Then David arose from the earth, and washed 1
24 Then David comforted his wife, Bathshe'ba 1
27 Jo'ab sent messengers to David, and said 1
29 David gathered all the people together and went 1
30 the crown . . and it was placed on David's head. 1
31 David and all the people returned to Jerusalem. 1
13: 1 Now Ab'salom, David's son, had a beautiful sister 1
1 after a time Amnon, David's son, loved her. 1
3 the son of Shim'e-ah, David's brother 1
7 Then David sent home to Tamar, saying, "Go 1
21 When King David heard of all these things 1
30 While they were on the way, tidings came to David 1
32 Jon'adab the son of Shim'e-ah, David's brother, said 1
37 And David mourned for his son day after day. 2
15:12 for Ahith'opel the Gi'lonite, David's counselor 1
13 And a messenger came to David, saying 1
14 David said to all his servants who were with him 1
22 And David said to It'tai, "Go then, pass on. 1
30 David went up the ascent of the Mount of Olives 1
31 And it was told David, "Ahith'ophel is among 1
31 David said, "O LORD, I pray thee, turn the counsel 1
32 David came to the summit, where God was worshiped 1
33 David said to him, "If you go on with me, you will be 1
37 So Hushai, David's friend, came into the city 1
16: 1 When David had passed a little beyond the summit 1
5 When King David came to Bahu'rim, there came out 1
6 he threw stones at David, and at all the servants 1
6 at David, and at all the servants of King David; 1
10 because the LORD has said to him, 'Curse David,' 1
11 David said to Abi'shai and to all his servants 1
13 So David and his men went on the road 1
16 And when Hushai the Archite, David's friend, came 1
23 so was . . esteemed, both by David and by Ab'salom. 1
17: 1 and I will set out and pursue David tonight. 1

16 Now therefore send quickly and tell David, 'Do not 1
17 tell them, and they would go and tell King David; 1
21 the men came up . . and went and told King David. 1
21 They said to David, "Arise, and go quickly over 1
22 David arose, and all the people who were with him 1
24 Then David came to Mahana'im. 1
27 When David came to Mahana'im, Shobi 1
29 for David and the people with him to eat; 1
18: 1 Then David mustered the men who were with him 1
2 And David sent forth the army 1
7 were defeated there by the servants of David 1
9 Ab'salom chanced to meet the servants of David. 1
24 Now David was sitting between the two gates; 1
19:11 David sent this message to Zadok and Abi'athar 1
16 come down with the men of Judah to meet King David 1
22 But David said, "What have I to do with you 1
41 brought the king . . and all David's men with him? 1
43 We have . . and in David also we have more than you. 1
20: 1 We have no portion in David, and . . no inheritance 1
2 the men of Israel withdrew from David 1
3 And David came to his house at Jerusalem; 1
6 And David said to Abi'shai, "Now Sheba . . will do 1
11 and whoever is for David, let him follow Jo'ab. 1
21 a man . . has lifted up his hand against King David; 1
26 and Ira the Ja'irite was also David's priest. 1
21: 1 a famine in the days of David for three years 1
1 and David sought the face of the LORD. 1
3 And David said to the Gib'eonites, "What shall I do 1
7 oath . . between them, between David and Jonathan 1
11 When David was told what Rizpah . . had done 1
12 David went and took the bones of Saul 1
15 and David went down together with his servants 1
15 and they fought against . . and David grew weary. 1
16 And Ish'bi-be'nob . . thought to kill David. 1
17 Then David's men adjured him, "You shall no more go 1
21 Jonathan, the son of Shim'e-i, David's brother 1
22 fell by the hand of David and . . his servants. 1
22: 1 And David spoke to the LORD the words of this song 1
51 shows steadfast love to his anointed, to David 1
23: 1 Now these are the last words of David 1
1 The oracle of David, the son of Jesse 1
8 the names of the mighty men whom David had 1
9 He was with David when they defied 1
13 and came . . to David at the cave of Adullam 1
14 David was then in the stronghold; 1
15 And David said longingly, "O that some one would 1
16 drew water . . and took and brought it to David. 1
23 And David set him over his bodyguard. 1
24: 1 and he incited David against them, saying, "Go 1
10 But David's heart smote him after he had numbered 1
10 And David said to the LORD, "I have sinned greatly 1
11 when David arose in the morning, the word . . came 1
11 the word . . came to the prophet Gad, David's seer 1
12 Go and say to David, 'Thus says the LORD 1
13 Gad came to David and told him, and said to him 1
14 Then David said to Gad, "I am in great distress 1
17 Then David spoke to the LORD when he saw the angel 1
18 Gad came that day to David, and said to him, "Go up 1
19 David went up at Gad's word, as . . commanded. 1
21 David said, "To buy the threshing floor of you 1
22 Arau'nah said to David, "Let my lord the king take 1
24 David bought the threshing floor and the oxen 1
25 And David built there an altar to the LORD 1
1Kg 1: 1 King David was old and advanced in years; 1
8 and David's mighty men were not with Adoni'jah. 1
11 has become king and David our lord does not know 1
13 Go in at once to King David, and say to him, 'Did you 1
28 Then King David answered, "Call Bathshe'ba to me. 1
31 and said, "May my lord King David live for ever. 1
32 King David said, "Call to me Zadok the priest 1
37 greater than the throne of my lord King David. 1
38 and caused Solomon to ride on King David's mule 1
43 No, for our lord King David has made Solomon king; 1
47 to congratulate our lord King David, saying, 'Your 1
2: 1 When David's time to die drew near, he charged 1
10 David slept with his fathers, and was buried 1
10 his fathers, and was buried in the city of David. 1
11 time that David reigned over Israel was 40 years; 1
12 Solomon sat upon the throne of David his father; 1
24 me, and placed me on the throne of David my father 1
26 you bore the ark . . before David my father 1
32 without the knowledge of my father David 1
33 to David, and to his . . there shall be peace 1
44 all the evil that you did to David my father; 1
45 the throne of David shall be established before 1
3: 1 daughter, and brought her into the city of David 1
3 LORD, walking in the statutes of David his father; 1
6 steadfast love to thy servant David my father 1
7 made thy servant king in place of David my father 1
14 walk in my ways . . as your father David walked 1
5: 1 for Hiram always loved David. 1
3 David my father could not build a house 1
5 as the LORD said to David my father, 'Your son 1
7 the LORD . . who has given to David a wise son 1
6:12 my word . . which I spoke to David your father. 1
7:51 the things which David his father had dedicated 1
8: 1 the ark . . out of the city of David, which is Zion. 1
15 what he promised . . to David my father, saying 1
16 but I chose David to be over my people Israel.' 1
17 Now it was in the heart of David my father to build 1
18 the LORD said to David my father, 'Whereas 1
20 I have risen in the place of David my father 1
24 hast kept with thy servant David my father 1
25 keep with thy servant David my father what thou 1
26 thou hast spoken to thy servant David my father. 1
66 that the LORD had shown to David his servant 1
9: 4 you . . walk before me, as David your father walked 1
5 as I promised David your father, saying 1
24 went up from the city of David to her own house 1
11: 4 true . . as was the heart of David his father. 1
6 follow the LORD, as David his father had done. 1
12 for the sake of David your father I will not do it 1
13 I will give one tribe . . for the sake of David 1
15 when David was in Edom, and Jo'ab . . went up 1
21 Hadad heard . . that David slept with his fathers 1
24 he gathered men . . after the slaughter by David; 1
27 the breach of the city of David his father. 1
32 he shall have . . for the sake of my servant David 1
33 keeping my statutes . . as David his father did. 1
34 for the sake of David my servant whom I chose 1
36 that David my servant may always have a lamp 1
38 do what is right . . as David my servant did 1
38 a sure house, as I built for David 1
39 I will for this afflict the descendants of David 1
43 and was buried in the city of David his father; 1
12:16 What portion have we in David? 1
16 Look now to your own house, David. 1
19 in rebellion against the house of David 1
20 There was none that followed the house of David 1
26 the kingdom will turn back to the house of David; 1
13: 2 a son shall be born to the house of David, Josi'ah 1
14: 8 tore the kingdom away from the house of David 1
8 and yet you have not been like my servant David 1
31 was buried with his fathers in the city of David. 1
15: 3 wholly true . . as the heart of David his father. 1
4 for David's sake the LORD his God gave him a lamp 1
5 David did what was right in the eyes of the LORD 1
8 and they buried him in the city of David. 1
11 right in the eyes of the LORD, as David . . had done. 1
24 was buried with his fathers in the city of David 1
22:50 was buried with his fathers in the city of David 1
2Kg 8:19 LORD would . . for the sake of David his servant 1
24 was buried with his fathers in the city of David; 1
9:28 buried . . with his fathers in the city of David. 1
11:10 the spears and shields that had been King David's 1
12:21 buried him with his fathers in the city of David 1
14: 3 And he did . . yet not like David his father; 1
20 was buried in Jerusalem . . in the city of David. 1
15: 7 buried him with his fathers in the city of David 1
38 and was buried . . in the city of David his father; 1
16: 2 he did not do . . as his father David had done 1
20 was buried with his fathers in the city of David; 1
17:21 When he had torn Israel from the house of David 1
18: 3 according to all that David his father had done. 1
19:34 my own sake and for the sake of my servant David. 1
20: 5 Thus says the LORD, the God of David your father 1
6 for my own sake and for my servant David's sake. 1
21: 7 the LORD said to David and to Solomon his son 1
22: 2 and walked in all the way of David his father 1
1Ch 2:15 Ozem the sixth, David the seventh; 1
3: 1 the sons of David that were born to him in Hebron 1
9 All these were David's sons 1
4:31 These were their cities until David reigned. 1
6:31 These are the men whom David put in charge 1
7: 2 their number in the days of David being 22,600 1
9:22 David and Samuel the seer established them 1
10:14 the kingdom over to David the son of Jesse. 1
11: 1 all Israel gathered together to David at Hebron 1
3 David made a covenant with them at Hebron 1
3 they anointed David king over Israel 1
4 David and all Israel went to Jerusalem 1
5 The inhabitants of Jebus said to David 1
5 Nevertheless David took the stronghold of Zion 1
5 stronghold of Zion, that is, the city of David. 1
6 David said, "Whoever shall smite the Jeb'usites 1
7 David dwelt in the stronghold; 1
7 therefore it was called the city of David. 1
9 David became greater and greater 1
10 Now these are the chiefs of David's mighty men 1
11 This is an account of David's mighty men 1
13 He was with David at Pas-dam'mim 1
15 to the rock to David at the cave of Adullam 1
16 David was then in the stronghold; 1
17 David said longingly, "O that some one 1
18 drew water . . and took and brought it to David. 1
18 But David would not drink of it; 1
25 And David set him over his bodyguard. 1
12: 1 Now these are the men who came to David at Ziklag 1
8 to David at the stronghold in the wilderness 1
16 men of Benjamin and Judah came . . to David 1
17 David went out to meet them and said to them 1
18 We are yours, O David; and with you, O son of Jesse! 1
18 Then David received them, and made them officers 1
19 deserted to David when he came 1
21 They helped David against the band of raiders; 1
22 men kept coming to David to help him 1
23 armed troops, who came to David in Hebron 1
31 were expressly named to come and make David king. 1
33 to help David with singleness of purpose. 2
38 to make David king over all Israel; 1
38 were of a single mind to make David king. 1
39 they were there with David for three days 1
13: 1 David consulted with the commanders 1
2 David said to all the assembly of Israel 1
5 David assembled all Israel 1
6 David and all Israel went up to Ba'alah 1
8 David and all Israel were making merry 1
11 David was angry because the LORD 1
12 David was afraid of God that day; 1
13 David did not take the ark home into the city 1
13 did not take the ark home into the city of David 1
14: 1 Hiram king of Tyre sent messengers to David 1
2 David perceived that the LORD had established 1
3 David took more wives in Jerusalem 1
3 and David begot more sons and daughters. 1
8 Philistines heard that David had been anointed 1
8 all the Philistines went up in search of David; 1
8 David heard of it and went out against them. 1
10 David inquired of God, "Shall I go up against 1
11 went up to Ba'al-pera'zim, and David defeated them 1
11 David said, "God has broken through my enemies 1
12 left their gods there, and David gave command 1
14 when David again inquired of God, God said to him 1
16 David did as God commanded him 1
17 the fame of David went out into all lands 1
15: 1 David built houses for himself in the city •
1 built houses for himself in the city of David; 1
2 Then David said, "No one but the Levites may carry 1
3 David assembled all Israel at Jerusalem 1
4 David gathered together the sons of Aaron 1
11 David summoned the priests Zadok and Abi'athar 1
16 David also commanded the chiefs of the Levites 1
25 David and the elders of Israel 1
27 David was clothed with a robe of fine linen 1
27 and David wore a linen ephod. 1
29 ark . . of the LORD came to the city of David 1
29 Michal . . saw King David dancing 1
16: 1 inside the tent which David had pitched for it; 1
2 when David had finished offering 1
7 David first appointed that thanksgiving be sung 1
37 David left Asaph and his brethren there •
43 and David went home to bless his household. 1
17: 1 Now when David dwelt in his house 1
1 David said to Nathan the prophet 1
2 Nathan said to David, "Do all that is in your heart 1
4 Go and tell my servant David, 'Thus says the LORD 1
7 therefore thus shall you say to my servant David 1
15 In accordance with . . Nathan spoke to David. 1
16 Then King David went in and sat before the LORD 1
18 can David say to thee for honoring thy servant? 1
24 house of thy servant David will be established 1
18: 1 David defeated the Philistines and subdued 1
2 the Mo'abites became servants to David 1
3 David also defeated Hadade'zer king of Zobah 1
4 And David took from him a 1,000 chariots 1
4 David hamstrung all the chariot horses 1
5 David slew 22,000 men of the Syrians. 1
6 Then David put garrisons in Syria of Damascus; 1
6 the Syrians became servants to David 1
6 LORD gave victory to David wherever he went. 1
7 David took the shields of gold 1
8 and from Cun . . David took very much bronze; 1
9 David had defeated the whole army of Hadade'zer 1
10 he sent his son Hador'am to King David, to greet him 1
11 these also King David dedicated to the LORD 1
13 and all the E'domites became David's servants. 1
13 the LORD gave victory to David wherever he went. 1
14 David reigned over all Israel; 1
17 David's sons were the chief officials 1
19: 2 David said, "I will deal loyally with Hanun 1
2 David sent messengers to console him 1
2 David's servants came to Hanun . . to console 1
3 because David has sent comforters to you •
4 Hanun took David's servants, and shaved them 1
5 When David was told concerning the men 1
6 that they had made themselves odious to David 1
8 When David heard of it, he sent Jo'ab 1
17 when it was told David, he gathered all Israel 1
17 when David set the battle in array against 1
18 David slew of the Syrians the men of 7,000 chariots 1
19 made peace with David, and became subject to him. 1
20: 1 But David remained at Jerusalem. 1
2 David took the crown of their king from his head; 1
2 the crown . . was placed on David's head. 1
3 David did to all the cities of the Ammonites. 1
3 David and all the people returned to Jerusalem. 1
7 Jonathan the son of Shim'e-a, David's brother 1
8 they fell by the hand of David and by the hand 1
21: 1 Satan . . incited David to number Israel. 1
2 David said to Jo'ab and the commanders of the army 1
5 the sum of the numbering of the people to David. 1
8 David said to God, "I have sinned greatly 1
9 the LORD spoke to Gad, David's seer, saying 1
10 Go and say to David, 'Thus says the LORD 1
11 Gad came to David and said . . "Thus says the LORD 1
13 Then David said to Gad, "I am in great distress; 1
16 David lifted his eyes and saw the angel 1

16 David and the elders, clothed in sackcloth 1
17 David said to God, "Was it not I who gave command 1
18 angel of the LORD commanded Gad to say to David 1
18 David should go up and rear an altar to the LORD 1
19 David went up at Gad's word, which he had spoken 1
21 As David came to Ornan, Ornan looked and saw David 1
21 Ornan looked and saw David and went forth 1
21 did obeisance to David with his face to the ground 1
22 David said to Ornan, "Give me the site 1
23 Ornan said to David, "Take it; and let my lord 1
24 King David said to Ornan, "No, but I will buy it 1
25 David paid Ornan 600 shekels of gold by weight 1
26 David built there an altar to the LORD 1
28 when David saw that the LORD had answered him 1
30 David could not go before it to inquire of God 1
22: 1 David said, "Here shall be the house of the LORD God 1
2 David commanded to gather together the aliens 1
3 David also provided great stores of iron 1
4 brought great quantities of cedar to David. 1
5 For David said, "Solomon my son is young 1
5 David provided materials in great quantity 1
7 David said to Solomon, "My son, I had it in my heart 1
17 David also commanded all the leaders of Israel 1
23: 1 When David was old and full of days 1
2 David assembled all the leaders of Israel •
4 24,000 of these," David said, "shall have charge •
6 David organized them in divisions 1
25 For David said, "The LORD, the God of Israel 1
27 for by the last words of David these were 1
24: 3 David organized them according 1
31 in the presence of King David, Zadok, Ahim'elech 1
25: 1 David and the chiefs of the service . . set apart 1
26:26 the dedicated gifts which David the king 1
31 In the 40th year of David's reign search was made 1
32 King David appointed him and his brethren 1
27:18 for Judah, Eli'hu, one of David's brothers; 1
23 David did not number those below twenty years 1
24 was not entered in the chronicles of King David. 1
31 these were stewards of King David's property. 1
32 Jonathan, David's uncle, was a counselor 1
28: 1 David assembled at Jerusalem all the officials 1
2 Then King David rose to his feet and said 1
11 David gave Solomon his son the plan 1
20 David said to Solomon . . "Be strong and of good 1
29: 1 David the king said to all the assembly 1
9 David the king also rejoiced greatly. 1
10 David blessed the LORD in the presence of all 1
10 David said: "Blessed art thou, O LORD 1
20 David said to all the assembly, "Bless the LORD 1
22 Solomon the son of David king the second time 1
23 Solomon sat . . as king instead of David 1
24 the mighty men, and also all the sons of King David 1
26 David the son of Jesse reigned over all Israel. 1
29 acts of King David, from first to last, are written 1
2Ch 1: 1 Solomon the son of David established himself 1
4 David had brought up the ark of God 1
4 to the place that David had prepared for it 1
8 great and steadfast love to David my father 1
9 thy promise to David my father be now fulfilled 1
2: 3 As you dealt with David . . so deal with me. 1
7 workers . . whom David my father provided. 1
12 who has given King David a wise son 1
14 the craftsmen of my lord, David your father. 1
17 census of them which David his father had taken; 1
3: 1 where the LORD had appeared to David his father 1
1 at the place that David had appointed 1
5: 1 the things which David his father had dedicated 1
2 to bring up the ark . . out of the city of David 1
6: 4 promised with his mouth to David . . saying 1
6 I have chosen David to be over my people Israel.' 1
7 in the heart of David my father to build a house 1
8 the LORD said to David my father, 'Whereas it was 1
10 for I have risen in the place of David my father 1
15 who hast kept with thy servant David my father 1
16 O LORD . . keep with thy servant David my father 1
17 which thou hast spoken to thy servant David. 1
42 Remember thy steadfast love for David 1
7: 6 instruments . . which King David had made 1
6 David offered praises by their ministry; 1
10 goodness that the LORD had shown to David 1
17 if you walk before me, as David your father walked 1
18 I will establish . . as I covenanted with David 1
8:11 up Pharoah's daughter from the city of David 1
11 My wife shall not live in the house of David 1
14 According to the ordinance of David his father 1
14 for so David the man of God had commanded. 1
9:31 Solomon . . was buried in the city of David 1
10:16 What portion have we in David? 1
16 Look now to your own house, David. 1
19 been in rebellion against the house of David 1
11:17 they walked . . in the way of David and Solomon. 1
18 Jer'imoth the son of David 1
12:16 Rehobo'am . . was buried in the city of David; 1
13: 5 gave the kingship over Israel for ever to David 1
6 son of Nebat, a servant of Solomon the son of David 1
8 kingdom . . in the hand of the sons of David 1
14: 1 they buried him in the city of David; 1
16:14 hewn out for himself in the city of David. 1
21: 1 buried with his fathers in the city of David; 1
7 Yet the LORD would not destroy the house of David 1
7 the covenant which he had made with David 1
12 Thus says the LORD, the God of David your father 1
20 buried him in the city of David 1
23: 3 as the LORD spoke concerning the sons of David. 1
9 spears and . . shields that had been King David's 1
18 whom David had organized to be in charge 1
18 according to the order of David. 1
24:16 buried him in the city of David among the kings 1
25 he died; and they buried him in the city of David 1
25:28 buried with his fathers in the city of David. 1
27: 9 they buried him in the city of David; 1
28: 1 not do what was right . . like his father David. 1
29: 2 according to all that David his father had done. 1
25 according to the commandment of David and of Gad 1
26 The Levites stood with the instruments of David 1
27 accompanied by the instruments of David 1
30 praises . . with the words of David and of Asaph 1
30:26 time of Solomon the son of David king of Israel 1
32: 5 he strengthened the Millo in the city of David. 1
30 down to the west side of the city of David. 1
33 the ascent of the tombs of the sons of David; 1
33: 7 house of God, of which God said to David 1
14 built an outer wall for the city of David 1
34: 2 walked in the ways of David his father; 1
3 he began to seek the God of David his father; 1
35: 3 house which Solomon the son of David . . built; 1
4 following the directions of David king 1
15 in their place according to the command of David 1
Ezr 3:10 directions of David king of Israel; 1
8: 2 Of the sons of David, Hattush 1
20 temple servants, whom David and his officials 1
Neh 3:15 stairs that go down from the City of David. 1
16 point opposite the sepulchres of David 1
12:24 commandment of David the man of God 1
36 musical instruments of David the man of God; 1
37 went up . . by the stairs of the city of David 1
37 above the house of David, to the Water Gate 1
45 command of David and his son Solomon. 1
46 For in the days of David and Asaph of old there was 1
Ps 3: 0 A Psalm of David, when he fled from Absalom 1
4: 0 with stringed instruments. A Psalm of David. 1
5: 0 for the flutes. A Psalm of David. 1
6: 0 according to The Sheminith. A Psalm of David. 1
7: 0 A Shiggaion of David, which he sang to the LORD 1
8: 0 according to The Gittith. A Psalm of David. 1
9: 0 according to Muth-labben. A Psalm of David. 1
11: 0 To the choirmaster. Of David. 1
12: 0 according to The Sheminith. A Psalm of David. 1
13: 0 To the choirmaster. A Psalm of David. 1
14: 0 To the choirmaster. Of David. 1
15: 0 A Psalm of David. 1
16: 0 A Miktam of David. 1
17: 0 A Prayer of David. 1
18: 0 To the choirmaster. A Psalm of David 1
50 to David and his descendants for ever. 1
19: 0 To the choirmaster. A Psalm of David. 1
20: 0 To the choirmaster. A Psalm of David. 1
21: 0 To the choirmaster. A Psalm of David. 1
22: 0 The Hind of the Dawn. A Psalm of David. 1
23: 0 A Psalm of David. 1
24: 0 A Psalm of David. 1
25: 0 A Psalm of David. 1
26: 0 A Psalm of David. 1
27: 0 A Psalm of David. 1
28: 0 A Psalm of David. 1
29: 0 A Psalm of David. 1
30: 0 A Psalm of David. 1
31: 0 To the choirmaster. A Psalm of David. 1
32: 0 A Psalm of David. A Maskil. 1
34: 0 A Psalm of David, when he feigned madness 1
35: 0 A Psalm of David. 1
36: 0 To the choirmaster. A Psalm of David 1
37: 0 A Psalm of David. 1
38: 0 A Psalm of David, for the memorial offering. 1
39: 0 To Jeduthun. A Psalm of David. 1
40: 0 To the choirmaster. A Psalm of David. 1
41: 0 To the choirmaster. A Psalm of David. 1
51: 0 To the choirmaster. A Psalm of David 1
52: 0 To the choirmaster. A Maskil of David 1
0 David has come to the house of Ahimelech. 1
53: 0 according to Mahalath. A Maskil of David. 1
54: 0 with stringed instruments. A Maskil of David 1
0 went and told Saul, "David is in hiding among us. 1
55: 0 with stringed instruments. A Maskil of David. 1
56: 0 Miktam of David, when the Philistines seized him 1
57: 0 A Miktam of David, when he fled from Saul 1
58: 0 according to Do Not Destroy. A Miktam of David. 1
59: 0 according to Do Not Destroy. A Miktam of David 1
60: 0 according to Shushan Eduth. A Miktam of David; 1
61: 0 with stringed instruments. A Psalm of David. 1
62: 0 according to Jeduthun. A Psalm of David. 1
63: 0 A Psalm of David, when he was in the Wilderness 1
64: 0 To the choirmaster. A Psalm of David. 1
65: 0 To the choirmaster. A Psalm of David. A Song. 1
68: 0 To the choirmaster. A Psalm of David. A Song. 1
69: 0 according to Lilies. A Psalm of David. 1
70: 0 A Psalm of David, for the memorial offering. 1
72:20 The prayers of David, the son of Jesse, are ended. 1
78:70 He chose David his servant 1
86: 0 A Prayer of David. 1
89: 3 I have sworn to David my servant 1
20 I have found David, my servant; 1
35 I will not lie to David. 1
49 by thy faithfulness thou didst swear to David? 1
101: 0 A Psalm of David. 1
103: 0 A Psalm of David. 1
108: 0 A Song. A Psalm of David. 1
109: 0 To the choirmaster. A Psalm of David. 1
110: 0 A Psalm of David. 1
122: 0 A Song of Ascents. Of David. 1
5 thrones of the house of David. 1
124: 0 A Song of Ascents. Of David. 1
131: 0 A Song of Ascents. Of David. 1
132: 1 Remember, O LORD, in David's favor 1
10 For thy servant David's sake do not turn away 1
11 The LORD swore to David a sure oath 1
17 There I will make a horn to sprout for David; 1
138: 0 A Psalm of David. 1
139: 0 To the choirmaster. A Psalm of David. 1
140: 0 To the choirmaster. A Psalm of David. 1
141: 0 A Psalm of David. 1
142: 0 A Maskil of David, when he was in the cave. 1
143: 0 A Psalm of David. 1
144: 0 A Psalm of David. 1
10 who rescuest David thy servant. 1
145: 0 A Song of Praise. Of David. 1
Prv 1: 1 proverbs of Solomon, son of David, king of Israel 1
Ecc 1: 1 The words of the Preacher, the son of David 1
Sng 4: 4 Your neck is like the tower of David 1
Isa 7: 2 the house of David was told, "Syria is in league 1
13 O house of David! is it too little for you to weary men 1
9: 7 upon the throne of David, and over his kingdom 1
16: 5 sit in faithfulness in the tent of David 1
22: 9 the breaches of the city of David were many 1
22 on his shoulder the key of the house of David; 1
29: 1 Ho Ariel, Ariel, the city where David encamped! 1
37:35 and for the sake of my servant David. 1
38: 5 Thus says the LORD, the God of David your father 1
55: 3 covenant, my steadfast, sure love for David. 1
Jer 13:13 the kings who sit on David's throne, the priests 1
17:25 kings who sit on the throne of David 1
21:12 O house of David! Thus says the LORD 1
22: 2 O King of Judah, who sit on the throne of David 1
4 kings who sit on the throne of David 1
30 shall succeed in sitting on the throne of David 1
23: 5 when I will raise up for David a righteous Branch 1
29:16 the king who sits on the throne of David 1
30: 9 and David their king, whom I will raise up for them. 1
33:15 a righteous Branch to spring forth for David; 1
17 David shall never lack a man to sit on the throne 1
21 my covenant with David my servant may be broken 1
22 I will multiply the descendants of David 1
26 the descendants of Jacob and David my servant 1
36:30 He shall have none to sit upon the throne of David 1
Ezk 34:23 shepherd, my servant David, and he shall feed them 1
24 my servant David shall be prince among them; 1
37:24 My servant David shall be king over them; 1
25 David my servant shall be their prince for ever. 1
Hos 3: 5 and seek the LORD their God, and David their king; 1
Ams 6: 5 and like David invent . . instruments of music; 1
9:11 I will raise up the booth of David that is fallen 1
Zec 12: 7 Judah first, that the glory of the house of David 1
8 the feeblest . . on that day shall be like David 1
8 the house of David shall be like God 1
10 I will pour out on the house of David 1
12 the family of the house of David by itself 1
13: 1 shall be a fountain opened for the house of David 1
Mat 1: 1 Jesus Christ, the son of David, the son of Abraham. 2
6 Jesse the father of David the king. 2
6 And David was the father of Solomon by the wife 2
17 So all the generations from Abraham to David 2
17 and from David to the deportation to Babylon 2
20 saying, "Joseph, son of David, do not fear to take 2
9:27 Have mercy on us, Son of David. 2
12: 3 He said to them, "Have you not read what David did 2
23 Can this be the Son of David? 2
15:22 Have mercy on me, O Lord, Son of David 2
20:30 Have mercy on us, Son of David! 2
31 Lord, have mercy on us, Son of David! 2
21: 9 shouted, "Hosanna to the Son of David! 2
15 Hosanna to the Son of David! 2
22:42 They said to him, "The son of David. 2
43 How is it then that David, inspired by the Spirit 2
45 If David thus calls him Lord, how is he his son? 2
Mrk 2:25 he said to them, "Have you never read what David did 2
10:47 Jesus, Son of David, have mercy on me! 2
48 Son of David, have mercy on me! 2
11:10 Blessed is the kingdom of our father David 2
12:35 scribes say that the Christ is the son of David? 2
36 David himself, inspired by the Holy Spirit 2
37 David himself calls him Lord; so how is he his son? 2
Lke 1:27 of the house of David 2
32 give to him the throne of his father David 2
69 in the house of his servant David 2
2: 4 to the city of David, which is called Bethlehem 2
4 because he was of the house and lineage of David 2
11 born this day in the city of David a Savior 2

3:31 the son of Nathan, the son of David 2
6: 3 Jesus answered, "Have you not read what David did 2
18:38 he cried, "Jesus, Son of David, have mercy on me! 2
39 Son of David, have mercy on me! 2
20:41 How can they say that the Christ is David's son? 2
42 For David himself says in the Book of Psalms 2
44 David thus calls him Lord; so how is he his son? 2
Joh 7:42 the Christ is descended from David 2
42 comes from Bethlehem, the village where David was? 2
Act 1:16 spoke beforehand by the mouth of David 2
2:25 David says concerning him, 'I saw the Lord 2
29 the patriarch David 2
34 David did not ascend into the heavens 2
4:25 by the mouth of our father David, thy servant 2
7:45 So it was until the days of David 2
13:22 he raised up David to be their king 2
22 I have found in David the son of Jesse a man 2
34 give you the holy and sure blessings of David.' 2
36 David . . fell asleep, and was laid with his fathers 2
15:16 rebuild the dwelling of David, which has fallen 2
Rom 1: 3 descended from David according to the flesh 2
4: 6 So also David pronounces a blessing upon the man 2
11: 9 And David says, "Let their table become a snare 2
2Ti 2: 8 descended from David, as preached in my gospel 2
Heb 4: 7 saying through David so long afterward 2
11:32 to tell of Gideon, Barak, Samson, Jephthah, of David 2
Rev 3: 7 the holy one, the true one, who has the key of David 2
5: 5 the Lion . . the Root of David, has conquered 2
22:16 I am the root and the offspring of David 2
1Es 1: 3 Solomon the king, the son of David 2
5 in accordance with the directions of David 2
15 according to the arrangement made by David 2
5: 5 of the house of David, of the lineage of Phares 2
60 according to . . David king of Israel 2
8:29 Of the sons of David, Hattush 2
49 David and the leaders 2
2Es 3:23 raise up for thyself a servant, named David. 3
7:108 and David for the plague 3
12:32 who will arise from the posterity of David ‡
Sir 45:25 A covenant was also established with David 2
47: 1 Nathan rose up to prophesy in the days of David. 2
2 so David was selected from the sons of Israel. 2
22 he gave . . to David a root of his stock. 2
48:15 with rulers from the house of David. 2
22 he held strongly to the ways of David his father 2
49: 4 Except David and Hezekiah and Josiah 2
1Mc 1:33 Then they fortified the city of David 2
2:31 the troops in Jerusalem the city of David 2
57 David . . inherited the throne of the kingdom 2
4:30 by the hand of thy servant David 2
7:32 the rest fled into the city of David. 2
14:36 the men in the city of David in Jerusalem 2
2Mc 2:13 the writings of David 2
4Mc 3: 6 the story of King David's thirst. 2
7 David had been attacking the Philistines 2
15 David, although he was burning with thirst •
18:15 songs of the psalmist David, who said 2

Debir 1. דְּבִיר 2. Δαβιρ
Jos 10: 3 Japhi'a king of Lachish, and to Debir king of Eglon 1
38 Joshua . . turned back to Debir and assaulted it 1
39 as he had done . . so he did to Debir and to its king. 1
11:21 from the hill country, from Hebron, from Debir 1
12:13 the king of Debir, one; the king of Geder, one; 1
13:26 from Mahana'im to the territory of Debir 2
15: 7 and the boundary goes up to Debir from the Valley 1
15 he went up . . against the inhabitants of Debir; 1
15 the name of Debir formerly was Kir'iath-se'pher. 1
49 Dannah, Kir'iath-san'nah (that is, Debir) 1
21:15 Holon with its . . Debir with its pasture lands 1
Jdg 1:11 they went against the inhabitants of Debir. 1
11 The name of Debir was formerly Kir'iath-se'pher. 1
1Ch 6:58 Debir with its pasture lands 1

Deborah 1. דְּבוֹרָה 2. Δεββωρα
Gen 35: 8 Deb'orah, Rebekah's nurse, died 1
Jdg 4: 4 Now Deb'orah, a prophetess, the wife of Lapp'idoth 1
5 the palm of Deb'orah between Ramah and Bethel 1
9 Deb'orah arose, and went with Barak to Kedesh. 1
10 went up at his heels; and Deb'orah went up with him. 1
14 Deb'orah said to Barak, "Up! For this is the day 1
5: 1 Then sang Deb'orah and Barak . . on that day 1
7 ceased until you arose, Deb'orah, arose as a mother 1
12 Awake, awake, Deb'orah! Awake, awake, utter a song 1
15 the princes of Is'sachar came with Deb'orah 1
Tob 1: 8 as Deborah my father's mother had commanded me 2

Decapolis 1. Δεκάπολις
Mat 4:25 from Galilee and the Decap'olis and Jerusalem 1
Mrk 5:20 began to proclaim in the Decap'olis 1
7:31 through the region of the Decap'olis. 1

Dedan 1. דְּדָן
Gen 10: 7 The sons of Ra'amah: Sheba and Dedan. 1
25: 3 Jokshan was the father of Sheba and Dedan. 1
3 The sons of Dedan were Asshu'rim, Letu'shim 1
1Ch 1: 9 The sons of Ra'amah: Sheba and Dedan. 1
32 Shu'ah. The sons of Jokshan: Sheba and Dedan. 1
Jer 25:23 Dedan, Tema, Buz 1
49: 8 dwell in the depths, O inhabitants of Dedan! 1
Ezk 25:13 I will make it desolate; from Teman even to Dedan 1
27:20 Dedan traded with you in saddlecloths 1
38:13 Sheba and Dedan and the merchants of Tarshish 1

Dedanite 1. דְּדָנִי
Isa 21:13 Arabia you will lodge, O caravans of De'danites. 1

feast of the Dedication 1. ἐγκαίνια
Joh 10:22 the feast of the Dedication at Jerusalem; 1

Delaiah 1. דְּלָיָהוּ 2. Δαλαιας
1Ch 3:24 sons of Eli-o-e'nai . . Joha'nan, Delai'ah, and Ana'ni 1
24:18 23rd to Delai'ah, the 24th to Ma-azi'ah. 1
Ezr 2:60 sons of Delai'ah, the sons of Tobi'ah 1
Neh 6:10 Shemai'ah the son of Delai'ah, son of Mehet'abel 1
7:62 sons of Delai'ah, the sons of Tobi'ah 1
Jer 36:12 Delai'ah the son of Shemai'ah 1
25 even when Elna'than and Delai'ah and Gemari'ah 1
1Es 5:37 the sons of Delaiah the son of Tobiah 2

Delilah 1. דְּלִילָה
Jdg 16: 4 he loved a woman . . whose name was Deli'lah. 1
6 Deli'lah said to Samson, "Please tell me wherein 1
10 Deli'lah said to Samson, "Behold, you have mocked me 1
12 Deli'lah took new ropes and bound him with them 1
13 Deli'lah said to Samson, "Until now you have mocked 1
14 Deli'lah took the seven locks of his head and wove •
18 When Deli'lah saw that he had told her all his mind 1

Delos 1. Δηλος
1Mc 15:23 to the Spartans, and to Delos, and to Myndos 1

Demas 1. Δημᾶς
Col 4:14 Luke the beloved physician and Demas greet you. 1
2Ti 4:10 Demas, in love with this present world 1
Phm 1:24 so do Mark, Aristar'chus, Demas, and Luke 1

Demetrius 1. Δημήτριος
Act 19:24 a man named Deme'trius, a silversmith 1
38 Deme'trius and the craftsmen with him 1
3Jn 1:12 Deme'trius has testimony from every one 1
1Mc 7: 1 In the 151st year Demetrius the son of Seleucus 1
4 Demetrius took his seat upon the throne 1
8:31 the wrongs which King Demetrius is doing 1
9: 1 When Demetrius heard 1
10: 2 When Demetrius the king heard of it 1
3 Demetrius sent Jonathan a letter 1
6 Demetrius gave him authority to recruit troops •
15 promises which Demetrius had sent to Jonathan 1
22 When Demetrius heard of these things 1
25 King Demetrius to the nation of the Jews, greeting 1
46 great wrongs which Demetrius had done in Israel •
48 encamped opposite Demetrius. 1
49 the army of Demetrius fled 1
50 Demetrius fell on that day. 1
52 I crushed Demetrius 1
67 Demetrius the son of Demetrius came from Crete 1
67 Demetrius the son of Demetrius came from Crete 1
69 Demetrius appointed Apollonius 1
11: 9 He sent envoys to Demetrius the king, saying, "Come 1
12 gave her to Demetrius 1
19 So Demetrius became king in the 167th year. 1
30 King Demetrius to Jonathan his brother 1
32 'King Demetrius to Lasthenes his father 1
38 Now when Demetrius the king saw 1
39 the troops were murmuring against Demetrius. 1
40 He also reported to Imalkue what Demetrius had done 1
40 the hatred which the troops of Demetrius had •
41 Jonathan sent to Demetrius the king the request 1
42 Demetrius sent this message to Jonathan 1
52 So Demetrius the king sat on the throne 1
55 All the troops that Demetrius had cast off 1
55 they fought against Demetrius •
63 the officers of Demetrius had come to Kadesh 1
12:24 the commanders of Demetrius had returned 1
34 the men whom Demetrius had sent 1
13:34 Simon also chose men and sent them to Demetrius 1
35 Demetrius the king sent him a favorable reply 1
36 King Demetrius to Simon, the high priest 1
14: 1 Demetrius the king assembled his forces 1
2 heard that Demetrius had invaded his territory 1
3 he went and defeated the army of Demetrius 1
38 Demetrius confirmed him in the high priesthood 1
15: 1 Antiochus, the son of Demetrius the king 1
22 The consul wrote the same thing to Demetrius 1
2Mc 1: 7 In the reign of Demetrius, in the 169th year 1
14: 1 Demetrius, the son of Seleucus 1
4 went to King Demetrius in about the 151st year 1
5 he was invited by Demetrius to a meeting 1
11 the rest . . quickly inflamed Demetrius still more. 1
26 went to Demetrius 1

Demophon 1. Δημοφων
2Mc 12: 2 as well as Hieronymus and Demophon 1

Derbe 1. Δερβαῖος 2. Δέρβη
Act 14: 6 fled to Lystra and Derbe, cities of Lycao'nia 2
20 on the next day he went on with Barnabas to Derbe. 2
16: 1 he came also to Derbe and to Lystra 2
20: 4 and Ga'ius of Derbe, and Timothy 1

Dessau 1. Δεσσαου
2Mc 14:16 at a village called Dessau. 1

Destiny 1. מְנִי
Isa 65:11 and fill cups of mixed wine for Destiny; 1

Deuel 1. דְּעוּאֵל
Num 1:14 from Gad, Eli'asaph the son of Deu'el; 1
7:42 Eli'asaph the son of Deu'el, the leader of the men 1
47 was the offering of Eli'asaph the son of Deu'el. 1
10:20 over the host . . was Eli'asaph the son of Deu'el. 1

Di-zahab 1. דִּי זָהָב
Deu 1: 1 Paran and Tophel, Laban, Haze'roth, and Di'zahab. 1

Diblaim 1. דִּבְלָיִם
Hos 1: 3 he went and took Gomer the daughter of Dibla'im 1

Dibon 1. דִּיבֹן
Num 21:30 posterity perished from Heshbon, as far as Dibon 1
32: 3 At'aroth, Dibon, Jazer, Nimrah, Heshbon, Elea'leh 1
34 the sons of Gad built Dibon, At'aroth, Aro'er 1
Jos 13: 9 and all the tableland of Med'eba as far as Dibon; 1
17 with Heshbon . . Dibon, and Ba'moth-ba'al 1
Neh 11:25 some . . lived . . in Dibon and its villages 1
Isa 15: 2 Dibon has gone up to the high places to weep; 1
9 For the waters of Dibon are full of blood; 1
9 yet I will bring upon Dibon even more 1
Jer 48:18 sit on the parched ground, O inhabitant of Dibon! 1
22 and Dibon, and Nebo, and Beth-diblatha'im 1

Dibon-gad 1. דִּיבֹן גָּד
Num 33:45 they set out from I'yim, and encamped at Dibon-gad. 1
46 set out from Dibon-gad, and encamped 1

Dibri 1. דִּבְרִי
Lev 24:11 name was Shelo'mith, the daughter of Dibri, 1

Diklah 1. דִּקְלָה
Gen 10:27 Hador'am, Uzal, Diklah 1
1Ch 1:21 Hador'am, Uzal, Diklah 1

Dilean 1. דִּלְעָן
Jos 15:38 Di'lean, Mizpeh, Jok'theel 1

Dimnah 1. דִּמְנָה
Jos 21:35 Dimnah with its pasture lands, Na'halal with its 1

Dimonah 1. דִּימוֹנָה
Jos 15:22 Kinah, Dimo'nah, Ada'dah 1

Dinah 1. דִּינָה
Gen 30:21 bore a daughter, and called her name Dinah. 1
34: 1 Dinah the daughter of Leah, whom she had borne 1
3 his soul was drawn to Dinah the daughter of Jacob; 1
5 heard that he had defiled his daughter Dinah; 1
13 because he had defiled their sister Dinah. 1
25 sons of Jacob, Simeon and Levi, Dinah's brothers 1
26 his son Shechem with the sword, and took Dinah out 1
46:15 to Jacob . . together with his daughter Dinah; 1

Dinhabah 1. דִּנְהָבָה
Gen 36:32 Edom, the name of his city being Din'habah. 1
1Ch 1:43 Bela . . the name of whose city was Din'habah. 1

Dionysius 1. Διονύσιος
Act 17:34 believed, among them Dionys'ius the Are-op'agite 1

Dionysus 1. Διονυσια 2. Διονυσος
2Mc 6: 7 when the feast of Dionysus came 1
7 to walk in the procession in honor of Dionysus 2
14:33 will build here a splendid temple to Dionysus. 2
3Mc 2:29 the ivy-leaf symbol of Dionysus 2

Dioscorinthius 1. Ζεῦς Κορίνθιος
2Mc 11:21 Farewell. The 148th year, Dioscorinthius 24th. 1

Diotrephes 1. Διοτρεφης
3Jn 1: 9 Diot'rephes, who likes to put himself first 1

Diphath 1. דִּיפַת
1Ch 1: 6 sons of Gomer: Ash'kenaz, Diphath, and To-gar'mah. 1

Dishan 1. דִּישָׁן 2. דִּישָׁן
Gen 36:21 Dishon, Ezer, and Dishan; these are the chiefs 2
28 These are the sons of Dishan: Uz and Aran. 2
30 Dishon, Ezer, and Dishan; these are the chiefs 2
1Ch 1:38 sons of Se'ir . . Dishon, Ezer, and Dishan. 2
42 The sons of Dishan: Uz and Aran. 1

Dishon 1. דִּישֹׁן 2. דִּישׁוֹן
Gen 36:21 Dishon, Ezer, and Dishan; these are the chiefs 2
25 of Anah: Dishon and Oholiba'mah the daughter 2
26 These are the sons of Dishon: Hemdan, Eshban 1
30 Dishon, Ezer, and Dishan; these are the chiefs 2

1Ch 1:38 sons of Se'ir . . Dishon, Ezer, and Dishan. 2
41 The sons of Anah: Dishon. The sons of Dishon 2
41 The sons of Anah: Dishon. The sons of Dishon 2

Dodai 1. דּוֹדַי
1Ch 27: 4 Dodai . . was in charge of the division 1

Dodanim 1. דֹּדָנִים
Gen 10: 4 of Javan: Eli'shah, Tarshish . . and Do'danim. 1

Dodavahu 1. דֹּדָוָהוּ
2Ch 20:37 Then Elie'zer the son of Do-dav'ahu of Mare'shah 1

Dodo 1. דּוֹדוֹ
Jdg 10: 1 Tola the son of Pu'ah, son of Dodo, a man of Is'sachar 1
2Sm 23: 9 next . . was Elea'zar the son of Dodo, son of Aho'hi. 1
24 As'ahel . . Elha'nan the son of Dodo of Bethlehem 1
1Ch 11:12 next to him . . was Elea'zar the son of Dodo 1
26 mighty men . . Elha'nan the son of Dodo 1

Doeg 1. דֹּאֵג
1Sm 21: 7 his name was Do'eg the E'domite 1
22: 9 Then answered Do'eg the E'domite . . "I saw the son 1
18 the king said to Do'eg, "You turn and fall upon 1
18 And Do'eg . . turned and fell upon the priests 1
22 I knew . . when Do'eg the E'domite was there 1
Ps 52: 0 when Doeg, the Edomite, came and told Saul 1

Dok 1. Δωκ
1Mc 16:15 in the little stronghold called Dok 1

Dophkah 1. דָּפְקָה
Num33:12 wilderness of Sin, and encamped at Dophkah. 1
13 they set out from Dophkah, and encamped at Alush. 1

Dor 1. דֹּאר 2. Δωρα
Jos 12:23 the king of Dor in Naphath-dor, one; 1
17:11 and the inhabitants of Dor and its villages 1
Jdg 1:27 not drive out . . or the inhabitants of Dor 1
1Ch 7:29 Megid'do and its towns, Dor and its towns. 1
1Mc 15:11 he came in his flight to Dor, which is by the sea; 2
13 So Antiochus encamped against Dor 2
25 Antiochus the king besieged Dor anew 2

Dorcas 1. Δορκάς
Act 9:36 a disciple named Tabitha, which means Dorcas. 1
39 tunics and other garments which Dorcas made 1

Dorymenes 1. Δορυμενης
1Mc 3:38 Lysias chose Ptolemy the son of Dorymenes 1
2Mc 4:45 Ptolemy son of Dorymenes 1

Dositheus 1. Δοσιθεος
AEs 11: 1 Dositheus, who said that he was a priest 1
2Mc 12:19 Dositheus and Sosipater, who were captains 1
24 Dositheus and Sosipater and their men 1
35 a certain Dositheus, one of Bacenor's men 1
3Mc 1: 3 Dositheus, known as the son of Drimylus 1

Dothan 1. דֹּתָן דֹּתַן 2. Δωθαιμ 3. Δωταια
Gen 37:17 away, for I heard them say, 'Let us go to Dothan.' 1
17 after his brothers, and found them at Dothan. 1
2Kg 6:13 It was told him, "Behold, he is in Dothan. 1
Jdt 3: 9 Then he came to the edge of Esdraelon, near Dothan 3
4: 6 opposite the plain near Dothan 2
7: 3 they spread out in breadth over Dothan 2
18 and encamped in the hill country opposite Dothan 2
8: 3 the field between Dothan and Balamon. 2

Drimylus 1. Δριμυλος
3Mc 1: 3 Dositheus, known as the son of Drimylus 1

Drusilla 1. Δρούσιλλα
Act 24:24 Felix came with his wife Drusil'la 1

Dumah 1. דּוּמָה
Gen 25:14 Mishma, Dumah, Massa 1
Jos 15:52 Arab, Dumah, Eshan 1
1Ch 1:30 Mishma, Dumah, Massa, Hadad, Tema 1
Isa 21:11 The oracle concerning Dumah. 1

Dung Gate 1. שַׁעַר הָאַשְׁפֹּת
Neh 2:13 went . . to the Jackal's Well and to the Dung Gate 1
3:13 repaired . . the wall, as far as the Dung Gate. 1
14 Malchi'jah . . repaired the Dung Gate; 1
12:31 One went to the right upon the wall to the Dung Gate; 1

Dura 1. דּוּרָא (A)
Dan 3: 1 plain of Dura, in the province of Babylon. 1

East Gate 1. שַׁעַר הַמִּזְרָח
Neh 3:29 Shemai'ah . . the keeper of the East Gate 1

Ebal 1. עֵיבָל
Gen 36:23 of Shobal . . Man'ahath, Ebal, Shepho, and Onam. 1
Deu 11:29 set the blessing . . and the curse on Mount Ebal. 1
27: 4 set up these stones . . on Mount Ebal 1
13 stand upon Mount Ebal for the curse: Reuben, Gad 1
Jos 8:30 Joshua built an altar in Mount Ebal to the LORD 1
33 half . . and half of them in front of Mount Ebal 1
1Ch 1:22 Ebal, Abim'a-el, Sheba 1
40 The sons of Shobal: Al'ian, Man'ahath, Ebal, Shephi 1

Ebed 1. עֶבֶד
Jdg 9:26 Ga'al the son of Ebed moved into Shechem 1
28 Ga'al the son of Ebed said, "Who is Abim'elech 1
30 Zebul . . heard the words of Ga'al the son of Ebed 1
31 Ga'al the son of Ebed and his kinsmen have come 1
35 Ga'al the son of Ebed went out and stood 1
Ezr 8: 6 Of the sons of Adin, Ebed the son of Jonathan 1

Ebed-melech 1. עֶבֶד מֶלֶךְ
Jer 38: 7 When E'bed-mel'ech the Ethiopian, a eunuch 1
8 E'bed-mel'ech went from the king's house and said 1
10 Then the king commanded E'bed-mel'ech 1
11 E'bed-mel'ech took the men with him and went 1
12 Then E'bed-mel'ech the Ethiopian said to Jeremiah 1
39:16 Go, and say to E'bed-mel'ech the Ethiopian 1

Eben-ezer 1. אֶבֶן הָעֵזֶר
1Sm 4: 1 Israel went out . . they encamped at Ebene'zer 1
5: 1 they carried it from Ebene'zer to Ashdod; 1
7:12 took a stone . . and called its name Ebene'zer; 1

Eber 1. עֵבֶר 2. Ἔβερ
Gen 10:21 Shem also, the father of all the children of Eber 1
24 and Shelah became the father of Eber. 1
25 To Eber were born two sons 1
11:14 Shelah . . became the father of Eber; 1
15 Shelah lived after the birth of Eber 403 years 1
16 When Eber had lived 34 years 1
17 Eber lived after the birth of Peleg 430 years 1
Num24:24 ships . . shall afflict Asshur and Eber; 1
1Ch 1:18 and Shelah was the father of Eber. 1
19 To Eber were born two sons: the name of the one was 1
25 Eber, Peleg, Re'u; 1
5:13 Michael . . Jo'rai, Jacan, Zi'a, and Eber, seven. 1
8:12 The sons of Elpa'al: Eber, Misham, and Shemed 1
22 Ishpan, Eber, Eli'el 1
Neh 12:20 of Sal'lai, Kal'lai; of Amok, Eber; 1
Lke 3:35 son of Peleg, the son of Eber, the son of Shelah 2

Ebez 1. אֶבֶץ
Jos 19:20 Rabbith, Kish'ion, Ebez 1

Ebiasaph 1. אֶבְיָאָסָף
1Ch 6:23 Elka'nah his son, Ebi'asaph his son, Assir his son 1
37 son of Assir, son of Ebi'asaph, son of Korah 1
9:19 Shallum the son of Ko're, son of Ebi'asaph 1

Ebron 1. עֶבְרֹן
Jos 19:28 Ebron, Rehob, Hammon, Kanah, as far as Sidon 1

Ecbatana 1. אַחְמְתָא (A) 2. Εκβατανα
Ezr 6: 2 Ecbat'ana, the capital which is in . . Media 1
1Es 6:23 in Ecbatana . . a scroll was found 2
Tob 3: 7 On the same day, at Ecbatana in Media 2
6: 5 until they came near to Ecbatana. 2
9 When they approached Ecbatana 2
7: 1 When they reached Ecbatana 2
14:12 Tobias returned with . . his sons to Ecbatana 2
14 He died in Ecbatana of Media 2
Jdt 1: 1 who ruled over the Medes in Ecbatana– 2
2 he is the king who built walls about Ecbatana 2
14 came to Ecbatana, captured its towers 2
2Mc 9: 3 While he was in Ecbatana 2

Eddinus 1. Εδδινους
1Es 1:15 Asaph, Zechariah, and Eddinus 1

Eden 1. עֵדֶן
Gen 2: 8 the LORD God planted a garden in Eden, in the east; 1
10 A river flowed out of Eden to water the garden 1
15 put him in the garden of Eden to till it and keep it. 1
3:23 God sent him forth from the garden of Eden 1
24 at the east of the garden of Eden 1
4:16 Cain . . dwelt in the land of Nod, east of Eden. 1
2Kg 19:12 Rezeph, and the people of Eden who were 1
2Ch 29:12 Levites arose . . Eden the son of Jo'ah; 1
31:15 Eden, Mini'amin, Jeshua, Shemai'ah, Amari'ah 1
Isa 37:12 and the people of Eden who were in Tel-assar? 1
51: 3 and will make her wilderness like Eden 1
Ezk 27:23 Canneh, Eden, Asshur, and Chilmad traded with you. 1
28:13 You were in Eden, the garden of God; 1
31: 9 the trees of Eden envied it 1
16 the trees of Eden, the choice and best of Lebanon 1
18 in glory and in greatness among the trees of Eden? 1
18 You shall be brought down with the trees of Eden 1
36:35 desolate has become like the garden of Eden 1
Jol 2: 3 The land is like the garden of Eden before them 1

Eder 1. עֵדֶר 2. עֶדֶר
Gen 35:21 and pitched his tent beyond the tower of Eder. 1
Jos 15:21 cities belonging to . . were Kabzeel, Eder, Jagur 1
1Ch 8:15 Zebadi'ah, Arad, Eder 2
23:23 The sons of Mushi: Mahli, Eder, and Jer'emoth, three. 1
24:30 The sons of Mushi: Mahli, Eder, and Jer'i-moth. 1

Edna 1. Εδνα
Tob 7: 2 Then Raguel said to his wife Edna 1
8 his wife Edna and his daughter Sarah wept 1
14 Next he called his wife Edna 1
16 Raguel called his wife Edna and said to her 1
8:12 said to his wife Edna, "Send one of the maids 1
10:12 Edna said to Tobias 1
11: 1 he blessed Raguel and his wife Edna 1

Edom 1. אֱדוֹם
Gen 25:30 Therefore his name was called Edom. 1
32: 3 in the land of Se'ir, the country of Edom 1
36: 1 These are the descendants of Esau (that is, Edom) 1
8 in the hill country of Se'ir; Esau is Edom. 1
16 the chiefs of El'iphaz in the land of Edom; 1
17 these are the chiefs of Reu'el in the land of Edom; 1
19 These are the sons of Esau (that is, Edom) 1
21 the Horites, the sons of Se'ir in the land of Edom. 1
31 the kings who reigned in the land of Edom, before 1
32 Bela the son of Be'or reigned in Edom 1
43 Mag'diel, and Iram; these are the chiefs of Edom 1
43 of Edom (that is, Esau, the father of Edom), according 1
Exd 15:15 Now are the chiefs of Edom dismayed; 1
Num20:14 Moses sent messengers . . to the king of Edom 1
18 Edom said to him, "You shall not pass through 1
20 Edom came out against them with many men 1
21 Thus Edom refused to give Israel passage 1
23 Mount Hor, on the border of the land of Edom 1
21: 4 set out . . to go around the land of Edom; 1
24:18 Edom shall be dispossessed, Se'ir also 1
33:37 at Mount Hor, on the edge of the land of Edom. 1
34: 3 from the wilderness of Zin along the side of Edom 1
Jos 15: 1 lot . . reached southward to the boundary of Edom 1
21 in the extreme South, toward the boundary of Edom 1
Jdg 5: 4 from Se'ir . . march from the region of Edom 1
11:17 Israel then sent messengers to the king of Edom 1
17 your land'; but the king of Edom would not listen. 1
18 went around the land of Edom and the land of Moab 1
1Sm 14:47 against the Ammonites, against Edom 1
2Sm 8:12 from Edom, Moab, the Ammonites, the Philistines 1
14 And he put garrisons in Edom; throughout all Edom 1
14 throughout all Edom he put garrisons 1
1Kg 9:26 E'zion-ge'ber . . in the land of Edom. 1
11:14 Hadad . . he was of the royal house in Edom. 1
15 when David was in Edom, and Jo'ab . . went up 1
15 Jo'ab the commander . . slew every male in Edom 1
16 until he had cut off every male in Edom); 1
22:47 There was no king in Edom; a deputy was king. 1
2Kg 3: 8 answered, "By the way of the wilderness of Edom. 1
9 king of Israel went with . . and the king of Edom. 1
12 and Jehosh'aphat and the king of Edom went down 1
20 water came from the direction of Edom 1
26 to break through, opposite the king of Edom; 1
8:20 In his days Edom revolted from the rule of Judah 1
22 Edom revolted from the rule of Judah to this day. 1
14:10 You have indeed smitten Edom 1
16: 6 At that time the king of Edom recovered Elath •
6 the king of Edom recovered Elath for Edom •
1Ch 1:43 These are the kings who reigned in the land of Edom 1
51 chiefs of Edom were: chiefs Timna, Al'iah, Jetheth 1
54 Mag'di-el, and Iram; these are the chiefs of Edom. 1
18:11 all the nations, from Edom, Moab, the Ammonites 1
13 he put garrisons in Edom; 1
2Ch 8:17 to E'zion-Ge-ber and Eloth . . in the land of Edom. 1
20: 2 great multitude is coming against you from Edom 1
21: 8 In his days Edom revolted from the rule of Judah 1
10 Edom revolted from the rule of Judah to this day. 1
25:19 You say, 'See, I have smitten Edom,' 1
20 because they had sought the gods of Edom. 1
Ps 60: 0 when Joab . . killed 12,000 of Edom 1
8 Moab is my washbasin; upon Edom I cast my shoe; 1
9 to the fortified city? Who will lead me to Edom? 1
83: 6 the tents of Edom and the Ish'maelites 1
108: 9 Moab is my washbasin; upon Edom I cast my shoe; 1
10 Who will lead me to Edom? 1
Isa 11:14 shall put forth their hand against Edom and Moab 1
34: 5 behold, it descends for judgment upon Edom 1
6 LORD has . . a great slaughter in the land of Edom. 1
9 the streams of Edom shall be turned into pitch •
63: 1 this that comes from Edom, in crimsoned garments 1
Jer 9:26 Egypt, Judah, Edom, the sons of Ammon, Moab 1
25:21 Edom, Moab, and the sons of Ammon; 1
27: 3 Send word to the king of Edom, the king of Moab 1
40:11 in Moab and among the Ammonites and in Edom 1
49: 7 Concerning Edom. Thus says the LORD of hosts 1
17 Edom shall become a horror; 1
20 the plan which the LORD has made against Edom 1
22 heart of the warriors of Edom shall be in that day 1
Lam 4:21 Rejoice and be glad, O daughter of Edom 1

22 your iniquity, O daughter of Edom, he will punish 1
Ezk 16:57 an object of reproach for the daughters of Edom 1
25:12 Because Edom acted revengefully 1
13 I will stretch out my hand against Edom 1
14 I will lay my vengeance upon Edom 1
14 they shall do in Edom according to my anger 1
27:16 Edom trafficked with you 1
32:29 Edom is there, her kings and all her princes 1
35:15 be desolate, Mount Se'ir, and all Edom, all of it. 1
36: 5 against all Edom, who gave my land to themselves 1
Dan 11:41 Edom and Moab and the main part of the Ammonites. 1
Jol 3:19 and Edom a desolate wilderness, 1
Ams 1: 6 exile a whole people to deliver them up to Edom. 1
9 because they delivered up a whole people to Edom 1
11 For three transgressions of Edom, and for four 1
2: 1 he burned to lime the bones of the king of Edom. 1
9:12 that they may possess the remnant of Edom 1
Obd 1: 1 Thus says the Lord GOD concerning Edom 1
8 destroy the wise men out of Edom 1
Mal 1: 4 If Edom says, "We are shattered but we will rebuild 1

Edomite 1. אֲדוֹם 2. אֲדֹמִי 3. אִישׁ אֲדֹמִי 4. בֶּן אֱדוֹם
5. Ιδουμαια 6. Ιδουμαιος

Gen 36: 9 the E'domites in the hill country of Se'ir. 1
Deu 23: 7 shall not abhor an E'domite, for he is your brother; 2
1Sm 21: 7 Do'eg the E'domite, the chief of Saul's herdsmen. 2
22: 9 Then answered Do'eg the E'domite . . "I saw the son 2
18 Do'eg the E'domite turned and fell upon 2
22 I knew . . when Do'eg the E'domite was there 2
2Sm 8:13 When he returned, he slew 18,000 E'domites 5
14 and all the E'domites became David's servants. 1
1Kg 11: 1 Moabite, Ammonite, E'domite, Sido'nian, and Hittite 2
14 an adversary against Solomon, Hadad the E'domite; 2
17 with certain E'domites of his father's servants 3
2Kg 8:21 he . . smote the E'domites who had surrounded him; 1
14: 7 He killed 10,000 E'domites in the Valley of Salt 1
16: 6 and the E'domites came to Elath, where they dwell 2
1Ch 18:12 Abi'shai, the son of Zeru'iah, slew 18,000 E'domites 1
13 and all the E'domites became David's servants. 1
2Ch 21: 9 Jeho'ram . . rose by night and smote the E'domites 1
25:14 Amazi'ah came from the slaughter of the E'domites 2
28:17 E'domites had again invaded and defeated Judah 2
Ps 52: 0 when Doeg, the Edomite, came and told Saul 2
137: 7 O LORD, against the E'domites the day of Jerusalem 4
1Es 4:45 which the Edomites burned 6
8:69 Moabites, the Egyptians, and the Edomites. 6

Edrei 1. אֶדְרֶעִי

Num21:33 came out against them . . to battle at Ed're-i. 1
Deu 1: 4 king of Bashan, who lived in . . Ed're-i. 1
3: 1 Og . . came out against us, . . to battle at Ed're-i. 1
10 as far as Sal'ecah and Ed're-i, cities of the kingdom 1
Jos 12: 4 and Og . . who dwelt at Ash'taroth and at Ed're-i 1
13:12 of Og . . who reigned in Ash'taroth and in Ed're-i 1
31 and half Gilead, and Ash'taroth, and Ed're-i 1
19:37 Kedesh, Ed're-i, En-ha'zor 1

Eduth 1. עֵדוּת

Ps 60: 0 To the choirmaster: according to Shushan Eduth. 1

Eglah 1. עֶגְלָה

2Sm 3: 5 and the sixth, Ith're-am, of Eglah, David's wife. 1
1Ch 3: 3 the sixth Ith'ream, by his wife Eglah; 1

Eglaim 1. אֶגְלַיִם

Isa 15: 8 the wailing reaches to Egla'im 1

Eglath-shelishiyah 1. עֶגְלַת שְׁלִשִׁיָּה

Isa 15: 5 to Eg'lath-shelish'iyah. 1
Jer 48:34 from Zo'ar to Horona'im and Eg'lath-shelish'iyah. 1

Eglon 1. עֶגְלוֹן

Jos 10: 3 Japhi'a king of Lachish, and to Debir king of Eglon 1
5 the king of Lachish, and the king of Eglon 1
23 the king of Lachish, and the king of Eglon. 1
34 And Joshua passed on . . from Lachish to Eglon; 1
36 Then Joshua went up . . from Eglon to Hebron; 1
37 he left none remaining, as he had done to Eglon 1
12:12 the king of Eglon, one; the king of Gezer, one; 1
15:39 Lachish, Bozkath, Eglon 1
Jdg 3:12 and the LORD strengthened Eglon the king of Moab 1
14 Israel served Eglon the king of Moab eighteen 1
15 sent tribute by him to Eglon the king of Moab. 1
17 he presented the tribute to Eglon king of Moab. 1
17 Eglon king of Moab. Now Eglon was a very fat man. 1

Egypt 1. מָצוֹר 2. מִצְרִי 3. מִצְרַיִם 4. Αἴγυπτος
5. Aegyptus

Gen 10: 6 The sons of Ham: Cush, Egypt, Put, and Canaan. 3
13 Egypt became the father of Ludim, An'amim 3
12:10 So Abram went down to Egypt to sojourn there 3
11 When he was about to enter Egypt, he said to Sar'ai 3
14 When Abram entered Egypt the Egyptians saw that 3
13: 1 Abram went up from Egypt, he and his wife 3
10 like the land of Egypt, in the direction of Zo'ar; 3
15:18 from the river of Egypt to the great river 3
21:21 took a wife for him from the land of Egypt. 3
25:18 from Hav'ilah to Shur, which is opposite Egypt 3
26: 2 Do not go down to Egypt; dwell in the land of which I 3
37:25 on their way to carry it down to Egypt. 3
28 shekels of silver; and they took Joseph to Egypt. 3
36 Meanwhile the Mid'ianites had sold him in Egypt 3
39: 1 Now Joseph was taken down to Egypt 3
40: 1 after this, the butler of the king of Egypt 3
1 his baker offended their lord the king of Egypt. 3
5 the baker of the king of Egypt, who were confined 3
41: 8 sent and called for all the magicians of Egypt 3
19 such as I had never seen in all the land of Egypt. 3
29 plenty throughout all the land of Egypt 3
30 plenty will be forgotten in the land of Egypt; 3
33 let Pharaoh . . set him over the land of Egypt. 3
34 the produce of the land of Egypt during the seven 3
36 famine which are to befall the land of Egypt 3
41 Behold, I have set you over all the land of Egypt. 3
43 Thus he set him over all the land of Egypt. 3
44 lift up hand or foot in all the land of Egypt. 3
45 Joseph went out over the land of Egypt. 3
46 entered the service of Pharaoh king of Egypt. 3
46 Joseph . . went through all the land of Egypt. 3
48 years when there was plenty in the land of Egypt 3
53 plenty that prevailed in the land of Egypt came 3
54 but in all the land of Egypt there was bread. 3
55 When all the land of Egypt was famished 3
56 for the famine was severe in the land of Egypt. 3
57 Moreover, all the earth came to Egypt to Joseph 3
42: 1 When Jacob learned that there was grain in Egypt 3
2 I have heard that there is grain in Egypt; 3
3 brothers went down to buy grain in Egypt. 3
43: 2 the grain which they had brought from Egypt 3
15 and they arose and went down to Egypt 3
45: 4 Joseph, whom you sold into Egypt. 3
8 made me . . ruler over all the land of Egypt. 3
9 God has made me lord of all Egypt; come down to me 3
13 tell my father of all my splendor in Egypt 3
18 and I will give you the best of the land of Egypt 3
19 from the land of Egypt for your little ones 3
20 for the best of all the land of Egypt is yours.' 3
23 asses loaded with the good things of Egypt 3
25 they went up out of Egypt, and came to the land 3
26 Joseph is . . ruler over all the land of Egypt. 3
46: 3 do not be afraid to go down to Egypt; 3
4 I will go down with you to Egypt 3
6 took . . goods . . and came into Egypt 3
7 his offspring he brought with him into Egypt. 3
8 the descendants of Israel, who came into Egypt 3
20 to Joseph in the land of Egypt were born Manas'seh 3
26 persons belonging to Jacob who came into Egypt 3
27 the sons of Joseph, who were born to him in Egypt 3
27 all the persons . . that came into Egypt, were 70. 3
47: 6 The land of Egypt is before you; 3
11 and gave them a possession in the land of Egypt 3
13 land of Egypt and the land of Canaan languished 3
14 all the money that was found in the land of Egypt 3
15 in the land of Egypt and in the land of Canaan 3
20 Joseph bought all the land of Egypt for Pharaoh; 3
21 from one end of Egypt to the other. 3
26 made it a statute concerning the land of Egypt 3
27 Thus Israel dwelt in the land of Egypt 3
28 Jacob lived in the land of Egypt seventeen years; 3
29 Do not bury me in Egypt 3
30 carry me out of Egypt and bury me in their burying 3
48: 5 were born to you in the land of Egypt before I came 3
5 in the land of Egypt before I came to you in Egypt 3
50: 7 went up . . all the elders of the land of Egypt 3
14 Joseph returned to Egypt with his brothers 3
22 Joseph dwelt in Egypt, he and his father's house; 3
25 he was put in a coffin in Egypt. 3
Exd 1: 1 sons of Israel who came to Egypt with Jacob 3
5 Joseph was already in Egypt. 3
8 Now there arose a new king over Egypt 3
15 the king of Egypt said to the Hebrew midwives 3
17 did not do as the king of Egypt commanded them 3
18 the king of Egypt called the midwives, and said 3
2:23 the king of Egypt died. And the people of Israel 3
3: 7 affliction of my people who are in Egypt 3
10 my people, the sons of Israel, out of Egypt. 3
11 bring the sons of Israel out of Egypt? 3
12 you have brought forth the people out of Egypt 3
16 observed . . what has been done to you in Egypt; 3
17 I will bring you up out of the affliction of Egypt 3
18 you . . shall go to the king of Egypt and say to him 3
19 I know that the king of Egypt will not let you go 3
20 I will . . smite Egypt with all the wonders 3
4:18 Let me go back, I pray, to my kinsmen in Egypt 3
19 Go back to Egypt; for all the men who were seeking 3
20 Moses . . went back to the land of Egypt; 3
21 the LORD said to Moses, "When you go back to Egypt 3
5: 4 the king of Egypt said to them, "Moses and Aaron 3
12 scattered . . throughout all the land of Egypt 3
6:11 Go in, tell Pharaoh king of Egypt to let the people 3
13 a charge . . to Pharaoh king of Egypt to bring 3
13 the people of Israel out of the land of Egypt. 3
26 Bring out . . Israel from the land of Egypt 3
27 It was they who spoke to Pharaoh king of Egypt 3
27 bringing out the people of Israel from Egypt 3
28 when the LORD spoke to Moses in the land of Egypt 3
29 tell Pharaoh king of Egypt all that I say to you. 3
7: 3 multiply my . . wonders in the land of Egypt 3
4 then I will lay my hand upon Egypt and bring forth 3
4 bring forth my hosts . . out of the land of Egypt 3
5 stretch forth my hand upon Egypt and bring out 3
11 the magicians of Egypt, did the same by their 3
19 stretch out your hand over the waters of Egypt 3
19 shall be blood throughout all the land of Egypt 3
21 was blood throughout all the land of Egypt. 3
22 the magicians of Egypt did the same 3
8: 5 cause frogs to come upon the land of Egypt!' 3
6 stretched out his hand over the waters of Egypt; 3
6 the frogs came up and covered the land of Egypt. 3
7 brought frogs upon the land of Egypt. 3
16 gnats throughout all the land of Egypt.' 3
17 gnats throughout all the land of Egypt. 3
24 and in all the land of Egypt the land was ruined 3
9: 4 the cattle of Israel and the cattle of Egypt 3
9 become fine dust over all the land of Egypt 3
9 throughout all the land of Egypt. 3
18 heavy hail . . such as never has been in Egypt 3
22 that there may be hail in all the land of Egypt 3
22 hail . . throughout the land of Egypt. 3
23 the LORD rained hail upon the land of Egypt; 3
24 never been in . . Egypt since it became a nation. 3
25 in the field throughout all the land of Egypt 3
10: 7 do you not yet understand that Egypt is ruined? 3
12 Stretch out your hand over the land of Egypt 3
12 that they may come upon the land of Egypt 3
13 stretched forth his rod over the land of Egypt 3
14 the locusts came up over all the land of Egypt 3
14 settled on the whole country of Egypt 3
15 through all the land of Egypt. 3
19 locust was left in all the country of Egypt. 3
21 darkness over the land of Egypt, a darkness to be 3
22 darkness in all the land of Egypt three days; 3
11: 1 I will bring upon Pharaoh and upon Egypt; 3
3 Moses was very great in the land of Egypt 3
4 midnight I will go forth in the midst of Egypt; 3
5 all the first-born in the land of Egypt shall die 3
6 be a great cry throughout all the land of Egypt 3
9 that my wonders may be multiplied in . . Egypt. 3
12: 1 LORD said to Moses and Aaron in the land of Egypt 3
12 For I will pass through the land of Egypt 3
12 I will smite all the first-born in . . Egypt 3
12 on all the gods of Egypt I will execute judgments 3
13 pass over you . . when I smite the land of Egypt. 3
17 I brought your hosts out of the land of Egypt 3
27 the houses of the people of Israel in Egypt 3
29 smote all the first-born in the land of Egypt 3
30 and there was a great cry in Egypt 3
39 of the dough which they had brought out of Egypt 3
39 because they were thrust out of Egypt and could 3
40 The time that the people of Israel dwelt in Egypt 3
41 hosts of the LORD went out from the land of Egypt. 3
42 by the LORD, to bring them out of the land of Egypt; 3
51 Israel out of the land of Egypt by their hosts. 3
13: 3 this day, in which you came out from Egypt, 3
8 the LORD did for me when I came out of Egypt.' 3
9 the LORD has brought you out of Egypt. 3
14 strength of hand the LORD brought us out of Egypt 3
15 slew all the first-born in the land of Egypt 3
16 strong hand the LORD brought us out of Egypt. 3
17 Lest the people repent . . and return to Egypt. 3
18 Israel went up out of the land of Egypt equipped 3
14: 5 When the king of Egypt was told that the people 3
7 took . . all the other chariots of Egypt 3
8 king of Egypt and he pursued the people of Israel 3
11 Is it because there are no graves in Egypt 3
11 you done to us, in bringing us out of Egypt? 3
12 Is not this what we said to you in Egypt 3
20 between the host of Egypt and the host of Israel. 3
16: 1 after they had departed from the land of Egypt. 3
3 that we had died by the hand of the LORD in . . Egypt 3
6 who brought you out of the land of Egypt 3
32 when I brought you out of the land of Egypt.' 3
17: 3 Why did you bring us up out of Egypt 3
18: 1 how the LORD had brought Israel out of Egypt. 3
19: 1 Israel had gone forth out of the land of Egypt 3
20: 2 God, who brought you out of the land of Egypt 3
22:21 for you were strangers in the land of Egypt. 3
23: 9 for you were strangers in the land of Egypt. 3
15 in the month of Abib, for in it you came out of Egypt. 3
29:46 who brought them forth out of the land of Egypt 3
32: 1 who brought us up out of the land of Egypt 3
4 who brought you up out of the land of Egypt! 3
7 whom you brought up out of the land of Egypt 3
8 who brought you up out of the land of Egypt!' 3
11 thou has brought forth out of the land of Egypt 3
23 who brought us up out of the land of Egypt 3
33: 1 whom you have brought up out of the land of Egypt 3
34:18 for in the month Abib you came out from Egypt. 3
Lev 11:45 who brought you up out of the land of Egypt 3
18: 3 not . . as they do in the land of Egypt 3
19:34 for you were strangers in the land of Egypt 3
36 your God, who brought you out of the land of Egypt 3
22:33 who brought you out of the land of Egypt 3
23:43 when I brought them out of the land of Egypt 3
25:38 God, who brought you forth out of the land of Egypt 3
42 whom I brought forth out of the land of Egypt 3

55 whom I brought forth out of the land of Egypt 3
26:13 God, who brought you forth out of the land of Egypt 3
45 whom I brought forth out of the land of Egypt 3
Num 1: 1 after they had come out of the land of Egypt 3
3:13 I slew all the first-born in the land of Egypt 3
8:17 slew all the first-born in the land of Egypt 3
9: 1 after they had come out of the land of Egypt, saying 3
11: 5 We remember the fish we ate in Egypt for nothing 3
18 For it was well with us in Egypt. 3
20 Why did we come forth out of Egypt?"' 3
13:22 built seven years before Zo'an in Egypt.) 3
14: 2 Would that we had died in the land of Egypt! 3
3 would it not be better for us to go back to Egypt? 3
4 Let us choose a captain, and go back to Egypt. 3
19 forgiven this people, from Egypt even until now. 3
22 seen . . my signs which I wrought in Egypt 3
15:41 LORD . . who brought you out of the land of Egypt 3
20: 5 why have you made us come up out of Egypt 3
15 how our fathers went down to Egypt 3
15 we dwelt in Egypt a long time; 3
16 sent an angel and brought us forth out of Egypt; 3
21: 5 Why have you brought us up out of Egypt to die 3
22: 5 Behold, a people has come out of Egypt; they cover 3
11 'Behold, a people has come out of Egypt 3
23:22 God brings them out of Egypt; 3
24: 8 God brings him out of Egypt; 3
26: 4 who came forth out of the land of Egypt, were 3
59 Joch'ebed . . who was born to Levi in Egypt; 3
32:11 Surely none of the men who came up out of Egypt 3
33: 1 when they went forth out of the land of Egypt 3
38 after . . Israel had come out of the land of Egypt 3
34: 5 boundary . . turn from Azmon to the Brook of Egypt 3
Deu 1:27 he has brought us forth out of the land of Egypt 3
30 just as he did for you in Egypt before your eyes 3
4:20 out of the iron furnace, out of Egypt, to be a people 3
34 LORD . . did for you in Egypt before your eyes? 3
37 brought you out of Egypt with his own presence 3
45 spoke to . . Israel when they came out of Egypt 3
46 Israel defeated when they came out of Egypt. 3
5: 6 LORD . . who brought you out of the land of Egypt 3
15 remember that you were a servant in . . Egypt 3
6:12 LORD, who brought you out of the land of Egypt 3
21 We were Pharaoh's slaves in Egypt; 3
21 LORD brought us out of Egypt with a mighty hand; 3
22 signs . . against Egypt and against Pharaoh 3
7: 8 redeemed . . from the hand of Pharaoh king of Egypt. 3
15 none of the evil diseases of Egypt . . will he inflict 3
18 remember what the LORD . . did to . . all Egypt 3
8:14 LORD . . who brought you out of the land of Egypt 3
9: 7 from the day you came out of the land of Egypt 3
12 for your people whom you have brought from Egypt 3
26 brought out of Egypt with a mighty hand. 3
10:19 for you were sojourners in the land of Egypt. 3
22 Your fathers went down to Egypt 70 persons; 3
11: 3 signs and his deeds which he did in Egypt 3
3 which he did in Egypt to Pharaoh the king of Egypt 3
4 what he did to the army of Egypt, to their horses 3
10 land . . is not like the land of Egypt 3
13: 5 LORD . . who brought you out of the land of Egypt 3
10 LORD . . who brought you out of the land of Egypt 3
15:15 remember . . you were a slave in the land of Egypt 3
16: 1 LORD your God brought you out of Egypt by night. 3
3 came out of the land of Egypt in hurried flight 3
3 remember the day . . came out of the land of Egypt. 3
6 passover . . at the time you came out of Egypt. 3
12 You shall remember that you were a slave in Egypt; 3
17:16 must not . . cause the people to return to Egypt 3
20: 1 LORD . . brought you up out of the land of Egypt. 3
23: 4 on the way, when you came forth out of Egypt 3
24: 9 Miriam on the way as you came forth out of Egypt. 3
18 remember that you were a slave in Egypt 3
22 remember that you were a slave in the land of Egypt; 3
25:17 Am'alek did to you . . as you came out of Egypt 3
26: 5 went down into Egypt and sojourned there 3
8 LORD brought us out of Egypt with a mighty hand 3
28:27 LORD will smite you with the boils of Egypt 3
60 bring upon you again all the diseases of Egypt 3
68 LORD will bring you back in ships to Egypt 3
29: 2 LORD did before your eyes in the land of Egypt 3
16 You know how we dwelt in the land of Egypt 3
25 when he brought them out of the land of Egypt 3
34:11 LORD sent him to do in the land of Egypt, to Pharaoh 3
Jos 2:10 dried up the water . . when you came out of Egypt 3
5: 4 all the males of the people who came out of Egypt 3
4 on the way . . after they had come out of Egypt. 3
5 born on the way . . after they had come out of Egypt 3
6 the men of war that came forth out of Egypt 3
9 I . . rolled away the reproach of Egypt from you. 3
9: 9 heard a report of him, and all that he did in Egypt 3
13: 3 from the Shihor, which is east of Egypt, northward 3
15: 4 passes . . to Azmon, goes out by the Brook of Egypt 3
47 to the Brook of Egypt, and the Great Sea 3
24: 4 but Jacob and his children went down to Egypt. 3
5 I plagued Egypt with what I did in the midst of it; 3
6 I brought your fathers out of Egypt, and you came 3
7 and your eyes saw what I did to Egypt; 3
14 fathers served beyond the River, and in Egypt 3
17 our God who brought us . . up from the land of Egypt 3
32 which . . Israel brought up from Egypt 3
Jdg 2: 1 I brought you up from Egypt, and brought you 3
12 who had brought them out of the land of Egypt; 3
6: 8 I led you up from Egypt . . the house of bondage 3
13 Did not the LORD bring us up from Egypt?' 3
11:13 Israel on coming from Egypt took away my land 3
16 when they came up from Egypt, Israel went through 3
19:30 people of Israel came up out of the land of Egypt 3
1Sm 2:27 they were in Egypt subject to the house 3
8: 8 from the day I brought them up out of Egypt even 3
10:18 I brought up Israel out of Egypt, and I delivered 3
12: 6 brought your fathers up out of the land of Egypt. 3
8 Jacob went into Egypt and the Egyptians 3
8 who brought forth your fathers out of Egypt 3
15: 2 opposing them . . when they came up out of Egypt. 3
6 to . . Israel when they came up out of Egypt. 3
7 Hav'ilah as far as Shur, which is east of Egypt. 3
27: 8 of the land . . as far as Shur, to the land of Egypt. 3
30:13 I am a young man of Egypt, servant to an Amal'ekite; 2
2Sm 7: 6 I brought up the people of Israel from Egypt 3
1Kg 3: 1 a marriage alliance with Pharaoh king of Egypt; 3
4:21 the Euphra'tes to . . and to the border of Egypt; 3
30 the wisdom of all . . and all the wisdom of Egypt. 3
6: 1 after . . Israel came out of the land of Egypt 3
8: 9 of Israel, when they came out of the land of Egypt. 3
16 day that I brought my people Israel out of Egypt 3
21 when he brought them out of the land of Egypt. 3
51 heritage, which thou didst bring out of Egypt 3
53 thou didst bring our fathers out of Egypt, O Lord 3
65 from the entrance of Hamath to the Brook of Egypt 3
9: 9 brought their fathers out of the land of Egypt 3
16 Pharaoh king of Egypt had gone up and captured 3
10:28 Solomon's import of horses was from Egypt and Ku'e 3
29 A chariot could be imported from Egypt 3
11:17 but Hadad fled to Egypt 3
18 They . . came to Egypt, to Pharaoh king of Egypt 3
18 They . . came to Egypt, to Pharaoh king of Egypt 3
21 Hadad heard in Egypt that David slept 3
40 Jerobo'am arose, and fled into Egypt, to Shishak 3
40 Jerobo'am . . fled . . to Shishak king of Egypt 3
40 and was in Egypt until the death of Solomon. 3
12: 2 he was still in Egypt, whither he had fled 3
2 then Jerobo'am returned from Egypt. 3
28 who brought you up out of the land of Egypt. 3
14:25 Shishak king of Egypt came up against Jerusalem; 3
2Kg 7: 6 Hittites and the kings of Egypt to come upon us. 3
17: 4 he had sent messengers to So, king of Egypt 3
7 who had brought them up out of the land of Egypt 3
7 from under the hand of Pharaoh king of Egypt 3
36 the LORD, who brought you out of the land of Egypt 3
18:21 Behold, you are relying now on Egypt 3
21 Such is Pharaoh king of Egypt to all who rely 3
24 you rely on Egypt for chariots and for horsemen? 3
19:24 I dried up . . all the streams of Egypt.' 1
21:15 since the day their fathers came out of Egypt 3
23:29 Neco king of Egypt went up to the king of Assyria 3
34 and he came to Egypt, and died there. 3
24: 7 king of Egypt did not come again out of his land 3
7 had taken all that belonged to the king of Egypt 3
7 from the Brook of Egypt to the river Euphra'tes. 3
25:26 all the people . . arose, and went to Egypt; 3
1Ch 1: 8 The sons of Ham: Cush, Egypt, Put, and Canaan. 3
11 Egypt was the father of Ludim, An'amim, Le'habim 3
13: 5 from the Shihor of Egypt to the entrance of Hamath 3
17:21 thy people whom thou didst redeem from Egypt? 3
2Ch 1:16 Solomon's import of horses was from Egypt and Ku'e 3
17 imported a chariot from Egypt for 600 3
5:10 people of Israel, when they came out of Egypt. 3
6: 5 I brought my people out of the land of Egypt 3
7: 8 the entrance of Hamath to the Brook of Egypt. 3
22 LORD . . who brought them out of the land of Egypt 3
9:26 he ruled . . and to the border of Egypt. 3
28 horses were imported for Solomon from Egypt 3
10: 2 for he was in Egypt, whither he had fled 3
2 then Jerobo'am returned from Egypt. 3
12: 2 Shishak king of Egypt came up against Jerusalem 3
3 without number who came with him from Egypt- 3
9 Shishak king of Egypt came up against Jerusalem; 3
20:10 when they came from the land of Egypt 3
26: 8 his fame spread even to the border of Egypt 3
35:20 Neco king of Egypt went up to fight at Car'chemish 3
36: 3 Then the king of Egypt deposed him in Jerusalem 3
4 the king of Egypt made Eli'akim his brother king 3
4 Neco took Jeho'ahaz . . and carried him to Egypt. 3
Neh 9: 9 didst see the affliction of our fathers in Egypt 3
17 leader to return to their bondage in Egypt. 3
18 'This is your God who brought you up out of Egypt,' 3
Ps 68:31 Let bronze be brought from Egypt; 3
78:12 he wrought marvels in the land of Egypt 3
43 when he wrought his signs in Egypt 3
51 He smote all the first-born in Egypt 3
80: 8 Thou didst bring a vine out of Egypt; 3
81: 5 when he went out over the land of Egypt. 3
10 who brought you up out of the land of Egypt. 3
105:23 Then Israel came to Egypt; 3
38 Egypt was glad when they departed 3
106: 7 Our fathers, when they were in Egypt 3
21 Savior, who had done great things in Egypt 3
114: 1 When Israel went forth from Egypt 3
135: 8 He it was who smote the first-born of Egypt 3
9 who in thy midst, O Egypt, sent signs and wonders 3
136:10 to him who smote the first-born of Egypt 3
Isa 7:18 the fly . . at the sources of the streams of Egypt 3
10:26 his rod . . and he will lift it as he did in Egypt. 3
11:11 remnant . . of his people, from Assyria, from Egypt 3
15 utterly destroy the tongue of the sea of Egypt; 3
16 Israel when they came up from the land of Egypt. 3
19: 1 An oracle concerning Egypt. 3
1 LORD is riding on a swift cloud and comes to Egypt; 3
1 the idols of Egypt will tremble at his presence 3
6 branches of Egypt's Nile will diminish and dry up 1
12 what the LORD . . has purposed against Egypt. 3
13 cornerstones of her tribes . . led Egypt astray. 3
14 they have made Egypt stagger in all her doings 3
15 nothing for Egypt which head or tail . . may do. 3
18 five cities in the land of Egypt which speak 3
19 altar to the LORD in the midst of the land of Egypt 3
20 a sign . . in the land of Egypt; 3
22 the LORD will smite Egypt, smiting and healing 3
23 there will be a highway from Egypt to Assyria 3
23 the Assyrian will come into Egypt 3
24 Israel will be the third with Egypt and Assyria 3
25 Blessed be Egypt my people 3
20: 3 as a sign and a portent against Egypt and Ethiopia 3
4 with buttocks uncovered, to the shame of Egypt. 3
5 Ethiopia their hope and of Egypt their boast. 3
23: 5 the report comes to Egypt, they will be in anguish 3
27:12 from the river Euphra'tes to the Brook of Egypt 3
13 those who were driven out to the land of Egypt 3
30: 2 who set out to go down to Egypt 3
2 and to seek shelter in the shadow of Egypt! 3
3 shelter in . . of Egypt to your humiliation. 3
7 For Egypt's help is worthless and empty 3
31: 1 Woe to those who go down to Egypt for help 3
36: 6 Behold, you are relying on Egypt, that broken reed 3
6 Such is Pharaoh . . of Egypt to all who rely on him. 3
9 when you rely on Egypt for chariots 3
37:25 I dried up with . . my foot all the streams of Egypt. 1
43: 3 I give Egypt as your ransom 3
45:14 wealth of Egypt and the merchandise of Ethiopia 3
52: 4 went down at the first into Egypt to sojourn 3
Jer 2: 6 the LORD who brought us up from the land of Egypt 3
18 And now what do you gain by going to Egypt 3
36 You shall be put to shame by Egypt 3
7:22 day that I brought them out of the land of Egypt 3
25 that your fathers came out of the land of Egypt 3
9:26 Egypt, Judah, Edom, the sons of Ammon, Moab 3
11: 4 when I brought them out of the land of Egypt 3
7 when I brought them up out of the land of Egypt 3
16:14 the people of Israel out of the land of Egypt 3
23: 7 the people of Israel out of the land of Egypt 3
24: 8 and those who dwell in the land of Egypt. 3
25:19 Pharoah king of Egypt, his servants, his princes 3
26:21 he was afraid and fled and escaped to Egypt. 3
22 Then King Jehoi'akim sent to Egypt certain men 3
23 they fetched Uri'ah from Egypt and brought him 3
31:32 to bring them out of the land of Egypt 3
32:20 hast shown signs and wonders in the land of Egypt 3
21 bring thy people Israel out of the land of Egypt 3
34:13 when I brought them out of the land of Egypt 3
37: 5 The army of Pharaoh had come out of Egypt; 3
7 is about to return to Egypt, to its own land. 3
41:17 near Bethlehem, intending to go to Egypt 3
42:14 saying, 'No, we will go to the land of Egypt 3
15 If you set your faces to enter Egypt 3
16 shall overtake you there in the land of Egypt; 3
16 famine . . shall follow hard after you to Egypt; 3
17 All the men who set their faces to go to Egypt 3
18 will be poured out on you when you go to Egypt. 3
19 said to you, O remnant of Judah, 'Do not go to Egypt. 3
43: 2 not send you to say, 'Do not go to Egypt to live there'; 3
7 And they came into the land of Egypt 3
11 He shall come and smite the land of Egypt 3
12 kindle a fire in the temples of the gods of Egypt; 3
12 he shall clean the land of Egypt, as a shepherd 3
13 Heliop'olis which is in the land of Egypt; 3
13 the temples of the gods of Egypt he shall burn 3
44: 1 all the Jews that dwelt in the land of Egypt 3
8 in the land of Egypt where you have come to live 3
12 have set their faces to come to the land of Egypt 3
12 in the land of Egypt they shall fall; 3
13 I will punish those who dwell in the land of Egypt 3
14 who have come to live in the land of Egypt 3
15 people who dwelt in Pathros in the land of Egypt 3
24 all you of Judah who are in the land of Egypt 3
26 all you of Judah who dwell in the land of Egypt 3
26 of any man of Judah in all the land of Egypt, saying 3
27 all the men of Judah who are in the land of Egypt 3
28 return from the land of Egypt to the land of Judah 3
28 the remnant of Judah, who came to the land of Egypt 3
30 Behold, I will give Pharaoh Hophra king of Egypt 3
46: 2 About Egypt. Concerning the army of Pharaoh 3
2 the army of Pharaoh Neco, king of Egypt 3
8 Egypt rises like the Nile 3
11 and take balm, O virgin daughter of Egypt! 3
13 king of Babylon to smite the land of Egypt 3
14 Declare in Egypt, and proclaim in Migdol; 3
17 Call the name of Pharaoh, king of Egypt, 'Noisy one 3
19 baggage for exile, O inhabitants of Egypt! 3

20 A beautiful heifer is Egypt 3
24 The daughter of Egypt shall be put to shame 3
25 and Pharaoh, and Egypt and her gods and her kings 3
26 Egypt shall be inhabited as in the days of old •
Lam 5: 6 We have given the hand to Egypt, and to Assyria 3
Ezk 17:15 rebelled . . by sending ambassadors to Egypt 3
19: 4 they brought him with hooks to the land of Egypt. 3
20: 5 making myself known to them in the land of Egypt 3
6 that I would bring them out of the land of Egypt 3
7 do not defile yourselves with the idols of Egypt; 3
8 nor did they forsake the idols of Egypt. 3
8 against them in the midst of the land of Egypt. 3
9 in bringing them out of the land of Egypt. 3
10 So I led them out of the land of Egypt 3
36 in the wilderness of the land of Egypt 3
23: 3 they played the harlot in Egypt; 3
8 which she had practiced since her days in Egypt; 3
19 when she played the harlot in the land of Egypt 3
27 your harlotry brought from the land of Egypt; 3
27: 7 fine embroidered linen from Egypt was your sail 3
29: 2 set your face against Pharaoh king of Egypt 3
2 and prophesy against him and against all Egypt; 3
3 Behold, I am against you, Pharaoh king of Egypt 3
6 Then all the inhabitants of Egypt shall know 3
9 land of Egypt shall be a desolation and a waste. 3
10 I will make the land of Egypt an utter waste 3
12 I will make the land of Egypt a desolation 3
14 I will restore the fortunes of Egypt 3
19 I will give the land of Egypt to Nebuchadrez'zar 3
20 I have given him the land of Egypt 3
30: 4 A sword shall come upon Egypt 3
4 shall be in Ethiopia, when the slain fall in Egypt 3
6 says the LORD: Those who support Egypt shall fall 3
8 when I have set fire to Egypt, and all her helpers 3
9 shall come upon them on the day of Egypt's doom; 3
10 I will put an end to the wealth of Egypt 3
11 and they shall draw their swords against Egypt 3
13 shall no longer be a prince in the land of Egypt; 3
13 I will put fear in the land of Egypt. 3
15 my wrath upon Pelusium, the stronghold of Egypt 3
16 I will set fire to Egypt; 3
18 when I break there the dominion of Egypt 3
19 Thus I will execute acts of judgment upon Egypt. 3
21 I have broken the arm of Pharaoh king of Egypt; 3
22 Behold, I am against Pharaoh king of Egypt 3
25 he shall stretch it out against the land of Egypt; 3
31: 2 say to Pharaoh king of Egypt and to his multitude 3
32: 2 raise a lamentation over Pharaoh king of Egypt 3
12 They shall bring to nought the pride of Egypt 3
15 I make the land of Egypt desolate and when the land 3
16 chant it; over Egypt, and over all her multitude 3
18 Son of man, wail over the multitude of Egypt 3
47:19 thence along the Brook of Egypt to the Great Sea. •
48:28 thence along the Brook of Egypt to the Great Sea. •
Dan 9:15 didst bring thy people out of the land of Egypt 3
11: 8 He shall also carry off to Egypt their gods 3
42 land of Egypt shall not escape. 3
43 ruler of . . all the precious things of Egypt; 3
Hos 2:15 at the time when she came out of the land of Egypt. 3
7:11 calling to Egypt, going to Assyria. 3
16 shall be their derision in the land of Egypt. 3
8:13 they shall return to Egypt. 3
9: 3 but E'phraim shall return to Egypt 3
6 Egypt shall gather them 3
11: 1 and out of Egypt I called my son. 3
5 They shall return to the land of Egypt 3
11 they shall come trembling like birds from Egypt 3
12: 1 and oil is carried to Egypt. 3
9 I am the LORD your God from the land of Egypt; 3
13 the LORD brought Israel up from Egypt 3
13: 4 I am the LORD your God from the land of Egypt; 3
Jol 3:19 Egypt shall become a desolation 3
Ams 2:10 Also I brought you up out of the land of Egypt 3
3: 1 family which I brought up out of the land of Egypt 3
9 to the strongholds in the land of Egypt, and say 3
4:10 among you a pestilence after the manner of Egypt; 3
8: 8 and sink again, like the Nile of Egypt? 3
9: 5 and sinks again, like the Nile of Egypt; 3
7 Did I not bring up Israel from the land of Egypt 3
Mic 6: 4 For I brought you up from the land of Egypt 3
7:12 they will come to you, from Assyria to Egypt 1
12 and from Egypt to the River, from sea to sea 1
15 in the days when you came out of the land of Egypt 3
Nah 3: 9 Ethiopia was her strength, Egypt too 3
Hag 2: 5 that I made you when you came out of Egypt. 3
Zec 10:10 I will bring them home from the land of Egypt 3
11 They shall pass through the sea of Egypt •
11 the scepter of Egypt shall depart. 3
14:18 if the family of Egypt do not go up and present 3
19 This shall be the punishment to Egypt 3
Mat 2:13 take the child and his mother, and flee to Egypt 4
14 his mother by night, and departed to Egypt 4
15 the prophet, "Out of Egypt have I called my son. 4
19 in a dream to Joseph in Egypt, saying 4
Act 2:10 Egypt and the parts of Libya belonging to Cyre'ne 4
7: 9 the patriarchs . . sold him into Egypt 4
10 favor and wisdom before Pharaoh, king of Egypt 4
10 who made him governor over Egypt 4
11 came a famine throughout all Egypt and Canaan 4
12 when Jacob heard that there was grain in Egypt 4
15 Jacob went down into Egypt 4
17 the people grew and multiplied in Egypt 4
18 till there arose over Egypt another king 4
34 ill-treatment of my people that are in Egypt 4
34 now come, I will send you to Egypt.' 4
36 wonders and signs in Egypt and at the Red Sea 4
39 in their hearts they turned to Egypt 4
40 this Moses who led us out from the land of Egypt 4
13:17 during their stay in the land of Egypt 4
Heb 3:16 left Egypt under the leadership of Moses. 4
8: 9 to lead them out of the land of Egypt 4
11:26 greater wealth than the treasures of Egypt 4
27 By faith he left Egypt 4
Jde 1: 5 he who saved a people out of the land of Egypt 4
Rev 11: 8 city . . allegorically called Sodom and Egypt 4
1Es 1:25 Pharaoh, king of Egypt, went to make war 4
26 the king of Egypt sent word to him saying 4
35 Then the king of Egypt deposed him from reigning 4
37 the king of Egypt made Jehoiakim . . king 4
38 brought him up out of Egypt. 4
2Es 1: 7 not I who brought them out of the land of Egypt 5
3:17 thou didst lead his descendants out of Egypt 5
9:29 when they came out from Egypt 5
14: 3 when my people were in bondage in Egypt; 5
4 I sent him and led my people out of Egypt 5
29 At first our fathers dwelt as aliens in Egypt 5
15:10 to live any longer in the land of Egypt 5
11 and will smite Egypt with plagues 5
12 Let Egypt mourn, and its foundations 5
16: 1 Woe to you, Egypt and Syria! 5
Tob 8: 3 he fled to the remotest parts of Egypt 4
Jdt 1: 9 Kadesh and the river of Egypt 4
10 all who lived in Egypt 4
12 all Judea, and every one in Egypt 4
5:10 they went down to Egypt 4
11 the king of Egypt became hostile to them 4
12 he afflicted the whole land of Egypt 4
6: 5 take revenge on this race that came out of Egypt. 4
AEs 11: 1 brought to Egypt the preceding Letter of Purim •
13:16 redeem for thyself out of the land of Egypt. 4
Sir 0: 3 When I came to Egypt in the . . reign of Euergetes 4
Bar 1:19 Lord brought our fathers out of the land of Egypt 4
20 he brought our fathers out of the land of Egypt 4
2:11 didst bring thy people out of the land of Egypt 4
1Mc 1:16 he determined to become king of the land of Egypt 4
17 So he invaded Egypt with a strong force 4
18 He engaged Ptolemy king of Egypt in battle 4
18 the fortified cities in the land of Egypt 4
19 he plundered the land of Egypt. 4
20 After subduing Egypt, Antiochus returned 4
2:53 kept the commandment, and became lord of Egypt. 4
3:32 from the river Euphrates to the borders of Egypt. 4
10:51 sent ambassadors to Ptolemy king of Egypt 4
57 So Ptolemy set out from Egypt 4
11: 1 Then the king of Egypt gathered great forces 4
13 the crown of Egypt and that of Asia. 4
59 from the Ladder of Tyre to the borders of Egypt. 4
2Mc 1: 1 To their Jewish brethren in Egypt 4
10 to the Jews in Egypt, Greeting, and good health. 4
4:21 When Apollonius . . was sent to Egypt 4
5: 1 Antiochus made his second invasion of Egypt. 4
8 he was cast ashore in Egypt; 4
11 raging inwardly, he left Egypt 4
9:29 betook himself to Ptolemy Philometor in Egypt. 4
3Mc 2:25 When he arrived in Egypt 4
3:12 soldiers in Egypt and all its districts 4
20 when we arrived in Egypt victorious 4
4:18 was impossible for all the generals in Egypt. 4
6: 4 the former ruler of this Egypt 4
7: 1 Ptolemy Philopator to the generals in Egypt 4
4Mc 4:22 For when he was warring against Ptolemy in Egypt 4

Egyptian 1. אִישׁ מִצְרִי 2. בֶּן מִצְרִים 3. מִצְרִי 4. מִצְרַיִם
5. Αἰγύπτιος 6. Αιγυπτος 7. Agyptius

Gen 12:12 when the Egyptians see you, they will say 4
14 When Abram entered Egypt the Egyptians saw that 4
16: 1 Sar'ai . . had an Egyptian maid whose name was 3
3 Sar'ai . . took Hagar the Egyptian, her maid 3
21: 9 Sarah saw the son of Hagar the Egyptian 3
25:12 whom Hagar the Egyptian, Sarah's maid, bore 3
39: 1 the captain of the guard, an Egyptian 1
2 he was in the house of his master the Egyptian 3
5 the LORD blessed the Egyptian's house 3
41:55 said to all the Egyptians, "Go to Joseph; 4
56 Joseph . . sold to the Egyptians, for the famine 4
43:32 served . . the Egyptians who ate with him 4
32 because the Egyptians might not eat bread 4
32 for that is an abomination to the Egyptians. 4
45: 2 he wept aloud, so that the Egyptians heard it 4
46:34 shepherd is an abomination to the Egyptians. 4
47:15 all the Egyptians came to Joseph, and said, 4
20 for all the Egyptians sold their fields 4
50: 3 And the Egyptians wept for him 70 days. 4
11 This is a grievous mourning to the Egyptians. 4
Exd 1:12 And the Egyptians were in dread of the people 6
19 the Hebrew women are not like the Egyptian women; 3
2:11 and he saw an Egyptian beating a Hebrew 1
12 seeing no one he killed the Egyptian and hid him 3
14 Do you mean to kill me as you killed the Egyptian? 3
19 They said, "An Egyptian delivered us out 1
3: 8 deliver them out of the hand of the Egyptians 4
9 oppression with which the Egyptians oppress 4
21 give . . favor in the sight of the Egyptians; 4
22 thus you shall despoil the Egyptians. 4
6: 5 people . . whom the Egyptians hold in bondage 4
6 out from under the burdens of the Egyptians 4
7 out from under the burdens of the Egyptians. 4
7: 5 the Egyptians shall know that I am the LORD 4
18 and the Egyptians will loathe to drink water 4
21 the Egyptians could not drink water 4
24 all the Egyptians dug round about the Nile 4
8:21 and the houses of the Egyptians shall be filled 4
26 offerings abominable to the Egyptians. 4
26 offerings abominable to the Egyptians. 4
9: 6 all the cattle of the Egyptians died 4
11 the magicians and upon all the Egyptians. 4
10: 2 tell . . how I have made sport of the Egyptians 4
6 fill . . the houses . . of all the Egyptians; 4
11: 3 favor in the sight of the Egyptians. 4
7 a distinction between the Egyptians and Israel. 4
12:23 the LORD will pass through to slay the Egyptians; 4
27 when he slew the Egyptians but spared our 4
30 he, and all his servants, and all the Egyptians; 4
33 the Egyptians were urgent with the people 4
35 they had asked of the Egyptians jewelry 4
36 favor in the sight of the Egyptians, so that they 4
36 Thus they despoiled the Egyptians. 4
14: 4 the Egyptians shall know that I am the LORD. 4
9 The Egyptians pursued them, all Pharaoh's horses 4
10 behold, the Egyptians were marching after them; 4
12 Let us alone and let us serve the Egyptians'? 4
12 better for us to serve the Egyptians than to die 4
13 the Egyptians whom you see today, you shall never 4
17 I will harden the hearts of the Egyptians 4
18 the Egyptians shall know that I am the LORD 4
23 The Egyptians pursued, and went in after them 4
24 looked down upon the host of the Egyptians 4
24 discomfited the host of the Egyptians 4
25 the Egyptians said, "Let us flee 4
25 the LORD fights for them against the Egyptians. 4
26 the water may come back upon the Egyptians 4
27 the Egyptians fled into it, and the LORD routed 4
27 the LORD routed the Egyptians in the midst 4
30 saved . . from the hand of the Egyptians; 4
30 Israel saw the Egyptians dead upon the seashore. 4
31 which the LORD did against the Egyptians 4
15:26 diseases upon you which I put upon the Egyptians; 4
18: 8 Pharaoh and to the Egyptians for Israel's sake 4
9 delivered them out of the hand of the Egyptians. 4
10 delivered you out of the hand of the Egyptians 4
11 people from under the hand of the Egyptians 4
19: 4 You have seen what I did to the Egyptians 4
32:12 Why should the Egyptians say, 'With evil intent 4
Lev 24:10 woman's son, whose father was an Egyptian 3
Num14:13 Then the Egyptians will hear of it 4
20:15 Egyptians dealt harshly with us and our fathers; 4
33: 3 triumphantly in the sight of all the Egyptians 4
4 Egyptians were burying all their first-born 4
Deu 23: 7 you shall not abhor an Egyptian 3
26: 6 Egyptians treated us harshly, and afflicted us 4
Jos 24: 6 and the Egyptians pursued your fathers 4
7 he put darkness between you and the Egyptians 4
Jdg 6: 9 I delivered you from the hand of the Egyptians 4
10:11 Did I not deliver you from the Egyptians 4
1Sm 4: 8 the gods who smote the Egyptians with every sort 4
6: 6 Egyptians and Pharaoh hardened their hearts? 4
10:18 I delivered you from the hand of the Egyptians 4
12: 8 Jacob went . . and the Egyptians oppressed them 6
30:11 They found an Egyptian in the open country 1
2Sm 23:21 And he slew an Egyptian, a handsome man. 1
21 The Egyptian had a spear in his hand; 3
21 and snatched the spear out of the Egyptian's hand 3
1Ch 2:34 but Sheshan had an Egyptian slave, whose name was 3
11:23 he slew an Egyptian, a man of great stature 3
23 Egyptian had in his hand a spear 3
23 and snatched the spear out of the Egyptian's hand 3
Ezr 9: 1 Moabites, the Egyptians, and the Amorites. 3
Prv 7:16 colored spreads of Egyptian linen; 4
Isa 10:24 lift up their staff against you as the Egyptians 4
19: 1 heart of the Egyptians will melt within them. 4
2 I will stir up Egyptians against Egyptians 4
2 I will stir up Egyptians against Egyptians 4
3 spirit of the Egyptians . . will be emptied out 4
4 give over the Egyptians into the hand of a hard 4
16 In that day the Egyptians will be like women 4
17 Judah will become a terror to the Egyptians; 4
21 LORD will make himself known to the Egyptians; 4
21 the Egyptians will know the LORD in that day 4
23 Assyrian . . into Egypt, and the Egyptian 4
23 the Egyptians will worship with the Assyrians. 4
20: 4 Assyria lead away the Egyptians captives 4
31: 3 The Egyptians are men, and not God; 4
Ezk 16:26 You also played the harlot with the Egyptians 2
23:21 when the Egyptians handled your bosom 4
27 you shall not lift up your eyes to the Egyptians 4
29:12 I will scatter the Egyptians among the nations 4

13 I will gather the Egyptians from the peoples 4
30:23 I will scatter the Egyptians among the nations 4
26 I will scatter the Egyptians among the nations 4
Act 7:22 instructed in all the wisdom of the Egyptians 5
24 avenged him by striking the Egyptian. 5
28 kill me as you killed the Egyptian yesterday?' 5
21:38 Are you not the Egyptian, then, who . . 5
Heb 11:29 the Egyptians, when they attempted to do the same 5
1Es 8:69 the Jebusites, the Moabites, the Egyptians 5
2Es 1:18 better . . to serve the Egyptians than to die 7
Jdt 5:12 the Egyptians drove them out of their sight. 5

Ehi 1. אֵחִי
Gen 46:21 Becher, Ashbel, Gera, Na'aman, Ehi, Rosh, Muppim 1

Ehud 1. אֵהוּד 2. אֵחוּד
Jdg 3:15 a deliverer, Ehud, the son of Gera, the Benjaminite 1
16 And Ehud made for himself a sword with two edges 1
18 when Ehud had finished presenting the tribute •
20 Ehud came to him, as he was sitting alone 1
20 And Ehud said, "I have a message from God for you. 1
21 Ehud reached with his left hand, took the sword 1
23 Ehud went out into the vestibule, and closed 1
26 Ehud escaped while they delayed, and passed 1
4: 1 in the sight of the LORD, after Ehud died. 1
1Ch 7:10 sons of Bilhan: Je'ush, Benjamin, Ehud, Chena'anah 1
8: 6 These are the sons of Ehud 2

Eker 1. עֵקֶר
1Ch 2:27 The sons of Ram . . Ma'az, Jamin, and Eker. 1

Ekron 1. עֶקְרוֹן 2. עֶקְרוֹנִי 3. Ακκαρων
Jos 13: 3 from . . northward to the boundary of Ekron 1
3 those of Gaza, Ashdod, Ash'kelon, Gath, and Ekron 2
15:11 out to the shoulder of the hill north of Ekron 1
45 Ekron, with its towns and its villages; 1
46 from Ekron to the sea, all . . by the side of Ashdod 1
19:43 Elon, Timnah, Ekron 1
Jdg 1:18 its territory, and Ekron with its territory. 1
1Sm 5:10 So they sent the ark of God to Ekron. 1
10 when the ark of God came to Ekron 1
6:16 they returned that day to Ekron. 1
17 Gaza, one for Ash'kelon, one for Gath, one for Ekron; 1
7:14 were restored to Israel, from Ekron to Gath; 1
17:52 pursued . . as far as Gath and the gates of Ekron 1
52 on the way from Sha-ara'im as far as Gath and Ekron. 1
2Kg 1: 2 Go, inquire of Ba'al-ze'bub, the god of Ekron, whether 1
3 going to inquire of Ba'al-ze'bub, the god of Ekron?' 1
6 to inquire of Ba'al-ze'bub, the god of Ekron? 1
16 to inquire of Ba'al-ze'bub, the god of Ekron 1
Jer 25:20 the Philistines (Ash'kelon, Gaza, Ekron 1
Ams 1: 8 I will turn my hand against Ekron; 1
Zep 2: 4 and Ekron shall be uprooted. 1
Zec 9: 5 Ekron also, because its hopes are confounded. 1
7 Ekron shall be like the Jeb'usites. 1
1Mc 10:89 He also gave him Ekron and all its environs 3

people of Ekron 1. עֶקְרוֹנִי
1Sm 5:10 when the ark . . the people of Ekron cried out 1

El-berith 1. אֵל בְּרִית
Jdg 9:46 the stronghold of the house of El-be'rith. 1

El-bethel 1. אֵל בֵּית אֵל
Gen 35: 7 built an altar, and called the place El-bethel 1

El-Elohe-Israel 1. אֵל אֱלֹהֵי יִשְׂרָאֵל
Gen 33:20 erected an altar and called it El-El'ohe-Israel 1

El-paran 1. אֵיל פָּארָן
Gen 14: 6 in their Mount Se'ir as far as El-paran 1

Ela 1. אֵלָא
1Kg 4:18 Shim'e-i the son of Ela, in Benjamin; 1

Elah 1. אֵלָה
Gen 36:41 Oholiba'mah, Elah, Pinon 1
1Sm 17: 2 were gathered, and encamped in the valley of Elah 1
19 all . . Israel, were in the valley of Elah 1
21: 9 Goliath . . whom you killed in the valley of Elah 1
1Kg 16: 6 and Elah his son reigned in his stead. 1
8 Elah the son of Ba'asha began to reign over Israel 1
13 the sins of Ba'asha and the sins of Elah his son 1
14 the rest of the acts of Elah, and all that he did 1
2Kg 15:30 Hoshe'a the son of Elah made a conspiracy against 1
17: 1 Hoshe'a the son of Elah began to reign in Sama'ria 1
18: 1 In the third year of Hoshe'a son of Elah 1
9 which was the seventh year of Hoshe'a son of Elah 1
1Ch 1:52 Oholiba'mah, Elah, Pinon 1
4:15 The sons of Caleb . . Iru, Elah, and Na'am; 1
15 and the sons of Elah: Kenaz. 1
9: 8 Elah the son of Uzzi, son of Michri 1

Elam 1. עֵילָם 2. Ηλαμ 3. Καλαμωλαλος
Gen 10:22 The sons of Shem: Elam, Asshur, Arpach'shad 1
14: 1 king of Ella'sar, Ched-or-lao'mer king of Elam 1
9 with Ched-or-lao'mer king of Elam 1
1Ch 1:17 sons of Shem: Elam, Asshur, Arpach'shad, Lud 1
8:24 Hanani'ah, Elam, Anthothi'jah 1
26: 3 Elam the fifth, Jehoha'nan the sixth, Eli-e-ho-e'nai 1
Ezr 2: 7 sons of Elam, 1,254. 1
31 sons of the other Elam, 1,254. 1
8: 7 Of the sons of Elam, Jeshai'ah the son of Athali'ah 1
10: 2 Shecani'ah the son of Jehi'el, of the sons of Elam 1
26 Of the sons of Elam: Mattani'ah, Zechari'ah, Jehi'el 1
Neh 7:12 sons of Elam, 1,254. 1
34 sons of the other Elam, 1,254. 1
10:14 chiefs . . Parosh, Pa'hath-mo'ab, Elam, Zattu, Bani 1
12:42 Jehoha'nan, Malchi'jah, Elam, and Ezer. 1
Isa 11:11 remnant . . from Ethiopia, from Elam, from Shinar 1
21: 2 Go up, O Elam, lay siege, O Media; 1
22: 6 Elam bore the quiver with chariots and horsemen 1
Jer 25:25 all the kings of Zimri, all the kings of Elam 1
49:34 came to Jeremiah the prophet concerning Elam 1
35 Behold, I will break the bow of Elam 1
36 I will bring upon Elam the four winds 1
36 to which those driven out of Elam shall not come. 1
37 I will terrify Elam before their enemies 1
38 I will set my throne in Elam 1
39 I will restore the fortunes of Elam, says the LORD. 1
Ezk 32:24 Elam is there, and all her multitude about her 1
Dan 8: 2 Susa the capital, which is in the province of Elam; 1
1Es 5:12 The sons of Elam, 1,254. The sons of Zattu, 945. 2
22 The sons of the other Elam and Ono, 725. 3
8:33 Of the sons of Elam, Jeshaiah the son of Gotholiah 2
9:27 Of the sons of Elam: Mattaniah and Zechariah 2

Elamite 1. עֵלְמָיֵא (A) 2. Ἐλαμίτης
Ezr 4: 9 men of Susa, that is, the Elamites 1
Act 2: 9 Par'thians and Medes and E'lamites 2

Elasa 1. Ελασα
1Mc 9: 5 Now Judas was encamped in Elasa 1

Elasah 1. אֶלְעָשָׂה 2. Σαλθας
Ezr 10:22 of Pashhur . . Nethan'el, Jo'zabad, and Ela'sah. 1
Jer 29: 3 was sent by the hand of Ela'sah the son of Shaphan 1
1Es 9:22 Ishmael, and Nathanael, and Gedaliah, and Elasah. 2

Elath 1. אֵילוֹת 2. אֵילַת
Deu 2: 8 from the Arabah road from Elath and E'zi-on-ge'ber. 2
2Kg 14:22 He built Elath and restored it to Judah 2
16: 6 the king of Edom recovered Elath for Edom 2
6 the king . . and drove the men of Judah from Elath; 1
6 and the E'domites came to Elath, where they dwell 2

Eldaah 1. אֶלְדָּעָה
Gen 25: 4 Hanoch, Abi'da, and Elda'ah. All these were 1
1Ch 1:33 Mid'ian: Ephah, Epher, Hanoch, Abida, and Elda'ah. 1

Eldad 1. אֶלְדָּד
Num 11:26 Now two men remained in the camp, one named Eldad 1
27 Eldad and Medad are prophesying in the camp. 1

Elead 1. אֶלְעָד
1Ch 7:21 Ezer and E'le-ad, whom the men of Gath . . slew 1

Eleadah 1. אֶלְעָדָה
1Ch 7:20 Tahath his son, Ele-a'dah his son, Tahath his son 1

Elealeh 1. אֶלְעָלֵא 2. אֶלְעָלֵה
Num 32: 3 Nimrah, Heshbon, Elea'leh, Sebam, Nebo, and Be'on 1
37 sons of Reuben built Heshbon, Elea'leh, Kiriatha'im 1
Isa 15: 4 Heshbon and Ele-a'leh cry out 2
16: 9 Heshbon and Ele-a'leh; for upon your fruit 2
Jer 48:34 Heshbon and Ele-a'leh cry out; 2

Eleasah 1. אֶלְעָשָׂה
1Ch 2:39 the father of Helez, and Helez of Ele-a'sah. 1
40 Ele-a'sah . . father of Sismai, and Sismai 1
8:37 Raphah was his son, Ele-a'sah his son, Azel his son. 1
9:43 Rephai'ah . . Ele-a'sah his son, Azel his son. 1

Eleazar 1. אֶלְעָזָר 2. Ἐλεάζαρ 3. Ελεαζαρος 4. Eleazar
Exd 6:23 she bore him Nadab, Abi'hu, Elea'zar, and Ith'amar. 1
25 Elea'zar, Aaron's son, took to wife one 1
28: 1 Nadab and Abi'hu, Elea'zar and Ith'amar. 1
Lev 10: 6 Moses said to Aaron and to Elea'zar and Ith'amar 1
12 Moses said to Aaron and to Elea'zar and Ith'amar 1
16 he was angry with Elea'zar and Ith'amar 1
Num 3: 2 Nadab . . and Abi'hu, Elea'zar, and Ith'amar; 1
4 Elea'zar and Ith'amar served as priests 1
32 Elea'zar . . was to be chief over the leaders 1
4:16 Elea'zar . . the priest shall have charge 1
16:37 Tell Elea'zar . . to take up the censers 1
39 Elea'zar the priest took the bronze censers 1
40 as the LORD said to Elea'zar through Moses. •
19: 3 you shall give her to Elea'zar the priest 1
4 Elea'zar the priest shall take some of her blood 1
20:25 Take Aaron and Elea'zar his son, and bring them up 1
26 garments, and put them upon Elea'zar his son; 1
28 garments, and put them upon Elea'zar his son; 1
28 Moses and Elea'zar came down from the mountain. 1
25: 7 When Phin'ehas the son of Elea'zar . . saw it 1
11 Phin'ehas the son of Elea'zar, son of Aaron 1
26: 1 LORD said to Moses and to Elea'zar the son of Aaron 1
3 Moses and Elea'zar the priest spoke with them 1
60 to Aaron were born Nadab, Abi'hu, Elea'zar 1
63 those numbered by Moses and Elea'zar the priest 1
27: 2 stood . . before Elea'zar the priest 1
19 cause him to stand before Elea'zar the priest 1
21 he shall stand before Elea'zar the priest 1
22 caused him to stand before Elea'zar the priest 1
31: 6 with Phin'ehas the son of Elea'zar the priest 1
12 brought . . to Moses, and to Elea'zar the priest 1
13 Moses, and Elea'zar the priest, and all the leaders 1
21 Elea'zar the priest said to the men of war 1
26 you and Elea'zar the priest and the heads 1
29 give it to Elea'zar the priest as an offering 1
31 Moses and Elea'zar the priest did as the LORD 1
41 Moses gave the tribute . . to Elea'zar the priest 1
51 Moses and Elea'zar . . received from them the gold 1
54 Moses and Elea'zar the priest received the gold 1
32: 2 came and said to Moses and to Elea'zar the priest 1
28 command concerning them to Elea'zar the priest 1
34:17 Elea'zar the priest and Joshua the son of Nun. 1
Deu 10: 6 his son Elea'zar ministered as priest in his stead 1
Jos 14: 1 Elea'zar the priest, and Joshua the son of Nun 1
17: 4 They came before Elea'zar the priest and Joshua 1
19:51 which Elea'zar . . and Joshua . . distributed 1
21: 1 Levites came to Elea'zar the priest and to Joshua 1
22:13 Phin'ehas the son of Elea'zar the priest 1
31 Phin'ehas the son of Elea'zar the priest said 1
32 Then Phin'ehas the son of Elea'zar the priest 1
24:33 Elea'zar the son of Aaron died; and they buried him 1
Jdg 20:28 Phin'ehas the son of Elea'zar, son of Aaron 1
1Sm 7: 1 they consecrated his son, Elea'zar, to have charge 1
2Sm 23: 9 next . . was Elea'zar the son of Dodo, son of Aho'hi. 1
1Ch 6: 3 sons of Aaron . . Abi'hu, Elea'zar, and Ith'amar. 1
4 Elea'zar was the father of Phin'ehas 1
50 sons of Aaron: Elea'zar his son, Phin'ehas his son 1
9:20 Phin'ehas the son of Elea'zar 1
11:12 next to him . . was Elea'zar the son of Dodo 1
23:21 The sons of Mahli: Elea'zar and Kish. 1
22 Elea'zar died having no sons, but only daughters; 1
24: 1 sons of Aaron: Nadab, Abi'hu, Elea'zar, and Ith'amar. 1
2 Elea'zar and Ith'amar became the priests. 1
3 With the help of Zadok of the sons of Elea'zar 1
4 chief men were found among the sons of Elea'zar 1
4 heads of fathers' houses of the sons of Elea'zar 1
5 officers . . among both the sons of Elea'zar 1
6 one father's house being chosen for Elea'zar 1
28 Of Mahli: Elea'zar, who had no sons. 1
Ezr 7: 5 Phin'ehas, son of Elea'zar, son of Aaron the chief 1
8:33 Mer'emoth . . Elea'zar the son of Phin'ehas 1
10:25 of Parosh . . Elea'zar, Hashabi'ah, and Benai'ah. 1
Neh 12:42 Ma-asei'ah, Shemai'ah, Elea'zar, Uzzi, Jehoha'nan 1
Mat 1:15 Eli'ud the father of Elea'zar 2
15 and Elea'zar the father of Matthan 2
1Es 8: 2 son of Phineas, son of Eleazar, son of Aaron 2
63 with him was Eleazar the son of Phinehas 2
9:26 Malchijah, Mijamin, and Eleazar, and Asibias 3
2Es 1: 2 son of Phinehas, son of Eleazar 4
Sir 45:23 Phinehas the son of Eleazar is the third in glory 2
50:27 the son of Sirach, son of Eleazar, of Jerusalem 2
1Mc 2: 5 Eleazar called Avaran 2
6:43 Eleazar, called Avaran, saw 3
8:17 and Jason the son of Eleazar 3
2Mc 6:18 Eleazar, one of the scribes in high position 3
24 Eleazar in his 90th year 3
8:23 Besides, he appointed Eleazar to read aloud 3
3Mc 6: 1 Then a certain Eleazar . . prayed as follows 3
16 Just as Eleazar was ending his prayer 3
4Mc 1: 8 Eleazar and the seven brothers and their mother. 3
5: 4 one man, Eleazar by name, leader of the flock 3
14 Eleazar asked to have a word. 3
6: 1 When Eleazar . . had made eloquent response 3
5 the courageous and noble man, as a true Eleazar 3
14 Eleazar, why are you . . destroying yourself 3
16 Eleazar . . cried out 3
7: 1 the reason of our father Eleazar 3
5 our father Eleazar broke the maddening waves 3
10 O supreme king over the passions, Eleazar! 3
12 the descendant of Aaron, Eleazar 3
9: 5 you learned nothing from Eleazar. 3
16:15 you stood and watched Eleazar being tortured 3
17:13 Eleazar was the first contestant 3

Eleutherus 1. Ελευθερος
1Mc 11: 7 as far as the river called Eleutherus 1
12:30 they had crossed the Eleutherus river. 1

Elhanan 1. אֶלְחָנָן
2Sm 21:19 Elha'nan the son of Ja'areor'egim . . slew Goliath 1
23:24 As'ahel . . Elha'nan the son of Dodo of Bethlehem 1
1Ch 11:26 mighty men . . Elha'nan the son of Dodo 1
20: 5 Elha'nan the son of Ja'ir slew Lahmi 1

Eli 1. עֵלִי 2. Heli
1Sm 1: 3 two sons of Eli, Hophni and Phin'ehas, were priests 1
9 Now Eli the priest was sitting on the seat beside 1
12 As she continued . . Eli observed her mouth. 1
13 therefore Eli took her to be a drunken woman. 1
14 Eli said to her, "How long will you be drunken? 1
17 Then Eli answered, "Go in peace 1

25 slew the bull, and they brought the child to Eli. 1
2:11 And the boy . . in the presence of Eli the priest. 1
12 Now the sons of Eli were worthless men; 1
20 Then Eli would bless Elka'nah and his wife, and say 1
22 Now Eli was very old, and he heard all that his sons 1
27 And there came a man of God to Eli, and said to him 1
3: 1 Samuel was ministering to the LORD under Eli. 1
2 At that time Eli . . was lying down in his own place; 1
5 and ran to Eli, and said, "Here I am 1
6 Samuel arose and went to Eli, and said, "Here I am 1
8 And he arose and went to Eli, and said, "Here I am 1
8 Eli perceived that the LORD was calling the boy. 1
9 Therefore Eli said to Samuel, "Go, lie down; 1
12 I will fulfil against Eli all that I have spoken 1
14 I swear to the house of Eli that the iniquity 1
14 the iniquity of Eli's house shall not be expiated 1
15 And Samuel was afraid to tell the vision to Eli. 1
16 But Eli called Samuel and said, "Samuel, my son. 1
17 Eli said, "What was it that he told you? Do not hide it •
4: 4 the two sons of Eli . . were there with the ark 1
11 two sons of Eli, Hophni and Phin'ehas, were slain. 1
13 Eli was sitting upon his seat by the road 1
14 When Eli heard the sound of the outcry, he said 1
14 Then the man hastened and came and told Eli. 1
15 Now Eli was 98 years old and his eyes were set 1
16 the man said to Eli, "I . . come from the battle; 1
18 Eli fell over backward . . and his neck was broken •
14: 3 son of Eli, the priest of the LORD in Shiloh 1
1Kg 2:27 spoken concerning the house of Eli in Shiloh. 1
2Es 1: 2 son of Ahijah, son of Phinehas, son of Eli 2

Eliab 1. אֱלִיאָב 2. Ελιαβ

Num 1: 9 from Zeb'ulun, Eli'ab the son of Helon; 1
2: 7 the leader . . being Eli'ab the son of Helon 1
7:24 Eli'ab the . . leader of the men of Zeb'ulun 1
29 This was the offering of Eli'ab the son of Helon. 1
10:16 over the host . . was Eli'ab the son of Helon. 1
16: 1 Dathan and Abi'ram the sons of Eli'ab, and On 1
12 sent to call Dathan and Abi'ram the sons of Eli'ab; 1
26: 8 the sons of Pallu: Eli'ab. 1
9 The sons of Eli'ab: Nem'uel, Dathan, and Abi'ram. 1
Deu 11: 6 what he did to Dathan and Abi'ram the sons of Eli'ab 1
1Sm 16: 6 When they came, he looked on Eli'ab and thought 1
17:13 sons who went . . were Eli'ab the first-born 1
28 Now Eli'ab . . heard when he spoke to the men; 1
28 and Eli'ab's anger was kindled against David 1
1Ch 2:13 Jesse was the father of Eli'ab his first-born 1
6:27 Eli'ab his son, Jero'ham his son, Elka'nah his son. 1
12: 9 Ezer the chief, Obadi'ah second, Eli'ab third 1
15:18 Eli'ab, Benai'ah, Ma-asei'ah, Mattithi'ah, 1
20 Jehi'el, Unni, Eli'ab, Ma-asei'ah, and Benai'ah 1
16: 5 second to him were . . Jehi'el, Mattithi'ah, Eli'ab 1
2Ch 11:18 Ab'ihail the daughter of Eli'ab the son of Jesse; 1
Jdt 8: 1 son of Hilkiah, son of Eliab, son of Nathanael 2

Eliada 1. אֶלְיָדָע

2Sm 5:16 Eli'shama, Eli'ada, and Eliph'elet. 1
1Kg 11:23 as an adversary to him, Rezon the son of Eli'ada 1
1Ch 3: 8 Eli'shama, Eli'ada, and Eliph'elet, nine. 1
2Ch 17:17 Of Benjamin: Eli'ada, a mighty man of valor 1

Eliahba 1. אֶלְיַחְבָּא

2Sm 23:32 Eli'ahba of Sha-al'bon, the sons of Jashen, Jonathan 1
1Ch 11:33 Az'maveth of Baha'rum, Eli'ahba of Sha-al'bon 1

Eliakim 1. אֶלְיָקִים 2. Ἐλιακίμ

2Kg 18:18 there came out to them Eli'akim the son of Hilki'ah 1
26 Then Eli'akim . . and Shebnah, and Jo'ah, said 1
37 Eli'akim the son of Hilki'ah, who was over 1
19: 2 he sent Eli'akim . . and Shebna the secretary 1
23:34 Pharaoh Neco made Eli'akim the son of Josi'ah king 1
2Ch 36: 4 the king of Egypt made Eli'akim his brother king 1
Neh 12:41 priests Eli'akim, Ma-asei'ah, Mini'amin, Micai'ah 1
Isa 22:20 I will call my servant Eli'akim the son of Hilki'ah 1
36: 3 there came out to him Eli'akim the son of Hilki'ah 1
11 Eli'akim, Shebna, and Jo'ah said to the Rab'shakeh 1
22 Then Eli'akim the son of Hilki'ah 1
37: 2 he sent Eli'akim, who was over the household 1
Mat 1:13 and Abi'ud the father of Eli'akim 2
13 and Eli'akim the father of Azor 2
Lke 3:30 the son of Jonam, the son of Eli'akim 2

Elialis 1. Ελιαλις

1Es 9:34 Machnadebai, Eliasis, Binnui, Elialis, Shimei 1

Eliam 1. אֱלִיעָם

2Sm 11: 3 Is not this Bathshe'ba, the daughter of Eli'am 1
23:34 Eli'am the son of Ahith'ophel of Gilo 1

Eliasaph 1. אֶלְיָסָף

Num 1:14 from Gad, Eli'asaph the son of Deu'el; 1
2:14 the leader . . Eli'asaph the son of Reu'el 1
3:24 with Eli'asaph . . as head of the fathers' house 1
7:42 Eli'asaph the . . leader of the men of Gad 1
47 was the offering of Eli'asaph the son of Deu'el. 1
10:20 over the host . . was Eli'asaph the son of Deu'el. 1

Eliashib 1. אֶלְיָשִׁיב 2. Ελιασιβος 3. Ελιασιμος

1Ch 3:24 sons of Eli-o-e'nai: Hod'avi'ah, Eli'ashib, Pelai'ah 1
24:12 the eleventh to Eli'ashib, the twelfth to Jakim 1
Ezr 10: 6 Jehoha'nan the son of Eli'ashib 1
24 Of the singers: Eli'ashib. 1
27 of Zattu: Eli-o-e'nai, Eli'ashib, Mattani'ah 1
36 Vani'ah, Mer'emoth, Eli'ashib 1
Neh 3: 1 Then Eli'ashib the high priest rose up 1
20 door of the house of Eli'ashib the high priest. 1
21 section from the door of the house of Eli'ashib 1
21 from . . to the end of the house of Eli'ashib. 1
12:10 Joi'akim the father of Eli'ashib 1
10 Eli'ashib the father of Joi'ada 1
22 Levites, in the days of Eli'ashib, Joi'ada, Joha'nan 1
23 until the days of Joha'nan the son of Eli'ashib. 1
13: 4 Eli'ashib the priest, who was appointed 1
7 evil that Eli'ashib had done for Tobi'ah 1
28 Jehoi'ada, the son of Eli'ashib the high priest 1
1Es 9: 1 the chamber of Jehohanan the son of Eliashib 2
24 Of the temple singers: Eliashib and Zaccur. 2
28 Of the sons of Zattu: Elioenai, Eliashib, Othoniah 3
34 Carabasion and Eliashib and Machnadebai 2

Eliasis 1. Ελιασις

1Es 9:34 Eliashib and Machnadebai, Eliasis, Binnui 1

Eliathah 1. אֱלִיאָתָה

1Ch 25: 4 sons of Heman . . Hanani'ah, Hana'ni, Eli'athah 1
27 twentieth, to Eli'athah, his sons and his brethren 1

Elidad 1. אֱלִידָד

Num34:21 tribe of Benjamin, Eli'dad the son of Chislon. 1

Eliehoenai 1. אֶלְיְהוֹעֵינַי 2. Ελιαωνιας

1Ch 26: 3 Jehoha'nan the sixth, Eli-e-ho-e'nai the seventh. 1
Ezr 8: 4 Of the sons of Pa'hath-mo'ab, Eli-e-ho-e'nai the son 1
1Es 8:31 Eliehoenai the son of Zerahiah 2

Eliel 1. אֱלִיאֵל

1Ch 5:24 heads of their fathers' houses . . Ishi, Eli'el 1
6:34 son of Jero'ham, son of Eli'el, son of To'ah 1
8:20 Eli-e'nai, Zil'lethai, Eli'el 1
22 Ishpan, Eber, Eli'el 1
11:46 Eli'el the Ma'havite, and Jer'ibai, 1
47 Eli'el, and Obed, and Ja-asi'el the Mezo'ba-ite 1
12:11 Attai sixth, Eli'el seventh 1
15: 9 of the sons of Hebron, Eli'el the chief 1
11 Levites . . Shemai'ah, Eli'el, and Ammin'adab 1
2Ch 31:13 Eli'el, Ismachi'ah, Mahath . . were overseers 1

Elienai 1. אֱלִיעֵינַי

1Ch 8:20 Eli-e'nai, Zil'lethai, Eli'el 1

Eliezar 1. Ελεαζαρος

1Es 8:43 I sent word to Eliezar, Iduel, Maasmas 1
9:19 Maaseiah, Eliezar, Jarib, and Jodan. 1

Eliezer 1. אֱלִיעֶזֶר 2. Ἐλιέζερ

Gen 15: 2 heir of my house is Elie'zer of Damascus? 1
Exd 18: 4 the name of the other was Elie'zer 1
1Ch 7: 8 The sons of Becher: Zemi'rah, Jo'ash, Elie'zer 1
15:24 Ama'sai, Zechari'ah, Benai'ah, and Elie'zer 1
23:15 The sons of Moses: Gershom and Elie'zer. 1
17 The sons of Elie'zer: Rehabi'ah the chief; 1
17 Elie'zer had no other sons 1
26:25 His brethren: from Elie'zer were his son Rehabi'ah 1
27:16 for the Reubenites Elie'zer the son of Zichri 1
2Ch 20:37 Elie'zer . . prophesied against Jehosh'aphat 1
Ezr 8:16 Then I sent for Elie'zer, Ar'i-el, Shemai'ah, 1
10:18 found Ma-asei'ah, Elie'zer, Jarib, and Gedali'ah 1
23 Of the Levites . . Petha-hi'ah, Judah, and Elie'zer. 1
31 of Harim: Elie'zer, Isshi'jah, Malchi'jah, Shemai'ah 1
Lke 3:29 the son of Joshua, the son of Elie'zer 2

Elihoreph 1. אֱלִיחֹרֶף

1Kg 4: 3 Elihor'eph and Ahi'jah the sons of Shisha were 1

Elihu 1. אֱלִיהוּ

1Sm 1: 1 of Jero'ham, son of Eli'hu, son of Tohu, son of Zuph 1
1Ch 12:20 men of Manas'seh . . Michael, Joz'abad, Eli'hu 1
26: 7 brethren were able men, Eli'hu and Semachi'ah. 1
27:18 for Judah, Eli'hu, one of David's brothers; 1
Job 32: 2 Then Eli'hu the son of Bar'achel the Buzite 1
4 Now Eli'hu had waited to speak to Job 1
5 when Eli'hu saw that there was no answer 1
6 Eli'hu the son of Bar'achel the Buzite answered 1
34: 1 Then Eli'hu said 1
35: 1 Eli'hu said 1
36: 1 Eli'hu continued, and said 1

Elijah 1. אֵלִיָּהוּ 2. Ἠλίας 3. Ηλιου 4. Helias

1Kg 17: 1 Now Eli'jah the Tishbite . . said to Ahab 1
13 Eli'jah said to her, "Fear not; go and do 1
15 she went and did as Eli'jah said; 1
16 the word of the LORD which he spoke by Eli'jah. 1
18 she said to Eli'jah, "What have you against me 1
22 the LORD hearkened to the voice of Eli'jah; 1
23 Eli'jah took the child, and brought him down 1
23 and Eli'jah said, "See, your son lives. 1
24 the woman said to Eli'jah, "Now I know 1
18: 1 the word of the LORD came to Eli'jah . . saying, "Go 1
2 So Eli'jah went to show himself to Ahab. 1
7 as Obadi'ah was on the way, behold, Eli'jah met him; 1
7 and said, "Is it you, my lord Eli'jah? 1
8 Go, tell your lord, 'Behold, Eli'jah is here.' 1
11 'Go, tell your lord, "Behold, Eli'jah is here."' 1
14 'Go, tell your lord, "Behold, Eli'jah is here"'; 1
15 Eli'jah said, "As the LORD of hosts lives 1
16 Obadi'ah . . told him; and Ahab went to meet Eli'jah. 1
17 When Ahab saw Eli'jah, Ahab said to him, "Is it you 1
21 Eli'jah came near to all the people, and said 1
22 Eli'jah said to the people, "I, even I only, am left 1
25 Then Eli'jah said to the prophets of Ba'al, "Choose 1
27 at noon Eli'jah mocked them, saying, "Cry aloud 1
30 Then Eli'jah said to all the people, "Come near to me"; 1
31 Eli'jah took twelve stones 1
36 Eli'jah the prophet came near and said, "O LORD 1
40 Eli'jah said to them, "Seize the prophets of Ba'al; 1
40 Eli'jah brought them down to the brook Kishon 1
41 Eli'jah said to Ahab, "Go up, eat and drink; 1
42 And Eli'jah went up to the top of Carmel; 1
46 the hand of the LORD was on Eli'jah; 1
19: 1 Ahab told Jez'ebel all that Eli'jah had done 1
2 Then Jez'ebel sent a messenger to Eli'jah saying 1
9 and he said to him, "What are you doing here, Eli'jah? 1
13 when Eli'jah heard it, he wrapped his face in his 1
13 and said, "What are you doing here, Eli'jah? 1
19 Eli'jah passed by him and cast his mantle 1
20 he left the oxen, and ran after Eli'jah, and said 1
21 he arose and went after Eli'jah, and ministered 1
21:17 the word of the LORD came to Eli'jah the Tishbite 1
20 Ahab said to Eli'jah, "Have you found me, 1
28 the word of the LORD came to Eli'jah the Tishbite 1
2Kg 1: 3 the angel of the LORD said to Eli'jah the Tishbite 1
4 So Eli'jah went. 1
8 And he said, "It is Eli'jah the Tishbite. 1
9 He went up to Eli'jah . . and said to him, "O man of God •
10 Eli'jah answered the captain of 50 1
12 Eli'jah answered them, "If I am a man of God 1
13 and came and fell on his knees before Eli'jah 1
15 the angel of the LORD said to Eli'jah, "Go down 1
17 the word of the LORD which Eli'jah had spoken. 1
2: 1 about to take Eli'jah up to heaven by a whirlwind 1
1 Eli'jah and Eli'sha were on their way from Gilgal. 1
2 Eli'jah said to Eli'sha, "Tarry here, I pray you; 1
4 Eli'jah said to him, "Eli'sha, tarry here, I pray you; 1
6 Then Eli'jah said to him, "Tarry here, I pray you; 1
8 Eli'jah took his mantle, and rolled it up 1
9 Eli'jah said to Eli'sha, "Ask what I shall do for you 1
11 And Eli'jah went up by a whirlwind into heaven. 1
13 he took up the mantle of Eli'jah that had fallen 1
14 the mantle of Eli'jah that had fallen from him 1
14 saying, "Where is the LORD, the God of Eli'jah? 1
15 The spirit of Eli'jah rests on Eli'sha. 1
3:11 Eli'jah . . poured water on the hands of Eli'jah. 1
9:36 he spoke by his servant Eli'jah the Tishbite 1
10:10 LORD has done what he said by his servant Eli'jah. 1
17 the word of the LORD which he spoke to Eli'jah. 1
1Ch 8:27 Ja-areshi'ah, Eli'jah, and . . sons of Jero'ham. 1
2Ch 21:12 a letter came to him from Eli'jah . . saying 1
Ezr 10:21 of Harim: Ma-asei'ah, Eli'jah, Shemai'ah, Jehi'el 1
26 of Elam . . Abdi, Jer'emoth, and Eli'jah. 1
Mal 4: 5 Behold, I will send you Eli'jah the prophet 1
Mat 11:14 he is Eli'jah who is to come. 2
16:14 Some say John the Baptist, others say Eli'jah 2
17: 3 behold, there appeared to them Moses and Eli'jah 2
4 one for you and one for Moses and one for Eli'jah. 2
10 the scribes say that first Eli'jah must come? 2
11 He replied, "Eli'jah does come 2
12 I tell you that Eli'jah has already come 2
27:47 This man is calling Eli'jah. 2
49 let us see whether Eli'jah will come to save him. 2
Mrk 6:15 others said, "It is Eli'jah. 2
8:28 others say, Eli'jah; and others one of the prophets 2
9: 4 there appeared to them Eli'jah with Moses; 2
5 one for you and one for Moses and one for Eli'jah. 2
11 the scribes say that first Eli'jah must come 2
12 Eli'jah does come first to restore all things 2
13 I tell you that Eli'jah has come 2
15:35 Behold, he is calling Eli'jah. 2
36 let us see whether Eli'jah will come 2
Lke 1:17 go before him in the spirit and power of Eli'jah 2
4:25 were many widows in Israel in the days of Eli'jah 2
26 Eli'jah was sent to none of them 2
9: 8 by some that Eli'jah had appeared 2
19 others say, Eli'jah 2
30 behold, two men talked with him, Moses and Eli'jah 2
33 one for you and one for Moses and one for Eli'jah 2
Joh 1:21 And they asked him, "What then? Are you Elijah? 2
25 if you are neither the Christ, nor Elijah 2
Rom 11: 2 Do you not know what the scripture says of Eli'jah 2
Jas 5:17 Eli'jah was a man of like nature with ourselves 2
1Es 9:27 Jehiel and Abdi, and Jeremoth and Elijah. 2
2Es 7:109 Elijah for those who received the rain 4
Jdt 8: 1 son of Ahitub, son of Elijah, son of Hilkiah 3
Sir 48: 1 Then the prophet Elijah arose like a fire 2
4 How glorious you were, O Elijah 2
12 It was Elijah who was covered by the whirlwind 2
1Mc 2:58 Elijah . . was taken up into heaven. 2

Elika 1. אֱלִיקָא
2Sm 23:25 Shammah of Harod, Eli'ka of Harod 1

Elim 1. אֵילִם
Exd 15:27 Then they came to Elim, where there were twelve 1
16: 1 They set out from Elim, and all the congregation 1
1 Sin, which is between Elim and Sinai 1
Num33: 9 they set out from Marah, and came to Elim; 1
9 at Elim there were twelve springs of water 1
10 set out from Elim, and encamped by the Red Sea. 1

Elimelech 1. אֱלִימֶלֶךְ
Rut 1: 2 The name of the man was Elim'elech 1
3 But Elim'elech, the husband of Na'omi, died 1
2: 1 a man of wealth, of the family of Elim'elech 1
3 Bo'az, who was of the family of Elim'elech. 1
4: 3 land which belonged to our kinsman Elim'elech. 1
9 I have bought . . all that belonged to Elim'elech 1

Elioenai 1. אֶלְיוֹעֵינַי 2. Ελιαδας 3. Ελιωναις
1Ch 3:23 sons of Neari'ah: Eli-o-e'nai, Hizki'ah, and Azri'kam 1
24 sons of Eli-o-e'nai: Hod'avi'ah, Eli'ashib, Pelai'ah 1
4:36 Eli-o-e'nai, Ja-ako'bah, Jeshohai'ah, Asai'ah 1
7: 8 sons of Becher . . Eli-o-e'nai, Omri, Jer'emoth 1
Ezr 10:22 of Pashhur: Eli-o-e'nai, Ma-asei'ah, Ish'mael 1
27 of Zattu: Eli-o-e'nai, Eli'ashib, Mattani'ah 1
Neh 12:41 priests . . Eli-o-e'nai, Zechari'ah, and Hanani'ah 1
1Es 9:22 Of the sons of Pashhur: Elioenai, Maaseiah 3
28 Of the sons of Zattu: Elioenai, Eliashib, Othoniah 2

Elionas 1. Ελιωνας
1Es 9:32 Of the sons of Annan, Elionas and Asaias 1

Eliphal 1. אֱלִיפַל
1Ch 11:35 Eli'phal the son of Ur 1

Eliphaz 1. אֱלִיפַז
Gen 36: 4 Adah bore to Esau, El'iphaz; 1
10 Esau's sons: El'iphaz the son of Adah the wife 1
11 The sons of El'iphaz were Teman, Omar, Zepho 1
12 (Timna was a concubine of El'iphaz, Esau's son; 1
12 she bore Am'alek to El'iphaz.) These are the sons 1
15 The sons of El'iphaz the first-born of Esau 1
16 these are the chiefs of El'iphaz in the land 1
1Ch 1:35 The sons of Esau: Eli'phaz, Reu'el, Je'ush 1
36 The sons of Eli'phaz: Teman, Omar, Zephi, Gatam 1
Job 2:11 Eli'phaz the Te'manite, Bildad the Shuhite 1
4: 1 Then Eli'phaz the Te'manite answered 1
15: 1 Then Eli'phaz the Te'manite answered 1
22: 1 Then Eli'phaz the Te'manite answered 1
42: 7 the LORD said to Eli'phaz the Te'manite 1
9 Eli'phaz the Te'manite and Bildad the Shuhite 1

Eliphelehu 1. אֱלִיפְלֵהוּ
1Ch 15:18 Eliph'elehu, and Miknei'ah, and the gatekeepers 1
21 Mattithi'ah, Eliph'elehu, Miknei'ah, O'bed-e'dom 1

Eliphelet 1. אֱלִיפֶלֶט 2. Ελιφαλατ 3. Ελιφαλατος
2Sm 5:16 Eli'shama, Eli'ada, and Eliph'elet. 1
23:34 Eliph'elet the son of Ahas'bai of Ma'acah 1
1Ch 3: 6 then Ib-har, Eli'shama, Eliph'elet 1
8 Eli'shama, Eli'ada, and Eliph'elet, nine. 1
8:39 sons of Eshek . . and Eliph'elet the third. 1
14: 7 Eli'shama, Beeli'ada, and Eliph'elet. 1
Ezr 8:13 names being Eliph'elet, Jeu'el, and Shemai'ah 1
10:33 of Hashum: Matte'nai, Mat'tattah, Zabad, Eliph'elet 1
1Es 8:39 their names being Eliphelet, Jeuel, and Shemaiah 3
9:33 Mattenai and Mattattah and Zabad and Eliphelet 2

Elisha 1. אֱלִישָׁע 2. 'Ελισαῖος
1Kg 19:16 Eli'sha . . you shall anoint to be prophet 1
17 him who escapes from . . Jehu shall Eli'sha slay. 1
19 departed . . and found Eli'sha the son of Shaphat 1
2Kg 2: 1 Eli'jah and Eli'sha were on their way from Gilgal. 1
2 Eli'jah said to Eli'sha, "Tarry here, I pray you; 1
2 Eli'sha said, "As the LORD lives, and as you yourself 1
3 the sons of the prophets . . came out to Eli'sha 1
4 Eli'jah said to him, "Eli'sha, tarry here, I pray you; 1
5 The sons of the prophets . . drew near to Eli'sha 1
9 Eli'jah said to Eli'sha, "Ask what I shall do for you 1
9 Eli'sha said, "I pray you, let me inherit 1
12 Eli'sha saw it and he cried, "My father, my father! 1
14 water was parted . . and Eli'sha went over. 1
15 The spirit of Eli'jah rests on Eli'sha. 1
19 Now the men of the city said to Eli'sha, "Behold 1
22 according to the word which Eli'sha spoke. 1
3:11 Eli'sha the son of Shaphat is here 1
13 Eli'sha said to the king of Israel 1
14 Eli'sha said, "As the LORD of hosts lives 1
4: 1 the wife of one . . cried to Eli'sha 1
2 Eli'sha said to her, "What shall I do for you? Tell me; 1
8 One day Eli'sha went on to Shunem 1
17 she bore a son . . as Eli'sha had said to her. 1
32 When Eli'sha came into the house, he saw the child 1
38 Eli'sha came again to Gilgal 1
42 Eli'sha said, "Give to the men, that they may eat. •
5: 8 Eli'sha . . heard that the king of Israel had rent 1
9 Na'aman . . halted at the door of Eli'sha's house. 1
10 Eli'sha sent a messenger to him, saying, "Go and wash 1
20 Geha'zi, the servant of Eli'sha the man of God, said 1
25 Eli'sha said to him, "Where have you been, Geha'zi? 1
6: 1 Now the sons of the prophets said to Eli'sha, "See 1
12 Eli'sha, the prophet who is in Israel, tells 1
17 Then Eli'sha prayed, and said, "O LORD, I pray thee 1
17 horses and chariots of fire round about Eli'sha. 1
18 when the Syrians . . Eli'sha prayed to the LORD 1
18 in accordance with the prayer of Eli'sha. 1
19 Eli'sha said to them, "This is not the way 1
20 Eli'sha said, "O LORD, open the eyes of these men 1
21 When the king of Israel saw them he said to Eli'sha 1
31 if the head of Eli'sha . . remains on his shoulders 1
32 Eli'sha was sitting in his house 1
32 Eli'sha said to the elders, "Do you see •
7: 1 Eli'sha said, "Hear the word of the LORD 1
8: 1 Now Eli'sha had said to the woman . . "Arise 1
4 Tell me all the great things . . Eli'sha has done. 1
5 telling . . how Eli'sha had restored the dead •
5 and here is her son whom Eli'sha restored to life. 1
7 Eli'sha came to Damascus. Ben-ha'dad . . was sick; 1
10 Eli'sha said to him, "Go, say to him, 'You shall 1
13 Eli'sha answered, "The LORD has shown me 1
14 he departed from Eli'sha, and came to his master 1
14 said to him, "What did Eli'sha say to you? 1
9: 1 Eli'sha . . called one of the sons of the prophets 1
13:14 Now when Eli'sha had fallen sick with the illness 1
15 Eli'sha said to him, "Take a bow and arrows"; 1
16 And Eli'sha laid his hands upon the king's hands. 1
17 he opened it. Then Eli'sha said, "Shoot"; and he shot. 1
20 So Eli'sha died, and they buried him. 1
21 and the man was cast into the grave of Eli'sha; 1
21 and as soon as the man touched the bones of Eli'sha 1
Lke 4:27 lepers in Israel in the time of the prophet Eli'sha 2
Sir 48:12 Elisha was filled with his spirit 2

Elishah 1. אֱלִישָׁה
Gen 10: 4 The sons of Javan: Eli'shah, Tarshish, Kittim 1
1Ch 1: 7 The sons of Javan: Eli'shah, Tarshish, Kittim 1
Ezk 27: 7 blue and purple from the coasts of Eli'shah was 1

Elishama 1. אֱלִישָׁמָע
Num 1:10 from E'phraim, Eli'shama the son of Ammi'hud 1
2:18 leader of the people of E'phraim being Eli'shama 1
7:48 Eli'shama the . . leader of the men of E'phraim 1
53 was the offering of Eli'shama the son of Ammi'hud. 1
10:22 over their host was Eli'shama the son of Ammi'hud. 1
2Sm 5:16 Eli'shama, Eli'ada, and Eliph'elet. 1
2Kg 25:25 Ish'mael the son of Nethani'ah, son of Eli'shama 1
1Ch 2:41 father of Jeka-mi'ah, and Jekami'ah of Eli'shama. 1
3: 6 then Ib-har, Eli'shama, Eliph'elet 1
8 Eli'shama, Eli'ada, and Eliph'elet, nine. 1
7:26 Ladan his son, Ammi'hud his son, Eli'shama his son 1
14: 7 Eli'shama, Beeli'ada, and Eliph'elet. 1
2Ch 17: 8 with these Levites, the priests Eli'shama 1
Jer 36:12 were sitting there: Eli'shama the secretary 1
20 having put the scroll in the chamber of Eli'shama 1
21 he took it from the chamber of Eli'shama 1
41: 1 Ish'mael the son of Nethani'ah, son of Eli'shama 1

Elishaphat 1. אֱלִישָׁפָט
2Ch 23: 1 commanders . . Elisha'phat the son of Zichri. 1

Elisheba 1. אֱלִישֶׁבַע
Exd 6:23 Aaron took to wife Eli'sheba, the daughter 1

Elishua 1. אֱלִישׁוּעַ
2Sm 5:15 Ibhar, Eli'shu-a, Nepheg, Japhi'a 1
1Ch 14: 5 Ibhar, Eli'shu-a, El'pelet 1

Eliud 1. 'Ελιούδ
Mat 1:14 and Achim the father of Eli'ud 1
15 Eli'ud the father of Elea'zar 1

Elizabeth 1. 'Ελισάβετ
Lke 1: 5 her name was Elizabeth. 1
7 they had no child, because Elizabeth was barren 1
13 your wife Elizabeth will bear you a son 1
24 After these days his wife Elizabeth conceived 1
36 behold, your kinswoman Elizabeth in her old age 1
40 greeted Elizabeth. 1
41 when Elizabeth heard the greeting of Mary 1
41 Elizabeth was filled with the Holy Spirit 1
57 Now the time came for Elizabeth to be delivered 1

Elizaphan 1. אֱלִיצָפָן
Num 3:30 Eli-za'phan . . head of the fathers' house 1
34:25 of Zeb'ulun a leader, Eli-za'phan the son of Parnach. 1
1Ch 15: 8 of the sons of Eli-za'phan, Shemai'ah the chief 1
2Ch 29:13 of the sons of Eli-za'phan, Shimri and Jeu'el; 1

Elizur 1. אֱלִיצוּר
Num 1: 5 From Reuben, Eli'zur the son of Shed'eur; 1
2:10 the leader of the people of Reuben being Eli'zur 1
7:30 Eli'zur the . . leader of the men of Reuben 1
35 was the offering of Eli'zur the son of Shed'eur. 1
10:18 over their host was Eli'zur the son of Shed'eur. 1

Elkanah 1. אֶלְקָנָה
Exd 6:24 The sons of Korah: Assir, Elka'nah, and Abi'asaph; 1
1Sm 1: 1 whose name was Elka'nah the son of Jero'ham 1
4 when Elka'nah sacrificed, he would give portions 1
8 Elka'nah, her husband, said to her, "Hannah, why 1
19 And Elka'nah knew Hannah his wife, and the LORD 1
21 the man Elka'nah and all his house went up to offer 1
23 Elka'nah her husband said . . "Do what seems best 1
2:11 Then Elka'nah went home to Ramah. 1
20 Then Eli would bless Elka'nah and his wife, and say 1
1Ch 6:23 Elka'nah his son, Ebi'asaph his son, Assir his son 1
25 The sons of Elka'nah: Ama'sai and Ahi'moth 1
26 Elka'nah his son, Zophai his son, Nahath his son 1
27 Eli'ab his son, Jero'ham his son, Elka'nah his son. 1
34 son of Elka'nah, son of Jero'ham, son of Eli'el, son 1
35 son of Elka'nah, son of Mahath, son of Ama'sai 1
36 son of Elka'nah, son of Jo'el, son of Azari'ah 1
9:16 Berechi'ah the son of Asa, son of Elka'nah 1
12: 6 Elka'nah, Isshi'ah, Az'arel, Jo-e'zer, and Jasho'be-am 1
15:23 and Elka'nah were to be gatekeepers for the ark. 1
2Ch 28: 7 Elka'nah the next in authority to the king. 1

Elkiah 1. Ελκια
Jdt 8: 1 son of Joseph, son of Oziel, son of Elkiah 1

Elkosh 1. אֶלְקֹשִׁי
Nah 1: 1 The book of the vision of Nahum of Elkosh. 1

Ellasar 1. אֶלָּסָר
Gen 14: 1 Am'raphel king of Shinar, Ar'ioch king of Ella'sar 1
9 Ar'ioch king of Ella'sar, four kings against five. 1

Elmadam 1. 'Ελμαδάμ
Lke 3:28 son of Cosam, the son of Elma'dam, the son of Er 1

Elnaam 1. אֶלְנָעַם
1Ch 11:46 Jer'ibai, and Joshavi'ah, the sons of El'na-am 1

Elnathan 1. אֶלְנָתָן 2. 'Ελναθαν 3. 'Εvvαταv
2Kg 24: 8 name was Nehush'ta the daughter of Elna'than 1
Ezr 8:16 Then I sent for . . Jarib, Elna'than, Nathan 1
16 Then I sent for . . Jarib, Elna'than, Nathan 1
16 Then I sent . . for Joi'arib and Elna'than 1
Jer 26:22 Elna'than the son of Achbor and others with him 1
36:12 Elna'than the son of Achbor 1
25 even when Elna'than and Delai'ah and Gemari'ah 1
1Es 8:44 Elnathan, Shemaiah, Jarib, Nathan, Elnathan 2
44 Elnathan, Shemaiah, Jarib, Nathan, Elnathan 3

Elon 1. אֵלוֹן
Gen 26:34 Bas'emath the daughter of Elon the Hittite; 1
36: 2 Adah the daughter of Elon the Hittite 1
46:14 The sons of Zeb'ulun: Sered, Elon, and Jah'leel 1
Num26:26 of Elon, the family of the E'lonites; 1
Jos 19:43 Elon, Timnah, Ekron 1
Jdg 12:11 After him Elon the Zeb'ulunite judged Israel; 1
12 Then Elon the Zeb'ulunite died, and was buried 1

Elon-beth-hanan 1. אֵילוֹן בֵּית חָנָן
1Kg 4: 9 Shaal'bim, Beth-she'mesh, and E'lonbeth-ha'nan; 1

Elonite 1. אֵלֹנִי
Num26:26 of Elon, the family of the E'lonites; 1

Eloth 1. אֵילוֹת
1Kg 9:26 E'zion-ge'ber, which is near Eloth on the shore 1
2Ch 8:17 went to E'zion-ge'ber and Eloth on . . the sea 1
26: 2 He built Eloth and restored it to Judah 1

Elpaal 1. אֶלְפַּעַל
1Ch 8:11 He also had sons by Hushim: Abi'tub and Elpa'al. 1
12 The sons of Elpa'al: Eber, Misham, and Shemed 1
18 Ish'merai, Izli'ah, and Jobab . . sons of Elpa'al. 1

Elpelet 1. אֶלְפָּלֶט
1Ch 14: 5 Ibhar, Eli'shu-a, El'pelet 1

Elteke 1. אֶלְתְּקֵא
Jos 21:23 El'teke with its pasture lands, Gib'bethon 1

Eltekeh 1. אֶלְתְּקֵה
Jos 19:44 El'tekeh, Gib'bethon, Ba'alath 1

Eltekon 1. אֶלְתְּקוֹן
Jos 15:59 Ma'arath, Beth-anoth, and El'tekon 1

Eltolad 1. אֶלְתּוֹלַד
Jos 15:30 Elto'lad, Chesil, Hormah 1
19: 4 Elto'lad, Bethul, Hormah 1

Elul 1. אֱלוּל 2. Ελουλ
Neh 6:15 finished on the 25th day of . . Elul 1
1Mc 14:27 On the eighteenth day of Elul, in the 172nd year 2

Eluzai 1. אֶלְעוּזַי
1Ch 12: 5 Elu'zai, Jer'imoth, Beali'ah, Shemari'ah, Shephati'ah 1

Elymaean 1. Ελυμαιος
Jdt 1: 6 the plain where Arioch ruled the Elymaeans. 1

Elymais 1. Ελυμαις
Tob 2:10 took care of me until he went to Elymais. 1
1Mc 6: 1 Elymais in Persia was a city famed for its wealth 1

Elymas 1. Ἐλύμας
Act 13: 8 El'ymas the magician . . withstood them 1

Elzabad 1. אֶלְזָבָד
1Ch 12:12 Joha'nan eighth, Elza'bad ninth 1
26: 7 of Shemai'ah: Othni, Reph'a-el, Obed, and Elza'bad 1

Elzaphan 1. אֶלְצָפָן
Exd 6:22 the sons of Uz'ziel: Mi'sha-el, Elza'phan, and Sithri. 1
Lev 10: 4 Moses called Mish'a-el and Elza'phan 1

Emadabun 1. Ημαδαβουν
1Es 5:58 the sons of Jeshua Emadabun 1

Emathis 1. Εμαθις
1Es 9:29 Jehohanan and Hananiah and Zabbai and Emathis. 1

Emek-keziz 1. עֵמֶק קְצִיץ
Jos 18:21 cities . . were Jericho, Beth-hoglah, Emek-ke'ziz 1

Emim 1. אֵימִים
Gen 14: 5 Zuzim in Ham, the Emim in Sha'veh-kiriatha'im 1
Deu 2:10 Emim formerly lived there, a people great and many 1
11 as Reph'idim, but the Moabites call them Emim. 1

Emmanuel 1. Ἐμμανουήλ
Mat 1:23 his name shall be called Emman'u-el 1

Emmaus 1. Αμμαους 2. Ἐμμαοῦς
Lke 24:13 two of them were going to a village named Emma'us 2
1Mc 3:40 they encamped near Emmaus in the plain. 1
57 encamped to the south of Emmaus. 1
4: 3 to attack the king's force in Emmaus 1
9:50 the fortress in Jericho, and Emmaus 1

En-dor 1. עֵין דֹּאר 2. עֵין דֹּר
Jos 17:11 and the inhabitants of En-dor and its villages 2
1Sm 28: 7 Behold, there is a medium at Endor. 2
Ps 83:10 who were destroyed at En-dor 1

En-eglaim 1. עֵין עֶגְלַיִם
Ezk 47:10 from En-ge'di to En-eg'laim it will be a place 1

En-gannim 1. עֵין גַּנִּים
Jos 15:34 Zano'ah, En-gan'nim, Tap'puah, Enam 1
19:21 Remeth, En-gan'nim, En-had'dah, Beth-paz'zez; 1
21:29 Jarmuth with . . En-gan'nim with its pasture lands 1

En-gedi 1. עֵין גֶּדִי 2. Ενγαδδοι
Jos 15:62 Nibshan, the City of Salt, and En-ge'di 1
1Sm 23:29 David . . dwelt in the strongholds of En-ge'di. 1
24: 1 Behold, David is in the wilderness of En-ge'di. 1
2Ch 20: 2 they are in Haz'azon-ta'mar" (that is, En-ge'di). 1
Sng 1:14 cluster of henna . . in the vineyards of En-ge'di 1
Ezk 47:10 from En-ge'di to En-eg'laim it will be a place 1
Sir 24:14 I grew tall like a palm tree in En-ge'di 2

En-haddah 1. עֵין חַדָּה
Jos 19:21 Remeth, En-gan'nim, En-had'dah, Beth-paz'zez; 1

En-hakkore 1. עֵין הַקּוֹרֵא
Jdg 15:19 the name of it was called En-hakkor'e; it is at Lehi 1

En-hazor 1. עֵין חָצוֹר
Jos 19:37 Kedesh, Ed're-i, En-ha'zor 1

En-rimmon 1. עֵין רִמּוֹן
Jos 19: 7 En-rimmon, Ether, and Ashan 1
Neh 11:29 in En-rim'mon, in Zorah, in Jarmuth 1

En-rogel 1. עֵין רֹגֵל
Jos 15: 7 passes along to . . and ends at En-ro'gel; 1
18:16 it then goes . . and downward to En-rogel; 1
2Sm 17:17 Jonathan and Ahim'a-az were waiting at En-ro'gel; 1
1Kg 1: 9 the Serpent's Stone, which is beside En-ro'gel 1

En-shemesh 1. עֵין שֶׁמֶשׁ
Jos 15: 7 boundary passes . . to the waters of En-she'mesh 1
18:17 then it bends . . going on to En-she'mesh 1

En-tappuah 1. עֵין תַּפּוּחַ
Jos 17: 7 southward to the inhabitants of En-tap'puah. 1

Enaim 1. עֵינַיִם
Gen 38:14 she . . sat at the entrance to Enaim, which is 1
21 harlot who was at Enaim by the wayside? 1

Enam 1. עֵינָם
Jos 15:34 Zano'ah, En-gan'nim, Tap'puah, Enam 1

Enan 1. עֵינָן
Num 1:15 from Naph'tali, Ahi'ra the son of Enan. 1
2:29 the leader . . being Ahi'ra the son of Enan 1
7:78 Ahi'ra the son of Enan, the leader of the men 1
83 This was the offering of Ahi'ra the son of Enan. 1
10:27 over the host . . was Ahi'ra the son of Enan. 1

Enmishpat 1. עֵין מִשְׁפָּט
Gen 14: 7 came to Enmish'pat (that is, Kadesh) 1

Enoch 1. חֲנוֹךְ 2. Ἑνώχ
Gen 4:17 she conceived and bore Enoch; and he built a city 1
17 name of the city after the name of his son, Enoch. 1
18 To Enoch was born Irad; and Irad was the father 1
5:18 Jared . . became the father of Enoch. 1
19 Jared lived after the birth of Enoch 800 years 1
21 When Enoch had lived 65 years 1
22 Enoch walked with God after the birth 1
23 Thus all the days of Enoch were 365 years. 1
24 Enoch walked with God; 1
1Ch 1: 3 Enoch, Me-thu'selah, Lamech; 1
Lke 3:37 the son of Methuselah, the son of Enoch 2
Heb 11: 5 By faith Enoch was taken up 2
Jde 1:14 It was of these also that Enoch . . prophesied 2
Sir 44:16 Enoch pleased the Lord, and was taken up 2
49:14 No one like Enoch has been created on earth 2

Enos 1. Ἐνώς
Lke 3:38 the son of Enos, the son of Seth, the son of Adam 1

Enosh 1. אֱנוֹשׁ
Gen 4:26 was born, and he called his name Enosh. 1
5: 6 he became the father of Enosh. 1
7 Seth lived after the birth of Enosh 807 years 1
9 When Enosh had lived 90 years 1
10 Enosh lived after the birth of Kenan 815 years 1
11 Thus all the days of Enosh were 905 years; 1
1Ch 1: 1 Adam, Seth, Enosh; 1

Epaenetus 1. Ἐπαίνετος
Rom 16: 5 Epae'netus, who was the first convert in Asia 1

Epaphras 1. Ἐπαφρᾶς
Col 1: 7 Ep'aphras our beloved fellow servant 1
4:12 Ep'aphras, who is one of yourselves 1
Phm 1:23 Ep'aphras, my fellow prisoner in Christ Jesus 1

Epaphroditus 1. Ἐπαφρόδιτος
Php 2:25 to send to you Epaphrodi'tus my brother 1
4:18 I am filled, having received from Epaphrodi'tus 1

Epeiph 1. Επιφι
3Mc 6:38 the fourth of Epeiph 1
38 was set for the fifth to the seventh of Epeiph 1

Ephah 1. עֵיפָה
Gen 25: 4 sons of Mid'ian were Ephah, Epher, Hanoch 1
1Ch 1:33 The sons of Mid'ian: Ephah, Epher, Hanoch, Abida 1
2:46 Ephah also, Caleb's concubine, bore Haran, Moza 1
47 sons of Jah'dai . . Pelet, Ephah, and Sha'aph. 1
Isa 60: 6 cover you, the young camels of Mid'ian and Ephah; 1

Ephai 1. עֵיפַי
Jer 40: 8 the sons of Ephai the Netoph'athite 1

Epher 1. עֵפֶר
Gen 25: 4 sons of Mid'ian were Ephah, Epher, Hanoch 1
1Ch 1:33 of Mid'ian: Ephah, Epher, Hanoch, Abida, 1
4:17 The sons of Ezrah: Jether, Mered, Epher, and Jalon. 1
5:24 heads of their fathers' houses: Epher 1

Ephes-dammim 1. אֶפֶס דַּמִּים
1Sm 17: 1 between Socoh and Aze'kah, in E'phes-dam'mim. 1

Ephesian 1. Ἐφέσιος
Act 19:28 Great is Ar'temis of the Ephesians! 1
34 Great is Ar'temis of the Ephesians! 1
35 the city of the Ephesians is temple keeper 1
21:29 had previously seen Troph'imus the Ephesian 1

Ephesus 1. Ἐφέσιος 2. Ἔφεσος
Act 18:19 they came to Ephesus, and he left them there 2
21 and he set sail from Ephesus. 2
24 a Jew named Apol'los . . came to Ephesus 2
19: 1 came to Ephesus 2
17 this became known to all residents of Ephesus 2
26 not only at Ephesus but . . throughout all Asia 2
35 Men of Ephesus, what man is there who does not 1
20:16 Paul had decided to sail past Ephesus 2
17 from Mile'tus he sent to Ephesus 2
1Co 15:32 I fought with beasts at Ephesus 2
16: 8 I will stay in Ephesus until Pentecost 2
1Ti 1: 3 remain at Ephesus 2
2Ti 1:18 all the service he rendered at Ephesus. 2
4:12 Tych'icus I have sent to Ephesus. 2
Rev 1:11 to the seven churches, to Ephesus and to Smyrna 2
2: 1 To the angel of the church in Ephesus write 2

Ephlal 1. אֶפְלָל
1Ch 2:37 Zabad . . father of Ephlal, and Ephlal of Obed. 1
37 Zabad . . father of Ephlal, and Ephlal of Obed. 1

Ephod 1. אֵפֹד
Num 34:23 of Manas'seh a leader, Han'niel the son of Ephod. 1

Ephraim 1. אֶפְרַיִם 2. Ἐφραίμ
Gen 41:52 The name of the second he called E'phraim 1
46:20 in . . Egypt were born Manas'seh and E'phraim 1
48: 1 with him his two sons, Manas'seh and E'phraim. 1
5 E'phraim and Manas'seh shall be mine 1
13 Joseph took them both, E'phraim in his right hand 1
14 right hand and laid it upon the head of E'phraim 1
17 laid his right hand upon the head of E'phraim 1
17 to remove it from E'phraim's head to Manas'seh's 1
20 God make you as E'phraim and as Manas'seh 1
20 and thus he put E'phraim before Manas'seh. 1
50:23 saw E'phraim's children of the third generation 1
Num 1:10 from the sons of Joseph, from E'phraim, Eli'shama 1
32 Joseph, namely, of the people of E'phraim 1
33 the number of the tribe of E'phraim was 40,500 1
2:18 shall be the standard of the camp of E'phraim 1
18 leader of the people of E'phraim being Eli'shama 1
24 The whole number of the camp of E'phraim 1
7:48 Eli'shama the . . leader of the men of E'phraim 1
10:22 standard of the camp of the men of E'phraim set out 1
13: 8 from the tribe of E'phraim, Hoshe'a the son of Nun; 1
26:28 sons of Joseph . . Manas'seh and E'phraim. 1
35 sons of E'phraim according to their families 1
37 These are the families of the sons of E'phraim 1
34:24 of the tribe of the sons of E'phraim a leader, Kemu'el 1
Deu 33:17 such are the ten thousands of E'phraim 1
34: 2 all Naph'tali, the land of E'phraim and Manas'seh 1
Jos 14: 4 of Joseph were two tribes, Manas'seh and E'phraim; 1
16: 4 The people of Joseph, Manas'seh and E'phraim 1
10 Canaanites have dwelt in the midst of E'phraim 1
17: 8 Tap'puah . . belonged to the sons of E'phraim. 1
9 The cities here . . belong to E'phraim. 1
10 the land to the south being E'phraim's 1
15 the hill country of E'phraim is too narrow for you. 1
17 to the house of Joseph, to E'phraim and Manas'seh 1
19:50 Tim'nath-se'rah in the hill country of E'phraim; 1
20: 7 and Shechem in the hill country of E'phraim 1
21: 5 by lot from the families of the tribe of E'phraim 1
20 the cities . . were out of the tribe of E'phraim. 1
21 pasture lands in the hill country of E'phraim 1
24:30 Tim'nath-se'rah . . in the hill country of E'phraim 1
33 been given him in the hill country of E'phraim. 1
Jdg 1:29 E'phraim did not drive out the Canaanites who 1
2: 9 Tim'nath-he'res, in the hill country of Ephraim 1
3:27 trumpet in the hill country of E'phraim; 1
4: 5 Ramah and Bethel in the hill country of E'phraim; 1
5:14 From E'phraim they set out . . into the valley 1
7:24 throughout all the hill country of E'phraim 1
24 So all the men of E'phraim were called out 1
8: 1 the men of E'phraim said to him, "What is this 1
2 the grapes of E'phraim better than the vintage 1
10: 1 lived at Shamir in the hill country of E'phraim. 1
9 Benjamin and against the house of E'phraim; 1
12: 1 The men of E'phraim were called to arms 1
4 gathered all . . Gilead and fought with E'phraim; 1
4 and the men of Gilead smote E'phraim 1
4 You are fugitives of E'phraim, you Gileadites 1
4 Gileadites, in the midst of E'phraim and Manas'seh 1
5 the fugitives of E'phraim said, "Let me go over 1
15 at Pira'thon in the land of E'phraim, in the hill 1
17: 1 There was a man of the hill country of E'phraim 1
8 he came to the hill country of E'phraim 1
18: 2 they came to the hill country of E'phraim 1
13 on from there to the hill country of E'phraim 1
19: 1 the remote parts of the hill country of E'phraim 1
16 the man was from the hill country of E'phraim 1
18 to the remote parts of the hill country of E'phraim 1
1Sm 1: 1 Ramatha'im-zo'phim of the hill country of E'phraim 1
9: 4 they passed through the hill country of E'phraim 1
14:22 hid themselves in the hill country of E'phraim 1
2Sm 2: 9 Jezreel and E'phraim and Benjamin and . . Israel. 1
13:23 at Ba'al-ha'zor, which is near E'phraim 1
18: 6 the battle was fought in the forest of E'phraim. 1
20:21 a man of the hill country of E'phraim, called Sheba 1
1Kg 4: 8 names: Ben-hur, in the hill country of E'phraim; 1
12:25 built Shechem in the hill country of E'phraim 1
2Kg 5:22 come to me from the hill country of E'phraim 1
1Ch 6:66 of their territory out of the tribe of E'phraim. 1
67 Shechem . . in the hill country of E'phraim 1
7:20 The sons of E'phraim: Shuthe'lah, and Bered his son 1
22 E'phraim their father mourned many days 1
23 E'phraim went in to his wife, and she conceived •
9: 3 some of the people of Judah, Benjamin, E'phraim 1
27:10 Helez the Pel'onite, of the sons of E'phraim; 1
14 Benai'ah of Pira'thon, of the sons of E'phraim; 1
2Ch 13: 4 which is in the hill country of E'phraim 1
15: 8 cities . . taken in the hill country of E'phraim 1
9 gathered . . those from E'phraim, Manas'seh 1
17: 2 set garrisons . . in the cities of E'phraim 1
19: 4 from Beer-sheba to the hill country of E'phraim 1
25:10 the army that had come to him from E'phraim 1

28: 7 Zichri, a mighty man of E'phraim, slew Ma-asei'ah 1
12 Certain chiefs also of the men of E'phraim 1
30: 1 Hezeki'ah . . wrote letters also to E'phraim 1
10 through the country of E'phraim and Manas'seh 1
18 many of them from E'phraim, Manas'seh, Is'sachar 1
31: 1 Judah and Benjamin, and in E'phraim and Manas'seh 1
34: 6 in the cities of Manas'seh, E'phraim, and Simeon 1
9 collected from Manas'seh and E'phraim 1
Ps 60: 7 E'phraim is my helmet; Judah is my scepter. 1
78:67 he did not choose the tribe of E'phraim; 1
80: 2 before E'phraim and Benjamin and Manas'seh! 1
108: 8 E'phraim is my helmet; Judah my scepter. 1
Isa 7: 2 was told, "Syria is in league with E'phraim 1
5 Syria, with E'phraim and the son of Remali'ah 1
8 Within 65 years E'phraim will be broken 1
9 the head of E'phraim is Sama'ria 1
17 the day that E'phraim departed from Judah– 1
9: 9 people will know, E'phraim and the inhabitants 1
21 Manas'seh E'phraim, and E'phraim Manas'seh 1
21 Manas'seh E'phraim, and E'phraim Manas'seh 1
11:13 The jealousy of E'phraim shall depart 1
13 E'phraim shall not be jealous of Judah 1
13 and Judah shall not harass E'phraim. 1
17: 3 The fortress will disappear from E'phraim 1
28: 1 the proud crown of the drunkards of E'phraim 1
3 The proud crown of the drunkards of E'phraim 1
Jer 4:15 from Dan and proclaims evil from Mount E'phraim. 1
7:15 all your kinsmen, all the offspring of E'phraim. 1
31: 6 will call in the hill country of E'phraim: 1
9 a father to Israel, and E'phraim is my first-born. 1
18 I have heard E'phraim bemoaning 1
20 Is E'phraim my dear son? Is he my darling child? 1
50:19 shall be satisfied on the hills of E'phraim 1
Ezk 37:16 For Joseph (the stick of E'phraim) and all the house 1
19 stick of Joseph (which is in the hand of E'phraim) 1
48: 5 the east side to the west, E'phraim, one portion. 1
6 Adjoining the territory of E'phraim 1
Hos 4:17 E'phraim is joined to idols, let him alone. 1
5: 3 I know E'phraim, and Israel is not hid from me; 1
3 for now, O E'phraim, you have played the harlot 1
5 E'phraim shall stumble in his guilt; 1
9 E'phraim shall become a desolation 1
11 E'phraim is oppressed, crushed in judgment 1
12 Therefore I am like a moth to E'phraim 1
13 When E'phraim saw his sickness 1
13 then E'phraim went to Assyria 1
14 For I will be like a lion to E'phraim 1
6: 4 What shall I do with you, O E'phraim? 1
10 E'phraim's harlotry is there, Israel is defiled. 1
7: 1 the corruption of E'phraim is revealed 1
8 E'phraim mixes himself with the peoples; 1
8 E'phraim is a cake not turned. 1
11 E'phraim is like a dove, silly and without sense 1
8: 9 E'phraim has hired lovers. 1
11 E'phraim has multiplied altars for sinning 1
9: 3 but E'phraim shall return to Egypt 1
8 The prophet is the watchman of E'phraim 1
11 E'phraim's glory shall fly away like a bird– 1
13 E'phraim's sons . . are destined for a prey; 1
13 E'phraim must lead forth his sons to slaughter. 1
16 E'phraim is stricken, their root is dried up 1
10: 6 E'phraim shall be put to shame 1
11 E'phraim was a trained heifer 1
11 but I will put E'phraim to the yoke 1
11: 3 Yet it was I who taught E'phraim to walk 1
8 How can I give you up, O E'phraim! 1
9 I will not again destroy E'phraim; 1
12 E'phraim has encompassed me with lies 1
12: 1 E'phraim herds the wind, and pursues the east wind 1
8 E'phraim has said, "Ah, but I am rich 1
14 E'phraim has given bitter provocation; 1
13: 1 When E'phraim spoke, men trembled; 1
12 The iniquity of E'phraim is bound up 1
14: 8 O E'phraim, what have I to do with idols? 1
Obd 1:19 they shall possess the land of E'phraim 1
Zec 9:10 I will cut off the chariot from E'phraim 1
13 Judah as my bow; I have made E'phraim its arrow. 1
10: 7 Then E'phraim shall become like a mighty warrior 1
Joh 11:54 but went . . to a town called E'phraim 2
Jdt 6: 2 who are you, Achior, and you hirelings of Ephraim 2
Sir 47:21 a disobedient kingdom arose out of Ephraim. 2
23 gave Ephraim a sinful way. 2

Ephraim Gate 1. שַׁעַר אֶפְרַיִם
2Kg 14:13 from the E'phraim Gate to the Corner Gate. 1
2Ch 25:23 from the E'phraim Gate to the Corner Gate. 1

Gate of Ephraim 1. שַׁעַר אֶפְרַיִם
Neh 8:16 booths . . in the square at the Gate of E'phraim. 1
12:39 above the Gate of E'phraim, and by the Old Gate 1

Ephraimite 1. אֶפְרַיִם 2. אֶפְרָתִי 3. בֶּן אֶפְרַיִם
Jos 16: 5 The territory of the E'phraimites . . as follows 1
8 the inheritance of the tribe of the E'phraimites 3
9 towns which were set apart for the E'phraimites 3
Jdg 12: 5 took the fords . . against the E'phraimites. 1
5 Are you an E'phraimite?" When he said, "No 2
6 there fell at that time 42,000 of the E'phraimites 1
1Sm 1: 1 Elka'nah the son of . . an E'phraimite. 2
1Kg 11:26 Jerobo'am . . an E'phraimite of Zer'edah 2
1Ch 12:30 Of the E'phraimites 20,800, mighty men of valor 1
27:20 for the E'phraimites, Hoshe'a the son of Azazi'ah; 1
2Ch 25: 7 LORD is not . . with all these E'phraimites. 1
Ps 78: 9 The E'phraimites, armed with the bow, turned back 3

Ephrath 1. אֶפְרָת
Gen 35:16 still some distance from Ephrath, Rachel 1
19 on the way to Ephrath (that is, Bethlehem) 1
48: 7 there was still some distance to go to Ephrath; 1
7 and I buried her there on the way to Ephrath 1
1Ch 2:19 Caleb married Ephrath, who bore him Hur. 1

Ephrathah 1. אֶפְרָתָה
Rut 4:11 May you prosper in Eph'rathah and be renowned 1
1Ch 2:24 Eph'rathah, the wife of Hezron his father 1
50 sons of Hur the first-born of Eph'rathah 1
4: 4 Eph'rathah, the father of Bethlehem. 1
Ps 132: 6 heard of it in Eph'rathah, we found it in the fields 1
Mic 5: 2 But you, O Bethlehem Eph'rathah, who are little 1

Ephrathite 1. אִישׁ אֶפְרָתִי 2. אֶפְרָתִי
Rut 1: 2 they were Eph'rathites from Bethlehem in Judah. 2
1Sm 17:12 David was the son of an Eph'rathite of Bethlehem 1

Ephron 1. עֶפְרוֹן 2. Εφρων
Gen 23: 8 and entreat for me Ephron the son of Zohar 1
10 Now Ephron was sitting among the Hittites; 1
10 Ephron the Hittite answered Abraham 1
13 he said to Ephron in the hearing of the people 1
14 Ephron answered Abraham 1
16 Abraham agreed with Ephron; 1
16 Abraham weighed out for Ephron the silver 1
17 the field of Ephron in Mach-pe'lah 1
25: 9 in the cave of Mach-pe'lah, in the field of Ephron 1
49:29 cave that is in the field of Ephron the Hittite 1
30 Abraham bought . . from Ephron the Hittite 1
50:13 Abraham bought . . from Ephron the Hittite 1
Jos 15: 9 and from there to the cities of Mount Ephron; 1
18:15 and the boundary goes from there to Ephron •
2Ch 13:19 took cities . . Ephron with its villages. 1
1Mc 5:46 So they came to Ephron 2
2Mc 12:27 he marched also against Ephron 2

Epicurean 1. Ἐπικούρειος
Act 17:18 Epicurean and Stoic philosophers met him 1

Epiphanes 1. Επιφανης
1Mc 1:10 a sinful root, Antiochus Epiphanes 1
10: 1 Alexander Epiphanes, the son of Antiochus 1
2Mc 2:20 further the wars against Antiochus Epiphanes 1
4: 7 Antiochus who was called Epiphanes 1
10: 9 Antiochus, who was called Epiphanes. 1
13 and had gone over to Antiochus Epiphanes. 1
4Mc 4:15 Antiochus Epiphanes succeeded to the throne 1

Er 1. עֵר 2. Ἤρ
Gen 38: 3 bore a son, and he called his name Er. 1
6 Judah took a wife for Er his first-born 1
7 Er, Judah's first-born, was wicked in the sight 1
46:12 sons of Judah: Er, Onan, Shelah, Perez, and Zerah 1
12 but Er and Onan died in the land of Canaan 1
Num26:19 The sons of Judah were Er and Onan; 1
19 Er and Onan died in the land of Canaan. 1
1Ch 2: 3 The sons of Judah: Er, Onan, and Shelah; 1
3 Now Er, Judah's first-born was wicked in the sight 1
4:21 sons of Shelah . . Er the father of Lecah 1
Lke 3:28 son of Cosam, the son of Elma'dam, the son of Er 2

Eran 1. עֵרָן
Num26:36 of Eran, the family of the E'ranites. 1

Eranite 1. עֵרָנִי
Num26:36 of Eran, the family of the E'ranites. 1

Erastus 1. Ἔραστος
Act 19:22 two of his helpers, Timothy and Eras'tus 1
Rom16:23 Eras'tus, the city treasurer, and . . greet you. 1
2Ti 4:20 Eras'tus remained at Corinth 1

Erech 1. אֶרֶךְ
Gen 10:10 his kingdom was Ba'bel, Erech, and Accad 1

man of Erech 1. אַרְכְּוָי
Ezr 4: 9 Persians, the men of Erech, the Babylonians 1

Eri 1. עֵרִי
Gen 46:16 sons of Gad: Ziph'ion . . Eri, Aro'di, and Are'li 1
Num26:16 of Eri, the family of the Erites; 1

Erite 1. עֵרִי
Num26:16 of Eri, the family of the Erites; 1

Esar-haddon 1. אֵסַר חַדֹּן
2Kg 19:37 Esarhad'don his son reigned in his stead. 1
Ezr 4: 2 since the days of E'sar-had'don king of Assyria 1
Isa 37:38 E'sar-had'don his son reigned in his stead. 1

Esarhaddon 1. Ασβασαρεθ 2. Σαχερδονος
1Es 5:69 the days of Esarhaddon king of the Assyrians 1
Tob 1:21 Then Esarhaddon, his son, reigned in his place 2
22 Esarhaddon had appointed him 2

Esau 1. עֵשָׂו 2. Ἡσαύ 3. Esau
Gen 25:25 like a hairy mantle; so they called his name Esau. 1
26 his hand had taken hold of Esau's heel; 1
27 When the boys grew up, Esau was a skilful hunter 1
28 Isaac loved Esau, because he ate of his game; 1
29 Once when Jacob was boiling pottage, Esau came 1
30 Esau said to Jacob, "Let me eat some of that red 1
32 Esau said, "I am about to die; 1
33 Esau swore to him, and sold his birthright •
34 Then Jacob gave Esau bread and pottage 1
34 Thus Esau despised his birthright. 1
26:34 When Esau was 40 years old, he took to wife Judith 1
27: 1 called Esau his older son, and said to him 1
5 was listening when Isaac spoke to his son Esau. 1
5 when Esau went to the field to hunt for game 1
6 I heard your father speak to your brother Esau 1
11 Behold, my brother Esau is a hairy man 1
15 Then Rebekah took the best garments of Esau 1
19 Jacob said to his father, "I am Esau 1
21 know whether you are really my son Esau or not. 1
22 Jacob's voice, but the hands are the hands of Esau 1
23 his hands were hairy like his brother Esau's 1
24 He said, "Are you really my son Esau? 1
30 Esau his brother came in from his hunting. 1
32 I am your son, your first-born, Esau. 1
34 When Esau heard the words of his father, he cried 1
36 Esau said, "Is he not rightly named Jacob? •
37 Isaac answered Esau, "Behold, I have made him 1
38 Esau said to his father, "Have you but one 1
38 And Esau lifted up his voice and wept. 1
41 Now Esau hated Jacob because of the blessing 1
41 Esau said to himself, "The days of mourning 1
42 words of Esau her older son were told to Rebekah; 1
42 Behold, your brother Esau comforts himself 1
28: 5 the brother of Rebekah, Jacob's and Esau's mother. 1
6 Esau saw that Isaac had blessed Jacob 1
8 when Esau saw that the Canaanite women 1
9 Esau went to Ish'mael and took to wife 1
32: 3 Jacob sent messengers before him to Esau 1
4 you shall say to my lord Esau: Thus says 1
6 We came to your brother Esau 1
8 thinking, "If Esau comes to the one company 1
11 Deliver me . . from the hand of Esau, for I fear him 1
13 had with him a present for his brother Esau 1
17 When Esau my brother meets you, and asks you 1
18 they are a present sent to my lord Esau; 1
19 shall say the same thing to Esau when you meet him 1
33: 1 looked, and behold, Esau was coming 1
4 Esau ran to meet him, and embraced him 1
5 when Esau raised his eyes and saw the women •
8 Esau said, "What do you mean by all his company •
9 Esau said, "I have enough, my brother; 1
12 Then Esau said, "Let us journey on our way •
15 Esau said, "Let me leave with you some of the men 1
16 Esau returned that day on his way to Se'ir. 1
35: 1 to you when you fled from your brother Esau. 1
29 and his sons Esau and Jacob buried him. 1
36: 1 These are the descendants of Esau (that is, Edom) 1
2 Esau took his wives from the Canaanites 1
4 Adah bore to Esau, El'iphaz; 1
5 These are the sons of Esau who were born 1
6 Then Esau took his wives, his sons, his daughters 1
8 Esau dwelt in the hill country of Se'ir; 1
8 in the hill country of Se'ir; Esau is Edom. 1
9 These are the descendants of Esau the father 1
10 These are the names of Esau's sons 1
10 El'iphaz the son of Adah the wife of Esau 1
10 Reu'el the son of Bas'emath the wife of Esau. 1
12 (Timna was a concubine of El'iphaz, Esau's son; 1
12 These are the sons of Adah, Esau's wife. 1
13 These are the sons of Bas'emath, Esau's wife. 1
14 daughter of Anah the son of Zib'eon, Esau's wife 1
14 she bore to Esau Je'ush, Jalam, and Korah. 1
15 These are the chiefs of the sons of Esau. 1
15 The sons of El'iphaz the first-born of Esau 1
17 These are the sons of Reu'el, Esau's son 1
17 Edom; they are the sons of Bas'emath, Esau's wife 1
18 These are the sons of Oholiba'mah, Esau's wife 1
18 the daughter of Anah, Esau's wife. 1
19 These are the sons of Esau (that is, Edom) 1
40 These are the names of the chiefs of Esau 1
43 of Edom (that is, Esau, the father of Edom), according 1
Deu 2: 4 territory of your brethren the sons of Esau 1
5 I have given Mount Se'ir to Esau as a possession. 1
8 we went on, away from our brethren the sons of Esau 1
12 sons of Esau dispossessed them, and destroyed 1
22 he did for the sons of Esau, who live in Se'ir 1
29 as the sons of Esau who live in Se'ir . . did for me 1
Jos 24: 4 and to Isaac I gave Jacob and Esau. 1
4 I gave Esau the hill country of Se'ir to possess 1
1Ch 1:34 The sons of Isaac: Esau and Israel. 1
35 The sons of Esau: Eli'phaz, Reu'el, Je'ush 1
Jer 49: 8 For I will bring the calamity of Esau upon him 1

10 But I have stripped Esau bare 1
Obd 1: 6 How Esau has been pillaged 1
8 out of Edom, and understanding out of Mount Esau? 1
9 every man from Mount Esau will be cut off 1
18 of Joseph a flame, and the house of Esau stubble; 1
18 there shall be no survivor to the house of Esau; 1
19 Those of the Negeb shall possess Mount Esau 1
21 shall go up to Mount Zion to rule Mount Esau; 1
Mal 1: 2 Is not Esau Jacob's brother?" says the LORD. 1
3 I have hated Esau; I have laid waste his hill 1
Rom 9:13 As it is written, "Jacob I loved, but Esau I hated. 2
Heb 11:20 invoked future blessings on Jacob and Esau. 2
12:16 that no one be immoral or irreligious like Esau 2
2Es 3:15 and to Isaac thou gavest Jacob and Esau. 3
16 but Esau thou didst reject 3
6: 8 because from him were born Jacob and Esau 3
8 Jacob's hand held Esau's heel from the beginning. 3
9 For Esau is the end of this age 3
Jdt 7: 8 Then all the chieftains of the people of Esau 2
18 the sons of Esau and the sons of Ammon went up 2
1Mc 5: 3 Judas made war on the sons of Esau in Idumea 2
65 fought the sons of Esau in the land to the south 2

Esdraelon 1. Εσδρηλων
Jdt 1: 8 Upper Galilee and the great Plain of Esdraelon 1
3: 9 Then he came to the edge of Esdraelon, near Dothan 1
4: 6 Betomesthaim, which faces Esdraelon 1
7: 3 from Bethulia to Cyamon, which faces Esdraelon. 1

Esdris 1. Εσδρις
2Mc 12:36 Esdris and his men 1

Esek 1. עֵשֶׂק
Gen 26:20 he called the name of the well Esek 1

Eshan 1. אֶשְׁעָן
Jos 15:52 Arab, Dumah, Eshan 1

Eshbaal 1. אֶשְׁבַּעַל
1Ch 8:33 Saul of . . Mal'chishu'a, Abin'adab, and Eshba'al; 1
9:39 Saul of Jonathan . . Abin'adab, and Eshba'al; 1

Eshban 1. אֶשְׁבָּן
Gen 36:26 sons of Dishon . . Eshban, Ithran, and Cheran. 1
1Ch 1:41 sons of Dishon: Hamran, Eshban, Ithran, and Cheran. 1

Eshcol 1. אֶשְׁכֹּל
Gen 14:13 the oaks of Mamre the Amorite, brother of Eshcol 1
24 let Aner, Eshcol, and Mamre take their share. 1
Num13:23 they came to the Valley of Eshcol, and cut down 1
24 That place was called the Valley of Eshcol 1
32: 9 For when they went up to the Valley of Eshcol 1
Deu 1:24 came to the Valley of Eshcol and spied it out. 1

Eshek 1. עֵשֶׁק
1Ch 8:39 The sons of Eshek his brother: Ulam his first-born 1

Eshtaol 1. אֶשְׁתָּאוֹל
Jos 15:33 And in the lowland, Eshta'ol, Zorah, Ashnah 1
19:41 included Zorah, Esh'ta-ol, Ir-she'mesh 1
Jdg 13:25 in Ma'haneh-dan, between Zorah and Esh'ta-ol. 1
16:31 and buried him between Zorah and Esh'ta-ol 1
18: 2 from the . . tribe, from Zorah and from Esh'ta-ol 1
8 they came to their brethren at Zorah and Esh'ta-ol 1
11 600 men . . set forth from Zorah and Esh'ta-ol 1

Eshtaolite 1. אֶשְׁתָּאֻלִי
1Ch 2:53 came the Zo'rathites and the Esh'taolites. 1

Eshtemoa 1. אֶשְׁתְּמוֹעַ
Jos 21:14 Jattir with . . Eshtemo'a with its pasture lands 1
1Sm 30:28 for those . . in Aro'er, in Siphmoth, in Eshtemo'a 1
1Ch 4:17 Ishbah, the father of Eshtemo'a. 1
19 Kei'lah the Garmite and Eshtemo'a the Ma-ac'athite. 1
6:57 of refuge . . Eshtemo'a with its pasture lands 1

Eshtemoh 1. אֶשְׁתְּמֹה
Jos 15:50 Anab, Esh'temoh, Anim 1

Eshton 1. אֶשְׁתּוֹן
1Ch 4:11 Mehir, who was the father of Eshton. 1
12 Eshton was the father of Bethra'pha, Pase'ah 1

Esli 1. Ἑσλί
Lke 3:25 the son of Nahum, the son of Esli, the son of Nag'gai 1

Esther 1. אֶסְתֵּר 2. Εσθηρ
Est 2: 7 He had brought up Hadas'sah, that is Esther 1
8 Esther also was taken into the king's palace 1
10 Esther had not made known her people or kindred 1
11 Mor'decai walked . . to learn how Esther was 1
15 the turn came for Esther . . to go in to the king 1
15 Esther found favor in the eyes of all who saw her. 1
16 And when Esther was taken to King Ahasu-e'rus 1
17 the king loved Esther more than all the women 1
18 gave a great banquet . . it was Esther's banquet. 1
20 Now Esther had not made known her kindred 1
20 Esther obeyed Mor'decai just as when she was 1
22 Mor'decai, and he told it to Queen Esther 1
22 and Esther told the king in the name of Mor'decai. 1
4: 4 Esther's maids and her eunuchs came and told her 1
5 Esther called for Hathach . . and ordered him 1
8 that he might show it to Esther and explain it 1
9 Hathach went and told Esther what Mor'decai had 1
10 Esther spoke to Hathach and gave him a message 1
12 And they told Mor'decai what Esther had said. 1
13 Mor'decai told them to return answer to Esther 1
15 Then Esther told them to reply to Mor'decai 1
17 went . . and did everything as Esther had ordered 1
5: 1 Esther put on her royal robes and stood 1
2 the king saw Queen Esther standing in the court 1
2 and he held out to Esther the golden scepter 1
2 Then Esther approached and touched the top 1
3 What is it, Queen Esther? What is your request? 1
4 And Esther said, "If it please the king, 1
5 Bring Haman . . that we may do as Esther desires. 1
5 came to the dinner that Esther had prepared. 1
6 the king said to Esther, "What is your petition? 1
7 But Esther said, "My petition and my request is 1
12 Even Queen Esther let no one come . . but myself. 1
6:14 to the banquet that Esther had prepared. 1
7: 1 and Haman went in to feast with Queen Esther. 1
2 king again said to Esther, "What is your petition 1
2 What is your petition, Queen Esther? 1
3 Then Queen Esther answered, "If I have found favor 1
5 King Ahasu-e'rus said to Queen Esther, "Who is he 1
6 Esther said, "A foe and enemy! This wicked Haman! 1
7 Haman stayed to beg his life from Queen Esther 1
8 Haman was falling on the couch where Esther was; 1
8: 1 King Ahasu-e'rus gave . . Esther the house of Haman 1
1 Mor'decai . . for Esther had told what he was to her; 1
2 And Esther set Mor'decai over the house of Haman. 1
3 Then Esther spoke again to the king; 1
4 the king held out the golden scepter to Esther 1
5 and Esther rose and stood before the king. 1
7 Ahasu-e'rus said to Queen Esther and to Mor'decai 1
7 Behold, I have given Esther the house of Haman 1
9:12 And the king said to Queen Esther, "In Susa 1
13 And Esther said, "If it please the king, let the Jews 1
25 when Esther came before the king, he gave orders •
29 Queen Esther, the daughter of Ab'ihail 1
31 as Mor'decai the Jew and Queen Esther enjoined 1
32 The command of Queen Esther fixed . . Purim 1
AEs 10: 6 the river is Esther 2
14: 1 Esther the queen, seized with deathly anxiety 2
15: 9 What is it, Esther? I am your brother. Take courage; 2
16:13 of Esther, the blameless partner of our kingdom 2

Etam 1. עֵיטָם
Jdg 15: 8 down and stayed in the cleft of the rock of Etam. 1
11 Judah went down to the cleft of the rock of Etam 1
1Ch 4: 3 the sons of Etam: Jezreel, Ishma, and Idbash; 1
32 villages were Etam, A'in, Rimmon, Tochen, 1
2Ch 11: 6 He built Bethlehem, Etam, Teko'a 1

Eth-kazin 1. עִתָּה קָצִין
Jos 19:13 it passes along . . to Gath-hepher, to Eth-kazin 1

Etham 1. אֵתָם
Exd 13:20 they moved on from Succoth, and encamped at Etham 1
Num33: 6 they set out from Succoth, and encamped at Etham 1
7 they set out from Etham, and turned back 1
8 went a three days' journey in the wilderness of Etham 1

Ethan 1. אֵיתָן
1Kg 4:31 wiser than Ethan the Ez'rahite, and Heman, Calcol 1
1Ch 2: 6 sons of Zerah: Zimri, Ethan, Heman, Calcol, and Dara 1
8 Ethan's son was Azari'ah. 1
6:42 son of Ethan, son of Zimmah, son of Shim'e-i 1
44 Ethan the son of Kishi, son of Abdi, son of Malluch 1
15:17 their brethren, Ethan the son of Kusha'iah 1
19 The singers, Heman, Asaph, and Ethan 1
Ps 89: 0 A Maskil of Ethan the Ezrahite. 1

Ethanim 1. אֵיתָנִים
1Kg 8: 2 feast in the month Eth'anim, which is the seventh 1

Ethanus 1. Ethanus
2Es 14:24 with you Sarea, Dabria, Selemia, Ethanus, and Asiel- 1

Ethbaal 1. אֶתְבַּעַל
1Kg 16:31 he took for wife Jez'ebel the daughter of Ethba'al 1

Ether 1. עֶתֶר
Jos 15:42 Libnah, Ether, Ashan 1
19: 7 En-rimmon, Ether, and Ashan 1

Ethiopia 1. כּוּשׁ 2. Αιθιοπια
2Kg 19: 9 heard concerning Tirha'kah king of Ethiopia 1
Est 1: 1 Ahasu-e'rus who reigned from India to Ethiopia 1
8: 9 princes of the provinces from India to Ethiopia 1
Job 28:19 The topaz of Ethiopia cannot compare with it 1
Ps 68:31 Ethiopia hasten to stretch out her hands to God. 1
87: 4 behold, Philistia and Tyre, with Ethiopia- 1
Isa 11:11 remnant . . from Ethiopia, from Elam, from Shinar 1
18: 1 whirring wings . . beyond the rivers of Ethiopia; 1
20: 3 as a sign and a portent against Egypt and Ethiopia 1
5 confounded because of Ethiopia their hope 1
37: 9 heard concerning Tirha'kah king of Ethiopia 1
43: 3 Ethiopia and Seba in exchange for you. 1
45:14 wealth of Egypt and the merchandise of Ethiopia 1
Jer 46: 9 Let the warriors go forth: men of Ethiopia and Put 1
Ezk 29:10 to Syene, as far as the border of Ethiopia. 1
30: 4 anguish shall be in Ethiopia 1
5 Ethiopia, and Put, and Lud, and all Arabia, and Libya 1
Nah 3: 9 Ethiopia was her strength, Egypt too 1
Zep 3:10 From beyond the rivers of Ethiopia 1
1Es 3: 2 the 127 satrapies from India to Ethiopia. 2
Jdt 1:10 as far as the borders of Ethiopia. 2
AEs 13: 1 the 127 provinces from India to Ethiopia 2
16: 1 rulers of the provinces from India to Ethiopia 2

Ethiopian 1. בֶּן כּוּשִׁי 2. כּוּשׁ 3. כּוּשִׁי 4. Αἰθίοψ
2Ch 12: 3 from Egypt-Libyans, Suk'ki-im, and Ethiopians. 3
14: 9 Zerah the Ethiopian came out against them 3
12 the LORD defeated the Ethiopians before Asa 3
12 and the Ethiopians fled. 3
13 the Ethiopians fell until none remained alive; 3
16: 8 the Ethiopians and the Libyans a huge army 3
21:16 of the Arabs who are near the Ethiopians; 3
Isa 20: 4 Egyptians captives and the Ethiopians exiles 2
Jer 13:23 Can the Ethiopian change his skin 3
38: 7 When E'bed-mel'ech the Ethiopian, a eunuch 3
10 the king commanded E'bed-mel'ech, the Ethiopian 3
12 Then E'bed-mel'ech the Ethiopian said to Jeremiah 3
39:16 Go, and say to E'bed-mel'ech the Ethiopian 3
Ezk 30: 9 from me to terrify the unsuspecting Ethiopians; 2
Dan 11:43 Libyans . . Ethiopians . . follow in his train. 3
Ams 9: 7 Are you not like the Ethiopians to me 1
Zep 2:12 You also, O Ethiopians, shall be slain by my sword. 3
Act 8:27 an Ethiopian, a eunuch, a minister of the Can'dace 4
27 the Can'dace, queen of the Ethiopians 4

Ethnan 1. אֶתְנָן
1Ch 4: 7 The sons of Helah: Zereth, Izhar, and Ethnan. 1

Ethni 1. אֶתְנִי
1Ch 6:41 son of Ethni, son of Zerah, son of Adai'ah 1

Eubulus 1. Εὔβουλος
2Ti 4:21 Eubu'lus sends greetings to you 1

Euergetes 1. Ευεργετης
Sir 0: 3 in the 38th year of the reign of Euergetes 1

Eumenes 1. Ευμενης
1Mc 8: 8 took from him and gave to Eumenes the king. 1

Eunice 1. Εὐνίκη
2Ti 1: 5 your grandmother Lo'is and your mother Eunice 1

Euodia 1. Εὐοδία
Php 4: 2 I entreat Eu-o'dia and I entreat Syn'tyche to agree 1

Eupator 1. Ευπατωρ
1Mc 6:17 he named him Eupator. 1
2Mc 2:20 Antiochus Epiphanes and his son Eupator 1
10:10 tell what took place under Antiochus Eupator 1
13 he was accused before Eupator by the king's friends 1
13: 1 Antiochus Eupator was coming with a great army 1

Euphrates 1. נָהָר 2. נְהַר פְּרָת 3. פְּרָת 4. Εὐφράτης
5. Eufrates
Gen 2:14 And the fourth river is the Euphra'tes. 3
15:18 of Egypt to the great river, the river Euphra'tes 3
31:21 and arose and crossed the Euphra'tes 1
36:37 Shaul of Reho'both on the Euphra'tes reigned 1
Exd 23:31 from the wilderness to the Euphra'tes; 1
Deu 1: 7 as far as the great river, the river Euphra'tes. 3
11:24 from the River, the river Euphra'tes 3
Jos 1: 4 as far as the great river, the river Euphra'tes 3
24: 2 Your fathers lived of old beyond the Euphra'tes 1
2Sm 8: 3 to restore his power at the river Euphra'tes. 3
10:16 the Syrians who were beyond the Euphra'tes; 1
1Kg 4:21 kingdoms from the Euphra'tes to the land 1
24 region west of the Euphra'tes from Tiphsah 1
24 over all the kings west of the Euphra'tes; 1
14:15 and scatter them beyond the Euphra'tes 1
2Kg 23:29 king of Egypt went up . . to the river Euphra'tes. 3
24: 7 from the Brook of Egypt to the river Euphra'tes. 3
1Ch 1:48 Sha'ul of Reho'both on the Euphra'tes reigned 1
5: 9 the desert this side of the Euphra'tes 2
18: 3 to set up his monument at the river Euphra'tes. 3
19:16 the Syrians who were beyond the Euphra'tes 1
2Ch 9:26 he ruled over all the kings from the Euphra'tes 1
35:20 to fight at Car'chemish on the Euphra'tes 3
Jer 2:18 to Assyria, to drink the waters of the Euphra'tes? 1
13: 4 and arise, go to the Euphra'tes, and hide it there 3
5 I went, and hid it by the Euphra'tes 3
6 the LORD said to me, "Arise, go to the Euphra'tes 3
7 Then I went to the Euphra'tes, and dug 3
46: 2 which was by the river Euphra'tes at Car'chemish 3
6 by the river Euphra'tes they have stumbled 3
10 in the north country by the river Euphra'tes. 3
51:63 and cast it into the midst of the Euphra'tes 3
Rev 9:14 angels . . bound at the great river Euphra'tes. 4

16:12 angel poured his bowl on the river Euphra'tes 4
1Es 1:25 went to make war at Carchemish on the Euphrates 4
27 my war is at the Euphrates 4
2Es 13:43 the narrow passages of the Euphrates river. 5
Jdt 1: 6 all those who lived along the Euphrates 4
2:24 Then he followed the Euphrates 4
Sir 24:26 full of understanding, like the Euphrates 4
1Mc 3:32 from the river Euphrates to the borders of Egypt. 4
37 He crossed the Euphrates river 4

river Euphrates 1. נָהָר
Isa 27:12 from the river Euphra'tes to the Brook of Egypt 1

Eupolemus 1. Ευπολεμος
1Mc 8:17 So Judas chose Eupolemus the son of John 1
2Mc 4:11 secured through John the father of Eupolemus 1

Eutychus 1. Εὔτυχος
Act 20: 9 Eu'tychus was sitting in the window 1

Eve 1. חַוָּה 2. Εὔα
Gen 3:20 The man called his wife's name Eve 1
4: 1 Adam knew Eve his wife, and she conceived 1
2Co 11: 3 as the serpent deceived Eve by his cunning 2
1Ti 2:13 For Adam was formed first, then Eve; 2
Tob 8: 6 gavest him Eve his wife as a helper and support. 2

Evi 1. אֱוִי
Num31: 8 Evi, Rekem, Zur, Hur, and Reba, the five kings 1
Jos 13:21 leaders . . Evi and Rekem and Zur and Hur and Reba 1

Evil-merodach 1. אֱוִיל מְרֹדַךְ
2Kg 25:27 Evil-mero'dach . . graciously freed Jehoi'achin 1
Jer 52:31 E'vil-mer'odach king of Babylon 1

Ezbai 1. אֶזְבָּי
1Ch 11:37 Hezro of Carmel, Na'arai the son of Ezbai 1

Ezbon 1. אֶצְבּוֹן
Gen 46:16 sons of Gad: Ziph'ion, Haggi, Shuni, Ezbon, Eri 1
1Ch 7: 7 sons of Bela: Ezbon, Uzzi, Uz'ziel, Jer'imoth, and Iri 1

Ezekiel 1. יְחֶזְקֵאל 2. Ιεζεκιηλ
Ezk 1: 3 the word of the LORD came to Ezekiel the priest 1
24:24 Thus shall Ezekiel be to you a sign; 1
Sir 49: 8 It was Ezekiel who saw the vision of glory 2
4Mc 18:17 He confirmed the saying of Ezekiel 2

Ezem 1. עֶצֶם
Jos 15:29 Ba'alah, I'im, Ezem 1
19: 3 Hazar-shu'al, Balah, Ezem 1
1Ch 4:29 Bilhah, Ezem, Tolad 1

Ezer 1. אֵצֶר 2. עֵזֶר 3. עֶזֶר
Gen 36:21 Dishon, Ezer, and Dishan; these are the chiefs 1
27 These are the sons of Ezer: Bilhan, Za'avan 1
30 Dishon, Ezer, and Dishan; these are the chiefs 1
1Ch 1:38 sons of Se'ir . . Dishon, Ezer, and Dishan. 1
42 The sons of Ezer: Bilhan, Za'avan, and Ja'akan. 1
4: 4 and Ezer the father of Hushah. 2
7:21 Ezer and E'le-ad, whom the men of Gath . . slew 3
12: 9 Ezer the chief, Obadi'ah second, Eli'ab third 2
Neh 3:19 next to him Ezer the son of Jeshua, ruler of Mizpah 2
12:42 Jehoha'nan, Malchi'jah, Elam, and Ezer. 3

Ezion-geber 1. עֶצְיוֹן גֶּבֶר
Num33:35 from Abro'nah, and encamped at E'zion-ge'ber. 1
36 they set out from E'zion-ge'ber, and encamped 1
Deu 2: 8 from the Arabah road from Elath and E'zi-on-ge'ber. 1
1Kg 9:26 Solomon built a fleet of ships at E'zion-ge'ber 1
22:48 the ships were wrecked at E'zion-ge'ber. 1
2Ch 8:17 went to E'zion-ge'ber and Eloth on . . the sea 1
20:36 they built the ships in E'zion-ge'-ber. 1

Ezora 1. Εζωρα
1Es 9:34 Of the sons of Ezora: Shashai, Azarel, Azael 1

Ezra 1. עֶזְרָא 2. עֶזְרָא (A) 3. Εζωρα 4. Ezra
Ezr 7: 1 Ezra the son of Serai'ah, son of Azari'ah 1
6 this Ezra went up from Babylonia. He was a scribe 1
10 Ezra had set his heart to study the law of the LORD 1
11 letter . . Ar-ta-xerx'es gave to Ezra the priest 1
12 Ar-ta-xerx'es, king of kings, to Ezra the priest 2
21 Whatever Ezra the priest . . requires of you 2
25 you, Ezra, according to the wisdom of your God 2
10: 1 While Ezra prayed and made confesssion 1
2 Shecani'ah . . addressed Ezra: "We have broken 1
5 Then Ezra arose and made the leading priests 1
6 Then Ezra withdrew from before the house of God 1
10 Ezra the priest stood up and said to them, 1
16 Ezra the priest selected men, heads of fathers' 1
Neh 8: 1 told Ezra the scribe to bring the book of the law 1
2 Ezra the priest brought the law before 1
4 Ezra the scribe stood on a wooden pulpit 1
5 Ezra opened the book in the sight of all 1
6 Ezra blessed the Lord, the great God; 1
9 Nehemi'ah . . and Ezra the priest and scribe 1
13 came . . to Ezra the scribe in order to study 1
9: 6 Ezra said: "Thou art the LORD, thou alone; •
12: 1 priests and the Levites . . Serai'ah, Jeremiah, Ezra 1
13 of Ezra, Meshul'lam; of Amari'ah, Jehoha'nan; 1
26 days of Nehemi'ah . . of Ezra the priest the scribe. 1
33 Azari'ah, Ezra, Meshul'lam 1
36 Ezra the scribe went before them. 1
1Es 8: 1 Ezra came, the son of Seraiah, son of Azariah 3
92 Then Shecaniah . . called out, and said to Ezra 3
2Es 1: 1 The second book of the prophet Ezra 4
2:10 Thus says the Lord to Ezra: "Tell my people 4
33 I, Ezra, received a command from the Lord 4
42 I, Ezra, saw on Mount Zion a great multitude 4
3: 1 I Salathiel, who am also called Ezra 4
6:10 seek for nothing else, Ezra! 4
7: 2 he said to me, "Rise, Ezra, and listen to the words 4
25 Therefore, Ezra, empty things are for the empty 4
49 He answered me and said, "Listen to me, Ezra ‡
8: 2 I tell you a parable, Ezra 4
19 The beginning of the words of Ezra's prayer 4
14: 1 a voice . . said, "Ezra, Ezra. 4
1 a voice . . said, "Ezra, Ezra. 4
38 Ezra, open your mouth and drink what I give you 4

Ezrah 1. עֶזְרָה
1Ch 4:17 The sons of Ezrah: Jether, Mered, Epher, and Jalon. 1

Ezrahite 1. אֶזְרָחִי
1Kg 4:31 wiser than Ethan the Ez'rahite, and Heman, Calcol 1
Ps 88: 0 Maskil of Heman the Ezrahite. 1
89: 0 A Maskil of Ethan the Ezrahite. 1

Ezri 1. עֶזְרִי
1Ch 27:26 over those . . for tilling the soil was Ezri 1

Fair Havens 1. καλοὺς λιμένας
Act 27: 8 we came to a place called Fair Havens 1

Felix 1. Φῆλιξ
Act 23:24 and bring him safely to Felix the governor. 1
26 to his Excellency the governor Felix, greeting. 1
24: 2 by your provision, most excellent Felix 1
22 Felix . . put them off, saying 1
24 Felix came with his wife Drusil'la 1
25 Felix was alarmed and said 1
27 Felix was succeeded by Porcius Festus; 1
27 Felix left Paul in prison. 1
25:14 There is a man left prisoner by Felix; 1

Festus 1. Φῆστος
Act 24:27 Felix was succeeded by Porcius Festus; 1
25: 1 Now when Festus had come into his province 1
4 Festus replied that Paul was being kept 1
9 Festus, wishing to do the Jews a favor, said to Paul 1
12 Then Festus . . answered 1
13 Agrippa . . arrived at Caesare'a to welcome Festus. 1
14 Festus laid Paul's case before the king, saying 1
22 Agrippa said to Festus, "I should like to hear 1
23 Then by command of Festus Paul was brought in. 1
24 Festus said, "King Agrippa 1
26:24 Festus said with a loud voice, "Paul, you are mad 1
25 Paul said, "I am not mad, most excellent Festus 1
32 Agrippa said to Festus 1

Fish Gate 1. שַׁעַר הַדָּגִים
Neh 3: 3 sons of Hassena'ah built the Fish Gate; 1
12:39 by the Old Gate, and by the Fish Gate and the Tower 1

Fortunatus 1. Φορτουνᾶτος
1Co 16:17 at the coming of Steph'anas and Fortuna'tus 1

Fountain Gate 1. שַׁעַר הָעַיִן
Neh 2:14 went on to the Fountain Gate and to the King's Pool; 1
3:15 Shallum . . repaired the Fountain Gate; 1
12:37 At the Fountain Gate they went up straight 1

Friend of Strangers 1. ξένιος
2Mc 6: 2 the temple of Zeus the Friend of Strangers 1
2 the temple of Zeus the Friend of Strangers 1

Fuller's Field 1. שְׂדֵה כוֹבֵס
2Kg 18:17 which is on the highway to the Fuller's Field. 1
Isa 7: 3 upper pool on the highway to the Fuller's Field 1
36: 2 upper pool on the highway to the Fuller's Field. 1

Gaal 1. גַּעַל
Jdg 9:26 Ga'al the son of Ebed moved into Shechem 1
28 Ga'al the son of Ebed said, "Who is Abim'elech 1
30 Zebul . . heard the words of Ga'al the son of Ebed 1
31 Ga'al the son of Ebed and his kinsmen have come 1
35 Ga'al the son of Ebed went out and stood 1
36 when Ga'al saw the men, he said to Zebul, "Look, 1
37 Ga'al spoke again and said, "Look, men are coming 1
39 Ga'al went out at the head of the men of Shechem 1
41 Zebul drove out Ga'al and his kinsmen 1

Gaash 1. גַּעַשׁ
Jos 24:30 Tim'nath-se'rah . . north of the mountain of Ga'ash. 1
Jdg 2: 9 of E'phraim, north of the mountain of Ga'ash. 1
2Sm 23:30 Benai'ah of . . Hid'dai of the brooks of Ga'ash 1
1Ch 11:32 Hurai of the brooks of Ga'ash 1

Gabael 1. Γαβαηλ 2. Γαβάηλος
Tob 1: 1 son of Ananiel, son of Aduel, son of Gabael 1
14 I left ten talents of silver in trust with Gabael 2
4: 1 left in trust with Gabael at Rages in Media 1
20 Gabael the son of Gabrias at Rages in Media. 2
5: 6 I have stayed with our brother Gabael. 1
9: 2 go to Gabael at Rages in Media and get the money 1
5 Raphael . . stayed over night with Gabael 2
5 Gabael brought out the money bags •
6 Gabael blessed Tobias and his wife. •
10: 2 is it possible that Gabael has died 1

Gabatha 1. Γαβαθα
AEs 12: 1 took his rest . . with Gabatha and Tharra 1

Gabbai 1. גַּבַּי
Neh 11: 8 after him Gabba'i, Salla'i, 928. 1

Gabbatha 1. Γαββαθᾶ
Joh 19:13 and in Hebrew, Gab'batha. 1

Gabrias 1. Γαβριας
Tob 1:14 Gabael, the brother of Gabrias. 1
4:20 Gabael the son of Gabrias at Rages in Media. 1

Gabriel 1. גַּבְרִיאֵל 2. Γαβριήλ
Dan 8:16 Gabriel, make this man understand the vision. 1
9:21 man Gabriel, whom I had seen in the vision 1
Lke 1:19 I am Gabriel, who stand in the presence of God 2
26 the angel Gabriel was sent from God 2

Gad 1. גָּד 2. גָּדִי 3. Γάδ
Gen 30:11 Good fortune!" so she called his name Gad. 1
35:26 The sons of Zilpah, Leah's maid: Gad and Asher. 1
46:16 sons of Gad: Ziph'ion, Haggi, Shuni, Ezbon, Eri 1
49:19 Raiders shall raid Gad 1
Exd 1: 4 Dan and Naph'tali, Gad and Asher. 1
Num 1:14 from Gad, Eli'asaph the son of Deu'el; 1
24 Of the people of Gad, their generations 1
25 the number of the tribe of Gad was 45,650 1
2:14 Then the tribe of Gad, the leader of the people 1
14 leader of the people of Gad being Eli'asaph 1
7:42 Eli'asaph the . . leader of the men of Gad 1
10:20 over the host of the tribe of the men of Gad 1
13:15 from the tribe of Gad, Geu'el the son of Machi. 1
26:15 The sons of Gad according to their families 1
18 These are the families of the sons of Gad 1
32: 1 sons of Gad had a very great multitude of cattle; 1
2 sons of Gad and the sons of Reuben came and said 1
6 Moses said to the sons of Gad and . . of Reuben 1
25 sons of Gad and the sons of Reuben said to Moses 1
29 If the sons of Gad and the sons of Reuben 1
31 sons of Gad and the sons of Reuben answered, "As 1
33 Moses gave to them, to the sons of Gad 1
34 the sons of Gad built Dibon, At'aroth, Aro'er 1
34:14 tribe of the sons of Gad by their fathers' houses 2
Deu 27:13 stand upon Mount Ebal . . Reuben, Gad, Asher 1
33:20 of Gad he said, "Blessed be he who enlarges Gad! 1
20 of Gad he said, "Blessed be he who enlarges Gad! 1
20 Gad couches like a lion, he tears the arm •
Jos 4:12 The sons of Reuben and the sons of Gad 1
18: 7 and Gad and Reuben and half the tribe of Manas'seh 1
20: 8 and Ramoth in Gilead, from the tribe of Gad 1
21: 7 Reuben, the tribe of Gad, and the tribe of Zeb'ulun 1
38 and out of the tribe of Gad, Ramoth in Gilead 1
1Sm 13: 7 crossed . . Jordan to the land of Gad and Gilead. 1
22: 5 Then the prophet Gad said to David, "Do not remain 1
2Sm 24: 5 began from Aro'er . . toward Gad and on to Jazer. 1
11 the word of the LORD came to the prophet Gad 1
13 Gad came to David and told him, and said to him 1
14 Then David said to Gad, "I am in great distress 1
18 Gad came that day to David, and said to him, "Go up 1
19 David went up at Gad's word, as . . commanded. 1
1Ch 2: 2 Dan, Joseph, Benjamin, Naph'tali, Gad, and Asher. 1
5:11 The sons of Gad dwelt . . in the land of Bashan 1
6:63 out of the tribes of Reuben, Gad, and Zeb'ulun. 1
80 out of the tribe of Gad: Ramoth in Gilead 1
21: 9 the LORD spoke to Gad, David's seer, saying 1
11 Gad came to David and said . . "Thus says the LORD 1
13 Then David said to Gad, "I am in great distress; 1
18 angel of the LORD commanded Gad to say to David 1
19 David went up at Gad's word, which he had spoken 1
29:29 and in the Chronicles of Gad the seer 1
2Ch 29:25 commandment of David and of Gad the king's seer 1
Jer 49: 1 Why then has Milcom dispossessed Gad 1
Ezk 48:27 from the east side to the west, Gad, one portion. 1
28 And adjoining the territory of Gad to the south 1
34 three gates, the gate of Gad, the gate of Asher 1
Rev 7: 5 12,000 of the tribe of Gad 3

Gadarene 1. Γαδαρηνός
Mat 8:28 to the country of the Gadarenes 1

Gaddi 1. גַּדִּי 2. Γαδδι
Num13:11 from the tribe of Joseph . . Gaddi the son of Susi; 1
1Mc 2: 2 He had five sons, John surnamed Gaddi 2

Gaddiel 1. גַּדִּיאֵל
Num13:10 from the tribe of Zeb'ulun, Gad'diel the son of Sodi; 1

Gadi 1. גָּדִי
2Kg 15:14 Then Men'ahem the son of Gadi came up from Tirzah 1
17 Men'ahem the son of Gadi began to reign 1

Gadite 1. בֶּן גָּד 2. גָּד 3. גָּדִי
Deu 3:12 I gave to the Reubenites and the Gadites 3
16 to the Reubenites and the Gadites I gave 3
4:43 Reubenites, and Ramoth in Gilead for the Gadites 3
29: 8 gave it for an inheritance to . . the Gadites 3
Jos 1:12 to the Reubenites, the Gadites, and the half-tribe 3
12: 6 gave . . to the Reubenites and the Gadites 3
13: 8 the Reubenites and the Gadites received their 3
24 Moses gave . . also to the tribe of the Gadites 1
28 This is the inheritance of the Gadites 1
22: 1 Joshua summoned the Reubenites, and the Gadites 3
9 the Reubenites and the Gadites . . returned home 1
10 the Reubenites and the Gadites . . built 1
11 the Reubenites and the Gadites . . have built 1
13 Israel sent to the Reubenites and the Gadites 1
15 And they came to the Reubenites, the Gadites 1
21 the Reubenites, the Gadites . . said in answer 1
25 between us and you, you Reubenites and Gadites; 1
30 the Reubenites and the Gadites 1
31 said to the Reubenites and the Gadites 1
32 returned from the Reubenites and the Gadites 1
33 the land where the Reubenites and the Gadites 1
34 The Reubenites and the Gadites called the altar 1
2Sm 23:36 Igal the son of Nathan of Zobah, Bani the Gadite 3
2Kg 10:33 land of Gilead, the Gadites, and the Reubenites 3
1Ch 5:18 the Gadites . . had valiant men 3
26 carried them away, namely . . the Gadites 3
12: 8 From the Gadites there went over to David 3
14 These Gadites were officers of the army 2
37 Of the Reubenites and Gadites and the half-tribe 3
26:32 the Gadites, and the half-tribe of the Manas'sites 1

Gaham 1. גַּחַם
Gen 22:24 whose name was Reumah, bore Tebah, Gaham, 1

Gahar 1. גַּחַר 2. Γεδδουρ
Ezr 2:47 sons of Giddel, the sons of Gahar 1
Neh 7:49 sons of Hanan, the sons of Giddel, the sons of Gahar 1
1Es 5:30 sons of Hana, the sons of Cathua, the sons of Gahar 2

Gaius 1. Γάϊος
Act 19:29 dragging with them Ga'ius and Aristar'chus 1
20: 4 and Ga'ius of Derbe, and Timothy 1
Rom16:23 Ga'ius, who is host to me and to the whole church 1
1Co 1:14 baptized none of you except Crispus and Ga'ius; 1
3Jn 1: 1 The elder to the beloved Ga'ius, whom I love 1

Galal 1. גָּלָל
1Ch 9:15 Bakbak'kar, Heresh, Galal, and Mattani'ah 1
16 Shemai'ah, son of Galal, son of Jedu'thun 1
Neh 11:17 son of Sham'mua, son of Galal, son of Jedu'thun. 1

Galatia 1. Γαλατία 2. Γαλατικός
Act 16: 6 they went through the region of Phry'gia and Galatia 2
18:23 the region of Galatia and Phryg'ia 2
1Co 16: 1 as I directed the churches of Galatia 1
Gal 1: 2 To the churches of Galatia 1
2Ti 4:10 Crescens has gone to Galatia, Titus to Dalmatia. 1
1Pe 1: 1 the Dispersion in Pontus, Galatia, Cappado'cia 1

Galatian 1. Γαλαται 2. Γαλάτης
Gal 3: 1 O foolish Galatians! Who has bewitched you 2
2Mc 8:20 the time of the battle with the Galatians 1

Galeed 1. גַּלְעֵד
Gen 31:47 Je'gar-sahadu'tha: but Jacob called it Galeed. 1
48 Therefore he named it Galeed 1

Galilean 1. Γαλιλαῖος
Mat 26:69 You also were with Jesus the Galilean. 1
Mrk 14:70 you are one of them; for you are a Galilean. 1
Lke 13: 1 the Galileans whose blood Pilate had mingled 1
2 you think that these Galileans were worse 1
2 worse sinners than all the other Galileans 1
22:59 he is a Galilean. 1
23: 6 he asked whether the man was a Galilean. 1
Joh 4:45 he came to Galilee, the Galileans welcomed him 1
Act 2: 7 Are not all these who are speaking Galileans? 1
5:37 Judas the Galilean arose 1

Galilee 1. הַגָּלִיל 2. Γαλιλαία 3. Γαλιλαῖος
Jos 12:23 king of Dor . . one; the king of Goi'im in Galilee, one; 2
20: 7 set apart Kedesh in Galilee in the hill country 1
21:32 Kedesh in Galilee with its pasture lands 1
1Kg 9:11 gave to Hiram . . cities in the land of Galilee. 1
2Kg 15:29 Kedesh, Hazor, Gilead, and Galilee, all . . Naph'tali; 1
1Ch 6:76 Kedesh in Galilee with its pasture lands 1
Isa 9: 1 land beyond the Jordan, Galilee of the nations. 1
Mat 2:22 he withdrew to the district of Galilee. 2
3:13 Jesus came from Galilee to the Jordan to John 2
4:12 had been arrested, he withdrew into Galilee; 2
15 sea, across the Jordan, Galilee of the Gentiles- 2
18 As he walked by the Sea of Galilee, he saw two 2
23 And he went about all Galilee teaching 2
25 And great crowds followed him from Galilee 2
15:29 and passed along the Sea of Galilee 2
17:22 As they were gathering in Galilee 2
19: 1 he went away from Galilee and entered 2
21:11 the prophet Jesus from Nazareth of Galilee. 2
26:32 I will go before you to Galilee. 2
27:55 who had followed Jesus from Galilee 2
28: 7 behold, he is going before you to Galilee 2
10 go and tell my brethren to go to Galilee 2
16 Now the eleven disciples went to Galilee 2
Mrk 1: 9 In those days Jesus came from Nazareth of Galilee 2
14 after John was arrested Jesus came into Galilee 2
16 And passing along by the Sea of Galilee 2
28 all the surrounding region of Galilee. 2
39 he went throughout all Galilee 2
3: 7 a great multitude from Galilee followed 2
6:21 and the leading men of Galilee. 2
7:31 went through Sidon to the Sea of Galilee 2
9:30 They went on . . and passed through Galilee 2
14:28 I will go before you to Galilee. 2
15:41 who, when he was in Galilee, followed him 2
16: 7 he is going before you to Galilee; 2
Lke 1:26 to a city of Galilee named Nazareth 2
2: 4 Joseph also went up from Galilee 2
39 they returned into Galilee, to their own city 2
3: 1 Herod being tetrarch of Galilee 2
4:14 Jesus returned . . into Galilee 2
31 he went down to Caper'na-um, a city of Galilee. 2
5:17 had come from every village of Galilee and Judea 2
8:26 which is opposite Galilee. 2
17:11 passing along between Sama'ria and Galilee. 2
23: 5 from Galilee even to this place. 2
49 the women who had followed him from Galilee 2
55 The women who had come with him from Galilee 2
24: 6 while he was still in Galilee 2
Joh 1:43 The next day Jesus decided to go to Galilee. 2
2: 1 there was a marriage at Cana in Galilee 2
11 first of his signs, Jesus did at Cana in Galilee 2
4: 3 he left Judea and departed again to Galilee. 2
43 After the two days he departed to Galilee. 2
45 he came to Galilee, the Galileans welcomed him 2
46 So he came again to Cana in Galilee 2
47 heard that Jesus had come from Judea to Galilee 2
54 when he had come from Judea to Galilee. 2
6: 1 Jesus went to the other side of the Sea of Galilee 2
7: 1 After this Jesus went about in Galilee 2
9 So saying, he remained in Galilee. 2
41 But some said, "Is the Christ to come from Galilee? 2
52 They replied, "Are you from Galilee too? 2
52 no prophet is to rise from Galilee. 2
12:21 was from Beth-sa'ida in Galilee 2
21: 2 Nathan'a-el of Cana in Galilee, the sons of Zeb'edee 2
Act 1:11 said, "Men of Galilee, why do you stand looking 3
9:31 the church throughout all Judea and Galilee 2
10:37 beginning from Galilee 2
13:31 came up with him from Galilee to Jerusalem 2
Tob 1: 2 in Galilee above Asher. 2
Jdt 1: 8 Upper Galilee and the great Plain of Esdraelon 2
15: 5 those in Gilead and in Galilee outflanked them 2
1Mc 5:14 behold, other messengers . . came from Galilee 2
15 all Galilee of the Gentiles 2
17 go and rescue your brethren in Galilee 2
20 assigned to Simon to go to Galilee 2
21 so Simon went to Galilee 2
23 Then he took the Jews of Galilee and Arbatta 2
55 Simon . . was in Galilee before Ptolemais 2
10:30 from Samaria and Galilee 2
11:63 had come to Kadesh in Galilee with a large army 2
12:47 2,000 of whom he left in Galilee 2
49 Trypho sent troops and cavalry into Galilee 2

Gallim 1. גַּלִּים
1Sm 25:44 Palti the son of La'ish, who was of Gallim. 1
Isa 10:30 Cry aloud, O daughter of Gallim! 1

Gallio 1. Γαλλίων
Act 18:12 when Gallio was proconsul of Acha'ia 1
14 Gallio said to the Jews 1
17 But Gallio paid no attention to this. 1

man of Gamad 1. גַּמָּדִים
Ezk 27:11 men of Gamad were in your towers; 1

Gamael 1. Γαμηλος
1Es 8:29 Of the sons of Ithamar, Gamael 1

Gamaliel 1. גַּמְלִיאֵל 2. Γαμαλιήλ
Num 1:10 from Manas'seh, Gama'liel the son of Pedah'zur; 1
2:20 the leader . . Gama'liel the son of Pedah'zur 1
7:54 Gama'liel the . . leader of the men of Manas'seh 1
59 offering of Gama'liel the son of Pedah'zur. 1
10:23 Gama'liel the son of Pedah'zur. 1
Act 5:34 a Pharisee in the council named Gama'li-el 2
22: 3 but brought up in this city at the feet of Gama'li-el 2

Gamul 1. גָּמוּל
1Ch 24:17 the 21st to Jachin, the 22nd to Gamul 1

Gareb 1. גָּרֵב
2Sm 23:38 Ira the Ithrite, Gareb the Ithrite 1
1Ch 11:40 Ira the Ithrite, Gareb the Ithrite 1
Jer 31:39 shall go out farther, straight to the hill Gareb 1

Garmite 1. גַּרְמִי
1Ch 4:19 Kei'lah the Garmite and Eshtemo'a the Ma-ac'athite. 1

Gas 1. Γας
1Es 5:34 the sons of Gas, the sons of Addus, the sons of Subas 1

Gatam 1. גַּעְתָּם
Gen 36:11 were Teman, Omar, Zepho, Gatam, and Kenaz. 1
16 Korah, Gatam, and Am'alek; these are the chiefs 1
1Ch 1:36 The sons of Eli'phaz: Teman, Omar, Zephi, Gatam 1

Gath 1. גַּת 2. גִּתִּי 3. Γεθ
Jos 11:22 in Gaza, in Gath, and in Ashdod, did some remain. 1
13: 3 those of Gaza, Ashdod, Ash'kelon, Gath, and Ekron 2
1Sm 5: 8 Let the ark . . be brought around to Gath. 1
6:17 Ashdod, one for Gaza, one for Ash'kelon, one for Gath 1
7:14 were restored to Israel, from Ekron to Gath; 1
17: 4 there came . . a champion named Goliath, of Gath 1
23 the Philistine of Gath, Goliath by name, came up 1
52 pursued . . as far as Gath and the gates of Ekron 3
52 on the way from Sha-ara'im as far as Gath and Ekron. 1
21:10 David rose . . and went to A'chish the king of Gath. 1
12 and was much afraid of A'chish the king of Gath. 1
27: 2 went . . to A'chish the son of Ma'och, king of Gath. 1
3 David dwelt with A'chish at Gath, he and his men 1
4 when it was told Saul that David had fled to Gath 1
11 neither man nor woman . . to bring tidings to Gath 1
2Sm 1:20 Tell it not in Gath, publish it not in . . Ash'kelon; 1
15:18 the . . Gittites who had followed him from Gath 1
21:20 And there was again war at Gath 1
22 These . . were descended from the giants in Gath; 1
1Kg 2:39 ran away to Achish, son of Ma'acah, king of Gath. 1
39 it was told Shim'e-i, "Behold, your slaves are in Gath 1
40 Shim'e-i arose . . and went to Gath to Achish 1
40 Shim'e-i went and brought his slaves from Gath. 1
41 Shim'e-i had gone from Jerusalem to Gath 1
2Kg 12:17 Haz'ael . . went up and fought against Gath 1
1Ch 7:21 the men of Gath who were born in the land slew 1
8:13 who put to flight the inhabitants of Gath 1
18: 1 he took Gath and its villages out of the hand 1
20: 6 there was again war at Gath 1
8 These were descended from the giants in Gath; 1
2Ch 11: 8 Gath, Mare'shah, Ziph 1
26: 6 broke down the wall of Gath and the wall of Jabneh 1
Ps 56: 0 David, when the Philistines seized him in Gath. 1
Ams 6: 2 then go down to Gath of the Philistines. 1
Mic 1:10 Tell it not in Gath, weep not at all; 1

Gath-hepher 1. גַּת חֵפֶר
Jos 19:13 it passes along . . to Gath-hepher, to Eth-kazin 1
2Kg 14:25 Jonah . . the prophet, who was from Gath-he'pher. 1

Gath-rimmon 1. גַּת רִמּוֹן
Jos 19:45 Jehud, Bene-be'rak, Gath-rim'mon 1
21:24 Gath-rim'mon with its pasture lands 1
25 and Gath-rim'mon with its pasture lands 1
1Ch 6:69 Gath-rim'mon with its pasture lands 1

Gaul 1. Γαλαται
1Mc 8: 2 brave deeds which they were doing among the Gauls 1

Gaza 1. עַזָּה 2. Γάζα
Gen 10:19 in the direction of Gerar, as far as Gaza 1
Deu 2:23 for the Avvim, who lived in villages as far as Gaza 1
Jos 10:41 Joshua defeated them from Ka'desh-bar'nea to Gaza 1
11:22 only in Gaza, in Gath, and in Ashdod, did some remain 1
13: 3 there are five . . those of Gaza, Ashdod, Ash'kelon 1
15:47 Gaza, its towns and its villages; 1
Jdg 1:18 Judah also took Gaza with its territory 1
6: 4 of the land, as far as the neighborhood of Gaza 1
16: 1 Samson went to Gaza, and there he saw a harlot 1
21 seized him . . and brought him down to Gaza 1
1Sm 6:17 the golden tumors . . one for Ashdod, one for Gaza 1
1Kg 4:24 west of the Euphra'tes from Tiphsah to Gaza, over 1
2Kg 18: 8 the Philistines as far as Gaza and its territory 1
Jer 25:20 the Philistines (Ash'kelon, Gaza, Ekron 1
47: 1 the Philistines, before Pharaoh smote Gaza. 1
5 Baldness has come upon Gaza 1
Ams 1: 6 For three transgressions of Gaza, and for four 1
7 I will send a fire upon the wall of Gaza 1
Zep 2: 4 For Gaza shall be deserted 1
Zec 9: 5 be afraid; Gaza too, and shall writhe in anguish; 1
5 The king shall perish from Gaza; 1
Act 8:26 the road that goes down from Jerusalem to Gaza. 2
1Mc 11:61 From there he departed to Gaza 2
61 the men of Gaza shut him out 2
62 Then the people of Gaza pleaded with Jonathan 2

Gazara 1. Γαζαρα 2. Γαζηρα 3. Γαζηρων
1Mc 4:15 They pursued them to Gazara 3

7:45 from Adasa as far as Gazara 2
9:52 He also fortified the city of Beth-zur, and Gazara 1
13:43 In those days Simon encamped against Gazara 1
53 he dwelt in Gazara. 1
14: 7 he ruled over Gazara and Beth-zur and the citadel 1
34 Gazara, which is on the borders of Azotus 1
15:28 You hold control of Joppa and Gazara 1
35 As for Joppa and Gazara, which you demand 1
16: 1 John went up from Gazara and reported to Simon 1
19 He sent other men to Gazara to do away with John 1
21 some one ran ahead and reported to John at Gazara 1
2Mc 10:32 Timothy . . fled to a stronghold called Gazara 1

Gazez 1. גָּזֵז

1Ch 2:46 Ephah . . bore Haran, Moza, and Gazez; 1
46 and Haran was the father of Gazez. 1

Gazite 1. עַזָּתִי

Jdg 16: 2 The Gazites were told, "Samson has come here 1

Gazzam 1. גַּזָּם 2. Γαζηρα

Ezr 2:48 the sons of Neko'da, the sons of Gazzam 1
Neh 7:51 sons of Gazzam, the sons of Uzza, the sons of Pase'ah 1
1Es 5:31 sons of Chezib, the sons of Gazzam, the sons of Uzza 2

Ge-harashim 1. גֵּיא חֲרָשִׁים

1Ch 4:14 Ge-har'ashim . . because they were craftsmen. 1

Geba 1. גֶּבַע 2. Γαββης 3. Γαιβαι

Jos 18:24 Che'phar-am'moni, Ophni, Geba 1
21:17 Gibeon with its . . Geba with its pasture lands 1
Jdg 20:33 in ambush rushed out of their place west of Geba. 1
1Sm 13: 3 Jonathan defeated the garrison . . at Geba; 1
16 Saul, and Jonathan . . stayed in Geba of Benjamin; 1
14: 5 and the other on the south in front of Geba. 1
2Sm 5:25 and smote the Philistines from Geba to Gezer. 1
1Kg 15:22 King Asa built Geba of Benjamin and Mizpah. 1
2Kg 23: 8 the high places . . from Geba to Beer-sheba; 1
1Ch 6:60 Geba with its pasture lands, Al'emeth 1
8: 6 of fathers' houses of the inhabitants of Geba 1
2Ch 16: 6 with them he built Geba and Mizpah. 1
Ezr 2:26 sons of Ramah and Geba, 621. 1
Neh 7:30 men of Ramah and Geba, 621. 1
11:31 people of Benjamin also lived from Geba onward 1
12:29 from the region of Geba and Az'maveth; 1
Isa 10:29 at Geba they lodge for the night; Ramah trembles 1
Zec 14:10 a plain from Geba to Rimmon south of Jerusalem. 1
1Es 5:20 The men of Ramah and Geba, 621. 2
Jdt 3:10 here he camped between Geba and Scythopolis 3

Gebal 1. גְּבָל 2. גְּבַל

Ps 83: 7 Gebal and Ammon and Am'alek 2
Ezk 27: 9 elders of Gebal and her skilled men were in you 1

man of Gebal 1. גִּבְלִי

1Kg 5:18 builders and the men of Gebal did the hewing 1

Gebalite 1. גִּבְלִי

Jos 13: 5 the land of the Geb'alites, and all Lebanon 1

Geber 1. גֶּבֶר

1Kg 4:19 Geber the son of Uri, in the land of Gilead 1

Gebim 1. גֵּבִים

Isa 10:31 the inhabitants of Gebim flee for safety. 1

Gedaliah 1. גְּדַלְיָהוּ 2. Ωκιδηλος

2Kg 25:22 he appointed Gedali'ah the son of . . governor. 1
23 the king . . had appointed Gedali'ah governor 1
23 they came with their men to Gedali'ah at Mizpah 1
24 Gedali'ah swore to them and their men, saying 1
25 attacked and killed Gedali'ah and the Jews 1
1Ch 25: 3 sons of Jedu'thun: Gedali'ah, Zeri, Jeshai'ah, 1
9 second to Gedali'ah, to him and his brethren 1
Ezr 10:18 found Ma-asei'ah, Elie'zer, Jarib, and Gedali'ah 1
Jer 38: 1 Gedali'ah the son of Pashhur 1
39:14 They entrusted him to Gedali'ah the son of Ahi'kam 1
40: 5 then return to Gedali'ah the son of Ahi'kam 1
6 Then Jeremiah went to Gedali'ah the son of Ahi'kam 1
7 had appointed Gedali'ah the son of Ahi'kam 1
8 they went to Gedali'ah at Mizpah 1
9 Gedali'ah the son of Ahi'kam, son of Shaphan, swore 1
11 and had appointed Gedali'ah the son of Ahi'kam 1
12 came to the land of Judah, to Gedali'ah at Mizpah; 1
13 the leaders . . came to Gedali'ah at Mizpah 1
14 But Gedali'ah the son of Ahi'kam would not believe 1
15 Joha'nan . . spoke secretly to Gedali'ah at Mizpah 1
16 But Gedali'ah the son of Ahi'kam said to Joha'nan 1
41: 1 came . . to Gedali'ah the son of Ahi'kam, at Mizpah. 1
2 ten men with him rose up and struck down Gedali'ah 1
3 slew . . the Jews who were with Gedali'ah at Mizpah 1
4 On the day after the murder of Gedali'ah 1
6 he met them, he said to them, "Come in to Gedali'ah 1
10 had committed to Gedali'ah the son of Ahi'kam. 1
16 after he had slain Gedali'ah the son of Ahi'kam 1
18 Ish'mael the son of Nethani'ah had slain Gedali'ah 1
43: 6 guard had left with Gedali'ah the son of Ahi'kam 1
Zep 1: 1 Zephani'ah the son of Cushi, son of Gedali'ah 1
1Es 9:22 Ishmael, and Nathanael, and Gedaliah, and Elasah. 2

Geder 1. גֶּדֶר

Jos 12:13 the king of Debir, one; the king of Geder, one; 1

Gederah 1. גְּדֵרָה 2. גְּדֵרָתִי

Jos 15:36 Shaara'im, Aditha'im, Gede'rah, Gederotha'im 1
1Ch 4:23 potters and inhabitants of Neta'im and Gede'rah; 1
12: 4 Jeremiah, Jaha'ziel, Joha'nan, Joz'abad of Gede'rah 2

Gederite 1. גְּדֵרִי

1Ch 27:28 Over the . . was Ba'al-ha'nan the Gede'rite; 1

Gederoth 1. גְּדֵרוֹת

Jos 15:41 Gede'roth, Beth-da'gon, Na'amah, and Makke'dah 1
2Ch 28:18 had taken Beth-she'mesh, Ai'jalon, Gede'roth 1

Gederothaim 1. גְּדֵרֹתַיִם

Jos 15:36 Shaara'im, Aditha'im, Gede'rah, Gederotha'im 1

Gedor 1. גְּדוֹר

Jos 15:58 Halhul, Beth-zur, Gedor 1
1Ch 4: 4 Penu'el was the father of Gedor 1
18 his Jewish wife bore Jered the father of Gedor 1
39 They journeyed to the entrance of Gedor 1
8:31 Gedor, Ahi'o, Zecher 1
9:37 Gedor, Ahi'o, Zechari'ah and Mikloth; 1
12: 7 and Zebadi'ah, the sons of Jero'ham of Gedor. 1

Gehazi 1. גֵּיחֲזִי

2Kg 4:12 he said to Geha'zi his servant 1
14 Geha'zi answered, "Well, she has no son 1
25 he said to Geha'zi his servant, "Look 1
27 And Geha'zi came to thrust her away. 1
29 He said to Geha'zi, "Gird up your loins 1
31 Geha'zi went on ahead and laid the staff 1
36 Then he summoned Geha'zi and said 1
5:20 Geha'zi, the servant of Eli'sha the man of God, said 1
21 So Geha'zi followed Na'aman. And when Na'aman 1
23 and they carried them before Geha'zi. *
25 Eli'sha said to him, "Where have you been, Geha'zi? 1
8: 4 Now the king was talking with Geha'zi the servant 1
5 And Geha'zi said, "My lord, O king, here is the woman 1

Gehenna 1. gehenna

2Es 2:29 that your sons may not see Gehenna. 1

Geliloth 1. גְּלִילוֹת

Jos 18:17 it bends . . and thence goes to Geli'loth 1

Gemalli 1. גְּמַלִּי

Num13:12 from the tribe of Dan, Am'miel the son of Gemal'li; 1

Gemariah 1. גְּמַרְיָהוּ

Jer 29: 3 son of Shaphan and Gemari'ah the son of Hilki'ah 1
36:10 in the chamber of Gemari'ah the son of Shaphan 1
11 When Micai'ah the son of Gemari'ah, son of Shaphan 1
12 Gemari'ah the son of Shaphan 1
25 even when Elna'than and Delai'ah and Gemari'ah 1

Gennaeus 1. Γενναίος

2Mc 12: 2 Timothy and Apollonius the son of Gennaeus 1

Gennesaret 1. Γεννησαρ 2. Γεννησαρέτ

Mat 14:34 they came to land at Gennesaret. 2
Mrk 6:53 they came to land at Gennes'aret 2
Lke 5: 1 he was standing by the lake of Gennes'aret. 2
1Mc 11:67 his army encamped by the waters of Gennesaret. 1

Gentile 1. ἀλλόφυλος 2. ἐθνικός 3. ἔθνος 4. gens

Mat 4:15 sea, across the Jordan, Galilee of the Gentiles– 3
5:47 than others? Do not even the Gentiles do the same? 2
6: 7 heap up empty phrases as the Gentiles do; 2
32 For the Gentiles seek all these things; 3
10: 5 Go nowhere among the Gentiles 3
18 to bear testimony before them and the Gentiles. 3
12:18 he shall proclaim justice to the Gentiles. 3
21 in his name will the Gentiles hope. 3
18:17 let him be to you as a Gentile and a tax collector. 2
20:19 deliver him to the Gentiles to be mocked 3
25 the rulers of the Gentiles lord it over them 3
Mrk 10:33 deliver him to the Gentiles; 3
42 those who are supposed to rule over the Gentiles 3
Lke 2:32 a light for revelation to the Gentiles 3
18:32 For he will be delivered to the Gentiles 3
21:24 Jerusalem will be trodden down by the Gentiles 3
24 until the times of the Gentiles are fulfilled. 3
22:25 he said to them, "The kings of the Gentiles 3
Act 4:25 Why did the Gentiles rage 3
27 with the Gentiles and the peoples of Israel 3
9:15 to carry my name before the Gentiles and kings 3
10:45 had been poured out even on the Gentiles. 3
11: 1 heard that the Gentiles also had received 3
18 Then to the Gentiles also God has granted 3
13:46 behold, we turn to the Gentiles. 3
47 I have set you to be a light for the Gentiles 3
48 when the Gentiles heard this, they were glad 3
14: 2 the unbelieving Jews stirred up the Gentiles 3
5 an attempt was made by both Gentiles and Jews 3
27 how he had opened a door of faith to the Gentiles. 3
15: 3 reporting the conversion of the Gentiles 3
7 by my mouth the Gentiles should hear the word 3
12 God had done through them among the Gentiles. 3
14 how God first visited the Gentiles 3
17 all the Gentiles who are called by my name 3
19 not trouble those of the Gentiles who turn to God 3
23 the brethren who are of the Gentiles in Antioch 3
18: 6 From now on I will go to the Gentiles. 3
21:11 deliver him into the hands of the Gentiles.' 3
19 things that God had done among the Gentiles 3
21 you teach all the Jews who are among the Gentiles 3
25 as for the Gentiles who have believed 3
22:21 I will send you far away to the Gentiles.' 3
26:17 delivering you . . from the Gentiles 3
20 also to the Gentiles 3
23 both to the people and to the Gentiles 3
28:28 salvation of God has been sent to the Gentiles; 3
Rom 1:13 as well as among the rest of the Gentiles 3
2:14 When Gentiles who have not the law 3
24 The name of God is blasphemed among the Gentiles 3
3:29 Is he not the God of Gentiles also? 3
29 God of Gentiles also? Yes, of Gentiles also 3
9:24 not from the Jews only but also from the Gentiles? 3
30 That Gentiles who did not pursue righteousness 3
11:11 salvation has come to the Gentiles 3
12 if their failure means riches for the Gentiles 3
13 Now I am speaking to you Gentiles. 3
13 Inasmuch then as I am an apostle to the Gentiles 3
25 until the full number of the Gentiles come in 3
15: 9 the Gentiles might glorify God for his mercy. 3
9 Therefore I will praise thee among the Gentiles 3
10 Rejoice, O Gentiles, with his people"; 3
11 and again, "Praise the Lord, all Gentiles 3
12 he who rises to rule the Gentiles; 3
12 in him shall the Gentiles hope. 3
16 to be a minister of Christ Jesus to the Gentiles 3
16 the offering of the Gentiles may be acceptable 3
18 to win obedience from the Gentiles 3
27 the Gentiles . . share in their spiritual blessings 3
16: 4 all the churches of the Gentiles give thanks; 3
1Co 1:23 a stumbling block to Jews and folly to Gentiles 3
2Co 11:26 danger from Gentiles, danger in the city 3
Gal 1:16 I might preach him among the Gentiles 3
2: 2 the gospel which I preach among the Gentiles 3
8 worked through me also for the Gentiles) 3
9 should go to the Gentiles and they to the circumcised; 3
12 he ate with the Gentiles 3
14 how can you compel the Gentiles to live like Jews? 3
15 who are Jews by birth and not Gentile sinners 3
3: 8 God would justify the Gentiles by faith 3
14 Abraham might come upon the Gentiles 3
Eph 2:11 at one time you Gentiles in the flesh 3
3: 1 prisoner for Christ Jesus on behalf of you Gentiles– 3
6 that is, how the Gentiles are fellow heirs 3
8 to preach to the Gentiles 3
4:17 you must no longer live as the Gentiles do 3
Col 1:27 how great among the Gentiles 3
1Th 2:16 by hindering us from speaking to the Gentiles 3
1Ti 2: 7 a teacher of the Gentiles in faith and truth. 3
2Ti 4:17 all the Gentiles might hear it 3
1Pe 2:12 Maintain good conduct among the Gentiles 3
4: 3 for doing what the Gentiles like to do 3
2Es 4:23 given over to the Gentiles as a reproach 4
Tob 1:10 my relatives ate the food of the Gentiles; 3
14: 6 all the Gentiles will turn to fear the Lord God 3
7 All the Gentiles will praise the Lord 3
Jdt 4:12 to the malicious joy of the Gentiles. 3
8:22 he will bring upon our heads among the Gentiles 3
1Mc 1:11 Let us . . make a covenant with the Gentiles 3
13 observe the ordinances of the Gentiles. 3
14 a gymnasium . . according to Gentile custom 3
15 They joined with the Gentiles 3
43 the Gentiles accepted the command of the king. 3
2:12 the Gentiles have profaned it. 3
18 as all the Gentiles and the men of Judah 3
40 refuse to fight with the Gentiles for our lives 3
44 the survivors fled to the Gentiles for safety. 3
48 rescued the law out of the hands of the Gentiles 3
68 Pay back the Gentiles in full 3
3:10 Apollonius gathered together Gentiles 3
25 terror fell upon the Gentiles round about them. 3
26 the Gentiles talked of the battles of Judas. 3
45 it was a lodging place for the Gentiles 3
48 the Gentiles were consulting the images 3
52 Gentiles are assembled against us to destroy us; 3
58 to fight with these Gentiles 3
4: 7 they saw the camp of the Gentiles 3
11 Then all the Gentiles will know 3
14 The Gentiles were crushed and fled into the plain 3
45 the Gentiles had defiled it 3
54 on the very day that the Gentiles had profaned it 3
58 the reproach of the Gentiles was removed. 3
60 to keep the Gentiles from coming 3
5: 1 When the Gentiles round about heard 3
9 Now the Gentiles in Gilead gathered together 3
10 The Gentiles around us have gathered together 3
15 all Galilee of the Gentiles 1
19 do not engage in battle with the Gentiles 3
21 fought many battles against the Gentiles 3

21 the Gentiles were crushed before him. 3
22 as many as 3,000 of the Gentiles fell 3
38 All the Gentiles around us have gathered to him 3
43 All the Gentiles were defeated before him 3
57 let us go and make war on the Gentiles around us. 3
63 in all Israel and among all the Gentiles 3
6:18 strengthen the Gentiles. 3
53 found safety in Judea from the Gentiles 3
7:23 it was more than the Gentiles had done. 3
13:41 the yoke of the Gentiles was removed from Israel 3
14:36 so that the Gentiles were put out of the country 3
2Mc 1:27 let the Gentiles know that thou art our God. 3
27 set free those who are slaves among the Gentiles 3
6: 4 filled with . . reveling by the Gentiles 3
8: 5 the Gentiles could not withstand him 3
9 no fewer than 20,000 Gentiles of all nations 3
16 not to fear the great multitude of Gentiles 3
17 which the Gentiles had committed •
12:13 and inhabited by all sorts of Gentiles 3
13:11 fall into the hands of the blasphemous Gentiles. 3
14:14 the Gentiles throughout Judea 3
15 the gathering of the Gentiles 3
38 when there was no mingling with the Gentiles •
15: 8 not to fear the attack of the Gentiles 3
10 pointing out the perfidy of the Gentiles 3
3Mc 4: 1 was arranged for the Gentiles 3
5: 6 to the Gentiles it appeared that . . 3
13 to show . . to the arrogant Gentiles. 3
6: 9 the abominable and lawless Gentiles. 3
13 let the Gentiles cower today in fear of your . . might 3
15 Let it be shown to all the Gentiles 3

like a Gentile 1. ἐθνικῶς
Gal 2:14 If you, though a Jew, live like a Gentile 1

Genubath 1. גְּנֻבַת
1Kg 11:20 the sister of Tah'penes bore him Genu'bath his son 1
20 Genu'bath was in Pharaoh's house 1

Gera 1. גֵּרָא
Gen 46:21 Benjamin: Bela, Becher, Ashbel, Gera, Na'aman, Ehi 1
Jdg 3:15 a deliverer, Ehud, the son of Gera, the Benjaminite 1
2Sm 16: 5 a man . . whose name was Shim'e-i, the son of Gera; 1
19:16 Shim'e-i the son of Gera . . made haste to come down 1
18 Shim'e-i the son of Gera fell down before the king 1
1Kg 2: 8 with you Shim'e-i the son of Gera, the Benjaminite 1
1Ch 8: 3 Bela had sons: Addar, Gera, Abi'hud 1
5 Gera, Shephu'phan, and Huram. 1
7 Na'aman, Ahi'jah, and Gera, that is, Heglam 1

Gerar 1. גְּרָר 2. Γερρηνοι
Gen 10:19 from Sidon, in the direction of Gerar 1
20: 1 Kadesh and Shur; and he sojourned in Gerar. 1
2 And Abim'elech king of Gerar sent and took Sarah. 1
26: 1 And Isaac went to Gerar, to Abim'elech 1
6 Isaac dwelt in Gerar. 1
17 Isaac . . encamped in the valley of Gerar 1
20 the herdsmen of Gerar quarreled with Isaac's 1
26 Then Abim'elech went to him from Gerar 1
2Ch 14:13 pursued them as far as Gerar 1
14 they smote all the cities round about Gerar 1
2Mc 13:24 governor from Ptolemais to Gerar 2

Gerasene 1. Γερασηνοs
Mrk 5: 1 to the country of the Ger'asenes. 1
Lke 8:26 they arrived at the country of the Ger'asenes 1
37 the surrounding country of the Ger'asenes 1

Gergesite 1. Γεργεσαιος
Jdt 5:16 Shechemites and all the Gergesites 1

Gerizim 1. גְּרִזִים 2. Γαριζιν
Deu 11:29 set the blessing on Mount Ger'izim and the curse 1
27:12 these shall stand upon Mount Ger'izim to bless 1
Jos 8:33 Israel . . half of them in front of Mount Ger'izim 1
Jdg 9: 7 he went and stood on the top of Mount Ger'izim 1
2Mc 5:23 at Gerizim, Andronicus 2
6: 2 to call the one in Gerizim the temple of Zeus 2

Gershom 1. גֵּרְשׁוֹן 2. גֵּרְשֹׁם 3. Γαρσομος 4. Gerson
Exd 2:22 She bore a son, and he called his name Gershom; 2
18: 3 two sons, of whom the name of the one was Gershom 2
Jdg 18:30 Jonathan the son of Gershom, son of Moses 2
1Ch 6: 1 The sons of Levi: Gershom, Kohath, and Merar'i. 1
16 The sons of Levi: Gershom, Kohath, and Merar'i. 2
17 names of the sons of Gershom: Libni and Shim'e-i. 2
20 Of Gershom: Libni his son, Jahath his son, Zimmah 2
43 son of Jahath, son of Gershom, son of Levi. 2
15: 7 of the sons of Gershom, Jo'el the chief 2
23: 6 the sons of Levi: Gershom, Kohath, and Merar'i. 1
7 The sons of Gershom were Ladan and Shim'e-i. 4
15 The sons of Moses: Gershom and Elie'zer. 2
16 The sons of Gershom: Sheb'uel the chief. 2
26:24 Sheb'uel the son of Gershom, son of Moses 2
Ezr 8: 2 Of the sons of Phin'ehas, Gershom. 2
1Es 8:29 Of the sons of Phineas, Gershom 3

Gershomite 1. גֵּרְשֻׁם
1Ch 6:62 Gershomites . . were allotted thirteen cities 1
71 To the Gershomites were given 1

Gershon 1. גֵּרְשׁוֹן
Gen 46:11 The sons of Levi: Gershon, Kohath, and Merar'i. 1
Exd 6:16 sons of Levi . . Gershon, Kohath, and Merar'i 1
17 The sons of Gershon: Libni and Shim'e-i 1
Num 3:17 sons of Levi . . Gershon and Kohath and Merar'i. 1
18 these are the names of the sons of Gershon 1
21 Of Gershon were the family of the Libnites 1
25 the charge of the sons of Gershon in the tent 1
4:22 Take a census of the sons of Gershon also 1
38 number of the sons of Gershon, by their families 1
41 number of the families of the sons of Gershon 1
7: 7 gave to the sons of Gershon 1
10:17 sons of Gershon and the sons of Merar'i 1
26:57 of Gershon, the family of the Gershonites; 1

Gershonite 1. בֶּן גֵּרְשׁוֹן 2. גֵּרְשֻׁנִּי
Num 3:21 these were the families of the Gershonites. 2
23 The families of the Gershonites were to encamp 2
24 as head of the fathers' house of the Gershonites. 2
4:24 the service of the families of the Gershonites 2
27 All the service of the sons of the Gershonites 2
28 service of . . the sons of the Gershonites 2
26:57 of Gershon, the family of the Gershonites; 2
Jos 21:27 And to the Gershonites . . two cities; 1
33 cities of the . . families of the Gershonites 2
1Ch 26:21 sons of the Gershonites belonging to Ladan 2
21 belonging to Ladan the Gershonite: Jehi'eli. 2
29: 8 in the care of Jehi'el the Gershonite. 2
2Ch 29:12 Levites arose . . of the Gershonites, 2

Gersonite 1. בֶּן גֵּרְשׁוֹן
Jos 21: 6 Gersonites received by lot . . thirteen cities. 1

Geruth 1. גֵּרוּת
Jer 41:17 and stayed at Geruth Chimham near Bethlehem 1

Geshan 1. גֵּישָׁן
1Ch 2:47 Jah'dai:sons of Jah'dai . . Jotham, Geshan, Pelet 1

Geshem 1. גֶּשֶׁם
Neh 2:19 Sanbal'lat . . Tobi'ah . . , and Geshem the Arab 1
6: 1 reported to Sanbal'lat and Tobi'ah and to Geshem 1
2 Sanbal'lat and Geshem sent to me, saying, "Come 1
6 reported among the nations, and Geshem also says 1

Geshur 1. גְּשׁוּר
Jos 13:13 Geshur and Ma'acath dwell in the midst of Israel 1
2Sm 3: 3 of Ma'acah the daughter of Talmai king of Geshur; 1
13:37 went to Talmai the son of Ammi'hud, king of Geshur. 1
38 So Ab'salom fled, and went to Geshur 1
14:23 So Jo'ab arose and went to Geshur 1
32 Why have I come from Geshur? It would be better 1
15: 8 vowed a vow while I dwelt at Geshur in Aram, saying 1
1Ch 2:23 Geshur and Aram took . . Havvoth-ja'ir, Kenath 1
3: 2 Ma'acah, the daughter of Talmai, king of Geshur; 1

Geshurite 1. גְּשׁוּרִי
Deu 3:14 as far as the border of the Gesh'urites 1
Jos 12: 5 and all Bashan to the boundary of the Gesh'urites 1
13: 2 the regions of . . all those of the Gesh'urites 1
11 the region of the Gesh'urites and Ma-ac'athites 1
13 Yet . . Israel did not drive out the Gesh'urites 1
1Sm 27: 8 and made raids upon the Gesh'urites, and Gir'zites 1

Gether 1. גֶּתֶר
Gen 10:23 The sons of Aram: Uz, Hul, Gether, and Mash. 1
1Ch 1:17 The sons of Shem . . Lud, Aram, Uz, Hul, Gether 1

Gethsemane 1. Γεθσημανί
Mat 26:36 to a place called Gethsem'ane 1
Mrk 14:32 they went to a place which was called Gethsem'ane; 1

Geuel 1. גְּאוּאֵל
Num13:15 from the tribe of Gad, Geu'el the son of Machi. 1

Gezer 1. גֶּזֶר
Jos 10:33 Then Horam king of Gezer came up to help Lachish; 1
12:12 the king of Eglon, one; the king of Gezer, one; 1
16: 3 it goes . . then to Gezer, and it ends at the sea. 1
10 not drive out the Canaanites that dwelt in Gezer 1
21:21 given Shechem . . Gezer with its pasture lands 1
Jdg 1:29 not drive out the Canaanites who dwelt in Gezer; 1
29 but the Canaanites dwelt in Gezer among them. 1
2Sm 5:25 and smote the Philistines from Geba to Gezer. 1
1Kg 9:15 to build . . Hazor and Megid'do and Gezer 1
16 gone up and captured Gezer and burnt it with fire 1
17 so Solomon rebuilt Gezer) 1
1Ch 6:67 of refuge . . Gezer with its pasture lands 1
7:28 westward Gezer and its towns 1
14:16 smote the Philistine army from Gibeon to Gezer. 1
20: 4 there arose war with the Philistines at Gezer; 1

Giah 1. גִּיחַ
2Sm 2:24 came to the hill of Ammah, which lies before Gi'ah 1

Gibbar 1. גִּבָּר
Ezr 2:20 sons of Gibbar, 95. 1

Gibbethon 1. גִּבְּתוֹן
Jos 19:44 El'tekeh, Gib'bethon, Ba'alath 1
21:23 El'teke with . . Gib'bethon with its pasture lands 1
1Kg 15:27 Ba'asha struck him down at Gib'bethon 1
27 and all Israel were laying siege to Gib'bethon. 1
16:15 Now the troops were encamped against Gib'bethon 1
17 Omri went up from Gib'bethon, and all Israel 1

Gibea 1. גִּבְעָא
1Ch 2:49 She also bore . . Sheva . . the father of Gib'e-a; 1

Gibeah 1. גִּבְעָה 2. גִּבְעָתִי
Jos 15:57 Kain, Gib'e-ah, and Timnah 1
18:28 Ha-eleph, Jebus . . Gib'e-ah and Kir'iath-je'arim 1
24:33 Elea'zar . . died; and they buried him at Gib'e-ah 1
Jdg 19:12 not turn aside . . but we will pass on to Gib'e-ah. 1
13 and spend the night at Gib'e-ah or at Ramah. 1
14 on them near Gib'e-ah, which belongs to Benjamin 1
15 to go in and spend the night at Gib'e-ah. 1
16 and he was sojourning in Gib'e-ah 1
20: 4 I came to Gib'e-ah that belongs to Benjamin 1
5 the men of Gib'e-ah rose against me, and beset 1
9 what we will do to Gib'e-ah: we will go up against it 1
10 that . . they may requite Gib'e-ah of Benjamin 1
13 give up the men, the base fellows in Gib'e-ah 1
14 Benjaminites came together . . to Gib'e-ah 1
15 besides the inhabitants of Gib'e-ah, who mustered 1
19 in the morning, and encamped against Gib'e-ah. 1
20 drew up the battle line against them at Gib'e-ah. 1
21 Benjaminites came out of Gib'e-ah, and felled 1
25 Benjamin went against them out of Gib'e-ah 1
29 Israel set men in ambush round about Gib'e-ah. 1
30 and set themselves in array against Gib'e-ah 1
31 one . . goes up to Bethel and the other to Gib'e-ah 1
34 there came against Gib'e-ah 10,000 picked men 1
36 men in ambush whom they had set against Gib'e-ah. 1
37 men in ambush made haste and rushed upon Gib'e-ah 1
43 from Nohah as far as opposite Gib'e-ah on the east. 1
1Sm 10:10 When they came to Gib'e-ah . . prophets met him; 1
26 Saul also went to his home at Gib'e-ah 1
11: 4 When the messengers came to Gib'e-ah of Saul 1
13: 2 and 1,000 were with Jonathan in Gib'e-ah 1
15 and went up from Gilgal to Gib'e-ah of Benjamin. 1
14: 2 Saul was staying in the outskirts of Gib'e-ah 1
16 watchmen of Saul in Gib'e-ah of Benjamin looked; 1
15:34 and Saul went up to his house in Gib'e-ah of Saul. 1
22: 6 Saul was sitting at Gib'e-ah, under the tamarisk 1
23:19 the Ziphites went up to Saul at Gib'e-ah, saying 1
26: 1 Then the Ziphites came to Saul at Gib'e-ah, saying 1
2Sm 23:29 the son of Ri'bai of Gib'e-ah of the Benjaminites. 1
1Ch 11:31 son of Ribai of Gib'e-ah of the Benjaminites 1
12: 3 both sons of Shema'ah of Gib'e-ah; 2
2Ch 13: 2 Micai'ah the daughter of U'riel of Gib'e-ah. 1
Isa 10:29 Ramah trembles, Gib'e-ah of Saul has fled. 1
Hos 5: 8 Blow the horn in Gib'e-ah, the trumpet in Ramah. 1
9: 9 corrupted themselves as in the days of Gib'e-ah 1
10: 9 From the days of Gib'e-ah, you have sinned, O Israel; 1
9 Shall not war overtake them in Gib'e-ah? 1

Gibeath-elohim 1. גִּבְעַת הָאֱלֹהִים
1Sm 10: 5 After that you shall come to Gib'e-ath-elo'him 1

Gibeath-haaraloth 1. גִּבְעַת הָעֲרָלוֹת
Jos 5: 3 circumcised . . Israel at Gibeath-haaraloth. 1

Gibeon 1. גִּבְעוֹן 2. גִּבְעֹנִי 3. Γαβαων
Jos 9: 3 the inhabitants of Gibeon heard what Joshua had 1
17 Now their cities were Gibeon, Chephi'rah 1
10: 1 and how the inhabitants of Gibeon had made peace 1
2 Gibeon was a great city, like . . the royal cities 1
4 Come up to me, and help me, and let us smite Gibeon; 1
5 went up with all . . and encamped against Gibeon 1
6 And the men of Gibeon sent to Joshua . . in Gilgal 1
10 who slew them with a great slaughter at Gibeon 1
12 Sun, stand thou still at Gibeon, and thou Moon 1
41 and all the country of Goshen, as far as Gibeon. 1
11:19 except the Hivites, the inhabitants of Gibeon; 1
18:25 Gibeon, Ramah, Be-er'oth 1
21:17 Gibeon with its pasture lands, Geba with its 1
2Sm 2:12 Abner . . went out from Mahana'im to Gibeon. 1
13 went out and met them at the pool of Gibeon; 1
16 was called Hel'kath-hazzu'rim, which is at Gibeon. 1
24 lies . . on the way to the wilderness of Gibeon. 1
3:30 he had killed . . As'ahel in the battle at Gibeon. 1
20: 8 they were at the great stone which is in Gibeon 1
21: 6 that we may hang them up before the LORD at Gibeon 3
1Kg 3: 4 the king went to Gibeon to sacrifice there 1
5 At Gibeon the LORD appeared to Solomon in a dream 1
9: 2 a second time, as he had appeared to him at Gibeon. 1
1Ch 8:29 Je-i'el the father of Gibeon dwelt in Gibeon 1
29 Je-i'el the father of Gibeon dwelt in Gibeon 1
9:35 In Gibeon dwelt the father of Gibeon, Je-i'el 1
35 In Gibeon dwelt the father of Gibeon, Je-i'el 1
12: 4 Ishma'iah of Gibeon, a mighty man among the 30 2
14:16 smote the Philistine army from Gibeon to Gezer. 1

16:39 in the high place that was at Gibeon 1
21:29 were at that time in the high place at Gibeon; 1
2Ch 1: 3 Solomon . . went to the high place . . at Gibeon; 1
13 Solomon came from the high place at Gibeon 1
Neh 3: 7 repaired . . the men of Gibeon and of Mizpah 1
7:25 sons of Gibeon, 95. 1
Isa 28:21 he will be wroth as in the valley of Gibeon; 1
Jer 28: 1 Hanani'ah . . the prophet from Gibeon, spoke to me 1
41:12 at the great pool which is in Gibeon. 1
16 eunuchs, whom Joha'nan brought back from Gibeon. 1

Gibeonite 1. גִּבְעֹנִי

2Sm 21: 1 because he put the Gib'eonites to death. 1
2 the king called the Gib'eonites. 1
2 the Gib'eonites were not of the people of Israel 1
3 And David said to the Gib'eonites, "What shall I do 1
4 The Gib'eonites said to him, "It is not a matter 1
9 and he gave them into the hands of the Gib'eonites 1
Neh 3: 7 repaired Melati'ah the Gib'eonite and Jadon 1

Giddalti 1. גִּדַּלְתִּי

1Ch 25: 4 sons of Heman . . Giddal'ti, and Romam'ti-e'zer 1
29 to Giddal'ti, his sons and his brethren, twelve; 1

Giddel 1. גִּדֵּל 2. Ισδαηλ

Ezr 2:47 sons of Giddel, the sons of Gahar 1
56 the sons of Darkon, the sons of Giddel 1
Neh 7:49 sons of Hanan, the sons of Giddel, the sons of Gahar 1
58 Ja'ala, the sons of Darkon, the sons of Giddel 1
1Es 5:33 the sons of Giddel, the sons of Shephatiah 2

Gideon 1. גִּדְעוֹן 2. Γεδεών

Jdg 6:11 Gideon was beating out wheat in the wine press 1
13 Gideon said to him, "Pray, sir, if the LORD is with us 1
19 So Gideon went into his house and prepared a kid 1
22 Gideon perceived that he was the angel of the LORD 1
22 Gideon said, "Alas, O Lord GOD! For now I have seen 1
24 Then Gideon built an altar there to the LORD 1
27 Gideon took ten men . . and did as the LORD had 1
29 they said, "Gideon the son of Jo'ash has done this 1
34 the Spirit of the LORD took possession of Gideon; 1
36 Gideon said to God, "If thou wilt deliver Israel 1
39 Gideon said to God, "Let not thy anger burn against 1
7: 1 Then Jerubba'al (that is, Gideon) and all the people 1
2 The LORD said to Gideon, "The people with you are 1
3 Gideon tested them; 22,000 returned •
4 LORD said to Gideon, "The people are still too many; 1
5 and the LORD said to Gideon, "Every one that laps 1
7 the LORD said to Gideon, "With the 300 men 1
13 When Gideon came, behold, a man was telling a dream 1
14 no other than the sword of Gideon the son of Jo'ash 1
15 When Gideon heard the telling of the dream 1
18 the camp, and shout, 'For the LORD and for Gideon.' 1
19 Gideon . . came to the outskirts of the camp 1
20 they cried, "A sword for the LORD and for Gideon! 1
24 Gideon sent messengers throughout all the hill 1
25 of Oreb and Zeeb to Gideon beyond the Jordan. 1
8: 4 Gideon came to the Jordan and passed over 1
7 Gideon said, "Well then, when the LORD has given 1
11 Gideon went up . . and attacked the army; 1
13 Gideon the son of Jo'ash returned from the battle 1
21 And Gideon arose and slew Zebah and Zalmun'na; 1
22 Then the men of Israel said to Gideon, "Rule over us 1
23 Gideon said to them, "I will not rule over you 1
24 Gideon said to them, "Let me make a request of you; 1
27 Gideon made an ephod of it and put it in his city 1
27 and it became a snare to Gideon and to his family. 1
28 the land had rest 40 years in the days of Gideon 1
30 Gideon had 70 sons, his own offspring 1
32 Gideon the son of Jo'ash died in a good old age 1
33 As soon as Gideon died, the people of Israel 1
35 to the family of Jerrubba'al (that is, Gideon) 1
Heb 11:32 time would fail me to tell of Gideon, Barak, Samson 2
Jdt 8: 1 son of Elkiah, son of Ananias, son of Gideon 2

Gideoni 1. גִּדְעֹנִי

Num 1:11 from Benjamin, Abi'dan the son of Gideo'ni; 1
2:22 the leader . . Abi'dan the son of Gideo'ni 1
7:60 Abi'dan the son of Gideo'ni, the leader of the men 1
65 was the offering of Abi'dan the son of Gideo'ni. 1
10:24 over the host . . was Abi'dan the son of Gideo'ni. 1

Gidom 1. גִּדְעֹם

Jdg 20:45 they were pursued hard to Gidom, and 2,000 men 1

Gihon 1. גִּיחוֹן 2. Γηων

Gen 2:13 The name of the second river is Gihon; 1
1Kg 1:33 to ride on my own mule, and bring him down to Gihon; 1
38 on King David's mule, and brought him to Gihon. 1
45 and Nathan . . have anointed him king at Gihon; 1
2Ch 32:30 closed the upper outlet of the waters of Gihon 1
33:14 outer wall for the city of David west of Gihon 1
Sir 24:27 like the Gihon at the time of vintage. 2

Gilalai 1. גִּלֲלַי

Neh 12:36 kinsmen, Shemai'ah, Az'arel, Mil'alai, Gil'alai, Ma'ai 1

Gilboa 1. גִּלְבֹּעַ

1Sm 28: 4 gathered . . Israel, and they encamped at Gilbo'a. 1
31: 1 Israel fled . . and fell slain on Mount Gilbo'a. 1
8 Saul and his three sons fallen on Mount Gilbo'a. 1
2Sm 1: 6 By chance I happened to be on Mount Gilbo'a; 1
21 Ye mountains of Gilbo'a, let there be no dew or rain 1
21:12 on the day the Philistines killed Saul on Gilbo'a; 1
1Ch 10: 1 men of Israel . . fell slain on Mount Gilbo'a. 1
8 found Saul and his sons fallen on Mount Gilbo'a. 1

Gilead 1. גִּלְעָד 2. Γαλααδ 3. Γαλααδιτις

Gen 31:21 set his face toward the hill country of Gilead. 1
23 after him into the hill country of Gilead. 1
25 kinsmen encamped in the hill country of Gilead. 1
37:25 a caravan of Ish'maelites coming from Gilead 1
Num26:29 Machir was the father of Gilead; 1
29 of Gilead, the family of the Gileadites. 1
30 These are the sons of Gilead: of Ie'zer . . of Helek 1
27: 1 Hepher, son of Gilead, son of Machir 1
32: 1 they saw the land of Jazer and the land of Gilead 1
26 shall remain there in the cities of Gilead; 1
29 give them the land of Gilead for a possession; 1
39 sons of Machir the son of Manas'seh went to Gilead 1
40 Moses gave Gilead to Machir the son of Manas'seh 1
36: 1 heads . . of the families of the sons of Gilead 1
Deu 2:36 From Aro'er . . as far as Gilead, there was not 1
3:10 tableland and all Gilead and all Bashan, as far 1
12 half the hill country of Gilead with its cities; 1
13 rest of Gilead, and all Bashan, the kingdom of Og 1
15 To Machir I gave Gilead 1
16 territory from Gilead as far as the valley 1
4:43 Reubenites, and Ramoth in Gilead for the Gadites 1
34: 1 LORD showed him all the land, Gilead as far as Dan 1
Jos 12: 2 ruled from . . as far as.., that is, half of Gilead 1
5 half of Gilead to the boundary of Sihon 1
13:11 and Gilead, and the region of the Gesh'urites 1
25 territory was Jazer, and all the cities of Gilead 1
31 and half Gilead, and Ash'taroth, and Ed're-i 1
17: 1 Machir the first-born . . the father of Gilead 1
1 To Machir . . were allotted Gilead and Bashan 1
3 Zeloph'ehad the son of Hepher, son of Gilead 1
5 ten . . besides the land of Gilead and Bashan 1
6 The land of Gilead was allotted to the rest 1
20: 8 appointed . . and Ramoth in Gilead, from the tribe 1
21:38 of Gad, Ramoth in Gilead with its pasture lands 1
22: 9 parting . . to go to the land of Gilead 1
13 the Gadites and . . Manas'seh, in the land of Gilead 1
15 the Gadites, and . . Manas'seh, in the land of Gilead 1
32 Reubenites and the Gadites in the land of Gilead 1
Jdg 5:17 Gilead stayed beyond the Jordan; 1
10: 4 30 cities . . which are in the land of Gilead. 1
8 in the land of the Amorites, which is in Gilead. 1
17 were called to arms, and they encamped in Gilead; 1
18 people, the leaders of Gilead, said one to another 1
18 be head over all the inhabitants of Gilead. 1
11: 1 of a harlot. Gilead was the father of Jephthah. 1
2 Gilead's wife also bore him sons; 1
5 the elders of Gilead went to bring Jephthah 1
7 Jephthah said to the elders of Gilead, "Did you not 1
8 the elders of Gilead said to Jephthah, "That is why 1
8 be our head over all the inhabitants of Gilead. 1
9 Jephthah said to the elders of Gilead 1
10 the elders of Gilead said to Jephthah, "The LORD 1
11 Jephthah went with the elders of Gilead 1
29 and he passed through Gilead and Manas'seh 1
29 Manas'seh, and passed on to Mizpah of Gilead 1
29 Gilead, and from Mizpah of Gilead he passed 1
12: 4 Then Jephthah gathered all the men of Gilead 1
4 and the men of Gilead smote E'phraim 1
5 men of Gilead said to him, "Are you an E'phraimite? 1
7 died, and was buried in his city in Gilead. 1
20: 1 people of Israel . . including the land of Gilead 1
1Sm 13: 7 crossed . . Jordan to the land of Gad and Gilead. 1
2Sm 2: 9 he made him king over Gilead and the Ash'urites 1
17:26 and Ab'salom encamped in the land of Gilead. 1
24: 6 Then they came to Gilead, and to Kadesh 1
1Kg 4:13 villages of Ja'ir . . which are in Gilead 1
19 land of Gilead, the country of Sihon . . and of Og 1
17: 1 Eli'jah the Tishbite, of Tishbe in Gilead, said 1
2Kg 10:33 from the Jordan eastward, all the land of Gilead 1
33 from Aro'er . . that is, Gilead and Bashan. 1
15:29 Kedesh, Hazor, Gilead, and Galilee, all . . Naph'tali; 1
1Ch 2:21 the daughter of Machir the father of Gilead 1
22 Ja'ir, who had 23 cities in the land of Gilead 1
23 descendants of Machir, the father of Gilead. 1
5: 9 cattle had multiplied in the land of Gilead. 1
10 tents throughout all the region east of Gilead. 1
14 sons of Ab'ihail . . son of Jaro'ah, son of Gilead 1
16 they dwelt in Gilead, in Bashan and in its towns 1
6:80 Ramoth in Gilead with its pasture lands 1
7:14 she bore Machir the father of Gilead. 1
17 These were the sons of Gilead the son of Machir 1
26:31 men . . among them were found at Jazer in Gilead. 1
27:21 for the half-tribe of Manas'seh in Gilead, 1
Ps 60: 7 Gilead is mine; Manas'seh is mine; 1
108: 8 Gilead is mine; Manas'seh is mine; 1
Sng 4: 1 flock of goats, moving down the slopes of Gilead. 1
6: 5 flock of goats, moving down the slopes of Gilead. 1
Jer 8:22 Is there no balm in Gilead? Is there no physician 1
22: 6 You are as Gilead to me, as the summit of Lebanon 1
46:11 Go up to Gilead, and take balm, O virgin daughter 1
50:19 satisfied on the hills of E'phraim and in Gilead. 1
Ezk 47:18 the Jordan between Gilead and the land of Israel; 1
Hos 6: 8 Gilead is a city of evildoers 1
12:11 If there is iniquity in Gilead 1
Ams 1: 3 threshed Gilead with threshing sledges of iron. 1
13 they have ripped up women with child in Gilead 1
Obd 1:19 and Benjamin shall possess Gilead. 1
Mic 7:14 let them feed in Bashan and Gilead 1
Zec 10:10 I will bring them to the land of Gilead 1
Jdt 1: 8 those among the nations of Carmel and Gilead 2
15: 5 those in Gilead and in Galilee outflanked them 2
1Mc 5: 9 Now the Gentiles in Gilead gathered together 2
17 I and Jonathan my brother will go to Gilead. 3
20 and 8,000 to Judas for Gilead. 3
25 happened to their brethren in Gilead 3
27 have been shut up in the other cities of Gilead; 3
36 Bosor, and the other cities of Gilead. 3
45 gathered together all the Israelites in Gilead 3
55 Now while Judas and Jonathan were in Gilead 2
13:22 He marched off and went into the land of Gilead. 3

Gileadite 1. בֶּן גִּלְעָדִי 2. גִּלְעָד 3. גִּלְעָדִי

Num26:29 of Gilead, the family of the Gileadites. 3
Jdg 10: 3 arose Ja'ir the Gileadite, who judged Israel 3
11: 1 Now Jephthah the Gileadite was a mighty warrior 3
40 lament the daughter of Jephthah the Gileadite 3
12: 4 You are fugitives of E'phraim, you Gileadites 2
5 the Gileadites took the fords of the Jordan 2
7 six years. Then Jephthah the Gileadite died 3
2Sm 17:27 and Barzil'lai the Gileadite from Ro'gelim 3
19:31 Now Barzil'lai the Gileadite had come down 3
1Kg 2: 7 with the sons of Barzil'lai the Gileadite, and let 3
2Kg 15:25 conspired . . with 50 men of the Gileadites 1
Ezr 2:61 from the daughters of Barzil'lai the Gileadite 3
Neh 7:63 daughters of Barzil'lai the Gileadite 3

Gilgal 1. גִּלְגָּל 2. Γαλγαλα

Deu 11:30 over against Gilgal, beside the oak of Moreh? 1
Jos 4:19 The people came up . . and they encamped in Gilgal 1
20 those twelve stones . . Joshua set up in Gilgal. 1
5: 9 name of this place is called Gilgal to this day. 1
10 the people of Israel were encamped in Gilgal 1
9: 6 they went to Joshua in the camp at Gilgal, and said 1
10: 6 the men . . sent to Joshua at the camp in Gilgal 1
7 So Joshua went up from Gilgal 1
9 having marched up all night from Gilgal. 1
15 Then Joshua returned . . to the camp at Gilgal. 1
43 Then Joshua returned . . to the camp at Gilgal. 1
14: 6 Then the people of Judah came to Joshua at Gilgal; 1
15: 7 goes . . and so northward, turning toward Gilgal 1
Jdg 2: 1 the angel of the LORD went up from Gilgal 1
3:19 back at the sculptured stones near Gilgal 1
1Sm 7:16 went on a circuit . . to Bethel, Gilgal, and Mizpah; 1
10: 8 And you shall go down before me to Gilgal; 1
11:14 let us go to Gilgal and there renew the kingdom. 1
15 all the people went to Gilgal . . made Saul king 1
15 they made Saul king before the LORD in Gilgal. 1
13: 4 people were called out to join Saul at Gilgal. 1
7 Saul was still at Gilgal, and all the people 1
8 He waited . . but Samuel did not come to Gilgal 1
12 the Philistines will come down upon me at Gilgal 1
15 and went up from Gilgal to Gib'e-ah of Benjamin. 1
15:12 and turned, and passed on, and went down to Gilgal. 1
21 to sacrifice to the LORD your God in Gilgal. 1
33 And Samuel hewed Agag in pieces . . in Gilgal. 1
2Sm 19:15 and Judah came to Gilgal to meet the king 1
40 The king went on to Gilgal, and Chimham went 1
2Kg 2: 1 Eli'jah and Eli'sha were on their way from Gilgal. 1
4:38 Eli'sha came again to Gilgal 1
Hos 4:15 Enter not into Gilgal, nor go up to Beth-a'ven 1
9:15 Every evil of theirs is in Gilgal; 1
12:11 if in Gilgal they sacrifice bulls 1
Ams 4: 4 to Gilgal, and multiply transgression; 1
5: 5 do not seek Bethel, and do not enter into Gilgal 1
5 for Gilgal shall surely go into exile 1
Mic 6: 5 and what happened from Shittim to Gilgal 1
1Mc 9: 2 They went by the road which leads to Gilgal 2

Gilo 1. גִּילֹנִי

2Sm 23:34 Eli'am the son of Ahith'ophel of Gilo 1

Giloh 1. גִּלֹה

Jos 15:51 Goshen, Holon, and Giloh 1
2Sm 15:12 he sent for Ahith'opel . . from his city Giloh. 1

Gilonite 1. גִּילֹנִי

2Sm 15:12 he sent for Ahith'opel the Gi'lonite 1

Gimzo 1. גִּמְזוֹ

2Ch 28:18 had taken . . and Gimzo with its villages; 1

Ginath 1. גִּינַת

1Kg 16:21 half . . followed Tibni the son of Ginath 1
22 the people who followed Tibni the son of Ginath; 1

Ginnethoi 1. גִּנְּתוֹי

Neh 12: 4 Iddo, Gin'nethoi, Abi'jah 1

Ginnethon 1.גִּנְּתוֹן
Neh 10: 6 Daniel, Gin'nethon, Baruch 1
12:16 of Iddo, Zechari'ah; of Gin'nethon, Meshul'lam; 1

Girgashite 1.גִּרְגָּשִׁי
Gen 10:16 the Jeb'usites, the Amorites, the Gir'gashites 1
15:21 the Amorites, the Canaanites, the Gir'gashites 1
Deu 7: 1 Hittites, the Gir'gashites, the Amorites 1
Jos 3:10 the Hivites, the Per'izzites, the Gir'gashites 1
24:11 the Canaanites, the Hittites, the Gir'gashites 1
1Ch 1:14 the Jeb'usites, the Am'orites, the Gir'gashites 1
Neh 9: 8 land of . . the Jeb'usite, and the Gir'gashite; 1

Girzite 1.גִּרְזִי
1Sm 27: 8 and made raids upon the Gesh'urites, and Gir'zites 1

Gishpa 1.גִּשְׁפָּא
Neh 11:21 Ziha and Gishpa were over the temple servants. 1

Gittaim 1.גִּתַּיִם
2Sm 4: 3 the Be-er'othites fled to Gitta'im 1
Neh 11:33 Hazor, Ramah, Git'taim 1

Gittite 1.גִּתִּי
2Sm 6:10 took it . . to the house of O'bed-e'dom the Gittite. 1
11 remained in the house of O'bed-e'dom the Gittite 1
15:18 all the 600 Gittites who had followed him 1
19 Then the king said to It'tai the Gittite 1
22 It'tai the Gittite passed on, with all his men 1
18: 2 third under the command of It'tai the Gittite. 1
21:19 and Elha'nan . . slew Goliath the Gittite 1
1Ch 13:13 to the house of O'bed-e'dom the Gittite. 1
20: 5 Lahmi the brother of Goliath the Gittite 1

Gittith 1.גִּתִּית
Ps 8: 0 To the choirmaster: according to The Gittith. 1
81: 0 To the choirmaster: according to The Gittith. 1
84: 0 To the choirmaster: according to The Gittith. 1

Gizonite 1.גִּזוֹנִי
1Ch 11:34 Hashem the Gi'zonite 1

Goah 1.גֹּעָה
Jer 31:39 to the hill Gareb, and shall then turn to Go'ah. 1

Gob 1.גּוֹב
2Sm 21:18 there was again war with the Philistines at Gob; 1
19 there was again war with the Philistines at Gob; 1

GOD 1.אֱלֹהִים 2.יָהּ 3.יְהוִה
Gen 15: 2 Abram said, "O Lord GOD, what wilt thou give me 3
8 he said, "O Lord GOD, how am I to know 3
Deu 3:24 'O Lord GOD, thou hast only begun to show 3
9:26 O Lord GOD, destroy not thy people and thy heritage 3
Jos 7: 7 And Joshua said, "Alas, O Lord GOD, why hast thou 3
Jdg 6:22 "Alas, O Lord GOD! For now I have seen the angel 3
16:28 O Lord GOD, remember me, I pray thee, 3
2Sm 7:18 Who am I, O Lord GOD . . that thou hast brought me 3
19 yet this was a small thing in thy eyes, O Lord GOD; 3
19 and . . shown me future generations, O Lord GOD! 3
20 For thou knowest thy servant, O Lord GOD! 3
28 O Lord GOD, thou art God, and thy words are true 3
29 for thou, O Lord GOD, hast spoken 3
1Kg 2:26 you bore the ark of the Lord GOD before David my 3
8:53 bring our fathers out of Egypt, O Lord GOD. 3
2Ch 32:16 servants said still more against the Lord GOD 1
Ps 69: 6 be put to shame through me, O Lord GOD of hosts; 3
71:16 With the mighty deeds of the Lord GOD I will come 3
73:28 I have made the Lord GOD my refuge 3
109:21 O GOD my Lord, deal on my behalf for thy name's 3
Isa 3:15 What do you mean . . ?" says the Lord GOD of hosts. 3
7: 7 thus says the Lord GOD: It shall not stand 3
12: 2 for the LORD GOD is my strength and my song 2
22: 5 For the Lord GOD of hosts has a day of tumult 3
12 Lord GOD of hosts called to weeping and mourning 3
14 till you die." says the Lord GOD of hosts. 3
15 Thus says the Lord GOD of hosts, "Come, go to this 3
25: 8 the Lord GOD will wipe away tears from all faces 3
26: 4 for ever, for the LORD GOD is an everlasting rock. 3
28:16 thus says the Lord GOD, "Behold, I am laying in Zion 3
22 destruction from the Lord GOD of hosts 3
30:15 For thus said the Lord GOD, the Holy One of Israel 3
40:10 Behold, the Lord GOD comes with might 3
48:16 And now the Lord GOD has sent me and his Spirit. 3
49:22 says the Lord GOD: "Behold, I will lift up my hand 3
50: 4 The Lord GOD has given me the tongue 3
5 The Lord GOD has opened my ear 3
7 For the Lord GOD helps me; 3
9 Behold, the Lord GOD helps me; 3
52: 4 For thus says the Lord GOD: My people went down 3
56: 8 the Lord GOD, who gathers the outcasts of Israel 3
61: 1 The Spirit of the Lord GOD is upon me 3
11 the Lord GOD will cause righteousness 3
65:13 says the Lord GOD: "Behold, my servants shall eat 3
15 for a curse, and the Lord GOD will slay you; 3
Jer 1: 6 "Ah, Lord GOD! Behold, I do not know how to speak 3
2:19 says the Lord GOD of hosts. 3
22 guilt is still before me, says the Lord GOD. 3
4:10 Then I said, "Ah, Lord GOD 3
7:20 Therefore thus says the Lord GOD: Behold, my anger 3
14:13 said: "Ah, Lord GOD, behold, the prophets say to them 3
32:17 'Ah Lord GOD! It is thou who hast made the heavens 3
25 Yet thou, O Lord GOD, hast said to me, "Buy the field 3
44:26 saying, 'As the Lord GOD lives.' 3
46:10 That day is the day of the Lord GOD of hosts 3
10 Lord GOD of hosts holds a sacrifice in the north 3
49: 5 bring terror upon you, says the Lord GOD of hosts 3
50:25 for the Lord GOD of hosts has a work to do 3
31 against you, O proud one, says the Lord GOD of hosts; 3
Ezk 2: 4 you shall say to them, 'Thus says the Lord GOD.' 3
3:11 say to them, 'Thus says the Lord GOD' 3
27 and you shall say to them, 'Thus says the Lord GOD' 3
4:14 Then I said, "Ah Lord GOD! 3
5: 5 Thus says the Lord GOD: This is Jerusalem; 3
7 Therefore thus says the Lord GOD 3
8 therefore thus says the Lord GOD: Behold, I, even I 3
11 Wherefore, as I live, says the Lord GOD 3
6: 3 mountains of Israel, hear the word of the Lord GOD! 3
3 Thus says the Lord GOD to the mountains 3
11 Thus says the Lord GOD: "Clap your hands 3
7: 2 thus says the Lord GOD to the land of Israel: An end! 3
5 Thus says the Lord GOD: Disaster after disaster! 3
8: 1 the hand of the Lord GOD fell there upon me. 3
9: 8 I fell upon my face, and cried, "Ah Lord GOD! 3
11: 7 Therefore thus says the Lord GOD 3
8 I will bring the sword upon you, says the Lord GOD. 3
13 and said, "Ah Lord GOD! wilt thou make a full end 3
16 Therefore say, 'Thus says the Lord GOD 3
17 say, 'Thus says the Lord GOD: 3
21 upon their own heads, says the Lord GOD. 3
12:10 Say to them, 'Thus says the Lord GOD: This oracle 3
19 says the Lord GOD concerning the inhabitants 3
23 Tell them therefore, 'Thus says the Lord GOD 3
25 speak the word and perform it, says the Lord GOD. 3
28 Therefore say to them, Thus says the Lord GOD 3
28 will be performed, says the Lord GOD. 3
13: 3 Thus says the Lord GOD, Woe to the foolish 3
8 Therefore thus says the Lord GOD 3
8 behold, I am against you, says the Lord GOD. 3
9 you shall know that I am the Lord GOD. 3
13 Therefore thus says the Lord GOD 3
16 when there was no peace, says the Lord GOD. 3
18 and say, Thus says the Lord GOD 3
20 Wherefore thus says the Lord GOD 3
14: 4 and say to them, Thus says the Lord GOD 3
6 Thus says the Lord GOD: Repent and turn away 3
11 and I may be their God, says the Lord GOD. 3
14 by their righteousness, says the Lord GOD. 3
16 as I live, says the Lord GOD, they would deliver 3
18 as I live, says the Lord GOD, they would deliver 3
20 as I live, says the Lord GOD, they would deliver 3
21 For thus says the Lord GOD 3
23 all that I have done in it, says the Lord GOD. 3
15: 6 Therefore thus says the Lord GOD 3
8 they have acted faithlessly, says the Lord GOD. 3
16: 3 and say, Thus says the Lord GOD to Jerusalem 3
8 into a covenant with you, says the Lord GOD 3
14 which I had bestowed upon you, says the Lord GOD. 3
19 for a pleasing odor, says the Lord GOD. 3
23 woe, woe to you! says the Lord GOD 3
30 How lovesick is your heart, says the Lord GOD 3
36 Thus says the Lord GOD, Because your shame was 3
43 your deeds upon your head, says the Lord GOD. 3
48 As I live, says the Lord GOD 3
59 Yea, thus says the Lord GOD: I will deal with you 3
63 all that you have done, says the Lord GOD. 3
17: 3 say, Thus says the Lord GOD 3
9 Say, Thus says the Lord GOD: Will it thrive? 3
16 As I live, says the Lord GOD 3
19 Therefore thus says the Lord GOD: As I live, surely 3
22 Thus says the Lord GOD: "I myself will take a sprig 3
18: 3 As I live, says the Lord GOD 3
9 he shall surely live, says the Lord GOD. 3
23 in the death of the wicked, says the Lord GOD 3
30 according to his ways, says the Lord GOD. 3
32 says the Lord GOD; so turn, and live. 3
20: 3 and say to them, Thus says the Lord GOD 3
3 As I live, says the Lord GOD 3
5 and say to them, Thus says the Lord GOD 3
27 and say to them, Thus says the Lord GOD 3
30 Thus says the Lord GOD: Will you defile 3
31 As I live, says the Lord GOD 3
33 As I live, says the Lord GOD 3
36 enter into judgment with you, says the Lord GOD. 3
39 As for you, O house of Israel, thus says the Lord GOD 3
40 mountain height of Israel, says the Lord GOD 3
44 O house of Israel, says the Lord GOD. 3
47 Hear the word of the LORD: Thus says the Lord GOD 3
49 Then I said, "Ah Lord GOD! 3
21: 7 it will be fulfilled,'" says the Lord GOD. 3
13 if you despise the rod?" says the Lord GOD. 3
24 Therefore thus says the Lord GOD 3
26 thus says the Lord GOD: Remove the turban 3
28 prophesy, and say, Thus says the Lord GOD 3
22: 3 You shall say, Thus says the Lord GOD 3
12 you have forgotten me, says the Lord GOD. 3
19 Therefore thus says the Lord GOD 3
28 says the Lord GOD,' when the LORD has not spoken. 3
31 requited upon their heads, says the Lord GOD. 3
23:22 Therefore, O Oholi'bah, thus says the Lord GOD 3
28 For thus says the Lord GOD: Behold, I will deliver 3
32 Thus says the Lord GOD: "You shall drink 3
34 for I have spoken, says the Lord GOD. 3
35 Therefore thus says the Lord GOD 3
46 thus says the Lord GOD: "Bring up a host 3
49 you shall know that I am the Lord GOD. 3
24: 3 say to them, Thus says the Lord GOD: Set on the pot 3
6 Therefore thus says the Lord GOD 3
9 Therefore thus says the Lord GOD 3
14 I will judge you, says the Lord GOD. 3
21 Say to the house of Israel, Thus says the Lord GOD 3
24 then you will know that I am the Lord GOD. 3
25: 3 Say to the Ammonites, Hear the word of the Lord GOD 3
3 Thus says the Lord GOD, Because you said, 'Aha!' 3
6 For thus says the Lord GOD 3
8 Thus says the Lord GOD: Because Moab said, Behold 3
12 Thus says the Lord GOD: Because Edom acted 3
13 therefore thus says the Lord GOD 3
14 they shall know my vengeance, says the Lord GOD. 3
15 Thus says the Lord GOD: Because the Philistines 3
16 therefore thus says the Lord GOD, Behold 3
26: 3 therefore thus says the Lord GOD 3
5 for I have spoken, says the Lord GOD; 3
7 says the Lord GOD: Behold, I will bring upon Tyre 3
14 for I the LORD have spoken, says the Lord GOD. 3
15 Thus says the Lord GOD to Tyre 3
19 For thus says the Lord GOD: When I make you a city 3
21 you will never be found again, says the Lord GOD. 3
27: 3 thus says the Lord GOD: "O Tyre, you have said 3
28: 2 to the prince of Tyre, Thus says the Lord GOD 3
6 therefore thus says the Lord GOD 3
10 for I have spoken, says the Lord GOD. 3
12 king of Tyre, and say to him, Thus says the Lord GOD 3
22 Thus says the Lord GOD: "Behold, I am against you 3
24 Then they will know that I am the Lord GOD. 3
25 Thus says the Lord GOD 3
29: 3 Thus says the Lord GOD: "Behold, I am against you 3
8 thus says the Lord GOD: Behold, I will bring a sword 3
13 thus says the Lord GOD: At the end of 40 years 3
16 Then they will know that I am the Lord GOD. 3
19 thus says the Lord GOD: Behold, I will give the land 3
20 because they worked for me, says the Lord GOD. 3
30: 2 prophesy, and say, Thus says the Lord GOD 3
6 fall within her by the sword, says the Lord GOD. 3
10 says the Lord GOD: I will put an end to the wealth 3
13 Thus says the Lord GOD: I will destroy the idols 3
22 Therefore thus says the Lord GOD: Behold, I am 3
31:10 Therefore thus says the Lord GOD 3
15 Thus says the Lord GOD: When it goes down to Sheol 3
18 Pharaoh and all his multitude, says the Lord GOD. 3
32: 3 Thus says the Lord GOD: I will throw my net over you 3
8 put darkness upon your land, says the Lord GOD. 3
11 says the Lord GOD: The sword of the king of Babylon 3
14 their rivers to run like oil, says the Lord GOD. 3
16 shall they chant it, says the Lord GOD. 3
31 all his army, slain by the sword, says the Lord GOD. 3
32 Pharaoh and all his multitude, says the Lord GOD. 3
33:11 Say to them, As I live, says the Lord GOD 3
25 Therefore say to them, Thus says the Lord GOD 3
27 Say this to them, Thus says the Lord GOD: As I live 3
34: 2 Thus says the Lord GOD: Ho, shepherds of Israel 3
8 As I live, says the Lord GOD 3
10 Thus says the Lord GOD, Behold 3
11 For thus says the Lord GOD: Behold 3
15 I will make them lie down, says the Lord GOD. 3
17 As for you, my flock, thus says the Lord GOD: Behold 3
20 Therefore, thus says the Lord GOD to them: Behold 3
30 house of Israel, are my people, says the Lord GOD. 3
31 and I am your God, says the Lord GOD. 3
35: 3 and say to it, Thus says the Lord GOD: Behold 3
6 therefore, as I live, says the Lord GOD 3
11 as I live, says the Lord GOD, I will deal with you 3
14 says the Lord GOD: For the rejoicing of the whole 3
36: 2 Thus says the Lord GOD: Because the enemy said 3
3 prophesy, and say, Thus says the Lord GOD: 3
4 hear the word of the Lord GOD: Thus says the Lord 3
4 Thus says the Lord GOD to the mountains 3
5 thus says the Lord GOD: I speak in my hot jealousy 3
6 Thus says the Lord GOD: Behold, I speak 3
7 thus says the Lord GOD: I swear that the nations 3
13 Thus says the Lord GOD: Because men say to you 3
14 your nation of children, says the Lord GOD; 3
15 cause your nation to stumble, says the Lord GOD. 3
22 Thus says the Lord GOD: It is not for your sake 3
23 will know that I am the LORD, says the Lord GOD 3
32 not for your sake that I will act, says the Lord GOD; 3
33 Thus says the Lord GOD: On the day that I cleanse 3
37 Thus says the Lord GOD: This also I will let 3
37: 3 And I answered, "O Lord GOD, thou knowest. 3
5 Thus says the Lord GOD to these bones 3
9 and say to the breath, Thus says the Lord GOD 3
12 prophesy, and say to them, Thus says the Lord GOD 3
19 say to them, Thus says the Lord GOD 3
21 then say to them, Thus says the Lord GOD 3
38: 3 Thus says the Lord GOD: Behold, I am against you 3
10 says the Lord GOD: On that day thoughts will come 3

14 Thus says the Lord GOD: On that day when my people 3
17 Thus says the Lord GOD: Are you he of whom I spoke 3
18 says the Lord GOD, my wrath will be roused. 3
21 kind of terror against Gog, says the Lord GOD; 3
39: 1 says the Lord GOD: Behold, I am against you, O Gog 3
5 for I have spoken, says the Lord GOD. 3
8 and it will be brought about, says the Lord GOD. 3
10 those who plundered them, says the Lord GOD. 3
13 on the day that I show my glory, says the Lord GOD. 3
17 As for you, son of man, thus says the Lord GOD 3
20 men and all kinds of warriors,' says the Lord GOD. 3
25 Therefore thus says the Lord GOD 3
29 upon the house of Israel, says the Lord GOD. 3
43:18 he said to me, "Son of man, thus says the Lord GOD 3
19 says the Lord GOD, a bull for a sin offering. 3
27 I will accept you, says the Lord GOD. 3
44: 6 Thus says the Lord GOD: O house of Israel 3
9 Therefore thus says the Lord GOD: No foreigner 3
12 I have sworn concerning them, says the Lord GOD 3
15 to offer me the fat and the blood, says the Lord GOD; 3
27 he shall offer his sin offering, says the Lord GOD 3
45: 9 Thus says the Lord GOD: Enough, O princes of Israel! 3
9 your evictions of my people, says the Lord GOD. 3
15 to make atonement for them, says the Lord GOD. 3
18 Thus says the Lord GOD: In the first month 3
46: 1 Thus says the Lord GOD: The gate of the inner court 3
16 Thus says the Lord GOD: If the prince makes a gift 3
47:13 Thus says the Lord GOD: "These are the boundaries 3
23 assign him his inheritance, says the Lord GOD. 3
48:29 are their several portions, says the Lord GOD. 3
Ams 1: 8 the Philistines shall perish," says the Lord GOD 3
3: 7 the Lord GOD does nothing, without revealing his 3
8 The Lord GOD has spoken; who can but prophesy? 3
11 says the Lord GOD: "An adversary shall surround 3
13 against the house of Jacob," says the Lord GOD 3
4: 2 The Lord GOD has sworn by his holiness 3
5 O people of Israel!" says the Lord GOD. 3
5: 3 For thus says the Lord GOD: "The city that went 3
6: 8 The Lord GOD has sworn by himself (says the LORD 3
7: 1 Thus the Lord GOD showed me 3
2 I said, "O Lord GOD, forgive, I beseech thee! 3
4 Thus the Lord GOD showed me 3
4 the Lord GOD was calling for a judgment by fire 3
5 Then I said, "O Lord GOD, cease, I beseech thee! 3
6 This also shall not be," said the Lord GOD. 3
8: 1 Thus the Lord GOD showed me 3
3 become wailings in that day," says the Lord GOD; 3
9 And on that day," says the Lord GOD 3
11 Behold, the days are coming," says the Lord GOD 3
9: 5 The Lord, GOD of hosts, he who touches the earth 3
8 eyes of the Lord GOD are upon the sinful kingdom 3
Obd 1: 1 Thus says the Lord GOD concerning Edom 3
Mic 1: 2 and let the Lord GOD be a witness against you 3
Hab 3:19 GOD, the Lord, is my strength; 3
Zep 1: 7 Be silent before the Lord GOD! 3
Zec 9:14 the Lord GOD will sound the trumpet, and march 3

God 1. אֲדוֹנָי 2. אֵל 3. אֱלָה 4. אֱלֹהַּ 5. אֱלֹהִים 6. יְהוָה
7. אֱלָהּ (A) 8. *θεῖος* 9. *θεός* 10. deus

Gen 1: 1 In the beginning God created the heavens 5
2 and the Spirit of God was moving over the face 5
3 God said, "Let there be light"; and there was light 5
4 God saw that the light was good 5
4 and God separated the light from the darkness 5
5 God called the light Day 5
6 God said, "Let there be a firmament 5
7 God made the firmament and separated the waters 5
8 God called the firmament Heaven. 5
9 God said, "Let the waters under the heavens 5
10 God called the dry land Earth 5
10 And God saw that it was good 5
11 God said, "Let the earth put forth vegetation 5
12 And God saw that it was good 5
14 God said, "Let there be lights in the firmament 5
16 God made the two great lights 5
17 God set them in the firmament of the heavens 5
18 And God saw that it was good 5
20 God said, "Let the waters bring forth swarms 5
21 God created the great sea monsters 5
21 And God saw that it was good 5
22 God blessed them, saying, "Be fruitful 5
24 God said, "Let the earth bring forth living 5
25 God made the beasts of the earth 5
25 And God saw that it was good 5
26 God said, "Let us make man in our image 5
27 God created man in his own image 5
27 in the image of God he created him; male and female 5
28 God blessed them, and God said to them, "Be fruitful 5
28 God blessed them, and God said to them, "Be fruitful 5
29 God said, "Behold, I have given you every plant 5
31 God saw everything that he had made 5
2: 2 on the seventh day God finished his work 5
3 God blessed the seventh day and hallowed it 5
3 and hallowed it, because on it God rested 5
4 In the day that the LORD God made the earth 5
5 for the LORD God had not caused it to rain 5
7 the LORD God formed man of dust from the ground 5
8 the LORD God planted a garden in Eden, in the east; 5
9 out of the ground the LORD God made to grow 5
15 The LORD God took the man and put him in the garden 5
16 the LORD God commanded the man, saying 5
18 the LORD God said, "It is not good that the man 5
19 out of the ground the LORD God formed every beast 5
21 the LORD God caused a deep sleep to fall upon 5
22 rib which the LORD God had taken from the man 5
3: 1 other wild creature that the LORD God had made. 5
1 He said to the woman, "Did God say, 'You shall not eat 5
3 God said, 'You shall not eat of the fruit of the tree 5
5 For God knows that when you eat of it 5
5 your eyes will be opened, and you will be like God 5
8 they heard the sound of the LORD God walking 5
8 hid themselves from the presence of the LORD God 5
9 the LORD God called to the man 5
13 the LORD God said to the woman 5
14 The LORD God said to the serpent 5
21 the LORD God made for Adam and for his wife 5
22 the LORD God said, "Behold, the man has become 5
23 the LORD God sent him forth from the garden 5
4:25 name Seth, for she said, "God has appointed for me 5
5: 1 When God created man, he made him in the likeness 5
1 man, he made him in the likeness of God. 5
22 Enoch walked with God after the birth 5
24 Enoch walked with God; 5
24 Enoch walked with God; 5
6: 2 the sons of God saw that the daughters of men 5
4 afterward, when the sons of God came 5
9 in his generation; Noah walked with God. 5
11 Now the earth was corrupt in God's sight 5
12 God saw the earth, and behold, it was corrupt; 5
13 God said to Noah, "I have determined to make an end 5
22 Noah did this; he did all that God commanded him. 5
7: 9 into the ark with Noah, as God had commanded Noah. 5
16 of all flesh, went in as God had commanded him; 5
8: 1 God remembered Noah and all the beasts 5
1 God made a wind blow over the earth, and the waters 5
15 Then God said to Noah 5
9: 1 God blessed Noah and his sons, and said to them 5
6 for God made man in his own image. 5
8 Then God said to Noah and to his sons with him 5
12 God said, "This is the sign of the covenant 5
16 the everlasting covenant between God 5
17 God said to Noah, "This is the sign of the covenant 5
26 He also said, "Blessed by the LORD my God be Shem; 5
27 God enlarge Japheth, and let him dwell 5
14:18 he was priest of God Most High. 2
19 Blessed be Abram by God Most High, maker of heaven 2
20 blessed be God Most High 2
22 I have sworn to the LORD God Most High 2
16:13 LORD who spoke to her, "Thou art a God of seeing"; 2
13 of seeing"; for she said, "Have I really seen God •
17: 1 "I am God Almighty; walk before me, and be blameless. 2
3 Then Abram fell on his face; and God said to him 5
7 everlasting covenant, to be God to you 5
8 possession; and I will be their God. 5
9 God said to Abraham, "As for you 5
15 God said to Abraham, "As for Sar'ai your wife 5
18 Abraham said to God, "O that Ish'mael might live 5
19 God said, "No, but Sarah your wife shall bear 5
22 talking with him, God went up from Abraham. 5
23 foreskins that very day, as God had said to him. 5
19:29 it was that, when God destroyed the cities 5
29 God remembered Abraham, and sent Lot out 5
20: 3 God came to Abim'elech in a dream by night 5
6 Then God said to him in the dream 5
11 There is no fear of God at all in this place 5
13 when God caused me to wander 5
17 Abraham prayed to God; and God healed Abim'elech 5
17 Abraham prayed to God; and God healed Abim'elech 5
21: 2 in his old age at the time of which God had spoken 5
4 he was eight days old, as God had commanded him. 5
6 Sarah said, "God has made laughter for me; 5
12 God said to Abraham, "Be not displeased 5
17 God heard the voice of the lad; 5
17 and the angel of God called to Hagar from heaven 5
17 Fear not; for God has heard the voice of the lad 5
19 Then God opened her eyes, and she saw a well 5
20 God was with the lad, and he grew up; 5
22 God is with you in all that you do; 5
23 now therefore swear to me here by God 5
33 the name of the LORD, the Everlasting God. 2
22: 1 After these things God tested Abraham 5
3 went to the place of which God had told him. 5
8 Abraham said, "God will provide himself the lamb 5
9 came to the place of which God had told him 5
12 for now I know that you fear God 5
24: 3 I will make you swear by the LORD, the God of heaven 5
7 The LORD, the God of heaven, who took me 5
12 he said, "O LORD, God of my master Abraham 5
27 Blessed be the LORD, the God of my master Abraham 5
42 and said, 'O LORD, the God of my master Abraham 5
48 blessed the LORD, the God of my master Abraham 5
25:11 After the death of Abraham God blessed Isaac 5
26:24 I am the God of Abraham your father; fear not 5
27:20 Because the LORD your God granted me success. 5
28 May God give you of the dew of heaven 5
28: 3 God Almighty bless you and make you fruitful 2
4 of your sojournings which God gave to Abraham! 5
12 and behold, the angels of God were ascending 5
13 I am the LORD, the God of Abraham your father 5
13 the God of Isaac; the land on which you lie I will 5
17 This is none other than the house of God 5
20 Jacob made a vow, saying, "If God will be with me 5
21 house in peace, then the LORD shall be my God 5
22 stone . . shall be God's house; 5
30: 2 and he said, "Am I in the place of God 5
6 Then Rachel said, "God has judged me 5
17 God hearkened to Leah, and she conceived and bore 5
18 Leah said, "God has given me my hire 5
20 Then Leah said, "God has endowed me 5
22 God remembered Rachel . . hearkened to her 5
22 God hearkened to her and opened her womb. 5
23 and said, "God has taken away my reproach"; 5
31: 5 But the God of my father has been with me. 5
7 but God did not permit him to harm me. 5
9 Thus God has taken away the cattle of your father 5
11 the angel of God said to me in the dream, 'Jacob,' 5
13 I am the God of Bethel, where you anointed a pillar 2
16 All the property which God has taken away 5
16 now then, whatever God has said to you, do. 5
24 God came to Laban the Aramean in a dream by night 5
29 but the God of your father spoke to me last night 5
42 If the God of my father, the God of Abraham 5
42 If the God of my father, the God of Abraham 5
42 God saw my affliction and the labor of my hands 5
50 remember, God is witness between you and me. 5
53 The God of Abraham and the God of Nahor 5
53 The God of Abraham and the God of Nahor 5
53 God of Nahor, the God of their father 5
32: 1 Jacob went on his way and the angels of God met him; 5
2 when Jacob saw them he said, "This is God's army! 5
9 Jacob said, "O God of my father Abraham 5
9 God of my father Abraham and God of my father 5
28 Israel, for you have striven with God and with men 5
30 saying, "For I have seen God face to face 5
33: 5 The children whom God has graciously given 5
10 to see your face is like seeing the face of God 5
11 Accept . . because God has dealt graciously 5
35: 1 God said to Jacob, "Arise, go up to Bethel 5
1 make there an altar to the God who appeared to you 2
3 an altar to the God who answered me in the day of my 2
5 as they journeyed, a terror from God fell upon 5
7 there God had revealed himself to him when he 5
9 God appeared to Jacob again, when he came 5
10 God said to him, "Your name is Jacob; 5
11 God said to him, "I am God Almighty 5
11 God said to him, "I am God Almighty 2
13 Then God went up from him in the place where he had 5
15 name of the place where God had spoken with him 5
39: 9 I do this great wickedness, and sin against God? 5
40: 8 Do not interpretations belong to God? 5
41:16 God will give Pharaoh a favorable answer. 5
25 God has revealed to Pharaoh what he is about 5
28 It is as I told Pharaoh, God has shown to Pharaoh 5
32 dream means that the thing is fixed by God 5
32 and God will shortly bring it to pass. 5
38 such a man as this, in whom is the Spirit of God? 5
39 Pharaoh said to Joseph, "Since God has shown you 5
51 "For," he said, "God has made me to forget all my 5
52 For God has made me fruitful in the land of my 5
42:18 Do this and you will live, for I fear God 5
28 "What is this that God has done to us? 5
43:14 may God Almighty grant you mercy before the man 2
23 not be afraid; your God and the God of your father 5
23 your God and the God of your father must have put 5
29 God be gracious to you, my son! 5
44:16 God has found out the guilt of your servants; 5
45: 5 for God sent me before you to preserve life. 5
7 God sent me before you to preserve for you 5
8 it was not you who sent me here, but God; 5
9 God has made me lord of all Egypt; come down to me 5
46: 1 offered sacrifices to the God of his father 5
2 God spoke to Israel in visions of the night 5
3 Then he said, "I am God, the God of your father; 5
3 Then he said, "I am God, the God of your father; 5
48: 3 Jacob said to Joseph, "God Almighty appeared 2
9 "They are my sons, whom God has given me here. 5
11 and lo, God has let me see your children also. 5
15 he blessed Joseph, and said, "The God before 5
15 the God who has led me all my life long to this day 5
20 will pronounce blessings, saying, 'God make you 5
21 Behold, I am about to die, but God will be with you 5
49:25 by the God of your father who will help you 2
25 by God Almighty who will bless you 2
50:17 the servants of the God of your father. 5
19 Fear not, for am I in the place of God? 5
20 but God meant it for good, to bring it about 5
24 but God will visit you, and bring you up out of this 5
25 God will visit you, and you shall carry up 5
Exd 1:17 the midwives feared God 5
20 So God dealt well with the midwives; 5
21 because the midwives feared God 5
2:23 and their cry under bondage came up to God. 5
24 God heard their groaning, and God remembered 5
24 and God remembered his covenant with Abraham 5
25 God saw the people of Israel 5
25 people of Israel, and God knew their condition. 5

3: 1 and came to Horeb, the mountain of God. 5
4 God called to him out of the bush, "Moses, Moses! 5
6 he said, "I am the God of your father 5
6 I am the God of your father, the God of Abraham 5
6 God of Abraham, the God of Isaac, and the God 5
6 of Abraham, the God of Isaac, and the God of Jacob. 5
6 hid his face, for he was afraid to look at God. 5
11 Moses said to God, "Who am I that I should go 5
12 you shall serve God upon this mountain. 5
13 Moses said to God, "If I come to the people of Israel 5
13 If I . . say to them, 'The God of your fathers 5
14 God said to Moses, "I AM WHO I AM." And he said, 5
15 God also said to Moses, "Say this to the people 5
15 Say this . . 'The LORD, the God of your fathers 5
15 God of Abraham, the God of Isaac, and the God 5
15 God of Abraham, the God of Isaac, and the God 5
15 God of Isaac, and the God of Jacob, has sent me to you' 5
16 LORD, the God of your fathers, the God of Abraham 5
16 LORD, the God of your fathers, the God of Abraham 5
18 The LORD, the God of the Hebrews, has met with us; 5
18 that we may sacrifice to the LORD our God.' 5
4: 5 believe that the LORD, the God of their fathers 5
5 LORD . . the God of Abraham, the God of Isaac 5
5 LORD . . the God of Abraham, the God of Isaac 5
5 and the God of Jacob, has appeared to you. 5
7 Then God said, "Put your hand back into your bosom. •
8 "If they will not believe you," God said, "or heed •
16 mouth for you, and you shall be to him as God. 5
20 and in his hand Moses took the rod of God. 5
27 met him at the mountain of God and kissed him. 5
5: 1 Thus says the LORD, the God of Israel 5
3 they said, "The God of the Hebrews has met with us; 5
3 let us . . sacrifice to the LORD our God 5
8 Let us go and offer sacrifice to our God.' 5
6: 2 God said to Moses, "I am the LORD. 5
3 I appeared . . as God Almighty, but by my name 2
7 I will take you for my people, and I will be your God; 5
7 and you shall know that I am the LORD your God 5
7: 1 to Moses, "See, I make you as God to Pharaoh; 5
16 The LORD, the God of the Hebrews, sent me to you 5
8:10 know that there is no one like the LORD our God. 5
19 said to Pharaoh, "This is the finger of God. 5
25 "Go, sacrifice to your God within the land. 5
26 shall sacrifice to the LORD our God offerings 5
27 sacrifice to the LORD our God as he will command 5
28 sacrifice to the LORD your God in the wilderness; 5
9: 1 Thus says the LORD, the God of the Hebrews 5
13 Thus says the LORD, the God of the Hebrews 5
30 I know that you do not yet fear the LORD God. 5
10: 3 Thus says the LORD, the God of the Hebrews, 'How long 5
7 that they may serve the LORD their God; 5
8 Go, serve the LORD your God; but who are to go? 5
16 I have sinned against the LORD your God 5
17 entreat the LORD your God only to remove this 5
25 that we may sacrifice to the LORD our God. 5
26 to serve the LORD our God, and we do not know 5
13:17 God did not lead them by way of the land 5
17 for God said, "Lest the people repent when they see 5
18 God led the people round by the way 5
19 solemnly sworn . . saying, "God will visit you; 5
14:19 angel of God who went before the host of Israel 5
15: 2 this is my God, and I will praise him 2
2 this is . . my father's God, and I will exalt him. 5
26 hearken to the voice of the LORD your God 5
16:12 then you shall know that I am the LORD your God.' 5
17: 9 I will stand . . with the rod of God in my hand. 5
18: 1 Jethro . . heard of all that God had done 5
4 for he said, "The God of father was my help 5
5 he was encamped at the mountain of God. 5
12 offered a burnt offering and sacrifices to God; 5
12 bread with Moses' father-in-law before God. 5
15 Because the people come to me to inquire of God; 5
16 I make them know the statutes of God 5
19 give you counsel, and God be with you! 5
19 You shall represent the people before God 5
19 You shall . . bring their cases to God; 5
21 choose able men . . such as fear God 5
23 If you do this, and God so commands you, then you 5
19: 3 Moses went up to God, and the LORD called to him 5
17 brought the people out . . to meet God; 5
19 Moses spoke, and God answered him in thunder. 5
20: 1 God spoke all these words, saying 5
2 I am the LORD your God, who brought you out 5
5 for I the LORD your God am a jealous God 5
5 for I the LORD your God am a jealous God 2
7 take the name of the LORD your God in vain; 5
10 the seventh day is a sabbath to the LORD your God; 5
12 the land which the LORD your God gives you. 5
19 but let not God speak to us, lest we die. 5
20 Do not fear; for God has come to prove you 5
21 drew near to the thick darkness where God was. 5
21: 6 then his master shall bring him to God 5
13 if he did not lie in wait for him, but God let him 5
22: 8 the owner of the house shall come near to God 5
9 the case of both parties shall come before God; 5
9 he whom God shall condemn shall pay double 5
28 You shall not revile God, nor curse a ruler 5
23:17 shall all your males appear before the LORD God. 9
19 shall bring into the house of the LORD your God. 5
25 You shall serve the LORD your God, and I will bless 5
24:10 they saw the God of Israel; 5
11 they beheld God, and ate and drank. 5
13 Moses went up into the mountain of God. 5
29:45 I . . will be their God. 5
46 they shall know that I am the LORD their God, who 5
46 dwell among them; I am the LORD their God. 5
31: 3 I have filled him with the Spirit of God 5
18 tables of stone, written with the finger of God. 5
32:11 Moses besought the LORD his God, and said, "O LORD 5
16 the tables were the work of God, and the writing 5
16 and the writing was the writing of God 5
27 he said to them, "Thus says the LORD God of Israel 5
34: 6 proclaimed, "The LORD, the LORD, a God merciful 2
14 the LORD, whose name is Jealous, is a jealous God) 2
23 appear before the LORD God, the God of Israel. 5
23 appear before the LORD God, the God of Israel. 5
24 before the LORD your God three times in the year. 5
26 you shall bring to the house of the LORD your God. 5
29 face shone because he had been talking with God. •
35:31 he has filled him with the Spirit of God 5
Lev 2:13 salt of the covenant with your God be lacking 5
4:22 the things which the LORD his God has commanded 5
11:44 For I am the LORD your God: consecrate yourselves 5
45 who brought you up . . to be your God 5
18: 2 "Say to the people of Israel, I am the LORD your God 5
4 I am the LORD your God 5
21 fire to Molech, and so profane the name of your God 5
30 I am the LORD your God 5
19: 2 You shall be holy; for I the LORD your God am holy 5
3 you shall keep my sabbaths: I am the LORD your God 5
4 I am LORD your God 5
10 I am the LORD your God 5
12 and so profane the name of your God: I am the LORD 5
14 but you shall fear your God: I am the LORD 5
25 may yield more richly for you: I am the LORD your God 5
31 I am the LORD your God 5
32 you shall fear your God; I am the LORD 5
34 I am the LORD your God 5
36 I am the LORD your God, who brought you out 5
20: 7 be holy; for I am the LORD your God 5
24 I am the LORD your God, who have separated you 5
21: 6 They shall be holy to their God, and not profane 5
6 shall . . not profane the name of their God 5
6 for they offer . . the bread of their God 5
7 for the priest is holy to his God 5
8 for he offers the bread of your God 5
12 nor profane the sanctuary of his God 5
12 the anointing oil of his God is upon him 5
17 may approach to offer the bread of his God 5
21 not come near to offer the bread of his God 5
22 He may eat the bread of his God 5
22:25 neither shall you offer as the bread of your God 5
33 who brought you . . to be your God: I am the LORD 5
23:14 until you have brought the offering of your God 5
22 I am the LORD your God 5
28 to make atonement for you before the LORD your God 5
40 you shall rejoice before the LORD your God 5
43 I am the LORD your God 5
24:15 Whoever curses his God shall bear his sin 5
22 for I am the LORD your God 5
25:17 fear your God; for I am the LORD your God 5
17 fear your God; for I am the LORD your God 5
36 fear your God; that your brother may live 5
38 I am the LORD your God, who brought you forth 5
38 to give you the land of Canaan, and to be your God 5
43 You shall not rule . . but shall fear your God 5
55 out of the land of Egypt: I am the LORD your God 5
26: 1 to bow down to them, for I am the LORD your God 5
12 I will walk among you, and will be your God 5
13 I am the LORD your God, who brought you forth 5
44 for I am the LORD their God 5
45 that I might be their God: I am the LORD 5
Num 6: 7 because his separation to God is upon his head. 5
10: 9 you may be remembered before the LORD your God 5
10 shall serve you for remembrance before your God 5
10 I am the LORD your God. 5
12:13 Moses cried . . "Heal her, O God, I beseech thee. 2
15:40 do all my commandments, and be holy to your God. 5
41 I am the LORD your God, who brought you out 5
41 brought you out of the land of Egypt, to be your God 5
41 I am the LORD your God. 5
16: 9 that the God of Israel has separated you 5
22 said, "O God, the God of the spirits of all flesh 2
22 said, "O God, the God of the spirits of all flesh 5
21: 5 the people spoke against God and against Moses 5
22: 9 God came to Balaam and said, "Who are these men 5
10 Balaam said to God, "Balak the son of Zippor 5
12 God said to Balaam, "You shall not go with them; 5
18 could not go beyond the command of the LORD my God 5
20 God came to Balaam at night and said to him 5
22 God's anger was kindled because he went; 5
38 word that God puts in my mouth, that must I speak. 5
23: 4 God met Balaam; and Balaam said to him 5
8 How can I curse whom God has not cursed? 2
19 God is not man, that he should lie 2
21 The LORD their God is with them 5
22 God brings them out of Egypt; 2
23 be said of Jacob and Israel, 'What has God wrought!' 2
27 perhaps it will please God that you may curse 5
24: 2 And the Spirit of God came upon him 5
4 oracle of him who hears the words of God 2
8 God brings him out of Egypt; 2
16 the oracle of him who hears the words of God 2
23 Alas, who shall live when God does this? 2
25:13 because he was jealous for his God 5
27:16 Let the LORD, the God of the spirits of all flesh 5
Deu 1: 6 LORD our God said to us in Horeb, 'You have stayed 5
10 the LORD your God has multiplied you, and behold 5
11 May the LORD, the God of your fathers, make you 5
17 not be afraid . . for the judgment is God's; 5
19 we set out . . as the LORD our God commanded us; 5
20 hill country . . which the LORD our God gives us. 5
21 LORD your God has set the land before you; go up 5
21 as the LORD, the God of your fathers, has told you; 5
25 'It is a good land which the LORD our God gives us.' 5
26 rebelled against the command of the LORD your God; 5
30 The LORD your God . . will himself fight for you 5
31 where you have seen how the LORD your God bore you 5
32 you did not believe the LORD your God 5
41 go up and fight, just as the LORD our God commanded 5
2: 7 LORD your God has blessed you in all the work 5
7 these 40 years the LORD your God has been with you 5
29 into the land which the LORD our God gives to us.' 5
30 for the LORD your God hardened his spirit 5
33 LORD our God gave him over to us; and we defeated 5
36 LORD our God gave all into our hands. 5
37 wherever the LORD our God forbade us. 5
3: 3 LORD our God gave into our hand Og also, the king 5
18 LORD your God has given you this land to possess; 5
20 land which the LORD your God gives them beyond 5
21 eyes have seen all that the LORD your God has done 5
22 for it is the LORD your God who fights for you.' 5
4: 1 land which the LORD, the God of your fathers, gives 5
2 may keep the commandments of the LORD your God 5
3 LORD your God destroyed from among you all 5
4 held fast to the LORD your God are all alive 5
5 taught you . . as the LORD my God commanded me 5
7 has a god so near to it as the LORD our God is to us 5
10 day that you stood before the LORD your God at Horeb 5
19 LORD your God has allotted to all the peoples 5
21 good land which the LORD your God gives you 5
23 lest you forget the covenant of the LORD your God 5
23 anything which the LORD your God has forbidden 5
24 LORD your God is a devouring fire, a jealous God. 5
24 LORD your God is a devouring fire, a jealous God. 2
25 doing . . evil in the sight of the LORD your God 5
29 from there you will seek the LORD your God 5
30 return to the LORD your God and obey his voice 5
31 for the LORD your God is a merciful God; 5
31 for the LORD your God is a merciful God; 2
32 since the day that God created man upon the earth 5
34 all that the LORD your God did for you in Egypt 5
35 shown, that you might know that the LORD is God; 5
39 know . . that the LORD is God in heaven above 5
40 land which the LORD your God gives you for ever. 5
5: 2 The LORD our God made a covenant with us in Horeb. 5
6 I am the LORD your God, who brought you out 5
9 for I the LORD your God am a jealous God 5
9 for I the LORD your God am a jealous God 2
11 not take the name of the LORD your God in vain 5
12 keep it holy, as the LORD your God commanded you. 5
14 seventh day is a sabbath to the LORD your God; 5
15 servant in the land of Egypt, and the LORD your God 5
15 LORD your God commanded you to keep the sabbath 5
16 "'Honor . . as the LORD your God commanded you; 5
16 in the land which the LORD your God gives you. 5
24 LORD our God has shown us his glory and greatness 5
24 day seen God speak with man and man still live. 5
25 if we hear the voice of the LORD our God any more 5
26 heard the voice of the living God speaking 5
27 Go near, and hear all that the LORD our God will say; 5
27 speak to us all that the LORD our God will speak 5
32 do . . as the LORD your God has commanded you; 5
33 all the way which the LORD your God has commanded 5
6: 1 which the LORD your God commanded me to teach you 5
2 that you may fear the LORD your God 5
3 as the LORD, the God of your fathers, has promised 5
4 "Hear, O Israel: The LORD our God is one LORD; 5
5 shall love the LORD your God with all your heart 5
10 when the LORD your God brings you into the land 5
13 shall fear the LORD your God; you shall serve him 5
15 LORD your God in the midst of you is a jealous God; 5
15 LORD your God in the midst of you is a jealous God; 2
15 anger of the LORD your God be kindled against you 5
16 You shall not put the LORD your God to the test 5
17 keep the commandments of the LORD your God 5
20 which the LORD our God has commanded you?' 5
24 LORD commanded us . . to fear the LORD our God 5
25 do all this commandment before the LORD our God 5
7: 1 "When the LORD your God brings you into the land 5
2 when the LORD your God gives them over to you 5
6 For you are a people holy to the LORD your God; 5
6 For you are a people holy to the LORD your God; 5
9 Know therefore that the LORD your God is God 5
9 Know therefore that the LORD your God is God 5

9 LORD . . the faithful God who keeps covenant 2
12 LORD your God will keep with you the covenant 5
16 all the peoples that the LORD your God will give 5
18 remember what the LORD your God did to Pharaoh 5
19 by which the LORD your God brought you out; 5
19 so will the LORD your God do to all the peoples 5
20 LORD your God will send hornets among them 5
21 LORD your God is in the midst of you 5
21 in the midst of you, a great and terrible God. 2
22 LORD your God will clear away these nations 5
23 LORD your God will give them over to you 5
25 for it is an abomination to the LORD your God. 5
8: 2 way which the LORD your God has led you 5
5 as a man . . the LORD your God disciplines you. 5
6 shall keep the commandments of the LORD your God 5
7 LORD your God is bringing you into a good land 5
10 shall bless the LORD your God for the good land 5
11 Take heed lest you forget the LORD your God, by not 5
14 then . . you forget the LORD your God, who brought 5
18 You shall remember the LORD your God, for it is he 5
19 forget the LORD your God and go after other gods 5
20 you would not obey the voice of the LORD your God. 5
9: 3 who goes over before you . . is the LORD your God; 5
4 after the LORD your God has thrust them out 5
5 LORD your God is driving them out from before you 5
6 Know . . that the LORD your God is not giving you 5
7 how you provoked the LORD your God to wrath 5
10 tables of stone written with the finger of God; 5
16 behold, you had sinned against the LORD your God; 5
23 against the commandment of the LORD your God 5
10: 9 as the LORD your God said to him.) 5
12 now, Israel, what does the LORD your God require 5
12 require . . but to fear the LORD your God, to walk 5
12 to serve the LORD your God with all your heart 5
14 Behold, to the LORD your God belong heaven 5
17 For the LORD your God is God of gods 5
17 LORD your God is God of gods and Lord of lords 5
17 great, the mighty, and the terrible God 2
20 fear the LORD your God; you shall serve him 5
21 your God, who has done for you these great 5
22 now the LORD your God has made you as the stars 5
11: 1 You shall therefore love the LORD your God 5
2 consider the discipline of the LORD your God 5
12 land which the LORD your God cares for; 5
12 eyes of the LORD your God are always upon it 5
13 my commandments . . to love the LORD your God 5
22 commandment . . loving the LORD your God 5
25 LORD your God will lay the fear of you 5
27 if you obey the commandments of the LORD your God 5
28 not obey the commandments of the LORD your God 5
29 when the LORD your God brings you into the land 5
31 land which the LORD your God gives you; 5
12: 1 which the LORD, the God of your fathers, has given 5
4 You shall not do so to the LORD your God. 5
5 LORD your God will choose out of all your tribes 5
7 there you shall eat before the LORD your God 5
7 in which the LORD your God has blessed you. 5
9 to the rest . . which the LORD your God gives you. 5
10 land which the LORD your God gives you to inherit 5
11 place which the LORD your God will choose 5
12 rejoice before the LORD your God 5
15 according to the blessing of the LORD your God 5
18 eat them before the LORD your God in the place 5
18 place which the LORD your God will choose 5
18 rejoice before the LORD your God in all that you 5
20 When the LORD your God enlarges your territory 5
21 If the place which the LORD your God will choose 5
27 offer . . on the altar of the LORD your God; 5
27 poured out on the altar of the LORD your God 5
28 good and right in the sight of the LORD your God. 5
29 When the LORD your God cuts off before you 5
31 You shall not do so to the LORD your God; 5
13: 3 LORD your God is testing you, to know whether 5
3 to know whether you love the LORD your God 5
4 shall walk after the LORD your God and fear him 5
5 taught rebellion against the LORD your God 5
5 way in which the LORD your God commanded you 5
10 sought to draw you away from the LORD your God 5
12 cities, which the LORD your God gives you to dwell 5
16 whole burnt offering to the LORD your God; 5
18 if you obey the voice of the LORD your God, keeping 5
18 doing . . right in the sight of the LORD your God. 5
14: 1 You are the sons of the LORD your God; you shall not 5
2 For you are a people holy to the LORD your God 5
21 for you are a people holy to the LORD your God. 5
23 before . . your God, . . , you shall eat the tithe 5
23 may learn to fear the LORD your God always. 5
24 when the LORD your God blesses you 5
24 place . . which the LORD your God chooses, to set 5
25 go to the place which the LORD your God chooses 5
26 eat there before the LORD your God and rejoice 5
29 LORD your God may bless you in all the work 5
15: 4 land which the LORD your God gives you 5
5 if . . you will obey the voice of the LORD your God 5
6 LORD your God will bless you, as he promised you 5
7 land which the LORD your God gives you 5
10 because for this the LORD your God will bless you 5
14 as the LORD your God has blessed you 5
15 LORD your God redeemed you; therefore I command 5
18 LORD your God will bless you in all that you do. 5
19 you shall consecrate to the LORD your God; 5
20 eat it . . before the LORD your God year by year 5
21 you shall not sacrifice it to the LORD your God. 5
16: 1 keep the passover to the LORD your God; 5
1 in the month of Abib the LORD your God brought you 5
2 passover sacrifice to the LORD your God 5
5 within any . . towns which the LORD your God gives 5
6 at the place which the LORD your God will choose 5
7 at the place which the LORD your God will choose; 5
8 shall be a solemn assembly to the LORD your God; 5
10 keep the feast of weeks to the LORD your God 5
10 which you shall give as the LORD your God blesses 5
11 rejoice before the LORD your God, you and your son 5
11 at the place which the LORD your God will choose 5
15 keep the feast to the LORD your God at the place 5
15 because the LORD your God will bless you in all 5
16 appear before the LORD your God at the place 5
17 blessing of the LORD your God which he has given 5
18 in all your towns which the LORD your God gives 5
20 inherit the land which the LORD your God gives 5
21 beside the altar of the LORD your God 5
22 not set up a pillar which the LORD your God hates. 5
17: 1 not sacrifice to the LORD your God an ox or a sheep 5
1 for that is an abomination to the LORD your God. 5
2 any of your towns which the LORD your God gives 5
2 does . . evil in the sight of the LORD your God 5
8 go up to the place . . LORD your God will choose 5
12 stands to minister . . before the LORD your God 5
14 come to the land which the LORD your God gives you 5
15 set as king . . whom the LORD your God will choose. 5
19 learn to fear the LORD his God, by keeping all 5
18: 5 your God has chosen him out of all your tribes 5
7 may minister in the name of the LORD his God 5
9 come into the land which the LORD your God gives 5
12 practices the LORD your God is driving them out 5
13 You shall be blameless before the LORD your God. 5
14 LORD your God has not allowed you so to do. 5
15 LORD your God will raise up for you a prophet 5
16 desired of the LORD your God at Horeb on the day 5
16 'Let me not hear again the voice of the LORD my God 5
19: 1 When the LORD your God cuts off the nations whose 5
1 whose land the LORD your God gives you 5
2 land which . . your God gives you to possess. 5
3 area of the land which the LORD your God gives you 5
8 if the LORD your God enlarges your border 5
9 by loving the LORD your God and by walking 5
10 land which the LORD your God gives you 5
14 land that the LORD your God gives you to possess 5
20: 1 not be afraid . . LORD your God is with you 5
4 LORD your God is he that goes with you, to fight 5
13 when the LORD your God gives it into your hand 5
14 spoil . . which the LORD your God has given you. 5
16 cities . . your God gives you for an inheritance 5
17 destroy . . as the LORD your God has commanded; 5
18 so to sin against the LORD your God. 5
21: 1 in the land . . LORD your God gives you to possess 5
5 LORD your God has chosen them to minister to him 5
10 LORD your God gives them into your hands 5
23 hanged man is accursed by God; 5
23 your land which the LORD your God gives you 5
22: 5 does . . is an abomination to the LORD your God. 5
23: 5 LORD your God would not hearken to Balaam; 5
5 LORD your God turned the curse into a blessing 5
5 because the LORD your God loved you. 5
14 LORD your God walks in the midst of your camp 5
18 not bring . . into the house of the LORD your God 5
18 both . . are an abomination to the LORD your God. 5
20 that the LORD your God may bless you in all 5
21 When you make a vow to the LORD your God 5
21 LORD your God will surely require it of you 5
23 voluntarily vowed to the LORD your God 5
24: 4 land . . LORD your God gives you for an inheritance. 5
9 Remember what the LORD your God did to Miriam 5
13 righteousness to you before the LORD your God. 5
18 and the LORD your God redeemed you from there; 5
19 God may bless you in all the work of your hands. 5
25:15 in the land which the LORD your God gives you. 5
16 dishonestly . . abomination to the LORD your God. 5
18 how he attacked you . . and he did not fear God. 5
19 when the LORD your God has given you rest from all 5
19 land . . LORD your God gives you for an inheritance 5
26: 1 land . . LORD your God gives you for an inheritance 5
2 harvest from your land . . LORD your God gives 5
2 go to the place . . LORD your God will choose 5
3 I declare this day to the LORD your God 5
4 set it down before the altar of the LORD your God. 5
5 make response before the LORD your God 5
7 Then we cried to the LORD the God of our fathers 5
10 set it down before the LORD your God, and worship 5
10 set it down . . worship before the LORD your God; 5
11 good which the LORD your God has given to you 5
13 then you shall say before the LORD your God, 'I have 5
14 I have obeyed the voice of the LORD my God 5
16 This day the LORD your God commands you to do 5
17 declared this day . . that he is your God 5
19 you shall be a people holy to the LORD your God 5
27: 2 Jordan to the land which the LORD your God gives 5
3 enter the land which the LORD your God gives you 5
3 as the LORD, the God of your fathers, has promised 5
5 there . . build an altar to the LORD your God 5
6 altar to the LORD your God of unhewn stones; 5
6 offer burnt offerings on it to the LORD your God; 5
7 you shall rejoice before the LORD your God. 5
9 you have become the people of the LORD your God. 5
10 therefore obey the voice of the LORD your God 5
28: 1 if you obey the voice of the LORD your God 5
1 your God will set you high above all the nations 5
2 if you obey the voice of the LORD your God. 5
8 land which the LORD your God gives you. 5
9 if you keep the commandments of the LORD your God 5
13 if you obey the commandments of the LORD your God 5
15 if you will not obey the voice of the LORD your God 5
45 you did not obey the voice of the LORD your God 5
47 Because you did not serve the LORD your God 5
52 all your land, which the LORD your God has given 5
53 sons and daughters . . LORD your God has given 5
58 glorious and awful name, the LORD your God 5
62 you did not obey the voice of the LORD your God. 5
29: 6 that you may know that I am the LORD your God. 5
10 stand this day all of you before the LORD your God; 5
12 enter . . the sworn covenant of the LORD your God 5
12 sworn covenant . . LORD your God makes with you 5
13 that he may be your God, as he promised you 5
15 stands here . . this day before the LORD our God. 5
18 heart turns away this day from the LORD our God 5
25 covenant of the LORD, the God of their fathers 5
29 secret things belong to the LORD our God; 5
30: 1 nations where the LORD your God has driven you 5
2 return to the LORD your God, you and your children 5
3 LORD your God will restore your fortunes 5
3 peoples where the LORD your God has scattered 5
4 from there the LORD your God will gather you 5
5 LORD your God will bring you into the land 5
6 LORD your God will circumcise your heart 5
6 love the LORD your God with all your heart 5
7 LORD your God will put all these curses 5
9 your God will make you abundantly prosperous 5
10 if you obey the voice of the LORD your God, to keep 5
10 turn to the LORD your God with all your heart 5
16 If you obey the commandments of the LORD your God 9
16 obey . . by loving the LORD your God 5
16 LORD your God will bless you in the land 5
20 loving the LORD your God, obeying his voice 5
31: 3 LORD your God himself will go over before you; 5
6 for it is the LORD your God who goes with you; 5
11 Israel comes to appear before the LORD your God 5
12 may hear and learn to fear the LORD your God 5
13 may hear and learn to fear the LORD your God 5
17 evils come upon us because our God is not among us?' 5
26 ark of the covenant of the LORD your God 5
32: 3 Ascribe greatness to our God! 5
4 God of faithfulness and without iniquity, just 2
8 according to the number of the sons of God. •
15 then he forsook God who made him 4
18 you forgot the God who gave you birth. 2
33: 1 blessing with which Moses the man of God blessed 5
26 There is none like God, O Jesh'urun, who rides 2
27 The eternal God is your dwelling place 5
Jos 1: 9 for the LORD your God is with you wherever you go. 5
11 land . . the LORD your God gives you to possess. 5
13 The LORD your God is providing you a place of rest 5
15 the land which the LORD your God is giving them; 5
17 may the LORD your God be with you, as . . with Moses! 5
2:11 the LORD your God is he who is God in heaven above 5
11 the LORD your God is he who is God in heaven above 5
3: 3 see the ark of the covenant of the LORD your God 5
9 Come . . and hear the words of the LORD your God. 5
10 you shall know that the living God is among you 2
4: 5 Pass on before the ark of the LORD your God 5
23 the LORD your God dried up the . . Jordan for you 5
23 as the LORD your God did to the Red Sea 5
24 that you may fear the LORD your God for ever. 5
7:13 for thus says the LORD, God of Israel 5
19 My son, give glory to the LORD God of Israel 5
20 I have sinned against the LORD God of Israel 5
8: 7 for the LORD your God will give it into your hand. 5
30 built an altar . . to the LORD, the God of Israel 5
9: 9 have come, because of the name of the LORD your God; 5
18 had sworn to them by the LORD, the God of Israel. 5
19 We have sworn to them by the LORD, the God of Israel 5
23 and drawers of water for the house of my God. 5
24 the LORD your God had commanded his servant 5
10:19 the LORD your God has given them into your hand. 5
40 left none . . as the LORD God of Israel commanded. 5
42 the LORD God of Israel fought for Israel. 5
13:14 the offerings by fire to the LORD God of Israel 5
33 the LORD God of Israel is their inheritance 5
14: 6 You know what the LORD said to Moses the man of God 5
8 yet I wholly followed the LORD my God. 5
9 you have wholly followed the LORD my God. 5
14 he wholly followed the LORD, the God of Israel. 5
18: 3 the land, which the LORD, the God of your fathers 5
6 I will cast lots . . here before the LORD our God. 5

22: 3 careful to keep the charge of the LORD your God. 5
4 the LORD your God has given rest to your brethren 5
5 and the law . . to love the LORD your God 5
16 you have committed against the God of Israel 5
19 an altar other than the altar of the LORD our God. 5
22 The Mighty One, God, the LORD! The Mighty One, God 5
22 God, the LORD! The Mighty One, God, the LORD! 5
24 What have you to do with the LORD, the God of Israel? 5
29 the altar of the LORD our God that stands 5
33 and the people of Israel blessed God 5
34 it is a witness between us that the LORD is God. 5
23: 3 you have seen all that the LORD your God has done 5
3 for it is the LORD your God who has fought for you. 5
5 The LORD your God will push them back before you 5
5 possess their land, as the LORD your God promised 5
8 but cleave to the LORD your God as you have done 5
10 since it is the LORD your God who fights for you 5
11 Take good heed . . to love the LORD your God. 5
13 the LORD your God will not continue to drive out 5
13 good land which the LORD your God has given you. 5
14 good things which the LORD your God promised 5
15 good things which the LORD your God has promised 5
15 good land which the LORD your God has given you 5
16 transgress the covenant of the LORD your God 5
24: 1 and they presented themselves before God. 5
2 Thus says the LORD, the God of Israel, 'Your fathers 5
17 the LORD our God . . brought us and our fathers up 5
18 we also will serve the LORD, for he is our God. 5
19 You cannot serve the LORD; for he is a holy God; 5
19 he is a holy God; he is a jealous God; 2
23 incline your heart to the LORD, the God of Israel. 5
24 The LORD our God we will serve, and his voice we 5
26 Joshua wrote these . . in the book of the law of God; 5
27 lest you deal falsely with your God. 5
Jdg 1: 7 as I have done, so God has requited me." And they 5
2:12 they forsook the LORD, the God of their fathers 5
3: 7 forgetting the LORD their God, and serving 5
20 And Ehud said, "I have a message from God for you. 5
4: 6 LORD, the God of Israel, commands you, 'Go, gather 5
23 on that day God subdued Jabin the king of Canaan 5
5: 3 I will make melody to the LORD, the God of Israel. 5
5 quaked . . before the LORD, the God of Israel. 5
6: 8 Thus says the LORD, the God of Israel: I led you up 5
10 I am the LORD your God; you shall not pay reverence 5
20 the angel of God said to him, "Take the meat 5
26 build an altar to the LORD your God on the top 5
36 Gideon said to God, "If thou wilt deliver Israel 5
39 Gideon said to God, "Let not thy anger burn against 5
40 God did so that night; for it was dry on the fleece 5
7:14 Israel; into his hand God has given Mid'ian and all 5
8: 3 God has given into your hands the princes 5
34 Israel did not remember the LORD their God 5
9: 7 Listen to me . . that God may listen to you. 5
23 God sent an evil spirit between Abim'elech 5
56 Thus God requited the crime of Abim'elech 5
57 God also made all the wickedness of the men 5
10:10 we have forsaken our God and have served 5
11:21 the LORD, the God of Israel, gave Sihon and all his 5
23 then the LORD, the God of Israel, dispossessed 5
24 And all that the LORD our God has dispossessed 5
13: 5 for the boy shall be a Nazirite to God from birth; 5
6 A man of God came to me, and his countenance was 5
6 countenance of the angel of God, very terrible; 5
7 for the boy shall be a Nazirite to God from birth 5
8 let the man of God whom thou didst send come again 5
9 God listened to the voice of Mano'ah, and the angel 5
9 the angel of God came again to the woman as she sat 5
22 his wife, "We shall surely die, for we have seen God. 5
15:19 God split open the hollow place that is at Lehi 5
16:17 I have been a Nazirite to God from my mother's 5
28 and strengthen me . . O God, that I may be avenged 5
18: 5 Inquire of God, we pray thee, that we may know 5
10 land is broad; yea, God has given it into your hands 5
31 he made, as long as the house of God was at Shiloh. 5
20: 2 themselves in the assembly of the people of God 5
18 Israel . . went up to Bethel, and inquired of God 5
27 for the ark of the covenant of God was there 5
21: 2 to Bethel, and sat there till evening before God 5
3 O LORD, the God of Israel, why has this come to pass 5
Rut 1:16 your people shall be my people, and your God my God; 5
16 your people shall be my people, and your God my God; 5
2:12 a full reward . . by the LORD, the God of Israel 5
1Sm 1:17 Go . . and the God of Israel grant your petition 5
2: 2 none besides thee; there is no rock like our God. 5
3 the LORD is a God of knowledge 2
25 If a man sins against a man, God will mediate 5
27 And there came a man of God to Eli, and said to him 5
30 Therefore the LORD the God of Israel declares 5
3: 3 the lamp of God had not yet gone out 5
3 the temple of the LORD, where the ark of God was. 5
13 because his sons were blaspheming God 9
17 May God do so to you and more also, if you hide 5
4: 4 were there with the ark of the covenant of God. 5
11 And the ark of God was captured; 5
13 for his heart trembled for the ark of God. 5
17 and the ark of God has been captured. 5
18 When he mentioned the ark of God, Eli fell over 5
19 the tidings that the ark of God was captured 5
21 because the ark of God had been captured 5
22 glory has . . for the ark of God has been captured. 5
5: 1 When the Philistines captured the ark of God 5
2 Philistines took the ark of God . . and set it up 5
7 The ark of the God of Israel must not remain 5
8 What shall we do with the ark of the God of Israel? 5
8 Let the ark of the God of Israel be brought around 5
8 they brought the ark of the God of Israel there. 5
10 So they sent the ark of God to Ekron. 5
10 when the ark of God came to Ekron 5
10 brought . . the ark of the God of Israel to slay us 5
11 Send away the ark of the God of Israel 5
11 The hand of God was very heavy there; 5
6: 3 If you send away the ark of the God of Israel 5
5 make images . . and give glory to the God of Israel; 5
20 Who is able to stand before the LORD, this holy God? 5
7: 8 cry to the LORD our God for us, that he may save us 5
9: 6 there is a man of God in this city 5
7 and there is no present to bring to the man of God. 5
8 I have . . silver, and I will give it to the man of God 5
9 when a man went to inquire of God, he said, "Come 5
10 they went to the city where the man of God was. 5
27 that I may make known to you the word of God. 5
10: 3 three men going up to God at Bethel will meet you 5
7 do whatever . . for God is with you. 5
9 When he turned . . God gave him another heart; 5
10 and the spirit of God came mightily upon him 5
18 Thus says the LORD, the God of Israel, 'I brought up 5
19 you have this day rejected your God, who saves you 5
26 went men of valor whose hearts God had touched. 5
11: 6 And the spirit of God came mightily upon Saul 5
12: 9 they forgot the LORD their God; and he sold them 5
12 you said . . when the LORD your God was your king. 5
14 both you and the king . . follow the LORD your God 5
19 Pray for your servants to the LORD your God 5
13:13 not kept the commandment of the LORD your God 5
14:18 Saul said to Ahi'jah, "Bring hither the ark of God. 5
18 the ark of God went at that time with the people 5
36 the priest said, "Let us draw near hither to God. 5
37 Saul inquired of God, "Shall I go down 5
41 O LORD God of Israel, why hast thou not answered 5
41 O LORD, God of Israel, give Urim; 9
44 God do so to me and more also; you shall surely die 5
45 for he has wrought with God this day. 5
15:15 the best . . to sacrifice to the LORD your God; 5
21 people took . . to sacrifice to the LORD your God 5
30 return . . that I may worship the LORD your God. 5
16:15 an evil spirit from God is tormenting you. 5
16 when the evil spirit from God is upon you 5
23 whenever the evil spirit from God was upon Saul 5
17:26 who . . should defy the armies of the living God? 5
36 he has defied the armies of the living God. 5
45 the LORD of hosts, the God of the armies of Israel 5
46 that all . . may know that there is a God in Israel 5
18:10 an evil spirit from God rushed upon Saul 5
19:20 the Spirit of God came upon the messengers 5
23 and the Spirit of God came upon him also 5
20:12 The LORD, the God of Israel, be witness! 5
22: 3 let . . till I know what God will do for me. 5
13 and have inquired of God for him, so that he 5
15 the first time that I have inquired of God for him? 5
23: 7 And Saul said, "God has given him into my hand; 5
10 Then said David, "O LORD, the God of Israel 5
11 O LORD, the God of Israel, I beseech thee 5
14 but God did not give him into his hand. 5
16 Jonathan . . and strengthened his hand in God. 5
25:22 God do so to David and more also 5
29 of the living in the care of the LORD your God; 5
32 Blessed be the LORD, the God of Israel, who sent you 5
34 For as surely as the LORD the God of Israel lives 5
26: 8 God has given your enemy into your hand this day; 5
28:15 God has turned away from me and answers me no more 5
29: 9 you are as blameless in my sight as an angel of God; 5
30: 6 David strengthened himself in the LORD his God. 5
15 he said, "Swear to me by God, that you will not kill me 5
2Sm 2:27 As God lives, if you had not spoken, surely the men 5
3: 9 God do so to Abner, and more also, if I do not 5
35 God do so to me and more also, if I taste bread 5
5:10 for the LORD, the God of hosts, was with him. 5
6: 2 went . . to bring up from there the ark of God 5
3 And they carried the ark of God upon a new cart 5
4 were driving the new cart with the ark of God; 5
6 Uzzah put out his hand to the ark of God 5
7 God smote him there because he put forth his hand 5
7 and he died there beside the ark of God. 5
12 The LORD has blessed . . because of the ark of God. 5
12 David went and brought up the ark of God 5
7: 2 I dwell . . but the ark of God dwells in a tent. 5
22 Therefore thou art great, O LORD God; 6
22 is none like thee, and there is no God besides thee 5
23 Israel, whom God went to redeem to be his people 5
24 and thou, O LORD, didst become their God. 5
25 And now, O LORD God, confirm for ever the word 5
26 saying, 'The LORD of hosts is God over Israel,' 5
27 thou, O LORD of hosts, the God of Israel, hast made 5
28 now, O Lord GOD, thou art God, and thy words are true 5
9: 3 that I may show the kindness of God to him? 5
10:12 for our people, and for the cities of our God; 5
12: 7 Thus says the LORD, the God of Israel, 'I anointed 5
16 David therefore besought God for the child; 5
14:11 Pray let the king invoke the LORD your God 5
13 planned such a thing against the people of God? 5
14 but God will not take away the life of him 5
16 destroy me and my son . . from the heritage of God.' 5
17 the king is like the angel of God to discern good 5
17 good and evil. The LORD your God be with you! 5
20 the wisdom of the angel of God to know all things 5
15:24 Levites, bearing the ark of the covenant of God; 5
24 and they set down the ark of God 5
25 Carry the ark of God back into the city. 5
29 So Zadok and Abi'athar carried the ark of God back 5
32 David came to the summit, where God was worshiped 5
16:23 was as if one consulted the oracle of God; 5
18:28 Blessed be the LORD your God, who has delivered up 5
19:13 God do so to me, and more also, if you are not 5
27 But my lord the king is like the angel of God; 5
21:14 And . . God heeded supplications for the land. 5
22: 3 my God, my rock, in whom I take refuge, my shield 5
7 I called upon the LORD; to my God I called. 5
22 and have not wickedly departed from my God. 5
29 Yea, thou art . . and my God lightens my darkness. 6
30 Yea, by thee . . and by my God I can leap over a wall. 5
31 This God-his way is perfect; 2
32 For who is God, but the LORD? 2
32 For who is God . . ? And who is a rock, except our God? 5
33 This God is my strong refuge, and has made my way 2
47 and exalted be my God, the rock of my salvation 5
48 the God who gave me vengeance 2
23: 1 David . . the anointed of the God of Jacob 5
3 The God of Israel has spoken, the Rock of Israel 5
3 When one rules justly . . ruling in the fear of God 5
5 Yea, does not my house stand so with God? 2
24: 3 May the LORD your God add to the people 5
23 And Arau'nah said . . "The LORD your God accept you. 5
24 I will not offer burnt offerings to the LORD my God 5
1Kg 1:17 you swore . . by the LORD your God, saying, 'Solomon 5
30 I swore to you by the LORD, the God of Israel, saying 5
36 May the LORD, the God of my lord the king, say so. 5
47 Your God make the name of Solomon more famous 5
48 Blessed be the LORD, the God of Israel, who has 5
2: 3 keep the charge of the LORD your God, walking 5
23 God do so to me and more also if this word does not 5
3: 5 in a dream by night; and God said, "Ask what I shall 5
7 now, O LORD my God, thou hast made thy servant king 5
11 God said to him, "Because you have asked this 5
28 the wisdom of God was in him, to render justice. 5
4:29 God gave Solomon wisdom and understanding 5
5: 3 not build a house for the name of the LORD his God 5
4 now the LORD my God has given me rest on every side; 5
5 to build a house for the name of the LORD my God 5
8:15 Blessed be the LORD, the God of Israel, who 5
17 a house for the name of the LORD, the God of Israel. 5
20 house for the name of the LORD, the God of Israel. 5
23 O LORD, God of Israel, there is no God like thee 5
23 LORD . . there is no God like thee, in heaven above 5
25 O LORD, God of Israel, keep with thy servant David 5
26 O God of Israel, let thy word be confirmed 5
27 But will God indeed dwell on the earth? 5
28 have regard . . O LORD my God, hearkening 5
57 The LORD our God be with us 5
59 words . . be near to the LORD our God day and night 5
60 may know that the LORD is God; there is no other. 5
61 your heart . . be wholly true to the LORD our God 5
65 the feast . . before the LORD our God, seven days. 5
9: 9 they forsook the LORD their God who brought 5
10: 9 Blessed be the LORD your God, who has delighted 5
24 hear his wisdom, which God had put into his mind. 5
11: 4 his heart was not wholly true to the LORD his God 5
9 turned away from the LORD, the God of Israel 5
23 God also raised up as an adversary to him, Rezon 5
31 thus says the LORD, the God of Israel 5
12:22 the word of God came to Shemai'ah the man of God 5
22 the word of God came to Shemai'ah the man of God 5
13: 1 behold, a man of God came out of Judah 5
4 when the king heard the saying of the man of God 5
5 the sign which the man of God had given 5
6 the king said to the man of God, "Entreat now 5
6 Entreat now the favor of the LORD your God 5
6 the man of God entreated the LORD; 5
7 the king said to the man of God, "Come home with me 5
8 the man of God said to the king 5
11 came and told him all that the man of God had done 5
12 the way which the man of God . . had gone. 5
14 he went after the man of God, and found him 5
14 Are you the man of God who came from Judah? 5
21 he cried to the man of God who came from Judah 5
21 commandment which the LORD your God commanded 5
26 It is the man of God, who disobeyed the word 5
29 the prophet took up the body of the man of God 5
31 the grave in which the man of God is buried; 5
14: 7 Thus says the LORD, the God of Israel 5
13 something pleasing to the LORD, the God of Israel 5
15: 3 his heart was not wholly true to the LORD his God 5
4 the LORD his God gave him a lamp in Jerusalem 5
30 he provoked the LORD, the God of Israel. 5
16:13 to sin, provoking the LORD God of Israel to anger 5

26 provoking the LORD, the God of Israel, to anger 5
33 to provoke the LORD, the God of Israel, to anger 5
17: 1 As the LORD the God of Israel lives 5
12 As the LORD your God lives, I have nothing baked 5
14 For thus says the LORD the God of Israel 5
18 What have you against me, O man of God? 5
20 O LORD my God, hast thou brought calamity even 5
21 O LORD my God, let this child's soul come into him 5
24 Now I know that you are a man of God 5
18:10 As the LORD your God lives, there is no nation 5
21 If the LORD is God, follow him; 5
24 the God who answers by fire, he is God. 5
24 the God who answers by fire, he is God. 5
36 O LORD, God of Abraham, Isaac, and Israel, let it be 5
36 LORD . . let it be known this day that thou art God 5
37 that this people may know that thou, O LORD, art God 5
39 they said, "The LORD, he is God; the LORD, he is God. 5
39 they said, "The LORD, he is God; the LORD, he is God. 5
19: 8 ate and drank, and went . . to Horeb the mount of God. 5
10 very jealous for the LORD, the God of hosts; 5
14 very jealous for the LORD, the God of hosts; 5
20:28 a man of God came near and said to the king 5
21:10 saying, 'You have cursed God and the king.' 5
13 saying, "Naboth cursed God and the king. 5
22:53 and provoked the LORD, the God of Israel, to anger 5
2Kg 1: 3 Is it because there is no God in Israel that you 5
6 Is it because there is no God in Israel that you 5
9 O man of God, the king says, 'Come down.' 5
10 If I am a man of God, let fire come down from heaven 5
11 O man of God, this is the king's order, 'Come down 5
12 If I am a man of God, let fire come down from heaven 5
12 Then the fire of God came down from heaven 5
13 O man of God, I pray you, let my life . . be precious 5
16 there is no God in Israel to inquire of his word? 5
2:14 saying, "Where is the LORD, the God of Eli'jah? 5
4: 7 She came and told the man of God, and he said, "Go 5
9 I perceive that this is a holy man of God 5
16 she said, "No, my lord, O man of God; do not lie 5
21 she went up and laid him on the bed of the man of God 5
22 Send . . that I may quickly go to the man of God 5
25 So she . . came to the man of God at Mount Carmel. 5
25 When the man of God saw her coming, he said 5
27 when she came to the mountain to the man of God 5
27 But the man of God said, "Let her alone 5
40 cried out, "O man of God, there is death in the pot! 5
42 A man came . . bringing the man of God bread 5
5: 7 Am I God, to kill and to make alive 5
8 when Eli'sha the man of God heard . . he sent 5
11 and stand, and call on the name of the LORD his God 5
14 dipped . . according to the word of the man of God; 5
15 Then he returned to the man of God 5
15 there is no God in all the earth but in Israel; 5
20 Geha'zi, the servant of Eli'sha the man of God, said 5
6: 6 Then the man of God said, "Where did it fall? 5
9 the man of God sent word to the king of Israel 5
10 sent to the place of which the man of God told him. 5
15 When the servant of the man of God rose early 5
31 May God do so to me, and more also, if the head 5
7: 2 the captain . . said to the man of God, "If the LORD 5
17 so that he died, as the man of God had said 5
18 when the man of God had said to the king 5
19 the captain had answered the man of God 5
8: 2 and did according to the word of the man of God; 5
4 talking with Geha'zi the servant of the man of God 5
7 when it was told him, "The man of God has come here 5
8 Take a present . . and go to meet the man of God 5
11 And the man of God wept. 5
9: 6 Thus says the LORD the God of Israel, I anoint you 5
10:31 to walk in the law of the LORD the God of Israel 5
13:19 Then the man of God was angry with him, and said 5
14:25 word of the LORD, the God of Israel, which he spoke 5
16: 2 do what was right in the eyes of the LORD his God 5
17: 7 Israel had sinned against the LORD their God 5
9 Israel did secretly against the LORD their God 5
14 who did not believe in the LORD their God. 5
16 all the commandments of the LORD their God 5
19 keep the commandments of the LORD their God 5
39 but you shall fear the LORD your God, and he will 5
18: 5 He trusted in the LORD the God of Israel; 5
12 they did not obey the voice of the LORD their God 5
22 if you say . . "We rely on the LORD our God," 5
19: 4 the LORD your God heard all the words 5
4 whom his master . . has sent to mock the living God 5
4 the words which the LORD your God has heard; 5
10 Do not let your God on whom you rely deceive you 5
15 O LORD the God of Israel, who art enthroned above 5
15 O LORD . . thou art the God, thou alone, of all 5
16 words . . which he has sent to mock the living God. 5
19 So now, O LORD our God, save us, I beseech thee 5
19 know that thou, O LORD, art God alone. 5
20 Thus says the LORD, the God of Israel 5
20: 5 Thus says the LORD, the God of David your father 5
21:12 thus says the LORD, the God of Israel 5
22 he forsook the LORD, the God of his fathers 5
22:15 Thus says the LORD, the God of Israel: 'Tell the man 5
18 Thus says the LORD, the God of Israel 5
23:16 word of the LORD which the man of God proclaimed 5
17 It is the tomb of the man of God who came from Judah 5
21 Keep the passover to the LORD your God 5
1Ch 4:10 Jabez called on the God of Israel, saying 5
10 And God granted what he asked. 5
5:20 for they cried to God in the battle 5
22 For many fell slain, because the war was of God. 5
25 transgressed against the God of their fathers 5
25 peoples . . whom God had destroyed before them. 5
26 So the God of Israel stirred up the spirit of Pul 5
6:48 service of the tabernacle of the house of God. 5
49 all that Moses the servant of God had commanded. 5
9:11 Ahi'tub . . chief officer of the house of God; 5
13 for the work of the service of the house of God. 5
26 chambers and the treasures of the house of God. 5
27 they lodged round about the house of God; 5
11: 2 LORD your God said to you, 'You shall be shepherd 5
19 Far be it from me before my God that I should do 5
12:17 may the God of our fathers see and rebuke you. 5
18 peace to you . . For your God helps you. 5
22 until there was a great army, like an army of God. 5
13: 2 good to you, and if it is the will of the LORD our God 5
3 Then let us bring again the ark of our God to us; 5
5 to bring the ark of God from Kir'iath-je'arim. 5
6 to bring up from there the ark of God 5
7 they carried the ark of God upon a new cart 5
8 making merry before God with all their might 5
10 and he died there before God. 5
12 David was afraid of God that day; 5
12 he said, "How can I bring the ark of God home to me? 5
14 the ark of God remained with the household 5
14:10 David inquired of God, "Shall I go up against 5
11 God has broken through my enemies by my hand 5
14 when David again inquired of God, God said to him 5
14 when David again inquired of God, God said to him 5
15 God has gone out before you to smite the army 5
16 David did as God commanded him 5
15: 1 he prepared a place for the ark of God 5
2 No one but the Levites may carry the ark of God 5
12 bring up the ark of the LORD, the God of Israel 5
13 LORD our God broke forth upon us 5
14 to bring up the ark of the LORD, the God of Israel. 5
15 carried the ark of God upon their shoulders 5
24 should blow the trumpets before the ark of God. 5
26 God helped the Levites who were carrying 5
16: 1 brought the ark of God, and set it inside the tent 5
1 offered . . and peace offerings before God. 5
4 to thank, and to praise the LORD, the God of Israel. 5
6 before the ark of the covenant of God. 5
14 LORD our God; his judgments are in all the earth. 5
35 Deliver us, O God of our salvation, and gather 5
36 Blessed be the LORD, the God of Israel 5
17: 2 Do all that is in your heart, for God is with you. 5
16 said, "Who am I, O LORD God, and what is my house 5
17 this was a small thing in thy eyes, O God; 5
17 and hast shown me future generations, O LORD God! 5
20 O LORD, and there is no God besides thee 5
21 Israel, whom God went to redeem to be his people 5
22 and thou, O LORD, didst become their God. 5
24 LORD of hosts, the God of Israel, is Israel's God 5
24 LORD of hosts, the God of Israel, is Israel's God 5
25 For thou, my God, hast revealed to thy servant that 5
26 now, O LORD, thou art God, and thou hast promised 5
19:13 play the man . . for the cities of our God; 5
21: 7 God was displeased with this thing, and he smote 5
8 David said to God, "I have sinned greatly 5
15 God sent the angel to Jerusalem to destroy it; 5
17 David said to God, "Was it not I who gave command 5
17 Let thy hand, I pray thee, O LORD my God, 5
30 David could not go before it to inquire of God 5
22: 1 David said, "Here shall be the house of the LORD God 5
2 dressed stones for building the house of God. 5
6 to build a house for the LORD, the God of Israel. 5
7 to build a house to the name of the LORD my God. 5
11 in building the house of the LORD your God 5
12 you may keep the law of the LORD your God. 5
18 Is not the LORD your God with you? 5
19 set your mind and heart to seek the LORD your God. 5
19 Arise and build the sanctuary of the LORD God 5
19 so that the ark . . and the holy vessels of God 5
23:14 sons of Moses the man of God were named among 5
25 The LORD, the God of Israel, has given peace 5
28 and any work for the service of the house of God; 5
24: 5 there were . . the sanctuary and officers of God 5
19 as the LORD God of Israel had commanded him. 5
25: 5 according to the promise of God to exalt him; 5
5 God had given Heman fourteen sons 5
6 the music . . for the service of the house of God. 5
26: 5 Pe-ul'lethai the eighth; for God blessed him. 5
20 had charge of the treasuries of the house of God 5
32 oversight . . for everything pertaining to God 5
28: 2 house . . and for the footstool of our God; 5
3 God said to me, 'You may not build a house for my name 5
4 LORD God of Israel chose me from all my father's 5
8 and in the hearing of our God 5
8 all the commandments of the LORD your God; 5
9 you, Solomon my son, know the God of your father 5
12 treasuries of the house of God 5
20 for the LORD God, even my God, is with you. 5
20 for the LORD God, even my God, is with you. 5
21 for all the service of the house of God; 5
29: 1 Solomon my son, whom alone God has chosen, is young 5
1 will not be for man but for the LORD God. 5
2 I have provided for the house of my God 5
3 because of my devotion to the house of my God 5
3 I give it to the house of my God 5
7 They gave for the service of the house of God 5
10 O LORD, the God of Israel our father 5
13 thank thee, our God, and praise thy glorious name 5
16 O LORD our God, all this abundance that we have 5
17 I know, my God, that thou triest the heart 5
18 O LORD, the God of Abraham, Isaac, and Israel 5
20 said to all the assembly, "Bless the LORD your God. 5
20 blessed the LORD, the God of their fathers 5
2Ch 1: 1 LORD his God was with him and made him 5
3 at Gibeon; for the tent of meeting of God 5
4 David had brought up the ark of God 5
7 In that night God appeared to Solomon 5
8 Solomon said to God, "Thou hast shown great 5
9 O LORD God, let thy promise . . be now fulfilled 5
11 God answered Solomon, "Because this was 5
2: 4 to build a house for the name of the LORD my God 5
4 appointed feasts of the LORD our God 5
5 house . . will be great, for our God is greater 5
12 Huram also said, "Blessed be the LORD God of Israel 5
3: 3 measurements for building the house of God 5
4:11 that he did for King Solomon on the house of God 5
19 all the things that were in the house of God 5
5: 1 stored . . in the treasuries of the house of God. 5
14 for the glory of the LORD filled the house of God. 5
6: 4 he said, "Blessed be the LORD, the God of Israel, who 5
7 build a house for . . the LORD, the God of Israel. 5
10 built the house for . . LORD, the God of Israel. 5
14 said, "O LORD, God of Israel, there is no God like thee 5
14 said, "O LORD, God of Israel, there is no God like thee 5
16 O LORD, God of Israel, keep with thy servant David 5
17 O LORD, God of Israel, let thy word be confirmed 5
18 will God dwell indeed with man on the earth? 5
19 have regard to the prayer . . O LORD my God 5
40 Now, O my God, let thy eyes be open and thy ears 5
41 now arise, O LORD God, and go to thy resting place 5
41 priests, O LORD God, be clothed with salvation 5
42 O LORD God, do not turn away the face of thy 5
7: 5 king and . . people dedicated the house of God. 5
22 they forsook the LORD the God of their fathers 5
8:14 for so David the man of God had commanded. 5
9: 8 Blessed be the LORD your God, who has delighted 5
8 set you on his throne as king for the LORD your God! 5
8 Because your God loved Israel 5
23 his wisdom, which God had put into his mind. 5
10:15 for it was a turn of affairs brought about by God 5
11: 2 word of the LORD came to Shemai'ah the man of God 5
16 set their hearts to seek the LORD God of Israel 5
16 sacrifice to the LORD, the God of their fathers. 5
13: 5 LORD God of Israel gave the kingship over Israel 5
10 as for us, the LORD is our God 5
11 for we keep the charge of the LORD our God 5
12 Behold, God is with us at our head 5
12 do not fight . . the LORD, the God of your fathers; 5
15 God defeated Jerobo'am and all Israel 5
16 God gave them into their hand. 5
18 relied upon the LORD, the God of their fathers. 5
14: 2 good and right in the eyes of the LORD his God. 5
4 to seek the LORD, the God of their fathers 5
7 because we have sought the LORD our God; 5
11 Asa cried to the LORD his God 5
11 Help us, O LORD our God, for we rely on thee 5
11 O LORD, thou art our God; let not man prevail 5
15: 1 Spirit of God came upon Azari'ah the son of Oded 5
3 For a long time Israel was without the true God 5
4 they turned to the LORD, the God of Israel 5
6 God troubled them with every sort of distress. 5
9 when they saw that he LORD his God was with him. 5
12 to seek the LORD, the God of their fathers 5
13 whoever would not seek the LORD, the God of Israel 5
18 he brought into the house of God the votive gifts 5
16: 7 did not rely on the LORD your God 5
17: 4 sought the God of his father 5
18: 5 God will give it into the hand of the king. 5
13 what my God says, that I will speak. 5
31 God drew them away from him 5
19: 3 have set your heart to seek God. 5
4 back to the LORD, the God of their fathers. 5
7 is no perversion of justice with the LORD our God 5
20: 6 LORD, God of our fathers, art thou not God in heaven? 5
6 LORD, God of our fathers, art thou not God in heaven? 5
7 O our God, drive out the inhabitants of this land 5
12 our God, wilt thou not execute judgment upon them? 5
15 Fear not . . for the battle is not yours but God's. 5
19 stood up to praise the LORD, the God of Israel 5
20 Believe in the LORD your God 5
29 fear of God came on all the kingdoms 5
30 for his God gave him rest round about. 5
33 not yet set . . upon the God of their fathers. 5
21:10 he had forsaken the LORD, the God of his fathers. 5
12 Thus says the LORD, the God of David your father 5
22: 7 ordained by God that the downfall of Ahazi'ah 5

12 remained with them . . hid in the house of God 5
23: 3 made a covenant with the king in the house of God. 5
9 which were in the house of God; 5
24: 5 money to repair the house of your God 5
7 had broken into the house of God; 5
9 tax that Moses the servant of God 5
13 they restored the house of God 5
16 done good in Israel, and toward God and his house. 5
18 house of the LORD, the God of their fathers 5
20 the Spirit of God took possession of Zechari'ah 5
20 Thus says God, 'Why do you transgress 5
24 forsaken the LORD, the God of their fathers. 5
27 the rebuilding of the house of God 5
25: 7 a man of God came to him and said 5
8 God will cast you down before the enemy; 5
8 for God has power to help or to cast down. 5
9 Amazi'ah said to the man of God 5
9 man of God answered, "The LORD is able to give you 5
16 I know that God has determined to destroy you 5
20 Amazi'ah would not listen; for it was of God 5
24 the vessels that were found in the house of God 5
26: 5 set himself to seek God in the days of Zechari'ah 5
5 Zechari'ah, who instructed him in the fear of God; 5
5 as long as he sought the LORD, God made him prosper. 5
7 God helped him against the Philistines 5
16 For he was false to the LORD his God 5
18 it will bring you no honor from the LORD God. 5
27: 6 ordered his ways before the LORD his God. 5
28: 5 LORD his God gave him into the hand of the king 5
6 forsaken the LORD, the God of their fathers. 5
9 LORD, the God of your fathers, was angry with Judah 5
10 sins of your own against the LORD your God? 5
24 gathered . . the vessels of the house of God 5
24 cut in pieces the vessels of the house of God 5
25 provoking to anger . . the God of his fathers. 5
29: 5 house of the LORD, the God of your fathers 5
6 done what was evil in the sight of the LORD our God; 5
7 in the holy place to the God of Israel. 5
10 to make a covenant with the LORD, the God of Israel 5
36 people rejoiced because of what God had done 5
30: 1 to keep the passover to the LORD the God of Israel. 5
5 keep the passover to the LORD the God of Israel 5
6 the LORD, the God of Abraham, Isaac, and Israel 5
7 faithless to the LORD God of their fathers 5
8 serve the LORD your God, that his fierce anger may 5
9 For the LORD your God is gracious and merciful 5
12 The hand of God was also upon Judah to give them 5
16 according to the law of Moses the man of God; 5
19 who sets his heart to seek God, the LORD 5
19 to seek God, the LORD the God of his fathers 5
22 giving thanks to the LORD the God 5
31: 6 been consecrated to the LORD their God 5
13 Azari'ah the chief officer of the house of God. 5
14 Ko're . . was over the freewill offerings to God 5
20 right and faithful before the LORD his God. 5
21 he undertook in the service of the house of God 5
21 law and the commandments, seeking his God 5
32: 8 with us is the LORD our God, to help us and to fight 5
11 The LORD our God will deliver us from the hand 5
14 God should be able to deliver you from my hand? 5
15 How . . will your God deliver you out of my hand!' 5
17 cast contempt on the LORD the God of Israel 5
17 God of Hezeki'ah will not deliver his people 5
19 spoke of the God of Jerusalem as . . the gods 5
29 God had given him very great possessions. 5
31 God left him to himself, in order to try him 5
33: 7 the image of the idol . . he set in the house of God 5
7 house of God, of which God said to David 5
12 he entreated the favor of the LORD his God 5
12 humbled . . before the God of his fathers. 5
13 He prayed to him, and God received his entreaty •
13 God . . heard his supplication and brought him 5
16 Judah to serve the LORD the God of Israel. 5
17 at the high places, but only to the LORD their God. 5
18 acts of Manas'seh, and his prayer to his God 5
18 spoke . . in the name of the LORD the God of Israel 5
19 his prayer, and how God received his entreaty •
34: 3 he began to seek the God of David his father; 5
8 to repair the house of the LORD his God. 5
9 money that had been brought into the house of God 5
23 Thus says the LORD, the God of Israel: 'Tell the man 5
26 Thus says the LORD, the God of Israel: Regarding 5
27 because . . you humbled yourself before God 5
32 Jerusalem did according to the covenant of God 5
32 covenant of God, the God of their fathers. 5
33 made all . . in Israel serve the LORD their God. 5
33 following the LORD the God of their fathers. 5
35: 3 Now serve the LORD your God and his people Israel. 5
8 the chief officers of the house of God 5
21 God has commanded me to make haste. 5
21 Cease opposing God, who is with me, lest he destroy 5
22 did not listen to the words of Neco from . . God 5
36: 5 did what was evil in the sight of the LORD his God. 5
12 did what was evil in the sight of the LORD his God. 5
13 Nebuchadnez'zar, who had made him swear by God; 5
13 against turning to the LORD, the God of Israel. 5
15 LORD, the God of their fathers, sent persistently 5
16 they kept mocking the messengers of God 5
18 vessels of the house of God, great and small 5
19 burned the house of God, and broke down the wall 5
23 LORD, the God of heaven, has given me all 5
23 may the LORD his God be with him. Let him go up. 5

Ezr 0: 4 the work on the house of God which is in Jerusalem 7
1: 2 LORD, the God of heaven, has given me all 5
3 Whoever is among you . . may his God be with him 5
3 rebuild the house of the LORD, the God of Israel– 5
3 LORD . . –he is the God who is in Jerusalem; 5
4 besides freewill offerings for the house of God 5
5 every one whose spirit God had stirred to go up 5
2:68 made freewill offerings for the house of God 5
3: 2 built the altar of the God of Israel 5
2 as it is written in the law of Moses the man of God. 5
8 their coming to the house of God at Jerusalem 5
9 oversight of the workmen in the house of God 5
4: 1 building a temple to the LORD, the God of Israel 5
2 for we worship your God as you do, and we have been 5
3 building a house to our God; but we alone 5
3 we alone will build to the LORD, the God of Israel 5
5: 1 prophesied . . in the name of the God of Israel 7
2 arose and began to rebuild the house of God 3
2 with them were the prophets of God, helping them. 3
5 eye of their God was upon the elders of the Jews 3
8 went to . . Judah, to the house of the great God. 3
11 'We are the servants of the God of heaven and earth 7
12 our fathers had angered the God of heaven 7
13 decree that this house of God should be rebuilt. 3
14 gold and silver vessels of the house of God 3
15 let the house of God be rebuilt on its site. 3
16 came and laid the foundations of the house of God 3
17 rebuilding of this house of God in Jerusalem. 3
6: 3 Concerning the house of God at Jerusalem 3
5 gold and silver vessels of the house of God 3
5 you shall put them in the house of God. 3
7 let the work on this house of God alone; 3
7 Jews rebuild this house of God on its site. 3
8 do . . for the rebuilding of this house of God; 3
9 burnt offerings to the God of heaven 7
10 offer pleasing sacrifices to the God of heaven 7
12 May the God who has caused his name to dwell there 7
12 put forth a hand . . to destroy this house of God 3
14 finished their building by command of the God 7
16 celebrated the dedication of this house of God 3
17 offered at the dedication of this house of God 3
18 set . . for the service of God at Jerusalem 3
21 separated . . to worship the LORD, the God of Israel. 5
22 aided them in the work of the house of God 5
22 work of the house of God, the God of Israel. 5
7: 6 law of Moses . . LORD the God of Israel had given; 5
6 for the hand of the LORD his God was upon him. 5
9 for the good hand of his God was upon him. 5
12 Ezra . . scribe of the law of the God of heaven. 7
14 according to the law of your God 3
15 freely offered to the God of Israel 7
16 vowed willingly for the house of their God 3
17 offer them upon the altar of the house of your God 3
18 you may do, according to the will of your God. 3
19 given you for the service of the house of your God 3
19 you shall deliver before the God of Jerusalem. 3
20 else is required for the house of your God 3
21 Ezra . . scribe of the law of the God of heaven 7
23 Whatever is commanded by the God of heaven 7
23 be done in full for the house of the God of heaven 7
24 or other servants of this house of God. 3
25 you, Ezra, according to the wisdom of your God 3
25 all such as know the laws of your God; 3
26 not obey the law of your God and the law of the king 3
27 Blessed be the LORD, the God of our fathers 5
28 hand of the LORD my God was upon me 5
8:17 to send us ministers for the house of our God. 5
18 by the good hand of our God upon us, they brought us 5
21 that we might humble ourselves before our God 5
22 hand of our God is for good upon all that seek him 5
23 fasted and besought our God for this 5
25 offering for the house of our God which the king 5
28 offering to the LORD, the God of your fathers. 5
30 to bring them to Jerusalem, to the house of our God. 5
31 hand of our God was upon us, and he delivered us 5
33 On the fourth day, within the house of our God 5
35 offered burnt offerings to the God of Israel 5
36 aided the people and the house of God. 5
9: 4 all who trembled at the words of the God of Israel 5
5 fell . . and spread out my hands to the LORD my God 5
6 O my God, I am ashamed and blush to lift my face 5
6 my God, for our iniquities have risen higher 5
8 favor has been shown by the LORD our God 5
8 that our God may brighten our eyes and grant us 5
9 yet our God has not forsaken us in our bondage 5
9 grant us some reviving to set up the house of our God 5
10 now, O our God, what shall we say after this? 5
13 seeing that thou, our God, hast punished us less 5
15 O LORD the God of Israel, thou art just 5
10: 1 casting himself down before the house of God 5
2 We have broken faith with our God 5
3 Therefore let us make a covenant with our God 5
3 those who tremble at the commandment of our God; 5
6 Then Ezra withdrew from before the house of God 5
9 sat in the open square before the house of God 5
11 make confession to the LORD the God of your fathers 5
14 till the fierce wrath of our God over this matter 5

Neh 1: 4 fasting and praying before the God of heaven. 5
5 I said, "O LORD God of heaven, the great and terrible 5
5 O LORD God of heaven, the great and terrible God 2
2: 4 I prayed to the God of heaven. 5
8 for the good hand of my God was upon me. 5
12 told no one what my God had put into my heart to do 5
18 I told them of the hand of my God which had been 5
20 The God of heaven will make us prosper 5
4: 4 Hear, O our God, for we are despised; 5
9 we prayed to our God, and set a guard 5
15 heard . . that God had frustrated their plan 5
20 rally to us there. Our God will fight for us. 5
5: 9 Ought you not to walk in the fear of our God 5
13 So may God shake out every man from his house 5
15 I did not do so, because of the fear of God. 5
19 Remember for my good, O my God, all that I have done 5
6: 9 But now, O God, strengthen thou my hands. •
10 Let us meet together in the house of God 5
12 I understood, and saw that God had not sent him 5
14 Remember Tobi'ah and Sanbal'lat, O my God 5
16 work . . accomplished with the help of our God. 5
7: 5 Then God put it into my mind to assemble 5
8: 6 Ezra blessed the Lord, the great God; 5
8 read from the book, from the law of God, clearly 5
9 This day is holy to the LORD your God; 5
16 made booths . . in the courts of the house of God 5
18 by day . . he read from the book of the law of God. 5
9: 3 read from the book of the law of the LORD their God 5
3 for another fourth . . worshiped the LORD their God. 5
4 cried with a loud voice to the LORD their God. 5
5 bless the LORD your God from everlasting 5
7 LORD, the God who didst choose Abram and bring him 5
17 But thou art a God ready to forgive 4
18 'This is your God who brought you up out of Egypt,' 5
31 for thou art a gracious and merciful God. 2
32 our God, the great and mighty and terrible God 5
32 our God, the great and mighty and terrible God 2
10:28 separated themselves . . to the law of God 5
29 enter into a curse and an oath to walk in God's law 5
29 God's law . . given by Moses the servant of God 5
32 third part . . for the service of the house of our God 5
33 for all the work of the house of our God. 5
34 offering, to bring it into the house of our God 5
34 to burn upon the altar of the LORD our God 5
36 also to bring to the house of our God 5
36 priests who minister in the house of our God 5
37 priests, to the chambers of the house of our God; 5
38 tithes to the house of our God, to the chambers 5
39 We will not neglect the house of our God. 5
11:11 Merai'oth, son of Ahi'tub, ruler of the house of God 5
16 who were over the outside work of the house of God; 5
22 singers, over the work of the house of God. 5
12:24 commandment of David the man of God 5
36 musical instruments of David the man of God; 5
40 both companies . . stood in the house of God 5
43 God had made them rejoice with great joy; 5
45 performed the service of their God 5
46 songs of praise and thanksgiving to God. 5
13: 1 no Ammonite . . ever enter the assembly of God; 5
2 yet our God turned the curse into a blessing. 5
4 chambers of the house of our God 5
7 chamber in the courts of the house of God. 5
9 brought back..the vessels of the house of God 5
11 Why is the house of God forsaken? 5
14 Remember me, O my God, concerning this 5
14 good deeds that I have done for the house of my God 5
18 did not our God bring all this evil on us 5
22 Remember this also in my favor, O my God 5
25 I made them take oath in the name of God, saying 5
26 beloved by his God, and God made him king 5
26 God made him king over all Israel; 5
27 evil and act treacherously against our God 5
29 Remember them, O my God, because they have defiled 5
31 Remember me, O my God, for good. 5

Job 1: 1 one who feared God, and turned away from evil. 5
5 sons have sinned, and cursed God in their hearts. 5
6 when the sons of God came to present themselves 5
8 a blameless and upright man, who fears God 5
9 answered the LORD, "Does Job fear God for nought? 5
16 another, and said, "The fire of God fell from heaven 5
22 Job did not sin or charge God with wrong. 5
2: 1 when the sons of God came to present themselves 5
3 a blameless and upright man, who fears God 5
9 hold fast your integrity? Curse God, and die. 5
10 Shall we receive good at the hand of God 5
3: 4 Let that day be darkness! May God above not seek it 4
23 a man whose way is hid, whom God has hedged in? 4
4: 6 Is not your fear of God your confidence •
9 By the breath of God they perish, and by the blast 4
17 Can mortal man be righteous before God? 4
5: 8 I would seek God, and to God would I commit my cause; 5
8 I would seek God, and to God would I commit my cause; 5
17 Behold, happy is the man whom God reproves; 4
6: 4 the terrors of God are arrayed against me. 4
8 and that God would grant my desire; 4

9 that it would please God to crush me 4
8: 3 Does God pervert justice? 2
5 If you will seek God and make supplication 2
13 Such are the paths of all who forget God; 2
20 Behold, God will not reject a blameless man 2
9: 2 it is so: but how can a man be just before God? 2
13 God will not turn back his anger; 4
10: 2 I will say to God, Do not condemn me; 4
11: 4 My doctrine is pure, and I am clean in God's eyes.' •
5 oh, that God would speak, and open his lips to you 4
6 God exacts of you less than your guilt deserves. 4
7 Can you find out the deep things of God? 4
12: 4 I, who called upon God and he answered me 4
6 those who provoke God are secure 2
13 With God are wisdom and might; •
13: 3 I desire to argue my case with God. 2
7 Will you speak falsely for God 2
8 will you plead the case for God? 2
15: 4 But you are doing away with the fear of God •
4 and hindering meditation before God. 2
8 Have you listened in the council of God? 4
11 Are the consolations of God too small for you 2
13 that you turn your spirit against God 2
15 Behold, God puts no trust in his holy ones •
25 he has stretched forth his hand against God 2
16: 7 Surely now God has worn me out; •
11 God gives me up to the ungodly 2
20 My friends scorn me; my eye pours out tears to God 4
21 he would maintain the right of a man with God 4
18:21 such is the place of him who knows not God. 2
19: 6 know then that God has put me in the wrong 4
21 for the hand of God has touched me! 4
22 Why do you, like God, pursue me? 2
26 thus destroyed, then from my flesh I shall see God 4
20:15 God casts them out of his belly. 2
23 God will send his fierce anger into him •
28 dragged off in the day of God's wrath. •
29 This is the wicked man's portion from God 5
29 the heritage decreed for him by God. 2
21: 9 safe from fear, and no rod of God is upon them. 4
14 They say to God, 'Depart from us! 2
17 That God distributes pains in his anger? •
19 God stores up their iniquity for their sons.' 4
22 Will any teach God knowledge 2
22: 2 Can a man be profitable to God? 2
12 Is not God high in the heavens? 4
13 Therefore you say, 'What does God know? 2
17 They said to God, 'Depart from us,' 2
21 Agree with God, and be at peace; •
26 in the Almighty, and lift up your face to God. 4
29 For God abases the proud, but he saves the lowly. •
23:16 God has made my heart faint; 2
24:12 yet God pays no attention to their prayer. 4
22 God prolongs the life of the mighty by his power; •
25: 2 Dominion and fear are with God; •
4 How then can man be righteous before God? 2
26: 6 Sheol is naked before God •
27: 2 As God lives, who has taken away my right 2
3 the spirit of God is in my nostrils; 4
8 the hope of the godless when God cuts him off •
8 when God cuts him off, when God takes away his life? 4
9 Will God hear his cry, when trouble comes upon him? 2
10 Will he call upon God at all times? 4
11 I will teach you concerning the hand of God; 2
13 This is the portion of a wicked man with God 2
28:23 God understands the way to it 5
29: 2 as in the days when God watched over me; 4
4 when the friendship of God was upon my tent; 4
30:11 Because God has loosed my cord and humbled me •
19 God has cast me into the mire •
31: 2 What would be my portion from God above 4
6 in a just balance, and let God know my integrity! 4
14 what then shall I do when God rises up? 2
23 For I was in terror of calamity from God 2
28 for I should have been false to God above. 2
32: 2 because he justified himself rather than God; 5
13 have found wisdom; God may vanquish him, not man. 2
33: 4 The spirit of God has made me 2
6 Behold, I am toward God as you are; 2
12 I will answer you. God is greater than man. 4
14 For God speaks in one way, and in two 2
26 then man prays to God, and he accepts him 4
29 Behold, God does all these things, 2
34: 5 I am innocent, and God has taken away my right; 2
9 that he should take delight in God 5
10 far be it from God that he should do wickedness 2
12 Of a truth, God will not do wickedly 2
23 a time for any man to go before God in judgment. 2
31 any one said to God, 'I have borne chastisement; 2
37 among us, and multiplies his words against God. 2
35: 2 Do you say, 'It is my right before God,' 2
10 Where is God my Maker, who gives songs in the night 4
13 Surely God does not hear an empty cry 2
36: 2 for I have yet something to say on God's behalf. 4
5 Behold, God is mighty, and does not despise any; 2
22 Behold, God is exalted in his power; 2
26 Behold, God is great, and we know him not; 2
37: 5 God thunders wondrously with his voice; 2
10 By the breath of God ice is given 2
14 stop and consider the wondrous works of God. 2
15 Do you know how God lays his command upon them 4
22 God is clothed with terrible majesty. 4
38: 7 all the sons of God shouted for joy? 5
41 the raven its prey, when its young ones cry to God 2
39:17 because God has made her forget wisdom 4
40: 2 He who argues with God, let him answer it. 4
9 Have you an arm like God, and can you thunder 2
19 He is the first of the works of God; 2
Ps 3: 2 are saying of me, there is no help for him in God. 5
7 Arise, O LORD! Deliver me, O my God! 5
4: 1 Answer me when I call, O God of my right! 5
5: 2 Hearken to the sound of my cry, my King and my God 5
4 thou art not a God who delights in wickedness; 2
10 Make them bear their guilt, O God; 5
7: 1 O LORD my God, in thee do I take refuge; 5
3 O LORD my God, if I have done this 5
6 awake, O my God; thou hast appointed a judgment. 2
9 triest the minds and hearts, thou righteous God. 5
10 My shield is with God, who saves the upright 5
11 God is a righteous judge 5
11 a God who has indignation every day. 2
12 If a man does not repent, God will whet his sword; •
8: 5 Yet thou hast made him little less than God 5
9:17 depart to Sheol, all the nations that forget God. 5
10: 4 all his thoughts are, "There is no God. 5
11 He thinks in his heart, "God has forgotten 2
12 Arise, O LORD; O God, lift up thy hand; 2
13 Why does the wicked renounce God 5
13: 3 Consider and answer me, O LORD my God; 5
14: 1 The fool says in his heart, "There is no God. 5
2 any that act wisely, that seek after God. 5
5 for God is with the generation of the righteous. 5
16: 1 Preserve me, O God, for in thee I take refuge. 2
17: 6 I call upon thee, for thou wilt answer me, O God; 2
18: 2 my fortress, and my deliverer, my God, my rock 2
6 I called upon the LORD; to my God I cried for help. 5
21 and have not wickedly departed from my God. 5
28 the LORD my God lightens my darkness. 5
29 by my God I can leap over a wall. 5
30 This God-his way is perfect; 2
31 For who is God, but the LORD? 4
31 who is a rock, except our God?- 5
32 the God who girded me with strength 2
46 exalted be the God of my salvation 5
47 the God who gave me vengeance 2
19: 1 The heavens are telling the glory of God; 2
20: 1 The name of the God of Jacob protect you! 5
5 in the name of our God set up our banners! 5
7 we boast of the name of the LORD our God. 5
22: 1 My God, my God, why hast thou forsaken me? 2
1 My God, my God, why hast thou forsaken me? 2
2 O my God, I cry by day, but thou dost not answer; 5
10 since my mother bore me thou hast been my God. 2
24: 5 and vindication from the God of his salvation. 5
6 who seek him, who seek the face of the God of Jacob. 9
25: 2 O my God, in thee I trust, let me not be put to shame; 5
5 teach me, for thou art the God of my salvation; 5
22 Redeem Israel, O God, out of all his troubles. 5
27: 9 Cast me not off, forsake me not, O God of my salvation! 5
29: 3 God of glory thunders, the LORD, upon many waters. 2
30: 2 O LORD my God, I cried to thee for help 5
12 O LORD my God, I will give thanks to thee for ever. 5
31: 5 thou hast redeemed me, O LORD, faithful God. 2
14 I trust in thee, O LORD, I say, "Thou art my God. 5
33:12 Blessed is the nation whose God is the LORD 5
35:23 awake for my right, for my cause, my God and my Lord! 5
24 Vindicate me, O LORD, my God 5
36: 1 there is no fear of God before his eyes. 5
6 Thy righteousness is like the mountains of God 2
7 How precious is thy steadfast love, O God! 5
37:31 The law of his God is in his heart; 5
38:15 it is thou, O LORD my God, who wilt answer. 5
21 Do not forsake me, O LORD! O my God, be not far 5
40: 3 a new song in my mouth, a song of praise to our God. 5
5 O LORD my God, thy wondrous deeds and thy thoughts 5
8 I delight to do thy will, O my God; 5
17 my help and my deliverer; do not tarry, O my God! 5
41:13 Blessed be the LORD, the God of Israel 5
42: 1 so longs my soul for thee, O God. 5
2 My soul thirsts for God, for the living God. 5
2 My soul thirsts for God, for the living God. 2
2 When shall I come and behold the face of God? 5
3 while men say to me continually, "Where is your God? 5
4 led them in procession to the house of God 5
5 Hope in God; for I shall again praise him, my help 5
6 and my God. 5
8 his song is with me, a prayer to the God of my life. 2
9 I say to God, my rock: "Why hast thou forgotten me? 2
10 they say to me continually, "Where is your God? 5
11 Hope in God; for I shall again praise him 5
11 I shall again praise him, my help and my God. 5
43: 1 Vindicate me, O God, and defend my cause 5
2 For thou art the God in whom I take refuge; 5
4 Then I will go to the altar of God 5
4 will go to the altar of God, to God my exceeding joy; 2
4 I will praise thee with the lyre, O God, my God. 5
4 I will praise thee with the lyre, O God, my God. 5
5 why are you disquieted within me? Hope in God; 5
5 for I shall again praise him, my help and my God. 5
44: 1 We have heard with our ears, O God 5
4 Thou art my King and my God 5
8 In God we have boasted continually 5
20 If we had forgotten the name of our God 5
21 would not God discover this? 5
45: 2 therefore God has blessed you for ever. 5
7 Therefore God, your God, has anointed you 5
7 Therefore God, your God, has anointed you 5
46: 1 God is our refuge and strength 5
4 a river whose streams make glad the city of God 5
5 God is in the midst of her, she shall not be moved; 5
5 God will help her right early. 5
7 the God of Jacob is our refuge. Selah 5
10 Be still, and know that I am God. 5
11 the God of Jacob is our refuge. Selah 5
47: 1 all peoples! Shout to God with loud songs of joy! 5
5 God has gone up with a shout 5
6 Sing praises to God, sing praises! 5
7 For God is the king of all the earth; 5
8 God reigns over the nations; 5
8 God sits on his holy throne. 5
9 gather as the people of the God of Abraham. 5
9 For the shields of the earth belong to God; 5
48: 1 and greatly to be praised in the city of our God! 5
3 God has shown himself a sure defense. 5
8 city of the LORD of hosts, in the city of our God 5
8 city of our God, which God establishes for ever. 5
9 We have thought on thy steadfast love, O God 5
10 As thy name, O God, so thy praise reaches to the ends 5
14 that this is God, our God for ever and ever. 5
14 that this is God, our God for ever and ever. 5
49: 7 or give to God the price of his life 5
15 God will ransom my soul from the power of Sheol 5
50: 1 The Mighty One, God the LORD, speaks and summons 5
2 the perfection of beauty, God shines forth. 5
3 Our God comes, he does not keep silence 5
6 his righteousness, for God himself is judge! 5
7 I will testify against you. I am God, your God. 5
7 I will testify against you. I am God, your God. 5
14 Offer to God a sacrifice of thanksgiving 5
16 But to the wicked God says: "What right have you 5
22 Mark this, then, you who forget God 4
23 I will show the salvation of God! 5
51: 1 Have mercy on me, O God, according to thy steadfast 5
10 Create in me a clean heart, O God 5
14 Deliver me from blood guiltiness, O God 5
14 O God, thou God of my salvation 5
17 sacrifice acceptable to God is a broken spirit; 5
17 a..contrite heart, O God, thou wilt not despise. 5
52: 5 God will break you down for ever; 2
7 See the man who would not make God his refuge 5
8 I am like a green olive tree in the house of God. 5
8 I trust in the steadfast love of God for ever 5
53: 1 The fool says in his heart, "There is no God. 5
2 God looks down from heaven upon the sons of men 5
2 any that are wise, that seek after God. 5
4 as they eat bread, and do not call upon God? 5
5 For God will scatter the bones of the ungodly; 5
5 will be put to shame, for God has rejected them. 5
6 When God restores the fortunes of his people 5
54: 1 Save me, O God, by thy name, and vindicate me 5
2 Hear my prayer, O God; 5
3 they do not set God before them. Selah 5
4 Behold, God is my helper; 5
55: 1 Give ear to my prayer, O God; and hide not thyself 5
14 within God's house we walked in fellowship. 5
16 I call upon God; and the LORD will save me. 5
19 God will give ear, and humble them 2
19 because they keep no law, and do not fear God. 5
23 thou, O God, wilt cast them down into the lowest pit; 5
56: 1 Be gracious to me, O God, for men trample upon me; 5
4 In God, whose word I praise, in God I trust 5
4 whose word I praise, in God I trust without a fear. 5
7 in wrath cast down the peoples, O God! 5
9 This I know, that God is for me. 5
10 In God, whose word I praise 5
11 in God I trust without fear. What can man do to me? 5
12 My vows to thee I must perform, O God; 5
13 that I may walk before God in the light of life. 5
57: 1 Be merciful to me, O God, be merciful to me 5
2 I cry to God Most High, to God who fulfils 5
2 to God who fulfils his purpose for me. 2
3 God will send forth his steadfast love 5
5 Be exalted, O God, above the heavens! 5
7 My heart is steadfast, O God, my heart is steadfast! 5
11 Be exalted, O God, above the heavens! 5
58: 6 O God, break the teeth in their mouths; 5
11 surely there is a God who judges on earth. 5
59: 1 Deliver me from my enemies, O my God 5
5 Thou, LORD God of hosts, art God of Israel. 5
5 Thou, LORD God of hosts, art God of Israel. 5
9 praises to thee; for thou, O God, art my fortress. 5
10 My God in his steadfast love will meet me; 5
10 my God will let me look in triumph on my enemies. 5
13 that men may know that God rules over Jacob 5

17 praises to thee, for thou, O God, art my fortress 5
17 my fortress, the God who shows me steadfast love. 5
60: 1 O God, thou hast rejected us, broken our defenses; 5
6 God has spoken in his sanctuary 5
10 Hast thou not rejected us, O God? 5
10 Thou dost not go forth, O God, with our armies. 5
12 With God we shall do valiantly; 5
61: 1 Hear my cry, O God, listen to my prayer; 5
5 For thou, O God, hast heard my vows 5
7 May he be enthroned for ever before God; 5
62: 1 For God alone my soul waits in silence; 5
5 For God alone my soul waits in silence 5
7 On God rests my deliverance and my honor; 5
7 my mighty rock, my refuge is God. 5
8 God is a refuge for us. Selah 5
11 Once God has spoken; twice have I heard this 5
11 I heard this: that power belongs to God; 5
63: 1 O God, thou art my God, I seek thee 5
1 my God, I seek thee, my soul thirsts for thee; 2
11 the king shall rejoice in God; 5
64: 1 Hear my voice, O God, in my complaint; 5
7 God will shoot his arrow at them; 5
9 men will fear; they will tell what God has wrought 5
65: 1 Praise is due to thee, O God, in Zion; 5
5 O God of our salvation, who art the hope of all 5
9 the river of God is full of water; 5
66: 1 Make a joyful noise to God, all the earth; 5
3 Say to God, "How terrible are thy deeds! 5
5 Come and see what God has done 5
8 Bless our God, O peoples 5
10 For thou, O God, hast tested us; thou hast tried us 5
16 Come and hear, all you who fear God 5
19 But truly God has listened; he has given heed 5
20 Blessed be God, because he has not rejected my 5
67: 1 May God be gracious to us and bless us 5
3 Let the peoples praise thee, O God; 5
5 Let the peoples praise thee, O God; 5
6 God, our God, has blessed us. 5
6 God, our God, has blessed us. 5
7 God has blessed us; 5
68: 1 Let God arise, let his enemies be scattered; 5
2 as wax melts . . , let the wicked perish before God! 5
3 righteous be joyful; let them exult before God; 5
4 Sing to God, sing praises to his name; 5
5 Father . . and protector . . is God in his holy 5
6 God gives the desolate a home to dwell in; 5
7 O God, when thou didst go forth before thy people 5
8 heavens poured down rain, at the presence of God; 5
8 yon Sinai quaked at the presence of God 5
8 Sinai quaked at the presence of . . God of Israel. 5
9 Rain in abundance, O God, thou didst shed abroad; 5
10 goodness, O God, thou didst provide for the needy. 5
16 at the mount which God desired for his abode 5
18 that the LORD God may dwell there. 5
19 Lord . . bears us up; God is our salvation. Selah 2
20 Our God is a God of salvation; 2
20 Our God is a God of salvation; 2
20 to God, the Lord, belongs escape from death. 6
21 But God will shatter the heads of his enemies 5
24 Thy solemn processions are seen, O God 5
24 processions of my God, my King, into the sanctuary- 2
26 Bless God in the great congregation, the LORD 5
28 Summon thy might, O God; show thy strength, O God 5
28 Summon thy might, O God; show thy strength, O God 5
31 Ethiopia hasten to stretch out her hands to God. 5
32 Sing to God, O kingdoms of the earth; sing praises 5
34 Ascribe power to God, whose majesty 5
35 Terrible is God in his sanctuary 5
35 God of Israel, he gives power and strength 2
35 Blessed be God! 5
69: 1 Save me, O God! For the waters have come up 5
3 My eyes grow dim with waiting for my God. 5
5 O God, thou knowest my folly; the wrongs I have done 5
6 brought to dishonor through me, O God of Israel. 5
13 O God, in the abundance of thy steadfast love 5
29 let thy salvation, O God, set me on high! 5
30 I will praise the name of God with a song; 5
32 you who seek God, let your hearts revive. 5
35 God will save Zion and rebuild the cities 5
70: 1 Be pleased, O God, to deliver me! 5
4 who love thy salvation say evermore, "God is great! 5
5 I am poor and needy; hasten to me, O God! 5
71: 4 Rescue me, O my God, from the hand of the wicked 5
11 and say, "God has forsaken him; pursue and seize him 5
12 O God, be not far from me; O my God, make haste 5
12 be not far from me; O my God, make haste to help me! 5
17 O God, from my youth thou hast taught me 5
18 to old age and gray hairs, O God, do not forsake me 5
19 thy righteousness, O God, reach the high heavens. 5
19 O God, who is like thee? 5
22 for thy faithfulness, O my God; I will sing praises 5
72: 1 Give the king thy justice, O God 5
18 Blessed be the LORD, the God of Israel 5
73: 1 Truly God is good to the upright 5
11 they say, "How can God know? 2
17 until I went into the sanctuary of God; 2
26 God is the strength of my heart and my portion 5
28 for me it is good to be near God; 5
74: 1 O God, why dost thou cast us off for ever? 5
8 burned all the meeting places of God in the land. 2
10 How long, O God, is the foe to scoff? 5
12 Yet God my King is from of old, working salvation 5
22 Arise, O God, plead thy cause; 5
75: 1 We give thanks to thee, O God; we give thanks; 5
7 it is God who executes judgment, putting down one 5
9 for ever, I will sing praises to the God of Jacob. 5
76: 1 In Judah God is known, his name is great in Israel. 5
6 At thy rebuke, O God of Jacob, both rider and horse 5
9 when God arose to establish judgment to save all 5
11 Make your vows to the LORD your God 5
77: 1 I cry aloud to God, aloud to God, that he may hear me. 5
1 I cry aloud to God, aloud to God, that he may hear me. 5
3 I think of God, and I moan; I meditate 5
9 Has God forgotten to be gracious? 2
13 Thy way, O God, is holy. 5
13 What god is great like our God? 5
14 Thou art the God who workest wonders 2
16 When the waters saw thee, O God 5
78: 7 that they should set their hope in God 5
7 hope in God, and not forget the works of God 2
8 whose spirit was not faithful to God. 2
10 They did not keep God's covenant, but refused 5
18 tested God in their heart by demanding the food 2
19 They spoke against God, saying 5
19 Can God spread a table in the wilderness? 2
22 because they had no faith in God 5
31 the anger of God rose against them and he slew 5
34 they repented and sought God earnestly. 2
35 They remembered that God was their rock 5
35 was their rock, the Most High God their redeemer. 2
56 tested and rebelled against the Most High God 5
59 When God heard, he was full of wrath 5
79: 1 O God, the heathen have come into thy inheritance; 5
9 Help us, O God of our salvation 5
10 Why should the nations say, "Where is their God? 5
80: 3 Restore us, O God; 5
4 O LORD God of hosts, how long wilt thou be angry 5
7 Restore us, O God of hosts; let thy face shine 5
14 Turn again, O God of hosts! Look down from heaven 5
19 Restore us, O LORD God of hosts! let thy face shine 5
81: 1 Sing aloud to God our strength; 5
1 shout for joy to the God of Jacob! 5
4 an ordinance of the God of Jacob. 5
10 I am the LORD your God, who brought you up 5
82: 1 God has taken his place in the divine council; 5
8 Arise, O God, judge the earth; 5
83: 1 O God, do not keep silence; do not hold thy peace 5
1 do not hold thy peace or be still, O God! 2
12 take . . for ourselves of the pastures of God. 5
13 O my God, make them like whirling dust 5
84: 2 my heart and flesh sing for joy to the living God. 2
3 at thy altars, O LORD of hosts, my King and my God. 5
7 God of gods will be seen in Zion. 5
8 O LORD God of hosts, hear my prayer; 5
8 give ear, O God of Jacob! Selah 5
9 Behold our shield, O God; 5
10 rather be a doorkeeper in the house of my God than 5
11 For the LORD God is a sun and shield; 5
85: 4 Restore us again, O God of our salvation 5
8 Let me hear what God the LORD will speak 2
86: 2 Thou art my God; 5
10 thou alone art God. 5
12 I give thanks to thee, O Lord my God 5
14 O God, insolent men have risen up against me; 5
15 O Lord, art a God merciful and gracious 2
87: 3 Glorious things are spoken of you, O city of God. 5
88: 1 O LORD, my God, I call for help by day; 5
89: 7 God feared in the council of the holy ones 2
8 O LORD God of hosts, who is mighty as thou art, 5
26 my Father, my God, and the Rock of my salvation.' 2
90: 0 A Prayer of Moses, the man of God. 5
2 from everlasting to everlasting thou art God. 2
17 Let the favor of the Lord our God be upon us 5
91: 2 My refuge and my fortress; my God, in whom I trust. 5
92:13 they flourish in the courts of our God. 5
94: 1 O LORD, thou God of vengeance 2
1 thou God of vengeance, shine forth! 2
7 does not see; the God of Jacob does not perceive. 5
22 my God the rock of my refuge. 5
23 LORD our God will wipe them out. 5
95: 3 For the LORD is a great God, and a great King 2
7 he is our God, and we are the people of his pasture 5
97: 8 rejoice, because of thy judgments, O God 6
98: 3 ends of the earth have seen the victory of our God. 5
99: 5 Extol the LORD our God; worship at his footstool! 5
8 O LORD our God, thou didst answer them; 5
8 forgiving God to them, but an avenger 2
9 Extol the LORD our God, and worship at his holy 5
9 Extol the LORD . . ; for the LORD our God is holy! 5
100: 3 Know that the LORD is God! It is he that made us 5
102:24 O my God," I say, "take me not hence in the midst 2
104: 1 O LORD my God, thou art very great! 5
21 lions roar . . , seeking their food from God. 2
33 I will sing praise to my God while I have being. 5
105: 7 LORD our God; his judgments are in all the earth. 5
106:14 put God to the test in the desert; 2
20 exchanged the glory of God for the image of an ox •
21 forgot God, their Savior, who had done great 2
47 Save us, O LORD our God, and gather us from among 5
48 Blessed be the LORD, the God of Israel 5
107:11 for they had rebelled against the words of God 2
108: 1 My heart is steadfast, O God, my heart is steadfast! 5
5 Be exalted, O God, above the heavens! 5
7 God has promised in his sanctuary 5
11 Hast thou not rejected us, O God? 5
11 Thou dost not go forth, O God, with our armies. 5
13 With God we shall do valiantly; 5
109: 1 Be not silent, O God of my praise! 5
26 Help me, O LORD my God! 5
113: 5 Who is like the LORD our God, who is seated on high 5
114: 7 Tremble, . . , at the presence of the God of Jacob 4
115: 2 Why should the nations say, "Where is their God? 5
3 Our God is in the heavens; 5
116: 5 Gracious . . , and righteous; our God is merciful. 5
118:27 The LORD is God, and he has given us light. 2
28 Thou art my God, and I will give thanks to thee; 2
28 thou art my God, I will extol thee. 5
119:115 that I may keep the commandments of my God. 5
122: 9 For the sake of the house of the LORD our God 5
123: 2 so our eyes look to the LORD our God 5
135: 2 that stand in . . courts of the house of our God! 5
5 For I know . . that our Lord is above all gods. 5
136: 2 O give thanks to the God of gods 5
26 O give thanks to the God of heaven 2
139:17 How precious to me are thy thoughts, O God! 2
19 O that thou wouldst slay the wicked, O God 4
23 Search me, O God, and know my heart! 2
140: 6 I say to the LORD, Thou art my God; give ear 2
141: 8 my eyes are toward thee, O LORD God; 1
143:10 Teach me to do thy will, for thou art my God! 5
144: 9 I will sing a new song to thee, O God; 5
15 Happy the people whose God is the LORD! 5
145: 1 I will extol thee, my God and King, and bless 5
146: 2 I will sing praises to my God while I have being. 5
5 Happy is he whose help is the God of Jacob 2
5 Happy is he whose . . hope is in the LORD his God 5
10 reign for ever, thy God, O Zion, to all generations. 5
147: 1 For it is good to sing praises to our God; 5
7 make melody to our God upon the lyre! 5
12 LORD, O Jerusalem! Praise your God, O Zion! 5
149: 6 Let the high praises of God be in their throats 2
150: 1 Praise the LORD! Praise God in his sanctuary; 2
Prv 2: 5 then you will . . find the knowledge of God. 5
17 who . . forgets the covenant of her God; 5
3: 4 favor and good repute in the sight of God and man. 5
14: 9 God scorns the wicked, but the upright enjoy •
25: 2 It is the glory of God to conceal things 5
30: 5 Every word of God proves true; 4
9 I be poor, and steal, and profane the name of my God. 5
Ecc 1:13 it is an unhappy business that God has given 5
2:24 This also, I saw, is from the hand of God; 5
26 God gives wisdom and knowledge and joy; •
26 he gives.., only to give to one who pleases God. 5
3:10 the business that God has given to the sons of men 5
11 find out what God has done from the beginning 5
13 it is God's gift to man that every one should eat 5
14 I know that whatever God does endures for ever; 5
14 God has made it so, in order that men should fear 5
15 and God seeks what has been driven away. 5
17 God will judge the righteous and the wicked 5
18 I said..that God is testing them to show them 5
5: 1 Guard your steps when you go to the house of God; 5
2 let your heart be hasty to utter a word before God 5
2 for God is in heaven, and you upon earth; 5
4 When you vow a vow to God, do not delay paying it; 5
6 why should God be angry at your voice, and destroy 5
7 empty words grow many: but do you fear God. 5
18 the few days of his life which God has given him 5
19 to whom God has given wealth and possessions 5
19 to accept his lot and..-this is the gift of God. 5
20 God keeps him occupied with joy in his heart. 5
6: 2 to whom God gives wealth, possessions, and honor 5
2 yet God does not give him power to enjoy them 5
7:13 Consider the work of God; 5
14 God has made the one as well as the other 5
18 he who fears God shall come forth from them all. 5
26 he who pleases God escapes her 5
29 God made man upright, but they have sought out 5
8:12 I know that it will be well with those who fear God 5
13 because he does not fear before God. 5
15 days of life which God gives him under the sun. 5
17 then I saw all the work of God, that man cannot find 5
9: 1 the wise and their deeds are in the hand of God; 5
7 God has already approved what you do. 5
11: 5 do not know the work of God who makes everything. 5
9 know that..God will bring you into judgment. 5
12: 7 and the spirit returns to God who gave it. 5
13 Fear God, and keep his commandments; 5
14 For God will bring every deed into judgment 5
Isa 1:10 Give ear to the teaching of our God . . Gomor'rah! 5
2: 3 mountain of the LORD . . house of the God of Jacob; 5
5:16 the Holy God shows himself holy in righteousness 2
7:11 Ask a sign of the LORD your God; 5
13 for you to weary men, that you weary my God also? 5

8:10 it will not stand, for God is with us. 2
19 should not a people consult their God? 5
21 enraged and will curse their king and their God 5
9: 6 be called "Wonderful Counselor, Mighty God 2
10:21 return, the remnant of Jacob, to the mighty God. 2
12: 2 Behold, God is my salvation; 2
13:19 Sodom and Gomor'rah when God overthrew them. 5
14:13 above the stars of God I will set my throne on high; 2
17: 6 of a fruit tree, says the LORD God of Israel. 5
10 For you have forgotten the God of your salvation 5
21:10 LORD of hosts, the God of Israel, I announce to you 5
17 for the LORD, the God of Israel, has spoken. 5
24:15 glory . . to the name of the LORD, the God of Israel. 5
25: 1 O LORD, thou art my God; I will exalt thee 5
9 It will be said on that day, "Lo, this is our God; 5
26:13 O LORD our God, other lords besides thee have 5
28:26 For he is instructed aright; his God teaches him. 5
29:23 and will stand in awe of the God of Israel. 5
30:18 For the LORD is a God of justice; 5
31: 3 The Egyptians are men, and not God; 2
35: 2 the glory of the LORD, the majesty of our God. 5
4 Behold, your God will come with vengeance 5
4 come with vengeance, with the recompense of God. 5
36: 7 if you say to me, "We rely on the LORD our God 5
37: 4 may be . . God heard the words of the Rab'shakeh 5
4 king of Assyria has sent to mock the living God 5
4 words which the LORD your God has heard; 5
10 Do not let your God on whom you rely deceive you 5
16 O LORD of hosts, God of Israel, who art enthroned 5
16 thou art the God, thou alone, of all the kingdoms 5
17 words . . which he has sent to mock the living God. 5
20 now, O LORD our God, save us from his hand 5
21 Thus says the LORD, the God of Israel 5
38: 5 Thus says the LORD, the God of David your father 5
40: 1 Comfort, comfort my people, says your God. 5
3 make straight in the desert a highway for our God. 5
8 fades; but the word of our God will stand for ever. 5
9 say to the cities of Judah, "Behold your God! 5
18 To whom then will you liken God 2
27 and my right is disregarded by my God"? 5
28 The LORD is the everlasting God 5
41:10 be not dismayed, for I am your God; 5
13 For I, the LORD your God, hold your right hand; 5
17 I the God of Israel will not forsake them. 5
42: 5 Thus says God, the LORD, who created the heavens 2
43: 3 For I am the LORD your God, the Holy One 5
13 I am God, and also henceforth I am He; 2
44: 8 you are my witnesses! Is there a God besides me? 4
45: 3 I . . the God of Israel, who call you by your name. 5
5 there is no other, besides me there is no God; 5
14 God is with you only, and there is no other 2
15 Truly, thou art a God who hidest thyself 2
15 who hidest thyself, O God of Israel, the Savior. 5
18 says the LORD, who created the heavens (he is God!) 5
21 god besides me, a righteous God and a Savior; 2
22 Turn to me . . For I am God, and there is no other. 2
46: 9 for I am God, and there is no other; 2
9 there is no other; I am God, and there is none like me 5
48: 1 and confess the God of Israel, but not in truth 5
2 and stay themselves on the God of Israel; 5
17 I am the LORD your God, who teaches you to profit 5
49: 4 is with the LORD, and my recompense with my God. 5
5 the LORD, and my God has become my strength- 5
50:10 trusts in the . . LORD and relies upon his God? 5
51:15 For I am the LORD your God, who stirs up the sea 5
20 the wrath of the LORD, the rebuke of your God. 5
22 thus says your Lord, the LORD, your God 5
52: 7 salvation, who says to Zion, "Your God reigns. 5
10 the earth shall see the salvation of our God. 5
12 and the God of Israel will be your rear guard. 5
53: 4 him stricken, smitten by God, and afflicted. 5
54: 5 Redeemer, the God of the whole earth he is called. 5
6 a wife of youth when she is cast off, says your God. 5
55: 5 the LORD your God, and of the Holy One of Israel 5
7 and to our God, for he will abundantly pardon. 5
57:21 There is no peace, says my God, for the wicked. 5
58: 2 and did not forsake the ordinance of their God; 5
2 they delight to draw near to God. 5
59: 2 a separation between you and your God 5
13 the LORD, and turning away from following our God 5
60: 9 for the name of the LORD your God, and for the Holy 5
19 and your God will be your glory. 5
61: 2 and the day of vengeance of our God; 5
6 men shall speak of you as the ministers of our God; 5
10 rejoice in the LORD, my soul shall exult in my God; 5
62: 3 and a royal diadem in the hand of your God. 5
5 over . . bride, so shall your God rejoice over you. 5
64: 4 no eye has seen a God besides thee 5
65:16 shall bless himself by the God of truth 5
16 in the land shall swear by the God of truth; 5
66: 9 I, who . . bring forth, shut the womb? says your God. 5
Jer 2:17 upon yourself by forsaking the LORD your God 5
19 and bitter for you to forsake the LORD your God; 5
3:13 that you rebelled against the LORD your God 5
21 they have forgotten the LORD their God. 5
22 we come to thee; for thou art the LORD our God. 5
23 in the LORD our God is the salvation of Israel. 5
25 for we have sinned against the LORD our God 5
25 we have not obeyed the voice of the LORD our God.". 5
5: 4 not know the way of the LORD, the law of their God. 5
5 they know the way of the LORD, the law of their God. 5
14 Therefore thus says the LORD, the God of hosts 5
19 Why has . . our God done all these things to us?' 5
24 Let us fear the LORD our God, who gives the rain 5
7: 3 Thus says the LORD of hosts, the God of Israel 5
21 Thus says the LORD of hosts, the God of Israel 5
23 I will be your God, and you shall be my people; 5
28 that did not obey the voice of the LORD their God 5
8:14 for the LORD our God has doomed us to perish 5
9:15 thus says the LORD of hosts, the God of Israel 5
10:10 the LORD is the true God; he is the living God 5
10 the LORD is the true God; he is the living God 5
11: 3 Thus says the LORD, the God of Israel 5
4 shall you be my people, and I will be your God 5
13:12 Thus says the LORD, the God of Israel 5
16 Give glory to the LORD your God 5
14:22 Art thou not he, O LORD our God? 5
15:16 for I am called by thy name, O LORD, God of hosts. 5
16: 9 For thus says the LORD of hosts, the God of Israel 5
10 that we have committed against the LORD our God? 5
19: 3 Thus says the LORD of hosts, the God of Israel 5
15 Thus says the LORD of hosts, the God of Israel 5
21: 4 Thus says the LORD, the God of Israel 5
22: 9 they forsook the covenant of the LORD their God 5
23: 2 Therefore thus says the LORD, the God of Israel 5
23 Am I a God at hand, says the LORD 5
23 a God at hand, says the LORD, and not a God afar off? 5
36 and you pervert the words of the living God 5
36 words of the living God, the LORD of hosts, our God. 5
24: 5 Thus says the LORD, the God of Israel 5
7 and they shall be my people and I will be their God 5
25:15 Thus the LORD, the God of Israel, said to me 5
27 Thus says the LORD of hosts, the God of Israel 5
26:13 and obey the voice of the LORD your God 5
16 he has spoken to us in the name of the LORD our God. 5
27: 4 Thus says the LORD of hosts, the God of Israel 5
21 thus says the LORD of hosts, the God of Israel 5
28: 2 Thus says the LORD of hosts, the God of Israel 5
14 For thus says the LORD of hosts, the God of Israel 5
29: 4 Thus says the LORD of hosts, the God of Israel 5
8 For thus says the LORD of hosts, the God of Israel 5
21 Thus says the LORD of hosts, the God of Israel 5
25 Thus says the LORD of hosts, the God of Israel 5
30: 2 Thus says the LORD, the God of Israel 5
9 But they shall serve the LORD their God and David 5
22 And you shall be my people, and I will be your God. 5
31: 1 I will be the God of all the families of Israel 5
6 Arise, and let us go up to Zion, to the LORD our God. 5
18 I may be restored, for thou art the LORD my God. 5
23 Thus says the LORD of hosts, the God of Israel 5
33 I will be their God, and they shall be my people. 5
32:14 Thus says the LORD of hosts, the God of Israel 5
15 For thus says the LORD of hosts, the God of Israel 5
18 O great and mighty God whose name is the LORD 2
27 Behold, I am the LORD, the God of all flesh; 5
36 therefore thus says the LORD, the God of Israel 5
38 they shall be my people, and I will be their God. 5
33: 4 For thus says the LORD, the God of Israel 5
34: 2 Thus says the LORD, the God of Israel: Go and speak 5
13 Thus says the LORD, the God of Israel 5
35: 4 sons of Hanan the son of Igdali'ah, the man of God 5
13 Thus says the LORD of hosts, the God of Israel 5
17 Therefore, thus says the LORD, the God of hosts 5
17 says the LORD, the God of hosts, the God of Israel 5
18 Thus says the LORD of hosts, the God of Israel 5
19 thus says the LORD of hosts, the God of Israel 5
37: 3 saying, "Pray for us to the LORD our God. 5
7 Thus says the LORD, God of Israel 5
38:17 Thus says the LORD, the God of hosts 5
17 says the LORD, the God of hosts, the God of Israel 5
39:16 Thus says the LORD of hosts, the God of Israel 5
40: 2 The LORD your God pronounced this evil 5
42: 2 and pray to the LORD your God for us 5
3 that the LORD your God may show us the way 5
4 behold, I will pray to the LORD your God 5
5 word with which the LORD your God sends you to us. 5
6 we will obey the voice of the LORD our God 5
6 when we obey the voice of the LORD our God. 5
9 said to them, "Thus says the LORD, the God of Israel 5
13 disobeying the voice of the LORD your God 5
15 Thus says the LORD of hosts, the God of Israel 5
18 For thus says the LORD of hosts, the God of Israel 5
20 you sent me to the LORD your God, saying, 'Pray for us 5
20 Pray for us to the LORD your God 5
20 whatever the LORD our God says declare to us 5
21 you have not obeyed the voice of the LORD your God 5
43: 1 speaking . . all these words of the LORD their God 5
1 with which the LORD their God had sent him to them 5
2 The LORD our God did not send you to say 5
10 Thus says the LORD of hosts, the God of Israel 5
44: 2 Thus says the LORD of hosts, the God of Israel 5
7 thus says the LORD God of hosts, the God of Israel 5
7 thus says the LORD God of hosts, the God of Israel 5
11 thus says the LORD of hosts, the God of Israel 5
25 Thus says the LORD of hosts, the God of Israel 5
45: 2 Thus says the LORD, the God of Israel, to you 5
46:25 The LORD of hosts, the God of Israel, said: "Behold 5
48: 1 Thus says the LORD of hosts, the God of Israel 5
50: 4 and they shall seek the LORD their God. 5
18 thus says the LORD of hosts, the God of Israel 5
28 in Zion the vengeance of the LORD our God 5
40 As when God overthrew Sodom and Gomor'rah 5
51: 5 and Judah have not been forsaken by their God 5
10 let us declare in Zion the work of the LORD our God. 5
33 For thus says the LORD of hosts, the God of Israel 5
56 the LORD is a God of recompense 2
Lam 3:41 lift up our hearts and hands to God in heaven 2
Ezk 1: 1 the heavens were opened, and I saw visions of God. 5
8: 3 and brought me in visions of God to Jerusalem 5
4 behold, the glory of the God of Israel was there 5
9: 3 Now the glory of the God of Israel had gone up 5
10: 5 like the voice of God Almighty when he speaks. 2
19 the glory of the God of Israel was over them. 5
20 underneath the God of Israel by the river Chebar; 5
11:20 they shall be my people, and I will be their God. 5
22 and the glory of the God of Israel was over them. 5
24 by the Spirit of God into Chalde'a, to the exiles. 5
14:11 that they may be my people and I may be their God 5
20: 5 I swore to them, saying, I am the LORD your God. 5
7 I am the LORD your God. 5
19 I the LORD am your God; walk in my statutes 5
20 that you may know that I the LORD am your God. 5
28:13 You were in Eden, the garden of God; 5
14 you were on the holy mountain of God; 5
16 as a profane thing from the mountain of God 5
26 Then they will know that I am the LORD their God. 5
31: 8 The cedars in the garden of God could not rival it 5
8 no tree in the garden of God was like it in beauty. 5
9 trees..envied it, that were in the garden of God. 5
34:24 I, the LORD, will be their God 5
30 shall know that I, the LORD their God, am with them 5
31 and I am your God, says the Lord GOD. 5
36:28 you shall be my people, and I will be your God. 5
37:23 they shall be my people, and I will be their God. 5
27 I will be their God, and they shall be my people. 5
39:22 I am the LORD their God, from that day forward. 5
28 Then they shall know that I am the LORD their God 5
40: 2 and brought me in the visions of God into the land 5
43: 2 the glory of the God of Israel came from the east; 5
44: 2 for the LORD, the God of Israel, has entered by it; 5
Dan 1: 9 God gave Daniel favor and compassion 5
17 God gave them learning and skill in all letters 5
2:18 told them to seek mercy of the God of heaven 7
19 Then Daniel blessed the God of heaven. 7
20 Blessed be the name of God for ever and ever. 7
23 O God of my fathers, I give thanks and praise 7
28 there is a God in heaven who reveals mysteries 7
37 to whom the God of heaven has given the kingdom 7
44 God of heaven will set up a kingdom 7
45 great God has made known to the king what shall be 7
47 Truly, your God is God of gods and Lord of kings 7
47 Truly, your God is God of gods and Lord of kings 7
3:17 God whom we serve is able to deliver us 7
26 servants of the Most High God, come forth 3
28 Blessed be the God of Shadrach, Meshach 3
28 serve and worship any god except their own God. 7
29 speaks anything against the God of Shadrach 3
4: 2 signs . . Most High God has wrought toward me. 3
5: 3 out of the temple, the house of God in Jerusalem; 3
18 O king, the Most High God gave Nebuchadnez'zar 3
21 knew . . Most High God rules the kingdom of men 3
23 but the God in whose hand is your breath 7
26 MENE, God has numbered the days of your kingdom 3
6: 5 find it in connection with the law of his God. 3
10 prayed and gave thanks before his God 3
11 petition and supplication before his God. 3
16 May your God, whom you serve contintually 3
20 O Daniel, servant of the living God, 3
20 has your God, whom you serve continually 3
22 My God sent his angel and shut the lions' mouths 3
23 because he had trusted in his God. 7
26 men tremble and fear before the God of Daniel 3
26 before the God of Daniel, for he is the living God 3
9: 3 Then I turned my face to the Lord God, seeking him 5
4 prayed to the LORD my God and made confession 5
4 O Lord, the great and terrible God 2
9 To the Lord our God belong mercy and forgiveness; 5
10 not obeyed the voice of the LORD our God 5
11 written in the law of Moses the servant of God 5
13 have not entreated the favor of the LORD our God 5
14 for the LORD our God is righteous in all the works 5
15 now, O Lord our God, who didst bring thy people out 5
17 Now therefore, O our God, hearken to the prayer 5
18 O my God, incline thy ear and hear; open thy eyes 5
19 delay not, for thy own sake, O my God 5
20 supplication before the LORD my God for the holy 5
20 before the LORD my God for the holy hill of my God; 5
10:12 day that you . . humbled yourself before your God 5
11:32 people who know their God shall stand firm 5
36 astonishing things against the God of gods. 2
0: 1 some of the vessels of the house of God; 5
Hos 1: 7 and I will deliver them by the LORD their God; 5
9 for you are not my people and I am not your God. •
10 it shall be said to them, "Sons of the living God. 2

2:23 and he shall say 'Thou art my God.' 5
3: 5 Israel shall return and seek the LORD their God 5
4: 1 There is..no knowledge of God in the land; 5
6 And since you have forgotten the law of your God 5
12 and they have left their God to play the harlot. 5
5: 4 deeds do not permit them to return to their God. 5
6: 6 knowledge of God, rather than burnt offerings. 5
7:10 yet they do not return to the LORD their God 5
8: 2 To me they cry, My God, we Israel know thee. 5
6 in Israel? A workman made it; it is not God. 5
9: 1 you have played the harlot, forsaking your God. 5
8 the watchman of E'phraim, the people of my God 5
8 and hatred in the house of his God. 5
17 My God will cast them off 5
11: 9 for I am God and not man, the Holy One in your midst 2
12 but Judah is still known by God, and is faithful 2
12: 3 and in his manhood he strove with God. 5
4 He met God at Bethel, and there God spoke with him- •
4 He met God at Bethel, and there God spoke with him- •
5 the LORD the God of hosts, the LORD is his name 5
6 by the help of your God, return, hold fast to love 5
6 and wait continually for your God. 5
9 I am the LORD your God from the land of Egypt; 5
13: 4 I am the LORD your God from the land of Egypt; 5
4 you know no God but me 5
16 guilt, because she has rebelled against her God; 5
14: 1 Return, O Israel, to the LORD your God 5
3 will say no more, 'Our God,' to the work of our hands. 5
Jol 1:13 pass the night in sackcloth, O ministers of my God! 5
13 are withheld from the house of your God. 5
14 Gather..to the house of the LORD your God; 5
16 joy and gladness from the house of our God? 5
2:13 Return to the LORD, your God, for he is gracious 5
14 and a drink offering for the LORD, your God? 5
17 they say among the peoples, 'Where is their God?' 5
23 O sons of Zion, and rejoice in the LORD, your God; 5
26 and praise the name of the LORD your God 5
27 that I, the LORD, am your God and there is none else. 5
3:17 you shall know that I am the LORD your God 5
Ams 2: 8 and in the house of their God they drink the wine 5
3:13 Jacob," says the Lord GOD, the God of hosts 5
4:11 as when God overthrew Sodom and Gomor'rah 5
12 do this to you, prepare to meet your God, O Israel! 5
13 of the earth- the LORD, the God of hosts, is his name! 5
5:14 the LORD, the God of hosts, will be with you 5
15 that the LORD, the God of hosts, will be gracious 5
16 thus says the LORD, the God of hosts, the Lord 5
27 says the LORD, whose name is the God of hosts. 5
6: 8 says the LORD, the God of hosts): "I abhor the pride 5
14 O house of Israel," says the LORD, the God of hosts; 5
9:15 which I have given them," says the LORD your God. 5
Jon 1: 9 I fear the LORD, the God of heaven, 5
2: 1 Then Jonah prayed to the LORD his God 5
6 my life from the Pit, O LORD my God. 5
3: 5 the people of Nin'eveh believed God; 5
8 with sackcloth, and let them cry mightily to God; 5
9 God may yet repent and turn from his fierce anger 5
10 When God saw what they did 5
10 God repented of the evil which he had said 5
4: 2 for I knew that thou art a gracious God 2
6 the LORD God appointed a plant, and made it come up 5
7 God appointed a worm which attacked the plant 5
8 the sun rose, God appointed a sultry east wind 5
9 God said to Jonah, "Do you do well to be angry 5
Mic 3: 7 cover their lips, for there is no answer from God. 5
4: 2 let us go up..to the house of the God of Jacob; 5
5 but we will walk in the name of the LORD our God 5
5: 4 in the majesty of the name of the LORD his God. 5
6: 6 and bow myself before God on high? 5
8 to love kindness, and to walk humbly with your God? 5
7: 7 I will wait for the God of my salvation; 5
7 my God will hear me. 5
10 her who said to me, "Where is the LORD your God? 5
17 they shall turn in dread to the LORD our God 5
18 Who is a God like thee, pardoning inquity 2
Nah 1: 2 The LORD is a jealous God and avenging 2
Hab 1: 1 oracle of God which Habak'kuk the prophet saw. •
12 Art thou not from everlasting, O LORD my God 5
3: 3 God came from Teman 4
18 I will joy in the God of my salvation. 5
Zep 2: 7 For the LORD their God will be mindful of them 5
9 says the LORD of hosts, the God of Israel 5
3: 2 she does not draw near to her God. 5
17 The LORD, your God, is in your midst, 5
Hag 1:12 the people, obeyed the voice of the LORD their God 5
12 the prophet, as the LORD their God had sent him; 5
14 the house of the LORD of hosts, their God 5
Zec 6:15 diligently obey the voice of the LORD your God. 5
8: 8 they shall be my people and I will be their God 5
23 for we have heard that God is with you. 5
9: 7 it too shall be a remnant for our God; 5
16 On that day the LORD their God will save them 5
10: 6 for I am the LORD their God and I will answer them. 5
11: 4 said the LORD my God: "Become shepherd of the flock 5
12: 5 strength through the LORD of hosts, their God. 5
8 the house of David shall be like God 5
13: 9 they will say, 'The LORD is my God.' 5
14: 5 Then the LORD your God will come 5
Mal 1: 9 now entreat the favor of God 2
2:10 Has not one God created us? 2
15 Has not the one God made and sustained for us •
16 For I hate divorce, says the LORD the God of Israel 5
17 Or by asking, "Where is the God of justice? 5
3: 8 Will man rob God? Yet you are robbing me. 5
14 You have said 'It is vain to serve God. 5
15 but when they put God to the test they escape. 5
18 between one who serves God and one who does not 5
Mat 1:23 be called Emman'u-el" (which means, God with us). 9
3: 9 for I tell you, God is able from these stones 9
16 heavens were opened and he saw the Spirit of God 9
4: 3 If you are the Son of God, command these stones 9
4 word that proceeds from the mouth of God.' 9
6 If you are the Son of God, throw yourself down; 9
7 written, 'You shall not tempt the Lord your God.' 9
10 You shall worship the Lord your God and him only 9
5: 8 are the pure in heart, for they shall see God. 9
9 for they shall be called sons of God. 9
34 at all, either by heaven, for it is the throne of God 9
6:24 the other. You cannot serve God and mammon. 9
30 But if God so clothes the grass of the field 9
8:29 What have you to do with us, O Son of God? 9
9: 8 they glorified God, who had given such authority 9
12: 4 how he entered the house of God and ate the bread 9
28 if it is by the Spirit of God that I cast out demons 9
28 then the kingdom of God has come upon you. 9
14:33 Truly you are the Son of God. 9
15: 3 And why do you transgress the commandment of God 9
4 For God commanded 'Honor your father 9
5 What you would have gained from me is given to God •
6 you have made void the word of God. 9
31 and they glorified the God of Israel. 9
16:16 You are the Christ, the Son of the living God. 9
23 are not on the side of God, but of men. 9
19: 6 What therefore God has joined together 9
24 than for a rich man to enter the kingdom of God. 9
26 but with God all things are possible. 9
21:12 Jesus entered the temple of God •
31 go into the kingdom of God before you. 9
43 the kingdom of God will be taken away from you 9
22:16 you are true, and teach the way of God truthfully 9
21 and to God the things that are God's 9
21 and to God the things that are God's 9
29 neither the scriptures nor the power of God. 9
31 have you not read what was said to you by God 9
32 'I am the God of Abraham, and the God of Isaac 9
32 'I am the God of Abraham, and the God of Isaac 9
32 the God of Isaac, and the God of Jacob 9
32 He is not God of the dead, but of the living. 9
37 love the Lord your God with all your heart 9
23:22 swears by the throne of God 9
26:61 I am able to destroy the temple of God 9
63 I adjure you by the living God 9
63 tell us if you are the Christ, the Son of God. 9
27:40 If you are the Son of God, come down from the cross. 9
43 He trusts in God; let God deliver him now 9
43 He trusts in God; let God deliver him now •
43 he said, 'I am the Son of God.' 9
46 My God, my God, why hast thou forsaken me? 9
46 My God, my God, why hast thou forsaken me? 9
54 Truly this was the Son of God! 9
Mrk 1: 1 the Son of God. 9
14 preaching the gospel of God 9
15 the kingdom of God is at hand 9
24 I know who you are, the Holy One of God. 9
2: 7 Who can forgive sins but God alone? 9
12 so that they were all amazed and glorified God 9
26 how he entered the house of God 9
3:11 You are the Son of God. 9
35 Whoever does the will of God is my brother 9
4:11 given the secret of the kingdom of God 9
26 The kingdom of God is as if a man should scatter 9
30 With what can we compare the kingdom of God 9
5: 7 Jesus, Son of the Most High God? 9
7 I adjure you by God, do not torment me. 9
7: 8 You leave the commandment of God 9
9 a fine way of rejecting the commandment of God 9
13 thus making void the word of God. 9
8:33 you are not on the side of God, but of men. 9
9: 1 the kingdom of God has come with power. 9
47 to enter the kingdom of God with one eye 9
10: 6 'God made them male and female.' •
9 What therefore God has joined together 9
14 to such belongs the kingdom of God. 9
15 receive the kingdom of God like a child 9
18 Why do you call me good? No one is good but God alone 9
23 to enter the kingdom of God! 9
24 how hard it is to enter the kingdom of God! 9
25 than for a rich man to enter the kingdom of God. 9
27 With men it is impossible, but not with God 9
27 for all things are possible with God. 9
11:22 Jesus answered them, "Have faith in God. 9
12:14 truly teach the way of God 9
17 and to God the things that are God's. 9
17 and to God the things that are God's. 9
24 you know neither the scriptures nor the power of God? 9
26 how God said to him, 'I am the God of Abraham 9
26 I am the God of Abraham, and the God of Isaac 9
26 I am the God of Abraham, and the God of Isaac 9
26 the God of Isaac, and the God of Jacob'? 9
27 He is not God of the dead, but of the living; 9
29 The Lord our God, the Lord is one; 9
30 shall love the Lord your God with all your heart 9
34 You are not far from the kingdom of God. 9
13:19 the creation which God created until now 9
14:25 when I drink it new in the kingdom of God. 9
15:34 means, "My God, my God, why hast thou forsaken 9
34 My God, my God, why hast thou forsaken me? 9
39 he said, "Truly this man was the Son of God! 9
43 who was also himself looking for the kingdom of God 9
16:19 Jesus . . sat down at the right hand of God. 9
Lke 1: 6 they were both righteous before God 9
8 Now while he was serving as priest before God 9
16 sons of Israel to the Lord their God 9
19 I am Gabriel, who stand in the presence of God 9
26 the angel Gabriel was sent from God 9
30 you have found favor with God. 9
32 the Lord God will give to him the throne 9
35 the child to be born will be called holy, the Son of God 9
37 For with God nothing will be impossible. 9
47 my spirit rejoices in God my Savior 9
64 he spoke, blessing God. 9
68 Blessed be the Lord God of Israel 9
78 through the tender mercy of our God 9
2:13 praising God and saying 9
14 Glory to God in the highest 9
20 glorifying and praising God 9
28 he took him up in his arms and blessed God and said 9
38 coming up at that very hour she gave thanks to God 9
40 the favor of God was upon him. 9
52 increased . . in favor with God and man. 9
3: 2 the word of God came to John the son of Zechari'ah 9
6 all flesh shall see the salvation of God. 9
8 God is able from these stones to raise up children 9
38 son of Seth, the son of Adam, the son of God. 9
4: 3 The devil said to him, "If you are the Son of God 9
8 It is written, 'You shall worship the Lord your God 9
9 said to him, "If you are the Son of God 9
12 'You shall not tempt the Lord your God.' 9
34 I know who you are, the Holy One of God. 9
41 You are the Son of God! 9
43 I must preach the good news of the kingdom of God 9
5: 1 people pressed upon him to hear the word of God 9
21 Who can forgive sins but God only? 9
25 and went home, glorifying God. 9
26 they glorified God and were filled with awe 9
6: 4 how he entered the house of God 9
12 and all night he continued in prayer to God. 9
20 yours is the kingdom of God. 9
7:16 God has visited his people! 9
16 they glorified God, saying, "A great prophet 9
28 who is least in the kingdom of God is greater than he. 9
29 the people and the tax collectors justified God 9
30 the lawyers rejected the purpose of God 9
8: 1 bringing the good news of the kingdom of God 9
10 given to know the secrets of the kingdom of God; 9
11 the parable is this: The seed is the word of God. 9
21 those who hear the word of God and do it. 9
28 Jesus, Son of the Most High God 9
39 and declare how much God has done for you 9
9: 2 to preach the kingdom of God and to heal. 9
11 spoke to them of the kingdom of God 9
20 Peter answered, "The Christ of God. 9
27 before they see the kingdom of God. 9
43 all were astonished at the majesty of God 9
60 as for you, go and proclaim the kingdom of God.". 9
62 fit for the kingdom of God. 9
10: 9 'The kingdom of God has come near to you.' 9
11 the kingdom of God has come near.' 9
27 shall love the Lord your God with all your heart 9
11:20 if it is by the finger of God that I cast out demons 9
20 then the kingdom of God has come upon you. 9
28 those who hear the word of God and keep it! 9
42 neglect justice and the love of God 9
49 Therefore also the Wisdom of God said, 'I will send 9
12: 6 not one of them is forgotten before God. 9
8 also will acknowledge before the angels of God; 9
9 will be denied before the angels of God. 9
20 God said to him, 'Fool! 9
21 is not rich toward God. 9
24 yet God feeds them 9
28 if God so clothes the grass 9
13:13 she was made straight, and she praised God. 9
18 He said therefore, "What is the kingdom of God like? 9
20 To what shall I compare the kingdom of God? 9
28 all the prophets in the kingdom of God 9
29 and sit at table in the kingdom of God. 9
14:15 he who shall eat bread in the kingdom of God! 9
15:10 there is joy before the angels of God 9
16:13 You cannot serve God and mammon. 9
15 God knows your hearts 9
15 God knows your hearts 9
16 the good news of the kingdom of God is preached 9
17:15 turned back, praising God with a loud voice; 9
18 Was no one found to return and give praise to God 9

20 asked . . when the kingdom of God was coming 9
20 asked . . when the kingdom of God was coming 9
21 behold, the kingdom of God is in the midst of you. 9
18: 2 who neither feared God nor regarded man 9
7 will not God vindicate his elect 9
11 God, I thank thee that I am not like other 9
13 beat his breast, saying, 'God, be merciful to me 9
16 to such belongs the kingdom of God. 9
17 whoever does not receive the kingdom of God 9
19 Why do you call me good? No one is good but God alone. 9
24 How hard it is . . to enter the kingdom of God! 9
25 for a rich man to enter the kingdom of God. 9
27 impossible with men is possible with God. 9
29 left house . . for the sake of the kingdom of God 9
43 and followed him, glorifying God 9
43 all the people, when they saw it, gave praise to God. 9
19:11 the kingdom of God was to appear immediately. 9
37 began to rejoice and praise God with a loud voice 9
20:21 truly teach the way of God. 9
25 to God the things that are God's. 9
25 to God the things that are God's. 9
36 they are equal to angels and are sons of God 9
37 where he calls the Lord the God of Abraham 9
37 where he calls the Lord the God of Abraham 9
37 where he calls the Lord the God of Abraham 9
38 Now he is not God of the dead, but of the living 9
21:31 you know that the kingdom of God is near. 9
22:16 until it is fulfilled in the kingdom of God. 9
18 until the kingdom of God comes. 9
69 seated at the right hand of the power of God. 9
70 they all said, "Are you the Son of God, then? 9
23:35 if he is the Christ of God, his Chosen One! 9
40 the other rebuked him, saying, "Do you not fear God 9
47 he praised God, and said 9
51 he was looking for the kingdom of God. 9
24:19 a prophet mighty in deed and word before God 9
53 were continually in the temple blessing God. 9
Joh 1: 1 and the Word was with God, and the Word was God. 9
1 and the Word was with God, and the Word was God. 9
2 He was in the beginning with God; 9
6 There was a man sent from God, whose name was John 9
12 he gave power to become children of God; 9
13 born, not of blood nor of the will of man, but of God. 9
18 No one has ever seen God; 9
29 Behold, the Lamb of God, who takes away the sin 9
34 borne witness that this is the Son of God. 9
36 and said, "Behold, the Lamb of God! 9
49 Rabbi, you are the Son of God! 9
51 the angels of God ascending and descending 9
3: 2 Rabbi, we know that you are a teacher come from God; 9
2 no one can do these signs . . unless God is with him. 9
3 he cannot see the kingdom of God. 9
5 he cannot enter the kingdom of God. 9
16 God so loved the world that he gave his only Son 9
17 For God sent the Son into the world 9
18 not believed in the name of the only Son of God. 9
21 seen that his deeds have been wrought in God. 9
33 sets his seal to this, that God is true. 9
34 For he whom God has sent utters the words of God 9
34 For he whom God has sent utters the words of God 9
36 but the wrath of God rests upon him. 9
4:10 Jesus answered her, "If you knew the gift of God 9
24 God is spirit, and those who worship him 9
5:18 also called God his Father 9
18 making himself equal with God. 9
25 when the dead will hear the voice of the Son of God 9
42 you have not the love of God within you. 9
44 do not seek the glory that comes from the only God?. 9
6:27 for on him has God the Father set his seal. 9
28 What must we do, to be doing the works of God? 9
29 Jesus answered them, "This is the work of God 9
33 bread of God is that which comes down from heaven 9
45 they shall all be taught by God 9
46 except him who is from God 9
69 . . come to know, that you are the Holy One of God 9
7:17 he shall know whether the teaching is from God 9
8:40 has told you the truth which I heard from God 9
41 we have one Father, even God. 9
42 If God were your Father, you would love me 9
42 I proceeded and came forth from God 9
47 He who is of God hears the words of God 9
47 He who is of God hears the words of God 9
47 you are not of God. 9
54 of whom you say that he is your God. 9
9: 3 that the works of God might be made manifest in him. 9
16 This man is not from God 9
24 Give God the praise 9
29 We know that God has spoken to Moses 9
31 We know that God does not listen to sinners 9
31 God listens to him •
33 If this man were not from God, he could do nothing. 9
10:33 because you, being a man, make yourself God. 9
35 If he called them gods to whom the word of God came 9
36 because I said, 'I am the Son of God'? 9
11: 4 it is for the glory of God 9
4 it is for the glory of God 9
22 whatever you ask from God, God will give you. 9
22 whatever you ask from God, God will give you. 9
27 I believe that you are the Christ, the Son of God 9

40 if you would believe you would see the glory of God? 9
52 to gather into one the children of God 9
12:43 more than the praise of God. 9
13: 3 he had come from God and was going to God 9
3 he had come from God and was going to God 9
31 in him God is glorified; 9
32 if God is glorified in him 9
32 if God is glorified in him 9
14: 1 believe in God, believe also in me. 9
16: 2 will think he is offering service to God. 9
30 by this we believe that you came from God. 9
17: 3 they know thee the only true God 9
19: 7 because he has made himself the Son of God. 9
20:17 I am ascending . . to my God and your God. 9
17 I am ascending . . to my God and your God. 9
28 Thomas answered him, "My Lord and my God! 9
31 Jesus is the Christ, the Son of God 9
21:19 to show by what death he was to glorify God 9
Act 1: 3 speaking of the kingdom of God. 9
2:11 the mighty works of God 9
17 in the last days it shall be, God declares 9
22 Jesus of Nazareth, a man attested to you by God 9
22 signs which God did through him in your midst 9
23 the definite plan and foreknowledge of God 9
24 But God raised him up 9
30 knowing that God had sworn with an oath to him 9
32 This Jesus God raised up 9
33 Being therefore exalted at the right hand of God 9
36 know assuredly that God has made him . . Lord 9
39 every one whom the Lord our God calls to him. 9
47 praising God and having favor 9
3: 8 walking and leaping and praising God. 9
9 all the people saw him walking and praising God 9
13 The God of Abraham and of Isaac and of Jacob 9
13 the God of our fathers 9
15 the Author of life, whom God raised from the dead. 9
18 what God foretold 9
21 God spoke by the mouth of his holy prophets 9
22 The Lord God will raise up for you a prophet 9
25 the covenant which God gave to your fathers 9
26 God, having raised up his servant 9
4:10 whom you crucified, whom God raised from the dead 9
19 Whether it is right in the sight of God 9
19 to listen to you rather than to God 9
21 all men praised God for what had happened. 9
24 lifted their voices together to God and said 9
31 spoke the word of God with boldness. 9
5: 4 You have not lied to men but to God. 9
29 We must obey God rather than men. 9
30 God of our fathers raised Jesus whom you killed 9
31 God exalted him at his right hand as Leader 9
32 whom God has given to those who obey him. 9
39 if it is of God 9
6: 2 give up preaching the word of God to serve tables. 9
7 the word of God increased 9
11 blasphemous words against Moses and God. 9
7: 2 The God of glory appeared to our father Abraham 9
4 after his father died, God removed him from there •
6 God spoke to this effect 9
7 I will judge the nation which they serve,' said God 9
9 but God was with him 9
17 which God had granted to Abraham 9
20 Moses . . was beautiful before God 9
25 God was giving them deliverance by his hand 9
32 I am the God of your fathers 9
32 the God of Abraham and of Isaac and of Jacob 9
35 God sent as both ruler and deliverer 9
37 God will raise up for you a prophet 9
42 God turned 9
45 the nations . . God thrust out before our fathers 9
46 who found favor in the sight of God 9
46 find a habitation for the God of Jacob. 9
55 saw the glory of God 9
55 Jesus standing at the right hand of God; 9
56 the Son of man standing at the right hand of God. 9
8:10 that power of God which is called Great. 9
12 as he preached good news about the kingdom of God 9
14 Sama'ria had received the word of God 9
20 you could obtain the gift of God with money! 9
21 your heart is not right before God. 9
9:20 He is the Son of God. 9
10: 2 a devout man who feared God 9
2 prayed constantly to God. 9
3 angel of God coming in and saying to him 9
4 have ascended as a memorial before God. 9
15 What God has cleansed, you must not call common. 9
22 a centurion, an upright and God-fearing man 9
28 God has shown me that I should not call any man 9
31 your alms have been remembered before God. 9
33 we are all here present in the sight of God 9
34 Truly I perceive that God shows no partiality 9
38 how God anointed Jesus of Nazareth 9
38 doing good and healing . . for God was with him. 9
40 God raised him on the third day 9
41 to us who were chosen by God as witnesses 9
42 the one ordained by God to be judge of the living 9
46 speaking in tongues and extolling God 9
11: 1 the Gentiles also had received the word of God. 9

9 'What God has cleansed you must not call common.' 9
17 If then God gave the same gift to them 9
17 who was I that I could withstand God? 9
18 they glorified God, saying 9
18 God has granted repentance unto life. 9
23 When he came and saw the grace of God, he was glad; 9
12: 5 prayer for him was made to God by the church. 9
23 because he did not give God the glory 9
24 the word of God grew and multiplied. 9
13: 5 proclaimed the word of God in the synagogues 9
7 sought to hear the word of God. 9
16 Men of Israel, and you that fear God, listen. 9
17 The God of this people Israel chose our fathers 9
21 Then they asked for a king; and God gave them Saul 9
23 God has brought to Israel a Savior 9
26 those among you that fear God 9
30 God raised him from the dead; 9
32 what God promised to the fathers •
36 served the counsel of God in his own generation 9
37 he whom God raised up saw no corruption. 9
43 urged them to continue in the grace of God. 9
44 gathered together to hear the word of God. 9
46 the word of God should be spoken first to you. 9
48 they were glad and glorified the word of God; 9
14:15 a living God who made the heaven and the earth 9
22 saying that . . we must enter the kingdom of God. 9
26 where they had been commended to the grace of God 9
27 declared all that God had done with them 9
15: 4 they declared all that God had done with them. 9
7 in the early days God made choice among you 9
8 God who knows the heart bore witness to them 9
10 Now therefore why do you make trial of God 9
12 what signs and wonders God had done through them 9
14 how God first visited the Gentiles 9
19 not trouble those of the Gentiles who turn to God 9
16:10 concluding that God had called us 9
14 who was a worshiper of God 9
17 These men are servants of the Most High God 9
25 were praying and singing hymns to God 9
34 rejoiced . . that he had believed in God. 9
17:13 the word of God was proclaimed by Paul at Beroe'a also 9
24 The God who made the world and everything in it 9
27 that they should seek God 9
29 Being then God's offspring 9
30 The times of ignorance God overlooked 9
18: 7 Titius Justus, a worshiper of God 9
11 teaching the word of God among them. 9
13 worship God contrary to the law. 9
21 I will return to you if God wills 9
26 and expounded to him the way of God more accurately. 9
19: 8 arguing and pleading about the kingdom of God; 9
11 God did extraordinary miracles 9
20:21 testifying . . of repentance to God 9
24 testify to the gospel of the grace of God. 9
27 declaring to you the whole counsel of God. 9
28 to care for the church of God 9
32 now I commend you to God 9
21:19 things that God had done among the Gentiles 9
20 when they heard it, they glorified God 9
22: 3 being zealous for God as you all are this day. 9
14 he said, 'The God of our fathers appointed you 9
23: 1 I have lived before God in all good conscience 9
3 God shall strike you, you whitewashed wall! 9
4 Would you revile God's high priest? 9
24:14 I admit to you . . I worship the God of our fathers 9
15 having a hope in God which these . . accept 9
16 a clear conscience toward God and toward men. 9
26: 6 hope in the promise made by God to our fathers 9
8 thought incredible . . that God raises the dead? 9
18 turn . . from the power of Satan to God 9
20 they should repent and turn to God 9
22 To this day I have had the help that comes from God 9
29 Paul said, "Whether short or long, I would to God 9
27:23 the God to whom I belong and whom I worship 9
24 lo, God has granted you all those who sail with you.' 9
25 I have faith in God 9
35 giving thanks to God in the presence of all 9
28:15 Paul thanked God and took courage. 9
23 testifying to the kingdom of God 9
28 salvation of God has been sent to the Gentiles; 9
31 preaching the kingdom of God 9
Rom 1: 1 Paul . . set apart for the gospel of God 9
4 designated Son of God in power 9
7 To all God's beloved in Rome 9
7 Grace to you and peace from God our Father 9
8 I thank my God through Jesus Christ for all of you 9
9 For God is my witness, whom I serve with my spirit 9
10 by God's will I may now at last succeed in coming 9
16 it is the power of God for salvation to every one 9
17 For in it the righteousness of God is revealed 9
18 For the wrath of God is revealed from heaven 9
19 For what can be known about God is plain to them 9
19 plain to them, because God has shown it to them. 9
21 for although they knew God they did not honor him 9
21 they did not honor him as God or give thanks to him 9
23 exchanged the glory of the immortal God 9
24 God gave them up in the lusts of their hearts 9
25 they exchanged the truth about God for a lie 9

26 God gave them up to dishonorable passions. 9
28 since they did not see fit to acknowledge God 9
28 God gave them up to a base mind 9
32 Though they know God's decree 9
2: 2 the judgment of God rightly falls upon those 9
3 you will escape the judgment of God? 9
4 God's kindness is meant to lead you to repentance? 9
5 when God's righteous judgment will be revealed. 9
11 For God shows no partiality. 9
13 hearers of the law who are righteous before God 9
16 God judges the secrets of men by Christ Jesus. 9
17 and boast of your relation to God 9
23 do you dishonor God by breaking the law? 9
24 The name of God is blasphemed among the Gentiles 9
29 His praise is not from men but from God. 9
3: 2 the Jews are entrusted with the oracles of God. 9
3 faithlessness nullify the faithfulness of God? 9
4 Let God be true though every man be false 9
5 our wickedness serves to show the justice of God 9
5 That God is unjust to inflict wrath on us? 9
6 By no means! For then how could God judge the world? 9
7 if . . God's truthfulness abounds to his glory 9
11 no one understands, no one seeks for God. 9
18 There is no fear of God before their eyes. 9
19 the whole world may be held accountable to God. 9
21 the righteousness of God has been manifested 9
22 the righteousness of God through faith in Jesus 9
23 all have sinned and fall short of the glory of God 9
25 whom God put forward as an expiation by his blood 9
25 This was to show God's righteousness •
29 Or is God the God of Jews only? •
29 Or is God the God of Jews only? 9
29 Is he not the God of Gentiles also? •
30 since God is one; and he will justify 9
4: 2 something to boast about, but not before God. 9
3 Abraham believed God, and it was reckoned to him 9
6 the man to whom God reckons righteousness 9
17 –in the presence of the God in whom he believed 9
20 made him waver concerning the promise of God 9
20 grew strong in his faith as he gave glory to God 9
21 that God was able to do what he had promised. •
5: 1 peace with God through our Lord Jesus Christ. 9
2 we rejoice in our hope of sharing the glory of God. 9
5 God's love has been poured into our hearts 9
8 But God shows his love for us 9
9 shall we be saved by him from the wrath of God. •
10 while we were enemies we were reconciled to God 9
11 rejoice in God through our Lord Jesus Christ 9
15 the grace of God . . abounded for many. 9
6:10 but the life he lives he lives to God. 9
11 dead to sin and alive to God in Christ Jesus. 9
13 yield . . your members to God as instruments 9
13 but yield yourselves to God 9
17 But thanks be to God 9
22 set free from sin and have become slaves of God 9
23 but the free gift of God is eternal life in Christ 9
7: 4 in order that we may bear fruit for God. 9
22 For I delight in the law of God, in my inmost self. 9
25 Thanks be to God through Jesus Christ our Lord! 9
25 I of myself serve the law of God with my mind 9
8: 3 For God has done what the law . . could not do 9
7 the mind that is set on the flesh is hostile to God; 9
7 it does not submit to God's law, indeed it cannot; 9
8 and those who are in the flesh cannot please God. 9
9 if in fact the Spirit of God dwells in you. 9
14 all who are led by the Spirit of God are sons of God 9
14 all who are led by the Spirit of God are sons of God 9
16 bearing witness . . that we are children of God 9
17 heirs of God and fellow heirs with Christ 9
19 waits . . for the revealing of the sons of God; 9
21 the glorious liberty of the children of God. 9
27 the Spirit intercedes . . according to the will of God. 9
28 God works for good with those who love him 9
31 If God is for us, who is against us? 9
33 Who shall bring any charge against God's elect? 9
33 It is God who justifies; 9
34 Christ Jesus . . who is at the right hand of God 9
39 will be able to separate us from the love of God 9
9: 5 God who is over all be blessed for ever. Amen. 9
6 But it is not as though the word of God had failed. 9
8 children of the flesh who are the children of God 9
11 that God's purpose of election might continue 9
14 Is there injustice on God's part? By no means! 9
16 upon man's will or exertion, but upon God's mercy. 9
20 But who are you, a man, to answer back to God? 9
22 What if God, desiring to show his wrath 9
26 they will be called 'sons of the living God.' 9
10: 1 Brethren, my heart's desire and prayer to God 9
2 I bear them witness that they have a zeal for God 9
3 the righteousness that comes from God 9
3 they did not submit to God's righteousness. 9
9 and believe . . that God raised him from the dead 9
11: 1 I ask, then, has God rejected his people? By no means! 9
2 God has not rejected his people 9
2 of Eli'jah, how he pleads with God against Israel? 9
8 as it is written, "God gave them a spirit of stupor 9
21 For if God did not spare the natural branches 9
22 Note then the kindness and the severity of God 9
22 severity toward those . . but God's kindness to you 9
23 for God has the power to graft them in again. 9
28 As regards the gospel they are enemies of God •
29 For the gifts and the call of God are 9
30 Just as you were once disobedient to God 9
32 For God has consigned all men to disobedience 9
33 the riches and wisdom and knowledge of God! 9
12: 1 I appeal to you . . by the mercies of God 9
1 as a living sacrifice, holy and acceptable to God 9
2 that you may prove what is the will of God 9
3 the measure of faith which God has assigned him. 9
19 but leave it to the wrath of God; •
13: 1 For there is no authority except from God 9
1 those that exist have been instituted by God. 9
2 resists what God has appointed 9
4 for he is God's servant for your good. 9
4 he is the servant of God to execute his wrath 9
5 one must be subject, not only to avoid God's wrath •
6 for the authorities are ministers of God 9
14: 3 for God has welcomed him. 9
6 in honor of the Lord, since he gives thanks to God; 9
6 abstains in honor of the Lord and gives thanks to God. 9
10 shall all stand before the judgment seat of God; 9
11 and every tongue shall give praise to God. 9
12 each of us shall give account of himself to God. 9
17 For the kingdom of God is not food and drink 9
18 he who thus serves Christ is acceptable to God 9
20 Do not . . destroy the work of God 9
22 The faith . . keep between yourself and God; 9
15: 5 May the God of steadfastness and encouragement 9
6 the God and Father of our Lord Jesus Christ. 9
7 Welcome one another . . for the glory of God. 9
8 to the circumcised to show God's truthfulness 9
9 the Gentiles might glorify God for his mercy. 9
13 May the God of hope fill you with all joy and peace 9
15 because of the grace given me by God 9
16 in the priestly service of the gospel of God 9
17 I have reason to be proud of my work for God. 9
30 with me in your prayers to God on my behalf 9
32 that by God's will I may come to you with joy 9
33 The God of peace be with you all. Amen. 9
16:20 then the God of peace will soon crush Satan 9
26 according to the command of the eternal God 9
27 to the only wise God be glory for evermore 9
1Co 1: 1 by the will of God to be an apostle of Christ Jesus 9
2 To the church of God which is at Corinth 9
3 Grace to you and peace from God our Father 9
4 I give thanks to God always for you 9
4 because of the grace of God which was given you 9
9 God is faithful, by whom you were called 9
18 to us who are being saved it is the power of God. 9
20 Has not God made foolish the wisdom of the world? 9
21 since, in the wisdom of God, the world did not know 9
21 the world did not know God through wisdom 9
21 it pleased God through the folly 9
24 Christ the power of God and the wisdom of God. 9
24 Christ the power of God and the wisdom of God. 9
25 For the foolishness of God is wiser than men 9
25 the weakness of God is stronger than men. 9
27 God chose what is foolish in the world 9
27 God chose what is weak in the world 9
28 God chose what is low and despised in the world 9
29 boast in the presence of God. 9
30 whom God made our wisdom, our righteousness 9
2: 1 the testimony of God in lofty words or wisdom. 9
5 in the power of God. 9
7 we impart a secret and hidden wisdom of God 9
7 which God decreed before the ages 9
9 what God has prepared for those who love him 9
10 God has revealed to us through the Spirit 9
10 even the depths of God. 9
11 So also no one comprehends the thoughts of God 9
11 except the Spirit of God. 9
12 the Spirit which is from God 9
12 understand the gifts bestowed on us by God. 9
14 does not receive the gifts of the Spirit of God 9
3: 6 Apol'los watered, but God gave the growth. 9
7 but only God who gives the growth. 9
9 For we are God's fellow workers; you are God's field 9
9 For we are God's fellow workers; you are God's field 9
9 you are God's field, God's building. 9
10 According to the grace of God given to me 9
16 Do you not know that you are God's temple 9
16 God's Spirit dwells in you? 9
17 If any one destroys God's temple 9
17 God will destroy him 9
17 God's temple is holy, and that temple you are. 9
19 For the wisdom of this world is folly with God. 9
23 you are Christ's; and Christ is God's. 9
4: 1 stewards of the mysteries of God. 9
5 will receive his commendation from God. 9
9 I think that God has exhibited us apostles 9
20 For the kingdom of God does not consist in talk 9
5:13 God judges those outside 9
6: 9 unrighteous will not inherit the kingdom of God? 9
10 inherit the kingdom of God. 9
11 in the Spirit of our God. 9
13 God will destroy both one and the other 9
14 God raised the Lord and will also raise us up 9
19 Holy Spirit within you, which you have from God? 9
20 So glorify God in your body. 9
7: 7 each has his own special gift from God 9
15 God has called us to peace. 9
17 in which God has called him 9
19 keeping the commandments of God. 9
24 there let him remain with God. 9
40 I think that I have the Spirit of God. 9
8: 3 if one loves God, one is known by him. 9
4 there is no God but one. 9
6 yet for us there is one God, the Father 9
8 Food will not commend us to God 9
9: 9 Is it for oxen that God is concerned? 9
21 not being without law toward God 9
10: 5 with most of them God was not pleased 9
13 God is faithful, and he will not let you be tempted 9
20 they offer to demons and not to God 9
31 do all to the glory of God. 9
32 to Jews or to Greeks or to the church of God 9
11: 3 the head of Christ is God. 9
7 since he is the image and glory of God 9
12 And all things are from God.) 9
13 for a woman to pray to God with her head uncovered? 9
16 nor do the churches of God. 9
22 do you despise the church of God 9
12: 3 no one speaking by the Spirit of God ever says 9
6 the same God who inspires them all in every one. 9
18 as it is, God arranged the organs in the body 9
24 God has so composed the body 9
28 God has appointed in the church first apostles 9
14: 2 who speaks in a tongue speaks not to men but to God; 9
18 I thank God that I speak in tongues 9
25 and so, falling on his face, he will worship God 9
25 declare that God is really among you. 9
28 speak to himself and to God. 9
33 For God is not a God of confusion but of peace 9
33 For God is not a God of confusion but of peace 9
36 What! Did the word of God originate with you 9
15: 9 because I persecuted the church of God. 9
10 by the grace of God I am what I am 9
10 the grace of God which is with me. 9
15 We are even found to be misrepresenting God 9
15 we testified of God that he raised Christ 9
24 when he delivers the kingdom to God the Father 9
27 For God has put all things in subjection •
28 that God may be everything to every one. 9
34 For some have no knowledge of God 9
38 God gives it a body as he has chosen 9
50 cannot inherit the kingdom of God 9
57 thanks be to God, who gives us the victory 9
2Co 1: 1 Paul, an apostle of Christ Jesus by the will of God 9
1 To the church of God which is at Corinth 9
2 Grace to you and peace from God our Father 9
3 Blessed be the God and Father of our Lord Jesus 9
3 Father of mercies and God of all comfort 9
4 with which we ourselves are comforted by God. 9
9 not on ourselves but on God who raises the dead; 9
12 not by earthly wisdom but by the grace of God. 9
18 As surely as God is faithful 9
19 For the Son of God, Jesus Christ, whom we preached 9
20 For all the promises of God find their Yes in him. 9
20 the Amen through him, to the glory of God. 9
21 it is God who establishes us with you in Christ 9
23 I call God to witness against me 9
2:14 thanks be to God 9
15 For we are the aroma of Christ to God 9
17 For we are not, like so many, peddlers of God's word; 9
17 as men of sincerity, as commissioned by God 9
17 in the sight of God we speak in Christ. 9
3: 3 not with ink but with the Spirit of the living God 9
4 that we have through Christ toward God. 9
5 our competence is from God 9
4: 1 having this ministry by the mercy of God •
2 practice cunning or to tamper with God's word 9
2 to every man's conscience in the sight of God. 9
4 the glory of Christ, who is the likeness of God. 9
6 the God who said, "Let light shine out of darkness 9
6 the glory of God in the face of Christ. 9
7 transcendent power belongs to God and not to us. 9
15 increase thanksgiving, to the glory of God. 9
5: 1 we have a building from God 9
5 He who has prepared us for this very thing is God 9
11 what we are is known to God 9
13 For if we are beside ourselves, it is for God 9
18 All this is from God 9
19 in Christ God was reconciling the world 9
20 God making his appeal through us 9
20 on behalf of Christ, be reconciled to God. 9
21 in him we might become the righteousness of God. 9
6: 1 not to accept the grace of God in vain. 9
4 as servants of God we commend ourselves 9
7 truthful speech, and the power of God 9
16 What agreement has the temple of God with idols? 9
16 For we are the temple of the living God; as God said 9
16 For we are the temple of the living God; as God said 9
16 I will be their God, and they shall be my people. 9
7: 1 make holiness perfect in the fear of God. 9

6 God, who comforts the downcast 9
12 be revealed to you in the sight of God. 9
8: 1 the grace of God which has been shown 9
5 to the Lord and to us by the will of God. 9
16 thanks be to God who puts the same earnest care 9
9: 7 God loves a cheerful giver. 9
8 God is able to provide you with every blessing 9
11 through us will produce thanksgiving to God; 9
12 also overflows in many thanksgivings to God. 9
13 glorify God by your obedience 9
14 because of the surpassing grace of God in you. 9
15 Thanks be to God for his inexpressible gift! 9
10: 5 every proud obstacle to the knowledge of God 9
13 keep to the limits God has apportioned us 9
11: 7 because I preached God's gospel without cost 9
11 why? Because I do not love you? God knows I do! 9
31 The God and Father of the Lord Jesus 9
12: 2 I do not know, God knows. 9
3 I do not know, God knows- 9
19 It is in the sight of God 9
21 my God may humble me before you 9
13: 4 lives by the power of God 9
4 we shall live with him by the power of God. 9
7 we pray God that you may not do wrong 9
11 the God of love and peace will be with you. 9
14 the love of God 9
Gal 1: 1 through Jesus Christ and God the Father 9
3 Grace to you and peace from God the Father 9
4 according to the will of our God and Father; 9
10 Am I now seeking the favor of men, or of God? 9
13 how I persecuted the church of God violently 9
20 In what I am writing to you, before God, I do not lie!) 9
24 they glorified God because of me. 9
2: 6 God shows no partiality 9
19 that I might live to God. 9
20 I live by faith in the Son of God 9
21 I do not nullify the grace of God 9
3: 6 Thus Abraham "believed God 9
8 God would justify the Gentiles by faith 9
11 no man is justified before God by the law 9
17 annul a covenant previously ratified by God 9
18 God gave it to Abraham by a promise. 9
20 but God is one. 9
21 Is the law then against the promises of God? 9
26 you are all sons of God, through faith. 9
4: 4 God sent forth his Son 9
6 God has sent the Spirit of his Son into our hearts 9
7 So through God you are no longer a slave but a son 9
8 Formerly, when you did not know God 9
9 now that you have come to know God 9
9 rather to be known by God 9
14 as an angel of God, as Christ Jesus. 9
5:21 shall not inherit the kingdom of God. 9
6: 7 Do not be deceived; God is not mocked 9
16 upon the Israel of God. 9
Eph 1: 1 Paul, an apostle of Christ Jesus by the will of God 9
2 Grace to you and peace from God our Father 9
3 Blessed be the God and Father of our Lord Jesus 9
17 God of our Lord Jesus Christ, the Father of glory 9
2: 4 God, who is rich in mercy 9
8 this is not your own doing, it is the gift of God- 9
10 for good works, which God prepared beforehand 9
16 might reconcile us both to God in one body 9
19 you are . . members of the household of God 9
22 a dwelling place of God in the Spirit. 9
3: 2 the stewardship of God's grace that was given to me 9
7 according to the gift of God's grace 9
9 plan of the mystery hidden for ages in God 9
10 the manifold wisdom of God 9
19 you may be filled with all the fulness of God. 9
4: 6 one God and Father of us all, who is above all 9
13 the knowledge of the Son of God 9
18 alienated from the life of God 9
24 created after the likeness of God 9
30 do not grieve the Holy Spirit of God 9
32 forgiving one another, as God in Christ forgave 9
5: 1 be imitators of God, as beloved children. 9
2 a fragrant offering and sacrifice to God. 9
5 in the kingdom of Christ and of God. 9
6 the wrath of God comes 9
20 giving thanks . . to God the Father. 9
6: 6 doing the will of God from the heart 9
11 Put on the whole armor of God 9
13 Therefore take the whole armor of God 9
17 the sword of the Spirit, which is the word of God. 9
23 God the Father and the Lord Jesus Christ. 9
Php 1: 2 Grace to you and peace from God our Father 9
3 I thank my God in all my remembrance of you 9
8 For God is my witness 9
11 to the glory and praise of God. 9
14 bold to speak the word of God without fear. •
28 of your salvation, and that from God. 9
2: 6 who, though he was in the form of God, did not count 9
6 not count equality with God a thing to be grasped 9
9 Therefore God has highly exalted him 9
11 to the glory of God the Father. 9
13 for God is at work in you, both to will and to work 9
15 be blameless and innocent, children of God 9
27 God had mercy on him, and not only on him but on me 9
3: 3 who worship God in spirit, and glory in Christ 9
9 righteousness from God that depends on faith 9
14 prize of the upward call of God in Christ Jesus. 9
15 God will reveal that also to you. 9
4: 6 let your requests be made known to God. 9
7 the peace of God, which passes all understanding 9
9 the God of peace will be with you. 9
18 a sacrifice acceptable and pleasing to God. 9
19 my God will supply every need of yours 9
20 To our God and Father be glory for ever and ever. 9
Col 1: 1 Paul, an apostle of Christ Jesus by the will of God 9
2 Grace to you and peace from God our Father. 9
3 We always thank God, the Father of our Lord Jesus 9
6 heard and understood the grace of God in truth 9
10 increasing in the knowledge of God. 9
15 He is the image of the invisible God 9
19 in him all the fulness of God was pleased to dwell •
25 to make the word of God fully known 9
27 To them God chose to make known 9
2: 2 the knowledge of God's mystery, of Christ 9
12 through faith in the working of God 9
13 God made alive together with him •
19 grows with a growth that is from God. 9
3: 1 where Christ is, seated at the right hand of God. 9
3 your life is hid with Christ in God. 9
6 On account of these the wrath of God is coming. 9
12 as God's chosen ones, holy and beloved 9
16 sing . . with thankfulness in your hearts to God. 9
17 giving thanks to God the Father through him. 9
4: 3 God may open to us a door for the word 9
11 fellow workers for the kingdom of God 9
12 fully assured in all the will of God. 9
1Th 1: 1 in God the Father and the Lord Jesus Christ 9
2 We give thanks to God always for you all 9
3 remembering before our God and Father your work 9
4 For we know, brethren beloved by God 9
8 your faith in God has gone forth everywhere 9
9 how you turned to God from idols 9
9 to serve a living and true God 9
2: 2 as you know, we had courage in our God 9
2 to declare to you the gospel of God 9
4 just as we have been approved by God 9
4 not to please men, but to please God 9
5 never used . . a cloak for greed, as God is witness; 9
8 ready to share with you not only the gospel of God 9
9 while we preached to you the gospel of God. 9
10 You are witnesses, and God also 9
12 to lead a life worthy of God 9
13 we also thank God constantly for this 9
13 when you received the word of God 9
13 but as what it really is, the word of God 9
14 became imitators of the churches of God in Christ 9
15 drove us out, and displease God and oppose all men 9
16 God's wrath has come upon them at last! •
3: 2 we sent Timothy, our brother and God's servant 9
9 what thanksgiving can we render to God for you 9
9 which we feel for your sake before our God 9
11 Now may our God and Father himself 9
13 unblamable in holiness before our God and Father 9
4: 1 how you ought to live and to please God 9
3 For this is the will of God, your sanctification 9
5 like heathen who do not know God; 9
7 God has not called us for uncleanness 9
8 disregards not man but God 9
14 God will bring with him those who have fallen 9
16 with the sound of the trumpet of God 9
5: 9 For God has not destined us for wrath 9
18 for this is the will of God in Christ Jesus 9
23 May the God of peace himself sanctify you wholly; 9
2Th 1: 1 God our Father and the Lord Jesus Christ 9
2 Grace to you and peace from God the Father 9
3 We are bound to give thanks to God always for you 9
4 boast of you in the churches of God 9
5 is evidence of the righteous judgment of God 9
5 you may be made worthy of the kingdom of God 9
6 since indeed God deems it just 9
8 those who do not know God 9
11 that our God may make you worthy of his call 9
12 according to the grace of our God 9
2: 4 he takes his seat in the temple of God 9
4 proclaiming himself to be God. 9
11 Therefore God sends upon them a strong delusion 9
13 we are bound to give thanks to God always for you 9
13 God chose you from the beginning to be saved 9
16 Jesus Christ himself, and God our Father 9
3: 5 May the Lord direct your hearts to the love of God 9
1Ti 1: 1 by command of God our Savior 9
2 Grace, mercy, and peace from God the Father 9
11 glorious gospel of the blessed God 9
17 the King of ages, immortal, invisible, the only God 9
2: 3 it is acceptable in the sight of God our Savior 9
5 For there is one God 9
5 there is one mediator between God and men 9
3: 5 how can he care for God's church? 9
15 how one ought to behave in the household of God 9
15 which is the church of the living God 9
4: 3 and enjoin abstinence from foods which God created 9
4 For everything created by God is good 9
5 is consecrated by the word of God and prayer. 9
10 because we have our hope set on the living God 9
5: 4 for this is acceptable in the sight of God. 9
5 a real widow . . has set her hope on God 9
21 In the presence of God and of Christ Jesus 9
6: 1 name of God and the teaching may not be defamed. 9
11 as for you, man of God, shun all this 9
13 God who gives life to all things 9
17 set their hopes . . on God 9
2Ti 1: 1 Paul, an apostle of Christ Jesus by the will of God 9
2 Grace, mercy, and peace from God the Father 9
3 I thank God whom I serve with a clear conscience 9
6 rekindle the gift of God that is within you 9
7 for God did not give us a spirit of timidity 9
8 in the power of God 9
2: 9 the word of God is not fettered. 9
15 Do your best to present yourself to God as . . 9
19 God's firm foundation stands, bearing this seal 9
25 his opponents with gentleness. God may perhaps 9
3:17 that the man of God may be complete 9
4: 1 I charge you in the presence of God 9
Tit 1: 1 Paul, a servant of God and an apostle of Jesus 9
1 to further the faith of God's elect 9
2 eternal life which God, who never lies, promised 9
3 by command of God our Savior; 9
4 Grace and peace from God the Father 9
7 For a bishop, as God's steward, must be blameless 9
16 They profess to know God 9
2: 5 the word of God may not be discredited. 9
10 they may adorn the doctrine of God our Savior. 9
11 the grace of God has appeared 9
13 glory of our great God and Savior Jesus Christ 9
3: 4 loving kindness of God our Savior appeared 9
8 those who have believed in God may be careful 9
Phm 1: 3 Grace to you and peace from God our Father 9
4 I thank my God always 9
Heb 1: 1 God spoke of old to our fathers by the prophets; 9
3 He reflects the glory of God •
5 For to what angel did God ever say, "Thou art my Son •
6 he says, "Let all God's angels worship him. 9
8 Thy throne, O God, is for ever and ever 9
9 therefore God, thy God, has anointed thee 9
9 therefore God, thy God, has anointed thee 9
2: 4 while God also bore witness by signs and wonders 9
5 God subjected the world to come •
9 that by the grace of God he might taste death 9
13 again, "Here am I, and the children God has given me. 9
17 faithful high priest in the service of God 9
3: 2 just as Moses also was faithful in God's house. •
4 but the builder of all things is God.) 9
5 Now Moses was faithful in all God's house •
6 Christ was faithful over God's house as a son •
12 leading you to fall away from the living God. 9
4: 4 God rested on the seventh day from all his works. 9
8 God would not speak later of another day. •
9 remains a sabbath rest for the people of God; 9
10 whoever enters God's rest •
10 ceases from his labors as God did from his. 9
12 For the word of God is living and active 9
14 a great high priest . . Jesus, the Son of God 9
5: 1 to act on behalf of men in relation to God 9
4 he is called by God, just as Aaron was. 9
10 being designated by God a high priest 9
12 teach you . . the first principles of God's word. 9
6: 1 foundation . . of faith toward God 9
3 this we will do if God permits. 9
5 have tasted the goodness of the word of God 9
6 since they crucify the Son of God 9
7 receives a blessing from God. 9
10 For God is not so unjust as to overlook your work 9
13 For when God made a promise to Abraham 9
17 when God desired to show more convincingly 9
18 it is impossible that God should prove false 9
7: 1 king of Salem, priest of the Most High God 9
3 resembling the Son of God 9
19 through which we draw near to God. 9
25 to save those who draw near to God through him 9
8: 5 he was instructed by God, saying •
10 I will be their God, and they shall be my people. 9
9:14 offered himself without blemish to God 9
14 to serve the living God. 9
20 the covenant which God commanded you. 9
24 now to appear in the presence of God on our behalf. 9
10: 7 I said, 'Lo, I have come to do thy will, O God,' 9
12 he sat down at the right hand of God 9
21 since we have a great priest over the house of God 9
29 the man who has spurned the Son of God 9
31 to fall into the hands of the living God. 9
36 do the will of God and receive what is promised. 9
11: 3 the world was created by the word of God 9
4 Abel offered to God a more acceptable sacrifice 9
4 God bearing witness by accepting his gifts 9
5 he was not found, because God had taken him 9
5 he was attested as having pleased God. 9
6 whoever would draw near to God 9
7 being warned by God concerning events as yet unseen •
10 the city . . whose builder and maker is God. 9

16 God is not ashamed to be called their God 9
16 God is not ashamed to be called their God 9
19 God was able to raise men even from the dead 9
25 share ill-treatment with the people of God 9
40 since God had foreseen something better for us 9
12: 2 seated at the right hand of the throne of God. 9
7 God is treating you as sons 9
15 no one fail to obtain the grace of God 9
22 the city of the living God 9
23 a judge who is God of all 9
28 thus let us offer to God acceptable worship 9
29 for our God is a consuming fire. 9
13: 4 God will judge the immoral and adulterous. 9
7 those who spoke to you the word of God 9
15 offer up a sacrifice of praise to God 9
16 such sacrifices are pleasing to God. 9
20 the God of peace who brought again from the dead 9
Jas 1: 1 servant of God and of the Lord Jesus Christ 9
5 If any of you lacks wisdom, let him ask God 9
12 the crown of life which God has promised •
13 Let no one say . . "I am tempted by God 9
13 for God cannot be tempted with evil 9
20 anger of man does not work the righteousness of God. 9
27 pure and undefiled before God and the Father 9
2: 5 Has not God chosen those who are poor in the world 9
19 You believe that God is one; you do well. 9
23 Abraham believed God 9
23 and he was called the friend of God. 9
3: 9 we curse men, who are made in the likeness of God. 9
4: 4 friendship with the world is enmity with God? 9
4 makes himself an enemy of God. 9
6 God opposes the proud, but gives grace 9
7 Submit yourselves therefore to God. 9
8 Draw near to God and he will draw near to you. 9
1Pe 1: 2 chosen and destined by God the Father 9
3 Blessed be the God and Father of our Lord Jesus 9
5 who by God's power are guarded through faith 9
21 Through him you have confidence in God 9
21 so that your faith and hope are in God. 9
23 through the living and abiding word of God; 9
2: 4 in God's sight chosen and precious; 9
5 offer spiritual sacrifices acceptable to God 9
9 you are . . a holy nation, God's own people •
10 but now you are God's people; 9
12 and glorify God on the day of visitation. 9
15 For it is God's will that by doing right 9
16 but live as servants of God. 9
17 Honor all men. Love the brotherhood. Fear God. 9
19 one is approved if, mindful of God, he endures pain 9
20 you have God's approval. 9
3: 4 spirit, which in God's sight is very precious. 9
5 women who hoped in God used to adorn themselves 9
17 to suffer . . if that should be God's will 9
18 Christ also died . . that he might bring us to God 9
20 when God's patience waited in the days of Noah 9
21 but as an appeal to God for a clear conscience 9
22 who . . is at the right hand of God 9
4: 2 no longer by human passions but by the will of God 9
6 they might live in the spirit like God. 9
10 as good stewards of God's varied grace 9
11 whoever speaks, as one who utters oracles of God; 9
11 one who renders it by the strength which God supplies 9
11 God may be glorified through Jesus Christ. 9
14 the spirit of glory and of God rests upon you. 9
16 but under that name let him glorify God. 9
17 for judgement to begin with the household of God; 9
17 the end of those who do not obey the gospel of God? 9
19 let those who suffer according to God's will 9
5: 2 Tend the flock of God that is your charge 9
5 God opposes the proud, but gives grace 9
6 under the mighty hand of God 9
10 the God of all grace, who has called you 9
12 and declaring that this is the true grace of God; 9
2Pe 1: 1 the righteousness of our God and Savior Jesus 9
2 in the knowledge of God and of Jesus our Lord. 9
17 he received honor and glory from God the Father 9
21 men moved by the Holy Spirit spoke from God. 9
2: 4 if God did not spare the angels when they sinned 9
3: 5 by the word of God heavens existed long ago 9
12 and hastening the coming of the day of God 9
1Jn 1: 5 God is light and in him is no darkness at all. 9
2: 5 in him truly love for God is perfected. 9
14 and the word of God abides in you 9
17 but he who does the will of God abides for ever. 9
3: 1 we should be called children of God; and so we are. 9
2 Beloved, we are God's children now; 9
8 The reason the Son of God appeared 9
9 No one born of God commits sin; 9
9 for God's nature abides in him, and he cannot sin •
9 and he cannot sin because he is born of God. 9
10 whoever does not do right is not of God 9
10 By this it may be seen who are the children of God 9
17 how does God's love abide in him? 9
20 for God is greater than our hearts 9
21 we have confidence before God; 9
4: 1 test the spirits to see whether they are of God; 9
2 By this you know the Spirit of God 9
2 that Jesus Christ has come in the flesh is of God 9
3 spirit which does not confess Jesus is not of God 9
4 Little children, you are of God 9
6 We are of God. Whoever knows God listens to us 9
6 We are of God. Whoever knows God listens to us 9
6 and he who is not of God does not listen to us. 9
7 let us love one another; for love is of God 9
7 and he who loves is born of God and knows God. 9
7 and he who loves is born of God and knows God. 9
8 He who does not love does not know God; 9
8 for God is love. 9
9 In this the love of God was made manifest among us 9
9 that God sent his only Son into the world 9
10 not that we loved God but that he loved us 9
11 Beloved, if God so loved us, we also ought to love 9
12 No man has ever seen God; 9
12 if we love one another, God abides in us 9
15 Whoever confesses that Jesus is the Son of God 9
15 God abides in him, and he in God. 9
15 God abides in him, and he in God. 9
16 So we know and believe the love God has for us. 9
16 God is love, and he who abides in love abides in God 9
16 God is love, and he who abides in love abides in God 9
16 and God abides in him. 9
20 cannot love God whom he has not seen. 9
20 If any one says, "I love God," and hates his brother 9
21 he who loves God should love his brother also. 9
5: 1 Every one who believes . . is a child of God 9
2 when we love God and obey his commandments. 9
2 when we love God and obey his commandments. 9
3 the love of God, that we keep his commandments. 9
4 For whatever is born of God overcomes the world; 9
5 he who believes that Jesus is the Son of God? 9
9 testimony of men, the testimony of God is greater; 9
9 for this is the testimony of God 9
10 He who believes in the Son of God 9
10 He who does not believe God has made him a liar 9
10 the testimony that God has borne to his Son. 9
11 the testimony, that God gave us eternal life 9
12 he who has not the Son of God has not life. 9
13 to you who believe in the name of the Son of God 9
16 he will ask, and God will give him life •
18 We know that any one born of God does not sin 9
18 but He who was born of God keeps him 9
19 We know that we are of God 9
20 we know that the Son of God has come 9
20 This is the true God and eternal life. 9
2Jn 1: 3 from God the Father and from Jesus Christ 9
9 Any one who . . does not have God; 9
3Jn 1: 6 to send them on . . as befits God's service. 9
11 He who does good is of God; 9
11 he who does evil has not seen God. 9
Jde 1: 1 To those who are called, beloved in God the Father 9
4 ungodly persons who pervert the grace of our God 9
21 keep yourselves in the love of God; 9
25 to the only God, our Savior through Jesus Christ 9
Rev 1: 1 The revelation of Jesus Christ, which God gave 9
2 who bore witness to the word of God 9
6 made us a kingdom, priests to his God and Father 9
8 I am the Alpha and the Omega," says the Lord God 9
9 on account of the word of God 9
2: 7 the tree of life, which is in the paradise of God.' 9
18 words of the Son of God, who has eyes like a flame 9
3: 1 the seven spirits of God and the seven stars. 9
2 not found your works perfect in the sight of God. 9
12 the temple of my God; never shall he go out of it 9
12 and I will write on him the name of my God 9
12 the new Jerusalem which comes down from my God 9
12 the new Jerusalem which comes down from my God 9
14 the Amen . . the beginning of God's creation 9
4: 5 torches . . which are the seven spirits of God; 9
8 the Lord God Almighty, who was and is and is to come! 9
11 Worthy art thou, our Lord and God, to receive glory 9
5: 6 seven spirits of God sent out into all the earth; 9
9 ransom men for God from every tribe and tongue 9
10 hast made them a kingdom and priests to our God 9
6: 9 slain for the word of God and for the witness 9
7: 2 another angel . . with the seal of the living God 9
3 till we have sealed the servants of our God 9
10 Salvation . . to our God who sits upon the throne 9
11 they fell on their faces . . and worshiped God 9
12 might be to our God for ever and ever! Amen. 9
15 Therefore are they before the throne of God 9
17 and God will wipe away every tear from their eyes. 9
8: 2 Then I saw the seven angels who stand before God 9
4 rose . . from the hand of the angel before God. 9
9: 4 who have not the seal of God upon their foreheads; 9
13 the four horns of the golden altar before God 9
10: 7 the mystery of God, as he announced to his 9
11: 1 the temple of God . . and those who worship there 9
11 a breath of life from God entered them 9
13 t rrified and gave glory to the God of heaven. 9
16 elders . . fell on their faces and worshiped God 9
16 elders . . fell on their faces and worshiped God 9
17 saying, "We give thanks to thee, Lord God Almighty 9
19 Then God's temple in heaven was opened 9
12: 5 her child was caught up to God and to his throne 9
6 wilderness, where she has a place prepared by God 9
10 salvation . . power and the kingdom of our God 9
10 who accuses them day and night before our God. 9
17 war . . on those who keep the commandments of God 9
13: 6 to utter blasphemies against God, blaspheming 9
14: 4 redeemed . . as first fruits for God and the Lamb 9
7 Fear God and give him glory 9
10 he also shall drink the wine of God's wrath 9
12 saints, those who keep the commandments of God 9
19 into the great wine press of the wrath of God; 9
15: 1 for with them the wrath of God is ended. 9
2 standing . . with harps of God in their hands. 9
3 And they sing the song of Moses, the servant of God 9
3 wonderful are thy deeds, O Lord God the Almighty! 9
7 seven golden bowls full of the wrath of God 9
8 smoke from the glory of God and from his power 9
16: 1 pour out . . the seven bowls of the wrath of God. 9
7 I heard the altar cry, "Yea, Lord God the Almighty 9
9 and they cursed the name of God 9
11 cursed the God of heaven for their pain and sores 9
14 for battle on the great day of God the Almighty. 9
19 and God remembered great Babylon 9
21 till men cursed God for the plague of the hail 9
17:17 for God has put it into their hearts 9
17 until the words of God shall be fulfilled. 9
18: 5 and God has remembered her iniquities. 9
8 for mighty is the Lord God who judges her. 9
20 for God has given judgment for you against her! 9
19: 1 Salvation and glory and power belong to our God 9
4 living creatures fell down and worshiped God 9
5 Praise our God, all you his servants 9
6 For the Lord our God the Almighty reigns. 9
9 And he said to me, "These are true words of God. 9
10 Worship God. 9
13 the name by which he is called is The Word of God. 9
15 of the fury of the wrath of God the Almighty. 9
17 Come, gather for the great supper of God 9
20: 4 for . . testimony to Jesus and for the word of God 9
6 but they shall be priests of God and of Christ 9
21: 2 new Jerusalem, coming down out of heaven from God 9
3 and God himself will be with them; 9
3 Behold, the dwelling of God is with men. 9
7 and I will be his God and he shall be my son. 9
10 Jerusalem coming down out of heaven from God 9
11 having the glory of God 9
22 for its temple is the Lord God the Almighty 9
23 for the glory of God is its light 9
22: 1 flowing from the throne of God and of the Lamb 9
3 but the throne of God and of the Lamb shall be in it 9
5 for the Lord God will be their light 9
6 the Lord, the God of the spirits of the prophets 9
9 who keep the words of this book. Worship God. 9
18 God will add to him the plagues 9
19 God will take away his share in the tree of life 9
1Es 1: 4 worship the Lord your God and serve his people 9
27 I was not sent against you by the Lord God 9
48 the laws of the Lord, the God of Israel. 9
50 the God of their fathers sent by his messenger 9
4:36 All God's works quake and tremble •
40 Blessed be the God of truth! 9
62 they praised the God of their fathers 9
5:44 to the temple of God which is in Jerusalem 9
48 prepared the altar of the God of Israel 9
49 the directions in the book of Moses the man of God. 9
53 all who had made any vow to God 9
53 began to offer sacrifices to God 9
53 though the temple of God was not yet built. 9
56 after their coming to the temple of God 9
57 they laid the foundation of the temple of God 9
58 the work on the house of God 9
67 the temple for the Lord God of Israel. 9
70 building the house for the Lord our God 9
6: 1 in the name of the Lord God of Israel. 9
31 libations may be made to the Most High God 9
7: 4 the command of the Lord God of Israel 9
9 for the services of the Lord God of Israel 9
15 for the service of the Lord God of Israel. 9
8: 3 which was given by the God of Israel; 9
16 perform it in accordance with the will of your God; 9
17 given you for the use of the temple of your God 9
18 as necessary for the temple of your God 9
19 reader of the law of the Most High God 9
21 all things prescribed in the law of God 9
21 scrupulously fulfilled for the Most High God 9
23 according to the wisdom of God 9
23 all those who know the law of your God 9
24 all who transgress the law of your God 9
27 I was encouraged by the help of the Lord my God 9
65 offered sacrifices to the Lord, the God of Israel 9
79 the house of the Lord our God •
9: 8 give glory to the Lord the God of our fathers 9
39 which had been given by the Lord God of Israel. 9
46 Ezra blessed the Lord God Most High 9
46 God Most High, the God of hosts, the Almighty; 9
2Es 1:29 you should be my people and I should be your God 10
2: 3 because you have sinned before the Lord God 10
45 and they have confessed the name of God 10
47 He answered and said to me, "He is the Son of God 10
48 wonders of the Lord God which you have seen. 10
7:19 he said to me, "You are not a better judge than God 10

20 the law of God which is set before them 10
21 For God strictly commanded those 10
48 which has alienated us from God •
79 and who have hated those who fear God- 10
8:58 said in their hearts that there is not God 10
9:45 after 30 years God heard your handmaid 10
10:16 if you acknowledge the decree of God to be just 10
15:20 Behold," says God, "I call together all the kings 10
21 Thus says the Lord God 10
27 for God will not deliver you 10
48 therefore God says 10
56 so God will do to you 10
16: 8 The Lord God sends calamities 10
53 for God will burn coals of fire on the head of him •
53 I have not sinned before God and his glory. 10
62 the spirit of Almighty God 10
66 will you hide your sins before God and his angels? 10
67 Behold, God is the judge, fear him! 10
67 so God will lead you forth 10
75 Do not fear or doubt, for God is your guide. 10
76 says the Lord God, "do not let your sins 10
Tob 1:12 because I remembered God with all my heart. 9
3:11 Blessed art thou, O Lord my God 9
16 in the presence of the glory of the great God. 9
4: 5 Remember the Lord our God all your days, my son 9
7 the face of God will not be turned away from you. 9
14 if you serve God you will receive payment 9
19 Bless the Lord God on every occasion 9
21 You have great wealth if you fear God 9
5:16 God who dwells in heaven will prosper your way 9
6:17 and cry out to the merciful God, and he will save you 9
7:12 The merciful God will guide you both for the best. 9
8: 5 Blessed art thou, O God of our fathers 9
15 Then Raguel blessed God and said 9
15 Blessed art thou, O God 9
10:11 The God of heaven will prosper you, my children 9
11: 1 Tobias went on his way, praising God 9
14 he wept and said, "Blessed art thou, O God 9
16 rejoicing and praising God 9
17 God had been merciful to him 9
17 Blessed is God who has brought you to us 9
12: 6 Praise God and give thanks to him 9
6 It is good to praise God and to exalt his name 9
6 worthily declaring the works of God 9
7 gloriously to reveal the works of God 9
11 gloriously to reveal the works of God.' 9
14 now God sent me to heal you 9
17 But praise God for ever. 9
18 by the will of our God 9
20 now give thanks to God 9
22 confessed the great and wonderful works of God 9
13: 1 Blessed is God who lives for ever 9
4 because he is our Lord and God 9
7 I exalt my God; my soul exalts the King of heaven 9
11 will come from afar to the name of the Lord God 9
15 Let my soul praise God the great King. 9
18 and will give praise, saying, 'Blessed is God 9
14: 2 continued to fear the Lord God and to praise him. 9
4 The house of God in it will be burned down 9
5 God will again have mercy on them 9
5 they will rebuild the house of God •
5 the house of God will be rebuilt there 9
6 the Gentiles will turn to fear the Lord God in truth 9
7 his people will give thanks to God 9
7 who love the Lord God in truth and righteousness 9
Jdt 4: 2 the temple of the Lord their God. 9
9 cried out to God with great fervor 9
12 praying earnestly to the God of Israel 9
5: 8 they worshiped the God of heaven 9
8 the God of heaven, the God they had come to know 9
9 Then their God commanded them to leave 9
12 Then they cried out to their God 9
13 Then God dried up the Red Sea before them 9
17 As long as they did not sin against their God 9
17 the God who hates iniquity is with them. 9
18 the temple of their God was razed to the ground 9
19 now they have returned to their God 9
20 they sin against their God 9
21 their God will protect them 9
6: 2 because their God will defend them 9
2 Who is God except Nebuchadnezzar? 9
3 their God will not deliver them 9
18 fell down and worshiped God, and cried out to him 9
19 O Lord God of heaven, behold their arrogance 9
21 they called on the God of Israel for help. 9
7:19 The people of Israel cried out to the Lord their God 9
24 God be judge between you and us! 9
25 God has sold us into their hands 9
28 heaven and earth and our God 9
29 they cried out to the Lord God with a loud voice. 9
30 the Lord our God will restore to us his mercy 9
8: 8 she feared God with great devotion. 9
11 pronounced this oath between God and you 9
12 that have put God to the test this day 9
12 setting yourselves up in the place of God 9
14 how do you expect to search out God 9
14 do not provoke the Lord our God to anger. 9
16 Do not try to bind the purposes of the Lord our God; 9
16 God is not like man, to be threatened 9
23 the Lord our God will turn it to dishonor. 9
25 let us give thanks to the Lord our God 9
35 may the Lord God go before you 9
9: 1 being offered in the house of God in Jerusalem 9
2 O Lord God of my father Simeon 9
4 O God, my God, hear me also, a widow. 9
4 O God, my God, hear me also, a widow. 9
11 thou art God of the lowly, helper of the oppressed 9
12 Hear, O hear me, God of my father 9
12 God of my father, God of the inheritance of Israel 9
14 to know and understand that thou art God 9
14 thou art God, the God of all power and might 9
10: 1 Judith had ceased crying out to the God of Israel 9
8 she worshiped God. 9
8 May the God of our fathers grant you favor 9
11: 6 God will accomplish something through you 9
10 unless they sin against their God. 9
11 they are about to provoke their God to anger 9
12 all that God by his laws has forbidden them to eat. 9
13 minister in the presence of our God at Jerusalem 9
16 God has sent me to accomplish with you things 9
17 serves the God of heaven day and night 9
17 I will pray to God and he will tell me 9
22 God has done well to send you before the people 9
23 if you do as you have said, your God shall be my God 9
23 if you do as you have said, your God shall be my God 9
12: 8 prayed the Lord God of Israel to direct her way 9
13: 4 O Lord God of all might 9
7 Give me strength this day, O Lord God of Israel! 9
11 God, our God, is still with us, to show his power 9
11 God, our God, is still with us, to show his power 9
14 Then she said to them with a loud voice, "Praise God 9
14 Praise God, O praise him! Praise God 9
17 and said with one accord, "Blessed art thou, our God 9
17 and said with one accord, "Blessed art thou, our God 9
18 you are blessed by the Most High God 9
18 blessed be the Lord God, who created the heavens 9
19 they remember the power of God. 9
20 May God grant this to be a perpetual honor to you 9
20 walking in the straight path before our God 9
14:10 Achior saw all that the God of Israel had done 9
10 he believed firmly in God, and was circumcised 9
15:10 God is well pleased with it 9
16: 2 Begin a song to my God with tambourines 9
3 For God is the Lord who crushes wars 9
13 I will sing to my God a new song 9
18 they worshiped God 9
19 Judith also dedicated to God all the vessels •
AEs 10: 4 Mordecai said, "These things have come from God. 9
9 God has done great signs and wonders 9
9 Israel, who cried out to God and were saved 9
10 one for the people of God 9
11 before God and among all the nations. 9
12 God remembered his people 9
13 with an assembly and joy and gladness before God 9
11:10 Then they cried to God 9
12 saw in this dream what God had determined to do 9
13:14 not set the glory of man above the glory of God 9
15 now, O Lord God and King, God of Abraham 9
15 now, O Lord God and King, God of Abraham 9
14: 3 she prayed to the Lord God of Israel, and said 9
18 except in thee, O Lord God of Abraham. 9
19 O God, whose might is over all 9
15: 2 invoking the aid of the all-seeing God and Savior 9
8 God changed the spirit of the king to gentleness 9
13 I saw you, my lord, like an angel of God 9
16: 4 they will escape the evil-hating justice of God 9
16 sons of the Most High, the most mighty living God 9
18 God, who rules over all things 9
21 God, who rules over all things 9
Wis 1: 3 For perverse thoughts separate men from God 9
6 because God is witness of his inmost feelings 9
13 because God did not make death 9
2:13 He professes to have knowledge of God 9
16 boasts that God is his father. 9
18 for if the righteous man is God's son 9
22 they did not know the secret purposes of God 9
23 for God created man for incorruption 9
3: 1 the souls of the righteous are in the hand of God 9
5 God tested them and found them worthy of himself; 9
13 she will have fruit when God examines souls. •
4: 1 because it is known both by God and by men. 9
6 when God examines them. •
10 There was one who pleased God and was loved by him 9
15 God's grace and mercy are with his elect •
5: 5 Why has he been numbered among the sons of God? 9
6: 4 nor walk according to the purpose of God 9
19 immortality brings one near to God; 9
7: 7 I called upon God •
14 those who get it obtain friendship with God 9
15 May God grant that I speak with judgment 9
25 For she is a breath of the power of God 9
26 a spotless mirror of the working of God 9
27 makes them friends of God, and prophets; 9
28 for God loves nothing 9
8: 3 She glorifies her noble birth by living with God 9
4 For she is an initiate in the knowledge of God 9
21 would not possess wisdom unless God gave her 9
9: 1 O God of my fathers and Lord of mercy 9
13 For what man can learn the counsel of God? 9
10: 5 and preserved him blameless before God 9
10 she showed him the kingdom of God 9
12: 7 receive a worthy colony of the servants of God. 9
26 will experience the deserved judgment of God. 9
27 they saw and recognized as the true God 9
13: 1 all men who were ignorant of God 9
6 perhaps they go astray while seeking God 9
14: 9 equally hateful to God 9
11 though part of what God created 9
22 to err about the knowledge of God 9
30 because they thought wickedly of God 9
15: 1 thou, our God, art kind and true 9
19 escaped both the praise of God and his blessing 9
16:18 they were being pursued by the judgment of God; 9
18:13 they acknowledged thy people to be God's son. 9
19: 1 God knew in advance even their future actions •
Sir 4:28 the Lord God will fight for you. 9
7: 9 when I make an offering to the Most High God 9
11:22 quickly God causes his blessing to flourish. •
21: 5 goes from his lips to the ears of God •
23: 4 O Lord, Father and God of my life 9
24:23 is the book of the covenant of the Most High God 9
36: 1 Have mercy upon us, O Lord, the God of all 9
5 there is not God but thee, O Lord. 9
17 thou art the Lord, the God of the ages. 9
39:17 in God's time all things will be sought after •
41: 8 who have forsaken the law of the Most High God! 9
19 before the truth of God and his covenant 9
45: 1 was beloved by God and man 9
46: 1 He became . . a great savior of God's elect •
47:10 while they praised God's holy name •
13 God gave him rest on every side 9
18 In the name of the Lord God 9
18 the Lord God, who is called the God of Israel 9
48:10 calm the wrath of God before it breaks out in fury •
16 Some of them did what was pleasing to God •
49: 8 which God showed him •
9 For God remembered his enemies with storm •
50:17 to worship their Lord, the Almighty, God Most High. 9
22 now bless the God of all 9
51: 1 will praise thee as God my Savior 9
30 in God's time he will give you your reward. •
Bar 1:10 offer them upon the altar of the Lord our God; 9
13 And pray for us to the Lord our God 9
13 for we have sinned against the Lord our God 9
15 Righteousness belongs to the Lord our God 9
18 have not heeded the voice of the Lord our God 9
19 we have been disobedient to the Lord our God 9
21 We did not heed the voice of the Lord our God 9
21 what is evil in the sight of the Lord our God. 9
2: 5 because we sinned against the Lord our God 9
6 Righteousness belongs to the Lord our God 9
11 O Lord God of Israel, who didst bring thy people 9
12 O Lord our God, against all thy ordinances. 9
15 earth may know that thou art the Lord our God 9
19 before thee our prayer for mercy, O Lord our God. 9
27 'Yet thou hast dealt with us, O Lord our God 9
31 they will know that I am the Lord their God. 9
35 them to be their God and they shall be my people; 9
3: 1 'O Lord Almighty, God of Israel, the soul in anguish 9
4 O Lord Almighty, God of Israel, hear now the prayer 9
4 who did not heed the voice of the Lord their God 9
6 For thou art the Lord our God, and thee, O Lord, will 9
8 our fathers who forsook the Lord our God.' 9
13 If you had walked in the way of God, you would be 9
24 O Israel, how great is the house of God! And how vast 9
27 God did not choose them, nor give them the way 9
35 This is our God; no other can be compared to him! 9
4: 1 She is the book of the commandments of God 9
4 for we know what is pleasing to God. 9
6 you were handed over . . because you angered God 9
7 by sacrificing to demons and not to God. 9
8 You forgot the everlasting God 9
9 For she saw the wrath that came upon you from God 9
9 God has brought great sorrow upon me; 9
12 because they turned away from the law of God. 9
13 walk in the ways of God's commandments 9
21 cry to God, and he will deliver you 9
23 God will give you back to me with joy and gladness 9
24 so they soon will see your salvation by God 9
25 the wrath that has come upon you from God 9
27 Take courage, my children, and cry to God 9
28 For just as you purposed to go astray from God 9
36 see the joy that is coming to you from God! 9
37 they are . . rejoicing in the glory of God. 9
5: 1 put on for ever the beauty of the glory from God. 9
2 Put on the robe of the righteousness from God 9
3 For God will show your splendor everywhere 9
4 For your name will for ever be called by God 9
5 rejoicing that God has remembered them. 9
6 God will bring them back to you, carried in glory 9
7 For God has ordered that every high mountain 9
7 so that Israel may walk safely in the glory of God 9
8 tree have shaded Israel at God's command. 9
9 For God will lead Israel with joy 9

LJr 1: 1 to give them the message which God had commanded 9
2 the sins which you have committed before God 9
51 there is no work of God in them. 9
57 Gods made of wood and overlaid with silver 9
62 God commands the clouds to go over the whole world 9
Aza 1: 1 singing hymns to God and blessing the Lord. 9
3 Blessed art thou, O Lord, God of our fathers 9
22 Let them know that thou art the Lord, the only God 9
28 glorified and blessed God in the furnace, saying 9
29 Blessed art thou, O Lord, God of our fathers 9
68 Bless him, all who worship the Lord, the God of gods 9
Sus 1:42 O eternal God, who dost discern what is secret 9
45 God aroused the holy spirit of a young lad 9
50 and inform us, for God has given you that right. 9
55 the angel of God has received the sentence 9
55 angel of God has received the sentence from God 9
59 for the angel of God is waiting with his sword 9
60 all the assembly shouted loudly and blessed God 9
63 Hilkiah and his wife praised God 9
Bel 1: 4 Daniel worshiped his own God. 9
5 the living God, who created heaven and earth 9
6 Do you not think that Bel is a living God? 9
25 Daniel said, "I will worship the Lord my God 9
25 he is the living God. 9
37 Take the dinner which God has sent you. 9
38 Daniel said, "Thou hast remembered me, O God 9
39 the angel of God immediately returned Habakkuk 9
41 Thou art great, O Lord God of Daniel 9
Man 1: 1 O Lord Almighty, God of our fathers, of Abraham 9
8 Therefore thou, O Lord, God of the righteous 9
13 thou, O Lord, art the God of those who repent 9
2Mc 1: 2 May God do good to you 9
11 Having been saved by God out of grave dangers 9
17 Blessed in every way be our God 9
20 when it pleased God 9
24 O Lord, Lord God, Creator of all things 9
27 let the Gentiles know that thou art our God. 9
2: 4 had seen the inheritance of God. 9
7 until God gathers his people together again 9
17 It is God who has saved all his people 9
18 we have hope in God 9
3:24 were astounded by the power of God 9
28 recognized clearly the sovereign power of God. 9
34 report to all men the majestic power of God. 9
36 the deeds of the supreme God 9
38 certainly is about the place some power of God. 9
6: 1 and cease to live by the laws of God 9
7: 6 The Lord God is watching over us 9
14 cherish the hope that God gives 9
16 do not think that God has forsaken our people. 9
18 because of our sins against our own God. 9
28 God did not make them out of things that existed. 9
29 in God's mercy I may get you back again •
31 you . . will certainly not escape the hands of God. 9
35 the judgment of the almighty, all-seeing God. 9
36 drunk of everflowing life under God's covenant; 9
36 by the judgment of God 9
37 appealing to God to show mercy soon to our nation 9
37 to make you confess that he alone is God 9
8:13 were cowardly and distrustful of God's justice 9
18 we trust in the Almighty God 9
23 gave the watchword, "God's help 9
9: 5 the all-seeing Lord, the God of Israel 9
8 making the power of God manifest to all. 9
11 to come to his senses under the scourge of God 8
12 It is right to be subject to God 9
17 to proclaim the power of God. 9
18 the judgment of God had justly come upon him 9
10:16 making solemn supplication and beseeching God 9
25 in supplication to God. 9
11: 4 He took no account whatever of the power of God 9
9 they all together praised the merciful God 9
13 because the mighty God fought on their side 9
12: 6 calling upon God the righteous Judge 9
11 won the victory, by the help of God 9
16 They took the city by the will of God 9
13:13 march out and decide the matter by the help of God 9
15 He gave his men the watchword, "God's victory 9
14:33 I will level this precinct of God to the ground 9
15:14 Jeremiah, the prophet of God. 9
16 Take this holy sword, a gift from God 9
26 with invocation to God and prayers. •
27 praying to God in their hearts 9
27 were greatly gladdened by God's manifestation. 9
3Mc 1: 9 he offered sacrifice to the supreme God 9
16 entreated the supreme God 9
2:21 God, who oversees all things 9
3: 4 because they worshiped God 9
11 not considering the might of the supreme God 9
4:16 improper words against the supreme God. 9
5: 7 their merciful God and Father 9
13 Then the Jews . . praised their holy God 9
25 implored the supreme God to help them again 9
28 This was the act of God who rules over all things 9
30 by the providence of God 9
35 praised the manifest Lord God, King of kings 9
6: 1 directed . . to cease calling upon the holy God 9
2 Almighty God Most High 9
18 the most glorious, almighty, and true God 9
28 the sons of the almighty and living God of heaven 9
29 the Jews . . praised their holy God and Savior 9
32 praising God, their Savior 9
36 had come to them through God. 9
7: 2 the great God guiding our affairs 9
6 the God of heaven surely defends the Jews 9
9 the Most High God 9
10 who had willfully transgressed against the holy God 9
10 transgressed against . . the law of God 9
12 who had transgressed the law of God. 9
16 those who had held fast to God even to death 9
16 giving thanks to the one God of their fathers 9
22 the supreme God . . performed great deeds 9
4Mc 1:12 giving glory to the all-wise God. 9
2:21 Now when God fashioned man 9
3:16 he poured out the drink as an offering to God. 9
4: 9 While the priests . . were imploring God 9
5:24 we worship the only real God. 9
25 we believe that the law was established by God 9
6:26 he lifted up his eyes to God and said 9
27 You know, O God 9
7:19 do not die to God, but live in God. 9
19 do not die to God, but live in God. 9
21 trusts in God 9
9: 8 shall be with God, for whom we suffer; 9
10:18 God hears also those who are mute. 9
20 Gladly, for the sake of God 9
21 God will visit you swiftly 9
12:11 you have received . . also your kingdom from God 9
14 by dying nobly fulfilled their service to God 9
17 I call on the God of our fathers 9
13: 3 by reason, which is praised before God 9
13 with all our hearts consecrate ourselves to God 9
15 who transgress the commandment of God. 9
22 our discipline in the law of God. 9
15: 3 for eternal life according to God's promise. 9
8 yet because of the fear of God 9
24 disregarded all these because of faith in God. 9
16:14 O mother, soldier of God in the cause of religion 9
18 Remember that it is through God 9
19 to endure any suffering for the sake of God. 9
21 and endured it for the sake of God. 9
22 have the same faith in God and not be grieved. 9
24 die rather than violate God's commandment. 9
25 those who die for the sake of God live in God 9
25 those who die for the sake of God live in God 9
17: 4 maintaining firm an enduring hope in God. 9
5 who . . stand in honor before God 9
10 looking to God and enduring torture 9
20 who have been consecrated for the sake of God 9
18:23 have received pure and immortal souls from God 9

God accepts 1. δεκτός
Sir 3:17 then you will be loved by those whom God accepts. 1

God-fearing 1. יְרֵא אֶת אֱלֹהִים 2. θεοσεβής
Neh 7: 2 more faithful and God-fearing man than many. 1
4Mc 15:28 as the daughter of God-fearing Abraham 2
16:12 the sacred and God-fearing mother did not wail 2

God-fearing man 1. ἔμφοβος
Sir 19:24 Better is the God-fearing man 1

God forbid 1. ἵλεώς σοι 2. μὴ γίγνομαι
Mat 16:22 rebuke him, saying, "God forbid, Lord! 1
Lke 20:16 When they heard this, they said, "God forbid! 2

God-given 1. θεόκτιστος
2Mc 6:23 moreover according to the holy God-given law 1

God's reply 1. χρηματισμός
Rom 11: 4 But what is God's reply to him? 1

without God 1. ἄθεος
Eph 2:12 having no hope and without God in the world. 1

Gog 1. גּוֹג 2. Γώγ
1Ch 5: 4 sons of Jo'el: Shemai'ah his son, Gog his son, Shim'e-i 1
Ezk 38: 2 set your face toward Gog, of the land of Magog 1
3 O Gog, chief prince of Meshech and Tubal; 1
14 Therefore, son of man, prophesy, and say to Gog 1
16 when through you, O Gog, I vindicate my holiness 1
18 on that day, when Gog shall come against the land 1
21 I will summon every kind of terror against Gog •
39: 1 And you, son of man, prophesy against Gog, 1
1 says the Lord GOD: Behold, I am against you, O Gog 1
11 I will give to Gog a place for burial in Israel 1
11 there Gog and all his multitude will be buried; 1
Rev 20: 8 to deceive the nations . . that is, Gog and Magog 2

Goiim 1. גּוֹיִם
Gen 14: 1 king of Elam, and Tidal king of Goi'im 1
9 Tidal king of Goi'im, Am'raphel king of Shinar 1
Jos 12:23 king of Dor . . one; the king of Goi'im in Galilee, one; 1

Golan 1. גּוֹלָן
Deu 4:43 Gadites, and Golan in Bashan for the Manas'sites. 1
Jos 20: 8 appointed . . and Golan in Bashan, from the tribe 1
21:27 given . . Golan in Bashan with its pasture lands 1
1Ch 6:71 given . . Golan in Bashan with its pasture lands 1

Golgotha 1. Γολγοθᾶ
Mat 27:33 when they came to a place called Gol'gotha 1
Mrk 15:22 they brought him to the place called Gol'gotha 1
Joh 19:17 the place . . which is called in Hebrew Gol'gotha. 1

Goliath 1. גָּלְיָת 2. Γολιαθ
1Sm 17: 4 there came . . a champion named Goliath, of Gath 1
23 the Philistine of Gath, Goliath by name, came up 1
21: 9 The sword of Goliath the Philistine . . is here 1
22:10 gave him the sword of Goliath the Philistine. 1
2Sm 21:19 and Elha'nan . . slew Goliath the Gittite 1
1Ch 20: 5 Elha'nan . . slew Lahmi the brother of Goliath 1
Sir 47: 4 struck down the boasting of Goliath? 2

Gomer 1. גֹּמֶר
Gen 10: 2 sons of Japheth: Gomer, Magog, Madai, Javan 1
3 The sons of Gomer: Ash'kenaz, Riphath 1
1Ch 1: 5 The sons of Japheth: Gomer, Magog, Madai, Javan 1
6 sons of Gomer: Ash'kenaz, Diphath, and To-gar'mah. 1
Ezk 38: 6 Gomer and all his hordes; 1
Hos 1: 3 he went and took Gomer the daughter of Dibla'im 1

Gomorrah 1. עֲמֹרָה 2. Γόμορρα 3. Gomorra
Gen 10:19 and in the direction of Sodom, Gomor'rah, Admah 1
13:10 before the LORD destroyed Sodom and Gomor'rah. 1
14: 2 Bera king of Sodom, Birsha king of Gomor'rah 1
8 Then the king of Sodom, the king of Gomor'rah 1
10 and as the kings of Sodom and Gomor'rah fled 1
11 all the goods of Sodom and Gomor'rah 1
18:20 Because the outcry against Sodom and Gomor'rah 1
19:24 Then the LORD rained on Sodom and Gomor'rah 1
28 he looked down toward Sodom and Gomor'rah 1
Deu 29:23 an overthrow like that of Sodom and Gomor'rah 1
32:32 their vine comes from . . the field of Gomor'rah; 1
Isa 1: 9 been like Sodom, and become like Gomor'rah. 1
10 Give ear . . you people of Gomor'rah! 1
13:19 like Sodom and Gomor'rah when God overthrew 1
Jer 23:14 Sodom to me, and its inhabitants like Gomor'rah. 1
49:18 As when Sodom and Gomor'rah . . were overthrown 1
50:40 As when God overthrew Sodom and Gomor'rah 1
Ams 4:11 as when God overthrew Sodom and Gomor'rah 1
Zep 2: 9 and the Ammonites like Gomor'rah 1
Mat 10:15 for the land of Sodom and Gomor'rah 2
Rom 9:29 fared like Sodom and been made like Gomor'rah. 2
2Pe 2: 6 the cities of Sodom and Gomor'rah to ashes 2
Jde 1: 7 Sodom and Gomor'rah and the surrounding cities 2
2Es 2: 8 remember what I did to Sodom and Gomorrah 3

Gorgias 1. Γοργιας
1Mc 3:38 Nicanor and Gorgias 1
4: 1 Now Gorgias took 5,000 infantry 1
5 When Gorgias entered the camp of Judas by night 1
18 Gorgias and his force are near us in the hills. 1
5:59 Gorgias and his men came out of the city 1
2Mc 8: 9 He associated with him Gorgias 1
10:14 When Gorgias became governor of the region 1
12:32 they hastened against Gorgias 1
35 Dositheus . . caught hold of Gorgias 1
35 Gorgias escaped and reached Marisa. 1
37 then he charged against Gorgias' men 1

Gortyna 1. Γορτυνα
1Mc 15:23 to Aradus and Gortyna and Cnidus and Cyprus 1

Goshen 1. גֹּשֶׁן 2. Γεσεμ
Gen 45:10 you shall dwell in the land of Goshen 1
46:28 sent Judah . . to appear before him in Goshen; 1
28 and they came into the land of Goshen. 1
29 went up to meet Israel his father in Goshen; 1
34 in order that you may dwell in the land of Goshen; 1
47: 1 they are now in the land of Goshen. 1
4 let your servants dwell in the land of Goshen. 1
6 let them dwell in the land of Goshen; 1
27 Thus Israel dwelt . . in the land of Goshen; 1
50: 8 their herds were left in the land of Goshen. 1
Exd 8:22 on that day I will set apart the land of Goshen 1
9:26 Only in the land of Goshen, where the people 1
Jos 10:41 and all the country of Goshen, as far as Gibeon. 1
11:16 all the Negeb and all the land of Goshen 1
15:51 Goshen, Holon, and Giloh 1
Jdt 1: 9 Raamses and the whole land of Goshen 2

Gotholiah 1. Γοθολιας
1Es 8:33 Of the sons of Elam, Jeshaiah the son of Gotholiah 1

Gothoniel 1. Γοθονιηλ
Jdt 6:15 Chabris the son of Gothoniel 1

Gozan 1. גּוֹזָן
2Kg 17: 6 in Halah, and on the Habor, the river of Gozan 1
18:11 put them . . on the Habor, the river of Gozan 1

19:12 which my fathers destroyed, Gozan, Haran, Rezeph 1
1Ch 5:26 brought them to . . Hara, and the river Gozan 1
Isa 37:12 which my fathers destroyed, Gozan, Haran, Rezeph 1

Greece 1. יָוָן 2. Ἑλλάς
Dan 8:21 he-goat is the king of Greece; 1
10:20 lo, the prince of Greece will come. 1
11: 2 shall stir up all against the kingdom of Greece. 1
Zec 9:13 brandish your sons, O Zion, over your sons, O Greece 1
Act 20: 2 he came to Greece. 2
1Mc 1: 1 (He had previously become king of Greece.) 2

Greek 1. בֶּן הַיְּוָנִים 2. Ἑλλάς 3. Ἕλλην 4. Ἑλληνικός 5. Ἑλληνίς 6. Ἑλληνιστί
Jol 3: 6 sold . . Judah and Jerusalem to the Greeks 1
Mrk 7:26 the woman was a Greek, a Syrophoeni'cian by birth. 5
Joh 7:35 to go to the Dispersion among the Greeks 3
35 Does he intend to . . teach the Greeks? 3
12:20 among those who went up . . were some Greeks. 3
19:20 it was written in Hebrew, in Latin, and in Greek. 6
Act 11:20 who on coming to Antioch spoke to the Greeks also 3
14: 1 a great company . . both of Jews and of Greeks. 3
16: 1 his father was a Greek. 3
3 they all knew that his father was a Greek. 3
17: 4 as did a great many of the devout Greeks 3
12 with not a few Greek women of high standing 5
18: 4 persuaded Jews and Greeks. 3
19:10 both Jews and Greeks. 3
17 all residents of Ephesus, both Jews and Greeks 3
20:21 testifying both to Jews and to Greeks 3
21:28 moreover he also brought Greeks into the temple 3
37 he said, "Do you know Greek? 6
Rom 1:14 obligation both to Greeks and to barbarians 3
16 to the Jew first and also to the Greek. 3
2: 9 the Jew first and also the Greek. 3
10 the Jew first and also the Greek. 3
3: 9 all men, both Jews and Greeks, are under . . sin 3
10:12 there is no distinction between Jew and Greek; 3
1Co 1:22 For Jews demand signs and Greeks seek wisdom 3
24 to those who are called, both Jews and Greeks 3
10:32 to Jews or to Greeks or to the church of God 3
12:13 Jews or Greeks, slaves or free 3
Gal 2: 3 though he was a Greek. 3
3:28 There is neither Jew nor Greek 3
Col 3:11 Here there cannot be Greek and Jew 3
Rev 9:11 and in Greek he is called Apol'lyon. 4
1Mc 1:10 the kingdom of the Greeks. 3
6: 2 the . . king who first reigned over the Greeks. 3
8: 9 The Greeks planned to come and destroy them 2
10 they sent a general against the Greeks •
18 the kingdom of the Greeks was . . enslaving 3
2Mc 4:10 he at once shifted . . over to the Greek way of life. 4
15 the highest value upon Greek forms of prestige. 4
36 the Greeks shared their hatred of the crime. 3
6: 8 was issued to the neighboring Greek cities 5
9 who did not choose to change over to Greek customs 4
11: 2 He intended to make the city a home for Greeks 3
24 our father's change to Greek customs 4
13: 2 Each of them had a Greek force of 110,000 infantry 4
3Mc 3: 8 The Greeks in the city, though wronged in no way 3
4Mc 8: 8 by adopting the Greek way of life 4
18:20 that bitter tyrant of the Greeks 3

Greek hat 1. πέτασος
2Mc 4:12 he induced . . the young men to wear the Greek hat. 1

Gate of the Guard 1. שַׁעַר הַמַּטָּרָה
Neh 12:39 came to a halt at the Gate of the Guard. 1

Gudgodah 1. גֻּדְגֹּדָה
Deu 10: 7 From there they journeyed to Gud'godah 1
7 journeyed . . from Gud'godah to Jot'bathah, a land 1

Guni 1. גּוּנִי
Gen 46:24 The sons of Naph'tali: Jahzeel, Guni, Jezer 1
Num26:48 of Guni, the family of the Gunites; 1
1Ch 5:15 Ahi the son of Ab'di-el, son of Guni 1
7:13 sons of Naph'tali: Jah'zi-el, Guni, Jezer, and Shallum 1

Gunite 1. גּוּנִי
Num26:48 of Guni, the family of the Gunites; 1

Gur 1. גּוּר
2Kg 9:27 they shot him in the chariot at the ascent of Gur 1

Gur-baal 1. גּוּר בַּעַל
2Ch 26: 7 against the Arabs that dwelt in Gurba'al 1

Haahashtari 1. אֲחַשְׁתָּרִי
1Ch 4: 6 Na'arah bore him . . Te'meni, and Ha-ahash'tari. 1

Habaiah 1. חֲבָיָה 2. Οββια
Ezr 2:61 of the sons of the priests: the sons of Habai'ah 1
1Es 5:38 the sons of Habaiah, the sons of Hakkoz 2

Habakkuk 1. חֲבַקּוּק 2. Αμβακουμ 3. Abacuc
Hab 1: 1 oracle of God which Habak'kuk the prophet saw. 1
3: 1 A prayer of Habak'kuk the prophet 1
2Es 1:40 Nahum and Habakkuk, Zephaniah, Haggai, Zechariah 3
Bel 1:33 Now the prophet Habakkuk was in Judea 2
34 the angel of the Lord said to Habakkuk 2
35 Habakkuk said, "Sir, I have never seen Babylon 2
37 Then Habakkuk shouted, "Daniel, Daniel! 2
39 the angel of God immediately returned Habakkuk 2

Habazziniah 1. חֲבַצִּנְיָה
Jer 35: 3 the son of Jeremiah, son of Habazzini'ah 1

Habor 1. חָבוֹר
2Kg 17: 6 in Halah, and on the Habor, the river of Gozan 1
18:11 put them in Halah, and on the Habor, the river 1
1Ch 5:26 brought them to . . Habor . . and the river Gozan 1

Hacaliah 1. חֲכַלְיָה
Neh 1: 1 The words of Nehemi'ah the son of Hacali'ah. 1
10: 1 Nehemi'ah the governor, the son of Hacali'ah 1

Hachilah 1. חֲכִילָה
1Sm 23:19 the hill of Hachi'lah, which is south of Jeshi'mon? 1
26: 1 Is not David hiding . . on the hill of Hachi'lah 1
3 Saul encamped on the hill of Hachi'lah 1

Hachmoni 1. חַכְמוֹנִי
1Ch 27:32 he and Jehi'el the son of Hach'moni attended 1

Hachmonite 1. חַכְמוֹנִי
1Ch 11:11 Jasho'be-am, a Hach'monite, was chief of the three; 1

Hadad 1. הֲדַד 2. חֲדַד
Gen 25:15 Hadad, Tema, Jetur, Naphish, and Ked'emah. 2
36:35 Husham died, and Hadad the son of Bedad 1
36 Hadad died, and Samlah of Masre'kah reigned 1
1Kg 11:14 an adversary against Solomon, Hadad the E'domite; 1
17 but Hadad fled to Egypt 1
17 Hadad fled . . Hadad being yet a little child. 1
19 Hadad found great favor in the sight of Pharaoh 1
21 Hadad heard . . that David slept with his fathers 1
21 Hadad said to Pharaoh, "Let me depart 1
25 an adversary . . doing mischief as Hadad did; 1
1Ch 1:30 Mishma, Dumah, Massa, Hadad, Tema 2
46 When Husham died, Hadad the son of Bedad 1
47 When Hadad died, Samlah of Masre'kah reigned 1
50 When Ba'al-ha'nan died, Hadad reigned in his stead; 1
51 Hadad died. The chiefs of Edom were: chiefs Timna 1

Hadadezer 1. הֲדַדְעֶזֶר
2Sm 8: 3 David also defeated Hadade'zer the son of Rehob 1
5 Syrians . . came to help Hadade'zer king of Zobah 1
7 shields . . carried by the servants of Hadade'zer 1
8 from Betah and . . Bero'thai, cities of Hadade'zer 1
9 David had defeated the whole army of Hadade'zer 1
10 had fought against Hadade'zer and defeated him; 1
10 Hadade'zer had often been at war with To'i. 1
12 and from the spoil of Hadade'zer the son of Rehob 1
10:16 Hadade'zer sent, and brought out the Syrians 1
16 Shobach the commander of the army of Hadade'zer 1
19 all the kings who were servants of Hadade'zer saw 1
1Kg 11:23 fled from his master Hadade'zer king of Zobah. 1
1Ch 18: 3 David also defeated Hadade'zer king of Zobah 1
5 Syrians . . came to help Hadade'zer king of Zobah 1
7 which were carried by the servants of Hadade'zer 1
8 And from Tibhath and from Cun, cities of Hadade'zer 1
9 the whole army of Hadade'zer, king of Zobah 1
10 because he had fought against Hadade'zer 1
10 for Hadade'zer had often been at war with To'u. 1
19:16 Shophach the commander of the army of Hadade'zer 1
19 when the servants of Hadade'zer saw that 1

Hadadrimmon 1. הֲדַדְרִמּוֹן
Zec 12:11 as great as the mourning for Hadadrim'mon 1

Hadar 1. הֲדַר
Gen 36:39 son of Achbor died, and Hadar reigned in his stead 1

Hadashah 1. חֲדָשָׁה
Jos 15:37 Zenan, Hadash'ah, Mig'dal-gad 1

Hadassah 1. הֲדַסָּה
Est 2: 7 He had brought up Hadas'sah, that is Esther 1

Hades 1. ᾅδης 2. infernus
Mat 11:23 You shall be brought down to Hades. 1
Lke 10:15 You shall be brought down to Hades. 1
16:23 in Hades, being in torment, he lifted up his eyes 1
Act 2:27 thou wilt not abandon my soul to Hades 1
31 he was not abandoned to Hades 1
Rev 6: 8 its rider's name was Death, and Hades followed him; 1
20:13 Death and Hades gave up the dead in them 1
14 Death and Hades were thrown into the lake of fire 1
2Es 4:41 In Hades the chambers of the souls 2
Tob 13: 2 he leads down to Hades, and brings up again 1
AEs 13: 7 may in one day go down in violence to Hades 1
Wis 1:14 the dominion of Hades is not on earth. 1
2: 1 no one has been known to return from Hades. 1
16:13 lead men down to the gates of Hades and back again. 1
17:14 beset them from the recesses of powerless Hades 1
Sir 14:12 the decree of Hades has not been shown to you. 1
16 because in Hades one cannot look for luxury. 1
17:27 Who will sing praises to the Most High in Hades 1
21:10 at its end is the pit of Hades. 1
28:21 Hades is preferable to it. 1
41: 4 there is no inquiry about it in Hades. 1
48: 5 You who raised a corpse from death and from Hades 1
51: 5 from the depths of the belly of Hades 1
6 my life was very near to Hades beneath. 1
Bar 2:17 for the dead who are in Hades, whose spirit 1
3:11 that you are counted among those in Hades? 1
19 They have vanished and gone down to Hades 1
Aza 1:66 he has rescued us from Hades 1
2Mc 6:23 telling them to send him to Hades. 1

Hadid 1. חָדִיד
Ezr 2:33 sons of Lod, Hadid, and Ono, 725. 1
Neh 7:37 sons of Lod, Hadid, and Ono, 721. 1
11:34 Hadid, Zebo'im, Nebal'lat 1

Hadlai 1. חַדְלָי
2Ch 28:12 chiefs . . and Ama'sa the son of Had-lai 1

Hadoram 1. הֲדוֹרָם 2. הֲדֹרָם
Gen 10:27 Hador'am, Uzal, Diklah 1
1Ch 1:21 Hador'am, Uzal, Diklah 1
18:10 he sent his son Hador'am to King David, to greet him 1
2Ch 10:18 Then King Rehobo'am send Hador'am 2

Hadrach 1. חַדְרָךְ
Zec 9: 1 word of the LORD is against the land of Hadrach 1

Haeleph 1. הָאֶלֶף
Jos 18:28 Zela, Ha-eleph, Jebus (that is, Jerusalem) 1

Hagab 1. חָגָב 2. Αγαβα
Ezr 2:46 sons of Hagab, the sons of Shamlai 1
1Es 5:30 sons of Uthai, the sons of Ketab, the sons of Hagab 2

Hagaba 1. חֲגָבָא
Neh 7:48 sons of Leba'na, the sons of Hag'aba 1

Hagabah 1. חֲגָבָה 2. Αγγαβα
Ezr 2:45 sons of Leba'nah, the sons of Hag'abah 1
1Es 5:29 the sons of Lebanah, the sons of Hagabah 2

Hagar 1. הָגָר 2. Ἁγάρ
Gen 16: 1 had an Egyptian maid whose name was Hagar; 1
3 Sar'ai, Abram's wife, took Hagar the Egyptian 1
4 he went in to Hagar, and she conceived; 1
8 he said "Hagar, maid of Sar'ai, where have you 1
15 Hagar bore Abram a son; and Abram called the name 1
15 the name of his son, whom Hagar bore, Ish'mael. 1
16 when Hagar bore Ish'mael to Abram. 1
21: 9 Sarah saw the son of Hagar the Egyptian 1
14 Abraham . . gave it to Hagar 1
17 and the angel of God called to Hagar from heaven 1
17 said to her, "What troubles you, Hagar? Fear not; 1
25:12 Abraham's son, whom Hagar the Egyptian 1
Gal 4:24 bearing children for slavery; she is Hagar. 2
25 Now Hagar is Mount Sinai in Arabia 2
Bar 3:23 the sons of Hagar, who seek for understanding 2

Haggai 1. חַגַּי 2. חַגַּי (A) 3. Αγγαιος 4. Aggei
Ezr 5: 1 prophets, Haggai and Zechari'ah the son of Iddo 2
6:14 through the prophesying of Haggai the prophet 2
Hag 1: 1 the word of the LORD came by Haggai the prophet 1
3 the word of the LORD came by Haggai the prophet 1
12 the LORD their God, and the words of Haggai 1
13 Then Haggai, the messenger of the LORD, spoke 1
2: 1 the word of the LORD came by Haggai the prophet 1
10 the word of the LORD came by Haggai the prophet 1
13 Then said Haggai, "If one who is unclean by contact 1
14 Then Haggai said, "So is it with this people 1
20 The word of the LORD came a second time to Haggai 1
1Es 6: 1 the prophets Haggai and Zechariah the son of Iddo 3
7: 3 the prophets Haggai and Zechariah prophesied; 3
2Es 1:40 Nahum and Habakkuk, Zephaniah, Haggai, Zechariah 4

Haggedolim 1. הַגְּדוֹלִים
Neh 11:14 overseer was Zab'diel the son of Haggedo'lim. 1

Haggi 1. חַגִּי
Gen 46:16 sons of Gad: Ziph'ion, Haggi, Shuni, Ezbon, Eri 1
Num26:15 of Haggi, the family of the Haggites; 1

Haggiah 1. חַגִּיָּה
1Ch 6:30 Shim'e-a his son, Haggi'ah his son, and Asai'ah his 1

Haggite 1. חַגִּי
Num26:15 of Haggi, the family of the Haggites; 1

Haggith 1. חַגִּית
2Sm 3: 4 and the fourth, Adoni'jah the son of Haggith; 1
1Kg 1: 5 Adoni'jah the son of Haggith exalted himself 1
11 that Adoni'jah the son of Haggith has become king 1
2:13 Adoni'jah the son of Haggith came to Bathshe'ba 1
1Ch 3: 2 the fourth Adoni'jah, whose mother was Haggith; 1

Hagri 1. הַגְרִי
1Ch 11:38 Mibhar the son of Hagri 1

Hagrite 1. הַגְרִי
1Ch 5:10 in the days of Saul they made war on the Hagrites 1
19 made war upon the Hagrites, Jetur, Naphish 1
20 the Hagrites and all . . with them were given 1
27:30 Over the flocks was Jaziz the Hagrite. 1
Ps 83: 6 tents of . . Moab and the Hagrites 1

Hahiroth 1. הַחִירֹת
Num33: 8 they set out from before Hahi'roth 1

Hakkatan 1. הַקָּטָן 2. Ακαταν
Ezr 8:12 Of the sons of Azgad, Joha'nan the son of Hak'katan 1
1Es 8:38 Of the sons of Azgad, Johanan the son of Hakkatan 2

Hakkoz 1. הַקּוֹץ 2. Ακκως
1Ch 24:10 the seventh to Hakkoz, the eighth to Abi'jah 1
Ezr 2:61 of the sons of the priests: the . . sons of Hakkoz 1
Neh 3: 4 the son of Uri'ah, son of Hakkoz repaired. 1
21 Mer'emoth the son of Uri'ah, son of Hakkoz repaired 1
7:63 priests: the sons of Hobai'ah, the sons of Hakkoz 1
1Es 5:38 the sons of Habaiah, the sons of Hakkoz 2

Hakupha 1. חֲקוּפָא 2. Αχιβα
Ezr 2:51 sons of Bakbuk, the sons of Haku'pha 1
Neh 7:53 sons of Bakbuk, the sons of Haku'pha 1
1Es 5:31 the sons of Bakbuk, the sons of Hakupha 2

Halah 1. חֲלַח
2Kg 17: 6 and placed them in Halah, and on the Habor 1
18:11 put them in Halah, and on the Habor, the river 1
1Ch 5:26 brought them to Halah . . and the river Gozan 1
Obd 1:20 exiles in Halah who are of the people of Israel •

Halak 1. חָלָק
Jos 11:17 lowland from Mount Halak, that rises toward Se'ir 1
12: 7 from Ba'al-gad in the valley . . to Mount Halak 1

Halhul 1. חַלְחוּל
Jos 15:58 Halhul, Beth-zur, Gedor 1

Hali 1. חֲלִי
Jos 19:25 Its territory included Helkath, Hali, Beten 1

Halicarnassus 1. Αλικαρνασσος
1Mc 15:23 to Lycia, and to Halicarnassus, and to Rhodes 1

Hallohesh 1. הַלּוֹחֵשׁ
Neh 3:12 Next to him Shallum the son of Hallo'hesh 1
10:24 Hallo'hesh, Pi'lha, Shobek 1

Ham 1. הָם 2. חָם
Gen 5:32 Noah became the father of Shem, Ham, and Japheth. 2
6:10 Noah had three sons, Shem, Ham, and Japheth. 2
7:13 Noah and his sons, Shem and Ham and Japheth 2
9:18 from the ark were Shem, Ham, and Japheth. 2
18 Ham was the father of Canaan. 2
22 Ham, the father of Canaan, saw the nakedness 2
10: 1 the sons of Noah, Shem, Ham, and Japheth; 2
6 The sons of Ham: Cush, Egypt, Put, and Canaan. 2
20 These are the sons of Ham, by their families 2
14: 5 Zuzim in Ham, the Emim in Sha'veh-kiriatha'im 1
1Ch 1: 4 Noah, Shem, Ham, and Japheth. 2
8 The sons of Ham: Cush, Egypt, Put, and Canaan. 2
4:40 the former inhabitants there belonged to Ham. 2
Ps 78:51 first issue of their strength in the tents of Ham. 2
105:23 Jacob sojourned in the land of Ham. 2
27 wrought his signs . . miracles in the land of Ham. 2
106:22 wondrous works in the land of Ham 2

Haman 1. הָמָן 2. Αμαν
Est 3: 1 King Ahasu-e'rus promoted Haman the Ag'agite 1
2 And all . . bowed down and did obeisance to Haman; 1
4 they told Haman, in order to see whether 1
5 Haman saw that Mor'decai did not bow down 1
5 And when Haman saw . . Haman was filled with fury. 1
6 Haman sought to destroy all the Jews 1
7 they cast Pur . . before Haman day after day; 1
8 Then Haman said to King Ahasu-e'rus 1
10 signet ring . . and gave it to Haman the Ag'agite 1
11 the king said to Haman, "The money is given to you 1
12 an edict, according to all that Haman commanded 1
15 And the king and Haman sat down to drink; 1
4: 7 exact sum of money that Haman had promised to pay 1
5: 4 let the king and Haman come this day to a dinner 1
5 Bring Haman quickly, that we may do as Esther 1
5 the king and Haman came to the dinner 1
8 let the king and Haman come . . to the dinner 1
9 Haman went out that day joyful and glad of heart. 1
9 But when Haman saw Mor'decai in the king's gate 1
10 Haman restrained himself, and went home; 1
11 Haman recounted to them the splendor of his 1
12 Haman added, "Even Queen Esther let no one come 1
14 This counsel pleased Haman, 1
6: 4 Haman had just entered the outer court 1
5 Haman is there, standing in the court. 1
6 Haman came in, and the king said to him 1
6 And Haman said to himself, "Whom would the king 1
7 Haman said to the king, "For the man whom the king 1
10 Then the king said to Haman, "Make haste 1
11 Haman took the robes and the horse 1
12 But Haman hurried to his house, mourning 1
13 Haman told . . everything that had befallen him. 1
14 eunuchs arrived and brought Haman in haste 1
7: 1 the king and Haman went in to feast 1
6 Esther said, "A foe and enemy! This wicked Haman! 1
6 Haman was in terror before the king and the queen. 1
7 Haman stayed to beg his life from Queen Esther 1
8 Haman was falling on the couch where Esther was; 1
8 As the words left . . they covered Haman's face. 1
9 gallows which Haman has prepared for Mor'decai 1
9 the gallows . . is standing in Haman's house 1
10 Hang him on that." So they hanged Haman 1
8: 1 King Ahasu-e'rus gave . . Esther the house of Haman 1
2 his signet ring, which he had taken from Haman 1
2 And Esther set Mor'decai over the house of Haman. 1
3 to avert the evil design of Haman the Ag'agite 1
5 order . . to revoke the letters devised by Haman 1
7 Behold, I have given Esther the house of Haman 1
9:10 the ten sons of Haman the son of Hammeda'tha 1
12 Jews have slain . . and also the ten sons of Haman. 1
13 let the . . sons of Haman be hanged on the gallows. 1
14 and the ten sons of Haman were hanged. 1
24 Haman . . had plotted against the Jews to destroy 1
AEs 10: 7 The two dragons are Haman and myself. 2
12: 6 Haman, the son of Hammedatha, a Bougaean 2
13: 3 Haman, who excels among us in sound judgment 2
6 those indicated to you in the letters of Haman 2
12 I . . refused to bow down to this proud Haman. 2
14:17 thy servant has not eaten at Haman's table 2
16:10 Haman, the son of Hammedatha, a Macedonian 2
17 letters sent by Haman the son of Hammedatha 2

Hamath 1. חֲמָת 2. Ἀμαθῖτις 3. Ημαθ
Num13:21 Zin to Rehob, near the entrance of Hamath. 1
34: 8 from Mount Hor . . to the entrance of Hamath 1
Jos 13: 5 from Ba'al-gad . . to the entrance of Hamath 1
Jdg 3: 3 Ba'al-her'mon as far as the entrance of Hamath. 1
2Sm 8: 9 When To'i king of Hamath heard that David had 1
1Kg 8:65 from the entrance of Hamath to the Brook of Egypt 1
2Kg 14:25 from the entrance of Hamath as far as the Sea 1
28 how he recovered for Israel Damascus and Hamath 1
17:24 brought people from Babylon, Cuthah, Avva, Hamath 1
30 Cuth made Nergal, the men of Hamath made Ashi'ma 1
18:34 Where are the gods of Hamath and Arpad? 1
19:13 Where is the king of Hamath, the king of Arpad 1
23:33 put him in bonds at Riblah in the land of Hamath 1
25:21 put them to death at Riblah in the land of Hamath. 1
1Ch 13: 5 from the Shihor of Egypt to the entrance of Hamath 1
18: 3 defeated Hadade'zer . . toward Hamath 1
9 To'u king of Hamath heard that David had defeated 1
2Ch 7: 8 the entrance of Hamath to the Brook of Egypt. 1
8: 4 all the store-cities which he built in Hamath. 1
Isa 10: 9 Is not Hamath like Arpad? 1
11:11 remnant . . from Hamath, and from the coastlands 1
36:19 Where are the gods of Hamath and Arpad? 1
37:13 Where is the king of Hamath, the king of Arpad 1
Jer 39: 5 king of Babylon, at Riblah, in the land of Hamath; 1
49:23 Hamath and Arpad are confounded 1
52: 9 king of Babylon at Riblah in the land of Hamath 1
27 put them to death at Riblah in the land of Hamath. 1
Ezk 47:15 by way of Hethlon to the entrance of Hamath 3
16 lies on the border between Damascus and Hamath) 1
17 Damascus, with the border of Hamath to the north. 1
20 to a point opposite the entrance of Hamath. 1
48: 1 to the entrance of Hamath, as far as Hazar-e'non 1
1 border of Damascus over against Hamath), 1
Ams 6: 2 Calneh, and see; and thence go to Hamath the great; 1
14 from the entrance of Hamath to the Brook 1
Zec 9: 2 Hamath also, which borders thereon 1
1Mc 12:25 met them in the region of Hamath 2

Hamath-zobah 1. חֲמַת צוֹבָה
2Ch 8: 3 Solomon went to Ha'math-zo'bah, and took it. 1

Hamathite 1. חֲמָתִי
Gen 10:18 the Zem'arites, and the Ha'mathites. 1
1Ch 1:16 Ar'vadites, the Zem'arites, and the Ha'mathites. 1

Hammath 1. חַמַּת
Jos 19:35 are Ziddim, Zer, Hammath, Rakkath, Chin'nereth 1
1Ch 2:55 Hammath, the father of the house of Rechab. 1

Hammedatha 1. הַמְּדָתָא 2. Αμαδαθος
Est 3: 1 Haman the Ag'agite, the son of Hammeda'tha 1
10 to Haman the Ag'agite, the son of Hammeda'tha 1
8: 5 by Haman the Ag'agite, the son of Hammeda'tha 1
9:10 the ten sons of Haman the son of Hammeda'tha 1
24 For Haman the Ag'agite, the son of Hammeda'tha 1
AEs 12: 6 Haman, the son of Hammedatha, a Bougaean 2
16:10 Haman, the son of Hammedatha, a Macedonian 2
17 letters sent by Haman the son of Hammedatha 2

Hammolecheth 1. הַמֹּלֶכֶת
1Ch 7:18 sister Hammo'lecheth bore Ishhod, Abi-e'zer 1

Hammon 1. חַמּוֹן
Jos 19:28 Ebron, Rehob, Hammon, Kanah, as far as Sidon 1
1Ch 6:76 Ham'mon with its pasture lands, and Kiria-tha'im 1

Hammoth-dor 1. חַמֹּת דֹּאר
Jos 21:32 Ham'moth-dor with its pasture lands 1

Hammuel 1. חַמּוּאֵל
1Ch 4:26 sons of Mishma: Ham'mu-el his son, Zac'cur 1

Hamon-gog 1. הֲמוֹן גּוֹג
Ezk 39:11 it will be called the Valley of Hamon-gog. 1
15 have buried it in the Valley of Hamon-gog. 1

Hamonah 1. הֲמוֹנָה
Ezk 39:16 A city Hamo'nah is there also. 1

Hamor 1. חֲמוֹר 2. Ἐμμώρ
Gen 33:19 from the sons of Hamor, Shechem's father 1
34: 2 when Shechem the son of Hamor the Hivite 1
4 spoke to his father Hamor, saying, "Get me this 1
6 Hamor the father of Shechem went out to Jacob 1
8 Hamor spoke with them, saying, "The soul of my son 1
13 answered Shechem and his father Hamor 1
18 Their words pleased Hamor and Hamor's son 1
18 Their words pleased Hamor and Hamor's son 1
20 Hamor and his son Shechem came to the gate 1
24 all . . hearkened to Hamor and his son Shechem; 1
26 They slew Hamor and his son Shechem 1
Jos 24:32 ground which Jacob bought from the sons of Hamor 1
Jdg 9:28 serve the men of Hamor the father of Shechem? 1
Act 7:16 bought . . from the sons of Hamor in Shechem. 2

Hamran 1. חַמְרָן
1Ch 1:41 sons of Dishon: Hamran, Eshban, Ithran, and Cheran. 1

Hamul 1. חָמוּל
Gen 46:12 and the sons of Perez were Hezron and Hamul. 1
Num26:21 of Hamul, the family of the Hamu'lites. 1
1Ch 2: 5 The sons of Perez: Hezron and Hamul. 1

Hamulite 1. חָמוּלִי
Num26:21 of Hamul, the family of the Hamu'lites. 1

Hamutal 1. חֲמוּטַל
2Kg 23:31 name was Hamu'tal the daughter of Jeremiah 1
24:18 His mother's name was Hamu'tal the daughter 1
Jer 52: 1 Hamu'tal the daughter of Jeremiah of Libnah. 1

Hana 1. Αναν
1Es 5:30 sons of Hagab, the sons of Shamlai, the sons of Hana 1

Hanamel 1. חֲנַמְאֵל
Jer 32: 7 Behold, Han'amel the son of Shallum your uncle 1
8 Then Han'amel my cousin came to me in the court 1
9 And I bought the field at An'athoth from Han'amel 1
12 in the presence of Han'amel my cousin 1

Hanan 1. חָנָן 2. Ανανιας
1Ch 8:23 Abdon, Zichri, Hanan 1
38 Azel had six sons . . Obadi'ah, and Hanan. 1
9:44 Azel had six sons . . Obadi'ah, and Hanan; 1
11:43 Hanan the son of Ma'acah 1
Ezr 2:46 the sons of Shamlai, the sons of Hanan 1
Neh 7:49 sons of Hanan, the sons of Giddel, the sons of Gahar 1
8: 7 Also . . Hanan, Pelai'ah, the Levites 1
10:10 their brethren . . Keli'ta, Pelai'ah, Hanan 1
22 Pelati'ah, Hanan, Anai'ah 1
26 Ahi'ah, Hanan, Anan 1
13:13 as their assistant Hanan the son of Zaccur, 1
Jer 35: 4 into the chamber of the sons of Hanan 1
1Es 9:48 Hanan, Pelaiah, the Levites 2

Hananel 1. חֲנַנְאֵל
Jer 31:38 from the tower of Han'anel to the Corner Gate. 1
Hananel *See also* Tower.

Hanani 1. חֲנָנִי 2. Ἀνανίας
1Kg 16: 1 the word of the LORD came to Jehu the son of Hana'ni 1
7 word of the LORD came by . . Jehu the son of Hana'ni 1
1Ch 25: 4 sons of Heman . . Hanani'ah, Hana'ni, Eli'athah 1
25 eighteenth, to Hana'ni, his sons and his brethren 1
2Ch 16: 7 Hana'ni the seer came to Asa king of Judah 1
19: 2 Jehu the son of Hana'ni the seer went out 1
20:34 chronicles of Jehu the son of Hana'ni 1
Ezr 10:20 Of the sons of Immer: Hana'ni and Zebadi'ah. 1
Neh 1: 2 Hana'ni, one of my brethren, came with certain men 1
7: 2 I gave my brother Hana'ni and Hanani'ah 1
12:36 kinsmen . . Ma'ai, Nethan'el, Judah, and Hana'ni 1
1Es 9:21 Of the sons of Immer: Hanani and Zebadiah 2

Hananiah 1. חֲנַנְיָה 2. חֲנַנְיָהוּ (A) 3. Ανανιας
4. Χανουναιος
1Ch 3:19 the sons of Zerub'babel: Meshul'lam and Hanani'ah 1

21 The sons of Hanani'ah: Pelati'ah and Jeshai'ah 1
8:24 Hanani'ah, Elam, Anthothi'jah 1
25: 4 sons of Heman . . Hanani'ah, Hana'ni, Eli'athah 1
23 sixteenth, to Hanani'ah, his sons and his brethren 1
2Ch 26:11 under the direction of Hanani'ah 1
Ezr 10:28 of Be'bai were Jehoha'nan, Hanani'ah, Zab'bai 1
Neh 3: 8 Next to him Hanani'ah, one of the perfumers 1
30 Hanani'ah the son of Shelemi'ah and Hanun 1
7: 2 I gave . . Hanani'ah the governor of the castle 1
10:23 Ho-she'a, Hanani'ah, Hasshub 1
12:12 heads of fathers' houses: of . . Jeremiah, Hanani'ah; 1
41 priests . . Eli-o-e'nai, Zechari'ah, and Hanani'ah 1
Jer 28: 1 Hanani'ah the son of Azzur 1
5 Then the prophet Jeremiah spoke to Hanani'ah 1
10 Then the prophet Hanani'ah took the yoke-bars 1
11 Hanani'ah spoke in the presence of all the people 1
12 the prophet Hanani'ah had broken the yoke-bars 1
13 Go, tell Hanani'ah, 'Thus says the LORD 1
15 And Jeremiah . . said to the prophet Hanani'ah 1
15 Listen, Hanani'ah, the LORD has not sent you 1
17 in the seventh month, the prophet Hanani'ah died. 1
36:12 Zedeki'ah the son of Hanani'ah, and all the princes. 1
37:13 Iri'jah the son of Shelemi'ah, son of Hanani'ah 1
Dan 1: 6 Daniel, Hanani'ah, Mish'a-el, and Azari'ah 1
7 Hanani'ah he called Shadrach 1
11 over Daniel, Hanani'ah, Mish'a-el, and Azari'ah; 1
19 like Daniel, Hanani'ah, Mish'a-el, and Azari'ah; 1
2:17 matter known to Hanani'ah, Mish'a-el, and Azari'ah 2
1Es 8:48 of the sons of Hananiah 4
9:29 Of the sons of Bebai: Jehohanan and Hananiah 3
Aza 1:66 Bless the Lord, Hananiah, Azariah, and Mishael 3
4Mc 16:21 Hananiah, Azariah, and Mishael 3
18:12 he taught you about Hananiah, Azariah, and Mishael 3

Hanes 1. חָנֵס
Isa 30: 4 officials are at Zo'an and his envoys reach Ha'nes 1

Hannah 1. חַנָּה
1Sm 1: 2 He had two wives; the name of the one was Hannah 1
2 but Hannah had no children. 1
5 although he loved Hannah, he would give . . only 1
5 he would give Hannah only one portion 1
7 Therefore Hannah wept and would not eat. •
8 Hannah, why do you weep? And why do you not eat? 1
9 After they had eaten and drunk . . Hannah rose. 1
13 Hannah was speaking in her heart; 1
15 But Hannah answered, "No, my lord 1
19 And Elka'nah knew Hannah his wife, and the LORD 1
20 in due time Hannah conceived and bore a son 1
22 Hannah did not go up, for she said to her husband 1
2: 1 Hannah also prayed and said, "My heart exults 1
21 And the LORD visited Hannah, and she conceived 1

Hannaniah 1. Ανανιας
1Mc 2:59 Hannaniah, Azariah, and Mishael believed 1

Hannathon 1. חַנָּתֹן
Jos 19:14 the boundary turns about to Han'nathon 1

Hanniel 1. חַנִּיאֵל
Num34:23 of Manas'seh a leader, Han'niel the son of Ephod. 1
1Ch 7:39 The sons of Ulla: Arah, Han'niel, and Rizi'a. 1

Hanoch 1. חֲנוֹךְ
Gen 25: 4 sons of Mid'ian were Ephah, Epher, Hanoch 1
46: 9 the sons of Reuben: Hanoch, Pallu, Hezron 1
Exd 6:14 sons of Reuben . . Hanoch, Pallu, Hezron 1
Num26: 5 of Hanoch, the family of the Ha'nochites; 1
1Ch 1:33 sons of Mid'ian: Ephah, Epher, Hanoch, Abida, 1
5: 3 sons of Reuben . . Hanoch, Pallu, Hezron 1

Hanochite 1. חֲנֹכִי
Num26: 5 of Hanoch, the family of the Ha'nochites; 1

Hanun 1. חָנוּן
2Sm 10: 1 and Hanun his son reigned in his stead. 1
2 I will deal loyally with Hanun the son of Nahash 1
3 But the princes of the Ammonites said to Hanun 1
4 Hanun took David's servants, and shaved off half 1
1Ch 19: 2 I will deal loyally with Hanun the son of Nahash 1
2 came to Hanun in the land of the Ammonites 1
3 the princes of the Ammonites said to Hanun 1
4 Hanun took David's servants, and shaved them 1
6 Hanun and the Ammonites sent 1,000 talents 1
Neh 3:13 Hanun and the inhabitants of Zano'ah repaired 1
30 Hanani'ah . . and Hanun the sixth son of Zalaph 1

Hapharaim 1. חֲפָרַיִם
Jos 19:19 Haph'ara-im, Shion, Ana'harath 1

Happizzez 1. הַפִּצֵּץ
1Ch 24:15 to Hezir, the eighteenth to Hap'pizzez 1

Har-heres 1. הַר חֶרֶס
Jdg 1:35 the Amorites persisted in dwelling in Har-heres 1

Hara 1. הָרָא
1Ch 5:26 brought them to . . Hara, and the river Gozan 1

Haradah 1. חֲרָדָה
Num33:24 out from Mount Shepher, and encamped at Hara'dah. 1
25 set out from Hara'dah, and encamped at Makhe'loth. 1

Haran 1. הָרָן 2. חָרָן 3. Χαρράν
Gen 11:26 Terah . . the father of Abram, Nahor, and Haran. 1
27 Terah was the father of Abram, Nahor, and Haran; 1
27 Nahor, and Haran; and Haran was the father of Lot. 1
28 Haran died before his father Terah in the land 1
29 Milcah, the daughter of Haran 1
31 Terah took Abram his son and Lot the son of Haran 1
31 but when they came to Haran, they settled there. 2
32 and Terah died in Haran. 2
12: 4 75 years old when he departed from Haran. 2
5 and the persons that they had gotten in Haran; 2
27:43 arise, flee to Laban my brother in Haran 2
28:10 Jacob left Beer-sheba, and went toward Haran. 2
29: 4 you come from?" They said, "We are from Haran. 2
2Kg 19:12 which my fathers destroyed, Gozan, Haran, Rezeph 2
1Ch 2:46 Ephah . . bore Haran, Moza, and Gazez; 2
46 and Haran was the father of Gazez. 2
23: 9 sons of Shim'e-i: Shelo'moth, Ha'zi-el, and Haran 1
Isa 37:12 which my fathers destroyed, Gozan, Haran, Rezeph 2
Ezk 27:23 Haran, Canneh, Eden, Asshur, and Chilmad traded 2
Act 7: 2 in Mesopota'mia, before he lived in Haran 3
4 Then he departed . . and lived in Haran 3

Hararite 1. הֲרָרִי
2Sm 23:11 next . . was Shammah, the son of Agee the Har'arite. 1
33 Shammah the Har'arite, Ahi'am the son of Sharar 1
33 Shammah . . Ahi'am the son of Sharar the Har'arite 1
1Ch 11:34 Jonathan the son of Shagee the Har'arite 1
35 Ahi'am the son of Sachar the Har'arite 1

Harbona 1. חַרְבוֹנָא 2. חַרְבוֹנָה
Est 1:10 he commanded Mehu'man, Biztha, Harbo'na, Bigtha 1
7: 9 Then said Harbo'na, one of the eunuchs 2

Hareph 1. חָרֵף
1Ch 2:51 and Hareph the father of Beth-gader. 1

Harhaiah 1. חַרְהֲיָה
Neh 3: 8 Uz'ziel the son of Harhai'ah, goldsmiths 1

Harhas 1. חַרְחַס
2Kg 22:14 wife of Shallum the son of Tikvah, son of Harhas 1

Harhur 1. חַרְחוּר
Ezr 2:51 the sons of Haku'pha, the sons of Harhur 1
Neh 7:53 Bakbuk, the sons of Haku'pha, the sons of Harhur 1

Harim 1. חָרִם 2. Χαρμη
1Ch 24: 8 the third to Harim, the fourth to Se-o'rim 1
Ezr 2:32 sons of Harim, 320. 1
39 sons of Harim, 1,017. 1
10:21 Of the sons of Harim: Ma-asei'ah, Eli'jah, Shemai'ah 1
31 Of the sons of Harim: Elie'zer, Isshi'jah, Malchi'jah 1
Neh 3:11 Malchi'jah the son of Harim and Hasshub 1
7:35 sons of Harim, 320. 1
42 sons of Harim, 1,017. 1
10: 5 Harim, Mer'emoth, Obadi'ah 1
27 Malluch, Harim, Ba'anah. 1
12:15 of Harim, Adna; of Merai'oth, Hel'kai; 1
1Es 5:25 The sons of Harim, 1,017. 2

Hariph 1. חָרִף
Neh 7:24 sons of Hariph, 112. 1
10:19 Hariph, An'athoth, Ne'bai 1

Harmon 1. הַרְמוֹן
Ams 4: 3 be cast forth into Harmon," says the LORD. 1

Harnepher 1. חַרְנֶפֶר
1Ch 7:36 sons of Zophah: Su'ah, Har'nepher, Shu'al, Beri, 1

Harod 1. חֲרֹד 2. חֲרֹדִי
Jdg 7: 1 early and encamped beside the spring of Harod; 1
2Sm 23:25 Shammah of Harod, Eli'ka of Harod 2
25 Shammah of Harod, Eli'ka of Harod 2
1Ch 11:27 Shammoth of Harod, Helez the Pel'onite •

Haroeh 1. הָרֹאֶה
1Ch 2:52 other sons: Haro'eh, half of the Menu'hoth. 1

Harosheth-hagoiim 1. חֲרֹשֶׁת הַגּוֹיִם
Jdg 4: 2 army was Sis'era, who dwelt in Haro'sheth-ha-goiim. 1
13 from Haro'sheth-ha-goiim to the river Kishon. 1
16 army to Haro'sheth-ha-goiim 1

Harsha 1. חַרְשָׁא
Ezr 2:52 the sons of Mehi'da, the sons of Harsha 1
Neh 7:54 Bazlith, the sons of Mehi'da, the sons of Harsha 1

Harum 1. הָרֻם
1Ch 4: 8 the families of Ahar'hel the son of Harum. 1

Harumaph 1. חֲרוּמַף
Neh 3:10 Jedai'ah the son of Haru'maph repaired opposite 1

Haruphite 1. חֲרוּפִי
1Ch 12: 5 Beali'ah, Shemari'ah, Shephati'ah the Har'uphite; 1

Haruz 1. חָרוּץ
2Kg 21:19 Meshul'lemeth the daughter of Haruz of Jotbah. 1

Hasadiah 1. חֲסַדְיָה 2. Ασαδιας
1Ch 3:20 Berechi'ah, Hasadi'ah, and Ju'shab-he'sed, five. 1
Bar 1: 1 son of Zedekiah, son of Hasadiah, son of Hilkiah 2

Hashabiah 1. חֲשַׁבְיָהוּ 2. Ασαβιας 3. Ασιβιας
1Ch 6:45 son of Hashabi'ah, son of Amazi'ah, son of Hilki'ah 1
9:14 Hasshub, son of Azri'kam, son of Hashabi'ah 1
25: 3 sons of Jedu'thun . . Shim'e-i, Hashabi'ah 1
19 twelfth to Hashabi'ah, his sons and his brethren 1
26:30 Of the He'bronites, Hashabi'ah and his brethren 1
27:17 for Levi, Hashabi'ah the son of Kem'uel; 1
2Ch 35: 9 Hashabi'ah and Je-i'el and Jo'zabad 1
Ezr 8:19 Hashabi'ah and . . Jeshai'ah of the sons of Merar'i 1
24 Sherebi'ah, Hashabi'ah, and ten of their kinsmen 1
10:25 of Parosh . . Elea'zar, Hashabi'ah, and Benai'ah. 3
Neh 3:17 next to him Hashabi'ah, ruler of half the district 1
10:11 Mica, Rehob, Hashabi'ah 1
11:15 son of Azri'kim, son of Hashabi'ah, son of Bunni; 1
22 son of Bani, son of Hashabi'ah, son of Mattani'ah 1
12:21 of Hilki'ah, Hashabi'ah; of Jedai'ah, Nethan'el 1
24 chiefs of the Levites: Hashabi'ah, Sherebi'ah 1
1Es 1: 9 Hashabiah and Ochiel and Joram 2
8:48 also Hashabiah and Annunus and Jeshaiah 2
54 leaders of the priests, Sherebiah and Hashabiah 2

Hashabnah 1. חֲשַׁבְנָה
Neh 10:25 Rehum, Hashab'nah, Ma-asei'ah 1

Hashabneiah 1. חֲשַׁבְנְיָה
Neh 3:10 Hattush the son of Hashabnei'ah repaired. 1
9: 5 Levites . . Bani, Hashabnei'ah, Sherebi'ah, Hodi'ah 1

Hashbaddanah 1. חַשְׁבַּדָּנָה
Neh 8: 4 Hashum, Hash-bad'danah . . on his left hand. 1

Hashem 1. הָשֵׁם
1Ch 11:34 Hashem the Gi'zonite 1

Hashmonah 1. חַשְׁמֹנָה
Num33:29 set out from Mithkah, and encamped at Hashmo'nah. 1
30 set out from Hashmo'nah, and encamped at Mose'roth 1

Hashubah 1. חֲשֻׁבָה
1Ch 3:20 Hashu'bah, Ohel, Berechi'ah, Hasadi'ah 1

Hashum 1. חָשֻׁם 2. Ασομ
Ezr 2:19 sons of Hashum, 223. 1
10:33 Of the sons of Hashum: Matte'nai, Mat'tattah, Zabad 1
Neh 7:22 sons of Hashum, 328. 1
8: 4 Hashum, Hash-bad'danah . . on his left hand. 1
10:18 Hodi'ah, Hashum, Be'zai 1
1Es 9:33 Of the sons of Hashum: Mattenai and Mattattah 2

Hasidean 1. Ασιδαιος
1Mc 2:42 there united with them a company of Hasideans 1
7:13 The Hasideans were first 1
2Mc 14: 6 Those of the Jews who are called Hasideans 1

Hasrah 1. חַסְרָה 2. Ασαρα
2Ch 34:22 Tokhath, son of Hasrah, keeper of the wardrobe 1
1Es 5:31 sons of Uzza, the sons of Paseah, the sons of Hasrah 2

Hassenaah 1. הַסְּנָאָה
Neh 3: 3 sons of Hassena'ah built the Fish Gate; 1

Hassenuah 1. הַסְּנוּאָה
1Ch 9: 7 Meshul'lam, son of Hodavi'ah, son of Hassenu'ah. 1
Neh 11: 9 Judah . . of Hassen'u-ah was second over the city. 1

Hasshub 1. חַשּׁוּב
1Ch 9:14 Of the Levites: Shemai'ah the son of Hasshub 1
Neh 3:11 Malchi'jah . . and Hasshub the son of Pa'hath-mo'ab 1
23 Hasshub repaired opposite their house. 1
10:23 Ho-she'a, Hanani'ah, Hasshub 1
11:15 Shemai'ah the son of Hasshub, son of Azri'kim 1

Hassophereth 1. הַסֹּפֶרֶת 2. Ασσαφιωθ
Ezr 2:55 sons of Solomon's servants . . sons of Hasso'phereth 1
1Es 5:33 the sons of Hassophereth, the sons of Peruda 2

Hasupha 1. חֲשׂוּפָא 2. Ασουφα
Ezr 2:43 temple servants: the . . sons of Hasu'pha 1
Neh 7:46 temple servants: the sons . . Hasu'pha 1
1Es 5:29 the sons of Hasupha, the sons of Tabbaoth 2

Hathach 1. הֲתָךְ
Est 4: 5 Esther called for Hathach . . and ordered him 1
6 Hathach went out to Mor'decai in the open square 1
9 Hathach went and told Esther what Mor'decai had 1
10 Esther spoke to Hathach and gave him a message 1

Hathath 1.חֲתַת
1Ch 4:13 and the sons of Oth'ni-el: Hathath and Meo'nothai. 1

Hatipha 1.חֲטִיפָא 2.Ατιφα
Ezr 2:54 sons of Nezi'ah, and the sons of Hati'pha. 1
Neh 7:56 sons of Nezi'ah, the sons of Hati'pha. 1
1Es 5:32 the sons of Neziah, the sons of Hatipha. 2

Hatita 1.חֲטִיטָא 2.Ατητα
Ezr 2:42 sons of the gatekeepers: the . . sons of Hati'ta 1
Neh 7:45 gatekeepers . . sons of Hati'ta 1
1Es 5:28 the sons of Akkub, the sons of Hatita 2

Hattil 1.חַטִּיל 2.Αγια
Ezr 2:57 sons of Shephati'ah, the sons of Hattil 1
Neh 7:59 sons of Shephati'ah, the sons of Hattil 1
1Es 5:34 the sons of Hattil 2

Hattush 1.חַטּוּשׁ 2.Αττους
1Ch 3:22 And the sons of Shemai'ah: Hattush, Igal, Bari'ah 1
Ezr 8: 2 Of the sons of David, Hattush 1
Neh 3:10 next to him Hattush the son of Hashabnei'ah 1
10: 4 Hattush, Shebani'ah, Malluch 1
12: 2 Amari'ah, Malluch, Hattush 1
1Es 8:29 Of the sons of David, Hattush 2

Hauran 1.חַוְרָן
Ezk 47:16 Hazer-hatticon, which is on the border of Hauran. 1
18 from Hazar-e'non between Hauran and Damascus; 1

Havilah 1.חֲוִילָה
Gen 2:11 the whole land of Havilah, where there is gold; 1
10: 7 sons of Cush: Seba, Hav'ilah, Sabtah, Ra'amah 1
29 Ophir, Hav'ilah, and Jobab; 1
25:18 They dwelt from Hav'ilah to Shur 1
1Sm 15: 7 Saul defeated . . from Hav'ilah as far as Shur 1
1Ch 1: 9 sons of Cush: Seba, Hav'ilah, Sabta, Ra'ama 1
23 Ophir, Hav'ilah, and Jobab . . the sons of Joktan 1

Havvoth-jair 1.חַוֹּת יָאִיר
Num32:41 their villages, and called them Hav'voth-ja'ir. 1
Deu 3:14 villages after his own name, Hav'voth-ja'ir 1
Jdg 10: 4 30 cities, called Hav'voth-ja'ir to this day 1
1Ch 2:23 Havvoth-ja'ir, Kenath and its villages 1

Hazael 1.חֲזָאֵל 2.חֲזָהאֵל
1Kg 19:15 you shall anoint Haz'ael to be king over Syria; 1
17 him who escapes from . . Haz'ael shall Jehu slay; 1
2Kg 8: 8 the king said to Haz'ael, "Take a present with you 2
9 So Haz'ael went to meet him, and took a present 1
12 Haz'ael said, "Why does my lord weep? 1
13 Haz'ael said, "What is your servant, who is but a dog 2
15 And Haz'ael became king in his stead. 2
28 He went with Joram . . to make war against Haz'ael 2
29 when he fought against Haz'ael king of Syria. 2
9:14 been on guard at Ramoth-gilead against Haz'ael 1
15 when he fought with Haz'ael king of Syria.) 1
10:32 Haz'ael defeated them throughout . . Israel 1
12:17 Haz'ael . . went up and fought against Gath 1
17 But when Haz'ael set his face to go up 1
18 took . . and sent these to Haz'ael king of Syria. 1
18 Then Haz'ael went away from Jerusalem. •
13: 3 he gave them continually into the hand of Haz'ael 1
3 and into the hand of Ben-ha'dad the son of Haz'ael. 1
22 Now Haz'ael king of Syria oppressed Israel 1
24 Haz'ael king of Syria died . . his son became king 1
25 took again from Ben-ha'dad the son of Haz'ael 1
2Ch 22: 5 went with Jeho'ram . . to make war against Haz'ael 1
6 when he fought against Haz'ael king of Syria. 2
Ams 1: 4 I will send a fire upon the house of Haz'ael 1

Hazaiah 1.חֲזָיָה
Neh 11: 5 Col-ho'zeh, son of Hazai'ah, son of Adai'ah 1

Hazar-addar 1.חֲצַר אַדָּר
Num34: 4 Ka'desh-bar'nea; then it shall go on to Ha'zar-ad'dar 1

Hazar-enan 1.חֲצַר עֵינָן
Num34: 9 Ziphron, and its end shall be at Ha'zar-e'nan; 1
10 eastern boundary from Ha'zar-e'nan to Shepham; 1

Hazar-enon 1.חֲצַר עֵינוֹן 2.חֲצַר עֵינָן
Ezk 47:17 the boundary shall run from the sea to Hazar-e'non 1
18 the boundary shall run from Hazar-e'non •
48: 1 to the entrance of Hamath, as far as Hazar-e'non 2

Hazar-gaddah 1.חֲצַר גַּדָּה
Jos 15:27 Ha'zar-gad'dah, Heshmon, Beth-pel'et 1

Hazar-shual 1.חֲצַר שׁוּעָל
Jos 15:28 Hazar-shu'al, Beer-sheba, Biziothi'ah 1
19: 3 Hazar-shu'al, Balah, Ezem 1
1Ch 4:28 They dwelt in Beer-sheba, Mola'dah, Ha'zar-shu'al 1
Neh 11:27 in Ha'zar-shu'al, in Beer-sheba and its villages 1

Hazar-susah 1.חֲצַר סוּסָה
Jos 19: 5 Ziklag, Beth-mar'caboth, Ha'zar-su'sah 1

Hazar-susim 1.חֲצַר סוּסִים
1Ch 4:31 Ha'zar-su'sim, Beth-biri, and Sha-ara'im. 1

Hazarmaveth 1.חֲצַרְמָוֶת
Gen 10:26 father of Almo'dad, Sheleph, Hazarma'veth, Jerah 1
1Ch 1:20 father of Almo'dad, Sheleph, Hazarma'veth, Jerah 1

Hazazon-tamar 1.חַצְצוֹן תָּמָר
Gen 14: 7 also the Amorites who dwelt in Haz'azon-ta'mar. 1
2Ch 20: 2 they are in Haz'azon-ta'mar" (that is, En-ge'di). 1

Hazer-hatticon 1.חָצֵר הַתִּיכוֹן
Ezk 47:16 Damascus and Hamath), as far as Hazer-hatticon 1

Hazeroth 1.חֲצֵרוֹת
Num11:35 From . . the people journeyed to Haze'roth; 1
35 people . . remained at Haze'roth. 1
12:16 After that the people set out from Haze'roth 1
33:17 Kib'roth-hatta'avah, and encamped at Haze'roth. 1
18 set out from Haze'roth, and encamped at Rithmah. 1
Deu 1: 1 Paran and Tophel, Laban, Haze'roth, and Di'zahab. 1

Haziel 1.חֲזִיאֵל
1Ch 23: 9 sons of Shim'e-i: Shelo'moth, Ha'zi-el, and Haran 1

Hazo 1.חֲזוֹ
Gen 22:22 Chesed, Hazo, Pildash, Jidlaph, and Bethu'el. 1

Hazor 1.חָצוֹר 2.Ασωρ
Jos 11: 1 When Jabin king of Hazor heard of this, he sent 1
10 Joshua turned back at that time, and took Hazor 1
10 for Hazor . . was the head of all those kingdoms. 1
11 put to the sword . . and he burned Hazor with fire. 1
13 none . . did Israel burn, except Hazor only; 1
12:19 the king of Madon, one; the king of Hazor, one; 1
15:23 Kedesh, Hazor, Ithnan 1
25 Ker'i-oth-hezron (that is, Hazor) 1
19:36 Ad'amah, Ramah, Hazor 1
Jdg 4: 2 hand of Jabin king of Canaan, who reigned in Hazor; 1
17 there was peace between Jabin the king of Hazor 1
1Sm 12: 9 commander of the army of Jabin king of Hazor 1
1Kg 9:15 build . . the wall of Jerusalem and Hazor 1
2Kg 15:29 A'bel-beth-ma'acah, Jan-o'ah, Kedesh, Hazor, Gilead 1
Neh 11:33 Hazor, Ramah, Git'taim 1
Jer 49:28 Concerning Kedar and the kingdoms of Hazor 1
30 dwell in the depths, O inhabitants of Hazor! 1
33 Hazor shall become a haunt of jackals 1
1Mc 11:67 they marched to the plain of Hazor 2

Hazor-hadattah 1.חָצוֹר חֲדַתָּה
Jos 15:25 Ha'zor-hadat'tah, Ker'i-oth-hezron 1

Hazzelelponi 1.הַצְלֶלְפּוֹנִי
1Ch 4: 3 and the name of their sister was Hazzelelpo'ni. 1

Heber 1.חֶבֶר
Gen 46:17 And the sons of Beri'ah: Heber and Mal'chi-el 1
Num26:45 of Heber, the family of the He'berites; 1
Jdg 4:11 Heber the Ken'ite had separated from the Ken'ites 1
17 to the tent of Ja'el, the wife of Heber the Ken'ite; 1
17 king of Hazor and the house of Heber the Ken'ite. 1
21 Ja'el the wife of Heber took a tent peg 1
5:24 blessed . . be Ja'el, the wife of Heber the Ken'ite 1
1Ch 4:18 his Jewish wife bore . . Heber the father of Soco 1
7:31 The sons of Beri'ah: Heber and Mal'chi-el 1
32 Heber was the father of Japhlet, Shomer, Hotham 1
8:17 Zebadi'ah, Meshul'lam, Hizki, Heber 1

Heberite 1.חֶבְרִי
Num26:45 of Heber, the family of the He'berites; 1

Hebrew 1.אִישׁ עִבְרִי 2.עִבְרִי 3.עִבְרִי עִבְרִיָּה
4.῾Εβραῖος 5.῾Εβραΐς 6.῾Εβραϊστί
Gen 14:13 one . . came, and told Abram the Hebrew 2
39:14 See, he has brought among us a Hebrew to insult us; 2
17 The Hebrew servant, whom you have brought 2
40:15 I was indeed stolen out of the land of the Hebrews; 2
41:12 A young Hebrew was there with us, a servant 2
43:32 Egyptians might not eat bread with the Hebrews 2
Exd 1:15 the king of Egypt said to the Hebrew midwives 2
22 Every son that is born to the Hebrews 4
2: 6 This is one of the Hebrews' children. 2
11 an Egyptian beating a Hebrew, one of his people. 1
13 behold, two Hebrews were struggling together; 1
3:18 The LORD, the God of the Hebrews, has met with us; 2
5: 3 they said, "The God of the Hebrews has met with us; 2
7:16 The LORD, the God of the Hebrews, sent me to you 2
9: 1 Thus says the LORD, the God of the Hebrews 2
13 Thus says the LORD, the God of the Hebrews 2
10: 3 says the LORD, the God of the Hebrews, 'How long 2
21: 2 When you buy a Hebrew slave, he shall serve six 2
1Sm 4: 6 this great shouting in the camp of the Hebrews 2
9 lest you become slaves to the Hebrews 2
13: 3 blew the trumpet . . saying, "Let the Hebrews hear. 2
19 Lest the Hebrews make . . swords or spears"; 2
14:11 Look, Hebrews are coming out of the holes 2
21 the Hebrews who had been with the Philistines 2
29: 3 What are these Hebrews doing here? 2
Jer 34: 9 that every one should set free his Hebrew slaves 3
14 each of you must set free the fellow Hebrew 2
Jon 1: 9 And he said to them, "I am a Hebrew; 2
Joh 5: 2 a pool, in Hebrew called Beth-za'tha 6
19:13 and in Hebrew, Gab'batha. 6
17 the place . . which is called in Hebrew Gol'gotha. 6
20 it was written in Hebrew, in Latin, and in Greek. 6
20:16 She turned and said to him in Hebrew, "Rab-bo'ni! 6
Act 6: 1 the Hellenists murmured against the Hebrews 4
21:40 he spoke to them in the Hebrew language, saying 5
22: 2 he addressed them in the Hebrew language 5
26:14 heard a voice saying to me in the Hebrew language 5
2Co 11:22 Are they Hebrews? So am I 4
Php 3: 5 a Hebrew born of Hebrews; as to the law a Pharisee 4
5 a Hebrew born of Hebrews; as to the law a Pharisee 4
Rev 9:11 his name in Hebrew is Abad'don 6
16:16 the place which is called in Hebrew Armaged'don. 6
Jdt 10:12 She replied, "I am a daughter of the Hebrews 4
12:11 Go now and persuade the Hebrew woman 4
14:18 One Hebrew woman has brought disgrace 4
Sir 0: 2 what was originally expressed in Hebrew 6
2Mc 7:31 contrived all sorts of evil against the Hebrews 4
11:13 realized that the Hebrews were invincible 4
15:37 the city has been in the possession of the Hebrews 4
4Mc 4:11 with tears besought the Hebrews to pray for him 4
5: 2 to seize each and every Hebrew 4
8: 2 others of the Hebrew captives be brought 4
9: 6 if the aged men of the Hebrews . . lived piously 4
18 sons of the Hebrews alone are invincible 4
12: 7 exhorted him in the Hebrew language 5
16:15 said to your sons in the Hebrew language 5
17: 9 wished to destroy the way of life of the Hebrews. 4

Hebrew man 1.עִבְרִי
Deu 15:12 brother, a Hebrew man, or a Hebrew woman, is sold 1

Hebrew woman 1.עִבְרִי
Exd 1:16 When you serve as midwife to the Hebrew women 1
19 the Hebrew women are not like the Egyptian women; 1
2: 7 call . . a nurse from the Hebrew women 1
Deu 15:12 brother, a Hebrew man, or a Hebrew woman, is sold 1

Hebron 1.חֶבְרוֹן 2.Χεβρων
Gen 13:18 the oaks of Mamre, which are at Hebron; 1
23: 2 Sarah died at Kir'iath-ar'ba (that is, Hebron) 1
19 of Mamre (that is, Hebron) in the land of Canaan. 1
35:27 Mamre, or Kir'iath-ar'ba (that is, Hebron) 1
37:14 from the valley of Hebron, and he came to Shechem. 1
Exd 6:18 sons of Kohath: Amram, Izhar, Hebron, and Uz'ziel 1
Num 3:19 sons of Kohath . . Amram, Izhar, Hebron 1
13:22 They went up into the Negeb, and came to Hebron; 1
22 (Hebron was built seven years before Zo'an 1
Jos 10: 3 Ado'ni-ze'dek . . sent to Hoham king of Hebron 1
5 the king of Jerusalem, the king of Hebron, the king 1
23 king of Jerusalem, the king of Hebron 1
36 Then Joshua went up . . from Eglon to Hebron; 1
39 as he had done to Hebron and to Libnah and its king 1
11:21 from the hill country, from Hebron, from Debir 1
12:10 king of Jerusalem, one; the king of Hebron, one; 1
14:13 Joshua blessed him; and he gave Hebron to Caleb 1
14 Hebron became the inheritance of Caleb 1
15 Now the name of Hebron formerly was Kir'iath-ar'ba; 1
15:13 he gave to Caleb . . Kir'iath-ar'ba, that is, Hebron 1
54 Humtah, Kir'iath-ar'ba (that is, Hebron), and Zi'or 1
20: 7 set apart . . and Kir'iath-ar'ba (that is, Hebron) 1
21:11 They gave them Kir'iath-ar'ba . . that is Hebron 1
13 to the descendants of Aaron . . they gave Hebron 1
Jdg 1:10 went against the Canaanites who dwelt in Hebron 1
10 now the name of Hebron was formerly Kir'iath-ar'ba 1
20 Hebron was given to Caleb, as Moses had said; 1
16: 3 to the top of the hill that is before Hebron. 1
1Sm 30:31 for those . . in Hebron, for all the places 1
2Sm 2: 1 To which shall I go up?" And he said, "To Hebron. 1
3 and they dwelt in the towns of Hebron. 1
11 David was king in Hebron over the house of Judah 1
32 all night, and the day broke upon them at Hebron. 1
3: 2 And sons were born to David at Hebron 1
5 These were born to David in Hebron. 1
12 Abner sent messengers to David at Hebron, saying 2
19 then Abner went to tell David at Hebron 1
20 Abner came with twenty men to David at Hebron 1
22 But Abner was not with David at Hebron 1
27 when Abner returned to Hebron, Jo'ab took him 1
32 They buried Abner at Hebron; 1
4: 1 Saul's son . . heard that Abner had died at Hebron 1
8 and brought the head . . to David at Hebron. 1
12 and hanged them beside the pool at Hebron. 1
12 and buried it in the tomb of Abner at Hebron. 1
5: 1 the tribes of Israel came to David at Hebron 1
3 the elders . . came to the king at Hebron; 1
3 King David made a covenant with them at Hebron 1
5 At Hebron he reigned . . seven years 1
13 David took more . . after he came from Hebron; 1
15: 7 Pray let me go and pay my vow . . in Hebron. 1
9 Go in peace." So he arose, and went to Hebron. 1
10 As soon as . . then say, 'Ab'salom is king at Hebron!' 1
1Kg 2:11 he reigned seven years in Hebron 1
1Ch 2:42 The sons of Mare'shah: Hebron. 1
43 sons of Hebron: Korah, Tap'puah, Rekem, and Shema. 1

3: 1 the sons of David that were born to him in Hebron 1
4 born to him in Hebron, where he reigned 1
6: 2 sons of Kohath: Amram, Izhar, Hebron, and Uz'ziel. 1
18 sons of Kohath: Amram, Izhar, Hebron, and Uz'ziel. 1
55 to them they gave Hebron in the land of Judah 1
57 the cities of refuge: Hebron, Libnah 1
11: 1 all Israel gathered together to David at Hebron 1
3 the elders of Israel came to the king at Hebron; 1
3 a covenant with them at Hebron before the LORD 1
12:23 armed troops, who came to David in Hebron 1
38 All these . . came to Hebron with full intent 1
15: 9 of the sons of Hebron, Eli'el the chief 1
23:12 sons of Kohath: Amram, Izhar, Hebron, and Uz'ziel 1
19 sons of Hebron: Jeri'ah the chief, Amari'ah 1
24:23 sons of Hebron: Jeri'ah the chief, Amari'ah •
29:27 reigned seven years in Hebron, and 33 in Jerusalem 1
2Ch 11:10 Zorah, Ai'jalon, and Hebron, fortified cities 1
1Mc 5:65 He struck Hebron and its villages 2

Hebronite 1. חֶבְרוֹנִי
Num 3:27 Of Kohath . . the family of the He'bronites 1
26:58 of Levi . . the family of the He'bronites 1
1Ch 26:23 Of the Am'ramites, the Iz'harites, the He'bronites 1
30 Of the He'bronites, Hashabi'ah and his brethren 1
31 Of the He'bronites, Jeri'jah was chief 1
31 Jeri'jah was chief of the He'bronites 1

Hegai 1. הֵגָא
Est 2: 3 Hegai the king's eunuch . . in charge of the women; 1
8 maidens were gathered . . in custody of Hegai 1
8 Esther also was . . and put in custody of Hegai 1
15 asked for nothing except what Hegai . . advised. 1

Hegemonides 1. Ηεγεμονιδης
2Mc 13:24 left Hegemonides as governor 1

Heglam 1. הֶגְלָם
1Ch 8: 7 Gera, that is, Heglam . . father of Uzza and Ahi'hud. 1

Helah 1. חֶלְאָה
1Ch 4: 5 Asshur . . had two wives, Helah and Na'arah; 1
7 The sons of Helah: Zereth, Izhar, and Ethnan. 1

Helam 1. חֵילָם
2Sm 10:16 they came to Helam, with Shobach . . at their head. 1
17 and crossed the Jordan, and came to Helam. 1

Helbah 1. חֶלְבָּה
Jdg 1:31 inhabitants . . of Achzib, or of Helbah 1

Helbon 1. חֶלְבּוֹן
Ezk 27:18 great wealth . . wine of Helbon, and white wool 1

Heldai 1. חֶלְדַּי
1Ch 27:15 Twelfth . . was Heldai the Netoph'athite 1
Zec 6:10 Take from the exiles Heldai, Tobi'jah, and Jedai'ah 1
14 as a reminder to Heldai, Tobi'jah, Jedai'ah •

Heleb 1. חֵלֶב
2Sm 23:29 Heleb the son of Ba'anah of Netoph'ah 1

Helech 1. חֵילֵךְ
Ezk 27:11 The men of Arvad and Helech were upon your walls 1

Heled 1. חֵלֶד
1Ch 11:30 Heled the son of Ba'anah of Netoph'ah 1

Helek 1. בְּנֵי חֵלֶק 2. חֵלֶק
Num26:30 of Helek, the family of the He'lekites; 2
Jos 17: 2 their families Abi-e'zer, Helek, As'ri-el 1

Helekite 1. חֶלְקִי
Num26:30 of Helek, the family of the He'lekites; 1

Helem 1. חֵלֶם
1Ch 7:35 sons of Helem . . Zophah, Imna, Shelesh, and Amal. 1

Heleph 1. חֵלֶף
Jos 19:33 its boundary ran from Heleph, from the oak 1

Helez 1. חֶלֶץ
2Sm 23:26 Helez the Paltite, Ira the son of Ikkesh of Teko'a 1
1Ch 2:39 Azari'ah was the father of Helez 1
39 the father of Helez, and Helez of Ele-a'sah. 1
11:27 Shammoth of Harod, Helez the Pel'onite 1
27:10 Seventh . . was Helez the Pel'onite 1

Heli 1. Ἡλί
Lke 3:23 Joseph, the son of Heli 1

Heliodorus 1. Ηλιοδωρος
2Mc 3: 7 The king chose Heliodorus 1
8 Heliodorus at once set out on his journey 1
13 Heliodorus . . said 1
23 Heliodorus went on with what had been decided. 1
25 it rushed furiously at Heliodorus 1
31 Quickly some of Heliodorus' friends asked Onias 1
32 some foul play . . with regard to Heliodorus 1
33 the same young men appeared again to Heliodorus 1
35 Then Heliodorus offered sacrifice to the Lord 1
37 When the king asked Heliodorus . . he replied 1
40 Heliodorus and the protection of the treasury. 1
4: 1 saying that it was he who had incited Heliodorus 1
5:18 just as Heliodorus was 1

Heliopolis 1. בֵּית שֶׁמֶשׁ
Jer 43:13 He shall break the obelisks of Heliop'olis 1

Helkai 1. חֶלְקָי
Neh 12:15 of Harim, Adna; of Merai'oth, Hel'kai; 1

Helkath 1. חֶלְקַת
Jos 19:25 Its territory included Helkath, Hali, Beten 1
21:31 Helkath with its pasture lands, and Rehob 1

Helkath-hazzurim 1. חֶלְקַת הַצֻּרִים
2Sm 2:16 that place was called Hel'kath-hazzu'rim 1

Hellenist 1. Ἑλληνιστής
Act 6: 1 the Hellenists murmured against the Hebrews 1
9:29 he spoke and disputed against the Hellenists; 1

Hellenization 1. Ελληνισμος
2Mc 4:13 There was such an extreme of Hellenization 1

Helon 1. חֵלֹן
Num 1: 9 from Zeb'ulun, Eli'ab the son of Helon; 1
2: 7 the leader . . being Eli'ab the son of Helon 1
7:24 Eli'ab the son of Helon, the leader of the men 1
29 This was the offering of Eli'ab the son of Helon. 1
10:16 over the host . . was Eli'ab the son of Helon. 1

Heman 1. הֵימָם 2. הֵימָן
Gen 36:22 The sons of Lotan were Hori and Heman; 1
1Kg 4:31 wiser than Ethan . . and Heman, Calcol, and Darda 2
1Ch 2: 6 sons of Zerah: Zimri, Ethan, Heman, Calcol, and Dara 2
6:33 Of the sons of the Ko'hathites: Heman the singer 2
15:17 the Levites appointed Heman the son of Jo'el; 2
19 The singers, Heman, Asaph, and Ethan 2
16:41 Heman and Jedu'thun, and the rest of those chosen 2
42 Heman and Jedu'thun had trumpets and cymbals 2
25: 1 set apart for the service . . and of Heman 2
4 Of Heman, the sons of Heman: Bukki'ah, Mattani'ah 2
4 sons of Heman: Bukki'ah, Mattani'ah, Uz'ziel, 2
5 All these were the sons of Heman the king's seer 2
5 God had given Heman fourteen sons 2
6 and Heman were under the order of the king. 2
2Ch 5:12 Levitical singers, Asaph, Heman, and Jedu'thun 2
29:14 of the sons of Heman, Jehu'el and Shim'e-i; 2
35:15 command of David, and Asaph, and Heman 2
Ps 88: 0 Maskil of Heman the Ezrahite. 2

Hemdan 1. חֶמְדָּן
Gen 36:26 These are the sons of Dishon: Hemdan, Eshban 1

Hena 1. הֵנַע
2Kg 18:34 Where are the gods of Sepharva'im, Hena, and Ivvah? 1
19:13 Sepharva'im, the king of Hena, or the king of Ivvah?' 1
Isa 37:13 the king of Hena, or the king of Ivvah?' 1

Henadad 1. חֵנָדָד
Ezr 3: 9 along with the sons of Hen'adad and the Levites 1
Neh 3:18 brethren repaired: Bav'vai the son of Hen'adad 1
24 After him Bin'nui the son of Hen'adad repaired 1
10: 9 Levites: Jeshua . . Bin'nui of the sons of Hen'adad 1

Hepher 1. בְּנֵי חֵפֶר 2. חֵפֶר
Num26:32 of Hepher, the family of the He'pherites. 2
33 Now Zeloph'ehad the son of Hepher had no sons 2
27: 1 daughters of Zeloph'ehad the son of Hepher 2
Jos 12:17 the king of Tap'puah, one; the king of Hepher, one; 2
17: 2 Helek, As'ri-el, Shechem, Hepher, and Shemi'da 1
3 Zeloph'ehad the son of Hepher, son of Gilead 2
1Kg 4:10 (to him belonged Socoh and all the land of Hepher); 2
1Ch 4: 6 Na'arah bore him Ahuz'zam, Hepher, Te'meni 2
11:36 Hepher the Meche'rathite, Ahi'jah the Pel'onite 2

Hepherite 1. חֶפְרִי
Num26:32 of Hepher, the family of the He'pherites. 1

Hephzi-bah 1. חֶפְצִי בָהּ
2Kg 21: 1 His mother's name was Heph'zibah. 1

Hercules 1. Ηρακλης
2Mc 4:19 for the sacrifice to Hercules 1
20 intended . . for the sacrifice to Hercules 1

Heres 1. חֶרֶס
Jdg 8:13 returned from the battle by the ascent of Heres. 1

Heresh 1. חֶרֶשׁ
1Ch 9:15 Bakbak'kar, Heresh, Galal, and Mattani'ah 1

Hereth 1. חֶרֶת
1Sm 22: 5 David . . went into the forest of Hereth. 1

Hermas 1. Ἑρμᾶς
Rom16:14 Greet . . Hermes, Pat'robas, Hermas 1

Hermes 1. Ἑρμῆς
Act 14:12 Paul . . they called Hermes. 1
Rom16:14 Greet Asyn'critus, Phlegon, Hermes, Pat'robas 1

Hermogenes 1. Ἑρμογένης
2Ti 1:15 among them Phy'gelus and Hermog'enes. 1

Hermon 1. חֶרְמוֹן 2. חֶרְמוֹנִים 3. Αερμων 4. Ερμων
Deu 3: 8 from the valley of the Arnon to Mount Hermon 1
9 (the Sido'nians call Hermon Si'rion, while 1
4:48 as far as Mount Si'rion (that is, Hermon) 1
Jos 11: 3 the Hivites under Hermon in the land of Mizpah. 1
17 in the valley of Lebanon below Mount Hermon. 1
12: 1 from the valley of the Arnon to Mount Hermon 1
5 and ruled over Mount Hermon and Sal'ecah 1
13: 5 from Ba'al-gad below Mount Hermon to the entrance 1
11 and all Mount Hermon, and all Bashan to Sal'ecah; 1
1Ch 5:23 very numerous from Bashan to . . Mount Hermon. 1
Ps 42: 6 land of Jordan and of Hermon, from Mount Mizar. 2
89:12 Tabor and Hermon joyously praise thy name. 1
133: 3 It is like the dew of Hermon 1
Sng 4: 8 Depart from . . from the peak of Senir and Hermon 1
Sir 24:13 like a cypress on the heights of Hermon. 3
3Mc 5: 1 he summoned Hermon, keeper of the elephants 4
4 Hermon, keeper of the elephants 4
10 Hermon, however . . presented himself 4
18 the king summoned Hermon 4
23 Hermon . . began to move them along in . . colonnade 4
26 Hermon arrived and invited him to come out 4
29 Hermon and all the king's friends pointed out 4
33 Hermon suffered an unexpected . . threat 4
37 After summoning Hermon 4

Herod 1. Ἡρῴδης
Mat 2: 1 Bethlehem of Judea in the days of Herod the king 1
3 When Herod the king heard this, he was troubled 1
7 Then Herod summoned the wise men secretly 1
12 being warned in a dream not to return to Herod 1
13 Herod is about to search for the child, to destroy 1
15 remained there until the death of Herod. 1
16 Then Herod, when he saw that he had been tricked 1
19 when Herod died, behold, an angel of the Lord 1
22 in place of his father Herod, he was afraid to go 1
14: 1 At that time Herod the tetrarch heard 1
3 For Herod had seized John and bound him 1
6 when Herod's birthday came 1
6 Hero'di-as danced . . and pleased Herod 1
Mrk 6:14 King Herod heard of it; 1
16 when Herod heard of it he said 1
17 For Herod had sent and seized John 1
18 For John said to Herod, "It is not lawful for you 1
20 for Herod feared John . . and kept him safe 1
21 when Herod on his birthday gave a banquet 1
22 she pleased Herod and his guests 1
8:15 the leaven of Herod. 1
Lke 1: 5 In the days of Herod, king of Judea 1
3: 1 Herod being tetrarch of Galilee 1
19 Herod the tetrarch, who had been reproved by him 1
19 for all the evil things that Herod had done 1
8: 3 Joan'na, the wife of Chuza, Herod's steward 1
9: 7 Now Herod the tetrarch heard of all that was done 1
9 Herod said, "John I beheaded 1
13:31 Get away from here, for Herod wants to kill you. 1
23: 7 he belonged to Herod's jurisdiction 1
7 he sent him over to Herod 1
8 When Herod saw Jesus, he was very glad 1
11 Herod with his soldiers 1
12 Herod and Pilate became friends with each other 1
15 neither did Herod, for he sent him back to us. 1
Act 4:27 both Herod and Pontius Pilate, with the Gentiles 1
12: 1 Herod the king laid violent hands upon some 1
6 when Herod was about to bring him out 1
11 and rescued me from the hand of Herod 1
19 Herod had sought for him and could not find him 1
20 Herod was angry with the people of Tyre and Sidon; •
21 On an appointed day Herod put on his royal robes 1
13: 1 a member of the court of Herod the tetrarch 1
23:35 to be guarded in Herod's praetorium. 1

Herodian 1. Ἡρῳδιανοί
Mat 22:16 disciples to him, along with the Hero'dians 1
Mrk 3: 6 held counsel with the Hero'di-ans against him 1
12:13 some of the Pharisees and some of the Hero'di-ans 1

Herodias 1. Ἡρῳδιάς
Mat 14: 3 for the sake of Hero'di-as 1
6 the daughter of Hero'di-as danced 1
Mrk 6:17 bound him in prison for the sake of Hero'di-as 1
19 Hero'di-as had a grudge against him 1
22 For when Hero'di-as' daughter came in and danced 1
Lke 3:19 who had been reproved by him for Hero'di-as 1

Herodion 1. Ἡρῳδίων
Rom16:11 Greet my kinsman Hero'dion. 1

Heshbon 1. חֶשְׁבּוֹן 2. Εσεβωνιτης
Num21:25 settled in . . Heshbon, and in all its villages. 1

26 For Heshbon was the city of Sihon the king 1
27 Come to Heshbon, let it be built, let the city 1
28 For fire went forth from Heshbon 1
30 posterity perished from Heshbon, as far as Dibon 1
34 as you did to Sihon . . who dwelt at Heshbon. 1
32: 3 Nimrah, Heshbon, Elea'leh, Sebam, Nebo, and Be'on 1
37 sons of Reuben built Heshbon, Elea'leh, Kiriatha'im 1
Deu 1: 4 king of the Amorites, who lived in Heshbon 1
2:24 Sihon the Amorite, king of Heshbon, and his land; 1
26 sent messengers . . to Sihon the king of Heshbon 1
30 Sihon the king of Heshbon would not let us pass 1
3: 2 king of the Amorites, who dwelt at Heshbon.' 1
6 as we did to Sihon the king of Heshbon, destroying 1
4:46 king of the Amorites, who lived at Heshbon 1
29: 7 Sihon the king of Heshbon and Og the king 1
Jos 9:10 to the two kings . . Sihon the king of Heshbon 1
12: 2 Sihon king of the Amorites who dwelt at Heshbon 1
5 Gilead to the boundary of Sihon king of Heshbon. 1
13:10 Sihon . . of the Amorites, who reigned in Heshbon 1
17 territory was . . with Heshbon, and all its cities 1
21 Sihon . . of the Amorites, who reigned in Heshbon 1
26 and from Heshbon to Ra'math-miz'peh and Bet'onim 1
27 the rest of the kingdom of Sihon king of Heshbon 1
21:39 Heshbon with its pasture lands, Jazer with its 1
Jdg 11:19 Sihon king of the Amorites, king of Heshbon 1
26 While Israel dwelt in Heshbon and its villages 1
1Ch 6:81 Heshbon with its pasture lands, and Jazer 1
Neh 9:22 possession of the land of Sihon king of Heshbon 1
Sng 7: 4 Your eyes are pools in Heshbon, by the gate 1
Isa 15: 4 Heshbon and Ele-a'leh cry out 1
16: 8 For the fields of Heshbon languish 1
9 I drench you with my tears, O Heshbon and Ele-a'leh; 1
Jer 48: 2 In Heshbon they planned evil against her 1
34 Heshbon and Ele-a'leh cry out; 1
45 In the shadow of Heshbon fugitives stop 1
45 for a fire has gone forth from Heshbon 1
49: 3 Wail, O Heshbon, for Ai is laid waste! 1
Jdt 5:15 their might destroyed all the inhabitants of Heshbon 2

Heshmon 1. חֶשְׁמוֹן
Jos 15:27 Ha'zar-gad'dah, Heshmon, Beth-pel'et 1

Heth 1. חֵת
Gen 10:15 father of Sidon his first-born, and Heth 1
1Ch 1:13 Canaan was the father of Sidon . . and Heth 1

Hethlon 1. חֶתְלֹן
Ezk 47:15 by way of Hethlon to the entrance of Hamath 1
48: 1 from the sea by way of Hethlon to the entrance 1

Hezekiah 1. חִזְקִיָּהוּ חִזְקִיָּה 2. יְחִזְקִיָּהוּ 3. Ἐζεκίας
4. Ezechias
2Kg 16:20 Ahaz slept . . and Hezeki'ah his son reigned 1
18: 1 Hezeki'ah the son of Ahaz . . began to reign. 1
9 In the fourth year of King Hezeki'ah 1
10 In the sixth year of Hezeki'ah . . Sama'ria was 1
13 In the fourteenth year of King Hezeki'ah 1
14 Hezeki'ah . . to the king of Assyria at Lachish 1
14 the king . . required of Hezeki'ah king of Judah 1
15 Hezeki'ah gave him all the silver that was found 1
16 Hezeki'ah stripped the gold from the doors 1
16 the doorposts which Hezeki'ah . . had overlaid 1
17 Assyria sent . . from Lachish to King Hezeki'ah 1
19 the Rab'shakeh said to them, "Say to Hezeki'ah, 'Thus 1
22 high places and altars Hezeki'ah has removed 1
29 Do not let Hezeki'ah deceive you, for he will not be 1
30 Do not let Hezeki'ah make you to rely on the LORD 1
31 Do not listen to Hezeki'ah; for thus says the king 1
32 do not listen to Hezeki'ah when he misleads you 1
37 came to Hezeki'ah with their clothes rent 1
19: 1 When King Hezeki'ah heard it, he rent his clothes 1
3 Thus says Hezeki'ah, This day is a day of distress 1
5 When the servants of . . Hezeki'ah came to Isaiah 1
9 he sent messengers again to Hezeki'ah, saying 1
10 Thus shall you speak to Hezeki'ah king of Judah 1
14 Hezeki'ah received the letter from the hand 1
14 and Hezeki'ah went up to the house of the LORD 1
15 Hezeki'ah prayed before the LORD, and said: "O LORD 1
20 Amoz sent to Hezeki'ah, saying, "Thus says the LORD 1
20: 1 Hezeki'ah became sick and was at the point 1
2 Hezeki'ah turned his face to the wall, and prayed 1
3 And Hezeki'ah wept bitterly. 1
5 and say to Hezeki'ah the prince of my people 1
8 Hezeki'ah said to Isaiah, "What shall be the sign 1
10 Hezeki'ah answered, "It is an easy thing 2
12 sent . . letters and a present to Hezeki'ah; 1
12 for he heard that Hezeki'ah had been sick. 1
13 Hezeki'ah welcomed them, and he showed them all 1
13 there was nothing . . Hezeki'ah did not show them. 1
14 Isaiah . . came to King Hezeki'ah, and said to him 1
14 Hezeki'ah said, "They have come from a far country 1
15 Hezeki'ah answered, "They have seen all that is 1
16 Isaiah said to Hezeki'ah, "Hear the word of the LORD 1
19 Then said Hezeki'ah to Isaiah, "The word . . is good. 1
20 rest of the deeds of Hezeki'ah, and all his might 1
21 And Hezeki'ah slept with his fathers; 1
21: 3 the high places which Hezeki'ah . . had destroyed; 1
1Ch 3:13 Ahaz his son, Hezeki'ah his son, Manas'seh his son 1
4:41 These . . came in the days of Hezeki'ah 2
2Ch 28:27 And Hezeki'ah his son reigned in his stead. 2
29: 1 Hezeki'ah began to reign when he was 25 1
18 Then they went in to Hezeki'ah the king and said 1
20 Then Hezeki'ah the king rose early and gathered 2
27 Hezeki'ah commanded that the burnt offering 1
30 Hezeki'ah the king and the princes commanded 2
31 Then Hezeki'ah said, "You have now consecrated 2
36 Hezeki'ah and all the people rejoiced 2
30: 1 Hezeki'ah sent to all Israel and Judah 2
18 Hezeki'ah had prayed for them, saying 2
20 the LORD heard Hezeki'ah, and healed the people. 2
22 Hezeki'ah spoke encouragingly 2
24 Hezeki'ah . . gave the assembly 1,000 bulls 1
31: 2 Hezeki'ah appointed the divisions 2
8 Hezeki'ah and the princes came and saw the heaps 2
9 Hezeki'ah questioned . . about the heaps. 2
11 Hezeki'ah commanded them to prepare chambers 2
13 by the appointment of Hezeki'ah . . and Azari'ah 2
20 Thus Hezeki'ah did throughout all Judah; 2
32: 2 when Hezeki'ah saw that Sennach'erib had come 2
8 took confidence from the words of Hezeki'ah 2
9 sent his servants to Jerusalem to Hezeki'ah 2
11 Is not Hezeki'ah misleading you . . when he tells 2
12 this same Hezeki'ah taken away his high places 2
15 do not let Hezeki'ah deceive you or mislead you 1
16 said . . against his servant Hezeki'ah. 2
17 God of Hezeki'ah will not deliver his people 2
20 Then Hezeki'ah . . and Isaiah . . , prayed 2
22 LORD saved Hezeki'ah and the inhabitants 2
23 many brought . . precious things to Hezeki'ah 2
24 In those days Hezeki'ah became sick 2
25 Hezeki'ah did not make return 2
26 Hezeki'ah humbled himself for the pride 2
26 did not come upon them in the days of Hezeki'ah. 2
27 Hezeki'ah had very great riches and honor; 2
30 Hezeki'ah closed the upper outlet of the waters 2
30 Hezeki'ah prospered in all his works. 2
32 rest of the acts of Hezeki'ah, and his good deeds 2
33 Hezeki'ah slept with his fathers, and they buried 2
33: 3 which his father Hezeki'ah had broken down 2
Ezr 2:16 sons of Ater, namely of Hezeki'ah, 98. 2
Neh 7:21 sons of Ater, namely of Hezeki'ah, 98. 1
10:17 Ater, Hezeki'ah, Azzur 1
Prv 25: 1 proverbs of Solomon which the men of Hezeki'ah 1
Isa 1: 1 in the days of Uzzi'ah, Jotham, Ahaz, and Hezeki'ah 2
36: 1 In the fourteenth year of King Hezeki'ah 1
2 from Lachish to King Hezeki'ah at Jerusalem 1
4 the Rab'shakeh said to them, "Say to Hezeki'ah 1
7 high places and altars Hezeki'ah has removed 1
14 says the king: 'Do not let Hezeki'ah deceive you 1
15 Do not let Hezeki'ah make you rely on the LORD 1
16 Do not listen to Hezeki'ah; 1
18 Beware lest Hezeki'ah mislead you by saying 1
22 came to Hezeki'ah with their clothes rent 1
37: 1 When King Hezeki'ah heard it, he rent his clothes 1
3 Thus says Hezeki'ah, 'This day is a day of distress 1
5 the servants of King Hezeki'ah came to Isaiah 1
9 when he heard it, he sent messengers to Hezeki'ah 1
10 Thus shall you speak to Hezeki'ah king of Judah 1
14 Hezeki'ah received the letter . . and read it; 1
14 and Hezeki'ah went up to the house of the LORD •
15 Hezeki'ah prayed to the LORD 1
21 Isaiah the son of Amoz sent to Hezeki'ah, saying 1
38: 1 In those days Hezeki'ah became sick 1
2 Then Hezeki'ah turned his face to the wall 1
3 And Hezeki'ah wept bitterly. 1
5 Go and say to Hezeki'ah, Thus says the LORD 1
9 A writing of Hezeki'ah king of Judah 1
22 Hezeki'ah also had said, "What is the sign 1
39: 1 envoys with letters and a present to Hezeki'ah 1
2 Hezeki'ah welcomed them; 1
2 nothing . . that Hezeki'ah did not show them. 1
3 Then Isaiah the prophet came to King Hezeki'ah 1
3 Hezeki'ah said, "They have come to me from a far 1
4 Hezeki'ah answered, "They have seen all 1
5 Isaiah said to Hezeki'ah, "Hear the word of the LORD 1
8 Then said Hezeki'ah to Isaiah, "The word of the LORD 1
Jer 15: 4 Manas'seh the son of Hezeki'ah, king of Judah 2
26:18 prophesied in the days of Hezeki'ah king of Judah 1
19 Did Hezeki'ah king of Judah 1
Hos 1: 1 in the days of Uzzi'ah, Jotham, Ahaz, and Hezeki'ah 2
Mic 1: 1 Jotham, Ahaz, and Hezeki'ah, kings of Judah 2
Zep 1: 1 son of Gedali'ah, son of Amari'ah, son of Hezeki'ah 1
Mat 1: 9 and Ahaz the father of Hezeki'ah 3
10 Hezeki'ah the father of Manas'seh 3
1Es 5:15 The sons of Ater, namely of Hezekiah, 92. 3
9:43 Azariah, Uriah, Hezekiah 3
2Es 7:110 Hezekiah for the people 4
Sir 48:17 Hezekiah fortified his city 3
22 For Hezekiah did what was pleasing to the Lord 3
49: 4 Except David and Hezekiah and Josiah 3
2Mc 15:22 in the time of Hezekiah king of Judea 3

Hezion 1. חֶזְיוֹן
1Kg 15:18 Tabrim'mon, the son of He'zion, king of Syria 1

Hezir 1. חֵזִיר
1Ch 24:15 the seventeenth to Hezir, the eighteenth 1
Neh 10:20 Mag'piash, Meshul'lam, He-zir 1

Hezro 1. חֶצְרוֹ
2Sm 23:35 Hezro of Carmel, Pa'arai the Arbite 1
1Ch 11:37 Hezro of Carmel, Na'arai the son of Ezbai 1

Hezron 1. חֶצְרוֹן 2. Ἑσρώμ
Gen 46: 9 sons of Reuben: Hanoch, Pallu, Hezron, and Carmi 1
12 and the sons of Perez were Hezron and Hamul. 1
Exd 6:14 Hanoch, Pallu, Hezron, and Carmi; these are 1
Num26: 6 of Hezron, the family of the Hez'ronites; 1
21 of Hezron, the family of the Hez'ronites; 1
Jos 15: 3 goes up south of Ka'desh-bar'nea, along by Hezron 1
Rut 4:18 descendants of . . Perez was the father of Hezron 1
19 Hezron of Ram, Ram of Ammin'adab 1
1Ch 2: 5 The sons of Perez: Hezron and Hamul. 1
9 The sons of Hezron, that were born to him 1
18 Caleb the son of Hezron had children by his wife 1
21 Hezron went in to the daughter of Machir 1
24 After the death of Hezron, Caleb went 1
24 Eph'rathah, the wife of Hezron his father 1
25 The sons of Jerah'meel, the first-born of Hezron 1
4: 1 sons of Judah: Perez, Hezron, Carmi, Hur, and Shobal. 1
5: 3 sons of Reuben . . Pallu, Hezron, and Carmi. 1
Mat 1: 3 Perez the father of Hezron 2
3 and Hezron the father of Ram 2
Lke 3:33 the son of Arni, the son of Hezron, the son of Perez 2

Hezronite 1. חֶצְרוֹנִי
Num26: 6 of Hezron, the family of the Hez'ronites; 1
21 of Hezron, the family of the Hez'ronites; 1

Hiddai 1. הִדַּי
2Sm 23:30 Benai'ah . . Hid'dai of the brooks of Ga'ash 1

Hiel 1. חִיאֵל
1Kg 16:34 In his days Hi'el of Bethel built Jericho; 1

Hierapolis 1. Ἱεράπολις
Col 4:13 for those in La-odice'a and in Hi-erap'olis. 1

Hieronymus 1. Ιερωνυμος
2Mc 12: 2 as well as Hieronymus and Demophon 1

Higgaion 1. הִגָּיוֹן
Ps 9:16 in the work of their own hands. Higgaion. Selah 1

Hilen 1. חִילֵן
1Ch 6:58 Hilen with its pasture lands 1

Hilkiah 1. חִלְקִיָּהוּ חִלְקִיָּה 2. Χελκιας 3. Helchia
2Kg 18:18 the son of Hilki'ah, who was over the household 1
26 Eli'akim the son of Hilki'ah, and . . said 1
37 Eli'akim the son of Hilki'ah, who was over 1
22: 4 Go up to Hilki'ah the high priest 1
8 And Hilki'ah the high priest said to Shaphan 1
8 Hilki'ah gave the book to Shaphan, and he read it. 1
10 Hilki'ah the priest has given me a book. 1
12 king commanded Hilki'ah the priest, and Ahi'kam 1
14 Hilki'ah the priest, and Ahi'kam, and Achbor 1
23: 4 And the king commanded Hilki'ah the high priest 1
24 book that Hilki'ah the priest found in the house 1
1Ch 6:13 Shallum of Hilki'ah, Hilki'ah of Azari'ah 1
13 Shallum of Hilki'ah, Hilki'ah of Azari'ah 1
45 son of Hashabi'ah, son of Amazi'ah, son of Hilki'ah 1
9:11 Azari'ah the son of Hilki'ah, son of Meshul'lam 1
26:11 Hilki'ah the second, Tebali'ah the third 1
2Ch 34: 9 came to Hilki'ah the high priest and delivered 1
14 Hilki'ah the priest found the book of the law 1
15 Then Hilki'ah said to Shaphan the secretary 1
15 Hilki'ah gave the book to Shaphan. 1
18 Hilki'ah the priest has given me a book. 1
20 king commanded Hilki'ah, Ahi'kam the son 1
22 Hilki'ah and those whom the king had sent went 1
35: 8 Hilki'ah, Zechari'ah, and Jehi'el, the chief 1
Ezr 7: 1 son of Serai'ah, son of Azari'ah, son of Hilki'ah 1
Neh 8: 4 beside him stood . . Uri'ah, Hilki'ah, and Ma-asei'ah 1
11:11 Serai'ah the son of Hilki'ah, son of Meshul'lam 1
12: 7 Sallu, Amok, Hilki'ah, Jedai'ah. 1
21 of Hilki'ah, Hashabi'ah; of Jedai'ah, Nethan'el. 1
Isa 22:20 I will call my servant Eli'akim the son of Hilki'ah 1
36: 3 the son of Hilki'ah, who was over the household 1
22 the son of Hilki'ah, who was over the household 1
Jer 1: 1 The words of Jeremiah, the son of Hilki'ah 1
29: 3 son of Shaphan and Gemari'ah the son of Hilki'ah 1
1Es 1: 8 Hilkiah, Zechariah, and Jehiel 2
8: 1 the son of Seraiah, son of Azariah, son of Hilkiah 2
2Es 1: 1 son of Hilkiah, son of Shallum, son of Zadok 3
Jdt 8: 1 son of Ahitub, son of Elijah, son of Hilkiah 2
Bar 1: 1 son of Zedekiah, son of Hasadiah, son of Hilkiah 2
7 Jehoiakim . . the son of Hilkiah, son of Shallum 2
Sus 1: 2 a wife named Susanna, the daughter of Hilkiah 2
29 Send for Susanna, the daughter of Hilkiah 2
63 Hilkiah and his wife praised God 2

Hillel 1. הֵלֵל
Jdg 12:13 Abdon the son of Hillel the Pira'thonite judged 1
15 Abdon the son of Hillel the Pira'thonite died 1

Hinnom 1. הִנֹּם
Jos 15: 8 goes up by the valley of the son of Hinnom 1
8 over against the valley of Hinnom, on the west 1
18:16 that overlooks the valley of the son of Hinnom 1
16 and it then goes down the valley of Hinnom 1
2Kg 23:10 which is in the valley of the sons of Hinnom 1
2Ch 28: 3 burned incense in the valley of the son of Hinnom 1
33: 6 as an offering in the valley of the son of Hinnom 1
Neh 11:30 from Beer-sheba to the valley of Hinnom. 1
Jer 7:31 which is in the valley of the son of Hinnom 1
32 called Topheth, or the valley of the son of Hinnom 1
19: 2 the valley of the son of Hinnom at the entry 1
6 called Topheth, or the valley of the son of Hinnom 1
32:35 high places . . in the valley of the son of Hinnom 1

Hirah 1. חִירָה
Gen 38: 1 to a certain Adullamite, whose name was Hirah. 1
12 he and his friend Hirah the Adullamite. 1

Hiram 1. חִירָם
2Sm 5:11 And Hiram king of Tyre sent messengers to David 1
1Kg 5: 1 Hiram king of Tyre sent his servants to Solomon 1
1 for Hiram always loved David. 1
2 Solomon sent word to Hiram 1
7 When Hiram heard the words . . he rejoiced 1
8 Hiram sent to Solomon, saying, "I have heard 1
10 So Hiram supplied Solomon with all the timber 1
11 Solomon gave Hiram . . wheat as food 1
11 Solomon gave this to Hiram year by year. 1
12 there was peace between Hiram and Solomon; 1
18 and Hiram's builders and the men of Gebal did 1
7:13 King Solomon sent and brought Hiram from Tyre. 1
40 Hiram also made the pots, the shovels 1
40 Hiram finished all the work that he did 1
45 vessels . . which Hiram made for King Solomon 1
9:11 Hiram king of Tyre had supplied Solomon 1
11 Solomon gave to Hiram twenty cities in the land 1
12 when Hiram came from Tyre to see the cities 1
14 Hiram had sent to the king 120 talents of gold. 1
27 Hiram sent with the fleet his servants 1
10:11 the fleet of Hiram, which brought gold from Ophir 1
22 ships of Tarshish at sea with the fleet of Hiram. 1
1Ch 14: 1 Hiram king of Tyre sent messengers to David 1
Ps 90:10 they are soon gone, and we fly away. 1

Hittite 1. בֶּן חֵת 2. חֵת 3. חִתִּי 4. Χετταιος 5. Χεττιειμ
Gen 15:20 the Hittites, the Per'izzites, the Reph'aim 3
23: 3 Abraham . . said to the Hittites 1
5 The Hittites answered Abraham 1
7 bowed to the Hittites, the people of the land. 1
10 Now Ephron was sitting among the Hittites; 1
10 Ephron the Hittite answered Abraham 3
10 answered Abraham in the hearing of the Hittites 1
16 which he had named in the hearing of the Hittites 1
18 a possession in the presence of the Hittites 1
20 possession for a burying place by the Hittites. 1
25: 9 the field of Ephron the son of Zohar the Hittite 3
10 Abraham purchased from the Hittites. 1
26:34 Judith the daughter of Be-e'ri the Hittite 3
34 Bas'emath the daughter of Elon the Hittite; 3
27:46 weary of my life because of the Hittite women. 2
46 If Jacob marries one of the Hittite women 2
36: 2 Adah the daughter of Elon the Hittite 3
49:29 cave that is in the field of Ephron the Hittite 3
30 Abraham bought . . from Ephron the Hittite 3
32 cave . . were purchased from the Hittites. 1
50:13 Abraham bought . . from Ephron the Hittite 3
Exd 3: 8 of the Canaanites, the Hittites, the Amorites 3
17 to the land of . . the Hittites, the Amorites 3
13: 5 Canaanites, the Hittites, the Amorites 3
23:23 brings you in to the Amorites, and the Hittites 3
28 shall drive out Hivite, Canaanite, and Hittite 3
33: 2 the Canaanites, the Amorites, the Hittites 3
34:11 the Canaanites, the Hittites, the Per'izzites 3
Num13:29 Hittites, the Jeb'usites, and the Amorites dwell 3
Deu 7: 1 Hittites, the Gir'gashites, the Amorites 3
20:17 utterly destroy . . Hittites and the Amorites 3
Jos 1: 4 land of the Hittites . . shall be your territory. 3
3:10 drive out . . the Canaanites, the Hittites 3
9: 1 When all . . the Hittites, the Amorites 3
11: 3 the Amorites, the Hittites, the Per'izzites 3
12: 8 the land of the Hittites, the Amorites 3
24:11 the Canaanites, the Hittites, the Gir'gashites 3
Jdg 1:26 the man went to the land of the Hittites and built 3
3: 5 among the Canaanites, the Hittites, the Amorites 3
1Sm 26: 6 Then David said to Ahim'elech the Hittite 3
2Sm 11: 3 Bathshe'ba . . the wife of Uri'ah the Hittite? 3
6 David sent word . . "Send me Uri'ah the Hittite. 3
17 Uri'ah the Hittite was slain also. 3
21 say, 'Your servant Uri'ah the Hittite is dead also.' 3
24 and your servant Uri'ah the Hittite is dead also. 3
12: 9 have smitten Uri'ah the Hittite with the sword 3
10 taken the wife of Uri'ah the Hittite to . . wife. 3
23:39 Uri'ah the Hittite: 37 in all. 3
24: 6 came . . and to Kadesh in the land of the Hittites; 5
1Kg 9:20 All . . who were left of the Amorites, the Hittites 3
10:29 exported to all the kings of the Hittites 3
11: 1 Ammonite, E'domite, Sido'nian, and Hittite women 3
15: 5 except in the matter of Uri'ah the Hittite. 3
2Kg 7: 6 Israel has hired . . the kings of the Hittites 3
1Ch 11:41 Uri'ah the Hittite, Zabad the son of Ahlai 3
2Ch 1:17 exported to all the kings of the Hittites 3
8: 7 All the people who were left of the Hittites 3
Ezr 9: 1 from the Canaanites, the Hittites 3
Neh 9: 8 land of the Canaanite, the Hittite, the Amorite 3
Ezk 16: 3 father was an Amorite, and your mother a Hittite. 3
45 mother was a Hittite and your father an Amorite. 3
1Es 8:69 the Canaanites, the Hittites, the Perizzites 4

Hivite 1. חִוִּי 2. Ευαιος
Gen 10:17 the Hivites, the Arkites, the Sinites 1
34: 2 son of Hamor the Hivite, the prince of the land 1
36: 2 daughter of Anah the son of Zib'eon the Hivite 1
Exd 3: 8 the Per'izzites, the Hivites, and the Jeb'usites. 1
17 the Amorites, the Per'izzites, the Hivites 1
13: 5 the Amorites, the Hivites, and the Jeb'usites 1
23:23 the Per'izzites, and the Canaanites, the Hivites 1
28 which shall drive out Hivite, Canaanite 1
33: 2 the Per'izzites, the Hivites, and the Jeb'usites. 1
34:11 the Per'izzites, the Hivites, and the Jeb'usites. 1
Deu 7: 1 Per'izzites, the Hivites, and the Jeb'usites, seven 1
20:17 utterly destroy . . Hivites and the Jeb'usites 1
Jos 3:10 the Canaanites, the Hittites, the Hivites 1
9: 1 the Per'izzites, the Hivites, and the Jeb'usites 1
7 But the men of Israel said to the Hivites 1
11: 3 the Jeb'usites . . and the Hivites under Hermon 1
19 There was not a city that . . except the Hivites 1
12: 8 the Canaanites, the Per'izzites, the Hivites 1
24:11 the Gir'gashites, the Hivites, and the Jeb'usites; 1
Jdg 3: 3 and the Hivites who dwelt on Mount Lebanon 1
5 the Per'izzites, the Hivites, and the Jeb'usites; 1
2Sm 24: 7 to all the cities of the Hivites and Canaanites; 1
1Kg 9:20 the Per'izzites, the Hivites, and the Jeb'usites 1
1Ch 1:15 the Hivites, the Arkites, the Sinites 1
2Ch 8: 7 All the people who were left of . . the Hivites 1
Isa 17: 9 deserted places of the Hivites and the Amorites 2

Hizki 1. חִזְקִי
1Ch 8:17 Zebadi'ah, Meshul'lam, Hizki, Heber 1

Hizkiah 1. חִזְקִיָּהוּ
1Ch 3:23 sons of Neari'ah: Eli-o-e'nai, Hizki'ah, and Azri'kam 1

Hobab 1. חֹבָב
Num10:29 Moses said to Hobab the son of Reu'el 1
Jdg 4:11 descendants of Hobab the father-in-law of Moses 1

Hobah 1. חוֹבָה
Gen 14:15 pursued them to Hobah, north of Damascus. 1

Hobaiah 1. חֲבָיָה
Neh 7:63 priests: the sons of Hobai'ah, the sons of Hakkoz 1

Hod 1. הוֹד
1Ch 7:37 Bezer, Hod, Shamma, Shilshah, Ithran, and Be-e'ra. 1

Hodaviah 1. הוֹדַוְיָהוּ
1Ch 3:24 sons of Eli-o-e'nai: Hod'avi'ah, Eli'ashib, Pelai'ah 1
5:24 heads of their fathers' houses . . Hodavi'ah 1
9: 7 Meshul'lam, son of Hodavi'ah, son of Hassenu'ah. 1
Ezr 2:40 and Kad'mi-el, of the sons of Ho-davi'ah, 74. 1

Hodesh 1. חֹדֶשׁ
1Ch 8: 9 sons by Hodesh his wife: Jobab, Zib'i-a, Mesha, 1

Hodevah 1. הוֹדְוָה
Neh 7:43 Jeshua, namely of Kad'mi-el of the sons of Ho'devah 1

Hodiah 1. הוֹדִיָּה 2. Αυταιας
1Ch 4:19 The sons of the wife of Hodi'ah, the sister of Naham 1
Neh 8: 7 Also . . Akkub, Shab'bethai, Hodi'ah, Ma-asei'ah 1
9: 5 Levites . . Bani, Hashabnei'ah, Sherebi'ah, Hodi'ah 1
10:10 their brethren, Shebani'ah, Hodi'ah, Keli'ta 1
13 Hodi'ah, Bani, Beni'nu. 1
18 Hodi'ah, Hashum, Be'zai 1
1Es 9:48 Sherebiah, Jamin, Akkub, Shabbethai, Hodiah 2

Hoglah 1. חָגְלָה
Num26:33 daughters of Zeloph'ehad . . Hoglah, Milcah 1
27: 1 names of his daughters were: Mahlah, Noah, Hoglah 1
36:11 Tirzah, Hoglah, Milcah, and Noah, the daughters 1
Jos 17: 3 the names of his daughters: Mahlah, Noah, Hoglah 1

Hoham 1. הוֹהָם
Jos 10: 3 Ado'ni-ze'dek . . sent to Hoham king of Hebron 1

Holofernes 1. Ολοφερνης
Jdt 2: 4 Holofernes, the chief general of his army 1
14 Holofernes left the presence of his master 1
22 From there Holofernes took his whole army •
3: 5 The men came to Holofernes and told him all this. 1
4: 1 Holofernes, the general of Nebuchadnezzar 1
5: 1 Holofernes, the general of the Assyrian army 1
22 Holofernes' officers 1
24 Therefore let us go up, Lord Holofernes 1
6: 1 Holofernes, the commander of the Assyrian army 1
10 Then Holofernes ordered his slaves 1
17 the council of Holofernes 1
17 all that Holofernes had said so boastfully 1
7: 1 The next day Holofernes ordered his whole army 1
6 Holofernes led out all his cavalry 1
16 These words pleased Holofernes 1
26 to the army of Holofernes and to all his forces 1
10:13 I am on my way to the presence of Holofernes 1
17 they brought them to the tent of Holofernes. 1
18 she waited outside the tent of Holofernes 1
20 Holofernes' companions and all his servants 1
21 Holofernes was resting on his bed 1
23 Judith came into the presence of Holofernes •
11: 1 Then Holofernes said to her, "Take courage, woman 1
20 Her words pleased Holofernes 1
22 Holofernes said to her, "God has done well 1
12: 3 Holofernes said to her 1
5 Then the servants of Holofernes brought her 1
6 sent to Holofernes and said 1
7 Holofernes commanded his guards not to hinder 1
10 Holofernes held a banquet for his slave only 1
13 Bagoas went out from the presence of Holofernes 1
15 on the ground . . before Holofernes the soft fleeces 1
16 Holofernes' heart was ravished with her 1
17 Holofernes said to her. "Drink now 1
20 Holofernes was greatly pleased with her 1
13: 2 with Holofernes stretched out on his bed 1
6 above Holofernes' head 1
9 gave Holofernes' head to her maid 1
15 here is the head of Holofernes 1
14: 3 they will rush into the tent of Holofernes 1
6 when he came and saw the head of Holofernes 1
11 they hung the head of Holofernes on the wall 1
13 they came to Holofernes' tent 1
18 For look, here is Holofernes lying on the ground 1
15:11 They gave Judith the tent of Holofernes 1
16:19 all the vessels of Holofernes 1

Holon 1. חֹלוֹן
Jos 15:51 Goshen, Holon, and Giloh 1
21:15 Holon with its pasture lands, Debir with its 1
Jer 48:21 Judgment has come upon the tableland, upon Holon 1

Homam 1. הוֹמָם
1Ch 1:39 The sons of Lotan: Hori and Homam; and Lotan's 1

Hophni 1. חָפְנִי
1Sm 1: 3 two sons of Eli, Hophni and Phin'ehas, were priests 1
2:34 shall befall your two sons, Hophni and Phin'ehas 1
4: 4 two sons of Eli, Hophni and Phin'ehas, were there 1
11 two sons of Eli, Hophni and Phin'ehas, were slain. 1
17 your two sons also, Hophni and Phin'ehas, are dead 1

Hophra 1. חָפְרַע
Jer 44:30 Behold, I will give Pharaoh Hophra king of Egypt 1

Hor 1. הֹר
Num20:22 people of Israel . . came to Mount Hor. 1
23 the LORD said to Moses and Aaron at Mount Hor 1
25 Aaron and Elea'zar . . bring them up to Mount Hor; 1
27 they went up Mount Hor in the sight of all 1
21: 4 From Mount Hor they set out . . to the Red Sea 1
33:37 set out from Kadesh, and encamped at Mount Hor 1
38 went up Mount Hor at the command of the LORD 1
39 Aaron was 123 years old when he died on Mount Hor. 1
41 set out from Mount Hor, and encamped at Zalmo'nah. 1
34: 7 you shall mark out your line to Mount Hor 1
8 from Mount Hor you shall mark it out 1
Deu 32:50 as Aaron your brother died in Mount Hor 1

Hor-haggidgad 1. חֹר הַגִּדְגָּד
Num33:32 from Bene-ja'akan, and encamped at Hor-haggid'gad. 1
33 set out from Hor-haggid'gad, and encamped 1

Horam 1. הֹרָם
Jos 10:33 Then Horam king of Gezer came up to help Lachish; 1

Horeb 1. חֹרֵב 2. Χωρηβ 3. Horeb
Exd 3: 1 and came to Horeb, the mountain of God. 1
17: 6 stand before you there on the rock at Horeb; 1
33: 6 stripped themselves . . from Mount Horeb onward. 1
Deu 1: 2 from Horeb by the way of Mount Se'ir 1
6 LORD our God said to us in Horeb, 'You have stayed 1
19 we set out from Horeb, and went through 1
4:10 that you stood before the LORD your God at Horeb 1
15 spoke to you at Horeb out of the midst of the fire 1
5: 2 The LORD our God made a covenant with us in Horeb. 1
9: 8 Even at Horeb you provoked the LORD to wrath 1
18:16 desired of the LORD your God at Horeb on the day 1
29: 1 covenant which he had made with them at Horeb. 1
1Kg 8: 9 which Moses put there at Horeb, where the LORD 1
19: 8 ate and drank, and went . . to Horeb the mount of God. 1
2Ch 5:10 the two tables which Moses put there at Horeb 1
Ps 106:19 made a calf in Horeb and worshiped 1
Mal 4: 4 that I commanded him at Horeb for all Israel. 1

2Es 2:33 from the Lord on Mount Horeb to go to Israel 3
Sir 48: 7 heard . . judgments of vengeance at Horeb; 2

Horem 1. חֳרֵם
Jos 19:38 Yiron, Mig'dal-el, Horem, Beth-anath 1

Horesh 1. חֹרֶשׁ
1Sm 23:15 David was in the Wilderness of Ziph at Horesh. 1
16 Jonathan . . rose, and went to David at Horesh 1
18 David remained at Horesh, and Jonathan went home. 1
19 David hide among us in the strongholds at Horesh 1

Hori 1. חֹרִי
Gen 36:22 The sons of Lotan were Hori and Heman; 1
Num13: 5 from the tribe of Simeon, Shaphat the son of Hori; 1
1Ch 1:39 The sons of Lotan: Hori and Homam; and Lotan's 1

Horite 1. חֹרִי
Gen 14: 6 the Horites in their Mount Se'ir 1
36:20 These are the sons of Se'ir the Horite 1
21 these are the chiefs of the Horites 1
29 These are the chiefs of the Horites 1
30 Dishan; these are the chiefs of the Horites 1
Deu 2:12 The Horites also lived in Se'ir formerly 1
22 when he destroyed the Horites before them 1

Hormah 1. חָרְמָה
Num14:45 defeated them and pursued them, even to Hormah. 1
21: 3 so the name of the place was called Hormah. 1
Deu 1:44 Amorites . . beat you down in Se'ir as far as Hormah. 1
Jos 12:14 the king of Hormah, one; the king of Arad, one; 1
15:30 Elto'lad, Chesil, Hormah 1
19: 4 Elto'lad, Bethul, Hormah 1
Jdg 1:17 So the name of the city was called Hormah. 1
1Sm 30:30 for those . . in Hormah, in Borash'an, in A'thach 1
1Ch 4:30 Bethu'el, Hormah, Ziklag 1

Horonaim 1. חֹרוֹנַיִם
2Sm 13:34 many people were coming from the Horona'im road •
Isa 15: 5 on the road to Horona'im they raise a cry 1
Jer 48: 3 Hark! a cry from Horona'im, 'Desolation 1
5 at the descent of Horona'im they have heard 1
34 from Zo'ar to Horona'im and Eg'lath-shelish'iyah. 1

Horonite 1. חֹרֹנִי
Neh 2:10 when Sanbal'lat the Hor'onite and Tobi'ah 1
19 when Sanbal'lat the Hor'onite and Tobi'ah 1
13:28 the son-in-law of Sanbal'lat the Hor'onite; 1

Horse Gate 1. שַׁעַר הַסּוּסִים
Neh 3:28 Above the Horse Gate the priests repaired 1

Hosah 1. חֹסָה
Jos 19:29 the boundary turns to Hosah, and it ends at the sea; 1
1Ch 16:38 O'bed-e'dom . . and Hosah were to be gatekeepers. 1
26:10 Hosah . . of Merar'i, had sons: Shimri the chief 1
11 the sons and brethren of Hosah were thirteen. 1
16 For Shuppim and Hosah it came out for the west 1

Hosea 1. הוֹשֵׁעַ 2. Ὡσηέ 3. Osee
Hos 1: 1 The word . . that came to Hose'a the son of Be-e'ri 1
2 When the LORD first spoke through Hose'a 1
2 the LORD said to Hose'a, "Go, take to yourself a wife 1
Rom 9:25 As indeed he says in Hose'a 2
2Es 1:39 Jacob and Hosea and Amos and Micah and Joel 3

Hoshaiah 1. הוֹשַׁעְיָה
Neh 12:32 went Hoshai'ah and half of the princes of Judah 1
Jer 42: 1 Azari'ah the son of Hoshai'ah, and all the people 1
43: 2 Azari'ah the son of Hoshai'ah 1

Hoshama 1. הוֹשָׁמָע
1Ch 3:18 Shenaz'zar, Jekami'ah, Hosh'ama, and Nedabi'ah; 1

Hoshea 1. הוֹשֵׁעַ 2. Iosiae
Num13: 8 from the tribe of E'phraim, Hoshe'a the son of Nun; 1
16 Moses called Hoshe'a the son of Nun Joshua. 1
2Kg 15:30 Then Hoshe'a . . made a conspiracy against Pekah 1
17: 1 Hoshe'a the son of Elah began to reign in Sama'ria 1
3 Hoshe'a became his vassal, and paid him tribute. 1
4 the king of Assyria found treachery in Hoshe'a; 1
6 In the ninth year of Hoshe'a 1
18: 1 In the third year of Hoshe'a son of Elah 1
9 which was the seventh year of Hoshe'a son of Elah 1
10 which was the ninth year of Hoshe'a king of Israel 1
1Ch 27:20 for the E'phraimites, Hoshe'a the son of Azazi'ah; 1
Neh 10:23 Ho-she'a, Hanani'ah, Hasshub 1
2Es 13:40 in the days of King Hoshea 2

Hotham 1. חוֹתָם
1Ch 7:32 father of . . Hotham, and their sister Shu'a. 1
11:44 Shama and Je-i'el the sons of Hotham the Aro'erite 1

Hothir 1. הוֹתִיר
1Ch 25: 4 sons of Heman . . Mallo'thi, Hothir, Maha'zi-oth. 1
28 to Hothir, his sons and his brethren, twelve; 1

Hukkok 1. חֻקֹק
Jos 19:34 boundary turns . . and goes from there to Hukkok 1

Hukok 1. חוּקֹק
1Ch 6:75 Hukok with its pasture lands, and Rehob 1

Hul 1. חוּל
Gen 10:23 The sons of Aram: Uz, Hul, Gether, and Mash. 1
1Ch 1:17 The sons of Shem . . Lud, Aram, Uz, Hul, Gether 1

Huldah 1. חֻלְדָּה
2Kg 22:14 So . . and Asai'ah went to Huldah the prophetess 1
2Ch 34:22 Hilki'ah . . went to Huldah the prophetess 1

Humtah 1. חֻמְטָה
Jos 15:54 Humtah, Kir'iath-ar'ba (that is, Hebron), and Zi'or 1

Hundred *See also* Tower.

Hupham 1. חוּפָם
Num26:39 of Hupham, the family of the Hu'phamites. 1

Huphamite 1. חוּפָמִי
Num26:39 of Hupham, the family of the Hu'phamites. 1

Huppah 1. חֻפָּה
1Ch 24:13 the thirteenth to Huppah, the fourteenth 1

Huppim 1. חֻפִּים
Gen 46:21 Gera, Na'aman, Ehi, Rosh, Muppim, Huppim, and Ard 1
1Ch 7:12 And Shuppim and Huppim were the sons of Ir 1
15 Machir took a wife for Huppim and for Shuppim. 1

Hur 1. חוּר
Exd 17:10 and Moses, Aaron, and Hur went up to the top 1
12 and Aaron and Hur held up his hands, one on one side 1
24:14 and, behold, Aaron and Hur are with you; 1
31: 2 called by name Bez'alel and son of Uri, son of Hur 1
35:30 the son of Uri, son of Hur, of the tribe of Judah; 1
38:22 Bez'alel the son of Uri, son of Hur, of the tribe 1
Num31: 8 Evi, Rekem, Zur, Hur, and Reba, the five kings 1
Jos 13:21 leaders . . Evi and Rekem and Zur and Hur and Reba 1
1Ch 2:19 Caleb married Ephrath, who bore him Hur. 1
20 Hur was the father of Uri 1
50 sons of Hur the first-born of Eph'rathah 1
4: 1 sons of Judah: Perez, Hezron, Carmi, Hur, and Shobal. 1
4 the sons of Hur, the first-born of Eph'rathah 1
2Ch 1: 5 that Bez'alel the son of Uri, son of Hur, had made 1
Neh 3: 9 Rephai'ah the son of Hur . . repaired. 1

Hurai 1. חוּרַי
1Ch 11:32 Hurai of the brooks of Ga'ash 1

Huram 1. חוּרָם
1Ch 8: 5 Gera, Shephu'phan, and Huram. 1
2Ch 2: 3 Solomon sent word to Huram the king of Tyre 1
11 Then Huram the king of Tyre answered in a letter 1
12 Huram also said, "Blessed be the LORD God of Israel 1
4:11 Huram also made the pots, the shovels 1
11 Huram finished the work that he did for King 1
8: 2 rebuilt the cities which Huram had given to him 1
18 Huram sent him . . ships and servants familiar 1
9:10 servants of Huram and the servants of Solomon 1
21 went to Tarshish with the servants of Huram; 1

Huram-abi 1. חוּרָם אָבִי
2Ch 2:13 man, endued with understanding, Huram-abi. 1
4:16 for these Huram-abi made of burnished bronze 1

Huri 1. חוּרִי
1Ch 5:14 the sons of Ab'ihail the son of Huri, son of Jaro'ah 1

Hushah 1. חוּשָׁה
1Ch 4: 4 and Ezer the father of Hushah. 1

Hushai 1. חוּשַׁי
2Sm 15:32 Hushai the Archite came to meet him 1
37 So Hushai, David's friend, came into the city 1
16:16 And when Hushai the Archite, David's friend, came 1
16 Hushai said to Ab'salom, "Long live the king! 1
17 And Ab'salom said to Hushai, "Is this your loyalty 1
18 And Hushai said to Ab'salom, "No; 1
17: 5 Call Hushai the Archite also, and let us hear 1
6 And when Hushai came to Ab'salom, Ab'salom said 1
7 Then Hushai said to Ab'salom 1
8 Hushai said moreover, "You know that 1
14 The counsel of Hushai the Archite is better 1
15 Hushai said to Zadok and Abi'athar the priests 1
1Kg 4:16 Ba'ana the son of Hushai, in Asher and Bealoth; 1
1Ch 27:33 and Hushai the Archite was the king's friend. 1

Husham 1. חֻשָׁם
Gen 36:34 Husham of the land of the Te'manites reigned 1
35 Husham died, and Hadad the son of Bedad 1
1Ch 1:45 When Jobab died, Husham of the land 1
46 When Husham died, Hadad the son of Bedad 1

Hushathite 1. חֻשָׁתִי
2Sm 21:18 then Sib'becai the Hu'shathite slew Saph 1
23:27 Abi-e'zer, of An'athoth, Mebun'nai the Hu'shathite 1
1Ch 11:29 Sib'becai the Hu'shathite, I'lai the Aho'hite 1
20: 4 then Sib'becai the Hu'shathite slew Sip'pai 1
27:11 Eighth . . was Sib'becai the Hu'shathite 1

Hushim 1. חוּשִׁים
Gen 46:23 The sons of Dan: Hushim. 1
1Ch 7:12 Hushim the sons of Aher. 1
8: 8 he had sent away Hushim and Ba'ara his wives. 1
11 He also had sons by Hushim: Abi'tub and Elpa'al. 1

Hydaspes 1. Υδασπης
Jdt 1: 6 the Euphrates and the Tigris and the Hydaspes 1

Hymenaeus 1. Ὑμέναιος
1Ti 1:20 among them Hymenae'us and Alexander 1
2Ti 2:17 Among them are Hymenae'us and Phile'tus 1

Hyrcanus 1. Υρκανος
2Mc 3:11 also some money of Hyrcanus, son of Tobias 1

Ibhar 1. יִבְחָר
2Sm 5:15 Ibhar, Eli'shu-a, Nepheg, Japhi'a 1
1Ch 3: 6 then Ib-har, Eli'shama, Eliph'elet 1
14: 5 Ibhar, Eli'shu-a, El'pelet 1

Ibleam 1. יִבְלְעָם 2. Ιεβλααμ
Jos 17:11 Manas'seh had . . and Ibleam and its villages 1
Jdg 1:27 drive out . . or the inhabitants of Ibleam 1
2Kg 9:27 at the ascent of Gur, which is by Ibleam. 1
15:10 conspired . . and struck him down at Ibleam 2

Ibneiah 1. יִבְנְיָה
1Ch 9: 8 Ibne'iah the son of Jero'ham, Elah the son of Uzzi 1

Ibnijah 1. יִבְנִיָּה
1Ch 9: 8 Shephati'ah, son of Reu'el, son of Ibni'jah; 1

Ibri 1. עִבְרִי
1Ch 24:27 of Ja-azi'ah, Beno, Shoham, Zaccur, and Ibri. 1

Ibsam 1. יִבְשָׂם
1Ch 7: 2 sons of Tola . . Je'ri-el, Jah'mai, Ibsam, and Shem'uel 1

Ibzan 1. אִבְצָן
Jdg 12: 8 After him Ibzan of Bethlehem judged Israel. 1
10 Then Ibzan died, and was buried at Bethlehem. 1

Ichabod 1. אִי כָבוֹד
1Sm 4:21 And she named the child Ich'abod, saying 1
14: 3 Ahi'jah the son of Ahi'tub, Ich'abod's brother 1

Iconium 1. Ἰκόνιον
Act 13:51 and went to Ico'nium. 1
14: 1 at Ico'nium they entered . . the Jewish synagogue 1
19 Jews came there from Antioch and Ico'nium; 1
21 they returned . . to Ico'nium and to Antioch 1
16: 2 He was well spoken of . . at Lystra and Ico'nium. 1
2Ti 3:11 at Antioch, at Ico'nium, and at Lystra 1

Idalah 1. יִדְאֲלָה
Jos 19:15 Kattath, Nahal'al, Shimron, I'dalah, and Bethlehem 1

Idbash 1. יִדְבָּשׁ
1Ch 4: 3 the sons of Etam: Jezreel, Ishma, and Idbash; 1

Iddo 1. אִדּוֹ 2. יִדּוֹ 3. יֶעְדּוֹ 4. עִדּוֹ 5. עִדּוֹא (A) 6. Αδδαι 7. Εδδι 8. Ηδος
1Kg 4:14 Ahin'adab the son of Iddo, in Mahana'im; 4
1Ch 6:21 Jo'ah . . Iddo his son, Zerah . . Je-ath'erai 4
27:21 Manas'seh in Gilead, Iddo the son of Zechari'ah; 2
2Ch 9:29 and in the visions of Iddo the seer 3
12:15 chronicles of Shemai'ah . . and of Iddo the seer? 4
13:22 written in the story of the prophet Iddo. 4
Ezr 5: 1 prophets, Haggai and Zechari'ah the son of Iddo 5
6:14 prophesying of . . Zechari'ah the son of Iddo. 5
8:17 sent them to Iddo, the leading man at . . Casiphi'a 1
17 telling them what to say to Iddo and his brethren 1
Neh 12: 4 Iddo, Gin'nethoi, Abi'jah 4
16 of Iddo, Zechari'ah; of Gin'nethon, Meshul'lam; 4
Zec 1: 1 to Zechari'ah the son of Berechi'ah, son of Iddo 4
7 the son of Berechi'ah, son of Iddo, the prophet; 4
1Es 6: 1 the prophets Haggai and Zechariah the son of Iddo 7
8:45 I told them to go to Iddo 6
46 ordered them to tell Iddo and his brethren 6
9:35 Mattithiah, Zabad, Iddo, Joel, Benaiah. 8

Iduel 1. Ἰδουηλος
1Es 8:43 I sent word to Eliezar, Iduel, Maasmas 1

Idumea 1. Ἰδουμαία
Mrk 3: 8 Jerusalem and Idume'a and from beyond the Jordan 1
1Mc 4:15 to the plains of Idumea, and to Azotus and Jamnia; 1
29 They came into Idumea and encamped at Beth-zur 1
61 a stronghold that faced Idumea. 1
5: 3 Judas made war on the sons of Esau in Idumea 1

6:31 They came through Idumea 1
2Mc 12:32 Gorgias, the governor of Idumea. 1

Idumean 1. Ιδουμαιος
1Es 4:50 the Idumeans should give up the villages 1
2Mc 10:15 the Idumeans . . were harassing the Jews 1
16 rushed to the strongholds of the Idumeans. 1

Iezer 1. אִיעֶזֶר
Num26:30 of Ie'zer, the family of the Ie'zerites; 1

Iezerite 1. אִיעֶזְרִי
Num26:30 of Ie'zer, the family of the Ie'zerites; 1

Igal 1. יִגְאָל
Num13: 7 from the tribe of Is'sachar, Igal the son of Joseph; 1
2Sm 23:36 Igal the son of Nathan of Zobah, Bani the Gadite 1
1Ch 3:22 And the sons of Shemai'ah: Hattush, Igal, Bari'ah 1

Igdaliah 1. יִגְדַּלְיָהוּ
Jer 35: 4 sons of Hanan the son of Igdali'ah, the man of God 1

Iim 1. עִיִּים
Jos 15:29 Ba'alah, I'im, Ezem 1

Ijon 1. עִיּוֹן
1Kg 15:20 Ben-ha'dad . . conquered Ijon, Dan, 1
2Kg 15:29 came and captured I'jon, A'bel-beth-ma'acah, 1
2Ch 16: 4 conquered I'jon, Dan, A'bel-ma'im 1

Ikkesh 1. עִקֵּשׁ
2Sm 23:26 Helez the Paltite, Ira the son of Ikkesh of Teko'a 1
1Ch 11:28 Ira the son of Ikkesh of Teko'a, Abi-e'zer of An'athoth 1
27: 9 Sixth . . was Ira, the son of Ikkesh the Teko'ite; 1

Ilai 1. עִילַי
1Ch 11:29 Sib'becai the Hu'shathite, I'lai the Aho'hite 1

Iliadun 1. Ιλιαδουν
1Es 5:58 the sons of Joda son of Iliadun 1

Illyricum 1. Ἰλλυρικόν
Rom15:19 from Jerusalem and as far round as Illyr'icum 1

Imalkue 1. Ιμαλκουε
1Mc 11:39 So he went to Imalkue the Arab 1
40 He also reported to Imalkue what Demetrius had done •

Imlah 1. יִמְלָא
1Kg 22: 8 by whom we may inquire . . Micai'ah the son of Imlah; 1
9 and said, "Bring quickly Micai'ah the son of Imlah. 1
2Ch 18: 7 Micai'ah the son of Imlah; 1
8 Bring quickly Micai'ah the son of Imlah. 1

Immanu-el 1. עִמָּנוּ אֵל
Isa 7:14 bear a son, and shall call his name Imman'u-el. 1
8: 8 fill the breadth of your land, O Imman'u-el. 1

Immer 1. אִמֵּר 2. Εμμηρ 3. Ημμερ
1Ch 9:12 Meshul'lam, son of Meshil'lemith, son of Immer; 1
24:14 the fifteenth to Bilgah, the sixteenth to Immer 1
Ezr 2:37 sons of Immer, 1,052. 1
59 those who came up from . . Cherub, Addan, and Immer 1
10:20 Of the sons of Immer: Hana'ni and Zebadi'ah. 1
Neh 3:29 Zadok the son of Immer repaired opposite his own 1
7:40 sons of Immer, 1,052. 1
61 came up from . . Cherub, Addon, and Immer 1
11:13 son of Ah'zai, son of Meshil'lemoth, son of Immer 1
Jer 20: 1 Now Pashhur the priest, the son of Immer 1
1Es 5:24 The sons of Immer, 1,052. 2
36 under the leadership of Cherub, Addan, and Immer 3
9:21 Of the sons of Immer: Hanani and Zebadiah 2

Imna 1. יִמְנָע
1Ch 7:35 sons of Helem . . Zophah, Imna, Shelesh, and Amal. 1

Imnah 1. יִמְנָה
Gen 46:17 The sons of Asher: Imnah, Ishvah, Ishvi, Beri'ah 1
Num26:44 of Imnah, the family of the Imnites; 1
1Ch 7:30 The sons of Asher: Imnah, Ishvah, Ishvi, Beri'ah 1
2Ch 31:14 Ko're the son of Imnah the Levite 1

Imnite 1. יִמְנָה
Num26:44 of Imnah, the family of the Imnites; 1

Imrah 1. יִמְרָה
1Ch 7:36 sons of Zophah: Su'ah, Har'nepher, Shu'al . . Imrah 1

Imri 1. אִמְרִי
1Ch 9: 4 son of Ammi'hud, son of Omri, son of Imri, son of Bani 1
Neh 3: 2 next to them Zaccur the son of Imri built. 1

India 1. הֹדּוּ 2. Ινδικη
Est 1: 1 Ahasu-e'rus who reigned from India to Ethiopia 1
8: 9 princes of the provinces from India to Ethiopia 1
1Es 3: 2 the 127 satrapies from India to Ethiopia. 2
AEs 13: 1 the 127 provinces from India to Ethiopia 2
16: 1 rulers of the provinces from India to Ethiopia 2
1Mc 8: 8 the country of India and Media and Lydia 2

Indian 1. Ινδος
1Mc 6:37 also its Indian driver. 1

Iob 1. יוֹב
Gen 46:13 sons of Is'sachar: Tola, Puvah, Iob, and Shimron 1

Iphdeiah 1. יִפְדְיָה
1Ch 8:25 Iphdei'ah, and Penu'el were the sons of Shashak. 1

Iphtah 1. יִפְתָּח
Jos 15:43 Iphtah, Ashnah, Nezib 1

Iphtah-el 1. יִפְתַּח אֵל
Jos 19:14 boundary . . and it ends at the valley of Iph'tahel; 1
27 and touches Zeb'ulun and the valley of Iph'tahel 1

Ir 1. עִיר
1Ch 7:12 And Shuppim and Huppim were the sons of Ir 1

Ir-shemesh 1. עִיר שֶׁמֶשׁ
Jos 19:41 included Zorah, Esh'ta-ol, Ir-she'mesh 1

Ira 1. עִירָא
2Sm 20:26 and Ira the Ja'irite was also David's priest. 1
23:26 Helez the Paltite, Ira the son of Ikkesh of Teko'a 1
38 Ira the Ithrite, Gareb the Ithrite 1
1Ch 11:28 Ira the son of Ikkesh of Teko'a, Abi-e'zer of An'athoth 1
40 Ira the Ithrite, Gareb the Ithrite 1
27: 9 Sixth . . was Ira, the son of Ikkesh the Teko'ite; 1

Irad 1. עִירָד
Gen 4:18 To Enoch was born Irad; and Irad was the father 1
18 and Irad was the father of Me-hu'ja-el 1

Iram 1. עִירָם
Gen 36:43 Mag'diel, and Iram; these are the chiefs of Edom 1
1Ch 1:54 Mag'di-el, and Iram; these are the chiefs of Edom. 1

Iri 1. עִירִי
1Ch 7: 7 sons of Bela: Ezbon, Uzzi, Uz'ziel, Jer'imoth, and Iri 1

Irijah 1. יִרְאִיָּה
Jer 37:13 a sentry there named Iri'jah the son of Shelemi'ah 1
14 But Iri'jah would not listen to him 1

Irnahash 1. עִיר נָחָשׁ
1Ch 4:12 Tehin'nah the father of Irna'hash. 1

Irpeel 1. יִרְפְּאֵל
Jos 18:27 Rekem, Irpeel, Tar'alah 1

Iru 1. עִירוּ
1Ch 4:15 sons of Caleb . . Iru, Elah, and Na'am; 1

Isaac 1. יִצְחָק 2. Ἰσαάκ 3. Ισακιος 4. Isaac
Gen 17:19 and you shall call his name Isaac. 1
21 I will establish my covenant with Isaac 1
21: 3 was born to him, whom Sarah bore him, Isaac. 1
4 Abraham circumcised his son Isaac 1
5 years old when his son Isaac was born to him. 1
8 great feast on the day that Isaac was weaned. 1
9 the son . . playing with her son Isaac. 2
10 shall not be heir with my son Isaac. 1
12 through Isaac shall your descendants be named. 1
22: 2 your only son Isaac, whom you love 1
3 Abraham . . took . . his son Isaac; 1
6 wood of the burnt offering, and laid it on Isaac 1
7 Isaac said to his father Abraham, "My father! 1
9 Abraham . . bound Isaac his son 1
24: 4 to my kindred, and take a wife for my son Isaac. 1
14 thou hast appointed for thy servant Isaac. 1
62 Now Isaac had come from Beer-la'hai-roi 1
63 Isaac went out to meditate in the field 1
64 when she saw Isaac, she alighted from the camel 1
66 the servant told Isaac all the things 1
67 Isaac brought her into the tent, and took Rebekah 1
67 Isaac was comforted after his mother's death. 1
25: 5 Abraham gave all he had to Isaac. 1
6 he sent them away from his son Isaac 1
9 Isaac and Ish'mael his sons buried him in the cave 1
11 After the death of Abraham God blessed Isaac 1
11 And Isaac dwelt at Beer-la'hai-roi. 1
19 the descendants of Isaac, Abraham's son 1
19 Abraham was the father of Isaac 1
20 Isaac was 40 years old when he took to wife Rebekah 1
21 Isaac prayed to the LORD for his wife 1
26 Isaac was 60 years old when she bore them. 1
28 Isaac loved Esau, because he ate of his game; 1
26: 1 And Isaac went to Gerar, to Abim'elech 1
6 Isaac dwelt in Gerar. 1
8 Abim'elech . . saw Isaac fondling Rebekah 1
9 Abim'elech called Isaac, and said 1
9 you say, 'She is my sister'?" Isaac said to him 1
12 Isaac sowed in that land, and reaped 1
16 Abim'elech said to Isaac, "Go away from us; 1
17 Isaac departed from there, and encamped 1
18 Isaac dug again the wells of water 1
19 when Isaac's servants dug in the valley 1
20 herdsmen . . quarreled with Isaac's herdsmen 1
25 And there Isaac's servants dug a well. 1
27 Isaac said to them, "Why have you come to me 1
31 and Isaac set them on their way, and they departed 1
32 That same day Isaac's servants came and told him 1
35 they made life bitter for Isaac and Rebekah. 1
27: 1 When Isaac was old and his eyes were dim 1
5 Now Rebekah was listening when Isaac spoke 1
20 Isaac said to his son, "How is it 1
21 Isaac said to Jacob, "Come near, that I may feel 1
22 Jacob went near to Isaac his father 1
26 Then his father Isaac said to him, "Come near 1
30 As soon as Isaac had finished blessing Jacob 1
30 gone out from the presence of Isaac his father 1
32 His father Isaac said to him, "Who are you? 1
33 Isaac trembled violently, and said, "Who was it 1
37 Isaac answered Esau, "Behold, I have made him 1
39 Then Isaac his father answered him 1
46 Rebekah said to Isaac, "I am weary of my life 1
28: 1 Then Isaac called Jacob and blessed him 1
5 Thus Isaac sent Jacob away; 1
6 Esau saw that Isaac had blessed Jacob 1
8 Canaanite women did not please Isaac his father 1
13 the God of Isaac; the land on which you lie I will 1
31:18 to go to the land of Canaan to his father Isaac. 1
42 God of Abraham and the Fear of Isaac 1
53 Jacob swore by the Fear of his father Isaac 1
32: 9 God of my father Isaac, O LORD who didst say to me 1
35:12 The land which I gave to Abraham and Isaac I will 1
27 Jacob came to his father Isaac at Mamre 1
27 where Abraham and Isaac had sojourned. 1
28 Now the days of Isaac were 180 years. 1
29 Isaac breathed his last; and he died 1
46: 1 sacrifices to the God of his father Isaac. 1
48:15 my fathers Abraham and Isaac walked, the God who 1
16 the name of my fathers Abraham and Isaac; 1
49:31 there they buried Isaac and Rebekah his wife; 1
50:24 swore to Abraham, to Isaac, and to Jacob. 1
Exd 2:24 his covenant with Abraham, with Isaac 1
3: 6 of Abraham, the God of Isaac, and the God of Jacob. 1
15 God of Abraham, the God of Isaac, and the God 1
16 God of Abraham, of Isaac, and of Jacob, has appeared 1
4: 5 Abraham, the God of Isaac, and the God of Jacob, has 1
6: 3 I appeared to Abraham, to Isaac, and to Jacob, as God 1
8 swore to give to Abraham, to Isaac, and to Jacob; 1
32:13 Remember Abraham, Isaac, and Israel, thy servants 1
33: 1 I swore to Abraham, Isaac, and Jacob, saying 1
Lev 26:42 I will remember my covenant with Isaac 1
Num32:11 I swore to give to Abraham, to Isaac, and to Jacob 1
Deu 1: 8 to your fathers, to Abraham, to Isaac, and to Jacob 1
6:10 to your fathers, to Abraham, to Isaac, and to Jacob 1
9: 5 to your fathers, to Abraham, to Isaac, and to Jacob. 1
27 Remember thy servants, Abraham, Isaac, and Jacob; 1
29:13 as he swore to . . Abraham, to Isaac, and to Jacob. 1
30:20 to your fathers, to Abraham, to Isaac, and to Jacob 1
34: 4 land . . I swore to Abraham, to Isaac, and to Jacob 1
Jos 24: 3 and made his offspring many. I gave him Isaac; 1
4 and to Isaac I gave Jacob and Esau. 1
1Kg 18:36 O LORD, God of Abraham, Isaac, and Israel, let it be 1
2Kg 13:23 his covenant with Abraham, Isaac, and Jacob 1
1Ch 1:28 The sons of Abraham: Isaac and Ish'mael. 1
34 was the father of Isaac. The sons of Isaac 1
34 The sons of Isaac: Esau and Israel. 1
16:16 his sworn promise to Isaac 1
29:18 O LORD, the God of Abraham, Isaac, and Israel 1
2Ch 30: 6 the LORD, the God of Abraham, Isaac, and Israel 1
Ps 105: 9 covenant . . Abraham, his sworn promise to Isaac 1
Jer 33:26 to rule over the seed of Abraham, Isaac, and Jacob. 1
Ams 7: 9 the high places of Isaac shall be made desolate 1
16 and do not preach against the house of Isaac.' 1
Mat 1: 2 Abraham was the father of Isaac 2
2 and Isaac the father of Jacob 2
8:11 sit at table with Abraham, Isaac, and Jacob 2
22:32 'I am the God of Abraham, and the God of Isaac 2
Mrk 12:26 the God of Isaac, and the God of Jacob'? 2
Lke 3:34 the son of Jacob, the son of Isaac 2
13:28 when you see Abraham and Isaac and Jacob 2
20:37 the God of Isaac and the God of Jacob. 2
Act 3:13 The God of Abraham and of Isaac and of Jacob 2
7: 8 so Abraham became the father of Isaac 2
8 Isaac became the father of Jacob 2
32 the God of Abraham and of Isaac and of Jacob 2
Rom 9: 7 Through Isaac shall your descendants be named. 2
10 conceived . . by one man, our forefather Isaac 2
Gal 4:28 we, brethren, like Isaac, are children of promise. 2
Heb 11: 9 living in tents with Isaac and Jacob 2
17 Abraham, when he was tested, offered up Isaac 2
18 Through Isaac shall your descendants be named. 2
20 By faith Isaac invoked future blessings 2
Jas 2:21 when he offered his son Isaac upon the altar? 2
2Es 1:39 to them I will give as leaders Abraham, Isaac 4
3:15 and thou gavest to him Isaac 4
15 and to Isaac thou gavest Jacob and Esau. 4
6: 8 He said to me, "From Abraham to Isaac 4
Tob 4:12 Noah, Abraham, Isaac, and Jacob, our fathers of old 2
Jdt 8:26 how he tested Isaac 2
Sir 44:22 To Isaac also he gave the same assurance 2
Bar 2:34 fathers, to Abraham and to Isaac and to Jacob 2
Aza 1:12 for the sake of Isaac thy servant 2

Man 1: 1 God . . of Abraham and Isaac and Jacob 2
8 repentance . . for Abraham and Isaac and Jacob 2
2Mc 1: 2 his covenant with Abraham and Isaac and Jacob 2
4Mc 7:14 by reason like that of Isaac 3
19 like our patriarchs Abraham and Isaac and Jacob 2
13:12 Isaac would have submitted to being slain 2
17 Abraham and Isaac and Jacob will welcome us 2
16:20 Abraham was zealous to sacrifice his son Isaac 2
20 when Isaac saw his father's hand wielding a sword •
25 as do Abraham and Isaac and Jacob 2
18:11 Isaac who was offered as a burnt offering 2

Isaiah 1. יְשַׁעְיָהוּ 2. Ἠσαΐας 3. Esaia
2Kg 19: 2 he sent . . to the prophet Isaiah the son of Amoz. 1
5 When the servants of . . Hezeki'ah came to Isaiah 1
6 Isaiah said to them, "Say to your master, 'Thus says 1
20 Then Isaiah the son of Amoz sent to Hezeki'ah 1
20: 1 Isaiah the prophet . . came to him, and said to him 1
4 before Isaiah had gone out of the middle court 1
7 Isaiah said, "Bring a cake of figs. 1
8 Hezeki'ah said to Isaiah, "What shall be the sign 1
9 Isaiah said, "This is the sign to you from the LORD 1
11 Isaiah the prophet cried to the LORD 1
14 Then Isaiah the prophet came to King Hezeki'ah 1
16 Isaiah said to Hezeki'ah, "Hear the word of the LORD 1
19 Then said Hezeki'ah to Isaiah, "The word . . is good. 1
2Ch 26:22 Isaiah the prophet the son of Amoz wrote. 1
32:20 Then Hezeki'ah . . and Isaiah . . , prayed 1
32 written in the vision of Isaiah the prophet 1
Isa 1: 1 The vision of Isaiah the son of Amoz, which he saw 1
2: 1 The word which Isaiah the son of Amoz saw 1
7: 3 the LORD said to Isaiah, "Go forth to meet Ahaz 1
13: 1 oracle concerning Babylon which Isaiah . . saw. 1
20: 2 the LORD had spoken by Isaiah the son of Amoz 1
3 my servant Isaiah has walked naked and barefoot 1
37: 2 he sent . . to the prophet Isaiah the son of Amoz. 1
5 the servants of King Hezeki'ah came to Isaiah 1
6 Isaiah said to them, "Say to your master 1
21 Then Isaiah the son of Amoz sent to Hezeki'ah 1
38: 1 Isaiah the prophet the son of Amoz came to him 1
4 Then the word of the LORD came to Isaiah 1
21 Now Isaiah had said, "Let them take a cake of figs 1
39: 3 Then Isaiah the prophet came to King Hezeki'ah 1
5 Isaiah said to Hezeki'ah, "Hear the word of the LORD 1
8 Then said Hezeki'ah to Isaiah, "The word of the LORD 1
Mat 3: 3 by the prophet Isaiah when he said, "The voice 2
4:14 spoken by the prophet Isaiah might be fulfilled 2
8:17 to fulfil what was spoken by the prophet Isaiah 2
12:17 to fulfil what was spoken by the prophet Isaiah 2
13:14 indeed is fulfilled the prophecy of Isaiah 2
15: 7 You hypocrites! Well did Isaiah prophesy of you 2
Mrk 1: 2 As it is written in Isaiah the prophet 2
7: 6 Well did Isaiah prophesy of you hypocrites 2
Lke 3: 4 the book of the words of Isaiah the prophet 2
4:17 was given to him the book of the prophet Isaiah. 2
Joh 1:23 'Make straight . . ' as the prophet Isaiah said. 2
12:38 the word spoken by the prophet Isaiah 2
39 For Isaiah again said 2
41 Isaiah said this because he saw his glory 2
Act 8:28 he was reading the prophet Isaiah. 2
30 heard him reading Isaiah the prophet 2
28:25 saying . . through Isaiah the prophet 2
Rom 9:27 And Isaiah cries out concerning Israel 2
29 And as Isaiah predicted, "If the Lord of hosts had 2
10:16 for Isaiah says, "Lord, who has believed 2
20 Then Isaiah is so bold as to say, "I have been found 2
15:12 further Isaiah says, "The root of Jesse shall come 2
2Es 2:18 send you help, my servants Isaiah and Jeremiah. 3
Sir 48:20 delivered them by the hand of Isaiah. 2
22 which Isaiah the prophet commanded 2
4Mc 18:14 He reminded you of the scripture of Isaiah 2

Iscah 1. יִסְכָּה
Gen 11:29 of Haran the father of Milcah and Iscah. 1

Iscariot 1. Ἰσκαριώθ 2. Ἰσκαριώτης
Mat 10: 4 Simon the Cananaean, and Judas Iscariot 2
26:14 one of the twelve, who was called Judas Iscariot 2
Mrk 3:19 Judas Iscariot, who betrayed him. 1
14:10 Then Judas Iscariot, who was one of the twelve 1
Lke 6:16 Judas Iscariot, who became a traitor. 1
22: 3 Then Satan entered into Judas called Iscariot 2
Joh 6:71 He spoke of Judas the son of Simon Iscariot 1
12: 4 Judas Iscariot, one of his disciples 2
13: 2 the heart of Judas Iscariot, Simon's son 1
26 he gave it to Judas, the son of Simon Iscariot. 1
14:22 Judas (not Iscariot) said to him, "Lord, how is it 2

Ish-bosheth 1. אִישׁ בֹּשֶׁת
2Sm 2: 8 Abner . . had taken Ish-bo'sheth the son of Saul 1
10 Ish-bo'sheth, Saul's son, was 40 years old 1
12 and the servants of Ish-bo'sheth the son of Saul 1
15 for Benjamin and Ish-bo'sheth the son of Saul 1
3: 7 and Ish-bo'sheth said to Abner, "Why have you gone •
8 Abner was . . angry over the words of Ish-bo'sheth 1
11 Ish-bo'sheth could not answer Abner another word •
14 David sent messengers to Ish-bo'sheth Saul's son 1
15 Ish-bo'sheth sent, and took her from her husband 1
4: 1 Ish-bo'sheth, Saul's son, heard that Abner had died •
5 they came to the house of Ish-bo'sheth, as he was 1
8 and brought the head of Ish-bo'sheth to David 1
8 Here is the head of Ish-bo'sheth, the son of Saul 1
12 they took the head of Ish-bo'sheth, and buried it 1

Ishbah 1. יִשְׁבַּח
1Ch 4:17 Bith'i-ah . . conceived and bore . . Ishbah 1

Ishbak 1. יִשְׁבָּק
Gen 25: 2 Jokshan, Medan, Mid'ian, Ishbak, and Shuah. 1
1Ch 1:32 Jokshan, Medan, Mid'ian, Ishbak, and Shu'ah. 1

Ishbi-benob 1. יִשְׁבִּי בְּנֹב
2Sm 21:16 And Ish'bi-be'nob . . thought to kill David. 1

Ishhod 1. אִישְׁהוֹד
1Ch 7:18 sister Hammo'lecheth bore Ishhod, Abi-e'zer 1

Ishi 1. יִשְׁעִי
1Ch 2:31 The sons of Ap'pa-im: Ishi. 1
31 The sons of Ishi: Sheshan. 1
4:20 The sons of Ishi: Zoheth and Ben-zo'heth. 1
42 Pelati'ah . . and Uz'ziel, the sons of Ishi; 1
5:24 heads of their fathers' houses . . Ishi, Eli'el 1

Ishma 1. יִשְׁמָא
1Ch 4: 3 the sons of Etam: Jezreel, Ishma, and Idbash; 1

Ishmael 1. יִשְׁמָעֵאל 2. Ισμαηλος
Gen 16:11 you shall call his name Ish'mael; 1
15 the name of his son, whom Hagar bore, Ish'mael. 1
16 when Hagar bore Ish'mael to Abram. 1
17:18 O that Ish'mael might live in thy sight! 1
20 As for Ish'mael, I have heard you; 1
23 Then Abraham took Ish'mael his son 1
25 Ish'mael his son was thirteen years old 1
26 Abraham and his son Ish'mael were circumcised; 1
25: 9 Isaac and Ish'mael his sons buried him in the cave 1
12 These are the descendants of Ish'mael 1
13 These are the names of the sons of Ish'mael 1
13 Neba'ioth, the first-born of Ish'mael; 1
16 These are the sons of Ish'mael 1
17 These are the years of the life of Ish'mael 1
28: 9 Esau went to Ish'mael and took to wife 1
9 the daughter of Ish'mael Abraham's son 1
36: 3 Bas'emath, Ish'mael's daughter, the sister 1
2Kg 25:23 they came . . namely, Ish'mael the son of Nethani'ah 1
25 Ish'mael . . came with ten men, and attacked 1
1Ch 1:28 The sons of Abraham: Isaac and Ish'mael. 1
29 the first-born of Ish'mael, Neba'ioth; and Kedar 1
31 Ked'emah. These are the sons of Ish'mael. 1
8:38 Azel had six sons . . Azri'kam, Bo'cheru, Ish'mael 1
9:44 Azel had six sons . . Azri'kam, Bo'cheru, Ish'mael 1
2Ch 19:11 Zebadi'ah the son of Ish'mael 1
23: 1 commanders . . Ish'mael the son of Jehoha'nan 1
Ezr 10:22 of Pashhur: Eli-o-e'nai, Ma-asei'ah, Ish'mael 1
Jer 40: 8 Ish'mael the son of Nethani'ah 1
14 Ba'alis . . has sent Ish'mael the son of Nethani'ah 1
15 Let me go and slay Ish'mael the son of Nethani'ah 1
16 for you are speaking falsely of Ish'mael. 1
41: 1 In the seventh month, Ish'mael . . came 1
2 Ish'mael the son of Nethani'ah and the ten men 1
3 Ish'mael also slew all the Jews 1
6 And Ish'mael the son of Nethani'ah came out 1
7 When they came into the city, Ish'mael . . slew them 1
8 there were ten men among them who said to Ish'mael 1
9 cistern into which Ish'mael cast all the bodies 1
9 Ish'mael . . filled it with the slain. 1
10 Then Ish'mael took captive all the rest 1
10 Ish'mael the son of Nethani'ah took them captive 1
11 heard of all the evil which Ish'mael . . had done 1
12 and went to fight against Ish'mael 1
13 all the people who were with Ish'mael saw Joha'nan 1
14 all the people whom Ish'mael had carried away 1
15 But Ish'mael the son of Nethani'ah escaped 1
16 whom Ish'mael the son of Nethani'ah had carried 1
18 Ish'mael the son of Nethani'ah had slain Gedali'ah 1
1Es 9:22 Ishmael, and Nathanael, and Gedaliah, and Elasah. 2

Ishmaelite 1. יִשְׁמְעֵאלִי 2. υἱὸς Ισμαηλ
Gen 37:25 a caravan of Ish'maelites coming from Gilead 1
27 Come, let us sell him to the Ish'maelites 1
28 sold him to the Ish'maelites for twenty shekels 1
39: 1 Pot'i-phar . . bought him from the Ish'maelites 1
Jdg 8:24 had . . earrings, because they were Ish'maelites. 1
2Sm 17:25 was the son of a man named Ithra the Ish'maelite •
1Ch 2:17 the father of Ama'sa was Jether the Ish'maelite. 1
27:30 Over the camels was Obil the Ish'maelite; 1
Ps 83: 6 the tents of Edom and the Ish'maelites 1
Jdt 2:23 the Ishmaelites who lived along the desert 2

Ishmaiah 1. יִשְׁמַעְיָהוּ
1Ch 12: 4 Ishma'iah of Gibeon, a mighty man among the 30 1
27:19 for Zeb'ulun, Ishma'iah the son of Obadi'ah; 1

Ishmerai 1. יִשְׁמְרַי
1Ch 8:18 Ish'merai, Izli'ah, and Jobab . . sons of Elpa'al. 1

Ishpah 1. יִשְׁפָּה
1Ch 8:16 Michael, Ishpah, and Joha were sons of Beri'ah. 1

Ishpan 1. יִשְׁפָּן
1Ch 8:22 Ishpan, Eber, Eli'el 1

Ishvah 1. יִשְׁוָה
Gen 46:17 The sons of Asher: Imnah, Ishvah, Ishvi, Beri'ah 1
1Ch 7:30 The sons of Asher: Imnah, Ishvah, Ishvi, Beri'ah 1

Ishvi 1. יִשְׁוִי
Gen 46:17 The sons of Asher: Imnah, Ishvah, Ishvi, Beri'ah 1
Num26:44 of Ishvi, the family of the Ishvites; 1
1Sm 14:49 sons of Saul were Jonathan, Ishvi, and Mal'chishu'a; 1
1Ch 7:30 The sons of Asher: Imnah, Ishvah, Ishvi, Beri'ah 1

Ishvite 1. יִשְׁוִי
Num26:44 of Ishvi, the family of the Ishvites; 1

Ismachiah 1. יִסְמַכְיָהוּ
2Ch 31:13 Ismachi'ah, Mahath, and Benai'ah were overseers 1

Israel 1. בְּנֵי יִשְׂרָאֵל 2. יִשְׂרָאֵל 3. יִשְׂרְאֵלִי 4. יִשְׂרָאֵל (A) 5. Ἰσραήλ 6. Ἰσραηλίτης 7. Israhel
Gen 32:28 be called Jacob, but Israel, for you have striven 2
34: 7 because he had wrought folly in Israel by lying 2
35:10 be called Jacob, but Israel shall be your name. 2
10 his name was called Israel. 2
21 Israel journeyed on, and pitched his tent beyond 2
22 While Israel dwelt in that land Reuben went 2
22 Bilhah his father's concubine; and Israel heard 2
37: 3 Now Israel loved Joseph more than any other 2
13 Israel said to Joseph, "Are not your brothers 2
42: 5 Thus the sons of Israel came to buy among 2
43: 6 Israel said, "Why did you treat me so ill 2
8 Judah said to Israel his father, "Send the lad 2
11 Then their father Israel said to them 2
45:21 The sons of Israel did so; 2
28 Israel said, "It is enough; Joseph my son is still 2
46: 1 Israel took his journey with all that he had 2
2 God spoke to Israel in visions of the night 2
5 and the sons of Israel carried Jacob their 2
8 the names of the descendants of Israel, who came 2
29 went up to meet Israel his father in Goshen; 2
30 Israel said to Joseph, "Now let me die 2
47:27 Thus Israel dwelt in the land of Egypt 2
29 when the time drew near that Israel must die 2
31 Israel bowed himself upon the head of his bed. 2
48: 2 then Israel summoned his strength, and sat up 2
8 When Israel saw Joseph's sons, he said, 2
10 Now the eyes of Israel were dim with age 2
11 Israel said to Joseph, "I had not thought to see 2
13 E'phraim in his right hand toward Israel's left 2
13 Manas'seh in his left hand toward Israel's right 2
14 Israel stretched out his right hand and laid it 2
20 By you Israel will pronounce blessings, saying 2
21 Then Israel said to Joseph, "Behold, I am 2
49: 2 Assemble . . and hearken to Israel your father. 2
7 I will . . scatter them in Israel. 2
16 judge his people as one of the tribes of Israel. 2
24 by the name of the Shepherd, the Rock of Israel 2
28 All these are the twelve tribes of Israel; 2
50: 2 the physicians embalmed Israel; 2
25 Then Joseph took an oath of the sons of Israel 2
Exd 1: 1 the names of the sons of Israel who came to Egypt 2
7 the descendants of Israel were fruitful 2
9 Behold, the people of Israel are too many 2
12 Egyptians were in dread of the people of Israel. 2
13 they made the people of Israel serve with rigor 2
2:23 people of Israel groaned under their bondage 2
25 God saw the people of Israel 2
3: 9 the cry of the people of Israel has come to me 2
10 my people, the sons of Israel, out of Egypt. 2
11 bring the sons of Israel out of Egypt? 2
13 I come to the people of Israel and say to them 2
14 Say this to the people of Israel, 'I AM has sent me 2
15 Say this to the people of Israel, 'The LORD 2
16 Go and gather the elders of Israel together 2
18 you and the elders of Israel shall go to the king 2
4:22 Thus says the LORD, Israel is my first-born son 2
29 all the elders of the people of Israel. 2
31 that the LORD had visited the people of Israel 2
5: 1 Thus says the LORD, the God of Israel 2
2 that I should . . let Israel go? 2
2 and moreover I will not let Israel go. 2
14 the foremen of the people of Israel 2
15 Then the foremen of the people of Israel came 2
19 The foremen of the people of Israel saw that they 2
6: 5 I have heard the groaning of the people of Israel 2
6 Say therefore to the people of Israel 2
9 Moses spoke thus to the people of Israel; 2
11 tell Pharaoh . . to let the people of Israel go 2
12 the people of Israel have not listened to me; 2
13 a charge to the people of Israel and to Pharaoh 2
13 a charge . . to bring the people of Israel out 2
14 the sons of Reuben, the first-born of Israel 2
26 Bring out the people of Israel from the land 2
27 bringing out the people of Israel from Egypt 2

7: 2 let the people of Israel go out of his land. 2
4 bring forth . . my people the sons of Israel 2
5 when I . . bring out the people of Israel 2
9: 4 the cattle of Israel and the cattle of Egypt 2
4 of all that belongs to the people of Israel. 2
6 of the cattle of . . Israel not one died. 2
26 Goshen, where the people of Israel were, there was 2
35 he did not let the people of Israel go; 2
10:20 he did not let the children of Israel go. 2
23 but all the people of Israel had light 2
11: 7 against any of the people of Israel 2
7 a distinction between the Egyptians and Israel. 2
10 did not let the people of Israel go out 2
12: 3 Tell all the congregation of Israel that 2
6 congregation of Israel shall kill their lambs 2
15 that person shall be cut off from Israel. 2
19 cut off from the congregation of Israel 2
21 Moses called all the elders of Israel, and said 2
27 the houses of the people of Israel in Egypt 2
28 Then the people of Israel went and did so; 2
31 go forth . . both you and the people of Israel; 2
35 The people of Israel had also done as Moses told 2
37 the people of Israel journeyed from Ram'eses 2
40 The time that the people of Israel dwelt in Egypt 2
42 kept to the LORD by all the people of Israel 2
47 All the congregation of Israel shall keep it. 2
50 Thus did all the people of Israel; 2
51 brought the people of Israel out of the land 2
13: 2 first to open the womb among the people of Israel 2
18 the people of Israel went up out of the land 2
19 Joseph had solemnly sworn the people of Israel 2
14: 2 Tell the people of Israel to turn back and encamp 2
3 For Pharaoh will say of the people of Israel 2
5 that we have let Israel go from serving us? 2
8 king of Egypt and he pursued the people of Israel 2
10 the people of Israel lifted up their eyes 2
10 the people of Israel cried out to the LORD; 2
15 Tell the people of Israel to go forward. 2
16 the people of Israel may go on dry ground through 2
19 angel of God who went before the host of Israel 2
20 between the host of Egypt and the host of Israel. 2
22 the people of Israel went into the midst 2
25 Egyptians said, "Let us flee from before Israel; 2
29 the people of Israel walked on dry ground 2
30 Thus the LORD saved Israel that day from the hand 2
30 Israel saw the Egyptians dead upon the seashore. 2
31 Israel saw the great work which the LORD did 2
15: 1 Moses and the people of Israel sang this song 2
19 the people of Israel walked on dry ground 2
22 Then Moses led Israel onward from the Red Sea 2
16: 1 people of Israel came to the wilderness of Sin 2
2 the whole congregation of the people of Israel 2
6 Moses and Aaron said to all the people of Israel 2
9 the whole congregation of the people of Israel 2
10 whole congregation of the people of Israel 2
12 the murmurings of the people of Israel; 2
15 When the people of Israel saw it, they said to one 2
17 the people of Israel did so; they gathered 2
31 Now the house of Israel called its name manna; 2
35 the people of Israel ate the manna forty years 2
17: 1 All the congregation of the people of Israel 2
5 taking with you some of the elders of Israel; 2
6 did so, in the sight of the elders of Israel. 2
7 the faultfinding of the children of Israel 2
8 came Am'alek and fought with Israel at Reph'idim. 2
11 Moses held up his hand, Israel prevailed; 2
18: 1 God had done for Moses and for Israel his people 2
1 how the LORD had brought Israel out of Egypt. 2
8 Pharaoh and to the Egyptians for Israel's sake 2
9 the good which the LORD had done to Israel 2
12 and Aaron came with all the elders of Israel 2
25 Moses chose able men out of all Israel 2
19: 1 after the people of Israel had gone forth 2
2 there Israel encamped before the mountain. 2
3 Thus you shall . . tell the people of Israel 2
6 you shall speak to the children of Israel. 2
20:22 Moses, "Thus you shall say to the people of Israel 2
24: 1 Abi'hu, and 70 of the elders of Israel 2
4 according to the twelve tribes of Israel. 2
5 he sent young men of the people of Israel 2
9 Abi'hu, and 70 of the elders of Israel went up 2
10 they saw the God of Israel; 2
11 on the chief men of the people of Israel; 2
17 in the sight of the people of Israel. 2
25: 2 Speak to the people of Israel, that they take 2
22 in commandment for the people of Israel. 2
27:20 you shall command the people of Israel 2
21 observed . . by the people of Israel. 2
28: 1 from among the people of Israel, to serve me 2
9 engrave on them the names of the sons of Israel 2
11 stones with the names of the sons of Israel; 2
12 as stones of remembrance for the sons of Israel; 2
21 according to the names of the sons of Israel; 2
29 Aaron shall bear all the names of the sons of Israel 2
30 bear the judgment of the people of Israel 2
38 holy offering which the people of Israel hallow 2
29:28 perpetual due from the people of Israel 2
28 portion to be offered by the people of Israel 2
43 There I will meet with the people of Israel 2
45 I will dwell among the people of Israel 2
30:12 When you take the census of the people of Israel 2
16 atonement money from the people of Israel 2
16 it may bring the people of Israel to remembrance 2
31 you shall say to the people of Israel, 'This shall 2
31:13 Say to the people of Israel 2
16 people of Israel shall keep the sabbath 2
17 sign for ever between me and the people of Israel 2
32: 4 they said, "These are your gods, O Israel, who 2
8 These are your gods, O Israel, who brought you up 2
13 Remember Abraham, Isaac, and Israel, thy servants 2
20 and made the people of Israel drink it. 2
27 he said to them, "Thus says the LORD God of Israel 2
33: 5 Say to the people of Israel, 'You are a stiff-necked 2
6 the people of Israel stripped themselves 2
34:23 appear before the LORD God, the God of Israel. 2
27 I have made a covenant with you and with Israel. 2
30 when Aaron and all the people of Israel saw Moses 2
32 afterward all the people of Israel came near 2
34 told the people of Israel what he was commanded 2
35 the people of Israel saw the face of Moses 2
35: 1 the people of Israel, and said to them 2
4 all the congregation of the people of Israel 2
20 Israel departed from the presence of Moses. 2
29 All the men and women, the people of Israel 2
30 Moses said to the people of Israel, "See, the LORD 2
36: 3 freewill offering which the people of Israel 2
39: 6 according to the names of the sons of Israel. 2
7 stones of remembrance for the sons of Israel; 2
14 according to the names of the sons of Israel; 2
32 the people of Israel had done according to all 2
42 so the people of Israel had done all the work. 2
40:36 the people of Israel would go onward; 2
38 by night, in the sight of all the house of Israel. 2
Lev 1: 2 Speak to the people of Israel, and say to them 2
4: 2 Say to the people of Israel, If any one sins 2
13 If the whole congregation of Israel commits a sin 2
7:23 Say to the people of Israel, You shall eat no fat 2
29 Say to the people of Israel, He that offers 2
34 I have taken from the people of Israel 2
34 as a perpetual due from the people of Israel 2
36 to be given them by the people of Israel 2
38 on the day that he commanded the people of Israel 2
9: 1 Aaron and his sons and the elders of Israel 2
3 say to the people of Israel, 'Take a male goat 2
10: 6 but your brethren, the whole house of Israel 2
11 you are to teach the people of Israel 2
14 the peace offerings of the people of Israel 2
11: 2 Say to the people of Israel 2
12: 2 Say to the people of Israel, If a woman conceives 2
15: 2 Say to the people of Israel 2
31 you shall keep the people of Israel separate 2
16: 5 from the congregation of the people of Israel 2
16 the uncleannesses of the people of Israel 2
17 for his house and for all the assembly of Israel 2
19 from the uncleannesses of the people of Israel 2
21 all the iniquities of the people of Israel 2
34 atonement may be made for the people of Israel 2
17: 2 Say to Aaron . . and to all the people of Israel 2
3 If any man of the house of Israel kills an ox 2
5 the people of Israel may bring their sacrifices 2
8 Any man of the house of Israel 2
10 If any man of the house of Israel 2
12 Therefore I have said to the people of Israel 2
13 Any man also of the people of Israel 2
14 therefore I have said to the people of Israel 2
18: 2 Say to the people of Israel, I am the LORD your God 2
19: 2 to all the congregation of the people of Israel 2
20: 2 Say to the people of Israel, Any man of the people 2
2 Any man of the people of Israel, or of the strangers 2
2 Any . . of the strangers that sojourn in Israel 2
21:24 spoke . . to all the people of Israel 2
22: 2 the holy things of the people of Israel 2
3 holy things, which the people of Israel dedicate 2
15 profane the holy things of the people of Israel 2
18 Say to . . all the people of Israel, When any one 2
18 When any one of the house of Israel . . presents 2
18 When any one . . of the sojourners in Israel 2
32 I will be hallowed among the people of Israel 2
23: 2 Say to the people of Israel, The appointed feasts 2
10 Say to the people of Israel, When you come 2
24 Say to the people of Israel, In the seventh month 2
34 Say to the people of Israel, On the fifteenth day 2
42 all that are native in Israel shall dwell 2
43 may know that I made the people of Israel dwell 2
44 Thus Moses declared to the people of Israel 2
24: 2 Command the people of Israel to bring you . . oil 2
8 on behalf of the people of Israel as a covenant 2
10 went out among the people of Israel 2
10 woman's son and a man of Israel quarreled 3
15 say to the people of Israel, Whoever curses 2
23 So Moses spoke to the people of Israel 2
23 the people of Israel did as the LORD commanded 2
25: 2 Say to the people of Israel, When you come 2
33 their possession among the people of Israel 2
46 over . . the people of Israel you shall not rule 2
55 For to me the people of Israel are servants 2
26:46 between him and the people of Israel on Mount 2
27: 2 Say to the people of Israel 2
34 commandments . . for the people of Israel 2
Num 1: 2 all the congregation of the people of Israel 2
3 all in Israel who are able to go forth to war 2
16 These were . . the heads of the clans of Israel. 2
20 The people of Reuben, Israel's first-born 2
44 the help of the leaders of Israel, twelve men 2
45 So the whole number of the people of Israel 2
45 every man able to go forth to war in Israel– 2
49 take a census of them among the people of Israel; 2
52 The people of Israel shall pitch their tents 2
53 upon the congregation of the people of Israel; 2
54 Thus did the people of Israel; they did according 2
2: 2 The people of Israel shall encamp each by his own 2
32 These are the people of Israel as numbered 2
33 not numbered among the people of Israel 2
34 Thus did the people of Israel. 2
3: 8 for the people of Israel as they minister 2
9 given to him from among the people of Israel. 2
12 the Levites from among the people of Israel 2
12 that opens the womb among the people of Israel. 2
13 consecrated . . the first-born in Israel 2
38 whatever had to be done for the people of Israel; 2
40 all the first-born males of the people of Israel 2
41 all the first-born among the people of Israel 2
41 firstlings among the cattle of . . Israel. 2
42 all the first-born among the people of Israel 2
45 all the first-born among the people of Israel 2
46 273 of the first-born of the people of Israel 2
50 from the first-born of the people of Israel 2
4:46 whom Moses and Aaron and the leaders of Israel 2
5: 2 Command the people of Israel that they put out 2
4 people of Israel did so, and drove them outside 2
4 as the LORD said . . so the people of Israel did. 2
6 Say to the people of Israel, When a man or woman 2
9 all the holy things of the people of Israel 2
12 Say to the people of Israel, If any man's wife 2
6: 2 Say to the people of Israel, When either a man 2
23 Thus you shall bless the people of Israel 2
27 shall they put my name upon the people of Israel 2
7: 2 leaders of Israel, heads of their fathers' houses 2
84 offering . . from the leaders of Israel 2
8: 6 Take the Levites from among the people of Israel 2
9 assemble the whole . . of the people of Israel. 2
10 people of Israel shall lay their hands upon 2
11 as a wave offering from the people of Israel 2
14 Levites from among the people of Israel 2
16 given to me from among the people of Israel; 2
16 first-born of all the people of Israel 2
17 first-born among the people of Israel are mine 2
18 all the first-born among the people of Israel. 2
19 as a gift . . from among the people of Israel 2
19 to do the service for the people of Israel 2
19 to make atonement for the people of Israel 2
19 there may be no plague among the people of Israel 2
19 in case the people of Israel should come near 2
20 all the congregation of the people of Israel 2
20 people of Israel did to them. 2
9: 2 Let the people of Israel keep the passover 2
4 Moses told the people of Israel that they should 2
5 so the people of Israel did. 2
7 among the people of Israel? 2
10 Say to the people of Israel, If any man of you 2
17 after that the people of Israel set out; 2
17 there the people of Israel encamped. 2
18 command of the LORD the people of Israel set out 2
19 people of Israel kept the charge of the LORD 2
22 the people of Israel remained in camp 2
10: 4 leaders, the heads of the tribes of Israel 2
12 people of Israel set out by stages 2
28 was the order of march of the people of Israel 2
29 for the LORD has promised good to Israel. 2
36 O LORD, to the ten thousand thousands of Israel. 2
11: 4 people of Israel also wept again 2
16 Gather for me 70 men of the elders of Israel 2
30 elders of Israel returned to the camp. 2
13: 2 Canaan, which I give to the people of Israel; 2
3 men who were heads of the people of Israel. 2
24 which the men of Israel cut down from there. 2
26 all the congregation of the people of Israel 2
32 brought to the people of Israel an evil report 2
14: 2 all the people of Israel murmured against Moses 2
5 all . . congregation of the people of Israel. 2
7 said to all . . of the people of Israel 2
10 appeared . . to all the people of Israel. 2
27 heard the murmurings of the people of Israel 2
39 Moses told these words to all . . Israel 2
15: 2 Say to the people of Israel, When you come 2
18 Say to the people of Israel, When you come 2
25 for all the congregation of the people of Israel 2
26 all the congregation of the people of Israel 2
29 for him who is native among the people of Israel 2
32 people of Israel were in the wilderness 2
38 Speak to the people of Israel, and bid them to make 2
16: 2 rose up . . with a number of the people of Israel 2
9 that the God of Israel has separated you 2
9 separated you from the congregation of Israel 2
25 elders of Israel followed him. 2
34 all Israel that were round about them fled 2
38 Thus they shall be a sign to the people of Israel. 2

40 to be a reminder to the people of Israel 2
41 all . . the people of Israel murmured against 2
17: 2 Speak to the people of Israel, and get from them 2
5 murmurings of the people of Israel 2
6 Moses spoke to the people of Israel; 2
9 all the rods . . to all the people of Israel; 2
12 people of Israel said to Moses, "Behold, we perish 2
18: 5 there be wrath no more upon the people of Israel. 2
6 Levites from among the people of Israel; 2
8 consecrated things of the people of Israel; 2
11 all the wave offerings of the people of Israel; 2
14 Every devoted thing in Israel shall be yours. 2
19 offerings which the people of Israel present 2
20 portion and your inheritance among . . Israel. 2
21 To the Levites I have given every tithe in Israel 2
22 henceforth the people of Israel shall not come 2
23 among the people of Israel they shall have no 2
24 For the tithe of the people of Israel 2
24 have no inheritance among the people of Israel. 2
26 When you take from the people of Israel the tithe 2
28 tithes . . you receive from the people of Israel; 2
32 holy things of the people of Israel 2
19: 2 Tell the people of Israel to bring you 2
9 for the congregation of the people of Israel 2
10 be to the people of Israel, and to the stranger 2
13 that person shall be cut off from Israel; 2
20: 1 people of Israel . . came into the wilderness 2
12 to sanctify me in the eyes of the people of Israel 2
13 Mer'ibah, where the people of Israel contended 2
14 Thus says your brother Israel: You know 2
19 people of Israel said to him, "We will go up 2
21 Edom refused to give Israel passage through 2
21 so Israel turned away from him. 2
22 people of Israel . . came to Mount Hor. 2
24 land which I have given to the people of Israel 2
29 all the house of Israel wept for Aaron 30 days 2
21: 1 Canaanite . . heard that Israel was coming 2
1 he fought against Israel, and took some 2
2 Israel vowed a vow to the LORD, and said 2
3 LORD hearkened to the voice of Israel, and gave 2
6 so that many people of Israel died. 2
10 people of Israel set out, and encamped in Oboth. 2
17 Israel sang this song: "Spring up, O well!–Sing to it!– 2
21 Then Israel sent messengers to Sihon king 2
23 Sihon would not allow Israel to pass through 2
23 went out against Israel to the wilderness 2
23 came to Jahaz, and fought against Israel. 2
24 Israel slew him with the edge of the sword 2
25 Israel took all these cities, and Israel settled 2
25 Israel settled in all the cities of the Amorites 2
31 Thus Israel dwelt in the land of the Amorites. 2
22: 1 Then the people of Israel set out, and encamped 2
2 Balak . . saw all that Israel had done 2
3 overcome with fear of the people of Israel. 2
23: 7 Come, curse Jacob for me, and come, denounce Israel!' 2
10 dust of Jacob, or number the fourth part of Israel? 2
21 nor has he seen trouble in Israel. 2
23 For there is . . no divination against Israel; 2
23 be said of Jacob and Israel, 'What has God wrought!' 2
24: 1 saw that it pleased the LORD to bless Israel 2
2 Balaam . . saw Israel encamping tribe by tribe. 2
5 how fair are you . . encampments, O Israel! 2
17 scepter shall rise out of Israel; 2
18 be dispossessed, while Israel does valiantly. 2
25: 1 While Israel dwelt in Shittim the people 2
3 Israel yoked himself to Ba'al of Pe'or. 2
3 anger of the LORD was kindled against Israel; 2
4 anger of the LORD may turn away from Israel. 2
5 Moses said to the judges of Israel, "Every one 2
6 one of the people of Israel came and brought 2
6 whole congregation of the people of Israel 2
8 went after the man of Israel into the inner room 2
8 both of them, the man of Israel and the woman 2
8 plague was stayed from the people of Israel. 2
11 turned back my wrath from the people of Israel 2
11 not consume the people of Israel in my jealousy. 2
13 made atonement for the people of Israel.' 2
14 The name of the slain man of Israel . . was Zimri 2
26: 2 all the congregation of the people of Israel 2
2 all in Israel who are able to go forth to war. 2
4 people of Israel, who came forth out of . . Egypt 2
5 Reuben, the first-born of Israel; 2
51 number of the people of Israel, 601,730. 2
62 not numbered among the people of Israel 2
62 no inheritance . . among the people of Israel. 2
63 numbered the people of Israel in the plains 2
64 numbered the people of Israel in the wilderness 2
27: 8 you shall say to the people of Israel, 'If a man dies 2
11 to the people of Israel a statute and ordinance 2
12 land which I have given to the people of Israel. 2
20 congregation of the people of Israel may obey. 2
21 both he and all the people of Israel with him 2
28: 2 Command the people of Israel, and say to them 2
29:40 Moses told the people of Israel everything 2
30: 1 heads of the tribes of the people of Israel 2
31: 2 Avenge the people of Israel on the Mid'ianites; 2
4 send 1,000 from each of the tribes of Israel to the war 2
5 provided, out of the thousands of Israel 2
9 people of Israel took captive the women 2

12 the congregation of the people of Israel 2
16 these caused the people of Israel . . to act 2
30 from the people of Israel's half you shall take 2
42 From the people of Israel's half, which Moses 2
47 from the people of Israel's half Moses took 2
54 memorial for the people of Israel before 2
32: 4 land . . LORD smote before the congregation of Israel 2
7 you discourage the heart of the people of Israel 2
9 discouraged the heart of the people of Israel 2
13 the LORD'S anger was kindled against Israel 2
14 fierce anger of the LORD against Israel! 2
17 take up arms, ready to go before the people of Israel 2
18 until the people of Israel have inherited 2
22 and be free of obligation to the LORD and to Israel 2
28 tribes of the people of Israel. 2
33: 1 These are the stages of the people of Israel 2
3 people of Israel went out triumphantly 2
5 the people of Israel set out from Ram'eses 2
38 after the people of Israel had come out 2
40 heard of the coming of the people of Israel. 2
51 Say to the people of Israel, When you pass over 2
34: 2 Command the people of Israel, and say to them 2
13 Moses commanded the people of Israel, saying 2
29 divide the inheritance for the people of Israel 2
35: 2 Command the people of Israel, that they give 2
8 give from the possession of the people of Israel 2
10 Say to the people of Israel, When you cross 2
15 cities . . for refuge for the people of Israel 2
34 LORD dwell in the midst of the people of Israel. 2
36: 1 leaders, the heads . . of the people of Israel; 2
2 give the land . . by lot to the people of Israel; 2
3 sons of the other tribes of the people of Israel 2
4 when the jubilee of the people of Israel comes 2
5 Moses commanded the people of Israel 2
7 inheritance of the people of Israel shall not 2
7 every one of the people of Israel shall cleave 2
8 inheritance in any tribe of the people of Israel 2
8 every one of the people of Israel may possess 2
9 for each of the tribes of the people of Israel 2
13 LORD commanded by Moses to the people of Israel 2
Deu 1: 1 Moses spoke to all Israel beyond the Jordan 2
3 Moses spoke to the people of Israel according 2
38 for he shall cause Israel to inherit it. 2
2:12 as Israel did to the land of their possession 2
3:18 before your brethren the people of Israel. 2
4: 1 now, O Israel, give heed to the statutes 2
44 law . . Moses set before the children of Israel; 2
45 which Moses spoke to the children of Israel 2
46 whom Moses and the children of Israel defeated 2
5: 1 Moses summoned all Israel, and said to them, "Hear 2
1 Hear, O Israel, the statutes and the ordinances 2
6: 3 Hear therefore, O Israel, and be careful to do them; 2
4 Hear, O Israel: The LORD our God is one LORD; 2
9: 1 Hear, O Israel; you are to pass over the Jordan 2
10: 6 Israel journeyed from Be-er'oth Bene-ja'akan 2
12 now, Israel, what does the LORD your God require 2
11: 6 swallowed them up . . in the midst of all Israel; 2
13:11 all Israel shall hear, and fear, and never again do 2
17: 4 such an abominable thing has been done in Israel 2
12 so you shall purge the evil from Israel. 2
20 continue long in his kingdom . . in Israel. 2
18: 1 Levi . . no portion or inheritance with Israel; 2
6 Levite comes from any of your towns out of all Israel 2
19:13 purge the guilt of innocent blood from Israel 2
20: 3 say to them, 'Hear, O Israel, you draw near this day 2
21: 8 Forgive, O LORD, thy people Israel, whom thou hast 2
8 not the guilt . . in the midst of thy people Israel; 2
21 all Israel shall hear, and fear. 2
22:19 brought an evil name upon a virgin of Israel; 2
21 wrought folly in Israel by playing the harlot 2
22 so you shall purge the evil from Israel. 2
23:17 no cult prostitute of the daughters of Israel 2
17 neither . . a cult prostitute of the sons of Israel. 2
24: 7 one of his brethren, the people of Israel 2
25: 6 that his name may not be blotted out of Israel. 2
7 perpetuate his brother's name in Israel; 2
10 the name of his house shall be called in Israel 2
26:15 bless thy people Israel and the ground 2
27: 1 Now Moses and the elders of Israel commanded 2
9 Moses and the . . priests said to all Israel 2
9 Keep silence and hear, O Israel 2
14 Levites shall declare to all the men of Israel 2
29: 1 Moses to make with the people of Israel in . . Moab 2
2 Moses summoned all Israel and said to them 2
10 stand this day all of you . . all the men of Israel 2
21 single him out from all the tribes of Israel 2
31: 1 continued to speak these words to all Israel. 2
7 Joshua, and said to him in the sight of all Israel 2
9 gave it to . . and to all the elders of Israel. 2
11 when all Israel comes to appear before the LORD 2
11 read this law before all Israel in their hearing. 2
19 this song, and teach it to the people of Israel; 2
19 witness for me against the people of Israel. 2
22 song . . and taught it to the people of Israel. 2
23 shall bring the children of Israel into the land 2
30 in the ears of all the assembly of Israel 2
32:45 finished speaking all these words to all Israel 2
49 give to the people of Israel for a possession; 2
51 broke faith . . in the midst of the people of Israel 2

51 holy in the midst of the people of Israel. 2
52 land which I give to the people of Israel. 2
33: 1 Moses . . blessed the children of Israel 2
5 gathered, all the tribes of Israel together. 2
10 They shall teach . . Israel thy law; 2
21 with Israel he executed the commands and just 2
28 Israel dwelt in safety, the fountain of Jacob 2
29 Happy are you, O Israel! Who is like you, a people 2
34: 8 people of Israel wept for Moses in . . Moab 2
9 so the people of Israel obeyed him, and did 2
10 not arisen a prophet since in Israel like Moses 2
12 which Moses wrought in the sight of all Israel. 2
Jos 1: 2 which I am giving to them, to the people of Israel. 2
2: 2 certain men of Israel have come here tonight 2
3: 1 rose and set out . . with all the people of Israel; 2
7 I will begin to exalt you in the sight of Israel 2
9 Joshua said to the people of Israel, "Come hither 2
12 Now . . take twelve men from the tribes of Israel 2
17 while all Israel were passing over on dry ground 2
4: 4 called the twelve men from the people of Israel 2
5 to the number of the tribes of the people of Israel 2
7 be to the people of Israel a memorial for ever. 2
8 And the men of Israel did as Joshua commanded 2
8 the number of the tribes of the people of Israel 2
12 passed over armed before the people of Israel 2
14 LORD exalted Joshua in the sight of all Israel; 2
21 And he said to the people of Israel 2
22 'Israel passed over this Jordan on dry ground.' 2
5: 1 dried up . . the Jordan for the people of Israel 2
1 heart melted . . because of the people of Israel. 2
2 and circumcise the people of Israel again 2
3 Joshua . . and circumcised the people of Israel 2
6 the people of Israel walked 40 years 2
10 the people of Israel were encamped in Gilgal 2
12 and the people of Israel had manna no more 2
6: 1 was shut up . . because of the people of Israel; 2
18 make the camp of Israel a thing for destruction 2
23 and set them outside the camp of Israel. 2
25 and she dwelt in Israel to this day 2
7: 1 But the people of Israel broke faith in regard 2
1 of the LORD burned against the people of Israel. 2
6 Then Joshua rent . . he and the elders of Israel; 2
8 what can I say, when Israel has turned their backs 2
11 Israel has sinned; they have transgressed 2
12 Therefore the people of Israel cannot stand 2
13 for thus says the LORD, God of Israel 2
13 are devoted things in the midst of you, O Israel; 2
15 because he has done a shameful thing in Israel 2
16 Joshua . . brought Israel near tribe by tribe 2
19 My son, give glory to the LORD God of Israel 2
20 I have sinned against the LORD God of Israel 2
23 brought . . to Joshua and all the people of Israel; 2
24 Joshua and all Israel with him took Achan 2
25 And all Israel stoned him with stones; 2
8:10 and went up, with the elders of Israel . . to Ai. 2
14 made haste and went . . to meet Israel in battle; 2
15 and all Israel made a pretense of being beaten 2
17 not a man left . . who did not go out after Israel; 2
17 they left the city open, and pursued Israel. 2
21 Joshua and all Israel saw that the ambush had 2
22 they were in the midst of Israel, some on this side 2
22 and Israel smote them, until there was left none •
24 When Israel had finished slaughtering . . Ai 2
24 all Israel returned to Ai, and smote it 2
27 the spoil of that city Israel took as their booty 2
30 built an altar . . to the LORD, the God of Israel 2
31 as Moses . . had commanded the people of Israel 2
32 in the presence of the people of Israel, he wrote 2
33 all Israel . . stood on opposite sides of the ark 2
33 that they should bless the people of Israel. 2
35 Joshua . . read before all the assembly of Israel 2
9: 2 they gathered . . to fight Joshua and Israel. 2
6 and said to him and to the men of Israel 2
7 But the men of Israel said to the Hivites 2
17 And the people of Israel set out 2
18 But the people of Israel did not kill them 2
18 had sworn to them by the LORD, the God of Israel. 2
19 have sworn to them by the LORD, the God of Israel 2
26 out of the hand of the people of Israel; 2
10: 1 had made peace with Israel and were among them 2
4 peace with Joshua and with the people of Israel. 2
10 the LORD threw them into a panic before Israel 2
11 And as they fled before Israel 2
11 the men of Israel killed with the sword. 2
12 LORD gave the Amorites over to the men of Israel; 2
12 spoke Joshua . . and he said in the sight of Israel 2
14 for the LORD fought for Israel. 2
15 Joshua returned, and all Israel . . to the camp 2
20 When Joshua and the men of Israel had finished 2
21 against any of the people of Israel. 2
24 Joshua summoned all the men of Israel, and said 2
29 Joshua passed on . . and all Israel with him 2
30 gave it also and its king into the hand of Israel; 2
31 Joshua passed on . . and all Israel with him 2
32 and the LORD gave Lachish into the hand of Israel 2
34 Joshua passed on with all Israel from Lachish 2
36 Joshua went up with all Israel from Eglon 2
38 Then Joshua, with all Israel, turned back to Debir 2
40 left none . . as the LORD God of Israel commanded. 2

42 the LORD God of Israel fought for Israel. 2
42 the LORD God of Israel fought for Israel. 2
43 Joshua returned, and all Israel with him 2
11: 5 and came and encamped . . to fight with Israel. 2
6 I will give over all of them, slain, to Israel; 2
8 And the LORD gave them into the hand of Israel 2
13 none of the cities . . on mounds did Israel burn 2
14 spoil . . and the cattle, the people of Israel took 2
16 and the hill country of Israel and its lowland 2
19 a city that made peace with the people of Israel 2
20 that they should come against Israel in battle 2
21 and from all the hill country of Israel; 2
22 none . . left in the land of the people of Israel; 2
23 and Joshua gave it for an inheritance to Israel 2
12: 1 the kings . . whom the people of Israel defeated 2
6 Moses . . and the people of Israel defeated them; 2
7 whom Joshua and the people of Israel defeated 2
7 Joshua gave their land to the tribes of Israel 2
13: 6 drive them out from before the people of Israel; 2
6 only allot the land to Israel for an inheritance 2
13 the people of Israel did not drive out 2
13 Geshur and Ma'acath dwell in the midst of Israel 2
14 the offerings by fire to the LORD God of Israel 2
22 Balaam also . . the people of Israel killed 2
33 the LORD God of Israel is their inheritance 2
14: 1 the inheritances which the people of Israel 2
1 houses of the tribes of the people of Israel 2
5 The people of Israel did as the LORD commanded 2
10 since . . while Israel walked in the wilderness; 2
14 he wholly followed the LORD, the God of Israel. 2
17:13 when the people of Israel grew strong 2
18: 1 Then . . the people of Israel assembled at Shiloh 2
2 There remained among the people of Israel seven 2
3 Joshua said to the people of Israel, "How long 2
10 to the people of Israel, to each his portion. 2
19:49 people of Israel gave an inheritance among them 2
51 houses of the tribes of the people of Israel 2
20: 2 Say to the people of Israel, 'Appoint the cities 2
9 cities designated for all the people of Israel 2
21: 1 houses of the tribes of the people of Israel; 2
3 the people of Israel gave to the Levites 2
8 These . . the people of Israel gave by lot 2
41 midst of the possession of the people of Israel 2
43 the LORD gave to Israel all the land . . he swore 2
45 which the LORD had made to the house of Israel 2
22: 9 parting from the people of Israel at Shiloh 2
11 And the people of Israel heard say 2
11 on the side that belongs to the people of Israel. 2
12 when the people of Israel heard of it 2
12 whole assembly of the people of Israel gathered 2
13 Then the people of Israel sent . . Phin'ehas 2
14 one from each of the tribal families of Israel 2
14 the head of a family among the clans of Israel. 2
16 you have committed against the God of Israel 2
18 angry with the whole congregation of Israel 2
20 wrath fell upon all the congregation of Israel? 2
21 in answer to the heads of the families of Israel 2
22 God, the LORD! He knows; and let Israel itself know! 2
24 What have you to do with the LORD, the God of Israel 2
30 heads of the families of Israel who were with him 2
31 you have saved the people of Israel from the hand 2
32 to the land of Canaan, to the people of Israel 2
33 And the report pleased the people of Israel; 2
33 and the people of Israel blessed God 2
23: 1 the LORD had given rest to Israel from all their 2
2 Joshua summoned all Israel, their elders 2
24: 1 Then Joshua gathered all the tribes of Israel 2
1 the heads, the judges, and the officers of Israel; 2
2 Thus says the LORD, the God of Israel, 'Your fathers 2
9 Then Balak . . arose and fought against Israel; 2
23 incline your heart to the LORD, the God of Israel. 2
31 And Israel served the LORD all the days of Joshua 2
31 known all the work which the LORD did for Israel. 2
32 bones . . which the people of Israel brought up 2
Jdg 1: 1 the people of Israel inquired of the LORD 2
28 When Israel grew strong, they put the Canaanites 2
2: 4 spoke these words to all the people of Israel 2
6 the people of Israel went each to his 2
7 great work which the LORD had done for Israel. 2
10 the LORD or the work which he had done for Israel. 2
11 the people of Israel did what was evil 2
14 the anger of the LORD was kindled against Israel 2
20 the anger of the LORD was kindled against Israel; 2
22 that by them I may test Israel, whether they will 2
3: 1 which the LORD left, to test Israel by them, that is 2
1 all in Israel who had no experience of any war •
2 generations of the people of Israel might know 2
4 for the testing of Israel, to know whether Israel 2
4 to know whether Israel would obey •
5 the people of Israel dwelt among the Canaanites 2
7 the people of Israel did what was evil 2
8 the anger of the LORD was kindled against Israel 2
8 the people of Israel served Cu'shan-rishatha'im 2
9 But when the people of Israel cried to the LORD 2
9 raised up a deliverer for the people of Israel 2
10 of the LORD came upon him, and he judged Israel; 2
12 the people of Israel again did what was evil 2
12 Eglon the king of Moab against Israel 2
13 and went and defeated Israel; and they took 2

14 people of Israel served Eglon the king of Moab 2
15 when the people of Israel cried to the LORD 2
15 The people of Israel sent tribute by him to Eglon 2
27 and the people of Israel went down with him 2
30 was subdued that day under the hand of Israel. 2
31 with an oxgoad; and he too delivered Israel. 2
4: 1 the people of Israel again did what was evil 2
3 the people of Israel cried to the LORD for help; 2
3 he . . oppressed the people of Israel cruelly 2
4 Deb'orah . . was judging Israel at that time. 2
5 the people of Israel came up to her for judgment. 2
6 LORD, the God of Israel, commands you, 'Go, gather 2
23 the king of Canaan before the people of Israel. 2
24 the hand of the people of Israel bore harder 2
5: 2 That the leaders took the lead in Israel 2
3 I will make melody to the LORD, the God of Israel. 2
5 quaked . . before the LORD, the God of Israel. 2
7 The peasantry ceased in Israel, they ceased 2
7 you arose, Deb'orah, arose as a mother in Israel. 2
8 Was shield or spear to be seen . . in Israel? 2
9 commanders of Israel who offered themselves 2
11 LORD, the triumphs of his peasantry in Israel. 2
6: 1 people of Israel did what was evil in the sight 2
2 And the hand of Mid'ian prevailed over Israel; 2
2 people of Israel made for themselves the dens 2
4 they would . . leave no sustenance in Israel 2
6 Israel was brought very low because of Mid'ian; 2
6 the people of Israel cried for help to the LORD. 2
7 When the people of Israel cried to the LORD 2
8 the LORD sent a prophet to the people of Israel; 2
8 Thus says the LORD, the God of Israel: I led you up 2
14 Go . . and deliver Israel from the hand of Mid'ian; 2
15 Lord, how can I deliver Israel? Behold, my clan is 2
36 said to God, "If thou wilt deliver Israel by my hand 2
37 know that thou wilt deliver Israel by my hand 2
7: 2 hand, lest Israel vaunt themselves against me 2
8 he sent all the rest of Israel every man to his 2
14 sword of Gideon the son of Jo'ash, a man of Israel; 2
15 he returned to the camp of Israel, and said, "Arise; 2
23 the men of Israel were called out from Naph'tali 2
8:22 Then the men of Israel said to Gideon, "Rule over us 2
27 and all Israel played the harlot after it there 2
28 Mid'ian was subdued before the people of Israel 2
33 the people of Israel turned again and played 2
34 the people of Israel did not remember the LORD 2
35 for all the good that he had done to Israel. 2
9:22 Abim'elech ruled over Israel three years. 2
55 the men of Israel saw that Abim'elech was dead 2
10: 1 arose to deliver Israel Tola the son of Pu'ah 2
2 And he judged Israel 23 years. Then he died 2
3 Ja'ir the Gileadite, who judged Israel 22 years. 2
6 the people of Israel again did what was evil 2
7 the anger of the LORD was kindled against Israel 2
8 crushed and oppressed the children of Israel 2
8 the people of Israel that were beyond the Jordan 2
9 so that Israel was sorely distressed. 2
10 the people of Israel cried to the LORD 2
11 the LORD said to the people of Israel, "Did I not 2
15 the people of Israel said to the LORD, "We have 2
16 he became indignant over the misery of Israel. 2
17 and the people of Israel came together 2
11: 4 a time the Ammonites made war against Israel. 2
5 when the Ammonites made war against Israel 2
13 Israel on coming from Egypt took away my land 2
15 Israel did not take away the land of Moab 2
16 from Egypt, Israel went through the wilderness 2
17 Israel then sent messengers to the king of Edom 2
17 not consent. So Israel remained at Kadesh. 2
19 Israel then sent messengers to Sihon king 2
19 Israel said to him, 'Let us pass, we pray, through 2
20 Sihon did not trust Israel to pass through his 2
20 and encamped at Jahaz, and fought with Israel. 2
21 the LORD, the God of Israel, gave Sihon and all his 2
21 LORD . . gave Sihon . . into the hand of Israel 2
21 Israel took possession of all the land 2
23 then the LORD, the God of Israel, dispossessed 2
23 the Amorites from before his people Israel; 2
25 Did he ever strive against Israel, or did he ever 2
26 While Israel dwelt in Heshbon and its villages 2
27 decide this day between the people of Israel 2
33 were subdued before the people of Israel. 2
39 it became a custom in Israel . . to lament 2
40 the daughters of Israel went . . to lament 2
12: 7 Jephthah judged Israel six years. 2
8 After him Ibzan of Bethlehem judged Israel. 2
9 And he judged Israel seven years. 2
11 After him Elon the Zeb'ulunite judged Israel; 2
11 Elon . . and he judged Israel ten years. 2
13 After him Abdon the son of Hillel . . judged Israel. 2
14 rode on 70 asses; and he judged Israel eight years. 2
13: 1 the people of Israel again did what was evil 2
5 he shall begin to deliver Israel from the hand 2
14: 4 time the Philistines had dominion over Israel. 2
15:20 he judged Israel in the days of the Philistines 2
16:31 He had judged Israel twenty years. 2
17: 6 there was no king in Israel; every man did what was 2
18: 1 In those days there was no king in Israel. 2
1 no inheritance among the tribes of Israel had 2
19 or to be priest to a tribe and family in Israel? 2

29 name of Dan their ancestor, who was born to Israel; 2
19: 1 In those days, when there was no king in Israel 2
12 who do not belong to the people of Israel; 2
29 her throughout all the territory of Israel. 2
30 from the day that the people of Israel came up out 2
20: 1 all the people of Israel came out, from Dan 2
2 of all the people, of all the tribes of Israel 2
3 heard that the people of Israel had gone up 2
3 the people of Israel said, "Tell us, how was this 2
6 all the country of the inheritance of Israel; 2
6 abomination and wantonness in Israel. 2
7 people of Israel, all of you, give your advice 2
10 of a 100 throughout all the tribes of Israel 2
10 crime which they have committed in Israel. 2
11 all the men of Israel gathered against the city 2
12 the tribes of Israel sent men through all 2
13 put them to death, and put away evil from Israel. 2
13 voice of their brethren, the people of Israel. 2
14 to go out to battle against the people of Israel 2
17 the men of Israel, apart from Benjamin, mustered 2
18 The people of Israel arose and went up to Bethel 2
19 the people of Israel rose in the morning 2
20 the men of Israel went out to battle against 2
20 the men of Israel drew up the battle line against 2
22 But the people, the men of Israel, took courage 2
23 the people of Israel went up and wept 2
24 the people of Israel came near against 2
25 felled . . 18,000 men of the people of Israel 2
26 all the people of Israel, the whole army, went up 2
27 the people of Israel inquired of the LORD 2
29 Israel set men in ambush round about Gib'e-ah. 2
30 the people of Israel went up against 2
31 and kill some . . about 30 men of Israel. 2
32 the men of Israel said, "Let us flee, and draw them 2
33 all the men of Israel rose up out of their place 2
33 the men of Israel who were in ambush rushed out 2
34 came . . 10,000 picked men out of all Israel 2
35 the LORD defeated Benjamin before Israel; 2
35 men of Israel destroyed 25,100 men of Benjamin 2
36 The men of Israel gave ground to Benjamin 2
38 signal between the men of Israel and the men 2
39 the men of Israel should turn in battle. 2
39 to smite and kill about 30 men of Israel; 2
41 the men of Israel turned, and the men of Benjamin 2
42 they turned their backs before the men of Israel 2
48 the men of Israel turned back against 2
21: 1 the men of Israel had sworn at Mizpah, "No one of us 2
3 O LORD, the God of Israel, why has this come to pass 2
3 why has this come to pass in Israel 2
3 there . . be today one tribe lacking in Israel? 2
5 the people of Israel said, "Which of all the tribes 2
5 Which of all the tribes of Israel did not come up 2
6 the people of Israel had compassion 2
6 One tribe is cut off from Israel this day. 2
8 What one is there of the tribes of Israel that did 2
15 LORD had made a breach in the tribes of Israel. 2
17 that a tribe be not blotted out from Israel. 2
18 the people of Israel had sworn, "Cursed be he who 2
24 the people of Israel departed from there 2
25 In those days there was no king in Israel; 2
Rut 2:12 a full reward . . by the LORD, the God of Israel 2
4: 7 Now this was the custom in former times in Israel 2
7 this was the manner of attesting in Israel. 2
11 who together built up the house of Israel. 2
14 and may his name be renowned in Israel! 2
1Sm 1:17 Go . . and the God of Israel grant your petition 2
2:22 heard all that his sons were doing to all Israel 2
28 chose him out of all the tribes of Israel to be my 2
28 my offerings by fire from the people of Israel. 2
29 parts of every offering of my people Israel? 2
30 Therefore the LORD the God of Israel declares 2
32 prosperity which shall be bestowed upon Israel; 2
3:11 I am about to do a thing in Israel 2
20 And all Israel from Dan to Beer-sheba knew that 2
4: 1 And the word of Samuel came to all Israel. 2
1 Now Israel went out to battle . . the Philistines; 2
2 The Philistines drew up in line against Israel 2
2 Israel was defeated by the Philistines 2
3 the elders of Israel said, "Why has the LORD 2
5 When the ark . . all Israel gave a mighty shout 2
10 the Philistines fought, and Israel was defeated 2
10 there fell of Israel 30,000 foot soldiers. 2
17 Israel has fled before the Philistines 2
18 Eli fell . . He had judged Israel 40 years. 2
21 The glory has departed from Israel! 2
22 And she said, "The glory has departed from Israel 2
5: 7 ark of the God of Israel must not remain with us; 2
8 What shall we do with the ark of the God of Israel? 2
8 Let the ark of the God of Israel be brought around 2
8 they brought the ark of the God of Israel there. 2
10 brought . . the ark of the God of Israel to slay us 2
11 Send away the ark of the God of Israel 2
6: 3 If you send away the ark of the God of Israel 2
5 make images . . and give glory to the God of Israel; 2
7: 2 all the house of Israel lamented after the LORD. 2
3 Then Samuel said to all the house of Israel 2
4 So Israel put away the Ba'als and the Ash'taroth 1
5 Gather all Israel at Mizpah, and I will pray 2
6 Samuel judged the people of Israel at Mizpah. 2

7 that the people of Israel had gathered at Mizpah 2
7 the Philistines went up against Israel. 2
7 when the people of Israel heard of it they were 2
8 the people of Israel said to Samuel, "Do not cease 2
9 and Samuel cried to the LORD for Israel 2
10 the Philistines drew near to attack Israel; 2
10 and they were routed before Israel. 2
11 the men of Israel went out of Mizpah and pursued 2
13 and did not again enter the territory of Israel. 2
14 cities . . the Philistines had taken from Israel 2
14 The cities . . were restored to Israel, from Ekron 2
14 Israel rescued their territory from the hand 2
14 was peace also between Israel and the Amorites. 2
15 Samuel judged Israel all the days of his life. 2
16 and he judged Israel in all these places. 2
17 there also he administered justice to Israel. 2
8: 1 Samuel . . made his sons judges over Israel. 2
4 Then all the elders of Israel gathered together 2
22 Samuel then said to the men of Israel 2
9: 2 a man among the people of Israel more handsome 2
9 Formerly in Israel, when a man went to inquire 2
16 anoint him to be prince over my people Israel. 2
20 And for whom is all that is desirable in Israel? 2
21 Am I not . . from the least of the tribes of Israel? 2
10: 1 anointed you to be prince over his people Israel? 5
18 he said to the people of Israel, "Thus says the LORD 2
18 Thus says the LORD, the God of Israel, 'I brought up 2
18 I brought up Israel out of Egypt, and I delivered 2
20 Samuel brought all the tribes of Israel near 2
11: 2 and thus put disgrace upon all Israel. 2
3 send . . through all the territory of Israel. 2
7 sent them through . . all the territory of Israel 2
8 the men of Israel were 300,000 2
13 the LORD has wrought deliverance in Israel. 2
15 Saul and all the men of Israel rejoiced greatly. 2
12: 1 Samuel said to all Israel, "Behold, I have 2
13: 1 and he reigned . . and two years over Israel. 2
2 Saul chose 3,000 men of Israel; 2
4 Israel heard . . Saul had defeated the garrison 2
4 Israel had become odious to the Philistines. 2
5 the Philistines mustered to fight with Israel 2
6 the men of Israel saw that they were in straits 2
13 established your kingdom over Israel for ever. 2
19 no smith . . throughout all the land of Israel; 2
14:12 the LORD has given them into the hand of Israel. 2
18 the ark of God went . . with the people of Israel. 2
22 when all the men of Israel who had hid themselves 2
23 So the LORD delivered Israel that day; 2
24 And the men of Israel were distressed that day; 2
37 Wilt thou give them into the hand of Israel? 2
39 as the LORD lives who saves Israel . . he shall 2
40 Then he said to all Israel, "You shall be on one side 2
41 O LORD God of Israel, why hast thou not answered 2
41 O LORD, God of Israel, give Urim; 5
41 if . . guilt is in thy people Israel, give Thummim. 5
45 who has wrought this great victory in Israel? 2
47 When Saul had taken the kingship over Israel 2
48 and smote the Amal'ekites, and delivered Israel 2
15: 1 sent me to anoint you king over his people Israel; 2
2 I will punish what Am'alek did to Israel 2
6 you showed kindness to all the people of Israel 2
17 are you not the head of the tribes of Israel? 2
17 The LORD anointed you king over Israel. 2
26 has rejected you from being king over Israel. 2
28 The LORD has torn the kingdom of Israel from you 2
29 the Glory of Israel will not lie or repent; 2
30 before the elders of my people and before Israel 2
35 repented that he had made Saul king over Israel. 2
16: 1 I have rejected him from being king over Israel? 2
17: 2 And Saul and the men of Israel were gathered 2
3 Israel stood on the mountain on the other side 2
8 He stood and shouted to the ranks of Israel 2
10 I defy the ranks of Israel this day; give me a man 2
11 When Saul and all Israel heard . . the Philistine 2
19 all the men of Israel, were in the valley of Elah 2
21 Israel and the Philistines drew up for battle 2
24 All the men of Israel, when they saw the man, fled 2
25 And the men of Israel said, "Have you seen this man 2
25 Surely he has come up to defy Israel; 2
25 make his father's house free in Israel. 2
26 and takes away the reproach from Israel? 2
45 the LORD of hosts, the God of the armies of Israel 2
46 that all . . may know that there is a God in Israel 2
52 And the men of Israel and Judah rose with a shout 2
18: 6 the women came out of all the cities of Israel 2
16 But all Israel and Judah loved David; 2
18 Who am I, and . . my father's family in Israel 2
28 LORD was with David, and that all Israel loved him 5
19: 5 the LORD wrought a great victory for all Israel. 2
20:12 The LORD, the God of Israel, be witness! 2
23:10 Then said David, "O LORD, the God of Israel 2
11 O LORD, the God of Israel, I beseech thee 2
17 you shall be king over Israel 2
24: 2 Then Saul took 3,000 chosen men out of all Israel 2
14 After whom has the king of Israel come out? 2
20 the kingdom of Israel shall be established 2
25: 1 all Israel assembled and mourned for him 2
30 and has appointed you prince over Israel 2
32 Blessed be the LORD, the God of Israel, who sent you 2
34 For as surely as the LORD the God of Israel lives 2
26: 2 Saul arose and . . with 3,000 chosen men of Israel 2
15 Are you not a man? Who is like you in Israel? 2
20 the king of Israel has come out to seek my life 2
27: 1 of seeking me . . within the borders of Israel 2
12 made himself . . abhorred by his people Israel; 2
28: 1 gathered . . for war, to fight against Israel. 2
3 Samuel . . died, and all Israel had mourned for him 2
4 Saul gathered all Israel, and they encamped 2
19 the LORD will give Israel also . . into the hand 2
19 LORD will give the army of Israel . . into the hand 2
29: 3 this David, the servant of Saul, king of Israel 2
30:25 he made it a statute and an ordinance for Israel 2
31: 1 Now the Philistines fought against Israel; 2
1 the men of Israel fled before the Philistines 2
7 men of Israel . . on the other side of the valley 2
7 saw that the men of Israel had fled and that Saul 2
2Sm 1: 3 he said . . "I have escaped from the camp of Israel. 2
12 for the people . . and for the house of Israel 2
19 Thy glory, O Israel, is slain upon thy high places! 2
24 Ye daughters of Israel, weep over Saul 2
2: 9 and E'phraim and Benjamin and all Israel. 2
10 was 40 . . when he began to reign over Israel 2
17 Abner and the men of Israel were beaten before 2
28 all the men stopped, and pursued Israel no more 2
3:10 the throne of David over Israel and over Judah 2
12 shall be with you to bring over all Israel to you. 2
17 Abner conferred with the elders of Israel 2
18 I will save my people Israel from . . Philistines 2
19 all that Israel and . . Benjamin thought good 2
21 I . . will gather all Israel to my lord the king 2
37 the people and all Israel understood that day 2
38 a prince . . has fallen this day in Israel? 2
4: 1 his courage failed, and all Israel was dismayed. 2
5: 1 the tribes of Israel came to David at Hebron 2
2 it was you that led out and brought in Israel; 2
2 You shall be shepherd of my people Israel 2
2 and you shall be prince over Israel.' 2
3 elders of Israel came to the king 2
3 and they anointed David king over Israel. 2
5 he reigned over all Israel and Judah 2
12 the LORD had established him king over Israel 2
12 LORD had . . for the sake of his people Israel. 2
17 that David had been anointed king over Israel 2
6: 1 David . . gathered all the chosen men of Israel 2
5 David and all the house of Israel were . . merry 2
15 the house of Israel brought up the ark 2
19 all the people, the whole multitude of Israel 2
20 How the king of Israel honored himself today 2
21 who chose . . to appoint me as prince over Israel 2
7: 6 I brought up the people of Israel from Egypt 2
7 where I have moved with all the people of Israel 2
7 did I speak a word with any of the judges of Israel 2
7 whom I commanded to shepherd my people Israel 2
8 that you should be prince over my people Israel; 2
10 And I will appoint a place for my people Israel 2
11 that I appointed judges over my people Israel; 2
23 What . . nation on earth is like thy people Israel 2
24 thou didst establish . . thy people Israel 2
26 saying, 'The LORD of hosts is God over Israel,' 2
27 thou, O LORD of hosts, the God of Israel, hast made 2
8:15 David reigned over all Israel; 2
10: 9 Jo'ab . . chose some of the picked men of Israel 2
15 Syrians saw . . they had been defeated by Israel 2
17 was told David, he gathered all Israel together 2
18 And the Syrians fled before Israel; 2
19 saw that they had been defeated by Israel 2
19 when all the kings . . they made peace with Israel 2
11: 1 sent Jo'ab, and his servants . . and all Israel; 2
11 The ark and Israel and Judah dwell in booths; 2
12: 7 Thus says the LORD, the God of Israel, 'I anointed 2
7 I anointed you king over Israel, and I delivered 2
8 gave you the house of Israel and of Judah; 2
12 but I will do this thing before all Israel 2
13:12 for such a thing is not done in Israel; 2
13 you would be as one of the wanton fools in Israel. 2
14:25 Now in all Israel there was no one . . as Ab'salom; 2
15: 2 Your servant is of such and such a tribe in Israel 2
6 to all of Israel who came to the king for judgment; 2
6 so Ab'salom stole the hearts of the men of Israel. 2
10 sent . . throughout all the tribes of Israel 2
13 The . . men of Israel have gone after Ab'salom. 2
16: 3 the house of Israel will give me back the kingdom 2
15 Ab'salom and all the people, the men of Israel, came 2
18 the LORD and this people and all the men of Israel 2
21 all Israel will hear that you have made yourself 2
22 Ab'salom went in to . . in the sight of all Israel. 2
17: 4 pleased Ab'salom and all the elders of Israel. 2
10 all Israel knows that your father is a mighty man 2
11 my counsel is that all Israel be gathered to you 2
13 all Israel will bring ropes to that city 2
14 And Ab'salom and all the men of Israel said 2
15 counsel Ab'salom and the elders of Israel; 2
24 Ab'salom crossed . . with all the men of Israel. 2
26 And Israel and Ab'salom encamped in the land 2
18: 6 the army went out into the field against Israel; 2
7 And the men of Israel were defeated there 2
16 and the troops came back from pursuing Israel; 2
17 and all Israel fled every one to his own home. 2
19: 8 Now Israel had fled every man to his own home. 2
9 at strife throughout all the tribes of Israel 2
11 when the word of all Israel has come to the king? 2
22 Shall any one be put to death in Israel this day? 2
22 do I not know that I am this day king over Israel? 2
40 all . . of Judah, and also half the people of Israel 2
41 all the men of Israel came to the king, and said 2
42 All the men of Judah answered the men of Israel 2
43 And the men of Israel answered the men of Judah 2
43 were fiercer than the words of the men of Israel. 2
20: 1 every man to his tents, O Israel! 2
2 the men of Israel withdrew from David 2
14 Sheba passed through all the tribes of Israel 2
19 those who are peaceable and faithful in Israel; 2
19 to destroy a city which is a mother in Israel; 2
23 Now Jo'ab was in command of all the army of Israel; 2
21: 2 the Gib'eonites were not of the people of Israel 2
2 the people of Israel had sworn to spare them 2
2 in his zeal for the people of Israel and Judah. 2
4 is it for us to put any man to death in Israel. 2
5 have no place in all the territory of Israel 2
15 The Philistines had war again with Israel 2
17 no more . . lest you quench the lamp of Israel. 2
21 when he taunted Israel, Jonathan . . slew him. 2
23: 1 oracle of David . . the sweet psalmist of Israel 2
3 The God of Israel has spoken, the Rock of Israel 2
3 the Rock of Israel has said to me: When one rules 2
9 and the men of Israel withdrew. 2
24: 1 the anger of the LORD was kindled against Israel 2
1 he incited David . . "Go, number Israel and Judah. 2
2 Go through all the tribes of Israel, from Dan 2
4 went out . . to number the people of Israel. 2
9 in Israel there were 800,000 valiant men 2
15 the LORD sent a pestilence upon Israel 2
25 and the plague was averted from Israel. 2
1Kg 1: 3 throughout all the territory of Israel 2
20 the eyes of all Israel are upon you, to tell them 2
30 I swore to you by the LORD, the God of Israel, saying 2
34 there anoint him king over Israel; then blow 2
35 him to be ruler over Israel and over Judah. 2
48 Blessed be the LORD, the God of Israel, who has 2
2: 4 shall not fail you a man on the throne of Israel.' 2
5 the two commanders of the armies of Israel, Abner 2
11 time that David reigned over Israel was 40 years; 2
15 and that all Israel fully expected me to reign; 2
32 Abner . . commander of the army of Israel 2
3:28 all Israel heard of the judgment which the king 2
4: 1 King Solomon was king over all Israel 2
7 Solomon had twelve officers over all Israel, who 2
20 Judah and Israel were as many as the sand 2
25 Judah and Israel dwelt in safety, from Dan even 2
5:13 raised a levy of forced labor out of all Israel; 2
6: 1 after the people of Israel came out of . . Egypt 2
1 in the fourth year of Solomon's reign over Israel 2
13 I will dwell among the children of Israel 2
13 I will . . and will not forsake my people Israel. 2
8: 1 assembled the elders of Israel and all the heads 2
1 of the fathers' houses of the people of Israel 2
2 all the men of Israel assembled to King Solomon 2
3 all the elders of Israel came 2
5 King Solomon and all the congregation of Israel 2
9 LORD made a covenant with the people of Israel 2
14 king . . blessed all the assembly of Israel 2
14 while all the assembly of Israel stood. 2
15 Blessed be the LORD, the God of Israel, who 2
16 day that I brought my people Israel out of Egypt 2
16 I chose no city in all the tribes of Israel 2
16 but I chose David to be over my people Israel.' 2
17 a house for the name of the LORD, the God of Israel. 2
20 I have risen . . and sit on the throne of Israel 2
20 house for the name of the LORD, the God of Israel. 2
22 in the presence of all the assembly of Israel 2
23 O LORD, God of Israel, there is no God like thee 2
25 O LORD, God of Israel, keep with thy servant David 2
25 a man before me to sit upon the throne of Israel 2
26 O God of Israel, let thy word be confirmed 2
30 of thy servant and of thy people Israel 2
33 When thy people Israel are defeated . . if they 2
34 hear . . and forgive the sin of thy people Israel 2
36 forgive . . thy servants, thy people Israel 2
38 prayer . . by any man or by all thy people Israel 2
41 a foreigner, who is not of thy people Israel, comes 2
43 thy name and fear thee, as do thy people Israel 2
52 open . . to the supplication of thy people Israel 2
55 he stood, and blessed all the assembly of Israel 2
56 the LORD who has given rest to his people Israel 2
59 maintain . . and the cause of his people Israel 2
62 king, and all Israel with him, offered sacrifice 2
63 the king and all the people of Israel dedicated 2
65 Solomon held the feast . . and all Israel with him 2
66 LORD had shown to . . and to Israel his people. 2
9: 5 I will establish your royal throne over Israel 2
5 not fail you a man upon the throne of Israel.' 2
7 I will cut off Israel from the land 2
7 Israel will become a proverb and a byword 2
20 the people . . who were not of the people of Israel– 2
21 whom the people of Israel were unable to destroy 2
22 of the people of Israel Solomon made no slaves; 2
10: 9 and set you on the throne of Israel! 2

9 Because the LORD loved Israel for ever 2
11: 2 the LORD had said to the people of Israel 2
9 turned away from the LORD, the God of Israel 2
16 Jo'ab and all Israel remained there six months 2
25 He was an adversary of Israel 2
25 and he abhorred Israel, and reigned over Syria. 2
31 thus says the LORD, the God of Israel 2
32 I have chosen out of all the tribes of Israel) 2
37 and you shall be king over Israel. 2
38 I will be with you . . and I will give Israel to you. 2
42 Solomon reigned in Jerusalem over all Israel 2
12: 1 all Israel had come to Shechem to make him king. 2
3 Jerobo'am and all the assembly of Israel came 2
16 all Israel saw that the king did not hearken 2
16 To your tents, O Israel! Look now to your own house 2
16 So Israel departed to their tents. 2
17 But Rehobo'am reigned over the people of Israel 2
18 and all Israel stoned him to death with stones. 2
19 So Israel has been in rebellion 2
20 when all Israel heard that Jerobo'am had returned 2
20 and made him king over all Israel. 2
21 to fight against the house of Israel 2
24 against your kinsmen the people of Israel. 2
28 Behold your gods, O Israel, who brought you up 2
33 he ordained a feast for the people of Israel 2
14: 7 Thus says the LORD, the God of Israel 2
7 and made you leader over my people Israel 2
10 cut off . . every male, both bond and free in Israel 2
13 all Israel shall mourn for him, and bury him; 2
13 something pleasing to the LORD, the God of Israel 2
14 LORD will raise up for himself a king over Israel 2
15 the LORD will smite Israel, as a reed is shaken 2
15 LORD will . . root up Israel out of this good land 2
16 he will give Israel up because of the sins 2
16 sins of Jerobo'am . . which he made Israel to sin. 2
18 all Israel buried him and mourned for him 2
19 Book of the Chronicles of the Kings of Israel. 2
21 LORD had chosen out of all the tribes of Israel 2
24 the LORD drove out before the people of Israel. 2
15: 9 In the twentieth year of Jerobo'am king of Israel 2
16 was war between Asa and Ba'asha king of Israel 2
17 Ba'asha king of Israel went up against Judah 2
19 go, break your league with Ba'asha king of Israel 2
20 sent . . his armies against the cities of Israel 2
25 Nadab . . began to reign over Israel 2
25 Nadab . . and he reigned over Israel two years. 2
26 and in his sin which he made Israel to sin. 2
27 Nadab and all Israel were laying siege 2
30 sins . . he sinned and which he made Israel to sin 2
30 he provoked the LORD, the God of Israel. 2
31 the Book of the Chronicles of the Kings of Israel? 2
32 war between Asa and Ba'asha king of Israel 2
33 Ba'asha . . began to reign over all Israel 2
34 and in his sin which he made Israel to sin. 2
16: 2 and made you leader over my people Israel 2
2 and have made my people Israel to sin 2
5 the Book of the Chronicles of the Kings of Israel? 2
8 Elah . . began to reign over Israel in Tirzah 2
13 they sinned, and which they made Israel to sin 2
13 to sin, provoking the LORD God of Israel to anger 2
14 the Book of the Chronicles of the Kings of Israel? 2
16 all Israel made Omri . . king over Israel 2
16 Israel made Omri . . king over Israel that day 2
17 Omri went up . . and all Israel with him 2
19 his sin which he committed, making Israel to sin. 2
20 the Book of the Chronicles of the Kings of Israel? 2
21 the people of Israel were divided into two parts; 2
23 Omri began to reign over Israel 2
26 walked . . in the sins which he made Israel to sin 2
26 provoking the LORD, the God of Israel, to anger 2
27 the Book of the Chronicles of the Kings of Israel? 2
29 Ahab the son of Omri began to reign over Israel 2
29 Ahab . . reigned over Israel in Sama'ria 22 years. 2
33 to provoke the LORD, the God of Israel, to anger 2
33 than all the kings of Israel who were before him. 2
17: 1 As the LORD the God of Israel lives 2
14 For thus says the LORD the God of Israel 2
18:17 Ahab said to him, "Is it you, you troubler of Israel? 2
18 I have not troubled Israel; but you have 2
19 send and gather all Israel to me at Mount Carmel 2
20 So Ahab sent to all the people of Israel 2
31 word of the LORD came . . "Israel shall be your name"; 2
36 O LORD, God of Abraham, Isaac, and Israel, let it be 2
36 be known this day that thou art God in Israel 2
19:10 the people of Israel have forsaken thy covenant 2
14 the people of Israel have forsaken thy covenant 2
16 Jehu . . you shall anoint to be king over Israel; 2
18 Yet I will leave 7,000 in Israel 2
20: 2 he sent messengers . . to Ahab king of Israel 2
4 the king of Israel answered, "As you say, my lord 2
7 the king of Israel called all the elders 2
11 the king of Israel answered, "Tell him 2
13 behold, a prophet came near to Ahab king of Israel 2
15 after them he mustered all the people of Israel 2
20 the Syrians fled and Israel pursued them 2
21 the king of Israel went out, and captured 2
22 the prophet came near to the king of Israel 2
26 and went up to Aphek, to fight against Israel. 2
27 the people of Israel were mustered 2
27 the people of Israel encamped before them 2
28 a man of God came . . and said to the king of Israel 2
29 the people of Israel smote . . 100,000 foot soldiers 2
31 the kings of the house of Israel are merciful 2
31 put sackcloth . . and go out to the king of Israel; 2
32 and went to the king of Israel and said 2
40 The king of Israel said to him 2
41 the king of Israel recognized him 2
43 the king of Israel went to his house resentful 2
21: 7 Do you now govern Israel? Arise, and eat bread 2
18 go . . to meet Ahab king of Israel, who is in Sama'ria; 2
21 cut off from Ahab every male . . in Israel; 2
22 I will . . and because you have made Israel to sin. 2
26 the LORD cast out before the people of Israel.) 2
22: 1 Syria and Israel continued without war. 2
2 Jehosh'aphat . . came down to the king of Israel. 2
3 the king of Israel said to his servants 2
4 Jehosh'aphat said to the king of Israel, "I am as you 2
5 Jehosh'aphat said to the king of Israel 2
6 the king of Israel gathered the prophets 2
8 the king of Israel said to Jehosh'aphat, "There is 2
9 the king of Israel summoned an officer and said 2
10 Now the king of Israel and Jehosh'aphat the king 2
17 I saw all Israel scattered upon the mountains 2
18 the king of Israel said to Jehosh'aphat 2
26 the king of Israel said, "Seize Micai'ah 2
29 the king of Israel and Jehosh'aphat . . went up 2
30 the king of Israel said to Jehosh'aphat 2
30 the king of Israel disguised himself and went 2
31 small nor great, but only with the king of Israel. 2
32 they said, "It is surely the king of Israel. 2
33 captains . . saw that it was not the king of Israel 2
34 drew his bow . . and struck the king of Israel 2
39 the Book of the Chronicles of the Kings of Israel? 2
41 in the fourth year of Ahab king of Israel. 2
44 made peace with the king of Israel. 2
51 Ahazi'ah . . began to reign over Israel in Sama'ria 2
51 and he reigned two years over Israel. 2
52 Jerobo'am the son of Nebat, who made Israel to sin. 2
53 and provoked the LORD, the God of Israel, to anger 2
2Kg 1: 1 Moab rebelled against Israel. 2
3 Is it because there is no God in Israel that you 2
6 Is it because there is no God in Israel that you 2
16 there is no God in Israel to inquire of his word? 2
18 the Book of the Chronicles of the Kings of Israel? 2
2:12 father! the chariots of Israel and its horsemen! 2
3: 1 Jeho'ram . . became king over Israel in Sama'ria 2
3 the sin of Jerobo'am . . which he made Israel to sin; 2
4 he had to deliver annually to the king of Israel 2
5 Moab rebelled against the king of Israel. 2
6 Jeho'ram marched out . . and mustered all Israel. 2
9 So the king of Israel went with the king of Judah 2
10 Then the king of Israel said, "Alas! 2
11 one of the king of Israel's servants answered 2
12 the king of Israel and Jehosh'aphat . . went down 2
13 Eli'sha said to the king of Israel 2
13 But the king of Israel said to him, "No; it is the LORD 2
24 they came to the camp of Israel 2
27 And there came great wrath upon Israel; 2
5: 2 carried off a little maid from the land of Israel 2
4 so spoke the maiden from the land of Israel. 2
5 I will send a letter to the king of Israel. 2
6 he brought the letter to the king of Israel 2
7 when the king of Israel read the letter 2
8 that the king of Israel had rent his clothes 2
8 he may know that there is a prophet in Israel. 2
12 Are not . . better than all the waters of Israel? 2
15 there is no God in all the earth but in Israel; 2
6: 8 the king of Syria was warring against Israel 2
9 the man of God sent word to the king of Israel 2
10 the king of Israel sent to the place 2
11 show me who of us is for the king of Israel? 2
12 Eli'sha, the prophet who is in Israel, tells 2
12 Eli'sha . . tells the king of Israel the words 2
21 When the king of Israel saw them he said to Eli'sha 2
23 Syrians came no more . . into the land of Israel. 2
26 as the king of Israel was passing by upon the wall 2
7: 6 the king of Israel has hired against us the kings 2
13 multitude of Israel that have already perished; 2
8:12 the evil that you will do to the people of Israel; 2
16 of Joram the son of Ahab, king of Israel 2
18 he walked in the way of the kings of Israel 2
25 year of Joram the son of Ahab, king of Israel 2
26 she was a granddaughter of Omri king of Israel. 2
9: 3 'Thus says the LORD, I anoint you king over Israel.' 2
6 Thus says the LORD the God of Israel, I anoint you 2
6 king over the people of the LORD, over Israel. 2
8 cut off . . every male, bond or free, in Israel. 2
12 Thus says the LORD, I anoint you king over Israel.' 2
14 Now Joram with all Israel had been on guard 2
21 Joram king of Israel and Ahazi'ah . . set out 2
10:21 Jehu sent throughout all Israel; 2
28 Thus Jehu wiped out Ba'al from Israel. 2
29 the sins . . which he made Israel to sin 2
30 your sons . . shall sit on the throne of Israel. 2
31 to walk in the law of the LORD the God of Israel 2
31 the sins of Jerobo'am, which he made Israel to sin. 2
32 the LORD began to cut off parts of Israel. 2
32 defeated . . throughout the territory of Israel 2
34 the Book of the Chronicles of the Kings of Israel? 2
36 time that Jehu reigned over Israel in Sama'ria 2
13: 1 Jeho'ahaz . . began to reign over Israel 2
2 the sins of . . which he made Israel to sin; 2
3 the anger of the LORD was kindled against Israel 2
4 for he saw the oppression of Israel 2
5 Therefore the LORD gave Israel a savior 2
5 and the people of Israel dwelt in their homes 2
6 sins . . of Jerobo'am, which he made Israel to sin 2
8 the Book of the Chronicles of the Kings of Israel? 2
10 Jeho'ash . . began to reign over Israel in Sama'ria 2
11 sins of Jerobo'am . . which he made Israel to sin 2
12 the Book of the Chronicles of the Kings of Israel? 2
13 Jo'ash was buried . . with the kings of Israel. 2
14 Jo'ash king of Israel went down to him, and wept 2
14 father! The chariots of Israel and its horsemen! 2
16 Then he said to the king of Israel, "Draw the bow"; 2
18 he said to the king of Israel, "Strike the ground 2
22 Haz'ael . . oppressed Israel all the days 2
25 and recovered the cities of Israel. 2
14: 1 In the second year of Jo'ash . . king of Israel 2
8 sent messengers to Jeho'ash . . king of Israel 2
9 Jeho'ash king of Israel sent word to Amazi'ah 2
11 Jeho'ash king of Israel went up, and he and Amazi'ah 2
12 Judah was defeated by Israel, and every man fled 2
13 Jeho'ash king of Israel captured Amazi'ah 2
15 the Book of the Chronicles of the Kings of Israel? 2
16 was buried in Sama'ria with the kings of Israel; 2
17 death of Jeho'ash son of Jeho'ahaz, king of Israel. 2
23 Jerobo'am the son of Jo'ash, king of Israel, began 2
24 sins of Jerobo'am . . which he made Israel to sin. 2
25 He restored the border of Israel 2
25 word of the LORD, the God of Israel, which he spoke 2
26 the LORD saw that the affliction of Israel was 2
26 none left . . and there was none to help Israel. 2
27 that he would blot out the name of Israel 2
28 how he recovered for Israel Damascus and Hamath 2
28 the Book of the Chronicles of the Kings of Israel? 2
29 slept with his fathers, the kings of Israel 2
15: 1 In the 27th year of Jerobo'am king of Israel 2
8 Zechari'ah . . reigned over Israel in Sama'ria 2
9 sins of Jerobo'am . . which he made Israel to sin. 2
11 Book of the Chronicles of the Kings of Israel. 2
12 Your sons shall sit upon the throne of Israel 2
15 Book of the Chronicles of the Kings of Israel. 2
17 Men'ahem . . began to reign over Israel 2
18 sins of Jerobo'am . . which he made Israel to sin. 2
20 Men'ahem exacted the money from Israel 2
21 the Book of the Chronicles of the Kings of Israel? 2
23 Pekahi'ah . . began to reign over Israel 2
24 sins of Jerobo'am . . which he made Israel to sin. 2
26 Book of the Chronicles of the Kings of Israel. 2
27 Pekah . . began to reign over Israel in Sama'ria 2
28 sins of Jerobo'am . . which he made Israel to sin. 2
29 In the days of Pekah king of Israel 2
31 Book of the Chronicles of the Kings of Israel. 2
32 In the second year of Pekah . . king of Israel 2
16: 3 but he walked in the way of the kings of Israel. 2
3 the LORD drove out before the people of Israel. 2
5 Pekah the son of Remali'ah, king of Israel, came up 2
7 rescue me . . from the hand of the king of Israel 2
17: 1 Hoshe'a . . began to reign in Sama'ria over Israel 2
2 not as the kings of Israel who were before him. 2
7 the people of Israel had sinned against the LORD 2
8 the LORD drove out before the people of Israel 2
8 which the kings of Israel had introduced. 2
9 And the people of Israel did secretly 2
13 Yet the LORD warned Israel and Judah 2
18 Therefore the LORD was very angry with Israel 2
19 the customs which Israel had introduced. 2
20 the LORD rejected all the descendants of Israel 2
21 When he had torn Israel from the house of David 2
21 Jerobo'am drove Israel from following the LORD 2
22 The people of Israel walked in all the sins 2
23 the LORD removed Israel out of his sight 2
23 Israel was exiled from their own land to Assyria 2
24 placed them in . . instead of the people of Israel; 2
34 the children of Jacob, whom he named Israel. 2
18: 1 third year of Hoshe'a son of Elah, king of Israel 2
4 the people of Israel had burned incense to it; 2
5 He trusted in the LORD the God of Israel; 2
9 seventh year of Hoshe'a son of Elah, king of Israel 2
10 which was the ninth year of Hoshe'a king of Israel 2
19:15 O LORD the God of Israel, who art enthroned above 2
20 Thus says the LORD, the God of Israel 2
22 Against the Holy One of Israel! 2
21: 2 the LORD drove out before the people of Israel. 2
3 made an Ashe'rah, as Ahab king of Israel had done 2
7 I have chosen out of all the tribes of Israel 2
8 I will not cause the feet of Israel to wander 2
9 the LORD destroyed before the people of Israel. 2
12 thus says the LORD, the God of Israel 2
22:15 Thus says the LORD, the God of Israel: 'Tell the man 2
18 Thus says the LORD, the God of Israel 2
23:13 which Solomon the king of Israel had built 2
15 Jerobo'am the son of Nebat, who made Israel to sin 2
19 the shrines . . which kings of Israel had made 2
22 since the days of the judges who judged Israel 2
22 or during all the days of the kings of Israel 2

27 I will remove Judah . . as I have removed Israel 2
24:13 vessels . . which Solomon king of Israel had made 2
1Ch 1:34 The sons of Isaac: Esau and Israel. 2
2: 1 These are the sons of Israel: Reuben, Simeon, Levi 2
7 The sons of Carmi: Achar, the troubler of Israel 2
4:10 Jabez called on the God of Israel, saying 2
5: 1 The sons of Reuben the first-born of Israel 2
1 sons of Joseph the son of Israel 2
3 the sons of Reuben, the first-born of Israel 2
17 in the days of Jerobo'am king of Israel. 2
26 So the God of Israel stirred up the spirit of Pul 2
6:38 son of Kohath, son of Levi, son of Israel; 2
49 and to make atonement for Israel 2
64 the people of Israel gave the Levites the cities 2
7:29 the sons of Joseph the son of Israel. 2
9: 1 all Israel was enrolled by genealogies; 2
1 written in the Book of the Kings of Israel. 2
2 Israel, the priests, the Levites 2
10: 1 Now the Philistines fought against Israel; 2
1 men of Israel fled before the Philistines 2
7 when all the men of Israel who were in the valley 2
11: 1 all Israel gathered together to David at Hebron 2
2 it was you that led out and brought in Israel; 2
2 You shall be shepherd of my people Israel 2
2 you shall be prince over my people Israel 2
3 the elders of Israel came to the king at Hebron; 2
3 they anointed David king over Israel 2
4 David and all Israel went to Jerusalem 2
10 together with all Israel, to make him king 2
10 the word of the LORD concerning Israel. 2
12:32 to know what Israel ought to do 2
38 to make David king over all Israel; 2
38 all the rest of Israel were of a single mind 2
40 for there was joy in Israel. 2
13: 2 David said to all the assembly of Israel 2
2 our brethren who remain in all the land of Israel 2
5 David assembled all Israel 2
6 David and all Israel went up to Ba'alah 2
8 David and all Israel were making merry 2
14: 2 the LORD had established him king over Israel 2
2 exalted for the sake of his people Israel. 2
8 David had been anointed king over all Israel 2
15: 3 David assembled all Israel at Jerusalem 2
12 bring up the ark of the LORD, the God of Israel 2
14 to bring up the ark of the LORD, the God of Israel. 2
25 David and the elders of Israel 2
28 all Israel brought up the ark of the covenant 2
16: 3 distributed to all Israel, both men and women 2
4 to thank, and to praise the LORD, the God of Israel. 2
17 as an everlasting covenant to Israel 2
36 Blessed be the LORD, the God of Israel 2
40 the law of the LORD which he commanded Israel. 2
17: 5 not dwelt in a house since the day I led up Israel 2
6 In all places where I have moved with Israel 2
6 did I speak a word with any of the judges of Israel 2
7 that you should be prince over my people Israel; 2
9 I will appoint a place for my people Israel 2
10 I appointed judges over my people Israel; 2
21 What other nation . . is like thy people Israel 2
22 didst make thy people Israel to be thy people 2
24 LORD of hosts, the God of Israel, is Israel's God 2
24 LORD of hosts, the God of Israel, is Israel's God 2
18:14 David reigned over all Israel; 2
19:10 he chose some of the picked men of Israel 2
16 Syrians saw . . they had been defeated by Israel 2
17 he gathered all Israel together 2
18 the Syrians fled before Israel; 2
19 saw that they had been defeated by Israel 2
20: 7 when he taunted Israel, Jonathan . . slew him. 2
21: 1 Satan stood up against Israel 2
1 Satan . . incited David to number Israel. 2
2 Go, number Israel, from Beer-sheba to Dan 2
3 Why should he bring guilt upon Israel? 2
4 Jo'ab departed and went throughout all Israel 2
5 In all Israel there were 1,100,000 men who drew 2
7 God was displeased . . and he smote Israel. 2
12 destroying . . all the territory of Israel. 2
14 the LORD sent a pestilence upon Israel; 2
14 and there fell 70,000 men of Israel. 2
22: 1 and here the altar of burnt offering for Israel. 2
2 the aliens who were in the land of Israel 2
6 to build a house for the LORD, the God of Israel. 2
9 I will give peace and quiet to Israel in his days. 2
10 establish his royal throne in Israel for ever. 2
12 that when he gives you charge over Israel 2
13 which the LORD commanded Moses for Israel. 2
17 David also commanded all the leaders of Israel 2
23: 1 David . . made Solomon his son king over Israel. 2
2 David assembled all the leaders of Israel 2
25 The LORD, the God of Israel, has given peace 2
24:19 as the LORD God of Israel had commanded him. 2
26:29 appointed to outside duties for Israel 2
30 the oversight of Israel westward of the Jordan 2
27: 1 This is the list of the people of Israel 2
16 Over the tribes of Israel, for the Reubenites 2
22 These were the leaders of the tribes of Israel. 2
23 to make Israel as many as the stars of heaven. 2
24 yet wrath came upon Israel for this 2
28: 1 David assembled . . all the officials of Israel 2
4 LORD God of Israel chose me from all my father's 2
4 chose me . . to be king over Israel for ever; 2
4 took pleasure in me to make me king over all Israel 2
5 throne of the kingdom of the LORD over Israel. 2
8 Now therefore in the sight of all Israel 2
29:10 O LORD, the God of Israel our father 2
18 O LORD, the God of Abraham, Isaac, and Israel 2
21 sacrifices in abundance for all Israel; 2
23 and he prospered, and all Israel obeyed him. 2
25 Solomon great repute in the sight of all Israel 2
25 not been on any king before him in Israel. 2
26 David the son of Jesse reigned over all Israel. 2
27 time that he reigned over Israel was 40 years; 2
30 circumstances that came . . and upon Israel 2
2Ch 1: 2 Solomon spoke to all Israel 2
2 to the judges, and to all the leaders in all Israel 2
13 And he reigned over Israel. 2
2: 4 the LORD our God, as ordained for ever for Israel. 2
12 Huram also said, "Blessed be the LORD God of Israel 2
17 who were in the land of Israel 2
5: 2 Then Solomon assembled the elders of Israel 2
2 of the fathers' houses of the people of Israel 2
3 all the men of Israel assembled before the king 2
4 all the elders of Israel came 2
6 King Solomon and all the congregation of Israel 2
10 LORD made a covenant with the people of Israel 2
6: 3 king . . and blessed all the assembly of Israel 2
3 while all the assembly of Israel stood. 2
4 he said, "Blessed be the LORD, the God of Israel, who 2
5 I chose no city in all the tribes of Israel 2
5 I chose no man as prince over my people Israel; 2
6 I have chosen David to be over my people Israel.' 2
7 build a house for . . the LORD, the God of Israel. 2
10 I have risen . . and sit on the throne of Israel 2
10 built the house for . . LORD, the God of Israel. 2
11 covenant of the LORD . . made with . . Israel. 2
12 in the presence of all the assembly of Israel 2
13 in the presence of all the assembly of Israel 2
14 said, "O LORD, God of Israel, there is no God like thee 2
16 O LORD, God of Israel, keep with thy servant David 2
16 never fail you a man . . upon the throne of Israel 2
17 O LORD, God of Israel, let thy word be confirmed 2
21 supplications . . and of thy people Israel 2
24 If . . Israel are defeated before the enemy 2
25 hear . . and forgive the sin of thy people Israel 2
27 the sin of thy servants, thy people Israel 2
29 prayer . . made by . . or by all thy people Israel 2
32 when a foreigner, who is not of thy people Israel 2
33 may know . . and fear thee, as do thy people Israel 2
7: 3 all the children of Israel saw the fire come down 2
6 priests sounded trumpets; and all Israel stood. 2
8 held the feast . . and all Israel with him 2
10 goodness that the LORD had shown to . . Israel his 2
18 'There shall not fail you a man to rule Israel.' 2
8: 2 and settled the people of Israel in them. 2
7 people who were left . . who were not of Israel 2
8 whom the people of Israel had not destroyed- 2
9 of the people of Israel Solomon made no slaves 2
11 not live in the house of David king of Israel 2
9: 8 Because your God loved Israel 2
30 Solomon reigned in Jerusalem over all Israel 2
10: 1 all Israel had come to Shechem to make him king. 2
3 Jerobo'am and all Israel came and said 2
16 Israel saw that the king did not hearken to them 2
16 Each of you to your tents, O Israel! 2
16 So all Israel departed to their tents. 2
17 Rehobo'am reigned over the people of Israel 2
18 people of Israel stoned him to death 2
19 Israel has been in rebellion 2
11: 1 180,000 chosen warriors, to fight against Israel 2
3 Say . . to all Israel in Judah and Benjamin 2
13 priests and the Levites that were in all Israel 2
16 set their hearts to seek the LORD God of Israel 2
16 came after them from all the tribes of Israel 2
12: 1 he forsook the law . . and all Israel with him. 2
6 Then the princes of Israel and the king 2
13 out of all the tribes of Israel to put his name 2
13: 4 Abi'jah . . said, "Hear me, O Jerobo'am and all Israel! 2
5 LORD God of Israel gave the kingship over Israel 2
5 LORD . . gave the kingship over Israel for ever 2
12 O sons of Israel, do not fight against the LORD 2
15 God defeated Jerobo'am and all Israel 2
16 The men of Israel fled before Judah 2
17 there fell slain of Israel 500,000 picked men. 2
18 Thus the men of Israel were subdued at that time 2
15: 3 For a long time Israel was without the true God 2
4 they turned to the LORD, the God of Israel 2
9 great numbers had deserted to him from Israel 2
13 whoever would not seek the LORD, the God of Israel 2
17 the high places were not taken out of Israel. 2
16: 1 Ba'asha king of Israel went up against Judah 2
3 go, break your league with Ba'asha king of Israel 2
4 his armies against the cities of Israel 2
11 the Book of the Kings of Judah and Israel. 2
17: 1 strengthened himself against Israel. 2
4 walked . . not according to the ways of Israel. 2
18: 3 Ahab king of Israel said to Jehosh'aphat 2
4 Jehosh'aphat said to the king of Israel 2
5 king of Israel gathered the prophets together 2
7 the king of Israel said to Jehosh'aphat 2
8 the king of Israel summoned an officer and said 2
9 king of Israel and Jehosh'aphat the king of Judah 2
16 I saw all Israel scattered upon the mountains 2
17 the king of Israel said to Jehosh'aphat 2
19 LORD said, 'Who will entice Ahab the king of Israel 2
25 the king of Israel said, "Seize Micai'ah 2
28 king of Israel and Jehosh'aphat the king of Judah 2
29 the king of Israel said to Jehosh'aphat 2
29 king of Israel disguised himself; 2
30 Fight . . only with the king of Israel. 2
31 It is the king of Israel. 2
32 saw that it was not the king of Israel 2
33 struck the king of Israel between 2
34 king of Israel propped himself up in his chariot 2
19: 8 certain . . heads of families of Israel 2
20: 7 drive out . . before thy people Israel 2
10 whom thou wouldest not let Israel invade 2
19 stood up to praise the LORD, the God of Israel 2
29 LORD had fought against the enemies of Israel. 2
34 are recorded in the Book of the Kings of Israel. 2
35 Ahazi'ah king of Israel, who did wickedly. 2
21: 4 he slew . . also some of the princes of Israel. 2
6 he walked in the way of the kings of Israel 2
13 have walked in the way of the kings of Israel 2
13 house of Ahab led Israel into unfaithfulness •
22: 5 went with Jeho'ram the son of Ahab king of Israel 2
23: 2 the heads of fathers' houses of Israel 2
24: 5 gather from all Israel money to repair 2
6 tax levied . . on the congregation of Israel 2
9 tax that Moses . . laid upon Israel 2
16 because he had done good in Israel 2
25: 6 hired . . 100,000 mighty men of valor from Israel 2
7 O king, do not let the army of Israel go with you 2
7 LORD is not with Israel 2
9 talents which I have given to the army of Israel? 2
17 son of Jeho'ahaz, son of Jehu, king of Israel 2
18 Jo'ash the king of Israel sent word to Amazi'ah 2
21 Jo'ash king of Israel went up; 2
22 Judah was defeated by Israel 2
23 Jo'ash king of Israel captured Amazi'ah 2
25 Jo'ash the son of Jeho'ahaz, king of Israel. 2
26 the Book of the Kings of Judah and Israel? 2
27: 7 in the Book of the Kings of Israel and Judah. 2
28: 2 walked in the ways of the kings of Israel. 2
3 the LORD drove out before the people of Israel. 2
5 also given into the hand of the king of Israel 2
8 The men of Israel took captive 200,000 2
13 there is fierce wrath against Israel. 2
19 brought Judah low because of Ahaz king of Israel 2
23 But they were the ruin of him, and of all Israel. 2
26 the Book of the Kings of Judah and Israel. 2
27 into the tombs of the kings of Israel. 2
29: 7 in the holy place to the God of Israel. 2
10 to make a covenant with the LORD, the God of Israel 2
24 to make atonement for all Israel. 2
24 sin offering should be made for all Israel. 2
27 by the instruments of David king of Israel. 2
30: 1 Hezeki'ah sent to all Israel and Judah 2
1 to keep the passover to the LORD the God of Israel. 2
5 to make a proclamation throughout all Israel 2
5 keep the passover to the LORD the God of Israel 2
6 couriers went throughout all Israel and Judah 2
6 O people of Israel, return to the LORD 2
6 the LORD, the God of Abraham, Isaac, and Israel 2
21 people of Israel . . kept the feast 2
25 whole assembly that came out of Israel 2
25 sojourners who came out of the land of Israel 2
26 time of Solomon the son of David king of Israel 2
31: 1 Israel who were present went out to the cities 2
1 people of Israel returned to their cities 2
5 people of Israel gave in abundance 2
6 people of Israel and Judah 2
8 blessed the LORD and his people Israel. 2
32:17 cast contempt on the LORD the God of Israel 2
32 in the Book of the Kings of Judah and Israel. 2
33: 2 LORD drove out before the people of Israel. 2
7 I have chosen out of all the tribes of Israel 2
8 no more remove the foot of Israel from the land 2
9 LORD destroyed before the people of Israel. 2
16 Judah to serve the LORD the God of Israel. 2
18 spoke . . in the name of the LORD the God of Israel 2
18 the Chronicles of the Kings of Israel. 2
34: 7 throughout all the land of Israel. 2
9 collected . . from all the remnant of Israel 2
21 for those who are left in Israel and in Judah 2
23 Thus says the LORD, the God of Israel: 'Tell the man 2
26 Thus says the LORD, the God of Israel: Regarding 2
33 territory that belonged to the people of Israel 2
33 made all . . in Israel serve the LORD their God. 2
35: 3 he said to the Levites who taught all Israel 2
3 house which Solomon . . king of Israel, built; 2
3 Now serve the LORD your God and his people Israel. 2
4 the directions of David king of Israel 2
17 people of Israel . . present kept the passover 2
18 No passover like it had been kept in Israel since 2
18 none of the kings of Israel had kept such 2
18 by . . all Judah and Israel who were present 2
25 They made these an ordinance in Israel; 2

27 in the Book of the Kings of Israel and Judah. 2
36: 8 Book of the Kings of Israel and Judah; 2
13 against turning to the LORD, the God of Israel. 2
Ezr 1: 3 rebuild the house of the LORD, the God of Israel- 2
2: 2 number of the men of the people of Israel 2
59 not prove . . whether they belonged to Israel 2
70 all Israel in their towns. 2
3: 1 When the . . sons of Israel were in the towns 2
2 built the altar of the God of Israel 2
10 directions of David king of Israel; 2
11 steadfast love endures for ever toward Israel. 2
4: 1 building a temple to the LORD, the God of Israel 2
3 rest of the heads of fathers' houses in Israel 2
3 we alone will build to the LORD, the God of Israel 2
5: 1 prophesied . . in the name of the God of Israel 4
11 which a great king of Israel built and finished. 4
6:14 finished . . by command of the God of Israel 4
16 people of Israel, the priests and the Levites 4
17 sin offering for all Israel twelve he-goats 4
17 according to the number of the tribes of Israel. 4
21 eaten by the people of Israel who had returned 2
21 separated . . to worship the LORD, the God of Israel. 2
22 work of the house of God, the God of Israel. 2
7: 6 law of Moses . . LORD the God of Israel had given; 2
7 some of the people of Israel 2
10 to teach his statutes and ordinances in Israel. 2
11 learned in . . his statutes for Israel 2
13 any one of the people of Israel or their priests 4
15 freely offered to the God of Israel 4
28 gathered leading men from Israel to go up 2
8:18 sons of Mahli the son of Levi, son of Israel 2
25 all Israel there present had offered; 2
29 heads of fathers' houses in Israel at Jerusalem 2
35 offered burnt offerings to the God of Israel 2
35 twelve bulls for all Israel, 96 rams 2
9: 1 people of Israel and the priests and the Levites 2
4 all who trembled at the words of the God of Israel 2
15 O LORD the God of Israel, thou art just 2
10: 1 great assembly . . gathered to him out of Israel; 2
2 there is hope for Israel in spite of this. 2
5 made the . . Levites and all Israel take oath 2
10 so increased the guilt of Israel. 2
25 of Israel: of the sons of Parosh: Rami'ah, Izzi'ah 2
Neh 1: 6 prayer . . for the people of Israel thy servants 2
6 confessing the sins of the people of Israel 2
2:10 seek the welfare of the children of Israel. 2
7: 7 number of the men of the people of Israel 2
61 their descent, whether they belonged to Israel 2
73 people, the temple servants, and all Israel 2
73 children of Israel were in their towns. 2
8: 1 law of Moses which the LORD had given to Israel. 2
14 people of Israel should dwell in booths during 2
17 from . . Jeshua . . people of Israel had not done 2
9: 1 people of Israel were assembled with fasting 2
10:33 sin offerings to make atonement for Israel 2
39 For the people of Israel and the sons of Levi 2
11: 3 Israel, the priests, the Levites 2
20 rest of Israel, and of the priests and the Levites 2
12:47 all Israel in the days of Zerub'babel 2
13: 2 not meet the children of Israel with bread 2
3 separated from Israel all those of foreign 2
18 wrath upon Israel by profaning the sabbath. 2
26 not Solomon king of Israel sin on account of such 2
26 God made him king over all Israel; 2
Ps 14: 7 O that deliverance for Israel would come 2
7 Jacob shall rejoice, Israel shall be glad. 2
22: 3 art holy, enthroned on the praises of Israel. 2
23 stand in awe of him, all you sons of Israel! 2
25:22 Redeem Israel, O God, out of all his troubles. 2
41:13 Blessed be the LORD, the God of Israel 2
50: 7 O Israel, I will testify against you. 2
53: 6 O that deliverance for Israel would come 2
6 Jacob will rejoice and Israel be glad. 2
59: 5 Thou, LORD God of hosts, art God of Israel. 2
68: 8 Sinai quaked at the presence of . . God of Israel. 2
26 Bless . . LORD, O you who are of Israel's fountain! 2
34 God, whose majesty is over Israel 2
35 God of Israel, he gives power and strength 2
69: 6 brought to dishonor through me, O God of Israel. 2
71:22 sing praises to thee . . O Holy One of Israel. 2
72:18 Blessed be the LORD, the God of Israel 2
76: 1 In Judah God is known, his name is great in Israel. 2
78: 5 testimony in Jacob, and appointed a law in Israel 2
21 against Jacob, his anger mounted against Israel; 2
31 and laid low the picked men of Israel. 2
41 and provoked the Holy One of Israel. 2
55 settled the tribes of Israel in their tents. 2
59 full of wrath, and he utterly rejected Israel. 2
71 of Jacob his people, of Israel his inheritance. 2
80: 1 Give ear, O Shepherd of Israel 2
81: 4 For it is a statute for Israel 2
8 O Israel, if you would but listen to me! 2
11 Israel would have none of me. 2
13 O that . . Israel would walk in my ways! 2
83: 4 let the name of Israel be remembered no more! 2
89:18 our king to the Holy One of Israel. 2
98: 3 love and faithfulness to the house of Israel. 2
103: 7 made known his . . acts to the people of Israel. 2
105:10 to Israel as an everlasting covenant 2
23 Then Israel came to Egypt; 2
37 Then he led forth Israel with silver and gold •
106:48 Blessed be the LORD, the God of Israel 2
114: 1 When Israel went forth from Egypt 2
2 Judah . . his sanctuary, Israel his dominion. 2
115: 9 O Israel, trust in the LORD! 2
12 he will bless the house of Israel; 2
118: 2 Israel say, "His steadfast love endures for ever. 2
121: 4 keeps Israel will neither slumber nor sleep. 2
122: 4 as was decreed for Israel, to give thanks 2
124: 1 If . . the LORD who was on our side, let Israel now say- 2
125: 5 Peace be in Israel! 2
128: 6 Peace be upon Israel! 2
129: 1 let Israel now say- 2
130: 7 O Israel, hope in the LORD! 2
8 he will redeem Israel from all his iniquities. 2
131: 3 O Israel, hope in the LORD from this time forth 2
135: 4 chosen Jacob . . Israel as his own possession. 2
12 as a heritage, a heritage to his people Israel. 2
19 O house of Israel, bless the LORD! O house of Aaron 2
136:11 brought Israel out from among them 2
14 made Israel pass through the midst of it 2
22 a heritage to Israel his servant 2
147: 2 LORD . . gathers the outcasts of Israel. 2
19 his statutes and ordinances to Israel. 2
148:14 his saints, for the people of Israel who are near 2
149: 2 Let Israel be glad in his Maker 2
Prv 1: 1 proverbs of Solomon, son of David, king of Israel 2
Ecc 1:12 I . . have been king over Israel in Jerusalem. 2
Sng 3: 7 About it are 60 . . of the mighty men of Israel 2
Isa 1: 3 The ox knows its owner . . but Israel does not know 2
4 they have despised the Holy One of Israel 2
24 the LORD of hosts, the Mighty One of Israel 2
4: 2 the pride and glory of the survivors of Israel. 2
5: 7 the vineyard of the LORD . . is the house of Israel 2
19 the purpose of the Holy One of Israel draw near 2
24 have despised the word of the Holy One of Israel. 2
7: 1 Pekah the son of Remali'ah the king of Israel came 2
8:14 a rock of stumbling to both houses of Israel 2
18 the children . . are signs and portents in Israel 2
9: 8 a word . . and it will light upon Israel; 2
12 Philistines . . devour Israel with open mouth. 2
14 So the LORD cut off from Israel head and tail 2
10:17 The light of Israel will become a fire 2
20 In that day the remnant of Israel 2
20 but will lean upon the LORD, the Holy One of Israel 2
22 For though your people Israel be as the sand 2
11:12 and will assemble the outcasts of Israel 2
16 highway . . as there was for Israel when the came 2
12: 6 for great in your midst is the Holy One of Israel. 2
14: 1 The LORD . . will again choose Israel 2
2 the house of Israel will possess them 2
17: 3 Syria . . like the glory of the children of Israel 2
6 of a fruit tree, says the LORD God of Israel. 2
7 and their eyes will look to the Holy One of Israel; 2
9 deserted because of the children of Israel 2
19:24 Israel will be the third with Egypt and Assyria 2
25 Blessed be Egypt . . and Israel my heritage. 2
21:10 LORD of hosts, the God of Israel, I announce to you 2
17 for the LORD, the God of Israel, has spoken. 2
24:15 glory . . to the name of the LORD, the God of Israel. 2
27: 6 Israel shall blossom and put forth shoots 2
12 be gathered one by one, O people of Israel. 2
29:19 men shall exult in the Holy One of Israel. 2
23 and will stand in awe of the God of Israel. 2
30:11 let us hear no more of the Holy One of Israel. 2
12 Therefore thus says the Holy One of Israel 2
15 For thus said the Lord GOD, the Holy One of Israel 2
29 to the mountain of the LORD, to the Rock of Israel. 2
31: 1 but do not look to the Holy One of Israel 2
6 you have deeply revolted, O people of Israel. 2
37:16 O LORD of hosts, God of Israel, who art enthroned 2
21 Thus says the LORD, the God of Israel 2
23 Against whom . . ? Against the Holy One of Israel! 2
40:27 Why do you say, O Jacob, and speak, O Israel 2
41: 8 you, Israel, my servant, Jacob, whom I have chosen 2
14 Fear not, you worm Jacob, you men of Israel! 2
14 your Redeemer is the Holy One of Israel. 2
16 in the Holy One of Israel you shall glory. 2
17 I the God of Israel will not forsake them. 2
20 the Holy One of Israel has created it. 2
42:24 Jacob to the spoiler, and Israel to the robbers? 2
43: 1 created you, O Jacob, he who formed you, O Israel 2
3 your God, the Holy One of Israel, your Savior. 2
14 the LORD, your Redeemer, the Holy One of Israel 2
15 your Holy One, the Creator of Israel, your King. 2
22 but you have been weary of me, O Israel! 2
28 I delivered . . Israel to reviling. 2
44: 1 O Jacob my servant, Israel whom I have chosen! 2
5 and surname himself by the name of Israel. 2
6 says the LORD, the King of Israel and his Redeemer 2
21 Remember these things, O Jacob, and Israel 2
21 O Israel, you will not be forgotten by me. 2
23 redeemed Jacob, and will be glorified in Israel. 2
45: 3 LORD, the God of Israel, who call you by your name. 2
4 the sake of my servant Jacob, and Israel my chosen 2
11 the LORD, the Holy One of Israel, and his Maker 2
15 who hidest thyself, O God of Israel, the Savior. 2
17 Israel is saved by the LORD with everlasting 2
25 the offspring of Israel shall triumph and glory. 2
46: 3 all the remnant of the house of Israel 2
13 I will put salvation in Zion, for Israel my glory. 2
47: 4 Our Redeemer . . is the Holy One of Israel. 2
48: 1 of Jacob, who are called by the name of Israel 2
1 and confess the God of Israel, but not in truth 2
2 and stay themselves on the God of Israel; 2
12 Hearken to me, O Jacob, and Israel, whom I called! 2
17 the LORD, your Redeemer, the Holy One of Israel 2
49: 3 my servant, Israel, in whom I will be glorified. 2
5 to him, and that Israel might be gathered to him 2
6 of Jacob and to restore the preserved of Israel; 2
7 Thus says the LORD, the Redeemer of Israel 2
7 the Holy One of Israel, who has chosen you. 2
52:12 and the God of Israel will be your rear guard. 2
54: 5 and the Holy One of Israel is your Redeemer 2
55: 5 the LORD your God, and of the Holy One of Israel 2
56: 8 the Lord GOD, who gathers the outcasts of Israel 2
60: 9 Holy One of Israel, because he has glorified you. 2
14 of the LORD, the Zion of the Holy One of Israel. 2
63: 7 and the great goodness to the house of Israel 2
16 not know us and Israel does not acknowledge us; 2
Jer 2: 3 Israel was holy to the LORD, the first fruits 2
4 and all the families of the house of Israel. 2
14 Is Israel a slave? Is he a homeborn servant? 2
26 the house of Israel shall be shamed 2
31 Have I been a wilderness to Israel 2
3: 6 seen what she did, that faithless one, Israel 2
8 all the adulteries of that faithless one, Israel 2
11 Faithless Israel has shown herself less guilty 2
12 Return, faithless Israel, says the LORD. 2
18 the house of Judah shall join the house of Israel 2
20 have you been faithless to me, O house of Israel 2
21 the weeping and pleading of Israel's sons 2
23 in the LORD our God is the salvation of Israel. 2
4: 1 If you return, O Israel, says the LORD 2
5:11 For the house of Israel and the house of Judah 2
15 upon you a nation from afar, O house of Israel 2
6: 9 Glean thoroughly as a vine the remnant of Israel; 2
7: 3 Thus says the LORD of hosts, the God of Israel 2
12 did to it for the wickedness of my people Israel. 2
21 Thus says the LORD of hosts, the God of Israel 2
9:15 thus says the LORD of hosts, the God of Israel 2
26 the house of Israel is uncircumcised in heart. 2
10: 1 the LORD speaks to you, O house of Israel. 2
16 and Israel is the tribe of his inheritance; 2
11: 3 Thus says the LORD, the God of Israel 2
10 the house of Israel and the house of Judah have 2
17 because of the evil which the house of Israel 2
12:14 which I have given my people Israel to inherit 2
13:11 I made the whole house of Israel . . cling to me 2
12 Thus says the LORD, the God of Israel 2
14: 8 O thou hope of Israel, its savior 2
16: 9 For thus says the LORD of hosts, the God of Israel 2
14 LORD lives who brought up the people of Israel 2
15 LORD lives who brought up the people of Israel 2
17:13 O LORD, the hope of Israel 2
18: 6 O house of Israel, can I not do with you as this 2
6 so are you in my hand, O house of Israel. 2
13 virgin Israel has done a very horrible thing. 2
19: 3 Thus says the LORD of hosts, the God of Israel 2
15 Thus says the LORD of hosts, the God of Israel 2
21: 4 Thus says the LORD, the God of Israel 2
23: 2 Therefore thus says the LORD, the God of Israel 2
6 and Israel will dwell securely. 2
7 LORD lives who brought up the people of Israel 2
8 and led the descendants of the house of Israel 2
13 by Ba'al and led my people Israel astray. 2
24: 5 Thus says the LORD, the God of Israel 2
25:15 Thus the LORD, the God of Israel, said to me 2
27 Thus says the LORD of hosts, the God of Israel 2
27: 4 Thus says the LORD of hosts, the God of Israel 2
21 thus says the LORD of hosts, the God of Israel 2
28: 2 Thus says the LORD of hosts, the God of Israel 2
14 For thus says the LORD of hosts, the God of Israel 2
29: 4 Thus says the LORD of hosts, the God of Israel 2
8 For thus says the LORD of hosts, the God of Israel 2
21 Thus says the LORD of hosts, the God of Israel 2
23 because they have committed folly in Israel 2
25 Thus says the LORD of hosts, the God of Israel 2
30: 2 Thus says the LORD, the God of Israel 2
3 my people, Israel and Judah, says the LORD 2
4 the LORD spoke concerning Israel and Judah 2
10 says the LORD, nor be dismayed, O Israel; 2
31: 1 I will be the God of all the families of Israel 2
2 in the wilderness; when Israel sought for rest 2
4 and you shall be built, O virgin Israel! 2
7 LORD has saved his people, the remnant of Israel. 2
9 for I am a father to Israel 2
10 say, 'He who scattered Israel will gather him 2
21 Return, O virgin Israel 2
23 Thus says the LORD of hosts, the God of Israel 2
27 says the LORD, when I will sow the house of Israel 2
31 will make a new covenant with the house of Israel 2
33 make with the house of Israel after those days 2
36 then shall the descendants of Israel cease 2
37 I will cast off all the descendants of Israel 2
32:14 Thus says the LORD of hosts, the God of Israel 2
15 For thus says the LORD of hosts, the God of Israel 2

20 and to this day in Israel and among all mankind 2
21 bring thy people Israel out of the land of Egypt 2
30 the sons of Israel . . have done nothing but evil 2
30 the sons of Israel have done nothing but provoke 2
32 because of all the evil of the sons of Israel 2
36 therefore thus says the LORD, the God of Israel 2
33: 4 For thus says the LORD, the God of Israel 2
7 the fortunes of Judah and the fortunes of Israel 2
14 fulfil the promise I made to the house of Israel 2
17 a man to sit on the throne of the house of Israel 2
34: 2 Thus says the LORD, the God of Israel: Go and speak 2
13 Thus says the LORD, the God of Israel 2
35:13 Thus says the LORD of hosts, the God of Israel 2
17 says the LORD, the God of hosts, the God of Israel 2
18 Thus says the LORD of hosts, the God of Israel 2
19 thus says the LORD of hosts, the God of Israel 2
36: 2 against Israel and Judah and all the nations 2
37: 7 Thus says the LORD, God of Israel 2
38:17 says the LORD, the God of hosts, the God of Israel 2
39:16 Thus says the LORD of hosts, the God of Israel 2
41: 9 made for defense against Ba'asha king of Israel; 2
42: 9 said to them, "Thus says the LORD, the God of Israel 2
15 Thus says the LORD of hosts, the God of Israel 2
18 For thus says the LORD of hosts, the God of Israel 2
43:10 Thus says the LORD of hosts, the God of Israel 2
44: 2 Thus says the LORD of hosts, the God of Israel 2
7 thus says the LORD God of hosts, the God of Israel 2
11 thus says the LORD of hosts, the God of Israel 2
25 Thus says the LORD of hosts, the God of Israel 2
45: 2 Thus says the LORD, the God of Israel, to you 2
46:25 The LORD of hosts, the God of Israel, said: "Behold 2
27 nor be dismayed, O Israel; 2
48: 1 Thus says the LORD of hosts, the God of Israel 2
13 as the house of Israel was ashamed of Bethel 2
27 Was not Israel a derision to you? 2
49: 1 says the LORD: "Has Israel no sons? Has he no heir? 2
2 then Israel shall dispossess those 2
50: 4 the people of Israel and the people of Judah 2
17 Israel is a hunted sheep driven away by lions. 2
18 thus says the LORD of hosts, the God of Israel 2
19 I will restore Israel to his pasture 2
20 says the LORD, iniquity shall be sought in Israel 2
29 she has . . defied the LORD, the Holy One of Israel. 2
33 The people of Israel are oppressed 2
51: 5 For Israel and Judah have not been forsaken 2
5 is full of guilt against the Holy One of Israel. 2
19 and Israel is the tribe of his inheritance; 2
33 For thus says the LORD of hosts, the God of Israel 2
49 Babylon must fall for the slain of Israel 2
Lam 2: 1 has cast down . . to earth the splendor of Israel; 2
3 He has cut down in . . anger all the might of Israel; 2
5 Lord . . like an enemy, he has destroyed Israel; 2
Ezk 2: 3 Son of man, I send you to the people of Israel 2
3: 1 and go, speak to the house of Israel. 2
4 Son of man, go, get you to the house of Israel 2
5 not sent to a people . . but to the house of Israel 2
7 But the house of Israel will not listen to you; 2
7 all the house of Israel are of a hard forehead 2
17 I have made you a watchman for the house of Israel; 2
4: 3 This is a sign for the house of Israel. 2
4 the punishment of the house of Israel upon you; 2
5 you bear the punishment of the house of Israel. 2
13 Thus shall the people of Israel eat their bread 2
5: 4 will come forth into all the house of Israel. 2
6: 2 set your face toward the mountains of Israel 2
3 You mountains of Israel, hear the word of the Lord 2
5 I will lay the dead bodies of the people of Israel 2
11 all the evil abominations of the house of Israel; 2
7: 2 thus says the Lord GOD to the land of Israel: An end! 2
8: 4 behold, the glory of the God of Israel was there 2
6 the great abominations that the house of Israel 2
10 and all the idols of the house of Israel. 2
11 70 men of the elders of the house of Israel 2
12 what the elders of the house of Israel are doing 2
9: 3 Now the glory of the God of Israel had gone up 2
8 wilt thou destroy all that remains of Israel 2
9 The guilt of the house of Israel and Judah is 2
10:19 the glory of the God of Israel was over them. 2
20 underneath the God of Israel by the river Chebar; 2
11: 5 Thus says the LORD: So you think, O house of Israel; 2
10 I will judge you at the border of Israel; 2
11 I will judge you at the border of Israel; 2
13 wilt thou make a full end of the remnant of Israel? 2
15 your fellow exiles, the whole house of Israel 2
17 I will give you the land of Israel. 2
22 and the glory of the God of Israel was over them. 2
12: 6 I have made you a sign for the house of Israel. 2
9 has not the house of Israel, the rebellious house 2
10 and all the house of Israel who are in it. 2
19 inhabitants of Jerusalem in the land of Israel 2
22 proverb that you have about the land of Israel 2
23 they shall no more use it as a proverb in Israel. 2
24 no . . divination within the house of Israel. 2
27 Son of man, behold, they of the house of Israel say 2
13: 2 prophesy against the prophets of Israel 2
4 have been like foxes among ruins, O Israel. 2
5 or built up a wall for the house of Israel 2
9 enrolled in the register of the house of Israel 2
9 nor shall they enter the land of Israel; 2
16 the prophets of Israel who prophesied 2
14: 1 Then came certain of the elders of Israel to me; 2
4 Any man of the house of Israel who takes his idols 2
5 I may lay hold of the hearts of the house of Israel 2
6 Therefore say to the house of Israel 2
7 For any one of the house of Israel 2
7 or of the strangers that sojourn in Israel 2
9 destroy him from the midst of my people Israel. 2
11 that the house of Israel may go no more astray 2
17: 2 speak an allegory to the house of Israel; 2
23 on the mountain height of Israel will I plant it 2
18: 2 this proverb concerning the land of Israel 2
3 proverb shall no more be used by you in Israel. 2
6 or lift up his eyes to the idols . . of Israel 2
15 or lift up his eyes to the idols . . of Israel 2
25 Hear now, O house of Israel: Is my way not just? 2
29 Yet the house of Israel says, 'The way of the Lord is 2
29 O house of Israel, are my ways not just? 2
30 Therefore I will judge you, O house of Israel 2
31 Why will you die, O house of Israel? 2
19: 1 take up a lamentation for the princes of Israel 2
9 no more be heard upon the mountains of Israel. 2
20: 1 certain of the elders of Israel came to inquire 2
3 Son of man, speak to the elders of Israel 2
5 On the day when I chose Israel 2
13 But the house of Israel rebelled against me 2
27 Therefore, son of man, speak to the house of Israel 2
30 Wherefore say to the house of Israel 2
31 And shall I be inquired of by you, O house of Israel? 2
38 but they shall not enter the land of Israel. 2
39 As for you, O house of Israel, thus says the Lord GOD 2
40 my holy mountain, the mountain height of Israel 2
40 there all the house of Israel, all of them 2
42 when I bring you into the land of Israel 2
44 your corrupt doings, O house of Israel 2
21: 2 prophesy against the land of Israel 2
3 say to the land of Israel, Thus says the LORD 2
12 it is against all the princes of Israel; 2
25 you, O unhallowed wicked one, prince of Israel 2
22: 6 Behold, the princes of Israel in you, every one 2
18 the house of Israel has become dross to me; 2
24:21 Say to the house of Israel, Thus says the Lord GOD 2
25: 3 over the land of Israel when it was made desolate 2
6 the malice within you against the land of Israel 2
14 upon Edom by the hand of my people Israel; 2
27:17 Judah and the land of Israel traded with you; 2
28:24 for . . Israel there shall be no more a brier 2
25 When I gather the house of Israel 2
29: 6 have been a staff of reed to the house of Israel; 2
16 again be the reliance of the house of Israel 2
21 a horn to spring forth to the house of Israel 2
33: 7 I have made a watchman for the house of Israel; 2
10 And you, son of man, say to the house of Israel 2
11 for why will you die, O house of Israel? 2
20 O house of Israel, I will judge each of you 2
24 waste places in the land of Israel keep saying 2
28 the mountains of Israel shall be so desolate 2
34: 2 prophesy against the shepherds of Israel 2
2 Thus says the Lord GOD: Ho, shepherds of Israel 2
13 I will feed them on the mountains of Israel 2
14 upon the mountain heights of Israel 2
14 they shall feed on the mountains of Israel. 2
30 the house of Israel, are my people, says the Lord 2
35: 5 and gave over the people of Israel 2
12 you uttered against the mountains of Israel 2
15 over the inheritance of the house of Israel 2
36: 1 son of man, prophesy to the mountains of Israel 2
1 O mountains of Israel, hear the word of the LORD. 2
4 O mountains of Israel, hear the word of the Lord 2
6 prophesy concerning the land of Israel, 2
8 you, O mountains of Israel, shall shoot forth 2
8 and yield your fruit to my people Israel; 2
10 men upon you, the whole house of Israel, all of it; 2
12 I will let men walk upon you, even my people Israel; 2
17 when the house of Israel dwelt in their own land 2
21 which the house of Israel caused to be profaned 2
22 Therefore say to the house of Israel 2
22 It is not for your sake, O house of Israel 2
32 and confounded for your ways, O house of Israel. 2
37 I will let the house of Israel ask me to do for them 2
37:11 these bones are the whole house of Israel. 2
12 I will bring you home into the land of Israel. 2
16 and the children of Israel associated with him 2
16 all the house of Israel associated with him 2
19 and the tribes of Israel associated with him; 2
21 I will take the people of Israel from the nations 2
22 nation in the land, upon the mountains of Israel; 2
28 will know that I the LORD sanctify Israel 2
38: 8 from many nations upon the mountains of Israel 2
14 when my people Israel are dwelling securely 2
16 you will come up against my people Israel 2
17 by my servants the prophets of Israel 2
18 when Gog shall come against the land of Israel 2
19 shall be a great shaking in the land of Israel; 2
39: 2 and lead you against the mountains of Israel; 2
4 You shall fall upon the mountains of Israel 2
7 I will make known in the midst of my people Israel; 2
7 know that I am the LORD, the Holy One in Israel. 2
9 those who dwell in the cities of Israel will go 2
11 I will give to Gog a place for burial in Israel 2
12 the house of Israel will be burying them 2
17 sacrificial feast upon the mountains of Israel 2
22 The house of Israel shall know that I am the LORD 2
23 that the house of Israel went into captivity 2
25 and have mercy upon the whole house of Israel; 2
29 when I pour out my Spirit upon the house of Israel 2
40: 2 in the visions of God into the land of Israel, 2
4 declare all that you see to the house of Israel. 2
43: 2 the glory of the God of Israel came from the east; 2
7 I will dwell in the midst of the people of Israel 2
7 house of Israel shall no more defile my holy name 2
10 describe to the house of Israel the temple 2
44: 2 for the LORD, the God of Israel, has entered by it; 2
6 to the rebellious house, to the house of Israel 2
6 O house of Israel, let there be an end 2
9 foreigners who are among the people of Israel 2
10 after their idols when Israel went astray 2
12 of iniquity to the house of Israel 2
15 when the people of Israel went astray from me 2
22 a virgin of the stock of the house of Israel 2
28 you shall give them no possession in Israel; 2
29 every devoted thing in Israel shall be theirs. 2
45: 6 it shall belong to the whole house of Israel. 2
8 It is to be his property in Israel. 2
8 they shall let the house of Israel have the land 2
9 Thus says the Lord GOD: Enough, O princes of Israel! 2
15 from the families of Israel. 2
16 give this offering to the prince in Israel. 2
17 all the appointed feasts of the house of Israel 2
17 to make atonement for the house of Israel. 2
47:13 inheritance among the twelve tribes of Israel. 2
18 the Jordan between Gilead and the land of Israel; 2
21 among you according to the tribes of Israel. 2
22 They shall be to you as native-born sons of Israel; 2
22 an inheritance among the tribes of Israel. 2
48:11 go astray when the people of Israel went astray 2
19 workers of the city, from all the tribes of Israel 2
29 as an inheritance among the tribes of Israel 2
31 gates . . being named after the tribes of Israel. 2
Dan 9: 7 all Israel . . near and those that are far away 2
11 All Israel has transgressed thy law and turned 2
20 confessing my sin and the sin of my people Israel 2
Hos 1: 1 Jerobo'am the son of Jo'ash, king of Israel. 2
4 put an end to the kingdom of the house of Israel. 2
5 break the bow of Israel in the valley of Jezreel. 2
6 for I will no more have pity on the house of Israel 2
10 people of Israel shall be like the sand of the sea 2
11 and the people of Israel shall be gathered 2
3: 1 even as the LORD loves the people of Israel 2
4 For the children of Israel shall dwell many days 2
5 Afterward the children of Israel shall return 2
4: 1 Hear the word of the LORD, O people of Israel; 2
15 Though you play the harlot, O Israel 2
16 Like a stubborn heifer, Israel is stubborn; 2
5: 1 Hear this, O priests! Give heed, O house of Israel! 2
3 I know E'phraim, and Israel is not hid from me; 2
3 you have played the harlot, Israel is defiled. 2
5 The pride of Israel testifies to his face; 2
9 among the tribes of Israel I declare what is sure. 2
6:10 In the house of Israel I have seen a horrible 2
10 E'phraim's harlotry is there, Israel is defiled. 2
7: 1 when I would heal Israel 2
10 The pride of Israel witnesses against him; 2
8: 2 To me they cry, My God, we Israel know thee. 2
3 Israel has spurned the good; 2
6 in Israel? A workman made it; it is not God. 2
8 Israel is swallowed up; 2
14 For Israel has forgotten his Maker 2
9: 1 Rejoice not, O Israel! Exult not like the peoples; 2
7 Israel shall know it. 2
10 Like grapes in the wilderness, I found Israel. 2
10: 1 Israel is a luxuriant vine that yields 2
6 and Israel shall be ashamed of his idol. 2
8 The high places of Aven, the sin of Israel 2
9 From the days of Gib'e-ah, you have sinned, O Israel; 2
15 Thus it shall be done to you, O house of Israel 5
15 the king of Israel shall be utterly cut off. 2
11: 1 When Israel was a child, I loved him 2
8 How can I hand you over, O Israel! 2
12 and the house of Israel with deceit; 2
12:12 land of Aram, there Israel did service for a wife 2
13 the LORD brought Israel up from Egypt 2
13: 1 he was exalted in Israel; but he incurred guilt 2
9 I will destroy you, O Israel; who can help you? 2
14: 1 Return, O Israel, to the LORD your God 2
5 I will be as the dew to Israel; 2
Jol 2:27 You shall know that I am in the midst of Israel 2
3: 2 on account of my people and my heritage Israel 2
16 a stronghold to the people of Israel. 2
Ams 1: 1 words of Amos . . which he saw concerning Israel 2
1 Jerobo'am the son of Jo'ash, king of Israel 2
2: 6 For three transgressions of Israel, and for four 2
11 it not indeed so, O people of Israel?" says the LORD. 2
3: 1 has spoken against you, O people of Israel 2
12 shall the people of Israel who dwell in Sama'ria 2
14 the day I punish Israel for his transgressions 2
4: 5 for so you love to do, O people of Israel! 2
12 Therefore thus I will do to you, O Israel; 2

12 do this to you, prepare to meet your God, O Israel! 2
5: 1 take up over you in lamentation, O house of Israel 2
2 Fallen, no more to rise, is the virgin Israel; 2
3 have ten left to the house of Israel. 2
4 thus says the LORD to the house of Israel 2
25 40 years in the wilderness, O house of Israel? 2
6: 1 of the nations, to whom the house of Israel come! 2
14 raise up against you a nation, O house of Israel 2
7: 8 a plumb line in the midst of my people Israel; 2
9 the sanctuaries of Israel shall be laid waste 2
10 Amazi'ah . . sent to Jerobo'am king of Israel 2
10 against you in the midst of the house of Israel; 2
11 and Israel must go into exile away from his land 2
15 LORD said to me, 'Go, prophesy to my people Israel.' 2
16 You say, 'Do not prophesy against Israel 2
17 and Israel shall surely go into exile 2
8: 2 The end has come upon my people Israel; 2
9: 7 O people of Israel?" says the LORD. 2
7 Did I not bring up Israel from the land of Egypt 2
9 shake the house of Israel among all the nations 2
14 I will restore the fortunes of my people Israel 2
Obd 1:20 exiles in Halah who are of the people of Israel 2
Mic 1: 5 this is . . for the sins of the house of Israel. 2
13 in you were found the transgressions of Israel. 2
14 be a deceitful thing to the kings of Israel. 2
15 the glory of Israel shall come to Adullam. 2
2:12 O Jacob, I will gather the remnant of Israel; 2
3: 1 Hear, you . . rulers of the house of Israel! 2
8 to declare . . to Israel his sin. 2
9 Hear this, you . . rulers of the house of Israel 2
5: 1 they strike upon the cheek the ruler of Israel. 2
2 for me one who is to be ruler in Israel 2
3 brethren shall return to the people of Israel. 2
6: 2 and he will contend with Israel. 2
Nah 2: 2 the majesty of Jacob as the majesty of Israel 2
Zep 2: 9 says the LORD of hosts, the God of Israel 2
3:13 those who are left in Israel; 2
14 Sing aloud, O daughter of Zion; shout, O Israel! 2
15 The King of Israel, the LORD, is in your midst; 2
Zec 1:19 have scattered Judah, Israel, and Jerusalem. 2
8:13 house of Israel, so will I save you 2
9: 1 of Aram, even as all the tribes of Israel; 2
11:14 the brotherhood between Judah and Israel. 2
12: 1 An Oracle The word of the LORD concerning Israel 2
Mal 1: 1 the word of the LORD to Israel by Mal'achi. 2
5 Great is the LORD, beyond the border of Israel! 2
2:11 abomination has been committed in Israel 2
16 For I hate divorce, says the LORD the God of Israel 2
4: 4 that I commanded him at Horeb for all Israel. 2
Mat 2: 6 a ruler who will govern my people Israel.' 5
20 his mother, and go to the land of Israel, for those 5
21 his mother, and went to the land of Israel. 5
8:10 not even in Israel have I found such faith. 5
9:33 Never was anything like this seen in Israel. 5
10: 6 to the lost sheep of the house of Israel. 5
23 gone through all the towns of Israel 5
15:24 only to the lost sheep of the house of Israel. 5
31 and they glorified the God of Israel. 5
19:28 judging the twelve tribes of Israel. 5
27: 9 a price had been set by some of the sons of Israel 5
42 He is the King of Israel 5
Mrk 12:29 Jesus answered, "The first is, 'Hear, O Israel 5
15:32 Let the Christ, the King of Israel, come down now 5
Lke 1:16 he will turn many of the sons of Israel to the Lord 5
54 He has helped his servant Israel 5
68 Blessed be the Lord God of Israel 5
80 till the day of his manifestation to Israel. 5
2:25 looking for the consolation of Israel 5
32 for glory to thy people Israel. 5
34 the fall and rising of many in Israel 5
4:25 were many widows in Israel in the days of Eli'jah 5
27 there were many lepers in Israel 5
7: 9 not even in Israel have I found such faith. 5
22:30 judging the twelve tribes of Israel. 5
24:21 we had hoped that he was the one to redeem Israel. 5
Joh 1:31 that he might be revealed to Israel. 5
49 you are the Son of God! You are the King of Israel! 5
3:10 Jesus answered him, "Are you a teacher of Israel 5
12:13 even the King of Israel! 5
Act 1: 6 at this time restore the kingdom to Israel? 5
2:22 Men of Israel, hear these words 6
36 Let all the house of Israel therefore know 5
3:12 Men of Israel, why do you wonder at this 6
4:10 to all the people of Israel 5
27 with the Gentiles and the peoples of Israel 5
5:21 the council and all the senate of Israel 5
31 give repentance to Israel 5
35 he said to them, "Men of Israel 6
7:23 to visit his brethren, the sons of Israel. 5
42 40 years in the wilderness, O house of Israel? 5
9:15 Gentiles and kings and the sons of Israel; 5
10:36 You know the word which he sent to Israel 5
13:16 Men of Israel, and you that fear God, listen. 6
17 The God of this people Israel chose our fathers 5
23 brought to Israel a Savior, Jesus, as he promised. 5
24 preached . . to all the people of Israel. 5
21:28 crying out, "Men of Israel, help! 6
28:20 since it is because of the hope of Israel 5
Rom 9: 6 For not all who are descended from Israel 5

6 are descended from Israel belong to Israel 5
27 And Isaiah cries out concerning Israel 5
27 Though the number of the sons of Israel be 5
31 but that Israel who pursued the righteousness 5
10:19 Again I ask, did Israel not understand? 5
21 But of Israel he says, "All day long I have held out 5
11: 2 of Eli'jah, how he pleads with God against Israel? 5
7 Israel failed to obtain what it sought. 5
11 so as to make Israel jealous. •
25 a hardening has come upon part of Israel 5
26 so all Israel will be saved; as it is written 5
1Co 10:18 Consider the people of Israel 5
Gal 6:16 upon the Israel of God. 5
Eph 2:12 alienated from the commonwealth of Israel 5
Php 3: 5 of the people of Israel, of the tribe of Benjamin 5
Heb 8: 8 with the house of Israel 5
10 with the house of Israel after those days 5
Rev 2:14 put a stumbling block before the sons of Israel 5
7: 4 sealed, out of every tribe of the sons of Israel 5
21:12 names of the twelve tribes of the sons of Israel 5
1Es 1: 3 told the Levites, the temple servants of Israel 5
4 serve his people Israel 5
5 the directions of David king of Israel 5
5 before your brethren the people of Israel 5
19 people of Israel who were present at that time 5
20 No passover like it had been kept in Israel 5
21 none of the kings of Israel 5
21 all of Israel who were dwelling in Jerusalem. 5
24 the words of the Lord rose up against Israel. 5
32 throughout the whole nation of Israel. 5
33 in the book of the kings of Israel and Judah. 5
48 the laws of the Lord, the God of Israel. 5
2: 3 The Lord of Israel, the Lord Most High 5
5 build the house of the Lord of Israel 5
5:37 could not prove . . that they belonged to Israel 5
41 All those of Israel, twelve or more years of age 5
46 the gatekeepers, and all Israel in their towns. 5
47 the sons of Israel were each in his own home 5
48 prepared the altar of the God of Israel 5
60 according to . . David king of Israel 5
61 his glory are for ever upon all Israel. 5
67 the temple for the Lord God of Israel. 5
70 the heads of the fathers' houses in Israel said 5
71 for we alone will build it for the Lord of Israel 5
6: 1 in the name of the Lord God of Israel. 5
14 a king of Israel who was great and strong 5
15 the Lord of Israel who is in heaven 5
7: 4 the command of the Lord God of Israel 5
6 the people of Israel, the priests, the Levites 5
8 twelve he-goats for the sin of all Israel 5
8 the twelve leaders of the tribes of Israel; 5
9 for the services of the Lord God of Israel 5
10 The people of Israel who came from the captivity 5
13 the people of Israel who came from the captivity 5
15 for the service of the Lord God of Israel. 5
8: 3 which was given by the God of Israel; 5
5 some of the people of Israel 5
7 taught all Israel all the ordinances 5
13 the gifts for the Lord of Israel 5
27 I gathered men from Israel to go up with me. 5
47 the son of Levi, son of Israel, namely Sherebiah 5
55 the nobles and all Israel had given. 5
59 the heads of the fathers' houses of Israel 5
65 offered sacrifices to the Lord, the God of Israel 5
65 12 bulls for all Israel, 96 rams 5
69 The people of Israel and the leaders 5
72 the word of the Lord of Israel 5
89 O Lord of Israel, thou art true 5
92 the son of Jehiel, one of the men of Israel 5
92 even now there is hope for Israel. 5
96 leaders of the priests and Levites of all Israel 5
9: 7 have increased the sin of Israel. 5
26 Of Israel: of the sons of Parosh: Ramiah, Izziah 5
37 The priests and the Levites and the men of Israel 5
37 the sons of Israel were in their settlements 5
39 which had been given by the Lord God of Israel. 5
2Es 2:10 which I was going to give to Israel. 7
11 which I had prepared for Israel. •
33 a command . . to go to Israel 7
3:19 thy commandment to the posterity of Israel. 7
32 Or has another nation known thee besides Israel? 7
4:23 why Israel has been given over to the Gentiles 7
5:17 Israel has been entrusted to you 7
33 Are you greatly disturbed in mind over Israel? 7
35 and the exhaustion of the people of Israel? 7
7:10 And he said to me, "So also is Israel's portion. 7
107 Joshua after him for Israel in the days of Achan 7
8:16 and about Israel, for whom I am sad 7
9:30 thou didst say, 'Hear me, O Israel 7
12:46 Take courage, O Israel 7
14:28 Hear these words, O Israel 7
Tob 1: 4 in the land of Israel, while I was still a young man 5
4 chosen from among all the tribes of Israel 5
6 as it is ordained for all Israel 5
13: 3 Acknowledge him . . O sons of Israel 5
Jdt 4: 1 the people of Israel living in Judea 5
8 the senate of the whole people of Israel 5
9 every man of Israel cried out to God 5
11 the men and women of Israel, and their children 5

12 praying earnestly to the God of Israel 5
15 to look with favor upon the whole house of Israel. 5
5: 1 the people of Israel had prepared for war 5
6: 2 not to make war against the people of Israel 5
10 and hand him over to the men of Israel. 5
14 Then the men of Israel came down from their city 5
17 said so boastfully against the house of Israel. 5
21 they called on the God of Israel for help. 5
7:19 The people of Israel cried out to the Lord their God 5
8: 1 son of Salamiel, son of Sarasadai, son of Israel. 5
6 and days of rejoicing of the house of Israel. 5
33 the Lord will deliver Israel by my hand. 5
9:12 God of my father, God of the inheritance of Israel 5
14 no other who protects the people of Israel 5
10: 1 Judith had ceased crying out to the God of Israel 5
8 the people of Israel may glory 5
12: 8 prayed the Lord God of Israel to direct her way 5
13: 7 Give me strength this day, O Lord God of Israel! 5
11 to show his power in Israel 5
14 not withdrawn his mercy from the house of Israel 5
14: 4 you and all who live within the borders of Israel 5
5 the man who despised the house of Israel 5
10 Achior saw all that the God of Israel had done 5
10 was circumcised, and joined the house of Israel 5
15: 3 the men of Israel, every one that was a soldier 5
4 to all the frontiers of Israel 5
8 the senate of the people of Israel 5
8 which the Lord had done for Israel 5
9 you are the great glory of Israel 5
10 you have done great good to Israel 5
12 Then all the women of Israel gathered to see her 5
13 while all the men of Israel followed 5
16: 1 began this thanksgiving before all Israel 5
8 to exalt the oppressed in Israel 5
24 the house of Israel mourned for her seven days. 5
25 spread terror among the people of Israel 5
AEs 10: 9 my nation, this is Israel, who cried out to God 5
13 for ever among his people Israel. 5
13: 9 if it is thy will to save Israel. 5
13 kiss the soles of his feet, to save Israel! 5
18 all Israel cried out mightily 5
14: 3 she prayed to the Lord God of Israel, and said 5
5 didst take Israel out of all the nations 5
Sir 0: 1 should praise Israel for instruction and wisdom; 5
17:17 Israel is the Lord's own portion. 5
24: 8 in Israel receive your inheritance.' 5
36:12 Have mercy . . upon Israel 5
37:25 the days of Israel are without number. 5
45: 5 to teach . . Israel his judgments. 5
11 according to the number of the tribes of Israel; 5
17 to enlighten Israel with his law. 5
23 made atonement for Israel. 5
46: 1 that he might give Israel its inheritance. 5
10 that all the sons of Israel might see 5
47: 2 so David was selected from the sons of Israel. 5
11 a throne of glory in Israel. 5
18 the Lord God, who is called the God of Israel 5
23 who caused Israel to sin 5
50:13 before the whole congregation of Israel. 5
20 whole congregation of the sons of Israel 5
23 grant that peace may be in our days in Israel 5
Bar 2: 1 against our judges who judged Israel 5
1 princes and against the men of Israel and Judah. 5
11 O Lord God of Israel, who didst bring thy people 5
15 Israel and his descendants are called by thy 5
26 wickedness of the house of Israel and the house 5
28 in the presence of the people of Israel, saying 5
35 I will never again remove my people Israel 5
3: 1 'O Lord Almighty, God of Israel, the soul in anguish 5
4 O Lord Almighty, God of Israel, hear now the prayer 5
4 hear now the prayer of the dead of Israel 5
9 Hear the commandments of life, O Israel; give ear 5
10 Why is it, O Israel, why is it that you are in the land 5
24 O Israel, how great is the house of God! And how vast 5
36 Jacob his servant and to Israel whom he loved. 5
4: 4 Happy are we, O Israel, for we know what is pleasing 5
5 Take courage, my people, O memorial of Israel! 5
5: 7 so that Israel may walk safely in the glory of God 5
8 tree have shaded Israel at God's command. 5
9 For God will lead Israel with joy 5
Aza 1:12 Isaac thy servant and Israel thy holy one 5
61 Bless the Lord, O Israel 5
Sus 1:48 Are you such fools, you sons of Israel? 5
48 Have you condemned a daughter of Israel 5
57 have been dealing with the daughters of Israel 5
1Mc 1:11 In those days lawless men came forth from Israel 5
20 He went up against Israel and came to Jerusalem 5
25 Israel mourned deeply in every community 5
30 destroyed many people of Israel. 5
36 an evil adversary of Israel continually. 5
43 Many even from Israel 5
53 they drove Israel into hiding 5
58 They kept using violence against Israel 5
62 many in Israel stood firm 5
64 very great wrath came upon Israel. 5
2:16 Many from Israel came to them 5
42 Hasideans, mighty warriors of Israel 5
46 that they found within the borders of Israel. 5
55 Joshua . . became a judge in Israel. 5

70 Israel mourned for him with great lamentation. 5
3: 2 they gladly fought for Israel. 5
8 thus he turned away wrath from Israel. 5
10 a large force . . to fight against Israel. 5
15 to take vengeance on the sons of Israel. 5
35 to wipe out and destroy the strength of Israel 5
41 to the camp to get the sons of Israel for slaves. 5
46 Israel formerly had a place of prayer in Mizpah. 5
4:11 there is one who redeems and saves Israel. 5
25 Thus Israel had a great deliverance that day. 5
27 had not happened to Israel as he had intended 5
30 Blessed art thou, O Savior of Israel 5
31 hem in this army by the hand of thy people Israel 5
59 all the assembly of Israel determined 5
5: 3 because they kept lying in wait for Israel 5
60 as many as 2,000 of the people of Israel 5
62 through whom deliverance was given to Israel. 5
63 his brothers were greatly honored in all Israel 5
6:18 Now the men in the citadel kept hemming Israel 5
7: 5 the lawless and ungodly men of Israel 5
9 take vengeance on the sons of Israel. 5
13 Hasideans were first among the sons of Israel 5
22 did great damage in Israel. 5
23 the evil . . done among the sons of Israel 5
26 Nicanor . . who hated and detested Israel 5
8:18 was completely enslaving Israel. 5
9:20 all Israel made great lamentation for him 5
21 How is the mighty fallen, the savior of Israel! 5
23 the lawless emerged in all parts of Israel 5
27 Thus there was great distress in Israel 5
51 he placed garrisons in them to harass Israel. 5
73 Thus the sword ceased from Israel 5
73 he destroyed the ungodly out of Israel. 5
10:46 great wrongs which Demetrius had done in Israel 5
61 A group of pestilent men from Israel, lawless men 5
11:23 he chose some of the elders of Israel 5
41 they kept fighting against Israel. 5
12:52 all Israel mourned deeply. 5
13: 4 perished for the sake of Israel 5
26 All Israel bewailed him with great lamentation 5
41 the yoke of the Gentiles was removed from Israel 5
51 crushed and removed from Israel. 5
14:11 Israel rejoiced with great joy. 5
26 they have fought and repulsed Israel's enemies 5
16: 2 have fought the wars of Israel from our youth 5
2 so that we have delivered Israel many times. 5
2Mc 1:25 who dost rescue Israel from every evil 5
26 on behalf of all thy people Israel 5
9: 5 the all-seeing Lord, the God of Israel 5
10:38 who shows great kindness to Israel 5
11: 6 to send a good angel to save Israel. 5
3Mc 2: 6 who had enslaved your holy people Israel. 5
10 because you love the house of Israel 5
16 bestowed your glory upon your people Israel 5
6: 4 light of your mercy upon the nation of Israel. 5
9 those of the nation of Israel 5
7:16 the eternal Savior of Israel 5
23 Blessed be the Deliverer of Israel 5
4Mc 17:22 divine Providence preserved Israel 5
151 1: 7 removed reproach from the people of Israel. 5

Israelite 1. בֶּן יִשְׂרָאֵל 2. יִשְׂרָאֵל 3. יִשְׂרְאֵלִי
4. Ἰσραήλ 5. Ἰσραηλίτης 6. υἱὸς Ἰσραήλ

Gen 32:32 Therefore to this day the Israelites do not eat 1
36:31 before any king reigned over the Israelites. 1
Exd 9: 7 not one of the cattle of the Israelites was dead. 2
Lev 24:10 Now an Israelite woman's son, whose father was 3
11 the Israelite woman's son blasphemed the Name 3
Jdg 6: 3 For whenever the Israelites put in seed 2
20:21 felled . . 22,000 men of the Israelites. 2
1Sm 2:14 they did . . to all the Israelites who came 2
13:20 the Israelites went down to the Philistines 2
14:21 even they also turned to be with the Israelites 2
17:53 And the Israelites came back from chasing 1
29: 1 the Israelites were encamped by the fountain 2
2Kg 3:24 the Israelites rose and attacked the Moabites 2
17: 6 and he carried the Israelites away to Assyria 2
18:11 The king of Assyria carried the Israelites away 2
1Ch 1:43 before any king reigned over the Israelites 1
Neh 9: 2 Israelites separated . . from all foreigners 2
Isa 66:20 as the Israelites bring their cereal offering 1
Joh 1:47 Behold, an Israelite indeed, in whom is no guile! 5
Act 7:37 This is the Moses who said to the Israelites 6
Rom 9: 4 They are Israelites, and to them belong 5
11: 1 I myself am an Israelite, a descendant of Abraham 5
2Co 3: 7 the Israelites could not look 6
13 so that the Israelites might not see 6
11:22 Are they Israelites? So am I 5
Heb 11:22 made mention of the exodus of the Israelites 6
Jdt 4: 8 the Israelites did as Joakim . . had given order 6
5:23 they said, "we will not be afraid of the Israelites; 6
7: 1 make war on the Israelites. 6
4 When the Israelites saw their vast numbers 6
6 in full view of the Israelites in Bethulia 6
10 these people, the Israelites 6
17 the springs of the Israelites 6
10:19 they . . admired the Israelites 6
15: 5 when the Israelites heard it 6
7 the Israelites . . took possession of what remained 6
1Mc 5: 9 the Gentiles . . gathered together against the Israelites 4
45 Judas gathered together all the Israelites 4
6:21 some of the ungodly Israelites joined them. 4
4Mc 18: 1 O Israelite children 5
5 able to compel the Israelites to become pagans *

Israelite woman 1. יִשְׂרְאֵלִי

Lev 24:10 the Israelite woman's son and a man of Israel 1

Issachar 1. יִשָּׂשכָר 2. Ἰσσαχάρ

Gen 30:18 she called his name Is'sachar. 1
35:23 Simeon, Levi, Judah, Is'sachar, and Zeb'ulun. 1
46:13 sons of Is'sachar: Tola, Puvah, Iob, and Shimron 1
49:14 Is'sachar is a strong ass, crouching between 1
Exd 1: 3 Is'sachar, Zeb'ulun, and Benjamin 1
Num 1: 8 from Is'sachar, Nethan'el the son of Zu'ar; 1
28 Of the people of Is'sachar, their generations 1
29 the number of the tribe of Is'sachar was 54,400 1
2: 5 the tribe of Is'sachar, the leader of the people 1
5 the leader of the people of Is'sachar 1
7:18 Nethan'el the son of Zu'ar, the leader of Is'sachar 1
10:15 over the host of the tribe of the men of Is'sachar 1
13: 7 from the tribe of Is'sachar, Igal the son of Joseph; 1
26:23 sons of Is'sachar according to their families 1
25 families of Is'sachar according to their number 1
34:26 Of the tribe of the sons of Is'sachar a leader 1
Deu 27:12 stand upon Mount Ger'izim . . Is'sachar, Joseph 1
33:18 Rejoice, Zeb'ulun . . and Is'sachar, in your tents. 1
Jos 17:10 on the north Asher . . and on the east Is'sachar. 1
11 in Is'sachar and in Asher Manas'seh had Beth-she'an 1
19:17 The fourth lot came out for Is'sachar 1
17 fourth lot . . for the tribe of Is'sachar 1
23 This is the inheritance of the tribe of Is'sachar 1
21: 6 by lot from the families of the tribe of Is'sachar 1
28 and out of the tribe of Is'sachar, Ki'shion 1
Jdg 5:15 the princes of Is'sachar came with Deb'orah 1
15 with Deb'orah, and Is'sachar faithful to Barak; 1
10: 1 Tola the son of Pu'ah, son of Dodo, a man of Is'sachar 1
1Kg 4:17 Jehosh'aphat the son of Paru'ah, in Is'sachar; 1
15:27 Ba'asha the son of Ahi'jah, of the house of Is'sachar 1
1Ch 2: 1 sons of Israel . . Levi, Judah, Is'sachar, Zeb'ulun 1
6:62 out of the tribes of Is'sachar, Asher, Naph'tali 1
72 out of the tribe of Is'sachar: Kedesh . . Dab'erath 1
7: 1 sons of Is'sachar: Tola, Pu'ah, Jashub, and Shimron 1
5 belonging to all the families of Is'sachar 1
12:32 Is'sachar men who had understanding of the times 1
40 from as far as Is'sachar and Zeb'ulun and Naph'tali 1
26: 5 Is'sachar the seventh, Pe-ul'lethai the eighth; 1
27:18 for Is'sachar, Omri the son of Michael; 1
2Ch 30:18 many of them from E'phraim, Manas'seh, Is'sachar 1
Ezk 48:25 the east side to the west, Is'sachar, one portion. 1
26 Adjoining the territory of Is'sachar 1
33 the gate of Is'sachar, and the gate of Zeb'ulun. 1
Rev 7: 7 12,000 of the tribe of Is'sachar 2

Isshiah 1. יִשִּׁיָּהוּ

1Ch 7: 3 sons of Izrahi'ah . . Obadi'ah, Jo'el, and Isshi'ah 1
12: 6 Elka'nah, Isshi'ah, Az'arel, Jo-e'zer, and Jasho'be-am 1
23:20 sons of Uz'ziel: Micah . . and Isshi'ah the second. 1
24:21 of the sons of Rehabi'ah, Isshi'ah the chief. 1
25 The brother of Micah, Isshi'ah; 1
25 of the sons of Isshi'ah, Zechari'ah. 1

Isshijah 1. יִשִּׁיָּהוּ

Ezr 10:31 of Harim: Elie'zer, Isshi'jah, Malchi'jah, Shemai'ah 1

Istalcurus 1. Ισταλκουρος

1Es 8:40 Of the sons of Bigvai, Uthai the son of Istalcurus 1

Italian 1. Ἰταλικός

Act 10: 1 what was known as the Italian Cohort 1

Italy 1. Ἰταλία

Act 18: 2 lately come from Italy with his wife Priscilla 1
27: 1 when it was decided that we should sail for Italy 1
6 a ship of Alexandria sailing for Italy 1
Heb 13:24 Those who come from Italy send you greetings. 1

Ithai 1. אִיתַי

1Ch 11:31 Ithai the son of Ribai of Gib'e-ah 1

Ithamar 1. אִיתָמָר 2. Ιθαμαρ

Exd 6:23 she bore him Nadab, Abi'hu, Elea'zar, and Ith'amar. 1
28: 1 Nadab and Abi'hu, Elea'zar and Ith'amar. 1
38:21 the Levites under the direction of Ith'amar 1
Lev 10: 6 Moses said to Aaron and to Elea'zar and Ith'amar 1
12 Moses said to Aaron and to Elea'zar and Ith'amar 1
16 he was angry with Elea'zar and Ith'amar 1
Num 3: 2 Nadab . . and Abi'hu, Elea'zar, and Ith'amar; 1
4 Elea'zar and Ith'amar served as priests 1
4:28 work is to be under the oversight of Ith'amar 1
33 under the hand of Ith'amar the son of Aaron 1
7: 8 under the direction of Ith'amar the son of Aaron 1
26:60 to Aaron were born Nadab, Abi'hu . . and Ith'amar. 1
1Ch 6: 3 sons of Aaron . . Abi'hu, Elea'zar, and Ith'amar. 1
24: 1 sons of Aaron: Nadab, Abi'hu, Elea'zar, and Ith'amar. 1
2 Elea'zar and Ith'amar became the priests. 1
3 help of . . Ahim'elech of the sons of Ith'amar 1
4 more . . than among the sons of Ith'amar 1
4 and eight of the sons of Ith'amar. 1
5 among both . . the sons of Ith'amar. 1
6 for Elea'zar and one chosen for Ith'amar. 1
Ezr 8: 2 Of the sons of Ith'amar, Daniel. 1
1Es 8:29 Of the sons of Ithamar, Gamael 2

Ithiel 1. אִיתִיאֵל

Neh 11: 7 Ma-asei'ah, son of I'thi-el, son of Jeshai'ah. 1
Prv 30: 1 The man says to Ith'i-el, to Ith'i-el and Ucal 1
1 The man says to Ith'i-el, to Ith'i-el and Ucal 1

Ithlah 1. יִתְלָה

Jos 19:42 Sha-alab'bin, Ai'jalon, Ithlah 1

Ithmah 1. יִתְמָה

1Ch 11:46 and Ithmah the Mo'abite 1

Ithnan 1. יִתְנָן

Jos 15:23 Kedesh, Hazor, Ithnan 1

Ithra 1. יִתְרָא

2Sm 17:25 was the son of a man named Ithra the Ish'maelite 1

Ithran 1. יִתְרָן

Gen 36:26 sons of Dishon . . Eshban, Ithran, and Cheran. 1
1Ch 1:41 sons of Dishon: Hamran, Eshban, Ithran, and Cheran. 1
7:37 Bezer, Hod, Shamma, Shilshah, Ithran, and Be-e'ra. 1

Ithream 1. יִתְרְעָם

2Sm 3: 5 and the sixth, Ith're-am, of Eglah, David's wife. 1
1Ch 3: 3 the sixth Ith'ream, by his wife Eglah; 1

Ithrite 1. יִתְרִי

2Sm 23:38 Ira the Ithrite, Gareb the Ithrite 1
38 Ira the Ithrite, Gareb the Ithrite 1
1Ch 2:53 the Ithrites, the Puthites, the Shu'mathites 1
11:40 Ira the Ithrite, Gareb the Ithrite 1
40 Ira the Ithrite, Gareb the Ithrite 1

Ittai 1. אִתַּי

2Sm 15:19 Then the king said to It'tai the Gittite 1
21 But It'tai answered the king, "As the LORD lives 1
22 And David said to It'tai, "Go then, pass on. 1
22 It'tai the Gittite passed on, with all his men 1
18: 2 third under the command of It'tai the Gittite. 1
5 And the king ordered Jo'ab and Abi'shai and It'tai 1
12 the king commanded you and Abi'shai and It'tai 1
23:29 It'tai the son of Ri'bai of Gib'e-ah 1

Ituraea 1. Ἰτουραῖος

Lke 3: 1 the region of Iturae'a and Trachoni'tis 1

Ivvah 1. עִוָּה

2Kg 18:34 Where are the gods of Sepharva'im, Hena, and Ivvah? 1
19:13 Sepharva'im, the king of Hena, or the king of Ivvah?' 1
Isa 37:13 the king of Hena, or the king of Ivvah?' 1

Iye-abarim 1. עִיֵּי עֲבָרִים

Num21:11 set out from Oboth, and encamped at I'ye-ab'arim 1
33:44 set out from Oboth, and encamped at I'ye-ab'arim 1

Iyim 1. עִיִּים

Num33:45 they set out from I'yim, and encamped at Dibon-gad. 1

Izhar 1. יִצְהָר 2. יִצְחָר

Exd 6:18 sons of Kohath: Amram, Izhar, Hebron, and Uz'ziel 1
21 The sons of Izhar: Korah, Nepheg, and Zichri. 1
Num 3:19 sons of Kohath . . Amram, Izhar, Hebron 1
16: 1 Korah the son of Izhar, son of Kohath, son of Levi 1
1Ch 4: 7 The sons of Helah: Zereth, Izhar, and Ethnan. 2
6: 2 sons of Kohath: Amram, Izhar, Hebron, and Uz'ziel. 1
18 sons of Kohath: Amram, Izhar, Hebron, and Uz'ziel. 1
38 son of Izhar, son of Kohath, son of Levi 1
23:12 sons of Kohath: Amram, Izhar, Hebron, and Uz'ziel 1
18 The sons of Izhar: Shelo'mith the chief. 1

Izharite 1. יִצְהָרִי

Num 3:27 Of Kohath . . the family of the Izhar'ites 1
1Ch 24:22 Of the Iz'harites, Shelo'moth; 1
26:23 Of the Am'ramites, the Iz'harites, the He'bronites 1
29 Of the Iz'harites, Chenani'ah and his sons 1

Izliah 1. יִזְלִיאָה

1Ch 8:18 Ish'merai, Izli'ah, and Jobab . . sons of Elpa'al. 1

Izrahiah 1. יִזְרַחְיָה

1Ch 7: 3 The sons of Uzzi: Izrahi'ah. 1
3 sons of Izrahi'ah: Michael, Obadi'ah, Jo'el 1

Izrahite 1. יִזְרָח

1Ch 27: 8 fifth commander . . was Shamhuth, the Iz'rahite; 1

Izri 1. יִצְרִי

1Ch 25:11 fourth to Izri, his sons and his brethren, twelve; 1

Izziah 1. יִזִּיָּה 2. Ιεζιας
Ezr 10:25 of Parosh: Rami'ah, Izzi'ah, Malchi'jah, Mi'jamin 1
1Es 9:26 Of Israel: of the sons of Parosh: Ramiah, Izziah 2

Jaakan 1. יַעֲקָן
1Ch 1:42 The sons of Ezer: Bilhan, Za'avan, and Ja'akan. 1

Jaakobah 1. יַעֲקֹבָה
1Ch 4:36 Eli-o-e'nai, Ja-ako'bah, Jeshohai'ah, Asai'ah 1

Jaala 1. יַעֲלָא
Neh 7:58 sons of Ja'ala, the sons of Darkon 1

Jaalah 1. יַעֲלָה 2. Ιεηλι
Ezr 2:56 sons of Ja'alah, the sons of Darkon 1
1Es 5:33 the sons of Jaalah, the sons of Lozon 2

Jaar 1. יַעַר
Ps 132: 6 in Eph'rathah, we found it in the fields of Ja'ar. 1

Jaare-oregim 1. יַעְרֵי אֹרְגִים
2Sm 21:19 Elha'nan the son of Ja'areor'egim . . slew Goliath 1

Jaareshiah 1. יַעֲרֶשְׁיָה
1Ch 8:27 Ja-areshi'ah, Eli'jah, and . . sons of Jero'ham. 1

Jaasiel 1. יַעֲשִׂיאֵל
1Ch 11:47 Eli'el, and Obed, and Ja-asi'el the Mezo'ba-ite. 1
27:21 for Benjamin, Ja-a'si-el the son of Abner; 1

Jaasu 1. יַעֲשׂוּ
Ezr 10:37 Mattani'ah, Matte'nai, Ja'asu. 1

Jaazaniah 1. יַאֲזַנְיָהוּ
2Kg 25:23 and Ja-azani'ah the son of the Ma-ac'athite. 1
Jer 35: 3 So I took Ja-azani'ah the son of Jeremiah 1
Ezk 8:11 with Ja-azani'ah the son of Shaphan standing among 1
11: 1 I saw among them Ja-azani'ah the son of Azzur 1

Jaaziah 1. יַעֲזִיָּהוּ
1Ch 24:26 The sons of Ja-azi'ah: Beno. 1
27 of Ja-azi'ah, Beno, Shoham, Zaccur, and Ibri. 1

Jaaziel 1. יַעֲזִיאֵל
1Ch 15:18 Zechari'ah, Ja-a'ziel, Shemi'ramoth, Jehi'el, Unni 1

Jabal 1. יָבָל
Gen 4:20 Adah bore Jabal; he was the father 1

Jabbok 1. יַבֹּק
Gen 32:22 children, and crossed the ford of the Jabbok. 1
Num21:24 took . . his land from the Arnon to the Jabbok 1
Deu 2:37 banks of the river Jabbok and the cities 1
3:16 as far over as the river Jabbok, the boundary 1
Jos 12: 2 from . . the valley as far as the river Jabbok 1
Jdg 11:13 my land, from the Arnon to the Jabbok 1
22 territory . . from the Arnon to the Jabbok 1

Jabesh 1. יָבֵשׁ
1Sm 11: 1 all the men of Jabesh said to Nahash, "Make a treaty 1
3 The elders of Jabesh said . . "Give us seven days 1
5 they told him the tidings of the men of Jabesh. 1
9 the messengers came and told the men of Jabesh 1
10 Therefore the men of Jabesh said 1
31:12 they came to Jabesh and burnt them there. 1
13 buried them under the tamarisk tree in Jabesh 1
2Kg 15:10 Shallum the son of Jabesh conspired against him 1
13 Shallum the son of Jabesh began to reign 1
14 and he struck down Shallum the son of Jabesh 1
1Ch 10:12 the bodies . . and brought them to Jabesh. 1
12 the bodies . . and brought them to Jabesh. 1

Jabesh-gilead 1. יָבֵשׁ גִּלְעָד
Jdg 21: 8 no one had come to the camp from Ja'besh-gil'ead 1
9 of the inhabitants of Ja'besh-gil'ead was there. 1
10 Go and smite the inhabitants of Ja'besh-gil'ead 1
12 found among the inhabitants of Ja'besh-gil'ead 1
14 had saved alive of the women of Ja'besh-gil'ead; 1
1Sm 11: 1 Nahash . . went up and besieged Ja'besh-gil'ead; 1
9 Thus shall you say to the men of Ja'besh-gil'ead 1
31:11 when the inhabitants of Ja'besh-gil'ead heard 1
2Sm 2: 4 It was the men of Ja'besh-gil'ead who buried Saul 1
5 sent messengers to the men of Ja'besh-gil'ead 1
21:12 took the bones . . from the men of Ja'besh-gil'ead 1
1Ch 10:11 Ja'besh-gil'ead heard all that the Philistines 1

Jabez 1. יַעְבֵּץ
1Ch 2:55 families also of the scribes that dwelt at Jabez 1
4: 9 Jabez was more honorable than his brothers; 1
9 and his mother called his name Jabez, saying 1
10 Jabez called on the God of Israel, saying 1

Jabin 1. יָבִין 2. Ιαβιν
Jos 11: 1 When Jabin king of Hazor heard of this, he sent 1
Jdg 4: 2 hand of Jabin king of Canaan, who reigned in Hazor; 1
7 Sis'era, the general of Jabin's army, to meet you 1
17 there was peace between Jabin the king of Hazor 1
23 God subdued Jabin the king of Canaan before 1
24 harder and harder on Jabin the king of Canaan 1
24 until they destroyed Jabin king of Canaan. 1
1Sm 12: 9 commander of the army of Jabin king of Hazor 2
Ps 83: 9 as to Sis'era and Jabin at the river Kishon 1

Jabneel 1. יַבְנְאֵל
Jos 15:11 passes . . to Mount Ba'alah, and goes out to Jabneel; 1
19:33 Za-anan'nim, and Ad'ami-nekeb, and Jabneel 1

Jabneh 1. יַבְנֶה
2Ch 26: 6 broke down the wall of Gath and the wall of Jabneh 1

Jacan 1. יַעְכָּן
1Ch 5:13 Michael, Meshul'lam, Sheba, Jo'rai, Jacan, Zi'a 1

Jachin 1. יָכִין
Gen 46:10 The sons of Simeon: Jemu'el, Jamin, Ohad, Jachin 1
Exd 6:15 Simeon: Jemu'el, Jamin, Ohad, Jachin, Zohar 1
Num26:12 of Jachin, the family of the Ja'chinites; 1
1Kg 7:21 pillar on the south and called its name Jachin; 1
1Ch 9:10 Of the priests: Jedai'ah, Jehoi'arib, Jachin 1
24:17 the 21st to Jachin, the 22nd to Gamul 1
2Ch 3:17 pillars . . that on the south he called Jachin 1
Neh 11:10 Of the priests: Jedai'ah the son of Joi'arib, Jachin 1

Jachinite 1. יָכִינִי
Num26:12 of Jachin, the family of the Ja'chinites; 1

Jacob 1. יַעֲקֹב 2. 'Ιακώβ 3. Iacob
Gen 25:26 hold of Esau's heel; so his name was called Jacob. 1
27 man of the field, while Jacob was a quiet man 1
28 ate of his game; but Rebekah loved Jacob. 1
29 Once when Jacob was boiling pottage, Esau came 1
30 Esau said to Jacob, "Let me eat some of that red 1
31 Jacob said, "First sell me your birthright. 1
33 Jacob said, "Swear to me first. 1
33 swore to him, and sold his birthright to Jacob. 1
34 Then Jacob gave Esau bread and pottage 1
27: 6 Rebekah said to her son Jacob, "I heard your father 1
11 Jacob said to Rebekah his mother 1
15 and put them on Jacob her younger son; 1
17 had prepared, into the hand of her son Jacob. 1
19 Jacob said to his father, "I am Esau 1
21 Isaac said to Jacob, "Come near, that I may feel 1
22 Jacob went near to Isaac his father 1
22 who felt him and said, "The voice is Jacob's voice 1
30 As soon as Isaac had finished blessing Jacob 1
30 when Jacob had scarcely gone out 1
36 Esau said, "Is he not rightly named Jacob? 1
41 Now Esau hated Jacob because of the blessing 1
41 then I will kill my brother Jacob. 1
42 she sent and called Jacob her younger son 1
46 If Jacob marries one of the Hittite women 1
28: 1 Then Isaac called Jacob and blessed him 1
5 Isaac sent Jacob away; and he went to Paddan-aram 1
5 the brother of Rebekah, Jacob's and Esau's mother. 1
6 Esau saw that Isaac had blessed Jacob 1
7 that Jacob had obeyed his father and his mother 1
10 Jacob left Beer-sheba, and went toward Haran. 1
16 Then Jacob awoke from his sleep and said 1
18 Jacob rose early in the morning 1
20 Jacob made a vow, saying, "If God will be with me 1
29: 1 Then Jacob went on his journey 1
4 Jacob said to them, "My brothers 1
10 Now when Jacob saw Rachel the daughter of Laban 1
10 Jacob went up and rolled the stone from the well's 1
11 Then Jacob kissed Rachel, and wept aloud. 1
12 Jacob told Rachel that he was her father's 1
13 When Laban heard the tidings of Jacob 1
13 Jacob told Laban all these things •
15 Laban said to Jacob, "Because you are my kinsman 1
18 Jacob loved Rachel; and he said 1
20 Jacob served seven years for Rachel 1
21 Then Jacob said to Laban, "Give me my wife 1
23 took his daughter Leah and brought her to Jacob; 2
25 Jacob said to Laban, "What is this you have done 2
28 Jacob did so, and completed her week; 1
30 Jacob went in to Rachel also, and he loved Rachel •
30: 1 When Rachel saw that she bore Jacob no children 1
1 said to Jacob, "Give me children, or I shall die! 1
2 Jacob's anger was kindled against Rachel 1
4 Bilhah as a wife; and Jacob went in to her. 1
5 Bilhah conceived and bore Jacob a son. 1
7 conceived again and bore Jacob a second son. 1
9 she took her maid Zilpah and gave her to Jacob 1
10 Then Leah's maid Zilpah bore Jacob a son. 1
12 Leah's maid Zilpah bore Jacob a second son. 1
16 When Jacob came from the field in the evening 1
17 she conceived and bore Jacob a fifth son. 1
19 conceived again, and she bore Jacob a sixth son. 1
25 When Rachel had borne Joseph, Jacob said to Laban 1
29 Jacob said to him, "You yourself know how I have 2
31 I give you?" Jacob said, "You shall not give me 1
36 three days' journey between himself and Jacob; 1
36 and Jacob fed the rest of Laban's flock. 1
37 Then Jacob took fresh rods of poplar and almond 1
40 Jacob separated the lambs, and set the faces 1
41 Jacob laid the rods in the runnels 1
42 feebler were Laban's, and the stronger Jacob's. 1
31: 1 Now Jacob heard that the sons of Laban 2
1 Jacob has taken all that was our father's; 1
2 Jacob saw that Laban did not regard him 1
3 Then the LORD said to Jacob, "Return to the land 1
4 Jacob sent and called Rachel and Leah 1
11 in the dream, 'Jacob,' and I said, 'Here I am!' 1
17 Jacob arose, and set his sons and his wives 1
20 Jacob outwitted Laban the Aramean, in that he did 1
22 told Laban on the third day that Jacob had fled 1
24 say not a word to Jacob, either good or bad. 1
25 Laban overtook Jacob. Now Jacob had pitched 1
25 Jacob had pitched his tent in the hill country 1
26 Laban said to Jacob, "What have you done 1
29 Take heed that you speak to Jacob neither good 1
31 Jacob answered Laban, "Because I was afraid 1
32 Now Jacob did not know that Rachel had stolen 1
33 Laban went into Jacob's tent, and into Leah's 1
36 Then Jacob became angry, and upbraided Laban; 1
36 Jacob said to Laban, "What is my offense? 1
43 Then Laban answered and said to Jacob 1
45 Jacob took a stone, and set it up as a pillar. 1
46 Jacob said to his kinsmen, "Gather stones 1
47 Je'gar-sahadu'tha: but Jacob called it Galeed. 1
51 Then Laban said to Jacob, "See this heap 1
53 Jacob swore by the Fear of his father Isaac 1
54 Jacob offered a sacrifice on the mountain 1
32: 1 Jacob went on his way and the angels of God met him; 1
2 when Jacob saw them he said, "This is God's army! 1
3 Jacob sent messengers before him to Esau 1
4 Thus says your servant Jacob, 'I have sojourned 1
6 the messengers returned to Jacob, saying 1
7 Then Jacob was greatly afraid and distressed; 1
9 Jacob said, "O God of my father Abraham 1
18 They belong to your servant Jacob; 1
20 you shall say, 'Moreover your servant Jacob is 1
24 Jacob was left alone; and a man wrestled with him 1
25 saw that he did not prevail against Jacob •
25 of his thigh; and Jacob's thigh was put out of joint 1
26 But Jacob said, "I will not let you go •
27 and he said, "Jacob. 1
28 he said, "Your name shall no more be called Jacob 1
29 Then Jacob asked him, "Tell me, I pray, your name. 1
30 Jacob called the name of the place Peni'el 1
32 touched the hollow of Jacob's thigh on the sinew 1
33: 1 Jacob lifted up his eyes and looked 1
5 Jacob said, "The children whom God has graciously •
8 Jacob answered, "To find favor in the sight of my •
10 Jacob said, "No, I pray you, if I have found favor 1
13 Jacob said to him, "My lord knows that the children •
17 Jacob journeyed to Succoth 1
18 Jacob came safely to the city of Shechem 1
34: 1 the daughter of Leah, whom she had borne to Jacob 1
3 his soul was drawn to Dinah the daughter of Jacob; 1
5 Now Jacob heard that he had defiled his daughter 1
5 so Jacob held his peace until they came. 1
6 Shechem went out to Jacob to speak with him. 1
7 The sons of Jacob came in from the field 1
7 folly in Israel by lying with Jacob's daughter 1
13 The sons of Jacob answered Shechem 1
19 because he had delight in Jacob's daughter. 1
25 when they were sore, two of the sons of Jacob 1
27 the sons of Jacob came upon the slain 1
30 Then Jacob said to Simeon and Levi 1
35: 1 God said to Jacob, "Arise, go up to Bethel 1
2 Jacob said to his household 1
4 they gave to Jacob all the foreign gods 1
4 and Jacob hid them under the oak which was near 1
5 that they did not pursue the sons of Jacob. 1
6 Jacob came to Luz (that is, Bethel) 1
9 God appeared to Jacob again, when he came 1
10 God said to him, "Your name is Jacob; 1
10 no longer shall your name be called Jacob 1
14 Jacob set up a pillar in the place where he had 1
15 Jacob called the name of the place where God 1
20 Jacob set up a pillar upon her grave; 1
22 Now the sons of Jacob were twelve. 1
23 sons of Leah: Reuben (Jacob's first-born) 1
26 These were the sons of Jacob who were born to him 1
27 Jacob came to his father Isaac at Mamre 1
29 and his sons Esau and Jacob buried him. 1
36: 6 he went into a land away from his brother Jacob. 1
37: 1 Jacob dwelt in the land of his father's 1
2 This is the history of the family of Jacob. 1
34 Then Jacob rent his garments, and put sackcloth 1
42: 1 When Jacob learned that there was grain in Egypt 1
4 Jacob did not send Benjamin, Joseph's brother 1
29 When they came to Jacob their father in the land 1
36 Jacob their father said to them 1
45:25 to the land of Canaan to their father Jacob. 1
27 the spirit of their father Jacob revived; 1
46: 2 said, "Jacob, Jacob." And he said, "Here am I. 1
2 said, "Jacob, Jacob." And he said, "Here am I. 1
5 Then Jacob set out from Beer-sheba; 1
5 the sons of Israel carried Jacob their father 1
6 came into Egypt, Jacob and all his offspring 1
8 who came into Egypt, Jacob and his sons. 1
8 Jacob and his sons. Reuben, Jacob's first-born 1
15 whom she bore to Jacob in Paddan-aram, 1
18 and these she bore to Jacob–sixteen persons. 1

19 of Rachel, Jacob's wife: Joseph and Benjamin. 1
22 who were born to Jacob–fourteen persons in all. 1
25 and these she bore to Jacob–seven persons in all 1
26 persons belonging to Jacob who came into Egypt 1
26 own offspring, not including Jacob's sons' wives 1
27 the persons of the house of Jacob, that came 1
47: 7 Then Joseph brought in Jacob his father, 1
7 and Jacob blessed Pharaoh. 1
8 Pharaoh said to Jacob, "How many are the days 1
9 Jacob said to Pharaoh, "The days of the years of my 1
10 Jacob blessed Pharaoh, and went out 1
28 Jacob lived in the land of Egypt seventeen years; 1
28 the days of Jacob, the years of his life, 1
48: 2 it was told to Jacob, "Your son Joseph has come 1
3 Jacob said to Joseph, "God Almighty appeared 1
49: 1 Jacob called his sons, and said, "Gather 1
2 Assemble and hear, O sons of Jacob 1
7 I will divide them in Jacob and scatter them 1
24 by the hands of the Mighty One of Jacob 1
33 When Jacob finished charging his sons 1
50:24 swore to Abraham, to Isaac, and to Jacob. 1
Exd 1: 1 sons of Israel who came to Egypt with Jacob 1
5 All the offspring of Jacob were 70 persons; 1
2:24 with Abraham, with Isaac, and with Jacob. 1
3: 6 of Abraham, the God of Isaac, and the God of Jacob. 1
15 God of Isaac, and the God of Jacob, has sent me to you 1
16 God of Abraham, of Isaac, and of Jacob, has appeared 1
4: 5 and the God of Jacob, has appeared to you. 1
6: 3 I appeared to Abraham, to Isaac, and to Jacob, as God 1
8 swore to give to Abraham, to Isaac, and to Jacob; 1
19: 3 Thus you shall say to the house of Jacob, and tell 1
33: 1 I swore to Abraham, Isaac, and Jacob, saying 1
Lev 26:42 then I will remember my covenant with Jacob 1
Num23: 7 Come, curse Jacob for me, and come, denounce Israel!' 1
10 Who can count the dust of Jacob, or number 1
21 He has not beheld misfortune in Jacob; 1
23 For there is no enchantment against Jacob 1
23 be said of Jacob and Israel, 'What has God wrought!' 1
24: 5 how fair are your tents, O Jacob 1
17 star shall come forth out of Jacob, and a scepter 1
19 By Jacob shall dominion be exercised 1
32:11 I swore to give to Abraham, to Isaac, and to Jacob 1
Deu 1: 8 to your fathers, to Abraham, to Isaac, and to Jacob 1
6:10 to your fathers, to Abraham, to Isaac, and to Jacob 1
9: 5 to your fathers, to Abraham, to Isaac, and to Jacob. 1
27 Remember thy servants, Abraham, Isaac, and Jacob; 1
29:13 as he swore to . . Abraham, to Isaac, and to Jacob. 1
30:20 to your fathers, to Abraham, to Isaac, and to Jacob 1
32: 9 LORD'S portion . . Jacob his allotted heritage. 1
33: 4 law, as a possession for the assembly of Jacob. 1
10 They shall teach Jacob thy ordinances 1
28 Israel dwelt . . the fountain of Jacob alone 1
34: 4 land . . I swore to Abraham, to Isaac, and to Jacob 1
Jos 24: 4 and to Isaac I gave Jacob and Esau. 1
4 but Jacob and his children went down to Egypt. 1
32 ground which Jacob bought from the sons of Hamor 1
1Sm 12: 8 When Jacob went into Egypt . . then your fathers 1
2Sm 23: 1 David . . the anointed of the God of Jacob 1
1Kg 18:31 the number of the tribes of the sons of Jacob 1
2Kg 13:23 his covenant with Abraham, Isaac, and Jacob 1
17:34 which the LORD commanded the children of Jacob 1
1Ch 16:13 sons of Jacob, his chosen ones! 1
17 which he confirmed as a statute to Jacob 1
Ps 14: 7 Jacob shall rejoice, Israel shall be glad. 1
20: 1 The name of the God of Jacob protect you! 1
22:23 all you sons of Jacob, glorify him, and stand in awe 1
24: 6 who seek him, who seek the face of the God of Jacob. 1
44: 4 my God, who ordainest victories for Jacob. 1
46: 7 the God of Jacob is our refuge. Selah 1
11 the God of Jacob is our refuge. Selah 1
47: 4 heritage for us, the pride of Jacob whom he loves. 1
53: 6 Jacob will rejoice and Israel be glad. 1
59:13 that men may know that God rules over Jacob 1
75: 9 for ever, I will sing praises to the God of Jacob. 1
76: 6 At thy rebuke, O God of Jacob, both rider and horse 1
77:15 redeem thy people, the sons of Jacob and Joseph. 1
78: 5 He established a testimony in Jacob 1
21 a fire was kindled against Jacob 1
71 to be the shepherd of Jacob his people, of Israel 1
79: 7 devoured Jacob, and laid waste his habitation. 1
81: 1 shout for joy to the God of Jacob! 1
4 an ordinance of the God of Jacob. 1
84: 8 give ear, O God of Jacob! Selah 1
85: 1 thou didst restore the fortunes of Jacob. 1
87: 2 more than all the dwelling places of Jacob. 1
94: 7 does not see; the God of Jacob does not perceive. 1
99: 4 executed justice and righteousness in Jacob. 1
105: 6 sons of Jacob, his chosen ones! 1
10 which he confirmed to Jacob as a statute 1
23 Jacob sojourned in the land of Ham. 1
114: 1 house of Jacob from a people of strange language 1
7 Tremble . . at the presence of the God of Jacob 1
132: 2 to the LORD and vowed to the Mighty One of Jacob 1
5 dwelling place for the Mighty One of Jacob. 1
135: 4 For the LORD has chosen Jacob for himself 1
146: 5 Happy is he whose help is the God of Jacob 1
147:19 He declares his word to Jacob 1
Isa 2: 3 mountain of the LORD . . house of the God of Jacob; 1
5 O house of Jacob, come, let us walk in the light 1

6 thou hast rejected thy people, the house of Jacob 1
8:17 LORD . . hiding his face from the house of Jacob 1
9: 8 The Lord has sent a word against Jacob 1
10:20 of Israel and the survivors of the house of Jacob 1
21 return, the remnant of Jacob, to the mighty God. 1
14: 1 The LORD will have compassion on Jacob 1
1 aliens . . will cleave to the house of Jacob. 1
17: 4 in that day the glory of Jacob will be brought low 1
27: 6 In days to come Jacob shall take root 1
9 by this the guilt of Jacob will be expiated 1
29:22 says the LORD . . concerning the house of Jacob 1
22 Jacob shall no more be ashamed 1
23 they will sanctify the Holy One of Jacob 1
40:27 Why do you say, O Jacob, and speak, O Israel 1
41: 8 you, Israel, my servant, Jacob, whom I have chosen 1
14 Fear not, you worm Jacob, you men of Israel! 1
21 bring your proofs, says the King of Jacob. 1
42:24 Who gave up Jacob to the spoiler 1
43: 1 created you, O Jacob, he who formed you, O Israel 1
22 Yet you did not call upon me, O Jacob; 1
28 I delivered Jacob to utter destruction 1
44: 1 But now hear, O Jacob my servant 1
2 Fear not, O Jacob my servant 1
5 another will call himself by the name of Jacob 1
21 Remember these things, O Jacob, and Israel 1
23 For the LORD has redeemed Jacob 1
45: 4 For the sake of my servant Jacob 1
19 I did not say to . . Jacob, 'Seek me in chaos.' 1
46: 3 Hearken to me, O house of Jacob 1
48: 1 Hear this, O house of Jacob, who are called 1
12 Hearken to me, O Jacob, and Israel, whom I called! 1
20 say, "The LORD has redeemed his servant Jacob! 1
49: 5 to be his servant, to bring Jacob back to him 1
6 be my servant to raise up the tribes of Jacob 1
26 and your Redeemer, the Mighty One of Jacob. 1
58: 1 declare . . to the house of Jacob their sins. 1
14 I will feed you with the heritage of Jacob 1
59:20 to those in Jacob who turn from transgression 1
60:16 and your Redeemer, the Mighty One of Jacob. 1
65: 9 I will bring forth descendants from Jacob 1
Jer 2: 4 Hear the word of the LORD, O house of Jacob 1
5:20 Declare this in the house of Jacob 1
10:16 Not like these is he who is the portion of Jacob 1
25 for they have devoured Jacob; 1
30: 7 it is a time of distress for Jacob; 1
10 Then fear not, O Jacob my servant, says the LORD 1
10 Jacob shall return and have quiet and ease 1
18 I will restore the fortunes of the tents of Jacob 1
31: 7 Sing aloud with gladness for Jacob 1
11 the LORD has ransomed Jacob, and has redeemed him 1
33:26 then I will reject the descendants of Jacob 1
26 to rule over the seed of Abraham, Isaac, and Jacob. 1
46:27 But fear not, O Jacob my servant, nor be dismayed 1
27 Jacob shall return and have quiet and ease 1
28 Fear not, O Jacob my servant, says the LORD 1
51:19 Not like these is he who is the portion of Jacob 1
Lam 1:17 the LORD has commanded against Jacob that 1
2: 2 has destroyed . . all the habitations of Jacob; 1
3 he has burned like a flaming fire in Jacob 1
Ezk 20: 5 I swore to the seed of the house of Jacob 1
28:25 their own land which I gave to my servant Jacob. 1
37:25 in the land . . that I gave to my servant Jacob; 1
39:25 Now I will restore the fortunes of Jacob 1
Hos 10:11 Judah must plow, Jacob must harrow for himself. 1
12: 2 and will punish Jacob according to his ways 1
12 (Jacob fled to the land of Aram 1
Ams 3:13 Hear, and testify against the house of Jacob 1
6: 8 I abhor the pride of Jacob, and hate his 1
7: 2 How can Jacob stand? He is so small! 1
5 How can Jacob stand? He is so small"! 1
8: 7 The LORD has sworn by the pride of Jacob 1
9: 8 I will not utterly destroy the house of Jacob 1
Obd 1:10 For the violence done to your brother Jacob 1
17 the house of Jacob shall possess their own 1
18 The house of Jacob shall be a fire 1
Mic 1: 5 All this is for the transgression of Jacob 1
5 What is the transgression of Jacob? 1
2: 7 Should this be said, O house of Jacob? 1
12 I will surely gather all of you, O Jacob 1
3: 1 And I said: Hear, you heads of Jacob 1
8 to declare to Jacob his transgression 1
9 Hear this, you heads of the house of Jacob 1
4: 2 let us go up . . to the house of the God of Jacob; 1
5: 7 the remnant of Jacob shall be in the midst of many 1
8 the remnant of Jacob shall be among the nations 1
7:20 Thou wilt show faithfulness to Jacob 1
Nah 2: 2 For the LORD is restoring the majesty of Jacob 1
Mal 1: 2 Is not Esau Jacob's brother?" says the LORD. 1
2 Yet I have loved Jacob 1
2:12 May the LORD cut off from the tents of Jacob 1
3: 6 therefore you, O sons of Jacob, are not consumed. 1
Mat 1: 2 and Isaac the father of Jacob 2
2 and Jacob the father of Judah 2
15 Matthan, and Matthan the father of Jacob 2
16 Jacob the father of Joseph the husband of Mary 2
8:11 sit at table with Abraham, Isaac, and Jacob 2
22:32 the God of Isaac, and the God of Jacob 2
Mrk 12:26 the God of Isaac, and the God of Jacob'? 2
Lke 1:33 he will reign over the house of Jacob for ever; 2

3:34 the son of Jacob, the son of Isaac 2
13:28 Abraham and Isaac and Jacob and all the prophets 2
20:37 the God of Isaac and the God of Jacob. 2
Joh 4: 5 near the field that Jacob gave to his son Joseph. 2
6 Jacob's well was there, and so Jesus . . sat down 2
12 Are you greater than our father Jacob 2
Act 3:13 The God of Abraham and of Isaac and of Jacob 2
7: 8 Isaac became the father of Jacob 2
8 Jacob of the twelve patriarchs. 2
12 when Jacob heard that there was grain in Egypt 2
14 Joseph sent and called to him Jacob his father 2
15 Jacob went down into Egypt 2
32 the God of Abraham and of Isaac and of Jacob 2
46 find a habitation for the God of Jacob. 2
Rom 9:13 As it is written, "Jacob I loved, but Esau I hated. 2
11:26 he will banish ungodliness from Jacob"; 2
Heb 11: 9 living in tents with Isaac and Jacob 2
20 invoked future blessings on Jacob and Esau. 2
21 Jacob, when dying, blessed . . the sons of Joseph 2
2Es 1:24 What shall I do to you, O Jacob? 3
39 Jacob and Hosea and Amos and Micah and Joel 3
3:15 and to Isaac thou gavest Jacob and Esau. 3
16 thou didst set apart Jacob for thyself 3
16 and Jacob became a great multitude. 3
19 to give the law to the descendants of Jacob 3
32 as these tribes of Jacob? 3
5:35 that I might not see the travail of Jacob 3
6: 8 because from him were born Jacob and Esau 3
8 Jacob's hand held Esau's heel from the beginning. 3
9 Jacob is the beginning of the age that follows. 3
8:16 about the seed of Jacob, for whom I am troubled. 3
9:30 and give heed to my words, O descendants of Jacob. 3
12:46 do not be sorrowful, O house of Jacob; 3
Tob 4:12 Noah, Abraham, Isaac, and Jacob, our fathers of old 2
Jdt 8:26 what happened to Jacob in Mesopotamia in Syria 2
Sir 23:12 may it never be found in the inheritance of Jacob! 2
24: 8 he said, 'Make your dwelling in Jacob 2
23 an inheritance for the congregations of Jacob. 2
36:11 Gather all the tribes of Jacob 2
44:23 he made to rest upon the head of Jacob 2
45: 5 to teach Jacob the covenant 2
17 to teach Jacob the testimonies 2
46:14 the Lord watched over Jacob. 2
47:22 he gave a remnant to Jacob 2
48:10 to restore the tribes of Jacob. 2
49:10 they comforted the people of Jacob 2
Bar 2:34 fathers, to Abraham and to Isaac and to Jacob 2
3:36 gave her to Jacob his servant and to Israel whom 2
4: 2 Turn, O Jacob, and take her 2
Man 1: 1 God . . of Abraham and Isaac and Jacob 2
8 repentance . . for Abraham and Isaac and Jacob 2
1Mc 1:28 all the house of Jacob was clothed with shame. 2
3: 7 he made Jacob glad by his deeds 2
45 Joy was taken from Jacob 2
5: 2 to destroy the descendants of Jacob 2
2Mc 1: 2 his covenant with Abraham and Isaac and Jacob 2
3Mc 6: 3 look . . upon the children of the sainted Jacob 2
13 who have power to save the nation of Jacob. 2
4Mc 2:19 Why else did Jacob, our most wise father, censure 2
7:19 like our patriarchs Abraham and Isaac and Jacob 2
13:17 Abraham and Isaac and Jacob will welcome us 2
16:25 as do Abraham and Isaac and Jacob 2

Jada 1. יָדָע
1Ch 2:28 The sons of Onam: Sham'mai and Jada. 1
32 sons of Jada, Sham'mai's brother: Jether 1

Jaddai 1. יַדַּי
Ezr 10:43 of Nebo . . Zebi'na, Jaddai, Jo'el, and Benai'ah. 1

Jaddua 1. יַדּוּעַ
Neh 10:21 Meshez'abel, Zadok, Jad'du-a 1
12:11 Jonathan the father of Jad'du-a. 1
22 Levites, in the days of . . Joha'nan, and Jad'du-a 1

Jaddus 1. Ιοδδους
1Es 5:38 the sons of Jaddus who had married Agia 1

Jadon 1. יָדוֹן
Neh 3: 7 repaired Melati'ah . . and Jadon the Mero'nothite 1

Jael 1. יָעֵל
Jdg 4:17 to the tent of Ja'el, the wife of Heber the Ken'ite; 1
18 Ja'el came out to meet Sis'era, and said to him 1
21 Ja'el the wife of Heber took a tent peg 1
22 as Barak pursued Sis'era, Ja'el went out to meet him 1
5: 6 In the days of Shamgar . . in the days of Ja'el 1
24 blessed . . be Ja'el, the wife of Heber the Ken'ite 1

Jagur 1. יָגוּר
Jos 15:21 cities belonging to . . were Kabzeel, Eder, Jagur 1

Jahath 1. יַחַת
1Ch 4: 2 Re-ai'ah the son of Shobal was the father of Jahath 1
2 and Jahath was the father of Ahu'mai and Lahad. 1
6:20 Of Gershom: Libni his son, Jahath his son, Zimmah 1
43 son of Jahath, son of Gershom, son of Levi. 1
23:10 sons of Shim'e-i: Jahath, Zina, and Je'ush 1

11 Jahath was the chief, and Zizah the second; 1
24:22 of the sons of Shelo'moth, Jahath. 1
2Ch 34:12 Over them were set Jahath and Obadi'ah 1

Jahaz 1. יַהַץ
Num21:23 came to Jahaz, and fought against Israel. 1
Deu 2:32 Sihon came out against us . . to battle at Jahaz. 1
Jos 13:18 Jahaz, and Ked'emoth, and Meph'aath 1
21:36 Bezer with its . . Jahaz with its pasture lands 1
Jdg 11:20 Sihon gathered . . and encamped at Jahaz 1
Isa 15: 4 cry out, their voice is heard as far as Jahaz; 1
Jer 48:34 as far as Jahaz they utter their voice 1

Jahaziel 1. יַחֲזִיאֵל 2. Ιεζηλος
1Ch 12: 4 Jeremiah, Jaha'ziel, Joha'nan, Joz'abad of Gede'rah 1
16: 6 Benai'ah and Jaha'ziel the priests were to blow 1
23:19 sons of Hebron . . Jaha'ziel the third 1
24:23 sons of Hebron . . Jaha'ziel the third, Jeka-me'am 1
2Ch 20:14 the Spirit of the LORD came upon Jaha'ziel 1
Ezr 8: 5 Shecani'ah the son of Jaha'ziel 1
1Es 8:32 Shecaniah the son of Jahaziel 2

Jahdai 1. יָהְדַּי
1Ch 2:47 sons of Jah'dai: Regem, Jotham, Geshan, Pelet, 1

Jahdiel 1. יַחְדִּיאֵל
1Ch 5:24 heads of their fathers' houses . . and Jah'di-el 1

Jahdo 1. יַחְדּוֹ
1Ch 5:14 sons of Ab'ihail . . son of Jeshish'ai, son of Jahdo 1

Jahleel 1. יַחְלְאֵל
Gen 46:14 The sons of Zeb'ulun: Sered, Elon, and Jah'leel 1
Num26:26 of Jahleel, the family of the Jah'leelites. 1

Jahleelite 1. יַחְלְאֵלִי
Num26:26 of Jahleel, the family of the Jah'leelites. 1

Jahmai 1. יַחְמַי
1Ch 7: 2 sons of Tola . . Je'ri-el, Jah'mai, Ibsam, and Shem'uel 1

Jahzah 1. יַהְצָה
1Ch 6:78 Jahzah with its pasture lands 1
Jer 48:21 upon the tableland, upon Holon, and Jahzah 1

Jahzeel 1. יַחְצְאֵל
Gen 46:24 The sons of Naph'tali: Jahzeel, Guni, Jezer 1
Num26:48 of Jahzeel, the family of the Jah'zeelites; 1

Jahzeelite 1. יַחְצְאֵלִי
Num26:48 of Jahzeel, the family of the Jah'zeelites; 1

Jahzeiah 1. יַחְזְיָה 2. Ιεζιας
Ezr 10:15 Only Jonathan . . and Jahzei'ah the son of Tikvah 1
1Es 9:14 Jahzeiah the son of Tikvah 2

Jahzerah 1. יַחְזֵרָה
1Ch 9:12 Ad'i-el, son of Jah'zerah, son of Meshul'lam 1

Jahziel 1. יַחֲצִיאֵל
1Ch 7:13 sons of Naph'tali: Jah'zi-el, Guni, Jezer, and Shallum 1

Jair 1. יָאִיר 2. יָעִיר 3. Ἰάϊρος
Num32:41 Ja'ir . . went and took their villages 1
Deu 3:14 Ja'ir the Manas'site took all the region of Argob 1
Jos 13:30 all Bashan . . and all the towns of Ja'ir 1
Jdg 10: 3 arose Ja'ir the Gileadite, who judged Israel 1
5 Ja'ir died, and was buried in Kamon. 1
1Kg 4:13 he had the villages of Ja'ir the son of Manas'seh 1
1Ch 2:22 Ja'ir, who had 23 cities in the land of Gilead 1
20: 5 Elha'nan the son of Ja'ir slew Lahmi 2
Est 2: 5 name was Mor'decai, the son of Ja'ir, son of Shim'e-i 1
AEs 11: 2 Mordecai the son of Jair, son of Shimei, son of Kish 3

Jairite 1. יָאִרִי
2Sm 20:26 and Ira the Ja'irite was also David's priest. 1

Jairus 1. Ἰάϊρος
Mrk 5:22 Ja'irus by name 1
Lke 8:41 there came a man named Ja'irus 1

Jakeh 1. יָקֶה
Prv 30: 1 The words of Agur son of Jakeh of Massa. 1

Jakim 1. יָקִים
1Ch 8:19 Jakim, Zichri, Zabdi 1
24:12 the eleventh to Eli'ashib, the twelfth to Jakim 1

Jalam 1. יַעְלָם
Gen 36: 5 Oholiba'mah bore Je'ush, Jalam, and Korah. 1
14 she bore to Esau Je'ush, Jalam, and Korah. 1
18 Esau's wife: the chiefs Je'ush, Jalam, and Korah 1
1Ch 1:35 sons of Esau: Eli'phaz, Reu'el, Je'ush, Jalam, 1

Jalon 1. יָלוֹן
1Ch 4:17 The sons of Ezrah: Jether, Mered, Epher, and Jalon. 1

Jambres 1. Ἰαμβρῆς
2Ti 3: 8 As Jannes and Jambres opposed Moses 1

Jambri 1. Ιαμβρι
1Mc 9:36 the sons of Jambri from Medeba came out 1
37 sons of Jambri are celebrating a great wedding 1

James 1. Ἰάκωβος
Mat 4:21 saw two other brothers, James the son of Zeb'edee 1
10: 2 James the son of Zeb'edee, and John his brother; 1
3 James the son of Alphaeus, and Thaddaeus; 1
13:55 are not his brothers James and Joseph and Simon 1
17: 1 Jesus took with him Peter and James and John 1
27:56 Mary the mother of James and Joseph 1
Mrk 1:19 he saw James the son of Zeb'edee 1
29 entered the house . . with James and John 1
3:17 James the son of Zeb'edee 1
17 John the brother of James 1
18 and Thomas, and James the son of Alphaeus 1
5:37 Peter and James and John the brother of James. 1
37 Peter and James and John the brother of James. 1
6: 3 brother of James and Joses and Judas and Simon 1
9: 2 Jesus took with him Peter and James and John 1
10:35 James and John, the sons of Zeb'edee, came forward 1
41 they began to be indignant at James and John. 1
13: 3 Peter and James and John and Andrew asked him 1
14:33 he took with him Peter and James and John 1
15:40 Mary the mother of James the younger and of Joses 1
16: 1 Mary Mag'dalene, and Mary the mother of James 1
Lke 5:10 so also were James and John, sons of Zeb'edee 1
6:14 Andrew his brother, and James and John, and Philip 1
15 and Thomas, and James the son of Alphaeus 1
16 Judas the son of James, and Judas Iscariot 1
8:51 except Peter and John and James 1
9:28 he took with him Peter and John and James 1
54 when his disciples James and John saw it 1
24:10 Mary the mother of James and the other women 1
Act 1:13 Peter and John and James and Andrew 1
13 James the son of Alphaeus and Simon the Zealot 1
13 Simon the Zealot and Judas the son of James. 1
12: 2 killed James the brother of John with the sword; 1
17 he said, "Tell this to James and to the brethren. 1
15:13 After they finished speaking, James replied 1
21:18 On the following day Paul went in with us to James; 1
1Co 15: 7 he appeared to James, then to all the apostles. 1
Gal 1:19 except James the Lord's brother. 1
2: 9 James and Cephas and John 1
12 For before certain men came from James 1
Jas 1: 1 James, a servant of God and of the Lord Jesus 1
Jde 1: 1 Jude, a servant of Jesus . . and brother of James 1

Jamin 1. יָמִין 2. Ιαδινος
Gen 46:10 The sons of Simeon: Jemu'el, Jamin, Ohad, Jachin 1
Exd 6:15 The sons of Simeon: Jemu'el, Jamin, Ohad, Jachin 1
Num26:12 of Jamin, the family of the Ja'minites; 1
1Ch 2:27 The sons of Ram . . Ma'az, Jamin, and Eker. 1
4:24 sons of Simeon: Nem'uel, Jamin, Jarib, Zerah, Sha'ul; 1
Neh 8: 7 Also Jesh'ua, Bani, Sherebi'ah, Jamin, Akkub 1
1Es 9:48 Jeshua and Anniuth and Sherebiah, Jamin, Akkub 2

Jaminite 1. יָמִינִי
Num26:12 of Jamin, the family of the Ja'minites; 1

Jamlech 1. יַמְלֵךְ
1Ch 4:34 Mesho'bab, Jamlech, Joshah the son of Amazi'ah 1

Jamnia 1. Ιαμνια 2. Ιαμνιτης 3. Ιεμνααa
Jdt 2:28 all who lived in Jamnia 3
1Mc 4:15 to the plains of Idumea, and to Azotus and Jamnia; 1
5:58 they marched against Jamnia. 1
10:69 encamped against Jamnia 1
15:40 So Cendebeus came to Jamnia 1
2Mc 12: 8 the men in Jamnia meant . . to wipe out the Jews 1
9 he attacked the people of Jamnia by night 2
40 they found sacred tokens of the idols of Jamnia 1

Janai 1. יַעְנַי
1Ch 5:12 Jo'el . . Shapham . . Ja'nai, and Shaphat in Bashan. 1

Janim 1. יָנִים
Jos 15:53 Janim, Beth-tap'puah, Aphe'kah 1

Jannai 1. Ἰανναί
Lke 3:24 son of Melchi, the son of Jan'nai, the son of Joseph 1

Jannes 1. Ἰάννης
2Ti 3: 8 As Jannes and Jambres opposed Moses 1

Janoah 1. יָנוֹחַ 2. יָנוֹחָה
Jos 16: 6 and passes along beyond it on the east to Jan-o'ah 2
7 goes down from Jan-o'ah to At'aroth and to Na'arah 2
2Kg 15:29 captured I'jon, A'bel-beth-ma'acah, Jan-o'ah, Kedesh 1

Japheth 1. יֶפֶת 2. Ιαφεθ
Gen 5:32 Noah became the father of Shem, Ham, and Japheth. 1
6:10 Noah had three sons, Shem, Ham, and Japheth. 1
7:13 Noah and his sons, Shem and Ham and Japheth 1
9:18 from the ark were Shem, Ham, and Japheth. 1
23 Then Shem and Japheth took a garment 1
27 God enlarge Japheth, and let him dwell 1
10: 1 the sons of Noah, Shem, Ham, and Japheth; 1
2 sons of Japheth: Gomer, Magog, Madai, Javan 1
5 These are the sons of Japheth in their lands •
21 the elder brother of Japheth, children were born 1
1Ch 1: 4 Noah, Shem, Ham, and Japheth. 1
5 The sons of Japheth: Gomer, Magog, Madai, Javan 1
Jdt 2:25 came to the southern borders of Japheth 2

Japhia 1. יָפִיעַ
Jos 10: 3 to Japhi'a king of Lachish, and to Debir . . of Eglon 1
19:12 thence it goes to Dab'erath, then up to Japhi'a; 1
2Sm 5:15 Ibhar, Eli'shu-a, Nepheg, Japhi'a 1
1Ch 3: 7 Nogah, Nepheg, Japhi'a 1
14: 6 Nogah, Nepheg, Japhi'a 1

Japhlet 1. יַפְלֵט
1Ch 7:32 Heber was the father of Japhlet, Shomer, Hotham 1
33 The sons of Japhlet: Pasach, Bimhal, and Ashvath. 1
33 These are the sons of Japhlet. 1

Japhletite 1. יַפְלֵטִי
Jos 16: 3 goes down . . to the territory of the Japh'letites 1

Jarah 1. יַעְרָה
1Ch 9:42 Ahaz was the father of Jarah 1
42 and Jarah of Al'emeth, Az'maveth, and Zimri; 1

Jared 1. יֶרֶד 2. Ἰάρετ
Gen 5:15 Ma-hal'alel . . became the father of Jared. 1
16 Ma-hal'alel lived after the birth of Jared 1
18 When Jared had lived 162 years 1
19 Jared lived after the birth of Enoch 800 years 1
20 Thus all the days of Jared were 962 years; 1
1Ch 1: 2 Kenan, Ma-hal'alel, Jared; 1
Lke 3:37 the son of Jared, the son of Maha'lele-el 2

Jarha 1. יַרְחָע
1Ch 2:34 had an Egyptian slave, whose name was Jarha. 1
35 gave his daughter . . to Jarha his slave; 1

Jarib 1. יָרִיב 2. Ιωριβος
1Ch 4:24 sons of Simeon: Nem'uel, Jamin, Jarib, Zerah, Sha'ul; 1
Ezr 8:16 Then I sent for . . Jarib, Elna'than, Nathan 1
10:18 found Ma-asei'ah, Elie'zer, Jarib, and Gedali'ah 1
1Es 8:44 Elnathan, Shemaiah, Jarib, Nathan, Elnathan 2
9:19 Maaseiah, Eliezar, Jarib, and Jodan. 2

Jarmuth 1. יַרְמוּת
Jos 10: 3 to Hoham king of Hebron, to Piram king of Jarmuth 1
5 the king of Hebron, the king of Jarmuth, the king 1
23 king of Hebron, the king of Jarmuth 1
12:11 the king of Jarmuth, one; the king of Lachish, one; 1
15:35 Jarmuth, Adullam, Socoh, Aze'kah 1
21:29 Jarmuth with its pasture lands, En-gan'nim 1
Neh 11:29 in En-rim'mon, in Zorah, in Jarmuth 1

Jaroah 1. יָרוֹחַ
1Ch 5:14 the sons of Ab'ihail the son of Huri, son of Jaro'ah 1

Jashar 1. יָשָׁר
Jos 10:13 Is this not written in the Book of Jashar? 1
2Sm 1:18 it is written in the Book of Jashar. He said 1

Jashen 1. יָשֵׁן
2Sm 23:32 Eli'ahba of Sha-al'bon, the sons of Jashen, Jonathan 1

Jashobeam 1. יָשָׁבְעָם
1Ch 11:11 Jasho'be-am, a Hach'monite, was chief of the three; 1
12: 6 Az'arel, Jo-e'zer, and Jasho'be-am, the Ko'rahites; 1
27: 2 Jasho'beam . . in charge of the first division 1

Jashub 1. יָשׁוּב 2. Ιασουβος
Num26:24 of Jashub, the family of the Jash'ubites; 1
1Ch 7: 1 sons of Is'sachar: Tola, Pu'ah, Jashub, and Shimron 1
Ezr 10:29 of Bani were . . Jashub, She'al, and Jer'emoth. 1
1Es 9:30 Adaiah, Jashub, and Sheal and Jeremoth. 2

Jashubite 1. יָשֻׁבִי
Num26:24 of Jashub, the family of the Jash'ubites; 1

Jason 1. Ἰάσων
Act 17: 5 attacked the house of Jason 1
6 they dragged Jason and some of the brethren 1
7 Jason has received them 1
9 they had taken security from Jason and the rest 1
Rom 16:21 so do Lucius and Jason and Sosip'ater, my kinsmen. 1
1Mc 8:17 and Jason the son of Eleazar 1
12:16 Antipater the son of Jason 1
14:22 Antipater the son of Jason 1
2Mc 1: 7 after Jason and his company revolted 1
2:23 which has been set forth by Jason of Cyrene 1
4: 7 Jason the brother of Onias 1
10 When the king assented and Jason came to office •
13 because of the surpassing wickedness of Jason 1
19 the vile Jason sent envoys 1
22 welcomed magnificently by Jason and the city 1
23 Jason sent Menelaus 1

24 outbidding Jason by 300 talents of silver. 1
26 Jason . . was driven as a fugitive 1
5: 5 Jason took no less than 1,000 men 1
6 Jason kept relentlessly slaughtering 1
4Mc 4:16 and appointed Onias's brother Jason as high priest. 1
17 Jason agreed *
19 Jason changed the nation's way of life *

Jathan 1. Ιαθαν
Tob 5:13 I used to know Ananias and Jathan 1

Jathniel 1. יַתְנִיאֵל
1Ch 26: 2 Meshelemi'ah had sons . . Jath'ni-el the fourth 1

Jattir 1. יַתִּיר
Jos 15:48 And in the hill country, Shamir, Jattir, Socoh 1
21:14 Jattir with its pasture lands, Eshtemo'a with its 1
1Sm 30:27 those in Bethel, in Ramoth of the Negeb, in Jattir 1
1Ch 6:57 cities of refuge . . Jattir, Eshtemo'a 1

Javan 1. יָוָן
Gen 10: 2 sons of Japheth: Gomer, Magog, Madai, Javan 1
4 The sons of Javan: Eli'shah, Tarshish, Kittim 1
1Ch 1: 5 The sons of Japheth: Gomer, Magog, Madai, Javan 1
7 The sons of Javan: Eli'shah, Tarshish, Kittim 1
Isa 66:19 to Tubal and Javan, to the coastlands afar off 1
Ezk 27:13 Javan, Tubal, and Meshech traded with you; 1

Jazer 1. יַעְזֵר 2. Ιαζηρ
Num21:24 for Jazer was the boundary of the Ammonites. 2
32 Moses sent to spy out Jazer; 1
32: 1 they saw the land of Jazer and the land of Gilead 1
3 At'aroth, Dibon, Jazer, Nimrah, Heshbon, Elea'leh 1
35 At'roth-sho'phan, Jazer, Jog'behah 1
Jos 13:25 Their territory was Jazer, and all the cities 1
21:39 Heshbon with its . . Jazer with its pasture lands 1
2Sm 24: 5 began from Aro'er . . toward Gad and on to Jazer. 1
1Ch 6:81 Heshbon . . and Jazer with its pasture lands. 1
26:31 ability among them were found at Jazer in Gilead. 1
Isa 16: 8 struck down its branches, which reached to Jazer 1
9 with the weeping of Jazer for the vine of Sibmah; 1
Jer 48:32 More than for Jazer I weep for you, O vine of Sibmah! 1
32 Your branches . . reached as far as Jazer; 1
1Mc 5: 8 He also took Jazer and its villages 2

Jaziz 1. יָזִיז
1Ch 27:30 Over the flocks was Jaziz the Hagrite. 1

Jearim 1. יְעָרִים
Jos 15:10 along to the northern shoulder of Mount Je'arim 1

Jeatherai 1. יְאָתְרַי
1Ch 6:21 Jo'ah . . Iddo . . Zerah . . Je-ath'erai his son. 1

Jeberechiah 1. יְבֶרֶכְיָהוּ
Isa 8: 2 Zechari'ah the son of Jeberechi'ah, to attest 1

Jebus 1. יְבוּס 2. יְבוּסִי
Jos 18:28 Zela, Ha-eleph, Jebus (that is, Jerusalem) 2
Jdg 19:10 and arrived opposite Jebus (that is, Jerusalem). 1
11 When they were near Jebus, the day was far spent 1
1Ch 11: 4 and all Israel went to Jerusalem, that is Jebus 1
5 The inhabitants of Jebus said to David 1

Jebusite 1. יְבוּסִי 2. Ιεβουσαιος
Gen 10:16 the Jeb'usites, the Amorites, the Gir'gashites 1
15:21 the Gir'gashites and the Jeb'usites. 1
Exd 3: 8 the Per'izzites, the Hivites, and the Jeb'usites. 1
17 the Hivites, and the Jeb'usites, a land flowing 1
13: 5 land of . . the Jeb'usites, which he swore 1
23:23 the Hivites, and the Jeb'usites, and I blot them out 1
33: 2 the Per'izzites, the Hivites, and the Jeb'usites. 1
34:11 the Per'izzites, the Hivites, and the Jeb'usites. 1
Num13:29 Hittites, the Jeb'usites, and the Amorites dwell 1
Deu 7: 1 Per'izzites, the Hivites, and the Jeb'usites, seven 1
20:17 utterly destroy . . Hivites and the Jebusites 1
Jos 3:10 Gir'gashites, the Amorites, and the Jeb'usites. 1
9: 1 the Per'izzites, the Hivites, and the Jeb'usites 1
11: 3 the Hittites, the Per'izzites, and the Jeb'usites 1
12: 8 Per'izzites, the Hivites, and the Jeb'usites 1
15: 8 goes . . at the southern shoulder of the Jeb'usite 1
63 But the Jeb'usites . . Judah could not drive out; 1
63 so the Jeb'usites dwell with the people of Judah 1
18:16 valley . . south of the shoulder of the Jeb'usites 1
24:11 the Gir'gashites, the Hivites, and the Jeb'usites; 1
Jdg 1:21 Benjamin did not drive out the Jeb'usites who 1
21 so the Jeb'usites have dwelt with the people 1
3: 5 the Per'izzites, the Hivites, and the Jeb'usites; 1
19:11 let us turn aside to this city of the Jeb'usites 1
2Sm 5: 6 king and his men went . . against the Jeb'usites 1
8 Whoever would smite the Jeb'usites, let him get up 1
24:16 by the threshing floor of Arau'nah the Jeb'usite. 1
18 on the threshing floor of Arau'nah the Jeb'usite. 1
1Kg 9:20 the Per'izzites, the Hivites, and the Jeb'usites 1
1Ch 1:14 the Jeb'usites, the Am'orites, the Gir'gashites 1
11: 4 Jebus, where the Jeb'usites were 1
6 David said, "Whoever shall smite the Jeb'usites 1
21:15 the threshing floor of Ornan the Jeb'usite. 1
18 on the threshing floor of Ornan the Jeb'usite. 1
28 at the threshing floor of Ornan the Jeb'usite 1
2Ch 3: 1 on the threshing floor of Ornan the Jeb'usite. 1
8: 7 the people who were left of . . and the Jeb'usites 1
Ezr 9: 1 Per'izzites, the Jeb'usites, the Ammonites 1
Neh 9: 8 land of . . the Per'izzite, the Jeb'usite 1
Zec 9: 7 Ekron shall be like the Jeb'usites. 1
1Es 8:69 the Jebusites, the Moabites, the Egyptians 2
Jdt 5:16 the Jebusites and the Shechemites 2

Jechoniah 1. Ἰεχονίας
Mat 1:11 Josi'ah the father of Jechoni'ah and his brothers 1
12 Jechoni'ah was the father of She-al'ti-el 1

Jecoliah 1. יְכָלְיָהוּ
2Kg 15: 2 His mother's name was Jecoli'ah of Jerusalem. 1
2Ch 26: 3 His mother's name was Jecoli'ah of Jerusalem. 1

Jeconiah 1. יְכוֹנְיָה 2. Ἰεχονίας
1Ch 3:16 descendants of Jehoi'akim: Jeconi'ah his son 1
17 sons of Jeconi'ah, the captive: Sheal'tiel his son 1
Est 2: 6 among the captives carried away with Jeconi'ah 1
Jer 24: 1 taken into exile from Jerusalem Jeconi'ah 1
27:20 Jeconi'ah the son of Jehoi'akim, king of Judah 1
28: 4 I will also bring back to this place Jeconi'ah 1
29: 2 This was after King Jeconi'ah, and the queen 1
1Es 1: 9 Jeconiah and Shemaiah and Nethanel his brother 2
34 men of the nation took Jeconiah the son of Josiah 2
AEs 11: 4 Jeconiah king of Judea 2
Bar 1: 3 Jeconiah the son of Jehoiakim, king of Judah 2
9 Jeconiah and the princes and the prisoners 2

Jedaiah 1. יְדָיָה 2. יְדַעְיָה 3. Ιεδδος
1Ch 4:37 Ziza . . son of Jedai'ah, son of Shimri 1
9:10 Of the priests: Jedai'ah, Jehoi'arib, Jachin 2
24: 7 The first lot fell to . . the second to Jedai'ah 2
Ezr 2:36 priests: the sons of Jedai'ah, of the house 2
Neh 3:10 Next to them Jedai'ah the son of Haru'maph 1
7:39 sons of Jedai'ah, namely the house of Jeshua, 973. 2
11:10 Of the priests: Jedai'ah the son of Joi'arib, Jachin 2
12: 6 Shemai'ah, Joi'arib, Jedai'ah 2
7 Sallu, Amok, Hilki'ah, Jedai'ah. 2
19 of Joi'arib, Matte'nai; of Jedai'ah, Uzzi; 2
21 of Hilki'ah, Hashabi'ah; of Jedai'ah, Nethan'el. 2
Zec 6:10 Take from the exiles Heldai, Tobi'jah, and Jedai'ah 2
14 as a reminder to Heldai, Tobi'jah, Jedai'ah 2
1Es 5:24 the sons of Jedaiah the son of Jeshua 3

Jediael 1. יְדִיעֲאֵל
1Ch 7: 6 sons of Benjamin: Bela, Becher, and Jedi'a-el, three. 1
10 The sons of Jedi'a-el: Bilhan. 1
11 All these were the sons of Jedi'a-el 1
11:45 Jedi'a-el the son of Shimri, and Joha his brother 1
12:20 men of Manas'seh . . Adnah, Joz'abad, Jedi'a-el 1
26: 2 Meshelemi'ah had sons . . Jedi'a-el the second 1

Jedidah 1. יְדִידָה
2Kg 22: 1 mother's name was Jedi'dah the daughter of Adai'ah 1

Jedidiah 1. יְדִידְיָה
2Sm 12:25 he called his name Jedidi'ah, because of the LORD. 1

Jeduthun 1. ידותון
1Ch 9:16 Shemai'ah, son of Galal, son of Jedu'thun 1
16:38 while O'bed-e'dom, the son of Jedu'thun, and Hosah 1
41 Heman and Jedu'thun, and the rest of those chosen 1
42 Heman and Jedu'thun had trumpets and cymbals 1
42 The sons of Jedu'thun were appointed to the gate. 1
25: 1 set apart for the service . . of Jedu'thun 1
3 Of Jedu'thun, the sons of Jedu'thun: Gedali'ah, Zeri 1
3 sons of Jedu'thun: Gedali'ah, Zeri, Jeshai'ah, 1
3 under the direction of their father Jedu'thun 1
6 Asaph, Jedu'thun, and Heman were under the order 1
2Ch 5:12 Levitical singers, Asaph, Heman, and Jedu'thun 1
29:14 of the sons of Jedu'thun, Shemai'ah and Uz'ziel. 1
35:15 command of David . . and Jedu'thun the king's seer 1
Neh 11:17 son of Sham'mua, son of Galal, son of Jedu'thun. 1
Ps 39: 0 To the choirmaster: To Jeduthun. 1
62: 0 To the choirmaster: according to Jeduthun. 1
77: 0 To the choirmaster: according to Jeduthun. 1

Jegar-sahadutha 1. יְגַר שָׂהֲדוּתָא
Gen 31:47 Laban called it Je'gar-sahadu'tha: but Jacob 1

Jehallelel 1. יְהַלֶּלְאֵל
1Ch 4:16 sons of Jehal'lelel: Ziph, Ziphah, Tir'i-a 1
2Ch 29:12 Levites arose . . Azari'ah the son of Jehal'lelel; 1

Jehdeiah 1. יֶחְדְּיָהוּ
1Ch 24:20 of the sons of Shu'ba-el, Jehde'iah. 1
27:30 the she-asses was Jehde'iah the Meron'othite. 1

Jehezkel 1. יְחֶזְקֵאל
1Ch 24:16 to Pethahi'ah, the twentieth to Jehez'kel 1

Jehiah 1. יְחִיָּה
1Ch 15:24 Jehi'ah also were to be gatekeepers for the ark. 1

Jehiel 1. יְחִיאֵל 2. Ησυηλος 3. Ιεζριηλος 4. Ιεηλος 5. Ιειηλ
1Ch 15:18 Zechari'ah, Ja-a'ziel, Shemi'ramoth, Jehi'el, Unni 1
20 Zechari'ah, A'zi-el, Shemi'ramoth, Jehi'el, Unni 1
16: 5 second to him were . . Jehi'el, Mattithi'ah, Eli'ab 1
23: 8 of Ladan: Jehi'el the chief, and Zetham, and Jo'el 1
27:32 he and Jehi'el the son of Hach'moni attended 1
29: 8 in the care of Jehi'el the Gershonite. 1
2Ch 21: 2 sons of Jehosh'aphat: Azari'ah, Jehi'el, Zechari'ah 1
31:13 while Jehi'el, Azazi'ah, Nahath . . were overseers 1
35: 8 Hilki'ah, Zechari'ah, and Jehi'el, the chief 1
Ezr 8: 9 Of the sons of Jo'ab, Obadi'ah the son of Jehi'el 1
10: 2 Shecani'ah the son of Jehi'el, of the sons of Elam 1
21 of Harim . . Eli'jah, Shemai'ah, Jehi'el, and Uzzi'ah. 1
26 of Elam: Mattani'ah, Zechari'ah, Jehi'el, Abdi 1
1Es 1: 8 Hilkiah, Zechariah, and Jehiel 2
8:35 Of the sons of Joab, Obadiah the son of Jehiel 5
92 Shecaniah the son of Jehiel 4
9:21 Maaseiah and Shemaiah and Jehiel and Azariah. 5
27 Jehiel and Abdi, and Jeremoth and Elijah. 3

Jehieli 1. יְחִיאֵלִי
1Ch 26:21 belonging to Ladan the Gershonite: Jehi'eli. 1
22 The sons of Jehi'eli . . were in charge 1

Jehizkiah 1. יְחִזְקִיָּהוּ
2Ch 28:12 chiefs . . Jehizki'ah the son of Shallum 1

Jehoaddah 1. יְהוֹעַדָּה
1Ch 8:36 Ahaz was the father of Jeho'addah; 1
36 Jeho'addah . . father of Al'emeth, Az'maveth 1

Jehoaddan 1. יְהוֹעַדָּן
2Ch 25: 1 His mother's name was Jeho-ad'dan of Jerusalem. 1

Jehoaddin 1. יְהוֹעַדִּין
2Kg 14: 2 His mother's name was Jeho-ad'din of Jerusalem. 1

Jehoahaz 1. יְהוֹאָחָז
2Kg 10:35 And Jeho'ahaz his son reigned in his stead. 1
13: 1 Jeho'ahaz . . began to reign over Israel 1
4 Then Jeho'ahaz besought the LORD 1
7 there was not left to Jeho'ahaz an army 1
8 the rest of the acts of Jeho'ahaz and all . . he did 1
9 So Jeho'ahaz slept with his fathers 1
10 Jeho'ash the son of Jeho'ahaz began to reign 1
22 oppressed Israel all the days of Jeho'ahaz. 1
25 Jeho'ash the son of Jeho'ahaz took . . the cities 1
25 the cities which he had taken from Jeho'ahaz 1
14: 8 sent messengers to Jeho'ash the son of Jeho'ahaz 1
17 death of Jeho'ash son of Jeho'ahaz, king of Israel. 1
23:30 the people . . took Jeho'ahaz the son of Josi'ah 1
31 Jeho'ahaz was 23 years old when he began to reign 1
34 But he took Jeho'ahaz away; and he came to Egypt 1
2Ch 21:17 so that no son was left to him except Jeho'ahaz 1
25:17 Jo'ash the son of Jeho'ahaz, son of Jehu, 1
25 after the death of Jo'ash the son of Jeho'ahaz 1
36: 1 people . . took Jeho'ahaz the son of Josi'ah 1
2 Jeho'ahaz was 23 . . when he began 1
4 Neco took Jeho'ahaz . . and carried him to Egypt. 1

Jehoash 1. יְהוֹאָשׁ
2Kg 11:21 Jeho'ash was seven . . when he began to reign. 1
12: 1 seventh year of Jehu Jeho'ash began to reign 1
2 Jeho'ash did what was right in the eyes of the LORD 1
4 Jeho'ash said to the priests, "All the money 1
6 But by the 23rd year of King Jeho'ash 1
7 King Jeho'ash summoned Jehoi'ada . . and the other 1
18 Jeho'ash king of Judah took all the votive gifts 1
13:10 Jeho'ash . . began to reign over Israel in Sama'ria 1
25 Jeho'ash the son of Jeho'ahaz took . . the cities 1
14: 8 Then Amazi'ah sent messengers to Jeho'ash 1
9 Jeho'ash king of Israel sent word to Amazi'ah 1
11 Jeho'ash king of Israel went up, and he and Amazi'ah 1
13 Jeho'ash king of Israel captured Amazi'ah 1
13 Amazi'ah . . the son of Jeho'ash, son of Ahazi'ah 1
15 Now the rest of the acts of Jeho'ash which he did 1
16 Jeho'ash slept with his fathers, and was buried 1
17 lived fifteen years after the death of Jeho'ash 1

Jehohanan 1. יְהוֹחָנָן 2. Ἰωάννης
1Ch 26: 3 Elam the fifth, Jehoha'nan the sixth, Eli-e-ho-e'nai 1
2Ch 17:15 next to him Jehoha'nan the commander, with 280,000 1
23: 1 commanders . . Ish'mael the son of Jehoha'nan 1
Ezr 10: 6 Ezra . . went to the chamber of Jehoha'nan 1
28 of Be'bai were Jehoha'nan, Hanani'ah, Zab'bai 1
Neh 6:18 Jehoha'nan had taken the daughter of Meshul'lam 1
12:13 of Ezra, Meshul'lam; of Amari'ah, Jehoha'nan; 1
42 Jehoha'nan, Malchi'jah, Elam, and Ezer. 1
1Es 9:29 Of the sons of Bebai: Jehohanan and Hananiah 2

Jehoiachin 1. יְהוֹיָכִין 2. Ἰωακίμ
2Kg 24: 6 Jehoi'akim . . and Jehoi'achin his son reigned 1
8 Jehoi'achin was eighteen . . when he became king 1
12 Jehoi'achin the king of Judah gave himself up 1
15 And he carried away Jehoi'achin to Babylon; 1
17 king . . made Mattani'ah, Jehoi'achin's uncle, king *
25:27 And in the 37th year of the exile of Jehoi'achin 1
27 Evil-mero'dach . . graciously freed Jehoi'achin 1
29 So Jehoi'achin put off his prison garments. *
2Ch 36: 8 Jehoi'achin his son reigned in his stead. 1

9 Jehoi'achin was eight . . when he began to reign 1
Jer 52:31 of the captivity of Jehoi'achin king of Judah 1
31 lifted up the head of Jehoi'achin king of Judah 1
33 Jehoi'achin put off his prison garments. •
Ezk 1: 2 the fifth year of the exile of King Jehoi'achin 1
1Es 1:43 Jehoiachin his son became king in his stead 2

Jehoiada 1. יְהוֹיָדָע
2Sm 8:18 Benai'ah the son of Jehoi'ada was over 1
20:23 Benai'ah the son of Jehoi'ada was in command 1
23:20 Benai'ah the son of Jehoi'ada was a valiant man 1
22 These things did Benai'ah the son of Jehoi'ada 1
1Kg 1: 8 Benai'ah the son of Jehoi'ada, and Nathan 1
26 Zadok the priest, and Benai'ah the son of Jehoi'ada 1
32 the prophet, and Benai'ah the son of Jehoi'ada." So 1
36 Benai'ah the son of Jehoi'ada answered the king 1
38 and Benai'ah the son of Jehoi'ada 1
44 Nathan . . and Benai'ah the son of Jehoi'ada 1
2:25 So King Solomon sent Benai'ah the son of Jehoi'ada; 1
29 the son of Jehoi'ada, saying, "Go, strike him down. 1
34 Benai'ah the son of Jehoi'ada went up, and struck 1
35 king put Benai'ah the son of Jehoi'ada over 1
46 the king commanded Benai'ah the son of Jehoi'ada; 1
4: 4 Benai'ah the son of Jehoi'ada was in command 1
2Kg 11: 4 Jehoi'ada sent and brought the captains 1
9 did according to all that Jehoi'ada . . commanded 1
9 each brought his men . . and came to Jehoi'ada 1
15 Jehoi'ada the priest commanded the captains 1
17 Jehoi'ada made a covenant between the LORD 1
12: 2 because Jehoi'ada the priest instructed him. 1
7 King Jeho'ash summoned Jehoi'ada . . and the other 1
9 Jehoi'ada the priest took a chest, and bored a hole 1
1Ch 11:22 Benai'ah the son of Jehoi'ada was a valiant man 1
24 did Benai'ah the son of Jehoi'ada, and won a name 1
12:27 prince Jehoi'ada, of the house of Aaron 1
18:17 Benai'ah the son of Jehoi'ada 1
27: 5 Benai'ah, the son of Jehoi'ada the priest, as chief; 1
34 was succeeded by Jehoi'ada the son of Benai'ah 1
2Ch 22:11 Jeho-shab'e-ath . . wife of Jehoi'ada the priest 1
23: 1 in the seventh year Jehoi'ada took courage 1
3 Jehoi'ada said to them, "Behold, the king's son! •
8 did according to all that Jehoi'ada the priest 1
8 for Jehoi'ada . . did not dismiss the divisions. 1
9 Jehoi'ada the priest delivered to the captains 1
11 Jehoi'ada and his sons anointed him, 1
14 Jehoi'ada the priest brought out the captains 1
16 Jehoi'ada made a covenant between himself 1
18 Jehoi'ada posted watchmen 1
24: 2 all the days of Jehoi'ada the priest. 1
3 Jehoi'ada got for him two wives, and he had sons 1
6 king summoned Jehoi'ada the chief, and said to him 1
12 king and Jehoi'ada gave it to those who had charge 1
14 the rest of the money before . . Jehoi'ada 1
14 continually all the days of Jehoi'ada. 1
15 Jehoi'ada grew old and full of days, and died; 1
17 Now after the death of Jehoi'ada 1
20 Zechari'ah the son of Jehoi'ada the priest; 1
22 kindness which Jehoi'ada . . had shown him 1
25 blood of the son of Jehoi'ada the priest 1
Neh 13:28 one of the sons of Jehoi'ada, the son of Eli'ashib 1
Jer 29:26 The LORD has made you priest instead of Jehoi'ada 1

Jehoiakim 1. יְהוֹיָקִים 2. Ἰωακίμ
2Kg 23:34 and changed his name to Jehoi'akim. 1
35 Jehoi'akim gave the silver and . . to Pharaoh 1
36 Jehoi'akim was 25 years old when he began to reign 1
24: 1 and Jehoi'akim became his servant three years; 1
5 rest of the deeds of Jehoi'akim, and all that he did 1
6 So Jehoi'akim slept with his fathers 1
19 according to all that Jehoi'akim had done. 1
1Ch 3:15 sons of Josi'ah . . the second Jehoi'akim 1
16 descendants of Jehoi'akim: Jeconi'ah his son 1
2Ch 36: 4 changed his name to Jehoi'akim; 1
5 Jehoi'akim was 25 . . when he began to reign 1
8 Now the rest of the acts of Jehoi'akim 1
Jer 1: 3 It came also in the days of Jehoi'akim 1
22:18 thus says the LORD concerning Jehoi'akim 1
24 though Coni'ah the son of Jehoi'akim, king of Judah 1
24: 1 Jeconi'ah the son of Jehoi'akim, king of Judah 1
25: 1 in the fourth year of Jehoi'akim the son of Josi'ah 1
26: 1 In the beginning of the reign of Jehoi'akim 1
21 And when King Jehoi'akim, with all his warriors 1
22 Then King Jehoi'akim sent to Egypt certain men 1
23 from Egypt and brought him to King Jehoi'akim 1
27:20 Jeconi'ah the son of Jehoi'akim, king of Judah 1
28: 4 Jeconi'ah the son of Jehoi'akim, king of Judah 1
35: 1 in the days of Jehoi'akim the son of Josi'ah 1
36: 1 In the fourth year of Jehoi'akim the son of Josi'ah 1
9 In the fifth year of Jehoi'akim the son of Josi'ah 1
28 which Jehoi'akim the king of Judah has burned. 1
29 And concerning Jehoi'akim king of Judah 1
30 the LORD concerning Jehoi'akim king of Judah 1
32 scroll which Jehoi'akim king of Judah had burned 1
37: 1 reigned instead of Coni'ah the son of Jehoi'akim. 1
45: 1 in the fourth year of Jehoi'akim the son of Josi'ah 1
46: 2 defeated in the fourth year of Jehoi'akim 1
52: 2 according to all that Jehoi'akim had done. 1
1Es 1:37 made Jehoiakim his brother king of Judea 2
38 Jehoiakim put the nobles in prison 2
39 Jehoiakim was 25 years old 2
42 the things that are reported about Jehoiakim •
Bar 1: 3 Jeconiah the son of Jehoiakim, king of Judah 2
7 Jehoiakim the high priest, the son of Hilkiah 2

Jehoiarib 1. יְהוֹיָרִיב
1Ch 9:10 Of the priests: Jedai'ah, Jehoi'arib, Jachin 1
24: 7 The first lot fell to Jehoi'arib 1

Jehonadab 1. יְהוֹנָדָב
2Kg 10:15 he met Jehon'adab the son of Rechab 1
15 Jehon'adab answered, "It is." Jehu said, "If it is 1
23 Jehu went . . with Jehon'adab the son of Rechab; 1

Jehonathan 1. יְהוֹנָתָן
2Ch 17: 8 the Levites . . Jehon'athan, Adoni'jah, Tobi'jah 1
Neh 12:18 of Bilgah, Sham'mu-a; of Shemai'ah, Jehon'athan; 1

Jehoram 1. יְהוֹרָם
1Kg 22:50 and Jeho'ram his son reigned in his stead. 1
2Kg 1:17 Jeho'ram, his brother, became king in his stead 1
17 became king . . in the second year of Jeho'ram 1
3: 1 Jeho'ram the son of Ahab became king over Israel 1
6 King Jeho'ram marched out of Sama'ria at that time 1
8 Jeho'ram answered, "By the way of the wilderness •
8:16 Jeho'ram the son of Jehosh'aphat, king of Judah 1
25 Ahazi'ah the son of Jeho'ram . . began to reign. 1
29 Ahazi'ah the son of Jeho'ram king of Judah went 1
9:15 King Joram had returned to be healed in Jezreel 1
12:18 gifts that Jehosh'aphat and Jeho'ram and Ahazi'ah 1
2Ch 17: 8 with these Levites, the priests . . Jeho'ram. 1
21: 1 Jeho'ram his son reigned in his stead. 1
3 but he gave the kingdom to Jeho'ram 1
4 Jeho'ram had ascended the throne of his father 1
5 Jeho'ram was 32 . . when he became king 1
9 Then Jeho'ram passed over with his commanders 1
16 LORD stirred up against Jeho'ram the anger 1
22: 1 Ahazi'ah the son of Jeho'ram . . reigned. 1
5 went with Jeho'ram . . to make war against Haz'ael 1
6 Ahazi'ah the son of Jeho'ram king of Judah 1
7 came there he went out with Jeho'ram to meet Jehu 1
11 Jeho-shab'e-ath, the daughter of King Jeho'ram 1

Jehoshabeath 1. יְהוֹשַׁבְעַת
2Ch 22:11 Jeho-shab'e-ath . . took Jo'ash . . and stole him away 1
11 Thus Jeho-shab'e-ath . . hid him from Athali'ah 1

Jehoshaphat 1. יְהוֹשָׁפָט 2. Ἰωσαφάτ
2Sm 8:16 Jehosh'aphat the son of Ahi'lud was recorder; 1
20:24 Jehosh'aphat the son of Ahi'lud was the recorder; 1
1Kg 4: 3 Jehosh'aphat the son of Ahi'lud was recorder; 1
17 Jehosh'aphat the son of Paru'ah, in Is'sachar; 1
15:24 and Jehosh'aphat his son reigned in his stead. 1
22: 2 Jehosh'aphat . . came down to the king of Israel. 1
4 he said to Jehosh'aphat, "Will you go with me 1
4 Jehosh'aphat said to the king of Israel, "I am as you 1
5 Jehosh'aphat said to the king of Israel 1
7 Jehosh'aphat said, "Is there not here another 1
8 the king of Israel said to Jehosh'aphat, "There is 1
8 Jehosh'aphat said, "Let not the king say so. 1
10 Now the king of Israel and Jehosh'aphat the king 1
18 the king of Israel said to Jehosh'aphat 1
29 the king of Israel and Jehosh'aphat . . went up 1
30 the king of Israel said to Jehosh'aphat 1
32 when the captains . . saw Jehosh'aphat, they said 1
32 to fight against him; and Jehosh'aphat cried out. 1
41 Jehosh'aphat . . began to reign over Judah 1
42 Jehosh'aphat was 35 years old when he began 1
44 Jehosh'aphat also made peace with . . Israel. 1
45 the rest of the acts of Jehosh'aphat, and his might 1
48 Jehosh'aphat made ships . . to go to Ophir for gold; 1
49 Ahazi'ah the son of Ahab said to Jehosh'aphat, "Let 1
49 but Jehosh'aphat was not willing. 1
50 Jehosh'aphat slept with his fathers 1
51 seventeenth year of Jehosh'aphat king of Judah 1
2Kg 1:17 second year of Jeho'ram the son of Jehosh'aphat 1
3: 1 In the eighteenth year of Jehosh'aphat 1
7 he went and sent word to Jehosh'aphat 1
11 Jehosh'aphat said, "Is there no prophet 1
12 Jehosh'aphat said, "The word of the LORD is 1
12 the king of Israel and Jehosh'aphat . . went down 1
14 were it not that I have regard for Jehosh'aphat 1
8:16 Jeho'ram the son of Jehosh'aphat, king of Judah 1
9: 2 look there for Jehu the son of Jehosh'aphat 1
14 Jehu the son of Jehosh'aphat the son of Nimshi 1
12:18 gifts that Jehosh'aphat and Jeho'ram and Ahazi'ah 1
1Ch 3:10 descendants of Solomon . . Jehosh'aphat his son 1
18:15 Jehosh'aphat the son of Ahi'lud was recorder; 1
2Ch 17: 1 Jehosh'aphat his son reigned in his stead 1
3 The LORD was with Jehosh'aphat 1
5 all Judah brought tribute to Jehosh'aphat; 1
10 they made no war against Jehosh'aphat. 1
11 Philistines brought Jehosh'aphat presents 1
12 Jehosh'aphat grew steadily greater. 1
18: 1 Now Jehosh'aphat had great riches and honor; 1
3 Ahab . . said to Jehosh'aphat king of Judah 1
4 Jehosh'aphat said to the king of Israel 1
6 Jehosh'aphat said, "Is there not here another 1
7 the king of Israel said to Jehosh'aphat 1
7 Jehosh'aphat said, "Let not the king say so. 1
9 king of Israel and Jehosh'aphat the king of Judah 1
17 the king of Israel said to Jehosh'aphat 1
28 king of Israel and Jehosh'aphat the king of Judah 1
29 the king of Israel said to Jehosh'aphat 1
31 when the captains . . saw Jehosh'aphat, they said 1
31 Jehosh'aphat cried out, and the LORD helped him. 1
19: 1 Jehosh'aphat . . returned in safety to his house 1
2 Jehu . . said to King Jehosh'aphat 1
4 Jehosh'aphat dwelt at Jerusalem; 1
8 Jehosh'aphat appointed certain Levites 1
20: 1 came against Jehosh'aphat for battle. 1
2 Some men came and told Jehosh'aphat 1
3 Then Jehosh'aphat feared, and set himself to seek 1
5 Jehosh'aphat stood in the assembly of Judah 1
15 Hearken, all Judah . . and King Jehosh'aphat 1
18 Then Jehosh'aphat bowed his head 1
20 as they went out, Jehosh'aphat stood and said 1
25 When Jehosh'aphat and his people came to take 1
27 Jehosh'aphat at their head 1
30 the realm of Jehosh'aphat was quiet 1
31 Thus Jehosh'aphat reigned over Judah. 1
34 Now the rest of the acts of Jehosh'aphat 1
35 Jehosh'aphat king of Judah joined with Ahazi'ah 1
37 Elie'zer . . prophesied against Jehosh'aphat 1
21: 1 Jehosh'aphat slept with his fathers 1
2 He had brothers, the sons of Jehosh'aphat 1
2 sons of Jehosh'aphat king of Judah. 1
12 not walked in the ways of Jehosh'aphat 1
22: 9 He is the grandson of Jehosh'aphat 1
Jol 3: 2 and bring them down to the valley of Jehosh'aphat 1
12 and come up to the valley of Jehosh'aphat; 1
Mat 1: 8 Asa the father of Jehosh'aphat 2
8 and Jehosh'aphat the father of Joram 2

Jehosheba 1. יְהוֹשֶׁבַע
2Kg 11: 2 Jehosh'eba . . took Jo'ash the son of Ahazi'ah 1

Jehozabad 1. יְהוֹזָבָד
2Kg 12:21 It was Jo'zacar . . and Jeho'zabad..who struck him 1
1Ch 26: 4 O'bed-e'dom had sons . . Jehoz'abad the second, Jo'ah 1
2Ch 17:18 Jeho'zabad with a 180,000 armed for war. 1
24:26 who conspired against him were . . Jeho'zabad 1

Jehozadak 1. יְהוֹצָדָק
1Ch 6:14 Azari'ah of Serai'ah, Serai'ah of Jehoz'adak; 1
15 Jehoz'adak went into exile when the LORD sent 1
Hag 1: 1 to Joshua the son of Jehoz'adak, the high priest 1
12 Joshua the son of Jehoz'adak, the high priest 1
14 the spirit of Joshua the son of Jehoz'adak 1
2: 2 to Joshua the son of Jehoz'adak, the high priest 1
4 take courage, O Joshua, son of Jehoz'adak 1
Zec 6:11 of Joshua, the son of Jehoz'adak, the high priest; 1

Jehu 1. יֵהוּא 2. Ἰού
1Kg 16: 1 word of the LORD came to Jehu . . against Ba'asha 1
7 the word of the LORD came by the prophet Jehu 1
12 he spoke against Ba'asha by Jehu the prophet 1
19:16 Jehu the son of Nimshi you shall anoint to be king 1
17 him who escapes from . . Haz'ael shall Jehu slay; 1
17 him who escapes from . . Jehu shall Eli'sha slay. 1
2Kg 9: 2 look there for Jehu the son of Jehosh'aphat 1
5 And Jehu said, "To which of us all?" And he said, 1
11 When Jehu came out to the servants of his master 1
13 blew the trumpet, and proclaimed, "Jehu is king. 1
14 Thus Jehu . . conspired against Joram. 1
15 Jehu said, "If this is your mind, then let no one slip 1
16 Jehu mounted his chariot, and went to Jezreel 1
17 he spied the company of Jehu as he came, and said 1
18 And Jehu said, "What have you to do with peace? 1
19 Jehu answered, "What have you to do with peace? 1
20 is like the driving of Jehu the son of Nimshi; 1
21 set out, each in his chariot, and went to meet Jehu 1
22 when Joram saw Jehu, he said, "Is it peace, Jehu? 1
22 when Joram saw Jehu, he said, "Is it peace, Jehu? 1
24 Jehu drew his bow . . and shot Joram 1
25 Jehu said to Bidkar his aide, "Take him up •
27 And Jehu pursued him, and said, "Shoot him also"; 1
30 When Jehu came to Jezreel, Jez'ebel heard of it; 1
31 as Jehu entered the gate, she said, "Is it peace 1
10: 1 Jehu wrote letters, and sent them to Sama'ria 1
5 So he who was over the palace, and . . sent to Jehu 1
11 Jehu slew all that remained of the house of Ahab 1
13 Jehu met the kinsmen of Ahazi'ah . . and he said 1
15 Jehu said, "If it is, give me your hand. 2
15 And Jehu took him up with him into the chariot. •
18 Jehu assembled all the people, and said to them 1
18 served Ba'al . . but Jehu will serve him much. 1
19 Jehu did it . . in order to destroy the worshipers 1
20 Jehu ordered, "Sanctify a solemn assembly 1
21 Jehu sent throughout all Israel; 1
23 Jehu went into the house of Ba'al with Jehon'adab 1
24 Now Jehu had stationed 80 men outside 1
25 Jehu said to the guard and to the officers, "Go 1
28 Thus Jehu wiped out Ba'al from Israel. 1
29 Jehu did not turn aside from the sins of Jerobo'am 1
30 the LORD said to Jehu, "Because you have done well 1
31 Jehu was not careful to walk in the law of the LORD 1
34 Now the rest of the acts of Jehu, and all that he did 1

35 Jehu slept with his fathers, and they buried him 1
36 time that Jehu reigned over Israel in Sama'ria 1
12: 1 In the seventh year of Jehu Jeho'ash began 1
13: 1 Jeho'ahaz the son of Jehu began to reign 1
14: 8 to Jeho'ash the son of Jeho'ahaz, son of Jehu 1
15:12 the promise of the LORD which he gave to Jehu 1
1Ch 2:38 Obed was the father of Jehu, and Jehu of Azari'ah. 1
38 Obed was the father of Jehu, and Jehu of Azari'ah. 1
4:35 Jo'el, Jehu the son of Joshibi'ah, son of Serai'ah 1
12: 3 Ber'acah, Jehu of An'athoth 1
2Ch 19: 2 Jehu the son of Hana'ni the seer went out 1
20:34 written in the chronicles of Jehu 1
22: 7 came there he went out with Jeho'ram to meet Jehu 1
8 when Jehu was executing judgment 1
9 Ahazi'ah . . was brought to Jehu and put to death. 1
25:17 Jo'ash the son of Jeho'ahaz, son of Jehu, 1
Hos 1: 4 a little while, and I will punish the house of Jehu 1

Jehubbah 1. יְחֻבָּה
1Ch 7:34 sons of Shemer . . Rohgah, Jehub'bah, and Aram. 1

Jehucal 1. יְהוּכַל
Jer 37: 3 King Zedeki'ah sent Jehu'cal the son of Shelemi'ah 1

Jehud 1. יְהֻד
Jos 19:45 Jehud, Bene-be'rak, Gath-rim'mon 1

Jehudi 1. יְהוּדִי
Jer 36:14 all the princes sent Jehu'di the son of Nethani'ah 1
21 Then the king sent Jehu'di to get the scroll 1
21 and Jehu'di read it to the king and all the princes 1
23 As Jehu'di read three or four columns 1

Jehuel 1. יְחוּאֵל
2Ch 29:14 of the sons of Heman, Jehu'el and Shim'e-i; 1

Jeiel 1. יְעִיאֵל
1Ch 5: 7 his kinsmen . . the chief, Je-i'el, and Zechari'ah 1
8:29 Je-i'el the father of Gibeon dwelt in Gibeon *
9:35 In Gibeon dwelt the father of Gibeon, Je-i'el 1
11:44 Shama and Je-i'el the sons of Hotham the Aro'erite 1
15:18 and the gatekeepers O'bed-e'dom and Je-i'el. 1
21 Miknei'ah, O'bed-e'dom, Je-i'el, and Azazi'ah 1
16: 5 second to him were Zechari'ah, Je-i'el, Shemi'ramoth 1
5 second to him . . Benai'ah, O'bed-e'dom, and Je-i'el 1
2Ch 20:14 Benai'ah, son of Je-i'el, son of Mattani'ah 1
26:11 in the muster made by Je-i'el the secretary 1
35: 9 Hashabi'ah and Je-i'el and Jo'zabad 1
Ezr 10:43 of Nebo: Je-i'el, Mattithi'ah, Zabad, Zebi'na, Jaddai 1

Jekabzeel 1. יְקַבְצְאֵל
Neh 11:25 some . . lived . . in Jekab'zeel and its villages 1

Jekameam 1. יְקַמְעָם
1Ch 23:19 sons of Hebron . . and Jekame'am the fourth. 1
24:23 sons of Hebron . . Jeka-me'am the fourth. 1

Jekamiah 1. יְקַמְיָה
1Ch 2:41 Shallum . . father of Jekami'ah, and Jekami'ah 1
41 father of Jeka-mi'ah, and Jekami'ah of Eli'shama. 1
3:18 Shenaz'zar, Jekami'ah, Hosh'ama, and Nedabi'ah; 1

Jekuthiel 1. יְקוּתִיאֵל
1Ch 4:18 wife bore . . Jeku'thiel the father of Zano'ah. 1

Jemimah 1. יְמִימָה
Job 42:14 he called the name of the first Jemi'mah; 1

Jemuel 1. יְמוּאֵל
Gen 46:10 The sons of Simeon: Jemu'el, Jamin, Ohad, Jachin 1
Exd 6:15 The sons of Simeon: Jemu'el, Jamin, Ohad, Jachin 1

Jephthah 1. יִפְתָּח 2. Ἰεφθάε
Jdg 11: 1 Now Jephthah the Gileadite was a mighty warrior 1
1 of a harlot. Gilead was the father of Jephthah. 1
2 sons grew up, they thrust Jephthah out, and said 1
3 Jephthah fled from his brothers, and dwelt 1
3 worthless fellows collected round Jephthah 1
5 of Gilead went to bring Jephthah from the land 1
6 they said to Jephthah, "Come and be our leader 1
7 Jephthah said to the elders of Gilead, "Did you not 1
8 the elders of Gilead said to Jephthah, "That is why 1
9 Jephthah said to the elders of Gilead 1
10 the elders of Gilead said to Jephthah, "The LORD 1
11 Jephthah went with the elders of Gilead 1
11 Jephthah spoke all his words before the LORD 1
12 Then Jephthah sent messengers to the king 1
13 king . . answered the messengers of Jephthah 1
14 Jephthah sent messengers again to the king 1
15 Thus says Jephthah: Israel did not take away 1
28 the king . . did not heed the message of Jephthah 1
29 the Spirit of the LORD came upon Jephthah 1
30 Jephthah made a vow to the LORD, and said, "If thou 1
32 Jephthah crossed over to the Ammonites to fight 1
34 Then Jephthah came to his home at Mizpah; 1
40 lament the daughter of Jephthah the Gileadite 1
12: 1 and they crossed to Zaphon and said to Jephthah 1
2 Jephthah said to them, "I and my people had a great 1
4 Then Jephthah gathered all the men of Gilead 1
7 Jephthah judged Israel six years. 1
7 six years. Then Jephthah the Gileadite died 1
1Sm 12:11 the LORD sent Jerubba'al and Barak, and Jephthah 1
Heb 11:32 to tell of Gideon, Barak, Samson, Jephthah, of David 2

Jephunneh 1. יְפֻנֶּה 2. Ιεφοννη
Num13: 6 from the tribe of Judah, Caleb . . of Jephun'neh; 1
14: 6 Joshua . . of Nun and Caleb the son of Jephun'neh 1
30 except Caleb the son of Jephun'neh and Joshua 1
38 Joshua . . of Nun and Caleb the son of Jephun'neh 1
26:65 except Caleb the son of Jephun'neh 1
32:12 except Caleb the son of Jephun'neh the Ken'izzite 1
34:19 Of the tribe of Judah, Caleb the son of Jephun'neh. 1
Deu 1:36 except Caleb the son of Jephun'neh; he shall see it 1
Jos 14: 6 and Caleb the son of Jephun'neh the Ken'izzite 1
13 and he gave Hebron to Caleb the son of Jephun'neh 1
14 of Caleb the son of Jephun'neh the Ken'izzite 1
15:13 he gave to Caleb the son of Jephun'neh a portion 1
21:12 had been given to Caleb the son of Jephun'neh 1
1Ch 4:15 Caleb the son of Jephun'neh 1
6:56 they gave to Caleb the son of Jephun'neh. 1
7:38 The sons of Jether: Jephun'neh, Pispa, and Ara. 1
Sir 46: 7 he and Caleb the son of Jephunneh 2

Jerah 1. יֶרַח
Gen 10:26 father of Almo'dad, Sheleph, Hazarma'veth, Jerah 1
1Ch 1:20 father of Almo'dad, Sheleph, Hazarma'veth, Jerah 1

Jerahmeel 1. יְרַחְמְאֵל
1Ch 2: 9 sons of Hezron . . Jerah'meel, Ram, and Chelu'bai. 1
25 The sons of Jerah'meel, the first-born of Hezron 1
26 Jerah'meel also had another wife, whose name was 1
27 The sons of Ram, the first-born of Jerah'meel: Ma'az 1
33 These were the descendants of Jerah'meel. 1
42 The sons of Caleb the brother of Jerah'meel 1
24:29 Of Kish, the sons of Kish: Jerah'meel. 1
Jer 36:26 And the king commanded Jerah'meel the king's son 1

Jerahmeelite 1. יְרַחְמְאֵלִי
1Sm 27:10 Against the Negeb of the Jerah'meelites 1
30:29 in Racal, in the cities of the Jerah'meelites 1

Jered 1. יֶרֶד
1Ch 4:18 his Jewish wife bore Jered the father of Gedor 1

Jeremai 1. יְרֵמַי 2. Ἰερεμίας
Ezr 10:33 of Hashum . . Jer'emai, Manas'seh, and Shim'e-i. 1
1Es 9:34 Of the sons of Bani: Jeremai, Maadai, Amram, Joel 2

Jeremiah 1. יִרְמְיָהוּ 2. Ἰερεμίας 3. Hieremia
2Kg 23:31 was Hamu'tal the daughter of Jeremiah of Libnah. 1
24:18 was Hamu'tal the daughter of Jeremiah of Libnah. 1
1Ch 5:24 heads of their fathers' houses . . Jeremiah 1
12: 4 Jeremiah, Jaha'ziel, Joha'nan, Joz'abad of Gede'rah 1
10 Mishman'nah fourth, Jeremiah fifth 1
13 Jeremiah tenth, Mach'bannai eleventh. 1
2Ch 35:25 Jeremiah also uttered a lament for Josi'ah; 1
36:12 not humble himself before Jeremiah the prophet 1
21 to fulfil the word of the LORD by . . Jeremiah 1
22 that the word of the LORD by the mouth of Jeremiah 1
Ezr 1: 1 that the word of the LORD by the mouth of Jeremiah 1
Neh 10: 2 Serai'ah, Azari'ah, Jeremiah 1
12: 1 priests and the Levites . . Serai'ah, Jeremiah, Ezra 1
12 heads of fathers' houses: of . . Jeremiah, Hanani'ah; 1
34 Judah, Benjamin, Shemai'ah, and Jeremiah 1
Jer 1: 1 The words of Jeremiah, the son of Hilki'ah 1
11 came to me, saying, "Jeremiah, what do you see? 1
7: 1 The word that came to Jeremiah from the LORD 1
11: 1 The word that came to Jeremiah from the LORD 1
14: 1 The word of the LORD which came to Jeremiah 1
18: 1 The word that came to Jeremiah from the LORD 1
18 Come, let us make plots against Jeremiah 1
19:14 Then Jeremiah came from Topheth 1
20: 1 heard Jeremiah prophesying these things. 1
2 Then Pashhur beat Jeremiah the prophet 1
3 On the morrow, when Pashhur released Jeremiah 1
3 Jeremiah said to him, "The LORD does not call 1
21: 1 the word which came to Jeremiah from the LORD 1
3 Then Jeremiah said to them 1
24: 3 the LORD said to me, "What do you see, Jeremiah? 1
25: 1 The word that came to Jeremiah 1
2 which Jeremiah the prophet spoke to all 1
13 written in this book, which Jeremiah prophesied 1
26: 7 the people heard Jeremiah speaking these words 1
8 And when Jeremiah had finished speaking 1
9 And all the people gathered about Jeremiah 1
12 Then Jeremiah spoke to all the princes 1
20 prophesied . . in words like those of Jeremiah. 1
24 Ahi'kam the son of Shaphan was with Jeremiah 1
27: 1 this word came to Jeremiah from the LORD. 1
28: 5 Then the prophet Jeremiah spoke to Hanani'ah 1
6 prophet Jeremiah said, "Amen! May the LORD do so; 1
10 took the yoke-bars from the neck of Jeremiah 1
11 But Jeremiah the prophet went his way. 1
12 from off the neck of Jeremiah the prophet 1
12 the word of the LORD came to Jeremiah 1
15 And Jeremiah the prophet said to . . Hanani'ah 1
29: 1 the letter which Jeremiah the prophet sent 1
27 why have you not rebuked Jeremiah of An'athoth 1
29 read this letter in the hearing of Jeremiah 1
30 Then the word of the LORD came to Jeremiah 1
30: 1 The word that came to Jeremiah from the LORD 1
32: 1 The word that came to Jeremiah from the LORD 1
2 and Jeremiah the prophet was shut up in the court 1
6 Jeremiah said, "The word of the LORD came to me 1
26 The word of the LORD came to Jeremiah 1
33: 1 word of the LORD came to Jeremiah a second time 1
19 The word of the LORD came to Jeremiah 1
23 The word of the LORD came to Jeremiah 1
34: 1 The word which came to Jeremiah from the LORD 1
6 Then Jeremiah the prophet spoke all these words 1
8 The word which came to Jeremiah from the LORD 1
12 word of the LORD came to Jeremiah from the LORD 1
35: 1 The word which came to Jeremiah from the LORD 1
3 So I took Ja-azani'ah the son of Jeremiah 1
12 Then the word of the LORD came to Jeremiah 1
18 to the house of the Re'chabites Jeremiah said 1
36: 1 this word came to Jeremiah from the LORD 1
4 Then Jeremiah called Baruch the son of Neri'ah 1
4 wrote upon a scroll at the dictation of Jeremiah 1
5 And Jeremiah ordered Baruch, saying 1
8 did all that Jeremiah the prophet ordered him 1
10 read the words of Jeremiah from the scroll 1
19 Go and hide, you and Jeremiah 1
26 Baruch the secretary and Jeremiah the prophet 1
27 which Baruch wrote at Jeremiah's dictation 1
27 the word of the LORD came to Jeremiah 1
32 Then Jeremiah took another scroll 1
32 who wrote on it at the dictation of Jeremiah 1
37: 2 which he spoke through Jeremiah the prophet. 1
3 Zedeki'ah sent . . to Jeremiah the prophet, saying 1
4 Now Jeremiah was still going in and out among 1
6 the word of the LORD came to Jeremiah the prophet 1
12 Jeremiah set out from Jerusalem to go to the land 1
13 seized Jeremiah the prophet, saying 1
14 And Jeremiah said, "It is false; I am not deserting 1
14 and seized Jeremiah and brought him 1
15 And the princes were enraged at Jeremiah 1
16 When Jeremiah had come to the dungeon cells 1
17 any word from the LORD?" Jeremiah said, "There is. 1
18 Jeremiah also said to King Zedeki'ah 1
21 committed Jeremiah to the court of the guard; 1
21 Jeremiah remained in the court of the guard. 1
38: 1 heard the words that Jeremiah was saying 1
6 they took Jeremiah and cast him into the cistern 1
6 and Jeremiah sank in the mire. 1
6 the guard, letting Jeremiah down by ropes. 1
7 that they had put Jeremiah into the cistern 1
9 have done evil in all that they did to Jeremiah 1
10 and lift Jeremiah the prophet out of the cistern 1
11 he let down to Jeremiah in the cistern by ropes. 1
12 Then E'bed-mel'ech the Ethiopian said to Jeremiah 1
12 your armpits and the ropes." Jeremiah did so. 1
13 Then they drew Jeremiah up with ropes 1
13 And Jeremiah remained in the court of the guard. 1
14 King Zedeki'ah sent for Jeremiah the prophet 1
14 The king said to Jeremiah 1
15 Jeremiah said to Zedeki'ah, "If I tell you 1
16 Then King Zedeki'ah swore secretly to Jeremiah 1
17 Then Jeremiah said to Zedeki'ah 1
19 King Zedeki'ah said to Jeremiah 1
20 Jeremiah said, "You shall not be given to them. 1
24 Then Zedeki'ah said to Jeremiah, "Let no one know 1
27 all the princes came to Jeremiah and asked him 1
28 Jeremiah remained in the court of the guard 1
39:11 Babylon gave command concerning Jeremiah 1
14 and took Jeremiah from the court of the guard. 1
15 The word of the LORD came to Jeremiah 1
40: 1 The word that came to Jeremiah from the LORD 1
2 The captain of the guard took Jeremiah and said 1
6 Then Jeremiah went to Gedali'ah the son of Ahi'kam 1
42: 2 and said to Jeremiah the prophet 1
4 Jeremiah the prophet said to them, "I have heard 1
5 Then they said to Jeremiah 1
7 the word of the LORD came to Jeremiah. 1
43: 1 Jeremiah finished speaking to all the people 1
2 and all the insolent men said to Jeremiah 1
6 also Jeremiah the prophet and Baruch 1
8 word of the LORD came to Jeremiah in Tah'panhes 1
44: 1 The word that came to Jeremiah 1
15 in the land of Egypt, answered Jeremiah 1
20 Then Jeremiah said to all the people 1
24 Jeremiah said to all the people and all the women 1
45: 1 The word that Jeremiah the prophet spoke 1
1 words in a book at the dictation of Jeremiah 1
46: 1 The word of the LORD which came to Jeremiah 1
13 The word which the LORD spoke to Jeremiah 1
47: 1 The word of the LORD that came to Jeremiah 1
49:34 The word of the LORD that came to Jeremiah 1
50: 1 land of the Chalde'ans, by Jeremiah the prophet 1
51:59 The word which Jeremiah the prophet commanded 1
60 Jeremiah wrote in a book all the evil 1
61 And Jeremiah said to Serai'ah 1
64 Thus far are the words of Jeremiah. 1
52: 1 Hamu'tal the daughter of Jeremiah of Libnah. 1
Dan 9: 2 word of the LORD to Jeremiah the prophet 1
Mat 2:17 what was spoken by the prophet Jeremiah 2
16:14 others say Eli'jah, and others Jeremiah 2

27: 9 spoken by the prophet Jeremiah, saying 2
1Es 1:28 did not heed the words of Jeremiah the prophet 2
32 Jeremiah the prophet lamented for Josiah 2
47 words that were spoken by Jeremiah the prophet 2
57 the word of the Lord by the mouth of Jeremiah 2
2: 1 the word of the Lord by the mouth of Jeremiah 2
2Es 2:18 send you help, my servants Isaiah and Jeremiah. 2
Sir 49: 6 according to the word of Jeremiah. 2
LJr 1: 1 A copy of a letter which Jeremiah sent 2
2Mc 2: 1 Jeremiah the prophet ordered . . 2
5 Jeremiah came and found a cave 2
7 When Jeremiah learned of it 2
15:14 Jeremiah, the prophet of God. 2
15 Jeremiah stretched out his right hand 2

Jeremiel 1. Hieremihel

2Es 4:36 Jeremiel the archangel answered them and said 1

Jeremoth 1. יְרֵמוֹת 2. Ιαριμωθ 3. Ιερεμωθ

1Ch 7: 8 sons of Becher . . Eli-o-e'nai, Omri, Jer'emoth 1
8:14 Ahi'o, Shashak, and Jer'emoth. 1
23:23 The sons of Mushi: Mahli, Eder, and Jer'emoth, three. 1
25:22 fifteenth, to Jer'emoth, his sons and his brethren 1
27:19 for Naph'tali, Jer'emoth the son of Az'riel; 1
Ezr 10:26 of Elam . . Abdi, Jer'emoth, and Eli'jah. 1
27 of Zattu . . Jer'emoth, Zabad, and Azi'za. 1
29 of Bani were . . Jashub, She'al, and Jer'emoth. 1
1Es 9:27 Jehiel and Abdi, and Jeremoth and Elijah. 3
28 Jeremoth, and Zabad and Zerdaiah. 2
30 Adaiah, Jashub, and Sheal and Jeremoth. 3

Jeriah 1. יְרִיָּהוּ

1Ch 23:19 sons of Hebron: Jeri'ah the chief, Amari'ah 1
24:23 sons of Hebron: Jeri'ah the chief, Amari'ah 1

Jeribai 1. יְרִיבַי

1Ch 11:46 Jer'ibai, and Joshavi'ah, the sons of El'na-am 1

Jericho 1. יְרִיחוֹ 2. Ιερεχος 3. Ἰεριχώ

Num22: 1 encamped in the plains of Moab . . at Jericho. 1
26: 3 in the plains of Moab by the Jordan at Jericho 1
63 plains of Moab by the Jordan at Jericho. 1
31:12 on the plains of Moab by the Jordan at Jericho. 1
33:48 in the plains of Moab by the Jordan at Jericho; 1
50 in the plains of Moab by the Jordan at Jericho 1
34:15 beyond the Jordan at Jericho eastward 1
35: 1 in the plains of Moab by the Jordan at Jericho 1
36:13 in the plains of Moab by the Jordan at Jericho. 1
Deu 32:49 Nebo . . in the land of Moab, opposite Jericho; 1
34: 1 top of Pisgah, which is opposite Jericho. 1
3 valley of Jericho the city of palm trees 1
Jos 2: 1 saying, "Go, view the land, especially Jericho. 1
2 And it was told the king of Jericho, "Behold 1
3 Then the king of Jericho sent to Rahab, saying 1
3:16 and the people passed over opposite Jericho. 1
4:13 passed . . for battle, to the plains of Jericho. 1
19 in Gilgal on the east border of Jericho. 1
5:10 kept the passover . . in the plains of Jericho. 1
13 When Joshua was by Jericho, he lifted up his eyes 1
6: 1 Jericho was shut up from within and from without 1
2 I have given into your hand Jericho, with its king 1
25 messengers whom Joshua sent to spy out Jericho. 1
26 that rises up and rebuilds this city, Jericho. 1
7: 2 Joshua sent men from Jericho to Ai . . and said 1
8: 2 shall do to Ai . . as you did to Jericho and its king; 1
9: 3 heard what Joshua had done to Jericho and to Ai 1
10: 1 doing . . as he had done to Jericho and its king 1
28 he did to . . as he had done to the king of Jericho. 1
30 he did to . . as he had done to the king of Jericho. 1
12: 9 the king of Jericho, one, the king of Ai 1
13:32 of Moab, beyond the Jordan east of Jericho. 1
16: 1 allotment . . went from the Jordan by Jericho 1
1 allotment . . went . . east of the waters of Jericho 1
1 up from Jericho into the hill country to Bethel; 1
7 then it goes down . . and touches Jericho 1
18:12 boundary goes up the shoulder north of Jericho 1
21 cities of the tribe . . were Jericho, Beth-hoglah 1
20: 8 And beyond the Jordan east of Jericho 1
24:11 And you went over the Jordan and came to Jericho 1
11 and the men of Jericho fought against you 1
2Sm 10: 5 Remain at Jericho until your beards have grown 1
1Kg 16:34 In his days Hi'el of Bethel built Jericho; 1
2Kg 2: 4 tarry here . . the LORD has sent me to Jericho. 1
4 So they came to Jericho. 1
5 prophets who were at Jericho drew near to Eli'sha 1
15 the sons of the prophets who were at Jericho saw 1
18 they came back to him, while he tarried at Jericho 1
25: 5 and overtook him in the plains of Jericho; 1
1Ch 6:78 at Jericho, on the east side of the Jordan 1
19: 5 Remain at Jericho until your beards have grown 1
2Ch 28:15 brought them to their kinsfolk at Jericho 1
Ezr 2:34 sons of Jericho, 345. 1
Neh 3: 2 next to him the men of Jericho built. 1
7:36 sons of Jericho, 345. 1
Jer 39: 5 and overtook Zedeki'ah in the plains of Jericho; 1
52: 8 and overtook Zedeki'ah in the plains of Jericho; 1
Mat 20:29 as they went out of Jericho 3
Mrk 10:46 they came to Jericho 3
46 as he was leaving Jericho with his disciples 3
Lke 10:30 A man was going down from Jerusalem to Jericho 3
18:35 As he drew near to Jericho 3
19: 1 He entered Jericho and was passing through. 3
Heb 11:30 By faith the walls of Jericho fell down 3
1Es 5:22 The sons of Jericho, 345 2
Jdt 4: 4 Kona and Beth-horon and Belmain and Jericho 3
Sir 24:14 like rose plants in Jericho 3
1Mc 9:50 the fortress in Jericho, and Emmaus 3
16:11 appointed governor over the plain of Jericho 3
14 he went down to Jericho with Mattathias and Judas 3
2Mc 12:15 overthrew Jericho in the days of Joshua 3

Jeriel 1. יְרִיאֵל

1Ch 7: 2 sons of Tola: Uzzi, Rephai'ah, Je'ri-el, Jah'mai, Ibsam 1

Jerijah 1. יְרִיָּהוּ

1Ch 26:31 Jeri'jah was chief of the He'bronites 1

Jerimoth 1. יְרִימוֹת

1Ch 7: 7 sons of Bela: Ezbon, Uzzi, Uz'ziel, Jer'imoth, and Iri 1
12: 5 Elu'zai, Jer'imoth, Beali'ah, Shemari'ah, Shephati'ah 1
24:30 The sons of Mushi: Mahli, Eder, and Jer'i-moth. . 1
25: 4 sons of Heman . . Shebu'el, and Jer'imoth, Hanani'ah 1
2Ch 11:18 took as wife Ma'halath the daughter of Jer'imoth 1
31:13 As'ahel, Jer'imoth, Jo'zabad . . were overseers 1

Jerioth 1. יְרִיעוֹת

1Ch 2:18 Caleb . . had children . . by Jer'ioth; 1

Jeroboam 1. יָרָבְעָם 2. Ιεροβοαμ

1Kg 11:26 Jerobo'am . . lifted up his hand against the king. 1
28 The man Jerobo'am was very able 1
29 at that time, when Jerobo'am went out of Jerusalem 1
31 he said to Jerobo'am, "Take for yourself ten pieces; 1
40 Solomon sought therefore to kill Jerobo'am; 1
40 Jerobo'am arose, and fled into Egypt, to Shishak 1
12: 2 when Jerobo'am the son of Nebat heard of it 1
2 then Jerobo'am returned from Egypt. 1
3 Jerobo'am and all the assembly of Israel came 1
12 Jerobo'am and all the people came to Rehobo'am 1
15 the LORD spoke . . to Jerobo'am the son of Nebat. 1
20 when all Israel heard that Jerobo'am had returned 1
25 Jerobo'am built Shechem in the hill country 1
26 Jerobo'am said in his heart 1
32 Jerobo'am appointed a feast on the fifteenth day 1
13: 1 Jerobo'am was standing by the altar 1
4 Jerobo'am stretched out his hand from the altar 1
33 Jerobo'am did not turn from his evil way 1
34 this thing became sin to the house of Jerobo'am 1
14: 1 Abi'jah the son of Jerobo'am fell sick. 1
2 Jerobo'am said to his wife, "Arise 1
2 it be not known that you are the wife of Jerobo'am 1
4 Jerobo'am's wife did so; she arose, and went 1
5 the wife of Jerobo'am is coming to inquire of you 1
6 Come in, wife of Jerobo'am; why do you pretend 1
7 Go, tell Jerobo'am, 'Thus says the LORD 1
10 I will bring evil upon the house of Jerobo'am 1
10 and will cut off from Jerobo'am every male 1
10 and will utterly consume the house of Jerobo'am 1
11 Any one belonging to Jerobo'am who dies 1
13 he only of Jerobo'am shall come to the grave 1
13 something pleasing . . in the house of Jerobo'am. 1
14 the house of Jerobo'am today. And henceforth 1
16 give Israel up because of the sins of Jerobo'am 1
17 Jerobo'am's wife arose, and departed 1
19 the rest of the acts of Jerobo'am . . are written 1
20 the time that Jerobo'am reigned was 22 years; 1
30 there was war between Rehobo'am and Jerobo'am 1
15: 1 in the . . year of King Jerobo'am the son of Nebat 1
6 Rehobo'am and Jerobo'am all the days of his life. 1
7 there was war between Abi'jam and Jerobo'am. 1
9 In the twentieth year of Jerobo'am king of Israel 1
25 Nadab the son of Jerobo'am began to reign 1
29 he killed all the house of Jerobo'am; 1
29 he left to . . Jerobo'am not one that breathed 1
30 the sins of Jerobo'am which he sinned and which he 1
34 and walked in the way of Jerobo'am and in his sin 1
16: 2 and you have walked in the way of Jerobo'am 1
3 I will make your house like the house of Jerobo'am 1
7 in being like the house of Jerobo'am 1
19 his sins . . walking in the way of Jerobo'am 1
26 For he walked in all the way of Jerobo'am 1
31 to walk in the sins of Jerobo'am the son of Nebat 1
21:22 I will make your house like the house of Jerobo'am 1
22:52 walked . . in the way of Jerobo'am the son of Nebat 1
2Kg 3: 3 he clung to the sin of Jerobo'am the son of Nebat 1
9: 9 make the house of Ahab like the house of Jerobo'am 1
10:29 Jehu did not turn aside from the sins of Jerobo'am 1
31 he did not turn from the sins of Jerobo'am 1
13: 2 the sins of Jerobo'am the son of Nebat 1
6 depart from the sins of the house of Jerobo'am 1
11 from all the sins of Jerobo'am the son of Nebat 1
13 Jo'ash slept . . and Jerobo'am sat upon his throne; 1
14:16 Jeho'ash slept . . and Jerobo'am his son reigned 1
23 Jerobo'am . . began to reign in Sama'ria 1
24 he did not depart from all the sins of Jerobo'am 1
27 saved . . by the hand of Jerobo'am the son of Jo'ash. 1
28 rest of the acts of Jerobo'am and all that he did 1
29 And Jerobo'am slept with his fathers, the kings 1
15: 1 In the 27th year of Jerobo'am king of Israel 1
8 Zechari'ah the son of Jerobo'am reigned over 1
9 depart from the sins of Jerobo'am the son of Nebat 1
18 from all the sins of Jerobo'am the son of Nebat 1
24 away from the sins of Jerobo'am the son of Nebat 1
28 depart from the sins of Jerobo'am the son of Nebat 1
17:21 When . . they made Jerobo'am the son of Nebat king. 1
21 Jerobo'am drove Israel from following the LORD 1
22 Israel walked in all the sins which Jerobo'am did; 1
23:15 high place erected by Jerobo'am the son of Nebat 1
1Ch 5:17 enrolled . . in the days of Jerobo'am 1
2Ch 9:29 concerning Jerobo'am the son of Nebat? 1
10: 2 when Jerobo'am the son of Nebat heard of it 1
2 then Jerobo'am returned from Egypt. 1
3 Jerobo'am and all Israel came and said 1
12 Jerobo'am and all the people came to Rehobo'am 1
15 spoke by Ahi'jah . . to Jerobo'am the son of Nebat. 1
11: 4 returned and did not go against Jerobo'am. 1
14 Jerobo'am and his sons cast them out 1
12:15 continual wars between Rehobo'am and Jerobo'am. 1
13: 1 In the eighteenth year of King Jerobo'am 1
2 Now there was war between Abi'jah and Jerobo'am. 1
3 Jerobo'am drew up his line of battle against him 1
4 Abi'jah . . said, "Hear me, O Jerobo'am and all Israel! 1
6 Yet Jerobo'am . . rose up and rebelled against 1
8 golden calves which Jerobo'am made you for gods. 1
13 Jerobo'am had sent an ambush around 1
15 God defeated Jerobo'am and all Israel 1
19 Abi'jah pursued Jerobo'am, and took cities 1
20 Jerobo'am did not recover his power 1
Hos 1: 1 and in the days of Jerobo'am the son of Jo'ash 1
Ams 1: 1 and in the days of Jerobo'am the son of Jo'ash, 1
7: 9 against the house of Jerobo'am with the sword. 1
10 Amazi'ah the priest of Bethel sent to Jerobo'am 1
11 Amos has said, 'Jerobo'am shall die by the sword 1
Sir 47:23 Also Jeroboam the son of Nebat 2

Jeroham 1. יְרֹחָם

1Sm 1: 1 whose name was Elka'nah the son of Jero'ham 1
1Ch 6:27 Eli'ab his son, Jero'ham his son, Elka'nah his son. 1
34 of Elka'nah, son of Jero'ham, son of Eli'el, 1
8:27 Eli'jah, and Zichri were the sons of Jero'ham. 1
9: 8 Ibne'iah the son of Jero'ham, Elah the son of Uzzi 1
12 Adai'ah the son of Jero'ham, son of Pashhur 1
12: 7 and Zebadi'ah, the sons of Jero'ham of Gedor. 1
27:22 for Dan, Az'arel the son of Jero'ham. 1
2Ch 23: 1 commanders . . Azari'ah the son of Jero'ham 1
Neh 11:12 Adai'ah the son of Jero'ham, son of Pelali'ah 1

Jerrubbaal 1. יְרֻבַּעַל

Jdg 8:35 to the family of Jerrubba'al (that is, Gideon) 1

Jerubbaal 1. יְרֻבַּעַל

Jdg 6:32 on that day he was called Jerubba'al, that is to say 1
7: 1 Then Jerubba'al (that is, Gideon) and all the people 1
8:29 Jerubba'al the son of Jo'ash went and dwelt in his 1
9: 1 Abim'elech the son of Jerubba'al went to Shechem 1
2 that all 70 of the sons of Jerubba'al rule over you 1
5 and slew his brothers the sons of Jerubba'al 1
5 Jotham the youngest son of Jerubba'al was left 1
16 you have dealt well with Jerubba'al and his house 1
19 acted in good faith and honor with Jerubba'al 1
24 the violence done to the 70 sons of Jerubba'al 1
28 Did not the son of Jerubba'al and Zebul 1
57 came the curse of Jotham the son of Jerubba'al. 1
1Sm 12:11 the LORD sent Jerubba'al and Barak, and Jephthah 1

Jerubbesheth 1. יְרֻבֶּשֶׁת

2Sm 11:21 Who killed Abim'elech the son of Jerub'besheth? 1

Jeruel 1. יְרוּאֵל

2Ch 20:16 the valley, east of the wilderness of Jeru'el. 1

Jerusalem 1. יְרוּשָׁלַם 2. יְרוּשְׁלֵם (A) 3. Ἱεροσόλυμα 4. Ἱεροσολυμίτης 5. Ἰερουσαλήμ 6. Hierusalem

Jos 10: 1 When Ado'ni-ze'dek king of Jerusalem heard 1
3 Ado'ni-ze'dek king of Jerusalem sent to Hoham 1
5 the king of Jerusalem, the king of Hebron, the king 1
23 five kings . . the king of Jerusalem 1
12:10 king of Jerusalem, one; the king of Hebron, one; 1
15: 8 shoulder of the Jeb'usite (that is, Jerusalem); 1
63 But the Jeb'usites, the inhabitants of Jerusalem 1
63 the Jeb'usites dwell with . . Judah at Jerusalem 1
18:28 Zela, Ha-eleph, Jebus (that is, Jerusalem) 1
Jdg 1: 7 they brought him to Jerusalem, and he died there. 1
8 Judah fought against Jerusalem, and took it 1
21 drive out the Jeb'usites who dwelt in Jerusalem; 1
21 dwelt with the people of Benjamin in Jerusalem 1
19:10 and arrived opposite Jebus (that is, Jerusalem). 1
1Sm 17:54 took the head . . and brought it to Jerusalem; 1
2Sm 5: 5 at Jerusalem he reigned . . 33 years. 1
6 And the king and his men went to Jerusalem 1
13 took more concubines and wives from Jerusalem 1
14 names of those who were born to him in Jerusalem 1
8: 7 David took . . and brought them to Jerusalem. 1
9:13 Mephib'osheth dwelt in Jerusalem; 1
10:14 Jo'ab returned . . and came to Jerusalem. 1
11: 1 But David remained at Jerusalem. 1

12 Uri'ah remained in Jerusalem that day 1
12:31 David and all the people returned to Jerusalem. 1
14:23 Jo'ab arose . . and brought Ab'salom to Jerusalem. 1
28 Ab'salom dwelt two full years in Jerusalem 1
15: 8 the LORD will indeed bring me back to Jerusalem 1
11 200 men from Jerusalem who were invited guests 1
14 to . . his servants who were with him at Jerusalem 1
29 carried the ark of God back to Jerusalem; 1
37 just as Ab'salom was entering Jerusalem. 1
16: 3 he remains in Jerusalem; for he said 1
15 Ab'salom and all the people . . came to Jerusalem 1
17:20 could not find them, they returned to Jerusalem. 1
19:19 on the day my lord the king left Jerusalem; 1
25 And when he came from Jerusalem to meet the king 1
33 I will provide for you with me in Jerusalem. 1
34 that I should go up with the king to Jerusalem? 1
20: 2 Judah followed . . from the Jordan to Jerusalem. 1
3 And David came to his house at Jerusalem; 1
7 they went out from Jerusalem to pursue Sheba 1
22 And Jo'ab returned to Jerusalem to the king. 1
24: 8 they came to Jerusalem at the end of nine months 1
16 angel stretched . . his hand toward Jerusalem 1
1Kg 2:11 David . . reigned . . 33 years in Jerusalem. 1
36 Build yourself a house in Jerusalem, and dwell 1
38 So Shim'e-i dwelt in Jerusalem many days. 1
41 Shim'e-i had gone from Jerusalem to Gath 1
3: 1 house of the LORD and the wall around Jerusalem. 1
15 he came to Jerusalem, and stood before the ark 1
8: 1 assembled . . before King Solomon in Jerusalem 1
9:15 build . . the Millo and the wall of Jerusalem 1
19 whatever Solomon desired to build in Jerusalem 1
10: 2 She came to Jerusalem with a very great retinue 1
26 and with the king in Jerusalem. 1
27 king made silver as common in Jerusalem as stone 1
11: 7 high place . . on the mountain east of Jerusalem. 1
13 I will give one tribe . . for the sake of Jerusalem 1
29 at that time, when Jerobo'am went out of Jerusalem 1
32 he shall have . . for the sake of Jerusalem 1
36 that David . . have a lamp before me in Jerusalem 1
42 Solomon reigned in Jerusalem over all Israel 1
12:18 King Rehobo'am made haste . . to flee to Jerusalem. 1
21 When Rehobo'am came to Jerusalem, he assembled 1
27 sacrifices in the house of the LORD at Jerusalem 1
28 You have gone up to Jerusalem long enough. 1
14:21 and he reigned seventeen years in Jerusalem 1
25 Shishak king of Egypt came up against Jerusalem; 1
15: 2 He reigned for three years in Jerusalem. 1
4 the LORD his God gave him a lamp in Jerusalem 1
4 gave him a lamp . . and establishing Jerusalem; 1
10 he reigned 41 years in Jerusalem. 1
22:42 and he reigned 25 years in Jerusalem. 1
2Kg 8:17 and he reigned eight years in Jerusalem. 1
26 and he reigned one year in Jerusalem. 1
9:28 His servants carried him . . to Jerusalem 1
12: 1 Jeho'ash . . reigned 40 years in Jerusalem. 1
17 Haz'ael set his face to go up against Jerusalem 1
18 Then Haz'ael went away from Jerusalem. 1
14: 2 and he reigned 29 years in Jerusalem. 1
2 His mother's name was Jeho-ad'din of Jerusalem. 1
13 and came to Jerusalem, and broke down the wall 1
13 and broke down the wall of Jerusalem 1
19 they made a conspiracy against him in Jerusalem 1
20 and he was buried in Jerusalem with his fathers 1
15: 2 and he reigned 52 years in Jerusalem. 1
2 His mother's name was Jecoli'ah of Jerusalem. 1
33 and he reigned sixteen years in Jerusalem. 1
16: 2 and he reigned sixteen years in Jerusalem. 1
5 came up to wage war on Jerusalem 1
18: 2 and he reigned 29 years in Jerusalem. 1
17 from Lachish to King Hezeki'ah at Jerusalem. 1
17 And they went up and came to Jerusalem. 1
22 has removed, saying to Judah and to Jerusalem 1
22 shall worship before this altar in Jerusalem"? 1
35 the LORD should deliver Jerusalem out of my hand?' 1
19:10 that Jerusalem will not be given into the hand 1
21 she wags her head . . -the daughter of Jerusalem. 1
31 for out of Jerusalem shall go forth a remnant 1
21: 1 and he reigned 55 years in Jerusalem. 1
4 the LORD had said, "In Jerusalem will I put my name. 1
7 this house, and in Jerusalem . . I will put my name 1
12 I am bringing upon Jerusalem and Judah such evil 1
13 stretch over Jerusalem the . . line of Sama'ria 1
13 I will wipe Jerusalem as one wipes a dish 1
16 he had filled Jerusalem from one end to another 1
19 Amon . . and he reigned two years in Jerusalem. 1
22: 1 and he reigned 31 years in Jerusalem. 1
14 (now she dwelt in Jerusalem in the Second Quarter); 1
23: 1 the elders of Judah and Jerusalem were gathered 1
2 men of Judah and . . the inhabitants of Jerusalem 1
4 he burned them outside Jerusalem in the fields 1
5 at the cities of Judah and round about Jerusalem; 1
6 outside Jerusalem to the brook Kidron 1
9 come up to the altar of the LORD in Jerusalem 1
13 the high places that were east of Jerusalem 1
20 Then he returned to Jerusalem. 1
23 this passover was kept to the LORD in Jerusalem. 1
24 were seen in the land of Judah and in Jerusalem 1
27 cast off this city which I have chosen, Jerusalem 1
30 carried him . . and brought him to Jerusalem 1
31 and he reigned three months in Jerusalem. 1
33 put him . . that he might not reign in Jerusalem 1
36 and he reigned eleven years in Jerusalem. 1
24: 4 for he filled Jerusalem with innocent blood 1
8 and he reigned three months in Jerusalem. 1
8 the daughter of Elna'than of Jerusalem. 1
10 the servants of . . came up to Jerusalem 1
14 He carried away all Jerusalem, and . . the princes 1
15 took into captivity from Jerusalem to Babylon. 1
18 and he reigned eleven years in Jerusalem. 1
20 it came to the point in Jerusalem and Judah that 1
25: 1 came with all his army against Jerusalem 1
8 Nebu'zarad'an . . came to Jerusalem. 1
9 the king's house and all the houses of Jerusalem; 1
10 all . . broke down the walls around Jerusalem. 1
1Ch 3: 4 And he reigned 33 years in Jerusalem. 1
5 were born to him in Jerusalem: Shim'e-a, Shobab 1
6:10 in the house that Solomon built in Jerusalem 1
15 the LORD sent Judah and Jerusalem into exile 1
32 built the house of the LORD in Jerusalem; 1
8:28 These dwelt in Jerusalem. 1
32 dwelt opposite their kinsmen in Jerusalem 1
9: 3 some of the people . . dwelt in Jerusalem 1
34 leaders, who lived in Jerusalem. 1
38 dwelt opposite their kinsmen in Jerusalem 1
11: 4 and all Israel went to Jerusalem, that is Jebus 1
14: 3 David took more wives in Jerusalem 1
4 names of the children whom he had in Jerusalem 1
15: 3 David assembled all Israel at Jerusalem 1
18: 7 and brought them to Jerusalem. 1
19:15 Then Jo'ab came to Jerusalem. 1
20: 1 But David remained at Jerusalem. 1
3 David and all the people returned to Jerusalem. 1
21: 4 Jo'ab departed . . and came back to Jerusalem. 1
15 God sent the angel to Jerusalem to destroy it; 1
16 a drawn sword stretched out over Jerusalem. 1
23:25 and he dwells in Jerusalem for ever. 1
28: 1 David assembled at Jerusalem all the officials 1
29:27 reigned seven years in Hebron, and 33 in Jerusalem 1
2Ch 1: 4 for he had pitched a tent for it in Jerusalem. 1
13 came from the high place . . to Jerusalem. 1
14 stationed in . . and with the king in Jerusalem. 1
15 silver and gold as common in Jerusalem as stone 1
2: 7 workers who are with me in Judah and Jerusalem 1
16 to Joppa, so that you may take it up to Jerusalem. 1
3: 1 build the house of the LORD in Jerusalem 1
5: 2 Solomon assembled . . of Israel, in Jerusalem 1
6: 6 I have chosen Jerusalem that my name may be there 1
8: 6 whatever Solomon desired to build in Jerusalem 1
9: 1 she came to Jerusalem to test him 1
25 stationed . . with the king in Jerusalem. 1
27 king made silver as common in Jerusalem as stone 1
30 Solomon reigned in Jerusalem over all Israel 1
10:18 to mount his chariot, to flee to Jerusalem. 1
11: 1 When Rehobo'am came to Jerusalem 1
5 Rehobo'am dwelt in Jerusalem 1
14 +evites left . . and came to Judah and Jerusalem 1
16 came . . to Jerusalem to sacrifice to the LORD 1
12: 2 Shishak king of Egypt came up against Jerusalem 1
4 came as far as Jerusalem. 1
5 had gathered at Jerusalem because of Shishak 1
7 my wrath shall not be poured out upon Jerusalem 1
9 Shishak king of Egypt came up against Jerusalem; 1
13 Rehobo'am established himself in Jerusalem 1
13 he reigned seventeen years in Jerusalem 1
13: 2 He reigned for three years in Jerusalem. 1
14:15 Then they returned to Jerusalem. 1
15:10 They were gathered at Jerusalem 1
17:13 He had soldiers . . in Jerusalem. 1
19: 1 returned in safety to his house in Jerusalem. 1
4 Jehosh'aphat dwelt at Jerusalem; 1
8 Moreover in Jerusalem Jehosh'aphat appointed 1
8 They had their seat at Jerusalem. 1
20: 5 stood in the assembly of Judah and Jerusalem 1
15 Hearken, all Judah and inhabitants of Jerusalem 1
17 on your behalf, O Judah and Jerusalem.' 1
18 all Judah and the inhabitants of Jerusalem fell 1
20 Hear me, Judah and inhabitants of Jerusalem! 1
27 returned, every man of Judah and Jerusalem 1
27 returning to Jerusalem with joy 1
28 They came to Jerusalem with harps and lyres 1
31 he reigned 25 years in Jerusalem. 1
21: 5 Jeho'ram . . reigned eight years in Jerusalem. 1
11 inhabitants of Jerusalem into unfaithfulness 1
13 led Judah and the inhabitants of Jerusalem 1
20 he reigned eight years in Jerusalem; 1
22: 1 inhabitants of Jerusalem made Ahazi'ah . . king 1
2 Ahazi'ah . . reigned one year in Jerusalem. 1
23: 2 and they came to Jerusalem. 1
24: 1 Jo'ash . . reigned 40 years in Jerusalem; 1
6 to bring in from Judah and Jerusalem the tax 1
9 throughout Judah and Jerusalem 1
18 wrath came upon Judah and Jerusalem for this 1
23 They came to Judah and Jerusalem 1
25: 1 he reigned 29 years in Jerusalem. 1
1 His mother's name was Jeho-ad'dan of Jerusalem. 1
23 Jo'ash . . brought him to Jerusalem 1
23 broke down the wall of Jerusalem for 400 cubits 1
27 they made a conspiracy against him in Jerusalem 1
26: 3 reigned 52 years in Jerusalem. 1
3 His mother's name was Jecoli'ah of Jerusalem. 1
9 built towers in Jerusalem at the Corner Gate 1
15 In Jerusalem he made engines 1
27: 1 Jotham . . reigned sixteen years in Jerusalem. 1
8 he reigned sixteen years in Jerusalem. 1
28: 1 Ahaz . . reigned sixteen years in Jerusalem. 1
10 subjugate the people of Judah and Jerusalem 1
24 Ahaz . . made himself altars in . . Jerusalem. 1
27 buried him in the city, in Jerusalem 1
29: 1 reigned 29 years in Jerusalem. 1
8 the wrath of the LORD came on Judah and Jerusalem 1
30: 1 come to the house of the LORD at Jerusalem, to keep 1
2 king and . . all the assembly in Jerusalem 1
3 nor had the people assembled in Jerusalem 1
5 keep the passover to the LORD . . at Jerusalem; 1
11 humbled themselves and came to Jerusalem. 1
13 many people came together in Jerusalem to keep 1
14 removed the altars that were in Jerusalem 1
21 people of Israel that were present at Jerusalem 1
26 there was great joy in Jerusalem 1
26 there had been nothing like this in Jerusalem. 1
31: 4 commanded the people who lived in Jerusalem 1
32: 2 intended to fight against Jerusalem 1
9 sent his servants to Jerusalem to Hezeki'ah 1
9 to all the people of Judah that were in Jerusalem 1
10 that you stand siege in Jerusalem? 1
12 Hezeki'ah . . commanded Judah and Jerusalem 1
18 the people of Jerusalem who were upon the wall 1
19 spoke of the God of Jerusalem as . . the gods 1
22 LORD saved . . the inhabitants of Jerusalem 1
23 many brought gifts to the LORD to Jerusalem 1
25 wrath came upon him and Judah and Jerusalem. 1
26 both he and the inhabitants of Jerusalem 1
33 all Judah and the inhabitants of Jerusalem did 1
33: 1 he reigned 55 years in Jerusalem. 1
4 In Jerusalem shall my name be for ever. 1
7 Jerusalem, which I have chosen out of all 1
9 Manas'seh seduced . . inhabitants of Jerusalem 1
13 brought him again to Jerusalem into his kingdom. 1
15 altars that he had built . . in Jerusalem 1
21 Amon . . reigned two years in Jerusalem. 1
34: 1 he reigned 31 years in Jerusalem. 1
3 purge Judah and Jerusalem of the high places 1
5 purged Judah and Jerusalem. 1
7 Then he returned to Jerusalem. 1
9 from the inhabitants of Jerusalem. 1
22 now she dwelt in Jerusalem in the Second Quarter 1
29 gathered . . the elders of Judah and Jerusalem. 1
30 men of Judah and the inhabitants of Jerusalem 1
32 all . . present in Jerusalem and in Benjamin 1
32 inhabitants of Jerusalem did according 1
35: 1 Josi'ah kept a passover to the LORD in Jerusalem; 1
18 by Josi'ah . . and the inhabitants of Jerusalem. 1
24 his servants . . brought him to Jerusalem. 1
24 All Judah and Jerusalem mourned for Josi'ah. 1
36: 1 made him king in his father's stead in Jerusalem. 1
2 he reigned three months in Jerusalem. 1
3 Then the king of Egypt deposed him in Jerusalem 1
4 made Eli'akim . . king over Judah and Jerusalem 1
5 he reigned eleven years in Jerusalem. 1
9 reigned three months and ten days in Jerusalem. 1
10 made . . Zedeki'ah king over Judah and Jerusalem. 1
11 he reigned eleven years in Jerusalem. 1
14 house . . which he had hallowed in Jerusalem. 1
19 broke down the wall of Jerusalem, and burned all 1
23 charged me to build him a house at Jerusalem 1
Ezr 1: 2 charged me to build him a house at Jerusalem 1
3 let him go up to Jerusalem, which is in Judah 1
3 LORD . . -he is the God who is in Jerusalem; 1
4 for the house of God which is in Jerusalem. 1
5 house of the LORD which is in Jerusalem; 1
7 carried away from Jerusalem and placed 1
11 brought up from Babylonia to Jerusalem. 1
2: 1 returned to Jerusalem and Judah, each to his own 1
68 house of the LORD which is in Jerusalem 1
70 some . . lived in Jerusalem and its vicinity; 5
3: 1 people gathered as one man to Jerusalem. 1
8 their coming to the house of God at Jerusalem 1
8 who had come to Jerusalem from the captivity. 1
4: 6 against the inhabitants of Judah and Jerusalem. 1
8 wrote a letter against Jerusalem to Ar-ta-xerx'es 2
12 Jews who came up . . have gone to Jerusalem. 2
20 mighty kings have been over Jerusalem, who ruled 2
23 they went in haste to the Jews at Jerusalem 2
24 the work on the house of God which is in Jerusalem 2
5: 1 prophesied to the Jews . . in Judah and Jerusalem 2
2 rebuild the house of God which is in Jerusalem; 2
14 taken out of the temple that was in Jerusalem 2
15 put them in the temple which is in Jerusalem 2
16 foundations of the house of God . . in Jerusalem; 2
17 rebuilding of this house of God in Jerusalem. 2
6: 3 Concerning the house of God at Jerusalem 2
5 took out of the temple that is in Jerusalem 2
5 brought back to the temple which is in Jerusalem 2
9 wine, or oil, as the priests at Jerusalem require- 2
12 destroy this house of God which is in Jerusalem. 2
18 set . . for the service of God at Jerusalem 2
7: 7 there went up also to Jerusalem 1

8 came to Jerusalem in the fifth month 1
9 first day of the fifth month he came to Jerusalem 1
13 freely offers to go to Jerusalem, may go with you. 2
14 to make inquiries about Judah and Jerusalem 2
15 God of Israel, whose dwelling is in Jerusalem 2
16 house of their God which is in Jerusalem. 2
17 house of your God which is in Jerusalem. 2
19 you shall deliver before the God of Jerusalem. 2
27 to beautify the house of the LORD . . in Jerusalem 1
8:29 heads of fathers' houses in Israel at Jerusalem 1
30 to bring them to Jerusalem, to the house of our God. 1
31 twelfth day of the first month, to go to Jerusalem; 1
32 came to Jerusalem . . remained three days. 1
9: 9 to give us protection in Judea and Jerusalem. 1
10: 7 proclamation was made throughout . . Jerusalem 1
7 returned exiles . . should assemble at Jerusalem 1
9 assembled at Jerusalem within the three days; 1
Neh 1: 2 I asked them . . concerning Jerusalem. 1
3 wall of Jerusalem is broken down, and its gates 1
2:11 I came to Jerusalem and was there three days. 1
12 my God had put into my heart to do for Jerusalem. 1
13 I inspected the walls of Jerusalem 1
17 Jerusalem lies in ruins with its gates burned. 1
17 Come, let us build the wall of Jerusalem 1
20 no portion or right or memorial in Jerusalem. 1
3: 8 restored Jerusalem as far as the Broad Wall. 1
9 ruler of half the district of Jerusalem 1
12 ruler of half the district of Jerusalem 1
4: 7 repairing of the walls of Jerusalem was going 1
8 together to come and fight against Jerusalem 1
22 every man . . pass the night within Jerusalem 1
6: 7 set up prophets to proclaim . . in Jerusalem 1
7: 2 I gave . . charge over Jerusalem 1
3 Let not the gates of Jerusalem be opened 1
3 guards from among the inhabitants of Jerusalem 1
6 returned to Jerusalem and Judah, each to his town. 1
8:15 proclaim in all their towns and in Jerusalem, "Go 1
11: 1 Now the leaders of the people lived in Jerusalem; 1
1 one out of ten to live in Jerusalem the holy city 1
2 men who willingly offered to live in Jerusalem. 1
3 chiefs of the province who lived in Jerusalem; 1
4 Jerusalem lived certain of the sons of Judah 1
6 sons of Perez who lived in Jerusalem were 468 1
22 overseer of the Levites in Jerusalem was Uzzi 1
12:27 dedication of the wall of Jerusalem they sought 1
27 bring them to Jerusalem to celebrate 1
28 gathered . . from the circuit round Jerusalem 1
29 built . . villages around Jerusalem. 1
43 joy of Jerusalem was heard afar off. 1
13: 6 not in Jerusalem, for in the 32nd year 1
7 came to Jerusalem, and I then discovered the evil 1
15 brought into Jerusalem on the sabbath day; 1
16 sold them on the sabbath . . in Jerusalem. 1
19 When it began to be dark at the gates of Jerusalem 1
20 lodged outside Jerusalem once or twice. 1
Est 2: 6 a Jew . . who had been carried away from Jerusalem 1
Ps 51:18 rebuild the walls of Jerusalem 1
68:29 Because of thy temple at Jerusalem 1
79: 1 heathen . . have laid Jerusalem in ruins. 1
3 blood like water round about Jerusalem 1
102:21 that men may declare . . in Jerusalem his praise 1
116:19 house of the LORD, in your midst, O Jerusalem. 1
122: 2 feet . . standing within your gates, O Jerusalem! 1
3 Jerusalem, built as a city which is bound firmly 1
6 Pray for the peace of Jerusalem! 1
125: 2 As the mountains are round about Jerusalem 1
128: 5 May you see the prosperity of Jerusalem 1
135:21 Blessed . . from Zion, he who dwells in Jerusalem! 1
137: 5 If I forget you, O Jerusalem, let my right hand 1
6 if I do not set Jerusalem above my highest joy! 1
7 O LORD, against the E'domites the day of Jerusalem 1
147: 2 LORD builds up Jerusalem; 1
12 Praise the LORD, O Jerusalem! 1
Ecc 1: 1 the Preacher, the son of David, king in Jerusalem. 1
12 I . . have been king over Israel in Jerusalem. 1
16 wisdom, surpassing all who were over Jerusalem 1
2: 7 any who had been before me in Jerusalem. 1
9 surpassed all who were before me in Jerusalem; 1
Sng 1: 5 dark, but comely, O daughters of Jerusalem 1
2: 7 I adjure you, O daughters of Jerusalem 1
3: 5 I adjure you, O daughters of Jerusalem . . stir not 1
10 wrought within by the daughters of Jerusalem. 1
5: 8 I adjure you, O daughters of Jerusalem 1
16 This is my beloved . . O daughters of Jerusalem. 1
6: 4 beautiful as Tirzah, my love, comely as Jerusalem 1
8: 4 I adjure you, O daughters of Jerusalem 1
Isa 1: 1 which he saw concerning Judah and Jerusalem 1
2: 1 Isaiah . . saw concerning Judah and Jerusalem. 1
3 the law, and the word of the LORD from Jerusalem. 1
3: 1 is taking away from Jerusalem and from Judah 1
8 For Jerusalem has stumbled, and Judah has fallen; 1
4: 3 he who . . remains in Jerusalem will be called 1
3 one who has been recorded for life in Jerusalem 1
4 cleansed the bloodstains of Jerusalem 1
5: 3 now, O inhabitants of Jerusalem and men of Judah 1
14 nobility of Jerusalem and her multitude go down *
7: 1 came up to Jerusalem to wage war against it 1
8:14 snare to the inhabitants of Jerusalem. 1
10:10 images were greater than those of Jerusalem 1
11 shall I not do to Jerusalem and her idols as I have 1
12 all his work on Mount Zion and on Jerusalem 1
32 the daughter of Zion, the hill of Jerusalem. 1
22:10 you counted the houses of Jerusalem 1
21 a father to the inhabitants of Jerusalem 1
24:23 in Jerusalem and before his elders he will 1
27:13 worship . . on the holy mountain at Jerusalem. 1
28:14 you scoffers, who rule this people in Jerusalem! 1
30:19 Yea, O people in Zion who dwell at Jerusalem; 1
31: 5 the LORD of hosts will protect Jerusalem; 1
9 the LORD . . whose furnace is in Jerusalem. 1
33:20 Your eyes will see Jerusalem, a quiet habitation 1
36: 2 to King Hezeki'ah at Jerusalem, with a great army. 1
7 Hezeki'ah . . saying to Judah and to Jerusalem 1
20 the LORD should deliver Jerusalem out of my hand?' 1
37:10 that Jerusalem will not be given into the hand 1
22 her head behind you–the daughter of Jerusalem. 1
32 for out of Jerusalem shall go forth a remnant 1
40: 2 Speak tenderly to Jerusalem, and cry to her 1
9 lift up your voice with strength, O Jerusalem 1
41:27 and I give to Jerusalem a herald of good tidings. 1
44:26 who says of Jerusalem, 'She shall be inhabited,' 1
28 saying of Jerusalem, 'She shall be built,' 1
51:17 rouse yourself, stand up, O Jerusalem 1
52: 1 put on your beautiful garments, O Jerusalem 1
2 from the dust, arise, O captive Jerusalem; 1
9 into singing, you waste places of Jerusalem; 1
9 his people, he has redeemed Jerusalem. 1
62: 1 and for Jerusalem's sake I will not rest 1
6 Upon your walls, O Jerusalem, I have set watchmen; 1
7 give him no rest until he establishes Jerusalem 1
64:10 Zion . . a wilderness, Jerusalem a desolation. 1
65:18 for behold, I create Jerusalem a rejoicing 1
19 I will rejoice in Jerusalem, and be glad 1
66:10 Rejoice with Jerusalem, and be glad for her 1
13 you shall be comforted in Jerusalem. 1
20 upon dromedaries, to my holy mountain Jerusalem 1
Jer 1: 3 the captivity of Jerusalem in the fifth month. 1
15 at the entrance of the gates of Jerusalem 1
2: 2 Go and proclaim in the hearing of Jerusalem 1
3:17 Jerusalem shall be called the throne of the LORD 1
17 to the presence of the LORD in Jerusalem 1
4: 3 says . . to the inhabitants of Jerusalem 1
4 O men of Judah and inhabitants of Jerusalem; 1
5 Declare in Judah, and proclaim in Jerusalem 1
10 utterly deceived this people and Jerusalem 1
11 it will be said to this people and to Jerusalem 1
14 O Jerusalem, wash your heart from wickedness 1
16 announce to Jerusalem, "Besiegers come 1
5: 1 Run to and fro through the streets of Jerusalem 1
6: 1 Flee for safety . . from the midst of Jerusalem! 1
6 cast up a siege mound against Jerusalem. 1
8 Be warned, O Jerusalem 1
7:17 cities of Judah and in the streets of Jerusalem? 1
34 from the streets of Jerusalem the voice of mirth 1
8: 1 and the bones of the inhabitants of Jerusalem 1
9:11 I will make Jerusalem a heap of ruins 1
11: 2 men of Judah and the inhabitants of Jerusalem. 1
6 cities of Judah, and in the streets of Jerusalem 1
9 men of Judah and the inhabitants of Jerusalem. 1
12 and the inhabitants of Jerusalem will go and cry 1
13 as many as the streets of Jerusalem 1
13: 9 pride of Judah and the great pride of Jerusalem. 1
13 prophets, and all the inhabitants of Jerusalem. 1
27 Woe to you, O Jerusalem! 1
14: 2 and the cry of Jerusalem goes up. 1
16 shall be cast out in the streets of Jerusalem 1
15: 4 son of Hezeki'ah, king of Judah, did in Jerusalem. 1
5 Who will have pity on you, O Jerusalem 1
17:19 they go out, and in all the gates of Jerusalem 1
20 all Judah, and all the inhabitants of Jerusalem 1
21 or bring it in by the gates of Jerusalem. 1
25 men of Judah and the inhabitants of Jerusalem; 1
26 Judah and the places round about Jerusalem 1
27 and enter by the gates of Jerusalem 1
27 and it shall devour the palaces of Jerusalem 1
18:11 men of Judah and the inhabitants of Jerusalem 1
19: 3 O kings of Judah and inhabitants of Jerusalem. 1
7 I will make void the plans of Judah and Jerusalem 1
13 houses of Jerusalem and the houses of the kings 1
22:19 and cast forth beyond the gates of Jerusalem. 1
23:14 But in the prophets of Jerusalem I have seen 1
15 for from the prophets of Jerusalem ungodliness 1
24: 1 Babylon had taken into exile from Jerusalem 1
8 the remnant of Jerusalem who remain in this land 1
25: 2 Judah and all the inhabitants of Jerusalem 1
18 Jerusalem and the cities of Judah 1
26:18 Jerusalem shall become a heap of ruins 1
27: 3 the envoys who have come to Jerusalem 1
18 in the house of the king of Judah, and in Jerusalem 1
20 took into exile from Jerusalem to Babylon 1
20 and all the nobles of Judah and Jerusalem– 1
21 in the house of the king of Judah, and in Jerusalem 1
29: 1 the prophet sent from Jerusalem to the elders 1
1 had taken into exile from Jerusalem to Babylon. 1
2 the eunuchs, the princes of Judah and Jerusalem 1
2 and the smiths had departed from Jerusalem. 1
4 I have sent into exile from Jerusalem to Babylon 1
20 whom I sent away from Jerusalem to Babylon 1
25 to all the people who are in Jerusalem 1
32: 2 the king of Babylon was besieging Jerusalem 1
32 men of Judah and the inhabitants of Jerusalem. 1
44 in the places about Jerusalem, and in the cities 1
33:10 and the streets of Jerusalem that are desolate 1
13 the land of Benjamin, the places about Jerusalem 1
16 and Jerusalem will dwell securely. 1
34: 1 the peoples were fighting against Jerusalem 1
6 to Zedeki'ah king of Judah, in Jerusalem 1
7 king of Babylon was fighting against Jerusalem 1
8 made a covenant with all the people in Jerusalem 1
19 the princes of Judah, the princes of Jerusalem 1
35:11 we said, 'Come, and let us go to Jerusalem 1
11 So we are living in Jerusalem. 1
13 men of Judah and the inhabitants of Jerusalem 1
17 on Judah and all the inhabitants of Jerusalem 1
36: 9 in the ninth month, all the people in Jerusalem 1
9 from the cities of Judah to Jerusalem 1
31 upon them, and upon the inhabitants of Jerusalem 1
37: 5 the Chalde'ans who were besieging Jerusalem 1
5 they withdrew from Jerusalem. 1
11 the Chalde'an army had withdrawn from Jerusalem 1
12 Jeremiah set out from Jerusalem to go to the land 1
38:28 until the day that Jerusalem was taken. 1
39: 1 his army came against Jerusalem and besieged it; 1
3 When Jerusalem was taken 1
8 and broke down the walls of Jerusalem. 1
40: 1 along with all the captives of Jerusalem 1
42:18 were poured out on the inhabitants of Jerusalem 1
44: 2 all the evil that I brought upon Jerusalem 1
6 cities of Judah and in the streets of Jerusalem; 1
9 the land of Judah and in the streets of Jerusalem? 1
13 as I have punished Jerusalem, with the sword 1
17 cities of Judah and in the streets of Jerusalem; 1
21 cities of Judah and in the streets of Jerusalem 1
51:35 My blood be upon . . Chalde'a," let Jerusalem say. 1
50 let Jerusalem come into your mind 1
52: 1 and he reigned eleven years in Jerusalem. 1
3 things came to such a pass in Jerusalem and Judah 1
4 came with all his army against Jerusalem 1
12 Nebu'zarad'an . . entered Jerusalem. 1
13 the king's house and all the houses of Jerusalem; 1
14 broke down all the walls round about Jerusalem. 1
29 he carried away captive from Jerusalem 1
Lam 1: 7 Jerusalem remembers . . all the precious things 1
8 Jerusalem sinned grievously 1
17 Jerusalem has become a filthy thing among them. 1
2:10 the maidens of Jerusalem have bowed their heads 1
13 What can I say for you . . O daughter of Jerusalem? 1
15 and wag their heads at the daughter of Jerusalem; 1
4:12 foe or enemy could enter the gates of Jerusalem. 1
Ezk 4: 1 and portray upon it a city, even Jerusalem; 1
7 set your face toward the siege of Jerusalem 1
16 I will break the staff of bread in Jerusalem; 1
5: 5 Thus says the Lord GOD: This is Jerusalem; 1
8: 3 and brought me in visions of God to Jerusalem 1
9: 4 Go through the city, through Jerusalem 1
8 in the outpouring of thy wrath upon Jerusalem? 1
11:15 of whom the inhabitants of Jerusalem have said 1
12:10 This oracle concerns the prince in Jerusalem 1
19 concerning the inhabitants of Jerusalem 1
13:16 who prophesied concerning Jerusalem and saw 1
14:21 upon Jerusalem my four sore acts of judgment 1
22 for the evil that I have brought upon Jerusalem 1
15: 6 so will I give up the inhabitants of Jerusalem. 1
16: 2 make known to Jerusalem her abominations 1
3 and say, Thus says the Lord GOD to Jerusalem 1
17:12 Behold, the king of Babylon came to Jerusalem 1
21: 2 Son of man, set your face toward Jerusalem 1
20 and to Judah and to Jerusalem the fortified. 1
22 Into his right hand comes the lot for Jerusalem 1
22:19 I will gather you into the midst of Jerusalem. 1
23: 4 Oho'lah is Sama'ria, and Ohol'ibah is Jerusalem. 1
24: 2 The king of Babylon has laid siege to Jerusalem 1
26: 2 because Tyre said concerning Jerusalem 1
33:21 a man who had escaped from Jerusalem came to me 1
36:38 for sacrifices, like the flock at Jerusalem 1
Dan 5: 2 vessels . . taken out of the temple in Jerusalem 2
3 out of the temple, the house of God in Jerusalem; 2
6:10 where he had windows . . open toward Jerusalem; 2
9: 2 before the end of the desolations of Jerusalem 1
7 men of Judah, to the inhabitants of Jerusalem 1
12 like of what has been done against Jerusalem. 1
16 anger . . wrath turn away from thy city Jerusalem 1
16 Jerusalem and thy people have become a byword 1
25 forth of the word to restore and build Jerusalem 1
Jol 2:32 and in Jerusalem there shall be those who escape 1
3: 1 restore the fortunes of Judah and Jerusalem 1
6 You have sold the people of Judah and Jerusalem 1
16 and utters his voice from Jerusalem 1
17 And Jerusalem shall be holy 1
20 and Jerusalem to all generations. 1
Ams 1: 2 from Zion, and utters his voice from Jerusalem; 1
2: 5 it shall devour the strongholds of Jerusalem. 1
Obd 1:11 and foreigners . . cast lots for Jerusalem 1
20 the exiles of Jerusalem who are in Sephar'ad 1
Mic 1: 1 which he saw concerning Sama'ria and Jerusalem. 1
5 the sin of the house of Judah? Is it not Jerusalem? 1
9 reached to the gate of my people, to Jerusalem. 1

12 evil has come down . . to the gate of Jerusalem. 1
3:10 build Zion with blood and Jerusalem with wrong. 1
12 Jerusalem shall become a heap of ruins 1
4: 2 the law, and the word of the LORD from Jerusalem. 1
8 come, the kingdom of the daughter of Jerusalem. 1
Zep 1: 4 and against all the inhabitants of Jerusalem; 1
12 At that time I will search Jerusalem with lamps 1
3:14 with all your heart, O daughter of Jerusalem! 1
16 On that day it shall be said to Jerusalem 1
Zec 1:12 how long wilt thou have no mercy on Jerusalem 1
14 I am exceedingly jealous for Jerusalem 1
16 I have returned to Jerusalem with compassion; 1
16 line shall be stretched out over Jerusalem. 1
17 again comfort Zion and again choose Jerusalem. 1
19 have scattered Judah, Israel, and Jerusalem. 1
2: 2 To measure Jerusalem, to see what is its breadth 1
4 Jerusalem shall be inhabited as villages 1
12 and will again choose Jerusalem. 1
3: 2 The LORD who has chosen Jerusalem rebuke you! 1
7: 7 When Jerusalem was inhabited and in prosperity 1
8: 3 to Zion, and will dwell in the midst of Jerusalem 1
3 Jerusalem shall be called the faithful city 1
4 shall again sit in the streets of Jerusalem 1
8 bring them to dwell in the midst of Jerusalem; 1
15 to do good to Jerusalem and to the house of Judah; 1
22 shall come to seek the LORD of hosts in Jerusalem 1
9: 9 Shout aloud, O daughter of Jerusalem! 1
10 from E'phraim and the war horse from Jerusalem; 1
12: 2 Lo, I am about to make Jerusalem a cup of reeling 1
2 Judah also in the siege against Jerusalem. 1
3 On that day I will make Jerusalem a heavy stone 1
5 The inhabitants of Jerusalem have strength 1
6 Jerusalem shall still be inhabited in its place 1
6 be inhabited in its place, in Jerusalem. 1
7 the inhabitants of Jerusalem may not be exalted 1
8 put a shield about the inhabitants of Jerusalem 1
9 all the nations that come against Jerusalem. 1
10 of David and the inhabitants of Jerusalem 1
11 the mourning in Jerusalem will be as great 1
13: 1 house of David and the inhabitants of Jerusalem 1
14: 2 all the nations against Jerusalem to battle 1
4 the Mount of Olives which lies before Jerusalem 1
8 living waters shall flow out from Jerusalem 1
10 a plain from Geba to Rimmon south of Jerusalem. 1
10 But Jerusalem shall remain aloft upon its site •
11 Jerusalem shall dwell in security. 1
12 the peoples that wage war against Jerusalem 1
14 even Judah will fight against Jerusalem. 1
16 the nations that have come against Jerusalem 1
17 do not go up to Jerusalem to worship the King 1
21 every pot in Jerusalem and Judah shall be sacred 1
Mal 2:11 has been committed in Israel and in Jerusalem; 1
3: 4 Judah and Jerusalem will be pleasing to the LORD 1
Mat 2: 1 wise men from the East came to Jerusalem, saying 3
3 he was troubled, and all Jerusalem with him; 3
3: 5 Then went out to him Jerusalem and all Judea 3
4:25 from Galilee and the Decap'olis and Jerusalem 3
5:35 his footstool, or by Jerusalem, for it is the city 3
15: 1 scribes came to Jesus from Jerusalem and said 3
16:21 he must go to Jerusalem and suffer many things 3
20:17 as Jesus was going up to Jerusalem 3
18 Behold, we are going up to Jerusalem 3
21: 1 they drew near to Jerusalem 3
10 when he entered Jerusalem 3
23:37 O Jerusalem, Jerusalem, killing the prophets 5
37 O Jerusalem, Jerusalem, killing the prophets 5
Mrk 1: 5 and all the people of Jerusalem 4
3: 8 Jerusalem and Idume'a and from beyond the Jordan 3
22 the scribes who came down from Jerusalem said 3
7: 1 some of the scribes, who had come from Jerusalem 3
10:32 they were on the road, going up to Jerusalem 3
33 saying, "Behold, we are going up to Jerusalem; 3
11: 1 when they drew near to Jerusalem, to Beth'phage 3
11 he entered Jerusalem, and went into the temple; 3
15 they came to Jerusalem 3
27 they came again to Jerusalem 3
15:41 women who came up with him to Jerusalem. 3
Lke 2:22 they brought him up to Jerusalem to present him 3
25 was a man in Jerusalem, whose name was Simeon 5
38 all who were looking for the redemption of Jerusalem 5
41 Now his parents went to Jerusalem every year 5
43 the boy Jesus stayed behind in Jerusalem 5
45 they returned to Jerusalem, seeking him. 5
4: 9 he took him to Jerusalem 5
5:17 who had come . . from Jerusalem 5
6:17 Judea and Jerusalem and the seacoast of Tyre 5
9:31 which he was to accomplish at Jerusalem. 5
51 he set his face to go to Jerusalem. 5
53 because his face was set toward Jerusalem. 5
10:30 A man was going down from Jerusalem to Jericho 5
13: 4 all the others who dwelt in Jerusalem? 5
22 teaching, and journeying toward Jerusalem. 3
33 that a prophet should perish away from Jerusalem.' 5
34 O Jerusalem, Jerusalem, killing the prophets 5
34 O Jerusalem, Jerusalem, killing the prophets 5
17:11 On the way to Jerusalem 5
18:31 Behold, we are going up to Jerusalem 5
19:11 because he was near to Jerusalem 5
28 he went on ahead, going up to Jerusalem. 3
21:20 when you see Jerusalem surrounded by armies 5
24 Jerusalem will be trodden down by the Gentiles 5
23: 7 who was himself in Jerusalem at that time. 3
28 Daughters of Jerusalem, do not weep for me 5
24:13 Emma'us, about seven miles from Jerusalem 5
18 the only visitor to Jerusalem who does not know 5
33 rose that same hour and returned to Jerusalem; 5
47 beginning from Jerusalem. 5
52 they returned to Jerusalem with great joy, 5
Joh 1:19 Jews sent priests and Levites from Jerusalem 3
2:13 and Jesus went up to Jerusalem. 3
23 when he was in Jerusalem at the Passover feast 3
4:20 Jerusalem is . . where men ought to worship. 3
21 neither on this mountain nor in Jerusalem 3
45 all that he had done in Jerusalem at the feast 3
5: 1 and Jesus went up to Jerusalem. 3
2 Now there is in Jerusalem by the Sheep Gate a pool 3
7:25 Some of the people of Jerusalem therefore said 4
10:22 the feast of the Dedication at Jerusalem; 3
11:18 Bethany was near Jerusalem, about two miles off 3
55 many went up from the country to Jerusalem 3
12:12 heard that Jesus was coming to Jerusalem. 3
Act 1: 4 he charged them not to depart from Jerusalem 3
8 you shall be my witnesses in Jerusalem 5
12 Then they returned to Jerusalem from the mount 5
12 the mount called Olivet, which is near Jerusalem 5
19 known to all the inhabitants of Jerusalem 5
2: 5 Now there were dwelling in Jerusalem Jews 5
14 Men of Judea and all who dwell in Jerusalem 5
4: 5 scribes were gathered together in Jerusalem 5
16 is manifest to all the inhabitants of Jerusalem 5
5:16 gathered from the towns around Jerusalem 5
28 you have filled Jerusalem with your teaching 5
6: 7 the disciples multiplied greatly in Jerusalem 5
8: 1 against the church in Jerusalem 3
14 Now when the apostles at Jerusalem heard 3
25 they returned to Jerusalem 3
26 the road that goes down from Jerusalem to Gaza. 5
27 had come to Jerusalem to worship 5
9: 2 he might bring them bound to Jerusalem. 5
13 evil he has done to thy saints at Jerusalem; 5
21 Is not this the man who made havoc in Jerusalem 5
26 when he had come to Jerusalem 5
28 So he went in and out among them at Jerusalem 5
10:39 both in the country of the Jews and in Jerusalem. 5
11: 2 when Peter went up to Jerusalem 5
22 came to the ears of the church in Jerusalem 5
27 prophets came down from Jerusalem to Antioch. 3
12:25 Barnabas and Saul returned from Jerusalem 5
13:13 John left them and returned to Jerusalem; 3
27 For those who live in Jerusalem and their rulers 5
31 came up with him from Galilee to Jerusalem 5
15: 2 appointed to go up to Jerusalem to the apostles 5
4 When they came to Jerusalem 5
16: 4 the apostles and elders who were at Jerusalem. 3
19:21 resolved . . to . . go to Jerusalem, saying 3
20:16 he was hastening to be at Jerusalem 3
22 I am going to Jerusalem, bound in the Spirit 5
21: 4 they told Paul not to go on to Jerusalem. 3
11 So shall the Jews at Jerusalem bind the man 5
12 begged him not to go up to Jerusalem. 5
13 die at Jerusalem for the name of the Lord Jesus. 5
15 we made ready and went up to Jerusalem. 3
17 When we had come to Jerusalem 5
31 all Jerusalem was in confusion. 5
22: 5 and bring them in bonds to Jerusalem to be punished. 5
17 When I had returned to Jerusalem 5
18 Make haste and get quickly out of Jerusalem 5
23:11 as you have testified about me at Jerusalem 5
24:11 since I went up to worship at Jerusalem; 5
25: 1 he went up to Jerusalem from Caesare'a. 3
3 to have the man sent to Jerusalem 5
7 the Jews who had gone down from Jerusalem 3
9 Do you wish to go up to Jerusalem 3
15 when I was at Jerusalem 3
20 I asked whether he wished to go to Jerusalem 3
24 both at Jerusalem and here 3
26: 4 among my own nation and at Jerusalem 3
10 I did so in Jerusalem 3
20 then at Jerusalem 3
28:17 yet I was delivered prisoner from Jerusalem 3
Rom 15:19 from Jerusalem and as far round as Illyr'icum 5
25 I am going to Jerusalem with aid for the saints. 5
26 for the poor among the saints at Jerusalem; 5
31 that my service for Jerusalem may be acceptable 5
1Co 16: 3 to carry your gift to Jerusalem. 5
Gal 1:17 nor did I go up to Jerusalem 3
18 I went up to Jerusalem to visit Cephas 3
2: 1 I went up again to Jerusalem with Barnabas 3
4:25 she corresponds to the present Jerusalem 5
26 Jerusalem above is free, and she is our mother. 5
Heb 12:22 the heavenly Jerusalem 5
Rev 3:12 the new Jerusalem which comes down from my God 5
21: 2 new Jerusalem, coming down out of heaven from God 5
10 Jerusalem coming down out of heaven from God 5
1Es 1: 1 kept the passover to his Lord in Jerusalem; 5
21 all of Israel who were dwelling in Jerusalem. 5
31 after he was brought back to Jerusalem he died 5
35 he reigned three months in Judah and Jerusalem. 5
35 deposed him from reigning in Jerusalem 5
37 made Jehoiakim . . king of Judea and Jerusalem. 5
39 when he began to reign in Judea and Jerusalem 5
44 reigned three months and ten days in Jerusalem. 5
46 made Zedekiah king of Judea and Jerusalem. 5
49 which had been hallowed in Jerusalem. 5
55 broke down the walls of Jerusalem 3
2: 4 commanded me to build him a house at Jerusalem 5
5 let him go up to Jerusalem, which is in Judea 5
5 he is the Lord who dwells in Jerusalem 5
7 the temple of the Lord which is in Jerusalem. 5
8 go up to build the house in Jerusalem for the Lord; 5
10 had carried away from Jerusalem 5
15 the returning exiles from Babylon to Jerusalem. 5
16 those who were living in Judea and Jerusalem 5
18 have gone to Jerusalem 5
27 mighty and cruel kings ruled in Jerusalem 5
30 went in haste to Jerusalem 5
30 the building of the temple in Jerusalem ceased 5
4:43 the vow which you made to build Jerusalem 5
44 the vessels that were taken from Jerusalem 5
47 all who were going up with him to build Jerusalem. 5
48 to bring cedar timber from Lebanon to Jerusalem 5
55 until the day when . . Jerusalem built 5
57 to be done and to be sent to Jerusalem. 5
58 he lifted up his face to heaven toward Jerusalem 5
63 to go up and build Jerusalem and the temple 5
5: 2 to take them back to Jerusalem in safety 5
8 who returned to Jerusalem and the rest of Judea 5
44 to the temple of God which is in Jerusalem 5
46 some of the people settled in Jerusalem 5
56 the temple of God in Jerusalem 5
56 all who had come to Jerusalem from the captivity; 5
57 after they came to Judea and Jerusalem. 5
6: 1 the Jews who were in Judea and Jerusalem 5
2 the house of the Lord which is in Jerusalem 5
8 when we . . entered the city of Jerusalem 5
9 in the city of Jerusalem 5
18 taken out of the house in Jerusalem 5
19 put them in the temple at Jerusalem 5
20 the house of the Lord which is in Jerusalem 5
22 building of the house of the Lord in Jerusalem 5
24 the building of the house of the Lord in Jerusalem 5
26 took out of the house in Jerusalem 5
26 should be restored to the house in Jerusalem 5
30 as the priests in Jerusalem may indicate 5
33 damage that house of the Lord in Jerusalem. 5
8: 5 There came up with him to Jerusalem 5
6 arrived in Jerusalem on the new moon 5
10 may go with you to Jerusalem. 5
12 look into matters in Judea and Jerusalem 5
13 to carry to Jerusalem the gifts 5
13 to collect for the Lord in Jerusalem all the gold 5
14 the temple of their Lord which is in Jerusalem 5
15 altar of their Lord which is in Jerusalem. 5
17 the temple of your God which is in Jerusalem. 5
25 to glorify his house which is in Jerusalem 5
59 in Jerusalem, in the chambers of the house 5
60 the vessels which had been in Jerusalem 5
61 we arrived in Jerusalem 5
61 so we came to Jerusalem. 5
81 to give us a stronghold in Judea and Jerusalem. 5
91 a very great throng from Jerusalem 5
9: 3 throughout Judea and Jerusalem 5
3 they should assemble at Jerusalem 5
5 the men of . . Benjamin assembled at Jerusalem 5
37 settled in Jerusalem and in the country 5
2Es 2:10 that I will give them the kingdom of Jerusalem 6
10:20 be consoled because of the sorrow of Jerusalem. 6
47 that was the period of residence in Jerusalem. 6
48 the destruction which befell Jerusalem. 6
Tob 1: 4 deserted the house of Jerusalem. 3
6 I alone went often to Jerusalem for the feasts 3
7 sons of Levi who ministered at Jerusalem 5
7 and spend the proceeds each year at Jerusalem; 3
5:13 when we went together to Jerusalem to worship 3
13: 8 and give him thanks in Jerusalem. 3
9 O Jerusalem, the holy city, he will afflict you 3
16 Jerusalem will be built with sapphires 5
17 The streets of Jerusalem will be paved 5
14: 4 Jerusalem will be desolate 3
5 and will rebuild Jerusalem in splendor 5
Jdt 1: 9 and beyond the Jordan as far as Jerusalem 5
4: 2 alarmed both for Jerusalem and for the temple 5
6 Joakim . . who was in Jerusalem at the time 5
8 the senate . . of Israel, in session at Jerusalem 5
11 their children, living at Jerusalem 5
13 in Jerusalem before the sanctuary of the Lord 5
5:19 have occupied Jerusalem 5
9: 1 being offered in the house of God in Jerusalem 5
10: 8 Jerusalem may be exalted 5
11:13 minister in the presence of our God at Jerusalem 5
14 They have sent men to Jerusalem 5
19 till you come to Jerusalem 5
13: 4 for the exaltation of Jerusalem. 5
15: 5 Those in Jerusalem and all the hill country 5
8 who lived at Jerusalem 5
9 You are the exaltation of Jerusalem 5
16:18 When they arrived at Jerusalem 5

20 the people continued feasting in Jerusalem 5
AEs 11: 1 one of the residents of Jerusalem. 5
4 had brought from Jerusalem 5
Sir 24:11 in Jerusalem was my dominion. 5
36:13 Have pity on the city of thy sanctuary, Jerusalem 5
50:27 the son of Sirach, son of Eleazar, of Jerusalem 4
Bar 1: 2 at the time when the Chaldeans took Jerusalem 5
7 they sent it to Jerusalem to Jehoiakim the high 5
7 people who were present with him in Jerusalem. 5
9 had carried away from Jerusalem Jeconiah 5
15 to the inhabitants of Jerusalem 5
2: 2 done the like of what he has done in Jerusalem 5
23 to cease . . from the region about Jerusalem 5
4: 8 and you grieved Jerusalem, who reared you. 5
30 Take courage, O Jerusalem 5
36 Look toward the east, O Jerusalem 5
5: 1 Take off the garment . . O Jerusalem 5
5 Arise, O Jerusalem, stand upon the height and look 5
Aza 1: 5 thou hast brought upon us and upon Jerusalem 5
1Mc 1:14 So they built a gymnasium in Jerusalem 3
20 came to Jerusalem with a strong force. 3
29 he came to Jerusalem with a large force. 5
35 collecting the spoils of Jerusalem 5
38 Because of them the residents of Jerusalem fled; 5
44 the king sent letters by messengers to Jerusalem 5
2: 1 moved from Jerusalem and settled in Modein. 5
6 in Judah and Jerusalem 5
18 as . . those . . left in Jerusalem have done. 5
31 the troops in Jerusalem the city of David 5
3:34 As for the residents of Judea and Jerusalem 5
35 the remnant of Jerusalem 5
45 Jerusalem was uninhabited like a wilderness; 5
46 went to Mizpah, opposite Jerusalem 5
6: 7 which he had erected upon the altar in Jerusalem; 5
12 now I remember the evils I did in Jerusalem 5
26 have encamped against the citadel in Jerusalem 5
48 the king's army went up to Jerusalem against them 5
7:17 their blood they poured out round about Jerusalem 5
19 Then Bacchides departed from Jerusalem 5
27 So Nicanor came to Jerusalem with a large force 5
39 Now Nicanor went out from Jerusalem 5
47 and displayed them just outside Jerusalem. 5
8:22 sent to Jerusalem to remain with them there 5
9: 3 they encamped against Jerusalem; 5
50 Bacchides then returned to Jerusalem 5
53 put them under guard in the citadel at Jerusalem. 5
10: 7 Then Jonathan came to Jerusalem 5
10 Jonathan dwelt in Jerusalem 5
31 let Jerusalem and her environs . . be holy 5
32 the citadel in Jerusalem 5
39 the sanctuary in Jerusalem 5
43 whoever takes refuge at the temple in Jerusalem 3
45 the cost of rebuilding the walls of Jerusalem 5
66 Jonathan returned to Jerusalem in peace 5
74 and set out from Jerusalem 5
87 returned to Jerusalem with much booty. 5
11: 7 then he returned to Jerusalem. 5
20 to attack the citadel in Jerusalem 5
34 To all those who offer sacrifice in Jerusalem 3
41 he remove the troops of the citadel from Jerusalem 5
51 they returned to Jerusalem with much spoil. 5
62 sent them to Jerusalem 5
74 Jonathan returned to Jerusalem. 5
12:25 So he marched away from Jerusalem 5
36 to build the walls of Jerusalem still higher 5
13: 2 So he went up to Jerusalem 5
10 hastened to complete the walls of Jerusalem 5
39 other tax has been collected in Jerusalem 5
49 The men in the citadel at Jerusalem 5
14:19 read before the assembly in Jerusalem. 5
36 the men in the city of David in Jerusalem 5
37 and built the walls of Jerusalem higher. 5
15: 7 I grant freedom to Jerusalem and the sanctuary. 5
28 Gazara and the citadel in Jerusalem 5
32 Athenobius . . came to Jerusalem 5
16:20 he sent other men to take possession of Jerusalem 5
2Mc 1: 1 The Jewish brethren in Jerusalem 3
10 Those in Jerusalem and those in Judea 3
3: 6 the treasury in Jerusalem 3
9 When he had arrived at Jerusalem 3
37 to send on another mission to Jerusalem 3
4: 9 to enrol the men of Jerusalem 3
19 being Antiochian citizens from Jerusalem 3
21 arriving at Joppa he proceeded to Jerusalem. 3
5:22 at Jerusalem, Philip, by birth a Phrygian 3
25 When this man arrived in Jerusalem 3
6: 2 also to pollute the temple in Jerusalem 3
8:31 carried the rest of the spoils to Jerusalem. 3
36 the capture of the people of Jerusalem 3
9: 4 I will make Jerusalem a cemetery of Jews. 3
10:15 those who were banished from Jerusalem 3
11: 5 about five leagues from Jerusalem 3
8 while they were still near Jerusalem 3
12: 9 the glow of the light was seen in Jerusalem 3
29 Scythopolis, which is 75 miles from Jerusalem. 3
31 Then they went up to Jerusalem 3
43 sent it to Jerusalem 3
14:23 Nicanor stayed on in Jerusalem 3
37 A certain Razis, one of the elders of Jerusalem 3
15:30 carry them to Jerusalem. 3
3Mc 1: 9 After he had arrived in Jerusalem 3
3:16 we came on to Jerusalem also 3
4Mc 4: 3 in the Jerusalem treasuries 3
22 the people of Jerusalem . . rejoiced greatly 4
18: 5 he left Jerusalem 3

people of Jerusalem 1. Ἱεροσολυμίτης
Joh 7:25 Some of the people of Jerusalem therefore said 1

Jerusha 1. יְרוּשָׁא
2Kg 15:33 mother's name was Jeru'sha the daughter of Zadok. 1

Jerushah 1. יְרוּשָׁה
2Ch 27: 1 His mother's name was Jeru'shah 1

Jeshaiah 1. יְשַׁעְיָה 2. Ιεσιας 3. Ωσαιας
1Ch 3:21 sons of Hanani'ah . . Jeshai'ah, his son Rephai'ah 1
25: 3 sons of Jedu'thun: Gedali'ah, Zeri, Jeshai'ah, 1
15 eighth to Jeshai'ah, his sons and his brethren 1
26:25 from Elie'zer were . . his son Jeshai'ah 1
Ezr 8: 7 Of the sons of Elam, Jeshai'ah the son of Athali'ah 1
19 Hashabi'ah and . . Jeshai'ah of the sons of Merar'i 1
Neh 11: 7 Ma-asei'ah, son of I'thi-el, son of Jeshai'ah. 1
1Es 8:33 Of the sons of Elam, Jeshaiah the son of Gotholiah 2
48 Hashabiah and Annunus and Jeshaiah his brother 3

Jeshanah 1. יְשָׁנָה
1Sm 7:12 a stone and set it up between Mizpah and Jesha'nah •
2Ch 13:19 took cities . . Jesha'nah with its villages 1

Jesharelah 1. יְשַׂרְאֵלָה
1Ch 25:14 seventh to Jeshare'lah, his sons and his brethren 1

Jeshebeab 1. יֶשֶׁבְאָב
1Ch 24:13 to Huppah, the fourteenth to Jesheb'e-ab 1

Jesher 1. יֵשֶׁר
1Ch 2:18 these were her sons: Jesher, Shobab, and Ardon. 1

Jeshimon 1. יְשִׁימוֹן
1Sm 23:19 the hill of Hachi'lah, which is south of Jeshi'mon? 1
24 of Ma'on, in the Arabah to the south of Jeshi'mon. 1
26: 1 hill of Hachi'lah, which is on the east of Jeshi'mon? 1
3 Hachi'lah, which is . . on the east of Jeshi'mon. 1

Jeshishai 1. יְשִׁישַׁי
1Ch 5:14 sons of Ab'ihail . . son of Jeshish'ai, son of Jahdo 1

Jeshohaiah 1. יְשׁוֹחָיָה
1Ch 4:36 Eli-o-e'nai, Ja-ako'bah, Jeshohai'ah, Asai'ah 1

Jeshua 1. יֵשׁוּעַ 2. יְהוֹשׁוּעַ(A) 3. Ἰησοῦς
1Ch 24:11 the ninth to Jeshua, the tenth to Shecani'ah 1
2Ch 31:15 Jeshua, Shemai'ah, Amari'ah, and Shecani'ah 1
Ezr 2: 2 They came with Zerub'babel, Jeshua, Nehemi'ah 1
6 Pa'hath-moab, namely the sons of Jeshua and Jo'ab 1
36 sons of Jedai'ah, of the house of Jeshua, 973. 1
40 The Levites: the sons of Jeshua and Kad'mi-el 1
3: 2 Then arose Jeshua . . with his fellow priests 1
8 Zerub'babel . . and Jeshua . . made a beginning 1
9 Jeshua with his sons and his kinsmen, and Kad'mi-el 1
4: 3 Zerub'babel, Jeshua, and the rest of the heads 1
5: 2 Zerub'babel . . and Jeshua the son of Jo'zadak 2
8:33 Levites, Jo'zabad the son of Jeshua and No-adi'ah 1
10:18 of the sons of Jeshua the son of Jo'zadak 1
Neh 3:19 next to him Ezer the son of Jeshua, ruler of Mizpah 1
7: 7 came with Zerub'babel, Jeshua, Nehemi'ah, Azari'ah 1
11 Pa'hath-mo'ab, namely the sons of Jeshua and Jo'ab 1
39 sons of Jedai'ah, namely the house of Jeshua, 973. 1
43 sons of Jeshua, namely of Kad'mi-el of the sons 1
8: 7 Also Jesh'ua, Bani, Sherebi'ah, Jamin, Akkub 1
17 from the days of Jeshua the son of Nun to that day 1
9: 4 stood Jeshua, Bani, Kad'mi-el, Shebani'ah, Bunni 1
5 Levites, Jeshua, Kad'mi-el, Bani, Hashabnei'ah 1
10: 9 Levites: Jeshua the son of Azani'ah, Bin'nui 1
11:26 in Jeshua and in Mola'dah and Beth-pelet 1
12: 1 who came up with Zerub'babel . . and Jeshua 1
7 chiefs of the priests . . in the days of Jeshua. 1
8 Levites: Jeshua, Bin'nui, Kad'mi-el 1
10 Jeshua was the father of Joi'akim 1
24 chiefs of the Levites . . Jeshua the son 1
26 days of Joi'akim the son of Jeshua son of Jo'zadak 1
1Es 5: 5 Jeshua the son of Jozadak, son of Seraiah 3
8 They came with Zerubbabel and Jeshua 3
11 sons of Pahathmoab, of the sons of Jeshua and Joab 3
24 the sons of Jedaiah the son of Jeshua 3
26 sons of Jeshua and Kadmiel and Bannas and Sudias 3
48 Jeshua the son of Jozadak 3
56 Jeshua the son of Jozadak 3
58 Jeshua arose, and his sons and brethren 3
58 the sons of Jeshua Emadabun 3
68 So they approached Zerubbabel and Jeshua 3
70 Jeshua and the heads of the fathers' houses 3
6: 2 Jeshua the son of Jozadak arose 3
8:63 with them were Jozabad the son of Jeshua 3
9:19 of the sons of Jeshua the son of Jozadak 3
48 Jeshua and Anniuth and Sherebiah, Jamin, Akkub 3
Sir 49:12 so was Jeshua the son of Jozadak 3

Jeshurun 1. יְשֻׁרוּן
Deu 32:15 Jesh'urun waxed fat, and kicked; 1
33: 5 Thus the LORD became king in Jesh'urun 1
26 There is none like God, O Jesh'urun, who rides 1
Isa 44: 2 O Jacob my servant, Jeshu'run whom I have chosen. 1

Jesimiel 1. יְשִׂימִאֵל
1Ch 4:36 Asai'ah, Ad'i-el, Jesim'iel, Benai'ah 1

Jesse 1. יִשַׁי 2. Ἰεσσαί
Rut 4:17 They named him Obed; he was the father of Jesse 1
22 Obed of Jesse, and Jesse of David. 1
22 Obed of Jesse, and Jesse of David. 1
1Sm 16: 1 and go; I will send you to Jesse the Bethlehemite 1
3 invite Jesse to the sacrifice, and I will show you 1
5 And he consecrated Jesse and his sons 1
8 Jesse called Abin'adab, and made him pass before 1
9 Then Jesse made Shammah pass by. 1
10 Jesse made seven of his sons pass before Samuel. 1
10 And Samuel said to Jesse, "The LORD has not chosen 1
11 And Samuel said to Jesse, "Are all your sons here? 1
11 And Samuel said to Jesse, "Send and fetch him; 1
18 I have seen a son of Jesse the Bethlehemite 1
19 Saul sent messengers to Jesse, and said, "Send me 1
20 Jesse took an ass laden with bread 1
22 And Saul sent to Jesse, saying, "Let David remain 1
17:12 an Eph'rathite of Bethlehem in Judah, named Jesse 1
13 The three eldest sons of Jesse had followed Saul 1
17 And Jesse said to David his son, "Take 1
20 David rose . . and went, as Jesse had commanded him; 1
58 I am the son of . . Jesse the Bethlehemite. 1
20:27 Why has not the son of Jesse come to the meal 1
30 do I not know that you have chosen the son of Jesse 1
31 as long as the son of Jesse lives upon the earth 1
22: 7 will the son of Jesse give every one of you fields 1
8 when my son makes a league with the son of Jesse 1
9 I saw the son of Jesse coming to Nob, to Ahim'elech 1
13 Why have you conspired . . you and the son of Jesse 1
25:10 Who is David? Who is the son of Jesse? 1
2Sm 20: 1 and we have no inheritance in the son of Jesse; 1
23: 1 The oracle of David, the son of Jesse 1
1Kg 12:16 We have no inheritance in the son of Jesse. 1
1Ch 2:12 Bo'az of Obed, Obed of Jesse. 1
13 Jesse was the father of Eli'ab his first-born 1
10:14 the kingdom over to David the son of Jesse. 1
12:18 We are yours, O David; and with you, O son of Jesse! 1
29:26 David the son of Jesse reigned over all Israel. 1
2Ch 10:16 We have no inheritance in the son of Jesse. 1
11:18 Ab'ihail the daughter of Eli'ab the son of Jesse; 1
Ps 72:20 The prayers of David, the son of Jesse, are ended. 1
Isa 11: 1 shall come forth a shoot from the stump of Jesse 1
10 the root of Jesse shall stand as an ensign 1
Mat 1: 5 and Obed the father of Jesse 2
6 Jesse the father of David the king. 2
Lke 3:32 the son of Jesse, the son of Obed, the son of Bo'az 2
Act 13:22 I have found in David the son of Jesse a man 2
Rom 15:12 further Isaiah says, "The root of Jesse shall come 2
Sir 45:25 David, the son of Jesse, of the tribe of Judah 2

Jesus 1. Ἰησοῦς
Mat 1: 1 The book of the genealogy of Jesus Christ 1
16 Joseph the husband of Mary, of whom Jesus was born 1
18 the birth of Jesus Christ took place in this way. 1
21 you shall call his name Jesus, for he will save his 1
25 she had borne a son; and he called his name Jesus. 1
2: 1 Now when Jesus was born in Bethlehem of Judea 1
3:13 Jesus came from Galilee to the Jordan to John 1
15 But Jesus answered him, "Let it be so now; 1
16 when Jesus was baptized, he went up immediately 1
4: 1 Then Jesus was led up by the Spirit 1
7 Jesus said to him, "Again it is written, 'You shall 1
10 Jesus said to him, "Begone, Satan! for it is written 1
17 From that time Jesus began to preach, saying 1
7:28 And when Jesus finished these sayings 1
8: 4 Jesus said to him, "See that you say nothing 1
10 When Jesus heard him, he marveled 1
13 to the centurion Jesus said, "Go; be it done for you 1
14 when Jesus entered Peter's house 1
18 Now when Jesus saw great crowds around him 1
20 Jesus said to him, "Foxes have holes 1
22 Jesus said to him, "Follow me, and leave the dead 1
34 behold, all the city came out to meet Jesus 1
9: 2 and when Jesus saw their faith he said 1
4 Jesus, knowing their thoughts, said 1
9 As Jesus passed on from there, he saw a man 1
10 sat down with Jesus and his disciples. 1
15 Jesus said to them, "Can the wedding guests mourn 1
19 Jesus rose and followed him, with his disciples. 1
22 Jesus turned, and seeing her he said, "Take heart 1
23 when Jesus came to the ruler's house 1
27 as Jesus passed on from there 1
28 the blind men came to him; and Jesus said to them 1
30 And Jesus sternly charged them 1
35 Jesus went about all the cities and villages 1
10: 5 These twelve Jesus sent out, charging them 1
11: 1 when Jesus had finished instructing 1
4 Jesus answered them, "Go and tell John 1
7 As they went away, Jesus began to speak 1

25 At that time Jesus declared, "I thank thee, Father 1
12: 1 At that time Jesus went through the grainfields 1
15 Jesus, aware of this, withdrew from there 1
13: 1 That same day Jesus went out of the house and sat 1
34 All this Jesus said to the crowds in parables; 1
53 when Jesus had finished these parables 1
57 But Jesus said to them 1
14: 1 the tetrarch heard about the fame of Jesus; 1
12 and they went and told Jesus. 1
13 when Jesus heard this, he withdrew from there 1
16 Jesus said, "They need not go away 1
29 walked on the water and came to Jesus; 1
31 Jesus immediately reached out his hand 1
15: 1 scribes came to Jesus from Jerusalem and said 1
21 Jesus went away from there and withdrew 1
28 Then Jesus answered her 1
29 Jesus went on from there 1
32 Jesus called his disciples to him and said 1
34 Jesus said to them, "How many loaves have you? 1
16: 6 Jesus said to them 1
8 Jesus, aware of this, said 1
13 Now when Jesus came into the district 1
17 Jesus answered him 1
21 From that time Jesus began to show his disciples 1
24 Then Jesus told his disciples 1
17: 1 after six days Jesus took with him Peter 1
4 Peter said to Jesus 1
7 Jesus came and touched them, saying 1
8 they saw no one but Jesus only. 1
9 coming down the mountain, Jesus commanded them 1
17 Jesus answered 1
18 Jesus rebuked him, and the demon came out of him 1
19 Then the disciples came to Jesus privately 1
22 Jesus said to them 1
25 when he came home, Jesus spoke to him first, saying 1
26 Jesus said to him, "Then the sons are free. 1
18: 1 At that time the disciples came to Jesus, saying 1
22 Jesus said to him, "I do not say to you seven times 1
19: 1 Now when Jesus had finished these sayings 1
14 Jesus said, "Let the children come to me 1
18 And Jesus said, "You shall not kill 1
21 Jesus said to him, "If you would be perfect 1
23 Jesus said to his disciples, "Truly, I say to you 1
26 Jesus looked at them and said to them 1
28 Jesus said to them, "Truly, I say to you 1
20:17 as Jesus was going up to Jerusalem 1
22 Jesus answered, "You do not know 1
25 Jesus called them to him and said 1
30 when they heard that Jesus was passing by 1
32 Jesus stopped and called them, saying 1
34 Jesus in pity touched their eyes 1
21: 1 then Jesus sent two disciples 1
6 The disciples went and did as Jesus had directed 1
11 This is the prophet Jesus from Nazareth 1
12 Jesus entered the temple of God 1
16 Jesus said to them, "Yes 1
21 Jesus answered them, "Truly, I say to you 1
24 Jesus answered them, "I also will ask you 1
27 So they answered Jesus, "We do not know. 1
31 They said, "The first." Jesus said to them 1
42 Jesus said to them, "Have you never read 1
22: 1 again Jesus spoke to them in parables, saying 1
18 Jesus, aware of their malice, said 1
20 Jesus said to them •
29 Jesus answered them, "You are wrong 1
41 Jesus asked them a question 1
23: 1 Then said Jesus to the crowds 1
24: 1 Jesus left the temple and was going away 1
4 Jesus answered them, "Take heed that no one leads 1
26: 1 When Jesus had finished all these sayings 1
4 in order to arrest Jesus by stealth and kill him. 1
6 when Jesus was at Bethany in the house of Simon 1
10 Jesus, aware of this, said to them 1
17 the disciples came to Jesus, saying 1
19 the disciples did as Jesus had directed them 1
26 as they were eating, Jesus took bread, and blessed 1
31 Then Jesus said to them, "You will all fall away 1
34 Jesus said to him, "Truly, I say to you 1
36 Then Jesus went with them to a place 1
49 he came up to Jesus at once and said, "Hail, Master! 1
50 Jesus said to him, "Friend, why are you here? 1
50 came up and laid hands on Jesus and seized him. 1
51 those who were with Jesus stretched out his hand 1
52 Then Jesus said to him, "Put your sword back 1
55 At that hour Jesus said to the crowds 1
57 Then those who had seized Jesus 1
59 council sought false testimony against Jesus 1
63 Jesus was silent. And the high priest said to him 1
64 Jesus said to him, "You have said so. But I tell you 1
69 You also were with Jesus the Galilean. 1
71 This man was with Jesus of Nazareth. 1
75 Peter remembered the saying of Jesus 1
27: 1 elders of the people took counsel against Jesus 1
11 Now Jesus stood before the governor 1
11 Jesus said, "You have said so. 1
17 Barab'bas or Jesus who is called Christ? 1
20 to ask for Barab'bas and destroy Jesus. 1
22 what shall I do with Jesus who is called Christ? 1
26 having scourged Jesus 1
27 Then the soldiers of the governor took Jesus 1
37 This is Jesus the King of the Jews. 1
46 Jesus cried with a loud voice 1
50 Jesus cried again with a loud voice 1
54 keeping watch over Jesus, saw the earthquake 1
55 who had followed Jesus from Galilee 1
57 who also was a disciple of Jesus. 1
58 He went to Pilate and asked for the body of Jesus. 1
28: 5 I know that you seek Jesus who was crucified. 1
9 behold, Jesus met them and said, "Hail! 1
10 Then Jesus said to them, "Do not be afraid 1
16 to the mountain to which Jesus had directed 1
18 Jesus came and said to them 1
Mrk 1: 1 The beginning of the Gospel of Jesus Christ 1
9 In those days Jesus came from Nazareth of Galilee 1
14 after John was arrested Jesus came into Galilee 1
17 Jesus said to them, "Follow me 1
24 What have you to do with us, Jesus of Nazareth? 1
25 Jesus rebuked him, saying, "Be silent, and come out 1
45 so that Jesus could no longer openly enter a town •
2: 5 when Jesus saw their faith 1
8 immediately Jesus, perceiving in his spirit 1
15 sitting with Jesus and his disciples 1
17 when Jesus heard it, he said to them 1
19 Jesus said to them, "Can the wedding guests fast 1
3: 7 Jesus withdrew with his disciples to the sea 1
5: 6 when he saw Jesus from afar, he ran and worshiped 1
7 What have you to do with me, Jesus 1
9 Jesus asked him, "What is your name? •
15 they came to Jesus, and saw the demoniac sitting 1
17 they began to beg Jesus to depart •
20 how much Jesus had done for him 1
21 Jesus had crossed again in the boat to the other side 1
27 She had heard the reports about Jesus 1
30 Jesus, perceiving in himself that power had gone 1
36 Jesus said to the ruler of the synagogue 1
6: 4 Jesus said to them, "A prophet is not without honor 1
14 Jesus' name had become known •
30 The apostles returned to Jesus, and told him all 1
8:17 being aware of it, Jesus said to them •
27 Jesus went on with his disciples 1
9: 2 And after six days Jesus took with him Peter 1
4 they were talking to Jesus. 1
5 Peter said to Jesus, "Master, it is well 1
8 saw any one with them but Jesus only. 1
21 Jesus asked his father, "How long has he had this? •
23 Jesus said to him, "If you can! 1
25 Jesus saw that a crowd came running together 1
27 Jesus took him by the hand and lifted him up 1
39 Jesus said, "Do not forbid him 1
10: 5 Jesus said to them, "For your hardness of heart 1
14 when Jesus saw it he was indignant 1
18 Jesus said to him, "Why do you call me good? 1
21 Jesus looking upon him loved him, and said to him 1
23 Jesus looked around and said to his disciples 1
24 Jesus said to them again 1
27 Jesus looked at them and said 1
29 Jesus said, "Truly, I say to you, there is no one 1
32 Jesus was walking ahead of them 1
38 Jesus said to them, "You do not know 1
39 Jesus said to them, "The cup that I drink 1
42 Jesus called them to him and said to them 1
47 when he heard that it was Jesus of Nazareth 1
47 Jesus, Son of David, have mercy on me! 1
49 Jesus stopped and said, "Call him. 1
50 he sprang up and came to Jesus. 1
51 Jesus said .. "What do you want me to do for you? 1
52 Jesus said to him, "Go your way 1
11: 6 they told them what Jesus had said 1
7 they brought the colt to Jesus 1
22 Jesus answered them, "Have faith in God. 1
29 Jesus said to them, "I will ask you a question; 1
33 So they answered Jesus, "We do not know. 1
33 Jesus said to them, "Neither will I tell you 1
12:17 Jesus said to them, "Render to Caesar the things 1
24 Jesus said to them, "Is not this why you are wrong 1
29 Jesus answered, "The first is, 'Hear, O Israel 1
34 when Jesus saw that he answered wisely 1
35 as Jesus taught in the temple, he said 1
13: 2 Jesus said to him, "Do you see 1
5 Jesus began to say to them, "Take heed 1
14: 6 Jesus said, "Let her alone; why do you trouble her? 1
18 as they were at table eating, Jesus said 1
27 Jesus said to them, "You will all fall away 1
30 Jesus said to him, "Truly, I say to you 1
48 Jesus said to them, "Have you come out 1
53 they led Jesus to the high priest 1
55 sought testimony against Jesus 1
60 stood up in the midst, and asked Jesus 1
62 Jesus said, "I am; and you will see the Son of man 1
67 said, "You also were with the Nazarene, Jesus. 1
72 Peter remembered how Jesus had said to him 1
15: 1 they bound Jesus and led him away 1
5 Jesus made no further answer 1
15 having scourged Jesus 1
34 at the ninth hour Jesus cried with a loud voice 1
37 Jesus uttered a loud cry, and breathed his last. 1
43 went to Pilate, and asked for the body of Jesus. 1
16: 6 Do not be amazed; you seek Jesus of Nazareth 1
19 So then the Lord Jesus, after he had spoken to them 1
Lke 1:31 you shall call his name Jesus. 1
2:21 he was called Jesus, the name given by the angel 1
27 when the parents brought in the child Jesus 1
43 the boy Jesus stayed behind in Jerusalem 1
52 Jesus increased in wisdom and in stature 1
3:21 when Jesus also had been baptized 1
23 Jesus, when he began his ministry 1
4: 1 Jesus, full of the Holy Spirit, returned 1
4 Jesus answered him, "It is written 1
8 Jesus answered him, "It is written 1
12 Jesus answered him, "It is said, 'You shall not tempt 1
14 Jesus returned .. into Galilee 1
34 Ah! What have you to do with us, Jesus of Nazareth? 1
35 Jesus rebuked him, saying, "Be silent 1
5: 8 he fell down at Jesus' knees, saying 1
10 Jesus said to Simon, "Do not be afraid 1
12 when he saw Jesus 1
18 they sought to bring him in and lay him before Jesus; •
19 through the tiles into the midst before Jesus. 1
22 When Jesus perceived their questionings 1
31 Jesus answered them, "Those who are well 1
34 Jesus said to them, "Can you make wedding guests 1
6: 3 Jesus answered, "Have you not read what David did 1
9 Jesus said to them, "I ask you 1
11 what they might do to Jesus. 1
7: 3 When he heard of Jesus 1
4 when they came to Jesus 1
6 Jesus went with them 1
9 When Jesus heard this he marveled at him 1
40 Jesus answering said to him, "Simon 1
8:28 When he saw Jesus, he cried out and fell down 1
28 Jesus, Son of the Most High God 1
30 Jesus then asked him, "What is your name? 1
35 they came to Jesus 1
35 sitting at the feet of Jesus 1
39 proclaiming .. how much Jesus had done for him. 1
40 Now when Jesus returned, the crowd welcomed him 1
41 falling at Jesus' feet he besought him to come 1
45 Jesus said, "Who was it that touched me? 1
46 Jesus said, "Some one touched me 1
50 Jesus on hearing this answered him, "Do not fear; 1
9:33 Peter said to Jesus, "Master, it is well 1
36 when the voice had spoken, Jesus was found alone. 1
41 Jesus answered, "O faithless and perverse 1
42 But Jesus rebuked the unclean spirit 1
47 Jesus perceived the thought of their hearts 1
50 Jesus said to him, "Do not forbid him 1
58 Jesus said to him, "Foxes have holes 1
62 Jesus said to him, "No one 1
10:29 he, desiring to justify himself, said to Jesus 1
30 Jesus replied, "A man was going down 1
37 Jesus said to him "Go and do likewise. 1
13:12 when Jesus saw her, he called her and said to her 1
14 Jesus had healed on the sabbath 1
14: 3 Jesus spoke to the lawyers and Pharisees, saying 1
17:13 lifted up their voices and said, "Jesus, Master 1
16 he fell on his face at Jesus' feet •
17 Then said Jesus, "Were not ten cleansed? 1
18:16 Jesus called them to him, saying 1
19 Jesus said to him, "Why do you call me good? 1
22 when Jesus heard it, he said to him, "One thing 1
24 Jesus looking at him said, "How hard it is for those 1
37 They told him, "Jesus of Nazareth is passing by. 1
38 he cried, "Jesus, Son of David, have mercy on me! 1
40 Jesus stopped, and commanded him to be brought 1
42 Jesus said to him, "Receive your sight 1
19: 3 he sought to see who Jesus was, but could not 1
5 when Jesus came to the place, he looked up and said 1
9 Jesus said to him, "Today salvation has come 1
35 they brought it to Jesus 1
35 they set Jesus upon it. 1
20: 8 Jesus said to them, "Neither will I tell you 1
34 Jesus said to them, "The sons of this age marry 1
22: 8 So Jesus sent Peter and John, saying, "Go •
47 He drew near to Jesus to kiss him; 1
48 Jesus said to him, "Judas 1
51 Jesus said, "No more of this! 1
52 Then Jesus said to the chief priests 1
63 Now the men who were holding Jesus mocked him •
23: 8 When Herod saw Jesus, he was very glad 1
20 desiring to release Jesus; 1
25 Jesus he delivered up to their will. 1
26 and laid on him the cross, to carry it behind Jesus. 1
28 Jesus turning to them said 1
34 Jesus said, "Father, forgive them 1
42 he said, "Jesus, remember me 1
46 Then Jesus, crying with a loud voice, said, "Father 1
52 went to Pilate and asked for the body of Jesus. 1
24:15 Jesus himself drew near and went with them. 1
19 they said to him, "Concerning Jesus of Nazareth 1
36 Jesus himself stood among them 1
Joh 1:17 grace and truth came through Jesus Christ. 1
29 The next day he saw Jesus coming toward him 1
36 and he looked at Jesus as he walked, and said 1
37 heard him say this, and they followed Jesus. 1
38 Jesus turned, and saw them following, and said 1
42 He brought him to Jesus. Jesus looked at him 1
42 Jesus looked at him, and said, "So you are Simon 1

43 The next day Jesus decided to go to Galilee. 1
45 found him . . Jesus of Nazareth, the son of Joseph 1
47 Jesus saw Nathan'a-el coming to him, and said of him 1
48 Jesus answered him, "Before Philip called you 1
50 Jesus answered him, "Because I said to you 1
2: 1 at Cana . . and the mother of Jesus was there; 1
2 Jesus also was invited to the marriage 1
3 When the wine failed, the mother of Jesus said 1
4 Jesus said to her, "O woman 1
7 Jesus said to them, "Fill the jars with water. 1
11 first of his signs, Jesus did at Cana in Galilee 1
13 and Jesus went up to Jerusalem. 1
19 Jesus answered them, "Destroy this temple 1
22 believed . . the word which Jesus had spoken. 1
24 but Jesus did not trust himself to them 1
3: 2 This man came to Jesus by night and said to him •
3 Jesus answered him, "Truly, truly, I say to you 1
5 Jesus answered, "Truly, truly, I say to you 1
10 Jesus answered him, "Are you a teacher of Israel 1
22 Jesus and his disciples went into the land 1
4: 1 Jesus was making and baptizing more disciples 1
2 (although Jesus himself did not baptize 1
6 Jesus, wearied as he was with his journey, sat down 1
7 Jesus said to her, "Give me a drink. 1
10 Jesus answered her, "If you knew the gift of God 1
13 Jesus said to her, "Every one who drinks 1
16 Jesus said to her, "Go, call your husband •
17 Jesus said to her, "You are right in saying 1
21 Jesus said to her, "Woman, believe me 1
26 Jesus said to her, "I who speak to you am he. 1
34 Jesus said to them, "My food is to do the will of him 1
44 For Jesus himself testified that a prophet 1
47 heard that Jesus had come from Judea to Galilee 1
48 Jesus therefore said to him, "Unless you see signs 1
50 Jesus said to him, "Go; your son will live. 1
50 The man believed the word that Jesus spoke to him 1
53 knew that was the hour when Jesus had said to him 1
54 This was now the second sign that Jesus did 1
5: 1 and Jesus went up to Jerusalem. 1
6 When Jesus saw him 1
8 Jesus said to him, "Rise, take up your pallet 1
13 Jesus had withdrawn 1
14 Afterward, Jesus found him in the temple, and said 1
15 it was Jesus who had healed him. 1
16 this was why the Jews persecuted Jesus 1
17 Jesus answered them, "My Father is working still 1
19 Jesus said to them, "Truly, truly, I say to you 1
6: 1 Jesus went to the other side of the Sea of Galilee 1
3 Jesus went up on the mountain 1
5 Jesus said to Philip, "How are we to buy bread 1
10 Jesus said, "Make the people sit down. 1
11 Jesus then took the loaves 1
15 Jesus withdrew again to the mountain by himself. 1
17 and Jesus had not yet come to them. 1
19 they saw Jesus walking on the sea 1
22 Jesus had not entered the boat with his disciples 1
24 when the people saw that Jesus was not there 1
24 went to Caper'na-um, seeking Jesus. 1
26 Jesus answered them, "Truly, truly, I say to you 1
29 Jesus answered them, "This is the work of God 1
32 Jesus then said to them, "Truly, truly, I say to you 1
35 Jesus said to them, "I am the bread of life 1
42 They said, "Is not this Jesus, the son of Joseph 1
43 Jesus answered them, "Do not murmur 1
53 Jesus said to them, "Truly, truly, I say to you 1
61 Jesus . . said to them, "Do you take offense at this? 1
64 Jesus knew from the first 1
67 Jesus said to the twelve 1
70 Jesus answered them, "Did I not choose you 1
7: 1 After this Jesus went about in Galilee 1
6 Jesus said to them, "My time has not yet come 1
14 Jesus went up into the temple and taught. 1
16 Jesus answered them, "My teaching is not mine 1
21 Jesus answered them, "I did one deed 1
28 Jesus proclaimed, as he taught in the temple 1
33 Jesus then said, "I shall be with you 1
37 Jesus stood up and proclaimed, "If any one thirst 1
39 because Jesus was not yet glorified. 1
8: 1 Jesus went to the Mount of Olives. 1
6 Jesus bent down 1
9 Jesus was left alone with the woman •
10 Jesus looked up and said to her, "Woman 1
11 Jesus said, "Neither do I condemn you 1
12 Again Jesus spoke to them, saying, "I am the light 1
14 Jesus answered, "Even if I do bear witness 1
19 Jesus answered, "You know neither me nor my Father 1
25 Jesus said to them, "Even what I have told you 1
28 Jesus said, "When you have lifted up the Son of man 1
31 Jesus then said to the Jews who had believed 1
34 Jesus answered them, "Truly, truly, I say to you 1
39 Jesus said to them, "If you were Abraham's children 1
42 Jesus said to them, "If God were your Father 1
49 Jesus answered, "I have not a demon 1
54 Jesus answered, "If I glorify myself 1
58 Jesus said to them, "Truly, truly, I say to you 1
59 Jesus hid himself, and went out of the temple. 1
9: 3 Jesus answered, "It was not that this man sinned 1
11 He answered, "The man called Jesus made clay 1
14 Now it was a sabbath day when Jesus made the clay 1
35 Jesus heard that they had cast him out 1
37 Jesus said to him, "You have seen him 1
39 Jesus said, "For judgment I came into this world 1
41 Jesus said to them, "If you were blind 1
10: 6 This figure Jesus used with them 1
7 Jesus again said to them, "Truly, truly, I say to you 1
23 it was winter, and Jesus was walking in the temple 1
25 Jesus answered them, "I told you 1
32 Jesus answered them, "I have shown you 1
34 Jesus answered them, "Is it not written in your law 1
11: 4 when Jesus heard it he said 1
5 Jesus loved Martha and her sister and Laz'arus. 1
9 Jesus answered, "Are there not twelve hours 1
13 Now Jesus had spoken of his death 1
14 Jesus told them plainly, "Laz'arus is dead; 1
17 Now when Jesus came 1
20 When Martha heard that Jesus was coming 1
21 Martha said to Jesus, "Lord if you had been here 1
23 Jesus said to her, "Your brother will rise again. 1
25 Jesus said to her, "I am the resurrection 1
30 Now Jesus had not yet come to the village 1
32 Mary, when she came where Jesus was and saw him 1
33 When Jesus saw her weeping 1
35 Jesus wept. 1
38 Then Jesus, deeply moved again, came to the tomb 1
39 Jesus said, "Take away the stone. 1
40 Jesus said to her, "Did I not tell you 1
41 Jesus lifted up his eyes and said, "Father 1
44 Jesus said to them, "Unbind him, and let him go. 1
46 told them what Jesus had done. 1
51 Jesus should die for the nation 1
54 Jesus therefore no longer went about openly 1
56 They were looking for Jesus 1
12: 1 Jesus came to Bethany, where Laz'arus was 1
1 whom Jesus had raised from the dead. 1
3 anointed the feet of Jesus 1
7 Jesus said, "Let her alone 1
9 they came, not only on account of Jesus 1
11 Jews were going away and believing in Jesus. 1
12 heard that Jesus was coming to Jerusalem. 1
14 Jesus found a young ass and sat upon it 1
16 when Jesus was glorified, then they remembered 1
21 Sir, we wish to see Jesus. 1
22 Andrew went with Philip and they told Jesus. 1
23 Jesus answered them, "The hour has come 1
30 Jesus answered, "This voice has come for your sake 1
35 Jesus said to them, "The light is with you 1
36 When Jesus had said this 1
44 Jesus cried out and said, "He who believes in me 1
13: 1 when Jesus knew that his hour had come to depart 1
3 Jesus, knowing that . . •
7 Jesus answered . . "What I am doing you do not know 1
8 Jesus answered him, "If I do not wash you 1
10 Jesus said to him, "He who has bathed 1
21 When Jesus had thus spoken 1
23 One of his disciples, whom Jesus loved 1
23 was lying close to the breast of Jesus; 1
25 lying thus, close to the breast of Jesus, he said 1
26 Jesus answered, "It is he 1
27 Jesus said to him, "What you are going to do 1
29 Some thought that . . Jesus was telling him 1
31 When he had gone out, Jesus said 1
36 Jesus answered, "Where I am going 1
38 Jesus answered, "Will you lay down your life for me? 1
14: 6 Jesus said to him, "I am the way, and the truth 1
9 Jesus said to him, "Have I been with you so long 1
23 Jesus answered him, "If a man loves me 1
16:19 Jesus knew that they wanted to ask him 1
31 Jesus answered them, "Do you now believe? 1
17: 1 When Jesus had spoken these words 1
3 Jesus Christ whom thou hast sent. 1
18: 1 When Jesus had spoken these words 1
2 Jesus often met there with his disciples. 1
4 Jesus, knowing all that was to befall him 1
5 They answered him, "Jesus of Nazareth. 1
5 Jesus said to them, "I am he. •
7 And they said, "Jesus of Nazareth. 1
8 Jesus answered, "I told you that I am he 1
11 Jesus said to Peter 1
12 officers of the Jews seized Jesus and bound him. 1
15 Simon Peter followed Jesus 1
15 he entered the court . . along with Jesus 1
19 The high priest then questioned Jesus 1
20 Jesus answered him, "I have spoken openly 1
22 one of the officers . . struck Jesus with his hand 1
23 Jesus answered him, "If I have spoken wrongly 1
28 they led Jesus from the house of Ca'iaphas 1
32 to fulfil the word which Jesus had spoken 1
33 Pilate . . called Jesus, and said to him 1
34 Jesus answered, "Do you say this of your own accord 1
36 Jesus answered, "My kingship is not of this world; 1
37 Jesus answered, "You say that I am a king 1
19: 1 Pilate took Jesus and scourged him. 1
5 Jesus came out, wearing the crown of thorns 1
9 he . . said to Jesus, "Where are you from? 1
9 But Jesus gave no answer. 1
11 Jesus answered him, "You would have no power 1
13 he brought Jesus out 1
17 they took Jesus, and he went out 1
18 one on either side, and Jesus between them. 1
19 it read, "Jesus of Nazareth, the King of the Jews. 1
20 the place where Jesus was crucified 1
23 When the soldiers had crucified Jesus 1
25 standing by the cross of Jesus were his mother 1
26 When Jesus saw his mother 1
28 After this Jesus . . said . . "I thirst. 1
30 When Jesus had received the vinegar, he said 1
33 when they came to Jesus 1
38 was a disciple of Jesus, but secretly 1
38 that he might take away the body of Jesus 1
40 They took the body of Jesus 1
42 they laid Jesus there. 1
20: 2 the other disciple, the one whom Jesus loved 1
12 sitting where the body of Jesus had lain 1
14 she turned round and saw Jesus standing 1
14 she did not know that it was Jesus. 1
15 Jesus said to her, "Woman, why are you weeping? 1
16 Jesus said to her, "Mary. 1
17 Jesus said to her, "Do not hold me 1
19 Jesus came and stood among them and said to them 1
21 Jesus said to them again, "Peace be with you •
24 was not with them when Jesus came. 1
26 Jesus came and stood among them, and said 1
29 Jesus said to him, "Have you believed 1
30 Now Jesus did many other signs 1
31 Jesus is the Christ, the Son of God 1
21: 1 After this Jesus revealed himself again 1
4 Just as day was breaking, Jesus stood on the beach; 1
4 yet the disciples did not know that it was Jesus. 1
5 Jesus said to them, "Children have you any fish? 1
7 That disciple whom Jesus loved said to Peter 1
10 Jesus said to them, "Bring some of the fish 1
12 Jesus said to them, "Come and have breakfast. 1
13 Jesus came and took the bread and gave it to them 1
14 Jesus was revealed to the disciples 1
15 Jesus said to Simon Peter, "Simon, son of John 1
17 Jesus said to him, "Feed my sheep. •
20 following them the disciple whom Jesus loved 1
21 When Peter saw him, he said to Jesus, "Lord 1
22 Jesus said to him, "If it is my will that he remain 1
23 yet Jesus did not say to him that he was not to die 1
25 there are also many other things which Jesus did; 1
Act 1: 1 dealt with all that Jesus began to do and teach 1
11 This Jesus, who was taken up from you 1
14 Mary the mother of Jesus, and with his brothers. 1
16 Judas who was guide to those who arrested Jesus. 1
21 the Lord Jesus went in and out among us 1
2:22 Jesus of Nazareth, a man attested to you by God 1
23 this Jesus . . you crucified and killed •
32 This Jesus God raised up 1
36 Lord and Christ, this Jesus whom you crucified. 1
38 in the name of Jesus Christ 1
3: 6 in the name of Jesus Christ of Nazareth, walk. 1
13 glorified his servant Jesus 1
16 the faith which is through Jesus •
20 he may send the Christ appointed for you, Jesus 1
4: 2 in Jesus the resurrection from the dead. 1
10 by the name of Jesus Christ of Nazareth 1
13 they recognized that they had been with Jesus. 1
18 not to speak or teach at all in the name of Jesus. 1
27 thy holy servant Jesus, whom thou didst anoint 1
30 through the name of thy holy servant Jesus. 1
33 testimony to the resurrection of the Lord Jesus 1
5:30 God of our fathers raised Jesus whom you killed 1
40 charged them not to speak in the name of Jesus 1
42 preaching Jesus as the Christ. 1
6:14 Jesus of Nazareth will destroy this place 1
7:55 Jesus standing at the right hand of God; 1
59 Lord Jesus, receive my spirit. 1
8:12 the name of Jesus Christ 1
16 baptized in the name of the Lord Jesus. 1
35 he told him the good news of Jesus. 1
9: 5 he said, "I am Jesus, whom you are persecuting; 1
17 the Lord Jesus who appeared to you on the road 1
20 immediately he proclaimed Jesus, saying 1
22 by proving that Jesus was the Christ. •
27 he had preached boldly in the name of Jesus. 1
34 Peter said to him, "Aene'as, Jesus Christ heals you; 1
10:36 preaching good news of peace by Jesus Christ 1
38 how God anointed Jesus of Nazareth 1
48 baptized in the name of Jesus Christ 1
11:17 when we believed in the Lord Jesus Christ 1
20 preaching the Lord Jesus. 1
13:23 brought to Israel a Savior, Jesus, as he promised. 1
33 this he has fulfilled . . by raising Jesus 1
15:11 saved through the grace of the Lord Jesus 1
26 for the sake of our Lord Jesus Christ. 1
16: 7 the Spirit of Jesus did not allow them; 1
18 I charge you in the name of Jesus Christ 1
31 Believe in the Lord Jesus, and you will be saved 1
17: 3 This Jesus, whom I proclaim to you, is the Christ. 1
7 saying that there is another king, Jesus. 1
18 because he preached Jesus and the resurrection. 1
18: 5 testifying to the Jews that the Christ was Jesus. 1
25 and taught accurately the things concerning Jesus 1
28 showing . . that the Christ was Jesus. 1
19: 4 the one who was to come after him, that is, Jesus. 1
5 baptized in the name of the Lord Jesus. 1

13 to pronounce the name of the Lord Jesus 1
13 I adjure you by the Jesus whom Paul preaches. 1
15 Jesus I know, and Paul I know; but who are you? 1
17 the name of the Lord Jesus was extolled. 1
20:21 faith in our Lord Jesus Christ. 1
24 ministry which I received from the Lord Jesus 1
35 the words of the Lord Jesus, how he said 1
21:13 die at Jerusalem for the name of the Lord Jesus. 1
22: 8 'I am Jesus of Nazareth whom you are persecuting.' 1
24:24 and heard him speak upon faith in Christ Jesus. 1
25:19 dispute . . about one Jesus, who was dead 1
26: 9 in opposing the name of Jesus of Nazareth. 1
15 I am Jesus whom you are persecuting. 1
28:23 trying to convince them about Jesus 1
31 teaching about the Lord Jesus Christ 1
Rom 1: 1 Paul, a servant of Jesus Christ 1
4 Jesus Christ our Lord 1
6 who are called to belong to Jesus Christ 1
7 from God our Father and the Lord Jesus Christ. 1
8 I thank my God through Jesus Christ for all of you 1
2:16 God judges the secrets of men by Christ Jesus. 1
3:22 through faith in Jesus Christ for all 1
24 through the redemption which is in Christ Jesus 1
26 and that he justifies him who has faith in Jesus. 1
4:24 him that raised from the dead Jesus our Lord 1
5: 1 peace with God through our Lord Jesus Christ. 1
11 rejoice in God through our Lord Jesus Christ 1
15 in the grace of that one man Jesus Christ 1
17 reign in life through the one man Jesus Christ. 1
21 to eternal life through Jesus Christ our Lord. 1
6: 3 who have been baptized into Christ Jesus 1
11 dead to sin and alive to God in Christ Jesus. 1
23 is eternal life in Christ Jesus our Lord. 1
7:25 Thanks be to God through Jesus Christ our Lord! 1
8: 1 for those who are in Christ Jesus. 1
2 For the law of the Spirit of life in Christ Jesus 1
11 the Spirit of him who raised Jesus from the dead 1
11 he who raised Christ Jesus from the dead 1
34 who is to condemn? Is it Christ Jesus, who died, yes 1
39 from the love of God in Christ Jesus our Lord. 1
10: 9 if you confess with your lips that Jesus is Lord 1
13:14 But put on the Lord Jesus Christ 1
14:14 I know and am persuaded in the Lord Jesus 1
15: 5 in such harmony . . in accord with Christ Jesus 1
6 the God and Father of our Lord Jesus Christ. 1
16 to be a minister of Christ Jesus to the Gentiles 1
17 In Christ Jesus, then, I have reason to be proud 1
30 I appeal to you, brethren, by our Lord Jesus Christ 1
16: 3 my fellow workers in Christ Jesus 1
20 The grace of our Lord Jesus Christ be with you. 1
25 my gospel and the preaching of Jesus Christ 1
27 be glory for evermore through Jesus Christ! 1
1Co 1: 1 by the will of God to be an apostle of Christ Jesus 1
2 to those sanctified in Christ Jesus 1
2 call on the name of our Lord Jesus Christ 1
3 God our Father and the Lord Jesus Christ. 1
4 given you in Christ Jesus 1
7 for the revealing of our Lord Jesus Christ; 1
8 guiltless in the day of our Lord Jesus Christ. 1
9 the fellowship of his Son, Jesus Christ our Lord. 1
10 by the name of our Lord Jesus Christ 1
30 He is the source of your life in Christ Jesus 1
2: 2 except Jesus Christ and him crucified. 1
3:11 than that which is laid, which is Jesus Christ. 1
4:15 your father in Christ Jesus through the gospel. 1
5: 4 in the name of the Lord Jesus 1
4 with the power of our Lord Jesus 1
5 may be saved in the day of the Lord Jesus. •
6:11 justified in the name of the Lord Jesus Christ 1
8: 6 one Lord, Jesus Christ 1
9: 1 Have I not seen Jesus our Lord? 1
11:23 the Lord Jesus on the night when he was betrayed 1
12: 3 Jesus be cursed! 1
3 no one can say "Jesus is Lord 1
15:31 which I have in Christ Jesus our Lord 1
57 through our Lord Jesus Christ. 1
16:23 The grace of the Lord Jesus be with you. 1
24 My love be with you all in Christ Jesus. Amen. 1
2Co 1: 1 Paul, an apostle of Christ Jesus by the will of God 1
2 God our Father and the Lord Jesus Christ. 1
3 Father of our Lord Jesus Christ 1
14 on the day of the Lord Jesus. 1
19 For the Son of God, Jesus Christ, whom we preached 1
4: 5 Jesus Christ as Lord 1
5 with ourselves as your servants for Jesus' sake. 1
10 always carrying in the body the death of Jesus 1
10 so that the life of Jesus may also be manifested 1
11 always being given up to death for Jesus' sake 1
11 so that the life of Jesus may be manifested 1
14 knowing that he who raised the Lord Jesus 1
14 will raise us also with Jesus 1
8: 9 For you know the grace of our Lord Jesus Christ 1
11: 4 For if some one comes and preaches another Jesus 1
31 The God and Father of the Lord Jesus 1
13: 5 realize that Jesus Christ is in you 1
14 The grace of the Lord Jesus Christ 1
Gal 1: 1 through Jesus Christ and God the Father 1
3 God the Father and our Lord Jesus Christ 1
12 it came through a revelation of Jesus Christ. 1
2: 4 spy out our freedom which we have in Christ Jesus 1
16 through faith in Jesus Christ 1
16 even we have believed in Christ Jesus 1
3: 1 Jesus Christ was publicly portrayed 1
14 that in Christ Jesus the blessing of Abraham 1
22 what was promised to faith in Jesus Christ 1
26 for in Christ Jesus you are all sons of God 1
28 for you are all one in Christ Jesus. 1
4:14 as an angel of God, as Christ Jesus. 1
5: 6 in Christ Jesus neither circumcision 1
24 those who belong to Christ Jesus 1
6:14 except in the cross of our Lord Jesus Christ 1
17 I bear on my body the marks of Jesus. 1
18 The grace of our Lord Jesus Christ 1
Eph 1: 1 Paul, an apostle of Christ Jesus by the will of God 1
1 the saints who are also faithful in Christ Jesus 1
2 God our Father and the Lord Jesus Christ. 1
3 the God and Father of our Lord Jesus Christ 1
5 to be his sons through Jesus Christ 1
15 have heard of your faith in the Lord Jesus 1
17 God of our Lord Jesus Christ, the Father of glory 1
2: 6 in the heavenly places in Christ Jesus 1
7 in kindness toward us in Christ Jesus. 1
10 we are his workmanship, created in Christ Jesus 1
13 in Christ Jesus you . . have been brought near 1
20 Christ Jesus himself being the cornerstone 1
3: 1 Paul, a prisoner for Christ Jesus on behalf of you 1
6 partakers of the promise in Christ Jesus 1
11 which he has realized in Christ Jesus our Lord 1
21 to him be glory in the church and in Christ Jesus 1
4:21 as the truth is in Jesus. 1
5:20 in the name of our Lord Jesus Christ 1
6:23 God the Father and the Lord Jesus Christ. 1
24 Grace be with all who love our Lord Jesus Christ 1
Php 1: 1 Paul and Timothy, servants of Christ Jesus 1
1 To all the saints in Christ Jesus 1
2 God our Father and the Lord Jesus Christ. 1
6 at the day of Jesus Christ. 1
8 with the affection of Christ Jesus. 1
11 which come through Jesus Christ 1
19 the help of the Spirit of Jesus Christ 1
26 ample cause to glory in Christ Jesus 1
2: 5 which is yours in Christ Jesus 1
10 at the name of Jesus every knee should bow 1
11 every tongue confess that Jesus Christ is Lord 1
19 hope in the Lord Jesus to send Timothy to you soon 1
21 not those of Jesus Christ. 1
3: 3 worship God in spirit, and glory in Christ Jesus 1
8 the surpassing worth of knowing Christ Jesus 1
12 because Christ Jesus has made me his own. 1
14 prize of the upward call of God in Christ Jesus. 1
20 from it we await a Savior, the Lord Jesus Christ 1
4: 7 keep your hearts and your minds in Christ Jesus. 1
19 his riches in glory in Christ Jesus. 1
21 Greet every saint in Christ Jesus 1
23 grace of the Lord Jesus Christ 1
Col 1: 1 Paul, an apostle of Christ Jesus by the will of God 1
3 God, the Father of our Lord Jesus Christ 1
4 we have heard of your faith in Christ Jesus 1
2: 6 As therefore you received Christ Jesus the Lord 1
3:17 do everything in the name of the Lord Jesus 1
4:11 Jesus who is called Justus 1
12 Ep'aphras . . a servant of Christ Jesus 1
1Th 1: 1 in God the Father and the Lord Jesus Christ 1
3 steadfastness of hope in our Lord Jesus Christ. 1
10 Jesus who delivers us from the wrath to come. 1
2:14 imitators of the churches of God in Christ Jesus 1
15 who killed both the Lord Jesus and the prophets 1
19 crown of boasting before our Lord Jesus 1
3:11 our Lord Jesus, direct our way to you; 1
13 at the coming of our Lord Jesus 1
4: 1 we beseech and exhort you in the Lord Jesus 1
2 we gave you through the Lord Jesus. 1
14 since we believe that Jesus died and rose again 1
14 since we believe that Jesus died and rose again 1
5: 9 salvation through our Lord Jesus Christ 1
18 is the will of God in Christ Jesus for you. 1
23 at the coming of our Lord Jesus Christ. 1
28 The grace of our Lord Jesus Christ be with you. 1
2Th 1: 1 God our Father and the Lord Jesus Christ 1
2 God the Father and the Lord Jesus Christ. 1
7 when the Lord Jesus is revealed from heaven 1
8 who do not obey the gospel of our Lord Jesus. 1
12 that the name of our Lord Jesus may be glorified 1
12 the grace of our God and the Lord Jesus Christ. 1
2: 1 concerning the coming of our Lord Jesus Christ 1
8 the Lord Jesus will slay him 1
14 may obtain the glory of our Lord Jesus Christ. 1
16 Now may our Lord Jesus Christ himself 1
3: 6 in the name of our Lord Jesus Christ 1
12 exhort in the Lord Jesus Christ to do their work 1
18 The grace of our Lord Jesus Christ be with you 1
1Ti 1: 1 Paul, an apostle of Christ Jesus by command of God 1
1 God our Savior and of Christ Jesus our hope 1
2 God the Father and Christ Jesus our Lord. 1
12 Christ Jesus our Lord 1
14 the faith and love that are in Christ Jesus. 1
15 Jesus came into the world to save sinners 1
16 Jesus Christ might display . . 1
2: 5 the man Christ Jesus 1
3:13 the faith which is in Christ Jesus. 1
4: 6 you will be a good minister of Christ Jesus 1
5:21 of God and of Christ Jesus and of the elect angels 1
6: 3 sound words of our Lord Jesus Christ 1
13 In the presence of . . of Christ Jesus 1
14 until the appearing of our Lord Jesus Christ; 1
2Ti 1: 1 Paul, an apostle of Christ Jesus by the will of God 1
1 the promise of the life which is in Christ Jesus. 1
2 God the Father and Christ Jesus our Lord. 1
9 the grace which he gave us in Christ Jesus ages ago 1
10 the appearing of our Savior Christ Jesus 1
13 in the faith and love which are in Christ Jesus; 1
2: 1 be strong in the grace that is in Christ Jesus 1
3 as a good soldier of Christ Jesus. 1
8 Remember Jesus Christ, risen from the dead 1
10 they also may obtain salvation in Christ Jesus 1
3:12 desire to live a godly life in Christ Jesus 1
15 through faith in Christ Jesus. 1
4: 1 in the presence of God and of Christ Jesus 1
Tit 1: 1 a servant of God and an apostle of Jesus Christ 1
4 God the Father and Christ Jesus our Savior. 1
2:13 glory of our great God and Savior Jesus Christ 1
3: 6 through Jesus Christ our Savior 1
Phm 1: 1 Paul, a prisoner for Christ Jesus 1
3 God our Father and the Lord Jesus Christ. 1
5 the faith which you have toward the Lord Jesus 1
9 now a prisoner also for Christ Jesus- 1
23 Ep'aphras, my fellow prisoner in Christ Jesus 1
25 The grace of the Lord Jesus Christ 1
Heb 2: 9 we see Jesus 1
3: 1 Therefore, holy brethren . . consider Jesus 1
3 Yet Jesus has been counted worthy of . . glory •
4:14 a great high priest . . Jesus, the Son of God 1
5: 7 In the days of his flesh, Jesus offered up prayers •
6:20 Jesus has gone as a forerunner on our behalf 1
7:22 makes Jesus the surety of a better covenant. 1
10:10 the offering of the body of Jesus Christ 1
19 we have confidence . . by the blood of Jesus 1
12: 2 Jesus the pioneer and perfecter of our faith 1
24 to Jesus, the mediator of a new covenant 1
13: 8 Jesus Christ is the same yesterday and today 1
12 Jesus also suffered outside the gate 1
20 who brought again from the dead our Lord Jesus 1
21 through Jesus Christ; to whom be glory for ever 1
Jas 1: 1 servant of God and of the Lord Jesus Christ 1
2: 1 as you hold the faith of our Lord Jesus Christ 1
1Pe 1: 1 Peter, an apostle of Jesus Christ 1
2 sanctified . . for obedience to Jesus Christ 1
3 the God and Father of our Lord Jesus Christ 1
3 the resurrection of Jesus Christ from the dead 1
7 and honor at the revelation of Jesus Christ. 1
13 coming to you at the revelation of Jesus Christ. 1
2: 5 acceptable to God through Jesus Christ. 1
3:21 through the resurrection of Jesus Christ 1
4:11 God may be glorified through Jesus Christ. 1
2Pe 1: 1 Peter, a servant and apostle of Jesus Christ 1
1 righteousness of our . . Savior Jesus Christ 1
2 in the knowledge of God and of Jesus our Lord. 1
8 in the knowledge of our Lord Jesus Christ. 1
11 kingdom of our Lord and Savior Jesus Christ. 1
14 will be soon, as our Lord Jesus Christ showed me. 1
16 the power and coming of our Lord Jesus Christ 1
2:20 knowledge of our Lord and Savior Jesus Christ 1
3:18 knowledge of our Lord and Savior Jesus Christ. 1
1Jn 1: 3 with the Father and with his Son Jesus Christ. 1
7 blood of Jesus his Son cleanses us from all sin. 1
2: 1 an advocate . . Jesus Christ the righteous; 1
22 he who denies that Jesus is the Christ 1
3:23 believe in the name of his Son Jesus Christ 1
4: 2 every spirit which confesses that Jesus Christ 1
3 every spirit which does not confess Jesus 1
15 Whoever confesses that Jesus is the Son of God 1
5: 1 Every one who believes that Jesus is the Christ 1
5 he who believes that Jesus is the Son of God? 1
6 he who came by water and blood, Jesus Christ 1
20 we are in him who is true, in his Son Jesus Christ. 1
2Jn 1: 3 and from Jesus Christ the Father's Son 1
7 the coming of Jesus Christ in the flesh; 1
Jde 1: 1 Jude, a servant of Jesus Christ 1
1 To those who are . . and kept for Jesus Christ 1
4 and deny our only Master and Lord, Jesus Christ. 1
17 of the apostles of our Lord Jesus Christ; 1
21 wait for the mercy of our Lord Jesus Christ 1
25 God, our Savior through Jesus Christ our Lord 1
Rev 1: 1 The revelation of Jesus Christ, which God gave 1
2 bore witness . . to the testimony of Jesus Christ 1
5 and from Jesus Christ the faithful witness 1
9 I John, your brother, who share with you in Jesus 1
9 on account of . . the testimony of Jesus. 1
12:17 and bear testimony to Jesus 1
14:12 the commandments of God and the faith of Jesus. 1
17: 6 drunk with . . the blood of the martyrs of Jesus. 1
19:10 your brethren who hold the testimony of Jesus. 1
10 testimony of Jesus is the spirit of prophecy. 1
20: 4 beheaded for their testimony to Jesus 1
22:16 I Jesus have sent my angel to you 1
20 Surely I am coming soon." Amen. Come, Lord Jesus! 1

Sir 0: 1 my grandfather Jesus, after devoting himself 1
50:27 Jesus the son of Sirach, son of Eleazar 1

Jether 1. יֶתֶר

Jdg 8:20 he said to Jether his first-born, "Rise, and slay 1
1Kg 2: 5 Abner the son of Ner, and Ama'sa the son of Jether 1
32 Ama'sa the son of Jether, commander of the army 1
1Ch 2:17 the father of Ama'sa was Jether the Ish'maelite. 1
32 The sons of Jada . . Jether and Jonathan; 1
32 Jonathan; and Jether died childless. 1
4:17 The sons of Ezrah: Jether, Mered, Epher, and Jalon. 1
7:38 The sons of Jether: Jephun'neh, Pispa, and Ara. 1

Jetheth 1. יְתֵת

Gen 36:40 by their names: the chiefs Timna, Alvah, Jetheth 1
1Ch 1:51 chiefs of Edom were: chiefs Timna, Al'iah, Jetheth 1

Jethro 1. יֶתֶר 2. יִתְרוֹ

Exd 3: 1 his father-in-law, Jethro, the priest of Mid'ian; 2
4:18 Moses went back to Jethro his father-in-law 1
18 And Jethro said to Moses, "Go in peace. 2
18: 1 Jethro, the priest of Mid'ian, Moses' father-in-law 2
2 Now Jethro, Moses' father-in-law, had taken 2
5 Jethro, Moses' father-in-law, came with his sons 2
6 Lo, your father-in-law Jethro is coming to you 2
9 Jethro rejoiced for all the good which the LORD 2
10 Jethro said, "Blessed be the LORD, who has 2
12 Jethro, Moses' father-in-law, offered a burnt 2

Jetur 1. יְטוּר

Gen 25:15 Hadad, Tema, Jetur, Naphish, and Ked'emah. 1
1Ch 1:31 Jetur, Naphish, and Ked'emah. These are the sons 1
5:19 made war upon the Hagrites, Jetur, Naphish 1

Jeuel 1. יְעוּאֵל 2. Ιεουηλ

1Ch 9: 6 Of the sons of Zerah: Jeu'el and their kinsmen, 690. 1
2Ch 29:13 of the sons of Eli-za'phan, Shimri and Jeu'el; 1
Ezr 8:13 names being Eliph'elet, Jeu'el, and Shemai'ah 1
1Es 8:39 their names being Eliphelet, Jeuel, and Shemaiah 2

Jeush 1. יְעוּשׁ

Gen 36: 5 Oholiba'mah bore Je'ush, Jalam, and Korah. 1
14 she bore to Esau Je'ush, Jalam, and Korah. 1
18 Esau's wife: the chiefs Je'ush, Jalam, and Korah 1
1Ch 1:35 sons of Esau: Eli'phaz, Reu'el, Je'ush, Jalam . . 1
7:10 sons of Bilhan: Je'ush, Benjamin, Ehud, Chena'anah 1
8:39 sons of Eshek his brother . . Je'ush the second 1
23:10 sons of Shim'e-i: Jahath, Zina, and Je'ush 1
11 but Je'ush and Beri'ah had not many sons 1
2Ch 11:19 she bore him sons, Je'ush, Shemari'ah, and Zaham. 1

Jeuz 1. יְעוּץ

1Ch 8:10 Je'uz, Sachi'a, and Mirmah. 1

Jew 1. אִישׁ יְהוּדִי 2. יְהוּדָה 3. יְהוּדִי 4. יְהוּדָי (A) 5. Ἰουδαϊκός 6. Ἰουδαῖος

2Kg 25:25 killed Gedali'ah and the Jews and the Chalde'ans 3
Ezr 4:12 Jews who came up from you to us have gone 4
23 they went in haste to the Jews at Jerusalem 4
5: 1 prophesied to the Jews . . in Judah and Jerusalem 4
5 eye of their God was upon the elders of the Jews 4
6: 7 let the governor of the Jews and the elders 4
7 let the governor . . and the elders of the Jews 4
8 elders of the Jews for the rebuilding 4
14 elders of the Jews built and prospered 4
Neh 1: 2 I asked them concerning the Jews that survived 3
2:16 I had not yet told the Jews, the priests, the nobles 3
4: 1 Sanbal'lat . . ridiculed the Jews. 3
2 What are these feeble Jews doing? 3
12 When the Jews who lived by them came they said 3
5:17 there were at my table 150 men, Jews and officials 3
6: 6 that you and the Jews intend to rebel; 3
13:23 days also I saw the Jews who had married women 3
Est 2: 5 there was a Jew in Susa . . whose name was Mor'decai 1
3: 4 for he had told them that he was a Jew. 3
6 to destroy all the Jews, the people of Mor'decai 3
10 to Haman the Ag'agite . . the enemy of the Jews. 3
13 to destroy, to slay, and to annihilate all Jews 3
4: 3 there was great mourning among the Jews 3
7 pay into the . . for the destruction of the Jews. 3
13 you will escape any more than all the other Jews. 3
14 relief and deliverance will rise for the Jews 3
16 gather all the Jews to be found in Susa, and . . fast 3
5:13 I see Mor'decai the Jew sitting at the king's gate. 3
6:10 to Mor'decai the Jew who sits at the king's gate. 3
8: 1 the house of Haman, the enemy of the Jews. 3
3 the plot which he had devised against the Jews. 3
5 letters . . which he wrote to destroy the Jews 3
7 said to Queen Esther and to Mor'decai the Jew 3
7 hanged . . because he would lay hands on the Jews. 3
8 may write as you please with regard to the Jews 3
9 that Mor'decai commanded concerning the Jews 3
9 to the Jews in their script and their language. 3
11 the king allowed the Jews . . to gather and defend 3
13 the Jews were to be ready . . to avenge themselves 3
16 The Jews had light and gladness and joy 3
17 there was gladness and joy among the Jews, a feast 3
17 for the fear of the Jews had fallen upon them. 3
9: 1 the enemies of the Jews hoped to get the mastery 3
1 a day when the Jews should get the mastery over 3
2 the Jews gathered in their cities . . to lay hands 3
3 governors and . . officials also helped the Jews 3
5 the Jews smote all their enemies with the sword 3
6 the Jews slew and destroyed 500 men 3
10 the ten sons of Haman . . the enemy of the Jews; 3
12 In Susa . . the Jews have slain 500 men 3
13 let the Jews who are in Susa be allowed 3
15 The Jews . . gathered also on the fourteenth day 3
16 Now the other Jews . . also gathered to defend 3
18 Jews . . in Susa gathered on the thirteenth day 3
19 Jews of the villages . . hold the fourteenth day 3
20 and sent letters to all the Jews who were 3
22 days . . the Jews got relief from their enemies 3
23 the Jews undertook to do as they had begun 3
24 Haman . . the enemy of all the Jews, had plotted 3
24 Haman . . had plotted against the Jews to destroy 3
25 plot which he had devised against the Jews 3
27 the Jews ordained and took it upon themselves 3
28 Purim . . never fall into disuse among the Jews 3
29 Esther . . and Mor'decai the Jew gave full written 3
30 Letters were sent to all the Jews . . in words 3
31 as Mor'decai the Jew and Queen Esther enjoined 3
31 and Queen Esther enjoined upon the Jews •
10: 3 Mor'decai the Jew was next in rank to . . Ahasu-e'rus 3
3 and he was great among the Jews and popular 3
Jer 32:12 Jews who were sitting in the court of the guard. 3
34: 9 so that no one should enslave a Jew, his brother. 3
38:19 I am afraid of the Jews who have deserted 3
40:11 Likewise, when all the Jews who were in Moab 3
12 then all the Jews returned from all the places 3
15 all the Jews who are gathered about you 2
41: 3 Ish'mael also slew all the Jews 3
44: 1 that came to Jeremiah concerning all the Jews 3
52:28 carried away captive . . 3,023 Jews; 3
30 carried away captive of the Jews 745 persons; 3
Dan 3: 8 Chalde'ans . . maliciously accused the Jews. 4
12 There are certain Jews whom you have appointed 4
Zec 8:23 every tongue shall take hold of the robe of a Jew 1
Mat 2: 2 Where is he who has been born king of the Jews? 6
27:11 Are you the King of the Jews? 6
29 they mocked him, saying, "Hail, King of the Jews! 6
37 This is Jesus the King of the Jews. 6
28:15 story has been spread among the Jews to this day. 6
Mrk 7: 3 For the Pharisees, and all the Jews, do not eat 6
15: 2 Pilate asked him, "Are you the King of the Jews? 6
9 you want me to release for you the King of the Jews? 6
12 do with the man whom you call the King of the Jews? 6
18 they began to salute him, "Hail, King of the Jews! 6
26 The King of the Jews. 6
Lke 7: 3 he sent to him elders of the Jews 6
23: 3 Pilate asked him, "Are you the King of the Jews? 6
37 If you are the King of the Jews, save yourself! 6
38 This is the King of the Jews. 6
Joh 1:19 Jews sent priests and Levites from Jerusalem 6
2:13 The Passover of the Jews was at hand 6
18 The Jews then said to him, "What sign have you 6
20 The Jews then said, "It has taken 46 years to build 6
3: 1 Nicode'mus, a ruler of the Jews. 6
25 a discussion . . between John's disciples and a Jew 6
4: 9 you, a Jew, ask a drink of me, a woman of Samar'ia? 6
9 For Jews have no dealings with Samaritans. 6
22 for salvation is from the Jews. 6
5: 1 After this there was a feast of the Jews 6
10 the Jews said to the man who was cured 6
15 The man went away and told the Jews 6
16 this was why the Jews persecuted Jesus 6
18 This was why the Jews sought . . to kill him 6
6: 4 the Passover, the feast of the Jews, was at hand. 6
41 The Jews then murmured at him, because he said 6
52 The Jews then disputed among themselves, saying 6
7: 1 because the Jews sought to kill him. 6
2 Now the Jews' feast of Tabernacles was at hand. 6
11 The Jews were looking for him at the feast 6
13 Yet for fear of the Jews no one spoke openly 6
15 The Jews marveled at it, saying, "How is it 6
35 The Jews said to one another 6
8:22 Then said the Jews, "Will he kill himself 6
31 Jesus then said to the Jews who had believed 6
48 The Jews answered him, "Are we not right in saying 6
52 The Jews said to him, "Now we know 6
57 The Jews then said to him 6
9:18 The Jews did not believe that he had been blind 6
22 because they feared the Jews 6
22 the Jews had already agreed 6
10:19 There was again a division among the Jews 6
24 the Jews gathered round him and said to him 6
31 The Jews took up stones again to stone him. 6
33 The Jews answered him, "It is not for a good work 6
11: 8 the Jews were but now seeking to stone you 6
19 many of the Jews had come to Martha and Mary 6
31 the Jews who were with her in the house 6
33 and the Jews who came with her also weeping 6
36 the Jews said, "See how he loved him! 6
45 Many of the Jews therefore, who had come with Mary 6
54 no longer went about openly among the Jews 6
55 Now the Passover of the Jews was at hand 6
12: 9 great crowd of the Jews learned that he was there 6
11 on account of him many of the Jews were going away 6
13:33 as I said to the Jews so now I say to you 6
18:12 their captain and the officers of the Jews 6
14 It was Ca'iaphas who had given counsel to the Jews 6
20 where all Jews come together 6
31 The Jews said to him, "It is not lawful for us 6
33 Are you the King of the Jews? 6
35 Pilate answered, "Am I a Jew? 6
36 that I might not be handed over to the Jews 6
38 went out to the Jews again, and told them 6
39 release for you the King of the Jews? 6
19: 3 they came up to him, saying, "Hail, King of the Jews! 6
7 The Jews answered him. "We have a law 6
12 the Jews cried out, "If you release this man 6
14 He said to the Jews, "Behold your King! 6
19 it read, "Jesus of Nazareth, the King of the Jews. 6
20 Many of the Jews read this title 6
21 The chief priests of the Jews then said to Pilate 6
21 Do not write, 'The King of the Jews,' 6
21 but 'This man said, I am King of the Jews.' 6
31 the Jews asked Pilate 6
38 but secretly, for fear of the Jews 6
40 as is the burial custom of the Jews. 6
20:19 the doors being shut . . for fear of the Jews 6
Act 2: 5 Now there were dwelling in Jerusalem Jews 6
10 visitors from Rome, both Jews and proselytes 6
9:22 confounded the Jews who lived in Damascus 6
23 the Jews plotted to kill him 6
10:28 You yourselves know how unlawful it is for a Jew 6
39 both in the country of the Jews and in Jerusalem. 6
11:19 speaking the word to none except Jews. 6
12: 3 when he saw that it pleased the Jews 6
13: 5 in the synagogues of the Jews 6
43 many Jews and devout converts to Judaism 6
45 when the Jews saw the multitudes 6
50 the Jews incited the devout women of high standing 6
14: 1 a great company . . both of Jews and of Greeks. 6
2 the unbelieving Jews stirred up the Gentiles 6
4 some sided with the Jews 6
5 an attempt was made by both Gentiles and Jews 6
19 Jews came there from Antioch and Ico'nium; 6
16: 3 circumcised him because of the Jews 6
20 they said, "These men are Jews 6
17: 1 where there was a synagogue of the Jews. 6
5 the Jews were jealous 6
11 Now these Jews were more noble •
13 when the Jews of Thessaloni'ca learned 6
17 he argued in the synagogue with the Jews 6
18: 2 he found a Jew named Aq'uila, a native of Pontus 6
2 had commanded all the Jews to leave Rome 6
4 persuaded Jews and Greeks. 6
5 testifying to the Jews that the Christ was Jesus. 6
12 the Jews made a united attack upon Paul 6
14 Gallio said to the Jews 6
14 I should have reason to bear with you, O Jews; 6
19 went into the synagogue and argued with the Jews. 6
24 a Jew named Apol'los, a native of Alexandria, came 6
28 for he powerfully confuted the Jews in public 6
19:10 both Jews and Greeks. 6
17 all residents of Ephesus, both Jews and Greeks 6
33 Alexander, whom the Jews had put forward 6
34 when they recognized that he was a Jew 6
20: 3 when a plot was made against him by the Jews 6
19 which befell me through the plots of the Jews; 6
21 testifying both to Jews and to Greeks 6
21:11 So shall the Jews at Jerusalem bind the man 6
20 how many thousands there are among the Jews 6
21 you teach all the Jews who are among the Gentiles 6
27 the Jews from Asia . . stirred up all the crowd 6
39 Paul replied, "I am a Jew, from Tarsus in Cili'cia 6
22: 3 I am a Jew, born at Tarsus in Cili'cia 6
12 well spoken of by all the Jews who lived there 6
30 to know the real reason why the Jews accused him 6
23:12 When it was day, the Jews made a plot 6
20 The Jews have agreed to ask you to bring Paul down 6
27 This man was seized by the Jews 6
24: 5 an agitator among all the Jews 6
9 The Jews also joined in the charge 6
18 some Jews from Asia- 6
27 desiring to do the Jews a favor 6
25: 2 the chief priests and the principal men of the Jews 6
7 the Jews who had gone down from Jerusalem 6
8 the law of the Jews 6
9 Festus, wishing to do the Jews a favor, said to Paul 6
10 to the Jews I have done no wrong 6
15 the chief priests and the elders of the Jews 6
26: 2 against all the accusations of the Jews 6
3 all customs and controversies of the Jews 6
4 is known by all the Jews. 6
7 for this hope I am accused by Jews, O king! 6
21 Jews seized me in the temple and tried to kill me. 6
28:17 he called together the local leaders of the Jews 6
19 when the Jews objected 6
Rom 1:16 to the Jew first and also to the Greek. 6
2: 9 the Jew first and also the Greek. 6
10 the Jew first and also the Greek. 6
17 if you call yourself a Jew and rely upon the law 6
28 For he is not a real Jew who is one outwardly 6
29 He is a Jew who is one inwardly 6

3: 1 Then what advantage has the Jew? 6
2 the Jews are entrusted with the oracles of God. •
9 What then? Are we Jews any better off? No, not at all; •
9 all men, both Jews and Greeks, are under . . sin 6
29 Or is God the God of Jews only? 6
9:24 not from the Jews only but also from the Gentiles? 6
10:12 there is no distinction between Jew and Greek; 6
1Co 1:22 For Jews demand signs and Greeks seek wisdom 6
23 a stumbling block to Jews and folly to Gentiles 6
24 to those who are called, both Jews and Greeks 6
9:20 To the Jews I became as a Jew, in order to win Jews 6
20 To the Jews I became as a Jew, in order to win Jews 6
20 To the Jews I became as a Jew, in order to win Jews 6
10:32 Give no offense to Jews or to Greeks 6
12:13 Jews or Greeks, slaves or free 6
2Co 11:24 I have received at the hands of the Jews 6
Gal 2:13 with him the rest of the Jews acted insincerely 6
14 If you, though a Jew, live like a Gentile 6
15 who are Jews by birth and not Gentile sinners 6
3:28 There is neither Jew nor Greek 6
Col 3:11 Here there cannot be Greek and Jew 6
1Th 2:14 as they did from the Jews 6
Rev 2: 9 those who say that they are Jews and are not 6
3: 9 those . . who say that they are Jews and are not 6
1Es 2:18 the Jews who came up from you to us 6
23 the Jews were rebels 6
4:49 he wrote for all the Jews who were going up 6
50 should give up the villages of the Jews 6
6: 1 the Jews who were in Judea and Jerusalem 6
5 Yet the elders of the Jews were dealt with kindly 6
8 we found the elders of the Jews 6
27 the elders of the Jews 6
7: 2 assisting the elders of the Jews 6
AEs 10: 8 gathered to destroy the name of the Jews. 6
11: 3 He was a Jew, dwelling in the city of Susa 6
16:15 we find that the Jews . . are not evildoers 6
19 permit the Jews to live under their own laws. 6
Sus 1: 4 and the Jews used to come to him 6
Bel 1:28 The king has become a Jew; he has destroyed Bel 6
1Mc 2:23 a Jew came forward in the sight of all 6
4: 2 to fall upon the camp of the Jews 6
20 the Jews were burning the camp •
5:23 Then he took the Jews of Galilee and Arbatta •
30 and attacking the Jews within. •
6: 6 but had turned and fled before the Jews •
6 that the Jews had grown strong from the arms •
31 the Jews sallied out and burned these with fire •
47 when the Jews saw the royal might •
52 The Jews also made engines of war to match theirs •
60 he sent to the Jews an offer of peace •
61 the Jews evacuated the stronghold. •
7:45 The Jews pursued them a day's journey •
47 Then the Jews seized the spoils and the plunder •
8:20 his brothers and the people of the Jews 6
23 with the Romans and with the nation of the Jews 6
25 the nation of the Jews shall act as their allies 6
27 if war comes first to the nation of the Jews 6
31 our friends and allies the Jews? 6
10:23 forming a friendship with the Jews 6
25 King Demetrius to the nation of the Jews, greeting 6
29 and exempt all the Jews from payment of tribute 6
33 every one of the Jews taken as a captive 6
34 all the Jews who are in my kingdom. 6
36 Let Jews be enrolled in the king's forces 6
11:30 to the nation of the Jews, greeting. 6
33 To the nation of the Jews, who are our friends 6
47 So the king called the Jews to his aid 6
49 the Jews had gained control of the city 6
50 and make the Jews stop fighting against us 6
51 So the Jews gained glory in the eyes of the king 6
12:21 the Spartans and the Jews 6
26 to fall upon the Jews by night. •
13:36 to the elders and nation of the Jews, greeting. 6
42 commander and leader of the Jews. 6
51 the Jews entered it with praise and palm branches •
14:22 envoys of the Jews, have come to us 6
33 he placed there a garrison of Jews. 6
34 He settled Jews there 6
37 He settled Jews in it 6
40 the Jews were addressed by the Romans as friends 6
41 the Jews and their priests decided 6
47 be commander and ethnarch of the Jews and priests 6
15: 1 Simon, the priest and ethnarch of the Jews 6
2 to the nation of the Jews, greeting. 6
17 envoys of the Jews have come to us as our friends 6
17 sent . . by the people of the Jews 6
2Mc 1: 7 we Jews wrote to you . . in those years 6
10 to the Jews in Egypt, Greeting, and good health. 6
3:32 some foul play had been perpetrated by the Jews 6
4:11 the existing royal concessions to the Jews 6
35 For this reason not only Jews . . were grieved 6
36 the Jews in the city appealed to him 6
41 when the Jews became aware of Lysimachus' attack •
5:25 then, finding the Jews not at work 6
6: 1 to compel the Jews to forsake the laws 6
6 nor so much as confess himself to be a Jew. 6
7 the Jews were taken, under bitter constraint •
8 should adopt the same policy toward the Jews 6
8:10 by selling the captured Jews into slavery. 6
32 one who had greatly troubled the Jews. 6
34 who had brought the 1,000 merchants to buy the Jews 6
36 proclaimed that the Jews had a Defender 6
36 therefore the Jews were invulnerable 6
9: 4 turning upon the Jews the injury 6
4 I will make Jerusalem a cemetery of Jews. 6
7 breathing fire in his rage against the Jews 6
15 the Jews . . he would make . . citizens of Athens 6
17 he also would become a Jew 6
18 wrote to the Jews the following letter 6
10: 8 the whole nation of the Jews 6
12 Ptolemy . . took the lead in showing justice to the Jews 6
14 and at every turn kept on warring against the Jews. 6
15 the Idumeans . . were harassing the Jews 6
24 Timothy, who had been defeated by the Jews before 6
29 they were leading the Jews. 6
11: 2 came against the Jews 6
15 every request in behalf of the Jews 6
16 The letter written to the Jews by Lysias 6
16 Lysias to the people of the Jews, greeting 6
24 the Jews do not consent 6
27 King Antiochus to the senate of the Jews 6
27 King Antiochus . . to the other Jews, greeting. 6
31 for the Jews to enjoy their own food and laws 6
34 to the people of the Jews, greeting. 6
12: 1 the Jews went about their farming. 6
3 they invited the Jews . . to embark . . on boats 6
3 as though there were no ill will to the Jews; •
8 to wipe out the Jews who were living among them 6
17 to Charax, to the Jews who are called Toubiani. 6
28 the Jews called upon the Sovereign •
30 when the Jews who dwelt there bore witness 6
34 it happened that a few of the Jews fell. 6
40 which the law forbids the Jews to wear 6
13: 9 was coming to show the Jews things far worse 6
18 having had a taste of the daring of the Jews 6
19 Beth-zur, a strong fortress of the Jews 6
21 Rhodocus, a man from the ranks of the Jews 5
23 he was dismayed, called in the Jews, yielded 6
14: 5 the disposition and intentions of the Jews 6
6 Those of the Jews who are called Hasideans 6
14 the misfortunes and calamities of the Jews 6
15 When the Jews heard of Nicanor's coming •
37 for his good will was called father of the Jews. 6
39 to exhibit the enmity which he had for the Jews 6
15: 2 the Jews who were compelled to follow him said 6
12 praying . . for the whole body of the Jews. 6
3Mc 1: 3 a Jew by birth who later changed his religion 6
8 Since the Jews had sent some of their council 6
2:28 all Jews shall be subjected to a registration 6
3: 1 those Jews who lived in Alexandria •
3 The Jews . . continued to maintain good will 6
27 whoever shelters any of the Jews 6
29 Every place detected sheltering a Jew 6
4: 2 among the Jews there was incessant mourning 6
12 the Jews' compatriots from the city •
17 were no longer able to take the census of the Jews 6
21 who was aiding the Jews from heaven. 6
5: 2 so that the Jews might meet their doom. 6
3 who were especially hostile toward the Jews. 6
5 The servants in charge of the Jews went out •
6 the Jews were left without any aid 6
13 Then the Jews . . praised their holy God 6
18 why the Jews had been allowed to remain alive 6
20 the Jews were benefited by today's sleep •
20 the destruction of the lawless Jews! 6
25 the Jews . . implored the supreme God to help 6
31 I would have prepared them . . instead of the Jews 6
35 Then the Jews, upon hearing what the king had said 6
38 the destruction of the Jews tomorrow! 6
42 the protection of the Jews 6
48 the Jews saw the dust raised by the elephants 6
6:17 when the Jews observed this 6
18 visible to all but the Jews. 6
29 the Jews, immediately released, praised •
30 ordered him to provide to the Jews 6
34 the Jews would be destroyed •
35 the Jews . . passed the time in feasting 6
7: 3 friends . . persuaded us to gather together the Jews 6
6 the God of heaven surely defends the Jews 6
10 the Jews did not immediately hurry •
4Mc 5: 7 when you observe the religion of the Jews. 6

fellow Jew 1. σάρξ
Rom 11:14 in order to make my fellow Jews jealous, and thus 1

like a Jew 1. ἰουδαϊκῶς
Gal 2:14 live like a Gentile and not like a Jew 1

live like a Jew 1. ἰουδαΐζω
Gal 2:14 how can you compel the Gentiles to live like Jews? 1

Jewess 1. Ἰουδαῖος
Act 24:24 his wife Drusil'la, who was a Jewess 1

Jewish 1. יְהוּדִי 2. Ἰουδαϊκός 3. Ἰουδαῖος
1Ch 4:18 his Jewish wife bore Jered the father of Gedor 1
Neh 5: 1 great outcry . . against their Jewish brethren. 1
8 We . . have bought back our Jewish brethren 1
Lke 23:50 from the Jewish town of Arimathe'a 3
Joh 2: 6 jars . . for the Jewish rites of purification 3
19:42 because of the Jewish day of Preparation 3
Act 10:22 who is well spoken of by the whole Jewish nation 3
12:11 from all that the Jewish people were expecting. 3
13: 6 a certain magician, a Jewish false prophet 3
14: 1 entered together into the Jewish synagogue 3
16: 1 the son of a Jewish woman who was a believer 3
17:10 they went into the Jewish synagogue. 3
19:13 Then some of the itinerant Jewish exorcists 3
14 Seven sons of a Jewish high priest named Sceva 3
25:24 about whom the whole Jewish people petitioned 3
Tit 1:14 instead of giving heed to Jewish myths 2
1Es 8:10 of the Jewish nation and of the priests 3
1Mc 8:29 the Romans make a treaty with the Jewish people. 3
12: 3 Jonathan the high priest and the Jewish nation 3
6 the rest of the Jewish people 3
14:20 the priests and the rest of the Jewish people 3
2Mc 1: 1 The Jewish brethren in Jerusalem 3
1 To their Jewish brethren in Egypt 3
5:23 In his malice toward the Jewish citizens 3
8:11 inviting them to buy Jewish slaves 3
9:19 To his worthy Jewish citizens 3
3Mc 2:27 to inflict public disgrace upon the Jewish community •
33 to be enemies of the Jewish nation •
3: 2 a hostile rumor . . against the Jewish nation •
7:10 those of the Jewish nation 3

Jewish faith 1. Ἰουδαϊσμός
2Mc 8: 1 those who had continued in the Jewish faith 1

Jewish people 1. יְהוּדִי
Est 6:13 If Mor'decai . . is of the Jewish people, you will 1

Jezaniah 1. יְזַנְיָהוּ
Jer 40: 8 Jezani'ah the son of the Ma-ac'athite 1

Jezebel 1. אִיזֶבֶל 2. Ἰεζάβελ
1Kg 16:31 he took for wife Jez'ebel the daughter of Ethba'al 1
18: 4 when Jez'ebel cut off the prophets of the LORD 1
13 when Jez'ebel killed the prophets of the LORD 1
19 prophets of Ashe'rah, who eat at Jez'ebel's table. 1
19: 1 Ahab told Jez'ebel all that Eli'jah had done 1
2 Then Jez'ebel sent a messenger to Eli'jah saying 1
21: 5 Jez'ebel his wife came to him, and said to him 1
7 Jez'ebel his wife said to him, "Do you now govern 1
11 the men of his city . . did as Jez'ebel had sent word 1
14 they sent to Jez'ebel, saying 1
15 As soon as Jez'ebel heard . . Jea'ebel said to Ahab 1
15 Jez'ebel said to Ahab, "Arise, take possession 1
23 And of Jez'ebel the LORD also said 1
23 'The dogs shall eat Jez'ebel within . . Jezreel.' 1
25 like Ahab, whom Jez'ebel his wife incited. 1
2Kg 9: 7 I may avenge on Jez'ebel the blood of my servants 1
10 And the dogs shall eat Jez'ebel in . . Jezreel 1
22 the harlotries and . . of your mother Jez'ebel 1
30 When Jehu came to Jezreel, Jez'ebel heard of it; 1
36 the dogs shall eat the flesh of Jez'ebel; 1
37 and the corpse of Jez'ebel shall be as dung 1
37 so that no one can say, This is Jez'ebel.' 1
Rev 2:20 against you, that you tolerate the woman Jez'ebel 2

Jezer 1. יֵצֶר
Gen 46:24 sons of Naph'tali: Jahzeel . . Jezer, and Shillem 1
Num 26:49 of Jezer, the family of the Je'zerites; 1
1Ch 7:13 sons of Naph'tali: Jah'zi-el, Guni, Jezer, and Shallum 1

Jezerite 1. יִצְרִי
Num 26:49 of Jezer, the family of the Je'zerites; 1

Jeziel 1. יְזִיאֵל
1Ch 12: 3 also Je'zi-el and Pelet the sons of Az'maveth; 1

Jezrahiah 1. יִזְרַחְיָה
Neh 12:42 singers sang with Jezrahi'ah as their leader. 1

Jezreel 1. יִזְרְעֶאל 2. יִזְרְעֵאלִי
Jos 15:56 Jezreel, Jok'de-am, Zano'ah 1
17:16 those in . . and those in the Valley of Jezreel. 1
19:18 territory included Jezreel, Chesul'loth, Shunem 1
Jdg 6:33 Jordan they encamped in the Valley of Jezreel. 1
1Sm 25:43 David also took Ahin'o-am of Jezreel; 1
27: 3 his two wives, Ahin'o-am of Jezreel, and Ab'igail 2
29: 1 encamped by the fountain which is in Jezreel. 1
11 But the Philistines went up to Jezreel. 1
30: 5 David's two wives . . Ahin'o-am of Jezreel 2
2Sm 2: 2 his two wives . . Ahin'o-am of Jezreel, and Ab'igail 2
9 Jezreel and E'phraim and Benjamin and . . Israel. 1
3: 2 his first-born was Amnon, of Ahin'o-am of Jezreel; 2
4: 4 news about Saul and Jonathan came from Jezreel; 1
1Kg 4:12 which is beside Zarethan below Jezreel 1
18:45 And Ahab rode and went to Jezreel. 1
46 and ran before Ahab to the entrance of Jezreel. 1
21: 1 Naboth the Jezreelite had a vineyard in Jezreel 1
23 'The dogs shall eat Jez'ebel within . . Jezreel.' 1
2Kg 8:29 King Joram returned to be healed in Jezreel 1
29 went down to see Joram . . in Jezreel 1
9:10 dogs . . eat Jez'ebel in the territory of Jezreel 1

15 King Joram had returned to be healed in Jezreel 1
15 out of the city to go and tell the news in Jezreel. 1
16 Jehu mounted his chariot, and went to Jezreel 1
17 watchman was standing on the tower in Jezreel 1
30 When Jehu came to Jezreel, Jez'ebel heard of it; 1
36 In the territory of Jezreel the dogs shall eat 1
37 shall be as dung . . in the territory of Jezreel 1
10: 6 and come to me at Jezreel tomorrow at this time. 1
7 and sent them to him at Jezreel. 1
11 Jehu slew all that remained . . of Ahab in Jezreel 1
1Ch 4: 3 the sons of Etam: Jezreel, Ishma, and Idbash; 1
2Ch 22: 6 he returned to be healed in Jezreel of the wounds 1
6 went down to see Joram the son of Ahab in Jezreel 1
Hos 1: 4 And the LORD said to him, "Call his name Jezreel; 1
4 punish the house of Jehu for the blood of Jezreel 1
5 break the bow of Israel in the valley of Jezreel. 1
11 for great shall be the day of Jezreel. 1
2:22 the oil, and they shall answer Jezreel; 1

Jezreelite 1. יִזְרְעֵאלִי

1Kg 21: 1 Naboth the Jezreelite had a vineyard in Jezreel 1
4 what Naboth the Jezreelite had said to him; 1
6 I spoke to Naboth the Jezreelite, and said to him 1
7 the vineyard of Naboth the Jezreelite. 1
15 take . . the vineyard of Naboth the Jezreelite 1
16 go down to the vineyard of Naboth the Jezreelite 1
2Kg 9:21 met . . at the property of Naboth the Jezreelite. 1
25 ground belonging to Naboth the Jezreelite; 1

Jezreelitess 1. יִזְרְעֵאלִי

1Ch 3: 1 first-born Amnon, by Ahin'o-am the Jezreelitess; 1

Jidlaph 1. יִדְלָף

Gen 22:22 Chesed, Hazo, Pildash, Jidlaph, and Bethu'el. 1

Joab 1. יוֹאָב 2. Ιωαβ

1Sm 26: 6 David said . . to Jo'ab's brother Abi'shai 1
2Sm 2:13 Jo'ab . . and the servants of David, went out and met 1
14 Abner said to Jo'ab, "Let the young men arise 1
14 And Jo'ab said, "Let them arise. 1
18 sons of Zeru'iah . . Jo'ab, Abi'shai, and As'ahel. 1
22 How . . could I lift up my face to your brother Jo'ab? 1
24 But Jo'ab and Abi'shai pursued Abner; 1
26 Abner called to Jo'ab, "Shall the sword devour 1
27 Jo'ab said, "As God lives, if you had not spoken 1
28 Jo'ab blew the trumpet; and all the men stopped 1
30 Jo'ab returned from the pursuit of Abner; 1
32 And Jo'ab and his men marched all night 1
3:22 servants of David arrived with Jo'ab from a raid 1
23 When Jo'ab and all the army that was with him came 1
23 it was told Jo'ab, "Abner . . came to the king 1
24 Jo'ab went to the king and said, "What have you done 1
26 When Jo'ab came out from David's presence 1
27 Jo'ab took him aside into the midst of the gate 1
29 May it fall upon the head of Jo'ab 1
29 may the house of Jo'ab never be without one who has 1
30 Jo'ab and Abi'shai his brother slew Abner 1
31 Then David said to Jo'ab and to all the people 1
8:16 Jo'ab the son of Zeru'iah was over the army; 1
10: 7 he sent Jo'ab and all the host of the mighty men. 1
9 When Jo'ab saw that the battle was set against him 1
13 Jo'ab and the people . . drew near to battle 1
14 Jo'ab returned from fighting . . the Ammonites 1
11: 1 David sent Jo'ab, and his servants with him 1
6 David sent word to Jo'ab, "Send me Uri'ah 1
6 Send me Uri'ah . . And Jo'ab sent Uri'ah to David. 1
7 David asked how Jo'ab was doing, and how the people 1
11 my lord Jo'ab . . are camping in the open field; 1
14 David wrote a letter to Jo'ab, and sent it 1
16 as Jo'ab was besieging the city, he assigned Uri'ah 1
17 the men of the city came out and fought with Jo'ab; 1
18 Jo'ab sent and told David . . about the fighting; 1
22 and told David all that Jo'ab had sent him to tell. 1
25 David said . . "Thus shall you say to Jo'ab 1
12:26 Now Jo'ab fought against Rabbah of the Ammonites 1
27 Jo'ab sent messengers to David, and said 1
14: 1 Jo'ab . . perceived that the king's heart went out 1
2 Jo'ab sent to Teko'a, and fetched . . a wise woman 1
3 speak thus . . " So Jo'ab put the words in her mouth. 1
19 Is the hand of Jo'ab with you in all this? 1
19 It was your servant Jo'ab who bade me; 1
20 to change . . affairs your servant Jo'ab did this. 1
21 Then the king said to Jo'ab, "Behold now, I grant this; 1
22 And Jo'ab fell on his face to the ground 1
22 and Jo'ab said, "Today your servant knows 1
23 So Jo'ab arose and went to Geshur 1
29 Then Ab'salom sent for Jo'ab, to send him to the king; 1
29 Ab'salom sent for Jo'ab . . but Jo'ab would not come •
29 And he sent a second time, but Jo'ab would not come. •
30 See, Jo'ab's field is next to mine, and he has barley 1
31 Then Jo'ab arose and went to Ab'salom at his house 1
32 Ab'salom answered Jo'ab, "Behold, I sent word to you 1
33 Then Jo'ab went to the king, and told him; 1
17:25 had set Ama'sa over the army instead of Jo'ab. 1
25 of Nahash, sister of Zeru'iah, Jo'ab's mother. 1
18: 2 the army, one third under the command of Jo'ab 1
2 of Abi'shai the son of Zeru'iah, Jo'ab's brother 1
5 And the king ordered Jo'ab and Abi'shai and It'tai 1
10 a certain man saw it, and told Jo'ab, "Behold, I saw 1
11 Jo'ab said to the man who told him, "What, you saw 1
12 But the man said to Jo'ab, "Even if I felt in my hand 1
14 Jo'ab said, "I will not waste time like this 1
15 And ten young men, Jo'ab's armor-bearers 1
16 Jo'ab blew the trumpet, and the troops came back 1
16 troops came back . . for Jo'ab restrained them. 1
20 Jo'ab said to him, "You are not to carry tidings 1
21 Then Jo'ab said to the Cushite, "Go, tell the king 1
21 The Cushite bowed before Jo'ab, and ran. 1
22 Then Ahi'ma-az the son of Zadok said again to Jo'ab 1
22 And Jo'ab said, "Why will you run, my son 1
29 When Jo'ab sent your servant, I saw a great tumult 1
19: 1 It was told Jo'ab, "Behold, the king is weeping 1
5 Then Jo'ab came into the house to the king, and said 1
13 commander of my army . . in place of Jo'ab.' 1
20: 7 there went out . . Jo'ab and the Cher'ethites 1
8 Now Jo'ab was wearing a soldier's garment 1
9 Jo'ab said to Ama'sa, "Is it well with you, my brother? 1
9 And Jo'ab took Ama'sa by the beard . . to kiss him. 1
10 did not observe the sword which was in Jo'ab's hand; 1
10 so Jo'ab struck him with it in the body •
10 Then Jo'ab and Abi'shai his brother pursued Sheba 1
11 And one of Jo'ab's men took his stand by Ama'sa 1
11 Whoever favors Jo'ab, and whoever is for David 1
11 and whoever is for David, let him follow Jo'ab. 1
13 all the people went on after Jo'ab to pursue Sheba 1
15 all . . who were with Jo'ab came and besieged him 1
16 Hear! Tell Jo'ab, 'Come here, that I may speak to you.' 1
17 the woman said, "Are you Jo'ab?" He answered, "I am. 1
20 Jo'ab answered, "Far be it from me . . that I should 1
21 the woman said to Jo'ab, "Behold, his head shall be 1
22 they cut off the head . . and threw it out to Jo'ab. 1
22 And Jo'ab returned to Jerusalem to the king. 1
23 Now Jo'ab was in command of all the army of Israel; 1
23:18 Abi'shai, the brother of Jo'ab, the son of Zeru'iah 1
24 As'ahel the brother of Jo'ab was one of the 30; 1
37 the armor-bearer of Jo'ab the son of Zeru'iah 1
24: 2 the king said to Jo'ab and the commanders 1
3 Jo'ab said to the king, "May the LORD your God add 1
4 word prevailed against Jo'ab and the commanders 1
4 Jo'ab and the commanders of the army went out 1
9 Jo'ab gave the sum of the numbering . . to the king 1
1Kg 1: 7 He conferred with Jo'ab the son of Zeru'iah 1
19 Abi'athar . . and Jo'ab the commander of the army; 1
25 the king's sons, Jo'ab the commander of the army 2
41 when Jo'ab heard the sound of the trumpet, he said 1
2: 5 you know . . what Jo'ab the son of Zeru'iah did to me 1
22 Abi'athar the priest and Jo'ab the son of Zeru'iah. 1
28 When the news came to Jo'ab . . Jo'ab fled 1
28 Jo'ab had supported Adoni'jah 1
28 Jo'ab fled to the tent of the LORD and caught hold 1
29 Jo'ab has fled to the tent of the LORD, and behold 1
30 saying, "Thus said Jo'ab, and thus he answered me. 1
31 for the blood which Jo'ab shed without cause. 1
33 blood come back upon the head of Jo'ab and upon 1
35 king put Benai'ah . . over the army in place of Jo'ab •
11:15 Jo'ab the commander of the army went up 1
16 Jo'ab and all Israel remained there six months 1
21 Jo'ab the commander of the army was dead 1
1Ch 2:16 The sons of Zeru'iah: Abi'shai, Jo'ab, and As'ahel 1
4:14 Jo'ab the father of Ge-har'ashim 1
11: 6 Jo'ab . . went up first, so he became chief. 1
8 and Jo'ab repaired the rest of the city. 1
20 Abi'shai, the brother of Jo'ab, was chief of the 30 1
26 mighty men . . were As'ahel the brother of Jo'ab 1
39 the armor-bearer of Jo'ab the son of Zeru'iah 1
18:15 Jo'ab the son of Zeru'iah was over the army; 1
19: 8 he sent Jo'ab and all the army of the mighty men. 1
10 When Jo'ab saw that the battle was set against him 1
14 Jo'ab and the people who were with him drew near 1
15 likewise fled before Abi'shai, Jo'ab's brother •
15 Then Jo'ab came to Jerusalem. 1
20: 1 Jo'ab led out the army, and ravaged the country 1
1 And Jo'ab smote Rabbah, and overthrew it. 1
21: 2 David said to Jo'ab and the commanders of the army 1
3 Jo'ab said, "May the LORD add to his people 1
4 the king's word prevailed against Jo'ab. 1
4 Jo'ab departed and went throughout all Israel 1
5 Jo'ab gave the sum of the numbering of the people 1
6 for the king's command was abhorrent to Jo'ab. 1
26:28 Abner the son of Ner, and Jo'ab the son of Zeru'iah 1
27: 7 As'ahel the brother of Jo'ab was fourth 1
24 Jo'ab . . began to number, but did not finish; 1
34 Jo'ab was commander of the king's army. 1
Ezr 2: 6 Pa'hath-moab, namely the sons of Jeshua and Jo'ab 1
8: 9 Of the sons of Jo'ab, Obadi'ah the son of Jehi'el 1
Neh 7:11 Pa'hath-mo'ab, namely the sons of Jeshua and Jo'ab 1
Ps 60: 0 when Joab on his return killed 12,000 •
1Es 5:11 sons of Pahathmoab, of the sons of Jeshua and Joab 2
8:35 Of the sons of Joab, Obadiah the son of Jehiel 2

Joah 1. יוֹאָח

2Kg 18:18 and Jo'ah the son of Asaph, the recorder. 1
26 Then Eli'akim . . and Shebnah, and Jo'ah, said 1
37 Eli'akim . . and Shebna.., and Jo'ah the son of Asaph 1
1Ch 6:21 Jo'ah his son, Iddo . . Zerah . . Je-ath'erai 1
26: 4 O'bed-e'dom had sons . . Jo'ah the third, Sachar 1
2Ch 29:12 Levites arose . . Jo'ah the son of Zimmah, 1
12 Levites arose . . Eden the son of Jo'ah; 1
34: 8 he sent . . Jo'ah the son of Jo'ahaz, the recorder 1
Isa 36: 3 and Jo'ah the son of Asaph, the recorder. 1
11 Eli'akim, Shebna, and Jo'ah said to the Rab'shakeh 1
22 Jo'ah the son of Asaph, the recorder 1

Joahaz 1. יוֹאָחָז

2Kg 14: 1 In the second year of Jo'ash the son of Jo'ahaz 1
2Ch 34: 8 he sent . . Jo'ah the son of Jo'ahaz, the recorder 1

Joakim 1. Ἰωακίμ

1Es 5: 5 Joakim the son of Zerubbabel, son of Shealtiel 1
Jdt 4: 6 Joakim, the high priest 1
8 Joakim the high priest 1
14 Joakim the high priest 1
15: 8 Then Joakim the high priest . . came to witness 1
Sus 1: 1 a man living in Babylon whose name was Joakim. 1
4 Joakim was very rich, and had a spacious garden 1
6 These men were frequently at Joakim's house 1
28 gathered at the house of her husband Joakim 1
29 Send for Susanna . . who is the wife of Joakim. 1
63 so did Joakim her husband and all her kindred 1

Joanan 1. Ἰωανάν

Lke 3:27 the son of Joan'an, the son of Rhesa 1

Joanna 1. Ἰωάννα

Lke 8: 3 Joan'na, the wife of Chuza, Herod's steward 1
24:10 Now it was Mary Mag'dalene and Joan'na 1

Joarib 1. Ιωαριβ

1Mc 2: 1 son of Simeon, a priest of the sons of Joarib 1
14:29 a priest of the sons of Joarib 1

Joash 1. יוֹאָשׁ 2. יוֹעָשׁ

Jdg 6:11 at Ophrah, which belonged to Jo'ash the Abiez'rite 1
29 they said, "Gideon the son of Jo'ash has done this 1
30 men of the town said to Jo'ash, "Bring out your son 1
31 Jo'ash said to all who were arrayed against him 1
7:14 sword of Gideon the son of Jo'ash, a man of Israel; 1
8:13 Gideon the son of Jo'ash returned from the battle 1
29 the son of Jo'ash went and dwelt in his own house. 1
32 Gideon the son of Jo'ash died in a good old age 1
32 age, and was buried in the tomb of Jo'ash his father 1
1Kg 22:26 take him back . . to Jo'ash the king's son; 1
2Kg 11: 2 Jehosh'eba . . took Jo'ash the son of Ahazi'ah 1
12:19 the rest of the acts of Jo'ash, and all that he did 1
20 a conspiracy, and slew Jo'ash in the house of Millo 1
13: 1 In the 23rd year of Jo'ash the son of Ahazi'ah 1
9 and Jo'ash his son reigned in his stead. 1
10 In the 37th year of Jo'ash king of Judah 1
12 the rest of the acts of Jo'ash, and all that he did 1
13 So Jo'ash slept with his fathers, and Jerobo'am sat 1
13 Jo'ash was buried in Sama'ria with the kings 1
14 Jo'ash king of Israel went down to him, and wept 1
25 Jo'ash defeated him and recovered the cities 1
14: 1 In the second year of Jo'ash the son of Jo'ahaz 1
1 Amazi'ah the son of Jo'ash, king of Judah, began 1
3 he did in all things as Jo'ash his father had done. 1
17 Amazi'ah the son of Jo'ash, king of Judah, lived 1
23 In the fifteenth year of Amazi'ah the son of Jo'ash 1
23 Jerobo'am the son of Jo'ash, king of Israel, began 1
27 saved . . by the hand of Jerobo'am the son of Jo'ash. 1
1Ch 3:11 Joram his son, Ahazi'ah his son, Jo'ash his son 1
4:22 Jokim, and the men of Co-ze'ba, and Jo'ash, 1
7: 8 The sons of Becher: Zemi'rah, Jo'ash, Elie'zer 2
12: 3 The chief was Ahi-e'zer, then Jo'ash, both sons 1
27:28 and over the stores of oil was Jo'ash. 2
2Ch 18:25 take him back . . to Jo'ash the king's son; 1
22:11 Jeho-shab'e-ath . . took Jo'ash . . ,and stole him 1
24: 1 Jo'ash was seven years old when he began to reign 1
2 Jo'ash did what was right in the eyes of the LORD 1
4 Jo'ash decided to restore the house of the LORD. 1
22 Jo'ash the king did not remember the kindness 1
23 the army of the Syrians came up against Jo'ash. •
24 Thus they executed judgment on Jo'ash. 1
25:17 Amazi'ah . . sent to Jo'ash the son of Jeho'ahaz 1
18 Jo'ash the king of Israel sent word to Amazi'ah 1
21 Jo'ash king of Israel went up; 1
23 Jo'ash king of Israel captured Amazi'ah 2
23 Amazi'ah king of Judah, the son of Jo'ash 1
25 Amazi'ah the son of Jo'ash king of Judah 1
25 lived fifteen years after the death of Jo'ash 1
Hos 1: 1 and in the days of Jerobo'am the son of Jo'ash 1
Ams 1: 1 and in the days of Jerobo'am the son of Jo'ash, 1

Job 1. אִיּוֹב 2. Ἰώβ

Job 1: 1 was a man in the land of Uz, whose name was Job 1
5 Job would send and sanctify them 1
5 for Job said, "It may be that my sons have sinned 1
5 Thus Job did continually. 1
8 Have you considered my servant Job 1
9 answered the LORD, "Does Job fear God for nought? 1
14 there came a messenger to Job, and said 1
20 Then Job arose, and rent his robe 1
22 Job did not sin or charge God with wrong. 1
2: 3 said to Satan, "Have you considered my servant Job 1
7 Satan . . afflicted Job with loathsome sores 1
10 In all this Job did not sin with his lips. 1
11 when Job's three friends heard of all this evil 1

3: 1 Job opened his mouth and cursed the day of his 1
2 Job said 1
6: 1 Then Job answered 1
9: 1 Then Job answered 1
12: 1 Then Job answered 1
16: 1 Then Job answered 1
19: 1 Then Job answered 1
21: 1 Then Job answered 1
23: 1 Then Job answered 1
26: 1 Then Job answered 1
27: 1 Job again took up his discourse, and said 1
29: 1 Job again took up his discourse, and said 1
31:40 The words of Job are ended. 1
32: 1 these three men ceased to answer Job 1
2 He was angry at Job because he justified himself 1
3 he was angry also at Job's three friends *
3 although they had declared Job to be in the wrong. 1
4 Now Eli'hu had waited to speak to Job 1
12 behold, there was none that confuted Job 1
33: 1 hear my speech, O Job, and listen to all my words. 1
31 Give heed, O Job, listen to me; 1
34: 5 For Job has said, 'I am innocent 1
7 What man is like Job, who drinks up scoffing 1
35 Job speaks without knowledge 1
36 Would that Job were tried to the end 1
35:16 Job opens his mouth in empty talk 1
37:14 Hear this, O Job; stop and consider the wondrous 1
38: 1 Then the LORD answered Job out of the whirlwind 1
40: 1 the LORD said to Job 1
3 Then Job answered the LORD 1
6 Then the LORD answered Job out of the whirlwind 1
42: 1 Then Job answered the LORD 1
7 After the LORD had spoken these words to Job 1
7 spoken of me what is right, as my servant Job has. 1
8 go to my servant Job, and offer up for yourselves 1
8 my servant Job shall pray for you 1
8 spoken of me what is right, as my servant Job has. 1
9 the LORD accepted Job's prayer. 1
10 the LORD restored the fortunes of Job 1
10 the LORD gave Job twice as much as he had before. 1
12 the LORD blessed the latter days of Job 1
15 there were no women so fair as Job's daughters; 1
16 after this Job lived 140 years 1
17 Job died, an old man, and full of days. 1
Ezk 14:14 even if these three men, Noah, Daniel, and Job 1
20 even if Noah, Daniel, and Job were in it, as I live 1
Jas 5:11 You have heard of the steadfastness of Job 2

Jobab 1. יוֹבָב
Gen 10:29 Ophir, Hav'ilah, and Jobab; 1
36:33 Bela died, and Jobab the son of Zerah of Bozrah 1
34 Jobab died, and Husham of the land 1
Jos 11: 1 When Jabin . . he sent to Jobab king of Madon 1
1Ch 1:23 Ophir, Hav'ilah, and Jobab . . the sons of Joktan 1
44 When Bela died, Jobab the son of Zerah of Bozrah 1
45 When Jobab died, Husham of the land 1
8: 9 sons by Hodesh his wife: Jobab, Zib'i-a, Mesha, 1
18 Ish'merai, Izli'ah, and Jobab . . sons of Elpa'al. 1

Jochebed 1. יוֹכֶבֶד
Exd 6:20 Amram took to wife Joch'ebed his father's sister 1
Num26:59 Amram's wife was Joch'ebed the daughter of Levi 1

Joda 1. 'Ιωδά
Lke 3:26 son of Sem'ein, the son of Josech, the son of Joda 1
1Es 5:58 the sons of Joda son of Iliadun 1

Jodan 1. Ιωδανος
1Es 9:19 Maaseiah, Eliezar, Jarib, and Jodan. 1

Joed 1. יוֹעֵד
Neh 11: 7 Sallu the son of Meshul'lam, son of Jo'ed 1

Joel 1. יוֹאֵל 2. Ιουηλ 3. 'Ιωήλ 4. Iohel
1Sm 8: 2 The name of his first-born son was Jo'el 1
1Ch 4:35 Jo'el, Jehu the son of Joshibi'ah, son of Serai'ah 1
5: 4 sons of Jo'el: Shemai'ah his son, Gog his son, Shim'e-i 1
8 Bela the son of Azaz, son of Shema, son of Jo'el 1
12 Jo'el the chief, Shapham . . Ja'nai, and Shaphat 1
6:28 sons of Samuel: Jo'el his first-born . . Abi'jah. 3
33 Heman the singer the son of Jo'el, son of Samuel 1
36 son of Jo'el, son of Azari'ah, son of Zephani'ah 1
7: 3 sons of Izrahi'ah . . Obadi'ah, Jo'el, and Isshi'ah 1
11:38 Jo'el the brother of Nathan 1
15: 7 of the sons of Gershom, Jo'el the chief 1
11 Levites Uri'el, Asai'ah, Jo'el, Shemai'ah, Eli'el 1
17 the Levites appointed Heman the son of Jo'el; 1
23: 8 of Ladan: Jehi'el the chief, and Zetham, and Jo'el 1
26:22 sons of Jehi'eli, Zetham and Jo'el his brother 1
27:20 half-tribe of Manas'seh, Jo'el the son of Pedai'ah; 1
2Ch 29:12 Levites arose . . Jo'el the son of Azari'ah 1
Ezr 10:43 of Nebo . . Zebi'na, Jaddai, Jo'el, and Benai'ah. 1
Neh 11: 9 Jo'el the son of Zichri was their overseer; 1
Jol 1: 1 The word of the LORD that came to Joel 1
Act 2:16 this is what was spoken by the prophet Joel 3
1Es 9:34 Of the sons of Bani: Jeremai, Maadai, Amram, Joel 2
35 Mattithiah, Zabad, Iddo, Joel, Benaiah. 2
2Es 1:39 Amos and Micah and Joel and Obadiah and Jonah 4

Joelah 1. יוֹעֵאלָה
1Ch 12: 7 Joe'lah and Zebadi'ah, the sons of Jero'ham 1

Joezer 1. יוֹעֶזֶר
1Ch 12: 6 Az'arel, Jo-e'zer, and Jasho'be-am, the Ko'rahites; 1

Jogbehah 1. יָגְבְּהָה
Num32:35 At'roth-sho'phan, Jazer, Jog'behah 1
Jdg 8:11 by the caravan route east of Nobah and Jog'behah 1

Jogli 1. יָגְלִי
Num34:22 tribe . . of Dan a leader, Bukki the son of Jogli. 1

Joha 1. יוֹחָא
1Ch 8:16 Michael, Ishpah, and Joha were sons of Beri'ah. 1
11:45 Jedi'a-el . . and Joha his brother, the Tizite 1

Johanan 1. יוֹחָנָן 2. 'Ιωάνης
2Kg 25:23 namely, Ish'mael . . and Joha'nan the son of Kare'ah 1
1Ch 3:15 The sons of Josi'ah: Joha'nan the first-born 1
24 sons of Eli-o-e'nai . . Joha'nan, Delai'ah, and Ana'ni 1
6: 9 Ahim'a-az of Azari'ah, Azari'ah of Joha'nan 1
10 Joha'nan of Azari'ah (it was he who served as priest 1
12: 4 Jeremiah, Jaha'ziel, Joha'nan, Joz'abad of Gede'rah 1
12 Joha'nan eighth, Elza'bad ninth 1
2Ch 28:12 chiefs . . Azari'ah the son of Joha'nan, Berechi'ah 1
Ezr 8:12 Of the sons of Azgad, Joha'nan the son of Hak'katan 1
Neh 12:22 Levites, in the days of . . Joha'nan, and Jad'du-a 1
23 Book of the Chronicles until the days of Joha'nan 1
Jer 40: 8 Joha'nan the son of Kare'ah 1
13 Now Joha'nan the son of Kare'ah and all the leaders 1
15 Then Joha'nan the son of Kare'ah spoke secretly 1
16 But Gedali'ah the son of Ahi'kam said to Joha'nan 1
41:11 But when Joha'nan the son of Kare'ah . . heard 1
13 all the people who were with Ish'mael saw Joha'nan 1
14 came back, and went to Joha'nan the son of Kare'ah. 1
15 Ish'mael . . escaped from Joha'nan with eight men 1
16 Then Joha'nan the son of Kare'ah 1
16 eunuchs, whom Joha'nan brought back from Gibeon. *
42: 1 and Joha'nan the son of Kare'ah 1
8 Then he summoned Joha'nan the son of Kare'ah 1
43: 2 Joha'nan the son of Kare'ah 1
4 Joha'nan the son of Kare'ah and all the commanders 1
5 Joha'nan the son of Kare'ah and all the commanders 1
1Es 8:38 Of the sons of Azgad, Johanan the son of Hakkatan 2

John 1. 'Ιωάννης
Mat 3: 1 In those days came John the Baptist, preaching 1
4 Now John wore a garment of camel's hair 1
13 to the Jordan to John, to be baptized by him. 1
14 John would have prevented him, saying, "I need to be 1
4:12 Now when he heard that John had been arrested 1
21 son of Zeb'edee and John his brother, in the boat 1
9:14 Then the disciples of John came to him, saying 1
10: 2 James the son of Zeb'edee, and John his brother; 1
11: 2 when John heard in prison about the deeds 1
4 Go and tell John what you hear and see 1
7 began to speak to the crowds concerning John 1
11 has risen no one greater than John the Baptist 1
12 From the days of John the Baptist until now 1
13 the prophets and the law prophesied until John; 1
18 For John came neither eating nor drinking 1
14: 2 he said to this servants, "This is John the Baptist 1
3 For Herod had seized John and bound him 1
4 because John said to him 1
8 she said, "Give me the head of John the Baptist 1
10 he sent and had John beheaded in the prison 1
16:14 Some say John the Baptist, others say Eli'jah 1
17: 1 Peter and James and John his brother 1
13 he was speaking to them of John the Baptist. 1
21:25 The baptism of John, whence was it? 1
26 for all hold that John was a prophet. 1
32 For John came to you in the way of righteousness 1
Mrk 1: 4 John the baptizer appeared in the wilderness 1
6 Now John was clothed in camel's hair 1
9 baptized by John in the Jordan. 1
14 Now after John was arrested 1
19 James the son of Zeb'edee and John his brother 1
29 entered the house . . with James and John 1
2:18 John's disciples and the Pharisees were fasting; 1
18 Why do John's disciples . . fast 1
3:17 John the brother of James 1
5:37 Peter and James and John the brother of James. 1
6:14 John the baptizer has been raised from the dead; 1
16 John, whom I beheaded, has been raised. 1
17 For Herod had sent and seized John 1
18 For John said to Herod, "It is not lawful for you 1
20 for Herod feared John . . and kept him safe 1
24 she said, "The head of John the baptizer. 1
25 at once the head of John the Baptist on a platter. 1
8:28 they told him, "John the Baptist 1
9: 2 Jesus took with him Peter and James and John 1
38 John said to him, "Teacher, we saw a man 1
10:35 James and John, the sons of Zeb'edee, came forward 1
41 they began to be indignant at James and John. 1
11:30 Was the baptism of John from heaven or from men? 1
32 for all held that John was a real prophet. 1
13: 3 Peter and James and John and Andrew asked him 1
14:33 he took with him Peter and James and John 1
Lke 1:13 you shall call his name John. 1
60 his mother said, "Not so, he shall be called John. 1
63 for a writing tablet, and wrote, "His name is John. 1
3: 2 the word of God came to John the son of Zechari'ah 1
15 all men questioned in their hearts concerning John 1
16 John answered them all, "I baptize you with water; 1
20 he shut up John in prison. 1
5:10 so also were James and John, sons of Zeb'edee 1
33 disciples of John fast often and offer prayers 1
6:14 Andrew his brother, and James and John, and Philip 1
7:18 disciples of John told him of all these things. 1
19 John, calling to him two of his disciples 1
20 John the Baptist has sent us to you, saying 1
22 Go and tell John what you have seen and heard 1
24 When the messengers of John had gone 1
24 he began to speak to the crowds concerning John 1
28 none is greater than John 1
29 baptized with the baptism of John; 1
33 For John the Baptist has come eating no bread 1
8:51 except Peter and John and James 1
9: 7 John had been raised from the dead 1
9 Herod said, "John I beheaded 1
19 they answered, "John the Baptist 1
28 he took with him Peter and John and James 1
49 John answered, "Master, we saw a man 1
54 when his disciples James and John saw it 1
11: 1 teach us to pray, as John taught his disciples. 1
16:16 The law and the prophets were until John 1
20: 4 Was the baptism of John from heaven or from men? 1
6 they are convinced that John was a prophet. 1
22: 8 So Jesus sent Peter and John, saying, "Go 1
Joh 1: 6 was a man sent from God, whose name was John. 1
15 (John bore witness to him and cried 1
19 And this is the testimony of John 1
26 John answered them, "I baptize with water; 1
28 beyond the Jordan, where John was baptizing. 1
32 And John bore witness, "I saw the Spirit descend 1
35 John was standing with two of his disciples; 1
40 One of the two who heard John speak . . was Andrew 1
42 So you are Simon the son of John? 1
3:23 John also was baptizing at Ae'non near Salim 1
24 For John had not yet been put in prison. 1
25 a discussion . . between John's disciples and a Jew 1
26 And they came to John, and said to him, "Rabbi 1
27 John answered, "No one can receive anything 1
4: 1 making and baptizing more disciples than John 1
5:33 You sent to John 1
36 the testimony . . is greater than that of John 1
10:40 to the place where John at first baptized 1
41 many came to him; and they said, "John did no sign 1
41 everything . . John said about this man was true 1
21:15 Jesus said to Simon Peter, "Simon, son of John 1
16 A second time he said to him, "Simon, son of John 1
17 Simon, son of John, do you love me? 1
Act 1: 5 for John baptized with water 1
13 Peter and John and James and Andrew 1
22 beginning from the baptism of John 1
3: 1 Now Peter and John were going up to the temple 1
3 Seeing Peter and John about to go into the temple 1
4 Peter directed his gaze at him, with John, and said 1
11 While he clung to Peter and John 1
4: 6 Ca'iaphas and John and Alexander 1
13 Now when they saw the boldness of Peter and John 1
19 Peter and John answered them, "Whether it is right 1
8:14 they sent to them Peter and John 1
10:37 after the baptism which John preached 1
11:16 John baptized with water 1
12: 2 killed James the brother of John with the sword; 1
12 Mary, mother of John whose other name was Mark 1
25 John whose other name was Mark. 1
13: 5 they had John to assist them. 1
13 John left them and returned to Jerusalem; 1
24 Before his coming John had preached 1
25 as John was finishing his course, he said 1
15:37 wanted to take with them John called Mark. 1
18:25 though he knew only the baptism of John. 1
19: 3 They said, "Into John's baptism. 1
4 John baptized with the baptism of repentance 1
Gal 2: 9 James and Cephas and John 1
Rev 1: 1 by sending his angel to his servant John 1
4 John to the seven churches that are in Asia 1
9 I John, your brother, who share with you in Jesus 1
22: 8 I John am he who heard and saw these things. 1
1Mc 2: 1 Mattathias the son of John, son of Simeon 1
2 He had five sons, John surnamed Gaddi 1
8:17 Eupolemus the son of John, son of Accos 1
9:36 seized John and all that he had 1
38 they remembered the blood of John their brother 1
13:53 Simon saw that John his son had reached manhood 1
16: 1 John went up from Gazara and reported to Simon 1
2 Simon called in his two older sons Judas and John 1
4 So John chose . . 20,000 warriors *
9 Judas the brother of John was wounded 1
9 John pursued them 1
10 John burned it with fire *
19 He sent other men to Gazara to do away with John 1
21 some one ran ahead and reported to John at Gazara 1
23 The rest of the acts of John and his wars 1

2Mc 4:11 secured through John the father of Eupolemus 1
11:17 John and Absalom, who were sent by you 1

Joiada 1. יוֹיָדָע
Neh 3: 6 Joi'ada the son of Pase'ah and Meshul'lam 1
12:10 Eli'ashib the father of Joi'ada 1
11 Joi'ada the father of Jonathan 1
22 Levites, in the days of Eli'ashib, Joi'ada, Joha'nan 1

Joiakim 1. יוֹיָקִים
Neh 12:10 Jeshua was the father of Joi'akim 1
10 Joi'akim the father of Eli'ashib 1
12 days of Joi'akim were priests, heads of fathers' 1
26 days of Joi'akim the son of Jeshua son of Jo'zadak 1

Joiarib 1. יוֹיָרִיב
Ezr 8:16 Then I sent . . for Joi'arib and Elna'than 1
Neh 11: 5 Adai'ah, son of Joi'arib, son of Zechari'ah 1
10 Of the priests: Jedai'ah the son of Joi'arib, Jachin 1
12: 6 Shemai'ah, Joi'arib, Jedai'ah 1
19 of Joi'arib, Matte'nai; of Jedai'ah, Uzzi; 1

Jokdeam 1. יָקְדְעָם
Jos 15:56 Jezreel, Jok'de-am, Zano'ah 1

Jokim 1. יוֹקִים
1Ch 4:22 Jokim, and the men of Co-ze'ba, and Jo'ash, 1

Jokmeam 1. יָקְמְעָם
1Kg 4:12 A'bel-meho'lah, as far as the other side of Jok'meam; 1
1Ch 6:68 Jok'me-am with its pasture lands 1

Jokneam 1. יָקְנְעָם
Jos 12:22 of Kedesh, one; the king of Jok'ne-am in Carmel, one; 1
19:11 then the brook which is east of Jok'ne-am; 1
21:34 were given . . Jok'ne-am with its pasture lands 1

Jokshan 1. יָקְשָׁן
Gen 25: 2 She bore him Zimran, Jokshan, Medan, Mid'ian 1
3 Jokshan was the father of Sheba and Dedan. 1
1Ch 1:32 she bore Zimran, Jokshan, Medan, Mid'ian, Ishbak 1
32 Shu'ah. The sons of Jokshan: Sheba and Dedan. 1

Joktan 1. יָקְטָן
Gen 10:25 was divided, and his brother's name was Joktan. 1
26 Joktan became the father of Almo'dad, Sheleph 1
29 and Jobab; all these were the sons of Joktan. 1
1Ch 1:19 two sons . . the name of his brother Joktan. 1
20 Joktan was the father of Almo'dad, Sheleph 1
23 Jobab; all these were the sons of Joktan. 1

Joktheel 1. יָקְתְאֵל
Jos 15:38 Di'lean, Mizpeh, Jok'theel 1
2Kg 14: 7 and took Sela by storm, and called it Jok'the-el 1

Jonadab 1. יוֹנָדָב
2Sm 13: 3 But Amnon had a friend, whose name was Jon'adab 1
3 and Jon'adab was a very crafty man. 1
5 Jon'adab said to him, "Lie down on your bed 1
32 Jon'adab the son of Shim'e-ah, David's brother, said 1
35 Jon'adab said to the king, "Behold, the king's sons 1
Jer 35: 6 for Jon'adab the son of Rechab, our father 1
8 We have obeyed the voice of Jon'adab 1
10 done all that Jon'adab our father commanded us. 1
14 The command which Jon'adab the son of Rechab gave 1
16 The sons of Jon'adab the son of Rechab 1
18 Because you have obeyed the command of Jon'adab 1
19 Jon'adab the son of Rechab shall never lack a man 1

Jonah 1. יוֹנָה 2. Ἰωνας 3. Ἰωναν 4. Ἰωνᾶς 5. Iona
2Kg 14:25 he spoke by his servant Jonah the son of Amit'tai 1
Jon 1: 1 the LORD came to Jonah the son of Amit'tai, saying 1
3 Jonah rose to flee to Tarshish 1
5 Jonah had gone down into the inner part 1
7 So they cast lots, and the lot fell upon Jonah. 1
15 they took up Jonah and threw him into the sea; 1
17 LORD appointed a great fish to swallow up Jonah; 1
17 Jonah was in the belly of the fish three days 1
2: 1 Then Jonah prayed to the LORD his God 1
10 it vomited out Jonah upon the dry land. 1
3: 1 Then the word of the LORD came to Jonah 1
3 Jonah arose and went to Nin'eveh 1
4 Jonah began to go into the city 1
4: 1 it displeased Jonah exceedingly 1
5 Then Jonah went out of the city and sat to the east 1
6 appointed a plant, and made it come up over Jonah 1
6 Jonah was exceedingly glad 1
8 the sun beat upon the head of Jonah 1
9 God said to Jonah, "Do you do well to be angry 1
Mat 12:39 except the sign of the prophet Jonah. 4
40 For as Jonah was three days and three nights 4
41 for they repented at the preaching of Jonah 4
41 behold, something greater than Jonah is here. 4
16: 4 except the sign of Jonah 4
Lke 11:29 no sign . . except the sign of Jonah. 4
30 For as Jonah became a sign to the men of Nin'eveh 4
32 they repented at the preaching of Jonah 4
32 behold, something greater than Jonah is here. 4
1Es 9:23 Pethahiah and Judah and Jonah. 2
2Es 1:39 Amos and Micah and Joel and Obadiah and Jonah 5
Tob 14: 4 I fully believe what Jonah the prophet said 4
8 what the prophet Jonah said will surely happen. 4
3Mc 6: 8 Jonah . . you, Father, watched over 3

Jonam 1. Ἰωνάμ
Lke 3:30 the son of Joseph, the son of Jonam 1

Jonathan 1. יְהוֹנָתָן 2. יוֹנָתָן 3. Ιωναθαν 4. Ἰωνάθας 5. Ιωναθης 6. Ionatha
Jdg 18:30 Jonathan the son of Gershom, son of Moses 2
1Sm 13: 2 and 1,000 were with Jonathan in Gib'e-ah 2
3 Jonathan defeated the garrison . . at Geba; 2
16 And Saul, and Jonathan his son . . stayed in Geba 2
22 of any of the people with Saul and Jonathan; 2
22 but Saul and Jonathan his son had them. 2
14: 1 One day Jonathan the son of Saul said . . "Come 2
3 the people did not know that Jonathan had gone. 2
4 In the pass, by which Jonathan sought to go over 2
6 Jonathan said to the young man who bore his armor 2
8 Then said Jonathan, "Behold, we will cross over 2
12 the men . . hailed Jonathan and his armor-bearer 2
12 Jonathan said to his armor-bearer, "Come up 2
13 Then Jonathan climbed up on his hands and feet 2
13 they fell before Jonathan, and his armor-bearer 2
14 which Jonathan and his armor-bearer made 2
17 Jonathan and his armor-bearer were not there. 2
21 the Israelites who were with Saul and Jonathan. 2
27 Jonathan had not heard his father charge 2
29 Jonathan said, "My father has troubled the land; 2
39 though it be in Jonathan my son, he shall . . die. 2
40 I and Jonathan my son will be on the other side. 2
41 If this guilt is in me or in Jonathan my son, O LORD 6
41 Jonathan and Saul were taken, but the people 2
42 Cast the lot between me and my son Jonathan. 2
42 Saul said, "Cast the lot . . " And Jonathan was taken. 2
43 Saul said to Jonathan, "Tell me what you have done. 2
43 Tell me what you have done." And Jonathan told him 2
44 God do so to me . . you shall surely die, Jonathan. 2
45 Shall Jonathan die, who has wrought . . victory 2
45 the people ransomed Jonathan, that he . . not die. 2
49 sons of Saul were Jonathan, Ishvi, and Mal'chishu'a; 2
18: 1 the soul of Jonathan was knit to the soul of David 2
1 and Jonathan loved him as his own soul. 2
3 Then Jonathan made a covenant with David 2
4 Jonathan stripped himself of the robe 2
19: 1 Saul spoke to Jonathan . . and to all his servants 2
1 But Jonathan, Saul's son, delighted much in David. 2
2 Jonathan told David, "Saul . . seeks to kill you; 2
4 Jonathan spoke well of David to Saul his father 2
6 And Saul hearkened to the voice of Jonathan; 2
7 Jonathan called David, and . . showed him all 2
7 and Jonathan showed him all these things. 2
7 And Jonathan brought David to Saul, and he was 2
20: 1 David fled . . and came and said before Jonathan 2
3 'Let not Jonathan know this, lest he be grieved.' 2
4 Then said Jonathan to David, "Whatever . . I will do 2
5 David said to Jonathan, "Behold, tomorrow is 2
9 And Jonathan said, "Far be it from you! 2
10 Then said David to Jonathan, "Who will tell me 2
11 Jonathan said to David, "Come, let us go out 2
12 Jonathan said to David, "The LORD . . be witness! 2
13 the LORD do so to Jonathan, and more also 2
16 let not the name of Jonathan be cut off 2
17 Jonathan made David swear . . by his love for him; 2
18 Jonathan said to him, "Tomorrow is the new moon; 2
25 The king sat . . Jonathan sat opposite, and Abner 2
27 Saul said to Jonathan his son, "Why has not the son 2
28 Jonathan answered Saul, "David earnestly asked 2
30 Then Saul's anger was kindled against Jonathan 2
32 Jonathan answered Saul his father, "Why should he 2
33 Jonathan knew that his father was determined 2
34 And Jonathan rose from the table in fierce anger 2
35 In the morning Jonathan went ou into the field 2
37 the place of the arrow which Jonathan had shot 2
37 Jonathan called after the lad and said 2
38 Jonathan called after the lad, "Hurry, make haste 2
38 Jonathan's lad gathered up the arrows 2
39 only Jonathan and David knew the matter. 2
40 And Jonathan gave his weapons to his lad, and said 2
42 Then Jonathan said to David, "Go in peace 2
42 And he rose . . and Jonathan went into the city. 2
23:16 Jonathan, Saul's son, rose, and went to David 2
18 David remained at Horesh, and Jonathan went home. 2
31: 2 the Philistines slew Jonathan and Abin'adab 2
2Sm 1: 4 and Saul and his son Jonathan are also dead. 2
5 How do you know that Saul and . . Jonathan are dead? 2
12 they mourned and . . for Saul and for Jonathan 2
17 David lamented . . over Saul and Jonathan his son 2
22 the bow of Jonathan turned not back, and the sword 2
23 Saul and Jonathan, beloved and lovely! 2
25 Jonathan lies slain upon thy high places. 2
26 I am distressed for you, my brother Jonathan; 2
4: 4 Jonathan . . had a son who was crippled 2
4 news about Saul and Jonathan came from Jezreel; 2
9: 1 that I may show him kindness for Jonathan's sake? 2
3 There is still a son of Jonathan; he is crippled 2
6 Mephib'osheth the son of Jonathan, son of Saul 2
7 kindness for the sake of your father Jonathan 2
15:27 Ahim'a-az . . and Jonathan the son of Abi'athar. 2
36 their two sons . . and Jonathan, Abi'athar's son; 2
17:17 Jonathan and Ahim'a-az were waiting at En-ro'gel; 2
20 they said, "Where are Ahim'a-az and Jonathan? 2
21: 7 Mephib'osheth, the son of Saul's son Jonathan 2
7 oath . . between them, between David and Jonathan 2
12 took . . the bones of his son Jonathan 2
13 bones of Saul and the bones of his son Jonathan; 2
14 buried the bones of Saul and his son Jonathan 2
21 Jonathan the son of Shim'e-i, David's brother 2
23:32 Eli'ahba of Sha-al'bon, the sons of Jashen, Jonathan 2
1Kg 1:42 Jonathan the son of Abi'athar the priest came; 2
43 Jonathan answered Adoni'jah, "No, for our lord King 2
1Ch 2:32 The sons of Jada . . Jether and Jonathan; 2
33 The sons of Jonathan: Peleth and Zaza. 2
8:33 Saul of Jonathan, Mal'chishu'a, Abin'adab 2
34 the son of Jonathan was Mer'ib-ba'al; 2
9:39 Saul of Jonathan, Mal'chishu'a, Abin'adab 2
40 the son of Jonathan was Mer'ib-ba'al; 2
10: 2 Philistines slew Jonathan and Abin'adab 2
11:34 Jonathan the son of Shagee the Har'arite 2
20: 7 Jonathan the son of Shim'e-a . . slew him. 2
27:25 treasuries . . was Jonathan the son of Uzzi'ah; 2
32 Jonathan, David's uncle, was a counselor 2
Ezr 8: 6 Of the sons of Adin, Ebed the son of Jonathan 2
10:15 Only Jonathan the son of As'ahel and Jahzei'ah 2
Neh 12:11 Joi'ada the father of Jonathan 2
11 Jonathan the father of Jad'du-a. 2
14 of Mal'luchi, Jonathan; of Shebani'ah, Joseph; 2
35 Zechari'ah the son of Jonathan, son of Shemai'ah 2
Jer 37:15 in the house of Jonathan the secretary 1
20 do not send me back to the house of Jonathan 1
38:26 he would not send me back to the house of Jonathan 1
1Es 9:14 Jonathan the son of Asahel and Jahzeiah 4
1Mc 2: 5 Jonathan called Apphus. 5
4:30 didst give . . into the hands of Jonathan 4
5:17 I and Jonathan my brother will go to Gilead. 3
24 Judas Maccabeus and Jonathan his brother 3
55 Now while Judas and Jonathan were in Gilead 3
9:19 Jonathan and Simon took Judas their brother 3
28 assembled and said to Jonathan 3
31 Jonathan at that time accepted the leadership 3
33 Jonathan and Simon his brother 3
35 Jonathan sent his brother as leader •
37 was reported to Jonathan and Simon his brother 3
44 Jonathan said to those with him 3
47 Jonathan stretched out his hand to strike Bacchides 3
48 Then Jonathan and the men with him leaped 3
58 Jonathan and his men are living in quiet 3
60 telling them to seize Jonathan and his men 3
61 Jonathan's men seized about 50 of the men •
62 Then Jonathan with his men, and Simon 3
65 Jonathan left Simon his brother in the city 3
70 When Jonathan learned of this 3
71 he swore to Jonathan •
73 Jonathan dwelt in Michmash 3
73 Jonathan began to judge the people 3
10: 3 Demetrius sent Jonathan a letter 3
7 Then Jonathan came to Jerusalem 3
9 released the hostages to Jonathan 3
10 Jonathan dwelt in Jerusalem 3
15 promises which Demetrius had sent to Jonathan 3
15 the battles that Jonathan . . had fought •
18 King Alexander to his brother Jonathan, greeting 3
21 So Jonathan put on the holy garments 3
46 When Jonathan and the people heard these words 3
59 the king wrote to Jonathan to come to meet him. 3
62 The king gave orders to take off Jonathan's garments 3
66 Jonathan returned to Jerusalem in peace 3
69 Then he sent the following message to Jonathan 3
74 When Jonathan heard the words of Apollonius 3
76 Jonathan gained possession of Joppa. 3
78 Jonathan pursued him to Azotus •
80 Jonathan learned that there was an ambush 3
81 his men stood fast, as Jonathan commanded 3
84 Jonathan burned Azotus 3
86 Then Jonathan departed from there 3
87 Jonathan and those with him 3
88 he honored Jonathan still more; 3
11: 4 those whom Jonathan had burned in the war •
5 They also told the king what Jonathan had done 3
6 Jonathan met the king at Joppa with pomp 3
7 Jonathan went with the king as far as the river 3
20 In those days Jonathan assembled the men of Judea 3
21 Jonathan was besieging the citadel. 3
22 he wrote Jonathan not to continue the siege 3
23 When Jonathan heard this 3
28 Then Jonathan asked the king to free Judea 3
29 The king consented, and wrote a letter to Jonathan 3
30 King Demetrius to Jonathan his brother 3
37 let it be given to Jonathan 3
41 Jonathan sent to Demetrius the king the request 3
42 Demetrius sent this message to Jonathan 3
44 So Jonathan sent 3,000 stalwart men 3
53 he became estranged from Jonathan 3
53 did not repay the favors which Jonathan had done •

57 the young Antiochus wrote to Jonathan, saying 3
60 Then Jonathan set forth 3
62 Then the people of Gaza pleaded with Jonathan 3
63 Then Jonathan heard 3
67 Jonathan and his army encamped by the waters 3
70 All the men with Jonathan fled 3
71 Jonathan rent his garments 3
74 Jonathan returned to Jerusalem. 3
12: 1 Now when Jonathan saw 3
3 Jonathan the high priest and the Jewish nation 3
5 This is a copy of the letter which Jonathan wrote 3
6 Jonathan the high priest 3
24 Now Jonathan heard 3
27 Jonathan commanded his men to be alert 3
28 Jonathan and his men were prepared for battle 3
29 Jonathan and his men did not know it 3
30 Then Jonathan pursued them 3
31 So Jonathan turned aside against the Arabs 3
35 When Jonathan returned he convened the elders 3
40 He feared that Jonathan might not permit him 3
41 Jonathan went out to meet him 3
44 Then he said to Jonathan 3
46 Jonathan trusted him and did as he said •
48 when Jonathan entered Ptolemais 3
49 to destroy all Jonathan's soldiers. 3
50 they realized that Jonathan had been seized •
52 they mourned for Jonathan and his companions 3
13: 8 in place of Judas and Jonathan your brother. 3
11 He sent Jonathan the son of Absalom to Joppa 3
12 Jonathan was with him under guard. 3
14 had risen up in place of Jonathan his brother 3
15 the money that Jonathan your brother owed 3
19 broke his word and did not release Jonathan. 3
23 When he approached Baskama, he killed Jonathan 3
25 took the bones of Jonathan his brother 3
14:16 It was heard . . that Jonathan had died 3
18 Judas and Jonathan his brothers. 3
30 Jonathan rallied the nation 3
2Mc 1:23 Jonathan led, and the rest responded 4
8:22 Simon and Joseph and Jonathan 5

son of Jonathan 1. Βην Ιωναθου
1Es 8:32 Obed the son of Jonathan, and with him 250 men. 1

Joppa 1. יָפוֹ 2. Ἰόππη 3. Ιοππιτης
Jos 19:46 Rakkon with the territory over against Joppa. 1
2Ch 2:16 and bring it to you in rafts by sea to Joppa 1
Ezr 3: 7 cedar trees from Lebanon to the sea, to Joppa 1
Jon 1: 3 He went down to Joppa and found a ship 1
Act 9:36 Now there was at Joppa a disciple named Tabitha 2
38 Since Lydda was near Joppa 2
42 it became known throughout all Joppa 2
43 in Joppa for many days with one Simon, a tanner. 2
10: 5 now send men to Joppa 2
8 he sent them to Joppa. 2
23 some of the brethren from Joppa accompanied him. 2
32 Send therefore to Joppa and ask for Simon 2
11: 5 I was in the city of Joppa praying 2
13 'Send to Joppa and bring Simon called Peter; 2
1Es 5:55 convey them in rafts to the harbor of Joppa 2
1Mc 10:75 He encamped before Joppa 2
75 Apollonius had a garrison in Joppa. 2
76 Jonathan gained possession of Joppa. 2
11: 6 Jonathan met the king at Joppa with pomp 2
12:33 He turned aside to Joppa and took it by surprise 2
13:11 He sent Jonathan the son of Absalom to Joppa 2
14: 5 To crown all his honors he took Joppa for a harbor 2
34 He also fortified Joppa, which is by the sea 2
15:28 You hold control of Joppa and Gazara 2
35 As for Joppa and Gazara, which you demand 2
2Mc 4:21 upon arriving at Joppa 2
12: 3 some men of Joppa did so ungodly a deed as this 3
7 and root out the whole community of Joppa. 3

man of Joppa
2Mc 12: 4 the men of Joppa took them out to sea •

Jorah 1. יוֹרָה 2. Αρσιφουριθ
Ezr 2:18 sons of Jorah, 112. 1
1Es 5:16 The sons of Bezai, 323. The sons of Jorah, 112. 2

Jorai 1. יוֹרַי
1Ch 5:13 Michael, Meshul'lam, Sheba, Jo'rai, Jacan, Zi'a 1

Joram 1. יוֹרָם 2. Ἰωράμ
2Sm 8:10 To'i sent his son Joram to King David, to greet him 1
10 Joram brought with him articles of silver 1
2Kg 8:16 In the fifth year of Joram the son of Ahab 1
21 Joram passed over to Za'ir with all his chariots 1
23 the rest of the acts of Joram, and all that he did 1
24 So Joram slept with his fathers, and was buried 1
25 In the twelfth year of Joram the son of Ahab 1
28 He went with Joram . . to make war against Haz'ael 1
28 to make war . . where the Syrians wounded Joram. 1
29 King Joram returned to be healed in Jezreel 1
29 Ahazi'ah . . went down to see Joram the son of Ahab 1
9:14 Thus Jehu . . conspired against Joram. 1
14 Now Joram with all Israel had been on guard 1
16 Jehu . . and went to Jezreel, for Joram lay there. 1
16 And Ahazi'ah . . had come down to visit Joram. 1
17 Joram said, "Take a horseman, and send to meet them 1
21 Joram said, "Make ready." And they made ready 1
21 Joram king of Israel and Ahazi'ah . . set out 1
22 when Joram saw Jehu, he said, "Is it peace, Jehu? 1
23 Joram reined about and fled, saying to Ahazi'ah 1
24 Jehu . . and shot Joram between the shoulders 1
29 In the eleventh year of Joram . . Ahazi'ah began 1
11: 2 Jehosh'eba, the daughter of King Joram, sister 1
1Ch 3:11 Joram his son, Ahazi'ah his son, Jo'ash his son 1
26:25 from Elie'zer were . . his son Joram 1
2Ch 22: 5 And the Syrians wounded Joram 1
6 Ahazi'ah . . went down to see Joram the son of Ahab 1
7 come about through his going to visit Joram. 1
Mat 1: 8 and Jehosh'aphat the father of Joram 2
8 and Joram the father of Uzzi'ah 2
1Es 1: 9 Hashabiah and Ochiel and Joram 2

Jordan 1. יַרְדֵּן 2. Ἰορδάνης
Gen 13:10 the Jordan valley was well watered everywhere 1
11 Lot chose for himself all the Jordan valley 1
32:10 for with only my staff I crossed this Jordan; 1
50:10 floor of Atad, which is beyond the Jordan 1
11 named A'bel-mizraim; it is beyond the Jordan. 1
Num13:29 Canaanites dwell by the sea, and along the Jordan. 1
22: 1 plains of Moab beyond the Jordan at Jericho. 1
26: 3 in the plains of Moab by the Jordan at Jericho 1
63 plains of Moab by the Jordan at Jericho. 1
31:12 on the plains of Moab by the Jordan at Jericho. 1
32: 5 do not take us across the Jordan. 1
19 on the other side of the Jordan and beyond; 1
19 come to us on this side of the Jordan to the east. 1
21 pass over the Jordan before the LORD 1
29 every man . . will pass with you over the Jordan 1
32 inheritance shall remain with us beyond the Jordan. 1
33:48 in the plains of Moab by the Jordan at Jericho; 1
49 encamped by the Jordan from Beth-jes'himoth 1
50 in the plains of Moab by the Jordan at Jericho 1
51 pass over the Jordan into the land of Canaan 1
34:12 boundary shall go down to the Jordan, and its end 1
15 received their inheritance beyond the Jordan 1
35: 1 in the plains of Moab by the Jordan at Jericho 1
10 When you cross the Jordan into the land of Canaan 1
14 You shall give three cities beyond the Jordan 1
36:13 in the plains of Moab by the Jordan at Jericho. 1
Deu 1: 1 Moses spoke to all Israel beyond the Jordan 1
5 Beyond the Jordan, in the land of Moab 1
2:29 until I go over the Jordan into the land 1
3: 8 kings of the Amorites who were beyond the Jordan 1
17 the Arabah also, with the Jordan as the boundary 1
20 which the LORD . . gives them beyond the Jordan; 1
25 Let me . . see the good land beyond the Jordan 1
27 for you shall not go over this Jordan. 1
4:21 LORD . . swore that I should not cross the Jordan 1
22 must die in this land, I must not go over the Jordan; 1
26 land . . you are going over the Jordan to possess; 1
41 three cities in the east beyond the Jordan 1
46 beyond the Jordan in the valley 1
47 who lived to the east beyond the Jordan; 1
49 all the Arabah on the east side of the Jordan 1
9: 1 O Israel; you are to pass over the Jordan this day 1
11:30 Are they not beyond the Jordan, west of the road 1
31 pass over the Jordan to go in to take possession 1
12:10 when you go over the Jordan, and live in the land 1
27: 2 day you pass over the Jordan to the land 1
4 passed over the Jordan, you shall set up 1
12 passed over the Jordan, these shall stand upon 1
30:18 land . . going over the Jordan to enter and possess. 1
31: 2 said to me, 'You shall not go over this Jordan.' 1
13 land . . you are going over the Jordan to possess. 1
32:47 land . . going over the Jordan to possess. 1
Jos 1: 2 arise, go over this Jordan you and all this people 1
11 you are to pass over this Jordan, to go 1
14 the land which Moses gave you beyond the Jordan; 1
15 land which Moses . . gave you beyond the Jordan 1
2: 7 pursued . . them on the way to the Jordan as far 1
10 to the two kings . . that were beyond the Jordan 1
3: 1 and they came to the Jordan, and lodged there 1
8 you come to the brink of the waters of the Jordan 1
8 you shall stand still in the Jordan. 1
11 ark . . is to pass over before you into the Jordan. 1
13 soles . . shall rest in the waters of the Jordan 1
13 the waters of the Jordan shall be stopped 1
14 when the people set out . . to pass over the Jordan 1
15 when those who bore the ark had come to the Jordan 1
15 the Jordan overflows all its banks 1
17 stood on dry ground in the midst of the Jordan 1
17 the nation finished passing over the Jordan. 1
4: 1 When all . . had finished passing over the Jordan 1
3 Take . . from here out of the midst of the Jordan 1
5 Pass on . . into the midst of the Jordan, and take up 1
7 waters of the Jordan were cut off before the ark 1
7 when it passed over the Jordan, the waters 1
7 the waters of the Jordan were cut off. 1
8 twelve stones out of the midst of the Jordan 1
9 set up twelve stones in the midst of the Jordan 1
10 the priests . . stood in the midst of the Jordan 1
16 the priests . . to come up out of the Jordan. 1
17 commanded the priests, "Come up out of the Jordan. 1
18 priests . . came up from the midst of the Jordan 1
18 the waters of the Jordan returned to their place 1
19 The people came up out of the Jordan on the tenth 1
20 twelve stones, which they took out of the Jordan 1
22 'Israel passed over this Jordan on dry ground.' 1
23 LORD . . dried up the waters of the Jordan for you 1
5: 1 Amorites that were beyond the Jordan to the west 1
1 the LORD had dried up the waters of the Jordan 1
7: 7 brought this people over the Jordan at all 1
7 we had been content to dwell beyond the Jordan! 1
9: 1 who were beyond the Jordan in the hill country 1
10 kings of the Amorites who were beyond the Jordan 1
12: 1 took possession of their land beyond the Jordan 1
7 Joshua . . defeated on the west side of the Jordan 1
13: 8 which Moses gave . . beyond the Jordan eastward 1
23 the border . . was the Jordan as a boundary. 1
27 the kingdom of . . having the Jordan as a boundary 1
27 the lower end of . . eastward beyond the Jordan. 1
32 of Moab, beyond the Jordan east of Jericho. 1
14: 3 to the two and one-half tribes beyond the Jordan; 1
15: 5 east boundary is . . to the mouth of the Jordan. 1
5 from the bay of the sea at the mouth of the Jordan; 1
16: 1 allotment . . went from the Jordan by Jericho 1
7 it goes down . . ending at the Jordan. 1
17: 5 Bashan, which is on the other side of the Jordan; 1
18: 7 received their inheritance beyond the Jordan 1
12 their boundary began at the Jordan; 1
19 the northern bay . . at the south end of the Jordan 1
20 The Jordan forms its boundary on the eastern 1
19:22 and its boundary ends at the Jordan 1
33 ran . . as far as Lakkum; and it ended at the Jordan; 1
34 touching . . Judah on the east at the Jordan. 1
20: 8 And beyond the Jordan . . they appointed Bezer 1
22: 4 Moses . . gave you on the other side of the Jordan. 1
7 a possession . . in the land west of the Jordan. 1
10 And when they came to the region about the Jordan 1
10 Manas'seh built there an altar by the Jordan 1
11 the land of Canaan, in the region about the Jordan 1
25 For the LORD has made the Jordan a boundary 1
23: 4 nations . . from the Jordan to the Great Sea 1
24: 8 who lived on the other side of the Jordan; 1
11 And you went over the Jordan and came to Jericho 1
Jdg 3:28 they . . seized the fords of the Jordan 1
5:17 Gilead stayed beyond the Jordan; 1
6:33 and crossing the Jordan they encamped •
7:24 them, as far as Beth-bar'ah, and also the Jordan. 1
24 waters as far as Beth-bar'ah, and also the Jordan. 1
25 of Oreb and Zeeb to Gideon beyond the Jordan. 1
8: 4 Gideon came to the Jordan and passed over 1
10: 8 beyond the Jordan in the land of the Amorites 1
9 the Ammonites crossed the Jordan to fight also 1
11:13 from the Arnon to the Jabbok and to the Jordan; 1
22 Jabbok and from the wilderness to the Jordan. 1
12: 5 the Gileadites took the fords of the Jordan 1
6 him and slew him at the fords of the Jordan. 1
1Sm 13: 7 people hid . . or crossed the fords of the Jordan 1
31: 7 men of Israel who . . and those beyond the Jordan 1
2Sm 2:29 they crossed the Jordan, and . . came to Mahana'im. 1
10:17 he gathered all Israel . . and crossed the Jordan 1
16:14 the king . . arrived weary at the Jordan; 2
17:22 Then David arose . . and they crossed the Jordan; 1
22 not one was left who had not crossed the Jordan. 1
24 Ab'salom crossed the Jordan with all . . Israel. 1
19:15 So the king came back to the Jordan; and Judah came 1
15 Judah came . . to bring the king over the Jordan. 1
17 Ziba . . rushed down to the Jordan before the king 1
18 Shim'e-i . . as he was about to cross the Jordan 1
31 and he went on with the king to the Jordan 1
31 went on with the king . . to escort him over the Jordan. 1
36 Your servant will go a little way over the Jordan 1
39 Then all the people went over the Jordan 1
41 and brought the king and his . . over the Jordan 1
20: 2 Judah followed . . from the Jordan to Jerusalem. 1
24: 5 They crossed the Jordan, and began from Aro'er 1
1Kg 2: 8 when he came down to meet me at the Jordan, I swore 1
7:46 In the plain of the Jordan the king cast them 1
17: 3 the brook Cherith, that is east of the Jordan. 1
5 the brook Cherith that is east of the Jordan. 1
2Kg 2: 6 the LORD has sent me to the Jordan. 1
7 they both were standing by the Jordan. 1
13 went back and stood on the bank of the Jordan. 1
5:10 Go and wash in the Jordan seven times 1
14 and dipped himself seven times in the Jordan 1
6: 2 Let us go to the Jordan and each of us get . . a log 1
4 when they came to the Jordan, they cut down trees. 1
7:15 So they went after them as far as the Jordan; 1
10:33 from the Jordan eastward, all the land of Gilead 1
1Ch 6:78 beyond the Jordan at Jericho 1
78 at Jericho, on the east side of the Jordan 1
12:15 These are the men who crossed the Jordan 1
37 Of the Reubenites and . . from beyond the Jordan 1
19:17 crossed the Jordan, and came to them 1
26:30 the oversight of Israel westward of the Jordan 1
2Ch 4:17 In the plain of the Jordan the king cast them 1
Job 40:23 though Jordan rushes against his mouth. 1
Ps 42: 6 I remember thee from the land of Jordan 1
114: 3 The sea looked and fled, Jordan turned back. 1
5 What ails you . . O Jordan, that you turn back? 1

Isa 9: 1 will make glorious . . the land beyond the Jordan 1
Jer 12: 5 how will you do in the jungle of the Jordan? 1
49:19 lion coming up from the jungle of the Jordan 1
50:44 lion coming up from the jungle of the Jordan 1
Ezk 47:18 the Jordan between Gilead and the land of Israel; 1
Zec 11: 3 for the jungle of the Jordan is laid waste! 1
Mat 3: 5 Judea and all the region about the Jordan 2
6 they were baptized by him in the river Jordan 2
13 Jesus came from Galilee to the Jordan to John 2
4:15 Naph'tali, toward the sea, across the Jordan 2
25 Judea and from beyond the Jordan. 2
19: 1 entered the region of Judea beyond the Jordan; 2
Mrk 1: 5 and they were baptized by him in the river Jordan 2
9 baptized by John in the Jordan. 2
3: 8 from beyond the Jordan and from about Tyre 2
10: 1 went to the region of Judea and beyond the Jordan 2
Lke 3: 3 he went into all the region about the Jordan 2
4: 1 Jesus . . returned from the Jordan 2
Joh 1:28 This took place in Bethany beyond the Jordan 2
3:26 Rabbi, he who was with you beyond the Jordan 2
10:40 He went away again across the Jordan 2
Jdt 1: 9 and beyond the Jordan as far as Jerusalem 2
5:15 crossing over the Jordan 2
Sir 24:26 like the Jordan at harvest time. 2
1Mc 5:24 crossed the Jordan and went three days' journey 2
52 they crossed the Jordan into the large plain 2
9:34 he with all his army crossed the Jordan. 2
42 they returned to the marshes of the Jordan. 2
43 he came . . to the banks of the Jordan. 2
45 the water of the Jordan is on this side and on that 2
48 leaped into the Jordan 2
48 did not cross the Jordan to attack them. 2

Jorim 1. Ἰωρίμ
Lke 3:29 son of Elie'zer, the son of Jorim, the son of Matthat 1

Jorkeam 1. יָרְקְעָם
1Ch 2:44 Shema . . father of Raham, the father of Jor'ke-am; 1

Josech 1. Ἰωσήχ
Lke 3:26 the son of Sem'ein, the son of Josech, the son of Joda 1

Joseph 1. יוֹסֵף 2. Ιωσηπος 3. Ἰωσήφ
Gen 30:24 she called his name Joseph 1
25 When Rachel had borne Joseph, Jacob said to Laban 1
33: 2 children, and Rachel and Joseph last of all. 1
7 and last Joseph and Rachel drew near 1
35:24 The sons of Rachel: Joseph and Benjamin. 1
37: 2 and Joseph brought an ill report of them to their 1
2 and Joseph brought an ill report of them to their 1
3 Now Israel loved Joseph more than any other 1
5 Now Joseph had a dream, and when he told 1
13 Israel said to Joseph, "Are not your brothers 1
17 Joseph went after his brothers, and found them 1
23 when Joseph came to his brothers 1
28 and they drew Joseph up and lifted him out 1
28 shekels of silver; and they took Joseph to Egypt. 1
29 saw that Joseph was not in the pit 1
31 Then they took Joseph's robe, and killed a goat 1
33 Joseph is without doubt torn to pieces. 1
39: 1 Now Joseph was taken down to Egypt 1
2 The LORD was with Joseph 1
4 Joseph found favor in his sight and attended him 1
5 blessed the Egyptian's house for Joseph's sake; 1
6 he left all that he had in Joseph's charge; 1
6 Now Joseph was handsome and good-looking. 1
7 cast her eyes upon Joseph, and said, "Lie with me. 1
10 although she spoke to Joseph day after day 1
20 Joseph's master took him and put him 1
21 the LORD was with Joseph and showed him 1
22 the prison committed to Joseph's care 1
23 anything that was in Joseph's care 3
40: 3 in the prison where Joseph was confined. 1
4 captain of the guard charged Joseph with them 1
6 When Joseph came to them in the morning 1
8 And Joseph said to them, "Do not 1
9 told his dream to Joseph, and said to him 1
12 Then Joseph said to him, "This is its 1
16 favorable, he said to Joseph, "I also had a dream 1
18 Joseph answered, "This is its interpretation 1
22 as Joseph had interpreted to them. 1
23 butler did not remember Joseph, but forgot him. 1
41:14 Pharaoh sent and called Joseph, and they brought 1
15 Pharaoh said to Joseph, "I have had a dream 1
16 Joseph answered Pharaoh, "It is not in me; 1
17 Then Pharaoh said to Joseph, "Behold, in my dream 1
25 Joseph said to Pharaoh, "The dream of Pharaoh 1
39 Pharaoh said to Joseph, "Since God has shown you 1
41 Pharaoh said to Joseph, "Behold, I have set you 1
42 from his hand and put it on Joseph's hand 1
44 Moreover Pharaoh said to Joseph, "I am Pharaoh 1
45 Pharaoh called Joseph's name Zaph'enath-pane'ah 1
45 Joseph went out over the land of Egypt. 1
46 Joseph was 30 years old when he entered 1
46 Joseph went out from the presence of Pharaoh 1
49 Joseph stored up grain in great abundance 1
50 Joseph had two sons, whom As'enath 1
51 Joseph called the name of the first-born 1
54 years of famine began to come, as Joseph had said. 1
55 said to all the Egyptians, "Go to Joseph; 1
56 Joseph opened all the storehouses 1
57 Moreover, all the earth came to Egypt to Joseph 1
42: 3 ten of Joseph's brothers went down to buy grain 1
4 Jacob did not send Benjamin, Joseph's brother 1
6 Now Joseph was governor over the land; 1
6 Joseph's brothers came, and bowed themselves 1
7 Joseph saw his brothers, and knew them 1
8 Thus Joseph knew his brothers 1
9 Joseph remembered the dreams which he had 1
14 Joseph said to them, "It is as I said to you 1
18 On the third day Joseph said to them 1
23 They did not know that Joseph understood them 1
25 Joseph gave orders to fill their bags with grain 1
36 my children: Joseph is no more, and Simeon is no 1
43:15 went down to Egypt, and stood before Joseph. 1
16 When Joseph saw Benjamin with them, he said 1
17 man did as Joseph bade him, and brought the men 1
17 and brought the men to Joseph's house. 1
18 they were brought to Joseph's house 1
19 they went up to the steward of Joseph's house 1
24 the man had brought the men into Joseph's house 1
25 they made ready the present for Joseph's coming 1
26 When Joseph came home, they brought 1
30 Then Joseph made haste, for his heart yearned 1
34 Portions were taken to them from Joseph's table •
44: 2 And he did as Joseph told him. 1
4 Joseph said to his steward, "Up, follow after 1
14 Judah and his brothers came to Joseph's house 1
15 Joseph said to them, "What deed is this that you 1
45: 1 Then Joseph could not control himself 1
1 no one stayed . . when Joseph made himself known 1
3 Joseph said to his brothers, "I am Joseph; 1
3 Joseph said to his brothers, "I am Joseph; 1
4 Joseph said to his brothers, "Come near to me 1
4 Joseph, whom you sold into Egypt. 1
9 Thus says your son Joseph, God has made me lord 1
16 report was heard . . "Joseph's brothers have come 1
17 Pharaoh said to Joseph, "Say to your brothers 1
21 and Joseph gave them wagons 1
26 they told him, "Joseph is still alive 1
27 all the words of Joseph, which he had said to them 1
27 he saw the wagons which Joseph had sent to carry 1
28 It is enough; Joseph my son is still alive; 1
46: 4 and Joseph's hand shall close your eyes. 1
19 of Rachel, Jacob's wife: Joseph and Benjamin. 1
20 to Joseph in the land of Egypt were born Manas'seh 1
27 the sons of Joseph, who were born to him in Egypt 1
28 He sent Judah before him to Joseph, to appear 1
29 Then Joseph made ready his chariot and went up 1
30 Israel said to Joseph, "Now let me die 1
31 Joseph said to his brothers and to his father's 1
47: 1 Joseph went in and told Pharaoh, 1
5 Then Pharaoh said to Joseph, "Your father 1
7 Then Joseph brought in Jacob his father, 1
11 Then Joseph settled his father and his brothers 1
12 Joseph provided his father, his brothers, 1
14 Joseph gathered up all the money that was found 1
14 Joseph brought the money into Pharaoh's house. 1
15 all the Egyptians came to Joseph, and said, 1
16 Joseph answered, "Give your cattle, 1
17 they brought their cattle to Joseph; 1
17 Joseph gave them food in exchange for the horses 1
20 Joseph bought all the land of Egypt for Pharaoh; 1
23 Joseph said to the people, "Behold, I have 1
26 Joseph made it a statute concerning the land 1
29 Israel must die, he called his son Joseph 1
48: 1 Joseph was told, "Behold, your father is ill"; 1
2 it was told to Jacob, "Your son Joseph has come 1
3 Jacob said to Joseph, "God Almighty appeared 1
8 When Israel saw Joseph's sons, he said, 1
9 Joseph said to his father, "They are my sons 1
10 Joseph brought them near him; •
11 Israel said to Joseph, "I had not thought to see 1
12 Then Joseph removed them from his knees 1
13 Joseph took them both, E'phraim in his right hand 1
15 he blessed Joseph, and said, "The God before 1
17 Joseph saw that his father laid his right hand 1
18 Joseph said to his father, "Not so, my father; 1
21 Israel said to Joseph, "Behold, I am about to die 1
49:22 Joseph is a fruitful bough 1
26 may they be on the head of Joseph, and on the brow 1
50: 1 Then Joseph fell on his father's face, and wept 1
2 Joseph commanded his servants the physicians 1
4 Joseph spoke to the household of Pharaoh, saying 1
7 Joseph went up to bury his father; 1
8 as well as all the household of Joseph 1
14 After he had buried his father, Joseph returned 1
15 Joseph's brothers saw that their father was dead 1
15 It may be that Joseph will hate us and pay us back 1
16 sent a message to Joseph, saying, "Your father 1
17 'Say to Joseph, Forgive, I pray you 1
17 Joseph wept when they spoke to him. 1
19 Joseph said to them, "Fear not, 1
22 Joseph dwelt in Egypt, he and his father's house; 1
22 and Joseph lived 110 years. 1
23 Joseph saw E'phraim's children of the third 1
23 children . . were born upon Joseph's knees. 1
24 Joseph said to his brothers, "I am about to die; 1
25 Then Joseph took an oath of the sons of Israel 1
25 Joseph died, being 110 years old; 1
Exd 1: 5 Joseph was already in Egypt. 1
6 Then Joseph died, and all his brothers 1
8 a new king over Egypt, who did not know Joseph. 1
13:19 Moses took the bones of Joseph with him; 1
19 Joseph had solemnly sworn the people of Israel 3
Num 1:10 from the sons of Joseph, from E'phraim, Eli'shama 1
32 Of the people of Joseph, namely . . E'phraim 1
13: 7 from the tribe of Is'sachar, Igal the son of Joseph; 1
11 from the tribe of Joseph . . Gaddi the son of Susi; 1
26:28 The sons of Joseph according to their families 1
37 sons of Joseph according to their families. 1
27: 1 from the families of Manas'seh the son of Joseph. 1
32:33 to the half-tribe of Manas'seh the son of Joseph 1
34:23 sons of Joseph: of the tribe of the sons of Manas'seh 1
36: 1 of the fathers' houses of the sons of Joseph 1
5 The tribe of the sons of Joseph is right. 1
12 sons of Manas'seh the son of Joseph 1
Deu 27:12 stand upon Mount Ger'izim . . Is'sachar, Joseph 1
33:13 of Joseph he said, "Blessed by the LORD be his land 1
16 Let these come upon the head of Joseph 1
Jos 14: 4 For the people of Joseph were two tribes 1
16: 1 The allotment of the descendants of Joseph went 1
4 The people of Joseph, Manas'seh and E'phraim 1
17: 1 Manas'seh, for he was the first-born of Joseph. 1
2 male descendants of Manas'seh the son of Joseph 1
14 And the tribe of Joseph spoke to Joshua, saying 1
16 The tribe of Joseph said, "The hill country is not 1
17 to the house of Joseph, to E'phraim and Manas'seh 1
18: 5 and the house of Joseph in their territory 1
11 fell between . . Judah and the tribe of Joseph. 1
24:32 The bones of Joseph . . were buried at Shechem 1
32 an inheritance of the descendants of Joseph. 1
Jdg 1:22 The house of Joseph also went up against Bethel; 1
23 And the house of Joseph sent to spy out Bethel. 1
35 hand of the house of Joseph rested heavily upon 1
2Sm 19:20 I have come . . the first of all the house of Joseph 1
1Kg 11:28 over all the forced labor of the house of Joseph. 1
1Ch 2: 2 Dan, Joseph, Benjamin, Naph'tali, Gad, and Asher. 1
5: 1 his birthright was given to the sons of Joseph 1
2 yet the birthright belonged to Joseph 1
7:29 the sons of Joseph the son of Israel. 1
25: 2 sons of Asaph: Zaccur, Joseph, Nethani'ah 1
9 The first lot fell for Asaph to Joseph; 1
Ezr 10:42 Shallum, Amari'ah, and Joseph. 1
Neh 12:14 of Mal'luchi, Jonathan; of Shebani'ah, Joseph; 1
Ps 77:15 redeem thy people, the sons of Jacob and Joseph. 1
78:67 He rejected the tent of Joseph, he did not choose 1
80: 1 Shepherd . . who leadest Joseph like a flock! 1
81: 5 He made it a decree in Joseph, when he went out 1
105:17 he had sent a man ahead of them, Joseph 1
Ezk 37:16 For Joseph (the stick of E'phraim) and all the house 1
19 Behold, I am about to take the stick of Joseph 1
47:13 Joseph shall have two portions. 1
48:32 gates, the gate of Joseph, the gate of Benjamin 1
Ams 5: 6 lest he break out like fire in the house of Joseph 1
15 will be gracious to the remnant of Joseph. 1
6: 6 but are not grieved over the ruin of Joseph! 1
Obd 1:18 shall be a fire, and the house of Joseph a flame 1
Zec 10: 6 I will save the house of Joseph. 1
Mat 1:16 Jacob the father of Joseph the husband of Mary 3
18 his mother Mary had been betrothed to Joseph 3
19 her husband Joseph, being a just man 3
20 in a dream, saying, "Joseph, son of David, do not fear 3
24 When Joseph woke from sleep, he did as the angel 3
2:13 an angel of the Lord appeared to Joseph in a dream 3
19 in a dream to Joseph in Egypt, saying 3
13:55 are not his brothers James and Joseph and Simon 3
27:56 Mary the mother of James and Joseph 3
57 a rich man from Arimathe'a, named Joseph 3
59 Joseph took the body 3
Mrk 15:43 Joseph of Arimathe'a, a respected member 3
45 he granted the body to Joseph. 3
Lke 1:27 a virgin betrothed to a man whose name was Joseph 3
2: 4 Joseph also went up from Galilee 3
16 they went with haste, and found Mary and Joseph 3
3:23 being the son (as was supposed) of Joseph 3
24 son of Melchi, the son of Jan'nai, the son of Joseph 3
30 the son of Joseph, the son of Jonam 3
4:22 they said, "Is not this Joseph's son? 3
23:50 Now there was a man named Joseph 3
Joh 1:45 found him . . Jesus of Nazareth, the son of Joseph 3
4: 5 near the field that Jacob gave to his son Joseph. 3
6:42 They said, "Is not this Jesus, the son of Joseph 3
19:38 Joseph of Arimathe'a, who was a disciple of Jesus 3
Act 1:23 they put forward two, Joseph called Barsab'bas 3
4:36 Joseph who was surnamed . . Barnabas 3
7: 9 the patriarchs, jealous of Joseph 3
13 Joseph made himself known to his brothers 3
13 Joseph's family became known to Pharaoh. 3
14 Joseph sent and called to him Jacob his father 3
18 another king who had not known Joseph. 3
Heb 11:21 Jacob . . blessed each of the sons of Joseph 3
22 By faith Joseph . . made mention of the exodus 3
Rev 7: 8 12,000 of the tribe of Joseph 3
1Es 9:34 Shashai, Azarel, Azael, Shemaiah, Amariah, Joseph. 2
Jdt 8: 1 the daughter of Merari the son of Ox, son of Joseph 3
Sir 49:15 no man like Joseph has been born, and his bones are 1

1Mc 2:53 Joseph . . kept the commandment 3
5:18 he left Joseph, the son of Zechariah 2
56 Joseph, the son of Zechariah 3
60 Then Joseph and Azariah were routed 2
2Mc 8:22 Simon and Joseph and Jonathan 2
10:19 Maccabeus left Simon and Joseph 2
4Mc 2: 2 the temperate Joseph is praised 3
18:11 Joseph in prison. 3

Joses 1. Ἰωσῆς

Mrk 6: 3 brother of James and Joses and Judas and Simon 1
15:40 Mary the mother of James the younger and of Joses 1
47 Mary Mag'dalene and Mary the mother of Joses saw 1

Joshah 1. יוֹשָׁה

1Ch 4:34 Mesho'bab, Jamlech, Joshah the son of Amazi'ah 1

Joshaphat 1. יוֹשָׁפָט

1Ch 11:43 and Josh'aphat the Mithnite 1
15:24 Shebani'ah, Josh'aphat, Nethan'el, Ama'sai 1

Joshaviah 1. יוֹשַׁוְיָה

1Ch 11:46 Jer'ibai, and Joshavi'ah, the sons of El'na-am 1

Joshbekashah 1. יָשְׁבְּקָשָׁה

1Ch 25: 4 sons of Heman . . Joshbekash'ah, Mallo'thi, Hothir 1
24 to Joshbekash'ah, his sons and his brethren 1

Josheb-basshebeth 1. יֹשֵׁב בַּשֶּׁבֶת

2Sm 23: 8 the mighty men . . Josheb-basshe'beth 1

Joshibiah 1. יוֹשִׁבְיָה

1Ch 4:35 the son of Joshibi'ah, son of Serai'ah, son of As'i-el 1

Joshua 1. הוֹשֵׁעַ 2. יְהוֹשׁוּעַ 3. Ἰησοῦς 4. Iesus

Exd 17: 9 Moses said to Joshua, "Choose for us men, and go out 2
10 So Joshua did as Moses told him, and fought 2
13 Joshua mowed down Am'alek and his people 2
14 recite it in the ears of Joshua, that I will 2
24:13 So Moses rose with his servant Joshua 2
32:17 When Joshua heard the noise of the people 2
33:11 his servant Joshua the son of Nun, a young man 2
Num11:28 Joshua . . said, "My lord Moses, forbid them. 2
13:16 Moses called Hoshe'a the son of Nun Joshua. 2
14: 6 Joshua the son of Nun and Caleb . . of Jephun'neh 2
30 except Caleb . . and Joshua the son of Nun. 2
38 Joshua . . and Caleb . . remained alive 2
26:65 not left a man . . except Caleb . . and Joshua 2
27:18 Take Joshua the son of Nun . . and lay your hand 2
22 took Joshua and caused him to stand 2
32:12 none except Caleb . . and Joshua the son of Nun 2
28 command concerning them to . . Joshua the son of Nun 2
34:17 Elea'zar the priest and Joshua the son of Nun. 2
Deu 1:38 Joshua the son of Nun . . he shall enter; 2
3:21 I commanded Joshua at that time, 'Your eyes 2
28 charge Joshua, and encourage and strengthen him; 2
31: 3 Joshua will go over at your head, as the LORD 2
7 Then Moses summoned Joshua, and said to him 2
14 call Joshua, and present yourselves in the tent 2
14 Moses and Joshua went and presented themselves 2
23 LORD commissioned Joshua the son of Nun and said 2
32:44 Moses came and recited . . and Joshua the son of Nun. 1
34: 9 Joshua . . was full of the spirit of wisdom 2
Jos 1: 1 LORD said to Joshua the son of Nun, Moses' minister 2
10 Joshua commanded the officers of the people 2
12 to . . and the half-tribe of Manas'seh Joshua said 2
16 And they answered Joshua, "All that . . we will do 2
2: 1 And Joshua . . sent two men secretly from Shittim 2
23 and passed over and came to Joshua the son of Nun; 2
24 And they said to Joshua, "Truly the LORD has given 2
3: 1 Early in the morning Joshua rose and set out 2
5 Joshua said to the people, "Sanctify yourselves; 2
6 And Joshua said to the priests, "Take up the ark 2
7 And the LORD said to Joshua, "This day I will begin 2
9 Joshua said to the people of Israel, "Come hither 2
10 And Joshua said, "Hereby you shall know 2
4: 1 When all the nation had . . the LORD said to Joshua 2
4 Joshua called the twelve men from the people 2
5 and Joshua said to them, "Pass on before the ark 2
8 And the men of Israel did as Joshua commanded 2
8 took up twelve stones . . as the LORD told Joshua; 2
9 And Joshua set up twelve stones in the . . Jordan 2
10 everything . . that the LORD commanded Joshua 2
10 to all that Moses had commanded Joshua. 2
14 LORD exalted Joshua in the sight of all Israel; 2
15 And the LORD said to Joshua 2
17 Joshua therefore commanded the priests, "Come up 2
20 those twelve stones . . Joshua set up in Gilgal. 2
5: 2 the LORD said to Joshua, "Make flint knives 2
3 Joshua made flint knives, and circumcised 2
4 this is the reason why Joshua circumcised them 2
7 it was their children . . Joshua circumcised; 2
9 And the LORD said to Joshua, "This day I have rolled 2
13 When Joshua was by Jericho, he lifted up his eyes 2
13 and Joshua went to him and said to him, "Are you 2
14 And Joshua fell on his face to the earth 2
15 the commander of the LORD's army said to Joshua 2
15 Put off your shoes . . " And Joshua did so. 2
6: 2 LORD said to Joshua, "See, I have given . . Jericho 2
6 Joshua the son of Nun called the priests and said 2
8 And as Joshua had commanded the people 2
10 Joshua commanded the people, "You shall not shout 2
12 Then Joshua rose early in the morning 2
16 Joshua said to the people, "Shout; 2
22 Joshua said to the two men . . "Go into the harlot's 2
25 Rahab the harlot, and her . . Joshua saved alive; 2
25 messengers whom Joshua sent to spy out Jericho. 2
26 Joshua laid an oath upon them at that time, saying 2
27 the LORD was with Joshua; and his fame was in all 2
7: 2 Joshua sent men from Jericho to Ai . . and said 2
3 And they returned to Joshua, and said to him 2
6 Joshua rent his clothes, and fell to the earth 2
7 And Joshua said, "Alas, O Lord GOD, why hast thou 2
10 The LORD said to Joshua, "Arise 2
16 Joshua rose early in the morning 2
19 Joshua said to Achan, "My son, give glory to the LORD 2
20 Achan answered Joshua, "Of a truth I have sinned 2
22 Joshua sent messengers, and they ran to the tent; 2
23 And they took them . . and brought them to Joshua 2
24 Joshua and all Israel . . took Achan the son 2
25 And Joshua said, "Why did you bring trouble on us? 2
8: 1 the LORD said to Joshua, "Do not fear or be dismayed; 2
3 Joshua arose, and all the fighting men, to go up 2
3 and Joshua chose 30,000 mighty men of valor 2
9 Joshua sent them forth; and they went to the place 2
9 but Joshua spent that night among the people. 2
10 Joshua arose early . . and mustered the people 2
13 But Joshua spent that night in the valley. 2
15 Joshua and all . . made a pretense of being beaten 2
16 and as they pursued Joshua they were drawn away 2
18 the LORD said to Joshua, "Stretch out the javelin 2
18 Joshua stretched out the javelin . . in his hand 2
21 Joshua . . saw that the ambush had taken the city 2
23 But . . they took alive, and brought him to Joshua. 2
26 Joshua did not draw back his hand . . until he had 2
27 the word of the LORD which he commanded Joshua. 2
28 Joshua burned Ai, and made it . . a heap of ruins 2
29 and at the going down of the sun Joshua commanded 2
30 Joshua built an altar in Mount Ebal to the LORD 2
35 not a word . . which Joshua did not read before all 2
9: 2 they gathered . . to fight Joshua and Israel. 2
3 heard what Joshua had done to Jericho and to Ai 2
6 they went to Joshua in the camp at Gilgal, and said 2
8 They said to Joshua, "We are your servants. 2
8 We are your servants." And Joshua said to them 2
15 Joshua made peace with them, and made a covenant 2
22 Joshua summoned them, and he said to them 2
24 They answered Joshua, "Because it was told 2
27 But Joshua made them that day hewers of wood 2
10: 1 When Ado'ni-ze'dek . . heard how Joshua had taken Ai 2
4 for it has made peace with Joshua and . . Israel. 2
6 the men . . sent to Joshua at the camp in Gilgal 2
7 So Joshua went up from Gilgal 2
8 And the LORD said to Joshua, "Do not fear them 2
9 Joshua came upon them suddenly 2
12 Then spoke Joshua to the LORD in the day 2
15 Joshua returned, and all Israel . . to the camp 2
17 it was told Joshua, "The five kings have been found 2
18 And Joshua said, "Roll great stones against 2
20 When Joshua and the men of Israel had finished 2
21 the people returned safe to Joshua in the camp 2
22 Then Joshua said, "Open the mouth of the cave 2
24 when they brought those kings out to Joshua 2
24 Joshua summoned all the men of Israel, and said 2
25 Joshua said to them, "Do not be afraid or dismayed; 2
26 Joshua smote them and put them to death 2
27 Joshua commanded, and they took them down 2
28 And Joshua took Makke'dah on that day, and smote it 2
29 Then Joshua passed on from Makke'dah . . to Libnah 2
31 Joshua passed on from Libnah . . to Lachish 2
33 and Joshua smote him and his people 2
34 And Joshua passed on . . from Lachish to Eglon; 2
36 Then Joshua went up . . from Eglon to Hebron; 2
38 Joshua . . turned back to Debir and assaulted it 2
40 Joshua defeated the whole land 2
41 Joshua defeated them from Ka'desh-bar'nea to Gaza 2
42 And Joshua took all these kings and their land 2
43 Then Joshua returned . . to the camp at Gilgal. 2
11: 6 the LORD said to Joshua, "Do not be afraid of them 2
7 Joshua came suddenly upon them 2
9 And Joshua did to them as the LORD bade him; 2
10 Joshua turned back at that time, and took Hazor 2
12 all the cities . . and all their kings, Joshua took 2
13 none . . except Hazor only; that Joshua burned. 2
15 As the LORD had . . so Moses commanded Joshua 2
15 Moses commanded Joshua, and so Joshua did; 2
16 Joshua took all that land 2
18 Joshua made war a long time with all those kings. 2
21 Joshua came at that time, and wiped out the Anakim 2
21 Joshua . . destroyed them with their cities. 2
23 Joshua took the whole land 2
23 and Joshua gave it for an inheritance to Israel 2
12: 7 whom Joshua and the people of Israel defeated 2
7 and Joshua gave their land to the tribes 2
13: 1 Now Joshua was old and advanced in years; 2
14: 1 Elea'zar the priest, and Joshua the son of Nun 2
6 Then the people of Judah came to Joshua at Gilgal; 2
13 Joshua blessed him; and he gave Hebron to Caleb 2
15:13 the commandment of the LORD to Joshua 2
17: 4 came before Elea'zar . . and Joshua the son of Nun 2
14 And the tribe of Joseph spoke to Joshua, saying 2
15 Joshua said to them, "If you are a numerous people 2
17 Then Joshua said to the house of Joseph 2
18: 3 Joshua said to the people of Israel, "How long 2
8 and Joshua charged those who went . . saying, "Go up 2
9 then they came to Joshua in the camp at Shiloh 2
10 Joshua cast lots . . in Shiloh before the LORD; 2
10 there Joshua apportioned the land to the people 2
19:49 Israel gave an inheritance among them to Joshua 2
51 which Elea'zar . . and Joshua . . distributed 2
20: 1 Then the LORD said to Joshua 2
21: 1 to Elea'zar the priest and to Joshua the son of Nun 2
22: 1 Joshua summoned the Reubenites, and the Gadites 2
6 Joshua blessed them, and sent them away; 2
7 to the other half Joshua had given a possession 2
7 Joshua sent them away to their homes and blessed 2
23: 1 and Joshua was old and well advanced in years 2
2 Joshua summoned all Israel . . and said to them 2
24: 1 Then Joshua gathered all . . Israel to Shechem 2
2 Joshua said to all the people, "Thus says the LORD 2
19 But Joshua said to the people, "You cannot serve 2
21 the people said to Joshua, "Nay; but we will serve 2
22 Then Joshua said to the people, "You are witnesses 2
24 And the people said to Joshua, "The LORD our God 2
25 Joshua made a covenant with the people that day 2
26 Joshua wrote these words in the book of the law 2
27 Joshua said to all the people, "Behold, this stone 2
28 Joshua sent the people away, every man to his 2
29 Joshua the son of Nun, the servant of the LORD, died 2
31 And Israel served the LORD all the days of Joshua 2
31 all the days of the elders who outlived Joshua 2
Jdg 1: 1 After the death of Joshua the people of Israel 2
2: 6 When Joshua dismissed the people, the people 2
7 the people served the LORD all the days of Joshua 2
7 elders who outlived Joshua, who had seen all 2
8 Joshua the son of Nun, the servant of the LORD, died 2
21 any of the nations that Joshua left when he died 2
23 he did not give them into the power of Joshua. 2
1Sm 6:14 came into the field of Joshua of Beth-she'mesh 2
18 this day in the field of Joshua of Beth-she'mesh. 2
1Kg 16:34 word . . which he spoke by Joshua the son of Nun. 2
2Kg 23: 8 of the gate of Joshua the governor of the city 2
1Ch 7:27 Nun his son, Joshua his son. 2
Hag 1: 1 to Joshua the son of Jehoz'adak, the high priest 2
12 Joshua the son of Jehoz'adak, the high priest 2
14 the spirit of Joshua the son of Jehoz'adak 2
2: 2 to Joshua the son of Jehoz'adak, the high priest 2
4 take courage, O Joshua, son of Jehoz'adak 2
Zec 3: 1 Then he showed me Joshua the high priest 2
3 Now Joshua was standing before the angel 2
6 the angel of the LORD enjoined Joshua 2
8 Hear now, O Joshua the high priest 2
9 upon the stone which I have set before Joshua 2
6:11 make a crown, and set it upon the head of Joshua 2
Lke 3:29 the son of Joshua, the son of Elie'zer 3
Act 7:45 Our fathers in turn brought it in with Joshua 3
Heb 4: 8 For if Joshua had given them rest 3
2Es 7:107 Joshua after him for Israel in the days of Achan 4
Sir 46: 1 Joshua the son of Nun was mighty in war 3
1Mc 2:55 Joshua . . became a judge in Israel. 3
2Mc 12:15 overthrew Jericho in the days of Joshua 3

Josiah 1. יֹאשִׁיָּהוּ 2. Ἰωσίας

1Kg 13: 2 a son shall be born to . . David, Josi'ah by name; 1
2Kg 21:24 people . . made Josi'ah his son king in his stead. 1
26 and Josi'ah his son reigned in his stead. 1
22: 1 Josi'ah was eight years old when he began to reign 1
3 In the eighteenth year of King Josi'ah 1
23:16 as Josi'ah turned, he saw the tombs . . on the mount; 1
19 And all the shrines also . . Josi'ah removed; 1
23 but in the eighteenth year of King Josi'ah 1
24 Josi'ah put away the mediums and the wizards 1
28 the rest of the acts of Josi'ah, and all that he did 1
29 King Josi'ah went to meet him; and Pharaoh Neco 1
30 the people . . took Jeho'ahaz the son of Josi'ah 1
34 Pharaoh Neco made Eli'akim the son of Josi'ah king 1
34 made . . king in the place of Josi'ah his father 1
1Ch 3:14 Amon his son, Josi'ah his son. 1
15 The sons of Josi'ah: Joha'nan the first-born 1
2Ch 33:25 people of the land made Josi'ah his son king 1
34: 1 Josi'ah was eight years old when he began to reign 1
33 Josi'ah took away all the abominations 1
35: 1 Josi'ah kept a passover to the LORD in Jerusalem; 1
7 Then Josi'ah contributed to the lay people 1
16 according to the command of King Josi'ah. 1
18 such a passover as was kept by Josi'ah 1
19 In the eighteenth year of the reign of Josi'ah 1
20 when Josi'ah had prepared the temple 1
20 Neco . . went up . . and Josi'ah went out against him 1
22 Nevertheless Josi'ah would not turn away 1
23 the archers shot King Josi'ah; and the king said 1
24 All Judah and Jerusalem mourned for Josi'ah. 1
25 Jeremiah also uttered a lament for Josi'ah; 1
25 spoken of Josi'ah in their laments to this day. 1
26 the rest of the acts of Josi'ah, and his good deeds 1
36: 1 people . . took Jeho'ahaz the son of Josi'ah 1
Jer 1: 2 in the days of Josi'ah the son of Amon, king of Judah 1

3 days of Jehoi'akim the son of Josi'ah, king of Judah 1
3 year of Zedeki'ah, the son of Josi'ah, king of Judah 1
3: 6 The LORD said to me in the days of King Josi'ah 1
22:11 Shallum the son of Josi'ah, king of Judah 1
11 who reigned instead of Josi'ah his father 1
18 Jehoi'akim the son of Josi'ah, king of Judah 1
25: 1 in the fourth year of Jehoi'akim the son of Josi'ah 1
3 from the thirteenth year of Josi'ah the son of Amon 1
26: 1 Jehoi'akim the son of Josi'ah, king of Judah 1
27: 1 Zedeki'ah the son of Josi'ah, king of Judah 1
35: 1 in the days of Jehoi'akim the son of Josi'ah 1
36: 1 In the fourth year of Jehoi'akim the son of Josi'ah 1
2 spoke to you, from the days of Josi'ah until today. 1
9 In the fifth year of Jehoi'akim the son of Josi'ah 1
37: 1 Zedeki'ah the son of Josi'ah whom Nebuchadrez'zar 1
45: 1 in the fourth year of Jehoi'akim the son of Josi'ah 1
46: 2 Jehoi'akim the son of Josi'ah, king of Judah 1
Zep 1: 1 Hezeki'ah, in the days of Josi'ah the son of Amon 1
Zec 6:10 and go the same day to the house of Josi'ah 1
14 Jedai'ah, and Josi'ah the son of Zephani'ah. *
Mat 1:10 and Amos the father of Josi'ah 2
11 Josi'ah the father of Jechoni'ah and his brothers 2
1Es 1: 1 Josiah kept the passover to his Lord 2
7 Josiah gave to the people . . 30,000 lambs 2
18 according to the command of King Josiah. 2
21 such a passover as was kept by Josiah 2
22 In the eighteenth year of the reign of Josiah 2
23 the deeds of Josiah were upright 2
25 After all these acts of Josiah 2
25 Josiah went out against him. 2
28 Josiah did not turn back to his chariot 2
29 the commanders came down against King Josiah. 2
32 in all Judea they mourned for Josiah 2
32 Jeremiah the prophet lamented for Josiah 2
33 every one of the acts of Josiah 2
34 men of the nation took Jeconiah the son of Josiah 2
34 made him king in succession to Josiah his father. 2
Sir 49: 1 The memory of Josiah 2
4 Except David and Hezekiah and Josiah 2
Bar 1: 8 Zedekiah the son of Josiah, king of Judah 2

Josiphiah 1. יוֹסִפְיָה 2. Ιωσαφιας
Ezr 8:10 Shelo'mith the son of Josi-phi'ah, and with him 160 1
1Es 8:36 Shelomith the son of Josiphiah 2

Jotbah 1. יָטְבָה
2Kg 21:19 Meshul'lemeth the daughter of Haruz of Jotbah. 1

Jotbathah 1. יָטְבָתָה
Num33:33 from Hor-haggid'gad, and encamped at Jot'bathah. 1
34 set out from Jot'bathah, and encamped at Abro'nah. 1
Deu 10: 7 journeyed . . from Gud'godah to Jot'bathah, a land 1

Jotham 1. יוֹתָם 2. 'Ιωαθάμ
Jdg 9: 5 but Jotham the youngest son of Jerubba'al was 1
7 When it was told to Jotham, he went and stood 1
21 Jotham ran away and fled, and went to Beer 1
57 came the curse of Jotham the son of Jerubba'al. 1
2Kg 15: 5 And Jotham the king's son was over the household 1
7 Azari'ah slept . . and Jotham his son reigned 1
30 the twentieth year of Jotham the son of Uzzi'ah. 1
32 Jotham the son of Uzzi'ah . . began to reign. 1
36 the rest of the acts of Jotham, and all that he did 1
38 Jotham slept with his fathers, and was buried 1
16: 1 Ahaz the son of Jotham . . began to reign. 1
1Ch 2:47 sons of Jah'dai: Regem, Jotham, Geshan, Pelet, 1
3:12 Amazi'ah his son, Azari'ah his son, Jotham his son 1
5:17 enrolled . . in the days of Jotham king of Judah 1
2Ch 26:21 Jotham his son was over the king's household 1
23 Jotham his son reigned in his stead. 1
27: 1 Jotham was 25 . . when he began to reign 1
6 Jotham became mighty 1
7 Now the rest of the acts of Jotham, and all his wars 1
9 Jotham slept with his fathers 1
Isa 1: 1 in the days of Uzzi'ah, Jotham, Ahaz, and Hezeki'ah 1
7: 1 In the days of Ahaz the son of Jotham, son of Uzzi'ah 1
Hos 1: 1 in the days of Uzzi'ah, Jotham, Ahaz, and Hezeki'ah 1
Mic 1: 1 Micah of Mo'resheth in the days of Jotham, 1
Mat 1: 9 Uzzi'ah the father of Jotham 2
9 and Jotham the father of Ahaz 2

Jozabad 1. יוֹזָבָד 2. Ιωζαβδος
1Ch 12: 4 Jeremiah, Jaha'ziel, Joha'nan, Joz'abad of Gede'rah 1
20 men of Manas'seh . . Adnah, Joz'abad, Jedi'a-el 1
20 men of Manas'seh . . Michael, Joz'abad, Eli'hu 1
2Ch 31:13 As'ahel, Jer'imoth, Jo'zabad . . were overseers 1
35: 9 Hashabi'ah and Je-i'el and Jo'zabad 1
Ezr 8:33 Levites, Jo'zabad the son of Jeshua and No-adi'ah 1
10:22 of Pashhur . . Nethan'el, Jo'zabad, and Ela'sah. 1
23 Of the Levites: Jo'zabad, Shim'e-i, Kelai'ah 1
Neh 8: 7 Also . . Keli'ta, Azari'ah, Jo'zabad, Hanan 1
11:16 Shab'bethai and Jo'zabad, of the chiefs 1
1Es 8:63 with them were Jozabad the son of Jeshua 2
9:23 of the Levites: Jozabad and Shimei and Kelaiah 2
48 Maaseiah and Kelita, Azariah and Jozabad 2

Jozacar 1. יוֹזָכָר
2Kg 12:21 It was Jo'zacar . . and Jeho'zabad..who struck him 1

Jozadak 1. יוֹצָדָק 2. יוֹצָדָק (A) 3. Ιωσεδεκ
Ezr 3: 2 Then arose Jeshua the son of Jo'zadak 1
8 Zerub'babel . . and Jeshua the son of Jo'zadak 1
5: 2 Zerub'babel . . and Jeshua the son of Jo'zadak 2
10:18 Jeshua the son of Jo'zadak and his brethren. 1
Neh 12:26 days of Joi'akim the son of Jeshua son of Jo'zadak 1
1Es 5: 5 Jeshua the son of Jozadak, son of Seraiah 3
48 Jeshua the son of Jozadak 3
56 Jeshua the son of Jozadak 3
6: 2 Jeshua the son of Jozadak arose 3
9:19 the son of Jozadak and his brethren 3
Sir 49:12 so was Jeshua the son of Jozadak 3

Jubal 1. יוּבָל
Gen 4:21 His brother's name was Jubal; 1

Jucal 1. יוּכַל
Jer 38: 1 Jucal the son of Shelemi'ah 1

Judah 1. בְּנֵי יְהוּדָה 2. יְהוּדָה 3. יְהוּדִי 4. יְהוּד (A) 5. Ιουδα 6. 'Ιουδαῖος 7. 'Ιούδας 8. Ωουδας 9. Iuda
Gen 29:35 therefore she called his name Judah; 2
35:23 Simeon, Levi, Judah, Is'sachar, and Zeb'ulun. 2
37:26 Then Judah said to his brothers, "What profit is it 2
38: 1 It happened at that time that Judah went down 2
2 Judah saw the daughter of a certain Canaanite 2
6 Judah took a wife for Er his first-born 2
7 Er, Judah's first-born, was wicked in the sight 2
8 Judah said to Onan, "Go in to your brother's wife 2
11 Then Judah said to Tamar his daughter-in-law 2
12 of time the wife of Judah, Shua's daughter, died; 2
12 when Judah was comforted, he went up to Timnah 2
15 When Judah saw her, he thought her to be a harlot 2
20 When Judah sent the kid by his friend 2
22 he returned to Judah, and said, "I have not found 2
23 Judah replied, "Let her keep the things as her own 2
24 About three months later Judah was told 2
24 And Judah said, "Bring her out, and let her be 2
26 Judah acknowledged them and said, "She is more 2
43: 3 Judah said to him, "The man solemnly warned us 2
8 Judah said to Israel his father, "Send the lad 2
44:14 Judah and his brothers came to Joseph's house 2
16 Judah said, "What shall we say to my lord? 2
18 Then Judah went up to him and said, "O my lord 2
46:12 sons of Judah: Er, Onan, Shelah, Perez, and Zerah 2
28 He sent Judah before him to Joseph, to appear 2
49: 8 Judah, your brothers shall praise you; 2
9 Judah is a lion's whelp; 2
10 The scepter shall not depart from Judah 2
Exd 1: 2 Reuben, Simeon, Levi, and Judah 2
31: 2 Bez'alel and son . . of Hur, of the tribe of Judah 2
35:30 the son of Uri, son of Hur, of the tribe of Judah; 2
38:22 son of Uri, son of Hur, of the tribe of Judah 2
Num 1: 7 from Judah, Nahshon the son of Ammin'adab; 2
26 Of the people of Judah, their generations 2
27 the number of the tribe of Judah was 74,600 2
2: 3 of the standard of the camp of Judah 2
3 the leader of the people of Judah being Nahshon 2
9 The whole number of the camp of Judah 2
7:12 Nahshon . . of the tribe of Judah; 2
10:14 standard of the camp of the men of Judah set out 2
13: 6 from the tribe of Judah, Caleb . . of Jephun'neh; 2
26:19 The sons of Judah were Er and Onan; 2
20 sons of Judah according to their families were 2
22 families of Judah according to their number 2
34:19 Of the tribe of Judah, Caleb the son of Jephun'neh. 2
Deu 27:12 stand upon Mount Ger'izim . . Simeon, Levi, Judah 2
33: 7 this he said of Judah: "Hear, O LORD, the voice 2
7 Hear, O LORD, the voice of Judah, and bring him 2
34: 2 all the land of Judah as far as the Western Sea 2
Jos 7: 1 Achan the son of Carmi . . of the tribe of Judah 2
16 and the tribe of Judah was taken; 2
17 and he brought near the families of Judah 2
18 and Achan . . of the tribe of Judah, was taken. 2
11:21 from Anab, and from all the hill country of Judah 2
14: 6 Then the people of Judah came to Joshua at Gilgal; 2
15: 1 The lot for the tribe of the people of Judah 2
12 is the boundary round about the people of Judah 2
13 he gave . . a portion among the people of Judah 2
20 inheritance of the tribe of the people of Judah 2
21 belonging to the tribe of the people of Judah 2
63 Jeb'usites . . the people of Judah could not drive 2
63 so the Jeb'usites dwell with the people of Judah 2
18: 5 divide it . . Judah continuing in his territory 2
11 fell between the tribe of Judah and . . of Joseph. 2
14 a city belonging to the tribe of Judah. 2
19: 1 midst of the inheritance of the tribe of Judah. 2
9 formed part of the territory of Judah; 2
9 the portion of the tribe of Judah was too large 2
34 touching . . Judah on the east at the Jordan. 2
20: 7 Kir'iath-ar'ba . . in the hill country of Judah. 2
21: 4 from the tribes of Judah, Simeon, and Benjamin 2
9 Out of the tribe of Judah and . . Simeon they gave 1
11 Kir'iath-ar'ba . . in the hill country of Judah 2
Jdg 1: 2 LORD said, "Judah shall go up; behold, I have given 2
3 Judah said to Simeon his brother, "Come up with me 2
4 Judah went up and the LORD gave the Canaanites 2
8 the men of Judah fought against Jerusalem 2
9 the men of Judah went down to fight against 2
10 Judah went against the Canaanites who dwelt 2
16 went up with the people of Judah from the city 2
16 the city of palms into the wilderness of Judah 2
17 Judah went with Simeon his brother 2
18 Judah also took Gaza with its territory 2
19 the LORD was with Judah, and he took possession 2
10: 9 crossed the Jordan to fight also against Judah 2
15: 9 the Philistines came up and encamped in Judah 2
10 the men of Judah said, "Why have you come up 2
11 Then 3,000 men of Judah went down to the cleft 2
17: 7 there was a young man of Bethlehem in Judah 2
7 man of Bethlehem in Judah, of the family of Judah 2
8 departed from the town of Bethlehem in Judah 2
9 I am a Levite of Bethlehem in Judah, and I am going 2
18:12 went up and encamped at Kir'iath-je'arim in Judah. 2
19: 1 took . . a concubine from Bethlehem in Judah. 2
2 to her father's house at Bethlehem in Judah 2
18 passing from Bethlehem in Judah to the remote 2
18 I went to Bethlehem in Judah; and I am going to my 2
20:18 And the LORD said, "Judah shall go up first. 2
Rut 1: 1 a certain man of Bethlehem in Judah went 2
2 they were Eph'rathites from Bethlehem in Judah. 2
7 went on the way to return to the land of Judah. 2
4:12 Perez, whom Tamar bore to Judah 2
1Sm 11: 8 and the men of Judah 30,000. 2
15: 4 200,000 men on foot, and 10,000 men of Judah. 2
17: 1 were gathered at Socoh, which belongs to Judah 2
12 an Eph'rathite of Bethlehem in Judah, named Jesse 2
52 And the men of Israel and Judah rose with a shout 2
18:16 But all Israel and Judah loved David; 2
22: 5 depart, and go into the land of Judah. 2
23: 3 we are afraid here in Judah; how much more 2
23 search him out among all the thousands of Judah. 2
27: 6 Ziklag has belonged to the kings of Judah 2
10 David would say, "Against the Negeb of Judah 2
30:14 made a raid . . upon that which belongs to Judah 2
16 spoil they had taken . . from the land of Judah. 2
26 sent part . . to his friends, the elders of Judah 2
2Sm 1:18 he said it should be taught to the people of Judah; 2
2: 1 Shall I go up into any of the cities of Judah? 2
4 the men of Judah came, and . . anointed David king 2
4 anointed David king over the house of Judah. 2
7 and the house of Judah has anointed me king 2
10 But the house of Judah followed David. 2
11 David was king in Hebron over the house of Judah 2
3: 8 Am I a dog's head of Judah? This day I keep showing 2
10 the throne of David over Israel and over Judah 2
5: 5 he reigned over Judah seven years and six months 2
5 he reigned over all Israel and Judah 2
11:11 The ark and Israel and Judah dwell in booths; 2
12: 8 gave you the house of Israel and of Judah; 2
19:11 Say to the elders of Judah, 'Why should you be 2
14 he swayed the heart of all the men of Judah as one 2
15 and Judah came to Gilgal to meet the king 2
16 with the men of Judah to meet King David; 2
40 the people of Judah, and also half . . of Israel 2
41 Why have our brethren the men of Judah stolen you 2
42 All the men of Judah answered the men of Israel 2
43 And the men of Israel answered the men of Judah 2
43 But the words of the men of Judah were fiercer 2
20: 2 but the men of Judah followed their king 2
4 Call the men of Judah together to me 2
5 Ama'sa went to summon Judah; but he delayed 2
21: 2 in his zeal for the people of Israel and Judah. 2
24: 1 he incited David . . "Go, number Israel and Judah. 2
7 they went out to the Negeb of Judah at Beer-sheba. 2
9 and the men of Judah were 500,000. 2
1Kg 1: 9 king's sons, and all the royal officials of Judah 2
35 him to be ruler over Israel and over Judah. 2
2:32 and Ama'sa . . commander of the army of Judah. 2
4:19 And there was one officer in the land of Judah. 5
20 Judah and Israel were as many as the sand 2
25 Judah and Israel dwelt in safety, from Dan even 2
9:18 and Tamar in the wilderness, in the land of Judah *
12:17 people of Israel who dwelt in the cities of Judah. 2
20 but the tribe of Judah only. 2
21 Rehobo'am . . assembled all the house of Judah 2
23 Say to Rehobo'am the son of Solomon, king of Judah 2
23 Say to . . all the house of Judah and Benjamin 2
27 turn . . to their lord, to Rehobo'am king of Judah 2
27 kill me and return to Rehobo'am king of Judah. 2
32 a feast . . like the feast that was in Judah 2
13: 1 of God came out of Judah by the word of the LORD 2
12 the way which the man of God who came from Judah 2
14 Are you the man of God who came from Judah? 2
21 he cried to the man of God who came from Judah 2
14:21 Rehobo'am the son of Solomon reigned in Judah. 2
22 Judah did what was evil in the sight of the LORD 2
29 the Book of the Chronicles of the Kings of Judah? 2
15: 1 Abi'jam began to reign over Judah. 2
7 the Book of the Chronicles of the Kings of Judah? 2
9 Asa began to reign over Judah 2
17 Ba'asha king of Israel went up against Judah 2
17 no one to go out or come in to Asa king of Judah. 2
22 King Asa made a proclamation to all Judah 2
23 the Book of the Chronicles of the Kings of Judah? 2
25 to reign . . in the second year of Asa king of Judah; 2
28 killed him in the third year of Asa king of Judah 2

33 In the third year of Asa king of Judah 2
16: 8 In the 26th year of Asa king of Judah 2
10 in the 27th year of Asa king of Judah 2
15 In the 27th year of Asa king of Judah 2
23 In the 31st year of Asa king of Judah 2
29 In the 38th year of Asa king of Judah 2
19: 3 and came to Beer-sheba, which belongs to Judah 2
22: 2 Jehosh'aphat the king of Judah came down 2
10 and Jehosh'aphat the king of Judah were sitting 2
29 king of Israel and Jehosh'aphat the king of Judah 2
41 Jehosh'aphat . . began to reign over Judah 2
45 the Book of the Chronicles of the Kings of Judah? 2
51 seventeenth year of Jehosh'aphat king of Judah 2
2Kg 1:17 Jeho'ram the son of Jehosh'aphat, king of Judah 2
3: 1 eighteenth year of Jehosh'aphat king of Judah 2
7 went and sent word to Jehosh'aphat king of Judah 2
9 So the king of Israel went with the king of Judah 2
14 I have regard for Jehosh'aphat the king of Judah 2
8:16 Jeho'ram the son of Jehosh'aphat, king of Judah 2
19 Yet the LORD would not destroy Judah 2
20 In his days Edom revolted from the rule of Judah 2
22 Edom revolted from the rule of Judah to this day. 2
23 the Book of the Chronicles of the Kings of Judah? 2
25 Ahazi'ah the son of Jeho'ram, king of Judah 2
29 Ahazi'ah the son of Jeho'ram king of Judah went 2
9:16 Ahazi'ah king of Judah had come . . to visit Joram. 2
21 Then Joram . . and Ahazi'ah king of Judah set out 2
27 When Ahazi'ah the king of Judah saw this, he fled 2
29 Ahazi'ah began to reign over Judah. 2
10:13 Jehu met the kinsmen of Ahazi'ah king of Judah 2
12:18 Jeho'ash king of Judah took all the votive gifts 2
18 and Jeho'ram and Ahazi'ah . . the kings of Judah 2
19 the Book of the Chronicles of the Kings of Judah? 2
13: 1 year of Jo'ash the son of Ahazi'ah, king of Judah 2
10 In the 37th year of Jo'ash king of Judah 2
12 he fought against Amazi'ah king of Judah 2
14: 1 Amazi'ah . . king of Judah, began to reign. 2
9 Jeho'ash . . sent word to Amazi'ah king of Judah 2
10 so that you fall, you and Judah with you? 2
11 he and Amazi'ah king of Judah faced one another 2
11 battle at Beth-she'mesh, which belongs to Judah. 2
12 Judah was defeated by Israel, and every man fled 2
13 Jeho'ash . . captured Amazi'ah king of Judah 2
15 and how he fought with Amazi'ah king of Judah 2
17 Amazi'ah the son of Jo'ash, king of Judah, lived 2
18 the Book of the Chronicles of the Kings of Judah? 2
21 all the people of Judah took Azari'ah 2
22 He built Elath and restored it to Judah 2
23 fifteenth year of Amazi'ah . . king of Judah 2
28 Damascus and Hamath, which had belonged to Judah 2
15: 1 Azari'ah the son of Amazi'ah, king of Judah, began 2
6 the Book of the Chronicles of the Kings of Judah? 2
8 In the 38th year of Azari'ah king of Judah 2
13 in the 39th year of Uzzi'ah king of Judah 2
17 In the 39th year of Azari'ah the king of Judah 2
23 In the 50th year of Azari'ah king of Judah 2
27 In the 52nd year of Azari'ah king of Judah 2
32 Jotham the son of Uzzi'ah, king of Judah, began 2
36 the Book of the Chronicles of the Kings of Judah? 2
37 to send Rezin . . and Pekah . . against Judah. 2
16: 1 Ahaz the son of Jotham, king of Judah, began 2
19 the Book of the Chronicles of the Kings of Judah? 2
17: 1 In the twelfth year of Ahaz king of Judah 2
13 Yet the LORD warned Israel and Judah 2
18 none was left but the tribe of Judah only. 2
19 Judah also did not keep the commandments 2
18: 1 Hezeki'ah the son of Ahaz, king of Judah, began 2
5 was none like him among all the kings of Judah 2
13 against all the fortified cities of Judah 2
14 Hezeki'ah king of Judah sent to . . at Lachish 2
14 Assyria required of Hezeki'ah king of Judah 2
16 which Hezeki'ah king of Judah had overlaid 2
22 has removed, saying to Judah and to Jerusalem 2
19:10 Thus shall you speak to Hezeki'ah king of Judah 2
30 remnant of the house of Judah shall . . take root 2
20:20 the Book of the Chronicles of the Kings of Judah? 2
21:11 Manas'seh king of Judah has committed these 2
11 Manas'seh . . has made Judah also to sin 2
12 I am bringing upon Jerusalem and Judah such evil 2
16 the sin which he made Judah to sin so that they did 2
17 the Book of the Chronicles of the Kings of Judah? 2
25 the Book of the Chronicles of the Kings of Judah? 2
22:13 for me, and for the people, and for all Judah 2
16 of the book which the king of Judah has read. 2
18 But as to the king of Judah, who sent you to inquire 2
23: 1 the elders of Judah and Jerusalem were gathered 2
2 the king went . . and with him all the men of Judah 2
5 priests whom the kings of Judah had ordained 2
5 in the high places at the cities of Judah 2
8 brought . . the priests out of the cities of Judah 2
11 that the kings of Judah had dedicated to the sun 2
12 altars . . which the kings of Judah had made 2
17 the man of God who came from Judah and predicted 2
22 of the kings of Israel or of the kings of Judah; 2
24 abominations that were seen in the land of Judah 2
26 by which his anger was kindled against Judah 2
27 I will remove Judah also out of my sight 2
28 the Book of the Chronicles of the Kings of Judah? 2
24: 2 and sent them against Judah to destroy it 2
3 this came upon Judah at the command of the LORD 2
5 the Book of the Chronicles of the Kings of Judah? 2
12 Jehoi'achin the king of Judah gave himself up 2
20 it came to the point in Jerusalem and Judah that 2
25:21 So Judah was taken into exile out of its land. 2
22 over the people who remained in the land of Judah 2
27 year of the exile of Jehoi'achin king of Judah 2
27 freed Jehoi'achin king of Judah from prison; 2
1Ch 2: 1 sons of Israel . . Levi, Judah, Is'sachar, Zeb'ulun 2
3 The sons of Judah: Er, Onan, and Shelah; 2
3 Now Er, Judah's first-born was wicked in the sight 2
4 Judah had five sons in all. 2
10 Nahshon, prince of the sons of Judah. 2
4: 1 sons of Judah: Perez, Hezron, Carmi, Hur, and Shobal. 2
21 sons of Shelah the son of Judah 2
27 their family multiply like the men of Judah. 2
41 in the days of Hezeki'ah, king of Judah 2
5: 2 though Judah became strong among his brothers 2
17 enrolled . . in the days of Jotham king of Judah 2
6:15 the LORD sent Judah and Jerusalem into exile 2
55 to them they gave Hebron in the land of Judah 2
65 out of the tribes of Judah, Simeon, and Benjamin 2
9: 1 And Judah was taken into exile in Babylon 2
3 some of the people of Judah, Benjamin, E'phraim 2
4 from the sons of Perez the son of Judah. 2
12:16 some of the men of Benjamin and Judah 2
24 The men of Judah bearing shield and spear were 2
13: 6 Kir'iath-je'arim which belongs to Judah 2
21: 5 and in Judah 470,000 who drew the sword. 2
27:18 for Judah, Eli'hu, one of David's brothers; 2
28: 4 chose Judah as leader, and in the house of Judah 2
4 chose Judah as leader, and in the house of Judah 2
2Ch 2: 7 skilled workers who are with me in Judah 2
9:11 never . . the like of them before in . . Judah. 2
10:17 the people . . who dwelt in the cities of Judah. 2
11: 1 he assembled the house of Judah, and Benjamin 2
3 Say to Rehobo'am the son of Solomon king of Judah 2
3 Say . . to all Israel in Judah and Benjamin 2
5 Rehobo'am . . built cities for defense in Judah. 2
10 cities which are in Judah and in Benjamin. 2
12 strong. So he held Judah and Benjamin. 2
14 +evites left . . and came to Judah and Jerusalem 2
17 They strengthened the kingdom of Judah 2
23 through all the districts of Judah and Benjamin 2
12: 4 he took the fortified cities of Judah 2
5 Shemai'ah . . came . . to the princes of Judah 2
12 moreover, conditions were good in Judah. 2
13: 1 Abi'jah began to reigh over Judah. 2
13 thus his troops were in front of Judah 2
14 when Judah looked, behold, the battle was 2
15 Then the men of Judah raised the battle shout. 2
15 when the men of Judah shouted, God defeated 2
15 defeated Jerobo'am . . before Abi'jah and Judah. 2
16 The men of Israel fled before Judah 2
18 the men of Judah prevailed 2
14: 4 commanded Judah to seek the LORD 2
5 out of all the cities of Judah the high places 2
6 He built fortified cities in Judah 2
7 he said to Judah, "Let us build these cities 2
8 Asa had an army of 300,000 from Judah 2
12 LORD defeated the Ethiopians . . before Judah 2
13 The men of Judah carried away very much booty. •
15: 2 Hear me, Asa, and all Judah and Benjamin 2
8 from all the land of Judah and Benjamin 2
9 he gathered all Judah and Benjamin 2
15 all Judah rejoiced over the oath; 2
16: 1 Ba'asha king of Israel went up against Judah 2
1 no one to go out or come in to Asa king of Judah. 2
6 Then King Asa took all Judah 2
7 Hana'ni the seer came to Asa king of Judah 2
11 the Book of the Kings of Judah and Israel. 2
17: 2 forces in all the fortified cities of Judah 2
2 set garrisons in the land of Judah 2
5 all Judah brought tribute to Jehosh'aphat; 2
6 high places and the Ashe'rim out of Judah. 2
7 to teach in the cities of Judah; 2
9 they taught in Judah, having the book of the law 2
9 they went about through all the cities of Judah 2
10 lands that were round about Judah 2
12 He built in Judah fortresses and store-cities 2
13 he had great stores in the cities of Judah. 2
14 Of Judah, the commanders of thousands 2
19 in the fortified cities throughout all Judah. 2
18: 3 Ahab . . said to Jehosh'aphat king of Judah 2
9 king of Israel and Jehosh'aphat the king of Judah 2
28 king of Israel and Jehosh'aphat the king of Judah 2
19: 1 Jehosh'aphat the king of Judah returned 2
5 in the land in all the fortified cities of Judah 2
11 Zebedi'ah . . the governor of the house of Judah 2
20: 3 proclaimed a fast throughout all Judah. 2
4 Judah assembled to seek help from the LORD; 2
4 from all the cities of Judah they came to seek 2
5 Jehosh'aphat stood in the assembly of Judah 2
13 all the men of Judah stood before the LORD 2
15 Hearken, all Judah and inhabitants of Jerusalem 2
17 on your behalf, O Judah and Jerusalem.' 2
18 all Judah and the inhabitants of Jerusalem fell 2
20 Hear me, Judah and inhabitants of Jerusalem! 2
22 had come against Judah, so that they were routed. 2
24 Judah came to the watchtower of the wilderness 2
27 returned, every man of Judah and Jerusalem 2
31 Thus Jehosh'aphat reigned over Judah. 2
35 Jehosh'aphat king of Judah joined with Ahazi'ah 2
21: 2 sons of Jehosh'aphat king of Judah. 2
3 together with fortified cities in Judah; 2
8 In his days Edom revolted from the rule of Judah 2
10 Edom revolted from the rule of Judah to this day. 2
11 he made high places in the hill country of Judah 2
11 into unfaithfulness, and made Judah go astray. 2
12 not walked . . in the ways of Asa king of Judah 2
13 led Judah and the inhabitants of Jerusalem 2
17 they came up against Judah, and invaded it 2
22: 1 the son of Jeho'ram king of Judah reigned. 2
6 Ahazi'ah the son of Jeho'ram king of Judah 2
8 Jehu . . met the princes of Judah 2
10 destroyed all the royal family of . . Judah. 2
23: 2 they went about through Judah 2
2 Levites from all the cities of Judah 2
8 The Levites and all Judah did according to all 2
24: 5 Go out to the cities of Judah, and gather 2
6 to bring in from Judah and Jerusalem the tax 2
9 proclamation was made throughout Judah 2
17 th e princes of Judah came and did obeisance 2
18 wrath came upon Judah and Jerusalem for this 2
23 They came to Judah and Jerusalem 2
25: 5 under commanders . . for all Judah and Benjamin. 2
10 And they became very angry with Judah 2
12 The men of Judah captured another 10,000 alive 2
13 fell upon the cities of Judah 2
17 Amazi'ah king of Judah took counsel and sent 2
18 Jo'ash . . sent word to Amazi'ah king of Judah 2
19 so that you fall, you and Judah with you? 2
21 he and Amazi'ah king of Judah faced one another 2
21 Beth-she'mesh, which belongs to Judah. 2
22 Judah was defeated by Israel 2
23 Jo'ash . . captured Amazi'ah king of Judah 2
25 Amazi'ah the son of Jo'ash king of Judah 2
26 the Book of the Kings of Judah and Israel? 2
26: 1 all the people of Judah took Uzzi'ah 2
2 He built Eloth and restored it to Judah 2
27: 4 he built cities in the hill country of Judah 2
7 in the Book of the Kings of Israel and Judah. 2
28: 6 Pekah the son of Remali'ah slew 120,000 in Judah 2
9 because the LORD . . was angry with Judah 2
10 subjugate the people of Judah and Jerusalem 2
17 E'domites had again invaded and defeated Judah 2
18 made raids on the cities in . . the Negeb of Judah 2
19 For the LORD brought Judah low because of Ahaz 2
19 for he had dealt wantonly in Judah 2
25 In every city of Judah he made high places 2
26 the Book of the Kings of Judah and Israel. 2
29: 8 the wrath of the LORD came on Judah and Jerusalem 2
21 for a sin offering for . . Judah. 2
30: 1 Hezeki'ah sent to all Israel and Judah 2
6 couriers went throughout all Israel and Judah 2
12 The hand of God was also upon Judah to give them 2
24 Hezeki'ah king of Judah gave the assembly 2
25 whole assembly of Judah, and the priests 2
25 sojourners who dwelt in Judah 2
31: 1 all Israel . . went out to the cities of Judah 2
1 throughout all Judah and Benjamin 2
6 people of Israel and Judah 2
6 people . . who lived in the cities of Judah 2
20 Thus Hezeki'ah did throughout all Judah; 2
32: 1 Sennach'erib . . came and invaded Judah 2
8 from the words of Hezeki'ah king of Judah. 2
9 to Jerusalem to Hezeki'ah king of Judah 2
12 Hezeki'ah . . commanded Judah and Jerusalem 2
23 precious things to Hezeki'ah king of Judah 2
25 wrath came upon him and Judah and Jerusalem. 2
32 in the Book of the Kings of Judah and Israel. 2
33 all Judah and the inhabitants of Jerusalem did 2
33: 9 Manas'seh seduced Judah and . . Jerusalem 2
14 in all the fortified cities in Judah. 2
16 commanded Judah to serve the LORD the God 2
34: 3 purge Judah and Jerusalem of the high places 2
5 purged Judah and Jerusalem. 2
9 collected . . from all Judah and Benjamin 2
11 buildings . . kings of Judah had let go to ruin. 2
21 for those who are left in Israel and in Judah 2
24 book which was read before the king of Judah. 2
26 to the king of Judah . . thus shall you say to him 2
29 gathered . . the elders of Judah and Jerusalem. 2
30 king went up . . with all the men of Judah 2
35:18 by . . all Judah and Israel who were present 2
21 What have we to do with each other, king of Judah? 2
24 All Judah and Jerusalem mourned for Josi'ah. 2
27 in the Book of the Kings of Israel and Judah. 2
36: 4 made Eli'akim . . king over Judah and Jerusalem 2
8 Book of the Kings of Israel and Judah; 2
10 made . . Zedeki'ah king over Judah and Jerusalem. 2
23 build him a house at Jerusalem, which is in Judah. 2
Ezr 1: 2 build him a house at Jerusalem, which is in Judah. 2
3 let him go up to Jerusalem, which is in Judah 2
5 heads of the fathers' houses of Judah 2
8 out to Shesh-baz'zar the prince of Judah. 2
2: 1 returned to Jerusalem and Judah, each to his own 2
3: 9 Kad'mi-el and his sons, the sons of Judah 2

4: 1 Now when the adversaries of Judah and Benjamin 2
4 land discouraged the people of Judah 2
6 against the inhabitants of Judah and Jerusalem. 2
5: 1 prophesied to the Jews . . in Judah and Jerusalem 4
8 went to the province of Judah, to the house 4
7:14 to make inquiries about Judah and Jerusalem 4
10: 7 proclamation was made throughout Judah 2
9 Then all the men of Judah and Benjamin assembled 2
23 Of the Levites . . Petha-hi'ah, Judah, and Elie'zer. 2
Neh 1: 2 Hana'ni . . came with certain men out of Judah; 2
2: 5 send me to Judah . . that I may rebuild it. 2
7 let me pass through until I come to Judah; 2
4:10 Judah said, "The strength of the burden-bearers 2
16 leaders stood behind all the house of Judah 2
5:14 appointed . . governor in the land of Judah 2
6: 7 to proclaim . . 'There is a king in Judah.' 2
17 nobles of Judah sent many letters to Tobi'ah 2
18 For many in Judah were bound by oath to him 2
7: 6 returned to Jerusalem and Judah, each to his town. 2
11: 3 towns of Judah every one lived on his property 2
4 Jerusalem lived certain of the sons of Judah 2
4 Of the sons of Judah: Athai'ah the son of Uzzi'ah 2
9 Judah the son of Hassen'u-ah was second over 2
20 towns of Judah, every one in his inheritance. 2
24 Pethahi'ah . . of the sons of Zerah the son of Judah 2
25 some of the people of Judah lived in Kir'iath-ar'ba 2
36 Levites in Judah were joined to Benjamin. 2
12: 8 Levites . . Sherebi'ah, Judah, and Mattani'ah 2
31 I brought up the princes of Judah upon the wall 2
32 went Hoshai'ah and half of the princes of Judah 2
34 Judah, Benjamin, Shemai'ah, and Jeremiah 2
36 kinsmen . . Ma'ai, Nethan'el, Judah, and Hana'ni 2
44 Judah rejoiced over the priests and the Levites 2
13:12 Then all Judah brought the tithe of the grain 2
15 saw in Judah men treading wine presses 2
16 sold them on the sabbath to the people of Judah 2
17 I remonstrated with the nobles of Judah and said 2
Est 2: 6 carried away with Jeconi'ah king of Judah 2
Ps 48:11 Let the daughters of Judah rejoice 2
60: 7 E'phraim is my helmet; Judah is my scepter. 2
63: 0 of David, when he was in the Wilderness of Judah. 2
68:27 princes of Judah in their throng, the princes 2
69:35 will save Zion and rebuild the cities of Judah; 2
76: 1 In Judah God is known, his name is great in Israel. 2
78:68 he chose the tribe of Judah 2
97: 8 daughters of Judah rejoice 2
108: 8 E'phraim is my helmet; Judah my scepter. 2
114: 2 Judah became his sanctuary 2
Prv 25: 1 proverbs . . men of Hezeki'ah king of Judah copied. 2
Isa 1: 1 which he saw concerning Judah and Jerusalem 2
1 Jotham, Ahaz, and Hezeki'ah, kings of Judah. 2
2: 1 Isaiah . . saw concerning Judah and Jerusalem. 2
3: 1 from Jerusalem and from Judah stay and staff 2
8 For Jerusalem has stumbled, and Judah has fallen; 2
5: 3 inhabitants of Jerusalem and men of Judah, judge 2
7 the men of Judah are his pleasant planting; 2
7: 1 Ahaz the son of Jotham, son of Uzzi'ah, king of Judah 2
6 Let us go up against Judah and terrify it 2
17 the day that E'phraim departed from Judah– 2
8: 8 it will sweep on into Judah, it will overflow 2
9:21 and together they are against Judah. 2
11:12 the dispersed of Judah from the four corners 2
13 and those who harass Judah shall be cut off; 2
13 E'phraim shall not be jealous of Judah 2
13 and Judah shall not harass E'phraim. 2
19:17 Judah will become a terror to the Egyptians; 2
22: 8 He has taken away the covering of Judah. 2
21 a father . . to the house of Judah. 2
26: 1 this song will be sung in the land of Judah 2
36: 1 all the fortified cities of Judah and took them. 2
7 Hezeki'ah . . saying to Judah and to Jerusalem 2
37:10 Thus shall you speak to Hezeki'ah king of Judah 2
31 the surviving remnant of the house of Judah 2
38: 9 A writing of Hezeki'ah king of Judah 2
40: 9 say to the cities of Judah, "Behold your God! 2
44:26 and of the cities of Judah, 'They shall be built 2
48: 1 and who came forth from the loins of Judah; 2
65: 9 and from Judah inheritors of my mountains; 2
Jer 1: 2 in the days of Josi'ah the son of Amon, king of Judah 2
3 days of Jehoi'akim the son of Josi'ah, king of Judah 2
3 year of Zedeki'ah, the son of Josi'ah, king of Judah 2
15 and against all the cities of Judah. 2
18 against the kings of Judah, its princes 2
2:28 for as many as your cities are your gods, O Judah. 2
3: 7 and her false sister Judah saw it. 2
8 yet her false sister Judah did not fear 2
10 Yet . . her false sister Judah did not return to me 2
11 shown herself less guilty than false Judah. 2
18 the house of Judah shall join the house of Israel 2
4: 3 For thus says the LORD to the men of Judah 2
4 remove the foreskin of your hearts, O men of Judah 2
5 Declare in Judah, and proclaim in Jerusalem 2
16 they shout against the cities of Judah. 2
5:11 For the house of Israel and the house of Judah 2
20 in the house of Jacob, proclaim it in Judah 2
7: 2 all you men of Judah who enter these gates 2
17 see what they are doing in the cities of Judah 2
30 For the sons of Judah have done evil in my sight 2
34 And I will make to cease from the cities of Judah 2
8: 1 says the LORD, the bones of the kings of Judah 2
9:11 and I will make the cities of Judah a desolation 2
26 Egypt, Judah, Edom, the sons of Ammon, Moab 2
10:22 to make the cities of Judah a desolation 2
11: 2 and speak to the men of Judah 2
6 Proclaim all these words in the cities of Judah 2
9 There is revolt among the men of Judah 2
10 and the house of Judah have broken my covenant 2
12 Then the cities of Judah . . will go 2
13 gods have become as many as your cities, O Judah; 2
17 of Israel and the house of Judah have done 2
12:14 will pluck up the house of Judah from among them. 2
13: 9 Even so will I spoil the pride of Judah 2
11 I made . . the whole house of Judah cling to me 2
19 all Judah is taken into exile 2
14: 2 Judah mourns and her gates languish; 2
19 Hast thou utterly rejected Judah? 2
15: 4 Manas'seh the son of Hezeki'ah, king of Judah 2
17: 1 The sin of Judah is written with a pen of iron; 2
19 Benjamin Gate, by which the kings of Judah enter 2
20 say: 'Hear the word of the LORD, you kings of Judah 2
20 all Judah, and all the inhabitants of Jerusalem 2
25 men of Judah and the inhabitants of Jerusalem; 2
26 And people shall come from the cities of Judah 2
18:11 Now, therefore, say to the men of Judah 2
19: 3 O kings of Judah and inhabitants of Jerusalem. 2
4 their fathers nor the kings of Judah have known; 2
7 in this place I will make void the plans of Judah 2
13 and the houses of the kings of Judah 2
20: 4 all Judah into the hand of the king of Babylon; 2
5 and all the treasures of the kings of Judah 2
21: 7 give Zedeki'ah king of Judah, and his servants 2
11 And to the house of the king of Judah say 2
22: 1 Go down to the house of the king of Judah 2
2 and say, 'Hear the word of the LORD, O King of Judah 2
6 concerning the house of the king of Judah 2
11 Shallum the son of Josi'ah, king of Judah 2
18 Jehoi'akim the son of Josi'ah, king of Judah 2
24 though Coni'ah the son of Jehoi'akim, king of Judah 2
30 on the throne of David, and ruling again in Judah. 2
23: 6 In his days Judah will be saved 2
24: 1 Jeconi'ah the son of Jehoi'akim, king of Judah 2
1 king of Judah, together with the princes of Judah 2
5 I will regard as good the exiles from Judah 2
8 will I treat Zedeki'ah the king of Judah 2
25: 1 to Jeremiah concerning all the people of Judah 2
1 Jehoi'akim the son of Josi'ah, king of Judah 2
2 the prophet spoke to all the people of Judah 2
3 Josi'ah the son of Amon, king of Judah, to this day 2
18 Jerusalem and the cities of Judah 2
26: 1 Jehoi'akim the son of Josi'ah, king of Judah 2
2 and speak to all the cities of Judah which come 2
10 When the princes of Judah heard these things 2
18 prophesied in the days of Hezeki'ah king of Judah 2
18 and said to all the people of Judah 2
19 Did Hezeki'ah king of Judah 2
19 king of Judah and all Judah put him to death? 2
27: 1 Zedeki'ah the son of Josi'ah, king of Judah 2
3 come to Jerusalem to Zedeki'ah king of Judah. 2
12 To Zedeki'ah king of Judah I spoke in like manner 2
18 in the house of the king of Judah, and in Jerusalem 2
20 Jeconi'ah the son of Jehoi'akim, king of Judah 2
20 and all the nobles of Judah and Jerusalem– 2
21 in the house of the king of Judah, and in Jerusalem 2
28: 1 beginning of the reign of Zedeki'ah king of Judah 2
4 Jeconi'ah the son of Jehoi'akim, king of Judah 2
4 and all the exiles from Judah who went to Babylon 2
29: 2 the eunuchs, the princes of Judah and Jerusalem 2
3 whom Zedeki'ah king of Judah sent to Babylon 2
22 be used by all the exiles from Judah in Babylon 2
30: 3 my people, Israel and Judah, says the LORD 2
4 the LORD spoke concerning Israel and Judah 2
31:23 they shall use these words in the land of Judah 2
24 Judah and all its cities shall dwell there 2
27 sow the house of Israel and the house of Judah 2
31 with the house of Israel and the house of Judah 2
32: 1 in the tenth year of Zedeki'ah king of Judah 2
2 which was in the palace of the king of Judah. 2
3 For Zedeki'ah king of Judah had imprisoned him 2
4 Zedeki'ah king of Judah shall not escape 2
30 and the sons of Judah have done nothing but evil 2
32 evil of the sons of Israel and the sons of Judah 2
32 men of Judah and the inhabitants of Jerusalem. 2
35 this abomination, to cause Judah to sin. 2
44 about Jerusalem, and in the cities of Judah 2
33: 4 houses of the kings of Judah which were torn down 2
7 I will restore the fortunes of Judah 2
10 in the cities of Judah and the streets 2
13 about Jerusalem, and in the cities of Judah 2
14 the house of Israel and the house of Judah. 2
16 In those days Judah will be saved 2
34: 2 Go and speak to Zedeki'ah king of Judah 2
4 the word of the LORD, O Zedeki'ah king of Judah! 2
6 spoke all these words to Zedeki'ah king of Judah 2
7 against all the cities of Judah that were left 2
7 only fortified cities of Judah that remained. 2
19 the princes of Judah, the princes of Jerusalem 2
21 And Zedeki'ah king of Judah, and his princes 2
22 I will make the cities of Judah a desolation 2
35: 1 Jehoi'akim the son of Josi'ah, king of Judah 2
13 Go and say to the men of Judah 2
17 on Judah and all the inhabitants of Jerusalem 2
36: 1 Jehoi'akim the son of Josi'ah, king of Judah 2
2 against Israel and Judah and all the nations 2
3 It may be that the house of Judah will hear 2
6 all the men of Judah who come out of their cities. 2
9 Jehoi'akim the son of Josi'ah, king of Judah 2
9 the people who came from the cities of Judah 2
28 which Jehoi'akim the king of Judah has burned. 2
29 And concerning Jehoi'akim king of Judah 2
30 the LORD concerning Jehoi'akim king of Judah 2
31 and upon the men of Judah, all the evil 2
32 scroll which Jehoi'akim king of Judah had burned 2
37: 1 king of Babylon made king in the land of Judah 2
7 Thus shall you say to the king of Judah 2
38:22 the women left in the house of the king of Judah 2
39: 1 In the ninth year of Zedeki'ah king of Judah 2
4 Zedeki'ah king of Judah and all the soldiers saw 2
6 the king of Babylon slew all the nobles of Judah. 2
10 left in the land of Judah some of the poor people 2
40: 1 Jerusalem and Judah who were being exiled 2
5 appointed governor of the cities of Judah 2
11 the king of Babylon had left a remnant in Judah 2
12 they had been driven and came to the land of Judah 2
15 scattered, and the remnant of Judah would perish? 2
42:15 then hear the word of the LORD, O remnant of Judah. 2
19 The LORD has said to you, O remnant of Judah 2
43: 4 to remain in the land of Judah. 2
5 all the remnant of Judah who had returned to live 2
5 who had returned to live in the land of Judah 2
9 in the sight of the men of Judah 3
44: 2 upon Jerusalem and upon all the cities of Judah. 2
6 poured forth and kindled in the cities of Judah 2
7 from the midst of Judah, leaving you no remnant? 2
9 the wickedness of the kings of Judah 2
9 which they committed in the land of Judah 2
11 set my face against you . . to cut off all Judah. 2
12 I will take the remnant of Judah 2
14 so that none of the remnant of Judah who have come 2
14 or survive or return to the land of Judah 2
17 our kings and our princes, in the cities of Judah 2
21 incense that you burned in the cities of Judah 2
24 Hear the word of the LORD, all you of Judah 2
26 all you of Judah who dwell in the land of Egypt 2
26 no more be invoked by the mouth of any man of Judah 2
27 all the men of Judah who are in the land of Egypt 2
28 return from the land of Egypt to the land of Judah 2
28 the remnant of Judah, who came to the land of Egypt 2
30 as I gave Zedeki'ah king of Judah into the hand 2
45: 1 Jehoi'akim the son of Josi'ah, king of Judah 2
46: 2 Jehoi'akim the son of Josi'ah, king of Judah 2
49:34 of the reign of Zedeki'ah king of Judah. 2
50: 4 the people of Israel and the people of Judah 2
20 and sin in Judah, and none shall be found; 2
33 are oppressed, and the people of Judah with them; 2
51: 5 and Judah have not been forsaken by their God 2
59 he went with Zedeki'ah king of Judah to Babylon 2
52: 3 things came to such a pass in Jerusalem and Judah 2
10 and also slew all the princes of Judah at Riblah. 2
27 So Judah was carried captive out of its land. 2
31 of the captivity of Jehoi'achin king of Judah 2
31 lifted up the head of Jehoi'achin king of Judah 2
Lam 1: 3 Judah has gone into exile because of affliction 2
15 as in a . . press the virgin daughter of Judah. 2
2: 2 broken . . strongholds of the daughter of Judah; 2
5 he has multiplied in the daughter of Judah 2
5:11 ravished in Zion, virgins in the towns of Judah. 2
Ezk 4: 6 and bear the punishment of the house of Judah; 2
8: 1 sat . . with the elders of Judah sitting before me 2
17 Is it too slight a thing for the house of Judah 2
9: 9 The guilt of the house of Israel and Judah is 2
21:20 and to Judah and to Jerusalem the fortified. 2
25: 3 over the house of Judah when it went into exile; 2
8 the house of Judah is like all the other nations 2
12 acted revengefully against the house of Judah 2
27:17 Judah and the land of Israel traded with you; 2
37:16 Son of man, take a stick and write on it, 'For Judah 2
19 I will join with it the stick of Judah 2
48: 7 from the east side to the west, Judah, one portion. 2
8 Adjoining the territory of Judah, from the east 2
22 shall lie between the territory of Judah 2
31 three gates, the gate of Reuben, the gate of Judah 2
Dan 1: 6 Daniel . . and Azari'ah of the tribe of Judah. 2
2:25 I have found among the exiles from Judah a man 4
5:13 You are that Daniel, one of the exiles of Judah 4
13 exiles . . king my father brought from Judah. 4
6:13 That Daniel, who is one of the exiles from Judah 4
9: 7 men of Judah, to the inhabitants of Jerusalem 2
Hos 1: 1 Uzzi'ah, Jotham, Ahaz, and Hezeki'ah, kings of Judah 2
7 But I will have pity on the house of Judah 2
11 And the people of Judah . . shall be gathered 2
4:15 O Israel, let not Judah become guilty. 2
5: 5 Judah also shall stumble with them. 2
10 The princes of Judah have become like those 2
12 I am . . like dry rot to the house of Judah. 2
13 E'phraim saw his sickness, and Judah his wound 2
14 and like a young lion to the house of Judah. 2
6: 4 What shall I do with you, O Judah? 2

11 For you also, O Judah, a harvest is appointed. 2
8:14 and Judah has multiplied fortified cities; 2
10:11 Judah must plow, Jacob must harrow for himself. 2
11:12 but Judah is still known by God, and is faithful 2
12: 2 The LORD has an indictment against Judah 2
Jol 3: 1 when I restore the fortunes of Judah 2
6 You have sold the people of Judah and Jerusalem 2
8 your daughters into the hand of the sons of Judah 2
18 the stream beds of Judah shall flow with water; 2
19 for the violence done to the people of Judah 2
20 But Judah shall be inhabited for ever 2
Ams 1: 1 in the days of Uzzi'ah king of Judah 2
2: 4 For three transgressions of Judah, and for four 2
5 I will send a fire upon Judah 2
7:12 flee away to the land of Judah, and eat bread there 2
Obd 1:12 not have rejoiced over the people of Judah 2
Mic 1: 1 Jotham, Ahaz, and Hezeki'ah, kings of Judah 2
5 And what is the sin of the house of Judah? 2
9 her wound is incurable; and it has come to Judah 2
5: 2 who are little to be among the clans of Judah 2
Nah 1:15 Keep your feasts, O Judah, fulfil your vows 2
Zep 1: 1 days of Josi'ah the son of Amon, king of Judah. 2
4 I will stretch out my hand against Judah 2
2: 7 possession of the remnant of the house of Judah 2
Hag 1: 1 to Zerub'babel . . governor of Judah, 2
14 Zerub'babel . . governor of Judah 2
2: 2 Speak now to Zerub'babel . . governor of Judah 2
21 Speak to Zerub'babel, governor of Judah, saying 2
Zec 1:12 mercy on Jerusalem and the cities of Judah 2
19 These are the horns which have scattered Judah 2
21 These are the horns which scattered Judah 2
21 against the land of Judah to scatter it. 2
2:12 the LORD will inherit Judah as his portion 2
8:13 O house of Judah and house of Israel, so will I save 2
15 to do good to Jerusalem and to the house of Judah; 2
19 shall be to the house of Judah seasons of joy 2
9: 7 it shall be like a clan in Judah 2
13 I have bent Judah as my bow; I have made E'phraim 2
10: 3 cares for his flock, the house of Judah 2
6 I will strengthen the house of Judah 2
11:14 the brotherhood between Judah and Israel. 2
12: 2 it will be against Judah also in the siege 2
4 But upon the house of Judah I will open my eyes 2
5 Then the clans of Judah shall say to themselves 2
6 I will make the clans of Judah like a blazing pot 2
7 the LORD will give victory to the tents of Judah 2
7 Jerusalem may not be exalted over that of Judah. 2
14: 5 earthquake in the days of Uzzi'ah king of Judah. 2
14 even Judah will fight against Jerusalem. 2
21 every pot in Jerusalem and Judah shall be sacred 2
Mal 2:11 Judah has been faithless 2
11 Judah has profaned the sanctuary of the LORD 2
3: 4 Judah and Jerusalem will be pleasing to the LORD 2
Mat 1: 2 Jacob the father of Judah and his brothers 7
3 Judah the father of Perez and Zerah by Tamar 7
2: 6 you, O Bethlehem, in the land of Judah, are by no 7
6 are by no means least among the rulers of Judah; 7
Lke 1:39 into the hill country, to a city of Judah 7
3:30 the son of Simeon, the son of Judah 7
33 son of Hezron, the son of Perez, the son of Judah 7
Heb 7:14 evident that our Lord was descended from Judah 7
8: 8 with the house of Judah; 7
Rev 5: 5 lo, the Lion of the tribe of Judah . . has conquered 7
7: 5 12,000 sealed out of the tribe of Judah 7
1Es 1:21 the priests and Levites and the men of Judah 6
33 in the book of the kings of Israel and Judah. 7
35 he reigned three months in Judah and Jerusalem. 7
2: 8 the tribes of Judah and Benjamin 7
5: 5 of the lineage of Phares, of the tribe of Judah. 7
66 the enemies of the tribe of Judah and Benjamin 7
9: 5 the men of the tribe of Judah and Benjamin 7
23 Pethahiah and Judah and Jonah. 8
2Es 1:24 You would not obey me, O Judah. 9
Jdt 14: 7 Blessed are you in every tent of Judah! 7
Sir 45:25 David, the son of Jesse, of the tribe of Judah 7
49: 4 the kings of Judah came to an end; 7
Bar 1: 3 Jeconiah the son of Jehoiakim, king of Judah 7
8 to return them to the land of Judah–the silver 7
8 Zedekiah the son of Josiah, king of Judah 7
15 to the men of Judah, to the inhabitants 7
2: 1 princes and against the men of Israel and Judah. 7
23 I will make to cease from the cities of Judah 7
26 the house of Israel and the house of Judah. 7
Sus 1:56 You offspring of Canaan and not of Judah 7
57 but a daughter of Judah would not endure 7
1Mc 1:29 the cities of Judah 7
44 to Jerusalem and the cities of Judah 7
51 the cities of Judah to offer sacrifice 7
54 built altars in the surrounding cities of Judah 7
2: 6 He saw the blasphemies being committed in Judah 7
18 as all the Gentiles and the men of Judah 7
3: 8 He went through the cities of Judah; 7
39 to go into the land of Judah and destroy it 7
5:45 to go to the land of Judah. 7
53 till he came to the land of Judah. 7
68 returned to the land of Judah. 7
6: 5 the armies which had gone into the land of Judah 7
12 I sent to destroy the inhabitants of Judah 7
7:10 came with a large force into the land of Judah 7
22 They gained control of the land of Judah 7
50 the land of Judah had rest for a few days. 7
9: 1 sent . . into the land of Judah a second time 7
57 the land of Judah had rest for two years. 7
72 formerly taken from the land of Judah 7
10:30 I will not collect them from the land of Judah 7
33 taken as a captive from the land of Judah 7
37 in the land of Judah. 7
12: 4 safe conduct to the land of Judah. 7
46 they returned to the land of Judah. 7
52 So they all reached the land of Judah safely 7
13: 1 invade the land of Judah and destroy it 7
12 with a large army to invade the land of Judah 7

language of Judah 1. יְהוּדִית

2Kg 18:26 do not speak to us in the language of Judah 1
28 called . . in a loud voice in the language of Judah 1
2Ch 32:18 they shouted it . . in the language of Judah 1
Neh 13:24 they could not speak the language of Judah 1
Isa 36:11 do not speak to us in the language of Judah 1
13 in a loud voice in the language of Judah 1

man of Judah 1. יְהוּדָה 2. יְהוּדִי

2Kg 16: 6 the king . . and drove the men of Judah from Elath; 2
2Ch 25: 5 Then Amazi'ah assembled the men of Judah 1

people of Judah 1. יְהוּדָה

2Ch 32: 9 to all the people of Judah that were in Jerusalem 1

Judaism 1. Ἰουδαϊσμός

Act 13:43 many Jews and devout converts to Judaism *
Gal 1:13 For you have heard of my former life in Judaism 1
14 I advanced in Judaism beyond many of my own age 1
2Mc 2:21 those who strove zealously on behalf of Judaism 1
14:38 he had been accused of Judaism 1
38 for Judaism he had with all zeal risked body 1
4Mc 4:26 to eat defiling foods and to renounce Judaism. 1

Judas 1. Ἰούδας

Mat 10: 4 Simon the Cananaean, and Judas Iscariot 1
13:55 James and Joseph and Simon and Judas? 1
26:14 one of the twelve, who was called Judas Iscariot 1
25 Judas, who betrayed him, said, "Is it I, Master? 1
47 Judas came, one of the twelve 1
27: 3 When Judas, his betrayer, saw 1
Mrk 3:19 Judas Iscariot, who betrayed him. 1
6: 3 brother of James and Joses and Judas and Simon 1
14:10 Then Judas Iscariot, who was one of the twelve 1
43 while he was still speaking, Judas came 1
Lke 6:16 Judas the son of James, and Judas Iscariot 1
16 Judas Iscariot, who became a traitor. 1
22: 3 Then Satan entered into Judas called Iscariot 1
47 the man called Judas, one of the twelve, was leading 1
48 Jesus said to him, "Judas 1
Joh 6:71 He spoke of Judas the son of Simon Iscariot 1
12: 4 Judas Iscariot, one of his disciples 1
13: 2 the heart of Judas Iscariot, Simon's son 1
26 he gave it to Judas, the son of Simon Iscariot. 1
29 because Judas had the money box 1
14:22 Judas (not Iscariot) said to him, "Lord, how is it 1
18: 2 Now Judas, who betrayed him, also knew the place; 1
3 Judas, procuring a band of soldiers 1
5 Judas, who betrayed him, was standing with them. 1
Act 1:13 Simon the Zealot and Judas the son of James. 1
16 Judas who was guide to those who arrested Jesus. 1
25 the place . . from which Judas turned aside 1
5:37 Judas the Galilean arose 1
9:11 inquire in the house of Judas for a man of Tarsus 1
15:22 They sent Judas called Barsab'bas, and Silas 1
27 We have therefore sent Judas and Silas 1
32 Judas and Silas, who were themselves prophets 1
1Mc 2: 4 Judas called Maccabeus 1
66 Judas Maccabeus has been a mighty warrior 1
3: 1 Judas his son, who was called Maccabeus 1
11 When Judas learned of it, he went out to meet him 1
12 Judas took the sword of Apollonius 1
13 Judas had gathered a large company 1
14 I will make war on Judas and his companions 1
16 Judas went out to meet him with a small company. 1
17 they said to Judas, "How can we 1
18 Judas replied, "It is easy 1
25 Then Judas and his brothers began to be feared 1
26 the Gentiles talked of the battles of Judas. 1
42 Judas . . saw that misfortunes had increased 1
55 After this Judas appointed leaders of the people 1
58 Judas said, "Gird yourselves and be valiant 1
4: 3 Judas heard of it 1
5 When Gorgias entered the camp of Judas by night 1
6 At daybreak Judas appeared in the plain 1
8 Judas said to the men who were with him 1
13 Then the men with Judas blew their trumpets 1
16 Then Judas and his force turned back 1
19 Just as Judas was finishing this speech 1
21 when they also saw the army of Judas 1
23 Then Judas returned to plunder the camp 1
29 Judas met them with 10,000 men. 1
35 the boldness which inspired those of Judas 1
36 Then said Judas and his brothers, "Behold 1
41 Then Judas detailed men to fight 1
59 Then Judas and his brothers and all the assembly 1
5: 3 Judas made war on the sons of Esau in Idumea 1
10 sent to Judas and his brothers a letter 1
16 When Judas and the people heard these messages 1
17 Then Judas said to Simon his brother 1
20 and 8,000 to Judas for Gilead. 1
24 Judas Maccabeus and Jonathan his brother 1
28 Then Judas and his army quickly turned back 1
31 So Judas saw that the battle had begun 1
38 Judas sent men to spy out the camp 1
39 Judas went to meet them. 1
40 Now as Judas and his army drew near 1
42 When Judas approached the stream of water 1
44 they could stand before Judas no longer. 1
45 Then Judas gathered together 1
48 Judas sent them this friendly message 1
49 Then Judas ordered proclamation to be made 1
53 Judas kept rallying the laggards 1
55 Now while Judas and Jonathan were in Gilead 1
61 they did not listen to Judas and his brothers. 1
63 The man Judas and his brothers 1
65 Then Judas and his brothers went forth 1
68 Judas turned aside to Azotus 1
6:19 So Judas decided to destroy them 1
32 Then Judas marched away from the citadel 1
42 Judas and his army advanced to the battle 1
7: 6 Judas and his brothers have destroyed 1
7 see all the ruin which Judas has brought upon us *
10 he sent messengers to Judas and his brothers 1
23 Judas saw all the evil 1
24 So Judas went out into all the surrounding parts *
25 Judas and those with him had grown strong 1
27 treacherously sent to Judas and his brothers 1
29 So he came to Judas 1
29 the enemy were ready to seize Judas. 1
30 It became known to Judas 1
31 he went out to meet Judas in battle 1
35 Unless Judas and his army are delivered 1
40 Judas encamped in Adasa with 3,000 men 1
40 Then Judas prayed and said 1
8: 1 Now Judas heard of the fame of the Romans 1
17 So Judas chose Eupolemus the son of John 1
20 Judas, who is also called Maccabeus 1
9: 5 Now Judas was encamped in Elasa 1
7 When Judas saw that his army had slipped away 1
10 Judas said, "Far be it from us 1
12 the men with Judas also blew their trumpets. 1
14 Judas saw 1
16 they . . followed close behind Judas and his men. 1
18 Judas also fell, and the rest fled. 1
19 Jonathan and Simon took Judas their brother 1
22 Now the rest of the acts of Judas 1
23 After the death of Judas, the lawless emerged 1
26 They sought and searched for the friends of Judas 1
28 Then all the friends of Judas assembled and said 1
29 Since the death of your brother Judas 1
31 and took the place of Judas his brother. 1
11:70 Judas the son of Chalphi 1
13: 8 You are our leader in place of Judas 1
14:18 alliance which they had established with Judas 1
16: 2 Simon called in his two older sons Judas and John 1
9 Judas the brother of John was wounded 1
14 he went down to Jericho with Mattathias and Judas 1
2Mc 1:10 the senate and Judas 1
2:14 In the same way Judas also collected . . books 1
19 The story of Judas Maccabeus and his brothers 1
5:27 Judas Maccabeus, with about nine others, got away 1
8: 1 Judas, who was also called Maccabeus 1
12 Word came to Judas 1
12: 5 When Judas heard of the cruelty 1
11 Judas and his men won the victory 1
11 The defeated nomads besought Judas 1
12 Judas, thinking that they might really be useful 1
14 those . . behaved most insolently toward Judas 1
15 Judas and his men 1
21 When Timothy learned of the approach of Judas 1
22 when Judas' first division appeared 1
23 Judas pressed the pursuit with the utmost vigor 1
26 Then Judas marched against Carnaim *
36 Judas called upon the Lord 1
38 Then Judas assembled his army 1
39 Judas and his men went to take up the bodies 1
42 the noble Judas exhorted the people 1
13: 1 word came to Judas and his men 1
10 when Judas heard of this 1
12 Judas exhorted them 1
20 Judas sent in to the garrison whatever was necessary. 1
22 attacked Judas and his men, was defeated; 1
14: 1 Three years later, word came to Judas and his men 1
6 whose leader is Judas Maccabeus 1
10 For as long as Judas lives 1
11 who were hostile to Judas 1
13 with orders to kill Judas and scatter his men 1
14 the Gentiles . . who had fled before Judas 1
17 Simon, the brother of Judas 1
18 hearing of the valor of Judas and his men 1
22 Judas posted armed men in readiness 1
24 he kept Judas always in his presence 1
26 that conspirator against the kingdom, Judas 1

33 If you do not hand Judas over to me as a prisoner 1
15: 1 Judas and his men were in the region of Samaria 1
6 a public monument of victory over Judas and his men 1
15 gave to Judas a golden sword 1
17 Encouraged by the words of Judas 1
26 Judas and his men met the enemy in battle 1

Jude 1. Ἰούδας

Jde 1: 1 Jude, a servant of Jesus . . and brother of James 1

Judea 1. יְהוּדָה 2. Ἰουδαία 3. Ἰουδαῖος

Ezr 9: 9 to give us protection in Judea and Jerusalem. 1
Mat 2: 1 Now when Jesus was born in Bethlehem of Judea 2
5 They told him, "In Bethlehem of Judea; 2
22 when he heard that Archela'us reigned over Judea 2
3: 1 Baptist, preaching in the wilderness of Judea 2
5 to him Jerusalem and all Judea and all the region 2
4:25 Decap'olis and Jerusalem and Judea 2
19: 1 entered the region of Judea beyond the Jordan; 2
24:16 let those who are in Judea flee to the mountains; 2
Mrk 1: 5 there went out to him all the country of Judea 2
3: 7 also from Judea 2
10: 1 went to the region of Judea and beyond the Jordan 2
13:14 let those who are in Judea flee to the mountains; 2
Lke 1: 5 In the days of Herod, king of Judea 2
65 through all the hill country of Judea; 2
2: 4 from Galilee, from the city of Nazareth, to Judea 2
3: 1 Pontius Pilate being governor of Judea 2
4:44 he was preaching in the synagogues of Judea. 2
5:17 had come from every village of Galilee and Judea 2
6:17 Judea and Jerusalem and the seacoast of Tyre 2
7:17 through the whole of Judea 2
21:21 let those who are in Judea flee to the mountains 2
23: 5 teaching throughout all Judea 2
Joh 3:22 After this Jesus . . went into the land of Judea; 2
4: 3 he left Judea and departed again to Galilee. 2
47 heard that Jesus had come from Judea to Galilee 2
54 when he had come from Judea to Galilee. 2
7: 1 he would not go about in Judea 2
3 Leave here and go to Judea 2
11: 7 Let us go into Judea again. 2
Act 1: 8 in Jerusalem and in all Judea and Sama'ria 2
2: 9 residents of Mesopota'mia, Judea and Cappado'cia 2
14 Men of Judea and all who dwell in Jerusalem 3
8: 1 scattered throughout the region of Judea and 2
9:31 church throughout all Judea and Galilee and 2
10:37 word which was proclaimed throughout all Judea 2
11: 1 the apostles and the brethren who were in Judea 2
29 send relief to the brethren who lived in Judea; 2
12:19 Then he went down from Judea to Caesare'a 2
15: 1 some men came down from Judea 2
21:10 a prophet named Ag'abus came down from Judea. 2
26:20 throughout all the country of Judea 2
28:21 We have received no letters from Judea about you 2
Rom 15:31 I may be delivered from the unbelievers in Judea 2
2Co 1:16 and have you send me on my way to Judea. 2
Gal 1:22 the churches of Christ in Judea; 2
1Th 2:14 which are in Judea 2
1Es 1:26 What have we to do with each other, king of Judea? 2
32 in all Judea they mourned for Josiah 2
33 the book of the histories of the kings of Judea; 2
37 made Jehoiakim . . king of Judea and Jerusalem. 2
39 when he began to reign in Judea and Jerusalem 2
46 made Zedekiah king of Judea and Jerusalem. 2
2: 4 a house at Jerusalem, which is in Judea. 2
5 let him go up to Jerusalem, which is in Judea 2
12 given to Sheshbazzar the governor of Judea. 2
16 those who were living in Judea and Jerusalem 2
4:45 when Judea was laid waste by the Chaldeans. 2
49 Jews who were going up from his kingdom to Judea 2
5: 7 the men of Judea who came up out of . . captivity 2
8 who returned to Jerusalem and the rest of Judea 2
57 after they came to Judea and Jerusalem. 2
72 pressed hard upon those in Judea 2
6: 1 the Jews who were in Judea and Jerusalem 2
8 when we went to the country of Judea 2
27 the servant of the Lord and governor of Judea 2
28 who have returned from the captivity of Judea 2
8:12 look into matters in Judea and Jerusalem 2
81 to give us a stronghold in Judea and Jerusalem. 2
9: 3 a proclamation was made throughout Judea 2
Tob 1:18 put to death any who came fleeing from Judea 2
Jdt 1:12 the people of Ammon, and all Judea 2
3: 9 fronting the great ridge of Judea; 2
4: 1 the people of Israel living in Judea 2
3 all the people of Judea were newly gathered together 2
7 since by them Judea could be invaded 2
13 the people fasted many days throughout Judea 2
8:21 For if we are captured all Judea will be captured 2
11:19 Then I will lead you through the middle of Judea 2
AEs 11: 4 Jeconiah king of Judea 2
Bel 1:33 Now the prophet Habakkuk was in Judea 2
1Mc 3:34 As for the residents of Judea and Jerusalem 2
4:35 enlisted mercenaries, to invade Judea again 2
5: 8 then he returned to Judea. 2
18 he left Joseph . . in Judea to guard it; 2
23 led them to Judea with great rejoicing. 2
60 were pursued to the borders of Judea 2
6:48 the king encamped in Judea and at Mount Zion. 2
53 those who found safety in Judea 2
7:24 Judas went out . . the surrounding parts of Judea 2
46 men came out of all the villages of Judea round about 2
9:50 built strong cities in Judea 2
60 secretly sent letters to all his allies in Judea 2
63 and sent orders to the men of Judea. 2
10:38 three districts that have been added to Judea 2
38 let them be so annexed to Judea 2
45 the cost of rebuilding the walls in Judea 2
11:20 In those days Jonathan assembled the men of Judea 2
28 Judea and the three districts of Samaria 2
34 the territory of Judea 2
34 the latter . . were added to Judea from Samaria. 2
12:35 planned with them to build strongholds in Judea 2
13:33 Simon built up the strongholds of Judea 2
14:33 He fortified the cities of Judea, and Beth-zur 2
33 Beth-zur on the borders of Judea 2
15:30 outside the borders of Judea; 2
39 He commanded him to encamp against Judea 2
40 and invade Judea and take the people captive 2
41 go out and make raids along the highways of Judea 2
16:10 he returned to Judea safely. 2
2Mc 1: 1 those in the land of Judea 2
10 Those in Jerusalem and those in Judea 2
5:11 he took it to mean that Judea was in revolt 2
8: 9 to wipe out the whole race of Judea 2
10:24 He came on, intending to take Judea by storm. 2
11: 5 Invading Judea, he approached Beth-zur 2
13: 1 was coming with a great army against Judea 2
13 before the king's army could enter Judea 2
14:12 he . . appointed him governor of Judea . . sent him off 2
14 the Gentiles throughout Judea 2
15:22 in the time of Hezekiah king of Judea 2
3Mc 5:43 and would also march against Judea 2

Judith 1. יְהוּדִית 2. Ιουδιθ

Gen 26:34 When Esau was 40 years old, he took to wife Judith 1
Jdt 8: 1 At that time Judith heard about these things 2
4 Judith had lived at home as a widow 2
9 When Judith heard the wicked words 2
32 Judith said to them, "Listen to me 2
9: 1 Then Judith fell upon her face 2
1 Judith cried out to the Lord with a loud voice 2
10: 1 Judith had ceased crying out to the God of Israel •
10 When they had done this, Judith went out 2
23 Judith came into the presence of Holofernes 2
11: 5 Judith replied to him 2
12: 2 Judith said, "I cannot eat it, lest it be an offense; 2
4 Judith replied, "As your soul lives, my lord 2
14 Judith said, "Who am I, to refuse my lord? 2
16 Then Judith came in and lay down 2
18 Judith said, "I will drink now, my lord 2
13: 2 Judith was left alone in the tent 2
3 Now Judith had told her maid . . 2
4 Then Judith, standing beside his bed, said 2
11 Judith called out from afar to the watchmen 2
14: 1 Then Judith said to them, "Listen to me, my brethren 2
7 when they raised him up he fell at Judith's feet 2
8 Then Judith described . . all that she had done 2
14 he supposed that he was sleeping with Judith. 2
17 Then he went to the tent where Judith had stayed 2
15: 8 to see Judith and to greet her. 2
11 They gave Judith the tent of Holofernes 2
16: 1 Then Judith began this thanksgiving 2
2 Judith said, Begin a song to my God 2
7 Judith the daughter of Merari undid him 2
19 Judith also dedicated to God all the vessels 2
20 Judith remained with them. 2
21 Judith went to Bethulia 2
25 in the days of Judith 2

Julia 1. Ἰουλία

Rom 16:15 Greet Philol'ogus, Julia, Nereus and his sister 1

Julius 1. Ἰούλιος

Act 27: 1 a centurion of the Augustan Cohort, named Julius. 1
3 Julius treated Paul kindly 1

Junias 1. Ἰουνιᾶς

Rom 16: 7 Greet Androni'cus and Ju'nias, my kinsmen 1

Jushab-hesed 1. יוּשַׁב חֶסֶד

1Ch 3:20 Berechi'ah, Hasadi'ah, and Ju'shab-he'sed, five. 1

Justus 1. Ἰοῦστος

Act 1:23 Joseph called Barsab'bas, who was surnamed Justus 1
18: 7 went to the house of a man named Titius Justus 1
Col 4:11 Jesus who is called Justus 1

Juttah 1. יֻטָּה

Jos 15:55 Ma'on, Carmel, Ziph, Juttah 1
21:16 A'in with its . . Juttah with its pasture lands 1

Kabzeel 1. קַבְצְאֵל

Jos 15:21 cities belonging to . . were Kabzeel, Eder, Jagur 1
2Sm 23:20 Benai'ah . . was a valiant man of Kabzeel, a doer 1
1Ch 11:22 Benai'ah . . was a valiant man of Kabzeel 1

Kadesh 1. קָדֵשׁ 2. Καδης 3. Κηδες

Gen 14: 7 came to Enmish'pat (that is, Kadesh) 1
16:14 Beer-la'hai-roi; it lies between Kadesh and Bered. 1
20: 1 of the Negeb, and dwelt between Kadesh and Shur; 1
Num 13:26 in the wilderness of Paran, at Kadesh; 1
20: 1 people stayed in Kadesh; and Miriam died there 1
14 Moses sent messengers from Kadesh to the king 1
16 here we are in Kadesh, a city on the edge 1
22 journeyed from Kadesh, and . . came to Mount Hor. 1
27:14 Mer'ibah of Kadesh in the wilderness of Zin.) 1
33:36 in the wilderness of Zin (that is, Kadesh). 1
37 set out from Kadesh, and encamped at Mount Hor 1
Deu 1:46 you remained at Kadesh many days 1
Jdg 11:16 the wilderness to the Red Sea and came to Kadesh. 1
17 not consent. So Israel remained at Kadesh. 1
2Sm 24: 6 came . . and to Kadesh in the land of the Hittites; 2
Ps 29: 8 LORD shakes the wilderness of Kadesh. 1
Jdt 1: 9 Jerusalem and Bethany and Chelous and Kadesh 2
1Mc 11:63 the officers of Demetrius had come to Kadesh 3
73 as far as Kadesh, to their camp 2

Kadesh-barnea 1. קָדֵשׁ בַּרְנֵעַ 2. Καδης Βαρνη

Num 32: 8 sent them from Ka'desh-bar'nea to see the land. 1
34: 4 Zin, and its end shall be south of Ka'desh-bar'nea; 1
Deu 1: 2 from Horeb by . . Mount Se'ir to Ka'desh-bar'nea. 1
19 we set out . . and we came to Ka'desh-bar'nea. 1
2:14 the time from our leaving Ka'desh-bar'nea until 1
9:23 when the LORD sent you from Ka'desh-bar'nea, 1
Jos 10:41 Joshua defeated them from Ka'desh-bar'nea to Gaza 1
14: 6 in Ka'desh-bar'nea concerning you and me. 1
7 Moses . . sent me from Ka'desh-bar'nea to spy out 1
15: 3 along to Zin, and goes up south of Ka'desh-bar'nea 1
Jdt 5:14 he led them by the way of Sinai and Kadesh-barnea 2

Kadmiel 1. קַדְמִיאֵל 2. Καδμιηλ 3. Καδμιηλος

Ezr 2:40 The Levites: the sons of Jeshua and Kad'mi-el 1
3: 9 Jeshua . . and Kad'mi-el and his sons 1
Neh 7:43 Jeshua, namely of Kad'mi-el of the sons of Ho'devah 1
9: 4 stood Jeshua, Bani, Kad'mi-el, Shebani'ah, Bunni 1
5 Levites, Jeshua, Kad'mi-el, Bani, Hashabnei'ah 1
10: 9 Levites: Jeshua . . Bin'nui . . , Kad'mi-el; 1
12: 8 Levites . . Kad'mi-el, Sherebi'ah, Judah 1
24 Sherebi'ah, and Jeshua the son of Kad'mi-el 1
1Es 5:26 sons of Jeshua and Kadmiel and Bannas and Sudias 3
58 Kadmiel his brother 2

Kadmonite 1. קַדְמֹנִי

Gen 15:19 the Ken'ites, the Ken'izzites, the Kad'monites 1

Kain 1. קַיִן

Num 24:22 nevertheless Kain shall be wasted. 1
Jos 15:57 Kain, Gib'e-ah, and Timnah 1

Kaiwan 1. כִּיּוּן

Ams 5:26 Sakkuth your king, and Kaiwan your star-god 1

Kallai 1. קַלָּי

Neh 12:20 of Sal'lai, Kal'lai; of Amok, Eber; 1

Kamon 1. קָמוֹן

Jdg 10: 5 Ja'ir died, and was buried in Kamon. 1

Kanah 1. קָנָה

Jos 16: 8 the boundary goes westward to the brook Kanah 1
17: 9 Then the boundary went down to the brook Kanah. 1
19:28 Rehob, Hammon, Kanah, as far as Sidon the Great; 1

Kareah 1. קָרֵחַ

2Kg 25:23 namely, Ish'mael . . and Joha'nan the son of Kare'ah 1
Jer 40: 8 Joha'nan the son of Kare'ah 1
13 Now Joha'nan the son of Kare'ah and all the leaders 1
15 Then Joha'nan the son of Kare'ah spoke secretly 1
16 But Gedali'ah . . said to Joha'nan the son of Kare'ah 1
41:11 But when Joha'nan the son of Kare'ah . . heard 1
13 saw Joha'nan the son of Kare'ah and all the leaders 1
14 came back, and went to Joha'nan the son of Kare'ah. 1
16 Then Joha'nan the son of Kare'ah 1
42: 1 and Joha'nan the son of Kare'ah 1
8 Then he summoned Joha'nan the son of Kare'ah 1
43: 2 Jona'nan the son of Kare'ah 1
4 Joha'nan the son of Kare'ah and all the commanders 1
5 Joha'nan the son of Kare'ah and all the commanders 1

Karka 1. קַרְקַע

Jos 15: 3 along by Hezron, up to Addar, turns about to Karka 1

Karkor 1. קַרְקֹר

Jdg 8:10 Zebah and Zalmun'na were in Karkor with their 1

Karnaim 1. קַרְנַיִם

Ams 6:13 Have we not by our own strength taken Karnaim 1

Kartah 1. קַרְתָּה

Jos 21:34 Jok'ne-am . . Kartah with its pasture lands 1

Kartan 1. קַרְתָּן

Jos 21:32 and Kartan with its pasture lands 1

Kattath 1. קַטָּת
Jos 19:15 Kattath, Nahal'al, Shimron, I'dalah, and Bethlehem 1

Kedar 1. קֵדָר
Gen 25:13 first-born of Ish'mael; and Kedar, Adbeel, Mibsam 1
1Ch 1:29 Ish'mael, Neba'ioth; and Kedar, Adbeel, Mibsam 1
Ps 120: 5 Woe is me, that . . I dwell among the tents of Kedar! 1
Sng 1: 5 I am very dark . . like the tents of Kedar 1
Isa 21:16 year . . all the glory of Kedar will come to an end; 1
17 archers of the mighty men of the sons of Kedar 1
42:11 the villages that Kedar inhabits; 1
60: 7 All the flocks of Kedar shall be gathered to you 1
Jer 2:10 or send to Kedar and examine with care; 1
49:28 Concerning Kedar and the kingdoms of Hazor 1
28 says the LORD: "Rise up, advance against Kedar! 1
Ezk 27:21 the princes of Kedar were your favored dealers 1

Kedemah 1. קֵדְמָה
Gen 25:15 Hadad, Tema, Jetur, Naphish, and Ked'emah. 1
1Ch 1:31 Jetur, Naphish, and Ked'emah. These are the sons 1

Kedemoth 1. קְדֵמוֹת
Deu 2:26 messengers from the wilderness of Ked'emoth 1
Jos 13:18 Jahaz, and Ked'emoth, and Meph'aath 1
21:37 Ked'emoth with its pasture lands, and Meph'a-ath 1
1Ch 6:79 Ked'emoth with its pasture lands, and Meph'a-ath 1

Kedesh 1. קֶדֶשׁ 2. Κυδιως
Jos 12:22 the king of Kedesh, one; the king of Jok'ne-am . . one; 1
15:23 Kedesh, Hazor, Ithnan 1
19:37 Kedesh, Ed're-i, En-ha'zor 1
20: 7 set apart Kedesh in Galilee in the hill country 1
21:32 Kedesh in Galilee with its pasture lands 1
Jdg 4: 6 Barak the son of Abin'o-am from Kedesh in Naph'tali 1
9 Deb'orah arose, and went with Barak to Kedesh. 1
10 Barak summoned Zeb'ulun and Naph'tali to Kedesh; 1
11 the oak in Za-anan'nim, which is near Kedesh. 1
2Kg 15:29 A'bel-beth-ma'acah, Jan-o'ah, Kedesh, Hazor, Gilead 1
1Ch 6:72 tribe of Is'sachar: Kedesh with its pasture lands 1
76 Kedesh in Galilee with its pasture lands 1
Tob 1: 2 which is to the south of Kedesh Naphtali 2

Kedron 1. Κεδρών
1Mc 15:39 build up Kedron and fortify its gates 1
41 He built up Kedron and stationed there horsemen 1
16: 9 John pursued them until Cendebeus reached Kedron 1

Kehelathah 1. קְהֵלָתָה
Num33:22 set out from Rissah, and encamped at Kehela'thah. 1
23 set out from Kehela'thah, and encamped at Mount 1

Keilah 1. קְעִילָה
Jos 15:44 Kei'lah, Achzib, and Mare'shah 1
1Sm 23: 1 the Philistines are fighting against Kei'lah 1
2 Go and attack the Philistines and save Kei'lah. 1
3 if we go to Kei'lah against the . . Philistines? 1
4 Arise, go down to Kei'lah; for I will give 1
5 And David and his men went to Kei'lah, and fought 1
5 David delivered the inhabitants of Kei'lah. 1
6 When Abi'athar . . fled to David to Kei'lah 1
7 it was told Saul that David had come to Kei'lah. 1
8 go down to Kei'lah, to besiege David and his men. 1
10 Saul seeks to come to Kei'lah, to destroy the city 1
11 Will the men of Kei'lah surrender me into his hand? 1
12 Will the men of Kei'lah surrender me and my men 1
13 David and his . . arose and departed from Kei'lah 1
13 that David had escaped from Kei'lah 1
1Ch 4:19 Kei'lah the Garmite and Eshtemo'a the Ma-ac'athite. 1
Neh 3:17 Hashabi'ah, ruler of half the district of Kei'lah 1
18 Bav'vai . . ruler of half the district of Kei'lah; 1

Kelaiah 1. קֵלָיָה 2. Κωλιος
Ezr 10:23 Of the Levites . . Kelai'ah (that is, Keli'ta) 1
1Es 9:23 Jozabad and Shimei and Kelaiah, who was Kelita 2

Kelita 1. קְלִיטָא 2. Καλιτας
Ezr 10:23 Of the Levites . . Kelai'ah (that is, Keli'ta) 1
Neh 8: 7 Also . . Keli'ta, Azari'ah, Jo'zabad, Hanan 1
10:10 their brethren . . Keli'ta, Pelai'ah, Hanan 1
1Es 9:23 Jozabad and Shimei and Kelaiah, who was Kelita 2
48 Maaseiah and Kelita, Azariah and Jozabad 2

Kemuel 1. קְמוּאֵל
Gen 22:21 Buz his brother, Kemu'el the father of Aram 1
Num34:24 of E'phraim a leader, Kemu'el the son of Shiphtan. 1
1Ch 27:17 for Levi, Hashabi'ah the son of Kem'uel; 1

Kenan 1. קֵינָן
Gen 5: 9 he became the father of Kenan. 1
10 Enosh lived after the birth of Kenan 815 years 1
12 When Kenan had lived 70 years 1
13 Kenan lived after the birth of Ma-hal'alel 1
14 Thus all the days of Kenan were 910 years; 1
1Ch 1: 2 Kenan, Ma-hal'alel, Jared; 1

Kenath 1. קְנָת
Num32:42 Nobah went and took Kenath and its villages 1
1Ch 2:23 Kenath and its villages, 60 towns. 1

Kenaz 1. קְנַז
Gen 36:11 were Teman, Omar, Zepho, Gatam, and Kenaz. 1
15 the chiefs Teman, Omar, Zepho, Kenaz 1
42 Kenaz, Teman, Mibzar 1
Jos 15:17 Oth'ni-el the son of Kenaz, the brother of Caleb 1
Jdg 1:13 Oth'ni-el the son of Kenaz, Caleb's younger brother 1
3: 9 Oth'niel the son of Kenaz, Caleb's younger 1
11 40 years. Then Oth'ni-el the son of Kenaz died. 1
1Ch 1:36 The sons of Eli'phaz . . Gatam, Kenaz, Timna 1
53 Kenaz, Teman, Mibzar 1
4:13 The sons of Kenaz: Oth'ni-el and Serai'ah; 1
15 and the sons of Elah: Kenaz. 1

Kenite 1. קַיִן 2. קֵינִי
Gen 15:19 the land of the Ken'ites, the Ken'izzites 2
Num24:21 he looked on the Ken'ite, and took up his discourse 2
Jdg 1:16 descendants of the Ken'ite, Moses' father-in-law 2
4:11 Heber the Ken'ite had separated from the Ken'ites 2
11 Heber the Ken'ite had separated from the Ken'ites 1
17 to the tent of Ja'el, the wife of Heber the Ken'ite; 2
17 king of Hazor and the house of Heber the Ken'ite. 2
5:24 blessed . . be Ja'el, the wife of Heber the Ken'ite 2
1Sm 15: 6 Saul said to the Ken'ites, "Go, depart, go down 2
6 the Ken'ites departed from . . the Amal'ekites. 2
27:10 or, "Against the Negeb of the Ken'ites. 2
30:29 for those . . in the cities of the Ken'ites 2
1Ch 2:55 These are the Ken'ites who came from Hammath 2

Kenizzite 1. קְנִזִּי
Gen 15:19 the Ken'ites, the Ken'izzites, the Kad'monites 1
Num32:12 except Caleb the son of Jephun'neh the Ken'izzite 1
Jos 14: 6 and Caleb the son of Jephun'neh the Ken'izzite 1
14 of Caleb the son of Jephun'neh the Ken'izzite 1

Keren-happuch 1. קֶרֶן הַפּוּךְ
Job 42:14 and the name of the third Ker'en-hap'puch. 1

Kerioth 1. קְרִיּוֹת
Jer 48:24 Ker'i-oth, and Bozrah, and all the cities of the land 1
Ams 2: 2 and it shall devour the strongholds of Ker'ioth 1

Kerioth-hezron 1. קְרִיּוֹת חֶצְרוֹן
Jos 15:25 Ker'i-oth-hezron (that is, Hazor) 1

Keros 1. קֵרֹס 2. Κηρας
Ezr 2:44 sons of Keros, the sons of Si'aha, the sons of Padon 1
Neh 7:47 sons of Keros, the sons of Si'a, the sons of Padon 1
1Es 5:29 the sons of Keros, the sons of Siaha 2

Ketab 1. Κηταβ
1Es 5:30 sons of Uthai, the sons of Ketab, the sons of Hagab 1

Keturah 1. קְטוּרָה
Gen 25: 1 took another wife, whose name was Ketu'rah. 1
4 All these were the children of Ketu'rah. 1
1Ch 1:32 The sons of Ketu'rah, Abraham's concubine 1
33 All these were the descendants of Ketu'rah. 1

Keziah 1. קְצִיעָה
Job 42:14 first Jemi'mah; and the name of the second Kezi'ah; 1

Kibroth-hattaavah 1. קִבְרוֹת הַתַּאֲוָה
Num11:34 name of that place was called Kib'roth-hatta'avah 1
35 From Kib'roth-hatta'avah the people journeyed 1
33:16 Sinai, and encamped at Kib'roth-hatta'avah. 1
17 they set out from Kib'roth-hatta'avah, and encamped 1
Deu 9:22 also, and at Massah, and at Kib'roth-hatta'avah 1

Kibzaim 1. קִבְצַיִם
Jos 21:22 Kib'za-im with its pasture lands, Beth-hor'on 1

Kidron 1. קִדְרוֹן 2. Κεδρών
2Sm 15:23 and the king crossed the brook Kidron 1
1Kg 2:37 on the day you go forth, and cross the brook Kidron 1
15:13 down her image and burned it at the brook Kidron. 1
2Kg 23: 4 outside Jerusalem in the fields of the Kidron 1
6 outside Jerusalem to the brook Kidron 1
6 he brought . . and burned it at the brook Kidron 1
12 and cast the dust of them into the brook Kidron. 1
2Ch 15:16 crushed it, and burned it at the brook Kidron. 1
29:16 Levites . . carried it out to the brook Kidron. 1
30:14 they took away and threw into the Kidron valley. 1
Jer 31:40 and all the fields as far as the brook Kidron 1
Joh 18: 1 he went forth . . across the Kidron valley 2

Kilan 1. Κιλαν
1Es 5:15 The sons of Kilan and Azetas, 67. 1

Kinah 1. קִינָה
Jos 15:22 Kinah, Dimo'nah, Ada'dah 1

King's Pool 1. בְּרֵכַת הַמֶּלֶךְ
Neh 2:14 went on to the Fountain Gate and to the King's Pool; 1

Kir 1. קִיר
2Kg 16: 9 and took it, carrying its people captive to Kir 1
Isa 15: 1 because Kir is laid waste in a night 1
22: 6 bore the quiver . . and Kir uncovered the shield. 1
Ams 1: 5 and the people of Syria shall go into exile to Kir 1
9: 7 Did I not bring up . . and the Syrians from Kir? 1

Kir-hareseth 1. קִיר חֲרֶשֶׂת
2Kg 3:25 only its stones were left in Kir-har'eseth 1
Isa 16: 7 stricken, for the raisin-cakes of Kir-har'eseth. 1

Kir-heres 1. קִיר הֶרֶשׂ 2. קִיר חֶרֶשׂ
Isa 16:11 soul moans . . for Moab, and my heart for Kir-he'res. 1
Jer 48:31 for all Moab; for the men of Kir-he'res I mourn. 2
36 moans like a flute for the men of Kir-he'res; 2

Kiriath-arba 1. קִרְיַת אַרְבַּע
Gen 23: 2 Sarah died at Kir'iath-ar'ba (that is, Hebron) 1
35:27 his father Isaac at Mamre, or Kir'iath-ar'ba 1
Jos 14:15 Now the name of Hebron formerly was Kir'iath-ar'ba; 1
15:13 a portion among . . Judah, Kir'iath-ar'ba 1
54 Humtah, Kir'iath-ar'ba (that is, Hebron), and Zi'or 1
20: 7 set apart . . and Kir'iath-ar'ba (that is, Hebron) 1
21:11 They gave them Kir'iath-ar'ba . . that is Hebron 1
Jdg 1:10 (the name of Hebron was formerly Kir'iath-ar'ba); 1
Neh 11:25 some . . lived in Kir'iath-ar'ba and its villages 1

Kiriath-baal 1. קִרְיַת בַּעַל
Jos 15:60 Kir'iath-ba'al (that is, Kir'iath-je'arim) 1
18:14 boundary goes . . and it ends at Kir'iath-ba'al 1

Kiriath-huzoth 1. קִרְיַת חֻצוֹת
Num22:39 Balaam . . Balak . . came to Kir'iath-hu'zoth. 1

Kiriath-jearim 1. קִרְיַת יְעָרִים
Jos 9:17 Chephi'rah, Be-er'oth, and Kir'iath-je'arim. 1
15: 9 round to Ba'alah (that is, Kir'iath-je'arim); 1
60 Kir'iath-ba'al (that is, Kir'iath-je'arim) 1
18:14 at Kir'iath-ba'al (that is, Kir'iath-je'arim) 1
15 side begins at the outskirts of Kir'iath-je'arim; 1
28 Ha-eleph, Jebus . . Gib'e-ah and Kir'iath-je'arim •
Jdg 18:12 went up and encamped at Kir'iath-je'arim in Judah. 1
12 to this day; behold, it is west of Kir'iath-je'arim. 1
1Sm 6:21 sent . . to the inhabitants of Kir'iath-je'arim 1
7: 1 the men of Kir'iath-je'arim came and took up the ark 1
2 the day that the ark was lodged at Kir'iath-je'arim 1
1Ch 2:50 Shobal the father of Kir'iath-je'arim. 1
52 Shobal . . father of Kir'iath-je'arim had other 1
53 the families of Kir'iath-je'arim 1
13: 5 to bring the ark of God from Kir'iath-je'arim. 1
6 to Ba'alah, that is, to Kir'iath-je'arim 1
2Ch 1: 4 ark of God from Kir'iath-je'arim 1
Neh 7:29 men of Kir'iath-je'arim, Chephi'rah 1
Jer 26:20 Uri'ah the son of Shemai'ah from Kir'iath-je'arim. 1

Kiriath-sannah 1. קִרְיַת סַנָּה
Jos 15:49 Dannah, Kir'iath-san'nah (that is, Debir) 1

Kiriath-sepher 1. קִרְיַת סֵפֶר
Jos 15:15 the name of Debir formerly was Kir'iath-se'pher. 1
16 Whoever smites Kir'iath-se'pher, and takes it 1
Jdg 1:11 The name of Debir was formerly Kir'iath-se'pher. 1
12 He who attacks Kir'iath-se'pher and takes it, I will 1

Kiriathaim 1. קִרְיָתַיִם
Num32:37 sons of Reuben built Heshbon, Elea'leh, Kiriatha'im 1
Jos 13:19 and Kiriatha'im, and Sibmah, and Zer'eth-sha'har 1
1Ch 6:76 and Kiria-tha'im with its pasture lands. 1
Jer 48: 1 Kiriatha'im is put to shame, it is taken; 1
23 and Kiriatha'im, and Beth-ga'mul, and Beth-me'on 1
Ezk 25: 9 Beth-jesh'imoth, Ba'al-me'on, and Kiriatha'im. 1

Kiriatharim 1. קִרְיַת עָרִים 2. Καριαθιαριος
Ezr 2:25 sons of Kir'iathar'im, Chephi'rah, 1
1Es 5:19 The men of Kiriatharim, 25. 2

Kish 1. קִישׁ 2. Κίς 3. Κισαιας
1Sm 9: 1 There was a man of Benjamin whose name was Kish 1
3 Now the asses of Kish, Saul's father, were lost. 1
3 asses . . were lost. So Kish said to Saul his son 1
10:11 What has come over the son of Kish? 1
21 and Saul the son of Kish was taken by lot. 1
14:51 Kish was the father of Saul, and Ner the father 1
2Sm 21:14 And they buried . . in the tomb of Kish his father; 1
1Ch 8:30 His first-born son: Abdon, then Zur, Kish, Ba'al, 1
33 Ner was the father of Kish, Kish of Saul 1
33 Ner was the father of Kish, Kish of Saul 1
9:36 first-born son Abdon, then Zur, Kish, Ba'al, Ner, 1
39 Ner was the father of Kish, Kish of Saul 1
39 father of Kish, Kish of Saul, Saul of Jonathan 1
12: 1 could not move . . because of Saul the son of Kish; 1
23:21 The sons of Mahli: Elea'zar and Kish. 1
22 their kinsmen, the sons of Kish, married them. 1
24:29 Of Kish, the sons of Kish: Jerah'meel. 1
29 Of Kish, the sons of Kish: Jerah'meel. 1
26:28 all that Samuel the seer, and Saul the son of Kish 1
2Ch 29:12 Levites arose . . Kish the son of Abdi 1
Est 2: 5 the son of Ja'ir, son of Shim'e-i, son of Kish 1
Act 13:21 Saul the son of Kish, a man of the tribe of Benjamin 2
AEs 11: 2 Mordecai the son of Jair, son of Shimei, son of Kish 3

Kishi 1. קִישִׁי
1Ch 6:44 Ethan the son of Kishi, son of Abdi, son of Malluch 1

Kishion 1. קִשְׁיוֹן
Jos 19:20 Rabbith, Kish'ion, Ebez 1
21:28 of Is'sachar, Ki'shion with its pasture lands 1

Kishon 1. קִישׁוֹן
Jdg 4: 7 to meet you by the river Kishon with his chariots 1
13 from Haro'sheth-ha-goiim to the river Kishon. 1
5:21 The torrent Kishon swept them away 1
21 the onrushing torrent, the torrent Kishon. 1
1Kg 18:40 Eli'jah brought them down to the brook Kishon 1
Ps 83: 9 as to Sis'era and Jabin at the river Kishon 1

Kitron 1. קִטְרוֹן
Jdg 1:30 did not drive out the inhabitants of Kitron 1

Kittim 1. כִּתִּי 2. Χεττιμ
Gen 10: 4 The sons of Javan: Eli'shah, Tarshish, Kittim 1
Num24:24 ships shall come from Kittim and shall afflict 1
1Ch 1: 7 of Javan: Eli'shah, Tarshish, Kittim, and Ro'danim. 1
Dan 11:30 For ships of Kittim shall come against him 1
1Mc 1: 1 who came from the land of Kittim 2

Koa 1. קוֹעַ
Ezk 23:23 and Sho'a and Ko'a, and all the Assyrians with them 1

Kohath 1. קְהָת
Gen 46:11 The sons of Levi: Gershon, Kohath, and Merar'i. 1
Exd 6:16 sons of Levi . . Gershon, Kohath, and Merar'i 1
18 The sons of Kohath: Amram, Izhar, Hebron, 1
18 the years of the life of Kohath being 133 years. 1
Num 3:17 sons of Levi . . Gershon and Kohath and Merar'i. 1
19 the sons of Kohath by their families 1
27 Of Kohath were the family of the Amramites 1
29 The families of the sons of Kohath were to encamp 1
4: 2 Take a census of the sons of Kohath 1
4 This is the service of the sons of Kohath 1
15 sons of Kohath shall come to carry these 1
15 things . . which the sons of Kohath are to carry. 1
7: 9 to the sons of Kohath he gave none 1
16: 1 Korah the son of Izhar, son of Kohath, son of Levi 1
26:57 of Kohath, the family of the Ko'hathites; 1
58 Kohath was the father of Amram. 1
1Ch 6: 1 The sons of Levi: Gershom, Kohath, and Merar'i. 1
2 sons of Kohath: Amram, Izhar, Hebron, and Uz'ziel. 1
16 The sons of Levi: Gershom, Kohath, and Merar'i. 1
18 sons of Kohath: Amram, Izhar, Hebron, and Uz'ziel. 1
22 sons of Kohath: Ammin'adab . . Korah . . Assir 1
38 son of Kohath, son of Levi, son of Israel; 1
66 some of the families of the sons of Kohath 1
15: 5 of the sons of Kohath, Uri'el the chief 1
23: 6 the sons of Levi: Gershom, Kohath, and Merar'i. 1
12 sons of Kohath: Amram, Izhar, Hebron, and Uz'ziel 1

Kohathite 1. בֶּן קְהָת 2. קְהָתִי
Num 3:27 these are the families of the Ko'hathites. 2
30 house of the families of the Ko'hathites. 2
4:18 tribe of the families of the Ko'hathites 2
34 Moses . . numbered the sons of the Ko'hathites 2
37 number of the families of the Ko'hathites 2
10:21 Ko'hathites set out, carrying the holy things 2
26:57 of Kohath, the family of the Ko'hathites; 2
Jos 21: 4 lot came out for the families of the Ko'hathites. 2
5 And the rest of the Ko'hathites received by lot 1
10 one of the families of the Ko'hathites 2
20 the rest of the Ko'hathites . . of the Levites 1
20 the rest . . belonging to the Ko'hathite families 1
26 of the families of the rest of the Ko'hathites 1
1Ch 6:33 Of the sons of the Ko'hathites: Heman the singer 2
54 sons of Aaron of the families of Ko'hathites 2
61 To the rest of the Ko'hathites were given by lot 1
70 for the rest of the families of the Ko'hathites. 1
9:32 Also some of their kinsmen of the Ko'hathites 2
2Ch 20:19 Levites, of the Ko'hathites and the Kor'ahites 2
29:12 of the sons of the Ko'hathites; 2
34:12 of the sons of the Ko'hathites 2

Kola 1. Κωλα
Jdt 15: 4 Betomasthaim and Bebai and Choba and Kola 1

Kolaiah 1. קוֹלָיָה
Neh 11: 7 Jo'ed, son of Pedai'ah, son of Ko-lai'ah 1
Jer 29:21 concerning Ahab the son of Kola'iah and Zedeki'ah 1

Kona 1. Κωνα
Jdt 4: 4 Kona and Beth-horon and Belmain and Jericho 1

Korah 1. קֹרַח 2. Κόρε
Gen 36: 5 Oholiba'mah bore Je'ush, Jalam, and Korah. 1
14 she bore to Esau Je'ush, Jalam, and Korah. 1
16 Korah, Gatam, and Am'alek; these are the chiefs 1
18 Esau's wife: the chiefs Je'ush, Jalam, and Korah 1
Exd 6:21 The sons of Izhar: Korah, Nepheg, and Zichri. 1
24 The sons of Korah: Assir, Elka'nah, and Abi'asaph; 1
Num16: 1 Korah the son of Izhar, son of Kohath, son of Levi 1
5 said to Korah and all his company, "In the morning 1
6 Do this: take censers, Korah and all his company; 1
8 Moses said to Korah, "Hear now, you sons of Levi 1
16 Moses said to Korah, "Be present, you and all 1
19 Then Korah assembled all the congregation 1
24 Get away from about the dwelling of Korah, Dathan 1
27 got away from about the dwelling of Korah, Dathan 1
32 men that belonged to Korah and all their goods. 1
40 lest he become as Korah and as his company– 1
49 besides those who died in the affair of Korah. 1
26: 9 Dathan and Abi'ram . . in the company of Korah 1
10 earth . . swallowed them up together with Korah 1
11 Notwithstanding, the sons of Korah did not die. 1
27: 3 against the LORD in the company of Korah 1
1Ch 1:35 sons of Esau: Eli'phaz, Reu'el, Je'ush, and Korah 1
2:43 sons of Hebron: Korah, Tap'puah, Rekem, and Shema. 1
6:22 of Kohath: Ammin'adab . . Korah his son, Assir 1
37 son of Assir, son of Ebi'asaph, son of Korah 1
9:19 Ko're, son of Ebi'asaph, son of Korah 1
Ps 42: 0 A Maskil of the Sons of Korah. 1
44: 0 A Maskil of the Sons of Korah. 1
45: 0 A Maskil of the Sons of Korah; a love song. 1
46: 0 To the choirmaster. A Psalm of the Sons of Korah. 1
47: 0 To the choirmaster. A Psalm of the Sons of Korah. 1
48: 0 A Song. A Psalm of the Sons of Korah. 1
49: 0 To the choirmaster. A Psalm of the Sons of Korah. 1
84: 0 A Psalm of the Sons of Korah. 1
85: 0 To the choirmaster. A Psalm of the Sons of Korah. 1
87: 0 A Psalm of the Sons of Korah. A Song. 1
88: 0 A Song. A Psalm of the Sons of Korah. 1
Jde 1:11 and perish in Korah's rebellion. 2
Sir 45:18 their men and the company of Korah 2

Korahite 1. קָרְחִי
Exd 6:24 these are the families of the Ko'rahites. 1
Num26:58 of Levi . . the family of the Ko'rahites. 1
1Ch 9:19 kinsmen of his fathers' house, the Ko'rahites 1
31 the first-born of Shallum the Ko'rahite 1
12: 6 Az'arel, Jo-e'zer, and Jasho'be-am, the Ko'rahites; 1
26: 1 of the Ko'rahites, Meshelemi'ah the son of Ko're 1
19 among the Ko'rahites and the sons of Merar'i. 1
2Ch 20:19 Levites, of the Ko'hathites and the Kor'ahites 1

Kore 1. קוֹרֵא
1Ch 9:19 Shallum the son of Ko're, son of Ebi'asaph 1
26: 1 of the Ko'rahites, Meshelemi'ah the son of Ko're 1
2Ch 31:14 Ko're . . was over the freewill offerings to God 1

Koz 1. קוֹץ
1Ch 4: 8 Koz was the father of Anub, Zobe'bah 1

Kue 1. קְוֵה
1Kg 10:28 Solomon's import of horses was from Egypt and Ku'e 1
28 king's traders received them from Ku'e at a price. 1
2Ch 1:16 Solomon's import of horses was from Egypt and Ku'e 1
16 and the king's traders received them from Ku'e 1

Kushaiah 1. קוּשָׁיָהוּ
1Ch 15:17 their brethren, Ethan the son of Kusha'iah 1

Laadah 1. לַעְדָּה
1Ch 4:21 sons of Shelah . . La'adah the father 1

Laban 1. לָבָן 2. Λαβάν
Gen 24:29 Rebekah had a brother whose name was Laban; 1
29 name was Laban; and Laban ran out to the man 1
32 Laban ungirded the camels, and gave him straw 1
50 Laban and Bethu'el answered, "The thing comes 1
25:20 Rebekah . . the sister of Laban the Aramean. 1
27:43 arise, flee to Laban my brother in Haran 1
28: 2 daughters of Laban your mother's brother. 1
5 went to Paddan-aram to Laban, the son of Bethu'el 1
29: 5 said to them, "Do you know Laban the son of Nahor? 1
10 Now when Jacob saw Rachel the daughter of Laban 1
10 saw . . the sheep of Laban his mother's brother 1
10 watered the flock of Laban his mother's brother. 1
13 When Laban heard the tidings of Jacob 1
13 Jacob told Laban all these things 1
14 Laban said . . "Surely you are my bone and flesh! 1
15 Laban said to Jacob, "Because you are my kinsman 1
16 Now Laban had two daughters; 1
19 Laban said, "It is better that I give her to you 1
21 Then Jacob said to Laban, "Give me my wife 1
22 Laban gathered together all the men of the place 1
24 Laban gave his maid Zilpah to his daughter Leah 1
25 Jacob said to Laban, "What is this you have done 1
26 Laban said, "It is not so done in our country 1
28 then Laban gave him his daughter Rachel to wife. 2
29 Laban gave his maid Bilhah to his daughter 1
30 and served Laban for another seven years. 1
30:25 When Rachel had borne Joseph, Jacob said to Laban 1
27 Laban said to him, "If you will allow me to say so 1
34 Laban said, "Good! Let it be as you have said. 1
35 that day Laban removed the he-goats 1
36 and Jacob fed the rest of Laban's flock. 1
40 striped and all the black in the flock of Laban; 1
40 and did not put them with Laban's flock. 1
42 the feebler were Laban's, and the stronger 1
31: 1 Jacob heard that the sons of Laban were saying 1
2 Jacob saw that Laban did not regard him 1
12 for I have seen all that Laban is doing to you. 1
19 Laban had gone to shear his sheep 1
20 Jacob outwitted Laban the Aramean, in that he did 1
22 When it was told Laban on the third day that Jacob 1
24 God came to Laban the Aramean in a dream by night 1
25 Laban overtook Jacob. Now Jacob had pitched 1
25 Laban with his kinsmen encamped in the hill 1
26 Laban said to Jacob, "What have you done 1
31 Jacob answered Laban, "Because I was afraid 1
33 Laban went into Jacob's tent, and into Leah's 1
34 Laban felt all about the tent, but did not find 1
36 Then Jacob became angry, and upbraided Laban; 1
36 Jacob said to Laban, "What is my offense? 1
43 Then Laban answered and said to Jacob 1
47 Laban called it Je'gar-sahadu'tha: but Jacob 1
48 Laban said, "This heap is a witness 1
51 Then Laban said to Jacob, "See this heap 1
55 Early in the morning Laban arose 1
32: 4 I have sojourned with Laban, and stayed until now 1
46:18 the sons of Zilpah, whom Laban gave to Leah 1
25 Bilhah, whom Laban gave to Rachel his daughter 1
Deu 1: 1 Paran and Tophel, Laban, Haze'roth, and Di'zahab. 1
Jdt 8:26 while he was keeping the sheep of Laban 2

Laccunus 1. Λακκουνος
1Es 9:31 Laccunus and Naidus 1

Lacedaemonian 1. Λακαιδαιμονιοι
2Mc 5: 9 having embarked to go to the Lacedaemonians 1

Lachish 1. לָכִישׁ
Jos 10: 3 to Japhi'a king of Lachish, and to Debir . . of Eglon 1
5 of Jarmuth, the king of Lachish, and the king 1
23 king of Jarmuth, the king of Lachish 1
31 Joshua passed . . to Lachish, and laid siege to it 1
32 and the LORD gave Lachish into the hand of Israel 1
33 Then Horam king of Gezer came up to help Lachish; 1
34 And Joshua passed on . . from Lachish to Eglon; 1
35 utterly destroyed . . as he had done to Lachish. 1
12:11 the king of Jarmuth, one; the king of Lachish, one; 1
15:39 Lachish, Bozkath, Eglon 1
2Kg 14:19 they made a conspiracy . . and he fled to Lachish. 1
19 But they sent after him to Lachish, and slew him 1
18:14 sent to the king of Assyria at Lachish, saying 1
17 Assyria sent . . with a great army from Lachish 1
19: 8 for he heard that the king had left Lachish. 1
2Ch 11: 9 Adora'im, Lachish, Aze'kan 1
25:27 made a conspiracy . . and he fled to Lachish. 1
27 they sent after him to Lachish, and slew him there. 1
32: 9 Sennach'erib . . who was besieging Lachish 1
Neh 11:30 Lachish and its fields 1
Isa 36: 2 from Lachish to King Hezeki'ah at Jerusalem 1
37: 8 for he had heard that the king had left Lachish. 1
Jer 34: 7 the cities . . that were left, Lachish and Aze'kah; 1
Mic 1:13 Harness the steeds . . inhabitants of Lachish; 1

Ladan 1. לַעְדָּן
1Ch 7:26 Ladan his son, Ammi'hud his son, Eli'shama his son 1
23: 7 The sons of Gershom were Ladan and Shim'e-i. 1
8 sons of Ladan: Jehi'el . . and Zetham, and Jo'el 1
9 the heads of the fathers' houses of Ladan. 1
26:21 The sons of Ladan, the sons of the Gershonites 1
21 sons of the Gershonites belonging to Ladan 1
21 belonging to Ladan the Gershonite: Jehi'eli. 1

Lael 1. לָאֵל
Num 3:24 son of La'el as head of the fathers' house 1

Lahad 1. לָהַד
1Ch 4: 2 and Jahath was the father of Ahu'mai and Lahad. 1

Lahmam 1. לַחְמָם
Jos 15:40 Cabbon, Lahmam, Chitlish 1

Lahmi 1. לַחְמִי
1Ch 20: 5 Elha'nan . . slew Lahmi the brother of Goliath 1

Laish 1. לַיִשׁ
Jdg 18: 7 came to La'ish, and saw the people who were there 1
14 men who had gone to spy out the country of La'ish 1
27 the Danites came to La'ish, to a people quiet 1
29 but the name of the city was La'ish at the first. 1
1Sm 25:44 Palti the son of La'ish, who was of Gallim. 1
2Sm 3:15 and took her from . . Pal'ti-el the son of La'ish. 1

Laishah 1. לַיְשָׁה
Isa 10:30 O daughter of Gallim! Hearken, O La'ishah! 1

Lakkum 1. לַקּוּם
Jos 19:33 ran . . as far as Lakkum; and it ended at the Jordan; 1

Lamech 1. לֶמֶךְ 2. Λάμεχ
Gen 4:18 and Me-thu'sha-el the father of Lamech. 1
19 Lamech took two wives . . name of the one was Adah 1
23 Lamech said to his wives: "Adah and Zillah 1
23 hear my voice; you wives of Lamech 1
24 truly Lamech seventy-sevenfold. 1
5:25 Methu'selah . . became the father of Lamech. 1

26 Methu'selah lived after the birth of Lamech 1
28 When Lamech had lived 182 years 1
30 Lamech lived after the birth of Noah 595 years 1
31 Thus all the days of Lamech were 777 years; 1
1Ch 1: 3 Enoch, Me-thu'selah, Lamech; 1
Lke 3:36 the son of Shem, the son of Noah, the son of Lamech 2

Laodicea 1. Λαοδίκεια
Col 2: 1 and for those at La-odice'a 1
4:13 for those in La-odice'a and in Hi-erap'olis. 1
15 Give my greetings to the brethren at La-odice'a 1
16 see that you read also the letter from La-odice'a. 1
Rev 1:11 seven churches, to Ephesus . . and to La-odice'a 1
3:14 And to the angel of the church in La-odice'a write 1

Laodicean 1. Λαοδικεύς
Col 4:16 have it read also in the church of the La-odice'ans; 1

Lappidoth 1. לַפִּידוֹת
Jdg 4: 4 Now Deb'orah, a prophetess, the wife of Lapp'idoth 1

Lasea 1. Λασαία
Act 27: 8 Fair Havens, near which was the city of Lase'a. 1

Lasha 1. לֶשַׁע
Gen 10:19 Gomor'rah, Admah, and Zeboi'im, as far as Lasha. 1

Lasharon 1. לַשָּׁרוֹן
Jos 12:18 the king of Aphek, one; the king of Lashar'on, one; 1

Lasthenes 1. Λασθενης
1Mc 11:31 wrote concerning you to Lasthenes our kinsman 1
32 'King Demetrius to Lasthenes his father 1

Latin 1. Ῥωμαϊστί
Joh 19:20 it was written in Hebrew, in Latin, and in Greek. 1

Lazarus 1. Λάζαρος
Lke 16:20 at his gate lay a poor man named Laz'arus 1
23 and saw Abraham far off and Laz'arus in his bosom. 1
24 send Laz'arus to dip the end of his finger in water 1
25 Laz'arus in like manner evil things 1
Joh 11: 1 Now a certain man was ill, Laz'arus of Bethany 1
2 It was Mary . . whose brother Laz'arus was ill. 1
5 Jesus loved Martha and her sister and Laz'arus. 1
11 Our friend Laz'arus has fallen asleep 1
14 Jesus told them plainly, "Laz'arus is dead; 1
17 Laz'arus had already been in the tomb four days. •
43 Laz'arus, come out. 1
12: 1 Jesus came to Bethany, where Laz'arus was 1
2 Laz'arus was one of those at table with him. 1
9 to see Laz'arus, whom he had raised from the dead. 1
10 planned to put Laz'arus also to death 1
17 when he called Laz'arus out of the tomb 1

Leah 1. לֵאָה
Gen 29:16 had two daughters; the name of the older was Leah 1
17 Leah's eyes were weak, but Rachel was beautiful 1
23 in the evening he took his daughter Leah 1
24 Laban gave his maid Zilpah to his daughter Leah 1
25 in the morning, behold, it was Leah; 1
30 he loved Rachel more than Leah, and served Laban 1
31 When the LORD saw that Leah was hated 1
32 Leah conceived and bore a son 1
30: 9 Leah saw that she had ceased bearing children 1
10 Then Leah's maid Zilpah bore Jacob a son. 1
11 And Leah said, "Good fortune! 1
12 Leah's maid Zilpah bore Jacob a second son. 1
13 Leah said, "Happy am I! For the women will call me 1
14 in the field, and brought them to his mother Leah. 1
14 Then Rachel said to Leah, "Give me, I pray 1
16 Leah went out to meet him, and said 1
17 God hearkened to Leah, and she conceived and bore 1
18 Leah said, "God has given me my hire 1
19 Leah conceived again, and she bore Jacob a sixth 1
20 Then Leah said, "God has endowed me 1
31: 4 Jacob . . called Rachel and Leah into the field 1
14 Then Rachel and Leah answered him 1
33 Laban went into Jacob's tent, and into Leah's 1
33 he did not find them. And he went out of Leah's tent 1
33: 1 he divided the children among Leah and Rachel 1
2 in front, then Leah with her children, 1
7 Leah likewise and her children drew near 1
34: 1 Dinah the daughter of Leah, whom she had borne 1
35:23 sons of Leah: Reuben (Jacob's first-born) 1
26 The sons of Zilpah, Leah's maid: Gad and Asher. 1
46:15 these are the sons of Leah, whom she bore to Jacob 1
18 the sons of Zilpah, whom Laban gave to Leah 1
49:31 Rebekah his wife; and there I buried Leah– 1
Rut 4:11 the LORD make the woman . . like Rachel and Leah 1

Leannoth 1. לְעַנּוֹת
Ps 88: 0 choirmaster: according to Mahalath Leannoth 1

Lebana 1. לְבָנָה
Neh 7:48 sons of Leba'na, the sons of Hag'aba 1

Lebanah 1. לְבָנָה 2. Λαβανα
Ezr 2:45 sons of Leba'nah, the sons of Hag'abah 1
1Es 5:29 the sons of Padon, the sons of Lebanah 2

Lebanon 1. לְבָנוֹן 2. Λίβανος 3. Libanus
Deu 1: 7 land of the Canaanites, and Lebanon, as far 1
3:25 see . . that goodly hill country, and Lebanon.' 1
11:24 from the wilderness and Lebanon 1
Jos 1: 4 From the wilderness and this Lebanon as far 1
9: 1 along the coast of the Great Sea toward Lebanon 1
11:17 as far as Ba'al-gad in the valley of Lebanon 1
12: 7 from Ba'al-gad in the valley of Lebanon 1
13: 5 and all Lebanon, toward the sunrising 1
6 hill country from Lebanon to Mis'rephoth-ma'im 1
Jdg 3: 3 Hivites who dwelt on Mount Lebanon, from Mount 1
9:15 of the bramble and devour the cedars of Lebanon.' 1
1Kg 4:33 trees, from the cedar that is in Lebanon 1
5: 6 command that cedars of Lebanon be cut for me; 1
9 servants . . bring it down to the sea from Lebanon; 1
14 he sent them to Lebanon . . in relays; 1
14 be a month in Lebanon and two months at home; 1
7: 2 He built the House of the Forest of Lebanon; 1
9:19 build in Jerusalem, in Lebanon, and in all the land 1
10:17 put them in the House of the Forest of Lebanon. 1
21 the vessels of the House of the Forest of Lebanon 1
2Kg 14: 9 A thistle on Lebanon sent to a cedar on Lebanon 1
9 A thistle on Lebanon sent to a cedar on Lebanon 1
9 a wild beast of Lebanon passed by and trampled 1
19:23 I have gone up . . to the far recesses of Lebanon; 1
2Ch 2: 8 cedar, cypress, and algum timber from Lebanon 1
8 your servants know how to cut timber in Lebanon. 1
16 will cut whatever timber you need from Lebanon 1
8: 6 desired to build in Jerusalem, in Lebanon 1
9:16 put them in the House of the Forest of Lebanon. 1
20 vessels of the House of the Forest of Lebanon 1
25:18 A thistle on Lebanon sent to a cedar on Lebanon 1
18 A thistle on Lebanon sent to a cedar on Lebanon 1
18 wild beast of Lebanon passed by and trampled 1
Ezr 3: 7 cedar trees from Lebanon to the sea, to Joppa 1
Ps 29: 5 LORD breaks the cedars of Lebanon. 1
6 He makes Lebanon to skip like a calf 1
37:35 towering like a cedar of Lebanon. 2
72:16 may its fruit be like Lebanon; and may men blossom 1
92:12 The righteous . . grow like a cedar in Lebanon. 1
104:16 cedars of Lebanon which he planted. 1
Sng 3: 9 made . . a palanquin from the wood of Lebanon. 1
4: 8 Come with me from Lebanon, my bride; come with me 1
8 from Lebanon, my bride; come with me from Lebanon. 1
11 of your garments is like the scent of Lebanon. 1
15 living water, and flowing streams from Lebanon. 1
5:15 His appearance is like Lebanon 1
7: 4 Your nose is like a tower of Lebanon 1
Isa 2:13 all the cedars of Lebanon, lofty and lifted up; 1
10:34 and Lebanon with its majestic trees will fall. 1
14: 8 rejoice at you, the cedars of Lebanon, saying 1
29:17 Lebanon shall be turned into a fruitful field 1
33: 9 Lebanon is confounded and withers away; 1
35: 2 The glory of Lebanon shall be given to it 1
37:24 I have gone up . . to the far recesses of Lebanon; 1
40:16 Lebanon would not suffice for fuel 1
60:13 The glory of Lebanon shall come to you 1
Jer 18:14 Does the snow of Lebanon leave the crags 1
22: 6 You are as Gilead to me, as the summit of Lebanon 1
20 Go up to Lebanon, and cry out, and lift up your voice 1
23 O inhabitant of Lebanon, nested among the cedars 1
Ezk 17: 3 came to Lebanon and took the top of the cedar; 1
27: 5 they took a cedar from Lebanon to make a mast 1
31: 3 Behold, I will liken you to a cedar in Lebanon 1
15 I will clothe Lebanon in gloom for it 1
16 the trees of Eden, the choice and best of Lebanon 1
Hos 14: 6 and his fragrance like Lebanon. 1
7 fragrance shall be like the wine of Lebanon. 1
Nah 1: 4 the bloom of Lebanon fades. 1
Hab 2:17 The violence done to Lebanon will overwhelm you; 1
Zec 10:10 and to Lebanon, till there is no room for them. 1
11: 1 Open your doors, O Lebanon 1
1Es 4:48 wrote letters . . to those in Lebanon 2
48 to bring cedar timber from Lebanon to Jerusalem 2
5:55 to bring cedar logs from Lebanon 2
2Es 15:20 from the east and from Lebanon 3
Jdt 1: 7 Cilicia and Damascus and Lebanon 2
Sir 24:13 I grew tall like a cedar in Lebanon 2
50: 8 like a green shoot on Lebanon on a summer day; 2
12 like a young cedar on Lebanon 2

Lebaoth 1. לְבָאוֹת
Jos 15:32 Leba'oth, Shilhim, A'in, and Rimmon 1

Lebonah 1. לְבוֹנָה
Jdg 21:19 is north of Bethel . . and south of Lebo'nah. 1

Lecah 1. לֵכָה
1Ch 4:21 sons of Shelah . . Er the father of Lecah 1

Lehabim 1. לְהָבִים
Gen 10:13 father of . . An'amim, Leha'bim, Naph-tu'him 1
1Ch 1:11 father of Ludim, An'amim, Le'habim, Naph-tu'him 1

Lehem 1. לֶחֶם
1Ch 4:22 Saraph, who ruled in Moab and returned to Lehem 1

Lehi 1. לֶחִי
Jdg 15: 9 up and encamped in Judah, and made a raid on Lehi. 1
14 When he came to Lehi, the Philistines came 1
19 God split open the hollow place that is at Lehi 1
19 it was called En-hakkor'e; it is at Lehi to this day. 1
2Sm 23:11 The Philistines gathered together at Lehi 1

Lemuel 1. לְמוּאֵל
Prv 31: 1 The words of Lemuel, king of Massa 1
4 not for kings, O Lemuel, it is not for kings to drink 1

Leshem 1. לֶשֶׁם
Jos 19:47 the Danites went up and fought against Leshem 1
47 settled . . calling Leshem, Dan, after the name 1

Letushim 1. לְטוּשִׁם
Gen 25: 3 The sons of Dedan were Asshu'rim, Letu'shim 1

Leummim 1. לְאֻמִּים
Gen 25: 3 Dedan were Asshu'rim, Letu'shim, and Le-um'mim 1

Levi 1. לֵוִי 2. Λευί 3. Λευις 4. Levi
Gen 29:34 therefore his name was called Levi. 1
34:25 sons of Jacob, Simeon and Levi, Dinah's brothers 1
30 Then Jacob said to Simeon and Levi 1
35:23 sons of Leah . . Simeon, Levi, Judah, Is'sachar 1
46:11 The sons of Levi: Gershon, Kohath, and Merar'i. 1
49: 5 Simeon and Levi are brothers; 1
Exd 1: 2 Reuben, Simeon, Levi, and Judah 1
2: 1 Now a man from the house of Levi went and took 1
1 a man . . went and took to wife a daughter of Levi. 1
6:16 These are the names of the sons of Levi according 1
16 the years of the life of Levi being 137 years. 1
32:26 Come to me." And all the sons of Levi gathered 1
28 the sons of Levi did according to the word of Moses; 1
Num 1:49 Only the tribe of Levi you shall not number 1
3: 6 Bring the tribe of Levi near, and set them before 1
15 Number the sons of Levi, by fathers' houses 1
17 these were the sons of Levi by their names 1
4: 2 sons of Kohath from among the sons of Levi 1
16: 1 Korah the son of Izhar, son of Kohath, son of Levi 1
7 You have gone too far, sons of Levi! 1
8 Moses said to Korah, "Hear now, you sons of Levi 1
10 all your brethren the sons of Levi with you? 1
17: 3 write Aaron's name upon the rod of Levi. 1
8 rod of Aaron for the house of Levi had sprouted 1
18: 2 brethren also, the tribe of Levi 1
26:58 families of Levi: the family of the Libnites 1
59 Amram's wife was Joch'ebed the daughter of Levi 1
59 Joch'ebed . . who was born to Levi in Egypt; 1
Deu 10: 8 LORD set apart the tribe of Levi to carry the ark 1
9 Therefore Levi has no portion or inheritance 1
18: 1 Levitical priests, that is, all the tribe of Levi 1
21: 5 priests the sons of Levi shall come forward 1
27:12 stand upon Mount Ger'izim . . Simeon, Levi, Judah 1
31: 9 Moses . . gave it to the priests the sons of Levi 1
33: 8 of Levi he said, "Give to Levi thy Thummim 1
8 Give to Levi thy Thummim, and thy Urim to thy godly 2
Jos 13:14 To the tribe of Levi . . Moses gave no inheritance; 1
33 to the tribe of Levi Moses gave no inheritance; 1
1Ch 2: 1 These are the sons of Israel: Reuben, Simeon, Levi 1
6: 1 The sons of Levi: Gershom, Kohath, and Merar'i. 1
16 The sons of Levi: Gershom, Kohath, and Merar'i. 1
38 son of Kohath, son of Levi, son of Israel; 1
43 son of Jahath, son of Gershom, son of Levi. 1
47 son of Mahli, son of Mushi, son of Merar'i, son of Levi; 1
21: 6 not include Levi and Benjamin in the numbering 1
23: 6 divisions corresponding to the sons of Levi 1
14 sons of Moses . . named among the tribe of Levi. 1
24 were the sons of Levi by their fathers' houses 1
24:20 And of the rest of the sons of Levi 1
27:17 for Levi, Hashabi'ah the son of Kem'uel; 1
Ezr 8:15 I found there none of the sons of Levi. 1
18 sons of Mahli the son of Levi, son of Israel 1
Neh 10:39 For the people of Israel and the sons of Levi 1
12:23 sons of Levi, heads of fathers' houses 1
Ps 135:20 O house of Levi, bless the LORD! 1
Ezk 40:46 sons of Zadok, who alone among the sons of Levi may 1
48:31 of Reuben, the gate of Judah, and the gate of Levi 1
Zec 12:13 the family of the house of Levi by itself 1
Mal 2: 4 that my covenant with Levi may hold, says the LORD 1
8 you have corrupted the covenant of Levi 1
3: 3 he will purify the sons of Levi and refine them 1
Mrk 2:14 as he passed on, he saw Levi the son of Alphaeus 2
Lke 3:24 the son of Matthat, the son of Levi 2
29 the son of Matthat, the son of Levi 2
5:27 he went out, and saw a tax collector, named Levi 2
29 Levi made him a great feast in his house 2
Heb 7: 5 those descendants of Levi 2
9 Levi himself . . paid tithes through Abraham 2
Rev 7: 7 12,000 of the tribe of Levi 2
1Es 8:47 the son of Levi, son of Israel, namely Sherebiah 2
9:14 Meshullam and Levi and Shabbethai 3
2Es 1: 3 son of Aaron, of the tribe of Levi 4
Tob 1: 7 I would give a tenth to the sons of Levi 2

Sir 45: 6 a holy man like him, of the tribe of Levi. 2
4Mc 2:19 censure the households of Simeon and Levi 3

Leviathan 1. לִוְיָתָן 2. Leviathan

Job 3: 8 who are skilled to rouse up Leviathan. 1
41: 1 Can you draw out Levi'athan with a fishhook 1
Ps 74:14 Thou didst crush the heads of Leviathan 1
104:26 There go the ships, and Leviathan which thou 1
Isa 27: 1 will punish Leviathan the fleeing serpent 1
1 Leviathan the twisting serpent 1
2Es 6:49 and the name of the other Leviathan. 2
52 to Leviathan thou didst give the seventh part 2

Levite 1. אִישׁ לֵוִי 2. בֶּן לֵוִי 3. לֵוִי 4. לֵוִי (A) 5. Λευίτης 6. Levites

Exd 4:14 Is there not Aaron, your brother, the Levite? 3
6:19 These are the families of the Levites according 3
25 heads . . of the Levites by their families. 3
38:21 for the work of the Levites under the direction 3
Lev 25:32 Nevertheless the cities of the Levites 3
32 houses . . the Levites may redeem at any time 3
33 if one of the Levites does not exercise his right 3
33 for the houses in the cities of the Levites are 3
Num 1:47 the Levites were not numbered by their 3
50 appoint the Levites over the tabernacle 3
51 When the tabernacle is to set out, the Levites 3
51 the Levites shall set it up. 3
53 the Levites shall encamp around the tabernacle 3
53 the Levites shall keep charge of the tabernacle 3
2:17 with the camp of the Levites in the midst 3
33 the Levites were not numbered among the people 3
3: 9 you shall give the Levites to Aaron and his sons; 3
12 Behold, I have taken the Levites from among 3
12 The Levites shall be mine 3
20 These are the families of the Levites 3
32 chief over the leaders of the Levites 3
39 All who were numbered of the Levites 3
41 you shall take the Levites for me–I am the LORD 3
41 cattle of the Levites instead of all 3
45 Take the Levites instead of all the first-born 3
45 Take . . the cattle of the Levites instead 3
45 Levites shall be mine: I am the LORD. 3
49 over and above those redeemed by the Levites; 3
4:18 Ko'hathites be destroyed from among the Levites; 3
46 All those who were numbered of the Levites 3
7: 5 Accept these . . and give them to the Levites 3
6 wagons and the oxen, and gave them to the Levites. 3
8: 6 Take the Levites from among the people of Israel 3
9 present the Levites before the tent of meeting 3
10 When you present the Levites before the LORD 3
10 Israel shall lay their hands upon the Levites 3
11 Aaron shall offer the Levites before the LORD 3
12 Then the Levites shall lay their hands upon 3
12 to make atonement for the Levites. 3
13 you shall cause the Levites to attend Aaron 3
14 Thus you shall separate the Levites from among 3
14 Levites shall be mine. 3
15 Levites shall go in to do service at the tent 3
18 taken the Levites instead of all the first-born 3
19 given the Levites as a gift to Aaron and his sons 3
20 Thus did Moses and Aaron . . to the Levites; 3
20 LORD commanded Moses concerning the Levites 3
21 the Levites purified themselves from sin 3
22 after that the Levites went in to do 3
22 commanded Moses concerning the Levites 3
24 This is what pertains to the Levites; 3
26 Thus shall you do to the Levites in assigning 3
18: 6 behold, I have taken your brethren the Levites 3
21 To the Levites I have given every tithe in Israel 3
23 Levites shall do the service of the tent 3
24 I have given to the Levites for an inheritance; 3
26 Moreover you shall say to the Levites, 'When you 3
30 then the rest shall be reckoned to the Levites 3
26:57 These are the Levites as numbered according 3
31:30 take . . and give them to the Levites 3
47 the Levites who had charge of the tabernacle 3
35: 2 Command . . Israel, that they give to the Levites 3
2 you shall give to the Levites pasture lands 3
4 pasture lands . . you shall give to the Levites 3
6 cities which you give to the Levites shall be 3
7 the cities which you give to the Levites shall be 48 3
8 each . . shall give of its cities to the Levites. 3
Deu 12:12 rejoice . . you . . and the Levite . . within your towns 3
18 eat . . you and . . the Levite who is within your towns; 3
19 Take heed that you do not forsake the Levite 3
14:27 not forsake the Levite who is within your towns 3
29 Levite, because he has no portion or inheritance 3
16:11 rejoice . . you and . . the Levite who is within 3
14 rejoice . . you and . . the Levite, the sojourner 3
18: 6 Levite comes from any of your towns out of all Israel 3
26:11 rejoice . . you, and the Levite, and the sojourner 3
12 giving it to the Levite, the sojourner 3
13 given it to the Levite, the sojourner 3
27:14 Levites shall declare to all the men of Israel 3
31:25 Moses commanded the Levites who carried the ark 3
Jos 14: 3 but to the Levites he gave no inheritance 3
4 no portion was given to the Levites in the land 3
18: 7 The Levites have no portion among you 3
21: 1 the heads of the fathers' houses of the Levites 3
3 Israel gave to the Levites the following cities 3
4 those Levites . . received by lot from the tribes 3
8 These . . Israel gave by lot to the Levites 3
10 of the Ko'hathites who belonged to the Levites; 2
20 to the Ko'hathite families of the Levites 3
27 Gershonites, one of the families of the Levites 3
34 the rest of the Levites, the Merar'ite families 3
40 the remainder of the families of the Levites 3
41 cities of the Levites . . were in all 48 3
Jdg 17: 7 was a young man of Bethlehem . . who was a Levite; 3
9 I am a Levite of Bethlehem in Judah, and I am going 3
11 And the Levite was content to dwell with the man; 3
12 Micah installed the Levite, and the young man 3
13 prosper me, because I have a Levite as priest. 3
18: 3 they recognized the voice of the young Levite; 3
15 and came to the house of the young Levite 3
19: 1 a certain Levite was sojourning in the remote 3
20: 4 the Levite, the husband of the woman 1
1Sm 6:15 And the Levites took down the ark of the LORD 3
2Sm 15:24 Zadok . . with all the Levites, bearing the ark 3
1Kg 8: 4 the priests and the Levites brought them up. 3
12:31 priests . . who were not of the Levites. 2
1Ch 6:19 families of the Levites according to their 3
48 their brethren the Levites were appointed 3
64 the people of Israel gave the Levites the cities 3
9: 2 the priests, the Levites, and the temple servants. 3
14 Of the Levites: Shemai'ah the son of Hasshub 3
18 the gatekeepers of the camp of the Levites. 3
26 for the four chief gatekeepers, who were Levites 3
31 Mattithi'ah, one of the Levites, the first-born 3
33 the heads of fathers' houses of the Levites 3
34 heads of fathers' houses of the Levites 3
12:26 Of the Levites 4,600. 3
13: 2 priests and Levites in the cities 3
15: 2 No one but the Levites may carry the ark of God 3
4 together the sons of Aaron and the Levites 3
11 David summoned the priests . . and the Levites 3
12 the heads of the fathers' houses of the Levites; 3
14 priests and the Levites sanctified themselves 3
15 Levites carried the ark of God 3
16 David also commanded the chiefs of the Levites 3
17 the Levites appointed Heman the son of Jo'el; 3
22 Chenani'ah, leader of the Levites in music 3
26 God helped the Levites who were carrying 3
27 all the Levites who were carrying the ark 3
16: 4 appointed certain of the Levites as ministers 3
23: 2 assembled . . and the priests and the Levites. 3
3 Levites . . were numbered, and the total was 3
26 Levites no longer need to carry the tabernacle 3
27 number of the Levites from twenty years old 3
24: 6 scribe Shemai'ah the son of Nethan'el, a Levite 3
6 heads of fathers' houses of . . the Levites; 3
30 These were the sons of the Levites according 3
31 heads of fathers' houses . . and of the Levites. 3
26:20 of the Levites, Ahi'jah had charge 3
28:13 the divisions of the priests and of the Levites 3
21 divisions of the priests and the Levites 3
2Ch 5: 4 and the Levites took up the ark. 3
5 the priests and the Levites brought them up. 3
7: 6 priests stood at their posts; the Levites also 3
8:14 he appointed . . the Levites for their offices 3
15 commanded the priests and Levites concerning 3
11:13 priests and the Levites that were in all Israel 3
14 For the Levites left their common lands 3
13: 9 the priests . . the sons of Aaron, and the Levites 3
10 We have . . and Levites for their service. 3
17: 8 with them the Levites, Shemai'ah, Nethani'ah 3
8 with these Levites, the priests Eli'shama 3
19: 8 appointed certain Levites and priests 3
11 the Levites will serve you as officers. 3
20:14 Mattani'ah, a Levite of the sons of Asaph 3
19 the Levites . . stood up to praise the LORD 3
23: 2 went about . . and gathered the Levites 3
4 of you priests and Levites who come off duty 3
6 priests and ministering Levites; they may enter 3
7 The Levites shall surround the king 3
8 The Levites and all Judah did according to all 3
18 under the direction of . . the Levites 3
24: 5 he gathered the priests and the Levites 3
5 But the Levites did not hasten it. 3
6 Why have you not required the Levites to bring 3
11 the chest was brought . . by the Levites 3
29: 4 He brought in the priests and the Levites 3
5 Hear me, Levites! Now sanctify yourselves 3
12 Then the Levites arose, Mahath the son of Ama'sai 3
16 Levites took it and carried it out to the brook 3
25 he stationed the Levites in the house of the LORD 3
26 The Levites stood with the instruments of David 3
30 king and the princes commanded the Levites 3
34 their brethren the Levites helped them 3
34 for the Levites were more upright in heart 3
30:15 priests and the Levites were put to shame 3
16 blood which they received from . . the Levites. 3
17 Levites had to kill the passover lamb 3
21 Levites and the priests praised the LORD 3
22 spoke encouragingly to all the Levites 3
25 Judah, and the priests and the Levites 3
27 the priests and the Levites arose and blessed 3
31: 2 the divisions of the priests and of the Levites 3
2 priests and the Levites, for burnt offerings 3
4 to give the portion due to the . . Levites 3
9 questioned the priests and the Levites 3
12 chief officer . . was Conani'ah the Levite 3
14 Ko're the son of Imnah the Levite 3
17 Levites . . was according to their offices 3
19 portions . . to every one among the Levites 3
34: 9 money . . which the Levites, . . , had collected 3
12 Jahath and Obadi'ah the Levites, of . . Merar'i 3
12 The Levites, all who were skilful 3
13 some of the Levites were scribes, and officials 3
30 king went up . . with . . priests and the Levites 3
35: 3 he said to the Levites who taught all Israel 3
5 a part of a father's house of the Levites. 3
8 to the people, to the priests, and to the Levites. 3
9 chiefs of the Levites, gave to the Levites 3
9 gave to the Levites for the passover offerings 3
10 Levites in their divisions according 3
11 while the Levites flayed the victims. 3
14 Levites prepared for themselves 3
15 their brethren the Levites prepared for them. 3
18 by Josi'ah, and the priests and the Levites 3
Ezr 1: 5 rose up the . . priests and the Levites 3
2:40 The Levites: the sons of Jeshua and Kad'mi-el 3
70 priests, the Levites, and some of the people lived 3
3: 8 priests and the Levites and all who had come 3
8 appointed the Levites, from twenty years old 3
9 along with the sons of Hen'adad and the Levites 3
10 Levites, the sons of Asaph, with cymbals 3
12 many of the priests and Levites and heads 3
6:16 people of Israel, the priests and the Levites 4
18 set . . the Levites in their courses 4
20 priests and the Levites had purified 3
7: 7 went up . . some of the priests and Levites 3
13 Israel or their priests or Levites in my kingdom 4
24 upon any one of the priests, the Levites 4
8:20 David . . had set apart to attend the Levites. 3
29 chief priests and the Levites and the heads 3
30 priests and the Levites took over the weight 3
33 with them were the Levites, Jo'zabad 3
9: 1 people of Israel and the priests and the Levites 3
10: 5 made the . . Levites and all Israel take oath 3
15 Meshul'lam and Shab'bethai the Levite supported 3
23 Of the Levites: Jo'zabad, Shim'e-i, Kelai'ah 3
Neh 3:17 After him the Levites repaired: Rehum the son 3
7: 1 gatekeepers, the singers, and the Levites 3
43 Levites: the sons of Jeshua, namely of Kad'mi-el 3
73 priests, the Levites, the gatekeepers 3
8: 7 Also . . Hanan, Pelai'ah, the Levites 3
9 Nehemi'ah . . Ezra . . , and the Levites who taught 3
11 Levites stilled all the people, saying, "Be quiet 3
13 heads . . with the priests and the Levites, came 3
9: 4 Upon the stairs of the Levites stood Jeshua, Bani 3
5 Then the Levites, Jeshua, Kad'mi-el, Bani 3
38 princes, our Levites, and our priests set 3
10: 9 Levites: Jeshua the son of Azani'ah, Bin'nui 3
28 The rest of the people, the priests, the Levites 3
34 cast lots, the priests, the Levites, and the people 3
37 bring to the Levites the tithes from our ground 3
37 for it is the Levites who collect the tithes 3
38 priest . . shall be with the Levites 3
38 with . . when the Levites receive the tithes; 3
38 Levites shall bring up the tithe of the tithes 3
11: 3 Israel, the priests, the Levites 3
15 Levites: Shemai'ah the son of Hasshub 3
16 Shab'bethai . . of the chiefs of the Levites 3
18 All the Levites in the holy city were 284. 3
20 rest of Israel, and of the priests and the Levites 3
22 overseer of the Levites in Jerusalem was Uzzi 3
36 certain divisions of the Levites in Judah 3
12: 1 These are the priests and the Levites who came up 3
8 Levites . . Kad'mi-el, Sherebi'ah, Judah 3
22 Levites, in the days of Eli'ashib, Joi'ada, Joha'nan 3
24 chiefs of the Levites: Hashabi'ah, Sherebi'ah 3
27 sought the Levites in all their places 3
30 priests and the Levites purified themselves; 3
44 required . . for the priests and for the Levites 3
44 Judah rejoiced over the priests and the Levites 3
47 set apart that which was for the Levites; 3
47 Levites set apart that which was for the sons 3
13: 5 given by commandment to the Levites, singers 3
10 portions of the Levites had not been given 3
10 Levites and the singers, who did the work, 3
13 appointed . . Pedai'ah of the Levites 3
22 I commanded the Levites that they should purify 3
29 covenant of the priesthood and the Levites. 3
30 duties of the priests and Levites 3
Isa 66:21 take for priests and for Levites, says the LORD. 3
Ezk 44:10 the Levites who went far from me, going astray 3
45: 5 shall be for the Levites who minister 3
48:11 people of Israel went astray, as the Levites did. 3
12 adjoining the territory of the Levites. 3
13 Levites shall have an allotment 25,000 cubits 3
22 the property of the Levites and the property 3
Lke 10:32 So likewise a Levite, when he came to the place 5
Joh 1:19 Jews sent priests and Levites from Jerusalem 5
Act 4:36 a Levite, a native of Cyprus 5
1Es 1: 3 he told the Levites . . sanctify themselves 5

5 groupings of the fathers' houses of you Levites 5
7 the people and the priests and Levites. 5
9 gave the Levites for the passover 5,000 sheep 5
10 The priests and the Levites 5
14 the Levites prepared it for themselves 5
16 their brethren the Levites 5
21 the priests and Levites and the men of Judah 5
2: 8 the priests and the Levites 5
4:55 the support for the Levites should be provided 5
5:26 The Levites: the sons of Jeshua and Kadmiel 5
46 The priests, the Levites, and some of the people 5
58 the Levites who were twenty or more years of age 5
58 all the Levites 5
59 the Levites, the sons of Asaph, with cymbals 5
7: 6 the people of Israel, the priests, the Levites 5
9 the priests and the Levites stood 5
10 after the priests and the Levites were purified 5
11 the Levites were all purified together 5
8: 5 some of the priests and Levites 5
10 the priests and Levites and others in our realm 5
22 to be laid on any of the priests or Levites 5
42 of the sons of the priests or of the Levites 5
49 had given for the service of the Levites 5
59 the leaders of the priests and the Levites 5
60 the priests and the Levites who took the silver 5
63 Jozabad . . and Moeth . . , the Levites. 5
69 the leaders and the priests and the Levites 5
96 leaders of the priests and Levites of all Israel 5
9:23 of the Levites: Jozabad and Shimei and Kelaiah 5
37 The priests and the Levites and the men of Israel 5
48 Hanan, Pelaiah, the Levites 5
49 the Levites who were teaching the multitude 5
53 the Levites commanded all the people, saying 5
2Es 10:22 our Levites have gone into captivity 6
AEs 11: 1 who said that he was a priest and a Levite 5

fellow Levite 1. אָח לֵוִי
Deu 18: 7 he may minister . . like all his fellow-Levites 1

male Levite 1. לֵוִי
Num 3:46 over and above the number of the male Levites 1

Levitical 1. לֵוִי 2. Λευίτης 3. Λευιτικός
Deu 17: 9 coming to the Levitical priests, and to the judge 1
18 which is in the charge of the Levitical priests; 1
18: 1 Levitical priests, that is, all the tribe of Levi 1
24: 8 all that the Levitical priests shall direct you; 1
27: 9 Moses and the Levitical priests said to all 1
Jos 3: 3 ark . . being carried by the Levitical priests 1
8:33 the Levitical priests who carried the ark 1
2Ch 5:12 Levitical singers, Asaph, Heman, and Jedu'thun 1
23:18 under the direction of the Levitical priests 1
Jer 33:18 and the Levitical priests shall never lack a man 1
21 and my covenant with the Levitical priests 1
22 and the Levitical priests who minister to me. 1
Ezk 43:19 to the Levitical priests of the family of Zadok 1
44:15 But the Levitical priests, the sons of Zadok 1
Heb 7:11 attainable through the Levit'ical priesthood 3
1Es 5:56 their brethren and the Levitical priests 2
63 Some of the Levitical priests 2

Libnah 1. לִבְנָה
Num33:20 from Rim'mon-per'ez, and encamped at Libnah. 1
21 they set out from Libnah, and encamped at Rissah. 1
Jos 10:29 Joshua passed on . . and fought against Libnah 1
29 Joshua passed on . . and fought against Libnah 1
31 Joshua passed on from Libnah . . to Lachish 1
32 and smote it . . as he had done to Libnah. 1
39 as he had done to Hebron and to Libnah and its king 1
12:15 the king of Libnah, one; the king of Adullam, one; 1
15:42 Libnah, Ether, Ashan 1
21:13 gave Hebron . . Libnah with its pasture lands 1
2Kg 8:22 Then Libnah revolted at the same time. 1
19: 8 and found the king . . fighting against Libnah; 1
23:31 was Hamu'tal the daughter of Jeremiah of Libnah. 1
24:18 was Hamu'tal the daughter of Jeremiah of Libnah. 1
1Ch 6:57 of refuge . . Libnah with its pasture lands 1
2Ch 21:10 At that time Libnah also revolted from his rule 1
Isa 37: 8 the king of Assyria fighting against Libnah; 1
Jer 52: 1 Hamu'tal the daughter of Jeremiah of Libnah. 1

Libni 1. לִבְנִי
Exd 6:17 The sons of Gershon: Libni and Shim'e-i 1
Num 3:18 sons of Gershon . . Libni and Shim'e-i. 1
1Ch 6:17 names of the sons of Gershom: Libni and Shim'e-i. 1
20 Of Gershom: Libni his son, Jahath his son, Zimmah 1
29 sons of Merar'i: Mahli, Libni his son, Shim'e-i 1

Libnite 1. לִבְנִי
Num 3:21 Of Gershon were the family of the Libnites 1
26:58 families of Levi: the family of the Libnites 1

Libya 1. Λίβυες 2. Λιβύη
Ezk 30: 5 Ethiopia, and Put, and Lud, and all Arabia, and Libya 1
Act 2:10 Egypt and the parts of Libya belonging to Cyre'ne 2

Libyan 1. לוּב
2Ch 12: 3 from Egypt–Libyans, Suk'ki-im, and Ethiopians. 1
16: 8 the Ethiopians and the Libyans a huge army 1
Dan 11:43 Libyans . . Ethiopians . . follow in his train. 1
Nah 3: 9 Put and the Libyans were her helpers. 1

Likhi 1. לִקְחִי
1Ch 7:19 sons of Shemi'da were . . Likhi, and Ani'am. 1

Lilies 1. שׁוֹשָׁן
Ps 45: 0 To the choirmaster: according to Lilies. 1
0 To the choirmaster: according to Lilies. 1
80: 0 To the choirmaster: according to Lilies. 1
0 To the choirmaster: according to Lilies. 1

Linus 1. Λίνος
2Ti 4:21 as do Pudens and Linus and Claudia 1

Lo-debar 1. לֹא דְבָר
2Sm 9: 4 He is in the house of Machir . . at Lo-debar. 1
5 the house of Machir the son of Am'miel, at Lo-debar. 1
17:27 and Machir the son of Am'miel from Lo'debar 1
Ams 6:13 you who rejoice in Lo-debar, who say 1

Lod 1. לֹד
1Ch 8:12 Shemed, who built Ono and Lod with its towns. 1
Ezr 2:33 sons of Lod, Hadid, and Ono, 725. 1
Neh 7:37 sons of Lod, Hadid, and Ono, 721. 1
11:35 Lod, and Ono, the valley of craftsmen. 1

Lois 1. Λωΐς
2Ti 1: 5 dwelt first in your grandmother Lo'is 1

LORD 1. אָדוֹן 2. אֲדֹנָי 3. יָהּ 4. יְהוָה 5. יֱהוִה 6. κύριος
Gen 2: 4 In the day that the LORD God made the earth 4
5 for the LORD God had not caused it to rain 4
7 the LORD God formed man of dust from the ground 4
8 the LORD God planted a garden in Eden, in the east; 4
9 out of the ground the LORD God made to grow 4
15 LORD God took the man and put him in the garden 4
16 the LORD God commanded the man, saying 4
18 the LORD God said, "It is not good that the man 4
19 out of the ground the LORD God formed every beast 4
21 the LORD God caused a deep sleep to fall upon 4
22 rib which the LORD God had taken from the man 4
3: 1 other wild creature that the LORD God had made. 4
8 they heard the sound of the LORD God walking 4
8 hid themselves from the presence of the LORD God 4
9 the LORD God called to the man 4
13 the LORD God said to the woman 4
14 The LORD God said to the serpent 4
21 the LORD God made for Adam and for his wife 4
22 the LORD God said, "Behold, the man has become 4
23 the LORD God sent him forth from the garden 4
4: 1 I have gotten a man with the help of the LORD. 4
3 In the course of time Cain brought to the LORD 4
4 And the LORD had regard for Abel and his offering 4
6 The LORD said to Cain, "Why are you angry 4
9 the LORD said to Cain, "Where is Abel your brother? 4
10 the LORD said, "What have you done? •
13 Cain said to the LORD, "My punishment is greater 4
15 Then the LORD said to him, "Not so! If any one slays 4
15 And the LORD put a mark on Cain 4
16 Cain went away from the presence of the LORD 4
26 time men began to call upon the name of the LORD. 4
5:29 Out of the ground which the LORD has cursed 4
6: 3 Then the LORD said, "My spirit shall not abide 4
5 The LORD saw that the wickedness of man was great 4
6 the LORD was sorry that he had made man 4
7 the LORD said, "I will blot out man 4
8 Noah found favor in the eyes of the LORD. 4
7: 1 Then the LORD said to Noah, "Go into the ark 4
5 Noah did all that the LORD had commanded him. 4
16 and the LORD God shut him in. 4
8:20 Then Noah built an altar to the LORD 4
21 when the LORD smelled the pleasing odor 4
21 the LORD said in his heart, "I will never again 4
9:26 He also said, "Blessed by the LORD my God be Shem; 4
10: 9 He was a mighty hunter before the LORD; 4
9 Like Nimrod a mighty hunter before the LORD. 4
11: 5 the LORD came down to see the city and the tower 4
6 the LORD said, "Behold, they are one people 4
8 the LORD scattered them abroad 4
9 because there the LORD confused the language 4
9 and from there the LORD scattered them abroad 4
12: 1 Now the LORD said to Abram, "Go from your country 4
4 Abram went, as the LORD had told him; 4
7 Then the LORD appeared to Abram, and said 4
7 he built there an altar to the LORD 4
8 and there he built an altar to the LORD 4
8 to the LORD and called on the name of the LORD. 4
17 the LORD afflicted Pharaoh and his house 4
13: 4 there Abram called on the name of the LORD. 4
10 watered everywhere like the garden of the LORD 4
10 before the LORD destroyed Sodom and Gomor'rah. 4
13 were wicked, great sinners against the LORD. 4
14 The LORD said to Abram, after Lot had separated 4
18 Hebron; and there he built an altar to the LORD. 4
14:22 I have sworn to the LORD God Most High 4
15: 1 the word of the LORD came to Abram in a vision 4
4 behold, the word of the LORD came to him 4
6 he believed the LORD; and he reckoned it to him 4
7 said to him, "I am the LORD who brought you from Ur 4
13 Then the LORD said to Abram, "Know of a surety •
18 On that day the LORD made a covenant with Abram 4
16: 2 Sar'ai said to Abram, "Behold now, the LORD has 4
5 May the LORD judge between you and me! 4
7 The angel of the LORD found her by a spring 4
9 The angel of the LORD said to her 4
10 The angel of the LORD also said to her 4
11 the angel of the LORD said to her 4
11 name Ish'mael; because the LORD has given heed 4
13 she called the name of the LORD who spoke to her 4
17: 1 the LORD appeared to Abram, and said to him 4
18: 1 the LORD appeared to him by the oaks of Mamre 4
10 The LORD said, "I will surely return to you •
13 The LORD said to Abraham, "Why did Sarah laugh 4
14 Is anything too hard for the LORD? 4
17 The LORD said, "Shall I hide from Abraham 4
19 household after him to keep the way of the LORD 4
19 and justice; so that the LORD may bring to Abraham 4
20 Then the LORD said, "Because the outcry 4
22 Sodom; but Abraham still stood before the LORD. 4
26 the LORD said, "If I find at Sodom 50 righteous 4
33 the LORD went his way, when he had finished 4
19:13 the outcry . . has become great before the LORD 4
13 and the LORD has sent us to destroy it. 4
14 for the LORD is about to destroy the city. 4
16 by the hand, the LORD being merciful to him 4
24 Then the LORD rained on Sodom and Gomor'rah 4
24 fire from the LORD out of heaven; 4
27 to the place where he had stood before the LORD; 4
20:18 For the LORD had closed all the wombs of the house 4
21: 1 The LORD visited Sarah as he had said 4
1 and the LORD did to Sarah as he had promised. 4
33 and called there on the name of the LORD 4
22:11 the angel of the LORD called to him from heaven 4
14 name of that place The LORD will provide; 4
14 On the mount of the LORD it shall be provided. 4
15 the angel of the LORD called to Abraham 4
16 By myself I have sworn, says the LORD 4
24: 1 the LORD had blessed Abraham in all things. 4
3 I will make you swear by the LORD, the God 4
7 The LORD, the God of heaven, who took me 4
12 he said, "O LORD, God of my master Abraham 4
21 whether the LORD had prospered his journey 4
26 The man bowed his head and worshiped the LORD 4
27 Blessed be the LORD, the God of my master Abraham 4
27 the LORD has led me in the way to the house 4
31 He said, "Come in, O blessed of the LORD; 4
35 The LORD has greatly blessed my master 4
40 he said to me, 'The LORD, before whom I walk 4
42 and said, 'O LORD, the God of my master Abraham 4
44 let her be the woman whom the LORD has appointed 4
48 Then I bowed my head and worshiped the LORD 4
48 worshiped the LORD, and blessed the LORD 4
50 The thing comes from the LORD; we cannot speak 4
51 wife of your master's son, as the LORD has spoken. 4
52 bowed himself to the earth before the LORD. 4
56 since the LORD has prospered my way; let me go 4
25:21 Isaac prayed to the LORD for his wife 4
21 and the LORD granted his prayer 4
22 why do I live?" So she went to inquire of the LORD. 4
23 the LORD said to her, "Two nations are in your womb 4
26: 2 the LORD appeared to him and said, Do not go down 4
12 The LORD blessed him 4
22 For now the LORD has made room for us 4
24 the LORD appeared to him the same night and said 4
25 and called upon the name of the LORD 4
28 They said, "We see plainly that the LORD is 4
29 You are now the blessed of the LORD. 4
27: 7 and bless you before the LORD before I die. 4
20 He answered, "Because the LORD your God 4
27 the smell of a field which the LORD has blessed! 4
28:13 behold, the LORD stood above it and said 4
13 I am the LORD, the God of Abraham your father 4
16 Surely the LORD is in this place 4
21 house in peace, then the LORD shall be my God 4
29:31 When the LORD saw that Leah was hated 4
32 Because the LORD has looked upon my affliction; 4
33 Because the LORD has heard that I am hated 4
35 This time I will praise the LORD"; 4
30:24 name Joseph, saying, "May the LORD add to me 4
27 by divination that the LORD has blessed me 4
30 and the LORD has blessed you wherever I turned. 4
31: 3 Then the LORD said to Jacob, "Return to the land 4
49 The LORD watch between you and me 4
32: 9 God of my father Isaac, O LORD who didst say to me 4
38: 7 Er . . was wicked in the sight of the LORD; 4
7 Er . . was wicked . . and the LORD slew him. 4
10 he did was displeasing in the sight of the LORD 4
39: 2 The LORD was with Joseph 4
3 his master saw that the LORD was with him 4
3 the LORD caused all that he did to prosper 4
5 the LORD blessed the Egyptian's house 4
5 the blessing of the LORD was upon all that he had 4
21 the LORD was with Joseph and showed him 4
23 in Joseph's care, because the LORD was with him; 4
23 and whatever he did, the LORD made it prosper. 4
49:18 I wait for thy salvation, O LORD. 4
Exd 3: 2 the angel of the LORD appeared to him in a flame 4

4 When the LORD saw that he turned aside to see 4
7 Then the LORD said, "I have seen the affliction 4
15 Say this . . 'The LORD, the God of your fathers 4
16 say to them, 'The LORD, the God of your father 4
18 say to him, 'The LORD, the God of the Hebrews, 4
18 that we may sacrifice to the LORD our God.' 4
4: 1 for they will say, 'The LORD did not appear to you.' 4
2 The LORD said to him, "What is that in your hand? 4
4 the LORD said to Moses, "Put out your hand, and take 4
5 believe that the LORD, the God of their fathers 4
6 Again, the LORD said to him, "Put your hand 4
10 Moses said to the LORD, "Oh, my Lord, I am not 4
11 the LORD said to him, "Who has made man's mouth? 4
11 Who makes him dumb . . Is it not I, the LORD? 4
14 the anger of the LORD was kindled against Moses 4
19 the LORD said to Moses in Mid'ian, "Go back to Egypt; 4
21 the LORD said to Moses, "When you go back to Egypt 4
22 Thus says the LORD, Israel is my first-born son 4
24 on the way the LORD met him and sought to kill him. 4
27 The LORD said to Aaron, "Go into the wilderness 4
28 the words of the LORD with which he had sent him 4
30 Aaron spoke all the words which the LORD had 4
31 and when they heard that the LORD had visited 4
5: 1 Thus says the LORD, the God of Israel 4
2 Pharaoh said, "Who is the LORD, that I should heed 4
2 I do not know the LORD, and moreover I will not let 4
3 let us . . sacrifice to the LORD our God 4
17 'Let us go and sacrifice to the LORD,' 4
21 they said to them, "The LORD look upon you 4
22 Then Moses turned again to the LORD and said 4
22 Moses . . said, "O LORD, why hast thou done evil 2
6: 1 the LORD said to Moses, "Now you shall see what I 4
2 God said to Moses, "I am the LORD. 4
3 by my name the LORD I did not make myself known 4
6 Say therefore . . 'I am the LORD, and I will bring 4
7 and you shall know that I am the LORD your God 4
8 I am the LORD.' 4
10 the LORD said to Moses 4
12 Moses said to the LORD, "Behold, the people 4
13 the LORD spoke to Moses and Aaron, and gave them 4
26 the Aaron and Moses to whom the LORD said 4
28 when the LORD spoke to Moses in the land of Egypt 4
29 the LORD said to Moses, "I am the LORD; tell Pharaoh 4
29 the LORD said to Moses, "I am the LORD; tell Pharaoh 4
30 Moses said to the LORD, "Behold, I am 4
7: 1 the LORD said to Moses, "See, I make you as God 4
5 the Egyptians shall know that I am the LORD 4
6 Moses and Aaron . . did as the LORD commanded 4
8 the LORD said to Moses and Aaron 4
10 Moses and Aaron . . did as the LORD commanded; 4
13 would not listen to them; as the LORD had said. 4
14 LORD said to Moses, "Pharaoh's heart is hardened 4
16 you shall say to him, 'The LORD, the God 4
17 says the LORD, "By this you shall know that I am 4
17 By this you shall know that I am the LORD 4
19 the LORD said to Moses, "Say to Aaron, 'Take your rod 4
20 Moses and Aaron did as the LORD commanded; 4
22 would not listen to them; as the LORD had said. 4
25 days passed after the LORD had struck the Nile. 4
8: 1 Then the LORD said to Moses, "Go in to Pharaoh 4
1 say to him, 'Thus says the LORD, "Let my people go 4
5 the LORD said to Moses, "Say to Aaron, 'Stretch out 4
8 Pharaoh . . said, "Entreat the LORD to take away 4
8 I will let the people go to sacrifice to the LORD. 4
10 know that there is no one like the LORD our God. 4
12 and Moses cried to the LORD concerning the frogs 4
13 the LORD did according to the word of Moses; 4
15 would not listen to them; as the LORD had said. 4
16 Then the LORD said to Moses, "Say to Aaron, 'Stretch 4
19 would not listen to them; as the LORD had said. 4
20 Then the LORD said to Moses, "Rise up early 4
20 say to him, 'Thus says the LORD, "Let my people go 4
22 that I am the LORD in the midst of the earth. 4
24 the LORD did so; there came great swarms of flies 4
26 shall sacrifice to the LORD our God offerings 4
27 sacrifice to the LORD our God as he will command 4
28 will let you go, to sacrifice to the LORD your God 4
29 I will pray to the LORD that the swarms of flies 4
29 letting the people go to sacrifice to the LORD. 4
30 Moses went out . . and prayed to the LORD. 4
31 the LORD did as Moses asked, and removed 4
9: 1 Then the LORD said to Moses, "Go in to Pharaoh 4
1 Thus says the LORD, the God of the Hebrews 4
3 the hand of the LORD will fall with a very severe 4
4 the LORD will make a distinction between 4
5 the LORD set a time, saying, "Tomorrow the LORD 4
5 the LORD will do this thing in the land. 4
6 on the morrow the LORD did this thing; 4
8 the LORD said to Moses and Aaron, "Take handfuls 4
12 the LORD hardened the heart of Pharaoh 4
12 as the LORD had spoken to Moses. 4
13 Then the LORD said to Moses, "Rise up early 4
13 Thus says the LORD, the God of the Hebrews 4
20 Then he who feared the word of the LORD among 4
21 he who did not regard the word of the LORD 4
22 the LORD said to Moses, "Stretch forth your hand 4
23 the LORD sent thunder and hail, and fire ran down 4
23 the LORD rained hail upon the land of Egypt; 4
27 the LORD is in the right, and I and my people are 4
28 Entreat the LORD; for there has been enough 4
29 I will stretch out my hands to the LORD; 4
29 that you may know that the earth is the LORD'S. 4
30 I know that you do not yet fear the LORD God. 4
33 Moses . . stretched out his hands to the LORD; 4
35 as the LORD had spoken through Moses. 4
10: 1 Then the LORD said to Moses, "Go in to Pharaoh; 4
2 that you may know that I am the LORD. 4
3 Thus says the LORD, the God of the Hebrews, 4
7 that they may serve the LORD their God; 4
8 Go, serve the LORD your God; but who are to go? 4
9 for we must hold a feast to the LORD. 4
10 he said to them, "The LORD be with you, if ever I let 4
11 No! Go, the men among you, and serve the LORD 4
12 Then the LORD said to Moses, "Stretch out your hand 4
13 the LORD brought an east wind upon the land 4
16 I have sinned against the LORD your God 4
17 entreat the LORD your God only to remove this 4
18 he went out from Pharaoh, and entreated the LORD. 4
19 the LORD turned a very strong west wind 4
20 the LORD hardened Pharaoh's heart, and he did not 4
21 Then the LORD said to Moses, "Stretch out your hand 4
24 Go, serve the LORD; your children also may go 4
25 that we may sacrifice to the LORD our God. 4
26 to serve the LORD our God, and we do not know 4
26 with what we must serve the LORD until we arrive 4
27 the LORD hardened Pharaoh's heart, and he would 4
11: 1 The LORD said to Moses, "Yet one plague more I will 4
3 the LORD gave the people favor in the sight 4
4 Moses said, "Thus says the LORD: About midnight 4
7 you may know that the LORD makes a distinction 4
9 the LORD said to Moses, "Pharaoh will not listen 4
10 the LORD hardened Pharaoh's heart 4
12: 1 The LORD said to Moses and Aaron in the land 4
11 It is the LORD'S passover. 4
12 I will execute judgments: I am the LORD. 4
14 and you shall keep it as a feast to the LORD; 4
23 For the LORD will pass through to slay 4
23 the LORD will pass over the door, and will not 4
25 when you come to the land which the LORD will give 4
27 It is the sacrifice of the LORD'S passover 4
28 as the LORD had commanded Moses and Aaron 4
29 At midnight the LORD smote all the first-born 4
31 go, serve the LORD, as you have said. 4
36 the LORD had given the people favor in the sight 4
41 all the hosts of the LORD went out from the land 4
42 It was a night of watching by the LORD, to bring 4
42 is a night of watching kept to the LORD by all 4
43 the LORD said to Moses and Aaron, "This is 4
48 stranger . . would keep the passover to the LORD 4
50 the LORD commanded Moses and Aaron, so they did. 4
51 the LORD brought the people of Israel out 4
13: 1 The LORD said to Moses 4
3 for by strength of hand the LORD brought you out 4
5 when the LORD brings you into the land 4
6 seventh day there shall be a feast to the LORD. 4
8 It is because of what the LORD did for me 4
9 that the law of the LORD may be in your mouth; 4
9 the LORD has brought you out of Egypt. 4
11 when the LORD brings you into the land 4
12 set apart to the LORD all that first opens 4
12 your cattle that are males shall be the LORD'S. 4
14 strength of hand the LORD brought us out of Egypt 4
15 the LORD slew all the first-born in the land 4
15 Therefore I sacrifice to the LORD all the males 4
16 strong hand the LORD brought us out of Egypt. 4
21 the LORD went before them by day in a pillar 4
14: 1 Then the LORD said to Moses 4
4 the Egyptians shall know that I am the LORD. 4
8 the LORD hardened the heart of Pharaoh 4
10 the people of Israel cried out to the LORD; 4
13 stand firm, and see the salvation of the LORD 4
14 The LORD will fight for you 4
15 The LORD said to Moses, "Why do you cry to me? 4
18 the Egyptians shall know that I am the LORD 4
21 the LORD drove the sea back by a strong east wind 4
24 the LORD in the pillar of fire and of cloud looked 4
25 the LORD fights for them against the Egyptians. 4
26 Then the LORD said to Moses, "Stretch out your hand 4
27 the Egyptians fled into it, and the LORD routed 4
30 Thus the LORD saved Israel that day from the hand 4
31 Israel saw the great work which the LORD did 4
31 Israel saw . . and the people feared the LORD; 4
31 they believed in the LORD and in his servant 4
15: 1 Israel sang this song to the LORD, saying 4
1 I will sing to the LORD, for he has triumphed 4
2 The LORD is my strength and my song, and he has 3
3 The LORD is a man of war; the LORD is his name. 4
3 The LORD is a man of war; the LORD is his name. 4
6 Thy right hand, O LORD, glorious in power 4
6 thy right hand, O LORD, shatters the enemy. 4
11 Who is like thee, O LORD, among the gods? 4
16 still as a stone, till thy people, O LORD, pass 4
17 place, O LORD, which thou has made for thy abode 4
17 the sanctuary, O LORD, which thy hands have 4
18 The LORD will reign for ever and ever. 4
19 the LORD brought back the waters of the sea upon 4
21 Sing to the LORD, for he has triumphed gloriously; 4
25 he cried to the LORD; and the LORD showed him 4
25 he cried to the LORD; and the LORD showed him 4
25 There the LORD made for them a statute •
26 hearken to the voice of the LORD your God 4
26 for I am the LORD, your healer. 4
16: 3 that we had died by the hand of the LORD in the land 4
4 Then the LORD said to Moses, "Behold, I will rain 4
6 At evening you shall know that it was the LORD who 4
7 in the morning you shall see the glory of the LORD 4
7 he has heard your murmurings against the LORD. 4
8 the LORD gives you in the evening flesh to eat 4
8 because the LORD has heard your murmurings 4
8 are not against us but against the LORD. 4
9 Say . . 'Come near before the LORD, for he has heard 4
10 the glory of the LORD appeared in the cloud. 4
11 the LORD said to Moses 4
12 then you shall know that I am the LORD your God.' 4
15 the bread which the LORD has given you to eat. 4
16 This is what the LORD has commanded 4
23 This is what the LORD has commanded: 'Tomorrow is 4
23 Tomorrow is . . a holy sabbath to the LORD; 4
25 Eat it today, for today is a sabbath to the LORD; 4
28 the LORD said to Moses, "How long do you refuse 4
29 See! The LORD has given you the sabbath, therefore 4
32 Moses said, "This is what the LORD has commanded 4
33 a jar . . and place it before the LORD, to be kept 4
34 As the LORD commanded Moses, so Aaron placed it 4
17: 1 according to the commandment of the LORD 4
2 Why do you put the LORD to the proof? 4
4 Moses cried to the LORD, "What shall I do with this 4
5 the LORD said to Moses, "Pass on before the people 4
7 and because they put the LORD to the proof 4
7 by saying, "Is the LORD among us or not? 4
14 the LORD said to Moses, "Write this as a memorial 4
15 the name of it, The LORD is my banner 4
16 saying, "A hand upon the banner of the LORD! 3
16 The LORD will have war with Am'alek 4
18: 1 how the LORD had brought Israel out of Egypt. 4
8 Moses told . . all that the LORD had done 4
8 Moses told . . how the LORD had delivered them. 4
9 the good which the LORD had done to Israel 4
10 Blessed be the LORD, who has delivered you 4
11 Now I know that the LORD is greater than all gods 4
19: 3 Moses went up to God, and the LORD called to him 4
7 these words which the LORD had commanded him. 4
8 All that the LORD has spoken we will do. 4
8 reported the words of the people to the LORD. 4
9 the LORD said to Moses, "Lo, I am coming to you 4
9 Moses told the words of the people to the LORD. 4
10 the LORD said to Moses, "Go to the people 4
11 for on the third day the LORD will come down 4
18 was wrapped in smoke, because the LORD descended 4
20 the LORD came down upon Mount Sinai, to the top 4
20 the LORD called Moses to the top of the mountain 4
21 LORD said to Moses, "Go down and warn the people 4
21 lest they break through to the LORD 4
22 the priests who come near to the LORD consecrate 4
22 lest the LORD break out upon them. 4
23 Moses said to the LORD, "The people cannot come up 4
24 the LORD said to him, "Go down, and come up 4
24 the people break through to come up to the LORD 4
20: 2 I am the LORD your God, who brought you out 4
5 for I the LORD your God am a jealous God 4
7 You shall not take the name of the LORD your God 4
7 the LORD will not hold him guiltless 4
10 the seventh day is a sabbath to the LORD your God; 4
11 for in six days the LORD made heaven and earth 4
11 therefore the LORD blessed the sabbath day 4
12 the land which the LORD your God gives you. 4
22 the LORD said to Moses, "Thus you shall say 4
22:11 an oath by the LORD shall be between them both 4
20 sacrifices to any god, save to the LORD only 4
23:17 shall all your males appear before the LORD God. 4
19 shall bring into the house of the LORD your God. 4
25 You shall serve the LORD your God, and I will bless 4
24: 1 said to Moses, "Come up to the LORD, you and Aaron 4
2 Moses alone shall come near to the LORD; 4
3 told the people all the words of the LORD 4
3 the words which the LORD has spoken we will do. 4
4 Moses wrote all the words of the LORD. 4
5 sacrificed peace offerings of oxen to the LORD. 4
7 they said, "All that the LORD has spoken we will do 4
8 the covenant which the LORD has made with you 4
12 The LORD said to Moses, "Come up to me 4
16 The glory of the LORD settled on Mount Sinai 4
17 the appearance of the glory of the LORD was like 4
25: 1 The LORD said to Moses 4
27:21 tend it from evening to morning before the LORD. 4
28:12 Aaron shall bear their names before the LORD 4
29 them to continual remembrance before the LORD. 4
30 when he goes in before the LORD; 4
30 upon his heart before the LORD continually. 4
35 when he goes into the holy place before the LORD 4
36 engrave on it . . 'Holy to the LORD.' 4
38 that they may be accepted before the LORD. 4
29:11 you shall kill the bull before the LORD 4
18 it is a burnt offering to the LORD; 4
18 it is . . an offering by fire to the LORD. 4
23 out of the basket . . that is before the LORD; 4
24 wave them for a wave offering before the LORD. 4

25 burn them . . as a pleasing odor before the LORD; 4
25 it is an offering by fire to the LORD. 4
26 for a wave offering before the LORD; 4
28 it is their offering to the LORD. 4
41 an offering by fire to the LORD. 4
42 door of the tent of meeting before the LORD 4
46 they shall know that I am the LORD their God, who 4
46 dwell among them; I am the LORD their God. 4
30: 8 a perpetual incense before the LORD 4
10 it is most holy to the LORD. 4
11 The LORD said to Moses 4
12 each shall give a ransom for himself to the LORD 4
13 half a shekel as an offering to the LORD. 4
14 Every one . . shall give the LORD'S offering. 4
15 give the LORD'S offering to make atonement 4
16 bring . . to remembrance before the LORD 4
17 The LORD said to Moses 4
20 to burn an offering by fire to the LORD 4
22 Moreover, the LORD said to Moses 4
34 the LORD said to Moses, "Take sweet spices, stacte 4
37 it shall be for you holy to the LORD. 4
31: 1 LORD said to Moses 4
12 LORD said to Moses 4
13 that you may know that I, the LORD, sanctify you. 4
15 sabbath of solemn rest, holy to the LORD; 4
17 in six days the LORD made heaven and earth 4
32: 5 Tomorrow shall be a feast to the LORD. 4
7 the LORD said to Moses, "Go down; for your people 4
9 the LORD said to Moses, "I have seen this people 4
11 Moses besought the LORD his God, and said, "O LORD 4
11 and said, "O LORD, why does thy wrath burn hot 4
14 the LORD repented of the evil which he thought 4
26 Who is on the LORD'S side? Come to me. 4
27 he said to them, "Thus says the LORD God of Israel 4
29 ordained yourselves for the service of the LORD 4
30 I will go up to the LORD; 4
31 So Moses returned to the LORD and said 4
33 the LORD said to Moses, "Whoever has sinned 4
35 the LORD sent a plague upon the people 4
33: 1 The LORD said to Moses, "Depart, go up hence 4
5 For the LORD had said to Moses, "Say to the people 4
7 And every one who sought the LORD would go out 4
9 the tent, and the LORD would speak with Moses. *
11 Thus the LORD used to speak to Moses face to face 4
12 Moses said to the LORD, "See, thou sayest to me 4
17 the LORD said to Moses, "This very thing 4
19 will proclaim before you my name 'The LORD'; 4
21 the LORD said, "Behold, there is a place by me 4
34: 1 The LORD said to Moses, "Cut two tables of stone 4
4 went up on Mount Sinai, as the LORD had commanded 4
5 the LORD descended in the cloud and stood 4
5 the LORD . . proclaimed the name of the LORD. 4
6 The LORD passed before him, and proclaimed 4
6 The LORD passed before him, and proclaimed 4
6 proclaimed, "The LORD, the LORD, a God merciful 4
10 all the people . . shall see the work of the LORD; 4
14 the LORD, whose name is Jealous, is a jealous God) 4
23 appear before the LORD God, the God of Israel. 4
24 when you go up to appear before the LORD your God 4
26 you shall bring to the house of the LORD your God. 4
27 the LORD said to Moses, "Write these words; 4
28 he was there with the LORD 40 days and 40 nights; 4
32 gave . . all that the LORD had spoken with him 4
34 whenever Moses went in before the LORD to speak 4
35: 1 the things which the LORD has commanded you 4
2 a holy sabbath of solemn rest to the LORD; 4
4 This is the thing which the LORD has commanded. 4
5 Take from among you an offering to the LORD; 4
5 let him bring the LORD'S offering: gold, silver 4
10 come and make all that the LORD has commanded 4
21 brought the LORD'S offering to be used 4
22 dedicating an offering of gold to the LORD. 4
24 brought it as the LORD'S offering; 4
29 work which the LORD had commanded by Moses to be 4
29 as their freewill offering to the LORD. 4
30 See, the LORD has called by name Bez'alel 4
36: 1 every able man in whom the LORD has put ability 4
1 with all that the LORD has commanded. 4
2 man in whose mind the LORD had put ability 4
5 the work which the LORD has commanded us to do. 4
38:22 made all that the LORD commanded Moses; 4
39: 1 as the LORD had said to Moses. 4
5 twined linen; as the LORD had commanded Moses. 4
7 sons of Israel; as the LORD had commanded Moses. 4
21 as the LORD had commanded Moses. 4
26 as the LORD had commanded Moses. 4
29 as the LORD had commanded Moses. 4
30 the engraving of a signet, "Holy to the LORD. 4
31 as the LORD had commanded Moses. 4
32 all that the LORD had commanded Moses; 4
42 According to all that the LORD had commanded 4
43 as the LORD had commanded, so had they done it. 4
40: 1 The LORD said to Moses 4
16 according to all that the LORD commanded him 4
19 the tent over it, as the LORD had commanded Moses. 4
21 as the LORD had commanded Moses. 4
23 set the bread in order on it before the LORD; 4
23 set the bread . . as the LORD had commanded Moses. 4
25 set up the lamps before the LORD; 4
25 as the LORD had commanded Moses. 4
27 as the LORD had commanded Moses. 4
29 as the LORD had commanded Moses. 4
32 as the LORD commanded Moses. 4
34 the glory of the LORD filled the tabernacle. 4
35 the glory of the LORD filled the tabernacle. 4
38 the cloud of the LORD was upon the tabernacle 4
Lev 1: 1 The LORD called Moses, and spoke to him 4
2 When any man of you brings an offering to the LORD 4
3 that he may be accepted before the LORD 4
5 Then he shall kill the bull before the LORD 4
9 an offering by fire, a pleasing odor to the LORD 4
11 he shall kill it . . before the LORD 4
13 offering by fire, a pleasing odor to the LORD 4
14 If his offering to the LORD is a burnt offering 4
17 offering by fire, a pleasing odor to the LORD 4
2: 1 cereal offering as an offering to the LORD 4
2 an offering by fire, a pleasing odor to the LORD 4
3 part of the offerings by fire to the LORD 4
8 bring the cereal offering . . to the LORD 4
9 an offering by fire, a pleasing odor to the LORD 4
10 part of the offerings by fire to the LORD 4
11 No cereal offering which you bring to the LORD 4
11 honey as an offering by fire to the LORD 4
12 first fruits you may bring them to the LORD 4
14 cereal offering of first fruits to the LORD 4
16 it is an offering by fire to the LORD 4
3: 1 shall offer it without blemish before the LORD 4
3 as an offering by fire to the LORD 4
5 offering by fire, a pleasing odor to the LORD 4
6 a sacrifice of peace offering to the LORD 4
7 then he shall offer it before the LORD 4
9 peace offering as an offering by fire to the LORD 4
11 on he altar as food offered by fire to the LORD 4
12 then he shall offer it before the LORD 4
14 for an offering by fire to the LORD 4
16 All fat is the LORD'S 4
4: 1 the LORD said to Moses 4
2 in any of the things which the LORD has commanded 4
3 a young bull . . to the LORD for a sin offering 4
4 to the door of the tent of meeting before the LORD 4
4 he shall . . kill the bull before the LORD 4
6 sprinkle . . seven times before the LORD 4
7 altar of fragrant incense before the LORD 4
13 If . . they do any one of the things which the LORD 4
15 upon the head of the bull before the LORD 4
15 the bull shall be killed before the LORD 4
17 blood . . sprinkle it seven times before the LORD 4
18 in the tent of meeting before the LORD 4
22 the things which the LORD his God has commanded 4
24 kill the burnt offering before the LORD 4
27 the things which the LORD has commanded not to be 4
31 upon the altar for a pleasing odor to the LORD 4
35 upon the offerings by fire to the LORD 4
5: 6 he shall bring his guilt offering to the LORD 4
7 he shall bring, as his guilt offering to the LORD 4
12 the altar, upon the offerings by fire to the LORD 4
14 The LORD said to Moses 4
15 sins . . in any of the holy thing of the LORD 4
15 he shall bring, as his guilt offering to the LORD 4
17 the things which the LORD has commanded not to be 4
19 guilt offering he is guilty before the LORD 4
6: 1 The LORD said to Moses 4
2 a breach of faith against the LORD by deceiving 4
6 guilt offering to the LORD, a ram without blemish 4
7 make atonement for him before the LORD 4
8 The LORD said to Moses 4
14 The sons of Aaron shall offer it before the LORD 4
15 on the altar, a pleasing odor to the LORD 4
18 from the LORD'S offerings by fire 4
19 The LORD said to Moses 4
20 offer to the LORD on the day when he is anointed 4
21 offer it for a pleasing odor to the LORD 4
22 priest . . shall offer it to the LORD as decreed 4
24 The LORD said to Moses 4
25 be killed before the LORD; it is most holy 4
7: 5 as an offering by fire to the LORD 4
11 peace offerings which one may offer to the LORD 4
14 as an offering to the LORD; it shall belong 4
20 the sacrifice of the LORD'S peace offerings 4
21 the sacrifice of the LORD'S peace offerings 4
22 The LORD said to Moses 4
25 offering by fire is made to the LORD shall be cut 4
28 The LORD said to Moses 4
29 the sacrifice of his peace offerings to the LORD 4
29 He shall bring his offering to the LORD 4
30 bring . . offerings by fire to the LORD 4
30 be waved as a wave offering before the LORD 4
35 the offerings made by fire to the LORD 4
35 were presented to them as priests of the LORD 4
36 the LORD commanded this to be given them 4
38 which the LORD commanded Moses on Mount Sinai 4
38 commanded . . bring their offerings to the LORD 4
8: 1 The LORD said to Moses 4
4 Moses did as the LORD commanded him 4
5 the thing which the LORD has commanded 4
9 the holy crown, as the LORD commanded Moses 4
13 bound caps on them, as the LORD commanded Moses 4
17 outside the camp, as the LORD commanded Moses 4
21 offering by fire to the LORD, as the LORD commanded 4
21 to the LORD, as the LORD commanded Moses 4
26 unleavened bread which was before the LORD 4
27 waved them as a wave offering before the LORD 4
28 a pleasing odor, an offering by fire to the LORD 4
29 waved it for a wave offering before the LORD 4
29 ram of ordination, as the LORD commanded Moses 4
34 As has been done today, the LORD has commanded 4
35 performing what the LORD has charged 4
36 all the things which the LORD commanded by Moses 4
9: 2 without blemish, and offer them before the LORD 4
4 sacrifice before the LORD, and a cereal offering 4
4 for today the LORD will appear to you.' 4
5 drew near and stood before the LORD 4
6 the thing which the LORD commanded you to do 4
6 the glory of the LORD will appear to you 4
7 make atonement . . as the LORD has commanded 4
10 upon the altar, as the LORD commanded Moses 4
21 for a wave offering before the LORD 4
23 the glory of the LORD appeared to all the people 4
24 fire came forth from before the LORD 4
10: 1 and offered unholy fire before the LORD 4
2 fire came forth from the presence of the LORD 4
2 devoured them, and they died before the LORD 4
3 This is what the LORD has said, 'I will show myself 4
6 bewail the burning which the LORD has kindled 4
7 for the anointing oil of the LORD is upon you 4
8 the LORD spoke to Aaron, saying 4
11 the statutes which the LORD has spoken to them 4
12 remains of the offerings by fire to the LORD 4
13 due, from the offerings by fire to the LORD 4
15 to wave for a wave offering before the LORD 4
15 a due for ever; as the LORD has commanded 4
17 to make atonement for them before the LORD 4
19 their burnt offering before the LORD 4
19 acceptable in the sight of the LORD 4
11: 1 the LORD said to Moses and Aaron 4
44 For I am the LORD your God: consecrate yourselves 4
45 I am the LORD who brought you up out of the land 4
12: 1 The LORD said to Moses 4
7 he shall offer it before the LORD 4
13: 1 The LORD said to Moses and Aaron 4
14: 1 The LORD said to Moses 4
11 shall set . . these things before the LORD 4
12 wave them for a wave offering before the LORD 4
16 with his finger seven times before the LORD 4
18 make atonement for him before the LORD 4
23 bring them . . before the LORD 4
24 for a wave offering before the LORD 4
27 sprinkle . . seven times before the LORD 4
29 to make atonement for him before the LORD 4
31 the priest shall make atonement before the LORD 4
33 The LORD said to Moses and Aaron 4
15: 1 The LORD said to Moses and Aaron 4
14 before the LORD to the door of the tent of meeting 4
15 shall make atonement for him before the LORD 4
30 shall make atonement for her before the LORD 4
16: 1 The LORD spoke to Moses after the death of the two 4
1 when they drew near before the LORD and died 4
2 the LORD said to Moses, "Tell Aaron your brother 4
7 set them before the LORD at the door of the tent 4
8 one lot for the LORD and the other lot for Aza'zel 4
9 the goat on which the lot fell for the LORD 4
10 goat . . shall be presented alive before the LORD 4
12 coals of fire from the altar before the LORD 4
13 put the incense on the fire before the LORD 4
18 shall go out to the altar which is before the LORD 4
30 you shall be clean before the LORD 4
34 And Moses did as the LORD commanded him 4
17: 1 the LORD said to Moses 4
2 This is the thing which the LORD has commanded 4
4 as a gift to the LORD before the tabernacle 4
4 bring it . . before the tabernacle of the LORD 4
5 that they may bring them to the LORD, to the priest 4
5 as sacrifices of peace offerings to the LORD 4
6 sprinkle the blood on the altar of the LORD 4
6 and burn the fat for a pleasing odor to the LORD 4
9 bring it . . to sacrifice it to the LORD 4
18: 1 the LORD said to Moses 4
2 Say to the people of Israel, I am the LORD your God 4
4 I am the LORD your God 4
5 I am the LORD 4
6 I am the LORD 4
21 and so profane the name of your God: I am the LORD 4
30 I am the LORD your God 4
19: 1 And the LORD said to Moses 4
2 You shall be holy; for I the LORD your God am holy 4
3 you shall keep my sabbaths: I am the LORD your God 4
4 I am LORD your God 4
5 offer a sacrifice of peace offerings to the LORD 4
8 because he has profaned a holy thing of the LORD 4
10 I am the LORD your God 4
12 and so profane the name of your God: I am the LORD 4
14 but you shall fear your God: I am the LORD 4
16 I am the LORD 4
18 love your neighbor as yourself: I am the LORD 4
21 bring a guilt offering for himself to the LORD 4
22 make atonement for him . . before the LORD 4
24 holy, an offering of praise to the LORD 4

25 yield more richly for you: I am the LORD your God 4
28 or tattoo any marks upon you: I am the LORD 4
30 reverence my sanctuary: I am the LORD 4
31 I am the LORD your God 4
32 you shall fear your God; I am the LORD 4
34 I am the LORD your God 4
36 I am the LORD your God, who brought you out 4
37 my ordinances, and do them: I am the LORD 4
20: 1 The LORD said to Moses 4
7 be holy; for I am the LORD your God 4
8 do them; I am the LORD who sanctify you 4
24 I am the LORD your God, who have separated you 4
26 You shall be holy to me; for I the LORD am holy 4
21: 1 the LORD said to Moses, "Speak to the priests 4
6 for they offer the offerings by fire to the LORD 4
8 he shall be holy to you; for I the LORD, who sanctify 4
12 I am the LORD 4
15 for I am the LORD who sanctify him 4
16 And the LORD said to Moses 4
21 come near to offer the LORD'S offerings by fire 4
23 for I am the LORD who sanctify them 4
22: 1 And the LORD said to Moses 4
2 may not profane my holy name: I am the LORD 4
3 which the people of Israel dedicate to the LORD 4
3 shall be cut off from my presence; I am the LORD 4
8 I am the LORD.' 4
9 they profane it: I am the LORD who sanctify them 4
15 holy things . . which they offer to the LORD 4
16 holy thing: for I am the LORD who sanctify them 4
17 And the LORD said to Moses 4
18 freewill offering which is offered to the LORD 4
21 of peace offerings to the LORD, to fulfil a vow 4
22 Animals . . you shall not offer to the LORD 4
22 an offering by fire upon the altar to the LORD 4
24 you shall not offer to the LORD or sacrifice 4
26 And the LORD said to Moses 4
27 as an offering by fire to the LORD 4
29 sacrifice of thanksgiving to the LORD 4
30 I am the LORD 4
31 keep my commandments and do them: I am the LORD 4
32 I am the LORD who sanctify you 4
33 who brought you . . to be your God: I am the LORD 4
23: 1 The LORD said to Moses 4
2 The appointed feasts of the LORD 4
3 a sabbath to the LORD in all your dwellings 4
4 These are the appointed feasts of the LORD 4
5 In the first month . . is the LORD'S passover 4
6 the feast of unleavened bread to the LORD 4
8 you shall present an offering by fire to the LORD 4
9 And the LORD said to Moses 4
11 he shall wave the sheaf before the LORD 4
12 a male lamb . . as a burnt offering to the LORD 4
13 to be offered by fire to the LORD, a pleasing odor 4
16 a cereal offering of new grain to the LORD 4
17 baked with leaven, as first fruits to the LORD 4
18 they shall be a burnt offering to the LORD 4
18 an offering by fire, a pleasing odor to the LORD 4
20 first fruits as a wave offering before the LORD 4
20 they shall be holy to the LORD for the priest 4
22 I am the LORD your God 4
23 And the LORD said to Moses 4
25 you shall present an offering by fire to the LORD 4
26 And the LORD said to Moses 4
27 present an offering by fire to the LORD 4
28 to make atonement for you before the LORD your God 4
33 And the LORD said to Moses 4
34 for seven days is the feast of booths to the LORD 4
36 shall present offerings by fire to the LORD 4
36 and present an offering by fire to the LORD 4
37 These are the appointed feasts of the LORD 4
37 for presenting to the LORD offerings by fire 4
38 besides the sabbaths of the LORD 4
38 freewill offerings, which you give to the LORD 4
39 you shall keep the feast of the LORD seven days 4
40 you shall rejoice before the LORD your God 4
41 You shall keep it as a feast to the LORD seven days 4
43 I am the LORD your God 4
44 declared . . the appointed feasts of the LORD 4
24: 1 The LORD said to Moses 4
3 keep it in order . . before the LORD continually 4
4 lampstand of pure gold before the LORD 4
7 memorial portion to be offered by fire to the LORD 4
8 Aaron shall set it in order before the LORD 4
9 offerings by fire to the LORD, a perpetual due 4
12 they put him in custody, till the will of the LORD 4
13 And the LORD said to Moses 4
16 He who blasphemes the name of the LORD 4
22 for I am the LORD your God 4
23 Israel did as the LORD commanded Moses 4
25: 1 The LORD said to Moses on Mount Sinai 4
2 the land shall keep a sabbath to the LORD 4
4 solemn rest for the land, a sabbath to the LORD 4
17 fear your God; for I am the LORD your God 4
38 I am the LORD your God, who brought you forth 4
55 out of the land of Egypt: I am the LORD your God 4
26: 1 to bow down to them, for I am the LORD your God 4
2 reverence my sanctuary: I am the LORD 4
13 I am the LORD your God, who brought you forth 4
44 for I am the LORD their God 4

45 that I might be their God: I am the LORD 4
46 which the LORD made between him and the people 4
27: 1 The LORD said to Moses 4
2 vow of persons to the LORD at your valuation 4
9 offer as an offering to the LORD 4
9 all of such that any man gives to the LORD is holy 4
11 such as is not offered as an offering to the LORD 4
14 dedicates his house to be holy to the LORD 4
16 If a man dedicates to the LORD part of the land 4
21 field . . shall be holy to the LORD 4
22 If he dedicates to the LORD a field 4
23 on that day as a holy thing to the LORD 4
26 which as a firstling belongs to the LORD 4
26 whether ox or sheep, it is the LORD'S 4
28 no devoted thing that a man devotes to the LORD 4
28 every devoted thing is most holy to the LORD 4
30 All the tithe of the land . . is holy to the LORD 4
30 All the tithe of the land . . is holy to the LORD 4
32 All the tithe . . shall be holy to the LORD 4
34 These are the commandments which the LORD 4
Num 1: 1 The LORD spoke to Moses in the wilderness 4
19 the LORD commanded Moses. So he numbered them 4
48 For the LORD said to Moses 4
54 according to all that the LORD commanded Moses. 4
2: 1 The LORD said to Moses and Aaron 4
33 not numbered . . as the LORD commanded Moses. 4
34 According to all that the LORD commanded Moses 4
3: 1 at the time when the LORD spoke with Moses 4
4 Nadab and Abi'hu died before the LORD 4
4 they offered unholy fire before the LORD 4
5 the LORD said to Moses 4
11 the LORD said to Moses 4
13 they shall be mine: I am the LORD. 4
14 the LORD said to Moses in the wilderness of Sinai 4
16 the word of the LORD, as he was commanded. 4
39 numbered at the commandment of the LORD 4
40 LORD said to Moses, "Number all the first-born 4
41 you shall take the Levites for me–I am the LORD 4
42 Moses numbered . . as the LORD commanded him. 4
44 the LORD said to Moses 4
45 Levites shall be mine: I am the LORD. 4
51 according to the word of the LORD, as the LORD 4
51 word of the LORD, as the LORD commanded Moses. 4
4: 1 The LORD said to Moses and Aaron 4
17 The LORD said to Moses and Aaron 4
21 The LORD said to Moses 4
37 commandment of the LORD by Moses. 4
41 according to the commandment of the LORD. 4
45 commandment of the LORD by Moses. 4
49 commandment of the LORD through Moses 4
49 numbered by him, as the LORD commanded Moses. 4
5: 1 The LORD said to Moses 4
4 as the LORD said to Moses, so . . Israel did. 4
5 the LORD said to Moses 4
6 men commit by breaking faith with the LORD 4
8 restitution for wrong shall go to the LORD 4
11 the LORD said to Moses 4
16 priest shall . . set her before the LORD; 4
18 the priest shall set the woman before the LORD 4
21 then . . LORD make you an execration and an oath 4
21 when the LORD makes your thigh fall away 4
25 shall wave the cereal offering before the LORD 4
30 then he shall set the woman before the LORD 4
6: 1 the LORD said to Moses 4
2 vow of a Nazirite, to separate himself to the LORD 4
5 for which he separates himself to the LORD 4
6 days that he separates himself to the LORD 4
8 days of his separation he is holy to the LORD. 4
12 separate himself to the LORD for the days 4
14 he shall offer his gift to the LORD 4
16 the priest shall present them before the LORD 4
17 ram as a sacrifice of peace offering to the LORD 4
20 for a wave offering before the LORD; 4
21 offering to the LORD shall be according 4
22 The LORD said to Moses 4
24 The LORD bless you and keep you 4
25 The LORD make his face to shine upon you 4
26 The LORD lift up his countenance upon you 4
7: 3 brought their offerings before the LORD 4
4 Then the LORD said to Moses 4
11 LORD said to Moses, "They shall offer 4
89 into the tent of meeting to speak with the LORD •
8: 1 Now the LORD said to Moses 4
3 set up its lamps . . as the LORD commanded Moses. 4
4 pattern which the LORD had shown Moses 4
5 the LORD said to Moses 4
10 When you present the Levites before the LORD 4
11 Aaron shall offer the Levites before the LORD 4
11 may be theirs to do the service of the LORD. 4
12 other for a burnt offering to the LORD 4
13 shall offer them as a wave offering to the LORD. 4
20 according to all that the LORD commanded Moses 4
21 offered them as a wave offering before the LORD 4
22 as the LORD had commanded Moses concerning 4
23 the LORD said to Moses 4
9: 1 LORD spoke to Moses in the wilderness of Sinai 4
5 according to all that the LORD commanded Moses 4
7 why are we kept from offering the LORD'S offering 4
8 hear what the LORD will command concerning you. 4

9 The LORD said to Moses 4
10 he shall still keep the passover to the LORD. 4
13 offer the LORD'S offering at its appointed time; 4
14 stranger . . will keep the passover to the LORD 4
18 At the command of the LORD the people of Israel 4
18 at the command of the LORD they encamped; 4
19 people of Israel kept the charge of the LORD 4
20 then according to the command of the LORD 4
20 according to the command of the LORD they set out. 4
23 At the command of the LORD they encamped 4
23 at the command of the LORD they set out; 4
23 they kept the charge of the LORD 4
23 at the command of the LORD by Moses. 4
10: 1 The LORD said to Moses 4
9 you may be remembered before the LORD your God 4
10 I am the LORD your God. 4
13 set out . . at the command of the LORD by Moses. 4
29 place of which the LORD said, 'I will give it to you'; 4
29 for the LORD has promised good to Israel. 4
32 whatever good the LORD will do to us 4
33 set out from the mount of the LORD three days' 4
33 ark of the covenant of the LORD went before them 4
34 the cloud of the LORD was over them by day 4
35 Arise, O LORD, and let thy enemies be scattered; 4
36 Return, O LORD, to the ten thousand thousands 4
11: 1 people complained in the hearing of the LORD 4
1 when the LORD heard it, his anger was kindled 4
1 fire of the LORD burned among them, and consumed 4
2 Moses prayed to the LORD, and the fire abated. 4
3 Tab'erah, because the fire of the LORD burned 4
10 anger of the LORD blazed hotly 4
11 Moses said to the LORD, "Why has thou dealt ill 4
16 the LORD said to Moses, "Gather for me 70 men 4
18 you have wept in the hearing of the LORD, saying 4
18 Therefore the LORD will give you meat 4
20 you have rejected the LORD who is among you 4
23 LORD said to Moses, "Is the LORD'S hand shortened? 4
23 LORD said to Moses, "Is the LORD'S hand shortened? 4
24 Moses . . told the people the words of the LORD; 4
25 LORD came down in the cloud and spoke to him 4
29 Would that all the LORD'S people were prophets 4
29 that the LORD would put his spirit upon them! 4
31 there went forth a wind from the LORD 4
33 anger of the LORD was kindled against the people 4
33 LORD smote the people with a very great plague. 4
12: 2 Has the LORD indeed spoken only through Moses? 4
2 And the LORD heard it. 4
4 suddenly the LORD said to Moses and to Aaron 4
5 LORD came down in a pillar of cloud, and stood 4
6 I the LORD make myself known to him in a vision 4
8 beholds the form of the LORD. 4
9 anger of the LORD was kindled against them 4
13 Moses cried to the LORD, "Heal her, O God, I beseech 4
14 LORD said to Moses, "If her father had but spit 4
13: 1 The LORD said to Moses 4
3 sent . . according to the command of the LORD 4
14: 3 Why does the LORD bring us into this land, to fall 4
8 If the LORD delights in us, he will bring us 4
9 Only do not rebel against the LORD; and do not fear 4
9 LORD is with us; do not fear them. 4
10 Then the glory of the LORD appeared at the tent 4
11 LORD said to Moses, "How long will this people 4
13 Moses said to the LORD, "Then the Egyptians 4
14 They have heard that thou, O LORD, art in the midst 4
14 for thou, O LORD, art seen face to face, and thy cloud 4
16 'Because the LORD was not able to bring 4
17 let the power of the LORD be as great as thou hast 4
18 LORD is slow to anger, and abounding in steadfast 4
20 Then the LORD said, "I have pardoned 4
21 earth shall be filled with the glory of the LORD 4
26 the LORD said to Moses and to Aaron 4
28 Say to them, 'As I live,' says the LORD 4
35 I, the LORD, have spoken; surely this will I do 4
37 died by plague before the LORD. 4
40 go up to the place which the LORD has promised; 4
41 Why . . you trangressing the command of the LORD 4
42 Do not go up . . for the LORD is not among you. 4
43 you have turned back from following the LORD 4
43 LORD will not be with you. 4
44 neither the ark of the covenant of the LORD 4
15: 1 Then the LORD said to Moses 4
3 offer to the LORD from the herd or from the flock 4
3 to make a pleasing odor to the LORD 4
4 who brings his offering shall offer to the LORD 4
7 a pleasing odor to the LORD. 4
8 a bull for . . peace offerings to the LORD 4
10 offering by fire, a pleasing odor to the LORD. 4
13 offering by fire, a pleasing odor to the LORD. 4
14 pleasing odor to the LORD, he shall do as you do. 4
15 so shall the sojourner be before the LORD. 4
17 The LORD said to Moses 4
19 you shall present an offering to the LORD. 4
21 you shall give to the LORD an offering 4
22 commandments which the LORD has spoken to Moses 4
23 all that the LORD has commanded you by Moses 4
23 from the day the the LORD gave commandment 4
24 a burnt offering, a pleasing odor to the LORD 4
25 their offering, an offering by fire to the LORD 4
25 brought . . their sin offering before the LORD 4

28 the priest shall make atonement before the LORD 4
30 anything with a high hand . . reviles the LORD 4
31 Because he has despised the word of the LORD 4
35 LORD said to Moses, "The man shall be put to death; 4
36 stoned him . . as the LORD commanded Moses. 4
37 The LORD said to Moses 4
39 remember all the commandments of the LORD, to do 4
41 I am the LORD your God, who brought you out 4
41 I am the LORD your God. 4
16: 3 LORD is among them; why then do you exalt 4
3 exalt yourselves above the assembly of the LORD? 4
5 In the morning the LORD will show who is his 4
7 put incense upon them before the LORD tomorrow 4
7 man whom the LORD chooses shall be the holy one. 4
9 to do service in the tabernacle of the LORD 4
11 against the LORD that you and all your company 4
15 Moses was very angry, and said to the LORD 4
16 Be present . . before the LORD 4
17 every one of you bring before the LORD his censer 4
19 glory of the LORD appeared to all 4
20 the LORD said to Moses and to Aaron 4
23 the LORD said to Moses 4
28 Hereby you shall know that the LORD has sent me 4
29 then the LORD has not sent me. 4
30 if the LORD creates something new 4
30 know that these men have despised the LORD. 4
35 fire came forth from the LORD, and consumed 4
36 Then the LORD said to Moses 4
38 for they offered them before the LORD 4
40 should draw near to burn incense before the LORD 4
40 as the LORD said to Elea'zar through Moses. 4
41 You have killed the people of the LORD. 4
42 covered it, and the glory of the LORD appeared. 4
44 the LORD said to Moses 4
46 for wrath has gone forth from the LORD, the plague 4
17: 1 The LORD said to Moses 4
7 rods before the LORD in the tent of the testimony. 4
9 brought out all the rods from before the LORD 4
10 the LORD said to Moses, "Put back the rod of Aaron 4
11 did Moses; as the LORD commanded him, so he did. 4
13 near to the tabernacle of the LORD, shall die. 4
18: 1 LORD said to Aaron, "You and your sons 4
6 Levites . . are a gift to you, given to the LORD 4
8 Then the LORD said to Aaron, "And behold 4
12 the first fruits of what they give to the LORD 4
13 ripe fruits . . which they bring to the LORD 4
15 which they offer to the LORD, shall be yours; 4
17 offering by fire, a pleasing odor to the LORD; 4
19 which the people of Israel present to the LORD 4
19 it is a covenant of salt for ever before the LORD 4
20 LORD said to Aaron, "You shall have no inheritance 4
24 tithe . . they present as an offering to the LORD 4
25 the LORD said to Moses 4
26 you shall present an offering from it to the LORD 4
28 shall you also present an offering to the LORD 4
28 give the LORD'S offering to Aaron the priest. 4
29 you shall present every offering due to the LORD 4
19: 1 Now the LORD said to Moses and to Aaron 4
2 statute of the law which the LORD has commanded 4
13 defiles the tabernacle of the LORD 4
20 since he has defiled the sanctuary of the LORD; 4
20: 3 died when our brethren died before the LORD! 4
4 Why have you brought the assembly of the LORD 4
6 And the glory of the LORD appeared to them 4
7 the LORD said to Moses 4
9 Moses took the rod from before the LORD 4
12 LORD said to Moses and Aaron, "Because you did not 4
13 where . . Israel contended with the LORD 4
16 when we cried to the LORD, he heard our voice 4
23 the LORD said to Moses and Aaron at Mount Hor 4
27 Moses did as the LORD commanded; 4
21: 2 Israel vowed a vow to the LORD, and said 4
3 LORD hearkened to the voice of Israel, and gave 4
6 LORD sent fiery serpents among the people 4
7 we have spoken against the LORD and against you; 4
7 We have sinned . . pray to the LORD 4
8 the LORD said to Moses, "Make a fiery serpent 4
14 Where it is said in the Book of the Wars of the LORD 4
16 Beer . . the well of which the LORD said to Moses 4
34 the LORD said to Moses, "Do not fear him; 4
22: 8 bring back word to you, as the LORD speaks to me"; 4
13 for the LORD has refused to let me go with you. 4
18 could not go beyond the command of the LORD 4
19 that I may know what more the LORD will say to me. 4
22 the angel of the LORD took his stand in the way 4
23 ass saw the angel of the LORD standing in the road 4
24 Then the angel of the LORD stood in a narrow path 4
25 when the ass saw the angel of the LORD, she pushed 4
26 Then the angel of the LORD went ahead, and stood 4
27 the ass saw the angel of the LORD, she lay down 4
28 LORD opened the mouth of the ass, and she said 4
31 the LORD opened the eyes of Balaam, and he saw 4
31 he saw the angel of the LORD standing in the way 4
32 angel of the LORD said to him, "Why have you struck 4
34 Balaam said to the angel of the LORD, "I have sinned 4
35 angel of the LORD said to Balaam, "Go with the men; 4
23: 3 perhaps the LORD will come to meet me; 4
5 the LORD put a word in Balaam's mouth, and said 4
8 can I denounce whom the LORD has not denounced? 4
12 take heed to speak what the LORD puts in my mouth? 4
15 Stand here . . while I meet the LORD yonder. *
16 LORD met Balaam, and put a word in his mouth 4
17 Balak said to him, "What has the LORD spoken? 4
21 The LORD their God is with them 4
26 All that the LORD says, that I must do'? 4
24: 1 Balaam saw that it pleased the LORD to bless 4
6 like aloes that the LORD has planted 4
11 but the LORD has held you back from honor. 4
13 I would not be able to go beyond the word of the LORD 4
13 what the LORD speaks, that will I speak'? 4
25: 3 anger of the LORD was kindled against Israel; 4
4 LORD said to Moses, "Take all the chiefs 4
4 hang them in the sun before the LORD 4
4 that the fierce anger of the LORD may turn away 4
10 the LORD said to Moses 4
16 the LORD said to Moses 4
26: 1 LORD said to Moses and to Elea'zar the son of Aaron 4
4 Take a census . . " as the LORD commanded Moses. 4
9 Korah, when they contended against the LORD 4
52 The LORD said to Moses 4
61 when they offered unholy fire before the LORD. 4
65 For the LORD had said of them, "They shall die 4
27: 3 gathered themselves together against the LORD 4
5 Moses brought their case before the LORD. 4
6 the LORD said to Moses 4
11 as the LORD commanded Moses.' 4
12 LORD said to Moses, "Go up into this mountain 4
15 Moses said to the LORD 4
16 LORD . . appoint a man over the congregation 4
17 congregation of the LORD may not be as sheep 4
18 LORD said to Moses, "Take Joshua the son of Nun 4
21 by the judgment of the Urim before the LORD; 4
22 Moses did as the LORD commanded him; 4
23 commissioned him as the LORD directed 4
28: 1 The LORD said to Moses 4
3 offering by fire . . you shall offer to the LORD 4
6 pleasing odor, an offering by fire to the LORD. 4
7 drink offering of strong drink to the LORD. 4
8 offering by fire, a pleasing odor to the LORD. 4
11 you shall offer a burnt offering to the LORD 4
13 pleasing odor, an offering by fire to the LORD. 4
15 Also one male goat for a sin offering to the LORD; 4
16 On the fourteenth day . . is the LORD'S passover. 4
19 an offering by fire, a burnt offering to the LORD 4
24 offering by fire, a pleasing odor to the LORD; 4
26 offering . . to the LORD at your feast of weeks 4
27 burnt offering, a pleasing odor to the LORD; 4
29: 2 a burnt offering, a pleasing odor to the LORD 4
6 a pleasing odor, an offering by fire to the LORD. 4
8 you shall offer a burnt offering to the LORD 4
12 you shall keep a feast to the LORD seven days; 4
13 offering by fire, a pleasing odor to the LORD 4
36 offering by fire, a pleasing odor to the LORD 4
39 shall offer to the LORD at your appointed feasts 4
40 just as the LORD had commanded Moses. 4
30: 1 This is what the LORD has commanded. 4
2 a man vows a vow to the LORD, or swears an oath 4
3 Or when a woman vows a vow to the LORD 4
5 the LORD will forgive her, because her father 4
8 LORD will forgive her. 4
12 made them void, and the LORD will forgive her. 4
16 statutes which the LORD commanded Moses 4
31: 1 The LORD said to Moses 4
3 to execute the LORD'S vengeance on Mid'ian. 4
7 against Mid'ian, as the LORD commanded Moses 4
16 to act treacherously against the LORD 4
16 plague came among the congregation of the LORD. 4
21 statute of the law which the LORD has commanded 4
25 The LORD said to Moses 4
28 levy for the LORD a tribute from the men of war 4
29 give it to Elea'zar . . as an offering to the LORD. 4
30 have charge of the tabernacle of the LORD. 4
31 Moses and Elea'zar . . did as the LORD commanded 4
37 the LORD'S tribute of sheep was 675. 4
38 36,000, of which the LORD'S tribute was 72. 4
39 30,500, of which the LORD'S tribute was 61. 4
40 16,000, of which the LORD'S tribute was 32 4
41 tribute, which was the offering for the LORD 4
41 gave the tribute . . as the LORD commanded Moses. 4
47 had charge of the tabernacle of the LORD; 4
47 as the LORD commanded Moses. 4
50 we have brought the LORD'S offering 4
50 make atonement for ourselves before the LORD. 4
52 offering that they offered to the LORD 4
54 for the people of Israel before the LORD. 4
32: 4 land which the LORD smote before . . Israel 4
7 going over into the land which the LORD has given 4
9 from going into the land which the LORD had given 4
10 LORD'S anger was kindled on that day, and he swore 4
12 they have wholly followed the LORD.' 4
13 the LORD'S anger was kindled against Israel 4
13 generation that had done evil in the sight of the LORD 4
14 increase still more the fierce anger of the LORD 4
20 take up arms to go before the LORD for war 4
21 pass over the Jordan before the LORD 4
22 and the land is subdued before the LORD 4
22 return and be free of obligation to the LORD 4
22 land shall be your possession before the LORD 4
23 behold, you have sinned against the LORD; 4
27 pass over . . before the LORD to battle 4
29 every man who is armed to battle before the LORD 4
31 As the LORD has said to your servants, so we will do. 4
32 pass over armed before the LORD into . . Canaan 4
33: 2 wrote down . . by command of the LORD; 4
4 first-born, whom the LORD had struck down among 4
4 upon their gods . . LORD executed judgments. 4
38 went up Mount Hor at the command of the LORD 4
50 LORD said to Moses in the plains of Moab 4
34: 1 The LORD said to Moses 4
13 land . . which the LORD has commanded to give 4
16 The LORD said to Moses 4
29 the LORD commanded to divide the inheritance 4
35: 1 LORD said to Moses in the plains of Moab 4
9 the LORD said to Moses 4
34 LORD dwell in the midst of the people of Israel. 4
36: 2 LORD commanded my lord to give the land 4
2 my lord was commanded by the LORD to give 4
5 Israel according to the word of the LORD, saying 4
6 This is what the LORD commands concerning 4
10 daughters . . did as the LORD commanded Moses; 4
13 which the LORD commanded by Moses to . . Israel 4
Deu 1: 3 all that the LORD had given him in commandment 4
6 LORD our God said to us in Horeb, 'You have stayed 4
8 land which the LORD swore to your fathers 4
10 the LORD your God has multiplied you, and behold 4
11 May the LORD, the God of your fathers, make you 4
19 we set out . . as the LORD our God commanded us; 4
20 hill country . . which the LORD our God gives us. 4
21 LORD your God has set the land before you; go up 4
21 as the LORD, the God of your fathers, has told you; 4
25 'It is a good land which the LORD our God gives us.' 4
26 rebelled against the command of the LORD your God; 4
27 'Because the LORD hated us he has brought us forth 4
30 The LORD your God . . will himself fight for you 4
31 you have seen how the LORD your God bore you 4
32 in spite of this word you did not believe the LORD 4
34 LORD heard your words, and was angered, 4
36 because he has wholly followed the LORD!' 4
37 The LORD was angry with me also on your account 4
41 'We have sinned against the LORD; we will go up 4
41 go up and fight, just as the LORD our God commanded 4
42 the LORD said to me, 'Say to them, Do not go up 4
43 you rebelled against the command of the LORD 4
45 returned and wept before the LORD; 4
45 LORD did not hearken to your voice or give ear 4
2: 1 in the direction of the Red Sea, as the LORD told me 4
2 Then the LORD said to me 4
7 LORD . . blessed you in all the work of your hands; 4
7 these 40 years the LORD your God has been with you 4
9 LORD said to me, 'Do not harass Moab or contend 4
12 their possession, which the LORD gave to them.) 4
14 perished from the camp, as the LORD had sworn 4
15 For indeed the hand of the LORD was against them 4
17 the LORD said to me 4
21 but the LORD destroyed them before them; 4
29 into the land which the LORD our God gives to us.' 4
30 for the LORD your God hardened his spirit 4
31 LORD said to me, 'Behold, I have begun to give Sihon 4
33 LORD our God gave him over to us; and we defeated 4
36 LORD our God gave all into our hands. 4
37 wherever the LORD our God forbade us. 4
3: 2 LORD said to me, 'Do not fear him; for I have given 4
3 LORD our God gave into our hand Og also, the king 4
18 LORD your God has given you this land to possess; 4
20 until the LORD gives rest to your brethren 4
20 land which the LORD your God gives them beyond 4
21 eyes have seen all that the LORD your God has done 4
21 so will the LORD do to all the kingdoms 4
22 for it is the LORD your God who fights for you.' 4
23 I besought the LORD at that time, saying 4
26 LORD was angry with me on your account 4
26 LORD said to me, 'Let it suffice you; speak no more 4
4: 1 possession of the land which the LORD . . gives 4
2 may keep the commandments of the LORD your God 4
3 eyes have seen what the LORD did at Ba'al-pe'or; 4
3 LORD your God destroyed from among you all 4
4 you who held fast to the LORD . . are all alive 4
5 taught you . . as the LORD my God commanded me 4
7 has a god so near to it as the LORD our God is to us 4
10 day that you stood before the LORD your God at Horeb 4
10 LORD said to me, 'Gather the people to me 4
12 LORD spoke to you out of the midst of the fire; 4
14 LORD commanded me at that time to teach you 4
15 no form on the day that the LORD spoke to you 4
19 LORD your God has allotted to all the peoples 4
20 LORD has taken you, and brought you forth 4
21 LORD was angry with me on your account 4
21 good land which the LORD your God gives you 4
23 lest you forget the covenant of the LORD your God 4
23 anything which the LORD your God has forbidden 4
24 LORD your God is a devouring fire, a jealous God. 4
25 doing . . evil in the sight of the LORD your God 4
27 LORD will scatter you among the peoples 4
27 among the nations where the LORD will drive you. 4
29 from there you will seek the LORD your God 4
30 return to the LORD your God and obey his voice 4
31 for the LORD your God is a merciful God; 4

34 all that the LORD your God did for you in Egypt 4
35 shown, that you might know that the LORD is God; 4
39 know . . that the LORD is God in heaven above 4
40 land which the LORD your God gives you for ever. 4
5: 2 The LORD our God made a covenant with us in Horeb. 4
3 Not with . . did the LORD make this covenant 4
4 LORD spoke with you face to face at the mountain 4
5 I stood between the LORD and you at that time 4
5 I stood . . to declare to you the word of the LORD; 4
6 I am the LORD your God, who brought you out 4
9 for I the LORD your God am a jealous God 4
11 not take the name of the LORD your God in vain 4
11 for the LORD will not hold him guiltless 4
12 keep it holy, as the LORD your God commanded you. 4
14 seventh day is a sabbath to the LORD your God; 4
15 servant in the land of Egypt, and the LORD your God 4
15 LORD your God commanded you to keep the sabbath 4
16 'Honor . . as the LORD your God commanded you; 4
16 in the land which the LORD your God gives you. 4
22 These words the LORD spoke to all your assembly 4
24 LORD our God has shown us his glory and greatness 4
25 if we hear the voice of the LORD our God any more 4
27 Go near, and hear all that the LORD our God will say; 4
27 speak to us all that the LORD our God will speak 4
28 LORD heard your words, when you spoke to me; 4
28 LORD said to me, 'I have heard the words 4
32 do . . as the LORD your God has commanded you; 4
33 the way which the LORD your God has commanded 4
6: 1 which the LORD your God commanded me to teach 4
2 that you may fear the LORD your God 4
3 as the LORD, the God of your fathers, has promised 4
4 Hear, O Israel: The LORD our God is one LORD; 4
4 Hear, O Israel: The LORD our God is one LORD; 4
5 shall love the LORD your God with all your heart 4
10 when the LORD your God brings you into the land 4
12 then take heed lest you forget the LORD 4
13 shall fear the LORD your God; you shall serve him 4
15 LORD your God in the midst of you is a jealous God; 4
15 lest the anger of the LORD your God be kindled 4
16 You shall not put the LORD your God to the test 4
17 keep the commandments of the LORD your God 4
18 do what is right and good in the sight of the LORD 4
18 land which the LORD swore to give to your fathers 4
19 thrusting out . . as the LORD has promised. 4
20 which the LORD our God has commanded you?' 4
21 LORD brought us out of Egypt with a mighty hand; 4
22 LORD showed signs and wonders 4
24 LORD commanded us to do all these statutes 4
24 LORD commanded us . . to fear the LORD our God 4
25 do all this commandment before the LORD our God 4
7: 1 When the LORD your God brings you into the land 4
2 when the LORD your God gives them over to you 4
4 anger of the LORD would be kindled against you 4
6 For you are a people holy to the LORD your God; 4
6 For you are a people holy to the LORD your God; 4
7 that the LORD set his love upon you and chose you 4
8 because the LORD loves you, and is keeping 4
8 the LORD has brought you out with a mighty hand 4
9 Know therefore that the LORD your God is God 4
12 LORD your God will keep with you the covenant 4
15 LORD will take away from you all sickness; 4
16 all the peoples that the LORD your God will give 4
18 remember what the LORD your God did to Pharaoh 4
19 by which the LORD your God brought you out; 4
19 so will the LORD your God do to all the peoples 4
20 LORD your God will send hornets among them 4
21 LORD your God is in the midst of you 4
22 LORD your God will clear away these nations 4
23 LORD your God will give them over to you 4
25 for it is an abomination to the LORD your God. 4
8: 1 possess the land which the LORD swore to give 4
2 way which the LORD your God has led you 4
3 that proceeds out of the mouth of the LORD. 4
5 as a man . . the LORD your God disciplines you. 4
6 shall keep the commandments of the LORD your God 4
7 LORD your God is bringing you into a good land 4
10 shall bless the LORD your God for the good land 4
11 Take heed lest you forget the LORD your God, by not 4
14 then . . you forget the LORD your God, who brought 4
18 You shall remember the LORD your God, for it is he 4
19 forget the LORD your God and go after other gods 4
20 nations that the LORD makes to perish before you 4
20 you would not obey the voice of the LORD your God. 4
9: 3 who goes over before you . . is the LORD your God; 4
3 perish quickly, as the LORD has promised you. 4
4 after the LORD your God has thrust them out 4
4 LORD has brought me in to possess this land'; 4
4 that the LORD is driving them out before you. 4
5 LORD your God is driving them out from before you 4
5 word which the LORD swore to your fathers 4
6 Know . . that the LORD your God is not giving you 4
7 how you provoked the LORD your God to wrath 4
7 you have been rebellious against the LORD. 4
8 Even at Horeb you provoked the LORD to wrath 4
8 LORD was so angry with you that he was ready 4
9 tables of the covenant which the LORD made 4
10 LORD gave me the two tables of stone written 4
10 all the words which the LORD had spoken with you 4
11 at the end . . LORD gave me the two tables of stone 4
12 Then the LORD said to me, 'Arise, go down quickly 4
13 Furthermore the LORD said to me, 'I have seen 4
16 behold, you had sinned against the LORD your God; 4
16 from the way which the LORD had commanded 4
18 Then I lay prostrate before the LORD as before 4
18 in doing what was evil in the sight of the LORD 4
19 the anger and hot displeasure which the LORD bore 4
19 But the LORD hearkened to me that time also. 4
20 LORD was so angry with Aaron that he was ready 4
22 At Tab'erah . . you provoked the LORD to wrath. 4
23 when the LORD sent you from Ka'desh-bar'nea, 4
23 against the commandment of the LORD your God 4
24 rebellious against the LORD from the day 4
25 I lay prostrate before the LORD for these 40 days 4
25 because the LORD had said he would destroy you. 4
26 I prayed to the LORD, 'O Lord GOD, destroy not 4
28 Because the LORD was not able to bring them 4
10: 1 At that time the LORD said to me, 'Hew two tables 4
4 ten commandments which the LORD had spoken 4
4 wrote on the tables . . and the LORD gave them to me. 4
5 there they are, as the LORD commanded me. 4
8 At that time the LORD set apart the tribe of Levi 4
8 Levi to carry the ark of the covenant of the LORD 4
8 to stand before the LORD to minister to him 4
9 LORD is his inheritance, as the LORD your God said 4
9 as the LORD your God said to him.) 4
10 LORD hearkened to me that time also; 4
10 LORD was unwilling to destroy you. 4
11 LORD said to me, 'Arise, go on your journey 4
12 now, Israel, what does the LORD your God require 4
12 require . . but to fear the LORD your God, to walk 4
12 to serve the LORD your God with all your heart 4
13 keep the commandments and statutes of the LORD 4
14 Behold, to the LORD your God belong heaven 4
15 yet the LORD set his heart in love upon 4
17 For the LORD your God is God of gods 4
20 fear the LORD your God; you shall serve him 4
22 now the LORD your God has made you as the stars 4
11: 1 You shall therefore love the LORD your God 4
2 consider the discipline of the LORD your God 4
4 how the LORD has destroyed them to this day; 4
7 all the great work of the LORD which he did. 4
9 LORD swore to your fathers to give to them 4
12 land which the LORD your God cares for; 4
12 eyes of the LORD your God are always upon it 4
13 my commandments . . to love the LORD your God 4
17 anger of the LORD be kindled against you 4
17 perish . . off the good land which the LORD gives 4
21 land which the LORD swore to your fathers to give 4
22 commandment . . loving the LORD your God 4
23 LORD will drive out all these nations before you 4
25 LORD your God will lay the fear of you 4
27 if you obey the commandments of the LORD your God 4
28 not obey the commandments of the LORD your God 4
29 when the LORD your God brings you into the land 4
31 land which the LORD your God gives you; 4
12: 1 do in the land which the LORD . . has given you 4
4 You shall not do so to the LORD your God. 4
5 LORD your God will choose out of all your tribes 4
7 there you shall eat before the LORD your God 4
7 in which the LORD your God has blessed you. 4
9 to the rest . . which the LORD your God gives you. 4
10 land which the LORD your God gives you to inherit 4
11 then to the place which the LORD . . will choose 4
11 votive offerings which you vow to the LORD. 4
12 rejoice before the LORD your God 4
14 at the place which the LORD will choose 4
15 according to the blessing of the LORD your God 4
18 eat them before the LORD your God in the place 4
18 place which the LORD your God will choose 4
18 rejoice before the LORD your God in all that you 4
20 When the LORD your God enlarges your territory 4
21 If the place which the LORD your God will choose 4
21 herd or your flock, which the LORD has given you 4
25 when you do what is right in the sight of the LORD. 4
26 shall go to the place which the LORD will choose 4
27 offer . . on the altar of the LORD your God; 4
27 poured out on the altar of the LORD your God 4
28 good and right in the sight of the LORD your God. 4
29 When the LORD your God cuts off before you 4
31 You shall not do so to the LORD your God; 4
31 for every abominable thing which the LORD hates 4
13: 3 LORD your God is testing you, to know whether 4
3 to know whether you love the LORD your God 4
4 shall walk after the LORD your God and fear him 4
5 taught rebellion against the LORD your God 4
5 way in which the LORD your God commanded you 4
10 sought to draw you away from the LORD your God 4
12 which the LORD your God gives you to dwell there 4
16 whole burnt offering to the LORD your God; 4
17 LORD may turn from the fierceness of his anger 4
18 if you obey the voice of the LORD your God, keeping 4
18 doing . . right in the sight of the LORD your God. 4
14: 1 You are the sons of the LORD your God; you shall not 4
2 For you are a people holy to the LORD your God 4
2 LORD has chosen you to be a people 4
21 for you are a people holy to the LORD your God. 4
23 before the LORD . . you shall eat the tithe 4
23 may learn to fear the LORD your God always. 4
24 when the LORD your God blesses you 4
24 place . . which the LORD your God chooses, to set 4
25 go to the place which the LORD your God chooses 4
26 eat there before the LORD your God and rejoice 4
29 LORD your God may bless you in all the work 4
15: 2 because the LORD'S release has been proclaimed. 4
4 (for the LORD will bless you in the land 4
4 land which the LORD your God gives you 4
5 if only you will obey the voice of the LORD 4
6 LORD your God will bless you, as he promised you 4
7 land which the LORD your God gives you 4
9 cry to the LORD against you, and it be sin in you. 4
10 because for this the LORD your God will bless you 4
14 as the LORD your God has blessed you 4
15 LORD your God redeemed you; therefore I command 4
18 LORD your God will bless you in all that you do. 4
19 you shall consecrate to the LORD your God; 4
20 eat it . . before the LORD your God year by year 4
20 eat . . at the place which the LORD will choose. 4
21 you shall not sacrifice it to the LORD your God. 4
16: 1 keep the passover to the LORD your God; 4
1 in the month of Abib the LORD your God brought you 4
2 passover sacrifice to the LORD your God 4
2 place . . LORD will choose, to make his name dwell 4
5 within any . . towns which the LORD your God gives 4
6 at the place which the LORD your God will choose 4
7 at the place which the LORD your God will choose; 4
8 shall be a solemn assembly to the LORD your God; 4
10 keep the feast of weeks to the LORD your God 4
10 which you shall give as the LORD your God blesses 4
11 rejoice before the LORD your God, you and your son 4
11 at the place which the LORD your God will choose 4
15 keep the feast to the LORD your God at the place 4
15 feast . . at the place which the LORD will choose; 4
15 because the LORD your God will bless you in all 4
16 appear before the LORD your God at the place 4
16 shall not appear before the LORD empty-handed; 4
17 blessing of the LORD your God which he has given 4
18 in all your towns which the LORD your God gives 4
20 inherit the land which the LORD your God gives 4
21 beside the altar of the LORD your God 4
22 not set up a pillar which the LORD your God hates. 4
17: 1 not sacrifice to the LORD your God an ox or a sheep 4
1 for that is an abomination to the LORD your God. 4
2 any of your towns which the LORD your God gives 4
2 does . . evil in the sight of the LORD your God 4
8 go up to the place . . LORD your God will choose 4
10 from that place which the LORD will choose; 4
12 stands to minister . . before the LORD your God 4
14 come to the land which the LORD your God gives you 4
15 set as king . . whom the LORD your God will choose. 4
16 since the LORD has said to you, 'You shall never 4
19 learn to fear the LORD his God, by keeping all 4
18: 1 eat the offerings by fire to the LORD 4
2 LORD is their inheritance, as he promised them. 4
5 LORD . . has chosen him out of all your tribes 4
5 stand and minister in the name of the LORD 4
6 comes . . to the place which the LORD will choose 4
7 may minister in the name of the LORD his God 4
7 who stand to minister there before the LORD. 4
9 come into the land which the LORD your God gives 4
12 does these things is an abomination to the LORD; 4
12 practices the LORD your God is driving them out 4
13 You shall be blameless before the LORD your God. 4
14 LORD your God has not allowed you so to do. 4
15 LORD your God will raise up for you a prophet 4
16 desired of the LORD your God at Horeb on the day 4
16 'Let me not hear again the voice of the LORD my God 4
17 LORD said to me, 'They have rightly said all 4
21 we know the word which the LORD has not spoken 4
22 when a prophet speaks in the name of the LORD 4
22 that is a word which the LORD has not spoken; 4
19: 1 When the LORD your God cuts off the nations whose 4
1 whose land the LORD your God gives you 4
2 land which the LORD . . gives you to possess. 4
3 area of the land which the LORD your God gives you 4
8 if the LORD your God enlarges your border 4
9 by loving the LORD your God and by walking 4
10 land which the LORD your God gives you 4
14 land that the LORD your God gives you to possess 4
17 both parties . . shall appear before the LORD 4
20: 1 not be afraid . . LORD your God is with you 4
4 LORD your God is he that goes with you, to fight 4
13 when the LORD your God gives it into your hand 4
14 spoil . . which the LORD your God has given you. 4
16 cities . . LORD . . gives you for an inheritance 4
17 destroy . . as the LORD your God has commanded; 4
18 so to sin against the LORD your God. 4
21: 1 in the land . . LORD your God gives you to possess 4
5 LORD your God has chosen them to minister to him 4
5 chosen them . . to bless in the name of the LORD 4
8 Forgive, O LORD, thy people Israel, whom thou hast 4
9 when you do what is right in the sight of the LORD. 4
10 LORD your God gives them into your hands 4
23 your land which the LORD your God gives you 4
22: 5 does . . is an abomination to the LORD your God. 4
23: 1 shall not enter the assembly of the LORD. 4
2 No bastard shall enter the assembly of the LORD; 4
2 none . . shall enter the assembly of the LORD. 4

3 No Ammonite . . shall enter the assembly of the LORD; 4
3 none . . shall enter the assembly of the LORD 4
5 LORD your God would not hearken to Balaam; 4
5 LORD your God turned the curse into a blessing 4
5 because the LORD your God loved you. 4
8 born to them may enter the assembly of the LORD. 4
14 LORD your God walks in the midst of your camp 4
18 not bring . . into the house of the LORD your God 4
18 both . . are an abomination to the LORD your God. 4
20 that the LORD your God may bless you in all 4
21 When you make a vow to the LORD your God 4
21 LORD your God will surely require it of you 4
23 voluntarily vowed to the LORD your God 4
24: 4 for that is an abomination before the LORD 4
4 land . . LORD your God gives you for an inheritance. 4
9 Remember what the LORD your God did to Miriam 4
13 righteousness to you before the LORD your God. 4
15 lest he cry against you to the LORD, and it be sin 4
18 the LORD your God redeemed you from there; 4
19 LORD . . bless you in all the work of your hands. 4
25:15 in the land which the LORD your God gives you. 4
16 act dishonestly, are an abomination to the LORD 4
19 when the LORD your God has given you rest from all 4
19 land . . LORD your God gives you for an inheritance 4
26: 1 land . . LORD your God gives you for an inheritance 4
2 harvest from your land . . LORD your God gives 4
2 go to the place . . LORD your God will choose 4
3 I declare this day to the LORD your God 4
3 land . . LORD swore to our fathers to give us.' 4
4 set it down before the altar of the LORD your God. 4
5 make response before the LORD your God 4
7 Then we cried to the LORD the God of our fathers 4
7 LORD heard our voice, and saw our affliction 4
8 LORD brought us out of Egypt with a mighty hand 4
10 first of the fruit . . which thou, O LORD, has given 4
10 set it down before the LORD your God, and worship 4
10 set it down . . worship before the LORD your God; 4
11 good which the LORD your God has given to you 4
13 then you shall say before the LORD your God, 'I have 4
14 I have obeyed the voice of the LORD my God 4
16 This day the LORD your God commands you to do 4
17 declared this day concerning the LORD 4
18 LORD has declared this day concerning you 4
19 you shall be a people holy to the LORD your God 4
27: 2 Jordan to the land which the LORD your God gives 4
3 enter the land which the LORD your God gives you 4
3 as the LORD, the God of your fathers, has promised 4
5 there . . build an altar to the LORD your God 4
6 altar to the LORD your God of unhewn stones; 4
6 offer burnt offerings on it to the LORD your God; 4
7 you shall rejoice before the LORD your God. 4
9 you have become the people of the LORD your God. 4
10 therefore obey the voice of the LORD your God 4
15 graven . . image, an abomination to the LORD 4
28: 1 if you obey the voice of the LORD your God 4
1 LORD . . will set you high above all the nations 4
2 if you obey the voice of the LORD your God. 4
7 LORD will cause your enemies who rise against 4
8 LORD will command the blessing upon you 4
8 land which the LORD your God gives you. 4
9 LORD will establish you as a people holy 4
9 if you keep the commandments of the LORD your God 4
10 see that you are called by the name of the LORD; 4
11 LORD will make you abound in prosperity 4
11 land which the LORD swore to your fathers to give 4
12 LORD will open to you his good treasury 4
13 LORD will make you the head, and not the tail; 4
13 if you obey the commandments of the LORD your God 4
15 if you will not obey the voice of the LORD your God 4
20 LORD will send upon you curses, confusion 4
21 LORD will make the pestilence cleave to you 4
22 LORD will smite you with consumption . . fever 4
24 LORD will make the rain of your land powder 4
25 LORD will cause you to be defeated before 4
27 LORD will smite you with the boils of Egypt 4
28 LORD will smite you with madness and blindness 4
35 LORD will smite you on the knees and on the legs 4
36 LORD will bring you, and your king . . to a nation 4
37 among . . peoples where the LORD will lead you away. 4
45 you did not obey the voice of the LORD your God 4
47 Because you did not serve the LORD your God 4
48 your enemies whom the LORD will send against you 4
49 LORD will bring a nation against you from afar 4
52 all your land, which the LORD your God has given 4
53 sons and daughters . . LORD your God has given 4
58 glorious and awful name, the LORD your God 4
59 LORD will bring on you and your offspring 4
61 LORD will bring upon you, until you are destroyed. 4
62 you did not obey the voice of the LORD your God. 4
63 as the LORD took delight in doing you good 4
63 LORD will take delight in bringing ruin upon you 4
64 LORD will scatter you among all peoples 4
65 LORD will give you there a trembling heart 4
68 LORD will bring you back in ships to Egypt 4
29: 1 covenant which the LORD commanded Moses to make 4
2 seen all that the LORD did before your eyes 4
4 LORD has not given you a mind to understand 4
6 that you may know that I am the LORD your God. 4
10 stand this day all of you before the LORD your God; 4
12 enter . . the sworn covenant of the LORD your God 4
12 sworn covenant . . LORD your God makes with you 4
15 stands here . . this day before the LORD our God. 4
18 heart turns away this day from the LORD our God 4
20 LORD would not pardon him, but rather the anger 4
20 rather the anger of the LORD and his jealousy 4
20 LORD would blot out his name from under heaven. 4
21 LORD would single him out . . for calamity 4
22 sicknesses with which the LORD has made it sick- 4
23 which the LORD overthrew in his anger and wrath- 4
24 'Why has the LORD done thus to this land? 4
25 because they forsook the covenant of the LORD 4
27 therefore the anger of the LORD was kindled 4
28 LORD uprooted them from their land in anger 4
29 secret things belong to the LORD our God; 4
30: 1 nations where the LORD your God has driven you 4
2 return to the LORD your God, you and your children 4
3 LORD your God will restore your fortunes 4
3 peoples where the LORD your God has scattered 4
4 from there the LORD your God will gather you 4
5 LORD your God will bring you into the land 4
6 LORD your God will circumcise your heart 4
6 love the LORD your God with all your heart 4
7 LORD your God will put all these curses 4
8 again obey the voice of the LORD, and keep all 4
9 LORD . . will make you abundantly prosperous 4
9 LORD will again take delight in prospering you 4
10 if you obey the voice of the LORD your God, to keep 4
10 turn to the LORD your God with all your heart 4
16 If you obey the commandments of the LORD your God 6
16 obey . . by loving the LORD your God 4
16 LORD your God will bless you in the land 4
20 loving the LORD your God, obeying his voice 4
20 land which the LORD swore to your fathers 4
31: 2 LORD has said to me, 'You shall not go over 4
3 LORD your God himself will go over before you; 4
3 Joshua . . at your head, as the LORD has spoken. 4
4 LORD will do to them as he did to Sihon and Og 4
5 LORD will give them over to you, and you shall do 4
6 for it is the LORD your God who goes with you; 4
7 land . . LORD has sworn to their fathers to give 4
8 LORD who goes before you; he will be with you 4
9 carried the ark of the covenant of the LORD 4
11 Israel comes to appear before the LORD your God 4
12 may hear and learn to fear the LORD your God 4
13 may hear and learn to fear the LORD your God 4
14 LORD said to Moses, "Behold, the days approach 4
15 LORD appeared in the tent in a pillar of cloud; 4
16 LORD said to Moses, "Behold, you are about to sleep 4
23 LORD commissioned Joshua the son of Nun and said •
25 who carried the ark of the covenant of the LORD 4
26 ark of the covenant of the LORD your God 4
27 today you have been rebellious against the LORD; 4
29 will do what is evil in the sight of the LORD 4
32: 3 For I will proclaim the name of the LORD. 4
6 Do you thus requite the LORD, you foolish 4
9 For the LORD'S portion is his people 4
12 LORD alone did lead him, and there was no foreign 4
19 LORD saw it, and spurned them 4
27 LORD has not wrought all this. 4
30 unless . . LORD had given them up? 4
36 For the LORD will vindicate his people 4
48 LORD said to Moses that very day 4
33: 2 LORD came from Sinai, and dawned from Se'ir 4
5 Thus the LORD became king in Jesh'urun •
7 Hear, O LORD, the voice of Judah, and bring him 4
11 Bless, O LORD, his substance, and accept the work 4
12 The beloved of the LORD, he dwells in safety by him; 4
13 of Joseph he said, "Blessed by the LORD be his land 4
21 executed the commands and just decrees of the LORD. 4
23 O Naph'tali . . full of the blessing of the LORD 4
29 O Israel! Who is like you, a people saved by the LORD 4
34: 1 LORD showed him all the land. Gilead as far as Dan 4
4 LORD said to him, "This is the land of which I swore 4
5 Moses the servant of the LORD died there 4
5 died there . . according to the word of the LORD 4
9 Israel . . did as the LORD had commanded Moses. 4
10 like Moses, whom the LORD knew face to face 4
11 signs . . which the LORD sent him to do in the land 4
Jos 1: 1 After the death of Moses the servant of the LORD 4
1 the LORD said to Joshua the son of Nun 4
9 for the LORD your God is with you wherever you go. 4
11 land . . the LORD your God gives you to possess. 4
13 Moses the servant of the LORD commanded you 4
13 The LORD your God is providing you a place of rest 4
15 until the LORD gives rest to your brethren 4
15 the land which the LORD your God is giving them; 4
15 land which Moses the servant of the LORD gave you 4
17 may the LORD your God be with you, as . . with Moses! 4
2: 9 I know that the LORD has given you the land 4
10 the LORD dried up the water of the Red Sea 4
11 the LORD your God is he who is God in heaven above 4
12 swear to me by the LORD that as I have dealt kindly 4
14 we will deal . . when the LORD gives us the land. 4
24 the LORD has given all the land into our hands; 4
3: 3 see the ark of the covenant of the LORD your God 4
5 for tomorrow the LORD will do wonders among you. 4
7 And the LORD said to Joshua, "This day I will begin 4
9 Come . . and hear the words of the LORD your God. 4
13 feet of the priests who bear the ark of the LORD 4
17 who bore the ark of the covenant of the LORD 4
4: 1 When all the nation had . . the LORD said to Joshua 4
5 Pass on before the ark of the LORD your God 4
7 cut off before the ark of the covenant of the LORD; 4
8 took up twelve stones . . as the LORD told Joshua; 4
10 everything . . that the LORD commanded Joshua 4
11 the ark of the LORD and the priests passed over 4
13 40,000 . . passed over before the LORD 4
14 the LORD exalted Joshua in the sight of all 4
15 And the LORD said to Joshua 4
18 bearing the ark of the covenant of the LORD 4
23 the LORD your God dried up the . . Jordan for you 4
23 as the LORD your God did to the Red Sea 4
24 all . . may know that the hand of the LORD is mighty; 4
24 that you may fear the LORD your God for ever. 4
5: 1 the LORD had dried up the waters of the Jordan 4
2 the LORD said to Joshua, "Make flint knives 4
6 they did not hearken to the voice of the LORD; 4
6 LORD swore that he would not let them see the land 4
6 land which the LORD had sworn to their fathers 4
9 And the LORD said to Joshua, "This day I have rolled 4
14 as commander of the army of the LORD I . . now come. 4
15 the commander of the LORD's army said to Joshua 4
6: 2 the LORD said to Joshua, "See, I have 4
6 seven . . rams' horns before the ark of the LORD. 4
7 the armed men pass on before the ark of the LORD. 4
8 bearing the seven trumpets . . before the LORD 4
8 ark of the covenant of the LORD following them. 4
11 he caused the ark of the LORD to compass the city 4
12 and the priests took up the ark of the LORD. 4
13 bearing the . . horns before the ark of the LORD 4
13 and the rear guard came after the ark of the LORD 4
16 Shout; for the LORD has given you the city. 4
17 shall be devoted to the LORD for destruction; 4
19 all silver and gold, and . . are sacred to the LORD; 4
19 they shall go into the treasury of the LORD. 4
24 put into the treasury of the house of the LORD. 4
26 Cursed before the LORD be the man that rises up 4
27 the LORD was with Joshua; and his fame was in all 4
7: 1 the anger of the LORD burned against the people 4
6 fell . . upon his face before the ark of the LORD 4
10 The LORD said to Joshua, "Arise 4
13 Sanctify yourselves . . for thus says the LORD 4
14 the tribe which the LORD takes shall come near 4
14 the family which the LORD takes shall come near 4
14 the household which the LORD takes shall come 4
15 he has transgressed the covenant of the LORD 4
19 My son, give glory to the LORD God of Israel 4
20 I have sinned against the LORD God of Israel 4
23 and they laid them down before the LORD. 4
25 The LORD brings trouble on you today. 4
26 then the LORD turned from his burning anger. 4
8: 1 the LORD said to Joshua, "Do not fear or be dismayed; 4
7 for the LORD your God will give it into your hand. 4
8 set the city on fire, doing as the LORD has bidden; 4
18 the LORD said to Joshua, "Stretch out the javelin 4
27 Israel took . . according to the word of the LORD 4
30 Joshua built an altar in Mount Ebal to the LORD 4
31 as Moses the servant of the LORD had commanded 4
31 they offered on it burnt offerings to the LORD 4
33 who carried the ark of the covenant of the LORD 4
33 as Moses the servant of the LORD had commanded 4
9: 9 come, because of the name of the LORD your God; 4
14 and did not ask direction from the LORD. 4
18 the leaders . . had sworn to them by the LORD 4
19 We have sworn to them by the LORD, the God of Israel 4
24 the LORD your God had commanded his servant 4
27 for the congregation and . . the altar of the LORD 4
10: 8 And the LORD said to Joshua, "Do not fear them 4
10 the LORD threw them into a panic before Israel 4
11 the LORD threw down great stones from heaven 4
12 Then spoke Joshua to the LORD in the day 4
12 when the LORD gave the Amorites over to . . Israel; 4
14 when the LORD hearkened to the voice of a man; 4
14 for the LORD fought for Israel. 4
19 the LORD your God has given them into your hand. 4
25 thus the LORD will do to all your enemies 4
30 the LORD gave it also . . into the hand of Israel; 4
32 and the LORD gave Lachish into the hand of Israel 4
40 left none . . as the LORD God of Israel commanded. 4
42 the LORD God of Israel fought for Israel. 4
11: 6 the LORD said to Joshua, "Do not be afraid of them 4
8 And the LORD gave them into the hand of Israel 4
9 And Joshua did to them as the LORD bade him; 4
12 as Moses the servant of the LORD had commanded. 4
15 As the LORD had commanded Moses his servant 4
15 of all that the LORD had commanded Moses. 4
20 For it was the LORD's doing to harden their hearts 4
20 be exterminated, as the LORD commanded Moses. 4
23 according to all . . the LORD had spoken to Moses; 4
12: 6 Moses, the servant of the LORD 4
6 and Moses the servant of the LORD gave their land 4
13: 1 Joshua was old . . and the LORD said to him 4
8 as Moses the servant of the LORD gave them 4
14 the offerings by fire to the LORD God of Israel 4
33 the LORD God of Israel is their inheritance 4
14: 2 inheritance was by lot, as the LORD had commanded 4

5 people of Israel did as the LORD commanded Moses; 4
6 know what the LORD said to Moses the man of God 4
7 Moses the servant of the LORD sent me . . to spy out 4
8 yet I wholly followed the LORD my God. 4
9 you have wholly followed the LORD my God. 4
10 And now . . the LORD has kept me alive, as he said 4
10 the time that the LORD spoke this word to Moses 4
12 hill country of which the LORD spoke on that day; 4
12 it may be that the LORD will be with me, and I shall 4
12 and I shall drive them out as the LORD said. 4
14 he wholly followed the LORD, the God of Israel. 4
15:13 According to the commandment of the LORD 4
17: 4 The LORD commanded Moses to give us 4
4 according to the commandment of the LORD he gave 4
14 I am . . since hitherto the LORD has blessed me? 4
18: 3 the land, which the LORD, the God of your fathers 4
6 I will cast lots . . here before the LORD our God. 4
7 for the priesthood of the LORD is their heritage; 4
7 which Moses the servant of the LORD gave them. 4
8 I will cast lots . . before the LORD in Shiloh. 4
10 Joshua cast lots . . in Shiloh before the LORD; 4
19:50 By command of the LORD they gave him the city 4
51 distributed by lot at Shiloh before the LORD 4
20: 1 Then the LORD said to Joshua 4
21: 2 The LORD commanded through Moses that we be 4
3 by command of the LORD the people . . gave 4
8 as the LORD had commanded through Moses. 4
43 the LORD gave to Israel all the land . . he swore 4
44 And the LORD gave them rest on every side 4
44 LORD had given all . . enemies into their hands. 4
45 promises which the LORD had made to . . Israel 4
22: 2 all that Moses the servant of the LORD commanded 4
3 careful to keep the charge of the LORD your God. 4
4 the LORD your God has given rest to your brethren 4
4 which Moses the servant of the LORD gave you 4
5 which Moses the servant of the LORD commanded 4
5 and the law . . to love the LORD your God 4
9 had possessed themselves by command of the LORD 4
16 Thus says the whole congregation of the LORD 4
16 in turning away this day from following the LORD 4
16 by building . . in rebellion against the LORD? 4
17 came a plague upon the congregation of the LORD 4
18 you must turn away . . from following the LORD? 4
18 And if you rebel against the LORD today 4
19 the LORD's land where the . . tabernacle stands 4
19 LORD's land where the LORD's tabernacle stands 4
19 do not rebel against the LORD, or make us as rebels 4
19 an altar other than the altar of the LORD our God. 4
22 The Mighty One, God, the LORD! The Mighty One, God 4
22 the LORD! The Mighty One, God, the LORD! He knows 4
22 rebellion or in breach of faith toward the LORD 4
23 an altar to turn away from following the LORD; 4
23 if we did . . may the LORD himself take vengeance. 4
24 What have you to do with the LORD, the God 4
25 For the LORD has made the Jordan a boundary 4
25 you have no portion in the LORD. 4
25 make our children cease to worship the LORD. 4
27 perform the service of the LORD in his presence 4
27 You have no portion in the LORD. 4
28 Behold the copy of the altar of the LORD 4
29 rebel against the LORD, and turn away this day 4
29 and turn away this day from following the LORD 4
29 the altar of the LORD our God that stands 4
31 Today we know that the LORD is in the midst of us 4
31 not committed this treachery against the LORD; 4
31 saved . . Israel from the hand of the LORD. 4
34 it is a witness between us that the LORD is God. 4
23: 1 the LORD had given rest to Israel from all their 4
3 you have seen all that the LORD your God has done 4
3 for it is the LORD your God who has fought for you. 4
5 The LORD your God will push them back before you 4
5 possess their land, as the LORD your God promised 4
8 but cleave to the LORD your God as you have done 4
9 the LORD has driven out before you . . nations; 4
10 since it is the LORD your God who fights for you 4
11 Take good heed . . to love the LORD your God. 4
13 the LORD your God will not continue to drive out 4
13 good land which the LORD your God has given you. 4
14 good things which the LORD your God promised 4
15 good things which the LORD your God has promised 4
15 the LORD will bring upon you all the evil things 4
15 good land which the LORD your God has given you 4
16 transgress the covenant of the LORD your God 4
16 the anger of the LORD will be kindled against you 4
24: 2 Thus says the LORD, the God of Israel, 'Your fathers 4
7 And when they cried to the LORD, he put darkness 4
14 fear the LORD, and serve him in sincerity 4
14 put away the gods . . and serve the LORD. 4
15 And if you be unwilling to serve the LORD 4
15 but as for me and my house, we will serve the LORD. 4
16 Far be it from us that we should forsake the LORD 4
17 the LORD our God . . brought us and our fathers up 4
18 and the LORD drove out before us all the peoples 4
18 we also will serve the LORD, for he is our God. 4
19 You cannot serve the LORD; for he is a holy God; 4
20 If you forsake the LORD and serve foreign gods 4
21 the people said . . "Nay; but we will serve the LORD. 4
22 that you have chosen the LORD, to serve him. 4
23 put away . . and incline your heart to the LORD 4
24 The LORD our God we will serve, and his voice we 4
26 set it up there . . in the sanctuary of the LORD. 4
27 it has heard all the words of the LORD 4
29 Joshua the son of Nun, the servant of the LORD, died 4
31 And Israel served the LORD all the days of Joshua 4
31 and had known all the work which the LORD did 4
Jdg 1: 1 Israel inquired of the LORD, "Who shall go up first 4
2 The LORD said, "Judah shall go up; behold, I have 4
4 LORD gave the Canaanites and the Per'izzites 4
19 the LORD was with Judah, and he took possession 4
22 up against Bethel; and the LORD was with them. 4
2: 1 the angel of the LORD went up from Gilgal 4
4 When the angel of the LORD spoke these words 4
5 Bochim; and they sacrificed there to the LORD. 4
7 the people served the LORD all the days of Joshua 4
7 great work which the LORD had done for Israel. 4
8 Joshua the son of Nun, the servant of the LORD, died 4
10 who did not know the LORD or the work which he had 4
11 evil in the sight of the LORD and served the Ba'als; 4
12 they forsook the LORD, the God of their fathers 4
12 and they provoked the LORD to anger. 4
13 They forsook the LORD, and served the Ba'als 4
14 the anger of the LORD was kindled against Israel 4
15 the hand of the LORD was against them for evil 4
15 against them for evil, as the LORD had warned 4
15 LORD had warned, and as the LORD had sworn 4
16 the LORD raised up judges, who saved them 4
17 who had obeyed the commandments of the LORD 4
18 Whenever the LORD raised up judges for them 4
18 the LORD was with the judge, and he saved them 4
18 for the LORD was moved to pity by their groaning 4
20 the anger of the LORD was kindled against Israel; 4
22 to walk in the way of the LORD as their fathers did 4
23 the LORD left those nations, not driving them out 4
3: 1 the nations which the LORD left, to test Israel 4
4 Israel would obey the commandments of the LORD 4
7 Israel did what was evil in the sight of the LORD 4
7 forgetting the LORD their God, and serving 4
8 the anger of the LORD was kindled against Israel 4
9 Israel cried to the LORD, the LORD raised up 4
9 cried to the LORD, the LORD raised up a deliverer 4
10 The Spirit of the LORD came upon him, and he judged 4
10 to war, and the LORD gave Cu'shan-rishatha'im king 4
12 again did what was evil in the sight of the LORD; 4
12 and the LORD strengthened Eglon the king of Moab 4
12 had done what was evil in the sight of the LORD. 4
15 Israel cried to the LORD, the LORD raised up 4
15 Israel cried to the LORD, the LORD raised up 4
28 for the LORD has given your enemies the Moabites 4
4: 1 again did what was evil in the sight of the LORD 4
2 the LORD sold them into the hand of Jabin king 4
3 the people of Israel cried to the LORD for help; 4
6 said to him, "The LORD, the God of Israel, commands 4
9 for the LORD will sell Sis'era into the hand 4
14 day in which the LORD has given Sis'era 4
14 Does not the LORD go out before you?" So Barak went 4
15 the LORD routed Sis'era and all his chariots 4
5: 2 people offered themselves . . bless the LORD! 4
3 to the LORD I will sing . . make melody to the LORD 4
3 I will make melody to the LORD, the God of Israel. 4
4 LORD, when thou didst go forth from Se'ir 4
5 The mountains quaked before the LORD, yon Sinai 4
5 quaked . . before the LORD, the God of Israel. 4
9 among the people. Bless the LORD. 4
11 there they repeat the triumphs of the LORD 4
11 down to the gates marched the people of the LORD. 4
13 the people of the LORD marched down for him 4
23 Curse Meroz, says the angel of the LORD 4
23 because they came not to the help of the LORD 4
23 to the help of the LORD against the mighty. 4
31 So perish all thine enemies, O LORD! 4
6: 1 Israel did what was evil in the sight of the LORD; 4
1 the LORD gave them into the hand of Mid'ian 4
6 the people of Israel cried for help to the LORD. 4
7 When . . Israel cried to the LORD on account 4
8 the LORD sent a prophet to the people of Israel; 4
8 Thus says the LORD, the God of Israel: I led you up 4
10 I am the LORD your God; you shall not pay reverence 4
11 the angel of the LORD came and sat under the oak 4
12 angel of the LORD appeared to him and said to him 4
12 him, "The LORD is with you, you mighty man of valor. 4
13 if the LORD is with us, why then has all this 4
13 Did not the LORD bring us up from Egypt?' 4
13 us up from Egypt?' But now the LORD has cast us off 4
14 the LORD turned to him and said, "Go in this might 4
16 the LORD said to him, "But I will be with you 4
21 the angel of the LORD reached out the tip 4
21 the angel of the LORD vanished from his sight. 4
22 Gideon perceived that he was the angel of the LORD 4
22 now I have seen the angel of the LORD face to face. 4
23 the LORD said to him, "Peace be to you; do not fear 4
24 Then Gideon built an altar there to the LORD 4
24 Gideon built . . and called it, The LORD is peace. 4
25 night the LORD said to him, "Take your father's bull 4
26 build an altar to the LORD your God on the top 4
27 Gideon took . . and did as the LORD had told him; 4
34 the Spirit of the LORD took possession of Gideon; 4
7: 2 The LORD said to Gideon, "The people with you are 4
4 LORD said to Gideon, "The people are still too many; 4
5 and the LORD said to Gideon, "Every one that laps 4
7 the LORD said to Gideon, "With the 300 men 4
9 same night the LORD said to him, "Arise, go down 4
15 Arise; for the LORD has given the host of Mid'ian 4
18 the camp, and shout, 'For the LORD and for Gideon.' 4
20 they cried, "A sword for the LORD and for Gideon! 4
22 the LORD set every man's sword against his fellow 4
8: 7 Well then, when the LORD has given Zebah 4
19 as the LORD lives, if you had saved them alive 4
23 not rule over you; the LORD will rule over you. 4
34 Israel did not remember the LORD their God 4
10: 6 Israel again did . . evil in the sight of the LORD 4
6 they forsook the LORD, and did not serve him. 4
7 the anger of the LORD was kindled against Israel 4
10 Israel cried to the LORD, saying, "We have sinned 4
11 the LORD said to the people of Israel, "Did I not 4
15 Israel said to the LORD, "We have sinned; do to us 4
16 put away the foreign gods . . and served the LORD; 4
11: 9 the Ammonites, and the LORD gives them over to me 4
10 The LORD will be witness between us; we will 4
11 spoke all his words before the LORD at Mizpah. 4
21 the LORD, the God of Israel, gave Sihon and all his 4
23 then the LORD, the God of Israel, dispossessed 4
24 And all that the LORD our God has dispossessed 4
27 the LORD, the Judge, decide this day between 4
29 the Spirit of the LORD came upon Jephthah 4
30 Jephthah made a vow to the LORD, and said, "If thou 4
31 whoever . . shall be the LORD'S, and I will offer 4
32 them; and the LORD gave them into his hand. 4
35 I have opened my mouth to the LORD, and I cannot 4
36 father, if you have opened your mouth to the LORD 4
36 now that the LORD has avenged you on your enemies 4
12: 3 and the LORD gave them into my hand; 4
13: 1 Israel again did . . evil in the sight of the LORD; 4
1 and the LORD gave them into the hand 4
3 the angel of the LORD appeared to the woman 4
8 Mano'ah entreated the LORD, and said, "O LORD, 4
8 O LORD, I pray thee, let the man of God whom thou 2
13 the angel of the LORD said to Mano'ah, "Of all that I 4
15 Mano'ah said to the angel of the LORD, "Pray, let us 4
16 the angel of the LORD said to Mano'ah, "If you detain 4
16 ready a burnt offering, then offer it to the LORD. 4
16 did not know that he was the angel of the LORD. 4
17 Mano'ah said to the angel of the LORD, "What is 4
18 the angel of the LORD said to him, "Why do you ask 4
19 offered . . to the LORD, to him who works wonders. 4
20 the angel of the LORD ascended in the flame 4
21 The angel of the LORD appeared no more to Mano'ah 4
21 Mano'ah knew that he was the angel of the LORD. 4
23 If the LORD had meant to kill us, he would not have 4
24 Samson; and the boy grew, and the LORD blessed him. 4
25 And the Spirit of the LORD began to stir him 4
14: 4 and mother did not know that it was from the LORD; 4
6 the Spirit of the LORD came mightily upon him 4
19 the Spirit of the LORD came mightily upon him 4
15:14 and the Spirit of the LORD came mightily upon him 4
18 very thirsty, and he called on the LORD and said 4
16:20 And he did not know that the LORD had left him. 4
28 Samson called to the LORD and said, "O Lord GOD 4
17: 2 his mother said, "Blessed be my son by the LORD. 4
3 I consecrate the silver to the LORD from my hand 4
13 Now I know that the LORD will prosper me, because I 4
18: 6 The journey . . is under the eye of the LORD. 4
20: 1 congregation assembled as one man to the LORD 4
18 And the LORD said, "Judah shall go up first. 4
23 people of Israel went up and wept before the LORD 4
23 they inquired of the LORD, "Shall we again draw 4
23 And the LORD said, "Go up against them. 4
26 they sat there before the LORD, and fasted 4
26 burnt . . and peace offerings before the LORD. 4
27 the people of Israel inquired of the LORD 4
28 And the LORD said, "Go up; for tomorrow 4
35 the LORD defeated Benjamin before Israel; 4
21: 3 O LORD, the God of Israel, why has this come to pass 4
5 did not come up in the assembly to the LORD? 4
5 him who did not come up to the LORD to Mizpah 4
7 we have sworn by the LORD that we will not give 4
8 What one . . did not come up to the LORD to Mizpah? 4
15 the LORD had made a breach in the tribes 4
19 there is the yearly feast of the LORD at Shiloh 4
Rut 1: 6 had heard . . that the LORD had visited his people 4
8 Go, return . . May the LORD deal kindly with you 4
9 The LORD grant that you may find a home, 4
13 the hand of the LORD has gone forth against me. 4
17 May the LORD do so to me and more also if even death 4
21 and the LORD has brought me back empty. 4
21 Why call me Na'omi, when the LORD has afflicted me 4
2: 4 and he said to the reapers, "The LORD be with you! 4
4 And they answered, "The LORD bless you. 4
12 The LORD recompense you for what you have done 4
12 and a full reward be given you by the LORD 4
20 And Na'omi said . . "Blessed be he by the LORD 4
3:10 said, "May you be blessed by the LORD, my daughter; 4
13 as the LORD lives, I will do the part . . for you. 4
4:11 May the LORD make the woman . . like Rachel 4
12 because of the children that the LORD will give 4
13 he went in to her, and the LORD gave her conception 4
14 Blessed be the LORD, who has not left you this day 4
1Sm 1: 3 to worship and to sacrifice to the LORD of hosts 4

3 Hophni and Phin'ehas, were priests of the LORD. 4
5 only one . . because the LORD had closed her womb. 4
6 because the LORD had closed her womb. 4
7 as often as she went up to the house of the LORD 4
9 beside the doorpost of the temple of the LORD. 4
10 She was deeply distressed and prayed to the LORD 4
11 O LORD of hosts, if thou wilt . . then I will give him 4
11 I will give him to the LORD all the days of his life 4
12 As she continued praying before the LORD 4
15 I have been pouring out my soul before the LORD. 4
19 rose early . . and worshiped before the LORD; 4
19 knew Hannah . . and the LORD remembered her; 4
20 Samuel, for she said, "I have asked him of the LORD. 4
21 went up to offer to the LORD the yearly sacrifice 4
22 that he may appear in the presence of the LORD 4
23 wait . . only, may the LORD establish his word. 4
24 she brought him to the house of the LORD at Shiloh; 4
26 woman who was standing . . praying to the LORD. 4
27 I prayed; and the LORD has granted me my petition 4
28 Therefore I have lent him to the LORD; 4
28 as long as he lives, he is lent to the LORD. 4
28 And they worshiped the LORD there. 4
2: 1 My heart exults in the LORD; 4
1 my strength is exalted in the LORD. 4
2 There is none holy like the LORD 4
3 the LORD is a God of knowledge 4
6 The LORD kills and brings to life; 4
7 The LORD makes poor and makes rich; 4
8 For the pillars of the earth are the LORD's 4
10 The adversaries of the LORD shall be broken 4
10 The LORD will judge the ends of the earth; 4
11 And the boy ministered to the LORD 4
12 they had no regard for the LORD. 4
17 the sin . . was very great in the sight of the LORD; 4
17 treated the offering of the LORD with contempt. 4
18 Samuel was ministering before the LORD 4
20 The LORD give you children by this woman 4
20 for the loan which she lent to the LORD"; 4
21 And the LORD visited Hannah, and she conceived 4
21 the boy Samuel grew in the presence of the LORD. 4
24 that I hear the people of the LORD spreading 4
25 if a man sins against the LORD, who can intercede 4
25 for it was the will of the LORD to slay them. 4
26 to grow . . in favor with the LORD and with men. 4
27 Thus the LORD has said, 'I revealed myself 4
30 Therefore the LORD the God of Israel declares 4
30 I promised . . '; but now the LORD declares: 'Far be it 4
3: 1 Samuel was ministering to the LORD under Eli. 4
1 And the word of the LORD was rare in those days; 4
3 Samuel was lying . . within the temple of the LORD 4
4 Then the LORD called, "Samuel! Samuel! 4
6 the LORD called again, "Samuel!" And Samuel arose 4
7 Now Samuel did not yet know the LORD 4
7 the word of the LORD had not yet been revealed 4
8 And the LORD called Samuel again the third time. 4
8 Eli perceived that the LORD was calling the boy. 4
9 you shall say, 'Speak, LORD, for thy servant hears.' 4
10 And the LORD came and stood forth, calling 4
11 the LORD said to Samuel, "Behold, I am about to do 4
15 then he opened the doors of the house of the LORD. 4
18 It is the LORD; let him do what seems good to him. 4
19 And Samuel grew, and the LORD was with him 4
20 Samuel was established as a prophet of the LORD. 4
21 And the LORD appeared again at Shiloh 4
21 the LORD revealed himself to Samuel at Shiloh 4
21 LORD revealed himself . . by the word of the LORD. 4
4: 3 Why has the LORD put us to rout today 4
3 bring the ark of the covenant of the LORD here 4
4 the ark of the covenant of the LORD of hosts 4
5 the ark of the covenant of the LORD came 4
6 the ark of the LORD had come to the camp 4
5: 3 face downward . . before the ark of the LORD. 4
4 face downward . . before the ark of the LORD 4
6 The hand of the LORD was heavy upon the people 4
9 the hand of the LORD was against the city 4
6: 1 The ark of the LORD was in the country 4
2 What shall we do with the ark of the LORD? 4
8 take the ark of the LORD and place it on the cart 4
11 And they put the ark of the LORD on the cart 4
14 offered the cows as a burnt offering to the LORD. 4
15 Levites took down the ark of the LORD and the box 4
15 sacrificed sacrifices on that day to the LORD. 4
17 returned as a guilt offering to the LORD 4
18 stone, beside which they set . . the ark of the LORD 4
19 because they looked into the ark of the LORD; 4
19 LORD had made a . . slaughter among the people. 4
20 Who is able to stand before the LORD, this holy God? 4
21 Philistines have returned the ark of the LORD. 4
7: 1 the men . . came and took up the ark of the LORD 4
1 Elea'zar, to have charge of the ark of the LORD. 4
2 all the house of Israel lamented after the LORD. 4
3 you are returning to the LORD with all your heart 4
3 put away . . and direct your heart to the LORD 4
4 Israel put away . . and they served the LORD only. 4
5 Gather . . and I will pray to the LORD for you. 4
6 and drew water and poured it out before the LORD 4
6 and said there, "We have sinned against the LORD. 4
8 cry to the LORD our God for us, that he may save us 4
9 offered it as a whole burnt offering to the LORD; 4
9 and Samuel cried to the LORD for Israel 4
9 Samuel cried to the LORD . . and the LORD answered 4
10 the LORD thundered with a mighty voice that day 4
12 for he said, "Hitherto the LORD has helped us. 4
13 the hand of the LORD was against the Philistines 4
17 And he built there an altar to the LORD. 4
8: 6 And Samuel prayed to the LORD. 4
7 the LORD said to Samuel, "Hearken to the . . people 4
10 Samuel told all the words of the LORD 4
18 you will cry . . but the LORD will not answer you 4
21 he repeated them in the ears of the LORD. 4
22 the LORD said to Samuel, "Hearken to their voice 4
9:15 before Saul came, the LORD had revealed to Samuel 4
17 the LORD told him, "Here is the man of whom I spoke 4
10: 1 Has not the LORD anointed you to be prince 6
1 And you shall reign over the people of the LORD 6
1 the LORD has anointed you to be prince over his 4
6 the spirit of the LORD will come mightily upon 4
17 Samuel called the people together to the LORD 4
18 Thus says the LORD, the God of Israel, 'I brought up 4
19 present yourselves before the LORD by . . tribes 4
22 they inquired again of the LORD, "Did the man come 4
22 the LORD said, "Behold, he has hidden himself 4
24 Do you see him whom the LORD has chosen? 4
25 wrote . . in a book and laid it up before the LORD. 4
11: 7 Then the dread of the LORD fell upon the people 4
13 the LORD has wrought deliverance in Israel. 4
15 they made Saul king before the LORD in Gilgal. 4
15 sacrificed peace offerings before the LORD 4
12: 3 Here I am; testify against me before the LORD 4
5 The LORD is witness against you, and his anointed 4
6 The LORD is witness, who appointed Moses 4
7 stand . . that I may plead with you before the LORD 4
7 the saving deeds of the LORD which he performed 4
8 your fathers cried to the LORD and the LORD sent 4
8 the LORD sent Moses and Aaron, who brought forth 4
9 they forgot the LORD their God; and he sold them 4
10 they cried to the LORD, and said, "We have sinned 4
10 We have sinned, because we have forsaken the LORD 4
11 the LORD sent Jerubba'al and Barak, and Jephthah 4
12 you said . . when the LORD your God was your king. 4
13 behold, the LORD has set a king over you. 4
14 If you will fear the LORD and serve him 4
14 not rebel against the commandment of the LORD 4
14 both you and the king . . follow the LORD your God 4
15 if you will not hearken to the voice of the LORD 4
15 but rebel against the commandment of the LORD 4
15 the hand of the LORD will be against you 4
16 which the LORD will do before your eyes. 4
17 I will call upon the LORD, that he may send thunder 4
17 which you have done in the sight of the LORD 4
18 Samuel called upon the LORD, and the LORD sent 4
18 and the LORD sent thunder and rain that day; 4
18 the people greatly feared the LORD and Samuel. 4
19 Pray for your servants to the LORD your God 4
20 do not turn aside from following the LORD 4
20 but serve the LORD with all your heart; 4
22 the LORD will not cast away his people 4
22 it has pleased the LORD to make you a people 4
23 far be it . . that I should sin against the LORD 4
24 Only fear the LORD, and serve him faithfully 4
13:12 and I have not entreated the favor of the LORD'; 4
13 not kept the commandment of the LORD your God 4
13 the LORD would have established your kingdom 4
14 the LORD has sought out a man after his own heart; 4
14 the LORD has appointed him to be prince 4
14 you have not kept what the LORD commanded you. 4
14: 3 son of Eli, the priest of the LORD in Shiloh 4
6 it may be that the LORD will work for us; 4
6 nothing can hinder the LORD from saving 4
10 the LORD has given them into our hand. 4
12 the LORD has given them into the hand of Israel. 4
23 So the LORD delivered Israel that day; 4
33 the people are sinning against the LORD 4
34 sin against the LORD by eating with the blood.' 4
35 And Saul built an altar to the LORD; 4
35 it was the first altar that he built to the LORD. 4
39 For as the LORD lives . . he shall surely die. 4
41 O LORD God of Israel, why hast thou not answered 4
41 O LORD, God of Israel, give Urim; 6
45 As the LORD lives, there shall not one hair . . fall 4
15: 1 The LORD sent me to anoint you king over . . Israel; 4
1 now therefore hearken to the words of the LORD. 4
2 Thus says the LORD of hosts, 'I will punish 4
10 The word of the LORD came to Samuel 4
11 was angry; and he cried to the LORD all night. 4
13 Blessed be you to the LORD; I have performed 4
13 I have performed the commandment of the LORD. 4
15 spared the best . . to sacrifice to the LORD 4
16 tell you what the LORD said to me on this night. 4
17 The LORD anointed you king over Israel. 4
18 And the LORD sent you on a mission, and said 4
19 Why then did you not obey the voice of the LORD? 4
19 and do what was evil in the sight of the LORD? 4
20 I have obeyed the voice of the LORD, I have gone 4
20 have gone on the mission on which the LORD sent me 4
21 people took . . to sacrifice to the LORD your God 4
22 Has the LORD as great delight in burnt offerings 4
22 as in obeying the voice of the LORD? 4
23 Because you have rejected the word of the LORD 4
24 I have transgressed the commandment of the LORD 4
25 and return with me, that I may worship the LORD. 4
26 for you have rejected the word of the LORD 4
26 and the LORD has rejected you from being king 4
28 The LORD has torn the kingdom of Israel from you 4
30 return . . that I may worship the LORD your God. 4
31 and Saul worshiped the LORD. 4
33 And Samuel hewed Agag in pieces before the LORD 4
35 And the LORD repented that he had made Saul king 4
16: 1 The LORD said to Samuel, "How long will you grieve 4
2 And the LORD said, "Take a heifer with you, and say 4
2 and say, 'I have come to sacrifice to the LORD.' 4
4 Samuel did what the LORD commanded, and came 4
5 I have come to sacrifice to the LORD; 4
6 Surely the LORD's anointed is before him. 4
7 But the LORD said to Samuel, "Do not look on his 4
7 for the LORD sees not as man sees; *
7 man looks on . . but the LORD looks on the heart. 4
8 And he said, "Neither has the LORD chosen this one. 4
9 And he said, "Neither has the LORD chosen this one. 4
10 Samuel said . . "The LORD has not chosen these. 4
12 And the LORD said, "Arise, anoint him; for this is he. 4
13 the Spirit of the LORD came mightily upon David 4
14 Now the Spirit of the LORD departed from Saul 4
14 and an evil spirit from the LORD tormented him. 4
18 a man of good presence; and the LORD is with him. 4
17:37 The LORD who delivered me from the paw of the lion 4
37 Saul said to David, "Go, and the LORD be with you! 4
45 but I come to you in the name of the LORD of hosts 4
46 This day the LORD will deliver you into my hand 4
47 know that the LORD saves not with sword and spear; 4
47 the battle is the LORD's and he will give you 4
18:12 the LORD was with him but had departed from Saul. 4
14 David had success . . for the LORD was with him. 4
17 be valiant . . and fight the LORD's battles. 4
28 Saul saw and knew that the LORD was with David 4
19: 5 the LORD wrought a great victory for all Israel. 4
6 As the LORD lives, he shall not be put to death. 4
9 Then an evil spirit from the LORD came upon Saul 4
20: 3 But truly, as the LORD lives . . there is but a step 4
12 The LORD, the God of Israel, be witness! 4
13 the LORD do so to Jonathan, and more also 4
13 the LORD be with you, as he has been with my father. 4
14 show me the loyal love of the LORD 4
15 When the LORD cuts off every one of the enemies 4
16 may the LORD take vengeance on David's enemies. 4
21 for, as the LORD lives, it is safe for you 4
22 if I say . . then go; for the LORD has sent you away. 4
23 as for . . the LORD is between you and me for ever. 4
42 we have sworn both of us in the name of the LORD 4
42 'The LORD shall be between me and you . . for ever.' 4
21: 6 which is removed from before the LORD 4
7 was there that day, detained before the LORD; 4
22:10 and he inquired of the LORD for him 4
17 king said . . "Turn and kill the priests of the LORD; 4
17 to fall upon the priests of the LORD. 4
21 that Saul had killed the priests of the LORD. 4
23: 2 David inquired of the LORD, "Shall I go and attack 4
2 Therefore David inquired of the LORD, "Shall I go 4
4 Then David inquired of the LORD again. 4
4 the LORD answered him, "Arise, go down to Kei'lah; 4
10 Then said David, "O LORD, the God of Israel 4
11 O LORD, the God of Israel, I beseech thee 4
11 And the LORD said, "He will come down. 4
12 And the LORD said, "They will surrender you. 4
18 the two of them made a covenant before the LORD; 4
21 And Saul said, "May you be blessed by the LORD; 4
24: 4 Here is the day of which the LORD said to you 4
6 The LORD forbid that I . . do this thing to my lord 4
6 do this thing to my lord, the LORD's anointed 4
6 LORD forbid . . seeing he is the LORD's anointed. 4
10 the LORD gave you today into my hand in the cave; 4
10 'I will not . . for he is the LORD's anointed.' 4
12 May the LORD judge between me and you 4
12 May the LORD judge . . may the LORD avenge me 4
15 May the LORD therefore be judge 4
18 not kill me when the LORD put me into your hands. 4
19 may the LORD reward you with good 4
21 Swear to me therefore by the LORD that you will 4
25:26 as the LORD lives, and as your soul lives 4
26 the LORD has restrained you from bloodguilt 4
28 the LORD will certainly make my lord a sure house 4
28 my lord is fighting the battles of the LORD; 4
29 of the living in the care of the LORD your God; 4
30 when the LORD has done to my lord 4
31 And when the LORD has dealt well with my lord 4
32 Blessed be the LORD, the God of Israel, who sent you 4
34 For as surely as the LORD the God of Israel lives 4
38 ten days later the LORD smote Nabal; and he died. 4
39 Blessed be the LORD who has avenged the insult 4
39 LORD has returned the evil . . upon his own head. 4
26: 9 put forth his hand against the LORD's anointed 4
10 As the LORD lives, the LORD will smite him; 4
10 As the LORD lives, the LORD will smite him; 4
11 The LORD forbid that I should put forth my hand 4
11 put forth my hand against the LORD's anointed; 4
12 a deep sleep from the LORD had fallen upon them. 4
16 As the LORD lives, you deserve to die 4

16 kept watch over your lord, the LORD's anointed. 4
19 If it is the LORD who has stirred you up against me 4
19 but if it is men, may they be cursed before the LORD 4
19 I should have no share in the heritage of the LORD 4
20 away from the presence of the LORD; 4
23 LORD rewards every man for his righteousness 4
23 the LORD gave you into my hand today 4
23 put forth my hand against the LORD's anointed. 4
24 so may my life be precious in the sight of the LORD 4
28: 6 when Saul inquired of the LORD, the LORD did not 4
6 the LORD did not answer him, either by dreams 4
10 Saul swore to her by the LORD, "As the LORD lives 4
10 Saul swore to her by the LORD, "As the LORD lives 4
16 the LORD has turned . . and become your enemy? 4
17 The LORD has done to you as he spoke by me; 4
17 The LORD has done to you as he spoke by me; 4
18 Because you did not obey the voice of the LORD 4
18 therefore the LORD has done this thing to you 4
19 the LORD will give Israel also . . into the hand 4
19 the LORD will give the army . . into the hand 4
29: 6 As the LORD lives, you have been honest 4
30: 6 David strengthened himself in the LORD his God. 4
8 And David inquired of the LORD, "Shall I pursue 4
23 shall not do so . . with what the LORD has given us; 4
26 for you from the spoil of the enemies of the LORD"; 4
2Sm 1:12 for the people of the LORD and for the house 4
14 put . . your hand to destroy the LORD's anointed? 4
16 saying, 'I have slain the LORD's anointed.' 4
2: 1 David inquired of the LORD, "Shall I go up into any 4
1 And the LORD said to him, "Go up. 4
5 May you be blessed by the LORD, because you showed 4
6 the LORD show steadfast love and faithfulness 4
3: 9 accomplish for David what the LORD has sworn 4
18 the LORD has promised David, saying, 'By the hand 4
28 I and my kingdom are . . guiltless before the LORD 4
39 The LORD requite the evildoer according to his 4
4: 8 the LORD has avenged my lord the king . . on Saul 4
9 As the LORD lives, who has redeemed my life 4
5: 2 the LORD said to you, 'You shall be shepherd 4
3 made a covenant with them . . before the LORD 4
10 for the LORD, the God of hosts, was with him. 4
12 the LORD had established him king over Israel 4
19 And David inquired of the LORD, "Shall I go up 4
19 And the LORD said to David, "Go up; for I will 4
20 The LORD has broken through my enemies before me 4
23 And when David inquired of the LORD, he said 4
24 for then the LORD has gone out before you to smite 4
25 And David did as the LORD commanded him 4
6: 2 which is called by the name of the LORD of hosts 4
5 making merry before the LORD with all . . might 4
7 the anger of the LORD was kindled against Uzzah; 4
8 because the LORD had broken forth upon Uzzah; 4
9 And David was afraid of the LORD that day; 4
9 he said, "How can the ark of the LORD come to me? 4
10 David was not willing to take the ark of the LORD 4
11 the ark of the LORD remained . . three months; 4
11 LORD blessed O'bed-e'dom and all his household. 4
12 The LORD has blessed the household of O'bed-e'dom 4
13 who bore the ark of the LORD had gone six paces 4
14 David danced before the LORD with all his might; 4
15 David and . . Israel brought up the ark of the LORD 4
16 As the ark of the LORD came into the city of David 4
16 saw . . David leaping and dancing before the LORD; 4
17 And they brought in the ark of the LORD, and set it 4
17 burnt . . and peace offerings before the LORD. 4
18 he blessed . . in the name of the LORD of hosts 4
21 It was before the LORD, who chose me 4
21 as prince over Israel, the people of the LORD 4
21 and I will make merry before the LORD. 4
7: 1 the LORD had given him rest from all his enemies 4
3 Go, do all . . in your heart; for the LORD is with you. 4
4 that . . night the word of the LORD came to Nathan 4
5 Thus says the LORD: Would you build me a house 4
8 Thus says the LORD of hosts, I took you 4
11 the LORD declares to you that the LORD will make 4
11 declares . . that the LORD will make you a house. 4
18 David went in and sat before the LORD, and said 4
22 Therefore thou art great, O LORD God; 4
24 and thou, O LORD, didst become their God. 4
25 And now, O LORD God, confirm for ever the word 4
26 saying, 'The LORD of hosts is God over Israel,' 4
27 thou, O LORD of hosts, the God of Israel, hast made 4
8: 6 the LORD gave victory to David wherever he went. 4
11 these also King David dedicated to the LORD 4
14 the LORD gave victory to David wherever he went. 4
10:12 and may the LORD do what seems good to him. 4
11:27 the thing . . David had done displeased the LORD. 4
12: 1 And the LORD sent Nathan to David. 4
5 As the LORD lives, the man . . deserves to die; 4
7 Thus says the LORD, the God of Israel, 'I anointed 4
9 you despised the word of the LORD, to do . . evil 4
11 Thus says the LORD, 'Behold, I will raise up evil 4
13 David said . . "I have sinned against the LORD. 4
13 The LORD . . put away your sin; you shall not die. 4
14 by this deed you have utterly scorned the LORD 4
15 the LORD struck the child . . and it became sick. 4
20 he went into the house of the LORD, and worshiped; 4
22 Who knows whether the LORD will be gracious to me 4
24 called his name Solomon. And the LORD loved him 4
25 he called his name Jedidi'ah, because of the LORD. 4
14:11 Pray let the king invoke the LORD your God 4
11 As the LORD lives, not one hair . . shall fall 4
17 good and evil. The LORD your God be with you! 4
15: 7 let me . . pay my vow, which I have vowed to the LORD 4
8 If the LORD will . . bring me back to Jerusalem 4
8 then I will offer worship to the LORD.' 4
20 may the LORD show steadfast love and . . to you. 6
21 As the LORD lives, and as my lord the king lives 4
25 If I find favor in the eyes of the LORD 4
31 O LORD, I pray thee, turn the counsel of Ahith'ophel 4
16: 8 LORD has avenged . . the blood of the house of Saul 4
8 the LORD has given the kingdom into the hand 4
10 If he is cursing because the LORD has said to him 4
11 and let him curse; for the LORD has bidden him. 4
12 may be that the LORD will look upon my affliction 4
12 the LORD will repay me with good for this cursing 4
18 the LORD and this people and all the men of Israel 4
17:14 the LORD had ordained to defeat the good counsel 4
14 so that the LORD might bring evil upon Ab'salom. 4
18:19 the LORD has delivered him from . . his enemies. 4
28 Blessed be the LORD your God, who has delivered up 4
31 the LORD has delivered you this day from . . all 4
19: 7 I swear by the LORD, if you do not go, not a man will 4
21 to death . . because he cursed the LORD's anointed? 4
20:19 why will you swallow up the heritage of the LORD? 4
21: 1 and David sought the face of the LORD. 4
1 And the LORD said, "There is bloodguilt on Saul 4
3 that you may bless the heritage of the LORD? 4
6 that we may hang them up before the LORD at Gibeon 4
6 hang . . at Gibeon on the mountain of the LORD. 4
7 the oath of the LORD which was between them 4
9 they hanged them on the mountain before the LORD 4
22: 1 And David spoke to the LORD the words of this song 4
1 David . . on the day when the LORD delivered him 4
2 The LORD is my rock . . my fortress . . my deliverer 4
4 I call upon the LORD, who is worthy to be praised 4
7 In my distress I called upon the LORD; 4
14 The LORD thundered from heaven 4
16 were laid bare, at the rebuke of the LORD 4
19 They came upon me . . but the LORD was my stay. 4
21 The LORD rewarded me according to my 4
22 For I have kept the ways of the LORD, and have not 4
25 Therefore the LORD has recompensed me 4
29 Yea, thou art my lamp, O LORD 4
31 the promise of the LORD proves true; 4
32 For who is God, but the LORD? 4
42 they cried to the LORD, but he did not answer them. 4
47 The LORD lives; and blessed be my rock, and exalted 4
50 I will extol thee, O LORD, among the nations 4
23: 2 The Spirit of the LORD speaks by me 4
10 and the LORD wrought a great victory that day; 4
12 and the LORD wrought a great victory. 4
16 would not drink of it; he poured it out to the LORD 4
17 Far be it from me, O LORD, that I should do this. 4
24: 1 the anger of the LORD was kindled against Israel 4
3 May the LORD your God add to the people 4
10 And David said to the LORD, "I have sinned greatly 4
10 But now, O LORD, I pray thee, take away the iniquity 4
11 the word of the LORD came to the prophet Gad 4
12 Thus says the LORD, Three things I offer you; 4
14 let us fall into the hand of the LORD 4
15 the LORD sent a pestilence upon Israel 4
16 the LORD repented of the evil, and said 4
16 the angel of the LORD was by the threshing floor 4
17 Then David spoke to the LORD when he saw the angel 4
18 rear an altar to the LORD on the threshing floor 4
19 David went up . . as the LORD commanded. 4
21 To buy the . . in order to build an altar to the LORD 4
23 And Arau'nah said . . "The LORD your God accept you. 4
24 I will not offer burnt offerings to the LORD my God 4
25 And David built there an altar to the LORD 4
25 So the LORD heeded supplications for the land 4
1Kg 1:17 you swore . . by the LORD your God, saying, 'Solomon 4
29 As the LORD lives, who has redeemed my soul 4
30 I swore to you by the LORD, the God of Israel, saying 4
36 May the LORD, the God of my lord the king, say so. 4
37 As the LORD has been with my lord the king, even 4
48 Blessed be the LORD, the God of Israel, who has 4
2: 3 keep the charge of the LORD your God, walking 4
4 that the LORD may establish his word which he 4
8 when he came . . I swore to him by the LORD, saying 4
15 become my brother's, for it was his from the LORD. 4
23 Solomon swore by the LORD, saying, "God do so to me 4
24 as the LORD lives, who has established me 4
27 expelled Abi'athar from being priest to the LORD 4
27 thus fulfilling the word of the LORD which he had 4
28 Jo'ab fled to the tent of the LORD and caught hold 4
29 Jo'ab has fled to the tent of the LORD, and behold 4
30 Benai'ah came to the tent of the LORD, and said 4
32 The LORD will bring back his bloody deeds upon 4
33 to David . . there shall be peace from the LORD 4
42 Did I not make you swear by the LORD, and solemnly 4
43 Why then have you not kept your oath to the LORD 4
44 the LORD will bring back your evil upon your own 4
45 of David shall be established before the LORD 4
3: 1 building his own house and the house of the LORD 4
2 house had yet been built for the name of the LORD. 4
3 Solomon loved the LORD, walking in the statutes 4
5 At Gibeon the LORD appeared to Solomon in a dream 4
7 O LORD my God, thou hast made thy servant king 4
15 stood before the ark of the covenant of the LORD 4
5: 3 not build a house for the name of the LORD his God 4
3 could not build . . until the LORD put them under 4
4 the LORD my God has given me rest on every side; 4
5 to build a house for the name of the LORD my God 4
5 to build a house . . as the LORD said to David 4
7 Blessed be the LORD . . who has given to David 4
12 the LORD gave Solomon wisdom, as he promised him; 4
6: 1 he began to build the house of the LORD. 4
2 The house which King Solomon built for the LORD 4
11 Now the word of the LORD came to Solomon 4
19 to set there the ark of the covenant of the LORD. 4
37 the foundation of the house of the LORD was laid 4
7: 9 from the court of the house of the LORD •
12 so had the inner court of the house of the LORD 4
40 all the work that he did . . on the house of the LORD 4
45 all these vessels in the house of the LORD 4
48 made all the vessels . . in the house of the LORD 4
51 work that . . Solomon did on the house of the LORD 4
51 them in the treasuries of the house of the LORD. 4
8: 1 bring up the ark of the covenant of the LORD 4
4 they brought up the ark of the LORD, the tent 4
6 brought the ark of the covenant of the LORD 4
9 LORD made a covenant with the people of Israel 4
10 a cloud filled the house of the LORD 4
11 glory of the LORD filled the house of the LORD. 4
11 glory of the LORD filled the house of the LORD. 4
12 The LORD has set the sun in the heavens 4
15 Blessed be the LORD, the God of Israel, who 4
17 a house for the name of the LORD, the God of Israel. 4
18 the LORD said to David my father, 'Whereas 4
20 the LORD has fulfilled his promise which he made; 4
20 sit on the throne of Israel, as the LORD promised 4
20 house for the name of the LORD, the God of Israel. 4
21 in which is the covenant of the LORD which he made 4
22 Then Solomon stood before the altar of the LORD 4
23 O LORD, God of Israel, there is no God like thee 4
25 O LORD, God of Israel, keep with thy servant David 4
28 have regard . . O LORD my God, hearkening 4
44 they pray to the LORD toward the city 4
54 offering . . prayer and supplication to the LORD 4
54 he arose from before the altar of the LORD 4
56 Blessed be the LORD who has given rest 4
57 The LORD our God be with us 4
59 I have made supplication before the LORD 4
59 words . . be near to the LORD our God day and night 4
60 may know that the LORD is God; there is no other. 4
61 your heart . . be wholly true to the LORD our God 4
62 Israel . . offered sacrifice before the LORD. 4
63 Solomon offered as peace offerings to the LORD 4
63 the king and . . dedicated the house of the LORD. 4
64 the court that was before the house of the LORD; 4
64 the bronze altar that was before the LORD 4
65 the feast . . before the LORD our God, seven days. 4
66 the goodness that the LORD had shown to David 4
9: 1 finished building the house of the LORD 4
2 the LORD appeared to Solomon a second time 4
3 the LORD said to him, "I have heard 4
8 Why has the LORD done thus to this land 4
9 they forsook the LORD their God who brought 4
9 the LORD has brought all this evil upon them.' 4
10 Solomon had built . . the house of the LORD 4
15 forced labor . . to build the house of the LORD 4
25 upon the altar which he built to the LORD 4
25 offer up . . burning incense before the LORD. 4
10: 1 fame of Solomon concerning the name of the LORD 4
5 which he offered at the house of the LORD 4
9 Blessed be the LORD . . who has delighted in you 4
9 Because the LORD loved Israel for ever 4
12 king made . . supports for the house of the LORD 4
11: 2 the nations concerning which the LORD had said 4
4 his heart was not wholly true to the LORD his God 4
6 Solomon did what was evil in the sight of the LORD 4
6 Solomon . . did not wholly follow the LORD 4
9 the LORD was angry with Solomon 4
9 his heart had turned away from the LORD 4
10 he did not keep what the LORD commanded. 4
11 Therefore the LORD said to Solomon 4
14 the LORD raised up an adversary against Solomon 4
31 Take . . ten pieces; for thus says the LORD 4
12:15 it was a turn of affairs brought about by the LORD 4
15 fulfil his word, which the LORD spoke by Ahi'jah 4
24 'Thus says the LORD, You shall not go up or fight 4
24 they hearkened to the word of the LORD 4
24 went home . . according to the word of the LORD. 4
27 go up to offer sacrifices in the house of the LORD 4
13: 1 came out of Judah by the word of the LORD 4
2 cried against the altar by the word of the LORD 4
2 thus says the LORD: 'Behold, a son shall be born 4
3 This is the sign that the LORD has spoken: 'Behold 4
5 which the man . . had given by the word of the LORD. 4
6 Entreat now the favor of the LORD your God 4
6 the man of God entreated the LORD; 4
9 so was it commanded me by the word of the LORD 4
17 it was said to me by the word of the LORD 4
18 an angel spoke to me by the word of the LORD, saying 4
20 the word of the LORD came to the prophet 4

21 Thus says the LORD, 'Because you have disobeyed 4
21 Because you have disobeyed the word of the LORD 4
21 commandment which the LORD your God commanded 4
26 the man of God, who disobeyed the word of the LORD; 4
26 the LORD has given him to the lion, which has torn 4
26 the word which the LORD spoke to him. 4
32 the saying which he cried by the word of the LORD 4
14: 5 the LORD said to Ahi'jah, "Behold 4
7 Go, tell Jerobo'am, 'Thus says the LORD 4
11 the birds . . shall eat; for the LORD has spoken it."' 4
13 there is found something pleasing to the LORD 4
14 the LORD will raise up for himself a king 4
15 the LORD will smite Israel, as a reed is shaken 4
15 made their Ashe'rim, provoking the LORD to anger. 4
18 mourned for him, according to the word of the LORD 4
21 in Jerusalem, the city which the LORD had chosen 4
22 Judah did what was evil in the sight of the LORD 4
24 the nations which the LORD drove out 4
26 took away the treasures of the house of the LORD 4
28 as the king went into the house of the LORD 4
15: 3 his heart was not wholly true to the LORD his God 4
4 the LORD his God gave him a lamp in Jerusalem 4
5 David did what was right in the eyes of the LORD 4
11 Asa did what was right in the eyes of the LORD 4
14 Asa was wholly true to the LORD all his days. 4
15 he brought into the house of the LORD the . . gifts 4
18 left in the treasures of the house of the LORD 4
26 He did what was evil in the sight of the LORD 4
29 destroyed it, according to the word of the LORD 4
30 he provoked the LORD, the God of Israel. 4
34 He did what was evil in the sight of the LORD 4
16: 1 the word of the LORD came to Jehu the son of Hana'ni 4
7 the word of the LORD came by the prophet Jehu 4
7 all the evil that he did in the sight of the LORD 4
12 Thus Zimri . . according to the word of the LORD 4
13 to sin, provoking the LORD God of Israel to anger 4
19 his sins . . doing evil in the sight of the LORD 4
25 Omri did what was evil in the sight of the LORD 4
26 provoking the LORD . . to anger by their idols. 4
30 Ahab . . did evil in the sight of the LORD 4
33 Ahab did more to provoke the LORD . . to anger 4
34 the word of the LORD, which he spoke by Joshua 4
17: 1 As the LORD the God of Israel lives 4
2 And the word of the LORD came to him 4
5 he went and did according to the word of the LORD; 4
8 Then the word of the LORD came to him 4
12 As the LORD your God lives, I have nothing baked 4
14 For thus says the LORD the God of Israel 4
14 until the day that the LORD sends rain 4
16 the word of the LORD which he spoke by Eli'jah. 4
20 he cried to the LORD, "O LORD my God 4
20 O LORD my God, hast thou brought calamity even 4
21 and cried to the LORD, "O LORD my God 4
21 O LORD my God, let this child's soul come into him 4
22 the LORD hearkened to the voice of Eli'jah; 4
24 the word of the LORD in your mouth is truth. 4
18: 1 the word of the LORD came to Eli'jah . . saying, "Go 4
3 Now Obadi'ah revered the LORD greatly; 4
4 when Jez'ebel cut off the prophets of the LORD 4
10 As the LORD your God lives, there is no nation 4
12 the Spirit of the LORD will carry you 4
12 I . . have revered the LORD from my youth. 4
13 when Jez'ebel killed the prophets of the LORD 4
13 how I hid 100 men of the LORD's prophets 4
15 As the LORD of hosts lives . . I will surely show 4
18 you have forsaken the commandments of the LORD 4
21 If the LORD is God, follow him; 4
22 I, even I only, am left a prophet of the LORD; 4
24 I will call on the name of the LORD; 4
30 he repaired the altar of the LORD 4
31 Jacob, to whom the word of the LORD came, saying 4
32 he built an altar in the name of the LORD. 4
36 O LORD, God of Abraham, Isaac, and Israel, let it be 4
37 Answer me, O LORD . . that this people may know 4
37 that this people may know that thou, O LORD, art God 4
38 the fire of the LORD fell, and consumed 4
39 they said, "The LORD, he is God; the LORD, he is God. 4
39 they said, "The LORD, he is God; the LORD, he is God. 4
46 the hand of the LORD was on Eli'jah; 4
19: 4 It is enough; now, O LORD, take away my life; 4
7 the angel of the LORD came again a second time 4
9 the word of the LORD came to him, and he said to him 4
10 He said, "I have been very jealous for the LORD 4
11 stand upon the mount before the LORD. 4
11 the LORD passed by, and a great and strong wind 4
11 and broke in pieces the rocks before the LORD 4
11 but the LORD was not in the wind; 4
11 but the LORD was not in the earthquake; 4
12 a fire, but the LORD was not in the fire; 4
14 He said, "I have been very jealous for the LORD 4
15 the LORD said to him, "Go, return on your way 4
20:13 Thus says the LORD, Have you seen all this 4
13 I will . . and you shall know that I am the LORD. 4
14 Thus says the LORD, By the servants 4
28 Thus says the LORD, 'Because the Syrians have said 4
28 The LORD is a god of the hills but he is not a god 4
28 and you shall know that I am the LORD.' 4
35 said to his fellow at the command of the LORD 4
36 Because you have not obeyed the voice of the LORD 4
42 Thus says the LORD, 'Because you have let go 4
21: 3 The LORD forbid that I should give you 4
17 the word of the LORD came to Eli'jah the Tishbite 4
19 'Thus says the LORD, "Have you killed, and also taken 4
19 'Thus says the LORD: "In the place where dogs licked 4
20 to do what is evil in the sight of the LORD. 4
23 And of Jez'ebel the LORD also said 4
25 to do what was evil in the sight of the LORD 4
26 as the Amorites . . whom the LORD cast out 4
28 the word of the LORD came to Eli'jah the Tishbite 4
22: 5 Inquire first for the word of the LORD. 4
7 Is there not here another prophet of the LORD 4
8 yet one man by whom we may inquire of the LORD 4
11 Thus says the LORD, 'With these you shall push 4
12 the LORD will give it into the hand of the king. 4
14 Micai'ah said, "As the LORD lives . . that I will 4
14 what the LORD says to me, that I will speak. 4
15 the LORD will give it into the hand of the king. 4
16 that you speak . . the truth in the name of the LORD? 4
17 the LORD said, 'These have no master; 4
19 Therefore hear the word of the LORD: I saw the LORD 4
19 I saw the LORD sitting on his throne 4
20 the LORD said, 'Who will entice Ahab 4
21 a spirit came forward and stood before the LORD 4
22 the LORD said to him, 'By what means?' 4
23 the LORD has put a lying spirit in the mouth 4
23 the LORD has spoken evil concerning you. 4
24 How did the Spirit of the LORD go from me 4
28 If you return . . the LORD has not spoken by me. 4
38 the word of the LORD which he had spoken. 4
43 doing what was right in the sight of the LORD; 4
52 He did what was evil in the sight of the LORD 4
53 and provoked the LORD, the God of Israel, to anger 4
2Kg 1: 3 the angel of the LORD said to Eli'jah the Tishbite 4
4 thus says the LORD, 'You shall not come down 4
6 Thus says the LORD, Is it because there is no God 4
15 the angel of the LORD said to Eli'jah, "Go down 4
16 Thus says the LORD, 'Because you have sent 4
17 So he died according to the word of the LORD 4
2: 1 the LORD was about to take Eli'jah up to heaven 4
2 the LORD has sent me as far as Bethel. 4
2 As the LORD lives, and as you yourself live, I will 4
3 the LORD will take away your master from over you? 4
4 tarry here . . the LORD has sent me to Jericho. 4
4 As the LORD lives, and as you yourself live, I will 4
5 the LORD will take away your master from over you? 4
6 the LORD has sent me to the Jordan. 4
6 As the LORD lives, and as you yourself live, I will 4
14 saying, "Where is the LORD, the God of Eli'jah? 4
16 the Spirit of the LORD has caught him up 4
21 Thus says the LORD, I have made this 4
24 he cursed them in the name of the LORD. 4
3: 2 He did what was evil in the sight of the LORD 4
10 The LORD has called these three kings to give 4
11 Is there no prophet of the LORD here 4
11 through whom we may inquire of the LORD? 4
12 said, "The word of the LORD is with him. 4
13 No; it is the LORD who has called these three kings 4
14 As the LORD of hosts lives, whom I serve, were it not 4
15 the power of the LORD came upon him. 4
16 Thus says the LORD, 'I will make this dry stream-bed 4
17 For thus says the LORD, 'You shall not see wind 4
18 This is a light thing in the sight of the LORD; 4
4: 1 you know that your servant feared the LORD 4
27 the LORD has hidden it from me, and has not told me. 4
30 As the LORD lives, and as you yourself live, I will 4
33 and shut the door . . and prayed to the LORD. 4
43 that they may eat, for thus says the LORD 4
44 had some left, according to the word of the LORD. 4
5: 1 by him the LORD had given victory to Syria. 4
11 and stand, and call on the name of the LORD his God 4
16 As the LORD lives, whom I serve, I will receive 4
17 will not . . sacrifice to any god but the LORD. 4
18 In this matter may the LORD pardon your servant 4
18 when I . . the LORD pardon your servant in this 4
20 As the LORD lives, I will run after him 4
6:17 O LORD, I pray thee, open his eyes that he may see. 4
17 So the LORD opened the eyes of the young man 4
18 when the Syrians . . Eli'sha prayed to the LORD 4
20 Eli'sha said, "O LORD, open the eyes of these men 4
20 So the LORD opened their eyes, and they saw; 4
27 If the LORD will not help you, whence shall I help 4
33 This trouble is from the LORD! Why should I wait 4
33 Why should I wait for the LORD any longer? 4
7: 1 Hear the word of the LORD: thus says the LORD 4
1 thus says the LORD, Tomorrow about this time 4
2 If the LORD . . should make windows in heaven 4
16 for a shekel, according to the word of the LORD. 4
19 If the LORD himself should make windows 4
8: 1 the LORD has called for a famine, and it will come 4
8 go to meet . . and inquire of the LORD through him 4
10 the LORD has shown me that he shall . . die. 4
13 The LORD has shown me that you are to be king 4
18 And he did what was evil in the sight of the LORD. 4
19 Yet the LORD would not destroy Judah 4
27 and did what was evil in the sight of the LORD 4
9: 3 'Thus says the LORD, I anoint you king over Israel.' 4
6 Thus says the LORD the God of Israel, I anoint you 4
6 I anoint you king over the people of the LORD 4
7 and the blood of the all the servants of the LORD. 4
12 Thus says the LORD, I anoint you king over Israel.' 4
25 remember . . how the LORD uttered this oracle 4
26 As surely as I saw . . -says the LORD-I will requite 4
26 in accordance with the word of the LORD. 4
36 This is the word of the LORD, which he spoke 4
10:10 shall fall . . nothing of the word of the LORD 4
10 word . . which the LORD spoke concerning 4
10 the LORD has done what he said by his servant 4
16 Come with me, and see my zeal for the LORD. 4
17 he slew all . . according to the word of the LORD 4
23 there is no servant of the LORD here among you 4
30 the LORD said to Jehu, "Because you have done well 4
31 to walk in the law of the LORD the God of Israel 4
32 the LORD began to cut off parts of Israel. 4
11: 3 he remained . . hid in the house of the LORD, while 4
4 and had them come to him in the house of the LORD; 4
4 and put them under oath in the house of the LORD 4
7 which come on . . and guard the house of the LORD 4
10 and shields . . which were in the house of the LORD; 4
13 she went into the house of the LORD to the people; 4
15 Let her not be slain in the house of the LORD. 4
17 between the LORD and the king and people 4
17 covenant . . that they should be the LORD's people; 4
18 posted watchmen over the house of the LORD. 4
19 brought the king down from the house of the LORD 4
12: 2 Jeho'ash did what was right in the eyes of the LORD 4
4 the money . . brought into the house of the LORD 4
4 prompts him to bring into the house of the LORD 4
9 right side as one entered the house of the LORD; 4
9 the money . . brought into the house of the LORD. 4
10 the money that was found in the house of the LORD. 4
11 who had the oversight of the house of the LORD; 4
11 builders who worked upon the house of the LORD 4
12 stone for making repairs on the house of the LORD 4
13 were not made for the house of the LORD basins 4
13 money that was brought into the house of the LORD 4
14 workmen who were repairing the house of the LORD 4
16 was not brought into the house of the LORD; it 4
18 found in the treasuries of the house of the LORD 4
13: 2 He did what was evil in the sight of the LORD 4
3 the anger of the LORD was kindled against Israel 4
4 Then Jeho'ahaz besought the LORD 4
4 Jeho'ahaz besought . . and the LORD hearkened 4
5 Therefore the LORD gave Israel a savior 4
11 He also did what was evil in the sight of the LORD; 4
17 The LORD's arrow of victory, the arrow of victory 4
23 the LORD was gracious to them and had compassion 4
14: 3 And he did what was right in the eyes of the LORD 4
6 what is written . . where the LORD commanded 4
14 vessels that were found in the house of the LORD 4
24 And he did what was evil in the sight of the LORD; 4
25 word of the LORD, the God of Israel, which he spoke 4
26 For the LORD saw that the affliction of Israel 4
27 the LORD had not said . . he would blot out the name 4
15: 3 he did what was right in the eyes of the LORD 4
5 the LORD smote the king, so that he was a leper 4
9 And he did what was evil in the sight of the LORD 4
12 the promise of the LORD which he gave to Jehu 4
18 And he did what was evil in the sight of the LORD; 4
24 And he did what was evil in the sight of the LORD; 4
28 And he did what was evil in the sight of the LORD; 4
34 And he did what was right in the eyes of the LORD 4
35 He built the upper gate of the house of the LORD. 4
37 the LORD began to send Rezin . . and Pekah 4
16: 2 do what was right in the eyes of the LORD his God 4
3 practices of the nations whom the LORD drove out 4
8 silver and gold . . found in the house of the LORD 4
14 the bronze altar . . before the LORD he removed 4
14 place between his altar and the house of the LORD 4
18 he removed from the house of the LORD 4
17: 2 And he did what was evil in the sight of the LORD 4
7 Israel had sinned against the LORD their God 4
8 nations whom the LORD drove out before . . Israel 4
9 Israel did secretly against the LORD their God 4
11 as the nations did whom the LORD carried away 4
11 did wicked things, provoking the LORD to anger 4
12 served idols, of which the LORD had said to them 4
13 Yet the LORD warned Israel and Judah 4
14 who did not believe in the LORD their God. 4
15 concerning whom the LORD had commanded them 4
16 all the commandments of the LORD their God 4
17 to do evil in the sight of the LORD, provoking him 4
18 Therefore the LORD was very angry with Israel 4
19 keep the commandments of the LORD their God 4
20 the LORD rejected all the descendants of Israel 4
21 Jerobo'am drove Israel from following the LORD 4
23 the LORD removed Israel out of his sight 4
25 at the beginning . . they did not fear the LORD; 4
25 the LORD sent lions among them, which killed some 4
28 and taught them how they should fear the LORD. 4
32 They also feared the LORD 4
33 they feared the LORD but also served their own 4
34 They do not fear the LORD, and they do not follow 4
34 commandment which the LORD commanded . . Jacob 4
35 The LORD made a covenant with them, 4
36 you shall fear the LORD, who brought you out 4
39 but you shall fear the LORD your God, and he will 4
41 these nations feared the LORD and also served 4

18: 3 And he did what was right in the eyes of the LORD 4
5 He trusted in the LORD the God of Israel; 4
6 commandments which the LORD commanded Moses. 4
6 For he held fast to the LORD; he did not depart 4
7 the LORD was with him; wherever . . he prospered. 4
12 they did not obey the voice of the LORD their God 4
12 all that Moses the servant of the LORD commanded; 4
15 the silver that was found in the house of the LORD 4
16 the gold from the doors of the temple of the LORD 4
22 if you say . . "We rely on the LORD our God," is it not 4
25 is it without the LORD that I have come up 4
25 The LORD said to me, Go up against this land 4
30 Do not let . . make you to rely on the LORD by saying 4
30 The LORD will surely deliver us 4
32 misleads you by saying, The LORD will deliver us. 4
35 the LORD should deliver Jerusalem out of my hand?' 4
19: 1 and went into the house of the LORD. 4
4 the LORD . . heard all the words of the Rab'shakeh 4
4 the words which the LORD your God has heard; 4
6 Thus says the LORD: Do not be afraid 4
14 and Hezeki'ah went up to the house of the LORD 4
14 Hezeki'ah went . . and spread it before the LORD. 4
15 Hezeki'ah prayed before the LORD, and said: "O LORD 4
15 O LORD the God of Israel, who art enthroned above 4
16 Incline thy ear, O LORD, and hear; open thy eyes 4
16 open thy eyes, O LORD, and see; and hear the words 4
17 Of a truth, O LORD, the kings . . have laid waste 4
19 So now, O LORD our God, save us, I beseech thee 4
19 know that thou, O LORD, art God alone. 4
20 Thus says the LORD, the God of Israel 4
21 This is the word that the LORD has spoken 4
31 The zeal of the LORD will do this. 4
32 thus says the LORD concerning the king 4
33 he shall not come into this city, says the LORD. 4
35 the angel of the LORD went forth, and slew 4
20: 1 Thus says the LORD, 'Set your house in order; 4
2 Hezeki'ah turned . . and prayed to the LORD, saying 4
3 Remember now, O LORD . . how I have walked before 4
4 the word of the LORD came to him 4
5 Thus says the LORD, the God of David your father 4
5 you shall go up to the house of the LORD. 4
8 What shall be the sign that the LORD will heal me 4
8 I . . go up to the house of the LORD on the third day? 4
9 This is the sign . . that the LORD will do the thing 4
9 the LORD will do the thing that he has promised 4
11 Isaiah . . cried to the LORD, and he brought 4
16 Isaiah said to Hezeki'ah, "Hear the word of the LORD 4
17 nothing shall be left, says the LORD. 4
19 The word of the LORD which you have spoken is good. 4
21: 2 And he did what was evil in the sight of the LORD 4
2 nations whom the LORD drove out before . . Israel. 4
4 And he built altars in the house of the LORD 4
4 the house of the LORD, of which the LORD had said 4
5 the two courts of the house of the LORD. 4
6 He did much evil in the sight of the LORD 4
7 the house of which the LORD said to David 4
9 the nations . . whom the LORD destroyed 4
10 And the LORD said by his servants the prophets 4
12 thus says the LORD, the God of Israel 4
16 they did what was evil in the sight of the LORD. 4
20 And he did what was evil in the sight of the LORD 4
22 he forsook the LORD . . and did not walk in the way 4
22 and did not walk in the way of the LORD. 4
22: 2 And he did what was right in the eyes of the LORD 4
3 the king sent Shaphan . . to the house of the LORD 4
4 the money . . brought into the house of the LORD 4
5 who have the oversight of the house of the LORD; 4
5 give it to the workmen . . at the house of the LORD 4
8 found the book of the law in the house of the LORD. 4
9 who have the oversight of the house of the LORD. 4
13 Go, inquire of the LORD for me, and for the people 4
13 great is the wrath of the LORD that is kindled 4
15 Thus says the LORD, the God of Israel: 'Tell the man 4
16 Thus says the LORD, Behold, I will bring evil 4
18 king of Judah, who sent you to inquire of the LORD 4
18 Thus says the LORD, the God of Israel 4
19 and you humbled yourself before the LORD 4
19 I also have heard you, says the LORD. 4
23: 2 And the king went up to the house of the LORD 4
2 which had been found in the house of the LORD. 4
3 king stood . . and made a covenant before the LORD 4
3 a covenant . . to walk after the LORD and to keep 4
4 to bring out of the temple of the LORD all 4
6 brought . . the Ashe'rah from the house of the LORD 4
7 the houses . . which were in the house of the LORD 4
9 priests . . did not come up to the altar of the LORD 4
11 horses . . at the entrance to the house of the LORD 4
12 had made in the two courts of the house of the LORD 4
16 and defiled it, according to the word of the LORD 4
19 which kings . . made, provoking the LORD to anger 6
21 Keep the passover to the LORD your God 4
23 this passover was kept to the LORD in Jerusalem. 4
24 the book . . found in the house of the LORD. 4
25 who turned to the LORD with all his heart 4
26 the LORD did not turn from . . his great wrath 4
27 the LORD said, "I will remove Judah also 4
32 And he did what was evil in the sight of the LORD 4
37 And he did what was evil in the sight of the LORD 4
24: 2 the LORD sent against him bands of the Chalde'ans 4
2 to destroy it, according to the word of the LORD 4
3 this came upon Judah at the command of the LORD 4
4 innocent blood, and the LORD would not pardon. 4
9 And he did what was evil in the sight of the LORD 4
13 all the treasures of the house of the LORD 4
13 all the vessels of gold in the temple of the LORD 4
13 as the LORD had foretold. 4
19 And he did what was evil in the sight of the LORD 4
20 because of the anger of the LORD . . he cast them 4
25: 9 burned the house of the LORD, and the king's house 4
13 the pillars of bronze . . in the house of the LORD 4
13 the bronze sea that were in the house of the LORD 4
16 which Solomon had made for the house of the LORD 4
1Ch 2: 3 Er . . was wicked in the sight of the LORD 4
6:15 the LORD sent Judah and Jerusalem into exile 4
31 put in charge . . in the house of the LORD 4
32 until Solomon had built the house of the LORD 4
9:19 had been in charge of the camp of the LORD 4
20 Phin'ehas . . the LORD was with him. 4
23 in charge of the gates of the house of the LORD 4
10:13 Saul . . was unfaithful to the LORD 4
13 Saul . . was unfaithful to the LORD 4
14 did not seek guidance from the LORD. 4
14 Therefore the LORD slew him •
11: 2 LORD your God said to you, 'You shall be shepherd 4
3 a covenant with them at Hebron before the LORD 4
3 according to the word of the LORD by Samuel. 4
9 and greater, for the LORD of hosts was with him. 4
10 to make him king, according to the word of the LORD 4
14 and the LORD saved them by a great victory. 4
18 would not drink of it; he poured it out to the LORD 4
12:23 according to the word of the LORD. 4
13: 2 good to you, and if it is the will of the LORD our God 4
6 the LORD who sits enthroned above the cherubim. 4
10 the anger of the LORD was kindled against Uzzah; 4
11 because the LORD had broken forth upon Uzzah; 4
14 the LORD blessed the household of O'bed-e'dom 4
14: 2 the LORD had established him king over Israel 4
10 LORD said to him, "Go up, and I will give them 4
17 LORD brought the fear of him upon all nations. 4
15: 2 LORD chose them to carry the ark of the LORD 4
2 LORD chose them to carry the ark of the LORD 4
3 to bring up the ark of the LORD to its place 4
12 bring up the ark of the LORD, the God of Israel 4
13 LORD our God broke forth upon us 4
14 to bring up the ark of the LORD, the God of Israel. 4
15 commanded according to the word of the LORD. 4
25 to bring up the ark of the covenant of the LORD 4
26 carrying the ark of the covenant of the LORD 4
28 brought up the ark of the covenant of the LORD 4
29 ark of the covenant of the LORD came to the city 4
16: 2 he blessed the people in the name of the LORD 4
4 Levites as ministers before the ark of the LORD 4
4 to invoke, to thank, and to praise the LORD 4
7 thanksgiving be sung to the LORD by Asaph 4
8 O give thanks to the LORD, call on his name 4
10 let the hearts of those who seek the LORD rejoice! 4
11 Seek the LORD and his strength, seek his presence 4
14 LORD our God; his judgments are in all the earth. 4
23 Sing to the LORD, all the earth! 4
25 For great is the LORD, and greatly to be praised 4
26 are idols; but the LORD made the heavens. 4
28 Ascribe to the LORD, O families of the peoples 4
28 ascribe to the LORD glory and strength! 4
29 Ascribe to the LORD the glory due his name; 4
29 Worship the LORD in holy array; 4
31 let them say among the nations, "The LORD reigns! 4
33 the trees of the wood sing for joy before the LORD 4
34 O give thanks to the LORD, for he is good; 4
36 Blessed be the LORD, the God of Israel 4
36 all the people said "Amen!" and praised the LORD. 4
37 there before the ark of the covenant of the LORD 4
39 tabernacle of the LORD in the high place 4
40 to the LORD upon the altar of burnt offering 4
40 all that is written in the law of the LORD 4
41 expressly named to give thanks to the LORD 4
17: 1 ark of the covenant of the LORD is under a tent. 4
3 same night the word of the LORD came to Nathan 6
4 Thus says the LORD: You shall not build me a house 4
7 Thus says the LORD of hosts 4
10 that the LORD will build you a house. 4
16 Then King David went in and sat before the LORD 4
16 said, "Who am I, O LORD God, and what is my house 4
17 and hast shown me future generations, O LORD God! 4
19 For thy servant's sake, O LORD 4
20 There is none like thee, O LORD 4
22 and thou, O LORD, didst become their God. 4
23 now, O LORD, let the word which thou hast spoken 4
24 LORD of hosts, the God of Israel, is Israel's God 4
26 now, O LORD, thou art God, and thou hast promised 4
27 what thou, O LORD, hast blessed is blessed for ever 4
18: 6 LORD gave victory to David wherever he went. 4
11 these also King David dedicated to the LORD 4
13 the LORD gave victory to David wherever he went. 4
19:13 and may the LORD do what seems good to him. 4
21: 3 May the LORD add to his people 100 times 4
9 the LORD spoke to Gad, David's seer, saying 4
10 'Thus says the LORD, Three things I offer you; 4
11 Thus says the LORD, 'Take which you will 4
12 or else three days of the sword of the LORD 4
12 angel of the LORD destroying . . Israel. 4
13 let me fall into the hand of the LORD 4
14 the LORD sent a pestilence upon Israel; 4
15 when he was about to destroy it, the LORD saw 4
15 the angel of the LORD was standing 4
16 and saw the angel of the LORD standing between 4
17 Let thy hand, I pray thee, O LORD my God, be against 4
18 angel of the LORD commanded Gad to say to David 4
18 David should go up and rear an altar to the LORD 4
19 word, which he had spoken in the name of the LORD. 4
22 that I may build on it an altar to the LORD 4
24 I will not take for the LORD what is yours 4
26 David built there an altar to the LORD 4
26 called upon the LORD, and he answered him 4
27 Then the LORD commanded the angel; 4
28 when David saw that the LORD had answered him 4
29 tabernacle of the LORD, which Moses had made 4
30 afraid of the sword of the angel of the LORD. 4
22: 1 David said, "Here shall be the house of the LORD God 4
5 the house that is to be built for the LORD 4
6 to build a house for the LORD, the God of Israel. 4
7 to build a house to the name of the LORD my God. 4
8 the word of the LORD came to me, saying 4
11 the LORD be with you, so that you may succeed 4
11 in building the house of the LORD your God 4
12 LORD grant you discretion and understanding 4
12 you may keep the law of the LORD your God. 4
13 which the LORD commanded Moses for Israel. 4
14 I have provided for the house of the LORD 4
16 Arise and be doing! The LORD be with you! 4
18 Is not the LORD your God with you? 4
18 land is subdued before the LORD and his people. 4
19 set your mind and heart to seek the LORD your God. 4
19 Arise and build the sanctuary of the LORD God 4
19 so that the ark of the covenant of the LORD 4
19 into a house built for the name of the LORD. 4
23: 4 have charge of the work in the house of the LORD 4
5 4,000 shall offer praises to the LORD 4
13 for ever should burn incense before the LORD 4
24 the work for the service of the house of the LORD. 4
25 The LORD, the God of Israel, has given peace 4
28 for the service of the house of the LORD 4
30 every morning, thanking and praising the LORD 4
31 burnt offerings are offered to the LORD 4
31 required of them, continually before the LORD. 4
32 for the service of the house of the LORD. 4
24:19 duty . . to come into the house of the LORD 4
19 as the LORD God of Israel had commanded him. 4
25: 3 in thanksgiving and praise to the LORD. 4
6 in the music in the house of the LORD 4
7 brethren, who were trained in singing to the LORD 4
26:12 ministering in the house of the LORD; 4
22 of the treasuries of the house of the LORD. 4
27 for the maintenance of the house of the LORD. 4
30 for all the work of the LORD and for the service 4
27:23 LORD had promised to make Israel as many • 4
28: 2 house . . for the ark of the covenant of the LORD 4
4 LORD God of Israel chose me from all my father's 4
5 of all my sons (for the LORD has given me many sons 4
5 throne of the kingdom of the LORD over Israel. 4
8 in the sight of . . the assembly of the LORD 4
8 all the commandments of the LORD your God; 4
9 LORD searches all hearts, and understands every 4
10 LORD has chosen you to build a house 4
12 for the courts of the house of the LORD 4
13 the work of the service in the house of the LORD; 4
13 vessels for the service in the house of the LORD 4
18 and covered the ark of the covenant of the LORD. 4
19 clear by the writing from the hand of the LORD 4
20 for the LORD God, even my God, is with you. 4
20 work for the service of the house of the LORD 4
29: 1 will not be for man but for the LORD God. 4
5 consecrating himself today to the LORD? 4
8 gave them to the treasury of the house of the LORD 4
9 they had offered freely to the LORD; 4
10 David blessed the LORD in the presence of all 4
10 David said: "Blessed art thou, O LORD 4
11 Thine, O LORD, is the greatness, and the power 4
11 thine is the kingdom, O LORD, and thou art exalted 4
16 O LORD our God, all this abundance that we have 4
18 O LORD . . keep for ever such purposes 4
20 said to all the assembly, "Bless the LORD your God. 4
20 And all the assembly blessed the LORD, the God 4
20 bowed their heads, and worshipped the LORD 4
21 they performed sacrifices to the LORD 4
21 the next day offered burnt offerings to the LORD 4
22 they ate and drank before the LORD on that day 4
22 and they anointed him as prince for the LORD 4
23 Then Solomon sat on the throne of the LORD as king 4
25 LORD gave Solomon great repute in the sight 4
2Ch 1: 1 LORD his God was with him and made him 4
3 which Moses the servant of the LORD had made 4
5 was there before the tabernacle of the LORD. 4
5 And Solomon and the assembly sought the LORD. •
6 went up there to the bronze altar before the LORD 4
9 O LORD God, let thy promise . . be now fulfilled 4
2: 1 to build a temple for the name of the LORD 4

4 to build a house for the name of the LORD my God 4
4 appointed feasts of the LORD our God 4
11 Because the LORD loves his people he has made you 4
12 Huram also said, "Blessed be the LORD God of Israel 4
12 a wise son . . who will build a temple for the LORD 4
3: 1 Then Solomon began to build the house of the LORD 4
1 Mori'ah, where the LORD had appeared to David •
4:16 for King Solomon for the house of the LORD. 4
5: 1 work that Solomon did for the house of the LORD 4
2 to bring up the ark of the covenant of the LORD 4
7 brought the ark of the covenant of the LORD 4
10 Horeb, where the LORD made a covenant 4
13 in unison in praise and thanksgiving to the LORD 4
13 when the song was raised . . in praise to the LORD 4
13 the house of the LORD, was filled with a cloud. 4
14 for the glory of the LORD filled the house of God. 4
6: 1 The LORD has said that he would dwell in thick 4
4 he said, "Blessed be the LORD, the God of Israel, who 4
7 David . . to build a house for the name of the LORD 4
8 the LORD said to David my father, 'Whereas it was 4
10 the LORD has fulfilled his promise which he made; 4
10 I sit on the throne of Israel, as the LORD promised 4
10 I have built the house for the name of the LORD 4
11 the ark, in which is the covenant of the LORD 4
12 Then Solomon stood before the altar of the LORD 4
14 said, "O LORD, God of Israel, there is no God like thee 4
16 O LORD, God of Israel, keep with thy servant David 4
17 O LORD, God of Israel, let thy word be confirmed 4
19 have regard to the prayer . . O LORD my God 4
41 now arise, O LORD God, and go to thy resting place 4
41 priests, O LORD God, be clothed with salvation 4
42 O LORD God, do not turn away the face of thy 4
7: 1 and the glory of the LORD filled the temple. 4
2 the priests could not enter the house of the LORD 4
2 the glory of the LORD filled the LORD's house. 4
2 the glory of the LORD filled the LORD's house. 4
3 saw . . and the glory of the LORD upon the temple 4
3 worshiped and gave thanks to the LORD, saying 4
4 the people offered sacrifice before the LORD. 4
6 with the instruments for music to the LORD 4
6 King David had made for giving thanks to the LORD 4
7 the court that was before the house of the LORD; 4
10 joyful and . . for the goodness that the LORD 4
11 Thus Solomon finished the house of the LORD 4
11 planned to do in the house of the LORD and in his 4
12 Then the LORD appeared to Solomon in the night 4
21 'Why has the LORD done thus to this land and to this 4
22 they forsook the LORD the God of their fathers 4
8: 1 in which Solomon had built the house of the LORD 4
11 the places to which the ark of the LORD has come 4
12 Solomon offered up burnt offerings to the LORD 4
12 offerings to the LORD upon the altar of the LORD 4
16 foundation of the house of the LORD was laid 4
16 So the house of the LORD was completed. 4
9: 4 which he offered at the house of the LORD 4
8 Blessed be the LORD your God, who has delighted 4
8 set you on his throne as king for the LORD your God! 4
11 algum wood steps for the house of the LORD 4
10:15 that the LORD might fulfil his word 4
11: 2 word of the LORD came to Shemai'ah the man of God 4
4 'Thus says the LORD, You shall not go up or fight 4
4 So they hearkened to the word of the LORD 4
14 cast them out from serving as priests of the LORD 4
16 set their hearts to seek the LORD God of Israel 4
16 came . . to Jerusalem to sacrifice to the LORD 4
12: 1 he forsook the law of the LORD, and all Israel 4
2 because they had been unfaithful to the LORD 4
5 Thus says the LORD, 'You abandoned me 4
6 said, "The LORD is righteous. 4
7 When the LORD saw that they humbled themselves 4
7 word of the LORD came to Shemai'ah 4
9 took away the treasures of the house of the LORD 4
11 often as the king went into the house of the LORD 4
12 when he humbled himself the wrath of the LORD 4
13 Jerusalem, the city which the LORD had chosen 4
14 for he did not set his heart to seek the LORD. 4
13: 5 know that the LORD . . gave the kingship 4
8 you think to withstand the kingdom of the LORD 4
9 Have you not driven out the priests of the LORD 4
10 as for us, the LORD is our God 4
10 We have priests ministering to the LORD 4
11 They offer to the LORD . . burnt offerings 4
11 for we keep the charge of the LORD our God 4
12 O sons of Israel, do not fight against the LORD 4
14 and they cried to the LORD 4
18 because they relied upon the LORD 4
20 the LORD smote him, and he died. 4
14: 2 what was good and right in the eyes of the LORD 4
4 commanded Judah to seek the LORD 4
6 no war in those years, for the LORD gave him peace. 4
7 because we have sought the LORD our God; 4
11 Asa cried to the LORD his God 4
11 O LORD, there is none like thee to help 4
11 Help us, O LORD our God, for we rely on thee 4
11 O LORD, thou art our God; let not man prevail 4
12 the LORD defeated the Ethiopians before Asa 4
13 they were broken before the LORD and his army. 4
14 for the fear of the LORD was upon them. 4
15: 2 The LORD is with you, while you are with him. 4
4 when in their distress they turned to the LORD 4
8 he repaired the altar of the LORD 4
8 the vestibule of the house of the LORD. 4
9 when they saw that he LORD his God was with him. 4
11 They sacrificed to the LORD on that day 4
12 they entered into a covenant to seek the LORD 4
13 whoever would not seek the LORD, the God of Israel 4
14 They took oath to the LORD with a loud voice 4
15 the LORD gave them rest round about. 4
16: 2 from the treasures of the house of the LORD 4
7 did not rely on the LORD your God 4
8 Yet because you relied on the LORD 4
9 the eyes of the LORD run to and fro 4
12 yet even in his disease he did not seek the LORD 4
17: 3 The LORD was with Jehosh'aphat 4
5 the LORD established the kingdom in his hand; 4
6 His heart was courageous in the ways of the LORD; 4
9 taught . . having the book of the law of the LORD 4
10 the fear of the LORD fell upon all the kingdoms 4
16 a volunteer for the service of the LORD 4
18: 4 Inquire first for the word of the LORD. 4
6 Is there not here another prophet of the LORD 4
7 yet one man by whom we may inquire of the LORD 4
10 Zedekiah . . said, "Thus says the LORD 4
11 LORD will give it into the hand of the king. 4
13 Micai'ah said, "As the LORD lives, what my God says 4
15 nothing but the truth in the name of the LORD? 4
16 LORD said, 'These have no master; 4
18 Micai'ah said, "Therefore hear the word of the LORD 4
18 I saw the LORD sitting on his throne 4
19 LORD said, 'Who will entice Ahab the king of Israel 4
20 a spirit came forward and stood before the LORD 4
20 And the LORD said to him, 'By what means?' 4
22 LORD has put a lying spirit in the mouth of these 4
22 the LORD has spoken evil concerning you. 4
23 Which way did the Spirit of the LORD go 4
27 If you return . . the LORD has not spoken by me. 4
31 Jehosh'aphat cried out, and the LORD helped him. 4
19: 2 Should you . . love those who hate the LORD? 4
2 wrath has gone out against you from the LORD. 4
4 Jehosh'aphat . . brought them back to the LORD 4
6 you judge not for man but for the LORD; 4
7 Now then, let the fear of the LORD be upon you; 4
7 is no perversion of justice with the LORD our God 4
8 to give judgment for the LORD 4
9 Thus you shall do in the fear of the LORD 4
10 that they may not incure guilt before the LORD 4
11 Amari'ah . . is over you in all matters of the LORD; 4
11 may the LORD be with the upright! 4
20: 3 Jehosh'aphat . . set himself to seek the LORD 4
4 Judah assembled to seek help from the LORD; 4
4 they came to seek the LORD. 4
5 Jehosh'aphat stood . . in the house of the LORD 4
6 LORD, God of our fathers, art thou not God in heaven? 4
13 all the men of Judah stood before the LORD 4
14 the Spirit of the LORD came upon Jaha'ziel 4
15 Thus says the LORD to you, 'Fear not 4
17 see the victory of the LORD on your behalf, O Judah 4
17 and the LORD will be with you. 4
18 fell down before the LORD, worshiping the LORD. 4
18 fell down before the LORD, worshiping the LORD. 4
19 the Levites . . stood up to praise the LORD 4
20 Believe in the LORD your God 4
21 he appointed those who were to sing to the LORD 4
21 Give thanks to the LORD, for his steadfast love 4
22 LORD set an ambush against the men of Ammon, 4
26 Bera'cah, for there they blessed the LORD; 4
27 LORD had made them rejoice over their enemies. 4
28 to the house of the LORD. 4
29 LORD had fought against the enemies of Israel. 4
32 did what was right in the sight of the LORD. 4
37 LORD will destroy what you have made. 4
21: 6 And he did what was evil in the sight of the LORD. 4
7 Yet the LORD would not destroy the house of David 4
10 because he had forsaken the LORD 4
12 Thus says the LORD, the God of David your father 4
14 LORD will bring a great plague on your people 4
16 LORD stirred up against Jeho'ram the anger 4
18 after all this the LORD smote him in his bowels 4
22: 4 He did what was evil in the sight of the LORD 4
7 LORD had anointed to destroy the house of Ahab. 4
9 who sought the LORD with all his heart. 4
23: 3 the king's son! Let him reign, as the LORD spoke 4
5 shall be in the courts of the house of the LORD. 4
6 Let no one enter the house of the LORD 4
6 all the people shall keep the charge of the LORD. 4
12 she went into the house of the LORD to the people; 4
14 Do not slay her in the house of the LORD. 4
16 that they should be the LORD'S people. 4
18 posted watchmen for the house of the LORD 4
18 organized to be in charge of the house of the LORD 4
18 to offer burnt offerings to the LORD 4
19 gatekeepers at the gates of the house of the LORD 4
20 brought the king down from the house of the LORD 4
24: 2 Jo'ash did what was right in the eyes of the LORD 4
4 Jo'ash decided to restore the house of the LORD. 4
6 the tax levied by Moses, the servant of the LORD 4
7 all the dedicated things of the house of the LORD 4
8 set it outside the gate of the house of the LORD. 4
9 to bring in for the LORD the tax that Moses 4
12 charge of the work of the house of the LORD 4
12 hired masons . . to restore the house of the LORD 4
12 workers . . to repair the house of the LORD. 4
14 made utensils for the house of the LORD 4
14 offered burnt offerings in the house of the LORD 4
18 they forsook the house of the LORD 4
19 sent prophets . . to bring them back to the LORD; 4
20 do you transgress the commandments of the LORD 4
20 you have forsaken the LORD, he has forsaken you.' 4
21 with stones in the court of the house of the LORD. 4
22 he was dying, he said, "May the LORD see and avenge! 4
24 LORD delivered into their hand a very great army 4
24 forsaken the LORD, the God of their fathers. 4
25: 2 he did what was right in the eyes of the LORD 4
4 in the book of Moses, where the LORD commanded 4
7 LORD is not with Israel 4
9 The LORD is able to give you much more than this. 4
15 Therefore the LORD was angry with Amazi'ah 4
27 From the time he turned away from the LORD 4
26: 4 he did what was right in the eyes of the LORD 4
5 as long as he sought the LORD, God made him prosper. 4
16 For he was false to the LORD his God 4
16 entered the temple of the LORD to burn incense 4
17 80 priests of the LORD who were men of valor; 4
18 is not for you, Uzzi'ah, to burn incense to the LORD 4
18 it will bring you no honor from the LORD God. 4
19 the priests in the house of the LORD 4
20 to go out, because the LORD had smitten him. 4
21 for he was excluded from the house of the LORD. 4
27: 2 he did what was right in the eyes of the LORD 4
2 only he did not invade the temple of the LORD. 4
3 He built the upper gate of the house of the LORD 4
6 ordered his ways before the LORD his God. 4
28: 1 he did not do what was right in the eyes of the LORD 4
3 nations whom the LORD drove out 4
5 LORD his God gave him into the hand of the king 4
6 because they had forsaken the LORD 4
9 prophet of the LORD was there, whose name was Oded 4
9 Behold, because the LORD . . was angry with Judah 4
10 Have you not sins of your own against the LORD 4
11 for the fierce wrath of the LORD is upon you. 4
13 propose to bring upon us guilt against the LORD 4
19 For the LORD brought Judah low because of Ahaz 4
19 Ahaz . . had been faithless to the LORD. 4
21 For Ahaz took from the house of the LORD 4
22 he became yet more faithless to the LORD 4
24 Ahaz . . shut up the doors of the house of the LORD; 4
25 provoking to anger the LORD, the God 4
29: 2 he did what was right in the eyes of the LORD 4
3 opened the doors of the house of the LORD 4
5 sanctify the house of the LORD, the God 4
6 done what was evil in the sight of the LORD our God; 4
6 turned away . . from the habitation of the LORD 4
8 the wrath of the LORD came on Judah and Jerusalem 4
10 it is in my heart to make a covenant with the LORD 4
11 not now be negligent, for the LORD has chosen you 4
15 the king had commanded, by the words of the LORD 4
15 went in . . to cleanse the house of the LORD. 4
16 went into the inner part of the house of the LORD 4
16 that they found in the temple of the LORD 4
16 into the court of the house of the LORD; 4
17 they came to the vestibule of the LORD; 4
17 eight days they sanctified the house of the LORD 4
18 We have cleansed all the house of the LORD 4
19 behold, they are before the altar of the LORD. 4
20 Hezeki'ah . . went up to the house of the LORD. 4
21 to offer them on the altar of the LORD. 4
25 he stationed the Levites in the house of the LORD 4
25 commandment was from the LORD 4
27 burnt offering began, the song to the LORD began 4
30 Levites to sing praises to the LORD 4
31 You have now consecrated yourselves to the LORD; 4
31 bring sacrifices . . to the house of the LORD. 4
32 all these were for a burnt offering to the LORD. 4
35 service of the house of the LORD was restored. 4
30: 1 come to the house of the LORD at Jerusalem, to keep 4
1 to keep the passover to the LORD the God of Israel. 4
5 should come and keep the passover to the LORD 4
6 O people of Israel, return to the LORD 4
7 faithless to the LORD God of their fathers 4
8 but yield yourselves to the LORD, and come 4
8 serve the LORD your God, that his fierce anger may 4
9 For if you return to the LORD 4
9 For the LORD your God is gracious and merciful 4
12 commanded by the word of the LORD. 4
15 burnt offerings into the house of the LORD. 4
17 to make it holy to the LORD. 4
18 The good LORD pardon every one 4
19 to seek God, the LORD the God of his fathers 4
20 the LORD heard Hezeki'ah, and healed the people. 4
21 Levites and the priests praised the LORD 4
21 singing with all their might to the LORD. 4
22 showed good skill in the service of the LORD. 4
22 giving thanks to the LORD the God 4
31: 2 minister in the gates of the camp of the LORD 4
3 as it is written in the law of the LORD. 4
4 might give themselves to the law of the LORD. 4
6 been consecrated to the LORD their God 4

8 blessed the LORD and his people Israel. 4
10 contributions into the house of the LORD 4
10 for the LORD has blessed his people 4
11 to prepare chambers in the house of the LORD; 4
14 the contribution reserved for the LORD 4
16 all who entered the house of the LORD as the duty 4
20 good and right and faithful before the LORD 4
32: 8 With him is an arm of flesh; but with us is the LORD 4
11 The LORD our God will deliver us from the hand 4
17 cast contempt on the LORD the God of Israel 4
21 LORD sent an angel, who cut off all the mighty 4
22 LORD saved Hezeki'ah and the inhabitants 4
23 many brought gifts to the LORD to Jerusalem 4
24 Hezeki'ah became sick . . he prayed to the LORD 4
26 wrath of the LORD did not come upon them 4
33: 2 He did what was evil in the sight of the LORD 4
2 nations whom the LORD drove out 4
4 he built altars in the house of the LORD 4
4 house of the LORD, of which the LORD had said 4
5 in the two courts of the house of the LORD. 4
6 He did much evil in the sight of the LORD 4
9 evil than the nations whom the LORD destroyed 4
10 The LORD spoke to Manas'seh and to his people 4
11 LORD brought upon them the commanders 4
12 he entreated the favor of the LORD his God 4
13 Then Manas'seh knew that the LORD was God. 4
15 gods and the idol from the house of the LORD 4
15 built on the mountain of the house of the LORD 4
16 He also restored the altar of the LORD 4
16 Judah to serve the LORD the God of Israel. 4
17 at the high places, but only to the LORD their God. 4
18 seers who spoke to him in the name of the LORD 4
22 He did what was evil in the sight of the LORD 4
23 he did not humble himself before the LORD 4
34: 2 He did what was right in the eyes of the LORD 4
8 to repair the house of the LORD his God. 4
10 who had the oversight of the house of the LORD; 4
10 workmen who were working in the house of the LORD 4
14 money . . brought into the house of the LORD 4
14 Hilki'ah . . found the book of the law of the LORD 4
15 found the book of the law in the house of the LORD"; 4
17 the money that was found in the house of the LORD 4
21 Go, inquire of the LORD for me and for those who are 4
21 great is the wrath of the LORD that is poured out 4
21 our fathers have not kept the word of the LORD 4
23 Thus says the LORD, the God of Israel: 'Tell the man 4
24 Thus says the LORD, Behold, I will bring evil 4
26 king of Judah, who sent you to inquire of the LORD 4
26 Thus says the LORD . . Regarding the words 4
27 I also have heard you, says the LORD 4
30 the king went up to the house of the LORD 4
30 which had been found in the house of the LORD. 4
31 king . . made a covenant before the LORD 4
31 made a covenant . . to walk after the LORD 4
33 made all . . in Israel serve the LORD their God. 4
33 they did not turn away from following the LORD 4
35: 1 Josi'ah kept a passover to the LORD in Jerusalem; 4
2 in the service of the house of the LORD. 4
3 said to the Levites . . who were holy to the LORD 4
3 Now serve the LORD your God and his people Israel. 4
6 to do according to the word of the LORD by Moses. 4
12 burnt offerings . . to offer to the LORD 4
16 all the service of the LORD was prepared that day 4
16 to offer burnt offerings on the altar of the LORD 4
26 what is written in the law of the LORD 4
36: 5 did what was evil in the sight of the LORD his God. 4
7 part of the vessels of the house of the LORD 4
9 He did what was evil in the sight of the LORD. 4
10 precious vessels of the house of the LORD 4
12 did what was evil in the sight of the LORD his God. 4
12 Jeremiah . . spoke from the mouth of the LORD. 4
13 hardened his heart against turning to the LORD 4
14 polluted the house of the LORD which he had 4
15 LORD . . sent persistently to them 4
16 till the wrath of the LORD rose against his people 4
18 treasures of the house of the LORD 4
21 to fulfil the word of the LORD by . . Jeremiah 4
22 that the word of the LORD by the mouth of Jeremiah 4
22 LORD stirred up the spirit of Cyrus king 4
23 LORD . . has given me all the kingdoms 4
23 may the LORD his God be with him. Let him go up. 4
Ezr 1: 1 that the word of the LORD by the mouth of Jeremiah 4
1 LORD stirred up the spirit of Cyrus king of Persia 4
2 LORD . . has given me all the kingdoms 4
3 Jerusalem . . and rebuild the house of the LORD 4
5 stirred to go up to rebuild the house of the LORD 4
7 brought out the vessels of the house of the LORD 4
2:68 when they came to the house of the LORD 4
3: 3 offered burnt offerings upon it to the LORD 4
5 at all the appointed feasts of the LORD 4
5 every one who made a freewill offering to the LORD. 4
6 began to offer burnt offerings to the LORD. 4
6 foundation of the temple of the LORD was not yet 4
8 oversight of the work of the house of the LORD. 4
10 laid the foundation of the temple of the LORD 4
10 came forward . . to praise the LORD 4
11 praising and giving thanks to the LORD 4
11 great shout, when they praised the LORD 4
11 foundation of the house of the LORD was laid. 4
4: 1 exiles were building a temple to the LORD 4
3 we alone will build to the LORD, the God of Israel 4
6:21 separated . . to worship the LORD, the God of Israel. 4
22 LORD had made them joyful, and had turned 4
7: 6 law of Moses . . LORD the God of Israel had given; 4
6 for the hand of the LORD his God was upon him. 4
10 Ezra had set his heart to study the law of the LORD 4
11 commandments of the LORD and his statutes 4
27 Blessed be the LORD, the God of our fathers 4
27 to beautify the house of the LORD . . in Jerusalem 4
28 hand of the LORD my God was upon me 4
8:28 You are holy to the LORD, and the vessels are holy; 4
28 freewill offering to the LORD, 4
29 within the chambers of the house of the LORD. 4
35 all this was a burnt offering to the LORD. 4
9: 5 fell . . and spread out my hands to the LORD my God 4
8 favor has been shown by the LORD our God 4
15 O LORD the God of Israel, thou art just 4
10:11 make confession to the LORD the God of your fathers 4
Neh 1: 5 I said, "O LORD God of heaven, the great and terrible 4
5:13 all the assembly said "Amen" and praised the LORD. 4
8: 1 law of Moses which the LORD had given to Israel. 4
6 Ezra blessed the LORD, the great God; 4
6 worshiped the LORD . . faces to the ground. 4
9 This day is holy to the LORD your God; 4
10 for the joy of the LORD is your strength. 4
14 LORD had commanded by Moses that the people 4
9: 3 read from the book of the law of the LORD their God 4
3 for another fourth . . worshiped the LORD their God. 4
4 cried with a loud voice to the LORD their God. 4
5 bless the LORD your God from everlasting 4
6 Thou art the LORD, thou alone; thou hast made 4
7 Thou art the LORD, the God who didst choose Abram 4
10:29 do all the commandments of the LORD our Lord 4
34 to burn upon the altar of the LORD our God 4
35 first fruits . . year by year, to the house of the LORD; 4
Job 1: 6 came to present themselves before the LORD 4
7 The LORD said to Satan, "Whence have you come? 4
7 Satan answered the LORD, "From going to and fro 4
8 the LORD said to Satan, "Have you considered 4
9 Then Satan answered the LORD, "Does Job fear God 4
12 the LORD said to Satan, "Behold, all that he has 4
12 Satan went forth from the presence of the LORD. 4
21 the LORD gave, and the LORD has taken away; 4
21 the LORD gave, and the LORD has taken away; 4
21 blessed be the name of the LORD. 4
2: 1 came to present themselves before the LORD 4
1 among them to present himself before the LORD. 4
2 the LORD said to Satan, "Whence have you come? 4
2 Satan answered the LORD, "From going to and fro 4
3 the LORD said to Satan, "Have you considered 4
4 Then Satan answered the LORD, "Skin for skin! 4
6 the LORD said to Satan, "Behold, he is in your power; 4
7 Satan went forth from the presence of the LORD 4
12: 9 not know that the hand of the LORD has done this? 4
38: 1 Then the LORD answered Job out of the whirlwind 4
40: 1 the LORD said to Job 4
3 Then Job answered the LORD 4
6 Then the LORD answered Job out of the whirlwind 4
42: 1 Then Job answered the LORD 4
7 After the LORD had spoken these words to Job 4
7 the LORD said to Eli'phaz the Te'manite 4
9 went and did what the LORD had told them; 4
9 the LORD accepted Job's prayer. 4
10 the LORD restored the fortunes of Job 4
10 the LORD gave Job twice as much as he had before. 4
11 all the evil that the LORD had brought upon him; 4
12 the LORD blessed the latter days of Job 4
Ps 1: 2 his delight is in the law of the LORD 4
6 for the LORD knows the way of the righteous 4
2: 2 rulers take counsel together, against the LORD 4
4 laughs; the LORD has them in derision. 4
7 I will tell of the decree of the LORD: He said to me 4
11 Serve the LORD with fear, with trembling 4
3: 1 O LORD, how many are my foes! 4
3 But thou, O LORD, art a shield about me 4
4 I cry aloud to the LORD, and he answers me 4
5 I wake again, for the LORD sustains me. 4
7 Arise, O LORD! Deliver me, O my God! 4
8 Deliverance belongs to the LORD; 4
4: 3 But know that the LORD has set apart the godly 4
3 the LORD hears when I call to him. 4
5 sacrifices, and put your trust in the LORD. 4
6 the light of thy countenance upon us, O LORD! 4
8 for thou alone, O LORD, makest me dwell in safety. 4
5: 1 Give ear to my words, O LORD; 4
3 O LORD, in the morning thou dost hear my voice; 4
6 LORD abhors bloodthirsty and deceitful men. 4
8 Lead me, O LORD, in thy righteousness 4
12 For thou dost bless the righteous, O LORD; 4
6: 1 O LORD, rebuke me not in thy anger, nor chasten me 4
2 Be gracious to me, O LORD, for I am languishing; 4
2 O LORD, heal me, for my bones are troubled. 4
3 sorely troubled. But thou, O LORD–how long? 4
4 Turn, O LORD, save my life; deliver me 4
8 for the LORD has heard the sound of my weeping. 4
9 The LORD has heard my supplication; 4
9 The LORD has heard . . the LORD accepts my prayer. 4
7: 0 A Shiggaion of David, which he sang to the LORD 4
1 O LORD my God, in thee do I take refuge; 4
3 O LORD my God, if I have done this 4
6 Arise, O LORD, in thy anger, lift thyself up 4
8 The LORD judges the peoples; 4
8 judge me, O LORD, according to my righteousness 4
17 I will give to the LORD the thanks due 4
17 sing praise to the name of the LORD, the Most High. 4
8: 1 O LORD, our Lord, how majestic is thy name 4
9 O LORD, our Lord, how majestic is thy name 4
9: 1 I will give thanks to the LORD with my whole heart; 4
7 the LORD sits enthroned for ever 4
9 The LORD is a stronghold for the oppressed 4
10 thou, O LORD, hast not forsaken those who seek 4
11 Sing praises to the LORD, who dwells in Zion! 4
13 Be gracious to me, O LORD! Behold what I suffer 4
16 The LORD has made himself known 4
19 Arise, O LORD! Let not man prevail; 4
20 Put them in fear, O LORD! 4
10: 1 Why dost thou stand afar off, O LORD? 4
3 man greedy for gain curses and renounces the LORD. 4
12 Arise, O LORD; O God, lift up thy hand; 4
16 The LORD is king for ever and ever; 4
17 O LORD, thou wilt hear the desire of the meek; 4
11: 1 In the LORD I take refuge; how can you say to me, 4
4 The LORD is in his holy temple 4
4 in his holy temple, the LORD'S throne is in heaven; 4
5 The LORD tests the righteous and the wicked 4
7 the LORD is righteous, he loves righteous deeds; 4
12: 1 Help, LORD; for there is no longer any that is godly; 4
3 May the LORD cut off all flattering lips 4
5 I will now arise," says the LORD; 4
6 promises of the LORD are promises that are pure 4
7 Do thou, O LORD, protect us, guard us ever 4
13: 1 How long, O LORD? Wilt thou forget me for ever? 4
3 Consider and answer me, O LORD my God; 4
6 I will sing to the LORD 4
14: 2 The LORD looks down from heaven 4
4 as they eat bread, and do not call upon the LORD? 4
6 confound . . the poor, but the LORD is his refuge. 4
7 the LORD restores the fortunes of his people 4
15: 1 O LORD, who shall sojourn in thy tent? 4
4 but who honors those who fear the LORD; 4
16: 2 I say to the LORD, "Thou art my Lord; 4
5 The LORD is my chosen portion and my cup; 4
7 I bless the LORD who gives me counsel; 4
8 I keep the LORD always before me; 4
17: 1 Hear a just cause, O LORD; attend to my cry! 4
13 Arise, O LORD! confront them, overthrow them! 4
14 from men by thy hand, O LORD, from men 4
18: 0 A Psalm of David the servant of the LORD 4
0 who addressed the words of this song to the LORD 4
0 on the day when the LORD delivered him 4
1 I love thee, O LORD, my strength. 4
2 The LORD is my rock, and my fortress 4
3 I call upon the LORD, who is worthy to be praised 4
6 In my distress I called upon the LORD; 4
13 The LORD also thundered in the heavens 4
15 O LORD, at the blast of the breath of thy nostrils. 4
18 in the day of my calamity; but the LORD was my stay. 4
20 LORD rewarded me according to my righteousness; 4
21 For I have kept the ways of the LORD 4
24 Therefore the LORD has recompensed me 4
28 the LORD my God lightens my darkness. 4
30 the promise of the LORD proves true; he is a shield 4
31 For who is God, but the LORD? 4
41 they cried to the LORD, but he did not answer them. 4
46 The LORD lives; and blessed be my rock 4
49 For this I will extol thee, O LORD 4
19: 7 The law of the LORD is perfect, reviving the soul; 4
7 the testimony of the LORD is sure 4
8 the precepts of the LORD are right 4
8 the commandment of the LORD is pure 4
9 the fear of the LORD is clean, enduring for ever; 4
9 the ordinances of the LORD are true, and righteous 4
14 my heart be acceptable in thy sight, O LORD, my rock 4
20: 1 The LORD answer you in the day of trouble! 4
5 May the LORD fulfil all your petitions! 4
6 Now I know that the LORD will help his anointed; 4
7 we boast of the name of the LORD our God. 4
9 Give victory to the king, O LORD; 4
21: 1 In thy strength the king rejoices, O LORD; 4
7 For the king trusts in the LORD; 4
9 The LORD will swallow them up in his wrath; 4
13 Be exalted, O LORD, in thy strength! 4
22: 8 He committed his cause to the LORD; 4
19 But thou, O LORD, be not far off! 4
23 You who fear the LORD, praise him! 4
26 those who seek him shall praise the LORD! 4
27 of the earth shall remember and turn to the LORD; 4
28 For dominion belongs to the LORD, and he rules 4
23: 1 The LORD is my shepherd, I shall not want; 4
6 I shall dwell in the house of the LORD for ever. 4
24: 1 The earth is the LORD'S and the fulness thereof 4
3 Who shall ascend the hill of the LORD? 4
5 He will receive blessing from the LORD 4
8 Who is the King of glory? The LORD 4
8 LORD, strong and mighty, the LORD, mighty in battle! 4
10 The LORD of hosts, he is the King of glory! Selah 4
25: 1 To thee, O LORD, I lift up my soul. 4

4 Make me to know thy ways, O LORD; teach me 4
6 Be mindful of thy mercy, O LORD 4
7 remember me, for thy goodness' sake, O LORD! 4
8 Good and upright is the LORD; 4
10 All the paths of the LORD are steadfast love 4
11 For thy name's sake, O LORD, pardon my guilt 4
12 Who is the man that fears the LORD? 4
14 friendship of the LORD is for those who fear him 4
15 My eyes are ever toward the LORD 4
26: 1 Vindicate me, O LORD 4
1 I have trusted in the LORD without wavering. 4
2 Prove me, O LORD, and try me; test my heart 4
6 in innocence, and go about thy altar, O LORD 4
8 O LORD, I love the habitation of thy house 4
12 in the great congregation I will bless the LORD. 4
27: 1 The LORD is my light and my salvation; 4
1 The LORD is the stronghold of my life; 4
4 One thing have I asked of the LORD, that will I seek 4
4 that I may dwell in the house of the LORD 4
4 to behold the beauty of the LORD 4
6 I will sing and make melody to the LORD. 4
7 Hear, O LORD, when I cry aloud, be gracious to me 4
8 My heart says to thee, "Thy face, LORD, do I seek. 4
10 have forsaken me, but the LORD will take me up. 4
11 Teach me thy way, O LORD; and lead me 4
13 believe that I shall see the goodness of the LORD 4
14 Wait for the LORD; be strong 4
14 let your heart take courage; yea, wait for the LORD! 4
28: 1 To thee, O LORD, I call; my rock, be not deaf to me 4
5 they do not regard the works of the LORD 4
6 Blessed be the LORD! for he has heard 4
7 The LORD is my strength and my shield; 4
8 The LORD is the strength of his people 4
29: 1 Ascribe to the LORD, O heavenly beings 4
1 ascribe to the LORD glory and strength. 4
2 Ascribe to the LORD the glory of his name; 4
2 worship the LORD in holy array. 4
3 The voice of the LORD is upon the waters; 4
3 God of glory thunders, the LORD, upon many waters. 4
4 The voice of the LORD is powerful 4
4 voice of the LORD is full of majesty. 4
5 The voice of the LORD breaks the cedars 4
5 LORD breaks the cedars of Lebanon. 4
7 voice of the LORD flashes forth flames of fire. 4
8 The voice of the LORD shakes the wilderness 4
8 LORD shakes the wilderness of Kadesh. 4
9 voice of the LORD makes the oaks to whirl 4
10 The LORD sits enthroned over the flood; 4
10 LORD sits enthroned as king for ever. 4
11 May the LORD give strength to his people! 4
11 May the LORD bless his people with peace! 4
30: 1 I will extol thee, O LORD, for thou hast drawn me up 4
2 O LORD my God, I cried to thee for help 4
3 O LORD, thou hast brought up my soul from Sheol 4
4 Sing praises to the LORD, O you his saints 4
7 By thy favor, O LORD, thou hadst established me 4
8 To thee, O LORD, I cried; 4
8 to the LORD I made supplication 4
10 Hear, O LORD, and be gracious to me! 4
10 be gracious to me! O LORD, be thou my helper! 4
12 O LORD my God, I will give thanks to thee for ever. 4
31: 1 In thee, O LORD, do I seek refuge; 4
5 thou hast redeemed me, O LORD, faithful God. 4
6 pay regard to vain idols; but I trust in the LORD. 4
9 Be gracious to me, O LORD, for I am in distress; 4
14 I trust in thee, O LORD, I say, "Thou art my God. 4
17 Let me not be put to shame, O LORD, for I call on thee; 4
21 Blessed be the LORD, for he has wondrously shown 4
23 Love the LORD, all you his saints! 4
23 The LORD preserves the faithful 4
24 take courage, all you who wait for the LORD! 4
32: 2 the man to whom the LORD imputes no iniquity 4
5 I will confess my transgressions to the LORD"; 4
10 love surrounds him who trusts in the LORD. 4
11 Be glad in the LORD, and rejoice, O righteous 4
33: 1 Rejoice in the LORD, O you righteous! 4
2 Praise the LORD with the lyre, make melody to him 4
4 For the word of the LORD is upright; 4
5 earth is full of the steadfast love of the LORD. 4
6 By the word of the LORD the heavens were made 4
8 Let all the earth fear the LORD 4
10 LORD brings the counsel of the nations to nought; 4
11 The counsel of the LORD stands for ever 4
12 Blessed is the nation whose God is the LORD 4
13 The LORD looks down from heaven, he sees all 4
18 Behold, the eye of the LORD is on those who fear him 4
20 soul waits for the LORD; he is our help and shield. 4
22 Let thy steadfast love, O LORD, be upon us 4
34: 1 I will bless the LORD at all times; 4
2 My soul makes its boast in the LORD; 4
3 O magnify the LORD with me, and let us exalt 4
4 I sought the LORD, and he answered me 4
6 This poor man cried, and the LORD heard him 4
7 The angel of the LORD encamps around those who 4
8 O taste and see that the LORD is good! 4
9 O fear the LORD, you his saints 4
10 but those who seek the LORD lack no good thing. 4
11 listen to me, I will teach you the fear of the LORD. 4
15 The eyes of the LORD are toward the righteous 4
16 The face of the LORD is against evildoers 4
17 When the righteous cry for help, the LORD hears 4
18 The LORD is near to the brokenhearted, and saves 4
19 but the LORD delivers him out of them all. 4
22 The LORD redeems the life of his servants; 4
35: 1 Contend, O LORD, with those who contend with me; 4
5 with the angel of the LORD driving them on! 4
6 with the angel of the LORD pursuing them! 4
9 Then my soul shall rejoice in the LORD 4
10 All my bones shall say, "O LORD, who is like thee 4
17 How long, O LORD, wilt thou look on? Rescue me 4
22 Thou hast seen, O LORD; be not silent! 4
24 Vindicate me, O LORD, my God 4
27 be glad, and say evermore, "Great is the LORD 4
36: 0 A Psalm of David, the servant of the LORD. 4
5 Thy steadfast love, O LORD, extends to the heavens 4
6 man and beast thou savest, O LORD. 4
37: 3 Trust in the LORD, and do good; 4
4 Take delight in the LORD 4
5 Commit your way to the LORD; trust in him 4
7 Be still before the LORD, and wait patiently 4
9 who wait for the LORD shall possess the land. 4
13 the LORD laughs at the wicked 4
17 the LORD upholds the righteous. 4
18 The LORD knows the days of the blameless 4
20 enemies of the LORD are like the glory 4
22 those blessed by the LORD shall possess the land •
23 The steps of a man are from the LORD 4
24 for the LORD is the stay of his hand. 4
28 For the LORD loves justice; 4
33 The LORD will not abandon him to his power 4
34 Wait for the LORD, and keep to his way 4
39 The salvation of the righteous is from the LORD; 4
40 The LORD helps them and delivers them; 4
38: 1 O LORD, rebuke me not in thy anger, nor chasten me 4
15 But for thee, O LORD, do I wait; it is thou, O LORD 4
15 it is thou, O LORD my God, who wilt answer. 4
21 Do not forsake me, O LORD! O my God, be not far 4
39: 4 LORD, let me know my end 4
12 Hear my prayer, O LORD, and give ear to my cry; 4
40: 1 I waited patiently for the LORD; 4
3 see and fear, and put their trust in the LORD. 4
4 Blessed is the man who makes the LORD his trust 4
5 O LORD my God, thy wondrous deeds and . . thoughts 4
9 not restrained my lips, as thou knowest, O LORD. 4
11 Do not thou, O LORD, withhold thy mercy from me 4
13 Be pleased, O LORD, to deliver me! 4
13 deliver me! O LORD, make haste to help me! 4
16 say continually, "Great is the LORD! 4
41: 1 The LORD delivers him in the day of trouble; 4
2 the LORD protects him and keeps him alive; 4
3 The LORD sustains him on his sickbed; 4
4 As for me, I said, "O LORD, be gracious to me; 4
10 do thou, O LORD, be gracious to me, and raise me up 4
13 Blessed be the LORD, the God of Israel 4
42: 8 By day the LORD commands his steadfast love; 4
46: 7 The LORD of hosts is with us; 4
8 Come, behold the works of the LORD 4
11 The LORD of hosts is with us; 4
47: 2 the LORD, the Most High, is terrible, a great king 4
5 the LORD with the sound of a trumpet. 4
48: 1 Great is the LORD and greatly to be praised 4
8 so have we seen in the city of the LORD of hosts 4
50: 1 The Mighty One, God the LORD, speaks and summons 4
54: 6 I will give thanks to thy name, O LORD, for it is good. 4
55:16 I call upon God; and the LORD will save me. 4
22 Cast your burden on the LORD, and he will sustain 4
56:10 in the LORD, whose word I praise 4
58: 6 tear out the fangs of the young lions, O LORD! 4
59: 3 For no transgression or sin of mine, O LORD 4
5 Thou, LORD God of hosts, art God of Israel. 4
8 But thou, O LORD, dost laugh at them; 4
64:10 Let the righteous rejoice in the LORD 4
68: 4 his name is the LORD, exult before him! 3
16 yea, where the LORD will dwell for ever! 4
18 that the LORD God may dwell there. 3
26 Bless God in the great congregation, the LORD 4
69:13 But as for me, my prayer is to thee, O LORD. 4
16 Answer me, O LORD, for thy steadfast love is good; 4
31 This will please the LORD more than an ox or a bull 4
33 For the LORD hears the needy, and does not despise 4
70: 1 O LORD, make haste to help me! 4
5 my help and my deliverer, O LORD, do not tarry! 4
71: 1 In thee O LORD, do I take refuge; 4
5 thou . . art my hope, my trust, O LORD, from my youth. 4
72:18 Blessed be the LORD, the God of Israel 4
74:18 Remember this, O LORD, how the enemy scoffs 4
75: 8 For in the hand of the LORD there is a cup 4
76:11 Make your vows to the LORD your God 4
77:11 I will call to mind the deeds of the LORD; 3
78: 4 but tell . . the glorious deeds of the LORD 4
21 when the LORD heard, he was full of wrath; 4
79: 5 How long, O LORD? Wilt thou be angry for ever? 4
80: 4 O LORD God of hosts, how long wilt thou be angry 4
19 Restore us, O LORD God of hosts! let thy face shine 4
81:10 I am the LORD your God, who brought you up 4
15 Those who hate the LORD would cringe toward him 4
83:16 shame, that they may seek thy name, O LORD. 4
18 them know that thou alone, whose name is the LORD 4
84: 1 How lovely is thy dwelling place, O LORD of hosts! 4
2 soul longs, yea, faints for the courts of the LORD; 4
3 at thy altars, O LORD of hosts, my King and my God. 4
8 O LORD God of hosts, hear my prayer; 4
11 For the LORD God is a sun and shield; 4
11 No good thing does the LORD withhold 4
12 O LORD of hosts, blessed is the man who trusts 4
85: 1 LORD, thou wast favorable to thy land; 4
7 Show us thy steadfast love, O LORD 4
8 Let me hear what God the LORD will speak 4
12 Yea, the LORD will give what is good 4
86: 1 Incline thy ear, O LORD, and answer me 4
6 Give ear, O LORD, to my prayer; 4
11 Teach me thy way, O LORD, that I may walk 4
17 LORD, hast helped me and comforted me. 4
87: 2 LORD loves the gates of Zion more than all 4
6 LORD records as he registers the peoples 4
88: 1 O LORD, my God, I call for help by day; 4
9 Every day I call upon thee, O LORD; 4
13 I, O LORD, cry to thee; 4
14 O LORD, why dost thou cast me off? 4
89: 1 I will sing of thy steadfast love, O LORD, for ever; 4
5 Let the heavens praise thy wonders, O LORD 4
6 For who in the skies can be compared to the LORD? 4
6 Who among the heavenly beings is like the LORD 4
8 O LORD God of hosts, who is mighty as thou art, 4
8 LORD God of hosts, who is mighty as thou art, O LORD 3
15 who walk, O LORD, in the light of thy countenance 4
18 For our shield belongs to the LORD 4
46 How long, O LORD? Wilt thou hide thyself for ever? 4
51 with which thy enemies taunt, O LORD 4
52 Blessed be the LORD for ever! Amen and Amen. 4
90:13 Return, O LORD! How long? Have pity on thy servants! 4
91: 2 will say to the LORD, "My refuge and my fortress; 4
9 Because you have made the LORD your refuge 4
92: 1 It is good to give thanks to the LORD 4
4 For thou, O LORD, hast made me glad by thy work; 4
5 How great are thy works, O LORD! 4
8 but thou, O LORD, art on high for ever. 4
9 For, lo, thy enemies, O LORD, for, lo, thy enemies 4
13 They are planted in the house of the LORD 4
15 to show that the LORD is upright; 4
93: 1 The LORD reigns; he is robed in majesty; 4
1 LORD is robed, he is girded with strength. 4
3 floods have lifted up, O LORD 4
4 LORD on high is mighty! 4
5 holiness befits thy house, O LORD, for evermore. 4
94: 1 O LORD, thou God of vengeance 4
3 O LORD, how long shall the wicked 4
5 They crush thy people, O LORD 4
7 LORD does not see; the God of Jacob does not 3
11 the LORD, knows the thoughts of man 4
12 Blessed is the man whom thou dost chasten, O LORD 3
14 For the LORD will not forsake his people; 4
17 If the LORD had not been my help, my soul would 4
18 foot slips," thy steadfast love, O LORD, held me up. 4
22 the LORD has become my stronghold 4
23 LORD our God will wipe them out. 4
95: 1 O come, let us sing to the LORD; 4
3 For the LORD is a great God, and a great King 4
6 bow down, let us kneel before the LORD, our Maker! 4
96: 1 O sing to the LORD a new song; 4
1 sing to the LORD, all the earth! 4
2 Sing to the LORD, bless his name; 4
4 For great is the LORD, and greatly to be praised; 4
5 but the LORD made the heavens. 4
7 Ascribe to the LORD, O families of the peoples 4
7 ascribe to the LORD glory and strength! 4
8 Ascribe to the LORD the glory due his name; 4
9 Worship the LORD in holy array; 4
10 Say among the nations, "The LORD reigns! 4
13 before the LORD, for he comes, for he comes to judge 4
97: 1 The LORD reigns; let the earth rejoice; 4
5 The mountains melt like wax before the LORD 4
9 For thou, O LORD, art most high over all the earth; 4
10 The LORD loves those who hate evil; 4
12 Rejoice in the LORD, O you righteous 4
98: 1 O sing to the LORD a new song 4
2 The LORD has made known his victory 4
4 Make a joyful noise to the LORD, all the earth; 4
5 Sing praises to the LORD with the lyre 4
6 make a joyful noise before the King, the LORD! 4
9 before the LORD, for he comes to judge the earth. 4
99: 1 The LORD reigns; let the peoples tremble! 4
2 The LORD is great in Zion; 4
5 Extol the LORD our God; worship at his footstool! 4
6 They cried to the LORD, and he answered them. 4
8 O LORD our God, thou didst answer them; 4
9 Extol the LORD our God, and worship at his holy 4
9 Extol the LORD . . for the LORD our God is holy! 4
100: 1 Make a joyful noise to the LORD, all the lands! 4
2 Serve the LORD with gladness! 4
3 Know that the LORD is God! It is he that made us 4
5 LORD is good; his steadfast love endures for ever 4
101: 1 loyalty and of justice; to thee, O LORD, I will sing. 4
8 off all the evildoers from the city of the LORD. 4
102: 0 pours out his complaint before the LORD. 4
1 Hear my prayer, O LORD; let my cry come to thee! 4
12 But thou, O LORD, art enthroned for ever; 4

15 The nations will fear the name of the LORD 4
16 For the LORD will build up Zion 4
18 so that a people yet unborn may praise the LORD 3
19 from heaven the LORD looked at the earth 4
21 that men may declare in Zion the name of the LORD 4
22 peoples . . and kingdoms, to worship the LORD. 4
103: 1 Bless the LORD, O my soul; and all that is within me 4
2 Bless the LORD, O my soul, and forget not 4
6 LORD works vindication and justice for all 4
8 The LORD is merciful and gracious 4
13 As a father . . so the LORD pities those who fear 4
17 steadfast love of the LORD is from everlasting 4
19 LORD has established his throne in the heavens 4
20 Bless the LORD, O you his angels, you mighty ones 4
21 Bless the LORD, all his hosts, his ministers 4
22 Bless the LORD, all his works, in all places 4
22 Bless the LORD, O my soul! 4
104: 1 Bless the LORD, O my soul! 4
1 O LORD my God, thou art very great! 4
16 The trees of the LORD are watered abundantly 4
24 O LORD, how manifold are thy works! 4
31 May the glory of the LORD endure for ever 4
31 may the LORD rejoice in his works 4
33 I will sing to the LORD as long as I live; 4
34 for I rejoice in the LORD. 4
35 Bless the LORD, O my soul! Praise the LORD! 4
35 Bless the LORD, O my soul! Praise the LORD! 3
105: 1 O give thanks to the LORD, call on his name 4
3 let the hearts of those who seek the LORD rejoice! 4
4 Seek the LORD and his strength 4
7 LORD our God; his judgments are in all the earth. 4
19 until . . came to pass the word of the LORD tested 4
24 LORD made his people very fruitful •
45 Praise the LORD! 3
106: 1 Praise the LORD! O give thanks to the LORD 3
1 O give thanks to the LORD, for he is good; 4
2 Who can utter the mighty doings of the LORD 4
4 Remember me, O LORD, when thou showest favor 4
16 Moses and Aaron, the holy one of the LORD 4
25 murmured . . did not obey the voice of the LORD. 4
29 provoked the LORD to anger with their doings •
34 not destroy the peoples, as the LORD commanded 4
40 anger of the LORD was kindled against his people 4
47 Save us, O LORD our God, and gather us from among 4
48 Blessed be the LORD, the God of Israel 4
48 let all the people say, "Amen!" Praise the LORD! 3
107: 1 O give thanks to the LORD, for he is good; 4
2 Let the redeemed of the LORD say so 4
6 Then they cried to the LORD in their trouble 4
8 Let them thank the LORD for his steadfast love 4
13 Then they cried to the LORD in their trouble 4
15 Let them thank the LORD for his steadfast love 4
19 Then they cried to the LORD in their trouble 4
21 Let them thank the LORD for his steadfast love 4
24 saw the deeds of the LORD, his wondrous works 4
28 Then they cried to the LORD in their trouble 4
31 Let them thank the LORD for his steadfast love 4
43 let men consider the steadfast love of the LORD. 4
108: 3 give thanks to thee, O LORD, among the peoples 4
109:14 iniquity of his . . remembered before the LORD 4
15 Let them be before the LORD continually; 4
20 this be the reward of my accusers from the LORD 4
26 Help me, O LORD my God! 4
27 thou, O LORD, hast done it! 4
30 With my mouth I will give great thanks to the LORD; 4
110: 1 LORD says to my lord: "Sit at my right hand 4
2 LORD sends forth from Zion your mighty scepter. 4
4 The LORD has sworn and will not change his mind 4
111: 1 Praise the LORD. I will give thanks to the LORD 3
1 I will give thanks to the LORD with my whole heart 4
2 Great are the works of the LORD 4
4 LORD is gracious and merciful. 4
10 The fear of the LORD is the beginning of wisdom; 4
112: 1 Praise the LORD. Blessed is the man who fears 3
1 Blessed is the man who fears the LORD 4
4 LORD is gracious, merciful, and righteous. 6
7 his heart is firm, trusting in the LORD. 4
113: 1 Praise the LORD! Praise, O servants of the LORD 3
1 O servants of the LORD, praise the name of the LORD! 4
1 O servants of the LORD, praise the name of the LORD! 4
2 Blessed be the name of the LORD from this time 4
3 name of the LORD is to be praised! 4
4 The LORD is high above all nations 4
5 Who is like the LORD our God, who is seated on high 4
9 Praise the LORD! 3
114: 7 Tremble, O earth, at the presence of the LORD 1
115: 1 Not to us, O LORD, not to us, but to thy name 4
9 O Israel, trust in the LORD! 4
10 O house of Aaron, put your trust in the LORD! 4
11 You who fear the LORD, trust in the LORD! 4
11 You who fear the LORD, trust in the LORD! 4
12 The LORD has been mindful of us; he will bless us; 4
13 he will bless those who fear the LORD 4
14 May the LORD give you increase . . your children! 4
15 May you be blessed by the LORD 4
16 The heavens are the LORD's heavens 4
17 The dead do not praise the LORD 3
18 we will bless the LORD from this time forth 3
18 Praise the LORD! 3
116: 1 I love the LORD, because he has heard my voice •
4 Then I called on the name of the LORD: "O LORD 4
4 O LORD, I beseech thee, save my life! 4
5 Gracious is the LORD, and righteous; 4
6 The LORD preserves the simple; 4
7 for the LORD has dealt bountifully with you. 4
9 I walk before the LORD in the land of the living. 4
12 What shall I render to the LORD for all his bounty 4
13 I will . . call on the name of the LORD 4
14 I will pay my vows to the LORD in the presence 4
15 Precious in the sight of the LORD is the death 4
16 O LORD, I am thy servant; I am thy servant, the son 4
17 I will . . call on the name of the LORD. 4
18 I will pay my vows to the LORD in the presence 4
19 in the courts of the house of the LORD 4
19 Praise the LORD! 3
117: 1 Praise the LORD, all nations! 4
2 faithfulness of the LORD endures for ever. 4
2 Praise the LORD! 3
118: 1 O give thanks to the LORD, for he is good; 4
4 who fear the LORD say, "His steadfast love endures 4
5 Out of my distress I called on the LORD; 3
5 LORD answered me and set me free. 3
6 With the LORD on my side I do not fear. 4
7 The LORD is on my side to help me; 4
8 It is better to take refuge in the LORD 4
9 better to take refuge in the LORD 4
10 in the name of the LORD I cut them off! 4
11 in the name of the LORD I cut them off! 4
12 in the name of the LORD I cut them off! 4
13 pushed hard . . falling, but the LORD helped me. 4
14 The LORD is my strength and my song; 3
15 The right hand of the LORD does valiantly 4
16 the right hand of the LORD is exalted 4
16 the right hand of the LORD does valiantly! 4
17 I shall live, and recount the deeds of the LORD. 3
18 The LORD has chastened me sorely 3
19 enter through them and give thanks to the LORD. 3
20 This is the gate of the LORD; 4
23 This . . LORD's doing; it is marvelous in our eyes. 4
24 This is the day which the LORD has made; 4
25 Save us, we beseech thee, O LORD! 4
25 O LORD, we beseech thee, give us success! 4
26 Blessed be he who enters in the name of the LORD! 4
26 We bless you from the house of the LORD 4
27 The LORD is God, and he has given us light. 4
29 O give thanks to the LORD, for he is good; 4
119: 1 Blessed are those . . who walk in the law of the LORD! 4
12 Blessed be thou, O LORD; teach me thy statutes! 4
31 I cleave to thy testimonies, O LORD; 4
33 Teach me, O LORD, the way of thy statutes; 4
41 Let thy steadfast love come to me, O LORD 4
52 thy ordinances from of old, I take comfort, O LORD. 4
55 I remember thy name in the night, O LORD 4
57 The LORD is my portion; 4
64 The earth, O LORD, is full of thy steadfast love; 4
65 Thou hast dealt well with thy servant, O LORD 4
75 I know, O LORD, that thy judgments are right 4
89 O LORD, thy word is firmly fixed in the heavens. 4
107 I am sorely afflicted; give me life, O LORD 4
108 O LORD, and teach me thy ordinances. 4
126 It is time for the LORD to act 4
137 Righteous art thou, O LORD 4
145 With my whole heart I cry; answer me, O LORD! 4
149 O LORD, in thy justice preserve my life. 4
151 thou art near, O LORD 4
156 Great is thy mercy, O LORD; 4
166 I hope for thy salvation, O LORD 4
169 Let my cry come before thee, O LORD; 4
174 I long for thy salvation, O LORD 4
120: 1 In my distress I cry to the LORD, that he may answer 4
2 Deliver me, O LORD, from lying lips 4
121: 2 My help comes from the LORD, who made heaven 4
5 The LORD is your keeper; the LORD is your shade 4
5 LORD is your shade on your right hand. 4
7 The LORD will keep you from all evil; 4
8 LORD will keep your going out and your coming 4
122: 1 Let us go to the house of the LORD! 4
4 to which the tribes go up, the tribes of the LORD 3
4 for Israel, to give thanks to the name of the LORD. 4
9 For the sake of the house of the LORD our God 4
123: 2 so our eyes look to the LORD our God 4
3 Have mercy upon us, O LORD, have mercy upon us 4
124: 1 If it had not been the LORD who was on our side 4
2 if it had not been the LORD who was on our side 4
6 Blessed be the LORD, who has not given us as prey 4
8 help is in the name of the LORD, who made heaven 4
125: 1 Those who trust in the LORD are like Mount Zion 4
2 so the LORD is round about his people 4
4 Do good, O LORD, to those who are good 4
5 who turn . . LORD will lead away with evildoers! 4
126: 1 When the LORD restored the fortunes of Zion 4
2 The LORD has done great things for them. 4
3 The LORD has done great things for us; we are glad. 4
4 Restore our fortunes, O LORD 4
127: 1 Unless the LORD builds the house, those who build 4
1 Unless the LORD watches over the city 4
3 Lo, sons are a heritage from the LORD 4
128: 1 Blessed is every one who fears the LORD 4
4 thus shall the man be blessed who fears the LORD. 4
5 The LORD bless you from Zion! 4
129: 4 The LORD is righteous; 4
8 do not say, "The blessing of the LORD be upon you! 4
8 do not say . . We bless you in the name of the LORD! 4
130: 1 Out of the depths I cry to thee, O LORD! 4
3 If thou, O LORD, shouldst mark iniquities 3
5 I wait for the LORD, my soul waits 4
6 my soul waits for the LORD more than watchmen 4
7 O Israel, hope in the LORD! 4
7 For with the LORD there is steadfast love 4
131: 1 O LORD, my heart is not lifted up, my eyes are not 4
3 O Israel, hope in the LORD from this time forth 4
132: 1 Remember, O LORD, in David's favor 4
2 swore to the LORD and vowed to the Mighty One 4
5 until I find a place for the LORD, a dwelling place 4
8 Arise, O LORD, and go to thy resting place 4
11 The LORD swore to David a sure oath 4
13 For the LORD has chosen Zion; he has desired it 4
133: 3 there the LORD has commanded the blessing 4
134: 1 Come, bless the LORD, all you servants of the LORD 4
1 Come, bless the LORD, all you servants of the LORD 4
1 who stand by night in the house of the LORD! 4
2 hands to the holy place, and bless the LORD! 4
3 May the LORD bless you from Zion 4
135: 1 Praise the LORD. Praise the name of the LORD 3
1 Praise the name of the LORD, give praise 4
1 give praise, O servants of the LORD 4
2 you that stand in the house of the LORD 4
3 Praise the LORD, for the LORD is good; 3
3 Praise the LORD, for the LORD is good; 4
4 For the LORD has chosen Jacob for himself 3
5 For I know that the LORD is great 4
6 Whatever the LORD pleases he does 4
13 Thy name, O LORD, endures for ever, thy renown, 4
13 thy renown, O LORD, throughout all ages. 4
14 For the LORD will vindicate his people 4
19 O house of Israel, bless the LORD! O house of Aaron 4
19 Israel . . O house of Aaron, bless the LORD! 4
20 O house of Levi, bless the LORD! 4
20 You that fear the LORD, bless the LORD! 4
20 You that fear the LORD, bless the LORD! 4
21 Blessed be the LORD from Zion, he who dwells 4
21 Praise the LORD! 3
136: 1 O give thanks to the LORD, for he is good 4
137: 4 How shall we sing the LORD'S song in a foreign land? 4
7 Remember, O LORD, against the E'domites the day 4
138: 1 I give thee thanks, O LORD, with my whole heart; 4
4 kings of the earth shall praise thee, O LORD 4
5 they shall sing of the ways of the LORD 4
5 for great is the glory of the LORD. 4
6 For though the LORD is high, he regards the lowly; 4
8 The LORD will fulfil his purpose for me; 4
8 thy steadfast love, O LORD, endures for ever. 4
139: 1 O LORD, thou hast searched me and known me! 4
4 lo, O LORD, thou knowest it altogether. 4
21 Do I not hate them that hate thee, O LORD? 4
140: 1 Deliver me, O LORD, from evil men; 4
4 Guard me, O LORD, from the hands of the wicked; 4
6 I say to the LORD, Thou art my God; give ear 4
6 give ear to the voice of my supplications, O LORD! 4
7 O LORD, my Lord, my strong deliverer 4
8 Grant not, O LORD, the desires of the wicked; 4
12 LORD maintains the cause of the afflicted 4
141: 1 I call upon thee, O LORD; make haste to me! 4
3 Set a guard over my mouth, O LORD 4
6 then . . learn that the word of the LORD is true. •
8 my eyes are toward thee, O LORD God; 4
142: 1 I cry with my voice to the LORD 4
1 with my voice I make supplication to the LORD 4
5 I cry to thee, O LORD; I say, Thou art my refuge 4
143: 1 Hear my prayer, O LORD; give ear 4
7 Make haste to answer me, O LORD! My spirit fails! 4
9 Deliver me, O LORD, from my enemies! 4
11 For thy name's sake, O LORD, preserve my life! 4
144: 1 Blessed be the LORD, my rock, who trains my hands 4
3 O LORD, what is man that thou dost regard him 4
5 Bow thy heavens, O LORD, and come down! 4
15 Happy the people whose God is the LORD! 4
145: 3 Great is the LORD, and greatly to be praised 4
8 The LORD is gracious and merciful 4
9 The LORD is good to all, and his compassion 4
10 All thy works shall give thanks to thee, O LORD 4
13 The LORD is faithful in all his words 4
14 The LORD upholds all who are falling 4
17 LORD is just in all his ways, and kind in all 4
18 The LORD is near to all who call upon him 4
20 LORD preserves all who love him; 4
21 My mouth will speak the praise of the LORD 4
146: 1 Praise the LORD! Praise the LORD, O my soul! 3
1 Praise the LORD! Praise the LORD, O my soul! 4
2 I will praise the LORD as long as I live; 4
5 Happy is he whose . . hope is in the LORD his God 4
7 The LORD sets the prisoners free; 4
8 the LORD opens the eyes of the blind. 4
8 The LORD lifts up those who are bowed down; 4
8 the LORD loves the righteous. 4
9 The LORD watches over the sojourners 4
10 The LORD will reign for ever, thy God, O Zion 4

10 Praise the LORD! 3
147: 1 Praise the LORD! For it is good to sing praises 3
2 LORD builds up Jerusalem; 4
5 Great is our LORD, and abundant in power; 1
6 LORD lifts up the downtrodden 4
7 Sing to the LORD with thanksgiving; make melody 4
11 the LORD takes pleasure in those who fear him 4
12 Praise the LORD, O Jerusalem! 4
20 Praise the LORD! 3
148: 1 Praise the LORD! Praise the LORD from the heavens 3
1 Praise the LORD from the heavens, praise him 4
5 Let them praise the name of the LORD! 4
7 Praise the LORD from the earth, you sea monsters 4
13 Let them praise the name of the LORD 4
14 Praise the LORD! 3
149: 1 Praise the LORD! Sing to the LORD a new song 3
1 Sing to the LORD a new song, his praise 4
4 For the LORD takes pleasure in his people; 4
9 Praise the LORD! 3
150: 1 Praise the LORD! Praise God in his sanctuary; 3
6 Let everything that breathes praise the LORD! 3
6 Praise the LORD! 3
Prv 1: 7 fear of the LORD is the beginning of knowledge; 4
29 did not choose the fear of the LORD 4
2: 5 then you will understand the fear of the LORD 4
6 For the LORD gives wisdom; 4
3: 5 Trust in the LORD with all your heart 4
7 fear the LORD, and turn away from evil. 4
9 Honor the LORD with your substance 4
11 My son, do not despise the LORD'S discipline 4
12 for the LORD reproves him whom he loves 4
19 LORD by wisdom founded the earth; 4
26 for the LORD will be your confidence 4
32 perverse man is an abomination to the LORD 4
33 LORD'S curse is on the house of the wicked 4
5:21 For a man's ways are before the eyes of the LORD 4
6:16 There are six things which the LORD hates 4
8:13 The fear of the LORD is hatred of evil. 4
22 The LORD created me at the beginning of his work 4
35 he who finds me . . obtains favor from the LORD; 4
9:10 The fear of the LORD is the beginning of wisdom 4
10: 3 The LORD does not let the righteous go hungry 4
22 The blessing of the LORD makes rich 4
27 The fear of the LORD prolongs life 4
29 LORD is a stronghold to him whose way is upright 4
11: 1 A false balance is an abomination to the LORD 4
20 perverse mind are an abomination to the LORD 4
12: 2 A good man obtains favor from the LORD 4
22 Lying lips are an abomination to the LORD 4
14: 2 He who walks in uprightness fears the LORD 4
26 In the fear of the LORD one has strong confidence 4
27 The fear of the LORD is a fountain of life 4
15: 3 The eyes of the LORD are in every place 4
8 sacrifice of . . is an abomination to the LORD 4
9 way of the wicked is an abomination to the LORD 4
11 Sheol and Abaddon lie open before the LORD 4
16 Better is a little with the fear of the LORD 4
25 The LORD tears down the house of the proud 4
26 thoughts of . . are an abomination to the LORD 4
29 The LORD is far from the wicked 4
33 The fear of the LORD is instruction in wisdom 4
16: 1 but the answer of the tongue is from the LORD. 4
2 but the LORD weighs the spirit. 4
3 Commit your work to the LORD 4
4 The LORD has made everything for its purpose 4
5 who is arrogant is an abomination to the LORD; 4
6 by the fear of the LORD a man avoids evil. 4
7 When a man's ways please the LORD 4
9 but the LORD directs his steps. 4
11 A just balance and scales are the LORD'S; 4
20 happy is he who trusts in the LORD. 4
33 but the decision is wholly from the LORD. 4
17: 3 furnace is for gold, and the LORD tries hearts. 4
15 both alike an abomination to the LORD. 4
18:10 The name of the LORD is a strong tower; 4
22 finds a wife . . obtains favor from the LORD. 4
19: 3 way to ruin, his heart rages against the LORD. 4
14 but a prudent wife is from the LORD. 4
17 He who is kind to the poor lends to the LORD 4
21 purpose of the LORD that will be established. 4
23 The fear of the LORD leads to life; 4
20:10 both alike an abomination to the LORD. 4
12 ear and the . . eye, the LORD has made them both. 4
22 wait for the LORD, and he will help you. 4
23 Diverse weights are an abomination to the LORD 4
24 A man's steps are ordered by the LORD; 4
27 The spirit of man is the lamp of the LORD 4
21: 1 heart is a stream of water in the hand of the LORD; 4
2 but the LORD weighs the heart. 4
3 do . . justice is more acceptable to the LORD 4
30 No . . counsel, can avail against the LORD. 4
31 but the victory belongs to the LORD. 4
22: 2 rich and the poor . . LORD is the maker of them all. 4
4 reward for humility and fear of the LORD is 4
12 The eyes of the LORD keep watch over knowledge 4
14 he with whom the LORD is angry will fall into it. 4
19 That your trust may be in the LORD 4
23 for the LORD will plead their cause and despoil 4
23:17 but continue in the fear of the LORD all the day. 4
24:18 lest the LORD see it, and be displeased 4
21 My son, fear the LORD and the king 4
25:22 for . . the LORD will reward you. 4
28: 5 who seek the LORD understand it completely. 4
14 Blessed is the man who fears the LORD always; *
25 but he who trusts in the LORD will be enriched. 4
29:13 LORD gives light to the eyes of both. 4
25 but he who trusts in the LORD is safe. 4
26 but from the LORD a man gets justice. 4
30: 9 I be full, and deny thee, and say, "Who is the LORD? 4
31:30 but a woman who fears the LORD is to be praised. 4
Isa 1: 2 Hear . . for the LORD has spoken: "Sons have I reared 4
4 They have forsaken the LORD . . the Holy One 4
9 If the LORD of hosts had not left . . survivors 4
10 Hear the word of the LORD, you rulers of Sodom! 4
11 What to me is . . your sacrifices? says the LORD; 4
18 Come now, let us reason together, says the LORD 4
20 for the mouth of the LORD has spoken. 4
24 Therefore the Lord says, the LORD of hosts 4
28 those who forsake the LORD shall be consumed. 4
2: 2 the mountain of the house of the LORD shall be 4
3 mountain of the LORD . . house of the God of Jacob; 4
3 the law, and the word of the LORD from Jerusalem. 4
5 come, let us walk in the light of the LORD. 4
10 hide in the dust from . . the terror of the LORD 4
11 the LORD alone will be exalted in that day. 4
12 the LORD of hosts has a day against all . . proud 4
17 the LORD alone will be exalted in that day. 4
19 from before the terror of the LORD 4
21 from before the terror of the LORD 4
3: 1 behold, the Lord, the LORD of hosts, is taking away 4
8 deeds are against the LORD, defying his glorious 4
13 The LORD has taken his place to contend 4
14 The LORD enters into judgment with the elders 4
16 The LORD said: Because the daughters of Zion are 4
17 the LORD will lay bare their secret parts. 4
4: 2 the branch of the LORD shall be beautiful 4
5 Then the LORD will create over . . Mount Zion 4
5: 7 For the vineyard of the LORD of hosts is . . Israel 4
9 The LORD of hosts has sworn in my hearing 4
12 the deeds of the LORD, or see the work of his hands. 4
16 the LORD of hosts is exalted in justice 4
24 they have rejected the law of the LORD of hosts 4
25 Therefore the anger of the LORD was kindled 4
6: 3 Holy, holy, holy is the LORD of hosts; 4
5 for my eyes have seen the King, the LORD of hosts! 4
12 the LORD removes men far away 4
7: 3 the LORD said to Isaiah, "Go forth to meet Ahaz 4
10 Again the LORD spoke to Ahaz 4
11 Ask a sign of the LORD your God; 4
12 not ask, and I will not put the LORD to the test. 4
17 The LORD will bring upon you and upon your people 4
18 In that day the LORD will whistle for the fly 4
8: 1 the LORD said to me, "Take a large tablet and write 4
3 conceived and bore a son. Then the LORD said to me 4
5 The LORD spoke to me again 4
11 For the LORD spoke thus to me with his strong hand 4
13 the LORD of hosts, him you shall regard as holy; 4
17 I will wait for the LORD, who is hiding his face 4
18 I and the children whom the LORD has given me 4
18 I and the children whom the LORD has given me 4
9: 7 The zeal of the LORD of hosts will do this. 4
11 So the LORD raises adversaries against them 4
13 did not turn . . nor seek the LORD of hosts. 4
14 So the LORD cut off from Israel head and tail 4
19 Through the wrath of the LORD of hosts 4
10:16 the LORD of hosts, will send wasting sickness 4
18 his fruitful land the LORD will destroy *
20 but will lean upon the LORD, the Holy One of Israel 4
23 For the Lord, the LORD of hosts, will make a full end 4
24 Therefore thus says the Lord, the LORD of hosts 4
26 the LORD of hosts will wield against them 4
33 Behold . . the LORD of hosts will lop the boughs 4
11: 2 the Spirit of the LORD shall rest upon him 4
2 the spirit of knowledge and the fear of the LORD. 4
3 his delight shall be in the fear of the LORD. 4
9 earth shall be full of the knowledge of the LORD 4
15 the LORD will . . destroy the tongue of the sea 4
12: 1 I will give thanks to thee, O LORD 4
2 for the LORD GOD is my strength and my song 4
4 you will say in that day: "Give thanks to the LORD 4
5 Sing praises to the LORD 4
13: 4 The LORD of hosts is mustering a host for battle. 4
5 the LORD and the weapons of his indignation 4
6 Wail, for the day of the LORD is near; 4
9 Behold, the day of the LORD comes, cruel 4
13 tremble . . at the wrath of the LORD of hosts 4
14: 1 The LORD will have compassion on Jacob 4
2 Israel will possess them in the LORD'S land 4
3 When the LORD has given you rest from your pain 4
5 The LORD has broken the staff of the wicked 4
22 I will rise up against them," says the LORD of hosts 4
22 remnant, offspring and posterity, says the LORD. 4
23 I will sweep it . . says the LORD of hosts. 4
24 The LORD of hosts has sworn: "As I have planned 4
27 For the LORD of hosts has purposed 4
32 The LORD has founded Zion 4
16:13 the LORD spoke concerning Moab in the past. 4
14 now the LORD says, "In three years 4
17: 3 of the children of Israel, says the LORD of hosts. 4
6 of a fruit tree, says the LORD God of Israel. 4
18: 4 For thus the LORD said to me: "I will quietly look 4
7 brought to the LORD . . from a people tall 4
7 Zion, the place of the name of the LORD of hosts. 4
19: 1 Behold, the LORD is riding on a swift cloud 4
4 rule over them, says the Lord, the LORD of hosts. 4
12 what the LORD . . has purposed against Egypt. 4
14 LORD . . mingled within her a spirit of confusion; 4
16 the hand . . the LORD of hosts shakes over them. 4
17 the purpose which the LORD of hosts has purposed 4
18 swear allegiance to the LORD of hosts. 4
19 an altar to the LORD in . . the land of Egypt 4
19 of Egypt, and a pillar to the LORD at its border. 4
20 It will be a sign and a witness to the LORD of hosts 4
20 when they cry to the LORD because of oppressors 4
21 the LORD will make himself known 4
21 the Egyptians will know the LORD in that day 4
21 they will make vows to the LORD and perform them. 4
22 the LORD will smite Egypt, smiting and healing 4
22 they will return to the LORD, and he will heed 4
25 whom the LORD of hosts has blessed, saying 4
20: 2 the LORD had spoken by Isaiah the son of Amoz 4
3 the LORD said, "As my servant Isaiah has walked 4
21:10 what I have heard from the LORD of hosts 4
17 for the LORD, the God of Israel, has spoken. 4
22:14 The LORD of hosts has revealed himself in my ears 4
17 Behold, the LORD will hurl you away violently 4
25 In that day, says the LORD of hosts 4
25 burden . . be cut off, for the LORD has spoken. 4
23: 9 The LORD of hosts has purposed it 4
11 the LORD has given command concerning Canaan 4
17 the end of 70 years, the LORD will visit Tyre 4
18 her hire will be dedicated to the LORD; 4
18 clothing for those who dwell before the LORD. 4
24: 1 Behold, the LORD will lay waste the earth 4
3 earth . . despoiled; for the LORD has spoken this 4
14 over the majesty of the LORD they shout 4
15 Therefore in the east give glory to the LORD; 4
15 glory . . to the name of the LORD, the God of Israel. 4
21 that day the LORD will punish the host of heaven 4
23 for the LORD of hosts will reign on Mount Zion 4
25: 1 O LORD, thou art my God; I will exalt thee 4
6 the LORD of hosts will make for all peoples 4
8 all the earth; for the LORD has spoken. 4
9 This is the LORD; we have waited for him; 4
10 the hand of the LORD will rest on this mountain 4
11 the LORD will lay low his pride *
26: 4 Trust in the LORD for ever 4
4 for ever, for the LORD GOD is an everlasting rock. 3
8 In the path of thy judgments, O LORD, we wait 4
10 and does not see the majesty of the LORD. 4
11 O LORD, thy hand is lifted up, but they see it not 4
12 O LORD, thou wilt ordain peace for us 4
13 O LORD our God, other lords besides thee have 4
15 thou hast increased the nation, O LORD 4
16 O LORD, in distress they sought thee 4
17 were we because of thee, O LORD; 4
21 the LORD is coming forth out of his place 4
27: 1 the LORD with his hard and great and strong sword 4
3 I, the LORD, am its keeper; every moment I water it 4
12 the LORD will thresh out the grain 4
13 come and worship the LORD on the holy mountain 4
28: 5 the LORD of hosts will be a crown of glory 4
11 alien tongue the LORD will speak to this people *
13 Therefore the word of the LORD will be to them 4
14 Therefore hear the word of the LORD, you scoffers 4
21 For the LORD will rise up as on Mount Pera'zim 4
29 This also comes from the LORD of hosts; 4
29: 6 be visited by the LORD of hosts with thunder 4
10 the LORD has poured out upon you a spirit 4
15 those who hide deep from the LORD their counsel 4
19 The meek shall obtain fresh joy in the LORD 4
22 thus says the LORD, who redeemed Abraham 4
30: 1 Woe to the rebellious children," says the LORD 4
9 who will not hear the instruction of the LORD; 4
18 Therefore the LORD waits to be gracious to you; 4
18 For the LORD is a God of justice; 4
26 when the LORD binds up the hurt of his people 4
27 Behold, the name of the LORD comes from far 4
29 to the mountain of the LORD, to the Rock of Israel. 4
30 the LORD will cause his majestic voice to be heard 4
31 will be terror-stricken at the voice of the LORD 4
32 punishment which the LORD lays upon them 4
33 the breath of the LORD, like a stream of brimstone 4
31: 1 do not look to . . or consult the LORD! 4
3 When the LORD stretches out his hand 4
4 For thus the LORD said to me, As a lion 4
4 the LORD of hosts will come down to fight 4
5 Like birds hovering, so the LORD . . will protect 4
9 says the LORD, whose fire is in Zion 4
32: 6 to utter error concerning the LORD 4
33: 2 O LORD, be gracious to us; we wait for thee. 4
5 The LORD is exalted, for he dwells on high; 4
6 the fear of the LORD is his treasure. 4
10 Now I will arise," says the LORD 4
21 there the LORD in majesty will be for us 4
22 For the LORD is our judge, the LORD is our ruler 4
22 For the LORD is our judge, the LORD is our ruler 4

22 the LORD is our king; he will save us. 4
34: 2 For the LORD is enraged against all the nations 4
6 The LORD has a sword; it is sated with blood 4
6 For the LORD has a sacrifice in Bozrah 4
8 For the LORD has a day of vengeance 4
16 Seek and read from the book of the LORD 4
16 For the mouth of the LORD has commanded 4
35: 2 They shall see the glory of the LORD 4
10 the ransomed of the LORD shall return 4
36: 7 if you say to me, "We rely on the LORD our God 4
10 Moreover, is it without the LORD that I have come 4
10 The LORD said to me, Go up against this land 4
15 Do not let Hezeki'ah make you rely on the LORD 4
15 by saying, "The LORD will surely deliver us; 4
18 mislead you by saying, "The LORD will deliver us. 4
20 that the LORD should deliver Jerusalem out of my 4
37: 1 and went into the house of the LORD. 4
4 may be . . the LORD your God heard the words 4
4 rebuke the words which the LORD . . has heard; 4
6 Say to your master, 'Thus says the LORD 4
14 and Hezeki'ah went up to the house of the LORD 4
14 went up . . and spread it before the LORD. 4
15 Hezeki'ah prayed to the LORD 4
16 O LORD of hosts, God of Israel, who art enthroned 4
17 Incline thy ear, O LORD, and hear; 4
17 open thy eyes, O LORD, and see; 4
18 Of a truth, O LORD, the kings of Assyria have 4
20 now, O LORD our God, save us from his hand 4
20 the earth may know that thou alone art the LORD. 4
21 Thus says the LORD, the God of Israel 4
22 the word that the LORD has spoken concerning him 4
32 zeal of the LORD of hosts will accomplish this. 4
33 says the LORD concerning the king of Assyria 4
34 he shall not come into this city, says the LORD. 4
36 the angel of the LORD went forth 4
38: 1 Thus says the LORD: Set your house in order; 4
2 turned his face to the wall, and prayed to the LORD 4
3 said, "Remember now, O LORD, I beseech thee 4
4 Then the word of the LORD came to Isaiah 4
5 Thus says the LORD, the God of David your father 4
7 This is the sign to you from the LORD 4
7 the LORD will do this thing that he has promised 4
11 I shall not see the LORD in the land of the living; 5
20 The LORD will save me, and we will sing 4
20 all the days of our life, at the house of the LORD. 4
22 sign that I shall go up to the house of the LORD 4
39: 5 Hear the word of the LORD of hosts 4
6 nothing shall be left, says the LORD. 4
8 word of the LORD which you have spoken is good. 4
40: 2 from the LORD'S hand double for all her sins. 4
3 In the wilderness prepare the way of the LORD 4
5 And the glory of the LORD shall be revealed 4
5 together, for the mouth of the LORD has spoken. 4
7 fades, when the breath of the LORD blows upon it; 4
13 Who has directed the Spirit of the LORD 4
27 My way is hid from the LORD 4
28 The LORD is the everlasting God 4
31 who wait for the LORD shall renew their strength 4
41: 4 I, the LORD, the first, and with the last; I am He. 4
13 For I, the LORD your God, hold your right hand; 4
14 I will help you, says the LORD; 4
16 And you shall rejoice in the LORD; 4
17 I the LORD will answer them 4
20 that the hand of the LORD has done this 4
21 Set forth your case, says the LORD; 4
42: 5 Thus says God, the LORD, who created the heavens 4
6 I am the LORD, I have called you in righteousness 4
8 I am the LORD, that is my name; 4
10 Sing to the LORD a new song 4
12 Let them give glory to the LORD 4
13 The LORD goes forth like a mighty man 4
19 or blind as the servant of the LORD? 4
21 The LORD was pleased, for his righteousness' sake 4
24 Was it not the LORD, against whom we have sinned 4
43: 1 now thus says the LORD, he who created you 4
3 For I am the LORD your God, the Holy One 4
10 You are my witnesses," says the LORD 4
11 I, I am the LORD, and besides me there is no savior. 4
12 and you are my witnesses," says the LORD. 4
14 Thus says the LORD, your Redeemer 4
15 I am the LORD, your Holy One, the Creator 4
16 Thus says the LORD, who makes a way in the sea 4
44: 2 Thus says the LORD who made you, who formed you 4
5 This one will say 'I am the LORD'S,' 4
5 and another will write on his hand, 'The LORD'S,' 4
6 Thus says the LORD, the King of Israel 4
6 King of Israel and his Redeemer, the LORD of hosts 4
23 Sing, O heavens, for the LORD has done it; 4
23 For the LORD has redeemed Jacob 4
24 Thus says the LORD, your Redeemer, who formed you 4
24 I am the LORD, who made all things 4
45: 1 Thus says the LORD to his anointed, to Cyrus 4
3 that you may know that it is I, the LORD 4
5 I am the LORD, and there is no other 4
6 I am the LORD, and there is no other. 4
7 I am the LORD, who do all these things. 4
8 I the LORD have created it. 4
11 Thus says the LORD, the Holy One of Israel 4
13 not for price or reward," says the LORD of hosts. 4
14 Thus says the LORD: "The wealth of Egypt 4
17 saved by the LORD with everlasting salvation; 4
18 For thus says the LORD, who created the heavens 4
18 I am the LORD, and there is no other. 4
19 I the LORD speak the truth 4
21 Who declared it of old? Was it not I, the LORD? 4
24 Only in the LORD, it shall be said of me 4
25 In the LORD all . . Israel shall triumph 4
47: 4 Our Redeemer-the LORD of hosts is his name 4
48: 1 who swear by the name of the LORD, and confess 4
2 God of Israel; the LORD of hosts is his name. 4
14 LORD loves him; he shall perform his purpose 4
17 Thus says the LORD, your Redeemer, the Holy One 4
17 I am the LORD your God, who teaches you to profit 4
20 say, "The LORD has redeemed his servant Jacob! 4
22 There is no peace," says the LORD, "for the wicked. 4
49: 1 The LORD called me from the womb 4
4 yet surely my right is with the LORD 4
5 now the LORD says, who formed me from the womb 4
5 for I am honored in the eyes of the LORD 4
7 Thus says the LORD, the Redeemer of Israel 4
7 shall prostrate themselves; because of the LORD 4
8 Thus says the LORD: "In a time of favor 4
13 For the LORD has comforted his people 4
14 But Zion said, "The LORD has forsaken me 4
18 As I live, says the LORD, you shall put them 4
23 Then you will know that I am the LORD; 4
25 Surely, thus says the LORD: "Even the captives 4
26 flesh shall know that I am the LORD your Savior 4
50: 1 Thus says the LORD: "Where is your mother's bill 4
10 fears the LORD and obeys the voice of his servant 4
10 has no light, yet trusts in the name of the LORD 4
51: 1 who pursue deliverance, you who seek the LORD; 4
3 For the LORD will comfort Zion; 4
3 like Eden, her desert like the garden of the LORD; 4
9 Awake, awake, put on strength, O arm of the LORD; 4
11 And the ransomed of the LORD shall return 4
13 and have forgotten the LORD, your Maker 4
15 For I am the LORD your God, who stirs up the sea 4
15 that its waves roar-the LORD of hosts is his name 4
17 drunk at the hand of the LORD the cup of his wrath 4
20 they are full of the wrath of the LORD 4
22 thus says your Lord, the LORD, your God 4
52: 3 For thus says the LORD: "You were sold for nothing 4
5 Now therefore what have I here, says the LORD 4
5 Their rulers wail, says the LORD 4
8 eye to eye they see the return of the LORD to Zion. 4
9 Jerusalem; for the LORD has comforted his people 4
10 The LORD has bared his holy arm before the eyes 4
11 purify . . you who bear the vessels of the LORD. 4
12 not go in flight, for the LORD will go before you 4
53: 1 to whom has the arm of the LORD been revealed? 4
6 the LORD has laid on him the iniquity of us all. 4
10 Yet it was the will of the LORD to bruise him; 4
10 the will of the LORD shall prosper in his hand; 4
54: 1 children of her that is married, says the LORD. 4
5 is your husband, the LORD of hosts is his name; 4
6 For the LORD has called you like a wife forsaken 4
8 compassion on you, says the LORD, your Redeemer. 4
10 not be removed, says the LORD, who has compassion 4
13 All your sons shall be taught by the LORD 4
17 This is the heritage of the servants of the LORD 4
17 and their vindication from me, says the LORD. 4
55: 5 shall run to you, because of the LORD your God 4
6 Seek the LORD while he may be found 4
7 let him return to the LORD 4
8 neither are your ways my ways, says the LORD. 4
13 and it shall be to the LORD for a memorial 4
56: 1 Thus says the LORD: "Keep justice 4
3 the foreigner who has joined himself to the LORD 4
3 LORD will surely separate me from his people"; 4
4 thus says the LORD: "To the eunuchs who keep my 4
6 the foreigners who join themselves to the LORD 4
6 to minister to him, to love the name of the LORD 4
57:19 peace, to the far and to the near, says the LORD; 4
58: 5 call this a fast, and a day acceptable to the LORD? 4
8 the glory of the LORD shall be your rear guard. 4
9 Then you shall call, and the LORD will answer; 4
11 And the LORD will guide you continually 4
13 a delight and the holy day of the LORD honorable; 4
14 then you shall take delight in the LORD 4
14 your father, for the mouth of the LORD has spoken. 4
59: 1 Behold, the LORD'S hand is not shortened 4
13 transgressing, and denying the LORD 4
15 The LORD saw it, and it displeased him 4
19 they shall fear the name of the LORD from the west 4
19 stream, which the wind of the LORD drives. 4
20 who turn from transgression, says the LORD. 4
21 this is my covenant with them, says the LORD 4
21 of your children's children, says the LORD 4
60: 1 and the glory of the LORD has risen upon you. 4
2 but the LORD will arise upon you 4
6 and shall proclaim the praise of the LORD. 4
9 for the name of the LORD your God, and for the Holy 4
14 they shall call you the City of the LORD, 4
16 and you shall know that I, the LORD, am your Savior 4
19 but the LORD will be your everlasting light 4
20 for the LORD will be your everlasting light 4
22 I am the LORD; in its time I will hasten it. 4
61: 1 the LORD has anointed me to bring good tidings 4
2 to proclaim the year of the LORD'S favor 4
3 oaks of righteousness, the planting of the LORD 4
6 but you shall be called the priests of the LORD 4
8 I the LORD love justice, I hate robbery and wrong; 4
9 that they are a people whom the LORD has blessed. 4
10 I will greatly rejoice in the LORD 4
62: 2 a new name which the mouth of the LORD will give. 4
3 shall be a crown of beauty in the hand of the LORD 4
4 your land Married; for the LORD delights in you 4
6 You who put the LORD in remembrance, take no rest 4
8 The LORD has sworn by his right hand 4
9 who garner it shall eat it and praise the LORD 4
11 the LORD has proclaimed to the end of the earth 4
12 called The holy people, The redeemed of the LORD; 4
63: 7 I will recount the steadfast love of the LORD 4
7 love of the LORD, the praises of the LORD 4
7 according to all that the LORD has granted us 4
14 the Spirit of the LORD gave them rest. 4
16 thou, O LORD, art our Father, our Redeemer 4
17 O LORD, why dost thou make us err from thy ways 4
64: 8 Yet, O LORD, thou art our Father; we are the clay 4
9 Be not exceedingly angry, O LORD 4
12 thou restrain thyself at these things, O LORD? 4
65: 7 fathers' iniquities together, says the LORD; 4
8 Thus says the LORD: "As the wine is found 4
11 you who forsake the LORD, who forget my holy 4
23 shall be the offspring of the blessed of the LORD 4
25 in all my holy mountain, says the LORD. 4
66: 1 Thus says the LORD: "Heaven is my throne 4
2 all these things are mine, says the LORD. 4
5 Hear the word of the LORD, 4
5 said, 'Let the LORD be glorified, 4
6 voice from the temple! The voice of the LORD 4
9 and not cause to bring forth? says the LORD; 4
12 For thus says the LORD: "Behold, I will extend 4
14 that the hand of the LORD is with his servants 4
15 For behold, the LORD will come in fire 4
16 For by fire will the LORD execute judgment 4
16 and those slain by the LORD shall be many. 4
17 shall come to an end together, says the LORD. 4
20 from all the nations as an offering to the LORD 4
20 to my holy mountain Jerusalem, says the LORD 4
20 in a clean vessel to the house of the LORD. 4
21 take for priests and for Levites, says the LORD. 4
22 shall remain before me, says the LORD; 4
23 shall come to worship before me, says the LORD. 4
Jer 1: 2 to whom the word of the LORD came 4
4 Now the word of the LORD came to me saying 4
7 the LORD said to me, "Do not say, 'I am only a youth' 4
8 for I am with you to deliver you, says the LORD. 4
9 the LORD put forth his hand and touched my mouth; 4
9 the LORD said to me, "Behold, I have put my words 4
11 the word of the LORD came to me, saying, "Jeremiah 4
12 Then the LORD said to me, "You have seen well 4
13 The word of the LORD came to me a second time 4
14 Then the LORD said to me 4
15 tribes of the kingdoms of the north, says the LORD; 4
19 for I am with you, says the LORD, to deliver you. 4
2: 1 The word of the LORD came to me, saying 4
2 Thus says the LORD, I remember the devotion 4
3 Israel was holy to the LORD, the first fruits 4
3 evil came upon them, says the LORD. 4
4 Hear the word of the LORD, O house of Jacob 4
5 Thus says the LORD 4
6 the LORD who brought us up from the land of Egypt 4
8 The priests did not say, 'Where is the LORD?' 4
9 Therefore I still contend with you, says the LORD 4
12 be shocked, be utterly desolate, says the LORD 4
17 upon yourself by forsaking the LORD your God 4
19 and bitter for you to forsake the LORD your God; 4
29 You have all rebelled against me, says the LORD. 4
31 And you, O generation, heed the word of the LORD. 4
37 for the LORD has rejected those in whom you trust 4
3: 1 and would you return to me? says the LORD. 4
6 The LORD said to me in the days of King Josi'ah 4
10 but in pretense, says the LORD. 4
11 And the LORD said to me 4
12 Return, faithless Israel, says the LORD. 4
12 for I am merciful, says the LORD; 4
13 that you rebelled against the LORD your God 4
13 that you have not obeyed my voice, says the LORD. 4
14 Return, O faithless children, says the LORD; 4
16 in those days, says the LORD, they shall no more say 4
16 no more say, "The ark of the covenant of the LORD. 4
17 Jerusalem shall be called the throne of the LORD 4
17 to the presence of the LORD in Jerusalem 4
20 faithless to me, O house of Israel, says the LORD.' 4
21 they have forgotten the LORD their God. 4
22 we come to thee; for thou art the LORD our God. 4
23 in the LORD our God is the salvation of Israel. 4
25 for we have sinned against the LORD our God 4
25 we have not obeyed the voice of the LORD our God.". 4
4: 1 If you return, O Israel, says the LORD 4
2 if you swear, 'As the LORD lives,' in truth, in justice 4
3 For thus says the LORD to the men of Judah 4
4 Circumcise yourselves to the LORD 4
8 the fierce anger of the LORD has not turned back 4
9 In that day, says the LORD, courage shall fail 4

17 she has rebelled against me, says the LORD. 4
26 all its cities were laid in ruins before the LORD 4
27 For thus says the LORD 4
5: 2 Though they say, "As the LORD lives 4
3 O LORD, do not thy eyes look for truth? 4
4 for they do not know the way of the LORD 4
5 for they know the way of the LORD 4
9 not punish them for these things? says the LORD; 4
10 her branches, for they are not the LORD'S. 4
11 have been utterly faithless to me, says the LORD. 4
12 They have spoken falsely of the LORD 4
14 Therefore thus says the LORD, the God of hosts 4
15 upon you a nation from afar . . says the LORD. 4
18 But even in those days, says the LORD 4
19 Why has the LORD . . done all these things to us?' 4
22 Do you not fear me? says the LORD; 4
24 Let us fear the LORD our God, who gives the rain 4
29 not punish them for these things? says the LORD 4
6: 6 thus says the LORD of hosts: "Hew down her trees; 4
9 Thus says the LORD of hosts 4
10 the word of the LORD is to them an object of scorn 4
11 Therefore I am full of the wrath of the LORD; 4
12 hand against the inhabitants . . " says the LORD. 4
15 they shall be overthrown," says the LORD. 4
16 Thus says the LORD: "Stand by the roads, and look 4
21 Therefore thus says the LORD: 'Behold 4
22 Thus says the LORD: "Behold, a people is coming 4
30 for the LORD has rejected them. 4
7: 1 The word that came to Jeremiah from the LORD 4
2 Stand in the gate of the LORD'S house, and proclaim 4
2 and say, Hear the word of the LORD 4
2 who enter these gates to worship the LORD. 4
3 Thus says the LORD of hosts, the God of Israel 4
4 deceptive words: 'This is the temple of the LORD 4
4 the temple of the LORD, the temple of the LORD.' 4
4 the temple of the LORD, the temple of the LORD.' 4
11 Behold, I myself have seen it, says the LORD. 4
13 you have done all these things, says the LORD 4
19 Is it I whom they provoke? says the LORD. 4
21 Thus says the LORD of hosts, the God of Israel 4
28 the nation that did not obey the voice of the LORD 4
29 for the LORD has rejected and forsaken 4
30 Judah have done evil in my sight, says the LORD; 4
32 behold, the days are coming, says the LORD 4
8: 1 At that time, says the LORD 4
3 where I have driven them, says the LORD of hosts. 4
4 You shall say to them, Thus says the LORD 4
7 but my people know not the ordinance of the LORD. 4
8 say, 'We are wise, and the law of the LORD is with us 4
9 lo, they have rejected the word of the LORD 4
12 they shall be overthrown, says the LORD. 4
13 When I would gather them, says the LORD 4
14 for the LORD our God has doomed us to perish 4
14 because we have sinned against the LORD. 4
17 and they shall bite you," says the LORD. 4
19 Is the LORD not in Zion? Is her King not in her? 4
9: 3 they do not know me, says the LORD. 4
6 they refuse to know me, says the LORD. 4
7 Therefore thus says the LORD of hosts: "Behold 4
9 not punish them for these things? says the LORD; 4
12 To whom has the mouth of the LORD spoken 4
13 the LORD says: "Because they have forsaken my law 4
15 Therefore thus says the LORD of hosts 4
17 Thus says the LORD of hosts: "Consider, and call 4
20 Hear, O women, the word of the LORD 4
22 Speak, "Thus says the LORD 4
23 Thus says the LORD: "Let not the wise man glory 4
24 that I am the LORD who practice steadfast love 4
24 for in these things I delight, says the LORD. 4
25 Behold, the days are coming, says the LORD 4
10: 1 Hear the word which the LORD speaks to you 4
2 Thus says the LORD 4
6 There is none like thee, O LORD; thou art great 4
10 the LORD is the true God; he is the living God 4
16 the LORD of hosts is his name. 4
18 For thus says the LORD 4
21 are stupid, and do not inquire of the LORD; 4
23 I know, O LORD, that the way of man is not in himself 4
24 Correct me, O LORD, but in just measure; 4
11: 1 The word that came to Jeremiah from the LORD 4
3 You shall say to them, Thus says the LORD 4
5 Then I answered, "So be it, LORD. 4
6 And the LORD said to me, "Proclaim all these words 4
9 Again the LORD said to me 4
11 Therefore, thus says the LORD, Behold 4
16 The LORD once called you, 'A green olive tree 4
17 The LORD of hosts, who planted you 4
18 The LORD made it known to me and I knew; 4
20 But, O LORD of hosts, who judgest righteously 4
21 Therefore thus says the LORD 4
21 and say, "Do not prophesy in the name of the LORD 4
22 therefore thus says the LORD of hosts: "Behold 4
12: 1 Righteous art thou, O LORD, when I complain to thee; 4
3 But thou, O LORD, knowest me; thou seest me 4
12 for the sword of the LORD devours from one end 4
13 because of the fierce anger of the LORD. 4
14 Thus says the LORD 4
16 my people, to swear by my name, 'As the LORD lives 4
17 utterly pluck it up and destroy it, says the LORD. 4
13: 1 Thus said the LORD to me 4
2 a waistcloth according to the word of the LORD 4
3 the word of the LORD came to me a second time 4
5 hid it by the Euphra'tes, as the LORD commanded me. 4
6 And after many days the LORD said to me 4
8 Then the word of the LORD came to me 4
9 Thus says the LORD: Even so will I spoil the pride 4
11 whole house of Judah cling to me, says the LORD 4
12 Thus says the LORD, the God of Israel 4
13 Then you shall say to them, 'Thus says the LORD 4
14 fathers and sons together, says the LORD. 4
15 give ear; be not proud, for the LORD has spoken. 4
16 Give glory to the LORD your God 4
17 because the LORD'S flock has been taken captive. 4
25 portion I have measured out to you, says the LORD 4
14: 1 The word of the LORD which came to Jeremiah 4
7 act, O LORD, for thy name's sake; 4
9 Yet thou, O LORD, art in the midst of us 4
10 Thus says the LORD concerning this people 4
10 therefore the LORD does not accept them 4
11 The LORD said to me: "Do not pray for the welfare 4
14 And the LORD said to me 4
15 Therefore thus says the LORD 4
20 We acknowledge our wickedness, O LORD 4
22 Art thou not he, O LORD our God? 4
15: 1 Then the LORD said to me 4
2 you shall say to them, 'Thus says the LORD 4
3 over them four kinds of destroyers, says the LORD 4
6 You have rejected me, says the LORD 4
9 before their enemies, says the LORD. 4
11 So let it be, O LORD, if I have not entreated thee 4
15 O LORD, thou knowest; remember me and visit me 4
16 for I am called by thy name, O LORD, God of hosts. 4
19 Therefore thus says the LORD: "If you return 4
20 to save you and deliver you, says the LORD. 4
16: 1 The word of the LORD came to me 4
3 For thus says the LORD concerning the sons 4
5 says the LORD: Do not enter the house of mourning 4
5 my peace from this people, says the LORD 4
9 For thus says the LORD of hosts, the God of Israel 4
10 Why has the LORD pronounced all this great evil 4
10 the sin that we have committed against the LORD 4
11 your fathers have forsaken me, says the LORD 4
14 behold, the days are coming, says the LORD 4
14 As the LORD lives who brought up the people 4
15 but 'As the LORD lives who brought up the people 4
16 I am sending for many fishers, says the LORD 4
19 O LORD, my strength and my stronghold, my refuge 4
21 they shall know that my name is the LORD. 4
17: 5 Thus says the LORD 4
5 whose heart turns away from the LORD. 4
7 Blessed is the man who trusts in the LORD 4
7 who trusts in the LORD, whose trust is the LORD. 4
10 I the LORD search the mind and try the heart 4
13 O LORD, the hope of Israel 4
13 for they have forsaken the LORD 4
14 Heal me, O LORD, and I shall be healed; 4
15 they say to me, "Where is the word of the LORD? 4
19 Thus said the LORD to me 4
20 say: 'Hear the word of the LORD, you kings of Judah 4
21 Thus says the LORD 4
24 But if you listen to me, says the LORD 4
26 thank offerings to the house of the LORD. 4
18: 1 The word that came to Jeremiah from the LORD 4
5 Then the word of the LORD came to me 4
6 do with you as this potter has done? says the LORD. 4
11 Thus says the LORD, Behold, I am shaping evil 4
13 thus says the LORD: Ask among the nations 4
19 Give heed to me, O LORD, and hearken to my plea. 4
23 Yet, thou, O LORD, knowest all their plotting 4
19: 1 Thus said the LORD, "Go, buy a potter's earthen flask 4
3 You shall say, 'Hear the word of the LORD 4
3 Thus says the LORD of hosts, the God of Israel 4
6 therefore, behold, days are coming, says the LORD 4
11 and shall say to them, 'Thus says the LORD of hosts 4
12 Thus will I do to this place, says the LORD 4
14 Topheth, where the LORD had sent him to prophesy 4
14 and he stood in the court of the LORD'S house 4
15 Thus says the LORD of hosts, the God of Israel 4
20: 1 who was chief officer in the house of the LORD 4
2 the upper Benjamin Gate of the house of the LORD. 4
3 The LORD does not call your name Pashhur 4
4 thus says the LORD: Behold, I will make you a terror 4
7 O LORD, thou hast deceived me, and I was deceived; 4
8 the word of the LORD has become for me a reproach 4
11 But the LORD is with me as a dread warrior; 4
12 O LORD of hosts, who triest the righteous 4
13 Sing to the LORD; praise the LORD! 4
13 Sing to the LORD; praise the LORD! 4
16 like the cities which the LORD overthrew 4
21: 1 the word which came to Jeremiah from the LORD 4
2 Inquire of the LORD for us 4
2 perhaps the LORD will deal with us 4
4 Thus you shall say to Zedeki'ah, 'Thus says the LORD 4
7 Afterward, says the LORD, I will give Zedeki'ah 4
8 to this people you shall say: 'Thus says the LORD 4
10 for evil and not for good, says the LORD 4
11 to . . Judah say, 'Hear the word of the LORD 4
12 O house of David! Thus says the LORD 4
13 against you . . O rock of the plain, says the LORD; 4
14 the fruit of your doings, says the LORD; 4
22: 1 says the LORD: "Go down to the house of the king 4
2 and say, 'Hear the word of the LORD, O King of Judah 4
3 Thus says the LORD: Do justice and righteousness 4
5 I swear by myself, says the LORD 4
6 For thus says the LORD concerning the house 4
8 Why has the LORD dealt thus with this great city? 4
9 Because they forsook the covenant of the LORD 4
11 For thus says the LORD concerning Shallum 4
16 Is not this to know me? says the LORD. 4
18 thus says the LORD concerning Jehoi'akim 4
24 As I live, says the LORD 4
29 O land, land, land, hear the word of the LORD! 4
30 Thus says the LORD: "Write this man down 4
23: 1 the sheep of my pasture!" says the LORD. 4
2 Therefore thus says the LORD, the God of Israel 4
2 attend to you for your evil doings, says the LORD. 4
4 neither shall any be missing, says the LORD. 4
5 Behold, the days are coming, says the LORD 4
6 he will be called: 'The LORD is our righteousness.' 4
7 behold, the days are coming, says the LORD 4
7 when men shall no longer say, 'As the LORD lives 4
8 'As the LORD lives who brought up and led 4
9 because of the LORD and because of his holy words. 4
11 I have found their wickedness, says the LORD. 4
12 in the year of their punishment, says the LORD. 4
15 Therefore thus says the LORD of hosts 4
16 Thus says the LORD of hosts 4
16 of their own minds, not from the mouth of the LORD. 4
17 to those who despise the word of the LORD 4
18 For who . . has stood in the council of the LORD 4
19 Behold, the storm of the LORD! Wrath has gone forth 4
20 The anger of the LORD will not turn back 4
23 a God at hand, says the LORD, and not a God afar off? 4
24 places so that I cannot see him? says the LORD. 4
24 Do I not fill heaven and earth? says the LORD. 4
28 has straw in common with wheat? says the LORD. 4
29 Is not my word like fire, says the LORD 4
30 behold, I am against the prophets, says the LORD 4
31 Behold, I am against the prophets, says the LORD 4
31 who use their tongues and say, 'Says the LORD.' *
32 those who prophesy lying dreams, says the LORD 4
32 not profit this people at all, says the LORD. 4
33 a priest asks you, 'What is the burden of the LORD? 4
33 and I will cast you off, says the LORD. 4
34 one of the people who says, 'The burden of the LORD 4
35 What has the LORD answered? 4
35 or 'What has the LORD spoken?' 4
36 'the burden of the LORD' you shall mention no more 4
36 words of the living God, the LORD of hosts, our God. 4
37 to the prophet, 'What has the LORD answered you? 4
37 LORD answered you?' or 'What has the LORD spoken? 4
38 But if you say, 'The burden of the LORD,' 4
38 says the LORD, 'Because you have said these words 4
38 you have said these words, "The burden of the LORD 4
38 saying, "You shall not say, 'The burden of the LORD,' 4
24: 1 the LORD showed me this vision 4
1 figs placed before the temple of the LORD. 4
3 the LORD said to me, "What do you see, Jeremiah? 4
4 Then the word of the LORD came to me 4
5 Thus says the LORD, the God of Israel 4
7 I will give them a heart to know that I am the LORD; 4
8 But thus says the LORD 4
25: 3 to this day, the word of the LORD has come to me 4
4 although the LORD persistently sent to you 4
5 and dwell upon the land which the LORD has given 4
7 Yet you have not listened to me, says the LORD 4
8 Therefore thus says the LORD of hosts: 4
9 send for all the tribes of the north, says the LORD 4
12 punish . . for their iniquity, says the LORD 4
15 Thus the LORD, the God of Israel, said to me 4
17 I took the cup from the LORD'S hand 4
27 you shall say to them, 'Thus says the LORD of hosts 4
28 you shall say to them, 'Thus says the LORD of hosts 4
29 inhabitants of the earth, says the LORD of hosts. 4
30 The LORD will roar from on high 4
31 the LORD has an indictment against the nations; 4
31 the wicked he will put to the sword, says the LORD. 4
32 Thus says the LORD of hosts 4
33 those slain by the LORD on that day 4
36 For the LORD is despoiling their pasture 4
37 because of the fierce anger of the LORD. 4
26: 1 this word came from the LORD 4
2 Thus says the LORD: Stand in the court of the LORD'S 4
2 Stand in the court of the LORD'S house, and speak 4
2 which come to worship in the house of the LORD 4
4 You shall say to them, 'Thus says the LORD 4
7 speaking these words in the house of the LORD. 4
8 all that the LORD had commanded him to speak 4
9 Why have you prophesied in the name of the LORD 4
9 about Jeremiah in the house of the LORD. 4
10 to the house of the LORD and took their seat 4
10 the entry of the New Gate of the house of the LORD. 4
12 The LORD sent me to prophesy against this house 4
13 and obey the voice of the LORD your God 4
13 and the LORD will repent of the evil 4
15 for in truth the LORD sent me to you to speak 4
16 he has spoken to us in the name of the LORD our God. 4

18 Thus says the LORD of hosts, Zion shall be plowed 4
19 Did he not fear the LORD 4
19 fear the LORD and entreat the favor of the LORD 4
19 did not the LORD repent of the evil 4
20 another . . who prophesied in the name of the LORD 4
27: 1 this word came to Jeremiah from the LORD. 4
2 Thus the LORD said to me: "Make yourself thongs 4
4 Thus says the LORD of hosts, the God of Israel 4
8 with famine, and with pestilence, says the LORD 4
11 to till it and dwell there, says the LORD. 4
13 and by pestilence, as the LORD has spoken 4
15 I have not sent them, says the LORD 4
16 Thus says the LORD: Do not listen to the words 4
16 saying, 'Behold, the vessels of the LORD'S house 4
18 and if the word of the LORD is with them 4
18 then let them intercede with the LORD of hosts 4
18 vessels which are left in the house of the LORD 4
19 For thus says the LORD of hosts 4
21 thus says the LORD of hosts, the God of Israel 4
21 vessels which are left in the house of the LORD 4
22 when I give attention to them, says the LORD. 4
28: 1 Hanani'ah . . spoke to me in the house of the LORD 4
2 Thus says the LORD of hosts, the God of Israel 4
3 to this place all the vessels of the LORD'S house 4
4 from Judah who went to Babylon, says the LORD 4
5 people who were standing in the house of the LORD; 4
6 prophet Jeremiah said, "Amen! May the LORD do so; 4
6 LORD make the words which you have prophesied 4
6 from Babylon the vessels of the house of the LORD 4
9 then it will be known that the LORD has truly sent 4
11 Thus says the LORD: Even so will I break the yoke 4
12 the word of the LORD came to Jeremiah 4
13 Go, tell Hanani'ah, 'Thus says the LORD 4
14 For thus says the LORD of hosts, the God of Israel 4
15 Listen, Hanani'ah, the LORD has not sent you 4
16 Therefore thus says the LORD 4
16 you have uttered rebellion against the LORD. 4
29: 4 Thus says the LORD of hosts, the God of Israel 4
7 and pray to the LORD on its behalf 4
8 For thus says the LORD of hosts, the God of Israel 4
9 I did not send them, says the LORD. 4
10 For thus says the LORD 4
11 For I know the plans I have for you, says the LORD 4
14 I will be found by you, says the LORD 4
14 the places where I have driven you, says the LORD 4
15 The LORD has raised up prophets for us in Babylon, 4
16 Thus says the LORD concerning the king 4
17 Thus says the LORD of hosts, Behold 4
19 because they did not heed my words, says the LORD 4
19 but you would not listen, says the LORD. 4
20 Hear the word of the LORD, all you exiles 4
21 Thus says the LORD of hosts, the God of Israel 4
22 The LORD make you like Zedeki'ah and Ahab 4
23 and I am witness, says the LORD. 4
25 Thus says the LORD of hosts, the God of Israel 4
26 The LORD has made you priest instead of Jehoi'ada 4
26 to have charge in the house of the LORD 4
30 Then the word of the LORD came to Jeremiah 4
31 Send to all the exiles, saying, 'Thus says the LORD 4
32 thus says the LORD: Behold, I will punish Shemai'ah 4
32 the good that I will do to my people, says the LORD 4
32 for he has talked rebellion against the LORD. 4
30: 1 The word that came to Jeremiah from the LORD 4
2 Thus says the LORD, the God of Israel 4
3 For behold, days are coming, says the LORD 4
3 my people, Israel and Judah, says the LORD 4
4 These are the words which the LORD spoke 4
5 Thus says the LORD: We have heard a cry of panic 4
8 come to pass in that day, says the LORD of hosts 4
9 But they shall serve the LORD their God and David 4
10 Then fear not, O Jacob my servant, says the LORD 4
11 For I am with you to save you, says the LORD; 4
12 For thus says the LORD: Your hurt is incurable 4
17 and your wounds I will heal, says the LORD 4
18 Thus says the LORD: Behold, I will restore 4
21 dare of himself to approach me? says the LORD. 4
23 Behold the storm of the LORD! Wrath has gone forth 4
24 The fierce anger of the LORD will not turn back 4
31: 1 says the LORD, I will be the God of all the families 4
2 Thus says the LORD 4
3 the LORD appeared to him from afar. 4
6 Arise, and let us go up to Zion, to the LORD our God. 4
7 For thus says the LORD: "Sing aloud with gladness 4
7 give praise, and say, 'The LORD has saved his people 4
10 Hear the word of the LORD, O nations, and declare it 4
11 the LORD has ransomed Jacob, and has redeemed him 4
12 shall be radiant over the goodness of the LORD 4
14 be satisfied with my goodness, says the LORD. 4
15 Thus says the LORD: "A voice is heard in Ramah 4
16 Thus says the LORD: "Keep your voice from weeping 4
16 for your work shall be rewarded, says the LORD 4
17 There is hope for your future, says the LORD 4
18 I may be restored, for thou art the LORD my God. 4
20 I will surely have mercy on him, says the LORD. 4
22 For the LORD has created a new thing on the earth 4
23 Thus says the LORD of hosts, the God of Israel 4
23 The LORD bless you 4
27 Behold, the days are coming, says the LORD 4
28 to build and to plant, says the LORD. 4
31 Behold, the days are coming, says the LORD 4
32 though I was their husband, says the LORD. 4
33 the covenant which I will make . . says the LORD 4
34 and each his brother, saying, 'Know the LORD,' 4
34 from the least . . to the greatest, says the LORD; 4
35 Thus says the LORD, who gives the sun for light 4
35 the LORD of hosts is his name 4
36 fixed order departs from before me, says the LORD 4
37 Thus says the LORD 4
37 for all that they have done, says the LORD. 4
38 Behold, the days are coming, says the LORD 4
38 when the city shall be rebuilt for the LORD 4
40 Gate toward the east, shall be sacred to the LORD. 4
32: 1 The word that came to Jeremiah from the LORD 4
3 Why do you prophesy and say, 'Thus says the LORD 4
5 shall remain until I visit him, says the LORD; 4
6 Jeremiah said, "The word of the LORD came to me 4
8 came . . in accordance with the word of the LORD 4
8 Then I knew that this was the word of the LORD. 4
14 Thus says the LORD of hosts, the God of Israel 4
15 For thus says the LORD of hosts, the God of Israel 4
16 I prayed to the LORD, saying 4
18 mighty God whose name is the LORD of hosts 4
26 The word of the LORD came to Jeremiah 4
27 Behold, I am the LORD, the God of all flesh; 4
28 Therefore, thus says the LORD 4
30 to anger by the work of their hands, says the LORD. 4
36 therefore thus says the LORD, the God of Israel 4
42 For thus says the LORD 4
44 for I will restore their fortunes, says the LORD. 4
33: 1 word of the LORD came to Jeremiah a second time 4
2 Thus says the LORD who made the earth 4
2 the LORD who formed it to establish it 4
2 formed it to establish it–the LORD is his name 4
4 For thus says the LORD, the God of Israel 4
10 Thus says the LORD: In this place of which you say 4
11 bring thank offerings to the house of the LORD 4
11 Give thanks to the LORD of hosts 4
11 the LORD is good, for his steadfast love endures 4
11 fortunes of the land as at first, says the LORD. 4
12 Thus says the LORD of hosts 4
13 hands of the one who counts them, says the LORD. 4
14 Behold, the days are coming, says the LORD 4
16 it will be called: 'The LORD is our righteousness 4
17 For thus says the LORD 4
19 The word of the LORD came to Jeremiah 4
20 Thus says the LORD: If you can break my covenant 4
23 The word of the LORD came to Jeremiah 4
24 The LORD has rejected the two families 4
25 Thus says the LORD 4
34: 1 The word which came to Jeremiah from the LORD 4
2 Thus says the LORD, the God of Israel: Go and speak 4
2 Thus says the LORD: Behold, I am giving this city 4
4 Yet hear the word of the LORD, O Zedeki'ah 4
4 O Zedeki'ah . . ! Thus says the LORD concerning you 4
5 For I have spoken the word, says the LORD. 4
8 The word which came to Jeremiah from the LORD 4
12 word of the LORD came to Jeremiah from the LORD 4
12 word of the LORD came to Jeremiah from the LORD 4
13 Thus says the LORD, the God of Israel 4
17 Therefore, thus says the LORD: You have not obeyed 4
17 to pestilence, and to famine, says the LORD 4
22 Behold, I will command, says the LORD 4
35: 1 The word which came to Jeremiah from the LORD 4
2 and bring them to the house of the LORD 4
4 I brought them to the house of the LORD 4
12 Then the word of the LORD came to Jeremiah 4
13 Thus says the LORD of hosts, the God of Israel 4
13 and listen to my words? says the LORD. 4
17 Therefore, thus says the LORD, the God of hosts 4
18 Thus says the LORD of hosts, the God of Israel 4
19 therefore thus says the LORD of hosts 4
36: 1 this word came to Jeremiah from the LORD 4
4 the words of the LORD which he had spoken to him. 4
5 I am debarred from going to the house of the LORD; 4
6 in the LORD'S house you shall read the words 4
6 you shall read the words of the LORD 4
7 their supplication will come before the LORD 4
7 the anger and wrath that the LORD has pronounced 4
8 reading from the scroll the words of the LORD 4
8 the words of the LORD in the LORD'S house. 4
9 Jerusalem proclaimed a fast before the LORD. 4
10 read . . from the scroll, in the house of the LORD 4
10 at the entry of the New Gate of the LORD'S house. 4
11 heard all the words of the LORD from the scroll 4
26 but the LORD hid them. 4
27 the word of the LORD came to Jeremiah 4
29 Thus says the LORD, You have burned this scroll 4
30 thus says the LORD concerning Jehoi'akim king 4
37: 2 listened to the words of the LORD which he spoke 4
3 saying, "Pray for us to the LORD our God. 4
6 the word of the LORD came to Jeremiah the prophet 4
7 Thus says the LORD, God of Israel 4
9 Thus says the LORD, Do not deceive yourselves 4
17 and said, "Is there any word from the LORD? 4
38: 2 Thus says the LORD 4
3 Thus says the LORD, This city shall . . be given 4
14 at the third entrance of the temple of the LORD. 4
16 to Jeremiah, "As the LORD lives, who made our souls 4
17 Thus says the LORD, the God of hosts 4
20 Obey now the voice of the LORD in what I say to you 4
21 this is the vision which the LORD has shown to me 4
39:15 The word of the LORD came to Jeremiah 4
16 Thus says the LORD of hosts, the God of Israel 4
17 But I will deliver you on that day, says the LORD 4
18 you have put your trust in me, says the LORD. 4
40: 1 The word that came to Jeremiah from the LORD 4
2 The LORD your God pronounced this evil 4
3 the LORD has brought it about 4
3 you sinned against the LORD, and did not obey 4
41: 5 and incense to present at the temple of the LORD. 4
42: 2 and pray to the LORD your God for us 4
3 that the LORD your God may show us the way 4
4 behold, I will pray to the LORD your God 4
4 and whatever the LORD answers you I will tell you; 4
5 May the LORD be a true and faithful witness 4
5 word with which the LORD your God sends you to us. 4
6 we will obey the voice of the LORD our God 4
6 when we obey the voice of the LORD our God. 4
7 the word of the LORD came to Jeremiah. 4
9 said to them, "Thus says the LORD, the God of Israel 4
11 do not fear him, says the LORD, for I am with you 4
13 disobeying the voice of the LORD your God 4
15 then hear the word of the LORD, O remnant of Judah. 4
15 Thus says the LORD of hosts, the God of Israel 4
18 For thus says the LORD of hosts, the God of Israel 4
19 The LORD has said to you, O remnant of Judah 4
20 sent me to the LORD your God, saying, 'Pray for us 4
20 Pray for us to the LORD your God 4
20 whatever the LORD our God says declare to us 4
21 you have not obeyed the voice of the LORD your God 4
43: 1 speaking . . all these words of the LORD their God 4
1 with which the LORD their God had sent him to them 4
2 The LORD our God did not send you to say 4
4 the people did not obey the voice of the LORD 4
7 for they did not obey the voice of the LORD. 4
8 Then the word of the LORD came to Jeremiah 4
10 Thus says the LORD of hosts, the God of Israel 4
44: 2 Thus says the LORD of hosts, the God of Israel 4
7 thus says the LORD God of hosts, the God of Israel 4
11 thus says the LORD of hosts, the God of Israel 4
16 which you have spoken to us in the name of the LORD 4
21 did not the LORD remember it? 4
22 The LORD could no longer bear your evil doings 4
23 and because you sinned against the LORD 4
23 and did not obey the voice of the LORD 4
24 Hear the word of the LORD, all you of Judah 4
25 Thus says the LORD of hosts, the God of Israel 4
26 Therefore hear the word of the LORD 4
26 I have sworn by my great name, says the LORD 4
29 This shall be the sign to you, says the LORD 4
30 Thus says the LORD 4
45: 2 Thus says the LORD, the God of Israel, to you 4
3 Woe is me! for the LORD has added sorrow to my pain; 4
4 Thus shall you say to him, Thus says the LORD 4
5 I am bringing evil upon all flesh, says the LORD; 4
46: 1 The word of the LORD which came to Jeremiah 4
5 terror on every side! says the LORD. 4
13 The word which the LORD spoke to Jeremiah 4
15 bull stand? Because the LORD thrust him down. 4
18 says the King, whose name is the LORD of hosts 4
23 They shall cut down her forest, says the LORD 4
25 The LORD of hosts, the God of Israel, said: "Behold 4
26 as in the days of old, says the LORD. 4
28 Fear not, O Jacob my servant, says the LORD 4
47: 1 The word of the LORD that came to Jeremiah 4
2 Thus says the LORD: Behold, waters are rising 4
4 For the LORD is destroying the Philistines 4
6 Ah, sword of the LORD! How long till you are quiet? 4
7 can it be quiet, when the LORD has given it a charge? 4
48: 1 Concerning Moab. Thus says the LORD of hosts 4
8 plain shall be destroyed, as the LORD has spoken. 4
10 he who does the work of the LORD with slackness; 4
12 behold, the days are coming, says the LORD 4
15 says the King, whose name is the LORD of hosts. 4
25 his arm is broken, says the LORD. 4
26 because he magnified himself against the LORD; 4
30 I know his insolence, says the LORD; 4
35 I will bring to an end in Moab, says the LORD 4
38 a vessel for which no one cares, says the LORD. 4
40 For thus says the LORD: "Behold, one shall fly 4
42 because he magnified himself against the LORD. 4
43 before you, O inhabitant of Moab! says the LORD. 4
44 in the year of their punishment, says the LORD. 4
47 of Moab in the latter days, says the LORD. 4
49: 1 Concerning the Ammonites. Thus says the LORD 4
2 behold, the days are coming, says the LORD 4
2 those who dispossessed him, says the LORD. 4
6 the fortunes of the Ammonites, says the LORD. 4
7 Concerning Edom. Thus says the LORD of hosts 4
12 thus says the LORD: "If those who did not deserve 4
13 For I have sworn by myself, says the LORD 4
14 I have heard tidings from the LORD 4
16 I will bring you down from there, says the LORD. 4
18 neighbor cities were overthrown, says the LORD 4
20 Therefore hear the plan which the LORD has made 4
26 destroyed in that day, says the LORD of hosts. 4
28 says the LORD: "Rise up, advance against Kedar! 4

30 O inhabitants of Hazor! says the LORD. 4
31 at ease, that dwells securely, says the LORD 4
32 calamity from every side of them, says the LORD. 4
34 The word of the LORD that came to Jeremiah 4
35 says the LORD of hosts: "Behold, I will break the bow 4
37 evil upon them, my fierce anger, says the LORD. 4
38 and destroy their king and princes, says the LORD. 4
39 I will restore the fortunes of Elam, says the LORD. 4
50: 1 word which the LORD spoke concerning Babylon 4
4 In those days and in that time, says the LORD 4
4 and they shall seek the LORD their God. 4
5 saying, 'Come, let us join ourselves to the LORD 4
7 for they have sinned against the LORD 4
7 the LORD, the hope of their fathers. 4
10 all who plunder her shall be sated, says the LORD. 4
13 Because of the wrath of the LORD she shall not be 4
14 for she has sinned against the LORD. 4
15 For this is the vengeance of the LORD 4
18 Therefore, thus says the LORD of hosts 4
20 In those days and in that time, says the LORD 4
21 and utterly destroy after them, says the LORD 4
24 caught, because you strove against the LORD. 4
25 The LORD has opened his armory 4
28 to declare in Zion the vengeance of the LORD 4
29 she has . . defied the LORD, the Holy One of Israel. 4
30 be destroyed on that day, says the LORD. 4
33 Thus says the LORD of hosts: The people of Israel 4
34 Redeemer is strong; the LORD of hosts is his name. 4
35 A sword upon the Chalde'ans, says the LORD 4
40 Sodom . . and their neighbor cities, says the LORD 4
45 Therefore hear the plan which the LORD has made 4
51: 1 Thus says the LORD: "Behold, I will stir up 4
5 not been forsaken by their God, the LORD of hosts; 4
6 for this is the time of the LORD'S vengeance 4
7 Babylon was a golden cup in the LORD'S hand 4
10 The LORD has brought forth our vindication; 4
10 let us declare in Zion the work of the LORD our God. 4
11 The LORD has stirred up the spirit of the kings 4
11 for that is the vengeance of the LORD 4
12 the LORD has both planned and done what he spoke 4
14 The LORD of hosts has sworn by himself 4
19 the LORD of hosts is his name. 4
24 that they have done in Zion, says the LORD. 4
25 against you, O destroying mountain, says the LORD 4
26 you shall be a perpetual waste, says the LORD. 4
29 for the LORD'S purposes against Babylon stand 4
33 For thus says the LORD of hosts, the God of Israel 4
36 Therefore thus says the LORD: "Behold, I will plead 4
39 a perpetual sleep and not wake, says the LORD. 4
45 save his life from the fierce anger of the LORD! 4
48 come against them out of the north, says the LORD. 4
50 go, stand not still! Remember the LORD from afar 4
51 come into the holy places of the LORD'S house.' 4
52 behold, the days are coming, says the LORD 4
53 would come from me upon her, says the LORD. 4
55 For the LORD is laying Babylon waste 4
56 the LORD is a God of recompense 4
57 says the King, whose name is the LORD of hosts. 4
58 Thus says the LORD of hosts 4
62 say, 'O LORD, thou hast said concerning this place 4
52: 2 he did what was evil in the sight of the LORD 4
3 Surely because of the anger of the LORD 4
13 he burned the house of the LORD 4
17 of bronze that were in the house of the LORD 4
17 the bronze sea that were in the house of the LORD 4
20 the king had made for the house of the LORD 4
Lam 1: 5 LORD has made her suffer for . . transgressions; 4
9 O LORD, behold my affliction 4
11 Look, O LORD, and behold, for I am despised. 4
12 like my sorrow . . which the LORD inflicted 4
17 the LORD has commanded against Jacob that 4
18 The LORD is in the right, for I have rebelled 4
20 Behold, O LORD, for I am in distress 4
2: 6 the LORD has brought to an end . . appointed feast 4
7 a clamor was raised in the house of the LORD 4
8 The LORD determined to lay in ruins the wall 4
9 and her prophets obtain no vision from the LORD. 4
17 The LORD has done what he purposed 4
20 Look, O LORD, and see! With whom hast thou dealt 4
22 on the day of the anger of the LORD none escaped 4
3:18 Gone is . . and my expectation from the LORD. 4
22 The steadfast love of the LORD never ceases 4
24 The LORD is my portion," says my soul 4
25 The LORD is good to those who wait for him 4
26 wait quietly for the salvation of the LORD. 4
40 test and examine our ways, and return to the LORD! 4
50 until the LORD from heaven looks down and sees; 4
55 I called on thy name, O LORD, from the depths 4
59 Thou hast seen the wrong done to me, O LORD; 4
61 Thou hast heard their taunts, O LORD 4
64 Thou wilt requite them, O LORD 4
66 and destroy them from under thy heavens, O LORD. 4
4:11 The LORD gave full vent to his wrath 4
16 The LORD himself has scattered them 4
20 The breath of our nostrils, the LORD'S anointed 4
5: 1 Remember, O LORD, what has befallen us; 4
19 But thou, O LORD, dost reign for ever; 4
21 Restore us to thyself, O LORD 4
Ezk 1: 3 the word of the LORD came to Ezekiel the priest 4
3 and the hand of the LORD was upon him there. 4
28 the likeness of the glory of the LORD. 4
3:12 and as the glory of the LORD arose from its place 4
14 the hand of the LORD being strong upon me; 4
16 the word of the LORD came to me 4
22 the hand of the LORD was there upon me; 4
23 and, lo, the glory of the LORD stood there 4
4:13 the LORD said, "Thus shall the people of Israel eat 4
5:13 they shall know that I, the LORD, have spoken 4
15 I, the LORD, have spoken 4
17 I, the LORD, have spoken. 4
6: 1 The word of the LORD came to me 4
7 and you shall know that I am the LORD. 4
10 And they shall know that I am the LORD; 4
13 And you shall know that I am the LORD 4
14 Then they will know that I am the LORD. 4
7: 1 The word of the LORD came to me 4
4 Then you will know that I am the LORD. 4
9 Then you will know that I am the LORD, who smite. 4
19 to deliver them in the day of the wrath of the LORD; 4
27 and they shall know that I am the LORD. 4
8:12 For they say, 'The LORD does not see us 4
12 For they say . . the LORD has forsaken the land. 4
14 the north gate of the house of the LORD; 4
16 me into the inner court of the house of the LORD; 4
16 and behold, at the door of the temple of the LORD 4
16 men, with their backs to the temple of the LORD 4
9: 4 And the LORD said to him, "Go through the city 4
9 for they say, 'The LORD has forsaken the land 4
9 has forsaken the land, and the LORD does not see. 4
10: 4 the glory of the LORD went up from the cherubim 4
4 full of the brightness of the glory of the LORD. 4
18 Then the glory of the LORD went forth 4
19 the door of the east gate of the house of the LORD; 4
11: 1 to the east gate of the house of the LORD 4
5 Spirit of the LORD fell upon me, and he said to me 4
5 Thus says the LORD: So you think, O house of Israel; 4
10 and you shall know that I am the LORD. 4
12 you shall know that I am the LORD; 4
14 the word of the LORD came to me 4
15 have said, 'They have gone far from the LORD; 4
23 And the glory of the LORD went up from the midst 4
25 all the things that the LORD had showed me. 4
12: 1 The word of the LORD came to me 4
8 In the morning the word of the LORD came to me 4
15 they shall know that I am the LORD 4
16 and may know that I am the LORD. 4
17 Moreover the word of the LORD came to me 4
20 and you shall know that I am the LORD. 4
21 the word of the LORD came to me 4
25 I the LORD will speak the word which I will speak 4
26 Again the word of the LORD came to me 4
13: 1 The word of the LORD came to me 4
2 prophesy and say . . 'Hear the word of the LORD!' 4
5 it might stand in battle in the day of the LORD. 4
6 they say, 'Says the LORD,' when the LORD has not 4
6 they say, 'Says the LORD,' when the LORD has not 4
7 whenever you have said, 'Says the LORD,' 4
14 you shall know that I am the LORD. 4
21 prey; and you shall know that I am the LORD. 4
23 Then you will know that I am the LORD. 4
14: 2 the word of the LORD came to me 4
4 I the LORD will answer him myself 4
7 I the LORD will answer him myself; 4
8 you shall know that I am the LORD. 4
9 I, the LORD, have deceived that prophet 4
12 the word of the LORD came to me 4
15: 1 the word of the LORD came to me 4
7 you will know that I am the LORD, when I set my face 4
16: 1 Again the word of the LORD came to me 4
35 Wherefore, O harlot, hear the word of the LORD 4
58 You bear the penalty . . says the LORD. 4
62 you shall know that I am the LORD 4
17: 1 The word of the LORD came to me 4
11 Then the word of the LORD came to me 4
21 you shall know that I, the LORD, have spoken. 4
24 shall know that I the LORD bring low the high tree 4
24 I the LORD have spoken, and I will do it. 4
18: 1 The word of the LORD came to me again 4
20: 1 came to inquire of the LORD, and sat before me. 4
2 the word of the LORD came to me 4
5 I swore to them, saying, I am the LORD your God. 4
7 I am the LORD your God. 4
12 they might know that I the LORD sanctify them. 4
19 I the LORD am your God; walk in my statutes 4
20 that you may know that I the LORD am your God. 4
26 that they might know that I am the LORD. 4
38 Then you will know that I am the LORD. 4
42 And you shall know that I am the LORD 4
44 you shall know that I am the LORD 4
45 the word of the LORD came to me 4
47 Hear the word of the LORD: Thus says the Lord GOD 4
48 flesh shall see that I the LORD have kindled it; 4
21: 1 The word of the LORD came to me 4
3 say to the land of Israel, Thus says the LORD 4
5 shall know that I the LORD have drawn my sword out 4
8 the word of the LORD came to me 4
17 I will satisfy my fury; I the LORD have spoken. 4
18 The word of the LORD came to me again 4
32 no more remembered; for I the LORD have spoken. 4
22: 1 Moreover the word of the LORD came to me, saying 4
14 I the LORD have spoken, and I will do it. 4
16 you shall know that I am the LORD. 4
17 the word of the LORD came to me 4
22 I the LORD have poured out my wrath upon you. 4
23 the word of the LORD came to me 4
28 says the Lord GOD,' when the LORD has not spoken. 4
23: 1 The word of the LORD came to me 4
36 The LORD said to me: "Son of man, will you judge 4
24: 1 the word of the LORD came to me 4
14 I the LORD have spoken; it shall come to pass 4
15 Also the word of the LORD came to me 4
20 I said to them, "The word of the LORD came to me 4
27 they will know that I am the LORD. 4
25: 1 The word of the LORD came to me 4
5 Then you will know that I am the LORD. 4
7 Then you will know that I am the LORD. 4
11 Then they will know that I am the LORD. 4
17 Then they will know that I am the LORD 4
26: 1 the word of the LORD came to me 4
6 Then they will know that I am the LORD. 4
14 for I the LORD have spoken, says the Lord GOD. 4
27: 1 The word of the LORD came to me 4
28: 1 The word of the LORD came to me 4
11 Moreover the word of the LORD came to me 4
20 The word of the LORD came to me 4
22 they shall know that I am the LORD when I execute 4
23 Then they will know that I am the LORD. 4
26 Then they will know that I am the LORD their God. 4
29: 1 the word of the LORD came to me 4
6 Egypt shall know that I am the LORD. 4
9 Then they will know that I am the LORD. 4
17 the word of the LORD came to me 4
21 Then they will know that I am the LORD. 4
30: 1 The word of the LORD came to me 4
3 For the day is near, the day of the LORD is near; 4
6 says the LORD: Those who support Egypt shall fall 4
8 Then they will know that I am the LORD 4
12 by the hand of foreigners; I, the LORD, have spoken. 4
19 Then they will know that I am the LORD. 4
20 the word of the LORD came to me 4
25 they shall know that I am the LORD. 4
26 Then they will know that I am the LORD. 4
31: 1 the word of the LORD came to me 4
32: 1 the word of the LORD came to me 4
15 then they will know that I am the LORD. 4
17 the word of the LORD came to me 4
33: 1 The word of the LORD came to me 4
22 Now the hand of the LORD had been upon me 4
23 The word of the LORD came to me 4
29 Then they will know that I am the LORD 4
30 what the word is that comes forth from the LORD 4
34: 1 The word of the LORD came to me 4
7 you shepherds, hear the word of the LORD 4
9 you shepherds, hear the word of the LORD 4
24 I, the LORD, will be their God 4
24 I, the LORD, have spoken. 4
27 they shall know that I am the LORD 4
30 shall know that I, the LORD their God, am with them 4
35: 1 The word of the LORD came to me 4
4 and you shall know that I am the LORD. 4
9 Then you will know that I am the LORD. 4
10 although the LORD was there 4
12 And you shall know that I, the LORD, have heard all 4
15 Then they will know that I am the LORD. 4
36: 1 O mountains of Israel, hear the word of the LORD. 4
11 Then you will know that I am the LORD. 4
16 The word of the LORD came to me 4
20 men said of them, 'These are the people of the LORD 4
23 the nations will know that I am the LORD 4
36 left round about you shall know that I, the LORD 4
36 I, the LORD, have spoken, and I will do it. 4
38 Then they will know that I am the LORD. 4
37: 1 The hand of the LORD was upon me, and he brought 4
1 he brought me out by the spirit of the LORD 4
4 say to them, O dry bones, hear the word of the LORD. 4
6 you shall know that I am the LORD. 4
13 you shall know that I am the LORD 4
14 then you shall know that I, the LORD, have spoken 4
14 have spoken, and I have done it, says the LORD. 4
15 The word of the LORD came to me 4
28 will know that I the LORD sanctify Israel 4
38: 1 The word of the LORD came to me 4
23 Then they will know that I am the LORD. 4
39: 6 they shall know that I am the LORD. 4
7 the nations shall know that I am the LORD 4
22 The house of Israel shall know that I am the LORD 4
28 Then they shall know that I am the LORD their God 4
40: 1 on that very day, the hand of the LORD was upon me 4
46 may come near to the LORD to minister to him. 4
41:22 This is the table which is before the LORD. 4
42:13 the priests who approach the LORD shall eat 4
43: 4 glory of the LORD entered the temple by the gate 4
5 behold, the glory of the LORD filled the temple. 4
24 You shall present them before the LORD 4
24 and offer them up as a burnt offering to the LORD. 4
44: 2 for the LORD, the God of Israel, has entered by it; 4
3 prince may sit in it to eat bread before the LORD; 4

4 glory of the LORD filled the temple of the LORD; 4
4 glory of the LORD filled the temple of the LORD; 4
5 And the LORD said to me, "Son of man, mark well 4
5 all the ordinances of the temple of the LORD 4
45: 1 you shall set apart for the LORD a portion 4
4 and approach the LORD to minister to him; 4
23 he shall provide as a burnt offering to the LORD 4
46: 3 at the entrance of that gate before the LORD 4
4 offering that the prince offers to the LORD 4
9 When the people of the land come before the LORD 4
12 offerings as a freewill offering to the LORD 4
13 for a burnt offering to the LORD daily; 4
14 the flour, as a cereal offering to the LORD; 4
48: 9 portion which you shall set apart for the LORD 4
10 with the sanctuary of the LORD in the midst of it. 4
14 portion of the land, for it is holy to the LORD. 4
35 name of the city . . shall be, The LORD is there. 4
Dan 9: 2 according to the word of the LORD to Jeremiah 4
4 prayed to the LORD my God and made confession 4
10 not obeyed the voice of the LORD our God 4
13 have not entreated the favor of the LORD our God 4
14 Therefore the LORD has kept ready the calamity 4
14 for the LORD our God is righteous in all the works 4
19 O LORD, hear; O LORD, forgive; 4
19 O LORD, hear; O LORD, forgive; 4
19 O LORD, give heed and act 4
20 supplication before the LORD my God for the holy 4
Hos 1: 1 The word of the LORD that came to Hose'a 4
2 When the LORD first spoke through Hose'a 4
2 the LORD said to Hose'a, "Go, take to yourself a wife 4
2 commits great harlotry by forsaking the LORD. 4
4 And the LORD said to him, "Call his name Jezreel; 4
6 the LORD said to him, "Call her name Not pitied •
7 and I will deliver them by the LORD their God; 4
9 And the LORD said, "Call his name Not my people •
2:13 after her lovers, and forgot me, says the LORD. 4
16 says the LORD, you will call me, 'My husband,' 4
20 and you shall know the LORD. 4
21 that day, says the LORD, I will answer the heavens 4
3: 1 And the LORD said to me, "Go again, love a woman 4
1 even as the LORD loves the people of Israel 4
5 Israel shall return and seek the LORD their God 4
5 and they shall come in fear to the LORD 4
4: 1 Hear the word of the LORD, O people of Israel; 4
1 the LORD has a controversy with the inhabitants 4
10 they have forsaken the LORD to cherish harlotry. 4
15 and swear not, "As the LORD lives. 4
16 can the LORD now feed them like a lamb in a broad 4
5: 4 and they know not the LORD. 4
6 they shall go to seek the LORD 4
7 They have dealt faithlessly with the LORD; 4
6: 1 Come, let us return to the LORD; 4
3 Let us know, let us press on to know the LORD; 4
7:10 yet they do not return to the LORD their God 4
8: 1 for a vulture is over the house of the LORD 4
13 but the LORD has no delight in them. 4
9: 3 They shall not remain in the land of the LORD; 4
4 They shall not pour libations of wine to the LORD; 4
4 it shall not come to the house of the LORD. 4
5 and on the day of the feast of the LORD? 4
14 Give them, O LORD-what wilt thou give? 4
10: 2 The LORD will break down their altars •
3 We have no king, for we fear not the LORD 4
12 for it is the time to seek the LORD 4
11:10 They shall go after the LORD 4
11 I will return them to their homes, says the LORD. 4
12: 2 The LORD has an indictment against Judah 4
5 the LORD the God of hosts, the LORD is his name 4
5 the LORD the God of hosts, the LORD is his name 4
9 I am the LORD your God from the land of Egypt; 4
13 the LORD brought Israel up from Egypt 4
14 so his LORD will leave his bloodguilt upon him 1
13: 4 I am the LORD your God from the land of Egypt; 4
15 the east wind, the wind of the LORD, shall come 4
14: 1 Return, O Israel, to the LORD your God 4
2 Take with you words and return to the LORD; 4
9 for the ways of the LORD are right 4
Jol 1: 1 The word of the LORD that came to Joel 4
9 offering are cut off from the house of the LORD. 4
9 The priests mourn, the ministers of the LORD. 4
14 Gather . . to the house of the LORD your God; 4
14 and cry to the LORD. 4
15 Alas for the day! For the day of the LORD is near 4
19 Unto thee, O LORD, I cry. 4
2: 1 for the day of the LORD is coming, it is near 4
11 The LORD utters his voice before his army 4
11 For the day of the LORD is great and very terrible; 4
12 Yet even now," says the LORD, "return to me 4
13 Return to the LORD, your God, for he is gracious 4
14 and a drink offering for the LORD, your God? 4
17 let the priests, the ministers of the LORD, weep 4
17 weep and say, "Spare thy people, O LORD 4
18 Then the LORD became jealous for his land 4
19 The LORD answered and said to his people 4
21 rejoice, for the LORD has done great things! 4
23 Be glad, O sons of Zion, and rejoice in the LORD 4
26 and praise the name of the LORD your God 4
27 that I, the LORD, am your God and there is none else. 4
31 before the great and terrible day of the LORD 4
32 that all who call upon the name of the LORD 4
32 those who escape, as the LORD has said 4
32 the survivors shall be those whom the LORD calls. 4
3: 8 for the LORD has spoken. 4
11 Bring down thy warriors, O LORD. 4
14 day of the LORD is near in the valley of decision. 4
16 And the LORD roars from Zion 4
16 But the LORD is a refuge to his people 4
17 you shall know that I am the LORD your God 4
18 shall come forth from the house of the LORD 4
21 for the LORD dwells in Zion. 4
Ams 1: 2 And he said: "The LORD roars from Zion 4
3 Thus says the LORD: "For three transgressions 4
5 shall go into exile to Kir," says the LORD. 4
6 says the LORD: "For three transgressions of Gaza 4
9 says the LORD: "For three transgressions of Tyre 4
11 says the LORD: "For three transgressions of Edom 4
13 Thus says the LORD: "For three transgressions 4
15 exile, he and his princes together," says the LORD. 4
2: 1 says the LORD: "For three transgressions of Moab 4
3 will slay all its princes with him," says the LORD. 4
4 says the LORD: "For three transgressions of Judah 4
4 because they have rejected the law of the LORD 4
6 Thus says the LORD: "For three transgressions 4
11 it not indeed so, O people of Israel?" says the LORD. 4
16 shall flee naked in that day," says the LORD. 4
3: 1 this word that the LORD has spoken against you 4
6 Does evil befall a city, unless the LORD has done it? 4
10 They do not know how to do right," says the LORD 4
12 Thus says the LORD: "As the shepherd rescues 4
15 houses shall come to an end," says the LORD. 4
4: 3 be cast forth into Harmon," says the LORD. 4
6 yet you did not return to me," says the LORD. 4
8 yet you did not return to me," says the LORD. 4
9 yet you did not return to me," says the LORD. 4
10 yet you did not return to me," says the LORD. 4
11 yet you did not return to me," says the LORD. 4
13 of the earth- the LORD, the God of hosts, is his name! 4
5: 4 thus says the LORD to the house of Israel 4
6 Seek the LORD and live, lest he break out like fire 4
8 surface of the earth, the LORD is his name 4
14 the LORD, the God of hosts, will be with you 4
15 that the LORD, the God of hosts, will be gracious 4
16 thus says the LORD, the God of hosts, the Lord 4
17 will pass through the midst of you," says the LORD. 4
18 Woe to you who desire the day of the LORD! 4
18 Why would you have the day of the LORD? 4
20 Is not the day of the LORD darkness, and not light 4
27 you into exile beyond Damascus," says the LORD 4
6: 8 The Lord GOD has sworn by himself (says the LORD 4
10 "Hush! We must not mention the name of the LORD. 4
11 For behold, the LORD commands 4
14 O house of Israel," says the LORD, the God of hosts; 4
7: 3 The LORD repented concerning this; 4
3 concerning this; "It shall not be," said the LORD. 4
6 The LORD repented concerning this; 4
15 the LORD took me from following the flock 4
15 and the LORD said to me, 'Go, prophesy to my people 4
16 Now therefore hear the word of the LORD. 4
17 thus says the LORD: 'Your wife shall be a harlot 4
8: 2 LORD said to me, "The end has come upon my people 4
7 The LORD has sworn by the pride of Jacob 4
11 but of hearing the words of the LORD. 4
12 run to and fro, to seek the word of the LORD 4
9: 1 I saw the LORD standing beside the altar 2
6 who calls . . the LORD is his name. 4
7 O people of Israel?" says the LORD. 4
8 not . . destroy the house of Jacob," says the LORD. 4
12 called by my name," says the LORD who does this. 4
13 Behold, the days are coming," says the LORD 4
15 which I have given them," says the LORD your God. 4
Obd 1: 1 We have heard tidings from the LORD 4
4 thence I will bring you down, says the LORD. 4
8 Will I not on that day, says the LORD, destroy 4
15 the day of the LORD is near upon all the nations. 4
18 for the LORD has spoken. 4
21 and the kingdom shall be the LORD'S. 4
Jon 1: 1 Now the word of the LORD came to Jonah 4
3 flee to Tarshish from the presence of the LORD. 4
3 to Tarshish, away from the presence of the LORD. 4
4 the LORD hurled a great wind upon the sea 4
9 I fear the LORD, the God of heaven, 4
10 he was fleeing from the presence of the LORD 4
14 Therefore they cried to the LORD, "We beseech thee 4
14 O LORD, let us not perish for this man's life 4
14 for thou, O LORD, hast done as it pleased thee. 4
16 Then the men feared the LORD exceedingly 4
16 they offered a sacrifice to the LORD 4
17 LORD appointed a great fish to swallow up Jonah; 4
2: 1 Then Jonah prayed to the LORD his God 4
2 saying, "I called to the LORD, out of my distress 4
6 yet thou didst bring up my life from the Pit, O LORD 4
7 my soul fainted within me, I remembered the LORD; 4
9 Deliverance belongs to the LORD! 4
10 the LORD spoke to the fish, and it vomited out 4
3: 1 Then the word of the LORD came to Jonah 4
3 to Nin'eveh, according to the word of the LORD. 4
4: 2 he prayed to the LORD and said, "I pray thee, LORD 4
2 he prayed to the LORD and said, "I pray thee, LORD 4
3 Therefore now, O LORD, take my life from me 4
4 the LORD said, "Do you do well to be angry? 4
6 the LORD God appointed a plant, and made it come up 4
10 the LORD said, "You pity the plant 4
Mic 1: 1 The word of the LORD that came to Micah 4
3 behold, the LORD is coming forth out of his place 4
12 evil has come down from the LORD to the gate 4
2: 3 Therefore thus says the LORD 4
5 cast the line by lot in the assembly of the LORD. 4
7 Is the Spirit of the LORD impatient? 4
13 will pass on before them, the LORD at their head. 4
3: 4 they will cry to the LORD, but he will not answer 4
5 Thus says the LORD concerning the prophets 4
8 am filled with power, with the Spirit of the LORD 4
11 yet they lean upon the LORD and say 4
11 Is not the LORD in the midst of us? 4
4: 1 the mountain of the house of the LORD shall be 4
2 Come, let us go up to the mountain of the LORD 4
2 the law, and the word of the LORD from Jerusalem. 4
4 for the mouth of the LORD of hosts has spoken. 4
5 but we will walk in the name of the LORD our God 4
6 In that day, says the LORD, I will assemble the lame 4
7 the LORD will reign over them in Mount Zion 4
10 the LORD will redeem you from the hand 4
12 But they do not know the thoughts of the LORD 4
13 and shall devote their gain to the LORD 4
5: 4 and feed his flock in the strength of the LORD 4
4 in the majesty of the name of the LORD his God. 4
7 the midst of many peoples like dew from the LORD 4
10 And in that day, says the LORD 4
6: 1 Hear what the LORD says: Arise, plead your case 4
2 Hear, you mountains, the controversy of the LORD 4
2 for the LORD has a controversy with his people 4
5 that you may know the saving acts of the LORD. 4
6 With what shall I come before the LORD 4
7 Will the LORD be pleased with thousands of rams 4
8 does the LORD require of you but to do justice 4
9 The voice of the LORD cries to the city 4
7: 7 But as for me, I will look to the LORD 4
8 I sit in darkness, the LORD will be a light to me. 4
9 I will bear the indignation of the LORD 4
10 her who said to me, "Where is the LORD your God? 4
17 they shall turn in dread to the LORD our God 4
Nah 1: 2 The LORD is a jealous God and avenging 4
2 the LORD is avenging and wrathful; 4
2 the LORD takes vengeance on his adversaries 4
3 The LORD is slow to anger and of great might 4
3 and the LORD will by no means clear the guilty. 4
7 The LORD is good, a stronghold 4
9 What do you plot against the LORD? 4
11 one . . who plotted evil against the LORD 4
12 says the LORD, "Though they be strong and many 4
14 The LORD has given commandment about you 4
2: 2 For the LORD is restoring the majesty of Jacob 4
13 Behold, I am against you, says the LORD of hosts 4
3: 5 Behold, I am against you, says the LORD of hosts 4
Hab 1: 2 O LORD, how long shall I cry for help 4
12 Art thou not from everlasting, O LORD my God 4
12 O LORD, thou hast ordained them as a judgment; 4
2: 2 And the LORD answered me: "Write the vision; 4
13 from the LORD . . that peoples labor only for fire 4
14 with the knowledge of the glory of the LORD 4
16 The cup in the LORD'S right hand will come around 4
20 But the LORD is in his holy temple; 4
3: 2 O LORD, I have heard the report of thee, and thy work 4
2 the report of thee, and thy work, O LORD, do I fear. 4
8 Was thy wrath against the rivers, O LORD? 4
18 yet I will rejoice in the LORD 4
Zep 1: 1 The word of the LORD which came to Zephani'ah 4
2 sweep away everything . . says the LORD. 4
3 I will cut off mankind . . says the LORD. 4
5 those who bow down and swear to the LORD 4
6 who have turned back from following the LORD 4
6 who do not seek the LORD or inquire of him. 4
7 For the day of the LORD is at hand; 4
7 the LORD has prepared a sacrifice 4
8 And on the day of the LORD'S sacrifice- 4
10 On that day," says the LORD, "a cry will be heard 4
12 The LORD will not do good, nor will he do ill.' 4
14 The great day of the LORD is near 4
14 the sound of the day of the LORD is bitter 4
17 because they have sinned against the LORD; 4
18 deliver them on the day of the wrath of the LORD. 4
2: 2 there comes upon you the fierce anger of the LORD 4
2 comes upon you the day of the wrath of the LORD. 4
3 Seek the LORD, all you humble of the land 4
3 may be hidden on the day of the wrath of the LORD. 4
5 The word of the LORD is against you, O Canaan 4
7 For the LORD their God will be mindful of them 4
9 Therefore, as I live," says the LORD of hosts 4
10 boasted against the people of the LORD of hosts. 4
11 The LORD will be terrible against them; 4
3: 2 She does not trust in the LORD 4
5 The LORD within her is righteous, he does no wrong; 4
8 Therefore wait for me," says the LORD 4
9 that all of them may call on the name of the LORD 4
12 They shall seek refuge in the name of the LORD 4
15 LORD has taken away the judgments against you 4
15 The King of Israel, the LORD, is in your midst; 4

17 The LORD, your God, is in your midst, 4
20 when I restore your fortunes . . says the LORD. 4
Hag 1: 1 the word of the LORD came by Haggai the prophet 4
2 Thus says the LORD of hosts: This people say 4
2 has not yet come to rebuild the house of the LORD. 4
3 the word of the LORD came by Haggai the prophet 4
5 Now therefore thus says the LORD of hosts 4
7 Thus says the LORD of hosts: Consider how you have 4
8 that I may appear in my glory, says the LORD. 4
9 Why? says the LORD of hosts. Because of my house 4
12 the people, obeyed the voice of the LORD their God 4
12 the prophet, as the LORD their God had sent him; 4
12 the people feared before the LORD. 4
13 Then Haggai, the messenger of the LORD, spoke 4
13 spoke to the people with the LORD's message 4
13 the LORD's message, "I am with you, says the LORD. 4
14 the LORD stirred up the spirit of Zerub'babel 4
14 they came and worked on the house of the LORD 4
2: 1 the word of the LORD came by Haggai the prophet 4
4 Yet now take courage, O Zerub'babel, says the LORD; 4
4 courage, all you people of the land, says the LORD; 4
4 work, for I am with you, says the LORD of hosts 4
6 For thus says the LORD of hosts 4
7 will fill this house with splendor, says the LORD 4
8 the gold is mine, says the LORD of hosts. 4
9 greater than the former, says the LORD of hosts; 4
9 I will give prosperity, says the LORD of hosts.' 4
10 the word of the LORD came by Haggai the prophet 4
11 Thus says the LORD of hosts: Ask the priests 4
14 and with this nation before me, says the LORD; 4
15 was placed upon a stone in the temple of the LORD 4
17 yet you did not return to me, says the LORD. 4
18 that the foundation of the LORD'S temple was laid 4
20 The word of the LORD came a second time to Haggai 4
23 On that day, says the LORD of hosts, I will take you 4
23 says the LORD, and make you like a signet ring; 4
23 for I have chosen you, says the LORD of hosts. 4
Zec 1: 1 the word of the LORD came to Zechari'ah 4
2 The LORD was very angry with your fathers. 4
3 Therefore say to them, Thus says the LORD of hosts 4
3 Return to me, says the LORD of hosts 4
3 and I will return to you, says the LORD of hosts. 4
4 Thus says the LORD of hosts, Return from your evil 4
4 But they did not hear or heed me, says the LORD. 4
6 As the LORD of hosts purposed to deal with us 4
7 the word of the LORD came to Zechari'ah 4
10 These are they whom the LORD has sent to patrol 4
11 they answered the angel of the LORD 4
12 Then the angel of the LORD said, 'O LORD of hosts 4
12 O LORD of hosts, how long wilt thou have no mercy 4
13 the LORD answered gracious and comforting 4
14 Thus says the LORD of hosts: I am exceedingly 4
16 Therefore, thus says the LORD, I have returned 4
16 my house shall be built in it, says the LORD 4
17 Cry again, Thus says the LORD of hosts 4
17 the LORD will again comfort Zion 4
20 Then the LORD showed me four smiths. 4
2: 5 says the LORD, and I will be the glory within her. 4
6 ho! Flee from the land of the north, says the LORD; 4
6 as the four winds of the heavens, says the LORD. 4
8 thus said the LORD of hosts, after his glory sent 4
9 you will know that the LORD of hosts has sent me. 4
10 I will dwell in the midst of you, says the LORD. 4
11 many nations shall join themselves to the LORD 4
11 you shall know that the LORD of hosts has sent me 4
12 the LORD will inherit Judah as his portion 4
13 Be silent, all flesh, before the LORD; 4
3: 1 priest standing before the angel of the LORD 4
2 the LORD said to Satan, "The LORD rebuke you, 4
2 the LORD said to Satan, "The LORD rebuke you, 4
2 The LORD who has chosen Jerusalem rebuke you! 4
5 the angel of the LORD was standing by. 4
6 the angel of the LORD enjoined Joshua 4
7 Thus says the LORD of hosts: If you will walk 4
9 I will engrave its inscription, says the LORD 4
10 In that day, says the LORD of hosts 4
4: 6 This is the word of the LORD to Zerub'babel 4
6 by my Spirit, says the LORD of hosts. 4
8 Moreover the word of the LORD came to me, saying 4
9 you will know that the LORD of hosts has sent me 4
10 These seven are the eyes of the LORD 4
5: 4 I will send it forth, says the LORD of hosts 4
6: 5 before the LORD of all the earth. 1
9 the word of the LORD came to me 4
12 say to him, 'Thus says the LORD of hosts 4
12 he shall build the temple of the LORD. 4
13 It is he who shall build the temple of the LORD 4
14 the crown shall be in the temple of the LORD 4
15 come and help to build the temple of the LORD; 4
15 you shall know that the LORD of hosts has sent me 4
15 if you will diligently obey the voice of the LORD 4
7: 1 the word of the LORD came to Zechari'ah 4
2 their men, to entreat the favor of the LORD 4
3 the house of the LORD of hosts and the prophets 4
4 Then the word of the LORD of hosts came to me; 4
7 the LORD proclaimed by the former prophets? 4
8 the word of the LORD came to Zechari'ah, saying 4
9 says the LORD of hosts, Render true judgments 4
12 law and the words which the LORD of hosts had sent 4
12 great wrath came from the LORD of hosts. 4
13 I would not hear," says the LORD of hosts 4
8: 1 the word of the LORD of hosts came to me, saying 4
2 Thus says the LORD of hosts: I am jealous for Zion 4
3 Thus says the LORD: I will return to Zion 4
3 the mountain of the LORD of hosts, the holy 4
4 Thus says the LORD of hosts: Old men and old women 4
6 Thus says the LORD of hosts: If it is marvelous 4
6 marvelous in my sight, says the LORD of hosts? 4
7 Thus says the LORD of hosts: Behold, I will save 4
9 says the LORD of hosts: "Let your hands be strong 4
9 the foundation of the house of the LORD of hosts 4
11 as in the former days, says the LORD of hosts. 4
14 For thus says the LORD of hosts: "As I purposed to do 4
14 I did not relent, says the LORD of hosts 4
17 for all these things I hate, says the LORD. 4
18 the word of the LORD of hosts came to me, saying 4
19 Thus says the LORD of hosts: The fast of the fourth 4
20 says the LORD of hosts: Peoples shall yet come 4
21 Let us go at once to entreat the favor of the LORD 4
21 to seek the LORD of hosts; I am going. 4
22 nations shall come to seek the LORD of hosts 4
22 to entreat the favor of the LORD. 4
23 Thus says the LORD of hosts: In those days ten men 4
9: 1 word of the LORD is against the land of Hadrach 4
1 For to the LORD belong the cities of Aram 4
14 Then the LORD will appear over them 4
15 The LORD of hosts will protect them 4
16 On that day the LORD their God will save them 4
10: 1 Ask rain from the LORD in the season of the spring 4
1 from the LORD who makes the storm clouds 4
3 the LORD of hosts cares for his flock 4
5 they shall fight because the LORD is with them 4
6 for I am the LORD their God and I will answer them. 4
7 their hearts shall exult in the LORD. 4
12 I will make them strong in the LORD 4
12 they shall glory in his name," says the LORD. 4
11: 4 said the LORD my God: "Become shepherd of the flock 4
5 those who sell them say, 'Blessed be the LORD 4
6 on the inhabitants of this land, says the LORD. 4
11 watching me, knew that it was the word of the LORD. 4
13 Then the LORD said to me, "Cast it into the treasury 4
13 into the treasury in the house of the LORD. 4
15 Then the LORD said to me, "Take once more 4
12: 1 An Oracle The word of the LORD concerning Israel 4
1 Thus says the LORD, who stretched out the heavens 4
4 On that day, says the LORD, I will strike 4
5 strength through the LORD of hosts, their God. 4
7 the LORD will give victory to the tents of Judah 4
8 the LORD will put a shield about the inhabitants 4
8 like God, like the angel of the LORD, at their head. 4
13: 2 says the LORD of hosts, I will cut off the names 4
3 not live, for you speak lies in the name of the LORD 4
7 who stands next to me," says the LORD of hosts. 4
8 says the LORD, two thirds shall be cut off 4
9 they will say, 'The LORD is my God.' 4
14: 1 Behold, a day of the LORD is coming 4
3 Then the LORD will go forth and fight 4
5 Then the LORD your God will come 4
7 continuous day (it is known to the LORD) 4
9 the LORD will become king over all the earth; 4
9 on that day the LORD will be one and his name one. 4
12 the plague with which the LORD will smite 4
13 a great panic from the LORD shall fall on them 4
16 to worship the King, the LORD of hosts 4
17 Jerusalem to worship the King, the LORD of hosts 4
18 plague with which the LORD afflicts the nations 4
20 on the bells of the horses, "Holy to the LORD. 4
20 pots in the house of the LORD shall be as the bowls 4
21 and Judah shall be sacred to the LORD of hosts 4
21 in the house of the LORD of hosts on that day. 4
Mal 1: 1 the word of the LORD to Israel by Mal'achi. 4
2 I have loved you," says the LORD. 4
2 Is not Esau Jacob's brother?" says the LORD. 4
4 the LORD of hosts says, "They may build 4
4 the people with whom the LORD is angry for ever. 4
5 Great is the LORD, beyond the border of Israel! 4
6 if I am a master, where is my fear? says the LORD 4
7 By thinking that the LORD'S table may be despised. 4
8 or show you favor? says the LORD of hosts. 4
9 show favor to any of you? says the LORD of hosts. 4
10 I have no pleasure in you, says the LORD of hosts 4
11 my name is great among the nations, says the LORD 4
12 when you say that the LORD'S table is polluted 2
13 you say, and you sniff at me, says the LORD of hosts. 4
13 Shall I accept that from your hand? says the LORD. 4
14 and yet sacrifices to the LORD what is blemished; 4
14 I am a great King, says the LORD of hosts 4
2: 2 to give glory to my name, says the LORD of hosts 4
4 with Levi may hold, says the LORD of hosts. 4
7 for he is the messenger of the LORD of hosts. 4
8 the covenant of Levi, says the LORD of hosts 4
11 Judah has profaned the sanctuary of the LORD 4
12 May the LORD cut off from the tents of Jacob 4
12 or to bring an offering to the LORD of hosts! 4
13 You cover the LORD'S altar with tears 4
14 Because the LORD was witness to the covenant 4
16 For I hate divorce, says the LORD the God of Israel 4
16 garment with violence, says the LORD of hosts. 4
17 You have wearied the LORD with your words. 4
17 one who does evil is good in the sight of the LORD 4
3: 1 behold, he is coming, says the LORD of hosts. 4
3 till they present right offerings to the LORD. 4
4 Judah and Jerusalem will be pleasing to the LORD 4
5 and do not fear me, says the LORD of hosts. 4
6 For I the LORD do not change; 4
7 Return to me, and I will return to you, says the LORD 4
10 thereby put me to the test, says the LORD of hosts 4
11 shall not fail to bear, says the LORD of hosts. 4
12 a land of delight, says the LORD of hosts. 4
13 words have been stout against me, says the LORD. 4
14 walking as in mourning before the LORD of hosts? 4
16 those who feared the LORD spoke with one another; 4
16 the LORD heeded and heard them 4
16 who feared the LORD and thought on his name. 4
17 They shall be mine, says the LORD of hosts 4
4: 1 shall burn them up, says the LORD of hosts 4
3 on the day when I act, says the LORD of hosts. 4
5 before the great and terrible day of the LORD 4

Lord 1. אָדוֹן 2. אֲדֹנָי 3. יְהוָה 4. מָרֵא (A) 5. *δεσπόζω* 6. *δέσποτα,* 7. *δεσπότης* 8. *δυνάστης* 9. *θεός* 10. *κυριακός* 11. *κυριεύω* 12. Κύριος 13. *κύριος* 14. dominus

Gen 15: 2 Abram said, "O Lord GOD, what wilt thou give me 2
8 he said, "O Lord GOD, how am I to know 2
18:27 taken upon myself to speak to the Lord 2
30 let not the Lord be angry, and I will speak. 2
31 I have taken upon myself to speak to the Lord. 2
32 Then he said, "Oh let not the Lord be angry 2
20: 4 he said, "Lord, wilt thou slay an innocent people? 2
Exd 4:10 Moses said to the LORD, "Oh, my Lord, I am not 2
13 he said, "Oh, my Lord, send, I pray, some other person. 2
34: 9 favor in thy sight, O Lord, let the Lord, I pray thee 2
9 favor in thy sight, O Lord, let the Lord, I pray thee 2
Deu 3:24 'O Lord GOD, thou hast only begun to show 2
9:26 Lord GOD, destroy not thy people and thy heritage 2
10:17 LORD your God is God of gods and Lord of lords 1
Jos 3:11 ark of the covenant of the Lord of all the earth 1
13 bear the ark of the LORD, the Lord of all the earth 1
7: 7 And Joshua said, "Alas, O Lord GOD, why hast thou 2
8 O Lord, what can I say, when Israel has turned 2
Jdg 6:15 he said to him, "Pray, Lord, how can I deliver Israel? 2
22 said, "Alas, O Lord GOD! For now I have seen the angel 2
16:28 O Lord GOD, remember me, I pray thee, and strengthen 2
2Sm 7:18 Who am I, O Lord GOD . . that thou hast brought me 2
19 yet this was a small thing in thy eyes, O Lord GOD; 2
19 and . . shown me future generations, O Lord GOD! 2
20 For thou knowest thy servant, O Lord GOD! 2
28 now, O Lord GOD, thou art God, and thy words are true 2
29 for thou, O Lord GOD, hast spoken 2
1Kg 2:26 you bore the ark of the Lord GOD before David my 2
3:10 It pleased the Lord that Solomon had asked this. 3
8:53 bring our fathers out of Egypt, O Lord GOD. 2
22: 6 the Lord will give it into the hand of the king. 2
2Kg 7: 6 the Lord had made the army . . hear the sound 2
19:23 you have mocked the LORD, and you have said 2
2Ch 32:16 servants said still more against the Lord GOD 3
Neh 1:11 O Lord, let thy ear be attentive to the prayer 2
3: 5 did not put their necks to the work of their Lord. 1
4:14 Remember the Lord, who is great and terrible 2
8:10 for this day is holy to our Lord; 1
10:29 do all the commandments of the LORD our Lord 1
Job 28:28 Behold, the fear of the Lord, that is wisdom; 2
Ps 8: 1 O LORD, our Lord, how majestic is thy name 2
9 our Lord, how majestic is thy name in all the earth! 2
16: 2 I say to the LORD, "Thou art my Lord; 2
22:30 shall tell of the Lord to the coming generation 2
35:22 O LORD; be not silent! O Lord, be not far from me! 2
23 awake for my right, for my cause, my God and my Lord! 2
38: 9 Lord, all my longing is known to thee 2
22 Make haste to help me, O Lord, my salvation! 2
39: 7 now, Lord, for what do I wait? My hope is in thee. 2
40:17 poor and needy; but the Lord takes thought for me. 2
44:23 Rouse thyself! Why sleepest thou, O Lord? Awake! 2
51:15 O Lord, open thou my lips 2
54: 4 the Lord is the upholder of my life. 2
55: 9 Destroy their plans, O Lord 2
57: 9 I will give thanks to thee, O Lord 2
59:11 bring them down, O Lord, our shield! 2
62:12 that to thee, O Lord, belongs steadfast love. 2
66:18 the Lord would not have listened. 2
68:11 The Lord gives the command; 2
17 the Lord came from Sinai into the holy place. 2
19 Blessed be the Lord, who daily bears us up; 2
20 to God, the Lord, belongs escape from death. 2
22 The Lord said, "I will bring them back from Bashan 2
32 O kingdoms . . sing praises to the Lord, Selah 2
69: 6 be put to shame through me, O Lord GOD of hosts; 2
71: 5 For thou, O Lord, art my hope 2
16 With the mighty deeds of the Lord GOD I will come 2
73:28 I have made the Lord GOD my refuge 2
77: 2 In the day of my trouble I seek the Lord; 2
7 Will the Lord spurn for ever 2

78:65 Then the Lord awoke as from sleep 2
79:12 taunts with which they have taunted thee, O Lord 2
86: 3 be gracious to me, O Lord 2
4 for to thee, O Lord, do I lift up my soul. 2
5 For thou, O Lord, art good and forgiving 2
8 There is none like thee among the gods, O Lord 2
9 come and bow down before thee, O Lord 2
12 I give thanks to thee, O Lord my God 2
15 O Lord, art a God merciful and gracious 2
89:47 Remember, O Lord, what the measure of life is *
49 Lord, where is thy steadfast love of old 2
50 Remember, O Lord, how thy servant is scorned; 2
90: 1 Lord, thou hast been our dwelling place 2
17 Let the favor of the Lord our God be upon us 2
109:21 O GOD my Lord, deal on my behalf for thy name's sake; 2
110: 5 The Lord is at your right hand; 2
130: 2 Lord, hear my voice! Let thy ears be attentive 2
3 LORD, . . mark iniquities, Lord, who could stand? 2
135: 5 For I know . . that our Lord is above all gods. 1
136: 3 O give thanks to the Lord of lords 1
140: 7 O LORD, my Lord, my strong deliverer 2
Isa 1:24 Therefore the Lord says, the LORD of hosts 1
3: 1 behold, the Lord, the LORD of hosts, is taking away 1
15 What do you mean . . ?" says the Lord GOD of hosts. 2
17 the Lord will smite with a scab the heads 2
18 the Lord will take away the finery of the anklets 2
4: 4 when the Lord shall have washed away the filth 2
6: 1 I saw the Lord sitting upon a throne 2
8 the voice of the Lord saying, "Whom shall I send 2
11 How long, O Lord?" And he said: "Until cities lie waste 2
7: 7 thus says the Lord GOD: It shall not stand 2
14 Therefore the Lord himself will give you a sign. 2
20 the Lord will shave with a razor which is hired 2
8: 7 the Lord is bringing up against them the waters 2
9: 8 The Lord has sent a word against Jacob 2
17 the Lord does not rejoice over their young men 2
10:12 When the Lord has finished all his work 2
16 the Lord, the LORD of hosts, will send wasting 1
23 For the Lord, the LORD of hosts, will make a full end 2
24 Therefore thus says the Lord, the LORD of hosts 2
33 Behold, the Lord . . will lop the boughs 1
11:11 the Lord will extend his hand yet a second time 2
19: 4 rule over them, says the Lord, the LORD of hosts. 1
21: 6 For thus the Lord said to me: "Go, set a watchman 2
8 who saw cried: "Upon a watchtower I stand, O Lord 2
16 For thus the Lord said to me, "Within a year 2
22: 5 For the Lord GOD of hosts has a day of tumult 2
12 the Lord GOD of hosts called to weeping 2
14 till you die." says the Lord GOD of hosts. 2
15 Thus says the Lord GOD of hosts, "Come, go to this 2
25: 8 the Lord GOD will wipe away tears from all faces 2
28: 2 Behold, the Lord has one who is mighty and strong; 2
16 thus says the Lord GOD, "Behold, I am laying in Zion 2
22 destruction from the Lord GOD of hosts 2
29:13 the Lord said: "Because this people draw near 2
30:15 For thus said the Lord GOD, the Holy One of Israel 2
20 though the Lord give you the bread of adversity 2
37:24 By your servants you have mocked the Lord 2
38:14 O Lord, I am oppressed; be thou my security! 2
16 O Lord, by these things men live 2
40:10 Behold, the Lord GOD comes with might 2
48:16 And now the Lord GOD has sent me and his Spirit. 2
49:14 But Zion said, " . . my Lord has forgotten me. 2
22 says the Lord GOD: "Behold, I will lift up my hand 2
50: 4 The Lord GOD has given me the tongue 2
5 The Lord GOD has opened my ear 2
7 For the Lord GOD helps me; 2
9 Behold, the Lord GOD helps me; 2
51:22 thus says your Lord, the LORD, your God 2
52: 4 For thus says the Lord GOD: My people went down 2
56: 8 the Lord GOD, who gathers the outcasts of Israel 2
61: 1 The Spirit of the Lord GOD is upon me 2
11 the Lord GOD will cause righteousness 2
65:13 says the Lord GOD: "Behold, my servants shall eat 2
15 for a curse, and the Lord GOD will slay you; 2
Jer 1: 6 I said, "Ah, Lord GOD! Behold, I do not know how 2
2:19 says the Lord GOD of hosts. 2
22 guilt is still before me, says the Lord GOD. 2
4:10 Then I said, "Ah, Lord GOD 2
7:20 Therefore thus says the Lord GOD: Behold, my anger 2
14:13 I said: "Ah, Lord GOD, behold, the prophets say to them 2
25:17 all the nations to whom the Lord sent me 3
32:17 'Ah Lord GOD! It is thou who hast made the heavens 2
25 Yet thou, O Lord GOD, hast said to me, "Buy the field 2
44:26 saying, 'As the Lord GOD lives.' 2
46:10 That day is the day of the Lord GOD of hosts 2
10 Lord GOD of hosts holds a sacrifice in the north 2
49: 5 bring terror upon you, says the Lord GOD of hosts 2
50:25 for the Lord GOD of hosts has a work to do 2
31 "Behold, I am against you, O proud one, says the Lord 2
Lam 1:14 the Lord gave me into the hands of those whom I 2
15 The Lord flouted all my mighty men in the midst 2
15 the Lord has trodden as in a wine press the virgin 2
2: 1 How the Lord in his anger has set..Zion under 2
2 The Lord has destroyed..all the habitations 2
5 The Lord has become like an enemy 2
7 The Lord has scorned his altar, ..his sanctuary; 2
18 Cry aloud to the Lord! O daughter of Zion! 2
19 Pour out..before the presence of the Lord! 2
20 priest . . be slain in the sanctuary of the Lord? 2
3:31 For the Lord will not cast off for ever 2
36 to subvert a man.., the Lord does not approve. 2
37 Who has.., unless the Lord has ordained it? 2
58 Thou hast taken up my cause, O Lord 2
Ezk 2: 4 you shall say to them, 'Thus says the Lord GOD.' 2
3:11 say to them, 'Thus says the Lord GOD' 2
27 and you shall say to them, 'Thus says the Lord GOD' 2
4:14 Then I said, "Ah Lord GOD! 2
5: 5 Thus says the Lord GOD: This is Jerusalem; 2
7 Therefore thus says the Lord GOD 2
8 therefore thus says the Lord GOD: Behold, I, even I 2
11 Wherefore, as I live, says the Lord GOD 2
6: 3 mountains of Israel, hear the word of the Lord GOD! 2
3 Thus says the Lord GOD to the mountains 2
11 Thus says the Lord GOD: "Clap your hands 2
7: 2 thus says the Lord GOD to the land of Israel: An end! 2
5 "Thus says the Lord GOD: Disaster after disaster! 2
8: 1 the hand of the Lord GOD fell there upon me. 2
9: 8 I fell upon my face, and cried, "Ah Lord GOD! 2
11: 7 Therefore thus says the Lord GOD 2
8 I will bring the sword upon you, says the Lord GOD. 2
13 and said, "Ah Lord GOD! wilt thou make a full end 2
16 Therefore say, 'Thus says the Lord GOD 2
17 Therefore say, 'Thus says the Lord GOD 2
21 upon their own heads, says the Lord GOD. 2
12:10 Say to them, 'Thus says the Lord GOD: This oracle 2
19 says the Lord GOD concerning the inhabitants 2
23 Tell them therefore, 'Thus says the Lord GOD 2
25 speak the word and perform it, says the Lord GOD. 2
28 Therefore say to them, Thus says the Lord GOD 2
28 will be performed, says the Lord GOD. 2
13: 3 Thus says the Lord GOD, Woe to the foolish 2
8 Therefore thus says the Lord God 2
8 behold, I am against you, says the Lord GOD. 2
9 you shall know that I am the Lord GOD. 2
13 Therefore thus says the Lord GOD 2
16 when there was no peace, says the Lord GOD. 2
18 and say, Thus says the Lord GOD 2
20 "Wherefore thus says the Lord GOD 2
14: 4 and say to them, Thus says the Lord GOD 2
6 Thus says the Lord GOD: Repent and turn away 2
11 and I may be their God, says the Lord GOD. 2
14 by their righteousness, says the Lord GOD. 2
16 as I live, says the Lord GOD, they would deliver 2
18 as I live, says the Lord GOD, they would deliver 2
20 as I live, says the Lord GOD, they would deliver 2
21 For thus says the Lord GOD 2
23 all that I have done in it, says the Lord GOD. 2
15: 6 Therefore thus says the Lord GOD 2
8 they have acted faithlessly, says the Lord GOD. 2
16: 3 and say, Thus says the Lord GOD to Jerusalem 2
8 into a covenant with you, says the Lord GOD 2
14 which I had bestowed upon you, says the Lord GOD. 2
19 for a pleasing odor, says the Lord GOD. 2
23 woe, woe to you! says the Lord GOD 2
30 "How lovesick is your heart, says the Lord GOD 2
36 Thus says the Lord GOD, Because your shame was 2
43 your deeds upon your head, says the Lord GOD. 2
48 As I live, says the Lord GOD 2
59 "Yea, thus says the Lord GOD: I will deal with you 2
63 all that you have done, says the Lord GOD. 2
17: 3 say, Thus says the Lord GOD 2
9 Say, Thus says the Lord GOD: Will it thrive? 2
16 As I live, says the Lord GOD 2
19 Therefore thus says the Lord GOD: As I live, surely 2
22 Thus says the Lord GOD: "I myself will take a sprig 2
18: 3 As I live, says the Lord GOD 2
9 he shall surely live, says the Lord GOD. 2
23 in the death of the wicked, says the Lord GOD 2
25 "Yet you say, 'The way of the Lord is not just.' 2
29 Israel says, 'The way of the Lord is not just. 2
30 every one according to his ways, says the Lord 2
32 says the Lord GOD; so turn, and live. 2
20: 3 and say to them, Thus says the Lord GOD 2
3 As I live, says the Lord GOD 2
5 and say to them, Thus says the Lord GOD 2
27 and say to them, Thus says the Lord GOD 2
30 Thus says the Lord GOD: Will you defile 2
31 As I live, says the Lord GOD 2
33 As I live, says the Lord GOD 2
36 enter into judgment with you, says the Lord GOD. 2
39 As for you, O house of Israel, thus says the Lord GOD 2
40 mountain height of Israel, says the Lord GOD 2
44 O house of Israel, says the Lord GOD. 2
47 Hear the word of the LORD: Thus says the Lord GOD 2
49 Then I said, "Ah Lord GOD! 2
21: 7 it will be fulfilled,'" says the Lord GOD. 2
9 "Son of man, prophesy and say, Thus says the Lord, Say 2
13 if you despise the rod?" says the Lord GOD. 2
24 "Therefore thus says the Lord GOD 2
26 thus says the Lord GOD: Remove the turban 2
28 son of man, prophesy, and say, Thus says the Lord GOD 2
22: 3 You shall say, Thus says the Lord GOD 2
12 you have forgotten me, says the Lord GOD. 2
19 Therefore thus says the Lord GOD 2
28 divining lies for them, saying, 'Thus says the Lord 2
31 requited upon their heads, says the Lord GOD. 2
23:22 Therefore, O Ohol'ibah, thus says the Lord GOD 2
28 For thus says the Lord GOD: Behold, I will deliver 2
32 Thus says the Lord GOD: "You shall drink 2
34 for I have spoken, says the Lord GOD. 2
35 Therefore thus says the Lord GOD 2
46 thus says the Lord GOD: "Bring up a host 2
49 you shall know that I am the Lord GOD. 2
24: 3 say to them, Thus says the Lord GOD: Set on the pot 2
6 "Therefore thus says the Lord GOD 2
9 Therefore thus says the Lord GOD 2
14 I will judge you, says the Lord GOD. 2
21 Say to the house of Israel, Thus says the Lord GOD 2
24 then you will know that I am the Lord GOD. 2
25: 3 Say to the Ammonites, Hear the word of the Lord GOD 2
3 Thus says the Lord GOD, Because you said, 'Aha!' 2
6 For thus says the Lord GOD 2
8 "Thus says the Lord GOD: Because Moab said, Behold 2
12 "Thus says the Lord GOD: Because Edom acted 2
13 therefore thus says the Lord GOD 2
14 they shall know my vengeance, says the Lord GOD. 2
15 Thus says the Lord GOD: Because the Philistines 2
16 therefore thus says the Lord GOD, Behold 2
26: 3 therefore thus says the Lord GOD 2
5 for I have spoken, says the Lord GOD; 2
7 For thus says the Lord GOD: Behold, I will bring 2
14 for I the LORD have spoken, says the Lord GOD. 2
15 "Thus says the Lord GOD to Tyre 2
19 For thus says the Lord GOD: When I make you a city 2
21 you will never be found again, says the Lord GOD. 2
27: 3 thus says the Lord GOD: "O Tyre, you have said 2
28: 2 to the prince of Tyre, Thus says the Lord GOD 2
6 therefore thus says the Lord GOD 2
10 for I have spoken, says the Lord GOD. 2
12 king of Tyre, and say to him, Thus says the Lord GOD 2
22 say, Thus says the Lord GOD: "Behold, I am against you 2
24 Then they will know that I am the Lord GOD. 2
25 "Thus says the Lord GOD 2
29: 3 Thus says the Lord GOD: "Behold, I am against you 2
8 thus says the Lord GOD: Behold, I will bring a sword 2
13 thus says the Lord GOD: At the end of 40 years 2
16 Then they will know that I am the Lord GOD. 2
19 thus says the Lord GOD: Behold, I will give the land 2
20 because they worked for me, says the Lord GOD. 2
30: 2 prophesy, and say, Thus says the Lord GOD 2
6 fall within her by the sword, says the Lord GOD. 2
10 says the Lord GOD: I will put an end to the wealth 2
13 "Thus says the Lord GOD: I will destroy the idols 2
22 Therefore thus says the Lord GOD: Behold, I am 2
31:10 "Therefore thus says the Lord GOD 2
15 "Thus says the Lord GOD: When it goes down to Sheol 2
18 Pharaoh and all his multitude, says the Lord GOD. 2
32: 3 Thus says the Lord GOD: I will throw my net over you 2
8 put darkness upon your land, says the Lord GOD. 2
11 For thus says the Lord GOD: The sword of the king 2
14 their rivers to run like oil, says the Lord GOD. 2
16 shall they chant it, says the Lord GOD. 2
31 all his army, slain by the sword, says the Lord GOD. 2
32 Pharaoh and all his multitude, says the Lord GOD. 2
33:11 Say to them, As I live, says the Lord GOD 2
17 Yet your people say, 'The way of the Lord is not just 2
20 Yet you say, 'The way of the Lord is not just.' 2
25 Therefore say to them, Thus says the Lord GOD 2
27 Say this to them, Thus says the Lord GOD: As I live 2
34: 2 Thus says the Lord GOD: Ho, shepherds of Israel 2
8 As I live, says the Lord GOD 2
10 Thus says the Lord GOD, Behold 2
11 For thus says the Lord GOD: Behold 2
15 I will make them lie down, says the Lord GOD. 2
17 As for you, my flock, thus says the Lord GOD: Behold 2
20 "Therefore, thus says the Lord GOD to them: Behold 2
30 house of Israel, are my people, says the Lord GOD. 2
31 and I am your God, says the Lord GOD. 2
35: 3 and say to it, Thus says the Lord GOD: Behold 2
6 therefore, as I live, says the Lord GOD 2
11 as I live, says the Lord GOD, I will deal with you 2
14 says the Lord GOD: For the rejoicing of the whole 2
36: 2 Thus says the Lord GOD: Because the enemy said 2
3 therefore prophesy, and say, Thus says the Lord 2
4 O mountains of Israel, hear the word of the Lord 2
4 Thus says the Lord GOD to the mountains 2
5 thus says the Lord GOD: I speak in my hot jealousy 2
6 Thus says the Lord GOD: Behold, I speak 2
7 thus says the Lord GOD: I swear that the nations 2
13 Thus says the Lord GOD: Because men say to you 2
14 bereave your nation of children, says the Lord 2
15 cause your nation to stumble, says the Lord GOD. 2
22 Thus says the Lord GOD: It is not for your sake 2
23 nations will know that I am the LORD, says the Lord 2
32 not for your sake that I will act, says the Lord GOD; 2
33 "Thus says the Lord GOD: On the day that I cleanse 2
37 "Thus says the Lord GOD: This also I will let 2
37: 3 And I answered, "O Lord GOD, thou knowest. 2
5 Thus says the Lord GOD to these bones 2
9 and say to the breath, Thus says the Lord GOD 2
12 prophesy, and say to them, Thus says the Lord GOD 2
19 say to them, Thus says the Lord GOD 2
21 then say to them, Thus says the Lord GOD 2

38: 3 say, Thus says the Lord GOD: Behold, I am against you 2
10 says the Lord GOD: On that day thoughts will come 2
14 Thus says the Lord GOD: On that day when my people 2
17 "Thus says the Lord GOD: Are you he of whom I spoke 2
18 says the Lord GOD, my wrath will be roused. 2
21 kind of terror against Gog, says the Lord GOD; 2
39: 1 says the Lord GOD: Behold, I am against you, O Gog 2
5 for I have spoken, says the Lord GOD. 2
8 and it will be brought about, says the Lord GOD. 2
10 those who plundered them, says the Lord GOD. 2
13 on the day that I show my glory, says the Lord GOD. 2
17 As for you, son of man, thus says the Lord GOD 2
20 men and all kinds of warriors,' says the Lord GOD. 2
25 "Therefore thus says the Lord GOD 2
29 upon the house of Israel, says the Lord GOD. 2
43:18 he said to me, "Son of man, thus says the Lord GOD 2
19 says the Lord GOD, a bull for a sin offering. 2
27 I will accept you, says the Lord GOD. 2
44: 6 Thus says the Lord GOD: O house of Israel 2
9 "Therefore thus says the Lord GOD: No foreigner 2
12 I have sworn concerning them, says the Lord GOD 2
15 to offer me the fat and the blood, says the Lord GOD; 2
27 he shall offer his sin offering, says the Lord GOD 2
45: 9 "Thus says the Lord GOD: Enough, O princes of Israel! 2
9 your evictions of my people, says the Lord GOD. 2
15 to make atonement for them, says the Lord GOD. 2
18 "Thus says the Lord GOD: In the first month 2
46: 1 "Thus says the Lord GOD: The gate of the inner court 2
16 "Thus says the Lord GOD: If the prince makes a gift 2
47:13 Thus says the Lord GOD: "These are the boundaries 2
23 assign him his inheritance, says the Lord GOD. 2
48:29 are their several portions, says the Lord GOD. 2
Dan 2:47 "Truly, your God is God of gods and Lord of kings 4
5:23 lifted up yourself against the Lord of heaven; 4
9: 3 Then I turned my face to the Lord God, seeking him 2
4 "O Lord, the great and terrible God 2
7 To thee, O Lord, belongs righteousness, but to us 2
8 To us, O Lord, belongs confusion of face 3
9 To the Lord our God belong mercy and forgiveness; 2
15 now, O Lord our God, who didst bring thy people out 2
16 O Lord, according to all thy righteous acts 2
17 for thy own sake, O Lord, cause thy face to shine 2
0: 1 Lord gave Jehoi'akim king of Judah into his hand 2
Ams 1: 8 the Philistines shall perish," says the Lord GOD 2
3: 7 the Lord GOD does nothing, without revealing his 2
8 The Lord GOD has spoken; who can but prophesy? 2
11 thus says the Lord GOD: "An adversary shall 2
13 against the house of Jacob," says the Lord GOD 2
4: 2 The Lord GOD has sworn by his holiness 2
5 O people of Israel!" says the Lord GOD. 2
5: 3 For thus says the Lord GOD: "The city that went 2
16 LORD, the God of hosts, the Lord: "In all the squares 2
6: 8 The Lord GOD has sworn by himself (says the LORD 2
7: 1 Thus the Lord GOD showed me 2
2 I said, "O Lord GOD, forgive, I beseech thee! 2
4 Thus the Lord GOD showed me 2
4 the Lord GOD was calling for a judgment by fire 2
5 Then I said, "O Lord GOD, cease, I beseech thee! 2
6 This also shall not be," said the Lord GOD. 2
7 behold, the Lord was standing beside a wall 2
8 the Lord said, "Behold, I am setting a plumb line 2
8: 1 Thus the Lord GOD showed me 2
3 become wailings in that day," says the Lord GOD; 2
9 And on that day," says the Lord GOD 2
11 "Behold, the days are coming," says the Lord GOD 2
9: 5 The Lord, GOD of hosts, he who touches the earth 2
8 eyes of the Lord GOD are upon the sinful kingdom 2
Obd 1: 1 Thus says the Lord GOD concerning Edom 2
Mic 1: 2 and let the Lord GOD be a witness against you 2
2 against you, the Lord from his holy temple. 2
4:13 their wealth to the Lord of the whole earth. 1
Hab 3:19 GOD, the Lord, is my strength; 2
Zep 1: 7 Be silent before the Lord GOD! 2
Zec 4:14 who stand by the Lord of the whole earth. 1
9: 4 But lo, the Lord will strip her of her possessions 2
14 the Lord GOD will sound the trumpet, and march 2
Mal 3: 1 the Lord whom you seek will suddenly come 1
Mat 1:20 an angel of the Lord appeared to him in a dream 13
22 to fulfil what the Lord had spoken by the prophet 13
24 he did as the angel of the Lord commanded him; he 13
2:13 an angel of the Lord appeared to Joseph in a dream 13
15 to fulfil what the Lord had spoken by the prophet 13
19 an angel of the Lord appeared in a dream to Joseph 13
3: 3 Prepare the way of the Lord, make his paths 13
4: 7 written, 'You shall not tempt the Lord your God.' 13
10 You shall worship the Lord your God and him only 13
5:33 shall perform to the Lord what you have sworn.' 13
7:21 Not every one who says to me, 'Lord, Lord,' shall enter 13
21 Not every one who says to me, 'Lord, Lord,' shall enter 13
22 On that day many will say to me, 'Lord, Lord 13
22 On that day many will say to me, 'Lord, Lord 13
8: 2 saying, "Lord, if you will, you can make me clean. 13
6 saying, "Lord, my servant is lying paralyzed 13
8 the centurion answered him, "Lord, I am not worthy 13
21 "Lord, let me first go and bury my father. 13
25 they went and woke him, saying, "Save, Lord 13
9:28 They said to him, "Yes, Lord. 13
38 pray therefore the Lord of the harvest 13
11:25 I thank thee, Father, Lord of heaven and earth 13
14:28 "Lord, if it is you, bid me come to you on the water. 13
30 beginning to sink he cried out, "Lord, save me. 13
15:22 "Have mercy on me, O Lord, Son of David 13
25 "Lord, help me. 13
27 She said, "Yes, Lord, yet even the dogs eat the crumbs 13
16:22 rebuke him, saying, "God forbid, Lord! 13
17: 4 "Lord, it is well that we are here 13
15 "Lord, have mercy on my son, for he is an epileptic 13
18:21 "Lord, how often shall my brother sin against me 13
26 'Lord, have patience with me, and I will pay you •
20:31 "Lord, have mercy on us, Son of David! 13
33 They said to him, "Lord, let our eyes be opened. 13
21: 3 'The Lord has need of them,' 13
9 Blessed is he who comes in the name of the Lord! 13
42 this was the Lord's doing 13
22:37 love the Lord your God with all your heart 13
43 inspired by the Spirit, calls him Lord, saying 13
44 'The Lord said to my Lord, Sit at my right hand 13
44 'The Lord said to my Lord, Sit at my right hand 13
45 If David thus calls him Lord, how is he his son? 13
23:39 'Blessed is he who comes in the name of the Lord.' 13
24:42 you do not know on what day your Lord is coming. 13
25:11 'Lord, lord, open to us.' 13
37 Lord, when did we see thee hungry and feed thee 13
44 Lord, when did we see thee hungry or thirsty 13
26:22 "Is it I, Lord? 13
27:10 as the Lord directed me. 13
28: 2 an angel of the Lord descended from heaven 13
Mrk 1: 3 Prepare the way of the Lord 13
5:19 tell them how much the Lord has done for you 13
7:28 Yes, Lord; yet even the dogs under the table eat 13
11: 3 say, 'The Lord has need of it 13
9 Blessed is he who comes in the name of the Lord! 13
12:11 this was the Lord's doing 13
29 The Lord our God, the Lord is one; 13
29 The Lord our God, the Lord is one; 13
30 shall love the Lord your God with all your heart 13
36 The Lord said to my Lord, Sit at my right hand 13
36 The Lord said to my Lord, Sit at my right hand 13
37 David himself calls him Lord; so how is he his son? 13
13:20 if the Lord had not shortened the days 13
16:19 So then the Lord Jesus, after he had spoken to them 13
20 while the Lord worked with them 13
Lke 1: 6 commandments and ordinances of the Lord 13
9 to enter the temple of the Lord and burn incense. 13
11 there appeared to him an angel of the Lord 13
15 for he will be great before the Lord 13
16 he will turn many of the sons of Israel to the Lord 13
17 to make ready for the Lord a people prepared. 13
25 Thus the Lord has done to me 13
28 "Hail, O favored one, the Lord is with you! 13
32 the Lord God will give to him the throne 13
38 Mary said, "Behold, I am the handmaid of the Lord 13
43 that the mother of my Lord should come to me? 13
45 what was spoken to her from the Lord 13
46 Mary said, "My soul magnifies the Lord 13
58 the Lord had shown great mercy to her 13
66 the hand of the Lord was with him. 13
68 "Blessed be the Lord God of Israel 13
76 you will go before the Lord to prepare his ways 13
2: 9 an angel of the Lord appeared to them 13
9 the glory of the Lord shone around them 13
11 a Savior, who is Christ the Lord. 13
15 this thing . . which the Lord has made known to us. 13
22 to present him to the Lord. 13
23 as it is written in the law of the Lord 13
23 shall be called holy to the Lord") 13
24 according to what is said in the law of the Lord 13
26 before he had seen the Lord's Christ. 13
29 "Lord, now lettest thou thy servant depart 7
39 according to the law of the Lord 13
3: 4 Prepare the way of the Lord 13
4: 8 It is written, 'You shall worship the Lord your God 13
12 'You shall not tempt the Lord your God.' 13
18 The Spirit of the Lord is upon me 13
19 to proclaim the acceptable year of the Lord. 13
5: 8 Depart from me, for I am a sinful man, O Lord. 13
12 "Lord, if you will, you can make me clean. 13
17 the power of the Lord was with him to heal. 13
6:46 "Why do you call me 'Lord, Lord,' and not do what I tell 13
46 "Why do you call me 'Lord, Lord,' and not do what I tell 13
7: 6 Lord, do not trouble yourself, for I am not worthy 13
13 when the Lord saw her 13
19 sent them to the Lord, saying, "Are you he 13
9:54 they said, "Lord, do you want us to bid fire come down 13
59 he said, "Lord, let me first go and bury my father. 13
61 Another said, "I will follow you, Lord 13
10: 1 After this the Lord appointed 70 others 13
2 pray therefore the Lord of the harvest 13
17 The 70 returned with joy, saying, "Lord 13
21 I thank thee, Father, Lord of heaven and earth 13
27 shall love the Lord your God with all your heart 13
39 a sister called Mary, who sat at the Lord's feet 13
40 she went to him and said, "Lord, do you not care 13
41 the Lord answered her, "Martha, Martha 13
11: 1 Lord teach us to pray 13
39 the Lord said to him, "Now you Pharisees cleanse 13
12:41 Peter said, "Lord, are you telling this parable 13
42 the Lord said, "Who then is the faithful and wise 13
13:15 Then the Lord answered him, "You hypocrites! 13
23 some one said to him, "Lord 13
25 to knock at the door, saying, 'Lord, open to us.' 13
35 'Blessed is he who comes in the name of the Lord!' 13
17: 5 The apostles said to the Lord, "Increase our faith! 13
6 the Lord said, "If you had faith 13
37 they said to him, "Where, Lord? 13
18: 6 the Lord said, "Hear 13
41 He said, "Lord, let me receive my sight. 13
19: 8 Zacchae'us stood and said to the Lord, "Behold 13
8 Zacchae'us stood and said to the Lord, "Behold 13
16 The first came before him, saying, 'Lord 13
18 the second came, saying, 'Lord 13
20 'Lord, here is your pound 13
25 they said to him, 'Lord, he has ten pounds!') 13
31 you shall say this, 'The Lord has need of it.' 13
34 they said, "The Lord has need of it. 13
38 the King who comes in the name of the Lord 13
20:37 where he calls the Lord the God of Abraham 13
42 The Lord said to my Lord, Sit at my right hand 13
42 The Lord said to my Lord, Sit at my right hand 13
44 David thus calls him Lord; so how is he his son? 13
22:33 he said to him, "Lord, I am ready to go with you 13
38 they said, "Look, Lord, here are two swords. 13
49 Lord, shall we strike with the sword? 13
61 the Lord turned and looked at Peter 13
61 Peter remembered the word of the Lord 13
24:34 who said, "The Lord has risen indeed 13
Joh 1:23 'Make straight the way of the Lord,' 13
4: 1 when the Lord knew that the Pharisees had heard 12
6:23 after the Lord had given thanks. 13
34 They said to him, "Lord, give us this bread always. 13
68 Peter answered him, "Lord, to whom shall we go? 13
8:11 She said, "No one, Lord. 13
9:38 He said, "Lord, I believe"; and he worshiped him. 13
11: 2 It was Mary who anointed the Lord with ointment 13
3 "Lord, he whom you love is ill. 13
12 The disciples said to him, "Lord 13
21 Martha said to Jesus, "Lord if you had been here 13
27 She said to him, "Yes, Lord; I believe 13
32 Mary . . fell at his feet, saying to him, "Lord 13
34 They said to him, "Lord, come and see. 13
39 Martha, the sister of the dead man, said to him, "Lord 13
12:13 Blessed is he who comes in the name of the Lord 13
38 Lord, who has believed our report 13
38 to whom has the arm of the Lord been revealed? 13
13: 6 Peter said to him, "Lord, do you wash my feet? 13
9 Simon Peter said to him, "Lord, not my feet only 13
13 You call me Teacher and Lord; and you are right 13
14 If I then, your Lord and Teacher, have washed 13
25 he said to him, "Lord, who is it? 13
36 Simon Peter said to him, "Lord, where are you going? 13
37 Peter said to him, "Lord, why cannot I follow you now? 13
14: 5 Thomas said to him, "Lord, we do not know 13
8 Philip said to him, "Lord, show us the Father 13
22 Judas (not Iscariot) said to him, "Lord, how is it 13
20: 2 They have taken the Lord out of the tomb 13
13 Because they have taken away my Lord 13
18 "I have seen the Lord 13
20 the disciples were glad when they saw the Lord. 13
25 "We have seen the Lord. 13
28 Thomas answered him, "My Lord and my God! 13
21: 7 "It is the Lord! 13
7 When Simon Peter heard that it was the Lord 13
12 They knew it was the Lord. 13
15 He said to him, "Yes, Lord; you know that I love you. 13
16 He said to him, "Yes, Lord; you know that I love you. 13
17 he said to him, "Lord, you know everything 13
20 "Lord, who is it that is going to betray you? 13
21 he said to Jesus, "Lord, what about this man? 13
Act 1: 6 Lord, will you at this time restore the kingdom 13
21 the Lord Jesus went in and out among us 13
24 Lord, who knowest the hearts of all men 13
2:20 before the day of the Lord comes 13
21 whoever calls on the name of the Lord 13
25 I saw the Lord always before me 13
34 The Lord said to my Lord, Sit at my right hand 13
34 The Lord said to my Lord, Sit at my right hand 13
36 God has made him both Lord and Christ 13
39 every one whom the Lord our God calls to him. 13
47 the Lord added to their number day by day 13
3:19 may come from the presence of the Lord 13
22 The Lord God will raise up for you a prophet 13
4:26 against the Lord and against his Anointed'- 13
29 now, Lord, look upon their threats 13
33 testimony to the resurrection of the Lord Jesus 13
5: 9 agreed together to tempt the Spirit of the Lord? 13
14 more than ever believers were added to the Lord 13
19 an angel of the Lord opened the prison doors 13
7:31 as he drew near to look, the voice of the Lord came 13
33 the Lord said to him, 'Take off the shoes 13
49 What house will you build for me, says the Lord 13
59 "Lord Jesus, receive my spirit. 13
60 "Lord, do not hold this sin against them. 13
8:16 baptized in the name of the Lord Jesus. 13
22 pray to the Lord 13

24 Simon answered, "Pray for me to the Lord 13
25 had testified and spoken the word of the Lord 13
26 an angel of the Lord said to Philip, "Rise and go 13
39 the Spirit of the Lord caught up Philip 13
9: 1 against the disciples of the Lord 13
5 he said, "Who are you, Lord? 13
10 The Lord said to him in a vision, "Anani'as. 13
10 he said, "Here I am, Lord. 13
11 the Lord said to him, "Rise and go 13
13 Anani'as answered, "Lord 13
15 the Lord said to him, "Go 13
17 the Lord Jesus who appeared to you on the road 13
27 on the road he had seen the Lord, who spoke to him 13
29 preaching boldly in the name of the Lord. 13
31 walking in the fear of the Lord 13
35 they turned to the Lord. 13
42 many believed in the Lord. 13
10: 4 stared at him in terror, and said, "What is it, Lord? 13
14 Peter said, "No, Lord 13
33 hear all that you have been commanded by the Lord 13
36 peace by Jesus Christ (he is Lord of all) 13
11: 8 I said, 'No, Lord 13
16 I remembered the word of the Lord, how he said 13
17 when we believed in the Lord Jesus Christ 13
20 preaching the Lord Jesus. 13
21 the hand of the Lord was with them 13
21 a great number that believed turned to the Lord. 13
23 he exhorted them all to remain faithful to the Lord 13
24 a large company was added to the Lord. 13
12: 7 behold, an angel of the Lord appeared 13
11 Now I am sure that the Lord has sent his angel 13
17 how the Lord had brought him out of the prison 13
23 Immediately an angel of the Lord smote him 13
13: 2 While they were worshiping the Lord and fasting 13
10 now, behold, the hand of the Lord is upon you 13
11 now, behold, the hand of the Lord is upon you 13
12 he was astonished at the teaching of the Lord. 13
47 so the Lord has commanded us, saying 13
49 the word of the Lord spread 13
14: 3 speaking boldly for the Lord 13
23 the Lord in whom they believed. 13
15:11 saved through the grace of the Lord Jesus 13
17 the rest of men may seek the Lord 13
18 says the Lord, who has made these things 13
26 for the sake of our Lord Jesus Christ. 13
35 teaching and preaching the word of the Lord 13
36 where we proclaimed the word of the Lord 13
40 commended . . to the grace of the Lord. 13
16:14 The Lord opened her heart to give heed 13
15 If you have judged me to be faithful to the Lord 13
31 Believe in the Lord Jesus, and you will be saved 13
32 they spoke the word of the Lord to him 13
17:24 being Lord of heaven and earth 13
18: 8 Crispus . . believed in the Lord 13
9 the Lord said to Paul one night in a vision 13
25 He had been instructed in the way of the Lord; 13
19: 5 baptized in the name of the Lord Jesus. 13
10 the residents of Asia heard the word of the Lord 13
13 to pronounce the name of the Lord Jesus 13
17 the name of the Lord Jesus was extolled. 13
20 the word of the Lord grew and prevailed 13
20:19 serving the Lord with all humility 13
21 faith in our Lord Jesus Christ. 13
24 ministry which I received from the Lord Jesus 13
35 the words of the Lord Jesus, how he said 13
21:13 die at Jerusalem for the name of the Lord Jesus. 13
14 "The will of the Lord be done. 13
22: 8 I answered, 'Who are you, Lord?' 13
10 I said, 'What shall I do, Lord?' 13
10 the Lord said to me, 'Rise, and go into Damascus 13
19 I said, 'Lord, they themselves know 13
23:11 the Lord stood by him and said, "Take courage 13
26:15 I said, 'Who are you, Lord?' 13
15 And the Lord said, 'I am Jesus 13
28:31 teaching about the Lord Jesus Christ 13
Rom 1: 4 Jesus Christ our Lord 13
7 from God our Father and the Lord Jesus Christ. 13
4: 8 the man . . whom the Lord will not reckon his sin. 13
24 him that raised from the dead Jesus our Lord 13
5: 1 peace with God through our Lord Jesus Christ. 13
11 rejoice in God through our Lord Jesus Christ 13
21 to eternal life through Jesus Christ our Lord. 13
6:23 is eternal life in Christ Jesus our Lord. 13
7:25 Thanks be to God through Jesus Christ our Lord! 13
8:39 from the love of God in Christ Jesus our Lord. 13
9:28 Lord will execute his sentence upon the earth 13
29 "If the Lord of hosts had not left us children 13
10: 9 if you confess with your lips that Jesus is Lord 13
12 the same Lord is Lord of all 13
12 the same Lord is Lord of all 13
13 For, "every one who calls upon the name of the Lord 13
16 "Lord, who has believed what he has heard from us? 13
11: 3 "Lord, they have killed thy prophets 13
34 For who has known the mind of the Lord 13
12:11 be aglow with the Spirit, serve the Lord. 13
19 "Vengeance is mine, I will repay, says the Lord. 13
13:14 But put on the Lord Jesus Christ 13
14: 6 the day, observes it in honor of the Lord. 13
6 He also who eats, eats in honor of the Lord 13
6 he who abstains, abstains in honor of the Lord 13
8 If we live, we live to the Lord 13
8 and if we die, we die to the Lord; 13
8 whether we live or whether we die, we are the Lord's. 13
9 be Lord both of the dead and of the living. 11
11 "As I live, says the Lord, every knee shall bow to me 13
14 I know and am persuaded in the Lord Jesus 13
15: 6 the God and Father of our Lord Jesus Christ. 13
11 and again, "Praise the Lord, all Gentiles 13
30 I appeal to you, brethren, by our Lord Jesus Christ 13
16: 2 receive her in the Lord as befits the saints 13
8 Greet Amplia'tus, my beloved in the Lord. 13
11 Greet those in the Lord who belong to the family 13
12 Greet those workers in the Lord 13
12 beloved Persis, who has worked hard in the Lord. 13
13 Greet Rufus, eminent in the Lord 13
18 For such persons do not serve our Lord Christ 13
20 The grace of our Lord Jesus Christ be with you. 13
22 I Tertius . . greet you in the Lord. 13
1Co 1: 2 call on the name of our Lord Jesus Christ 13
2 Lord Jesus Christ, both their Lord and ours 13
3 God our Father and the Lord Jesus Christ. 13
7 as you wait for the revealing of our Lord Jesus 13
8 guiltless in the day of our Lord Jesus Christ. 13
9 the fellowship of his Son, Jesus Christ our Lord. 13
10 by the name of our Lord Jesus Christ 13
31 "Let him who boasts, boast of the Lord. 13
2: 8 they would not have crucified the Lord of glory. 13
16 For who has known the mind of the Lord 13
3: 5 as the Lord assigned to each. 13
20 The Lord knows that the thoughts of the wise 13
4: 4 It is the Lord who judges me. 13
5 before the time, before the Lord comes 13
17 my beloved and faithful child in the Lord 13
19 I will come to you soon, if the Lord wills 13
5: 4 in the name of the Lord Jesus 13
4 with the power of our Lord Jesus 13
5 may be saved in the day of the Lord Jesus. 13
6:11 justified in the name of the Lord Jesus Christ 13
13 is not meant for immorality, but for the Lord 13
13 and the Lord for the body. 13
14 God raised the Lord and will also raise us up 13
17 he who is united to the Lord becomes one spirit 13
7:10 To the married I give charge, not I but the Lord 13
12 To the rest I say, not the Lord 13
17 which the Lord has assigned to him 13
22 who was called in the Lord as a slave is a freedman 13
22 a slave is a freedman of the Lord 13
25 I have no command of the Lord 13
25 one who by the Lord's mercy is trustworthy. 13
32 is anxious about the affairs of the Lord 13
32 how to please the Lord; 13
34 is anxious about the affairs of the Lord 13
35 secure your undivided devotion to the Lord. 13
39 married to whom she wishes, only in the Lord. 13
8: 6 one Lord, Jesus Christ 13
9: 1 Have I not seen Jesus our Lord? 13
1 Are not you my workmanship in the Lord? 13
2 you are the seal of my apostleship in the Lord. 13
5 the brothers of the Lord and Cephas? 13
14 In the same way, the Lord commanded 13
10: 9 We must not put the Lord to the test, as some of them 12
21 the cup of the Lord and the cup of demons 13
21 You cannot partake of the table of the Lord 13
22 Shall we provoke the Lord to jealousy? 13
26 For "the earth is the Lord's, and everything in it. 13
11:11 (Nevertheless, in the Lord 13
20 it is not the Lord's supper that you eat. 10
23 For I received from the Lord 13
23 the Lord Jesus on the night when he was betrayed 13
26 you proclaim the Lord's death until he comes. 13
27 drinks the cup of the Lord in an unworthy manner 13
27 be guilty of profaning the body and blood of the Lord. 13
32 when we are judged by the Lord, we are chastened 13
12: 3 no one can say "Jesus is Lord 13
5 there are varieties of service, but the same Lord; 13
14:21 they will not listen to me, says the Lord. 13
37 is a command of the Lord. 13
15:31 which I have in Christ Jesus our Lord 13
57 through our Lord Jesus Christ. 13
58 always abounding in the work of the Lord 13
58 in the Lord your labor is not in vain. 13
16: 7 some time with you, if the Lord permits. 13
10 he is doing the work of the Lord, as I am. 13
19 send you hearty greetings in the Lord. 13
22 If any one has no love for the Lord 13
23 The grace of the Lord Jesus be with you. 13
2Co 1: 2 God our Father and the Lord Jesus Christ. 13
3 Father of our Lord Jesus Christ 13
14 on the day of the Lord Jesus. 13
2:12 a door was opened for me in the Lord; 13
3:16 when a man turns to the Lord the veil is removed. 13
17 Now the Lord is the Spirit 13
17 where the Spirit of the Lord is, there is freedom. 13
18 this comes from the Lord who is the Spirit. 13
18 beholding the glory of the Lord 13
4: 5 Jesus Christ as Lord 13
14 knowing that he who raised the Lord Jesus 13
5: 6 we are away from the Lord 13
8 be away from the body and at home with the Lord. 13
11 Therefore, knowing the fear of the Lord 13
6:17 be separate from them, says the Lord 13
18 be my sons and daughters, says the Lord Almighty. 13
8: 5 first they gave themselves to the Lord and to us 13
9 For you know the grace of our Lord Jesus Christ 13
19 for the glory of the Lord and to show our good will. 13
21 not only in the Lord's sight 13
10: 8 which the Lord gave for building you up 13
17 Let him who boasts, boast of the Lord. 13
18 the man whom the Lord commends. 13
11:17 I say not with the Lord's authority but as a fool 13
31 The God and Father of the Lord Jesus 13
12: 1 go on to visions and revelations of the Lord. 13
8 Three times I besought the Lord about this 13
13:10 which the Lord has given me for building up 13
14 The grace of the Lord Jesus Christ 13
Gal 1: 3 God the Father and our Lord Jesus Christ 13
19 except James the Lord's brother. 13
5:10 I have confidence in the Lord 13
6:14 except in the cross of our Lord Jesus Christ 13
18 The grace of our Lord Jesus Christ 13
Eph 1: 2 God our Father and the Lord Jesus Christ. 13
3 the God and Father of our Lord Jesus Christ 13
15 have heard of your faith in the Lord Jesus 13
17 God of our Lord Jesus Christ, the Father of glory 13
2:21 grows into a holy temple in the Lord; 13
3:11 which he has realized in Christ Jesus our Lord 13
4: 1 I therefore, a prisoner for the Lord, beg you 13
5 one Lord, one faith, one baptism 13
17 Now this I affirm and testify in the Lord 13
5: 8 now you are light in the Lord 13
10 try to learn what is pleasing to the Lord. 13
17 but understand what the will of the Lord is. 13
19 singing and making melody to the Lord 13
20 in the name of our Lord Jesus Christ 13
22 Wives, be subject to your husbands, as to the Lord. 13
6: 1 Children, obey your parents in the Lord 13
4 in the discipline and instruction of the Lord. 13
7 as to the Lord and not to men 13
8 he will receive the same again from the Lord 13
10 Finally, be strong in the Lord 13
21 faithful minister in the Lord 13
23 God the Father and the Lord Jesus Christ. 13
24 Grace be with all who love our Lord Jesus Christ 13
Php 1: 2 God our Father and the Lord Jesus Christ. 13
14 in the Lord because of my imprisonment 13
2:11 every tongue confess that Jesus Christ is Lord 13
19 I hope in the Lord Jesus to send Timothy to you 13
24 I trust in the Lord 13
29 So receive him in the Lord with all joy 13
3: 1 Finally, my brethren, rejoice in the Lord 13
8 knowing Christ Jesus my Lord 13
20 from it we await a Savior, the Lord Jesus Christ 13
4: 1 stand firm thus in the Lord, my beloved. 13
2 I entreat Syn'tyche to agree in the Lord. 13
4 Rejoice in the Lord always 13
5 The Lord is at hand. 13
10 I rejoice in the Lord greatly 13
23 grace of the Lord Jesus Christ 13
Col 1: 3 God, the Father of our Lord Jesus Christ 13
10 to lead a life worthy of the Lord 13
2: 6 As therefore you received Christ Jesus the Lord 13
3:13 as the Lord has forgiven you 13
17 do everything in the name of the Lord Jesus 13
18 as is fitting in the Lord. 13
20 this pleases the Lord. 13
22 in singleness of heart, fearing the Lord. 13
23 work heartily, as serving the Lord and not men 13
24 from the Lord you will receive the inheritance 13
24 you are serving the Lord Christ. 13
4: 7 Tych'icus . . fellow servant in the Lord. 13
17 the ministry which you have received in the Lord. 13
1Th 1: 1 in God the Father and the Lord Jesus Christ 13
3 steadfastness of hope in our Lord Jesus Christ. 13
6 you became imitators of us and of the Lord 13
8 not only has the word of the Lord sounded forth 13
2:15 who killed both the Lord Jesus and the prophets 13
19 crown of boasting before our Lord Jesus 13
3: 8 for now we live, if you stand fast in the Lord. 13
11 our Lord Jesus, direct our way to you; 13
12 may the Lord make you increase and abound in love 13
13 the coming of our Lord Jesus with all his saints. 13
4: 1 we beseech and exhort you in the Lord Jesus 13
2 we gave you through the Lord Jesus. 13
6 because the Lord is an avenger 13
15 For this we declare to you by the word of the Lord 13
15 who are left until the coming of the Lord 13
16 For the Lord himself will descend from heaven 13
17 in the clouds to meet the Lord in the air 13
17 so we shall always be with the Lord. 13
5: 2 the day of the Lord will come like a thief 13
9 to obtain salvation through our Lord Jesus 13
12 are over you in the Lord and admonish you 13
23 blameless at the coming of our Lord Jesus 13
27 I adjure you by the Lord that this letter be read 13

28 The grace of our Lord Jesus Christ be with you. 13
2Th 1: 1 God our Father and the Lord Jesus Christ 13
2 God the Father and the Lord Jesus Christ. 13
7 when the Lord Jesus is revealed from heaven 13
8 who do not obey the gospel of our Lord Jesus. 13
9 and exclusion from the presence of the Lord 13
12 that the name of our Lord Jesus may be glorified 13
12 the grace of our God and the Lord Jesus Christ. 13
2: 1 concerning the coming of our Lord Jesus Christ 13
2 to the effect that the day of the Lord has come. 13
8 the Lord Jesus will slay him 13
13 brethren beloved by the Lord 13
14 may obtain the glory of our Lord Jesus Christ. 13
16 Now may our Lord Jesus Christ himself 13
3: 1 the word of the Lord may speed on and triumph 13
3 the Lord is faithful 13
4 we have confidence in the Lord about you 13
5 May the Lord direct your hearts to the love of God 13
6 in the name of our Lord Jesus Christ 13
12 exhort in the Lord Jesus Christ to do their work 13
16 Now may the Lord of peace himself give you peace 13
16 The Lord be with you all. 13
18 The grace of our Lord Jesus Christ be with you 13
1Ti 1: 2 God the Father and Christ Jesus our Lord. 13
12 Christ Jesus our Lord 13
14 the grace of our Lord overflowed for me 13
6: 3 sound words of our Lord Jesus Christ 13
14 until the appearing of our Lord Jesus Christ; 13
15 the King of kings and Lord of lords 13
2Ti 1: 2 God the Father and Christ Jesus our Lord. 13
8 Do not be ashamed then of testifying to our Lord 13
16 May the Lord grant mercy 13
18 may the Lord grant him to find mercy from the Lord 13
18 to find mercy from the Lord on that Day 13
2: 7 the Lord will grant you understanding 13
14 charge them before the Lord 9
19 "The Lord knows those who are his 13
19 every one who names the name of the Lord depart 13
22 those who call upon the Lord from a pure heart. 13
24 the Lord's servant must not be quarrelsome 13
3:11 yet from them all the Lord rescued me. 13
4: 8 which the Lord, the righteous judge, will award 13
14 the Lord will requite him for his deeds. 13
17 the Lord stood by me 13
18 The Lord will rescue me from every evil 13
22 The Lord be with your spirit. Grace be with you. 13
Phm 1: 3 God our Father and the Lord Jesus Christ. 13
5 the faith which you have toward the Lord Jesus 13
16 both in the flesh and in the Lord. 13
20 brother, I want some benefit from you in the Lord. 13
25 The grace of the Lord Jesus Christ 13
Heb 1:10 Thou, Lord, didst found the earth in the beginning 13
2: 3 It was declared at first by the Lord 13
7:14 evident that our Lord was descended from Judah 13
21 The Lord has sworn and will not change his mind 13
8: 2 which is set up not by man but by the Lord. 13
8 The days will come, says the Lord 13
9 so I paid no heed to them, says the Lord. 13
10 This is the covenant . . says the Lord 13
11 saying, 'Know the Lord,' for all shall know me 13
10:16 after those days, says the Lord 13
30 And again, "The Lord will judge his people. 13
12: 5 do not regard lightly the discipline of the Lord 13
6 For the Lord disciplines him whom he loves 13
14 holiness without which no one will see the Lord. 13
13: 6 The Lord is my helper, I will not be afraid 13
20 who brought again from the dead our Lord Jesus 13
Jas 1: 1 servant of God and of the Lord Jesus Christ 13
7 will receive anything from the Lord. 13
2: 1 as you hold the faith of our Lord Jesus Christ 13
1 our Lord Jesus Christ, the Lord of glory. •
3: 9 With it we bless the Lord and Father 13
4:10 Humble yourselves before the Lord 13
15 "If the Lord wills, we shall live 13
5: 4 reached the ears of the Lord of hosts. 13
7 Be patient . . until the coming of the Lord. 13
8 for the coming of the Lord is at hand. 13
10 the prophets who spoke in the name of the Lord. 13
11 and you have seen the purpose of the Lord 13
11 how the Lord is compassionate and merciful. 13
14 anointing him with oil in the name of the Lord; 13
15 and the Lord will raise him up 13
1Pe 1: 3 the God and Father of our Lord Jesus Christ 13
25 but the word of the Lord abides for ever. 13
2: 3 for you have tasted the kindness of the Lord. 13
13 Be subject for the Lord's sake 13
3:12 For the eyes of the Lord are upon the righteous 13
12 the face of the Lord is against those that do evil 13
15 in your hearts reverence Christ as Lord. 13
2Pe 1: 2 in the knowledge of God and of Jesus our Lord. 13
8 in the knowledge of our Lord Jesus Christ. 13
11 kingdom of our Lord and Savior Jesus Christ. 13
14 will be soon, as our Lord Jesus Christ showed me. 13
16 the power and coming of our Lord Jesus Christ 13
2: 9 the Lord knows how to rescue the godly from trial 13
11 a reviling judgment upon them before the Lord 13
20 knowledge of our Lord and Savior Jesus Christ 13
3: 2 the commandment of the Lord and Savior 13
8 with the Lord one day is as a 1,000 years 13
9 The Lord is not slow about his promise 13
10 But the day of the Lord will come like a thief 13
15 count the forbearance of our Lord as salvation. 13
18 knowledge of our Lord and Savior Jesus Christ. 13
Jde 1: 4 and deny our only Master and Lord, Jesus Christ. 13
9 but said, "The Lord rebuke you. 13
14 "Behold, the Lord came with his holy myriads 13
17 predictions of the apostles of our Lord Jesus 13
21 wait for the mercy of our Lord Jesus Christ 13
25 God, our Savior through Jesus Christ our Lord 13
Rev 1: 8 I am the Alpha and the Omega," says the Lord God 13
10 I was in the Spirit on the Lord's day, and I heard 10
4: 8 the Lord God Almighty, who was and is and is to come! 13
11 "Worthy art thou, our Lord and God, to receive glory 13
11: 4 two olive trees . . which stand before the Lord 13
8 great city . . where their Lord was crucified. 13
15 become the kingdom of our Lord and of his Christ 13
17 saying, "We give thanks to thee, Lord God Almighty 13
14:13 Blessed are the dead who die in the Lord 13
15: 3 wonderful are thy deeds, O Lord God the Almighty! 13
4 Who shall not fear and glorify thy name, O Lord? 13
16: 7 I heard the altar cry, "Yea, Lord God the Almighty 13
17:14 Lamb . . for he is Lord of lords and King of kings 13
18: 8 for mighty is the Lord God who judges her. 13
19: 6 For the Lord our God the Almighty reigns. 13
16 a name inscribed, King of kings and Lord of lords. 13
21:22 for its temple is the Lord God the Almighty 13
22: 5 for the Lord God will be their light 13
6 the Lord, the God of the spirits of the prophets 13
20 "Surely I am coming soon." Amen. Come, Lord Jesus! 13
1Es 1: 1 kept the passover to his Lord in Jerusalem; 13
2 in the temple of the Lord. 13
3 they should sanctify themselves to the Lord 13
3 put the holy ark of the Lord in the house 13
4 worship the Lord your God and serve his people 13
6 according to the commandment of the Lord 13
11 to make the offering to the Lord 13
17 the sacrifices to the Lord were accomplished 13
18 sacrifices were offered on the altar of the Lord 13
23 upright in the sight of the Lord 13
24 how they grieved the Lord deeply •
24 who sinned and acted wickedly toward the Lord 13
24 the words of the Lord rose up against Israel. 13
27 I was not sent against you by the Lord God 13
27 now the Lord is with me! 13
27 The Lord is with me, urging me on! 13
27 Stand aside, and do not oppose the Lord. 13
28 words . . from the mouth of the Lord. 13
33 his understanding of the law of the Lord 13
39 he did what was evil in the sight of the Lord. 13
41 also took some holy vessels of the Lord 13
44 He did what was evil in the sight of the Lord. 13
45 the holy vessels of the Lord 13
47 He also did what was evil in the sight of the Lord 13
47 words . . from the mouth of the Lord. 13
48 made him swear by the name of the Lord 13
48 transgressed the laws of the Lord 13
49 polluted the temple of the Lord 13
51 whenever the Lord spoke, they scoffed 13
54 all the holy vessels of the Lord, great and small 13
54 treasure chests of the Lord, and the royal stores 13
55 they burned the house of the Lord 13
57 in fulfillment of the word of the Lord 13
2: 1 the word of the Lord by the mouth of Jeremiah 13
2 the Lord stirred up the spirit of Cyrus 13
3 The Lord of Israel, the Lord Most High 13
3 The Lord of Israel, the Lord Most High 13
5 may his Lord be with him 13
5 build the house of the Lord of Israel 13
5 he is the Lord who dwells in Jerusalem 13
7 the temple of the Lord which is in Jerusalem. 13
8 all whose spirit the Lord had stirred 13
8 go up to build the house in Jerusalem for the Lord; 13
10 also brought out the holy vessels of the Lord 13
4:60 I give thee thanks, O Lord of our fathers. 7
5:50 they offered . . burnt offerings to the Lord 13
58 to have charge of the work of the Lord 13
58 So the builders built the temple of the Lord. 13
60 praising the Lord and blessing him 13
61 they sang hymns, giving thanks to the Lord 13
62 praising the Lord for the erection of the house 13
62 the erection of the house of the Lord. 13
67 the temple for the Lord God of Israel. 13
69 For we obey your Lord just as you do 13
70 building the house for the Lord our God 13
71 for we alone will build it for the Lord of Israel 13
6: 1 in the name of the Lord God of Israel. 13
2 the house of the Lord which is in Jerusalem 13
2 with the help of the prophets of the Lord 13
5 the providence of the Lord was over the captives; 13
9 building . . a great new house for the Lord 13
13 the servants of the Lord who created the heaven 13
15 our fathers sinned against the Lord of Israel 13
19 this temple of the Lord should be rebuilt 13
20 laid the foundations of the house of the Lord 13
22 building of the house of the Lord in Jerusalem 13
24 the building of the house of the Lord in Jerusalem 13
26 the holy vessels of the house of the Lord 13
27 the servant of the Lord and governor of Judea 13
27 to build this house of the Lord on its site. 13
28 until the house of the Lord is finished; 13
29 for sacrifices to the Lord 13
33 "Therefore may the Lord . . destroy every king 13
33 damage that house of the Lord in Jerusalem. 13
7: 4 the command of the Lord God of Israel 13
7 at the dedication of the temple of the Lord 13
9 for the services of the Lord God of Israel 13
13 all those who . . sought the Lord. 13
14 rejoicing before the Lord 13
15 for the service of the Lord God of Israel. 13
8: 6 the prosperous journey which the Lord gave them. 13
7 he omitted nothing from the law of the Lord 13
8 Ezra the priest and reader of the law of the Lord 13
9 Ezra the priest and reader of the law of the Lord 13
12 in accordance with what is in the law of the Lord 13
13 to collect for the Lord in Jerusalem all the gold 13
13 the gifts for the Lord of Israel 13
14 the temple of their Lord which is in Jerusalem 13
15 to offer sacrifices upon the altar of their Lord 13
17 deliver the holy vessels of the Lord 13
25 Blessed be the Lord alone 13
27 I was encouraged by the help of the Lord my God 13
46 to serve as priests in the house of our Lord. 13
47 by the mighty hand of our Lord 13
50 I proclaimed a fast . . before our Lord 13
52 power of our Lord will be with those who seek him 13
53 again we prayed to our Lord about these things 13
55 the holy vessels of the house of our Lord 13
58 I said to them, "You are holy to the Lord 13
58 the silver and the gold are vowed to the Lord 13
58 vowed to the Lord, the Lord of our fathers. 13
59 in the chambers of the house of our Lord. 13
60 carried them to the temple of the Lord. 13
61 by the mighty hand of our Lord 13
62 delivered in the house of our Lord to Meremoth 13
65 offered sacrifices to the Lord, the God of Israel 13
66 all as a sacrifice to the Lord. 13
67 the people and the temple of the Lord. 13
72 all who were ever moved at the word of the Lord 13
73 stretching forth my hands to the Lord 13
74 I said, "O Lord, I am ashamed and confounded 13
78 mercy has come to us from thee, O Lord 13
79 the house of the Lord our God 13
80 we were not forsaken by our Lord 13
81 glorified the temple of our Lord 13
82 now, O Lord, what shall we say 13
86 thou, O Lord, didst lift the burden of our sins 13
89 O Lord of Israel, thou art true 13
92 We have sinned against the Lord 13
93 Let us take an oath to the Lord about this 13
94 to you and to all who obey the law of the Lord. 13
9: 8 give glory to the Lord the God of our fathers 13
13 until we are freed from the wrath of the Lord 13
39 which had been given by the Lord God of Israel. 13
46 Ezra blessed the Lord God Most High 13
47 fell to the ground and worshiped the Lord. 13
48 the Levites, taught the law of the Lord 13
50 This day is holy to the Lord 13
52 for the day is holy to the Lord 13
52 do not be sorrowful, for the Lord will exalt you. 13
2Es 1: 4 The word of the Lord came to me, saying 14
12 speak to them and say, Thus says the Lord 14
14 Yet you have forgotten me, says the Lord. 14
15 "Thus says the Lord Almighty 14
21 What more can I do for you? says the Lord. 14
22 Thus says the Lord Almighty 14
27 you have forsaken yourselves, says the Lord. 14
28 "Thus says the Lord Almighty 14
32 their blood I will require of you, says the Lord. 14
33 "Thus says the Lord Almighty 14
40 who is also called the messenger of the Lord. 14
2: 1 "Thus says the Lord 14
3 because you have sinned before the Lord God 14
4 Go, my children, and ask for mercy from the Lord.' 14
9 So will I do to those . . says the Lord Almighty. 14
10 Thus says the Lord to Ezra: "Tell my people 14
14 because I live, says the Lord. 14
15 because I have chosen you, says the Lord. 14
17 for I have chosen you, says the Lord. 14
28 to do anything against you, says the Lord. 14
30 because I will deliver you, says the Lord. 14
31 for I am merciful, says the Lord Almighty. 14
33 I, Ezra, received a command from the Lord 14
33 and refused the Lord's commandment. 14
37 Receive what the Lord has entrusted to you 14
38 Rise and stand, and see at the feast of the Lord 14
39 have received glorious garments from the Lord. 14
40 who have fulfilled the law of the Lord. 14
41 beseech the Lord's power 14
42 they all were praising the Lord with songs. 14
47 who had stood valiantly for the name of the Lord. 14
48 how great and many are the wonders of the Lord God 14
3: 4 "O sovereign Lord, didst thou not speak 14
4:38 Then I answered and said, "O sovereign Lord 14
5:23 I said, "O sovereign Lord 14

28 now, O Lord, why hast thou given over the one 14
38 I said, "O sovereign Lord, who is able to know 14
41 I said, "Yet behold, O Lord 14
56 I said, "O Lord, I beseech thee 14
6:11 I answered and said, "O sovereign Lord 14
38 I said, "O Lord, thou didst speak at the beginning 14
55 All this I have spoken before thee, O Lord 14
57 now, O Lord, behold, these nations 14
7:17 Then I answered and said, "O sovereign Lord, behold 14
45 I answered and said, "O sovereign Lord, I said 14
53 I said, "Lord, how could that be? 14
58 I said, "O sovereign Lord, what is plentiful 14
75 If I have found favor in thy sight, O Lord 14
132I answered and said, "I know, O Lord 14
8: 6 O Lord who are over us, grant to thy servant 14
20 "O Lord who inhabitest eternity 14
24 hear, O Lord, the prayer of thy servant 14
36 For in this, O Lord, thy righteousness 14
45 No, O Lord who art over us! ‡
63 "Behold, O Lord, thou hast now shown me 14
9:29 "O Lord, thou didst show thyself among us 14
12: 7 I said, "O sovereign Lord, if I have found favor 14
13:51 I said, "O sovereign Lord, explain this to me 14
14: 2 I said, "Here I am, Lord," and I rose to my feet. 14
19 "Let me speak in thy presence, Lord. 14
15: 1 The Lord says, "Behold, speak in the ears 14
5 "Behold," says the Lord, "I bring evils upon the world 14
7 Therefore," says the Lord 14
9 I will surely avenge them," says the Lord 14
12 punishment that the Lord will bring upon it. 14
21 Thus says the Lord God 14
24 do not observe my commandments," says the Lord; 14
26 the Lord knows all who transgress against him; 14
52 dealt with you so violently," says the Lord 14
56 As you will do to my chosen people," says the Lord 14
16: 8 The Lord God sends calamities 14
11 The Lord will threaten 14
12 be troubled at the presence of the Lord 14
35 and understand them, O servants of the Lord. 14
36 Behold the word of the Lord, receive it 14
36 do not disbelieve what the Lord says. 14
48 the more angry I will be . . " says the Lord. 14
54 Behold, the Lord knows all the works of men 14
64 the Lord will strictly examine all their works 14
70 insurrection against those who fear the Lord. 14
71 destroying those who continue to fear the Lord. 14
74 "Hear, my elect," says the Lord. 14
76 says the Lord God, "do not let your sins 14
Tob 2: 2 who is mindful of the Lord 13
3: 2 "Righteous art thou, O Lord 13
11 Blessed art thou, O Lord my God 13
12 now, O Lord, I have turned my eyes . . toward thee. 13
14 Thou knowest, O Lord, that I am innocent 13
4: 5 "Remember the Lord our God all your days, my son 13
19 Bless the Lord God on every occasion 13
19 the Lord himself gives all good things 13
5:19 the life that is given to us by the Lord is enough 13
7:18 the Lord of heaven and earth grant you joy 13
8: 4 let us pray that the Lord may have mercy upon us. 13
7 now, O Lord, I am not taking this sister of mine 13
17 Show them mercy, O Lord 7
10:12 The Lord of heaven bring you back safely 13
12 that I may rejoice before the Lord 13
12:22 the angel of the Lord had appeared to them. 13
13: 4 because he is our Lord and God 13
6 Praise the Lord of righteousness 13
10 Give thanks worthily to the Lord 13
11 will come from afar to the name of the Lord God 13
13 will praise the Lord of the righteous. 13
14: 2 continued to fear the Lord God and to praise him. 13
6 the Gentiles will turn to fear the Lord God in truth 13
7 All the Gentiles will praise the Lord 13
7 the Lord will exalt his people 13
7 all who love the Lord God in truth 13
Jdt 4: 2 the temple of the Lord their God. 13
11 and spread out their sackcloth before the Lord. 13
13 the Lord heard their prayers 13
13 before the sanctuary of the Lord Almighty. 13
14 all the priests who stood before the Lord 13
14 the priests who . . ministered to the Lord 13
15 they cried out to the Lord with all their might 13
5:21 their Lord will defend them 13
24 Therefore let us go up, Lord Holofernes 7
6:19 "O Lord God of heaven, behold their arrogance 13
7:19 The people of Israel cried out to the Lord their God 13
28 our God, the Lord of our fathers 13
29 they cried out to the Lord God with a loud voice. 13
30 the Lord our God will restore to us his mercy 13
8:11 unless the Lord turns and helps us 13
13 You are putting the Lord Almighty to the test 13
14 do not provoke the Lord our God to anger. 13
16 Do not try to bind the purposes of the Lord our God; 13
23 the Lord our God will turn it to dishonor. 13
25 let us give thanks to the Lord our God 13
27 the Lord scourges those who draw near to him 13
31 the Lord will send us rain to fill our cisterns 13
33 the Lord will deliver Israel by my hand. 13
35 may the Lord God go before you 13
9: 1 Judith cried out to the Lord with a loud voice 13
2 "O Lord God of my father Simeon 13
7 the Lord is thy name. 13
7 know not that thou art the Lord 13
12 Lord of heaven and earth, Creator of the waters 7
12: 4 the Lord carries out . . what he has determined to do 13
8 prayed the Lord God of Israel to direct her way 13
13: 4 "O Lord God of all might 13
7 Give me strength this day, O Lord God of Israel! 13
15 The Lord has struck him down by the hand of a woman. 13
16 As the Lord lives, who has protected me 13
18 blessed be the Lord God, who created the heavens 13
15: 8 the good things which the Lord had done 13
10 May the Almighty Lord bless you for ever! 13
16: 2 sing to my Lord with cymbals 13
3 For God is the Lord who crushes wars 13
6 the Lord Almighty has foiled them 13
12 they perished before the army of my Lord. 13
13 O Lord, thou are great and glorious 13
16 he who fears the Lord shall be great for ever. 13
17 The Lord Almighty will take vengeance on them 13
19 the canopy . . she gave as a votive offering to the Lord. 9
AEs 10: 9 The Lord has saved his people 13
9 the Lord has delivered us from all these evils 13
13: 8 Then Mordecai prayed to the Lord 13
8 calling to remembrance all the works of the Lord 13
9 "O Lord, Lord, King who rulest over all things 13
9 "O Lord, Lord, King who rulest over all things 13
11 thou art Lord of all 13
11 is no one who can resist thee, who art the Lord. 13
12 thou knowest, O Lord, that it was not in insolence 13
14 who art my Lord 13
15 now, O Lord God and King, God of Abraham 13
17 that we may live and sing praise to thy name, O Lord; 13
14: 1 Esther the queen . . fled to the Lord; 13
3 she prayed to the Lord God of Israel, and said 13
3 O my Lord, thou only art our King 13
5 thou, O Lord, didst take Israel 13
7 Thou art righteous, O Lord! 13
11 O Lord, do not surrender thy scepter 13
12 Remember, O Lord; make thyself known in this time 13
14 am alone and have no helper but thee, O Lord. 13
18 except in thee, O Lord God of Abraham. 13
Wis 1: 1 think of the Lord with uprightness 13
7 the Spirit of the Lord has filled the world 13
9 a report of his words will come to the Lord 13
2:13 calls himself a child of the Lord. 13
3: 8 the Lord will reign over them for ever. 13
10 and rebelled against the Lord; 13
14 who has not devised wicked things against the Lord; 13
14 a place of great delight in the temple of the Lord. 13
4:14 for his soul was pleasing to the Lord 13
17 not understand what the Lord purposed for him 13
18 the Lord will laugh them to scorn 13
5: 7 the way of the Lord we have not known. 13
15 their reward is with the Lord 13
16 a beautiful diadem from the hand of the Lord 13
17 The Lord will take his zeal as his whole armor •
6: 3 For your dominion was given you from the Lord 13
7 For the Lord of all will not stand in awe of any one 7
8: 3 the Lord of all loves her. 7
21 so I appealed to the Lord and besought him 13
9: 1 "O God of my fathers and Lord of mercy 13
13 who can discern what the Lord wills? 13
10:16 She entered the soul of a servant of the Lord 13
20 they sang hymns, O Lord, to thy holy name 13
11:13 they perceived it was the Lord's doing. 13
26 O Lord who lovest the living. 7
12: 2 and put their trust in thee, O Lord. 13
13: 3 know how much better than these is their Lord 7
9 fail to find sooner the Lord of these things 7
16:12 it was thy word, O Lord, which heals all men. 13
26 thy sons, whom thou didst love, O Lord 13
19: 9 praising thee, O Lord, who didst deliver them. 13
22 O Lord, thou hast exalted . . thy people 13
Sir 1: 1 All wisdom comes from the Lord 13
9 The Lord himself created wisdom; 13
11 The fear of the Lord is glory and exultation 13
12 The fear of the Lord delights the heart 13
13 With him who fears the Lord it will go well 13
14 To fear the Lord is the beginning of wisdom 13
16 To fear the Lord is wisdom's full measure 13
18 The fear of the Lord is the crown of wisdom 13
20 To fear the Lord is the root of wisdom 13
26 the Lord will supply it for you. 13
27 the fear of the Lord is wisdom and instruction 13
28 Do not disobey the fear of the Lord; 13
30 The Lord will reveal your secrets 13
30 because you did not come in the fear of the Lord 13
2: 1 My son, if you come forward to serve the Lord 13
7 You who fear the Lord, wait for his mercy 13
8 You who fear the Lord, trust in him 13
9 you who fear the Lord, hope for good things 13
10 who ever trusted in the Lord and was put to shame? 13
10 persevered in the fear of the Lord and was forsaken? •
11 For the Lord is compassionate and merciful 13
14 What will you do when the Lord punishes you? 13
15 who fear the Lord will not disobey his words 13
16 Those who fear the Lord will seek his approval 13
17 who fear the Lord will prepare their hearts 13
18 Let us fall into the hands of the Lord 13
3: 2 For the Lord honored the father above 13
6 whoever obeys the Lord will refresh his mother; 13
16 whoever angers his mother is cursed by the Lord. 13
18 so you will find favor in the sight of the Lord. 13
20 For great is the might of the Lord 13
4:13 the Lord will bless the place she enters. 13
14 the Lord loves those who love her. 13
28 the Lord God will fight for you. 13
5: 3 the Lord will surely punish you. 13
4 the Lord is slow to anger. 13
7 Do not delay to turn to the Lord 13
7 suddenly the wrath of the Lord will go forth 13
6:16 those who fear the Lord will find him. 13
17 Whoever fears the Lord directs his friendship 13
37 Reflect on the statutes of the Lord 13
7: 4 not seek from the Lord the highest office 13
5 not assert your righteousness before the Lord 13
29 With all your soul fear the Lord 13
31 Fear the Lord and honor the priest 13
9:16 let your glorying be in the fear of the Lord. 13
10: 4 government . . is in the hands of the Lord 13
5 success . . is in the hands of the Lord 13
7 Arrogance is hateful before the Lord 13
12 pride is to depart from the Lord 13
13 the Lord brought upon them . . afflictions 13
14 The Lord has cast down . . rulers 13
15 The Lord has plucked up the roots of the nations 13
16 The Lord has overthrown the lands of the nations 13
19 Those who fear the Lord. 13
20 those who fear the Lord are worthy of honor 13
22 their glory is the fear of the Lord. 13
24 greater than the man who fears the Lord. 13
11: 4 the works of the Lord are wonderful 13
12 but the eyes of the Lord look upon him 13
14 Good things and bad . . come from the Lord 13
17 The gift of the Lord endures 13
21 trust in the Lord and keep at your toil 13
21 trust in the Lord and keep at your toil 13
22 blessing of the Lord is the reward of the godly 13
26 it is easy in the sight of the Lord to reward a man 13
14:11 present worthy offerings to the Lord. 13
15: 1 The man who fears the Lord will do this 13
9 for it has not been sent from the Lord. 13
10 the Lord will prosper it. 13
11 Do not say, "Because of the Lord I left the right way"; 13
13 The Lord hates all abominations 13
18 For great is the wisdom of the Lord 13
16: 2 unless the fear of the Lord is in them. 13
11 mercy and wrath are with the Lord •
17 Do not say, "I shall be hidden from the Lord 13
26 works of the Lord have existed 13
29 After this the Lord looked upon the earth 13
17: 1 The Lord created man out of earth 13
17 Israel is the Lord's own portion. 13
20 all their sins are before the Lord. 13
22 A man's almsgiving is like a signet with the Lord •
25 Turn to the Lord and forsake your sins 13
28 he who is alive and well sings the Lord's praises. 13
29 How great is the mercy of the Lord 13
18: 2 the Lord alone will be declared righteous. 13
6 is it possible to trace the wonders of the Lord. 13
11 Therefore the Lord is patient with them 13
13 the compassion of the Lord is for . . beings 13
23 do not be like a man who tempts the Lord. 13
26 all things move swiftly before the Lord. 13
19:20 All wisdom is the fear of the Lord 13
21: 6 he that fears the Lord will repent in his heart. 13
11 wisdom is the fulfilment of the fear of the Lord. 13
23: 1 O Lord, Father and Ruler of my life 13
4 O Lord, Father and God of my life 13
19 the eyes of the Lord 13
27 nothing is better than the fear of the Lord 13
27 to heed the commandments of the Lord. 13
24:12 in the portion of the Lord 13
25: 1 are beautiful in the sight of the Lord and of men; 13
6 their boast is the fear of the Lord. 13
10 no one superior to him who fears the Lord. 13
11 The fear of the Lord surpasses everything 13
26: 3 the blessings of the man who fears the Lord. 13
14 A silent wife is a gift of the Lord 13
16 Like the sun rising in the heights of the Lord 13
28 the Lord will prepare him for the sword! 13
27: 3 zealous in the fear of the Lord 13
24 even the Lord will hate him. 13
28: 1 suffer vengeance from the Lord 13
3 yet seek for healing from the Lord? 13
23 who forsake the Lord will fall into its power 13
30:19 So is he who is afflicted by the Lord; 13
32:14 He who fears the Lord will accept his discipline 13
16 Those who fear the Lord will form true judgments 13
24 he who trusts the Lord will not suffer loss. 13
33: 1 No evil will befall the man who fears the Lord 13
8 By the Lord's decision they were distinguished 13
11 the Lord distinguished them 13
16 by the blessing of the Lord I excelled 13

34:13 The spirit of those who fear the Lord will live 13
14 He who fears the Lord will not be timid 13
15 Blessed is the soul of the man who fears the Lord! 13
16 The eyes of the Lord are upon those who love him 13
24 to whose voice will the Lord listen? 7
35: 3 To keep from wickedness is pleasing to the Lord 13
4 Do not appear before the Lord empty-handed 13
8 Glorify the Lord generously 13
11 For the Lord is the one who repays 13
12 the Lord is the judge 13
16 He whose service is pleasing to the Lord •
17 he will not be consoled until it reaches the Lord; •
18 the Lord will not delay 13
36: 1 Have mercy upon us, O Lord, the God of all 7
5 there is not God but thee, O Lord. 13
12 Have mercy, O Lord, upon the people 13
17 thou art the Lord, the God of the ages. 13
17 Hearken, O Lord, to the prayer of thy servants 13
37:21 for grace was not given him by the Lord 13
38: 1 the Lord created him; 13
4 The Lord created medicines from the earth 13
9 pray to the Lord, and he will heal you. 13
12 the Lord created him 13
14 for they too will pray to the Lord 13
39: 5 to rise early to seek the Lord who made him 13
6 If the great Lord is willing 13
6 give thanks to the Lord in prayer. 13
8 will glory in the law of the Lord's covenant. 13
14 bless the Lord for all his works; 13
16 "All things are the works of the Lord 13
33 The works of the Lord are all good 13
35 bless the name of the Lord. 13
40:26 the fear of the Lord is better than both 13
26 There is no loss in the fear of the Lord 13
27 The fear of the Lord is like a garden of blessing 13
41: 3 this is the decree from the Lord for all flesh 13
42:15 I will now call to mind the works of the Lord 13
15 By the words of the Lord his works are done. 13
16 the work of the Lord is full of his glory. 13
17 The Lord has not enabled his holy ones to recount 13
17 which the Lord the Almighty has established 13
43: 5 Great is the Lord who made it 13
9 a gleaming array in the heights of the Lord. 13
29 Terrible is the Lord and very great 13
30 When you praise the Lord 13
33 For the Lord has made all things 13
44: 2 The Lord apportioned to them great glory 13
16 Enoch pleased the Lord, and was taken up 13
21 Therefore the Lord assured him by an oath •
45: 1 the Lord brought forth a man of mercy •
3 the Lord glorified him in the presence of kings. •
15 to minister to the Lord •
16 to offer sacrifice to the Lord 13
19 The Lord saw it and was not pleased 13
21 for they eat the sacrifices to the Lord 13
22 the Lord himself is his portion •
23 he was zealous in the fear of the Lord 13
26 May the Lord grant you wisdom in your heart •
46: 3 he waged the wars of the Lord. 13
6 the great Lord answered him 13
6 he was fighting in the sight of the Lord 13
9 the Lord gave Caleb strength 13
10 might see that it is good to follow the Lord. 13
11 who did not turn away from the Lord 13
13 Samuel, beloved by his Lord, a prophet of the Lord 13
13 Samuel, beloved by his Lord, a prophet of the Lord 13
14 By the law of the Lord he judged the congregation 13
14 the Lord watched over Jacob. 13
16 He called upon the Lord, the Mighty One 13
17 Then the Lord thundered from heaven 13
19 before the Lord and his anointed 13
47: 5 For he appealed to the Lord, the Most High 13
6 praised him for the blessings of the Lord 13
11 The Lord took away his sins, and exalted his power 13
18 In the name of the Lord God 13
22 the Lord will never give up his mercy 13
48: 3 By the word of the Lord he shut up the heavens 13
20 they called upon the Lord who is merciful 13
21 The Lord smote the camp of the Assyrians •
22 For Hezekiah did what was pleasing to the Lord 13
49: 3 He set his heart upon the Lord 13
12 raised a temple holy to the Lord 13
50:13 with the Lord's offering in their hands 13
17 to worship their Lord, the Almighty, God Most High. 13
19 the people besought the Lord Most High in prayer 13
19 till the order of worship of the Lord was ended 13
20 pronounce the blessing of the Lord with his lips 13
29 the light of the Lord is his path. 13
51: 1 I will give thanks to thee, O Lord and King 13
8 Then I remembered thy mercy, O Lord 13
10 I appealed to the Lord, the Father of my lord 13
12 I will bless the name of the Lord. 13
22 The Lord gave me a tongue as my reward 13
Bar 1: 5 they wept, and fasted, and prayed before the Lord; 13
8 Baruch took the vessels of the house of the Lord 13
10 offer them upon the altar of the Lord our God; 13
12 And the Lord will give us strength 13
13 And pray for us to the Lord our God 13
13 for we have sinned against the Lord our God 13
13 the anger of the Lord and his wrath have not 13
14 make your confession in the house of the Lord 13
15 Righteousness belongs to the Lord our God 13
17 because we have sinned before the Lord 13
18 have not heeded the voice of the Lord our God 13
18 statutes of the Lord which he set before us. 13
19 Lord brought our fathers out of the land of Egypt 13
19 we have been disobedient to the Lord our God 13
20 the curse which the Lord declared through Moses 13
21 We did not heed the voice of the Lord our God 13
21 what is evil in the sight of the Lord our God. 13
2: 1 "'So the Lord confirmed his word, which he spoke 13
4 peoples, where the Lord has scattered them. 13
5 because we sinned against the Lord our God 13
6 Righteousness belongs to the Lord our God 13
7 calamities with which the Lord threatened us 13
8 Yet we have not entreated the favor of the Lord 13
9 And the Lord has kept the calamities ready 13
9 calamities . . the Lord has brought them upon us 13
9 for the Lord is righteous in all his works 13
10 to walk in the statutes of the Lord which he set 13
11 O Lord God of Israel, who didst bring thy people 13
12 O Lord our God, against all thy ordinances. 13
14 Hear, O Lord, our prayer and our supplication 13
15 earth may know that thou art the Lord our God 13
16 O Lord, look down from thy holy habitation 13
16 Incline thy ear, O Lord, and hear; 13
17 open thy eyes, O Lord, and see; for the dead who are 13
17 will not ascribe glory or justice to the Lord 13
18 to thee glory and righteousness, O Lord. 13
19 before thee our prayer for mercy, O Lord our God. 13
21 "Thus says the Lord: Bend your shoulders and serve 13
22 But if you will not obey the voice of the Lord 13
27 "'Yet thou hast dealt with us, O Lord our God 13
31 they will know that I am the Lord their God. 13
33 their fathers, who sinned before the Lord. 13
3: 1 "'O Lord Almighty, God of Israel, the soul in anguish 13
2 Hear, O Lord, and have mercy, for we have sinned 13
4 O Lord Almighty, God of Israel, hear now the prayer 13
4 who did not heed the voice of the Lord their God 13
6 For thou art the Lord our God, and thee, O Lord, will 13
6 Lord our God, and thee, O Lord, will we praise. 13
8 our fathers who forsook the Lord our God.' 13
LJr 1: 6 "It is thou, O Lord, whom we must worship. 7
Aza 1: 1 singing hymns to God and blessing the Lord. 13
3 "Blessed art thou, O Lord, God of our fathers 13
14 For we, O Lord, have become fewer than any nation 6
20 give glory to thy name, O Lord! 13
22 Let them know that thou art the Lord, the only God 13
26 the angel of the Lord came down into the furnace 13
29 Blessed art thou, O Lord, God of our fathers 13
35 Bless the Lord, all works of the Lord 13
35 Bless the Lord, all works of the Lord 13
36 Bless the Lord, you heavens 13
37 Bless the Lord, you angels of the Lord 13
37 Bless the Lord, you angels of the Lord 13
38 Bless the Lord, all waters above the heaven 13
39 Bless the Lord, all powers 13
40 Bless the Lord, sun and moon 13
41 Bless the Lord, stars of heaven 13
42 Bless the Lord, all rain and dew 13
43 Bless the Lord, all winds 13
44 Bless the Lord, fire and heat 13
45 Bless the Lord, winter cold and summer heat 13
46 Bless the Lord, dews and snows 13
47 Bless the Lord, nights and days 13
48 Bless the Lord, light and darkness 13
49 Bless the Lord, ice and cold 13
50 Bless the Lord, frosts and snows 13
51 Bless the Lord, lightnings and clouds 13
52 Let the earth bless the Lord 13
53 Bless the Lord, mountains and hills 13
54 Bless the Lord, all things that grow on the earth 13
55 Bless the Lord, you springs 13
56 Bless the Lord, seas and rivers 13
57 Bless the Lord, you whales 13
58 Bless the Lord, all birds of the air 13
59 Bless the Lord, all beasts and cattle 13
60 Bless the Lord, you sons of men 13
61 Bless the Lord, O Israel 13
62 Bless the Lord, you priests of the Lord 13
62 Bless the Lord, you priests of the Lord 13
63 Bless the Lord, you servants of the Lord 13
63 Bless the Lord, you servants of the Lord 13
64 Bless the Lord, spirits . . of the righteous 13
65 Bless the Lord, you who are holy 13
66 Bless the Lord, Hananiah, Azariah, and Mishael 13
67 Give thanks to the Lord, for he is good 13
68 Bless him, all who worship the Lord, the God of gods 13
Sus 1: 2 and one who feared the Lord. 13
5 Concerning them the Lord had said 7
23 rather than to sin in the sight of the Lord. 13
35 for her heart trusted in the Lord. 13
44 The Lord heard her cry. 13
53 though the Lord said, 'Do not put to death 13
Bel 1:25 Daniel said, "I will worship the Lord my God 13
34 the angel of the Lord said to Habakkuk 13
36 Then the angel of the Lord took him 13
41 Thou art great, O Lord God of Daniel 13
Man 1: 1 O Lord Almighty, God of our fathers, of Abraham 13
7 thou art the Lord Most High, of great compassion 13
7 Thou, O Lord, according to thy great goodness 13
8 Therefore thou, O Lord, God of the righteous 13
9 my transgressions are multiplied, O Lord 13
12 I have sinned, O Lord, I have sinned 13
13 forgive me, O Lord, forgive me! 13
13 thou, O Lord, art the God of those who repent 13
2Mc 1: 8 We besought the Lord and we were heard 13
24 O Lord, Lord God, Creator of all things 13
24 O Lord, Lord God, Creator of all things 13
2: 2 not to forget the commandments of the Lord 13
8 then the Lord will disclose these things 13
8 the glory of the Lord and the cloud will appear 13
10 Just as Moses prayed to the Lord 13
22 while the Lord . . became gracious to them– 13
3:22 While they were calling upon the Almighty Lord 13
30 they praised the Lord who had acted marvelously 13
30 now that the Almighty Lord had appeared. 13
33 for his sake the Lord has granted you your life. 13
35 Then Heliodorus offered sacrifice to the Lord 13
4:38 The Lord thus repaid him 13
5:17 did not perceive that the Lord was angered 7
19 the Lord did not choose the nation 13
20 when the great Lord became reconciled. 7
6:14 the Lord waits patiently to punish them 7
30 It is clear to the Lord in his holy knowledge 13
7: 6 The Lord God is watching over us 13
20 because of her hope in the Lord. 13
33 if our living Lord is angry for a little while 13
40 putting his whole trust in the Lord. 13
8: 2 They besought the Lord to look upon the people 13
5 the wrath of the Lord had turned to mercy. 13
14 and at the same time besought the Lord 13
27 giving great praise and thanks to the Lord 13
29 besought the merciful Lord 13
35 having been humbled with the help of the Lord 13
9: 5 the all-seeing Lord, the God of Israel 13
13 Then the abominable fellow made a vow to the Lord 7
10: 1 the Lord leading them on, recovered the temple 13
4 they fell prostrate and besought the Lord 13
28 not only . . valor but their reliance upon the Lord 13
38 they blessed the Lord 13
11: 6 with lamentations and tears, besought the Lord 13
10 the Lord had mercy on them. 13
12:36 Judas called upon the Lord 13
41 they all blessed the ways of the Lord 13
13:10 to call upon the Lord day and night 13
12 besought the merciful Lord with weeping 13
17 because the Lord's help protected him. 13
14:35 "O Lord of all, who hast need of nothing 13
36 now, O holy One, Lord of all holiness 13
46 calling upon the Lord of life and spirit 5
15: 4 the living Lord himself, the Sovereign in heaven 13
7 he would get help from the Lord. 13
21 as the Lord decides •
21 and called upon the Lord who works wonders 13
22 O Lord, thou didst send thy angel 7
29 they blessed the Sovereign Lord •
34 they all, looking to heaven, blessed the Lord 13
35 sign to every one of the help of the Lord. 13
3Mc 2: 2 "Lord, Lord, king of the heavens 13
2 "Lord, Lord, king of the heavens 13
5: 7 they all called upon the Almighty Lord 13
11 the Lord sent upon the king a portion of sleep •
12 by the action of the Lord 7
35 praised the manifest Lord God, King of kings 13
6: 5 Sennacherib . . you, O Lord, broke in pieces 6
10 destroy us, Lord, by whatever fate you choose. 6
15 you are with us, O Lord 13
15 so accomplish it, O Lord. 13
39 the Lord of all . . revealed his mercy 8
151 1: 3 who will declare it to my Lord? The Lord himself; 13
3 who will declare it to my Lord? The Lord himself; 13
5 but the Lord was not pleased with them. 13

sovereign Lord 1. δεσπότης
Act 4:24 Sovereign Lord, who didst make the heaven 1
Rev 6:10 "O Sovereign Lord, holy and true, how long before 1

Lot 1. לוֹט 2. Λώτ
Gen 11:27 Nahor, and Haran; and Haran was the father of Lot. 1
31 Terah took Abram his son and Lot the son of Haran 1
12: 4 and Lot went with him. 1
5 Sar'ai his wife, and Lot his brother's son 1
13: 1 and Lot with him, into the Negeb. 1
5 Lot, who went with Abram, also had flocks and herds 1
7 Abram's cattle and the herdsmen of Lot's cattle. 1
8 Then Abram said to Lot, "Let there be no strife 1
10 Lot lifted up his eyes, and saw that the Jordan 1
11 Lot chose for himself all the Jordan valley 1
11 and Lot journeyed east; 1
12 while Lot dwelt among the cities of the valley 1
14 The LORD said to Abram, after Lot had separated 1
14:12 they also took Lot, the son of Abram's brother 1
16 also brought back his kinsman Lot with his goods 1
19: 1 and Lot was sitting in the gate of Sodom. 1
1 and Lot was sitting in the gate of Sodom. 1
5 they called to Lot, "Where are the men who came 1

6 Lot went out of the door to the men 1
9 Then they pressed hard against the man Lot 1
10 their hands and brought Lot into the house 1
12 the men said to Lot, "Have you any one else here? 1
14 Lot went out and said to his sons-in-law 1
15 When morning dawned, the angels urged Lot 1
18 Lot said to them, "Oh, no, my lords; 1
23 sun had risen on the earth when Lot came to Zo'ar. 1
26 Lot's wife behind him looked back •
29 God remembered Abraham, and sent Lot out 1
29 when he overthrew the cities in which Lot dwelt. 1
30 Lot went up out of Zo'ar, and dwelt in the hills 1
36 Thus both the daughters of Lot were with child 1
Deu 2: 9 have given Ar to the sons of Lot for a possession.' 1
19 given it to the sons of Lot for a possession.' 1
Ps 83: 8 are the strong arm of the children of Lot. Selah 1
Lke 17:28 Likewise as it was in the days of Lot 2
29 on the day when Lot went out from Sodom 2
32 Remember Lot's wife. 2
2Pe 2: 7 if he rescued the righteous Lot 2
Sir 16: 8 He did not spare the neighbors of Lot 2

Lotan 1. לוֹטָן
Gen 36:20 inhabitants of the land: Lotan, Shobal, Zib'eon 1
22 The sons of Lotan were Hori and Heman; 1
22 Hori and Heman; and Lotan's sister was Timna. 1
29 Horites: the chiefs Lotan, Shobal, Zib'eon, Anah 1
1Ch 1:38 The sons of Se'ir: Lotan, Shobal, Zib'eon, Anah 1
39 The sons of Lotan: Hori and Homam; and Lotan's 1
39 and Lotan's sister was Timna. 1

Lothasubus 1. Λωθασουβος
1Es 9:44 Lothasubus, Nabariah, and Zechariah. 1

Lozon 1. Λοζων
1Es 5:33 the sons of Jaalah, the sons of Lozon 1

Lucius 1. Λευκιος 2. Λούκιος
Act 13: 1 Lucius of Cyre'ne 2
Rom 16:21 so do Lucius and Jason and Sosip'ater, my kinsmen. 2
1Mc 15:16 Lucius, consul of the Romans, to King Ptolemy 1

Lud 1. לוּד 2. Λουδ
Gen 10:22 of Shem: Elam, Asshur, Arpach'shad, Lud, and Aram. 1
1Ch 1:17 sons of Shem . . Arpach'shad, Lud, Aram, Uz, Hul 1
Isa 66:19 to the nations, to Tarshish, Put, and Lud 1
Ezk 27:10 Persia and Lud and Put were in your army 1
30: 5 Ethiopia, and Put, and Lud, and all Arabia, and Libya 1
Jdt 2:23 ravaged Put and Lud 2

man of Lud 1. לוּד
Jer 46: 9 men of Lud, skilled in handling the bow. 1

Ludim 1. לוּדִים
Gen 10:13 Egypt became the father of Ludim, An'amim 1
1Ch 1:11 Egypt was the father of Ludim, An'amim, Le'habim 1

Luhith 1. לוּחִית
Isa 15: 5 For at the ascent of Luhith they go up weeping; 1
Jer 48: 5 For at the ascent of Luhith they go up weeping; 1

Luke 1. Λουκᾶς
Col 4:14 Luke the beloved physician and Demas greet you. 1
2Ti 4:11 Luke alone is with me 1
Phm 1:24 Aristar'chus, Demas, and Luke, my fellow workers. 1

Luz 1. לוּז
Gen 28:19 but the name of the city was Luz at the first. 1
35: 6 Jacob came to Luz (that is, Bethel) 1
48: 3 God Almighty appeared to me at Luz in the land 1
Jos 16: 2 from Bethel to Luz, it passes along to At'aroth 1
18:13 boundary passes along . . in the direction of Luz 1
13 passes along southward . . to the shoulder of Luz 1
Jdg 1:23 (Now the name of the city was formerly Luz.) 1
26 Hittites and built a city, and called its name Luz; 1

Lycaonia 1. Λυκαονία
Act 14: 6 fled to Lystra and Derbe, cities of Lycao'nia 1

Lycaonian 1. Λυκαονιστί
Act 14:11 they lifted up their voices, saying in Lycao'nian 1

Lycia 1. Λυκία
Act 27: 5 we came to Myra in Ly'cia. 1
1Mc 15:23 to Samos, and to Pamphylia, and to Lycia 1

Lydda 1. Λύδδα
Act 9:32 he came down also to the saints that lived at Lydda. 1
35 all the residents of Lydda and Sharon saw him 1
38 Since Lydda was near Joppa 1
1Mc 11:34 Aphairema and Lydda and Rathamin 1

Lydia 1. Λυδία
Act 16:14 One who heard us was a woman named Lydia 1
40 So they went out of the prison, and visited Lydia; 1
1Mc 8: 8 the country of India and Media and Lydia 1

Lysanias 1. Λυσανίας
Lke 3: 1 Lysa'nias tetrarch of Abile'ne 1

Lysias 1. Λυσίας
Act 23:26 Claudius Lys'ias to his Excellency the governor 1
24:22 When Lys'ias the tribune comes down 1
1Mc 3:32 Lysias, a distinguished man of royal lineage 1
33 Lysias was also to take care of Antiochus his son •
34 he turned over to Lysias half of his troops •
35 Lysias was to send a force against them •
38 Lysias chose Ptolemy the son of Dorymenes 1
4:26 went and reported to Lysias 1
34 there fell of the army of Lysias 5,000 men 1
35 when Lysias saw the rout of his troops 1
6: 6 that Lysias had gone first with a strong force 1
17 when Lysias learned that the king was dead 1
17 Lysias had brought him up as a boy •
55 Then Lysias heard 1
7: 2 the army seized Antiochus and Lysias 1
2Mc 10:11 appointed one Lysias 1
11: 1 Lysias, the king's guardian and kinsman 1
6 Lysias was besieging the strongholds •
12 Lysias himself escaped by disgraceful flight. 1
15 Maccabeus . . agreed to all that Lysias urged. 1
15 which Maccabeus delivered to Lysias in writing. 1
16 The letter written to the Jews by Lysias 1
16 Lysias to the people of the Jews, greeting 1
22 King Antiochus to his brother Lysias, greeting. 1
35 what Lysias the kinsman of the king has granted 1
12: 1 Lysias returned to the king 1
27 Ephron, a fortified city where Lysias dwelt 1
13: 2 with him Lysias, his guardian 1
4 when Lysias informed him 1
26 Lysias took the public platform 1
14: 2 Antiochus and his guardian Lysias. 1

Lysimachus 1. Λυσιμαχος
AEs 11: 1 translated by Lysimachus the son of Ptolemy 1
2Mc 4:29 his own brother Lysimachus 1
39 acts of sacrilege . . in the city by Lysimachus 1
39 the populace gathered against Lysimachus 1
40 Lysimachus armed about 3,000 men 1
41 when the Jews became aware of Lysimachus' attack 1
41 threw them . . at Lysimachus and his men. 1

Lystra 1. Λύστρα
Act 14: 6 they learned of it and fled to Lystra and Derbe 1
8 Now at Lystra there was a man sitting 1
21 returned to Lystra and to Ico'nium and to Antioch 1
16: 1 he came also to Derbe and to Lystra 1
2 He was well spoken of . . at Lystra and Ico'nium. 1
2Ti 3:11 at Antioch, at Ico'nium, and at Lystra 1

Maacah 1. מַעֲכָה 2. מַעֲכָתִי
Gen 22:24 Reumah, bore Tebah, Gaham, Tahash, and Ma'acah. 1
2Sm 3: 3 Ab'salom the son of Ma'acah the daughter of Talmai 1
10: 6 hired . . the king of Ma'acah with 1,000 men 1
8 Zobah and of Rehob, and the men of Tob and Ma'acah 1
23:34 Eliph'elet the son of Ahas'bai of Ma'acah 2
1Kg 2:39 ran away to Achish, son of Ma'acah, king of Gath. 1
15: 2 name was Ma'acah the daughter of Abish'alom. 1
10 name was Ma'acah the daughter of Abish'alom. 1
13 also removed Ma'acah . . from being queen mother 1
1Ch 2:48 Ma'acah, Caleb's concubine, bore Sheber 1
3: 2 whose mother was Ma'acah, the daughter of Talmai 1
7:15 The name of his sister was Ma'acah. 1
16 Ma'acah the wife of Machir bore a son 1
8:29 Je-i'el . . the name of his wife was Ma'acah. 1
9:35 Je-i'el, and the name of his wife was Ma'acah 1
11:43 Hanan the son of Ma'acah 1
19: 7 chariots and the king of Ma'acah with his army 1
27:16 for the Simeonites, Shephati'ah the son of Ma'acah; 1
2Ch 11:20 After her he took Ma'acah the daughter of Ab'salom 1
21 Rehobo'am loved Ma'acah . . above all his wives 1
22 Abi'jah the son of Ma'acah as chief prince 1
15:16 Even Ma'acah, his mother, King Asa removed 1

Maacath 1. מַעֲכָת
Jos 13:13 Geshur and Ma'acath dwell in the midst of Israel 1

Maacathite 1. מַעֲכָתִי
Deu 3:14 border of the Gesh'urites and the Ma-ac'athites 1
Jos 12: 5 boundary of the Gesh'urites and the Ma-ac'athites 1
13:11 the region of the Gesh'urites and Ma-ac'athites 1
13 drive out the Gesh'urites or the Ma-ac'athites 1
2Kg 25:23 and Ja-azani'ah the son of the Ma-ac'athite. 1
1Ch 4:19 Kei'lah the Garmite and Eshtemo'a the Ma-ac'athite. 1
Jer 40: 8 Jezani'ah the son of the Ma-ac'athite 1

Maadai 1. מַעֲדַי 2. Μομδιος
Ezr 10:34 Of the sons of Bani: Ma-ada'i, Amram, Uel 1
1Es 9:34 Of the sons of Bani: Jeremai, Maadai, Amram, Joel 2

Maadiah 1. מַעַדְיָה
Neh 12: 5 Mi'jamin, Ma-adi'ah, Bilgah 1

Maai 1. מָעַי
Neh 12:36 kinsmen . . Ma'ai, Nethan'el, Judah, and Hana'ni 1

Maarath 1. מַעֲרָת
Jos 15:59 Ma'arath, Beth-anoth, and El'tekon 1

Maasai 1. מַעְשַׂי
1Ch 9:12 Ma'asai the son of Ad'i-el, son of Jah'zerah 1

Maaseiah 1. מַעֲשֵׂיָהוּ 2. Μαασιας 3. Μαιαννας 4. Μασσιας
1Ch 15:18 Eli'ab, Benai'ah, Ma-asei'ah, Mattithi'ah, 1
20 Jehi'el, Unni, Eli'ab, Ma-asei'ah, and Benai'ah 1
2Ch 23: 1 commanders . . Ma-asei'ah the son of Adai'ah 1
26:11 in the muster made by . . Ma-asei'ah the officer 1
28: 7 Zichri . . slew Ma-asei'ah the king's son 1
34: 8 he sent . . Ma-asei'ah the governor of the city 1
Ezr 10:18 found Ma-asei'ah, Elie'zer, Jarib, and Gedali'ah 1
21 of Harim: Ma-asei'ah, Eli'jah, Shemai'ah, Jehi'el 1
22 of Pashhur: Eli-o-e'nai, Ma-asei'ah, Ish'mael 1
30 of Pa'hath-mo'ab: Adna, Chelal, Benai'ah, Ma-asei'ah 1
Neh 3:23 Azari'ah the son of Ma-asei'ah, son of Anani'ah 1
8: 4 beside him stood . . Uri'ah, Hilki'ah, and Ma-asei'ah 1
7 Also . . Akkub, Shab'bethai, Hodi'ah, Ma-asei'ah 1
10:25 Rehum, Hashab'nah, Ma-asei'ah 1
11: 5 Ma-asei'ah the son of Baruch, son of Col-ho'zeh 1
7 Ko-lai'ah, son of Ma-asei'ah, son of I'thi-el 1
12:41 priests Eli'akim, Ma-asei'ah, Mini'amin, Micai'ah 1
42 Ma-asei'ah, Shemai'ah, Elea'zar, Uzzi, Jehoha'nan 1
Jer 21: 1 Zephani'ah the priest, the son of Ma-asei'ah, saying 1
29:21 son of Kola'iah and Zedeki'ah the son of Ma-asei'ah 1
25 and to Zephani'ah the son of Ma-asei'ah the priest 1
35: 4 above the chamber of Ma-asei'ah the son of Shallum 1
37: 3 and Zephani'ah the priest, the son of Ma-asei'ah 1
1Es 9:19 Maaseiah, Eliezar, Jarib, and Jodan. 2
21 Hanani and Zebadiah and Maaseiah and Shemaiah 2
22 Of the sons of Pashhur: Elioenai, Maaseiah 4
48 Maaseiah and Kelita, Azariah and Jozabad 3

Maasmas 1. Μαασμαν
1Es 8:43 I sent word to Eliezar, Iduel, Maasmas 1

Maath 1. Μάαθ
Lke 3:26 the son of Ma'ath, the son of Mattathi'as 1

Maaz 1. מַעַץ
1Ch 2:27 The sons of Ram . . Ma'az, Jamin, and Eker. 1

Maaziah 1. מַעַזְיָהוּ
1Ch 24:18 23rd to Delai'ah, the 24th to Ma-azi'ah. 1
Neh 10: 8 Ma-azi'ah, Bil'gai, Shemai'ah; these are the priests. 1

Maccabeus 1. Μακκαβαιος
1Mc 2: 4 Judas called Maccabeus 1
66 Judas Maccabeus has been a mighty warrior 1
3: 1 Judas his son, who was called Maccabeus 1
5:24 Judas Maccabeus and Jonathan his brother 1
34 army of Timothy realized that it was Maccabeus 1
8:20 Judas, who is also called Maccabeus 1
2Mc 2:19 The story of Judas Maccabeus and his brothers 1
5:27 Judas Maccabeus, with about nine others, got away 1
8: 1 Judas, who was also called Maccabeus 1
5 As soon as Maccabeus got his army organized 1
16 Maccabeus gathered his men together 1
10: 1 Maccabeus and his followers 1
16 Maccabeus and his men 1
19 Maccabeus left Simon and Joseph 1
21 When word of what had happened came to Maccabeus 1
25 Maccabeus and his men 1
30 Surrounding Maccabeus 1
33 Then Maccabeus and his men were glad 1
35 twenty young men in the army of Maccabeus 1
11: 6 When Maccabeus and his men got word 1
7 Maccabeus himself was the first to take up arms 1
15 Maccabeus, having regard for the common good 1
15 which Maccabeus delivered to Lysias in writing. 1
12:19 who were captains under Maccabeus 1
20 Maccabeus arranged his army in divisions 1
13:24 He received Maccabeus 1
14: 6 whose leader is Judas Maccabeus 1
27 to send Maccabeus to Antioch as a prisoner 1
30 Maccabeus . . concluded that . . 1
15: 7 Maccabeus did not cease to trust 1
21 Maccabeus . . stretched out his hands toward heaven 1

Macedonia 1. Μακεδονία 2. Μακεδών
Act 16: 9 a man of Macedo'nia was standing beseeching him 2
9 Come over to Macedo'nia and help us. 1
10 immediately we sought to go on into Macedo'nia 1
12 the leading city of the district of Macedo'nia 1
18: 5 When Silas and Timothy arrived from Macedo'nia 1
19:21 to pass through Macedo'nia and Acha'ia 1
22 having sent into Macedo'nia two of his helpers 1
20: 1 took leave of them and departed for Macedo'nia. 1
3 he determined to return through Macedo'nia. 1
Rom 15:26 For Macedo'nia and Acha'ia have been pleased 1
1Co 16: 5 visit you after passing through Macedo'nia 1
5 for I intend to pass through Macedo'nia 1
2Co 1:16 I wanted to visit you on my way to Macedo'nia 1
16 to come back to you from Macedo'nia 1
2:13 So I took leave of them and went on to Macedo'nia. 1
7: 5 For even when we came into Macedo'nia 1
8: 1 shown in the churches of Macedo'nia 1
9: 2 I boast . . to the people of Macedo'nia, saying 2

11: 9 the brethren who came from Macedo'nia 1
Php 4:15 when I left Macedo'nia 1
1Th 1: 7 all the believers in Macedo'nia and in Acha'ia. 1
8 sounded forth from you in Macedo'nia and Acha'ia 1
4:10 love all the brethren throughout Macedo'nia. 1
1Ti 1: 3 As I urged you when I was going to Macedonia 1

Macedonian 1. Κιτιεις 2. Μακεδών
Act 19:29 Macedo'nians who were Paul's companions in travel 2
27: 2 Aristar'chus, a Macedo'nian from Thessaloni'ca. 2
2Co 9: 4 lest if some Macedo'nians come with me and find 2
AEs 16:10 Haman, the son of Hammedatha, a Macedonian 2
14 transfer the kingdom . . to the Macedonians. 2
1Mc 1: 1 After Alexander son of Philip, the Macedonian 2
6: 2 Alexander, the son of Philip, the Macedonian king 2
8: 5 Philip, and Perseus king of the Macedonians 1
2Mc 8:20 with 4,000 Macedonians 2
20 when the Macedonians were hard pressed 2

Machbannai 1. מַכְבַנָּי
1Ch 12:13 Jeremiah tenth, Mach'bannai eleventh. 1

Machbenah 1. מַכְבֵּנָה
1Ch 2:49 She also bore . . Sheva the father of Machbe'nah 1

Machi 1. מָכִי
Num13:15 from the tribe of Gad, Geu'el the son of Machi. 1

Machir 1. מָכִיר
Gen 50:23 the children also of Machir the son of Manas'seh 1
Num26:29 of Machir, the family of the Ma'chirites; 1
29 Machir was the father of Gilead; 1
27: 1 Hepher, son of Gilead, son of Machir 1
32:39 sons of Machir the son of Manas'seh went to Gilead 1
40 Moses gave Gilead to Machir the son of Manas'seh 1
36: 1 sons of Gilead the son of Machir, son of Manas'seh 1
Deu 3:15 To Machir I gave Gilead 1
Jos 13:31 these were allotted to the people of Machir 1
17: 1 To Machir the first-born . . were allotted Gilead 1
3 son of Gilead, son of Machir, son of Manas'seh 1
Jdg 5:14 from Machir marched down the commanders 1
2Sm 9: 4 He is in the house of Machir the son of Am'miel 1
5 David . . brought him from the house of Machir 1
17:27 and Machir the son of Am'miel from Lo'debar 1
1Ch 2:21 Hezron went in to the daughter of Machir 1
23 descendants of Machir, the father of Gilead. 1
7:14 she bore Machir the father of Gilead. 1
15 Machir took a wife for Huppim and for Shuppim. 1
16 Ma'acah the wife of Machir bore a son 1
17 sons of Gilead the son of Machir, son of Manas'seh. 1

Machirite 1. בֶּן מָכִיר 2. מָכִירִי
Num26:29 of Machir, the family of the Ma'chirites; 2
Jos 13:31 were allotted . . for the half of the Machirites 1

Machnadebai 1. מַכְנַדְבַי 2. Μαμνιταναιμος
Ezr 10:40 Machnad'ebai, Shashai, Sha'rai 1
1Es 9:34 Carabasion and Eliashib and Machnadebai 2

Machpelah 1. מַכְפֵּלָה
Gen 23: 9 that he may give me the cave of Mach-pe'lah 1
17 the field of Ephron in Mach-pe'lah 1
19 the cave of the field of Mach-pe'lah east of Mamre 1
25: 9 his sons buried him in the cave of Mach-pe'lah 1
49:30 in the cave that is in the field at Mach-pe'lah 1
50:13 buried him in the cave of the field at Mach-pe'lah 1

Macron 1. Μακρων
2Mc 10:12 Ptolemy, who was called Macron 1

Madai 1. מָדַי
Gen 10: 2 sons of Japheth: Gomer, Magog, Madai, Javan 1
1Ch 1: 5 The sons of Japheth: Gomer, Magog, Madai, Javan 1

Madmannah 1. מַדְמַנָּה
Jos 15:31 Ziklag, Madman'nah, Sansan'nah 1
1Ch 2:49 She also bore Sha'aph the father of Madman'nah 1

Madmen 1. מַדְמֵן
Jer 48: 2 You also, O Madmen, shall be brought to silence; 1

Madmenah 1. מַדְמֵנָה
Isa 10:31 Madme'nah is in flight, the inhabitants of Gebim flee 1

Madon 1. מָדוֹן
Jos 11: 1 When Jabin . . he sent to Jobab king of Madon 1
12:19 the king of Madon, one; the king of Hazor, one; 1

Magadan 1. Μαγαδάν
Mat 15:39 and went to the region of Magadan. 1

Magbish 1. מַגְבִּישׁ 2. Νιφις
Ezr 2:30 sons of Magbish, 156. 1
1Es 5:21 The men of Bethel, 52. The sons of Magbish, 156. 2

Magdalene 1. Μαγδαληνή
Mat 27:56 among whom were Mary Mag'dalene 1
61 Mary Magdalene and the other Mary were there 1
28: 1 Mary Mag'dalene and the other Mary 1
Mrk 15:40 among whom were Mary Mag'dalene . . and Salo'me 1
47 Mary Mag'dalene and Mary the mother of Joses saw 1
16: 1 Mary Mag'dalene, and Mary the mother of James 1
9 he appeared first to Mary Magdalene 1
Lke 8: 2 Mary, called Mag'dalene 1
24:10 Now it was Mary Mag'dalene and Joan'na 1
Joh 19:25 Mary the wife of Clopas, and Mary Mag'dalene. 1
20: 1 Mary Mag'dalene came to the tomb early 1
18 Mary Mag'dalene went and said to the disciples 1

Magdiel 1. מַגְדִּיאֵל
Gen 36:43 Mag'diel, and Iram; these are the chiefs of Edom 1
1Ch 1:54 Mag'di-el, and Iram; these are the chiefs of Edom. 1

Magog 1. מָגוֹג 2. Μαγώγ
Gen 10: 2 sons of Japheth: Gomer, Magog, Madai, Javan 1
1Ch 1: 5 The sons of Japheth: Gomer, Magog, Madai, Javan 1
Ezk 38: 2 set your face toward Gog, of the land of Magog 1
39: 6 I will send fire on Magog 1
Rev 20: 8 to deceive the nations . . that is, Gog and Magog 2

Magpiash 1. מַגְפִּיעָשׁ
Neh 10:20 Mag'piash, Meshul'lam, He-zir 1

Mahalab
Jos 19:29 and it ends at the sea; Mahalab, Achzib •

Mahalalel 1. מַהֲלַלְאֵל
Gen 5:12 he became the father of Ma-hal'alel. 1
13 Kenan lived after the birth of Ma-hal'alel 1
15 When Ma-hal'alel had lived 65 years 1
16 Ma-hal'alel lived after the birth of Jared 1
17 Thus all the days of Ma-hal'alel were 895 years; 1
1Ch 1: 2 Kenan, Ma-hal'alel, Jared; 1
Neh 11: 4 Shephati'ah, son of Mahal'alel, of the sons of Perez; 1

Mahalath 1. מַחֲלַת
Gen 28: 9 Esau . . took . . Ma'halath the daughter 1
2Ch 11:18 Rehobo'am took as wife Ma'halath 1
Ps 53: 0 To the choirmaster: according to Mahalath. 1
88: 0 choirmaster: according to Mahalath Leannoth. 1

Mahaleleel 1. Μαλελεήλ
Lke 3:37 the son of Jared, the son of Maha'lele-el 1

Mahanaim 1. מַחֲנַיִם
Gen 32: 2 he called the name of that place Mahana'im. 1
Jos 13:26 from Mahana'im to the territory of Debir 1
30 extended from Mahana'im, through all Bashan 1
2Sm 2: 8 and brought him over to Mahana'im; 1
12 Abner . . went out from Mahana'im to Gibeon. 1
29 they crossed the Jordan, and . . came to Mahana'im. 1
17:24 Then David came to Mahana'im. 1
27 When David came to Mahana'im, Shobi 1
19:32 provided . . food while he stayed at Mahana'im 1
1Kg 2: 8 cursed me . . on the day when I went to Mahana'im; 1
4:14 Ahin'adab the son of Iddo, in Mahana'im; 1
1Ch 6:80 Mahana'im with its pasture lands 1

Mahaneh-dan 1. מַחֲנֵה דָן
Jdg 13:25 began to stir him in Ma'haneh-dan, between Zorah 1
18:12 that place is called Ma'haneh-dan to this day; 1

Maharai 1. מַהֲרַי
2Sm 23:28 Zalmon the Aho'hite, Ma'harai of Netoph'ah 1
1Ch 11:30 Ma'harai of Netoph'ah 1
27:13 Tenth . . was Ma'harai of Netoph'ah 1

Mahath 1. מַחַת
1Ch 6:35 son of Elka'nah, son of Mahath, son of Ama'sai 1
2Ch 29:12 Then the Levites arose, Mahath the son of Ama'sai 1
31:13 Ismachi'ah, Mahath, and Benai'ah were overseers 1

Mahavite 1. מַחֲוִים
1Ch 11:46 Eli'el the Ma'havite, and Jer'ibai, and Joshavi'ah 1

Mahazioth 1. מַחֲזִיאוֹת
1Ch 25: 4 sons of Heman . . Mallo'thi, Hothir, Maha'zi-oth. 1
30 to Maha'zi-oth, his sons and his brethren, twelve; 1

Maher-shalal-hash-baz 1. מַהֵר שָׁלָל חָשׁ בַּז
Isa 8: 1 'Belonging to Ma'her-shal'al-hash-baz.' 1
3 Call his name Ma'her-shal'al-hash-baz; 1

Mahlah 1. מַחְלָה
Num26:33 daughters of Zeloph'ehad were Mahlah, Noah 1
27: 1 names of his daughters were: Mahlah, Noah, Hoglah 1
36:11 Mahlah, Tirzah, Hoglah, Milcah, and Noah, 1
Jos 17: 3 the names of his daughters: Mahlah, Noah, Hoglah 1
1Ch 7:18 Hammo'lecheth bore . . Abi-e'zer, and Mahlah. 1

Mahli 1. מַחְלִי 2. Μοολι
Exd 6:19 The sons of Merar'i: Mahli and Mushi. 1
Num 3:20 sons of Merar'i . . Mahli and Mushi. 1
1Ch 6:19 The sons of Merar'i: Mahli and Mushi. 1
29 sons of Merar'i: Mahli, Libni his son, Shim'e-i 1
47 son of Mahli, son of Mushi, son of Merar'i, son of Levi; 1
23:21 The sons of Merar'i: Mahli and Mushi. 1
21 The sons of Mahli: Elea'zar and Kish. 1
23 The sons of Mushi: Mahli, Eder, and Jer'emoth, three. 1
24:26 The sons of Merar'i: Mahli and Mushi. 1
28 Of Mahli: Elea'zar, who had no sons. 1
30 The sons of Mushi: Mahli, Eder, and Jer'i-moth. 1
Ezr 8:18 man of discretion, of the sons of Mahli . . of Levi 1
1Es 8:47 brought us competent men of the sons of Mahli 2

Mahlite 1. מַחְלִי
Num 3:33 Of Merar'i were the family of the Mahlites 1
26:58 of Levi . . the family of the Mahlites 1

Mahlon 1. מַחְלוֹן
Rut 1: 2 the names of his two sons were Mahlon and Chil'ion; 1
5 and both Mahlon and Chil'ion died 1
4: 9 and all that belonged to Chil'ion and to Mahlon. 1
10 Also Ruth the Moabitess, the widow of Mahlon 1

Mahol 1. מָחוֹל
1Kg 4:31 Heman, Calcol, and Darda, the sons of Mahol; and his 1

Mahseiah 1. מַחְסֵיָה 2. Μαασαιας
Jer 32:12 to Baruch the son of Neri'ah son of Mahsei'ah 1
51:59 Serai'ah the son of Neri'ah, son of Mahsei'ah 1
Bar 1: 1 son of Neraiah, son of Mahseiah, son of Zedekiah 2

Makaz 1. מָקַץ
1Kg 4: 9 Ben-deker, in Makaz, Shaal'bim, Beth-she'mesh 1

Maked 1. Μακεδ
1Mc 5:26 in Alema and Chaspho, Maked and Carnaim 1
36 marched on and took Chaspho, Maked, and Bosor 1

Makheloth 1. מַקְהֵלֹת
Num33:25 set out from Hara'dah, and encamped at Makhe'loth. 1
26 set out from Makhe'loth, and encamped at Tahath. 1

Makkedah 1. מַקֵּדָה
Jos 10:10 and smote them as far as Aze'kah and Makke'dah. 1
16 fled, and hid themselves in the cave at Makke'dah. 1
17 have been found, hidden in the cave at Makke'dah. 1
21 returned safe to Joshua in the camp at Makke'dah; 1
28 And Joshua took Makke'dah on that day, and smote it 1
28 he did to the king of Makke'dah as he had done 1
29 Then Joshua passed on from Makke'dah . . to Libnah 1
12:16 the king of Makke'dah, one; the king of Bethel, one; 1
15:41 Gede'roth, Beth-da'gon, Na'amah, and Makke'dah 1

Malachi 1. מַלְאָכִי 2. Malachia
Mal 1: 1 the word of the LORD to Israel by Mal'achi. 1
2Es 1:40 Malachi . . called the messenger of the Lord. 2

Malcam 1. מַלְכָּם
1Ch 8: 9 sons by Hodesh his wife: Jobab, Zib'i-a, . . Malcam 1

Malchi-shua 1. מַלְכִּי שׁוּעַ
1Sm 14:49 sons of Saul were Jonathan, Ishvi, and Mal'chishu'a; 1
31: 2 slew Jonathan and Abin'adab and Mal'chishu'a 1
1Ch 8:33 Saul of . . Mal'chishu'a, Abin'adab, and Eshba'al; 1
9:39 Saul of Jonathan, Mal'chishu'a, Abin'adab 1
10: 2 Philistines slew Jonathan . . and Mal'chishu'a 1

Malchiah 1. מַלְכִּיָּהוּ
Jer 21: 1 Pashhur the son of Malchi'ah 1
38: 1 and Pashhur the son of Malchi'ah heard the words 1
6 and cast him into the cistern of Malchi'ah 1

Malchiel 1. מַלְכִּיאֵל
Gen 46:17 And the sons of Beri'ah: Heber and Mal'chi-el 1
Num26:45 of Mal'chi-el, the family of the Mal'chi-elites. 1
1Ch 7:31 The sons of Beri'ah: Heber and Mal'chi-el 1

Malchielite 1. מַלְכִּיאֵלִי
Num26:45 of Mal'chi-el, the family of the Mal'chi-elites. 1

Malchijah 1. מַלְכִּיָּהוּ 2. Μελχιας
1Ch 6:40 son of Michael, son of Ba-ase'iah, son of Malchi'jah 1
9:12 Jero'ham, son of Pashhur, son of Malchi'jah 1
24: 9 the fifth to Malchi'jah, the sixth to Mij'amin 1
Ezr 10:25 of Parosh: Rami'ah, Izzi'ah, Malchi'jah, Mi'jamin 1
31 of Harim: Elie'zer, Isshi'jah, Malchi'jah, Shemai'ah 1
Neh 3:11 Malchi'jah the son of Harim and Hasshub 1
14 Malchi'jah the son of Rechab, ruler 1
31 Malchi'jah, one of the goldsmiths, repaired as far 1
8: 4 Pedai'ah, Mish'a-el, Malchi'jah . . on his left hand. 1
10: 3 Pashhur, Amari'ah, Malchi'jah 1
11:12 Zechari'ah, son of Pashhur, son of Malchi'jah 1
12:42 Jehoha'nan, Malchi'jah, Elam, and Ezer. 1
1Es 9:26 Malchijah, Mijamin, and Eleazar, and Asibias 2
44 on his left Pedaiah, Mishael, Malchijah 2

Malchiram 1. מַלְכִּירָם
1Ch 3:18 Malchi'ram, Pedai'ah, Shenaz'zar, Jekami'ah 1

Malchus 1. Μάλχος
Joh 18:10 The slave's name was Malchus. 1

Mallothi 1. מַלּוֹתִי
1Ch 25: 4 sons of Heman . . Joshbekash'ah, Mallo'thi, Hothir 1
26 to Mallo'thi, his sons and his brethren, twelve; 1

Malluch 1. מַלּוּךְ 2. Μαμουχος
1Ch 6:44 Ethan the son of Kishi, son of Abdi, son of Malluch 1
Ezr 10:29 of Bani were Meshul'lam, Malluch, Adai'ah, Jashub 1
32 Benjamin, Malluch, and Shemari'ah. 1
Neh 10: 4 Hattush, Shebani'ah, Malluch 1
27 Malluch, Harim, Ba'anah. 1
12: 2 Amari'ah, Malluch, Hattush 1
1Es 9:30 Of the sons of Bani: Meshullam, Malluch, Adaiah 2

Malluchi 1. מַלּוּכִי
Neh 12:14 of Mal'luchi, Jonathan; of Shebani'ah, Joseph; 1

Mallus 1. Μαλλωται
2Mc 4:30 the people of Tarsus and of Mallus revolted 1

Malta 1. Μελίτη
Act 28: 1 then learned that the island was called Malta. 1

Mamdai 1. Μαμδαι
1Es 9:34 Mamdai and Bedeiah and Vaniah 1

Mamre 1. מַמְרֵא
Gen 13:18 and came and dwelt by the oaks of Mamre 1
14:13 the Hebrew, who was living by the oaks of Mamre 1
24 let Aner, Eshcol, and Mamre take their share. 1
18: 1 the LORD appeared to him by the oaks of Mamre 1
23:17 the field . . which was to the east of Mamre 1
19 the cave of the field of Mach-pe'lah east of Mamre 1
25: 9 the son of Zohar the Hittite, east of Mamre 1
35:27 Jacob came to his father Isaac at Mamre 1
49:30 at Mach-pe'lah, to the east of Mamre 1
50:13 at Mach-pe'lah, to the east of Mamre 1

Manaen 1. Μαναήν
Act 13: 1 Man'a-en a member of the court of Herod 1

Manahath 1. מָנַחַת
Gen 36:23 the sons of Shobal: Alvan, Man'ahath, Ebal 1
1Ch 1:40 The sons of Shobal: Al'ian, Man'ahath, Ebal, Shephi 1
8: 6 they were carried into exile to Mana'hath); 1

Manahathite 1. מְנֻחָתִי
1Ch 2:54 sons of Salma . . half of the Man'aha'thites 1

Manasseas 1. Μανασσηας
1Es 9:31 Sesthel, and Belnuus and Manasseas. 1

Manasseh 1. מְנַשֶּׁה 2. Μανασση 3. Μανασσῆς
Gen 41:51 called the name of the first-born Manas'seh 1
46:20 to Joseph in the land of Egypt were born Manas'seh 1
48: 1 with him his two sons, Manas'seh and E'phraim. 1
5 E'phraim and Manas'seh shall be mine 1
13 Manas'seh in his left hand toward Israel's right 1
14 and his left hand upon the head of Manas'seh 1
14 for Manas'seh was the first-born. 1
17 from E'phraim's head to Manas'seh's head. 1
20 God make you as E'phraim and as Manas'seh 1
20 and thus he put E'phraim before Manas'seh. 1
50:23 children . . of Machir the son of Manas'seh were 1
Num 1:10 from Manas'seh, Gama'liel the son of Pedah'zur; 1
34 Of the people of Manas'seh, their generations 1
35 the number of the tribe of Manas'seh was 32,200 1
2:20 next to him shall be the tribe of Manas'seh 1
20 leader of the people of Manas'seh being Gama'liel 1
7:54 Gama'liel the . . leader of the men of Manas'seh 1
10:23 over the host of the tribe of the men of Manas'seh 1
13:11 Joseph (that is from the tribe of Manas'seh) 1
26:28 sons of Joseph . . Manas'seh and E'phraim. 1
29 sons of Manas'seh 1
34 These are the families of Manas'seh; 1
27: 1 Gilead, son of Machir, son of Manas'seh 1
1 from the families of Manas'seh the son of Joseph. 1
32:33 Moses gave . . to the half-tribe of Manas'seh 1
39 sons of Machir the son of Manas'seh went to Gilead 1
40 Moses gave Gilead to Machir the son of Manas'seh 1
41 Ja'ir the son of Manas'seh went and took 1
34:14 also the half-tribe of Manas'seh; 1
23 the tribe of the sons of Manas'seh a leader, Han'niel 1
36: 1 sons of Gilead the son of Machir, son of Manas'seh 1
12 into the families of sons of Manas'seh 1
Deu 3:13 the rest . . I gave to the half-tribe of Manas'seh. 1
33:17 such are the thousands of Manas'seh. 1
34: 2 all Naph'tali, the land of E'phraim and Manas'seh 1
Jos 1:12 the Gadites, and the half-tribe of Manas'seh 1
4:12 and the sons of Gad and the half-tribe of Manas'seh 1
12: 6 and the Gadites and the half-tribe of Manas'seh. 1
13: 7 the nine tribes and half the tribe of Manas'seh. 1
8 With the other half of the tribe of Manas'seh 2
29 Moses gave . . to the half-tribe of Manas'seh; 1
31 were allotted to . . Machir the son of Manas'seh 1
14: 4 of Joseph were two tribes, Manas'seh and E'phraim; 1
16: 4 The people of Joseph, Manas'seh and E'phraim 1
17: 1 Then allotment was made to the tribe of Manas'seh 1
1 To Machir the first-born of Manas'seh, the father 1
2 were made to the rest of the tribe of Manas'seh 1
2 male descendants of Manas'seh the son of Joseph 1
3 son of Gilead, son of Machir, son of Manas'seh 1
5 there fell to Manas'seh ten portions, besides 1
6 daughters of Manas'seh received an inheritance 1
7 The territory of Manas'seh reached from Asher 1
8 The land of Tap'puah belonged to Manas'seh 1
8 Tap'puah on the boundary of Manas'seh belonged 1
9 The cities here . . among the cities of Manas'seh 1
9 the boundary of Manas'seh goes on the north side 1
10 and that to the north being Manas'seh's 1
11 Manas'seh had Beth-she'an and its villages 1
12 the sons of Manas'seh could not take possession 1
17 to the house of Joseph, to E'phraim and Manas'seh 1
18: 7 and Gad and Reuben and half the tribe of Manas'seh 1
20: 8 and Golan in Bashan, from the tribe of Manas'seh. 1
21: 5 the tribe of Dan and the half-tribe of Manas'seh 1
6 and from the half-tribe of Manas'seh in Bashan 1
25 and out of the half-tribe of Manas'seh, Ta'anach 1
27 were given out of the half-tribe of Manas'seh 1
22: 1 and the Gadites, and the half-tribe of Manas'seh 1
7 one half of the tribe of Manas'seh Moses had given 1
9 the Gadites and the half-tribe of Manas'seh 1
10 the Gadites, and the half-tribe of Manas'seh built 1
11 and the half-tribe of Manas'seh have built 1
13 and the Gadites and the half-tribe of Manas'seh 1
15 to . . the Gadites, and the half-tribe of Manas'seh 1
21 the Gadites, and the half-tribe of Manas'seh said 1
Jdg 1:27 Manas'seh did not drive out the inhabitants 1
6:15 Behold, my clan is the weakest in Manas'seh 1
35 And he sent messengers throughout all Manas'seh; 1
7:23 Naph'tali and from Asher and from all Manas'seh 1
11:29 and he passed through Gilead and Manas'seh 1
12: 4 Gileadites, in the midst of E'phraim and Manas'seh 1
1Kg 4:13 he had the villages of Ja'ir the son of Manas'seh 1
2Kg 20:21 Hezeki'ah slept . . and Manas'seh his son reigned 1
21: 1 Manas'seh was twelve . . when he began to reign 1
9 they did not listen, and Manas'seh seduced them 1
11 Manas'seh . . has committed these abominations 1
16 Manas'seh shed very much innocent blood 1
17 the rest of the acts of Manas'seh . . all that he did 1
18 Manas'seh slept with his fathers, and was buried 1
20 evil . . as Manas'seh his father had done. 1
23:12 altars which Manas'seh had made in the two courts 1
26 provocations with which Manas'seh had provoked 1
24: 3 to remove them . . for the sins of Manas'seh 1
1Ch 3:13 Ahaz his son, Hezeki'ah his son, Manas'seh his son 1
5:18 the half-tribe of Manas'seh had valiant men 1
23 the half-tribe of Manas'seh dwelt in the land 1
26 them away . . and the half-tribe of Manas'seh 1
6:61 out of the half-tribe, the half of Manas'seh 1
62 tribes of . . Naph'tali, and Manas'seh in Bashan. 1
70 out of the half-tribe of Manas'seh, Aner 1
71 were given out of the half-tribe of Manas'seh 1
7:14 The sons of Manas'seh: As'ri-el 1
17 sons of Gilead the son of Machir, son of Manas'seh. 1
9: 3 some of the people of Judah . . and Manas'seh 1
12:19 Some of the men of Manas'seh deserted to David 1
20 to Ziklag these men of Manas'seh deserted to him 1
20 chiefs of thousands in Manas'seh 1
31 Of the half-tribe of Manas'seh 18,000 1
37 and Gadites and the half-tribe of Manas'seh 1
27:20 for the half-tribe of Manas'seh, Jo'el the son 1
21 for the half-tribe of Manas'seh in Gilead, 1
2Ch 15: 9 gathered . . those from E'phraim, Manas'seh 1
30: 1 Hezeki'ah . . wrote letters also to . . Manas'seh 1
10 through the country of E'phraim and Manas'seh 1
11 a few men of Asher, of Manas'seh, and of Zeb'ulun 1
18 many of them from E'phraim, Manas'seh, Is'sachar 1
31: 1 Judah and Benjamin, and in E'phraim and Manas'seh 1
32:33 Manas'seh his son reigned in his stead. 1
33: 1 Manas'seh was twelve . . when he began to reign 1
9 Manas'seh seduced Judah and . . Jerusalem 1
10 The LORD spoke to Manas'seh and to his people 1
11 who took Manas'seh with hooks and bound him 1
13 Then Manas'seh knew that the LORD was God. 1
18 the rest of the acts of Manas'seh, and his prayer 1
20 Manas'seh slept with his fathers and they buried 1
22 did what was evil . . as Manas'seh his father had 1
22 all the images that Manas'seh his father had made 1
23 as Manas'seh his father had humbled himself 1
34: 6 in the cities of Manas'seh, E'phraim, and Simeon 1
9 collected from Manas'seh and E'phraim 1
Ezr 10:30 of Pa'hath-mo'ab . . Bin'nui, and Manas'seh. 1
33 of Hashum . . Jer'emai, Manas'seh, and Shim'e-i. 1
Ps 60: 7 Gilead is mine; Manas'seh is mine; 1
80: 2 before E'phraim and Benjamin and Manas'seh! 1
108: 8 Gilead is mine; Manas'seh is mine; 1
Isa 9:21 Manas'seh E'phraim, and E'phraim Manas'seh 1
21 Manas'seh E'phraim, and E'phraim Manas'seh 1
Jer 15: 4 because of what Manas'seh . . did in Jerusalem. 1
Ezk 48: 4 the east side to the west, Manas'seh, one portion. 1
5 Adjoining the territory of Manas'seh 1
Mat 1:10 Hezeki'ah the father of Manas'seh 3
10 and Manas'seh the father of Amos 3
Rev 7: 6 12,000 of the tribe of Manas'seh 3
1Es 9:33 Zabad and Eliphelet and Manasseh and Shimei. 3
Jdt 8: 2 Her husband Manasseh, who belonged to her tribe 3
7 her husband Manasseh had left her gold 3
10: 3 while her husband Manasseh was living. 3
16:22 after Manasseh her husband died 3
23 buried her in the cave of her husband Manasseh 3
24 who were next of kin to her husband Manasseh 3

Manassite 1. בֶּן מְנַשֶּׁה 2. מְנַשֶּׁה 3. מְנַשִּׁי
Deu 3:14 Ja'ir the Manas'site took all the region of Argob 1
4:43 Gadites, and Golan in Bashan for the Manas'sites. 3
29: 8 inheritance . . half-tribe of the Manas'sites. 3
Jos 13:29 was allotted to the half-tribe of the Manas'sites 1
16: 9 within the inheritance of the Manas'sites 1
17: 6 Gilead was allotted to . . the Manas'sites. 1
22:30 Reubenites and the Gadites and the Manas'sites 1
31 Reubenites and the Gadites and the Manas'sites 1
2Kg 10:33 Gadites, and the Reubenites, and the Manas'sites 3
1Ch 7:29 also along the borders of the Manas'sites 2
26:32 the Gadites, and the half-tribe of the Manas'sites 3

Manius 1. Μανιος
2Mc 11:34 Quintus Memmius and Titus Manius 1

Manoah 1. מָנוֹחַ
Jdg 13: 2 a certain man of Zorah . . whose name was Mano'ah; 1
8 Then Mano'ah entreated the LORD, and said, "O 1
9 God listened to the voice of Mano'ah, and the angel 1
9 field; but Mano'ah her husband was not with her. 1
11 Mano'ah arose and went after his wife, and came 1
12 Mano'ah said, "Now when your words come true 1
13 the angel of the LORD said to Mano'ah, "Of all that I 1
15 Mano'ah said to the angel of the LORD, "Pray, let us 1
16 the angel of the LORD said to Mano'ah, "If you detain 1
16 For Mano'ah did not know that he was the angel 1
17 Mano'ah said to the angel of the LORD, "What is 1
19 So Mano'ah took the kid with the cereal offering 1
20 ascended . . while Mano'ah and his wife looked on; 1
21 angel . . appeared no more to Mano'ah and to his wife. 1
21 Mano'ah knew that he was the angel of the LORD. 1
22 Mano'ah said to his wife, "We shall surely die 1
16:31 buried him . . in the tomb of Mano'ah his father. 1

Maoch 1. מָעוֹךְ
1Sm 27: 2 went . . to A'chish the son of Ma'och, king of Gath. 1

Maon 1. מָעוֹן
Jos 15:55 Ma'on, Carmel, Ziph, Juttah 1
1Sm 23:24 David and his men were in the wilderness of Ma'on 1
25 to the rock which is in the wilderness of Ma'on. 1
25 pursued after David in the wilderness of Ma'on. 1
25: 2 a man in Ma'on, whose business was in Carmel. 1
1Ch 2:45 The son of Sham'mai: Ma'on; 1
45 and Ma'on was the father of Bethzur. 1

Maonite 1. מָעוֹן
Jdg 10:12 the Amal'ekites, and the Ma'onites, oppressed you; 1

Mara 1. מָרָא
Rut 1:20 said to them, "Do not call me Na'omi, call me Mara 1

Marah 1. מָרָה
Exd 15:23 When they came to Marah, they could not drink 1
23 drink the water of Marah because it was bitter; 1
23 it was bitter; therefore it was named Marah. 1
Num33: 8 wilderness of Etham, and encamped at Marah. 1
9 they set out from Marah, and came to Elim; 1

Mareal 1. מַרְעֲלָה
Jos 19:11 its boundary goes up westward, and on to Mar'eal 1

Mareshah 1. מָרֵשָׁה 2. Μαρισα
Jos 15:44 Kei'lah, Achzib, and Mare'shah 1
1Ch 2:42 sons of Caleb . . Mare'shah his first-born 2
42 The sons of Mare'shah: Hebron. 1
4:21 La'adah the father of Mare'shah 1
2Ch 11: 8 Gath, Mare'shah, Ziph 1
14: 9 came as far as Mare'shah. 1
10 battle in the valley of Zeph'athah at Mare'shah. 1
20:37 Then Elie'zer the son of Do-dav'ahu of Mare'shah 1
Mic 1:15 a conqueror upon you, inhabitants of Mare'shah; 1

Marisa 1. Μαρισα
1Mc 5:66 and passed through Marisa. 1
2Mc 12:35 Gorgias escaped and reached Marisa. 1

Mark 1. Μᾶρκος
Act 12:12 the mother of John whose other name was Mark 1
25 John whose other name was Mark. 1
15:37 wanted to take with them John called Mark. 1
39 Barnabas took Mark with him 1
Col 4:10 Mark the cousin of Barnabas 1
2Ti 4:11 Get Mark and bring him with you 1
Phm 1:24 so do Mark, Aristar'chus, Demas, and Luke 1
1Pe 5:13 sends you greetings; and so does my son Mark. 1

Maroth 1. מָרוֹת
Mic 1:12 inhabitants of Maroth wait anxiously for good 1

Marsena 1. מַרְסְנָא
Est 1:14 Adma'tha, Tarshish, Meres, Marse'na, and Memu'can 1

Martha 1. Μάρθα
Lke 10:38 a woman named Martha received him 1
40 Martha was distracted with much serving 1
41 the Lord answered her, "Martha, Martha 1

41 the Lord answered her, "Martha, Martha 1
Joh 11: 1 the village of Mary and her sister Martha. 1
5 Jesus loved Martha and her sister and Laz'arus. 1
19 many of the Jews had come to Martha and Mary 1
20 When Martha heard that Jesus was coming 1
21 Martha said to Jesus, "Lord if you had been here 1
24 Martha said to him, "I know that he will rise again 1
30 still in the place where Martha had met him. 1
39 Martha, the sister of the dead man, said to him, "Lord 1
12: 2 There they made him a supper; Martha served 1

Mary 1. Μαρία

Mat 1:16 Joseph the husband of Mary, of whom Jesus was born 1
18 When his mother Mary had been betrothed 1
20 do not fear to take Mary your wife, for that 1
2:11 saw the child with Mary his mother, and they fell 1
13:55 Is not his mother called Mary? 1
27:56 among whom were Mary Mag'dalene 1
56 Mary the mother of James and Joseph 1
61 Mary Mag'dalene and the other Mary were there 1
61 Mary Mag'dalene and the other Mary were there 1
28: 1 Mary Mag'dalene and the other Mary 1
1 Mary Mag'dalene and the other Mary 1
Mrk 6: 3 Is not this the carpenter, the son of Mary 1
15:40 among whom were Mary Mag'dalene . . and Salo'me 1
40 Mary the mother of James the younger and of Joses 1
47 Mary Mag'dalene and Mary the mother of Joses saw 1
47 Mary Mag'dalene and Mary the mother of Joses saw 1
16: 1 Mary Mag'dalene, and Mary the mother of James 1
1 Mary Mag'dalene, and Mary the mother of James 1
9 he appeared first to Mary Magdalene 1
Lke 1:27 and the virgin's name was Mary. 1
30 the angel said to her, "Do not be afraid, Mary 1
34 Mary said to the angel, "How shall this be 1
38 Mary said, "Behold, I am the handmaid of the Lord 1
39 In those days Mary arose 1
41 when Elizabeth heard the greeting of Mary 1
46 Mary said, "My soul magnifies the Lord 1
56 Mary remained with her about three months 1
2: 5 to be enrolled with Mary, his betrothed 1
16 they went with haste, and found Mary and Joseph 1
19 Mary kept all these things 1
34 Simeon blessed them and said to Mary his mother 1
8: 2 Mary, called Mag'dalene 1
10:39 she had a sister called Mary 1
42 Mary has chosen the good portion 1
24:10 Now it was Mary Mag'dalene and Joan'na 1
10 Mary the mother of James and the other women 1
Joh 11: 1 the village of Mary and her sister Martha. 1
2 It was Mary who anointed the Lord with ointment 1
19 many of the Jews had come to Martha and Mary 1
20 she went and met him, while Mary sat in the house. 1
28 went and called her sister Mary, saying quietly 1
31 the Jews . . saw Mary rise quickly and go out 1
32 Mary, when she came where Jesus was and saw him 1
45 who had come with Mary and had seen what he did 1
12: 3 Mary took a pound of costly ointment of pure nard 1
19:25 his mother's sister, Mary the wife of Clopas 1
25 Mary the wife of Clopas, and Mary Mag'dalene. 1
20: 1 Mary Mag'dalene came to the tomb early 1
11 Mary stood weeping outside the tomb 1
16 Jesus said to her, "Mary. 1
18 Mary Mag'dalene went and said to the disciples 1
Act 1:14 with the women and Mary the mother of Jesus 1
12:12 When he realized this, he went to the house of Mary 1
Rom16: 6 Greet Mary, who has worked hard among you. 1

Mash 1. מַשׁ

Gen 10:23 The sons of Aram: Uz, Hul, Gether, and Mash. 1

Mashal 1. מִשְׁאָל

1Ch 6:74 out of . . Asher: Mashal with its pasture lands 1

Masiah 1. Μασιας

1Es 5:34 the sons of Sarothie, the sons of Masiah 1

Maskil 1. מַשְׂכִּיל

Ps 32: 0 A Psalm of David. A Maskil. 1
42: 0 A Maskil of the Sons of Korah. 1
44: 0 A Maskil of the Sons of Korah. 1
45: 0 A Maskil of the Sons of Korah; a love song. 1
52: 0 To the choirmaster. A Maskil of David 1
53: 0 according to Mahalath. A Maskil of David. 1
54: 0 with stringed instruments. A Maskil of David 1
55: 0 with stringed instruments. A Maskil of David. 1
74: 0 A Maskil of Asaph. 1
78: 0 A Maskil of Asaph. 1
88: 0 Maskil of Heman the Ezrahite. 1
89: 0 A Maskil of Ethan the Ezrahite. 1
142: 0 A Maskil of David, when he was in the cave. 1

Masrekah 1. מַשְׂרֵקָה

Gen 36:36 Samlah of Masre'kah reigned in his stead. 1
1Ch 1:47 Samlah of Masre'kah reigned in his stead. 1

Massa 1. מַשָּׂא

Gen 25:14 Mishma, Dumah, Massa 1
1Ch 1:30 Mishma, Dumah, Massa, Hadad, Tema 1
Prv 30: 1 The words of Agur son of Jakeh of Massa. 1
31: 1 The words of Lemuel, king of Massa 1

Massah 1. מַסָּה

Exd 17: 7 called the name of the place Massah and Mer'ibah 1
Deu 6:16 to the test, as you tested him at Massah. 1
9:22 also, and at Massah, and at Kib'roth-hatta'avah 1
33: 8 godly one, whom thou didst test at Massah 1
Ps 95: 8 Mer'ibah, as on the day of Massah in the wilderness 1

Matred 1. מַטְרֵד

Gen 36:39 name was Mehet'abel, the daughter of Matred 1
1Ch 1:50 his wife's name Mehet'abel the daughter of Matred 1

Matrite 1. מַטְרִי 2. Ματταρι

1Sm 10:21 the family of the Matrites was taken by lot; 1
21 he brought the . . Matrites near man by man 2

Mattan 1. מַתָּן

2Kg 11:18 and they slew Mattan the priest of Ba'al 1
2Ch 23:17 slew Mattan the priest of Ba'al before the altars. 1
Jer 38: 1 Now Shephati'ah the son of Mattan 1

Mattanah 1. מַתָּנָה

Num21:18 from the wilderness they went on to Mat'tanah 1
19 from Mat'tanah to Nahal'iel, and from Nahal'iel 1

Mattaniah 1. מַתַּנְיָהוּ 2. Ματανιας

2Kg 24:17 the king of Babylon made Mattani'ah . . king 1
1Ch 9:15 Mattani'ah the son of Mica, son of Zichri 1
25: 4 sons of Heman: Bukki'ah, Mattani'ah, Uz'ziel, 1
16 ninth to Mattani'ah, his sons and his brethren 1
2Ch 20:14 Benai'ah, son of Je-i'el, son of Mattani'ah, a Levite 1
29:13 the sons of Asaph, Zechari'ah and Mattani'ah 1
Ezr 10:26 of Elam: Mattani'ah, Zechari'ah, Jehi'el, Abdi 1
27 of Zattu: Eli-o-e'nai, Eli'ashib, Mattani'ah 1
30 of Pa'hath-mo'ab . . Mattani'ah, Bez'alel, Bin'nui 1
37 Mattani'ah, Matte'nai, Ja'asu. 1
Neh 11:17 Mattani'ah the son of Mica, son of Zabdi 1
22 son of Bani, son of Hashabi'ah, son of Mattani'ah 1
12: 8 Levites . . Sherebi'ah, Judah, and Mattani'ah 1
25 Mattani'ah, Bakbuki'ah, Obadi'ah, Meshul'lam, 1
35 Shemai'ah, son of Mattani'ah, son of Micai'ah, 1
13:13 Hanan the son of Zaccur, son of Mattani'ah 1
1Es 9:27 Of the sons of Elam: Mattaniah and Zechariah 2

Mattatha 1. Ματταθά

Lke 3:31 son of Menna, the son of Mat'tatha, the son of Nathan 1

Mattathiah 1. Ματταθίας

1Es 9:43 beside him stood Mattathiah, Shema, Anaiah 1

Mattathias 1. Ματταθίας

Lke 3:25 the son of Mattathi'as, the son of Amos 1
26 the son of Ma'ath, the son of Mattathi'as 1
1Mc 2: 1 Mattathias the son of John, son of Simeon 1
14 Mattathias and his sons rent their clothes 1
16 Mattathias and his sons were assembled. 1
17 the king's officers spoke to Mattathias as follows 1
19 Mattathias answered and said in a loud voice 1
24 When Mattathias saw it, be burned with zeal 1
27 Then Mattathias cried out in the city 1
39 When Mattathias and his friends learned of it 1
45 Mattathias and his friends went about 1
49 Now the days drew near for Mattathias to die 1
11:70 Mattathias the son of Absalom 1
14:29 Simon the son of Mattathias . . and his brothers 1
16:14 he went down to Jericho with Mattathias and Judas 1
2Mc 14:19 Posidonius and Theodotus and Mattathias 1

Mattattah 1. מַתַּתָּה 2. Ματταθίας

Ezr 10:33 of Hashum: Matte'nai, Mat'tattah, Zabad, Eliph'elet 1
1Es 9:33 Of the sons of Hashum: Mattenai and Mattattah 2

Mattenai 1. מַתְּנַי 2. Μαλτανναιος

Ezr 10:33 of Hashum: Matte'nai, Mat'tattah, Zabad, Eliph'elet 1
37 Mattani'ah, Matte'nai, Ja'asu. 1
Neh 12:19 of Joi'arib, Matte'nai; of Jedai'ah, Uzzi; 1
1Es 9:33 Of the sons of Hashum: Mattenai and Mattattah 2

Matthan 1. Ματθάν

Mat 1:15 and Elea'zar the father of Matthan 1
15 father of Matthan, and Matthan the father 1

Matthat 1. Ματθάτ

Lke 3:24 the son of Matthat, the son of Levi 1
29 son of Elie'zer, the son of Jorim, the son of Matthat 1

Matthew 1. Μαθθαῖος

Mat 9: 9 he saw a man called Matthew 1
10: 3 Thomas and Matthew the tax collector 1
Mrk 3:18 Philip, and Bartholomew, and Matthew, and Thomas 1
Lke 6:15 Matthew, and Thomas, and James the son of Alphaeus 1
Act 1:13 Philip and Thomas, Bartholomew and Matthew 1

Matthias 1. Μαθθίας

Act 1:23 Joseph called Barsab'bas . . and Matthi'as. 1
26 the lot fell on Matthi'as 1

Mattithiah 1. מַתִּתְיָהוּ 2. Μαζιτιας

1Ch 9:31 Mattithi'ah, one of the Levites, the first-born 1
15:18 Benai'ah, Ma-asei'ah, Mattithi'ah, Eliph'elehu 1
21 Mattithi'ah, Eliph'elehu, Miknei'ah, O'bed-e'dom 1
16: 5 second to him were . . Jehi'el, Mattithi'ah, Eli'ab 1
25: 3 sons of Jedu'thun . . Hashabi'ah, and Mattithi'ah 1
21 Mattithi'ah, his sons and his brethren, twelve; 1
Ezr 10:43 of Nebo: Je-i'el, Mattithi'ah, Zabad, Zebi'na, Jaddai 1
Neh 8: 4 beside him stood Mattithi'ah, Shema, Anai'ah, Uri'ah 1
1Es 9:35 Of the sons of Nebo: Mattithiah, Zabad, Iddo, Joel 2

Mazzaroth 1. מַזָּרוֹת

Job 38:32 Can you lead forth the Maz'zaroth in their season 1

Me-jarkon 1. מֵי יַרְקוֹן

Jos 19:46 and Mejar'kon and Rakkon with the territory over 1

Me-zahab 1. מֵי זָהָב

Gen 36:39 the daughter of Matred, daughter of Me'zahab. 1
1Ch 1:50 daughter of Matred, the daughter of Me'zahab. 1

Mearah 1. מְעָרָה

Jos 13: 4 and Mear'ah which belongs to the Sido'nians 1

Mebunnai 1. מְבֻנַּי

2Sm 23:27 Abi-e'zer, of An'athoth, Mebun'nai the Hu'shathite 1

Mecherathite 1. מְכֵרָתִי

1Ch 11:36 Hepher the Meche'rathite, Ahi'jah the Pel'onite 1

Meconah 1. מְכֹנָה

Neh 11:28 in Ziklag, in Meco'nah and its villages 1

Medad 1. מֵידָד

Num11:26 two men remained . . the other named Medad 1
27 Eldad and Medad are prophesying in the camp. 1

Medan 1. מְדָן

Gen 25: 2 She bore him Zimran, Jokshan, Medan, Mid'ian 1
1Ch 1:32 she bore Zimran, Jokshan, Medan, Mid'ian, Ishbak 1

Mede 1. מָדַי 2. מָדַי 3. מָדַי (A) 4. Μῆδος 5. Medus

2Kg 17: 6 in Halah . . and in the cities of the Medes. 2
18:11 put them in Halah . . and in the cities of the Medes 2
Est 1:19 among the laws of the Persians and the Medes 2
Isa 13:17 Behold, I am stirring up the Medes against them 2
Jer 51:11 stirred up the spirit of the kings of the Medes 2
28 the kings of the Medes, with their governors 2
Dan 5:28 kingdom is . . given to the Medes and Persians. 3
31 Darius the Mede received the kingdom, 3
6: 8 law of the Medes and the Persians, 3
12 according to the law of the Medes and Persians 3
15 law of the Medes and Persians that no interdict 3
9: 1 Darius . . by birth a Mede, who became king 2
11: 1 as for me, in the first year of Darius the Mede 1
Act 2: 9 Par'thians and Medes and E'lamites 4
2Es 1: 3 who was a captive in the country of the Medes 5
Jdt 1: 1 who ruled over the Medes in Ecbatana– 4
16:10 the Medes were daunted at her daring. 4
1Mc 1: 1 Darius, king of the Persians and the Medes 4

Medeba 1. מֵידְבָא 2. Μηδαβα

Num21:30 we laid waste until fire spread to Med'eba. 1
Jos 13: 9 and all the tableland of Med'eba as far as Dibon; 1
16 and all the tableland by Med'eba; 1
1Ch 19: 7 who came and encamped before Med'eba. 1
Isa 15: 2 over Nebo and over Med'eba Moab wails. 1
1Mc 9:36 the sons of Jambri from Medeba came out 2

Media 1. מָדַי 2. מָדַי (A) 3. Μηδια

Ezr 6: 2 Ecbat'ana, the capital which is in . . Media 2
Est 1: 3 and servants, the army chiefs of Persia and Media 1
14 the seven princes of Persia and Media 1
18 the ladies of Persia and Media who have heard 1
10: 2 the Chronicles of the kings of Media and Persia? 1
Isa 21: 2 Go up, O Elam, lay siege, O Media; 1
Jer 25:25 all the kings of Elam, and all the kings of Media; 1
Dan 8:20 these are the kings of Media and Persia. 1
1Es 3: 1 all the nobles of Media and Persia 3
14 summoned all the nobles of Persia and Media 3
6:23 the fortress which is in the country of Media 3
Tob 1:14 I used to go into Media 3
14 once at Rages in Media 3
15 I could no longer go into Media. 3
3: 7 On the same day, at Ecbatana in Media 3
4: 1 left in trust with Gabael at Rages in Media 3
20 Gabael the son of Gabrias at Rages in Media. 3
5: 5 Can you go with me to Rages in Media? 3
9: 2 go to Gabael at Rages in Media and get the money 3
11:15 great things that had happened to him in Media. 3
14: 4 Go to Media, my son 3
4 in Media there will be peace for a time. 3
14 He died in Ecbatana of Media 3
1Mc 6:56 returned from Persia and Media with the forces 3
8: 8 the country of India and Media and Lydia 3
14: 1 marched into Media to secure help 3
2 When Arsaces the king of Persia and Media heard 3

Megiddo 1. מְגִדּוֹ 2. מְגִדּוֹן 3. Μαγεδδαων

Jos 12:21 the king of Ta'anach, one; the king of Megid'do, one; 1
17:11 and the inhabitants of Megid'do and its villages; 1
Jdg 1:27 drive out . . or the inhabitants of Megid'do 1
5:19 fought . . at Ta'anach, by the waters of Megid'do 1
1Kg 4:12 Ba'ana . . in Ta'anach, Megid'do, and all Beth-she'an 1
9:15 to build . . Hazor and Megid'do and Gezer 1
2Kg 9:27 And he fled to Megid'do, and died there. 1
23:29 Pharaoh Neco slew him at Megid'do, when he saw 1
30 his servants carried him dead . . from Megid'do 1
1Ch 7:29 Megid'do and its towns, Dor and its towns. 1
2Ch 35:22 but joined battle in the plain of Megid'do. 1
Zec 12:11 for Hadadrim'mon in the plain of Megid'do. 2
1Es 1:29 He joined battle with him in the plain of Megiddo 3

Mehanaim 1. מַחֲנַיִם

Jos 21:38 Mehana'im with its pasture lands 1

Mehetabel 1. מְהֵיטַבְאֵל

Gen 36:39 his wife's name was Mehet'abel 1
1Ch 1:50 his wife's name Mehet'abel the daughter of Matred 1
Neh 6:10 Shemai'ah the son of Delai'ah, son of Mehet'abel 1

Mehida 1. מְחִידָא 2. Μεεδδα

Ezr 2:52 sons of Bazluth, the sons of Mehi'da 1
Neh 7:54 sons of Bazlith, the sons of Mehi'da 1
1Es 5:32 the sons of Mehida, the sons of Cutha 2

Mehir 1. מְחִיר

1Ch 4:11 Chelub . . was the father of Mehir 1

Meholathite 1. מְחֹלָתִי

1Sm 18:19 she was given to A'driel the Meho'lathite 1
2Sm 21: 8 to A'driel the son of Barzil'lai the Meho'lathite; 1

Mehujael 1. מְחוּיָאֵל

Gen 4:18 and Irad was the father of Me-hu'ja-el 1
18 and Me-hu'ja-el the father of Me-thu'sha-el 1

Mehuman 1. מְהוּמָן

Est 1:10 he commanded Mehu'man, Biztha, Harbo'na, Bigtha 1

Melatiah 1. מְלַטְיָה

Neh 3: 7 repaired Melati'ah the Gib'eonite and Jadon 1

Melchi 1. Μελχί

Lke 3:24 the son of Levi, the son of Melchi 1
28 the son of Melchi, the son of Addi, the son of Cosam 1

Melchi-zedek 1. מַלְכִּי צֶדֶק

Gen 14:18 Mel-chiz'edek king of Salem brought out bread 1
Ps 110: 4 priest for ever after the order of Melchiz'edek. 1

Melchias 1. Μελχιας

1Es 9:32 Elionas and Asaias and Melchias and Sabbaias 1

Melchiel 1. Μελχιηλ

Jdt 6:15 Charmis the son of Melchiel. 1

Melchizedek 1. Μελχισέδεκ

Heb 5: 6 a priest for ever, after the order of Melchiz'edek. 1
10 a high priest after the order of Melchiz'edek. 1
6:20 after the order of Melchiz'edek. 1
7: 1 For this Melchiz'edek, king of Salem 1
10 when Melchiz'edek met him. 1
11 after the order of Melchiz'edek 1
15 in the likeness of Melchiz'edek 1
17 a priest for ever, after the order of Melchiz'edek. 1

Melea 1. Μελεά

Lke 3:31 the son of Me'le-a, the son of Menna 1

Melech 1. מֶלֶךְ

1Ch 8:35 The sons of Micah: Pithon, Melech, Tare'a, and Ahaz. 1
9:41 sons of Micah: Pithon, Melech, Tahr'e-a, and Ahaz 1

Memmius 1. Μεμμιος

2Mc 11:34 Quintus Memmius and Titus Manius 1

Memphis 1. מֹף 2. נֹף 3. Μεμφις

Isa 19:13 and the princes of Memphis are deluded; 2
Jer 2:16 the men of Memphis . . have broken the crown 2
44: 1 land of Egypt, at Migdol, at Tah'panhes, at Memphis 2
46:14 proclaim in Memphis and Tah'panhes; 2
19 For Memphis shall become a waste, a ruin 2
Ezk 30:13 and put an end to the images, in Memphis; 2
Hos 9: 6 Memphis shall bury them. 1
Jdt 1:10 even beyond Tanis and Memphis 3

Memucan 1. מְמוּכָן

Est 1:14 Adma'tha, Tarshish, Meres, Marse'na, and Memu'can 1
16 Then Memu'can said in presence of the king 1
21 and the king did as Memu'can proposed; 1

Menahem 1. מְנַחֵם

2Kg 15:14 Then Men'ahem the son of Gadi came up from Tirzah 1
16 Men'ahem sacked Tappuah and all who were in it 1
17 Men'ahem the son of Gadi began to reign 1
19 Men'ahem gave Pul 1,000 talents of silver 1
20 Men'ahem exacted the money from Israel 1
21 the rest of the deeds of Men'ahem, and all . . he did 1
22 And Men'ahem slept with his fathers 1
23 Pekahi'ah the son of Men'ahem began to reign 1

Menelaus 1. Μενελαος

2Mc 4:23 Jason sent Menelaus 1
27 Menelaus held the office 1
29 Menelaus left . . Lysimachus as deputy 1
32 Menelaus . . stole some of the gold vessels 1
34 Therefore Menelaus . . urged him to kill Onias. 1
39 by Lysimachus with the connivance of Menelaus 1
43 Charges were brought against Menelaus 1
45 Menelaus . . promised a substantial bribe 1
47 Menelaus, the cause of all the evil, he acquitted 1
50 Menelaus . . remained in office 1
5: 5 Menelaus took refuge in the citadel. 1
15 guided by Menelaus, who had become a traitor 1
23 besides these Menelaus 1
11:29 Menelaus has informed us that . . 1
32 I have also sent Menelaus to encourage you. 1
13: 3 Menelaus also joined them 1
7 it came about that Menelaus the lawbreaker died 1

Menestheus 1. Μενεσθευς 2. Mnestheus

2Mc 4: 4 Apollonius, the son of Menestheus 2
21 Apollonius the son of Menestheus 1

Menna 1. Μεννά

Lke 3:31 the son of Me'le-a, the son of Menna 1

Menuhoth 1. מְנֻחוֹת

1Ch 2:52 other sons: Haro'eh, half of the Menu'hoth. 1

Meonothai 1. מְעוֹנֹתַי 2. Μαωναθει

1Ch 4:13 and the sons of Oth'ni-el: Hathath and Meo'nothai. 2
14 Meo'nothai was the father of Ophrah; 1

Mephaath 1. מֵיפַעַת

Jos 13:18 Jahaz, and Ked'emoth, and Meph'aath 1
21:37 and Meph'a-ath with its pasture lands 1
1Ch 6:79 and Meph'a-ath with its pasture lands; 1
Jer 48:21 tableland, upon Holon, and Jahzah, and Meph'a-ath 1

Mephibosheth 1. מְפִיבֹשֶׁת

2Sm 4: 4 and became lame. And his name was Mephib'osheth. 1
9: 6 Mephib'osheth the son of Jonathan, son of Saul 1
6 And David said, "Mephib'osheth! 1
10 Mephib'osheth . . shall always eat at my table. 1
11 Mephib'osheth ate at David's table 1
12 Mephib'osheth had a young son, whose name was 1
12 all who . . became Mephib'osheth's servants. 1
13 Mephib'osheth dwelt in Jerusalem; 1
16: 1 Ziba the servant of Mephib'osheth met him 1
4 all that belonged to Mephib'osheth is now yours. 1
19:24 And Mephib'osheth . . came down to meet the king; 1
25 Why did you not go with me, Mephib'osheth? 1
30 Mephib'osheth said to the king, "Oh, let him take it 1
21: 7 But the king spared Mephib'osheth 1
8 two sons of Rizpah . . Armo'ni and Mephib'osheth; 1

Merab 1. מֵרַב

1Sm 14:49 the name of the first-born was Merab 1
18:17 Here is my elder daughter Merab; I will give her 1
19 when Merab . . should have been given to David 1
2Sm 21: 8 and the five sons of Merab the daughter of Saul 1

Meraiah 1. מְרָיָהוּ

Neh 12:12 heads of fathers' houses: of Serai'ah, Merai'ah; 1

Meraioth 1. מְרָיוֹת 2. Marimoth

1Ch 6: 6 Uzzi of Zerahi'ah, Zerahi'ah of Merai'oth 1
7 Merai'oth of Amari'ah, Amari'ah of Ahi'tub 1
52 Merai'oth his son, Amari'ah his son, Ahi'tub his son 1
9:11 son of Zadok, son of Merai'oth, son of Ahi'tub 1
Ezr 7: 3 son of Amari'ah, son of Azari'ah, son of Merai'oth 1
Neh 11:11 Meshul'lam, son of Zadok, son of Merai'oth 1
12:15 of Harim, Adna; of Merai'oth, Hel'kai; 1
2Es 1: 2 son of Meraioth, son of Arna, son of Uzzi 2

Merari 1. מְרָרִי 2. Μεραρι

Gen 46:11 The sons of Levi: Gershon, Kohath, and Merar'i. 1
Exd 6:16 sons of Levi . . Gershon, Kohath, and Merar'i 1
19 The sons of Merar'i: Mahli and Mushi. 1
Num 3:17 sons of Levi . . Gershon and Kohath and Merar'i. 1
20 the sons of Merar'i by their families 1
33 Of Merar'i were the family of the Mahlites 1
33 these are the families of Merar'i. 1
35 fathers' house of the families of Merar'i 1
36 the appointed charge of the sons of Merar'i 1
4:29 As for the sons of Merar'i, you shall number them 1
33 service of the families of the sons of Merar'i 1
42 The number of the families of the sons of Merar'i 1
45 numbered of the families of the sons of Merar'i 1
7: 8 gave to the sons of Merar'i 1
10:17 sons of Gershon and the sons of Merar'i 1
26:57 of Merar'i, the family of the Merar'ites. 1
1Ch 6: 1 The sons of Levi: Gershom, Kohath, and Merar'i. 1
16 The sons of Levi: Gershom, Kohath, and Merar'i. 1
19 The sons of Merar'i: Mahli and Mushi. 1
29 sons of Merar'i: Mahli, Libni his son, Shim'e-i 1
44 their brethren the sons of Merar'i: Ethan 1
47 son of Mahli, son of Mushi, son of Merar'i, son of Levi; 1
9:14 Azri'kam, son of Hashabi'ah, of the sons of Merar'i; 1
15: 6 of the sons of Merar'i, Asai'ah the chief 1
17 of the sons of Merar'i, their brethren, Ethan 1
23: 6 the sons of Levi: Gershom, Kohath, and Merar'i. 1
21 The sons of Merar'i: Mahli and Mushi. 1
24:26 The sons of Merar'i: Mahli and Mushi. 1
27 sons of Merar'i: of Ja-azi'ah, Beno, Shoham, Zaccur 1
26:10 Hosah, of the sons of Merar'i, had sons 1
19 among the Ko'rahites and the sons of Merar'i. 1
2Ch 29:12 Levites arose . . of the sons of Merar'i, 1
34:12 Jahath and Obadi'ah . . of the sons of Merar'i 1
Ezr 8:19 Hashabi'ah and . . Jeshai'ah of the sons of Merar'i 1
Jdt 8: 1 the daughter of Merari the son of Ox, son of Joseph 2
16: 7 Judith the daughter of Merari undid him 2

Merarite 1. בֶּן מְרָרִי 2. מְרָרִי

Num26:57 of Merar'i, the family of the Merar'ites. 2
Jos 21: 7 Merar'ites . . received from the tribe of Reuben 1
34 the rest of the Levites, the Merar'ite families 1
40 the cities of the several Merar'ite families 1
1Ch 6:63 the Merar'ites . . were allotted twelve cities 2
77 To the rest of the Merar'ites were allotted 2

Merathaim 1. מְרָתַיִם

Jer 50:21 Go up against the land of Meratha'im 1

Mered 1. מֶרֶד

1Ch 4:17 The sons of Ezrah: Jether, Mered, Epher, and Jalon. 1
17 Bith'i-ah . . whom Mered married; 1

Meremoth 1. מְרֵמוֹת 2. Μαρμωθι

Ezr 8:33 weighed into the hands of Mer'emoth the priest 1
10:36 Vani'ah, Mer'emoth, Eli'ashib 1
Neh 3: 4 next to them Mer'emoth the son of Uri'ah 1
21 After him Mer'emoth the son of Uri'ah, son of Hakkoz 1
10: 5 Harim, Mer'emoth, Obadi'ah 1
12: 3 Shecani'ah, Rehum, Mer'emoth. 1
1Es 8:62 Meremoth the priest, son of Uriah; 2

Meres 1. מֶרֶס

Est 1:14 Adma'tha, Tarshish, Meres, Marse'na, and Memu'can 1

Merib-baal 1. מְרִיב בַּעַל 2. מְרִי בַעַל

1Ch 8:34 the son of Jonathan was Mer'ib-ba'al; 1
34 Mer'ib-ba'al was the father of Micah. 1
9:40 the son of Jonathan was Mer'ib-ba'al; 1
40 Mer'ib-ba'al was the father of Micah. 2

Meribah 1. מְרִיבָה

Exd 17: 7 called the name of the place Massah and Mer'ibah 1
Num20:13 These are the waters of Mer'ibah, where the people 1
24 against my command at the waters of Mer'ibah. 1
27:14 (These are the waters of Mer'ibah of Kadesh 1
Deu 33: 8 whom thou didst strive at the waters of Mer'ibah; 1
Ps 81: 7 I tested you at the waters of Mer'ibah. Selah 1
95: 8 Harden not your hearts, as at Mer'ibah, as on the day 1
106:32 They angered him at the waters of Mer'ibah 1

Meribath-kadesh 1. מְרִיבַת קָדֵשׁ

Deu 32:51 broke faith . . at the waters of Mer'i-bath-ka'desh 1
Ezk 47:19 as far as the waters of Meribath-ka'desh 1
48:28 from Tamar to the waters of Meribath-ka'desh 1

Merodach 1. מְרֹדָךְ

Jer 50: 2 Bel is put to shame, Mer'odach is dismayed. 1

Merodach-baladan 1. מְרֹדַךְ בַּלְאֲדָן

2Kg 20:12 At that time Mero'dach-bal'adan . . sent envoys 1
Isa 39: 1 At that time Mer'odach-bal'adan the son of Bal'adan 1

Merom 1. מֵרוֹם

Jos 11: 5 and encamped together at the waters of Merom 1
7 Joshua came suddenly . . by the waters of Merom 1

Meronothite 1. מֵרֹנֹתִי

1Ch 27:30 the she-asses was Jehde'iah the Meron'othite. 1
Neh 3: 7 repaired Melati'ah . . and Jadon the Mero'nothite 1

Meroz 1. מֵרוֹז

Jdg 5:23 Curse Meroz, says the angel of the LORD 1

Merran 1. Μερραν

Bar 3:23 merchants of Merran and Teman, the story-tellers 1

Mesaloth 1. Μαισαλωθ

1Mc 9: 2 encamped against Mesaloth in Arbela 1

Mesha 1. מֵישָׁא 2. מֵישַׁע 3. מֵשָׁא

Gen 10:30 extended from Mesha in the direction of Sephar 3
2Kg 3: 4 Now Mesha king of Moab was a sheep breeder; 2
1Ch 8: 9 sons by Hodesh his wife: Jobab, Zib'i-a, Mesha, 1

Meshach 1. מֵישַׁךְ 2. מֵישַׁךְ (A)
Dan 1: 7 Mish'a-el he called Meshach 1
2:49 appointed Shadrach, Meshach, and Abed'nego. 2
3:12 Shadrach, Meshach, and Abed'nego. These men 2
13 commanded that Shadrach, Meshach, and Abed'nego 2
14 Is it true, O Shadrach, Meshach, and Abed'nego 2
16 Shadrach, Meshach, and Abed'nego answered 2
19 against Shadrach, Meshach, and Abed'nego. 2
20 bind Shadrach, Meshach, and Abed'nego, and to cast 2
22 men who took up Shadrach, Meshach, and Abed'nego. 2
23 these three men, Shadrach, Meshach, and Abed'nego 2
26 Shadrach, Meshach, and Abed'nego, servants 2
26 Then Shadrach, Meshach, and Abed'nego came out 2
28 Blessed be the God of Shadrach, Meshach 2
29 God of Shadrach, Meshach, and Abed'nego 2
30 king promoted Shadrach, Meshach, and Abed'nego 2

Meshech 1. מֶשֶׁךְ
Gen 10: 2 Magog, Madai, Javan, Tubal, Meshech, and Tiras. 1
1Ch 1: 5 sons of Japheth . . Tubal, Meshech, and Tiras. 1
17 The sons of Shem: Elam . . Hul, Gether, and Meshech. 1
Ps 120: 5 Woe is me, that I sojourn in Meshech 1
Ezk 27:13 Javan, Tubal, and Meshech traded with you; 1
32:26 Meshech and Tubal are there 1
38: 2 of Magog, the chief prince of Meshech and Tubal 1
3 O Gog, chief prince of Meshech and Tubal; 1
39: 1 O Gog, chief prince of Meshech and Tubal; 1

Meshelemiah 1. מְשֶׁלֶמְיָהוּ
1Ch 9:21 Zechari'ah the son of Meshelemi'ah 1
26: 1 of the Ko'rahites, Meshelemi'ah the son of Ko're 1
2 Meshelemi'ah had sons: Zechari'ah the first-born 1
9 Meshelemi'ah had sons and brethren, able men 1

Meshezabel 1. מְשֵׁיזַבְאֵל
Neh 3: 4 son of Berechi'ah, son of Meshez'abel repaired. 1
10:21 Meshez'abel, Zadok, Jad'du-a 1
11:24 Pethahi'ah the son of Meshez'abel, of the sons 1

Meshillemith 1. מְשִׁלֵּמִית
1Ch 9:12 Jah'zerah, son of Meshul'lam, son of Meshil'lemith 1

Meshillemoth 1. מְשִׁלֵּמוֹת
2Ch 28:12 chiefs . . Berechi'ah the son of Meshil'lemoth 1
Neh 11:13 son of Ah'zai, son of Meshil'lemoth, son of Immer 1

Meshobab 1. מְשׁוֹבָב
1Ch 4:34 Mesho'bab, Jamlech, Joshah the son of Amazi'ah 1

Meshullam 1. מְשֻׁלָּם 2. Μοσολλαμος 3. Ωλαμος
2Kg 22: 3 sent Shaphan the son of Azali'ah, son of Meshul'lam 1
1Ch 3:19 the sons of Zerub'babel: Meshul'lam and Hanani'ah 1
5:13 Michael, Meshul'lam, Sheba, Jo'rai, Jacan, Zi'a 1
8:17 Zebadi'ah, Meshul'lam, Hizki, Heber 1
9: 7 Of the Benjaminites: Sallu the son of Meshul'lam 1
8 Meshul'lam the son of Shephati'ah, son of Reu'el 1
11 Azari'ah the son of Hilki'ah, son of Meshul'lam 1
12 Jah'zerah, son of Meshul'lam, son of Meshil'lemith 1
2Ch 34:12 Zechari'ah and Meshul'lam, of . . the Ko'hathites 1
Ezr 8:16 Then I sent for . . Zechari'ah, and Meshul'lam 1
10:15 Meshul'lam and Shab'bethai the Levite supported 1
29 of Bani were Meshul'lam, Malluch, Adai'ah, Jashub 1
Neh 3: 4 next to them Meshul'lam the son of Berechi'ah 1
6 Joi'ada . . and Meshul'lam the son of Besodei'ah 1
30 Meshul'lam the son of Berechi'ah repaired 1
6:18 Jehoha'nan had taken the daughter of Meshul'lam 1
8: 4 Zechari'ah, and Meshul'lam on his left hand. 1
10: 7 Meshul'lam, Abi'jah, Mi'jamin 1
20 Mag'piash, Meshul'lam, He-zir 1
11: 7 Sallu the son of Meshul'lam, son of Jo'ed 1
11 Serai'ah the son of Hilki'ah, son of Meshul'lam 1
12:13 of Ezra, Meshul'lam; of Amari'ah, Jehoha'nan; 1
16 of Iddo, Zechari'ah; of Gin'nethon, Meshul'lam; 1
25 Bakbuki'ah, Obadi'ah, Meshul'lam, Talmon, 1
33 Azari'ah, Ezra, Meshul'lam 1
1Es 8:44 Nathan, Elnathan, Zechariah, and Meshullam 2
9:14 Meshullam and Levi and Shabbethai 2
30 Of the sons of Bani: Meshullam, Malluch, Adaiah 3

Meshullemeth 1. מְשֻׁלֶּמֶת
2Kg 21:19 His mother's name was Meshul'lemeth 1

Mesopotamia 1. אֲרַם 2. אֲרַם נַהֲרַיִם
3. Μεσοποταμία
Gen 24:10 and he arose, and went to Mesopota'mia 2
Deu 23: 4 Balaam . . of Be'or from Pethor of Mesopota'mia 2
Jdg 3: 8 hand of Cu'shan-rishatha'im king of Mesopota'mia; 2
10 Cu'shan-rishatha'im king of Mesopota'mia into his 1
1Ch 19: 6 to hire chariots and horsemen from Mesopota'mia 2
Act 2: 9 E'lamites and residents of Mesopota'mia 3
7: 2 our father Abraham, when he was in Mesopota'mia 3
Jdt 2:24 and passed through Mesopotamia 3
5: 7 At one time they lived in Mesopotamia 3
8 they fled to Mesopotamia 3
8:26 what happened to Jacob in Mesopotamia in Syria 3

Messiah 1. Μεσσίας 2. christus 3. ungo
Joh 1:41 We have found the Messiah" (which means Christ). 1
4:25 I know that Messiah is coming 1
2Es 7:28 For my son the Messiah shall be revealed ‡
29 after these years my son the Messiah shall die 2
12:32 this is the Messiah whom the Most High has kept 3

Metheg-ammah 1. מֶתֶג אַמָּה
2Sm 8: 1 David took Meth'eg-am'mah out of the hand 1

Methuselah 1. מְתוּשֶׁלַח 2. Μαθουσάλα
Gen 5:21 he became the father of Methu'selah. 1
22 walked with God after the birth of Methu'selah 1
25 When Methu'selah had lived 187 years 1
26 Methu'selah lived after the birth of Lamech 1
27 Thus all the days of Methu'selah were 969 years; 1
1Ch 1: 3 Enoch, Me-thu'selah, Lamech; 1
Lke 3:37 the son of Methuselah, the son of Enoch 2

Methushael 1. מְתוּשָׁאֵל
Gen 4:18 and Me-hu'ja-el the father of Me-thu'sha-el 1
18 and Me-thu'sha-el the father of Lamech. 1

Meunim 1. מְעוּנִים
1Ch 4:41 destroyed . . the Me-u'nim who were found there 1
Ezr 2:50 sons of Asnah, the sons of Me-u'nim 1
Neh 7:52 sons of Besai, the sons of Me-u'nim 1

Meunite 1. מְעוּנִים 2. Μαανι
2Ch 20: 1 with them some of the Me-u'nites •
26: 7 God helped him . . against the Me-u'nites. 1
1Es 5:31 the sons of the Meunites, the sons of Nephisim 2

Mezobaite 1. מְצֹבָיָה
1Ch 11:47 Eli'el, and Obed, and Ja-asi'el the Mezo'ba-ite. 1

Mibhar 1. מִבְחָר
1Ch 11:38 Mibhar the son of Hagri 1

Mibsam 1. מִבְשָׂם
Gen 25:13 first-born of Ish'mael; and Kedar, Adbeel, Mibsam 1
1Ch 1:29 Ish'mael, Neba'ioth; and Kedar, Adbeel, Mibsam 1
4:25 Shallum . . Mibsam his son, Mishma his son. 1

Mibzar 1. מִבְצָר
Gen 36:42 Kenaz, Teman, Mibzar 1
1Ch 1:53 Kenaz, Teman, Mibzar 1

Mica 1. מִיכָא 2. מִיכָה
2Sm 9:12 Mephib'osheth had a . . son, whose name was Mica. 1
1Ch 9:15 Mattani'ah the son of Mica, son of Zichri 1
Neh 10:11 Mica, Rehob, Hashabi'ah 1
11:17 Mattani'ah the son of Mica, son of Zabdi 2
22 son of Mattani'ah, son of Mica, of the sons of Asaph 1

Micah 1. מִיכָה 2. מִיכָיְהוּ 3. Μιχα 4. Micha
Jdg 17: 1 was a man of . . E'phraim, whose name was Micah. 2
4 a molten image; and it was in the house of Micah. 2
5 the man Micah had a shrine, and he made an ephod 1
8 hill country of E'phraim to the house of Micah. 1
9 Micah said to him, "From where do you come? 1
10 Micah said to him, "Stay with me, and be . . a father 1
12 Micah installed the Levite, and the young man 1
12 became his priest, and was in the house of Micah. 1
13 Then Micah said, "Now I know that the LORD will 1
18: 2 they came to . . E'phraim, to the house of Micah 1
3 When they were by the house of Micah 1
4 thus has Micah dealt with me: he has hired me 1
13 they passed on . . and came to the house of Micah. 1
15 the house of the young Levite, at the home of Micah 1
18 when these went into Micah's house and took 1
22 When they were a good way from the home of Micah 1
22 the men who were in the houses near Micah's house 1
23 Danites, who turned round and said to Micah 1
26 when Micah saw that they were too strong for him 1
27 taking what Micah had made, and the priest who 1
31 they set up Micah's graven image which he made 1
1Ch 5: 5 Micah his son, Re-ai'ah his son, Ba'al his son 1
8:34 Mer'ib-ba'al was the father of Micah. 1
35 The sons of Micah: Pithon, Melech, Tare'a, and Ahaz. 1
9:40 Mer'ib-ba'al was the father of Micah. 1
41 sons of Micah: Pithon, Melech, Tahr'e-a, and Ahaz 1
23:20 The sons of Uz'ziel: Micah the chief 1
24:24 sons of Uz'ziel, Micah; of the sons of Micah, Shamir. 1
24 sons of Uz'ziel, Micah; of the sons of Micah, Shamir. 1
25 The brother of Micah, Isshi'ah; 1
2Ch 34:20 king commanded . . Abdon the son of Micah 1
Jer 26:18 Micah . . prophesied in the days of Hezeki'ah 1
Mic 1: 1 The word of the LORD that came to Micah 1
2Es 1:39 Jacob and Hosea and Amos and Micah and Joel 4
Jdt 6:15 Uzziah the son of Micah, of the tribe of Simeon 3

Micaiah 1. מִיכָה 2. מִיכָיָה 3. מִיכָיְהוּ 4. מִיכָיְהוּ
5. מִכָיְהוּ 6. Μιχαιας
1Kg 22: 8 by whom we may inquire . . Micai'ah the son of Imlah; 4
9 and said, "Bring quickly Micai'ah the son of Imlah. 4
13 the messenger who went to summon Micai'ah said 4
14 Micai'ah said, "As the LORD lives . . that I will 4
15 Micai'ah, shall we go to Ramoth-gilead to battle 4
19 Micai'ah said, "Therefore hear the word of the LORD 6
24 came near and struck Micai'ah on the cheek 4
25 Micai'ah said, "Behold, you shall see on that day 4
26 Seize Micai'ah, and take him back to Amon 4
28 Micai'ah said, "If you return . . the LORD has not 4
2Kg 22:12 Ahi'kam the son of . . and Achbor the son of Micai'ah 4
2Ch 13: 2 mother's name was Micai'ah the daughter of U'riel 3
17: 7 he sent his princes . . Nethan'el, and Micai'ah 3
18: 7 man by whom we may inquire of the LORD, Micai'ah 4
8 Bring quickly Micai'ah the son of Imlah. 4
12 messenger who went to summon Micai'ah said to him 4
13 Micai'ah said, "As the LORD lives, what my God says 4
14 Micai'ah, shall we go to Ramoth-gilead to battle 1
18 Micai'ah said, "Therefore hear the word of the LORD •
23 Then Zedeki'ah . . came near and struck Micai'ah 4
24 Micai'ah said, "Behold, you shall see on that day 4
25 Seize Micai'ah, and take him back to Amon 4
27 Micai'ah said, "If you return in peace 4
Neh 12:35 Shemai'ah, son of Mattani'ah, son of Micai'ah, 2
41 priests Eli'akim, Ma-asei'ah, Mini'amin, Micai'ah 2
Jer 36:11 When Micai'ah the son of Gemari'ah, son of Shaphan 5
13 Micai'ah told them all the words that he had heard 5

Michael 1. מִיכָאֵל 2. Μιχαήλ 3. Μιχαηλος
Num13:13 from the tribe of Asher, Sethur the son of Michael; 1
1Ch 5:13 Michael, Meshul'lam, Sheba, Jo'rai, Jacan, Zi'a 1
14 sons of Ab'ihail . . son of Gilead, son of Michael 1
6:40 son of Michael, son of Ba-ase'iah, son of Malchi'jah 1
7: 3 sons of Izrahi'ah: Michael, Obadi'ah, Jo'el 1
8:16 Michael, Ishpah, and Joha were sons of Beri'ah. 1
12:20 men of Manas'seh . . Michael, Joz'abad, Eli'hu 1
27:18 for Is'sachar, Omri the son of Michael; 1
2Ch 21: 2 sons of Jehosh'aphat . . Azari'ah, Michael 1
Ezr 8: 8 sons of Shephati'ah, Zebadi'ah the son of Michael 1
Dan 10:13 but Michael, one of the chief princes, came to help 1
21 none who contends . . except Michael 1
12: 1 time shall arise Michael, the great prince 1
Jde 1: 9 archangel Michael, contending with the devil 2
Rev 12: 7 Michael and his angels fighting . . the dragon; 2
1Es 8:34 Zeraiah the son of Michael 3

Michal 1. מִיכַל
1Sm 14:49 and the name of the younger Michal; 1
18:20 Now Saul's daughter Michal loved David; 1
27 And Saul gave him his daughter Michal for a wife. 1
19:11 But Michal, David's wife, told him, "If you do not save 1
12 So Michal let David down through the window; 1
13 Michal took an image and laid it on the bed 1
17 Saul said to Michal, "Why have you deceived me thus 1
17 And Michal answered Saul, "He said to me, 'Let me go; 1
25:44 Saul had given Michal his daughter . . to Palti 1
2Sm 3:13 not see my face, unless you first bring Michal 1
14 Give me my wife Michal, whom I betrothed 1
6:16 Michal the daughter of Saul looked out 1
20 But Michal . . came out to meet David, and said 1
21 And David said to Michal, "It was before the LORD 1
23 And Michal the daughter of Saul had no child 1
1Ch 15:29 Michal the daughter of Saul looked out 1

Michmas 1. מִכְמָס 2. Μακαλων
Ezr 2:27 men of Michmas, 122. 1
Neh 7:31 men of Michmas, 122. 1
1Es 5:21 The men of Michmas, 122. The men of Bethel, 52. 2

Michmash 1. מִכְמָשׂ 2. Μαχμας
1Sm 13: 2 2,000 were with Saul in Michmash 1
5 they came up and encamped in Michmash 1
11 the Philistines had mustered at Michmash 1
16 but the Philistines encamped at Michmash. 1
23 Philistines went out to the pass of Michmash. 1
14: 5 one crag rose on the north in front of Michmash 1
31 They struck down . . from Michmash to Ai'jalon. 1
Neh 11:31 Michmash, Ai'ja, Bethel and its villages 1
Isa 10:28 at Michmash he stores his baggage; 1
1Mc 9:73 Jonathan dwelt in Michmash 2

Michmethath 1. מִכְמְתָת
Jos 16: 6 the boundary . . on the north is Mich-me'thath; 1
17: 7 Manas'seh reached from Asher to Mich-me'thath 1

Michri 1. מִכְרִי
1Ch 9: 8 Elah the son of Uzzi, son of Michri 1

Middin 1. מִדִּין
Jos 15:61 In the wilderness, Beth-arabah, Middin, Seca'cah 1

Midian 1. מִדְיָן 2. Μαδιάμ
Gen 25: 2 She bore him Zimran, Jokshan, Medan, Mid'ian 1
4 sons of Mid'ian were Ephah, Epher, Hanoch 1
36:35 Hadad . . who defeated Mid'ian in the country 1
Exd 2:15 Moses fled . . and stayed in the land of Mid'ian; 1
16 Now the priest of Mid'ian had seven daughters; 1
3: 1 his father-in-law, Jethro, the priest of Mid'ian; 1
4:19 the LORD said to Moses in Mid'ian, "Go back to Egypt; 1
18: 1 Jethro, the priest of Mid'ian, Moses' father-in-law 1
Num22: 4 Moab said to the elders of Mid'ian, "This horde 1
7 elders of Moab and the elders of Mid'ian departed 1
25:15 head of the people of a fathers' house in Mid'ian. 1
18 Cozbi, the daughter of the prince of Mid'ian 1
31: 3 Arm men . . that they may go against Mid'ian 1

3 to execute the LORD'S vengeance on Mid'ian. 1
7 warred against Mid'ian, as the LORD commanded 1
8 slew the kings of Mid'ian with the rest of their 1
8 Evi . . Hur, and Reba, the five kings of Mid'ian; 1
9 Israel took captive the women of Mid'ian 1
Jos 13:21 whom Moses defeated with the leaders of Mid'ian 1
Jdg 6: 1 the LORD gave them into the hand of Mid'ian 1
2 And the hand of Mid'ian prevailed over Israel; 1
2 because of Mid'ian the people of Israel made 1
6 Israel was brought very low because of Mid'ian; 1
13 cast us off, and given us into the hand of Mid'ian. 1
14 Go . . and deliver Israel from the hand of Mid'ian; 1
7: 1 the camp of Mid'ian was north of them, by the hill 1
8 the camp of Mid'ian was below him in the valley. 1
13 of barley bread tumbled into the camp of Mid'ian 1
14 his hand God has given Mid'ian and all the host. 1
15 LORD has given the host of Mid'ian into your hand. 1
23 called out . . and they pursued after Mid'ian. 1
25 they took the two princes of Mid'ian, Oreb and Zeeb; 1
25 at the wine press of Zeeb, as they pursued Mid'ian; 1
8: 1 not to call us when you went to fight with Mid'ian? 1
3 has given into your hands the princes of Mid'ian 1
5 after Zebah and Zalmun'na, the kings of Mid'ian. 1
12 took the two kings of Mid'ian, Zebah and Zalmun'na 1
22 you have delivered us out of the hand of Mid'ian. 1
26 the purple garments worn by the kings of Mid'ian 1
28 Mid'ian was subdued before the people of Israel 1
9:17 his life, and rescued you from the hand of Mid'ian; 1
1Kg 11:18 set out from Mid'ian and came to Paran, and took men 1
1Ch 1:32 Jokshan, Medan, Mid'ian, Ishbak, and Shu'ah. 1
33 The sons of Mid'ian: Ephah, Epher, Hanoch, Abida 1
46 who defeated Mid'ian in the country of Moab 1
Ps 83: 9 Do to them as thou didst to Mid'ian 1
Isa 9: 4 rod . . thou hast broken as on the day of Mid'ian. 1
10:26 as when he smote Mid'ian at the rock of Oreb; 1
60: 6 cover you, the young camels of Mid'ian and Ephah; 1
Hab 3: 7 the curtains of the land of Mid'ian did tremble. 1
Act 7:29 and became an exile in the land of Mid'ian 2

Midianite 1. מִדְיָן 2. מִדְיָנִי 3. υἱὸς Μαδιάμ

Gen 37:28 Then Mid'ianite traders passed by; 2
36 Meanwhile the Mid'ianites had sold him in Egypt 2
Num10:29 Hobab the son of Reu'el the Mid'ianite 2
25:15 name of the Mid'ianite woman who was slain 2
17 Harass the Mid'ianites, and smite them; 2
31: 2 Avenge the people of Israel on the Mid'ianites; 2
Jdg 6: 3 Mid'ianites and the Amal'ekites and the people 1
7 cried to the LORD on account of the Mid'ianites 1
11 in the wine press, to hide it from the Mid'ianites. 1
16 and you shall smite the Mid'ianites as one man. 1
33 all the Mid'ianites and the Amal'ekites 1
7: 2 for me to give the Mid'ianites into their hand 1
7 and give the Mid'ianites into your hand; 1
12 the Mid'ianites and the Amal'ekites and all 1
24 Come down against the Mid'ianites and seize 1
Jdt 2:26 He surrounded all the Midianites 3

Midianite woman 1. מִדְיָנִי

Num25: 6 came and brought a Mid'ianite woman to his family 1
14 man . . who was slain with the Mid'ianite woman 1

Migdal-el 1. מִגְדַּל אֵל

Jos 19:38 Yiron, Mig'dal-el, Horem, Beth-anath 1

Migdal-gad 1. מִגְדַּל גָּד

Jos 15:37 Zenan, Hadash'ah, Mig'dal-gad 1

Migdol 1. מִגְדֹּל

Exd 14: 2 encamp . . between Migdol and the sea 1
Num33: 7 set out from Etham . . encamped before Migdol. 1
Jer 44: 1 land of Egypt, at Migdol, at Tah'panhes, at Memphis 1
46:14 Declare in Egypt, and proclaim in Migdol; 1
Ezk 29:10 from Migdol to Syene, as far as the border 1
30: 6 from Migdol to Syene they shall fall within her 1

Migron 1. מִגְרוֹן

1Sm 14: 2 under the pomegranate tree which is at Migron; 1
Isa 10:28 he has come to Ai'ath; he has passed through Migron 1

Mijamin 1. מִיָּמִן 2. Μιαμινος

1Ch 24: 9 the fifth to Malchi'jah, the sixth to Mij'amin 1
Ezr 10:25 of Parosh: Rami'ah, Izzi'ah, Malchi'jah, Mi'jamin 1
Neh 10: 7 Meshul'lam, Abi'jah, Mi'jamin 1
12: 5 Mi'jamin, Ma-adi'ah, Bilgah 1
1Es 9:26 Malchijah, Mijamin, and Eleazar, and Asibias 2

Mikloth 1. מִקְלוֹת

1Ch 8:32 Mikloth (he was the father of Shime'e-ah). 1
9:37 Gedor, Ahi'o, Zechari'ah and Mikloth; 1
38 Mikloth was the father of Shim'e-am; 1

Mikneiah 1. מִקְנֵיָהוּ

1Ch 15:18 Eliph'elehu, and Miknei'ah, and the gatekeepers 1
21 Mattithi'ah, Eliph'elehu, Miknei'ah, O'bed-e'dom 1

Miktam 1. מִכְתָּם

Ps 16: 0 A Miktam of David. 1
56: 0 Miktam of David, when the Philistines seized him 1
57: 0 A Miktam of David, when he fled from Saul 1
58: 0 according to Do Not Destroy. A Miktam of David. 1
59: 0 according to Do Not Destroy. A Miktam of David 1
60: 0 according to Shushan Eduth. A Miktam of David; 1

Milalai 1. מִלֲלַי

Neh 12:36 kinsmen, Shemai'ah, Az'arel, Mil'alai, Gil'alai, Ma'ai 1

Milcah 1. מִלְכָּה

Gen 11:29 and the name of Nahor's wife, Milcah 1
29 of Haran the father of Milcah and Iscah. 1
22:20 Behold, Milcah also has borne children 1
23 These eight Milcah bore to Nahor 1
24:15 Bethu'el the son of Milcah, the wife of Nahor 1
24 the son of Milcah, whom she bore to Nahor. 1
47 Nahor's son, whom Milcah bore to him.' 1
Num26:33 daughters of Zeloph'ehad . . Milcah, and Tirzah. 1
27: 1 his daughters were . . Milcah, and Tirzah. 1
36:11 Tirzah, Hoglah, Milcah, and Noah, the daughters 1
Jos 17: 3 Mahlah, Noah, Hoglah, Milcah, and Tirzah. 1

Milcom 1. מִלְכֹּם

1Kg 11: 5 Solomon went . . after Milcom the abomination 1
33 Chemosh . . and Milcom the god of the Ammonites 1
2Kg 23:13 for Milcom the abomination of the Ammonites. 1
Jer 49: 1 Why then has Milcom dispossessed Gad 1
3 For Milcom shall go into exile, with his priests 1
Zep 1: 5 and swear to the LORD and yet swear by Milcom; 1

Miletus 1. Μίλητος

Act 20:15 the day after that we came to Mile'tus. 1
17 from Mile'tus he sent to Ephesus 1
2Ti 4:20 Troph'imus I left ill at Mile'tus. 1

Millo 1. מִלּוֹא

2Sm 5: 9 built . . round about from the Millo inward. 1
1Kg 9:15 build . . his own house and the Millo and the wall 1
24 then he built the Millo. 1
11:27 Solomon built the Millo, and closed up the breach 1
2Kg 12:20 a conspiracy, and slew Jo'ash in the house of Millo 1
1Ch 11: 8 he built the city round about from the Millo 1
2Ch 32: 5 he strengthened the Millo in the city of David. 1

Miniamin 1. מִנְיָמִן

2Ch 31:15 Eden, Mini'amin, Jeshua, Shemai'ah, Amari'ah 1
Neh 12:17 of Abi'jah, Zichri; of Mini'amin, of Moadi'ah, Pil'tai; 1
41 priests Eli'akim, Ma-asei'ah, Mini'amin, Micai'ah 1

Minni 1. מִנִּי

Jer 51:27 the kingdoms, Ar'arat, Minni, and Ash'kenaz; 1

Minnith 1. מִנִּית

Jdg 11:33 from Aro'er to the neighborhood of Minnith 1

Miriam 1. מִרְיָם

Exd 15:20 Then Miriam, the prophetess, the sister of Aaron 1
21 Miriam sang to them: "Sing to the LORD 1
Num12: 1 Miriam and Aaron spoke against Moses 1
4 LORD said to Moses and to Aaron and Miriam 1
5 LORD came down . . and called Aaron and Miriam; 1
10 behold, Miriam was leprous, as white as snow. 1
10 Aaron turned towards Miriam, and behold 1
15 Miriam was shut up outside the camp seven days; 1
15 till Miriam was brought in again. 1
20: 1 people stayed in Kadesh; and Miriam died there 1
26:59 she bore to Amram Aaron and Moses and Miriam 1
Deu 24: 9 Remember what the LORD your God did to Miriam 1
1Ch 4:17 Bith'i-ah . . conceived and bore Miriam, Sham'mai 1
6: 3 The children of Amram: Aaron, Moses, and Miriam. 1
Mic 6: 4 and I sent before you Moses, Aaron, and Miriam. 1

Mirmah 1. מִרְמָה

1Ch 8:10 Je'uz, Sachi'a, and Mirmah. 1

Mishael 1. מִישָׁאֵל 2. מִישָׁאֵל (A) 3. Μισαήλ

Exd 6:22 the sons of Uz'ziel: Mi'sha-el, Elza'phan, and Sithri. 1
Lev 10: 4 Moses called Mish'a-el and Elza'phan 1
Neh 8: 4 Pedai'ah, Mish'a-el, Malchi'jah . . on his left hand. 1
Dan 1: 6 Daniel, Hanani'ah, Mish'a-el, and Azari'ah 1
7 Mish'a-el he called Meshach 1
11 over Daniel, Hanani'ah, Mish'a-el, and Azari'ah; 1
19 like Daniel, Hanani'ah, Mish'a-el, and Azari'ah; 1
2:17 matter known to Hanani'ah, Mish'a-el, and Azari'ah 2
1Es 9:44 on his left Pedaiah, Mishael, Malchijah 3
Aza 1:66 Bless the Lord, Hananiah, Azariah, and Mishael 3
1Mc 2:59 Hannaniah, Azariah, and Mishael believed 3
4Mc 16: 3 the raging fiery furnace of Mishael 3
21 Hananiah, Azariah, and Mishael 3
18:12 he taught you about Hananiah, Azariah, and Mishael 3

Mishal 1. מִשְׁאָל

Jos 19:26 Allam'melech, Amad, and Mishal; on the west it 1
21:30 and out of . . Asher, Mishal with its pasture lands 1

Misham 1. מִשְׁעָם

1Ch 8:12 The sons of Elpa'al: Eber, Misham, and Shemed 1

Mishma 1. מִשְׁמָע

Gen 25:14 Mishma, Dumah, Massa 1
1Ch 1:30 Mishma, Dumah, Massa, Hadad, Tema 1
4:25 Shallum . . Mibsam his son, Mishma his son. 1
26 sons of Mishma: Ham'mu-el his son, Zac'cur 1

Mishmannah 1. מִשְׁמַנָּה

1Ch 12:10 Mishman'nah fourth, Jeremiah fifth 1

Mishraite 1. מִשְׁרָעִי

1Ch 2:53 the Shu'mathites, and the Mish'ra-ites; 1

Mispar 1. מִסְפָּר 2. Ασφαρασος

Ezr 2: 2 came with . . Bilshan, Mispar, Bigva'i, Rehum 1
1Es 5: 8 Resaiah, Bigvai, Mordecai, Bilshan, Mispar 2

Mispereth 1. מִסְפֶּרֶת

Neh 7: 7 came with . . Mor'decai, Bilshan, Mis'pereth, Bigva'i 1

Misrephoth-maim 1. מִשְׂרְפוֹת מַיִם

Jos 11: 8 chased them as far as . . Mis'rephoth-ma'im 1
13: 6 hill country from Lebanon to Mis'rephoth-ma'im 1

Mithkah 1. מִתְקָה

Num33:28 they set out from Terah, and encamped at Mithkah. 1
29 set out from Mithkah, and encamped at Hashmo'nah. 1

Mithnite 1. מִתְנִי

1Ch 11:43 and Josh'aphat the Mithnite 1

Mithredath 1. מִתְרְדָת

Ezr 1: 8 brought these out in charge of Mith'redath 1
4: 7 Bishlam and Mith'redath and Tab'eel and the rest 1

Mithridates 1. Μιθραδατης

1Es 2:11 he gave them to Mithridates his treasurer 1
16 Bishlam, Mithridates, Tabeel, Rehum, Beltethmus 1

Mitylene 1. Μιτυλήνη

Act 20:14 we took him on board and came to Mityle'ne. 1

Mizar 1. מִצְעָר

Ps 42: 6 land of Jordan and of Hermon, from Mount Mizar. 1

Mizpah 1. מִצְפָּה 2. Μασσηφα

Gen 31:49 the pillar Mizpah, for he said, "The LORD watch 1
Jos 11: 3 the Hivites under Hermon in the land of Mizpah. 1
Jdg 10:17 came together, and they encamped at Mizpah. 1
11:11 spoke all his words before the LORD at Mizpah. 1
29 Manas'seh, and passed on to Mizpah of Gilead 1
29 Gilead, and from Mizpah of Gilead he passed 1
34 Then Jephthah came to his home at Mizpah; 1
20: 1 assembled as one man to the LORD at Mizpah. 1
3 that the people of Israel had gone up to Mizpah. 1
21: 1 the men of Israel had sworn at Mizpah, "No one of us 1
5 him who did not come up to the LORD to Mizpah 1
8 What one . . did not come up to the LORD to Mizpah? 1
1Sm 7: 5 Gather all Israel at Mizpah, and I will pray 1
6 they gathered at Mizpah, and drew water 1
6 Samuel judged the people of Israel at Mizpah. 1
7 that the people of Israel had gathered at Mizpah 1
11 went out of Mizpah and pursued the Philistines 1
12 a stone and set it up between Mizpah and Jesha'nah 1
16 went on a circuit . . to Bethel, Gilgal, and Mizpah; 1
10:17 Samuel called the people together . . at Mizpah; 1
1Kg 15:22 King Asa built Geba of Benjamin and Mizpah. 1
2Kg 25:23 they came with their men to Gedali'ah at Mizpah 1
25 and the Chalde'ans who were with him at Mizpah. 1
2Ch 16: 6 with them he built Geba and Mizpah. 1
Neh 3: 7 repaired . . the men of Gibeon and of Mizpah 1
15 Shallum . . ruler of the district of Mizpah 1
19 next to him Ezer the son of Jeshua, ruler of Mizpah 1
Jer 40: 6 at Mizpah, and dwelt with him among the people 1
8 they went to Gedali'ah at Mizpah 1
10 As for me, I will dwell at Mizpah 1
12 came to the land of Judah, to Gedali'ah at Mizpah; 1
13 the leaders . . came to Gedali'ah at Mizpah 1
15 Joha'nan . . spoke secretly to Gedali'ah at Mizpah 1
41: 1 came . . to Gedali'ah the son of Ahi'kam, at Mizpah. 1
1 As they ate bread together there at Mizpah 1
3 slew . . the Jews who were with Gedali'ah at Mizpah 1
6 Ish'mael . . came out from Mizpah to meet them 1
10 all the rest of the people who were in Mizpah 1
10 and all the people who were left at Mizpah 1
14 Ish'mael had carried away captive from Mizpah 1
16 Ish'mael . . had carried away captive from Mizpah 1
Hos 5: 1 for you have been a snare at Mizpah 1
1Mc 3:46 So they assembled and went to Mizpah 2
46 Israel formerly had a place of prayer in Mizpah. 2

Mizpeh 1. מִצְפֶּה

Jos 11: 8 and eastward as far as the valley of Mizpeh; 1
15:38 Di'lean, Mizpeh, Jok'theel 1
18:26 Mizpeh, Chephi'rah, Mozah 1
1Sm 22: 3 And David went from there to Mizpeh of Moab; 1

Mizzah 1. מִזָּה

Gen 36:13 of Reu'el: Nahath, Zerah, Shammah, and Mizzah. 1
17 the chiefs Nahath, Zerah, Shammah, and Mizzah; 1
1Ch 1:37 The sons of Reu'el . . Zerah, Shammah, and Mizzah. 1

Mnason 1. Μνάσων
Act 21:16 bringing us to the house of Mnason of Cyprus 1

Moab 1. מוֹאָב 2. מוֹאָבִי 3. Μωαβ
Gen 19:37 first-born bore a son, and called his name Moab; 1
36:35 in the country of Moab, reigned in his stead 1
Exd 15:15 the leaders of Moab, trembling seizes them; 1
Num21:11 in the wilderness which is opposite Moab 1
13 Arnon is the boundary of Moab 1
13 boundary of Moab, between Moab and the Amorites. 1
15 Ar, and leans to the border of Moab. 1
20 Bamoth to the valley lying in the region of Moab 1
26 Sihon . . fought against the former king of Moab 1
28 It devoured Ar of Moab, the lords of the heights 1
29 Woe to you, O Moab! You are undone, O people 1
22: 1 Israel set out, and encamped in the plains of Moab 1
3 Moab was in great dread of the people 1
3 Moab was overcome with fear of the people 1
4 Moab said to the elders of Mid'ian, "This horde 1
4 So Balak . . who was king of Moab at that time 1
7 elders of Moab and the elders of Mid'ian departed 1
8 so the princes of Moab stayed with Balaam. 1
10 Balak the son of Zippor, king of Moab, has sent to me 1
14 princes of Moab rose and went to Balak, and said 1
21 Balaam . . went with the princes of Moab. 1
36 Balak . . went out to meet him at the city of Moab 1
23: 6 lo, he and all the princes of Moab were standing 1
7 king of Moab from the eastern mountains 1
17 standing . . and the princes of Moab with him. 1
24:17 it shall crush the forehead of Moab 1
25: 1 play the harlot with the daughters of Moab. 1
26: 3 in the plains of Moab by the Jordan at Jericho 1
63 numbered . . Israel in the plains of Moab 1
31:12 at the camp on the plains of Moab by the Jordan 1
33:44 encamped at I'ye-ab'arim, in the territory of Moab. 1
48 encamped in the plains of Moab by the Jordan 1
49 as far as Abel-shittim in the plains of Moab. 1
50 in the plains of Moab by the Jordan at Jericho 1
35: 1 said to Moses in the plains of Moab by the Jordan 1
36:13 in the plains of Moab by the Jordan at Jericho. 1
Deu 1: 5 Beyond the Jordan, in the land of Moab 1
2: 8 went in the direction of the wilderness of Moab. 1
9 'Do not harass Moab or contend with them in battle 1
18 day you are to pass over the boundary of Moab at Ar; 1
29: 1 make with . . Israel in the land of Moab 1
32:49 Nebo . . in the land of Moab, opposite Jericho; 1
34: 1 Moses went up from the plains of Moab to Mount Nebo 1
5 Moses . . died there in the land of Moab 1
6 buried him in the valley in the land of Moab 1
8 Israel wept for Moses in the plains of Moab 1
Jos 13:32 which Moses distributed in the plains of Moab 1
24: 9 Balak the son of Zippor, king of Moab, arose 1
Jdg 3:12 strengthened Eglon the king of Moab against 1
14 Israel served Eglon the king of Moab eighteen 1
15 sent tribute by him to Eglon the king of Moab. 1
17 he presented the tribute to Eglon king of Moab. 1
30 Moab was subdued that day under the hand 1
10: 6 Sidon, the gods of Moab, the gods of the Ammonites 1
11:15 Israel did not take away the land of Moab 1
17 And they sent also to the king of Moab, but he would 1
18 went around the land of Edom and the land of Moab 1
18 and arrived on the east side of the land of Moab 1
18 did not enter the territory of Moab, for the Arnon 1
18 for the Arnon was the boundary of Moab 1
25 better than Balak the son of Zippor, king of Moab? 1
Rut 1: 1 went to sojourn in the country of Moab 1
2 They went into the country of Moab and remained 1
6 she started . . to return from the country of Moab 1
6 she had heard in the country of Moab that the LORD 1
22 Ruth . . who returned from the country of Moab. 1
2: 6 came back with Na'omi from the country of Moab. 1
4: 3 Na'omi, who has come back from the country of Moab 1
1Sm 12: 9 he sold them . . into the hand of the king of Moab; 1
14:47 he fought . . against Moab, against the Ammonites 1
22: 3 And David went from there to Mizpeh of Moab; 1
3 David went . . and he said to the king of Moab 1
4 he left them with the king of Moab, and they stayed 1
2Sm 8: 2 he defeated Moab, and measured them with a line 1
12 from Edom, Moab, the Ammonites, the Philistines 1
23:20 a doer of great deeds; he smote two ariels of Moab. 1
1Kg 11: 7 a high place for Chemosh the abomination of Moab 1
33 Ash'toreth . . Chemosh the god of Moab, and Milcom 1
2Kg 1: 1 Moab rebelled against Israel. 1
3: 4 Now Mesha king of Moab was a sheep breeder; 1
5 the king of Moab rebelled against . . Israel. 1
7 The king of Moab has rebelled against me; 1
7 will you go with me to battle against Moab? 1
10 to give them into the hand of Moab. 1
13 to give them into the hand of Moab. 1
23 Now then, Moab, to the spoil! 1
26 When the king of Moab saw . . he took with him 1
23:13 for . . and for Chemosh the abomination of Moab 1
1Ch 1:46 who defeated Mid'ian in the country of Moab 1
4:22 Saraph, who ruled in Moab and returned to Lehem 1
8: 8 Shahara'im had sons in the country of Moab 1
11:22 doer of great deeds; he smote two ariels of Moab. 1
18: 2 defeated Moab, and the Mo'abites became servants 1
11 from all the nations, from Edom, Moab, 1
2Ch 20:10 behold, the men of Ammon and Moab and Mount Se'ir 1
22 set an ambush against the men of Ammon, Moab 1
23 For the men of Ammon and Moab rose against 1
Neh 13:23 married women of Ashdod, Ammon, and Moab; 2
Ps 60: 8 Moab is my washbasin; upon Edom I cast my shoe; 1
83: 6 tents of . . Moab and the Hagrites 1
108: 9 Moab is my washbasin; upon Edom I cast my shoe; 1
Isa 11:14 shall put forth their hand against Edom and Moab 1
15: 1 An oracle concerning Moab. 1
1 Because Ar is laid waste in a night Moab is undone; 1
1 Kir is laid waste in a night Moab is undone. 1
2 over Nebo and over Med'eba Moab wails. 1
4 therefore the armed men of Moab cry aloud; 1
5 My heart cries out for Moab; his fugitives flee 1
8 For a cry has gone round the land of Moab; 1
9 a lion for those of Moab who escape 1
16: 2 the daughters of Moab at the fords of the Arnon. 1
4 let the outcasts of Moab sojourn among you; 1
6 have heard of the pride of Moab, how proud he was; 1
7 Therefore let Moab wail, let every one wail 1
7 let Moab wail, let every one wail for Moab. 1
11 Therefore my soul moans like a lyre for Moab 1
12 when Moab presents himself 1
13 the LORD spoke concerning Moab in the past. 1
14 the glory of Moab will be brought into contempt 1
25:10 and Moab shall be trodden down in his place 1
Jer 9:26 Egypt, Judah, Edom, the sons of Ammon, Moab 1
25:21 Edom, Moab, and the sons of Ammon; 1
27: 3 Send word to the king of Edom, the king of Moab 1
40:11 Likewise, when all the Jews who were in Moab 1
48: 1 Concerning Moab. Thus says the LORD of hosts 1
2 the renown of Moab is no more. 1
4 Moab is destroyed; a cry is heard as far as Zo'ar. 1
9 Give wings to Moab, for she would fly away; 1
11 Moab has been at ease from his youth 1
13 Then Moab shall be ashamed of Chemosh 1
15 The destroyer of Moab and his cities has come up 1
16 The calamity of Moab is near at hand 1
18 For the destroyer of Moab has come up against you; 1
20 Moab is put to shame, for it is broken; wail and cry! 1
20 Tell it by the Arnon, that Moab is laid waste. 1
24 all the cities of the land of Moab, far and near. 1
25 The horn of Moab is cut off, and his arm is broken 1
26 so that Moab shall wallow in his vomit 1
28 dwell in the rock, O inhabitants of Moab! 1
29 have heard of the pride of Moab–he is very proud 1
31 Therefore I wail for Moab; I cry out for all Moab; 1
31 Therefore I wail for Moab; I cry out for all Moab; 1
33 been taken away from the fruitful land of Moab; 1
35 I will bring to an end in Moab, says the LORD 1
36 Therefore my heart moans for Moab like a flute 1
38 On all the housetops of Moab and in the squares 1
38 for I have broken Moab like a vessel 1
39 they wail! How Moab has turned his back in shame! 1
39 Moab has become a derision and a horror to all 1
40 like an eagle, and spread his wings against Moab; 1
41 The heart of the warriors of Moab 1
42 Moab shall be destroyed and be no longer a people 1
43 pit, and snare are before you, O inhabitant of Moab! 1
44 I will bring these things upon Moab 1
45 it has destroyed the forehead of Moab 1
46 Woe to you, O Moab! The people of Chemosh is undone; 1
47 Yet I will restore the fortunes of Moab 1
47 Thus far is the judgment on Moab. 1
Ezk 25: 8 Thus says the Lord GOD: Because Moab said, Behold 1
9 therefore I will lay open the flank of Moab 1
11 I will execute judgments upon Moab. 1
Dan 11:41 Edom and Moab and the main part of the Ammonites. 1
Ams 2: 1 For three transgressions of Moab, and for four 1
2 I will send a fire upon Moab, and it shall devour 1
2 and Moab shall die amid uproar, amid shouting 1
Mic 6: 5 remember what Balak king of Moab devised 1
Zep 2: 8 I have heard the taunts of Moab 1
9 Moab shall become like Sodom 1
Jdt 1:12 also all the inhabitants of the land of Moab 3
5: 2 he called together all the princes of Moab 3
22 all the men from the seacoast and from Moab 3

Moabite 1. מוֹאָב 2. מוֹאָבִי 3. λαὸς Μωαβ 4. Μωαβίτης 5. υἱὸς Μωαβ
Gen 19:37 Moab; he is the father of the Moabites to this day. 2
Deu 2:11 as Reph'idim, but the Moabites call them Emim. 1
29 as . . the Moabites who live in Ar did for me 2
23: 3 No Ammonite or Moabite shall enter the assembly 2
Jdg 3:28 for the LORD has given your enemies the Moabites 2
28 fords of the Jordan against the Moabites 2
29 about 10,000 of the Moabites, all strong 2
Rut 1: 4 These took Moabite wives; 2
2: 6 It is the Moabite maiden, who came back with Na'omi 2
2Sm 8: 2 And the Moabites became servants to David 2
1Kg 11: 1 and Moabite, Ammonite, E'domite, Sido'nian 2
2Kg 3:18 he will also give the Moabites into your hand 2
21 When all the Moabites heard . . all who were able 2
22 the Moabites saw the water . . as red as blood. 2
24 the Israelites rose and attacked the Moabites 2
24 they went forward, slaughtering the Moabites 2
13:20 bands of Moabites used to invade . . in the spring 2
24: 2 bands of the Syrians, and bands of the Moabites 2
1Ch 11:46 and Ithmah the Mo'abite 2
18: 2 the Mo'abites became servants to David 2
2Ch 20: 1 After this the Moabites and Ammonites 2
Ezr 9: 1 Moabites, the Egyptians, and the Amorites. 2
Neh 13: 1 no Ammonite or Moabite should ever enter 2
1Es 8:69 the Jebusites, the Moabites, the Egyptians 4
Jdt 6: 1 said to Achior and all the Moabites 5
7: 8 the leaders of the Moabites 3

Moabitess 1. מוֹאָבִי
Rut 1:22 Ruth the Moabitess her daughter-in-law with her 1
2: 2 And Ruth the Moabitess said to Na'omi, "Let me go 1
21 And Ruth the Moabitess said, "Besides, he said to me 1
4: 5 you are also buying Ruth the Moabitess, the widow 1
10 Ruth the Moabitess, the widow . . I have bought 1
2Ch 24:26 Jeho'zabad the son of Shimrith the Moabitess. 1

Moadiah 1. מוֹעַדְיָהוּ
Neh 12:17 of Abi'jah, Zichri; of Mini'amin, of Moadi'ah, Pil'tai; 1

Mochmur 1. Μοχμουρ
Jdt 7:18 which is near Chusi beside the brook Mochmur. 1

Modein 1. Μωδειν
1Mc 2: 1 moved from Jerusalem and settled in Modein. 1
15 the king's officers . . came to the city of Modein 1
23 to offer sacrifice upon the altar in Modein 1
70 was buried in the tomb of his fathers at Modein. 1
9:19 buried him in the tomb of their fathers at Modein 1
13:25 buried him in Modein, the city of his fathers. 1
30 This is the tomb which he built in Modein 1
16: 4 and camped for the night in Modein. 1
2Mc 13:14 he pitched his camp near Modein. 1

Moeth 1. Μωεθ
1Es 8:63 Jozabad . . and Moeth the son of Binnui 1

Moladah 1. מוֹלָדָה
Jos 15:26 Amam, Shema, Mola'dah 1
19: 2 for its inheritance Beer-sheba, Sheba, Mola'dah 1
1Ch 4:28 They dwelt in Beer-sheba, Mola'dah, Ha'zar-shu'al 1
Neh 11:26 in Jeshua and in Mola'dah and Beth-pelet 1

Molech 1. מֹלֶךְ
Lev 18:21 of your children to devote them by fire to Molech 1
20: 2 gives . . children to Molech shall be put to death 1
3 he has given one of his children to Molech 1
4 when he gives one of his children to Molech 1
5 who follow him in playing the harlot after Molech 1
1Kg 11: 7 Solomon built a high place . . for Molech 1
2Kg 23:10 burn his son or . . as an offering to Molech. 1
Isa 57: 9 You journeyed to Molech with oil and multiplied 1
Jer 32:35 to offer up their sons and daughters to Molech 1

Molid 1. מוֹלִיד
1Ch 2:29 Ab'ihail, and she bore him Ahban and Molid. 1

Moloch 1. Μολόχ
Act 7:43 you took up the tent of Moloch 1

Moossias 1. Μοοσσιας
1Es 9:31 Of the sons of Addi: Naathus and Moossias 1

Mordecai 1. מָרְדֳּכַי 2. Μαρδοχαικος 3. Μαρδοχαιος
Ezr 2: 2 came with . . Serai'ah, Re-el-ai'ah, Mor'decai 1
Neh 7: 7 came with . . Mor'decai, Bilshan, Mis'pereth, Bigva'i 1
Est 2: 5 there was a Jew in Susa . . whose name was Mor'decai 1
7 Mor'decai adopted her as his own daughter. 1
10 Esther had not . . for Mor'decai had charged her 1
11 Mor'decai walked in front of the court 1
15 the daughter of Ab'ihail the uncle of Mor'decai 1
19 Mor'decai was sitting at the king's gate. 1
20 Esther had not . . as Mor'decai had charged her; 1
20 Esther obeyed Mor'decai just as when she was 1
21 as Mor'decai was sitting at the king's gate 1
22 And this came to the knowledge of Mor'decai 1
22 and Esther told the king in the name of Mor'decai. 1
3: 2 But Mor'decai did not bow down or do obeisance. 1
3 Then the king's servants . . said to Mor'decai 1
4 to see whether Mor'decai's words would avail; 1
5 Mor'decai did not bow down or do obeisance to him 1
6 But he disdained to lay hands on Mor'decai alone. 1
6 they had made known to him the people of Mor'decai 1
6 to destroy all the Jews, the people of Mor'decai 1
4: 1 When Mor'decai learned all that had been done 1
1 Mor'decai rent his clothes and put on sackcloth 1
4 she sent garments to clothe Mor'decai 1
5 to go to Mor'decai to learn what this was and why 1
6 Hathach went out to Mor'decai in the open square 1
7 Mor'decai told him all that had happened to him 1
8 Mor'decai also gave him a copy of the . . decree •
9 went and told Esther what Mor'decai had said. 1
10 and gave him a message for Mor'decai, saying 1
12 And they told Mor'decai what Esther had said. 1
13 Mor'decai told them to return answer to Esther 1
15 Then Esther told them to reply to Mor'decai 1
17 Mor'decai then went away and did everything 1
5: 9 But when Haman saw Mor'decai in the king's gate 1
9 he was filled with wrath against Mor'decai. 1

13 I see Mor'decai the Jew sitting at the king's gate. 1
14 tell the king to have Mor'decai hanged upon it; 1
6: 2 how Mor'decai had told about Bigthana and Teresh 1
3 What . . has been bestowed on Mor'decai for this? 1
4 speak to the king about having Mor'decai hanged 1
10 to Mor'decai the Jew who sits at the king's gate. 1
11 he arrayed Mor'decai and made him ride through 1
12 Then Mor'decai returned to the king's gate. 1
13 If Mor'decai . . is of the Jewish people, you will 1
7: 9 gallows which Haman has prepared for Mor'decai 1
10 on the gallows . . he had prepared for Mor'decai. 1
8: 1 And Mor'decai came before the king 1
2 his signet ring . . and gave it to Mor'decai. 1
2 And Esther set Mor'decai over the house of Haman. 1
7 said to Queen Esther and to Mor'decai the Jew 1
9 according to all that Mor'decai commanded 1
15 Mor'decai went out from . . the king in royal robes 1
9: 3 for the fear of Mor'decai had fallen upon them. 1
4 For Mor'decai was great in the king's house 1
4 the man Mor'decai grew more and more powerful. 1
20 And Mor'decai recorded these things 1
23 to do as . . and as Mor'decai had written to them. 1
29 Esther . . and Mor'decai the Jew gave full written 1
31 as Mor'decai the Jew and Queen Esther enjoined 1
10: 2 the full account of the high honor of Mor'decai 1
3 Mor'decai the Jew was next in rank to . . Ahasu-e'rus 1
1Es 5: 8 Nehemiah, Seraiah, Resaiah, Bigvai, Mordecai 3
AEs 10: 4 Mordecai said, "These things have come from God. 3
11: 2 Mordecai the son of Jair, son of Shimei, son of Kish 3
12 Mordecai saw in this dream 3
12: 1 Now Mordecai took his rest in the courtyard 3
4 Mordecai wrote an account of them. 3
5 the king ordered Mordecai to serve in the court 3
6 he sought to injure Mordecai and his people 3
13: 8 Then Mordecai prayed to the Lord •
16:13 asked for the destruction of Mordecai 3
2Mc 15:36 Syrian language–the day before Mordecai's day. 2

Moreh 1.מוֹרֶה
Gen 12: 6 to the place at Shechem, to the oak of Moreh. 1
Deu 11:30 over against Gilgal, beside the oak of Moreh? 1
Jdg 7: 1 camp . . was . . by the hill of Moreh, in the valley. 1

Moresheth 1.מוֹרַשְׁתִּי 2.מֹרַשְׁתִּי
Jer 26:18 Micah of Mo'resheth prophesied in the days 1
Mic 1: 1 Micah of Mo'resheth in the days of Jotham, 2

Moresheth-gath 1.מוֹרֶשֶׁת גַּת
Mic 1:14 you shall give parting gifts to Mo'resheth-gath; 1

Moriah 1.מֹרִיָּה
Gen 22: 2 and go to the land of Mori'ah 1
2Ch 3: 1 house of the LORD in Jerusalem on Mount Mori'ah 1

Moserah 1.מוֹסֵרָה
Deu 10: 6 journeyed from Be-er'oth Bene-ja'akan to Mose'rah. 1

Moseroth 1.מֹסֵרוֹת
Num33:30 set out from Hashmo'nah, and encamped at Mose'roth 1
31 set out from Mose'roth, and encamped 1

Moses 1.מֹשֶׁה 2.מֹשֶׁה(A) 3.Μωϋσῆς 4.Moyses
Exd 2:10 her son; and she named him Moses, for she said 1
11 One day, when Moses had grown up, he went out 1
14 Then Moses was afraid, and thought, "Surely 1
15 When Pharaoh heard of it, he sought to kill Moses. 1
15 But Moses fled from Pharaoh, and stayed 1
17 drove them away; but Moses stood up and helped 1
21 Moses was content to dwell with the man 1
21 the man, and he gave Moses his daughter Zippo'rah. 1
3: 1 Moses was keeping the flock of his father-in-law 1
3 Moses said, "I will turn aside and see this 1
4 God called to him out of the bush, "Moses, Moses! 1
4 God called to him out of the bush, "Moses, Moses! 1
6 And Moses hid his face, for he was afraid to look 1
11 Moses said to God, "Who am I that I should go 1
13 Then Moses said to God, "If I come to the people 1
14 God said to Moses, "I AM WHO I AM." And he said, 1
15 God also said to Moses, "Say this to the people 1
4: 1 Moses answered, "But behold, they will not believe 1
3 it became a serpent; and Moses fled from it. 1
4 the LORD said to Moses, "Put out your hand, and take 1
10 Moses said to the LORD, "Oh, my Lord, I am not 1
14 the anger of the LORD was kindled against Moses 1
18 Moses went back to Jethro his father-in-law 1
18 And Jethro said to Moses, "Go in peace. 1
19 the LORD said to Moses in Mid'ian, "Go back to Egypt; 1
20 So Moses took his wife and his sons and set them 1
20 and in his hand Moses took the rod of God. 1
21 the LORD said to Moses, "When you go back to Egypt 1
25 her son's foreskin, and touched Moses' feet with it •
27 Aaron, "Go into the wilderness to meet Moses. 1
28 Moses told Aaron all the words of the LORD 1
29 Then Moses and Aaron went and gathered together 1
30 words which the LORD had spoken to Moses 1
5: 1 Afterward Moses and Aaron went to Pharaoh 1
4 the king of Egypt said to them, "Moses and Aaron 1
20 They met Moses and Aaron, who were waiting 1
22 Then Moses turned again to the LORD and said 1
6: 1 the LORD said to Moses, "Now you shall see what I 1
2 God said to Moses, "I am the LORD. 1
9 Moses spoke thus to the people of Israel; 1
9 did not listen to Moses, because of their broken 1
10 the LORD said to Moses 1
12 Moses said to the LORD, "Behold, the people 1
13 the LORD spoke to Moses and Aaron, and gave them 1
20 and she bore him Aaron and Moses 1
26 the Aaron and Moses to whom the LORD said 1
27 they who spoke . . this Moses and this Aaron. 1
28 when the LORD spoke to Moses in the land of Egypt 1
29 the LORD said to Moses, "I am the LORD; tell Pharaoh 1
30 Moses said to the LORD, "Behold, I am 1
7: 1 the LORD said to Moses, "See, I make you as God 1
6 Moses and Aaron did so; 1
7 Now Moses was 80 years old 1
8 the LORD said to Moses and Aaron 1
10 So Moses and Aaron went to Pharaoh and did 1
14 LORD said to Moses, "Pharaoh's heart is hardened 1
19 the LORD said to Moses, "Say to Aaron, 'Take your rod 1
20 Moses and Aaron did as the LORD commanded; 1
8: 1 Then the LORD said to Moses, "Go in to Pharaoh 1
5 the LORD said to Moses, "Say to Aaron, 'Stretch out 1
8 Then Pharaoh called Moses and Aaron, and said 1
9 Moses said to Pharaoh, "Be pleased to command me 1
10 he said, "Tomorrow." Moses said, "Be it as you say •
12 So Moses and Aaron went out from Pharaoh; 1
12 and Moses cried to the LORD concerning the frogs 1
13 the LORD did according to the word of Moses; 1
16 Then the LORD said to Moses, "Say to Aaron, 'Stretch 1
20 Then the LORD said to Moses, "Rise up early 1
25 Then Pharaoh called Moses and Aaron, and said, "Go 1
26 Moses said, "It would not be right to do so; 1
29 Then Moses said, "Behold, I am going out from you 1
30 So Moses went out from Pharaoh and prayed 1
31 the LORD did as Moses asked, and removed 1
9: 1 Then the LORD said to Moses, "Go in to Pharaoh 1
8 the LORD said to Moses and Aaron, "Take handfuls 1
8 ashes from the kiln, and let Moses throw them 1
10 and Moses threw them toward heaven, and it became 1
11 the magicians could not stand before Moses 1
12 as the LORD had spoken to Moses. 1
13 Then the LORD said to Moses, "Rise up early 1
22 the LORD said to Moses, "Stretch forth your hand 1
23 Then Moses stretched forth his rod 1
27 Then Pharaoh sent, and called Moses and Aaron 1
29 Moses said to him, "As soon as I have gone out 1
33 So Moses went out of the city from Pharaoh 1
35 as the LORD had spoken through Moses. 1
10: 1 Then the LORD said to Moses, "Go in to Pharaoh; 1
3 Moses and Aaron went in to Pharaoh, and said to him 1
8 So Moses and Aaron were brought back to Pharaoh; 1
9 Moses said, "We will go with our young and our old; 1
12 Then the LORD said to Moses, "Stretch out your hand 1
13 So Moses stretched forth his rod over the land 1
16 Then Pharaoh called Moses and Aaron in haste 1
21 Then the LORD said to Moses, "Stretch out your hand 1
22 So Moses stretched out his hand toward heaven 1
24 Pharaoh called Moses, and said, "Go, serve the LORD; 1
25 Moses said, "You must also let us have sacrifices 1
29 Moses said, "As you say! I will not see your face 1
11: 1 The LORD said to Moses, "Yet one plague more I will 1
3 Moreover, the man Moses was very great in the land 1
4 Moses said, "Thus says the LORD: About midnight 1
9 the LORD said to Moses, "Pharaoh will not listen 1
10 Moses and Aaron did all these wonders before 1
12: 1 The LORD said to Moses and Aaron in the land 1
21 Then Moses called all the elders of Israel 1
28 as the LORD had commanded Moses and Aaron 1
31 he summoned Moses and Aaron by night, and said 1
35 Israel had also done as Moses told them 1
43 the LORD said to Moses and Aaron, "This is 1
50 the LORD commanded Moses and Aaron, so they did. 1
13: 1 The LORD said to Moses 1
3 Moses said to the people, "Remember this day 1
19 Moses took the bones of Joseph with him; 1
14: 1 Then the LORD said to Moses 1
11 they said to Moses, "Is it because there are no 1
13 Moses said to the people, "Fear not, stand firm 1
15 The LORD said to Moses, "Why do you cry to me? 1
21 Then Moses stretched out his hand over the sea; 1
26 Then the LORD said to Moses, "Stretch out your hand 1
27 So Moses stretched forth his hand over the sea 1
31 they believed in the LORD and . . his servant Moses. 1
15: 1 Moses and the people of Israel sang this song 1
22 Then Moses led Israel onward from the Red Sea 1
24 the people murmured against Moses, saying, "What 1
16: 2 Israel murmured against Moses and Aaron 1
4 Then the LORD said to Moses, "Behold, I will rain 1
6 So Moses and Aaron said to all the people 1
8 Moses said, "When the LORD gives you in the evening 1
9 Moses said to Aaron, "Say to the whole 1
11 the LORD said to Moses 1
15 And Moses said to them, "It is the bread 1
19 Moses said to them, "Let no man leave any of it till 1
20 they did not listen to Moses; some left part of it 1
20 and Moses was angry with them. 1
22 leaders of the congregation came and told Moses 1
24 So they laid it by till the morning, as Moses bade 1
25 Moses said, "Eat it today, for today is a sabbath 1
28 the LORD said to Moses, "How long do you refuse 1
32 Moses said, "This is what the LORD has commanded 1
33 Moses said to Aaron, "Take a jar, and put an omer 1
34 As the LORD commanded Moses, so Aaron placed it 1
17: 2 Therefore the people found fault with Moses 1
2 And Moses said to them, "Why do you find fault 1
3 and the people murmured against Moses 1
4 Moses cried to the LORD, "What shall I do with this 1
5 the LORD said to Moses, "Pass on before the people 1
6 And Moses did so, in the sight of the elders 1
9 Moses said to Joshua, "Choose for us men, and go out 1
10 So Joshua did as Moses told him, and fought 1
10 and Moses, Aaron, and Hur went up to the top 1
11 Whenever Moses held up his hand, Israel 1
12 Moses' hands grew weary; so they took a stone 1
14 the LORD said to Moses, "Write this as a memorial 1
15 Moses built an altar and called the name of it 1
18: 1 Jethro, the priest of Mid'ian, Moses' father-in-law 1
1 God had done for Moses and for Israel his people 1
2 Jethro, Moses' father-in-law, had taken Zippo'rah 1
2 Jethro . . had taken Zippo'rah, Moses' wife 1
5 Jethro, Moses' father-in-law, came with his sons 1
5 Jethro . . came . . to Moses in the wilderness 1
6 when one told Moses, "Lo, your father-in-law Jethro 1
7 Moses went out to meet his father-in-law 1
8 Moses told his father-in-law all that the LORD had 1
12 Jethro, Moses' father-in-law, offered a burnt 1
12 came . . to eat bread with Moses' father-in-law 1
13 On the morrow Moses sat to judge the people 1
13 stood about Moses from morning till evening. 1
14 When Moses' father-in-law saw all that he was doing 1
15 Moses said to his father-in-law, "Because 1
17 Moses' father-in-law said to him, "What you are doing 1
24 Moses gave heed to the voice of his father-in-law 1
25 Moses chose able men out of all Israel 1
26 hard cases they brought to Moses 1
27 Then Moses let his father-in-law depart 1
19: 3 Moses went up to God, and the LORD called to him 1
7 So Moses came and called the elders of the people 1
8 And Moses reported the words of the people 1
9 the LORD said to Moses, "Lo, I am coming to you 1
9 Moses told the words of the people to the LORD. 1
10 the LORD said to Moses, "Go to the people 1
14 Moses went down from the mountain to the people 1
17 Then Moses brought the people out of the camp 1
19 sound of the trumpet grew louder, Moses spoke 1
20 the LORD called Moses to the top of the mountain 1
20 LORD called Moses . . and Moses went up. 1
21 LORD said to Moses, "Go down and warn the people 1
23 Moses said to the LORD, "The people cannot come up 1
25 So Moses went down to the people and told them. 1
20:19 said to Moses, "You speak to us, and we will hear; 1
20 Moses said to the people, "Do not fear; for God has 1
21 while Moses drew near to the thick darkness 1
22 the LORD said to Moses, "Thus you shall say 1
24: 1 said to Moses, "Come up to the LORD, you and Aaron 1
2 Moses alone shall come near to the LORD; 1
3 Moses came and told the people all the words 1
4 Moses wrote all the words of the LORD. 1
6 Moses took half of the blood and put it in basins 1
8 Moses took the blood and threw it upon the people 1
9 Then Moses and Aaron, Nadab, and Abi'hu, 1
12 The LORD said to Moses, "Come up to me 1
13 So Moses rose with his servant Joshua 1
13 Moses went up into the mountain of God. 1
15 Then Moses went up on the mountain, and the cloud 1
16 he called to Moses out of the midst of the cloud. 1
18 Moses entered the cloud, and went up 1
18 And Moses was on the mountain 40 days 1
25: 1 The LORD said to Moses 1
30:11 The LORD said to Moses 1
17 The LORD said to Moses 1
22 Moreover, the LORD said to Moses 1
34 the LORD said to Moses, "Take sweet spices, stacte 1
31: 1 LORD said to Moses 1
12 LORD said to Moses 1
18 gave to Moses, when he had made an end of speaking 1
32: 1 When the people saw that Moses delayed 1
1 as for this Moses, the man who brought us up out 1
7 the LORD said to Moses, "Go down; for your people 1
9 the LORD said to Moses, "I have seen this people 1
11 Moses besought the LORD his God, and said, "O LORD 1
15 Moses turned, and went down from the mountain 1
17 as they shouted, he said to Moses, "There is a noise 1
19 Moses' anger burned hot, and he threw the tables 1
21 Moses said to Aaron, "What did this people do to you 1
23 as for this Moses, the man who brought us up 1
25 when Moses saw that the people had broken loose 1
26 then Moses stood in the gate of the camp, and said 1
28 the sons of Levi did according to the word of Moses; 1
29 Moses said, "Today you have ordained yourselves 1
30 On the morrow Moses said to the people, "You have 1
31 So Moses returned to the LORD and said 1
33 the LORD said to Moses, "Whoever has sinned 1
33: 1 The LORD said to Moses, "Depart, go up hence 1
5 For the LORD had said to Moses, "Say to the people 1
7 Now Moses used to take the tent and pitch it 1
8 Whenever Moses went out to the tent 1

8 looked after Moses, until he had gone 1
9 When Moses entered the tent, the pillar of cloud 1
9 the tent, and the LORD would speak with Moses. 1
11 Thus the LORD used to speak to Moses face to face 1
11 When Moses turned again into the camp *
12 Moses said to the LORD, "See, thou sayest to me 1
17 the LORD said to Moses, "This very thing 1
18 Moses said, "I pray thee, show me thy glory. *
34: 1 The LORD said to Moses, "Cut two tables of stone 1
4 Moses cut two tables of stone like the first; *
8 And Moses made haste to bow his head 1
27 the LORD said to Moses, "Write these words; 1
29 When Moses came down from Mount Sinai 1
29 Moses did not know that the skin of his face shone 1
30 when Aaron and all the people of Israel saw Moses 1
31 Moses called to them; and Aaron and all 1
31 returned to him, and Moses talked with them. 1
33 when Moses had finished speaking with them 1
34 whenever Moses went in before the LORD to speak 1
35 the people of Israel saw the face of Moses 1
35 saw . . that the skin of Moses' face shone; 1
35 and Moses would put the veil upon his face again 1
35: 1 Moses assembled all the congregation 1
4 Moses said to all the congregation of the people 1
20 Israel departed from the presence of Moses. 1
29 work which the LORD had commanded by Moses to be 1
30 Moses said to the people of Israel, "See, the LORD 1
36: 2 Moses called Bez'alel and Oho'liab and every able 1
3 they received from Moses all the freewill 1
5 said to Moses, "The people bring much more 1
6 So Moses gave command, and word was proclaimed 1
38:21 as they were counted at the commandment of Moses 1
22 made all that the LORD commanded Moses; 1
39: 1 as the LORD had commanded Moses. 1
5 twined linen; as the LORD had commanded Moses. 1
7 sons of Israel; as the LORD had commanded Moses. 1
21 as the LORD had commanded Moses. 1
26 as the LORD had commanded Moses. 1
29 as the LORD had commanded Moses. 1
31 as the LORD had commanded Moses. 1
32 all that the LORD had commanded Moses; 1
33 they brought the tabernacle to Moses 1
42 all that the LORD had commanded Moses 1
43 Moses saw all the work, and behold, they had done it; 1
43 had they done it. And Moses blessed them. 1
40: 1 The LORD said to Moses 1
16 Thus did Moses; according to all that the LORD 1
18 Moses erected the tabernacle; he laid its bases 1
19 the tent over it, as the LORD had commanded Moses. 1
21 as the LORD had commanded Moses. 1
23 the LORD; as the LORD had commanded Moses. 1
25 as the LORD had commanded Moses. 1
27 as the LORD had commanded Moses. 1
29 as the LORD had commanded Moses. 1
31 with which Moses and Aaron and his sons washed 1
32 as the LORD commanded Moses. 1
33 So Moses finished the work. 1
35 Moses was not able to enter the tent of meeting 1
Lev 1: 1 and spoke to him from the tent of meeting 1
4: 1 the LORD said to Moses 1
5:14 The LORD said to Moses 1
6: 1 The LORD said to Moses 1
8 The LORD said to Moses 1
19 The LORD said to Moses 1
24 The LORD said to Moses 1
7:22 The LORD said to Moses 1
28 The LORD said to Moses 1
38 which the LORD commanded Moses on Mount Sinai 1
8: 1 The LORD said to Moses 1
4 Moses did as the LORD commanded him 1
5 Moses said to the congregation, "This is the thing 1
6 Moses brought Aaron and his sons, and washed them 1
9 the holy crown, as the LORD commanded Moses 1
10 The Moses took the anointing oil, and anointed 1
13 Moses brought Aaron's sons, and clothed them 1
13 bound caps on them, as the LORD commanded Moses 1
15 Moses killed it, and took the blood 1
16 and Moses burned them on the altar 1
17 outside the camp, as the LORD commanded Moses 1
19 Moses killed it, and threw the blood 1
20 Moses burned the head and the pieces and the fat 1
21 Moses burned the whole ram on the altar 1
21 to the LORD, as the LORD commanded Moses 1
23 Moses killed it, and took some of its blood 1
24 Aaron's sons were brought, and Moses put some 1
24 Moses threw the blood upon the altar round about 1
28 Then Moses took them from their hands, and burned 1
29 Moses took the breast, and waved it for a wave 1
29 it was Moses' portion of the ram of ordination 1
29 ram of ordination, as the LORD commanded Moses 1
30 Then Moses took some of the anointing oil 1
31 Moses said to Aaron and his sons, "Boil the flesh 1
36 all the things which the LORD commanded by Moses 1
9: 1 On the eighth day Moses called Aaron and his sons 1
5 they brought what Moses commanded 1
6 Moses said, "This is the thing which the LORD 1
7 Then Moses said to Aaron, "Draw near to the altar 1
10 upon the altar, as the LORD commanded Moses 1
21 wave offering . . as Moses commanded 1
23 Moses and Aaron went into the tent of meeting 1
10: 3 Then Moses said to Aaron, "This is what the LORD 1
4 Moses called Mish'a-el and Elza'phan 1
5 carried them . . as Moses had said 1
6 Moses said to Aaron and to Elea'zar and Ith'amar 1
7 And they did according to the word of Moses 1
11 the LORD has spoken to them by Moses 1
12 Moses said to Aaron and to Elea'zar and Ith'amar 1
16 Now Moses diligently inquired about the goat 1
19 Aaron said to Moses, "Behold, today they have 1
20 when Moses heard that, he was content 1
11: 1 the LORD said to Moses and Aaron 1
12: 1 The LORD said to Moses 1
13: 1 The LORD said to Moses and Aaron 1
14: 1 The LORD said to Moses 1
33 The LORD said to Moses and Aaron 1
15: 1 The LORD said to Moses and Aaron 1
16: 1 The LORD spoke to Moses after the death of the two 1
2 the LORD said to Moses, "Tell Aaron your brother 1
34 And Moses did as the LORD commanded him 1
17: 1 the LORD said to Moses 1
18: 1 the LORD said to Moses 1
19: 1 And the LORD said to Moses 1
20: 1 The LORD said to Moses 1
21: 1 the LORD said to Moses, "Speak to the priests 1
16 And the LORD said to Moses 1
24 So Moses spoke to Aaron and to his sons 1
22: 1 And the LORD said to Moses 1
17 And the LORD said to Moses 1
26 And the LORD said to Moses 1
23: 1 The LORD said to Moses 1
9 And the LORD said to Moses 1
23 And the LORD said to Moses 1
26 And the LORD said to Moses 1
33 And the LORD said to Moses 1
44 Thus Moses declared to the people of Israel 1
24: 1 The LORD said to Moses 1
11 And they brought him to Moses 1
13 And the LORD said to Moses 1
23 So Moses spoke to the people of Israel 1
23 Israel did as the LORD commanded Moses 1
25: 1 The LORD said to Moses on Mount Sinai 1
26:46 statutes . . on Mount Sinai by Moses 1
27: 1 The LORD said to Moses 1
34 commandments which the LORD commanded Moses 1
Num 1: 1 The LORD spoke to Moses in the wilderness 1
17 Moses and Aaron took these men who have been 1
19 the LORD commanded Moses. So he numbered them 1
44 whom Moses and Aaron numbered with the help 1
48 For the LORD said to Moses 1
54 according to all that the LORD commanded Moses. 1
2: 1 The LORD said to Moses and Aaron 1
33 not numbered . . as the LORD commanded Moses. 1
34 According to all that the LORD commanded Moses 1
3: 1 These are the generations of Aaron and Moses 1
1 when the LORD spoke with Moses on Mount Sinai. 1
5 the LORD said to Moses 1
11 the LORD said to Moses 1
14 the LORD said to Moses in the wilderness of Sinai 1
16 So Moses numbered them according to the word 1
38 Moses and Aaron and his sons, having charge 1
39 Levites, whom Moses and Aaron numbered 1
40 LORD said to Moses, "Number all the first-born 1
42 Moses numbered all the first-born 1
44 the LORD said to Moses 1
49 Moses took the redemption money from those 1
51 Moses gave the redemption money to Aaron 1
51 word of the LORD, as the LORD commanded Moses. 1
4: 1 The LORD said to Moses and Aaron 1
17 The LORD said to Moses and Aaron 1
21 The LORD said to Moses 1
34 Moses and Aaron and the leaders 1
37 Ko'hathites . . Moses and Aaron numbered 1
37 commandment of the LORD by Moses. 1
41 whom Moses and Aaron numbered according 1
45 Merar'i, whom Moses and Aaron numbered 1
45 commandment of the LORD by Moses. 1
46 whom Moses and Aaron and the leaders of Israel 1
49 commandment of the LORD through Moses 1
49 numbered by him, as the LORD commanded Moses. 1
5: 1 The LORD said to Moses 1
4 as the LORD said to Moses, so . . Israel did. 1
5 the LORD said to Moses 1
11 the LORD said to Moses 1
6: 1 the LORD said to Moses 1
22 The LORD said to Moses 1
7: 1 Moses had finished setting up the tabernacle 1
4 Then the LORD said to Moses 1
6 Moses took the wagons and the oxen, and gave them 1
11 LORD said to Moses, "They shall offer 1
89 when Moses went into the tent of meeting to speak 1
8: 1 Now the LORD said to Moses 1
3 set up its lamps . . as the LORD commanded Moses. 1
4 pattern which the LORD had shown Moses 1
5 the LORD said to Moses 1
20 Thus did Moses and Aaron . . to the Levites; 1
20 according to all that the LORD commanded Moses 1
22 commanded Moses concerning the Levites 1
23 the LORD said to Moses 1
9: 1 LORD spoke to Moses in the wilderness of Sinai 1
4 Moses told the people of Israel that they should 1
5 according to all that the LORD commanded Moses 1
6 they came before Moses and Aaron on that day; 1
8 Moses said to them, "Wait, that I may hear 1
9 The LORD said to Moses 1
23 at the command of the LORD by Moses. 1
10: 1 The LORD said to Moses 1
13 set out . . at the command of the LORD by Moses. 1
29 Moses said to Hobab the son of Reu'el 1
29 Moses said to Hobab . . Moses' father-in-law 1
35 whenever the ark set out, Moses said, "Arise, O LORD 1
11: 2 Then the people cried to Moses; and Moses prayed 1
2 Moses prayed to the LORD, and the fire abated. 1
10 Moses heard the people weeping throughout 1
10 LORD blazed hotly, and Moses was displeased. 1
11 Moses said to the LORD, "Why has thou dealt ill 1
16 the LORD said to Moses, "Gather for me 70 men 1
21 Moses said, "The people among whom I am number 1
23 LORD said to Moses, "Is the LORD'S hand shortened? 1
24 Moses went out and told the people the words 1
27 a young man ran and told Moses, "Eldad and Medad 1
28 Joshua the son of Nun, the minister of Moses 1
28 Joshua . . said, "My lord Moses, forbid them. 1
29 Moses said to him, "Are you jealous for my sake? 1
30 Moses and the elders . . returned to the camp. 1
12: 1 Miriam and Aaron spoke against Moses 1
2 Has the LORD indeed spoken only through Moses? 1
3 the man Moses was very meek, more than all men 1
4 LORD said to Moses and to Aaron and Miriam 1
7 Not so with my servant Moses; he is entrusted 1
8 not afraid to speak against my servant Moses? 1
11 Aaron said to Moses, "Oh, my lord, do not punish us 1
13 Moses cried to the LORD, "Heal her, O God, I beseech 1
14 LORD said to Moses, "If her father had but spit 1
13: 1 The LORD said to Moses 1
3 Moses sent them from the wilderness of Paran 1
16 men whom Moses sent to spy out the land. 1
16 Moses called Hoshe'a the son of Nun Joshua. 1
17 Moses sent them to spy out the land of Canaan 1
26 they came to Moses and Aaron and to all 1
30 Caleb quieted the people before Moses, and said 1
14: 2 people . . murmured against Moses and Aaron; 1
5 Then Moses and Aaron fell on their faces 1
11 LORD said to Moses, "How long will this people 1
13 Moses said to the LORD, "Then the Egyptians 1
26 the LORD said to Moses and to Aaron 1
36 men whom Moses sent to spy out the land 1
39 Moses told these words to all . . Israel 1
41 Moses said, "Why now are you trangressing 1
44 nor Moses, departed out of the camp. 1
15: 1 Then the LORD said to Moses 1
17 The LORD said to Moses 1
22 commandments which the LORD has spoken to Moses 1
23 all that the LORD has commanded you by Moses 1
33 who found him . . brought him to Moses and Aaron 1
35 LORD said to Moses, "The man shall be put to death; 1
36 stoned him . . as the LORD commanded Moses. 1
37 The LORD said to Moses 1
16: 2 took men; and they rose up before Moses 1
3 assembled . . against Moses and against Aaron 1
4 When Moses heard it, he fell on his face; 1
8 Moses said to Korah, "Hear now, you sons of Levi 1
12 Moses sent to call Dathan and Abi'ram 1
15 Moses was very angry, and said to the LORD 1
16 Moses said to Korah, "Be present, you and all 1
18 at . . the tent of meeting with Moses and Aaron. 1
20 the LORD said to Moses and to Aaron 1
23 the LORD said to Moses 1
25 Then Moses rose and went to Dathan and Abi'ram; 1
28 Moses said, "Hereby you shall know that the LORD 1
36 Then the LORD said to Moses 1
40 as the LORD said to Elea'zar through Moses. 1
41 all . . murmured against Moses 1
42 congregation had assembled against Moses 1
43 Moses and Aaron came to the front of the tent 1
44 the LORD said to Moses 1
46 Moses said to Aaron, "Take your censer, and put fire 1
47 Aaron took it as Moses said, and ran into the midst 1
50 Aaron returned to Moses at the entrance 1
17: 1 The LORD said to Moses 1
6 Moses spoke to the people of Israel; 1
7 Moses deposited the rods before the LORD 1
8 morrow Moses went into the tent of the testimony; 1
9 Moses brought out all the rods from before 1
10 the LORD said to Moses, "Put back the rod of Aaron 1
11 Thus did Moses; as the LORD commanded him 1
12 people of Israel said to Moses, "Behold, we perish 1
18:25 the LORD said to Moses 1
19: 1 Now the LORD said to Moses and to Aaron 1
20: 2 assembled themselves together against Moses 1
3 people contended with Moses, and said, "Would that 1
6 Then Moses and Aaron went from the presence 1
7 the LORD said to Moses 1
9 Moses took the rod from before the LORD 1
10 Moses and Aaron gathered the assembly together 1
11 Moses lifted up his hand and struck the rock 1
12 LORD said to Moses and Aaron, "Because you did not 1
14 Moses sent messengers from Kadesh to the king 1

23 the LORD said to Moses and Aaron at Mount Hor 1
27 Moses did as the LORD commanded; 1
28 Moses stripped Aaron of his garments 1
28 Moses and Elea'zar came down from the mountain. 1
21: 5 the people spoke against God and against Moses 1
7 people came to Moses, and said, "We have sinned 1
7 So Moses prayed for the people. 1
8 the LORD said to Moses, "Make a fiery serpent 1
9 Moses made a bronze serpent, and set it on a pole; 1
16 Beer . . the well of which the LORD said to Moses 1
32 Moses sent to spy out Jazer; 1
34 the LORD said to Moses, "Do not fear him; 1
25: 4 LORD said to Moses, "Take all the chiefs 1
5 Moses said to the judges of Israel, "Every one 1
6 in the sight of Moses and in the sight of the whole 1
10 the LORD said to Moses 1
16 the LORD said to Moses 1
26: 1 LORD said to Moses and to Elea'zar the son of Aaron 1
3 Moses and Elea'zar the priest spoke with them 1
4 Take a census . . " as the LORD commanded Moses. 1
9 who contended against Moses and Aaron 1
52 The LORD said to Moses 1
59 she bore to Amram Aaron and Moses and Miriam 1
63 those numbered by Moses and Elea'zar the priest 1
64 of those numbered by Moses and Aaron the priest 1
27: 2 stood before Moses, and before Elea'zar 1
5 Moses brought their case before the LORD. 1
6 the LORD said to Moses 1
11 as the LORD commanded Moses.' 1
12 LORD said to Moses, "Go up into this mountain 1
15 Moses said to the LORD 1
18 LORD said to Moses, "Take Joshua the son of Nun 1
22 Moses did as the LORD commanded him; 1
23 as the LORD directed through Moses. 1
28: 1 The LORD said to Moses 1
29:40 Moses told the people of Israel everything 1
40 just as the LORD had commanded Moses. 1
30: 1 Moses said to the heads of the tribes 1
16 statutes which the LORD commanded Moses 1
31: 1 The LORD said to Moses 1
3 Moses said to the people, "Arm men from among you 1
6 Moses sent them to the war, 1,000 from each tribe 1
7 against Mid'ian, as the LORD commanded Moses 1
12 brought . . to Moses, and to Elea'zar the priest 1
13 Moses, and Elea'zar the priest, and all the leaders 1
14 Moses was angry with the officers of the army 1
15 Moses said to them, "Have you let all the women live? 1
21 which the LORD has commanded Moses 1
25 The LORD said to Moses 1
31 Moses and Elea'zar the priest did as the LORD 1
31 did as the LORD commanded Moses. 1
41 Moses gave the tribute . . to Elea'zar the priest 1
41 gave the tribute . . as the LORD commanded Moses. 1
42 Israel's half, which Moses separated from that 1
47 from . . Israel's half Moses took one of every fifty 1
47 as the LORD commanded Moses. 1
48 officers . . of the army . . , came near to Moses 1
49 said to Moses, "Your servants have counted 1
51 Moses and Elea'zar . . received from them the gold 1
54 Moses and Elea'zar the priest received the gold 1
32: 2 came and said to Moses and to Elea'zar the priest 1
6 Moses said to the sons of Gad and . . of Reuben 1
20 Moses said to them, "If you will do this 1
25 sons of Gad and the sons of Reuben said to Moses 1
28 Moses gave command concerning them to Elea'zar 1
29 Moses said to them, "If the sons of Gad 1
33 Moses gave to them, to the sons of Gad 1
40 Moses gave Gilead to Machir the son of Manas'seh 1
33: 1 went . . under the leadership of Moses and Aaron. 1
2 Moses wrote down their starting places 1
50 LORD said to Moses in the plains of Moab 1
34: 1 The LORD said to Moses 1
13 Moses commanded the people of Israel, saying 1
16 The LORD said to Moses 1
35: 1 LORD said to Moses in the plains of Moab 1
9 the LORD said to Moses 1
36: 1 spoke before Moses and before the leaders 1
5 Moses commanded the people of Israel 1
10 daughters . . did as the LORD commanded Moses; 1
13 LORD commanded by Moses to the people of Israel 1
Deu 1: 1 words that Moses spoke to all Israel 1
3 Moses spoke to the people of Israel according 1
5 Moses undertook to explain this law, saying 1
4:41 Moses set apart three cities in the east 1
44 This is the law which Moses set before . . Israel; 1
45 which Moses spoke to the children of Israel 1
46 whom Moses and the children of Israel defeated 1
5: 1 Moses summoned all Israel, and said to them, "Hear 1
27: 1 Now Moses and the elders of Israel commanded 1
9 Moses and the Levitical priests said to all 1
11 Moses charged the people the same day, saying 1
29: 1 covenant which the LORD commanded Moses to make 1
2 Moses summoned all Israel and said to them 1
31: 1 Moses continued to speak these words 1
7 Then Moses summoned Joshua, and said to him 1
9 Moses wrote this law, and gave it to the priests 1
10 Moses commanded them, "At the end of every seven 1
14 LORD said to Moses, "Behold, the days approach 1
14 Moses and Joshua went and presented themselves 1

16 LORD said to Moses, "Behold, you are about to sleep 1
22 Moses wrote this song the same day, and taught it 1
24 When Moses had finished writing the words 1
25 Moses commanded the Levites who carried the ark 1
30 Then Moses spoke the words of this song 1
32:44 Moses came and recited all the words of this song 1
45 Moses had finished speaking all these words 1
48 LORD said to Moses that very day 1
33: 1 blessing with which Moses the man of God blessed 1
4 when Moses commanded us a law, as a possession 1
34: 1 Moses went up from the plains of Moab to Mount Nebo 1
5 Moses the servant of the LORD died there 1
7 Moses was 120 years old when he died; 1
8 Israel wept for Moses in the plains of Moab 1
8 days of . . mourning for Moses were ended. 1
9 for Moses had laid his hands upon him; 1
9 Israel . . did as the LORD had commanded Moses. 1
10 not arisen a prophet since in Israel like Moses 1
12 which Moses wrought in the sight of all Israel. 1
Jos 1: 1 After the death of Moses the servant of the LORD 1
1 LORD said to Joshua the son of Nun, Moses' minister 1
2 Moses my servant is dead; now therefore arise 1
3 I have given to you, as I promised to Moses. 1
5 as I was with Moses, so I will be with you; 1
7 all the law which Moses my servant commanded you; 1
13 Moses the servant of the LORD commanded you 1
14 shall remain in the land which Moses gave you 1
15 land which Moses the servant of the LORD gave you 1
17 we obeyed Moses in all things, so we will obey you; 1
17 LORD your God be with you, as he was with Moses! 1
3: 7 know that, as I was with Moses, so I will be with you. 1
4:10 to all that Moses had commanded Joshua. 1
12 passed over armed . . as Moses had bidden them; 1
14 as they had stood in awe of Moses, all . . his life. 1
8:31 as Moses the servant of the LORD had commanded 1
31 as it is written in the book of the law of Moses 1
32 he wrote upon the stones a copy of the law of Moses 1
33 as Moses the servant of the LORD had commanded 1
35 There was not a word of all that Moses commanded 1
9:24 LORD . . had commanded his servant Moses to give 1
11:12 as Moses the servant of the LORD had commanded. 1
15 As the LORD had commanded Moses his servant 1
15 As the LORD had . . so Moses commanded Joshua 1
15 of all that the LORD had commanded Moses. 1
20 be exterminated, as the LORD commanded Moses. 1
23 according to all . . the LORD had spoken to Moses; 1
12: 6 Moses . . and the people of Israel defeated them; 1
6 and Moses . . gave their land for a possession 1
13: 8 their inheritance, which Moses gave them 1
8 as Moses the servant of the LORD gave them 1
12 these Moses had defeated and driven out. 1
14 To the tribe of Levi . . Moses gave no inheritance; •
15 Moses gave an inheritance to the . . Reubenites 1
21 whom Moses defeated with the leaders of Mid'ian 1
24 Moses gave an inheritance also to the . . Gadites 1
29 Moses gave an inheritance to . . Manas'seh; 1
32 the inheritances which Moses distributed 1
33 to the tribe of Levi Moses gave no inheritance; 1
14: 2 as the LORD had commanded Moses for the nine 1
3 Moses had given an inheritance to the . . tribes 1
5 people of Israel did as the LORD commanded Moses; 1
6 You know what the LORD said to Moses 1
7 Moses the servant of the LORD sent me . . to spy out 1
9 And Moses swore on that day, saying 1
10 the time that the LORD spoke this word to Moses 1
11 as strong . . as I was in the day that Moses sent me; 1
17: 4 LORD commanded Moses to give us an inheritance 1
18: 7 which Moses the servant of the LORD gave them. 1
20: 2 cities . . of which I spoke to you through Moses 1
21: 2 The LORD commanded through Moses that we be 1
8 as the LORD had commanded through Moses. 1
22: 2 You have kept all that Moses . . commanded you 1
4 which Moses the servant of the LORD gave you 1
5 and the law which Moses . . commanded you 1
7 Moses had given a possession in Bashan; 1
9 by command of the LORD through Moses. 1
23: 6 all that is written in the book of the law of Moses 1
24: 5 And I sent Moses and Aaron, and I plagued Egypt 1
Jdg 1:16 descendants of the Ken'ite, Moses' father-in-law 1
20 Hebron was given to Caleb, as Moses had said; 1
3: 4 LORD, which he commanded their fathers by Moses. 1
4:11 Hobab the father-in-law of Moses, and had pitched 1
18:30 Jonathan the son of Gershom, son of Moses 1
1Sm 12: 6 The LORD . . who appointed Moses and Aaron 1
8 the LORD sent Moses and Aaron, who brought forth 1
1Kg 2: 3 the charge . . as it is written in the law of Moses 1
8: 9 tables of stone which Moses put there at Horeb 1
53 as thou didst declare through Moses, thy servant 1
56 promise, which he uttered by Moses his servant. 1
2Kg 14: 6 what is written in the book of the law of Moses 1
18: 4 broke . . the bronze serpent that Moses had made 1
6 commandments which the LORD commanded Moses. 1
12 his covenant, even all that Moses . . commanded; 1
21: 8 the law that my servant Moses commanded them. 1
23:25 who turned . . according to all the law of Moses; 1
1Ch 6: 3 The children of Amram: Aaron, Moses, and Miriam. 1
49 all that Moses the servant of God had commanded. 1
15:15 Moses had commanded according to the word 1
21:29 tabernacle of the LORD, which Moses had made 1

22:13 which the LORD commanded Moses for Israel. 1
23:13 The sons of Amram: Aaron and Moses. 1
14 sons of Moses . . named among the tribe of Levi. 1
15 The sons of Moses: Gershom and Elie'zer. 1
26:24 Sheb'uel the son of Gershom, son of Moses 1
2Ch 1: 3 which Moses the servant of the LORD had made 1
5:10 the two tables which Moses put there at Horeb 1
8:13 offering according to the commandment of Moses 1
23:18 as it is written in the law of Moses 1
24: 6 bring in . . the tax levied by Moses 1
9 tax that Moses . . laid upon Israel 1
25: 4 what is written . . in the book of Moses 1
30:16 accustomed posts according to the law of Moses 1
33: 8 all the law . . given through Moses. 1
34:14 book of the law of the LORD given through Moses. 1
35: 6 to do according to the word of the LORD by Moses. 1
12 as it is written in the book of Moses. 1
Ezr 3: 2 as it is written in the law of Moses the man of God. 1
6:18 as it is written in the book of Moses. 2
7: 6 Ezra . . was a scribe skilled in the law of Moses 1
Neh 1: 7 which thou didst command thy servant Moses. 1
8 word . . didst command thy servant Moses, saying 1
8: 1 Ezra . . to bring the book of the law of Moses 1
14 LORD had commanded by Moses that the people 1
9:14 commandments . . and a law by Moses thy servant. 1
10:29 God's law . . given by Moses the servant of God 1
13: 1 read from the book of Moses in the hearing 1
Ps 77:20 like a flock by the hand of Moses and Aaron. 1
90: 0 A Prayer of Moses, the man of God. 1
99: 6 Moses and Aaron were among his priests 1
103: 7 He made known his ways to Moses 1
105:26 sent Moses his servant, and Aaron 1
106:16 men in the camp were jealous of Moses and Aaron 1
23 destroy them-had not Moses, his chosen one 1
32 it went ill with Moses on their account; 1
Isa 63:11 remembered the days of old, of Moses his servant. 1
12 his glorious arm to go at the right hand of Moses 1
Jer 15: 1 Though Moses and Samuel stood before me 1
Dan 9:11 which are written in the law of Moses the servant 1
13 As it is written in the law of Moses 1
Mic 6: 4 and I sent before you Moses, Aaron, and Miriam. 1
Mal 4: 4 Remember the law of my servant Moses 1
Mat 8: 4 and offer the gift that Moses commanded 3
17: 3 behold, there appeared to them Moses and Eli'jah 3
4 one for you and one for Moses and one for Eli'jah. 3
19: 7 Why then did Moses command 3
8 Moses allowed you to divorce your wives 3
22:24 saying, "Teacher, Moses said 3
23: 2 The scribes and the Pharisees sit on Moses' seat; 3
Mrk 1:44 and offer for your cleansing what Moses commanded 3
7:10 For Moses said, 'Honor your father and your mother'; 3
9: 4 there appeared to them Eli'jah with Moses; 3
5 one for you and one for Moses and one for Eli'jah. 3
10: 3 He answered them, "What did Moses command you? 3
4 Moses allowed a man to write a certificate 3
12:19 Teacher, Moses wrote for us 3
26 have you not read in the book of Moses 3
Lke 2:22 purification according to the law of Moses 3
5:14 as Moses commanded, for a proof to the people. 3
9:30 behold, two men talked with him, Moses and Eli'jah 3
33 one for you and one for Moses and one for Eli'jah 3
16:29 Abraham said, 'They have Moses and the prophets; 3
31 If they do not hear Moses and the prophets 3
20:28 Moses wrote for us that if a man's brother dies 3
37 that the dead are raised, even Moses showed 3
24:27 beginning with Moses and all the prophets 3
44 everything written about me in the law of Moses 3
Joh 1:17 For the law was given through Moses; 3
45 We have found him of whom Moses in the law . . wrote 3
3:14 as Moses lifted up the serpent in the wilderness 3
5:45 it is Moses who accuses you 3
46 If you believed Moses, you would believe me 3
6:32 was not Moses who gave you the bread from heaven; 3
7:19 Did not Moses give you the law? 3
22 Moses gave you circumcision 3
22 not that it is from Moses, but from the fathers 3
23 so that the law of Moses may not be broken 3
8: 5 Now in the law Moses commanded us to stone such. 3
9:28 we are disciples of Moses. 3
29 We know that God has spoken to Moses 3
Act 3:22 Moses said, 'The Lord God will raise up 3
6:11 blasphemous words against Moses and God. 3
14 change the customs which Moses delivered to us. 3
7:20 At this time Moses was born 3
22 Moses was instructed 3
29 At this retort Moses fled 3
31 When Moses saw it he wondered at the sight 3
32 Moses trembled and did not dare to look. 3
35 This Moses whom they refused, saying 3
37 This is the Moses who said to the Israelites 3
40 this Moses who led us out from the land of Egypt 3
44 he who spoke to Moses directed him to make it 3
13:39 you could not be freed by the law of Moses. 3
15: 1 you are circumcised according to the custom of Moses 3
5 to charge them to keep the law of Moses. 3
21 Moses has had in every city those who preach him 3
21:21 you teach all the Jews . . to forsake Moses 3
26:22 what . . Moses said would come to pass 3

28:23 both from the law of Moses and from the prophets. 3
Rom 5:14 Yet death reigned from Adam to Moses 3
9:15 For he says to Moses, "I will have mercy 3
10: 5 Moses writes that the man who practices 3
19 First Moses says, "I will make you jealous of those 3
1Co 9: 9 For it is written in the law of Moses 3
10: 2 all were baptized into Moses in the cloud 3
2Co 3: 7 Israelites could not look at Moses' face 3
13 not like Moses, who put a veil over his face 3
15 Yes, to this day whenever Moses is read 3
2Ti 3: 8 As Jannes and Jambres opposed Moses 3
Heb 3: 2 just as Moses also was faithful in God's house. 3
3 counted worthy of . . much more glory than Moses 3
5 Now Moses was faithful in all God's house 3
16 left Egypt under the leadership of Moses. 3
7:14 Moses said nothing about priests. 3
8: 5 when Moses was about to erect the tent 3
9:19 had been declared by Moses to all the people 3
10:28 A man who has violated the law of Moses dies 3
11:23 By faith Moses . . was hid for three months 3
24 By faith Moses . . refused to be called the son 3
12:21 Moses said, "I tremble with fear. 3
Jde 1: 9 Michael . . disputed about the body of Moses 3
Rev 15: 3 And they sing the song of Moses, the servant of God 3
1Es 1: 6 the commandment . . which was given to Moses. 3
11 as it is written in the book of Moses 3
5:49 the directions in the book of Moses the man of God. 3
7: 6 what was written in the book of Moses. 3
9 in accordance with the book of Moses 3
8: 3 a scribe skilled in the law of Moses 3
9:39 they told Ezra . . to bring the law of Moses 3
2Es 1:13 I gave you Moses as leader and Aaron as priest; 4
7:106 and Moses for our fathers who sinned in the desert 4
129 For this is the way of which Moses . . spoke 4
14: 3 I revealed myself in a bush and spoke to Moses 4
Tob 6:12 according to the law of Moses 3
7:13 Here she is; take her according to the law of Moses 3
Sir 24:23 the law which Moses commanded us 3
45: 1 Moses, whose memory is blessed. 3
6 He exalted Aaron, the brother of Moses •
15 Moses ordained him 3
46: 1 the successor of Moses in prophesying 3
7 in the days of Moses he did a loyal deed 3
Bar 1:20 the Lord declared through Moses his servant 3
2: 2 what is written in the law of Moses 3
28 thou didst speak by thy servant Moses on the day 3
Sus 1: 3 taught . . according to the law of Moses. 3
62 acting in accordance with the law of Moses 3
2Mc 1:29 Plant thy people in thy holy place, as Moses said. 3
2: 4 to the mountain where Moses had gone up 3
8 as they were shown in the case of Moses 3
10 Just as Moses prayed to the Lord 3
11 Moses said, "They were consumed because . . 3
7: 6 as Moses declared in his song 3
30 was given to our fathers through Moses. 3
4Mc 2:17 When Moses was angry with Dathan and Abiram 3
9: 2 to the law and to Moses our counselor. 3
17:19 For Moses says 3
18:18 the song that Moses taught, which says 3

Moza 1. מוֹצָא
1Ch 2:46 Ephah . . bore Haran, Moza, and Gazez; 1
8:36 Zimri was the father of Moza. 1
37 Moza was the father of Bin'e-a; Raphah was his son 1
9:42 and Zimri was the father of Moza. 1
43 Moza . . father of Bin'e-a; and Rephai'ah was his son 1

Mozah 1. מֹצָה
Jos 18:26 Mizpeh, Chephi'rah, Mozah 1

Muppim 1. מֻפִּים
Gen 46:21 Gera, Na'aman, Ehi, Rosh, Muppim, Huppim, and Ard 1

Mushi 1. מוּשִׁי
Exd 6:19 The sons of Merar'i: Mahli and Mushi. 1
Num 3:20 sons of Merar'i . . Mahli and Mushi. 1
1Ch 6:19 The sons of Merar'i: Mahli and Mushi. 1
47 son of Mahli, son of Mushi, son of Merar'i, son of Levi; 1
23:21 The sons of Merar'i: Mahli and Mushi. 1
23 The sons of Mushi: Mahli, Eder, and Jer'emoth, three. 1
24:26 The sons of Merar'i: Mahli and Mushi. 1
30 The sons of Mushi: Mahli, Eder, and Jer'i-moth. 1

Mushite 1. מוּשִׁי
Num 3:33 Of Merar'i were . . the family of the Mushites 1
26:58 of Levi . . the family of the Mushites 1

Muster Gate 1. שַׁעַר הַמִּפְקָד
Neh 3:31 opposite the Muster Gate, and to the upper 1

Muth-labben 1. מוּת לַבֵּן
Ps 9: 0 To the choirmaster: according to Muth-labben. 1

Myndos 1. Μυνδος
1Mc 15:23 to the Spartans, and to Delos, and to Myndos 1

Myra 1. Μύρα
Act 27: 5 we came to Myra in Ly'cia. 1

Mysia 1. Μυσία
Act 16: 7 when they had come opposite My'sia 1
8 so, passing by My'sia, they went down to Tro'as. 1

Mysian 1. Μυσαρχης
2Mc 5:24 Apollonius, the captain of the Mysians 1

Naam 1. נַעַם
1Ch 4:15 The sons of Caleb . . Iru, Elah, and Na'am; 1

Naamah 1. נַעֲמָה
Gen 4:22 The sister of Tubal-cain was Na'amah. 1
Jos 15:41 Gede'roth, Beth-da'gon, Na'amah, and Makke'dah 1
1Kg 14:21 His mother's name was Na'amah the Ammonitess. 1
31 His mother's name was Na'amah the Ammonitess. 1
2Ch 12:13 His mother's name was Na'amah the Ammonitess. 1

Naaman 1. נַעֲמָן 2. Ναιμάν
Gen 46:21 Benjamin: Bela, Becher, Ashbel, Gera, Na'aman, Ehi 1
Num26:40 the sons of Bela were Ard and Na'aman 1
40 of Na'aman, the family of the Na'amites. 1
2Kg 5: 1 Na'aman . . was a great man with his master 1
2 a little maid . . and she waited on Na'aman's wife. 1
4 Na'aman went in and told his lord, "Thus and so spoke •
6 know that I have sent to you Na'aman my servant 1
9 So Na'aman came with his horses and chariots 1
11 Na'aman was angry, and went away, saying, "Behold 1
17 Then Na'aman said, "If not . . let there be given 1
19 when Na'aman had gone from him a short distance •
20 See, my master has spared this Na'aman the Syrian 1
21 Geha'zi followed Na'aman. And when Na'aman saw 1
21 when Na'aman saw some one running after him 1
23 Na'aman said, "Be pleased to accept two talents. 1
27 the leprosy of Na'aman shall cleave to you 1
1Ch 8: 4 Abishu'a, Na'aman, Aho'ah 1
7 Na'aman, Ahi'jah, and Gera, that is, Heglam 1
Lke 4:27 but only Na'aman the Syrian. 2

Naamathite 1. נַעֲמָתִי
Job 2:11 Bildad the Shuhite, and Zophar the Na'amathite. 1
11: 1 Then Zophar the Na'amathite answered 1
20: 1 Then Zophar the Na'amathite answered 1
42: 9 Bildad the Shuhite and Zophar the Na'amathite 1

Naamite 1. נַעֲמִי
Num26:40 of Na'aman, the family of the Na'amites. 1

Naarah 1. נַעֲרָה
Jos 16: 7 goes down from Jan-o'ah to At'aroth and to Na'arah 1
1Ch 4: 5 Asshur . . had two wives, Helah and Na'arah; 1
6 Na'arah bore him Ahuz'zam, Hepher, Te'meni 1
6 These were the sons of Na'arah. 1

Naarai 1. נַעֲרַי
1Ch 11:37 Hezro of Carmel, Na'arai the son of Ezbai 1

Naaran 1. נַעֲרָן
1Ch 7:28 Bethel and its towns, and eastward Na'aran 1

Naathus 1. Νααθος
1Es 9:31 Of the sons of Addi: Naathus and Moossias 1

Nabal 1. נָבָל
1Sm 25: 3 Now the name of the man was Nabal 1
4 David heard . . Nabal was shearing his sheep. 1
5 Go up to Carmel, and go to Nabal, and greet him 1
9 they said all this to Nabal in the name of David; 1
10 Nabal answered David's servants, "Who is David? 1
14 But one of the young men told Ab'igail, Nabal's wife 1
19 But she did not tell her husband Nabal. 1
25 Let not my lord regard this ill-natured . . Nabal; 1
25 Nabal is his name, and folly is with him; 1
26 now then let your enemies . . be as Nabal. 1
34 there had not been left to Nabal 1
36 And Ab'igail came to Nabal; 1
36 And Nabal's heart was merry within him 1
37 in the morning, when the wine had gone out of Nabal 1
38 ten days later the LORD smote Nabal; and he died. 1
39 When David heard that Nabal was dead, he said 1
39 the insult I received at the hand of Nabal 1
39 returned the evil-doing of Nabal upon his own 1
27: 3 Ahin'o-am . . and Ab'igail of Carmel, Nabal's widow. 1
30: 5 Ab'igail the widow of Nabal of Carmel. 1
2Sm 2: 2 Ab'igail the widow of Nabal of Carmel. 1
3: 3 Chil'e-ab, of Ab'igail the widow of Nabal of Carmel; 1

Nabariah 1. Ναβαριας
1Es 9:44 Lothasubus, Nabariah, and Zechariah. 1

Nabatean 1. Ναβαταιος
1Mc 5:25 They encountered the Nabateans 1
9:35 begged the Nabateans, who were his friends 1

Naboth 1. נָבוֹת
1Kg 21: 1 Naboth the Jezreelite had a vineyard in Jezreel 1
2 Ahab said to Naboth, "Give me your vineyard 1
3 Naboth said to Ahab, "The LORD forbid that I should 1
4 sullen because of what Naboth . . had said to him; 1
6 I spoke to Naboth the Jezreelite, and said to him 1
7 I will give you the vineyard of Naboth 1
8 the elders and the nobles who dwelt with Naboth 1
9 Proclaim a fast, and set Naboth on high 1
12 they proclaimed a fast, and set Naboth on high 1
13 base fellows brought a charge against Naboth 1
13 saying, "Naboth cursed God and the king. 1
14 saying, "Naboth has been stoned; he is dead. 1
15 Jez'ebel heard that Naboth had been stoned 1
15 Arise, take possession of the vineyard of Naboth 1
15 Arise, take . . for Naboth is not alive, but dead. 1
16 as soon as Ahab heard that Naboth was dead 1
16 Ahab arose to go down to the vineyard of Naboth 1
18 Ahab . . is in the vineyard of Naboth 1
19 where dogs licked up the blood of Naboth 1
2Kg 9:21 met . . at the property of Naboth the Jezreelite. 1
25 cast him on the . . ground belonging to Naboth 1
26 saw yesterday the blood of Naboth and . . his sons 1

Nacon 1. נָכוֹן
2Sm 6: 6 when they came to the threshing floor of Nacon 1

Nadab 1. נָדָב 2. Ναδαβ
Exd 6:23 and she bore him Nadab, Abi'hu, Elea'zar 1
24: 1 Come up . . you and Aaron, Nadab, and Abi'hu 1
9 Moses and Aaron, Nadab, and Abi'hu, . . went up. 1
28: 1 Nadab and Abi'hu, Elea'zar and Ith'amar. 1
Lev 10: 1 Now Nadab and Abi'hu, the sons of Aaron 1
Num 3: 2 Nadab the first-born, and Abi'hu, Elea'zar 1
4 Nadab and Abi'hu died before the LORD 1
26:60 Aaron was born Nadab, Abi'hu, Elea'zar 1
61 Nadab and Abi'hu died when they offered unholy 1
1Kg 14:20 and Nadab his son reigned in his stead. 1
15:25 Nadab the son of Jerobo'am began to reign 1
27 Nadab and all Israel were laying siege 1
31 the rest of the acts of Nadab, and all that he did 1
1Ch 2:28 The sons of Sham'mai: Nadab and Abi'shur. 1
30 sons of Nadab: Seled and Ap'pa-im; and Seled died 1
6: 3 The sons of Aaron: Nadab, Abi'hu, Elea'zar 1
8:30 first-born son: Abdon, then Zur, Kish, Ba'al, Nadab 1
9:36 son Abdon, then Zur, Kish, Ba'al, Ner, Nadab 1
24: 1 sons of Aaron: Nadab, Abi'hu, Elea'zar, and Ith'amar. 1
2 Nadab and Abi'hu died before their father 1
Ps 68: 9 Rain in abundance, O God, thou didst shed abroad; 1
Tob 11:18 Ahikar and his nephew Nadab came 2
14:10 See, my son, what Nadab did to Ahikar 2
10 escaped the deathtrap which Nadab had set •
10 Nadab fell into the trap and perished. 2

Nadabath 1. Ναδαβαθ
1Mc 9:37 from Nadabath with a large escort. 1

Naggai 1. Ναγγαί
Lke 3:25 the son of Nahum, the son of Esli, the son of Nag'gai 1

Nahalal 1. נַהֲלָל
Jos 19:15 Kattath, Nahal'al, Shimron, I'dalah, and Bethlehem 1
21:35 Dimnah with . . Na'halal with its pasture lands 1

Nahaliel 1. נַחֲלִיאֵל
Num21:19 from Mat'tanah to Nahal'iel, and from Nahal'iel 1
19 to Nahal'iel, and from Nahal'iel to Bamoth 1

Nahalol 1. נַהֲלֹל
Jdg 1:30 not drive out . . or the inhabitants of Na'halol; 1

Naham 1. נַחַם
1Ch 4:19 The sons of the wife of Hodi'ah, the sister of Naham 1

Nahamani 1. נַחֲמָנִי
Neh 7: 7 came with . . Azari'ah, Raami'ah, Naham'ani, 1

Naharai 1. נַחְרַי
2Sm 23:37 Na'harai of Be-er'oth, the armor-bearer of Jo'ab 1
1Ch 11:39 Na'harai of Be-er'oth, the armor-bearer of Jo'ab 1

Nahash 1. נָחָשׁ
1Sm 11: 1 Nahash . . went up and besieged Ja'besh-gil'ead; 1
1 all the men of Jabesh said to Nahash, "Make a treaty 1
2 But Nahash . . said to them, "On this condition 1
12:12 when you saw that Nahash . . came against you 1
2Sm 10: 2 I will deal loyally with Hanun the son of Nahash 1
17:25 who had married Ab'igal the daughter of Nahash 1
27 Shobi the son of Nahash from Rabbah 1
1Ch 19: 1 after this Nahash the king of the Ammonites died 1
2 I will deal loyally with Hanun the son of Nahash 1

Nahath 1. נַחַת
Gen 36:13 are the sons of Reu'el: Nahath, Zerah, Shammah 1
17 the chiefs Nahath, Zerah, Shammah, and Mizzah; 1
1Ch 1:37 sons of Reu'el: Nahath, Zerah, Shammah, and Mizzah. 1
6:26 Elka'nah his son, Zophai his son, Nahath his son 1
2Ch 31:13 while Jehi'el, Azazi'ah, Nahath . . were overseers 1

Nahbi 1. נַחְבִּי
Num13:14 from the tribe of Naph'tali, Nahbi . . of Vophsi; 1

Nahor 1. נָחוֹר 2. Ναχώρ
Gen 11:22 Serug . . became the father of Nahor; 1

23 Serug lived after the birth of Nahor 200 years 1
24 When Nahor had lived 29 years 1
25 Nahor lived after the birth of Terah 119 years 1
26 Terah . . became the father of Abram, Nahor, 1
27 Terah was the father of Abram, Nahor, and Haran; 1
29 Abram and Nahor took wives; 1
29 and the name of Nahor's wife, Milcah 1
22:20 has borne children to your brother Nahor 1
23 Milcah bore to Nahor, Abraham's brother. 1
24:10 went to Mesopota'mia, to the city of Nahor. 1
15 Bethu'el the son of Milcah, the wife of Nahor 1
24 the son of Milcah, whom she bore to Nahor. 1
47 She said, The daughter of Bethu'el, Nahor's son 1
29: 5 said to them, "Do you know Laban the son of Nahor? 1
31:53 The God of Abraham and the God of Nahor 1
Jos 24: 2 Terah, the father of Abraham and of Nahor; 1
1Ch 1:26 Serug, Nahor, Terah; 1
Lke 3:34 the son of Terah, the son of Nahor 2

Nahshon 1. נַחְשׁוֹן 2. Ναασσών

Exd 6:23 took . . the sister of Nahshon; 1
Num 1: 7 from Judah, Nahshon the son of Ammin'adab; 1
2: 3 the leader of the people of Judah being Nahshon 1
7:12 offered his offering the first day was Nahshon 1
17 was the offering of Nahshon the son of Ammin'adab 1
10:14 over their host was Nahshon . . of Ammin'adab. 1
Rut 4:20 Ammin'adab of Nahshon, Nahshon of Salmon 1
20 Ammin'adab of Nahshon, Nahshon of Salmon 1
1Ch 2:10 Ammin'adab was the father of Nahshon, prince 1
11 Nahshon was the father of Salma, Salma of Bo'az 1
Mat 1: 4 Ammin'adab the father of Nahshon 2
4 and Nahshon the father of Salmon 2
Lke 3:32 son of Bo'az, the son of Sala, the son of Nahshon 2

Nahum 1. נַחוּם 2. Ναούμ 3. Naum

Nah 1: 1 The book of the vision of Nahum of Elkosh. 1
Lke 3:25 the son of Nahum, the son of Esli, the son of Nag'gai 2
2Es 1:40 Nahum and Habakkuk, Zephaniah, Haggai, Zechariah 3

Naidus 1. Ναιδος

1Es 9:31 Naathus and Moossias, Laccunus and Naidus 1

Nain 1. Ναΐν

Lke 7:11 Soon afterward he went to a city called Na'in 1

Naioth 1. נָיוֹת

1Sm 19:18 And he and Samuel went and dwelt at Nai'oth. 1
19 Behold, David is at Nai'oth in Ramah. 1
22 And one said, "Behold, they are at Nai'oth in Ramah. 1
23 And he went from there to Nai'oth in Ramah; 1
23 he prophesied, until he came to Nai'oth in Ramah. 1
20: 1 David fled from Nai'oth in Ramah, and came and said 1

Nanea 1. Ναναια 2. Ναναιος

2Mc 1:13 they were cut to pieces in the temple of Nanea 1
13 a deception employed by the priests of Nanea. 1
15 the priests of the temple of Nanea 2

Naomi 1. נָעֳמִי

Rut 1: 2 man was Elim'elech and the name of his wife Na'omi 1
3 But Elim'elech, the husband of Na'omi, died 1
8 But Na'omi said to her two daughters-in-law 1
11 Na'omi said, "Turn back, my daughters, 1
18 Na'omi saw that she was determined to go with her *
19 and the women said, "Is this Na'omi? 1
20 said to them, "Do not call me Na'omi, call me Mara 1
21 Why call me Na'omi, when the LORD has afflicted me 1
22 Na'omi returned, and Ruth . . with her 1
2: 1 Now Na'omi had a kinsman . . whose name was Bo'az. 1
2 And Ruth the Moabitess said to Na'omi, "Let me go 1
6 came back with Na'omi from the country of Moab. 1
20 Na'omi said to her daughter-in-law, "Blessed be he 1
20 Na'omi also said to her, "The man is a relative 1
22 Na'omi said to Ruth, her daughter-in-law, "It is well 1
3: 1 Then Na'omi her mother-in-law said to her 1
4: 3 Na'omi, who has come back . . is selling the parcel 1
5 The day you buy the field from the hand of Na'omi 1
9 bought from the hand of Na'omi all that belonged 1
14 the women said to Na'omi, "Blessed be the LORD 1
16 Na'omi took the child and laid him in her bosom 1
17 gave . . a name, saying, "A son has been born to Na'omi. 1

Naphath 1. נֶפֶת

Jos 17:11 Manas'seh had . . the third is Naphath. 1

Naphath-dor 1. נָפַת דֹּאר 2. נָפַת דּוֹר

Jos 12:23 the king of Dor in Naphath-dor, one; 2
1Kg 4:11 Ben-abin'adab, in all Naphath-dor (he had Taphath 1

Naphish 1. נָפִישׁ

Gen 25:15 Hadad, Tema, Jetur, Naphish, and Ked'emah. 1
1Ch 1:31 Jetur, Naphish, and Ked'emah. These are the sons 1
5:19 made war upon . . Jetur, Naphish, and Nodab; 1

Naphoth-dor 1. נָפוֹת דּוֹר

Jos 11: 2 in the lowland, and in Naphoth-dor on the west 1

Naphtali 1. בְּנֵי נַפְתָּלִי 2. נַפְתָּלִי 3. Νεφθαλίμ

Gen 30: 8 have prevailed"; so she called his name Naph'tali. 2
35:25 sons of Bilhah, Rachel's maid: Dan and Naph'tali 2
46:24 The sons of Naph'tali: Jahzeel, Guni, Jezer 2
49:21 Naph'tali is a hind let loose 2
Exd 1: 4 Dan and Naph'tali, Gad and Asher. 2
Num 1:15 from Naph'tali, Ahi'ra the son of Enan. 2
42 Of the people of Naph'tali, their generations 2
43 the number of the tribe of Naph'tali was 53,400 2
2:29 Then the tribe of Naph'tali 2
29 leader of the people of Naph'tali being Ahi'ra 2
7:78 Ahi'ra the . . leader of the men of Naph'tali 2
10:27 over the host of the tribe of the men of Naph'tali 2
13:14 from the tribe of Naph'tali, Nahbi . . of Vophsi; 2
26:48 sons of Naph'tali according to their families 2
50 families of Naph'tali according 2
34:28 Of the tribe of the sons of Naph'tali a leader 2
Deu 27:13 stand upon Mount Ebal . . Dan and Naph'tali. 2
33:23 of Naph'tali he said, "O Naph'tali, satisfied 2
23 O Naph'tali, satisfied with favor, and full 2
34: 2 all Naph'tali, the land of E'phraim and Manas'seh 2
Jos 19:32 The sixth lot came out for the tribe of Naph'tali 2
32 sixth lot . . for the tribe of Naph'tali 2
39 This is the inheritance of the tribe of Naph'tali 1
20: 7 Kedesh . . in the hill country of Naph'tali 2
21: 6 the tribe of Asher, from the tribe of Naph'tali 2
32 and out of the tribe of Naph'tali, Kedesh 2
Jdg 1:33 Naph'tali did not drive out the inhabitants 2
4: 6 the tribe of Naph'tali and the tribe of Zeb'ulun. 2
6 Barak the son of Abin'o-am from Kedesh in Naph'tali 2
10 Barak summoned Zeb'ulun and Naph'tali to Kedesh; 2
5:18 Naph'tali too, on the heights of the field. 2
6:35 sent messengers to Asher, Zeb'ulun, and Naph'tali; 2
7:23 called out from Naph'tali and from Asher 2
1Kg 4:15 Ahi'ma-az, in Naph'tali (he had taken Bas'emath 2
7:14 He was the son of a widow of the tribe of Naph'tali 2
15:20 all Chin'neroth, with all the land of Naph'tali. 2
2Kg 15:29 Gilead, and Galilee, all the land of Naph'tali; 2
1Ch 2: 2 Dan, Joseph, Benjamin, Naph'tali, Gad, and Asher. 2
6:62 out of the tribes of Is'sachar, Asher, Naph'tali 2
76 out of the tribe of Naph'tali: Kedesh 2
7:13 sons of Naph'tali: Jah'zi-el, Guni, Jezer, and Shallum 2
12:34 Of Naph'tali 1,000 commanders 2
40 from as far as Is'sachar and Zeb'ulun and Naph'tali 2
27:19 for Naph'tali, Jer'emoth the son of Az'riel; 2
2Ch 16: 4 conquered . . all the store-cities of Naph'tali. 2
34: 6 as far as Naph'tali, in their ruins round about 2
Ps 68:27 princes of Zeb'ulun, the princes of Naph'tali. 2
Isa 9: 1 he brought into contempt . . the land of Naph'tali 2
Ezk 48: 3 the east side to the west, Naph'tali, one portion. 2
4 Adjoining the territory of Naph'tali 2
34 of Gad, the gate of Asher, and the gate of Naph'tali. 2
Mat 4:13 in the territory of Zeb'ulun and Naph'tali 3
15 The land of Zeb'ulun and the land of Naph'tali 3
Rev 7: 6 12,000 of the tribe of Naph'tali 3
Tob 1: 1 the tribe of Naphtali 3
2 which is to the south of Kedesh Naphtali 3
4 the whole tribe of Naphtali my forefather 3
5 so did the house of Naphtali my forefather. 3
7: 3 We belong to the sons of Naphtali 3

Naphtuhim 1. נַפְתֻּחִים

Gen 10:13 father of . . An'amim, Leha'bim, Naph-tu'him 1
1Ch 1:11 Egypt was the father of . . Le'habim, Naph-tu'him 1

Narcissus 1. Νάρκισσος

Rom 16:11 those . . who belong to the family of Narcis'sus. 1

Nathan 1. נָתָן 2. Ναθάμ 3. Ναθαν

2Sm 5:14 born to him . . Sham'mu-a, Shobab, Nathan, Solomon 1
7: 2 the king said to Nathan the prophet 1
3 Nathan said to the king, "Go, do all . . in your heart; 1
4 that . . night the word of the LORD came to Nathan 1
17 in accordance with all . . Nathan spoke to David. 1
12: 1 And the LORD sent Nathan to David. 1
5 and he said to Nathan, "As the LORD lives 1
7 Nathan said to David, "You are the man. 1
13 David said to Nathan, "I have sinned 1
13 Nathan said to David, "The LORD . . put away your 1
15 Then Nathan went to his house. 1
25 LORD . . sent a message by Nathan the prophet; 1
23:36 Igal the son of Nathan of Zobah, Bani the Gadite 1
1Kg 1: 8 of Jehoi'ada, and Nathan the prophet, and Shim'e-i 1
10 but he did not invite Nathan the prophet 1
11 Nathan said to Bathshe'ba the mother of Solomon 1
22 still speaking . . Nathan the prophet came in. 1
23 they told the king, "Here is Nathan the prophet. 1
24 Nathan said, "My lord the king, have you said 1
32 Zadok the priest, Nathan the prophet, and Benai'ah 1
34 let Zadok . . and Nathan the prophet . . anoint 1
38 Zadok . . Nathan the prophet, and Benai'ah . . went 1
44 sent . . Zadok . . Nathan the prophet, and Benai'ah 1
45 Zadok . . and Nathan the prophet have anointed 1
4: 5 Azari'ah the son of Nathan was over the officers; 1
5 Zabud the son of Nathan was priest and king's 1
1Ch 2:36 Attai . . father of Nathan and Nathan of Zabad. 1
36 Attai . . father of Nathan and Nathan of Zabad. 1
3: 5 were born to him in Jerusalem . . Nathan 1
11:38 Jo'el the brother of Nathan 1
14: 4 the children . . Shammu'a, Shobab, Nathan, Solomon 1
17: 1 David said to Nathan the prophet 1
2 Nathan said to David, "Do all that is in your heart 1
3 same night the word of the LORD came to Nathan 1
15 In accordance with . . Nathan spoke to David. 1
29:29 and in the Chronicles of Nathan the prophet 1
2Ch 9:29 are they not written in the history of Nathan 1
29:25 commandment of . . Nathan the prophet; 1
Ezr 8:16 Then I sent for . . Jarib, Elna'than, Nathan 1
10:39 Shelemi'ah, Nathan, Adai'ah 1
Ps 51: 0 when Nathan the prophet came to him 1
Zec 12:12 the family of the house of Nathan by itself 1
Lke 3:31 son of Menna, the son of Mat'tatha, the son of Nathan 2
1Es 8:44 Elnathan, Shemaiah, Jarib, Nathan, Elnathan 3
Sir 47: 1 after him Nathan rose up to prophesy 3

Nathan-melech 1. נְתַן מֶלֶךְ

2Kg 23:11 by the chamber of Nathan-melech the chamberlain 1

Nathanael 1. Ναθαναήλ 2. Ναθαναηλος

Joh 1:45 Philip found Nathan'a-el, and said to him 1
46 Nathan'a-el said to him, "Can anything good come out 1
47 Jesus saw Nathan'a-el coming to him, and said of him 1
48 Nathan'a-el said to him, "How do you know me? 1
49 Nathan'a-el answered him, "Rabbi 1
21: 2 Nathan'a-el of Cana in Galilee, the sons of Zeb'edee 1
1Es 9:22 Ishmael, and Nathanael, and Gedaliah, and Elasah. 2
Jdt 8: 1 son of Hilkiah, son of Eliab, son of Nathanael 1

Nazarene 1. Ναζαρηνός 2. Ναζωραῖος

Mat 2:23 fulfilled, "He shall be called a Nazarene. 2
Mrk 14:67 said, "You also were with the Nazarene, Jesus. 1
Act 24: 5 a ringleader of the sect of the Nazarenes. 2

Nazareth 1. Ναζαρά 2. Ναζαρέθ 3. Ναζαρέτ 4. Ναζαρηνός 5. Ναζωραῖος

Mat 2:23 he went and dwelt in a city called Nazareth 3
4:13 leaving Nazareth he went and dwelt in Caper'na-um 1
21:11 the prophet Jesus from Nazareth of Galilee. 2
26:71 This man was with Jesus of Nazareth. 5
Mrk 1: 9 In those days Jesus came from Nazareth of Galilee 3
24 What have you to do with us, Jesus of Nazareth? 4
10:47 when he heard that it was Jesus of Nazareth 4
16: 6 Do not be amazed; you seek Jesus of Nazareth 4
Lke 1:26 to a city of Galilee named Nazareth 2
2: 4 from Galilee, from the city of Nazareth, to Judea 2
39 into Galilee, to their own city, Nazareth. 2
51 he went down with them and came to Nazareth 2
4:16 he came to Nazareth, where he had been brought up; 1
34 Ah! What have you to do with us, Jesus of Nazareth? 4
18:37 They told him, "Jesus of Nazareth is passing by. 5
24:19 they said to him, "Concerning Jesus of Nazareth 4
Joh 1:45 found him . . Jesus of Nazareth, the son of Joseph 3
46 Can anything good come out of Nazareth? 3
18: 5 They answered him, "Jesus of Nazareth. 5
7 And they said, "Jesus of Nazareth. 5
19:19 it read, "Jesus of Nazareth, the King of the Jews. 5
Act 2:22 Jesus of Nazareth, a man attested to you by God 5
3: 6 in the name of Jesus Christ of Nazareth, walk. 5
4:10 Jesus Christ of Nazareth, whom you crucified 5
6:14 Jesus of Nazareth will destroy this place 5
10:38 how God anointed Jesus of Nazareth 2
22: 8 'I am Jesus of Nazareth whom you are persecuting.' 5
26: 9 in opposing the name of Jesus of Nazareth. 5

Nazirite 1. נָזִיר 2. Ναζιραιος

Num 6: 2 makes a special vow, the vow of a Nazirite 1
13 this is the law for the Nazirite 1
18 Nazirite shall shave his consecrated head 1
19 shall put them upon the hands of the Nazirite 1
20 after that the Nazirite may drink wine. 1
21 This is the law for the Nazirite who takes a vow. 1
Jdg 13: 5 for the boy shall be a Nazirite to God from birth; 1
7 for the boy shall be a Nazirite to God from birth 1
16:17 I have been a Nazirite to God from my mother's 1
Ams 2:11 and some of your young men for Nazirites. 1
12 But you made the Nazirites drink wine 1
1Mc 3:49 they stirred up the Nazirites 2

separation as a Nazirite 1. נֵזֶר

Num 6:21 law for his separation as a Nazirite. 1

vow as a Nazirite 1. נָזִיר

Num 6:21 shall be according to his vow as a Nazirite 1

Neah 1. נֵעָה

Jos 19:13 and going on to Rimmon it bends toward Ne'ah; 1

Neapolis 1. Νέα πόλις

Act 16:11 and the following day to Ne-ap'olis 1

Neariah 1. נְעַרְיָה

1Ch 3:22 sons of Shemai'ah . . Neari'ah and Shaphat, six. 1
23 sons of Neari'ah: Eli-o-e'nai, Hizki'ah, and Azri'kam 1
4:42 having as their leaders Pelati'ah, Ne-ari'ah 1

Nebai 1. נֵיבָי
Neh 10:19 Hariph, An'athoth, Ne'bai 1

Nebaioth 1. נְבָיוֹת
Gen 25:13 Neba'ioth, the first-born of Ish'mael; 1
28: 9 Ma'halath . . the sister of Neba'ioth. 1
36: 3 Ish'mael's daughter, the sister of Neba'ioth. 1
1Ch 1:29 Ish'mael, Neba'ioth; and Kedar, Adbeel, Mibsam 1
Isa 60: 7 the rams of Nebai'oth shall minister to you; 1

Neballat 1. נְבַלָּט
Neh 11:34 Hadid, Zebo'im, Nebal'lat 1

Nebat 1. נְבָט 2. Ναβατ
1Kg 11:26 Jerobo'am the son of Nebat, an E'phraimite 1
12: 2 when Jerobo'am the son of Nebat heard of it 1
15 the LORD spoke . . to Jerobo'am the son of Nebat. 1
15: 1 in the . . year of King Jerobo'am the son of Nebat 1
16: 3 the house of Jerobo'am the son of Nebat. 1
26 walked in all the way of Jerobo'am the son of Nebat 1
31 to walk in the sins of Jerobo'am the son of Nebat 1
21:22 like the house of Jerobo'am the son of Nebat 1
22:52 walked . . in the way of Jerobo'am the son of Nebat 1
2Kg 3: 3 he clung to the sin of Jerobo'am the son of Nebat 1
9: 9 like the house of Jerobo'am the son of Nebat 1
10:29 turn . . from the sins of Jerobo'am the son of Nebat 1
13: 2 the sins of Jerobo'am the son of Nebat 1
11 from all the sins of Jerobo'am the son of Nebat 1
14:24 all the sins of Jerobo'am the son of Nebat 1
15: 9 depart from the sins of Jerobo'am the son of Nebat 1
18 from all the sins of Jerobo'am the son of Nebat 1
24 away from the sins of Jerobo'am the son of Nebat 1
28 depart from the sins of Jerobo'am the son of Nebat 1
17:21 When . . they made Jerobo'am the son of Nebat king. 1
23:15 high place erected by Jerobo'am the son of Nebat 1
2Ch 9:29 concerning Jerobo'am the son of Nebat? 1
10: 2 when Jerobo'am the son of Nebat heard of it 1
15 spoke by Ahi'jah . . to Jerobo'am the son of Nebat. 1
13: 6 Jerobo'am the son of Nebat, a servant of Solomon 1
Sir 47:23 Also Jeroboam the son of Nebat 2

Nebo 1. נְבוֹ 2. Νοομα
Num32: 3 Nimrah, Heshbon, Elea'leh, Sebam, Nebo, and Be'on 1
38 Nebo, and Ba'al-me'on (their names to be changed) 1
33:47 encamped in the mountains of Ab'arim, before Nebo. 1
Deu 32:49 Ascend this mountain of the Ab'arim, Mount Nebo 1
34: 1 Moses went up from the plains of Moab to Mount Nebo 1
1Ch 5: 8 who dwelt in Aro'er, as far as Nebo and Ba'al-me'on. 1
Ezr 2:29 sons of Nebo, 52. 1
10:43 Of the sons of Nebo: Je-i'el, Mattithi'ah, Zabad 1
Neh 7:33 men of the other Nebo, 52. 1
Isa 15: 2 over Nebo and over Med'eba Moab wails. 1
46: 1 Bel bows down, Nebo stoops 1
Jer 48: 1 Woe to Nebo, for it is laid waste! 1
22 and Dibon, and Nebo, and Beth-diblatha'im 1
1Es 9:35 Of the sons of Nebo: Mattithiah, Zabad, Iddo, Joel 2

Nebuchadnezzar 1. נְבוּכַדְנֶאצַּר 2. נְבוּכַדְנֶצַּר (A) 3. Ναβουχοδονοσορ
2Kg 24: 1 Nebuchadnez'zar king of Babylon came up 1
10 the servants of Nebuchadnez'zar . . came up 1
11 Nebuchadnez'zar . . came to the city 1
25: 1 Nebuchadnez'zar . . came with all his army 1
8 was the nineteenth year of King Nebuchadnez'zar 1
22 whom Nebuchadnez'zar king of Babylon had left 1
1Ch 6:15 into exile by the hand of Nebuchadnez'zar. 1
2Ch 36: 6 Against him came up Nebuchadnez'zar 1
7 Nebuchadnez'zar also carried part 1
10 King Nebuchadnez'zar sent and brought him 1
13 He also rebelled against King Nebuchadnez'zar 1
Ezr 1: 7 vessels . . Nebuchadnez'zar had carried away 1
2: 1 exiles whom Nebuchadnez'zar the king of Babylon 2
5:12 gave them into the hand of Nebuchadnez'zar king 2
14 vessels . . which Nebuchadnez'zar had taken out 2
6: 5 which Nebuchadnez'zar took out of the temple 2
Neh 7: 6 exiles whom Nebuchadnez'zar the king of Babylon 2
Est 2: 6 Nebuchadnez'zar king of Babylon had carried 1
Jer 27: 6 all these lands into the hand of Nebuchadnez'zar 1
8 not serve this Nebuchadnez'zar king of Babylon 1
20 Nebuchadnez'zar king of Babylon did not take 1
28: 3 which Nebuchadnez'zar king of Babylon took away 1
11 Even so will I break the yoke of Nebuchadnez'zar 1
14 an iron yoke of servitude to Nebuchadnez'zar 1
29: 1 the people, whom Nebuchadnez'zar had taken 1
3 to Babylon to Nebuchadnez'zar king of Babylon. 1
Dan 1:18 chief . . brought them in before Nebuchadnez'zar. 2
2: 1 second year of the reign of Nebuchadnez'zar 2
1 second year . . Nebuchadnez'zar had dreams; 2
28 made known to King Nebuchadnez'zar what will be 2
46 Then King Nebuchadnez'zar fell upon his face 2
3: 1 King Nebuchadnez'zar made an image of gold 2
2 Then King Nebuchadnez'zar sent to assemble 2
2 image which King Nebuchadnez'zar had set up. 2
3 image that King Nebuchadnez'zar had set up; 2
3 image that Nebuchadnez'zar had set up. 2
5 golden image . . King Nebuchadnez'zar has set up; 2
7 golden image . . King Nebuchadnez'zar had set up. 2
9 said to King Nebuchadnez'zar, "O king 2
13 Then Nebuchadnez'zar in furious rage commanded 2
14 Nebuchadnez'zar said to them, "Is it true 2
16 O Nebuchadnez'zar, we have no need to answer you 2
19 Then Nebuchadnez'zar was full of fury 2
24 King Nebuchadnez'zar was astonished and rose up 2
26 Then Nebuchadnez'zar came near to the door 2
28 Nebuchadnez'zar said, "Blessed be the God 2
4: 1 King Nebuchadnez'zar to all peoples 2
4 Nebuchadnez'zar, was at ease in my house 2
18 This dream I, King Nebuchadnez'zar, saw. 2
28 All this came upon King Nebuchadnez'zar. 2
31 O King Nebuchadnez'zar, to you it is spoken 2
33 word was fulfilled upon Nebuchadnez'zar. 2
34 Nebuchadnez'zar, lifted my eyes to heaven 2
37 Now I, Nebuchadnez'zar, praise and extol and honor 2
5: 2 Nebuchadnez'zar his father had taken 2
11 King Nebuchadnez'zar, your father, made him chief 2
18 Most High God gave Nebuchadnez'zar your father 2
1Es 1:40 Nebuchadnezzar king of Babylon 3
41 Nebuchadnezzar also took some holy vessels 3
45 Nebuchadnezzar sent and removed him to Babylon 3
48 though King Nebuchadnezzar had made him swear 3
2:10 which Nebuchadnezzar had carried away 3
5: 7 Nebuchadnezzar king of Babylon 3
6:15 gave them over into the hands of Nebuchadnezzar 3
18 which Nebuchadnezzar had taken out of the house 3
26 which Nebuchadnezzar took out of the house 3
Tob 14:15 Nebuchadnezzar and Ahasuerus had captured. 3
Jdt 1: 1 the twelfth year of the reign of Nebuchadnezzar 3
5 Nebuchadnezzar made war against King Arphaxad 3
7 Then Nebuchadnezzar king of the Assyrians sent 3
11 disregarded the orders of Nebuchadnezzar 3
12 Then Nebuchadnezzar was very angry 3
2: 1 Nebuchadnezzar king of the Assyrians 3
4 Nebuchadnezzar king of the Assyrians 3
19 to go ahead of King Nebuchadnezzar 3
3: 2 the servants of Nebuchadnezzar, the Great King 3
8 all nations should worship Nebuchadnezzar 3
4: 1 Holofernes, the general of Nebuchadnezzar 3
6: 2 Who is God except Nebuchadnezzar? 3
4 So says King Nebuchadnezzar 3
11: 1 any one who chose to serve Nebuchadnezzar 3
4 the servants of my lord King Nebuchadnezzar. 3
7 Nebuchadnezzar the king of the whole earth 3
7 will live by your power under Nebuchadnezzar 3
23 shall live in the house of King Nebuchadnezzar 3
12:13 who serve in the house of Nebuchadnezzar. 3
14:18 the house of King Nebuchadnezzar 3
AEs 11: 4 Nebuchadnezzar king of Babylon 3
Bar 1: 9 after Nebuchadnezzar king of Babylon had 3
11 Nebuchadnezzar king of Babylon 3
12 Nebuchadnezzar king of Babylon 3
LJr 1: 2 Nebuchadnezzar, king of the Babylonians. 3

Nebuchadrezzar 1. נְבוּכַדְרֶאצַּר
Jer 21: 2 Nebuchadrez'zar king of Babylon is making war 1
7 into the hand of Nebuchadrez'zar king of Babylon 1
22:25 into the hand of Nebuchadrez'zar king of Babylon 1
24: 1 After Nebuchadrez'zar king of Babylon had taken 1
25: 1 the first year of Nebuchadrez'zar king of Babylon 1
9 and for Nebuchadrez'zar the king of Babylon 1
29:21 deliver them into the hand of Nebuchadrez'zar 1
32: 1 was the eighteenth year of Nebuchadrez'zar. 1
28 into the hand of Nebuchadrez'zar king of Babylon 1
34: 1 when Nebuchadrez'zar king of Babylon 1
35:11 when Nebuchadrez'zar king of Babylon came up 1
37: 1 whom Nebuchadrez'zar king of Babylon made king 1
39: 1 Nebuchadrez'zar king of Babylon and all his army 1
5 they brought him up to Nebuchadrez'zar 1
11 Nebuchadrez'zar king of Babylon gave command 1
43:10 and take Nebuchadrez'zar the king of Babylon 1
44:30 into the hand of Nebuchadrez'zar king of Babylon 1
46: 2 which Nebuchadrez'zar king of Babylon defeated 1
13 the coming of Nebuchadrez'zar king of Babylon 1
26 into the hand of Nebuchadrez'zar king of Babylon 1
49:28 Hazor which Nebuchadrez'zar . . smote. 1
30 Nebuchadrez'zar king of Babylon has made a plan 1
50:17 now at last Nebuchadrez'zar king of Babylon 1
51:34 Nebuchadrez'zar the king of Babylon 1
52: 4 Nebuchadrez'zar king of Babylon came 1
12 Nebuchadrez'zar, king of Babylon–Nebu'zarad'an 1
28 the people whom Nebuchadrez'zar carried away 1
29 in the eighteenth year of Nebuchadrez'zar 1
30 in the 23rd year of Nebuchadrez'zar 1
Ezk 26: 7 Nebuchadrez'zar king of Babylon, king of kings 1
29:18 Nebuchadrez'zar king of Babylon made his army 1
19 I will give the land of Egypt to Nebuchadrez'zar 1
30:10 by the hand of Nebuchadrez'zar king of Babylon. 1

Nebushazban 1. נְבוּשַׁזְבָּן
Jer 39:13 Nebushaz'ban the Rab'saris 1

Nebuzaradan 1. נְבוּזַרְאֲדָן
2Kg 25: 8 Nebu'zarad'an . . came to Jerusalem. 1
11 the rest . . Nebu'zarad'an..carried into exile. 1
20 Nebu'zarad'an . . took them, and brought them 1
Jer 39: 9 Then Nebu'zarad'an, the captain of the guard 1
10 Nebu'zarad'an, the captain of the guard, 1
11 concerning Jeremiah through Nebu'zarad'an 1
13 Nebu'zarad'an the captain of the guard 1
40: 1 after Nebu'zarad'an . . had let him go from Ramah 1
41:10 Nebu'zarad'an, the captain of the guard 1
43: 6 and every person whom Nebu'zarad'an . . had left 1
52:12 Nebu'zarad'an the captain of the bodyguard 1
15 Nebu'zarad'an the captain of the guard 1
16 Nebu'zarad'an the captain of the guard left some 1
26 Nebu'zarad'an the captain of the guard took them 1
30 Nebu'zarad'an the captain of the guard 1

Neco 1. נְכוֹ
2Kg 23:29 Pharaoh Neco . . went up to the king of Assyria 1
29 Josi'ah went to meet him; and Pharaoh Neco slew him •
33 Pharaoh Neco put him in bonds at Riblah 1
34 Pharaoh Neco made Eli'akim the son of Josi'ah king 1
35 He exacted . . to give it to Pharaoh Neco. 1
2Ch 35:20 Neco king of Egypt went up to fight at Car'chemish 1
22 did not listen to the words of Neco from . . God 1
36: 4 Neco took Jeho'ahaz . . and carried him to Egypt. 1
Jer 46: 2 Concerning the army of Pharaoh Neco 1

Nedabiah 1. נְדַבְיָה
1Ch 3:18 Shenaz'zar, Jekami'ah, Hosh'ama, and Nedabi'ah; 1

Negeb 1. נֶגֶב
Gen 12: 9 still going toward the Negeb. 1
13: 1 and Lot with him, into the Negeb. 1
3 he journeyed on from the Negeb as far as Bethel 1
20: 1 journeyed toward the territory of the Negeb 1
24:62 Isaac . . was dwelling in the Negeb. 1
Num13:17 Go up into the Negeb yonder, and go up into the hill 1
22 They went up into the Negeb, and came to Hebron; 1
29 Amal'ekites dwell in the land of the Negeb; 1
21: 1 Canaanite, the king of Arad, who dwelt in the Negeb 1
33:40 king of Arad, who dwelt in the Negeb in . . Canaan 1
Deu 1: 7 lowland, and in the Negeb, and by the seacoast 1
34: 3 Negeb, and the Plain, that is, the valley of Jericho 1
Jos 10:40 the whole land, the hill country and the Negeb 1
11:16 all that land, the hill country and all the Negeb 1
12: 8 in the slopes, in the wilderness, and in the Negeb 1
15:19 since you have set me in the land of the Negeb 1
19: 8 as far as Ba'alath-beer, Ramah of the Negeb. 1
Jdg 1: 9 dwelt in the hill country, in the Negeb 1
15 you have set me in the land of the Negeb, give me 1
16 of Judah, which lies in the Negeb near Arad; 1
1Sm 27:10 David would say, "Against the Negeb of Judah 1
10 Against the Negeb of the Jerah'meelites 1
10 or, "Against the Negeb of the Ken'ites. 1
30: 1 had made a raid upon the Negeb and upon Ziklag. 1
14 made a raid upon the Negeb of the Cher'ethites 1
14 made a raid . . and upon the Negeb of Caleb; 1
27 it was for those in Bethel, in Ramoth of the Negeb 1
2Sm 24: 7 they went out to the Negeb of Judah at Beer-sheba. 1
2Ch 28:18 made raids on the cities in . . the Negeb of Judah 1
Ps 126: 4 fortunes . . like the watercourses in the Negeb! 1
Isa 21: 1 As whirlwinds in the Negeb sweep on 1
30: 6 An oracle on the beasts of the Negeb. 1
Jer 13:19 The cities of Negeb are shut up, with none to open 1
17:26 from the hill country, and from the Negeb 1
32:44 of the Shephe'lah, and in the cities of the Negeb; 1
33:13 of the Shephe'lah, and in the cities of the Negeb 1
Ezk 20:46 and prophesy against the forest land in the Negeb 1
47 say to the forest of the Negeb, Hear the word 1
Obd 1:19 Those of the Negeb shall possess Mount Esau 1
20 exiles . . shall possess the cities of the Negeb. 1

Nehelam 1. נֶחֱלָמִי
Jer 29:24 To Shemai'ah of Nehel'am you shall say 1
31 says the LORD concerning Shemai'ah of Nehel'am 1
32 punish Shemai'ah of Nehel'am and his descendants; 1

Nehemiah 1. נְחֶמְיָה 2. Νεεμιας
Ezr 2: 2 They came with Zerub'babel, Jeshua, Nehemi'ah 1
Neh 1: 1 The words of Nehemi'ah the son of Hacali'ah. 1
3:16 After him Nehemi'ah the son of Azbuk, ruler of half 1
7: 7 came with Zerub'babel, Jeshua, Nehemi'ah, Azari'ah 1
8: 9 Nehemi'ah, who was the governor 1
10: 1 set their seal are Nehemi'ah the governor 1
12:26 days of Nehemi'ah the governor and of Ezra 1
47 all Israel . . in the days of Nehemi'ah 1
1Es 5: 8 Nehemiah, Seraiah, Resaiah, Bigvai, Mordecai 2
40 Nehemiah and Attharias told them . . 2
Sir 49:13 The memory of Nehemiah also is lasting 2
2Mc 1:18 Nehemiah, who built the temple and the altar 2
20 Nehemiah . . sent the descendants 2
21 Nehemiah ordered the priests to sprinkle 2
23 the rest responded, as did Nehemiah. 2
31 Nehemiah ordered that . . 2
33 Nehemiah and his associates 2
36 Nehemiah and his associates 2
2:13 in the memoirs of Nehemiah 2

Nehum 1. נְחוּם
Neh 7: 7 came with . . Bigva'i, Nehum, Ba'anah. 1

Nehushta 1. נְחֻשְׁתָּא
2Kg 24: 8 name was Nehush'ta the daughter of Elna'than 1

Nehushtan 1. נְחֻשְׁתָּן
2Kg 18: 4 the bronze serpent . . it was called Nehush'tan. 1

Neiel 1. נְעִיאֵל
Jos 19:27 touches . . northward to Beth-emek and Nei'el; 1

Nekoda 1. נְקוֹדָא 2. Νεκωδαν 3. Νοεβα
Ezr 2:48 sons of Rezin, the sons of Neko'da 1
60 the sons of Tobi'ah, and the sons of Neko'da 1
Neh 7:50 Re-ai'ah, the sons of Rezin, the sons of Neko'da 1
62 Delai'ah, the sons of Tobi'ah, the sons of Neko'da 1
1Es 5:31 the sons of Nekoda, the sons of Chezib 3
37 the son of Tobiah, the sons of Nekoda, 652. 2

Nemuel 1. נְמוּאֵל
Num26: 9 The sons of Eli'ab: Nem'uel, Dathan, and Abi'ram. 1
12 of Nem'uel, the family of the Nem'uelites; 1
1Ch 4:24 sons of Simeon: Nem'uel, Jamin, Jarib, Zerah, Sha'ul; 1

Nemuelite 1. נְמוּאֵלִי
Num26:12 of Nem'uel, the family of the Nem'uelites; 1

Nepheg 1. נֶפֶג
Exd 6:21 The sons of Izhar: Korah, Nepheg, and Zichri. 1
2Sm 5:15 Ibhar, Eli'shu-a, Nepheg, Japhi'a 1
1Ch 3: 7 Nogah, Nepheg, Japhi'a 1
14: 6 Nogah, Nepheg, Japhi'a 1

Nephilim 1. נְפִלִים
Gen 6: 4 The Nephilim were on the earth in those days 1
Num13:33 there we saw the Nephilim (the sons of Anak 1
33 (the sons of Anak, who come from the Nephilim); 1

Nephisim 1. נְפִיסִים 2. Ναφισι
Ezr 2:50 the sons of Me-u'nim, the sons of Nephi'sim 1
1Es 5:31 the sons of the Meunites, the sons of Nephisim 2

Nephtoah 1. נֶפְתּוֹחַ
Jos 15: 9 from . . to the spring of the Waters of Nephto'ah 1
18:15 to Ephron, to the spring of the Waters of Nephto'ah; 1

Nephushesim 1. נְפוּשְׁסִים
Neh 7:52 the sons of Me-u'nim, the sons of Nephush'esim 1

Ner 1. נֵר
1Sm 14:50 commander of his army was Abner the son of Ner 1
51 and Ner the father of Abner was the son of Abi'el. 1
26: 5 the place where Saul lay, with Abner the son of Ner 1
14 David called . . to Abner the son of Ner 1
2Sm 2: 8 Now Abner the son of Ner . . had taken Ish-bo'sheth 1
12 Abner the son of Ner . . went out from Mahana'im 1
3:23 Abner the son of Ner came to the king 1
25 You know that Abner the son of Ner came to deceive 1
28 for the blood of Abner the son of Ner. 1
37 not . . the king's will to slay Abner the son of Ner. 1
1Kg 2: 5 commanders . . Abner the son of Ner, and Ama'sa 1
32 slew . . Abner the son of Ner, commander of the army 1
1Ch 8:33 Ner was the father of Kish, Kish of Saul 1
9:36 first-born son Abdon, then Zur, Kish, Ba'al, Ner, 1
39 Ner was the father of Kish, Kish of Saul 1
26:28 Abner the son of Ner, and Jo'ab the son of Zeru'iah 1

Neraiah 1. Νηριας
Bar 1: 1 Baruch the son of Neraiah, son of Mahseiah 1

Nereus 1. Νηρεύς
Rom16:15 Greet Philol'ogus, Julia, Nereus and his sister 1

Nergal 1. נֵרְגַל
2Kg 17:30 the men of Cuth made Nergal, the men of Hamath 1

Nergal-shar-ezer 1. נֵרְגַל שַׂר אֶצֶר
Jer 39: 3 Ner'gal-share'zer, Sam'gar-ne'bo 1
3 Ner'gal-share'zer the Rabmag 1
13 Ner'gal-share'zer the Rabmag 1

Neri 1. Νηρί
Lke 3:27 the son of She-al'ti-el, the son of Neri 1

Neriah 1. נֵרִיָּהוּ
Jer 32:12 to Baruch the son of Neri'ah son of Mahsei'ah 1
16 the deed of purchase to Baruch the son of Neri'ah 1
36: 4 Then Jeremiah called Baruch the son of Neri'ah 1
8 Baruch the son of Neri'ah did all that 1
14 Baruch the son of Neri'ah took the scroll 1
32 and gave it to Baruch the scribe, the son of Neri'ah 1
43: 3 Baruch the son of Neri'ah has set you against us 1
6 also Jeremiah . . and Baruch the son of Neri'ah. 1
45: 1 the prophet spoke to Baruch the son of Neri'ah 1
51:59 the prophet commanded Serai'ah the son of Neri'ah 1

Netaim 1. נְטָעִים
1Ch 4:23 potters and inhabitants of Neta'im and Gede'rah; 1

Nethanel 1. נְתַנְאֵל 2. Ναθαναήλ
Num 1: 8 from Is'sachar, Nethan'el the son of Zu'ar; 1
2: 5 the leader . . being Nethan'el the son of Zu'ar 1
7:18 Nethan'el the son of Zu'ar, the leader of Is'sachar 1
23 was the offering of Nethan'el the son of Zu'ar. 1
10:15 over the host . . was Nethan'el the son of Zu'ar. 1
1Ch 2:14 Nethan'el the fourth, Raddai the fifth 1
15:24 Shebani'ah, Josh'aphat, Nethan'el, Ama'sai 1
24: 6 scribe Shemai'ah the son of Nethan'el, a Levite 1
26: 4 O'bed-e'dom had sons . . Nethan'el the fifth 1
2Ch 17: 7 he sent his princes . . Nethan'el, and Micai'ah 1
35: 9 Shemai'ah and Nethan'el his brothers 1
Ezr 10:22 of Pashhur . . Nethan'el, Jo'zabad, and Ela'sah. 1
Neh 12:21 of Hilki'ah, Hashabi'ah; of Jedai'ah, Nethan'el. 1
36 kinsmen . . Ma'ai, Nethan'el, Judah, and Hana'ni 1
1Es 1: 9 Jeconiah and Shemaiah and Nethanel his brother 2

Nethaniah 1. נְתַנְיָהוּ 2. Ναθανιας
2Kg 25:23 they came . . namely, Ish'mael the son of Nethani'ah 1
25 Ish'mael the son of Nethani'ah, son of Eli'shama 1
1Ch 25: 2 sons of Asaph . . Nethani'ah, and Ashare'lah 1
12 fifth to Nethani'ah, his sons and his brethren 1
2Ch 17: 8 with them the Levites, Shemai'ah, Nethani'ah 1
Ezr 2:22 men of Neto'phah, 56. 1
Jer 36:14 all the princes sent Jehu'di the son of Nethani'ah 1
40: 8 Ish'mael the son of Nethani'ah 1
14 Ba'alis . . has sent Ish'mael the son of Nethani'ah 1
15 Let me go and slay Ish'mael the son of Nethani'ah 1
41: 1 Ish'mael the son of Nethani'ah, son of Eli'shama 1
2 Ish'mael the son of Nethani'ah and the ten men 1
6 And Ish'mael the son of Nethani'ah came out 1
7 Ish'mael the son of Nethani'ah and the men with him 1
9 the son of Nethani'ah filled it with the slain. 1
10 Ish'mael the son of Nethani'ah took them captive 1
11 evil which Ish'mael the son of Nethani'ah had done 1
12 to fight against Ish'mael the son of Nethani'ah. 1
15 But Ish'mael the son of Nethani'ah escaped 1
16 whom Ish'mael the son of Nethani'ah had carried 1
18 Ish'mael the son of Nethani'ah had slain Gedali'ah 1
1Es 9:34 Binnui, Elialis, Shimei, Shelemiah, Nethaniah 2

Netophah 1. נְטֹפָה 2. נְטֹפָתִי 3. Νετωφα
2Sm 23:28 Zalmon the Aho'hite, Ma'harai of Netoph'ah 2
29 Heleb the son of Ba'anah of Netoph'ah 2
1Ch 11:30 Ma'harai of Netoph'ah 2
30 Heled the son of Ba'anah of Netoph'ah 2
27:13 Tenth . . was Ma'harai of Netoph'ah 2
Neh 7:26 men of Bethlehem and Neto'phah, 188. 1
1Es 5:18 The men of Netophah, 55. The men of Anathoth, 158. 3

Netophathite 1. נְטֹפָתִי
2Kg 25:23 Serai'ah the son of Tanhu'meth the Netoph'athite 1
1Ch 2:54 sons of Salma: Bethlehem, the Netoph'athites 1
9:16 who dwelt in the villages of the Netoph'athites. 1
27:15 Twelfth . . was Heldai the Netoph'athite 1
Neh 12:28 from the villages of the Netoph'athites; 1
Jer 40: 8 the sons of Ephai the Netoph'athite 1

Neziah 1. נְצִיחַ 2. Νασι
Ezr 2:54 sons of Nezi'ah, and the sons of Hati'pha. 1
Neh 7:56 sons of Nezi'ah, the sons of Hati'pha. 1
1Es 5:32 the sons of Neziah, the sons of Hatipha. 2

Nezib 1. נְצִיב
Jos 15:43 Iphtah, Ashnah, Nezib 1

Nibhaz 1. נִבְחַז
2Kg 17:31 and the Av'vites made Nibhaz and Tartak; 1

Nibshan 1. נִבְשָׁן
Jos 15:62 Nibshan, the City of Salt, and En-ge'di 1

Nicanor 1. Νικάνωρ
Act 6: 5 Philip, and Proch'orus, and Nica'nor, and Ti'mon 1
1Mc 3:38 Nicanor and Gorgias 1
7:26 the king sent Nicanor, one of his honored princes 1
27 So Nicanor came to Jerusalem with a large force 1
30 Nicanor had come to him with treacherous intent •
31 When Nicanor learned 1
32 About 500 men of the army of Nicanor fell 1
33 After these events Nicanor went up to Mount Zion 1
39 Now Nicanor went out from Jerusalem 1
42 Nicanor has spoken wickedly •
43 The army of Nicanor was crushed 1
44 When his army saw that Nicanor had fallen 1
47 they cut off Nicanor's head 1
9: 1 Nicanor and his army had fallen in battle 1
2Mc 8: 9 Ptolemy promptly appointed Nicanor 1
10 Nicanor determined to make up . . the tribute 1
12 Word came . . concerning Nicanor's invasion 1
14 who had been sold by the ungodly Nicanor 1
23 he joined battle with Nicanor. 1
24 wounded and disabled most of Nicanor's army 1
34 The thrice-accursed Nicanor 1
9: 3 news came to him of what had happened to Nicanor 1
12: 2 these Nicanor the governor of Cyprus 1
14:12 he immediately chose Nicanor 1
14 flocked to join Nicanor, thinking that . . 1
15 When the Jews heard of Nicanor's coming 1
17 Simon . . had encountered Nicanor 1
18 Nicanor . . shrank from deciding the issue 1
23 Nicanor stayed on in Jerusalem 1
26 Nicanor was disloyal to the government 1
27 The king . . wrote to Nicanor 1
28 When this message came to Nicanor 1
30 Nicanor was more austere in his dealings 1
30 and went into hiding from Nicanor. 1
37 was denounced to Nicanor 1
39 Nicanor . . sent more than 500 soldiers to arrest him; 1
15: 1 When Nicanor heard 1
6 Nicanor . . had determined to erect 1
25 Nicanor and his men advanced with trumpets 1
28 they recognized Nicanor, lying dead 1
30 ordered them to cut off Nicanor's head and arm 1
32 He showed them the vile Nicanor's head 1
33 he cut out the tongue of the ungodly Nicanor 1
35 he hung Nicanor's head from the citadel 1
37 This . . is how matters turned out with Nicanor. 1
4Mc 3:20 even Seleucus Nicanor, king of Asia 1

Nicodemus 1. Νικόδημος
Joh 3: 1 there was a man of the Pharisees, named Nicode'mus 1
4 Nicode'mus said to him, "How can a man be born 1
9 Nicode'mus said to him, "How can this be? 1
7:50 Nicode'mus, who had gone to him before 1
19:39 Nicode'mus also . . came 1

Nicolaitan 1. Νικολαΐτης
Rev 2: 6 you hate the works of the Nicola'itans 1
15 some who hold the teaching of the Nicola'itans. 1

Nicolaus 1. Νικόλαος
Act 6: 5 Par'menas, and Nicola'us, a proselyte of Antioch. 1

Nicopolis 1. Νικόπολις
Tit 3:12 do your best to come to me at Nicop'olis 1

Niger 1. Νίγερ
Act 13: 1 Barnabas, Simeon who was called Niger 1

Nile 1. יְאֹר 2. יָם 3. שִׁיחוֹר
Gen 41: 1 Pharaoh dreamed that he was standing by the Nile 1
2 behold, there came up out of the Nile seven cows 1
3 cows . . came up out of the Nile after them 1
3 stood by the other cows on the bank of the Nile. 1
17 dream I was standing on the banks of the Nile; 1
18 came up out of the Nile and fed in the reed grass; 1
Exd 1:22 Every son . . you shall cast into the Nile 1
4: 9 you shall take some water from the Nile and pour 1
9 and the water which you shall take from the Nile 1
7:17 I will strike the water that is in the Nile 1
18 the fish in the Nile shall die, and the Nile shall 1
18 and the Nile shall become foul 1
18 will loathe to drink water from the Nile. 1
20 he . . struck the water that was in the Nile 1
20 all the water . . in the Nile turned to blood. 1
21 the fish in the Nile died; and the Nile became foul 1
21 the fish in the Nile died; and the Nile became foul 1
21 Egyptians could not drink water from the Nile; 1
24 Egyptians dug round about the Nile for water 1
24 for they could not drink the water of the Nile. 1
25 days passed after the LORD had struck the Nile. 1
8: 3 the Nile shall swarm with frogs which shall come 1
9 the frogs . . be left only in the Nile. 1
11 they shall be left only in the Nile. 1
17: 5 take . . the rod with which you struck the Nile 1
Isa 18: 2 which sends ambassadors by the Nile 2
19: 5 the waters of the Nile will be dried up 2
7 There will be bare places by the Nile 1
7 bare places by the Nile, on the brink of the Nile 1
7 all that is sown by the Nile will dry up 1
8 mourn and lament, all who cast hook in the Nile; 1
23: 3 your revenue was . . the harvest of the Nile; 1
10 Overflow your land like the Nile 1
Jer 2:18 by going to Egypt, to drink the waters of the Nile? 3
46: 7 Who is this, rising like the Nile 1
8 Egypt rises like the Nile 1
Ezk 29: 3 dragon . . that says, 'My Nile is my own; I made it 1
9 Because you said, 'The Nile is mine, and I made it 1
30:12 I will dry up the Nile, and will sell the land 1
Ams 8: 8 and all of it rise like the Nile, and be tossed 1
8 and sink again, like the Nile of Egypt? 1
9: 5 and all of it rises like the Nile, and sinks again 1
5 and sinks again, like the Nile of Egypt; 1
Nah 3: 8 Are you better than Thebes that sat by the Nile 1
Zec 10:11 smitten, and all the depths of the Nile dried up. 1

branch of the Nile 1. יְאֹר
Isa 19: 6 the branches of Egypt's Nile will diminish 1

Nimrah 1. נִמְרָה
Num32: 3 At'aroth, Dibon, Jazer, Nimrah, Heshbon, Elea'leh 1

Nimrim 1. נִמְרִים
Isa 15: 6 the waters of Nimrim are a desolation; 1
Jer 48:34 the waters of Nimrim also have become desolate. 1

Nimrod 1. נִמְרֹד
Gen 10: 8 Cush became the father of Nimrod; 1
9 Like Nimrod a mighty hunter before the LORD. 1
1Ch 1:10 Cush was the father of Nimrod; 1
Mic 5: 6 rule . . the land of Nimrod with the drawn sword; 1

Nimshi 1. נִמְשִׁי
1Kg 19:16 Jehu the son of Nimshi you shall anoint to be king 1
2Kg 9: 2 for Jehu the son of Jehosh'aphat, son of Nimshi; 1
14 Jehu the son of Jehosh'aphat the son of Nimshi 1
20 is like the driving of Jehu the son of Nimshi; 1
2Ch 22: 7 with Jeho'ram to meet Jehu the son of Nimshi 1

Nineveh 1. נִינְוֵה 2. Νινευή 3. Νινευίτης
Gen 10:11 went . . and built Nin'eveh, Reho'both-Ir 1
12 Resen between Nin'eveh and Calah; 1
2Kg 19:36 Sennach'erib . . went home, and dwelt at Nin'eveh. 1
Isa 37:37 and went home and dwelt at Nin'eveh. 1
Jon 1: 2 Arise, go to Nin'eveh, that great city 1
3: 2 Arise, go to Nin'eveh, that great city, and proclaim 1
3 Jonah arose and went to Nin'eveh 1
3 Now Nin'eveh was an exceedingly great city 1
4 Yet 40 days, and Nin'eveh shall be overthrown! 1
5 the people of Nin'eveh believed God; 1
6 Then tidings reached the king of Nin'eveh 1
7 and published through Nin'eveh 1
4:11 should not I pity Nin'eveh, that great city 1
Nah 1: 1 An oracle concerning Nin'eveh. 1
2: 8 Nin'eveh is like a pool whose waters run away. 1
3: 7 Wasted is Nin'eveh; who will bemoan her? 1
Zep 2:13 and he will make Nin'eveh a desolation, a dry waste 1
Mat 12:41 The men of Nin'eveh will arise at the judgment 3
Lke 11:30 For as Jonah became a sign to the men of Nin'eveh 3
32 The men of Nin'eveh will arise at the judgment 3
Tob 1: 3 into the land of the Assyrians, to Nineveh. 2
10 Now when I was carried away captive to Nineveh 2
17 dead and thrown out behind the wall of Nineveh 2
19 Then one of the men of Nineveh went and informed 2
22 I returned to Nineveh 2
7: 3 who are captives in Nineveh. 2
11: 1 until they came near to Nineveh. 2
16 meet his daughter-in-law at the gate of Nineveh 2
17 rejoicing among all his brethren in Nineveh. 2
14: 4 what Jonah the prophet said about Nineveh 2
8 now, my son, leave Nineveh 2
10 do not live in Nineveh any longer 2
15 he heard of the destruction of Nineveh 2
15 Before his death he rejoiced over Nineveh. 2
Jdt 1: 1 the great city of Nineveh 2
16 Then he returned with them to Nineveh •
2:21 from Nineveh to the plain of Bectileth 2

Nisan 1. נִיסָן 2. Νισαν
Neh 2: 1 month of Nisan, in the twentieth year of King 1
Est 3: 7 In the first month, which is the month of Nisan 1
1Es 5: 6 in the month of Nisan, the first month. 2
AEs 11: 2 on the first day of Nisan 2

Nisroch 1. נִסְרֹךְ
2Kg 19:37 he was worshiping in the house of Nisroch his god 1
Isa 37:38 he was worshiping in the house of Nisroch his god 1

Noadiah 1. נוֹעַדְיָה
Ezr 8:33 Levites . . No-adi'ah the son of Bin'nui. 1
Neh 6:14 Remember . . also the prophetess No-adi'ah 1

Noah 1. נֹחַ 2. נֹעָה 3. Νῶε 4. Noe
Gen 5:29 called his name Noah, saying, "Out of the ground 1
30 Lamech lived after the birth of Noah 595 years 1
32 After Noah was 500 years old 1
32 Noah became the father of Shem, Ham, and Japheth. 1
6: 8 Noah found favor in the eyes of the LORD. 1
9 These are the generations of Noah. 1
9 Noah was a righteous man, blameless 1
9 in his generation; Noah walked with God. 1
10 Noah had three sons, Shem, Ham, and Japheth. 1
13 God said to Noah, "I have determined to make an end 1
22 Noah did this; he did all that God commanded him. 1
7: 1 Then the LORD said to Noah, "Go into the ark 1
5 Noah did all that the LORD had commanded him. 1
6 Noah was 600 years old when the flood . . came 1
7 Noah and his sons and his wife and his sons' wives 1
9 into the ark with Noah, as God had commanded Noah. 1
9 into the ark with Noah, as God had commanded Noah. 1
11 In the 600th year of Noah's life 1
13 Noah and his sons, Shem and Ham and Japheth 1
13 and Noah's wife and the three wives of his sons 1
15 They went into the ark with Noah 1
23 Only Noah was left, and those that were with him 1
8: 1 God remembered Noah and all the beasts 1
6 At the end of 40 days Noah opened the window 1
11 Noah knew that the waters had subsided 1
13 Noah removed the covering of the ark, and looked 1
15 Then God said to Noah 1
18 So Noah went forth, and his sons and his wife 1
20 Then Noah built an altar to the LORD 1
9: 1 God blessed Noah and his sons, and said to them 1
8 Then God said to Noah and to his sons with him 1
17 God said to Noah, "This is the sign of the covenant 1
18 The sons of Noah who went forth from the ark 1
19 These three were the sons of Noah; 1
20 Noah was the first tiller of the soil. 1
24 When Noah awoke from his wine 1
28 After the flood Noah lived 350 years; 1
29 All the days of Noah were 950 years; 1
10: 1 These are the generations of the sons of Noah 1
32 These are the families of the sons of Noah 1
Num26:33 daughters of Zeloph'ehad were Mahlah, Noah 2
27: 1 names of his daughters were: Mahlah, Noah, Hoglah 2
36:11 Tirzah, Hoglah, Milcah, and Noah, the daughters 2
Jos 17: 3 the names of his daughters: Mahlah, Noah, Hoglah 2
1Ch 1: 4 Noah, Shem, Ham, and Japheth. 1
Isa 54: 9 this is like the days of Noah to me: as I swore that 1
9 I swore that the waters of Noah should no more go 1
Ezk 14:14 even if these three men, Noah, Daniel, and Job 1
20 even if Noah, Daniel, and Job were in it, as I live 1
Mat 24:37 As were the days of Noah 3
38 until the day when Noah entered the ark 3
Lke 3:36 the son of Shem, the son of Noah, the son of Lamech 3
17:26 As it was in the days of Noah 3
27 until the day when Noah entered the ark 3
Heb 11: 7 By faith Noah . . took heed 3
1Pe 3:20 when God's patience waited in the days of Noah 3
2Pe 2: 5 preserved Noah, a herald of righteousness 3
2Es 3:11 one of them, Noah with his household 4
Tob 4:12 Noah, Abraham, Isaac, and Jacob, our fathers of old 3
Sir 44:17 Noah was found perfect and righteous 3
4Mc 15:31 Just as Noah's ark . . endured the waves 3

Nob 1. נֹב
1Sm 21: 1 Then came David to Nob to Ahim'elech the priest; 1
22: 9 I saw the son of Jesse coming to Nob, to Ahim'elech 1
11 all his father's house, the priests who were at Nob; 1
19 Nob, the city of the priests, he put to the sword; 1
Neh 11:32 An'athoth, Nob, Anani'ah 1
Isa 10:32 This very day he will halt at Nob 1

Nobah 1. נֹבַח
Num32:42 Nobah went and took Kenath and its villages 1
42 took Kenath . . and called it Nobah, after his own name. 1
Jdg 8:11 by the caravan route east of Nobah and Jog'behah 1

Nod 1. נוֹד
Gen 4:16 Cain . . dwelt in the land of Nod, east of Eden. 1

Nodab 1. נוֹדָב
1Ch 5:19 made war upon . . Jetur, Naphish, and Nodab; 1

Nogah 1. נֹגַהּ
1Ch 3: 7 Nogah, Nepheg, Japhi'a 1
14: 6 Nogah, Nepheg, Japhi'a 1

Nohah 1. נוֹחָה 2. Νουα
Jdg 20:43 trod them down from Nohah as far as opposite 2
1Ch 8: 2 Nohah the fourth, and Rapha the fifth. 1

Not my people 1. לֹא עַמִּי
Hos 1: 9 And the LORD said, "Call his name Not my people 1
2:23 and I will say to Not my people, 'You are my people'; 1

Not pitied 1. לֹא רֻחָמָה
Hos 1: 6 the LORD said to him, "Call her name Not pitied 1
8 When she had weaned Not pitied, she conceived 1
2:23 And I will have pity on Not pitied 1

Numenius 1. Νουμηνιος
1Mc 12:16 We . . have chosen Numenius the son of Antiochus 1
14:22 Numenius the son of Antiochus 1
24 After this Simon sent Numenius to Rome 1
15:15 Numenius and his companions arrived from Rome 1

Nun 1. נוּן 2. Ναυή
Exd 33:11 his servant Joshua the son of Nun, a young man 1
Num11:28 Joshua the son of Nun, the minister of Moses 1
13: 8 from the tribe of E'phraim, Hoshe'a the son of Nun; 1
16 Moses called Hoshe'a the son of Nun Joshua. 1
14: 6 Joshua the son of Nun and Caleb . . of Jephun'neh 1
30 except Caleb . . and Joshua the son of Nun. 1
38 Joshua the son of Nun and Caleb . . of Jephun'neh 1
26:65 except Caleb . . and Joshua the son of Nun. 1
27:18 Take Joshua the son of Nun . . and lay your hand 1
32:12 none except Caleb . . and Joshua the son of Nun 1
28 command concerning them to . . Joshua the son of Nun 1
34:17 Elea'zar the priest and Joshua the son of Nun. 1
Deu 1:38 Joshua the son of Nun . . he shall enter; 1
31:23 LORD commissioned Joshua the son of Nun and said 1
32:44 Moses came and recited . . and Joshua the son of Nun. 1
34: 9 Joshua the son of Nun was full of . . wisdom 1
Jos 1: 1 LORD said to Joshua the son of Nun, Moses' minister 1
2: 1 And Joshua the son of Nun sent two men secretly 1
23 and passed over and came to Joshua the son of Nun; 1
6: 6 Joshua the son of Nun called the priests and said 1
14: 1 Elea'zar the priest, and Joshua the son of Nun 1
17: 4 came before Elea'zar . . and Joshua the son of Nun 1
19:49 gave an inheritance . . to Joshua the son of Nun. 1
51 Elea'zar the priest and Joshua the son of Nun 1
21: 1 to Elea'zar the priest and to Joshua the son of Nun 1
24:29 Joshua the son of Nun, the servant of the LORD, died 1
Jdg 2: 8 Joshua the son of Nun, the servant of the LORD, died 1
1Kg 16:34 word . . which he spoke by Joshua the son of Nun. 1
1Ch 7:27 Nun his son, Joshua his son. 1
Neh 8:17 from the days of Jeshua the son of Nun to that day 1
Sir 46: 1 Joshua the son of Nun was mighty in war 2

Nympha 1. Νύμφα
Col 4:15 to Nympha and the church in her house. 1

Obadiah 1. עֹבַדְיָהוּ 2. Αβαδιας 3. Abdia
Gen 10:28 Obal, Abim'a-el, Sheba 1
1Kg 18: 3 Ahab called Obadi'ah, who was over the household. 1
3 Now Obadi'ah revered the LORD greatly; 1
4 Obadi'ah took 100 prophets and hid them 1
5 Ahab said to Obadi'ah, "Go through the land 1
6 Obadi'ah went in another direction by himself. 1
7 as Obadi'ah was on the way, behold, Eli'jah met him; 1
7 Eli'jah met him; and Obadi'ah recognized him •
16 Obadi'ah went to meet Ahab, and told him; 1
1Ch 3:21 sons of Hanani'ah . . Obadi'ah, his son Shecani'ah. 1
7: 3 sons of Izrahi'ah . . Obadi'ah, Jo'el, and Isshi'ah 1
8:38 Azel had six sons . . Obadi'ah, and Hanan. 1
9:16 Obadi'ah the son of Shemai'ah, son of Galal 1
44 Azel had six sons . . She-ari'ah, Obadi'ah 1
12: 9 Ezer the chief, Obadi'ah second, Eli'ab third 1
27:19 for Zeb'ulun, Ishma'iah the son of Obadi'ah; 1
2Ch 17: 7 he sent his princes, Ben-hail, Obadi'ah, Zechari'ah 1
34:12 Over them were set Jahath and Obadi'ah 1
Ezr 8: 9 Of the sons of Jo'ab, Obadi'ah the son of Jehi'el 1
Neh 10: 5 Harim, Mer'emoth, Obadi'ah 1
12:25 Mattani'ah, Bakbuki'ah, Obadi'ah, Meshul'lam, 1
Obd 1: 1 The vision of Obadi'ah. 1
1Es 8:35 Of the sons of Joab, Obadiah the son of Jehiel 2
2Es 1:39 Amos and Micah and Joel and Obadiah and Jonah 3

Obed 1. עוֹבֵד 2. Ἰωβήδ 3. Ωβηθ
Rut 4:17 They named him Obed; he was the father of Jesse 1
21 Salmon of Bo'az, Bo'az of Obed 1
22 Obed of Jesse, and Jesse of David. 1
1Ch 2:12 Salma of Bo'az, Bo'az of Obed 1
12 Nahshon was the father of Salma . . Obed of Jesse. 1
37 Zabad . . father of Ephlal, and Ephlal of Obed. 1
38 Obed was the father of Jehu, and Jehu of Azari'ah. 1
11:47 Eli'el, and Obed, and Ja-asi'el the Mezo'ba-ite. 1
26: 7 sons of Shemai'ah: Othni, Reph'a-el, Obed, 1
2Ch 23: 1 commanders . . Azari'ah the son of Obed, Ma-asei'ah 1
Mat 1: 5 Bo'az the father of Obed by Ruth 2
5 and Obed the father of Jesse 2
Lke 3:32 the son of Jesse, the son of Obed, the son of Bo'az 2
1Es 8:32 Of the sons of Adin, Obed the son of Jonathan 3

Obed-edom 1. עֹבֵד אֱדֹם
2Sm 6:10 took it . . to the house of O'bed-e'dom the Gittite. 1
11 ark . . remained in the house of O'bed-e'dom 1
11 LORD blessed O'bed-e'dom and all his household. 1
12 The LORD has blessed the household of O'bed-e'dom 1
12 of O'bed-e'dom to the city of David with rejoicing; 1
1Ch 13:13 to the house of O'bed-e'dom the Gittite. 1
14 remained with the household of O'bed-e'dom 1
14 the LORD blessed the household of O'bed-e'dom 1
15:18 and the gatekeepers O'bed-e'dom and Je-i'el. 1
21 Miknei'ah, O'bed-e'dom, Je-i'el, and Azazi'ah 1
24 O'bed-e'dom and . . to be gatekeepers for the ark. 1
25 to bring up the ark . . from the house of O'bed-e'dom 1
16: 5 second to him . . Benai'ah, O'bed-e'dom, and Je-i'el 1
38 and also O'bed-e'dom and his 68 brethren 1
38 O'bed-e'dom . . and Hosah were to be gatekeepers. 1
26: 4 O'bed-e'dom had sons: Shemai'ah the first-born 1
8 sons of O'bed-e'dom with their sons and brethren 1
8 able men qualified for the service; 62 of O'bed-e'dom 1
15 O'bed-e'dom's came out for the south 1
2Ch 25:24 seized all the gold and silver . . and O'bed-e'dom 1

Obil 1. אוֹבִיל
1Ch 27:30 Over the camels was Obil the Ish'maelite; 1

Oboth 1. אֹבֹת
Num21:10 people of Israel set out, and encamped in Oboth. 1
11 set out from Oboth, and encamped at I'ye-ab'arim 1
33:43 they set out from Punon, and encamped at Oboth. 1
44 set out from Oboth, and encamped at I'ye-ab'arim 1

Ochiel 1. Οχιηλος
1Es 1: 9 Hashabiah and Ochiel and Joram 1

Ochran 1. עָכְרָן
Num 1:13 from Asher, Pa'giel the son of Ochran; 1
2:27 the leader . . Pa'giel the son of Ochran 1
7:72 Pa'giel the son of Ochran, the leader of the men 1
77 was the offering of Pa'giel the son of Ochran. 1
10:26 over the host . . was Pa'giel the son of Ochran. 1

Ocina 1. Οκινα
Jdt 2:28 those who lived in Sur and Ocina 1

Oded 1. עוֹדֵד
2Ch 15: 1 Spirit of God came upon Azari'ah the son of Oded 1
8 the prophecy of Azari'ah the son of Oded 1
28: 9 prophet . . was there, whose name was Oded; 1

Odomera 1. Οδομηρα
1Mc 9:66 He struck down Odomera and his brothers 1

Og 1. עוֹג
Num21:33 Og the king of Bashan came out against them 1
32:33 Moses gave . . the kingdom of Og king of Bashan 1
Deu 1: 4 defeated . . Og the king of Bashan, who lived 1
3: 1 Og the king of Bashan came out against us 1
3 LORD our God gave into our hand Og also, the king 1
4 region of Argob, the kingdom of Og in Bashan. 1
10 Sal'ecah and Ed're-i, cities of the kingdom of Og 1
11 only Og . . was left of the remnant of the Reph'aim; 1
13 rest of Gilead, and all Bashan, the kingdom of Og 1
4:47 possession of . . the land of Og the king of Bashan 1
29: 7 Sihon . . of Heshbon and Og the king of Bashan 1
31: 4 LORD will do to them as he did to Sihon and Og 1
Jos 2:10 to the two kings of the Amorites . . to Sihon and Og 1
9:10 Sihon the king of Heshbon, and Og king of Bashan 1
12: 4 and Og king of Bashan, one of the . . Reph'aim 1
13:12 all the kingdom of Og in Bashan 1
30 all Bashan, the whole kingdom of Og king of Bashan 1
31 the cities of the kingdom of Og in Bashan; 1
1Kg 4:19 Gilead, the country . . and of Og king of Bashan. 1
Neh 9:22 took possession of . . the land of Og king 1
Ps 135:11 Sihon, king of the Amorites, and Og, king of Bashan 1
136:20 Og, king of Bashan, for his steadfast love endures 1

Ohad 1. אֹהַד
Gen 46:10 The sons of Simeon: Jemu'el, Jamin, Ohad, Jachin 1
Exd 6:15 The sons of Simeon: Jemu'el, Jamin, Ohad, Jachin 1

Ohel 1. אֹהֶל
1Ch 3:20 Hashu'bah, Ohel, Berechi'ah, Hasadi'ah 1

Oholah 1. אָהֳלָה
Ezk 23: 4 Oho'lah was the name of the elder 1
4 As for their names, Oho'lah is Sama'ria 1
5 Oho'lah played the harlot while she was mine; 1
36 Son of man, will you judge Oho'lah and Ohol'ibah? 1
44 Thus they went in to Oho'lah and to Ohol'ibah 1

Oholiab 1. אָהֳלִיאָב
Exd 31: 6 behold, I have appointed with him Oho'liab 1
35:34 he has inspired him to teach, both him and Oho'liab 1
36: 1 Bez'alel and Oho'liab and every able man in whom 1
2 Moses called Bez'alel and Oho'liab and every able 1
38:23 with him was Oho'liab the son of Ahis'amach 1

Oholibah 1. אָהֳלִיבָה
Ezk 23: 4 and Ohol'ibah the name of her sister. 1
4 Oho'lah is Sama'ria, and Ohol'ibah is Jerusalem. 1
11 Ohol'ibah saw this, yet she was more corrupt 1
22 Therefore, O Ohol'ibah, thus says the Lord GOD 1
36 Son of man, will you judge Oho'lah and Ohol'ibah? 1
44 Thus they went in to Oho'lah and to Ohol'ibah 1

Oholibamah 1. אָהֳלִיבָמָה
Gen 36: 2 Oholiba'mah the daughter of Anah 1
5 Oholiba'mah bore Je'ush, Jalam, and Korah. 1
14 These are the sons of Oholiba'mah 1
18 These are the sons of Oholiba'mah, Esau's wife 1
18 these are the chiefs born of Oholiba'mah 1
25 Dishon and Oholiba'mah the daughter of Anah. 1
41 Oholiba'mah, Elah, Pinon 1
1Ch 1:52 Oholiba'mah, Elah, Pinon 1

Old Gate 1. שַׁעַר הַיְשָׁנָה
Neh 3: 6 Joi'ada . . Meshul'lam . . repaired the Old Gate; 1
12:39 by the Old Gate, and by the Fish Gate and the Tower 1

Olives 1. זֵיתִים
Zec 14: 4 his feet shall stand on the Mount of Olives 1
4 the Mount of Olives shall be split in two 1

Olivet 1. Ελαία 2. Ελαιών
Lke 19:29 at the mount that is called Olivet 1
21:37 went out and lodged on the mount called Olivet. 1
Act 1:12 from the mount called Olivet 2

Olympas 1. Ὀλυμπᾶς
Rom16:15 and Olym'pas, and all the saints who are with them. 1

Olympian 1. Ὀλυμπιος
2Mc 6: 2 and call it the temple of Olympian Zeus 1

Omar 1. אוֹמָר
Gen 36:11 The sons of El'iphaz were Teman, Omar, Zepho 1
15 the chiefs Teman, Omar, Zepho, Kenaz 1
1Ch 1:36 The sons of Eli'phaz: Teman, Omar, Zephi, Gatam 1

Omri 1. עָמְרִי
1Kg 16:16 all Israel made Omri . . king over Israel 1
17 Omri went up from Gib'bethon, and all Israel 1
21 Tibni . . to make him king, and half followed Omri. 1
22 the people who followed Omri overcame 1
22 so Tibni died, and Omri became king. 1
23 Omri began to reign over Israel 1
25 Omri did what was evil in the sight of the LORD 1
27 the rest of the acts of Omri which he did 1
28 Omri slept with his fathers, and was buried 1
29 Ahab the son of Omri began to reign over Israel 1
29 Ahab the son of Omri reigned over Israel 1
30 Ahab the son of Omri did evil 1
2Kg 8:26 she was a granddaughter of Omri king of Israel. 1
1Ch 7: 8 sons of Becher . . Eli-o-e'nai, Omri, Jer'emoth 1
9: 4 son of Ammi'hud, son of Omri, son of Imri, son of Bani 1
27:18 for Is'sachar, Omri the son of Michael; 1
2Ch 22: 2 Athali'ah, the granddaughter of Omri. 1
Mic 6:16 For you have kept the statutes of Omri 1

Onam 1. אוֹנָם
Gen 36:23 of Shobal . . Man'ahath, Ebal, Shepho, and Onam. 1
1Ch 1:40 of Shobal: Al'ian, Man'ahath, Ebal, Shephi, and Onam 1
2:26 wife . . At'arah; she was the mother of Onam. 1
28 The sons of Onam: Sham'mai and Jada. 1

Onan 1. אוֹנָן
Gen 38: 4 bore a son, and she called his name Onan. 1
8 Judah said to Onan, "Go in to your brother's wife 1
9 Onan knew that the offspring would not be his; 1
46:12 sons of Judah: Er, Onan, Shelah, Perez, and Zerah 1
12 but Er and Onan died in the land of Canaan 1
Num26:19 The sons of Judah were Er and Onan; 1
19 Er and Onan died in the land of Canaan. 1
1Ch 2: 3 The sons of Judah: Er, Onan, and Shelah; 1

Onesimus 1. Ὀνήσιμος
Col 4: 9 Ones'imus, the faithful and beloved brother 1
Phm 1:10 I appeal to you for my child, Ones'imus 1

Onesiphorus 1. Ὀνησίφορος
2Ti 1:16 grant mercy to the household of Onesiph'orus 1
4:19 Greet . . the household of Onesiph'orus. 1

Onias 1. Ονιας
1Co 7:17 Only, let every one lead the life 1
Sir 50: 1 Simon the high priest, son of Onias 1
1Mc 12: 7 to Onias the high priest from Arius 1
8 Onias welcomed the envoy with honor 1
19 a copy of the letter which they sent to Onias 1
20 Arius . . to Onias the high priest, greeting. 1
2Mc 3: 1 because of the piety of the high priest Onias 1
5 when he could not prevail over Onias 1
31 Quickly some of Heliodorus' friends asked Onias 1
33 Be very grateful to Onias the high priest 1
35 having bidden Onias farewell 1
4: 1 Simon . . slandered Onias 1
4 Onias recognized that the rivalry was serious 1
7 Jason the brother of Onias 1
33 When Onias became fully aware of these acts 1
34 Therefore Menelaus . . urged him to kill Onias. 1
34 Andronicus came to Onias 1
34 Andronicus . . persuaded Onias to come out •
36 with regard to the unreasonable murder of Onias 1
38 he had committed the outrage against Onias 1
15:12 Onias, who had been high priest 1
14 Onias spoke, saying 1
4Mc 4: 1 the noble and good man, Onias 1
1 unable to injure Onias in the eyes of the nation •
13 Onias the high priest . . prayed for him 1
16 who removed Onias from the priesthood 1
16 and appointed Onias's brother Jason as high priest. •

Ono 1. אוֹנוֹ 2. Ωνω
1Ch 8:12 Shemed, who built Ono and Lod with its towns. 1
Ezr 2:33 sons of Lod, Hadid, and Ono, 725. 1
Neh 6: 2 meet . . in one of the villages in the plain of Ono. 1
7:37 sons of Lod, Hadid, and Ono, 721. 1
11:35 Lod, and Ono, the valley of craftsmen. 1
1Es 5:22 The sons of the other Elam and Ono, 725. 2

Ophel 1. עֹפֶל
2Ch 27: 3 did much building on the wall of Ophel. 1
33:14 carried it round Ophel, and raised it 1
Neh 3:26 temple servants living on Ophel repaired 1
27 another section . . as far as the wall of Ophel. 1
11:21 temple servants lived on Ophel; 1

Ophir 1. אוֹפִיר 2. Σουφιρ
Gen 10:29 Ophir, Hav'ilah, and Jobab; 1
1Kg 9:28 they went to Ophir, and brought from there gold 1
10:11 the fleet of Hiram, which brought gold from Ophir 1
11 fleet . . brought from Ophir a very great amount 1
22:48 Jehosh'aphat made ships . . to go to Ophir for gold; 1
1Ch 1:23 Ophir, Hav'ilah, and Jobab . . the sons of Joktan 1
29: 4 3,000 talents of gold, of the gold of Ophir 1
2Ch 8:18 went to Ophir . . with the servants of Solomon 1
9:10 the servants . . who brought gold from Ophir 1
Job 22:24 gold of Ophir among the stones of the torrent bed 1
28:16 It cannot be valued in the gold of Ophir 1
Ps 45: 9 stands the queen in gold of Ophir. 1
Isa 13:12 fine gold, and mankind than the gold of Ophir. 1
Tob 13:17 beryl and ruby and stones of Ophir; 2
Sir 7:18 a real brother for the gold of Ophir. 2

Ophni 1. עָפְנִי
Jos 18:24 Che'phar-am'moni, Ophni, Geba 1

Ophrah 1. עָפְרָה
Jos 18:23 Avvim, Parah, Ophrah 1
Jdg 6:11 the angel . . came and sat under the oak at Ophrah 1
24 at Ophrah, which belongs to the Abiez'rites. 1
8:27 made an ephod of it and put it in his city, in Ophrah; 1
32 tomb of Jo'ash . . at Ophrah of the Abiez'rites. 1
9: 5 he went to his father's house at Ophrah, and slew 1
1Sm 13:17 one company turned toward Ophrah, to the land 1
1Ch 4:14 Meo'nothai was the father of Ophrah; 1

Oreb 1. עֹרֵב
Jdg 7:25 they took the two princes of Mid'ian, Oreb and Zeeb; 1
25 they killed Oreb at the rock of Oreb, and Zeeb they 1
25 they killed Oreb at the rock of Oreb, and Zeeb they 1
25 they brought the heads of Oreb and Zeeb to Gideon 1
8: 3 your hands the princes of Mid'ian, Oreb and Zeeb; 1
Ps 83:11 Make their nobles like Oreb and Zeeb 1
Isa 10:26 as when he smote Mid'ian at the rock of Oreb; 1

Oren 1. אֹרֶן
1Ch 2:25 The sons of Jerah'meel . . Oren, Ozem, and Ahi'jah. 1

Orion 1. כְּסִיל
Job 9: 9 who made the Bear and Orion, the Plei'ades 1
38:31 the Plei'ades, or loose the cords of Orion? 1
Ams 5: 8 He who made the Plei'ades and Orion 1

Ornan 1. אָרְנָן
1Ch 21:15 the threshing floor of Ornan the Jeb'usite. 1
18 on the threshing floor of Ornan the Jeb'usite. 1
20 Now Ornan was threshing wheat; he turned and saw 1
21 As David came to Ornan, Ornan looked and saw David 1
21 Ornan looked and saw David and went forth 1
22 David said to Ornan, "Give me the site 1
23 Ornan said to David, "Take it; and let my lord 1
24 King David said to Ornan, "No, but I will buy it 1
25 David paid Ornan 600 shekels of gold by weight 1
28 at the threshing floor of Ornan the Jeb'usite 1
2Ch 3: 1 on the threshing floor of Ornan the Jeb'usite. 1

Orpah 1. עָרְפָּה
Rut 1: 4 the name of the one was Orpah 1
14 and Orpah kissed her mother-in-law, but Ruth clung 1

Orthosia 1. Ορθωσια
1Mc 15:37 embarked on a ship and escaped to Orthosia. 1

Osnappar 1. אָסְנַפַּר (A)
Ezr 4:10 nations whom the great and noble Osnap'par 1

Othni 1. עָתְנִי
1Ch 26: 7 sons of Shemai'ah: Othni, Reph'a-el, Obed, 1

Othniel 1. עָתְנִיאֵל
Jos 15:17 And Oth'ni-el . . took it; and he gave him Achsah 1
Jdg 1:13 Oth'ni-el the son of Kenaz, Caleb's younger brother 1
3: 9 who delivered them, Oth'niel the son of Kenaz 1
11 40 years. Then Oth'ni-el the son of Kenaz died. 1
1Ch 4:13 The sons of Kenaz: Oth'ni-el and Serai'ah; 1
13 and the sons of Oth'ni-el: Hathath and Meo'nothai. 1
27:15 Heldai the Netoph'athite, of Oth'ni-el; 1

Othoniah 1. Οθονιας
1Es 9:28 Of the sons of Zattu: Elioenai, Eliashib, Othoniah 1

Oven *See also* Tower.

Ox 1. Ωξ
Jdt 8: 1 the daughter of Merari the son of Ox, son of Joseph 1

Ozem 1. אֹצֶם
1Ch 2:15 Ozem the sixth, David the seventh; 1
25 The sons of Jerah'meel . . Oren, Ozem, and Ahi'jah. 1

Oziel 1. Οζιηλ
Jdt 8: 1 son of Joseph, son of Oziel, son of Elkiah 1

Ozni 1. אָזְנִי
Num26:16 of Ozni, the family of the Oznites; 1

Oznite 1. אָזְנִי
Num26:16 of Ozni, the family of the Oznites; 1

Paarai 1. פַּעֲרַי
2Sm 23:35 Hezro of Carmel, Pa'arai the Arbite 1

Pachon 1. Παχων
3Mc 6:38 from the 25th of Pachon to the fourth of Epeiph 1

Paddan 1. פַּדָּן
Gen 48: 7 For when I came from Paddan, Rachel to my sorrow 1

Paddan-aram 1. פַּדַּן אֲרָם
Gen 25:20 Bethu'el the Aramean of Paddan-aram 1
28: 2 Arise, go to Paddan-aram to the house of Bethu'el 1
5 Isaac sent Jacob away; and he went to Paddan-aram 1
6 blessed Jacob and sent him away to Paddan-aram 1
7 Jacob had . . gone to Paddan-aram. 1
31:18 possession which he had acquired in Paddan-aram 1
33:18 in the land of Canaan, on his way from Paddan-aram 1
35: 9 when he came from Paddan-aram, and blessed him. 1
26 sons of Jacob who were born to him in Paddan-aram. 1
46:15 whom she bore to Jacob in Paddan-aram, 1

Padon 1. פָּדוֹן 2. Φαδων
Ezr 2:44 sons of Keros, the sons of Si'aha, the sons of Padon 1
Neh 7:47 sons of Keros, the sons of Si'a, the sons of Padon 1
1Es 5:29 the sons of Padon, the sons of Lebanah 2

Pagiel 1. פַּגְעִיאֵל
Num 1:13 from Asher, Pa'giel the son of Ochran; 1
2:27 the leader . . Pa'giel the son of Ochran 1
7:72 Pa'giel the . . leader of the men of Asher 1
77 was the offering of Pa'giel the son of Ochran. 1
10:26 over the host . . was Pa'giel the son of Ochran. 1

Pahath-moab 1. פַּחַת מוֹאָב
Ezr 2: 6 sons of Pa'hath-moab, namely the sons of Jeshua 1
8: 4 Of the sons of Pa'hath-mo'ab, Eli-e-ho-e'nai the son 1
10:30 Of the sons of Pa'hath-mo'ab: Adna, Chelal, Benai'ah 1
Neh 3:11 Malchi'jah . . and Hasshub the son of Pa'hath-mo'ab 1
7:11 sons of Pa'hath-mo'ab, namely the sons of Jeshua 1
10:14 chiefs . . Parosh, Pa'hath-mo'ab, Elam, Zattu, Bani 1

Pahathmoab 1. Φααθμωαβ
1Es 5:11 sons of Pahathmoab, of the sons of Jeshua and Joab 1
8:31 Of the sons of Pahathmoab, Eliehoenai 1

Pai 1. פָּעִי
1Ch 1:50 Hadad . . and the name of his city was Pa'i 1

Palal 1. פָּלָל
Neh 3:25 Palal the son of Uzai repaired opposite 1

Pallu 1. פַּלּוּא
Gen 46: 9 sons of Reuben: Hanoch, Pallu, Hezron, and Carmi 1
Exd 6:14 sons of Reuben . . Hanoch, Pallu, Hezron 1
Num26: 5 of Pallu, the family of the Pal'luites; 1
8 the sons of Pallu: Eli'ab. 1
1Ch 5: 3 sons of Reuben . . Hanoch, Pallu, Hezron 1

Palluite 1. פַּלֻּאִי
Num26: 5 of Pallu, the family of the Pal'luites; 1

Palti 1. פַּלְטִי
Num13: 9 from the tribe of Benjamin, Palti the son of Raphu; 1
1Sm 25:44 Saul had given Michal . . to Palti the son of La'ish 1

Paltiel 1. פַּלְטִיאֵל
Num34:26 of Is'sachar a leader, Pal'tiel the son of Azzan. 1
2Sm 3:15 Ish-bo'sheth . . took her from her husband Pal'ti-el 1

Paltite 1. פַּלְטִי
2Sm 23:26 Helez the Paltite, Ira the son of Ikkesh of Teko'a 1

Pamphylia 1. Παμφυλία
Act 2:10 Phryg'ia and Pamphyl'ia 1
13:13 and came to Perga in Pamphyl'ia 1
14:24 passed through Pisid'ia, and came to Pamphyl'ia. 1
15:38 one who had withdrawn from them in Pamphyl'ia 1
27: 5 the sea which is off Cili'cia and Pamphyl'ia 1
1Mc 15:23 to Samos, and to Pamphylia, and to Lycia 1

Paphos 1. Πάφος
Act 13: 6 had gone through the whole island as far as Paphos 1
13 Now Paul and his company set sail from Paphos 1

Parah 1. פָּרָה
Jos 18:23 Avvim, Parah, Ophrah 1

Paran 1. פָּארָן
Gen 21:21 He lived in the wilderness of Paran; 1
Num10:12 cloud settled down in the wilderness of Paran. 1
12:16 people . . encamped in the wilderness of Paran. 1
13: 3 Moses sent them from the wilderness of Paran 1
26 in the wilderness of Paran, at Kadesh; 1
Deu 1: 1 between Paran and Tophel, Laban, Haze'roth 1
33: 2 he shone forth from Mount Paran 1
1Sm 25: 1 David . . went down to the wilderness of Paran. 1
1Kg 11:18 They set out from Mid'ian and came to Paran 1
18 took men with them from Paran and came to Egypt 1
Hab 3: 3 came from Teman . . the Holy One from Mount Paran. 1

Parmashta 1. פַּרְמַשְׁתָּא
Est 9: 9 Parmash'ta and Ar'isai and Ar'idai and Vaiza'tha 1

Parmenas 1. Παρμενᾶς
Act 6: 5 Par'menas, and Nicola'us, a proselyte of Antioch. 1

Parnach 1. פַּרְנָךְ
Num34:25 of Zeb'ulun a leader, Eli-za'phan the son of Parnach. 1

Parosh 1. פַּרְעֹשׁ 2. Φορος
Ezr 2: 3 sons of Parosh, 2,172. 1
8: 3 Of the sons of Parosh, Zechari'ah 1
10:25 of Israel: of the sons of Parosh: Rami'ah, Izzi'ah 1
Neh 3:25 After him Pedai'ah the son of Parosh 1
7: 8 sons of Parosh, 2,172. 1
10:14 chiefs . . Parosh, Pa'hath-mo'ab, Elam, Zattu, Bani 1
1Es 5: 9 the sons of Parosh, 2,172 2
8:30 Of the sons of Parosh, Zechariah 2
9:26 Of Israel: of the sons of Parosh: Ramiah, Izziah 2

Parshandatha 1. פַּרְשַׁנְדָּתָא
Est 9: 7 also slew Par-shan-da'tha and Dalphon and Aspa'tha 1

Parthian 1. Πάρθοι
Act 2: 9 Par'thians and Medes and E'lamites 1

Paruah 1. פָּרוּחַ
1Kg 4:17 Jehosh'aphat the son of Paru'ah, in Is'sachar; 1

Parvaim 1. פַּרְוָיִם
2Ch 3: 6 The gold was gold of Parva'im. 1

Pas-dammim 1. פַּס דַּמִּים
1Ch 11:13 He was with David at Pas-dam'mim 1

Pasach 1. פָּסַךְ
1Ch 7:33 The sons of Japhlet: Pasach, Bimhal, and Ashvath. 1

Paseah 1. פָּסֵחַ 2. Φινοε
1Ch 4:12 Eshton was the father of Bethra'pha, Pase'ah 1
Ezr 2:49 sons of Uzza, the sons of Pase'ah, the sons of Besai 1
Neh 3: 6 Joi'ada the son of Pase'ah and Meshul'lam 1
7:51 sons of Gazzam, the sons of Uzza, the sons of Pase'ah 1
1Es 5:31 sons of Uzza, the sons of Paseah, the sons of Hasrah 2

Pashhur 1. פַּשְׁחוּר 2. Φαισουρ 3. Φασσορος
1Ch 9:12 Jero'ham, son of Pashhur, son of Malchi'jah 1
Ezr 2:38 sons of Pashhur, 1,247. 1
10:22 Of the sons of Pashhur: Eli-o-e'nai, Ma-asei'ah 1
Neh 7:41 sons of Pashhur, 1,247. 1
10: 3 Pashhur, Amari'ah, Malchi'jah 1
11:12 Zechari'ah, son of Pashhur, son of Malchi'jah 1
Jer 20: 1 Now Pashhur the priest, the son of Immer 1
2 Then Pashhur beat Jeremiah the prophet 1
3 On the morrow, when Pashhur released Jeremiah 1
3 The LORD does not call your name Pashhur 1
6 And you, Pashhur, and all who dwell in your house 1
21: 1 when King Zedeki'ah sent to him Pashhur 1
38: 1 Gedali'ah the son of Pashhur 1
1 and Pashhur the son of Malchi'ah heard the words 1
1Es 5:25 The sons of Pashhur, 1,247. 3
9:22 Of the sons of Pashhur: Elioenai, Maaseiah 2

Patara 1. Πάταρα
Act 21: 1 the next day to Rhodes, . . from there to Pat'ara 1

Pathros 1. פַּתְרוֹס
Isa 11:11 remnant . . of his people.., from Pathros 1
Jer 44: 1 at Memphis, and in the land of Pathros 1
15 people who dwelt in Pathros in the land of Egypt 1
Ezk 29:14 and bring them back to the land of Pathros 1
30:14 I will make Pathros a desolation 1

Pathrusim 1. פַּתְרֻסִים
Gen 10:14 Pathru'sim, Caslu'him (whence came 1
1Ch 1:12 Pathru'sim, Caslu'him (whence came the Philis'tines 1

Patmos 1. Πάτμος
Rev 1: 9 I John . . was on the island called Patmos 1

Patrobas 1. Πατροβᾶς
Rom16:14 Greet Asyn'critus, Phlegon, Hermes, Pat'robas 1

Patroclus 1. Πατροκλος
2Mc 8: 9 appointed Nicanor the son of Patroclus 1

Pau 1. פָּעוּ
Gen 36:39 the name of his city being Pau; 1

Paul 1. Παῦλος
Act 13: 9 Saul, who is also called Paul 1
13 Now Paul and his company set sail from Paphos 1
16 So Paul stood up, and motioning with his hand said 1
43 many Jews . . followed Paul and Barnabas 1
45 contradicted what was spoken by Paul 1
46 Paul and Barnabas spoke out boldly, saying 1
50 and stirred up persecution against Paul 1
14: 9 He listened to Paul speaking 1
9 Paul, looking intently at him •
11 when the crowds saw what Paul had done 1
12 Paul . . they called Hermes. 1
14 when the apostles Barnabas and Paul heard of it 1
19 they stoned Paul and dragged him out of the city 1
15: 2 when Paul and Barnabas had no small dissension 1
2 Paul and Barnabas and some of the others 1
12 they listened to Barnabas and Paul 1
22 send them to Antioch with Paul and Barnabas 1
25 with our beloved Barnabas and Paul 1
35 Paul and Barnabas remained in Antioch 1
36 after some days Paul said to Barnabas, "Come 1
38 Paul thought best not to take with them one 1
40 Paul chose Silas and departed 1
16: 3 Paul wanted Timothy to accompany him 1
9 a vision appeared to Paul in the night 1
14 to give heed to what was said by Paul. 1
17 She followed Paul and us, crying 1
18 Paul was annoyed 1
19 they seized Paul and Silas 1
25 Paul and Silas were praying and singing hymns 1
28 Paul cried with a loud voice, "Do not harm yourself 1
29 he fell down before Paul and Silas 1
36 the jailer reported the words to Paul, saying 1
37 Paul said to them, "they have beaten us publicly 1
17: 2 Paul went in, as was his custom 1
4 joined Paul and Silas 1
10 The brethren immediately sent Paul and Silas away 1
13 the word of God was proclaimed by Paul at Beroe'a 1
14 Then the brethren immediately sent Paul off 1
15 who conducted Paul brought him as far as Athens; 1
16 Now while Paul was waiting for them at Athens 1
22 Paul, standing in the middle of the Are-op'agus 1
33 Paul went out from among them. 1
18: 5 Paul was occupied with preaching 1
8 many of the Corinthians hearing Paul believed •
9 the Lord said to Paul one night in a vision 1
12 the Jews made a united attack upon Paul 1
14 when Paul was about to open his mouth 1
18 After this Paul stayed many days longer 1
19: 1 Paul passed through the upper country 1
4 Paul said, "John baptized 1
6 when Paul had laid his hands upon them 1
11 did extraordinary miracles by the hands of Paul 1
13 I adjure you by the Jesus whom Paul preaches. 1
15 Jesus I know, and Paul I know; but who are you? 1
21 Paul resolved . . to pass through Macedo'nia 1
26 this Paul has persuaded 1
29 who were Paul's companions in travel. 1
30 Paul wished to go in among the crowd 1
20: 1 Paul sent for the disciples 1
7 Paul talked with them 1
9 as Paul talked still longer 1
10 Paul went down and bent over him 1
11 Paul had gone up and had broken bread and eaten •
13 intending to take Paul aboard there 1
16 Paul had decided to sail past Ephesus 1
37 they all wept and embraced Paul and kissed him. 1
21: 4 they told Paul not to go on to Jerusalem. 1
11 coming to us he took Paul's girdle 1
13 Then Paul answered, "What are you doing 1
18 On the following day Paul went in with us to James; 1
26 Then Paul took the men 1
29 Paul had brought him into the temple. 1
30 seized Paul and dragged him out of the temple 1
32 they stopped beating Paul. 1
37 As Paul was about to be brought into the barracks 1
39 Paul replied, "I am a Jew, from Tarsus in Cili'cia 1
40 Paul, standing on the steps 1
22:25 Paul said to the centurion who was standing by 1
28 Paul said, "But I was born a citizen. 1
29 he realized that Paul was a Roman citizen •
30 he brought Paul down and set him before them. 1
23: 1 Paul, looking intently at the council, said 1
3 Paul said to him, "God shall strike you 1
5 Paul said, "I did not know, brethren 1
6 when Paul perceived 1
10 afraid that Paul would be torn in pieces by them 1
12 till they had killed Paul. 1
14 an oath to taste no food till we have killed Paul. 1
16 Now the son of Paul's sister heard of their ambush; 1
16 he went and entered the barracks and told Paul. 1
17 Paul called one of the centurions and said 1
18 Paul the prisoner called me 1
20 to ask you to bring Paul down to the council 1
24 Also provide mounts for Paul to ride 1
31 according to their instructions, took Paul 1
33 they presented Paul also before him. 1
24: 1 their case against Paul; 1
10 Paul replied 1
24 he sent for Paul 1
26 he hoped that money would be given him by Paul 1
27 Felix left Paul in prison. 1
25: 2 informed him against Paul 1
4 Paul was being kept at Caesare'a 1
6 ordered Paul to be brought. 1
8 Paul said in his defense 1
9 Festus, wishing to do the Jews a favor, said to Paul 1
10 Paul said, "I am standing before Caesar's tribunal 1
14 Festus laid Paul's case before the king, saying 1
19 who was dead, but whom Paul asserted to be alive. 1
21 when Paul had appealed to be kept in custody 1
23 Then by command of Festus Paul was brought in. 1
26: 1 Agrippa said to Paul, "You have permission 1
1 Paul stretched out his hand and made his defense 1
24 Festus said with a loud voice, "Paul, you are mad 1
25 Paul said, "I am not mad, most excellent Festus 1
28 Agrippa said to Paul 1
29 Paul said, "Whether short or long, I would to God 1
27: 1 they delivered Paul . . to a centurion 1
3 Julius treated Paul kindly 1
9 Paul advised them 1
11 what Paul said. 1
21 Paul then came forward among them and said, "Men 1
24 he said, 'Do not be afraid, Paul 1
31 Paul said to the centurion and the soldiers 1
33 Paul urged them all to take some food, saying 1
43 the centurion, wishing to save Paul 1
28: 3 Paul had gathered a bundle of sticks 1

8 Paul visited him and prayed 1
15 Paul thanked God and took courage. 1
16 Paul was allowed to stay by himself 1
25 they departed, after Paul had made one statement 1
Rom 1: 1 Paul, a servant of Jesus Christ 1
1Co 1: 1 Paul, called by the will of God to be an apostle 1
12 I belong to Paul," or "I belong to Apol'los 1
13 Is Christ divided? Was Paul crucified for you? 1
13 were you baptized in the name of Paul? 1
3: 4 For when one says, "I belong to Paul 1
5 What then is Apol'los? What is Paul? 1
22 whether Paul or Apol'los or Cephas or the world 1
16:21 I, Paul, write this greeting with my own hand. 1
2Co 1: 1 Paul, an apostle of Christ Jesus by the will of God 1
10: 1 I, Paul, myself entreat you 1
Gal 1: 1 Paul an apostle–not from men nor through man 1
5: 2 Now I, Paul, say to you 1
Eph 1: 1 Paul, an apostle of Christ Jesus by the will of God 1
3: 1 Paul, a prisoner for Christ Jesus on behalf of you 1
Php 1: 1 Paul and Timothy, servants of Christ Jesus 1
Col 1: 1 Paul, an apostle of Christ Jesus by the will of God 1
23 of which I, Paul, became a minister. 1
4:18 I, Paul, write this greeting with my own hand. 1
1Th 1: 1 Paul, Silva'nus, and Timothy 1
2:18 I, Paul, again and again 1
2Th 1: 1 Paul, Silva'nus, and Timothy 1
3:17 I, Paul, write this greeting with my own hand 1
1Ti 1: 1 Paul, an apostle of Christ Jesus by command of God 1
2Ti 1: 1 Paul, an apostle of Christ Jesus by the will of God 1
Tit 1: 1 Paul, a servant of God and an apostle of Jesus 1
Phm 1: 1 Paul, a prisoner for Christ Jesus 1
9 I, Paul, an ambassador and now a prisoner also 1
19 I, Paul, write this with my own hand, I will repay 1
2Pe 3:15 So also our beloved brother Paul wrote to you 1

Paulus 1. Παῦλος
Act 13: 7 He was with the Proconsul, Sergius Paulus 1

Pedahel 1. פְּדַהְאֵל
Num34:28 of Naph'tali a leader, Pedah'el the son of Ammi'hud. 1

Pedahzur 1. פְּדָהצוּר
Num 1:10 from Manas'seh, Gama'liel the son of Pedah'zur; 1
2:20 the leader . . Gama'liel the son of Pedah'zur 1
7:54 Gama'liel the son of Pedah'zur, the leader 1
59 offering of Gama'liel the son of Pedah'zur 1
10:23 Gama'liel the son of Pedah'zur. 1

Pedaiah 1. פְּדָיָהוּ 2. Φαδαιος
2Kg 23:36 was Zebi'dah the daughter of Pedai'ah of Rumah. 1
1Ch 3:18 Malchi'ram, Pedai'ah, Shenaz'zar, Jekami'ah 1
19 and the sons of Pedai'ah: Zerub'babel and Shim'e-i; 1
27:20 half-tribe of Manas'seh, Jo'el the son of Pedai'ah; 1
Neh 3:25 After him Pedai'ah the son of Parosh 1
8: 4 Pedai'ah, Mish'a-el, Malchi'jah . . on his left hand. 1
11: 7 Jo'ed, son of Pedai'ah, son of Ko-lai'ah 1
13:13 appointed . . Pedai'ah of the Levites 1
1Es 9:44 on his left Pedaiah, Mishael, Malchijah 2

Pekah 1. פֶּקַח
2Kg 15:25 Pekah . . his captain, conspired against him 1
27 Pekah . . began to reign over Israel in Sama'ria 1
29 In the days of Pekah king of Israel 1
30 Then Hoshe'a . . made a conspiracy against Pekah 1
31 the rest of the acts of Pekah, and all that he did 1
32 In the second year of Pekah the son of Remali'ah 1
37 to send Rezin . . and Pekah . . against Judah. 1
16: 1 In the seventeenth year of Pekah the son 1
5 Then Rezin . . and Pekah . . came up to wage war 1
2Ch 28: 6 Pekah the son of Remali'ah slew 120,000 in Judah 1
Isa 7: 1 Pekah the son of Remali'ah the king of Israel came 1

Pekahiah 1. פְּקַחְיָה
2Kg 15:22 Men'ahem slept . . and Pekahi'ah his son reigned 1
23 Pekahi'ah the son of Men'ahem began to reign 1
26 the rest of the deeds of Pekahi'ah, and all . . he did 1

Pekod 1. פְּקוֹד
Jer 50:21 Go up . . against the inhabitants of Pekod. 1
Ezk 23:23 Pekod and Sho'a and Ko'a, and all the Assyrians 1

Pelaiah 1. פְּלָאיָה 2. פְּלָיָה 3. Φαλιας
1Ch 3:24 sons of Eli-o-e'nai . . Pelai'ah, Akkub, Joha'nan 2
Neh 8: 7 Also . . Hanan, Pelai'ah, the Levites 1
10:10 their brethren . . Keli'ta, Pelai'ah, Hanan 1
1Es 9:48 Hanan, Pelaiah, the Levites 3

Pelaliah 1. פְּלַלְיָה
Neh 11:12 Adai'ah the son of Jero'ham, son of Pelali'ah 1

Pelatiah 1. פְּלַטְיָהוּ
1Ch 3:21 The sons of Hanani'ah: Pelati'ah and Jeshai'ah 1
4:42 having as their leaders Pelati'ah, Ne-ari'ah 1
Neh 10:22 Pelati'ah, Hanan, Anai'ah 1
Ezk 11: 1 the son of Azzur, and Pelati'ah the son of Benai'ah 1
13 Pelati'ah the son of Benai'ah died. 1

Peleg 1. פֶּלֶג 2. Φάλεκ
Gen 10:25 born two sons: the name of the one was Peleg 1
11:16 Eber . . became the father of Peleg; 1
17 Eber lived after the birth of Peleg 430 years 1
18 When Peleg had lived 30 years 1
19 Peleg lived after the birth of Re'u 209 years 1
1Ch 1:19 To Eber . . two sons: the name of the one was Peleg 1
25 Eber, Peleg, Re'u; 1
Lke 3:35 the son of Serug, the son of Re'u, the son of Peleg 2

Pelet 1. פֶּלֶט
1Ch 2:47 sons of Jah'dai . . Geshan, Pelet, Ephah 1
12: 3 also Je'zi-el and Pelet the sons of Az'maveth; 1

Peleth 1. פֶּלֶת
Num16: 1 Dathan and Abi'ram . . and On the son of Peleth 1
1Ch 2:33 The sons of Jonathan: Peleth and Zaza. 1

Pelethite 1. פְּלֵתִי
2Sm 8:18 was over the Cher'ethites and the Pel'ethites; 1
15:18 all the Cher'ethites, and all the Pel'ethites 1
20: 7 Jo'ab and the Cher'ethites and the Pel'ethites 1
23 command of the Cher'ethites and the Pel'ethites; 1
1Kg 1:38 the Cher'ethites and the Pel'ethites, went down 1
44 and the Cher'ethites and the Pel'ethites; 1
1Ch 18:17 Benai'ah . . was over . . the Pel'ethites; 1

Pelonite 1. פְּלֹנִי
1Ch 11:27 Shammoth of Harod, Helez the Pel'onite 1
36 Hepher the Meche'rathite, Ahi'jah the Pel'onite 1
27:10 Seventh . . was Helez the Pel'onite 1

Pelusium 1. סִין
Ezk 30:15 I will pour my wrath upon Pelusium 1
16 fire to Egypt; Pelusium shall be in great agony; 1

Peniel 1. פְּנִיאֵל
Gen 32:30 Jacob called the name of the place Peni'el 1

Peninnah 1. פְּנִנָּה
1Sm 1: 2 was Hannah, and the name of the other Penin'nah. 1
2 Penin'nah had children, but Hannah had no 1
4 portions to Penin'nah his wife and to all her sons 1

Pentecost 1. πεντηκοστή
Act 2: 1 When the day of Pentecost had come 1
20:16 at Jerusalem, if possible, on the day of Pentecost 1
1Co 16: 8 I will stay in Ephesus until Pentecost 1
Tob 2: 1 at the feast of Pentecost 1
2Mc 12:32 After the feast called Pentecost 1

Penuel 1. פְּנוּאֵל
Gen 32:31 The sun rose upon him as he passed Penu'el 1
Jdg 8: 8 from there he went up to Penu'el, and spoke to them 1
8 and the men of Penu'el answered him as the men 1
9 he said to the men of Penu'el, "When I come again 1
17 the tower of Penu'el, and slew the men of the city. 1
1Kg 12:25 and he went out from there and built Penu'el. 1
1Ch 4: 4 Penu'el was the father of Gedor 1
8:25 Iphdei'ah, and Penu'el were the sons of Shashak. 1

Peor 1. פְּעוֹר
Num23:28 Balak took Balaam to the top of Pe'or 1
25:18 they beguiled you in the matter of Pe'or 1
18 slain on the day of the plague on account of Pe'or. 1
31:16 to act . . against the LORD in the matter of Pe'or 1
Deu 4: 3 destroyed . . men who followed the Ba'al of Pe'or; 1
Jos 22:17 Have we not had enough of the sin at Pe'or 1

Perazim 1. פְּרָצִים
Isa 28:21 For the LORD will rise up as on Mount Pera'zim 1

Peresh 1. פֶּרֶשׁ
1Ch 7:16 Ma'acah . . she called his name Peresh; 1

Perez 1. פֶּרֶץ 2. Φάρες
Gen 38:29 Therefore his name was called Perez. 1
46:12 and the sons of Perez were Hezron and Hamul. 1
12 and the sons of Perez were Hezron and Hamul. 1
Num26:20 of Perez, the family of the Per'ezites; 1
21 the sons of Perez were: of Hezron . . of Hamul 1
Rut 4:12 and may your house be like the house of Perez 1
18 Now these are the descendants of Perez 1
18 descendants of . . Perez was the father of Hezron 1
1Ch 2: 4 Tamar also bore him Perez and Zerah. 1
5 The sons of Perez: Hezron and Hamul. 1
4: 1 sons of Judah: Perez, Hezron, Carmi, Hur, and Shobal. 1
9: 4 from the sons of Perez the son of Judah. 1
27: 3 He was a descendant of Perez 1
Neh 11: 4 Shephati'ah, son of Mahal'alel, of the sons of Perez; 1
6 sons of Perez who lived in Jerusalem were 468 1
Mat 1: 3 Judah the father of Perez and Zerah by Tamar 2
3 Perez the father of Hezron 2
Lke 3:33 son of Hezron, the son of Perez, the son of Judah 2

Perez-uzza 1. פֶּרֶץ עֻזָּא
1Ch 13:11 and that place is called Pe'rez-uz'za to this day. 1

Perez-uzzah 1. פֶּרֶץ עֻזָּה
2Sm 6: 8 and that place is called Pe'rez-uz'zah, to this day. 1

Perezite 1. פַּרְצִי
Num26:20 of Perez, the family of the Per'ezites; 1

Perga 1. Πέργη
Act 13:13 and came to Perga in Pamphyl'ia 1
14 they passed on from Perga 1
14:25 when they had spoken the word in Perga 1

Pergamum 1. Πέργαμος
Rev 1:11 seven churches . . to Per'gamum and to Thyati'ra 1
2:12 And to the angel of the church in Per'gamum write 1

Perida 1. פְּרִידָא
Neh 7:57 the sons of So'phereth, the sons of Peri'da 1

Perizzite 1. פְּרִזִּי 2. Φερεζαιος 3. Ferezeus
Gen 13: 7 At that time the Canaanites and the Per'izzites 1
15:20 the Hittites, the Per'izzites, the Reph'aim 1
34:30 of the land, the Canaanites and the Per'izzites; 1
Exd 3: 8 the Amorites, the Per'izzites, the Hivites 1
17 the Amorites, the Per'izzites, the Hivites 1
23:23 and the Per'izzites, and the Canaanites 1
33: 2 the Hittites, the Per'izzites, the Hivites 1
34:11 the Per'izzites, the Hivites, and the Jeb'usites. 1
Deu 7: 1 Amorites, the Canaanites, the Per'izzites 1
20:17 destroy . . Canaanites and the Per'izzites 1
Jos 3:10 the Hivites, the Per'izzites, the Gir'gashites 1
9: 1 the Canaanites, the Per'izzites, the Hivites 1
11: 3 the Hittites, the Per'izzites, and the Jeb'usites 1
12: 8 the Canaanites, the Per'izzites, the Hivites 1
17:15 in the land of the Per'izzites and the Reph'aim 1
24:11 the Amorites, the Per'izzites, the Canaanites 1
Jdg 1: 4 LORD gave the Canaanites and the Per'izzites 1
5 defeated the Canaanites and the Per'izzites. 1
3: 5 the Amorites, the Per'izzites, the Hivites 1
1Kg 9:20 the Hittites, the Per'izzites, the Hivites 1
2Ch 8: 7 the people who were left of . . the Per'izzites 1
Ezr 9: 1 Per'izzites, the Jeb'usites, the Ammonites 1
Neh 9: 8 land of . . the Per'izzite, the Jeb'usite 1
1Es 8:69 the Canaanites, the Hittites, the Perizzites 2
2Es 1:21 I drove out the Canaanites, the Perizzites 3
Jdt 5:16 the Canaanites and the Perizzites 2

Persepolis 1. Περσεπολις
2Mc 9: 2 For he had entered the city called Persepolis 1

Perseus 1. Περσευς
1Mc 8: 5 Philip, and Perseus king of the Macedonians 1

Persia 1. פָּרַס 2. פָּרַס (A) 3. Περσικος 4. Περσις
2Ch 36:20 establishment of the kingdom of Persia 1
22 Now in the first year of Cyrus king of Persia 1
22 stirred up the spirit of Cyrus king of Persia 1
23 Thus says Cyrus king of Persia, 'The LORD, the God 1
Ezr 1: 1 In the first year of Cyrus king of Persia 1
1 LORD stirred up the spirit of Cyrus king of Persia 1
2 Thus says Cyrus king of Persia: The LORD 1
8 Cyrus king of Persia brought these out in charge 1
3: 7 grant which they had from Cyrus king of Persia. 1
4: 3 as King Cyrus the king of Persia has commanded us. 1
5 days of Cyrus king of Persia, even until the reign 1
5 even until the reign of Darius king of Persia. 1
7 wrote to Ar-ta-xerx'es king of Persia; 1
24 second year of the reign of Darius king of Persia 2
6:14 Cyrus and Darius and Ar-ta-xerx'es king of Persia; 2
7: 1 in the reign of Ar-ta-xerx'es king of Persia 1
9: 9 his steadfast love before the kings of Persia 1
Est 1: 3 and servants, the army chiefs of Persia and Media 1
14 the seven princes of Persia and Media 1
18 the ladies of Persia and Media who have heard 1
10: 2 the Chronicles of the kings of Media and Persia? 1
Ezk 27:10 Persia and Lud and Put were in your army 1
38: 5 Persia, Cush, an Put are with them, all of them 1
Dan 8:20 these are the kings of Media and Persia. 1
10: 1 In the third year of Cyrus king of Persia 1
13 prince of the kingdom of Persia withstood me 1
13 left . . with the prince of the kingdom of Persia 1
20 return to fight against the prince of Persia; 1
11: 2 Behold, three more kings shall arise in Persia; 1
1Es 3: 1 all the nobles of Media and Persia 4
9 the king and the three nobles of Persia 4
14 summoned all the nobles of Persia and Media 4
Jdt 1: 7 sent to all who lived in Persia 4
1Mc 3:31 determined to go to Persia 4
6: 1 Elymais in Persia was a city famed for its wealth 4
5 Then some one came to him in Persia 4
56 returned from Persia and Media with the forces 4
14: 2 When Arsaces the king of Persia and Media heard 4
2Mc 1:13 when the leader reached Persia 4
19 when our fathers were . . led captive to Persia 3
20 having been commissioned by the king of Persia 4
9: 1 retreated . . from the region of Persia. 4
21 On my way back from the region of Persia 4

Persian 1. פָּרַס 2. פַּרְסִי 3. אֲפָרְסַי (A) 4. פָּרַס (A) 5. פָּרְסַי (A) 6. Περσης 7. Perses
Ezr 4: 9 Persians, the men of Erech, the Babylonians 3
Neh 12:22 priests until the reign of Darius the Persian. 2

Est 1:19 among the laws of the Persians and the Medes 1
Dan 5:28 kingdom is . . given to the Medes and Persians. 4
6: 8 law of the Medes and the Persians, 4
12 according to the law of the Medes and Persians 4
15 law of the Medes and Persians that no interdict 4
28 during the . . reign of Cyrus the Persian. 5
1Es 1:57 until the Persians began to reign 6
2: 1 In the first year of Cyrus as king of the Persians 6
2 the spirit of Cyrus king of the Persians 6
3 Thus says Cyrus king of the Persians 6
11 When Cyrus king of the Persians brought these 6
16 in the time of Artaxerxes king of the Persians 6
30 the reign of Darius king of the Persians. 6
5: 6 Darius the king of the Persians 6
55 the decree . . from Cyrus king of the Persians. 6
71 as Cyrus the king of the Persians has commanded 6
7: 4 Darius and Artaxerxes, kings of the Persians,. 6
8: 1 Artaxerxes the king of the Persians 6
80 the kings of the Persians 6
2Es 1: 3 in the reign of Artaxerxes, king of the Persians. 7
Jdt 16:10 The Persians trembled at her boldness 6
AEs 16:10 really an alien to the Persian blood 6
14 would transfer the kingdom of the Persians 6
23 may mean salvation for us and the loyal Persians 6
Bel 1: 1 Cyrus the Persian received his kingdom. 6
1Mc 1: 1 Darius, king of the Persians and the Medes 6
2Mc 1:33 it was reported to the king of the Persians 6
4Mc 18: 5 marched against the Persians. 6

Persis 1. Περσίς

Rom 16:12 Greet the beloved Persis, who has worked hard 1

Peruda 1. פְּרוּדָא 2. Φαριδα

Ezr 2:55 sons of Solomon's servants: the . . sons of Peru'da 1
1Es 5:33 the sons of Hassophereth, the sons of Peruda 2

Peter 1. Πέτρος

Mat 4:18 Simon who is called Peter and Andrew his brother 1
8:14 when Jesus entered Peter's house 1
10: 2 first, Simon, who is called Peter 1
14:28 Peter answered him 1
29 He said, "Come." So Peter got out of the boat 1
15:15 Peter said to him, "Explain the parable to us. 1
16:16 Simon Peter replied, "You are the Christ 1
18 I tell you, you are Peter 1
22 Peter took him and began to rebuke him, saying 1
23 he turned and said to Peter, "Get behind me, Satan! 1
17: 1 Jesus took with him Peter and James and John 1
4 Peter said to Jesus 1
24 the collectors . . went up to Peter and said 1
18:21 Then Peter came up and said to him 1
19:27 Then Peter said in reply 1
26:33 Peter declared to him, "Though they all fall away 1
35 Peter said to him, "Even if I must die with you 1
37 taking with him Peter and the two sons of Zeb'edee 1
40 he said to Peter 1
58 Peter followed him at a distance 1
69 Now Peter was sitting outside in the courtyard. 1
73 bystanders came up and said to Peter 1
75 Peter remembered the saying of Jesus 1
Mrk 3:16 Simon whom he surnamed Peter; 1
5:37 he allowed no one to follow him except Peter 1
8:29 Peter answered him, "You are the Christ. 1
32 Peter took him, and began to rebuke him. 1
33 seeing his disciples, he rebuked Peter, and said 1
9: 2 Jesus took with him Peter and James and John 1
5 Peter said to Jesus, "Master, it is well 1
10:28 Peter began to say to him, "Lo, we have left 1
11:21 Peter remembered and said to him, "Master, look! 1
13: 3 Peter and James and John and Andrew asked him 1
14:29 Peter said to him, "Even though they all fall away 1
33 he took with him Peter and James and John 1
37 he said to Peter, "Simon, are you asleep? 1
54 Peter had followed him at a distance 1
66 as Peter was below in the courtyard 1
67 seeing Peter warming himself, she looked at him 1
70 again the bystanders said to Peter 1
72 Peter remembered how Jesus had said to him 1
16: 7 But go, tell his disciples and Peter that he is going 1
Lke 5: 8 when Simon Peter saw it 1
6:14 Simon, whom he named Peter, and Andrew 1
8:45 When all denied it, Peter said, "Master 1
51 except Peter and John and James 1
9:20 Peter answered, "The Christ of God. 1
28 he took with him Peter and John and James 1
32 Now Peter and those who were with him were heavy 1
33 Peter said to Jesus, "Master, it is well 1
12:41 Peter said, "Lord, are you telling this parable 1
18:28 Peter said, "Lo, we have left our homes 1
22: 8 So Jesus sent Peter and John, saying, "Go 1
34 I tell you, Peter, the cock will not crow this day 1
54 Peter followed at a distance; 1
55 Peter sat among them. 1
58 Peter said, "Man, I am not. 1
60 Peter said, "Man, I do not know what you are saying. 1
61 the Lord turned and looked at Peter 1
61 Peter remembered the word of the Lord 1
Joh 1:40 Andrew, Simon Peter's brother. 1
42 You shall be called Cephas" (which means Peter). 1
44 from Beth-sa'ida, the city of Andrew and Peter. 1
6: 8 Andrew, Simon Peter's brother, said to him 1
68 Simon Peter answered him, "Lord, to whom shall we 1
13: 6 He came to Simon Peter; and Peter said to him, "Lord 1
6 He came to Simon Peter; and Peter said to him, "Lord 1
8 Peter said to him, "You shall never wash my feet. 1
9 Simon Peter said to him, "Lord, not my feet only 1
24 Simon Peter beckoned to him and said, "Tell us 1
36 Simon Peter said to him, "Lord, where are you going? 1
37 Peter said to him, "Lord, why cannot I follow you now 1
18:10 Simon Peter, having a sword, drew it 1
11 Jesus said to Peter 1
15 Simon Peter followed Jesus 1
16 while Peter stood outside at the door 1
16 went out . . and brought Peter in. 1
17 The maid who kept the door said to Peter 1
18 Peter also was with them 1
25 Simon Peter was standing and warming himself. 1
26 a kinsman of the man whose ear Peter had cut off 1
27 Peter again denied it 1
20: 2 went to Simon Peter and the other disciple 1
3 Peter then came out with the other disciple 1
4 the other disciple outran Peter 1
6 Simon Peter came, following him 1
21: 2 Simon Peter, Thomas called the Twin 1
3 Simon Peter said to them, "I am going fishing. 1
7 That disciple whom Jesus loved said to Peter 1
7 When Simon Peter heard that it was the Lord 1
11 Simon Peter went aboard and hauled the net ashore 1
15 Jesus said to Simon Peter, "Simon, son of John 1
17 Peter was grieved 1
20 Peter turned 1
21 When Peter saw him, he said to Jesus, "Lord 1
Act 1:13 Peter and John and James and Andrew 1
15 In those days Peter stood up among the brethren 1
2:14 Peter, standing with the eleven 1
37 said to Peter and the rest of the apostles 1
38 Peter said to them, "Repent, and be baptized 1
3: 1 Now Peter and John were going up to the temple 1
3 Seeing Peter and John about to go into the temple 1
4 Peter directed his gaze at him, with John, and said 1
6 Peter said, "I have no silver and gold 1
11 While he clung to Peter and John 1
12 when Peter saw it he addressed the people 1
4: 8 Then Peter, filled with the Holy Spirit, said 1
13 Now when they saw the boldness of Peter and John 1
19 Peter and John answered them, "Whether it is right 1
5: 3 Peter said, "Anani'as 1
8 Peter said to her, "Tell me 1
9 Peter said to her, "How is it that you have agreed 1
15 as Peter came 1
29 Peter and the apostles answered, "We must obey God 1
8:14 they sent to them Peter and John 1
20 Peter said to him, "Your silver perish with you 1
9:32 Now as Peter went here and there among them all 1
34 Peter said to him, "Aene'as, Jesus Christ heals you; 1
38 hearing that Peter was there 1
39 So Peter rose and went with them 1
40 Peter put them all outside and knelt down 1
40 when she saw Peter she sat up. 1
10: 5 bring one Simon who is called Peter; 1
9 Peter went up on the housetop to pray 1
13 there came a voice to him, "Rise, Peter; kill and eat. 1
14 Peter said, "No, Lord 1
17 Now while Peter was inwardly perplexed 1
18 Simon who was called Peter was lodging there. 1
19 while Peter was pondering the vision 1
21 Peter went down to the men and said, "I am the one 1
25 When Peter entered, Cornelius met him 1
26 Peter lifted him up, saying, "Stand up; I too am a man. 1
32 ask for Simon who is called Peter 1
34 Peter opened his mouth and said: "Truly I perceive 1
44 While Peter was still saying this 1
45 from among the circumcised who came with Peter 1
46 Then Peter declared 1
11: 2 when Peter went up to Jerusalem 1
4 Peter began and explained to them in order 1
7 'Rise, Peter; kill and eat.' 1
13 'Send to Joppa and bring Simon called Peter; 1
12: 3 he proceeded to arrest Peter also 1
5 So Peter was kept in prison 1
6 Peter was sleeping between two soldiers 1
7 he struck Peter on the side and woke him, saying 1
11 Peter came to himself, and said 1
14 Recognizing Peter's voice 1
14 told that Peter was standing at the gate. 1
16 Peter continued knocking 1
18 no small stir . . over what had become of Peter. 1
15: 7 Peter rose and said to them, "Brethren 1
Gal 2: 7 just as Peter had been entrusted 1
8 for he who worked through Peter 1
1Pe 1: 1 Peter, an apostle of Jesus Christ 1
2Pe 1: 1 Simeon Peter, a servant and apostle of Jesus 1

Pethahiah 1. פְּתַחְיָה 2. Παθαιος

1Ch 24:16 the nineteenth to Pethahi'ah, the twentieth 1
Ezr 10:23 Of the Levites . . Petha-hi'ah, Judah, and Elie'zer. 1
Neh 9: 5 Levites . . Shebani'ah, and Pethahi'ah, said, "Stand 1
11:24 Pethahi'ah the son of Meshez'abel, of the sons 1
1Es 9:23 Pethahiah and Judah and Jonah. 2

Pethor 1. פְּתוֹר

Num22: 5 sent messengers to Balaam . . at Pethor 1
Deu 23: 4 Balaam . . of Be'or from Pethor of Mesopota'mia 1

Pethuel 1. פְּתוּאֵל

Jol 1: 1 The word . . that came to Joel, the son of Pethu'el 1

Peullethai 1. פְּעֻלְּתַי

1Ch 26: 5 Is'sachar the seventh, Pe-ul'lethai the eighth; 1

Phalaris 1. Φαλαρις

3Mc 5:20 a savagery worse than that of Phalaris 1
42 Phalaris in everything and filled with madness 1

Phaltiel 1. Phalthihel

2Es 5:16 Phaltiel, a chief of the people, came to me and said 1

Phanuel 1. Φανουήλ

Lke 2:36 a prophetess, Anna, the daughter of Phan'uel 1

Pharakim 1. Φαρακιμ

1Es 5:31 the sons of Asur, the sons of Pharakim 1

Pharaoh 1. פַּרְעֹה 2. Φαραώ 3. Pharao

Gen 12:15 when the princes of Pharaoh saw her 1
15 they praised her to Pharaoh. 1
15 And the woman was taken into Pharaoh's house. 1
17 the LORD afflicted Pharaoh and his house 1
18 Pharaoh called Abram, and said, "What is this 1
20 Pharaoh gave men orders concerning him; 1
37:36 sold him . . to Pot'i-phar, an officer of Pharaoh 1
39: 1 Pot'i-phar, an officer of Pharaoh, bought him 1
40: 2 Pharaoh was angry with his two officers 1
7 he asked Pharaoh's officers who were with him 1
11 Pharaoh's cup was in my hand; and I took the grapes 1
11 grapes and pressed them into Pharaoh's cup 1
11 and placed the cup in Pharaoh's hand. 1
13 within three days Pharaoh will lift up your head 1
13 and you shall place Pharaoh's cup in his hand 1
14 to make mention of me to Pharaoh, and so get me out 1
17 all sorts of baked food for Pharaoh 1
19 three days Pharaoh will lift up your head 1
20 On the third day, which was Pharaoh's birthday 1
21 and he placed the cup in Pharaoh's hand; 1
41: 1 After two whole years, Pharaoh dreamed 1
4 And Pharaoh awoke. 1
7 And Pharaoh awoke, and behold, it was a dream. 1
9 Then the chief butler said to Pharaoh 1
10 When Pharaoh was angry with his servants 1
14 Then Pharaoh sent and called Joseph 1
14 changed his clothes, he came in before Pharaoh. 1
15 Pharaoh said to Joseph, "I have had a dream 1
16 Joseph answered Pharaoh, "It is not in me; 1
16 God will give Pharaoh a favorable answer. 1
17 Then Pharaoh said to Joseph, "Behold, in my dream 1
25 Joseph said to Pharaoh, "The dream of Pharaoh 1
25 said to Pharaoh, "The dream of Pharaoh is one; 1
25 God has revealed to Pharaoh what he is about 1
28 It is as I told Pharaoh, God has shown to Pharaoh 1
28 God has shown to Pharaoh what he is about to do. 1
32 the doubling of Pharaoh's dream means that 1
33 Now therefore let Pharaoh select a man discreet 1
34 Let Pharaoh proceed to appoint overseers over 1
35 lay up grain under the authority of Pharaoh 1
37 This proposal seemed good to Pharaoh 1
38 Pharaoh said to his servants, "Can we find such 1
39 Pharaoh said to Joseph, "Since God has shown you 1
41 Pharaoh said to Joseph, "Behold, I have set you 1
42 Then Pharaoh took his signet ring from his hand 1
44 Moreover Pharaoh said to Joseph, "I am Pharaoh 1
44 to Joseph, "I am Pharaoh, and without your consent 1
45 Pharaoh called Joseph's name Zaph'enath-pane'ah 1
46 entered the service of Pharaoh king of Egypt. 1
46 Joseph went out from the presence of Pharaoh 1
55 the people cried to Pharaoh for bread; 1
55 and Pharaoh said to all the Egyptians 1
42:15 be tested: by the life of Pharaoh 1
16 by the life of Pharaoh, surely you are spies. 1
44:18 for you are like Pharaoh himself. 1
45: 2 and the household of Pharaoh heard it. 1
8 and he has made me a father to Pharaoh 1
16 When the report was heard in Pharaoh's house 1
16 it pleased Pharaoh and his servants well. 1
17 Pharaoh said to Joseph, "Say to your brothers 1
21 gave . . according to the command of Pharaoh 1
46: 5 carried . . in the wagons which Pharaoh had sent 1
31 I will go up and tell Pharaoh, and will say to him 1
33 When Pharaoh calls you, and says, 1
47: 1 Joseph went in and told Pharaoh, 1
2 he took five men and presented them to Pharaoh. 1
3 Pharaoh said to his brothers, "What is 1
3 said to Pharaoh, "Your servants are shepherds 1
4 They said to Pharaoh, "We have come to sojourn 1
5 Then Pharaoh said to Joseph, "Your father 1
7 Jacob his father, and set him before Pharaoh 1
7 and Jacob blessed Pharaoh. 1

8 Pharaoh said to Jacob, "How many are the days 1
9 Jacob said to Pharaoh, "The days of the years of my 1
10 Jacob blessed Pharaoh, and went out 1
10 Jacob . . went out from the presence of Pharaoh. 1
11 gave them . . as Pharaoh had commanded. 1
14 Joseph brought the money into Pharaoh's house. 1
19 we with our land will be slaves to Pharaoh; 1
20 Joseph bought all the land of Egypt for Pharaoh; 1
20 The land became Pharaoh's; 1
22 the priests had a fixed allowance from Pharaoh 1
22 lived on the allowance which Pharaoh gave them; 1
23 bought you and your land for Pharaoh. 1
24 at the harvests you shall give a fifth to Pharaoh 1
25 my lord, we will be slaves to Pharaoh. 1
26 a statute . . Pharaoh should have the fifth; 1
26 the land . . alone did not become Pharaoh's. 1
50: 4 Joseph spoke to the household of Pharaoh, saying 1
4 speak, I pray you, in the ears of Pharaoh, saying 1
6 Pharaoh answered, "Go up, and bury your father 1
7 with him went up all the servants of Pharaoh 1
Exd 1:11 and they built for Pharaoh store-cities 1
19 The midwives said to Pharaoh, "Because the Hebrew 1
22 Then Pharaoh commanded all his people 1
2: 5 Now the daughter of Pharaoh came down to bathe 1
7 his sister said to Pharaoh's daughter, "Shall I go 1
8 Pharaoh's daughter said to her, "Go. 1
9 Pharaoh's daughter said to her, "Take this child 1
10 and she brought him to Pharaoh's daughter 1
15 When Pharaoh heard of it, he sought to kill Moses. 1
15 Moses fled from Pharaoh, and stayed in the land 1
3:10 Come, I will send you to Pharaoh that you may bring 1
11 said to God, "Who am I that I should go to Pharaoh 1
4:21 see that you do before Pharaoh all the miracles 1
22 you shall say to Pharaoh, 'Thus says the LORD 1
5: 1 Aaron went to Pharaoh and said, "Thus says 1
2 Pharaoh said, "Who is the LORD, that I should heed 1
5 Pharaoh said, "Behold, the people of the land 1
6 The same day Pharaoh commanded the taskmasters 1
10 Thus says Pharaoh, 'I will not give you straw. 1
14 the foremen . . whom Pharaoh's taskmasters had 1
15 the foremen . . came and cried to Pharaoh, "Why do 1
20 met Moses . . as they came forth from Pharaoh; 1
21 have made us offensive in the sight of Pharaoh 1
23 For since I came to Pharaoh to speak in thy name 1
6: 1 Now you shall see what I will do to Pharaoh; 1
11 Go in, tell Pharaoh king of Egypt to let the people 1
12 how then shall Pharaoh listen to me, who am a man 1
13 a charge . . to Pharaoh king of Egypt to bring 1
27 It was they who spoke to Pharaoh king of Egypt 1
29 I am the LORD; tell Pharaoh king of Egypt all that I 1
30 how then shall Pharaoh listen to me? 1
7: 1 to Moses, "See, I make you as God to Pharaoh; 1
2 Aaron . . shall tell Pharaoh to let the people 1
3 I will harden Pharaoh's heart 1
4 Pharaoh will not listen to you; 1
7 was . . years old, when they spoke to Pharaoh. 1
9 When Pharaoh says to you, 'Prove yourselves 1
9 Take your rod and cast it down before Pharaoh 1
10 So Moses and Aaron went to Pharaoh and did 1
10 Aaron cast down his rod before Pharaoh 1
11 Pharaoh summoned the wise men and the sorcerers; 1
13 Still Pharaoh's heart was hardened 1
14 LORD said to Moses, "Pharaoh's heart is hardened 1
15 Go to Pharaoh in the morning, as he is going out 1
20 in the sight of Pharaoh and in the sight of his 1
22 so Pharaoh's heart remained hardened 1
23 Pharaoh turned and went into his house 1
8: 1 LORD said to Moses, "Go in to Pharaoh and say to him 1
8 Then Pharaoh called Moses and Aaron, and said 1
9 Moses said to Pharaoh, "Be pleased to command me 1
12 So Moses and Aaron went out from Pharaoh; 1
12 Moses cried to . . as he had agreed with Pharaoh. 1
15 when Pharaoh saw that there was a respite 1
19 the magicians said to Pharaoh, "This is the finger 1
19 But Pharaoh's heart was hardened, and he would not 1
20 Rise up early . . wait for Pharaoh, as he goes out 1
24 great swarms of flies into the house of Pharaoh 1
25 Then Pharaoh called Moses and Aaron, and said, "Go 1
28 So Pharaoh said, "I will let you go, to sacrifice 1
29 the swarms of flies may depart from Pharaoh 1
29 only let not Pharaoh deal falsely again by not 1
30 So Moses went out from Pharaoh and prayed 1
31 and removed the swarms of flies from Pharaoh 1
32 Pharaoh hardened his heart this time also 1
9: 1 Go in to Pharaoh, and say to him, 'Thus says 1
7 Pharaoh sent, and behold, not one of the cattle 1
7 But the heart of Pharaoh was hardened 1
8 throw them . . in the sight of Pharaoh. 1
10 So they . . stood before Pharaoh, and Moses threw 1
12 the LORD hardened the heart of Pharaoh 1
13 Rise up . . and stand before Pharaoh, and say 1
20 word of the LORD among the servants of Pharaoh 1
27 Then Pharaoh sent, and called Moses and Aaron 1
33 So Moses went out of the city from Pharaoh 1
34 when Pharaoh saw that the rain and the hail 1
35 the heart of Pharaoh was hardened, and he did not 1
10: 1 Then the LORD said to Moses, "Go in to Pharaoh; 1
3 Moses and Aaron went in to Pharaoh, and said to him 1
6 Then he turned and went out from Pharaoh. 1
7 Pharaoh's servants said to him, "How long shall 1
8 So Moses and Aaron were brought back to Pharaoh; 1
11 they were driven out from Pharaoh's presence. 1
16 Then Pharaoh called Moses and Aaron in haste 1
18 he went out from Pharaoh, and entreated the LORD. 1
20 the LORD hardened Pharaoh's heart, and he did not 1
24 Then Pharaoh called Moses, and said, "Go, serve 1
27 the LORD hardened Pharaoh's heart, and he would 1
28 Then Pharaoh said to him, "Get away from me; 1
11: 1 I will bring upon Pharaoh and upon Egypt; 1
3 in the sight of Pharaoh's servants 1
5 shall die, from the first-born of Pharaoh who sits 1
8 And he went out from Pharaoh in hot anger. 1
9 the LORD said to Moses, "Pharaoh will not listen 1
10 Moses . . did all these wonders before Pharaoh; 1
10 the LORD hardened Pharaoh's heart 1
12:29 from the first-born of Pharaoh who sat on his 1
30 Pharaoh rose up in the night, he, and all his 1
13:15 For when Pharaoh stubbornly refused to let us go 1
17 When Pharaoh let the people go, God did not lead 1
14: 3 For Pharaoh will say of the people of Israel 1
4 I will harden Pharaoh's heart, and he will pursue 1
4 I will get glory over Pharaoh and all his host; 1
5 the mind of Pharaoh and his servants was changed 1
8 the LORD hardened the heart of Pharaoh 1
9 pursued them, all Pharaoh's horses and chariots 1
10 When Pharaoh drew near, the people of Israel 1
17 I will get glory over Pharaoh and all his host 1
18 I have gotten glory over Pharaoh, his chariots 1
23 Pharaoh's horses, his chariots, and his horsemen. 1
28 covered . . all the host of Pharaoh that had 1
15: 4 Pharaoh's chariots and his host he cast 1
19 For when the horses of Pharaoh with his chariots 1
18: 4 God . . delivered me from the sword of Pharaoh"). 1
8 the LORD had done to Pharaoh and to the Egyptians 1
10 delivered you . . out of the hand of Pharaoh. 1
Deu 6:21 We were Pharaoh's slaves in Egypt; 1
22 signs . . against Egypt and against Pharaoh 1
7: 8 redeemed you . . from the hand of Pharaoh 1
18 remember what the LORD your God did to Pharaoh 1
11: 3 which he did in Egypt to Pharaoh the king of Egypt 1
29: 2 LORD did . . to Pharaoh and to all his servants 1
34:11 to do . . to Pharaoh and to all his servants 1
1Sm 2:27 were in Egypt subject to the house of Pharaoh. 1
6: 6 Egyptians and Pharaoh hardened their hearts? 1
1Kg 3: 1 Solomon made a marriage alliance with Pharaoh 1
1 he took Pharaoh's daughter, and brought her 1
7: 8 made a house . . for Pharaoh's daughter whom he 1
9:16 Pharaoh . . had gone up and captured Gezer 1
24 Pharaoh's daughter went up from the city of David 1
11: 1 Solomon loved . . the daughter of Pharaoh 1
18 They . . came to Egypt, to Pharaoh king of Egypt 1
19 Hadad found great favor in the sight of Pharaoh 1
20 his son, whom Tah'penes weaned in Pharaoh's house; 1
20 Genu'bath was in Pharaoh's house 1
20 Genu'bath was in . . among the sons of Pharaoh. 1
21 Hadad said to Pharaoh, "Let me depart 1
22 Pharaoh said to him, "What have you lacked with me 1
2Kg 17: 7 out of . . Egypt from under the hand of Pharaoh 1
18:21 Such is Pharaoh . . to all who rely on him. 1
23:29 Pharaoh Neco . . went up to the king of Assyria 1
29 Josi'ah went to meet him; and Pharaoh Neco slew him •
33 Pharaoh Neco put him in bonds at Riblah 1
34 Pharaoh Neco made Eli'akim the son of Josi'ah king 1
35 gave the silver and the gold to Pharaoh 1
35 He . . according to the command of Pharaoh. 1
35 He exacted . . to give it to Pharaoh Neco. 1
1Ch 4:17 Bith'i-ah, the daughter of Pharaoh 1
2Ch 8:11 Solomon brought Pharaoh's daughter up 1
Neh 9:10 perform signs and wonders against Pharaoh 1
Ps 135: 9 signs . . against Pharaoh and all his servants; 1
136:15 overthrew Pharaoh and his host in the Red Sea 1
Sng 1: 9 I compare you . . to a mare of Pharaoh's chariots. 1
Isa 19:11 the wise counselors of Pharaoh give stupid 1
11 How can you say to Pharaoh, "I am a son of the wise 1
30: 2 to take refuge in the protection of Pharaoh 1
3 the protection of Pharaoh turn to your shame 1
36: 6 Such is Pharaoh . . of Egypt to all who rely on him. 1
Jer 25:19 Pharaoh king of Egypt, his servants, his princes 1
37: 5 The army of Pharaoh had come out of Egypt; 1
7 Behold, Pharaoh's army which came to help you 1
11 withdrawn . . at the approach of Pharaoh's army 1
43: 9 which is at the entrance to Pharaoh's palace 1
44:30 Behold, I will give Pharaoh Hophra king of Egypt 1
46: 2 Concerning the army of Pharaoh Neco 1
17 Call the name of Pharaoh, king of Egypt, 'Noisy one 1
25 and Pharaoh, and Egypt and her gods and her kings 1
25 upon Pharaoh and those who trust in him. 1
47: 1 the Philistines, before Pharaoh smote Gaza. 1
Ezk 17:17 Pharaoh with his mighty army and great company 1
29: 2 set your face against Pharaoh king of Egypt 1
3 Behold, I am against you, Pharaoh king of Egypt 1
30:21 I have broken the arm of Pharaoh king of Egypt; 1
22 Behold, I am against Pharaoh king of Egypt 1
24 but I will break the arms of Pharaoh 1
25 but the arms of Pharaoh shall fall; 1
31: 2 say to Pharaoh king of Egypt and to his multitude 1
18 This is Pharaoh and all his multitude 1
32: 2 raise a lamentation over Pharaoh king of Egypt 1
31 When Pharaoh sees them, he will comfort himself 1
31 Pharaoh and all his army, slain by the sword 1
32 slain by the sword, Pharaoh and all his multitude 1
Act 7:10 favor and wisdom before Pharaoh, king of Egypt 2
13 Joseph's family became known to Pharaoh. 2
21 Pharaoh's daughter adopted him 2
Rom 9:17 For the scripture says to Pharaoh 2
Heb 11:24 refused to be called the son of Pharaoh's daughter 2
1Es 1:25 Pharaoh, king of Egypt, went to make war 2
2Es 1:10 I struck down Pharaoh with his servants 3
1Mc 4: 9 when Pharaoh with his forces pursued them. 2
3Mc 2: 6 varied punishments on the audacious Pharaoh 2
6: 4 Pharaoh with his abundance of chariots 2

Pharathon 1. Φαραθων

1Mc 9:50 Bethel, and Timnath, and Pharathon, and Tephon 1

Phares 1. Φαρες

1Es 5: 5 of the house of David, of the lineage of Phares 1

Pharisee 1. Φαρισαῖος

Mat 3: 7 when he saw many of the Pharisees and Sad'ducees 1
5:20 exceeds that of the scribes and Pharisees 1
9:11 when the Pharisees saw this, they said 1
14 Why do we and the Pharisees fast 1
34 But the Pharisees said, "He casts out demons 1
12: 2 when the Pharisees saw it, they said to him, "Look 1
14 the Pharisees went out and took counsel 1
24 when the Pharisees heard it they said 1
38 Then some of the scribes and Pharisees said 1
15: 1 Then Pharisees and scribes came to Jesus 1
12 Do you know that the Pharisees were offended 1
16: 1 the Pharisees and Sad'ducees came 1
6 the leaven of the Pharisees and Sadducees. 1
11 the leaven of the Pharisees and Sad'ducees. 1
12 the teaching of the Pharisees and Sadducees. 1
19: 3 Pharisees came up to him and tested him by asking 1
21:45 priests and the Pharisees heard his parables 1
22:15 Then the Pharisees went and took counsel 1
34 when the Pharisees heard 1
41 Now while the Pharisees were gathered together 1
23: 2 The scribes and the Pharisees sit on Moses' seat; 1
13 woe to you, scribes and Pharisees, hypocrites! 1
15 Woe to you, scribes and Pharisees, hypocrites! 1
23 Woe to you, scribes and Pharisees, hypocrites! 1
25 Woe to you, scribes and Pharisees, hypocrites! 1
26 You blind Pharisee! 1
27 Woe to you, scribes and Pharisees, hypocrites! 1
29 Woe to you, scribes and Pharisees, hypocrites! 1
27:62 the chief priests and the Pharisees gathered 1
Mrk 2:16 the scribes of the Pharisees 1
18 John's disciples and the Pharisees were fasting; 1
18 the disciples of the Pharisees fast 1
24 the Pharisees said to him, "Look, why are they doing 1
3: 6 The Pharisees went out 1
7: 1 Now when the Pharisees gathered together to him 1
3 For the Pharisees, and all the Jews, do not eat 1
5 the Pharisees and the scribes asked him 1
8:11 The Pharisees came and began to argue with him 1
15 Take heed, beware of the leaven of the Pharisees 1
10: 2 Pharisees came up and in order to test him asked 1
12:13 some of the Pharisees and some of the Hero'di-ans 1
Lke 5:17 Pharisees and teachers of the law sitting 1
21 the scribes and the Pharisees began to question 1
30 the Pharisees and their scribes murmured 1
33 so do the disciples of the Pharisees 1
6: 2 some of the Pharisees said, "Why are you doing 1
7 the scribes and the Pharisees watched him 1
7:30 the Pharisees and the lawyers rejected 1
36 One of the Pharisees asked him to eat with him 1
36 he went into the Pharisee's house 1
37 he was at table in the Pharisee's house 1
39 Now when the Pharisee who had invited him saw it 1
11:37 a Pharisee asked him to dine with him 1
38 The Pharisee was astonished to see 1
39 Now you Pharisees cleanse the outside of the cup 1
42 woe to you Pharisees! 1
43 Woe to you Pharisees! 1
53 the scribes and the Pharisees began to press him 1
12: 1 the leaven of the Pharisees, which is hypocrisy. 1
13:31 At that very hour some Pharisees came, and said 1
14: 1 a ruler who belonged to the Pharisees 1
3 Jesus spoke to the lawyers and Pharisees, saying 1
15: 2 the Pharisees and the scribes murmured, saying 1
16:14 The Pharisees, who were lovers of money, heard all 1
17:20 Being asked by the Pharisees 1
18:10 one a Pharisee and the other a tax collector. 1
11 The Pharisee stood and prayed thus with himself 1
19:39 some of the Pharisees in the multitude said 1
Joh 1:24 Now they had been sent from the Pharisees. 1
3: 1 there was a man of the Pharisees, named Nicode'mus 1
4: 1 when the Lord knew that the Pharisees had heard 1
7:32 The Pharisees heard the crowd thus muttering 1
32 the chief priests and Pharisees sent officers 1
45 went back to the chief priests and Pharisees 1
47 The Pharisees answered them, "Are you led astray 1
48 Have any . . of the Pharisees believed in him? 1
8: 3 The scribes and the Pharisees brought a woman 1
13 The Pharisees then said to him 1

9:13 They brought to the Pharisees the man 1
15 The Pharisees again asked him 1
16 Some of the Pharisees said 1
40 Some of the Pharisees near him heard this 1
11:46 some of them went to the Pharisees 1
47 the Pharisees gathered the council, and said 1
57 the Pharisees had given orders 1
12:19 The Pharisees then said to one another 1
42 for fear of the Pharisees they did not confess it 1
18: 3 chief priests and the Pharisees 1
Act 5:34 a Pharisee in the council named Gama'li-el 1
15: 5 who belonged to the party of the Pharisees 1
23: 6 one part were Sad'ducees and the other Pharisees 1
6 Brethren, I am a Pharisee, a son of Pharisees 1
6 Brethren, I am a Pharisee, a son of Pharisees 1
7 between the Pharisees and . . Sad'ducees 1
8 the Pharisees acknowledge them all. 1
9 some of the scribes of the Pharisees' party 1
26: 5 I have lived as a Pharisee. 1
Php 3: 5 a Hebrew born of Hebrews; as to the law a Pharisee 1

Pharpar 1. פַּרְפַּר

2Kg 5:12 Are not Aba'na and Pharpar, the rivers of Damascus 1

Phaselis 1. Φασηλις

1Mc 15:23 to Rhodes, and to Phaselis, and to Cos, and to Side 1

Phasiron 1. Φασιρων

1Mc 9:66 the sons of Phasiron in their tents. 1

Phicol 1. פִּיכֹל

Gen 21:22 At that time Abim'elech and Phicol the commander 1
32 Then Abim'elech and Phicol the commander 1
26:26 adviser and Phicol the commander of his army. 1

Philadelphia 1. Φιλαδέλφεια

Rev 1:11 seven churches . . to Sardis and to Philadelphia 1
3: 7 to the angel of the church in Philadelphia write 1

Philemon 1. Φιλήμων

Phm 1: 1 To Phile'mon our beloved fellow worker 1

Philetus 1. Φίλητος

2Ti 2:17 Among them are Hymenae'us and Phile'tus 1

Philip 1. Φίλιππος

Mat 10: 3 Philip and Bartholomew; Thomas and Matthew 1
14: 3 Hero'di-as, his brother Philip's wife; 1
Mrk 3:18 Andrew, and Philip, and Bartholomew, and Matthew 1
6:17 Hero'di-as, his brother Philip's wife 1
Lke 3: 1 Philip tetrarch of the region of Iturae'a 1
6:14 James and John, and Philip, and Bartholomew 1
Joh 1:43 And he found Philip and said to him, "Follow me. 1
44 Now Philip was from Beth-sa'ida, the city of Andrew 1
45 Philip found Nathan'a-el, and said to him 1
46 Philip said to him, "Come and see. 1
48 Jesus answered him, "Before Philip called you 1
6: 5 Jesus said to Philip, "How are we to buy bread 1
7 Philip answered him 1
12:21 these came to Philip, who was from Beth-sa'ida 1
22 Philip went and told Andrew 1
22 Andrew went with Philip and they told Jesus. 1
14: 8 Philip said to him, "Lord, show us the Father 1
9 yet you do not know me, Philip? 1
Act 1:13 Philip and Thomas, Bartholomew and Matthew 1
6: 5 Philip, and Proch'orus, and Nica'nor, and Ti'mon 1
8: 5 Philip went down to a city of Sama'ria 1
6 gave heed to what was said by Philip 1
12 when they believed Philip 1
13 after being baptized he continued with Philip. 1
26 an angel of the Lord said to Philip, "Rise and go 1
29 the Spirit said to Philip, "Go up 1
30 Philip ran to him, and heard him reading Isaiah 1
31 he invited Philip to come up and sit with him. 1
34 the eunuch said to Philip 1
35 Then Philip opened his mouth 1
38 Philip and the eunuch 1
39 the Spirit of the Lord caught up Philip 1
40 Philip was found at Azo'tus 1
21: 8 we entered the house of Philip the evangelist 1
1Mc 1: 1 After Alexander son of Philip, the Macedonian 1
6: 2 Alexander, the son of Philip, the Macedonian king 1
14 Then he called for Philip, one of his friends 1
55 Philip, whom King Antiochus . . had appointed 1
63 He found Philip in control of the city 1
8: 5 Philip, and Perseus king of the Macedonians 1
2Mc 5:22 at Jerusalem, Philip, by birth a Phrygian 1
6:11 were betrayed to Philip 1
8: 8 When Philip saw that the man was gaining ground 1
9:29 Philip, one of his courtiers, took his body home; 1
13:23 Philip . . had revolted in Antioch 1

Philippi 1. Φίλιπποι 2. Φίλιππος

Mat 16:13 into the district of Caesare'a Philip'pi 2
Mrk 8:27 to the villages of Caesare'a Philip'pi 2
Act 16:12 and from there to Philip'pi 1
20: 6 we sailed away from Philip'pi 1
Php 1: 1 saints in Christ Jesus who are at Philip'pi 1
1Th 2: 2 we had . . been shamefully treated at Philip'pi 1

Philippian 1. Φιλιππήσιος

Php 4:15 you Philippians yourselves know 1

Philistia 1. פְּלֶשֶׁת 2. פְּלִשְׁתִּי

Exd 15:14 pangs . . on the inhabitants of Philistia. 1
Ps 60: 8 over Philistia I shout in triumph. 1
83: 7 Philistia with the inhabitants of Tyre; 1
87: 4 behold, Philistia and Tyre, with Ethiopia- 1
108: 9 over Philistia I shout in triumph. 1
Isa 14:29 Rejoice not, O Philistia, all of you 1
31 O city; melt in fear, O Philistia, all of you! 1
Jol 3: 4 O Tyre and Sidon, and all the regions of Philistia? 1
Zec 9: 6 I will make an end of the pride of Philistia. 2

Philistine 1. פְּלִשְׁתִּי 2. ἀλλόφυλος 3. Φυλιστιμ 4. Philistheus

Gen 10:14 Caslu'him (whence came the Philistines) 1
21:32 returned to the land of the Philistines. 1
34 many days in the land of the Philistines. 1
26: 1 to Gerar, to Abim'elech king of the Philistines. 1
8 Abim'elech king of the Philistines looked out 1
14 a great household, so that the Philistines 1
15 Now the Philistines had stopped and filled 1
18 for the Philistines had stopped them 1
Exd 13:17 lead them by way of the land of the Philistines 1
23:31 from the Red Sea to the sea of the Philistines 1
Jos 13: 2 yet remains: all the regions of the Philistines 1
3 there are five rulers of the Philistines 1
Jdg 3: 3 nations: the five lords of the Philistines 1
31 Shamgar . . who killed 600 of the Philistines 1
10: 6 the Ammonites, and the gods of the Philistines; 1
7 he sold them into the hand of the Philistines 1
11 from the Ammonites and from the Philistines? 1
13: 1 gave them into the hand of the Philistines 1
5 to deliver . . from the hand of the Philistines. 1
14: 1 he saw one of the daughters of the Philistines. 1
2 I saw one of the daughters of the Philistines 1
3 take a wife from the uncircumcised Philistines? 1
4 seeking an occasion against the Philistines. 1
4 time the Philistines had dominion over Israel. 1
15: 3 shall be blameless in regard to the Philistines 1
5 go into the standing grain of the Philistines 1
6 the Philistines said, "Who has done this? 1
6 the Philistines came up, and burned her 1
9 the Philistines came up and encamped in Judah 1
11 not know that the Philistines are rulers over us? 1
12 give you into the hands of the Philistines. 1
14 the Philistines came shouting to meet him; 1
20 he judged Israel in the days of the Philistines 1
16: 5 the lords of the Philistines came to her and said 1
8 the lords of the Philistines brought her seven 1
9 said to him, "The Philistines are upon you, Samson! 1
12 said to him, "The Philistines are upon you, Samson! 1
14 said to him, "The Philistines are upon you, Samson! 1
18 she sent and called the lords of the Philistines 1
18 the lords of the Philistines came up to her 1
20 she said, "The Philistines are upon you, Samson! 1
21 Philistines seized him and gouged out his eyes 1
23 the lords of the Philistines gathered to offer 1
27 all the lords of the Philistines were there 1
28 be avenged upon the Philistines for one of my two 1
30 Samson said, "Let me die with the Philistines. 1
1Sm 4: 1 went out to battle against the Philistines; 1
1 and the Philistines encamped at Aphek. 1
2 The Philistines drew up in line against Israel 1
2 Israel was defeated by the Philistines 1
3 LORD put us to rout today before the Philistines? 1
6 when the Philistines heard . . they said 1
7 the Philistines were afraid; for they said 1
9 acquit yourselves like men, O Philistines 1
10 the Philistines fought, and Israel was defeated 1
17 Israel has fled before the Philistines 1
5: 1 When the Philistines captured the ark of God 1
2 the Philistines took the ark . . and set it up 1
8 gathered . . all the lords of the Philistines 1
11 and gathered . . all the lords of the Philistines 1
6: 1 The ark . . was in the country of the Philistines 1
2 the Philistines called for the priests 1
4 the number of the lords of the Philistines; 1
12 the lords of the Philistines went after them 1
16 when the five lords of the Philistines saw it 1
17 golden tumors, which the Philistines returned 1
18 the cities of the Philistines belonging 1
21 The Philistines have returned the ark 1
7: 3 deliver you out of the hand of the Philistines. 1
7 the Philistines heard . . Israel had gathered 1
7 the lords of the Philistines went up against 1
7 they were afraid of the Philistines. 1
8 he may save us from the hand of the Philistines. 1
10 the Philistines drew near to attack Israel; 1
10 the LORD thundered . . against the Philistines 1
11 went out of Mizpah and pursued the Philistines 1
13 the Philistines were subdued and did not again 1
13 the hand of the LORD was against the Philistines 1
14 cities which the Philistines had taken 1
14 rescued . . from the hand of the Philistines. 1
9:16 save my people from the hand of the Philistines; 1
10: 5 where there is a garrison of the Philistines; 1
12: 9 he sold them . . into the hand of the Philistines 1
13: 3 defeated the garrison of the Philistines 1
3 Jonathan defeated . . and the Philistines heard 1
4 had defeated the garrison of the Philistines 1
4 Israel had become odious to the Philistines. 1
5 the Philistines mustered to fight with Israel 1
11 the Philistines had mustered at Michmash 1
12 the Philistines will come down upon me at Gilgal 1
16 but the Philistines encamped at Michmash. 1
17 raiders came out of the camp of the Philistines 1
19 the Philistines said, "Lest the Hebrews make 1
20 the Israelites went down to the Philistines 1
23 And the garrison of the Philistines went out 1
14: 1 go . . to the Philistine garrison on yonder side. 1
4 sought to go over to the Philistine garrison 1
11 showed themselves to the . . Philistines; 1
11 the Philistines said, "Look, Hebrews are coming 1
19 tumult in the camp of the Philistines increased 1
21 the Hebrews who had been with the Philistines 1
22 all . . heard that the Philistines were fleeing 1
30 the slaughter among the Philistines has not 1
31 They struck down the Philistines that day 1
36 Let us go down after the Philistines by night 1
37 Shall I go down after the Philistines? 1
46 Then Saul went up from pursuing the Philistines; 1
46 and the Philistines went to their own place. 1
47 the kings of Zobah, and against the Philistines; 1
52 was hard fighting against the Philistines 1
17: 1 Now the Philistines gathered their armies 1
2 drew up in . . battle against the Philistines. 1
3 And the Philistines stood . . on the one side 1
4 there came out from the camp of the Philistines 1
8 Am I not a Philistine, and are you not . . of Saul? 1
10 the Philistine said, "I defy the ranks of Israel 1
11 all Israel heard these words of the Philistine 1
16 the Philistine came forward and took his stand 1
19 in the valley . . fighting with the Philistines. 1
21 Israel and the Philistines drew up for battle 1
23 the Philistine of Gath, Goliath by name, came up 1
23 came up out of the ranks of the Philistines 1
26 What . . for the man who kills this Philistine 1
26 For who is this uncircumcised Philistine 1
32 servant will go and fight with this Philistine. 1
33 You are not able to go against this Philistine 1
36 this uncircumcised Philistine shall be like 1
37 deliver me from the hand of this Philistine. 1
40 and he drew near to the Philistine. 1
41 the Philistine came on and drew near to David 1
42 And when the Philistine looked, and saw David 1
43 And the Philistine said to David, "Am I a dog 1
43 And the Philistine cursed David by his gods. 1
44 The Philistine said to David, "Come to me 1
45 Then David said to the Philistine 1
46 the dead bodies of the host of the Philistines 1
48 When the Philistine arose and came and drew near 1
48 David ran quickly . . to meet the Philistine. 1
49 and struck the Philistine on his forehead; 1
50 David prevailed over the Philistine 1
50 David prevailed . . and struck the Philistine 1
51 Then David ran and stood over the Philistine 1
51 the Philistines saw . . their champion was dead 1
52 rose with a shout and pursued the Philistines 1
52 the wounded Philistines fell on the way 1
53 came back from chasing the Philistines 1
54 David took the head of the Philistine 1
55 Saul saw David go forth against the Philistine 1
57 returned from the slaughter of the Philistine 1
57 with the head of the Philistine in his hand. 1
18: 6 David returned from slaying the Philistine 1
17 but let the hand of the Philistines be upon him. 1
21 the hand of the Philistines may be against him. 1
25 except 100 foreskins of the Philistines 1
25 make David fall by the hand of the Philistines. 1
27 David . . killed 200 of the Philistines; 1
30 Then the princes of the Philistines came out 1
19: 5 he slew the Philistine, and the LORD wrought 1
8 David went out and fought with the Philistines 1
21: 9 The sword of Goliath the Philistine . . is here 1
22:10 gave him the sword of Goliath the Philistine. 1
23: 1 the Philistines are fighting against Kei'lah 1
2 Shall I go and attack these Philistines? 1
2 Go and attack the Philistines and save Kei'lah. 1
3 we go . . against the armies of the Philistines? 1
4 I will give the Philistines into your hand. 1
5 David and his men . . fought with the Philistines 1
27 the Philistines have made a raid upon the land. 1
28 Saul . . went against the Philistines; 1
24: 1 Saul returned from following the Philistines 1
27: 1 I should escape to the land of the Philistines; 1
7 David dwelt in the country of the Philistines 1
11 he dwelt in the country of the Philistines. 1
28: 1 the Philistines gathered their forces for war 1
4 The Philistines assembled, and came 1
5 When Saul saw the army of the Philistines 1
15 the Philistines are warring against me 1
19 give Israel . . into the hand of the Philistines; 1

19 Israel also . . into the hand of the Philistines. 1
29: 1 Now the Philistines gathered all their forces 1
2 As the lords of the Philistines were passing 1
3 the commanders of the Philistines said 1
3 said to the commanders of the Philistines 1
4 the commanders of the Philistines were angry 1
4 the commanders of the Philistines said to him 1
7 not displease the lords of the Philistines. 1
9 the commanders of the Philistines have said 1
11 to return to the land of the Philistines. 1
11 But the Philistines went up to Jezreel. 1
30:16 taken from the land of the Philistines 1
31: 1 Now the Philistines fought against Israel; 1
1 the men of Israel fled before the Philistines 1
2 And the Philistines overtook Saul and his sons; 1
2 the Philistines slew Jonathan and Abin'adab 1
7 and the Philistines came and dwelt in them. 1
8 when the Philistines came to strip the slain 1
9 sent . . throughout the land of the Philistines 1
11 heard what the Philistines had done to Saul 1
2Sm 1:20 lest the daughters of the Philistines rejoice 1
3:14 of 100 foreskins of the Philistines. 1
18 save . . Israel from the hand of the Philistines 1
5:17 Philistines heard . . David had been anointed 1
17 all the Philistines went up in search of David; 1
18 Now the Philistines had come and spread out 1
19 Shall I go up against the Philistines? 1
19 I will . . give the Philistines into your hand. 1
21 And the Philistines left their idols there *
22 the Philistines came up yet again 1
24 gone out . . to smite the army of the Philistines. 1
25 and smote the Philistines from Geba to Gezer. 1
8: 1 David defeated the Philistines and subdued 1
1 David took . . out of the hand of the Philistines. 1
12 from Edom, Moab, the Ammonites, the Philistines 1
19: 9 and saved us from the hand of the Philistines; 1
21:12 Beth-shan, where the Philistines had hanged them 1
12 on the day the Philistines killed Saul on Gilbo'a; 1
15 The Philistines had war again with Israel 1
15 and they fought against the Philistines; 1
17 and attacked the Philistine and killed him. 1
18 there was again war with the Philistines at Gob; 1
19 there was again war with the Philistines at Gob; 1
23: 9 they defied the Philistines who were gathered 1
10 He rose and struck down the Philistines 1
11 The Philistines gathered together at Lehi 1
11 and the men fled from the Philistines. 1
12 But he took his stand . . and slew the Philistines; 1
13 a band of Philistines was encamped in the valley 1
14 and the garrison of the Philistines was 1
16 broke through the camp of the Philistines 1
1Kg 4:21 the Euphra'tes to the land of the Philistines 1
15:27 at Gib'bethon, which belonged to the Philistines; 1
16:15 Gib'bethon, which belonged to the Philistines 1
2Kg 8: 2 and sojourned in the land of the Philistines 1
3 woman returned from the land of the Philistines 1
18: 8 He smote the Philistines as far as Gaza and its 1
1Ch 1:12 Pathru'sim, Caslu'him (whence came the Philis'tines 1
10: 1 Now the Philistines fought against Israel; 1
1 men of Israel fled before the Philistines 1
2 the Philistines overtook Saul and his sons; 1
2 Philistines slew Jonathan and Abin'adab 1
7 the Philistines came and dwelt in them. 1
8 when the Philistines came to strip the slain 1
9 throughout the land of the Philistines 1
11 heard all that the Philistines had done to Saul 1
11:13 Philistines were gathered there for battle. 1
13 and the men fled from the Philistines. 1
14 defended it, and slew the Philistines; 1
15 when the army of Philistines was encamped 1
16 garrison of the Philistines was 1
18 broke through the camp of the Philistines 1
12:19 came with the Philistines for the battle 1
19 for the rulers of the Philistines took counsel 1
14: 8 Philistines heard that David had been anointed 1
8 all the Philistines went up in search of David; 1
9 Now the Philistines had come and made a raid 1
10 Shall I go up against the Philistines? 1
13 Philistines yet again made a raid in the valley. 1
15 before you to smite the army of the Philistines. 1
16 smote the Philistine army from Gibeon to Gezer. 1
18: 1 David defeated the Philistines and subdued 1
1 its villages out of the hand of the Philistines. 1
11 Moab, the Ammonites, the Philistines, and Am'alek. 1
20: 4 there arose war with the Philistines at Gezer; 1
4 and the Philistines were subdued. *
5 there was again war with the Philistines; 1
2Ch 9:26 he ruled . . to the land of the Philistines 1
17:11 Some of the Philistines brought Jehosh'aphat 1
21:16 against Jeho'ram the anger of the Philistines 1
26: 6 He went out and made war against the Philistines 1
6 elsewhere among the Philistines. 1
7 God helped him against the Philistines 1
28:18 the Philistines had made raids on the cities 1
Ps 56: 0 David, when the Philistines seized him in Gath. 1
Isa 2: 6 full . . of soothsayers like the Philistines 1
9:12 the Philistines on the west devour Israel 1
11:14 swoop down upon the shoulder of the Philistines 1
Jer 25:20 all the kings of the land of the Philistines 1
47: 1 to . . the prophet concerning the Philistines 1
4 that is coming to destroy all the Philistines 1
4 For the LORD is destroying the Philistines 1
Ezk 16:27 your enemies, the daughters of the Philistines 1
57 and for the daughters of the Philistines 1
25:15 Because the Philistines acted revengefully 1
16 stretch out my hand against the Philistines 1
Ams 1: 8 and the remnant of the Philistines shall perish 1
6: 2 then go down to Gath of the Philistines. 1
9: 7 bring up . . and the Philistines from Caphtor 1
Obd 1:19 of the Shephe'lah the land of the Philistines; 1
Zep 2: 5 is against you, O Canaan, land of the Philistines; 1
2Es 1:21 the Perizzites, and the Philistines before you. 4
Sir 46:18 all the rulers of the Philistines. 3
47: 7 annihilated his adversaries the Philistines 3
50:26 Those who live on Mount Seir, and the Philistines 3
1Mc 3:24 the rest fled into the land of the Philistines. 3
41 from Syria and the land of the Philistines 2
4:22 they all fled into the land of the Philistines. 2
30 didst give the camp of the Philistines 2
5:66 to go into the land of the Philistines 2
68 Azotus in the land of the Philistines 2
4Mc 3: 7 had been attacking the Philistines all day long 2
151 1: 6 I went out to meet the Philistine 2

Philologus 1. Φιλόλογος
Rom 16:15 Greet Philol'ogus, Julia, Nereus and his sister 1

Philometor 1. Φιλομητωρ
2Mc 4:21 for the coronation of Philometor as king 1
21 Philometor had become hostile *
9:29 betook himself to Ptolemy Philometor in Egypt. 1
10:13 which Philometor had entrusted to him 1

Philopator 1. Φιλοπατωρ
3Mc 1: 1 When Philopator learned 1
3:12 King Ptolemy Philopator to his generals 1
7: 1 King Ptolemy Philopator to the generals 1

Phinehas 1. פִּינְחָס 2. Φινεες 3. Finees
Exd 6:25 daughters of Pu'ti-el; and she bore him Phin'ehas. 1
Num 25: 7 When Phin'ehas the son of Elea'zar . . saw it 1
11 Phin'ehas . . has turned back my wrath 1
31: 6 together with Phin'ehas the son of Elea'zar 1
Jos 22:13 Israel sent . . Phin'ehas the son of Elea'zar 1
30 Phin'ehas the priest and the chiefs 1
31 Phin'ehas . . said to the Reubenites 1
32 Then Phin'ehas . . and the chiefs, returned 1
24:33 the town of Phin'ehas his son, which had been given 1
Jdg 20:28 Phin'ehas . . ministered before it in those days) 1
1Sm 1: 3 two sons of Eli, Hophni and Phin'ehas, were priests 1
2:34 shall befall your two sons, Hophni and Phin'ehas 1
4: 4 two sons of Eli, Hophni and Phin'ehas, were there 1
11 two sons of Eli, Hophni and Phin'ehas, were slain. 1
17 your two sons also, Hophni and Phin'ehas, are dead 1
19 Now his daughter-in-law, the wife of Phin'ehas 1
14: 3 Ahi'tub . . son of Phin'ehas, son of Eli, the priest 1
1Ch 6: 4 Elea'zar was the father of Phin'ehas 1
4 the father of Phin'ehas, Phin'ehas of Abishu'a 1
50 sons of Aaron: Elea'zar his son, Phin'ehas his son 1
9:20 Phin'ehas the son of Elea'zar 1
Ezr 7: 5 son of Abi'shu-a, son of Phin'ehas 1
8: 2 Of the sons of Phin'ehas, Gershom. 1
33 Mer'emoth . . Elea'zar the son of Phin'ehas 1
Ps 106:30 Then Phin'ehas stood up and interposed 1
1Es 5: 5 the priests, the sons of Phinehas, son of Aaron; 2
8:63 with him was Eleazar the son of Phinehas 2
2Es 1: 2 son of Ahijah, son of Phinehas, son of Eli 3
2 son of Borith, son of Abishua, son of Phinehas 3
Sir 45:23 Phinehas the son of Eleazar is the third in glory 2
1Mc 2:26 as Phinehas did against Zimri the son of Salu. 2
54 Phinehas our father 2

Phlegon 1. Φλέγων
Rom 16:14 Greet Asyn'critus, Phlegon, Hermes, Pat'robas 1

Phoebe 1. Φοίβη
Rom 16: 1 I commend to you our sister Phoebe 1

Phoenicia 1. כְּנַעֲנִי 2. Φοινίκη
Obd 1:20 the people of Israel shall possess Phoenicia 1
Act 11:19 those . . traveled as far as Phoeni'cia and Cyprus 2
15: 3 they passed through both Phoeni'cia and Sama'ria 2
21: 2 having found a ship crossing to Phoeni'cia 2
1Es 2:17 their council in Coelesyria and Phoenicia 2
24 have access to Coelesyria and Phoenicia. 2
25 living in Samaria and Syria and Phoenicia 2
27 exacted tribute from Coelesyria and Phoenicia. 2
4:48 all the governors in Coelesyria and Phoenicia 2
6: 3 Sisinnes the governor of Syria and Phoenicia 2
7 Sisinnes the governor of Syria and Phoenicia 2
7 the local rulers in Syria and Phoenicia 2
27 Sisinnes the governor of Syria and Phoenicia 2
27 appointed as local rulers in Syria and Phoenicia 2
29 out of the tribute of Coelesyria and Phoenicia 2
7: 1 governor of Coelesyria and Phoenicia 2
8:19 the treasurers of Syria and Phoenicia 2
23 throughout all Syria and Phoenicia 2
67 the governors of Coelesyria and Phoenicia 2
2Mc 3: 5 was governor of Coelesyria and Phoenicia. 2
8 the cities of Coelesyria and Phoenicia 2
4: 4 governor of Coelesyria and Phoenicia 2
22 Then he marched into Phoenicia. 2
8: 8 governor of Coelesyria and Phoenicia 2
10:11 to be chief governor of Coelesyria and Phoenicia. 2
3Mc 3:15 nations inhabiting Coele-Syria and Phoenicia 2
4Mc 4: 2 governor of Syria, Phoenicia, and Cilicia 2

Phoenix 1. Φοῖνιξ
Act 27:12 they could reach Phoenix, a harbor of Crete 1

Phrygia 1. Φρυγία
Act 2:10 Phryg'ia and Pamphyl'ia 1
16: 6 they went through the region of Phry'gia and Galatia 1
18:23 the region of Galatia and Phryg'ia 1

Phrygian 1. Φρυξ
2Mc 5:22 at Jerusalem, Philip, by birth a Phrygian 1

Phygelus 1. Φύγελος
2Ti 1:15 among them Phy'gelus and Hermog'enes. 1

Pi-beseth 1. פִּי בֶסֶת
Ezk 30:17 On and of Pibe'seth shall fall by the sword; 1

Pi-hahiroth 1. פִּי הַחִירֹת
Exd 14: 2 turn back and encamp in front of Pi-ha-hi'roth 1
9 at the sea, by Pi-ha-hi'roth, in front of Ba'al-ze'phon. 1
Num 33: 7 from Etham, and turned back to Pi-hahi'roth 1

Pilate 1. Πιλᾶτος
Mat 27: 2 delivered him to Pilate the governor. 1
13 Then Pilate said to him, "Do you not hear 1
17 So when they had gathered, Pilate said to them 1
22 Pilate said to them, "Then what shall I do 1
24 So when Pilate saw that he was gaining nothing 1
58 He went to Pilate and asked for the body of Jesus. 1
58 Then Pilate ordered it to be given to him. 1
62 the Pharisees gathered before Pilate 1
65 Pilate said to them, "You have a guard of soldiers; 1
Mrk 15: 1 led him away and delivered him to Pilate. 1
2 Pilate asked him, "Are you the King of the Jews? 1
4 Pilate again asked him, "Have you no answer to make? 1
5 so that Pilate wondered. 1
8 the crowd came up and began to ask Pilate *
12 Pilate again said to them, "Then what shall I do 1
14 Pilate said to them, "Why, what evil has he done? 1
15 So Pilate, wishing to satisfy the crowd 1
43 took courage and went to Pilate 1
44 Pilate wondered if he were already dead; 1
Lke 3: 1 Pontius Pilate being governor of Judea 1
13: 1 the Galileans whose blood Pilate had mingled 1
23: 1 brought him before Pilate. 1
3 Pilate asked him, "Are you the King of the Jews? 1
4 Pilate said to the chief priests 1
6 When Pilate heard this 1
11 he sent him back to Pilate. 1
12 Herod and Pilate became friends with each other 1
13 Pilate then called together the chief priests 1
20 Pilate addressed them once more 1
24 So Pilate gave sentence 1
52 This man went to Pilate 1
Joh 18:29 Pilate went out to them and said 1
31 Pilate said to them, "Take him yourselves 1
33 Pilate entered the praetorium again 1
35 Pilate answered, "Am I a Jew? 1
37 Pilate said to him, "So you are a king? 1
38 Pilate said to him, "What is truth? 1
19: 1 Pilate took Jesus and scourged him. 1
4 Pilate went out again, and said to them 1
5 Pilate said to them, "Behold the man! *
6 Pilate said to them, "Take him yourselves 1
8 When Pilate heard these words 1
10 Pilate therefore said to him, "You will not speak 1
12 Upon this Pilate sought to release him 1
13 When Pilate heard these words 1
15 Pilate said to them, "Shall I crucify your King? 1
19 Pilate also wrote a title and put it on the cross; 1
21 The chief priests of the Jews then said to Pilate 1
22 Pilate answered, "What I have written 1
31 the Jews asked Pilate 1
38 asked Pilate that he might take away the body 1
38 and Pilate gave him leave 1
Act 3:13 denied in the presence of Pilate 1
4:27 both Herod and Pontius Pilate, with the Gentiles 1
13:28 yet they asked Pilate to have him killed. 1
1Ti 6:13 in his testimony before Pontius Pilate 1

Pildash 1. פִּלְדָּשׁ
Gen 22:22 Chesed, Hazo, Pildash, Jidlaph, and Bethu'el. 1

Pilha 1. פִּלְחָא
Neh 10:24 Hallo'hesh, Pi'lha, Shobek 1

Piltai 1. פִּלְטָי
Neh 12:17 of Abi'jah, Zichri; of Mini'amin, of Moadi'ah, Pil'tai; 1

Pinon 1. פִּינֹן
Gen 36:41 Oholiba'mah, Elah, Pinon 1
1Ch 1:52 Oholiba'mah, Elah, Pinon 1

Piram 1. פִּרְאָם
Jos 10: 3 to Hoham king of Hebron, to Piram king of Jarmuth 1

Pirathon 1. פִּרְעָתוֹן 2. פִּרְעָתוֹנִי
Jdg 12:15 and was buried at Pira'thon in the land of E'phraim 1
2Sm 23:30 Benai'ah of Pira'thon, Hid'dai of the brooks 2
1Ch 11:31 Benai'ah of Pira'thon 2
27:14 Eleventh . . was Benai'ah of Pira'thon 2

Pirathonite 1. פִּרְעָתוֹנִי
Jdg 12:13 Abdon the son of Hillel the Pira'thonite judged 1
15 Abdon the son of Hillel the Pira'thonite died 1

Pisgah 1. פִּסְגָּה
Num21:20 in the region of Moab by the top of Pisgah 1
23:14 he took him to . . Zophim, to the top of Pisgah 1
Deu 3:17 Salt Sea, under the slopes of Pisgah on the east. 1
27 Go up to the top of Pisgah, and lift up your eyes 1
4:49 Sea of the Arabah, under the slopes of Pisgah. 1
34: 1 Mount Nebo, to the top of Pisgah . . opposite Jericho. 1
Jos 12: 3 southward to the foot of the slopes of Pisgah; 1
13:20 and Beth-pe'or, and the slopes of Pisgah 1

Pishon 1. פִּישׁוֹן 2. Φισων
Gen 2:11 The name of the first is Pishon; 1
Sir 24:25 It fills men with wisdom, like the Pishon 2

Pisidia 1. Πισιδία
Act 13:14 and came to Antioch of Pisid'ia 1
14:24 Then they passed through Pisid'ia 1

Pispa 1. פִּסְפָּה
1Ch 7:38 The sons of Jether: Jephun'neh, Pispa, and Ara. 1

Pithom 1. פִּתֹם
Exd 1:11 built . . store-cities, Pithom and Ra-am'ses. 1

Pithon 1. פִּיתוֹן
1Ch 8:35 The sons of Micah: Pithon, Melech, Tare'a, and Ahaz. 1
9:41 sons of Micah: Pithon, Melech, Tahr'e-a, and Ahaz 1

Pleiades 1. כִּימָה
Job 9: 9 Orion, the Plei'ades and the chambers of the south; 1
38:31 Can you bind the chains of the Plei'ades 1
Ams 5: 8 He who made the Plei'ades and Orion 1

Pochereth-hazzebaim 1. פֹּכֶרֶת הַצְּבָיִים
2. Φακαρεθ σαβιη
Ezr 2:57 the sons of Po'chereth-hazzeba'im 1
Neh 7:59 sons of Hattil, the sons of Po'chereth-hazzeba'im 1
1Es 5:34 the sons of Pochereth-hazzebaim 2

Pontius 1. Πόντιος
Lke 3: 1 Pontius Pilate being governor of Judea 1
Act 4:27 both Herod and Pontius Pilate, with the Gentiles 1
1Ti 6:13 in his testimony before Pontius Pilate 1

Pontus 1. Ποντικός 2. Πόντος
Act 2: 9 Judea and Cappado'cia, Pontus and Asia 2
18: 2 he found a Jew named Aq'uila, a native of Pontus 1
1Pe 1: 1 the Dispersion in Pontus, Galatia, Cappado'cia 2

Poratha 1. פּוֹרָתָא
Est 9: 8 and Pora'tha and Ada'lia and Arida'tha 1

Porcius 1. Πόρκιος
Act 24:27 Felix was succeeded by Porcius Festus; 1

Posidonius 1. Ποσιδωνιος
2Mc 14:19 Therefore he sent Posidonius and Theodotus 1

Poti-phera 1. פּוֹטִי פֶרַע
Gen 41:45 As'enath, the daughter of Poti'phera priest of On. 1
50 As'enath, the daughter of Poti'phera priest of On 1
46:20 As'enath, the daughter of Poti'phera the priest 1

Potiphar 1. פּוֹטִיפַר
Gen 37:36 sold him . . to Pot'i-phar, an officer of Pharaoh 1
39: 1 Pot'i-phar, an officer of Pharaoh, bought him 1

day of Preparation 1. παρασκευή
Mrk 15:42 since it was the day of Preparation 1
Joh 19:14 Now it was the day of Preparation of the Passover; 1
31 Since it was the day of Preparation 1
42 because of the Jewish day of Preparation 1

Prisca 1. Πρίσκα
Rom 16: 3 Greet Prisca and Aq'uila, my fellow workers 1
1Co 16:19 Aq'uila and Prisca, together with the church 1
2Ti 4:19 Greet Prisca and Aq'uila 1

Priscilla 1. πρίσκιλλα
Act 18: 2 lately come from Italy with his wife Priscilla 1
18 and with him Priscilla and Aq'uila 1
26 when Priscilla and Aq'uila heard him 1

Prochorus 1. Πρόχορος
Act 6: 5 Philip, and Proch'orus, and Nica'nor, and Ti'mon 1

Ptolemaic 1. Πτολεμαικος
3Mc 1: 2 took with him the best of the Ptolemaic arms 1

Ptolemais 1. Πτολεμαεις 2. Πτολεμαΐς
Act 21: 7 we arrived at Ptolema'is 2
1Mc 5:15 men of Ptolemais and Tyre and Sidon 2
22 He pursued them to the gate of Ptolemais 2
55 Simon . . was in Galilee before Ptolemais 2
10: 1 landed and occupied Ptolemais 2
39 Ptolemais and the land adjoining it 2
56 meet me at Ptolemais 2
57 came to Ptolemais 2
58 celebrated her wedding at Ptolemais 2
60 went with pomp to Ptolemais and met the two kings; 2
11:22 he set out and came to Ptolemais 2
22 to meet him for a conference at Ptolemais 2
24 for he went to the king at Ptolemais 2
12:45 come with me to Ptolemais 2
48 when Jonathan entered Ptolemais 2
48 the men of Ptolemais closed the gates 1
13:12 Then Trypho departed from Ptolemais 2
2Mc 13:24 governor from Ptolemais to Gerar 2
25 went to Ptolemais 2
25 The people of Ptolemais were indignant 1
3Mc 7:17 When they had arrived at Ptolemais 2

Ptolemy 1. Πτολεμαιος
AEs 11: 1 the reign of Ptolemy and Cleopatra 1
1 Dositheus . . and Ptolemy his son 1
1 translated by Lysimachus the son of Ptolemy 1
1Mc 1:18 He engaged Ptolemy king of Egypt in battle 1
18 Ptolemy turned and fled before him 1
3:38 Lysias chose Ptolemy the son of Dorymenes 1
10:51 sent ambassadors to Ptolemy king of Egypt 1
55 Ptolemy the king replied and said 1
57 So Ptolemy set out from Egypt 1
58 Ptolemy gave him Cleopatra . . in marriage •
11: 3 when Ptolemy entered the cities 1
8 King Ptolemy gained control of the coastal cities 1
13 Then Ptolemy entered Antioch 1
15 Ptolemy marched out 1
16 King Ptolemy was exalted. 1
17 sent it to Ptolemy. 1
18 But King Ptolemy died three days later 1
15:16 Lucius, consul of the Romans, to King Ptolemy 1
16:11 Ptolemy the son of Abubus 1
16 Ptolemy and his men rose up, took their weapons 1
18 Then Ptolemy wrote a report about these things 1
2Mc 1:10 teacher of Ptolemy the king 1
4:45 promised a substantial bribe to Ptolemy 1
46 Ptolemy . . induced the king to change his mind. 1
6: 8 At the suggestion of Ptolemy a decree was issued 1
8: 8 he wrote to Ptolemy, the governor of Coelesyria 1
9 Ptolemy promptly appointed Nicanor •
9:29 betook himself to Ptolemy Philometor in Egypt. 1
10:12 Ptolemy, who was called Macron 1
3Mc 1: 2 and crossed over by night to the tent of Ptolemy 1
6 Ptolemy decided to visit the . . cities 1
3:12 King Ptolemy Philopator to his generals 1
7: 1 King Ptolemy Philopator to the generals 1
4Mc 4:22 For when he was warring against Ptolemy in Egypt 1

Puah 1. פּוּאָה 2. פּוּעָה
Exd 1:15 one . . was named Shiphrah and the other Pu'ah 2
Jdg 10: 1 Tola the son of Pu'ah, son of Dodo, a man of Is'sachar 1
1Ch 7: 1 sons of Is'sachar: Tola, Pu'ah, Jashub, and Shimron 1

Publius 1. Πόπλιος
Act 28: 7 the chief man of the island, named Publius 1
8 It happened that the father of Publius lay sick 1

Pudens 1. Πούδης
2Ti 4:21 as do Pudens and Linus and Claudia 1

Pul 1. פּוּל
2Kg 15:19 Pul the king of Assyria came against the land; 1
19 Men'aham gave Pul 1,000 talents of silver 1
1Ch 5:26 stirred up the spirit of Pul king of Assyria 1

Punite 1. פּוּנִי
Num26:23 of Puvah, the family of the Punites; 1

Punon 1. פּוּנֹן
Num33:42 set out from Zalmo'nah, and encamped at Punon. 1
43 they set out from Punon, and encamped at Oboth. 1

Pur 1. פּוּר
Est 3: 7 they cast Pur, that is the lot, before Haman 1
9:24 and had cast Pur, that is the lot, 1
26 they called these days Purim, after the term Pur. 1

Purah 1. פֻּרָה
Jdg 7:10 down, go down to the camp with Purah your servant; 1
11 Then he went down with Purah his servant 1

Purim 1. פּוּרִים
Est 9:26 they called these days Purim, after the term Pur. 1
28 days of Purim should never fall into disuse 1
29 confirming this second letter about Purim. 1
31 that these days of Purim should be observed 1
32 Queen Esther fixed these practices of Purim 1

Letter of Purim 1. ἐπιστολή Φρουραι
AEs 11: 1 brought to Egypt the preceding Letter of Purim 1

Put 1. פּוּט 2. Φουδ
Gen 10: 6 The sons of Ham: Cush, Egypt, Put, and Canaan. 1
1Ch 1: 8 The sons of Ham: Cush, Egypt, Put, and Canaan. 1
Isa 66:19 to the nations, to Tarshish, Put, and Lud 2
Jer 46: 9 Let the warriors go forth: men of Ethiopia and Put 1
Ezk 27:10 Persia and Lud and Put were in your army 1
30: 5 Ethiopia, and Put, and Lud, and all Arabia, and Libya 1
38: 5 Persia, Cush, and Put are with them, all of them 1
Nah 3: 9 Put and the Libyans were her helpers. 1
Jdt 2:23 ravaged Put and Lud 2
23 Holofernes . . ravaged Put and Lud 2

Puteoli 1. Ποτίολοι
Act 28:13 on the second day we came to Pute'oli. 1

Puthite 1. פּוּתִי
1Ch 2:53 the Ithrites, the Puthites, the Shu'mathites 1

Putiel 1. פּוּטִיאֵל
Exd 6:25 took to wife one of the daughters of Pu'ti-el; 1

Puvah 1. פֻּוָּה
Gen 46:13 sons of Is'sachar: Tola, Puvah, Iob, and Shimron 1
Num26:23 of Puvah, the family of the Punites; 1

Pyrrhus 1. Πύρρος
Act 20: 4 Sop'ater of Beroe'a, the son of Pyrrhus 1

Quartus 1. Κούαρτος
Rom 16:23 Eras'tus . . and our brother Quartus, greet you. 1

Quintus 1. Κοιντος
2Mc 11:34 Quintus Memmius and Titus Manius 1

Quirinius 1. Κυρηναῖος
Lke 2: 2 when Quirin'ius was governor of Syria. 1

Raama 1. רַעְמָא
1Ch 1: 9 sons of Cush: Seba, Hav'ilah, Sabta, Ra'ama 1

Raamah 1. רַעְמָה
Gen 10: 7 Cush: Seba . . Sabtah, Ra'amah, and Sab'teca. 1
7 The sons of Ra'amah: Sheba and Dedan. 1
1Ch 1: 9 The sons of Ra'amah: Sheba and Dedan. 1
Ezk 27:22 The traders of Sheba and Ra'amah traded with you; 1

Raamiah 1. רַעַמְיָה
Neh 7: 7 came with . . Azari'ah, Raami'ah, Naham'ani, 1

Raamses 1. רַעְמְסֵס 2. ῾Ραμεσση
Exd 1:11 built . . store-cities, Pithom and Ra-am'ses. 1
Jdt 1: 9 the river of Egypt, and Tahpanhes and Raamses 2

Rab-mag 1. רַב מָג
Jer 39: 3 Ner'gal-share'zer the Rabmag 1
13 Ner'gal-share'zer the Rabmag 1

Rab-saris 1. רַב סָרִיס
2Kg 18:17 the king of Assyria sent the Tartan, the Rab'saris 1
Jer 39: 3 Sam'gar-ne'bo, Sar'sechim the Rab'saris 1
13 Nebushaz'ban the Rab'saris 1

Rab-shakeh 1. רַב שָׁקֵה 2. ῾Ραψακης
2Kg 18:17 sent the Tartan, the Rab'saris, and the Rab'shakeh 1
19 the Rab'shakeh said to them, "Say to Hezeki'ah, 1
26 Eli'akim . . and Shebnah.., said to the Rab'shakeh 1
27 the Rab'shakeh said to them, "Has my master sent me 1
28 the Rab'shakeh stood and called . . in a loud voice 1
37 came . . and told him the words of the Rab'shakeh. 1
19: 4 the LORD . . heard all the words of the Rab'shakeh 1
8 The Rab'shakeh returned, and found the king 1
Isa 36: 2 the king of Assyria sent the Rab'shakeh 1
4 the Rab'shakeh said to them, "Say to Hezeki'ah 1
11 Eli'akim, Shebna, and Jo'ah said to the Rab'shakeh 1
12 Rab'shakeh said, "Has my master sent me to speak 1
13 Then the Rab'shakeh stood and called out 1
22 and told him the words of the Rab'shakeh. 1
37: 4 may be . . God heard the words of the Rab'shakeh 1
8 The Rab'shakeh returned, and found the king 1
Sir 48:18 Sennacherib came up, and sent the Rabshakeh 2

Rabbah 1. רַבָּה
Deu 3:11 bedstead . . is it not in Rabbah of the Ammonites? 1
Jos 13:25 to Aro'er, which is east of Rabbah 1

15:60 Kir'iath-ba'al . . and Rabbah 1
2Sm 11: 1 ravaged the Ammonites, and besieged Rabbah. 1
12:26 Now Jo'ab fought against Rabbah of the Ammonites 1
27 Jo'ab . . said, "I have fought against Rabbah; 1
29 David . . went to Rabbah 1
17:27 the son of Nahash from Rabbah of the Ammonites 1
1Ch 20: 1 and came and besieged Rabbah. 1
1 And Jo'ab smote Rabbah, and overthrew it. 1
Jer 49: 2 cry to be heard against Rabbah of the Ammonites; 1
3 for Ai is laid waste! Cry, O daughters of Rabbah! 1
Ezk 21:20 the sword to come to Rabbah of the Ammonites 1
25: 5 I will make Rabbah a pasture for camels 1
Ams 1:14 I will kindle a fire in the wall of Rabbah 1

Rabbith 1. רַבִּית
Jos 19:20 Rabbith, Kish'ion, Ebez 1

Racal 1. רָכָל
1Sm 30:29 in Racal, in the cities of the Jerah'meelites 1

Rachel 1. רָחֵל 2. ῾Ραχήλ
Gen 29: 6 Rachel his daughter is coming with the sheep! 1
9 still speaking with them, Rachel came with her 1
10 Now when Jacob saw Rachel the daughter of Laban 1
11 Then Jacob kissed Rachel, and wept aloud. 1
12 Jacob told Rachel that he was her father's 1
16 was Leah, and the name of the younger was Rachel. 1
17 Leah's eyes were weak, but Rachel was beautiful 1
18 Jacob loved Rachel; and he said 1
18 seven years for your younger daughter Rachel. 1
20 Jacob served seven years for Rachel 1
25 Did I not serve with you for Rachel? 1
28 then Laban gave him his daughter Rachel to wife. 1
29 Bilhah to his daughter Rachel to be her maid. 1
30 Jacob went in to Rachel also, and he loved Rachel 1
30 Jacob went in to Rachel also, and he loved Rachel 1
31 he opened her womb; but Rachel was barren. 1
30: 1 When Rachel saw that she bore Jacob no children 1
2 Jacob's anger was kindled against Rachel 1
6 Then Rachel said, "God has judged me 1
7 Rachel's maid Bilhah conceived again 1
8 Then Rachel said, "With mighty wrestlings 1
14 Then Rachel said to Leah, "Give me, I pray 1
15 Rachel said, "Then he may lie with you tonight 1
22 God remembered Rachel . . hearkened to her 1
25 When Rachel had borne Joseph, Jacob said to Laban 1
31: 4 Jacob sent and called Rachel and Leah 1
14 Then Rachel and Leah answered him 1
19 and Rachel stole her father's household gods. 1
32 Jacob did not know that Rachel had stolen them. 1
33 went out of Leah's tent, and entered Rachel's. 1
34 Rachel had taken the household gods 1
33: 1 he divided the children among Leah and Rachel 1
2 children, and Rachel and Joseph last of all. 1
7 and last Joseph and Rachel drew near 1
35:16 Rachel travailed, and she had hard labor. 1
19 Rachel died, and she was buried on the way 1
20 it is the pillar of Rachel's tomb 1
24 The sons of Rachel: Joseph and Benjamin. 1
25 The sons of Bilhah, Rachel's maid: Dan 1
46:19 The sons of Rachel, Jacob's wife: Joseph 1
22 the sons of Rachel, who were born to Jacob– 1
25 Bilhah, whom Laban gave to Rachel his daughter 1
48: 7 Rachel to my sorrow died in the land of Canaan 1
Rut 4:11 the LORD make the woman . . like Rachel and Leah 1
1Sm 10: 2 you will meet two men by Rachel's tomb 1
Jer 31:15 Rachel is weeping for her children; 1
Mat 2:18 wailing and loud lamentation, Rachel weeping 2

Raddai 1. רַדַּי
1Ch 2:14 Nethan'el the fourth, Raddai the fifth 1

Ragae 1. ῾Ραγαύ
Jdt 1: 5 the great plain which is on the borders of Ragae. 1
15 He captured Arphaxad in the mountains of Ragae 1

Rages 1. ῾Ραγοι
Tob 1:14 once at Rages in Media 1
4: 1 left in trust with Gabael at Rages in Media 1
20 Gabael the son of Gabrias at Rages in Media. 1
5: 5 Can you go with me to Rages in Media? 1
6:12 and as soon as we return from Rages 1
9: 2 go to Gabael at Rages in Media and get the money 1

Raguel 1. ῾Ραγουηλ
Tob 3: 7 Sarah, the daughter of Raguel, was reproached 1
17 to give Sarah the daughter of Raguel in marriage 1
17 Sarah the daughter of Raguel came down 1
6:10 Brother, today we shall stay with Raguel 1
12 I know that Raguel . . cannot give her 1
7: 1 arrived at the house of Raguel 1
2 Then Raguel said to his wife Edna 1
3 Raguel asked them, "Where are you from, brethren? 1
6 Then Raguel sprang up and kissed him and wept. 1
9 he communicated the proposal to Raguel 1
9 Raguel said to Tobias, "Eat, drink, and be merry; 1
12 Raguel said, "Take her right now 1
16 Raguel called his wife Edna and said to her 1
8: 9 Raguel arose and went and dug a grave 1
11 Then Raguel went into his house 1
15 Then Raguel blessed God and said 1
20 Raguel declared by oath to Tobias 1
21 then he should take half of Raguel's property •
9: 3 For Raguel has sworn that I should not leave; 1
10: 7 which Raguel had sworn that he should spend 1
7 At that time Tobias said to Raguel, "Send me back 1
10 Raguel arose and gave him his wife Sarah 1
11: 1 he blessed Raguel and his wife Edna 1
14:12 Tobias returned . . to Raguel his father-in-law. 1

Rahab 1. רַהַב 2. רָחָב 3. ῾Ραάβ 4. ῾Ραχάβ
Jos 2: 1 into the house of a harlot whose name was Rahab 2
3 Then the king of Jericho sent to Rahab, saying 2
6:17 Rahab the harlot and . . in her house shall live 2
23 and brought out Rahab, and her father and mother 2
25 But Rahab the harlot, and . . Joshua saved alive; 2
Job 9:13 beneath him bowed the helpers of Rahab. 1
26:12 by his understanding he smote Rahab. 1
Ps 87: 4 know me I mention Rahab and Babylon; 1
89:10 Thou didst crush Rahab like a carcass 1
Isa 30: 7 therefore I have called her "Rahab who sits still. 1
51: 9 Was it not thou that didst cut Rahab in pieces 1
Mat 1: 5 Salmon the father of Bo'az by Rahab 4
Heb 11:31 By faith Rahab the harlot did not perish 3
Jas 2:25 was not also Rahab the harlot justified by works 3

Raham 1. רַחַם
1Ch 2:44 Shema . . father of Raham, the father of Jor'ke-am; 1

Rakem 1. רֶקֶם
1Ch 7:16 Peresh . . and his sons were Ulam and Rakem. 1

Rakkath 1. רַקַּת
Jos 19:35 are Ziddim, Zer, Hammath, Rakkath, Chin'nereth 1

Rakkon 1. רַקּוֹן
Jos 19:46 and Mejar'kon and Rakkon with the territory over 1

Ram 1. רָם 2. Ἀράμ
Rut 4:19 Hezron of Ram, Ram of Ammin'adab 1
19 Hezron of Ram, Ram of Ammin'adab 1
1Ch 2: 9 sons of Hezron . . Jerah'meel, Ram, and Chelu'bai. 1
10 Ram was the father of Ammin'adab 1
25 The sons of Jerah'meel . . Ram, his first-born 1
27 The sons of Ram, the first-born of Jerah'meel: Ma'az 1
Job 32: 2 of Bar'achel the Buzite, of the family of Ram 1
Mat 1: 3 and Hezron the father of Ram 2
4 Ram the father of Ammin'adab 2

Ramah 1. רָמָה 2. Κιραμας 3. ῾Ραμά
Jos 18:25 Gibeon, Ramah, Be-er'oth 1
19: 8 as far as Ba'alath-beer, Ramah of the Negeb. 1
29 then the boundary turns to Ramah, reaching 1
36 Ad'amah, Ramah, Hazor 1
Jdg 4: 5 of Deb'orah between Ramah and Bethel in the hill 1
19:13 and spend the night at Gib'e-ah or at Ramah. 1
1Sm 1:19 they went back to their house at Ramah. 1
2:11 Then Elka'nah went home to Ramah. 1
7:17 he would come back to Ramah, for his home was there 1
8: 4 gathered together and came to Samuel at Ramah 1
15:34 Samuel went to Ramah; and Saul went up to his house 1
16:13 And Samuel rose up, and went to Ramah. 1
19:18 David . . escaped, and he came to Samuel at Ramah 1
19 Behold, David is at Nai'oth in Ramah. 1
22 he himself went to Ramah, and came to . . Secu; 1
22 And one said, "Behold, they are at Nai'oth in Ramah. 1
23 And he went from there to Nai'oth in Ramah; 1
23 he prophesied, until he came to Nai'oth in Ramah. 1
20: 1 David fled from Nai'oth in Ramah, and came and said 1
25: 1 they buried him in his house at Ramah. 1
28: 3 Israel had mourned . . him and buried him in Ramah 1
1Kg 15:17 Ba'asha . . went up against Judah, and built Ramah 1
21 when Ba'asha heard . . he stopped building Ramah 1
22 carried away the stones of Ramah and its timber 1
2Kg 8:29 wounds which the Syrians had given him at Ramah 1
2Ch 16: 1 Ba'asha . . went up against Judah, and built Ramah 1
5 when Ba'asha heard . . he stopped building Ramah 1
6 carried away the stones of Ramah and its timber 1
22: 6 wounds which he had received at Ramah 1
Ezr 2:26 sons of Ramah and Geba, 621. 1
Neh 7:30 men of Ramah and Geba, 621. 1
11:33 Hazor, Ramah, Git'taim 1
Isa 10:29 Ramah trembles, Gib'e-ah of Saul has fled. 1
Jer 31:15 Thus says the LORD: "A voice is heard in Ramah 1
40: 1 the captain of the guard had let him go from Ramah 1
Hos 5: 8 Blow the horn in Gib'e-ah, the trumpet in Ramah. 1
Mat 2:18 A voice was heard in Ramah, wailing and loud 3
1Es 5:20 The men of Ramah and Geba, 621. 2

Ramath-lehi 1. רָמַת לֶחִי
Jdg 15:17 and that place was called Ra'math-le'hi. 1

Ramath-mizpeh 1. רָמַת הַמִּצְפֶּה
Jos 13:26 and from Heshbon to Ra'math-miz'peh and Bet'onim 1

Ramathaim-zophim 1. רָמָתַיִם צוֹפִים
1Sm 1: 1 There was a certain man of Ramatha'im-zo'phim 1

Ramathite 1. רָמָתִי
1Ch 27:27 over the vineyards was Shim'e-i the Ra'mathite; 1

Rameses 1. רַעְמְסֵס
Gen 47:11 the best of the land, in the land of Ram'eses 1
Exd 12:37 the people of Israel journeyed from Ram'eses 1
Num33: 3 They set out from Ram'eses in the first month 1
5 the people of Israel set out from Ram'eses 1

Ramiah 1. רַמְיָה 2. ῾Ραμίας
Ezr 10:25 of Parosh: Rami'ah, Izzi'ah, Malchi'jah, Mi'jamin 1
1Es 9:26 Of Israel: of the sons of Parosh: Ramiah, Izziah 2

Ramoth 1. רָמוֹת
Deu 4:43 Reubenites, and Ramoth in Gilead for the Gadites 1
Jos 20: 8 appointed . . and Ramoth in Gilead, from the tribe 1
21:38 of Gad, Ramoth in Gilead with its pasture lands 1
1Sm 30:27 it was for those in Bethel, in Ramoth of the Negeb 1
1Ch 6:73 Ramoth with its pasture lands, and Anem 1
80 Ramoth in Gilead with its pasture lands 1

Ramoth-gilead 1. רָמֹת גִּלְעָד
1Kg 4:13 in Ra'moth-gil'ead (he had the villages of Ja'ir 1
22: 3 Do you know that Ramoth-gilead belongs to us 1
4 Will you go with me to battle at Ramoth-gilead? 1
6 Shall I go to battle against Ramoth-gilead 1
12 Go up to Ramoth-gilead and triumph; 1
15 Micai'ah, shall we go to Ramoth-gilead to battle 1
20 that he may go up and fall at Ramoth-gilead?' 1
29 and . . the king of Judah went up to Ramoth-gilead. 1
2Kg 8:28 to make war against Haz'ael . . at Ramoth-gilead 1
9: 1 take this flask of oil . . and go to Ramoth-gilead. 1
4 the young man, the prophet, went to Ramoth-gilead. 1
14 Joram . . had been on guard at Ramoth-gilead 1
2Ch 18: 2 induced him to go up against Ramoth-gilead. 1
3 Will you go with me to Ramoth-gilead? 1
5 Shall we go to battle against Ramoth-gilead 1
11 Go up to Ramoth-gilead and triumph; 1
14 Micai'ah, shall we go to Ramoth-gilead to battle 1
19 that he(Ahab) may go up and fall at Ramoth-gilead?' 1
28 went up to Ramoth-gilead. 1
22: 5 to make war against Haz'ael . . at Ramoth-gilead. 1

Rapha 1. רָפָא
1Ch 8: 2 Nohah the fourth, and Rapha the fifth. 1

Raphael 1. ῾Ραφαηλ
Tob 3:17 Raphael was sent to heal the two of them •
5: 4 he found Raphael, who was an angel 1
7: 8 Then Tobias said to Raphael, "Brother Azarias 1
8: 2 As he went he remembered the words of Raphael 1
9: 1 Then Tobias called Raphael and said to him 1
5 Raphael made the journey and stayed over night 1
11: 2 Then Raphael said to Tobias 1
7 Raphael said, "I know, Tobias 1
12:15 I am Raphael, one of the seven holy angels 1

Raphah 1. רָפָה
1Ch 8:37 Raphah was his son, Ele-a'sah his son, Azel his son. 1

Raphaim 1. ῾Ραφαιν
Jdt 8: 1 son of Gideon, son of Raphaim, son of Ahitub 1

Raphia 1. ῾Ραφια
3Mc 1: 1 and marched out to the region near Raphia 1

Raphon 1. ῾Ραφων
1Mc 5:37 encamped opposite Raphon 1

Raphu 1. רָפוּא
Num13: 9 from the tribe of Benjamin, Palti the son of Raphu; 1

Rassis 1. ῾Ρασσις
Jdt 2:23 plundered all the people of Rassis 1

Rathamin 1. ῾Ραθαμιν
1Mc 11:34 Aphairema and Lydda and Rathamin 1

Razis 1. ῾Ραζις
2Mc 14:37 A certain Razis, one of the elders of Jerusalem 1
41 Being surrounded, Razis fell upon his own sword •

Reaiah 1. רְאָיָה 2. Ιαιρος
1Ch 4: 2 Re-ai'ah the son of Shobal was the father of Jahath 1
5: 5 Micah his son, Re-ai'ah his son, Ba'al his son 1
Ezr 2:47 the sons of Gahar, the sons of Re-ai'ah 1
Neh 7:50 sons of Re-ai'ah, the sons of Rezin 1
1Es 5:31 sons of Reaiah, the sons of Rezin 2

Reba 1. רֶבַע
Num31: 8 Evi, Rekem, Zur, Hur, and Reba, the five kings 1
Jos 13:21 leaders . . Evi and Rekem and Zur and Hur and Reba 1

Rebecca 1. ῾Ρεβέκκα
Rom 9:10 when Rebecca had conceived children by one man 1

Rebekah 1. רִבְקָה
Gen 22:23 Bethu'el became the father of Rebekah. 1

24:15 behold, Rebekah, who was born to Bethu'el 1
29 Rebekah had a brother whose name was Laban; 1
30 when he heard the words of Rebekah his sister 1
45 behold, Rebekah came out with her water jar on her 1
51 Behold, Rebekah is before you, take her and go 1
53 gold, and raiment, and gave them to Rebekah; 1
58 they called Rebekah, and said to her 1
59 they sent away Rebekah their sister 1
60 they blessed Rebekah, and said to her 1
61 Then Rebekah and her maids arose 1
61 thus the servant took Rebekah, and went his way. 1
64 Rebekah lifted up her eyes, and when she saw Isaac 1
67 Isaac brought her into the tent, and took Rebekah 1
25:20 Isaac was 40 years old when he took to wife Rebekah 1
21 his prayer, and Rebekah his wife conceived. 1
28 ate of his game; but Rebekah loved Jacob. 1
26: 7 the men . . should kill me for the sake of Rebekah 1
8 window and saw Isaac fondling Rebekah his wife. 1
35 they made life bitter for Isaac and Rebekah. 1
27: 5 Now Rebekah was listening when Isaac spoke 1
6 Rebekah said to her son Jacob, "I heard your father 1
11 Jacob said to Rebekah his mother 1
15 Then Rebekah took the best garments of Esau 1
42 words of Esau her older son were told to Rebekah; 1
46 Rebekah said to Isaac, "I am weary of my life 1
28: 5 Bethu'el the Aramean, the brother of Rebekah 1
29:12 he was Rebekah's son; and she ran and told her 1
35: 8 Deb'orah, Rebekah's nurse, died 1
49:31 there they buried Isaac and Rebekah his wife; 1

Recah 1. רֵכָה
1Ch 4:12 These are the men of Recah. 1

Rechab 1. רֵכָב
2Sm 4: 2 one was Ba'anah, and the name of the other Rechab 1
5 sons of Rimmon . . Rechab and Ba'anah, set out 1
6 so Rechab and Ba'anah his brother slipped in. 1
9 David answered Rechab and Ba'anah his brother 1
2Kg 10:15 he met Jehon'adab the son of Rechab 1
23 Jehu went . . with Jehon'adab the son of Rechab; 1
1Ch 2:55 Hammath, the father of the house of Rechab. 1
Neh 3:14 Malchi'jah the son of Rechab, ruler 1
Jer 35: 6 for Jon'adab the son of Rechab, our father 1
8 the voice of Jon'adab the son of Rechab, our father 1
14 which Jon'adab the son of Rechab gave to his sons 1
16 The sons of Jon'adab the son of Rechab 1
19 Jon'adab the son of Rechab shall never lack a man 1

Rechabite 1. בֵּן בֵּית רֵכָב 2. רֵכָבִי
Jer 35: 2 Go to the house of the Re'chabites 2
3 his sons, and the whole house of the Re'chabites. 2
5 set before the Re'chabites pitchers full of wine 1
18 to the house of the Re'chabites Jeremiah said 2

Red Sea 1. יַם סוּף 2. ἐρυθρὰ θάλασσα 3. θάλασσα ἐρυθρά
Exd 10:19 locusts and drove them into the Red Sea; 1
13:18 the way of the wilderness toward the Red Sea. 1
15: 4 his picked officers are sunk in the Red Sea. 1
22 Then Moses led Israel onward from the Red Sea 1
23:31 I will set your bounds from the Red Sea to the sea 1
Num14:25 out for the wilderness by the way to the Red Sea. 1
21: 4 Mount Hor they set out by the way to the Red Sea 1
Jos 2:10 LORD dried up the water of the Red Sea before you 1
4:23 as the LORD your God did to the Red Sea 1
24: 6 and the Egyptians pursued . . to the Red Sea. 1
Jdg 11:16 through the wilderness to the Red Sea and came 1
1Kg 9:26 which is near Eloth on the shore of the Red Sea 1
Act 7:36 wonders and signs in Egypt and at the Red Sea 2
Heb 11:29 the people crossed the Red Sea as if on dry land 2
Jdt 5:13 Then God dried up the Red Sea before them 2
Wis 10:18 She brought them over the Red Sea 3
19: 7 an unhindered way out of the Red Sea 2
1Mc 4: 9 how our fathers were saved at the Red Sea 3

Reelaiah 1. רְעֵלָיָה
Ezr 2: 2 came with . . Serai'ah, Re-el-ai'ah, Mor'decai 1

Reeliah 1. ῾Ρεελιας
1Es 5: 8 Mispar, Reeliah, Rehum, and Baanah, their leaders 1

Regem 1. רֶגֶם
1Ch 2:47 sons of Jah'dai: Regem, Jotham, Geshan, Pelet, 1

Regem-melech 1. רֶגֶם מֶלֶךְ
Zec 7: 2 sent Share'zer and Reg'em-mel'ech and their men 1

Rehabiah 1. רְחַבְיָה
1Ch 23:17 The sons of Elie'zer: Rehabi'ah the chief; 1
17 but the sons of Rehabi'ah were very many. 1
24:21 Of Rehabi'ah: of the sons of Rehabi'ah, Isshi'ah 1
21 of the sons of Rehabi'ah, Isshi'ah the chief. 1
26:25 His brethren: from Elie'zer were his son Rehabi'ah 1

Rehob 1. רְחוֹב
Num13:21 land from the wilderness of Zin to Rehob 1
Jos 19:28 Ebron, Rehob, Hammon, Kanah, as far as Sidon 1
30 Mahalab, Achzib, Ummah, Aphek and Rehob 1
21:31 Helkath with . . and Rehob with its pasture lands 1
Jdg 1:31 inhabitants . . of Helbah, or of Aphik, or of Rehob; 1
2Sm 8: 3 David also defeated Hadade'zer the son of Rehob 1
12 of Hadade'zer the son of Rehob, king of Zobah. 1
10: 8 the Syrians of Zobah and of Rehob, and the men 1
1Ch 6:75 Hukok . . and Rehob with its pasture lands; 1
Neh 10:11 Mica, Rehob, Hashabi'ah 1

Rehoboam 1. רְחַבְעָם 2. ῾Ροβοάμ
1Kg 11:43 and Rehobo'am his son reigned in his stead. 1
12: 1 Rehobo'am went to Shechem, for all Israel had come 1
3 Jerobo'am . . came and said to Rehobo'am 1
6 King Rehobo'am took counsel with the old men 1
12 Jerobo'am and all the people came to Rehobo'am 1
17 But Rehobo'am reigned over the people of Israel 1
18 Then King Rehobo'am sent Ador'am 1
18 King Rehobo'am made haste to mount his chariot 1
21 When Rehobo'am came to Jerusalem, he assembled 1
21 to restore the kingdom to Rehobo'am 1
23 Say to Rehobo'am the son of Solomon, king of Judah 1
27 turn . . to their lord, to Rehobo'am king of Judah 1
27 kill me and return to Rehobo'am king of Judah. 1
14:21 Rehobo'am the son of Solomon reigned in Judah. 1
21 Rehobo'am was 41 years old when he began to reign 1
25 In the fifth year of King Rehobo'am 1
27 Rehobo'am made in their stead shields of bronze 1
29 rest of the acts of Rehobo'am, and all that he did 1
30 there was war between Rehobo'am and Jerobo'am 1
31 Rehobo'am slept with his fathers and was buried 1
15: 6 there was war between Rehobo'am and Jerobo'am 1
1Ch 3:10 descendants of Solomon: Rehobo'am, Abi'jah his son 1
2Ch 9:31 Rehobo'am his son reigned in his stead. 1
10: 1 Rehobo'am went to Shechem 1
3 and all Israel came and said to Rehobo'am. 1
6 Then King Rehobo'am took counsel with the old men 1
12 Jerobo'am and all the people came to Rehobo'am 1
14 King Rehobo'am spoke to them •
17 Rehobo'am reigned over the people of Israel 1
18 Then King Rehobo'am send Hador'am 1
18 King Rehobo'am made haste to mount his chariot 1
11: 1 When Rehobo'am came to Jerusalem 1
1 to restore the kingdom to Rehobo'am. 1
3 Say to Rehobo'am the son of Solomon king of Judah 1
5 Rehobo'am dwelt in Jerusalem 1
17 for three years they made Rehobo'am . . secure 1
18 Rehobo'am took as wife Ma'halath 1
21 Rehobo'am loved Ma'acah . . above all his wives 1
22 Rehobo'am appointed Abi'jah . . as chief prince 1
12: 1 rule of Rehobo'am was established and was strong 1
2 In the fifth year of King Rehobo'am 1
5 Then Shemai'ah the prophet came to Rehobo'am 1
10 Rehobo'am made in their stead shields of bronze 1
13 Rehobo'am established himself in Jerusalem 1
13 Rehobo'am was 41 years old 1
15 Now the acts of Rehobo'am, from first to last 1
15 continual wars between Rehobo'am and Jerobo'am. 1
16 Rehobo'am slept with his fathers 1
13: 7 gathered about him and defied Rehobo'am 1
7 when Rehobo'am was young and irresolute 1
Mat 1: 7 Solomon the father of Rehoboam 2
7 and Rehoboam the father of Abi'jah 2
Sir 47:23 one of his sons . . Rehoboam 2

Rehoboth 1. רְחֹבוֹת
Gen 26:22 did not quarrel; so he called its name Reho'both 1
36:37 Shaul of Reho'both on the Euphra'tes reigned 1
1Ch 1:48 Sha'ul of Reho'both on the Euphra'tes reigned 1

Rehoboth-Ir 1. רְחֹבֹת עִיר
Gen 10:11 and built Nin'eveh, Reho'both-Ir, Calah 1

Rehum 1. רְחוּם 2. ῾Ραουμος 3. ῾Ροιμος
Ezr 2: 2 came with . . Bilshan, Mispar, Bigva'i, Rehum 1
4: 8 Rehum the commander and Shim'shai the scribe 1
9 then wrote Rehum the commander, Shim'shai 1
17 To Rehum the commander and Shim'shai the scribe 1
23 letter was read before Rehum and Shim'shai 1
Neh 3:17 Levites repaired: Rehum the son of Bani; 1
10:25 Rehum, Hashab'nah, Ma-asei'ah 1
12: 3 Shecani'ah, Rehum, Mer'emoth. 1
1Es 2:16 Bishlam, Mithridates, Tabeel, Rehum, Beltethmus 2
17 Rehum the recorder and Shimshai the scribe 2
25 Rehum the recorder and Beltethmus and Shimshai 2
30 Rehum and Shimshai the scribe 2
5: 8 Mispar, Reeliah, Rehum, and Baanah, their leaders 3

Rei 1. רֵעִי
1Kg 1: 8 Shim'e-i, and Re'i, and David's mighty men were not 1

Rekem 1. רֶקֶם
Num31: 8 Evi, Rekem, Zur, Hur, and Reba, the five kings 1
Jos 13:21 leaders . . Evi and Rekem and Zur and Hur and Reba 1
18:27 Rekem, Irpeel, Tar'alah 1
1Ch 2:43 sons of Hebron: Korah, Tap'puah, Rekem, and Shema. 1
44 and Rekem was the father of Sham'mai. 1

Remaliah 1. רְמַלְיָהוּ
2Kg 15:25 Pekah the son of Remali'ah . . conspired against 1
27 Pekah the son of Remali'ah began to reign over 1
30 a conspiracy against Pekah the son of Remali'ah 1
32 In the second year of Pekah the son of Remali'ah 1
37 send Rezin . . and Pekah the son of Remali'ah 1
16: 1 seventeenth year of Pekah the son of Remali'ah 1
5 Pekah the son of Remali'ah . . came up to wage war 1
2Ch 28: 6 Pekah the son of Remali'ah slew 120,000 in Judah 1
Isa 7: 1 Pekah the son of Remali'ah the king of Israel came 1
4 of Rezin and Syria and the son of Remali'ah. 1
5 the son of Remali'ah, has devised evil against you 1
9 the head of Sama'ria is the son of Remali'ah. 1
8: 6 melt in fear before Rezin and the son of Remali'ah; 1

Remeth 1. רֶמֶת
Jos 19:21 Remeth, En-gan'nim, En-had'dah, Beth-paz'zez; 1

Rephael 1. רְפָאֵל
1Ch 26: 7 sons of Shemai'ah: Othni, Reph'a-el, Obed, 1

Rephah 1. רֶפַח
1Ch 7:25 Rephah was his son, Resheph his son, Telah his son 1

Rephaiah 1. רְפָיָה
1Ch 3:21 sons of Hanani'ah . . Rephai'ah, his son Arnan 1
4:42 having as their leaders . . Rephai'ah, and Uz'ziel 1
7: 2 sons of Tola: Uzzi, Rephai'ah, Je'ri-el, Jah'mai, Ibsam 1
9:43 Bin'e-a; and Rephai'ah was his son, Ele-a'sah his son 1
Neh 3: 9 Next to them Rephai'ah the son of Hur, ruler of half 1

Rephaim 1. רְפָאִים
Gen 14: 5 with him came and subdued the Reph'aim 1
15:20 the Hittites, the Per'izzites, the Reph'aim 1
Deu 2:11 like the Anakim they were also known as Reph'aim 1
20 That also is known as a land of Reph'aim; 1
20 Reph'aim formerly lived there, but the Ammonites 1
3:11 only Og . . was left of the remnant of the Reph'aim; 1
13 whole of that Bashan is called the land of Reph'aim. 1
Jos 12: 4 Og . . of Bashan, one of the remnant of the Reph'aim 1
13:12 he alone was left of the remnant of the Reph'aim 1
15: 8 at the northern end of the valley of Reph'aim; 1
17:15 Per'izzites and the Reph'aim, since the hill 1
18:16 which is at the north end of the valley of Reph'aim; 1
2Sm 5:18 had come and spread out in the valley of Reph'aim. 1
22 spread out in the valley of Reph'aim. 1
23:13 a band . . was encamped in the valley of Reph'aim. 1
1Ch 11:15 was encamped in the valley of Reph'aim. 1
14: 9 had come and made a raid in the valley of Reph'aim. 1
Isa 17: 5 the ears of grain in the Valley of Reph'aim. 1

Rephan 1. ῾Ρεφάν
Act 7:43 the star of the god Rephan 1

Rephidim 1. רְפִידִים
Exd 17: 1 Israel . . camped at Reph'idim; 1
8 came Am'alek and fought with Israel at Reph'idim. 1
19: 2 when they set out from Reph'idim and came 1
Num33:14 they set out from Alush, and encamped at Reph'idim 1
15 they set out from Reph'idim, and encamped 1

Resaiah 1. ῾Ρησαιας
1Es 5: 8 Nehemiah, Seraiah, Resaiah, Bigvai, Mordecai 1

Resen 1. רֶסֶן
Gen 10:12 Resen between Nin'eveh and Calah; 1

Resheph 1. רֶשֶׁף
1Ch 7:25 Resheph his son, Telah his son, Tahan his son 1

Reu 1. רְעוּ 2. ῾Ραγαύ
Gen 11:18 Peleg . . became the father of Re'u; 1
19 Peleg lived after the birth of Re'u 209 years 1
20 When Re'u had lived 32 years 1
21 Re'u lived after the birth of Serug 207 years 1
1Ch 1:25 Eber, Peleg, Re'u; 1
Lke 3:35 the son of Serug, the son of Re'u, the son of Peleg 2

Reuben 1. רְאוּבֵן 2. רְאוּבֵנִי 3. ῾Ρουβήν
Gen 29:32 she called his name Reuben; for she said 1
30:14 In the days of wheat harvest Reuben went 1
35:22 While Israel dwelt in that land Reuben went 1
23 sons of Leah: Reuben (Jacob's first-born) 1
37:21 when Reuben heard it, he delivered him out 1
22 Reuben said to them, "Shed no blood; 1
29 When Reuben returned to the pit 1
42:22 Reuben answered them, "Did I not tell you 1
37 Reuben said to his father, "Slay my two sons if I do 1
46: 8 Jacob and his sons. Reuben, Jacob's first-born 1
9 the sons of Reuben: Hanoch, Pallu, Hezron 1
48: 5 Manas'seh shall be mine, as Reuben and Simeon are 1
49: 3 Reuben, you are my first-born, my might 1
Exd 1: 2 Reuben, Simeon, Levi, and Judah 1
6:14 the sons of Reuben, the first-born of Israel 1
14 Carmi; these are the families of Reuben. 1
Num 1: 5 From Reuben, Eli'zur the son of Shed'eur; 1
20 The people of Reuben, Israel's first-born 1
21 the number of the tribe of Reuben was 46,500 1
2:10 the standard of the camp of Reuben 1
10 the leader of the people of Reuben being Eli'zur 1
16 The whole number of the camp of Reuben 1
7:30 Eli'zur the . . leader of the men of Reuben 1

10:18 standard of the camp of Reuben set out by their 1
13: 4 From the tribe of Reuben, Sham'mu-a . . of Zaccur; 1
16: 1 Dathan and Abi'ram . . and On . . , sons of Reuben 1
26: 5 Reuben, the first-born of Israel; 1
5 sons of Reuben: of Hanoch . . of Pallu 1
32: 1 sons of Reuben . . had a very great multitude of cattle; 1
2 sons of Gad and the sons of Reuben came and said 1
6 Moses said to . . of Gad and to the sons of Reuben 1
25 sons of Gad and the sons of Reuben said to Moses 1
29 If the sons of Gad and the sons of Reuben 1
31 sons of Gad and the sons of Reuben answered, "As 1
33 Moses gave . . to the sons of Reuben 1
37 sons of Reuben built Heshbon, Elea'leh, Kiriatha'im 1
34:14 tribe of the sons of Reuben by fathers' houses 2
Deu 11: 6 Dathan and Abi'ram the sons of Eli'ab, son of Reuben; 1
27:13 stand upon Mount Ebal . . Reuben, Gad, Asher 1
33: 6 Let Reuben live, and not die, nor let his men be few. 1
Jos 4:12 The sons of Reuben and the sons of Gad 1
13:23 the border of the people of Reuben was the Jordan 1
15: 6 goes up to the stone of Bohan the son of Reuben; 1
18: 7 and Gad and Reuben and half the tribe of Manas'seh 1
17 it goes down to the Stone of Bohan the son of Reuben; 1
20: 8 Bezer . . from the tribe of Reuben, and Ramoth 1
21: 7 Merar'ites . . received from the tribe of Reuben 1
36 and out of the tribe of Reuben, Bezer with its 1
Jdg 5:15 Among the clans of Reuben there were great 1
16 Among the clans of Reuben there were great 1
1Ch 2: 1 These are the sons of Israel: Reuben, Simeon, Levi 1
5: 1 The sons of Reuben the first-born of Israel 1
3 the sons of Reuben, the first-born of Israel 1
6:63 out of the tribes of Reuben, Gad, and Zeb'ulun. 1
78 out of the tribe of Reuben: Bezer . . Jahzah 1
Ezk 48: 6 from the east side to the west, Reuben, one portion. 1
7 Adjoining the territory of Reuben, from the east 1
31 three gates, the gate of Reuben, the gate of Judah 1
Rev 7: 5 12,000 of the tribe of Reuben 3

Reubenite 1. רְאוּבֵנִי 2. בֶּן רְאוּבֵן 3. רְאוּבֵן
Num26: 7 These are the families of the Reubenites; 3
Deu 3:12 I gave to the Reubenites and the Gadites 3
16 to the Reubenites and the Gadites I gave 3
4:43 Bezer in the wilderness . . for the Reubenites 3
29: 8 gave it for an inheritance to the Reubenites 3
Jos 1:12 to the Reubenites, the Gadites, and the half-tribe 3
12: 6 gave . . to the Reubenites and the Gadites 3
13: 8 the Reubenites and the Gadites received their 3
15 an inheritance to the tribe of the Reubenites 1
23 This was the inheritance of the Reubenites 1
22: 1 Joshua summoned the Reubenites, and the Gadites 3
9 the Reubenites and the Gadites . . returned home 1
10 the Reubenites and the Gadites . . built 1
11 the Reubenites and the Gadites . . have built 1
13 Israel sent to the Reubenites and the Gadites 1
15 And they came to the Reubenites, the Gadites 1
21 the Reubenites, the Gadites . . said in answer 1
25 between us and you, you Reubenites and Gadites; 1
30 heard the words that the Reubenites . . spoke 1
31 said to the Reubenites and the Gadites 1
32 returned from the Reubenites and the Gadites 1
33 the land where the Reubenites and the Gadites 1
34 The Reubenites and the Gadites called the altar 1
2Kg 10:33 land of Gilead, the Gadites, and the Reubenites 3
1Ch 5: 6 Be-er'ah . . a chieftain of the Reubenites. 3
18 The Reubenites . . had valiant men 2
26 carried them away, namely, the Reubenites 3
11:42 Ad'ina the son of Shiza the Reubenite 3
42 a leader of the Reubenites, and 30 with him 3
12:37 Of the Reubenites and Gadites and the half-tribe 3
26:32 Reubenites, the Gadites, and the half-tribe 3
27:16 for the Reubenites Elie'zer the son of Zichri 3

Reuel 1. רְעוּאֵל
Gen 36: 4 Bas'emath bore Reu'el; 1
10 Reu'el the son of Bas'emath the wife of Esau. 1
13 are the sons of Reu'el: Nahath, Zerah, Shammah 1
17 These are the sons of Reu'el, Esau's son 1
17 these are the chiefs of Reu'el in the land of Edom; 1
Exd 2:18 When they came to their father Reu'el 1
Num 2:14 the leader . . Eli'asaph the son of Reu'el 1
10:29 Hobab the son of Reu'el the Mid'ianite 1
1Ch 1:35 The sons of Esau: Eli'phaz, Reu'el, Je'ush 1
37 The sons of Reu'el: Nahath, Zerah, Shammah 1
9: 8 Shephati'ah, son of Reu'el, son of Ibni'jah; 1

Reumah 1. רְאוּמָה
Gen 22:24 Moreover, his concubine, whose name was Reumah 1

Rezeph 1. רֶצֶף
2Kg 19:12 which my fathers destroyed, Gozan, Haran, Rezeph 1
Isa 37:12 which my fathers destroyed, Gozan, Haran, Rezeph 1

Rezin 1. רְצִין 2. Δαισαν
2Kg 15:37 to send Rezin . . and Pekah . . against Judah. 1
16: 5 Then Rezin . . and Pekah . . came up to wage war 1
9 king of Assyria marched . . and he killed Rezin. 1
Ezr 2:48 sons of Rezin, the sons of Neko'da 1
Neh 7:50 sons of Re-ai'ah, the sons of Rezin 1
Isa 7: 1 In the days of Ahaz . . Rezin the king of Syria 1
4 at the fierce anger of Rezin and Syria 1
8 the head of Damascus is Rezin. 1
8: 6 melt in fear before Rezin and the son of Remali'ah; 1
1Es 5:31 sons of Reaiah, the sons of Rezin 2

Rezon 1. רְזוֹן
1Kg 11:23 as an adversary to him, Rezon the son of Eli'ada 1

Rhegium 1. Ῥήγιον
Act 28:13 we made a circuit and arrived at Rhe'gium 1

Rhesa 1. Ῥησά
Lke 3:27 the son of Joan'an, the son of Rhesa 1

Rhoda 1. Ῥόδη
Act 12:13 a maid named Rhoda came to answer. 1

Rhodes 1. Ῥοδιοι 2. Ῥόδος
Ezk 27:15 The men of Rhodes traded with you; 1
Act 21: 1 the next day to Rhodes, . . from there to Pat'ara 2
1Mc 15:23 to Lycia, and to Halicarnassus, and to Rhodes 2

Rhodocus 1. Ῥοδοκος
2Mc 13:21 Rhodocus, a man from the ranks of the Jews 1

Ribai 1. רִיבַי
2Sm 23:29 It'tai the son of Ri'bai of Gib'e-ah 1
1Ch 11:31 Ithai the son of Ribai of Gib'e-ah 1

Riblah 1. רִבְלָה
Num34:11 the boundary shall go down from Shepham to Riblah 1
2Kg 23:33 put him in bonds at Riblah in the land of Hamath 1
25: 6 brought him up to the king of Babylon at Riblah 1
20 brought them to the king of Babylon at Riblah. 1
21 king . . smote them, and put them to death at Riblah 1
Jer 39: 5 up to Nebuchadrez'zar king of Babylon, at Riblah 1
6 the sons of Zedeki'ah at Riblah before his eyes; 1
52: 9 king of Babylon at Riblah in the land of Hamath 1
10 and also slew all the princes of Judah at Riblah. 1
26 and brought them to the king of Babylon at Riblah. 1
27 put them to death at Riblah in the land of Hamath. 1
Ezk 6:14 desolate . . from the wilderness to Riblah. 1

Rimmon 1. רִמּוֹן
Jos 15:32 Leba'oth, Shilhim, A'in, and Rimmon 1
19:13 and going on to Rimmon it bends toward Ne'ah; 1
Jdg 20:45 fled toward the wilderness to the rock of Rimmon; 1
47 fled toward the wilderness to the rock of Rimmon 1
47 and abode at the rock of Rimmon four months. 1
21:13 the Benjaminites who were at the rock of Rimmon 1
2Sm 4: 2 two men . . sons of Rimmon a man of Benjamin 1
5 sons of Rimmon . . Rechab and Ba'anah, set out 1
9 Rechab and Ba'anah . . the sons of Rimmon 1
2Kg 5:18 goes into the house of Rimmon to worship there 1
18 when . . and I bow myself in the house of Rimmon 1
18 when I bow myself in the house of Rimmon 1
1Ch 4:32 villages were Etam, A'in, Rimmon, Tochen, and Ashan 1
Isa 10:27 He has gone up from Rimmon •
Zec 14:10 a plain from Geba to Rimmon south of Jerusalem. 1

Rimmon-perez 1. רִמֹּן פֶּרֶץ
Num33:19 out from Rithmah, and encamped at Rim'mon-per'ez. 1
20 they set out from Rim'mon-per'ez, and encamped 1

Rimmono 1. רִמּוֹנוֹ
1Ch 6:77 of Zeb'ulun: Rim'mono with its pasture lands 1

Rinnah 1. רִנָּה
1Ch 4:20 sons of Shimon: Amnon, Rinnah, Ben-ha'nan, 1

Riphath 1. רִיפַת
Gen 10: 3 The sons of Gomer: Ash'kenaz, Riphath 1

Rissah 1. רִסָּה
Num33:21 they set out from Libnah, and encamped at Rissah. 1
22 set out from Rissah, and encamped at Kehela'thah. 1

Rithmah 1. רִתְמָה
Num33:18 set out from Haze'roth, and encamped at Rithmah. 1
19 out from Rithmah, and encamped at Rim'mon-per'ez 1

Rizia 1. רִצְיָא
1Ch 7:39 The sons of Ulla: Arah, Han'niel, and Rizi'a. 1

Rizpah 1. רִצְפָּה
2Sm 3: 7 Now Saul had a concubine, whose name was Rizpah 1
21: 8 took the two sons of Rizpah the daughter of Ai'ah 1
10 Then Rizpah the daughter of Ai'ah took sackcloth 1
11 When David was told what Rizpah . . had done 1

Rodanim 1. רוֹדָנִים
1Ch 1: 7 of Javan: Eli'shah, Tarshish, Kittim, and Ro'danim. 1

Rogelim 1. רֹגְלִים
2Sm 17:27 and Barzil'lai the Gileadite from Ro'gelim 1
19:31 Now Barzil'lai . . had come down from Ro'gelim; 1

Rohgah 1. רָהְגָּה
1Ch 7:34 sons of Shemer . . Rohgah, Jehub'bah, and Aram. 1

Romamti-ezer 1. רֹמַמְתִּי עֶזֶר
1Ch 25: 4 sons of Heman . . Giddal'ti, and Romam'ti-e'zer 1
31 Romam'ti-e'zer, his sons and his brethren, twelve. 1

Roman 1. Ῥωμαῖος
Joh 11:48 the Romans will come 1
Act 16:12 Philip'pi . . a Roman colony •
21 not lawful for us Romans to accept or practice. 1
25:16 was not the custom of the Romans to give up any one 1
28:17 from Jerusalem into the hands of the Romans. 1
1Mc 8: 1 Now Judas heard of the fame of the Romans 1
10 the Romans took captive their wives and children; •
23 May all go well with the Romans 1
27 the Romans shall willingly act as their allies 1
29 the Romans make a treaty with the Jewish people. 1
12: 4 the Romans gave them letters •
14:24 to confirm the alliance with the Romans. •
40 the Jews were addressed by the Romans as friends 1
40 the Romans had received the envoys of Simon •
15:16 Lucius, consul of the Romans, to King Ptolemy 1
2Mc 4:11 friendship and alliance with the Romans 1
8:10 to make up for the king the tribute due to the Romans 1
36 had undertaken to secure tribute for the Romans 1
11:34 The Romans also sent them a letter 1
34 envoys of the Romans 1

Roman citizen 1. Ῥωμαῖος
Act 16:37 uncondemned, men who are Roman citizens 1
38 when they heard that they were Roman citizens; 1
22:25 lawful . . to scourge a man who is a Roman citizen 1
26 this man is a Roman citizen. 1
27 Tell me, are you a Roman citizen?" And he said, "Yes. 1
29 he realized that Paul was a Roman citizen 1
23:27 having learned that he was a Roman citizen. 1

Rome 1. Ῥωμαῖος 2. Ῥώμη
Act 2:10 visitors from Rome, both Jews and proselytes 1
18: 2 had commanded all the Jews to leave Rome 2
19:21 After I have been there, I must also see Rome. 2
23:11 so you must bear witness also at Rome. 2
28:14 so we came to Rome. 2
16 when we came into Rome 2
Rom 1: 7 To all God's beloved in Rome 2
15 preach the gospel to you also who are in Rome. 2
2Ti 1:17 when he arrived in Rome he searched for me 2
1Mc 1:10 he had been a hostage in Rome 2
7: 1 Demetrius . . set forth from Rome 2
8:17 sent them to Rome to establish friendship 2
19 They went to Rome, a very long journey 2
24 If war comes first to Rome 2
26 as Rome has decided 2
28 as Rome has decided 2
12: 1 he chose men and sent them to Rome 2
3 they went to Rome and entered the senate chamber 2
16 sent them to Rome to renew our former friendship 1
14:16 It was heard in Rome, and as far away as Sparta 2
24 After this Simon sent Numenius to Rome 2
15:15 Numenius and his companions arrived from Rome 2

Rosh 1. רֹאשׁ
Gen 46:21 Becher, Ashbel, Gera, Na'aman, Ehi, Rosh, Muppim 1

Rufus 1. Ῥοῦφος
Mrk 15:21 the father of Alexander and Rufus 1
Rom16:13 Greet Rufus, eminent in the Lord 1

Rumah 1. רוּמָה
2Kg 23:36 was Zebi'dah the daughter of Pedai'ah of Rumah. 1

Ruth 1. רוּת 2. Ῥούθ
Rut 1: 4 the one was Orpah and the name of the other Ruth. 1
14 and Orpah kissed her . . but Ruth clung to her. 1
16 Ruth said, "Entreat me not to leave you or to return 1
22 Na'omi returned, and Ruth the Moabitess 1
2: 2 And Ruth the Moabitess said to Na'omi, "Let me go 1
8 Then Bo'az said to Ruth, "Now, listen, my daughter 1
21 And Ruth the Moabitess said, "Besides, he said to me 1
22 Na'omi said to Ruth, her daughter-in-law, "It is well 1
3: 9 "Who are you?" And she answered, "I am Ruth 1
4: 5 you are also buying Ruth the Moabitess, the widow 1
10 Ruth the Moabitess, the widow . . I have bought 1
13 Bo'az took Ruth and she became his wife; 1
Mat 1: 5 Bo'az the father of Obed by Ruth 2

Sabbaias 1. Σαββαιας
1Es 9:32 Elionas and Asaias and Melchias and Sabbaias 1

Sabean 1. סְבָאִים 2. שְׁבָא 3. שְׁבָאִי
Job 1:15 the Sabe'ans fell upon them and took them 2
Isa 45:14 the Sabe'ans, men of stature, shall come over to you 1
Jol 3: 8 and they will sell them to the Sabe'ans 3

Sabta 1. סַבְתָּא
1Ch 1: 9 sons of Cush: Seba, Hav'ilah, Sabta, Ra'ama 1

Sabtah 1. סַבְתָּה
Gen 10: 7 sons of Cush: Seba, Hav'ilah, Sabtah, Ra'amah 1

Sabteca 1. סַבְתְּכָא
Gen 10: 7 Cush: Seba . . Sabtah, Ra'amah, and Sab'teca. 1
1Ch 1: 9 sons of Cush . . Sabta, Ra'ama, and Sab'teca. 1

Sachar 1. שָׂכָר
1Ch 11:35 Ahi'am the son of Sachar the Har'arite 1
26: 4 O'bed-e'dom had sons . . Sachar the fourth 1

Sachia 1. שָׂכְיָה
1Ch 8:10 Je'uz, Sachi'a, and Mirmah. 1

Sadducee 1. Σαδδουκαῖος
Mat 3: 7 when he saw many of the Pharisees and Sad'ducees 1
16: 1 the Pharisees and Sad'ducees came 1
6 the leaven of the Pharisees and Sadducees. 1
11 the leaven of the Pharisees and Sad'ducees. 1
12 the teaching of the Pharisees and Sadducees. 1
22:23 The same day Sad'ducees came to him 1
34 that he had silenced the Sad'ducees 1
Mrk 12:18 Sad'ducees came to him 1
Lke 20:27 There came to him some Sadducees 1
Act 4: 1 the Sad'ducees came upon them 1
5:17 the party of the Sad'ducees 1
23: 6 one part were Sad'ducees and the other Pharisees 1
7 dissension . . between the Pharisees
and . . Sad'ducees 1
8 the Sad'ducees say that there is no resurrection 1

Sakkuth 1. סִכּוּת
Ams 5:26 You shall take up Sakkuth your king, and Kaiwan 1

Sala 1. Σαλά
Lke 3:32 son of Bo'az, the son of Sala, the son of Nahshon 1

Salamiel 1. Σαλαμιηλ
Jdt 8: 1 son of Salamiel, son of Sarasadai, son of Israel. 1

Salamis 1. Σαλαμίς
Act 13: 5 When they arrived at Sal'amis 1

Salathiel 1. Salathihel
2Es 3: 1 I Salathiel, who am also called Ezra 1

Salecah 1. סַלְכָה
Deu 3:10 as far as Sal'ecah and Ed're-i, cities of the kingdom 1
Jos 12: 5 and ruled over Mount Hermon and Sal'ecah 1
13:11 and all Mount Hermon, and all Bashan to Sal'ecah; 1
1Ch 5:11 in the land of Bashan as far as Sal'ecah 1

Salem 1. שָׁלֵם 2. Σαλήμ
Gen 14:18 Mel-chiz'edek king of Salem brought out bread 1
Ps 76: 2 His abode has been established in Salem 1
Heb 7: 1 For this Melchiz'edek, king of Salem 2
2 then he is also king of Salem, that is, king of peace. 2
Jdt 4: 4 Choba and Aesora and the valley of Salem 2

Salim 1. Σαλίμ
Joh 3:23 John also was baptizing at Ae'non near Salim 1

Sallai 1. סַלָּי
Neh 11: 8 after him Gabba'i, Salla'i, 928. 1
12:20 of Sal'lai, Kal'lai; of Amok, Eber; 1

Sallu 1. סַלּוּא
1Ch 9: 7 Of the Benjaminites: Sallu the son of Meshul'lam 1
Neh 11: 7 sons of Benjamin: Sallu the son of Meshul'lam 1
12: 7 Sallu, Amok, Hilki'ah, Jedai'ah. 1

Salma 1. שַׂלְמָא
1Ch 2:11 Nahshon was the father of Salma, Salma of Bo'az 1
11 Salma of Bo'az, Bo'az of Obed 1
51 Salma, the father of Bethlehem 1
54 sons of Salma: Bethlehem, the Netoph'athites 1

Salmon 1. שַׂלְמוֹן 2. Σαλμών
Rut 4:20 Ammin'adab of Nahshon, Nahshon of Salmon 1
21 Salmon of Bo'az, Bo'az of Obed 1
Mat 1: 4 and Nahshon the father of Salmon 2
5 Salmon the father of Bo'az by Rahab 2

Salmone 1. Σαλμώνη
Act 27: 7 sailed under the lee of Crete off Salmo'ne. 1

Salome 1. Σαλώμη
Mrk 15:40 among whom were Mary Mag'dalene . . and Salo'me 1
16: 1 Mary the mother of James, and Salo'me 1

Salu 1. סָלוּא 2. Σαλωμ
Num25:14 Zimri the son of Salu, head of a fathers' house 1
1Mc 2:26 as Phinehas did against Zimri the son of Salu. 2

Samaria 1. שֹׁמְרוֹן 2. שָׁמְרַיִן (A) 3. Σαμάρεια
4. Σαμαρῖτις
1Kg 13:32 high places which are in the cities of Sama'ria 1
16:24 He bought the hill of Sama'ria from Shemer 1
24 and called . . the city which he built, Sama'ria 1
28 Omri slept . . and was buried in Sama'ria 1
29 Ahab . . reigned over Israel in Sama'ria 22 years. 1
32 in the house of Ba'al, which he built in Sama'ria. 1
18: 2 Now the famine was severe in Sama'ria. 1
20: 1 he went up and besieged Sama'ria, and fought 1
10 the dust of Sama'ria shall suffice for handfuls 1
17 Men are coming out from Sama'ria. 1
34 you may establish . . as my father did in Sama'ria. 1
43 king of Israel . . came to Sama'ria. 1
21: 1 beside the palace of Ahab king of Sama'ria. 1
18 go . . to meet Ahab king of Israel, who is in Sama'ria; 1
22:10 at the entrance of the gate of Sama'ria; 1
37 So the king died, and was brought to Sama'ria; 1
37 and they buried the king in Sama'ria. 1
38 they washed the chariot by the pool of Sama'ria 1
51 Ahazi'ah . . began to reign over Israel in Sama'ria 1
2Kg 1: 2 the lattice in his upper chamber in Sama'ria 1
3 to meet the messengers of the king of Sama'ria 1
2:25 Mount Carmel, and thence he returned to Sama'ria. 1
3: 1 Jeho'ram . . became king over Israel in Sama'ria 1
6 King Jeho'ram marched out of Sama'ria at that time 1
5: 3 my lord were with the prophet who is in Sama'ria! 1
6:19 And he led them to Sama'ria. 1
20 As soon as they entered Sama'ria Eli'sha said 1
20 they saw; and lo, they were in the midst of Sama'ria. 1
24 Ben-ha'dad . . and went up, and besieged Sama'ria. 1
25 there was a great famine in Sama'ria 1
7: 1 meal shall be sold for . . at the gate of Sama'ria. 1
18 about this time tomorrow in the gate of Sama'ria 1
10: 1 Now Ahab had 70 sons in Sama'ria. 1
1 Jehu wrote letters, and sent them to Sama'ria 1
12 Then he set out and went to Sama'ria. 1
17 when he came to Sama'ria, he slew all that remained 1
17 he slew all that remained to Ahab in Sama'ria 1
35 Jehu slept . . and they buried him in Sama'ria. 1
36 time that Jehu reigned . . in Sama'ria was 28 years. 1
13: 1 began to reign over Israel in Sama'ria 1
6 and the Ashe'rah also remained in Sama'ria.) 1
9 Jeho'ahaz slept . . and they buried him in Sama'ria; 1
10 Jeho'ash . . began to reign over Israel in Sama'ria 1
13 Jo'ash was buried in Sama'ria with the kings 1
14:14 he seized all the . . and he returned to Sama'ria. 1
16 Jeho'ash slept . . and was buried in Sama'ria 1
23 Jerobo'am . . began to reign in Sama'ria 1
15: 8 Zechari'ah . . reigned over Israel in Sama'ria 1
13 Shallum . . and he reigned one month in Sama'ria. 1
14 Men'ahem . . from Tirzah and came to Sama'ria 1
14 he struck down Shallum . . in Sama'ria and slew him 1
17 Men'ahem . . and he reigned ten years in Sama'ria. 1
23 began to reign over Israel in Sama'ria 1
25 Pekah . . and slew him in Sama'ria, in the citadel 1
27 Pekah . . began to reign over Israel in Sama'ria 1
17: 1 Hoshe'a the son of Elah began to reign in Sama'ria 1
5 king of Assyria invaded . . and came to Sama'ria 1
6 the king of Assyria captured Sama'ria 1
24 and placed them in the cities of Sama'ria 1
24 they took possession of Sama'ria, and dwelt in its 1
26 carried away and placed in the cities of Sama'ria 1
28 priests whom they had carried away from Sama'ria 1
18: 9 Assyria came up against Sama'ria and besieged it 1
10 the sixth year of Hezeki'ah . . Sama'ria was taken. 1
34 Have they delivered Sama'ria out of my hand? 1
21:13 stretch over Jerusalem the . . line of Sama'ria 1
23:18 the bones of the prophet who came out of Sama'ria. 1
19 the shrines . . that were in the cities of Sama'ria 1
2Ch 18: 2 After some years he went down to Ahab in Sama'ria. 1
9 the entrance of the gate of Sama'ria; 1
22: 9 Ahazi'ah . . captured while hiding in Sama'ria 1
25:13 cities of Judah, from Sama'ria to Beth-hor'on 1
24 seized . . hostages, and he returned to Sama'ria. 1
28: 8 and brought the spoil to Sama'ria. 1
9 he went out to meet the army that came to Sama'ria 1
15 Then they returned to Sama'ria. 1
Ezr 4:10 deported and settled in the cities of Sama'ria 2
17 rest of their associates who live in Sama'ria 2
Neh 4: 2 said in the presence . . of the army of Sama'ria 1
Isa 7: 9 the head of E'phraim is Sama'ria 1
9 the head of Sama'ria is the son of Remali'ah. 1
8: 4 the spoil of Sama'ria will be carried away 1
9: 9 E'phraim and the inhabitants of Sama'ria 1
10: 9 Is not Sama'ria like Damascus? 1
10 images were greater than those of . . Sama'ria 1
11 her idols as I have done to Sama'ria and her images? 1
36:19 Have they delivered Sama'ria out of my hand? 1
Jer 23:13 In the prophets of Sama'ria I saw an unsavory 1
31: 5 plant vineyards upon the mountains of Sama'ria; 1
41: 5 arrived from Shechem and Shiloh and Sama'ria 1
Ezk 16:46 your elder sister is Sama'ria 1
51 Sama'ria has not committed half your sins; 1
53 and the fortunes of Sama'ria and her daughters 1
55 Sama'ria and her daughters shall return to their 1
23: 4 As for their names, Oho'lah is Sama'ria 1
33 desolation, is the cup of your sister Sama'ria; 1
Hos 7: 1 corruption . . and the wicked deeds of Sama'ria; 1
8: 5 I have spurned your calf, O Sama'ria. 1
6 The calf of Sama'ria shall be broken to pieces. 1
10: 5 The inhabitants of Sama'ria tremble 1
7 Sama'ria's king shall perish 1
13:16 Sama'ria shall bear her guilt 1
Ams 3: 9 Assemble . . upon the mountains of Sama'ria 1
12 people of Israel who dwell in Sama'ria be rescued 1
4: 1 cows of Bashan, who are in the mountain of Sama'ria 1
6: 1 those who feel secure on the mountain of Sama'ria 1
8:14 Those who swear by Ash'imah of Sama'ria, and say 1
Obd 1:19 the land of E'phraim and the land of Sama'ria 1
Mic 1: 1 to Micah . . which he saw concerning Sama'ria 1
5 is the transgression of Jacob? Is it not Sama'ria? 1
6 I will make Sama'ria a heap in the open country 1
Lke 17:11 passing along between Sama'ria and Galilee. 3
Joh 4: 4 He had to pass through Samar'ia. 3
5 So he came to a city of Samar'ia, called Sy'char 3
7 There came a woman of Samar'ia to draw water. 3
9 you, a Jew, ask a drink of me, a woman of Samar'ia? 4
Act 1: 8 all Judea and Sama'ria and to the end of the earth. 3
8: 1 throughout the region of Judea and Sama'ria 3
5 Philip went down to a city of Sama'ria 3
9 and amazed the nation of Sama'ria 3
14 Sama'ria had received the word of God 3
9:31 the church throughout all Judea . . and Sama'ria 3
15: 3 they passed through both Phoeni'cia and Sama'ria 3
1Es 2:16 living in Samaria and other places 3
25 living in Samaria and Syria and Phoenicia 3
Jdt 1: 9 who were in Samaria and its surrounding towns 3
4: 4 they sent to every district of Samaria 3
1Mc 3:10 a large force from Samaria 3
10:30 from Samaria and Galilee 4
38 added to Judea from the country of Samaria 3
11:28 Judea and the three districts of Samaria 4
34 the latter . . were added to Judea from Samaria. 4
2Mc 15: 1 Judas and his men were in the region of Samaria 3

Samaritan 1. שֹׁמְרֹנִי 2. Σαμαρίτης 3. Σαμαρῖτις
2Kg 17:29 the high places which the Samaritans had made 1
Mat 10: 5 and enter no town of the Samaritans 2
Lke 9:52 who went and entered a village of the Samaritans 2
10:33 a Samaritan, as he journeyed, came to where he was; 2
17:16 Now he was a Samaritan. 2
Joh 4: 9 The Samaritan woman said to him, "How is it that you 3
9 For Jews have no dealings with Samaritans. 2
39 Many Samaritans from that city believed in him 2
40 So when the Samaritans came to him, they asked him 2
8:48 you are a Samaritan and have a demon? 2
Act 8:25 many villages of the Samaritans. 2

Samgar-nebo 1. סַמְגַּר נְבוֹ
Jer 39: 3 Ner'gal-share'zer, Sam'gar-ne'bo 1

Samlah 1. שַׂמְלָה
Gen 36:36 Hadad died, and Samlah of Masre'kah reigned 1
37 Samlah died, and Shaul of Reho'both 1
1Ch 1:47 When Hadad died, Samlah of Masre'kah reigned 1
48 When Samlah died, Sha'ul of Reho'both 1

Samos 1. Σάμος
Act 20:15 the next day we touched at Samos 1
1Mc 15:23 to Myndos, and to Sicyon, and to Caria, and to Samos 1

Samothrace 1. Σαμοθρᾴκη
Act 16:11 we made a direct voyage to Sam'o-thrace 1

Sampsames 1. Σαμψαμης
1Mc 15:23 to all the countries, and to Sampsames 1

Samson 1. שִׁמְשׁוֹן 2. Σαμψών
Jdg 13:24 the woman bore a son, and called his name Samson; 1
14: 1 Samson went down to Timnah, and at Timnah he saw 1
3 But Samson said to his father, "Get her for me; 1
5 Samson went down with his father and mother 1
7 with the woman; and she pleased Samson well. 1
10 down to the woman, and Samson made a feast there; 1
12 Samson said to them, "Let me now put a riddle to you; 1
15 On the fourth day they said to Samson's wife 1
16 Samson's wife wept before him, and said, "You only 1
20 Samson's wife was given to his companion 1
15: 1 harvest, Samson went to visit his wife with a kid; 1
3 Samson said to them, "This time I shall be 1
4 Samson went and caught 300 foxes 1
6 they said, "Samson, the son-in-law of the Timnite 1
7 Samson said to them, "If this is what you do, I swear 1
10 We have come up to bind Samson, to do to him as he 1
11 men of Judah went down . . and said to Samson 1
12 Samson said to them, "Swear to me that you will not 1
16 Samson said, "With the jawbone of an ass 1
16: 1 Samson went to Gaza, and there he saw a harlot 1
2 The Gazites were told, "Samson has come here 1
3 Samson lay till midnight, and at midnight he 1
6 Deli'lah said to Samson, "Please tell me wherein 1
7 Samson said to her, "If they bind me with seven 1
9 said to him, "The Philistines are upon you, Samson! 1
10 Deli'lah said to Samson, "Behold, you have mocked me 1
12 said to him, "The Philistines are upon you, Samson! 1
13 Deli'lah said to Samson, "Until now you have mocked 1
14 said to him, "The Philistines are upon you, Samson! 1
20 she said, "The Philistines are upon you, Samson! 1
23 Our god has given Samson our enemy into our hand. 1
25 Call Samson, that he may make sport for us. 1
25 they called Samson out of the prison 1
26 Samson said to the lad who held him by the hand 1
27 and women, who looked on while Samson made sport. 1
28 Samson called to the LORD and said, "O Lord GOD 1

29 Samson grasped the two middle pillars 1
30 Samson said, "Let me die with the Philistines. 1
Heb 11:32 to tell of Gideon, Barak, Samson, Jephthah, of David 2

Samuel 1. שְׁמוּאֵל 2. Σαμουήλ 3. Samuhel

1Sm 1:20 and she called his name Samuel, for she said 1
2:18 Samuel was ministering before the LORD 1
21 the boy Samuel grew in the presence of the LORD. 1
26 the boy Samuel continued to grow both in stature 1
3: 1 Now the boy Samuel was ministering to the LORD 1
3 Samuel was lying down within the temple 1
4 LORD called, "Samuel! Samuel!" and he said, "Here I 1
4 LORD called, "Samuel! Samuel!" and he said, "Here I 2
6 the LORD called again, "Samuel!" And Samuel arose 1
6 Samuel arose and went to Eli, and said, "Here I am 1
7 Now Samuel did not yet know the LORD 1
8 And the LORD called Samuel again the third time. 1
9 Therefore Eli said to Samuel, "Go, lie down; 1
9 So Samuel went and lay down in his place. 1
10 calling as at other times, "Samuel! Samuel! 1
10 calling as at other times, "Samuel! Samuel! 1
10 And Samuel said, "Speak, for thy servant hears. 1
11 the LORD said to Samuel, "Behold, I am about to do 1
15 Samuel lay until morning; 1
15 And Samuel was afraid to tell the vision to Eli. 1
16 But Eli called Samuel and said, "Samuel, my son. 1
16 But Eli called Samuel and said, "Samuel, my son. 1
18 Samuel told him everything and hid nothing 1
19 And Samuel grew, and the LORD was with him 1
20 Samuel was established as a prophet of the LORD. 1
21 the LORD revealed himself to Samuel at Shiloh 1
4: 1 And the word of Samuel came to all Israel. 1
7: 3 Then Samuel said to all the house of Israel 1
5 Then Samuel said, "Gather all Israel at Mizpah 1
6 Samuel judged the people of Israel at Mizpah. 1
8 the people of Israel said to Samuel, "Do not cease 1
9 Samuel took a sucking lamb and offered it 1
9 and Samuel cried to the LORD for Israel 1
10 As Samuel was offering up the burnt offering 1
12 Then Samuel took a stone and set it up 1
13 against the Philistines all the days of Samuel. 1
15 Samuel judged Israel all the days of his life. 1
8: 1 When Samuel became old, he made his sons judges 1
4 elders . . gathered together and came to Samuel 1
6 But the thing displeased Samuel when they said 1
6 And Samuel prayed to the LORD. 1
7 the LORD said to Samuel, "Hearken to the . . people 1
10 Samuel told all the words of the LORD 1
19 people refused to listen to the voice of Samuel; 1
21 when Samuel had heard all the words of the people 1
22 the LORD said to Samuel, "Hearken to their voice 1
22 Samuel then said to the men of Israel 1
9:14 they saw Samuel coming out toward them on his way 1
15 before Saul came, the LORD had revealed to Samuel 1
17 When Samuel saw Saul, the LORD told him 1
18 Then Saul approached Samuel in the gate, and said 1
19 Samuel answered Saul, "I am the seer; go up before me 1
22 Samuel took Saul and his servant and brought 1
23 Samuel said to the cook, "Bring the portion 1
24 Samuel said, "See, what was kept is set before you. •
24 Saul ate with Samuel that day. 1
26 Samuel called to Saul upon the roof 1
26 Saul arose, and both he and Samuel went out 1
27 Samuel said to Saul, "Tell the servant to pass 1
10: 1 Samuel took a vial of oil and poured it on his head 1
9 When he turned his back to leave Samuel 1
14 when we saw they were not . . we went to Samuel. 1
15 Pray, tell me what Samuel said to you. 1
16 matter of the kingdom, of which Samuel had spoken 1
17 Samuel called the people together to the LORD 1
20 Samuel brought all the tribes of Israel near 1
24 Samuel said to all the people, "Do you see him 1
25 Samuel told the people the rights and duties 1
25 Then Samuel sent all the people away 1
11: 7 Whoever does not come out after Saul and Samuel 1
12 Then the people said to Samuel, "Who is it that said 1
14 Samuel said to the people, "Come, let us go to Gilgal 1
12: 1 Samuel said to all Israel, "Behold, I have 1
6 Samuel said to the people, "The LORD is witness 1
11 Jerubba'al and Barak, and Jephthah, and Samuel 1
18 Samuel called upon the LORD, and the LORD sent 1
18 the people greatly feared the LORD and Samuel. 1
19 the people said to Samuel, "Pray for your servants 1
20 And Samuel said to the people, "Fear not; 1
13: 8 waited seven days, the time appointed by Samuel; 1
8 He waited . . but Samuel did not come to Gilgal 1
10 As soon as he had finished . . behold, Samuel came; 1
11 Samuel said, "What have you done? 1
13 Samuel said to Saul, "You have done foolishly; 1
15 Samuel arose, and went up from Gilgal to Gib'e-ah 1
15: 1 Samuel said to Saul, "The LORD sent me to anoint you 1
10 The word of the LORD came to Samuel 1
11 Samuel was angry; and he cried to the LORD 1
12 And Samuel rose early to meet Saul in the morning; 1
12 and it was told Samuel, "Saul came to Carmel 1
13 Samuel came to Saul, and Saul said to him 1
14 And Samuel said, "What then is this bleating 1
16 Then Samuel said to Saul, "Stop! I will tell you 1
17 Samuel said, "Though you are little in your . . eyes 1
20 Saul said to Samuel, "I have obeyed the . . LORD 1
22 Samuel said, "Has the LORD as great delight 1
24 And Saul said to Samuel, "I have sinned; 1
26 And Samuel said to Saul, "I will not return with you 1
27 As Samuel turned to go away, Saul laid hold upon 1
28 Samuel said to him, "The LORD has torn the kingdom 1
31 Samuel turned back after Saul; 1
32 Then Samuel said, "Bring here to me Agag the king 1
33 Samuel said, "As your sword has made women 1
33 And Samuel hewed Agag in pieces before the LORD 1
34 Samuel went to Ramah; and Saul went up to his house 1
35 Samuel did not see Saul again until . . his death 1
35 did not see Saul . . but Samuel grieved over Saul. 1
16: 1 The LORD said to Samuel, "How long will you grieve 1
2 And Samuel said, "How can I go? 1
4 Samuel did what the LORD commanded, and came 1
7 But the LORD said to Samuel, "Do not look on his 1
8 Jesse called . . and made him pass before Samuel. 1
10 Jesse made seven of his sons pass before Samuel. 1
10 And Samuel said to Jesse, "The LORD has not chosen 1
11 And Samuel said to Jesse, "Are all your sons here? 1
11 And Samuel said to Jesse, "Send and fetch him; 1
13 Then Samuel took the horn of oil, and anointed him 1
13 And Samuel rose up, and went to Ramah. 1
19:18 David . . escaped, and he came to Samuel at Ramah 1
18 And he and Samuel went and dwelt at Nai'oth. 1
20 the prophets . . and Samuel standing as head 1
22 and he asked, "Where are Samuel and David? 1
24 and he too prophesied before Samuel 1
25: 1 Now Samuel died; and all Israel . . mourned for him 1
28: 3 Now Samuel had died, and all Israel had mourned 1
11 He said, "Bring up Samuel for me. 1
12 When the woman saw Samuel, she cried out 1
14 And Saul knew that it was Samuel, and he bowed 1
15 Samuel said to Saul, "Why have you disturbed me 1
16 And Samuel said, "Why then do you ask me 1
20 filled with fear because of the words of Samuel; 1
1Ch 6:28 sons of Samuel: Jo'el his first-born . . Abi'jah. 1
33 Heman the singer the son of Jo'el, son of Samuel 1
9:22 David and Samuel the seer established them 1
11: 3 according to the word of the LORD by Samuel. 1
26:28 all that Samuel the seer, and Saul the son of Kish 1
29:29 are written in the Chronicles of Samuel the seer 1
2Ch 35:18 since the days of Samuel the prophet; 1
Ps 99: 6 Samuel . . among those who called on his name. 1
Jer 15: 1 Though Moses and Samuel stood before me 1
Act 3:24 from Samuel and those who came afterwards 2
13:20 he gave them judges until Samuel the prophet. 2
Heb 11:32 David and Samuel and the prophets– 2
1Es 1:20 since the times of Samuel the prophet; 2
2Es 7:108 Samuel in the days of Saul 3
Sir 46:13 Samuel, beloved by his Lord, a prophet of the Lord 2
19 Samuel called men to witness before the Lord •

Sanballat 1. סַנְבַלַּט

Neh 2:10 when Sanbal'lat the Hor'onite and Tobi'ah 1
19 when Sanbal'lat the Hor'onite and Tobi'ah 1
4: 1 Sanbal'lat heard that we were building the wall 1
7 when Sanbal'lat and Tobi'ah and the Arabs 1
6: 1 reported to Sanbal'lat and Tobi'ah and to Geshem 1
2 Sanbal'lat and Geshem sent to me, saying, "Come 1
5 Sanbal'lat for the fifth time sent his servant 1
12 because Tobi'ah and Sanbal'lat had hired him. 1
14 Remember Tobi'ah and Sanbal'lat, O my God 1
13:28 the son-in-law of Sanbal'lat the Hor'onite; 1

Sansannah 1. סַנְסַנָּה

Jos 15:31 Ziklag, Madman'nah, Sansan'nah 1

Saph 1. סַף

2Sm 21:18 then Sib'becai the Hu'shathite slew Saph 1

Sapphira 1. Σάπφιρα

Act 5: 1 a man named Anani'as with his wife Sapphi'ra 1

Sar-sechim 1. שַׂר סְכִים

Jer 39: 3 Sam'gar-ne'bo, Sar'sechim the Rab'saris 1

Sarah 1. שָׂרָה 2. Σάρρα

Gen 17:15 her name Sar'ai, but Sarah shall be her name. 1
17 Shall Sarah, who is 90 years old, bear a child? 1
19 God said, "No, but Sarah your wife shall bear 1
21 Isaac, whom Sarah shall bear to you at this season 1
18: 6 Abraham hastened into the tent to Sarah, and said 1
9 They said to him, "Where is Sarah your wife? 1
10 and Sarah your wife shall have a son. 1
10 Sarah was listening at the tent door behind him 1
11 Now Abraham and Sarah were old, advanced in age; 1
11 it had ceased to be with Sarah after the manner 1
12 Sarah laughed to herself, saying 1
13 LORD said to Abraham, "Why did Sarah laugh, 1
14 to you, in the spring, and Sarah shall have a son. 1
15 Sarah denied, saying, "I did not laugh"; 1
20: 2 Abraham said of Sarah his wife, "She is my sister. 1
2 And Abim'elech king of Gerar sent and took Sarah. 1
14 to Abraham, and restored Sarah his wife to him. 1
16 Sarah he said, "Behold, I have given your brother 1
18 of Abim'elech because of Sarah, Abraham's wife. 1
21: 1 The LORD visited Sarah as he had said 1
1 and the LORD did to Sarah as he had promised. 1
2 Sarah conceived, and bore Abraham a son 1
3 was born to him, whom Sarah bore him, Isaac. 1
6 Sarah said, "God has made laughter for me; 1
7 to Abraham that Sarah would suckle children? 1
9 Sarah saw the son of Hagar the Egyptian 1
12 whatever Sarah says to you, do as she tells you 1
23: 1 Sarah lived 127 years; 1
1 these were the years of the life of Sarah. 1
2 Sarah died at Kir'iath-ar'ba (that is, Hebron) 1
2 and Abraham went in to mourn for Sarah and to weep 1
19 After this, Abraham buried Sarah his wife 1
24:36 Sarah my master's wife bore a son to my master 1
25:10 There Abraham was buried, with Sarah his wife. 1
12 whom Hagar the Egyptian, Sarah's maid, bore 1
49:31 There they buried Abraham and Sarah his wife; 1
Isa 51: 2 to Abraham your father and to Sarah who bore you; 1
Rom 4:19 he considered the barrenness of Sarah's womb. 2
9: 9 I will return and Sarah shall have a son. 2
Heb 11:11 By faith Sarah . . received power to conceive 2
1Pe 3: 6 as Sarah obeyed Abraham, calling him lord. 2
Tob 3: 7 Sarah, the daughter of Raguel, was reproached 2
17 to give Sarah the daughter of Raguel in marriage 2
17 Sarah the daughter of Raguel came down 2
6:10 he has an only daughter named Sarah 2
7: 1 Sarah met them and greeted them 2
8 his wife Edna and his daughter Sarah wept 2
13 Then he called his daughter Sarah 2
10:10 Raguel arose and gave him his wife Sarah 2
12 to see your children by my daughter Sarah 2
11:17 When Tobit came near to Sarah his daughter-in-law 2
12:12 when you and your daughter-in-law Sarah prayed 2
14 to heal you and your daughter-in-law Sarah. 2

Sarai 1. שָׂרַי

Gen 11:29 the name of Abram's wife was Sar'ai 1
30 Now Sar'ai was barren; she had no child. 1
31 his grandson, and Sar'ai his daughter-in-law 1
12: 5 Abram took Sar'ai his wife, and Lot 1
11 he said to Sar'ai his wife 1
17 his house with great plagues because of Sar'ai 1
16: 1 Now Sar'ai, Abram's wife, bore him no children. 1
2 Sar'ai said to Abram, "Behold now, the LORD has 1
2 And Abram hearkened to the voice of Sar'ai. 1
3 Sar'ai, Abram's wife, took Hagar the Egyptian 1
5 Sar'ai said to Abram, "May the wrong done to me be 1
6 Abram said to Sar'ai 1
6 Then Sar'ai dealt harshly with her 1
8 he said "Hagar, maid of Sar'ai, where have you 1
8 he said "Hagar, maid of Sar'ai, where have you 1
8 She said, "I am fleeing from my mistress Sar'ai. 1
17:15 God said to Abraham, "As for Sar'ai your wife 1
15 you shall not call her name Sar'ai, but Sarah 1

Saraph 1. שָׂרָף

1Ch 4:22 Saraph, who ruled in Moab and returned to Lehem 1

Sarasadai 1. Σαρασαδαι

Jdt 8: 1 son of Salamiel, son of Sarasadai, son of Israel. 1

Sardis 1. Σάρδεις

Rev 1:11 seven churches . . to Sardis and to Philadelphia 1
3: 1 And to the angel of the church in Sardis write 1
4 Yet you have still a few names in Sardis 1

Sarea 1. Sarea

2Es 14:24 and take with you Sarea, Dabria, Selemia, Ethanus 1

Sargon 1. סַרְגוֹן

Isa 20: 1 the commander in chief, who was sent by Sargon 1

Sarid 1. שָׂרִיד

Jos 19:10 its inheritance reached as far as Sarid; 1
12 from Sarid it goes . . eastward toward 1

Sarothie 1. Σαρωθιε

1Es 5:34 the sons of Sarothie, the sons of Masiah 1

Satan 1. שָׂטָן 2. Σατανᾶς

1Ch 21: 1 Satan stood up against Israel 1
Job 1: 6 before the LORD, and Satan also came among them. 1
7 The LORD said to Satan, "Whence have you come? 1
7 Satan answered the LORD, "From going to and fro 1
8 the LORD said to Satan, "Have you considered 1
9 Then Satan answered the LORD, "Does Job fear God 1
12 the LORD said to Satan, "Behold, all that he has 1
12 Satan went forth from the presence of the LORD. 1
2: 1 Satan also came among them to present himself 1
2 the LORD said to Satan, "Whence have you come? 1
2 Satan answered the LORD, "From going to and fro 1
3 the LORD said to Satan, "Have you considered 1
4 Then Satan answered the LORD, "Skin for skin! 1
6 the LORD said to Satan, "Behold, he is in your power; 1
7 Satan went forth from the presence of the LORD 1
Zec 3: 1 Satan standing at his right hand to accuse him. 1
2 LORD said to Satan, "The LORD rebuke you, O Satan! 1
2 LORD said to Satan, "The LORD rebuke you, O Satan! 1
Mat 4:10 Jesus said to him, "Begone, Satan! for it is written 2
12:26 if Satan casts out Satan, he is divided 2

26 if Satan casts out Satan, he is divided 2
16:23 he turned and said to Peter, "Get behind me, Satan! 2
Mrk 1:13 he was in the wilderness 40 days, tempted by Satan 2
3:23 How can Satan cast out Satan? 2
23 How can Satan cast out Satan? 2
26 if Satan has risen up against himself 2
4:15 when they hear, Satan immediately comes 2
8:33 Get behind me, Satan! 2
Lke 10:18 I saw Satan fall like lightning from heaven. 2
11:18 if Satan also is divided against himself 2
13:16 a daughter of Abraham whom Satan bound 2
22: 3 Then Satan entered into Judas called Iscariot 2
31 Simon, Simon, behold, Satan demanded to have you 2
Joh 13:27 after the morsel, Satan entered into him 2
Act 5: 3 why has Satan filled your heart to lie 2
26:18 turn . . from the power of Satan to God 2
Rom 16:20 God . . will soon crush Satan under your feet. 2
1Co 5: 5 you are to deliver this man to Satan 2
7: 5 then come together again, lest Satan tempt you 2
2Co 2:11 to keep Satan from gaining the advantage over us; 2
11:14 Satan disguises himself as an angel of light. 2
12: 7 a messenger of Satan, to harass me 2
1Th 2:18 but Satan hindered us. 2
2Th 2: 9 the activity of Satan 2
1Ti 1:20 whom I have delivered to Satan 2
5:15 For some have already strayed after Satan. 2
Rev 2: 9 but are a synagogue of Satan. 2
13 'I know where you dwell, where Satan's throne is; 2
13 who was killed among you, where Satan dwells. 2
24 learned what some call the deep things of Satan 2
3: 9 I will make those in the synagogue of Satan 2
12: 9 serpent, who is called the Devil and Satan 2
20: 2 that ancient serpent, who is the Devil and Satan 2
7 Satan will be loosed from his prison 2

Sathrabuzanes 1. Σαθραβουζανης

1Es 6: 3 Sathrabuzanes and their associates came to them 1
7 Sathrabuzanes, and their associates 1
27 and Sathrabuzanes, and their associates 1
7: 1 Sathrabuzanes, and their associates 1

Saul 1. שָׁאוּל 2. Σαούλ 3. Σαῦλος

1Sm 9: 2 he had a son whose name was Saul 1
3 Now the asses of Kish, Saul's father, were lost. 1
3 asses . . were lost. So Kish said to Saul his son 1
5 Saul said to his servant who was with him, "Come 1
7 Then Saul said to his servant, "But if we go, what can 1
8 The servant answered Saul again, "Here, I have 1
10 Saul said to his servant, "Well said; come, let us go. 1
15 before Saul came, the LORD had revealed to Samuel 1
17 When Samuel saw Saul, the LORD told him 1
18 Then Saul approached Samuel in the gate, and said 1
19 Samuel answered Saul, "I am the seer; go up 1
21 Saul answered, "Am I not a Benjaminite 1
22 took Saul and his servant and brought them 1
24 took up the leg and . . and set them before Saul; 1
24 Saul ate with Samuel that day. 1
25 a bed was spread for Saul upon the roof, and he lay 1
26 Samuel called to Saul upon the roof 1
26 Saul arose, and both he and Samuel went out 1
27 Samuel said to Saul, "Tell the servant to pass 1
10:11 Is Saul also among the prophets? 1
12 became a proverb, "Is Saul also among the prophets? 1
14 Saul's uncle said to him . . "Where did you go? 1
15 Saul's uncle said, "Pray, tell me what Samuel said 1
16 Saul said to his uncle, "He told us plainly that 1
21 and Saul the son of Kish was taken by lot. 1
26 Saul also went to his home at Gib'e-ah 1
11: 4 When the messengers came to Gib'e-ah of Saul 1
5 Saul was coming from the field behind the oxen; 1
5 and Saul said, "What ails the people 1
6 And the spirit of God came mightily upon Saul 1
7 Whoever does not come out after Saul and Samuel 1
11 Saul put the people in three companies; 1
12 Who is it that said, 'Shall Saul reign over us?' 1
13 Saul said, "Not a man shall be put to death this day 1
15 they made Saul king before the LORD in Gilgal. 1
15 Saul and all the men of Israel rejoiced greatly. 1
13: 1 Saul was . . years old when he began to reign; 1
2 Saul chose 3,000 men of Israel; 1
2 2,000 were with Saul in Michmash 1
3 Saul blew the trumpet throughout all the land 1
4 Israel heard . . Saul had defeated the garrison 1
4 people were called out to join Saul at Gilgal. 1
7 Saul was still at Gilgal, and all the people 1
9 Saul said, "Bring the burnt offering here to me 1
10 Samuel came; and Saul went out to meet him 1
11 Saul said, "When I saw that the people were 1
13 Samuel said to Saul, "You have done foolishly; 1
15 Saul numbered the people . . present with him 1
16 And Saul, and Jonathan his son . . stayed in Geba 1
22 of any of the people with Saul and Jonathan; 1
22 but Saul and Jonathan his son had them. 1
14: 1 One day Jonathan the son of Saul said . . "Come 1
2 Saul was staying in the outskirts of Gib'e-ah 1
16 the watchmen of Saul in Gib'e-ah . . looked; 1
17 Then Saul said to the people who were with him 1
18 Saul said to Ahi'jah, "Bring hither the ark of God. 1
19 while Saul was talking to the priest 1
19 and Saul said to the priest, "Withdraw your hand. 1
20 Saul and all the people who were with him rallied 1
21 the Israelites who were with Saul and Jonathan. 1
24 Saul laid an oath on the people, saying, "Cursed be 1
33 they told Saul, "Behold, the people are sinning 1
34 Saul said, "Disperse yourselves among the people 1
35 And Saul built an altar to the LORD; 1
36 Saul said, "Let us go down after the Philistines 1
37 Saul inquired of God, "Shall I go down 1
38 Saul said, "Come hither . . leaders of the people; 1
40 the people said to Saul, "Do what seems good to you. 1
41 Saul said, "O LORD God of Israel, why hast thou not 1
41 Jonathan and Saul were taken, but the people 1
42 Then Saul said, "Cast the lot between me and my son 1
43 Saul said to Jonathan, "Tell me what you have done. 1
44 Saul said, "God do so to me and more also; 1
45 Then the people said to Saul, "Shall Jonathan die 1
46 Then Saul went up from pursuing the Philistines; 1
47 When Saul had taken the kingship over Israel 1
49 sons of Saul were Jonathan, Ishvi, and Mal'chishu'a; 1
50 and the name of Saul's wife was Ahin'o-am 1
50 commander . . was Abner the son of Ner, Saul's uncle; 1
51 Kish was the father of Saul, and Ner the father 1
52 There was hard fighting . . all the days of Saul; 1
52 when Saul saw any strong man, or any valiant man 1
15: 1 Samuel said to Saul, "The LORD sent me to anoint you 1
4 Saul summoned the people, and numbered them 1
5 Saul came to the city of Am'alek, and lay in wait 1
6 Saul said to the Ken'ites, "Go, depart, go down 1
7 Saul defeated the Amal'ekites 1
9 But Saul and the people spared Agag, and the best 1
11 I repent that I have made Saul king; 1
12 And Samuel rose early to meet Saul in the morning; 1
12 Saul came to Carmel, and . . he set up a monument 1
13 Samuel came to Saul, and Saul said to him 1
13 Samuel came to Saul, and Saul said to him 1
15 Saul said, "They have brought them 1
16 Then Samuel said to Saul, "Stop! I will tell you 1
20 Saul said to Samuel, "I have obeyed the . . LORD 1
24 And Saul said to Samuel, "I have sinned; 1
26 And Samuel said to Saul, "I will not return with you 1
27 Saul laid hold upon the skirt of his robe •
31 Samuel turned back after Saul; 1
31 and Saul worshiped the LORD. 1
34 and Saul went up to his house in Gib'e-ah of Saul. 1
34 and Saul went up to his house in Gib'e-ah of Saul. 1
35 Samuel did not see Saul again until . . his death 1
35 did not see Saul . . but Samuel grieved over Saul. 1
35 And the LORD repented that he had made Saul king 1
16: 1 How long will you grieve over Saul 1
2 How can I go? If Saul hears it, he will kill me. 1
14 Now the Spirit of the LORD departed from Saul 1
15 Saul's servants said to him, "Behold now 1
17 Saul said to his servants, "Provide for me a man 1
19 Saul sent messengers to Jesse, and said, "Send me 1
20 and sent them by David his son to Saul. 1
21 And David came to Saul, and entered his service. 1
21 Saul loved him greatly, and he became his •
22 And Saul sent to Jesse, saying, "Let David remain 1
23 whenever the evil spirit from God was upon Saul 1
23 so Saul was refreshed, and was well 1
17: 2 And Saul and the men of Israel were gathered 1
8 I . . a Philistine, and are you not servants of Saul? 1
11 When Saul and all Israel heard . . the Philistine 1
12 In the days of Saul the man was already old 1
13 sons of Jesse had followed Saul to the battle; 1
14 the three eldest followed Saul 1
15 but David went back and forth from Saul 1
19 Saul, and they, and all . . Israel, were in the valley 1
31 When the words . . they repeated them before Saul; 1
32 David said to Saul, "Let no man's heart fail 1
33 And Saul said to David, "You are not able to go 1
34 But David said to Saul, "Your servant used to keep 1
37 Saul said to David, "Go, and the LORD be with you! 1
38 Then Saul clothed David with his armor; 1
39 Then David said to Saul, "I cannot go with these; 1
55 Saul saw David go forth against the Philistine 1
57 Abner took him, and brought him before Saul 1
58 Saul said to him, "Whose son are you, young man? 1
18: 1 When he had finished speaking to Saul 1
2 Saul took him . . and would not let him return 1
5 David . . was successful wherever Saul sent him; 1
5 David . . so that Saul set him over the men of war. 1
5 and also in the sight of Saul's servants. 1
6 the women came . . to meet King Saul, with timbrels 1
7 Saul has slain his thousands 1
8 Saul was very angry, and this saying displeased 1
9 Saul eyed David from that day on. 1
10 an evil spirit from God rushed upon Saul 1
10 Saul had his spear in his hand; 1
11 and Saul cast the spear, for he thought, "I will pin 1
12 Saul was afraid of David 1
12 the LORD was with him but had departed from Saul. 1
13 Saul removed him from his presence, and made him 1
15 And when Saul saw that he had great success 1
17 Saul said to David, "Here is my elder daughter Merab; 1
17 Saul thought, "Let not my hand be upon him 1
18 David said to Saul, "Who am I, and who are 1
19 Merab, Saul's daughter, should have been given 1
20 Now Saul's daughter Michal loved David; 1
20 and they told Saul, and the thing pleased him. 1
21 Saul thought, "Let me give her to him, 1
21 Therefore Saul said to David a second time 1
22 And Saul commanded his servants, "Speak to David 1
23 Saul's servants spoke those words in the ears 1
24 And the servants of Saul told him 1
25 Then Saul said, "Thus shall you say to David 1
25 Now Saul thought to make David fall by the hand 1
27 And Saul gave him his daughter Michal for a wife. 1
28 Saul saw and knew that the LORD was with David 1
29 Saul was still more afraid of David. 1
29 Saul was David's enemy continually. 1
30 David had more . . than all the servants of Saul; 1
19: 1 Saul spoke to Jonathan . . and to all his servants 1
1 But Jonathan, Saul's son, delighted much in David. 1
2 Saul my father seeks to kill you; 1
4 Jonathan spoke well of David to Saul his father 1
6 And Saul hearkened to the voice of Jonathan; 1
6 Saul swore, "As the LORD lives, he shall not be put 1
7 And Jonathan brought David to Saul, and he was 1
9 Then an evil spirit from the LORD came upon Saul 1
10 Saul sought to pin David to the wall 1
10 he eluded Saul, so that he struck the spear 1
11 Saul sent messengers to David's house to watch 1
14 when Saul sent messengers to take David, she said 1
15 Saul sent the messengers to see David, saying 1
17 Saul said to Michal, "Why have you deceived me thus 1
17 And Michal answered Saul, "He said to me, 'Let me go; 1
18 and told him all that Saul had done to him. 1
19 And it was told Saul, "Behold, David is at Nai'oth 1
20 Then Saul sent messengers to take David; 1
20 Spirit of God came upon the messengers of Saul 1
21 When it was told Saul, he sent other messengers 1
21 And Saul sent messengers again the third time 1
24 Hence it is said, "Is Saul also among the prophets? 1
20:25 The king sat . . and Abner sat by Saul's side 1
26 Saul did not say anything that day; for he thought 1
27 Saul said to Jonathan his son, "Why has not the son 1
28 Jonathan answered Saul, "David earnestly asked 1
30 Then Saul's anger was kindled against Jonathan 1
32 Jonathan answered Saul his father, "Why should he 1
33 But Saul cast his spear at him to smite him; 1
21: 7 a certain man of the servants of Saul was there 1
7 Do'eg the E'domite, the chief of Saul's herdsmen. 1
10 And David rose and fled that day from Saul 1
11 Saul has slain his thousands 1
22: 6 Now Saul heard that David was discovered 1
6 Saul was sitting at Gib'e-ah, under the tamarisk 1
7 Saul said to his servants who stood about him 1
9 Do'eg . . who stood by the servants of Saul 1
12 Saul said, "Hear now, son of Ahi'tub." 1
13 Saul said . . "Why have you conspired against me 1
21 that Saul had killed the priests of the LORD. 1
22 I knew . . that he would surely tell Saul. 1
23: 7 it was told Saul that David had come to Kei'lah. 1
7 And Saul said, "God has given him into my hand; 1
8 And Saul summoned all the people to war 1
9 David knew . . Saul was plotting evil against him; 1
10 Saul seeks to come to Kei'lah, to destroy the city 1
11 Will Saul come down, as thy servant has heard? 1
12 surrender me and my men into the hand of Saul? 1
13 Saul was told that David had escaped from Kei'lah 1
14 Saul sought him every day 1
15 Saul had come out to seek his life. 1
16 Jonathan, Saul's son, rose, and went to David 1
17 the hand of Saul my father shall not find you; 1
17 Saul my father also knows this. 1
19 the Ziphites went up to Saul at Gib'e-ah, saying 1
21 And Saul said, "May you be blessed by the LORD; 1
24 And they arose, and went to Ziph ahead of Saul. 1
25 And Saul and his men went to seek him. 1
25 And when Saul heard that, he pursued after David 1
26 Saul went on one side of the mountain 1
26 and David was making haste to get away from Saul 1
26 Saul and his men were closing in 1
27 a messenger came to Saul, saying, "Make haste 1
28 Saul returned from pursuing after David 1
24: 1 Saul returned from following the Philistines 1
2 Then Saul took 3,000 chosen men out of all Israel 1
3 a cave; and Saul went in to relieve himself. 1
4 David . . cut off the skirt of Saul's robe. 1
5 because he had cut off Saul's skirt. 1
7 David . . did not permit them to attack Saul. 1
7 Saul rose up and left the cave, and went . . his way. 1
8 David also arose . . and called after Saul, "My lord 1
8 And when Saul looked behind him, David bowed 1
9 David said to Saul, "Why do you listen 1
16 David had finished speaking these words to Saul 1
16 Saul said, "Is this your voice, my son David? 1
16 And Saul lifted up his voice and wept. 1
22 And David swore this to Saul. Then Saul went home; 1
22 And David swore this to Saul. Then Saul went home; 1
25:44 Saul had given Michal his daughter . . to Palti 1
26: 1 Then the Ziphites came to Saul at Gib'e-ah, saying 1
2 Saul arose and went down to the wilderness 1
3 Saul encamped on the hill of Hachi'lah 1
3 saw that Saul came after him into the wilderness 1
4 and learned of a certainty that Saul had come. 1

5 and came to the place where Saul had encamped; 1
5 and David saw the place where Saul lay, with Abner 1
5 Saul was lying within the encampment 1
6 Who will go down with me into the camp to Saul? 1
7 there lay Saul sleeping within the encampment 1
12 took the spear and the jar . . from Saul's head; 1
17 Saul recognized David's voice, and said 1
21 Saul said, "I have done wrong; return, my son David 1
25 Saul said to David, "Blessed be you, my son David! 1
25 David went his way, and Saul returned to his place. 1
27: 1 I shall now perish one day by the hand of Saul; 1
1 Saul will despair of seeking me any longer 1
4 when it was told Saul that David had fled to Gath 1
28: 3 And Saul had put the mediums and the wizards out 1
4 Saul gathered all Israel, and they encamped 1
5 When Saul saw the army of the Philistines 1
6 when Saul inquired of the LORD, the LORD did not 1
7 Saul said to his servants, "Seek out . . a medium 1
8 Saul disguised himself and put on other 1
9 Surely you know what Saul has done 1
10 Saul swore to her by the LORD, "As the LORD lives 1
12 the woman said to Saul, "Why have you deceived me? 1
12 Why have you deceived me? You are Saul. 1
13 the woman said to Saul, "I see a god coming up 1
14 And Saul knew that it was Samuel, and he bowed 1
15 Samuel said to Saul, "Why have you disturbed me 1
15 Saul answered, "I am in great distress; 1
20 Saul fell at once full length upon the ground 1
21 the woman came to Saul, and when she saw . . she said 1
25 put it before Saul and his servants; and they ate. 1
29: 3 this David, the servant of Saul, king of Israel 1
5 'Saul has slain his thousands 1
31: 2 And the Philistines overtook Saul and his sons; 1
2 and Abin'adab and Mal'chishu'a, the sons of Saul. 1
3 The battle pressed hard upon Saul 1
4 Saul said to his armor-bearer, "Draw your sword 1
4 Saul took his own sword, and fell upon it. 1
5 when his armor-bearer saw that Saul was dead 1
6 Saul died, and his three sons, and his armor-bearer 1
7 saw that . . and that Saul and his sons were dead 1
8 they found Saul and his three sons fallen 1
11 heard what the Philistines had done to Saul 1
12 took the body of Saul and the bodies of his sons 1
2Sm 1: 1 After the death of Saul, when David had returned 1
2 a man came from Saul's camp, with his clothes rent 1
4 and Saul and his son Jonathan are also dead. 1
5 How do you know that Saul and . . Jonathan are dead? 1
6 and there was Saul leaning upon his spear; 1
12 they mourned and . . for Saul and for Jonathan 1
17 David lamented . . over Saul and Jonathan his son 1
21 the mighty was defiled, the shield of Saul 1
22 and the sword of Saul returned not empty. 1
23 Saul and Jonathan, beloved and lovely! 1
24 Ye daughters of Israel, weep over Saul 1
2: 4 It was the men of Ja'besh-gil'ead who buried Saul 1
5 you showed this loyalty to Saul . . and buried him! 1
7 and be valiant; for Saul your lord is dead 1
8 Now Abner the son of Ner, commander of Saul's army 1
8 Abner . . had taken Ish-bo'sheth the son of Saul 1
10 Ish-bo'sheth, Saul's son, was 40 years old 1
12 and the servants of Ish-bo'sheth the son of Saul 1
15 for Benjamin and Ish-bo'sheth the son of Saul 1
3: 1 a long war between the house of Saul and . . David; 1
1 the house of Saul became weaker and weaker. 1
6 was war between the house of Saul and . . of David 1
6 Abner . . making himself strong in the house of Saul. 1
7 Now Saul had a concubine, whose name was Rizpah 1
8 showing loyalty to the house of Saul your father 1
10 to transfer the kingdom from the house of Saul 1
13 first bring Michal, Saul's daughter, when you come 1
14 David sent messengers to Ish-bo'sheth Saul's son 1
4: 1 Ish-bo'sheth, Saul's son, heard that Abner had died 1
2 Now Saul's son had two men who were captains 1
4 Jonathan, the son of Saul, had a son 1
4 news about Saul and Jonathan came from Jezreel; 1
8 Here is the head of Ish-bo'sheth, the son of Saul 1
8 avenged my lord . . on Saul and on his offspring. 1
10 when one told me, 'Behold, Saul is dead,' 1
5: 2 when Saul was king over us, it was you that led out 1
6:16 Michal the daughter of Saul looked out 1
20 Michal the daughter of Saul came . . to meet David 1
23 And Michal the daughter of Saul had no child 1
7:15 take my steadfast love . . as I took it from Saul 1
9: 1 Is there still any one left of the house of Saul 1
2 a servant of the house of Saul whose name was Ziba 1
3 Is there not still some one of the house of Saul 1
6 Mephib'osheth the son of Jonathan, son of Saul 1
7 I will restore . . all the land of Saul your father; 1
9 Then the king called Ziba, Saul's servant 1
9 All that belonged to Saul . . I have given 1
12: 7 and I delivered you out of the hand of Saul; 1
16: 5 came out a man of the family of the house of Saul 1
8 has avenged . . all the blood of the house of Saul 1
19:17 Ziba the servant of the house of Saul . . rushed 1
24 And Mephib'osheth the son of Saul came down 1
21: 1 There is bloodguilt on Saul and on his house 1
2 Saul had sought to slay them in his zeal 1
4 not a matter of . . between us and Saul or his house; 1
7 Mephib'osheth, the son of Saul's son Jonathan 1
7 between David and Jonathan the son of Saul. 1
8 the two sons of Rizpah . . whom she bore to Saul 1
8 and the five sons of Merab the daughter of Saul 1
11 Rizpah . . daughter of Ai'ah, the concubine of Saul 1
12 took the bones of Saul and the bones of his son 1
12 on the day the Philistines killed Saul on Gilbo'a; 1
13 and he brought up from there the bones of Saul 1
14 And they buried the bones of Saul and his son 1
22: 1 hand of all his enemies, and from the hand of Saul. 1
1Ch 5:10 in the days of Saul they made war on the Hagrites 1
8:33 Ner was the father of Kish, Kish of Saul 1
33 Saul of Jonathan, Mal'chishu'a, Abin'adab 1
9:39 father of Kish, Kish of Saul, Saul of Jonathan 1
39 Saul of Jonathan, Mal'chishu'a, Abin'adab 1
10: 2 the Philistines overtook Saul and his sons; 1
2 Jonathan . . and Mal'chishu'a, the sons of Saul. 1
3 The battle pressed hard upon Saul 1
4 Then Saul said to his armor-bearer 1
4 Saul took his own sword, and fell upon it. 1
5 when his armor-bearer saw that Saul was dead 1
6 Saul died; he and his three sons and all his house 1
7 saw . . that Saul and his sons were dead 1
8 found Saul and his sons fallen on Mount Gilbo'a. 1
11 heard all that the Philistines had done to Saul 1
12 took away the body of Saul and . . of his sons 1
13 Saul died for his unfaithfulness; 1
11: 2 In times past, even when Saul was king, it was you 1
12: 1 he could not move about freely because of Saul 1
2 they were Benjaminites, Saul's kinsmen. 1
19 the Philistines for the battle against Saul. 1
19 he will desert to his master Saul. 1
23 to turn the kingdom of Saul over to him 1
29 Of the Benjaminites, the kinsmen of Saul, 3,000 1
29 kept their allegiance to the house of Saul. 1
13: 3 for we neglected it in the days of Saul. 1
15:29 Michal the daughter of Saul looked out 1
26:28 all that Samuel the seer, and Saul the son of Kish 1
Ps 18: 0 hand of all his enemies, and from the hand of Saul. 1
52: 0 when Doeg, the Edomite, came and told Saul 1
54: 0 when the Ziphites went and told Saul 1
57: 0 of David, when he fled from Saul, in the cave. 1
59: 0 of David, when Saul sent men to watch his house 1
Isa 10:29 Ramah trembles, Gib'e-ah of Saul has fled. 1
Act 7:58 at the feet of a young man named Saul. 3
8: 1 Saul was consenting to his death 3
3 Saul was ravaging the church 3
9: 1 Saul, still breathing threats and murder 3
4 Saul, Saul, why do you persecute me? 2
4 Saul, Saul, why do you persecute me? 2
8 Saul arose from the ground 3
11 a man of Tarsus named Saul 3
17 laying his hands on him he said, "Brother Saul 2
22 Saul increased all the more in strength 3
24 their plot became known to Saul 3
11:25 Barnabas went to Tarsus to look for Saul; 3
30 by the hand of Barnabas and Saul. 3
12:25 Barnabas and Saul returned from Jerusalem 3
13: 1 Man'a-en . . and Saul. 3
2 Set apart for me Barnabas and Saul 3
7 who summoned Barnabas and Saul 3
9 Saul, who is also called Paul 3
21 Saul the son of Kish, a man of the tribe of Benjamin 2
22: 7 'Saul, Saul, why do you persecute me?' 2
7 'Saul, Saul, why do you persecute me?' 2
13 'Brother Saul, receive your sight.' 2
26:14 Saul, Saul, why do you persecute me? 2
14 Saul, Saul, why do you persecute me? 2
2Es 7:108 Samuel in the days of Saul ‡
1Mc 4:30 Jonathan, the son of Saul 2

Sceva 1. Σκευᾶς

Act 19:14 Seven sons of a Jewish high priest named Sceva 1

Schedia 1. Σχεδια

3Mc 4:11 men had been brought to the place called Schedia 1

Scythian 1. Σκύθης

Col 3:11 barbarian, Scyth'ian, slave, free man 1
2Mc 4:47 if they had pleaded even before Scythians. 1
3Mc 7: 5 a cruelty more savage than that of Scythian custom 1

scalp Scythian fashion 1. ἀποσκυθίζω

4Mc 10: 7 and scalped him . . in a Scythian fashion. 1

Scythopolis 1. Σκυθοπολιται 2. Σκυθῶν πόλις

Jdt 3:10 here he camped between Geba and Scythopolis 2
2Mc 12:29 they hastened to Scythopolis 2
30 which the people of Scythopolis had shown them 1

Seba 1. סְבָא

Gen 10: 7 sons of Cush: Seba, Hav'ilah, Sabtah, Ra'amah 1
1Ch 1: 9 sons of Cush: Seba, Hav'ilah, Sabta, Ra'ama 1
Ps 72:10 may the kings of Sheba and Seba bring gifts! 1
Isa 43: 3 Ethiopia and Seba in exchange for you. 1

Sebam 1. שְׂבָם

Num32: 3 Nimrah, Heshbon, Elea'leh, Sebam, Nebo, and Be'on 1

Secacah 1. סְכָכָה

Jos 15:61 In the wilderness, Beth-arabah, Middin, Seca'cah 1

Secu 1. שֶׂכוּ

1Sm 19:22 went to Ramah, and came to the great well . . in Secu; 1

Secundus 1. Σεκοῦνδος

Act 20: 4 of the Thessalo'nians, Aristar'chus and Secun'dus; 1

Segub 1. שְׂגוּב

1Kg 16:34 and set up its gates at the cost of . . Segub 1
1Ch 2:21 the daughter of Machir . . and she bore him Segub; 1
22 Segub was the father of Ja'ir 1

Seir 1. שֵׂעִיר

Gen 14: 6 the Horites in their Mount Se'ir 1
32: 3 in the land of Se'ir, the country of Edom 1
33:14 lead on slowly . . until I come to my lord in Se'ir. 1
16 Esau returned that day on his way to Se'ir. 1
36: 8 in the hill country of Se'ir; Esau is Edom. 1
9 the E'domites in the hill country of Se'ir. 1
20 These are the sons of Se'ir the Horite 1
21 the Horites, the sons of Se'ir in the land of Edom. 1
30 according to their clans in the land of Se'ir. 1
Num24:18 Se'ir also, his enemies, shall be dispossessed 1
Deu 1: 2 from Horeb by the way of Mount Se'ir 1
44 Amorites . . beat you down in Se'ir as far as Hormah. 1
2: 1 for many days we went about Mount Se'ir. 1
4 your brethren the sons of Esau, who live in Se'ir; 1
5 I have given Mount Se'ir to Esau as a possession. 1
8 our brethren the sons of Esau who live in Se'ir 1
12 The Horites also lived in Se'ir formerly 1
22 he did for the sons of Esau, who live in Se'ir 1
29 as the sons of Esau who live in Se'ir . . did for me 1
33: 2 LORD came from Sinai, and dawned from Se'ir 1
Jos 11:17 lowland from Mount Halak, that rises toward Se'ir 1
12: 7 Ba'al-gad . . to Mount Halak, that rises toward Se'ir 1
15:10 boundary circles west of Ba'alah to Mount Se'ir 1
24: 4 I gave Esau the hill country of Se'ir to possess 1
Jdg 5: 4 go forth from Se'ir . . from the region of Edom 1
1Ch 1:38 The sons of Se'ir: Lotan, Shobal, Zib'eon, Anah 1
4:42 some of them . . went to Mount Se'ir 1
2Ch 20:10 behold, the men of Ammon and Moab and Mount Se'ir 1
22 an ambush against the men of . . Mount Se'ir 1
23 rose against the inhabitants of Mount Se'ir 1
23 they had made an end of the inhabitants of Se'ir 1
25:11 to the Valley of Salt and smote 10,000 men of Se'ir. 1
14 he brought the gods of the men of Se'ir 1
Isa 21:11 One is calling to me from Se'ir 1
Ezk 35: 2 Son of man, set your face against Mount Se'ir 1
3 Behold, I am against you, mount Se'ir 1
7 I will make Mount Se'ir a waste and a desolation; 1
15 you shall be desolate, Mount Se'ir, and all Edom 1
Sir 50:26 Those who live on Mount Seir, and the Philistines 1

Seirah 1. שְׂעִירָה

Jdg 3:26 the sculptured stones, and escaped to Se-i'rah. 1

Sela 1. סֶלַע

Jdg 1:36 ran from the ascent of Akrab'bim, from Sela 1
2Kg 14: 7 He killed 10,000 E'domites . . and took Sela by storm 1
Isa 16: 1 sent lambs . . from Sela, by way of the desert 1
42:11 let the inhabitants of Sela sing for joy 1

Selah 1. סֶלָה

Ps 3: 2 saying of me, there is no help for him in God. Selah 1
4 he answers me from his holy hill. Selah 1
8 thy blessing be upon thy people! Selah 1
4: 2 love vain words, and seek after lies? Selah 1
4 your own hearts on your beds, and be silent. Selah 1
7: 5 lay my soul in the dust. Selah 1
9:16 in the work of their own hands. Higgaion. Selah 1
20 Let the nations know that they are but men! Selah 1
20: 3 regard with favor your burnt sacrifices! Selah 1
21: 2 hast not withheld the request of his lips. Selah 1
24: 6 who seek the face of the God of Jacob. Selah 1
10 The LORD of hosts, he is the King of glory! Selah 1
32: 4 dried up as by the heat of summer. Selah 1
5 thou didst forgive the guilt of my sin. Selah 1
7 thou dost encompass me with deliverance. Selah 1
39: 5 Surely every man stands as a mere breath! Selah 1
11 surely every man is a mere breath! Selah 1
44: 8 we will give thanks to thy name for ever. Selah 1
46: 3 the mountains tremble with its tumult. Selah 1
7 the God of Jacob is our refuge. Selah 1
11 the God of Jacob is our refuge. Selah 1
47: 4 for us, the pride of Jacob whom he loves. Selah 1
48: 8 which God establishes for ever. Selah 1
49:13 those who are pleased with their portion. Selah 1
15 for he will receive me. Selah 1
50: 6 for God himself is judge! Selah 1
52: 3 lying more than speaking the truth. Selah 1
5 uproot you from the land of the living. Selah 1
54: 3 they do not set God before them. Selah 1
55: 7 I would lodge in the wilderness, Selah 1
19 they keep no law, and do not fear God. Selah 1
57: 3 put to shame those who trample upon me. Selah 1
6 they have fallen into it themselves. Selah 1

59: 5 of those who treacherously plot evil. Selah 1
13 rules over Jacob to the ends of the earth. Selah 1
60: 4 to rally to it from the bow. Selah 1
61: 4 Oh to be safe under the shelter of thy wings! Selah 1
62: 4 They bless . . but inwardly they curse. Selah 1
8 God is a refuge for us. Selah 1
66: 4 praises to thee, sing praises to thy name." Selah 1
7 let not the rebellious exalt themselves. Selah 1
15 I will make an offering of bulls and goats. Selah 1
67: 1 and make his face to shine upon us, Selah 1
4 guide the nations upon earth. Selah 1
68: 7 thou didst march through the wilderness, Selah 1
19 Lord . . bears us up; God is our salvation. Selah 1
32 O kingdoms . . sing praises to the Lord, Selah 1
75: 3 it is I who keep steady its pillars. Selah 1
76: 3 the sword, and the weapons of war. Selah 1
9 to save all the oppressed of the earth. Selah 1
77: 3 I meditate, and my spirit faints. Selah 1
9 Has he in anger shut up his compassion?" Selah 1
15 thy people, the sons of Jacob and Joseph. Selah 1
81: 7 I tested you at the waters of Mer'ibah. Selah 1
82: 2 How long . . show partiality to the wicked? Selah 1
83: 8 are the strong arm of the children of Lot. Selah 1
84: 4 dwell in thy house, ever singing thy praise! Selah 1
8 give ear, O God of Jacob! Selah 1
85: 2 thou didst pardon all their sin. Selah 1
87: 3 Glorious things are spoken . . Selah 1
6 records . . "This one was born there." Selah 1
88: 7 thou dost overwhelm me with all thy waves. Selah 1
10 Do the shades rise up to praise thee? Selah 1
89: 4 build your throne for all generations.'" Selah 1
37 shall stand firm while the skies endure." Selah 1
45 thou hast covered him with shame. Selah 1
48 deliver his soul from the power of Sheol? Selah 1
140: 3 under their lips is the poison of vipers. Selah 1
5 by the wayside they have set snares for me. Selah 1
8 do not further his evil plot! Selah 1
143: 6 soul thirsts for thee like a parched land. Selah 1
Hab 3: 3 and the earth was full of his praise. Selah 1
9 and put the arrows to the string. Selah 1
13 laying him bare from thigh to neck. Selah 1

Seled 1. סֶלֶד
1Ch 2:30 sons of Nadab: Seled and Ap'pa-im; and Seled died 1
30 and Seled died childless. 1

Selemia 1. Selemia
2Es 14:24 with you Sarea, Dabria, Selemia, Ethanus, and Asiel- 1

Seleucia 1. Σελεύκεια
Act 13: 4 they went down to Seleu'cia 1
1Mc 11: 8 as far as Seleucia by the sea 1

Seleucus 1. Σελευκος
1Mc 7: 1 In the 151st year Demetrius the son of Seleucus 1
2Mc 3: 3 even Seleucus, the king of Asia 1
4: 7 When Seleucus died 1
5:18 whom Seleucus the king sent 1
14: 1 Demetrius, the son of Seleucus 1
4Mc 3:20 even Seleucus Nicanor, king of Asia 1
4: 3 belong to King Seleucus. 1
4 and went up to Seleucus to inform him 1
13 lest King Seleucus suppose 1
15 When King Seleucus died 1

Semachiah 1. סְמַכְיָהוּ
1Ch 26: 7 brethren were able men, Eli'hu and Semachi'ah. 1

Semein 1. Σεμεΐν
Lke 3:26 the son of Sem'ein, the son of Josech, the son of Joda 1

Senaah 1. סְנָאָה 2. Σαναας
Ezr 2:35 sons of Sena'ah, 3,630. 1
Neh 7:38 sons of Sena'ah, 3,930. 1
1Es 5:23 The sons of Senaah, 3,330. 2

Seneh 1. סֶנֶּה
1Sm 14: 4 the one was Bozez, and the name of the other Seneh. 1

Senir 1. שְׂנִיר
Deu 3: 9 Si'rion, while the Amorites call it Senir) 1
1Ch 5:23 were very numerous from Bashan to . . Senir 1
Sng 4: 8 Depart from . . from the peak of Senir and Hermon 1
Ezk 27: 5 They made all your planks of fir trees from Senir; 1

Sennacherib 1. סַנְחֵרִיב 2. Σενναχηριμ 3. Sennacherib
2Kg 18:13 Sennach'erib king of Assyria came up against all 1
19:16 hear the words of Sennach'erib, which he has sent 1
20 prayer to me about Sennach'erib king of Assyria 1
36 Sennach'erib king of Assyria departed, and went 1
2Ch 32: 1 Sennach'erib king of Assyria came and invaded 1
2 Sennach'erib had come and intended to fight 1
9 After this Sennach'erib king of Assyria 1
10 Thus says Sennach'erib king of Assyria 1
22 LORD saved . . from the hand of Sennach'erib 1
Isa 36: 1 Sennach'erib king of Assyria came up against all 1
37:17 hear all the words of Sennach'erib 1
21 you have prayed to me concerning Sennach'erib 1
37 Then Sennach'erib king of Assyria departed 1
2Es 7:110 for the people in the days of Sennacherib 3
Tob 1:15 Sennacherib his son reigned in his place 2
18 if Sennacherib the king put to death 2
21 before two of Sennacherib's sons killed him *
Sir 48:18 In his days Sennacherib came up 2
2Mc 8:19 both the time of Sennacherib 2
15:22 slew . . 185,000 in the camp of Sennacherib. 2
3Mc 6: 5 Sennacherib exulting in his countless forces 2

Seorim 1. שְׂעֹרִים
1Ch 24: 8 the third to Harim, the fourth to Se-o'rim 1

Sephar 1. סְפָר
Gen 10:30 extended from Mesha in the direction of Sephar 1

Sepharad 1. סְפָרַד
Obd 1:20 the exiles of Jerusalem who are in Sephar'ad 1

Sepharvaim 1. סְפַרְוַיִם
2Kg 17:24 brought people from . . Hamath, and Sephar-va'im 1
31 and Anam'melech, the gods of Sephar-va'im. 1
18:34 Where are the gods of Sepharva'im, Hena, and Ivvah? 1
19:13 king of Arpad, the king of the city of Sepharva'im 1
Isa 36:19 Where are the gods of Sepharva'im? 1
37:13 king of Arpad, the king of the city of Sepharva'im 1

Sepharvite 1. סְפַרְוִי
2Kg 17:31 and the Sephar'vites burned their children 1

Serah 1. שֶׂרַח
Gen 46:17 Ishvi, Beri'ah, with Serah their sister. 1
Num26:46 the name of the daughter of Asher was Serah. 1
1Ch 7:30 sons of Asher . . Beri'ah, and their sister Serah. 1

Seraiah 1. שְׂרָיָה 2. Σαραιας 3. Sarei
2Sm 8:17 Serai'ah was secretary; 1
2Kg 25:18 the captain . . took Serai'ah the chief priest 1
23 Serai'ah the son of Tanhu'meth the Netoph'athite 1
1Ch 4:13 The sons of Kenaz: Oth'ni-el and Serai'ah; 1
14 Serai'ah was the father of Jo'ab 1
35 the son of Joshibi'ah, son of Serai'ah, son of As'i-el 1
6:14 Azari'ah of Serai'ah, Serai'ah of Jehoz'adak; 1
14 Azari'ah of Serai'ah, Serai'ah of Jehoz'adak; 1
Ezr 2: 2 came with . . Serai'ah, Re-el-ai'ah, Mor'decai 1
7: 1 Ezra the son of Serai'ah, son of Azari'ah 1
Neh 10: 2 Serai'ah, Azari'ah, Jeremiah 1
11:11 Serai'ah the son of Hilki'ah, son of Meshul'lam 1
12: 1 priests and the Levites . . Serai'ah, Jeremiah, Ezra 1
12 heads of fathers' houses: of Serai'ah, Merai'ah; 1
Jer 36:26 the king commanded . . Serai'ah the son of Az'ri-el 1
40: 8 Serai'ah the son of Tanhu'meth 1
51:59 the prophet commanded Serai'ah the son of Neri'ah 1
59 Serai'ah was the quartermaster. 1
61 And Jeremiah said to Serai'ah 1
52:24 the guard took Serai'ah the chief priest 1
1Es 5: 5 Jeshua the son of Jozadak, son of Seraiah 2
8 Nehemiah, Seraiah, Resaiah, Bigvai, Mordecai 2
8: 1 Ezra came, the son of Seraiah, son of Azariah 2
2Es 1: 1 the son of Seraiah, son of Azariah, son of Hilkiah 3

Sered 1. סֶרֶד
Gen 46:14 The sons of Zeb'ulun: Sered, Elon, and Jah'leel 1
Num26:26 of Sered, the family of the Ser'edites; 1

Seredite 1. סַרְדִּי
Num26:26 of Sered, the family of the Ser'edites; 1

Sergius 1. Σέργιος
Act 13: 7 He was with the Proconsul, Sergius Paulus 1

Seron 1. Σηρων
1Mc 3:13 Seron, the commander of the Syrian army, heard 1
23 he rushed suddenly against Seron and his army 1

Serug 1. שְׂרוּג 2. Σερούχ
Gen 11:20 Re'u . . became the father of Serug; 1
21 Re'u lived after the birth of Serug 207 years 1
22 When Serug had lived 30 years 1
23 Serug lived after the birth of Nahor 200 years 1
1Ch 1:26 Serug, Nahor, Terah; 1
Lke 3:35 the son of Serug, the son of Re'u, the son of Peleg 2

Sesthel 1. Σεσθηλ
1Es 9:31 Bescaspasmys and Sesthel, and Belnuus 1

Seth 1. שֵׁת 2. Σήθ
Gen 4:25 she bore a son and called his name Seth 1
26 To Seth also a son was born 1
5: 3 a son . . after his image, and named him Seth. 1
4 after he became the father of Seth 1
6 When Seth had lived 105 years 1
7 Seth lived after the birth of Enosh 807 years 1
8 Thus all the days of Seth were 912 years; 1
1Ch 1: 1 Adam, Seth, Enosh; 1
Lke 3:38 the son of Enos, the son of Seth, the son of Adam 2
Sir 49:16 Shem and Seth were honored among men 2

Sethur 1. סְתוּר
Num13:13 from the tribe of Asher, Sethur the son of Michael; 1

Shaalabbin 1. שַׁעַלַבִּין
Jos 19:42 Sha-alab'bin, Ai'jalon, Ithlah 1

Shaalbim 1. שַׁעַלְבִים
Jdg 1:35 dwelling . . in Ai'jalon, and in Shaal'bim 1
1Kg 4: 9 Shaal'bim, Beth-she'mesh, and E'lonbeth-ha'nan; 1

Shaalbon 1. שַׁעַלְבֹנִי
2Sm 23:32 Eli'ahba of Sha-al'bon, the sons of Jashen, Jonathan 1
1Ch 11:33 Az'maveth of Baha'rum, Eli'ahba of Sha-al'bon 1

Shaalim 1. שַׁעֲלִים
1Sm 9: 4 they passed through the land of Sha'alim 1

Shaaph 1. שַׁעַף
1Ch 2:47 sons of Jah'dai . . Pelet, Ephah, and Sha'aph. 1
49 She also bore Sha'aph the father of Madman'nah 1

Shaaraim 1. שַׁעֲרַיִם
Jos 15:36 Shaara'im, Aditha'im, Gede'rah, Gederotha'im 1
1Sm 17:52 on the way from Sha-ara'im as far as Gath and Ekron. 1
1Ch 4:31 Ha'zar-su'sim, Beth-biri, and Sha-ara'im. 1

Shaashgaz 1. שַׁעַשְׁגַז
Est 2:14 to the second harem in custody of Sha-ash'gaz 1

Shabbethai 1. שַׁבְּתַי 2. Σαββαταιος
Ezr 10:15 Meshul'lam and Shab'bethai the Levite supported 1
Neh 8: 7 Also . . Akkub, Shab'bethai, Hodi'ah, Ma-asei'ah 1
11:16 Shab'bethai and Jo'zabad, of the chiefs 1
1Es 9:14 Meshullam and Levi and Shabbethai 2
48 Sherebiah, Jamin, Akkub, Shabbethai, Hodiah 2

Shadrach 1. שַׁדְרַךְ 2. שַׁדְרַךְ (A)
Dan 1: 7 Hanani'ah he called Shadrach 1
2:49 appointed Shadrach, Meshach, and Abed'nego 2
3:12 Shadrach, Meshach, and Abed'nego. These men 2
13 commanded that Shadrach, Meshach, and Abed'nego 2
14 Is it true, O Shadrach, Meshach, and Abed'nego 2
16 Shadrach, Meshach, and Abed'nego answered 2
19 against Shadrach, Meshach, and Abed'nego. 2
20 bind Shadrach, Meshach, and Abed'nego, and to cast 2
22 men who took up Shadrach, Meshach, and Abed'nego. 2
23 these three men, Shadrach, Meshach, and Abed'nego 2
26 Shadrach, Meshach, and Abed'nego, servants 2
26 Then Shadrach, Meshach, and Abed'nego came out 2
28 Blessed be the God of Shadrach, Meshach 2
29 God of Shadrach, Meshach, and Abed'nego 2
30 king promoted Shadrach, Meshach, and Abed'nego 2

Shagee 1. שָׁגֵה
1Ch 11:34 Jonathan the son of Shagee the Har'arite 1

Shaharaim 1. שַׁחֲרַיִם
1Ch 8: 8 Shahara'im had sons in the country of Moab 1

Shahazumah 1. שַׁחֲצוּמָה
Jos 19:22 touches Tabor, Shahazu'mah, and Beth-she'mesh 1

Shalishah 1. שָׁלִשָׁה
1Sm 9: 4 and passed through the land of Shal'ishah 1

Shallecheth 1. שַׁלֶּכֶת
1Ch 26:16 the gate of Shal'lecheth on the road that goes up. 1

Shallum 1. שַׁלּוּם 2. Σαλωμ 3. Σελλουμ 4. Salame
2Kg 15:10 Shallum the son of Jabesh conspired against him 1
13 Shallum the son of Jabesh began to reign 1
14 and he struck down Shallum the son of Jabesh 1
15 Now the rest of the deeds of Shallum 1
22:14 Huldah . . the wife of Shallum the son of Tikvah 1
1Ch 2:40 the father of Sismai, and Sismai of Shallum. 1
41 Shallum . . father of Jekami'ah, and Jekami'ah 1
3:15 sons of Josi'ah . . the fourth Shallum. 1
4:25 Shallum was his son, Mibsam his son 1
6:12 Ahi'tub of Zadok, Zadok of Shallum 1
13 Shallum of Hilki'ah, Hilki'ah of Azari'ah 1
7:13 sons of Naph'tali: Jah'zi-el, Guni, Jezer, and Shallum 1
9:17 gatekeepers . . Shallum, Akkub, Talmon, Ahi'man 1
17 Shallum being the chief 1
19 Shallum the son of Ko're, son of Ebi'asaph 1
31 Mattithi'ah . . the first-born of Shallum 1
2Ch 28:12 chiefs . . Jehizki'ah the son of Shallum 1
34:22 Huldah the . . wife of Shallum the son of Tokhath 1
Ezr 2:42 sons of the gatekeepers: the sons of Shallum 1
7: 2 son of Shallum, son of Za-dok, son of Ahi'tub 1
10:24 Of the gatekeepers: Shallum, Telem, and Uri. 1
42 Shallum, Amari'ah, and Joseph. 1
Neh 3:12 Next to him Shallum the son of Hallo'hesh 1
15 Shallum the son of Colho'zeh, ruler 1
7:45 gatekeepers: the sons of Shallum, the sons of Ater 1
Jer 22:11 For thus says the LORD concerning Shallum 1
32: 7 Behold, Han'amel the son of Shallum your uncle 1
35: 4 above the chamber of Ma-asei'ah the son of Shallum 1
1Es 5:28 The gatekeepers: the sons of Shallum 3

8: 1 son of Azariah, son of Hilkiah, son of Shallum 3
9:25 Of the gatekeepers: Shallum and Telem. 3
2Es 1: 1 son of Hilkiah, son of Shallum, son of Zadok 4
Bar 1: 7 Jehoiakim . . the son of Hilkiah, son of Shallum 2

Shalmai 1. שַׁלְמַי
Neh 7:48 Leba'na, the sons of Hag'aba, the sons of Shalmai 1

Shalman 1. שַׁלְמַן
Hos 10:14 as Shalman destroyed Beth-ar'bel 1

Shalmaneser 1. שַׁלְמַנְאֶסֶר 2. Ενεμεσσαρος
3. Salmanassar
2Kg 17: 3 Against him came up Shalmane'ser king of Assyria; 1
18: 9 Shalmane'ser . . came up against Sama'ria 1
2Es 13:40 Shalmaneser the king of the Assyrians 3
Tob 1: 2 days of Shalmaneser, king of the Assyrians 2
13 and good appearance in the sight of Shalmaneser 2
15 when Shalmaneser died 2
16 In the days of Shalmaneser 2

Shama 1. שָׁמָע
1Ch 11:44 Shama and Je-i'el the sons of Hotham the Aro'erite 1

Shamgar 1. שַׁמְגַּר
Jdg 3:31 After him was Shamgar the son of Anath, who killed 1
5: 6 In the days of Shamgar, son of Anath, in the days 1

Shamhuth 1. שַׁמְהוּת
1Ch 27: 8 fifth commander . . was Shamhuth, the Iz'rahite; 1

Shamir 1. שָׁמִיר
Jos 15:48 And in the hill country, Shamir, Jattir, Socoh 1
Jdg 10: 1 lived at Shamir in the hill country of E'phraim. 1
2 Then he died, and was buried at Shamir. 1
1Ch 24:24 sons of Uz'ziel, Micah; of the sons of Micah, Shamir. 1

Shamlai 1. שַׁמְלַי 2. Συβαι
Ezr 2:46 sons of Hagab, the sons of Shamlai 1
1Es 5:30 sons of Hagab, the sons of Shamlai, the sons of Hana 2

Shamma 1. שַׁמָּא
1Ch 7:37 Bezer, Hod, Shamma, Shilshah, Ithran, and Be-e'ra. 1

Shammah 1. שַׁמָּה
Gen 36:13 of Reu'el: Nahath, Zerah, Shammah, and Mizzah. 1
17 the chiefs Nahath, Zerah, Shammah, and Mizzah; 1
1Sm 16: 9 Then Jesse made Shammah pass by. 1
17:13 and next to him Abin'adab, and the third Shammah. 1
2Sm 23:11 And next to him was Shammah, the son of Agee 1
25 Shammah of Harod, Eli'ka of Harod 1
33 Shammah the Har'arite, Ahi'am the son of Sharar 1
1Ch 1:37 The sons of Reu'el . . Zerah, Shammah, and Mizzah. 1

Shammai 1. שַׁמַּי
1Ch 2:28 The sons of Onam: Sham'mai and Jada. 1
28 The sons of Sham'mai: Nadab and Abi'shur. 1
32 sons of Jada, Sham'mai's brother: Jether 1
44 and Rekem was the father of Sham'mai. 1
45 The son of Sham'mai: Ma'on; 1
4:17 Bith'i-ah . . conceived and bore Miriam, Sham'mai 1

Shammoth 1. שַׁמּוֹת
1Ch 11:27 Shammoth of Harod, Helez the Pel'onite 1

Shammua 1. שַׁמּוּעַ
Num13: 4 From the tribe of Reuben, Sham'mu-a . . of Zaccur; 1
2Sm 5:14 born to him . . Sham'mu-a, Shobab, Nathan, Solomon 1
1Ch 14: 4 the children . . Shammu'a, Shobab, Nathan, Solomon 1
Neh 11:17 Abda the son of Sham'mua, son of Galal 1
12:18 of Bilgah, Sham'mu-a; of Shemai'ah, Jehon'athan; 1

Shamsherai 1. שַׁמְשְׁרַי
1Ch 8:26 Sham'sherai, Shehari'ah, Athali'ah 1

Shapham 1. שָׁפָם
1Ch 5:12 Jo'el . . Shapham the second, Ja'nai, and Shaphat 1

Shaphan 1. שָׁפָן
2Kg 22: 3 the king sent Shaphan . . to the house of the LORD 1
8 And Hilki'ah . . said to Shaphan the secretary 1
8 Hilki'ah gave the book to Shaphan, and he read it. 1
9 And Shaphan the secretary came to the king 1
10 Then Shaphan the secretary told the king 1
10 And Shaphan read it before the king. 1
12 Hilki'ah the priest, and Ahi'kam the son of Shaphan 1
12 Achbor the son of . . and Shaphan the secretary 1
14 and Ahi'kam, and Achbor, and Shaphan, and Asai'ah 1
25:22 Gedali'ah the son of Ahi'kam, son of Shaphan 1
2Ch 34: 8 sent Shaphan the son of Azali'ah, and Ma-asei'ah 1
15 Then Hilki'ah said to Shaphan the secretary 1
15 Hilki'ah gave the book to Shaphan. 1
16 Shaphan brought the book to the king 1
18 Then Shaphan the secretary told the king 1
18 Shaphan read it before the king. 1
20 king commanded . . Ahi'kam the son of Shaphan 1
20 king commanded . . Shaphan the secretary 1
Jer 26:24 the hand of Ahi'kam the son of Shaphan 1
29: 3 was sent by the hand of Ela'sah the son of Shaphan 1
36:10 of Gemari'ah the son of Shaphan the secretary 1
11 When Micai'ah the son of Gemari'ah, son of Shaphan 1
12 Gemari'ah the son of Shaphan 1
39:14 Gedali'ah the son of Ahi'kam, son of Shaphan 1
40: 5 Gedali'ah the son of Ahi'kam, son of Shaphan 1
9 Gedali'ah the son of Ahi'kam, son of Shaphan, swore 1
11 Gedali'ah the son of Ahi'kam, son of Shaphan 1
41: 2 Gedali'ah the son of Ahi'kam, son of Shaphan 1
43: 6 Gedali'ah the son of Ahi'kam, son of Shaphan; 1
Ezk 8:11 with Ja-azani'ah the son of Shaphan standing among 1

Shaphat 1. שָׁפָט 2. Σαφατ
Num13: 5 from the tribe of Simeon, Shaphat the son of Hori; 1
1Kg 19:16 Eli'sha the son of Shaphat of A'bel-meho'lah 1
19 departed . . and found Eli'sha the son of Shaphat 1
2Kg 3:11 Eli'sha the son of Shaphat is here 1
6:31 if the head of Eli'sha the son of Shaphat remains 1
1Ch 3:22 sons of Shemai'ah . . Neari'ah and Shaphat, six. 1
5:12 Jo'el . . Shapham . . Ja'nai, and Shaphat in Bashan. 1
27:29 in the valleys was Shaphat the son of Adlai. 1
1Es 5:34 the sons of Shaphat, the sons of Ami. 2

Shaphir 1. שָׁפִיר
Mic 1:11 Pass on your way, inhabitants of Shaphir 1

Sharai 1. שָׁרַי
Ezr 10:40 Machnad'ebai, Shashai, Sha'rai 1

Sharar 1. שָׁרָר
2Sm 23:33 Shammah . . Ahi'am the son of Sharar the Har'arite 1

Sharezer 1. שַׂרְאֶצֶר
2Kg 19:37 Adram'melech and Share'zer, his sons, slew him 1
Isa 37:38 Adram'melech and Share'zer, his sons, slew him 1
Zec 7: 2 Now the people of Bethel had sent Share'zer 1

Sharon 1. שָׁרוֹן 2. Σαρων
1Ch 5:16 in all the pasture lands of Sharon to their limits 1
27:29 Over the herds that pastured in Sharon was 1
Sng 2: 1 I am a rose of Sharon, a lily of the valleys. 1
Isa 33: 9 Sharon is like a desert; 1
35: 2 the majesty of Carmel and Sharon. 1
65:10 Sharon shall become a pasture for flocks 1
Act 9:35 all the residents of Lydda and Sharon saw him 2

Sharonite 1. שָׁרוֹנִי
1Ch 27:29 pastured in Sharon was Shitrai the Shar'onite; 1

Sharuhen 1. שָׁרוּחֶן
Jos 19: 6 Beth-leba'oth, and Sharu'hen 1

Shashai 1. שָׁשַׁי 2. Σεσσις
Ezr 10:40 Machnad'ebai, Shashai, Sha'rai 1
1Es 9:34 Of the sons of Ezora: Shashai, Azarel, Azael 2

Shashak 1. שָׁשָׁק
1Ch 8:14 Ahi'o, Shashak, and Jer'emoth. 1
25 Iphdei'ah, and Penu'el were the sons of Shashak. 1

Shaul 1. שָׁאוּל
Gen 36:37 Samlah died, and Shaul of Reho'both 1
38 Shaul died, and Ba'al-ha'nan the son of Achbor 1
46:10 and Shaul, the son of a Canaanitish woman. 1
Exd 6:15 Zohar, and Shaul, the son of a Canaanite woman; 1
Num26:13 of Sha'ul, the family of the Sha'ulites. 1
1Ch 1:48 Sha'ul of Reho'both on the Euphra'tes reigned 1
49 When Sha'ul died, Ba'al-ha'nan, the son of Achbor 1
4:24 sons of Simeon: Nem'uel, Jamin, Jarib, Zerah, Sha'ul; 1
6:24 Uri'el his son, Uzzi'ah his son, and Sha'ul his son. 1

Shaulite 1. שָׁאוּלִי
Num26:13 of Sha'ul, the family of the Sha'ulites. 1

Shaveh 1. שָׁוֵה
Gen 14:17 meet him at the Valley of Shaveh 1

Shaveh-kiriathaim 1. שָׁוֵה קִרְיָתָיִם
Gen 14: 5 Zuzim in Ham, the Emim in Sha'veh-kiriatha'im 1

Shavsha 1. שַׁוְשָׁא
1Ch 18:16 and Shavsha was secretary; 1

Sheal 1. שְׁאָל 2. Ασαηλος
Ezr 10:29 of Bani were . . Jashub, She'al, and Jer'emoth. 1
1Es 9:30 Adaiah, Jashub, and Sheal and Jeremoth. 2

Shealtiel 1. שְׁאַלְתִּיאֵל 2. שַׁלְתִּיאֵל 3. שְׁאַלְתִּיאֵל (A)
4. Σαλαθιηλ
1Ch 3:17 sons of Jeconi'ah, the captive: Sheal'tiel his son 1
Ezr 3: 2 arose . . Zerub'babel the son of She-al'ti-el 1
8 Zerub'babel the son of She-al'ti-el and Jeshua 1
5: 2 Then Zerub'babel the son of She-al'ti-el and Jeshua 3
Neh 12: 1 who came up with Zerub'babel the son of She-al'ti-el 1
Hag 1: 1 to Zerub'babel the son of She-al'ti-el, governor 1
12 Then Zerub'babel the son of She-al'ti-el 2
14 spirit of Zerub'babel the son of She-al'ti-el 2
2: 2 Speak now to Zerub'babel the son of She-al'ti-el 2
23 O Zerub'babel my servant, the son of She-al'ti-el 1
Mat 1:12 Jechoni'ah was the father of She-al'ti-el •
12 and She-al'ti-el the father of Zerub'babel •
Lke 3:27 the son of Zerub'babel, the son of She-al'ti-el •
1Es 5: 5 Joakim the son of Zerubbabel, son of Shealtiel 4
48 Zerubbabel the son of Shealtiel 4
56 Zerubbabel the son of Shealtiel 4
6: 2 Zerubbabel the son of Shealtiel 4

Shear-jashub 1. שְׁאָר יָשׁוּב
Isa 7: 3 to Isaiah . . you and She'ar-jash'ub your son 1

Sheariah 1. שְׁעַרְיָה
1Ch 8:38 Azel had six sons . . She-ari'ah, Obadi'ah 1
9:44 Azel had six sons . . She-ari'ah, Obadi'ah 1

Sheba 1. שְׁבָא 2. שֶׁבַע
Gen 10: 7 The sons of Ra'amah: Sheba and Dedan. 1
28 Obal, Abim'a-el, Sheba 1
25: 3 Jokshan was the father of Sheba and Dedan. 1
Jos 19: 2 for its inheritance Beer-sheba, Sheba, Mola'dah 2
2Sm 20: 1 a . . fellow, whose name was Sheba, the son of Bichri 2
2 men of Israel . . followed Sheba the son of Bichri; 2
6 Now Sheba . . will do us more harm than Ab'salom; 2
7 they went out . . to pursue Sheba the son of Bichri. 2
10 Then Jo'ab and Abi'shai his brother pursued Sheba 2
13 all the people went on after Jo'ab to pursue Sheba 2
14 Sheba passed through all the tribes of Israel •
21 a man of . . E'phraim, called Sheba the son of Bichri 2
22 they cut off the head of Sheba the son of Bichri 2
1Kg 10: 1 the queen of Sheba heard of the fame of Solomon 1
4 when the queen of Sheba had seen all the wisdom 1
10 which the queen of Sheba gave to King Solomon. 1
13 King Solomon gave to the queen of Sheba 1
1Ch 1: 9 The sons of Ra'amah: Sheba and Dedan. 1
22 Ebal, Abim'a-el, Sheba 1
32 Shu'ah. The sons of Jokshan: Sheba and Dedan. 1
5:13 Michael, Meshul'lam, Sheba, Jo'rai, Jacan, Zi'a 2
2Ch 9: 1 the queen of Sheba heard of the fame of Solomon 1
3 queen of Sheba had seen the wisdom of Solomon 1
9 which the queen of Sheba gave to King Solomon. 1
12 King Solomon gave to the queen of Sheba 1
Job 6:19 of Tema look, the travelers of Sheba hope. 1
Ps 72:10 may the kings of Sheba and Seba bring gifts! 1
15 Long may he live, may gold of Sheba be given to him! 1
Isa 60: 6 all those from Sheba shall come. 1
Jer 6:20 does frankincense come to me from Sheba 1
Ezk 27:22 The traders of Sheba and Ra'amah traded with you; 1
38:13 Sheba and Dedan and the merchants of Tarshish 1

Shebaniah 1. שְׁבַנְיָהוּ
1Ch 15:24 Shebani'ah, Josh'aphat, Nethan'el, Ama'sai 1
Neh 9: 4 stood Jeshua, Bani, Kad'mi-el, Shebani'ah, Bunni 1
5 Levites . . Shebani'ah, and Pethahi'ah, said, "Stand 1
10: 4 Hattush, Shebani'ah, Malluch 1
10 their brethren, Shebani'ah, Hodi'ah, Keli'ta 1
12 Zaccur, Sherebi'ah, Shebani'ah 1
12:14 of Mal'luchi, Jonathan; of Shebani'ah, Joseph; 1

Shebarim 1. שְׁבָרִים
Jos 7: 5 chased them before the gate as far as Sheb'arim 1

Shebat 1. שְׁבָט 2. Σαβατ
Zec 1: 7 the eleventh month which is the month of Shebat 1
1Mc 16:14 in the eleventh month, which is the month of Shebat 2

Sheber 1. שֶׁבֶר
1Ch 2:48 Ma'acah . . bore Sheber and Tir'hanah. 1

Shebna 1. שֶׁבְנָא
2Kg 18:37 Eli'akim . . and Shebna the secretary, and Jo'ah 1
19: 2 he sent Eli'akim . . and Shebna the secretary 1
Isa 22:15 this steward, to Shebna, who is over the household 1
36: 3 Shebna the secretary, and Jo'ah the son of Asaph 1
11 Eli'akim, Shebna, and Jo'ah said to the Rab'shakeh 1
22 Shebna the secretary, and Jo'ah the son of Asaph 1
37: 2 and Shebna the secretary, and the senior priests 1

Shebnah 1. שֶׁבְנָה
2Kg 18:18 there came out . . and Shebnah the secretary 1
26 Then Eli'akim . . and Shebnah, and Jo'ah, said 1

Shebuel 1. שְׁבוּאֵל
1Ch 23:16 The sons of Gershom: Sheb'uel the chief. 1
25: 4 sons of Heman . . Shebu'el, and Jer'imoth, Hanani'ah 1
26:24 Sheb'uel . . was chief officer in charge 1

Shecaniah 1. שְׁכַנְיָהוּ שְׁכַנְיָה 2. Σεχενιας
1Ch 3:21 sons of Hanani'ah . . Obadi'ah, his son Shecani'ah. 1
22 The sons of Shecani'ah: Shemai'ah. 1
24:11 the ninth to Jeshua, the tenth to Shecani'ah 1
2Ch 31:15 Jeshua, Shemai'ah, Amari'ah, and Shecani'ah 1
Ezr 8: 3 of the sons of Shecani'ah. 1
5 Shecani'ah the son of Jaha'ziel 1
10: 2 Shecani'ah the son of Jehi'el, of the sons of Elam 1
Neh 3:29 Shemai'ah the son of Shecani'ah . . repaired. 1
6:18 son-in-law of Shecani'ah the son of Arah 1
12: 3 Shecani'ah, Rehum, Mer'emoth. 1
1Es 8:29 Hattush the son of Shecaniah. 2

32 Shecaniah the son of Jahaziel 2
92 Shecaniah the son of Jehiel 2

Shechem 1. בְּנֵי שְׁכֶם 2. שְׁכֶם 3. שְׁכֶם 4. Σικιμα 5. Συχέμ

Gen 12: 6 to the place at Shechem, to the oak of Moreh. 2
33:18 Jacob came safely to the city of Shechem 2
19 from the sons of Hamor, Shechem's father 2
34: 2 when Shechem the son of Hamor the Hivite 2
4 Shechem spoke to his father Hamor, saying 2
6 Hamor the father of Shechem went out to Jacob 2
8 The soul of my son Shechem longs 2
11 Shechem also said to her father 2
13 The sons of Jacob answered Shechem 2
18 words pleased Hamor and Hamor's son Shechem. 2
20 Hamor and his son Shechem came to the gate 2
24 all . . hearkened to Hamor and his son Shechem; 2
26 They slew Hamor and his son Shechem 2
26 took Dinah out of Shechem's house, and went away. 2
35: 4 hid them under the oak which was near Shechem. 2
37:12 to pasture their father's flock near Shechem. 2
13 your brothers pasturing the flock at Shechem? 2
14 from the valley of Hebron, and he came to Shechem. 2
Num26:31 of Shechem, the family of the She'chemites; 3
Jos 17: 2 Helek, As'ri-el, Shechem, Hepher, and Shemi'da 1
7 Asher to Mich-me'thath, which is east of Shechem; 2
20: 7 set apart . . and Shechem in the hill country 2
21:21 To them were given Shechem, the city of refuge 2
24: 1 Then Joshua gathered all . . Israel to Shechem 2
25 and made statutes . . for them at Shechem. 2
32 The bones of Joseph . . were buried at Shechem 2
32 from the sons of Hamor the father of Shechem 2
Jdg 8:31 his concubine who was in Shechem also bore him 2
9: 1 Abim'elech . . went to Shechem to his mother's 2
2 Say in the ears of all the citizens of Shechem 2
3 words . . in the ears of all the men of Shechem; 2
6 all the citizens of Shechem came together 2
6 made . . king, by the oak of the pillar at Shechem. 2
7 Listen to me, you men of Shechem, that God may 2
18 Abim'elech . . king over the citizens of Shechem 2
20 let fire . . devour the citizens of Shechem 2
20 let fire come out from the citizens of Shechem 2
23 spirit between Abim'elech and the men of Shechem; 2
23 and the men of Shechem dealt treacherously 2
24 blood be laid . . upon the men of Shechem 2
25 the men of Shechem put men in ambush against him 2
26 Ga'al . . moved into Shechem with his kinsmen; 2
26 and the men of Shechem put confidence in him. 2
28 Who is Abim'elech, and who are we of Shechem 2
28 serve the men of Hamor the father of Shechem? 2
31 Ga'al . . and his kinsmen have come to Shechem 2
34 rose up . . and laid wait against Shechem in four 2
39 Ga'al went out at the head of the men of Shechem 2
41 so that they could not live on at Shechem. 2
46 the people of the Tower of Shechem heard of it 2
47 told that all the people of the Tower of Shechem 2
49 all the people of the Tower of Shechem also died 2
57 all the wickedness of the men of Shechem 2
21:19 the highway that goes up from Bethel to Shechem 2
1Kg 12: 1 Rehobo'am went to Shechem, for all Israel had come 2
1 all Israel had come to Shechem to make him king. 2
25 Jerobo'am built Shechem in the hill country 2
1Ch 6:67 cities of refuge: Shechem with its pasture lands 2
7:19 sons of Shemi'da were Ahi'an, Shechem, Likhi 3
28 westward Gezer . . Shechem and its towns 2
2Ch 10: 1 Rehobo'am went to Shechem 2
1 all Israel had come to Shechem to make him king. 2
Ps 60: 6 With exultation I will divide up Shechem 2
108: 7 With exultation I will divide up Shechem 2
Jer 41: 5 80 men arrived from Shechem and Shiloh 2
Hos 6: 9 they murder on the way to Shechem 2
Act 7:16 they were carried back to Shechem 5
16 bought . . from the sons of Hamor in Shechem. 5
Sir 50:26 the foolish people that dwell in Shechem. 4

Shechemite 1. שִׁכְמִי 2. Σικιμιται 3. Συχέμ

Num26:31 of Shechem, the family of the She'chemites; 1
Jdt 5:16 the Jebusites and the Shechemites 3
4Mc 2:19 the entire tribe of the Shechemites 2

Shedeur 1. שְׁדֵיאוּר

Num 1: 5 From Reuben, Eli'zur the son of Shed'eur; 1
2:10 the leader . . Eli'zur the son of Shed'eur 1
7:30 Eli'zur the son of Shed'eur, the leader of the men 1
35 was the offering of Eli'zur the son of Shed'eur. 1
10:18 over their host was Eli'zur the son of Shed'eur. 1

Sheep Gate 1. שַׁעַר הַצֹּאן 2. προβατικός

Neh 3: 1 rose up . . and they built the Sheep Gate. 1
32 between the upper chamber . . and the Sheep Gate 1
12:39 above the Gate of E'phraim . . to the Sheep Gate; 1
Joh 5: 2 Now there is in Jerusalem by the Sheep Gate a pool 2

Sheerah 1. שֶׁאֱרָה

1Ch 7:24 She'erah, who built . . Lower and Upper Beth-hor'on 1

Shehariah 1. שְׁחַרְיָה

1Ch 8:26 Sham'sherai, Shehari'ah, Athali'ah 1

Shelah 1. שֵׁלָה 2. שֶׁלַח 3. Σαλά

Gen 10:24 Arpach'shad became the father of Shelah; 2
24 and Shelah became the father of Eber. 2
11:12 35 years, he became the father of Shelah; 2
13 Arpach'shad lived after the birth of Shelah 2
14 When Shelah had lived 30 years 2
15 Shelah lived after the birth of Eber 403 years 2
38: 5 bore a son, and she called his name Shelah. 1
11 Remain a widow . . till Shelah my son grows up 1
14 for she saw that Shelah was grown up 1
26 inasmuch as I did not give her to my son Shelah. 1
46:12 sons of Judah: Er, Onan, Shelah, Perez, and Zerah 1
Num26:20 of Shelah, the family of the Shela'nites; 1
1Ch 1:18 and Shelah was the father of Eber. 2
18 and Shelah was the father of Eber. 2
24 Shem, Arpach'shad, Shelah; 2
2: 3 The sons of Judah: Er, Onan, and Shelah; 1
4:21 sons of Shelah the son of Judah 1
Neh 3:15 built the wall of the Pool of Shelah of the king's 2
Lke 3:35 son of Peleg, the son of Eber, the son of Shelah 3

Shelanite 1. שֵׁלָנִי

Num26:20 of Shelah, the family of the Shela'nites; 1

Shelemiah 1. שֶׁלֶמְיָהוּ 2. Σελεμιας

1Ch 26:14 The lot for the east fell to Shelemi'ah. 1
Ezr 10:39 Shelemi'ah, Nathan, Adai'ah 1
41 Az'arel, Shelemi'ah, Shemari'ah 1
Neh 3:30 Hanani'ah the son of Shelemi'ah and Hanun 1
13:13 appointed . . Shelemi'ah the priest, Zadok 1
Jer 36:14 son of Nethani'ah, son of Shelemi'ah, son of Cushi 1
26 and Shelemi'ah the son of Abdeel to seize Baruch 1
37: 3 King Zedeki'ah sent Jehu'cal the son of Shelemi'ah 1
13 a sentry there named Iri'jah the son of Shelemi'ah 1
38: 1 Jucal the son of Shelemi'ah 1
1Es 9:34 Eliasis, Binnui, Elialis, Shimei, Shelemiah 2

Sheleph 1. שֶׁלֶף

Gen 10:26 Joktan became the father of Almo'dad, Sheleph 1
1Ch 1:20 father of Almo'dad, Sheleph, Hazarma'veth, Jerah 1

Shelesh 1. שֵׁלֶשׁ

1Ch 7:35 sons of Helem . . Zophah, Imna, Shelesh, and Amal. 1

Shelomi 1. שְׁלֹמִי

Num34:27 of Asher a leader, Ahi'hud the son of Shelo'mi. 1

Shelomith 1. שְׁלֹמִית 2. Ασσαλιμωθ

Lev 24:11 His mother's name was Shelo'mith, 1
1Ch 3:19 and Hanani'ah, and Shel-o'mith was their sister; 1
23:18 The sons of Izhar: Shelo'mith the chief. 1
2Ch 11:20 Ma'acah . . bore him . . , Ziza, and Shelo'mith. 1
Ezr 8:10 Of the sons of Bani, Shelo'mith the son 1
1Es 8:36 Shelomith the son of Josiphiah 2

Shelomoth 1. שְׁלֹמוֹת 2. Σαλωμωθ

1Ch 23: 9 sons of Shim'e-i: Shelo'moth, Ha'zi-el, and Haran 1
24:22 Of the Iz'harites, Shelo'moth; 1
22 of the sons of Shelo'moth, Jahath. 1
26:25 from Elie'zer were . . his son Shelo'moth. 1
26 This Shelo'moth and his brethren were in charge 1
28 were in the care of Shelo'moth and his brethren. 2

Shelumiel 1. שְׁלֻמִיאֵל

Num 1: 6 from Simeon, Shelu'mi-el the son of Zurishad'dai; 1
2:12 the leader . . Shelu'mi-el the son of Zurishad'dai 1
7:36 Shelu'mi-el the . . leader of the men of Simeon 1
41 offering of Shelu'mi-el the son of Zurishad'dai. 1
10:19 Shelu'mi-el the son of Zurishad'dai. 1

Shem 1. שֵׁם 2. Σήμ

Gen 5:32 Noah became the father of Shem, Ham, and Japheth. 1
6:10 Noah had three sons, Shem, Ham, and Japheth. 1
7:13 Noah and his sons, Shem and Ham and Japheth 1
9:18 from the ark were Shem, Ham, and Japheth. 1
23 Then Shem and Japheth took a garment 1
26 He also said, "Blessed by the LORD my God be Shem; 1
27 Japheth, and let him dwell in the tents of Shem; 1
10: 1 the sons of Noah, Shem, Ham, and Japheth; 1
21 To Shem also, the father of all the children 1
22 The sons of Shem: Elam, Asshur, Arpach'shad 1
31 These are the sons of Shem, by their families 1
11:10 These are the descendants of Shem. 1
10 When Shem was 100 years old 1
11 Shem lived after the birth of Arpach'shad 1
1Ch 1: 4 Noah, Shem, Ham, and Japheth. 1
17 sons of Shem: Elam, Asshur, Arpach'shad, Lud 1
24 Shem, Arpach'shad, Shelah; 1
Lke 3:36 the son of Shem, the son of Noah, the son of Lamech 2
Sir 49:16 Shem and Seth were honored among men 2

Shema 1. שְׁמַע 2. שֶׁמַע 3. Σαμμους

Jos 15:26 Amam, Shema, Mola'dah 1
1Ch 2:43 sons of Hebron: Korah, Tap'puah, Rekem, and Shema. 2
44 Shema . . father of Raham, the father of Jor'ke-am; 2
5: 8 Bela the son of Azaz, son of Shema, son of Jo'el 2
8:13 Beri'ah and Shema . . heads of fathers' houses 2
Neh 8: 4 beside him stood Mattithi'ah, Shema, Anai'ah, Uri'ah 2
1Es 9:43 beside him stood Mattathiah, Shema, Anaiah 3

Shemaah 1. שְׁמָעָה

1Ch 12: 3 Ahi-e'zer, then Jo'ash, both sons of Shema'ah 1

Shemaiah 1. שְׁמַעְיָהוּ 2. Σαμαιας 3. Σεμειας

1Kg 12:22 the word of God came to Shemai'ah the man of God 1
1Ch 3:22 The sons of Shecani'ah: Shemai'ah. 1
22 And the sons of Shemai'ah: Hattush, Igal, Bari'ah 1
4:37 Ziza . . son of Shimri, son of Shemai'ah 1
5: 4 sons of Jo'el: Shemai'ah his son, Gog his son, Shim'e-i 1
9:14 Of the Levites: Shemai'ah the son of Hasshub 1
16 Obadi'ah the son of Shemai'ah, son of Galal 1
15: 8 of the sons of Eli-za'phan, Shemai'ah the chief 1
11 Levites Uri'el, Asai'ah, Jo'el, Shemai'ah, Eli'el 1
24: 6 scribe Shemai'ah the son of Nethan'el, a Levite 1
26: 4 O'bed-e'dom had sons: Shemai'ah the first-born 1
6 Also to his son Shemai'ah were sons born who were 1
7 sons of Shemai'ah: Othni, Reph'a-el, Obed, 1
2Ch 11: 2 word of the LORD came to Shemai'ah the man of God 1
12: 5 Then Shemai'ah the prophet came to Rehobo'am 1
7 word of the LORD came to Shemai'ah 1
15 written in the chronicles of Shemai'ah 1
17: 8 with them the Levites, Shemai'ah, Nethani'ah 1
29:14 of the sons of Jedu'thun, Shemai'ah and Uz'ziel. 1
31:15 Jeshua, Shemai'ah, Amari'ah, and Shecani'ah 1
35: 9 Shemai'ah and Nethan'el his brothers 1
Ezr 8:13 names being Eliph'elet, Jeu'el, and Shemai'ah 1
16 Then I sent for Elie'zer, Ar'i-el, Shemai'ah, 1
10:21 of Harim . . Eli'jah, Shemai'ah, Jehi'el, and Uzzi'ah. 1
31 of Harim: Elie'zer, Isshi'jah, Malchi'jah, Shemai'ah 1
Neh 3:29 Shemai'ah the son of Shecani'ah . . repaired. 1
6:10 into the house of Shemai'ah the son of Delai'ah 1
10: 8 Ma-azi'ah, Bil'gai, Shemai'ah; these are the priests. 1
11:15 Levites: Shemai'ah the son of Hasshub 1
12: 6 Shemai'ah, Joi'arib, Jedai'ah 1
18 of Bilgah, Sham'mu-a; of Shemai'ah, Jehon'athan; 1
34 Judah, Benjamin, Shemai'ah, and Jeremiah 1
35 Zechari'ah the son of Jonathan, son of Shemai'ah 1
36 kinsmen, Shemai'ah, Az'arel, Mil'alai, Gil'alai, Ma'ai 1
42 Ma-asei'ah, Shemai'ah, Elea'zar, Uzzi, Jehoha'nan 1
Jer 26:20 Uri'ah the son of Shemai'ah from Kir'iath-je'arim. 1
29:24 To Shemai'ah of Nehel'am you shall say 1
31 says the LORD concerning Shemai'ah of Nehel'am 1
31 Because Shemai'ah has prophesied to you 1
32 thus says the LORD: Behold, I will punish Shemai'ah 1
36:12 Delai'ah the son of Shemai'ah 1
1Es 1: 9 Jeconiah and Shemaiah and Nethanel his brother 2
8:39 their names being Eliphelet, Jeuel, and Shemaiah 2
44 Elnathan, Shemaiah, Jarib, Nathan, Elnathan 2
9:21 Zebadiah and Maaseiah and Shemaiah and Jehiel 2
34 Shashai, Azarel, Azael, Shemaiah, Amariah, Joseph. 2
Tob 5:13 the sons of the great Shemaiah 3

Shemariah 1. שְׁמַרְיָהוּ

1Ch 12: 5 Beali'ah, Shemari'ah, Shephati'ah the Har'uphite; 1
2Ch 11:19 she bore him sons, Je'ush, Shemari'ah, and Zaham. 1
Ezr 10:32 Benjamin, Malluch, and Shemari'ah. 1
41 Az'arel, Shelemi'ah, Shemari'ah 1

Shemeber 1. שֶׁמְאֵבֶר

Gen 14: 2 Shinab king of Admah, Sheme'ber king of Zeboi'im 1

Shemed 1. שֶׁמֶד

1Ch 8:12 sons of Elpa'al . . Shemed, who built Ono and Lod 1

Shemer 1. שֶׁמֶר

1Kg 16:24 He bought the hill of Sama'ria from Shemer 1
24 Sama'ria, after the name of Shemer, the owner 1
1Ch 6:46 son of Amzi, son of Bani, son of Shemer 1
7:34 sons of Shemer . . Rohgah, Jehub'bah, and Aram. 1

Shemida 1. בְּנֵי שְׁמִידָע 2. שְׁמִידָע

Num26:32 of Shemi'da, the family of the Shemi'daites; 2
Jos 17: 2 Helek, As'ri-el, Shechem, Hepher, and Shemi'da 1
1Ch 7:19 sons of Shemi'da were Ahi'an, Shechem, Likhi 2

Shemidaite 1. שְׁמִידָעִי

Num26:32 of Shemi'da, the family of the Shemi'daites; 1

Sheminith 1. שְׁמִינִית

1Ch 15:21 lead with lyres according to the Shem'inith. 1
Ps 6: 0 according to The Sheminith. A Psalm of David 1
12: 0 To the choirmaster: according to The Sheminith. 1

Shemiramoth 1. שְׁמִירָמוֹת

1Ch 15:18 Zechari'ah, Ja-a'ziel, Shemi'ramoth, Jehi'el, Unni 1
20 Zechari'ah, A'zi-el, Shemi'ramoth, Jehi'el, Unni 1
16: 5 second to him were Zechari'ah, Je-i'el, Shemi'ramoth 1
2Ch 17: 8 with them the Levites . . Shemi'ramoth 1

Shemuel 1. שְׁמוּאֵל

Num34:20 tribe . . of Simeon, Shemu'el the son of Ammi'hud. 1
1Ch 7: 2 sons of Tola . . Je'ri-el, Jah'mai, Ibsam, and Shem'uel 1

Shenazzar 1. שֶׁנְאַצַּר

1Ch 3:18 Malchi'ram, Pedai'ah, Shenaz'zar, Jekami'ah 1

Sheol 1.שְׁאוֹל
Gen 37:35 No, I shall go down to Sheol to my son, mourning. 1
42:38 bring down my gray hairs with sorrow to Sheol. 1
44:29 bring down my gray hairs in sorrow to Sheol.' 1
31 your servant our father with sorrow to Sheol. 1
Num16:30 they go down alive into Sheol, then you shall know 1
33 they . . went down alive into Sheol; 1
Deu 32:22 fire is kindled . . burns to the depths of Sheol 1
1Sm 2: 6 The LORD . . he brings down to Sheol and raises up. 1
2Sm 22: 6 the cords of Sheol entangled me 1
1Kg 2: 6 do not let his gray head go down to Sheol in peace. 1
9 bring his gray head down with blood to Sheol. 1
Job 7: 9 he who goes down to Sheol does not come up; 1
11: 8 Deeper than Sheol-what can you know? 1
14:13 Oh that thou wouldest hide me in Sheol 1
17:13 If I look for Sheol as my house 1
16 Will it go down to the bars of Sheol? 1
21:13 and in peace they go down to Sheol. 1
24:19 does Sheol those who have sinned. 1
26: 6 Sheol is naked before God 1
Ps 6: 5 in Sheol who can give thee praise? 1
9:17 The wicked shall depart to Sheol 1
16:10 For thou dost not give me up to Sheol 1
18: 5 the cords of Sheol entangled me 1
30: 3 O LORD, thou hast brought up my soul from Sheol 1
31:17 let them go dumbfounded to Sheol. 1
49:14 Like sheep they are appointed for Sheol; 1
14 form shall waste away; Sheol shall be their home. 1
15 God will ransom my soul from the power of Sheol 1
55:15 let them go down to Sheol alive; 1
86:13 hast delivered my soul from the depths of Sheol. 1
88: 3 my life draws near to Sheol. 1
89:48 Who can deliver his soul from the power of Sheol? 1
116: 3 pangs of Sheol laid hold on me; 1
139: 8 If I make my bed in Sheol, thou art there! 1
141: 7 their bones be strewn at the mouth of Sheol. 1
Prv 1:12 like Sheol let us swallow them alive and whole 1
5: 5 her steps follow the path to Sheol; 1
7:27 Her house is the way to Sheol 1
9:18 that her guests are in the depths of Sheol. 1
15:11 Sheol and Abaddon lie open before the LORD 1
24 that he may avoid Sheol beneath. 1
23:14 beat him with the rod . . save his life from Sheol. 1
27:20 Sheol and Abaddon are never satisfied 1
30:16 Sheol, the barren womb, the earth ever thirsty 1
Ecc 9:10 work or thought or knowledge or wisdom in Sheol 1
Isa 5:14 Therefore Sheol has enlarged its appetite 1
7:11 a sign . . let it be deep as Sheol or high as heaven. 1
14: 9 Sheol beneath is stirred up to meet you 1
11 Your pomp is brought down to Sheol 1
15 you are brought down to Sheol 1
28:15 with death, and with Sheol we have an agreement; 1
18 and your agreement with Sheol will not stand; 1
38:10 I am consigned to the gates of Sheol 1
18 For Sheol cannot thank thee, death cannot praise 1
57: 9 your envoys far off, and sent down even to Sheol. 1
Ezk 31:15 Thus says the Lord GOD: When it goes down to Sheol 1
16 when I cast it down to Sheol with those who go down 1
17 They also shall go down to Sheol with it 1
32:21 with their helpers, out of the midst of Sheol 1
27 who went down to Sheol with their weapons of war 1
Hos 13:14 Shall I ransom them from the power of Sheol? 1
14 O Sheol, where is your destruction? 1
Ams 9: 2 Though they dig into Sheol 1
Jon 2: 2 he answered me; out of the belly of Sheol I cried 1
Hab 2: 5 His greed is as wide as Sheol; 1

Shepham 1.שְׁפָם
Num34:10 eastern boundary from Ha'zar-e'nan to Shepham; 1
11 the boundary shall go down from Shepham to Riblah 1

Shephatiah 1.שְׁפַטְיָהוּ 2.Σαφατια 3.Σαφατιας
2Sm 3: 4 and the fifth, Shephati'ah the son of Abi'tal; 1
1Ch 3: 3 the fifth Shephati'ah, by Abi'tal; 1
9: 8 Meshul'lam the son of Shephati'ah, son of Reu'el 1
12: 5 Beali'ah, Shemari'ah, Shephati'ah the Har'uphite; 1
27:16 for the Simeonites, Shephati'ah the son of Ma'acah; 1
2Ch 21: 2 sons of Jehosh'aphat . . Michael, and Shephati'ah; 1
Ezr 2: 4 sons of Shephati'ah, 372. 1
57 sons of Shephati'ah, the sons of Hattil 1
8: 8 Of the sons of Shephati'ah, Zebadi'ah the son 1
Neh 7: 9 sons of Shephati'ah, 372. 1
59 sons of Shephati'ah, the sons of Hattil 1
11: 4 Zechari'ah, son of Amari'ah, son of Shephati'ah 1
Jer 38: 1 Now Shephati'ah the son of Mattan 1
1Es 5: 9 The sons of Shephatiah, 472 2
33 the sons of Giddel, the sons of Shephatiah 2
8:34 Of the sons of Shephatiah, Zeraiah 3

Shephelah 1.שְׁפֵלָה 2.Σεφηλα
1Kg 10:27 as plentiful as the sycamore of the Shephe'lah. 1
1Ch 27:28 Over the . . trees in the Shephe'lah was 1
2Ch 1:15 as plentiful as the sycamore of the Shephe'lah. 1
9:27 as plentiful as the sycamore of the Shephe'lah. 1
26:10 he had large herds, both in the Shephe'lah 1
28:18 made raids on the cities in the Shephe'lah 1
Jer 17:26 from the land of Benjamin, from the Shephe'lah 1
32:44 in the cities of the Shephe'lah 1
33:13 the hill country, in the cities of the Shephe'lah 1
Obd 1:19 possess Mount Esau, and those of the Shephe'lah 1
1Mc 12:38 Simon built Adida in the Shephelah 2

Shepher 1.שֶׁפֶר
Num33:23 from Kehela'thah, and encamped at Mount Shepher. 1
24 set out from Mount Shepher, and encamped 1

Shephi 1.שְׁפִי
1Ch 1:40 The sons of Shobal: Al'ian, Man'ahath, Ebal, Shephi 1

Shepho 1.שְׁפוֹ
Gen 36:23 of Shobal . . Man'ahath, Ebal, Shepho, and Onam. 1

Shephupham 1.שְׁפוּפָם
Num26:39 of Shephu'pham, the family of the Shu'phamites; 1

Shephuphan 1.שְׁפוּפָן
1Ch 8: 5 Gera, Shephu'phan, and Huram. 1

Sherebiah 1.שֵׁרֵבְיָה 2.Ασεβηβιας 3.Σαραβιας
Ezr 8:18 Sherebi'ah with his sons and kinsmen, eighteen. 1
24 Sherebi'ah, Hashabi'ah, and ten of their kinsmen 1
Neh 8: 7 Also Jesh'ua, Bani, Sherebi'ah, Jamin, Akkub 1
9: 4 stood . . Bunni, Sherebi'ah, Bani, and Chena'ni; 1
5 Levites . . Bani, Hashabnei'ah, Sherebi'ah, Hodi'ah 1
10:12 Zaccur, Sherebi'ah, Shebani'ah 1
12: 8 Levites . . Sherebi'ah, Judah, and Mattani'ah 1
24 chiefs of the Levites: Hashabi'ah, Sherebi'ah 1
1Es 8:47 the son of Levi, son of Israel, namely Sherebiah 2
54 leaders of the priests, Sherebiah and Hashabiah 3
9:48 Jeshua and Anniuth and Sherebiah, Jamin, Akkub 3

Sheresh 1.שֶׁרֶשׁ
1Ch 7:16 Peresh; and the name of his brother was Sheresh; 1

Sheshai 1.שֵׁשַׁי
Num13:22 came to Hebron; and Ahi'man, She'shai, and Talmai 1
Jos 15:14 three sons of Anak, She'shai and Ahi'man and Talmai 1
Jdg 1:10 they defeated She'shai and Ahi'man and Talmai. 1

Sheshan 1.שֵׁשָׁן
1Ch 2:31 The sons of Ishi: Sheshan. 1
31 The sons of Sheshan: Ahlai. 1
34 Now Sheshan had no sons, only daughters; 1
34 but Sheshan had an Egyptian slave, whose name was 1
35 Sheshan gave his daughter in marriage to Jarha 1

Sheshbazzar 1.שֵׁשְׁבַּצַּר 2.שֵׁשְׁבַּצַּר (A) 3.Σαναβασσαρος
Ezr 1: 8 Mith'redath . . counted them out to Shesh-baz'zar 1
11 5,469. All these did Shesh-baz'zar bring up 1
5:14 delivered to one whose name was Shesh-baz'zar 2
16 Then this Shesh-baz'zar came and laid 2
1Es 2:12 by him they were given to Sheshbazzar 3
15 they were carried back by Sheshbazzar 3
6:18 delivered to . . Sheshbazzar the governor 3
20 Sheshbazzar . . laid the foundations 3

Sheth 1.שֵׁת
Num24:17 it shall . . break down all the sons of Sheth. 1

Shethar 1.שֵׁתָר
Est 1:14 the men next to him being Carshe'na, Shethar 1

Shethar-bozenai 1.שְׁתַר בּוֹזְנַי (A)
Ezr 5: 3 She'thar-boz'enai and their associates came 1
6 She'thar-boz'enai and his associates 1
6: 6 She'thar-boz'enai, and your associates 1
13 She'thar-boz'enai, and their associates 1

Sheva 1.שְׁוָא
2Sm 20:25 Sheva was secretary; and Zadok and Abi'athar were 1
1Ch 2:49 She also bore . . Sheva the father of Machbe'nah 1

Shibah 1.שִׁבְעָה
Gen 26:33 He called it Shibah; therefore the name 1

Shibboleth 1.שִׁבֹּלֶת
Jdg 12: 6 said to him, "Then say Shibboleth," and he said 1

Shiggaion 1.שִׁגָּיוֹן
Ps 7: 0 A Shiggaion of David, which he sang to the LORD 1

Shigionoth 1.שִׁגְיֹנוֹת
Hab 3: 1 prayer of Habak'kuk . . according to Shigion'oth. 1

Shihor 1.שִׁיחוֹר
Jos 13: 3 from the Shihor, which is east of Egypt, northward 1
1Ch 13: 5 from the Shihor of Egypt to the entrance of Hamath 1
Isa 23: 3 your revenue was the grain of Shihor 1

Shihor-libnath 1.שִׁיחוֹר לִבְנָת
Jos 19:26 on the west it touches . . Shihor-lib'nath 1

Shikkeron 1.שִׁכְּרוֹן
Jos 15:11 then the boundary bends round to Shik'keron 1

Shilhi 1.שִׁלְחִי
1Kg 22:42 mother's name was Azu'bah the daughter of Shilhi. 1
2Ch 20:31 Azu'bah the daughter of Shili. 1

Shilhim 1.שִׁלְחִים
Jos 15:32 Leba'oth, Shilhim, A'in, and Rimmon 1

Shillem 1.שִׁלֵּם
Gen 46:24 sons of Naph'tali: Jahzeel . . Jezer, and Shillem 1
Num26:49 of Shillem, the family of the Shil'lemites. 1

Shillemite 1.שִׁלֵּמִי
Num26:49 of Shillem, the family of the Shil'lemites. 1

Shiloah 1.שִׁלֹחַ
Isa 8: 6 refused the waters of Shilo'ah that flow gently 1

Shiloh 1.שִׁלוֹ
Jos 18: 1 Then . . the people of Israel assembled at Shiloh 1
8 I will cast lots . . before the LORD in Shiloh. 1
9 then they came to Joshua in the camp at Shiloh 1
10 Joshua cast lots . . in Shiloh before the LORD; 1
19:51 distributed by lot at Shiloh before the LORD 1
21: 2 they said to them at Shiloh in the land of Canaan 1
22: 9 parting from the people of Israel at Shiloh 1
12 whole assembly . . of Israel gathered at Shiloh 1
Jdg 18:31 he made, as long as the house of God was at Shiloh. 1
21:12 the camp at Shiloh, which is in the land of Canaan. 1
19 feast . . at Shiloh, which is north of Bethel 1
21 if the daughters of Shiloh come out to dance 1
21 each man his wife from the daughters of Shiloh 1
1Sm 1: 3 and to sacrifice to the LORD of hosts at Shiloh 1
9 they had eaten and drunk in Shiloh, Hannah rose. 1
24 she brought him to the house of the LORD at Shiloh; 1
2:14 they did at Shiloh to all the Israelites 1
3:21 And the LORD appeared again at Shiloh 1
21 the LORD revealed himself to Samuel at Shiloh 1
4: 3 bring the ark of the covenant . . here from Shiloh 1
4 the people sent to Shiloh, and brought . . the ark 1
12 and came to Shiloh the same day 1
14: 3 son of Eli, the priest of the LORD in Shiloh 1
1Kg 2:27 spoken concerning the house of Eli in Shiloh. 1
14: 2 Arise, and disguise yourself . . go to Shiloh; 1
4 she arose, and went to Shiloh, and came to the house 1
Ps 78:60 He forsook his dwelling at Shiloh, the tent 1
Jer 7:12 Go now to my place that was in Shiloh 1
14 to you and to your fathers, as I did to Shiloh. 1
26: 6 then I will make this house like Shiloh 1
9 the LORD, saying, 'This house shall be like Shiloh 1
41: 5 arrived from Shechem and Shiloh and Sama'ria 1

Shilonite 1.שִׁילֹנִי
1Kg 11:29 the prophet Ahi'jah the Shi'lonite found him 1
12:15 LORD spoke by Ahi'jah the Shi'lonite to Jerobo'am 1
15:29 he spoke by his servant Ahi'jah the Shi'lonite; 1
1Ch 9: 5 of the Shi'lonites: Asai'ah the first-born 1
2Ch 9:29 and in the prophecy of Ahi'jah the Shi'lonite 1
10:15 which he spoke by Ahi'jah the Shi'lonite 1
Neh 11: 5 Joi'arib, son of Zechari'ah, son of the Shi'lonite. 1

Shilshah 1.שִׁלְשָׁה
1Ch 7:37 Bezer, Hod, Shamma, Shilshah, Ithran, and Be-e'ra. 1

Shimea 1.שִׁמְעָא
1Ch 2:13 Jesse was the father of . . Shim'ea the third 1
3: 5 were born to him in Jerusalem: Shim'e-a, Shobab 1
6:30 Shim'e-a his son, Haggi'ah his son, and Asai'ah his 1
39 namely, Asaph the son of Berechi'ah, son of Shim'e-a 1
20: 7 Jonathan the son of Shim'e-a . . slew him. 1

Shimeah 1.שִׁמְעָה
2Sm 13: 3 whose name was Jon'adab, the son of Shim'e-ah 1
32 Jon'adab the son of Shim'e-ah, David's brother, said 1

Shimeam 1.שִׁמְאָם
1Ch 9:38 Mikloth was the father of Shim'e-am; 1

Shimeath 1.שִׁמְעָת
2Kg 12:21 Jo'zacar the son of Shim'e-ath and Jeho'zabad 1
2Ch 24:26 Zabad the son of Shim'e-ath the Ammonitess 1

Shimeathite 1.שִׁמְעָתִים
1Ch 2:55 the Shim'e-athites, and the Su'cathites. 1

Shimeeah 1.שִׁמְאָה
1Ch 8:32 Mikloth (he was the father of Shime'e-ah). 1

Shimei 1.שִׁמְעִי 2.Σεμει 3.Σεμεειας
Exd 6:17 of Gershon: Libni and Shim'e-i, by their families. 1
Num 3:18 sons of Gershon . . Libni and Shim'e-i. 1
2Sm 16: 5 man of the . . house of Saul, whose name was Shim'e-i 1
7 Shim'e-i said as he cursed, "Begone, begone, you man 1
13 Shim'e-i went along on the hillside opposite him 1
19:16 Shim'e-i the son of Gera . . made haste to come down 1
18 Shim'e-i the son of Gera fell down before the king 1
21 Shall not Shim'e-i be put to death for this 1
23 And the king said to Shim'e-i, "You shall not die. 1
21:21 the son of Shim'e-i, David's brother, slew him. 1

1Kg 1: 8 Nathan the prophet, and Shim'e-i, and Re'i, 1
2: 8 there is also with you Shim'e-i the son of Gera 1
36 the king sent and summoned Shim'e-i, and said to him 1
38 Shim'e-i said to the king, "What you say is good; 1
38 So Shim'e-i dwelt in Jerusalem many days. 1
39 two of Shim'e-i's slaves ran away to Achish, son 1
39 it was told Shim'e-i, "Behold, your slaves are in Gath 1
40 Shim'e-i arose and saddled an ass, and went to Gath 1
40 Shim'e-i went and brought his slaves from Gath. 1
41 Shim'e-i had gone from Jerusalem to Gath 1
42 the king sent and summoned Shim'e-i, and said to him 1
44 The king also said to Shim'e-i, "You know in your own 1
4:18 Shim'e-i the son of Ela, in Benjamin; 1
1Ch 3:19 and the sons of Pedai'ah: Zerub'babel and Shim'e-i; 1
4:26 sons of Mishma: Ham'mu-el . . Zac'cur . . Shim'e-i 1
27 Shim'e-i had sixteen sons and six daughters; 1
5: 4 sons of Jo'el . . Gog his son, Shim'e-i his son 1
6:17 names of the sons of Gershom: Libni and Shim'e-i. 1
29 of Merar'i: Mahli, Libni . . Shim'e-i his son 1
42 son of Ethan, son of Zimmah, son of Shim'e-i 1
8:21 Adai'ah, Berai'ah, and Shimrath . . sons of Shim'e-i. 1
23: 7 The sons of Gershom were Ladan and Shim'e-i. 1
9 sons of Shim'e-i: Shelo'moth, Ha'zi-el, and Haran 1
10 sons of Shim'e-i: Jahath, Zina, and Je'ush 1
10 These four were the sons of Shim'e-i. 1
25: 3 sons of Jedu'thun: Gedali'ah . . Jeshai'ah, Shim'e-i 1
17 tenth to Shim'e-i, his sons and his brethren, twelve; 1
27:27 over the vineyards was Shim'e-i the Ra'mathite; 1
2Ch 29:14 of the sons of Heman, Jehu'el and Shim'e-i; 1
31:12 Conani'ah . . with Shim'e-i his brother as second; 1
13 overseers assisting Conani'ah and Shim'e-i 1
Ezr 10:23 Of the Levites: Jo'zabad, Shim'e-i, Kelai'ah 1
33 of Hashum . . Jer'emai, Manas'seh, and Shim'e-i. 1
38 Of the sons of Bin'nui: Shim'e-i 1
Est 2: 5 the son of Ja'ir, son of Shim'e-i, son of Kish 1
1Es 9:23 of the Levites: Jozabad and Shimei and Kelaiah 2
33 Zabad and Eliphelet and Manasseh and Shimei. 2
34 Machnadebai, Eliasis, Binnui, Elialis, Shimei 2
AEs 11: 2 Mordecai the son of Jair, son of Shimei, son of Kish 3

Shimeite 1. שִׁמְעִי
Num 3:21 the Libnites and the family of the Shim'e-ites; 1
Zec 12:13 the family of the Shim'e-ites by itself 1

Shimeon 1. שִׁמְעוֹן
Ezr 10:31 of Harim . . Malchi'jah, Shemai'ah, Shim'e-on 1

Shimon 1. שִׁימוֹן
1Ch 4:20 sons of Shimon: Amnon, Rinnah, Ben-ha'nan, 1

Shimrath 1. שִׁמְרָת
1Ch 8:21 Adai'ah, Berai'ah, and Shimrath . . sons of Shim'e-i. 1

Shimri 1. שִׁמְרִי
1Ch 4:37 Ziza . . son of Shimri, son of Shemai'ah 1
11:45 Jedi'a-el the son of Shimri, and Joha his brother 1
26:10 Hosah . . of Merar'i, had sons: Shimri the chief 1
2Ch 29:13 of the sons of Eli-za'phan, Shimri and Jeu'el; 1

Shimrith 1. שִׁמְרִית
2Ch 24:26 Jeho'zabad the son of Shimrith the Moabitess. 1

Shimron 1. שִׁמְרוֹן
Gen 46:13 sons of Is'sachar: Tola, Puvah, Iob, and Shimron 1
Num26:24 of Shimron, the family of the Shim'ronites. 1
Jos 11: 1 he sent to . . the king of Shimron 1
19:15 Kattath, Nahal'al, Shimron, I'dalah, and Bethlehem 1
1Ch 7: 1 sons of Is'sachar: Tola, Pu'ah, Jashub, and Shimron 1

Shimron-meron 1. שִׁמְרוֹן מְראוֹן
Jos 12:20 the king of Shim'ron-me'ron, one; 1

Shimronite 1. שִׁמְרֹנִי
Num26:24 of Shimron, the family of the Shim'ronites. 1

Shimshai 1. שִׁמְשַׁי 2. Σαμσαιος
Ezr 4: 8 Rehum the commander and Shim'shai the scribe 1
9 Rehum . . Shim'shai the scribe 1
17 To Rehum the commander and Shim'shai the scribe 1
23 Rehum and Shim'shai the scribe 1
1Es 2:16 Shimshai the scribe 2
17 Rehum the recorder and Shimshai the scribe 2
25 Shimshai the scribe and the others 2
30 Rehum and Shimshai the scribe 2

Shinab 1. שִׁנְאָב
Gen 14: 2 Shinab king of Admah, Sheme'ber king of Zeboi'im 1

Shinar 1. שִׁנְעָר
Gen 10:10 Accad, all of them in the land of Shinar. 1
11: 2 they found a plain in the land of Shinar 1
14: 1 In the days of Am'raphel king of Shinar 1
9 Tidal king of Goi'im, Am'raphel king of Shinar 1
Jos 7:21 among the spoil a beautiful mantle from Shinar 1
Isa 11:11 remnant . . from Ethiopia, from Elam, from Shinar 1
Zec 5:11 To the land of Shinar, to build a house for it; 1

Shion 1. שִׁיאֹן
Jos 19:19 Haph'ara-im, Shion, Ana'harath 1

Shiphi 1. שִׁפְעִי
1Ch 4:37 Ziza the son of Shiphi, son of Allon, son of Jedai'ah 1

Shiphmite 1. שִׁפְמִי
1Ch 27:27 over the produce of . . was Zabdi the Shiphmite. 1

Shiphrah 1. שִׁפְרָה
Exd 1:15 one . . was named Shiphrah and the other Pu'ah 1

Shiphtan 1. שִׁפְטָן
Num34:24 of E'phraim a leader, Kemu'el the son of Shiphtan. 1

Shisha 1. שִׁישָׁא
1Kg 4: 3 Elihor'eph and Ahi'jah the sons of Shisha were 1

Shishak 1. שִׁישַׁק
1Kg 11:40 Jerobo'am . . fled . . to Shishak king of Egypt 1
14:25 Shishak king of Egypt came up against Jerusalem; 1
2Ch 12: 2 Shishak king of Egypt came up against Jerusalem 1
5 had gathered at Jerusalem because of Shishak 1
5 I have abandoned you to the hand of Shishak.' 1
7 by the hand of Shishak. 1
9 Shishak king of Egypt came up against Jerusalem; 1

Shitrai 1. שִׁטְרַי
1Ch 27:29 pastured in Sharon was Shitrai the Shar'onite; 1

Shittim 1. שִׁטִּים
Num25: 1 While Israel dwelt in Shittim the people 1
Jos 2: 1 sent two men secretly from Shittim as spies 1
3: 1 Early . . Joshua rose and set out from Shittim 1
Hos 5: 2 And they have made deep the pit of Shittim; 1
Jol 3:18 and water the valley of Shittim. 1
Mic 6: 5 and what happened from Shittim to Gilgal 1

Shiza 1. שִׁיזָא
1Ch 11:42 Ad'ina the son of Shiza the Reubenite 1

Shoa 1. שׁוֹעַ
Ezk 23:23 and Sho'a and Ko'a, and all the Assyrians with them 1

Shobab 1. שׁוֹבָב
2Sm 5:14 born to him . . Sham'mu-a, Shobab, Nathan, Solomon 1
1Ch 2:18 these were her sons: Jesher, Shobab, and Ardon. 1
3: 5 were born to him in Jerusalem: Shim'e-a, Shobab 1
14: 4 the children . . Shammu'a, Shobab, Nathan, Solomon 1

Shobach 1. שׁוֹבַךְ
2Sm 10:16 they came to Helam, with Shobach . . at their head. 1
18 David slew . . and wounded Shobach the commander 1

Shobai 1. שֹׁבָי 2. Σωβαι
Ezr 2:42 sons of the gatekeepers: the . . sons of Sho'bai 1
Neh 7:45 gatekeepers . . sons of Sho'bai 1
1Es 5:28 sons of Hatita, the sons of Shobai, in all 139. 2

Shobal 1. שׁוֹבָל
Gen 36:20 inhabitants of the land: Lotan, Shobal, Zib'eon 1
23 the sons of Shobal: Alvan, Man'ahath, Ebal 1
29 Horites: the chiefs Lotan, Shobal, Zib'eon, Anah 1
1Ch 1:38 The sons of Se'ir: Lotan, Shobal, Zib'eon, Anah 1
40 The sons of Shobal: Al'ian, Man'ahath, Ebal, Shephi 1
2:50 Shobal the father of Kir'iath-je'arim. 1
52 Shobal . . father of Kir'iath-je'arim had other 1
4: 1 sons of Judah: Perez, Hezron, Carmi, Hur, and Shobal. 1
2 Re-ai'ah the son of Shobal was the father of Jahath 1

Shobek 1. שׁוֹבֵק
Neh 10:24 Hallo'hesh, Pi'lha, Shobek 1

Shobi 1. שֹׁבִי
2Sm 17:27 Shobi the son of Nahash from Rabbah 1

Shoham 1. שֹׁהַם
1Ch 24:27 of Ja-azi'ah, Beno, Shoham, Zaccur, and Ibri. 1

Shomer 1. שֹׁמֵר
2Kg 12:21 Jo'zacar . . and Jeho'zabad the son of Shomer 1
1Ch 7:32 Heber was the father of Japhlet, Shomer, Hotham 1

Shophach 1. שׁוֹפַךְ
1Ch 19:16 with Shophach the commander of the army 1
18 also Shophach the commander of their army. 1

Shua 1. שׁוּעַ 2. שׁוּעָא
Gen 38: 2 a certain Canaanite whose name was Shua; 1
12 of time the wife of Judah, Shua's daughter, died; 1
1Ch 7:32 father of . . Hotham, and their sister Shu'a. 2

Shuah 1. שׁוּחַ
Gen 25: 2 Jokshan, Medan, Mid'ian, Ishbak, and Shuah. 1
1Ch 1:32 Mid'ian, Ishbak, and Shu'ah. The sons of Jokshan 1

Shual 1. שׁוּעָל
1Sm 13:17 one . . turned toward Ophrah, to the land of Shu'al 1
1Ch 7:36 sons of Zophah: Su'ah, Har'nepher, Shu'al, Beri, 1

Shubael 1. שְׁבוּאֵל
1Ch 24:20 sons of Levi: of the sons of Amram, Shu'ba-el; 1
20 of the sons of Shu'ba-el, Jehde'iah. 1
25:20 thirteenth, Shu'ba-el, his sons and his brethren 1

Shuhah 1. שׁוּחָה
1Ch 4:11 Chelub . . brother of Shuhah, . . father of Mehir 1

Shuham 1. שׁוּחָם
Num26:42 of Shuham, the family of the Shu'hamites. 1

Shuhamite 1. שׁוּחָמִי
Num26:42 of Shuham, the family of the Shu'hamites. 1
43 All the families of the Shu'hamites 1

Shuhite 1. שׁוּחִי
Job 2:11 Eli'phaz the Te'manite, Bildad the Shuhite 1
8: 1 Then Bildad the Shuhite answered 1
18: 1 Then Bildad the Shuhite answered 1
25: 1 Then Bildad the Shuhite answered 1
42: 9 Bildad the Shuhite and Zophar the Na'amathite 1

Shulammite 1. שׁוּלַמִּית
Sng 6:13 Return, return, O Shu'lammite . . that we may look 1
13 Why should you look upon the Shu'lammite 1

Shumathite 1. שֻׁמָתִי
1Ch 2:53 the Ithrites, the Puthites, the Shu'mathites 1

Shunammite 1. שׁוּנַמִּי
1Kg 1: 3 they sought . . and found Ab'ishag the Shu'nammite 1
15 Ab'ishag the Shu'nammite was ministering 1
2:17 to give me Ab'ishag the Shu'nammite as my wife. 1
21 Let Ab'ishag the Shu'nammite be given to Adoni'jah 1
22 why do you ask Ab'ishag the Shu'nammite 1
2Kg 4:12 he said to . . his servant, "Call this Shu'nammite. 1
25 he said . . "Look, yonder is the Shu'nammite; 1
36 summoned Geha'zi and said, "Call this Shu'nammite. 1

Shunem 1. שׁוּנֵם
Jos 19:18 territory included Jezreel, Chesul'loth, Shunem 1
1Sm 28: 4 Philistines . . came and encamped at Shunem; 1
2Kg 4: 8 One day Eli'sha went on to Shunem 1

Shuni 1. שׁוּנִי
Gen 46:16 sons of Gad: Ziph'ion, Haggi, Shuni, Ezbon, Eri 1
Num26:15 of Shuni, the family of the Shunites; 1

Shunite 1. שׁוּנִי
Num26:15 of Shuni, the family of the Shunites; 1

Shuphamite 1. שׁוּפָמִי
Num26:39 of Shephu'pham, the family of the Shu'phamites; 1

Shuppim 1. שֻׁפִּים
1Ch 7:12 And Shuppim and Huppim were the sons of Ir 1
15 Machir took a wife for Huppim and for Shuppim. 1
26:16 For Shuppim and Hosah it came out for the west 1

Shur 1. שׁוּר
Gen 16: 7 in the wilderness, the spring on the way to Shur. 1
20: 1 of the Negeb, and dwelt between Kadesh and Shur; 1
25:18 They dwelt from Hav'ilah to Shur 1
Exd 15:22 they went into the wilderness of Shur; 1
1Sm 15: 7 Saul defeated . . from Hav'ilah as far as Shur 1
27: 8 of the land . . as far as Shur, to the land of Egypt. 1

Shushan 1. שׁוּשַׁן
Ps 60: 0 To the choirmaster: according to Shushan Eduth. 1

Shuthelah 1. שׁוּתֶלַח
Num26:35 of Shuthe'lah, the family of the Shuthe'lahites; 1
36 these are the sons of Shuthe'lah: of Eran 1
1Ch 7:20 The sons of E'phraim: Shuthe'lah, and Bered his son 1
21 Shuthe'lah his son, and Ezer and E'le-ad 1

Shuthelahite 1. שֻׁתַלְחִי
Num26:35 of Shuthe'lah, the family of the Shuthe'lahites; 1

Sia 1. סִיעָא
Neh 7:47 sons of Keros, the sons of Si'a, the sons of Padon 1

Siaha 1. סִיעֲהָא 2. Σουα
Ezr 2:44 sons of Keros, the sons of Si'aha, the sons of Padon 1
1Es 5:29 the sons of Keros, the sons of Siaha 2

Sibbecai 1. סִבְּכַי
2Sm 21:18 then Sib'becai the Hu'shathite slew Saph 1
1Ch 11:29 Sib'becai the Hu'shathite, I'lai the Aho'hite 1
20: 4 then Sib'becai the Hu'shathite slew Sip'pai 1
27:11 Eighth . . was Sib'becai the Hu'shathite 1

Sibboleth 1. סִבֹּלֶת
Jdg 12: 6 Then say Shibboleth," and he said, "Sibboleth 1

Sibmah 1. שִׂבְמָה
Num32:38 Nebo, Ba'al-me'on . . and Sibmah; and they gave 1
Jos 13:19 and Kir'iatha'im, and Sibmah, and Zer'eth-sha'har 1
Isa 16: 8 fields . . languish, and the vine of Sibmah; 1
9 with the weeping of Jazer for the vine of Sibmah; 1
Jer 48:32 More than for Jazer I weep for you, O vine of Sibmah! 1

Sibraim 1. סִבְרַיִם
Ezk 47:16 Sib'raim (which lies on the border between 1

Sicyon 1. Σικυων
1Mc 15:23 to Myndos, and to Sicyon, and to Caria, and to Samos 1

Siddim 1. שִׂדִּים
Gen 14: 3 all these joined forces in the valley of Siddim 1
8 they joined battle in the Valley of Siddim 1
10 Now the Valley of Siddim was full of bitumen pits; 1

Side 1. Σιδη
1Mc 15:23 to Rhodes, and to Phaselis, and to Cos, and to Side 1

Sidon 1. צִידוֹן 2. Σιδών 3. Σιδώνιος 4. Sidon
Gen 10:15 Canaan became the father of Sidon 1
19 the Canaanites extended from Sidon 1
49:13 and his border shall be at Sidon. 1
Jos 11: 8 smote them and chased them as far as Great Sidon 1
19:28 Rehob, Hammon, Kanah, as far as Sidon the Great; 1
Jdg 1:31 did not drive out . . or the inhabitants of Sidon 1
10: 6 Syria, the gods of Sidon, the gods of Moab, the gods 1
18:28 was no deliverer because it was far from Sidon 1
2Sm 24: 6 came to Dan, and from Dan they went around to Sidon 1
1Kg 17: 9 go to Zar'ephath, which belongs to Sidon, and dwell 1
1Ch 1:13 was the father of Sidon his first-born, and Heth 1
Isa 23: 2 Be still . . O merchants of Sidon; 1
4 Be ashamed, O Sidon, for the sea has spoken 1
12 O oppressed virgin daughter of Sidon; 1
Jer 25:22 all the kings of Tyre, all the kings of Sidon 1
27: 3 and the king of Sidon by the hand of the envoys 1
47: 4 to cut off from Tyre and Sidon every helper 1
Ezk 27: 8 inhabitants of Sidon and Arvad were your rowers; 1
28:21 Son of man, set your face toward Sidon 1
22 says the Lord GOD: "Behold, I am against you, O Sidon 1
Jol 3: 4 What are you to me, O Tyre and Sidon 1
Zec 9: 2 Tyre and Sidon, though they are very wise. 1
Mat 11:21 had been done in Tyre and Sidon 2
22 day of judgment for Tyre and Sidon than for you. 2
15:21 and withdrew to the district of Tyre and Sidon. 2
Mrk 3: 8 from about Tyre and Sidon a great multitude 2
7:24 to the region of Tyre and Sidon *
31 went through Sidon to the Sea of Galilee 2
Lke 4:26 in the land of Sidon 3
6:17 Jerusalem and the seacoast of Tyre and Sidon 2
10:13 done in Tyre and Sidon 2
14 more tolerable . . for Tyre and Sidon 2
Act 12:20 Herod was angry with the people of Tyre and Sidon; 3
27: 3 The next day we put in at Sidon 2
2Es 1:11 the people of two provinces, Tyre and Sidon 4
Jdt 2:28 lived along the seacoast, at Sidon and Tyre 2
1Mc 5:15 men of Ptolemais and Tyre and Sidon 2

Sidonian 1. צִידוֹנִי 2. Σιδώνιος
Deu 3: 9 (the Sido'nians call Hermon Si'rion, while 1
Jos 13: 4 and Mear'ah which belongs to the Sido'nians 1
6 the inhabitants of . . even all the Sido'nians. 1
Jdg 3: 3 Canaanites, and the Sido'nians, and the Hivites 1
10:12 The Sido'nians also, and the Amal'ekites 1
18: 7 in security, after the manner of the Sido'nians 1
7 they were far from the Sido'nians and had no 1
1Kg 5: 6 who knows how to cut timber like the Sido'nians. 1
11: 1 Ammonite, E'domite, Sido'nian, and Hittite women 1
5 after Ash'toreth the goddess of the Sido'nians 1
33 Ash'toreth the goddess of the Sido'nians 1
16:31 the daughter of Ethba'al king of the Sido'nians 1
2Kg 23:13 for Ash'toreth the abomination of the Sido'nians 1
1Ch 22: 4 Sido'nians and Tyrians brought . . cedar 1
Ezr 3: 7 gave . . food, drink, and oil to the Sido'nians 1
Ezk 32:30 all the Sido'nians, who have gone down in shame 1
1Es 5:55 carts to the Sidonians and the Tyrians 2

Sihon 1. סִיחוֹן
Num21:21 sent messengers to Sihon king of the Amorites 1
23 Sihon would not allow Israel to pass through 1
26 city of Sihon the king of the Amorites 1
27 be built, let the city of Sihon be established. 1
28 from Heshbon, flame from the city of Sihon. 1
29 his sons fugitives . . to an Amorite king, Sihon. 1
34 do to him as you did to Sihon king of the Amorites 1
32:33 gave . . the kingdom of Sihon king of the Amorites 1
Deu 1: 4 defeated Sihon the king of the Amorites 1
2:24 I have given into your hand Sihon the Amorite 1
26 sent messengers . . to Sihon the king of Heshbon 1
30 Sihon the king of Heshbon would not let us pass 1
31 I have begun to give Sihon and his land over to you; 1
32 Sihon came out against us . . to battle at Jahaz. 1
3: 2 as you did to Sihon the king of the Amorites 1
6 as we did to Sihon the king of Heshbon, destroying 1
4:46 in the land of Sihon the king of the Amorites, who 1
29: 7 Sihon the king of Heshbon and Og the king 1
31: 4 LORD will do to them as he did to Sihon and Og 1
Jos 2:10 to the two kings of the Amorites . . to Sihon and Og 1
9:10 to the two kings . . Sihon the king of Heshbon 1
12: 2 these are the kings . . Sihon king of the Amorites 1
5 Gilead to the boundary of Sihon king of Heshbon. 1
13:10 all the cities of Sihon king of the Amorites 1
21 and all the kingdom of Sihon king of the Amorites 1
21 and Zur and Hur and Reba, the princes of Sihon 1
27 the rest of the kingdom of Sihon king of Heshbon 1
Jdg 11:19 sent messengers to Sihon king of the Amorites 1
20 Sihon did not trust Israel to pass through his 1
20 so Sihon gathered all his people together 1
21 the LORD . . gave Sihon and all his people 1
1Kg 4:19 Gilead, the country of Sihon king of the Amorites 1
Neh 9:22 possession of the land of Sihon king of Heshbon 1
Ps 135:11 Sihon, king of the Amorites, and Og, king of Bashan 1
136:19 Sihon, king of the Amorites 1
Jer 48:45 has gone forth . . a flame from the house of Sihon; 1

Silas 1. Σίλας
Act 15:22 They sent Judas called Barsab'bas, and Silas 1
27 We have therefore sent Judas and Silas 1
32 Judas and Silas, who were themselves prophets 1
40 Paul chose Silas and departed 1
16:19 they seized Paul and Silas 1
25 Paul and Silas were praying and singing hymns 1
29 he fell down before Paul and Silas 1
17: 4 joined Paul and Silas 1
10 The brethren immediately sent Paul and Silas away 1
14 Silas and Timothy remained there. 1
15 a command for Silas and Timothy to come to him 1
18: 5 When Silas and Timothy arrived from Macedo'nia 1

Silla 1. סִלָּא
2Kg 12:20 house of Millo, on the way that goes down to Silla. 1

Siloam 1. Σιλωάμ
Lke 13: 4 eighteen upon whom the tower in Silo'am fell 1
Joh 9: 7 Go, wash in the pool of Silo'am" (which means Sent) 1
11 'Go to Silo'am and wash'; so I went and washed 1

Silvanus 1. Σιλουανός
2Co 1:19 Silva'nus and Timothy and I 1
1Th 1: 1 Paul, Silva'nus, and Timothy 1
2Th 1: 1 Paul, Silva'nus, and Timothy 1
1Pe 5:12 By Silva'nus . . I have written briefly to you 1

Simeon 1. בְּנֵי שִׁמְעוֹן 2. שִׁמְעוֹן 3. שִׁמְעוֹנִי 4. Συμεών
Gen 29:33 this son also"; and she called his name Simeon. 2
34:25 sons of Jacob, Simeon and Levi, Dinah's brothers 2
30 Then Jacob said to Simeon and Levi 2
35:23 sons of Leah . . Simeon, Levi, Judah, Is'sachar 2
42:24 he took Simeon from them and bound him before 2
36 and Simeon is no more, and now you would take 2
43:23 Then he brought Simeon out to them. 2
46:10 The sons of Simeon: Jemu'el, Jamin, Ohad, Jachin 2
48: 5 Manas'seh shall be mine, as Reuben and Simeon are 2
49: 5 Simeon and Levi are brothers; 2
Exd 1: 2 Reuben, Simeon, Levi, and Judah 2
6:15 The sons of Simeon: Jemu'el, Jamin, Ohad, Jachin 2
15 these are the families of Simeon. 2
Num 1: 6 from Simeon, Shelu'mi-el the son of Zurishad'dai; 2
22 Of the people of Simeon, their generations 2
23 the number of the tribe of Simeon was 59,300 2
2:12 tribe of Simeon, the leader of the people 2
12 the leader . . of Simeon being Shelu'mi-el 2
7:36 Shelu'mi-el the . . leader of the men of Simeon 2
10:19 over the host of the tribe of the men of Simeon 2
13: 5 from the tribe of Simeon, Shaphat the son of Hori; 2
26:12 The sons of Simeon according to their families 2
34:20 Of the tribe of the sons of Simeon, Shemu'el 2
Deu 27:12 stand upon Mount Ger'izim . . Simeon, Levi, Judah 2
Jos 19: 1 lot came out for Simeon, for the tribe of Simeon 2
1 lot came out for Simeon, for the tribe of Simeon 2
8 This was the inheritance of the tribe of Simeon 2
9 inheritance . . of Simeon formed part 2
9 the tribe of Simeon obtained an inheritance 2
21: 4 from the tribes of Judah, Simeon, and Benjamin 3
9 Out of . . Judah and the tribe of Simeon they gave 1
Jdg 1: 3 Judah said to Simeon his brother, "Come up with me 2
3 So Simeon went with him. 2
17 Judah went with Simeon his brother 2
1Ch 2: 1 These are the sons of Israel: Reuben, Simeon, Levi 2
4:24 sons of Simeon: Nem'uel, Jamin, Jarib, Zerah, Sha'ul; 2
6:65 out of the tribes of Judah, Simeon, and Benjamin 2
2Ch 15: 9 gathered . . those from . . Manas'seh and Simeon 2
34: 6 in the cities of Manas'seh, E'phraim, and Simeon 2
Ezk 48:24 from the east side to the west, Simeon, one portion 2
25 Adjoining the territory of Simeon, from the east 2
33 the gate of Simeon, the gate of Is'sachar 2
Lke 2:25 was a man in Jerusalem, whose name was Simeon 4
34 Simeon blessed them and said to Mary his mother 4
3:30 the son of Simeon, the son of Judah 4
Act 13: 1 Barnabas, Simeon who was called Niger 4
15:14 Simeon has related how God first visited 4
2Pe 1: 1 Simeon Peter, a servant and apostle of Jesus 4
Rev 7: 7 12,000 of the tribe of Simeon 4
Jdt 6:15 Uzziah the son of Micah, of the tribe of Simeon 4
9: 2 O Lord God of my father Simeon 4
1Mc 2: 1 Mattathias the son of John, son of Simeon 4
65 Simeon your brother is wise in counsel 4
4Mc 2:19 censure the households of Simeon and Levi 4

Simeonite 1. שִׁמְעוֹן 2. שִׁמְעֹנִי
Num25:14 fathers' house belonging to the Simeonites. 2
26:14 These are the families of the Simeonites, 22,200. 2
1Ch 4:42 some of them, 500 men of the Simeonites 1
12:25 the Simeonites, mighty men of valor for war, 7,100 1
27:16 for the Simeonites, Shephati'ah the son of Ma'acah; 2

Simon 1. Σίμων
Mat 4:18 he saw two brothers, Simon who is called Peter 1
10: 2 first, Simon, who is called Peter 1
4 Simon the Cananaean, and Judas Iscariot 1
13:55 James and Joseph and Simon and Judas? 1
16:16 Simon Peter replied, "You are the Christ 1
17 Blessed are you, Simon Bar-Jona! 1
17:25 What do you think, Simon? 1
26: 6 at Bethany in the house of Simon the leper 1
27:32 they came upon a man of Cyre'ne, Simon by name 1
Mrk 1:16 he saw Simon and Andrew the brother of Simon 1
16 he saw Simon and Andrew the brother of Simon 1
29 entered the house of Simon and Andrew 1
30 Now Simon's mother-in-law lay sick with a fever 1
36 Simon and those who were with him pursued him 1
3:16 Simon whom he surnamed Peter; 1
18 Thaddaeus, and Simon the Cananaean 1
6: 3 brother of James and Joses and Judas and Simon 1
14: 3 at Bethany in the house of Simon the leper 1
37 he said to Peter, "Simon, are you asleep? 1
15:21 they compelled a passer-by, Simon of Cyre'ne 1
Lke 4:38 left the synagogue, and entered Simon's house. 1
38 Now Simon's mother-in-law was ill with a high fever 1
5: 3 Getting into one of the boats, which was Simon's 1
4 when he had ceased speaking, he said to Simon 1
5 Simon answered, "Master, we toiled all night 1
8 when Simon Peter saw it 1
10 sons of Zeb'edee, who were partners with Simon. 1
10 Jesus said to Simon, "Do not be afraid 1
6:14 Simon, whom he named Peter, and Andrew 1
15 Simon who was called the Zealot 1
7:40 Simon, I have something to say to you. 1
43 Simon answered, "The one, I suppose 1
44 Then turning toward the woman he said to Simon 1
22:31 Simon, Simon, behold, Satan demanded to have you 1
31 Simon, Simon, behold, Satan demanded to have you 1
23:26 they seized one Simon of Cyre'ne 1
24:34 has appeared to Simon! 1
Joh 1:40 Andrew, Simon Peter's brother. 1
41 He first found his brother Simon, and said to him 1
42 So you are Simon the son of John? 1
6: 8 Andrew, Simon Peter's brother, said to him 1
68 Simon Peter answered him, "Lord, to whom shall we 1
71 He spoke of Judas the son of Simon Iscariot 1
13: 2 the heart of Judas Iscariot, Simon's son 1
6 He came to Simon Peter; and Peter said to him, "Lord 1
9 Simon Peter said to him, "Lord, not my feet only 1
24 Simon Peter beckoned to him and said, "Tell us 1
26 he gave it to Judas, the son of Simon Iscariot. 1
36 Simon Peter said to him, "Lord, where are you going? 1
18:10 Simon Peter, having a sword, drew it 1
15 Simon Peter followed Jesus 1
25 Simon Peter was standing and warming himself. 1
20: 2 went to Simon Peter and the other disciple 1
6 Simon Peter came, following him 1
21: 2 Simon Peter, Thomas called the Twin 1
3 Simon Peter said to them, "I am going fishing. 1
7 When Simon Peter heard that it was the Lord 1
11 Simon Peter went aboard and hauled the net ashore 1
15 Jesus said to Simon Peter, "Simon, son of John 1
15 Jesus said to Simon Peter, "Simon, son of John 1
16 A second time he said to him, "Simon, son of John 1
17 He said to him the third time, "Simon, son of John 1
Act 1:13 James the son of Alphaeus and Simon the Zealot 1
8: 9 there was a man named Simon 1
13 Even Simon himself believed 1
18 Now when Simon saw 1
24 Simon answered, "Pray for me to the Lord 1
9:43 in Joppa for many days with one Simon, a tanner. 1
10: 5 bring one Simon who is called Peter; 1
6 he is lodging with Simon, a tanner 1
17 having made inquiry for Simon's house 1
18 ask whether Simon . . was lodging there. 1
32 ask for Simon who is called Peter 1
32 in the house of Simon, a tanner, by the seaside.' 1
11:13 'Send to Joppa and bring Simon called Peter; 1
1Es 9:32 Melchias and Sabbaias and Simon Chosamaeus. 1
Sir 50: 1 the pride of his people was Simon the high priest 1
20 Simon came down *
1Mc 2: 3 Simon called Thassi 1
5:17 Then Judas said to Simon his brother 1
20 assigned to Simon to go to Galilee 1
21 so Simon went to Galilee 1
55 Simon . . was in Galilee before Ptolemais 1
9:19 Jonathan and Simon took Judas their brother 1
33 Jonathan and Simon his brother 1
37 was reported to Jonathan and Simon his brother 1
62 Then Jonathan with his men, and Simon 1

65 Jonathan left Simon his brother in the city 1
67 Simon and his men sallied out from the city 1
10:74 Simon his brother met him to help him. 1
82 Then Simon brought forward his force 1
11:59 Simon his brother he made governor 1
64 left his brother Simon in the country. 1
65 Simon encamped before Beth-zur 1
12:33 Simon also went forth 1
38 Simon built Adida in the Shephelah 1
13: 1 Simon heard 1
13 Simon encamped in Adida, facing the plain. 1
14 Trypho learned that Simon had risen up 1
17 Simon knew that they were speaking deceitfully 1
18 Because Simon did not send him the money •
20 Simon and his army 1
25 Simon sent and took the bones of Jonathan 1
27 Simon built a monument over the tomb of his father 1
33 Simon built up the strongholds of Judea 1
34 Simon also chose men and sent them to Demetrius 1
36 Simon, the high priest and friend of kings 1
42 In the first year of Simon the great high priest 1
43 In those days Simon encamped against Gazara •
45 asking Simon to make peace with them; 1
47 So Simon reached an agreement with them 1
50 Then they cried to Simon to make peace with them 1
52 Simon decreed •
53 Simon saw that John his son had reached manhood 1
14: 4 The land had rest all the days of Simon 1
17 Simon his brother had become high priest 1
20 to Simon the high priest and to the elders 1
23 they have sent a copy of this to Simon the high priest.' 1
24 After this Simon sent Numenius to Rome 1
25 How shall we thank Simon and his sons? 1
27 which is the third year of Simon 1
29 Simon the son of Mattathias . . and his brothers 1
32 then Simon rose up and fought for his nation 1
35 The people saw Simon's faithfulness 1
40 had received the envoys of Simon with honor. 1
41 Simon should be their leader and high priest 1
46 agreed to grant Simon the right 1
47 So Simon accepted and agreed to be high priest 1
49 so that Simon and his sons might have them. 1
15: 1 sent a letter from the islands of the sea to Simon 1
2 King Antiochus to Simon the high priest 1
17 They had been sent by Simon the high priest 1
21 hand them over to Simon the high priest 1
24 They also sent a copy of these things to Simon 1
26 Simon sent to Antiochus 2,000 picked men 1
27 the agreements he formerly had made with Simon •
32 when he saw the splendor of Simon 1
33 Simon gave him this reply 1
36 reported . . the splendor of Simon 1
16: 1 John went up from Gazara and reported to Simon 1
2 Simon called in his two older sons Judas and John 1
13 made treacherous plans against Simon and his sons 1
14 Now Simon was visiting the cities of the country 1
16 When Simon and his sons were drunk, Ptolemy 1
16 and rushed in against Simon in the banquet hall 1
2Mc 3: 4 a man named Simon, of the tribe of Benjamin 1
11 the impious Simon had misrepresented the facts. 1
4: 1 The previously mentioned Simon 1
3 one of Simon's approved agents 1
4 was intensifying the malice of Simon. 1
6 Simon would not stop his folly. 1
23 the brother of the previously mentioned Simon 1
8:22 Simon and Joseph and Jonathan 1
10:19 Maccabeus left Simon and Joseph 1
20 the men with Simon, who were money-hungry 1
14:17 Simon, the brother of Judas 1
3Mc 2: 1 the high priest Simon, facing the sanctuary 1
4Mc 4: 1 Now there was a certain Simon 1
4 he praised Simon for his service to the king 1
5 he proceeded . . accompanied by the accursed Simon 1

Sin 1. סִין
Exd 16: 1 people of Israel came to the wilderness of Sin 1
17: 1 Israel moved on from the wilderness of Sin 1
Num33:11 encamped in the wilderness of Sin. 1
12 set out from the wilderness of Sin, and encamped 1

Sinai 1. סִינַי 2. Σινά 3. Sina
Exd 16: 1 Sin, which is between Elim and Sinai 1
19: 1 that day they came into the wilderness of Sinai. 1
2 came into the wilderness of Sinai 1
11 the LORD will come down upon Mount Sinai 1
18 Mount Sinai was wrapped in smoke 1
20 the LORD came down upon Mount Sinai, to the top 1
23 The people cannot come up to Mount Sinai; 1
24:16 The glory of the LORD settled on Mount Sinai 1
31:18 made an end of speaking with him upon Mount Sinai 1
34: 2 come up in the morning to Mount Sinai 1
4 went up on Mount Sinai, as the LORD had commanded 1
29 When Moses came down from Mount Sinai 1
32 the LORD had spoken with him in Mount Sinai. 1
Lev 7:38 which the LORD commanded Moses on Mount Sinai 1
38 to the LORD, in the wilderness of Sinai 1
25: 1 The LORD said to Moses on Mount Sinai 1
26:46 statutes . . on Mount Sinai by Moses 1
27:34 for the people of Israel on Mount Sinai. 1
Num 1: 1 in the wilderness of Sinai, in the tent of meeting 1
19 So he numbered them in the wilderness of Sinai. 1
3: 1 when the LORD spoke with Moses on Mount Sinai. 1
4 before the LORD in the wilderness of Sinai; 1
14 the LORD said to Moses in the wilderness of Sinai 1
9: 1 LORD spoke to Moses in the wilderness of Sinai 1
5 kept the passover . . in the wilderness of Sinai; 1
10:12 set out by stages from the wilderness of Sinai; 1
26:64 numbered . . Israel in the wilderness of Sinai. 1
28: 6 offering, which was ordained at Mount Sinai 1
33:15 encamped in the wilderness of Sinai. 1
16 they set out from the wilderness of Sinai 1
Deu 33: 2 LORD came from Sinai, and dawned from Se'ir 1
Jdg 5: 5 mountains quaked . . yon Sinai before the LORD 1
Neh 9:13 Thou didst come down upon Mount Sinai, and speak 1
Ps 68: 8 yon Sinai quaked at the presence of God 1
17 Lord came from Sinai into the holy place. 1
Act 7:30 in the wilderness of Mount Sinai 2
38 the angel who spoke to him at Mount Sinai 2
Gal 4:24 One is from Mount Sinai 2
25 Now Hagar is Mount Sinai in Arabia 2
2Es 3:17 thou didst bring them to Mount Sinai. 3
14: 4 and I led him up on Mount Sinai 3
Jdt 5:14 he led them by the way of Sinai and Kadesh-barnea 2
Sir 48: 7 who heard rebuke at Sinai 2

Sinite 1. סִינִי
Gen 10:17 the Hivites, the Arkites, the Sinites 1
1Ch 1:15 the Hivites, the Arkites, the Sinites 1

Siphmoth 1. שִׂפְמוֹת
1Sm 30:28 for those . . in Aro'er, in Siphmoth, in Eshtemo'a 1

Sippai 1. סִפַּי
1Ch 20: 4 then Sib'becai the Hu'shathite slew Sip'pai 1

Sirach 1. Σιραχ
Sir 50:27 Jesus the son of Sirach, son of Eleazar 1

Sirah 1. סִרָה
2Sm 3:26 they brought him back from the cistern of Sirah; 1

Sirion 1. שִׂרְיֹן
Deu 3: 9 (the Sido'nians call Hermon Si'rion, while 1
4:48 from Aro'er . . as far as Mount Si'rion ‡
Ps 29: 6 skip like a calf, and Si'rion like a young wild ox. 1
Jer 18:14 the snow of Lebanon leave the crags of Si'rion? •

Sisera 1. סִיסְרָא 2. Σεραρ
Jdg 4: 2 Jabin . . the commander of his army was Sis'era 1
7 I will draw out Sis'era, the general of Jabin's army 1
9 LORD will sell Sis'era into the hand of a woman. 1
12 When Sis'era was told that Barak the son 1
13 Sis'era called out all his chariots, 900 chariots 1
14 which the LORD has given Sis'era into your hand. 1
15 the LORD routed Sis'era and all his chariots 1
15 and Sis'era alighted from his chariot and fled 1
16 the army of Sis'era fell by the edge of the sword; 1
17 Sis'era fled away on foot to the tent of Ja'el 1
18 Ja'el came out to meet Sis'era, and said to him 1
22 behold, as Barak pursued Sis'era, Ja'el went out 1
22 there lay Sis'era dead, with the tent peg in his 1
5:20 from their courses they fought against Sis'era. 1
26 she struck Sis'era a blow, she crushed his head 1
28 the mother of Sis'era gazed through the lattice 1
30 spoil of dyed stuffs for Sis'era, spoil of dyed 1
1Sm 12: 9 and he sold them into the hand of Sis'era 1
Ezr 2:53 sons of Barkos, the sons of Sis'era 1
Neh 7:55 sons of Barkos, the sons of Sis'era 1
Ps 83: 9 as to Sis'era and Jabin at the river Kishon 1
1Es 5:32 the sons of Sisera, the sons of Temah 2

Sisinnes 1. Σισιννης
1Es 6: 3 Sisinnes the governor of Syria and Phoenicia 1
7 Sisinnes the governor of Syria and Phoenicia 1
27 Sisinnes the governor of Syria and Phoenicia 1
7: 1 Sisinnes the governor of Coelesyria 1

Sismai 1. סִסְמַי
1Ch 2:40 Ele-a'sah . . father of Sismai, and Sismai 1
40 the father of Sismai, and Sismai of Shallum. 1

Sithri 1. סִתְרִי
Exd 6:22 the sons of Uz'ziel: Mi'sha-el, Elza'phan, and Sithri. 1

Sitnah 1. שִׂטְנָה
Gen 26:21 he called its name Sitnah. 1

Sivan 1. סִיוָן 2. Σιουαν
Est 8: 9 in the third month, which is the month of Sivan 1
Bar 1: 8 At the same time, on the tenth day of Sivan, Baruch 2

Smyrna 1. Σμύρνα
Rev 1:11 to the seven churches, to Ephesus and to Smyrna 1
2: 8 And to the angel of the church in Smyrna write 1

Soco 1. שׂוֹכוֹ
1Ch 4:18 his Jewish wife bore . . Heber the father of Soco 1
2Ch 11: 7 Beth-zur, Soco, Adullam 1
28:18 had taken . . Soco with its villages, Timnah 1

Socoh 1. שׂוֹכֹה
Jos 15:35 Jarmuth, Adullam, Socoh, Aze'kah 1
48 And in the hill country, Shamir, Jattir, Socoh 1
1Sm 17: 1 were gathered at Socoh, which belongs to Judah 1
1 and encamped between Socoh and Aze'kah 1
1Kg 4:10 Ben-hesed . . (to him belonged Socoh and all 1

Sodi 1. סוֹדִי
Num13:10 from the tribe of Zeb'ulun, Gad'diel the son of Sodi; 1

Sodom 1. סְדֹם 2. Σόδομα 3. Σοδομιται 4. Sodoma 5. Sodomitus
Gen 10:19 and in the direction of Sodom, Gomor'rah, Admah 1
13:10 before the LORD destroyed Sodom and Gomor'rah. 1
12 of the valley and moved his tent as far as Sodom. 1
13 Now the men of Sodom were wicked, great sinners 1
14: 2 these kings made war with Bera king of Sodom 1
8 Then the king of Sodom, the king of Gomor'rah 1
10 and as the kings of Sodom and Gomor'rah fled 1
11 all the goods of Sodom and Gomor'rah 1
12 son of Abram's brother, who dwelt in Sodom 1
17 king of Sodom went out to meet him at the Valley 1
21 the king of Sodom said to Abram 1
22 Abram said to the king of Sodom 1
18:16 from there, and they looked toward Sodom; 1
20 Because the outcry against Sodom and Gomor'rah 1
22 the men turned from there, and went toward Sodom; 1
26 the LORD said, "If I find at Sodom 50 righteous 1
19: 1 The two angels came to Sodom in the evening; 1
1 and Lot was sitting in the gate of Sodom. 1
4 the men of Sodom, both young and old 1
24 Then the LORD rained on Sodom and Gomor'rah 1
28 he looked down toward Sodom and Gomor'rah 1
Deu 29:23 an overthrow like that of Sodom and Gomor'rah 1
32:32 For their vine comes from the vine of Sodom 1
Isa 1: 9 we should have been like Sodom, and . . Gomor'rah. 1
10 Hear the word of the LORD, you rulers of Sodom! 1
3: 9 they proclaim their sin like Sodom 1
13:19 like Sodom and Gomor'rah when God overthrew 1
Jer 23:14 all of them have become like Sodom to me 1
49:18 As when Sodom and Gomor'rah . . were overthrown 1
50:40 As when God overthrew Sodom and Gomor'rah 1
Lam 4: 6 the punishment of Sodom, which was overthrown 1
Ezk 16:46 south of you, is Sodom with her daughters. 1
48 your sister Sodom and her daughters have not 1
49 Behold, this was the guilt of your sister Sodom 1
53 both the fortunes of Sodom and her daughters 1
55 As for your sisters, Sodom and her daughters 1
56 Was not your sister Sodom a byword in your mouth 1
Ams 4:11 as when God overthrew Sodom and Gomor'rah 1
Zep 2: 9 Moab shall become like Sodom 1
Mat 10:15 for the land of Sodom and Gomor'rah 2
11:23 had been done in Sodom, it would have remained 2
24 day of judgment for the land of Sodom 2
Lke 10:12 it shall be more tolerable on that day for Sodom 2
17:29 on the day when Lot went out from Sodom 2
Rom 9:29 we would have fared like Sodom 2
2Pe 2: 6 the cities of Sodom and Gomor'rah to ashes 2
Jde 1: 7 Sodom and Gomor'rah and the surrounding cities 2
Rev 11: 8 city which is allegorically called Sodom 2
2Es 2: 8 remember what I did to Sodom and Gomorrah 4
5: 7 the sea of Sodom shall cast up fish 5
3Mc 2: 5 consumed with fire and sulphur the men of Sodom 3

people of Sodom 1. Sodomitae
2Es 7:106 first Abraham prayed for the people of Sodom 1

Solomon 1. שְׁלֹמֹה 2. Σολομών 3. Salomon
2Sm 5:14 born to him . . Sham'mu-a, Shobab, Nathan, Solomon 1
12:24 and she bore a son, and he called his name Solomon. 1
1Kg 1:10 did not invite . . or Solomon his brother. 1
11 Nathan said to Bathshe'ba the mother of Solomon 1
12 your own life and the life of your son Solomon. 1
13 Solomon your son shall reign after me 1
17 Solomon your son shall reign after me 1
19 but Solomon your servant he has not invited. 1
21 I and my son Solomon will be counted offenders. 1
26 and your servant Solomon, he has not invited. 1
30 Solomon your son shall reign after me 1
33 cause Solomon my son to ride on my own mule 1
34 blow the trumpet, and say, 'Long live King Solomon 1
37 even so may he be with Solomon, and make his throne 1
38 and caused Solomon to ride on King David's mule 1
39 took the horn of oil . . and anointed Solomon. 1
39 and all the people said, "Long live King Solomon! 1
43 No, for our lord King David has made Solomon king; 1
46 Solomon sits upon the royal throne. 1
47 make the name of Solomon more famous than yours 1
50 Adoni'jah feared Solomon; and he arose, and went 1
51 it was told Solomon, "Behold, Adoni'jah fears King 1
51 Adoni'jah fears King Solomon; for, lo, he has laid 1
51 Let King Solomon swear to me first that he will 1
52 Solomon said, "If he prove to be a worthy man, not one 1
53 King Solomon sent, and they brought him down 1
53 And he came and did obeisance to King Solomon; 1

53 and Solomon said to him, "Go to your house. 1
2: 1 drew near, he charged Solomon his son, saying 1
12 Solomon sat upon the throne of David his father; 1
13 came to Bathshe'ba the mother of Solomon. 1
17 ask King Solomon . . to give me Ab'ishag 1
19 Bathshe'ba went to King Solomon, to speak to him 1
22 King Solomon answered his mother, "And why do you 1
23 King Solomon swore by the LORD, saying, "God do 1
25 So King Solomon sent Benai'ah the son of Jehoi'ada; 1
27 Solomon expelled Abi'athar from being priest 1
29 when it was told King Solomon, "Jo'ab has fled 1
29 Solomon sent Benai'ah the son of Jehoi'ada, saying 1
41 when Solomon was told 1
45 King Solomon shall be blessed, and the throne 1
46 kingdom was established in the hand of Solomon. 1
3: 1 Solomon made a marriage alliance with Pharaoh 1
3 Solomon loved the LORD, walking in the statutes 1
4 Solomon used to offer . . burnt offerings 1
5 the LORD appeared to Solomon in a dream by night; 1
6 Solomon said, "Thou hast shown great 1
10 It pleased the Lord that Solomon had asked this. 1
15 Solomon awoke, and behold, it was a dream. Then he 1
4: 1 King Solomon was king over all Israel 1
7 Solomon had twelve officers over all Israel, who 1
11 (he had Taphath the daughter of Solomon as his 1
15 he had taken Bas'emath the daughter of Solomon 1
21 Solomon ruled over all the kingdoms 1
21 brought tribute and served Solomon all the days 1
22 Solomon's provision for one day was 30 cors 1
25 dwelt in safety . . all the days of Solomon. 1
26 Solomon also had 40,000 stalls of horses 1
27 officers supplied provisions for King Solomon 1
27 and for all who came to King Solomon's table, each 1
29 God gave Solomon wisdom and understanding 1
30 Solomon's wisdom surpassed the wisdom of all 1
34 men came . . to hear the wisdom of Solomon 1
5: 1 Hiram king of Tyre sent his servants to Solomon 1
2 Solomon sent word to Hiram 1
7 When Hiram heard the words of Solomon 1
8 Hiram sent to Solomon, saying, "I have heard 1
10 So Hiram supplied Solomon with all the timber 1
11 Solomon gave Hiram . . wheat as food 1
11 Solomon gave this to Hiram year by year. 1
12 the LORD gave Solomon wisdom, as he promised him; 1
12 there was peace between Hiram and Solomon; 1
13 King Solomon raised a levy of forced labor 1
15 Solomon also had . . burden-bearers 1
16 besides Solomon's . . chief officers 1
18 Solomon's builders and Hiram's builders 1
6: 1 in the fourth year of Solomon's reign over Israel 1
2 The house which King Solomon built for the LORD 1
11 Now the word of the LORD came to Solomon 1
14 So Solomon built the house, and finished it. 1
21 Solomon overlaid the inside of the house 1
7: 1 Solomon was building his own house 1
8 Solomon also made a house like this hall 1
13 King Solomon sent and brought Hiram from Tyre. 1
14 He came to King Solomon, and did all his work. 1
40 Hiram finished . . that he did for King Solomon 1
45 vessels . . which Hiram made for King Solomon 1
47 Solomon left all the vessels unweighed 1
48 So Solomon made all the vessels that were 1
51 all the work that King Solomon did on the house 1
51 Solomon brought in the things . . dedicated 1
8: 1 Solomon assembled the elders of Israel 1
1 assembled . . before King Solomon in Jerusalem 1
2 all the men of Israel assembled to King Solomon 1
5 King Solomon and all the congregation of Israel 1
12 Then Solomon said, "The LORD has set the sun 1
22 Then Solomon stood before the altar of the LORD 1
54 as Solomon finished offering all this prayer 1
63 Solomon offered . . to the LORD 22,000 oxen 1
65 Solomon held the feast . . and all Israel with him 1
9: 1 When Solomon had finished building the house 1
1 finished . . all that Solomon desired to build 1
2 the LORD appeared to Solomon a second time 1
10 years, in which Solomon had built the two houses 1
11 Hiram . . had supplied Solomon with cedar 1
11 King Solomon gave to Hiram twenty cities 1
12 to see the cities which Solomon had given him 1
15 forced labor which King Solomon levied to build 1
16 given it as dowry to his daughter, Solomon's wife; 1
17 so Solomon rebuilt Gezer) 1
19 build . . all the store-cities that Solomon had 1
19 to build . . whatever Solomon desired to build 1
21 Solomon made a forced levy of slaves 1
22 of the people of Israel Solomon made no slaves; 1
23 the chief officers who were over Solomon's work 1
24 to her own house which Solomon had built for her; •
25 Solomon used to offer up burnt offerings 1
26 King Solomon built a fleet of ships 1
27 seamen . . together with the servants of Solomon; 1
28 and they brought it to King Solomon. 1
10: 1 the queen of Sheba heard of the fame of Solomon 1
2 when she came to Solomon, she told him all 1
3 Solomon answered all her questions; 1
4 queen of Sheba had seen all the wisdom of Solomon 1
10 which the queen of Sheba gave to King Solomon. 1
13 King Solomon gave to the queen of Sheba 1
13 what was given her by the bounty of King Solomon. 1
14 the weight of gold that came to Solomon 1
16 King Solomon made 200 large shields of beaten gold; 1
21 All King Solomon's drinking vessels were of gold 1
21 was not considered . . in the days of Solomon. 1
23 King Solomon excelled all the kings of the earth 1
24 the whole earth sought the presence of Solomon 1
26 Solomon gathered . . chariots and horsemen; 1
28 Solomon's import of horses was from Egypt and Ku'e 1
11: 1 Now King Solomon loved many foreign women 1
2 Solomon clung to these in love. 1
4 when Solomon was old his wives turned away 1
5 Solomon went after Ash'toreth the goddess 1
6 Solomon did what was evil in the sight of the LORD 1
7 Solomon built a high place for Chemosh 1
9 the LORD was angry with Solomon 1
11 Therefore the LORD said to Solomon 1
14 the LORD raised up an adversary against Solomon 1
25 an adversary of Israel all the days of Solomon 1
26 Jerobo'am the son of Nebat . . a servant of Solomon 1
27 Solomon built the Millo, and closed up the breach 1
28 Solomon saw that the young man was industrious 1
31 to tear the kingdom from the hand of Solomon 1
40 Solomon sought therefore to kill Jerobo'am; 1
40 and was in Egypt until the death of Solomon. 1
41 the rest of the acts of Solomon, and all that he did 1
41 not written in the book of the acts of Solomon? 1
42 Solomon reigned in Jerusalem over all Israel 1
43 Solomon slept with his fathers, and was buried 1
12: 2 in Egypt, whither he had fled from King Solomon) 1
6 old men, who had stood before Solomon his father 1
21 the kingdom to Rehobo'am the son of Solomon. 1
23 Say to Rehobo'am the son of Solomon, king of Judah 1
14:21 Rehobo'am the son of Solomon reigned in Judah. 1
26 all the shields of gold which Solomon had made; 1
2Kg 21: 7 the LORD said to David and to Solomon his son 1
23:13 which Solomon the king of Israel had built 1
24:13 vessels . . which Solomon king of Israel had made 1
25:16 As for the . . which Solomon had made for the house 1
1Ch 3: 5 were born to him in Jerusalem . . and Solomon 1
10 descendants of Solomon: Rehobo'am, Abi'jah his son 1
6:10 in the house that Solomon built in Jerusalem 1
32 until Solomon had built the house of the LORD 1
14: 4 the children . . Shammu'a, Shobab, Nathan, Solomon 1
18: 8 with it Solomon made the bronze sea 1
22: 5 Solomon my son is young and inexperienced 1
6 called for Solomon his son, and charged him 1
7 David said to Solomon, "My son, I had it in my heart 1
9 for his name shall be Solomon 1
17 leaders of Israel to help Solomon his son, saying 1
23: 1 David . . made Solomon his son king over Israel. 1
28: 5 of all my sons . . he has chosen Solomon my son 1
6 Solomon your son who shall build my house 1
9 you, Solomon my son, know the God of your father 1
11 David gave Solomon his son the plan 1
20 David said to Solomon . . "Be strong and of good 1
29: 1 Solomon my son . . is young and inexperienced 1
19 Grant to Solomon my son that with a whole heart 1
22 Solomon the son of David king the second time 1
23 Then Solomon sat on the throne of the LORD as king 1
24 pledged their allegiance to King Solomon. 1
25 LORD gave Solomon great repute in the sight 1
28 and Solomon his son reigned in his stead. 1
2Ch 1: 1 Solomon . . established himself in his kingdom 1
2 Solomon spoke to all Israel 1
3 Solomon . . went to the high place . . at Gibeon; 1
5 And Solomon and the assembly sought the LORD. 1
6 Solomon went up there to the bronze altar 1
7 In that night God appeared to Solomon 1
8 Solomon said to God, "Thou hast shown great 1
11 God answered Solomon, "Because this was 1
13 Solomon came from the high place at Gibeon 1
14 Solomon gathered together chariots 1
16 Solomon's import of horses was from Egypt and Ku'e 1
2: 1 Solomon purposed to build a temple for . . LORD 1
2 Solomon assigned 70,000 men 1
3 Solomon sent word to Huram the king of Tyre 1
11 answered in a letter which he sent to Solomon 1
17 Solomon took a census of all the aliens who were 1
3: 1 Then Solomon began to build the house of the LORD 1
3 Solomon's measurements for building the house 1
4:11 finished the work that he did for King Solomon 1
16 Huram-abi made . . for King Solomon for the house 1
18 Solomon made all these things in great 1
19 Solomon made all the things that were 1
5: 1 work that Solomon did for the house of the LORD 1
1 Solomon brought in the things which David 1
2 Then Solomon assembled the elders of Israel 1
6 King Solomon and all the congregation of Israel 1
6: 1 Then Solomon said, "The LORD has said that he 1
12 Then Solomon stood before the altar of the LORD •
13 Solomon had made a bronze platform . . and set it 1
7: 1 When Solomon had ended his prayer, fire came down 1
5 King Solomon offered as a sacrifice 1
7 Solomon consecrated the middle of the court 1
7 bronze altar Solomon had made could not hold 1
8 Solomon held the feast for seven days 1
10 goodness that the LORD had shown to . . Solomon 1
11 Thus Solomon finished the house of the LORD 1
11 all that Solomon had planned to do in the house 1
12 Then the LORD appeared to Solomon in the night 1
8: 1 twenty years, in which Solomon had built 1
2 Solomon rebuilt the cities which Huram had 1
3 Solomon went to Ma'math-zo'bah, and took it. 1
6 Ba'alath, and all the store-cities . . Solomon had 1
6 whatever Solomon desired to build in Jerusalem 1
8 these Solomon made a forced levy and so they are 1
9 of the people of Israel Solomon made no slaves 1
10 these were the chief officers of King Solomon 1
11 Solomon brought Pharaoh's daughter up 1
12 Solomon offered up burnt offerings to the LORD 1
16 Thus was accomplished all the work of Solomon 1
17 Then Solomon went to E'zion-ge'ber and Eloth 1
18 went to Ophir . . with the servants of Solomon 1
18 talents of gold and brought it to King Solomon. 1
9: 1 the queen of Sheba heard of the fame of Solomon 1
1 When she came to Solomon, she told him all that was 1
2 Solomon answered all her questions; 1
2 there was nothing hidden from Solomon 1
3 queen of Sheba had seen the wisdom of Solomon 1
9 which the queen of Sheba gave to King Solomon. 1
10 servants of Huram and the servants of Solomon 1
12 King Solomon gave to the queen of Sheba 1
13 weight of gold that came to Solomon in one year 1
14 brought gold and silver to Solomon. 1
15 King Solomon made 200 large shields of . . gold; 1
20 All King Solomon's drinking vessels were of gold 1
20 not considered . . in the days of Solomon. 1
22 King Solomon excelled all the kings of the earth 1
23 all the kings . . sought the presence of Solomon 1
25 Solomon had 4,000 stalls for horses and chariots 1
28 horses were imported for Solomon from Egypt 1
29 Now the rest of the acts of Solomon 1
30 Solomon reigned in Jerusalem over all Israel 1
31 Solomon slept with his fathers, and was buried 1
10: 2 in Egypt, whither he had fled from King Solomon) 1
6 old men, who had stood before Solomon his father 1
11: 3 Say to Rehobo'am the son of Solomon king of Judah 1
17 they made Rehobo'am the son of Solomon secure 1
17 they walked . . in the way of David and Solomon. 1
12: 9 the shields of gold which Solomon had made; 1
13: 6 Jerobo'am the son of Nebat, a servant of Solomon 1
7 defied Rehobo'am the son of Solomon 1
30:26 since the time of Solomon . . there had been 1
33: 7 house of God, of which God said . . to Solomon 1
35: 3 house which Solomon the son of David . . built; 1
4 following . . directions of Solomon his son. 1
Ezr 2:55 sons of Solomon's servants: the sons of So'tai 1
58 servants and the sons of Solomon's servants 1
Neh 7:57 sons of Solomon's servants: the sons of So'tai 1
60 servants and the sons of Solomon's servants 1
11: 3 descendants of Solomon's servants. 1
12:45 command of David and his son Solomon. 1
13:26 not Solomon king of Israel sin on account of such 1
Ps 72: 0 A Psalm of Solomon. 1
127: 0 A Song of Ascents. Of Solomon. 1
Prv 1: 1 proverbs of Solomon, son of David, king of Israel 1
10: 1 The proverbs of Solomon. 1
25: 1 These also are proverbs of Solomon 1
Sng 1: 1 The Song of Songs, which is Solomon's. 1
5 I am very dark . . like the curtains of Solomon. 1
3: 7 Behold, it is the litter of Solomon! 1
9 King Solomon made himself a palanquin 1
11 Go . . O daughters of Zion, and behold King Solomon 1
8:11 Solomon had a vineyard at Ba'al-ha'mon; 1
12 you, O Solomon, may have the 1,000 1
Jer 52:20 and the stands, which Solomon the king had made 1
Mat 1: 6 And David was the father of Solomon by the wife 2
7 Solomon the father of Rehoboam 2
6:29 yet I tell you, even Solomon in all his glory was not 2
12:42 to hear the wisdom of Solomon 2
42 behold, something greater than Solomon is here. 2
Lke 11:31 to hear the wisdom of Solomon 2
31 behold, something greater than Solomon is here. 2
12:27 even Solomon in all his glory was not arrayed 2
Joh 10:23 in the temple, in the portico of Solomon. 2
Act 3:11 in the portico called Solomon's 2
5:12 they were all together in Solomon's Portico. 2
7:47 it was Solomon who built a house for him. 2
1Es 1: 3 the house which Solomon . . had built; 2
5 the magnificence of Solomon his son 2
5:33 The sons of Solomon's servants 2
35 the sons of Solomon's servants were 372. 2
2Es 7:108 and Solomon for those in the sanctuary 3
10:46 after 3,000 years Solomon built the city 3
Sir 47:13 Solomon reigned in days of peace 2
23 Solomon rested with his fathers 2
2Mc 2: 8 as Solomon asked that . . 2
9 Solomon offered sacrifice •
10 so also Solomon prayed 2
12 Likewise Solomon also kept the eight days. 2
4Mc 18:16 He recounted to you Solomon's proverb 2

Sopater 1. Σώπατρος

Act 20: 4 Sop'ater of Beroe'a, the son of Pyrrhus 1

Sophereth 1. סוֹפֶרֶת

Neh 7:57 sons of So'tai, the sons of So'phereth 1

Sorek 1. שֹׂרֵק
Jdg 16: 4 he loved a woman in the valley of Sorek, whose name 1

Sosipater 1. Σωσίπατρος
Rom 16:21 so do Lucius and Jason and Sosip'ater, my kinsmen. 1
2Mc 12:19 Dositheus and Sosipater, who were captains 1
24 Dositheus and Sosipater and their men 1

Sosthenes 1. Σωσθένης
Act 18:17 they all seized Sos'thenes, the ruler of the synagogue 1
1Co 1: 1 Paul . . and our brother Sos'thenes 1

Sostratus 1. Σωστρατος
2Mc 4:28 Sostratus the captain of the citadel 1
29 while Sostratus left Crates 1

Sotai 1. סוֹטַי
Ezr 2:55 sons of Solomon's servants: the sons of So'tai 1
Neh 7:57 sons of So'tai, the sons of So'phereth 1

Spain 1. Σπανία
Rom 15:24 I hope to see you in passing as I go to Spain 1
28 I shall go on by way of you to Spain; 1
1Mc 8: 3 what they had done in the land of Spain 1

Sparta 1. Σπαρτη
1Mc 14:16 It was heard in Rome, and as far away as Sparta 1

Spartan 1. Σπαρτιαται
1Mc 12: 2 to the Spartans and to other places. 1
5 the letter which Jonathan wrote to the Spartans 1
6 to their brethren the Spartans, greeting. 1
20 Arius, king of the Spartans 1
21 found in writing concerning the Spartans 1
14:20 a copy of the letter which the Spartans sent 1
20 The rulers and the city of the Spartans 1
23 the people of the Spartans may have a record 1
15:23 to the Spartans, and to Delos, and to Myndos 1

Stachys 1. Στάχυς
Rom 16: 9 Greet Urba'nus . . and my beloved Stachys. 1

Stephanas 1. Στεφανᾶς
1Co 1:16 I did baptize also the household of Steph'anas. 1
16:15 household of Steph'anas were the first converts 1
17 at the coming of Steph'anas and Fortuna'tus 1

Stephen 1. Στέφανος
Act 6: 5 they chose Stephen 1
8 Stephen, full of grace and power 1
9 some of those . . arose and disputed with Stephen. 1
7: 2 Stephen said: "Brethren and fathers, hear me. •
59 as they were stoning Stephen, he prayed 1
8: 2 Devout men buried Stephen 1
11:19 the persecution that arose over Stephen 1
22:20 when the blood of Stephen thy witness was shed 1

Stoic 1. Στοϊκός
Act 17:18 Epicurean and Stoic philosophers met him 1

Suah 1. סוּחַ
1Ch 7:36 sons of Zophah: Su'ah, Har'nepher, Shu'al, Beri, 1

Subas 1. Σουβας
1Es 5:34 the sons of Gas, the sons of Addus, the sons of Subas 1

Sucathite 1. שׂוּכָתִים
1Ch 2:55 the Shim'e-athites, and the Su'cathites. 1

Succoth 1. סֻכּוֹת
Gen 33:17 Jacob journeyed to Succoth 1
17 the name of the place is called Succoth. 1
Exd 12:37 the people . . journeyed from Ram'eses to Succoth 1
13:20 they moved on from Succoth, and encamped at Etham 1
Num33: 5 people of Israel . . encamped at Succoth. 1
6 they set out from Succoth, and encamped at Etham 1
Jos 13:27 of Beth-ha'ram, Beth-nim'rah, Succoth, and Zaphon 1
Jdg 8: 5 he said to the men of Succoth, "Pray, give loaves 1
6 the officials of Succoth said, "Are Zebah 1
8 answered him as the men of Succoth had answered. 1
14 he caught a young man of Succoth, and questioned 1
14 the officials and elders of Succoth, 77 men. 1
15 he came to the men of Succoth, and said, "Behold 1
16 briers and with them taught the men of Succoth. 1
1Kg 7:46 in the clay ground between Succoth and Zarethan. 1
2Ch 4:17 in the clay ground between Succoth and Zer'edah. 1
Ps 60: 6 and portion out the Vale of Succoth. 1
108: 7 I will . . portion out the Vale of Succoth. 1

Succoth-benoth 1. סֻכּוֹת בְּנוֹת
2Kg 17:30 the men of Babylon made Suc'coth-be'noth 1

Sud 1. Σουδ
Bar 1: 4 all who dwelt in Babylon by the river Sud. 1

Sudias 1. Σουδιας
1Es 5:26 sons of Jeshua and Kadmiel and Bannas and Sudias 1

Sukkiim 1. סֻכִּיִּים
2Ch 12: 3 from Egypt–Libyans, Suk'ki-im, and Ethiopians. 1

Suph 1. סוּף
Deu 1: 1 the wilderness, in the Arabah over against Suph 1

Suphah 1. סוּפָה
Num21:14 Waheb in Suphah, and the valleys of the Arnon 1

Sur 1. סוּר 2. Σουρ
2Kg 11: 6 another third being at the gate Sur and a third 1
Jdt 2:28 those who lived in Sur and Ocina 2

Susa 1. שׁוּשַׁן 2. Σουσα
Neh 1: 1 Now it happened . . as I was in Susa the capital 1
Est 1: 2 sat on his royal throne in Susa the capital 1
5 for all the people present in Susa the capital 1
2: 3 gather . . to the harem in Susa the capital 1
5 there was a Jew in Susa . . whose name was Mor'decai 1
8 many maidens were gathered in Susa the capital 1
3:15 and the decree was issued in Susa the capital. 1
15 but the city of Susa was perplexed. 1
4: 8 decree issued in Susa for their destruction 1
16 gather all the Jews to be found in Susa, and . . fast 1
8:14 and the decree was issued in Susa the capital. 1
15 while the city of Susa shouted and rejoiced. 1
9: 6 In Susa the capital itself the Jews slew 1
11 the number of those slain in Susa . . was reported 1
12 In Susa . . the Jews have slain 500 men 1
13 let the Jews who are in Susa be allowed 1
14 a decree was issued in Susa, and . . were hanged. 1
15 The Jews who were in Susa gathered also 1
15 and they slew 300 men in Susa; 1
18 Jews . . in Susa gathered on the thirteenth day 1
Dan 8: 2 vision; and when I saw, I was in Susa the capital 1
AEs 11: 3 He was a Jew, dwelling in the city of Susa 2
16:18 the man . . has been hanged at the gate of Susa 2

man of Susa 1. שׁוּשַׁנְכָיֵא (A)
Ezr 4: 9 men of Erech, the Babylonians, the men of Susa 1

Susanna 1. Σουσάννα
Lke 8: 3 Joan'na . . and Susanna, and many others 1
Sus 1: 2 a wife named Susanna, the daughter of Hilkiah 1
7 Susanna would go into her husband's garden 1
22 Susanna sighed deeply, and said, "I am hemmed 1
24 Then Susanna cried out with a loud voice 1
27 nothing like this had ever been said about Susanna. 1
28 their wicked plot to have Susanna put to death. 1
29 Send for Susanna, the daughter of Hilkiah 1
31 Now Susanna was a woman of great refinement 1
42 Then Susanna cried out with a loud voice, and said 1
63 praised God for their daughter Susanna 1

Susi 1. סוּסִי
Num13:11 from the tribe of Joseph . . Gaddi the son of Susi; 1

Sychar 1. Συχάρ
Joh 4: 5 So he came to a city of Samar'ia, called Sy'char 1

Syene 1. סְוֵן
Isa 49:12 from the west, and these from the land of Syene. •
Ezk 29:10 to Syene, as far as the border of Ethiopia. 1
30: 6 from Migdol to Syene they shall fall within her 1

Syntyche 1. Συντύχη
Php 4: 2 I entreat Eu-o'dia and I entreat Syn'tyche to agree 1

Syracuse 1. Συράκουσαι
Act 28:12 Putting in at Syracuse, we stayed there 1

Syria 1. אֲרָם 2. Συρία 3. Syria
Jdg 10: 6 the Ash'taroth, the gods of Syria, the gods of Sidon 1
1Kg 10:29 exported to all . . the kings of Syria. 1
11:25 and he abhorred Israel, and reigned over Syria. 1
15:18 Tabrim'mon, the son of He'zion, king of Syria 1
19:15 you shall anoint Haz'ael to be king over Syria; 1
20: 1 Ben-ha'dad the king of Syria gathered . . his army 1
20 Ben-ha'dad king of Syria escaped on a horse 1
22 the king of Syria will come up against you. 1
23 the servants of the king of Syria said to him 1
22: 1 Syria and Israel continued without war. 1
3 do not take it out of the hand of the king of Syria? 1
31 the king of Syria had commanded the . . captains 1
2Kg 5: 1 Na'aman, commander of the army of the king of Syria 1
1 by him the LORD had given victory to Syria. 1
5 the king of Syria said, "Go now 1
6: 8 the King of Syria was warring against Israel 1
11 the mind of the king of Syria was . . troubled 1
24 Ben-ha'dad king of Syria mustered his entire army 1
8: 7 Ben-ha'dad the king of Syria was sick; 1
9 Your son Ben-ha'dad king of Syria has sent me to you 1
13 LORD has shown me . . you are to be king over Syria. 1
28 to make war against Haz'ael king of Syria 1
29 when he fought against Haz'ael king of Syria. 1
9:14 been on guard . . against Haz'ael king of Syria; 1
15 when he fought with Haz'ael king of Syria.) 1
12:17 Haz'ael king of Syria went up . . against Gath 1
18 took . . and sent these to Haz'ael king of Syria. 1
13: 3 gave them . . into the hand of Haz'ael king of Syria 1
4 he saw . . how the king of Syria oppressed them. 1
7 the king of Syria had destroyed them 1
17 LORD's arrow . . the arrow of victory over Syria! 1
19 struck down Syria until you had made an end of it 1
19 now you will strike down Syria only three times. 1
22 Now Haz'ael king of Syria oppressed Israel 1
24 Haz'ael king of Syria died . . his son became king 1
15:37 send Rezin the king of Syria . . against Judah. 1
16: 5 Rezin king of Syria . . came up to wage war 1
7 and rescue me from the hand of the king of Syria 1
1Ch 18: 6 Then David put garrisons in Syria of Damascus; 1
2Ch 1:17 exported to . . and the kings of Syria. 1
16: 2 sent them to Ben-ha'dad king of Syria 1
7 Because you relied on the king of Syria 1
7 the army of the king of Syria has escaped you. 1
18:30 Now the king of Syria had commanded the captains 1
22: 5 to make war against Haz'ael king of Syria 1
6 when he fought against Haz'ael king of Syria. 1
28: 5 gave him into the hand of the king of Syria 1
23 Because the gods of the kings of Syria helped 1
Isa 7: 1 In the days of Ahaz . . Rezin the king of Syria 1
2 was told, "Syria is in league with E'phraim 1
4 at the fierce anger of Rezin and Syria 1
5 Syria, with E'phraim . . has devised evil 1
8 For the head of Syria is Damascus 1
17: 3 the remnant of Syria will be like the glory 1
Ams 1: 5 and the people of Syria shall go into exile to Kir 1
Mat 4:24 So his fame spread throughout all Syria 2
Lke 2: 2 when Quirin'ius was governor of Syria. 2
Act 15:23 the brethren . . in Antioch and Syria, and Cili'cia 2
41 he went through Syria and Cili'cia 2
18:18 took leave of the brethren and sailed for Syria 2
20: 3 as he was about to set sail for Syria 2
21: 3 leaving it on the left we sailed to Syria 2
Gal 1:21 I went into the regions of Syria and Cili'cia. 2
1Es 2:25 living in Samaria and Syria and Phoenicia 2
6: 3 Sisinnes the governor of Syria and Phoenicia 2
7 Sisinnes the governor of Syria and Phoenicia 2
7 the local rulers in Syria and Phoenicia 2
27 Sisinnes the governor of Syria and Phoenicia 2
27 appointed as local rulers in Syria and Phoenicia 2
8:19 the treasurers of Syria and Phoenicia 2
23 throughout all Syria and Phoenicia 2
2Es 16: 1 Woe to you, Egypt and Syria! 3
Jdt 1:12 Cilicia and Damascus and Syria 2
8:26 what happened to Jacob in Mesopotamia in Syria 2
1Mc 3:41 forces from Syria . . joined with them. 2
11: 2 He set out for Syria with peaceable words 2
60 all the army of Syria gathered to him as allies. 2
4Mc 4: 2 he came to Apollonius, governor of Syria 2

Syrian 1. אֲרָם 2. אֲרַמִּי 3. Συρία 4. Συριακος 5. Σύρος
2Sm 8: 5 when the Syrians of Damascus came to help 1
5 David slew 22,000 men of the Syrians. 1
6 the Syrians became servants to David 1
10: 6 Ammonites . . hired the Syrians of Beth-re'hob 1
6 hired . . the Syrians of Zobah 1
8 the Syrians of Zobah and of Rehob, and the men 1
9 he chose . . and arrayed them against the Syrians; 1
11 And he said, "If the Syrians are too strong for me 1
13 Jo'ab . . drew near to battle against the Syrians; 1
14 when the Ammonites saw that the Syrians fled 1
15 when the Syrians saw that they had been defeated 1
16 brought out the Syrians . . beyond the Euphra'tes; 1
17 the Syrians arrayed themselves against David 1
18 And the Syrians fled before Israel; 1
18 David slew of the Syrians the men of 700 chariots 1
19 the Syrians feared to help the Ammonites any 1
1Kg 20:20 the Syrians fled and Israel pursued them 1
21 and killed the Syrians with a great slaughter. 1
26 Ben-ha'dad mustered the Syrians, and went up 1
27 but the Syrians filled the country. 1
28 Because the Syrians have said, "The LORD is a god 1
29 Israel smote of the Syrians 100,000 foot soldiers 1
22:11 With these you shall push the Syrians 1
35 the king was propped up . . facing the Syrians 1
2Kg 5: 2 the Syrians . . had carried off a little maid 1
20 See, my master has spared this Na'aman the Syrian 2
6: 9 this place, for the Syrians are going down there. 1
18 when the Syrians came down . . Eli'sha prayed •
23 the Syrians came no more on raids into the land 1
7: 4 come, let us go over to the camp of the Syrians; 1
5 they arose . . to go to the camp of the Syrians; 1
5 they came to the edge of the camp of the Syrians 1
6 the Lord had made the army of the Syrians hear 1
10 We came to the camp of the Syrians 1
12 I will tell you what the Syrians have prepared 1
14 the king sent them after the army of the Syrians 1
15 and equipment which the Syrians had thrown away 1
16 went out, and plundered the camp of the Syrians. 1
8:28 to make war . . where the Syrians wounded Joram. 2
29 wounds which the Syrians had given him at Ramah 2
9:15 of the wounds which the Syrians had given him 2
13: 5 so that they escaped from the hand of the Syrians; 1
17 For you shall fight the Syrians in Aphek until 1

24: 2 bands of the Chalde'ans, and bands of the Syrians 1
1Ch 18: 5 Syrians of Damascus came to help Hadade'zer 1
5 David slew 22,000 men of the Syrians. 1
6 the Syrians became servants to David 1
19:10 and arrayed them against the Syrians; 1
12 he said, "If the Syrians are too strong for me 1
14 drew near before the Syrians for battle; 1
15 when the Ammonites saw that the Syrians fled 1
16 when the Syrians saw that they had been defeated 1
16 the Syrians who were beyond the Euphra'tes 1
17 David set the battle in array against the Syrians 1
18 the Syrians fled before Israel; 1
18 David slew of the Syrians the men of 7,000 chariots 1
19 Syrians were not willing to help the Ammonites 1
2Ch 18:10 With these you shall push the Syrians 1
34 in his chariot facing the Syrians until evening; 1
22: 5 And the Syrians wounded Joram 2
24:23 the army of the Syrians came up against Jo'ash. 1
24 the army of the Syrians had come with few men 1
Isa 9:12 The Syrians on the east and the Philistines 1
Jer 35:11 for fear of . . the army of the Syrians. 1
Ams 9: 7 Did I not bring up . . and the Syrians from Kir? 1
Lke 4:27 but only Na'aman the Syrian. 5
1Mc 3:13 Seron, the commander of the Syrian army, heard 3
7:39 the Syrian army joined him. 3
2Mc 15:36 which is called Adar in the Syrian language 4

Syrophoenician 1. Συροφοινίκισσα
Mrk 7:26 the woman was a Greek, a Syrophoeni'cian by birth. 1

Syrtis 1. Σύρτις
Act 27:17 then, fearing that they should run on the Syr'tis 1

Taanach 1. תַּעְנָךְ
Jos 12:21 the king of Ta'anach, one; the king of Megid'do, one; 1
17:11 and the inhabitants of Ta'anach and its villages 1
21:25 Ta'anach with its pasture lands, and Gath-rim'mon 1
Jdg 1:27 did not drive out . . or Ta'anach and its villages 1
5:19 fought . . at Ta'anach, by the waters of Megid'do 1
1Kg 4:12 Ba'ana . . in Ta'anach, Megid'do, and all Beth-she'an 1
1Ch 7:29 Beth-she'an and its towns, Ta'anach and its towns 1

Taanath-shiloh 1. תַּאֲנַת שִׁלֹה
Jos 16: 6 the boundary turns round toward Ta'anath-shi'loh 1

Tabbaoth 1. טַבָּעוֹת 2. Ταβαωθ
Ezr 2:43 temple servants: the . . sons of Tabba'oth 1
Neh 7:46 temple servants . . the sons of Tabba'oth 1
1Es 5:29 the sons of Hasupha, the sons of Tabbaoth 2

Tabbath 1. טַבַּת
Jdg 7:22 as far as the border of A'bel-meho'lah, by Tabbath. 1

Tabeel 1. טָבְאַל 2. טָבְאֵל 3. Ταβελλιος
Ezr 4: 7 Bishlam and Mith'redath and Tab'eel and the rest 2
Isa 7: 6 set up the son of Ta'be-el as king in the midst of it 1
1Es 2:16 Bishlam, Mithridates, Tabeel, Rehum, Beltethmus 3

Taberah 1. תַּבְעֵרָה
Num11: 3 name of that place was called Tab'erah 1
Deu 9:22 At Tab'erah also, and at Massah 1

Tabitha 1. Ταβιθά
Act 9:36 Now there was at Joppa a disciple named Tabitha 1
40 then turning to the body he said, "Tabitha, rise. 1

Tabor 1. תָּבוֹר
Jos 19:22 touches Tabor, Shahazu'mah, and Beth-she'mesh 1
Jdg 4: 6 Go, gather your men at Mount Tabor, taking 10,000 1
12 the son of Abin'o-am had gone up to Mount Tabor 1
14 Barak went down from Mount Tabor with 10,000 men 1
8:18 Where are the men whom you slew at Tabor? 1
1Sm 10: 3 go on . . further and come to the oak of Tabor; 1
1Ch 6:77 of Zeb'ulun . . Tabor with its pasture lands 1
Ps 89:12 Tabor and Hermon joyously praise thy name. 1
Jer 46:18 the LORD of hosts, like Tabor among the mountains 1
Hos 5: 1 a snare at Mizpah, and a net spread upon Tabor. 1

Tabrimmon 1. טַבְרִמּוֹן
1Kg 15:18 Asa sent them to Ben-ha'dad the son of Tabrim'mon 1

Tadmor 1. תַּדְמֹר
2Ch 8: 4 He built Tadmor in the wilderness 1

Tahan 1. תַּחַן
Num26:35 of Tahan, the family of the Ta'hanites. 1
1Ch 7:25 Resheph his son, Telah his son, Tahan his son 1

Tahanite 1. תַּחֲנִי
Num26:35 of Tahan, the family of the Ta'hanites. 1

Tahash 1. תַּחַשׁ
Gen 22:24 Reumah, bore Tebah, Gaham, Tahash, and Ma'acah. 1

Tahath 1. תַּחַת
Num33:26 set out from Makhe'loth, and encamped at Tahath. 1
27 they set out from Tahath, and encamped at Terah. 1
1Ch 6:24 Tahath his son, Uri'el his son, Uzzi'ah 1
37 son of Tahath, son of Assir, son of Ebi'asaph 1
7:20 Bered his son, Tahath his son, Ele-a'dah his son 1
20 Tahath his son, Ele-a'dah his son, Tahath his son 1

Tahchemonite 1. תַּחְכְּמֹנִי
2Sm 23: 8 men . . Josheb-basshe'beth a Tah-che'monite; 1

Tahpanhes 1. תַּחְפַּנְחֵס 2. Ταφνας
Jer 2:16 the men of . . Tah'panhes have broken the crown 1
43: 7 And they arrived at Tah'panhes. 1
8 word of the LORD came to Jeremiah in Tah'panhes 1
9 at the entrance to Pharaoh's palace in Tah'panhes 1
44: 1 land of Egypt, at Migdol, at Tah'panhes, at Memphis 1
46:14 proclaim in Memphis and Tah'panhes; 1
Jdt 1: 9 the river of Egypt, and Tahpanhes and Raamses 2

Tahpenes 1. תַּחְפְּנֵיס
1Kg 11:19 the sister of Tah'penes the queen. 1
20 the sister of Tah'penes bore him Genu'bath his son 1
20 his son, whom Tah'penes weaned in Pharaoh's house; 1

Tahrea 1. תַּחְרֵעַ
1Ch 9:41 sons of Micah: Pithon, Melech, Tahr'e-a, and Ahaz 1

Talmai 1. תַּלְמַי
Num13:22 came to Hebron; and Ahi'man, She'shai, and Talmai 1
Jos 15:14 three sons of Anak, She'shai and Ahi'man and Talmai 1
Jdg 1:10 they defeated She'shai and Ahi'man and Talmai. 1
2Sm 3: 3 Ab'salom the son of Ma'acah the daughter of Talmai 1
13:37 But Ab'salom fled, and went to Talmai 1
1Ch 3: 2 Ma'acah, the daughter of Talmai, king of Geshur; 1

Talmon 1. טַלְמוֹן 2. Τολμαν
1Ch 9:17 gatekeepers . . Shallum, Akkub, Talmon, Ahi'man 1
Ezr 2:42 sons of the gatekeepers: the . . sons of Talmon 1
Neh 7:45 gatekeepers . . sons of Talmon, the sons of Akkub 1
11:19 gatekeepers, Akkub, Talmon and their brethren 1
12:25 Obadi'ah, Meshul'lam, Talmon, and Akkub 1
1Es 5:28 the sons of Ater, the sons of Talmon 2

Tamar 1. תָּמָר 2. Θαμάρ
Gen 38: 6 took a wife . . and her name was Tamar. 1
11 Then Judah said to Tamar his daughter-in-law 1
11 Tamar went and dwelt in her father's house. 1
13 when Tamar was told, "Your father-in-law is going up 1
24 Judah was told, "Tamar your daughter-in-law has 1
Rut 4:12 Perez, whom Tamar bore to Judah 1
2Sm 13: 1 had a beautiful sister, whose name was Tamar; 1
2 he made himself ill because of his sister Tamar; 1
4 I love Tamar, my brother Ab'salom's sister. 1
5 Let my sister Tamar come and give me bread to eat 1
6 Pray let my sister Tamar come and make . . cakes 1
7 Then David sent home to Tamar, saying, "Go 1
8 Tamar went to her brother Amnon's house 1
10 Then Amnon said to Tamar, "Bring the food 1
10 And Tamar took the cakes she had made 1
19 Tamar put ashes on her head, and rent the long robe 1
20 Tamar dwelt, a desolate woman, in . . Ab'salom's 1
22 because he had forced his sister Tamar. 1
32 determined from the day he forced . . Tamar. 1
14:27 three sons, and one daughter whose name was Tamar; 1
1Kg 9:18 Ba'alath and Tamar in the wilderness 1
1Ch 2: 4 His daughter-in-law Tamar also bore him Perez 1
3: 9 David's sons . . and Tamar was their sister. 1
Ezk 47:18 to the eastern sea and as far as Tamar. •
19 it shall run from Tamar as far as the waters 1
48:28 from Tamar to the waters of Meribath-ka'desh 1
Mat 1: 3 Judah the father of Perez and Zerah by Tamar 2

Tammuz 1. תַּמּוּז
Ezk 8:14 and behold, there sat women weeping for Tammuz. 1

Tanhumeth 1. תַּנְחֻמֶת
2Kg 25:23 Serai'ah the son of Tanhu'meth the Netoph'athite 1
Jer 40: 8 Serai'ah the son of Tanhu'meth 1

Tanis 1. Τανις
Jdt 1:10 even beyond Tanis and Memphis 1

Taphath 1. טָפַת
1Kg 4:11 (he had Taphath the daughter of Solomon as his 1

Tappuah 1. תַּפּוּחַ
Jos 12:17 the king of Tap'puah, one; the king of Hepher, one; 1
15:34 Zano'ah, En-gan'nim, Tap'puah, Enam 1
16: 8 From Tap'puah the boundary goes westward 1
17: 8 The land of Tap'puah belonged to Manas'seh 1
8 but the town of Tap'puah . . belonged to the sons 1
2Kg 15:16 Men'ahem sacked Tappuah and all who were in it •
1Ch 2:43 sons of Hebron: Korah, Tap'puah, Rekem, and Shema. 1

Taralah 1. תַּרְאֲלָה
Jos 18:27 Rekem, Irpeel, Tar'alah 1

Tarea 1. תַּחְרֵעַ
1Ch 8:35 The sons of Micah: Pithon, Melech, Tare'a, and Ahaz. 1

Tarshish 1. תַּרְשִׁישׁ
Gen 10: 4 The sons of Javan: Eli'shah, Tarshish, Kittim 1
1Kg 10:22 For the king had a fleet of ships of Tarshish 1
22 the fleet of ships of Tarshish used to come 1
22:48 Jehosh'aphat made ships of Tarshish 1
1Ch 1: 7 of Javan: Eli'shah, Tarshish, Kittim, and Ro'danim. 1
7:10 sons of Bilhan . . Tarshish, and Ahish'ahar. 1
2Ch 9:21 king's ships went to Tarshish with the servants 1
21 ships of Tarshish used to come bringing gold 1
20:36 He joined him in building ships to go to Tarshish 1
37 ships . . were not able to go to Tarshish. 1
Est 1:14 Carshe'na, Shethar, Adma'tha, Tarshish, Meres 1
Ps 48: 7 thou didst shatter the ships of Tarshish. 1
72:10 May the kings of Tarshish . . render him tribute 1
Isa 2:16 against all the ships of Tarshish 1
23: 1 Wail, O ships of Tarshish, for Tyre is laid waste 1
6 Pass over to Tarshish, wail, O inhabitants 1
10 Overflow your land . . O daughter of Tarshish; 1
14 Wail, O ships of Tarshish 1
60: 9 the ships of Tarshish first, 1
66:19 to the nations, to Tarshish, Put, and Lud 1
Jer 10: 9 Beaten silver is brought from Tarshish 1
Ezk 27:12 Tarshish trafficked with you 1
25 The ships of Tarshish traveled for you 1
38:13 Sheba and Dedan and the merchants of Tarshish 1
Jon 1: 3 Jonah rose to flee to Tarshish 1
3 to Joppa and found a ship going to Tarshish; 1
3 went on board, to go with them to Tarshish, 1
4: 2 That is why I made haste to flee to Tarshish; 1

Tarsus 1. Θαρσεας 2. Ταρσεύς 3. Ταρσός
Act 9:11 a man of Tarsus named Saul 2
30 and sent him off to Tarsus. 3
11:25 Barnabas went to Tarsus to look for Saul; 3
21:39 from Tarsus in Cili'cia, a citizen of no mean city 2
22: 3 I am a Jew, born at Tarsus in Cili'cia 2
2Mc 3: 5 he went to Apollonius of Tarsus 1
4:30 the people of Tarsus and of Mallus revolted 2

people of Tarsus 1. Ταρσεῖς
2Mc 4:30 the people of Tarsus and of Mallus revolted 1

Tartak 1. תַּרְתָּק
2Kg 17:31 and the Av'vites made Nibhaz and Tartak; 1

Tartan 1. תַּרְתָּן
2Kg 18:17 the king of Assyria sent the Tartan, the Rab'saris 1

Tattenai 1. תַּתְּנַי (A)
Ezr 5: 3 Tat'tenai the governor of the province Beyond 1
6 letter which Tat'tenai the governor 1
6: 6 therefore, Tat'tenai, governor of the province 1
13 Tat'tenai, the governor of the province 1

Tebah 1. טֶבַח
Gen 22:24 name was Reumah, bore Tebah, Gaham, Tahash 1

Tebaliah 1. טְבַלְיָהוּ
1Ch 26:11 Tebali'ah the third, Zechari'ah the fourth 1

Tebeth 1. טֵבֵת
Est 2:16 in the tenth month, which is the month of Tebeth 1

Tehaphnehes 1. תְּחַפְנְחֵס
Ezk 30:18 At Tehaph'nehes the day shall be dark 1

Tehinnah 1. תְּחִנָּה
1Ch 4:12 Eshton was the father of . . Pase'ah, and Tehin'nah 1

Tekoa 1. תְּקוֹעַ 2. תְּקוֹעִי 3. Θεκωε
2Sm 14: 2 Jo'ab sent to Teko'a, and fetched . . a wise woman 1
4 When the woman of Teko'a came to the king 2
9 And the woman of Teko'a said to the king 2
23:26 Helez the Paltite, Ira the son of Ikkesh of Teko'a 2
1Ch 2:24 she bore him Ashhur, the father of Teko'a. 1
4: 5 Ashhur, the father of Teko'a, had two wives 1
11:28 Ira the son of Ikkesh of Teko'a, Abi-e'zer of An'athoth 2
2Ch 11: 6 He built Bethlehem, Etam, Teko'a 1
20:20 went out into the wilderness of Teko'a; 1
Jer 6: 1 Blow the trumpet in Teko'a, and raise a signal 1
Ams 1: 1 of Amos, who was among the shepherds of Teko'a 1
1Mc 9:33 they fled into the wilderness of Tekoa 3

Tekoite 1. תְּקוֹעִי
1Ch 27: 9 Sixth . . was Ira, the son of Ikkesh the Teko'ite; 1
Neh 3: 5 next to them the Teko'ites repaired; 1
27 Teko'ites repaired another section opposite 1

Tel-abib 1. תֵּל אָבִיב
Ezk 3:15 I came to the exiles at Tel-abib 1

Tel-harsha 1. תֵּל חַרְשָׁא 2. Θελερσας
Ezr 2:59 came up from Tel-me'lah, Tel-har'sha, Cherub 1
Neh 7:61 came up from Tel-me'lah, Tel-har'sha, Cherub, Addon 1
1Es 5:36 who came up from Telmelah and Telharsha 2

Tel-melah 1. תֵּל מֶלַח 2. Θερμελεθ
Ezr 2:59 came up from Tel-me'lah, Tel-har'sha, Cherub 1
Neh 7:61 came up from Tel-me'lah, Tel-har'sha, Cherub, Addon 1
1Es 5:36 who came up from Telmelah and Telharsha 2

Telah 1. תֶּלַח
1Ch 7:25 Resheph his son, Telah his son, Tahan his son 1

Telaim 1. טְלָאִים
1Sm 15: 4 summoned the people, and numbered them in Tela'im 1

Telassar 1. תְּלַאשָּׂר
2Kg 19:12 the people of Eden who were in Tel-assar? 1
Isa 37:12 and the people of Eden who were in Tel-assar? 1

Telem 1. טֶלֶם 2. Τολβανης
Jos 15:24 Ziph, Telem, Be-a'loth 1
Ezr 10:24 Of the gatekeepers: Shallum, Telem, and Uri. 1
1Es 9:25 Of the gatekeepers: Shallum and Telem. 2

Tema 1. תֵּימָא
Gen 25:15 Hadad, Tema, Jetur, Naphish, and Ked'emah. 1
1Ch 1:30 Mishma, Dumah, Massa, Hadad, Tema 1
Job 6:19 The caravans of Tema look, the travelers of Sheba 1
Isa 21:14 with bread, O inhabitants of the land of Tema. 1
Jer 25:23 Dedan, Tema, Buz 1

Temah 1. תֶּמַח 2. Θομει
Ezr 2:53 the sons of Sis'era, the sons of Temah 1
Neh 7:55 Barkos, the sons of Sis'era, the sons of Temah 1
1Es 5:32 the sons of Sisera, the sons of Temah 2

Teman 1. תֵּימָן 2. Θαιμαν
Gen 36:11 The sons of El'iphaz were Teman, Omar, Zepho 1
15 the chiefs Teman, Omar, Zepho, Kenaz 1
42 Kenaz, Teman, Mibzar 1
1Ch 1:36 The sons of Eli'phaz: Teman, Omar, Zephi, Gatam 1
53 Kenaz, Teman, Mibzar 1
Jer 49: 7 Is wisdom no more in Teman? Has counsel perished 1
20 purposes . . against the inhabitants of Teman 1
Ezk 25:13 I will make it desolate; from Teman even to Dedan 1
Ams 1:12 I will send a fire upon Teman 1
Obd 1: 9 And your mighty men shall be dismayed, O Teman 1
Hab 3: 3 God came from Teman 1
Bar 3:22 She has not been heard of . . nor seen in Teman; 2
23 merchants of Merran and Teman, the story-tellers 2

Temanite 1. תֵּימָנִי
Gen 36:34 Husham of the land of the Te'manites reigned 1
1Ch 1:45 Husham of the land of the Te'manites reigned 1
Job 2:11 Eli'phaz the Te'manite, Bildad the Shuhite 1
4: 1 Then Eli'phaz the Te'manite answered 1
15: 1 Then Eli'phaz the Te'manite answered 1
22: 1 Then Eli'phaz the Te'manite answered 1
42: 7 the LORD said to Eli'phaz the Te'manite 1
9 Eli'phaz the Te'manite and Bildad the Shuhite 1

Temeni 1. תֵּימְנִי
1Ch 4: 6 Na'arah bore him Ahuz'zam, Hepher, Te'meni 1

Tephon 1. Τεφων
1Mc 9:50 Bethel, and Timnath, and Pharathon, and Tephon 1

Terah 1. תֶּרַח 2. Θάρα
Gen 11:24 Nahor . . became the father of Terah; 1
25 Nahor lived after the birth of Terah 119 years 1
26 When Terah had lived 70 years 1
27 Now these are the descendants of Terah. 1
27 Terah was the father of Abram, Nahor, and Haran; 1
28 Haran died before his father Terah in the land 1
31 Terah took Abram his son and Lot the son of Haran 1
32 The days of Terah were 205 years; 1
32 and Terah died in Haran. 1
Num33:27 they set out from Tahath, and encamped at Terah. 1
28 they set out from Terah, and encamped at Mithkah. 1
Jos 24: 2 Your fathers . . Terah, the father of Abraham 1
1Ch 1:26 Serug, Nahor, Terah; 1
Lke 3:34 son of Isaac, the son of Abraham, the son of Terah 2

Teresh 1. תֶּרֶשׁ
Est 2:21 Bigthan and Teresh . . became angry and sought 1
6: 2 how Mor'decai had told about Bigthana and Teresh 1

Tertius 1. Τέρτιος
Rom 16:22 I Tertius, the writer of this letter, greet you 1

Tertullus 1. Τέρτυλλος
Act 24: 1 some elders and a spokesman, one Tertul'lus 1
2 when he was called, Tertul'lus began to accuse him 1

Thaddaeus 1. Θαδδαῖος
Mat 10: 3 James the son of Alphaeus, and Thaddaeus; 1
Mrk 3:18 Thaddaeus, and Simon the Cananaean 1

Tharra 1. Θαρρα
AEs 12: 1 took his rest . . with Gabatha and Tharra 1

Thassi 1. Θασσι
1Mc 2: 3 Simon called Thassi 1

Thebes 1. נֹא 2. נֹא אָמוֹן
Jer 46:25 I am bringing punishment upon Amon of Thebes 1
Ezk 30:14 and will execute acts of judgment upon Thebes. 1
15 and cut off the multitude of Thebes. 1
16 Thebes shall be breached, and its walls broken 1
Nah 3: 8 Are you better than Thebes that sat by the Nile 2

Thebez 1. תֵּבֵץ
Jdg 9:50 Then Abim'elech went to Thebez, and encamped 1
50 Abim'elech went . . and encamped against Thebez 1
2Sm 11:21 millstone upon him . . so that he died at Thebez 1

Theodotus 1. Θεοδοτος
2Mc 14:19 Therefore he sent Posidonius and Theodotus 1
3Mc 1: 2 a certain Theodotus . . crossed over by night 1

Theophilus 1. Θεόφιλος
Lke 1: 3 it seemed good to me . . most excellent Theoph'ilus 1
Act 1: 1 In the first book, O The-oph'ilus 1

Theras 1. Θερα
1Es 8:41 I assembled them at the river called Theras 1
61 We departed from the river Theras 1

Thessalonian 1. Θεσσαλονικεύς
Act 20: 4 and of the Thessalo'nians, Aristar'chus 1
1Th 1: 1 To the church of the Thessalo'nians 1
2Th 1: 1 To the church of the Thessalo'nians 1

Thessalonica 1. Θεσσαλονικεύς 2. Θεσσαλονίκη
Act 17: 1 they came to Thessaloni'ca 2
11 were more noble than those in Thessaloni'ca 2
13 when the Jews of Thessaloni'ca learned 2
27: 2 Aristar'chus, a Macedo'nian from Thessaloni'ca. 1
Php 4:16 for even in Thessaloni'ca you sent me help once 2
2Ti 4:10 has deserted me and gone to Thessaloni'ca; 2

Theudas 1. Θευδᾶς
Act 5:36 before these days Theu'das arose 1

Thisbe 1. Θισβη
Tob 1: 2 who . . was taken into captivity from Thisbe 1

Thomas 1. Θωμᾶς
Mat 10: 3 Philip and Bartholomew; Thomas and Matthew 1
Mrk 3:18 Philip, and Bartholomew, and Matthew, and Thomas 1
Lke 6:15 Matthew, and Thomas, and James the son 1
Joh 11:16 Thomas, called the Twin 1
14: 5 Thomas said to him, "Lord, we do not know 1
20:24 Now Thomas, one of the twelve, called the Twin 1
26 Thomas was with them 1
27 Then he said to Thomas, "Put your finger here 1
28 Thomas answered him, "My Lord and my God! 1
21: 2 Simon Peter, Thomas called the Twin 1
Act 1:13 Philip and Thomas, Bartholomew and Matthew 1

Thracian 1. Θραξ
2Mc 12:35 one of the Thracian horsemen bore down upon him 1

Three Taverns 1. τρεῖς ταβέρναι
Act 28:15 as far as the Forum of Ap'pius and Three Taverns 1

Thummim 1. תֻּמִּים 2. ἀλήθεια
Exd 28:30 judgment you shall put the Urim and Thummim 1
Lev 8: 8 in the breastpiece he put the Urim and the Thummim 1
Deu 33: 8 Give to Levi thy Thummim, and thy Urim to thy godly 1
1Sm 14:41 if . . guilt is in thy people Israel, give Thummim. •
Ezr 2:63 priest to consult Urim and Thummim. 1
Neh 7:65 priest with Urim and Thummim should arise. 1
1Es 5:40 a high priest . . wearing Urim and Thummim. 2
Sir 45:10 with the oracle of judgment, Urim and Thummim; 2

Thyatira 1. Θυάτιρα
Act 16:14 Lydia, from the city of Thyati'ra 1
Rev 1:11 seven churches . . to Per'gamum and to Thyati'ra 1
2:18 And to the angel of the church in Thyati'ra write 1
24 But to the rest of you in Thyati'ra 1

Tiberias 1. Τιβεριάς
Joh 6: 1 the Sea of Galilee, which is the Sea of Tiber'i-as. 1
23 However, boats from Tiber'i-as came near the place 1
21: 1 Jesus revealed himself . . by the Sea of Tibe'ri-as 1

Tiberius 1. Τιβέριος
Lke 3: 1 fifteenth year of the reign of Tiber'ius Caesar 1

Tibhath 1. טִבְחַת
1Ch 18: 8 And from Tibhath and from Cun, cities of Hadade'zer 1

Tibni 1. תִּבְנִי
1Kg 16:21 half . . followed Tibni the son of Ginath 1
22 overcame the people who followed Tibni 1
22 so Tibni died, and Omri became king. 1

Tidal 1. תִּדְעָל
Gen 14: 1 king of Elam, and Tidal king of Goi'im 1
9 Tidal king of Goi'im, Am'raphel king of Shinar 1

Tiglath-pileser 1. תִּגְלַת פִּלְאֶסֶר
2Kg 15:29 Tig'lath-pile'ser . . came and captured I'jon 1
16: 7 Ahaz sent . . to Tig'lath-pile'ser king of Assyria 1
10 to meet Tig'lath-pile'ser king of Assyria 1

Tigris 1. חִדֶּקֶל 2. Τιγρις
Gen 2:14 the name of the third river is Tigris 1
Dan 10: 4 bank of the great river, that is, the Tigris 1
Tob 6: 1 they came at evening to the Tigris river 2
Jdt 1: 6 the Euphrates and the Tigris and the Hydaspes 2
Sir 24:25 like the Tigris at the time of the first fruits. 2

Tikvah 1. תִּקְוָה 2. Θοκανος
2Kg 22:14 Huldah . . the wife of Shallum the son of Tikvah 1
Ezr 10:15 Only Jonathan . . and Jahzei'ah the son of Tikvah 1
1Es 9:14 Jahzeiah the son of Tikvah 2

Tilgath-pilneser 1. תִּלְגַת פִּלְנְאֶסֶר
1Ch 5: 6 Til'gath-pilne'ser king of Assyria 1
26 the spirit of Til'gath-pilne'ser king of Assyria 1
2Ch 28:20 Til'gath-pilne'ser king of Assyria came against 1

Tilon 1. תִּילוֹן
1Ch 4:20 of Shimon: Amnon, Rinnah, Ben-ha'nan, and Tilon. 1

Timaeus 1. Τιμαῖος
Mrk 10:46 Bartimae'us, a blind beggar, the son of Timae'us 1

Timna 1. תִּמְנָע
Gen 36:12 (Timna was a concubine of El'iphaz, Esau's son; 1
22 Hori and Heman; and Lotan's sister was Timna. 1
40 by their names: the chiefs Timna, Alvah, Jetheth 1
1Ch 1:36 The sons of Eli'phaz . . Gatam, Kenaz, Timna 1
39 and Lotan's sister was Timna. 1
51 chiefs of Edom were: chiefs Timna, Al'iah, Jetheth 1

Timnah 1. תִּמְנָה
Gen 38:12 he went up to Timnah to his sheepshearers 1
13 is going up to Timnah to shear his sheep 1
14 Enaim, which is on the road to Timnah; 1
Jos 15:10 down to Beth-she'mesh, and passes along by Timnah; 1
57 Kain, Gib'e-ah, and Timnah 1
19:43 Elon, Timnah, Ekron 1
Jdg 14: 1 Samson went down to Timnah, and at Timnah he saw 1
1 and at Timnah he saw one of the daughters 1
2 one of the daughters of the Philistines at Timnah; 1
5 Samson went down . . to Timnah, and he came 1
5 to Timnah, and he came to the vineyards of Timnah. 1
2Ch 28:18 had taken . . Timnah with its villages, and Gimzo 1

Timnath 1. Θαμναθα
1Mc 9:50 Emmaus, and Beth-horon, and Bethel, and Timnath 1

Timnath-heres 1. תִּמְנַת חֶרֶס
Jdg 2: 9 the bounds of his inheritance in Tim'nath-he'res 1

Timnath-serah 1. תִּמְנַת סֶרַח
Jos 19:50 gave him . . Tim'nath-se'rah in the hill country 1
24:30 in his own inheritance at Tim'nath-se'rah 1

Timnite 1. תִּמְנִי
Jdg 15: 6 they said, "Samson, the son-in-law of the Timnite 1

Timon 1. Τίμων
Act 6: 5 Philip, and Proch'orus, and Nica'nor, and Ti'mon 1

Timothy 1. Τιμόθεος
Act 16: 1 A disciple was there, named Timothy 1
3 Paul wanted Timothy to accompany him •
17:14 Silas and Timothy remained there. 1
15 a command for Silas and Timothy to come to him 1
18: 5 When Silas and Timothy arrived from Macedo'nia 1
19:22 two of his helpers, Timothy and Eras'tus 1
20: 4 and Ga'ius of Derbe, and Timothy 1
Rom 16:21 Timothy, my fellow worker, greets you; 1
1Co 4:17 Therefore I sent to you Timothy 1
16:10 When Timothy comes, see that you put him at ease 1
2Co 1: 1 Timothy our brother 1
19 Silva'nus and Timothy and I 1
Php 1: 1 Paul and Timothy, servants of Christ Jesus 1
2:19 hope in the Lord Jesus to send Timothy to you soon 1
22 Timothy's worth you know •
Col 1: 1 Paul, an apostle . . and Timothy our brother 1
1Th 1: 1 Paul, Silva'nus, and Timothy 1
3: 2 we sent Timothy, our brother and God's servant 1
6 now that Timothy has come to us from you 1
2Th 1: 1 Paul, Silva'nus, and Timothy 1
1Ti 1: 2 To Timothy, my true child in the faith 1
18 This charge I commit to you, Timothy, my son 1
6:20 O Timothy, guard what has been entrusted to you. 1
2Ti 1: 2 To Timothy, my beloved child 1
Phm 1: 1 Paul . . and Timothy our brother 1
Heb 13:23 our brother Timothy has been released 1
1Mc 5: 6 many people with Timothy as their leader. 1
11 Timothy is leading their forces. 1
34 army of Timothy realized that it was Maccabeus 1
37 Timothy gathered another army 1
40 Timothy said to the officers of his forces 1
2Mc 8:30 the forces of Timothy and Bacchides 1
32 They killed the commander of Timothy's forces 1
9: 3 to Nicanor and the forces of Timothy. 1
10:24 Timothy, who had been defeated by the Jews before 1
32 Timothy . . fled to a stronghold called Gazara 1

37 They killed Timothy, who was hidden in a cistern 1
12: 2 Timothy and Apollonius the son of Gennaeus 1
10 on their march against Timothy 1
18 They did not find Timothy in that region 1
19 whom Timothy had left in the stronghold 1
20 hastened after Timothy 1
21 When Timothy learned of the approach of Judas 1
24 Timothy himself fell into the hands of . . 1

Tiphsah 1. תִּפְסַח
1Kg 4:24 west of the Euphra'tes from Tiphsah to Gaza, over 1

Tiras 1. תִּירָס
Gen 10: 2 Magog, Madai, Javan, Tubal, Meshech, and Tiras. 1
1Ch 1: 5 sons of Japheth . . Tubal, Meshech, and Tiras. 1

Tirathite 1. תִּרְעָתִים
1Ch 2:55 the Ti'rathites, the Shim'e-athites 1

Tirhakah 1. תִּרְהָקָה
2Kg 19: 9 heard concerning Tirha'kah king of Ethiopia 1
Isa 37: 9 heard concerning Tirha'kah king of Ethiopia 1

Tirhanah 1. תִּרְחֲנָה
1Ch 2:48 Ma'acah . . bore Sheber and Tir'hanah. 1

Tiria 1. תִּירְיָא
1Ch 4:16 sons of Jehal'lelel . . Ziphah, Tir'i-a, and As'arel. 1

Tirzah 1. תִּרְצָה
Num26:33 daughters of Zeloph'ehad . . Milcah, and Tirzah. 1
27: 1 his daughters were . . Milcah, and Tirzah. 1
36:11 Tirzah, Hoglah, Milcah, and Noah, the daughters 1
Jos 12:24 the king of Tirzah, one: in all, 31 kings. 1
17: 3 Mahlah, Noah, Hoglah, Milcah, and Tirzah. 1
1Kg 14:17 wife arose, and departed, and came to Tirzah. 1
15:21 stopped building Ramah, and he dwelt in Tirzah. 1
33 began to reign over all Israel at Tirzah 1
16: 6 Ba'asha . . was buried at Tirzah; 1
8 Elah . . began to reign over Israel in Tirzah 1
9 When he was at Tirzah, drinking 1
9 Arza, who was over the household in Tirzah 1
15 Zimri reigned seven days in Tirzah. 1
17 Omri went up . . and they besieged Tirzah. 1
23 Omri . . reigned . . six years he reigned in Tirzah. 1
2Kg 15:14 came up from Tirzah and came to Sama'ria 1
16 Tappuah . . and its territory from Tirzah on; 1
Sng 6: 4 You are beautiful as Tirzah, my love 1

Tishbe 1. Θεσβων
1Kg 17: 1 Eli'jah the Tishbite, of Tishbe in Gilead, said 1

Tishbite 1. תִּשְׁבִּי
1Kg 17: 1 Now Eli'jah the Tishbite . . said to Ahab 1
21:17 the word of the LORD came to Eli'jah the Tishbite 1
28 the word of the LORD came to Eli'jah the Tishbite 1
2Kg 1: 3 the angel of the LORD said to Eli'jah the Tishbite 1
8 And he said, "It is Eli'jah the Tishbite. 1
9:36 he spoke by his servant Eli'jah the Tishbite 1

Titan 1. τιτανες
Jdt 16: 7 nor did the sons of the Titans smite him 1

Titius 1. Τίτιος
Act 18: 7 went to the house of a man named Titius Justus 1

Titus 1. Τίτος
2Co 2:13 because I did not find my brother Titus there 1
7: 6 comforted us by the coming of Titus 1
13 we rejoiced still more at the joy of Titus 1
14 so our boasting before Titus has proved true. 1
8: 6 Accordingly we have urged Titus 1
16 earnest care for you into the heart of Titus. 1
23 As for Titus, he is my partner and fellow worker 1
12:18 I urged Titus to go, and sent the brother with him. 1
18 Did Titus take advantage of you? 1
Gal 2: 1 taking Titus along with me 1
3 even Titus, who was with me, was not compelled 1
2Ti 4:10 Crescens has gone to Galatia, Titus to Dalmatia. 1
Tit 1: 4 To Titus, my true child in a common faith 1
2Mc 11:34 Quintus Memmius and Titus Manius 1

Tizite 1. תִּיצִי
1Ch 11:45 Jedi'a-el . . and Joha his brother, the Tizite 1

Toah 1. תּוֹחַ
1Ch 6:34 son of Jero'ham, son of Eli'el, son of To'ah 1

Tob 1. טוֹב 2. Τουβιας
Jdg 11: 3 Jephthah fled . . and dwelt in the land of Tob; 1
5 went to bring Jephthah from the land of Tob; 1
2Sm 10: 6 hired . . the men of Tob, 12,000 men. 1
8 and of Rehob, and the men of Tob and Ma'acah 1
1Mc 5:13 all our brethren who were in the land of Tob 2

Tob-adonijah 1. טוֹב אֲדוֹנִיָּה
2Ch 17: 8 with them the Levites . . and Tobadoni'jah; 1

Tobiah 1. טוֹבִיָּה 2. Τωβιας
Ezr 2:60 sons of Delai'ah, the sons of Tobi'ah 1
Neh 2:10 when Sanbal'lat . . and Tobi'ah the servant 1
19 when Sanbal'lat . . and Tobi'ah the servant 1
4: 3 Tobi'ah the Ammonite was by him, and he said 1
7 when Sanbal'lat and Tobi'ah and the Arabs 1
6: 1 reported to Sanbal'lat and Tobi'ah and to Geshem 1
12 because Tobi'ah and Sanbal'lat had hired him. 1
14 Remember Tobi'ah and Sanbal'lat, O my God 1
17 nobles of Judah sent many letters to Tobi'ah 1
17 Tobi'ah's letters came to them. 1
19 Tobi'ah sent letters to make me afraid. 1
7:62 sons of Delai'ah, the sons of Tobi'ah 1
13: 4 Eli'ashib . . who was connected with Tobi'ah 1
5 prepared for Tobi'ah a large chamber •
7 evil that Eli'ashib had done for Tobi'ah 1
8 threw all the household furniture of Tobi'ah 1
1Es 5:37 the sons of Delaiah the son of Tobiah 2

Tobias 1. Τωβιας
Tob 1: 9 by her I became the father of Tobias. 1
20 except my wife Anna and my son Tobias. 1
2: 1 my wife Anna and my son Tobias were restored to me 1
3:17 give . . in marriage to Tobias the son of Tobit 1
17 because Tobias was entitled to possess her. 1
4: 2 Why do I not call my son Tobias 1
5: 1 Then Tobias answered him 1
5 Tobias did not know it •
5 Tobias said to him •
7 Then Tobias said to him, "Wait for me 1
9 Tobias invited him •
16 Then he said to Tobias, "Get ready for the journey 1
6:17 When Tobias heard these things, he fell in love 1
7: 5 Tobias said, "He is my father. 1
8 Then Tobias said to Raphael, "Brother Azarias 1
9 Raguel said to Tobias, "Eat, drink, and be merry; 1
11 Tobias said, "I will eat nothing here 1
13 he gave her to Tobias to be his wife, saying 1
8: 1 they escorted Tobias in to her. 1
4 Tobias got up from the bed and said, "Sister, get up 1
5 Tobias began to pray 1
20 Raguel declared by oath to Tobias •
9: 1 Then Tobias called Raphael and said to him 1
6 Gabael blessed Tobias and his wife. 1
10: 7 she never stopped mourning for her son Tobias 1
7 At that time Tobias said to Raguel, "Send me back 1
9 Tobias replied, "No, send me back to my father. 1
12 Edna said to Tobias 1
11: 1 After this Tobias went on his way 1
2 Then Raphael said to Tobias 1
7 I know, Tobias, that your father will open his eyes. •
15 here I see my son Tobias! 1
19 Tobias' marriage was celebrated for seven days 1
12: 1 Tobit then called his son Tobias and said to him 1
14:11 Tobias gave him a magnificent funeral. •
12 Then Tobias returned with his wife 1
2Mc 3:11 also some money of Hyrcanus, son of Tobias 1

Tobiel 1. Τωβιηλ
Tob 1: 1 The book of the acts of Tobit the son of Tobiel 1

Tobijah 1. טוֹבִיָּהוּ
2Ch 17: 8 the Levites . . Jehon'athan, Adoni'jah, Tobi'jah 1
Zec 6:10 Take from the exiles Heldai, Tobi'jah, and Jedai'ah 1
14 as a reminder to Heldai, Tobi'jah, Jedai'ah 1

Tobit 1. Τωβιτ
Tob 1: 1 The book of the acts of Tobit the son of Tobiel 1
3 I, Tobit, walked in the ways of truth 1
3:17 to scale away the white films of Tobit's eyes 1
17 give . . in marriage to Tobias the son of Tobit 1
17 At that very moment Tobit returned 1
4: 1 On that day Tobit remembered the money 1
5: 3 Then Tobit gave him the receipt, and said to him •
10 Then Tobit said to him, "My brother 1
11 Tobit said to him, "I should like to know, my brother •
13 Tobit said to him, "You are welcome, my brother •
17 Anna, his mother, began to weep, and said to Tobit 1
20 Tobit said to her, "Do not worry, my sister 1
7: 2 How much the young man resembles my cousin Tobit! 1
4 he said to them, "Do you know our brother Tobit? 1
7 When he heard that Tobit had lost his sight 1
10: 1 Now his father Tobit was counting each day 1
6 Tobit said to her, "Be still and stop worrying 1
11:10 Tobit started toward the door, and stumbled 1
16 Then Tobit went out to meet his daughter-in-law 1
17 Tobit gave thanks before them 1
17 When Tobit came near to Sarah his daughter-in-law 1
12: 1 Tobit then called his son Tobias and said to him 1
13: 1 Then Tobit wrote a prayer of rejoicing, and said 1
14: 1 Here Tobit ended his words of praise. 1
13 their property and that of his father Tobit. 1

Tochen 1. תֹּכֶן
1Ch 4:32 villages were Etam, A'in, Rimmon, Tochen, 1

Togarmah 1. תֹּגַרְמָה
Gen 10: 3 The sons of Gomer: Ash'kenaz . . and Togar'mah. 1
1Ch 1: 6 sons of Gomer: Ash'kenaz, Diphath, and To-gar'mah. 1

Tohu 1. תֹּחוּ
1Sm 1: 1 of Jero'ham, son of Eli'hu, son of Tohu, son of Zuph 1

Toi 1. תֹּעוּ 2. תֹּעִי
2Sm 8: 9 To'i king of Hamath heard that David had defeated 2
10 To'i sent his son Joram to King David, to greet him 1
10 Hadade'zer had often been at war with To'i. 1

Tokhath 1. תָּקְהַת
2Ch 34:22 Huldah the . . wife of Shallum the son of Tokhath 1

Tola 1. תּוֹלָע
Gen 46:13 sons of Is'sachar: Tola, Puvah, Iob, and Shimron 1
Num26:23 of Tola, the family of the To'laites; 1
Jdg 10: 1 arose to deliver Israel Tola the son of Pu'ah 1
1Ch 7: 1 sons of Is'sachar: Tola, Pu'ah, Jashub, and Shimron 1
2 sons of Tola: Uzzi, Rephai'ah, Je'ri-el, Jah'mai, Ibsam 1
2 heads of their fathers' houses, namely of Tola 1

Tolad 1. תּוֹלָד
1Ch 4:29 Bilhah, Ezem, Tolad 1

Tolaite 1. תּוֹלָעִי
Num26:23 of Tola, the family of the To'laites; 1

Tophel 1. תֹּפֶל
Deu 1: 1 between Paran and Tophel, Laban, Haze'roth 1

Topheth 1. תֹּפֶת
2Kg 23:10 he defiled To'pheth . . that no one might burn his 1
Jer 7:31 And they have built the high place of Topheth 1
32 when it will no more be called Topheth 1
32 for they will bury in Topheth 1
19: 6 when this place shall no more be called Topheth 1
11 Men shall bury in Topheth 1
12 making this city like Topheth. 1
13 shall be defiled like the place of Topheth. 1
14 Then Jeremiah came from Topheth 1

Tou 1. תֹּעוּ
1Ch 18: 9 To'u king of Hamath heard that David had defeated 1
10 for Hadade'zer had often been at war with To'u. 1

Toubiani 1. Τουβιανοι
2Mc 12:17 to Charax, to the Jews who are called Toubiani. 1

Tower of Hananel 1. מִגְדַּל חֲנַנְאֵל
Neh 3: 1 consecrated . . as far as the Tower of Hanan'el. 1
12:39 Tower of Hanan'el and the Tower of the Hundred 1
Zec 14:10 the Tower of Hanan'el to the king's wine press 1

Tower of the Hundred 1. מִגְדַּל הַמֵּאָה
Neh 3: 1 consecrated it as far as the Tower of the Hundred 1
12:39 Tower of Hanan'el and the Tower of the Hundred 1

Tower of the Ovens 1. מִגְדַּל הַתַּנּוּרִים
Neh 3:11 repaired . . section and the Tower of the Ovens. 1
12:38 upon the wall, above the Tower of the Ovens 1

Trachonitis 1. Τραχωνῖτις
Lke 3: 1 the region of Iturae'a and Tracheni'tis 1

Tripolis 1. Τριπολις
2Mc 14: 1 Demetrius . . had sailed into the harbor of Tripolis 1

Troas 1. Τρῳάς
Act 16: 8 so, passing by My'sia, they went down to Tro'as. 1
11 Setting sail therefore from Tro'as 1
20: 5 These went on and were waiting for us at Tro'as 1
6 in five days we came to them at Tro'as 1
2Co 2:12 When I came to Tro'as 1
2Ti 4:13 bring the cloak that I left with Carpus at Tro'as 1

Trophimus 1. Τρόφιμος
Act 20: 4 and the Asians, Tych'icus and Troph'imus. 1
21:29 had previously seen Troph'imus the Ephesian 1
2Ti 4:20 Troph'imus I left ill at Mile'tus. 1

Tryphaena 1. Τρύφαινα
Rom 16:12 workers in the Lord, Tryphae'na and Trypho'sa. 1

Trypho 1. Τρυφων
1Mc 11:39 Now Trypho had formerly been one 1
54 After this Trypho returned 1
56 Trypho captured the elephants 1
12:39 Then Trypho attempted to become king in Asia 1
42 When Trypho saw that he had come with a large army 1
49 Trypho sent troops and cavalry into Galilee 1
13: 1 Trypho had assembled a large army 1
12 Then Trypho departed from Ptolemais 1
14 Trypho learned that Simon had risen up 1
19 Trypho broke his word •
20 Trypho came to invade the country and destroy it 1
21 the men in the citadel kept sending envoys to Trypho 1
22 So Trypho got all his cavalry ready to go 1

24 Trypho turned back and departed to his own land. 1
31 Trypho dealt treacherously with the young king 1
34 all that Trypho did was to plunder. 1
14: 1 so that he could make war against Trypho. 1
15:10 so that there were few with Trypho. 1
25 he shut Trypho up and kept him from going out or in. 1
37 Trypho embarked on a ship and escaped 1
39 the king pursued Trypho. 1

Tryphosa 1. Τρυφῶσα
Rom 16:12 workers in the Lord, Tryphae'na and Trypho'sa. 1

Tubal 1. תּוּבַל
Gen 10: 2 Magog, Madai, Javan, Tubal, Meshech, and Tiras. 1
1Ch 1: 5 sons of Japheth . . Tubal, Meshech, and Tiras. 1
Isa 66:19 to Tubal and Javan, to the coastlands afar off 1
Ezk 27:13 Javan, Tubal, and Meshech traded with you; 1
32:26 Meshech and Tubal are there 1
38: 2 of Magog, the chief prince of Meshech and Tubal 1
3 O Gog, chief prince of Meshech and Tubal; 1
39: 1 O Gog, chief prince of Meshech and Tubal; 1

Tubal-cain 1. תּוּבַל קַיִן
Gen 4:22 Zillah bore Tubal-cain; he was the forger of all 1
22 The sister of Tubal-cain was Na'amah. 1

Twin 1. Δίδυμος
Joh 11:16 Thomas, called the Twin 1
20:24 Now Thomas, one of the twelve, called the Twin 1
21: 2 Simon Peter, Thomas called the Twin 1

Twin Brothers 1. Διόσκουροι
Act 28:11 with the Twin Brothers as figurehead. 1

Tychicus 1. Τυχικός
Act 20: 4 and the Asians, Tych'icus and Troph'imus. 1
Eph 6:21 Tych'icus the beloved brother 1
Col 4: 7 Tych'icus will tell you all about my affairs 1
2Ti 4:12 Tych'icus I have sent to Ephesus. 1
Tit 3:12 When I send Artemas or Tych'icus to you 1

Tyrannus 1. Τύραννος
Act 19: 9 and argued daily in the hall of Tyran'nus. 1

Tyre 1. צֹר 2. Τύριος 3. Τύρος 4. Tyrus
Jos 19:29 turns . . reaching to the fortified city of Tyre; 1
2Sm 5:11 And Hiram king of Tyre sent messengers to David 1
24: 7 and came to the fortress of Tyre 1
1Kg 5: 1 Hiram king of Tyre sent his servants to Solomon 1
7:13 King Solomon sent and brought Hiram from Tyre. 1
9:11 Hiram king of Tyre had supplied Solomon 1
12 when Hiram came from Tyre to see the cities 1
1Ch 14: 1 Hiram king of Tyre sent messengers to David 1
2Ch 2: 3 Solomon sent word to Huram the king of Tyre 1
11 Then Huram the king of Tyre answered in a letter 1
Ps 45:12 the people of Tyre will sue your favor with gifts 1
83: 7 Philistia with the inhabitants of Tyre; 1
87: 4 behold, Philistia and Tyre, with Ethiopia– 1
Isa 23: 1 The oracle concerning Tyre. 1
1 Wail, O ships of Tarshish, for Tyre is laid waste •
5 Egypt . . in anguish over the report about Tyre. 1
8 Who has purposed this against Tyre 1
13 Chalde'ans . . destined Tyre for wild beasts. •
15 Tyre will be forgotten for 70 years 1
15 it will happen to Tyre as in the song of the harlot 1
17 the end of 70 years, the LORD will visit Tyre 1
Jer 25:22 all the kings of Tyre, all the kings of Sidon 1
27: 3 the king of the sons of Ammon, the king of Tyre 1
47: 4 to cut off from Tyre and Sidon every helper 1
Ezk 26: 2 because Tyre said concerning Jerusalem 1
3 says the Lord GOD: Behold, I am against you, O Tyre 1
4 They shall destroy the walls of Tyre 1
7 bring upon Tyre from the north Nebuchadrez'zar 1
15 Thus says the Lord GOD to Tyre 1
27: 2 Now you, son of man, raise a lamentation over Tyre 1
3 say to Tyre, who dwells at the entrance to the sea 1
3 O Tyre, you have said, 'I am perfect in beauty 1
32 destroyed like Tyre in the midst of the sea? 1
28: 2 Son of man, say to the prince of Tyre 1
12 raise a lamentation over the king of Tyre, and say 1
29:18 Babylon made his army labor hard against Tyre; 1
18 army got anything from Tyre to pay for the labor 1
Jol 3: 4 What are you to me, O Tyre and Sidon 1
Ams 1: 9 For three transgressions of Tyre, and for four 1
10 I will send a fire upon the wall of Tyre 1
Zec 9: 2 Tyre and Sidon, though they are very wise. 1
3 Tyre has built herself a rampart 1
Mat 11:21 had been done in Tyre and Sidon 3
22 day of judgment for Tyre and Sidon than for you. 3
15:21 and withdrew to the district of Tyre and Sidon. 3
Mrk 3: 8 from beyond the Jordan and from about Tyre 3
7:24 to the region of Tyre and Sidon 3
31 Then he returned from the region of Tyre 3
Lke 6:17 Jerusalem and the seacoast of Tyre and Sidon 3
10:13 if the mighty works . . had been done in Tyre 3
14 more tolerable . . for Tyre and Sidon 3
Act 12:20 Herod was angry with the people of Tyre and Sidon; 2
21: 3 sailed to Syria, and landed at Tyre 3
7 When we had finished the voyage from Tyre 3
2Es 1:11 the people of two provinces, Tyre and Sidon 4
Jdt 2:28 lived along the seacoast, at Sidon and Tyre 3
Sir 46:18 he wiped out the leaders of the people of Tyre 2
1Mc 5:15 men of Ptolemais and Tyre and Sidon 3
11:59 from the Ladder of Tyre to the borders of Egypt. 3
2Mc 4:18 the quadrennial games were being held at Tyre 3
32 he had sold to Tyre and the neighboring cities. 3
44 When the king came to Tyre 3

man of Tyre 1. צֹרִי
1Kg 7:14 his father was a man of Tyre, a worker in bronze; 1
2Ch 2:14 and his father was a man of Tyre. 1
Neh 13:16 Men of Tyre also, who lived in the city, 1

Tyrian 1. צֹרִי 2. Τύριος
1Ch 22: 4 Sido'nians and Tyrians brought . . cedar 1
Ezr 3: 7 gave . . food, drink, and oil to . . the Tyrians 1
1Es 5:55 carts to the Sidonians and the Tyrians 2
2Mc 4:49 Therefore even the Tyrians . . provided 2

Ucal 1. אֻכָל
Prv 30: 1 The man says to Ith'i-el, to Ith'i-el and Ucal 1

Uel 1. אוּאֵל
Ezr 10:34 Of the sons of Bani: Ma-ada'i, Amram, Uel 1

Ulai 1. אוּלָי
Dan 8: 2 saw in the vision, and I was at the river U'lai. 1
16 I heard a man's voice between the banks of the U'lai 1

Ulam 1. אוּלָם
1Ch 7:16 Peresh . . and his sons were Ulam and Rakem. 1
17 The sons of Ulam: Bedan. 1
8:39 The sons of Eshek his brother: Ulam his first-born 1
40 sons of Ulam were men who were mighty warriors 1

Ulla 1. עֻלָּא
1Ch 7:39 The sons of Ulla: Arah, Han'niel, and Rizi'a. 1

Ummah 1. עֻמָּה
Jos 19:30 Mahalab, Achzib, Ummah, Aphek and Rehob 1

feast of Unleavened Bread 1. ἄζυμος
Mrk 14: 1 Passover and the feast of Unleavened Bread 1

Unni 1. עֻנִּי
1Ch 15:18 Zechari'ah, Ja-a'ziel, Shemi'ramoth, Jehi'el, Unni 1
20 Jehi'el, Unni, Eli'ab, Ma-asei'ah, and Benai'ah 1

Unno 1. עֻנּוֹ
Neh 12: 9 Bakbuki'ah and Unno their brethren 1

Uphaz 1. אוּפָז
Jer 10: 9 silver . . from Tarshish, and gold from Uphaz. 1
Dan 10: 5 whose loins were girded with gold of Uphaz. 1

Ur 1. אוּר
Gen 11:28 land of his birth, in Ur of the Chalde'ans. 1
31 went forth together from Ur of the Chalde'ans 1
15: 7 said to him, "I am the LORD who brought you from Ur 1
1Ch 11:35 Eli'phal the son of Ur 1
Neh 9: 7 bring him forth out of Ur of the Chalde'ans 1

Urbanus 1. Οὐρβανός
Rom 16: 9 Greet Urba'nus, our fellow worker in Christ 1

Uri 1. אוּרִי
Exd 31: 2 called by name Bez'alel and son of Uri, son of Hur 1
35:30 has called by name Bez'alel the son of Uri 1
38:22 Bez'alel the son of Uri, son of Hur, of the tribe 1
1Kg 4:19 Geber the son of Uri, in the land of Gilead 1
1Ch 2:20 Hur was the father of Uri 1
20 and Uri was the father of Bez'alel. 1
2Ch 1: 5 that Bez'alel the son of Uri, son of Hur, had made 1
Ezr 10:24 Of the gatekeepers: Shallum, Telem, and Uri. 1

Uriah 1. אוּרִיָּה 2. אוּרִיָּהוּ 3. Οὐρίας
2Sm 11: 3 Bathshe'ba . . the wife of Uri'ah the Hittite? 1
6 David sent word . . "Send me Uri'ah the Hittite. 1
6 Send me Uri'ah . . And Jo'ab sent Uri'ah to David. 1
7 When Uri'ah came to him, David asked how Jo'ab was 1
8 Then David said to Uri'ah, "Go down to your house 1
8 Uri'ah went out of the king's house 1
9 Uri'ah slept at the door of the king's house 1
10 they told David, "Uri'ah did not go down to his house 1
10 David said to Uri'ah, "Have you not come 1
11 Uri'ah said to David, "The ark and Israel and Judah 1
12 Then David said to Uri'ah, "Remain here today also 1
12 Uri'ah remained in Jerusalem that day 1
14 David wrote . . and sent it by the hand of Uri'ah. 1
15 Set Uri'ah in the forefront of the . . fighting 1
16 Jo'ab . . assigned Uri'ah to the place 1
17 Uri'ah the Hittite was slain also. 1
21 say, 'Your servant Uri'ah the Hittite is dead also.' 1
24 and your servant Uri'ah the Hittite is dead also. 1
26 the wife of Uri'ah heard . . her husband was dead 1
26 the wife . . heard that Uri'ah her husband was dead 1
12: 9 have smitten Uri'ah the Hittite with the sword 1
10 taken the wife of Uri'ah the Hittite to . . wife. 1
15 the LORD struck the child that Uri'ah's wife bore 1
23:39 Uri'ah the Hittite: 37 in all. 1
1Kg 15: 5 except in the matter of Uri'ah the Hittite. 1
2Kg 16:10 King Ahaz sent to Uri'ah . . a model of the altar 1
11 And Uri'ah the priest built the altar; 1
11 in accordance with . . so Uri'ah the priest made it 1
15 King Ahaz commanded Uri'ah the priest, saying 1
16 Uri'ah the priest did all this 1
1Ch 11:41 Uri'ah the Hittite, Zabad the son of Ahlai 1
Ezr 8:33 Mer'emoth the priest, son of Uri'ah 1
Neh 3: 4 the son of Uri'ah, son of Hakkoz repaired. 1
21 Mer'emoth the son of Uri'ah, son of Hakkoz repaired 1
8: 4 beside him stood . . Uri'ah, Hilki'ah, and Ma-asei'ah 1
Isa 8: 2 witnesses, Uri'ah the priest and Zechari'ah 1
Jer 26:20 Uri'ah the son of Shemai'ah from Kir'iath-je'arim. 2
21 but when Uri'ah heard of it, he was afraid and fled 2
23 they fetched Uri'ah from Egypt and brought him 2
Mat 1: 6 David . . the father of Solomon by the wife of Uri'ah 3
1Es 8:62 Meremoth the priest, son of Uriah; 3
9:43 Azariah, Uriah, Hezekiah 3

Uriel 1. אוּרִיאֵל 2. Urihel
1Ch 6:24 Tahath his son, Uri'el his son, Uzzi'ah 1
15: 5 of the sons of Kohath, Uri'el the chief 1
11 Levites Uri'el, Asai'ah, Jo'el, Shemai'ah, Eli'el 1
2Ch 13: 2 Micai'ah the daughter of U'riel of Gib'e-ah. 1
2Es 4: 1 the angel . . whose name was Uriel, answered 2
5:20 as Uriel the angel had commanded me. 2
10:28 Where is the angel Uriel, who came to me at first? 2

Urim 1. אוּרִים 2. δῆλος 3. δήλωσις 4. ostensio
Exd 28:30 judgment you shall put the Urim and the Thummim 1
Lev 8: 8 in the breastpiece he put the Urim and the Thummim 1
Num 27:21 by the judgment of the Urim before the LORD; 1
Deu 33: 8 Give to Levi . . and thy Urim to thy godly one 1
1Sm 14:41 If this guilt is in me or in Jonathan . . give Urim; 4
28: 6 either by dreams, or by Urim, or by prophets. 1
Ezr 2:63 priest to consult Urim and Thummim. 1
Neh 7:65 priest with Urim and Thummim should arise. 1
1Es 5:40 a high priest . . wearing Urim and Thummim. 3
Sir 33: 3 as dependable as an inquiry by means of Urim. 2
45:10 with the oracle of judgment, Urim and Thummim; 2

Uthai 1. עוּתַי 2. Ουθι 3. Ουτα
1Ch 9: 4 Uthai the son of Ammi'hud, son of Omri, son of Imri 1
Ezr 8:14 Of the sons of Bigva'i, Uthai and Zaccur 1
1Es 5:30 the sons of Akkub, the sons of Uthai 3
8:40 Of the sons of Bigvai, Uthai the son of Istalcurus 2

Uz 1. עוּץ
Gen 10:23 The sons of Aram: Uz, Hul, Gether, and Mash. 1
22:21 Uz the first-born, Buz his brother 1
36:28 These are the sons of Dishan: Uz and Aran. 1
1Ch 1:17 The sons of Shem . . Lud, Aram, Uz, Hul, Gether 1
42 The sons of Dishan: Uz and Aran. 1
Job 1: 1 was a man in the land of Uz, whose name was Job 1
Jer 25:20 all the kings of the land of Uz 1
Lam 4:21 O daughter of Edom, dweller in the land of Uz; 1

Uzai 1. אוּזַי
Neh 3:25 Palal the son of Uzai repaired opposite 1

Uzal 1. אוּזָל
Gen 10:27 Hador'am, Uzal, Diklah 1
1Ch 1:21 Hador'am, Uzal, Diklah 1
Ezk 27:19 wine from Uzal they exchanged for your wares; 1

Uzza 1. עֻזָּא 2. 'Οζίας
2Kg 21:18 and was buried . . in the garden of Uzza; 1
26 And he was buried in his tomb in the garden of Uzza; 1
1Ch 8: 7 Gera, that is, Heglam . . father of Uzza and Ahi'hud. 1
Ezr 2:49 sons of Uzza, the sons of Pase'ah, the sons of Besai 1
Neh 7:51 sons of Gazzam, the sons of Uzza, the sons of Pase'ah 1
1Es 5:31 sons of Chezib, the sons of Gazzam, the sons of Uzza 2

Uzzah 1. עֻזָּה
2Sm 6: 3 and Uzzah and Ahi'o . . were driving the new cart 1
6 Uzzah put out his hand to the ark . . and took hold 1
7 the anger of the LORD was kindled against Uzzah; 1
8 because the LORD had broken forth upon Uzzah; 1
1Ch 6:29 of Merar'i . . Libni . . Shim'e-i . . Uzzah his son 1
13: 7 and Uzzah and Ahi'o were driving the cart. 1
9 Uzzah put out his hand to hold the ark 1
10 the anger of the LORD was kindled against Uzzah; 1
11 because the LORD had broken forth upon Uzzah; 1

Uzzen-sheerah 1. אֻזֵּן שֶׁאֱרָה
1Ch 7:24 She'erah, who built . . and Uz'zen-she'erah. 1

Uzzi 1. עֻזִּי 2. 'Οζίας 3. Ozia
1Ch 6: 5 Abishu'a of Bukki, Bukki of Uzzi 1
6 Uzzi of Zerahi'ah, Zerahi'ah of Merai'oth 1
51 Bukki his son, Uzzi his son, Zerahi'ah his son 1
7: 2 sons of Tola: Uzzi, Rephai'ah, Je'ri-el, Jah'mai, Ibsam 1
3 The sons of Uzzi: Izrahi'ah. 1
7 sons of Bela: Ezbon, Uzzi, Uz'ziel, Jer'imoth, and Iri 1
9: 8 Elah the son of Uzzi, son of Michri 1
Ezr 7: 4 son of Zerahi'ah, son of Uzzi, son of Bukki 1
Neh 11:22 overseer . . Uzzi the son of Bani 1

12:19 of Joi'arib, Matte'nai; of Jedai'ah, Uzzi; 1
42 Ma-asei'ah, Shemai'ah, Elea'zar, Uzzi, Jehoha'nan 1
1Es 8: 2 son of Uzzi, son of Bukki, son of Abishua 2
2Es 1: 2 son of Meraioth, son of Arna, son of Uzzi 3

Uzzia 1. עֻזִּיָּא
1Ch 11:44 Uzzi'a the Ash'terathite, Shama and Je-i'el 1

Uzziah 1. עֻזִּיָּהוּ 2. Ὀζίας
2Kg 15:13 in the 39th year of Uzzi'ah king of Judah 1
30 the twentieth year of Jotham the son of Uzzi'ah. 1
32 Jotham the son of Uzzi'ah . . began to reign. 1
34 to all that his father Uzzi'ah had done. 1
1Ch 6:24 Uri'el his son, Uzzi'ah his son, and Sha'ul his son. 1
27:25 treasuries . . was Jonathan the son of Uzzi'ah; 1
2Ch 26: 1 all the people of Judah took Uzzi'ah 1
3 Uzzi'ah was sixteen . . when he began to reign 1
8 The Ammonites paid tribute to Uzzi'ah 1
9 Moreover Uzzi'ah built towers in Jerusalem 1
11 Uzzi'ah had an army of soldiers, fit for war 1
14 Uzzi'ah prepared for all the army shields, spears 1
18 they withstood King Uzzi'ah, and said to him 1
18 is not for you, Uzzi'ah, to burn incense to the LORD 1
19 Then Uzzi'ah was angry. 1
21 King Uzzi'ah was a leper to the day of his death 1
22 the rest of the acts of Uzzi'ah, from first to last 1
23 Uzzi'ah slept with his fathers, and they buried him 1
27: 2 all that his father Uzzi'ah had done 1
Ezr 10:21 of Harim . . Eli'jah, Shemai'ah, Jehi'el, and Uzzi'ah. 1
Neh 11: 4 Athai'ah the son of Uzzi'ah, son of Zechari'ah 1
Isa 1: 1 in the days of Uzzi'ah, Jotham, Ahaz, and Hezeki'ah 1
6: 1 In the year that King Uzzi'ah died I saw the Lord 1
7: 1 In the days of Ahaz the son of Jotham, son of Uzzi'ah 1
Hos 1: 1 in the days of Uzzi'ah, Jotham, Ahaz, and Hezeki'ah 1
Ams 1: 1 in the days of Uzzi'ah king of Judah 1
Zec 14: 5 earthquake in the days of Uzzi'ah king of Judah. 1
Mat 1: 8 and Joram the father of Uzzi'ah 2
9 Uzzi'ah the father of Jotham 2
Jdt 6:15 Uzziah the son of Micah, of the tribe of Simeon 2
16 Uzziah asked him what had happened. 2
21 Uzziah took him from the assembly to his own house 2
7:23 gathered about Uzziah and the rulers of the city 2
30 Uzziah said to them, "Have courage, my brothers! 2
8: 9 when she heard all that Uzziah said to them 2
28 Then Uzziah said to her 2
35 Uzziah and the rulers said to her, "Go in peace 2
10: 6 found Uzziah standing there with the elders 2
13:18 Uzziah said to her, "O daughter . . 2
14: 6 they summoned Achior from the house of Uzziah. 2
15: 4 Uzziah sent men to Betomasthaim and Bebai 2

Uzziel 1. עֻזִּיאֵל
Exd 6:18 sons of Kohath: Amram, Izhar, Hebron, and Uz'ziel 1
22 the sons of Uz'ziel: Mi'sha-el, Elza'phan, and Sithri. 1
Lev 10: 4 Mish'a-el and Elza'phan, the sons of Uz'ziel 1
Num 3:19 Amram, Izhar, Hebron, and Uz'ziel. 1
30 Eli-za'phan the son of Uz'ziel as head 1
1Ch 4:42 having as their leaders . . Rephai'ah, and Uz'ziel 1
6: 2 sons of Kohath: Amram, Izhar, Hebron, and Uz'ziel. 1
18 sons of Kohath: Amram, Izhar, Hebron, and Uz'ziel. 1
7: 7 sons of Bela: Ezbon, Uzzi, Uz'ziel, Jer'imoth, and Iri 1
15:10 of the sons of Uz'ziel, Ammin'adab the chief 1
23:12 sons of Kohath: Amram, Izhar, Hebron, and Uz'ziel 1
20 The sons of Uz'ziel: Micah the chief 1
24:24 sons of Uz'ziel, Micah; of the sons of Micah, Shamir. 1
25: 4 sons of Heman: Bukki'ah, Mattani'ah, Uz'ziel, 1
2Ch 29:14 of the sons of Jedu'thun, Shemai'ah and Uz'ziel. 1
Neh 3: 8 Next to them Uz'ziel the son of Harhai'ah 1

Uzzielite 1. עָזִּיאֵלִי
Num 3:27 Of Kohath . . the family of the Uzzie'lites; 1
1Ch 26:23 the He'bronites, and the Uzzie'lites 1

Vaizatha 1. וַיְזָתָא
Est 9: 9 Parmash'ta and Ar'isai and Ar'idai and Vaiza'tha 1

Valley Gate 1. שַׁעַר הַגַּיְא
Neh 2:13 I went out by night by the Valley Gate 1
15 I turned back and entered by the Valley Gate 1
3:13 Hanun and . . Zano'ah repaired the Valley Gate; 1

Vaniah 1. וַנְיָה 2. Ανως
Ezr 10:36 Vani'ah, Mer'emoth, Eli'ashib 1
1Es 9:34 Mamdai and Bedeiah and Vaniah 2

Vashti 1. וַשְׁתִּי
Est 1: 9 Queen Vashti also gave a banquet for the women 1
11 to bring Queen Vashti before the king 1
12 But Queen Vashti refused to come 1
15 what is to be done to Queen Vashti, 1
16 Not only to the king has Queen Vashti done wrong 1
17 Ahasu-e'rus commanded Queen Vashti to be brought 1
19 a royal order . . that Vashti is to come no more 1
2: 1 he remembered Vashti and what she had done 1
4 let the maiden . . be queen instead of Vashti. 1
17 and made her queen instead of Vashti. 1

Vophsi 1. וָפְסִי
Num13:14 from the tribe of Naph'tali, Nahbi . . of Vophsi; 1

Waheb 1. וָהֵב
Num21:14 Waheb in Suphah, and the valleys of the Arnon 1

Water Gate 1. שַׁעַר הַמַּיִם
Neh 3:26 point opposite the Water Gate on the east 1
8: 1 gathered . . into the square before the Water Gate; 1
3 read . . facing the square before the Water Gate 1
16 made booths . . in the square at the Water Gate 1
12:37 house of David, to the Water Gate on the east. 1

Wildgoats' Rocks 1. צוּרֵי הַיְּעֵלִים
1Sm 24: 2 seek David . . in front of the Wildgoats' Rocks. 1

Xanthicus 1. Ξανθικός
2Mc 11:30 those who go home by the 30th day of Xanthicus 1
33 Farewell. The 148th year, Xanthicus fifteenth. 1
38 Farewell. The 148th year, Xanthicus fifteenth. 1

Yiron 1. יִרְאוֹן
Jos 19:38 Yiron, Mig'dal-el, Horem, Beth-anath 1

Zaanan 1. צַאֲנָן
Mic 1:11 the inhabitants of Za'anan do not come forth; 1

Zaanannim 1. צַעֲנַנִּים
Jos 19:33 its boundary ran . . from the oak in Za-anan'nim 1
Jdg 4:11 the oak in Za-anan'nim, which is near Kedesh. 1

Zaavan 1. זַעֲוָן
Gen 36:27 the sons of Ezer: Bilhan, Za'avan, and Akan. 1
1Ch 1:42 The sons of Ezer: Bilhan, Za'avan, and Ja'akan. 1

Zabad 1. זָבָד 2. Ζαβαδ 3. Ζαβδια
1Ch 2:36 Attai . . father of Nathan and Nathan of Zabad. 1
37 Zabad . . father of Ephlal, and Ephlal of Obed. 1
7:21 Zabad his son, Shuthe'lah his son, and Ezer 1
11:41 Uri'ah the Hittite, Zabad the son of Ahlai 1
2Ch 24:26 Those who conspired against him were Zabad 1
Ezr 10:27 of Zattu . . Jer'emoth, Zabad, and Azi'za. 1
33 of Hashum: Matte'nai, Mat'tattah, Zabad, Eliph'elet 1
43 of Nebo: Je-i'el, Mattithi'ah, Zabad, Zebi'na, Jaddai 1
1Es 9:28 Jeremoth, and Zabad and Zerdaiah. 2
33 Mattenai and Mattattah and Zabad and Eliphelet 3
35 Mattithiah, Zabad, Iddo, Joel, Benaiah. 2

Zabadean 1. Ζαβαδαιοι
1Mc 12:31 the Arabs who are called Zabadeans 1

Zabbai 1. זַבַּי 2. Ζαβδος
Ezr 10:28 of Be'bai were . . Hanani'ah, Zab'bai, and Ath'lai. 1
Neh 3:20 After him Baruch the son of Zab'bai repaired 1
1Es 9:29 Jehohanan and Hananiah and Zabbai and Emathis. 2

Zabdi 1. זַבְדִּי
Jos 7: 1 Achan the son of Carmi, son of Zabdi, son of Zerah 1
17 he brought near the family . . and Zabdi was taken; 1
18 Achan the son of Carmi, son of Zabdi, son of Zerah 1
1Ch 8:19 Jakim, Zichri, Zabdi 1
27:27 over the produce of the vineyards . . was Zabdi 1
Neh 11:17 Mattani'ah the son of Mica, son of Zabdi 1

Zabdiel 1. זַבְדִּיאֵל 2. Ζαβδιηλ
1Ch 27: 2 Jasho'beam the son of Zab'di-el was in charge 1
Neh 11:14 overseer was Zab'diel the son of Haggedo'lim. 1
1Mc 11:17 Zabdiel the Arab cut off the head of Alexander 2

Zabud 1. זָבוּד
1Kg 4: 5 Zabud the son of Nathan was priest and king's 1

Zaccai 1. זַכַּי
Ezr 2: 9 sons of Zac'cai, 760. 1
Neh 7:14 sons of Zac'cai, 760. 1

Zacchaeus 1. Ζακχαῖος
Lke 19: 2 there was a man named Zacchae'us; 1
5 Zacchae'us, make haste and come down 1
8 Zacchae'us stood and said to the Lord, "Behold 1
2Mc 10:19 left . . also Zacchaeus and his men 1

Zaccur 1. זַכּוּר 2. Βακχουρος
Num13: 4 tribe of Reuben, Sham'mu-a the son of Zaccur; 1
1Ch 4:26 sons of Mishma: Ham'mu-el . . Zac'cur his son 1
24:27 of Ja-azi'ah, Beno, Shoham, Zaccur, and Ibri. 1
25: 2 sons of Asaph: Zaccur, Joseph, Nethani'ah 1
10 third to Zaccur, his sons and his brethren, twelve; 1
Ezr 8:14 Of the sons of Bigva'i, Uthai and Zaccur 1
Neh 3: 2 next to them Zaccur the son of Imri built. 1
10:12 Zaccur, Sherebi'ah, Shebani'ah 1
12:35 son of Micai'ah, son of Zaccur, son of Asaph; 1
13:13 as their assistant Hanan the son of Zaccur, 1
1Es 9:24 Of the temple singers: Eliashib and Zaccur. 2

Zadok 1. צָדוֹק 2. Σαδδουκος 3. Σαδώκ 4. Sadoch
2Sm 8:17 Zadok the son of Ahi'tub . . were priests; 1
15:24 And Abi'athar came up, and lo, Zadok came also 1
25 Then the king said to Zadok, "Carry the ark of God 1
27 The king also said to Zadok the priest 1
29 So Zadok and Abi'athar carried the ark of God back 1
35 Are not Zadok and Abi'athar the priests with you 1
35 tell it to Zadok and Abi'athar the priests. 1
36 two sons . . Ahim'a-az, Zadok's son, and Jonathan 1
17:15 Hushai said to Zadok and Abi'athar the priests 1
18:19 Then said Ahi'ma-az the son of Zadok, "Let me run 1
22 Then Ahi'ma-az the son of Zadok said again to Jo'ab 1
27 is like the running of Ahi'ma-az the son of Zadok. 1
19:11 David sent . . to Zadok and Abi'athar the priests 1
20:25 and Zadok and Abi'athar were priests; 1
1Kg 1: 8 Zadok the priest, and Benai'ah the son of Jehoi'ada 1
26 me, your servant, and Zadok the priest, and Benai'ah 1
32 Call to me Zadok the priest, Nathan the prophet 1
34 let Zadok the priest and Nathan . . anoint him 1
38 Zadok the priest, Nathan . . and Benai'ah . . went 1
39 Zadok the priest took the horn of oil 1
44 sent . . Zadok the priest, Nathan . . and Benai'ah 1
45 Zadok the priest and Nathan . . have anointed him 1
2:35 the king put Zadok the priest in the place 1
4: 2 Azari'ah the son of Zadok was the priest; 1
4 of the army; Zadok and Abi'athar were priests; 1
2Kg 15:33 mother's name was Jeru'sha the daughter of Zadok. 1
1Ch 6: 8 Ahi'tub of Zadok, Zadok of Ahim'a-az 1
8 Ahi'tub of Zadok, Zadok of Ahim'a-az 1
12 Ahi'tub of Zadok, Zadok of Shallum 1
12 Ahi'tub of Zadok, Zadok of Shallum 1
53 Zadok his son, Ahim'a-az his son. 1
9:11 son of Zadok, son of Merai'oth, son of Ahi'tub 1
12:28 Zadok, a young man mighty in valor 1
15:11 David summoned the priests Zadok and Abi'athar 1
16:39 he left Zadok the priest and his brethren 1
18:16 Zadok . . and Ahim'elech . . were priests; 1
24: 3 With the help of Zadok of the sons of Elea'zar 1
6 in the presence of . . Zadok the priest 1
31 in the presence of King David, Zadok, Ahim'elech 1
27:17 for Levi, Hashabi'ah . . for Aaron, Zadok; 1
29:22 anointed him as prince . . and Zadok as priest. 1
2Ch 27: 1 name was Jeru'shah the daughter of Zadok. 1
31:10 Azari'ah . . who was of the house of Zadok 1
Ezr 7: 2 son of Shallum, son of Za-dok, son of Ahi'tub 1
Neh 3: 4 next to them Zadok the son of Ba'ana repaired. 1
29 Zadok the son of Immer repaired opposite his own 1
10:21 Meshez'abel, Zadok, Jad'du-a 1
11:11 Meshul'lam, son of Zadok, son of Merai'oth 1
13:13 appointed . . Zadok the scribe, and Pedai'ah 1
Ezk 40:46 these are the sons of Zadok 1
43:19 to the Levitical priests of the family of Zadok 1
44:15 But the Levitical priests, the sons of Zadok 1
48:11 for the consecrated priests, the sons of Zadok 1
Mat 1:14 Azor the father of Zadok 3
14 and Zadok the father of Achim 3
1Es 8: 2 son of Zadok, son of Ahitub, son of Amariah 2
2Es 1: 1 son of Shallum, son of Zadok, son of Ahitub 4

Zaham 1. זַהַם
2Ch 11:19 she bore him sons, Je'ush, Shemari'ah, and Zaham. 1

Zair 1. צָעִיר
2Kg 8:21 Joram passed over to Za'ir with all his chariots 1

Zalaph 1. צָלָף
Neh 3:30 Hanani'ah . . and Hanun the sixth son of Zalaph 1

Zalmon 1. צַלְמוֹן
Jdg 9:48 Abim'elech went up to Mount Zalmon 1
2Sm 23:28 Zalmon the Aho'hite, Ma'harai of Netoph'ah 1
Ps 68:14 scattered kings there, snow fell on Zalmon. 1

Zalmonah 1. צַלְמֹנָה
Num33:41 set out from Mount Hor, and encamped at Zalmo'nah. 1
42 set out from Zalmo'nah, and encamped at Punon. 1

Zalmunna 1. צַלְמֻנָּע
Jdg 8: 5 I am pursuing after Zebah and Zalmun'na, the kings 1
6 Are Zebah and Zalmun'na already in your hand 1
7 LORD has given Zebah and Zalmun'na into my hand 1
10 Zebah and Zalmun'na were in Karkor with their 1
12 Zebah and Zalmun'na fled; and he pursued them 1
12 took the two kings of Mid'ian, Zebah and Zalmun'na 1
15 Zebah and Zalmun'na, about whom you taunted me 1
15 Are Zebah and Zalmun'na already in your hand 1
18 he said to Zebah and Zalmun'na, "Where are the men 1
21 Then Zebah and Zalmun'na said, "Rise yourself 1
21 And Gideon arose and slew Zebah and Zalmun'na; 1
Ps 83:11 all their princes like Zebah and Zalmun'na 1

Zamzummim 1. זַמְזֻמִּים
Deu 2:20 but the Ammonites call them Zamzum'mim 1

Zanoah 1. זָנוֹחַ
Jos 15:34 Zano'ah, En-gan'nim, Tap'puah, Enam 1
56 Jezreel, Jok'de-am, Zano'ah 1
1Ch 4:18 wife bore . . Jeku'thiel the father of Zano'ah. 1
Neh 3:13 Hanun and the inhabitants of Zano'ah repaired 1
11:30 Zano'ah, Adullam, and their villages 1

Zaphenath-paneah 1. צָפְנַת פַּעְנֵחַ
Gen 41:45 Pharaoh called Joseph's name Zaph'enath-pane'ah 1

Zaphon 1. צָפוֹן
Jos 13:27 of Beth-ha'ram, Beth-nim'rah, Succoth, and Zaphon 1
Jdg 12: 1 and they crossed to Zaphon and said to Jephthah 1

Zarephath 1. צָרְפַת 2. Σάρεπτα
1Kg 17: 9 Arise, go to Zar'ephath . . and dwell there. 1
10 So he arose and went to Zar'ephath; 1
Obd 1:20 possess Phoenicia as far as Zar'ephath; 1
Lke 4:26 sent to none of them but only to Zar'ephath 2

Zarethan 1. צָרְתָן
Jos 3:16 far off, at Adam, the city that is beside Zar'ethan 1
1Kg 4:12 all Beth-she'an which is beside Zarethan below 1
7:46 in the clay ground between Succoth and Zarethan. 1

Zarius 1. Ζαριος
1Es 1:38 seized his brother Zarius 1

Zattu 1. זַתּוּא 2. Ζαθθουι 3. Ζαθοης 4. Ζαμοθ
Ezr 2: 8 sons of Zattu, 945. 1
8: 5 Of the sons of Zattu, Shecani'ah 3
10:27 Of the sons of Zattu: Eli-o-e'nai, Eli'ashib 1
Neh 7:13 sons of Zattu, 845. 1
10:14 chiefs . . Parosh, Pa'hath-mo'ab, Elam, Zattu, Bani 1
1Es 5:12 The sons of Zattu, 945. The sons of Chorbe, 705. 2
8:32 Of the sons of Zattu, Shecaniah 3
9:28 Of the sons of Zattu: Elioenai, Eliashib, Othoniah 4

Zaza 1. זָזָא
1Ch 2:33 The sons of Jonathan: Peleth and Zaza. 1

Zealot 1. ζηλωτής
Lke 6:15 Simon who was called the Zealot 1
Act 1:13 James the son of Alphaeus and Simon the Zealot 1

Zebadiah 1. זְבַדְיָהוּ 2. Ζαβδαιος
1Ch 8:15 Zebadi'ah, Arad, Eder 1
17 Zebadi'ah, Meshul'lam, Hizki, Heber 1
12: 7 Joe'lah and Zebadi'ah, the sons of Jero'ham 1
26: 2 Meshelemi'ah had sons . . Zebadi'ah the third 1
27: 7 his son Zebadi'ah after him; in his division were 1
2Ch 17: 8 with them the Levites . . Zebadi'ah, As'ahel 1
19:11 Zebadi'ah . . in all the king's matters; 1
Ezr 8: 8 sons of Shephati'ah, Zebadi'ah the son of Michael 1
10:20 Of the sons of Immer: Hana'ni and Zebadi'ah. 1
1Es 9:21 Of the sons of Immer: Hanani and Zebadiah 2

Zebah 1. זֶבַח
Jdg 8: 5 I am pursuing after Zebah and Zalmun'na, the kings 1
6 Are Zebah and Zalmun'na already in your hand 1
7 LORD has given Zebah and Zalmun'na into my hand 1
10 Zebah and Zalmun'na were in Karkor with their 1
12 Zebah and Zalmun'na fled; and he pursued them 1
12 took the two kings of Mid'ian, Zebah and Zalmun'na 1
15 Zebah and Zalmun'na, about whom you taunted me 1
15 Are Zebah and Zalmun'na already in your hand 1
18 he said to Zebah and Zalmun'na, "Where are the men 1
21 Then Zebah and Zalmun'na said, "Rise yourself 1
21 And Gideon arose and slew Zebah and Zalmun'na; 1
Ps 83:11 all their princes like Zebah and Zalmun'na 1

Zebedee 1. Ζεβεδαῖος
Mat 4:21 other brothers, James the son of Zeb'edee and John 1
21 in the boat with Zeb'edee their father, mending 1
10: 2 James the son of Zeb'edee, and John his brother; 1
20:20 the mother of the sons of Zeb'edee came up to him 1
26:37 taking with him Peter and the two sons of Zeb'edee 1
27:56 the mother of the sons of Zeb'edee. 1
Mrk 1:19 James the son of Zeb'edee and John his brother 1
20 they left their father Zeb'edee in the boat 1
3:17 James the son of Zeb'edee 1
10:35 James and John, the sons of Zeb'edee, came forward 1
Lke 5:10 so also were James and John, sons of Zeb'edee 1
Joh 21: 2 Nathan'a-el of Cana in Galilee, the sons of Zeb'edee 1

Zebidah 1. זְבִידָה
2Kg 23:36 name was Zebi'dah the daughter of Pedai'ah 1

Zebina 1. זְבִינָא
Ezr 10:43 of Nebo: Je-i'el, Mattithi'ah, Zabad, Zebi'na, Jaddai 1

Zeboiim 1. צְבֹיִים
Gen 10:19 direction of Sodom . . Admah,and Zeboi'im 1
14: 2 Shinab king of Admah, Sheme'ber king of Zeboi'im 1
8 the king of Admah, the king of Zeboi'im 1
Deu 29:23 an overthrow like that of . . Admah and Zeboi'im 1
Hos 11: 8 How can I treat you like Zeboi'im! 1

Zeboim 1. צְבֹעִים
1Sm 13:18 border that looks down upon the valley of Zebo'im 1
Neh 11:34 Hadid, Zebo'im, Nebal'lat 1

Zebul 1. זְבֻל
Jdg 9:28 the son of Jerubba'al and Zebul his officer 1
30 When Zebul the ruler of the city heard the words 1
36 when Ga'al saw the men, he said to Zebul, "Look, 1
36 And Zebul said to him, "You see the shadow 1
38 Zebul said to him, "Where is your mouth now 1
41 Zebul drove out Ga'al and his kinsmen 1

Zebulun 1. זְבוּלֻן 2. Ζαβουλών
Gen 30:20 she called his name Zeb'ulun. 1
35:23 Simeon, Levi, Judah, Is'sachar, and Zeb'ulun. 1
46:14 The sons of Zeb'ulun: Sered, Elon, and Jah'leel 1
49:13 Zeb'ulun shall dwell at the shore of the sea; 1
Exd 1: 3 Is'sachar, Zeb'ulun, and Benjamin 1
Num 1: 9 from Zeb'ulun, Eli'ab the son of Helon; 1
30 Of the people of Zeb'ulun, their generations 1
31 the number of the tribe of Zeb'ulun was 57,400 1
2: 7 Then the tribe of Zeb'ulun, the leader 1
7 leader of the people of Zeb'ulun being Eli'ab 1
7:24 Eli'ab the . . leader of the men of Zeb'ulun 1
10:16 over the host of the tribe of the men of Zeb'ulun 1
13:10 from the tribe of Zeb'ulun, Gad'diel the son of Sodi; 1
26:26 The sons of Zeb'ulun, according to their families 1
34:25 Of the tribe of the sons of Zeb'ulun a leader 1
Deu 27:13 stand upon Mount Ebal . . Zeb'ulun, Dan 1
33:18 of Zeb'ulun he said, "Rejoice, Zeb'ulun 1
18 Rejoice, Zeb'ulun, in your going out; and Is'sachar 1
Jos 19:10 The third lot came up for the tribe of Zeb'ulun 1
16 This is the inheritance of the tribe of Zeb'ulun 1
27 and touches Zeb'ulun and the valley of Iph'tahel 1
34 goes . . to Hukkok, touching Zeb'ulun at the south 1
21: 7 Reuben, the tribe of Gad, and the tribe of Zeb'ulun 1
34 the rest . . were given out of the tribe of Zeb'ulun 1
Jdg 1:30 Zeb'ulun did not drive out the inhabitants 1
4: 6 the tribe of Naph'tali and the tribe of Zeb'ulun. 1
10 Barak summoned Zeb'ulun and Naph'tali to Kedesh; 1
5:14 from Zeb'ulun those who bear the marshal's staff; 1
18 Zeb'ulun is a people that jeoparded their lives 1
6:35 sent messengers to Asher, Zeb'ulun, and Naph'tali; 1
12:12 and was buried at Ai'jalon in the land of Zeb'ulun. 1
1Ch 2: 1 sons of Israel . . Levi, Judah, Is'sachar, Zeb'ulun 1
6:63 out of the tribes of Reuben, Gad, and Zeb'ulun. 1
77 were allotted out of the tribe of Zeb'ulun 1
12:33 Of Zeb'ulun 50,000 seasoned troops 1
40 from as far as Is'sachar and Zeb'ulun and Naph'tali 1
27:19 for Zeb'ulun, Ishma'iah the son of Obadi'ah; 1
2Ch 30:10 couriers went . . as far as Zeb'ulun; 1
11 a few men of Asher, of Manas'seh, and of Zeb'ulun 1
18 many of them from E'phraim . . and Zeb'ulun 1
Ps 68:27 princes of Zeb'ulun, the princes of Naph'tali. 1
Isa 9: 1 he brought into contempt the land of Zeb'ulun 1
Ezk 48:26 the east side to the west, Zeb'ulun, one portion. 1
27 Adjoining the territory of Zeb'ulun 1
33 the gate of Is'sachar, and the gate of Zeb'ulun. 1
Mat 4:13 in the territory of Zeb'ulun and Naph'tali 2
15 The land of Zeb'ulun and the land of Naph'tali 2
Rev 7: 8 12,000 of the tribe of Zeb'ulun 2

Zebulunite 1. זְבוּלֹנִי
Num26:27 These are the families of the Zeb'ulunites 1
Jdg 12:11 After him Elon the Zeb'ulunite judged Israel; 1
12 Then Elon the Zeb'ulunite died, and was buried 1

Zechariah 1. זְכַרְיָהוּ 2. זְכַרְיָה (A) 3. Ζαχαρίας 4. Zaccharia
2Kg 14:29 Jerobo'am slept . . and Zechari'ah his son reigned 1
15: 8 Zechari'ah the son of Jerobo'am reigned over 1
11 Now the rest of the deeds of Zechari'ah 1
18: 2 mother's name was Abi the daughter of Zechari'ah. 1
1Ch 5: 7 his kinsmen . . the chief, Je-i'el, and Zechari'ah 1
9:21 Zechari'ah the son of Meshelemi'ah 1
37 Gedor, Ahi'o, Zechari'ah and Mikloth; 1
15:18 Zechari'ah, Ja-a'ziel, Shemi'ramoth, Jehi'el, Unni 1
20 Zechari'ah, A'zi-el, Shemi'ramoth, Jehi'el, Unni 1
24 Ama'sai, Zechari'ah, Benai'ah, and Elie'zer 1
16: 5 second to him were Zechari'ah, Je-i'el, Shemi'ramoth 1
24:25 of the sons of Isshi'ah, Zechari'ah. 1
26: 2 Meshelemi'ah had sons: Zechari'ah the first-born 1
11 Tebali'ah the third, Zechari'ah the fourth 1
14 They cast lots also for his son Zechari'ah 1
27:21 Manas'seh in Gilead, Iddo the son of Zechari'ah; 1
2Ch 17: 7 he sent his princes, Ben-hail, Obadi'ah, Zechari'ah 1
20:14 Jaha'ziel the son of Zechari'ah, son of Benai'ah 1
21: 2 sons of Jehosh'aphat: Azari'ah, Jehi'el, Zechari'ah 1
24:20 the Spirit of God took possession of Zechari'ah 1
22 Jehoi'ada, Zechari'ah's father, had shown him •
26: 5 set himself to seek God in the days of Zechari'ah 1
29: 1 Abi'jah the daughter of Zechari'ah. 1
13 the sons of Asaph, Zechari'ah and Mattani'ah 1
34:12 Zechari'ah and Meshul'lam, of . . the Ko'hathites 1
35: 8 Hilki'ah, Zechari'ah, and Jehi'el, the chief 1
Ezr 5: 1 prophets, Haggai and Zechari'ah the son of Iddo 2
6:14 through the prophesying of . . Zechari'ah 2
8: 3 Of the sons of Parosh, Zechari'ah 1
11 Of the sons of Be'bai, Zechari'ah, the son of Be'bai 1
16 Then I sent for . . Zechari'ah, and Meshul'lam 1
10:26 of Elam: Mattani'ah, Zechari'ah, Jehi'el, Abdi 1
Neh 8: 4 Zechari'ah, and Meshul'lam on his left hand. 1
11: 4 Athai'ah the son of Uzzi'ah, son of Zechari'ah 1
5 Joi'arib, son of Zechari'ah, son of the Shi'lonite. 1
12 Pelali'ah, son of Amzi, son of Zechari'ah 1
12:16 of Iddo, Zechari'ah; of Gin'nethon, Meshul'lam; 1
35 Zechari'ah the son of Jonathan, son of Shemai'ah 1
41 priests . . Eli-o-e'nai, Zechari'ah, and Hanani'ah 1
Isa 8: 2 the priest and Zechari'ah the son of Jeberechi'ah 1
Zec 1: 1 the word of the LORD came to Zechari'ah 1
7 the word of the LORD came to Zechari'ah 1
7 and Zechari'ah said •
7: 1 the word of the LORD came to Zechari'ah 1
8 the word of the LORD came to Zechari'ah, saying 1
Mat 23:35 to the blood of Zechari'ah the son of Barachi'ah 3
Lke 1: 5 there was a priest named Zechari'ah 3
12 Zechari'ah was troubled when he saw him 3
13 the angel said to him, "Do not be afraid, Zechari'ah 3
18 Zechari'ah said to the angel, "How shall I know this? 3
21 the people were waiting for Zechari'ah 3
40 she entered the house of Zechari'ah 3
59 would have named him Zechari'ah after his father 3
67 Zechari'ah was filled with the Holy Spirit 3
3: 2 John the son of Zechari'ah in the wilderness; 3
11:51 from the blood of Abel to the blood of Zechari'ah 3
1Es 1: 8 Hilkiah, Zechariah, and Jehiel 3
15 Asaph, Zechariah, and Eddinus 3
6: 1 the prophets Haggai and Zechariah the son of Iddo 3
7: 3 the prophets Haggai and Zechariah prophesied; 3
8:30 Of the sons of Parosh, Zechariah 3
37 Of the sons of Bebai, Zechariah the son of Bebai 3
44 Shemaiah, Jarib, Nathan, Elnathan, Zechariah 3
9:27 Of the sons of Elam: Mattaniah and Zechariah 3
44 Lothasubus, Nabariah, and Zechariah. 3
2Es 1:40 Nahum and Habakkuk, Zephaniah, Haggai, Zechariah 4
1Mc 5:18 he left Joseph, the son of Zechariah 3
56 Joseph, the son of Zechariah 3

Zecher 1. זֶכֶר
1Ch 8:31 Gedor, Ahi'o, Zecher 1

Zedad 1. צְדָד
Num34: 8 end of the boundary shall be at Zedad; 1
Ezk 47:15 to the entrance of Hamath, and on to Zedad 1

Zedekiah 1. צִדְקִיָּהוּ 2. Σεδεκιας
1Kg 22:11 Zedeki'ah . . made for himself horns of iron 1
24 Zedeki'ah . . came near and struck Micai'ah 1
2Kg 24:17 and changed his name to Zedeki'ah. 1
18 Zedeki'ah was 21 years old when he became king 1
20 Zedeki'ah rebelled against the king of Babylon. 1
25: 2 till the eleventh year of King Zedeki'ah. 1
7 They slew the sons of Zedeki'ah before his eyes 1
7 slew the sons . . and put out the eyes of Zedeki'ah 1
1Ch 3:15 sons of Josi'ah . . the third Zedeki'ah 1
16 descendants of Jehoi'akim . . Zedeki'ah his son; 1
2Ch 18:10 Zedeki'ah . . made for himself horns of iron 1
23 Then Zedeki'ah . . came near and struck Micai'ah 1
36:10 made . . Zedeki'ah king over Judah and Jerusalem. 1
11 Zedeki'ah was 21 . . when he began 1
Neh 10: 1 Nehemi'ah . . son of Hacali'ah, Zedeki'ah 1
Jer 1: 3 until the end of the eleventh year of Zedeki'ah 1
21: 1 when King Zedeki'ah sent to him Pashhur 1
4 Thus you shall say to Zedeki'ah, 'Thus says the LORD 1
7 Afterward, says the LORD, I will give Zedeki'ah 1
24: 8 will I treat Zedeki'ah the king of Judah 1
27: 1 In the beginning of the reign of Zedeki'ah 1
3 come to Jerusalem to Zedeki'ah king of Judah. 1
12 To Zedeki'ah king of Judah I spoke in like manner 1
28: 1 at the beginning of the reign of Zedeki'ah 1
29: 3 whom Zedeki'ah king of Judah sent to Babylon 1
21 son of Kola'iah and Zedeki'ah the son of Ma-asei'ah 1
22 The LORD make you like Zedeki'ah and Ahab 1
32: 1 in the tenth year of Zedeki'ah king of Judah 1
3 For Zedeki'ah king of Judah had imprisoned him 1
4 Zedeki'ah king of Judah shall not escape 1
5 and he shall take Zedeki'ah to Babylon 1
34: 2 Go and speak to Zedeki'ah king of Judah 1
4 hear the word of the LORD, O Zedeki'ah king of Judah 1
6 spoke all these words to Zedeki'ah king of Judah 1
8 after King Zedeki'ah had made a covenant 1
21 And Zedeki'ah king of Judah, and his princes 1
36:12 Zedeki'ah the son of Hanani'ah, and all the princes. 1
37: 1 Zedeki'ah the son of Josi'ah whom Nebuchadrez'zar 1
3 King Zedeki'ah sent Jehu'cal the son of Shelemi'ah 1
17 King Zedeki'ah sent for him, and received him. 1
18 Jeremiah also said to King Zedeki'ah 1
21 King Zedeki'ah gave orders 1
38: 5 King Zedeki'ah said, "Behold, he is in your hands; 1
14 King Zedeki'ah sent for Jeremiah the prophet 1
15 Jeremiah said to Zedeki'ah, "If I tell you 1
16 Then King Zedeki'ah swore secretly to Jeremiah 1
17 Then Jeremiah said to Zedeki'ah 1
19 King Zedeki'ah said to Jeremiah 1
24 Then Zedeki'ah said to Jeremiah, "Let no one know 1
39: 1 In the ninth year of Zedeki'ah king of Judah 1
2 in the eleventh year of Zedeki'ah 1
4 Zedeki'ah king of Judah and all the soldiers saw 1
5 Chalde'ans pursued them, and overtook Zedeki'ah 1
6 The king of Babylon slew the sons of Zedeki'ah 1
7 He put out the eyes of Zedeki'ah 1
44:30 as I gave Zedeki'ah king of Judah into the hand 1
49:34 of the reign of Zedeki'ah king of Judah. 1
51:59 he went with Zedeki'ah king of Judah to Babylon 1
52: 1 Zedeki'ah was 21 . . when he became king; 1
3 Zedeki'ah rebelled against the king of Babylon. 1

5 till the eleventh year of King Zedeki'ah. 1
8 and overtook Zedeki'ah in the plains of Jericho; 1
10 The king of Babylon slew the sons of Zedeki'ah 1
11 He put out the eyes of Zedeki'ah, and bound him 1
1Es 1:46 made Zedekiah king of Judea and Jerusalem. 2
46 Zedekiah was 21 years old 2
Bar 1: 1 son of Mahseiah, son of Zedekiah, son of Hasadiah 2
8 Zedekiah the son of Josiah, king of Judah 2

Zeeb 1. זְאֵב
Jdg 7:25 they took the two princes of Mid'ian, Oreb and Zeeb; 1
25 and Zeeb they killed at the wine press of Zeeb 1
25 and Zeeb they killed at the wine press of Zeeb 1
25 they brought the heads of Oreb and Zeeb to Gideon 1
8: 3 your hands the princes of Mid'ian, Oreb and Zeeb; 1
Ps 83:11 Make their nobles like Oreb and Zeeb 1

Zela 1. צֵלָע
Jos 18:28 Zela, Ha-eleph, Jebus (that is, Jerusalem) 1
2Sm 21:14 And they buried . . in the land of Benjamin in Zela 1

Zelek 1. צֶלֶק
2Sm 23:37 Zelek the Ammonite, Na'harai of Be-er'oth 1
1Ch 11:39 Zelek the Ammonite, Na'harai of Be-er'oth 1

Zelophehad 1. צְלָפְחָד
Num26:33 Now Zeloph'ehad the son of Hepher had no sons 1
33 names of the daughters of Zeloph'ehad were 1
27: 1 Then drew near the daughters of Zeloph'ehad 1
7 The daughters of Zeloph'ehad are right; 1
36: 2 give the inheritance of Zeloph'ehad our brother 1
6 commands concerning the daughters of Zeloph'ehad 1
10 daughters of Zeloph'ehad did as the LORD 1
11 daughters of Zeloph'ehad, were married to sons 1
Jos 17: 3 Now Zeloph'ehad . . had no sons, but only daughters; 1
1Ch 7:15 And the name of the second was Zeloph'ehad; 1
15 and Zeloph'ehad had daughters. 1

Zelzah 1. צֶלְצַח
1Sm 10: 2 tomb in the territory of Benjamin at Zelzah 1

Zemaraim 1. צְמָרַיִם
Jos 18:22 Beth-arabah, Zemara'im, Bethel 1
2Ch 13: 4 Then Abi'jah stood up on Mount Zemara'im 1

Zemarite 1. צְמָרִי
Gen 10:18 the Ar'vadites, the Zem'arites 1
1Ch 1:16 Ar'vadites, the Zem'arites, and the Ha'mathites. 1

Zemer
Ezk 27: 8 skilled men of Zemer were in you •

Zemirah 1. זְמִירָה
1Ch 7: 8 The sons of Becher: Zemi'rah, Jo'ash, Elie'zer 1

Zenan 1. צְנָן
Jos 15:37 Zenan, Hadash'ah, Mig'dal-gad 1

Zenas 1. Ζηνᾶς
Tit 3:13 speed Zenas the lawyer and Apol'los on their way 1

Zephaniah 1. צְפַנְיָהוּ 2. Sofonia
2Kg 25:18 took Serai'ah . . and Zephani'ah the second priest 1
1Ch 6:36 son of Jo'el, son of Azari'ah, son of Zephani'ah 1
Jer 21: 1 Zephani'ah the priest, the son of Ma-asei'ah, saying 1
29:25 and to Zephani'ah the son of Ma-asei'ah the priest 1
29 Zephani'ah the priest read this letter 1
37: 3 and Zephani'ah the priest, the son of Ma-asei'ah 1
52:24 chief priest, and Zephani'ah the second priest 1
Zep 1: 1 The word of the LORD which came to Zephani'ah 1
Zec 6:10 to the house of Josi'ah, the son of Zephani'ah. 1
14 Jedai'ah, and Josi'ah the son of Zephani'ah. 1
2Es 1:40 Nahum and Habakkuk, Zephaniah, Haggai, Zechariah 2

Zephath 1. צְפַת
Jdg 1:17 defeated the Canaanites who inhabited Zephath 1

Zephathah 1. צְפָתָה
2Ch 14:10 battle in the valley of Zeph'athah at Mare'shah. 1

Zephi 1. צְפִי
1Ch 1:36 The sons of Eli'phaz: Teman, Omar, Zephi, Gatam 1

Zepho 1. צְפוֹ
Gen 36:11 The sons of El'iphaz were Teman, Omar, Zepho 1
15 the chiefs Teman, Omar, Zepho, Kenaz 1

Zephon 1. צְפוֹן
Num26:15 of Zephon, the family of the Ze'phonites; 1

Zephonite 1. צְפוֹנִי
Num26:15 of Zephon, the family of the Ze'phonites; 1

Zer 1. צֵר
Jos 19:35 The fortified cities are Ziddim, Zer, Hammath 1

Zerah 1. זֶרַח 2. Ζάρα
Gen 36:13 are the sons of Reu'el: Nahath, Zerah, Shammah 1
17 the chiefs Nahath, Zerah, Shammah, and Mizzah; 1
33 Jobab the son of Zerah of Bozrah reigned 1
38:30 his hand; and his name was called Zerah. 1
46:12 sons of Judah: Er, Onan, Shelah, Perez, and Zerah 1
Num26:13 of Zerah, the family of the Zer'ahites; 1
20 of Zerah, the family of the Zer'ahites. 1
Jos 7: 1 Achan the son of Carmi, son of Zabdi, son of Zerah 1
18 son of Zabdi, son of Zerah, of the tribe of Judah 1
24 Joshua . . took Achan the son of Zerah 1
22:20 Did not Achan the son of Zerah break faith 1
1Ch 1:37 The sons of Reu'el . . Zerah, Shammah, and Mizzah. 1
44 When Bela died, Jobab the son of Zerah of Bozrah 1
2: 4 Tamar also bore him Perez and Zerah. 1
6 The sons of Zerah: Zimri, Ethan, Heman, Calcol 1
4:24 sons of Simeon: Nem'uel, Jamin, Jarib, Zerah, Sha'ul; 1
6:21 Jo'ah . . Iddo . . Zerah his son, Je-ath'erai 1
41 son of Ethni, son of Zerah, son of Adai'ah 1
9: 6 Of the sons of Zerah: Jeu'el and their kinsmen, 690. 1
2Ch 14: 9 Zerah the Ethiopian came out against them 1
Neh 11:24 Pethahi'ah . . of the sons of Zerah the son of Judah 1
Mat 1: 3 Judah the father of Perez and Zerah by Tamar 2

Zerahiah 1. זְרַחְיָה 2. Ζαραιας
1Ch 6: 6 Uzzi of Zerahi'ah, Zerahi'ah of Merai'oth 1
6 Uzzi of Zerahi'ah, Zerahi'ah of Merai'oth 1
51 Bukki his son, Uzzi his son, Zerahi'ah his son 1
Ezr 7: 4 son of Zerahi'ah, son of Uzzi, son of Bukki 1
8: 4 Eli-e-ho-e'nai the son of Zerahi'ah, and with him 200 1
1Es 8:31 Eliehoenai the son of Zerahiah 2

Zerahite 1. זַרְחִי
Num26:13 of Zerah, the family of the Zer'ahites; 1
20 of Zerah, the family of the Zer'ahites. 1
Jos 7:17 and the family of the Zer'ahites was taken; 1
17 and he brought near the family of the Zer'ahites 1
1Ch 27:11 Sib'becai the Hu'shathite, of the Ze'rahites; 1
13 Ma'harai of Netoph'ah, of the Ze'rahites; 1

Zeraiah 1. Ζαραιας
1Es 8:34 Zeraiah the son of Michael 1

Zerdaiah 1. Ζερδαιας
1Es 9:28 Jeremoth, and Zabad and Zerdaiah. 1

Zered 1. זֶרֶד
Num21:12 set out, and encamped in the Valley of Zered. 1
Deu 2:13 'Now rise up, and go over the brook Zered.' 1
13 So we went over the brook Zered. 1
14 Ka'desh-bar'nea until we crossed the brook Zered 1

Zeredah 1. צְרֵדָה
1Kg 11:26 Jerobo'am . . an E'phraimite of Zer'edah 1
2Ch 4:17 in the clay ground between Succoth and Zer'edah. 1

Zererah 1. צְרֵרָה
Jdg 7:22 army fled as far as Beth-shit'tah toward Zer'erah 1

Zeresh 1. זֶרֶשׁ
Est 5:10 he . . fetched his friends and his wife Zeresh. 1
14 his wife Zeresh and all his friends said to him 1
6:13 Haman told his wife Zeresh and all his friends 1
13 Then his wise men and his wife Zeresh said to him 1

Zereth 1. צֶרֶת
1Ch 4: 7 The sons of Helah: Zereth, Izhar, and Ethnan. 1

Zereth-shahar 1. צֶרֶת הַשַּׁחַר
Jos 13:19 and Kir'iatha'im, and Sibmah, and Zer'eth-sha'har 1

Zeri 1. צְרִי
1Ch 25: 3 sons of Jedu'thun: Gedali'ah, Zeri, Jeshai'ah, 1

Zeror 1. צְרוֹר
1Sm 9: 1 whose name was Kish, the son of Abi'el, son of Zeror 1

Zeruah 1. צְרוּעָה
1Kg 11:26 Jerobo'am . . whose mother's name was Zeru'ah 1

Zerubbabel 1. זְרֻבָּבֶל 2. זְרֻבָּבֶל (A) 3. Ζοροβαβέλ
1Ch 3:19 and the sons of Pedai'ah: Zerub'babel and Shim'e-i; 1
19 the sons of Zerub'babel: Meshul'lam and Hanani'ah 1
Ezr 2: 2 They came with Zerub'babel, Jeshua, Nehemi'ah 1
3: 2 arose Jeshua . . and Zerub'babel the son 1
8 Zerub'babel . . and Jeshua . . made a beginning 1
4: 2 approached Zerub'babel and the heads of fathers' 1
3 Zerub'babel, Jeshua, and the rest of the heads 1
5: 2 Then Zerub'babel the son of She-al'ti-el and Jeshua 2
Neh 7: 7 came with Zerub'babel, Jeshua, Nehemi'ah, Azari'ah 1
12: 1 who came up with Zerub'babel the son of She-al'ti-el 1
47 all Israel in the days of Zerub'babel 1
Hag 1: 1 to Zerub'babel the son of She-al'ti-el, governor 1
12 Then Zerub'babel the son of She-al'ti-el 1
14 the LORD stirred up the spirit of Zerub'babel 1
2: 2 Speak now to Zerub'babel the son of She-al'ti-el 1
4 Yet now take courage, O Zerub'babel, says the LORD; 1
21 Speak to Zerub'babel, governor of Judah, saying 1
23 I will take you, O Zerub'babel my servant 1
Zec 4: 6 This is the word of the LORD to Zerub'babel 1
7 Before Zerub'babel you shall become a plain; 1
9 hands of Zerub'babel have laid the foundation 1
10 shall see the plummet in the hand of Zerub'babel. 1
Mat 1:12 She-al'ti-el the father of Zerub'babel 3
13 Zerub'babel the father of Abi'ud 3
Lke 3:27 the son of Zerub'babel, the son of She-al'ti-el 3
1Es 4:13 the third, that is Zerubbabel 3
5: 5 Joakim the son of Zerubbabel, son of Shealtiel 3
8 They came with Zerubbabel and Jeshua 3
48 Zerubbabel the son of Shealtiel 3
56 Zerubbabel the son of Shealtiel 3
68 So they approached Zerubbabel and Jeshua 3
70 Zerubbabel and Jeshua 3
6: 2 Zerubbabel the son of Shealtiel 3
18 they were delivered to Zerubbabel 3
27 to permit Zerubbabel . . to build this house 3
29 Zerubbabel the governor 3
Sir 49:11 How shall we magnify Zerubbabel? 3

Zeruiah 1. צְרוּיָה
1Sm 26: 6 to Jo'ab's brother Abi'shai the son of Zeru'iah 1
2Sm 2:13 Jo'ab the son of Zeru'iah, and the servants . . went 1
18 And the three sons of Zeru'iah were there 1
3:39 these men the sons of Zeru'iah are too hard for me. 1
8:16 Jo'ab the son of Zeru'iah was over the army; 1
14: 1 Jo'ab the son of Zeru'iah perceived that 1
16: 9 Then Abi'shai the son of Zeru'iah said to the king 1
10 What have I to do with you, you sons of Zeru'iah? 1
17:25 of Nahash, sister of Zeru'iah, Jo'ab's mother. 1
18: 2 under the command of Abi'shai the son of Zeru'iah 1
19:21 Abi'shai the son of Zeru'iah answered 1
22 What have I to do with you, you sons of Zeru'iah 1
21:17 But Abi'shai the son of Zeru'iah came to his aid 1
23:18 Abi'shai, the brother of Jo'ab, the son of Zeru'iah 1
37 the armor-bearer of Jo'ab the son of Zeru'iah 1
1Kg 1: 7 He conferred with Jo'ab the son of Zeru'iah 1
2: 5 you know . . what Jo'ab the son of Zeru'iah did to me 1
22 Abi'athar the priest and Jo'ab the son of Zeru'iah. 1
1Ch 2:16 their sisters were Zeru'iah and Ab'igail. 1
16 The sons of Zeru'iah: Abi'shai, Jo'ab, and As'ahel 1
11: 6 Jo'ab the son of Zeru'iah went up first J
39 the armor-bearer of Jo'ab the son of Zeru'iah 1
18:12 Abi'shai, the son of Zeru'iah, slew 18,000 E'domites 1
15 Jo'ab the son of Zeru'iah was over the army; 1
26:28 Abner the son of Ner, and Jo'ab the son of Zeru'iah 1
27:24 Jo'ab the son of Zeru'iah began to number 1

Zetham 1. זֵתָם
1Ch 23: 8 of Ladan: Jehi'el the chief, and Zetham, and Jo'el 1
26:22 sons of Jehi'eli, Zetham and Jo'el his brother 1

Zethan 1. זֵיתָן
1Ch 7:10 sons of Bilhan . . Zethan, Tarshish 1

Zethar 1. זֵתַר
Est 1:10 Harbo'na, Bigtha and Abag'tha, Zethar and Carkas 1

Zeus 1. Ζεύς
Act 14:12 Barnabas they called Zeus 1
13 the priest of Zeus . . brought oxen and garlands 1
2Mc 6: 2 and call it the temple of Olympian Zeus 1
2 the temple of Zeus the Friend of Strangers 1

Zia 1. זִיעַ
1Ch 5:13 Michael, Meshul'lam, Sheba, Jo'rai, Jacan, Zi'a 1

Ziba 1. צִיבָא
2Sm 9: 2 a servant of the house of Saul whose name was Ziba 1
2 and the king said to him, "Are you Ziba? 1
3 Ziba said to the king, "There is still a son 1
4 Ziba said to the king, "He is in the house of Machir 1
9 Then the king called Ziba, Saul's servant 1
10 Now Ziba had fifteen sons and twenty servants. 1
11 Then Ziba said to the king, "According to all 1
12 all who dwelt in Ziba's house became 1
16: 1 Ziba the servant of Mephib'osheth met him 1
2 the king said to Ziba, "Why have you brought these? 1
2 Ziba answered, "The asses are for the king's 1
3 Ziba said to the king, "Behold, he remains 1
4 Then the king said to Ziba 1
4 And Ziba said, "I do obeisance; let me ever find 1
19:17 Ziba . . rushed down to the Jordan before the king 1
29 I have decided: you and Ziba shall divide the land. 1

Zibeon 1. צִבְעוֹן
Gen 36: 2 daughter of Anah the son of Zib'eon the Hivite 1
14 daughter of Anah the son of Zib'eon, Esau's wife 1
20 of the land: Lotan, Shobal, Zib'eon, Anah 1
24 These are the sons of Zib'eon: A'iah and Anah; 1
24 as he pastured the asses of Zib'eon his father. 1
29 Horites: the chiefs Lotan, Shobal, Zib'eon, Anah 1
1Ch 1:38 The sons of Se'ir: Lotan, Shobal, Zib'eon, Anah 1
40 The sons of Zib'eon: Ai'ah and Anah. 1

Zibia 1. צִבְיָא
1Ch 8: 9 sons by Hodesh his wife: Jobab, Zib'i-a, Mesha, 1

Zibiah 1. צִבְיָה
2Kg 12: 1 His mother's name was Zib'iah of Beer-sheba. 1
2Ch 24: 1 his mother's name was Zib'iah of Beer-sheba. 1

Zichri 1. זִכְרִי
Exd 6:21 The sons of Izhar: Korah, Nepheg, and Zichri. 1
1Ch 8:19 Jakim, Zichri, Zabdi 1
23 Abdon, Zichri, Hanan 1
27 Eli'jah, and Zichri were the sons of Jero'ham. 1
9:15 the son of Mica, son of Zichri, son of Asaph; 1
26:25 from Elie'zer were . . his son Zichri 1
27:16 for the Reubenites Elie'zer the son of Zichri 1
2Ch 17:16 next to him Amasi'ah the son of Zichri 1
23: 1 commanders . . Elisha'phat the son of Zichri. 1
28: 7 Zichri, a mighty man of E'phraim, slew Ma-asei'ah 1
Neh 11: 9 Jo'el the son of Zichri was their overseer; 1
12:17 of Abi'jah, Zichri; of Mini'amin, of Moadi'ah, Pil'tai; 1

Ziddim 1. צִדִּים
Jos 19:35 The fortified cities are Ziddim, Zer, Hammath 1

Ziha 1. צִיחָא 2. Ησαυ
Ezr 2:43 temple servants: the sons of Ziha 1
Neh 7:46 temple servants: the sons of Ziha 1
11:21 Ziha and Gishpa were over the temple servants. 1
1Es 5:29 The temple servants: the sons of Ziha 2

Ziklag 1. צִקְלַג
Jos 15:31 Ziklag, Madman'nah, Sansan'nah 1
19: 5 Ziklag, Beth-mar'caboth, Ha'zar-su'sah 1
1Sm 27: 6 that day A'chish gave him Ziklag; 1
6 Ziklag has belonged to . . Judah to this day. 1
30: 1 David and his men came to Ziklag on the third day 1
1 had made a raid upon the Negeb and upon Ziklag. 1
1 They had overcome Ziklag, and burned it with fire 1
14 and we burned Ziklag with fire. 1
26 When David came to Ziklag, he sent . . the spoil 1
2Sm 1: 1 David remained two days in Ziklag; 1
4:10 I seized him and slew him at Ziklag 1
1Ch 4:30 Bethu'el, Hormah, Ziklag 1
12: 1 Now these are the men who came to David at Ziklag 1
20 As he went to Ziklag these men of Manas'seh 1
Neh 11:28 in Ziklag, in Meco'nah and its villages 1

Zillah 1. צִלָּה
Gen 4:19 one was Adah, and the name of the other Zillah. 1
22 Zillah bore Tubal-cain; he was the forger of all 1
23 Lamech said to his wives: "Adah and Zillah 1

Zillethai 1. צִלְּתַי
1Ch 8:20 Eli-e'nai, Zil'lethai, Eli'el 1
12:20 men of Manas'seh . . Eli'hu, and Zil'lethai 1

Zilpah 1. זִלְפָּה
Gen 29:24 Laban gave his maid Zilpah to his daughter Leah 1
30: 9 she took her maid Zilpah and gave her to Jacob 1
10 Then Leah's maid Zilpah bore Jacob a son. 1
12 Leah's maid Zilpah bore Jacob a second son. 1
35:26 The sons of Zilpah, Leah's maid: Gad and Asher. 1
• 37: 2 he was a lad with the sons of Bilhah and Zilpah 1
46:18 these are the sons of Zilpah, whom Laban gave 1

Zimmah 1. זִמָּה
1Ch 6:20 Of Gershom: Libni . . Jahath . . , Zimmah his son 1
42 son of Ethan, son of Zimmah, son of Shim'e-i 1
2Ch 29:12 Levites arose . . Jo'ah the son of Zimmah, 1

Zimran 1. זִמְרָן
Gen 25: 2 She bore him Zimran, Jokshan, Medan, Mid'ian 1
1Ch 1:32 she bore Zimran, Jokshan, Medan, Mid'ian, Ishbak 1

Zimri 1. זִמְרִי 2. Ζαμβρι
Num25:14 The name of the slain man of Israel . . was Zimri 1
1Kg 16: 9 his servant Zimri . . conspired against him. 1
10 Zimri came in and struck him down and killed him 1
12 Thus Zimri destroyed all the house of Ba'asha 1
15 Zimri reigned seven days in Tirzah. 1
16 Zimri has conspired, and he has killed the king"; 1
18 when Zimri saw that the city was taken, he went 1
20 the rest of the acts of Zimri, and the conspiracy 1
2Kg 9:31 Is it peace, you Zimri, murderer of your master? 1
1Ch 2: 6 The sons of Zerah: Zimri, Ethan, Heman, Calcol 1
8:36 Jeho'addah . . father of Al'emeth . . , and Zimri; 1
36 Zimri was the father of Moza. 1
9:42 and Jarah of Al'emeth, Az'maveth, and Zimri; 1
42 and Zimri was the father of Moza. 1
Jer 25:25 all the kings of Zimri, all the kings of Elam 1
1Mc 2:26 as Phinehas did against Zimri the son of Salu. 2

Zin 1. צִן
Num13:21 land from the wilderness of Zin to Rehob 1
20: 1 Israel . . came into the wilderness of Zin 1
27:14 rebelled . . in the wilderness of Zin 1
14 Mer'ibah of Kadesh in the wilderness of Zin.) 1
33:36 set out . . and encamped in the wilderness of Zin 1
34: 3 south side shall be from the wilderness of Zin 1
4 boundary shall turn south . . and cross to Zin 1
Deu 32:51 Mer'i-bath-ka'desh, in the wilderness of Zin; 1
Jos 15: 1 to the boundary of Edom, to the wilderness of Zin 1
3 it goes out southward . . passes along to Zin 1

Zina 1. זִינָא
1Ch 23:10 sons of Shim'e-i: Jahath, Zina, and Je'ush 1

Zion 1. צִיּוֹן 2. Σιών 3. Sion
2Sm 5: 7 Nevertheless David took the stronghold of Zion 1
1Kg 8: 1 the ark . . out of the city of David, which is Zion. 1
2Kg 19:21 she scorns you–the virgin daughter of Zion; 1
31 and out of Mount Zion a band of survivors. 1
1Ch 11: 5 Nevertheless David took the stronghold of Zion 1
2Ch 5: 2 out of the city of David, which is Zion. 1
Ps 2: 6 I have set my king on Zion, my holy hill. 1
9:11 Sing praises to the LORD, who dwells in Zion! 1
14 in the gates of the daughter of Zion I may rejoice 1
14: 7 deliverance for Israel would come out of Zion! 1
20: 2 May he . . give you support from Zion! 1
48: 2 joy of all the earth, Mount Zion, in the far north 1
11 let Mount Zion be glad! 1
12 Walk about Zion, go round about her 1
50: 2 Out of Zion, the perfection of beauty, God shines 1
51:18 Do good to Zion in thy good pleasure; 1
53: 6 deliverance for Israel would come from Zion! 1
65: 1 Praise is due to thee, O God, in Zion; 1
69:35 God will save Zion and rebuild the cities 1
74: 2 Remember Mount Zion, where thou hast dwelt. 1
76: 2 in Salem, his dwelling place in Zion. 1
78:68 the tribe of Judah, Mount Zion, which he loves. 1
84: 5 in whose heart are the highways to Zion. •
7 God of gods will be seen in Zion. 1
87: 2 LORD loves the gates of Zion more than all 1
5 of Zion it shall be said, "This one and that one 1
97: 8 Zion hears and is glad, and the daughters of Judah 1
99: 2 The LORD is great in Zion; 1
102:13 Thou wilt arise and have pity on Zion; 1
16 For the LORD will build up Zion 1
21 that men may declare in Zion the name of the LORD 1
110: 2 LORD sends forth from Zion your mighty scepter. 1
125: 1 Those who trust in the LORD are like Mount Zion 1
126: 1 When the LORD restored the fortunes of Zion 1
128: 5 The LORD bless you from Zion! 1
129: 5 who hate Zion be put to shame and turned backward! 1
132:13 For the LORD has chosen Zion; he has desired it 1
133: 3 dew . . which falls on the mountains of Zion! 1
134: 3 May the LORD bless you from Zion 1
135:21 Blessed be the LORD from Zion, he who dwells 1
137: 1 sat down and wept, when we remembered Zion. 1
3 saying, "Sing us one of the songs of Zion! 1
146:10 reign for ever, thy God, O Zion, to all generations. 1
147:12 LORD, O Jerusalem! Praise your God, O Zion! 1
149: 2 let the sons of Zion rejoice in their King! 1
Sng 3:11 Go forth, O daughters of Zion, and behold 1
Isa 1: 8 And the daughter of Zion is left like a booth 1
27 Zion shall be redeemed by justice 1
2: 3 For out of Zion shall go forth the law 1
3:16 Because the daughters of Zion are haughty 1
17 smite . . the heads of the daughters of Zion 1
4: 3 he who is left in Zion and remains in Jerusalem 1
4 washed away the filth of the daughters of Zion 1
5 whole site of Mount Zion and over her assemblies 1
8:18 the LORD of hosts, who dwells on Mount Zion. 1
10:12 the Lord has finished all his work on Mount Zion 1
24 O my people, who dwell in Zion, be not afraid 1
32 shake . . fist at the mount of the daughter of Zion 1
12: 6 Shout, and sing for joy, O inhabitant of Zion 1
14:32 The LORD has founded Zion 1
16: 1 lambs . . to the mount of the daughter of Zion. 1
18: 7 to Mount Zion, the place of the name of the LORD 1
24:23 for the LORD of hosts will reign on Mount Zion 1
28:16 I am laying in Zion for a foundation a stone 1
29: 8 the nations be that fight against Mount Zion. 1
30:19 Yea, O people in Zion who dwell at Jerusalem; 1
31: 4 LORD . . will come down to fight upon Mount Zion 1
9 says the LORD, whose fire is in Zion 1
33: 5 he will fill Zion with justice 1
14 The sinners in Zion are afraid; 1
20 Look upon Zion, the city of our appointed feasts! 1
34: 8 a year of recompense for the cause of Zion. 1
35:10 shall return, and come to Zion with singing; 1
37:22 she scorns you–the virgin daughter of Zion; 1
32 and out of Mount Zion a band of survivors. 1
40: 9 to a high mountain, O Zion, herald of good tidings 1
41:27 I first have declared it to Zion 1
46:13 I will put salvation in Zion, for Israel my glory. 1
49:14 But Zion said, "The LORD has forsaken me 1
51: 3 For the LORD will comfort Zion; 1
11 shall return, and come to Zion with singing; 1
16 and saying to Zion, 'You are my people.' 1
52: 1 Awake, awake, put on your strength, O Zion; 1
2 bonds from your neck, O captive daughter of Zion. 1
7 salvation, who says to Zion, "Your God reigns. 1
8 eye to eye they see the return of the LORD to Zion. 1
59:20 And he will come to Zion as Redeemer 1
60:14 of the LORD, the Zion of the Holy One of Israel. 1
61: 3 to grant to those who mourn in Zion– 1
62: 1 For Zion's sake I will not keep silent 1
11 Say to the daughter of Zion, "Behold 1
64:10 Zion has become a wilderness, 1
66: 8 as Zion was in labor she brought forth her sons. 1
Jer 3:14 and I will bring you to Zion. 1
4: 6 Raise a standard toward Zion, flee for safety 1
31 cry of the daughter of Zion gasping for breath 1
6: 2 I will destroy, the daughter of Zion. 1
23 for battle, against you, O daughter of Zion! 1
8:19 Is the LORD not in Zion? Is her King not in her? 1
9:19 For a sound of wailing is heard from Zion 1
14:19 Does thy soul loathe Zion? 1
26:18 Zion shall be plowed as a field; 1
30:17 an outcast: 'It is Zion, for whom no one cares!' 1
31: 6 Arise, and let us go up to Zion, to the LORD our God. 1
12 shall come and sing aloud on the height of Zion 1
50: 5 They shall ask the way to Zion 1
28 to declare in Zion the vengeance of the LORD 1
51:10 let us declare in Zion the work of the LORD our God. 1
24 for all the evil that they have done in Zion 1
35 be upon Babylon," let the inhabitant of Zion say. 1
Lam 1: 4 The roads to Zion mourn, for none come to . . feasts; 1
6 From the daughter of Zion has departed all her 1
17 Zion stretches out her hands 1
2: 1 Lord . . has set the daughter of Zion under a cloud! 1
4 he has slain . . in the tent of the daughter of Zion; 1
6 brought to an end in Zion appointed feast 1
8 to lay in ruins the wall of the daughter of Zion; 1
10 elders of the daughter of Zion sit . . in silence; 1
13 that I may comfort you, O virgin daughter of Zion? 1
18 Cry aloud to the Lord! O daughter of Zion! 1
4: 2 The precious sons of Zion, worth their weight 1
11 and he kindled a fire in Zion 1
22 punishment of your iniquity, O daughter of Zion 1
5:11 Women are ravished in Zion, virgins in . . Judah. 1
18 for Mount Zion which lies desolate; 1
Jol 2: 1 Blow the trumpet in Zion; 1
15 Blow the trumpet in Zion; sanctify a fast; 1
23 Be glad, O sons of Zion, and rejoice in the LORD 1
32 for in Mount Zion and in Jerusalem there shall be 1
3:16 And the LORD roars from Zion 1
17 that I am the LORD your God, who dwell in Zion 1
21 for the LORD dwells in Zion. 1
Ams 1: 2 And he said: "The LORD roars from Zion 1
6: 1 Woe to those who are at ease in Zion 1
Obd 1:17 in Mount Zion there shall be those that escape 1
21 Saviors shall go up to Mount Zion to rule 1
Mic 1:13 were the beginning of sin to the daughter of Zion 1
3:10 who build Zion with blood and Jerusalem 1
12 because of you Zion shall be plowed as a field; 1
4: 2 For out of Zion shall go forth the law 1
7 the LORD will reign over them in Mount Zion 1
8 O tower of the flock, hill of the daughter of Zion 1
10 Writhe and groan, O daughter of Zion 1
11 and let our eyes gaze upon Zion. 1
13 Arise and thresh, O daughter of Zion 1
Zep 3:14 Sing aloud, O daughter of Zion; shout, O Israel! 1
16 Do not fear, O Zion; let not your hands grow weak. 1
Zec 1:14 jealous for Jerusalem and for Zion. 1
17 the LORD will again comfort Zion 1
2: 7 Ho! Escape to Zion 1
10 Sing and rejoice, O daughter of Zion; for lo, I come 1
8: 2 I am jealous for Zion with great jealousy 1
3 Thus says the LORD: I will return to Zion 1
9: 9 Rejoice greatly, O daughter of Zion! 1
13 I will brandish your sons, O Zion 1
Mat 21: 5 Tell the daughter of Zion 2
Joh 12:15 Fear not, daughter of Zion 2
Rom 9:33 Behold, I am laying in Zion a stone 2
11:26 it is written, "The Deliverer will come from Zion 2
Heb 12:22 you have come to Mount Zion 2
1Pe 2: 6 Behold, I am laying in Zion a stone, a cornerstone 2
Rev 14: 1 Then I looked, and lo, on Mount Zion stood the Lamb 2
1Es 8:81 raised Zion from desolation 2
2Es 2:40 Take again your full number, O Zion 3
42 I, Ezra, saw on Mount Zion a great multitude 3
3: 2 because I saw the desolation of Zion 3
28 Is that why she has gained dominion over Zion? 3
31 Are the deeds of Babylon better than those of Zion? 3
5:25 thou hast consecrated Zion for thyself 3
6: 4 before the footstool of Zion was established 3
19 and when the humiliation of Zion is complete 3
10: 7 For Zion, the mother of us all, is in deep grief 3
20 be persuaded because of the troubles of Zion 3
23 And, what is more than all, the seal of Zion 3
39 and mourned greatly over Zion. 3
44 This woman whom you saw . . is Zion. 3
12:44 we also had been consumed in the burning of Zion! 3
48 to pray on account of the desolation of Zion 3
13:35 he shall stand on the top of Mount Zion. 3
36 Zion will come and be made manifest to all people 3
14:31 to you for a possession in the land of Zion 3
Jdt 9:13 they have planned . . against the top of Zion 2
Sir 24:10 so I was established in Zion. 2
36:14 Fill Zion with the celebration 2
48:18 he lifted up his hand against Zion 2
24 comforted those who mourned in Zion. 2
Bar 4: 9 and she said: "Hearken, you neighbors of Zion 2
14 Let the neighbors of Zion come 2
24 the neighbors of Zion have now seen your capture 2
1Mc 4:37 they went up to Mount Zion. 2
60 At that time they fortified Mount Zion 2
5:54 they went up to Mount Zion with gladness and joy 2
6:48 the king encamped in Judea and at Mount Zion. 2

62 when the king entered Mount Zion 2
7:33 After these events Nicanor went up to Mount Zion 2
10:11 encircle Mount Zion with squared stones 2
14:27 and put it upon pillars on Mount Zion 2

Zior 1. צִיעֹר

Jos 15:54 Humtah, Kir'iath-ar'ba (that is, Hebron), and Zi'or 1

Ziph 1. זִיף

Jos 15:24 Ziph, Telem, Be-a'loth 1
55 Ma'on, Carmel, Ziph, Juttah 1
1Sm 23:14 in the hill country of the Wilderness of Ziph. 1
15 David was in the Wilderness of Ziph at Horesh. 1
24 And they arose, and went to Ziph ahead of Saul. 1
26: 2 Saul . . went down to the wilderness of Ziph 1
2 went . . to seek David in the wilderness of Ziph. 1
1Ch 2:42 Mare'shah . . who was the father of Ziph. 1
4:16 sons of Jehal'lelel: Ziph, Ziphah, Tir'i-a 1
2Ch 11: 8 Gath, Mare'shah, Ziph 1

Ziphah 1. זִיפָה

1Ch 4:16 sons of Jehal'lelel: Ziph, Ziphah, Tir'i-a 1

Ziphion 1. צִפְיוֹן

Gen 46:16 sons of Gad: Ziph'ion, Haggi, Shuni, Ezbon, Eri 1

Ziphite 1. זִיפִי

1Sm 23:19 the Ziphites went up to Saul at Gib'e-ah, saying 1
26: 1 Then the Ziphites came to Saul at Gib'e-ah, saying 1
Ps 54: 0 when the Ziphites went and told Saul 1

Ziphron 1. זִפְרֹן

Num34: 9 then the boundary shall extend to Ziphron 1

Zippor 1. צִפּוֹר

Num22: 2 Balak the son of Zippor saw all that Israel 1
4 So Balak the son of Zippor, who was king of Moab 1
10 Balak the son of Zippor, king of Moab, has sent to me 1
16 Thus says Balak the son of Zippor: 'Let nothing 1
23:18 Rise, Balak, and hear; hearken to me, O son of Zippor 1
Jos 24: 9 Balak the son of Zippor, king of Moab, arose 1
Jdg 11:25 better than Balak the son of Zippor, king of Moab? 1

Zipporah 1. צִפֹּרָה

Exd 2:21 the man, and he gave Moses his daughter Zippo'rah. 1
4:25 Then Zippo'rah took a flint and cut off her son's 1
18: 2 Jethro, Moses' father-in-law, had taken Zippo'rah 1

Ziv 1. זִו

1Kg 6: 1 in the month of Ziv, which is the second month 1
37 the foundation . . was laid, in the month of Ziv. 1

Ziz 1. צִיץ

2Ch 20:16 behold, they will come up by the ascent of Ziz; 1

Ziza 1. זִיזָא

1Ch 4:37 Ziza the son of Shiphi, son of Allon, son of Jedai'ah 1
2Ch 11:20 Ma'acah . . bore him Abi'jah, Attai, Ziza 1

Zizah 1. זִיזָה

1Ch 23:11 Jahath was the chief, and Zizah the second; 1

Zoan 1. צֹעַן

Num13:22 (Hebron was built seven years before Zo'an 1
Ps 78:12 in the land of Egypt, in the fields of Zo'an. 1
43 in Egypt, and his miracles in the fields of Zo'an. 1
Isa 19:11 The princes of Zo'an are utterly foolish; 1
13 The princes of Zo'an have become fools 1
30: 4 For though his officials are at Zo'an 1
Ezk 30:14 Pathros a desolation, and will set fire to Zo'an 1

Zoar 1. צֹעַר 2. Ζογορα

Gen 13:10 like the land of Egypt, in the direction of Zo'ar; 1
14: 2 of Zeboi'im, and the king of Bela (that is, Zo'ar). 1
8 of Zeboi'im, and the king of Bela (that is, Zo'ar) 1
19:22 Therefore the name of the city was called Zo'ar. 1
23 sun had risen on the earth when Lot came to Zo'ar. 1
30 Lot went up out of Zo'ar, and dwelt in the hills 1
30 for he was afraid to dwell in Zo'ar; 1
Deu 34: 3 Jericho the city of palm trees, as far as Zo'ar. 1
Isa 15: 5 his fugitives flee to Zo'ar 1
Jer 48: 4 Moab is destroyed; a cry is heard as far as Zo'ar. 2
34 from Zo'ar to Horona'im and Eg'lath-shelish'iyah. 1

Zobah 1. צוֹבָה

1Sm 14:47 against the kings of Zobah, and against 1
2Sm 8: 3 Hadade'zer the son of Rehob, king of Zobah 1
5 Syrians . . came to help Hadade'zer king of Zobah 1
12 of Hadade'zer the son of Rehob, king of Zobah. 1
10: 6 hired . . the Syrians of Zobah 1
8 the Syrians of Zobah and of Rehob, and the men 1
23:36 Igal the son of Nathan of Zobah, Bani the Gadite 1
1Kg 11:23 fled from his master Hadade'zer king of Zobah. 1
1Ch 18: 3 David also defeated Hadade'zer king of Zobah 1
5 Syrians . . came to help Hadade'zer king of Zobah 1
9 the whole army of Hadade'zer, king of Zobah 1
19: 6 from Aram-ma'acah, and from Zobah 1

Zobebah 1. צֹבֵבָה

1Ch 4: 8 Koz was the father of Anub, Zobe'bah 1

Zohar 1. צֹחַר

Gen 23: 8 and entreat for me Ephron the son of Zohar 1
25: 9 the field of Ephron the son of Zohar the Hittite 1
46:10 sons of Simeon: Jemu'el . . Zohar, and Shaul 1
Exd 6:15 Simeon: Jemu'el, Jamin, Ohad, Jachin, Zohar 1

Zoheth 1. זוֹחֵת

1Ch 4:20 The sons of Ishi: Zoheth and Ben-zo'heth. 1

Zophah 1. צוֹפַח

1Ch 7:35 sons of Helem . . Zophah, Imna, Shelesh, and Amal. 1
36 sons of Zophah: Su'ah, Har'nepher, Shu'al, Beri, 1

Zophai 1. צוֹפַי

1Ch 6:26 Elka'nah his son, Zophai his son, Nahath his son 1

Zophar 1. צֹפַר

Job 2:11 Bildad the Shuhite, and Zophar the Na'amathite. 1
11: 1 Then Zophar the Na'amathite answered 1
20: 1 Then Zophar the Na'amathite answered 1
42: 9 Bildad the Shuhite and Zophar the Na'amathite 1

Zophim 1. צֹפִים

Num23:14 he took him to the field of Zophim, to the top 1

Zorah 1. צָרְעָה

Jos 15:33 And in the lowland, Eshta'ol, Zorah, Ashnah 1
19:41 included Zorah, Esh'ta-ol, Ir-she'mesh 1
Jdg 13: 2 a certain man of Zorah, of the tribe of the Danites 1
25 in Ma'haneh-dan, between Zorah and Esh'ta-ol. 1
16:31 and buried him between Zorah and Esh'ta-ol 1
18: 2 from the . . tribe, from Zorah and from Esh'ta-ol 1
8 they came to their brethren at Zorah and Esh'ta-ol 1
11 600 men . . set forth from Zorah and Esh'ta-ol 1
2Ch 11:10 Zorah, Ai'jalon, and Hebron, fortified cities 1
Neh 11:29 in En-rim'mon, in Zorah, in Jarmuth 1

Zorathite 1. צָרְעָתִי

1Ch 2:53 came the Zo'rathites and the Esh'taolites. 1
4: 2 These were the families of the Zo'rathites. 1

Zorite 1. צָרְעִי

1Ch 2:54 sons of Salma . . the Zorites. 1

Zuar 1. צוּעָר

Num 1: 8 from Is'sachar, Nethan'el the son of Zu'ar; 1
2: 5 the leader . . being Nethan'el the son of Zu'ar 1
7:18 Nethan'el the son of Zu'ar, the leader of Is'sachar 1
23 was the offering of Nethan'el the son of Zu'ar. 1
10:15 over the host . . was Nethan'el the son of Zu'ar. 1

Zuph 1. צוּף

1Sm 1: 1 of Jero'ham, son of Eli'hu, son of Tohu, son of Zuph 1
9: 5 When they came to the land of Zuph, Saul said to his 1
1Ch 6:35 son of Zuph, son of Elka'nah, son of Mahath 1

Zur 1. צוּר

Num25:15 Cozbi the daughter of Zur, who was the head 1
31: 8 Evi, Rekem, Zur, Hur, and Reba, the five kings 1
Jos 13:21 leaders . . Evi and Rekem and Zur and Hur and Reba 1
1Ch 8:30 first-born son: Abdon, then Zur, Kish, Ba'al, Nadab 1
9:36 first-born son Abdon, then Zur, Kish, Ba'al, Ner, 1

Zuriel 1. צוּרִיאֵל

Num 3:35 head . . was Zu'riel the son of Ab'ihail; 1

Zurishaddai 1. צוּרִישַׁדָּי

Num 1: 6 from Simeon, Shelu'mi-el the son of Zurishad'dai; 1
2:12 Simeon being Shelu'mi-el the son of Zurishad'dai 1
7:36 Shelu'mi-el the son of Zurishad'dai, the leader 1
41 offering of Shelu'mi-el the son of Zurishad'dai. 1
10:19 Shelu'mi-el the son of Zurishad'dai. 1

Zuzim 1. זוּזִים

Gen 14: 5 Zuzim in Ham, the Emim in Sha'veh-kiriatha'im 1

Numbers

1/2 1. חֲצִי
Jos 14: 2 commanded . . for the nine and one-half tribes. 1
3 an inheritance to the two and one-half tribes 1

1/3 1. שְׁלִישִׁי 2. τρίτος
Num15: 6 fine flour mixed with a third of a hin of oil; 1
7 drink . . you shall offer a third of a hin of wine 1
28:14 drink offerings . . a third of a hin for a ram 1
1Sm 13:21 and a third of a shekel for sharpening the axes *
2Sm 18: 2 the army, one third under the command of Jo'ab 1
2 one third under the command of Abi'shai the son 1
2 and one third under the command of It'tai 1
2Kg 11: 5 one third of you, those who come off duty 1
6 another third being at the gate Sur and a third 1
6 and a third at the gate behind the guards) 1
2Ch 23: 4 one third shall be gatekeepers 1
5 one third shall be at the king's house 1
5 one third at the Gate of the Foundation; 1
Neh 10:32 charge . . yearly with the third part of a shekel 1
Ezk 5: 2 A third part you shall burn in the fire 1
2 a third part you shall take and strike 1
2 and a third part you shall scatter to the wind 1
12 A third part of you shall die of pestilence 1
12 a third part shall fall by the sword round about 1
12 and a third part I will scatter to all the winds 1
46:14 one third of a hin of oil to moisten the flour 1
Zec 13: 8 and perish, and one third shall be left alive. 1
9 I will put this third into the fire 1
Rev 8: 7 and a third of the earth was burnt up 2
7 and a third of the trees were burnt up 2
9 and a third of the sea became blood 2
9 a third of the living creatures in the sea died 2
9 and a third of the ships were destroyed. 2
10 star fell . . and it fell on a third of the rivers 2
11 A third of the waters became wormwood 2
12 blew his trumpet, and a third of the sun was struck 2
12 third of the sun was struck, and a third of the moon 2
12 and a third of the moon, and a third of the stars 2
12 so that a third of their light was darkened; 2
12 a third of the day was kept from shining 2
12 from shining, and likewise a third of the night. *
9:15 angels . . ready . . to kill a third of mankind. 2
18 By . . three plagues a third of mankind was killed 2
12: 4 His tail swept down a third of the stars of heaven 2
1Mc 10:30 instead of collecting the third of the grain 2

2/3 1. פִּי שְׁנַיִם
Zec 13: 8 two thirds shall be cut off and perish 1

1/4 1. רְבִיעִי 2. רֶבַע 3. τέταρτος
Exd 29:40 fine flour mingled with a fourth of a hin 2
40 a fourth of a hin of wine for a libation. 1
Lev 23:13 with it shall be of wine, a fourth of a hin 1
Num15: 4 fine flour, mixed with a fourth of a hin of oil; 1
5 wine for the drink offering, a fourth of a hin 1
28: 5 cereal offering, mixed with a fourth of a hin 1
7 offering shall be a fourth of a hin for each lamb; 1
14 drink offerings . . a fourth of a hin for a lamb; 1
Neh 9: 3 for another fourth of it they made confession 1
Rev 6: 8 they were given power over a fourth of the earth 3

1/4 part 1. רֶבַע 2. רֹבַע
Num23:10 dust of Jacob, or number the fourth part of Israel? 2
1Sm 9: 8 I have . . the fourth part of a shekel of silver 1
2Kg 6:25 the fourth part of a kab of dove's dung for 5 shekels 2

1/5 1. חֲמִישִׁי 2. חֹמֶשׁ
Gen 47:24 at the harvests you shall give a fifth to Pharaoh 1
26 a statute . . Pharaoh should have the fifth; 2
Lev 5:16 shall add a fifth to it and give it to the priest 1
6: 5 he shall restore it in full, and shall add a fifth 1
22:14 he shall add the fifth of its value to it 1
27:13 he shall add a fifth to the valuation 1
15 he shall add a fifth of the valuation in money 1
19 he shall add a fifth of the valuation in money 1
27 shall buy it back . . and add a fifth to it 1
31 redeem any of his tithe, he shall add a fifth to it 1
Num 5: 7 make full restitution . . adding a fifth to it 1

4/5 1. אַרְבַּע הַיָּדוֹת
Gen 47:24 and four fifths shall be your own, 1

1/6 1. שִׁשִּׁי
Ezk 45:13 one sixth of an ephah from each homer of wheat 1
13 one sixth of an ephah from each homer of barley 1
46:14 one sixth of an ephah, and one third of a hin of oil 1

1/10 1. מַעֲשֵׂר 2. עֲשִׂירִי 3. עִשָּׂרוֹן 4. δέκατος 5. decimus
Gen 14:20 And Abram gave him a tenth of everything. 1
Exd 16:36 (An omer is the tenth part of an ephah.) 2
Lev 5:11 bring . . a tenth of an ephah of fine flour 2
6:20 a tenth of an ephah of fine flour as a regular 2
14:21 to make atonement for him, and a tenth of an ephah 3
Num 5:15 offering . . a tenth of an ephah of barley meal; 2
15: 4 offering of a tenth of an ephah of fine flour 3
28: 5 also a tenth of an ephah of fine flour 2
13 a tenth of fine flour mixed with oil as a cereal 3
21 tenth shall you offer for each of the seven lambs; 3
29 a tenth for each of the seven lambs; 3
29: 4 one tenth for each of the seven lambs; 3
10 a tenth for each of the seven lambs 3
15 a tenth for each of the fourteen lambs; 3
Isa 6:13 though a tenth remain in it, it will be burned 2
Ezk 45:11 the bath containing one tenth of a homer 1
11 the ephah one tenth of a homer; 2
14 as the fixed portion of oil, one tenth of a bath 1
Heb 7: 2 to him Abraham apportioned a tenth part 4
Rev 11:13 great earthquake, and a tenth of the city fell; 4
2Es 14:12 as well as half of the tenth part 5
12 besides half of the tenth part. 5
Tob 1: 7 I would give a tenth to the sons of Levi 4
7 a second tenth I would sell 4
8 the third tenth I would give to those *
Sir 25: 7 a tenth I shall tell with my tongue 4

1/10 measure 1. עִשָּׂרוֹן
Exd 29:40 with the first lamb a tenth measure of fine flour 1

2/10 1. שְׁנֵי עֶשְׂרֹנִים
Lev 23:13 the cereal offering with it shall be two tenths 1
17 bread . . made of two tenths of an ephah 1
24: 5 two tenths of an ephah shall be in each cake 1
Num15: 6 offering two tenths of an ephah of fine flour 1
28: 9 two tenths of an ephah of fine flour 1
12 two tenths of fine flour for a cereal offering 1
20 offer for a bull, and two tenths for a ram; 1
28 ephah for each bull, two tenths for one ram 1
29: 3 of an ephah for the bull, two tenths for the ram 1
9 ephah for the bull, two tenths for the one ram 1
14 two tenths for each of the two rams 1

3/10 1. שְׁלֹשָׁה עֶשְׂרֹנִים
Lev 14:10 a cereal offering of three tenths of an ephah 1
Num15: 9 three tenths of an ephah of fine flour 1
28:12 three tenths of an ephah of fine flour 1
20 three tenths of an ephah shall you offer 1
28 three tenths of an ephah for each bull 1
29: 3 three tenths of an ephah for the bull 1
9 three tenths of an ephah for the bull 1
14 three tenths of an ephah for each of the . . bulls 1

9/10 1. תֵּשַׁע הַיָּדוֹת
Neh 11: 1 while nine tenths remained in the other towns. 1
1 while nine tenths remained in the other towns. †

1/10,000 1. decies millesima pars
2Es 7:138 not one 10,000th of mankind 1

21 1. עֶשְׂרִים וְאֶחָד 2. εἴκοσι εἷς
2Kg 24:18 Zedeki'ah was 21 years old when he became king 1
2Ch 36:11 21 years old when he began to reign 1
Jer 52: 1 Zedeki'ah 21 years old when he became king; 1
Dan 10:13 prince . . Persia withstood me 21 days; 1
1Es 1:46 Zedekiah was 21 years old 2

21st 1. אֶחָד וְעֶשְׂרִים 2. עֶשְׂרִים וְאֶחָד
Exd 12:18 so until the 21st day of the month 1
1Ch 24:17 the 21st to Jachin, the 22nd to Gamul 1
25:28 to the 21st, to Hothir, his sons and his brethren 1
Hag 2: 1 in the seventh month, on the 21st day of the month 2

22 1. עֶשְׂרִים וּשְׁנַיִם 2. εἴκοσι δύο
Jos 19:30 22 cities with their villages. 1
Jdg 10: 3 Ja'ir the Gileadite, who judged Israel 22 years. 1
1Kg 14:20 the time that Jerobo'am reigned was 22 years; 1
16:29 Ahab . . reigned over Israel in Sama'ria 22 years. 1
2Kg 8:26 Ahazi'ah was 22 years old when he began to reign 1
21:19 Amon was 22 years old when he began to reign 1
1Ch 12:28 and 22 commanders from his own father's house. 1
2Ch 13:21 took fourteen wives, and had 22 sons 1
33:21 Amon was 22 years old when he began to reign 1
2Mc 13: 2 5,300 cavalry, 22 elephants 2

22nd 1. שְׁנַיִם וְעֶשְׂרִים 2. δεύτερος καὶ εἰκάς
1Ch 24:17 the 21st to Jachin, the 22nd to Gamul 1
25:29 to the 22nd, to Giddal'ti, his sons and his brethren 1
Jdt 2: 1 on the 22nd day of the first month 2

23 1. עֶשְׂרִים וְשָׁלֹשׁ 2. שָׁלֹשׁ וְעֶשְׂרִים 3. εἴκοσι τρεῖς
Jdg 10: 2 And he judged Israel 23 years. Then he died 1
2Kg 23:31 Jeho'ahaz was 23 years old when he began to reign 1
1Ch 2:22 Ja'ir, who had 23 cities in the land of Gilead 1
2Ch 36: 2 Jeho'ahaz was 23 . . when he began 2
Jer 25: 3 For 23 years, from the thirteenth year of Josi'ah 2
1Es 1:34 who was 23 years old 3

23rd 1. שָׁלֹשׁ וְעֶשְׂרִים 2. עֶשְׂרִים וְשָׁלֹשׁ 3. τρίτος εἰκάς 4. τρίτος καὶ εἰκάς
2Kg 12: 6 But by the 23rd year of King Jeho'ash 1
13: 1 In the 23rd year of Jo'ash the son of Ahazi'ah 1
1Ch 24:18 23rd to Delai'ah, the 24th to Ma-azi'ah. 2
25:30 to the 23rd, to Maha'zi-oth, his sons and his brethren 2
2Ch 7:10 On the 23rd day of the seventh month he 1
Est 8: 9 in the third month . . on the 23rd day; 2
Jer 52:30 in the 23rd year of Nebuchadrez'zar 2
1Es 7: 5 the 23rd day of the month of Adar 4
1Mc 13:51 On the 23rd day of the second month 3

24 1. עֶשְׂרִים וְאַרְבַּע 2. εἴκοσι τέσσαρες
Num 7:88 for the sacrifice of peace offerings 24 bulls 1
2Sm 21:20 and six toes on each foot, 24 in number 1
1Kg 15:33 Ba'asha . . reigned 24 years. 1
1Ch 20: 6 on each hand, and six toes on each foot, 24 in number 1
Rev 4: 4 Round the throne were 24 thrones 2
4 and seated on the thrones were 24 elders 2
10 the 24 elders fall down before him 2
5: 8 the 24 elders fell down before the Lamb 2
11:16 the 24 elders who sit on their thrones before God 2
19: 4 the 24 elders and the four living creatures 2
2Es 14:45 Make public the 24 books that you wrote first ‡

24th 1. אַרְבָּעָה וְעֶשְׂרִים 2. עֶשְׂרִים וְאַרְבָּעָה 3. τετρὰς καὶ εἰκάς
1Ch 24:18 23rd to Delai'ah, the 24th to Ma-azi'ah. 1
25:31 the 24th, to Romam'ti-e'zer, his sons and his brethren 1
Neh 9: 1 Now on the 24th day of this month 2
Dan 10: 4 On the 24th day of the first month 2
Hag 1:15 on the 24th day of the month, in the sixth month 2
2:10 On the 24th day of the ninth month 2
18 from the 24th day of the ninth month. 2
20 on the 24th day of the month 2
Zec 1: 7 On the 24th day of the eleventh month 2
2Mc 11:21 Farewell. The 148th year, Dioscorinthius 24th. 3

25 1. עֶשְׂרִים וְחָמֵשׁ 2. חָמֵשׁ וְעֶשְׂרִים 3. εἴκοσι πέντε
Num 8:24 from 25 years old and upward they shall go 1
1Kg 22:42 and he reigned 25 years in Jerusalem. 2
2Kg 14: 2 He was 25 years old when he began to reign 2
15:33 He was 25 years old when he began to reign 2

18: 2 He was 25 years old when he began to reign 2
23:36 Jehoi'akim was 25 years old when he began to reign 2
2Ch 20:31 he reigned 25 years in Jerusalem. 2
25: 1 Amazi'ah was 25 years old when he began 2
27: 1 Jotham was 25 . . when he began to reign 2
8 He was 25 . . when he began to reign 2
29: 1 Hezeki'ah began to reign when he was 25 2
36: 5 Jehoi'akim was 25 . . when he began to reign 2
Ezk 8:16 behold, at the door . . were about 25 men 2
11: 1 at the door of the gateway there were 25 men; 2
40:13 25 cubits, from door to door. 2
21 and its breadth 25 cubits. 1
25 and its breadth 25 cubits. 1
29 and its breadth 25 cubits. 2
30 vestibules round about, 25 cubits long 1
33 and its breadth 25 cubits. 1
36 and its breadth 25 cubits. 1
1Es 1:39 Jehoiakim was 25 years old 3
5:19 The men of Kiriatharim, 25. 3

25th 1. עֶשְׂרִים וְחָמֵשׁ 2. *εἰκάς πέμπτος* 3. *πέμπτος εἰκάς* 4. *πέμπτος καὶ εἰκάς*

Neh 6:15 finished on the 25th day of . . Elul 1
Jer 52:31 on the 25th day of the month 1
Ezk 40: 1 In the 25th year of our exile 1
1Mc 1:59 And on the 25th day of the month 2
4:52 on the 25th day of the ninth month 3
59 beginning with the 25th day of the month 3
2Mc 1:18 on the 25th day of Chislev 3
10: 5 on the 25th day of the same month 4
3Mc 6:38 the 25th of Pachon 3

26th 1. עֶשְׂרִים וָשֵׁשׁ

1Kg 16: 8 In the 26th year of Asa king of Judah 1

27th 1. עֶשְׂרִים וָשֶׁבַע 2. שֶׁבַע וְעֶשְׂרִים

Gen 8:14 In the second month, on the 27th day of the month 2
1Kg 16:10 killed him, in the 27th year of Asa 1
15 In the 27th year of Asa king of Judah 1
2Kg 15: 1 In the 27th year of Jerobo'am king of Israel 1
25:27 in the twelfth month, on the 27th day of the month 1
Ezk 29:17 In the 27th year, in the first 1

28 1. עֶשְׂרִים וּשְׁמֹנֶה 2. שְׁמֹנֶה וְעֶשְׂרִים 3. *εἴκοσι ὀκτώ*

Exd 26: 2 The length of each curtain shall be 28 cubits 2
36: 9 The length of each curtain was 28 cubits 2
2Kg 10:36 time that Jehu reigned . . in Sama'ria was 28 years. 1
2Ch 11:21 had 28 sons and 60 daughters); 1
Ezr 8:11 son of Be'bai, and with him 28 men. 1
1Es 8:37 the son of Bebai, and with him 28 men. 3

29 1. עֶשְׂרִים וָתֵשַׁע 2. תֵּשַׁע וְעֶשְׂרִים 3. *εἴκοσι ἐννέα*

Gen 11:24 When Nahor had lived 29 years 2
Exd 38:24 the gold from the offering, was 29 talents 2
Jos 15:32 in all, 29 cities, with their villages. 1
2Kg 14: 2 and he reigned 29 years in Jerusalem. 1
18: 2 and he reigned 29 years in Jerusalem. 1
2Ch 25: 1 he reigned 29 years in Jerusalem. 1
29: 1 Hezeki'ah . . reigned 29 years 1
Ezr 1: 9 number . . 1,000 basins of silver, 29 censers 2
1Es 2:13 29 silver censers, 30 gold bowls, 2,410 silver bowls 3

30 1. שְׁלֹשִׁים 2. תְּלָתִין (A) 3. *τριάκοντα* 4. triginta

Gen 6:15 its breadth 50 cubits, and its height 30 cubits. 1
11:14 When Shelah had lived 30 years 1
18 When Peleg had lived 30 years 1
22 When Serug had lived 30 years 1
18:30 Suppose 30 are found there. 1
30 He answered, "I will not do it, if I find 30 there. 1
32:15 30 milch camels and their colts, 40 cows 1
41:46 Joseph was 30 years old when he entered 1
Exd 21:32 the owner shall give to the master 30 shekels 1
26: 8 The length of each curtain shall be 30 cubits 1
36:15 The length of each curtain was 30 cubits 1
Lev 27: 4 your valuation shall be 30 shekels 1
Num 4: 3 from 30 years old up to 50 years old 1
23 from 30 years old up to 50 years old 1
30 from 30 years old up to 50 years old 1
35 from 30 years old up to 50 years old 1
39 from 30 years old up to 50 years old 1
43 from 30 years old up to 50 years old 1
47 from 30 years old up to 50 years old 1
20:29 all the house of Israel wept for Aaron 30 days 1
Deu 34: 8 wept . . in the plains of Moab 30 days; 1
Jdg 10: 4 he had 30 sons who rode on 30 asses; 1
4 he had 30 sons who rode on 30 asses; 1
4 and they had 30 cities, called Hav'voth-ja'ir 1
12: 9 He had 30 sons; and 30 daughters he gave 1
9 30 sons; and 30 daughters he gave in marriage 1
9 and 30 daughters he brought in from outside 1
14 He had 40 sons and 30 grandsons, who rode 1
14:11 they brought 30 companions to be with him. 1
12 I will give you 30 linen garments and 30 festal 1
12 30 linen garments and 30 festal garments; 1
13 give me 30 linen garments and 30 festal garments 1
13 give me 30 linen garments and 30 festal garments 1
19 to Ash'kelon and killed 30 men of the town 1
20:31 and kill some . . about 30 men of Israel. 1
39 to smite and kill about 30 men of Israel; 1
1Sm 9:22 those . . invited, who were about 30 persons. 1
2Sm 5: 4 David was 30 years old when he began to reign 1
23:13 And three of the 30 chief men went down 1
18 Now Abi'shai . . was chief of the 30. 1
19 He was the most renowned of the 30 *
23 He was renowned among the 30 1
24 As'ahel the brother of Jo'ab was one of the 30; 1
1Kg 4:22 provision . . was 30 cors of fine flour 1
6: 2 The house . . twenty cubits wide, and 30 cubits high. 1
7: 2 its breadth 50 cubits, and its height 30 cubits 1
6 length was 50 cubits, and its breadth 30 cubits; 1
23 a line of 30 cubits measured its circumference. 1
24 Under its brim were gourds, for 30 cubits *
2Kg 18:14 300 talents of silver and 30 talents of gold. 1
1Ch 11:15 Three of the 30 chief men went down to the rock 1
20 Abi'shai, the brother of Jo'ab, was chief of the 30 ‡
21 He was the most renowned of the 30 ‡
25 He was renowned among the 30 1
42 a leader of the Reubenites, and 30 with him 1
12: 4 Ishma'iah of Gibeon, a mighty man among the 30 1
4 Ishma'iah of Gibeon . . a leader over the 30; 1
18 Then the Spirit came upon Ama'sai, chief of the 30 1
23: 3 The Levites, 30 years old and upward, were numbered 1
27: 6 Benai'ah who was a mighty man of the 30 1
6 Benai'ah who was . . in command of the 30; 1
2Ch 4: 2 round . . and a line of 30 cubits measured 1
3 were figures of gourds, for 30 cubits *
Ezr 1:10 30 bowls of gold, 2,410 bowls of silver 1
Est 4:11 I have not been called . . these 30 days. 1
Prv 22:20 Have I not written for you 30 sayings *
Ezk 40:17 30 chambers fronted on the pavement. 1
41: 6 stories, one over another, 30 in each story. 1
46:22 small courts, 40 cubits long and 30 broad; 1
Dan 6: 7 makes petition to any god or man for 30 days 2
12 god or man within 30 days except to you, O king 2
Zec 11:12 they weighed out as my wages 30 shekels 1
13 I took the 30 shekels of silver 1
Mat 13: 8 grain, some a hundredfold, some 60, some 30. 3
23 a hundredfold, in another 60, and in another 30. 3
26:15 And they paid him 30 pieces of silver. 3
27: 3 and brought back the 30 pieces of silver 3
9 they took the 30 pieces of silver 3
Lke 3:23 Jesus . . was about 30 years of age 3
1Es 2:13 29 silver censers, 30 gold bowls, 2,410 silver bowls 3
2Es 3:29 has seen many sinners during these 30 years ‡
9:43 though I lived with my husband 30 years. 4
44 every hour and every day during those 30 years 4
45 after 30 years God heard your handmaid 4
10:45 that she was barren for 30 years 4
Jdt 15:11 the people plundered the camp for 30 days. 3

30 *See also* thirtyfold.

30 gallons 1. *μετρητάς τρεῖς*

Joh 2: 6 jars . . each holding twenty or 30 gallons 1

30 miles 1. *στάδιοι διακόσιοι τεσσαράκοντα*

2Mc 12: 9 in Jerusalem, 30 miles distant. 1

30th 1. שְׁלֹשִׁים 2. *τριακάς* 3. tricesimus

Ezk 1: 1 In the 30th year, in the fourth month 1
2Es 3: 1 the 30th year after the destruction of our city 3
2Mc 11:30 those who go home by the 30th day of Xanthicus 2

31 1. שְׁלֹשִׁים וְאֶחָד

Jos 12:24 the king of Tirzah, one: in all, 31 kings. 1
2Kg 22: 1 and he reigned 31 years in Jerusalem. 1
2Ch 34: 1 Josi'ah . . reigned 31 years 1

31st 1. שְׁלֹשִׁים וְאַחַת

1Kg 16:23 In the 31st year of Asa king of Judah 1

32 1. שְׁלֹשִׁים וּשְׁנַיִם 2. שְׁנַיִם וּשְׁלֹשִׁים 3. *δύο τριάκοντα*

Gen 11:20 When Re'u had lived 32 years 2
Num31:40 of which the LORD'S tribute was 32 persons 2
1Kg 20: 1 32 kings were with him, and horses and chariots; 1
16 they went out . . he and the 32 kings who helped him. 2
22:31 king of Syria had commanded the 32 captains 1
2Kg 8:17 He was 32 years old when became king 1
2Ch 21: 5 Jeho'ram was 32 . . when he became king 1
20 He was 32 years old when he began to reign 1
1Mc 6:30 32 elephants accustomed to war. 3

32nd 1. שְׁלֹשִׁים וּשְׁנַיִם

Neh 5:14 20th year to the 32nd year 1
13: 6 32nd year of Ar-ta-xerx'es king 1

33 1. שְׁלֹשִׁים וְשָׁלֹשׁ

Gen 46:15 his sons and his daughters numbered 33 1
Lev 12: 4 Then she shall continue for 33 days in the blood 1
2Sm 5: 5 at Jerusalem he reigned . . 33 years. 1
1Kg 2:11 David . . reigned . . 33 years in Jerusalem. 1
1Ch 3: 4 And he reigned 33 years in Jerusalem. 1
29:27 reigned seven years in Hebron, and 33 in Jerusalem 1

34 1. אַרְבַּע וּשְׁלֹשִׁים 2. *τριάκοντα τέσσαρες*

Gen 11:16 When Eber had lived 34 years 1
Jdt 7:20 whole Assyrian army . . surrounded them for 34 days 2

35 1. חָמֵשׁ וּשְׁלֹשִׁים 2. שְׁלֹשִׁים וְחָמֵשׁ

Gen 11:12 When Arpach'shad had lived 35 years 1
1Kg 22:42 Jehosh'aphat was 35 years old when he began 2
2Ch 3:15 he made two pillars 35 cubits high 2
20:31 35 years old when he began to reign 2

35th 1. שְׁלֹשִׁים וְחָמֵשׁ

2Ch 15:19 there was no more war until the 35th year 1

36 1. שְׁלֹשִׁים וָשֵׁשׁ

Jos 7: 5 the men of Ai killed about 36 men of them 1

36th 1. שְׁלֹשִׁים וָשֵׁשׁ

2Ch 16: 1 In the 36th year of the reign of Asa 1

37 1. שְׁלֹשִׁים וָשֶׁבַע

2Sm 23:39 Uri'ah the Hittite: 37 in all. 1

37th 1. שְׁלֹשִׁים וָשֶׁבַע

2Kg 13:10 In the 37th year of Jo'ash king of Judah 1
25:27 And in the 37th year of the exile of Jehoi'achin 1
Jer 52:31 in the 37th year of the captivity 1

38 1. שְׁלֹשִׁים וּשְׁמֹנֶה 2. *τριάκοντα καὶ ὀκτώ*

Deu 2:14 until we crossed the brook Zered was 38 years 1
Joh 5: 5 One man was there, who had been ill for 38 years. 2

38th 1. שְׁלֹשִׁים וּשְׁמֹנֶה 2. *τριακοστὸς ὄγδοος*

1Kg 16:29 In the 38th year of Asa king of Judah 1
2Kg 15: 8 In the 38th year of Azari'ah king of Judah 1
Sir 0: 3 the 38th year of the reign of Euergetes 2

39th 1. שְׁלוֹשִׁים וָתֵשַׁע 2. שְׁלֹשִׁים וָתֵשַׁע

2Kg 15:13 Shallum . . began to reign in the 39th year 1
17 In the 39th year of Azari'ah the king of Judah 2
2Ch 16:12 In the 39th year of his reign Asa 1

40 1. אַרְבָּעִים 2. *τεσσαράκοντα* 3. quadraginta

Gen 7: 4 send rain upon the earth 40 days and 40 nights; 2
4 send rain upon the earth 40 days and 40 nights; 1
12 rain fell upon the earth 40 days and 40 nights. 1
12 rain fell upon the earth 40 days and 40 nights. 1
17 The flood continued 40 days upon the earth; 1
8: 6 At the end of 40 days Noah opened the window 1
18:29 Suppose 40 are found there. 1
29 He answered, "For the sake of 40 I will not do it. 1
25:20 Isaac was 40 years old when he took to wife Rebekah 1
26:34 When Esau was 40 years old, he took to wife Judith 1
32:15 40 cows and ten bulls, twenty she-asses 1
50: 3 40 days were required for it 1
Exd 16:35 the people of Israel ate the manna forty years 1
24:18 Moses was on the mountain 40 days and 40 nights. 1
18 Moses was on the mountain 40 days and 40 nights. 1
26:19 40 bases of silver you shall make 1
21 their 40 bases of silver, two bases under one 1
34:28 he was there with the LORD 40 days and 40 nights; 1
28 he was there with the LORD 40 days and 40 nights; 1
36:24 he made 40 bases of silver under the twenty frames 1
26 their 40 bases of silver, two bases under one 1
Num13:25 At the end of 40 days they returned from spying 1
14:33 shall be shepherds in the wilderness 40 years 1
34 40 days, for every day a year, you shall bear 1
34 you shall bear your iniquity, 40 years 1
32:13 he made them wander in the wilderness 40 years 1
Deu 2: 7 these 40 years the LORD your God has been with you 1
8: 2 which the LORD . . has led you these 40 years 1
4 your foot did not swell, these 40 years. 1
9: 9 I remained on the mountain 40 days and 40 nights 1
9 I remained on the mountain . . 40 nights; 1
11 at the end of 40 days . . LORD gave me the two tables 1
11 And at the end of . . 40 nights the LORD gave me 1
18 I lay prostrate before the LORD as before, 40 days 1
18 I lay prostrate before the LORD . . 40 nights 1
25 I lay prostrate before the LORD for these 40 days 1
25 before the LORD for these 40 days and 40 nights 1
10:10 I stayed on the mountain . . 40 days and 40 nights 1
10 on the mountain, as at the first time . . 40 nights 1
25: 3 Forty stripes may be given him, but not more; 1
29: 5 I have led you 40 years in the wilderness; 1
Jos 5: 6 the people of Israel walked 40 years 1
14: 7 I was 40 years old when Moses . . sent me 1
Jdg 3:11 the land had rest 40 years. Then Oth'ni-el the son 1
5:31 And the land had rest for 40 years. 1
8:28 the land had rest 40 years in the days of Gideon 1
12:14 He had 40 sons and 30 grandsons, who rode 1
13: 1 the hand of the Philistines for 40 years. 1
1Sm 4:18 Eli fell . . He had judged Israel 40 years. 1
17:16 For 40 days the Philistine came forward 1
2Sm 2:10 Ish-bo'shet . . was 40 years old when he began to reign 1
5: 4 David was 30 years old . . and he reigned 40 years. 1
1Kg 2:11 the time that David reigned . . was 40 years; 1
6:17 The house . . the nave . . was 40 cubits long. 1
7:38 he made ten lavers . . each laver held 40 baths 1
11:42 time that Solomon reigned . . was 40 years. 1
19: 8 and went . . 40 days and 40 nights to Horeb 1
8 and went . . 40 days and 40 nights to Horeb 1
2Kg 8: 9 all kinds of goods of Damascus, 40 camel loads. 1
12: 1 Jeho'ash . . reigned 40 years in Jerusalem. 1

1Ch 29:27 time that he reigned over Israel was 40 years; 1
2Ch 9:30 reigned . . over all Israel 40 years. 1
24: 1 Jo'ash . . reigned 40 years in Jerusalem; 1
Neh 5:15 food and wine, besides 40 shekels of silver. 1
9:21 40 years . . sustain them in the wilderness 1
Ps 95:10 40 years I loathed that generation and said 1
Ezk 4: 6 40 days I assign you, a day for each year. 1
29:11 it shall be uninhabited 40 years. 1
12 her cities shall be a desolation 40 years 1
13 thus says the Lord GOD: At the end of 40 years 1
41: 2 he measured the length of the nave 40 cubits 1
46:22 small courts, 40 cubits long and 30 broad; 1
Ams 2:10 and led you 40 years in the wilderness 1
5:25 and offerings the 40 years in the wilderness 1
Jon 3: 4 Yet 40 days, and Nin'eveh shall be overthrown! 1
Mat 4: 2 And he fasted 40 days and 40 nights 2
2 And he fasted 40 days and 40 nights 2
Mrk 1:13 he was in the wilderness 40 days, tempted by Satan 2
Lke 4: 2 for 40 days in the wilderness 2
Act 1: 3 appearing to them during 40 days 2
4:22 the man . . was more than 40 years old. 2
7:30 Now when 40 years had passed 2
36 and in the wilderness for 40 years. 2
42 40 years in the wilderness, O house of Israel? 2
13:21 God gave them Saul . . for 40 years. 2
23:13 There were more than 40 who made this conspiracy. 2
21 more than 40 of their men lie in ambush for him 2
2Co 11:24 I have received . . the 40 lashes less one. 2
Heb 3: 9 and saw my works for 40 years. 2
17 And with whom was he provoked 40 years? 2
2Es 14:23 and tell them not to seek you for 40 days. 3
36 and let no one seek me for 40 days. 3
42 They sat 40 days, and wrote during the daytime 3
44 during the 40 days 94 books were written. 3
45 when the 40 days were ended 3
Jdt 1: 4 70 cubits high and 40 cubits wide 2
Bel 1: 3 40 sheep and 12 gallons of wine. 2
2Mc 5: 2 over all the city, for almost 40 days 2
3Mc 4:15 though uncompleted it stopped after 40 days. 2
6:38 for 40 days 2

40th 1. אַרְבָּעִים
Num33:38 in the 40th year after the people of Israel 1
Deu 1: 3 In the 40th year, on the first day 1
1Ch 26:31 In the 40th year of David's reign search was made 1

40 years 1. *τεσσαρακονταετής*
Act 7:23 When he was 40 years old 1
13:18 for about 40 years he bore with them 1

41 1. אַרְבָּעִים וְאֶחָד
1Kg 14:21 Rehobo'am was 41 years old when he began to reign 1
15:10 he reigned 41 years in Jerusalem. 1
2Kg 14:23 began to reign in Sama'ria, and he reigned 41 years. 1
2Ch 12:13 41 years old when he began to reign 1

41st 1. אַרְבָּעִים וְאֶחָד
2Ch 16:13 dying in the 41st year of his reign. 1

42 1. אַרְבָּעִים וּשְׁנַיִם 2. *τεσσαράκοντα δύο*
Num35: 6 in addition to them you shall give 42 cities 1
2Kg 2:24 two shebears came . . and tore 42 of the boys. 1
10:14 slew them . . 42 persons, and he spared none of them. 1
2Ch 22: 2 Ahazi'ah was 42 . . when he began to reign 1
Ezr 2:24 sons of Az'maveth, 42. 1
Neh 7:28 men of Beth-az'maveth, 42. 1
Rev 11: 2 they will trample over the holy city for 42 months. 2
13: 5 it was allowed to exercise authority for 42 months; 2
1Es 5:18 The men of Bethasmoth, 42. 2

45 1. אַרְבָּעִים וְחָמֵשׁ
Gen 18:28 I will not destroy it if I find 45 there. 1
Jos 14:10 LORD has kept me alive . . these 45 years 1
1Kg 7: 3 above the chambers that were upon the 45 pillars 1

46 1. *τεσσεράκοντα καὶ ἕξ*
Joh 2:20 It has taken 46 years to build this temple 1

48 1. אַרְבָּעִים וּשְׁמֹנֶה
Num35: 7 the cities which you give to the Levites shall be 48 1
Jos 21:41 cities of the Levites . . were in all 48 1

49 1. תֵּשַׁע וְאַרְבָּעִים 2. *τεσσαράκοντα ἐννέα*
Lev 25: 8 seven weeks of years shall be to you 49 years 1
Aza 1:24 streamed out above the furnace 49 cubits 2
49 *See also* seven.

50 1. חֲמִשִּׁים 2. *πεντήκοντα*
Gen 6:15 its breadth 50 cubits, and its height 30 cubits. 1
18:24 Suppose there are 50 righteous within the city; 1
24 not spare it for the 50 righteous who are in it? 1
26 the LORD said, "If I find at Sodom 50 righteous 1
28 Suppose five of the 50 righteous are lacking? 1
Exd 26: 5 50 loops you shall make on the one curtain 1
5 50 loops you shall make on the edge 1
6 you shall make 50 clasps of gold 1
10 you shall make 50 loops on the edge 1
10 shall make 50 loops on the edge of the curtain 1
11 you shall make 50 clasps of bronze 1
27:12 there shall be hangings for 50 cubits 1
13 breadth of the court . . shall be 50 cubits. 1
18 the breadth 50, and the height five cubits 1
36:12 he made 50 loops on the one curtain 1
12 he made 50 loops on the edge of the curtain 1
13 he made 50 clasps of gold 1
17 he made 50 loops on the edge of the outmost 1
17 made . . 50 loops on the edge of the other 1
18 he made 50 clasps of bronze to couple the tent 1
38:12 for the west side were hangings of 50 cubits 1
13 for the front of the east, 50 cubits. 1
Lev 23:16 50 days to the morrow after the seventh sabbath 1
27: 3 valuation . . shall be 50 shekels of silver 1
16 barley shall be valued at 50 shekels of silver 1
Num 4: 3 from 30 years old up to 50 years old 1
23 from 30 years old up to 50 years old 1
30 from 30 years old up to 50 years old 1
35 from 30 years old up to 50 years old 1
39 from 30 years old up to 50 years old 1
43 from 30 years old up to 50 years old 1
47 from 30 years old up to 50 years old 1
8:25 from the age of 50 years they shall withdraw 1
31:30 take one drawn out of every 50, of the persons 1
47 from . . Israel's half Moses took one of every fifty 1
Deu 22:29 give to the father . . 50 shekels of silver 1
Jos 7:21 I saw . . and a bar of gold weighing 50 shekels 1
2Sm 15: 1 a chariot and horses, and 50 men to run before him. 1
24:24 David bought . . for 50 shekels of silver. 1
1Kg 1: 5 chariots . . and 50 men to run before him. 1
7: 2 its breadth 50 cubits, and its height 30 cubits 1
6 he made the Hall of Pillars; its length was 50 cubits 1
2Kg 1: 9 the king sent to him a captain of 50 men 1
9 a captain of 50 men with his 50. 1
10 Eli'jah answered the captain of 50 1
10 let fire come . . and consume you and your 50. 1
10 Then fire came . . and consumed him and his 50. 1
11 the king sent to him another captain of 50 men 1
11 sent to him another captain . . with his 50. 1
12 let fire come . . and consume you and your 50. 1
12 fire of God came . . and consumed him and his 50 1
13 Again the king sent the captain of a third 50 1
13 the king sent the captain of . . with his 50. 1
13 the third captain of 50 went up, and came 1
13 the life of these 50 servants of yours 1
14 and consumed the two former captains of 50 1
2: 7 50 men of the sons of the prophets also went 1
16 there are with your servants 50 strong men; 1
17 he said, "Send." They sent therefore 50 men; 1
13: 7 was not . . an army of more than 50 horsemen 1
15:20 exacted the money . . 50 shekels of silver 1
25 conspired . . with 50 men of the Gileadites 1
2Ch 3: 9 weight . . one shekel to 50 shekels of gold. 1
Ezr 8: 6 Ebed the son of Jonathan, and with him 50 men. 1
Neh 7:70 governor gave to the treasury . . 50 basins 1
Est 5:14 Let a gallows 50 cubits high be made 1
7: 9 gallows . . in Haman's house, 50 cubits high. 1
Isa 3: 3 the captain of 50 and the man of rank 1
Ezk 40:15 inner vestibule of the gate was 50 cubits. 1
21 its length was 50 cubits 1
25 its length was 50 cubits 1
29 its length was 50 cubits 1
33 its length was 50 cubits 1
36 windows round about; its length was 50 cubits 1
42: 2 100 cubits, and the breadth 50 cubits. 1
7 opposite the chambers, 50 cubits long. 1
8 chambers on the outer court were 50 cubits 1
45: 2 with 50 cubits for an open space around it. 1
12 your mina shall be 50 shekels. 2
Hag 2:16 when one came to the winevat to draw 50 measures 1
Lke 7:41 one owed 500 denarii, and the other 50. 2
9:14 Make them sit down in companies, about 50 each. 2
16: 6 and sit down quickly and write 50' 2
Joh 8:57 You are not yet 50 years old 2
Tob 1:21 not 50 days passed before . . 2
Jdt 1: 2 70 cubits high and 50 cubits wide; 2
1Mc 9:61 Jonathan's men seized about 50 of the men 2
2Mc 13: 5 there is a tower in that place, 50 cubits high 2
50 *See also* fifties.

50 gallons 1. *μετρηταὶ ἕξ*
Bel 1: 3 40 sheep and 50 gallons of wine. 1

50th 1. חֲמִשִּׁים
Lev 25:10 you shall hallow the 50th year, and proclaim 1
11 A jubilee shall that 50th year be to you 1
2Kg 15:23 In the 50th year of Azari'ah king of Judah 1

52 1. חֲמִשִּׁים וּשְׁנַיִם 2. *πεντήκοντα δύο*
2Kg 15: 2 and he reigned 52 years in Jerusalem. 1
2Ch 26: 3 reigned 52 years in Jerusalem. 1
Ezr 2:29 sons of Nebo, 52. 1
Neh 6:15 wall was finished . . in 52 days. 1
7:33 men of the other Nebo, 52. 1
1Es 5:21 The men of Bethel, 52. The sons of Magbish, 156. 2

52nd 1. חֲמִשִּׁים וּשְׁתַּיִם
2Kg 15:27 In the 52nd year of Azari'ah king of Judah 1

55 1. חֲמִשִּׁים וְחָמֵשׁ 2. *πεντήκοντα πέντε*
2Kg 21: 1 and he reigned 55 years in Jerusalem. 1
2Ch 33: 1 he reigned 55 years in Jerusalem. 1
1Es 5:18 The men of Netophah, 55. The men of Anathoth, 158. 2

56 1. חֲמִשִּׁים וָשֵׁשׁ
Ezr 2:22 men of Neto'phah, 56. 1

58 1. *πεντήκοντα ὀκτώ*
Tob 14: 2 He was 58 years old when he lost his sight 1

60 1. שִׁשִּׁים 2. שִׁתִּין (A) 3. *ἑξήκοντα*
Gen 25:26 Isaac was 60 years old when she bore them. 1
Lev 27: 3 a male from twenty years old up to 60 years old 1
7 if the person is 60 years old and upward 1
Num 7:88 sacrifice of peace offerings . . the rams 60 1
88 peace offerings . . the male goats 60 1
88 peace offerings . . male lambs a year old 60 1
Deu 3: 4 60 cities, the whole region . . the kingdom of Og 1
Jos 13:30 and all the towns of Ja'ir . . 60 cities 1
1Kg 4:13 he had . . 60 great cities with walls 1
22 provision for one day was . . and 60 cors of meal 1
6: 2 The house . . for the LORD was 60 cubits long 1
2Kg 25:19 and 60 men of the people of the land 1
1Ch 2:21 whom he married when he was 60 years old; 1
23 Kenath and its villages, 60 towns. 1
2Ch 3: 3 length, in cubits of the old standard, was 60 1
11:21 (he took eighteen wives and 60 concubines 1
21 had 28 sons and 60 daughters); 1
Ezr 6: 3 height shall be 60 cubits and its breadth 2
3 its height . . and its breadth 60 cubits 2
8:13 sons of Adoni'kam . . and with them 60 men. 1
Sng 3: 7 litter of Solomon! About it are 60 mighty men 1
6: 8 There are 60 queens and 80 concubines 1
Jer 52:25 60 men of the people of the land, who were found 1
Dan 3: 1 image of gold, whose height was 60 cubits 2
Mat 13: 8 grain, some a hundredfold, some 60, some 30. 3
23 in one case a hundredfold, in another 60 3
1Ti 5: 9 if she is not less than 60 years of age 3
1Es 6:25 its height to be 60 cubits 3
25 and its breadth 60 cubits 3
Jdt 1: 3 100 cubits high and 60 cubits wide 3
1Mc 7:16 he seized 60 of them and killed them in one day 3
60 *See also* sixtyfold, threescore.

61 1. אֶחָד וְשִׁשִּׁים
Num31:39 30,500, of which the LORD'S tribute was 61. 1

62 1. שִׁשִּׁים וּשְׁנַיִם 2. שִׁתִּין וְתַרְתֵּין (A)
1Ch 26: 8 able men qualified for the service; 62 of O'bed-e'dom 1
Dan 5:31 Darius . . being about 62 years old. 2
9:25 Then for 62 weeks it shall be built again 1
26 after the 62 weeks, an anointed one 1

65 1. שִׁשִּׁים וְחָמֵשׁ 2. חָמֵשׁ וְשִׁשִּׁים
Gen 5:15 When Ma-hal'alel had lived 65 years 1
21 When Enoch had lived 65 years 1
Isa 7: 8 Within 65 years E'phraim will be broken 2

66 1. שִׁשִּׁים וָשֵׁשׁ
Gen 46:26 belonging to Jacob . . were 66 persons in all; 1
Lev 12: 5 in the blood of her purifying for 66 days 1

67 1. שִׁשִּׁים וְשֶׁבַע 2. *ἑξήκοντα ἑπτά*
Neh 7:72 rest . . gave . . 67 priests' garments. 1
1Es 5:15 The sons of Kilan and Azetas, 67. 2

68 1. שִׁשִּׁים וּשְׁמֹנָה
1Ch 16:38 and also O'bed-e'dom and his 68 brethren 1

70 1. שִׁבְעִים 2. *ἑβδομήκοντα* 3. septuaginta
Gen 5:12 When Kenan had lived 70 years 1
11:26 When Terah had lived 70 years 1
46:27 all the persons . . that came into Egypt, were 70. 1
50: 3 And the Egyptians wept for him 70 days. 1
Exd 1: 5 All the offspring of Jacob were 70 persons; 1
15:27 12 springs of water and 70 palm trees; 1
24: 1 Abi'hu, and 70 of the elders of Israel 1
9 Abi'hu, and 70 of the elders of Israel went up 1
38:29 the bronze that was contributed was 70 talents 1
Num 7:13 one silver basin of 70 shekels 1
19 one silver basin of 70 shekels 1
25 one silver basin of 70 shekels 1
31 one silver basin of 70 shekels 1
37 one silver basin of 70 shekels 1
43 one silver basin of 70 shekels 1
49 one silver basin of 70 shekels 1
55 one silver basin of 70 shekels 1
61 one silver basin of 70 shekels 1
67 one silver basin of 70 shekels 1
73 one silver basin of 70 shekels 1
79 one silver basin of 70 shekels 1
85 weighing 130 shekels and each basin 70 1
11:16 Gather for me 70 men of the elders of Israel 1
24 he gathered 70 men of the elders of the people 1
25 the LORD came . . and put it upon the 70 elders; 1
33: 9 there were twelve springs of water and 70 palm trees 1
Deu 10:22 Your fathers went down to Egypt 70 persons; 1

Jdg 1: 7 70 kings with their thumbs and their great toes 1
8:30 Gideon had 70 sons, his own offspring 1
9: 2 that all 70 of the sons of Jerubba'al rule over you 1
4 they gave him 70 pieces of silver out of the house 1
5 slew his brothers the sons of Jerubba'al, 70 men 1
18 and have slain his sons, 70 men on one stone 1
24 the violence done to the 70 sons of Jerubba'al 1
56 against his father in killing his 70 brothers; 1
12:14 40 sons and 30 grandsons, who rode on 70 asses; 1
1Sm 6:19 he slew 70 men of them, and the people mourned 1
2Kg 10: 1 Now Ahab had 70 sons in Sama'ria. 1
6 the king's sons, 70 persons, were with the great men 1
7 took the king's sons, and slew them, 70 persons 1
2Ch 29:32 number of the burnt offerings . . 70 bulls 1
36:21 it kept sabbath, to fulfil 70 years. 1
Ezr 8: 7 Jeshai'ah the son of Athali'ah, and with him 70 men. 1
14 Uthai and Zaccur, and with them 70 men. 1
Isa 23:15 Tyre will be forgotten for 70 years 1
15 At the end of 70 years, it will happen to Tyre 1
17 At the end of 70 years, the LORD will visit 1
Jer 25:11 nations shall serve the king of Babylon 70 years. 1
12 Then after 70 years are completed 1
29:10 When 70 years are completed for Babylon 1
Ezk 8:11 And before them stood 70 men of the elders 1
41:12 yard on the west side was 70 cubits broad; 1
Dan 9: 2 number of years . . namely, 70 years. 1
24 70 weeks of years are decreed concerning 1
Zec 1:12 thou hast had indignation these 70 years? 1
7: 5 for these 70 years, was it for me that you fasted? 1
Lke 10: 1 After this the Lord appointed 70 others 2
17 The 70 returned with joy, saying, "Lord 2
Act 23:23 200 soldiers with 70 horsemen 2
1Es 1:58 until the completion of 70 years. 2
8:33 the son of Gotholiah, and with him 70 men. 2
34 the son of Michael, and with him 70 men. 2
39 Jeuel, and Shemaiah, and with them 70 men. 2
40 the son of Istalcurus, and with him 70 men. 2
2Es 14:46 but keep the 70 that were written last 3
Jdt 1: 2 he made the walls 70 cubits high 2
4 he made its gates, which were 70 cubits high 2
Bel 1:10 Now there were 70 priests of Bel 2

70 times 1. *ἑβδομηκοντάκις*

Mat 18:22 not . . seven times, but 70 times seven. 1

72 1. שְׁנַיִם וְשִׁבְעִים 2. *ἑβδομήκοντα δύο*

Num31:38 36,000, of which the LORD'S tribute was 72. 1
1Es 8:66 72 lambs, and as a thank offering twelve he-goats 2

74 1. שִׁבְעִים וְאַרְבַּע 2. *ἑβδομήκοντα τέσσαρες*

Ezr 2:40 Kad'mi-el, of the sons of Ho-davi'ah, 74. 1
Neh 7:43 Levites: the sons of Jeshua . . 74. 1
1Es 5:26 the sons of . . Bannas and Sudias, 74. 2

75 1. חָמֵשׁ וְשִׁבְעִים 2. *ἑβδομήκοντα πέντε*

Gen 12: 4 Abram was 75 years old when he departed 1
Act 7:14 all his kindred, 75 souls; 2

75 miles 1. *στάδιοι ἑξακόσιοι*

2Mc 12:29 Scythopolis, which is 75 miles from Jerusalem. 1

77 1. שִׁבְעִים וָשֶׁבַע

Jdg 8:14 the officials and elders of Succoth, 77 men. 1
Ezr 8:35 96 rams, 77 lambs 1

80 1. שְׁמֹנִים 2. *ὀγδοήκοντα*

Exd 7: 7 Now Moses was 80 years old 1
Jdg 3:30 And the land had rest for 80 years. 1
2Sm 19:32 Barzil'lai was a very aged man, 80 years old; 1
35 I am this day 80 years old; can I discern 1
2Kg 6:25 an ass's head was sold for 80 shekels of silver 1
10:24 Now Jehu had stationed 80 men outside 1
1Ch 15: 9 Eli'el the chief, with 80 of his brethren; 1
2Ch 26:17 80 priests of the LORD who were men of valor; 1
Ezr 8: 8 Zebadi'ah the son of Michael, and with him 80 men. 1
Sng 6: 8 There are 60 queens and 80 concubines 1
Jer 41: 5 80 men arrived from Shechem and Shiloh 1
Lke 16: 7 He said to him, 'Take your bill, and write 80.' 2
2Mc 4: 8 from another source of revenue, 80 talents. 2
11: 4 his thousands of cavalry, and his 80 elephants. 2

80 *See also* fourscore.

83 1. שָׁלֹשׁ וּשְׁמֹנִים

Exd 7: 7 Moses was 80 . . and Aaron 83 years old 1

84 1. *ὀγδοήκοντα τέσσαρες*

Lke 2:37 and as a widow till she was 84 1

85 1. חָמֵשׁ וּשְׁמֹנִים 2. שְׁמֹנִים וְחָמֵשׁ

Jos 14:10 and now, lo, I am this day 85 years old. 1
1Sm 22:18 Do'eg . . killed . . 85 persons who wore the linen 2

86 1. שְׁמֹנִים וָשֵׁשׁ

Gen 16:16 Abram was 86 years old when Hagar bore Ish'mael 1

90 1. תִּשְׁעִים 2. *ἐνενήκοντα*

Gen 5: 9 When Enosh had lived 90 years 1
17:17 Shall Sarah, who is 90 years old, bear a child? 1
Ezk 41:12 and its length 90 cubits. 1
2Mc 8:11 and promising to hand over 90 slaves for a talent 2

90th year 1. *ἐνενηκονταετής*

2Mc 6:24 Eleazar in his 90th year 1

92 1. *ἐνενήκοντα δύο*

1Es 5:15 The sons of Ater, namely of Hezekiah, 92. 1

94

2Es 14:44 during the 40 days 94 books were written. ‡

95 1. תִּשְׁעִים וְחָמֵשׁ

Ezr 2:20 sons of Gibbar, 95. 1
Neh 7:25 sons of Gibeon, 95. 1

95 miles 1. *στάδιοι ἑπτακόσιοι πεντήκοντα*

2Mc 12:17 When they had gone 95 miles from there 1

96 1. שֵׁשׁ 2. תִּשְׁעִים וָשֵׁשׁ 3. *ἐνενήκοντα ἕξ*

Ezr 8:35 96 rams, 77 lambs 1
Jer 52:23 There were 96 pomegranates on the sides; 1
1Es 8:65 12 bulls for all Israel, 96 rams 2

98 1. תִּשְׁעִים וּשְׁמֹנָה

1Sm 4:15 Now Eli was 98 years old and his eyes were set 1
Ezr 2:16 sons of Ater, namely of Hezeki'ah, 98. 1
Neh 7:21 sons of Ater, namely of Hezeki'ah, 98. 1

99 1. תִּשְׁעִים וָתֵשַׁע 2. *ἐνενήκοντα ἐννέα*

Gen 17: 1 When Abram was 99 years old the LORD appeared 1
24 Abraham was 99 years old 1
Mat 18:12 does he not leave the 99 on the mountains 2
13 more than over the 99 that never went astray. 2
Lke 15: 4 does not leave the 99 in the wilderness 2
7 sinner . . than over 99 righteous persons 2

100 1. מֵאָה 2. מְאָה (A) 3. *ἑκατόν*

Gen 11:10 When Shem was 100 years old 1
17:17 Shall a child be born to a man who is 100 years old? 1
21: 5 Abraham was 100 years old when . . Isaac was born 1
33:19 he bought for 100 pieces of money the . . land 1
Exd 27: 9 hangings . . 100 cubits long for one side; 1
11 there shall be hangings 100 cubits long 1
18 The length of the court shall be 100 cubits 1
38: 9 hangings . . were of fine twined linen, 100 cubits; 1
11 for the north side 100 cubits, their pillars 20 1
25 silver . . was 100 talents and 1,775 shekels 1
27 The 100 talents of silver were for casting 1
27 100 bases for the 100 talents, a talent for a base. 1
27 100 bases for the 100 talents, a talent for a base. 1
Lev 26: 8 Five of you shall chase 100 1
8 100 of you shall chase 10,000 1
Deu 22:19 they shall fine him 100 shekels of silver 1
Jos 24:32 Jacob bought . . for 100 pieces of money; 1
Jdg 7:19 Gideon and the 100 men who were with him came 1
20:10 take ten men of a 100 throughout all the tribes 1
10 and a 100 of a 1,000, and a 1,000 of 10,000 1
1Sm 18:25 except 100 foreskins of the Philistines 1
25:18 parched grain, and 100 clusters of raisins 1
2Sm 3:14 I betrothed at the price of 100 foreskins 1
8: 4 David . . left enough for 100 chariots. 1
16: 1 200 loaves of bread, 100 bunches of raisins 1
1 bunches of raisins, 100 of summer fruits 1
24: 3 God add . . 100 times as many as they are 1
1Kg 4:23 twenty pasture-fed cattle, 100 sheep 1
7: 2 its length was 100 cubits 1
18: 4 Obadi'ah took 100 prophets and hid them 1
13 how I hid 100 men of the LORD's prophets 1
2Kg 4:43 How am I to set this before 100 men? 1
23:33 laid upon the land a tribute of 100 talents of silver 1
1Ch 12:14 the lesser over 100 and the greater over 1,000. 1
18: 4 but left enough for 100 chariots. 1
21: 3 May the LORD add to his people 100 times 1
2Ch 3:16 made 100 pomegranates, and put them 1
4: 8 And he made 100 basins of gold. 1
25: 6 for 100 talents of silver. 1
9 But what shall we do about the 100 talents 1
27: 5 gave him that year 100 talents of silver 1
29:32 number of the burnt offerings . . 100 rams 1
36: 3 tribute of 100 talents of silver and a talent 1
Ezr 2:69 gave to . . the work . . 100 priests' garments. 1
6:17 offered . . 100 bulls, 200 rams 2
7:22 up to 100 talents of silver 2
22 up to . . 100 cors of wheat 2
22 up to . . 100 baths of wine 2
22 up to . . 100 baths of oil, and salt 2
8:26 silver vessels worth 100 talents 1
26 silver vessels . . and 100 talents of gold 1
Prv 17:10 than 100 blows into a fool. 1
Ecc 6: 3 If a man begets 100 children . . but he does 1
8:12 Though a sinner does evil 100 times 1
Isa 65:20 for the child shall die 100 years old 1
20 sinner 100 years old shall be accursed. 1
Jer 52:23 pomegranates were 100 upon the network 1
Ezk 40:19 outer front of the inner court, 100 cubits. 1
23 he measured from gate to gate, 100 cubits. 1
27 gate to gate toward the south, 100 cubits. 1
47 he measured the court, 100 cubits long 1
47 and 100cubits broad, foursquare; 1
41:13 he measured the temple, 100 cubits long; 1
13 building with its walls, 100 cubits long; 1
14 the temple and the yard, 100 cubits. 1
15 and its walls on either side, 100 cubits. 1
42: 2 which was on the north side was 100 cubits 1
4 ten cubits wide and 100 cubits long 3
8 opposite the temple were 100 cubits long. 1
Ams 5: 3 went forth 1,000 shall have 100 left 1
3 which went forth 100 shall have ten left 1
Mat 18:12 If a man has a 100 sheep 3
28 fellow servants who owed him a 100 denarii 3
Lke 15: 4 What man of you, having 100 sheep 3
16: 6 He said, 'A 100 measures of oil.' 3
7 He said, 'A 100 measures of wheat.' 3
Joh 19:39 about a 100 pounds' weight. 3
1Es 1:36 fined the nation 100 talents of silver 3
5:45 100 priests' garments. 3
7: 7 They offered . . 100 bulls, 200 rams, 400 lambs 3
8:20 up to 100 talents of silver 3
20 likewise up to 100 cors of wheat 3
20 100 baths of wine, and salt in abundance. 3
56 silver vessels worth a 100 talents 3
56 a 100 talents of gold 3
Jdt 1: 3 he built towers 100 cubits high 3
10:17 They chose from their number 100 men 3
Sir 18: 9 is great if he reaches 100 years. 3
41: 4 for ten or 100 or 1,000 years 3
1Mc 13:16 Send now 100 talents of silver 3
19 So he sent the sons and the 100 talents 3
15:35 for them we will give you 100 talents. 3

100 *See also* hundredfold, hundreds, hundredweight.

100th 1. מֵאָה

Neh 5:11 Return . . 100th of money, grain, wine, and oil 1

100 yards 1. *πήχεις διακόσιοι*

Joh 21: 8 about 100 yards off. 1

100 years 1. *ἑκατονταετής*

Rom 4:19 because he was about a 100 years old 1

101 1. *ἑκατὸν εἷς*

1Es 5:16 The sons of Annias,101. The sons of Arom. 1

105 1. חָמֵשׁ וּמֵאָה 2. *ἑκατὸν πέντε*

Gen 5: 6 When Seth had lived 105 years 1
Jdt 16:23 until she was 105 years old 2

110 1. מֵאָה וָעֶשֶׂר 2. *ἑκατὸν δέκα*

Gen 50:22 and Joseph lived 110 years. 1
25 Joseph died, being 110 years old; 1
Jos 24:29 Joshua . . died, being 110 years old. 1
Jdg 2: 8 Joshua . . died at the age of 110 years. 1
Ezr 8:12 Joha'nan the son of Hak'katan, and with him 110 men 1
1Es 8:38 the son of Hakkatan, and with him 110 men. 2

112 1. מֵאָה וּשְׁתֵּים עֶשְׂרֵה 2. מֵאָה שְׁתֵּים עֶשְׂרֵה 3. *ἑκατὸν δέκα δύο*

1Ch 15:10 Ammin'adab the chief, with 112 of his brethren. 1
Ezr 2:18 sons of Jorah, 112. 1
Neh 7:24 sons of Hariph, 112. 2
1Es 5:16 The sons of Bezai, 323. The sons of Jorah, 112. 3

119 1. תְּשַׁע עֶשְׂרֵה וּמֵאָה

Gen 11:25 Nahor lived after the birth of Terah 119 years 1

120 1. מֵאָה וְעֶשְׂרִים 2. עֶשְׂרִים וּמֵאָה 3. מְאָה וְעֶשְׂרִין (A) 4. *ἑκατὸν εἴκοσι*

Gen 6: 3 he is flesh, but his days shall be 120 years. 1
Num 7:86 all the gold of the dishes being 120 shekels; 2
Deu 31: 2 said to them, "I am 120 years old this day; 1
34: 7 Moses was 120 years old when he died; 1
1Kg 9:14 Hiram had sent to the king 120 talents of gold. 1
10:10 she gave the king 120 talents of gold 1
1Ch 15: 5 Uri'el the chief, with 120 of his brethren; 1
2Ch 3: 4 its height was 120 cubits. 1
5:12 stood . . with 120 priests who 1
9: 9 she gave . . 120 talents of gold 1
Dan 6: 1 Darius to set over the kingdom 120 satraps 3
Act 1:15 in all about 120 4
Jdt 1:16 and feasted for 120 days. 4
1Mc 8: 6 to fight against them with 120 elephants 4

122 1. מֵאָה וְעֶשְׂרִים וּשְׁנָיִם 2. מֵאָה עֶשְׂרִים וּשְׁנָיִם 3. *ἑκατὸν εἴκοσι δύο*

Ezr 2:27 men of Michmas, 122. 2
Neh 7:31 men of Michmas, 122. 1
1Es 5:21 The men of Michmas, 122. The men of Bethel, 52. 3

123 1. מֵאָה עֶשְׂרִים וְשָׁלֹשׁ 2. שָׁלֹשׁ וְעֶשְׂרִים וּמֵאָה 3. *ἑκατὸν εἴκοσι τρεῖς*

Num33:39 Aaron was 123 years old when he died on Mount Hor. 2
Ezr 2:21 sons of Bethlehem, 123. 1
Neh 7:32 men of Bethel and Ai, 123. 1
1Es 5:17 The sons of Bethlehem, 123. 3

127 1. מֵאָה וְעֶשְׂרִים וָשֶׁבַע 2. שֶׁבַע וְעֶשְׂרִים וּמֵאָה
3. *ἑκατὸν εἴκοσι ἑπτά*
Gen 23: 1 Sarah lived 127 years; 1
Est 1: 1 Ahasu-e'rus who reigned . . over 127 provinces 2
8: 9 provinces from India to Ethiopia, 127 provinces 2
9:30 to the 127 provinces of the kingdom of Ahasu-e'rus 2
1Es 3: 2 the 127 satrapies from India to Ethiopia. 3
Tob 14:14 at the age of a 127 years. 3
AEs 13: 1 the 127 provinces from India to Ethiopia 3
16: 1 127 satrapies 3

128 1. מֵאָה עֶשְׂרִים וּשְׁמֹנֶה 2. *ἑκατὸν εἴκοσι ὀκτώ*
Ezr 2:23 men of An'athoth, 128. 1
41 singers: the sons of Asaph, 128. 1
Neh 7:27 men of An'athoth, 128. 1
11:14 their brethren, mighty men of valor, 128; 1
1Es 5:27 The temple singers: the sons of Asaph, 128. 2

130 1. מֵאָה וּשְׁלֹשִׁים 2. שְׁלֹשִׁים וּמֵאָה
Gen 5: 3 When Adam had lived 130 years 2
47: 9 The days . . of my sojourning are 130 years; 2
Num 7:13 one silver plate whose weight was 130 shekels 2
19 one silver plate, whose weight was 130 shekels 2
25 one silver plate, whose weight was 130 shekels 2
31 one silver plate whose weight was 130 shekels 2
37 one silver plate, whose weight was 130 shekels 2
43 one silver plate, whose weight was 130 shekels 2
49 one silver plate, whose weight was 130 shekels 2
55 one silver plate, whose weight was 130 shekels 2
61 one silver plate, whose weight was 130 shekels 2
67 one silver plate, whose weight was 130 shekels 2
73 one silver plate, whose weight was 130 shekels 2
79 one silver plate, whose weight was 130 shekels 2
85 each silver plate weighing 130 shekels 2
1Ch 15: 7 Jo'el the chief, with 130 of his brethren; 1
2Ch 24:15 Jehoi'ada . . was 130 years old at his death. 1

133 1. שְׁלֹשׁ וּשְׁלֹשִׁים וּמֵאָה
Exd 6:18 the years of the life of Kohath being 133 years. 1

137 1. מֵאָה וּשְׁלֹשִׁים וָשֶׁבַע 2. שֶׁבַע וּשְׁלֹשִׁים וּמֵאָה
Gen 25:17 years of the life of Ish'mael, 137 years; 1
Exd 6:16 the years of the life of Levi being 137 years. 2
20 the years of the life of Amram being 137 years. 2

137th 1. *ἑκατοστός τριακοστός ἕβδομος*
1Mc 1:10 He began to reign in the 137th year 1

138 1. מֵאָה שְׁלֹשִׁים וּשְׁמֹנֶה
Neh 7:45 gatekeepers: the sons of . . of Sho'bai, 138. 1

139 1. מֵאָה שְׁלֹשִׁים וָתֵשַׁע 2. *ἑκατὸν τριάκοντα ἐννέα*
Ezr 2:42 sons of the gatekeepers . . in all 139. 1
1Es 5:28 sons of Hatita, the sons of Shobai, in all 139. 2

140 1. מֵאָה וְאַרְבָּעִים
Job 42:16 after this Job lived 140 years 1

143rd 1. *ἑκατοστὸς τεσσαρακοστὸς τρίτος*
1Mc 1:20 Antiochus returned in the 143rd year 1

144 1. *ἑκατὸν τεσσαράκοντα τέσσαρες*
Rev 21:17 its wall, 144 cubits by a man's measure 1

145th 1. *ἑκατοστὸς τεσσαρακοστὸς πέμπτος*
1Mc 1:54 fifteenth day of Chislev, in the 145th year 1

146th 1. *ἑκατοστὸς ἕκτος τεσσαρακοστός*
2Mc 2:70 He died in the 146th year 1

147 1. שֶׁבַע וְאַרְבָּעִים וּמֵאָה
Gen 47:28 Jacob, the years of his life, were 147 years. 1

147th 1. *ἑκατοστὸς ἕβδομος τεσσαρακοστός*
1Mc 3:37 from Antioch his capital in the 147th year 1

148 1. מֵאָה אַרְבָּעִים וּשְׁמֹנֶה
Neh 7:44 singers: the sons of Asaph, 148. 1

148th 1. *ἑκατοστὸς ὄγδοος τεσσαρακοστός*
2. *ἑκατοστὸς τεσσαρακοστὸς ὄγδοος*
1Mc 4:52 the month of Chislev, in the 148th year 1
2Mc 11:21 Farewell. The 148th year, Dioscorinthius 24th. 2
33 Farewell. The 148th year, Xanthicus fifteenth. 2
38 Farewell. The 148th year, Xanthicus fifteenth. 2

149th 1. *ἑκατοστὸς ἔνατος τεσσαρακοστός*
2. *ἔνατος τεσσαρακοστὸς ἑκατοστός*
1Mc 6:16 in the 149th year. 1
2Mc 13: 1 In the 149th year 2

150 1. חֲמִשִּׁים וּמֵאָה 2. מֵאָה וַחֲמִשִּׁים
3. *ἑκατὸν πεντήκοντα* 4. *πεντήκοντα πρὸς ἑκατόν*
Gen 7:24 the waters prevailed upon the earth 150 days. 1
8: 3 At the end of 150 days the waters had abated; 1
1Kg 10:29 could be imported . . a horse for 150; 1
1Ch 8:40 bowmen, having many sons and grandsons, 150. 2
2Ch 1:17 imported . . a horse for 150; 1
Ezr 8: 3 Zechari'ah, with whom were registered 150 men. 2
Neh 5:17 there were at my table 150 men, Jews and officials 2
1Es 8:30 Zechariah, and with him 150 men enrolled. 3
2Mc 4: 9 he promised to pay 150 more 4

150th 1. *ἑκατοστὸς πεντηκοστός*
1Mc 6:20 besieged the citadel in the 150th year 1

151st 1. *ἑκατοστὸς εἷς πεντηκοστός*
2. *πρῶτος πεντηκοστὸς ἑκατοστός*
1Mc 7: 1 In the 151st year Demetrius the son of Seleucus 1
2Mc 14: 4 went to King Demetrius in about the 151st year 2

152nd 1. *ἑκατοστὸς δεύτερος πεντηκοστός*
1Mc 9: 3 In the first month of the 152nd year 1

153 1. *ἑκατὸν πεντήκοντα τρεῖς*
Joh 21:11 hauled the net ashore, full of large fish, 153 1

153rd 1. *ἑκατοστὸς τρίτος πεντηκοστός*
1Mc 9:54 In the 153rd year, in the second month 1

156 1. מֵאָה חֲמִשִּׁים וָשֵׁשׁ 2. *ἑκατὸν πεντήκοντα ἕξ*
Ezr 2:30 sons of Magbish, 156. 1
1Es 5:21 The men of Bethel, 52. The sons of Magbish, 156. 2

158 1. *ἑκατὸν πεντήκοντα ὀκτώ*
1Es 5:18 The men of Netophah, 55. The men of Anathoth, 158. 1
Tob 14:11 He was 158 years old 1

160 1. מֵאָה וְשִׁשִּׁים 2. *ἑκατὸν ἑξήκοντα*
Ezr 8:10 Shelo'mith . . of Josi-phi'ah, and with him 160 men. 1
1Es 8:36 the son of Josiphiah, and with him 160 men. 2

160th 1. *ἑκατοστὸς ἑξηκοστός*
1Mc 10: 1 In the 160th year 1
21 the 160th year 1

162 1. שְׁנַיִם וְשִׁשִּׁים וּמֵאָה
Gen 5:18 When Jared had lived 162 years 1

162nd 1. *ἑκατοστὸς δεύτερος ἑξηκοστός*
1Mc 10:57 in the 162nd year. 1

165th 1. *ἑκατοστὸς πέμπτος ἑξηκοστός*
1Mc 10:67 In the 165th year 1

167th 1. *ἑκατοστὸς ἕβδομος ἑξηκοστός*
1Mc 11:19 in the 167th year. 1

169th 1. *ἑκατοστὸς ἑξηκοστὸς ἔνατος*
2Mc 1: 7 In the reign of Demetrius, in the 169th year 1

170th 1. *ἑκατοστὸς ἑβδομηκοστός*
1Mc 13:41 In the 170th year 1

171st 1. *ἑκατοστὸς πρῶτος ἑβδομηκοστός*
1Mc 13:51 the 23rd day of the second month, in the 171st year 1

172 1. מֵאָה שִׁבְעִים וּשְׁנָיִם
Neh 11:19 brethren, who kept watch at the gates, were 172. 1

172nd 1. *ἑκατοστὸς δεύτερος ἑβδομηκοστός*
1Mc 14: 1 In the 172nd year Demetrius the king 1
27 On the eighteenth day of Elul, in the 172nd year 1

174th 1. *ἑκατοστὸς τέταρτος ἑβδομηκοστός*
1Mc 15:10 In the 174th year Antiochus set out and invaded 1

175 1. מְאַת וְשִׁבְעִים וְחָמֵשׁ
Gen 25: 7 days of the years of Abraham's life, 175 years. 1

177th 1. *ἑκατοστὸς ἕβδομος ἑβδομηκοστός*
1Mc 16:14 his sons, in the 177th year, in the eleventh month 1

180 1. שְׁמֹנִים וּמְאַת 2. מֵאָה וּשְׁמֹנִים
Gen 35:28 Now the days of Isaac were 180 years. 1
Est 1: 4 he showed the riches . . for many days, 180 days. 2

182 1. שְׁנַיִם וּשְׁמֹנִים וּמֵאָה
Gen 5:28 When Lamech had lived 182 years 1

187 1. שֶׁבַע וּשְׁמֹנִים וּמֵאָה
Gen 5:25 When Methu'selah had lived 187 years 1

188 1. מֵאָה שְׁמֹנִים וּשְׁמֹנָה
Neh 7:26 men of Bethlehem and Neto'phah, 188. 1

188th 1. *ἑκατοστὸς ὀγδοηκοστὸς ὄγδοος*
2Mc 1: 9 in the month of Chislev, in the 188th year. 1

200 1. מָאתַיִם 2. מָאתַיִן (A) 3. *διακόσιοι*
Gen 11:23 Serug lived after the birth of Nahor 200 years 1
32:14 200 she-goats and twenty he-goats 1
14 200 ewes and twenty rams 1
Jos 7:21 I saw among the spoil . . 200 shekels of silver 1
Jdg 17: 4 his mother took 200 pieces of silver 1
1Sm 18:27 David . . killed 200 of the Philistines; 1
25:13 while 200 remained with the baggage. 1
18 clusters of raisins, and 200 cakes of figs 1
18 Ab'igail made haste, and took 200 loaves 1
30:10 200 stayed behind, who were too exhausted 1
21 Then David came to the 200 men 1
2Sm 14:26 he weighed the hair of his head, 200 shekels 1
15:11 200 men from Jerusalem who were invited guests 1
16: 1 a couple of asses . . bearing 200 loaves of bread 1
1Kg 7:20 there were 200 pomegranates, in two rows 1
10:16 King Solomon made 200 large shields of beaten gold; 1
1Ch 12:32 200 chiefs, and all their kinsmen 1
15: 8 Shemai'ah the chief, with 200 of his brethren; 1
2Ch 9:15 Solomon made 200 large shields of beaten gold; 1
29:32 number of the burnt offerings . . 200 lambs; 1
Ezr 2:65 7,337; and they had 200 male and female singers. 1
6:17 They offered . . 100 bulls, 200 rams 2
8: 4 son of Zerahi'ah, and with him 200 men. 1
Sng 8:12 and the keepers of the fruit 200. 1
Ezk 45:15 one sheep from every flock of 200 1
Mrk 6:37 we go and buy 200 denarii worth of bread 3
Joh 6: 7 200 denarii would not buy enough bread 3
Act 23:23 200 soldiers with 70 horsemen 3
23 70 horsemen and 200 spearmen 3
1Es 7: 7 They offered . . 100 bulls, 200 rams, 400 lambs 3
8:31 the son of Zerahiah, and with him 200 men. 3
2Mc 3:11 400 talents of silver and 200 of gold 3
12: 4 not less than 200. 3

205 1. חָמֵשׁ וּמָאתַיִם
Gen 11:32 The days of Terah were 205 years; 1

207 1. שֶׁבַע וּמָאתַיִם
Gen 11:21 Re'u lived after the birth of Serug 207 years 1

209 1. תֵּשַׁע וּמָאתַיִם
Gen 11:19 Peleg lived after the birth of Re'u 209 years 1

212 1. מָאתַיִם וּשְׁנֵים עָשָׂר 2. *διακόσιοι δέκα δύο*
1Ch 9:22 chosen as gatekeepers at the thresholds, were 212 1
1Es 8:35 the son of Jehiel, and with him 212 men. 2

218 1. מָאתַיִם וּשְׁמֹנָה עָשָׂר
Ezr 8: 9 Obadi'ah the son of Jehi'el, and with him 218 men. 1

220 1. מָאתַיִם וְעֶשְׂרִים 2. *διακόσιοι εἴκοσι*
1Ch 15: 6 Asai'ah the chief, with 220 of his brethren; 1
Ezr 8:20 besides 220 of the temple servants, whom David 1
1Es 8:49 220 temple servants 2

223 1. מָאתַיִם עֶשְׂרִים וְשָׁלֹשׁ
Ezr 2:19 sons of Hashum, 223. 1
28 men of Bethel and Ai, 223. 1

232 1. מָאתַיִם שְׁנַיִם וּשְׁלֹשִׁים
1Kg 20:15 he mustered the servants . . and they were 232; 1

242 1. מָאתַיִם אַרְבָּעִים וּשְׁנָיִם
Neh 11:13 his brethren, heads of fathers' houses, 242; 1

245 1. מָאתַיִם אַרְבָּעִים וְחָמֵשׁ 2. מָאתַיִם וְאַרְבָּעִים וְחָמֵשׁ
3. *διακόσιοι τεσσαράκοντα πέντε*
Ezr 2:66 Their horses were 736, their mules were 245 1
Neh 7:67 they had 245 singers, male and female. 2
68 Their horses were 736, their mules 245 1
1Es 5:42 245 musicians and singers. 3
43 245 mules, and 5,525 asses. 3

250 1. חֲמִשִּׁים וּמָאתָיִם 2. *διακόσιοι πεντήκοντα*
Exd 30:23 of . . cinnamon half as much, that is, 250 1
23 Take . . of aromatic cane 250 1
Num16: 2 with . . 250 leaders of the congregation 1
17 bring . . before the LORD his censer, 250 censers; 1
35 consumed the 250 men offering the incense. 1
26:10 when the fire devoured 250 men; 1
2Ch 8:10 chief officers . . 250, who exercised authority 1
Ezk 48:17 open land: on the north 250 cubits, on the south 250 1
17 on the south 250, on the east 250 1
17 on the east 250, and on the west 250. 1
17 on the east 250, and on the west 250 1
1Es 8:32 Obed the son of Jonathan, and with him 250 men. 2

273 1. שְׁלֹשָׁה וְשִׁבְעִים וּמָאתָיִם
Num 3:46 for the redemption of the 273 of the first-born 1

276 1. *διακόσιοι ἑβδομήκοντα ἕξ*
Act 27:37 We were in all 276 persons in the ship. 1

284 1. מָאתַיִם שְׁמֹנִים וְאַרְבַּע
Neh 11:18 All the Levites in the holy city were 284. 1

288 1. מָאתַיִם שְׁמוֹנִים וּשְׁמוֹנֶה
1Ch 25: 7 singing to the LORD, all who were skilful, was 288. 1

300 1. שְׁלֹשׁ מֵאוֹת 2. *τριακόσιοι*
Gen 5:22 after the birth of Methu'selah 300 years 1
6:15 the length of the ark 300 cubits 1
45:22 but to Benjamin he gave 300 shekels of silver 1
Jdg 7: 6 of those that lapped . . was 300 men; 1

7 With the 300 men . . I will deliver you 1
8 every man to his tent, but retained the 300 men; 1
16 he divided the 300 men into three companies 1
22 When they blew the 300 trumpets 1
8: 4 he and the 300 men who were with him 1
11:26 While Israel dwelt . . 300 years, why did you not 1
15: 4 Samson went and caught 300 foxes 1
2Sm 21:16 whose spear weighed 300 shekels of bronze 1
23:18 he wielded his spear against 300 men 1
1Kg 10:17 he made 300 shields of beaten gold; 1
11: 3 He had 700 wives . . and 300 concubines; 1
2Kg 18:14 king of Assyria required of Hezeki'ah . . 300 talents 1
1Ch 11:11 he wielded his spear against 300 whom he slew 1
20 he wielded his spear against 300 men and slew them 1
2Ch 9:16 he made 300 shields of beaten gold; 1
16 300 shekels of gold went into each shield; 1
14: 9 with an army of 1,000,000 men and 300 chariots 1
35: 8 for the passover offerings . . 300 bulls. 1
Ezr 8: 5 son of Jaha'ziel, and with him 300 men. 1
Est 9:15 and they slew 300 men in Susa; 1
Mrk 14: 5 ointment . . sold for more than 300 denarii 2
Joh 12: 5 Why was this ointment not sold for 300 denarii 2
1Es 1: 8 for the passover 2,600 sheep and 300 calves. 2
8:32 Shecaniah . . and with him 300 men 2
1Mc 11:28 and promised him 300 talents. 2
2Mc 4:19 to carry 300 silver drachmas for the sacrifice 2
24 outbidding Jason by 300 talents of silver. 2
13: 2 300 chariots armed with scythes. 2
3Mc 7:15 In that day they put to death more than 300 men 2

318 1. שְׁמֹנֶה עָשָׂר וּשְׁלֹשׁ מֵאוֹת
Gen 14:14 his trained men, born in his house, 318 of them 1

320 1. שְׁלֹשׁ מֵאוֹת וְעֶשְׂרִים 2. τριακόσιοι εἴκοσι
Ezr 2:32 sons of Harim, 320. 1
Neh 7:35 sons of Harim, 320. 1
1Mc 8:15 every day 320 senators constantly deliberate 2

323 1. שְׁלֹשׁ מֵאוֹת עֶשְׂרִים וְשָׁלֹשׁ 2. τριακόσιοι εἴκοσι τρεῖς
Ezr 2:17 sons of Be'zai, 323. 1
1Es 5:16 The sons of Bezai, 323. The sons of Jorah, 112. 2

324 1. שְׁלֹשׁ מֵאוֹת עֶשְׂרִים וְאַרְבָּעָה
Neh 7:23 sons of Be'zai, 324. 1

328 1. שְׁלֹשׁ מֵאוֹת עֶשְׂרִים וּשְׁמֹנָה
Neh 7:22 sons of Hashum, 328. 1

345 1. שְׁלֹשׁ מֵאוֹת אַרְבָּעִים וְחָמֵשׁ 2. τριακόσιοι τεσσαράκοντα πέντε
Ezr 2:34 sons of Jericho, 345. 1
Neh 7:36 sons of Jericho, 345. 1
1Es 5:22 The sons of Jericho, 345 2

350 1. שְׁלֹשׁ מֵאוֹת וַחֲמִשִּׁים
Gen 9:28 After the flood Noah lived 350 years; 1

360 1. שְׁלֹשׁ מֵאוֹת וְשִׁשִּׁים 2. ἑξήκοντα πρὸς τοῖς τριακοσίοις
2Sm 2:31 servants . . had slain of Benjamin 360 of Abner's men. 1
2Mc 4: 8 360 talents of silver 2

365 1. חָמֵשׁ וְשִׁשִּׁים וּשְׁלֹשׁ מֵאוֹת
Gen 5:23 Thus all the days of Enoch were 365 years. 1

372 1. שְׁלֹשׁ מֵאוֹת שִׁבְעִים וּשְׁנַיִם 2. τριακόσιοι ἑβδομήκοντα δύο
Ezr 2: 4 sons of Shephati'ah, 372. 1
Neh 7: 9 sons of Shephati'ah, 372. 1
1Es 5:35 the sons of Solomon's servants were 372. 2

390 1. שְׁלֹשׁ מֵאוֹת וְתִשְׁעִים
Ezk 4: 5 For I assign to you a number of days, 390 days 1
9 days that you lie upon your side, 390 days 1

392 1. שְׁלֹשׁ מֵאוֹת תִּשְׁעִים וּשְׁנָיִם
Ezr 2:58 All the temple servants and the sons . . were 392. 1
Neh 7:60 All the temple . . servants were 392. 1

400 1. אַרְבַּע מֵאוֹת 2. אַרְבַּע מְאָה (A) 3. τετρακόσιοι 4. quadringenti
Gen 15:13 they will be oppressed for 400 years; 1
23:15 a piece of land worth 400 shekels of silver 1
16 weighed out for Ephron . . 400 shekels of silver 1
32: 6 he is coming to meet you, and 400 men with him. 1
33: 1 Esau was coming, and 400 men with him. 1
Jdg 21:12 found . . 400 young virgins who had not known man 1
1Sm 22: 2 And there were with him about 400 men. 1
25:13 and about 400 men went up after David 1
30:10 David went on with the pursuit, he and 400 men; 1
17 not a man of them escaped, except 400 young men 1
1Kg 7:42 400 pomegranates for the two networks 1
18:19 gather . . and the 400 prophets of Ashe'rah 1
22: 6 king . . gathered the prophets . . about 400 men 1
2Kg 14:13 broke down the wall of Jerusalem for 400 cubits 1
2Ch 4:13 400 pomegranates for the two networks 1
18: 5 gathered the prophets together, 400 men 1
25:23 broke down the wall of Jerusalem for 400 cubits 1
Ezr 6:17 offered . . 200 rams, 400 lambs 2
Act 5:36 a number of men, about 400, joined him 3
7: 6 and ill-treat them 400 years. 3
1Es 7: 7 They offered . . 100 bulls, 200 rams, 400 lambs 3
2Es 7:28 and those who remain shall rejoice 400 years. 4
2Mc 3:11 totaled in all 400 talents of silver 3
12:33 he came out with 3,000 infantry and 400 cavalry. 3

403 1. שָׁלֹשׁ וְאַרְבַּע מֵאוֹת
Gen 11:13 Arpach'shad lived after the birth . . 403 years 1
15 Shelah lived after the birth of Eber 403 years 1

420 1. אַרְבַּע מֵאוֹת וְעֶשְׂרִים
1Kg 9:28 gold, to the amount of 420 talents; 1

422 1. τετρακόσιοι εἴκοσι δύο
1Es 5:20 The Chadiasans and Ammidians, 422. 1

430 1. שְׁלֹשִׁים וְאַרְבַּע מֵאוֹת 2. τετρακόσιοι καὶ τριάκοντα
Gen 11:17 Eber lived after the birth of Peleg 430 years 1
Exd 12:40 time that the people . . dwelt in Egypt was 430 years. 1
41 at the end of 430 years, on that very day 1
Gal 3:17 the law, which came 430 years afterward 2

432 1. τετρακόσιοι τριάκοντα δύο
1Es 5:15 The sons of Azaru, 432 1

435 1. אַרְבַּע מֵאוֹת שְׁלֹשִׁים וְחָמֵשׁ 2. τετρακόσιοι τριάκοντα πέντε
Ezr 2:67 their camels were 435, and their asses were 6,720. 1
Neh 7:69 their camels 435, and their asses 6,720. 1
1Es 5:43 435 camels, and 7,036 horses 2

450 1. אַרְבַּע מֵאוֹת וַחֲמִשִּׁים 2. τετρακοσίοι πεντήκοντα
1Kg 18:19 send and gather . . and the 450 prophets of Ba'al 1
22 Ba'al's prophets are 450 men. 1
2Ch 8:18 fetched from there . . 450 talents of gold 1
Act 13:19 for about 450 years 2

454 1. אַרְבַּע מֵאוֹת חֲמִשִּׁים וְאַרְבָּעָה 2. τετρακόσιοι πεντήκοντα τέσσαρες
Ezr 2:15 sons of Adin, 454. 1
1Es 5:14 The sons of Bigvai, 2,066. The sons of Adin, 454 2

468 1. אַרְבַּע מֵאוֹת שִׁשִּׁים וּשְׁמֹנָה
Neh 11: 6 All the sons of Perez . . were 468 valiant men. 1

472 1. τετρακόσιοι ἑβδομήκοντα δύο
1Es 5: 9 The sons of Shephatiah, 472 1

480th 1. שְׁמוֹנִים וְאַרְבַּע מֵאוֹת
1Kg 6: 1 the 480th year after . . Israel came out of . . Egypt 1
490 *See* 70 times.

500 1. חֲמֵשׁ מֵאוֹת 2. πεντακόσιοι
Gen 5:32 After Noah was 500 years old 1
11:11 Shem lived after the birth . . 500 years 1
Exd 30:23 Take . . of liquid myrrh 500 shekels 1
24 of cassia 500, according to the shekel 1
Num31:28 one out of 500, of the persons and of the oxen 1
1Ch 4:42 some of them, 500 men of the Simeonites 1
2Ch 35: 9 for the passover offerings . . 500 bulls. 1
Est 9: 6 the Jews slew and destroyed 500 men 1
12 In Susa . . the Jews have slain 500 men 1
Job 1: 3 3,000 camels, 500 yoke of oxen 1
3 500 she-asses, and very many servants; 1
Ezk 42:16 500 cubits by the measuring reed. 1
17 500 cubits by the measuring reed. 1
17 500 cubits by the measuring reed. 1
18 500 cubits by the measuring reed. 1
18 500 cubits by the measuring reed. 1
19 500 cubits by the measuring reed. 1
19 500 cubits by the measuring reed. 1
20 It had a wall around it, 500 cubits long 1
20 It had a wall around it, 500 cubits long 1
20 cubits long and 500 cubits broad 1
20 cubits long and 500 cubits broad 1
45: 2 a square plot of 500 by 500 cubits 1
2 a square plot of 500 by 500 cubits 1
Lke 7:41 one owed 500 denarii, and the other 50. 2
1Co 15: 6 Then he appeared to more than 500 brethren 2
1Mc 6:35 500 picked horsemen 2
7:32 About 500 men of the army of Nicanor fell 2
15:31 or else give me for them 500 talents of silver 2
31 500 talents more 2
2Mc 12:10 not less than 5,000 Arabs with 500 horsemen 2
14:39 Nicanor . . sent more than 500 soldiers to arrest him; 2
3Mc 5: 2 all the elephants–500 in number 2

530 1. שְׁלֹשִׁים וַחֲמֵשׁ מֵאוֹת
Neh 7:70 governor gave . . 530 priests' garments. 1

550 1. חֲמִשִּׁים וַחֲמֵשׁ מֵאוֹת
1Kg 9:23 chief officers who were over Solomon's work: 550 1

595 1. חָמֵשׁ וְתִשְׁעִים וַחֲמֵשׁ מֵאוֹת
Gen 5:30 Lamech lived after the birth of Noah 595 years 1

600 1. שֵׁשׁ מֵאוֹת 2. ἑξακόσιοι
Gen 7: 6 Noah was 600 years old when the flood . . came 1
Exd 14: 7 and took 600 picked chariots 1
Jdg 3:31 Shamgar . . who killed 600 of the Philistines 1
18:11 600 men of the tribe of Dan, armed . . set forth 1
16 the 600 men . . stood by the entrance of the gate 1
17 with the 600 men armed with weapons of war 1
20:47 600 men turned and fled toward the wilderness 1
1Sm 13:15 people who were present with him, about 600 men. 1
14: 2 the people who were with him were about 600 men 1
17: 7 and his spear's head weighed 600 shekels of iron; 1
23:13 David and his men, who were about 600 1
27: 2 David . . and the 600 men who were with him 1
30: 9 David set out, and the 600 men who were with him 1
2Sm 15:18 all the 600 Gittites who had followed him 1
1Kg 10:16 600 shekels of gold went into each shield. 1
29 imported from Egypt for 600 shekels of silver 1
1Ch 21:25 David paid Ornan 600 shekels of gold by weight 1
2Ch 1:17 chariot . . for 600 shekels of silver 1
3: 8 he overlaid it with 600 talents of fine 1
9:15 600 shekels of . . gold went into each shield. 1
29:33 offerings were 600 bulls and 3,000 sheep 1
1Mc 6:42 600 men of the king's army fell. 2
2Mc 10:31 20,500 were slaughtered, besides 600 horsemen. 2

600th 1. שֵׁשׁ מֵאוֹת
Gen 7:11 In the 600th year of Noah's life 1

601st 1. אַחַת וְשֵׁשׁ מֵאוֹת
Gen 8:13 In the 601st year, in the first month 1

621 1. שֵׁשׁ מֵאוֹת עֶשְׂרִים וְאֶחָד 2. ἑξακόσιοι εἴκοσι εἷς
Ezr 2:26 sons of Ramah and Geba, 621. 1
Neh 7:30 men of Ramah and Geba, 621. 1
1Es 5:20 The men of Ramah and Geba, 621. 2

623 1. שֵׁשׁ מֵאוֹת עֶשְׂרִים וְשָׁלֹשׁ 2. ἑξακόσιοι εἴκοσι τρεῖς
Ezr 2:11 sons of Be'bai, 623. 1
1Es 5:13 The sons of Bebai, 623 The sons of Azgad, 1,322 2

628 1. שֵׁשׁ מֵאוֹת עֶשְׂרִים וּשְׁמֹנָה
Neh 7:16 sons of Be'bai, 628. 1

642 1. שֵׁשׁ מֵאוֹת אַרְבָּעִים וּשְׁנַיִם 2. שֵׁשׁ מֵאוֹת וְאַרְבָּעִים וּשְׁנָיִם
Ezr 2:10 sons of Bani, 642. 1
Neh 7:62 Delai'ah . . Tobi'ah, the sons of Neko'da, 642. 2

648 1. שֵׁשׁ מֵאוֹת אַרְבָּעִים וּשְׁמֹנָה 2. ἑξακόσιοι τεσσαράκοντα ὀκτώ
Neh 7:15 sons of Bin'nui, 648. 1
1Es 5:12 The sons of Chorbe, 705. The sons of Bani, 648. 2

650 1. שֵׁשׁ מֵאוֹת וַחֲמִשִּׁים 2. ἑξακόσιοι πεντήκοντα
Ezr 8:26 I weighed out . . 650 talents of silver 1
1Es 8:56 I weighed and gave to them 650 talents of silver 2

652 1. שֵׁשׁ מֵאוֹת חֲמִשִּׁים וּשְׁנָיִם 2. ἑξακόσιοι πεντήκοντα δύο
Ezr 2:60 sons of Delai'ah . . and the sons of Neko'da, 652. 1
Neh 7:10 sons of Arah, 652. 1
1Es 5:37 the son of Tobiah, the sons of Nekoda, 652. 2

655 1. שֵׁשׁ מֵאוֹת חֲמִשִּׁים וְחָמֵשׁ
Neh 7:20 sons of Adin, 655. 1

666 1. שֵׁשׁ מֵאוֹת וְשִׁשִּׁים וָשֵׁשׁ 2. שֵׁשׁ מֵאוֹת שִׁשִּׁים וָשֵׁשׁ 3. ἑξακόσιοι ἑξήκοντα ἕξ
1Kg 10:14 the weight of gold that came . . was 666 talents 2
2Ch 9:13 weight of gold . . was 666 talents of gold 2
Ezr 2:13 sons of Adoni'kam, 666. 2
Rev 13:18 the number of the beast . . its number is 666. 3

667 1. שֵׁשׁ מֵאוֹת שִׁשִּׁים וְשִׁבְעָה 2. ἑξακόσιοι ἑξήκοντα ἑπτά
Neh 7:18 sons of Adoni'kam, 667. 1
1Es 5:14 The sons of Adonikam, 667. 2

675 1. שֵׁשׁ מֵאוֹת חָמֵשׁ וְשִׁבְעִים
Num31:37 the LORD'S tribute of sheep was 675. 1

690 1. שֵׁשׁ מֵאוֹת וְתִשְׁעִים
1Ch 9: 6 Of the sons of Zerah: Jeu'el and their kinsmen, 690. 1

700 1. שְׁבַע מֵאוֹת 2. ἑπτακόσιοι
Jdg 20:15 Gib'e-ah, who mustered 700 picked men. 1
16 were 700 picked men who were left-handed 1
2Sm 10:18 David slew of the Syrians the men of 700 chariots 1
1Kg 11: 3 He had 700 wives, princesses 1
2Kg 3:26 he took with him 700 swordsmen to break through 1
2Ch 15:11 They sacrificed . . 700 oxen and 7,000 sheep. 1
1Es 1: 9 5,000 sheep and 700 calves. 2

705 1. ἑπτακόσιοι πέντε
1Es 5:12 The sons of Chorbe, 705. The sons of Bani, 648. 1

721 1. שְׁבַע מֵאוֹת וְעֶשְׂרִים וְאֶחָד
Neh 7:37 sons of Lod, Hadid, and Ono, 721. 1

725 1. שְׁבַע מֵאוֹת עֶשְׂרִים וְחָמֵשׁ 2. ἑπτακόσιοι εἴκοσι πέντε
Ezr 2:33 sons of Lod, Hadid, and Ono, 725. 1
1Es 5:22 The sons of the other Elam and Ono, 725. 2

730 1. שְׁבַע מֵאוֹת וּשְׁלֹשִׁים
Exd 38:24 gold . . 29 talents and 730 shekels 1

736 1. שְׁבַע מֵאוֹת שְׁלֹשִׁים שֵׁשׁ 2. שְׁבַע מֵאוֹת שְׁלֹשִׁים וְשֵׁשׁ
Ezr 2:66 Their horses were 736, their mules were 245 2
Neh 7:68 Their horses were 736, their mules 245 1

743 1. שְׁבַע מֵאוֹת אַרְבָּעִים וְשָׁלֹשׁ 2. שְׁבַע מֵאוֹת וְאַרְבָּעִים וְשָׁלֹשׁ 3. ἑπτακόσιοι τεσσαράκοντα τρεῖς
Ezr 2:25 sons of Kir'iathar'im . . and Be-er'oth, 743. 2
Neh 7:29 men of . . Chephi'rah, and Be-er'oth, 743 1
1Es 5:19 The men of Chephirah and Beeroth, 743 3

745 1. שְׁבַע מֵאוֹת אַרְבָּעִים וְחָמֵשׁ
Jer 52:30 carried away captive of the Jews 745 persons; 1

756 1. ἑπτακόσιοι πεντήκοντα ἕξ
1Es 5:10 The sons of Arah, 756 1

760 1. שְׁבַע מֵאוֹת וְשִׁשִּׁים
Ezr 2: 9 sons of Zac'cai, 760. 1
Neh 7:14 sons of Zac'cai, 760. 1

775 1. שְׁבַע מֵאוֹת חָמֵשׁ וְשִׁבְעִים
Ezr 2: 5 sons of Arah, 775. 1

777 1. שֶׁבַע וְשִׁבְעִים וּשְׁבַע מֵאוֹת
Gen 5:31 Thus all the days of Lamech were 777 years; 1

782 1. שְׁנַיִם וּשְׁמוֹנִים וּשְׁבַע מֵאוֹת
Gen 5:26 Methu'selah lived after the birth . . 782 years 1

800 1. שְׁמֹנֶה מֵאוֹת 2. ὀκτακοσίος
Gen 5: 4 The days of Adam . . were 800 years; 1
19 Jared lived after the birth of Enoch 800 years 1
2Sm 23: 8 he wielded his spear against 800 whom he slew 1
1Mc 3:24 800 of them fell 2
9: 6 until no more than 800 of them were left. 2

807 1. שֶׁבַע וּשְׁמֹנֶה מֵאוֹת
Gen 5: 7 Seth lived after the birth of Enosh 807 years 1

815 1. חָמֵשׁ עֶשְׂרֵה וּשְׁמֹנֶה מֵאוֹת
Gen 5:10 Enosh lived after the birth of Kenan 815 years 1

822 1. שְׁמֹנֶה מֵאוֹת עֶשְׂרִים וּשְׁנָיִם
Neh 11:12 their brethren who did the work of the house, 822; 1

830 1. שְׁלֹשִׁים וּשְׁמֹנֶה מֵאוֹת
Gen 5:16 Ma-hal'alel lived after the birth . . 830 years 1

832 1. שְׁמֹנֶה מֵאוֹת שְׁלֹשִׁים וּשְׁנָיִם
Jer 52:29 carried away captive from Jerusalem . . 832 persons; 1

840 1. אַרְבָּעִים וּשְׁמֹנֶה מֵאוֹת
Gen 5:13 lived after the birth of Ma-hal'alel 840 years 1

845 1. שְׁמֹנֶה מֵאוֹת אַרְבָּעִים וְחָמֵשׁ
Neh 7:13 sons of Zattu, 845. 1

895 1. חָמֵשׁ וְתִשְׁעִים וּשְׁמֹנֶה מֵאוֹת
Gen 5:17 Thus all the days of Ma-hal'alel were 895 years; 1

900 1. תְּשַׁע מֵאוֹת
Jdg 4: 3 he had 900 chariots of iron 1
13 called out all his chariots, 900 chariots of iron 1

905 1. חָמֵשׁ וּתְשַׁע מֵאוֹת
Gen 5:11 Thus all the days of Enosh were 905 years; 1

910 1. עֶשֶׂר וּתְשַׁע מֵאוֹת
Gen 5:14 Thus all the days of Kenan were 910 years; 1

912 1. שְׁתֵּים עֶשְׂרֵה וּתְשַׁע מֵאוֹת
Gen 5: 8 Thus all the days of Seth were 912 years; 1

928 1. תְּשַׁע מֵאוֹת עֶשְׂרִים וּשְׁמֹנָה
Neh 11: 8 after him Gabba'i, Salla'i, 928. 1

930 1. תְּשַׁע מֵאוֹת וּשְׁלֹשִׁים
Gen 5: 5 days . . Adam lived were 930 years; and he died. 1

945 1. תְּשַׁע מֵאוֹת וְאַרְבָּעִים וְחָמֵשׁ 2. ἐννακόσιοι τεσσαράκοντα πέντε
Ezr 2: 8 sons of Zattu, 945. 1
1Es 5:12 The sons of Elam, 1,254. The sons of Zattu, 945. 2

950 1. תְּשַׁע מֵאוֹת וַחֲמִשִּׁים
Gen 9:29 All the days of Noah were 950 years; 1

956 1. תְּשַׁע מֵאוֹת וַחֲמִשִּׁים וְשִׁשָּׁה
1Ch 9: 9 kinsmen according to their generations, 956 1

962 1. שְׁנַיִם וְשִׁשִּׁים וּתְשַׁע מֵאוֹת
Gen 5:20 Thus all the days of Jared were 962 years; 1

969 1. תֵּשַׁע וְשִׁשִּׁים וּתְשַׁע מֵאוֹת
Gen 5:27 Thus all the days of Methu'selah were 969 years; 1

972 1. ἐννακόσιοι ἑβδομήκοντα δύο
1Es 5:24 of the sons of Anasib, 972 1

973 1. תְּשַׁע מֵאוֹת שִׁבְעִים וְשָׁלֹשׁ
Ezr 2:36 sons of Jedai'ah, of the house of Jeshua, 973. 1
Neh 7:39 sons of Jedai'ah, namely the house of Jeshua, 973. 1

1,000 1. אֶלֶף 2. אֶלֶף אֶחָד 3. אֲלַף (A) 4. χιλιαρχία 5. χίλιοι 6. mille
Gen 20:16 I have given your brother 1,000 pieces of silver; 1
Num31: 4 send 1,000 from each of the tribes of Israel to the war 1
5 out of . . Israel, 1,000 from each tribe, 12,000 armed 1
6 Moses sent them to the war, 1,000 from each tribe 1
35: 4 wall of the city outward a 1,000 cubits all round. 1
Deu 1:11 the LORD . . make you a 1,000 times as many as you are 1
7: 9 God who keeps covenant . . to 1,000 generations 1
32:30 How should one chase 1,000, and two 1
Jos 23:10 One man of you puts to flight 1,000 1
Jdg 9:49 of Shechem also died, about 1,000 men and women. 1
15:15 jawbone of an ass . . and with it he slew 1,000 men. 1
16 with the jawbone of an ass have I slain 1,000 men 1
20:10 and a 100 of a 1,000, and a 1,000 of 10,000 1
10 and a 100 of a 1,000, and a 1,000 of 10,000 1
1Sm 13: 2 and 1,000 were with Jonathan in Gib'e-ah 1
17:18 ten cheeses to the commander of their 1,000. 1
18:13 and made him a commander of 1,000; 1
25: 2 he had 3,000 sheep and 1,000 goats. 1
2Sm 10: 6 hired . . the king of Ma'acah with 1,000 men 1
18:12 Even if I felt in my hand the weight of 1,000 1
19:17 and with him were 1,000 men from Benjamin. 1
1Kg 3: 4 Solomon used to offer 1,000 burnt offerings 1
2Kg 15:19 Men'aham gave Pul 1,000 talents of silver 1
24:16 and the craftsmen and the smiths, 1,000 1
1Ch 29:21 burnt offerings to the LORD, 1,000 bulls, 1,000 rams 1
21 burnt offerings to the LORD, 1,000 bulls, 1,000 rams 1
21 and 1,000 lambs, with their drink offerings 1
2Ch 1: 6 offered 1,000 burnt offerings upon it. 1
30:24 Hezeki'ah . . gave the assembly 1,000 bulls 1
24 princes gave the assembly 1,000 bulls and 10,000 1
Ezr 1: 9 number . . 1,000 basins of gold 5
Ps 50:10 is mine, the cattle on 1,000 hills. 1
84:10 thy courts is better than 1,000 elsewhere. 1
90: 4 1,000 years in thy sight are but as yesterday 1
91: 7 1,000 may fall at your side 1
105: 8 He is mindful . . for 1,000 generations 1
Ecc 6: 6 though he . . live 1,000 years twice told 1
Isa 7:23 every place where there used to be 1,000 vines 1
23 vines, worth 1,000 shekels of silver 1
30:17 1,000 shall flee at the threat of one 2
Ezk 47: 3 the man measured 1,000 cubits 1
4 Again he measured 1,000, and led me through 1
4 Again he measured 1,000, and led me through 1
5 Again he measured 1,000, and it was a river 1
Dan 5: 1 made a great feast for 1,000 of his lords 3
Ams 5: 3 The city that went forth 1,000 shall have 1
2Pe 3: 8 with the Lord one day is as a 1,000 years 5
8 and a 1,000 years as one day. 5
Rev 20: 2 seized the dragon . . and bound him for a 1,000 years 5
3 no more, till the 1,000 years were ended. 5
4 and reigned with Christ a 1,000 years. 5
5 until the 1,000 years were ended. 5
6 and they shall reign with him a 1,000 years. 5
7 And when the 1,000 years are ended 5
1Es 2:13 1,000 gold cups . . silver cups 5
13 1,000 gold cups, 1,000 silver cups 5
13 2,410 silver bowls, and 1,000 other vessels. 5
5: 2 Darius sent with them 1,000 horsemen 5
45 1,000 minas of gold, 5,000 minas of silver 5
2Es 6:51 to live in it, where there are 1,000 mountains; 6
Sir 6: 6 let your advisers be one in 1,000 5
16: 3 one is better than 1,000 5
39:11 he will leave a name greater than 1,000 5
41: 4 for ten or 100 or 1,000 years 5
12 longer than 1,000 great stores of gold. 5
1Mc 2:38 to the number of 1,000 persons. 5
4: 1 and 1,000 picked cavalry 5
5:13 and have destroyed about 1,000 men there. 4
6:35 with each elephant they stationed 1,000 men 5
9:49 about 1,000 of Bacchides' men fell that day. 5
10:79 had secretly left 1,000 cavalry behind them. 5
12:47 while 1,000 accompanied him. 5
14:24 a large gold shield weighing 1,000 minas 5
15:18 have brought a gold shield weighing 1,000 minas. 5
2Mc 5: 5 Jason took no less than 1,000 men 5
8:34 who had brought the 1,000 merchants to buy the Jews 5
1,000 *See also* thousands.

1,000 times 1. אֶלֶף
Job 9: 3 could not answer him once in 1,000 times. 1

1,005 1. חֲמֵשׁ וָאָלֶף
1Kg 4:32 and his songs were 1,005. 1

1,017 1. אֶלֶף וְשִׁבְעָה עָשָׂר 2. אֶלֶף שְׁבַע עֶשְׂרֵה 3. χίλιοι δέκα ἑπτά
Ezr 2:39 sons of Harim, 1,017. 1
Neh 7:42 sons of Harim, 1,017. 2
1Es 5:25 The sons of Harim, 1,017. 3

1,052 1. אֶלֶף חֲמִשִּׁים וּשְׁנָיִם 2. χίλιοι πεντήκοντα δύο
Ezr 2:37 sons of Immer, 1,052. 1
Neh 7:40 sons of Immer, 1,052. 1
1Es 5:24 The sons of Immer, 1,052. 2

1,100 1. אֶלֶף וּמֵאָה
Jdg 16: 5 we will each give you 1,100 pieces of silver. 1
17: 2 The 1,100 pieces of silver which were taken 1
3 he restored the 1,100 pieces of silver 1

1,200 1. אֶלֶף וּמָאתַיִם
2Ch 12: 3 with 1,200 chariots and 60,000 horsemen. 1

1,222 1. אֶלֶף מָאתַיִם עֶשְׂרִים וּשְׁנָיִם
Ezr 2:12 sons of Azgad, 1,222. 1

1,247 1. אֶלֶף מָאתַיִם אַרְבָּעִים וְשִׁבְעָה 2. χίλιοι διακόσιοι τεσσαράκοντα ἑπτά
Ezr 2:38 sons of Pashhur, 1,247. 1
Neh 7:41 sons of Pashhur, 1,247. 1
1Es 5:25 The sons of Pashhur, 1,247. 2

1,254 1. אֶלֶף מָאתַיִם חֲמִשִּׁים וְאַרְבָּעָה 2. χίλιοι διακόσιοι πεντήκοντα τέσσαρες
Ezr 2: 7 sons of Elam, 1,254. 1
31 sons of the other Elam, 1,254. 1
Neh 7:12 sons of Elam, 1,254. 1
34 sons of the other Elam, 1,254. 1
1Es 5:12 The sons of Elam, 1,254. The sons of Zattu, 945. 2

1,260 1. χιλίας διακοσίας ἑξήκοντα
Rev 11: 3 to prophesy for 1,260 days, clothed in sackcloth. 1
12: 6 to be nourished for 1,260 days. 1

1,290 1. אֶלֶף מָאתַיִם וְתִשְׁעִים
Dan 12:11 there shall be 1,290 days. 1

1,322 1. χίλιοι τριακόσιοι εἴκοσι δύο
1Es 5:13 The sons of Bebai, 623 The sons of Azgad, 1,322 1

1,335 1. אֶלֶף שְׁלֹשׁ מֵאוֹת שְׁלֹשִׁים וַחֲמִשָּׁה
Dan 12:12 he who waits and comes to the 1,335 days. 1

1,365 1. חֲמִשָּׁה וְשִׁשִּׁים וּשְׁלֹשׁ מֵאוֹת וָאֶלֶף
Num 3:50 took . . 1,365 shekels, reckoned by . . the sanctuary; 1

1,400 1. אֶלֶף וְאַרְבַּע מֵאוֹת
1Kg 10:26 he had 1,400 chariots and 12,000 horsemen 1
2Ch 1:14 he had 1,400 chariots 1

1,500 1. χίλιοι πρὸς πεντακοσίοις
2Mc 8:22 to command a division, putting 1,500 men under each. 1

1,600 1. ἑξακόσιοι πρὸς χιλίοις 2. χίλιοι ἑξακόσιοι
Rev 14:20 blood flowed . . for 1,600 stadia 2
2Mc 11:11 slew . . 1,600 horsemen 1

1,700 1. אֶלֶף וּשְׁבַע מֵאוֹת 2. אֶלֶף שְׁבַע מֵאוֹת
Jdg 8:26 the weight . . was 1,700 shekels of gold; 1
2Sm 8: 4 David took from him 1,700 horsemen 2
1Ch 26:30 Hashabi'ah and his brethren, 1,700 men of ability 1

1,760 1. אֶלֶף וּשְׁבַע מֵאוֹת וְשִׁשִּׁים
1Ch 9:13 kinsmen, heads of their fathers' houses, 1,760 1

1,775 1. אֶלֶף וּשְׁבַע הַמֵּאוֹת חָמֵשׁ וְשִׁבְעִים 2. אֶלֶף וּשְׁבַע מֵאוֹת וַחֲמִשָּׁה וְשִׁבְעִים
Exd 38:25 silver . . was 100 talents and 1,775 shekels 2
28 of the 1,775 shekels he made hooks 1

1,800 1. ὀκτακόσιοι πρὸς τοῖς χιλίοις
2Mc 5:21 Antiochus carried off 1,800 talents 1

2,000 1. אַלְפַּיִם 2. δισχίλιοι
Num35: 5 shall measure . . for the east side 2,000 cubits 1
5 shall measure . . for the south side 2,000 cubits 1
5 shall measure . . for the west side 2,000 cubits 1
5 shall measure . . for the north side 2,000 cubits 1
Jos 3: 4 shall be a space . . a distance of about 2,000 cubits; 1
7: 3 but let about 2,000 or 3,000 men go up 1
Jdg 20:45 to Gidom, and 2,000 men of them were slain. 1
1Sm 13: 2 2,000 were with Saul in Michmash 1

1Kg 7:26 it held 2,000 baths. 1
2Kg 18:23 I will give you 2,000 horses 1
1Ch 5:21 50,000 camels, 250,000 sheep, 2,000 asses 1
Neh 7:72 rest of the people gave . . 2,000 minas of silver 1
Isa 36: 8 I will give you 2,000 horses 1
Mrk 5:13 and the herd, numbering about 2,000 2
1Mc 5:60 as many as 2,000 of the people of Israel 2
9: 4 20,000 foot soldiers and 2,000 cavalry. 2
12:47 2,000 of whom he left in Galilee 2
15:26 Simon sent to Antiochus 2,000 picked men 2
16:10 about 2,000 of them fell 2
2Mc 8:10 tribute due to the Romans, 2,000 talents 2
12:43 to the amount of 2,000 drachmas of silver 2
13:15 slew as many as 2,000 men in the camp 2
3Mc 3:28 2,000 drachmas from the royal treasury 2

2,056 1. אַלְפַּיִם חֲמִשִּׁים וְשֵׁשׁ
Ezr 2:14 sons of Bigva'i, 2,056. 1

2,066 1. *δισχίλιοι ἑξήκοντα ἕξ*
1Es 5:14 The sons of Bigvai, 2,066. The sons of Adin, 454 1

2,067 1. אַלְפַּיִם שִׁשִּׁים וְשֶׁבַע
Neh 7:19 sons of Bigva'i, 2,067. 1

2,172 1. אַלְפַּיִם מֵאָה וְשִׁבְעִים וּשְׁנָיִם
2. אַלְפַּיִם מֵאָה שִׁבְעִים וּשְׁנָיִם
3. *δύο χιλιάδες ἑκατὸν ἑβδομήκοντα δύο*
Ezr 2: 3 sons of Parosh, 2,172. 2
Neh 7: 8 sons of Parosh, 2,172. 1
1Es 5: 9 the sons of Parosh, 2,172 3

2,200 1. אַלְפַּיִם וּמָאתָיִם
Neh 7:71 gave into the treasury . . 2,200 minas of silver. 1

2,300 1. אַלְפַּיִם וּשְׁלֹשׁ מֵאוֹת
Dan 8:14 said to him, "For 2,300 evenings and mornings; 1

2,322 1. אַלְפַּיִם שְׁלֹשׁ מֵאוֹת עֶשְׂרִים וּשְׁנָיִם
Neh 7:17 sons of Azgad, 2,322. 1

2,400 1. אַלְפַּיִם וְאַרְבַּע מֵאוֹת
Exd 38:29 the bronze . . was 70 talents, and 2,400 shekels; 1
Num 7:85 all the silver of the vessels 2,400 shekels 1

2,410 1. *δισχίλιοι τετρακόσιοι δέκα*
Ezr 1:10 30 bowls of gold, 2,410 bowls of silver 1
1Es 2:13 2,410 silver bowls, and 1,000 other vessels. 1

2,500 1. *δισχίλιοι πρὸς πεντακόσιοι*
2Mc 12:20 120,000 infantry and 2,500 cavalry. 1

2,600 1. אַלְפַּיִם וְשֵׁשׁ מֵאוֹת 2. *δισχίλιοι ἑξακοσίοι*
2Ch 26:12 whole number of the heads . . was 2,600. 1
35: 8 for the passover offerings 2,600 lambs and kids 1
1Es 1: 8 gave to the priests for the passover 2,600 sheep 2

2,630 1. אַלְפַּיִם וְשֵׁשׁ מֵאוֹת וּשְׁלֹשִׁים
Num 4:40 their number . . was 2,630. 1

2,700 1. אַלְפַּיִם וּשְׁבַע מֵאוֹת
1Ch 26:32 2,700 men of ability, heads of fathers' houses 1

2,750 1. אַלְפַּיִם שְׁבַע מֵאוֹת וַחֲמִשִּׁים
Num 4:36 their number by families was 2,750. 1

2,812 1. אַלְפַּיִם שְׁמֹנֶה מֵאוֹת וּשְׁנֵים עָשָׂר
2. *δισχίλιοι ὀκτακόσιοι δέκα δύο*
Ezr 2: 6 sons of Pa'hath-moab . . of Jeshua and Jo'ab, 2,812. 1
1Es 5:11 The sons of Pahathmoab . . 2,812 2

2,818 1. אַלְפַּיִם וּשְׁמֹנֶה מֵאוֹת שְׁמֹנָה עָשָׂרָה
Neh 7:11 sons of Pa'hath-mo'ab . . 2,818. 1

3,000 1. שְׁלֹשֶׁת אֲלָפִים 2. *τρισχίλιοι*
Exd 32:28 there fell of the people that day about 3,000 men. 1
Jos 7: 3 but let about 2,000 or 3,000 men go up 1
4 about 3,000 went up there from the people; 1
Jdg 15:11 Then 3,000 men of Judah went down to the cleft 1
16:27 on the roof there were about 3,000 men and women 1
1Sm 13: 2 Saul chose 3,000 men of Israel; 1
24: 2 Then Saul took 3,000 chosen men out of all Israel 1
25: 2 The man was very rich; he had 3,000 sheep 1
26: 2 Saul arose and . . with 3,000 chosen men of Israel 1
1Kg 4:32 He also uttered 3,000 proverbs; 1
1Ch 12:29 Of the Benjaminites, the kinsmen of Saul, 3,000 1
29: 4 3,000 talents of gold, of the gold of Ophir 1
2Ch 4: 5 it held over 3,000 baths. 1
25:13 killed 3,000 people in them, and took much spoil. 1
29:33 offerings were 600 bulls and 3,000 sheep 1
35: 7 Josi'ah contributed . . 3,000 bulls; 1
Job 1: 3 7,000 sheep, 3,000 camels 1
Act 2:41 there were added that day about 3,000 souls. 2
1Es 1: 7 30,000 lambs and kids, and 3,000 calves 2
2Es 10:45 it is because there were 3,000 years in the world ‡
46 after 3,000 years Solomon built the city ‡
1Mc 4: 6 Judas appeared in the plain with 3,000 men 2
15 3,000 of them fell. 2
5:20 Then 3,000 men were assigned to Simon 2
22 as many as 3,000 of the Gentiles fell 2
7:40 Judas encamped in Adasa with 3,000 men 2
9: 5 with him were 3,000 picked men. 2
10:77 he mustered 3,000 cavalry 2
11:44 So Jonathan sent 3,000 stalwart men 2
74 As many as 3,000 of the foreigners fell 2
12:47 He kept with himself 3,000 men 2
2Mc 12:33 he came out with 3,000 infantry and 400 cavalry. 2

3,000 men 1. *τρισχίλιοι*
2Mc 4:40 Lysimachus armed about 3,000 men 1

3,005 1. *τρισχίλιοι πέντε*
1Es 5:17 The sons of Baiterus, 3,005. 1

3,023 1. שְׁלֹשֶׁת אֲלָפִים וְעֶשְׂרִים וּשְׁלֹשָׁה
Jer 52:28 carried away captive . . 3,023 Jews; 1

3,200 1. שְׁלֹשֶׁת אֲלָפִים וּמָאתָיִם
Num 4:44 their number by families was 3,200. 1

3,300 1. שְׁלֹשֶׁת אֲלָפִים וּשְׁלֹשׁ מֵאוֹת
1Kg 5:16 besides Solomon's 3,300 chief officers 1

3,330 1. *τρισχίλιοι τριακόσιοι τριάκοντα*
1Es 5:23 The sons of Senaah, 3,330. 1

3,600 1. שְׁלֹשֶׁת אֲלָפִים וְשֵׁשׁ מֵאוֹת
2Ch 2: 2 assigned . . and 3,600 to oversee them. 1
18 assigned . . 3,600 as overseers 1

3,630 1. שְׁלֹשֶׁת אֲלָפִים וְשֵׁשׁ מֵאוֹת וּשְׁלֹשִׁים
Ezr 2:35 sons of Sena'ah, 3,630. 1

3,660 1. *τρισχίλιοι ἑξακοσίοι ἑξήκοντα*
4Mc 4:17 he would pay the king 3,660 talents annually. 1

3,700 1. שְׁלֹשֶׁת אֲלָפִים וּשְׁבַע מֵאוֹת
1Ch 12:27 Jehoi'ada, of the house of Aaron, and with him 3,700 1

3,930 1. שְׁלֹשֶׁת אֲלָפִים תְּשַׁע מֵאוֹת וּשְׁלֹשִׁים
Neh 7:38 sons of Sena'ah, 3,930. 1

4,000 1. אַרְבַּעַת אֲלָפִים 2. *τετρακισχίλιοι*
1Sm 4: 2 Philistines, who slew about 4,000 men 1
1Ch 23: 5 4,000 gatekeepers 1
5 4,000 shall offer praises to the LORD 1
2Ch 9:25 Solomon had 4,000 stalls for horses and chariots 1
Mat 15:38 Those who ate were 4,000 men 2
16:10 Or the seven loaves of the 4,000 2
Mrk 8: 9 there were about 4,000 people 2
20 And the seven for the 4,000 2
Act 21:38 and led the 4,000 men of the Assassins out 2
2Mc 8:20 with 4,000 Macedonians 2

4,500 1. חֲמֵשׁ מֵאוֹת וְאַרְבַּעַת אֲלָפִים
Ezk 48:16 its dimensions: the north side 4,500 cubits 1
16 the north side 4,500 cubits, the south side 4,500 1
16 the east side 4,500, and the west side 4,500. 1
16 the east side 4,500, and the west side 4,500. 1
30 north side, which is to be 4,500 cubits by measure 1
32 On the east side, which is to be 4,500 cubits 1
33 south side, which is to be 4,500 cubits by measure 1
34 On the west side, which is to be 4,500 cubits 1

4,600 1. אַרְבַּעַת אֲלָפִים וְשֵׁשׁ מֵאוֹת
1Ch 12:26 Of the Levites 4,600. 1
Jer 52:30 all the persons were 4,600. 1

5,000 1. חֲמֵשֶׁת אֲלָפִים 2. *πεντακισχίλιοι*
3. *πέντε χιλιάδες*
Jos 8:12 he took about 5,000 men, and set them in ambush 1
Jdg 20:45 5,000 men of them were cut down in the highways 1
1Sm 17: 5 weight of the coat was 5,000 shekels of bronze. 1
1Ch 29: 7 5,000 talents and 10,000 darics of gold 1
2Ch 35: 9 for the passover offerings 5,000 lambs and kids 1
Ezr 2:69 gave to . . the work . . gold, 5,000 minas of silver 1
Ezk 45: 6 of the city an area 5,000 cubits broad 1
48:15 5,000 cubits in breadth and 25,000 in length 1
Mat 14:21 those who ate were about 5,000 men 2
16: 9 remember the five loaves of the 5,000 2
Mrk 6:44 those who ate the loaves were 5,000 men. 2
8:19 I broke the five loaves for the 5,000 2
Lke 9:14 For there were about 5,000 men. 2
Joh 6:10 the men sat down, in number about 5,000. 2
Act 4: 4 the number of the men came to about 5,000 3
1Es 1: 9 gave the Levites for the passover 5,000 sheep 2
5:45 1,000 minas of gold, 5,000 minas of silver 2
Jdt 7:17 together with 5,000 Assyrians 3
1Mc 4: 1 Now Gorgias took 5,000 infantry 2
28 and 5,000 cavalry to subdue them. 2
34 there fell of the army of Lysias 5,000 men 2
10:42 Moreover, the 5,000 shekels of silver 2
2Mc 12:10 not less than 5,000 Arabs with 500 horsemen 2

5,300 1. *πεντακισχίλιοι τριακόσιοι*
2Mc 13: 2 5,300 cavalry, 22 elephants 1

5,469 1. *πεντακισχίλιοι τετρακόσιοι ἑξήκοντα ἐννέα*
Ezr 1:11 all the vessels of gold and of silver were 5,469. 1
1Es 2:14 All the vessels were handed over . . 5,469 1

5,525 1. *πεντακισχίλιοι πεντακόσιοι εἴκοσι πέντε*
1Es 5:43 245 mules, and 5,525 asses. 1

6,000 1. שֵׁשֶׁת אֲלָפִים 2. *ἑξακισχίλιοι*
1Sm 13: 5 30,000 chariots, 6,000 horsemen, and troops 1
2Kg 5: 5 taking with him . . silver, 6,000 shekels of gold 1
1Ch 23: 4 6,000 shall be officers and judges 1
Job 42:12 had 14,000 sheep, 6,000 camels, 1,000 yoke of oxen 1
2Mc 8:16 to the number 6,000 2

6,000 men 1. *ἑξακισχίλιοι*
2Mc 8: 1 so they gathered about 6,000 men. 1

6,200 1. שֵׁשֶׁת אֲלָפִים מָאתָיִם
Num 3:34 males from a month old and upward was 6,200. 1

6,720 1. שֵׁשֶׁת אֲלָפִים שְׁבַע מֵאוֹת וְעֶשְׂרִים
Ezr 2:67 their camels were 435, and their asses were 6,720. 1
Neh 7:69 their camels 435, and their asses 6,720. 1

6,800 1. שֵׁשֶׁת אֲלָפִים וּשְׁמוֹנֶה מֵאוֹת
1Ch 12:24 bearing shield and spear were 6,800 armed troops 1

7,000 1. שִׁבְעַת אֲלָפִים 2. *ἑπτακισχίλιοι*
3. *χιλιάδες ἑπτά*
1Kg 19:18 Yet I will leave 7,000 in Israel 1
20:15 he mustered all the people of Israel, 7,000. 1
2Kg 24:16 brought captive . . all the men of valor, 7,000 1
1Ch 18: 4 David took from him . . 7,000 horsemen 1
19:18 David slew of the Syrians the men of 7,000 chariots 1
29: 4 and 7,000 talents of refined silver 1
2Ch 15:11 They sacrificed . . 700 oxen and 7,000 sheep. 1
30:24 Hezeki'ah . . gave the assembly . . 7,000 sheep 1
Job 1: 3 He had 7,000 sheep 1
Rom 11: 4 I have kept for myself 7,000 men who have not bowed 2
Rev 11:13 7,000 people were killed in the earthquake 3
1Mc 3:39 and 7,000 cavalry 2

7,036 1. *ἑπτακισχίλιοι τριάκοντα ἕξ*
1Es 5:43 435 camels, and 7,036 horses 1

7,100 1. שִׁבְעַת אֲלָפִים וּמֵאָה
1Ch 12:25 the Simeonites, mighty men of valor for war, 7,100 1

7,337 1. שִׁבְעַת אֲלָפִים שְׁלֹשׁ מֵאוֹת שְׁלֹשִׁים וְשֶׁבַע
2. *ἑπτακισχίλιοι τριακόσιοι τριάκοντα ἑπτά*
Ezr 2:65 menservants and . . of whom there were 7,337; 1
Neh 7:67 menservants . . of whom there were 7,337; 1
1Es 5:42 their menservants..were 7,337 2

7,500 1. שִׁבְעַת אֲלָפִים וַחֲמֵשׁ מֵאוֹת
Num 3:22 all the males from a month old and upward was 7,500 1

7,700 1. שִׁבְעַת אֲלָפִים וּשְׁבַע מֵאוֹת
2Ch 17:11 Arabs also brought him 7,700 rams 1
11 Arabs also brought him . . 7,700 he-goats. 1

8,000 1. *ὀκτακισχίλιοι*
1Mc 5:20 and 8,000 to Judas for Gilead. 1
34 As many as 8,000 of them fell that day. 1
10:85 The number . . came to 8,0,000 men. 1
15:13 with him were 120,000 warriors and 8,000 cavalry. 1
2Mc 8:20 when 8,000 in all went into the affair 1
20 the 8,000 . . destroyed 120,000 1

8,580 1. שְׁמֹנַת אֲלָפִים וַחֲמֵשׁ מֵאוֹת וּשְׁמֹנִים
Num 4:48 those who were numbered of them were 8,580. 1

8,600 1. שְׁמֹנַת אֲלָפִים שֵׁשׁ מֵאוֹת
Num 3:28 males, from a month old and upward, there were 8,600 1

9,000 1. *ἐνακισχίλιοι*
2Mc 8:24 they slew more than 9,000 of the enemy 1
10:18 When no less than 9,000 took refuge 1

10,000 1. עֲשֶׂרֶת אֲלָפִים 2. רְבָבָה 3. רִבּוֹ 4. רִבּוֹ(A)
5. *δέκα χιλιάδες* 6. *δέκα χίλιοι* 7. *μυριάς* 8. *μύριοι*
9. *μυριότης*
Lev 26: 8 100 of you shall chase 10,000 2
Deu 32:30 How should . . two put 10,000 to flight 2
Jdg 1: 4 and they defeated 10,000 of them at Bezek. 1
3:29 killed at that time about 10,000 of the Moabites 1
4: 6 men . . taking 10,000 from the tribe of Naph'tali 1
10 and 10,000 men went up at his heels; 1
14 down from Mount Tabor with 10,000 men following 1
7: 3 tested them; 22,000 returned, and 10,000 remained 1
20:10 and a 100 of a 1,000, and a 1,000 of 10,000 2
34 there came against Gib'e-ah 10,000 picked men 1
1Sm 15: 4 200,000 men on foot, and 10,000 men of Judah. 1
2Sm 18: 3 But you are worth 10,000 of us; 1
1Kg 5:14 he sent them to Lebanon, 10,000 a month in relays; 1
2Kg 13: 7 an army of . . and ten chariots and 10,000 footmen; 1
14: 7 He killed 10,000 E'domites in the Valley of Salt 1
24:14 He carried away . . 10,000 captives 1

1Ch 29: 7 5,000 talents and 10,000 darics of gold 3
7 10,000 talents of silver, 18,000 talents of bronze 1
2Ch 25:11 to the Valley of Salt and smote 10,000 men of Se'ir. 1
12 The men of Judah captured another 10,000 alive 1
27: 5 gave him that year . . and 10,000 cors of wheat 1
5 gave him that year . . and 10,000 of barley. 1
30:24 princes gave the assembly . . 10,000 sheep. 1
Est 3: 9 I will pay 10,000 talents of silver 1
Ps 91: 7 fall at your side, 10,000 at your right hand; 2
Sng 5:10 and ruddy, distinguished among 10,000. 2
Ezk 45: 3 cubits long and 10,000 broad 1
5 cubits long and 10,000 cubits broad 1
48:10 10,000 cubits in breadth on the western side 1
10 10,000 in breadth on the eastern side 1
13 cubits in length and 10,000 in breadth. 1
18 holy portion shall be 10,000 cubits to the east 1
18 10,000 cubits to the east, and 10,000 to the west 1
Dan 7:10 10,000 times 10,000 stood before 4
10 10,000 times 10,000 stood before 4
Mat 18:24 one was brought to him who owed him 10,000 talents; 8
Lke 14:31 whether he is able with 10,000 to meet him 6
1Co 14:19 than 10,000 words in a tongue. 8
Rev 9:16 cavalry was twice 10,000 times 10,000 7
Wis 12:22 thou scourgest our enemies 10,000 times more 9
1Mc 4:29 Judas met them with 10,000 men. 5
10:74 He chose 10,000 men 5
2Mc 12:19 more than 10,000 men. 8

10,000 times 1. μυριοπλασίως
Sir 23:19 10,000 times brighter than the sun 1

twice 10,000 1. רִבֹּתַיִם 2. δισμυριάς
Ps 68:17 With mighty chariotry, twice 10,000 1
Rev 9:16 cavalry was twice 10,000 times 10,000 2

11,000 1. χίλιοι πρὸς μυρίοις
2Mc 11:11 slew 11,000 of them 1

12,000 1. שְׁנֵים עָשָׂר אֶלֶף 2. δώδεκα χιλιάδες 3. μυρίοι δισχιλίοι 4. χιλιάδες δέκα δύο
Num31: 5 Israel, 1,000 from each tribe, 12,000 armed for war 1
Jos 8:25 both men and women, were 12,000 1
Jdg 21:10 sent thither 12,000 of their bravest men 1
2Sm 10: 6 hired . . the men of Tob, 12,000 men. 1
17: 1 Let me choose 12,000 men 1
1Kg 4:26 Solomon also had . . 12,000 horsemen. 1
10:26 he had 1,400 chariots and 12,000 horsemen 1
2Ch 1:14 chariots and 12,000 horsemen 1
9:25 had . . horses and chariots, and 12,000 horsemen 1
Ps 60: 0 when Joab on his return killed 12,000 1
Rev 7: 5 12,000 sealed out of the tribe of Judah 2
5 12,000 of the tribe of Reuben 2
5 12,000 of the tribe of Gad 2
6 12,000 of the tribe of Asher 2
6 12,000 of the tribe of Naph'tali 2
6 12,000 of the tribe of Manas'seh 2
7 12,000 of the tribe of Simeon 2
7 12,000 of the tribe of Levi 2
7 12,000 of the tribe of Is'sachar 2
8 12,000 of the tribe of Zeb'ulun 2
8 12,000 of the tribe of Joseph 2
8 12,000 . . out of the tribe of Benjamin 2
21:16 he measured the city with his rod, 12,000 stadia; 2
Jdt 2: 5 120,000 foot soldiers and 12,000 cavalry. 4
15 together with 12,000 archers on horseback 3
7: 2 170,000 infantry and 12,000 cavalry 4

14,000 1. אַרְבָּעָה עָשָׂר אֶלֶף
Job 42:12 had 14,000 sheep, 6,000 camels, 1,000 yoke of oxen 1

14,700 1. אַרְבָּעָה עָשָׂר אֶלֶף וּשְׁבַע מֵאוֹת
Num16:49 Now those who died by the plague were 14,700 1

15,000 1. חֲמֵשֶׁת עָשָׂר אֶלֶף 2. δέκα πέντε χιλιάδες
Jdg 8:10 were in Karkor with their army, about 15,000 men 1
1Mc 10:40 I also grant 15,000 shekels of silver 2

16,000 1. שִׁשָּׁה עָשָׂר אֶלֶף
Num31:40 persons were 16,000, of which the LORD'S tribute 1
46 16,000 persons 1

16,750 1. שִׁשָּׁה עָשָׂר אֶלֶף שְׁבַע מֵאוֹת וַחֲמִשִּׁים
Num31:52 gold of the offering . . was 16,750 shekels. 1

17,200 1. שִׁבְעָה עָשָׂר אֶלֶף וּמָאתָיִם
1Ch 7:11 mighty warriors, 17,200, ready for service in war. 1

18,000 1. שְׁמֹנָה עָשָׂר אֶלֶף 2. רִבּוֹ וּשְׁמֹנַת אֲלָפִים
Jdg 20:25 and felled to the ground 18,000 men 2
44 18,000 men of Benjamin fell, all of them men 2
2Sm 8:13 When he returned, he slew 18,000 E'domites 2
1Ch 12:31 Of the half-tribe of Manas'seh 18,000 2
18:12 Abi'shai, the son of Zeru'iah, slew 18,000 E'domites 2
29: 7 10,000 talents of silver, 18,000 talents of bronze 1
Ezk 48:35 circumference of . . city shall be 18,000 cubits. 2

20,000 1. עֶשְׂרִים אֶלֶף 2. שְׁתֵּי רִבּוֹת 3. δισμύριοι 4. εἴκοσι χιλιάδες 5. ἔικοσι χιλιάδες
2Sm 8: 4 David took . . 20,000 foot soldiers; 1
10: 6 the Syrians of Zobah, 20,000 foot soldiers 1
18: 7 the slaughter there was great . . 20,000 men. 1
1Kg 5:11 Solomon gave Hiram 20,000 cors of wheat as food 1
11 Solomon gave . . and 20,000 cors of beaten oil. 5
1Ch 18: 4 David took from him . . 20,000 foot soldiers; 1
2Ch 2:10 20,000 cors of crushed wheat 1
10 crushed wheat, 20,000 cors of barley 1
10 cors of barley, 20,000 baths of wine 1
10 baths of wine, and 20,000 baths of oil. 1
Neh 7:71 gave into the treasury . . 20,000 darics of gold 2
72 rest of the people gave was 20,000 darics of gold 2
Ezk 45: 1 cubits long and 20,000 cubits broad; 1
48: 9 in length, and 20,000 in breadth. 1
13 cubits and the breadth 20,000. 1
Lke 14:31 who comes against him with 20,000? 4
1Mc 6:30 20,000 horsemen 4
9: 4 went to Berea with 20,000 foot soldiers 4
16: 4 20,000 warriors and horsemen 4
2Mc 8: 9 no fewer than 20,000 Gentiles of all nations 3
30 they killed more than 20,000 of them 3
10:17 killing no fewer than 20,000. 3
23 he destroyed more than 20,000 3

20,200 1. עֶשְׂרִים אֶלֶף וּמָאתָיִם
1Ch 7: 9 their enrollment by genealogies . . was 20,200 1

20,500 1. δισμύριοι πρὸς πεντακοσίοις
2Mc 10:31 20,500 were slaughtered, besides 600 horsemen. 1

20,800 1. עֶשְׂרִים אֶלֶף וּשְׁמֹנֶה מֵאוֹת
1Ch 12:30 Of the E'phraimites 20,800, mighty men of valor 1

22,000 1. עֶשְׂרִים וּשְׁנַיִם אֶלֶף 2. עֶשְׂרִים שְׁנַיִם אֶלֶף 3. שְׁנַיִם וְעֶשְׂרִים אֶלֶף 4. δισμύριοι πρὸς τοῖς δισχιλίοις
Num 3:39 the males from a month old and upward, were 22,000 3
Jdg 7: 3 Gideon tested them; 22,000 returned 1
20:21 felled to the ground on that day 22,000 men 3
2Sm 8: 5 David slew 22,000 men of the Syrians. 2
1Kg 8:63 Solomon offered . . 22,000 oxen 1
1Ch 18: 5 David slew 22,000 men of the Syrians. 1
2Ch 7: 5 offered as a sacrifice 22,000 oxen 1
2Mc 5:24 with an army of 22,000 4

22,034 1. עֶשְׂרִים וּשְׁנַיִם אֶלֶף וּשְׁלֹשִׁים וְאַרְבָּעָה
1Ch 7: 7 their enrollment by genealogies was 22,034. 1

22,200 1. שְׁנַיִם וְעֶשְׂרִים אֶלֶף וּמָאתָיִם
Num26:14 These are the families of the Simeonites, 22,200. 1

22,273 1. שְׁנַיִם וְעֶשְׂרִים אֶלֶף שְׁלֹשָׁה וְשִׁבְעִים וּמָאתָיִם
Num 3:43 all the first-born males . . were 22,273. 1

22,600 1. עֶשְׂרִים וּשְׁנַיִם אֶלֶף וְשֵׁשׁ מֵאוֹת
1Ch 7: 2 their number in the days of David being 22,600 1

23,000 1. שְׁלֹשָׁה וְעֶשְׂרִים אֶלֶף 2. εἴκοσι τρεῖς χιλιάδες
Num26:62 those numbered of them were 23,000 1
1Co 10: 8 and 23,000 fell in a single day. 2

24,000 1. עֶשְׂרִים וְאַרְבָּעָה אֶלֶף 2. אַרְבָּעָה וְעֶשְׂרִים אֶלֶף
Num25: 9 those that died by the plague were 24,000. 1
1Ch 23: 4 24,000 of these," David said, "shall have charge 2
27: 1 each division numbering 24,000 2
2 in his division were 24,000. 2
4 in his division were 24,000. 2
5 in his division were 24,000. 2
7 in his division were 24,000. 2
8 in his division were 24,000. 2
9 in his division were 24,000. 2
10 in his division were 24,000. 2
11 in his division were 24,000. 2
12 in his division were 24,000. 2
13 in his division were 24,000. 2
14 in his division were 24,000. 2
15 in his division were 24,000. 2

25,000 1. עֶשְׂרִים חֲמִשָּׁה אֶלֶף 2. חֲמִשָּׁה וְעֶשְׂרִים אֶלֶף 3. μυριάδες δύο πεντακισχίλιοι
Jdg 20:46 fell . . 25,000 men that drew the sword 2
Ezk 45: 1 holy district, 25,000 cubits long 1
3 a section 25,000 cubits long 1
5 Another section, 25,000 cubits 1
6 25,000 cubits long; 1
48: 8 25,000 cubits in breadth 1
9 be 25,000 cubits in length, 1
10 shall have an allotment measuring 25,000 cubits 1
10 and 25,000 in length on the southern side 1
13 Levites shall have an allotment 25,000 cubits 1
13 The whole length shall be 25,000 cubits 1
15 5,000 cubits in breadth and 25,000 in length 1
20 set apart shall be 25,000 cubits square 1
21 from the 25,000 cubits of the holy portion 1
21 from the 25,000 cubits to the west border 1
2Mc 12:26 slaughtered 25,000 people. 3
28 25,000 of those who were within it. 3

25,100 1. עֶשְׂרִים וַחֲמִשָּׁה אֶלֶף וּמֵאָה
Jdg 20:35 men of Israel destroyed 25,100 men of Benjamin 1

26,000 1. עֶשְׂרִים וְשִׁשָּׁה אֶלֶף
Jdg 20:15 mustered . . 26,000 men that drew the sword 1
1Ch 7:40 Their number . . for service in war, was 26,000 men. 1

27,000 1. עֶשְׂרִים וְשִׁבְעָה אֶלֶף
1Kg 20:30 the wall fell upon 27,000 men that were left. 1

28,600 1. עֶשְׂרִים וּשְׁמוֹנָה אֶלֶף וְשֵׁשׁ מֵאוֹת
1Ch 12:35 Of the Danites 28,600 men equipped for battle. 1

30,000 1. שְׁלֹשִׁים אֶלֶף 2. μυριάδες τρεῖς 3. τριάκοντα χιλιάδες
Jos 8: 3 and Joshua chose 30,000 mighty men of valor 1
1Sm 4:10 there fell of Israel 30,000 foot soldiers. 1
11: 8 and the men of Judah 30,000. 1
13: 5 Philistines mustered . . 30,000 chariots 1
2Sm 6: 1 all the chosen men of Israel, 30,000. 1
1Kg 5:13 the levy numbered 30,000 men. 1
2Ch 35: 7 lambs and kids . . to the number of 30,000 1
1Es 1: 7 gave to the people . . 30,000 lambs and kids 3
1Mc 10:36 to the number of 30,000 men 3
2Mc 12:23 and destroyed as many as 30,000 men. 2

30,500 1. שְׁלֹשִׁים אֶלֶף וַחֲמֵשׁ מֵאוֹת
Num31:39 asses were 30,500, of which the LORD'S tribute 1
45 30,500 asses 1

32,000 1. שְׁנַיִם וּשְׁלֹשִׁים אֶלֶף
Num31:35 32,000 persons in all, women who had not known man 1
1Ch 19: 7 They hired 32,000 chariots and the king of Ma'acah 1

32,200 1. שְׁנַיִם וּשְׁלֹשִׁים אֶלֶף וּמָאתָיִם
Num 1:35 the number of the tribe of Manas'seh was 32,200 1
2:21 his host as numbered being 32,200 1

32,500 1. שְׁנַיִם וּשְׁלֹשִׁים אֶלֶף וַחֲמֵשׁ מֵאוֹת
Num26:37 E'phraim according to their number, 32,500. 1

35,000 1. μυριάδες τρεῖς πεντακισχίλιοι
2Mc 15:27 they laid low no less than 35,000 men 1

35,400 1. חֲמִשָּׁה וּשְׁלֹשִׁים אֶלֶף וְאַרְבַּע מֵאוֹת
Num 1:37 the number of the tribe of Benjamin was 35,400 1
2:23 his host as numbered being 35,400 1

36,000 1. שְׁלֹשִׁים וְשִׁשָּׁה אֶלֶף 2. שִׁשָּׁה וּשְׁלֹשִׁים אֶלֶף
Num31:38 The cattle were 36,000, of which the LORD'S tribute 2
44 36,000 cattle 2
1Ch 7: 4 were units of the army for war, 36,000 1

37,000 1. שְׁלֹשִׁים וְשִׁבְעָה אֶלֶף
1Ch 12:34 1,000 commanders with whom were 37,000 men 1

38,000 1. שְׁלֹשִׁים וּשְׁמוֹנָה אֶלֶף
1Ch 23: 3 numbered, and the total was 38,000 men. 1

40,000 1. אַרְבָּעִים אֶלֶף 2. τεσσαράκοντα χιλιάδες 3. τέσσαρες μυριάδες
Jos 4:13 about 40,000 ready armed for war passed over 1
Jdg 5: 8 shield or spear to be seen among 40,000 in Israel? 1
2Sm 10:18 David slew of the Syrians . . 40,000 horsemen 1
1Kg 4:26 Solomon also had 40,000 stalls of horses 1
1Ch 12:36 Of Asher 40,000 seasoned troops ready for battle. 1
19:18 David slew of the Syrians . . 40,000 foot soldiers 1
1Mc 3:39 and sent with them 40,000 infantry 2
2Mc 5:14 40,000 in hand-to-hand fighting 3

40,500 1. אַרְבָּעִים אֶלֶף וַחֲמֵשׁ מֵאוֹת
Num 1:33 the number of the tribe of E'phraim was 40,500 1
2:19 his host as numbered being 40,500 1
26:18 sons of Gad according to their number, 40,500. 1

41,500 1. אֶחָד וְאַרְבָּעִים אֶלֶף וַחֲמֵשׁ מֵאוֹת
Num 1:41 the number of the tribe of Asher was 41,500 1
2:28 his host as numbered being 41,500 1

42,000 1. אַרְבָּעִים וּשְׁנַיִם אֶלֶף
Jdg 12: 6 there fell at that time 42,000 of the E'phraimites 1

42,360 1. אַרְבַּע רִבּוֹא אַלְפַּיִם שְׁלֹשׁ מֵאוֹת וְשִׁשִּׁים 2. אַרְבַּע רִבּוֹא אַלְפַּיִם שְׁלֹשׁ מֵאוֹת שִׁשִּׁים 3. μυριάδες τέσσαρες δισχίλιοι τριακόσιοι ἑξήκοντα
Ezr 2:64 whole assembly together was 42,360 2
Neh 7:66 The whole assembly together was 42,360 1
1Es 5:41 All . . were 42,360; 3

43,730 1. שְׁלֹשָׁה וְאַרְבָּעִים אֶלֶף וּשְׁבַע מֵאוֹת וּשְׁלֹשִׁים
Num26: 7 Reubenites; and their number was 43,730. 1

44,760 1. אַרְבָּעָה וְאַרְבָּעִים אֶלֶף וּשְׁבַע מֵאוֹת וְשִׁשִּׁים
1Ch 5:18 expert in war, 44,760, ready for service. 1

45,400 1. חֲמִשָּׁה וְאַרְבָּעִים אֶלֶף וְאַרְבַּע מֵאוֹת
Num26:50 Naph'tali . . their number was 45,400. 1

45,600 1. חֲמִשָּׁה וְאַרְבָּעִים אֶלֶף וְשֵׁשׁ מֵאוֹת
Num26:41 sons of Benjamin . . and their number was 45,600. 1

45,650 1. חֲמִשָּׁה וְאַרְבָּעִים אֶלֶף וְשֵׁשׁ מֵאוֹת וַחֲמִשִּׁים
Num 1:25 the number of the tribe of Gad was 45,650 1
2:15 his host as numbered being 45,650 1

46,500 1. שִׁשָּׁה וְאַרְבָּעִים אֶלֶף וַחֲמֵשׁ מֵאוֹת
Num 1:21 the number of the tribe of Reuben was 46,500 1
2:11 his host as numbered being 46,500. 1

50,000 1. חֲמִשִּׁים אֶלֶף 2. πέντε μυριάδες
1Ch 5:21 their livestock: 50,000 of their camels 1
12:33 Of Zeb'ulun 50,000 seasoned troops 1
Act 19:19 and found it came to 50,000 pieces of silver. 2

52,700 1. שְׁנַיִם וַחֲמִשִּׁים אֶלֶף וּשְׁבַע מֵאוֹת
Num26:34 Manas'seh; and their number was 52,700. 1

53,400 1. שְׁלֹשָׁה וַחֲמִשִּׁים אֶלֶף וְאַרְבַּע מֵאוֹת
Num 1:43 the number of the tribe of Naph'tali was 53,400 1
2:30 his host as numbered being 53,400 1
26:47 sons of Asher according to their number, 53,400. 1

54,400 1. אַרְבָּעָה וַחֲמִשִּׁים אֶלֶף וְאַרְבַּע מֵאוֹת
Num 1:29 the number of the tribe of Is'sachar was 54,400 1
2: 6 his host as numbered being 54,400. 1

57,400 1. שִׁבְעָה וַחֲמִשִּׁים אֶלֶף וְאַרְבַּע מֵאוֹת
Num 1:31 the number of the tribe of Zeb'ulun was 57,400 1
2: 8 his host as numbered being 57,400. 1

59,300 1. תִּשְׁעָה וַחֲמִשִּׁים אֶלֶף וּשְׁלֹשׁ מֵאוֹת
Num 1:23 the number of the tribe of Simeon was 59,300 1
2:13 his host as numbered being 59,300 1

60,000 1. שִׁשִּׁים אֶלֶף 2. ἑξήκοντα χιλιάδες
2Ch 12: 3 with 1,200 chariots and 60,000 horsemen. 1
1Mc 4:28 he mustered 60,000 picked infantrymen 2

60,500 1. שִׁשִּׁים אֶלֶף וַחֲמֵשׁ מֵאוֹת
Num26:27 Zeb'ulunites according to their number, 60,500. 1

61,000 1. שֵׁשׁ רִבּוֹא וָאָלֶף 2. אֶחָד וְשִׁשִּׁים אֶלֶף
Num31:34 61,000 asses 1
Ezr 2:69 gave to . . the work 61,000 darics of gold 2

62,700 1. שְׁנַיִם וְשִׁשִּׁים אֶלֶף וּשְׁבַע מֵאוֹת
Num 1:39 the number of the tribe of Dan was 62,700 1
2:26 his host as numbered being 62,700 1

64,300 1. אַרְבָּעָה וְשִׁשִּׁים אֶלֶף וּשְׁלֹשׁ מֵאוֹת
Num26:25 families of Is'sachar . . their number, 64,300. 1

64,400 1. אַרְבָּעָה וְשִׁשִּׁים אֶלֶף וְאַרְבַּע מֵאוֹת
Num26:43 according to their number, were 64,400. 1

70,000 1. שִׁבְעִים אֶלֶף 2. ἑπτάκις μυρίας
2Sm 24:15 died . . from Dan to Beer-sheba 70,000 men. 1
1Kg 5:15 Solomon also had 70,000 burden-bearers 1
1Ch 21:14 and there fell 70,000 men of Israel. 1
2Ch 2: 2 Solomon assigned 70,000 men 1
18 70,000 . . assigned to bear burdens 1
2Mc 10:20 on receiving 70,000 drachmas 2

72,000 1. שְׁנַיִם וְשִׁבְעִים אֶלֶף
Num31:33 72,000 cattle 1

74,600 1. אַרְבָּעָה וְשִׁבְעִים אֶלֶף וְשֵׁשׁ מֵאוֹת
Num 1:27 the number of the tribe of Judah was 74,600 1
2: 4 his host as numbered being 74,600 1

75,000 1. חֲמִשָּׁה וְשִׁבְעִים אֶלֶף
Est 9:16 slew 75,000 of those who hated them 1

76,500 1. שִׁשָּׁה וְשִׁבְעִים אֶלֶף וַחֲמֵשׁ מֵאוֹת
Num26:22 families of Judah . . their number, 76,500. 1

80,000 1. שְׁמֹנִים אֶלֶף 2. ὀκτὼ μυριάδες
1Kg 5:15 Solomon also had . . and 80,000 hewers of stone 1
2Ch 2: 2 assigned . . and 80,000 to quarry 1
18 80,000 to quarry in the hill country 1
2Mc 5:14 80,000 were destroyed 2
11: 2 gathered about 80,000 men and all his cavalry 2

87,000 1. שְׁמוֹנִים וְשִׁבְעָה אֶלֶף
1Ch 7: 5 of Is'sachar were in all 87,000 mighty warriors 1

100,000 1. מֵאָה אֶלֶף 2. ἑκατὸν χιλιάδες
3. μυριάδες δέκα
1Kg 20:29 Israel smote of the Syrians 100,000 foot soldiers 1
2Kg 3: 4 Moab . . had to deliver . . 100,000 lambs 1
4 had to deliver . . and the wool of 100,000 rams. 1
1Ch 5:21 They carried off . . 100,000 men alive. 1
22:14 for the house of the LORD 100,000 talents of gold 1
29: 7 bronze, and 100,000 talents of iron. 1
2Ch 25: 6 hired . . 100,000 mighty men of valor from Israel 1
1Mc 6:30 100,000 foot soldiers 2
11:47 they killed . . as many as 100,000 men. 3

108,100 1. אֶלֶף וּשְׁמֹנַת אֲלָפִים וּמֵאָה
Num 2:24 camp of E'phraim, by their companies, is a 108,100 1

110,000 1. μυριάδες ἕνδεκα
2Mc 13: 2 Each of them had a Greek force of 110,000 infantry 1

120,000 1. שְׁתֵּים עֶשְׂרֵה רִבּוֹ 2. מֵאָה וְעֶשְׂרִים אֶלֶף
3. δώδεκα μυριάδες 4. μυριάδες δέκα δύο
5. μυριάδες δώδεκα 6. χιλιάδες ἑκατὸν εἴκοσι
Jdg 8:10 there had fallen 120,000 men who drew the sword. 1
1Kg 8:63 Solomon offered . . and 120,000 sheep. 1
1Ch 12:37 120,000 men armed with all the weapons of war. 1
2Ch 7: 5 as a sacrifice . . 120,000 sheep. 1
28: 6 Pekah the son of Remali'ah slew 120,000 in Judah 1
Jon 4:11 city, in which there are more than 120,000 persons 2
Jdt 2: 5 120,000 foot soldiers and 12,000 cavalry. 6
15 120,000 of them 4
1Mc 11:45 to the number of 120,000 3
15:13 with him were 120,000 warriors and 8,000 cavalry. 3
2Mc 8:20 destroyed 120,000 and took much booty. 3
12:20 120,000 infantry and 2,500 cavalry. 5

144,000 1. ἑκατὸν τεσσεράκοντα τέσσαρες χιλιάδες
Rev 7: 4 144,000 sealed, out of every tribe 1
14: 1 stood the Lamb, and with him a 144,000 1
3 144,000 who had been redeemed from the earth. 1

151,450 1. מְאַת אֶלֶף וְאֶחָד וַחֲמִשִּׁים אֶלֶף וְאַרְבַּע מֵאוֹת וַחֲמִשִּׁים
Num 2:16 camp of Reuben, by their companies, is 151,450 1

153,600 1. מֵאָה וַחֲמִשִּׁים אֶלֶף וּשְׁלֹשֶׁת אֲלָפִים וְשֵׁשׁ מֵאוֹת
2Ch 2:17 and there were found 153,600. 1

157,600 1. מְאַת אֶלֶף וְשִׁבְעָה וַחֲמִשִּׁים אֶלֶף וְשֵׁשׁ מֵאוֹת
Num 2:31 The whole number of the camp of Dan is 157,600 1

170,000 1. χιλιάδες ἑκατὸν ἑβδομήκοντα
Jdt 7: 2 their force of men of war was 170,000 infantry 1

180,000 1. מֵאָה וּשְׁמֹנִים אֶלֶף
1Kg 12:21 he assembled . . 180,000 chosen warriors 1
2Ch 11: 1 180,000 chosen warriors, to fight against Israel 1
17:18 Jeho'zabad with a 180,000 armed for war. 1

185,000 1. מֵאָה וּשְׁמֹנִים וַחֲמִשָּׁה אֶלֶף
2. מֵאָה שְׁמֹנִים וַחֲמִשָּׁה אֶלֶף
3. ἑκατὸν ὀγδοήκοντα πέντε χιλιάδες
2Kg 19:35 slew 185,000 in the camp of the Assyrians; 2
Isa 37:36 and slew 185,000 in the camp 1
1Mc 7:41 thy angel . . struck down 185,000 of the Assyrians. 3
2Mc 8:19 when 185,000 perished 3
15:22 he slew fully 185,000 3

186,400 1. מְאַת אֶלֶף וּשְׁמֹנִים אֶלֶף וְשֵׁשֶׁת אֲלָפִים וְאַרְבַּע מֵאוֹת
Num 2: 9 the camp of Judah, by their companies, is 186,400 1

200,000 1. מָאתַיִם אֶלֶף
1Sm 15: 4 numbered them . . 200,000 men on foot 1
2Ch 17:16 Amasi'ah . . with 200,000 mighty men of valor. 1
17 with 200,000 men armed with bow and shield 1
28: 8 took captive 200,000 of their kinsfolk, women, sons 1

250,000 1. מָאתַיִם וַחֲמִשִּׁים אֶלֶף
1Ch 5:21 50,000 camels, 250,000 sheep, 2,000 asses 1

280,000 1. מָאתַיִם וּשְׁמֹנִים אֶלֶף
2Ch 14: 8 280,000 men from Benjamin,that carried shields 1
17:15 next to him Jehoha'nan the commander, with 280,000 1

300,000 1. שְׁלֹשׁ מֵאוֹת אֶלֶף
1Sm 11: 8 the men of Israel were 300,000 1
2Ch 14: 8 Asa had an army of 300,000 from Judah 1
17:14 Adnah . . with 300,000 mighty men of valor 1
25: 5 found that they were 300,000 picked men 1

307,500 1. שְׁלֹשׁ מֵאוֹת אֶלֶף וְשִׁבְעַת אֲלָפִים וַחֲמֵשׁ מֵאוֹת
2Ch 26:13 Under their command was an army of 307,500 1

337,500 1. שְׁלֹשׁ מֵאוֹת אֶלֶף וּשְׁלֹשִׁים אֶלֶף שִׁבְעַת אֲלָפִים וַחֲמֵשׁ מֵאוֹת
2. שְׁלֹשׁ מֵאוֹת אֶלֶף וּשְׁלֹשִׁים אֶלֶף וְשִׁבְעַת אֲלָפִים וַחֲמֵשׁ מֵאוֹת
Num31:36 the half . . was in number 337,500 sheep 2
43 now the congregation's half was 337,500 sheep 1

400,000 1. אַרְבַּע מֵאוֹת אֶלֶף
Jdg 20: 2 of God, 400,000 men on foot that drew the sword. 1
17 Israel . . mustered 400,000 men that drew sword 1
2Ch 13: 3 army of valiant men of war, 400,000 picked men; 1

470,000 1. אַרְבַּע מֵאוֹת וְשִׁבְעִים אֶלֶף
1Ch 21: 5 and in Judah 470,000 who drew the sword. 1

500,000 1. חֲמֵשׁ מֵאוֹת אֶלֶף
2Sm 24: 9 and the men of Judah were 500,000. 1
2Ch 13:17 there fell slain of Israel 500,000 picked men. 1

600,000 1. שֵׁשׁ מֵאוֹת אֶלֶף 2. ἑξακοσίοι χιλιάδες
Exd 12:37 about 600,000 men on foot, besides women 1
Num11:21 The people among whom I am number 600,000 on foot; 1
Sir 16:10 nor for the 600,000 men on foot 2
46: 8 out of 600,000 people on foot 2

601,730 1. שֵׁשׁ מֵאוֹת אֶלֶף וָאֶלֶף שְׁבַע מֵאוֹת וּשְׁלֹשִׁים
Num26:51 number of the people of Israel, 601,730. 1

603,550 1. שֵׁשׁ מֵאוֹת אֶלֶף וּשְׁלֹשֶׁת אֲלָפִים וַחֲמֵשׁ מֵאוֹת וַחֲמִשִּׁים
Exd 38:26 from twenty years old and upward, 603,550 men. 1
Num 1:46 their whole number was 603,550. 1
2:32 all . . numbered by their companies were 603,550 1

675,000 1. שֵׁשׁ מֵאוֹת אֶלֶף וְשִׁבְעִים אֶלֶף וַחֲמֵשֶׁת אֲלָפִים
Num31:32 booty remaining of the spoil . . 675,000 sheep 1

800,000 1. שְׁמֹנֶה מֵאוֹת אֶלֶף
2Sm 24: 9 in Israel there were 800,000 valiant men 1
2Ch 13: 3 with 800,000 picked mighty warriors. 1

1,000,000 1. אֶלֶף אֲלָפִים
1Ch 22:14 house of the LORD . . 1,000,000 talents of silver 1
2Ch 14: 9 with an army of 1,000,000 men and 300 chariots 1

1,100,000 1. אֶלֶף אֲלָפִים וּמֵאָה אֶלֶף
1Ch 21: 5 Israel there were 1,100,000 men who drew the sword 1

Indexes

Hebrew

אָב, ancestor, ancestral, family, father, *father's* house, patrimony
אָב רִאשׁוֹן, forefather
אֵב, blossom, flower
אֶבְיָסָף, Ebiasaph
אֲבַגְתָא, Abagtha
אבד, annihilate, banish, break, bring *ruin*, *cause to* perish, come *to nought*, corrupt, destroy, destruction, drive *out*, fail, go, lose, *make* perish, *no* remain, perish, ruin, squander, still, undo, vanish, void, wander, wipe *out*
אֲבֵדָה, lose, lost *thing*
אֲבַדּוֹן, Abaddon
אַבְדָן, destroy, destruction
אבה, appease, consent, will, willing, yield
אֵבֶה, reed
אֲבוֹי, sorrow
אֵבוּס, crib
אִבְחָה, glitter
אֲבַטִּחִים, melon
אֲבִי אָב, grandfather
אֲבִי הָעֶזְרִי, Abiezrite
אֲבִי עַלְבוֹן, Abi-albon
אֲבִיאֵל, Abiel
אֲבִיאָסָף, Abiasaph
אָבִיב, Abib, ear, *fresh* ear
אֲבִיגַיִל, Abigail
אֲבִיגַל, Abigail, Abigal
אֲבִידָן, Abidan
אֲבִידָע, Abida
אֲבִיָּהוּ, Abi, Abijah
אֲבִיהוּא, Abihu
אֲבִיהוּד, Abihud
אֶבְיוֹן, needy, poor, poor *man*
אֲבִיּוֹנָה, desire
אֲבִיחַיִל, Abihail
אֲבִיטוּב, Abitub
אֲבִיטַל, Abital
אֲבִיָּם, Abijam
אֲבִימָאֵל, Abimael
אֲבִימֶלֶךְ, Abimelech
אֲבִינָדָב, Abinadab
אֲבִינֹעַם, Abinoam
אֲבִינֵר, Abner
אֲבִיעַד, *everlasting* father
אֲבִיעֶזֶר, Abiezer, Abiezrite
אַבִּיר, angel, bull, chief, mighty, *mighty* bull, mighty *man*, stallion, steed, strong, stubborn
אַבִּיר לֵב, stouthearted
אָבִיר, mighty *one*
אֲבִירָם, Abiram
אֲבִישַׁג, Abishag
אֲבִישׁוּעַ, Abishua
אֲבִישׁוּר, Abishur
אֲבִישַׁי, Abishai
אֲבִישָׁלוֹם, Abishalom, Absalom
אֶבְיָתָר, Abiathar
אבך, roll *upward*
אבל, *cause to* lament, grieve, lament, *make* mourn, mourn, pretend *to be a mourner*
אָבֵל, Abel, lament, mourn, mourner
אָבֵל בֵּית מַעֲכָה, Abel-beth-maacah
אָבֵל הַשִּׁטִּים, Abel-shittim
אָבֵל כְּרָמִים, Abel-keramim
אָבֵל מְחוֹלָה, Abel-meholah
אָבֵל מַיִם, Abel-maim
אָבֵל מִצְרַיִם, Abel-mizraim
אֲבָל, alas, nevertheless, no, truth, well
אֵבֶל, mourn, mourner
אֶבֶן, jewel, ore, plummet, rock, stone, stony, vessel *of stone*, weight
אֶבֶן אֶלְגָּבִישׁ, hailstone
אֶבֶן אֶקְדָּח, carbuncle
אֶבֶן בְּדִיל, plummet
אֶבֶן בָּרָד, hailstone
אֶבֶן גִּר, chalkstone
אֶבֶן הָעֵזֶר, Eben-ezer
אֶבֶן סַפִּיר, sapphire
אֶבֶן פּוּךְ, antimony
אֶבֶן פִּנָּה, cornerstone
אֶבֶן קֶלַע, slingstone
אֶבֶן שֹׁהַם, onyx
אֶבֶן שֵׁשׁ, marble
אֶבֶן תַּרְשִׁישׁ, chrysolite
אֹבֶן, birthstool, wheel
אֲבָנָה, Abana
אַבְנֵט, girdle
אבס, fatted
אֲבַעְבֻּעֹת, sore
אֶבֶץ, Ebez
אִבְצָן, Ibzan
אבק, wrestle
אָבָק, dust, *fine* dust, powder
אֲבָקָה, *fragrant* powder
אבר, soar
אֵבֶר, pinion, wing
אֶבְרָה, pinion
אַבְרָהָם, Abraham
אַבְרֵךְ, bow *the knee*
אַבְרָם, Abram
אֹבֹת, Oboth
אָגֵא, Agee
אֲגָג, Agag
אֲגָגִי, Agagite
אֲגֻדָּה, band, bunch, thong, vault
אֱגוֹז, nut
אָגוּר, Agur
אֲגוֹרָה, piece
אֵגֶל, drop
אֶגְלַיִם, Eglaim
אגם, grieve
אֲגַם, bulwark, pond, pool
אַגְמוֹן, reed, rope, rush
אַגָּן, basin, bowl
אֲגַף, horde, troop
אגר, gather
אֲגַרְטָל, basin
אֶגְרֹף, fist
אִגֶּרֶת, letter
אֵד, mist
אדב, grieve
אַדְבְּאֵל, Adbeel
אִדּוֹ, Iddo
אֱדוֹם, Edom, Edomite
אַדּוֹן, Addon
אָדוֹן, husband, lord, LORD, Lord, master, owner
אָדוֹן, sir
אֲדוֹנָי, God, Lord
אֲדוֹרַיִם, Adoraim
אֹדוֹת, account
אַדִּיר, famous, glorious, lord, lordly, majestic, majesty, mighty, noble, officer, prince, stately
אֲדַלְיָא, Adalia
אדם, red, ruddy, tan
אָדָם, Adam, any *one*, human, man, mankind, ordinary *man*, person, some *one*
אָדֹם, red, *red* pottage, ruddy
אֹדֶם, carnelian, sardius
אֲדַמְדָּם, reddish
אַדְמָה, Admah
אֲדָמָה, Adamah, country, earth, ground, land, soil
אַדְמוֹנִי, red, ruddy
אֲדָמִי הַנֶּקֶב, Adami-nekeb
אֲדֹמִי, Edomite
אֲדֻמִּים, Adummim
אַדְמָתָא, Admatha
אַדָּן, Addan
אֶדֶן, base, socket
אֲדֹנָי, LORD, Lord
אֲדֹנִי בֶזֶק, Adoni-bezek
אֲדֹנִי צֶדֶק, Adoni-zedek
אֲדֹנִיָּהוּ, Adonijah
אֲדֹנִיקָם, Adonikam
אֲדֹנִירָם, Adoniram
אדר, glorious, majestic, make *glorious*
אַדָּר, Addar
אֶדֶר, lordly, robe
אֲדָר, Adar
אֲדֹרָם, Adoram
אַדְרַמֶּלֶךְ, Adrammelech
אֶדְרֶעִי, Edrei
אַדֶּרֶת, glory, mantle, robe
אהב, beloved, covet, friend, like, love, lover, take *pleasure*
אַהַב, lovely, lover
אֹהַב, love, loved *thing*
אַהֲבָה, love, loved *one*, lover, lovingly
אֹהַד, Ohad
אֲהָהּ, ah, alas
אַהֲוָא, Ahava
אֵהוּד, Ehud
אהל, bright, move *tent*, pitch *a tent*
אֹהֶל, home, Ohel, tent
אָהֳלָה, Oholah
אֲהָלוֹת, aloe
אָהֳלִיאָב, Oholiab
אָהֳלִיבָה, Oholibah
אָהֳלִיבָמָה, Oholibamah
אַהֲרֹן, Aaron, *house of* Aaron
אוֹ, either, else, if, nor, *other* hand, whether
אוּאֵל, Uel
אוֹב, ghost, medium, spirit, wineskin
אוֹבִיל, Obil
אוּבָל, river
אוּד, brand, firebrand
אוֹדָה, account, sake
אוה, covet, crave, desire, longingly, *strong* craving, *wanton* craving, wish, yearn
אוּזַי, Uzai
אוּזָל, Uzal
אוֹי, alas, woe
אֱוִי, Evi
אוֹיָה, woe
אֱוִיל, fool, foolish
אֱוִיל מְרֹדַךְ, Evil-merodach
אוּל, body
אֱוִלִי, worthless
אוּלַי, if, perhaps, suppose, yet
אוּלַי, Ulai
אוּלָם, hall, nevertheless, now, porch, surely, truly, Ulam, vestibule
אִוֶּלֶת, folly, fool, foolishly, foolishness
אוֹמָר, Omar
אָוֶן, affliction, Aven, calamity, crime, delusion, evil, godless, idol, ill, iniquitous, iniquity, mischief, misfortune, mourn, mourner, nonsense, nought, trouble, unrighteous, wicked, wickedness, wrong
אוֹן, manhood, might, power, strength, strong, wealth
אוֹנוֹ, Ono
אוֹנָם, Onam
אוֹנָן, Onan
אוּפָז, Uphaz
אוֹפִיר, Ophir
אוֹפָן, wheel
אוץ, hasten, hasty, labor, make *haste*, narrow, press, urge, urgent
אוֹצָר, armory, cellar, store, storehouse, treasure, treasury
אור, *become* bright, bright, brighten, *cause to* shine, day *break*, enlighten, give *light*, glorious, kindle *fire*, light, light *up*, lighten, make *a fire*, *make* shine, shine
אוֹר, bright, dawn, *early* morning, light, lightning, shine, sunshine
אוֹר הַבֹּקֶר, morning
אוּר, fire, Ur
אוֹרָה, herb, light
אוּרִי, Uri
אוּרִיאֵל, Uriel
אוּרִיָּה, Uriah

אוּרִיָּהוּ, Uriah
אוּרִים, Urim
אות, agree, consent
אַוַּת נֶפֶשׁ, heat
אוֹת, ensign, mark, omen, sign, testimony
אָז, after, early, now, old, past, *that* time, then, time, yet
אֶזְבַּי, Ezbai
אֵזוֹב, hyssop
אֵזוֹר, belt, girdle, waistcloth
אַזְכָּרָה, *memorial* portion
אזל, fail, gad *about*, go, go *away*
אזן, give *ear*, give *heed*, hear, hearken, listen, perceive *by ear*, weigh
אָזֵן, weapon
אֹזֶן, ear, hear
אֻזֵּן שֶׁאֱרָה, Uzzen-sheerah
אַזְנוֹת תָּבוֹר, Aznoth-tabor
אָזְנִי, Ozni, Oznite
אֲזַנְיָהוּ, Azaniah
אָזִק, chain
אזר, bind *about*, gird, gird *up*
אֶזְרָח, homeborn, native, native-born
אֶזְרָחִי, Ezrahite
אָח, ah, alas, another, brazier, brother, brotherhood, companion, family, fellow, kinsfolk, kinsman, other, people
אָח לֵוִי, *fellow* Levite
אֹחַ, *howling* creature
אַחְאָב, Ahab
אַחְבָּן, Ahban
אחד, cut *sharply*
אַחַד עָשָׂר, eleven, eleventh
אֶחָד, alone, another, any, any *one*, *any* other, apiece, certain, continuous, darling, each, every, every *one*, fellow, few, first, man, once, once *for all*, one, one *man*, one *thing*, one *way*, other, person, same, single, some, some *other*, such *and such*
אֶחָד אֶל אֶחָד, together
אֶחָד לַכֹּל, same
אָחוּ, reed, *reed* grass
אֵהוּד, Ehud
אַחֲוָה, brotherhood, declaration
אֲחוֹחַ, Ahoah
אֲחוֹחִי, Ahohi, Ahohite
אֲחוּמַי, Ahumai
אָחוֹר, away, back, backward, behind, hinder *part*, rear, time *to come*, west
אָחוֹת, another, other, sister
אחז, attach, bar, catch, catch *up*, choose, cover, draw, gain *possessions*, get *property*, girt, handle, hold, hold *fast*, hold *out*, insert, join, lay *hold*, look, possess, possession, seize, support, take, take *a possession*, take *hold*
אָחָז, Ahaz
אֲחֻזָּה, holding, inherit, inheritance, possess, possession, possession *by inheritance*, property
אֲחַזְיָהוּ, Ahaziah, Ahzai
אֲחֻזָּם, Ahuzzam
אֲחֻזַּת, Ahuzzath
אֵחִי, Ehi
אֲחִיאָם, Ahiam
אֲחִיָּהוּ, Ahi, Ahiah, Ahijah
אֲחִיהוּד, Ahihud
אַחְיוֹ, Ahio
אֲחִיחוּד, Ahihud
אֲחִיטוּב, Ahitub
אֲחִילוּד, Ahilud
אֲחִימוֹת, Ahimoth
אֲחִימֶלֶךְ, Ahimelech
אֲחִימַן, Ahiman
אֲחִימַעַץ, Ahimaaz
אַחְיָן, Ahian
אֲחִינָדָב, Ahinadab
אֲחִינֹעַם, Ahinoam
אֲחִיסָמָךְ, Ahisamach
אֲחִיעֶזֶר, Ahiezer
אֲחִיקָם, Ahikam
אֲחִירָם, Ahiram
אֲחִירָמִי, Ahiramite
אֲחִירַע, Ahira
אֲחִישַׁחַר, Ahishahar
אֲחִישָׁר, Ahishar
אֲחִיתֹפֶל, Ahithophel
אַחְלָב, Ahlab
אַחֲלַי, O *that*, would *that*
אַחְלַי, Ahlai
אַחְלָמָה, amethyst
אֲחַסְבַּי, Ahasbai
אחר, delay, go *late*, slack, stay, tarry, tarry *late*, tarry *long*
אַחַר, after, afterward, afterwards, behind, besides, follow, hereafter, last, then, *west* side
אַחֵר, Aher, alien, another, another *man*, any, *any* other, different, first, next, other, other *man*, second
אַחֲרוֹן, afterward, afterwards, come, come *later*, end, last, late, later *thing*, latter, next, rear, time, west, western
אַחְרַח, Aharah
אֲחַרְחֵל, Aharhel
אַחֲרֵי, after, afterward, again, around, back, behind, butt, end, *ever* again, follow, join, leave, next, now, onward, pursue, pursuit, rear, see, since, succeed, train, west, when
אַחֲרֵי אֲשֶׁר, since
אַחֲרֵי כֵן, afterward, afterwards
אַחֲרֵי מָתַי, *how* long
אַחֲרִית, come, doom, end, end *of life*, future, issue, last, latter, *latter* day, *latter* days, *latter* end, leave, outcome, posterity, survivor, uttermost *part*
אֲחֹרַנִּית, back, backward, turn *away*
אֲחַשְׁדַּרְפְּנִים, satrap
אֲחַשְׁוֵרוֹשׁ, Ahasuerus
אֲחַשְׁתָּרִי, Haahashtari
אֲחַשְׁתְּרָן, use *in the king's service*
אַט, dejectedly
אָטָד, Atad, bramble, thorn
אֵטוּן, linen
אִטִּי, sorcerer
אטם, close, narrow, recess, stop
אטר, close
אָטֵר, Ater
אִטֵּר יַד יְמִינוֹ, left-handed
אֵי, how, what, where
אִי, coast, coastland, hyena, island, isle, land, woe
אִי כָבוֹד, Ichabod
אֵי זֶה, what, where
אֵי מִזֶּה, whence
איב, attack, enemy, foe
אֵיבָה, enmity
אֵיד, calamity, destruction, disaster
אַיָּה, Aiah, falcon, kite
אַיֵּה, where
אַיֵּה אֵפוֹא, where
אִיּוֹב, Job
אִיזֶבֶל, Jezebel
אֵיךְ, else, how, what
אֵיכָה, how, what, where
אֵיכָכָה, how
אַיִל, chief, chief *man*, jamb, leader, lintel, mighty, mighty *one*, oak, ram, terebinth
אַיָּל, hart, stag
אֱיָל, strength
אֵיל פָּארָן, El-paran
אַיָּלָה, hind
אַיָּלוֹן, Aijalon
אֵילוֹן בֵּית חָנָן, Elon-beth-hanan
אֱיָלוּת, help
אֵילוֹת, Elath, Eloth
אֵילָם, vestibule
אֵילִם, Elim
אֵילַת, Elath
אָיֹם, dread, terrible
אֵימָה, dread, *dread* wrath, fear, idol, terrible, terror
אֵימִים, Emim
אַיִן, any, anything, before, beyond, fail, failure, go, here, lack, neither, never, no, no *more*, no *one*, none, nor, nothing, nought, vain, want, where, without
אֵין אֶפֶס, nothing *at all*
אֵין אָב, fatherless
אֵין אֶחָד, none
אֵין אִישׁ, no *one*, nobody
אֵין דָּבָר, nothing
אֵין חֵפֶץ, useless
אֵין חֵקֶר, unsearchable
אֵין כֹּחַ, powerless, weak
אֵין כֹּל, nothing
אֵין לֵב, senseless
אֵין מְאוּמָה, nothing
אֵין מַיִם, waterless
אֵין מִסְפָּר, innumerable
אֵין מַרְפֵּא, incurable
אִיעֶזֶר, Iezer
אִיעֶזְרִי, Iezerite
אֵיפָה, ephah, measure
אֵיפֹה, whence, where
אִישׁ, another, any, any *man*, any *one*, certain, common, cub, each, each *man*, each *one*, every, every *man*, every *one*, fellow, friend, *human* semblance, husband, keeper, kind, male, man, number, one, other, party, people, person, soldier, some, some *one*
אִישׁ אֶבְיוֹן, needy
אִישׁ אֲדֹמִי, Edomite
אִישׁ אֹיֵב, enemy
אִישׁ אֱוִיל, fool
אִישׁ אָח, kinsman
אִישׁ אֶחָד, alone
אִישׁ אִישׁ, any *one*
אִישׁ אֶל אָח, one *another*
אִישׁ אֶל רֵעַ, one *another*
אִישׁ אֳנִיּוֹת, seaman
אִישׁ אֶפְרָתִי, Ephrathite
אִישׁ אֹרֵחַ, wayfarer
אִישׁ אֲשֶׁר, whoever
אִישׁ אֲשֶׁר עַל, steward
אִישׁ אֶת רֵעַ, one *another*
אִישׁ בְּלִיַּעַל, base *fellow*
אִישׁ בֶּן בְּלִיַּעַל, base *fellow*
אִישׁ בֵּנַיִם, champion
אִישׁ בְּרִית, ally
אִישׁ בֹּשֶׁת, Ish-bosheth
אִישׁ גֵּר, sojourner
אִישׁ הַתָּרִים, trader
אִישׁ וְאִישׁ, every *man*
אִישׁ זָר, stranger
אִישׁ חַיִל, soldier
אִישׁ חָסִיד, godly *one*
אִישׁ יְהוּדִי, Jew
אִישׁ יְמִינִי, Benjaminite
אִישׁ כְּאָח, equally
אִישׁ כָּזָב, liar
אִישׁ כְּסִיל, fool
אִישׁ לֵוִי, Levite
אִישׁ לָצוֹן, scoffer
אִישׁ לְרֵעַ, one *another*
אִישׁ לָשׁוֹן, slanderer
אִישׁ מִלְחָמָה, expert *in war*, soldier, war, warrior
אִישׁ מִצְרִי, Egyptian
אִישׁ נָכְרִי, foreigner
אִישׁ נָקִי, innocent *man*
אִישׁ סָרִיס, eunuch
אִישׁ עֹבֵד, tiller
אִישׁ עִבְרִי, Hebrew
אִישׁ עֲמָלֵקִי, Amalekite
אִישׁ עָנִי, poor
אִישׁ עֵצָה, counselor
אִישׁ עָצֵל, sluggard
אִישׁ צְבָא לַמִּלְחָמָה, *experienced* warrior
אִישׁ צַר, foe
אִישׁ רַגְלִי, foot *soldier*
אִישׁ רִיב, adversary
אִישׁ שַׂר, prince
אִישׁ שָׁלוֹם, *bosom* friend, confederate, *trusted* friend
אִישׁ שֹׁלֵף חֶרֶב, swordsman
אִישׁ תְּכָכִים, oppressor
אִישְׁהוֹד, Ishhod
אִישׁוֹן, utter
אִיתוֹן, entrance
אִיתַי, Ithai
אִיתִיאֵל, Ithiel
אִיתָמָר, Ithamar
אֵיתָן, continual, endure, Ethan, mighty
אֵתָנִים, Ethanim
אַךְ, ah, all, alone, altogether, how, however, indeed, just, mere, nevertheless, nothing, nought, now, only, scarcely, still, surely, truly, utterly, when, wholly, yea, yet
אַכַּד, Accad
אַכְזָב, deceitful, deceitful *thing*
אַכְזִיב, Achzib
אַכְזָר, cruel, fierce
אַכְזָרִי, cruel, cruel *man*, merciless, *merciless* foe
אַכְזְרִיּוּת, cruel
אֲכִילָה, food
אָכִישׁ, Achish
אכל, consume, destroy, devour, devourer, dine, eat, eat *up*, eater, enjoy, feast, feed, food, fuel, give *to eat*, live, *make* eat, partake, provide *with food*, provision, table, take *away*, taste, use *up*
אכל לֶחֶם, dine
אֹכֶל, food, prey, victual
אֻכָל, Ucal
אָכֵן, all *the more*, nevertheless, surely, truly
אכף, urge
אֶכֶף, pressure
אִכָּר, farmer, plowman, tiller *of the soil*
אַכְשָׁף, Achshaph
אַל, instead, neither, never, no, no *one*, none, nothing
אַל אִישׁ, no *one*, none
אַל דָּבָר, nothing
אַל יֹסֵף, never *again*
אַל כֹּל, none, nothing
אַל לְעוֹלָם, never
אַל פְּלֹנִי, no *one*
אֶל, about, according, addition, adjoin, after, against, along, among, because, before, beside, concerning, face, follow, front, inside, near, opposite, over, round, thing, through, toward, under, unto, upon, within
אֶל אֲשֶׁר, where
אֶל דֶּרֶךְ, toward
אֶל הַיָּמִין, southward
אֶל הַפְּנִימִית, inward
אֶל יַד, next, over *against*
אֶל כָּל אֲשֶׁר, wherever
אֶל כֹּל אֲשֶׁר שָׁם, wherever
אֶל מִבֵּית, between, within
אֶל מוּל, before, front, toward
אֶל מוּל פָּנִים, front
אֶל מוֹסֵרִים, fast
אֶל מִנֶּגֶב, southward
אֶל עֵבֶר, next
אֶל עֵבֶר פָּנִים, straight *forward*
אֶל פָּנִים, against, alongside, before, beyond, extend, face, opposite
אֶל תּוֹךְ, within
אֵל, divine, god, God, here, mighty, mighty *one*, power, prince
אֵל אֱלֹהֵי יִשְׂרָאֵל, El-Elohe-Israel
אֵל בֵּית אֵל, El-bethel
אֵל בְּרִית, El-berith
אֵל יַד, power
אֵלָא, Ela
אַלְגּוּמִּים, algum
אֶלְדָּד, Eldad
אֶלְדָּעָה, Eldaah
אלה, lament, lay *an oath*, swear, swear *an oath*, utter *a curse*
אֵלָה, oak

אָלָה, curse, execration, oath, swear, *sworn* covenant, testify
אֱלָהּ, God
אֱלֹהַּ, god, God
אֵלָה, Elah, oak, terebinth
אֵלֶּה, another, follow, here, other, same, some, such, such *a thing*, thing
אֵלֶּה עִם אֵלֶּה, *all* alike
אֱלֹהִים, divine, exceedingly, god, GOD, God, goddess, godly, mighty, sacred, *very* great
אִלּוּ, even *though*, if
אֱלוּל, Elul
אַלּוֹן, Allon, oak
אַלּוֹן בָּכוּת, Allon-bacuth
אֵלוֹן, Elon, oak
אַלּוּף, cattle, chief, clan, *close* friend, companion, friend, gentle
אָלוּשׁ, Alush
אֶלְזָבָד, Elzabad
אלח, corrupt, deprave
אֶלְחָנָן, Elhanan
אֱלִיאָב, Eliab
אֱלִיאֵל, Eliel
אֱלִיאָתָה, Eliathah
אֱלִידָד, Elidad
אֶלְיָדָע, Eliada
אַלְיָה, *fat* tail
אֱלִיהוּ, Elihu
אֵלִיָּהוּ, Elijah
אֶלְיְהוֹעֵינַי, Eliehoenai
אֶלְיוֹעֵינַי, Elioenai
אֶלְיַחְבָּא, Eliahba
אֱלִיחֹרֶף, Elihoreph
אֱלִיל, idol, image, worthless, *worthless* idol
אֱלִימֶלֶךְ, Elimelech
אֶלְיָסָף, Eliasaph
אֱלִיעֶזֶר, Eliezer
אֱלִיעָם, Eliam
אֶלְיְעֵינַי, Elienai
אֱלִיפַז, Eliphaz
אֱלִיפָל, Eliphal
אֱלִיפְלֵהוּ, Eliphelehu
אֱלִיפֶלֶט, Eliphelet
אֱלִיצוּר, Elizur
אֱלִיצָפָן, Elizaphan
אֱלִיקָא, Elika
אֶלְיָקִים, Eliakim
אֱלִישֶׁבַע, Elisheba
אֱלִישָׁה, Elishah
אֱלִישׁוּעַ, Elishua
אֶלְיָשִׁיב, Eliashib
אֱלִישָׁמָע, Elishama
אֱלִישָׁע, Elisha
אֱלִישָׁפָט, Elishaphat
אַלְלַי, woe
אלם, bind, dumb
אִלֵּם, dumb, dumb *man*
אַלְמֻגִּים, almug
אֲלֻמָּה, sheaf
אַלְמוֹדָד, Almodad
אַלַּמֶּלֶךְ, Allammelech
אַלְמָן, forsake
אַלְמֹן, widowhood
אַלְמָנָה, tower, widow
אַלְמָנוּת, widow, widowhood
אֵלֹנִי, Elonite
אֶלְנַעַם, Elnaam
אֶלְנָתָן, Elnathan
אֶלָּסָר, Ellasar
אֶלְעָד, Elead
אֶלְעָדָה, Eleadah
אֶלְעוּזַי, Eluzai
אֶלְעָזָר, Eleazar
אֶלְעָלֵא, Elealeh
אֶלְעָלֵה, Elealeh
אֶלְעָשָׂה, Elasah, Eleasah
אלף, bring *forth thousands*, learn, teach
אֶלֶף, cattle, clan, family, ox, thousand, tribe

אֶלְפֶּלֶט, Elpelet
אֶלְפַּעַל, Elpaal
אלץ, urge
אֶלְצָפָן, Elzaphan
אַלְקוּם, stride
אֶלְקָנָה, Elkanah
אֶלְקֹשִׁי, Elkosh
אֶלְתּוֹלַד, Eltolad
אֶלְתְּקֵא, Elteke
אֶלְתְּקֵה, Eltekeh
אֶלְתְּקֹן, Eltekon
אִם, either, else, even, except, if, neither, no, none, nor, oh *that*, since, surely, than, though, when, whenever, whether, yet
אִם לֹא, else, unless
אֵם, dam, mother, parting
אַמָּה, Ammah, cubit, foundation
אָמָה, bondmaid, bondwoman, *female* slave, handmaid, maid, maiden, maidservant, servant, slave, slave *woman*
אֻמָּה, people, tribe
אָמוֹן, Amon, artisan, *master* workman
אֵמוּן, faithful
אֱמוּנָה, faith, faithful, faithfully, faithfulness, honestly, office *of trust*, security, stability, steady, sure, truth
אָמוֹץ, Amoz
אָמִי, Ami
אַמִּיץ, mighty, stout, strength, strong
אָמִיר, *high* bough
אמל, fade, forlorn, languish, lovesick, wither
אֻמְלַל, languish
אֲמֵלָל, feeble
אֲמָם, Amam
אמן, assurance, believe, bring *up*, carry, confidence, confirm, entrust, establish, faith, faithful, foster *father*, fulfil, guardian, keep *faith*, last, make *sure*, nurse, put *trust*, reliable, stand *firm*, stand *still*, sure, true, trust, trustworthy, verify
אָמֵן, amen, truth
אָמָּן, master
אֹמֶן, sure
אֵמֻן, faith, faithfulness
אָמְנָה, bring *up*, indeed, truth
אֹמְנָה, doorpost
אָמְנָה, indeed
אֲמָנָה, Amana, *firm* covenant, *settled* provision
אַמְנוֹן, Amnon
אָמְנָם, indeed, *no* doubt, true, truly
אמץ, collect, courageous, determine, *good* courage, grow *strong*, harden, make *firm*, make *haste*, make *obstinate*, make *secure*, make *strong*, mighty, prevail, retain, strengthen, strong, take *courage*
אמץ עַל, defy
אָמֹץ, steed
אַמִּץ, strong
אַמְצָה, strength
אַמְצִי, Amzi
אֲמַצְיָהוּ, Amaziah
אמר, add, address, advise, agree, answer, ask, assign, bid, boast, call, claim, command, commune, cry, decide, declare, desire, fear, give *a command*, give *orders*, glory, intend, mean, name, order, pray, proclaim, promise, pronounce, propose, publish, purpose, read, repeat, reply, say, set, shout, sing, speak, suppose, swear, tell, term, think, thought, use, utter, wish
אמר אֶל, bid
אמר לְ, bid
אמר לְחַי, salute
אמר לְלֵב, consider
אִמֵּר, Immer
אֹמֶר, command, matter, promise, speech, word
אֵמֶר, answer, decree, fawn, saying, speech, word
אִמְרָה, threat
אִמְרָה, command, promise, say, speech, word
אִמְרִי, Imri
אֱמֹרִי, Amorite
אֲמַרְיָהוּ, Amariah

אַמְרָפֶל, Amraphel
אֶמֶשׁ, *last* night, yesterday
אֱמֶת, act *of faithfulness*, assure, equity, faith, faithful, faithfully, faithfulness, *good* faith, pure, right, security, sure, true, truly, trustworthy, truth, truthful
אַמְתַּחַת, sack
אֲמִתַּי, Amittai
אָן, where, whither
אָנָּא, alas, beseech, now, pray
אנה, befall, fall, lament, mourn, seek *a quarrel*
אָנָה, where, whither
אָנָה וָאָנָה, any *place whatever*, nowhere
אָנָּה, beseech
אֱנוֹשׁ, common, Enosh, man
אֱנוֹשׁ כְּעֶרְכִּי, equal
אֱנוֹשׁ שְׁלוֹם, *familiar* friend
אנח, groan, sigh
אֲנָחָה, groan, groaning, moan, sigh
אֲנָחֲרָת, Anaharath
אֲנִי, I *am*
אֳנִי, fleet, fleet *of ships*, galley
אֲנִיָּה, lamentation
אֳנִיָּה, ship, skiff
אֲנִיעָם, Aniam
אֲנָךְ, plumb *line*
אָנֹכִי, I *am*
אנן, complain
אנס, compel
אנף, angry
אֲנָפָה, heron
אנק, groan, sigh
אֲנָקָה, gecko, groan
אנשׁ, *become* sick, despair, *desperately* corrupt, disaster, incurable
אַנְשֵׁי מִסְפָּר, few
אָסָא, Asa
אָסוּךְ, jar
אָסוֹן, harm
אֵסוּר, bond
אָסִיף, ingathering
אַסִּיר, Assir, captive, prisoner
אָסִיר, bond, captive, prisoner
אָסָם, barn
אַסְנָה, Asnah
אָסְנַת, Asenath
אסף, assemble, attach, bring, bring *together*, collect, come *together*, consume, cure, destroy, draw *up*, garner, gather, gather *together*, gather *up*, get *away*, heap, lose, make *an ingathering*, muster, put, put *together*, *rear* guard, remove, return, store *up*, sweep *away*, take, take *away*, take *into*, take *up*, withdraw
אָסָף, Asaph
אָסֹף, storehouse
אֹסֶף, gather, harvest
אֲסֵפָה, collect
אֲסֻפָּה, together
אֲסַפְסֻף, rabble
אַסְפָּתָא, Aspatha
אסר, begin, bind, capture, confine, fetter, gird, go *out*, harness, hold *captive*, make *ready*, prepare, prisoner, put *in bonds*, *remain* confined, remain *in prison*, tie, yoke
אֱסָר, bind, pledge
אֵסַר חַדֹּן, Esar-haddon
אֶסְתֵּר, Esther
אַף, anger, breath, countenance, even, even *if*, face, head, how, *how much* more, *how much* rather, indeed, indignation, moreover, nay, nose, nostril, now, snout, temper, then, truly, wrath, yea, yet
אַף אַיִן, nor
אַף בַּל, scarcely
אַף כִּי, even, *how much* better, *how much* less, *how much* more, moreover, much *less*, still *less*
אפד, bind, gird
אֵפֹד, Ephod
אֲפֻדָּה, gird, plate
אַפֶּדֶן, palatial
אפה, bake, baker

אֵפוֹ, now, then
אֵפוֹד, ephod
אֵפוּנָה, helpless
אֲפִיחַ, Aphiah
אָפִיל, late
אַפַּיִם, Appaim
אָפִיק, brook, channel, flow, fountain, ravine, row, spring, stream *bed*, strong, tube, watercourse
אֲפִיק, Aphik
אֲפִיק נַחַל, freshet
אֹפֶל, gloom
אֹפֶל, dark, darkness, gloom, *thick* darkness
אֲפֵלָה, darkness, *deep* darkness, gloom, thick, *thick* darkness
אֶפְלָל, Ephlal
אֹפֶן, fitly
אפס, cease, come *to nought*, go, no *more*
אֶפֶס, besides, end, except, lack, nevertheless, no, no *more*, no *one*, none, *none* remaining, nothing, only, without, yet
אֶפֶס דַּמִּים, Ephes-dammim
אֶפֶס כִּי, although, nevertheless
אֹפֶס, ankle-deep
אֶפְעֶה, viper
אפף, close, encompass
אפק, control, force, restrain, withhold
אֲפֵק, Aphek
אֲפֵקָה, Aphekah
אֲפֵר, bandage
אֵפֶר, ash
אֶפְרֹחַ, young, young *one*
אַפִּרְיוֹן, palanquin
אֶפְרַיִם, Ephraim, Ephraimite
אֶפְרָת, Ephrath
אֶפְרָתָה, Ephrathah
אֶפְרָתִי, Ephraimite, Ephrathite
אֶצְבּוֹן, Ezbon
אֶצְבַּע, finger, toe
אַצִּיל, long, wrist
אַצִּיל יָד, armpit
אָצִיל, chief *man*, *far* corner
אצל, keep, reserve, set *back*, take
אָצֵל, Azel, side
אֵצֶל, beside, close, near
אֲצַלְיָהוּ, Azaliah
אֹצֶם, Ozem
אֶצְעָדָה, armlet
אצר, appoint *as treasurer*, store, store *up*
אֵצֶר, Ezer
אַקּוֹ, wild *goat*
אָרָא, Ara
אֲרִיאֵל, *altar* hearth
אֶרְאֵל, valiant *one*
אַרְאֵלִי, Areli, Arelite
ארב, ambush, lay *wait*, lie *in ambush*, lie *in wait*, lurk, man *in ambush*
אֶרֶב, lair, wait
אֹרֶב, ambush, intrigue
אֲרָב, Arab
אַרְבֶּה, grasshopper, locust, *swarming* locust
אָרְבָּה, skill
אֲרֻבָּה, window
אֲרֻבּוֹת, Arubboth
אַרְבִּי, Arbite
אַרְבַּע, four, four *things*, fourfold, fourth
אַרְבַּע עֶשְׂרֵה, fourteen, fourteenth
ארג, weave, weaver
אֶרֶג, loom, *weaver's* shuttle
אַרְגֹּב, Argob
אַרְגָּז, box
אַרְגָּמָן, purple, *purple* fabric
אַרְדְּ, Ard
אַרְדּוֹן, Ardon
אַרְדִּי, Ardite
ארה, gather, pluck
אַרְוָד, Arvad
אֲרוֹד, Arod
אַרְוָדִי, Arvadite

אֲרוֹדִי, Arodi, Arodite
אֲרוּכָה, heal, health, repair
ארוּמָה, Arumah
אָרוֹן, ark, chest, coffin
אֲרַוְנָה, Araunah
אֶרֶז, cedar, cedar *tree*
אַרְזָה, *cedar* work
ארח, go, wayfarer
אָרַח, Arah
אֹרַח, caravan, course, manner, path, way, wayfarer
אֹרַח עֲקַלְקַלָּה, byway
אֹרְחָה, caravan
אֲרֻחָה, allowance, dinner
אֲרִי, lion
אֲרִיאֵל, ariel, Ariel
אֲרִידַי, Aridai
אֲרִידָתָא, Aridatha
אַרְיֵה, lion
אֻרְיָה, stall
אַרְיוֹךְ, Arioch
אֲרִים, east
אֲרִיסַי, Arisai
ארך, continue, continue *long*, defer, grow *long*, lengthen, live *long*, long, make *long*, make *slow*, prolong, put *out*
ארך יָמִים, continue *long*, live *long*
ארך יָמִים אַחֲרֵי, outlive
ארך נֶפֶשׁ, patient
אֹרֶךְ, long
אָרֵךְ, long, patient, slow
אֶרֶךְ, Erech
אֶרֶךְ אַף, forbearance
אֹרֶךְ, breadth, extend, length, long
אֹרֶךְ אַפַּיִם, patience
אֹרֶךְ יָמִים, evermore, long
אַרְכְּוָי, *man of* Erech
אַרְכִּי, Archite
אֲרַם מַעֲכָה, Aram-maacah
אֲרַם נַהֲרַיִם, Aram-naharaim, Mesopotamia
אֲרַם צוֹבָה, Aram-zobah
אֲרָם, Aram, Mesopotamia, Syria, Syrian
אַרְמוֹן, castle, citadel, palace, stronghold, tower
אֲרַמִּי, Aramean, Syrian
אֲרָמִי, Aramaic
אֲרָמִית, Aramaic
אַרְמֹנִי, Armoni
אֹרֶן, cedar, Oren
אֲרָן, Aran
אַרְנֶבֶת, hare
אַרְנוֹן, Arnon
אַרְנָן, Arnan
אָרְנָן, Ornan
אַרְפָּד, Arpad
אַרְפַּכְשַׁד, Arpachshad
אֶרֶץ, country, district, dust, earth, field, floor, ground, land, nation, path, people, piece *of land*, shore, territory, world
אֶרֶץ מִישׁוֹר, tableland
אֶרֶץ עֵמֶק, plain
אַרְצָא, Arza
ארר, accursed, bring *the curse*, curse, cursed *woman*
אֲרָרַט, Ararat
ארשׂ, betroth
אֲרֶשֶׁת, request
אַרְתַּחְשַׁסְתְּא, Artaxerxes
אַרְתַּחְשַׁשְׁתָּא, Artaxerxes
אֲשַׂרְאֵל, Asarel
אֲשַׂרְאֵלָה, Asharelah
אַשְׂרִאֵלִי, Asrielite
אַשְׂרִיאֵל, Asriel
אֵשׁ, blaze, burn, fiery, fire, flame, hot, lightning
אַשְׁבֵּל, Ashbel
אַשְׁבֵּלִי, Ashbelite
אֶשְׁבָּן, Eshban
אֶשְׁבַּעַל, Eshbaal
אֶשֶׁד, slope
אֲשֵׁדָה, slope
אַשְׁדּוֹד, Ashdod, *territory of* Ashdod
אַשְׁדּוֹדִי, Ashdod, Ashdodite, *people of* Ashdod
אַשְׁדּוֹדִית, Ashdod
אִשָּׁה, each, each *one*, each *woman*, girl, mate, widow, wife, woman
אִשָּׁה אַלְמָנָה, widow
אִשָּׁה זוֹנָה, harlot
אִשָּׁה ינק, nurse
אִשָּׁה נאף, adulteress
אִשָּׁה נְבִיאָה, prophetess
אִשָּׁה פִּלֶגֶשׁ, concubine
אִשֶּׁה, fire, offer *by fire*, offering *by fire*
אִישׁוֹן, apple, time
אַשּׁוּר, Asshur, Assyria, Assyrian
אֲשׁוּר, go, step
אֲשׁוּרִי, Ashurite
אַשּׁוּרִם, Asshurim
אַשְׁחוּר, Ashhur
אֻשִׁיָּה, bulwark
אֲשִׁימָא, Ashima
אֲשִׁישָׁה, cake, cake *of raisins*, raisin, raisin-cake
אֶשֶׁךְ, testicle
אֶשְׁכּוֹל, cluster
אֶשְׁכֹּל, Eshcol
אַשְׁכְּנַז, Ashkenaz
אֶשְׁכָּר, gift, payment
אֵשֶׁל, tamarisk *tree*
אשׁם, acknowledge *guilt*, bear *guilt*, *become* guilty, condemn, dismay, *do* wrong, guilty, guilty *man*, hold *guilty*, incur *guilt*, *make* bear *guilt*, offend, suffer *for guilt*
אָשָׁם, convict, guilt, *guilt* offering, guilty *way*, offering *for sin*, restitution *for wrong*, wrong
אַשְׁמָה, Ashimah, bring *guilt*, guilt, *guilt* offering, incur *guilt*, sin, wrong
אַשְׁמוּרָה, watch, watch *of the night*
אַשְׁמַנִּים, *full* vigor
אֶשְׁנָב, lattice
אַשְׁנָה, Ashnah
אֶשְׁעָן, Eshan
אַשָּׁף, enchanter
אַשְׁפָּה, quiver
אַשְׁפֹּת, ash *heap*
אַשְׁקְלוֹן, Ashkelon
אֶשְׁקְלוֹנִי, Ashkelon
אשׁר, call *blessed*, call *happy*, correct, deem *blessed*, direct, lead, leader, walk
אשׁר, step, track *down*
אָשֵׁר, Asher
אָשַׁר, bless, happy
אֶשֶׁר, happy
אֲשֶׁר, account, any *man*, any *one*, because, concerning *whom*, forasmuch, here, how, if, see, such, therefore, though, what, whatever, when, where, wherewith, while, whither, whoever, why
אֲשֶׁר בְּ, where
אֲשֶׁר בַּשָּׂדֶה, wild
אֲשֶׁר יצא, outlay
אֲשֶׁר יצא מִמֵּעִים, son
אֲשֶׁר לֹא, lest
אֲשֶׁר נשׁא בְּ, debtor
אֲשֶׁר עַל, steward, where, whither
אֲשֶׁר פלל, prayer
אֲשֶׁר שָׁם, where, whereever, wherever, whither
אֲשֶׁר שָׁמָּה, where, wherever
אֲשֵׁרָה, Asherah, Asherim, Asheroth
אָשֵׁרִי, Asherite
אשׁשׁ, consider
אֵשֶׁת אִישׁ, adulteress
אֶשְׁתָּאוֹל, Eshtaol
אֶשְׁתָּאֻלִי, Eshtaolite
אֶשְׁתּוֹן, Eshton
אֶשְׁתְּמֹה, Eshtemoh
אֶשְׁתְּמוֹעַ, Eshtemoa
אֵת, according, against, among, before, behalf, beside, care, company, mattock, near, plowshare, side, through, together, toward, upon
אֵת אֲשֶׁר, how
אֵת כֹּל אֲשֶׁר, how
אֵת פְּנֵי, sight
אֵת פָּנִים, before
אֶתְבַּעַל, Ethbaal
אתה, bring, come, come *upon*, *thing to* come
אָתוֹן, ass, she-ass
אִתַּי, Ittai
אַתִּיק, gallery
אֵתָם, Etham
אֶתְמוֹל שִׁלְשׁוֹם, before
אֵיתָן, ever-flowing, *running* water, strong, unmoved, *wonted* flow
אֶתְנָה, hire
אֶתְנִי, Ethni
אֶתְנַן, harlot's *hire*, hire
אֶתְנָן, Ethnan
אֲתָרִים, Atharim

בְּ, about, accordance, according, after, against, along, amid, among, because, before, beneath, beside, between, concerning, cost, despite, during, exchange, fact, follow, full, if, inside, lack, like, long, near, one *piece*, over, reason, regard, since, some, soon, spite, though, through, throughout, toward, under, up, upon, whenever, where, whether, within, worth
בִּאָה, entrance
בְּאֶחָד, both, unchangeable
בָּאַחֲרוֹנָה, afterward
בְּאַיִן, without
בֶּאֱמוּנָה, faithful, faithfully, honestly
בֶּאֱמֶת, faithfully, truly
בְּאַף, before
בְּאֶפֶס, without
באר, explain, make *plain*, plainly
בֹּאר, cistern, pit, well
בְּאֵר, Beer, pit, well
בְּאֵר אֵילִים, Beer-elim
בְּאֵר לַחַי רֹאִי, Beer-lahai-roi
בְּאֵר שֶׁבַע, Beer-sheba
בְּאֵר שַׁחַת, *low* pit
בְּאֵרָא, Beera
בְּאֵרָה, Beerah
בְּאֵרוֹת, Beeroth
בְּאֵרִי, Beeri
בְּאֵרֹת בְּנֵי יַעֲקָן, Beeroth *Bene-jaakan*
בְּאֵרֹתִי, Beeroth, Beerothite
באשׁ, *act* shamefully, *become* foul, *become* odious, *evil* odor, grow *foul*, *make* abhor, make *odious*, stink
באשׁ רֵיחַ, make *offensive*
בְּאֹשׁ, burn
בְּאשׁ, stench
בָּאְשָׁה, *foul* weed
בְּאֻשִׁים, *wild* grape
בַּאֲשֶׁר, because, where, wherever
בָּבָה, apple
בְּבֶטֶן, within
בֵּבַי, Bebai
בְּבֵין, amid
בְּבַיִת, within
בִּבְכִי, weep *tears*
בִּבְכִי, weep
בָּבֶל, Babel, Babylon, Babylonia
בִּבְלִי דַעַת, unintentionally, unwittingly
בְּגַאֲוֹת, arrogantly
בגד, *act* treacherously, deal *faithlessly*, deal *treacherously*, faithless, faithless *man*, false, plunder, plunderer, treacherous, treacherous *man*, treacherous *one*, *treacherously* plot, untrue
בֶּגֶד, apparel, cloak, cloth, clothes, clothing, garment, lap, raiment, robe, wardrobe
בֶּגֶד חֹפֶשׁ, saddlecloth
בֹּגְדוֹת, faithless
בָּגוֹד, false
בִּגְוַי, Bigvai
בִּגְלַל, account, because, sake
בְּגַף, alone
בְּגָרוֹן, aloud
בִּגְתָא, Bigtha
בִּגְתָן, Bigthan
בִּגְתָנָא, Bigthana
בַּד, babble, bar, boast, branch, diviner, *equal* part, liar, limb, linen, pole
בדא, devise, invent
בַּדָּבָר הַזֶּה, thereby
בדד, alone, lonely, straggler
בָּדָד, alone, lonely, solitary
בְּדַד, Bedad
בְּדֵי, only
בֵּדְיָה, Bedeiah
בְּדִיל, alloy, tin
בדל, ban, discharge, distinguish, divide *asunder*, go *over*, make *a distinction*, *make a* distinction, make *a separation*, separate, separation, set *apart*, sever, single *out*
בָּדָל, piece
בְּדֹלַח, bdellium
בְּדָן, Bedan
בדק, repair
בֶּדֶק, need *of repair*, repair, seam
בִּדְקַר, Bidkar
בדר עַל לֵב, comfort
בְּדֶרֶךְ, away
בָּהּ, therein, thereon
בָּה, here, there, thereby
בֹּהוּ, chaos, void
בַּהַט, porphyry
בָּהִיר, bright
בהל, alarm, dismay, get *hastily*, haste, hasten, make *afraid*, make *haste*, overwhelm, palsy *by terror*, panic, quickly, rash, sudden, terrify, thrust *out quickly*, trouble
בהל בָּרוּחַ, quick
בֶּהָלָה, calamity, *sudden* terror, terror
בָּהֶם, thereby, therein
בְּהֵמָה, animal, beast, cattle
בְּהֵמוֹת, Behemoth
בְּהֶמַת שָׂדֶה, *wild* beast
בֹּהַן, Bohan
בֹּהֶן, *great* toe, thumb
בֹּהֶן יָד, thumb
בֹּהֶן רֶגֶל, *great* toe
בָּהֵנָּה, therein
בֹּהַק, tetter
בַּהֶרֶת, spot
בּוֹ, thereby, therewith, wherein
בוא, admit, advance, alight, apply, approach, arrival, arrive, attain, attendant, back, befall, break, bring, bring *about*, bring *back*, bring *home*, bring *into*, bring *out*, bring *to pass*, carry, carry *off*, *cause to* come, *cause to* enter, come, come *back*, *come* bringing, come *by*, come *into*, come *near*, come *out*, *come to* pass, come *true*, come *up*, come *upon*, consort, dip, down, drive, enter, enter *into*, entrance, escape, escort, fall *upon*, fetch, fulfil, get, get *into*, give, go, go *back*, go *down*, go *forward*, go *into*, go *near*, go *through*, go *up*, grant, harvest, hear, invade, join, lead, *make* come, *make* go *down*, march, meet, mention, occupy, pass, penetrate, present, put, reach, resound, run, run *down*, send, set, soak, spring, stand, strike, take, *thing to* come, tread, way, *well* advanced, yet *to be*
בוא אַחֲרֵי, follow
בוא אֶל, befall, enter, invade, marry, receive
בוא אֶל קֶרֶב, eat
בוא אַף אַחֲרֵי, follow
בוא בְּ, enter, marry, mix
בוא בִּצְדָקָה, acquittal
בוא בְּרֶגֶל, follow
בוא בְּתוֹךְ, enter
בוא הַשֶּׁמֶשׁ, sunset
בוא לְ, enter
בוא לִפְנֵי, determine, report
בוא עַל, befall
בוא עַל לֵב, plan
בּוֹאֲךָ, far, neighborhood
בּוֹאֲכָה, direction, entrance

בוז, belittle, despise, scorn
בּוּז, Buz, contempt
בּוּזִי, Buzi, Buzite
בַּוַּי, Bavvai
בוך, entangle, perplex
בּוּל, block, Bul, food
בּוּנָה, Bunah
בוס, loathe, trample, trample *down*, trample *under foot*, tread *down*, tread *under foot*, welter
בּוּץ, *fine* linen, linen
בּוֹצֵץ, Bozez
בּוּקָה, desolate
בּוֹקֵר, herdsman
בור, examine
בּוֹר, cistern, death, dungeon, pit, well
בּוֹר עָשָׁן, Bor-ashan
בוש, *act* shamefully, ashamed, bring *shame*, *cause* shame, come *to shame*, confound, cover *with shame*, delay, despair, disappoint, disgrace, long, put *to confusion*, put *to shame*, shame, *utterly at a* loss
בּוּשָׁה, shame
בַּז, booty, plunder, prey, spoil
בזא, divide
בְּזָדוֹן, presumptuously
בזה, contemptible *person*, despise, disdain
בזה בְּעֵינַיִם, disdain
בָּזֶה, here, thereby
בִּזָּה, plunder, spoil
בָּזֹה, hereby, yet
בזז, carry *off*, despoil, make *a prey*, make *prey*, plunder, prey, rob, robber, seize, take, take *as booty*, take *as spoil*, take *booty*, take *for booty*, take *prey*
בִּזָּיוֹן, contempt
בִּזְיוֹתְיָה, Biziothiah
בְּזִמָּה, lewdly
בָּזָק, flash *of lightning*
בֶּזֶק, Bezek
בזר, scatter
בִּזְּתָא, Biztha
בַּחוּן, *siege* tower
בַּחוּץ, outside, without
בָּחוּר, picked *man*, young *man*, youth
בְּחוּרִים, youth
בְּחָזְקָה, cruelly, mightily, violently
בְּחֵיק, within
בָּחִיר, choose, chosen *one*
בחל, detest
בחן, assay, assayer, prove, put *to the proof*, put *to the test*, test, try
בַּחַן, watchtower
בֹּחַן, test
בחר, acceptable, choice, choose, chosen *man*, chosen *one*, *chosen* warrior, decide, desire, pick, picked *man*, prefer, rather
בַּחֲרוּמִי, Baharum
בַּחֻרִים, Bahurim
בְּחֶרְפָּה, insolently
בטא, rash, speak *a word that is rash*, swear
בטה, *rash* word
בְּטוֹב, joyful
בטח, bold, careless, complacent, complacent *one*, complacent *woman*, confidence, confident, depend, fall *down*, feel *secure*, keep *safe*, *make* rely, *make* trust, put *confidence*, put *trust*, rely, rest, secure, trust, unsuspecting
בֶּטַח, Betah, off *guard*, safety, secure, securely, security, trust, trustingly, unawares, unsuspecting
בַּטֻּחָה, secure
בִּטְחָה, trust
בִּטָּחוֹן, confidence, hope
בטל, cease
בֶּטֶן, bear, belly, Beten, birth, body, greed, heart, man, mother, part, pregnancy, *rounded* projection, within, womb
בָּטְנִים, pistachio *nut*
בְּטֹנִים, Betonim
בְּטֶרֶם, before, sooner *than*

בִּי, oh, pray
בְּיַד, *under the* leadership
בְּיַד, convey, through
בְּיַד, beside, hold, take
בְּיָד רָמָה, defiantly, triumphantly
בַּיּוֹם, once, today
בַּיּוֹם הַזֶּה, today
בְּיוֹם, when
ביי, would *that*
בְּיָמִים, long
בין, care, comprehend, consider, deal *wisely*, discern, discerning *man*, discover, discreet, enlightenment, examine, expert, explain, feel, gain, get *understanding*, give *attention*, give *heed*, give *insight*, give *understanding*, heed, impart *understanding*, instruct, intelligent, learn, look, look *closely*, look *well*, *make* understand, man *of discernment*, man *of insight*, man *of understanding*, mark, observe, perceive, ponder, prudent, regard, review, shrewd, skilful, teach, teacher, understand, understanding, wise
בין דַּעַת, *good* judgment
בין לֵב, pay *attention*
בַּיִן, among, between, either, every, midst, whether
בֵּין יָדַיִם, back
בֵּין לְ, concerning
בֵּין עֵינַיִם, forehead
בִּינָה, clearly, discernment, insight, understand, wisdom, wise
בְּיַעַן, because
בֵּיצָה, egg
בִּיצק, freeze *fast*
בִּירָה, capital, castle, fortress, palace
בִּירָנִית, fort, fortress
בֵּית הַשִּׁטָּה, Beth-shittah
בַּיִת, box, building, contain, enclose, family, fortress, hall, hanging, holder, home, house, household, *inner* end, inside, inward, nave, palace, place, room, shrine, temple, tomb, web
בַּיִת גָּדוֹל, nave
בֵּית אָב, family
בֵּית אָוֶן, Beth-aven
בֵּית אוֹצָר, storehouse
בֵּית אֱלֹהִים, shrine
בֵּית אֲסוּרִים, prison
בֵּית אֲסֻפִּים, storehouse
בֵּית אַרְבֵּאל, Beth-arbel
בֵּית אַשְׁבֵּעַ, Beth-ashbea
בֵּית בַּעַל מְעוֹן, Beth-baal-meon
בֵּית בִּרְאִי, Beth-biri
בֵּית בָּרָה, Beth-barah
בֵּית גָּדֵר, Beth-gader
בֵּית גִּלְגָּל, Beth-gilgal
בֵּית גָּמוּל, Beth-gamul
בֵּית דִּבְלָתַיִם, Beth-diblathaim
בֵּית דָּגוֹן, Beth-dagon
בֵּית הָאֵצֶל, Beth-ezel
בֵּית הַבּוֹר, dungeon
בֵּית הַגָּן, Beth-haggan
בֵּית הַכֶּרֶם, Beth-haccherem
בֵּית הַמְבַשְּׁלִים, kitchen
בֵּית הָעֵמֶק, Beth-emek
בֵּית הָעֲרָבָה, Beth-arabah
בֵּית הָרָם, Beth-haram
בֵּית הָרָן, Beth-haran
בֵּית הַשִּׁמְשִׁי, Beth-shemesh
בֵּית חָגְלָה, Beth-hoglah
בֵּית חוֹרוֹן, Beth-horon
בֵּית יְשִׁימוֹת, Beth-jeshimoth
בֵּית כֶּלֶא, prison
בֵּית כְּלוּא, prison
בֵּית כֵּלִים, armory
בֵּית כָּר, Beth-car
בֵּית לְבָאוֹת, Beth-lebaoth
בֵּית לֶחֶם, Bethlehem
בֵּית לַחְמִי, Bethlehemite
בֵּית לְעַפְרָה, Beth-leaphrah
בֵּית מִלּוֹא, Beth-millo
בֵּית מַלְכוּת, palace

בֵּית מְעוֹן, Beth-meon
בֵּית מַעֲכָה, Beth-maacah
בֵּית מַרְכָּבוֹת, Beth-marcaboth
בֵּית מִשְׁמָר, prison
בֵּית נִמְרָה, Beth-nimrah
בֵּית נָשִׁים, harem
בֵּית סֹהַר, prison
בֵּית עֶדֶן, Beth-eden
בֵּית עַזְמָוֶת, Beth-azmaveth
בֵּית עֲנוֹת, Beth-anoth
בֵּית עֲנָת, Beth-anath
בֵּית עֵקֶד, Beth-eked
בֵּית פֶּלֶט, Beth-pelet
בֵּית פְּעוֹר, Beth-peor
בֵּית פַּצֵּץ, Beth-pazzez
בֵּית פְּקֻדּוֹת, prison
בֵּית צוּר, Beth-zur
בֵּית רְחוֹב, Beth-rehob
בֵּית רָפָא, Beth-rapha
בֵּית שְׁאָן, Beth-shean
בֵּית שֶׁמֶשׁ, Beth-shemesh, Heliopolis
בֵּית שַׁן, Beth-shan
בֵּית תּוֹגַרְמָה, Beth-togarmah
בֵּית תַּפּוּחַ, Beth-tappuah
בֵּיתְאֵל, Bethel
בַּיְתָה, inside, inward, within
בִּיתָן, palace
בָּכָא, Baca, balsam *tree*
בכה, bewail, cry, make *lamentation*, mourn, tear, weep, weep *bitterly*
בֶּכֶה, another, one *thing*
בְּכוֹר, first, *first* son, first-born, firstling, old
בִּכּוּרָה, *first* fruit, *first* ripe, *first-ripe* fig
בִּכּוּרִים, first, *first* fruit, *first ripe* fruit, *first-ripe* fig
בְּכוֹרַת, Becorath
בַּכֹּחַ, qualify
בְּכִי, tear, trickle, weep
בֹּכִים, Bochim
בְּכִירָה, first-born
בְּכִית, weep
בְּכָל עֵת, always, continually, long
בְּכֹל, anywhere, throughout, whenever, wherever
בְּכֹל אֲשֶׁר, whenever, wherever
בכר, bear *fresh fruit*, bring *forth one's first*, firstling, treat *as a first-born*
בֶּכֶר, Becher
בִּכְרָה, *young* camel
בְּכֹרָה, birthright, first-born
בֹּכְרוּ, Bocheru
בַּכְרִי, Becherite
בִּכְרִי, Bichri
בַּל, lest, neither, never, no, no *more*, none
בַּל לָנֶצַח, never
בַּל לְעוֹלָם, never
בַּל מוט, immovable
בַּל צען, immovable
בֵּל, Bel
בְּלֹא, although, before, free, otherwise *than*, without
בַּלְאֲדָן, Baladan
בֵּלְאשַׁצַּר, Belshazzar
בִּלְבוּשׁ, clothe
בלג, find *comfort*, flash *forth*, *good* cheer, know *gladness*
בִּלְגָּה, Bilgah
בִּלְגַּי, Bilgai
בִּלְדַּד, Bildad
בלה, grow *old*, *long* enjoy, *make* waste *away*, waste, waste *away*, wear *off*, wear *out*
בָּלָה, Balah
בָּלֶה, worn-out
בַּלָּהָה, *dreadful* end, terror
בִּלְהָה, Bilhah
בִּלְהָן, Bilhan
בְּלוֹא, old
בְּלוֹאֵי מְלָחִים, *worn-out* clothes
בְּלוֹאֵי סְחָבוֹת, rag

בַּלָּט, softly, stealthily
בֵּלְטְשַׁאצַּר, Belteshazzar
בְּלִי, destruction, lack, no, no *more*, none, nothing, want, without
בְּלִי חָשַׂךְ, unrelenting
בְּלִי מָה, nothing
בְּלִי שֵׁם, disreputable
בְּלִיל, fodder, provender
בְּלִיַּעַל, base, deadly, godless, ill-natured, perdition, villainy, wicked, worthless, worthless *one*
בלל, confuse, fade, give *provender*, mingle, mix
בלם, curb
בלס, dresser
בלע, confound, confuse, consume, destroy, devour, eat *up*, end, moment, swallow, swallow *down*, swallow *up*
בֶּלַע, Bela, swallow
בִּלְעֲדֵי, besides, other *than*, without
בַּלְעִי, Belaite
בִּלְעָם, Balaam, Bileam
בלק, make *desolate*, ruin
בָּלָק, Balak
בִּלְשָׁן, Bilshan
בֵּלֶת, besides
בִּלְתִּי אִישׁ, no *one*
בִּלְתִּי, besides, except, lest, neither, never *again*, no, no *more*, no *one*, none, nothing, other, save, unless, until
בִּלְתִּי אִם, unless
בִּלְתִּי סָרָה, unceasing
בִּלְתִּי שָׂבְעָה, insatiable
בִּלְתִּי שמע, disobey
בָּם, therein, thereon
בִּמְאֹד מְאֹד, exceedingly
בַּמֶּה, how, wherein, why
בָּמָה, Bamah, height, high *place*, shrine, wave
בִּמְהָל, Bimhal
בִּמְהֵרָה, quickly
בְּמוֹ, through
בָּמוֹת, Bamoth
בָּמוֹת בַּעַל, Bamoth-baal
בִּמְחִיר בוא, buy
בַּמָּצוֹר, besiege
בִּמְקוֹם אֲשֶׁר שָׁם, wherever
בְּמִרְמָה, deceitfully
בֶּן אֶבְיוֹן, needy
בֶּן אֲבִינָדָב, Ben-abinadab
בֶּן אֱדוֹם, Edomite
בֶּן אָדָם, low, man, man *of low estate*
בֶּן אוֹנִי, Ben-oni
בֶּן אִישׁ, high, man, man *of high estate*
בֶּן אִישׁ יְמִינִי, Benjaminite
בֶּן אֵלִים, *heavenly* being
בֶּן אֶפְרַיִם, Ephraimite
בֶּן אַשּׁוּר, Assyrian
בֶּן בָּבֶל, Babylonian
בֶּן בַּיִת, slave
בֶּן בֵּית רֵכָב, Rechabite
בֶּן בְּלִיַּעַל, base *fellow*, ill-natured, scoundrel, worthless *fellow*, worthless *man*
בֶּן בֵּן, grandchild, grandson
בֶּן בִּנְיָמִן, Benjaminite
בֶּן בָּקָר, bull, calf, young, *young* bull
בֶּן גֶּבֶר, Ben-geber
בֶּן גָּד, Gadite
בֶּן גִּלְעָדִי, Gileadite
בֶּן גֹּרֶן, winnowed *one*
בֶּן גֵּרְשׁוֹן, Gershonite, Gersonite
בֶּן דּוֹד, cousin
בֶּן דָּן, Danite
בֶּן דֶּקֶר, Ben-deker
בֶּן הֲדַד, Ben-hadad
בֶּן הַיְּוָנִים, Greek
בֶּן זוֹחֵת, Ben-zoheth
בֶּן חוּר, Ben-hur
בֶּן חַיִל, able, Ben-hail, brave, strong, valiant, valiant *man*
בֶּן חֲלוֹף, desolate

בֶּן חָנָן, Ben-hanan
בֶּן חֶסֶד, Ben-hesed
בֶּן חֵת, Hittite
בֶּן יְמִינִי, Benjaminite
בֶּן יִצְהָר, anoint
בֶּן יִשְׂרָאֵל, Israelite
בֶּן כּוּשִׁי, Ethiopian
בֶּן לֵוִי, Levite
בֶּן מָוֶת, deserve *to die*, die
בֶּן מָכִיר, Machirite
בֶּן מֶלֶךְ, *royal* prince
בֶּן מְנַשֶּׁה, Manassite
בֶּן מִצְרַיִם, Egyptian
בֶּן מְרִי, rebel
בֶּן מְרָרִי, Merarite
בֶּן מֶשֶׁק, heir
בֶּן נֵכָר, alien, foreigner
בֶּן נֶשֶׁר, vulture
בֶּן עַוְלָה, violent *man*, wicked
בֶּן עֵז, kid
בֶּן עַם, countryman
בֶּן עַמּוֹן, Ammonite
בֶּן עַמִּי, Ben-ammi
בֶּן עֲמָלֵק, Amalekite
בֶּן עָנִי, afflict
בֶּן צֹאן, lamb
בֶּן קְהָת, Kohathite
בֶּן קֶלַע, slinger
בֶּן קֶשֶׁת, arrow
בֶּן רְאוּבֵן, Reubenite
בֶּן רְאֵמִים, *young* wild ox
בֶּן רצח, murderer
בֶּן רֶשֶׁף, spark
בֶּן שֶׁמֶן, *very* fertile
בֶּן תּוֹשָׁב, stranger
בֶּן תְּמוּתָה, doom *to die*
בֶּן תַּעֲרֻבָה, hostage
בֵּן, age, arrow, beast, bough, breed, brood, calf, child, colt, descendant, deserve, fellow, foal, grandchild, grandson, herd, man, member, offspring, old, people, son, tribe, whelp, young, young *man*, young *one*, youth
בנה, build, build *up*, builder, child, establish, fortify, line, make, obtain *a child*, prosper, rebuild, restore, set *up*, work
בנה עַל, besiege
בָּנוֹ, Beno
בִּנּוּי, Binnui
בָּנִי, Bani
בֻּנִּי, Bunni
בְּנֵי אֲבִיעֶזֶר, Abiezer
בְּנֵי אַשְׂרִיאֵל, Asriel
בְּנֵי אָשֵׁר, Asher
בְּנֵי בִנְיָמִן, Benjamin
בְּנֵי בְרַק, Bene-berak
בְּנֵי דָן, Dan
בְּנֵי הָעָם, common *people*, lay *people*
בְּנֵי חֵלֶק, Helek
בְּנֵי חֵפֶר, Hepher
בְּנֵי יְהוּדָה, Judah
בְּנֵי יַעֲקָן, Bene-jaakan
בְּנֵי יִשְׂרָאֵל, Israel
בְּנֵי נַפְתָּלִי, Naphtali
בְּנֵי עַם, people
בְּנֵי שָׁמוֹ, Amaw
בְּנֵי שְׁכֶם, Shechem
בְּנֵי שְׁמִידָע, Shemida
בְּנֵי שִׁמְעוֹן, Simeon
בִּנְיָה, building
בְּנָיָהוּ, Benaiah
בִּנְיָמִין, Benjamin, Benjaminite
בִּנְיָן, building, wall
בְּנִינוּ, Beninu
בִּנְעָא, Binea
בִּנְעָלִים, dryshod
בְּנֶפֶשׁ, deadly, inwardly
בְּנָקָם, revengefully
בִּנְקָמָה, revengefully
בְּסַאסְּאָה, measure *by measure*
בְּסוֹדְיָה, Besodeiah
בְּסוּס, mount
בֵּסַי, Besai
בֹּסֶר, grape, *sour* grapes, *unripe* grape
בְּסֵתֶר, secretly
בַּעֲבוּר, account, because, end, order, purpose, sake, while
בְּעֵבֶר, across, beyond, *other* side
בְּעַד, about, behalf, behind, out, over, through, upon, when
בְּעַד, about
בעה, bulge *out*, *cause to* boil, inquire, seek *out*
בְּעוֹד, long, soon, while, while *yet*, within
בְּעוֹר, Beor
בִּעוּתִים, *dread* assault, terror
בֹּעַז, Boaz
בעט, kick
בְּעֵינַיִם, think
בְּעֵינַיִם, before, look, seem
בְּעִיר, beast, cattle
בעל, get *a husband*, husband, marry, master, rule, rule *over*, wife
בַּעַל, Baal, bridegroom, citizen, due, husband, lord, man, master, owner, people, possessor
בַּעַל אִשָּׁה, marry
בַּעַל בְּרִית, ally, Baal-berith
בַּעַל גָּד, Baal-gad
בַּעַל הָמוֹן, Baal-hamon
בַּעַל זְבוּב, Baal-zebub
בַּעַל חֲלֹמוֹת, dreamer
בַּעַל חֵמָה, wrathful
בַּעַל חָנָן, Baal-hanan
בַּעַל חָצוֹר, Baal-hazor
בַּעַל חִצִּים, archer
בַּעַל חֶרְמוֹן, Baal-hermon
בַּעַל כָּנָף, bird
בַּעַל כְּנָפַיִם, *winged* creature
בַּעַל לָשׁוֹן, charmer
בַּעַל מְזִמּוֹת, mischief-maker
בַּעַל מְעוֹן, Baal-meon
בַּעַל מַשֵּׁה יָד, creditor
בַּעַל מִשְׁפָּט, adversary
בַּעַל פְּעוֹר, Baal *of Peor*, Baal-peor
בַּעַל פְּקִדֻת, sentry
בַּעַל פְּרָצִים, Baal-perazim
בַּעַל פָּרָשׁ, horseman
בַּעַל צְפוֹן, Baal-zephon
בַּעַל שָׁלִשָׁה, Baal-shalishah
בַּעַל תָּמָר, Baal-tamar
בַּעֲלָה, Baalah, mistress
בְּעָלוֹת, Bealoth
בַּעֲלֵי יְהוּדָה, Baale-judah
בְּעֶלְיָדָע, Beeliada
בְּעַלְיָה, Bealiah
בְּעָלִים, Baalis
בַּעֲלַת אוֹב, medium
בַּעֲלַת בְּאֵר, Baalath-beer
בַּעֲלָת, Baalath
בְּעֹן, Beon
בַּעֲנָא, Baana
בַּעֲנָה, Baanah
בְּעֶצֶם, very
בער, blaze, break *out*, brutal, burn, burn *up*, catch *fire*, *cause to* graze over, consume, destroy, devour, dull, exterminate, feed, flame *forth*, fuel, heat, kindle, make, make *a fire*, purge, put *away*, remove, set *fire*, stupid, *utterly* sweep *away*, *utterly* consume, waste
בער אַחֲרֵי, sweep *away*
בַּעַר, dull, stupid
בַּעֲרָא, Baara
בְּעֵרָה, fire
בַּעֲשֵׂיָה, Baaseiah
בַּעְשָׁא, Baasha
בְּעֶשְׁתְּרָה, Beeshterah
בעת, afraid, appall, assail, frighten, terrify, terror, torment
בְּעֵת, when, whenever
בְּעָתָה, terror
בְּפֶה, eat
בְּפִי, say
בִּפְנֵי, before
בְּפֶתַע, suddenly
בֹּץ, mire
בִּצְדָקָה, right
בִּצָּה, marsh, swamp
בְּצַוָּאר, stubbornly
בָּצוּר, fortify, thick
בֵּצָי, Bezai
בָּצִיר, vintage
בָּצָל, onion
בְּצַלְאֵל, Bezalel
בַּצְלוּת, Bazluth
בַּצְלִית, Bazlith
בצע, carry *out*, complete, cut *off*, finish, get *dishonest gain*, get *gain*, greedy, halt, make *gain*, man *greedy for gain*, shatter
בֶּצַע, bribe, covetousness, cut, *dishonest* gain, gain, gain *by violence*, good, profit, spoil, *unjust* gain
בצק, swell
בָּצֵק, dough
בָּצְקַת, Bozkath
בצר, cut *off*, fortify, gather, gather *grapes*, *grape* gatherer, hidden *thing*, impossible, thwart
בֶּצֶר, Bezer, gold
בַּצָּרָה, drought, trouble
בָּצְרָה, Bozrah, fold
בִּצָּרוֹן, stronghold
בַּצֹּרֶת, drought
בַּקְבּוּק, Bakbuk, flask, jar
בַּקְבֻּקְיָה, Bakbukiah
בַּקְבַּקַּר, Bakbakkar
בְּקוֹל, aloud
בְּקוֹל גָּדוֹל, aloud
בֻּקִּי, Bukki
בֻּקִּיָּהוּ, Bukkiah
בְּקִיעַ, bit, breach
בקע, breach, break, break *forth*, break *out*, break *through*, burst, burst *forth*, cleave, cleave *open*, conquer, cut, cut *out*, dash *to pieces*, divide, hatch, invade, make *a breach*, *make a* breach, *make* break *out*, rend, rip *open*, rip *up*, shatter, split, split *asunder*, split *in two*, split *open*, split *up*, tear, win
בֶּקַע, beka, half *shekel*
בִּקְעָה, plain, valley
בקק, empty, empty *out*, lay *waste*, luxuriant, make *void*, plunderer, strip
בקר, inquire, reflect, search, seek, seek *out*
בָּקָר, bull, cattle, cow, herd, ox
בֹּקֶר, morning, morrow
בְּקֶרֶב, among, deep, inwardly, there, through, within
בִּקֹּרֶת, inquiry
בקשׁ, ask, beg, beseech, demand, desire, impatient, inquire, investigate, look, make *a request*, make *search*, require, search, seek, seek *after*, seek *out*, snare, take *vengeance*
בקשׁ מִיַּד, take *vengeance*
בקשׁ מִלִּפְנֵי, entreat
בַּקָּשָׁה, ask, request
בַּר, bright, clean, flawless, food, grain, pure, son, wheat
בַּר, open
בֹּר, cleanness, lye
ברא, clear, clear *ground*, create, creation, creator, dispatch, fatten, make, wrought, *yet* unborn
בְּרָאיָה, Beraiah
בְּרֹאשׁ, first, full
בָּרִאשֹׁנָה, *first* time
בָּרִאשֹׁנָה, before, first, formerly
בַּרְבֻּרִים, fowl
בְּרֶגֶל, follow
בְּרַגְלֵ, after
בָּרָד, hail, hailstone
בָּרֹד, dapple, mottle
בֶּרֶד, Bered
ברה, eat, give *to eat*, persuade *to eat*
בָּרוּךְ, Baruch
בְּרוֹשׁ, cypress, fir *tree*
בָּרוּת, food
בְּרוֹת, pine
בֵּרוֹתָה, Berothah
בִּרְזָוִת, Birzaith
בַּרְזֶל, axe, *axe* head, head, iron, *iron* tool, *thing of* iron
בַּרְזִלַּי, Barzillai
ברח, chase, chase *away*, flee, flee *away*, *make* flee, make *haste*, pass *through*, put *to flight*, run *away*, take *to flight*
בְּרָחֹק, afar *off*
בֵּרִי, Beri
בָּרִיא, fat, fatling, plump, rich, sleek
בְּרִיא בָּשָׂר, fat
בְּרִיאָה, *something* new
בִּרְיָה, food
בָּרִיחַ, Bariah, flee, fugitive
בְּרִיחַ, bar, pole
בְּרִיעָה, Beriah
בְּרִיעִי, Beriite
בֹּרִית, soap
בְּרִית, bargain, compact, covenant, league, term, treaty
ברך, bless, congratulate, count *happy*, curse, give *blessing*, greet, invoke *a blessing*, kneel, *make* kneel *down*, pronounce *a blessing*, salute
בֶּרֶךְ, knee, knee-deep, lap
בָּרַכְאֵל, Barachel
בְּרָכָה, Beracah, bless, blessing, gift, peace, present
בְּרֵכָה, pool
בֶּרֶכְיָהוּ, Berechiah
בְּרֵכַת הַמֶּלֶךְ, King's *Pool*
בְּרֹמִים, colored *stuff*
בֶּרַע, Bera
ברק, flash *forth*
בָּרָק, Barak, glitter, *glittering* point, lightning
בַּרְקוֹס, Barkos
בַּרְקָנִים, brier
בָּרֶקֶת, carbuncle, emerald
ברר, approve, choice, choose, cleanse, polish, pure, purge *out*, purify, sharpen, *show oneself* pure, sincerely, test
בִּרְשַׁע, Birsha
בֵּרֹתַי, Berothai
בְּשׂוֹר, Besor
בְּשֵׂכֶל, shrewd
בֹּשֶׂם, aromatic, fragrance, perfume, spice, sweet-smelling
בָּשְׂמַת, Basemath
בשׂר, bear *tidings*, bring *good news*, bring *good tidings*, bring *news*, bring *tidings*, carry *good news*, carry *tidings*, *good tidings*, herald *of good tidings*, proclaim, publish, tell, tell *glad news*
בָּשָׂר, body, creature, flesh, meat, member
בְּשַׂר אִישׁ, mankind
בְּשׂרָה, *good* news, news, reward *for tidings*, tidings
בְּשֶׁ, seeing *that*
בַּשֶּׁבִי, captive
בִּשְׁגָגָה, unwittingly, *without* intent
בְּשִׁגָּעוֹן, furiously
בשׁל, bake, boil, hearth, ripe, ripen, roast, seethe
בָּשֵׁל, boil
בְּשֶׁל, because
בְּשֶׁל אֲשֶׁר, *however* much
בְּשַׁלְוָה, *without* warning
בְּשָׁלוֹם, peaceably, safe, safely, victorious
בַּשֶּׁלִי, privately
בִּשְׁלָם, Bishlam
בְּשֵׁם, expressly
בָּשָׁן, Bashan
בְּשָׁנָה, annual, yearly
בָּשְׁנָה, shame
בַּשֶּׁקֶר, falsely
בִּשְׁרִרוּת, stubbornly
בֹּשֶׁת, confusion, shame, shameful *thing*
בֹּשֶׁת פָּנִים, confusion

בַּת, bath, branch, daughter, female, granddaughter, maiden, old, people, town, village, woman
בַּת בְּלִיַּעַל, base *woman*
בַּת יַעֲנָה, ostrich
בַּת מֶלֶךְ, princess
בַּת רַבִּים, Bath-rabbim
בַּת שֶׁבַע, Bathsheba
בַּת שׁוּעַ, Bath-shua
בָּתָה, steep
בָּתָה, waste
בְּתוּאֵל, Bethuel
בְּתוֹךְ, along, along *with*, amid, among, between, halfway *up*, inside, there, through, within
בְּתוּל, Bethul
בְּתוּלָה, maiden, virgin
בְּתוּלִים, token *of virginity*, virgin, virginity
בַּתְּחִלָּה, first
בִּתְיָה, Bithiah
בתק, cut *to pieces*
בתר, cut *in two*
בֶּתֶר, half, part, rugged
בִּתְרוֹן, forenoon

גאה, grow, lift *up*, rise, triumph
גֵּאָה, pride
גֵּאֶה, arrogant *man*, proud
גְּאוּאֵל, Geuel
גַּאֲוָה, arrogance, haughtily, haughtiness, majesty, pride, proudly, triumph, tumult
גְּאוּלִים, redemption
גָּאוֹן, arrogance, jungle, majestic, majesty, pomp, pride, proud, vainglory
גֵּאוּת, column, gloriously, majesty, proud, rage
גַּאֲיוֹן, proud
גאל, avenger, claim, defile, deliver, *do* part *of next of kin*, exclude *as unclean*, *right of redemption*, kinsman, *near* kin, *near* kinsman, next *of kin*, pollute, redeem, redeemer, stain, take *a right of redemption*
גֹּאַל, defile
גְּאֻלָּה, money *for redemption*, price *for redemption*, redeem, redemption, right *of redemption*
גַּב, back, defense, height, rim, *vaulted* chamber
גַּב עַיִן, eyebrow
גֵּב, beam, cistern, locust, pool
גֶּבֶא, cistern, marsh
גָּבֹהַּ, great, haughty, height, high, *high* official, high *one*, lofty, proud, proudly, tall
גֹּבַהּ, dignity, haughty, height, high, loftiness, pride, raise
גְּבַהּ לֵב, arrogant
גבה, courageous, exalt, grow, grow *proud*, haughty, high, lift *up*, make *high*, *make* high, mount *up*, proud, raise *to a great height*, soar *aloft*, tall, tower, upward
גַּבְהוּת, haughtiness, haughty
גְּבוּל, area, barrier, border, bound, boundary, coast, coast-line, country, frontier, land, landmark, place *where lives*, region, rim, territory, wall
גְּבוּל סָבִיב, extent
גְּבוּלָה, border, bound, boundary, *full* extent, landmark, territory
גִּבּוֹר, champion, chief, hero, man, mighty, mighty *man*, mighty *one*, *mighty* warrior, strong, strong *man*, warrior
גְּבוּרָה, might, mighty, mighty *act*, mighty *deed*, *mighty* doing, mighty *man*, *mighty* power, *mighty* strength, power, strength, victory
גַּבַּחַת, baldness *of the forehead*
גַּבַּחַת, *bald* forehead, forehead, front
גַּבַּי, Gabbai
גֵּבִי, locust
גֵּבִים, Gebim
גְּבִינָה, cheese
גָּבִיעַ, cup, pitcher
גְּבִיר, lord
גְּבִירָה, queen, queen *mother*
גָּבִישׁ, crystal

גבל, form *a boundary*, set, set *a bound*, set *bounds*
גְּבַל, Gebal
גְּבָל, Gebal
גִּבְלִי, Gebalite, *man of* Gebal
גַּבְלֻת, twist
גִּבֵּן, hunchback
גַּבְנֹן, many-peaked
גֶּבַע, Geba
גִּבְעָא, Gibea
גִּבְעָה, Gibeah, hill
גִּבְעוֹן, Gibeon
גִּבְעֹל, bud
גִּבְעֹנִי, Gibeon, Gibeonite
גִּבְעַת הָאֱלֹהִים, Gibeath-elohim
גִּבְעַת הָעֲרָלוֹת, Gibeath-haaraloth
גִּבְעָתִי, Gibeah
גבר, *become* strong, behave *arrogantly*, bid *defiance*, gain *an advantage*, great, grow *mighty*, make *strong*, mighty, prevail, put *forth more*, *show* mighty, strengthen, strong
גֶּבֶר, each, Geber, man, man-child, strong *man*
גֶּבֶר אִישׁ מִלְחָמָה, soldier
גִּבָּר, Gibbar
גַּבְרִיאֵל, Gabriel
גְּבֶרֶת, mistress
גִּבְּתוֹן, Gibbethon
גָּג, housetop, roof, top
גַּד, coriander, fortune
גָּד, Gad, Gadite, *good* fortune
גֻּדְגֹּדָה, Gudgodah
גדד, band *together*, cut, gash, troop
גְּדָה, bank
גְּדוּד, army, band, band *of men*, band *of raiders*, bandit, division, gash, marauder, *marauding* band, raid, raider, *raiding* band, ridge, robber, troop, unit
גָּדוֹל, abound, bitterly, chief, elder, exceedingly, great, great *deed*, great *man*, *great* number, great *one*, great *thing*, greatly, greatness, hard, high, huge, large, leader, loud, many, mighty, more, much, noble, old, powerful, rich, severe, strong, vast, very, wealthy, wide
גָּדוֹל עַד מְאֹד, violently
גדול, great
גְּדוּלָּה, dignity, great *thing*, greatness, *high* honor, honor, majesty
גִּדּוּפָה, taunt
גִּדּוּפִים, revile
גְּדוֹר, Gedor
גַּדִּי, Gaddi
גָּדִי, Gad, Gadi, Gadite
גְּדִי, kid
גְּדִי עִזִּים, kid
גַּדִּיאֵל, Gaddiel
גְּדִיָּה, kid
גָּדִישׁ, shock, shock *of grain*, *stacked* grain, tomb
גדל, advance, *become* great, *become* rich, *become* tall, *become* wealthy, boast, bring *up*, deal *insolently*, *do a* great *thing*, educate, exalt, excel, excellent, *full* grown, gain, give *great*, give *repute*, great, great *thing*, grow, grow *great*, grow *in stature*, grow *long*, grow *up*, honor, increase, lift, magnificent, magnify, make *a boast*, make *great*, *make* great, *make* grow, make *much*, mount, nourish, precious, promote, rear, recover, *show* great, *show* greatness, triumph, yield
גדל פֶּה, boast
גְּדַל בָּשָׂר, lustful
גִּדֵּל, Giddel
גֹּדֶל, arrogance, arrogant, great, greatness
גְּדַלְיָהוּ, Gedaliah
גְּדִלִים, tassel, wreath
גִּדַּלְתִּי, Giddalti
גדע, break, cut *asunder*, cut *down*, cut *in two*, cut *off*, hew *down*
גִּדְעוֹן, Gideon
גִּדְעֹם, Gidom
גִּדְעֹנִי, Gideoni
גדף, blaspheme, revile, reviler

גדר, block, build, build *up*, mason, repair, repairer, wall, wall *up*
גָּדֵר, fence, protection, wall
גֶּדֶר, Geder
גְּדֵרָה, fence, fold, Gederah, hedge, wall
גְּדֵרוֹת, Gederoth
גְּדֵרִי, Gederite
גִּדְרֹת צֹאן, sheepfold
גְּדֵרָתִי, Gederah
גְּדֵרֹתַיִם, Gederothaim
גהה, heal
גֵּהָה, medicine
גהר, bow *down*, stretch
גַּו, back
גֵּו, among, back, bowels
גוב, Gob, locust
גּוֹג, Gog
גוד, invade, raid
גֵּוָה, body, pride, proud
גוז, bring, go
גּוֹזָל, young, *young* pigeon
גּוֹזָן, Gozan
גוח, take
גּוֹי, heathen, nation, people
גְּוִיָּה, body, carcass, corpse, *dead* body
גּוֹיִם, Goiim
גּוֹלָה, captive, captivity, carry *away*, exile
גּוֹלָן, Golan
גּוּמָּץ, pit
גּוּנִי, Guni, Gunite
גוע, breathe *one's last*, close *to death*, dead, die, expire, perish
גוף, shut
גּוּפָה, body
גור, abide, afraid, band, band *together*, dread, dwell, fear, guest, live, reside, settle, sojourn, sojourner, stand *in awe*, stay, stir *up*, stir *up strife*, strife, tremble
גּוּר, whelp
גּוּר, cub, Gur, whelp, young
גּוּר בַּעַל, Gur-baal
גּוֹרָל, allot, allotment, *allotted* land, allotted *place*, lot, territory *allotted*
גּוּשׁ, dirt
גֵּז, fleece, mow, *mown* grass
גִּזְבָּר, treasurer
גזה, take
גִּזָּה, fleece
גִּזוֹנִי, Gizonite
גזז, cut *off*, shave, shear, shearer, sheepshearer
גזז צֹאן, sheepshearer
גָּזֵז, Gazez
גָּזִית, dress, *dressed* stone, hew, *hewn* stone
גזל, carry *off*, commit, despoil, rob, seize, snatch, snatch *away*, steal, take *away*, take *away violently*, take *by force*, take *by violence*, tear
גֵּזֶל, robbery, take *away violently*
גְּזֵלָה, robbery, spoil, take *by robbery*
גַּזָּם, Gazzam
גָּזָם, cutter, *cutting* locust, locust
גֶּזַע, stem, stump
גזר, cut *down*, cut *off*, decide, decree, divide, exclude, lost, snatch
גֶּזֶר, Gezer, piece, sunder
גִּזְרָה, beauty *of form*, *temple* yard, yard
גְּזֵרָה, solitary
גָּחוֹן, belly
גַּחֶלֶת, coal, coal *of fire*, *glowing* coal, *hot* coal, *hot* ember
גַּחַם, Gaham
גַּחַר, Gahar
גַּיְא, ravine, valley
גֵּיא חֲרָשִׁים, Ge-harashim
גִּיד, sinew
גיח, burst *forth*, rush
גִּיחַ, Giah
גִּיחוֹן, Gihon
גֵּיחֲזִי, Gehazi
גיל, delight, exult, glad, joy, rejoice

גִּיל, age, joy
גִּילָה, joy, rejoicing
גִּילֹנִי, Gilo, Gilonite
גִּינַת, Ginath
גֵּישָׁן, Geshan
גַּל, billow, heap, heap *of ruins*, stone *heap*, stoneheap, wave
גֵּל, dung
גַּלָּב, barber
גִּלְבֹּעַ, Gilboa
גַּלְגַּל, wagon, wheel, *whirling* dust, *whirling* wheel, whirlwind
גִּלְגַּל, wheel
גִּלְגָּל, Gilgal
גֻּלְגֹּלֶת, apiece, head, individual, skull
גֶּלֶד, skin
גלה, appear, banish, betray, captive, captivity, carry, carry *away*, carry *away captive*, carry *away into exile*, carry *captive*, carry *into exile*, carry *on openly*, commit, depart, deport, disclose, exile, expose, express, flaunt, go, go *into captivity*, go *into exile*, go *like an exile*, lay *bare*, lie *uncovered*, lift *up*, open, proclamation, put *off*, remove, reveal, send *into exile*, show, strip, strip *off*, take *away*, take *into exile*, *thing* revealed, uncover
גלה אֹזֶן, disclose, make *a revelation*, reveal, tell
גִּלֹה, Giloh
גֻּלָּה, bowl, spring
גִּלּוּל, idol, idolatry
גְּלוֹם, clothes
גָּלוּת, captive, captivity, exile
גלח, cut, cut *hair*, shave, shave *off*, shave *the hair*
גִּלָּיוֹן, garment *of gauze*, tablet
גָּלִיל, fold, ring, round
גְּלִילָה, region, region *about*
גְּלִילוֹת, Geliloth
גַּלִּים, Gallim
גָּלְיָת, Goliath
גלל, commit, lie *wallowing*, roll, roll *away*, roll *down*, roll *up*, seek *occasion*, start *rolling*
גָּלָל, dung, Galal
גִּלֲלַי, Gilalai
גלם, roll *up*
גֹּלֶם, *unformed* substance
גַּלְמוּד, barren, hard
גלע, break *out*, quarrel
גַּלְעֵד, Galeed
גִּלְעָד, Gilead, Gileadite
גִּלְעָדִי, Gileadite
גלשׁ, move *down*
גַּם, again, alike, already, although, another, *at* all, besides, both, either, even, even *though*, indeed, just, likewise, moreover, now, oh, really, still, then, therefore, though, together, too, very, well, when, yea, yes, yet
גַּם אַיִן, neither
גַּם אֶתְמוֹל גַּם שִׁלְשׁוֹם, time *past*
גַּם כִּי, besides, though
גַּם לֹא, neither, nor
גַּם מִתְּמוֹל גַּם מִשִּׁלְשֹׁם, heretofore
גַּם שְׁנַיִם, both
גַּם תְּמוֹל גַּם שִׁלְשׁוֹם, *some* time past
גמא, give *to drink*, swallow
גֹּמֶא, bulrush, papyrus, rush
גֹּמֶד, cubit
גַּמָּדִים, *man of* Gamad
גָּמוּל, Gamul
גְּמוּל, benefit, deed, desert, deserve, do, *due* reward, recompense, requital, work
גְּמוּלָה, deed, recompense, reward
גִּמְזוֹ, Gimzo
גמל, bear, benefit, bring, deal *bountifully*, do, grant, pay *back*, quiet, recompense, repay, requite, reward, ripen, wean, *weaned* child
גָּמָל, camel
גְּמַלִּי, Gemalli
גַּמְלִיאֵל, Gamaliel
גמר, come *to an end*, end, fulfil, fulfil *purpose*, no longer
גֹּמֶר, Gomer

גְּמַרְיָהוּ, Gemariah
גַּן, garden
גנב, bring *stealthily*, carry *away*, carry *off*, cheat, count *stolen*, steal, steal *away*
גנב לֵב, outwit
גנב לֵבָב, cheat
גַּנָּב, thief
גְּנֵבָה, *stolen* beast, theft
גְּנֻבַת, Genubath
גַּנָּה, garden, orchard
גְּנָזִים, carpet, treasury
גִּנְזַךְ, treasury
גנן, defend, protect, put *a shield*
גִּנְּתוֹי, Ginnethoi
גִּנְּתוֹן, Ginnethon
געה, low
גֹּעָה, Goah
געל, abhor, defile, fail, loathe
גַּעַל, Gaal
גֹּעַל, abhor
גער, rebuke
גְּעָרָה, rebuke, threat
געש, quake, reel, shake, stagger, surge, toss
גַּעַשׁ, Gaash
גַּעְתָּם, Gatam
גַּף, single
גַּף מְרוֹם, high *place*
גֶּפֶן, vine
גֶּפֶן יַיִן, vine
גֶּפֶן יַיִן, grapevine
גֹּפֶר, gopher
גָּפְרִית, brimstone
גֵּר, alien, *passing* guest, sojourner, stranger
גֵּרָא, Gera
גָּרָב, itch, *itching* disease, scurvy
גָּרֵב, Gareb
גַּרְגַּר, berry
גַּרְגְּרוֹת, neck
גִּרְגָּשִׁי, Girgashite
גרד, scrape
גרה, carry *the war*, contend, provoke, stir *up*, strive, wage, wage *war*
גֵּרָה, cud, gerah
גָּרוֹן, neck, throat
גְּרוּשָׁה, eviction
גֵּרוּת, Geruth
גִּרְזִי, Girzite
גְּרִזִּים, Gerizim
גַּרְזֶן, axe
גרם, break *in pieces*, leave
גֶּרֶם, bare, bone, limb, strong
גַּרְמִי, Garmite
גֹּרֶן, *threshing* floor
גֹּרֶן דָּגָן, *threshing* floor
גרס, consume, *make* grind
גרע, cut *down*, cut *off*, diminish, draw *up*, hinder, hold *back*, keep, lessen, limit, make *a deduction*, shear, take, take *away*, withdraw
גרף, sweep *away*
גרר, chew, drag *out*, saw, sweep *away*, whirl
גְּרָר, Gerar
גֶּרֶשׂ, crush, *crushed* grain
גרשׁ, cast *out*, divorce, divorced *woman*, drive, drive *away*, drive *far*, drive *out*, expell, thrust *out*, toss, toss *about*, toss *up*
גֶּרֶשׁ, yield
גֵּרְשׁוֹן, Gershom, Gershon
גֵּרְשֹׁם, Gershom, Gershomite
גֵּרְשֻׁנִּי, Gershonite
גְּשׁוּר, Geshur
גְּשׁוּרִי, Geshurite
גשׁם, bring *rain*, rain *upon*
גֶּשֶׁם, *abundant* rain, Geshem, *heavy* rain, rain, shower
גֹּשֶׁן, Goshen
גִּשְׁפָּא, Gishpa
גשׁשׁ, grope
גַּת, Gath, wine *press*
גַּת חֵפֶר, Gath-hepher
גַּת רִמּוֹן, Gath-rimmon
גִּתִּי, Gath, Gittite
גִּתַּיִם, Gittaim
גִּתִּית, Gittith
גֶּתֶר, Gether

דאב, grow *dim*, languish
דְּאָבָה, terror
דְּאָבוֹן, languish
דאג, afraid, anxious, *become* anxious, dread, sorry
דֹּאֵג, Doeg
דְּאָגָה, anxiety, fear, fearfulness, trouble
דאה, come *swiftly*, fly
דָּאָה, buzzard, kite
דֹּאר, Dor
דֹּב, bear, she-bear
דֹּבֶא, strength
דבב, glide *over*
דִּבָּה, *evil* report, gossip, *ill* repute, report, slander, whisper
דְּבוֹרָה, bee, Deborah
דְּבִיר, Debir, *inner* sanctuary, sanctuary
דְּבֵלָה, cake, cake *of figs*
דִּבְלַיִם, Diblaim
דבק, cleave, cleave *together*, cling, close *upon*, draw, follow *close after*, follow *hard*, hold *fast*, join, keep *close*, *make* cleave, *make* cling, *make* stick, overtake, pursue *hard*, stick
דבק אַחֲרֵי, overtake
דבק בְּ, join
דבק בְּ, follow *steadfastly*
דָּבֵק, hold *fast*, join, stick *close*
דֶּבֶק, *scale* armor, soldering
דבר, address, announce, bid, command, declare, decree, direct, foretell, give, make, make *a boast*, man *who utters*, mention, name, order, pass, plea, plead, plot, promise, pronounce, recite, repeat, report, say, say *a word*, speak, speak *out*, speech, subdue, talk, talk *together*, teach, tell, think, threaten, use, utter, warn, woo, word
דבר אֶל, bid
דבר בְּאָזְנַיִם, explain, tell
דבר לֵאמֹר, say
דבר שֶׁקֶר, liar
דָּבָר, account, act, advice, advise, affair, answer, anything, ask, behavior, bid, business, case, cause, charge, chronicle, claim, command, commandment, concern, condition, conduct, conversation, counsel, danger, deal, decision, deed, desire, dispute, duty, each, eloquent, errand, favor, fulfilment, give, history, idly, least, manner, matter, message, more, much, need, news, number, one, oracle, order, part, pertain, plan, portion, practice, prayer, procedure, promise, proposal, propose, provision, purpose, question, reason, record, regard, report, request, require, rite, say, saying, sentence, something, speak, speech, story, talk, task, tell, term, theme, thing, thought, tidings, transaction, verdict, vision, way, what, whisper, word, work, write
דָּבָר אֲשֶׁר, what
דָּבָר טוֹב, promise
דָּבָר רֵיק, trifle
דָּבָר רָע, defect, harm
דֶּבֶר, pestilence, plague
דֹּבֶר, pasture
דָּבָר כָּזָב, lie
דָּבָר מָה, whatever
דָּבָר מִשְׁפָּט, decision
דָּבָר שְׂפָתַיִם, talk
דָּבָר שְׂפָתַיִם, word
דָּבָר שֶׁקֶר, falsehood
דִּבְרָה, cause, order
דֹּבְרוֹת, raft
דִּבְרִי, Dibri
דִּבְרֵי יָמִים, chronicle
דִּבְרֵי רִיבוֹת, case
דִּבְרֵי שִׁיר, song
דִּבֶּרֶת, direction
דָּבְרַת, Daberath
דְּבַשׁ, honey
דַּבֶּשֶׁת, Dabbesheth, hump
דָּג, fish
דגה, grow
דָּגָה, fish
דָּגוֹן, Dagon
דגל, banner, distinguish, set *up a banner*
דֶּגֶל, banner, standard
דָּגָן, bread, grain
דגר, gather
דַּד, bosom
דדה, lead *in procession*
דּוֹדָה, aunt, *father's* sister, *uncle's* wife
דֹּדָוָהוּ, Dodavahu
דְּדָן, Dedan
דְּדָנִי, Dedanite
דֹּדָנִים, Dodanim
דהם, confuse
דהר, gallop
דַּהֲרָה, gallop
דוב, *cause to* pine *away*
דוג, catch
דָּוִד, David
דּוֹד, affection, beloved, cousin, *father's* brother, kinsman, love, lover, uncle
דּוּד, basket, caldron, kettle, pot
דּוֹדוֹ, Dodo
דּוֹדַי, Dodai
דּוּדַי, mandrake
דָּוֶה, faint, sick, sickness, unclean *thing*
דוח, cleanse, rinse *off*, rinse *out*, wash
דְּוַי, sick
דַּוָּי, faint
דְּוַי, loathsome
דוך, beat
דּוּכִיפַת, hoopoe
דּוּמָה, Dumah, land *of silence*, silence
דּוּמִיָּה, rest, silence, silent
דּוּמָם, dumb, quietly, silence
דון, abide
דּוֹנַג, wax
דוץ, dance
דור, dwell, pile
דּוֹר, age, descendant, dwelling, generation, time
דּוּר, ball
דושׁ, flail, grass, thresh, trample, tread *down*, tread *out*
דחה, drive, overthrow, push, thrust *down*, totter, trip *up*
דְּחִי, fall, stumble
דֹּחַן, millet
דחף, haste, hasten, hurry, urge
דחק, jostle, oppress
דַּי, enough, plenty, proportion, suffice, sufficient, *sufficient* means
דִּי זָהָב, Di-zahab
דִּיבֹן גָּד, Dibon-gad
דִּיבֹן, Dibon
דַּיָּג, fisher, fisherman
דַּיָּה, kite
דְּיוֹ, ink
דִּימוֹנָה, Dimonah
דין, bring *judgment*, dispute, execute *judgment*, execute *justice*, judge, maintain *rights*, rule, strife, uphold, vindicate
דַּיָּן, judge, protector
דִּין, case, cause, judgment, justice, *legal* right, quarrel, right
דִּינָה, Dinah
דִּיפַת, Diphath
דָּיֵק, *siege* tower, *siege* wall, siegework
דַּיִשׁ, thresh
דִּישָׁן, Dishan, Dishon
דִּישֹׁן, Dishan, Dishon, ibex
דַּךְ, downtrodden, oppress, victim
דכא, break *in pieces*, bruise, contrite, crush, humble
דַּכָּא, contrite, crush, dust
דכה, break, contrite, crush
דַּכָּה, crush
דֳּכִי, roar
דכע, crush
דִּכְרָן, record
דַּל, haggard, lowly, needy, poor, poor *man*, weak
דַּל, door
דלג, leap, leap *over*
דלה, draw *out*, draw *water*, drawn *up*, hang *useless*
דַּלָּה, loom, poor
דלח, trouble
דְּלִי, bucket
דְּלָיָהוּ, Delaiah
דָּלִיּוֹת, branch
דְּלִילָה, Delilah
דלל, bring *low*, diminish, hang, weary
דִּלְעָן, Dilean
דלף, leak, melt *away*, pour *out tears*
דֶּלֶף, drip
דַּלְפוֹן, Dalphon
דלק, burn, chase, *fiery* shaft, *hotly* pursue, inflame, kindle
דלק אַחֲרֵי, chase
דַּלֶּקֶת, inflammation
דַּלַּת רֹאשׁ, *flowing* locks
דֶּלֶת, column, door, gate, leaf, lid
דַּם נְפָשׁוֹת, lifeblood
דָּם, blood, blood *guiltiness*, bloodguilt, bloodshed, bloodstain, bloodthirsty, bloody, death, guilt *of blood*, guilt *of bloodshed*, homicide, life, lifeblood, murder
דַּם לְנַפְשׁוֹת, lifeblood
דמה, alike, *become* like, cease, compare, consider, cut *off*, destroy, equal, give *a parable*, intend, like, liken, lost, make *like*, mean, no *more*, perish, plan, think, undone
דמה בְּנֶפֶשׁ, think
דְּמוּת, figure, form, likeness, model, picture, semblance
דֳּמִי, keep *silence*, noontide, rest
דמם, aloud, bring *to silence*, cease, cut *off*, destroy, devastate, doom, give *respite*, go *dumbfounded*, hold *one's peace*, keep *silence*, keep *silent*, perish, quiet, silence, silent, stand *still*, still, wait, wait *in silence*
דְּמָמָה, silence, still
דֹּמֶן, dung
דִּמְנָה, Dimnah
דמע, weep
דֶּמַע, outflow *of press*
דִּמְעָה, tear, weep
דַּמֶּשֶׂק, Damascus
דָּן, Dan
דָּנִאֵל, Daniel
דַּנָּה, Dannah
דִּנְהָבָה, Dinhabah
דָּנִי, Dan, Danite
דֵּעַ, knowledge, opinion
דֵּעָה, knowledge
דְּעוּאֵל, Deuel
דעך, extinguish, put *out*, vanish
דַּעַת, judgment, know, knowledge, skill
דפק, beat, knock, overdrive
דָּפְקָה, Dophkah
דַּק, beaten *small*, dwarf, fine, *fine* dust, powder, small, thin
דַּק בָּשָׂר, thin
דֹּק, curtain
דִּקְלָה, Diklah
דקק, beat, beat *in pieces*, crush, make *dust*, powder, *very* small
דקר, pierce, strike, thrust *through*, wound, wounded *man*
דַּר, mother-of-pearl
דֵּרָאוֹן, abhorrence, contempt
דָּרְבָן, goad
דָּרְבֹנָה, goad
דַּרְדַּע, Darda
דַּרְדַּר, thistle

דָּרוֹם, south, *south* wind
דְּרוֹר, liberty, liquid, swallow
דָּרְיָוֶשׁ, Darius
דרך, aim, archer, bend, come *forth*, cross, draw, go, guide, handle, lead, *make* tread, march, trample, tread, tread *down*, tread *out*, treader
דרך קֶשֶׁת, bowman
דֶּרֶךְ, behavior, come, conduct, course, deed, direction, fare, fate, go, highway, journey, life, manner, march, mid-course, mission, passage, path, road, road *side*, route, siegework, street, through, toward, track, undertaking, walk, way, wayside, work
דֶּרֶךְ אֲשֶׁר, wherever
דֶּרֶךְ מָבוֹא, entrance
דֶּרֶךְ סלל, highway
דַּרְכְּמוֹן, daric
דָּרַע, Dara
דַּרְקוֹן, Darkon
דרשׁ, ask, avenge, call *to account*, care, consult, examine, inquire, inquire *about*, inquirer, make *search*, question, reckoning *come*, require, resort, search, search *after*, seek, seek *after*, seek *guidance*, seek *out*, study, worship
דרשׁ אֶל הַמֵּתִים, necromancer
דרשׁ מִיַּד, avenge
דשׁא, green, put *forth*
דֶּשֶׁא, grass, green, herb, *new* growth, *tender* grass, vegetation
דשׁן, anoint, enrich, gorge, grow *fat*, make *rich*, receive *ash*, refresh, regard *with favor*, *richly* supply, take *away the ash*
דָּשֵׁן, full *of sap*, plenteous, proud
דֶּשֶׁן, abundance, ash, fat, fatness
דָּת, commission, decree, edict, law, regulation
דָּתָן, Dathan
דֹּתָן, Dothan

הֵא, behold, here, now
הֶאָח, aha
הָאֶלֶף, Haeleph
הָאֵם, truth
הבל, *become* false, *become* vain, *become* worthless, fill *with vain hope*, set *vain hope*
הֶבֶל, Abel, breath, empty, *empty* nothing, *empty* talk, false, *false* god, *false* idol, idol, nought, vain, vainly, vanity, vapor, worthless, worthless *thing*, worthlessness
הָבְנִי, ebony
הבר, divide
הֵגֶא, Hegai
הַגְּדוֹלִים, Haggedolim
הגה, devise, growl, make *a sound*, meditate, moan, mourn, muse, mutter, plot, ponder, remove, take *away*, talk, tell, utter
הֶגֶה, mourn, rumble, sigh
הָגוּת, meditation
הָגִיג, groan, muse
הִגָּיוֹן, Higgaion, meditation, melody, thought
הַגָּלִיל, Galilee
הֶגְלָם, Heglam
הָגָר, Hagar
הַגְרִי, Hagri, Hagrite
הֵד, *joyful* shouting
הדד, sharpen
הֲדַד, Hadad
הֲדַדְעֶזֶר, Hadadezer
הֲדַדְרִמּוֹן, Hadadrimmon
הדה, put
הֹדּוּ, India
הֲדוֹרָם, Hadoram
הִדַּי, Hiddai
הדך, tread *down*
הֲדֹם לְרַגְלַיִם, footstool
הֲדֹם רַגְלַיִם, footstool
הֲדַס, myrtle, myrtle *tree*
הֲדַסָּה, Hadassah
הדף, push, push *back*, stab, thrust, thrust *away*, thrust *down*, thrust *out*, thwart
הדר, glorious, honor, partial, put *forward*, respect
הדר פָּנִים, defer
הָדָר, beauty, comeliness, dignity, *glorious* power, glory, goodly, honor, majesty, nobility, splendor
הֶדֶר, glory
הֲדַר, Hadar
הֲדָרָה, array, glory
הֲדֹרָם, Hadoram
הָהּ, alas
הוֹ, alas
הוא, fall
הוּא, same, such, whatever
הוֹד, authority, beauty, glory, Hod, honor, majestic, majesty, proud, *radiant* appearance, splendor
הוֹדַוְיָה, Hodevah
הוֹדַוְיָהוּ, Hodaviah
הוֹדִיָּה, Hodiah
הוה, become, lie
הַוָּה, calamity, deadly, destruction, disaster, *evil* desire, lust, mischievous, ruin, storm *of destruction*, wicked
הוֹהָם, Hoham
הוֹי, ah, alas, ho, woe
הוֹלֵלָה, madness
הוֹלֵלוּת, madness
הום, distraught, *noisy* multitude, resound, stir, throw *into confusion*, uproar
הוֹמָם, Homam
הון, think *it easy*
הוֹן, afford, enough, goods, riches, substance, wealth
הוֹשָׁמָע, Hoshama
הוֹשֵׁעַ, Hosea, Hoshea, Joshua
הוֹשַׁעְיָה, Hoshaiah
הות, set
הוֹתִיר, Hothir
הזה, dream
הַחִירֹת, Hahiroth
הִי, woe
הִיא, same, such
הֵידָד, shout, shout *of joy*, shout *of victory*, *vintage* shout
הֻיְּדוֹת, song *of thanksgiving*
היה, abide, accomplish, acquit, allot, arise, *at* hand, become, befall, begin, behave, belong, bring, bring *about*, bring *to pass*, carry, cause, come, come *about*, come *into being*, *come to* pass, continue, count, do, due, endure, extend, fall, fall *upon*, fare, find, follow, form, fulfil, get, give, go, go *down*, grow, hand, happen, hold, I *am*, include, keep, last, lay, lie, make, marry, meet, number, overcome, place, present, prevail, put, reach, redound, remain, rest, run, serve, set, show, some, spread, supply, take *place*, tend, turn, use, used, wait
היה אַחֲרֵי, follow
היה אֶל, inherit
היה בְּעֵינַיִם, seem
היה דָּבָר, confer
היה הלך, continue
היה טוֹב, prosper
היה יָד אֵת, help
היה יָרֵא, fear, revere
היה כְּ, seem
היה כְּ, compare
היה לְ, become, keep, provide, receive, take
היה לְ, befall, come *over*, possess
היה לְאִישׁ, marry
היה לְאִשָּׁה, marry
היה לִישׁוּעָה, help
היה לִפְנֵי, enter *service*, precede, serve, wait
היה לְשַׁמָּה, destroy
היה עַל, drive *back*
היה עִם, join
היה עִם לֵב, decide
היה שׁרת, minister
היה תּוֹצָאָה, end
הַיּוֹם, *just* now, now, nowadays, recently, then, today
הַיּוֹם הַזֶּה, now, today
הַיִּים, life
הֵיךְ, how
הֵיכָל, nave, palace, temple
הֵילֵל, day *star*
הֵימָם, Heman
הֵימָן, Heman
הִין, hin
הכר, wrong
הַכָּרַת פָּנִים, partiality
הלא, cast *off*
הָלְאָה, back, beyond, far, far *and wide*, forward, onward
הָלְאָה מִן, beyond
הַלּוֹחֵשׁ, Hallohesh
הִלּוּל, festival, offering *of praise*
הַלָּז, yonder
הַלָּזֶה, yonder
הֵלִיךְ, step
הֲלִיכָה, go, procession, *solemn* procession, traveler, way
הלך, about, about *to go*, again, along, apace, bear, become, blow, bring, carry, carry *away*, *cause to* go, *cause to* run, come, come *away*, conduct, continually, continue, depart, dissolve, drive *back*, flash *on every side*, flee, float, flow, get, get *away*, get *off*, glide *away*, go, go *about*, go *along*, go *away*, go *back*, go *down*, go *forth*, go *forward*, go *in and out*, go *out*, go *up*, go *up and down*, grow, grow *more and more*, hie, intend, journey, keep, lead, lead *away*, live, make *a journey*, *make a* journey, *make* walk, march, march *forth*, more *and more*, move, move *about*, move *to and fro*, occupy, part, pass, patrol, prowl, reach, return, ride, roam, robber, run, run *away*, seek, send, set, set *forth*, set *out*, speed, spend, spread, spread *out*, stalk, stay *away*, stride, strut, take, take *away*, travel, vagabond, vanish, walk, walk *about*, walk *abroad*, walk *through*, walk *up and down*, wander, wander *about*, way
הלך אַחַר, follow
הלך אַחֲרֵי, follow, pursue
הלך בְּ, follow
הלך בְּרֶגֶל, follow
הלך וּברח, flee *away*
הלך וְגָדוֹל, *become* great
הלך והלך, go *up and down*
הלך וְקָשֶׁה, harder *and harder*
הלך וָשׁוֹב, continually
הלך לְרֶגֶל, attend
הלך מִן, leave, withdraw
הלך מֵעִם, leave
הלך נְתִיבָה, traveler
הלך עַל, join, overflow
הֵלֶךְ, drop, traveler
הלל, arrogant, boast, boastful, celebration, commend, craze, deride, feign *mad*, flash *forth*, give *light*, give *praise*, glory, *go* mad, mad, make *a boast*, make *a fool*, make *foolish*, offer *praise*, praise, rage, renowned, shine, sing *praise*, worthy *to be praised*
הִלֵּל, Hillel
הלם, beat, beat *loud*, break *down*, overcome, strike, strike *a blow*, strike *down*
הֶלֶם, Helem
הֲלֹם, far, here, hither, thither
הַלְמוּת, mallet
הָם, Ham
הֵם, here, other, such
הַמְּדָתָא, Hammedatha
המה, beat *wildly*, brawler, disquiet, growl, howl, loud, moan, noisy, rage, roar, thrill, thunder, tumult, tumultuous, turmoil, uproar, yearn
הָמוֹן, abundance, herd, horde, multitude, music, noise, orgy, populous, rumble, rush, thunder, thunderous, troop, tumult, tumultuous, uproar, wealth, yearn
הֲמוֹן גּוֹג, Hamon-gog
הֲמוֹנָה, Hamonah
הֶמְיָה, sound
הֲמֻלָּה, tempest, tumult
הַמֹּלֶכֶת, Hammolecheth
המם, crush, destroy, discomfit, drive, rout, throw *into a panic*, throw *into confusion*, trouble
המן, turbulent
הָמָן, Haman
הֵמֶס, brushwood
הַמַּעֲשֶׂה אֲשֶׁר, what
הֵן, behold, even, good, if, lo, when
הִנֵּה, behold, come, find, hark, here, how, if, indeed, just *then*, know, lo, look, now, see, surely, then, there, what, when, while, yea
הֵנָּה, way
הֵנָּה וְהֵנָּה, to *and fro*
הֵנָּה, here, hither, now, other, side, there, toward
הֵנָּה הֵנָּה, much *more*
הֲנָחָה, remission *of tax*
הִנֹּם, Hinnom
הִנְנִי, I *am*
הִנֵּנִי, I *am*
הֵנַע, Hena
הס, quiet
הַס, hush, keep *silence*, quiet, silence, silent
הַסְּנָאָה, Hassenaah
הַסְּנוּאָה, Hassenuah
הַסֹּפֶרֶת, Hassophereth
הֲפוּגָה, respite
הפך, change, come, dry *up*, give, overthrow, overturn, overwhelm, perverse, pervert, recoil, rein *about*, tumble, turn, turn *back*, turn *every way*, turn *over*, turn *up*, twist, wring
הפך יָד, turn *about*
הפך לְדֶרֶךְ, turn *away*
הֶפֶךְ, different, turn *upside down*
הֲפֵכָה, overthrow
הֲפַכְפַּךְ, crooked
הַפִּצֵּץ, Happizzez
הַצָּה, strive
הַצָּלָה, deliverance
הַצְלֶלְפּוֹנִי, Hazzelelponi
הַקּוֹץ, Hakkoz
הַקָּטָן, Hakkatan
הַר, hill, *hill* country, mount, mountain, *mountain* country, slope
הַר חֶרֶס, Har-heres
הֹר, Hor
הָרָא, Hara
הָרֹאֶה, Haroeh
הַרְבֵּה, many, more
הַרְבָּה, abundance
הרג, death, destroy, kill, make, murder, murderer, slaughter, slay, slayer
הֶרֶג, slaughter
הֲרֵגָה, slaughter, slay
הרה, child, conceive
הָרָה, child, conceive, great, pregnant, *woman with* child
הָרִיָּה, pregnant *woman*
הֵרָיוֹן, childbearing, conception
הֲרִיסָה, ruins
הֲרִיסוּת, devastate
הָרֻם, Harum
הֹרָם, Horam
הַרְמוֹן, Harmon
הָרָן, Haran
הרס, break, break *down*, break *through*, cast *down*, demolish, destroy, destroyer, overthrow, pull *down*, ruin, tear *down*, throw *down*
הרע, hurt
הֲרָרִי, Hararite
הָשֵׁם, Hashem
הַשְׁמָעוּת, report
הִתּוּךְ, melt
הֲתָךְ, Hathach
התל, mock
הֲתֻלִּים, mocker

וְ, after, afterward, again, along, although, because, before, besides, both, either, especially, even, even *though*, furthermore, how, however, if, include, lest, likewise, meanwhile, moreover, namely, neither, nevertheless, nor, notwithstanding, only, otherwise, see, since, soon, thence, therefore,

though, thus, till, together, too, until, well, whenever, where, whereas, yea, yet
וְאַיִן, neither
וְאַיִן, nor, unless
וְאַל, lest, neither, nor, rather *than*
וְאִם, nor
וְאִם לֹא, nay
וְכֹל, nor
וְגַם, moreover, nor, yet
וְגַם לֹא, nor
וָהֵב, Waheb
והיה, thus
וָו, hook
וָזָר, guilty
וַיְזָתָא, Vaizatha
וְלֹא, instead, lest, neither, never, nor, without
וָלָד, child
וָמָה, nor
וַנְיָה, Vaniah
וָעַד, well
וְעוֹד, moreover
וְעַל, along
וְעַתָּה, henceforth, moreover, therefore, yet
וְעַתָּה לָכֵן, then
וָפְסִי, Vophsi
וְשָׁם, where
וַשְׁתִּי, Vashti

זְאֵב, wolf, Zeeb
זבד, endow
זָבָד, Zabad
זֶבֶד, dowry
זַבְדִּי, Zabdi
זַבְדִּיאֵל, Zabdiel
זְבַדְיָהוּ, Zebadiah
זְבוּב, fly
זָבוּד, Zabud
זְבוּלֻן, Zebulun
זְבוּלֹנִי, Zebulunite
זבח, bring *a sacrifice*, *keep* sacrificing, kill, make *a sacrifice*, offer, offer *a sacrifice*, perform, prepare, sacrifice, sacrifice *an offering*, slaughter, slay
זֶבַח, feast, offer, offering, sacrifice, sacrificial, Zebah
זֶבַח שֶׁלֶם, sacrifice
זַבַּי, Zabbai
זְבִידָה, Zebidah
זְבִינָא, Zebina
זבל, honor
זְבֻל, exalt, habitation, Zebul
זָג, skin
זֵד, arrogant, godless, godless *man*, insolent, insolent *man*, *presumptuous* sin, proud *man*
זָדוֹן, insolence, presumption, presumptuously, pride, proud *one*
זֶה, another, first, follow, here, now, other, *other* side, really, same, *same* amount, same *way*, side, such, such *a thing*, there, thus, what, where, yon, yonder
זָהָב, gold, golden, *golden* splendor, *thing of* gold
זהם, loathe
זַהַם, Zaham
זהר, beware, give *a warning*, give *warning*, instruct, shine, take *advice*, take *warning*, teach, warn
זֹהַר, brightness
זִו, Ziv
זוּ, where
זוב, discharge, flow, gush *forth*, gush *out*, pine *away*
זוֹב, discharge
זוּזִים, Zuzim
זוֹחֵת, Zoheth
זָוִית, corner, *corner* pillar
זול, lavish
זוּלָה, besides, except
זוּלַת, only
זון, well-fed
זוע, *make* tremble, tremble
זְוָעָה, terror
זור, alien, another, any *one else*, crush, else, estrange, foreign, foreigner, go *astray*, loose, loose *woman*, outsider, press *out*, repulsive, squeeze, strange, *strange* god, strange *thing*, stranger, unholy
זָזָא, Zaza
זחח, come *loose*
זחל, crawling *thing*, timid
זֹחֶלֶת, serpent
זיד, *act* insolently, *act* presumptuously, boil, deal *arrogantly*, presume, presumptuous, proudly *defy*, *willfully* attack
זֵידוֹן, rage
זִיז, abundance, *all that* move, *all that* moves
זִיזָא, Ziza
זִיזָה, Zizah
זִינָא, Zina
זִיעַ, Zia
זִיף, Ziph
זִיפָה, Ziphah
זִיפִי, Ziphite
זַיִת, olive, *olive* leaf, *olive* orchard, olive *tree*, oliveyard
זֵית יִצְהָר, olive *tree*
זֵיתִים, Olives
זֵיתָן, Zethan
זַךְ, clean, pure
זכה, acquit, blameless, clean, keep *clean*, keep *pure*, make *clean*, pure
זְכוֹכִית, glass
זַכּוּר, Zaccur
זָכוּר, male
זַכַּי, Zaccai
זכך, clean, cleanse
זכר, acknowledge, boast, bring *to remembrance*, call *to mind*, *cause to* celebrate, *cause to* remember, come *to remembrance*, confess, extol, invoke, keep *in mind*, keep *in remembrance*, make *a memorial offering*, make *mention*, *make* remember, *memorial* offering, mention, mindful, name, praise, proclaim, put *in remembrance*, recall, recorder, recount, remember, summon, take *thought*, think, warn
זָכָר, male, man, son
זֶכֶר, Zecher
זֵכֶר, commemoration, fame, fragrance, memorial, memory, name, remember, remembrance, renown
זִכָּרוֹן, maxim, memorable *deed*, memorial, remembrance, reminder, symbol
זִכְרִי, Zichri
זְכַרְיָהוּ, Zechariah
זַלְזַל, shoot
זלל, despise, glutton, *gluttonous* eater, quake, worthless
זַלְעָפָה, *burning* heat, *hot* indignation, scorch
זִלְפָּה, Zilpah
זֻלּוּת, vileness
זִמָּה, abomination, devise, *evil* device, *evil* intent, *evil* purpose, *heinous* crime, lewd, lewdness, plan, villainy, *wicked* device, wickedness, wrong, Zimmah
זְמוֹרָה, branch, slip, *vine* branch
זַמְזֻמִּים, Zamzummim
זָמִיר, psalmist, sing, song, song *of praise*
זְמִירָה, Zemirah
זמם, consider, devise *evil*, mean, plan, plot, propose, purpose
זָמָם, *evil* plot
זמן, appoint
זְמָן, *appointed* season, *appointed* time, season, time
זמר, make *melody*, play, praise, prune, sing, sing *praise*
זֶמֶר, mountain-sheep
זִמְרָה, *choice* fruit, melody, song
זִמְרִי, Zimri
זִמְרָן, Zimran
זַן, store, various *kinds*
זנב, cut *off at rear*, fall *upon rear*
זָנָב, stump, tail
זנה, commit *harlotry*, fall *into harlotry*, false, give *to harlotry*, go *astray*, go *wantonly*, harlot, lead *into unfaithfulness*, make *a harlot*, *make* play *the harlot*, play *the harlot*, practice *harlotry*, solicit *to play the harlot*, turn *wantonly*, wanton
זָנוֹחַ, Zanoah
זְנוּנִים, harlotry
זְנוּת, faithlessness, harlotry, idolatry
זנח, *become* foul, bereft, cast *off*, cast *out*, discard, reject, scorn, spurn
זנק, leap *forth*
זֵעָה, sweat
זַעֲוָה, horror, object *of horror*, terror
זַעֲוָן, Zaavan
זְעֵיר, little
זעך, extinct
זעם, abhor, accursed, angry, denounce, enrage, indignation
זַעַם, fierce, fury, indignation, insolence, wrath
זעף, angry, poor, rage, trouble
זַעַף, furious, indignation, rage, wrath
זָעֵף, sullen
זעק, call, call *out*, call *together*, come, cry, cry *aloud*, cry *for help*, cry *out*, cry *out for help*, make *proclamation*, rally, summon, wail
זְעָקָה, cry, cry *out*, distress, lament, outcry, shout
זִפְרֹן, Ziphron
זֶפֶת, pitch
זֵק, brand, chain, fetter, firebrand
זקן, *become* old, grow *old*, old
זָקָן, beard
זָקֵן, age, aged *man*, elder, old, *old* folks, old *man*, old *woman*, senior
זָקֵן לְיָמִים, old
זֹקֶן, age
זִקְנָה, old, *old* age
זְקֻנִים, *old* age
זקף, lift *up*, raise *up*
זקק, distil, purify, refine
זֵר, molding
זָרָא, loathsome
זרב, heat
זְרֻבָּבֶל, Zerubbabel
זֶרֶד, Zered
זרה, disperse, scatter, *scattering* wind, search *out*, spread, winnow, winnower
זְרוֹעַ, arm, army, force, might, power, shoulder, strength, *strong* arm
זְרוֹעַ יָד, arm
זֵרוּעַ, sow
זרח, arise, break *out*, dawn, rise, shine, shine *forth*, up
זֶרַח, rise, Zerah
זַרְחִי, Zerahite
זְרַחְיָה, Zerahiah
זרם, pour *out*, sweep *away*
זֶרֶם, rage, rain, storm, tempest
זִרְמָה, issue
זרע, conceive, perpetuate, put *in seed*, scatter, set *out*, sow, sower, yield, yield *seed*
זֶרַע, birth, child, crop, descendant, descent, family, fertile, grain, house, kind, line, offspring, people, posterity, race, seed, seedtime, son, sow, stock
זֶרַע אֲנָשִׁים, son
זֵרֹעַ, vegetable
זֵרְעֹן, vegetable
זַרְזִיף, water
זרק, scatter, sow, sprinkle, strew, throw
זרר, sneeze
זֶרֶשׁ, Zeresh
זֶרֶת, span
זַתּוּא, Zattu
זֵתָם, Zetham
זֵתַר, Zethar

חֹב, bosom
חבא, *become* hard, hide, hush, secretly, withdraw
חבב, love
חֹבָב, Hobab
חבה, conceal, hide
חָבוֹר, Habor
חַבּוּרָה, blow, sore, strike, stripe, wound
חבט, beat, beat *out*, thresh *out*
חֲבַיָּה, Habaiah
חֳבַיָּה, Hobaiah
חֶבְיוֹן, veil
חבל, *act* corruptly, break, bring *destruction*, conceive, destroy, exact *a pledge*, hold *in pledge*, offend, pledge, ruin, spoil, take *for a pledge*, take *in pledge*, travail, union
חֶבֶל, allot, band, coil, cord, destruction, line, portion, region, rope, seacoast, snare, tackle, territory
חֶבֶל הַיָּם, seacoast
חִבֵּל, mast
חֹבֵל, pilot
חֵבֶל, agony, pain, pang, sorrow, young
חֲבֹלָה, pledge
חֲבַצֶּלֶת, crocus, rose
חֲבַצִּנְיָה, Habazziniah
חבק, cling, embrace, fold, lie
חִבֻּק, fold
חֲבַקּוּק, Habakkuk
חבר, ally, attach, bind *firmly*, binder, charmer, couple, couple *together*, enchanter, join, join *forces*, join *together*, make *an alliance*, touch
חַבָּר, trader
חָבֵר, associate, companion, fellow, unite
חֶבֶר, enchantment, Heber, share
חֲבַרְבֻּרָה, spot
חֶבְרָה, company
חֶבְרוֹן, Hebron
חֶבְרוֹנִי, Hebronite
חֶבְרִי, Heberite
חֹבֶרֶת, connect, set
חֲבֶרֶת, companion
חבשׁ, bind, bind *up*, govern, healer, make *secure*, saddle, swathe, wrap
חֲבִתִּים, *flat* cake
חַג, feast, *festal* procession, festival, offering
חָגָא, terror
חָגָב, grasshopper, Hagab, locust
חֲגָבָה, Hagaba, Hagabah
חגג, dance, hold *a feast*, keep, *keep* a feast, keep *festival*, observe, reel
חֲגָוִים, cleft
חָגוּר, gird
חֲגוֹר, girdle
חֲגוֹרָה, apron, armor, girdle
חַגַּי, Haggai
חַגִּי, Haggi, Haggite
חַגִּיָּה, Haggiah
חַגִּית, Haggith
חָגְלָה, Hoglah
חגר, arm, gird, gird *up*, gird *upon*, girdle, put, put *on armor*, wear
חַד, sharp
חדד, fierce
חֲדַד, Hadad
חדה, make *glad*, rejoice
חִדּוּד, sharp
חֶדְוָה, joy
חָדִיד, Hadid
חדל, cease, desist, fail, forbear, give *up*, keep, lack, leave, leave *off*, no *more*, quit, refrain, refuse, reject, stop, turn *away*
חדל לְעוֹלָם, *never* suffice
חדל מִן, let *alone*
חָדֵל, fleeting
חַדְלָי, Hadlai
חֵדֶק, brier, thorn
חִדֶּקֶל, Tigris
חדר, encompass
חֶדֶר, chamber, closet, *inner* chamber, inner *part*, innermost, room
חֶדֶר בְּחֶדֶר, *inner* chamber
חֲדַר מִטּוֹת, bedchamber

חֲדַר מִשְׁכָּב, bedchamber
חַדְרָךְ, Hadrach
חדשׁ, *new* moon, put *new*, renew, repair, restore
חָדָשׁ, fresh, new, *new* god, *new* grain, new *thing*, newly
חֹדֶשׁ, Hodesh, month, *new* moon
חֲדָשָׁה, Hadashah
חוב, endanger
חוֹבָה, Hobah
חוג, describe
חוּג, circle, vault
חוד, propound *a riddle*, put, put *a riddle*, sharpen
חוה, declare, show
חַוָּה, Eve, town, village
חוֹחַ, bramble, hole, hook, thistle, thorn
חוּט, cord, line, thread
חִוִּי, Hivite
חֲוִילָה, Havilah
חול, afraid, agony, anguish, bear, bring *forth*, burst, calve, dance, dancer, distress, endure, fall, feel *anguish*, form, give *birth*, labor, lay, *make* whirl, prosper, rage, shake, travail, tremble, wait, wait *anxiously*, wait *patiently*, whirl, woman *in travail*, wound, writhe, writhe *in pain*
חוֹל, sand
חוּל, Hul
חוּם, black
חוֹמָה, wall
חוס, pity, spare
חוֹף, coast, haven, shore
חוֹף הַיָּם, seacoast, seashore
חוּפָם, Hupham
חוּפָמִי, Huphamite
חוּץ, abroad, apart, bazaar, field, open, out, outer, outside, outward, street, without
חוּצָה, abroad, without
חוּקֹק, Hukok
חור, grow *pale*
חוּר, Hur, white, *white* curtain
חוֹרִי, *white* cotton
חוּרַי, Hurai
חוּרִי, Huri
חוּרָם, Huram
חוּרָם אָבִי, Huram-abi
חַוְרָן, Hauran
חושׁ, come *swiftly*, enjoyment, haste, hasten, make *haste*, *ready to* go, speed, swift
חוּשָׁה, Hushah
חוּשַׁי, Hushai
חוּשִׁים, Hushim
חַוֹּת יָאִיר, Havvoth-jair
חוֹתָם, Hotham
חֲזָאֵל, Hazael
חזה, behold, choose, gaze, look, look *upon*, prophesy, see, see *a vision*, see *an oracle*, speak
חָזֶה, breast
חֹזֶה, agreement, prophet, seer
חֲזָהאֵל, Hazael
חֲזוֹ, Hazo
חָזוֹן, prophecy, vision
חָזוּת, vision
חָזוּת, agreement, conspicuous, vision
חֲזִיאֵל, Haziel
חֲזָיָה, Hazaiah
חֶזְיוֹן, Hezion
חִזָּיוֹן, vision
חֲזִיז, lightning, storm *cloud*
חֲזִיז קוֹלוֹת, thunderbolt
חֲזִיר, boar, swine
חֵזִיר, Hezir
חזק, aid, *become* mighty, *become* strong, bind, catch, catch *fast*, catch *hold*, caulk, confirm, contend, courageous, courageously, encourage, establish, fasten, firmly, force, fortify, gird, give, give *strength*, give *strong support*, *good* courage, good *courage*, grasp, grow *mighty*, grow *strong*, harden, help, hold, *hold* fast, hold *fast*, hold *firm*, join, keep *hold*, lay *hold*, loud, maintain, maintenance, *make* hard, *make* stay, make *strong*, obtain, overcome, play *the man*, prevail, recover, repair, resolute, restore, retain, seize, *set to* work *resolutely*, severe, *show* might, stand *firm*, steadfast, stout, strengthen, strong, summon *strength*, sure, take, take *courage*, take *hold*, urgent, withstand
חזק בְּ, urge
חזק בֶּדֶק, caulker, make *repairs*, repair
חזק יָד, aid, encourage
חזק מִן, go *against*
חָזָק, hard, loud, might, mighty, severe, strong
חָזָק מְאֹד, severe
חָזֵק, strength, strong
חֲזַק לֵב, stubborn
חֵזֶק, strength
חֶזְקָה, *become* strong, strong
חִזְקִי, Hizki
חִזְקִיָּהוּ, Hezekiah, Hizkiah
חָח, brooch, hook
חטא, bear *blame*, bear *loss*, beside, bring *guilt upon*, *cause to* sin, cleanse, commit, commit *sin*, *do* amiss, *do* wrong, fault, forfeit, lead *into sin*, make *a sin offering*, *make* commit *sin*, make *out to be an offender*, *make* sin, miss, miss *the way*, offend, offer *a sin offering*, offer *for sin*, purge, purify, purify *from sin*, sin, sinful, sinner
חַטָּא, man *who sins*, offender, sinful, sinner
חֵטְא, crime, fault, incur, offense, punishment, sin, sinful, sinfully
חֲטָאָה, sin
חַטָּאָה, sin, *sin* offering
חַטָּאת, expiation, punishment, sin, *sin* offering, sinful *thing*, wrong
חטב, cut, cut *down*, fell, hew, hewer
חֲטֻבוֹת, *colored* spread
חִטָּה, wheat
חַטּוּשׁ, Hattush
חֲטִיטָא, Hatita
חַטִּיל, Hattil
חֲטִיפָא, Hatipha
חטם, restrain
חטף, seize
חֹטֶר, rod, shoot
חַי, alive, come *round*, green, kinsfolk, life, live, *living* creature, living *man*, living *thing*, raw, run, spring
חִיאֵל, Hiel
חִידָה, *dark* saying, *dark* speech, derision, *hard* question, riddle
חיה, bring *to life*, bring *up*, give *life*, heal, keep *alive*, leave *alive*, life, live, live *long*, make *alive*, *make* live, permit *to live*, preserve, preserve *life*, recover, *remain* alive, renew, repair, restore *to life*, revive, save, save *alive*, save *life*, spare, spare *life*
חַיָּה, animal, appetite, band, beast, flock, life, live, *living* creature, living *thing*, spring, *wild* beast, *wild* creature
חָיֶה, vigorous
חַיּוּת, live
חַיִּים, alive, life, lifetime, live, maintenance, wholesome
חַיִל, ability, able, able-bodied, *armed* force, army, band *of soldiers*, excellently, force, *full* yield, good, goods, *great* ability, host, might, mighty, power, profit, retinue, riches, season, strength, strong, substance, valiant, valiantly, valor, *very* able, war, wealth, wealthy, worth, worthy
חִיל, anguish, pain, pang
חִילָה, pain
חֵילֵךְ, Helech
חֵילָם, Helam
חִילֵן, Hilen
חִין, goodly
חַיִץ, wall
חִיצוֹן, outer, outside
חֵיק, base, bosom, bottom, embrace, lap
חִירָה, Hirah
חִירָם, Hiram
חַיַּת הַשָּׂדֶה, *wild* beast
חֵךְ, kiss, lip, mouth, palate, roof *of mouth*, speech, taste
חכה, lie *in wait*, long, tarry, wait
חַכָּה, fishhook, hook
חֲכִילָה, Hachilah
חֲכַלְיָה, Hacaliah
חַכְלִלוּת, redness
חַכְלִילִי, red
חכם, *become* wise, cunning, deal *shrewdly*, gain *wisdom*, make *wise*, teach *wisdom*, use *wisdom*, wise
חכם יוֹתֵר, make *overwise*
חָכָם, ability, able, able *man*, craftsman, crafty, skilful, skilful *woman*, skilled, skilled *man*, *skilled* worker, wisdom, wise, wise *man*, wise *one*, *wise* son
חֲכַם לֵב, ability, able, able *man*, wise
חָכְמָה, ability, able, skill, wisdom, *wise* conduct, wit
חַכְמוֹנִי, Hachmoni, Hachmonite
חֹל, common, ordinary
חֵל, bound, bulwark, rampart, wall
חלא, diseased
חֶלְאָה, Helah, rust
חלב, milk, suck
חֵלֶב, fat, fat *part*, *fat* piece, *fat* portion, fatness, fine, good, heart, Heleb, marrow
חֵלֶב כְּלָיוֹת, fine
חֶלְבָּה, Helbah
חֶלְבּוֹן, Helbon
חֶלְבְּנָה, galbanum
חֶלֶד, life, lifetime, measure *of life*, world
חֹלֶד, weasel
חֵלֶד, Heled
חֻלְדָּה, Huldah
חֶלְדַּי, Heldai
חלה, *become* ill, *become* sick, *become* weak, beseech, diseased, entreat, entreat *favor*, faint, fall *sick*, grief, grieve, grievous, hurt, ill, lie *sick*, make *ill*, make *sick*, pretend *to be ill*, put *to grief*, seek *favor*, sick, sorry, sue, tire *out*, weak, wound
חלה פָּנִים, beseech, entreat *favor*
חַלָּה, cake
חֲלוֹם, dream
חַלּוֹן, window
חֹלוֹן, Holon
חֲלוּשָׁה, defeat
חֲלַח, Halah
חַלְחוּל, Halhul
חַלְחָלָה, anguish
חלט, take *up*
חֲלִי, Hali, jewel, ornament
חֳלִי, affliction, disease, grief, illness, sick, sickness
חֶלְיָה, jewelry
חָלִיל, flute, pipe
חָלִילָה, far *be it*, far *from it*, forbid, no
חֲלִיפָה, release
חֲלִיפָה, festal, *festal* garment, relay
חֲלִיצָה, spoil
חֵלְכָה, hapless
חלל, begin, beginning, break, *cause to* profane, defile, desecrate, dishonor, enjoy, enjoy *fruit*, first, *first* time, make *a beginning*, pierce, play, pollute, profane, profane *thing*, slay, strike, undertake, use *the fruit*, violate, wound
חָלָל, carcass, defile, kill, lie *slain*, slain *man*, slaughter, slay, unhallowed, victim, wound, wounded *man*
חלם, *become* strong, dream, dreamer, restore *to health*
חַלָּמוּת, purslane
חַלָּמִישׁ, flint, flinty, flinty *rock*
חֵלֹן, Helon
חלף, change, *ever* new, glide *past*, go, move, over, pass *away*, pass *through*, pierce, put *in place*, renew, sprout, strike *through*, substitute, sweep, violate
חֵלֶף, Heleph, return
חלץ, arm, armed *man*, army, deliver, division, give, make *strong*, plunder, pull *off*, *ready* armed, rescue, save, take *off*, take *out*, take *up arms*, withdraw
חָלָץ, loin
חֶלֶץ, Helez
חלק, allot, apportion, distribute, divide, divide *up*, false, flatter, organize, parcel *out*, partner, portion *out*, receive *a portion*, scatter, share, smooth, take
חָלָק, smooth
חָלָק, flatter, Halak, smooth
חֵלֶק, answer, division, field, Helek, land, lot, portion, reward, share, smooth, territory
חֶלְקָה, field, flatter, parcel, part, piece, piece *of land*, plot, portion, property, slippery *place*, smooth, smooth *part*, smooth *thing*
חֲלַקָּה, flattery
חֲלֻקָּה, part
חֶלְקַי, Helkai
חֶלְקִי, Helekite
חִלְקִיָּהוּ, Hilkiah
חֲלַקְלַקּוֹת, flattery, slippery, *slippery* path
חֶלְקַת הַצֻּרִים, Helkath-hazzurim
חֶלְקַת, Helkath
חלשׁ, lay *low*, mow *down*
חַלָּשׁ, weak
חָם, father-in-law, Ham, hot
חֹם, heat, hot, warm
חֵמָא, fury
חֶמְאָה, butter, curd, milk
חמד, covet, dear, delight, desire, *great* delight, *greatly* beloved, pleasant, precious
חֶמֶד, desirable, pleasant
חֶמְדָּה, beautiful, beloved, choice, costly, desirable, pleasant, precious, regret, treasure
חֶמְדָּן, Hemdan
חַמָּה, heat, sun
חֵמָה, anger, angry, furious, fury, heat, *hot* displeasure, *hot* tempered, poison, rage, venom, wrath, wrathful
חַמּוּאֵל, Hammuel
חֲמוּדָה, *costly* gift, good, *greatly* beloved, precious, precious *thing*
חֲמוּטַל, Hamutal
חָמוּל, Hamul
חָמוּלִי, Hamulite
חַמּוֹן, Hammon
חָמוֹץ, oppression
חַמּוּק, round
חֲמוֹר, ass, Hamor, heap
חַמּוֹת דֹּאר, Hammoth-dor
חָמוֹת, mother-in-law
חֹמֶט, sand *lizard*
חֻמְטָה, Humtah
חָמִיץ, salt
חֲמִישִׁי, fifth, pentagon
חמל, compassion, concern, mercy, pity, spare, take *pity*, unwilling
חֶמְלָה, merciful, pity
חמם, *become* hot, *become* warm, breed, burn *with lust*, get *warm*, grow *hot*, hot, inflame, warm
חַמָּן, altar *of incense*, *incense* altar
חמס, break *down*, *do* violence, injure, shake *off*, suffer *violence*, wrong
חָמָס, malicious, violence, violent, wrong
חמץ, crimson, cruel *man*, embitter, leaven
חָמֵץ, leaven, *leavened* bread
חֹמֶץ, vinegar, wine
חמק, turn, waver
חמר, daub, foam, red *with weeping*, tumult
חֶמֶר, wine
חֹמֶר, clay, heap, homer, mire, mortar, surge
חֵמָר, bitumen
חַמְרָן, Hamran
חמשׁ, take *a fifth part*
חָמֵשׁ, fifth, five
חֹמֶשׁ, belly, body
חֲמֵשׁ עֶשְׂרֵה, fifteen, fifteenth
חֲמִשִּׁים, fifty
חֲמֻשִׁים, arm, armed *man*, equip *for battle*
חַמַּת, Hammath
חֲמָת, Hamath
חֲמַת צוֹבָה, Hamath-zobah
חֵמֶת, skin

חֲמָתִי, Hamathite
חֵן, adornment, charm, compassion, fair, favor, grace, graceful, gracious, magic
חֵנָדָד, Henadad
חנה, besiege, camp, draw *to close*, encamp, lay *siege*, pitch, pitch *a tent*, remain *in camp*, settle, supplication
חַנָּה, Hannah
חֲנוֹךְ, Enoch, Hanoch
חַנּוּן, compassionate, gracious
חָנוּן, Hanun
חָנוּת, cell
חנט, embalm, put *forth*
חֲנֻטִים, embalm
חַנִּיאֵל, Hanniel
חָנִיךְ, trained *man*
חֲנִינָה, favor
חֲנִית, spear
חנך, dedicate, train *up*
חֲנֻכָּה, dedication, *dedication* offering
חֲנֹכִי, Hanochite
חִנָּם, causeless, cost *nothing*, *no* reason, nothing, nought, vain, wantonly, *without* cause
חֲנַמְאֵל, Hanamel
חֲנָמַל, frost
חנן, appeal *for mercy*, beseech, deal *generously*, deal *graciously*, entreat, favor, find *mercy*, generous, give *graciously*, give *liberally*, gracious, graciously, kind, loathsome, make *supplication*, merciful, mercy, mercy *upon*, pity, seek *favor*, *show* favor, *show* mercy, spare, take *pity*
חָנָן, Hanan
חֲנַנְאֵל, Hananel
חֲנָנִי, Hanani
חֲנַנְיָהוּ, Hananiah
חָנֵס, Hanes
חנף, lie *polluted*, pollute, profane, seduce, ungodly
חָנֵף, godless, godless *man*
חֹנֶף, ungodliness
חֲנֻפָּה, ungodliness
חנק, hang, strangle
חַנָּתֹן, Hannathon
חסד, bring *shame upon*, *show oneself* loyal
חֶסֶד, beauty, devotion, devout, faithfulness, favor, good *deed*, kind, kindly, kindness, love, *loyal* love, loyally, loyalty, merciful, mercy, reproach, shameful *thing*, *steadfast* love, true *loyalty*, *true* loyalty
חֲסַדְיָה, Hasadiah
חסה, find *refuge*, flee *for refuge*, safe, seek *refuge*, seek *shelter*, take *refuge*
חֹסָה, Hosah
חָסוּת, shelter
חָסִיד, faithful, faithful *one*, godly, godly *man*, godly *one*, gracious, kind, love, loyal, merciful, saint
חֲסִידָה, stork
חָסִיל, caterpillar, destroyer, *destroying* locust
חָסִין, mighty
חסל, consume
חסם, block, muzzle
חסן, hoard
חָסֹן, strong
חֹסֶן, abundance, riches, treasure, wealth
חסף, strip *off*
חספס, flake-like
חסר, abate, deprive, fail, lack, make *less*, suffer *want*, want
חָסֵר, lack, no, without
חֶסֶר, want
חֹסֶר, lack, want
חַסְרָה, Hasrah
חֶסְרוֹן, lack
חַף, pure
חפה, cover, line, overlay
חֻפָּה, canopy, chamber, Huppah
חפז, alarm, consternation, frighten, haste, make *haste*, take *to flight*, tremble
חִפָּזוֹן, haste, *hurried* flight
חֻפִּים, Huppim
חֹפֶן, fist, hand, handful
חָפְנִי, Hophni
חפף, encompass
חפץ, care, delight, desire, like, make *stiff*, mean, please, pleasure, purpose, take *pleasure*, will, willing, wish
חפץ בְּ, favor
חָפֵץ, delight, desire, pleasure, will, willing
חֵפֶץ, care, delight, desire, matter, please, pleasure, precious, purpose, will, wish
חֶפְצִי בָהּ, Hephzi-bah
חפר, *act* disgracefully, ashamed, blush, bring *reproach*, confound, dig, dig *out*, disgrace, explore, protect, put *to confusion*, put *to shame*, search *out*, spy *out*
חֵפֶר, Hepher
חֶפְרִי, Hepherite
חֲפָרַיִם, Hapharaim
חָפְרַע, Hophra
חֲפַרְפֵּרָה, mole
חפשׂ, *cunningly* conceive, disguise, hide, pillage, search, search *out*, test
חֵפֶשׂ, plot
חפשׁ, free
חֻפְשָׁה, freedom
חָפְשִׁי, forsake, free
חָפְשִׁית, separate
חֵץ, arrow, wound
חצב, cut *in pieces*, dig, flash *forth*, graven, hew, hew *out*, hewer, mason, prepare, quarry, stonecutter
חצב אֶבֶן, stonecutter
חצה, divide, divide *into two parts*, divide *up*, live *out half*, part, reach, separate
חָצוֹר, Hazor
חָצוֹר חֲדַתָּה, Hazor-hadattah
חֲצוֹת הַלַּיְלָה, midnight
חֲצוֹת לַיְלָה, midnight
חֵצִי, half, halfway, middle, midst, two *parts*
חֲצִי הַלַּיְלָה, midnight
חֵצִי, arrow
חָצִיר, abode, grass, leek, plant
חֲצִיר גַּגּוֹת, housetop
חֹצֶן, bosom, lap
חֵצֶן, bosom
חצץ, cut *off*, musician, rank
חָצָץ, gravel
חַצְצוֹן תָּמָר, Hazazon-tamar
חצצר, sound, sound *a trumpet*, trumpeter
חֲצֹצְרָה, trumpet, trumpeter
חצק, confirm, get *possession*, hold, hold *fast*, take
חָצֵר, court, courtyard, village
חָצֵר הַתִּיכוֹן, Hazer-hatticon
חֲצַר אַדָּר, Hazar-addar
חֲצַר גַּדָּה, Hazar-gaddah
חֲצַר סוּסָה, Hazar-susah
חֲצַר סוּסִים, Hazar-susim
חֲצַר עֵינוֹן, Hazar-enon
חֲצַר עֵינָן, Hazar-enan, Hazar-enon
חֲצַר שׁוּעָל, Hazar-shual
חֶצְרוֹ, Hezro
חֶצְרוֹן, Hezron
חֶצְרוֹנִי, Hezronite
חֲצֵרוֹת, Hazeroth
חֲצַרְמָוֶת, Hazarmaveth
חֹק, *allotted* portion, allowance, appoint, barrier, bound, boundary, circle, condition, custom, decree, due, fix, *fixed* allowance, *fixed* order, limit, measure, needful, ordinance, search, *set* time, statute, task
חקה, *carved* work, portray, set *a bound*
חֻקָּה, statute
חֻקָּה, appoint, custom, due, *fixed* order, ordinance, statute
חֲקוּפָא, Hakupha
חקק, carve, commander, decree, draw, grave, inscribe, mark *out*, portray, ruler, *ruler's* staff, scepter
חֻקֹּק, Hukkok
חקר, ascertain, discover, examine, explore, find *out*, make *search*, search, search *out*, sound, study, try
חֵקֶר, search
חֵקֶר, deep *thing*, find, investigation, recess, understanding
חֹר, cave, free *man*, hole, latch, noble, socket
חֹר הַגִּדְגָּד, Hor-haggidgad
חֹר, hole
חֲרָא, dung
חרב, *become* dry, desolate, dry, dry *up*, fight *together*, lay *waste*, lie *waste*, parch, ravager, slay, waste, waste *away*
חָרֵב, dry, lie *in ruins*, lie *waste*, ruins, waste
חֶרֶב, axe, knife, sword, tool, war
חֹרֶב, drought, dry, heat, ruin, waste
חֹרֵב, Horeb
חָרָבָה, *dry* ground, *dry* land
חָרְבָּה, desert, desolate, desolation, ruin, ruins, waste, waste *place*
חֲרָבוֹן, heat
חַרְבוֹנָא, Harbona
חַרְבוֹנָה, Harbona
חרג, *come* trembling
חַרְגֹּל, cricket
חרד, afraid, *come* trembling, disturb, frighten *away*, make *afraid*, quake, startle, take *trouble*, terrify, throw *into a panic*, tremble, turn *trembling*
חָרֵד, tremble
חֲרֹד, Harod
חֲרָדָה, fear, Haradah, panic, tremble, trouble
חֲרֹדִי, Harod
חרה, angry, *become* angry, blaze, burn, burn *hot*, compete, fret, hot, incense, kindle, wrath
חרה אַף, angry, *become* angry
חרה לְ, angry
חַרְהֲיָה, Harhaiah
חָרוּז, string *of jewels*
חָרוּל, nettle
חֲרוּמַף, Harumaph
חָרוֹן, ablaze, burn, wrath
חָרוֹן, fierce, fierceness, fury, heat, hot
חֲרוֹן אַף, *fierce* anger, *fierce* wrath
חֹרוֹנַיִם, Horonaim
חֲרוּפִי, Haruphite
חָרוּץ, decision, diligent, gold, Haruz, moat, sharp, *threshing* sledge
חַרְחוּר, Harhur
חַרְחַס, Harhas
חַרְחֻר, *fiery* heat
חֶרֶט, character, graving *tool*
חַרְטֹם, magician
חֹרִי, cake, Hori, Horite
חֳרִי, fierce, heat, hot
חֳרִי אַף, *fierce* anger
חָרִיט, bag, handbag
חָרִיץ, pick
חֲרִיץ חָלָב, cheese
חָרִישׁ, ground, plow, *plowing* time, sultry
חֲרַכִּים, lattice
חרם, destroy, devote, doom, exterminate, forfeit, mutilate, *utterly* destroy
חָרִם, Harim
חֹרֵם, Horem
חֵרֶם, accursed, accursed *thing*, curse, devote, devote *for destruction*, devote *to destruction*, devoted *thing*, doom, dragnet, net, *thing* devoted *to destruction*, *thing for* destruction, *utter* destruction
חָרְמָה, Hormah
חֶרְמוֹן, Hermon
חֶרְמוֹנִים, Hermon
חֶרְמֵשׁ, sickle
חָרָן, Haran
חֹרֹנִי, Horonite
חַרְנֶפֶר, Harnepher
חֶרֶס, Heres, itch, sun
חַרְסִית, potsherd
חרף, betroth, cast *contempt*, defy, insult, jeopard, mock, put *to shame*, reproach, revile, scoff, taunt, taunter, winter
חָרִיף, Hariph
חָרֵף, Hareph
חֹרֶף, autumn, winter
חֶרְפָּה, byword, disgrace, humiliation, insolence, insult, object *of scorn*, reproach, scoff, scorn, shame, suffer *disgrace*, taunt
חרץ, bestir, decide, decree, determine, growl, move, mutilate
חַרְצֻבָּה, bond, pang
חַרְצַנִּים, seed
חרק, gnash
חרר, angry, burn, burn *up*, char, kindle, parch, scorch
חֲרֵר, parched *place*
חֶרֶשׂ, earthen, *earthen* vessel, earthenware, potsherd, sherd
חרשׁ, cease, deaf, declare, devise, engrave, hold *one's peace*, instrument, keep *quiet*, keep *silence*, keep *silent*, keep *still*, leave *off speaking*, listen *in silence*, plan, plot, plow, plower, plowman, *remain* silent, say *nothing*, silence, silent, still, worker
חָרַשׁ אֶבֶן, jeweler, mason
חָרַשׁ אֶבֶן קִיר, mason
חָרַשׁ בַּרְזֶל, ironsmith
חָרַשׁ עֵץ, carpenter
חָרַשׁ קִיר, mason
חָרָשׁ, carpenter, craftsman, magician, maker, skilful, smith, worker, workman
חֶרֶשׁ, Heresh, secretly
חֹרֶשׁ, forest, Horesh, *wooded* hill
חֵרֵשׁ, deaf, deaf *man*
חַרְשָׁא, Harsha
חֲרֹשֶׁת, carve, cut
חֲרֹשֶׁת הַגּוֹיִם, Harosheth-hagoiim
חרת, grave
חֶרֶת, Hereth
חֲשׂוּפָא, Hasupha
חֲשִׂף, *little* flock
חשׂך, assuage, hesitate, hold *back*, keep, keep *back*, punish, reserve, restrain, spare, withhold
חשׂף, bare, dip *up*, draw, lift *up*, strip *bare*, strip *off* bark, uncover
חשׁב, account, ask *an accounting*, compute, conceive, consider, count, credit, deem, designer, determine, devise, esteem, execute, form, hold, imagine, impute, intend, invent, know, make *a plot*, make *a reckoning*, mean, plan, plot, reckon, regard, seem, skilful *man*, skilfully, skilled, take, take *thought*, think, threaten
חֵשֶׁב, skilfully *woven band*
חַשְׁבַּדָּנָה, Hashbaddanah
חֲשֻׁבָה, Hashubah
חֶשְׁבּוֹן, Heshbon, sum, sum *of things*, thought
חִשָּׁבוֹן, device, engine
חֲשַׁבְיָהוּ, Hashabiah
חֲשַׁבְנָה, Hashabnah
חֲשַׁבְנְיָה, Hashabneiah
חשׁה, *do* nothing, hold *one's peace*, hush, keep *quiet*, keep *silence*, keep *silent*, silent, still
חַשּׁוּב, Hasshub
חָשׁוּק, fillet
חִשּׁוּק, spoke
חשׁך, black, bring *darkness*, dark, darken, dim, grow *dim*, make *dark*
חָשֹׁךְ, obscure *man*
חֹשֶׁךְ, dark, darken, darkness, gloom
חֲשֵׁכָה, dark, darkness
חשׁל, lag *behind*
חָשֻׁם, Hashum
חֻשָׁם, Husham
חֶשְׁמוֹן, Heshmon
חַשְׁמַל, bronze, *gleaming* bronze
חַשְׁמַן, bronze
חַשְׁמֹנָה, Hashmonah
חֹשֶׁן, breastpiece
חשׁק, cleave *in love*, desire, long, make *fillets*, set, set *one's love*

חֵשֶׁק, desire, long
חִשֻּׁר, hub
חַשְׁרָה, gather
חֲשַׁשׁ, chaff, *dry* grass
חשת, bronze
חֻשָׁתִי, Hushathite
חַת, break, dismay, dread, fear
חֵת, Heth, Hittite
חתה, carry, heap, snatch, take
חִתּוּל, bandage
חַתְחַת, terror
חִתִּי, Hittite
חִתִּית, terror
חתך, decree
חתל, swathe *with bands*
חֲתֻלָּה, *swaddling* band
חֶתְלֹן, Hethlon
חתם, seal, seal *up*, set *a seal*, shut *up*, signet, stop
חתם בְּעַד, seal *up*
חֹתָם, seal, signet, *signet* ring
חֹתֶמֶת, signet
חתן, *become a* son-in-law, intermarry, make *a marriage alliance*, make *marriage*, son-in-law
חָתָן, bridegroom, son-in-law
חֹתֵן, father-in-law, mother-in-law
חֲתֻנָּה, wedding
חתף, snatch *away*
חֶתֶף, robber
חתר, dig, dig *through*, row
חתת, break, break *down*, break *in pieces*, break *to pieces*, desert *in panic*, destroy, discomfit, dismay, end, scare, stand *in awe*, terrify, terror-stricken
חַתַּת, terror
חֲתַת, calamity, Hathath

טָבְאַל, Tabeel
טָבְאֵל, Tabeel
טְבוּל, turban
טַבּוּר, center
טבח, kill, slaughter, slay
טַבָּח, bodyguard, cook, guard
טֶבַח, animal, beast, slaughter, Tebah
טַבָּחָה, cook
טִבְחָה, meat, slaughter
טִבְחַת, Tibhath
טבל, dip, plunge
טְבַלְיָהוּ, Tebaliah
טבע, shape, sink
טַבָּעוֹת, Tabbaoth
טַבַּעַת, ring, *signet* ring
טַבְרִמּוֹן, Tabrimmon
טַבָּת, Tabbath
טֵבֵת, Tebeth
טָהוֹר, clean, clean *person*, clean *thing*, pure, *pure* gold, purity
טהר, clean, cleanse, clear, *make* clean, pronounce *clean*, pure, purge, purifier, purify
טֹהַר, clearness, purify
טָהֳרָה, cleanse, purification, purify, rule *of cleanness*
טוב, *do* well, fair, go *well*, good, grow *in favor*, please
טוֹב, beautiful, blameless, bountiful, cheerful, enjoyment, fair, *fair* word, favor, favorable, favorably, feast, fertile, fine, glad, good, good *man*, good *place*, good *thing*, goodly, *goodly* child, goodness, goods, gracious, handsome, happiness, happy, improve, kind, merry, more, pleasant, please, pleasure, precious, profitable, prosper, prosperity, pure, rich, right, safe, sweet, Tob, upright, welfare, well, *well* disposed, well *off*
טוֹב אֲדוֹנִיָּה, Tob-adonijah
טוֹב בְּעֵינַיִם, please, pleasure
טוֹב בְּעֵינַיִם, approve
טוֹב חֵן, graceful
טוֹב לִפְנֵי, please
טוֹב מַרְאֶה, beautiful, lovely
טוֹב עַל, please, save
טוֹב רֳאִי, handsome
טוֹב תֹּאַר, handsome
טוּב, *choice* gift, gladness, go *well*, good, *good* gift, good *thing*, goodness, goods, prosperity
טוֹבָה, bounty, good, good *deed*, goodness, kindly, prosperity
טוֹבִיָּהוּ, Tobiah, Tobijah
טוה, spin
טוח, daub, overlay, plaster
טוֹטָפוֹת, frontlet
טול, cast, cast *headlong*, fling, hurl, hurl *away*, lay *low*, throw
טוּר, course, row
טוש, swoop
טחה, distance
טְחוֹן, mill
טְחוֹר, tumor, ulcer
טֻחוֹת, *inward* being
טחח, shut
טחן, grind, grinder
טַחֲנָה, grind
טִיחַ, daubing
טִיט, bog, clay, dirt, mire, mud
טִירָה, battlement, camp, encampment, row, settlement
טַל, dew
טלא, gaily *deck*, patch, spot
טְלָאִים, Telaim
טָלֶה, lamb
טַלְטֵלָה, violently
טלל, cover
טֶלֶם, Telem
טַלְמֹן, Talmon
טמא, *become* defiled, *become* unclean, declare *unclean*, defile, hold *unclean*, make *unclean*, pollute, pronounce *unclean*, *remain* unclean, take *uncleanness*, unclean
טָמֵא, defile, impurity, unclean, unclean *person*, unclean *thing*
טֻמְאָה, uncleanness
טֻמְאָה, filthiness, filthy, pollution, rust, unclean, unclean *thing*, uncleanness
טְמֵאַת שֵׁם, infamous *one*
טמה, stupid
טמן, bury, hide, lay, lay *up*, world *below*
טֶנֶא, basket
טנף, soil
טעם, perceive, taste
טַעַם, behavior, decree, discernment, discreetly, discretion, judgment, taste
טען, load, pierce
טַף, child, dependent, *little* child, little *one*, young
טפח, dandle, spread *out*
טֶפַח, coping, handbreadth
טֹפַח, handbreadth
טִפֻּחִים, *tender* care
טפל, besmear, cover, whitewash
טִפְסָר, marshal, scribe
טפף, mince
טפש, gross
טָפַת, Taphath
טרד, continual
טרח, load
טֹרַח, burden, weight
טָרִי, bleed, fresh
טֶרֶם, before, yet, *yet* no
טרף, catch, feed, raven, ravenous, rend, tear, tear *in pieces*, tear *to pieces*, torn *by beast*
טָרָף, *freshly* plucked
טֶרֶף, food, *fresh* leaf, plunder, prey
טְרֵפָה, tear, torn *by beast*, torn *by wild beast*, torn flesh

יאב, long
יאה, due
יַאֲזַנְיָהוּ, Jaazaniah
יָאִיר, Jair
יָאִרִי, Jairite
יאל, *become a* fool, content, determine, *do* foolishly, *no* sense, persist, please, take *upon*, try *in vain*, undertake
יְאֹר, *branch of the* Nile, canal, channel, Nile, river, stream
יאש, despair, give *up to despair*, hopeless, vain
יֹאשִׁיָּהוּ, Josiah
יְאָתְרַי, Jeatherai
יְבוּל, crop, fruit, increase, possession, produce
יְבוּס, Jebus
יְבוּסִי, Jebus, Jebusite
יִבְחָר, Ibhar
יָבִין, Jabin
יבל, bear, bring, carry, lead, lead *along*, lead *forth*, rescue
יַבֶּל, discharge
יָבָל, flow, Jabal, run
יִבְלְעָם, Ibleam
יבם, perform *duty of a brother-in-law*, perform *duty of a husband's brother*
יָבָם, *husband's* brother
יְבֶמֶת, *brother's* wife, sister-in-law
יַבְנְאֵל, Jabneel
יַבְנֶה, Jabneh
יִבְנִיָּה, Ibnijah
יִבְנִיָּה, Ibneiah
יַבֹּק, Jabbok
יְבֶרֶכְיָהוּ, Jeberechiah
יִבְשָׂם, Ibsam
יבשׁ, dry, dry *up*, fail, make *dry*, *make* dry, parch, wither, wither *away*
יָבֵשׁ, dry, dry *up*, Jabesh
יָבֵשׁ גִּלְעָד, Jabesh-gilead
יַבָּשָׁה, *dry* ground, *dry* land, land
יַבֶּשֶׁת, *dry* land
יִגְאָל, Igal
יגב, plowman
יָגֵב, field
יָגְבְּהָה, Jogbehah
יִגְדַּלְיָהוּ, Igdaliah
יגה, *cause* grief, grieve, inflict, *make* suffer, take *out*, torment, tormentor
יָגוֹן, anguish, grief, sorrow
יָגוֹר, afraid
יָגוּר, Jagur
יְגִיעַ, fruit, gain, labor, toil, wealth, work
יְגִיעַ כֹּחַ, weary
יְגִיעַ כַּפַּיִם, labor
יְגִיעָה, weariness
יָגְלִי, Jogli
יגע, grow *weary*, labor, *make* toil, toil, weary
יָגָע, fruit *of toil*
יָגֵעַ, full *of weariness*, weary
יגר, afraid, *become* afraid, dread
יְגַר שָׂהֲדוּתָא, Jegar-sahadutha
יַד מַעְגָּל, wayside
יַד צַר, trouble
יָד, allegiance, arm, arm *rest*, authority, axle, bank, border, bounty, care, charge, command, courage, custody, deed, direction, division, favor, fist, force, hand, handle, liberality, ministry, monument, nakedness, order, oversight, paw, place, position, possession, power, present, rule, service, share, side, signpost, special, spoke, stay, strength, tenon, time, toil, violence, work
יָד לְיָד, assure
ידא, make *confession*
יִדְאֲלָה, Idalah
יִדְבָּשׁ, Idbash
ידד, cast
יְדִדוּת, beloved
ידה, acknowledge, cast, cast *down*, confess, extol, get *praise*, give *praise*, give *thanks*, make *confession*, praise, shoot, thank, thanksgiving
יִדּוֹ, Iddo
יָדוֹן, Jadon
יַדּוּעַ, Jaddua
יְדוּתוּן, Jeduthun
יַדַּי, Jaddai
יָדִיד, beloved, love, lovely
יְדִידָה, Jedidah
יְדִידְיָה, Jedidiah
יְדָיָה, Jedaiah
יְדִיעֲאֵל, Jediael
יִדְלָף, Jidlaph
ידע, acknowledge, acquaint, acquaintance, aware, *become* known, *cause to* know, certain, choose, *close* friend, come, *come to* know, come *to knowledge*, companion, comprehend, concern, consider, declare, determine, discover, endue, experience, familiar, *familiar* friend, feel, find *out*, gain, heed, instruct, know, know *how*, knowledge, lead, learn, lie, *make* know, make *known*, *make* known, man *of skill*, manifest, mark, meet, observe, perceive, predict, proclaim, regard, show, show *how*, skilful, skilled, sure, take *heed*, take *knowledge*, take *note*, teach, tell, train, understand, understanding, versed
ידע בִּין, discern
ידע בִּינָה, man *who has understanding*
ידע וראה, consider *well*
ידע מִשְׁכָּב, lie
ידע סֵפֶר, read
יָדָע, Jada
יְדַעְיָה, Jedaiah
יִדְּעֹנִי, wizard
יָהּ, GOD, LORD
יָהּ יָהּ, LORD
יהב, ascribe, bring, choose, come, give, grant, make *a gift*, provide, set
יהד, declare *a Jew*
יְהֻד, Jehud
יָהְדַּי, Jahdai
יֵהוּא, Jehu
יְהוֹאָחָז, Jehoahaz
יְהוֹאָשׁ, Jehoash
יְהוּדָה, Jew, Judah, Judea, *man of* Judah, *people of* Judah
יְהוּדִי, Jehudi, Jew, Jewish, Jewish *people*, Judah, *man of* Judah
יְהוּדִית, Judith, *language of* Judah
יְהוָה, GOD, God, LORD, Lord, sacred
יְהוֹזָבָד, Jehozabad
יְהוֹחָנָן, Jehohanan
יְהוֹיָדָע, Jehoiada
יְהוֹיָכִין, Jehoiachin
יְהוֹיָקִים, Jehoiakim
יְהוֹיָרִיב, Jehoiarib
יְהוּכַל, Jehucal
יְהוֹנָדָב, Jehonadab
יְהוֹנָתָן, Jehonathan, Jonathan
יְהוֹעַדָּה, Jehoaddah
יְהוֹעַדִּין, Jehoaddin
יְהוֹעַדָּן, Jehoaddan
יְהוֹצָדָק, Jehozadak
יְהוֹרָם, Jehoram
יְהוֹשֶׁבַע, Jehosheba
יְהוֹשַׁבְעַת, Jehoshabeath
יְהוֹשֻׁעַ, Jeshua, Joshua
יְהוֹשָׁפָט, Jehoshaphat
יָהִיר, arrogant, haughty *man*
יְהַלֶּלְאֵל, Jehallelel
יַהֲלֹם, diamond, jasper
יַהַץ, Jahaz
יַהְצָה, Jahzah
יוֹאָב, Joab
יוֹאָח, Joah
יוֹאָחָז, Joahaz
יוֹאֵל, Joel
יוֹאָשׁ, Joash
יוֹב, Iob
יוֹבָב, Jobab
יוֹבֵל, jubilee, ram, ram's *horn*, trumpet
יוּבַל, stream
יוּבָל, Jubal
יוֹזָבָד, Jozabad
יוֹזָכָר, Jozacar
יוֹחָא, Joha
יוֹחָנָן, Johanan

יוֹיָדָע, Joiada
יוֹיָקִים, Joiakim
יוֹיָרִיב, Joiarib
יוֹכֶבֶד, Jochebed
יוּכַל, Jucal
יוֹלֵדָה, childbirth
יוֹם, age, chronicle, daily, day, ever, first, full, *full* year, immediately, life, live, *long* time, period, season, *some* time, time, today, when, while, whole, year, yearly
יוֹם אוֹר, daylight
יוֹם אֶתְמוֹל, yesterday
יוֹם בְּיוֹם, daily, *every* day
יוֹם הַשַּׁבָּת, sabbath
יוֹם טוֹב, holiday, holiday-making
יוֹם יוֹם, daily
יוֹם יֶלֶד, birthday
יוֹם מָחָר, late, tomorrow
יוֹמָם, *all the* day, day, daytime
יָוָן, Greece, Javan
יָוֵן, mire, miry
יוֹנָדָב, Jonadab
יוֹנָה, dove, Jonah, pigeon
יוֹנֶקֶת, shoot, *young* plant, *young* twig
יוֹנָתָן, Jonathan
יוֹסֵף עוֹד, again
יוֹסֵף, Joseph
יוֹסִפְיָה, Josiphiah
יוֹעֵאלָה, Joelah
יוֹעֵד, Joed
יוֹעֶזֶר, Joezer
יוֹעָשׁ, Joash
יוֹצָדָק, Jozadak
יוֹקִים, Jokim
יוֹרָה, Jorah
יוֹרֶה, *autumn* rain, *early* rain
יוֹרַי, Jorai
יוֹרָם, Joram
יוּשַׁב חֶסֶד, Jushab-hesed
יוֹשִׁבְיָה, Joshibiah
יוֹשָׁה, Joshah
יוֹשַׁוְיָה, Joshaviah
יוֹשָׁפָט, Joshaphat
יוֹתָם, Jotham
יוֹתֵר, besides
יוֹתֵר מִן, beyond
יְזִיאֵל, Jeziel
יִזִּיָּה, Izziah
יָזִיז, Jaziz
יִזְלִיאָה, Izliah
יְזַנְיָהוּ, Jezaniah
יֶזַע, sweat
יִזְרָח, Izrahite
יִזְרַחְיָה, Izrahiah, Jezrahiah
יִזְרְעֶאל, Jezreel
יִזְרְעֶאלִי, Jezreel, Jezreelite, Jezreelitess
יְחֻבָּה, Jehubbah
יחד, join, unite
יַחַד, alike, all, alone, altogether, knit, together, unity, utterly
יַחְדָּו, alike, all, *all* alike, alone, altogether, both, join, one, together
יַחְדָּו תַּמִּים, join
יַחְדּוֹ, Jahdo
יַחְדִּיאֵל, Jahdiel
יֶחְדְּיָהוּ, Jehdeiah
יַחְדָּיו, together
יְחוּאֵל, Jehuel
יַחֲזִיאֵל, Jahaziel
יַחְזְיָה, Jahzeiah
יְחֶזְקֵאל, Ezekiel, Jehezkel
יְחִזְקִיָּהוּ, Hezekiah, Jehizkiah
יַחְזֵרָה, Jahzerah
יְחִיאֵל, Jehiel
יְחִיאֵלִי, Jehieli
יָחִיד, desolate, life, lonely, only, *only* child, *only* one, *only* son
יְחִיָּה, Jehiah
יָחִיל, wait
יחל, expect, hope, *make* hope, wait, waste *time*
יַחְלְאֵל, Jahleel
יַחְלְאֵלִי, Jahleelite
יחם, breed, conceive, mate
יַחְמוּר, roebuck
יַחְמַי, Jahmai
יָחֵף, barefoot, unshod
יַחְצְאֵל, Jahzeel
יַחְצְאֵלִי, Jahzeelite
יַחֲצִיאֵל, Jahziel
יחשׂ, enrol, enrol *by genealogy*, enrol *in the genealogy*, enrollment, enrollment *by genealogy*, genealogy, keep *a genealogical record*, reckon *genealogy*, register
יַחַשׂ, genealogy
יַחַת, Jahath
יטב, acceptable, adorn, amend, bestow *prosperity upon*, cheer, cheerful, content, deal *well*, diligently, direct *well*, do, *do* diligently, *do* good, *do* well, dress, find *favor*, glad, go *well*, good, improve, make *cheerful*, make *famous*, make *glad*, make *great*, make *merry*, make *prosperous*, merry, please, prosper, rightly, *seem* good, skillfully, stately, very, well
יטב בְּעֵינַיִם, please, please *well*
יטב לִפְנֵי, please
יטב נגן, make *sweet melody*
יָטְבָה, Jotbah
יָטְבָתָה, Jotbathah
יטה, bow, go *over*, turn
יֻטָּה, Juttah
יְטוּר, Jetur
יַיִן, banquet, wine
יְכוֹנְיָה, Jeconiah
יכח, accuse, appoint, argue, chasten, chastise, chastisement, complain, confute, contend, decide, defend, maintain *right*, make *an argument*, reason, reason *together*, rebuke, reproof, reprove, reprover, right, umpire
יָכִין, Jachin
יָכִינִי, Jachinite
יכל, able, attain, can, endure, overcome, overpower, power, prevail, prevail *over*, succeed
יְכָלְיָהוּ, Jecoliah
ילד, bear, bear *a child*, *become* father, beget, birth, bring *forth*, bring *forth young*, *cause to* bring *forth*, child, deliver, delivery, descend, father, give *birth*, hatch, labor, *make* bring *forth*, midwife, newborn, register, serve *as midwife*, son, time, travail, *woman in* labor, woman *in travail*, *yet* unborn
יֶלֶד, boy, child, lad, *male* child, offspring, son, young, young *man*, young *one*, youth
יֶלֶד נָכְרִי, foreigner
יַלְדָּה, girl, maiden
יַלְדוּת, youth
יִלּוֹד, bear
יָלוֹן, Jalon
יָלִיד, bear, descendant
יְלִיד בַּיִת, homeborn
ילל, *become* wailings, wail
יְלֵל, howl
יְלָלָה, wail
יַלֶּפֶת, scab
יֶלֶק, hopper, *hopping* locust, locust, *young* locust
יַלְקוּט, wallet
יַם סוּף, Red Sea
יָם, lake, Nile, sea, west, *west* side, western, westward
יָמָּה, western, westward
יְמוּאֵל, Jemuel
יְמֵי שְׁנוֹת, years *of life*
יָמִים אֲחָדִים, while
יָמִים לְיָמִים, *every* year
יָמִים מִיָּמִים, course *of time*
יָמִים רַבִּים, *long* time
יְמִימָה, Jemimah
יָמִין, Jamin, right, *right* hand, *right* side, south, *south* side
יָמִינִי, Jaminite
יְמִינִי, Benjamin
יִמְלָא, Imlah
יַמְלֵךְ, Jamlech
יֵמִם, *hot* spring
ימן, *go* right, right, *right* hand, turn *to the right*, turn *to the right hand*
יִמְנָה, Imnah, Imnite
יְמָנִי, right, south
יְמָנִית קֵדְמָה, southeast
יִמְנָע, Imna
יִמְרָה, Imrah
ינה, *do* wrong, oppress, oppressor, subdue, thrust, wrong
יָנוֹחַ, Janoah
יָנוֹחָה, Janoah
יָנִים, Janim
יְנִיקָה, *young* twig
ינק, babe, child, infant, *make* suck, milch, nurse, *nursing* mother, nursling, suck, *sucking* child, suckle, suckling
ינק שָׁדַיִם, *nursing* infant
יַנְשׁוּף, great *owl*, ibis, owl
יסד, appoint, begin, destine, establish, found, foundation, give *orders*, lay, lay *a foundation*, pile *up*, rebuild, scheme, set, sure, take *counsel*
יְסוֹד, base, establish, foundation, thigh
יִסּוֹר, faultfinder
יִסְכָּה, Iscah
יִסְמַכְיָהוּ, Ismachiah
יסף, acquire, add, addition, again, another, any, *any* more, bring, bring *more*, carry *further*, continue, *do* again, *do* much, even *more*, extend, far, further, give, give *increase*, go, grow, henceforth, increase, join, keep, long, make, more, more *also*, more *and more*, *more* richly, obtain *fresh*, proceed *further*, prolong, say, surpass, yet, *yet* more
יסף עבר, go *ahead*
יסף עוֹד, again, *any* more, long, more
יסר, chasten, chastise, correct, direct, discipline, instruct, take *warning*, teach, train, turn, warn, whip
יָע, shovel
יַעְבֵּץ, Jabez
יעד, appoint, appointment, assemble, designate, direct, gather, gather *together*, join *forces*, make *an appointment*, meet, meet *together*, place, summon
יֶעְדּוֹ, Iddo
יעה, sweep *away*
יְעוּאֵל, Jeuel
יְעוּץ, Jeuz
יְעוּשׁ, Jeush
יעז, insolent
יַעֲזִיאֵל, Jaaziel
יַעֲזִיָּהוּ, Jaaziah
יַעְזֵר, Jazer
יעט, cover
יְעִיאֵל, Jeiel
יָעִיר, Jair
יַעְכָּן, Jacan
יעל, avail, *do* good, get *profit*, help, profit, profitable, promote, succeed, well *off*
יָעֵל, goat
יָעֵל, Jael, wild *goat*
יַעֲלָא, Jaala
יַעֲלָה, doe, Jaalah
יַעְלָם, Jalam
יַעַן, because
יַעַן אֲשֶׁר, because, since, whereas
יַעַן כִּי, because
יַעַן מָה, why
יָעֵן, ostrich
יַעְנַי, Janai
יעף, faint, grow *weary*, weariness, weary
יָעֵף, faint
יעץ, advise, adviser, agree *together*, conspire, consult, consult *together*, counsel, counselor, determine, devise, give, give *counsel*, know, make, plan, purpose, take *advice*, take *counsel*
יַעֲקֹב, Jacob
יַעֲקֹבָה, Jaakobah
יַעֲקָן, Jaakan
יַעַר, forest, honeycomb, Jaar, thicket, wood, wooded
יַעְרָה, Jarah
יַעְרֵי אֹרְגִים, Jaare-oregim
יְעָרִים, Jearim
יַעֲרֶשְׁיָה, Jaareshiah
יַעֲרַת דְּבַשׁ, honeycomb
יַעֲשׂוּ, Jaasu
יַעֲשִׂיאֵל, Jaasiel
יִפְדְּיָה, Iphdeiah
יפה, beautiful, beautify, deck, fair, graceful, grow *beautiful*, sweet
יָפֶה, beautiful, beauty, comely, fair, fair *one*, fitting, good, sleek
יְפֵה פִּי, beautiful
יְפֵה תֹאַר, handsome
יָפוֹ, Joppa
יפח, gasp *for breath*
יָפֵחַ, breathe *out*
יֳפִי, beauty, fair
יָפִיעַ, Japhia
יַפְלֵט, Japhlet
יַפְלֵטִי, Japhletite
יְפֻנֶּה, Jephunneh
יפע, *cause to* shine, light, shine, shine *forth*
יפע עַל, favor
יִפְעָה, splendor
יֶפֶת, Japheth
יְפַת מַרְאֶה, beautiful, lovely, sleek
יְפַת תֹאַר, beautiful, sleek
יִפְתַּח אֵל, Iphtah-el
יִפְתָּח, Iphtah, Jephthah
יצא, bear, begone, break *out*, bring, bring *forth*, bring *forward*, bring *out*, bring *up*, carry, carry *away*, carry *forth*, carry *out*, clear *out*, come, come *away*, come *forth*, come *forward*, come *out*, continue, deliver, depart, draw *forth*, draw *out*, emission, end, escape, exact, expedition, export, extend, fail, fall, fetch, fit, flow, flow *forth*, flow *out*, follow, get *out*, give *up*, give *vent*, go, go *away*, go *beyond*, go *forth*, go *forward*, go *on an expedition*, go *out*, go *thence*, grow, grow *out*, import, issue, lead *forth*, lead *out*, leave, lose, *make* come, *make* go *out*, make *known*, *make* known, march, march *out*, pass, pay *out*, pierce, pluck *out*, proceed, proceed *out*, produce, project, put *away*, put *forth*, put *out*, ready, release, remove, report, ride *out*, rise, send, send *forth*, send *out*, set *forth*, set *out*, slip *out*, spread, spring, surrender, swell *out*, take, take *out*, utter
יצא אַחֲרֵי, follow
יצא וָשׁוֹב, to *and fro*
יצא יֶלֶד, miscarriage
יצא יָרֵךְ, offspring
יצא מֵחֲלָצַיִם, bear
יצא מִפֶּה, promise, vow
יצא מֵרֶחֶם, bear
יצא מִתַּחַת, escape
יצא צָבָא, *seasoned* troop, service
יצב, place, present, resort, set, stand, stand *firm*, stand *forth*, stand *ready*, stand *still*, stand *up*, station, take *a position*, take *a stand*, take *a station*, wait, withstand
יצג, establish, lay, leave, make, present, put, *remain* behind, set, set *up*
יִצְהָר, Izhar, oil
יִצְהָרִי, Izharite
יָצוּעַ, bed, couch
יִצְחָק, Isaac
יִצְחַר, Izhar
יְצִיא מֵעִים, son
יָצִיעַ, story, structure
יצע, bed, lie, make *a bed*, spread
יצק, cast, empty *out*, fasten, *firmly* cast, flow, hard, lay *down*, molten, pour, pour *out*, run, secure, set *down*, wash *away*
יצר, earthen, fashion, form, frame, make, maker, plan, potter, purpose, shape, *thing* formed, workman
יֵצֶר, member

יֵצֶר, creation, frame, imagination, Jezer, mind, plan, purpose
יִצְרִי, Izri, Jezerite
יצת, burn, burn *up*, destroy, fire, kindle, lay *waste*, ruin, ruins, set, set *on fire*
יצת בָּאֵשׁ, burn
יֶקֶב, press, vat, wine *press*, wine *vat*, winevat
יְקַבְצְאֵל, Jekabzeel
יקד, burn, hearth, *keep* burning, kindle
יָקְדְעָם, Jokdeam
יָקֶה, Jakeh
יְקָהָה, obedience, obey
יְקוֹד, burn
יְקוּם, living *thing*
יָקוֹשׁ, fowler
יָקוּשׁ, fowler
יְקוּתִיאֵל, Jekuthiel
יָקְטָן, Joktan
יָקִים, Jakim
יַקִּיר, dear
יְקַמְיָה, Jekamiah
יָקְמְעָם, Jokmeam
יְקַמְעָם, Jekameam
יָקְנְעָם, Jokneam
יקע, alienate, hang, hang *up*, put *out of joint*, turn *in disgust*
יקע נֶפֶשׁ, turn *in disgust*
יקץ, awake, awaken
יקר, costly, esteem, make *rare*, pay *off*, precious, *prized* belongings, seldom
יָקָר, costly, glory, lady *of honor*, precious, rare, splendor
יָקָר מִן, outweigh
יְקָר, honor, pomp, precious, precious *thing*, price, splendor
יקשׁ, ensnare, fowler, lay, set *a snare*, snare
יָקְשָׁן, Jokshan
יָקְתְאֵל, Joktheel
ירא, afraid, awesome, awful, cautious, dismay, dread *deed*, fear, fearful, frighten, hold *in awe*, make *afraid*, pay *reverence*, respect, revere, reverence, shoot, shun, stand *in awe*, terrible, terrible *act*, terrible *thing*, terrify, water, worship
ירא אֶת אֱלֹהִים, God-fearing
ירא מְאֹד, fill *with fear*
ירא מִפְּנֵי, afraid, stand *in awe*
יִרְאָה, fear
יִרְאוֹן, Yiron
יִרְאִיָּה, Irijah
יְרֻבַּעַל, Jerrubbaal, Jerubbaal
יָרָבְעָם, Jeroboam
יְרֻבֶּשֶׁת, Jerubbesheth
ירד, alight, bow, break *down*, bring *down*, carry *down*, cast *down*, *cause to* flow down, come, come *down*, decline, descend, downward, fall, flow, flow *down*, go, go *down*, lay *low*, let *down*, lower, *make* descend, march *down*, melt, pour *down*, pour *out*, put *off*, run *down*, send *down*, shed, sink *down*, step *down*, stream *down*, take *down*, thrust *down*
יֶרֶד, Jared, Jered
יַרְדֵּן, Jordan
ירה, archer, cast, direct, give, give *revelation*, instruct, instruction, lay, point, rain, set, shoot, show, teach, teacher, throw, water
ירה אִישׁ בַּקֶּשֶׁת, archer
יְרוּאֵל, Jeruel
יָרוֹחַ, Jaroah
יָרוֹק, green *thing*
יְרוּשָׁא, Jerusha
יְרוּשָׁה, Jerushah
יְרוּשָׁלַםִ, Jerusalem
יָרֵחַ, moon
יֶרַח, Jerah, month
יֶרַח יָמִים, month
יְרֹחָם, Jeroham
יְרַחְמְאֵל, Jerahmeel
יְרַחְמְאֵלִי, Jerahmeelite
יַרְחָע, Jarha
ירט, cast, perverse
יְרִיאֵל, Jeriel
יָרִיב, contend, Jarib
יְרִיבַי, Jeribai
יְרִיָּהוּ, Jeriah, Jerijah
יְרִיחוֹ, Jericho
יְרִימוֹת, Jeremoth, Jerimoth
יְרִיעָה, curtain, tent
יְרִיעוֹת, Jerioth
יָרֵךְ, base, side, thigh
יַרְכָה, depth, *extreme* end, far, far *part*, *far* recess, inner *part*, innermost *part*, rear, remote *part*, uttermost *part*
יַרְכָה, border
יַרְמוּת, Jarmuth
יְרֵמַי, Jeremai
יִרְמְיָהוּ, Jeremiah
ירע, tremble
יָרֵעַ, moon
יִרְפְּאֵל, Irpeel
ירק, spit
יָרָק, herb, tender, *tender* grass, vegetable
יֶרֶק, grass, green, green *thing*, verdure
יֵרָקוֹן, mildew, pale
יָרְקְעָם, Jorkeam
יְרַקְרַק, green, greenish
ירשׁ, cast, cast *out*, come *to poverty*, conqueror, destroy, disinherit, dispossess, drive *out*, get *possession*, give *to inherit*, give *to possess*, heir, impoverish, inherit, inheritor, *make* inherit, make *poor*, occupy, poor, possess, seize, strip *of possessions*, succeed, take *possession*, win
יְרֻשָּׁה, heritage, inheritance, possession
יְרֵשָׁה, dispossess
יְשִׂימְאֵל, Jesimiel
יִשָּׂשכָר, Issachar
יִשְׂרָאֵל, Israel, Israelite
יְשַׂרְאֵלָה, Jesharelah
יִשְׂרְאֵלִי, Israel, Israelite, Israelite *woman*
יֵשׁ, already, wealth
יֵשׁ אֲשֶׁר, sometimes
יֵשׁ אֶת נֶפֶשׁ, willing
יֵשׁ יִתְרוֹן לְ, excel
יֵשׁ לְ, possession
ישׁב, abide, abode, bring *back*, *cause to* inhabit, continue, council, dwell, dweller, enthrone, enthrone *upon*, find *a dwelling*, give, habitable, inhabit, inhabitant, keep *aloof*, leave, lie, live, lodge, loss *of time*, lurk, *make* dwell, *make* sit, marry, people, place, reign, remain, rest, restore, return, seat, set, settle, sit, sit *down*, sit *enthroned*, sit *enthroned upon*, sit *on a throne*, sit *still*, sit *up*, stand, stay, take, take *a seat*, tarry, wait, *whoever* sits
יֹשֵׁב בַּשֶּׁבֶת, Josheb-basshebeth
יֶשֶׁבְאָב, Jeshebeab
יִשְׁבָּח, Ishbah
יִשְׁבִּי בְּנֹב, Ishbi-benob
יָשָׁבְעָם, Jashobeam
יִשְׁבָּק, Ishbak
יָשְׁבְּקָשָׁה, Joshbekashah
יָשׁוּב, Jashub
יָשֻׁבִי, Jashubite
יִשְׁוָה, Ishvah
יְשׁוֹחָיָה, Jeshohaiah
יִשְׁוִי, Ishvi, Ishvite
יְשׁוּעָה, deliver, deliverance, deliverer, help, prosperity, salvation, save, *saving* power, triumph, victory, vindication
יֶשַׁח, hunger
ישׁט, hold *out*
יִשַׁי, Jesse
יִשִּׁיָּהוּ, Isshiah, Isshijah
יְשִׁימוֹן, desert, Jeshimon, wilderness
יָשִׁישׁ, age
יְשִׁישַׁי, Jeshishai
ישׁם, desolate, ruin, strip
יִשְׁמָא, Ishma
יִשְׁמָעֵאל, Ishmael
יִשְׁמְעֵאלִי, Ishmaelite
יִשְׁמַעְיָהוּ, Ishmaiah
יִשְׁמְרַי, Ishmerai
ישׁן, chronic, fall *asleep*, grow *old*, keep *long*, *make* sleep, sleep
יָשָׁן, old, *old* store
יָשֵׁן, asleep, Jashen, sleep, smolder
יְשָׁנָה, Jeshanah
ישׁע, avenge, bring *victory*, defend, deliver, deliverer, get *victory*, give *deliverance*, give *help*, give *victory*, help, rescue, safe, save, savior, spare, take *vengeance*, victorious
יֶשַׁע, deliverance, help, safety, salvation, victory
יִשְׁעִי, Ishi
יְשַׁעְיָה, Jeshaiah
יְשַׁעְיָהוּ, Isaiah
יָשְׁפֵה, jasper, onyx
יִשְׁפָּה, Ishpah
יִשְׁפָּן, Ishpan
ישׁר, aright, direct, direct *one's step*, *evenly* applied, go *straight*, honest, keep *straight*, level, make *straight*, right, *seem* good, straight, upright
ישׁר בְּעֵינַיִם, please, please *well*
יָשָׁר, equity, fit, Jashar, pure, right, righteous, straight, true, upright, upright *man*, uprightly, uprightness
יָשָׁר בְּעֵינַיִם, please
יֹשֶׁר, give, honest, upright, uprightly, uprightness
יֵשֶׁר, Jesher
יְשָׁרָה, uprightness
יְשֻׁרוּן, Jeshurun
יָשֵׁשׁ, age
יָתֵד, peg, pin, *secure* hold, stake, stick, *tent* peg
יָתוֹם, fatherless, *fatherless* child, orphan
יַתִּיר, Jattir
יִתְלָה, Ithlah
יִתְמָה, Ithmah
יַתְנִיאֵל, Jathniel
יִתְנָן, Ithnan
יתר, advantage, anything, escape, good, leave, leave *behind*, leave *over*, leave *remaining*, *make* abound, make *prosperous*, more, pre-eminence, preserve, remain, remainder, rest, survive, very
יֶתֶר, beyond, bowstring, cord, exceedingly, fine, Jether, Jethro, last, leave, measure, pre-eminent, remain, remnant, residue, rest, *something* over, string, survivor, tent-cord
יֶתֶר הַפְּלֵטָה, leave
יִתְרָא, Ithra
יִתְרָה, abundance, riches
יִתְרוֹ, Jethro
יִתְרוֹן, advantage, excel, gain, help
יִתְרוֹן לְ, gain
יִתְרִי, Ithrite
יִתְרָן, Ithran
יִתְרְעָם, Ithream
יֹתֶרֶת, appendage, fat
יְתֵת, Jetheth

—

כְּ, about, accordance, according, after, alike, although, because, before, compare, comparison, due, else, equal, equivalent, even, if, just, like, now, order, over, return, same, some *sort*, soon, such, suitable, though, time, under, well, when, whenever, while, within
כְּ כְּ, alike
כאב, dishearten, feel *pain*, hurt, pain, ruin, sad, sore, wound
כְּאֵב, distress, pain, suffer
כאה, afraid, dishearten
כאה לֵב, brokenhearted
כְּאֶחָד, alike, together
כְּאַיִן, *well* nigh
כָּאֵלֶּה, same *way*
כַּאֲשֶׁר, according, after, because, even, how, if, just, like, much, since, soon, such, what, when, whenever, while
כְּאֶתְמוֹל שִׁלְשֹׁם, *before that* time
כבד, abound, appear *in glory*, boastfulness, burdensome, come *to honor*, dim, dull, get *glory*, give *glory*, glorify, glorious, glorious *thing*, glory, grave, harden, *heavily* laden, heavy, hold *in honor*, honor, honorable, honored *man*, lay *a heavy burden*, lay *heavy*, lie *heavy*, load, make *glorious*, make *heavy*, *make* honored, manifest *one's glory*, multiply, noble, play *the great man*, press *hard*, renowned, rest *heavily*, *show* glory, stop, wealth, weigh
כָּבֵד, dense, entrails, great, grievous, grow *weary*, hard, heart, heavy, laden, liver, many, rich, severe, slow, sorrowful, thick
כֹּבֶד, heap, heavy, press, thick
כְּבֵדֻת, heavily
כבה, blot *out*, go *out*, put *out*, quench
כָּבוֹד, glorious, glory, goods, honor, riches, soul, spirit, splendid, splendor, stately, wealth, weight
כָּבוּל, Cabul
כַּבּוֹן, Cabbon
כַּבִּיר, great, mighty, much
כַּבִּיר יָמִים, old
כְּבִיר, pillow
כֶּבֶל, fetter
כבס, fuller, wash
כבר, abundance, multiply
כְּבָר, already, Chebar, long
כְּבָרָה, sieve
כִּבְרַת אֶרֶץ, *short* distance, *some* distance
כֶּבֶשׂ, lamb, *male* lamb, sheep
כִּבְשָׂה, ewe *lamb*, lamb
כבשׁ, assault, bring *into subjection*, enslave, force, lie *subdued*, subdue, subjugate, tread *down*, tread *under foot*
כֶּבֶשׁ, footstool
כִּבְשָׁן, furnace, kiln
כַּד, jar, pitcher, *water* jar
כַּדָּבָר הַזֶּה, thus
כַּדְּבָרִים הָאֵלֶּה, thus
כַּדּוּר, round *about*
כַּדְכֹּד, agate
כִּדְמוּת, like
כְּדָר לָעֹמֶר, Chedor-laomer
כְּדָרְלָעֹמֶר, Chedorlaomer
כֹּה, any, here, more, such, thus, way, yonder
כהה, blind, dim, fail, faint, grow *dim*, restrain
כֵּהָה, assuage
כֵּהֶה, dim, dimly, dull, faint, grow *dim*
כְּהֵמָּה, similar
כהן, *become a* priest, deck, minister *as priest*, minister *in the priest's office*, priest, priesthood, serve *as priest*, service *as priest*
כְּהַן, likewise
כֹּהֵן, priest
כְּהֻנָּה, priest's *place*, priesthood
כּוֹבַע, helmet
כוה, burn, scorch
כְּוִיָּה, burn
כּוֹכָב, star
כול, bear, conduct, contain, enclose, endure, feed, hold, make *provision*, nourish, nourisher, provide, provide *food*, provide *with food*, provision, receive, supply *provision*, sustain
כּוּמָז, armlet, bead
כון, accomplish, aim, appoint, certain, certainty, consider, continue, count, direct, do, endure, establish, *ever* abide, fashion, fasten, find, firm, fit, fix, form, full, keep *ready*, keep *steady*, make *preparation*, make *provision*, make *ready*, make *secure*, make *sure*, mark *off*, mete *out*, muster *in array*, order, pile *up*, place, prepare, provide, readiness, ready, rest, restore, right, set, *set* aright, set *up*, stand *firm*, steadfast, strengthen, string, sure, truth
כַּוָּן, cake
כּוּן, Cun
כּוֹנַנְיָהוּ, Conaniah
כּוֹס, cup, *little* owl, owl
כּוּר, furnace
כּוֹרֶשׁ, Cyrus
כּוּשׁ, Cush, Ethiopia, Ethiopian
כּוּשִׁי, Cushi, Cushite, Ethiopian
כּוּשַׁן רִשְׁעָתַיִם, Cushan-rishathaim
כּוּשָׁן, Cushan
כּוֹשָׁרָה, prosperity
כּוּתָה, Cuth, Cuthah

כזב, count *a liar*, disappoint, fail, find *a liar*, lie, prove *a liar*, utter, *vain* hope
כָּזָב, deceptive, delusion, false, *false* god, falsehood, lie
כֹּזֵבָא, Cozeba
כָּזְבִּי, Cozbi
כָּזֹה, effect, fashion, such, such *a thing*, thus, what
כְּזִיב, Chezib
כֹּחַ, ability, able, competent, contest, *land* crocodile, might, mighty, power, powerful, strength, strong, wealth, yield
כחד, blot *out*, conceal, cut *off*, deny, desolate, destroy, hide, perish, wipe *out*
כחל, paint
כחשׁ, *become* gaunt, *come* cringing, *come* fawning, cringe, deal *falsely*, deceive, deny, fail, false, lie, speak *falsely*
כַּחַשׁ, leanness, lie, treachery
כֶּחָשׁ, lie
כִּי, although, because, either, else, even, even *though*, except, how, if, nay, nevertheless, no, provided, rather, reason, say, see, since, such, surely, than, then, though, truly, when, whenever, while, yea, yes, yet
כִּי אָז, surely
כִּי אִם, except, however, more *than*, nevertheless, nothing, only, other *than*, surely, than, though, truly, truth, unless, without
כִּי גַם, yet
כִּי לֹא, neither
כִּי לוּלֵי, unless
כִּי עַל כֵּן, because, inasmuch, since
כִּיד, destruction
כִּידוֹד, spark
כִּידוֹן, javelin, spear
כִּידוֹר, battle
כִּידֹן, Chidon
כִּיּוֹם, first
כִּיּוּן, Kaiwan
כִּילַי, knave
כֵּילַפּוֹת, hammer
כִּימָה, Pleiades
כִּימִים, long
כִּיס, bag, purse
כִּיר, stove
כִּיּוֹר, laver, pan, platform, pot
כִּישׁוֹר, distaff
כָּכָה, another, even *so*, manner, one *thing*, such, thus, way
כְּכֹל, far, such, whatever
כְּכֹל אֲשֶׁר, just
כְּכֹל הַדְּבָרִים הָאֵלֶּה, *like* manner
כִּכָּר, circuit, cover, loaf, plain, talent, valley
כֹּל, all, all *kinds*, all *sorts*, all *things*, altogether, any, any *kind*, any *one*, *any* other, anything, completely, each, enough, entire, every, every *kind*, every *man*, every *one*, every *person*, every *sort*, everybody, everything, everywhere, far, full, main, much, open, other, rest, same, several, throughout, utter, utterly, whatever, whenever, wherever, whoever, whole, wholly
כֹּל אִישׁ, whoever
כֹּל אֲשֶׁר, any *one*, anything, whatever, wherever, whoever
כֹּל אֲשֶׁר שָׁם, wherever
כֹּל דָּבָר, anything, everything
כֹּל דָּבָר לֹא, nothing
כֹּל הָאָדָם, every *man*, every *one*
כֹּל הַדָּבָר, whatever
כֹּל הַיָּמִים, continual, day *after day*, ever, henceforth, life
כֹּל חֹזֶה, Col-hozeh
כֹּל יוֹם, continually
כֹּל יָמִים, always, long, remain, while
כֹּל כְּלִי, anything
כֹּל לֹא, none, nothing
כֹּל לֵב, wholehearted
כֹּל מְאוּמָה, anything
כֹּל נֶפֶשׁ, whoever
כֹּל עוֹד, long
כֹּל עוֹלָמִים, everlasting
כֹּל קֻמַּת שֶׁ, just
כלא, finish, forbid, hold *back*, imprison, keep, restrain, retain, shut, shut *up*, stop, withhold
כֶּלֶא, prison
כִּלְאָב, Chileab
כִּלְאַיִם, different *kind*
כִּלְאַיִם, two *kinds*
כָּלֵב, Caleb
כֶּלֶב, dog
כָּלִבִּי, Calebite
כלה, accomplish, bring *to pass*, *cause to* fail, cease, come *to an end*, *come to* end, complete, consume, destroy, *utterly* destroy, determine, do, *do* all, end, fade, fail, faint, finish, finish *up*, give *full vent*, go, grow *dim*, languish, long, make *a full end*, make *an end*, *make* vanish, pass *away*, perish, reap, settle, shut *up*, spend, strip, vanish, vanish *away*, waste, waste *away*, weep *out*, withhold
כלה טְעֵם, determine
כַּלָּה, bride, daughter-in-law
כָּלָה, accomplish, altogether, complete, destroy, destruction, end, full, *full* end, make *an end*
כְּלֻהַי, Cheluhi
כְּלוּב, basket, Chelub
כְּלוּבַי, Chelubai
כְּלוּלָה, bride
כֶּלַח, Calah, *ripe old* age, vigor
כֵּלַי, knavery
כְּלִי, accessory, anything, armor, article, bag, baggage, equipment, figure, furnishing, furniture, goblet, goods, implement, instrument, jewel, jewelry, object, pertain, sack, stuff, thing, tool, utensil, vessel, ware, weapon, yoke
כְּלִי אַגָּן, cup
כְּלִי נֶבֶל, flagon, harp
כְּלִי בַיִת, *household* goods
כִּלְיָה, heart, inward *part*, kidney, soul
כִּלְיוֹן, Chilion
כִּלָּיוֹן, destruction, fail
כָּלִיל, all, perfect, perfection, utterly, whole, *whole burnt* offering, wholly
כַּלְכֹּל, Calcol
כלל, make *perfect*
כְּלָל, Chelal
כלם, abase, ashamed, blush, bring *to dishonor*, cast *reproach upon*, confound, disgrace, dishonor, *do* harm, put *to shame*, reproach, shame, suffer *harm*
כִּלְמַד, Chilmad
כְּלִמָּה, confusion, disgrace, dishonor, humiliation, insult, reproach, shame
כְּלִמּוּת, shame
כַּלְנוֹ, Calno
כַּלְנֵה, Calneh
כמה, faint
כַּמָּה, *how* long, *how* many, *how* often, what
כַּמָּה יָמִים, *how* long
כִּמְהָם, Chimham
כְּמוֹ, such, well, whether
כְּמוֹ, according, like, thus
כְּמוֹשׁ, Chemosh
כַּמֹּן, cummin
כמס, lay *up in store*
כִּמְעַט, almost, easily, quickly, soon
כִּמְעַט שֶׁ, scarcely
כמר, grow *warm and tender*, hot, yearn
כֹּמֶר, *idolatrous* priest
כְּמַרְאָה, resemble, similar
כִּמְרִיר, blackness
כְּמִשְׁפָּט, require
כֵּן, account, aright, base, both, even *so*, faithful, gnat, honest *man*, like, likewise, more, office, place, right, same, stability, steadfast, such, such *a thing*, therefore, thus, time, true
כֵּן דבר, right
כְּנֶגֶד, fit
כנה, flatter, surname, use *flattery*
כַּנָּה, stock
כַּנֵּה, Canneh
כִּנּוֹר, harp, lyre
כָּנְיָהוּ, Coniah
כְּנָנִי, Chenani
כְּנַנְיָהוּ, Chenaniah
כנס, gather, gather *together*, heap, wrap
כנע, bow *down*, bring *into subjection*, bring *low*, humble, subdue
כִּנְעָה, bundle
כְּנַעַן, Canaan, Canaanite, merchant, trade, trader
כְּנַעֲנָה, Chenaanah
כְּנַעֲנִי, Canaanite, Canaanite *woman*, Canaanitess, Canaanitish *woman*, merchant, Phoenicia, trader, trafficker
כנף, hide
כָּנָף, corner, end, fly, much, robe, skirt, sort, wing, winged
כִּנֶּרֶת, Chinnereth, Chinneroth
כֶּסֶא, *full* moon
כִּסֵּא, chair, jurisdiction, ruler, seat, throne
כסה, clad, close, clothe, conceal, cover, cover *up*, covering, forgive, hide, ignore, keep *hidden*, *make* cover, overwhelm, pardon, put
כָּסוּי, covering
כְּסוּלוֹת, Chesulloth
כְּסוּת, cloak, clothing, covering, vindication
כסח, cut *down*
כְּסִיל, Chesil, constellation, fool, foolish, foolish *man*, Orion, stupid, *stupid* son
כְּסִילוּת, foolish
כסל, foolish
כֶּסֶל, confidence, folly, *foolish* confidence, hope, loin, trust
כִּסְלָה, confidence
כִּסְלֵו, Chislev
כִּסְלוֹן, Chislon
כְּסָלוֹן, Chesalon
כַּסְלֻחִים, Casluhim
כִּסְלֹת תָּבוֹר, Chisloth-tabor
כסם, trim
כֻּסֶּמֶת, spelt
כסס, count
כסף, eager, long
כֶּסֶף, money, money-value, payment, price, silver, *thing of* silver, tribute
כָּסִפְיָא, Casiphia
כֶּסֶת, *magic* band
כעס, provoke
כְּעַל, according
כעס, anger, angry, enrage, give *provocation*, provoke, provoke *to anger*, trouble, vexation
כַּעַס, anger, fretful, grief, indignation, provocation, sorely, sorrow, vexation
כַּעַשׂ, grief, vexation
כְּעֵת, now, when
כַּף, branch, dish, dish *for incense*, grasp, hand, handful, handle, hollow, palm, paw, power, reach, sole
כַּף יָד, hand
כַּף רֶגֶל, foot
כפה, avert
כִּפָּה, branch, palm *branch*
כְּפָה, according, much, proportion
כְּפוֹר, bowl, hoarfrost
כְּפִי, accordance, according
כְּפִי אֲשֶׁר, inasmuch
כָּפִיס, beam
כְּפִיר, lion, *young* lion
כְּפִיר אֲרָיוֹת, *young* lion
כְּפִירָה, Chephirah
כְּפִירִים, village
כפל, double, double *over*, twice
כֶּפֶל, double, manifold
כפן, bend
כָּפָן, famine, hunger
כפף, bow, bow *down*
כפר, annul, appease, atone, cover, expiate, forgive, make *atonement*, *make* atonement, make *expiation*, *make* expiation, pardon
כפר נֶפֶשׁ, ransom
כָּפָר, village
כֹּפֶר, bribe, compensation, henna, henna *blossom*, pitch, price *of life*, ransom, village
כְּפַר הָעַמּוֹנִי, Chephar-ammoni
כִּפֻּרִים, atonement
כַּפֹּרֶת, mercy *seat*
כפשׁ, *make* cower
כַּפְתּוֹר, Caphtor, capital
כַּפְתֹּרִי, Caphtorim
כַּר, *battering* ram, lamb, meadow, pasture, saddle
כֹּר, cor
כרבל, clothe
כרה, bargain, buy, delve, dig, hew *out*, plot, prepare *a feast*
כָּרָה, meadow
כֵּרָה, feast
כְּרוּב, cherub, Cherub
כָּרִי, Carite
כְּרִית, Cherith
כְּרִיתוּת, divorce
כַּרְכֹּב, ledge
כַּרְכֹּם, saffron
כַּרְכְּמִישׁ, Carchemish
כַּרְכַּס, Carkas
כִּרְכָּרָה, dromedary
כרם, vinedresser
כֶּרֶם, orchard, vineyard
כַּרְמִי, Carmi, Carmite
כַּרְמִיל, *crimson* fabric
כַּרְמֶל, Carmel, dense, *fertile* land, fresh, *fresh* ear *of grain*, fruitful, *fruitful* field, *fruitful* land, *garden* land, *new* grain, plentiful
כַּרְמְלִי, Carmel, Carmelitess
כְּרָן, Cheran
כרסם, ravage
כרע, bow, bow *down*, bring *low*, collapse, couch, crouch, fall, feeble, kneel, kneel *down*, lay *low*, *make* sink, overthrow, sink, stoop *down*
כֶּרַע, leg
כַּרְפַּס, cotton
כרר, dance
כָּרֵשׂ, belly
כַּרְשְׁנָא, Carshena
כרת, beam, consume, covenant, cut, cut *down*, cut *off*, destroy, destruction, fail, fell, hew *down*, hewer, lack, lose, make, make *a covenant*, make *a league*, make *a treaty*, make *an end*, perish, stop, wipe *out*
כרת מִן, without
כְּרֵתִי, Cherethite
כֶּשֶׂב, lamb, sheep
כִּשְׂבָּה, lamb
כֶּשֶׂד, Chesed
כַּשְׂדִּים, Chaldea, Chaldean
כשׂה, *become* sleek
כְּשֶׁ, when
כַּשִּׁיל, hatchet
כשׁל, bring *to ruin*, cast *down*, *cause to* fail, *cause to* stumble, exhaust, fail, fall, fall *down*, feeble, *make* stumble, overthrow, ruin, stagger, stumble, weak
כִּשָּׁלוֹן, fall
כשׁף, practice *sorcery*, sorcerer, sorceress
כַּשָּׁף, sorcerer
כֶּשֶׁף, charm, *deadly* charm, sorcery
כשׁר, prosper, *seem* right, succeed
כִּשְׁרוֹן, gain, skill
כְּתֹאַר, resemble
כתב, decree, describe, enrol, give *written*, prescribe, record, register, set *down*, sign, write, write *down*, writer, writing
כְּתָב, book, direction, document, edict, letter, register, registration, script, write
כְּתֹבֶת, mark
כִּתִּי, Cyprus, Kittim
כָּתִית, beat
כֹּתֶל, wall
כִּתְלִישׁ, Chitlish
כתם, stain
כֶּתֶם, *fine* gold, gold, *pure* gold
כֻּתֹּנֶת, coat, garment, *long* robe, robe, tunic

כָּתֵף, back, corner, end, flank, shoulder, shoulder *blade*, shoulder-piece, side, sidewall, support
כָּתֵף מִחוּץ, outside
כתר, bear, crown, cut *down*, surround
כֶּתֶר, crown
כֹּתֶרֶת, capital, crown
כתש, crush
כתת, batter, beat, beat *down*, beat *to pieces*, break *in pieces*, crush, destroy, pursue, smash

לְ, about, above, accordance, according, account, after, against, among, because, become, before, behalf, belong, besides, between, concerning, correspond, every, favor, inasmuch, like, namely, near, order, out, over, part, point, possess, regard, represent, require, sake, side, sight, soon, through, throughout, thus, till, toward, under, until, upon, when, whenever, within
לֹא, before, beyond, *by no* means, lest, more *than*, nay, neither, never, nevermore, no, none, nor, nothing, unless, without
לֹא אבה, unwilling
לֹא אוֹר, dark
לֹא אֶחָד, none
לֹא אִישׁ, no *one*, none
לֹא אמן, despair, fail
לֹא אִשָּׁה, none
לֹא אשם, go *unpunished*
לֹא בְּ, without
לֹא בֵּן, childless
לֹא דָּבָר, nothing
לֹא דְּבָר, Lo-debar
לֹא דֶרֶךְ, pathless
לֹא דֶּרֶךְ, trackless
לֹא דרשׁ, neglect
לֹא הוֹן, trifle
לֹא היה לְאִישׁ, unmarried
לֹא וְ, nor
לֹא וְ, neither
לֹא זרע, unsown
לֹא חָכָם, senseless, unwise
לֹא חמל, mercilessly, ruthlessly, unsparing, *without* pity
לֹא חָסִיד, ungodly
לֹא חקר, impenetrable
לֹא חֵקֶר, unsearchable
לֹא ידע, ignorant, ignore, unawares, unknown, unseen
לֹא יכל, cannot, unable
לֹא ילד, childless
לֹא יסף, never, *no* longer, no *more*
לֹא ישׁב, uninhabited
לֹא כְּ, against
לֹא כַּבִּיר, feeble
לֹא כִּי, rather
לֹא כִּי אִם, no *more than*
לֹא כֹּל, no, none
לֹא כָּל הַיָּמִים, never
לֹא כֵּן, false
לֹא כסף, shameless
לֹא כרת, always, spare
לֹא לֵב וָלֵב, singleness *of purpose*
לֹא לֶחֶם, nothing
לֹא למד, untrained
לֹא לָנֶצַח, never
לֹא לְעוֹלָם, never, never *again*
לֹא מְאוּמָה, nothing
לֹא מִכֹּל, none
לֹא מְלָאכָה, nothing
לֹא מִן, neither
לֹא מֵעוֹלָם, never
לֹא מִשְׁפָּט, injustice
לֹא נכר, disown
לֹא נקה, go *unpunished*
לֹא סְדָרִים, chaos
לֹא סכן, unprofitable
לֹא עָב, cloudless
לֹא עַד עוֹלָם, never
לֹא עוֹד, never, never *again*, no
לֹא עוֹלָם, never
לֹא עַמִּי, Not *my people*
לֹא ענה, go *unanswered*
לֹא פקד, miss
לֹא צֶדֶק, unrighteousness
לֹא צוה, forbid
לֹא רֻחָמָה, Not *pitied*
לֹא רחק, *short* distance
לֹא רַק, nothing
לֹא שׂבע, *ever* thirsty
לֹא שׁכח, unforgotten
לֹא שׁמע, disobey
לאה, impatient, languish, loathe, offend, wear *out*, weary
לֵאָה, Leah
לְאָחוֹר, hereafter
לְאַחֲרוֹנָה, after
לאט, cover
לְאַט, deal *gently*, gently, slowly
לְאֵל, fulness, fulness *of harvest*, *woman with* child
לְאֵל, Lael
לְאֹם, nation, people
לְאֻמִּים, Leummim
לֶאֱמֶת, faithfully
לְאַפַּיִם, before
לְאֹרֶךְ יָמִים, ever
לָאָרֶץ, grief
לְאִשָּׁה, marriage
לֵב, accord, attention, breast, conceit, conscience, courage, heart, midst, mind, opinion, sense, spirit, thought, understanding, wisdom, wise
לֵב קָמָי, Chaldea
לְבָאוֹת, Lebaoth
לבב, get *understanding*, make, make *a cake*, ravish *the heart*
לֵבָב, courage, heart, intent, mind, soul, understanding
לְבִבָה, cake
לְבַד, addition, alone, apart, besides, only
לְבַד מִן, besides, except
לְבָדָד, alone
לִבָּה, heart
לָבוֹא, *at* hand, hand
לְבוֹא, border, entrance
לְבוּז, laugh
לְבוֹנָה, Lebonah
לְבוּשׁ, apparel, clothing, deck, garment, raiment, robe, vestment
לבט, come *to ruin*
לָבֶטַח, secure, securely, trustingly
לָבֶטַח, secure, securely
לָבִי, lion, lioness
לָבִיא, lion, lioness
לְבִיָּא, lioness
לִבְלִי, beyond
לְבִלְתִּי, lest, never, no, no *one*, refuse
לבן, *make* brick, make *bricks*, make *white*, white
לָבָן, Laban, white
לִבְנָה, Libnah
לִבְנֶה, poplar
לְבָנָה, Lebana, Lebanah, moon
לְבֹנָה, frankincense, incense
לְבֵנָה, brick, stone
לְבָנוֹן, Lebanon
לִבְנִי, Libni, Libnite
לְבַעֲבוּר, order
לַבְּקָרִים, *every* morning, morning *by morning*
לבשׁ, arm, array, clad, clothe, come *upon*, dress, put, put *upon*, robe, take *possession*, vestment, wear, wrap
לֹג, log
לִגְבוּלוֹת, boundary *by boundary*
לִגְבָרִים, man *by man*
לְגֻלְגְּלוֹת, head *by head*
לְגֻלְגֹּלֶת, apiece
לֹד, Lod
לִדְגָלִים, standard *by standard*
לַהַב, aflame, blade, flame, flash
לֶהָבָה, blaze, flame, flash, head
לְהָבִים, Lehabim
לַהַג, study
לַהַד, Lahad
להה, languish
להט, burn, burn *up*, flame, kindle, *set* ablaze, set *on fire*
לַהַט, flame
להלה, madman
להם, delicious *morsel*
לָהֵן, therefore
להק, burn *up*
לַהֲקָה, company
לוּ, if, wish, would *that*
לוּב, Libyan
לוּד, Lud, *man of* Lud
לוּדִים, Ludim
לוה, borrow, borrower, go, join, lend, lender
לוה עַל, join
לוז, devious, escape, perverse *man*, perverseness
לוּז, almond, Luz
לוּחַ, board, plank, surface, table, tablet
לוּחִית, Luhith
לוט, cast, wrap
לוֹט, covering, Lot
לוֹטָן, Lotan
לֵוִי, Levi, Levite, Levitical, *male* Levite
לִוְיָה, garland
לִוְיָתָן, Leviathan
לוּל, stair
לוּלֵא, if *not*
לוּלִי, loop
לון, abide, *all* night, dwell, growl, leave, lie, lie *all night*, lodge, lodge *for the night*, *make* murmur, make *one's home*, murmur, pass *the night*, remain, *remain all* night, rest, spend *the night*, stay, stay *the night*, tarry, tarry *all night*, tarry *for a night*
לוע, rash, say *rashly*
לושׁ, knead
לָזוּת, devious
לַח, fresh, green
לֵחַ, *natural* force
לְחוּם, flesh
לַחוּץ, abroad, outside
לְחִי, cheek, jaw, jawbone, Lehi
לחך, lick, lick *up*
לחם, assault, attack, battle, conquer, devour, eat, fight, fight *against*, foeman, go *to war*, make *war*, war
לָחֶם, war
לֶחֶם, bread, bread *grain*, eat, food, *food* allowance, fruit, grain, Lehem, loaf, meal, provision
לֶחֶם הַמַּעֲרֶכֶת, showbread
לֶחֶם חמד, delicacy
לֶחֶם צַיִד, provision
לַחְמִי, Lahmi
לַחְמָס, Lahmam
לחץ, afflict, hold *fast*, oppress, oppressor, press, press *back*, push
לַחַץ, adversity, affliction, oppression, scant *fare*
לחשׁ, charmer, whisper, whisper *together*
לַחַשׁ, amulet, charm, prayer
לָט, private, *secret* art
לֹט, myrrh
לְטָאָה, lizard
לְטוֹבָה, abundantly
לְטוּשִׁם, Letushim
לטשׁ, forger, sharp, sharpen, whet
לְיַד, beside
לִוְיָה, wreath
לְיוֹם, daily, day *by day*
לַיְלָה, night, tonight
לִילִית, *night* hag
לְיָמָּה, westward
לִיץ, deride, envoy, interpreter, mediator, mock, mocker, scoff, scoffer, scorn, scorner, scornful
לַיִשׁ, Laish, lion
לַיְשָׁה, Laishah
לכד, capture, catch, clasp *each other*, ensnare, freeze, seize, take, take *by lot*, take *captive*, trap
לֶכֶד, catch
לֵכָה, Lecah
לָכִישׁ, Lachish
לְכֹל, before, far, much, throughout, wholly
לְכֹל אֲשֶׁר, wherever
לָכֵן, end, if, then, therefore, thus, *very* well, well, wherefore, why, yet
לְלֹא, without
לְמִבַּיִת, within
למד, accept, expert, instruction, instructor, learn, teach, teacher, train
לִמֻּד, accustom, disciple, teach, used
לִמְדַחֵפֹת, speedily
לָמָּה, good, what, *what* use, why
לָמָּה זֶּה, why
לְמוּאֵל, Lemuel
לְמִזְרָח, eastward
לְמַטָּה, below, beneath, down, downward, little
לְמֵישָׁרִים, smoothly
לֶמֶךְ, Lamech
לְמֶלֶךְ, royal
לְמִן, side, since
לְמִן עוֹלָם, old
לְמַסָּעִים, stage *by stage*
לִמְעַט, *too* few
לְמַעְלָה, above, exceedingly, great, high, highly, project *upward*, top, upside *down*, upward, very
לְמַעַן, account, because, end, only, order, purpose, result, sake, till
לְמַעַן לֹא, lest
לְמַעֲרָב, westward
לְמֵרָחוֹק, far, *long* ago
לְמִרְמָה, deceitfully
לְמַשְׂחִית, fearfully
לְמִשְׁפָּט, aright
לְנֶגֶד, before, opposite, over, over *against*, presence
לִנְדָבָה, willingly
לִנְחֻשְׁתַּיִם נגשׁ, fetter
לְנֹכַח, directly *forward*, front
לָנֶצַח, always, end, ever, everlasting
לִנְתָחִים, piece *by piece*
לֹעַ, throat
לעב, mock
לְעֵבֶר, beside
לעג, deride, derision, hold *in derision*, laugh, laugh *to scorn*, mock, ridicule, scorn, stammer
לַעַג, derision, hold *in derision*, mock, scoff, scorn, strange
לָעַד, ever, perpetually
לַעְדָּה, Laadah
לַעְדָּן, Ladan
לְעוֹלָם, again, endure, ever, evermore
לעז, *strange* language
לעט, eat
לְעֻמַּת, against, alike, along, alongside, beside, close, correspond, just, opposite, parallel, well
לַעֲנָה, *bitter* fruit, wormwood
לַעֲנוֹת, Leannoth
לַעֲצָמִים, limb *by limb*
לְעֵת, when
לְפִי, according, evidence, front, much, view, whenever
לַפִּיד, *flaming* torch, lightning, torch
לַפִּידוֹת, Lappidoth
לִפְנֵי, against, ahead, attend, attendance, attendance *upon*, before, charge, east, entrance, face, face *downward*, first, front, head, *into the* hand, *into the* hands, *into the* presence, long, meet, more *than*, open, over, presence, serve, service, sight, straight *before*, till, toward, under, upon
לְפָנִים, beforetime, former, formerly, forward, previously
לפת, grasp, turn *aside*, turn *over*
לְפֶתַע, suddenly
לֵץ, insolent
לִצְבָאוֹת, company *by company*

לִצְבִי, beautiful
לָצוֹן, scoff
לַקּוּם, Lakkum
לקח, accept, adopt, appoint, bring, buy, capture, carry *away*, catch, choose, entangle, enter, fetch, flash *continually*, flash *forth continually*, gain, get, heed, keep, marry, partake, put, raid, receive, seize, send, suffer, take, take *away*, take *to wife*, use
לקח אִשָּׁה, marry
לקח לְ, make
לקח לְאִשָּׁה, marry
לֶקַח, doctrine, instruction, learn, persuasiveness, precept, seductive *speech*, teach
לִקְחִי, Likhi
לקט, collect, gather, gather *up*, glean, pick *up*
לֶקֶט, gleanings
לְקֻמָּצִים, abundantly
לְקֵץ, after
לקק, lap, lick, lick *up*
לִקְרַאת, toward
לִקְרַאת, against, over *against*
לקשׁ, glean
לֶקֶשׁ, *latter* growth
לָרֹב, abundance, abundant, abundantly, great, *great* number, *great* quantity, *great* store, greatly, huge, much, plentiful, plenty
לִרְגָעִים, *every* moment
לְרֵיחַ, fragrant
לִשְׁבָטִים, tribe *by tribe*
לִשְׁגָגָה, unwittingly
לְשַׁד, cake, strength
לָשׁוֹן, bar, bay, language, speech, tongue
לִשְׁכָּה, chamber, hall
לְשָׁלוֹם, how *do*, how *fare*, *how* prosper
לֶשֶׁם, jacinth, Leshem
לשׁן, slander
לֶשַׁע, Lasha
לַשֶּׁקֶר, falsely
לַשָּׁרוֹן, Lasharon
לֶתֶךְ, lethech

מַאֲבוּס, granary
מְאֹד, all, apace, badly, care, deeply, diligently, ever, exceedingly, far, firmly, good, great, greatly, hard, highly, hotly, how, lightly, many, might, mightily, mighty, most, much, *right* well, sore, sorely, strongly, utterly, very, well
מֵאָה, hundred, hundredfold
מַאֲוַי, desire
מְאוּם, spot
מְאוּמָה, any *sort*, anything, else, fault, nothing, something
מָאוֹס, refuse
מָאוֹר, lamp, light, luminary
מְאוּרָה, den
מֵאָז, *long* ago, old, since, time *past*, when *once*
מֹאזְנַיִם, balance, scale
מֵאַחֲרֵי, after, away, behind, forsake
מֵאַחֲרֵי כֵן, afterward
מֵאַיִן, *from* whence, whence, where, without
מַאֲכָל, food, fruit, provision, slaughter, *something to* eat, sustenance
מַאֲכֶלֶת, knife
מַאֲכֹלֶת, fuel
מַאֲמָץ, force
מַאֲמָר, command
מאן, refuse
מאס, break *out afresh*, cast *away*, cast *off*, despise, disdain, loathe, refuse, reject, reprobate, spurn, vanish
מַאֲפֶה, bake
מַאֲפֵל, darkness
מַאְפֵּלְיָה, *thick* darkness
מֵאֵצֶל, away
מאר, malignant, prick
מַאֲרָב, ambush, place *of ambush*
מְאֵרָה, curse
מֵאֲשֶׁר, because, since, such, wherever

מֵאֵת, among, behalf
מֵאֶתְמוֹל שִׁלְשֹׁם, before
מָבוֹא, admit, come, enter, entrance, go *down*, set, time *for setting*, way *into*
מָבוֹא, haven
מְבוֹא הַשֶּׁמֶשׁ, west
מְבוּכָה, confusion
מַבּוּל, flood
מְבוּסָה, conquer, trample
מַבּוּעַ, fountain, spring
מְבוּקָה, desolation
מִבְחוֹר, choice
מִבְחָר, choice, Mibhar, pick
מַבָּט, hope
מִבְטָא, *thoughtless* utterance
מִבְטָח, confidence, hope, reliance, secure, trust
מִבֵּין, out
מִבַּיִת, back, beneath, inside, within
מִבְּלִי, because *no*, without, yet
מִבַּלְעֲדֵי, without
מִבַּלְעֲדֵי, besides, except, other *than*, without
מִבִּלְתִּי, because
מִבְנֶה, structure
מְבֻנַּי, Mebunnai
מִבַּעַד לְ, behind
מִבְצָר, fort, fortification, fortify, fortress, Mibzar, stronghold, fortified, tester, *well* fortified
מִבְשָׂם, Mibsam
מְבֻשׁ, private *part*
מַגְבִּישׁ, Magbish
מִגְבָּלֹת, cord
מִגְבָּעֹת, cap
מֶגֶד, abundance, choice, *choice* fruit, *choice* gift, *good* gift, rich
מְגִדּוֹ, Megiddo
מְגִדּוֹן, Megiddo
מַגְדִּיאֵל, Magdiel
מִגְדַּל אֵל, Migdal-el
מִגְדַּל גָּד, Migdal-gad
מִגְדַּל הַמֵּאָה, Tower *of the Hundred*
מִגְדַּל הַתַּנּוּרִים, Tower *of the Ovens*
מִגְדַּל חֲנַנְאֵל, Tower *of Hananel*
מִגְדַּל נצר, watchtower
מִגְדָּל, pulpit, tower, watchtower
מִגְדֹּל, Migdol
מִגְדָּנָה, *costly* ornament, *costly* ware, precious *thing*, *valuable* possession
מָגוֹג, Magog
מָגוֹר, sojourn, terror
מָגוּר, live, pilgrimage
מְגוֹרָה, dread, fear
מְגוּרָה, barn
מַגְזֵרָה, axe
מַגָּל, sickle
מְגִלָּה, roll, scroll
מְגִלַּת סֵפֶר, scroll
מגן, bestow, deliver, hand *over*
מָגֵן, arm, buckler, *large* shield, shield
מְגִנָּה, dullness
מִגְעֶרֶת, frustration
מַגֵּפָה, plague, slaughter, stroke
מַגְפִּיעָשׁ, Magpiash
מגר, cast, deliver *over*, terror
מְגֵרָה, saw
מִגְרוֹן, Migron
מִגְרָעָה, offset
מֶגְרָפָה, clod
מִגְרָשׁ, *common* land, countryside, *open* country, *open* land, *open* space, *pasture* land
מַד, armor, clothes, coat, garment, measure *out*, *rich* carpet, robe
מַד לְבוּשׁ, *soldier's* garment
מִדְבָּר, desert, *desert* waste, mouth, steppe, wilderness
מדד, long, measure, portion *out*, stretch
מדה, measure, measure *out*
מִדָּה, after, dimension, distance, district, great, *great* stature, measure, measure *of length*, measurement, section, size, standard, stature, tax

מַדּוּ, garment
מַדְוֶה, disease
מַדּוּחַ, mislead
מָדוֹן, contention, contentious, discord, Madon, quarrel, scorn, strife
מַדּוּעַ, how, what, why
מְדוּרָה, pile
מִדְחֶה, ruin
מִדַּי, *sufficient* number
מָדַי, Madai, Mede, Media
מָדַי, Mede
מִדֵּי, often, whenever
מִדְיָן, contentious, discord, dispute, Midian, Midianite, quarrel, quarrelsome
מִדִּין, Middin
מְדִינָה, city, district, province
מִדְיָנִי, Midianite, Midianite *woman*
מְדֹכָה, mortar
מַדְמֵן, Madmen
מַדְמַנָּה, Madmannah
מַדְמֵנָה, dung-pit, Madmenah
מְדָן, Medan
מַדָּע, knowledge, learning, thought
מֹדַעַת, kinsman
מַדְקָרָה, thrust
מַדְרֵגָה, cliff
מְדֻרָה, pyre
מִדְרָךְ, tread
מִדְרָשׁ, commentary, story
מְדֻשָׁה, thresh
מָה דַּרְכְּךָ, how
מָה, anything, how, *how* much, what, whatever, wherein, why
מָה זֶה, how, why
מָה שֶׁ, whatever
מֵהַבַּיִת, inner
מהה, delay, linger, *seem* slow, stupefy, wait
מהה, tarry
מָהוֹז, haven
מְהוּמָה, confusion, disturbance, panic, trouble, tumult
מְהוּמָן, Mehuman
מֵהַחוּץ, outside
מְהֵיטַבְאֵל, Mehetabel
מָהִיר, ready, skilful, skilled, swift
מהל, mix
מֵהָלְאָה, beyond
מַהֲלָךְ, access, go, journey, passage
מַהֲלָל, praise
מַהֲלַלְאֵל, Mahalalel
מַהֲלֻמוֹת, flog
מַהֲמֹרָה, pit
מַהְפֵּכָה, overthrow
מַהְפֶּכֶת, stocks
מהר, choose, fearful, give *a marriage present*, haste, hasten, hasty, make *haste*, *make* haste, outstrip, quick, quickly, rash, readily, rush, shortly, soon, speedily, swift
מַהֵר, hastily, once, soon, speedily, swift
מַהֵר מְאֹד, hasten *fast*
מַהֵר שָׁלָל חָשׁ בַּז, Maher-shalal-hash-baz
מֹהַר, *marriage* present
מְהֵרָה, hastily, hurry, quickly, shortly, soon, speedily, swiftly
מַהְרַי, Maharai
מַהֲתַלָּה, illusion
מוֹאָב, Moab, Moabite
מוֹאָבִי, Moab, Moabite, Moabitess
מוֹאל, left
מוֹבָא, come, entrance
מוג, dismay, fainthearted, flow, melt, melt *away*, melt *in fear*, soften, surge, toss *about*, totter
מוֹדָע, *intimate* friend, kinsman
מוט, fall, give *way*, move, remove, shake, slip, stumble, totter
מוט יָד, maintain
מוֹט, *carrying* frame, pole, yoke

מוֹטָה, bar, pole, yoke, yoke-bar
מוך, *become* poor, poor
מוֹכֵן, gnat
מול, circumcise, cut *off*
מוּל, before, front, frontier, opposite, over *against*
מוּל פְּנֵי, front
מוֹלָדָה, Moladah
מוֹלֶדֶת, birth, kindred, native, offspring
מוּלָה, circumcision
מוֹלִיד, Molid
מוּם, blemish, disfigurement, flaw, injury
מוּסָד, foundation
מוּסָד, foundation, lay *a foundation*
מוּסָדָה, foundation, punishment
מוּסָךְ, *covered* way
מוֹסֵר, bond, thong
מוּסָר, cease, censure, chasten, chastise, chastisement, correction, discipline, instruction, punishment, warn, warning
מוֹסֵרָה, Moserah
מוֹעֵד, rank
מוֹעֵד, appoint, *appointed* feast, *appointed* festival, *appointed* hour, *appointed* signal, *appointed* time, appointment, assembly, due *season*, feast, *feast* day, festival, holy *place*, hour, mark *the season*, meet, meeting *place*, place *of appointed feast*, season, *set* time, time
מוֹעַדְיָהוּ, Moadiah
מוּעָף, gloom
מוֹעֵצָה, admonition, counsel, device
מוּעָקָה, affliction
מוֹפֵת, miracle, omen, portent, sign, wonder
מוֹץ, chaff
מוֹצָא, come *out*, east, exclude, exit, go, go *forth*, go *out*, ground, import, Moza, outgoing, outlet, pass, proceed, proceed *out*, rise, spring, starting *place*, word *that goes forth*
מוֹצָאָה, latrine, origin
מוּצָק, anguish, cast, cramp, mass
מוּצֶקֶת, cast, lip
מוק, scoff
מוֹקֵד, burn, furnace
מוֹקְדָה, hearth
מוֹקֵשׁ, ensnare, lay *secretly*, snare, trap
מור, change, exchange, make *an exchange*
מוֹרָא, dread, fear, terrible *deed*, terror
מוֹרַג, *threshing* sledge
מוֹרָד, ascent, bevel, descent, steep *place*
מוֹרָה, fear, razor
מוֹרֶה, *early* rain, Moreh, teacher
מוֹרָשׁ, desire, possession
מוֹרָשָׁה, possess, possession
מוֹרֶשֶׁת גַּת, Moresheth-gath
מוֹרַשְׁתִּי, Moresheth
מושׁ, cease, depart, end, feel, give *way*, move, remove, withdraw
מוֹשָׁב, assembly, dwell, dwelling, dwelling *place*, habitation, inhabit, inhabited *place*, live, place *where dwells*, seat, settlement, situation, time
מוּשִׁי, Mushi, Mushite
מוֹשָׁעָה, salvation
מות, bring *about death*, bring *death*, *by no* means, *cause* death, *cause to* die, dead, *dead* beast, *dead* body, dead *man*, dead *person*, death, destroy, destruction, die, kill, murder, *one* dead, point *of death*, put *to death*, slay
מָוֶת, dead, deadly, death, deathly, die, pestilence, slay
מוּת לַבֵּן, Muth-labben
מוֹתָר, abundance, advantage, profit
מִזְבֵּחַ, altar
מֶזֶג, *mixed* wine
מָזֶה, waste
מִזָּה, Mizzah
מִזֶּה, hence, henceforth, other, side
מִזֶּה וּמִזֶּה, *opposite* sides
מָזוּ, garner
מְזוּזָה, beside, doorpost, post
מָזוֹן, provision
מָזוֹר, trap, wound

מֵזַח, belt, restraint
מְזִיחַ, belt
מַזְלֵג, fork
מִזְלָגָה, fork
מַזָּלוֹת, constellation
מְזִמָּה, discretion, *evil* device, intent, maliciously, mischief, purpose, scheme, thought, vile *deed*
מִזְמוֹר, psalm
מַזְמֵרָה, *pruning* hook
מְזַמֶּרֶת, snuffer
מִזְעָר, few, *very* little
מִזְרֶה, fork, *winnowing* fork
מַזָּרוֹת, Mazzaroth
מִזְרַח הַשֶּׁמֶשׁ, east, *east* side, eastward, sunrise, sunrising
מִזְרָח, east, east *side*, rise, sunrise
מִזְרָחָה, east, eastward, toward *the east*
מִזְרָע, sow
מִזְרָק, basin, bowl
מֹחַ, marrow
מֵחַ, fatling
מחא, clap
מַחֲבֹא, lurking *place*
מַחֲבֵא, hiding *place*
מְחַבְּרָה, clamp
מַחְבֶּרֶת, set
מַחְבֶּרֶת, join
מַחֲבַת, *baked* offering, griddle, plate
מַחֲגֹרֶת, girding
מחה, blot *out*, destroy, full *of marrow*, reach, sweep *away*, wash *off*, wipe, wipe *away*, wipe *out*
מְחוּגָה, compass
מְחוּיָאֵל, Mehujael
מַחֲוִים, Mahavite
מָחוֹל, dance, Mahol
מְחוֹלָה, dance
מִחוּץ, front, out, outer, outside, without
מַחֲזֶה, vision
מֶחֱזָה, window
מַחֲזִיאוֹת, Mahazioth
מְחִי, shock
מְחִידָא, Mehida
מִחְיָה, live, preserve *life*, quick, raw, *raw* flesh, *remain* alive, revive, sustenance
מְחִיר, hire, Mehir, price, value, wage
מַחֲלֶה, disease, sickness
מַחֲלָה, disease, sickness
מַחְלָה, Mahlah
מְחִלָּה, hole
מַחֲלוּי, wound
מַחְלוֹן, Mahlon
מַחְלִי, Mahli, Mahlite
מַחֲלָף, censer
מַחְלָפָה, lock
מַחֲלָצָה, *festal* robe, rich *apparel*
מַחֲלֹקֶת, allotment, division, escape, portion
מָחֲלַת, Mahalath
מְחֹלָתִי, Meholathite
מַחְמָד, delight, please, precious, precious *thing*
מַחְמַד בֶּטֶן, *beloved* child
מַחְמֹד, desirable, pleasant *place*, pride, treasure
מַחְמָל, desire
מַחְמֶצֶת, leaven
מַחֲנֶה, army, battle, camp, campaign, company, encampment, force, host, troop
מַחֲנֵה דָן, Mahaneh-dan
מַחֲנַיִם, Mahanaim, Mehanaim
מַחֲנָק, strangle
מַחְסֶה, refuge
מַחְסֶה, refuge, shelter
מַחְסוֹר, come *to want*, lack, need, poor, suffer *want*, want
מַחְסֵיָה, Mahseiah
מחץ, crush, pierce, shatter, smite, thrust *through*, wound
מַחַץ, wound
מַחְצֵב, quarry
מֶחֱצָה, half

מַחֲצִית, half, half *as much*
מַחֲצִית הַיּוֹם, midday
מחק, crush
מֶחְקָר, depth
מָחָר, time *to come*, tomorrow
מַחֲרֵשָׁה, plowshare
מָחֳרָת, day *after*, *following* day, morrow, next, *next* day, *next* morning
מַחְשֹׂף, expose
מַחֲשָׁבָה, *artistic* design, design, device, devise, invent, means, plan, plot, purpose, scheme, skilled, thought
מַחְשָׁךְ, dark, dark *place*, *dark* region, darkness
מַחַת, Mahath
מַחְתָּה, censer, firepan, tray
מְחִתָּה, destruction, dismay, horror, ruin, ruins, terror
מַחְתֶּרֶת, break
מַטְאֲטֵא, broom
מַטְבֵּחַ, slaughter
מַטָּה, below, beneath, low
מַטֶּה, dominion, rod, scepter, shaft, staff, stem, stick, tribal, tribe
מִטָּה, bed, bier, couch, litter
מֻטֶּה, outspread
מֻטֶּה, injustice
מַטְוֶה, spin
מְטִיל, bar
מַטְמוֹן, *hid* treasure, *hidden* store, *hidden* treasure, hoard, treasure
מַטָּע, plant, plantation
מַטְעַם, delicacy, *savory* food
מִטְפַּחַת, cloak, mantle
מטר, bring *rain*, *cause to* fall, *cause to* rain, rain, rain *down*, rain *upon*, send *rain*
מָטָר, rain
מַטְרֵד, Matred
מַטָּרָה, guard, mark, target
מַטְרִי, Matrite
מִטֶּרֶם, before
מַי, flood, pool, rain, sea, stream, tear, water
מִי, any *one*, how, some *one*, what, whoever
מִי אֲשֶׁר, whoever
מִי זֶה, what
מִי נתן, O *that*, oh *that*, would *that*
מֵי זָהָב, Me-zahab
מֵי יַרְקוֹן, Me-jarkon
מֵיד, assist
מֵידְבָא, Medeba
מֵידָד, Medad
מִיּוֹם, henceforth, since
מִיכָא, Mica
מִיכָאֵל, Michael
מִיכָה, Mica, Micah, Micaiah
מִיכָיָה, Micaiah
מִיכָיָהוּ, Micaiah
מִיכָיְהוּ, Micah, Micaiah
מִיכַל, Michal
מַיִם, brook
מִימֵי קֶדֶם, *long* ago
מִיָּמִים, *any* time
מִיָּמִים יָמִימָה, *each* year, yearly
מִיָּמִין, Mijamin, south
מִין, kind
מֵיפַעַת, Mephaath
מִיץ, press
מֵישָׁא, Mesha
מִישָׁאֵל, Mishael
מִישׁוֹר, equity, level, *level* ground, plain, tableland, uprightness
מֵישַׁךְ, Meshach
מֵישַׁע, Mesha
מֵישָׁר, equity, level, peace, right, rightly, smoothly, uprightly, uprightness
מֵיתָר, bow, cord
מַכְאוֹב, full *of pain*, pain, pang, sorrow, suffer, wound
מַכְבֵּנָה, Machbenah
מַכְבַּנַּי, Machbannai

מַכְבֵּר, coverlet
מִכְבָּר, grating
מַכָּה, affliction, blow, crush, disaster, plague, slaughter, stripe, stroke, wound
מִכְוָה, burn
מָכוֹן, dwelling, foundation, place, site
מְכוֹנָה, base, stand
מְכוּרָה, origin
מִכְוַת אֵשׁ, burn
מָכִי, Machi
מִכָיְהוּ, Micaiah
מָכִיר, Machir
מָכִירִי, Machirite
מכך, bring *low*, sink, wither
מִכֹּל, many, some
מִכְלְאֹת צֹאן, sheepfold
מִכְלָה, fold, pure
מִכְלוֹל, full
מַכְלֻל, *choice* garment
מִכְלָל, perfection
מַכֹּלֶת, food
מִכְמָן, treasure
מִכְמָס, Michmas
מִכְמֹר, net
מִכְמָר, net
מִכְמֶרֶת, seine
מִכְמֹרֶת, net
מִכְמָשׁ, Michmash
מִכְמְתָת, Michmethath
מַכְנַדְבַי, Machnadebai
מְכֹנָה, Meconah
מִכְנָס, breeches
מֶכֶס, tribute
מִכְסָה, number
מְכַסֶּה, covering
מִכְסֶה, awning, clothing, covering
מַכְפֵּלָה, Machpelah
מכר, betray, offer *for sale*, sell, seller
מַכָּר, acquaintance
מֶכֶר, precious, ware
מִכְרֶה, pit
מְכֵרָה, sword
מִכְרִי, Michri
מְכֵרָתִי, Mecherathite
מִכְשׁוֹל, fall, *make* stumble, obstruction, pang, ruin, stumble, *stumbling* block
מַכְשֵׁלָה, heap *of ruins*
מִכְתָּב, direction, inscription, letter, put *in writing*, write, writing
מְכִתָּה, fragment
מִכְתָּם, Miktam
מַכְתֵּשׁ, hollow *place*, mortar
מַל, before
מלא, arm, *become* full, come, complete, confirm, cover, draw, end, endow, expire, fill, fill *out*, fulfil, full, fully, fulness, give *in full number*, make, mass, number, ordain, overflow, pass, pay *in full*, replenish, require, sate, satisfy, set, take *up*, wet, wholly
מלא יָד, consecrate, install, ordain
מלא לֵב, presume
מָלֵא, full, fully, litter, rich, *too* full
מְלֹא, all, all *that fills*, band, everything, full, fulness, multitude
מְלֹא חָפְנַיִם, handful
מְלֹא כַף, handful
מְלֹא קֹמֶץ, handful
מְלֵא יָמִים, *very* aged
מְלֵאָה, row, set
מְלֵאָה, *whole* yield
מַלְאָךְ, ambassador, angel, envoy, messenger
מְלָאכָה, anything, business, cattle, construction, craft, craftsmanship, duty, goods, labor, make, occupation, property, purpose, royal, service, store, stuff, task, use, work, wrought
מַלְאֲכוּת, message
מַלְאָכִי, Malachi
מְלֶאכֶת עֲבֹדָה, *laborious* work
מִלֵּב, willingly

מִלְּבַד, addition, apart, besides, except, include, other *than*
מַלְבּוּשׁ, attire, clothing, raiment, vestment
מַלְבֵּן, brick *mold*, brickkiln, pavement
מִלָּה, anything, byword, say, speak, speech, talk, what, word
מִלּוֹא, Millo
מִלֻּא, consecration, ordination, *ordination* offering, set
מַלּוּחַ, mallow
מַלּוּךְ, Malluch
מְלוּכָה, dominion, kingdom, kingship, regal, *regal* estate, royal
מַלּוּכִי, Malluchi
מָלוֹן, lodging *place*, place, place *where lodges*, retreat
מְלוּנָה, hut, lodge
מַלּוֹתִי, Mallothi
מלח, rub *with salt*, season *with salt*, vanish
מַלָּח, mariner
מֶלַח, clothes, salt
מְלֵחָה, *salt* land, *salty* waste
מִלְחָמָה, attack, battle, *battle* array, *battle* line, combat, fight, storm, wage *war*, war, war *against*, *war* cry, warfare
מלט, deliver, escape, flee, get *away*, lay, leap *forth*, let *alone*, rescue, save
מֶלֶט, mortar
מְלַטְיָה, Melatiah
מְלִילָה, ear
מְלִיצָה, figure, scoff
מלך, *become* king, establishment, king, make *king*, make *queen*, proclaim *king*, queen, reign, reign *over*, set *up a king*, set *up as king*, take *counsel*, throne
מֶלֶךְ, king, Melech, royal
מֹלֶךְ, Molech
מַלְכֹּדֶת, trap
מַלְכָּה, queen
מִלְכָּה, Milcah
מַלְכוּת, *become* king, kingdom, realm, reign, royal, *royal* robe, rule
מַלְכִּי צֶדֶק, Melchi-zedek
מַלְכִּי שׁוּעַ, Malchi-shua
מַלְכִּיאֵל, Malchiel
מַלְכִּיאֵלִי, Malchielite
מַלְכִּיָּהוּ, Malchiah, Malchijah
מַלְכִּירָם, Malchiram
מַלְכָּם, Malcam
מִלְכֹּם, Milcom
מלל, cut *off*, fade, say, scrape, speak, utter, wither
מִלֲלַי, Milalai
מַלְמַד בָּקָר, oxgoad
מִלְמַטָּה, beneath, low
מִלְמַטָּה, deep
מִלְמַעְלָה, above
מִלִּפְנֵי, because, before, presence
מלץ, sweet
מֶלְצַר, steward
מלק, wring, wring *off*
מַלְקוֹחַ, booty, jaw, prey
מַלְקוֹשׁ, *later* rain, *latter* rain, spring *rain*
מֶלְקָח, tong
מַלְקָחַיִם, snuffer
מֶלְתָּחָה, wardrobe
מַמְּגֻרוֹת, granary
מֵמַד, measurement
מְמוּכָן, Memucan
מִמּוּל, opposite
מִמּוּל פְּנֵי, front
מָמוֹת, deadly, death
מַמְזֵר, bastard, mongrel
מִמְכָּר, release, sale, sell, ware
מַמְלָכָה, kingdom, kingship, reign, royal, *royal* power, throne
מַמְלְכוּת, kingdom
מַמְלָכוּת, reign
מִמְסָךְ, *mixed* wine
מִמְּעַיִם, bear
מִמַּעַל, above, upon

מִמַּעְלָה, above
מֶמֶר, bitterness
מַמְרֵא, Mamre
מִמָּרוֹם, loftily
מַמְרוֹר, bitterness
מִמֶּרְחָק, afar *off*
מִמְשַׁח, anoint
מִמְשָׁל, dominion
מֶמְשָׁלָה, authority, dominion, force, realm, rule
מֶמְשֶׁלֶת יָד, *under* dominion
מִמְשָׁק, possess
מַמְתַּקִּים, *most* sweet, *sweet* wine
מָן, manna
מִן, about, above, according, account, after, against, among, any, *any* part, any *part*, away, because, before, begin, beginning, belong, beside, besides, beyond, both, certain, either, even, ever *since*, expense, forth, instead, late, less *than*, lest, long, more *than*, most, neither, no, off, one *piece*, *one* piece, other, out, over, part, pass, rather *than*, reason, regard, respect, sake, *same* material, since, some, such, take *away*, than, through, throughout, till, too, toward, under, upon, what, when, where, whether, without, yet
מִן אָז, since
מִן הוּא, near
מִן הַרְבֵּה, no *more*
מֵן, portion, string, stringed *instrument*
מִנֶּגֶב, south, southern
מִנֶּגֶד, against, aloof, away, before, come, face, opposite, *out of* sight, over *against*
מְנַגִּינָה, song
מנה, appoint, apportion, assign, bid, count, destine, determine, muster, number
מָנָה, *choice* portion, *chosen* portion, contribution, portion, portion *of food*
מָנֶה, mina
מֹנֶה, time
מָנָה, prey
מִנְהָג, drive
מִנְהָרָה, den
מָנוֹחַ, home, Manoah, rest, resting *place*, set
מָנוֹחַ, home
מְנוּחָה, dwelling, peace, place *to rest*, rest, resting *place*, set *at rest*, still
מָנוֹן, heir
מָנוֹס, flight, refuge, way *of escape*
מָנוּס, refuge
מְנוּסָה, flee, flight
מָנוֹר, beam
מְנוֹרָה, lamp, lampstand
מִנְּזָר, prince
מִנְחָה, *burnt* offering, *cereal* offering, gift, *meal* offering, oblation, offering, present, sacrifice, tribute
מְנֻחוֹת, Menuhoth
מְנַחֵם, Menahem
מָנַחַת, Manahath
מָנַחְתִּי, Manahathite
מִנִּי, Minni
מְנִי, Destiny
מִנְיָמִן, Miniamin
מִנִּית, Minnith
מנם, truth
מנע, deny, hinder, hold, hold *back*, keep, keep *back*, refuse, restrain, withhold
מַנְעוּל, bolt
מִנְעָל, bar
מַנְעַמִּים, dainty
מְנַעַנְעַ, castanet
מְנַקִּיָּה, bowl, bowl *for libation*
מְנַשֶּׁה, Manasseh, Manassite
מְנַשִּׁי, Manassite
מְנָת, portion
מַס, *forced* labor, *forced* levy, levy, tribute, vassal
מֵסַב, couch, round *about*, round *and round*, surround
מְסִבִּיב, *every* side, round *about*
מַסְגֵּר, dungeon, prison, smith

מִסְגֶּרֶת, fastness, frame, panel, stronghold
מַסָּד, foundation
מִסְדְּרוֹן, vestibule
מסה, consume, drench, *make* melt, melt
מַסָּה, Massah, trial
מִסָּה, tribute
מַסְוֶה, veil
מְסוּכָה, *thorn* hedge
מִסְחָר, traffic
מסך, mingle, mix
מָסָךְ, covering, screen
מֶסֶךְ, mix
מַסֵּכָה, covering, league, *metal* image, molten, *molten* image, veil
מַסֵּכָה, covering
מִסְכֵּן, poor, poor *man*
מִסְכְּנוֹת, store, storehouse
מִסְכֵּנֻת, scarcity
מַסֶּכֶת, web
מְסִלָּה, course, highway, path, road
מַסְלוּל וְדֶרֶךְ, highway
מַסְמֵר, nail
מסס, faint, flow, *make* melt, melt, melt *away*, waste *away*
מַסָּע, break, journey
מַסָּע, dart, quarry
מִסְעָד, support
מִסְפֵּד, lament, lamentation, mourn, wail
מִסְפּוֹא, provender
מִסְפַּחַת, eruption
מִסְפָּחָה, veil
מִסְפַּר הַיָּמִים, time
מִסְפָּר, account, count, few, few *in number*, list, many, measure, Mispar, number, sum, tell, total
מִסְפֶּרֶת, Mispereth
מסר, act, provide
מֹסֵרוֹת, Moseroth
מִסְתּוֹר, shelter
מִסְתָּר, hide
מִסְתָּר, ambush, hide, hiding *place*, secret, secret *place*
מַעְבָּד, work
מַעֲבֶה, *clay* ground
מַעֲבָר, ford, pass, stroke
מֵעֵבֶר, across, beyond, *other* side, side
מַעְבָּרָה, ford, pass
מַעְגָּל, encampment, path, track, way
מַעְגָּלָה, path, way
מעד, *make* tremble, *set* time, slip, waver
מַעֲדַי, Maadai
מַעַדְיָה, Maadiah
מַעֲדָן, dainty, delight
מַעֲדַנּוֹת, chain, cheerfully
מַעְדֵּר, hoe
מָעָה, grain
מֵעָה, anguish, belly, body, bowels, breast, heart, soul, stomach, womb
מָעוֹג, bake
מָעוֹז, fortress, protection, refuge, strength, strengthen, strong, stronghold
מָעוֹז רֹאשׁ, helmet
מָעוּז, protection, refuge, stronghold
מָעוֹךְ, Maoch
מֵעוֹלָם, ancient, *long* ago, old, primeval
מָעוֹן, den, dwelling, dwelling *place*, habitation, haunt, lair, Maon, Maonite, refuge
מְעוּנִים, Meunim, Meunite
מְעוֹנֹתַי, Meonothai
מָעוּף, gloom
מָעוֹר, shame
מַעַזְיָהוּ, Maaziah
מעט, bring *to nothing*, decrease, diminish, dwindle, few, gather *little*, give *less*, give *small*, little, make *few in number*, make *small*, moment, *seem* little, small, take *few*, *too* few
מְעַט, almost, brief, enough, few, few *in number*, little, *little* account, *little* while, point, small, *small* matter, *small* tribe, some, while
מְעַט מִזְעָר, *very* few, *very* little

מַעֲטֶה, mantle
מַעֲטָפָה, mantle
מָעַי, Maai
מְעִי, heap
מְעִיל, mantle, robe
מַעְיָן, fountain, place *of springs*, spring, well
מעך, bruise, press, stick
מַעֲכָה, Maacah
מַעֲכַת, Maacath
מַעֲכָתִי, Maacah, Maacathite
מעל, act, *act* faithlessly, *act* treacherously, *act* unfaithfully, break *faith*, commit, commit *breach of faith*, commit *treachery*, commit *treason*, deal *treacherously*, *do* wrong, faithless, false, falsehood, practice, sin, transgress, trespass, unfaithful
מַעַל, above, breach *of faith*, deed, do, faithless, faithlessly, faithlessness, forward, guilty, high, project *upward*, treacherously, treachery, treason, unfaithfully, unfaithfulness, upward
מֹעַל, lift *up*
מַעַל, above, away, beside, beyond, forsake, high, off, out, presence, up, upon
מֵעַל הַחוּצָה, *out of the* presence
מַעַל לְ, over
מַעֲלָה, ascent, stair, stairway, step, thing, *upper* chamber
מַעֲלֶה, ascent, hill, stair, stairway, upward
מַעֲלָה, story, upward
מַעְלָה, above, heaven, high, onward, top
מַעֲלָל, act, behave, deed, do, practice, work
מֵעִם, before, suit, toward
מַעֲמָד, attendance, duty, place, station
מָעֳמָד, foothold
מַעֲמֵד, leave
מַעֲמָסָה, heavy
מַעֲמַקִּים, deep, depth
מַעַן, purpose
מַעֲנָה, furrow, *furrow's* length
מַעֲנֶה, answer, make *an answer*
מְעֹנָה, den, dwelling *place*, habitation
מַעַץ, Maaz
מַעֲצֵבָה, torment
מַעֲצָד, axe
מַעְצוֹר, hinder
מַעְצָר לְרוּחַ, self-control
מַעֲקֶה, parapet
מַעֲקַשׁ, rough *place*
מַעֲרָב, merchandise, ware, west
מַעֲרָבָה, *west* side, westward
מַעֲרֶה, nakedness, space
מְעָרָה, cave, den, Mearah
מַעֲרָךְ, plan
מַעֲרָכָה, army, battle, *battle* line, *battle* order, due *order*, rank, set
מַעֲרֶכֶת, row, showbread
מַעֲרֶכֶת לֶחֶם, showbread
מַעֲרֹם, naked
מַעֲרָצָה, *terrifying* power
מַעֲרָת, Maarath
מַעֲשֶׂה, act, art, blend, business, construction, deed, design, detail, do, effect, embroider, goods, labor, like, make, matter, needlework, occupation, pavement, produce, product, purpose, thing, *thing* made, use, verse, way, what, work, workmanship, wrought
מַעֲשֶׂה מִקְשֶׁה, *well-set* hair
מַעֲשֵׂה יָדַיִם, handiwork
מַעְשַׂי, Maasai
מַעֲשֵׂיָהוּ, Maaseiah
מַעֲשֵׂר, tithe
מַעֲשַׁקָּה, *cruel* oppressor, oppression
מֵעֵת עַד עֵת, once *a day*
מֹף, Memphis
מִפְגָּע, mark
מִפֹּה, inside, outside
מִפֹּה מִפֹּה, *either* side
מִפּוֹ, *other* side, side
מִפּוֹ מִפּוֹ, *each* side
מַפַּח, breathe

מַפֻּחַ, bellows
מְפִיבֹשֶׁת, Mephibosheth
מֻפִּים, Muppim
מַפָּל, fold, refuse
מִפְלָאָה, wondrous, work
מִפְלַגָּה, grouping
מַפָּלָה, ruins
מַפֵּלָה, ruin
מִפְלָט, shelter
מִפְלֶצֶת, *abominable* image, image
מִפְלָשׂ, balance
מַפֶּלֶת, carcass, downfall, fall, ruin
מִפְּנֵי, account, against, approach, away, because, before, fear, presence, reason, sake, sight, through, upon
מִפְּנִים, inside
מִפְּנִימָה, inside
מִפְעָל, act, do, work
מַפָּץ, slaughter
מַפֵּץ, hammer
מִפְקָד, appointed *place*, appointment, number
מִפְרָץ, landing
מַפְרֶקֶת, neck
מִפְרָשׂ, sail, spread
מִפְשָׂעָה, hip
מַפְתֵּחַ, key, open
מִפְתָּן, threshold
מֵץ, oppressor
מצא, befall, bring *forth*, catch, *cause to* fall, *cause to* happen, come, come *upon*, deliver, discover, enough, feel, find, find *out*, gain, get, give, grope, happen, here, lay *hold*, leave, *make* befall, meet, obtain, offer, overtake, present, reach, reap, seek, strike, suffer, suffice, use
מצא חֵן בְּעֵינַיִם, please
מצא טוֹב, prosper
מצא יָד, *at* hand, hand, occasion *offers*
מצא יָד דַּי, afford
מצא כֵּן, suffice
מַצָּב, garrison, office, place, place *where stands*
מֻצָּב, tower
מַצָּבָה, garrison
מַצֵּבָה, obelisk, pillar, stump
מִצָּבָה, guard
מְצֹבָיָה, Mezobaite
מִצַּד, beside
מְצָד, fortress, stronghold
מצה, drain *down*, drain *out*, wring
מַצָּה, fight, strife, unleavened, *unleavened* bread, *unleavened* cake
מֹצָה, Mozah
מִצְהָלָה, neigh
מָצוֹד, net, snare
מְצוּדָה, custody, net, stronghold
מְצוּדָה, fastness, fortress, net, prey, snare, strong, stronghold
מִצְוָה, charge, command, commandment, obligation, precept, term, *thing* commanded
מְצוֹלָה, *deep* region, depth
מְצוּלָה, deep
מָצוֹק, anguish, distress
מָצוּק, pillar, rise
מְצוּקָה, anguish, distress
מָצוֹר, besiege, defense, Egypt, fortify, rampart, siege, siegework, tower
מְצוּרָה, fortified, fortify, fortress, rampart, siegework
מַצּוּת, contend
מֵצַח, brow, forehead
מִצְחָה, greave
מְצִלָּה, bell
מְצֻלָּה, glen
מְצִלְתַּיִם, cymbal
מִצְנֶפֶת, turban
מַצָּע, bed
מִצְעָד, step, train
מִצְעָר, few, little *one*, *little* while, Mizar, small
מִצְפָּה, Mizpah
מִצְפֶּה, Mizpeh, watchtower

מַצְפּוּן, treasure
מִצְפּוֹן, *northerly* direction, northern
מצץ, drink *deeply*
מצצר, blow
מֵצַר, distress, pang
מִצְרִי, Egypt, Egyptian
מִצְרַיִם, Egypt, Egyptian
מַצְרֵף, crucible
מַק, rottenness
מַקֶּבֶת, hammer
מַקֶּבֶת בּוֹר, quarry
מַקֵּדָה, Makkedah
מִקֶּדֶם, east, *long* ago
מִקְדָּשׁ, hallowed *part*, holy *place*, holy *thing*, *sacred* area, sanctuary, temple
מַקְהֵל, congregation, *great* congregation
מַקְהֵלֹת, Makheloth
מִקְוָה, reservoir
מִקְוֶה, abide, gather *together*, hold *water*, hope, pool
מָקוֹם, country, direction, dwelling *place*, ground, home, part, place, post, quarter, resting *place*, room, side, site, space
מְקוֹם אֲשֶׁר, wherever
מְקוֹם אֲשֶׁר שָׁם, wherever
מְקוֹם שֶׁבֶת, seat
מָקוֹר, flow, fountain
מִקָּח, take
מַקָּחָה, ware
מַקְטֵר, burn
מֻקְטָר, incense
מִקְטֶרֶה, altar *for burning incense*
מִקְטֶרֶת, censer
מַקֵּל, staff, stick
מַקֵּל, rod, staff
מַקֵּל יָד, handpike
מִקְלוֹת, Mikloth
מִקְלָט, refuge
מִקְלַעַת, carve, carving
מִקְנָה, buy, pay, possession, price, purchase
מִקְנֶה, animal, cattle, flock, herd, livestock, possession, purchase
מִקְנֶה צֹאן, flock
מִקְנֵיָהוּ, Mikneiah
מִקְסָם, divination
מָקַץ, Makaz
מִקֵּץ, after
מִקְצָה, one *and all*
מִקְצֹעַ, Angle, corner
מַקְצֻעָה, plane
מִקְצֹעָה, corner
מִקְצָת, some
מקק, fester, pine *away*, rot, rot *away*, waste *away*
מִקְרָא, assembly, convocation, read, summon
מִקָּרֹב, *at* hand, hand, late, short, soon
מִקֶּרֶב, among, out
מִקְרֶה, befall, chance, fate
מְקָרֶה, roof
מְקֵרָה, cool
מִקְשָׁה, *cucumber* field, hammer, *hammered* work
מַר, bitter, bitterly, bitterness, *cause bitter* pain, distress, drop
מַר נֶפֶשׁ, angry, discontented, enrage
מֹר, myrrh
מרא, flee, rebellious
מָרָא, Mara
מַרְאָה, mirror, vision
מַרְאֶה, appear, appearance, beauty, behold, clearly, countenance, face, form, handsome, look, look *upon*, pattern, see, sight, something, vision
מֻרְאָה, crop
מְרַאֲשׁוֹת, head, *under the* head
מַרְאֶשֶׁת, head
מֵרַב, Merab
מֵרֹב, many
מַרְבָד, covering
מַרְבֶּה, abundance, increase
מִרְבָּה, much
מַרְבִּית, greatness, increase, majority, multitude, profit
מַרְבֵּץ, fold, lair
מַרְבֵּק, fatted, stall
מַרְגּוֹעַ, rest
מַרְגְּלוֹת, foot, leg
מַרְגֵּמָה, sling
מַרְגֵּעָה, repose
מרד, make *as rebel*, rebel
מֶרֶד, Mered, rebellion
מַרְדּוּת, rebellious, rebellious *woman*
מְרֹדַךְ בַּלְאֲדָן, Merodach-baladan
מְרֹדָךְ, Merodach
מָרְדֳּכַי, Mordecai
מֻרְדָּף, persecution
מרה, bitter, defy, disobedient, disobey, make *bitter*, rebel, rebel *against*, rebellious
מָרָה, bitterness, Marah
מֹרָה, bitter
מַרְהֵבָה, *insolent* fury
מָרוּד, homeless
מֵרוֹז, Meroz
מָרוֹחַ, crush
מָרוֹם, haughtily, heaven, height, high, *high* heaven, *high* mount, high *place*, proudly, upward
מֵרוֹם, Merom
מֵרוֹץ, race
מְרוּצָה, course, run, violence
מָרוּק, beautify
מָרוֹר, bitterness
מָרוֹת, Maroth
מַרְזֵחַ, mourn, revelry
מרח, apply
מֶרְחָב, *broad* pasture, broad *place*, *set* free
מֶרְחָב, breadth
מֵרָחוֹק, far *off*, *great* while to *come*, *long* ago
מֶרְחָק, afar, distant, far, far *away*, last, length *and breadth*, stretch *afar*
מֵרָחֹק, afar, afar *off*
מַרְחֶשֶׁת, pan
מרט, burnish, fall, polish, pull, pull *out*, pull *out hair*, rub *bare*, smooth
מְרִי, rebellion, rebellious
מְרִי בַעַל, Merib-baal
מְרִיא, fatling, *fatted* beast, *fed* beast
מְרִיב בַּעַל, Merib-baal
מְרִיבָה, Meribah, strife
מְרִיבַת קָדֵשׁ, Meribath-kadesh
מֹרִיָּה, Moriah
מְרָיָהוּ, Meraiah
מְרָיוֹת, Meraioth
מִרְיָם, Miriam
מְרִירוּת, *bitter* grief
מְרִירִי, poisonous
מֹרֶךְ, faintness
מֶרְכָּב, chariot, saddle, seat
מֶרְכָּבָה, chariot
מִרְמָה, betrayer, deceit, deceitful, deceitfully, deceive, false, fraud, guile, Mirmah, treacherous, treachery
מְרֵמוֹת, Meremoth
מִרְמָס, beat *down*, trample, trample *down*, tread, tread *down*
מֵרֹנֹתִי, Meronothite
מֶרֶס, Meres
מַרְסְנָא, Marsena
מֵרֵעַ, adviser, companion, friend
מִרְעֶה, pasture
מַרְעִית, flock, pasture
מַרְעֲלָה, Mareal
מַרְפֵּא, bring *healing*, deference, gentle, healing, health, remedy, tranquil
מִרְפָּשׂ, foul
מרץ, forceful, grievous, provoke
מַרְצֵעַ, awl
מַרְצֶפֶת, pediment
מרק, burnish, cleanse *away*, polish, scour
מָרָק, broth
מֶרְקָח, fragrance
מֶרְקָחָה, pot *of ointment*
מִרְקַחַת, mix
מרר, bitter, deal *bitterly*, enrage, *fiercely* attack, make *bitter*, move *with anger*, provocation, weep, weep *bitterly*
מָרֹר, *bitter* herb
מְרֹרָה, bitter, bitter *thing*, gall
מְרֵרָה, gall
מְרָרִי, Merari, Merarite
מָרֵשָׁה, Mareshah
מִרְשַׁעַת, wicked *woman*
מֹרַשְׁתִּי, Moresheth
מְרָתַיִם, Merathaim
מַשָּׂא, bear *a burden*, burden, carry, desire, load, Massa, music, oracle, tribute
מַשֹּׂא פָּנִים, partiality
מַשָּׂאָה, bear, present, *rising* smoke, signal
מַשְׂאֵת, cloud, exaction, gift, lift *up*, oracle, portion, present, tax
מִשְׂגָּב, fortress, high, place *of defense*, refuge, stronghold, *sure* defense
מַשּׂוֹר, see
מְשׂוּרָה, measure, quantity
מָשׂוֹשׂ, gladness, joy, joyous, mirth, rejoice
מִשְׂחָק, make *sport*
מִשְׂחֶקֶת, rejoice
מַשְׂטֵמָה, hatred
מְשֻׂכָּה, hedge
מַשְׂכִּיל, Maskil, psalm
מַשְׂכִּית, figure, figured *stone*, folly, picture, setting
מַשְׂכֹּרֶת, reward, wage
מִשְׂמֹאל, north
מִשְׂפָּח, bloodshed
מִשְׂרָה, government
מִשְׂרֵפָה, burn
מִשְׂרְפוֹת מַיִם, Misrephoth-maim
מַשְׂרֵקָה, Masrekah
מַשְׂרֵת, pan
מַשׁ, Mash
מַשָּׁא, interest
מַשָּׁא יָד, debt
מֵשָׁא, Mesha
מַשְׁאָב, watering *place*
מַשָּׁאָה, debt
מַשָּׁאוֹן, guile
מִשְׁאָל, Mashal, Mishal
מִשְׁאָלָה, desire, petition
מִשְׁאֶרֶת, *kneading* bowl, *kneading* trough
מִשְׁבְּצוֹת, setting, setting *of filigree*, weave
מַשְׁבֵּר, birth, mouth *of the womb*
מִשְׁבָּר, wave
מִשְׁבָּת, downfall
מִשְׁגֶּה, oversight
משה, draw, draw *out*
מֹשֶׁה, Moses
מְשׁוֹאָה, *desolate* ground, *desolate* land, devastation
מַשּׁוּאוֹת, ruin, ruins
מְשׁוֹבָב, Meshobab
מְשׁוּבָה, apostasy, backslide, faithless, faithless *one*, faithlessness, turn *away*
מְשׁוּגָה, error
מְשֻׁגָּע, madman
מָשׁוֹט, oar
משח, anoint, oil, paint, spread
מָשְׁחָה, portion
מִשְׁחָה, anoint, portion
מַשְׁחִית, corruption, destruction, ravage, trap, undo
מִשְׁחָר, morning
מָשְׁחָת, mutilation
מִשְׁחַת, mar
מִשְׁטוֹחַ, spread
מִשְׁטָח, spread
מִשְׁטָר, rule
מֶשִׁי, silk
מְשֵׁיזַבְאֵל, Meshezabel
מָשִׁיחַ, anoint, anointed *one*
משך, bear, cheer, continue, defer, delay, draw, draw *out*, draw *up*, extend, follow, gather, lead, make *a long blast*, move *out*, prolong, pull, select, sound, sow, stretch *out*, take *off*, tall
מֶשֶׁךְ, Meshech, price, sow
מִשְׁכָּב, bed, bier, couch, lie, rest
מִשְׁכָּן, abode, dwell, dwelling, dwelling *place*, encampment, habitation, tabernacle, tent
מֹשֶׁכֶת, cord
משל, *ballad* singer, *become* like, *become* ruler, byword, charge, compare, dominion, give *dominion*, governor, make *ruler*, maker, master, power, repeat, right, rule, rule *over*, ruler, sell, speak *an allegory*, use, use *a proverb*, utter
משל כְּ, like
משל עִם, like
מָשָׁל, allegory, byword, discourse, parable, proverb, taunt, *taunt* song
מֹשֶׁל, dominion, like, rule
מִשְׁלוֹחַ, put *forth*, send
מִשְׁלַח, let *loose*
מִשְׁלַח יָד, undertake
מִשְׁלַחַת, company, discharge
מְשֻׁלָּם, Meshullam
מְשִׁלֵּמוֹת, Meshillemoth
מְשֶׁלֶמְיָהוּ, Meshelemiah
מְשִׁלֵּמִית, Meshillemith
מְשֻׁלֶּמֶת, Meshullemeth
מִשָּׁם, off, out, thence, there, whence
מְשַׁמָּה, desolate, desolation, horror, waste
מַשְׁמָן, fat
מִשְׁמָן, fat, fatling, rich *part*, *stout* warrior, strong
מִשְׁמַנָּה, Mishmannah
מִשְׁמָע, hear, Mishma
מִשְׁמַעַת, bodyguard, obey
מִשְׁמָר, custody, duty, guard, prison, service, station, vigilance, watch
מִשְׁמֶרֶת, allegiance, appoint, attend, charge, do, duty, duty *of watching*, guard, keep, office, post, require, rite, safekeeping, service, *under* guard, watch, work
מִשְׁנֶה, copy, double, *double* portion, doubly, half, next, next *in authority*, next *in rank*, second, *second* order, *second* quarter, twice
משס, spoil
מְשִׁסָּה, booty, plunder
מִשְׁעוֹל, *narrow* path
מִשְׁעִי, cleanse
מִשְׁעָם, Misham
מַשְׁעֵן, stay, support
מִשְׁעָן, stay
מַשְׁעֵנָה, staff
מִשְׁעֶנֶת, staff, stave
מִשְׁפָּחָה, clan, family, kind, kindred, people, tribe
מִשְׁפָּט, accustom, appointment, arrangement, case, cause, charge, command, court, crime, custom, decision, deserve, duty, judge, judgment, just, *just* decree, *just* measure, justice, kind, law, lawful, manner, manner *of life*, ordinance, plan, prescribe, procedure, punishable, redress, right, rule, sentence, specification, trial, vindication, way, way *that is ordained*, *where it* used, wont
מִשְׁפְּתַיִם, sheepfold
מַשָּׁק, leap
מַשְׁקֶה, butler, butlership, cupbearer, drink
מִשְׁקוֹל, weight
מַשְׁקוֹף, lintel
מִשְׁקָל, *full* weight, shekel, weigh, weight
מִשְׁקֶלֶת, plummet
מִשְׁקָע, clear
מִשְׁרָה, juice
מִשְׁרָעִי, Mishraite
משש, feel, feel *about*, feel *through*, grope
מִשְׁתֶּה, banquet, dinner, drink, feast
מִשְׁתֵּה יַיִן, feast
מַת, few, man
מַת סוֹד, *intimate* friend
מֵת, dead
מַתְבֵּן, straw

מֶתֶג, bit, bridle
מֶתֶג אַמָּה, Metheg-ammah
מִתּוֹךְ, among, leave, out
מָתוֹק, *something* sweet, sweet, sweetness
מְתוּשָׁאֵל, Methushael
מְתוּשֶׁלַח, Methuselah
מתח, spread
מִתַּחַת, below, beneath, under, underneath
מָתַי, long, when
מִתֵּימָן, southward
מַתְכֹּנֶת, composition, measure, number, *proper* condition
מְתַלְּעוֹת, fang, tooth
מְתֹם, soundness
מִתְּמוֹל שִׁלְשֹׁם, before, time *past*
מַתָּן, gift, Mattan
מַתָּנָה, bribe, gift, Mattanah
מַתְּנַי, Mattenai
מִתְנִי, Mithnite
מַתַּנְיָהוּ, Mattaniah
מָתְנַיִם, heart, loin, side, waist
מַתְּנַת יָד, able
מתק, *become* sweet, hold *sweet*, sweet
מֶתֶק, pleasant
מִתְקָה, Mithkah
מִתְרְדָת, Mithredath
מַתָּת, gift, give, reward
מַתַּת יָד, much *as able*
מַתַּתָּה, Mattattah
מַתִּתְיָהוּ, Mattithiah

נָא, beg, beseech, come, now, oh, please, pray, raw, then, therefore, yet
נֹא, Thebes
נֹא אָמוֹן, Thebes
נֹאד, bottle, skin, wineskin
נֹאד יַיִן, wineskin
נאה, beautiful, comely
נָאוֶה, becoming, befit, comely, fitting, lovely, seemly
נאם, say
נְאֻם, declare, oracle, say, speak
נאף, adulterer, adulteress, adulterous, adultery, commit *adultery*, *woman who* breaks wedlock
נִאֻף, adultery
נַאֲפוּף, adultery
נאץ, despise, renounce, revile, scorn, spurn, treat *with contempt*
נְאָצָה, blasphemy, revile
נֶאָצָה, disgrace
נאק, groan
נְאָקָה, groan
נאר, disown, renounce
נֹב, Nob
נבא, appear *as prophet*, prophesy, rave
נבב, hollow, stupid
נְבוֹ, Nebo
נְבוּאָה, prophecy
נְבוּזַרְאֲדָן, Nebuzaradan
נְבוּכַדְנֶאצַּר, Nebuchadnezzar
נְבוּכַדְרֶאצַּר, Nebuchadrezzar
נְבוּשַׁזְבָּן, Nebushazban
נָבוֹת, Naboth
נבח, bark
נֹבַח, Nobah
נִבְחַז, Nibhaz
נבט, behold, consider, eye *fixed*, fix *one's eye*, gaze, look, look *down*, look *upon*, note, regard, see, stare
נְבָט, Nebat
נָבִיא, prophesy, prophet
נְבִיאָה, prophetess
נְבָיוֹת, Nebaioth
נֵבֶךְ, spring
נבל, crumble *away*, dishonor, fade, fall, foolish, lose *heart*, scoff, treat *with contempt*, wear *out*, wither
נָבָל, fool, foolish, foolish *woman*, impious, Nabal, senseless, *wanton* fool
נֵבֶל, harp, jar, lute, pot, skin, vessel, waterskin
נְבָלָה, folly, shameful *thing*, vile, vile *thing*, *wanton* crime, *wanton* folly, wantonness
נְבֵלָה, animal *that dies*, body, carcass, corpse, *dead* body, die
נַבְלוּת, lewdness
נְבַלָּט, Neballat
נבע, bellow, gush, *make* give *off*, pour *forth*, pour *out*, utter
נִבְשָׁן, Nibshan
נֶגֶב, Negeb, south, *south* side, southern, southward
נֶגֶב תֵּימָן, south
נגד, announce, answer, confess, declare, denounce, describe, disclose, explain, give, give *an oracle*, inform, make *clear*, make *known*, messenger, proclaim, prove, repeat, report, reveal, show, show *forth*, speak, tell, tell *about*, utter
נֶגֶד, adjoin, against, before, face, know, opposite, over *against*, presence, sight, straight, straight *before*
נֶגֶד עַיִן, sight
נֶגֶד פָּנִים, mind, sight
נֶגְדָּה לְ, presence
נֹגַהּ, bright, brightness, dawn, flash, light, Nogah, shine
נגה, lighten, shed *light*, shine
נְגֹהָה, brightness
נגח, attack, charge, gore, push, push *down*, thrust
נַגָּח, gore
נָגִיד, *chief* officer, commander, governor, leader, noble, noble *thing*, prince, ruler
נְגִינָה, music, song, stringed *instrument*
נגן, minstrel, play, play *on strings*, sing
נגע, about, afflict, arrive, attack, beat, bring *down*, cast, close, come, draw *near*, draw *nigh*, follow, happen, join, molest, reach, reach *up*, smite, strike, touch, *whoever* touches
נגע אֶל, befall
נגע יַד דַּי, afford
נֶגַע, afflict, affliction, assault, attack, disease, diseased, diseased *person*, *diseased* spot, diseased *thing*, plague, scourge, strike, stripe, stroke, wound
נגף, afflict, beat, bring *a plague*, dash, defeat, hurt, plague, put *to rout*, rout, send *a plague*, slay, smite, smite *down*, strike, strike *down*, stumble
נֶגֶף, offense, plague
נגר, drag *off*, flow, give, give *over*, pour, pour *down*, spill, stretch *out*
נגשׂ, distress, driver, exact, exactor, foreman, oppress, oppressor, press *hard*, ruler, taskmaster
נגשׁ, advance, approach, bring, bring *here*, bring *near*, come, come *forward*, come *near*, draw *near*, go, go *near*, go *up*, make *room*, near, offer, overtake, present, put, stand, touch
נגשׁ וָבוֹא, draw *near*
נֵד, heap
נדב, give *willingly*, make *a freewill offering*, make *willing*, move, offer *freely*, offer *willingly*, volunteer
נָדָב, Nadab
נְדָבָה, freely, *freewill* offering, offer *freely*, offering, voluntarily
נְדַבְיָה, Nedabiah
נדד, chase *away*, drive *out*, flee, flight, flutter, fly *away*, fugitive, move, shrink, stray, wander, wander *abroad*, wanderer
נדה, cast *out*, put *far away*
נֵדֶה, gift
נִדָּה, filth, filthy *thing*, impurity, menstrual, menstruation, pollution, unclean, unclean *thing*, uncleanness
נְדוּד, toss
נדח, banish, bring *down*, cast *out*, compel, disperse, draw *away*, drive, drive *away*, drive *out*, go *astray*, hunt, keep *outcast*, *make* go *astray*, *make* leave, outcast, stray, swing, thrust, thrust *down*, wield
נָדִיב, generous, generous *man*, noble, noble *man*, prince, queenly, willing, willing *man*
נְדִיבָה, honor, noble *thing*
נָדָן, gift, sheath
נדף, drive, drive *away*, fleeting, vanquish
נדר, make, make *a vow*, take, take *a vow*, vow
נֶדֶר, payment *of vow*, *votive* offering, vow
נֹהַּ, preeminence
נהג, bring, bring *away*, carry *away*, carry *off*, drive, drive *away*, guide, lament, lead, lead *away*, lead *out*
נהג וְהלך, urge
נהה, *bitter* lamentation, lament, wail
נְהִי, lament, lamentation, wail
נהל, carry, give *rest*, guide, lead, lead *gently*, supply
נַהֲלָל, Nahalal
נַהֲלֹל, Nahalol, pasture
נהם, groan, growl, roar
נְהָמָה, roar, tumult
נהק, bray
נהר, flow, radiant
נָהָר, canal, Euphrates, flood, river, *river* Euphrates, stream, water
נְהַר פְּרָת, Euphrates
נְהָרָה, light
נוא, discourage, express *disapproval*, frustrate, oppose
נוב, bring *forth*, bring *forth fruit*, increase, *make* flourish
נוד, bemoan, *cause to* wander, condole, drive *away*, flee, flee *away*, flit, pity, shake, *show* sympathy, sway, throw *away*, wag, wander *away*, wanderer, waver
נוד הלך, flee *away*
נוֹד, Nod, toss
נוֹדָב, Nodab
נוה, abide, praise
נָוֶה, fold, habitation, pasture
נָוֶה, abode, dwelling, fold, *grazing* land, habitation, haunt, pasture, sheepfold, woman
נוח, abandon, abide, allow, cast *down*, come, *come to* rest, deposit, find *rest*, get *relief*, give *peace*, give *rest*, lay, lay *down*, lay *up*, leave, leave *free*, let *alone*, lodge, lower, make *amends*, part *left free*, place, provide *a place of rest*, put, rest, satisfy, set, set *at rest*, set *down*, settle, station, tolerate, vent, wait, wait *quietly*, withhold
נוח עַל, league
נוֹחָה, Nohah
נוט, quake
נום, asleep, sink *into*, slumber
נוּמָה, drowsiness
נוּן, Nun
נוס, abate, drive, flee, flee *away*, flee *in haste*, fugitive, hide, *make* flee, put *to flight*, rally, run *away*, speed, speed *away*
נוע, *become a* wanderer, fugitive, *make* totter, *make* wander, move, roam *about*, *set* trembling, shake, stagger, sway, swing *to and fro*, tremble, wag, wander, wander *about*
נוֹעַדְיָה, Noadiah
נוף, dedicate, lift, lift *up*, offer, perfume, put, raise, shake, shed *abroad*, sift, wave, wield
נוֹף, elevation
נוֹצָה, feather, plumage
נזה, spatter, sprinkle, startle
נָזִיד, pottage
נָזִיר, Nazirite, prince, separate, *undressed* vine
נזל, distil, flood, flow, *flowing* stream, *flowing* water, gush, *make* flow, pour *down*, rain *down*, stream, waft
נֶזֶם, earring, ring
נֵזֶק, loss
נזר, consecrate, fast, keep *away*, keep *separate*, separate
נֵזֶר, consecrate, consecration, crown, hair, separation, *separation as a* Nazirite, *vow as a* Nazirite
נֹחַ, Noah
נַחְבִּי, Nahbi
נחה, bring, guide, lead, lead *away*
נַחוּם, Nahum
נִחוּם, comfort, compassion
נְחוּם, Nehum
נָחוֹר, Nahor
נָחוּשׁ, bronze
נְחוּשָׁה, brass, bronze, copper
נְחִילָה, flute
נְחִיר, nostril
נחל, acquire, allot, apportion, assign *as an inheritance*, belong, bequeath, *cause to* inherit, *cause to* possess, distribute, distribute *inheritance*, divide, divide *for inheritance*, divide *inheritance*, endow, give *an inheritance*, give *as a possession*, give *for a heritage*, give *to inherit*, hold, inherit, inheritance, leave *an inheritance*, leave *for an inheritance*, *make* inherit, obtain *an inheritance*, possess, put *in possession*, receive, receive *an inheritance*, receive *inheritance*, take *for inheritance*
נַחַל, brook, channel, *dry* stream-bed, flow, ravine, river, stream, stream-bed, torrent, *torrent* bed, valley
נַחֲלָה, inheritance
נַחֲלָה, heritage, inherit, inheritance, possession, *rightful* due
נַחֲלִיאֵל, Nahaliel
נֶחֱלָמִי, Nehelam
נחם, appease, *become a* consolation, bring *relief*, change *one's mind*, comfort, comforter, compassion, console, give *consolation*, move *to pity*, pity, reassure, relent, repent, satisfy, sorry, take *comfort*, vent *wrath*
נַחַם, Naham
נֹחַם, compassion
נֶחָמָה, comfort, consolation
נְחֶמְיָה, Nehemiah
נַחֲמָנִי, Nahamani
נחץ, require *haste*
נחר, blow *fiercely*
נַחַר, snort
נַחֲרָה, snort
נַחֲרַי, Naharai
נחשׁ, augur, divine, learn *by divination*, practice *augury*, sorcery, watch *for an omen*
נַחַשׁ, enchantment, omen
נָחָשׁ, Nahash, serpent
נַחְשׁוֹן, Nahshon
נְחֹשֶׁת, brass, bronze, *bronze* fetter, chain, copper, fetter, fetter *of bronze*, shame, *thing of* bronze
נְחֻשְׁתָּא, Nehushta
נְחֻשְׁתָּן, Nehushtan
נחת, bend, bring *down*, come *down*, descend, go *deep*, go *down*, settle, sink
נַחַת, descend, Nahath, quiet, quietness, rest, set
נָחֵת, go *down*
נטה, bend *down*, bow, cast, decline, depart, deprive, evening, extend, incline, lay *down*, lead *astray*, lean, lengthen, let *down*, mark *off*, offer, outstretched, persuade, pervert, pervert *justice*, pitch, plan, show, spread, spread *out*, stretch, stretch *forth*, stretch *out*, strike, stumble, sway, swerve, take *aside*, thrust, thrust *aside*, turn, turn *aside*, turn *aside upon*, turn *away*
נטה אַחֲרֵי, support
נְטִיל, weigh *out*
נָטִיעַ, plant
נְטִיפָה, pendant
נְטִישָׁה, branch, spread *branches*
נטל, lay, lift *up*, offer, take *up*
נֵטֶל, weighty
נטע, *firmly* fix, mislead, pitch, plant, planter, replant, stretch *out*
נֶטַע, plant, planting
נְטָעִים, Netaim
נטף, distil, drip, drop, pour *down rain*, preach, preacher
נָטָף, drop, stacte
נְטֹפָה, Netophah
נְטֹפָתִי, Netophah, Netophathite
נטר, bear *a grudge against*, keep, keep *anger*, keeper
נטשׁ, abandon, cast, cast *away*, cast *forth*, cast *off*, draw, fall, forego, forsake, hang *loose*, leave, lie *fallow*, make *a raid*, permit, quit, reject, spread, spread *abroad*, spread *out*
נטשׁ דְּבָרִים, cease *to care about*
נִי, wail
נִיב, fruit

נֵיבַי, Nebai
נִיד, solace
נִידָה, filthy
נָיוֹת, Naioth
נִיחֹחַ, please, soothe
נִין, offspring
נִינְוֵה, Nineveh
נִיסָן, Nisan
נִיצוֹץ, spark
ניר, break *up*
נִיר, *fallow* ground, lamp
נכא, whip
נָכָא, strike
נָכֵא, break, downcast
נְכֹאת, gum
נֶכֶד, descendant, posterity
נכה, afflict, attack, beat, blow, clap, conquer, cut *down*, deal *a blow*, defeat, destroy, fall, fight, flog, give, hit, hurl, kill, make, make *a slaughter*, manslayer, murderer, overcome, pin, put, put *to death*, receive, receive *a wound*, rout, ruin, sack, shoot, slaughter, slay, smite, smiter, strike, strike *down*, subdue, take, thrust, wound
נָכֶה, contrite, cripple
נָכֵה, cripple
נְכוֹ, Neco
נָכוֹן, Nacon
נָכֹחַ, right, straight, uprightness
נֹכַח, before, face, opposite, point *opposite*, straight *ahead*, *under the* eye
נֹכַח פָּנִים, front
נכל, beguile, cheat, conspire *against*, deal *craftily*
נֵכֶל, wile
נְכָסִים, possession, wealth
נכר, accept, acknowledge, acquaint, discern, dissemble, distinguish, friend, judge *amiss*, know, make *known*, mark, point *out*, pretend *to be another*, profane, recognize, regard, see, take *notice*, treat *like a stranger*, understand
נכר פָּנִים, partial, partiality, *show* partiality
נֵכֶר, disaster, misfortune
נֵכָר, foreign, foreigner, strange
נָכְרִי, adventuress, alien, foreign, foreigner, stranger, wild
נְכֹת, treasure
נלה, make *an end*
נְמוּאֵל, Nemuel
נְמוּאֵלִי, Nemuelite
נְמָלָה, ant
נִמְצָא, present
נָמֵר, leopard
נִמְרֹד, Nimrod
נִמְרָה, Nimrah
נִמְרִים, Nimrim
נִמְשִׁי, Nimshi
נֵס, banner, ensign, pole, sail, signal, standard, warning
נְסִבָּה, turn *of affairs*
נסג יַד, *become* rich
נסה, attempt, make *a test*, make *trial*, prove, put *to proof*, put *to the test*, test, try, used, venture
נסח, pluck, root *out*, tear, tear *down*
נָסִיךְ, *drink* offering, *molten* image, prince
נסך, cast, make, pour, pour *a libation*, pour *out*, set, set *up*, spread
נֶסֶךְ, *drink* offering, image, libation, *molten* image
נסס, shine, sick *man*
נסע, bring, *cause to* blow, depart, go, go *away*, go *forth*, go *forward*, go *onward*, journey, lead, lead *forth*, march, migrate, move, order *of march*, pluck *up*, pull *away*, pull *up*, quarry, quarry *out*, set *aside*, set *forth*, set *out*, set *out by stages*, stage, *take a* journey, take *a journey*, wander, withdraw
נסע וְהלך, depart
נסע מִן, leave
נִסְרֹךְ, Nisroch
נֹעָה, Noah
נֵעָה, Neah
נְעוּרוֹת, youth
נְעוּרִים, young, youth

נְעִיאֵל, Neiel
נָעִים, gracious, lovely, pleasant, pleasant *place*, pleasantness, pleasure, sweet
נעל, bolt, give *sandals*, lock, shoe
נַעַל, pair *of sandals*, pair *of shoes*, sandal, shoe
נעם, delight, pleasant, surpass *in beauty*, true
נַעַם, Naam
נֹעַם, beauty, favor, grace, pleasant, pleasantness, please
נַעֲמָה, Naamah
נַעֲמִי, Naamite
נָעֳמִי, Naomi
נַעֲמָן, Naaman, pleasant
נַעֲמָתִי, Naamathite
נַעֲצוּץ, thorn, *thorn* bush
נער, growl, overthrow, shake, shake *free*, shake *off*, shake *out*
נַעַר, babe, boy, child, lad, man, servant, son, young, young *man*, young *people*, youth
נֹעַר, childhood, youth
נַעֲרָה, girl, maid, maiden, Naarah, young, *young* maiden, young *woman*
נַעֲרָה בְּתוּלָה, virgin
נַעֲרַי, Naarai
נְעַרְיָה, Neariah
נַעֲרָן, Naaran
נְעֹרֶת, tow
נֹף, Memphis
נֶפֶג, Nepheg
נָפָה, sieve
נְפוּשְׁסִים, Nephushesim
נָפוֹת דּוֹר, Naphoth-dor
נפח, blow, blow *away*, blow *upon*, boil, breathe, sniff, spread, swoon *away*
נְפִיסִים, Nephisim
נָפִישׁ, Naphish
נֹפֶךְ, carbuncle, emerald
נפל, alight, allot, bring *down*, burst, cast, cast *down*, cast *lots*, *cause to* fall, *cause to* lie *down*, collapse, come, desert, deserter, drop, fail, fall, fall *away*, fall *down*, fall *out*, fall *over*, fall *upon*, fell, go *over*, inferior, keep, knock *out*, lay *flat*, lay *low*, leave *out*, lie, lie *prostrate*, light, lose, make, *make* drop, *make* fall, perish, plunge, present, settle, sink, slay, strike *down*, surrender, throw, throw *down*, tumble, turn *out*, void, wither
נפל בְּחֶבֶל, apportion
נפל פָּנִים, look *in anger*
נֵפֶל, *untimely* birth
נְפִלִים, Nephilim
נפץ, break, break *in pieces*, break *up*, crush *to pieces*, dash, dash *in pieces*, disperse, people, scatter, shatter, smash, spread *abroad*
נֶפֶץ, cloudburst
נפשׁ, refresh
נֶפֶשׁ, alive, another, any *one*, any *person*, appetite, being, body, breath, courage, crave, creature, dead, *dead* body, deeply, desire, distress, fancy, greed, heart, *heart's* desire, *human* life, hunger, last, life, *living* creature, man, member, mind, mortally, neck, perfume, peril *of life*, person, pleasure, risk *of life*, slave, soul, spirit, strength, thirst, utter, will, wish
נֶפֶשׁ אָדָם, person
נֶפֶשׁ בְּרָכָה, liberal *man*
נֶפֶשׁ מָרָה, *bitter* distress
נָפַת דּאר, Naphath-dor
נָפַת דּוֹר, Naphath-dor
נֶפֶת, Naphath
נֹפֶת, drippings *of honeycomb*, honey, nectar
נֶפְתּוֹחַ, Nephtoah
נַפְתֻּחִים, Naphtuhim
נַפְתָּלִי, Naphtali
נֵץ, blossom, hawk
נצא, fly *away*
נצב, chief, deputy, erect, fix, *firmly* fix, head, maintain, *make* stand, officer, present, raise, set, set *up*, sound, stand, stand *up*, stand *upright*, station, take *a stand*, take *one's place*, wait, *woman* attending
נצב לִקְרַאת, wait
נצב עַל, charge

נִצָּב, hilt
נצה, *become a* fugitive contend, fight *with one another*, quarrel, ruins, slay, strike, strive *together*, struggle *together*
נִצָּה, blossom, flower
נצח, choirmaster, direct, oversee, overseer, oversight, perpetual
נֵצַח, always, end, endure, ever, evermore, glory, lifeblood, never, perpetual, unceasing
נְצִיב, garrison, Nezib, officer, pillar
נְצִיחַ, Neziah
נצל, defend, deliver, deliverer, despoil, escape, pluck, pluck *out*, preserve, recover, rescue, safe, save, spare, strip, take, take *away*
נצל בֵּין, part
נִצָּן, flower
נצץ, bloom, blossom, sparkle
נצר, besiege, besieger, guard, hidden *thing*, keep, keep *watch*, keep *watch over*, keeper, man, observe, preserve, rout, secret *place*, tend, watch *over*, watcher, watchman, wily
נֵצֶר, branch, shoot
נקב, blaspheme, bore, designate, expressly, give, hole, mention, name, pierce
נקב שֵׁם, name
נֶקֶב, engraving
נְקֵבָה, female, woman
נָקֹד, speckle, spot
נֹקֵד, *sheep* breeder, shepherd
נקה, acquit, blameless, clear, clear *the guilty*, cut *off*, free, go *unpunished*, guiltless, hold *guiltless*, hold *innocent*, innocent, leave *unpunished*, ravage
נִקּוּד, cake, moldy
נְקוֹדָא, Nekoda
נָקִי, blameless, clean, clear, exempt, free, free *of obligation*, guiltless, innocent
נָקִיא, innocent
נִקָּיוֹן, cleanness, innocence, pure
נָקִיק, cleft
נקם, avenge, avenger, execute *vengeance*, punish, take *vengeance*
נָקָם, take *revenge*, vengeance
נְקָמָה, avenge, revenge, vengeance
נקע, turn
נקע נֶפֶשׁ, turn *in disgust*
נקף, close, cut *down*, destroy, encircle, envelope, go *about*, go *around*, go *round*, go *round about*, round *off*, run *a course*, run *round*, surround
נקף סָבִיב, surround
נֹקֶף, beat
נִקְפָּה, rope
נקר, dig, gouge *out*, pick *out*, put *out*, rack
נְקָרָה, cavern, cleft
נקשׁ, ensnare, lay *a snare*, seize
נֵר, lamp, light, Ner
נֵרְגַל, Nergal
נֵרְגַל שַׂר אֶצֶר, Nergal-shar-ezer
נֵרְדְּ, nard
נֵרִיָּהוּ, Neriah
נשׂא, accept, advance, aid, arise, arm, assist, bear, bear *a burden*, bear *away*, bear *up*, bearer, bring, bring *forth*, bring *upon*, carry, carry *about*, carry *away*, carry *off*, cast, catch *up*, *cause to* bear, contain, ease, exact, exalt, fetch, find, forgive, get, give *a gift*, grant, grind, help, high, lay, lift, lift *up*, load, lofty, *make* take, marry, move, offer, pardon, pay, pull, put *an end*, raise, raise *up*, receive, rise, rise *up*, set, set *up*, sing, spare, speak *out*, stir, stir *up*, suffer, supply, support, take, take *away*, take *up*, take *upon*, utter, wear, yield
נשׂא יָד, swear
נשׂא כַּף, revere
נשׂא לְ, forgive
נשׂא לִפְנֵי, win
נשׂא מִסְפָּר, number
נשׂא נֶפֶשׁ, desire, greedy, long
נשׂא עֵינַיִם, look *up*, see
נשׂא פָּנִים, accept, favored *man*, grant *petition*, *high* favor, honored *man*, man *of rank*, partial, regard, *show* favor, *show* partiality
נשׂא קוֹל, aloud

נשׂא רֹאשׁ, count, free, take *a census*
נשׂא רַגְלַיִם, go *on a journey*
נשׂג, attain, last, obtain, overtake, put, reach, regain
נשׂג יָד, ability, afford, *become* prosperous, grow *rich*
נָשִׂיא, chief, chieftain, cloud, head, leader, mist, prince, ruler
נשׁא, beguile, come, deceive, delude, outwit, yield
נשׁא לְ, debt
נשׂא פְּנֵימוֹ, *show* honor
נשׁב, blow, drive, drive *away*, *make* blow
נשׁה, borrow, creditor, exact, forget, lend, make *a loan*, *make* forget, unmindful
נשׁה מַשָּׁאָה, make *a loan*
נָשֶׁה, hip
נְשִׁי, debt
נְשִׁיָּה, forgetfulness
נְשִׁיקָה, kiss
נשׁך, bite, debtor, lend *for interest*, lend *upon interest*
נשׁך בְּשִׁנַּיִם, *something to* eat
נֶשֶׁךְ, interest
נִשְׁכָּה, chamber
נשׁל, clear *away*, drive, drop *off*, put *off*, slip
נשׁם, gasp
נְשָׁמָה, blast, breath, breath *of life*, breathe, spirit
נשׁף, blow
נֶשֶׁף, dawn, evening, twilight
נשׁק, arm, kiss, kiss *each other*, order, touch
נשׁק קֶשֶׁת, bowman
נֶשֶׁק, armory, arrow, battle, weapon
נֵשֶׁק, myrrh
נֶשֶׁר, eagle, vulture
נשׁת, dry *up*, fail, parch
נתח, cut, cut *in pieces*, cut *into pieces*, divide
נֵתַח, piece, piece *of flesh*
נָתִיב, path, wake
נְתִיבָה, bypath, path, road, street, way
נְתִינִים, *temple* servant
נתך, empty *out*, fall, melt, pour, pour *forth*, pour *out*
נתן, add, allow, apply, appoint, apportion, ascribe, assign, attach, bear, bestow, bring, cast, cause, chant, charge, choose, commit, consider, dedicate, deliver, deliver *up*, direct, distribute, entrust, exchange, execute, expose, fasten, fix, get, gift, give, give *forth*, give *over*, give *up*, grant, hand *over*, hang, hang *up*, hold, impose, inspire, invest, issue, join, lay, leave, lend, let *out*, lift *up*, make, *make* turn, offer, ordain, pay, pay *out*, perform, permit, place, plant, pledge, present, provide, put, put *out*, raise, render, requite, reward, send, set, set *apart*, set *out*, set *up*, share, shoot *forth*, show, sound, spend, spread, store, store *up*, strew, supply, take, thrust, tie, trade, treat, turn, utter, win, work, yield
נתן בְּיַד, commit, give *over*
נתן בֵּית הָאֵסוּר, imprison
נתן דֳּפִי, slander
נתן חָרְבָה, dry *up*
נתן יָד, pledge, surrender, yield
נתן לְאוֹר, show *forth*
נתן לְאִישׁ, give *in marriage*
נתן לֵב, give *heed*
נתן לִפְנֵי, give *over*, regard
נתן לָרֹב, make *common*, make *plentiful*
נתן מוּם, disfigure
נתן מֶכֶר, pay
נתן נְקָמוֹת, avenge
נתן עַל, punish
נתן עַל יָד, hand *over*
נתן פִּתְחוֹן, open
נתן קוֹל, aloud, cry *out*, roar *loudly*, shout, sing
נתן רְפָאָה, heal
נתן שְׁכָבָה, lie
נתן שְׁכָבָה לְזֶרַע, lie *carnally*
נתן תּוֹדָה, make *confession*
נָתָן, Nathan
נְתַן מֶלֶךְ, Nathan-melech

נְתַנְאֵל, Nethanel

נְתַנְיָהוּ, Nethaniah

נתס, break *up*

נתע, break

נתץ, break *asunder*, break *down*, break *in pieces*, demolish, destroy, lay *in ruins*, pull *down*, raze, tear *down*, tear *out*

נתק, break, break *asunder*, break *off*, burst, burst *asunder*, draw *away*, lift *up*, pull *out*, pull *up*, remove, snap, tear

נֶתֶק, itch, *itching* disease

נתר, leap, let *loose*, release, *set* free, shake, undo

נֶתֶר, lye

נתשׁ, pluck *up*, root *out*, root *up*, uproot

סְאָ, measure

סְאָה, measure

סאן, boot, tramp

סבא, drunkard, fill

סבא יַיִן, winebibber

סָבָא, drunkard

סֹבֶא, wine

סְבָא, Seba

סְבָאִים, Sabean

סבב, again, beset, beset *round about*, besiege, bring, bring *again*, bring *around*, bring *over*, carry, carry *round*, *cause to* compass, change, circle, circuit, circumference, come *around*, compass, dwell *apart*, enclose, encompass, entangle, flow *around*, gather *about*, gather *round*, go *about*, go *around*, go *home*, go *round*, lead *round*, make *a circuitous*, march *around*, measure, measure *circumference*, pass *over*, protect, prowl *about*, roll, round, round *about*, send *around*, surround, swing, transfer, turn, turn *about*, turn *aside*, turn *away*, turn *back*, turn *over*, turn *round*, walk *about*

סבב מִפְּנֵי, evade

סבב פָּנִים, face *about*, turn *round*

סִבָּה, turn *of affairs*

סָבִיב, about, all *around*, all *round*, *all* sides, around, band, circuit, circumference, *every* side, go *around*, guard, neighbor, place *about*, round, round *about*, surround, throughout, turn

סבך, entangle, twine

סְבַךְ, thicket

סֹבֶךְ, thicket, trellis

סִבְּכַי, Sibbecai

סבל, bear, carry, drag *along*, heavy

סַבָּל, bear *a burden*, burden, *burden* bearer

סֹבֶל, burden

סֵבֶל, burden, *forced* labor

סִבְלָה, burden, *heavy* burden

סִבֹּלֶת, Sibboleth

סִבְרַיִם, Sibraim

סַבְתָּא, Sabta

סַבְתָּה, Sabtah

סַבְתְּכָא, Sabteca

סגד, fall *down*

סְגוֹר, gold, javelin

סְגוֹר לֵב, breast

סְגֻלָּה, possession, treasure

סָגָן, chief *man*, commander, deputy, official, ruler

סגר, close, close *up*, deliver, deliver *up*, give, give *over*, give *up*, imprison, pure, put, shut, shut *up*, surrender

סַגְרִיר, rainy

סַד, stocks

סָדִין, *linen* garment

סְדֹם, Sodom

סַהַר, round

סוג, encircle, fall *away*, *make* grow, overtake, perverse *man*, put *away*, remove, turn, turn *away*, turn *back*

סוּגַר, cage

סוֹד, company, confidence, converse, council, counsel, friendship, gather, secret, *secret* plot

סוֹדִי, Sodi

סוח, flow, stretch

סוּחַ, Suah

סוּחָה, refuse

סוט, go *astray*

סוֹטַי, Sotai

סוך, anoint, hedge, pour, shut

סְוֵן, Syene

סוּס, horse, horseback, stallion, steed, swallow

סוּסָה, mare

סוּסִי, Susi

סוף, cease, come *to an end*, gather, sweep *away*

סוֹף, end, rear

סוּף, red, reed, rush, Suph, weed

סוּפָה, hurricane, storm, stormwind, Suphah, tempest, whirlwind

סוֹפֶרֶת, Sophereth

סור, avoid, away, call *back*, cut *off*, degenerate, depart, depose, deprive, escape, far, go, go *astray*, lead *off*, leave, leave *undone*, pass *away*, past, put *away*, put *far*, put *off*, put *out*, rebel, reject, relieve, removal, remove, return, set *aside*, strip *away*, sweep *away*, take, take *away*, take *home*, take *off*, take *out*, turn, turn *aside*, turn *away*, ward *off*, without

סור מֵעַל, avoid, take *off*

סור ראשׁ, behead

סור תיז, hew *away*

סוּר, Sur

סות, allure, deceive, draw *away*, entice, incite, induce, mislead, move, set, stir *up*, urge

סוּת, vesture

סחב, drag, drag *away*, tear

סְחָבָה, rag

סחה, scrape

סְחִי, offscouring

סָחִישׁ, spring *of the same*

סחף, beat

סחר, dealer, market, merchant, ply *a trade*, throb, trade, trader, traffic

סַחַר, gain, merchandise

סֹחֵרָה, buckler

סֹחֶרֶת, *precious* stone

סֵט, fall *away*

סִיג, dross, go *aside*

סִיוָן, Sivan

סִיחוֹן, Sihon

סִין, Pelusium, Sin

סִינַי, Sinai

סִינִי, Sinite

סִיסְרָא, Sisera

סִיעָא, Sia

סִיעֲהָא, Siaha

סִיר, caldron, kettle, pot, thorn

סִיר בָּשָׂר, fleshpot

סִיר דוּגָה, fishhook

סִיר רַחַץ, washbasin

סַךְ, throng

סֹךְ, abode, covert, shelter

סֻכָּה, booth, canopy, covert, pavilion, shelter, tabernacle

סִכּוּת, Sakkuth

סֻכּוֹת, Succoth

סֻכּוֹת בְּנוֹת, Succoth-benoth

סֻכִּיִּים, Sukkiim

סכך, anoint, cover, defend, guardian, knit *together*, make *a covering*, overshadow, screen, wrap

סכך רַגְלַיִם, relieve

סֹכֵךְ, mantelet

סְכָכָה, Secacah

סכל, *do* foolishly, make *foolish*, play *the fool*, turn *into foolishness*

סָכָל, folly, fool, foolish, stupid

סִכְלוּת, folly, foolishness

סכן, accustom, acquaint, advantage, agree, endanger, impoverish, nurse, profit, profitable, steward

סכר, close, give *over*, hire, stop

סכת, keep *silence*

סַל, basket

סלא, worth *weight*

סַלָּא, Silla

סלד, exult

סֶלֶד, Seled

סלה, flout, spurn, value

סֶלָה, Selah

סַלּוּא, Salu

סַלּוּא, Sallu

סִלּוֹן, brier, thorn

סלח, forgive, pardon

סַלָּח, forgive

סַלַּי, Sallai

סְלִיחָה, forgive, forgiveness

סַלְכָה, Salecah

סלל, build *up*, cast *up*, exalt, level, lift *up*, pile *up*, prize *highly*

סֹלְלָה, mound, *siege* mound

סֹלְלָה, siegework

סֻלָּם, ladder

סַלְסִלָּה, branch

סֶלַע, cliff, crag, mountain, rock, rocky, Sela

סָלְעָם, *bald* locust

סלף, bring *to ruin*, cast *down*, overthrow, subvert

סֶלֶף, crookedness, perverseness

סלק, ascend

סֹלֶת, fine, *fine* flour, *fine* meal, flour

סַם, fragrant, sweet, *sweet* spice

סַמְגַּר נְבוּ, Samgar-nebo

סְמָדַר, blossom

סמך, establish, lay, lay *siege*, lean, *lean* weight, lie *heavy*, stay, steady, support, sustain, take *confidence*, uphold

סְמַכְיָהוּ, Semachiah

סֶמֶל, figure, idol, image

סמן, proper *place*

סמר, stand *up*, tremble

סָמָר, bristle

סְנָאָה, Senaah

סַנְבַלַּט, Sanballat

סֶנֶּה, Seneh

סְנֶה, bush

סַנְוֵרִים, blindness

סַנְחֵרִיב, Sennacherib

סַנְסַנָּה, Sansannah

סַנְסִנִּים, branch

סְנַפִּיר, fin

סָס, worm

סִסְמַי, Sismai

סעד, give *support*, hold *up*, refresh, strengthen, support, sustain, uphold

סעה, rage

סָעִיף, branch, cleft

סעף, lop *the bough*

סֵעֵף, *double* minded m*an*

סְעַפָּה, bough

סְעִפָּה, different *opinion*

סער, come *like a whirlwind*, *greatly* trouble, scatter *with a whirlwind*, storm-tossed, swirl, tempestuous

סַעַר, storm, tempest

סְעָרָה, storm, stormy, tempest, whirlwind

סַף, basin, bowl, cup, frame, Saph, threshold

ספד, beat, lament, make *lamentation*, mourn, mourner

ספה, add, catch, consume, destroy, devastation, increase, perish, snatch *away*, sweep *away*

ספח, cleave, huddle *together*, put, share

סַפַּחַת, eruption

סִפַּי, Sippai

סָפִיחַ, grow, torrent

סְפִינָה, ship

סַפִּיר, sapphire

סֵפֶל, bowl

ספן, cover, finish, hide, make *the ceiling*, panel, reserve

סִפֻּן, ceiling

ספף, doorkeeper

ספק, clap, smite, strike, strike *hands*, strike *together*, wallow

ספר, assign, confess, count, count *out*, declare, keep *count*, learn, measure, number, recite, record, recount, set *forth*, speak, take, take *a census*, talk, tell, utter

סֹפֵר, marshal, scribe, secretary

סְפָר, census, Sephar

סֵפֶר, bill, book, decree, deed, indictment, letter, recite, scroll, write, writing

סֵפֶר מִלְחֲמוֹת יְהוָה, Book *of the Wars of the LORD*

סְפָרַד, Sepharad

סִפְרָה, book

סְפֹרָה, number

סְפַרְוִי, Sepharvite

סְפַרְוַיִם, Sepharvaim

סקל, clear, clear *of stone*, stone, throw *stone*

סַר, resentful, vex

סָרָב, brier

סַרְגוֹן, Sargon

סֶרֶד, Sered

סַרְדִּי, Seredite

סרה, rebellion, revolt, wrongdoing

סִרָה, Sirah

סרח, hang, spread, stretch, vanish

סֶרַח, part

סִרְיֹן, coat *of mail*

סָרִיס, chamberlain, eunuch, officer, official, *palace* official

סֶרֶן, axle, lord, ruler

סַרְעַפָּה, bough

סִרְפַּד, brier

סרר, rebel, rebellious, stubborn, stubbornly, wayward

סְתָו, winter

סְתוּר, Sethur

סתם, close, seal *up*, secret, *secret* heart, shut *up*, stop, stop *up*

סתר, absent, conceal, *hidden* fault, hide, hide *away*, secret *thing*, take *shelter*, undetected

סֵתֶר, backbiting, cover, covering, covert, enwrap, hiding *place*, refuge, secret, secret *place*, secretly, shelter

סִתְרָה, protection

סִתְרִי, Sithri

עָב, canopy, cloud, thick, *thick* cloud, thicket

עבד, *become a* slave, *become* subject, burden, cultivate, do, *do* service, *do* work, dress, enslave, give, hold *in bondage*, keep, labor, laborer, make, make *a servant*, make *a slave*, *make* labor, *make* serve, *make* work, minister, offer *worship*, perform, plow, serve, servitude, slave, spread *abroad*, till, tiller, work, worker, worship, worshiper

עבד לִפְנֵי, serve

עֶבֶד, bondage, bondman, Ebed, *female* slave, *male* slave, man, *man* slave, manservant, officer, official, servant, slave, vassal, work

עֶבֶד וְשִׁפְחָה, slave

עֶבֶד מֶלֶךְ, Ebed-melech

עֹבֵד אֱדֹם, Obed-edom

עֲבָד, deed

עֲבֵד נְגוֹ, Abed-nego

עַבְדָּא, Abda

עַבְדְּאֵל, Abdeel

עֲבֹדָה, accessory, attend, bondage, care, construction, cultivate, do, duty, labor, laborious, result, rural, serve, service, servitude, task, till, work, worker

עֲבֻדָּה, household, servant

עַבְדּוֹן, Abdon

עַבְדוּת, bondage

עַבְדִּי, Abdi

עַבְדִּיאֵל, Abdiel

עֹבַדְיָהוּ, Obadiah

עבה, grow *thick*, thick

עֲבוֹדָה, due *order*

עֲבוֹט, pledge

עָבוּר, produce

עָבוֹת, leafy

עבט, borrow, fetch, lend

עַבְטִיט, pledge

עָבֵי שְׁחָקִים, *thick* cloud

עֳבִי, thickness

עֲבִי גַּבִּי, thick-bossed
עבר, alienate, along, alter, angry, assess, avert, beyond, break, break *through*, breed, bring *on the way*, bring *over*, burn, *by all* means, carry *over*, *cause to* pass, charge, come, come *by*, come *over*, cross, cross *over*, current, devote, disregard, draw, drift, drive, enter, escape, fail, fall *into disuse*, ford, free, full *of wrath*, go, go *away*, go *beyond*, go *by*, go *down*, go *forward*, go *over*, go *through*, know *no bounds*, lead, liquid, make, *make* blow, *make* offer, *make* pass, march, meddle, move, number, offer *up*, offering, outrun, over, overcome, overflow, overlook, overrun, pass, pass *along*, pass *away*, pass *beyond*, pass *over*, pass *through*, pass *up and down*, passage, passer-by, past, perish, proclaim, provoke *to anger*, put *away*, remove, sacrifice, send, send *abroad*, send *across*, set *apart*, spare, sweep, take, take *across*, take *away*, take out, throw *off restraint*, transfer, transgress, travel, traveler, turn, turn *away*, vent *wrath*, walk
עבר בָּאֵשׁ, burn
עבר דֶּרֶךְ, pass
עבר וָשׁוּב, go *to and fro*
עבר מִן, leave
עבר מֵעַל, remove
עבר קוֹל, make *a proclamation*, proclaim
עֹבֵר אֹרַח, wayfaring *man*
עֵבֶר, beyond, direction, Eber, land *beyond*, *other* side, side, space, west
עֶבְרָה, arrogant, fury, indignation, insolence, overflow, wrath
עֲבָרָה, ford
עִבְרִי, Hebrew, Hebrew *man*, Hebrew *woman*, Ibri
עִבְרִי עִבְרִיָּה, Hebrew
עֲבָרִים, Abarim
עַבְרֹן, Ebron
עַבְרֹנָה, Abronah
עבשׁ, shrivel
עבת, weave *together*
עֲבֹת, band, branch, cord, rope, twist
עגב, dote, lover
עָגַב, love, *show much* love
עֲגָבָה, dote
עֻגָה, cake
עָגוֹל סָבִיב, round
עָגוּר, crane
עָגִיל, earring
עָגֹל, round
עֵגֶל, calf
עֶגְלָה, calf, Eglah, heifer
עֲגָלָה, cart, chariot, wagon
עֶגְלוֹן, Eglon
עֶגְלַת בָּקָר, heifer, *young* cow
עֶגְלַת שְׁלִשִׁיָּה, Eglath-shelishiyah
עגם, grieve
עגן לְבִלְתִּי, refrain
עַד, before, come, down, enough, eternal, eternity, even, ever, far, far *away*, far *over*, how, *how* long, inner, like, long, more, much, nor, old, over, prey, since, soon, spite, still, through, thus, till, toward, until, unto, up, when, whether, while, within, yet
עַד אַיִן, without
עַד אֵין, beyond
עַד אָן, *how* long
עַד אָנָה, *how* long, *how* long *till*
עַד אֲשֶׁר, till, until
עַד אֲשֶׁר לֹא, before
עַד בְּלִי דָי, overflow
עַד הַיּוֹם הַזֶּה, even *yet*
עַד הַיָּמִים הָהֵם, yet
עַד הֲלֹם, thus *far*
עַד הֵן, yet
עַד הֵנָּה, *all* along, here, since, thus *far*
עַד הֵנָּה, hitherto, still
עַד כֹּה, hitherto, yet, yonder
עַד כֹּה וְעַד כֹּה, *little* while
עַד כַּמֶּה, *how* many
עַד כֵּן, yet
עַד לְ, far
עַד לֹא, before
עַד לְמַעְלָה, severe
עַד לְמֵרָחוֹק, afar
עַד מְאֹד, exceedingly, sorely, utterly, very
עַד מָה, *how* long
עַד מָתַי, *how* long
עַד נֹכַח, opposite
עַד נֵצַח לֹא, never *more*
עַד עוֹלָם, ever, everlasting, evermore
עַד עַתָּה, yet
עַד פֹּה, thus *far*
עַד רָחֹק, afar *off*
עַד שֶׁ, till, until, when, while
עֵד, evidence, witness
עדה, adorn, deck, pass, take *off*
עָדָה, Adah
עֵדָה, pollute
עֵדָה, assembly, band, company, congregation, council, decree, herd, swarm, testimony, witness
עִדּוֹ, Iddo
עֵדוּת, decree, Eduth, testimony, warning
עֲדִי, ornament
עֲדֵי עַד, ever
עֲדִיאֵל, Adiel
עַדְיָה, thither
עֲדָיָהוּ, Adaiah
עֲדִין, Adin, lover *of pleasure*
עֲדִינָא, Adina
עֲדִיתַיִם, Adithaim
עַדְלַי, Adlai
עֲדֻלָּם, Adullam
עֲדֻלָּמִי, Adullamite
עדן, delight
עֵדֶן, delicacy, delight, Eden
עַדְנָא, Adna, Adnah
עַדְנָה, Adnah
עֶדְנָה, pleasure
עֲדֶנָה, still, yet
עַדְעָדָה, Adadah
עדף, *excess* number, leave *over*, over, over *and above*, overpayment, remain
עדר, fail, help, hoe, lack, lacking, leave, miss
עֵדֶר, Eder
עֵדֶר, drove, Eder, flock, herd
עַדְרִיאֵל, Adriel
עֲדָשָׁה, lentil
עוב, set *under a cloud*
עוֹבֵד, Obed
עוג, bake
עוֹג, Og
עוּגָב, pipe
עוד, admonish, approve, bring *a charge*, call *to witness*, charge, enjoin, ensnare, get, get *to attest*, give, give *warning*, lift *up*, say, stand *upright*, testify, uphold, warn, witness
עוֹד, add, again, *all* life *long*, another, *any* longer, any *more*, *any more*, before, being, besides, continually, continue, else, ever, far, further, furthermore, *good* while, henceforth, leave, long, more, moreover, once, once *more*, other, repeatedly, since, still, still *more*, though, very, while, yet, *yet* more
עוֹדֵד, Oded
עוה, *act* perversely, bow *down*, commit *iniquity*, *do* wickedly, *do* wrong, make *crooked*, perverse, pervert, twist
עַוָּה, Avva, Ivvah, ruin
עוז, flee *for safety*, get *into safe shelter*, seek *refuge*, take *refuge*
עַוִּי, Avvite
עֲוִיל, little *one*, ungodly, *young* child
עַוִּים, Avvim
עֲוִית, Avith
עול, deal *perversely*, ewe *that has young*, give *suck*, milch, unjust, young
עַוָּל, ungodly, unjust, unrighteous
עָוֶל, dishonestly, *do* wrong, iniquity, injustice, unjust, unjustly, unrighteousness, wrong
עוּל, infant, *sucking* child
עַוְלָה, crime, *do* wrong, falsehood, falsely, iniquity, injustice, perversion *of justice*, unjust, unrighteousness, violent, wayward, wickedness, wrong
עוֹלֵל, babe, child, infant, little *one*, *young* child
עוֹלֵלוֹת, glean, gleanings
עוֹלָם, again, age, always, ancient, *ancient* time, *any* time, eternal, eternity, ever, everlasting, evermore, future, life, long, *long* ago, *long* time, never-ending, old, perpetual
עוֹלָם עַד, *all* eternity
עָוֹן, chastisement, corruption, crime, fault, guilt, guilty, iniquity, punishment, punishment *of iniquity*, sin
עִוְעִים, confusion
עוּף, brandish, fly, fly *away*, light, swoop *down*
עוֹף, bird, fowl, winged, winged *thing*
עוץ, take *counsel*
עוּץ, Uz
עוק, press *down*
עור, arise, arouse, awake, awaken, bestir, blind, brandish, exult, put *out*, raise *a cry*, rouse, rouse *up*, stir, stir *up*, wake, waken, wield
עֹור, youth
עִוֵּר, blind, blind *man*
עוֹר, body, leather, skin
עוֹר הַבֹּקֶר, daybreak
עוֹר תַּחַשׁ, goatskin
עִוָּרוֹן, blindness
עַוֶּרֶת, blind
עוּשׁ, hasten
עות, bend, bring *to ruin*, crooked, deal *deceitfully*, make *crooked*, pervert, put *in the wrong*, subvert, sustain
עַוָּתָה, wrong
עוּתַי, Uthai
עַז, bold, fierce, fierce *man*, might, mighty, power, roughly, stern, strong
עֹז, bulwark, defense, hardness, might, mighty, power, strength, strong, stronghold
עֵז, flock, goat, *goat's* hair, kid, she-goat
עֻזָּא, Uzza
עֲזָאזֵל, Azazel
עזב, abandon, commit, desert, fail, forsake, free, give *free utterance*, give *up*, go, leave, leave *behind*, leave *off*, neglect, put *off*, reject, restore
עִזָּבוֹן, ware
עַזְבּוּק, Azbuk
עַזְגָּד, Azgad
עַזָּה, Gaza
עֻזָּה, Uzzah
עֲזוּבָה, Azubah, deserted *place*, forsaken *place*
עִזּוּז, strong, warrior
עֱזוּז, might
עַזּוּר, Azzur
עזז, establish, give *strength*, impudent, prevail, put *on bold*, *show* strength, strong
עָזָז, Azaz
עֲזַזְיָהוּ, Azaziah
עֻזִּי, Uzzi
עֻזִּיָּא, Uzzia
עֻזִּיאֵל, Uzziel
עֲזִיאֵל, Aziel
עָזִּיאֵלִי, Uzzielite
עֻזִּיָּהוּ, Uzziah
עֲזִיזָא, Aziza
עַזְמָוֶת, Azmaveth
עַזָּן, Azzan
עָזְנִיָּה, osprey
עזק, dig
עֲזֵקָה, Azekah
עזר, come *to aid*, come *to help*, further, help, helper, protect, receive *help*, support
עֵזֶר, Ezer
עֵזֶר, Ezer, help, helper
עֶזְרָא, Ezra
עֲזַרְאֵל, Azarel
עֶזְרָה, aid, Ezrah, help, helper
עֲזָרָה, court, ledge
עֶזְרִי, Ezri
עַזְרִיאֵל, Azriel
עֲזַרְיָהוּ, Azariah
עַזְרִיקָם, Azrikam
עַזָּתִי, Gazite
עֵט, pen
עטה, clean, cover, seize *firm hold*, wrap, wrap *round*
עָטִין, body
עֲטִישָׁה, sneeze
עֲטַלֵּף, bat
עטף, cover, deck, faint, feeble, proceed, turn
עטר, bestower *of crown*, close, cover, crown
עטר לְ, crown
עֲטָרָה, Atarah, crown
עַטְרוֹת אַדָּר, Ataroth-addar
עַטְרוֹת בֵּית יוֹאָב, Atroth-beth-joab
עֲטָרוֹת, Ataroth
עַטְרֹת שׁוֹפָן, Atroth-shophan
עַי, Ai
עִי, heap, heap *of ruins*, ruins
עֵיבָל, Ebal
עַיָּה, Aija, Ayyah
עִיּוֹן, Ijon
עִיט, fly, rail, swoop
עַיִט, bird *of prey*
עֵיטָם, Etam
עִיֵּי עֲבָרִים, Iye-abarim
עִיִּים, Iim, Iyim
עִילַי, Ilai
עֵילָם, Elam
עַיִם, scorch
עַיִן, Ain, appearance, color, esteem, eye, eyesight, face, facet, fountain, gleam, knowledge, look, look *with favor*, *outward* appearance, presence, shine, sight, sparkle, spring, well
עַיִן חוּס, give *thought*
עֵין גֶּדִי, En-gedi
עֵין גַּנִּים, En-gannim
עֵין דֹּאר, En-dor
עֵין דֹּר, En-dor
עֵין הַקּוֹרֵא, En-hakkore
עֵין חַדָּה, En-haddah
עֵין חָצוֹר, En-hazor
עֵין מִשְׁפָּט, Enmishpat
עֵין עֶגְלַיִם, En-eglaim
עֵין רֹגֵל, En-rogel
עֵין רִמּוֹן, En-rimmon
עֵין שֶׁמֶשׁ, En-shemesh
עֵין תַּפּוּחַ, En-tappuah
עֵינַיִם, Enaim
עֵינָם, Enam
עֵינָן, Enan
עיף, faint
עָיֵף, faint, famish, parch, thirsty, weary
עֵיפָה, darkness, Ephah, gloom
עֵיפַי, Ephai
עַיִר, ass, colt
עִיר, anguish, city, foal, Ir, town, village
עִיר וָעִיר, city
עִיר מִסְכְּנוֹת, store-city
עִיר נָחָשׁ, Irnahash
עִיר שֶׁמֶשׁ, Ir-shemesh
עִירָא, Ira
עִירָד, Irad
עִירוּ, Iru
עִירִי, Iri
עִירָם, Iram
עֵירֹם, naked, nakedness
עַיִשׁ, Bear
עַיָּת, Aiath
עַכְבּוֹר, Achbor
עַכָּבִישׁ, spider
עַכְבָּר, mouse
עַכּוֹ, Acco
עָכוֹר, Achor
עָכָן, Achan
עכס, tinkle
עֶכֶס, anklet
עַכְסָה, Achsah

עכר, bring *trouble*, cause *of great trouble*, grow *worse*, hurt, make *trouble*, trouble, troubler
עָכָר, Achar
עָכְרָן, Ochran
עַכְשׁוּב, viper
עַל, about, above, accordance, according, account, across, addition, adjoin, after, against, along, along *with*, although, among, bear, because, before, behalf, beside, besides, besiege, better *than*, beyond, care, charge, command, concerning, crown, deed, front, glad, ground, high, instead, more *than*, near, next, off, out, over, over *against*, oversight, presence, rather *than*, reason, regard, require, sake, spite, surpass, than, thereon, through, throughout, together, toward, under, until, up, upon, way, wear, whereon, whether, within
עַל אֹדוֹת, about, because, concerning
עַל אֲשֶׁר, because, much, whither
עַל דָּבָר, concerning
עַל דְּבַר, because
עַל דִּבְרָה, regard
עַל דִּבְרַת, because
עַל הָאָרֶץ, foot
עַל זֹאת, therefore, thereupon
עַל יַד, beside, charge, near
עַל יָד, accompany, along, assist, assistant, little *by little*, next
עַל יֹשֶׁר, wrong
עַל יֶתֶר, abundantly
עַל כִּי, because
עַל כֵּן, place
עַל כֵּן, because, hence, now, reason, then, therefore, truly, where, why
עַל לֵב, encouragingly, kindly, tenderly
עַל לֵבָב, encouragingly
עַל מָה, why
עַל מְלֵאת, fitly
עַל נְקַלָּה, lightly
עַל סָבִיב, around
עַל עֹמֶד, upright
עַל עֵקֶב, because
עַל פִּי, accordance, according, answer, commandment
עַל פְּנֵי, across, before, correspond, east, equal, front, lifetime, open, over, overlook, toward, upon, upside *down*
עַל פְּנֵי דֶרֶךְ, toward
עַל פָּנִים, opposite, over *against*, preference, presence, sight
עַל רֹאשׁ, over
עַל שָׂפָה, speech
עֹל, yoke
עֻלָּא, Ulla
עִלֵּג, stammerer
עלה, addition, advance, arrive, ascend, ascent, attack, break, bring, bring *back*, bring *up*, *burnt* offering, carry, carry *off*, carry *up*, cast, *cause to* come, *cause to* come *up*, charge, chew, climb, climb *up*, come, come *out*, come *up*, come *upon*, cut *off*, dawn, dial, draw *up*, enter, escape, exalt, fall, get, get *away*, get *up*, give *up*, go, go *away*, go *back*, go *forward*, go *up*, grow, grow *hot*, grow *over*, grow *up*, invade, *keep* burning, lead *up*, leap, levy, lift, make, *make* come *up*, *make* rise, *make* rise *up*, *make* withdraw, march, march *up*, mount, mount *up*, offer, offer *up*, overgrown, present, put, raise, raise *up*, record, restore, rise, rouse, scale, set, set *up*, shoot *forth*, shoot *up*, spring *up*, sprout, stand *up*, stir *up*, surpass, take, take *hence*, take *up*, up, way *up*, withdraw, work
עלה אַחֲרֵי, follow
עלה וְיָצָא, import
עלה לְמַעְלָה, go *upward*
עלה לַצָּבָא, make *war*
עלה מִן, withdraw
עלה עֵינַיִם, disregard
עלה עַל, prompt, touch
עָלֶה, branch, *green* leaf, leaf, leafy
עֹלָה, *burnt* offering, *burnt* sacrifice, offering
עֲלוֹ עַל, attack
עַלְוָה, Alvah
עֲלוּמִים, youth, *youthful* vigor
עַלְוָן, Alvan
עֲלוּקָה, leech
עֲלוֹת הַשַּׁחַר, dawn
עלז, exult, exultation, rejoice
עַלֵּז, exult
עֲלָטָה, dark
עִלִּי, upper
עֱלִי, pestle
עֵלִי, Eli
עַלְיָה, Aliah
עָלֶיהָ, therein
עֲלִיָּה, chamber, *lofty* abode, *roof* chamber, *upper* chamber, *upper* room
עָלָיו, there
עֶלְיוֹן, exalt, high, *most* high, top, upper, uppermost
עַלִּיז, exultant, exultant *one*, exulting *one*, joyful, jubilant
עֲלִיל, furnace
עֲלִילָה, act, action, deed, do, shameful, wrongdoing
עֲלִילִיָּה, deed
עֲלֵימוֹ, where
עַלְיָן, Alian
עֲלִיצוּת, rejoice
עלל, abuse, bring, busy, *cause* grief, child, cut *down*, deal, glean, lay, make *sport*, strip *bare*
עלם, blind, close, daze, dissembler, hide, secret, secret *thing*, withhold *help*
עֶלֶם, stripling, youth
עַלְמָה, girl, maiden, young *woman*
עַלְמוֹן, Almon
עֲלָמוֹת, Alamoth
עַלְמֹן דִּבְלָתָיְמָה, Almon-diblathaim
עָלֶמֶת, Alemeth
עלס, delight, get *enjoyment*, wave *proudly*
עלע, suck *up*
עלף, encrust, faint, wrap *up*
עלץ, exult, rejoice, triumph
עַם, army, force, host, kindred, kinsman, man, multitude, nation, other, people, population, soldier, throng, troop
עַם הָאָרֶץ, common *people*
עַם וָעָם, every *people*, people
עַם כְּנַעַן, trader
עִם, about, against, alike, along, among, aside, attend, because, before, behalf, beside, besides, between, both, *just* like, like, near, presence, purpose, side, together, toward, upon, well, when, while
עִם וְעִם, between
עִם נְקֻדּוֹת, stud
עִם עֵדֶן, daintily
עמד, abide, act, appear, appoint, arise, array, attend, attendant, avail, bring, *cause to* attend, *cause to* stand, cease, check, come *forward*, come *to a halt*, confirm, continue, delay, draw *up*, dwell, endure, enter, erect, establish, fix, fulfil, give, give *stability*, halt, join, last, lay, live, make *a stand*, *make* stand, man *who serves*, minister, perform, persist, place, present, prop *up*, put *in charge*, raise, reach *up*, remain, repair, resort, restore, rise, rise *up*, set, *set* secure, set *up*, stand, stand *fast*, stand *forth*, stand *still*, stand *up*, station, stay, stay *behind*, still, stop, stop *flowing*, survive, take, take *a stand*, tarry, upright, wait
עמד בִּפְנֵי, withstand
עמד דָּבָר, decree
עמד לְנֶגֶד, withstand
עמד לִפְנֵי, enter *service*, *remain in* service, serve, withstand
עמד מִן, cease
עמד נֶגֶד, withstand
עמד עַל, defend, oppose, withstand
עֹמֶד, place, post, station
עֲמַד לְ, consult
עֶמְדָּה לִפְנֵי, wait *upon*
עֶמְדָּה, standing *place*
עמד לִפְנֵי, attend
עֻמָּה, Ummah
עַמּוּד, column, pillar, post
עַמּוֹן, Ammon, Ammonite
עַמּוֹנִי, Ammon, Ammonite, Ammonitess
עָמוֹס, Amos
עָמוֹק, Amok
עַמִּיאֵל, Ammiel
עַמִּיהוּד, Ammihud
עַמִּיזָבָד, Ammizabad
עַמִּינָדָב, Amminadab
עָמִיר, sheaf
עַמִּישַׁדָּי, Ammishaddai
עָמִית, another, neighbor, stand *next*
עמל, labor, spend, toil, work
עָמָל, Amal, *hard* labor, hardship, mischief, miserable, misery, oppression, toil, travail, trouble, *wearisome* task, wrong
עָמֵל, misery, toil, worker, workman
עֲמָלֵק, Amalek, Amalekite
עֲמָלֵקִי, Amalekite
עמם, grow *dim*, hide, rival
עִמָּן, remain
עִמָּנוּ אֵל, Immanu-el
עמס, bear, bear *up*, lade, lay, lift, load
עֲמַסְיָה, Amasiah
עַמְעָד, Amad
עמק, deep, deeply, depth, make *deep*
עָמֹק, deep
עָמֵק, foreign, obscure
עֹמֶק, depth
עֵמֶק, plain, vale, valley
עֵמֶק קְצִיץ, Emek-keziz
עמר, binder *of sheaves*, treat *as a slave*
עֹמֶר, omer, sheaf
עֲמֹרָה, Gomorrah
עָמְרִי, Omri
עַמְרָם, Amram
עַמְרָמִי, Amramite
עֲמָשָׂא, Amasa
עֲמָשַׂי, Amasai
עֲמַשְׁסַי, Amashsai
עֲנָב, Anab
עֵנָב, grape, raisin, *ripe* grape
ענג, delicate, *delicately* bred, delight, make *sport*, take *delight*
עָנֹג, delicate, *delicately* bred, *delicately* bred *woman*
עֹנֶג, delight, pleasant
ענד, bind, tie
ענה, accuse, afflict, answer, bear, bear *witness*, break, busy, confront, cry, daunt, deal *harshly*, defile, endure *hardship*, force, give, give *answer*, give *heed*, hail, hear, humble, humiliate, hurt, ill-treat, keep *occupied*, make *answer*, make *response*, oppress, oppressor, overwhelm, raise, ravish, reply, respond, say, share *affliction*, shout, sing, sing *responsively*, sing *to one another*, speak, still, subdue, submit, suffer *affliction*, tell, testify, torment, violate, witness
ענה ואמר, answer
עֹנָה, *marital* right
עֲנָה, Anah
עָנָו, afflict, downtrodden, humble, meek, oppress, poor
עֻנּוֹ, Unno
עֲנוּב, Anub
עֲנָוָה, help, humility
עֱנוּת, affliction
עָנִי, afflict, afflicted *one*, humble, needy, poor, poor *man*, weak
עֻנִּי, Unni
עֳנִי, affliction, *great* pain, sorrow, suffer
עֲנָיָה, Anaiah
עָנִים, Anim
עִנְיָן, business, venture, work
עָנֵם, Anem
עֲנָמִים, Anamim
עֲנַמֶּלֶךְ, Anammelech
ענן, bring *a cloud*, diviner, practice *soothsaying*, practice *witchcraft*, soothsayer, sorceress
עָנָן, Anan, cloud, mist
עֲנָנָה, cloud
עֲנָנִי, Anani
עֲנַנְיָה, Ananiah
עָנָף, bough, branch
עָנֵף, full *of branches*
ענק, furnish
עֲנָק, Anak, Anakim, collar, jewel, necklace, pendant
עָנֵר, Aner
ענשׁ, fine, impose *a fine*, lay *a tribute*, punish, suffer
עֹנֶשׁ, penalty, tribute
עֲנָת, Anath
עֲנָתוֹת, Anathoth
עַנְּתֹתִי, Anathoth
עַנְתֹתִיָּה, Anthothijah
עָסִיס, juice, *sweet* wine, wine
עסס, tread *down*
עֳפָאִים, branch
עפל, presume
עֹפֶל, hill, Ophel
עָפְנִי, Ophni
עַפְעַף, eyelash, eyelid, gaze
עפר, fling *dust*
עָפָר, ash, dust, earth, ground, plaster, rubbish, soil
עֹפֶר, fawn, *young* stag
עֵפֶר, Epher
עָפְרָה, Ophrah
עֶפְרוֹן, Ephron
עֹפֶרֶת, lead, leaden
עֵץ, brushwood, forest, gallows, handle, log, shaft, stalk, stick, *thing of* wood, timber, tree, vessel *of wood*, wood, wooden, wooden *thing*, woodwork
עֵץ אֶרֶז, cedarwood
עֵץ בְּרוֹשִׁים, cypress
עֵץ שֶׁמֶן, olive, olivewood, *wild* olive
עצב, bear *an image*, displease, distress, fashion, grieve, hurt, indignant, seek *to injure*
עָצָב, idol, image
עָצֵב, worker
עֶצֶב, *anxious* toil, harsh, labor, pain, pot, sorrow, toil
עֹצֶב, idol, pain, wicked
עִצָּבוֹן, pain, toil
עַצֶּבֶת, sorrow, suffer, trouble, wound
עצה, wink
עָצֶה, backbone
עֵצָה, advice, counsel, design, order, plan, plot, purpose, scheme, strategy, understanding
עָצוּם, great, might, mighty, *mighty* host, mighty *man*, powerful, *powerful* contender, strong
עֶצְיוֹן גֶּבֶר, Ezion-geber
עצל, slow
עָצֵל, sluggard
עַצְלָה, sloth, slothfulness
עַצְלוּת, idleness
עצם, *become* strong, close, flagrant, gnaw *a bone*, great, grow *strong*, make *many*, make *strong*, many, mighty, shut, strong, vast
עֶצֶם, body, bone, Ezem, prosperity, same, very, *very* same
עֹצֶם, frame, might, strength
עָצְמָה, power, strength
עַצֻּמָה, proof
עַצְמוֹן, Azmon
עצר, able, avert, bond, close, debar, detain, keep, move *about freely*, prevail, prevent, recover, refrain, retain, rule, shut, shut *up*, slacken, stay, stop, withhold
עֶצֶר, wealth
עֹצֶר, barren, oppression
עֲצָרָה, company, *solemn* assembly
עֲצָרָה לְ, keep
עקב, restrain, supplant, supplanter, take *by the heel*
עָקֹב, deceitful, track, *uneven* ground
עָקֵב, footprint, footstep, heel, hoof, persecutor, *rear* guard, step, track
עֵקֶב, because, end, reward
עֵקֶב אֲשֶׁר, because
עֵקֶב כִּי, because
עָקְבָה, cunning

עקד, bind
עָקֹד, striped
עָקָה, oppression
עַקּוּב, Akkub
עקל, pervert
עֲקַלְקַל, crooked *way*
עֲקַלָּתוֹן, twist
עָקָן, Akan
עקר, hamstring, pluck *up*, uproot
עָקָר, barren, barren *female*, barren *male*, barren *woman*
עֵקֶר, Eker, member
עַקְרָב, scorpion
עַקְרַבִּים, Akrabbim
עֶקְרוֹן, Ekron
עֶקְרוֹנִי, Ekron, *people of* Ekron
עקשׁ, make *crooked*, perverse, pervert, prove *perverse*
עִקֵּשׁ, crooked, Ikkesh, perverse, perverseness
עִקְּשׁוּת, crooked
עָר, Ar, enemy
עֵר, Er
ערב, associate, barter, *become* surety, cross *over*, dare, dealer, evening, give *surety*, make *a wager*, mingle, mix, mortgage, pleasant, please, reach *eventide*, security, share, surety, sweet
ערב עֲרֻבָּה, *become* surety
עָרֹב, fly, swarm *of flies*
עָרֵב, sweet
עֶרֶב, afternoon, even, evening, night, twilight
עֹרֵב, Oreb, raven
עֲרָב, Arab, Arabia
עֵרֶב, *foreign* descent, *foreign* folk, *foreign* troop, mix, *mixed* tribes, woof
עֲרָבָה, Arabah, desert, plain, steppe, wilderness, willow
עֲרֻבָּה, token
עֵרָבוֹן, pledge
עֲרָבִי, Arab
עַרְבָתִי, Arbathite
ערג, cry, long
עֲרָד, Arad
ערה, empty, lay *bare*, leave *defenseless*, make *naked*, pour, pour *out*, rase, strip *oneself bare*, uncover
עָרָה, bare *place*
עֲרוּגָה, bed
עָרוֹד, *swift* ass
עֶרְוָה, flesh, indecent, naked, nakedness, shame, weakness
עָרוֹם, naked
עָרוּם, crafty, prudent, prudent *man*, subtle
עֲרוֹעֵר, shrub
עָרוּץ, gully
עֶרְוַת דָּבָר, indecency
עֵרִי, Eri, Erite
עֶרְיָה, bare, nakedness
עֲרִיסָה, *coarse* meal
עָרִיף, cloud
עָרִיץ, dread, oppressor, overbearing, ruthless, ruthless *man*, terrible, tyrant, violent *man*
עֲרִירִי, childless
ערך, array, avail, compare, direct, draw *up*, draw *up a case*, draw *up a line*, draw *up forces*, draw *up in array*, draw *up in line*, equal, equip, expert, form, join, keep *in order*, lay, lay *a charge*, lay *in order*, order, prepare, put *in order*, ready, set, set *forth*, set *in array*, set *in order*, spread, tax, tend, value
עֵרֶךְ, arrangement, assessment, fix, frame, order, suit, valuation, value
ערל, count *as forbidden*
עָרֵל, close, forbid, uncircumcised, uncircumcised *person*
עָרְלָה, foreskin, uncircumcised
ערם, cunning, learn *prudence*, pile *up*, prudent
ערם סוֹד, lay *a crafty plan*
עֹרֶם, craftiness
עָרְמָה, cunning, prudence, treacherously
עֲרֵמָה, heap

עַרְמוֹן, plane, plane *tree*
עֵרָן, Eran
עֵרָנִי, Eranite
עַרְעָר, destitute
עֲרֹעֵר, Aroer
עֲרֹעֵרִי, Aroerite
ערף, break *a neck*, break *down*, break *the neck*, drop, drop *down*
עֹרֶף, back, neck, necked
עֹרֶף קָשֶׁה, stubborn
עָרְפָּה, Orpah
עֲרָפֶל, *deep* darkness, gloom, *thick* darkness
ערץ, dread, fear, frighten, inspire *terror*, stand *in awe*, stand *in fear*, strike *terror*, terrify
ערק, gnaw
עַרְקִי, Arkite
ערר, level, make *bare*, raze
עֶרֶשׂ, bed, bedstead, couch
עֶרֶשׂ דְּוָי, sickbed
עֵשֶׂב, grass, herb, herbage, plant, vegetation
עשׂה, accomplish, achieve, act, administer, appoint, artificial, assign, bear, bestow, bring, bring *about*, bring *forth*, bring *to pass*, build, busy, carry, carry *out*, carve, cause, celebrate, charge, commit, creature, deal, deed, determine, do, doer, dress, earn, engage, erect, execute, fashion, fit, follow, form, fulfil, gain, gather, get, give, go, go *about*, grant, handle, hold, introduce, keep, labor, maintain, make, make *an offering*, make *ready*, maker, man *who practices*, mean, meet, obey, observance, observe, offer, ordain, pare, pass, perform, plot, practice, prepare, present, proceed, produce, provide, put, put *forth*, put *to use*, *ready* dressed, render, sacrifice, set, shape, show, suffer, take, take *action*, take *place*, treat, trim, try, use, wage, win, work, worker, workman, wreak, wrought, yield
עשׂה בְּ, fare
עשׂה דֶּרֶךְ, journey
עשׂה חַיִל, prosper
עשׂה טוֹב, enjoy
עשׂה יְקָר, honor
עשׂה כְּ, follow, requite
עשׂה מַאֲמָר, obey
עשׂה מְלָאכָה, industrious, official, use, work, workman
עשׂה מְלֶאכֶת, charge
עשׂה מְלוּכָה, govern
עשׂה מִלְחָמָה, soldier, warrior
עשׂה מִשְׁפָּט, judge
עשׂה נְקָמוֹת, avenge
עשׂה עַוְלָה, wrongdoer
עשׂה עֹמֶד, show
עשׂה רַע, evildoer
עשׂה רַע בְּעֵינַיִם, displease
עשׂה רָעָה, evildoer
עשׂה רִשְׁעָה, evildoer
עֲשָׂהאֵל, Asahel
עֵשָׂו, Esau
עָשׂוֹר, lute, ten, tenth
עֲשִׂי חֶסֶד, deal *kindly*
עֲשִׂיאֵל, Asiel
עֲשָׂיָה, Asaiah
עֲשִׂירִי, tenth
עשׂק, contend
עֵשֶׂק, Esek
עשׂר, collect *the tithe*, give *a tenth*, pay, receive *a tithe*, take *a tenth*, tithe
עֶשֶׂר, ten
עֶשְׂרִים, twentieth, twenty
עָשׁ, moth
עָשׁ אכל, moth-eaten
עָשׁוֹק, oppressor
עֲשׁוּקִים, oppression
עַשְׁוָת, Ashvath
עָשׁוֹת, wrought
עָשִׁיר, rich, rich *man*
עשׁן, angry, smoke, wrap *in smoke*
עָשָׁן, Ashan, smoke
עָשֵׁן, smolder

עשׁק, burden, defraud, extort, get, oppress, oppressor, practice *extortion*, turbulent
עֹשֶׁק, extortion, oppress, oppression
עֵשֶׁק, Eshek
עשׁר, acquire *wealth*, *become* rich, enrich, make *rich*, pretend *to be rich*, rich
עֹשֶׁר, possession, property, riches, wealth
עֹשֶׁר גָּדוֹל, rich
עשׁשׁ, waste, waste *away*
עשׁת, give *thought*, sleek
עֶשֶׁת, work
עֶשְׁתּוֹן, plan
עֶשְׁתּוּת, thought
עַשְׁתֵּי עָשָׂר, eleven, eleventh
עַשְׁתָּרוֹת, Ashtaroth, young
עַשְׁתֹּרֶת, Ashtaroth, Ashtoreth
עַשְׁתְּרֹת קַרְנַיִם, Ashteroth-karnaim
עַשְׁתְּרָתִי, Ashterathite
עֵת, age, circumstance, due *season*, fate, now, *proper* time, season, time, when
עֵת בּוֹא הַשֶּׁמֶשׁ, sunset
עֵת הָאֹכֶל, mealtime
עֵת הָעֶרֶב, evening
עֵת חַיָּה, spring
עֵת צָהֳרַיִם, noon
עֵת תְּשׁוּבָה, spring
עתד, destine, get *ready*
עַתָּה זֶה, *just* now
עַתָּה, already, more, moreover, now, now *then*, once, soon, then, therefore, time
עַתָּה זֶה, *just* now
עִתָּה קָצִין, Eth-kazin
עַתּוּד, goat, *he* goat, leader, *male* goat
עַתַּי, Attai
עִתִּי, readiness
עָתִיד, doom, prepare, ready, skilled, treasure
עֲתָיָה, Athaiah
עַתִּיק, ancient, take
עָתִיק, fine
עֲתָךְ, Athach
עַתְלַי, Athlai
עֲתַלְיָהוּ, Athaliah
עתם, burn
עָתְנִי, Othni
עָתְנִיאֵל, Othniel
עתק, copy, grow *weak*, move, reach *old age*, remove
עָתָק, arrogance, arrogant, insolent, insolently
עָתֵק, endure
עתר, entreat, grant *entreaty*, grant *prayer*, heed *a supplication*, make *a prayer*, make *entreaty*, multiply, pray, profuse, receive *entreaty*
עָתָר, smoke, suppliant
עֶתֶר, Ether
עֲתֶרֶת, abundance

פאה, scatter *afar*
פֵּאָה, border, corner, edge, forehead, side
פאר, adorn, beautify, glorify, go *over the boughs*, please, vaunt
פְּאֵר, cap, garland, headdress, turban
פֹּארָה, bough, branch, foliage
פֻּארָה, bough
פָּארוּר, pale
פָּארָן, Paran
פְּאַת פָּנִים, forehead, temple
פְּאַת רֹאשׁ, temple
פַּגָּה, fig
פִּגּוּל, abominable *thing*, abomination, foul
פגע, attack, come, entreat, fall *upon*, intercede, intervene, lay, make *intercession*, meet, molest, plead, pray, reach, spare, strike, strike *down*, urge
פגע בְּ, entreat, touch
פֶּגַע, chance
פֶּגַע רַע, misfortune
פַּגְעִיאֵל, Pagiel
פגר, exhaust
פֶּגֶר, body, carcass, corpse, *dead* body

פגשׁ, fall *upon*, meet, meet *together*
פדה, buy *back*, deliver, ransom, redeem, redemption, rescue, *set* free
פְּדַהְאֵל, Pedahel
פְּדָהצוּר, Pedahzur
פָּדוֹן, Padon
פְּדוּת, redeem, redemption
פְּדָיָהוּ, Pedaiah
פְּדוּיִם, redemption
פִּדְיוֹן, ransom
פִּדְיֹן, redemption
פַּדַּן אֲרָם, Paddan-aram
פַּדָּן, Paddan
פדע, deliver
פֶּדֶר, fat
פֶּה, accord, aloud, babble, brink, collar, command, commandment, dictation, direction, edge, end, evidence, face, lip, mouth, opening, portion, praise, share, sound, speech, talk, tooth, utter, word
פֹּה, here
פּוּאָה, Puah
פוג, faint, slack, spend, weary
פוּגַת, rest
פֻּוָּה, Puvah
פוח, blow, blow *upon*, breathe *out*, hasten, long, puff, *set* aflame, speak, utter
פוח נֶפֶשׁ, *cause* death
פּוּט, Put
פּוֹטִי פֶרַע, Poti-phera
פּוּטִיאֵל, Putiel
פּוֹטִיפַר, Potiphar
פּוּךְ, antimony, paint
פּוֹל, bean
פּוּל, Pul
פּוּנִי, Punite
פּוּנֹן, Punon
פּוּעָה, Puah
פוץ, chase, disperse, dispersed *ones*, dispossess, overflow, pour *forth*, scatter, scatter *abroad*, shatterer, spread
פוק, further, get, move, obtain, pour *out*, provide, stumble
פוּקָה, cause *of grief*
פּוּר, Pur
פּוּרָה, measure, wine *press*
פּוּרִים, Purim
פּוֹרָתָא, Poratha
פושׁ, leap, press *proudly*, scatter, wanton
פּוּתִי, Puthite
פָּז, *fine* gold, gold
פזז, fine, leap, make *agile*
פזר, distribute *freely*, give *freely*, hunt, scatter, strew
פַּח, leaf, plate, snare, trap
פחד, afraid, dread, fear, *great* terror, *make* shake, stand *in awe*, terrified, terror, thrill, turn *in dread*, turn *in fear*
פַּחַד, alarm, dread, fear, panic, terrify, terror, thigh
פַּחְדָּה, fear
פֶּחָה, captain, commander, governor
פחז, reckless, wanton
פַּחַז, unstable
פַּחֲזוּת, recklessness
פחח, trap
פֶּחָם, charcoal, coal
פַּחַת, gorge, pit, pitfall
פַּחַת מוֹאָב, Pahath-moab
פִּטְדָה, topaz
פַּטִּישׁ, hammer
פטר, dismiss, free, let *out*, open
פטר בְּשָׂפָה, make *mouths*
פטר מִפְּנֵי, elude
פֶּטֶר, firstling, open, open *first*
פֶּטֶר רֶחֶם, first-born
פֶּטֶר שֶׁגֶר, firstling
פִּטְרָה, open
פִּי, counsel
פִּי אִישׁ, word

פִּי בֶסֶת, Pi-beseth
פִּי הַחִירֹת, Pi-hahiroth
פִּי חֶרֶב, sword
פִּיד, disaster, misfortune, ruin
פִּיוֹת, two-edged
פִּיחַ, ash
פִּיכֹל, Phicol
פִּים, pim
פִּימָה, *gathered* fat
פִּינְחָס, Phinehas
פִּינֹן, Pinon
פִּיק, tremble
פִּישׁוֹן, Pishon
פִּיתוֹן, Pithon
פַּךְ, flask, vial
פכה, come *out*
פֹּכֶרֶת הַצְּבָיִים, Pochereth-hazzebaim
פלא, astonishing *thing*, bring *extraordinary*, difficult, *do a* marvelous *thing*, fearful, fulfil, hard, impossible, make *special*, marvel, marvelous, marvelous *thing*, *marvelous* work, marvelously, miracle, wonder, wonderful, wonderful *deed*, *wonderful* work, wondrous, wondrous *deed*, wondrous *thing*, *wondrous* work, wondrously, *wondrously* show, work *wonders*
פֶּלֶא, marvel, marvelous, terrible, wonder, wonderful, wonderful *thing*
פַּלֻּאִי, Palluite
פִּלְאִי, wonderful
פְּלָאיָה, Pelaiah
פלג, cleft, confuse, divide
פֶּלֶג, brook, Peleg, river, stream
פְּלַגָּה, clan, river
פְּלֻגָּה, grouping
פִּלֶגֶשׁ, concubine, paramour
פִּלְדָּשׁ, Pildash
פלה, distinct, make *a distinction*, set *apart*, *wondrously* show
פַּלּוּא, Pallu
פלח, bring *forth*, cleave, cut *up*, pierce, slash *open*
פֶּלַח, half, millstone, piece
פִּלְחָא, Pilha
פלט, acquit, calve, carry *off*, deliver, deliverer, escape, rescue, save
פַּלֵּט, deliverance
פְּלֵט, escape
פֶּלֶט, Pelet
פַּלְטִי, Palti, Paltite
פִּלְטָי, Piltai
פַּלְטִיאֵל, Paltiel
פְּלַטְיָהוּ, Pelatiah
פְּלָיָה, Pelaiah
פָּלִיט, escape, fugitive, survivor
פָּלֵיט, fugitive, survivor
פְּלֵיטָה, band *of survivors*, deliverance, escape, remnant, survive, survivor
פָּלִיל, judge
פְּלִילָה, justice
פְּלִילִי, judge
פְּלִילִיָּה, give *judgment*
פֶּלֶךְ, district, spindle
פלל, intercede, interpose, make *a prayer*, make *judgment*, make *supplication*, mediate, offer, offer *a prayer*, pray, prayer, think
פָּלָל, Palal
פְּלַלְיָה, Pelaliah
פְּלֹנִי, Pelonite
פְּלֹנִי אַלְמֹנִי, friend, such *and such*
פלס, deal *out*, make, make *smooth*, take *heed*
פֶּלֶס, balance, scale
פלץ, tremble
פַּלָּצוּת, horror, shudder
פלשׁ, roll, wallow
פְּלֶשֶׁת, Philistia
פְּלִשְׁתִּי, Philistia, Philistine
פֶּלֶת, Peleth
פְּלֵתִי, Pelethite
פֶּן, fear, lest, no, only
פַּנַּג, *early* fig

פנה, appear, cast *out*, clear, come, corner, decline, empty, face, look, look *back*, pass *away*, prepare, regard, respect, row, turn, turn *away*, turn *back*
פנה בְּ, consider
פנה בֹּקֶר, *right* early
פִּנָּה, battlement, chief, corner, cornerstone, leader
פְּנוּאֵל, Penuel
פְּנוֹת אַחֲרֵי, turn
פְּנֵי רֵעַ, another
פְּנִיאֵל, Peniel
פָּנִים, appear, bank, before, charge, condition, countenance, course, east, edge, eye, face, favor, forefront, *former* time, front, gaze, ground, head, inner, look, meet, mouth, old, open, outer, person, prayer, presence, regard, region, sight, surface, table, time *past*, utter, way, whole
פָּנִים דֶּרֶךְ, face
פָּנִים ל, intend
פָּנִים לְ, face
פְּנִימָה, chamber, inner, inner *part*, inside, inward, within
פְּנִימִי, inner, innermost, interior
פְּנִינִים, coral, *costly* stone, jewel, pearl
פְּנִנָּה, Peninnah
פנק, pamper
פַּס, long *with sleeves*
פַּס דַּמִּים, Pas-dammim
פסג, go *through*
פִּסְגָּה, Pisgah
פִּסָּה, abundance
פסח, *become* lame, go *limping*, limp, pass *over*, spare
פָּסֵחַ, Paseah
פֶּסַח, passover, *passover* lamb, *passover* offering, *passover* sacrifice
פִּסֵּחַ, lame, lame *man*
פְּסִיל, *graven* image, idol, image, *sculptured* stone
פָּסַךְ, Pasach
פסל, cut, *do* hewing, hew, shape
פֶּסֶל, *graven* image, idol, image
פסס, vanish
פִּסְפָּה, Pispa
פעה, cry *out*
פָּעוּ, Pau
פְּעוֹר, Peor
פָּעִי, Pai
פעל, accomplish, deal, devise, do, forge, make, maker, perform, work, worker, wrought
פֹּעֵל אָוֶן, evildoer
פֹּעַל, conduct, deed, do, get, toil, wage, work, wrought
פְּעֻלָּה, do, payment, recompense, reward, wage, work
פְּעֻלְּתַי, Peullethai
פעם, stir, trouble
פַּעַם, anvil, corner, foot, footstep, hoofbeat, last, moment, now, once, step, story, stroke, tier, time, twice, *twice* told
פַּעַם אַחַת, once
פַּעַם בְּפַעַם, *other* times
פַּעֲמֹן, bell
פער, gape, open
פַּעֲרַי, Paarai
פצה, open, open *wide*, rescue, utter
פצה פִּי, rail
פצח, break *forth*, break *in pieces*
פְּצִירָה, charge
פצל, peel
פְּצָלָה, streak
פצם, rend *open*
פצע, wound
פֶּצַע, bruise, wound
פצץ, break *in pieces*, dash *to pieces*
פצר, press, stubbornness, urge
פקד, appoint, assign, attend, bring *punishment*, care, census, charge, commit, consign, count, empty, enjoin, execute *judgment*, give *attention*, give *charge*, harm, help, inspect, lack, long, make, make *inquiry*, make *overseer*, mindful, miss, muster, number, observe, officer, overseer, oversight, prescribe, punish, put, regard, register, see, seek, set, set *over*, store, visit, without
פקד לְ, see *how*
פקד עַל, charge
פְּקֻדָּה, *appointed* duty, care, charge, executioner, fate, goods, lay *up*, muster, officer, overseer, oversight, punish, punishment, reckoning, watchman
פִּקָּדוֹן, deposit, reserve
פִּקּוּד, commandment, precept
פְּקוֹד, Pekod
פְּקוּדִים, sum
פקח, open
פֶּקַח, Pekah
פִּקֵּחַ, official
פִּקֵּחַ, see
פְּקַחְיָה, Pekahiah
פָּקִיד, charge, command, leader, officer, overseer
פָּקִיד נָגִיד, *chief* officer
פְּקָעִים, form *of gourd*, gourd
פַּקֻּעֹת, gourd
פַּר, bull, ox, *young* bull, *young* steer
פַּר בֶּן בָּקָר, bull, *young* bull
פַּר שׁוֹר, bull
פֶּרֶא, wild *ass*
פִּרְאָם, Piram
פרד, alienate, decide, desert, disperse, divide, estrange, go *aside*, *out of* joint, part, scatter, separate, spread, spread *abroad*, spread *out*
פֶּרֶד, mule
פִּרְדָּה, mule
פְּרֻדָה, seed
פַּרְדֵּס, forest, orchard, park
פרה, bear, flourish, *fruit* tree, fruitful, grow, increase, *make* fruitful, make *fruitful*
פָּרָה, cow, heifer, Parah
פֻּרָה, Purah
פְּרוּדָא, Peruda
פָּרוּחַ, Paruah
פַּרְוַיִם, Parvaim
פַּרְוָר, parbar, precinct
פָּרוּר, pot
פְּרָזָה, open, *unwalled* village, village *without a wall*
פִּרְזוֹן, peasantry
פְּרָזִי, unwalled, village
פְּרִזִּי, Perizzite
פרח, bird, blossom, break *out*, bud, flourish, *make* blossom, *make* flourish, put *forth a shoot*, spread, spring *up*, sprout, sprout *forth*
פֶּרַח, bloom, blossom, bud, flower
פִּרְחַח, rabble
פרט, sing *an idle song*
פֶּרֶט, *fallen* grape
פְּרִי, boast, fruit, fruitful, offspring, produce, reward, son
פְּרִידָא, Perida
פָּרִיץ, ravenous, robber, violence, violent
פֶּרֶךְ, harshness, rigor
פָּרֹכֶת, veil
פרם, rend, tear
פַּרְמַשְׁתָּא, Parmashta
פַּרְנָךְ, Parnach
פרס, break, chop *up*, cloven, give, hoof, part, share
פָּרַס, Persia, Persian
פֶּרֶס, vulture
פַּרְסָה, hoof
פַּרְסִי, Persian
פרע, avoid, break *loose*, cast *off restraint*, deal *wantonly*, go *back*, hang *loose*, ignore, neglect, take *away*, take *the lead*, unbind *the hair*
פֶּרַע, leader, lock, *long* haired
פַּרְעֹה, Pharaoh
פַּרְעֹשׁ, flea, Parosh
פִּרְעָתוֹן, Pirathon
פִּרְעָתוֹנִי, Pirathon, Pirathonite
פַּרְפַּר, Pharpar
פרץ, breach, break, break *away*, break *down*, break *forth*, break *into*, break *out*, break *through*, burst, destroy, distribute, frequent, grow *rich*, increase, *make a* breach, multiply, open, open *a shaft*, press, spread *abroad*, urge
פרץ פֶּרֶץ, break *forth*
פֶּרֶץ, breach, break, burst, mischance, Perez
פֶּרֶץ מַיִם, *bursting* flood
פֶּרֶץ עֻזָּא, Perez-uzza
פֶּרֶץ עֻזָּה, Perez-uzzah
פַּרְצִי, Perezite
פְּרָצִים, Perazim
פרק, break, deliver, drag *away*, rend, rescue, strip *off*, take *off*, tear *off*
פֶּרֶק, booty, parting *of ways*
פרר, annul, break, break *asunder*, bring *to nought*, come *to nought*, defeat, divide, do *away*, fail, frustrate, go *wrong*, make *null and void*, make *void*, put *away*, rend *asunder*
פרר מִשְׁפָּט, put *in the wrong*
פרשׂ, extend, flaunt, open, outstretched, scatter, spread, spread *abroad*, spread *forth*, spread *out*, spread *over*, stretch *out*, throw
פַּרְשֵׂז, spread
פרשׁ, clearly, declare, make *plain*, spread, sting
פָּרָשׁ, horse, horseman, *war* horse
פֶּרֶשׁ, dung, Peresh
פַּרְשְׁדֹנָה, dirt
פָּרָשָׁה, *exact* sum, *full* account
פַּרְשַׁנְדָּתָא, Parshandatha
פְּרָת, Euphrates
פַּרְתְּמִים, noble
פשׂה, spread
פשׂע, set *out*
פֶּשַׂע, step
פשׂק, offer, open *wide*
פשׁח, tear *to pieces*
פַּשְׁחוּר, Pashhur
פשׁט, fall, flay, make *a raid*, put *off*, raid, rush, spread, strip, strip *off*, take *off*
פשׁע, commit, *do* wrong, rebel, rebellion, revolt, transgress, transgression, transgressor
פֶּשַׁע, sinful
פֶּשַׁע, breach *of trust*, iniquity, offense, rebellion, transgress, transgression, treason, trespass
פֵּשֶׁר, diagnosis
פְּשַׁר, interpretation
פֵּשֶׁת, flax, linen
פִּשְׁתָּה, flax, wick
פַּת, morsel, piece
פַּת בַּג, *rich* food
פֹּת, secret *part*, socket
פִּתְאֹם, all *at once*, instant, sudden, suddenly
פַּתְבַּג, *rich* food
פִּתְגָם, decree, sentence
פתה, allure, deceive, enlarge, entice, flatter, foolishly, persuade, seduce, silly, simple
פְּתוּאֵל, Pethuel
פָּתוֹחַ נִפְתָּחוּ, *wide* open
פִּתּוּחַ, *carved* wood, engrave, figure, inscription
פְּתוֹר, Pethor
פְּתוֹת, piece
פתח, break *forth*, carve, draw, drawn, engrave, go, lay *open*, leave *open*, loose, offer, open, put *off*, release, *set* free, solve, spread *out*, ungird, unstop, vent
פֶּתַח, door, doorway, entrance, entry, gate, opening, portal
פֵּתַח, unfold
פִּתְחוֹן, open
פְּתַחְיָה, Pethahiah
פְּתִי, ignorance, simple, simple *one*, simpleness
פְּתִיגִיל, *rich* robe
פְּתִיחָה, *drawn* sword
פָּתִיל, cord, lace, line, string, thread
פתל, *show oneself* perverse, twist, wily, wrestle
פְּתַלְתֹּל, crooked
פִּתֹם, Pithom
פֶּתֶן, adder, asp
פֶּתַע, moment, suddenly
פתר, give *an interpretation*, interpret, interpretation, open
פִּתְרוֹן, meaning

פַּתְרוֹס, Pathros
פִּתְרֹן, interpretation
פַּתְרֻסִים, Pathrusim
פַּתְשֶׁגֶן, copy
פתת, break

צֹא, filthy
צֹאָה, filth, filthiness
צֵאָה, excrement
צֹאִי, filthy
צֶאֱלִים, lotus *plant*, lotus *tree*
צֹאן, flock, herd, lamb, sheep
צַאֲנָן, Zaanan, Zenan
צֶאֱצָא, grow, offspring
צֶאֱצָא מֵעֶה, descendant
צֶאֱצָאִים, child, come
צָב, cover, great *lizard*, litter
צבא, fight, go *to war*, minister, ministering *woman*, muster, perform, serve, service, wage *war*, war
צָבָא, *armed* troop, army, battle, company, conflict, gazelle, *hard* service, host, march, service, troop, war, warfare, work
צֹבֵבָה, Zobebah
צבה, *make* swell, swell
צָבוּעַ, speckle
צבט, pass
צְבִי, beauteous, beautiful, beauty, gazelle, glorious, glory
צִבְיָא, Zibia
צְבִיָּה, gazelle
צִבְיָהוּ, Zibiah
צְבֹיִים, Zeboiim
צֶבַע, dyed *stuff*, *dyed* work
צִבְעוֹן, Zibeon
צְבֹעִים, Zeboim
צבר, gather *together*, heap *up*, lay *up*, store *up*
צִבֻּר, heap
צֶבֶת, bundle
צַד, arm, hip, side
צְדָד, Zedad
צדה, hunt, make *desolate*
צָדוֹק, Zadok
צְדִיָּה, lie *in wait*
צִדִּים, Ziddim
צַדִּיק, good *man*, innocent, just, just *man*, justly, right, righteous, righteous *man*, triumphant, upright
צדק, acquit, clear, give *justice*, innocent, just, justify, maintain *right*, *make* account righteous, *make* appear righteous, prove *right*, restore *to rightful state*, right, righteous, say *one is right*, *show less* guilty, triumph, turn *one to righteousness*, vindicate
צֶדֶק, deliverance, *honest* evidence, just, *just* cause, justice, justly, right, righteous, righteously, righteousness, rightful, salvation, true, truth, victorious, victory, vindication
צְדָקָה, command, deliverance, equity, honesty, prosperity, right, righteous, righteous *act*, righteous *deed*, *righteous* help, righteously, righteousness, salvation, saving *act*, saving *deed*, *saving* help, triumph, uprightness, vindication
צִדְקִיָּהוּ, Zedekiah
צהב, baffle, bright
צָהֹב, yellow
צהל, cry *aloud*, *make* shine, neigh, raise *a shout*, shout
צהל קוֹל, cry *aloud*
צהר, make *oil*
צֹהַר, roof
צָהֳרַיִם, midday, noon, noonday
צַו, precept
צַוָּאר, neck
צוֹבָה, Zobah
צוד, dog, hunt, hunt *down*, lie *in wait*, stalk, take *in hunting*
צוה, appoint, bid, charge, command, commander, commission, forbid, give, give *a charge*, give *a command*, give *a message*, give *charge*, give *command*, give *commandment*, give *in commandment*, give *orders*, instruct, ordain, order, send *a message*, summon, tell, warn
צוה אֶל, set *in order*
צוה לְ, set *in order*
צוה לְ, appoint
צוה לֹא, forbid
צוה עַל, charge, order
צוח, shout
צְוָחָה, cry, cry *of distress*, outcry
צוּלָה, deep
צום, fast, hold *a fast*
צוֹם, fast
צוּעָר, Zuar
צוף, close, *make* float, *make* overflow
צוּף, honeycomb, Zuph
צוּף דְּבַשׁ, honeycomb
צוֹפֶה פְּנֵי, overlook
צוֹפַח, Zophah
צוֹפַי, Zophai
צוץ, blossom, blossom *forth*, flourish, look, produce *blossoms*, shed *luster*
צוק, afflict, constrain, distress, oppressor, pour *out*, press *hard*, smelt
צוֹק, trouble
צוּקָה, anguish
צור, adversary, afflict, attack, beset, besiege, bind, bind *up*, cast, fashion, harass, lay *siege*, press *the siege*, stir *up*, tie *up*
צור אֶל, besiege
צור עַל, besiege, enclose
צוּר, crag, edge, mountain, rock, stone, strength, Zur
צוּרָה, form
צַוְּרוֹן, necklace
צוּרֵי הַיְּעֵלִים, Wildgoats' *Rocks*
צוּרִיאֵל, Zuriel
צוּרִישַׁדָּי, Zurishaddai
צַח, clear, distinctly, hot, radiant
צִחֶה, parch
צחח, white
צְחִיחַ, bare, open *place*
צְחִיחָה, *parched* land
צַחֲנָה, *foul* smell
צחק, fondle, insult, jest, laugh, make *sport*, play
צְחֹק, laughter
צַחַר, white
צָחֹר, tawny
צֹחַר, Zohar
צִי, creature *of the wilderness*, ship, *wild* beast
צִיבָא, Ziba
ציד, make *ready provision*, take *as food*
צַיִד, food, game, hunt, hunter, prey, provision
צַיָּד, hunter
צֵידָה, food, provision
צִידוֹן, Sidon
צִידֹנִי, Sidonian
צִיָּה, desert, drought, dry, *dry* ground, *dry* land, *dry* waste, parch
צָיוֹן, dry *place*
צִיּוֹן, Zion
צִיּוּן, monument, sign, waymark
צִיחָא, Ziha
צִינֹק, collar
צִיעֹר, Zior
צִיץ, blossom, flower, plate, wing, Ziz
צִיצָה, flower
צִיצִת, lock, tassel
צִיר, ambassador, envoy, form, hinge, idol, messenger, pain, pang
צֵל, protection, shade, shadow, shelter
צלה, roast
צִלָּה, Zillah
צלח, avail, break *out*, *cause to* prosper, come, come *mightily*, give *success*, good, lame, *make* prosper, make *prosperous*, prosper, rush, rush *down*, succeed, successful, *successfully* accomplish, thrive, triumph, useful, victoriously
צֵלָחָה, pan
צְלֹחִית, bowl
צַלַּחַת, dish
צָלִי, meat
צְלִי אֵשׁ, roast
צְלִיל, cake
צלל, dark, quiver, shade, sink, tingle
צֶלֶם, image, phantom, shadow
צַלְמוֹן, Zalmon
צַלְמָוֶת, *deep* darkness, gloom, shadow *of death*
צַלְמֹנָה, Zalmonah
צַלְמֻנָּע, Zalmunna
צלע, limp
צֶלַע, fall, stumble
צֵלַע, story, Zela
צֵלַע הָהָר, hillside
צֵלָע, board, chamber, leaf, rib, side, *side* chamber
צָלָף, Zalaph
צְלָפְחָד, Zelophehad
צֶלְצַח, Zelzah
צִלְצָל, spear, whir
צְלָצַל, locust
צֶלְצְלִים, cymbal
צֶלֶק, Zelek
צִלְּתַי, Zillethai
צמא, suffer *thirst*, thirst, thirsty
צָמָא, *parched* ground, thirst, thirsty
צָמֵא, dry, thirst, thirsty, thirsty *man*
צִמְאָה, thirst
צִמָּאוֹן, *thirsty* ground
צמד, attach, fasten, frame, yoke
צֶמֶד, acre, couple, pair, side *by side*, team, two, yoke, yoke *of oxen*
צַמָּה, veil
צִמּוּק, bunch *of raisins*, cluster *of raisins*
צמח, bring *forth*, *cause to* grow, *cause to* prosper, *cause to* spring forth, *cause to* spring up, grow, grow *up*, *make* grow, *make* put forth, *make* sprout, spring, spring *forth*, spring *up*, sprout
צֶמַח, branch, grow, growth, head, plant, shoot, sprout
צָמִיד, bracelet, cover
צַמִּים, snare
צְמִיתֻת, perpetuity
צמק, dry
צֶמֶר, wool, woolen
צְמָרִי, Zemarite
צְמָרַיִם, Zemaraim
צַמֶּרֶת, top
צמת, consume, cut *off*, destroy, disappear, fling, hem, put *an end*, wipe *out*
צִן, Zin
צֵן, thorn
צנה, humbly
צִנָּה, buckler, cold, hook, *large* shield, shield, shield-bearer
צֹנֶה, sheep
צָנוּעַ, humble
צִנּוֹר, cataract, *water* shaft
צנח, alight, go *down*
צָנִין, thorn
צָנִיף, diadem, turban
צנם, wither
צנף, wear, whirl *round and round*
צְנֵפָה, throw
צִנְצֶנֶת, jar
צַנְתְּרוֹת, pipe
צעד, bestride, bring, go, march, run, take, walk
צַעַד, pace, step, tread
צְעָדָה, armlet, march
צעה, bow *down*, tilt, tilter
צָעִיף, veil
צָעִיר, humble, least, little, little *one*, servant, small, small *one*, young, *young* son, Zair
צָעִיר לְיָמִים, young
צְעִירָה, youth
צֹעַן, Zoan
צַעֲנַנִּים, Zaanannim
צעק, appeal, call, call *out*, call *together*, cry, cry *for help*, cry *out*
צְעָקָה, cry, outcry
צער, bring *low*, little *one*, small
צֹעַר, Zoar
צפד, shrivel
צפה, adorn, cover, destine, keep *watch*, look, look *forth*, overlay, spread, watch, watchman
צָפָה, flow
צְפוֹ, Zepho
צִפּוּי, cover, covering, overlay
צָפוֹן, north, *north* end, *north* side, *north* wind, northern, Zaphon
צְפוֹן, Zephon
צָפוֹנָה, northward, toward *the north*
צְפוֹנִי, northerner, Zephonite
צִפּוֹר, bird, fowl, *small* bird, sparrow, Zippor
צַפַּחַת, cruse, jar
צְפִי, Zephi
צְפִיָּה, watch
צִפְיוֹן, Ziphion
צַפִּיחִת, wafer
צֹפִים, Zophim
צָפִיעַ, dung
צָפִיר, goat, *he* goat
צָפִיר שָׂעִיר, *he* goat
צְפִיר עִזִּים, *he* goat
צְפִירָה, diadem, doom
צָפִית, rug
צפן, ambush, close, conceal, hide, hold *safe*, keep, keep *in store*, lay *up*, lurk, precious *place*, protected *one*, restrain, set *an ambush*, *stealthily* watch, store *up*, treasure, treasure *up*
צְפַנְיָהוּ, Zephaniah
צָפְנַת פַּעְנֵחַ, Zaphenath-paneah
צֶפַע, adder
צְפִעָה, issue
צִפְעוֹנִי, adder
צפף, chirp, clamor, whisper
צַפְצָפָה, willow
צֹפַר, Zophar
צְפַרְדֵּעַ, frog
צִפֹּרָה, Zipporah
צִפֹּרֶן, nail, point
צֶפֶת, capital
צְפַת, Zephath
צְפָתָה, Zephathah
צִקְלַג, Ziklag
צִקְלֹן, sack
צַר, adversary, adversity, affliction, anguish, closely, distress, enemy, flint, foe, narrow, rush, small, tribulation, trouble
צַר לְ, straits
צֹר, flint, Tyre
צֵר, Zer
צרב, scorch
צָרָב, scorch
צָרֶבֶת, scar
צְרֵדָה, Zeredah
צָרָה, adversity, affliction, anguish, distress, rival, *rival* wife, suffer, tribulation, trouble
צְרוּיָה, Zeruiah
צְרוּעָה, Zeruah
צְרוֹר, bag, bundle, pebble, Zeror
צרח, cry *aloud*, shout *aloud*
צֹרִי, *man of* Tyre, Tyrian
צֳרִי, balm
צְרִי, Zeri
צְרִיחַ, stronghold, tomb
צֹרֶךְ, need
צרע, leper, leprous, leprous *man*
צָרְעָה, Zorah
צִרְעָה, hornet
צָרְעִי, Zorite
צָרַעַת, leprosy, leprous
צָרְעָתִי, Zorathite
צרף, cast, goldsmith, prove *true*, refine, refiner, silversmith, smelt *away*, smith, test, try
צֹרְפִי, goldsmith
צָרְפַת, Zarephath
צרר, adversary, afflict, besiege, bind, bind *up*,

bring *distress*, distress, enemy, foe, hamper, harass, *make* suffer, mend, narrow, oppress, pang, shorten, shut *up*, straits, torment, trouble, wrap, wrap *up*
צְרֵרָה, Zererah
צרת, cut *off*
צֶרֶת, Zereth
צֶרֶת שַׁחַר, Zereth-shahar
צָרְתָן, Zarethan

קא, vomit
קאקא, sweep
קָאַת, hawk, pelican, vulture
קַב, kab
קבב, blaspheme, curse
קֻבָּה, *inner* room
קֵבָה, body, stomach
קִבּוּץ, collection
קְבוּרָה, burial
קבל, accept, opposite, receive, take, take *over*, take *upon*, undertake
קֹבֶל, *battering* ram
קבע, despoil, rob
קֻבַּעַת, dreg
קֻבַּעַת כּוֹס, bowl
קבץ, assemble, collect, come *together*, gather, gather *together*, gather *up*, grow, muster, rallv
קַבְצְאֵל, Kabzeel
קְבֻצָה, gather
קִבְצַיִם, Kibzaim
קבר, burier, bury
קֶבֶר, burial, burial *place*, burying *place*, grave, sepulchre, tomb
קְבֻרָה, burying *place*, grave, place *of burial*, tomb
קִבְרוֹת הַתַּאֲוָה, Kibroth-hattaavah
קדד, bow, bow *down*, bow *one's head*
קִדָּה, cassia
קְדוּמִים, onrushing
קָדוֹשׁ, consecrate, holy, holy *one*, holy *place*, saint
קדח, kindle
קַדַּחַת, fever
קָדִים, east, *east* wind, eastern, eastward, go *before*
קדם, awake *before*, come *before*, come *into*, *come to* meet, come *upon*, confront, front, go *before*, make *haste*, meet, receive
קדם פָּנִים, confront
קֶדֶם, ancient, *ancient* times, before, beginning, east, east *side*, eastern, eternal, everlasting, first, forward, long, old
קֵדֶם, east, east *side*, eastern, front
קֶדֶם מִמּוּל נֶגְבָּה, southeast
קַדְמָה, before, former, *former* estate, origin
קִדְמָה, east
קֵדְמָה, eastward, Kedemah
קַדְמוֹן, eastern
קַדְמִיאֵל, Kadmiel
קַדְמֹנִי, ancient, east, eastern, former, Kadmonite, *thing of* old
קְדֵמוֹת, Kedemoth
קָדְקֹד, brow, crown, crown *of head*, head, pate
קדר, black, blacken, clothe *in gloom*, dark, darken, grow *black*, lament, make *dark*, mourn
קֵדָר, Kedar
קִדְרוֹן, Kidron
קַדְרוּת, blackness
קְדֹרַנִּית, mourn
קדשׁ, *become* holy, communicate *holiness*, consecrate, consecrated *one*, declare, dedicate, *dedicated* gift, forfeit *to the sanctuary*, hallow, holy, keep *holy*, make *holy*, manifest *one's holiness*, prepare, purify, regard *as holy*, revere *as holy*, sanctify, set *apart*, *show* holiness, *show* holy, vindicate, vindicate *holiness*
קָדֵשׁ, *cult* prostitute, Kadesh, *male cult* prostitute
קָדֵשׁ בַּרְנֵעַ, Kadesh-barnea
קֶדֶשׁ, Kedesh
קֹדֶשׁ, consecrate, *consecrated* offering, consecrated *thing*, dedicate, *dedicated* gift, dedicated *thing*, hallowed *thing*, holiness, holy, *holy* offering, holy *one*, holy *place*, *holy* portion, holy *thing*, sacred, *sacred* portion, sacred *thing*, sacrificial, sanctuary, *votive* gift
קְדֵשָׁה, *cult* prostitute, harlot
קהה, blunt, set *on edge*
קהל, assemble, assemble *together*, call *to judgment*, gather, gather *together*
קָהָל, assemble, assembly, company, congregation, crew, horde, host, multitude
קְהִלָּה, assembly
קֹהֶלֶת, preacher
קְהֵלָתָה, Kehelathah
קְהָת, Kohath
קְהָתִי, Kohathite
קַו, line, *measuring* line
קַו קָו, mighty
קוֹבַע, helmet
קוה, gather, gather *together*, hope, lie *in wait*, long, look, set *one's hope*, tarry, vomit, wait
קְוֵה, Kue
קוט, break *in sunder*, disgust, loathe, loathsome
קוֹל, aloud, blast, bleat, clamor, command, crack, crackle, crash, cry, grind, hark, hear, loud, low, make *a sound*, moan, noise, plea, proclamation, *public* adjuration, report, roar, rumble, shout, song, sound, tell, thunder, thundering, voice, word
קוֹל אֶחָד, unison
קוֹל גָּדוֹל, aloud
קוֹל רַעַשׁ, rumble
קוֹלָיָה, Kolaiah
קום, accomplish, adversary, arise, ascend, assailant, attack, avail, bid *rise*, confirm, continue, dim, endure, enemy, enjoin, erect, establish, fix, fulfil, get *up*, go, grow *up*, grown, keep, lay *down*, leave, lift *up*, make, *make* come *true*, make *over*, *make* stand, make *sure*, observe, ordain, perform, perpetuate, prepare, prevail, provide, raise, raise *up*, rear, remain, *remain* standing, restore, rise, rise *up*, rise *up against*, rouse, rouse *up*, set, set *out*, *set to* work, set *up*, stand, stand *up*, start, stir *up*, strengthen, succeed, sustain, up, uphold, withdraw, withstand
קום אֶל, attack
קום וּבוֹא, set *out*
קום וְהלך, start *on the way*
קום עַל, attack, enjoin
קוֹמָה, aloft, height, high, length, stately, stature, tall
קוֹמְמִיּוּת, erect
קוֹעַ, Koa
קוֹף, ape
קוץ, abhor, dread, loathe, overcome *with fear*, terrify, weary
קוֹץ, Koz, thorn
קְוֻצּוֹת, lock
קור, dig, keep *fresh*
קוּר, web
קוֹרֵא, Kore
קוֹרָה, beam, log, roof
קושׁ, lay *a snare*
קוּשָׁיָהוּ, Kushaiah
קַט, very
קֶטֶב, destroy, destruction, pestilence
קְטוֹרָה, incense
קְטוּרָה, Keturah
קטל, kill, slay
קֶטֶל, slaughter
קטן, make *small*, small *thing*, worthy *of the least*
קָטָן, least, little, low, small, young
קָטֹן, brief, little, little *one*, small, small *thing*, young
קָטֹן וְגָדוֹל, all
קֹטֶן, *little* finger
קטף, break *off*, cut *down*, pick, pluck
קטר, burn, burn *a sacrifice*, burn *incense*, make *an offering*, offer, offer *a sacrifice*, offer *incense*, perfume
קִטֵּר, incense
קִטְרוֹן, Kitron
קְטֹרֶת, incense, perfume, smoke
קַטָּת, Kattath
קיא, vomit, vomit *out*, vomit *up*
קִיא, vomit
קִיטוֹר, frost, smoke
קִים, adversary
קִימָה, rise
קין, lament, mourning *woman*
קַיִן, Cain, Kain, Kenite, spear
קִינָה, dirge, Kinah, lament, lamentation
קֵינִי, Kenite
קֵינָן, Kenan
קיץ, awake, awaken, summer, wake
קַיִץ, fruit, summer, *summer* fruit
קִיצוֹן, outmost
קִיקָיוֹן, plant
קִיקָלוֹן, shame
קִיר, Kir, side, surface, wall
קִיר הַחוֹמָה, *city* wall
קִיר הֶרֶשׂ, Kir-heres
קִיר חֶרֶשׂ, Kir-heres
קִיר חֲרֶשֶׂת, Kir-hareseth
קִישׁ, Kish
קִישׁוֹן, Kishon
קִישִׁי, Kishi
קַל, restive, speedily, swift, swiftly
קֹל, light
קלה, base *fellow*, bring *into contempt*, burn, degrade, dishonor, *humble* standing, *no* repute, parch, *parched* grain, roast
קָלוֹן, abuse, contempt, disgrace, dishonor, insult, shame
קַלַּחַת, caldron
קלט, short
קַלַּי, Kallai
קָלִי, *parched* grain
קֵלָיָה, Kelaiah
קְלִיטָא, Kelita
קלל, accursed, blaspheme, bring *into contempt*, contempt, curse, despise, dishonor, easy, easy *thing*, light *thing*, lighten, *lightly* esteem, make *contemptible*, move *to and fro*, revile, *seem a* little *thing*, shake, slight *thing*, *small* account, subside, swift, treat *with contempt*, vile, whet
קָלָל, burnish
קְלָלָה, accursed, byword *of cursing*, curse
קלס, jeer, mock, scoff, scorn
קֶלֶס, deride, derision, scorn
קַלָּסָה, mock
קלע, carve, sling, sling *out*
קלע עַל, cover
קַלָּע, slinger
קֶלַע, hanging, sling
קְלֹקֵל, worthless
קֹלֹת אֱלֹהִים, thunder
קָמָה, standing *grain*
קְמוּאֵל, Kemuel
קָמוֹן, Kamon
קִמּוֹשׁ, nettle, thorn
קֶמַח, flour, meal
קמט, shrivel *up*, snatch *away*
קמל, rot *away*, wither *away*
קמץ, take *a handful*
קֹמֶץ, handful
קֵן, nest, nestling, room
קנא, *become* jealous, envious, envy, jealous, move *to jealousy*, provoke *to jealousy*, stir *to jealousy*, zeal
קַנָּא, jealous
קִנְאָה, envy, fury, indignation, jealous, *jealous* wrath, jealousy, passion, zeal
קנה, acquire, buy, buy *back*, buyer, create, form, gain, get, maker, owner, purchase, recover, win
קָנָה, Kanah
קָנֶה, branch, calamus, cane, reed, scale, shaft, socket, stalk, *sweet* cane
קַנּוֹא, jealous
קְנַז, Kenaz
קְנִזִּי, Kenizzite
קִנְיָן, creature, get, goods, possession, property, substance
קִנָּמוֹן, cinnamon
קנן, build *a nest*, chant, lament, *make a* nest, nest, utter *a lament*
קְנָת, Kenath
קסם, divination, divine, diviner, give *divination*, practice *divination*, soothsayer, use *divination*
קֶסֶם, divination, divine, fee *for divination*, *inspired* decision, lot
קסס, cut *off*
קֶסֶת, *writing* case
קֶסֶת סֹפֵר, *writing* case
קְעִילָה, Keilah
קַעֲקַע, tattoo
קְעָרָה, plate
קפא, congeal, curdle, thicken
קפד, roll *up*
קִפֹּד, hedgehog, porcupine
קְפָדָה, anguish
קִפּוֹז, owl
קפץ, bound, fade, shut, shut *up*, stop
קֵץ, course, end, far, final, limit, quarter, remote, some
קצב, cut *off*, shorn *ewe*
קֶצֶב, form, root
קצה, cut *off*, scrape, scrape *off*
קָצָה, among, corner, edge, end, outmost, outskirts, quarter, tip, *whole* number
קָצֶה, among, border, brink, edge, end, extreme, extremity, far, frontier, last *man*, mouth, near, *other* end, outlying *part*, outpost, outskirts, side, source, tip, uttermost *part*
קֵצֶה, end, limit
קְצוֹ, border, end
קֶצַח, dill
קָצִין, chief, commander, leader, ruler
קְצִיעָה, cassia, Keziah
קָצִיר, bough, branch, harvest, *harvest* time
קצע, *cause to* scrape
קצף, anger, angry, bear *anger*, *become* angry, enrage, provoke *to wrath*, wrath *come*
קצף מְאֹד, enrage
קֶצֶף, anger, chip, enrage, indignation, resentment, wrath
קְצָפָה, splinter
קצץ, cut, cut *in pieces*, cut *off*, shatter, strip
קצר, cut *short*, few, gather, harvest, impatient, narrow, reap, reaper, short, shorten, vex
קצר נֶפֶשׁ, *become* impatient, *become* indignant
קצר רוּחַ, impatient
קְצַר, hasty, quick, shorn
קֹצֶר, break
קְצָת, end, *far* bound
קַר, cold, cool
קֹר, cold
קרא, announce, appoint, befall, call, call *forth*, call *out*, call *upon*, chance, chance *to come upon*, chance *to meet*, chosen *one*, come, come *against*, come upon, cry, cry *out*, enter *suit*, follow *hard*, give *a name*, grasp, guest, happen, invite, invoke, look, make *a proclamation*, *make* come *upon*, make *proclamation*, meet, mention, name, offer, perpetuate, predict, proclaim, read, renowned, say, shout, summon
קרא בְּשֵׁם, name
קרא לְ, call, name
קרא מלא, cry *aloud*
קרא מִפֶּה, dictate
קרא שֵׁם, call, name, renowned
קֹרֵא, partridge
קרב, about, add, approach, *at* hand, bring, bring *near*, *cause to* come near, close, come, come *near*, come *together*, draw *near*, go, go *near*, hand, join, keep, make *an offering*, *make* draw *near*, meet, near, offer, present, remove, set *forth*
קרב אֶל, approach
קָרֵב, approach, connect, draw *near*, kinsfolk, kinsman, near, neighbor, next, next *of kin*, nigh, relative, soon
קְרֵב, approach, come, come *near*, draw *near*

קֶרֶב, among, body, entrails, heart, inner *part*, *inward* mind, inward *part*, midst, within
קְרָב, battle, war
קָרַב עַל, assail
קִרְבָה, draw *near*, near
קָרְבָּן, gift, offering
קַרְדֹּם, axe
קרה, attack, befall, come, come *true*, come *upon*, happen, lay *a beam*, make *a beam*, meet, select, summon
קרה לִפְנֵי, grant *success*
קָרָה, cold
קָרֶה, chance
קָרוֹב, warrior
קרח, make *a tonsure*, *make* bald, make *bald*
קָרֵחַ, baldhead, Kareah
קֶרַח, cold, crystal, frost, ice
קֹרַח, Korah
קֵרֵחַ, bald
קָרְחָה, bald, baldness, shave, tonsure
קָרְחִי, Korahite
קָרַחַת, back, *bald* head
קְרִי, contrary
קָרִיא, choose
קְרִיאָה, message
קִרְיָה, city, town
קְרִיּוֹת חֶצְרוֹן, Kerioth-hezron
קְרִיּוֹת, Kerioth
קִרְיַת אַרְבַּע, Kiriath-arba
קִרְיַת בַּעַל, Kiriath-baal
קִרְיַת חֻצוֹת, Kiriath-huzoth
קִרְיַת יְעָרִים, Kiriath-jearim
קִרְיַת סַנָּה, Kiriath-sannah
קִרְיַת סֵפֶר, Kiriath-sepher
קִרְיַת עָרִים, Kiriatharim
קִרְיָתַיִם, Kiriathaim
קרם, cover
קרן, horn, shine
קֶרֶן, hill, horn, might, power, ray, strength, tusk
קֶרֶן הַפּוּךְ, Keren-happuch
קַרְנַיִם, Karnaim
קרס, stoop
קֶרֶס, clasp, hook
קֵרֹס, Keros
קַרְסֹל, foot
קרע, cut *off*, cut *out*, enlarge, rend, slander, tear, tear *away*, tear *down*, tear *off*, tear *open*
קֶרַע, piece, rag
קרץ, compress, form, wink
קֶרֶץ, gadfly
קַרְקַע, bottom, floor
קַרְקַע, Karka
קַרְקֹר, Karkor
קרר, batter *down*, break *down*, keep *fresh*
קֶרֶשׁ, deck, frame
קֶרֶת, city, town
קַרְתָּה, Kartah
קַרְתָּן, Kartan
קַשְׂוָה, cup, flagon
קְשִׂיטָה, piece *of money*
קַשְׂקֶשֶׂת, mail, scale
קַשׁ, chaff, stubble
קִשֻּׁאָה, cucumber
קשב, attend, attentive, give *heed*, hearken, heed, incline, listen, listen *diligently*, make *attentive*
קַשָּׁב, attentive
קַשֻּׁב, attentive
קֶשֶׁב, diligently, heed, sign *of life*
קשה, cruel, fierce, *greatly* distress, hard, harden, heavy, make *heavy*, stiffen, *stubbornly* refuse
קשה עֹרֶף, stiff-necked, stubborn
קָשֶׁה, churlish, cruel, fierce, hard, hard *thing*, harshly, heavy, obstinate, roughly, stern, stiff, stubborn
קְשֵׁה עֹרֶף, stubborn
קְשֵׁה פָנִים, impudent
קשח, deal *cruelly*, harden
קֹשֶׁט, right
קְשִׁי, stubbornness
קִשְׁיוֹן, Kishion
קשר, bind, bind *up*, conspirator, conspire, join *together*, knit, make *a conspiracy*, plot, put *on a leash*, strong
קֶשֶׁר, conspiracy, revolt, treachery, treason
קִשֻּׁרִים, attire, sash
קשש, come *together*, gather, gather *straw*, gather *stubble*, hold *an assembly*
קֶשֶׁת, archer, bow, bowshot
קְשַׁת רוּחַ, *sorely* trouble

ראה, appear, approve, behold, cherish, choose, come, consider, decide, distinguish, enjoy, examine, experience, face, find, gaze, gleam, gloat, go, heed, here, learn, look, look *at one another*, look *one another*, look *upon*, make *an examination*, *make* see, *make* suffer, manifest, mark, observe, pay *heed*, perceive, present, provide, regard, remember, see, seem, seer, select, show, sight, spy, take *heed*, think, understand, view, visit, watch
ראה בְּ, behold
ראה בְּטוֹב, enjoy
ראה טוֹב, take *pleasure*
ראה נֶפֶשׁ, find
ראה פָּנִים, appear *before*, council, face *one another*
רֹאֶה, seer, vision
רְאוּבֵן, Reuben, Reubenite
רְאוּבֵנִי, Reuben, Reubenite
רְאוּמָה, Reumah
רֳאִי, gazingstock, see
רְאִי, mirror
רְאָיָה, Reaiah
רְאֵם, wild *ox*
רָאמוֹת, coral
ראשׁ, poor
רֵאשׁ, poverty
רֹאשׁ, beginning, bitterness, capital, captain, chief, chief *man*, company, count, end, every, fine, *fine* produce, first, front, full, gall, good, head, height, high, leader, leading *man*, officer, peak, poison, poisonous, *poisonous* fruit, *poisonous* weed, river, Rosh, sum, summit, temple, top, topmost, venom
רִאשָׁה, before
רֹאשָׁה, top
רִאשׁוֹן, before, beginning, bygone, chief, *chief* official, early, first, *first* month, *first* time, forefather, foremost, former, former *thing*, formerly, front, man *of old*, old, *old* son, *old* time, past
רֵאשִׁית, beginning, choice, choice *part*, *choice* portion, fine, first, *first* fruit, *first* issue, *first* season, good, main *part*, mainstay
רִאשֹׁנִי, first
רַב, abound, abundant, abundantly, archer, captain, *chief* officer, elder, enough, far, full, great, *great* multitude, greatly, high, increase, large, lavish, lie *heavy*, long, many, many *things*, mighty, more, much, multitude, numerous, official, populous, rich, severe, severely, sorely, suffice, thick, throng, vast, very, wide
רַב חֹבֵל, captain
רַב לָכֶם, end
רַב מָג, Rab-mag
רַב סָרִיס, Rab-saris
רַב עשה, multiply
רַב שָׁקֵה, Rab-shakeh
רַב כֹּחַ, violence
רֹב, abound, abundance, abundant, abundantly, all, common, countless, exceed, great, *great* number, *great* quantity, *great* store, greatness, hard, host, increase, length, long, many, mass, much, multitude, number, plentifully, plenty, quantity, very
רֹב מְאֹד מְאֹד, many
רבב, increase, manifold, many, *more* numerous, multiply, number, shoot, ten *thousands*
רְבָבָה, ten *thousands*
רִבְבוֹת אֲלָפִים, ten *thousand thousands*
רבד, deck
רבה, abound, abundance, abundantly, ask *much*, augment, authority, build *more*, continue, enlarge, exceedingly, expert, gather *much*, give *in abundance*, give *large*, great, greatly, grow *large*, grow *many*, grow *numerous*, grow *up*, heap, heap *up*, increase, large, lavish, long, magnify, make *abundant*, make *great*, make *many*, make *numerous*, many, more, much, much *more*, multiply, often, overmuch, pass, plenteous, rear, rich, rise, thoroughly, *very* numerous
רבה מְאֹד, *beyond* measure, exceedingly
רבה מִן, surpass
רַבָּה, Rabbah
רִבּוֹ, ten *thousands*, tens *of thousands*
רְבִיבִים, shower
רָבִיד, chain
רַבִּים, more
רְבִיעִי, fourth, square
רַבִּית, Rabbith
רבך, *mixed* offering, *well* mixed
רבך בלל, *well* mixed
רִבְלָה, Riblah
רבע, breed, foursquare, lie, lie *down*, square
רבע אֶל אַרְבַּעַת רִבְעִים, square
רֶבַע, direction, Reba, side
רֹבַע, fourth
רבץ, couch, crouch, lie, lie *down*, *make* lie down, rest, set, settle, sit
רֵבֶץ, fold, home, place *to lie down*
רִבְקָה, Rebekah
רֶגֶב, clod
רגז, angry, *come* trembling, *deeply* moved, disturb, enrage, *make* tremble, provoke, quake, quarrel, rage, shake, shudder, stir *up*, tremble, unrest, wroth
רַגָּז, tremble
רֹגֶז, rage, thunder, trouble, turmoil, wrath
רגל, *secret* messenger, slander, spy, spy *out*, teach *to walk*
רֶגֶל, close *behind*, foot, haunt, heel, leg, pace, step, time, traveler
רַגְלִי, foot, foot *soldier*, footman, man *on foot*
רֹגְלִים, Rogelim
רגם, stone
רֶגֶם, Regem
רֶגֶם מֶלֶךְ, Regem-melech
רִגְמָה, throng
רגן, murmur, whisperer
רגע, alight, find *ease*, give *rest*, harden, moment, rest, still, stir *up*, suddenly
רָגֵעַ, quiet
רֶגַע, moment, peace, time, while
רגשׁ, conspire
רֶגֶשׁ, fellowship
רִגְשָׁה, scheme
רדד, spread, subdue
רדה, charge, dominion, exercise *authority*, exercise *dominion*, lead, rule, scrape *out*, take, tread
רַדַּי, Raddai
רְדִיד, mantle, veil
רדם, *deep* sleep, fall *into a deep sleep*, fast *asleep*, lie *fast asleep*, lie *stunned*, sleep, sleeper
רדף, chase, drive *away*, drive *hard*, follow, follow *after*, go *in pursuit*, hunt, persecute, persecutor, press, pursue, pursuer, pursuit, put *to flight*, run *after*, subdue
רדף אַחַר, pursue
רדף אַחֲרֵי, follow, pursue, pursuer
רהב, disturb, importune, insolent
רַהַב, Rahab
רָהָב, proud
רֹהְגָּה, Rohgah
רַהַט, runnel, tress, trough
רָהִיט, rafter
רוד, break *loose*, free, overcome
רוֹדָנִים, Rodanim
רוה, drench, drink *one's fill*, feast, fill *with delight*, sate, satisfy, soak, take *one's fill*, water, water *abundantly*
רָוֶה, moist, water
רוח, find *relief*, refresh, spacious
רֶוַח, relief, space
רוּחַ, air, anger, blast, breath, cool, courage, mind, side, spirit, temper, thought, wind, windy
רְוָחָה, respite
רְוָיָה, overflow
רום, aloft, cease, contribute, direct, ease, exalt, extol, give, go *up*, great, haughty, high, hold *up*, levy, lift, lift *up*, lofty, loud, make *an offering*, *make* grow *tall*, make *on high*, mount *up*, offer, present, proud, raise, raise *high*, raise *up*, remove, rise, rise *high*, set *apart*, set *high*, set *up*, swear, take, take *away*, take *off*, take *up*, tall, triumph, triumphant, uplift
רום קוֹל, cry *aloud*, shout *aloud*
רום קֶרֶן, exalt
רוּם, high
רוּם, haughtiness, haughty, height, pride
רוֹמָה, haughtily
רוּמָה, Rumah
רוֹמָם, *high* praise
רוֹמֵמֻת, lift *up*
רוע, cry *aloud*, cry *out*, give *a shout*, make *a joyful noise*, raise *a shout*, raise *the battle shout*, shout, shout *aloud*, shout *for joy*, shout *in triumph*, sound *a call to battle*, sound *an alarm*, triumph
רוע רַע, cry *aloud*
רוץ, *bring* hastily, busy, carry *quickly*, charge, courier, dart, go *quickly*, guard, guardroom, hasten *to stretch out*, lust *after*, make *haste*, *make* run, race, run, runner
רושׁ, destitute, poor, poor *man*, pretend *to be poor*, suffer *want*
רוּת, Ruth
רזה, famish, grow *lean*
רָזֶה, lean, poor
רָזוֹן, prince, scant, *wasting* disease, *wasting* sickness
רְזוֹן, Rezon
רָזִי, pine *away*
רזם, flash
רזן, prince, ruler
רחב, *become* broad, broad, enlarge, give *a wide place*, give *room*, large, make *room*, make *wide*, open *wide*, rejoice, relieve, wide
רַחַב, broad *place*, expanse
רָחַב עַל, deride
רָחָב, ample, arrogant, broad, large, liberty, proud, Rahab, wide, *widely* spread
רֹחַב, breadth, broad, deep, distance, largeness, side, thick, thickness, wide, width
רְחַב יָדַיִם, broad
רְחַב נֶפֶשׁ, greedy *man*
רְחֹבוֹת, Rehoboth
רְחַבְיָה, Rehabiah
רְחַבְעָם, Rehoboam
רַחֲבַת יָדַיִם, large, wide
רְחֹבֹת עִיר, Rehoboth-Ir
רְחוֹב, market, market *place*, *open* square, *public* square, Rehob, square, street
רַחוּם, compassionate, merciful
רְחוּם, Rehum
רֵחַיִם, mill, millstone
רָחֵל, ewe, Rachel, sheep
רחם, compassion, compassion *upon*, find *mercy*, love, merciful, mercy, mercy *upon*, obtain *mercy*, obtain *pity*, pity, *show* mercy
רַחַם, Raham
רָחָם, *carrion* vulture
רֶחֶם, birth, maiden, womb
רַחֲמִים, compassion, heart, mercy, pity
רַחֲמָנִי, compassionate
רחף, flutter, move, shake
רחץ, bathe, cleanse, wash, wash *away*
רַחְצָה, wash
רחק, afar, *cause to* shun, drive *far*, enlarge, extend *far*, far, far *away*, far *off*, *go* far, go *far*, go *far away*, *good* way, *good* way *off*, keep *aloof*, keep *far*, old, put *far*, put *far away*, refrain, remove *far*, remove *far away*, remove *far off*, withdraw *far*
רחק מְאֹד, far *off*
רָחֹק, afar, afar *off*, distance, far, far *away*, far *off*, far-off, *great* while, long, space

רָחֵק, far
רחשׁ, overflow
רַחַת, shovel
רטב, wet
רָטֹב, thrive
רֶטֶט, panic
רטפשׁ, *become* fresh
רטשׁ, dash *in pieces*, slaughter
רִי, moisture
ריב, adversary, argue, avenge, bring *a charge*, bring *a complaint*, chide, complain, contend, court, defend, find *fault*, judgment, plead, plead *a case*, plead *a cause*, quarrel, remonstrate, strive, take *up a cause*, upbraid
רִיב, case, cause, contention, controversy, dispute, *disputed* case, faultfinding, feud, indictment, plead, quarrel, state *a case*, strife, strive *against*, suit
רִיב חֶרְפָּה, insult
רִיבַי, Ribai
ריח, accept, delight, smell, take *delight*, touch, use *as perfume*
רֵיחַ, fragrance, odor, scent, smell
רִיפָה, *crushed* grain, grain
רִיפַת, Riphath
ריק, cast *out*, draw, empty, lead *forth*, leave *unsatisfied*, pour *down*, pour *out*, unsheathe
רִיק, nought, vain, *vain* word
רֵיק, empty, satisfy, vulgar *fellow*, worthless, *worthless* pursuit
רֵיקָם, empty, empty-handed, wantonly, *without* cause
ריר, run
רִיר, slime, spittle
רֵישׁ, poverty
רַךְ, frail, inexperienced, penitent, soft, *soft* word, tender, tender *woman*, weak
רַךְ הַלֵּב, fainthearted
רַךְ לֵבָב, irresolute
רֹךְ, tender
רכב, carry, carry *in a chariot*, *cause to* ride, charioteer, conduct, *make* ride, mount, mount *a chariot*, pace, put *to the yoke*, ride, rider, set
רכב יָד, draw
רכב סוּס, horseman, man *on horseback*
רַכָּב, driver *of a chariot*, horseman
רֶכֶב, chariot, *chariot* horse, chariotry, rider, upper, *upper* millstone
רֶכֶב אִישׁ, rider
רֶכֶב סוּסִים, mounted *man*
רֵכָב, Rechab
רִכְבָּה, ride
רֵכָבִי, Rechabite
רֵכָה, Recah
רְכוּב, chariot
רְכוּשׁ, goods, livestock, possession, property, substance, supply
רָכִיל, gossip, slander, slanderer, talebearer
רכך, faint, make *faint*, soft, soften
רכל, merchant, trade, trader
רָכָל, Racal
רְכֻלָּה, merchandise, trade
רכס, bind
רֶכֶס, rough *place*
רֹכֶס, plot
רכשׁ, acquire, gain, gather
רֶכֶשׁ, steed, *swift* horse, *swift* steed
רָם, haughty
רָם, Ram
רמה, betray, deceive, throw, utter *deceit*
רָמָה, height, lofty *place*, Ramah
רִמָּה, maggot, worm
רֹמֵה קֶשֶׁת, archer
רִמּוֹן, pomegranate, pomegranate *tree*, Rimmon
רִמּוֹנוֹ, Rimmono
רָמוֹת, Ramoth
רֹמַח, lance, spear
רַמְיָה, Ramiah
רְמִיָּה, deceit, deceitful, deceitfully, idle, slack, slackness, slothful, slothful *man*, treacherous, treachery
רַמָּךְ, *royal* stud
רְמַלְיָהוּ, Remaliah
רמם, breed, bring *up*, decay, exalt, get *away*, mount *up*
רוֹמַמְתִּי עֶזֶר, Romamti-ezer
רִמֹּן פֶּרֶץ, Rimmon-perez
רמס, trample, trample *down*, trample *under foot*, trample *upon*, tread, tread *down*, tread *upon*
רמשׂ, crawl, creep, creep *forth*, move, teem
רֶמֶשׂ, crawling *thing*, creep, creeping *thing*, moving *thing*, reptile, teem *with things*
רָמַת הַמִּצְפֶּה, Ramath-mizpeh
רָמַת לְחִי, Ramath-lehi
רָמֹת גִּלְעָד, Ramoth-gilead
רֶמֶת, Remeth
רָמָתִי, Ramathite
רָמָתַיִם צוֹפִים, Ramathaim-zophim
רנה, rattle, sing
רִנָּה, cry, exult, *glad* shout, *glad* song, joy, *loud* singing, Rinnah, shout, shout *of gladness*, shout *of joy*, sing, song *of joy*
רנן, *cause to* sing *for joy*, cry *aloud*, cry *out*, *joyous* song, *joyously* praise, *make* shout *for joy*, praise, rejoice, shout, shout *for joy*, sing, sing *a song*, sing *aloud*, sing *for joy*
רְנָנָה, joyful, *joyful* cry, sing
רְנָנִים, ostrich
רִסָּה, Rissah
רְסִיס, drop, fragment
רֶסֶן, bridle, Resen, restraint
רסס, moisten
רַע, adversity, bad, calamity, cruel, deadly, destroy, disaster, downcast, evil, evil *man*, evildoer, gaunt, great, grievous, harm, heavy, hurt, ill, loathsome, malice, miserly, misfortune, plight, ruin, sad, severe, sore, trouble, unhappy, unpleasant, vile, wicked, wicked *deed*, wicked *man*, wickedness, woe, wrong
רַע בְּעַיִן, unwilling
רַע בְּעֵינַיִם, please
רַע מַרְאֶה, gaunt
רַע עַיִן, stingy
רַע תֹּאַר, gaunt
רֹעַ, bad, evil, sadness, wickedness, wrong
רֵעַ, another, companion, comrade, crash, fellow, friend, husband, lover, neighbor, opponent, other, paramour, shout, thought
רעב, famish, go *hungry*, hunger, hungry, suffer *hunger*
רָעָב, famine, hunger
רָעֵב, hunger-bitten, hungry, hungry *man*
רַעֲבוֹן, famine
רעד, tremble
רַעַד, tremble
רְעָדָה, tremble
רעה, *become a* shepherd, best *man*, care, companion, consume, eat, enjoy, feed, graze, herd, herdsman, keep, keep *company*, keeper, lead, make *friendship*, pasture, pasture *a flock*, rule, ruler, shepherd, tend
רעה צֹאן, shepherd
רָעָה, adversity, affliction, bad, calamity, crime, danger, disaster, discomfort, *do* evil, doom, evil, *evil* design, *evil* plight, *evil* purpose, evil *thing*, *evil* work, evil-doing, guilt, harm, hurt, mischief, misfortune, pain, ruin, sorrow, trouble, wicked *deed*, wicked *woman*, wickedness, wild, wretchedness, wrong
רָעָה מִן, bad
רֹעֶה בְּ, keep
רֵעָה, companion
רֵעֶה, friend
רְעוּ, Reu
רְעוּאֵל, Reuel
רְעוּת, another, mate, neighbor, strive *after*
רְעִי, pasture-fed
רֵעִי, Rei
רַעְיָה, love
רְעוּת, strive *after*
רַעְיוֹן לֵב, strain
רעל, *make* reel, prance
רַעַל, reel
רְעָלָה, scarf
רְעֵלָיָה, Reelaiah
רעם, convulse, irritate, roar, thunder
רַעַם, thunder
רַעְמָא, Raama
רַעְמָה, Raamah
רַעַמְיָה, Raamiah
רַעְמְסֵס, Raamses, Rameses
רַעֲנָן, evergreen, fresh, green
רעע, *act* wickedly, afflict, angry, bad, break, bring *calamity*, bring *evil*, consume, deal *harshly*, deal *ill*, deal *worse*, destroy, displease, *do a* wicked *thing*, *do* bad, *do* evil, *do* harm, *do* ill, *do* wickedly, *do* wrong, evil, evildoer, go *ill*, grudge, harm, hostile, hurt, make *evil*, mischief, sad, shatter, smart, suffer *harm*, treat *harshly*, treat *ill*, wicked, work *evil*
רעע בְּעֵינַיִם, displease, trouble
רעע בְּעֵנַיִם, displease
רעע עַיִן, grudge
רעף, drip, drop, drop *down*, shower
רעץ, crush, shatter
רעשׁ, *make* leap, *make* quake, quake, rock, shake, tremble, tremble stone, wave
רַעַשׁ, *battle* tumult, commotion, earthquake, fierceness, quake, rattle, rush, shake
רפא, *become* fresh, cure, heal, healer, make *wholesome*, mend, physician, repair, restore, weaken, wholesome
רָפָא, Rapha
רְפֻאָה, medicine
רִפְאוּת, heal
רְפָאִים, dead, giant, Rephaim, shade
רְפָאֵל, Rephael
רפד, refresh, spread
רפה, abate, *become* feeble, discourage, drop, fail, faint, fall *helpless*, feeble, forsake, give *respite*, grow *weak*, idle, leave, let *alone*, let *down*, let go, loose, refrain, relax, sink *down*, slack, stay, still, stop, wane, weak
רָפָה, Raphah
רָפֶה, weak
רְפֵה יָדַיִם, discourage
רָפוּא, Raphu
רֶפַח, Rephah
רְפִידָה, back
רְפִידִים, Rephidim
רְפָיָה, Rephaiah
רִפְיוֹן, feeble
רפס, foul, muddy
רַפְסֹדָה, raft
רפף, tremble
רפק, lean
רֶפֶשׁ, mire
רֶפֶת, stall
רצא, dart
רצד, look *with envy*
רצה, accept, acceptable, approve, delight, devotion, enjoy, favorable, favorite, friend, hold *dear*, make *amends*, pardon, please, pleasure, popular, receive *with favor*, reconcile, seek *favor*, take *delight*, take *pleasure*
רָצוֹן, accept, acceptable, acceptance, delight, desire, favor, find *acceptance*, *good* pleasure, please, pleasure, wantonness, will
רצח, kill, manslayer, murder, murderer, put *to death*, shatter, slay, slayer
רֶצַח, cry, *deadly* wound
רִצְיָא, Rizia
רְצִין, Rezin
רצע, bore *through*
רצף, wrought
רֶצֶף, Rezeph
רִצְפָּה, *mosaic* pavement, pavement
רִצְפָּה, *burning* coal, *hot* stone, Rizpah
רצץ, break, bruise, crush, discourage, inflict *cruelty*, oppress, struggle *together*
רַק, all, alone, except, however, lean, least, nevertheless, nothing, only, sheer, surely, thin, though, yet
רַק יָחִיד, only
רַק לֹא היה, none
רַק לְבַד, alone
רֹק, spit, spittle
רקב, rot
רָקָב, dry *rot*, rotten *thing*, rottenness
רִקָּבוֹן, rotten
רקד, bound, dance, leap, *make* skip, skip
רַקָּה, cheek, temple
רִקּוּחַ, perfume
רַקּוֹן, Rakkon
רִקּוּעַ, hammer
רַקּוֹת בָּשָׂר, thin
רקח, compound, perfumer, prepare
רַקָּח, perfumer
רֶקַח, spice
רֹקַח מַעֲשֶׂה, blend
רֹקַח מִרְקַחַת, blend
רַקָּחָה, perfumer
רָקִיעַ, firmament
רָקִיק, wafer
רקם, embroider, embroiderer, *intricately* wrought
רֶקֶם, Rakem, Rekem
רִקְמָה, *colored* stone, embroider, *embroidered* work, *many* colors, *many-colored* robe
רקע, beat, hammer, hammer *out*, overlay, spread *forth*, spread *out*, stamp, stamp *down*
רקק, spit
רַקַּת, Rakkath
רִשְׁיוֹן, grant
רשׁם, inscribe
רשׁע, *act* wickedly, condemn, confute, declare *guilty*, declare *wrong*, *do* wickedly, guilty, put *to the worse*, violate, wicked, wickedly
רָשָׁע, bad, guilty, guilty *man*, wicked, wicked *man*, wickedness, wrong
רֶשַׁע, evil, iniquity, wicked, wickedness
רִשְׁעָה, offense, wicked, wickedly, wickedness
רֶשֶׁף, *burning* heat, flash, plague, Resheph, thunderbolt
רשׁשׁ, destroy, shatter
רֶשֶׁת, net, network
רתח, bind, boil, *make* boil, turmoil
רתם, harness
רֹתֶם, broom, broom *tree*
רִתְמָה, Rithmah
רַתֻּקָה, chain
רְתֵת, tremble

שְׂאֹר, leaven
שְׂאֵת, dignity, eminence, majesty, pride, swell
שְׂבָכָה, checker, lattice, net, network, pitfall
שְׂבָם, Sebam
שִׂבְמָה, Sibmah
שׂבע, abundance, *become* weary, enough, feast, feed *to the full*, fill, full, get *enough*, get *one's fill*, give *in abundance*, gorge, more *than enough*, plenty, sate, satisfy, take *one's fill*, water *abundantly*
שׂבע מִן, enjoy
שָׂבָע, plenteous, plenty, surfeit
שָׂבֵעַ, fill, full, sate, satisfy
שֹׂבַע, abundance, fill, full, fulness, satisfy
שָׂבְעָה, abundant, enough, fill, satisfy, surfeit
שׂבר, hope, inspect, look, wait
שֵׂבֶר, hope
שׂגא, extol, flourish, make *great*
שׂגב, exalt, high, lift, lofty, protect, raise, raise *up*, safe, set *on high*
שׂגה, great, grow, increase
שְׂגוּב, Segub
שַׂגִּיא, great
שׂדד, harrow
שָׂדֶה, country, estate, field, forest, ground, land, mainland, open, *open* country, *open* field, region, soil, wild
שְׂדֵה כוֹבֵס, Fuller's *Field*
שָׂדַי, field
שִׂדִּים, Siddim
שְׂדֵרָה, plank, rank
שֶׂה, ewe, lamb, sheep

שֶׂה כְשָׂבִים, sheep
שֶׂה עִזִּים, goat
שָׂהֵד, vouch
שַׂהֲרוֹן, crescent
שׂוֹבֶךְ, *thick* branch
שׂוּךְ, hedge *up*, put *a hedge*
שׂוֹךְ, bundle
שׂוֹכָה, bundle
שׂוֹכֹה, Socoh
שׂוֹכוֹ, Soco
שׂוּכָתִים, Sucathite
שׂוּם, agree, appoint, assign, bear, bestow, bring, call, cast, change, charge, cherish, commit, consider, determine, do, establish, exact, fasten, form, give, give *heed*, grant, impute, inflict, keep, lay, lay *down*, lay *up*, leave, make, mark, ordain, order *aright*, pay *attention*, place, plan, plant, post, preserve, provide, put, put *in place*, regard, replace, reward, send *up*, serve, set, set *up*, show, stare, station, store, take, take *a position*, treat, turn, use, wield, wrought
שׂוּם בַּפּוּךְ, paint
שׂוּם דָּבָר, wrought
שׂוּם לְ, oppose
שׂוּם לֵב, consider, regard
שׂוּם סֵתֶר, disguise
שׂוּם עַיִן, look
שׂוּם עַל, require
שׂוּם עַל לֵב, resolve
שׂוּם קֵנֶץ, hunt
שׂוּם שֵׁם, name
שׂוֹרָה, row
שׂוּשׂ, delight, exult, glad, joy, joyfully, jubilant, make *mirth*, rejoice, take *delight*
שׂחה, flood, swim, swimmer
שׂחט, press
שָׂחִיף, panel
שׂחק, joke, laugh, laugh *to scorn*, make *merry*, make *sport*, merrymaker, mock, play, scorn, smile, sport
שְׂחֹק, derision, laughingstock, laughter, sport
שׂטה, go *astray*, turn *aside*, turn *away*
שׂטם, cherish *enmity against*, harass *sorely*, hate, persecute
שׂטן, accuse, accuser, adversary
שָׂטָן, accuser, adversary, Satan, withstand
שִׂטְנָה, accusation, Sitnah
שִׂיא, height
שׂיב, gray, *gray* haired
שֵׂיב, age
שֵׂיבָה, gray, *gray* hair, hoary, *hoary* head, *old* age
שׂיד, plaster
שִׂיד, lime, plaster
שׂיח, complain, consider, meditate, muse, talk, tell, utter *a complaint*
שִׂיחַ, anxiety, bush, complain, complaint, meditation, muse, plant, talk, thought, trouble
שִׂיחָה, meditation
שִׂים אֶל, take *back*
שִׂים בְּפֶה, tell
שִׂים לֵב, care
שִׂים פָּנִים עַל, expect
שֹׂךְ, booth
שֵׂךְ, prick
שֻׂכָּה, harpoon
שֶׂכוּ, Secu
שֶׂכְוִי, mist
שְׂכִיָה, Sachia
שְׂכִיָּה, craft
שַׂכִּין, knife
שָׂכִיר, hire, *hired* servant, hireling
שׂכך, cover, stir *up*
שׂכל, *act* wisely, consider, cross, deal *wisely*, give *heed*, give *wisdom*, *good* success, insight, instruct, make *judicious*, make *wise*, observe, ponder, prosper, prudent, regard, *show* skill, skill, skilled, study, succeed, success, successful, understand, understanding, wise, *wise* dealing, wise *man*
שֶׂכֶל, cunning, discretion, *good* sense, sense, skill, understand, understanding, wisdom

שׂכר, earn *a wage*, hire, hire *out*
שָׂכָר, cost, fare, hire, pay, reward, Sachar, wage
שֶׂכֶר, hire, reward
שְׂלָו, quail
שַׂלְמָא, Salma
שַׂלְמָה, cloak, clothes, clothing, garment
שַׂלְמוֹן, Salmon
שַׂלְמַי, Shalmai
שׂלק, burn, kindle
שׂמאל, *go* left, left *hand*, turn *left*, turn *to the left*
שְׂמֹאל, left, left *hand*, north, *north* side
שְׂמָאלִי, left, north
שׂמח, cheer, enjoy, find *enjoyment*, find *pleasure*, give *gladness*, glad, gladden, glee, happy, joy, joyful, make *glad*, make *joyful*, *make* rejoice, rejoice, welcome
שׂמח בְּ, enjoy
שָׂמֵחַ, cheerful, glad, happy, joyful, joyous, merrily, rejoice
שִׂמְחָה, delight, enjoyment, glad, gladness, joy, joyful, joyfulness, joyously, mirth, pleasure, rejoice, song *of joy*
שְׂמֵחַ לֵב, merry-hearted
שִׂמְחַת גִּיל, *exceeding* joy
שְׂמִיכָה, rug
שַׂמְלָה, Samlah
שִׂמְלָה, cloth, clothes, clothing, garb, garment, *good* clothes, mantle
שַׂמְלַי, Shamlai
שְׂמָמִית, lizard
שׂנא, adversary, dislike, enemy, enmity, foe, hate, hatred, loathe, spurn, unloved *woman*
שִׂנְאָה, hate, hatred
שְׂנִיר, Senir
שָׂעִיר, goat, *he* goat, *male* goat, satyr
שְׂעִיר עִזִּים, goat, *he* goat, *male* goat
שֵׂעִיר, Seir
שְׂעִירָה, Seirah
שְׂעִירִים, *gentle* rain
שְׂעִפִּים, thought
שׂער, afraid, dread, rush *like a whirlwind*, shock, shudder, sweep, sweep *away*, tempest
שַׂעַר, horror, tempest
שֵׂעָר, hairy
שֵׂעָר, hair, haircloth, hairy
שַׂעֲרָה, hair
שְׂעָרָה, storm, tempest
שְׂעֹרָה, barley
שְׂעֹרִים, Seorim
שָׂפָה, bank, binding, border, brim, brink, edge, full *of talk*, language, lip, mouth, prate, shore, speak, speech, talk, voice, word
שׂפח, smite *with a scab*
שָׂפָם, beard, lip, *upper* lip
שׂפק, suffice
שֶׂפֶק, scoff
שֵׂפֶק, sufficiency
שְׂפַת הַיָּם, seashore
שְׂפַת לָשׁוֹן, talk
שַׂק, sack, sackcloth
שׂקד, bind
שׂקר, glance *wantonly*
שַׂר, captain, charge, chief, commander, general, governor, head, keeper, lead, leader, lord, officer, official, prince, ruler, steward
שַׂר מֵאוֹת, captain
שַׂר מְנוּחָה, quartermaster
שַׂר מִסִּים, taskmaster
שַׂר סְכִים, Sar-sechim
שַׂר צְבָאוֹת, commander
שַׂרְאֶצֶר, Sharezer
שׂרג, fasten *together*, knit *together*
שׂרד, remain
שֶׂרֶד, pencil
שְׂרָד, *finely* wrought, work *finely*
שׂרה, strive
שָׂרָה, lady, princess, queen, Sarah
שְׂרוּג, Serug
שְׂרוֹךְ, thong
שֶׂרַח, Serah

שׂרט, hurt, make *a cutting*
שֶׂרֶט, cutting
שָׂרֶטֶת, cutting
שָׂרַי, Sarai
שָׂרִיג, branch
שָׂרִיד, leave, remain, remnant, Sarid, survive, survivor
שְׂרָיָה, Seraiah
שִׂרְיֹן, Sirion
שָׂרִיק, comb
שׂרך, interlace
שׂרע, limb *too long*, stretch, *too* long
שַׂרְעַפִּים, care, thought
שׂרף, burn, burn *down*, burned *one*, consume, kindle, make *a fire*
שׂרף בָּאֵשׁ, burn *up*
שָׂרָף, fiery, Saraph, seraphim, serpent
שְׂרֵפָה, blaze, burn, *burnt-out* waste, fire
שָׂרֹק, branch, sorrel
שֹׂרֵק, *choice* vine, Sorek
שֹׂרֵקָה, *choice* vine
שׂרר, lord, make *a prince*, rule, set *up a prince*
שָׂשׂוֹן, gladness, joy, mirth
שׂתם, shut *out*
שׂתר, break *out*

שֶׁ, order, see
שֶׁ שָׁם, where
שׁאב, draw, draw *out*, draw *water*, drawer
שׁאג, groan, roar
שְׁאָגָה, groan, roar
שׁאה, desolate, gaze, lie *waste*, *make* crash, roar, turn
שָׁאוּל, Saul, Shaul
שְׁאוֹל, grave, Sheol
שָׁאוּלִי, Shaulite
שָׁאוֹן, clamor, noise, noisy *one*, roar, throng, tumult, tumult *of war*, uproar
שְׁאָט, contempt
שְׁאָט, malice
שְׁאִיָּה, ruins
שׁאל, ask, beg, borrow, consult, crave, demand, desire, inquire, lend, make *a petition*, make *a request*, pray, question, request, require, seek
שׁאל אוֹב, medium
שׁאל לְשָׁלוֹם, greet, salute
שְׁאָל, Sheal
שְׁאֵלָה, ask, loan, petition, request
שְׁאַלְתִּיאֵל, Shealtiel
שׁאן, ease
שַׁאֲנָן, arrogance, ease, quiet
שׁאף, crush, hasten, long, pant, pant *after*, sniff, trample *upon*
שׁאר, escape, keep, leave, leave *behind*, remain, remnant, rest, spare, survive, survivor
שׁאר מִן, bereft
שְׁאָר, other, remainder, remnant, rest, survive
שְׁאָר יָשׁוּב, Shear-jashub
שְׁאֵר, body, flesh, food, kin, kinsman, kinswoman, meat, *near* kin
שְׁאֵר אָב, *near* kinswoman
שְׁאֵר אֵם, *near* kinswoman
שְׁאֵר בָּשָׂר, *near* kinsman, near *of kin*
שֶׁאֱרָה, Sheerah
שְׁאֵרִית, escape, leave, remain, remnant, residue, rest, survive
שֵׁאת, devastation
שְׁבָא, Sabean, Sheba
שְׁבָאִי, Sabean
שְׁבָבִים, piece
שׁבה, captive, captor, capture, carry *away*, carry *away captive*, carry *captive*, carry *off*, drive *away*, hold *captive*, lead *away*, lead *captive*, take, take *away captive*, take *captive*
שְׁבוֹ, agate
שְׁבוּאֵל, Shebuel, Shubael
שְׁבוּל, road
שָׁבוּעַ, feast *of weeks*, week
שְׁבוּעָה, curse, oath, *sworn* promise

שׁבח, commend, extol, glory, hold *quietly*, laud, praise, still
שַׁבֵּחַ מִן, think *more fortunate*
שְׁבָט, Shebat
שֵׁבֶט, bough, correction, dart, *herdsman's* staff, rod, scepter, staff, tribal, tribe
שְׁבִי, captive
שֹׁבַי, Shobai
שֹׁבִי, Shobi
שֶׁבִי, captive, captivity, exile, take
שְׁבִיב, flame
שִׁבְיָה, captive, captivity
שְׁבִיל, path
שְׁבִים לְ, again
שְׁבִיס, headband
שְׁבִיעִי, seventh
שְׁבִית, captive, fortune
שֹׁבֶל, robe
שַׁבְּלוּל, snail
שִׁבֹּלֶת, branch, ear, ear *of grain*, flood, grain, Shibboleth
שִׁבֹּלֶת מַיִם, flood
שֶׁבְנָא, Shebna
שֶׁבְנָה, Shebnah
שְׁבַנְיָהוּ, Shebaniah
שׁבע, adjure, charge *with an oath*, give *an oath*, lay *an oath upon*, *make* swear, *make* take *an oath*, plight *troth*, put *under oath*, swear, swear *allegiance*, swear *an oath*, take *an oath*, utter *an oath*
שׁבע בְּ, use *a name for a curse*
שֶׁבַע, seven, seven *men*, seven *times*, sevenfold, seventh, Sheba
שֶׁבַע וְעֶשֶׂר, seventeen
שְׁבַע עֶשְׂרֵה, seventeen, seventeenth
שִׁבְעָה, Shibah
שָׁבֻעִים יָמִים, week
שִׁבְעִים, threescore *and ten*
שִׁבְעִים וְשִׁבְעָה, seventy-sevenfold
שִׁבְעָתַיִם, seven *times*, sevenfold
שׁבץ, set *in filigree*, weave *in checker work*
שָׁבָץ, anguish
שׁבר, abolish, break, break *down*, break *in pieces*, break *up*, bring *to birth*, buy, buy *grain*, cripple, crush, dash *in pieces*, destroy, disable, hurt, lie *broken*, maim, prescribe, purchase, quench, sell, shatter, smite, tear, undo, wound, wreck
שׁבר לֵב, brokenhearted
שֶׁבֶר, anguish, breach, break, crash, destruction, disaster, fracture, grain, hurt, injure, interpretation, ruin, Sheber, wound
שִׁבָּרוֹן, break, destruction
שְׁבָרִים, Shebarim
שׁבת, banish, bring *to an end*, *cause to* cease, cease, come *to an end*, cut *off*, depose, destroy, disappear, keep *sabbath*, lacking, leave *without*, *make* cease, *make* rest, *make* stop, put *a stop*, put *an end*, put *away*, remove, rest, still, stop
שׁבת לְבִלְתִּי, *make* cease
שׁבת מִן, quit
שׁבת מִפְּנֵי, hear *no more*
שַׁבָּת, sabbath, week
שֶׁבֶת, dwelling, seat
שַׁבָּתוֹן, day *of solemn rest*, *solemn* rest
שַׁבְּתַי, Shabbethai
שׁגג, commit *an error*, commit *unwittingly*, deceive, go *astray*
שְׁגָגָה, error, mistake
שׁגה, commit *sin unwittingly*, deceiver, err, infatuate, lead *astray*, lost, mislead, reel, scatter, sin *through error*, stray, wander
שָׁגֵה, Shagee
שׁגח, gaze, look *forth*, stare
שְׁגִיאָה, error
שִׁגָּיוֹן, Shiggaion
שִׁגְיֹנוֹת, Shigionoth
שׁגל, ravish
שֵׁגָל, queen
שׁגע, drive *mad*, mad, mad *fellow*, madman, play *the madman*

שגעון, madness
שגר, increase
שד, breast
שד, breast, desolation, despoil, destroy, destruction, devastation, oppression, robbery, violence
שד, demon
שדד, bring *to nought*, dead, desolate, despoil, destroy, destroyer, devastator, *do* violence, lay *waste*, plunderer, robber, ruin, waste
שדי, almighty
שדיאור, Shedeur
שדמה, field
שדף, blight
שדפה, blight
שדפון, blast, blight
שדרך, Shadrach
שהם, beryl, onyx, Shoham
שוא, delusion, delusive, *delusive* vision, destruction, emptiness, empty, *empty* cry, *empty* word, evil, false, *false* god, falsehood, lie, nought, vain, vanity, worthless
שוא, ravage
שוא, Sheva
שואה, crash, destroy, ruin, storm, waste
שוב, again, again *and again*, answer, avenge, avert, back, backslide, bring, bring *again*, bring *back*, bring *home*, call, carry *back*, *cause to* return, come, come *again*, come *back*, deliver, deliver *again*, depart, draw *back*, drive, end, fro, further, get, get *back*, get *up again*, give, give *back*, go, go *again*, go *back*, go *home*, go *in the other direction*, hinder, hold *back*, lay, lead *astray*, *make* fall *back*, make *restitution*, make *return*, *make* turn, *make* turn *back*, *no* thought, once *more*, pass *again*, past, pay, pay *back*, put, put *again*, put *back*, recall, recede, recompense, recover, refresh, refund, render, repay, repent, replace, reply, report, requite, rescue, restore, restore *again*, restorer, restrain, return, revert, revive, revoke, reward, send *back*, sheathe, take, take *back*, turn, turn *about*, turn *again*, turn *around*, turn *aside*, turn *away*, turn *back*, withdraw, withhold
שוב אחור, withdraw
שוב אל, revive
שוב אל לב, consider
שוב את הפנים, repulse
שוב אתה, come *back again*
שוב גמול ל, requite
שוב דבר, answer, reply, report
שוב ובוא, go *back*
שוב ובוא, come *back*, go *again*
שוב ובנה, rebuild
שוב ונחם, repent
שוב ועשה, rework
שוב יד על, assail
שוב מלה, answer
שוב פנים, refuse
שובב, backslide, faithless, Shobab
שובב, faithless
שובך, Shobach
שובל, Shobal
שובק, Shobek
שוה, alike, bestow, calm, compare, *do one* good, keep, level, like, liken, make, make *equal*, profit, requite, set, yield
שוה, Shaveh
שוה קריתים, Shaveh-kiriathaim
שוח, bow *down*, sink *down*
שוח, Shuah
שוחה, pit, Shuhah
שוחי, Shuhite
שוחם, Shuham
שוחמי, Shuhamite
שוט, despise, go *about*, go *through*, go *to and fro*, range, rower, run *to and fro*, treat *with contempt*
שוט, disaster, scourge, whip
שול, skirt, train
שולל, strip
שולמית, Shulammite

שום, garlic
שוני, Shuni, Shunite
שונם, Shunem
שונמי, Shunammite
שוע, call, call *aloud*, call *for help*, cry, cry *for help*
שוע, honorable, rich, Shoa, shout
שוע, cry, cry *for help*, Shua
שועא, Shua
שועה, cry, cry *for help*
שועל, fox, jackal, Shual
שוף, bruise, cover, crush
שופך, Shophach
שופמי, Shuphamite
שוק, overflow, water
שוק, hip, leg, thigh
שוק, street
שור, behold, depart, journey, lie *in wait*, look *after*, lurk, perceive, regard, see, travel
שור, bull, cattle, cow, herd, ox
שור, Shur, wall
שורה, *olive* row, vine-row
שורר, enemy
שושא, Shavsha
שושן, Lilies
שושן, lily, Shushan, Susa
שותלח, Shuthelah
שזף, scorch, see
שזר, twine
שח עינים, lowly
שחד, bribe, offer *a bribe*
שחד, bribe, bribery, gift, present, reward
שחה, bow, bow *down*, *do* obeisance, fall, fall *down*, implore, make *obeisance*, prostrate, weigh *down*, worship
שחור, soot
שחות, pit
שחח, bend *low*, bow, bow *down*, bring *down*, bring *low*, cast *down*, crouch, humble, low, prostrate, sink *down*, sink *low*
שחט, beat, deadly, kill, offer, slaughter, slay
שחיטה, kill
שחין, boil, sore
שחיס, spring *of the same*
שחית, destruction, pit
שחל, lion
שחלת, onycha
שחף, sea *gull*
שחפת, consumption
שחץ, pride, proud
שחצומה, Shahazumah
שחק, beat, beat *fine*, wear *away*
שחק, cloud, dust, sky
שחר, diligent, seek, seek *diligently*, seek *eagerly*, seek *earnestly*, turn *black*
שחר, blackness, dawn, day, morning
שחר, black, dark
שחרות, dawn *of life*
שחרחר, swarthy
שחריה, Shehariah
שחרים, Shaharaim
שחת, *act* corruptly, batter, behave *badly*, blemish, cast *off*, *cause* destruction, corrupt, deal *corruptly*, destroy, destroyer, destruction, fell, follow *corrupt practices*, go *to ruin*, impair, lay *in ruins*, make *a destruction*, make *corrupt*, mar, pollute, raider, ravage, ravager, raven, ruin, slay, spill, spoil, waste, work *destruction*
שחת, hole, pit
שטה, acacia
שטח, enlarge, scatter, spread, spread *out*
שטט, scourge
שטים, Shittim
שטף, deluge, drown, flow, overflow, overwhelm, plunge *headlong*, rinse, sweep *away*, sweep *over*, torrential, wash, wash *away*, wash *off*
שטף, flood, overwhelm, rush, torrent
שטר, foreman, officer, official, taskmaster
שטרי, Shitrai
שי, gift
שיאון, Shion

שיבה, stay
שיזא, Shiza
שיחה, pit, pitfall
שיחור, Nile, Shihor
שיחור לבנת, Shihor-libnath
שיט, oar
שילני, Shilonite
שימון, Shimon
שין, urine
שיר, *female* singer, hoot, *male* singer, *man* singer, sing, singer, singing *man*, singing *woman*
שיר, music, musical, sing, sing *a song*, song
שירה, song
שישא, Shisha
שישק, Shishak
שית, apply, appoint, bear, bring, give, harbor, join, lay, make, place, prepare, put, set, set *up*, show, stay, take, take *a stand*
שית לב, consider, consider *well*, give *heed*
שית מן, let *alone*
שית על, close, punish
שית שכם, put *to flight*
שית, brier, thorn
שית, dress, garment
שכב, go *to bed*, lay, lay *low*, lie, lie *down*, lie *still*, lodge, *make* lie *down*, rest, sleep, stay, take *a rest*, tilt
שכבת זרע, carnally, semen
שכה, lusty
שכול, bereave, childless, rob
שכול, bereave
שכול, forlorn, loss *of a child*
שכח, bring *to an end*, forget, lose, *make* forget, pass
שכח, forget
שכך, abate, *make* cease, subside
שכל, bereave, bereave *of child*, bereft, cast, cast *one's young*, childless, fail *to bear*, make *childless*, miscarriage, miscarry, ravage, rob *of a child*, unfruitful
שכלים, time *of bereavement*
שכם, arise *early*, eager, early, go *early*, go *out early*, morning, persistently, rise *early*, rise *up early*, start *early*, urgently
שכם, Shechem
שכם, accord, back, *mountain* slope, Shechem, shoulder
שכמי, Shechemite
שכן, abide, *cause to* settle, couch, dwell, dwell *secure*, dweller, dwelling, encamp, habitation, inhabit, inhabitant, lay, live, make *a dwelling*, make *a habitation*, *make* dwell, nest, place, remain, rest, set *up*, settle, settle *down*, slumber, stand, stay
שכן באהלים, caravan
שכן, inhabitant, neighbor, *woman of the* neighborhood
שכניהו, Shecaniah
שכר, *become* drunk, drink *deeply*, drunk, drunken, fill, make *drunk*, make *drunken*, merry
שכר, drunk, drunkard, drunken, drunken *man*, drunken *woman*
שכר, *strong* drink
שכרון, drunk, drunkenness
שכרון, Shikkeron
של, account
שלאנן, ease
שלב, fit *together*
שלבים, frame
שלג, snow *fall*
שלג, snow
שלה, deceive, ease, negligent, peace, prosper, take *away*, thrive
שלה, Shelah
שלהבת, flame
שלהבתיה, *most vehement* flame
שלו, carefree, ease, peaceful, prosperity, rest, secure
שלו, prosperity
שלו, Shiloh
שלוה, complacence, prosperity, prosperous, quiet, security

שלוחה, shoot
שלוחים, dowry, *parting* gift, send *away*
שלום, Shallum
שלום, fare, favorable, friend, friendship, good, health, peace, peaceably, peaceful, prosperity, rest *assured*, safe, safely, safety, terms *of peace*, trust, visit, weal, welfare, well, whole, wholly
שלום, bribe, recompense
שלח, cast, cast *off*, cast *out*, charge, deliver, demand, depart, desert, dismiss, dispatch, divorce, drive, drive *forth*, escort *over*, exile, give, give *free rein*, give *over*, go, go *free*, grow *long*, lay, leave, let *down*, let *loose*, loose, *make* gush *forth*, point, put, put *away*, put *forth*, put *out*, range *free*, reach, reach *out*, remove, rush *forth*, scatter, send, send *abroad*, send *away*, send *back*, send *forth*, send *home*, send *off*, send *out*, send *word*, set, *set* free, set *on the way*, shoot, shoot *forth*, sow, spread, stretch *forth*, stretch *out*
שלח אל, direct
שלח יד, loot
שלח, Shelah, shoot, sword, weapon
שלח, Shiloah
שלחי, Shilhi
שלחים, Shilhim
שלחן, table
שלט, get *dominion*, get *mastery*, give *power*, lord, master
שלט, shield, *small* shield
שלטון, authority, supreme
שליה, afterbirth
שליט, brazen, governor, power, ruler
שליש, aide, captain, *full* measure, instrument *of music*, officer
שלישי, third, *third* day, *third* time, three, thrice
שלך, cast, cast *away*, cast *down*, cast *forth*, cast *off*, cast *out*, drop, hurl, *make* drop, overthrow, sprinkle, throw, throw *away*, throw *down*, throw *out*, thrust *back*, thrust *down*
שלך מנגד, risk
שלך, cormorant
שלכת, fell, Shallecheth
שלל, despoil, make *a prey*, make *a spoil*, plunder, pull *out*, seize, strip *of spoil*, take *spoil*
שלל שלל, despoil
שלל, booty, gain, goods, plunder, prize *of war*, spoil
שלם, bring *to an end*, complete, dedicated *one*, end, finish, friend, fulfil, give *back*, make *be at peace*, make *good*, make *peace*, make *requital*, make *restitution*, pay, pay *back*, peace, peaceable, perform, recompense, render, repay, requite, restore, return, reward, succeed
שלם, blameless, complete, friendly, full, just, prepare, safely, Salem, strong, unhewn, whole, *wholly* true
שלם, peace, *peace* offering
שלם, Shillem
שלמה, recompense
שלמה, Solomon
שלמות, Shelomoth
שלמי, Shillemite
שלמי, Shelomi
שלמיאל, Shelumiel
שלמיהו, Shelemiah
שלמית, Shelomith
שלמן, Shalman
שלמן, gift
שלמנאסר, Shalmaneser
שלני, Shelanite
שלף, draw, draw *forth*, draw *off*, draw *out*, grow *up*
שלף, Sheleph
שלש, divide *into three parts*, do *a third* time, third, three, three *years old*, threefold
שלש, measure
שלש, third, three, three *things*, three *times*
שלש, Shelesh
שלש, third, *third* generation
שלש עשרה, thirteen, thirteenth
שלשה, Shalishah

שִׁלְשָׁה, Shilshah
שְׁאַלְתִּיאֵל, Shealtiel
שָׁם, among *whom*, here, place, thence, there, thither, up *there*, where, wherever
שֵׁם, byword, call, fame, famous, honor, memorial, name, presence, renown, Shem, term, *well* known
שַׁמָּא, Shamma
שֶׁמְאֵבֶר, Shemeber
שִׁמְאָה, Shimeeah
שִׁמְאָם, Shimeam
שַׁמְגַּר, Shamgar
שמד, demolish, destroy, destruction, doom *to destruction*, exterminate, perish, wipe *out*
שֶׁמֶד, Shemed
שַׁמָּה, appall, desolate, desolation, dismay, horror, make *desolate*, object *of astonishment*, Shammah, terror, waste
שָׁמָּה, thither, wherever
שַׁמְהוּת, Shamhuth
שְׁמוּאֵל, Samuel, Shemuel
שַׁמּוּעַ, Shammua
שְׁמוּעָה, byword, hear, message, news, report, rumor, tidings
שַׁמּוֹת, Shammoth
שמט, give *over*, loosen, release, rest, stumble, throw *down*
שְׁמִטָּה, release
שַׁמַּי, Shammai
שְׁמֵי הַשָּׁמַיִם, *high* heaven
שְׁמִידָע, Shemida
שְׁמִידָעִי, Shemidaite
שָׁמַיִם, air, heaven, sky
שְׁמִינִי, eighth
שְׁמִינִית, Sheminith
שָׁמִיר, adamant, brier, diamond, Shamir, thorn
שְׁמִירָמוֹת, Shemiramoth
שמם, appall, astonish, *become* desolate, bring *desolation upon*, desolate, desolate *one*, desolate *place*, desolate *woman*, desolation, desolator, destroy, devastate, devastation, horrify, lay *desolate*, lay *waste*, lie *desolate*, lie *waste*, look *in dismay*, make *a desolation*, *make* appalled, make *desolate*, overwhelm, perish, ruin, ruins, strip, stun, terrify, wonder
שָׁמֵם, desolate
שְׁמָמָה, desolate, desolation, despair, lay *waste*, ruins, waste
שִׁמָּמוֹן, dismay
שמן, *become* fat, grow *fat*, make *fat*, wax *fat*
שֹׁמֶן, fatness
שָׁמֵן, fat, rich, strong
שֶׁמֶן חֵלֶק, live *in luxury*
שֶׁמֶן, *anointing* oil, fat *thing*, oil, ointment, rich
שְׁמֹנֶה, eight, eighth
שְׁמֹנֶה עֶשְׂרֵה, eighteen, eighteenth
שְׁמֹנִים, fourscore
שמע, agree, announce, attentively, *cause to* hear, comprehend, declare, discern, give *ear*, give *heed*, hear, hearken, heed, learn, listen, make *a proclamation*, *make* hear, *make* known, make *known*, make *loud music*, music, obedient, obey, overhear, proclaim, publish, report, show, show *forth*, sing, sound, summon, tell, understand, utter, wail, witness
שמע אֹזֶן, hear
שמע בְּקוֹל, hearken, listen
שמע לְקֹל, obey
שמע עַל, welcome
שָׁמָע, Shama
שֶׁמַע, Shema, sound
שֵׁמַע, fame, report
שֶׁמַע, Shema
שֹׁמַע, fame, hear, news, report, rumor, tidings
שִׁמְעָא, Shimea
שִׁמְעָה, Shimeah
שְׁמָעָה, Shemaah
שִׁמְעוֹן, Shimeon, Simeon, Simeonite
שִׁמְעוֹנִי, Simeon, Simeonite
שִׁמְעִי, Shimei, Shimeite
שְׁמַעְיָהוּ, Shemaiah
שִׁמְעָת, Shimeath
שִׁמְעָתִים, Shimeathite
שֵׁמֶץ, small, whisper
שִׁמְצָה, shame
שמר, attend, avoid, besiege, beware, care, careful, charge, cherish, give *heed*, guard, heed, herd, hold *fast*, keep, keep *charge*, keep *in mind*, keep *watch*, keeper, mark, obey, observe, pay *regard*, perform, preserve, protect, regard, save, secure, see, show, spare, spy, take *care*, take *heed*, wait, watch, watch *over*, watchman
שמר לְרֹאשׁ, bodyguard
שמר מִשְׁמֶרֶת, attend, charge
שֶׁמֶר, dreg, lees, Shemer, wine *on the lees*
שָׁמֶר, watch
שֹׁמֵר, Shomer
שְׁמֻרָה, eyelid
שִׁמְרוֹן, Shimron
שִׁמְרוֹן מְראוֹן, Shimron-meron
שֹׁמְרוֹן, Samaria
שִׁמְרִי, Shimri
שְׁמַרְיָהוּ, Shemariah
שִׁמְרִית, Shimrith
שִׁמְרֹנִי, Shimronite
שֹׁמְרֹנִי, Samaritan
שִׁמְרָת, Shimrath
שֶׁמֶשׁ, pinnacle, sun
שִׁמְשׁוֹן, Samson
שִׁמְשַׁי, Shimshai
שַׁמְשְׁרַי, Shamsherai
שֻׁמָתִי, Shumathite
שֵׁן, crag, ivory, prong, tooth
שִׁנְאָב, Shinab
שִׁנְאָן, thousand
שֶׁנְאַצַּר, Shenazzar
שנה, advance, again, alter, change, different, disguise, *do a second* time, *do* again, double, pervert, put *off*, repeat, second, twice
שנה טַעַם, feign *madness*
שָׁנָה, year
שֵׁנָה, *like a* dream, sleep
שֶׁנְהַבִּים, ivory
שָׁנִי, scarlet, *scarlet* thread
שְׁנִי תוֹלַעַת, scarlet *stuff*
שֵׁנִי, after, again, another, follow, more, next, other, second, *second* time
שְׁנֵיהֶם, one *another*
שְׁנַיִם, both, couple, double, *double* portion, pair, second, twice, two, two *men*, two *sons*, two *things*
שְׁנֵים עָשָׂר, twelfth, twelve
שְׁנִינָה, byword, taunt
שנן, make *sharp*, prick, sharp, teach *diligently*, whet
שנס, gird *up*
שִׁנְעָר, Shinar
שסה, despoil, get *spoil*, plunder, plunderer, rob, spoiler, strip
שסס, despoil, plunder
שסע, cloven, tear, tear *asunder*
שסע שֶׁסַע, cloven-footed
שסע שֶׁסַע פַּרְסָה, cloven-footed
שסף, hew *in pieces*
שעה, dismay, look, look *away*, pay *regard*, regard, shut
שַׁעֲטָה, stamp
שַׁעַטְנֵז, mingled *stuff*, stuff
שֹׁעַל, handful, hollow *of hand*
שַׁעַלְבִים, Shaalbim
שַׁעַלַבִּין, Shaalabbin
שַׁעַלְבֹנִי, Shaalbon
שַׁעֲלִים, Shaalim
שען, lean, rely, rest, support
שעע, blind, cheer, close, dandle, delight, find *delight*, play
שַׁעַף, Shaaph
שער, reckon
שַׁעַר, city, *city* gate, gate, gateway, town
שַׁעַר אֶפְרַיִם, Ephraim *Gate*, *Gate of* Ephraim
שַׁעַר בִּנְיָמִין, Benjamin *Gate*, *Gate of* Benjamin
שַׁעַר הָאַשְׁפֹּת, Dung *Gate*
שַׁעַר הַגַּיְא, Valley *Gate*
שַׁעַר הַדָּגִים, Fish *Gate*
שַׁעַר הַיְשָׁנָה, Old *Gate*
שַׁעַר הַמִּזְרָח, East *Gate*
שַׁעַר הַמַּטָּרָה, *Gate of the* Guard
שַׁעַר הַמַּיִם, Water *Gate*
שַׁעַר הַמִּפְקָד, Muster *Gate*
שַׁעַר הַסּוּסִים, Horse *Gate*
שַׁעַר הָעַיִן, Fountain *Gate*
שַׁעַר הַפִּנָּה, Corner *Gate*
שַׁעַר הַצֹּאן, Sheep *Gate*
שֹׁעָר, vile
שֹׁעֵר, gatekeeper, keeper *of the gate*
שֹׁעֵר הַסִּפִּים, gatekeeper
שַׁעֲרוּרָה, horrible *thing*
שַׁעֲרוּרִיָּה, horrible *thing*
שְׁעַרְיָה, Sheariah
שַׁעֲרַיִם, Shaaraim
שַׁעַשְׁגַּז, Shaashgaz
שַׁעֲשֻׁעִים, darling, delight, pleasant
שפה, bare, set, stick *out*
שְׁפוֹ, Shepho
שְׁפוֹט, judgment
שְׁפוּפָם, Shephupham
שְׁפוּפָן, Shephuphan
שְׁפוֹת, cheese
שִׁפְחָה, *female* slave, handmaid, maid, maidservant, servant, slave, *woman* slave
שפט, accuser, administer *justice*, argue, argument, bring *to judgment*, bring *to trial*, condemn, decide, defend, defend *the cause*, deliver, *do* justice, enter *into judgment*, execute *judgment*, give *judgment*, give *justice*, give *sentence*, go *to law*, govern, hold *judgment*, judge, judgment, pass *judgment*, play *the judge*, plead, pronounce *judgment*, punish, *render* judgment, rule, ruler, try, vindicate
שָׁפָט, Shaphat
שֶׁפֶט, act *of judgment*, condemnation, judgment
שְׁפַטְיָהוּ, Shephatiah
שִׁפְטָן, Shiphtan
שְׁפִי, *bare* height, Shephi
שֻׁפִּים, Shuppim
שְׁפִיפֹן, viper
שָׁפִיר, Shaphir
שפך, cast *up*, gush *out*, lavish, lie *scattered*, outpoured, outpouring, pour, pour *out*, pour *over*, shed, shedder, slip, throw *up*
שֶׁפֶךְ, pour *out*
שָׁפְכָה, *male* member
שפל, abase, bring *down*, bring *low*, cast, deep, far *down*, humble, lay *low*, lowly, make *low*, put *down*, put *low*, send *down*
שָׁפָל, abase, deep, humble, low, lowly
שֵׁפֶל, *low* estate, low *place*
שְׁפֵלָה, lowland, Shephelah
שִׁפְלוּת יָדַיִם, indolence
שָׁפָם, Shapham
שְׁפָם, Shepham
שִׁפְמוֹת, Siphmoth
שִׁפְמִי, Shiphmite
שָׁפָן, badger, rock *badger*, Shaphan
שֶׁפַע, affluence
שִׁפְעָה, company, flood, many, multitude
שִׁפְעִי, Shiphi
שפר, goodly
שֶׁפֶר, comely, Shepher
שׁוֹפָר, horn, trumpet, *trumpet* blast
שִׁפְרָה, fair, Shiphrah
שַׁפְרִיר, *royal* canopy
שפת, lay, ordain, set
שְׁפַתַּיִם, sheepfold
שְׁפַתַּיִם, hook
שֶׁצֶף, overflow
שקד, guard, keep *watch*, lie *awake*, make *like almond*, *stay* awake, watch
שָׁקֵד, almond, almond *tree*, *ripe* almond
שקה, drench, drink, give *drink*, give *to drink*, *make* drink, moist, offer *to drink*, provide *with drink*, serve *a drink*, water
שִׁקּוּי, drink, refreshment
שְׁקוּף, frame, *window* frame
שִׁקּוּץ, *abominable* idol, abomination, detestable, *detestable* idol, detestable *thing*, filth
שקט, calm, ease, give *respite*, quiet, quietly, quietness, rest, settle, still
שֶׁקֶט, quiet
שקל, feel *a weight*, pay, spend, weigh, weigh *out*
שֶׁקֶל, shekel
שִׁקְמָה, sycamore, sycamore *tree*
שקע, abate, *make* clear, make *clear*, press *down*, sink
שְׁקַעֲרוּרָה, spot
שקף, look, look *down*, look *forth*, look *out*, loom, overlook, peer
שֶׁקֶף, frame
שקץ, abhor, abomination, detest, make *abominable*
שֶׁקֶץ, abomination, insect, loathsome
שקק, charge, leap, quench, rush *to and fro*, thirsty
שקר, deal *falsely*, false, lie
שֶׁקֶר, deceit, deceitful, deceptive, delusion, false, falsehood, falsely, guile, liar, lie, pretense, treacherously, true, vain, *vain* hope, wrongfully
שֶׁקֶר כָּזָב, lie
שֹׁקֶת, trough, *watering* trough
שֹׁר, navel, *navel* string
שָׁרָב, *burning* sand, *scorching* wind
שֵׁרֵבְיָה, Sherebiah
שַׁרְבִיט, scepter
שרה, go, *woman* singer
שֵׁרָה, bracelet
שָׁרוּחֶן, Sharuhen
שָׁרוֹן, Sharon
שָׁרוֹנִי, Sharonite
שָׁרַי, Sharai
שִׁרְיָה, javelin
שִׁרְיוֹן, breastplate, coat, coat *of mail*
שְׁרִיקָה, pipe, *thing to* hiss *at*
שָׁרִיר, muscle
שְׁרִירוּת, stubborn, stubbornly, stubbornness
שרץ, breed *abundantly*, bring *forth*, bring *forth abundantly*, increase *greatly*, swarm
שֶׁרֶץ, creeping *thing*, insect, swarm, *swarming* creature, swarming *thing*
שרק, hiss, signal, whistle
שְׁרֵקָה, hiss, object *of hissing*, *thing to* hiss *at*
שָׁרָר, Sharar
שרשׁ, root, root *out*, take *root*, uproot
שֶׁרֶשׁ, Sheresh
שֹׁרֶשׁ, root, sole, take *root*
שַׁרְשְׁרָה, chain
שרת, attend, minister, ministry, official, servant, serve, service, supply, tend, use, wait, worship
שרת פָּנִים, serve
שָׁרֵת, service
שֵׁשׁ, alabaster, *fine* linen, *fine twined* linen, marble, six, six *things*, sixth, stuff
שֵׁשׁ עֶשְׂרֵה, sixteen, sixteenth
ששא, drive
שֵׁשְׁבַּצַּר, Sheshbazzar
שָׁשַׁי, Shashai
שִׁשִּׁי, sixth
שֵׁשַׁי, Sheshai
שֵׁשַׁךְ, Babylon
שֵׁשָׁן, Sheshan
שָׁשַׁק, Shashak
שָׁשַׁר, vermilion
שָׁת, foundation
שֵׁת, buttock, hip, Seth, Sheth
שתה, drink, drink *up*, drinker, feast
שתה שֵׁכָר, drunkard
שְׁתִי, drunkenness, warp
שְׁתִיָּה, drink
שְׁתֵּיהֶם, together
שָׁתִיל, shoot
שתל, plant, transplant
שֻׁתַלְחִי, Shuthelahite

שׁתם, open

שׁתן בְּקִיר, male

שׁתק, cease, quiet, quiet *down*

שֵׁתָר, Shethar

שׁתת, appoint, set

תָּא, room, side *room*

תָּא הָרָצִים, guardroom

תאב, abhor, long

תַּאֲבָה, long

תאה, mark *out*

תְּאוֹ, antelope

תַּאֲוָה, bounty, crave, dainty, delight, desire, long

תַּאֲלָה, curse

תאם, bear *twins*, separate

תַּאֲנָה, lust

תֹּאֲנָה, occasion

תְּאֵנָה, fig, fig *tree*

תַּאֲנִיָּה, moan, mourn

תַּאֲנַת שִׁלֹה, Taanath-shiloh

תאר, bend, bend *round*, extend, go *in another direction*, mark, mark *out*

תֹּאַר, appearance, form, *good* presence, goodly, visage

תְּאַשּׁוּר, pine

תֵּבָה, ark, basket

תְּבוּאָה, crop, fruit, gain, harvest, income, increase, produce, profit, revenue, yield

תְּבוּנָה, discernment, intelligence, skilful, skilfully, understand, understanding, *wise* saying

תְּבוּסָה, downfall

תָּבוֹר, Tabor

תֶּבֶל, incest, perversion

תֵּבֵל, inhabit, world

תֵּבֵל אֶרֶץ, habitable *world*

תַּבְלִית, destruction

תְּבַלֻּל, defect

תֶּבֶן, straw

תִּבְנִי, Tibni

תַּבְנִית, copy, figure, form, image, kind, likeness, pattern, plan, structure

תַּבְעֵרָה, Taberah

תֵּבֵץ, Thebez

תִּגְלַת פִּלְאֶסֶר, Tiglath-pileser

תַּגְמוּל, bounty

תִּגְרָה, blow

תֹּגַרְמָה, Togarmah

תִּדְהָר, plane

תַּדְמֹר, Tadmor

תִּדְעָל, Tidal

תֹּהוּ, chaos, confusion, emptiness, empty, *empty* plea, nothing, vain, vain *thing*, void, waste, *without* form

תְּהוֹם, deep, depth, flood, spring

תָּהֳלָה, error

תְּהִלָּה, famous, glorious *deed*, praise, renown, song *of praise*

תַּהֲלוּכָה, procession

תַּהְפֻּכָה, perverse, perverse *thing*, perversion, pervert

תָּו, mark, signature

תּוֹאָם, separate, twin

תּוּבַל קַיִן, Tubal-cain

תּוּבַל, Tubal

תּוּגָה, grief, sorrow

תּוֹדָה, give *thanks*, praise, song *of thanksgiving*, *thank* offering, thanksgiving

תוה, make *a mark*, provoke, put *a mark*

תּוֹחַ, Toah

תּוֹחֶלֶת, expectation, hope

תָּוֶךְ, among, center, height, middle, midst, within

תּוֹךְ, innermost *part*, presence

תּוֹךְ הַלַּיְלָה, midnight

תּוֹכֵחָה, chastisement, punishment, rebuke

תּוֹכַחַת, admonition, argument, chasten, chastisement, complaint, reasoning, rebuke, reproof, reprove

תּוֹלָד, Tolad

תּוֹלֵדוֹת, birth, descendant, genealogy, generation, history

תּוֹלָל, tormentor

תּוֹלָע, crimson, purple, Tola, worm

תּוֹלֵעָה, worm

תּוֹלָעִי, Tolaite

תּוֹלַעַת שָׁנִי, scarlet, scarlet *stuff*

תּוֹעֵבָה, abominable, abominable *deed*, *abominable* practice, abominable *thing*, abomination, *thing of* horror

תּוֹעָה, confusion, error

תּוֹעָפָה, height, horn, precious

תּוֹצָאָה, border, end, escape, exit, limit, spring, termination

תור, follow, range, search, search *out*, seek *out*, send *to spy out*, spy *out*

תּוֹר, ornament, turn

תּוֹרָה, decision, instruction, law, question, teaching

תּוֹשָׁב, sojourner

תּוּשִׁיָּה, resource, *sound* judgment, *sound* knowledge, *sound* wisdom, success, understanding, wisdom

תּוֹתָח, club

תַּזְנוּת, harlotry, lust

תַּחְבֻּלָה, counsel, guidance, skill, *wise* guidance

תֹּחוּ, Tohu

תַּחְכְּמֹנִי, Tahchemonite

תַּחֲלֻאִים, agony, disease, sickness

תְּחִלָּה, begin, beginning, first, *first* time

תַּחְמֹל עָלָי, spare

תַּחְמָס, nighthawk

תַּחַן, Tahan

תְּחִנָּה, favor, mercy, plea, supplication, Tehinnah

תַּחֲנוּן, entreaty, plead, supplication

תַּחֲנִי, Tahanite

תַּחְפַּנְחֵס, Tahpanhes

תְּחַפְנְחֵס, Tehaphnehes

תַּחְפְּנֵים, Tahpenes

תַּחְרָא, garment

תַּחֲרֵעַ, Tarea

תַּחְרֵעַ, Tahrea

תַּחַשׁ, goatskin, leather, Tahash

תַּחַת, amid, among, because, below, beneath, between, bottom, exchange, flat, foot, instead, one *place*, place, return, sake, site, stead, succeed, Tahath, under, *under* foot, underneath, underpart, where, *where one* stands, whereas, while

תַּחַת אֲשֶׁר, because, since, whereas

תַּחַת מָה, why

תַּחְתּוֹן, low

תַּחְתִּי, depth, foot, low, low *part*, nether

תַּחְתָּיו, there

תִּיכוֹן, middle

תִּילוֹן, Tilon

תֵּימָא, Tema

תֵּימָן, *south* side, *south* wind

תֵּימָן, south, southward, Teman

תֵּימָן נֶגֶב, south

תֵּימָנִי, Temanite

תֵּימְנִי, Temeni

תִּימָרָה, column

תִּיצִי, Tizite

תִּירוֹשׁ, grape, *new* wine, wine

תִּירְיָא, Tiria

תִּירָס, Tiras

תַּיִשׁ, *he* goat

תֹּךְ, oppression

תכה, follow

תְּכוּנָה, arrangement, seat, treasure

תֻּכִּיִּים, peacock

תִּכְלָה, perfection

תַּכְלִית, bound, boundary, end, limit, perfect

תְּכֵלֶת, blue, *blue* fabric, *blue* hanging, purple, violet

תכן, just, keep *steady*, weigh, weigh *out*

תֹּכֶן, measure, *same* number, Tochen

תָּכְנִית, perfection

תַּכְרִיךְ, mantle

תֵּל, heap, mound

תֵּל אָבִיב, Tel-abib

תֵּל חַרְשָׁא, Tel-harsha

תֵּל מֶלַח, Tel-melah

תלא, bend, hang

תַּלְאֻבָה, drought

תְּלָאָה, adversity, hardship, tribulation, weariness

תְּלַאשָּׂר, Telassar

תִּלְבֹּשֶׁת, clothing

תִּלְגַת פִּלְנְאֶסֶר, Tilgath-pilneser

תלה, hang, hang *up*, hanged *man*

תָּלוּל, lofty

תֶּלַח, Telah

תְּלִי, quiver

תלל, cheat, deal *falsely*, deceive, delude, mock

תֶּלֶם, furrow

תַּלְמַי, Talmai

תַּלְמִיד, pupil

תְּלֻנָּה, murmur

תלע, clothe *in scarlet*

תַּלְפִּיּוֹת, arsenal

תַּלְתַּלִּים, wavy

תָּם, blameless, perfect *one*, quiet

תֹּם, full, *full* measure, integrity, simplicity, upright, venture

תמה, amaze, astound, stupor, wonder

תֻּמָּה, integrity

תמהּ, astound, look *aghast*, look *in amazement*

תִּמָּהוֹן, confusion, panic

תַּמּוּז, Tammuz

תְּמוֹל, long, time *past*, yesterday

תְּמוֹל שִׁלְשׁוֹם, time *past*

תְּמוֹל שִׁלְשֹׁם, always, before, formerly, heretofore, hitherto, past

תְּמוּנָה, form, likeness

תְּמוּרָה, exchange, recompense, trade

תֶּמַח, Temah

תָּמִיד, always, continual, *continual burnt* offering, continually, daily, ever, evermore, perpetual, regular, regularly, unceasing

תָּמִיד לֹא, never

תָּמִים, blameless, blameless *man*, blamelessly, entire, full, honor, integrity, man *of integrity*, perfect, safe, sincerity, truth, uprightly, whole, *without* blemish, *without* defect

תֻּמִּים, Thummim

תמך, catch, follow *the path*, get, help, hold, hold *fast*, hold *up*, obtain, seize, take, uphold

תמם, accomplish, all, *all* gone, blameless, boil, cease, come *to a full end*, consume, destroy, *utterly* destroy, do, end, fail, finish, go, last, make *blameless*, over, perish, put *an end*, reckon, settle, *show* blameless, spend, think *out*, utterly, vanish, *very* end, *very* last, whole, wholly, wipe *out*

תמם לְ, finish

תִּמְנָה, Timnah

תִּמְנִי, Timnite

תִּמְנָע, Timna

תִּמְנַת חֶרֶס, Timnath-heres

תִּמְנַת סֶרַח, Timnath-serah

תֶּמֶס, slime

תָּמָר, palm, palm *tree*, Tamar

תֹּמֶר, palm, scarecrow

תִּמֹרָה, palm, palm *tree*

תַּמְרוּק, ointment

תַּמְרוּר, bitter, guidepost

תַּן, jackal

תנה, hire, lament, repeat

תְּנוּאָה, displeasure, occasion

תְּנוּבָה, fruit, increase, produce

תְּנוּךְ, tip

תְּנוּמָה, slumber

תְּנוּפָה, brandish, contribute, offering, wave, *wave* offering

תַּנּוּר, furnace, oven, pot

תַּנְחוּם, consolation, console

תַּנְחֻמֶת, Tanhumeth

תַּנִּין, dragon, monster, sea *monster*, serpent

תִּנְשֶׁמֶת, chameleon, water *hen*

תעב, abhor, abhorrent, abominable, *act* abominably, *do* abominable, *do* abominably, loathe, prostitute

תעה, *cause to* wander, deceive, err, go *astray*, lead *astray*, *make* err, *make* stagger, *make* wander, mislead, reel, seduce, stagger, stray, wander, wander *about*

תֹּעוּ, Toi, Tou

תְּעוּדָה, attest, testimony

תֹּעִי, Toi

תְּעָלָה, channel, conduit, healing, stream, trench

תַּעֲלוּלִים, affliction, babe

תַּעֲלֻמָה, secret

תַּעֲלֻמָּהּ, hide

תַּעֲנוּג, delight, luxury, pleasant

תַּעֲנִית, fast

תַּעְנָךְ, Taanach

תעע, mock, scoff

תְּעֻפָה, darkness

תַּעֲצֻמָה, strength

תַּעַר, penknife, razor, scabbard, sheath

תַּעְתֻּעִים, delusion

תֹּף, setting, tambourine, timbrel

תִּפְאָרָה, beautiful, beauty, boast, fair, fine, finery, glorious, glory, *haughty* pride, honor, pomp, pride, splendor

תַּפּוּחַ, apple, apple *tree*, Tappuah

תְּפוֹצָה, dispersion

תֻּפִינִים, bake

תָּפֵל, deceptive, tasteless, whitewash

תֹּפֶל, Tophel

תִּפְלָה, unsavory *thing*, wrong

תְּפִלָּה, pray, prayer, supplication

תִּפְלֶצֶת, horror

תִּפְסַח, Tiphsah

תפף, beat, play *a timbrel*

תפר, sew, sew *together*

תפש, capture, catch, grasp, handle, hold, lay *hold*, overlay, play, profane, seize, skilled, take, take *hold*, wield

תפש כַּבָּף, handle

תפש מִלְחָמָה, warrior

תֹּפֶת, spit, Topheth

תָּפְתֶּה, burning *place*

תָּקְהַת, Tokhath

תִּקְוָה, cord, desire, expectation, hope, Tikvah

תְּקוּמָה, power *to stand*

תָּקוֹעַ, trumpet

תְּקוֹעַ, Tekoa

תְּקוֹעִי, Tekoa, Tekoite

תְּקוּפָה, circuit, end

תְּקוּפוֹת הַיָּמִים, due *time*

תִּקְוַת חוּט, cord

תַּקִּיף, strong

תקן, arrange *with care*, make *straight*

תקע, blow, clap, drive, encamp, fasten, give *surety*, make *tight*, pitch, sound, suretyship, thrust

תקע כַּף, give *a pledge*

תֵּקַע, sound

תקף, prevail *against*

תֹּקֶף, authority, power, strength

תֹּר, dove, turtledove

תַּרְאֲלָה, Taralah

תַּרְבּוּת, brood

תַּרְבִּית, increase

תרגם, translate

תַּרְדֵּמָה, *deep* sleep

תִּרְהָקָה, Tirhakah

תְּרוּמָה, contribution, district, *freewill* offering, gift, offer, offering, portion, portion *set apart*

תְּרוּמִיָּה, portion

תְּרוּעָה, alarm, battle, *battle* cry, blast *of a trumpet*, cry, *festal* shout, joy, loud, *loud* clashing, *loud* shout, shout, shout *of joy*, trumpet

תְּרוּפָה, healing

תִּרְזָה, holm *tree*

תֶּרַח, Terah

תִּרְחֲנָה, Tirhanah

תַּרְמִית, cunning, deceit, deceitful

תֹּרֶן, flagstaff, mast
תַּרְעֵלָה, stagger
תִּרְעָתִים, Tirathite
תְּרָפִים, *household* god, idolatry, image, teraphim
תִּרְצָה, Tirzah
תֶּרֶשׁ, Teresh
תַּרְשִׁישׁ, beryl, chrysolite, jewel, Tarshish
תִּרְשָׁתָא, governor
תַּרְתָּן, commander *in chief*, Tartan
תַּרְתָּק, Tartak
תְּשׂוּמֶת יָד, security
תְּשֻׁאָה, shout, thundering
תִּשְׁבִּי, Tishbite
תַּשְׁבֵּץ, checker *work*
תְּשׁוּבָה, come *back*, spring
תְּשׁוּבַת הַשָּׁנָה, spring
תְּשֻׁוָּה, roar
תְּשׁוּעָה, deed *of salvation*, deliverance, help, safety, salvation, victory
תְּשׁוּקָה, desire
תְּשׁוּרָה, present
תְּשִׁיעִי, ninth
תְּשַׁלַּח בָּאֵשׁ, set *on fire*
תְּשַׁע עֶשְׂרֵה, nineteen, nineteenth
תֵּשַׁע, nine, ninth

Aramaic

אַב, father
אֵב, fruit
אבד, destroy, perish
אֶבֶן, stone
אִגֶּרֶת, letter
אֱדַיִן, then, time
אִדַּר, *threshing* floor
אֲדָר, Adar
אֲדַרְגָּזַר, counselor
אַדְרַזְדָּא, full
אֶדְרָע, force
אזא, heat, hot
אַזְדָּא, sure
אזל, go
אָח, brother
אֲחִידָה, riddle
אַחְמְתָא, Ecbatana
אַחֲרֵי, after
אַחֲרֵי דְנָה, hereafter
אַחֲרִית, latter
אָחֳרָן, another, other, yet
אָחֳרָן לָא, none
אֲחַשְׁדַּרְפְּנִין, satrap
אִילָן, tree
אֵימְתָן, dreadful
אִישׁ, man
אכל, devour, eat
אכל קְרַץ, accuse, *maliciously* accuse
אֱלָהּ, god, God
אֱלָהִים, god
אֲלוּ, behold
אֲלַף, thousand
אַמָּה, cubit
אֻמָּה, nation
אמן, faithful, sure, trust
אמר, ask, command, declare, order, require, say, speak, tell
אִמַּר, lamb, sheep
אנס, difficult
אֲנַף, face
אֱנָשׁ, man
אֱסוּר, band, imprisonment
אָסְנַפַּר, Osnappar
אָסְפַּרְנָא, *all* diligence, diligently, full, strictly
אֱסָר, interdict
אָע, beam, timber, wood
אֲפָרְסָי, Persian
אֲפַרְסְכָיֵא, governor
אֲפַרְסַתְכָיֵא, governor
אַפְּתֹם, revenue
אֶצְבַּע, finger, toe
אַרְבַּע, four
אַרְבַּע עֶשְׂרֵה, fourteenth
אַרְגְּוָן, purple, *purple* fabric
אֲרוּ, behold, lo
אֹרַח, way
אַרְיֵה, lion
אַרְיוֹךְ, Arioch
אֲרִיךְ, fitting
אַרְכֻבָּה, knee
אַרְכָה, lengthen
אֲרַע, earth, ground, inferior
אַרְעִי, bottom
אֲרַק, earth
ארתחשסתא, Artaxerxes
אַרְתַּחְשַׁשְׂתְּא, Artaxerxes
אֹשׁ, *burnt* offering, foundation
אֶשָּׁא, fire
אִשָּׁה, wife
אָשַׁף, enchanter
אֻשַּׁרְנָא, structure
אֶשְׁתַּדּוּר, sedition
אָת, sign
אתא, bring, come, go
אתה, bring
אַתּוּן, furnace
אֲתַר, place, site

בְּ, according, amid, because, concerning, connection, during, over, through, throughout, upon
בֵּאדַיִן, then
בְּאִישׁ, wicked
באשׁ עַל, distress
בָּאתַר, after
בָּבֶל, Babylon, Babylonia
בָּבְלָי, Babylonian
בְּגוֹא, within
בדר, scatter
בַּהּ שַׁעֲתָא, immediately
בַּהּ זִמְנָא כְּדִי, soon
בְּהִילוּ, haste
בהל, alarm, haste
בְּחַיִל, aloud
בטל, cease, delay, *make* cease, stop
בֵּין, among, between
בִּינָה, understand
בִּירָנְתָא, stronghold
בִּירְתָא, capital
בית, spend *the night*
בַּיִת, hall, house, residence, treasury
בֵּית גְּנַז, archive
בֵּית גִּנְזִין, treasury
בָּל, mind
בלא, wear *out*
בְּלוֹ, custom
בֵּלְטְשַׁאצַּר, Belteshazzar
בֵּלְשַׁאצַּר, Belshazzar
בֵּן אֱנָשׁ, man
בֵּן גָּלוּת, exile
בֵּן, child, people, young
בנא, build, rebuild
בנה, build
בִּנְיָן, building
בנס, angry
בעא, ask, make *a petition*, make *a request*, petition, seek
בְּעִדָּן, when
בעה, beseech
בָּעוּ, petition
בְּעֵל טְעֵם, commander
בִּקְעָא, plain
בקר, make *inquiry*, make *search*, search
בַּר, field, old, son
ברך, bless, get *down*
בְּרַךְ, knee
בְּרַם, however, nevertheless
בְּשַׂר, flesh
בַּת, bath

גַּב, back
גֹּב, den
גְּבוּרָה, might, strength
גְּבַר, man
גִּבַּר, certain, man
גְּדָבְרַיָּא, treasurer
גדד, hew *down*
גֵּו, midst
גֵּוָה, pride
גוח, stir *up*
גִּזְבַּר, treasurer
גזר, astrologer, cut, cut *out*
גְּזֵרָה, decree
גִּיר, plaster
גלא, reveal, revealer
גַּלְגַּל, wheel
גלה, carry *away*, reveal
גְּלָל, great, huge
גְּנַז, document
גַּף, wing
גְּרַם, bone
גֶּשֶׁם, body

דָּא, another
דָּא לְדָא, together
דֹּב, bear
דבח, offer
דְּבַח, sacrifice
דבק, hold
דִּבְרָה, end
דְּהַב, gold, golden
דור, dwell, find *shade*, inhabitant
דּוּרָא, Dura
דושׁ, trample *down*
דַּחֲוָה, diversion
דחל, fear, frighten, make *afraid*, terrible
דִּי, because, if, order, what, where, whereas
דִּי לָא, without
דִּי לְמָה, lest
דִּין, judge
דַּיָּן, judge
דִּין, court, judgment, just
דְּכַר, ram
דִּכְרוֹן, record
דלק, burn
דמה, like
דְּנָה עִם דְּנָה, together
דָּנִיֵּאל, Daniel
דקק, break, break *in pieces*, break *to pieces*
דָּר, generation
דָּרְיָוֶשׁ, Darius
דְּרָע, arm
דָּת, decree, law, sentence
דֶּתֶא, *tender* grass
דְּתָבָר, justice

הָא כְדִי, just
הַדָּבַר, counselor
הַדָּם, limb
הדר, honor
הֲדַר, majesty
הוא, become
היה לְ, become
הֵיכַל, palace, temple
הלך, bring *back*, go, reach, walk
הֲלָךְ, toll
הַמְנִכָא, chain
הֵן, if, perhaps, whether
הַרְהֹר, fancy

וְ, moreover, nor, therefore

זבן, gain
זהר, take *care*
זוד, deal *proudly*
זון, feed
זוע, tremble
זִיו, brightness, color, splendor
זָכוּ, blameless
זְכַרְיָהוּ, Zechariah
זמן, agree
זְמַן, season, time
זְמָן, time
זַמָּר, singer
זְמָר, music
זַן, kind
זְעֵיר, little *one*
זעק, cry *out*
זְרֻבָּבֶל, Zerubbabel

חֲבוּלָא, wrong
חבל, destroy, hurt
חֲבָל, damage, hurt
חֲבַר, companion
חַבְרָה, fellow
חַגַּי, Haggai
חַד, first, one, time
חֶדְוָה, joy
חֲדִי, breast
חוה, explain, meet, show
חוט, repair
חִוָּר, white
חזה, look, see, witness, wont
חזה הוה, see
חֵזוּ, seem, vision
חֲזוֹת, visible
חֲטָי, sin
חַטָּיא, *sin* offering
חַי, live
חיא, keep *alive*
חיה, live
חֵיוָא, beast
חַיִּין, life
חַיִל, army, host, mighty
חַכִּים, wise, wise *man*
חָכְמָה, wisdom
חֵלֶם, dream
חלף, pass
חֲלָק, lot, possession
חֱמָא, fury
חמה, beware
חֵמָה, furious
חֲמַר, wine
חִנְטָה, wheat
חֲנֻכָּה, dedication
חנן, *show* mercy, supplication
חֲנַנְיָה, Hananiah
חסן, possess, receive
חֱסֵן, power
חֲסַף, clay
חַסִּיר, want
חצף, severe, strict

חרב, lay *waste*
חַרְטֹם, magician
חרך, singe
חשב, account
חֲשׁוֹךְ, darkness
חשח, need
חַשְׁחָה, need
חַשְׁחוּ, require
חשל, shatter
חתם, seal

טאב, glad
טָב, fine, good
טַבָּח, guard
טוּר, mountain
טְוָת, fast
טִין, miry
טַל, dew
טלל, find *shade*
טעם, feed, *make* eat
טְעֵם, account, decree, report
טְעֵם, command, decree, discretion, heed, taste
טְפַר, claw, nail
טרד, drive
טַרְפְּלָיֵא, official

יבל, bring, convey
יַבֶּשֶׁת, earth
יַד, hand
יַד, power
ידא, give *thanks*
ידע, inform, information, know, learn, *make* known, make *known*, notify, teach
יהב, deliver, give, give *over*, lay, pay, restore, yield *up*
יְהוּד, Judah
יְהוּדָי, Jew
יְהוֹשׁוּעַ, Jeshua
יוֹם, day
יוֹמַת עָלְמָא, old
יוֹצָדָק, Jozadak
יטב, *seem* good
יכל, able, prevail
יַם, sea
יסף, add, fulfil
יעט, agree
יָעַט, counselor
יצב, know *the truth*
יַצִּיב, certain, stand *fast*, true, truth
יקד, burn
יְקֵדָה, burn
יַקִּיר, difficult, noble
יְקָר, glory, honor
יְרוּשְׁלֶם, Jerusalem
יְרַח, month
יַרְכָה, thigh
יִשְׂרָאֵל, Israel
יתב, live, settle, sit, take *a seat*
יַתִּיר, exceeding, exceedingly, excellent, still *more*, very

כְּ, about, according, after, like, such, when
כְּדַב, lie
כְּדִי, when
כִּדְנָה, thus
כָּה, here
כהל, able
כָּהֵן, priest
כַּוָּה, window
כּוֹר, cor
כּוֹרֶשׁ, Cyrus
כַּחֲדָה, together
כִּכַּר, talent
כָּל קֳבֵל דְּנָה, therefore
כָּל קֳבֵל דִּי, though
כֹּל, all, all *things*, any, every, kind, whole
כָּל אֱנָשׁ, whoever
כָּל דִּי, whatever, wherever, whoever
כָּל קֳבֵל, because
כָּל קֳבֵל דִּי, because
כָּל קֳבֵל דְּנָה, because
כָּל קֳבֵל דִּי, just
כָּל קֳבֵל דְּנָה, then
כלל, finish
כְּמָה, how
כֵּן, thus
כְּנֵמָא, follow, thus
כנש, assemble, gather *together*
כְּנָת, associate
כַּשְׂדַּי, Chaldean
כְּסַף, money
כְּסַף, silver
כְּעַן, now, therefore
כְּעֶנֶת, now
כֵּף, rock
כפת, bind
כַּרְבְּלָא, hat
כרה, anxious
כָּרוֹז, herald
כרז, make *proclamation*
כָּרְסֵא, throne
כַּשְׂדָּי, Chaldean
כתב, write, write *down*, writing
כְּתָב, document, prescribe, writing
כְּתַל, wall

לְ, according, against, like, over
לָא, never, no, none, nothing, without
לָא לְעָלְמִין, never
לָא צְבוּ, nothing
לֵב, heart, mind
לְבַב, mind
לְבוּשׁ, garment, raiment
לבש, clothe
לָהֵן, except, therefore, unless
לֵוִי, Levite
לְחֵם, feast
לְחֵנָה, concubine
לֵילְיָא, night
לְצַד, against
לָקֳבֵל, because, before, front, opposite, then
לִשָּׁן, language

מֹאזְנֵא, balance
מֵאמַר, word
מָאן, vessel
מְגִלָּה, scroll
מגר, overthrow
מַדְבַּח, altar
מְדוֹר, dwelling
מָדַי, Mede, Media
מְדִינָה, province
מְדָר, dwelling
מָה, what, whatever
מָה דִּי, what, whatever
מוֹת, death
מָזוֹן, food
מחא, impale, smite, stay, strike
מַחְלְקָת, course
מטא, come, reach
מִישָׁאֵל, Mishael
מֵישַׁךְ, Meshach
מלא, fill, full
מַלְאַךְ, angel
מִלָּה, command, demand, matter, order, thing, word
מלח, eat *salt*
מְלַח, salt
מֶלֶךְ, king, royal
מְלַךְ, counsel
מַלְכָּה, queen
מַלְכוּ, kingdom, kingly, kingship, royal, sovereignty
מַלְכוּת, kingdom, realm, reign, royal
מלל, say, speak
מַן דִּי, whoever
מַן, what
מִן, among, because, more *than*, out, partly, some, than, upon
מִן דִּי, because
מִן יַצִּיב, certainty
מִן קֳדָם, before
מִן קַדְמַת דְּנָה, previously
מִן קְצָת, partly
מִן קְשֹׁט דִּי, truly
מִנְדָּה, tribute
מַנְדַּע, knowledge, reason
מנה, appoint
מְנֵה, number
מִנְּהֵין, partly
מִנְחָה, *cereal* offering, offering
מִנְיָן, number
מְעֵא, belly
מַעְבָד, work
מֶעָל, go *down*
מִקַּדְמַת דְּנָה, ago
מָרֵא, lord, Lord
מָרָד, rebellious
מְרַד, rebellion
מרט, pluck *off*
מֹשֶׁה, Moses
מְשַׁח, oil
מִשְׁכַּב, bed
מִשְׁכַּן, dwelling
מַשְׁרוֹקִי, pipe
מִשְׁתֵּי, banquet
מַתַּן, gift
מַתְּנָה, gift

נבא, prophesy
נְבוּאָה, prophesy
נְבוּכַדְנֶצַּר, Nebuchadnezzar
נְבִזְבָּה, reward
נְבִיא, prophet
נֶבְרְשָׁה, lampstand
נגד, issue
נֶגֶד, toward
נדב, *freewill* offering, offer *freely*, vow *willingly*
נִדְבָּךְ, course
נדד, flee
נְהִיר, light
נַהִירוּ, light
נְהַר, stream
נְהַר, river
נוד, flee
נְוָלוּ, dunghill, ruins
נוּר, fiery, fire
נזק, hurt, hurtful, impair, suffer *loss*
נְחָשׁ, bronze
נחת, come *down*, depose, put, store
נטל, lift, lift *up*
נטר, keep
נִיחוֹחַ, incense, please
נְכַס, revenue
נְכַס, goods
נְמַר, leopard
נסח, pull
נסך, offer *up*
נְסַךְ, *drink* offering
נפל, fall, fall *down*
נפק, appear, come *forth*, go *forth*, go *out*, take
נִפְקָה, cost
נִצְבָּה, firmness
נצח, distinguish
נצל, deliver, rescue
נְקֵא, pure
נקש, knock
נשא, carry *away*, rise, take
נִשְׁמָה, breath
נְשַׁר, eagle
נִשְׁתְּוָן, letter
נְתִינִין, *temple* servant
נתן, appoint, give, provide
נתר, strip *off*

סבל, bring
סבר, think
סגד, *do* homage, worship
סְגַן, prefect
סגר, shut
סוּמְפֹּנְיָה, bagpipe
סוּף, bring *to an end*
סוֹף, end
סִיב, elder
סלק, come, come *up*, take *up*
סעד, help
סָפַר, scribe
סְפַר, archive, book
סֵפֶר, book
סַרְבָּל, mantle
סָרַךְ, president
סתר, destroy, mysterious *thing*

עבד, celebrate, do, execute, go, make, obey, stir *up*, tear, work, wrought
עֲבַד, servant
עֲבֵד נְגוֹ, Abed-nego
עֲבִידָה, affair, service, work
עֲבַר, beyond
עַד, till, until, up, within
עַד אָחֳרֵין, last
עַד דִּי, till
עדא, remove, revoke, take, take *away*
עדה, come, depart, pass *away*
עִדּוֹ, Iddo
עִדָּן, time
עוֹד, still
עֲוָיָה, iniquity
עוֹף, bird
עוּר, chaff
עִזְקָה, signet
עֶזְרָא, Ezra
עֲזַרְיָה, Azariah
עֵטָא, prudence
עַיִן, eye
עִיר, enemy, watcher
עַל, about, above, against, concerning, more, over, upon
עַל דִּבְרַת דִּי, order
עַל דְּנָה, therefore
עַל מָה, why
עלה, bring
עִלָּה, ground *for complaint*
עִלַּי, *most* high
עִלִּי, *upper* chamber
עֶלְיוֹן, *most* high
עלל, bring, come, come *into*, go
עָלַם, ever, everlasting
עֵלְמָיֵא, Elamite
עֲלַע, rib
עֲלָת, *burnt* offering
עַם, people
עִם, toward
עֲמִיק, deep
עֲמַר, wool
ענה, answer
עֲנֵה, oppress
עֲנָן, cloud
עֲנַף, branch
ענש, confiscation
עֳפִי, leaf
עצב, anguish
עקר, pluck *up by the roots*
עִקַּר, stump
ערב, mix
עֲרָד, wild *ass*
עַרְוָה, dishonor

עֲשַׂב, grass
עֲשַׂר, ten
עשׁת, plan
עֲתִיד, ready
עַתִּיק, ancient

פֶּחָה, governor
פֶּחָר, potter
פַּטִּשׁ, tunic
פלג, divide
פְּלַג, half
פְּלֻגָּה, division
פלח, servant, serve
פָּלְחָן, service
פֻּם, mouth
פְּסַנְטֵרִין, harp
פַּרְזֶל, iron
פרס, divide
פְּרַס, Persia, Persian
פָּרְסָי, Persian
פרק, break *off*
פרשׁ, plainly
פַּרְשֶׁגֶן, copy
פשׁר, give, interpret
פְּשַׁר, interpretation
פִּתְגָם, answer, edict, reply, report, sentence
פִּתְגָם הֲתָבוּת, answer
פתח, open
פְּתָי, breadth

צבא, will
צבע, wet
צַד, regard
צדא, ravage
צְדָא, true
צִדְקָה, righteousness
צַוַּאר, neck
צלא, pray
צלח, promote, prosper
צלל, finish
צְלֵם, expression, image
צְפִיר עִזִּין, *he* goat
צִפַּר, bird

קָאֵם, stand
קבל, receive
קַדִּישׁ, holy, holy *one*, saint
קֳדָם, before, presence
קַדְמָי, first, former *one*

קוֹל, sound, tone, voice
קום, arise, establish, make, *make* stand, raise *up*, rise *up*, set, set *up*, stand
קטל, slay
קְטַר, problem
קְטַר חֲרַץ, limb
קַיִט, summer
קַיָּם, endure, sure
קְיָם, ordinance
קנא, buy
קצף, furious
קְצַף, wrath
קצץ, cut *off*
קְצָת, end
קרא, call, cry, proclaim, read
קרב, approach, bring, come *forward*, come *near*, offer, offer *a sacrifice*, present, soon
קְרֵב, neighbor
קְרָב, war
קִרְיָה, city
קֶרֶן, horn
קְשֹׁט, right
קִתְרֹס, lyre

רֵאשׁ, head, sum
רַב, captain, chief, great, great *thing*, mighty
רבה, give *high honor*, greatness, grow, grow *long*
רְבוּ, greatness
רְבִיעָי, fourth
רַבְרְבָן, lord
רגז, anger
רְגַז, rage
רְגַל, foot
רגשׁ, come *by agreement*
רֵו, appearance
רוּחַ, spirit, wind
רום, extol, lift *up*, raise *up*
רוּם, height, top
רָז, mystery
רַחִיק, keep *away*
רַחֲמִין, mercy
רחץ, trust
רֵיחַ, smell
רמא, cast, impose, place
רְעוּ, pleasure, will
רַעְיוֹן, thought
רַעְנַן, prosper
רעע, crush
רפס, stamp
רשׁם, inscribe, sign

שַׂבְּכָא, trigon
שׂגא, grow, multiply
שַׂגִּיא, abundant, exceedingly, great, greatly, many, much, very
שׂוּם, give, issue, lay, make, pay, set
שׂוּם שְׂם, name
שְׂטַר, side
שִׂיב, elder
שׂכל, consider
שָׂכְלְתָנוּ, understanding
שׂנא, hate
שְׂעַר, hair

שׁאל, ask, require
שְׁאֵלָה, anything, decision
שְׁאַלְתִּיאֵל, Shealtiel
שׁאר, whatever *else*
שְׁאָר, residue, rest
שׁבח, praise
שְׁבַט, tribe
שְׁבִיב, flame
שְׁבַע, seven
שׁבק, leave, let *alone*
שׁבשׁ, perplex
שֵׁגַל, wife
שׁדר, labor
שַׁדְרַךְ, Shadrach
שׁוה, lay, make *like*
שׁוּר, wall
שׁוּשַׁנְכָיֵא, *man of* Susa
שׁחת, corrupt, fault
שׁיזב, deliver, save
שׁיציא, finish
שׁכח, find
שׁכן, *cause to* dwell, dwell
שָׁלֵה, ease
שָׁלוּ, error, fail, slack
שְׁלֵוָה, tranquillity
שׁלח, put *forth*, send
שׁלט, *make* rule, make *ruler*, overpower, power, rule, ruler
שִׁלְטוֹן, official
שָׁלְטָן, dominion
שַׁלִּיט, captain, lawful, powerful, rule, ruler
שׁלם, bring *to an end*, deliver, finish
שְׁלָם, greeting, peace
שֻׁם, name
שׁמד, consume
שְׁמַיִן, air, heaven
שׁמם, dismay
שׁמע, hear, obey
שָׁמְרַיִן, Samaria

שׁמשׁ, serve
שֶׁמֶשׁ, sun
שֵׁן, tooth
שׁנא, alter, change, different, harm, set *at nought*
שׁנה, different
שְׁנָה, sleep, year
שָׁעָה, moment
שׁפט, magistrate
שַׁפִּיר, fair
שׁפל, abase, humble, put *down*
שְׁפַל, lowly
שׁפר, acceptable, please, *seem* good
שְׁפַרְפָּר, break *of day*
שָׁק, leg
שׁרא, begin, dwell, give *way*, loose, solve
שֹׁרֶשׁ, root
שְׁרֹשִׁי, banishment
שֵׁשְׁבַּצַּר, Sheshbazzar
שֵׁת, six, sixth
שׁתה, drink
שְׁתַר בּוֹזְנַי, Shethar-bozenai

תבר, brittle
תְּדִירָא, continually
תוב, reply, return
תוה, astonish
תּוֹר, bull, ox
תְּחוֹת, under
תְּלַג, snow
תְּלִיתָי, third
תְּלָת, third
תְּלָת, three
תַּלְתִּי, third
תַּמָּה, there, wonder
תְּמַהּ, wonder
תִּנְיָן, second *one*
תִּנְיָנוּת, *second* time
תִּפְתָּיֵא, magistrate
תַּקִּיף, mighty, strong
תקל, weigh
תקן, establish
תקף, *become* strong, enforce, harden
תְּקִף, mighty
תְּקֹף, might
תְּרֵי עֲשַׂר, twelve
תִּרְיָן, second
תָּרָע, doorkeeper
תְּרַע, court, door
תַּתְּנַי, Tattenai
מְרַאֲשׁוֹת, *under the* head
אֲבִיאָסָף, Ebiasaph

Greek

Ἀαρών, Aaron
Ααρωνιδης, Aaron
Ἀβαδδών, Abaddon
Αβαδιας, Obadiah
Ἅβελ, Abel
Αβεσσαλωμ, Absalom
Ἀβιά, Abijah
Ἀβιαθάρ, Abiathar
Ἀβιληνή, Abilene
Ἀβιούδ, Abiud
Αβιρων, Abiram
Αβισουε, Abishua
Αβουβος, Abubus
Ἀβραάμ, Abraham
Αβρααμειτις, Abraham
Αβραμιαιος, Abraham
Αβρωνα, Abron
Αγαβα, Hagab
Ἅγαβος, Agabus
Ἁγάρ, Hagar

Αγγαβα, Hagabah
Αγγαιος, Haggai
Αγια, Hattil
Ἀγρίππας, Agrippa
Ἀδάμ, Adam
Αδαν, Addan
Αδαρ, Adar
Αδασα, Adasa
Αδδαι, Iddo
Ἀδδί, Addi
Αδδους, Addus
Αδιδα, Adida
Αδιν, Adin
Ἀδμίν, Admin
Αδουηλ, Aduel
Ἀδραμυττηνός, Adramyttium
Ἀδρίας, Adria
Αδωνικαμ, Adonikam
Αδωρα, Adora
Αερμων, Hermon

Ἀθῆναι, Athens
Ἀθηναῖος, Athenian, Athens
Αθηνοβιος, Athenobius
Αζαηλος, Asahel, Azael
Ἀζαρίας, Azariah, Azarias
Αζαρου, Azaru
Αζητας, Azetas
Ἀζώρ, Azor
Ἄζωτος, Azotus
Αἰγύπτιος, Egyptian
Αιγυπτος, Egyptian
Αἴγυπτος, Egypt
Αιθιοπια, Ethiopia
Αἰθίοψ, Ethiopian
Αἰνέας, Aeneas
Αἰνών, Aenon
Αισωρα, Aesora
Ακαταν, Hakkatan
Ἀκελδαμάχ, Akeldama
Ακκαρων, Ekron

Ακκουβ, Akkub
Ακκως, Accos, Hakkoz
Ακουβ, Akkub
Ακραβαττηνη, Akrabattene
Ἀκύλας, Aquila
Αλεμα, Alema
Αλεμοι, Alema
Ἀλεξάνδρεια, Alexandria
Ἀλεξάνδρειος, Alexandrian
Ἀλεξανδρεύς, Alexandria, Alexandrian
Ἀλεξανδρῖνος, Alexandria
Ἀλέξανδρος, Alexander
Αλικαρνασσος, Halicarnassus
Αλκιμος, Alcimus
Αλλων, Ami
Ἁλφαῖος, Alphaeus
Αμαδαθος, Hammedatha
Ἁμαθῖτις, Hamath
Αμαν, Haman
Αμαριας, Amariah

Αμβακουμ, Habakkuk
Ἀμιναδάβ, Amminadab
Αμμανιτις, Ammonite
Αμμαους, Emmaus
Αμμιδαιοι, Ammidian
Αμμωνιτης, Ammon, Ammonite
Αμορραιος, Amorite
Ἀμπλιᾶτος, Ampliatus
Ἀμφίπολις, Amphipolis
Ἀμών, Ammon, Ammonite
Ἀμώς, Amos
Αναηλ, Anael
Αναθωθ, Anathoth
Αναν, Hana
Ανανιας, Hanan, Hananiah, Hannaniah
Ἁνανίας, Anaiah, Ananias, Hanani
Ανανιηλ, Ananiel
Ανασιβ, Anasib
Ἀνδρέας, Andrew
Ἀνδρόνικος, Andronicus
Ἅννα, Anna
Ανναν, Annan
Ἅννας, Annas
Αννιας, Annias
Αννιουθ, Anniuth
Αννουνος, Annunus
Αντιλιβανος, Antilebanon
Ἀντιόχεια, Antioch
Ἀντιοχεύς, Antioch, Antiochian *citizen*
Αντιοχις, Antiochis
Αντιοχος, Antiochus
Ἀντιπᾶς, Antipas
Ἀντιπατρίς, Antipatris
Αντιπατρος, Antipater
Ανως, Vaniah
Απαμη, Apame
Ἀπελλῆς, Apelles
Απις, Apis
Απολλοφανης, Apollophanes
Ἀπολλύων, Apollyon
Ἀπολλωνία, Apollonia
Ἀπολλώνιος, Apollonius
Ἀπολλῶς, Apollos
Ἀππίος, Appius
Ἀπφία, Apphia
Απφους, Apphus
Ἀραβία, Arabia
Αραδος, Aradus
Ἀράμ, Ram
Αραρατ, Ararat
Αραψ, Arab
Ἄραψ, Arabian
Αρβαττα, Arbatta
Αρβηλα, Arbela
Ἄρειος, Arius
Ἄρειος πάγος, Areopagus
Ἀρεοπαγίτης, Areopagite
Αρες, Arah
Ἁρέτας, Aretas
Αριαραθης, Ariarathes
Ἁριμαθαία, Arimathea
Ἀρίσταρχος, Aristarchus
Ἀριστόβουλος, Aristobulus
Αριωχ, Arioch
Ἁρμαγεδών, Armageddon
Ἀρνί, Arni
Αρομ, Arom
Αρσακης, Arsaces
Αρσινοη, Arsinoe
Αρσιφουριθ, Jorah
Αρταξερξης, Artaxerxes
Ἀρτεμᾶς, Artemas
Ἀρτεμις, Artemis
Ἀρφαξάδ, Arphaxad
Ἀρχέλαος, Archelaus
Ἄρχιππος, Archippus

Ασαβιας, Hashabiah
Ασαδιας, Hasadiah
Ασαηλος, Sheal
Ασαιας, Asaias
Ασανα, Asnah
Ασαρα, Hasrah
Ἀσάφ, Asaph
Ασβασαρεθ, Esarhaddon
Ασγαδ, Azgad
Ασεβηβιας, Sherebiah
Ἀσήρ, Asher
Ἀσία, Asia
Ἀσιανός, Asian
Ἀσιάρχης, Asiarch
Ασιβιας, Asibias, Hashabiah
Ασιδαιος, Hasidean
Ἀσιηλ, Asiel
Ασκαλων, Ascalon, Askalon
Ασμοδαιος, Asmodeus
Ασομ, Hashum
Ασουρ, Asur
Ασουφα, Hasupha
Ασσαλιμωθ, Shelomith
Ασσαφιωθ, Hassophereth
Ἆσσος, Assos
Ασσουρ, Assyrian
Ασσυριος, Assyria, Assyrian
Αστυαγης, Astyages
Ἀσύγκριτος, Asyncritus
Ασυηρος, Ahasuerus
Ασφαρ, Asphar
Ασφαρασος, Mispar
Ασωρ, Hazor
Αταρ, Ater
Ατεργατιον, Atargatis
Ατηρ, Ater
Ατητα, Hatita
Ατθαριας, Attharias
Ατιφα, Hatipha
Ἀττάλεια, Attalia
Ἄτταλος, Attalus
Ατταρατης, Attharates
Αττους, Hattush
Αυαραν, Avaran
Αυγια, Agia
Αὔγουστος, Augustus
Αυρανος, Auranus
Αυταιας, Hodiah
Αφαιρεμα, Aphairema
Αφερρα, Apherra
Ἀχάζ, Ahaz
Ἀχαϊκός, Achaicus
Ἀχαΐα, Achaia
Αχιαχαρος, Ahikar
Αχιβα, Hakupha
Ἀχίμ, Achim
Αχιτωβ, Ahitub
Αχιωρ, Achior
Αψαλωμος, Absalom

Βάαλ, Baal
Βααλσαμος, Baalsamus
Βαανα, Baanah
Βααni, Bani
Βαβυλών, Babylon
Βαβυλωνια, Babylonia
Βαβυλωνιος, Babylonian
Βαγο, Bigvai
Βαγουαι, Bigvai
Βαγωας, Bagoas
Βαιαν, Baean
Βαιθαραβα, Beth-arabah
Βαιθβασι, Bethbasi
Βαιθηλ, Bethel
Βαιθζαχαρια, Beth-zechariah
Βαιθσαν, Beth-shan

Βαιθσουρα, Beth-zur
Βαιθωρων, Beth-horon
Βαιλμαιν, Belmain
Βαιτασμωθ, Bethasmoth
Βαιτηρους, Baiterus
Βαιτομασθαιμ, Betomasthaim
Βαιτομεσθαιμ, Betomesthaim
Βαιτυλουα, Bethulia
Βακβουκ, Bakbuk
Βακηνωρ, Bacenor
Βακχιδης, Bacchides
Βακχουρος, Zaccur
Βαλαάμ, Balaam
Βαλάκ, Balak
Βαλαμων, Balamon
Βαλνουος, Belnuus
Βαλτασαρ, Belshazzar
Βαναιας, Benaiah
Βανι, Bani
Βαννας, Bannas
Βαννους, Binnui
Βαραββᾶς, Barabbas
Βαράκ, Barak
Βαραχίας, Barachiah
Βαρθολομαῖος, Bartholomew
Βαριησοῦ, Bar-Jesus
Βαριωνᾶ, Bar-Jona
Βαρναβᾶς, Barnabas
Βαρουχ, Baruch
Βαρσαββᾶς, Barsabbas
Βαρτακος, Bartacus
Βαρτιμαῖος, Bartimaeus
Βαρχους, Barkos
Βαρωδις, Barodis
Βασαλωθ, Bazluth
Βασθαι, Besai
Βασκαμα, Baskama
Βασσαι, Bezai
Βατανη, Bethany
Βεελζεβούλ, Beelzebul
Βεελσαρος, Bilshan
Βεελτεθμος, Beltethmus
Βεκτιλεθ, Bectileth
Βελβαιμ, Balbaim
Βελιάλ, Belial
Βενιαμίν, Benjamin
Βερεα, Berea
Βερζελλει, Barzillai
Βερνίκη, Bernice
Βέροια, Beroea
Βεροιαῖος, Beroea
Βεσκασπασμυς, Bescaspasmys
Βεσλεμος, Bishlam
Βεώρ, Beor
Βηβαι, Bebai
Βηθανία, Bethany
Βηθδαγων, Beth-dagon
Βηθζαθά, Beth-zatha
Βηθζαιθ, Beth-zaith
Βηθλέεμ, Bethlehem
Βηθσαϊδά, Beth-saida
Βηθφαγή, Bethphage
Βηλ, Bel
Βην Ιωναθου, *son of* Jonathan
Βηροτ, Beeroth
Βιθλεεμ, Bethlehem
Βιθυνία, Bithynia
Βλάστος, Blastus
Βοανηργές, Boanerges
Βόες, Boaz
Βοκκα, Bukki
Βόος, Boaz
Βοσορ, Bosor
Βοσορρα, Bozrah
Βουγαῖος, Bougaean

Γαβαηλ, Gabael
Γαβάηλος, Gabael
Γαβαθα, Gabatha
Γαβαων, Gibeon
Γαββαθᾶ, Gabbatha
Γαββης, Geba
Γαβριας, Gabrias
Γαβριήλ, Gabriel
Γάδ, Gad
Γαδαρηνός, Gadarene
Γαδδι, Gaddi
Γάζα, Gaza
Γαζαρα, Gazara
Γαζηρα, Gazara, Gazzam
Γαζηρων, Gazara
Γάϊος, Gaius
Γαιβαι, Geba
Γαλααδ, Gilead
Γαλααδιτις, Gilead
Γαλαται, Galatian, Gaul
Γαλάτης, Galatian
Γαλατία, Galatia
Γαλατικός, Galatia
Γαλγαλα, Gilgal
Γαλιλαία, Galilee
Γαλιλαῖος, Galilean, Galilee
Γαλλίων, Gallio
Γαμαλιήλ, Gamaliel
Γαμηλος, Gamael
Γαριζιν, Gerizim
Γαρσομος, Gershom
Γας, Gas
Γεδδουρ, Gahar
Γεδεών, Gideon
Γεθ, Gath
Γεθσημανί, Gethsemane
Γενναίος, Gennaeus
Γεννησαρ, Gennesaret
Γεννησαρέτ, Gennesaret
Γερασηνὸς, Gerasene
Γεργεσαιος, Gergesite
Γερρηνοι, Gerar
Γεσεμ, Goshen
Γηων, Gihon
Γοθολιας, Gotholiah
Γοθονιηλ, Gothoniel
Γολγοθᾶ, Golgotha
Γολιαθ, Goliath
Γόμορρα, Gomorrah
Γοργιας, Gorgias
Γορτυνα, Gortyna
Γώγ, Gog

Δαβιρ, Debir
Δαγων, Dagon
Δαθαν, Dathan
Δαθεμα, Dathema
Δαισαν, Rezin
Δαλαιας, Delaiah
Δαλμανουθά, Dalmanutha
Δαλματία, Dalmatia
Δάμαρις, Damaris
Δαμασκηνός, Damascus
Δαμασκός, Damascus
Δανιήλ, Daniel
Δαρειος, Darius
Δαυίδ, David
Δαφνη, Daphne
Δεββωρα, Deborah
Δεκάπολις, Decapolis
Δερβαῖος, Derbe
Δέρβη, Derbe
Δεσσαου, Dessau
Δηλος, Delos
Δημᾶς, Demas
Δημήτριος, Demetrius

Δημοφων, Demophon
Δίδυμος, Twin
Διονυσια, Dionysus
Διονύσιος, Dionysius
Διονυσος, Dionysus
Διόσκουροι, Twin *Brothers*
Διοτρεφης, Diotrephes
Δορκάς, Dorcas
Δορυμενης, Dorymenes
Δοσιθεος, Dositheus
Δριμυλος, Drimylus
Δρούσιλλα, Drusilla
Δωθαιμ, Dothan
Δωκ, Dok
Δωρα, Dor
Δωταια, Dothan

Ἔβερ, Eber
Ἑβραϊστί, Hebrew
Ἑβραΐς, Hebrew
Ἑβραῖος, Hebrew
Εγρεβηλ, Acraba
Εδδι, Iddo
Εδδινους, Eddinus
Εδνα, Edna
Ἑζεκίας, Hezekiah
Εζριλ, Azarel
Εζωρα, Ezora, Ezra
Εκβατανα, Ecbatana
Ελαία, Olivet
Ελαιών, Olivet
Ἐλαμίτης, Elamite
Ελασα, Elasa
Ἐλεάζαρ, Eleazar
Ελεαζαρος, Eleazar, Eliezar
Ελευθερος, Eleutherus
Ελιαβ, Eliab
Ελιαδας, Elioenai
Ἐλιακίμ, Eliakim
Ελιαλις, Elialis
Ελιασιβος, Eliashib
Ελιασιμος, Eliashib
Ελιασις, Eliasis
Ελιαωνιας, Eliehoenai
Ἐλιέζερ, Eliezer
Ἐλιούδ, Eliud
Ἐλισάβετ, Elizabeth
Ἐλισαῖος, Elisha
Ελιφαλατ, Eliphelet
Ελιφαλατος, Eliphelet
Ελιωναις, Elioenai
Ελιωνας, Elionas
Ελκια, Elkiah
Ἑλλάς, Greece, Greek
Ἕλλην, Greek
Ἑλληνικός, Greek
Ἑλληνίς, Greek
Ελληνισμος, Hellenization
Ἑλληνιστής, Hellenist
Ἑλληνιστί, Greek
Ἐλμαδάμ, Elmadam
Ἐλναθαν, Elnathan
Ελουλ, Elul
Ελυμαιος, Elymaean
Ελυμαις, Elymais
Ἐλύμας, Elymas
Εμαθις, Emathis
Ἐμμανουήλ, Emmanuel
Ἐμμαοῦς, Emmaus
Εμμηρ, Immer
Ἑμμώρ, Hamor
Ενακιμ, Anakim
Ενγαδδοι, En-gedi
Ενεμεσσαρος, Shalmaneser
Ενηνιος, Bigvai
Ἐνναταν, Elnathan
Ἐνώς, Enos
Ἑνώχ, Enoch
Ἐπαίνετος, Epaenetus
Ἐπαφρᾶς, Epaphras
Ἐπαφρόδιτος, Epaphroditus
Ἐπικούρειος, Epicurean
Επιφανης, Epiphanes
Επιφι, Epeiph
Ἔραστος, Erastus
Ἑρμᾶς, Hermas
Ἑρμῆς, Hermes
Ἑρμογένης, Hermogenes
Ερμων, Hermon
Εσδρηλων, Esdraelon
Εσδρις, Esdris
Εσεβωνιτης, Heshbon
Εσθηρ, Esther
Ἑσλί, Esli
Ἑσρώμ, Hezron
Εὕα, Eve
Ευαιος, Hivite
Εὔβουλος, Eubulus
Ευεργετης, Euergetes
Ευμενης, Eumenes
Εὐνίκη, Eunice
Εὐοδία, Euodia
Ευπατωρ, Eupator
Ευπολεμος, Eupolemus
Εὔτυχος, Eutychus
Εὐφράτης, Euphrates
Ἐφέσιος, Ephesian, Ephesus
Ἔφεσος, Ephesus
Ἐφραίμ, Ephraim
Εφρων, Ephron

Ηδος, Iddo
Ηεγεμονιδης, Hegemonides
Ηλαμ, Elam
Ἠλί, Heli
Ἠλίας, Elijah
Ηλιοδωρος, Heliodorus
Ηλιου, Elijah
Ημαδαβουν, Emadabun
Ημαθ, Hamath
Ημμερ, Immer
Ἤρ, Er
Ηρακλης, Hercules
Ἡρῴδης, Herod
Ἡρῳδιανοί, Herodian
Ἡρῳδιάς, Herodias
Ἡρῳδίων, Herodion
Ἠσαΐας, Isaiah
Ησαυ, Ziha
Ἠσαύ, Esau
Ησυηλος, Jehiel

Θαδδαῖος, Thaddaeus
Θαιμαν, Teman
Θαμάρ, Tamar
Θαμναθα, Timnath
Θάρα, Terah
Θαρρα, Tharra
Θαρσεας, Tarsus
Θασσι, Thassi
Θεκωε, Tekoa
Θελερσας, Tel-harsha
Θεοδοτος, Theodotus
Θεόφιλος, Theophilus
Θερα, Theras
Θερμελεθ, Tel-melah
Θεσβων, Tishbe
Θεσσαλονικεύς, Thessalonian, Thessalonica
Θεσσαλονίκη, Thessalonica
Θευδᾶς, Theudas
Θισβη, Thisbe
Θοκανος, Tikvah
Θομει, Temah
Θραξ, Thracian
Θυάτιρα, Thyatira
Θωμᾶς, Thomas

Ζαβαδ, Zabad
Ζαβαδαιοι, Zabadean
Ζαβδαιος, Zebadiah
Ζαβδια, Zabad
Ζαβδιηλ, Zabdiel
Ζαβδος, Zabbai
Ζαβουλών, Zebulun
Ζαθθουι, Zattu
Ζαθοης, Zattu
Ζακχαῖος, Zacchaeus
Ζαμβρι, Zimri
Ζαμβρις, Amariah
Ζαμοθ, Zattu
Ζάρα, Zerah
Ζαραιας, Zerahiah, Zeraiah
Ζαριος, Zarius
Ζαχαρίας, Zechariah
Ζεβεδαῖος, Zebedee
Ζερδαιας, Zerdaiah
Ζεύς, Zeus
Ζεῦς Κορίνθιος, Dioscorinthius
Ζηνᾶς, Zenas
Ζογορα, Zoar
Ζοροβαβέλ, Zerubbabel

Ιαβιν, Jabin
Ιαδινος, Jamin
Ιαθαν, Jathan
Ιαζηρ, Jazer
Ἰάϊρος, Jair, Jairus
Ιαιρος, Reaiah
Ἰακώβ, Jacob
Ἰάκωβος, James
Ἰαμβρῆς, Jambres
Ιαμβρι, Jambri
Ιαμνια, Jamnia
Ιαμνιτης, Jamnia
Ἰανναί, Jannai
Ἰάννης, Jannes
Ἰάρετ, Jared
Ιαριμωθ, Jeremoth
Ιασουβος, Jashub
Ἰάσων, Jason
Ιαφεθ, Japheth
Ἰδουηλος, Iduel
Ιδουμαια, Edomite
Ἰδουμαία, Idumea
Ιδουμαιος, Edomite, Idumean
Ιεβλααμ, Ibleam
Ιεβουσαιος, Jebusite
Ιεδαιος, Adaiah
Ιεδδος, Jedaiah
Ιεηλι, Jaalah
Ιεηλος, Jehiel
Ἰεζάβελ, Jezebel
Ιεζεκιηλ, Ezekiel
Ιεζηλος, Jahaziel
Ιεζιας, Izziah, Jahzeiah
Ιεζριηλος, Jehiel
Ιειηλ, Jehiel
Ιεμναα, Jamnia
Ιεουηλ, Jeuel
Ἱεράπολις, Hierapolis
Ἰερεμίας, Jeremai, Jeremiah
Ιερεμωθ, Jeremoth
Ιερεχος, Jericho
Ἰεριχώ, Jericho
Ιεροβοαμ, Jeroboam
Ἱεροσόλυμα, Jerusalem
Ἱεροσολυμίτης, Jerusalem, *people of* Jerusalem
Ἰερουσαλήμ, Jerusalem
Ιερωνυμος, Hieronymus
Ιεσιας, Jeshaiah
Ἰεσσαί, Jesse
Ἰεφθάε, Jephthah
Ιεφοννη, Jephunneh
Ἰεχονίας, Jechoniah, Jeconiah
Ἰησοῦς, Jeshua, Jesus, Joshua
Ιθαμαρ, Ithamar
Ἰκόνιον, Iconium
Ιλιαδουν, Iliadun
Ἰλλυρικόν, Illyricum
Ιμαλκουε, Imalkue
Ινδικη, India
Ινδος, Indian
Ιοδδους, Jaddus
Ἰόππη, Joppa
Ιοππιτης, Joppa
Ἰορδάνης, Jordan
Ιου, Jehu
Ιουδα, Judah
Ἰουδαϊκός, Jew, Jewish
Ἰουδαϊσμός, Jewish *faith*, Judaism
Ἰουδαία, Judea
Ἰουδαῖος, Jew, Jewess, Jewish, Judah, Judea
Ἰούδας, Judah, Judas, Jude
Ιουδιθ, Judith
Ιουηλ, Joel
Ἰουλία, Julia
Ἰούλιος, Julius
Ἰουνιᾶς, Junias
Ἰοῦστος, Justus
Ἰσαάκ, Isaac
Ισακιος, Isaac
Ισδαηλ, Giddel
Ἰσκαριώθ, Iscariot
Ἰσκαριώτης, Iscariot
Ισμαηλος, Ishmael
Ἰσραήλ, Israel, Israelite
Ἰσραηλίτης, Israel, Israelite
Ἰσσαχάρ, Issachar
Ισταλκουρος, Istalcurus
Ἰταλία, Italy
Ἰταλικός, Italian
Ἰτουραῖος, Ituraea
Ιωαβ, Joab
Ἰωαθάμ, Jotham
Ἰωακίμ, Jehoiachin, Jehoiakim, Joakim
Ἰωανάν, Joanan
Ἰωανας, Jonah
Ἰωάνης, Johanan
Ἰωάννα, Joanna
Ἰωάννης, Jehohanan, John
Ιωαριβ, Joarib
Ἰώβ, Job
Ἰωβήδ, Obed
Ἰωδά, Joda
Ιωδανος, Jodan
Ἰωήλ, Joel
Ιωζαβδος, Jozabad
Ιωναθαν, Jonathan
Ἰωνάθας, Jonathan
Ιωναθης, Jonathan
Ἰωνάμ, Jonam
Ἰωναν, Jonah
Ἰωνᾶς, Jonah
Ἰωράμ, Joram
Ιωριβος, Jarib
Ἰωρίμ, Jorim
Ἰωσαφάτ, Jehoshaphat
Ιωσαφιας, Josiphiah
Ιωσεδεκ, Jozadak
Ιωσηπος, Joseph
Ἰωσῆς, Joses
Ἰωσήφ, Joseph
Ἰωσήχ, Josech
Ἰωσίας, Josiah

Καδης, Kadesh
Καδης Βαρνη, Kadesh-barnea
Καδμιηλ, Kadmiel
Καδμιηλος, Kadmiel
Καθουα, Cathua
Καϊάφας, Caiaphas
Καϊνάμ, Cainan
Κάϊν, Cain
Καῖσαρ, Caesar
Καισάρεια, Caesarea
Καλαμωλαλος, Elam
Καλιτας, Kelita
Καλλισθένης, Callisthenes
Κανά, Cana
Καναναῖος, Cananaean
Κανδάκη, Candace
Καπιρας, Chephirah
Καππαδοκία, Cappadocia
Καραβασιων, Carabasion
Καρια, Caria
Καριαθιαριος, Kiriatharim
Καρμηλος, Carmel
Καρναιν, Carnaim
Καρνιον, Carnaim
Κάρπος, Carpus
Κασπιν, Caspin
Καῦδα, Cauda
Καφαρναούμ, Capernaum
Κεγχρεαί, Cenchreae
Κεδρών, Kedron, Kidron
Κενδεβαιος, Cendebeus
Κηδες, Kadesh
Κηρας, Keros
Κηταβ, Ketab
Κηφᾶς, Cephas
Κιλαν, Kilan
Κιλικία, Cilicia
Κιραμας, Ramah
Κίς, Kish
Κισαιας, Kish
Κιτιεις, Macedonian
Κλαυδία, Claudia
Κλαύδιος, Claudius
Κλεοπᾶς, Cleopas
Κλεοπατρα, Cleopatra
Κλήμης, Clement
Κλωπᾶς, Clopas
Κνίδος, Cnidus
Κοιλη Συρια, Coele-Syria, Coelesyria
Κοιντος, Quintus
Κολοσσαί, Colossae
Κόρε, Korah
Κορίνθιος, Corinthian
Κόρινθος, Corinth
Κορνήλιος, Cornelius
Κούαρτος, Quartus
Κουθα, Cutha
Κρατης, Crates
Κρής, Cretan
Κρήσκης, Crescens
Κρήτη, Crete
Κρίσπος, Crispus
Κυαμων, Cyamon
Κυδιως, Kedesh
Κυπριαρχης, Cyprus
Κύπριος, Cyprian, Cyprus
Κύπρος, Cyprus
Κυρηναῖος, Cyrene, Cyrenian, Quirinius
Κυρήνη, Cyrene
Κύριος, Lord
Κυρος, Cyrus
Κῶ, Cos
Κωλα, Kola
Κωλιος, Kelaiah
Κωνα, Kona
Κωσάμ, Cosam

Λαβάν, Laban
Λαβανα, Lebanah
Λάζαρος, Lazarus
Λακαιδαιμονιοι, Lacedaemonian
Λακκουνος, Laccunus
Λάμεχ, Lamech
Λαοδίκεια, Laodicea
Λαοδικεύς, Laodicean
Λασαία, Lasea
Λασθενης, Lasthenes
Λευί, Levi
Λευις, Levi
Λευίτης, Levite, Levitical
Λευιτικός, Levitical
Λευκιος, Lucius
Λίβανος, Lebanon
Λιβυες, Libya
Λιβύη, Libya
Λίνος, Linus
Λοζων, Lozon
Λουδ, Lud
Λουκᾶς, Luke
Λούκιος, Lucius
Λύδδα, Lydda
Λυδία, Lydia
Λυκαονία, Lycaonia
Λυκαονιστί, Lycaonian
Λυκία, Lycia
Λυσανίας, Lysanias
Λυσίας, Lysias
Λυσιμαχος, Lysimachus
Λύστρα, Lystra
Λωθασουβος, Lothasubus
Λωΐς, Lois
Λώτ, Lot

Μάαθ, Maath
Μααν, Meunite
Μαασαιας, Mahseiah
Μαασιας, Maaseiah
Μαασμαν, Maasmas
Μαγαδάν, Magadan
Μαγδαληνή, Magdalene
Μαγεδδαων, Megiddo
Μαγώγ, Magog
Μαδιάμ, Midian
Μαηρος, Amram
Μαθουσάλα, Methuselah
Μαζιτιας, Mattithiah
Μαιαννας, Maaseiah
Μαισαλωθ, Mesaloth
Μακαλων, Michmas
Μακεδ, Maked
Μακεδονία, Macedonia
Μακεδών, Macedonia, Macedonian
Μακκαβαιος, Maccabeus
Μακρων, Macron
Μαλελεήλ, Mahaleleel
Μαλλωται, Mallus
Μαλτανναιος, Mattenai
Μάλχος, Malchus
Μαμδαι, Mamdai
Μαμνιταναιμος, Machnadebai
Μαμουχος, Malluch
Μαναήν, Manaen
Μανασση, Manasseh
Μανασσηας, Manasseas
Μανασσῆς, Manasseh
Μανι, Bani
Μανιος, Manius
Μαρδοχαικος, Mordecai
Μαρδοχαιος, Mordecai
Μάρθα, Martha
Μαρία, Mary
Μαρισα, Mareshah, Marisa

Μᾶρκος, Mark
Μαρμωθι, Meremoth
Μασιας, Masiah
Μασσηφα, Mizpah
Μασσιας, Maaseiah
Ματανιας, Mattaniah
Μαθθαῖος, Matthew
Μαθθάν, Matthan
Μαθθάτ, Matthat
Μαθθίας, Matthias
Ματταθά, Mattatha
Ματταθίας, Mattathiah, Mattathias, Mattattah
Ματταρι, Matrite
Μαχμας, Michmash
Μαωναθει, Meonothai
Μεεδδα, Mehida
Μελεά, Melea
Μελίτη, Malta
Μελχί, Melchi
Μελχιας, Malchijah, Melchias
Μελχιηλ, Melchiel
Μελχισέδεκ, Melchizedek
Μεμμιος, Memmius
Μεμφις, Memphis
Μενελαος, Menelaus
Μενεσθευς, Menestheus
Μεννά, Menna
Μεραρι, Merari
Μερραν, Merran
Μεσοποταμία, Mesopotamia
Μεσσίας, Messiah
Μηδαβα, Medeba
Μηδια, Media
Μῆδος, Mede
Μιαμινος, Mijamin
Μιθραδατης, Mithridates
Μίλητος, Miletus
Μισαήλ, Mishael
Μιτυλήνη, Mitylene
Μιχα, Micah
Μιχαήλ, Michael
Μιχαηλος, Michael
Μιχαιας, Micaiah
Μνάσων, Mnason
Μολόχ, Moloch
Μομδιος, Maadai
Μοολι, Mahli
Μοοσσιας, Moossias
Μοσολλαμος, Meshullam
Μοχμουρ, Mochmur
Μυνδος, Myndos
Μύρα, Myra
Μυσαρχης, Mysian
Μυσία, Mysia
Μωαβ, Moab
Μωαβιτης, Moabite
Μωδειν, Modein
Μωεθ, Moeth
Μωϋσῆς, Moses

Νααθος, Naathus
Ναασσών, Nahshon
Ναβαριας, Nabariah
Ναβατ, Nebat
Ναβαταιος, Nabatean
Ναβουχοδονοσορ, Nebuchadnezzar
Ναγγαί, Naggai
Ναδαβ, Nadab
Ναδαβαθ, Nadabath
Ναθάμ, Nathan
Ναθαν, Nathan
Ναθαναήλ, Nathanael, Nethanel
Ναθαναηλος, Nathanael
Ναθανιας, Nethaniah
Ναζαρά, Nazareth
Ναζαρέθ, Nazareth
Ναζαρέτ, Nazareth
Ναζαρηνός, Nazarene, Nazareth
Ναζιραιος, Nazirite
Ναζωραῖος, Nazarene, Nazareth
Ναΐν, Nain
Ναιδος, Naidus
Ναιμάν, Naaman
Ναναια, Nanea
Ναναιος, Nanea
Ναούμ, Nahum
Νάρκισσος, Narcissus
Νασι, Neziah
Ναυή, Nun
Ναφισι, Nephisim
Ναχώρ, Nahor
Νέα πόλις, Neapolis
Νεεμιας, Nehemiah
Νεκωδαν, Nekoda
Νετωφα, Netophah
Νεφθαλίμ, Naphtali
Νηρεύς, Nereus
Νηρί, Neri
Νηριας, Neraiah
Νίγερ, Niger
Νικάνωρ, Nicanor
Νικόδημος, Nicodemus
Νικολαΐτης, Nicolaitan
Νικόλαος, Nicolaus
Νικόπολις, Nicopolis
Νινευή, Nineveh
Νινευίτης, Nineveh
Νισαν, Nisan
Νιφις, Magbish
Νοεβα, Nekoda
Νοομα, Nebo
Νουα, Nohah
Νουμηνιος, Numenius
Νύμφα, Nympha
Νῶε, Noah

Ξανθικός, Xanthicus

Οββια, Habaiah
Οδολλαμ, Adullam
Οδομηρα, Odomera
Οθονιας, Othoniah
Ὀζίας, Uzza, Uzzi, Uzziah
Οζιηλ, Oziel
Οκινα, Ocina
Ολοφερνης, Holofernes
Ὀλυμπᾶς, Olympas
Ὀλυμπιος, Olympian
Ὀνήσιμος, Onesimus
Ὀνησίφορος, Onesiphorus
Ονιας, Onias
Ορθωσια, Orthosia
Ουθι, Uthai
Οὐρβανός, Urbanus
Οὐρίας, Uriah
Ουτα, Uthai
Οχιηλος, Ochiel

Παθαιος, Pethahiah
Παμφυλία, Pamphylia
Πάρθοι, Parthian
Παρμενᾶς, Parmenas
Πάταρα, Patara
Πάτμος, Patmos
Πατροβᾶς, Patrobas
Πατροκλος, Patroclus
Παῦλος, Paul, Paulus
Πάφος, Paphos
Παχων, Pachon

Πεδιας, Bedeiah
Πέργαμος, Pergamum
Πέργη, Perga
Περσεπολις, Persepolis
Περσευς, Perseus
Περσης, Persian
Περσικος, Persia
Περσις, Persia
Περσίς, Persis
Πέτρος, Peter
Πιλᾶτος, Pilate
Πισιδία, Pisidia
Ποντικός, Pontus
Πόντιος, Pontius
Πόντος, Pontus
Πόπλιος, Publius
Πόρκιος, Porcius
Ποσιδωνιος, Posidonius
Ποτίολοι, Puteoli
Πούδης, Pudens
Πρίσκα, Prisca
Πρόχορος, Prochorus
Πτολεμαεις, Ptolemais
Πτολεμαΐς, Ptolemais
Πτολεμαικος, Ptolemaic
Πτολεμαιος, Ptolemy
Πύρρος, Pyrrhus

Ῥαάβ, Rahab
Ῥαγαύ, Ragae, Reu
Ῥαγοι, Rages
Ῥαγουηλ, Raguel
Ῥαθαμιν, Rathamin
Ῥαζις, Razis
Ῥαμά, Ramah
Ῥαμεσση, Raamses
Ῥαμίας, Ramiah
Ῥαουμος, Rehum
Ῥασσις, Rassis
Ῥαφαηλ, Raphael
Ῥαφαιν, Raphaim
Ῥαφια, Raphia
Ῥαφων, Raphon
Ῥαχάβ, Rahab
Ῥαχήλ, Rachel
Ῥαψακης, Rab-shakeh
Ῥεβέκκα, Rebecca
Ῥεελιας, Reeliah
Ῥεφάν, Rephan
Ῥήγιον, Rhegium
Ῥησά, Rhesa
Ῥησαιας, Resaiah
Ῥοβοάμ, Rehoboam
Ῥόδη, Rhoda
Ῥοδιοι, Rhodes
Ῥοδοκος, Rhodocus
Ῥόδος, Rhodes
Ῥοιμος, Rehum
Ῥουβήν, Reuben
Ῥούθ, Ruth
Ῥοῦφος, Rufus
Ῥωμαϊστί, Latin
Ῥωμαῖος, Roman, Roman *citizen*, Rome
Ῥώμη, Rome

Σαβαννος, Binnui
Σαβατ, Shebat
Σαββαιας, Sabbaias
Σαββαταιος, Shabbethai
Σαδδουκαῖος, Sadducee
Σαδδουκος, Zadok
Σαδώκ, Zadok
Σαθραβουζανης, Sathrabuzanes
Σαλά, Sala, Shelah
Σαλαθιηλ, Shealtiel
Σαλαμιηλ, Salamiel
Σαλαμίς, Salamis
Σαλήμ, Salem
Σαλθας, Elasah
Σαλίμ, Salim
Σαλμών, Salmon
Σαλμώνη, Salmone
Σαλωμ, Salu, Shallum
Σαλώμη, Salome
Σαλωμωθ, Shelomoth
Σαμαιας, Shemaiah
Σαμάρεια, Samaria
Σαμαρίτης, Samaritan
Σαμαρῖτις, Samaria, Samaritan
Σαμμους, Shema
Σαμοθρᾴκη, Samothrace
Σάμος, Samos
Σαμουήλ, Samuel
Σαμσαιος, Shimshai
Σαμψαμης, Sampsames
Σαμψών, Samson
Σαναας, Senaah
Σαναβασσαρος, Sheshbazzar
Σαούλ, Saul
Σάπφιρα, Sapphira
Σαραβιας, Sherebiah
Σαραιας, Seraiah
Σαρασαδαι, Sarasadai
Σάρδεις, Sardis
Σάρεπτα, Zarephath
Σάρρα, Sarah
Σαρωθιε, Sarothie
Σαρων, Sharon
Σατανᾶς, Satan
Σαῦλος, Saul
Σαφατ, Shaphat
Σαφατια, Shephatiah
Σαφατιας, Shephatiah
Σαχερδονος, Esarhaddon
Σεβαστός, Augustan
Σεδεκιας, Zedekiah
Σεκοῦνδος, Secundus
Σελεμιας, Shelemiah
Σελεύκεια, Seleucia
Σελευκος, Seleucus
Σελλουμ, Shallum
Σεμει, Shimei
Σεμεΐν, Semein
Σεμειας, Shemaiah, Shimei
Σενναχηριμ, Sennacherib
Σεραρ, Sisera
Σέργιος, Sergius
Σερούχ, Serug
Σεσθηλ, Sesthel
Σεσσις, Shashai
Σεφηλα, Shephelah
Σεχενιας, Shecaniah
Σήθ, Seth
Σήμ, Shem
Σηρων, Seron
Σιδη, Side
Σιδών, Sidon
Σιδώνιος, Sidon, Sidonian
Σικιμα, Shechem
Σικιμιται, Shechemite
Σικυων, Sicyon
Σίλας, Silas
Σιλουανός, Silvanus
Σιλωάμ, Siloam
Σίμων, Simon
Σινά, Sinai
Σιουαν, Sivan
Σιραχ, Sirach
Σισιννης, Sisinnes
Σιών, Zion
Σκευᾶς, Sceva
Σκύθης, Scythian
Σκυθοπολιται, Scythopolis
Σκυθῶν πόλις, Scythopolis
Σμύρνα, Smyrna
Σόδομα, Sodom
Σοδομιται, Sodom
Σολομών, Solomon
Σουα, Siaha
Σουβας, Subas
Σουδ, Sud
Σουδιας, Sudias
Σουρ, Sur
Σουσα, Susa
Σουσάννα, Susanna
Σουφιρ, Ophir
Σπανία, Spain
Σπαρτη, Sparta
Σπαρτιαται, Spartan
Στάχυς, Stachys
Στεφανᾶς, Stephanas
Στέφανος, Stephen
Στοϊκός, Stoic
Συβαι, Shamlai
Συμεών, Simeon
Συντύχη, Syntyche
Συράκουσαι, Syracuse
Συρία, Syria, Syrian
Συριακος, Syrian
Σύρος, Syrian
Συροφοινίκισσα, Syrophoenician
Σύρτις, Syrtis
Συχάρ, Sychar
Συχέμ, Shechem, Shechemite
Σχεδια, Schedia
Σωβαι, Shobai
Σώπατρος, Sopater
Σωσθένης, Sosthenes
Σωσίπατρος, Sosipater
Σωστρατος, Sostratus

Ταβαωθ, Tabbaoth
Ταβελλιος, Tabeel
Ταβιθά, Tabitha
Τανις, Tanis
Ταρσεῖς, *people of* Tarsus
Ταρσεύς, Tarsus
Ταρσός, Tarsus
Ταφνας, Tahpanhes
Τέρτιος, Tertius
Τέρτυλλος, Tertullus
Τεφων, Tephon
Τιβεριάς, Tiberias
Τιβέριος, Tiberius
Τιγρις, Tigris
Τιμαῖος, Timaeus
Τιμόθεος, Timothy
Τίμων, Timon
Τίτιος, Titius
Τίτος, Titus
Τολβανης, Telem
Τολμαν, Talmon
Τουβιανοι, Toubiani
Τουβιας, Tob
Τραχωνῖτις, Trachonitis
Τριπολις, Tripolis
Τρόφιμος, Trophimus
Τρύφαινα, Tryphaena
Τρυφων, Trypho
Τρυφῶσα, Tryphosa
Τρῳάς, Troas
Τύραννος, Tyrannus
Τύριος, Tyre, Tyrian
Τύρος, Tyre
Τυχικός, Tychicus
Τωβιας, Tobiah, Tobias
Τωβιηλ, Tobiel
Τωβιτ, Tobit
Ὑδασπης, Hydaspes
Ὑμέναιος, Hymenaeus
Ὑρκανος, Hyrcanus

Φααθμωαβ, Pahathmoab
Φαδαιος, Pedaiah
Φαδων, Padon
Φαισουρ, Pashhur
Φακαρεθ σαβιη, Pochereth-hazzebaim
Φαλαρις, Phalaris
Φάλεκ, Peleg
Φαλιας, Pelaiah
Φανουήλ, Phanuel
Φαραθων, Pharathon
Φαρακιμ, Pharakim
Φαραώ, Pharaoh
Φαρες, Phares
Φάρες, Perez
Φαριδα, Peruda
Φαρισαῖος, Pharisee
Φασηλις, Phaselis
Φασιρων, Phasiron
Φασσορος, Pashhur
Φερεζαιος, Perizzite
Φῆλιξ, Felix
Φῆστος, Festus
Φιλαδέλφεια, Philadelphia
Φιλήμων, Philemon
Φίλητος, Philetus
Φιλιππήσιος, Philippian
Φίλιπποι, Philippi
Φίλιππος, Philip, Philippi
Φιλόλογος, Philologus
Φιλομητωρ, Philometor
Φιλοπατωρ, Philopator
Φινεες, Phinehas
Φινοε, Paseah
Φισων, Pishon
Φλέγων, Phlegon
Φοίβη, Phoebe
Φοινίκη, Phoenicia
Φοῖνιξ, Phoenix
Φορος, Parosh
Φορτουνᾶτος, Fortunatus
Φουδ, Put
Φρυγία, Phrygia
Φρυξ, Phrygian
Φύγελος, Phygelus
Φυλιστιιμ, Philistine

Χαβρις, Chabris
Χαδιασαι, Chadiasan
Χαιρεας, Chaereas
Χαλδαῖος, Chaldea, Chaldean
Χαλεβ, Caleb
Χαλφι, Chalphi
Χανάαν, Canaan
Χαναναῖος, Canaanite
Χανουναιος, Hananiah
Χαρααθ, Cherub
Χαραξ, Charax
Χαρεα, Charea
Χαρκαμυς, Carchemish
Χαρμη, Harim
Χαρμις, Charmis
Χαρράν, Haran
Χασεβα, Chezib
Χασελευ, Chislev
Χασφω, Chaspho
Χαφαρσαλαμα, Caphar-salama
Χαφεναθα, Chaphenatha
Χεβρων, Hebron
Χελεοι, Chellean
Χελκιας, Hilkiah
Χελους, Chelous
Χετταιος, Hittite

Χεττιειμ, Hittite
Χεττιμ, Kittim
Χίος, Chios
Χλόη, Chloe
Χοραζίν, Chorazin
Χορβε, Chorbe
Χοσαμαιος, Chosamaeus
Χουζᾶς, Chuza
Χουσι, Chusi
Χριστιανός, Christian
Χριστός, Christ
Χωβα, Choba
Χωρηβ, Horeb

Ωβαδιος, Abdi
Ωβηθ, Obed
Ωκιδηλος, Gedaliah
Ωλαμος, Meshullam,
Ωνω, Ono
Ωξ, Ox
Ωουδας, Judah
Ωσαιας, Jeshaiah
Ὡσηέ, Hosea

ἃ ὁράω, vision
ἀβαρής, burden
ἄβατος, desolation, impassable, inaccessible, trackless, unapproachable, untrodden
ἀβλαβής, harmless, unharmed
ἀβοηθησία, *no* help
ἀβοήθητος, helpless, unable *to help*
ἀβουλεύτως, unwisely
ἀβουλία, folly
ἄβρα, maid
ἀβροχία, drought
ἄβυσσος, abyss, bottomless *pit*, deep, *great* deep, pit, sea
ἀγαθοεργέω, *do* good, good
ἀγαθοποιέω, *do* good, *do* right, good *deed*
ἀγαθοποιΐα, *do* right
ἀγαθοποιός, *do* good, *do* right
ἀγαθός, blessing, brave, capable, clear, dinner, excellent, favor, fine, generosity, generous, glad, good, good *deed*, good *man*, good *people*, good *thing*, goodness, goods, great, happy, honest, honorable, kind, kindly, *most* skilful, noble, prosper, prosperity, pure, right, sound, true, welfare, well, well *off*, wise, worthily
ἀγαθότης, goodness, uprightness
ἀγαθουργέω, *do* good
ἀγαθόω, *do* good
ἀγαθύνω, please
ἀγαθωσύνη, good, goodness
ἀγαλλίαμα, gladness, joy, *joyful* praise, love, pride, rejoicing
ἀγαλλιάομαι, exult
ἀγαλλίασις, gladness, rejoicing
ἀγαλλιάω, exult, glad, glory, joy, rejoice, rejoicing
ἄγαλμα, statue
ἄγαμος, single, unmarried, unmarried *man*
ἀγανακτέω, anger, *become* incensed, indignant, indignantly, rage
ἀγανάκτησις, indignation
ἀγαπάω, beloved, love
ἀγάπη, beloved, love, *love* feast
ἀγάπησις, love
ἀγαπητός, beloved, dear, love, *very* dear
ἀγαυρίαμα, insolence
ἀγγαρεύω, compel, force
ἀγγεῖον, flask, jar, storage, vessel
ἀγγελία, message, rumor
ἀγγέλλω, say
ἄγγελος, angel, messenger
ἄγγος, vessel
ἀγείρω, stir, stir *up*
ἀγελαῖος, flock
ἀγέλη, flock, herd
ἀγεληδόν, crowd, flock

ἀγενεαλόγητος, *without* genealogy
ἀγενής, low
ἀγερωχία, insolence, revelry
ἀγέρωχος, arrogant
ἁγιάζω, consecrate, dedicate, hallow, make *holy*, make *sacred*, reverence, saint, sanctify
ἁγίασμα, holiness, holy, sanctuary
ἁγιασμός, consecration, holiness, holy, sanctification, sanctuary
ἁγιαστία, holiness
ἅγιος, angel, holiness, holy, holy *man*, holy *one*, holy *place*, holy *thing*, *most* holy, priest, sacred, saint, sanctuary, temple
ἁγιότης, holiness
ἁγιωσύνη, holiness
ἀγκάλη, arm
ἄγκιστρον, hook
ἄγκυρα, anchor
ἀγκών, elbow
ἄγναφος, unshrunk
ἁγνεία, purity
ἁγνίζω, burn, purify
ἁγνισμός, purification
ἀγνοέω, *act* amiss, commit *an offense*, *do in* ignorance, fail *to know*, ignorant, ignorantly, know, *no one* knows, recognize, stranger, unaware, understand, uninformed, unknown, *without* knowing
ἀγνόημα, error, ignorance, *unwitting* error, *unwitting* offense
ἄγνοια, error, ignorance, mistake
ἁγνός, chaste, guiltless, holy, pure, purity, sincerely
ἁγνότης, pure, purity
ἀγνωσία, ignorance, ignorant, incomprehension, *no* knowledge
ἄγνωστος, unknown
ἀγορά, market *place*, *public* square
ἀγοράζω, buy, buyer, ransom, redeem
ἀγοραῖος, court, rabble
ἀγορανομία, administration *of market*
ἀγορασμός, buy
ἀγοραστής, buyer *of provisions*
ἄγρα, catch
ἀγράμματος, uneducated
ἀγραυλέω, field
ἀγρεύω, entrap *in talk*
ἀγριέλαιος, *wild* olive, *wild* olive tree
ἄγριος, *more* savage, rage, savage, wild
ἀγριότης, savagery
ἀγριόω, madden
ἀγρίως, savagely
ἄγροικος, *more* rudely
ἀγρός, country, farm, field, land
ἀγρυπνέω, keep *alert*, keep *watch*, vigilant, watch, watchful
ἀγρυπνία, careful, loss *of sleep*, *sleepless* night, sleeplessness, wakeful, wakefulness, watch, watchfulness
ἀγυιά, street
ἄγχω, anguish, strangle
ἄγω, act, adopt, break *a spirit*, bring, bring *to trial*, bring *up*, carry *away*, carry *out*, celebrate, come, conduct, drag, drag *away*, drag *off*, drive, force, go, guide, hold, induce, keep, lead, lead *away*, make, *make* flow, move, observance, observe, open, subject, sway, take, take *away*, treat
ἄγω ἐπὶ πέρας, accomplish
ἀγωγή, conduct, policy, treatment, way *of living*
ἀγών, battle, conflict, contest, *deathly* anxiety, fight, game, opposition, race, struggle
ἀγῶνα ἔχω, strive
ἀγωνία, anguish, distress
ἀγωνιάω, alarm, anguish, distress
ἀγωνίζομαι, athlete, contend, fight, remember *earnestly*, strive
ἀγωνιστής, contestant
ἀδαμάντινος, *like* adamant
ἀδάμαστος, indomitable, untamed
ἀδάπανος, free *of charge*
ἀδεής, confidently

ἄδεια, *full* permission, license, unpunished
ἀδελφή, brother, sister
ἀδελφικῶς, *like a* brother
ἀδελφοκτόνος, slay *a brother*
ἀδελφοπρεπῶς, manner *worthy of a brother*
ἀδελφός, brother, brotherhood, fellow, husband, kinsman, man, relative
ἀδελφότης, brother, brotherhood
ἄδηλος, indistinct, see, *something* mysterious, uncertain
ἄδηλος καταστροφή, uncertainty
ἀδηλότης, uncertain
ἀδήλως, aimlessly
ἀδημονέω, distress, trouble
ᾅδης, Hades
ἀδιάκριτος, *without* uncertainty
ἀδιάλειπτος, constantly, unceasing
ἀδιαλείπτως, cease, constantly, continuously, unceasingly, *without* ceasing, *without* stopping
ἀδιάπτωτος, fail
ἀδιάστροφος, unswerving
ἀδιάτρεπτος, headstrong
ἀδιεξέταστος, unexamined
ἀδικέω, *do* evil, *do* wrong, evildoer, harm, hurt, offend, suffer *harm*, suffer *the wrong*, suffer *wrong*, wound, wrong, wrongdoer
ἀδίκημα, crime, iniquity, injury, wrong, wrongdoing
ἀδικία, dishonest, falsehood, iniquity, injury, injustice, *unjust* dealing, unrighteous, unrighteousness, wicked, wickedness, wrong, wrongdoing
ἄδικος, dishonest, iniquity, unjust, unrighteous, unrighteous *man*, unrighteous *thing*, unrighteousness, wrong, *wrongfully* obtain
ἀδίκως, deceit, unjustly, unrighteously, wickedly
ἀδόκητος, unexpected
ἀδόκιμος, base, counterfeit, disqualify, fail, fail *to meet the test*, unfit, worthless
ἀδολεσχέω, babble, commune, prattle
ἄδολος, pure
ἀδόλως, *without* guile
ἀδοξία, *not to* respect
ἄδοξος, dishonor, *without* honor
ἀδρανής, *no* strength
ἁδρότης, *liberal* gift
ἁδρύνω, mark *of pride*
ἀδυναμέω, imperfectly
ἀδυναμία, helplessness
ἀδυνατέω, impossible, unable
ἀδύνατος, do, helpless, impossible, *no* power, powerless, weak
ἀεί, all, always, regular
ἀείδω, sing
ἀέναος, ever-flowing, everflowing, everlasting
ἀετός, eagle
ἀήρ, air, breath
ἀθανασία, immortality
ἀθάνατος, immortal
ἀθέμιτος, forbid, lawless, unlawful, wicked
ἄθεος, *without* God,
ἀθεσία, act *of treachery*, perfidy
ἄθεσμος, lawless, lawless *man*, wicked
ἀθέσμως, lawlessly
ἀθετέω, annul, break, cancel, disregard, foil, make *light*, nullify, reject, thwart, trick, violate
ἀθέτησις, put *away*, set *aside*
ἀθεώρητος, unseen
ἀθλέω, athlete, compete
ἄθλησις, struggle
ἀθλητής, athlete
ἄθλιος, *most* miserable, *poor* wretch
ἀθλοθετέω, give *an award*
ἆθλον, prize
ἀθλοφόρος, carry *away the prize*, victorious
ἀθροίζω, assemble, crowd *together*, gather, gather *together*, rally
ἄθροισμα, *large* company
ἀθρόος, assemble

ἀθυμέω, *become* discouraged, discourage, lose *heart*
ἀθῷος, innocent
ἄζυμος, feast *of unleavened bread*, *feast of* Unleavened *Bread*, unleavened, *unleavened* bread
ἀϊδιότης, eternity
ἀΐδιος, eternal, everlasting
αἴγειος, goat
αἰγιαλός, beach
αἰδέομαι, ashamed, regard, respect
αἰδήμων, modest
αἴδης, death, grave, live
αἰδώς, modesty, shameful *manner*
αἴθριος, *open* air
αἰκία, outrage, *outrageous* treatment, torture
αἰκίζομαι, maltreat
αἰκίζω, mangle, torment, torture, torturer
αἰκισμός, agony, torture
αἰλαμμών, vestibule
αἴλουρος, cat
αἷμα, blood, bloodshed, juice
αἱματεκχυσία, shedding *of blood*
αἱμοβόρος, bloodthirsty
αἱμορροέω, hemorrhage
αἴνεσις, praise, song *of praise*, *thank* offering
αἰνετός, praise, worthy *of praise*
αἰνέω, give *praise*, praise, sing *praise*
αἴνιγμα, obscurity, riddle
αἶνος, hymn *of praise*, praise, word *of praise*
αἴξ, goat
αἵρεσις, discretion, faction, heresy, party, *party* spirit, sect
αἱρετίζω, choose, greet, prefer
αἱρετίζω μᾶλλον ἤ, prefer
αἱρετικός, factious
αἱρετίς, associate
αἱρετός, *cannot but* choose, choose, preferable, worthy
αἱρέω, choose
αἴρω, abolish, arouse, away, banish, bear *up*, carry, deny, destroy, do *away*, free, hoist *up*, lift, lift *up*, pick *up*, put *away*, raise, remove, set, sweep *away*, take, take *away*, take *up*, tear *away*, weigh
αἴρω τοὺς ὀφθαλμούς, look *up*
αἰσθάνομαι, feel, notice, perceive, please, see, understand
αἴσθησις, discernment, feel, pain, sense
αἰσθητήριον, faculty, sense
αἰσχροκερδής, greedy *for gain*
αἰσχροκερδῶς, *shameful* gain
αἰσχρολογία, *foul* talk
αἰσχρός, base, disgrace, disgraceful, *most* hateful, shame, shameful
αἰσχρότης, filthiness
αἰσχρῶς, disgraceful
αἰσχύνη, confusion, disgrace, disgraceful, sense *of shame*, shame
αἰσχύνομαι, shrink *in shame*
αἰσχυντηρός, modest, modest *man*, shame
αἰσχύνω, ashamed, bring *shame*, put *to shame*, respect, respectfully, shame
αἰτέω, ask, ask *leave*, beg, beseech, call, demand, make, request
αἴτημα, demand, request
αἰτία, case, cause, *cause to* question, charge, crime, deserve, issue, reason, result, why
αἰτιάομαι, censure, find *fault*
αἴτιος, attempt, blame, cause, crime, deserve, guilty, source
αἰτίωμα, charge
αἰφνίδιος, sudden, suddenly
αἰφνιδίως, sudden, suddenly
αἰχμαλωσία, captive, captivity, capture, exile, place *of captivity*, take *captive*
αἰχμαλωτεύω, bring *a captive*, carry *away captive*, lead *a host of captives*, lead *away captive*, take, take *into captivity*

αἰχμαλωτίζω, captivate, capture, carry *away captive*, lead *captive*, make *captive*, take *as captive*, take *captive*
αἰχμάλωτος, captive, captivity
αἰών, age, all, *all* time, beginning, end *of time*, eternal, eternity, ever, everlasting, evermore, future, old, time, world
αἰὼν χρόνου, beginning
αἰώνιος, age, eternal, eternal *one*, ever, everlasting, long, permanent, perpetual
ἀκαθαρσία, defilement, impurity, pollution, unclean, unclean *deed*, uncleanness
ἀκάθαρτος, foul, impure *man*, impurity, unclean, unclean *thing*, unhealthy
ἀκαιρέομαι, *no* opportunity
ἄκαιρος, *wrong* time
ἀκαίρως, *out of* season
ἄκακος, blameless, innocent, simple-minded
ἀκάλυπτος, uncover
ἀκαλύπτως, unveiled
ἄκανθα, thorn
ἀκάνθινος, thorn
ἀκάρδιος, weakling
ἀκαριαῖος, moment *longer*
ἄκαρπος, fruitless, unfruitful
ἀκατάγνωστος, censure, uncondemned
ἀκατακάλυπτος, uncover, unveiled
ἀκατάκριτος, uncondemned
ἀκατάλυτος, indestructible, unceasing
ἀκαταμάχητος, invincible
ἀκατάπαυστος, insatiable
ἀκαταστασία, confusion, disorder, tumult
ἀκαταστατέω, unsafe
ἀκατάστατος, restless, unstable
ἀκατάσχετος, uncontrollable
ἀκέραιος, guileless, innocent, sincere
ἀκηδία, unconcern, weary
ἀκηδιάω, weary
ἀκηλίδωτος, blameless, spotless
ἀκινάκης, sword
ἀκίνητος, immovable
ἀκλεής, ignoble
ἀκλεῶς, ignominiously
ἀκληρέω, misfortune
ἀκλινής, unswerving, *without* wavering
ἀκμάζω, prime, ripe
ἀκμαίας, prime
ἀκμή, critical, extreme, fierce, maturity, perfect, point
ἀκμήν, still
ἄκμονος, anvil
ἀκοή, ear, fame, hear, listen, report, rumor
ἀκοῇ ὠτίων, hear
ἀκοίμητος, *never* cease
ἀκοινώνητος, ought *not to share*
ἀκολασία, tempest
ἀκολουθέω, follow, obey, *thing* brought
ἀκολουθία, consequence
ἀκόλουθος, go, late
ἀκολούθως, accordance, according
ἀκοπιάστως, *without* toil
ἀκόσμως, disorder
ἀκούσιος, help
ἀκουστός, hear, hearer
ἀκουτίζω, *make* hear
ἀκούω, come, come *to ear*, give *a hearing*, hear, hearer, hearken, heed, listen, obey, overhear, report, think, understand, word
ἄκρα, citadel
ἄκρα δάκτυλου κορυφή, fingernail
ἀκρασία, lack *of self-control*, rapacity
ἀκρατής, profligate
ἄκρατος, unmixed
ἀκριβάζω, prove
ἀκρίβεια, accuracy, judge, *strict* manner, strictness
ἀκριβής, accurate, apt, *more* closely, *more* exactly, scrupulous, strict
ἀκριβόω, ascertain
ἀκριβῶς, accurately, carefully, clearly, closely, diligently, *more* accurately, *rather* accurate, well
ἀκρίς, locust
ἀκρίτως, unjustly
ἀκρόαμα, entertainment
ἀκροάομαι, hear, listen
ἀκρόασις, hear
ἀκροατήριον, *audience* hall
ἀκροατής, attentive, hearer
ἀκροβυστία, *before one* circumcises, uncircumcised, uncircumcision
ἀκρογωνιαῖος, cornerstone
ἀκρόδρυα, fruit *of a tree*
ἀκροθίνιον, spoil
ἀκρόπολις, citadel
ἄκρος, citadel, end, firm, head, point, top
ἀκρότομος, flinty, sheer
ἀκροφύλαξ, sentinel
ἀκρωτηριάζω, cut *off hands and feet*, mutilate
ἀκτίς, beam, ray
ἀκύματος, tranquillity
ἀκυρόω, annul, frustrate, invalidate, make *void*, nullify, *render* powerless
ἀκώλυτος, irresistible
ἀκωλύτως, unhindered
ἄκων, *against the* will, will
ἀλάβαστρον, alabaster, *alabaster* flask, flask
ἀλαζονεία, arrogance, boast, boastfulness, pride
ἀλαζονεύομαι, boast
ἀλαζών, boastful, proud
ἀλαλαγμός, shout
ἀλαλάζω, clang, raise *a shout*, shout *for joy*, wail
ἀλάλητος, *too* deep *for words*
ἄλαλος, dumb, speak
ἅλας, salt
ἀλάστωρ, accursed, *accursed* wretch, avenger
ἀλγέω, anguish
ἀλγηδών, agony, pain, suffer
ἄλγος, grief, pain
ἀλείφω, anoint
ἀλεκτοροφωνία, cockcrow
ἀλεκτρυών, cock
ἀλέκτωρ, cock
ἄλευρον, flour
ἀλήθεια, really, right, sincerity, Thummim, true, truth, truthful, truthfulness
ἀληθεύω, speak *the truth*, tell *the truth*, true
ἀληθής, indeed, *most* sincere, real, true, truly, truth
ἀληθινός, live, proper, true, true *one*, truly
ἀληθινῶς, truth
ἀλήθω, grind
ἀληθῶς, certainly, indeed, really, sure, truly, truth
ἄληκτον, incessant
ἁλιεύς, fisher, fisherman
ἁλιεύω, fish
ἁλίζω, restore *saltness*, salt
ἀλισγέω, pollute
ἀλίσγημα, pollution
ἁλίσκομαι, catch
ἁλίσκω, take *captive*
ἀλιτήριος, scoundrel, sinner, wicked
ἀλκή, might, power
ἀλλ᾽ ἤ, except, no *more than*, rather
ἀλλ᾽ ἰδού, no
ἀλλά, again, certainly, contrary, except, however, indeed, instead, mere, moreover, nevertheless, no, now, rather, rather *than*, then, what, why, yes, yet
ἀλλά γε, least, yes
ἀλλὰ καί, certainly, moreover
ἀλλαγή, alternation
ἄλλαγμα, change
ἀλλάσσω, change, exchange, prefer, take *one's place*
ἀλλαχῆ, another *there*
ἀλλαχόθεν, *another* way, various
ἀλληγορέω, allegory
ἀλλήλων, *both* sides, *each* other, one *another*, other
ἀλλογενής, alien, foreign, foreigner, outsider, stranger
ἀλλόγλωσσος, *strange* language
ἀλλοεθνής, heathen
ἀλλοῖος, change, confuse
ἀλλοιόω, alter, change, different, estrange, fade, make *a variety*, phase, work *further*
ἀλλοίωσις, change
ἅλλομαι, leap, spring *up*, well *up*
ἄλλος, additional, another, another *man*, *any* other, else, general, here, however, more, other, other *person*, other *thing*, rest, some
ἄλλος δέ, other
ἄλλος μέν, kind
ἄλλος οὐκ εἰ μή, only
ἀλλότρια φρονέω, disloyal
ἀλλοτριεπίσκοπος, mischief-maker
ἀλλότριος, alien, another, another *man*, belong *to another*, belong *to others*, foreign, *foreign* property, hostile, other, other *man*, other *people*, outsider, strange, stranger
ἀλλοτριόω, *become* estranged, *become* hostile, expell
ἀλλοφυλέω, *become a* pagan
ἀλλοφυλισμός, adoption *of foreign ways*, alien
ἀλλόφυλος, *another* nation, foreign, foreigner, Gentile, *other* race, Philistine
ἄλλως, addition, otherwise, wrongly
ἄλλως καὶ ἄλλως, here *and there*
ἅλμη, salt
ἀλοάω, thresher, tread *out grain*
ἀλογέω, *no* consideration
ἀλογιστία, folly, madness
ἀλόγιστος, irrational, irrationally, senseless, thoughtless, unreasonable
ἄλογος, idiot, irrational, senselessly, unreasonable, unreasoning
ἀλόη, aloe
ἅλς, salt
ἄλσος, *sacred* grove
ἁλυκός, salt
ἄλυπος, *less* anxious
ἁλυσιδωτός, coat *of mail*
ἅλυσις, chain
ἀλυσιτελής, *no* advantage
ἄλφιτον, *parched* grain
ἅλων, *threshing* floor
ἀλώπηξ, fox
ἅλωσις, catch
ἅμα, along, besides, *same* time, soon, together, when, yet
ἅμα αὐθωρί, soon
ἀμαθής, ignorant
ἅμαξα, cart
ἀμαράντινος, unfading
ἀμάραντος, unfading
ἁμαρτάνω, commit, commit *sin*, *do* wrong, guilty, offend, persist *in sin*, sin, sinful, sinfully
ἁμάρτημα, act *of sin*, offense, sin
ἁμαρτία, guilt, sin, sinful
ἀμάρτυρος, *without* witness
ἁμαρτωλός, sinful, sinner, wicked
ἀμαυρός, blind, obscure
ἄμαχος, avoid *quarreling*, quarrelsome
ἀμάω, mow
ἀμβλακία, error
ἀμβρόσιος, heavenly
ἀμέθυστος, amethyst
ἀμείδητος, gloomy
ἀμειξία, *no* mingling, separation
ἀμελέω, disregard, make *light*, neglect, pay *no heed*
ἄμεμπτος, blameless, faultless, unblamable
ἀμέμπτως, blameless, honorably
ἀμερής, run *out*
ἀμέριμνος, free *from anxiety*, free *from care*, *out of* trouble
ἀμετάθετος, inflexible, unchangeable
ἀμετακίνητος, immovable
ἀμεταμέλητος, bring *no regret*, irrevocable
ἀμετανόητος, impenitent
ἀμέτρητον, innumerable
ἀμέτρητος, boundless, countless, immeasurable
ἄμετρος, *beyond* limit
ἀμήν, amen, truly
ἀμητός, harvest
ἀμήτωρ, *without* mother
ἀμήχανος, impossible
ἀμίαντος, undefiled, unstained
ἄμμος, dust, grain *of sand*, sand
ἀμμώδης, sandy
ἀμνημονέω, unmindful
ἀμνησία, forget
ἀμνησικακία, amnesty
ἀμνηστία, forget, forgetfulness
ἀμνός, lamb
ἀμοιβή, return
ἄμοιρος, fail *to share*
ἀμόλυντος, unpolluted
ἄμορφος, formless
ἄμπελος, grapevine, vine, vintage
ἀμπελουργός, vinedresser
ἀμπελών, vineyard
ἀμύθητος, untold, *untold* number
ἄμυνα, repel
ἀμύνομαι, defend
ἀμύνω, beat *off*, defend, fight *off*, refuse
ἀμφιβάλλω, cast *a net*
ἀμφίβληστρον, net
ἀμφιέζω, clothes
ἀμφιέννυμι, clothe, clothes
ἀμφιλαφής, wide-spreading
ἄμφοδον, *open* street
ἀμφότεροι, two
ἀμφότερος, all, both
ἄμφω, both, either, two
ἀμώμητος, *without* blemish
ἄμωμον, spice
ἄμωμος, blameless, spotless, *without* blemish
ἄν, if, then
ἀνά, each
ἀνὰ μέρος, turn
ἀνὰ μέσον, among, between, midst, through
ἀναβαθμός, step
ἀναβαίνω, ascend, climb, climb *up*, come, come *back*, come *up*, conceive, get *into*, go, go *aboard*, go *into*, go *into battle*, go *up*, grow *up*, land, march *up*, return, rise, sail
ἀναβάλλω, place, put *off*, throw *up*
ἀνάβασις, approach, ascent, come *up*, go *up*, pass, pass *up*, step
ἀναβάτης, rider
ἀναβιβάζω, bring, draw
ἀναβιόω, renewal
ἀναβλέπω, look, look *up*, receive *sight*, regain, regain *sight*
ἀνάβλεψις, recovering *of sight*
ἀναβοάω, cry, cry *out*, shout
ἀναβολή, delay
ἀναβράσσω, cast *up*
ἀνάγαιον, *upper* room
ἀναγγέλλω, announce, declare, disclose, divulge, give *a message*, hear, inform, proclaim, report, show, tell, word *reach*
ἀναγεννάω, bear *anew*
ἀναγινώσκω, read, read *aloud*, reader
ἀναγκάζω, compel, compulsion, constrain, force, make, suffer
ἀναγκαῖος, close, essential, *highly* necessary, indispensable, *more* necessary, necessary, urgent
ἀναγκαστῶς, constraint
ἀνάγκη, affliction, coercive, compulsion, constraint, distress, drive, fate, forcibly, hardship, must, necessary, necessity, need, punishment, violence
ἀναγνεία, wickedness

ἀναγνωρίζω, make *known*
ἀνάγνωσιν ποιέω, read
ἀνάγνωσις, read
ἀναγνώστης, reader
ἀναγορεύω, call
ἀναγραφή, record
ἀναγράφω, enrol, inscribe, record, write
ἀνάγω, back *again*, bring, bring *again*, bring *back*, bring *out*, bring *up*, embark, haul *up*, lead, lead *up*, offer, put *to sea*, sail, set *out*, set *sail*, take, take *up*
ἀναγώγως, *most* insolently
ἀναδείκνυμι, appoint, declare, dedicate, disclose, make, make *king*, restore, show
ἀνάδειξις, manifestation, mark
ἀναδέχομαι, receive, undertake, welcome
ἀναδίδωμι, burst *forth*, deliver, give
ἀνάδυσις, emerge
ἀναθάλλω, *cause to* flourish, *make* flourish, put *forth*, revive
ἀνάθεμα, accursed, curse, *votive* offering
ἀναθεματίζω, bind *by oath*, invoke *a curse*, vow *complete destruction*
ἀναθεωρέω, consider, observe
ἀνάθημα, offering, *votive* offering
ἀναζάω, alive *again*, revive
ἀναζεύγνυμι, break *camp*, depart, departure, go, leave, march, move *camp*, return, return *home*, set *out*
ἀναζευγνύω, break *camp*
ἀναζέω, swarm
ἀναζητέω, look, seek
ἀναζυγή, retreat, withdrawal
ἀναζώννυμι, gird *up*
ἀναζωπυρέω, rekindle
ἀναίδεια, importunity, impudence
ἀναιδέομαι, shameless
ἀναιδής, impudent, shameless
ἀναίρεσις, death, destroy, kill
ἀναιρέω, abolish, adopt, destroy, kill, overcome, pick *up*, put *to death*, remove, slay
ἀναίρω, destroy
ἀναίτιος, guiltless, innocent, *without* cause
ἀνακαθίζω, sit *up*
ἀνακαινίζω, continually, restore
ἀνακαινόω, renew
ἀνακαίνωσις, renewal
ἀνακαίω, burn, kindle
ἀνακαλέω, warn
ἀνακαλύπτω, reveal, uncover, unlifted, unveiled
ἀνακάμπτω, return, turn *back*
ἀνάκειμαι, guest, lie, recline, seat, sit *at table*, table
ἀνακεφαλαιόω, sum *up*, unite
ἀνακηρύσσω, proclaim
ἀνακλάω, curl *back*
ἀνακλίνω, lay, recline, sit *at table*, sit *down*
ἀνακοινόω, inform
ἀνακομίζω, bring *back*, recover, return
ἀνακόπτω, check, hold *back*
ἀνακράζω, cry *out*, raise *a cry*, shout
ἀνακρίνω, call *to account*, discern, examination, examine, judge, raise *a question*
ἀνακρίσεως, inquiry
ἀνάκρισις, examine
ἀνακυλίω, roll *back*
ἀνακύπτω, look *up*, stand *up*, straighten
ἀναλαμβάνω, adopt, assemble, catch *up*, get, make, meet, put, raise *up*, seize, take, take *aboard*, take *on board*, take *up*
ἀναλάμπω, shine *forth*, shine *out*
ἀναλέγω, recover
ἀνάλημμα, retain
ἀναλημπτέος, *must* confiscate
ἀνάλημψις, receive *up*
ἀναλίσκομαι, use
ἀναλίσκω, burn, consume
ἀναλογία, proportion
ἀναλογίζομαι, consider, take *into account*
ἀναλόγως, correspond
ἄναλος, lose *saltness*
ἀναλόω, consume
ἀνάλυσις, departure
ἀναλύω, come *home*, come *together*, depart, go, go *away*, melt *away*, retreat, return, *set* free, withdraw
ἀναμάρτητος, free *from sin*, innocent, *without* sin
ἀναμείγνυμι, scatter
ἀναμένω, delay, remain, wait
ἀναμιμνήσκω, remember, remember *in favor*
ἀνάμνησις, remembrance, remind, reminder
ἀναμοχλεύω, pry *a limb*
ἀναμφισβητήτως, *without* quibbling
ἄνανδρος, cowardly, unmanly
ἀνανεάζω, *become* young *again*
ἀνανεόω, re-establish, renew, revive
ἀνανεύω, reject
ἀνανέωσις, renewal
ἀνανήφω, escape
ἀναντίρρητος, contradict
ἀναντιρρήτως, *without* objection
ἀναξηραίνω, parch, wither
ἀνάξιος, incompetent, inferior *man*, unworthily, unworthy
ἀναξίως, unworthy, *unworthy* manner
ἀνάπαλιν, contrary
ἀνάπαυσιν ἔχω, cease
ἀνάπαυσις, assuage, refresh, rest
ἀναπαύω, attain *rest*, give *rest*, go *to rest*, refresh, relief, remain, rest, set *at rest*, take *a rest*, take *ease*
ἀναπείθω, mislead, persuade
ἀναπείρω, pierce
ἀναπέμπω, send, send *back*, send *over*
ἀναπηδάω, leap *up*, spring, spring *up*
ἀνάπηρος, maim
ἀναπίπτω, lie, lie *close*, lie *down*, place, sit, sit *at table*, sit *down*, sit *down at table*, take *a meal*, take *one's place*
ἀναπλάσσω, fashion
ἀναπληρόω, fill *up*, fulfil, fulfilment, make *full*, make *up*
ἀναποδίζω, draw *back*, go *backward*
ἀναποδισμός, return
ἀναπολόγητος, *no* excuse, *without* excuse
ἀναπτερόω, give *wings*
ἀναπτύσσω, open
ἀνάπτω, blaze *up*, kindle, *set* ablaze
ἀναρίθμητος, *can not* reckon, countless, innumerable, reckon, *too* many *to count*, uncounted, *without* number
ἀνασείω, stir *up*
ἀνασκευάζω, unsettle
ἀνασπάω, drawn *up*, pull *out*
ἀνάστασις, resurrection, rise
ἀναστατόω, stir *up revolt*, turn *upside down*, unsettle
ἀνασταυρόω, crucify
ἀναστέλλω, prevent
ἀνάστεμα, arrogance
ἀναστενάζω, groan *aloud*, sigh, sigh *deeply*
ἀνάστημα, raise *up*
ἀναστρατοπεδεύω, march *off with forces*
ἀναστρέφω, act, behave, bring *back*, busy, concern, conduct, engage, home, join, live, occupy, overthrow, return, send *back*, treat, turn *back*, turn *out*
ἀναστροφή, behavior, conduct, life, live, manner *of life*, way
ἀνασώζω, find *safety*
ἀνατάσσομαι, compile
ἀνατείνω, lift *up*, stretch *out*
ἀνατέλλω, appear, dawn, *make* rise, rise
ἀνατέμνω, cut *open*
ἀνατίθημι, dedicate, lay *before*, make *a votive offering*, tell
ἀνατίκτω, give *rebirth*
ἀνατολή, dawn, east, rise
ἀνατολὴ ἡλίου, east
ἀνατρέπω, overthrow, throw, turn *back*, upset
ἀνατρέφω, breed, bring *up*, nurse, overturn
ἀνατρέχω, hasten *off*, run *up*
ἀνατροπή, drive
ἀνατροφή, upbringing
ἀνατυπόω, imagine
ἀναφαίνω, appear, clear, come *in sight*
ἀναφέρω, bear, bring *some*, carry *back*, carry *up*, give *vent*, lead *up*, offer, offer *up*, offering, pay, present
ἀναφωνέω, exclaim
ἀναχάσκω, open *one's mouth*
ἀνάχυσις, wild
ἀναχωρέω, depart, get *away*, go *aside*, go *over*, leave *home*, withdraw
ἀνάψυξις, refresh
ἀναψύχω, refresh, refreshment, revive
ἀνδραγαθέω, do, *do a brave* deed, strive
ἀνδραγαθία, brave *deed*, *noble* bravery, valor
ἀνδραποδιστής, kidnaper
ἀνδρεία, courage
ἀνδρεῖος, brave, courage, courageous, loyal, man, *more* manly
ἀνδρειόω, give *courage*
ἀνδρείως, manfully
ἀνδρίζω, courageous, valiant
ἀνδροφονέω, murderer
ἀνδροφόνος, manslayer, murderer
ἀνδρωδῶς, manfully
ἀνεγείρω, rebuild
ἀνέγκλητος, blameless, give *no ground for complaint*, guiltless, irreproachable, prove *blameless*
ἀνείκαστος, immense
ἀνεκδιήγητος, inexpressible
ἀνεκλάλητος, unutterable
ἀνέκλειπτος, fail
ἀνεκλιπής, unfailing
ἀνεκτός, *more* tolerable
ἀνελεήμων, cruel, merciless, merciless *man*, pitiless, ruthless, unmerciful
ἀνέλεος, *without* mercy
ἀνελπίστως, unexpectedly
ἀνεμίζω, driven *by the wind*
ἄνεμος, wind
ἄνεμος μέγας, gale
ἀνεμπόδιστος, unhindered
ἀνένδεκτος μή, sure
ἀνεξεραύνητος, unsearchable
ἀνεξικακία, forbearance
ἀνεξίκακος, forbear
ἀνεξιχνίαστος, inscrutable, unsearchable
ἀνεπαίσχυντος, *no need to be ashamed*
ἀνεπίλημπτος, *above* reproach, free *from reproach*, *without* reproach
ἀνεπιστρέπτως, *without a backward* look
ἀνερευνάω, search
ἀνέρχομαι, go *up*
ἄνεσις, ease, gain *in idleness*, liberty, permission, release, relief, rest
ἀνετάζω, examine, press
ἄνευ, apart, lack, no, without
ἄνευ γογγυσμοῦ, ungrudgingly
ἀνεύθετος, *not* suitable
ἀνευρίσκω, find, seek *out*
ἀνέφικτος, unapproachable
ἀνέχομαι, forbear, submit
ἀνέχω, bear, endure, restrain, shut *up*
ἀνεψιός, cousin
ἀνηβάω, boy
ἄνηθον, dill
ἀνήκεστος, irremediable, *no* relief, sure
ἀνηκέω, belong
ἀνήκω, appropriate, due, fitting, interest, pertain, require
ἀνηλεής, pitiless
ἀνήμερος, fierce
ἀνήνυτος, uncompleted
ἀνήρ, each, envoy, fellow, foot *soldier*, gentleman, husband, infantry, infantryman, man, manhood, officer, sir, troop, warrior
ἀνὴρ πολεμιστής, soldier, troop
ἀνὴρ ἁμαρτωλός, sinner
ἀνὴρ βουλῆς, wise *in counsel*
ἀνὴρ γλωσσώδης, babbler
ἀνὴρ δυνατός, warrior
ἀνὴρ πολεμιστής, warrior
ἀνὴρ σφενδονήτης, slinger
ἀνὴρ ψεύστης, liar
ἀνθ᾽ οὗ, therefore
ἀνθ᾽ ὧν, because, therefore
ἀνθέω, put *forth a blossom*
ἀνθίστημι, adversary, deny, offer *resistance*, oppose, opposition, outweigh, resist, rise *against*, rise *up*, withstand
ἀνθομολογέομαι, make *confession*
ἀνθομολογέω, confess *a fault*, give *thanks*
ἀνθομολόγησις, thanks
ἄνθος, blossom, flower
ἄνθος ῥόδων, rose
ἀνθρακιά, *burning* coal, *charcoal* fire, coal
ἄνθραξ, coal, ruby
ἀνθρωπάρεσκος, man-pleaser
ἀνθρώπινος, common *to man*, human, *human* term
ἀνθρωποκτόνος, murderer
ἄνθρωπος, another, any *one*, child, fellow, human, *human* being, life, man, mankind, nature, other, people, person, self
ἄνθρωπος ἁμαρτωλός, sinner
ἄνθρωπος ἀσθενής, cripple
ἄνθρωπος γλωσσώδης, chatterer
ἄνθρωπος εὐγενής, nobleman
ἄνθρωπος κριτής, ruler
ἄνθρωπος πόρνος, fornicator
ἄνθρωπος ψευδής, liar
ἀνθρώπων γένος, mankind
ἀνθύπατος, proconsul
ἀνίατος, incurable
ἀνιερόω, inscribe *as holy*, seize *for sacrifice*
ἀνίημι, fail, forbear, forgive, go, go *up*, leave, loosen, relax, unfasten, unrestrained
ἀνίκητος, invincible, unconquered
ἄνιπτος, unwashed
ἀνίστημι, appear, arise, build, finish, get *up*, leave, lift *up*, *make* stand, move, place, raise, raise *up*, repair, rise, rise *again*, rise *up*, rule, set *up*, stand *up*, stand *upright*, take *command*
ἀνίστημι ἀντί, take *place*
ἀνόητος, foolish, foolish *man*, *more* senseless, senseless, senseless *man*, stupid
ἄνοια, folly, foolish, fury, lack *of intelligence*, mad
ἀνοίγω, open
ἀνοίγω φάρυγγα, greedy
ἀνοίγω χεῖρας, generous
ἀνοικοδομέω, rebuild
ἄνοικτος, ruthless
ἄνοιξις, open
ἀνομβρέω, pour *forth*
ἀνομέω, break *the law*, lawlessly, lawlessness
ἀνόμημα, lawless *deed*
ἀνομία, iniquity, lawlessness, misdeed, transgression, wickedness
ἀνόμοιος, unlike
ἄνομος, lawless, lawless *man*, lawless *one*, outside *the law*, transgressor, unlawful, wicked, wicked *man*, *without* law
ἀνόμως, lawless, *without the* law
ἀνόνητος, profitless, unprofitable, *without* offspring
ἀνορθόω, lift, *make* stand *on end*, make *straight*, set *up*
ἀνορύσσω, paw
ἀνόσιος, evil, impious, *most* unholy, profane, unholy
ἀνοσίως, profanely, wickedly
ἄνους, *without* intelligence
ἀνοχή, forbearance, opportunity
ἀνταγωνίζομαι, antagonist, struggle

ἀνταγωνιστής, antagonist
ἀντάλλαγμα, precious, return, take *in exchange*
ἀνταναιρέω, take *away*
ἀντανακλάω, throw *back*
ἀνταναπληρόω, complete
ἀντανίστημι, arise
ἀνταποδίδωμι, do, give *back*, pay *back*, render, repay, requite, return
ἀνταποδίδωμι ἀνταπόδομα, pay *back in full*
ἀνταπόδομα, recompense, repay, repayment, retribution, return
ἀνταπόδοσις, reward
ἀνταποκρίνομαι, answer *back*, reply
ἀντεῖπον, contradict, oppose, say *in opposition*
ἀντερείδω, compete
ἀντερῶ, refuse
ἀντέχομαι, devote
ἀντέχω, endure, *firmly* hold, help, hold *firm*, hold *out*
ἀντηχέω, echo *back*
ἀντί, against, because, instead, *no* longer, place, rather *than*, reason, return, stead, succeed, succession, upon
ἀντιβάλλω, hold, ponder *over*
ἀντίγραφον, copy
ἀντιγράφω, write *in reply*, write *on one's part*
ἀντιδιατίθημι, opponent
ἀντίδικος, accuser, adversary
ἀντιδοκέω, oppose
ἀντίθεσις, contradiction
ἀντίθετος, contrary
ἀντίζηλος, envious, rival
ἀντικαθίστημι, resist
ἀντικαλέω, invite *in return*
ἀντικαταλλάσσω, live *again*, pay
ἀντίκειμαι, adversary, antagonist, contrary, enemy, opponent, oppose
ἄντικρυς, opposite
ἀντιλαμβάνομαι, benefit
ἀντιλαμβάνω, assist, help, lay *hold*, rescue, uphold
ἀντιλάμπω, shine *back*
ἀντιλέγω, contradict, contrary, object, protest, refractory, refuse, say, set *against*, speak *against*
ἀντιλήμπτωρ, upholder
ἀντίλημψις, assistance, help
ἀντιλήπτωρ, helper
ἀντίληψις, conduct, help, helper
ἀντιλογία, dispute, hostility, rebellion
ἀντιλοιδορέω, revile *in return*
ἀντίλυτρον, ransom
ἀντιμαρτυρέω, bear *witness against*
ἀντιμετρέω, get *back measure*
ἀντιμισθία, penalty, return
ἀντίπαλος, enemy
ἀντιπαραβάλλω, comparable
ἀντιπαράγω, march *along opposite*
ἀντιπαραγωγή, opposition
ἀντιπαρατάσσω, fight *against*
ἀντιπαρέρχομαι, come *to help*, pass *by on the other side*
ἀντιπέρα, opposite
ἀντιπίπτω, resist
ἀντιποιέω, lay *a claim*
ἀντιπολιτεύω, *political* opponent
ἀντιπράσσω, oppose
ἀντίπτωμα, hazard, stumble
ἀντιρρητορεύω, make *an eloquent response*
ἀντιστρατεύομαι, war
ἀντιτάσσω, oppose, resist
ἀντιτίθημι, oppose
ἀντίτυπος, copy, correspond
ἀντιφιλοσοφέω, oppose *with philosophy*
ἀντιφωνέω, send *a reply*
ἀντίχριστος, antichrist
ἀντιψύχω, exchange *for life*, ransom
ἀντλέω, draw, draw *out*, drawn
ἄντλημα, draw
ἀντοφθαλμέω, confront, face
ἄνυδρον, dry
ἄνυδρος, waterless
ἀνυπέρβλητος, invincible
ἀνυπερθέτως, *without* delay
ἀνυπόκριτος, authentic, genuine, impartial, sincere, *without* insincerity
ἀνυπονόητος, *never* think
ἀνυπόστατος, irresistible, withstand
ἀνυπότακτος, disobedient, insubordinate, insubordinate *man*, outside *one's control*
ἀνυψόω, exalt, extol, grow *tall*, heap *up*, heighten, lift *up*, raise, raise *up*, send *up*
ἀνύω, accomplish
ἄνω, above, brim, up, upper, upward
ἄνωθεν, above, anew, *long* time, *some* time *past*, top
ἀνώνυμος, name
ἀνωτερικός, upper
ἀνώτερος, above, high, remote
ἀνωφελής, unprofitable, useless, uselessness
ἀξία, deserve, keep *with a position*, merit, worth, worthy
ἀξίνη, axe
ἀξιόπιστος, worthy *of belief*
ἄξιος, advisable, appropriate, befit, beseech, deserve, due, fit, fitting, proper, qualification, think *good*, weigh *the value*, worth, worthy
ἄξιος εἰμί, deserve
ἄξιος θαυμασμοῦ, astounding *thing*
ἀξιόω, ask, attractive, beg, beseech, consider, consider *worthy*, count *worthy*, deserve, desire, intercede, make *worthy*, plead, pray, think *good*, worth
ἀξίωμα, *high* rank, request
ἀξίως, befit, deservedly, worthy
ἄξων, axle
ἀοίδιμος, glorious
ἀοίκητος, uninhabited
ἀορασία, blind, loss *of sight*
ἀόρατος, invisible, *invisible* nature, unseen
ἀπ' ἄρτι, again, henceforth, hereafter, now
ἀπ' ἐκείνου, afterward
ἀπ' οὐρανοῦ, heavenly
ἀπαγγέλλω, announce, bring *word*, declare, describe, explain, give *a report*, inform, make *a report*, proclaim, prove, report, say, tell
ἀπαγορεύω, forbid
ἀπάγχω, hang
ἀπάγω, bring, carry, lead, lead *astray*, lead *away*, lead *to execution*, put *to death*, sentence, take, take *away*
ἀπαγωγή, imprisonment
ἀπαιδευσία, ignorance, ill-mannered, vulgarity
ἀπαίδευτος, ignorant, ill-bred *person*, senseless, undisciplined, uninstructed, untaught
ἀπαίρω, depart, go *up*, leave, march, march *away*, march *forth*, march *off*, march *out*, move *forward*, move *out*, start, take, take *away*
ἀπαιτέω, ask *again*, ask *back*, make *a demand*, require, return
ἀπαίτησις, payment
ἀπαλγέω, *become* callous
ἀπαλείφω, wipe *away*
ἀπαλλάσσω, deliver, free, give *up*, leave, release, return, settle
ἀπαλλοτριόω, alienate, apostatize, estrange
ἁπαλός, soft, tender
ἀπαμύνω, defend
ἀπαναινέω, reject
ἀπανίστημι, rise *and depart*
ἀπαντάω, appear, befall, deal, handle, meet, overtake, receive, treat
ἀπάντησις, bearing, consideration, meet, treatment, *wedded* union
ἅπαξ, once, once *for all*
ἅπαξ καὶ δίς, again *and* again, before
ἀπαράβατος, permanently
ἀπαραίτητος, inexorable, relentless
ἀπαραλλάκτως, unchanging
ἀπαραπόδιστος, unimpeded
ἀπαρασήμαντος, unobserved
ἀπαρασκεύαστος, ready
ἀπαρέσκω, dislike
ἀπαρνέομαι, deny
ἀπαρτία, supply, *supply* train, transport
ἀπαρτισμός, complete
ἀπαρχή, *first* convert, *first* fruit
ἅπας, all, *all* men, all *things*, anything, every, everything, perfect, whole
ἀπασπάζομαι, bid *farewell*
ἀπατάω, beguile, deceive, delight, trick
ἀπάτη, deceit, deceitful, deceitfulness, deceive, deception, delight, dissipation
ἀπάτησις, entice
ἀπάτωρ, *without* father
ἀπαύγασμα, reflect, reflection
ἀπαυτομολέω, desert
ἀπείθεια, disobedience
ἀπειθέω, contrary, disbelieve, disobedient, disobey, obey, refuse, unbeliever, unbelieving
ἀπειθής, disobedience, disobedient
ἀπεικάζω, form *like*
ἀπείκασμα, likeness
ἀπειλέω, storm, threat, threaten, warn
ἀπειλή, threat, threaten
ἄπειμι, absent, absent *one*, away, depart, go, return, withdraw, without
ἀπεῖπον, forbid, reject, renounce
ἀπειράγαθος, know *nothing of goodness*
ἀπείραστος, tempt
ἀπείργω, forbid
ἄπειρος, unskilled, *utterly* inexperienced
ἀπεκδέχομαι, await, *eagerly* wait, wait
ἀπεκδύομαι, disarm, put *off*
ἀπέκδυσις, put *off*
ἀπελαύνω, drive, drive *off*
ἀπελεγμός, disrepute
ἀπελέγχω, *publicly* expose, rebuke
ἀπελεύθερος, freedman
ἀπελπίζω, despair, expect *in return*, give *up all hope*, *without* hope
ἀπέναντι, against, before, face, front, opposite, presence, toward
ἀπέναντι τῶν ὀφθαλμῶν, presence
ἀπένθητος, *no one to* mourn
ἀπέραντος, boundless, endless
ἀπερείδω, store
ἀπερίσπαστος, unresponsive, *without* distraction
ἀπερισπάστως, *undivided* devotion
ἀπερίτμητος, uncircumcised
ἀπέρχομαι, come, depart, draw *back*, get, go, go *aside*, go *away*, go *back*, go *home*, go *off*, go *out*, go *over*, go *up*, leave, pass, pass *away*, return, run *out*, spread
ἀπέρχομαι ὁδόν, march
ἀπέρχομαι ὀπίσω, follow, indulge
ἀπευθανατίζω, die *a good death*
ἀπεχθάνομαι, enemy, hateful
ἀπέχθεια, enmity
ἀπεχθῶς, hostile
ἀπέχω, abstain, abstinence, avoid, back, distant, enough, keep, keep *away*, receive, refrain
ἀπηλιώτης, east
ἀπήμαντος, invulnerable, unharmed
ἀπήνη, harsh
ἀπηνής, *most* savage
ἀπιστέω, believe, disbelieve, distrust, distrustful, doubt, faithless, unbelieving, unfaithful
ἀπιστία, distrust, faithlessness, unbelief, unbelieving
ἄπιστος, faithless, incredible, unbeliever, unbelieving, unfaithful
ἄπλατος, monstrous
ἀπληστεύομαι, insatiable, *insatiable* appetite
ἀπληστία, gluttony
ἄπληστος, glutton
ἁπλότης, generosity, innocence, liberality, sincere, sincerity, singleness
ἁπλοῦς, sound
ἁπλῶς, generously, much, simply
ἄπνοος, lifeless
ἀπό, accord, account, after, against, ago, any, authority, away, because, before, begin, belong, both, deprive, descendant, either, escape, ever *since*, instead, judge, leave, more, more *than*, off, opposite, out, *out of* sight, over, part, since, some, than, through, toward, upon, weigh, when, without
ἀπὸ μακρόθεν, far *off*
ἀπὸ μιᾶς, alike
ἀπὸ γραφῆς, enrol
ἀπὸ καλύψεως, reveal
ἀπὸ πέρυσι, year *ago*
ἀπὸ προσώπου, before, leave
ἀπὸ τῆς ψυχῆς, deprive
ἀπὸ τῆς ὥρας, instantly
ἀπὸ τοῦ νῦν, future, henceforth, *right* now
ἀποβαίνω, get *out*, go *out*, happen, time, turn, turn *out*
ἀποβάλλω, *cause to* fall *away*, loss, rejection, throw *away*, throw *off*
ἀποβάπτω, dip *out*
ἀποβλέπω, look
ἀπόβλημα, castoff *piece*
ἀπόβλητος, reject
ἀπογεύω, eat, taste
ἀπογίνομαι, die
ἀπογινώσκω, despair, forlorn
ἀπόγονος, child *of earth*, descend, offspring
ἀπογραφή, census, enrollment, record, registration
ἀπογράφω, carry *out registration*, enrol, register, registration
ἀποδείκνυμι, appoint, archive, attest, demonstrate, distinguish, exhibit, proclaim, prove
ἀπόδειξις, demonstration, prove
ἀποδειροτομέω, scalp
ἀποδεκατόω, give *a tithe*, take *a tithe*, tithe
ἀπόδεκτος, acceptable
ἀποδέχομαι, accept, acceptance, bid *farewell*, comfort, receive, recognize, welcome
ἀποδημέω, go *away*, go *into another country*, go *on a journey*, journey
ἀπόδημος, go *on a journey*
ἀποδιαστέλλω, *abominable* offering
ἀποδιδράσκω, flee
ἀποδίδωμι, bring, deliver, end, give, give *back*, inflict, keep, make, make *a payment*, *make* return, obtain *release*, pay, perform, receive *payment*, receive *repayment*, render, *render* account, repay, requite, restore, return, reward, sell, sprinkle, turn, yield
ἀποδίδωμι μαρτυρίαν, testify
ἀποδιορίζω, set *up divisions*
ἀποδοκιμάζω, reject
ἀπόδοσις, repayment
ἀποδοχεῖον, cistern, reservoir, storehouse
ἀποδράω, flee, run *away*
ἀποδύρομαι, lament *bitterly*
ἀποθαυμάζω, amaze, marvel, wonder
ἀποθήκη, barn, granary, store
ἀποθησαυρίζω, lay *up*, lay *up treasure*
ἀποθλίβω, press *upon*
ἀποθνῄσκω, die, perish
ἀποικία, colony, exile
ἀποικίζω, carry *away*, carry *into exile*, drive *into exile*
ἀποικισμός, exile
ἀποίχομαι, go, return
ἀποκαθαρίζω, purge *away*
ἀποκαθῆμαι, *woman in* menstruation
ἀποκαθίστημι, bring *back*, bring *back safely*, depose, lie, restore, return, station, take, take *back*
ἀποκαίω, burn
ἀποκαλύπτω, betray, disclose, make *a revelation*, reveal, unveiled
ἀποκάλυψις, disclosure, reveal, revelation
ἀποκαραδοκία, *eager* expectation, *eager* longing
ἀποκαταλλάσσω, reconcile
ἀποκατάστασις, establish

ἀπόκειμαι, appoint, lay *away*, lay *up*, remain
ἀποκενόω, drain
ἀποκεφαλίζω, behead
ἀποκλείω, close, shut, shut *out*
ἀποκλίνω, turn *aside*
ἀποκνίζω, prune
ἀποκομίζω, get
ἀποκόπτω, cut *away*, cut *off*, mutilate
ἀποκοσμέω, dispatch
ἀπόκρημνος, incline *precipitously*
ἀπόκριμα, sentence
ἀποκρίνομαι, address, answer, make *answer*, reply, say
ἀποκρίνω, again, declare, give *a reply*, make *answer*, speak, tell
ἀπόκρισις, answer
ἀποκρύπτω, go *unheard*, hide
ἀπόκρυφος, hidden *thing*, hide, secret, secretly
ἀποκτείνω, bring *to an end*, kill, murder, put *to death*, slay, strike, take *a life*
ἀποκνέω, bring *forth*, give *birth*
ἀποκυλίζω, tumble
ἀποκυλίω, roll *away*, roll *back*
ἀποκωλύω, prevent, withhold
ἀπολαμβάνω, capture, receive, receive *again*, take *aside*, win
ἀπόλαυσις, enjoy, enjoyment, pleasure
ἀπολαύω, enjoy
ἀπολείπω, cease, forsake, lack, leave, remain, *remain* behind
ἀπόλλυμι, *cause* ruin, cease, dead, destroy, destroyer, destruction, die, kill, lose, perish, perishable, put *to death*, ruin
ἀπολλύω, destroy, perish
ἀπόλλω, destroy
ἀπολογέομαι, answer, defend, excuse, make *a defense*, say *in defense*
ἀπολογία, defense, eagerness *to clear*, make *a defense*
ἀπολούω, wash, wash *away*
ἀπόλυσις, dismissal
ἀπολύτρωσις, redeem, redemption, release
ἀπολύω, acquit, allow *to escape*, deliver, depart, destroy, dismiss, divorce, divorced *woman*, forgive, free, go, go *free*, put *away*, release, save, send *away*, send *off*, *set at* liberty, *set* free
ἀπομαρτυρέω, bear *witness*
ἀπομάσσω, wipe *off*
ἀπομάχομαι, make *a defense*
ἀπομερίζω, show
ἀπονέμω, bestow, endow, grant
ἀπονίπτω, wash
ἀπονοέω, lose *one's mind*, revolt
ἀπόνοια, madness, *sheer* madness, stupidity
ἄπονος, painless
ἀποξαίνω, tear
ἀποξενόω, drive *into exile*
ἀποπαρθενόω, violate
ἀποπίπτω, fail *to achieve*, fall
ἀποπλανάω, deceive, go *astray*, lead *astray*, wander *away*
ἀποπλάνησις, travel
ἀποπλέω, sail
ἀποπνέω, breathe *one's last*
ἀποπνίγω, choke, drown, strangle
ἀποπρατίζομαι, sell
ἀποπτύω, spurn
ἀποργίζομαι, anger
ἀπορέω, break *the thread*, flow, lack *means*, loss, need, perplex, press *hard*, uncertain
ἀπορία, perplexity, want
ἀπορίπτω, cast *off*, throw *overboard*
ἄπορος, lack
ἀπορρέω, slip *away*
ἀπόρρητος, unseemly
ἀπόρροια, emanation
ἀπορρωγάς, precipitous
ἀπορρώξ, steep
ἀπορφανίζω, bereft
ἀποσβέννυμι, wither
ἀποσβέσις, extinguish
ἀποσκεδάννυμι, dispel
ἀποσκευή, baggage, goods
ἀποσκίασμα, shadow
ἀποσκοπεύω, watch
ἀποσκορακίζω, cast *off*
ἀποσκυθίζω, *scalp* Scythian *fashion*
ἀποσοβέω, scare *away*
ἀποσπάω, drag *away*, draw, draw *away*, go, part, withdraw
ἀποστασία, apostasy, forsake, rebellion
ἀποστάσιον, certificate *of divorce*, divorce
ἀπόστασις, rebellion
ἀποστατέω, revolt
ἀποστάτης, rebel, traitor
ἀποστάτις, rebellious
ἀποστεγάζω, remove
ἀποστέλλω, commission, dismiss, put, send, send *away*, send *forth*, send *out*, sender, set
ἀποστενόω, freeze
ἀποστερέω, bereft, defraud, deprive, refuse, rob
ἀποστολή, apostleship, gift, mission, pestilence, portion, present
ἀπόστολος, apostle, messenger, send
ἀποστοματίζω, provoke *to speak*
ἀποστρεβλόω, torture
ἀποστρέφω, abstain, avert, banish, bring *again*, cast, dissuade, drive *back*, lose, pervert, put *away*, put *back*, refuse, reject, remove, return, send *away*, spurn, turn, turn *away*, turn *back*
ἀποστροφή, reject, return, reverse, turn *away*
ἀποστυγέω, hate
ἀποσυνάγωγος, *out of the* synagogue, put *out of the synagogue*
ἀποσύρω, tear *out*
ἀποσφάζω, slaughter
ἀποσφενδονάω, hurl
ἀποτάσσομαι, renounce, say *farewell*, take *leave*
ἀποτάσσω, appoint, station
ἀποτελέω, enhance, *full* grown, perform
ἀποτέμνω, cut *off*, separate, sever
ἀποτίθημι, cast *off*, lay *aside*, lay *down*, put, put *away*, put *off*, removal, store, take *off*
ἀποτίκτω, bear, hatch
ἀποτινάσσω, shake *off*
ἀποτιννύω, pay
ἀποτίνω, pay, repay
ἀποτολμάω, bold
ἀποτομία, severity
ἀπότομος, severe, stern
ἀποτόμως, relentlessly, severe, sharply
ἀποτρέπω, avert, avoid, dissuade, restrain
ἀποτρέχω, depart, go, go *quickly*, return
ἀποτυμπανίζω, torture *to death*
ἀποτυφλόω, blind
ἀπουσία, absence
ἀποφαίνω, declare
ἀποφέρω, attain, bring *back*, carry, carry *away*, carry *off*, lead *away*, receive, take, take *back*
ἀποφεύγω, escape, flee
ἀποφθέγγομαι, address, speak, utterance
ἀποφορτίζομαι, unload
ἀποφράσσω, stop
ἀπόχρησις, use
ἀποχωρέω, depart, leave, separate, withdraw
ἀποχωρίζω, separate, vanish
ἀποψύχω, expire, faint
ἄπρακτος, frustrate *a purpose*, helpless, *without* accomplishing *anything*
ἀπρεπής, unbecoming
ἀπρονοήτως, heedlessly
ἀπρόπτωτος, deliberate
ἀπροσδεής, need *of nothing*, *no* need
ἀπροσδόκητος, unexpected
ἀπροσδοκήτως, expect, *without* warning
ἀπρόσιτος, unapproachable
ἀπρόσκοπος, blameless, clear, *no* offense, smooth, suddenly
ἀπροσωπολήμπτως, impartially
ἄπταιστος, fall, unharmed
ἅπτω, handle, hold, kindle, light, touch
ἀπωθέω, disdain, put *an end*, reject, repel, repulse, thrust, thrust *aside*
ἀπώλεια, death, destroy, destruction, destructive, lose, perdition, ruin, waste
ἀρά, case, curse, possible, then, therefore, thus, true
ἄρα οὖν, accordingly
ἆρα, then
ἀραρότως, faithfully
ἄραφος, *without* seam
ἀργέω, cease, idle, work
ἀργία, idleness, leisure
ἀργός, barren, careless, idle, idler, lazy, *no* use, *without* effect
ἀργυρικὴ ζημία, fine
ἀργύριον, fund, money, silver, treasury
ἀργυροκόπος, silversmith
ἀργυρολόγητος, levy *tribute*
ἄργυρος, silver
ἀργυροῦς, silver
ἀργυροχόος, silver
ἀργύρωμα, *silver* dish, *silver* plate
ἀργυρώνητος, purchase *a slave*
ἀρδαλόω, filthy
ἀρεσκεία, please
ἄρεσκος, please
ἀρέσκω, decide, please, satisfy
ἀρεστὰ ἐνώπιον, please
ἀρεστός, please, pleasure, right
ἀρέσω, please
ἀρεταλογία, celebration *of a wondrous deed*
ἀρετή, courage, excellence, praise, valor, virtue, virtuous, wonderful *deed*
ἀρήγω, come *to help*
ἀρθρέμβολον ὄργανον, instrument
ἀρθρέμβολον, joint-dislocator
ἄρθρον, joint
ἀριθμέω, count, muster, number
ἀριθμός, count, limit, number, only *a few men*, sum
ἀριστάω, breakfast, dine
ἀριστεία, excellent
ἀριστερός, left, left *hand*, north
ἀριστεύω, get *the better*
ἄριστον, dinner
ἀρίστου ὥρα, mealtime
ἀρκετός, enough, suffice, sufficient
ἀρκέω, content, enough, satisfy, suffice, sufficient
ἄρκος, bear
ἅρμα, chariot
ἁρματηλάτης, charioteer
ἁρμόζω, betroth, fashion, proper
ἁρμόνιος, suit
ἁρμός, fissure, joint, socket
ἀρνέομαι, deny, disown, refuse, renounce
ἀρνήν, lamb
ἀρνίον, lamb
ἄρξομαι, begin
ἀροτριάω, plow, plowman
ἄροτρον, plow
ἁρπαγή, extortion, plunder, seize
ἅρπαγμα, plunder
ἁρπαγμός, *thing to* grasp
ἁρπάζω, carry *off*, catch *up*, plunder, ravish, rob, snatch, snatch *away*, take *by force*
ἅρπαξ, extortioner, ravenous, robber
ἀρραβών, guarantee
ἀρρενωδῶς, bravely
ἄρρηκτος, unbreakable
ἄρρητος, tell
ἀρρωστέω, fall *ill*
ἀρρώστημα, illness, sick, sickness
ἀρρωστία, ill, sick
ἄρρωστος, ill, sick, sick *people*
ἀρσενικός, male
ἀρσενοκοίτης, *sexual* pervert, sodomite
ἄρσην, male, man
ἀρτάβη, bushel
ἀρτέμων, foresail
ἄρτι, just, now, once, present, soon, *very* time
ἀρτιγέννητος, newborn
ἄρτιος, complete
ἄρτος, bread, food, live, loaf, loaf *of bread*, meal
ἀρτύω, restore *saltness*, season
ἀρχάγγελος, archangel
ἀρχαῖος, ancient, early, man *of old*, old, *thing of* old
ἀρχή, authority, basic, beginning, company, corner, dominion, elementary, essential, first, good, government, kingdom, office, old, position, principality, rule, ruler, source, throne
ἀρχηγός, author, captain, first, head, leader, pioneer
ἀρχῆθεν, beginning
ἀρχιεράομαι, *high* priest
ἀρχιερατεύω, *high* priest
ἀρχιερατικός, *high* priestly
ἀρχιερεύς, *chief* priest, *high* priest, *high* priesthood
ἀρχιερωσύνη, *high* priesthood, priesthood
ἀρχιποίμην, *chief* shepherd
ἀρχιστράτηγος, *chief* general, commander, general
ἀρχισυνάγωγος, ruler, ruler *of the synagogue*
ἀρχιτέκτων, *master* builder, *master* workman
ἀρχιτελώνης, *chief tax* collector
ἀρχιτρίκλινος, steward *of the feast*
ἀρχίφυλος, head
ἄρχω, advance, arise, arrive, begin, beginning, come, come *up*, go, make *a beginning*, reign, rule, ruler, start
ἄρχων, authority, captain, chief, chieftain, command, commander, leader, magistrate, officer, prince, ruler
ἄρωμα, spice
ἀσάλευτος, immovable, shake
ἄσβεστος, unquenchable
ἀσέβεια, impiety, irreligion, ungodliness, ungodly
ἀσεβέω, *act* impiously, *act* wickedly, behave *impiously*, commit *an act of sacrilege*, commit *an outrage*, commit *in an ungodly way*, *show* irreverence, ungodly, ungodly *man*
ἀσεβής, impious, *most* impious, ungodly, ungodly *man*, wicked
ἀσέλγεια, debauchery, licentious, licentious *deed*, licentiousness
ἄσημος, insignificant, mean
ἀσθένεια, ailment, disease, illness, infirmity, limitation, weakness
ἀσθενέω, *become* faint, diseased, fail, feeble, ill, invalid, lack *strength*, sick, sick *man*, weak, weak *man*, weaken
ἀσθένημα, fail sick, weak, weak *thing*, weakness
ἀσθενόψυχος, *weaker* sex
ἆσθμα, breath
ἀσθμαίνω, breathe *heavily*
ἀσίδηρος, make *of iron*
ἀσινής, unharmed
ἀσιτέω, eat *nothing*
ἀσιτία, *without* food
ἄσιτος, *without* food
ἀσκέω, observe, take *pains*
ἄσκησις, discipline
ἀσκητός, practice
ἀσκοπυτίνη, bottle
ἀσκός, bottle, skin, wineskin
ἄσμενος, glad, readily
ἀσμένως, alacrity, gladly
ἄσοφος, unwise *man*, wise
ἀσπάζομαι, embrace, give *greetings*, greet, salute, send *greetings*, take *leave*, welcome
ἀσπάλαθος, camel's *thorn*
ἀσπασμός, greeting, salutation
ἀσπιδίσκη, *small* shield
ἄσπιλος, unstained, *without* spot
ἀσπίς, asp, shield
ἄσπονδος, implacable

ἀσσάριον, penny
ἆσσον, anchor, *close* inshore
ἀσταθή, instability
ἀστατέω, homeless
ἀστεῖος, beautiful, high
ἀστείως, honorably
ἄστεκτος, bear
ἀστήρ, star
ἀστήρικτος, unstable, unsteady
ἄστοργος, heartless, inhuman
ἀστοχέω, deprive, disregard, miss *the mark*, swerve
ἀστραπή, flash *of lightning*, lightning, ray
ἀστράπτω, dazzle, flash
ἄστρον, star, starry
ἀστυγείτων, neighbor
ἀσυλία, inviolability
ἄσυλος, sanctuary
ἀσύμφωνος, disagree, discordant
ἀσύνετος, foolish, ignorant, *no* understanding, senseless, stupid, stupid *people*, unintelligent *man*, *without* understanding
ἀσύνθετος, faithless
ἀσυρής, lewd
ἀσφάλεια, confidence, custody, keep *safe*, safety, secure, security, truth
ἀσφαλής, definite, fact, firm, *real* reason, safe, sure, surely
ἀσφαλίζω, fasten, keep *safe*, make *secure*
ἀσφαλῶς, assuredly, safely, steadily, sure, *under* guard
ἀσχημονέω, behave *properly*, rude
ἀσχημοσύνη, expose, nakedness, shame, shameless *act*, shamelessness
ἀσχήμων, shameful, unpresentable *part*
ἀσχολέω, concern
ἀσχολία, labor, occupation
ἀσωτία, debauchery, profligacy, profligate
ἀσώτως, loose
ἀτακτέω, idle
ἄτακτος, disorderly, idler
ἀτάκτως, idleness
ἀταξία, disorder
ἀταραξία, peace
ἀτάραχος, quiet, undisturbed, untroubled
ἄταφος, unburied
ἅτε, because
ἀτεκνία, childlessness
ἀτεκνίας καιρός, bereavement
ἄτεκνος, childless, *no* child, *without* child
ἀτελεία, immunity
ἀτέλεστος, *before one* comes to *maturity*, come *to maturity*
ἀτελής, irrevocable
ἀτελὴς ὥρα, ripen
ἀτενίζω, closely, direct *one's gaze*, fix, gaze, look, look *intently*, look *up*, make *a full effort*, observe *intently*, see, stare
ἄτερ, absence, no, without
ἀτιμάζω, despise, disdain, disgrace, dishonor, suffer *dishonor*, treat *shamefully*
ἀτίμητος, priceless
ἀτιμία, degrade, disgrace, dishonor, dishonorable, ignoble, *menial* use, shame, worthlessness
ἄτιμος, despise, dishonor, disrepute, *less* honorable, *less* worth, unworthy *of honor*, *without* honor
ἀτιμόω, despise
ἀτμίς, breath, fragrance, mist, smoke, vapor
ἄτομος, moment
ἀτοπία, wrong
ἄτοπος, misfortune, *out of the* way, wicked, wrong
ἀτραπός, path, track
ἄτρωτος, invulnerable, wound
ἀτυχία, misfortune
αὐγάζω, see
αὔγασμα, brightness
αὐγή, daybreak, glow
αὐθάδης, arrogant, wilful
αὐθαίρετος, accord, *free* will, voluntarily, willfully
αὐθαιρέτως, accord
αὐθεντέω, authority *over*
αὐθέντης, murder
αὐθεντία, status
αὐλαία, courtyard, door
αὖλαξ, furrow
αὐλέω, pipe
αὐλέω ἢ κιθαρίζω, play
αὐλή, court, courtyard, fold, gate, palace, pavilion
αὐλὴ προβάτων, sheepfold
αὐλητής, *flute* player
αὐλίζομαι, camp, hold *over till the next day*, live, lodge, spend *the night*, stay, stay *over night*
αὐλός, flute
αὐλών, valley
αὐξάνω, give *growth*, grow, grow *up*, honor, increase
αὔξησις, enhance, growth
αὔξω, grow
αὔριον, come, morrow, *next* day, tomorrow
αὐστηρία, austerity
αὐστηρός, severe
αὐτάρκεια, contentment, enough
αὐτάρκης, content, deservedly, enough, self-reliant, temperately
αὐτίκα, shortly, soon
αὐτοδέσποτος, sovereign
αὐτόθι, here, there
αὐτοκατάκριτος, self-condemned
αὐτοκράτωρ, dominant, sovereign
αὐτόματος, accord, self-kindled
αὐτομολέω, desert, fugitive
αὐτόπτης, eyewitness
αὐτός, alike, another, belong, body, descendant, *each* other, even, harmony, home, husband, man, one, people, right, same, same *thing*, self, too, very, *very* midst, well
αὐτοσχεδίως, *mere* chance
αὐτοῦ, here, there
αὐτόφωρος, act
αὐτόχειρ, hand
αὐχέω, boast
αὐχήν, neck
αὐχμηρός, dark
ἀφ' ἧς, ever *since*, since
ἀφ' ἧς ἡμέρας, after
ἀφ' οὗ, after, since
ἀφαίρεσις, seize, take *away*
ἀφαιρέω, cut *off*, delete, deletion, depose, lay *aside*, pull *down*, remove, rob, sever, take, take *away*, take *off*
ἀφάλλομαι, skip
ἀφανής, hide, unseen
ἀφανὴς γίνομαι, vanish
ἀφανίζω, consume, destroy, disfigure, perish, vanish
ἀφανισμός, annihilation, destroy, destruction, vanish *away*
ἄφαντος, vanish
ἀφασία, consternation
ἀφεγγής, dark
ἀφειδία, severity
ἀφειδῶς, relentlessly
ἀφελότης, generous
ἄφεμα, immunity, *tax* remission, tribute
ἄφεσις, forgiveness, liberty, permission, release, relief
ἀφεύκτως, inescapably
ἁφή, joint
ἀφηγέομαι, lead, leader, prince, ruler
ἀφήγημα, guidance
ἀφθαρσία, immortality, imperishable, incorruption, undying
ἄφθαρτος, immortal, imperishable
ἄφθονος, lavish, plentiful
ἀφθόνως, *without* grudging
ἀφθορία, integrity
ἀφιερόω, consecrate
ἀφίημι, abandon, allow, cancel, consent, desert, divorce, end, exempt, forgive, forsake, free *from tax*, give *up*, go, grant, grant *release*, leave, let *alone*, neglect, pardon, permit, release, set, *set* free, tolerate, utter, wait, yield *up*
ἀφικνέομαι, come, enough, go *down*, know, reach, reach *the end*
ἀφιλάγαθος, hater *of good*
ἀφιλάργυρος, free *from love of money*, *no* lover *of money*
ἄφιξις, departure, journey
ἀφίστημι, abandon, *cause to* revolt, depart, desert, desist, disappear, draw *away*, drive *away*, fall *away*, far, forsake, give *up*, keep, keep *away*, lead *astray*, leave, leave *the right* way, prevent, rebel, refrain, *remain at a* distance, remove, revolt, rob, stand *aside*, stay *away*, take, take *away*, take *out*, withdraw
ἄφνω, quickly, suddenly
ἄφοβος, confident, protect *from fear*
ἀφόβως, boldly, ease, *without* fear
ἀφοδεύω, droppings *fall*
ἄφοδος, departure
ἀφομοιόω, *become at all* like, compare, like
ἀφοράω, look, see, watch *over*
ἀφόρητος βάρος, intolerable
ἀφορίζω, appropriate, exclude, select, separate, set *apart*, take
ἀφορμή, cause, claim, occasion, opportunity, pretext
ἀφορολόγητος, free *from tribute*, *without* tribute
ἀφρίζω, foam, foam *at the mouth*
ἀφρός, boor, foam, fool, senseless
ἀφροσύνη, folly, foolishness
ἄφρων, fool, foolish, foolish *man*, *most* foolish
ἀφυπνόω, fall *asleep*
ἀφυστερέω, deprive, keep *back*
ἀφωμοιόω, resemble
ἄφωνος, dumb, speechless
ἀχανής, yawn
ἄχαρις, ungracious
ἀχάριστος, grateful, ungracious, ungrateful, ungrateful *man*
ἀχειροποίητος, make *with hands*, make *without hands*
ἄχι, reed
ἀχλύς, mist
ἀχρεῖος, unworthy, useless, worthless
ἀχρειότης, shiftlessness
ἀχρειόω, destroy, go *wrong*
ἄχρηστος, helpless, unprofitable, useless, waste
ἄχρι, all *the way*, before, down, even *unto*, far, high, long, till, until, unto, up
ἄχρι αἰῶνος, ever
ἄχρι τοῦ δεῦρο, thus *far*
ἄχρις, long, till
ἄχυρον, chaff
ἀψευδής, *never* lie, unerring
ἄψινθος, wormwood
ἄψυχος, lifeless, lifeless *thing*
ἀωρία, night
ἄωρος, ripe *enough*, untimely

βαδίζω, go, go *about*, go *one's way*, walk
βαθέως, dawn
βαθή, temper
βαθμός, standing
βαθμὸς θύρας, doorstep
βάθος, deep, depth, high
βαθύς, deep, deep *thing*, depth, profound
βαΐνη, palm *branch*
βαΐον, branch, palm *branch*
βαίνω, stand
βαλλάντιον, purse
βάλλω, bring, cast, contribute, fall, invest, lay, lie, place, pour, put, put *into*, scatter, shed, shoot, sow, strike, swing, throw, throw *down*
βάλλω ἑαυτόν, spring
βαπτίζω, baptize, baptizer, bathe, purify, wash
βάπτισμα, baptism
βαπτισμός, ablution, baptism, wash
βαπτιστής, Baptist
βάπτω, bathe, dip
βάρβαρος, barbarian, barbarous, foreigner, *more* barbarous, native, savage
βαρβαρόω, barbarous
βαρβάρως, barbarously
βαρέω, anxiety, burden, crush, heavy, weigh *down*
βαρέως, heavy
βαρέως φέρω, displease, vex
βάρος, burden, weight
βαρυηχής, loud
βαρύθυμος, sullen
βαρύνω, *become* desperate, burden, burdensome, feel *revulsion*, grieve, heavy, make *heavy*, overcome, weigh *down*
βαρύς, burden, burdensome, deep, fierce, force, fortress, great, grievous, hard *to bear*, heavy, large, *more* bitterly, oppressive, overpower, serious, severe, steadfastly, strong, *very* strong, weighty, *weighty* matter
βαρύτιμος, *very* expensive
βασανίζω, afflict, anguish, beat, distress, painfully, suffer *torment*, suffer *torture*, torment, torture, torturer, vex
βασανισμός, torment, torture
βασανιστήριον, instrument *of torture*
βασανιστής, jailer
βάσανος, agony,
cruelly, pain, torment, torture
βασιλεία, dominion, king, kingdom, kingship, realm, reign, royal, *royal* power, rule, sovereignty
βασίλειος, crown, dominion, king, kingship, palace, royal
βασιλεύς, dynasty, emperor, king, reign, royal, rule
βασιλεύω, *become* king, *begin to* reign, king, kingdom, make *king*, reign, rule
βασιλικός, forfeit *to the king*, king, *king's* possession, *king's* treasury, kingdom, money *to the king*, *more* royal, official, royal, *royal* tax, *royal* treasury
βασίλισσα, queen
βάσις, base, foot, hold, step
βασκαίνω, bewitch, grudge
βασκανία, fascination, malice
βάσκανος, envious, grudging *man*
βαστάζω, bear, bear *up*, bearer, carry, carry *away*, lift, support, take, take *up*
βάτος, bramble *bush*, bush, measure
βάτραχος, frog
βατταλογέω, heap *up empty phrases*
βδέλυγμα, abominable, abomination, sacrilege
βδελυκτός, despise, detestable
βδελυρός, abominable
βδελύσσομαι, abhor, abominable, abominate, loathe, loathing, make *abominable*, pollute
βεβαίαν ποιέω, confirm
βέβαιος, firm, firmly, guarantee, make *more sure*, steadfast, take *effect*, unshaken, valid
βεβαιόω, attest, confirm, establish, strengthen, sustain
βεβαίωσις, assurance, confirmation
βέβηλος, godless, irreligious, profane, profane *man*, profaner
βεβηλόω, defile, pollute, profane, profane *man*
βεβήλωσις, penalty *for desecration*, profanation, profane
βελόνη, needle
βέλος, arrow, dart, missile
βελόστασις, *siege* tower
βελτίων, good, well
βῆμα, *judgment* seat, length, manner *of walking*, platform, *public* platform, throne, tribunal, walk
βήρυλλος, beryl
βία, force, power, violence, violently
βία τῶν κυμάτων, surf
βιάζω, enter *violently*, force, overstuff, stop, struggle *against*, suffer *violence*

βίαιος, mighty, *more* powerful, *more* violent, rage, turbulent, violence
βιαίως, violence
βιαστής, man *of violence*
βιβλαρίδιον, *little* scroll
βιβλιοθήκη, library
βιβλίον, book, certificate, letter, record, scroll, volume
βιβλίον ἡμερῶν, chronicle
βιβλιοφυλάκιον, archive
βίβλος, book
βίβλος τῶν χρόνων, chronicle
βιβρώσκω, consume, eat
βίος, civilian, *common* life, existence, goods, life, live, livelihood, mankind, manner *of life*, race, way *of life*
βιοτεύω, live
βιόω, live
βίωσις, live, manner *of life*
βιωτικός, life, matter *pertaining to this life*, such
βλαβερός, hurtful
βλάβη, damage
βλάπτω, *do* harm, *do* injury, hinder, hurt, injure
βλαστάνω, bring *forth*, bud, *cause to* bud, come *up*, sprout
βλάστημα, young
βλαστός, blossom, *green* shoot
βλασφημέω, abuse, blaspheme, blasphemer, blasphemy, curse, defame, denounce, deride, discredit, rail, revile, slanderously, speak *evil*, speak *of as evil*, utter, utter *blasphemy*
βλασφημία, blasphemous, *blasphemous* word, blasphemy, revile, slander
βλάσφημος, abusive, blaspheme, blasphemer, blasphemous, revile
βλέμμα, see
βλέπω, behold, beware, consider, gaze, look, look *out*, regard, see, sight, take *care*, take *heed*, *thing* seen, *thing which one* sees
βλέφαρον, eyelid
βλητέος, put
βοάω, cry, cry *aloud*, cry *out*, give *a shout*, help, shout
βοή, cry, shout, uproar, voice
βοὴ ἰσχυρός, shout
βοὴ μέγας σφόδρα, shout
βοήθεια, aid, defense, help, measure, rescue
βοηθέω, aid, come *to help*, defend, help, helper
βοήθημα, help
βοηθός, bring *aid*, help, helper
βόθρος, pit
βόθυνος, pit
βολαί, ray
βόλβιτον, filth
βολή, hurl, throw
βολίζω, sound
βολίς, shaft
βόμβησις, multitude
βοοζύγιον, *ox* yoke
βορά, food
βόρβορος, mire
βορέας, north
βορρᾶς, north
βόσκημα, cattle
βόσκω, feed, herdsman
βοτάνη, herb, vegetation
βότρυς, cluster
βουκόλιον, cattle, herd
βουλευτήριον, *council* chamber, *senate* chamber
βουλευτής, member *of the council*
βουλεύω, consult, decide, deliberate, desire, determine, give *counsel*, intend, make *a decision*, make *a plan*, plan, plot, purpose, resolve, senator, take *counsel*, take *thought*, will
βουλή, council, counsel, decree, deliberation, desire, *good* counsel, intention, judgment, plan, plot, policy, purpose, understanding, will
βουλὴ ἀγαθή, good
βούλημα, design, like, purpose, resolve, will
βούλομα, direct
βούλομαι, choose, decide, desire, determine, freely, glad, intend, like, liking, mean, minded, please, ready, resolve, want, will, willing, wish
βουνός, hill
βοῦς, ox
βραβεῖον, prize
βραβεύω, give *victory*, rule
βραδέως, temporarily
βραδύνω, delay, slow
βραδυπλοέω, sail *slowly*
βραδύς, slow
βραδυτής, slowness
βραχέως, begin, *little* while
βραχίων, arm, shoulder, strength
βραχύς, brief, briefly, fleeting, little, *little* while, short, while
βραχύς τι, little
βραχυτελής, brief
βρέφος, babe, baby, child, childhood, infant
βρέχω, fall, rain, send *rain*, wet
βρίθω, burden
βρόμος, *thick* pall
βροντάω, thunder
βροντή, clap *of thunder*, peal *of thunder*, thunder, thunderpeal
βροχή, rain
βρόχος, restraint, rope
βρυγμός, gnash, gnashing *of teeth*
βρύχω, grind
βρύω, pour *forth*
βρῶμα, another, corrosion, devour, eat, food, *food* supply, meat, provision, *solid* food
βρῶμα θήρας, game
βρώσιμος, eat
βρῶσις, eat, food, meal, rust
βρωτός, food
βύβλος, book
βυθίζω, drown, plunge, sink
βυθός, sea
βυθοτρεφής, sea-born
βυρσεύς, tanner
βύσσινος, *fine* linen
βύσσος, *fine* linen
βῶλος, piece
βωμός, altar, high *place*

γάγγραινα, gangrene
γάζα, treasure
γαζοφυλάκιον, coffer, treasury
γαζοφύλαξ, treasurer
γαῖσος, spear
γάλα, milk
γαλαθηνός, suck
γαλακτοποτέω, drink *milk*
γαλακτοτροφία, nurse
γαλήνη, calm
γαληνός, calm
γαμβρός, son-in-law
γαμετή, wife
γαμέω, marriage, married *man*, married *woman*, marry
γαμίζω, give *in marriage*, marry
γαμικός, marry
γαμίσκω, give *in marriage*
γάμος, feast, marriage, *marriage* feast, *marriage* festival, wedding, *wedding* feast
γάρ, because, either, even, example, fact, indeed, now, say, since, then, though, thus, what, when, why, yet
γαστήρ, belly, child, glutton, stomach, womb
γαστριμαργία, gluttony
γαστρίμαργος, glutton
γαυρίαμα, boast, glory, pride
γαυριάω, glory
γαυρόω, boast, boastful, exult
γε, yea, yet
γε καί, really
γέ, certainly
γέ τοι, fact, then
γέεννα, hell
γειτνιάω, adjoin, neighbor
γείτων, neighbor
γελάω, laugh
γελοῖος, ridiculous
γέλως, derision, laugh, laughter, occasion *to laugh*
γεμίζω, fill
γέμω, full
γενεά, descendant, generation, lineage
γενεὰ γενεῶν, *all* generations
γενεαλογέω, genealogy
γενεαλογία, genealogy
γενέθλιος ἡμέρα, birthday
γένειον, chin
γενέσθαι πρός, *come to* see
γενέσια, birthday
γενεσιάρχης, author
γενεσιουργός, creator
γένεσις, bear, beginning, birth, child, come, creation, existence, genealogy, generation, *generative* force, natural, nature, offspring, origin, produce, production, sex
γενετή, bear, birth
γενέτις, mother
γένημα, child, crop, fruit, harvest, increase, offspring, produce
γενικῆς γραφή, genealogy
γενναῖος, brave, courageous, *more* noble, noble, nobly
γενναιότης, courage, nobility
γενναίως, bravely, cleverly, nobly
γεννάω, bear, bear *a child*, *become* father, beget, breed, bring, child, conceive, deliver, descendant, father, give *birth*, offspring, parent, parental, son
γέννημα, bear, brood
γέννησις, bear
γεννητός, bear
γένος, birth, descendant, different, family, kind, kindred, lineage, nation, native, nature, offspring, people, race, species
γεραιός, advanced *in years*, age, old *man*, old *people*
γεραίρω, celebrate
γέρας, place, prize
γερουσία, council, senate
γέρων, age, aged *man*, old, old *man*, senator
γεῦμα, taste
γεύομαι, eat, taste
γεῦσις, taste
γέφυρα, earthwork
γεώδης, earthy
γεωργέω, cultivate, till
γεωργία, farm, *farm* work
γεώργιον, field
γεώργιος, cultivation
γεωργός, farmer, tenant, tiller, vinedresser
γῆ, country, dirt, district, dust, earth, field, ground, land, region, soil, world
γῆ πεδινός, plain
γηγενής, descendant
γῆρας, age, man *of age*, *old* age
γηράσκω, grow *old*, old
γηράω, old, *old* age
γῆρος, *old* age
γήρως, age
γίγας, giant
γίνομαι, accomplish, acquire, act, appear, arise, arrive, bear, become, befall, begin, beginning, behavior, belong, birth, bring, certainly, come, come *about*, come *into being*, *come to* pass, come *upon*, commit, conduct, consider, consult, continue, dawn, do, draw, engage, experience, fall, fall *into*, fare, finish, follow, form, former, gain, get, give, go, grant, grow, happen, hold, inspire, introduce, join, last, lay, leave, lend, lie, live, look, make, marry, meet, now, occur, open, past, perform, prepare, proclaim, produce, promote, prove, put, rank, raze, reach, receive, recover, result, rise, secure, set, show, speak, spend, split, spring, stand, start, stray, suffer, take, take *place*, *thing that* happens, turn, turn *out*, use, visit, wrought
γίνομαι ἀντί, take *place*
γίνομαι γρηγορέω, awake
γίνομαι δίχα, divide
γίνομαι εἰς διαρπαγήν, capture
γίνομαι εἰς, supply
γίνομαι ἐκ σπέρματος, descend
γίνομαι ἡ διάνοια, purpose
γίνομαι κατήγορος, accuse
γίνομαι νεκρός, die
γίνομαι περί, make
γίνομαι πρός, look *after*
γινώσκω, aware, *become* known, comprehend, decide, discern, do, enter, feel, find *out*, grasp, hear, know, knowledge, learn, make *known*, news, notice, perceive, realize, recognize, regard, see, show, sure, understand
γλεῦκος, *new* wine
γλυκαίνω, make *sweet*, speak *sweetly*, sweet, sweetness
γλύκασμα, sweet, sweet *thing*
γλυκύς, delightful, fresh, pleasant, sweet
γλυκύτης, sweetness
γλύμμα, engrave, signet
γλυπτός, graven, *graven* image
γλυφή, engrave, mold
γλύφω, carve, cut
γλῶσσα, language, mouth, speak, speech, tongue, voice
γλῶσσα τρίτη, slander
γλωσσόκομον, *money* box
γλωσσοτομέω, cut *out the tongue*, make *speechless*
γλωσσώδης, garrulous
γναφεύς, fuller
γνήσιος, genuine, real, sincere, sincerely, true
γνησίως, genuinely
γνόφος, darkness, gloom, *thick* darkness
γνώμη, advice, connivance, consent, decision, determine, judgment, mind, opinion, purpose, wish
γνωρίζω, inform, know, make *known*, proclaim, remind, set, tell, tell *about*, want *one to know*, want *to understand*
γνώριμος, acquaintance, evidently, know
γνῶσιν ἔχω, know
γνῶσις, acquaintance, decision, discern, know, knowledge, learn, mind
γνωστέος, know
γνώστης, familiar
γνωστός, acquaintance, discern, know, notable
γνωστὸς εἰμί, know
γογγύζω, complain, grumble, murmur, mutter
γογγυσμός, grumble, murmur, mutter
γογγυστής, grumbler
γοερός, mournful
γόης, impostor
γοητεία, guile
γόμος, cargo
γομφιάζω, gnash
γονεύς, ancestor, parent, parental
γόνυ, knee
γονυπετέω, kneel
γόος, groan, lamentation, wail
γοῦν, certainly, now, thus
γράμμα, bill, learning, letter, literal, writing, *written* code
γράμματα οἶδα, learning
γραμματεία, learning
γραμματεύς, scribe, town *clerk*
γραπτός, write, writing
γραφή, decree, direction, letter, record, scripture, write, writing
γραφικός, write
γράφω, describe, enrol, inscribe, letter, make *a*

record, ordain, read, record, scripture, send, write, write *down*, write *out*, writer, writing
γράφω τὰ προσπίπτοντα, recorder
γραώδης, silly
γρηγορέω, alert, awake, keep *awake*, keep *ready*, wake, watch, watchful
γρύζω, growl
γυμνάζω, harass, train
γυμνασία, arena, train
γυμνάσιον, gymnasium
γυμνιτεύω, ill-clad
γυμνός, bare, body, ill-clad, naked, open, strip
γυμνότης, exposure, nakedness
γυμνόω, uncover
γυναικάριον, weak *woman*
γυναικεῖος, woman
γυνή, bride, marriage, widow, wife, woman
γῦρος, vault
γυρόω, encircle
γωνία, corner

δαιμονίζομαι, demon, demoniac, possessed *by a demon*, possessed *with a demon*
δαιμόνιον, demon
δαιμόνιος, demonic, divinity
δαιμονιώδης, devilish
δαίμων, demon
δάκνω, bite, smart
δάκρυον, tear
δακρύω, shed *tears*, weep
δακτυλήθρα, thumbscrew
δακτύλιος, ring, signet
δάκτυλος, finger
δαμάζω, subdue, tame
δάμαλις, calf, heifer
δανείζω, borrow, lend
δάνειον, debt
δανεισμός, borrow *money*
δανειστής, creditor, moneylender
δάνος, loan
δαπανάω, consume, devour, go *out*, pay, spend, use, use *up*
δαπάνη, cost, expense, provision, purpose
δαπάνημα, cost, expense, food
δασύς, spread
δαψιλῆ, rich
δαψιλής, abundant, large
δέ, although, besides, even, former, however, if, indeed, instead, moreover, now, only, other, *other* hand, rather, surely, then, therefore, though, thus, time, too, when, whereas, whether, while, yet
δὲ καί, besides
δὲ τοίνυν, then
δέησις, entreaty, petition, pray, prayer, supplication
δεῖ, due, must, necessary, need, ought, right
δεῖγμα, example
δειγματίζω, make *an example*, put *to shame*
δείκνυμι, inspire, make *manifest*, manifest, prove, see, show
δείκνυμι ἔκδηλος, show
δείκνυμι ἐπιστροφήν, turn *back*
δειλαίνω, *show* fear
δείλαιος, wretched
δειλανδρέω, cowardly, play *the coward*
δειλία, cowardice, terror, timidity
δειλιάζω, coward, play *the coward*, prove *a coward*
δειλιάω, afraid, fear
δειλινός, evening
δειλόομαι, afraid, frighten
δειλός, afraid, coward, cowardly, cowardly *thing*, dread, fainthearted, *late* afternoon, timid, worthless
δειλόψυχος, cowardly, fainthearted
δεῖμα, fear
δεῖνα, certain *one*
δεινάζω, angry, grieve
δεινός, dread, dreadful, fearfully, grievously, mighty, terrible
δεινῶς, hard, terrible, terribly
δειπνέω, eat, supper
δεῖπνον, banquet, feast, meal, supper
δεισιδαιμονία, superstition
δέκα, ten
δέκα δύο, twelve
δέκα καὶ ὀκτώ, eighteen
δέκα ὀκτώ, eighteen
δέκα τέσσαρες, fourteen
δεκαδάρχος, ten
δεκάμηνος, pregnancy
δεκαοκτώ, eighteen
δεκαπέντε, fifteen
δεκαπλασιάζω, tenfold
δεκατέσσαρες, fourteen
δέκατος, tenth, tithe
δέκατος γίνομαι, nine *others*
δεκατόω, pay *a tithe*, receive *a tithe*
δεκτός, acceptable, God *accepts*
δελεάζω, entice
δέλτος, tablet
δένδρον, tree
δενδροτομέω, cut *down*
δεξιά, peace
δεξιάζω, offer *a pledge*
δεξιολάβος, spearman
δεξιός, pledge, pledge *of friendship*, right, *right* hand, *right* side, south, terms *of peace*
δέομαι, beg, beseech, implore, pray, prayer
δέον, necessary
δέος, awe, fear, terror
δέρμα, skin
δερμάτινος, leather
δέρω, beat, receive *a beating*, strike
δέσις, setting
δεσμεύω, bind, man *binding*
δεσμή, bundle
δέσμιος, bond, captive, prison, prisoner, slave
δεσμός, bond, chain, fetter, imprison, imprisonment, prison
δεσμοφύλαξ, jailer
δεσμωτήριον, prison
δεσμώτης, prisoner
δεσπόζω, dominate, dominion *over*, Lord, master, ruler, sovereign, sovereignty
δέσποτα,, Lord
δεσποτεύω, rule
δεσπότης, lord, Lord, master, ruler, sovereign, *sovereign* Lord
δεῦρο, come, go, here
δεῦτε, come, come *away*
δεῦτε ὀπίσω, follow
δευτεραῖος, second
δευτέριον, second
δευτερολογέω, negotiate *a second time*
δεύτερος, afterward, double, next, once *more*, second, twice
δευτερόω, repeat, say *again*, *second* time
δευτέρωσις, repeat
δέχομαι, accept, give *welcome*, receive, take, take *up*, welcome
δέω, ask, beseech, bind, bond, doom, entreat, expense, fasten, fetter, frighten, imprison, make *supplication*, needy, prison, put, put *in prison*, tie
δέω δεξιάς, come *to terms*
δή, course, indeed, just, now, since, then
δὴ τοίνυν, next, then, therefore, turn
δῆγμα, bite
δῆλόν ποιέω, betray
δῆλος, clearly, evident, plain, Urim
δηλόω, disclose, explain, indicate, inform, make *clear*, make *known*, report, set *forth*, show, tell
δήλωσις, Urim
δημαγωγία, demagoguery
δημηγορέω, address *the people*, make *an oration*
δήμιος, butcher, executioner
δημιουργέω, administrator, build, make
δημιουργός, cause, maker
δῆμος, contingent, crowd, people, public, village
δημόσιος, common, public, *public* view, publicly
δημοτελής, *public* expense
δημότης, common *man*
δηνάριον, coin, denarius
δήπου, surely
δι᾽ αἰτίαν, why
δι᾽ αἰῶνος, ever
δι᾽ ἀκροβυστίας, *without being* circumcised
δι᾽ αὐτοῦ, therein
δι᾽ ἣν αἰτίαν, hence, therefore, why
δι᾽ ἧς, thus
δι᾽ ὅ, why
δι᾽ ὀλίγων, briefly
δι᾽ ὅλου, every *way*
δι᾽ ὅν, connection
δι᾽ οὗ, thereby
διά, abet, account, across, after, against, among, avoid, bear, because, before, behalf, benefit, cause, come, due, during, effect, example, fear, ground, intend, long, means, out, *out of* consideration, over, purpose, reason, reason *why*, sake, since, take, through, throughout, under, *under the* leadership, use, view, virtue, way, when, why
διά τινα αἰτίαν, why
διὰ βραχέων, briefly
διὰ κενῆς, needlessly, *without good* reason
διὰ μέσον, between
διὰ μνήμης ἀναλαμβάνω, memorize
διὰ παντός, always, constant, constantly, continually, ever, last, perpetual, perpetually
διὰ πυρός, fiery
διὰ ταύτης, thereby
διὰ τάχους, quickly, rapidly, soon, speedily
διὰ τέλους, completely
διὰ τί, why
διὰ τοῦτο, reason, *same* reason, then, therefore, why
διὰ τρόπον τοῦτον, therefore
διὰ χειρός, through
διαβαίνω, come *over*, cross, cross *over*, go *over*, pass, walk
διαβάλλω, bring *a charge*, misrepresent *a fact*, slander
διαβεβαιόομαι, insist, make *an assertion*
διαβιβάζω, bring *over*
διαβλέπω, look *intently*, see *clearly*
διαβοάω, report
διαβολή, criticism, enmity, *false* accusation, slander, slanderous
διάβολον, adversary
διάβολος, devil, slanderer
διαβούλιον, counsel, inclination
διαβουλία, deliberation
διαγγέλλω, give *notice*, make *proclamation*, proclaim, report
διαγίνομαι, go, lose, pass, past
διαγινώσκω, consider, decide, determine
διάγνωσις, decision
διαγογγύζω, complain, murmur
διαγορεύω, direction
διαγράφω, pay, portray
διαγρηγορέω, waken
διάγω, keep, labor, lead, lead *away*, lead *through*, pass *days*, pass *the time*, spend
διαγωγή, follow
διαδέχομαι, act *as a deputy*, receive, succeed, successor
διαδέω, bind
διάδηλος, notorious
διάδημα, crown, diadem
διαδιδράσκω, flee, run *off*
διαδίδωμι, distribute, divide, inflict, make *distribution*, scatter, spread, spread *abroad*, take
διάδοχος, deputy, succeed, successor
διάθεσις, disposition, live, malice, order, report, state, status, tendency
διαθήκη, covenant, decree, sentence, will
διαθρύπτω, break *in pieces*
διαζάω, keep *alive*
διαζώννυμι, gird, put
διαίρεσις, divide, variety
διαιρέω, apportion, distribute, divide, open *up*
δίαιτα, use
διαιτέω, control, win *over by pleading*
διακαθαρίζω, clear
διακαίω, burn *through*
διακαρτερέω, endure, hold *out*
διακατελέγχομαι, confute
διακατέχω, seize
διάκειμαι, dispose
διακεῖμαι, confine
διακινδυνεύω, risk *life*
διακινέω, move *along*
διακολυμβάω, swim *across*
διακομίζω, arrive, betake, carry *through*, cross *over*, hand *over*
διακονέω, administer, aid, carry, deliver, employ, helper, minister, provide, *render* service, serve, serve *as deacon*
διακονία, dispensation, distribution, ministry, mission, offering, relief, render, serve, service, *table* service
διάκονος, agent, attendant, deacon, deaconess, lackey, minister, servant
διακόπτω, break *open*, cut *to pieces*, ravage
διακόσμησις, adornment
διακούω, hear
διακρατέω, hold, keep
διακριβόω, responsibility, strict
διακρίνω, contend, criticize, decide, discern, doubt, hesitation, interpret, judge, judge *truly*, make *a distinction*, *make* waver, see *anything different*, weigh
διάκρισις, ability *to distinguish*, dispute, distinguish
διακυβερνάω, govern, steer
διακωλύω, hinder, prevent, stop
διαλαλέω, discuss, talk *about*
διαλαμβάνω, find *out*, opinion, sure, take *to mean*, understand
διαλανθάνω, slip
διαλέγομαι, address, argue, discuss, dispute, talk, tell
διαλέγω, confer, reason, speak
διαλείπω, cease
διάλεκτος, language
διάλημψις, notion
διαλιμπάνω, stop
διαλλαγή, reconciliation
διαλλάσσω, give *up*, reconcile, vary
διαλογίζομαι, argue, consider, consider *in mind*, devise, discuss, question, say, take *account*, think
διαλογισμός, argument, conversation, opinion, perplexity, plan, quarrel, question, reasoning, think, thought
διαλοιδόρησις, abuse
διαλύω, break *off*, consume, disperse, end, tear *loose*
διαμαρτυρία, witness
διαμαρτύρομαι, charge, solemnly, testify, warn
διαμασάομαι, chew *greedily*
διαμαχίζομαι, grapple
διαμάχομαι, argue, contend, waste *away*
διαμένω, continue, endure, persevere, preserve, remain, stand, stay
διαμερίζω, distribute, divide, part
διαμερισμός, division
διανέμω, spread
διανεύω, make *a sign*, wink
διανίστημι, get *up*
διανοέω, consider, design, determine, intend, meditate, plan, ponder, reflect, reflect *upon*, resolve, study, think, think *out*, think *upon*, thoughtful, thoughtful *people*, understand
διανόημα, idea, purpose, reasonable, thought, understanding

διάνοια, courage, feel, heart, imagination, intent, *mental* effort, mind, spirit, think, thought, understanding

διανοίγω, explain, open

διανυκτερεύω, continue *all night*

διανύω, come, finish

διαξαίνω, comb

διαπαρατριβή, wrangle

διαπειλέω, threaten

διαπειράζω, try

διαπείρω, pierce

διαπέμπω, send, send *on a mission*, send *word*

διαπεράομαι, cross

διαπεράω, cross, cross *over*

διαπίπτω, fail, lose, rot *away*

διαπλέω, sail *across*

διαπονέομαι, annoy

διαπονέω, devote *effort*

διαπορεύομαι, go, go *on one's way*, go *through*, pass, pass *through*, travel

διαπορεύω, cross

διαπορέω, perplex, perplex *much*

διαπραγματεύομαι, gain *by trading*

διαπράσσω, accomplish, do

διαπρεπής, resplendent

διαπρέπω, splendidly

διαπρίω, enrage

διάπυρος, fiery

διαπυρόω, burn

διαρήγνυμι, break

διαριθμέω, pay *heed*

διαρκέω, content

διαρπαγή, plunder, prey

διαρπάζω, confiscate, plunder, seize, tear *in pieces*

διαρρέω, slip *away*

διαρρήγνυμι, burst *open*, rend, tear, tear *off*

διαρρήσσω, break

διαρρυθμίζω, set *in order*

διασαφέω, *clear* declaration, declare, explain, inform, make *clear*, notify, report, state

διασεισθέντες, confiscation

διασείω, rob *by violence*

διασκεδάννυμι, abolish, break, derange, disperse, reject, scatter

διασκευάζω, make *ready*

διασκευή, *battle* order

διασκιρτάω, leap

διασκορπίζω, scatter, scatter *abroad*, squander, waste, winnow

διασπάω, tear *in pieces*, wrench *apart*

διασπείρω, scatter, spread *out*

διασπορά, dispersion, place *to which scattered*, scatter

διάσταλσις, term

διάστασις, difference

διαστέλλω, agreement, caution, charge, determine, forbid, give *instruction*, *given* order, open, *strictly* charge

διάστημα, interval, offset, period, space

διαστολή, distinct, distinction, division, surrender

διαστράπτω, flash

διαστρέφω, distort, make *crooked*, perverse, perverse *thing*, pervert, *tortuous* path, turn *away*, twist, upset

διαστρώννυμι, spread *a bed*

διασυρίζω, whistle

διασφάλλω, fail

διασχίζω, cut *off*

διασῴζω, bring *safely*, come *safely to land*, deliver, escape, heal, rescue, save

διαταγή, appoint, deliver

διάταγμα, decree, edict, ordinance

διάταξις, form *ranks*, plan, post

διαταράσσω, *greatly* trouble

διατάσσω, appoint, arrange, assign, command, direct, drawn *up*, give *directions*, give *orders*, instruct, instruction, ordain, organize, post, prepare, rule

διατείνω, reach

διατελέω, continually, continue

διατηρέω, *firmly* establish, hold, keep, maintain, preserve

διατίθημι, agree, appoint, assign, give, inflict, make, make *a covenant*, make *a will*, rouse

διατρέφω, food

διατρέχω, run

διατρίβω, live, remain, rub, stay

διατροφή, food, provision

διατυπόω, fashion

διαυγάζω, dawn

διαυγής, transparent

διαφαίνω, shine *through*

διαφαύσκω, come

διαφέρω, carry *through*, convey, differ, disagreement, distinguish, drift, excel, excellent, good, make *a difference*, *more* value, spread, spread *abroad*, steal, value, variance

διαφεύγω, escape, flee, way *of escape*

διαφημίζω, fame, spread

διαφθείρω, *cause to* perish, deprave, destroy, destroyer, rout, waste *away*

διαφθορά, corruption, destruction

διαφορά, difference, preference, variety

διάφορος, differ, excellent, fund, money, *more* excellent, profit, revenue, trifle, various

διαφυλάσσω, guard, keep, maintain, observe, preserve, protect, retain, set *aside*

διαφωνέω, lose

διαχειρίζω, kill

διαχέω, break, disperse, dissolve, stream *out*

διαχλευάζω, mock

διάχρυσος, golden

διαχωρίζομαι, parting

διαχωρίζω, distinguish, keep *far*, part, separate

διαψεύδω, break *a word*, frustrate

διαψιθυρίζω, whisper

δίγλωσσος, deceiver, *double* tongued

διδακτικός, *apt* teacher

διδακτός, teach, train

διδασκαλία, doctrine, instruction, teach, teaching

διδάσκαλος, teach, teacher

διδάσκω, direct, teach

διδαχή, doctrine, instruction, lesson, teach, teaching

δίδραχμον, half-shekel, tax

δίδωμι, allow, ascribe, assign, bear, bring, bring *forth*, cast, cause, come, commit, devote, do, expose, fill, gain, gift, give, give *over*, give *up*, grant, hand *over*, hold, impart, inflict, leave, make, make *a gift*, *make* drain, mingle, mix, offer, pay, permit, pronounce, provide, put, receive, seize, set, show, strike, surrender, turn, utter, yield

δίδωμι γίνομαι, make

δίδωμι δόματα, reward

δίδωμι ἑαυτόν, venture

δίδωμι εἰς ἀφανισμόν, destroy

δίδωμι εἰς στόμα, feed

δίδωμι ἐντολήν, command

δίδωμι ἐξομολόγησιν, praise

δίδωμι ἐξουσίαν, authorize

δίδωμι μισθόν, reward

δίδωμι ῥάπισμα, strike *with the hand*

δίδωμι τόπον, leave

δίδωμι χάραγμα, mark

διεγείρω, arouse, awake, fire, rise, rouse, wake

διεκκύπτω, peer *out*

διεμπίμπλημι, fill

διενθυμέομαι, ponder

διεξάγω, act, deal, maintain, perform

διεξέρχομαι, go *out*

διεξίημι, go

διέξοδος, outlet

διέξοδος τῶν ὁδῶν, thoroughfare

διέπω, rule

διερεθίζω, fan

διερευνάω, inquire, *keep* searching

διερμηνεύω, interpret, mean

διέρχομαι, advance, come, cross, expose, go, go *about*, go *abroad*, go *across*, go *here and there*, go *out*, go *over*, go *through*, pass, pass *along*, pass *through*, pierce, pierce *through*, run *through*, sail *through*, sever, spread, travel, visit

διερωτάω, make *inquiry*

δίεσις, indulgence

διετής, two *years*

διετία, two *years*

διευλαβέομαι, fear

διηγέομαι, declare, describe, proclaim, report, set *forth*, speak, tell, tell *a story*

διήγημα, discourse, narrative

διήγησις, discourse, discussion, narrative, story, tale, talk

διηκέω, pervade

διηνεκής, *all* time, constantly

διηνεκῶς, continually

διηχέω, spread

διϊκνέομαι, pierce

διϊσχυρίζομαι, insist

διΐστημι, depart, determine, devoid, farther, interval, part, scatter

διΐπταμαι, fly *through*

δικάζω, go *to law*, judge

δικαιοκρισία, *righteous* judgment

δικαιοκρίτης, *righteous* judge

δικαιολογία, case

δίκαιος, assert *righteousness*, innocent, just, just *man*, just *one*, *just* term, justice, justly, *more* fitting, *most* righteous, obligation, right, righteous, righteous *man*, righteous *one*, righteous *person*, sincere, upright

δικαιοσύνη, justice, justification, justify, piety, right, righteous *deed*, righteousness, uprightly

δικαιόω, acquit, declare *innocent*, declare *righteous*, deserve, free, hold *guiltless*, justify, release, vindicate

δικαίωμα, act *of righteousness*, custom, decree, judgment, *just* requirement, justice, justification, law, ordinance, plea, precept, principle, regulation, righteous, righteous *deed*, statute

δικαίως, just, justly, right, righteous, righteously, upright

δικαίωσις, acquittal, justification, justify

δικαστής, judge, justice

δίκη, judgment, *just* penalty, justice, penalty, punishment

δίκτυον, net

δίλογος, *double* tongued

διό, accordingly, consequently, reason *why*, then, therefore, why

διοδεύω, break *through*, go *far*, journey *through*, march *through*, pass *through*, traverse, voyage *over*, walk

δίοδος, *main* street, pass, passage *through*, pathway, way *through*

διοικέω, govern, order, rule

διοίκησις, administration

διοικητής, administration

διόλλυμι, kill, perish

διόλου, regularly

διόπερ, therefore

διοπετής, fall *from the sky*

διοργίζω, enrage, rage

διορθόω, *set* right

διόρθωμα, reform

διόρθωσις, reformation

διορθωτής, corrector

διορύσσω, break, break *into*

διότι, because, prove, since, therefore

διπλάσιος, double, twice *as much*

διπλοΐς, robe

διπλοῦς, bring *double*, double, twice *as much*, twofold

διπλόω, repay

δίς, again, twice, two *times*

δίσκος, discus

δισσός, divide, doubly, twofold

διστάζω, doubt

δίστομος, two-edged

διϋλίζω, strain *out*

δίφραξ, chariot

διφρεύω, sit

δίφρος, seat, seat *of honor*, throne

διχάζω, set *against*

διχομηνία, moon *at the full*

διχοστασία, dissension

διχοτομέω, punish

δίψα, thirst

διψάω, thirst, thirsty

δίψος, thirst, thirsty

δίψυχος, *double* minded, man *of double mind*

διωγμός, persecution, pursuit

διωδεύω, go *on through*

διώκτης, persecute

διώκω, aim, chase, drive *away*, follow, go *after*, hunt *down*, make *one's aim*, persecute, persecutor, practice, press, pursue, pursuer, pursuit, seek, strive

διῶρυξ, canal

δόγμα, decision, decree, *legal* demand, ordinance, teaching, tradition

δογματίζω, decree, submit *to regulation*

δοκέω, appear, convince, decide, determine, dispose, expect, extol, imagine, intend, judge, judgment, please, pleasure, presume, regard, repute, seem, *seem* good, suppose, think

δοκιμάζω, accredit, approve, examine, inflict, interpret, investigate, make *trial*, prove, see *fit*, test, try, try *to learn*

δοκιμασία, test

δοκιμή, character, proof, test, worth

δοκίμιον, genuineness, test

δόκιμος, accept, approve, genuine, meet *the test*, test

δοκός, beam, log, rafter, roof

δόλιος, crafty, deceitful, treacherous

δολιότης, deceit

δολιόω, deceive

δόλος, deceit, deceitfully, guile, stealth, treacherous, *treacherous* intent, treacherously, treachery, trickery

δολόω, tamper

δόμα, gift, give, offering, payment

δόμος, course

δόξα, another, brightness, dignity, expect, form *of prestige*, glorification, glorious, glorious *one*, gloriously, glory, honor, pomp, praise, pride, regard, reputation, respect, splendid, splendor, standing

δόξα προσώπου, partiality

δοξάζομαι, gain *glory*, gain *honor*, win *honor*

δοξάζω, bestow *honor*, boast, bring *glory*, exalt, famous *man*, give *glory*, glorify, glorious, honor, honorable *man*, magnify, make *glorious*, pay *honor*, praise, splendor, triumph

δοξικός, splendid

δοριάλωτος, captive, storm

δορκάς, gazelle

δόρυ, shaft, spear

δορυφορία, bodyguard

δορυφόρος, bodyguard, guard

δόσις, divide, endowment, gift, give, give *out*

δότης, giver

δουλαγωγέω, subdue

δουλεία, bondage, completely, servitude, slavery

δουλεύω, bondage, enslave, *render* service, servant, serve, serve *as slave*, slave, slavery

δούλη, handmaid, handmaiden, maid, maidservant, servant, slave

δοῦλος, manservant, servant, serve, slave, slavery

δουλόω, *become a* slave, bind, enslave, make *a slave*, slave

δοχή, banquet, feast

δράγμα, sheaf

δράκος, handful

δράκων, dragon, serpent

δρᾶμα, role

δραπέτης, *runaway* slave

δράσσομαι, catch, grasp, take *a handful*, take *hold*

δραχμή, coin, drachma, *silver* coin

δράω, act, do, make

δρεπανηφόρος, arm *with a scythe*
δρέπανον, sickle
δρόμος, course, race, run, rush
δροσίζω, moisten *with dew*
δρόσος, dew, moist
δρυμός, thicket, wood
δύναμαι, able, act, can, cannot, effective, enable, mighty, possible, power, ready
δύναμαι πρός, defeat
δύναμις, ability, arm, *armed* force, army, authority, division, force, garrison, host, intensely, meaning, means, might, mighty, *mighty* work, miracle, power, rage, strength, supply, troop, virtue, warrior, wealth, worker *of miracles*
δυναμόω, strengthen, win *strength*
δυναστεία, dominion, might, mighty, power, sovereignty
δυναστεύω, exercise *authority*, power *over*, rule, ruler, subdue
δυνάστης, commander, Lord, mighty, mighty *one*, minister, powerful, powerful *man*, prince, ruler, sovereign
δυνατέω, able, powerful
δυνατός, able, army, man *of authority*, mighty, mighty *man*, mighty *one*, *mighty* warrior, *more* powerful, officer, possible, power, powerful, strong, thoroughly, warrior, *well* versed
δυνατὸς ἰσχύς, stalwart, *very* strong
δυνατῶς, mightily
δύνω, set
δύνω ἥλιος, sundown
δύνω ὁ ἥλιος, sunset
δύο, both, two, two *things*
δύο δύο, pair
δυσάθλιος, *most* miserable
δυσαίακτος, lamentable
δυσάληκτος, inescapable
δυσβάστακτος, hard *to bear*
δυσδιήγητος, hard *to describe*
δυσεντερία, dysentery
δυσερμήνευτος, hard
δυσημερία, misfortune
δυσκλεής, infamous, shameful
δύσκολος, hard
δυσκόλως, hard
δυσμένεια, enmity, ill *will*, ill-will
δυσμενής, enemy, hostile
δυσμενῶς ἔχω, hostile
δυσμή, set, west
δυσνοέω, ill-disposed
δυσνόητος, hard *to understand*
δυσπέτημα, misfortune
δυσπολιόρκητος, hard *to besiege*
δυσπρόσιτος, difficult *of access*
δυσσέβεια, impiety
δυσσεβέω, impious
δυσσέβημα, ungodly, ungodly *deed*
δυσσεβής, impious, ungodly, ungodly *man*
δυσφημέω, slander, speak *blasphemy*
δυσφημία, blasphemy, *evil* report, *ill* repute
δύσφημος, blasphemous, profane *man*
δυσφορέω, displease, indignant
δυσφόρως, grieve
δυσφόρως φέρω, grieve
δυσχέρεια, annoy, difficulty
δυσχερής, grievous, hard, severe, unwelcome
δύσχρηστος, inconvenient
δυσώδης, stink
δύω, set
δώδεκα, twelve
δωδεκαετής, twelve *years*
δωδέκατος, twelfth
δωδεκάφυλον, twelve *tribes*
δῶμα, housetop, roof
δωρεά, bounty, *free* gift, gift
δωρεάν, needlessly, *no* purpose, present, *without* cause, *without* cost, *without* pay, *without* paying, *without* payment, *without* price
δωρέομαι, give, grant
δώρημα, *free* gift, gift
δωροκοπέω, bribe, offer *a bribe*
δῶρον, bribery, gift, give, give *to God*, offering, present

ἔα, ah
ἐάν, any *one*, even *if*, if, only *if*, provided, though, what, when, whether
ἐάν τε, either
ἐάν τε καί, whether
ἐάν τις, whatever
ἐὰν ἔχω, means
ἐὰν μή, except, only, unless, until, without
ἐάνπερ, if, if *at all*, if *only*
ἔαρ, spring
ἑαυτοῦ, conceit, conduct, *each* other, heart, life, natural, one *another*, person, property, same, together, various
ἑαυτοῦ ἀξιόω, presume
ἐάω, allow, go, leave, let, let *alone*, permit
ἐάω ἕως, no *more*
ἐβαθύνω, deep
ἑβδομάς, sevenfold, seventh, week
ἕβδομος, seven, seventh
ἐγγίζω, advance, approach, *at* hand, bring *near*, come, come *close*, come *near*, come *up*, draw *near*, hand, lead, reach
ἐγγλύφω, carve
ἐγγράφω, enrol, write
ἐγγυάω, give *surety*, surety
ἐγγύη, surety, suretyship
ἔγγυος, pledge, surety
ἐγγύς, *at* hand, close *at hand*, close *by*, hand, near, next, ready
ἐγείρω, arise, awake, bestir, come, erect, fulfil, lift *out*, lift *up*, make, raise, raise *up*, rise, rise *up*, rouse, wake, wake *up*
ἐγένετο ὡς, when
ἔγερσις, erection, resurrection
ἐγκάθετος, spy
ἐγκάθημαι, sit *along*
ἐγκαθίζω, lie, take *a seat*
ἐγκαίνια, *feast of the* Dedication, feast *of the Dedication*
ἐγκαινίζω, dedicate, open, ratify, restore, show *anew*
ἐγκαινισμός, dedication
ἐγκαίω, paint
ἐγκακέω, grow *weary*, lose *heart*, weary
ἐγκαλέω, accusation, accuse, bring *a charge against*, charge
ἐγκαρτερέω, bear *patiently*
ἐγκατά, mind
ἐγκαταλείπω, abandon, desert, fail, forsake, give *up*, leave, neglect
ἐγκατοικέω, live
ἐγκαυχάομαι, boast
ἐγκεντρίζω, bite, graft, graft *into*
ἐγκηδεύομαι, lie *buried*
ἔγκλημα, charge, lay *a charge against*
ἐγκομβόομαι, clothe
ἐγκοπή, obstacle
ἐγκόπτω, detain, hinder
ἐγκοσμέω, *remain* adorned
ἐγκράτεια, self-control
ἐγκρατεύομαι, exercise *self-control*
ἐγκρατής, chaste, control, get *hold*, hold, possess, possession, self-controlled
ἐγκρατὴς γίνομαι, get *possession*, hold
ἐγκρίνω, class
ἐγκρύπτω, hide
ἐγκυλίω, form, wallow
ἔγκυος, child, pregnant
ἐγχάσκω, gape
ἐγχειρίδιον, dagger
ἐγχρίω, anoint
ἐγχώριος, inhabitant, native
ἐγώ, I *am*
ἐδαφίζω, dash *to the ground*
ἔδαφος, earth *around*, floor, ground, pavement
ἔδεσμα, eat, food, luxurious
ἐδιδύσκω, clothe
ἑδράζω, settle, take
ἑδραῖος, firmly, steadfast
ἑδραίωμα, bulwark
ἐθελοθρησκία, rigor *of devotion*
ἐθελοκωφόω, pretend *not to hear*
ἐθέλω, desire, please, prefer, ready, seek, want, will, willing, wish, would *that*
ἐθίζω, accustom, custom
ἐθισμός, accustom, custom, habit
ἐθνάρχης, ethnarch, governor
ἐθνηδόν, entire *tribe*
ἐθνικός, Gentile, heathen
ἐθνικῶς, *like a* Gentile
ἐθνοπάτωρ, ancestor *of nation*
ἐθνοπλήθης, multitude *of the people*
ἔθνος, community, countryman, Gentile, heathen, nation, pagan, people
ἔθος, accustom, custom, habit
ἔθω, keep *well*
ἔθω ποιεῖν, custom
εἰ, although, chance, either, even, if, if *in fact*, never, no, only, provided, since, since *indeed*, such, though, when, whether, would *that*
εἰ ἄρα γε, hope
εἰ δὲ μή, else
εἰ μή, else, except, much, only, otherwise, unless
εἰ μή γε, then
εἰ μὴ οὐ, only
εἰ μὴ ὅταν, until
εἰ μήν, surely
εἰ μήτι, unless, unless *indeed*
εἰ μήτι ἄν, except *perhaps*
εἰ τυγχάνω, doubtless, perhaps
εἴ γε, assume
εἴ πως, order
εἴ τι, what
εἴ τις, whatever, whoever
εἰδέα, appearance
εἰδέχθεια, odious
εἰδέω, know
εἴδησις, know
εἶδον, behold, look, perceive, see
εἶδος, appearance, figure, form, kind, know, sight, sort
εἰδωλεῖον, *idol's* temple, temple *of idols*
εἰδώλιον, idol, shrine *for an idol*
εἰδωλόθυτος, food *offered to an idol*, food *sacrificed to an idol*, sacrifice *to idol*
εἰδωλολάτρης, idolater
εἰδωλολατρία, idolatry, worship *of an idol*
εἴδωλον, idol
εἴθε, then
εἰκάζω, guess, infer
εἰκάς, twentieth
εἰκοσαετής, twenty
εἴκοσι, twenty
εἰκότως, obviously
εἴκω, give *way*, yield
εἰκών, image, likeness, true *form*, *true* form
εἰλικρίνεια, sincerity
εἰλικρινής, pure, sincere
εἰμί, alive, alone, become, being, belong, bring, busy, come, consist, continue, count, depend, devote, do, dress, dwell, endure, exist, existence, fall, fare, find, follow, form, future, gather, give, go, go *out*, grant, grow, happen, hold, I *am*, imply, keep, leave, lie, life, like, live, make, mean, move, need, occur, own, plunge, possible, present, put, reach, real, remain, rest, result, serve, show, side, spring, stand, stay, store, supply, take *a position*, take *place*, thing, *thing that* exists, turn, whether
εἰμὶ ἀντί, take *one's place*
εἰμὶ ἐγκρατής, possess *wisdom*
εἰμὶ ἐκ, rely
εἰμὶ ἐν, keep, occupant, suffer
εἰμὶ ἐπί, governor, mark, wear, weigh *down*
εἰμὶ ἴσος, equality
εἰμὶ μνεία, remember
εἰμὶ παρά, give
εἰμὶ ποιέω, bring
εἰμὶ πρό, precede
εἴπερ, if, if *really*
εἶπον, add, answer, ask, bid, boast, call, call *out*, command, cry, declare, deny, direct, exclaim, give *a command*, insist, make, order, promise, quote, reply, say, serve, speak, state, tell, use, utter, what, word
εἰρηνεύω, gain *peace*, live *at peace*, live *in peace*, live *peaceably*, offer *of peace*, peace
εἰρήνη, health, peace, *peaceful* settlement, prosperous, safe, safety, welfare
εἰρηνικός, friendly, peace, peaceable, peaceably, *peaceably* disposed, peaceful, soothe
εἰρηνικῶς, peaceably, peaceful
εἰρηνοποιέω, make *peace*
εἰρηνοποιός, peacemaker
εἱρκτή, prison
εἰρωνεία, hypocrisy
εἷς, all, alone, another, any, anything, consistent, each, equal, first, man, once, one, one *man*, one *thing*, only, other, same, single
εἷς ἀπὸ τοῦ ἑνός, *each* other
εἷς ἕκαστος, each, everyone, one *by one*
εἷς καθ' ἕν, each
εἰς, about, accordingly, against, among, bear, because, become, before, bring, carry, cause, come, concerning, connection, contrive, cost, deal, down, fully, give, go, grant, gratify, ground, inflict, inside, interest, lead, like, make, many, meet, obtain, order, over, purpose, reach, refer, result, seek, serve, share, supply, through, throughout, thus, till, toward, turn, turn *into*, until, unto, upon, use, way, why
εἰς αἰῶνα, eternal, ever
εἰς αἰῶνας, ever
εἰς ἀλλήλους, mutual
εἰς ἄνδρας, man *by man*
εἰς ἅπαντα χρόνον, ever, forever
εἰς ἀπάντησιν, against
εἰς ἀπώλειαν, perish
εἰς ἀριθμόν, ordinary
εἰς αὔριον, tomorrow
εἰς ἀχάριστα, *without being* thanked
εἰς διακονίαν, relief
εἰς δόξαν, glorious
εἰς ἐπιτελοῦσαν ἡμέραν, tomorrow
εἰς ἔρχομαι, arouse
εἰς εὐθεῖαν, straight
εἰς εὐλογίαν, bless
εἰς θάνατον, mortal
εἰς καιρόν, never *amiss*
εἰς μέλλω, until
εἰς μέσον, among, within
εἰς μεταμέλον ἔρχομαι, repent
εἰς μετέπειτα χρόνον, hereafter
εἰς μή, keep
εἰς μνημόσυνον, permanent
εἰς ὁδόν, among
εἰς ὄλεθρον, destroy
εἰς πάντας αἰῶνας, ever
εἰς πάντας τοὺς αἰῶνας, ever
εἰς παράταξιν, fight
εἰς πᾶσαν, fully
εἰς περισσείαν, greatly
εἰς πλῆθος, plenty
εἰς πλοῖον ἐμβολή, embarkation
εἰς πόλεμον, attack
εἰς προκοπὴν ἔρχομαι, gain *ground*
εἰς πρόσωπον, before
εἰς στήριγμα, reinforce
εἰς συνάντησιν, against
εἰς συντέλειαν, utterly
εἰς τὰ ὀπίσω, back round
εἰς τέλος, completely, continual, hopelessly, last, utterly, wholly
εἰς τὴν γῆν, ashore
εἰς τὴν χρείαν, help

εἰς τί, why
εἰς τὸ διηνεκές, continually, ever
εἰς τὸ ἔμπροσθεν, ahead
εἰς τὸ ἕν, agree
εἰς τὸ λοιπόν, now *on*
εἰς τὸ μέσον, here
εἰς τὸ οὖς, whisper
εἰς τὸ παντελές, fully
εἰς τὸν αἰῶνα, ever, last
εἰς τὸν αἰῶνα χρόνον, ever
εἰς τὸν καιρόν, promptly
εἰς τὸν οἶκον, home
εἰς τοὺς αἰῶνας, ever
εἰς τοῦτο, reason, why
εἰς ὕψος, up
εἰς φθοράν, perish
εἰς ὦτα ἀκούω, *attentive* listener
εἰσάγω, bring, bring *back*, bring *into*, drive, escort, go, lead, take, take *into*
εἰσακούω, hear, hearken, listen, obey
εἰσβάλλω, enter, rush
εἰσδέχομαι, let, receive, usher, welcome
εἰσδύω, get
εἴσειμι, go, go *into*
εἰσέρχομαι, arise, arrive, come, come *into*, enter, enter *into*, get, go, go *into*, go *through*, invade, meet, reach, return
εἰσέρχομαι πρός, approach, visit
εἰσίημι, enter
εἰσκαλέομαι, call
εἰσκυκλέω, enter *upon*
εἴσοδος, come, enter, entrance, invade, visit, way, welcome
εἰσοράω, look *upon*
εἰσπέμπω, send
εἰσπηδάω, rush
εἰσπλέω, sail *into*
εἰσπορεύομαι, come, enter, go, go *into*, return
εἰσπορεύω, back, come
εἰστρέχω, run, rush *into*
εἰσφέρω, bring, bring *into*, carry, lead, put
εἶτα, if
εἶτα, afterward, then
εἶτα μέν, besides
εἴωθα, accustom, custom
ἐκ, accordance, according, adherent, after, against, among, answer, authority, away, base, basis, bear, because, before, begin, belong, between, come, commission, company, depend, depend *upon*, descend, do, ever *since*, flank, follow, ground, matter, means, off, origin, out, part, some, source, subject, through, time, under, upon, where
ἐκ γένους, kinsman, relative
ἐκ λύπης, reluctantly
ἐκ μέρους, imperfect, individually
ἐκ μέσου, aside
ἐκ μεταβολῆς ἀναλύω, revoke
ἐκ παλαιῶν χρόνων, long
ἐκ περιτομῆς, *circumcision* party
ἐκ σπέρματος, member
ἐκ τοῦ ὄπισθεν, follow
ἐκ τοῦ στόματος, say
ἐκ τούτου καὶ ἐκ τούτου, *both* sides
ἐκ τῶν ἀλλογενῶν, foreign
ἐκ φύσεως, physically
ἐκ ψυχῆς, heartily, willingly
ἕκαστος, all, another, any *one*, detail, each, each *man*, each *one*, each *woman*, every, every *man*, every *one*, *exact* detail, respective
ἕκαστος πάντων, every
ἕκαστος πρὸς τὸν πλησίον, one *another*
ἕκαστος τὸν πλησίον, one *another*
ἑκάστοτε, *any* time
ἑκάτερος, both, each, either, this *side and that*, two
ἑκατέρωθεν, *each* side
ἑκατόν, against, hundred, hundredfold
ἑκατονταπλασίων, hundredfold
ἑκατοντάρχης, centurion
ἑκατόνταρχος, hundred
ἑκατοστός, against
ἐκβαίνω, go *out*, leave, make *a landing*, result, turn *out*
ἐκβάλλω, bring, bring *forth*, bring *out*, cast, cast *out*, compel *to depart*, drive *away*, drive *out*, expell, pass, pluck *out*, put *away*, put *out*, put *outside*, remove, send *away*, send *out*, set, station, take, take *out*, throw, throw *out*, thrust *out*
ἐκβάλλω ἔξωθεν, leave *out*
ἔκβασις, end *of life*, event, outcome, way *of escape*
ἐκβιάζω, force
ἐκβολὴν ποιέω, throw *overboard cargo*
ἔκβολος, defeat
ἐκβράζω, cast *ashore*, drive *out*
ἐκγελάω, laugh *to scorn*
ἔκγονος, child, descendant, grandchildren
ἐκδαπανάω, spend
ἐκδειματόω, terror
ἐκδεκτέον, *must* admit
ἐκδέχομαι, accept, expect, gain, look *forward*, receive, take, wait
ἐκδέω, hang
ἔκδηλος, manifest, plain
ἐκδημέω, away
ἐκδιαιτάω, change *the way of life*
ἐκδιαιτέω, abandon
ἐκδιδάσκω, teach
ἐκδίδωμι, give, give *in marriage*, give *up*, let *out*, ordain, plow, publish, surrender, yield
ἐκδιηγέομαι, declare, describe, recount, relate, report, say, speak, tell
ἐκδικάζω, take *vengeance*
ἐκδικέω, avenge, carry *out revenge*, know, punish, take *revenge*, take *vengeance*, vindicate
ἐκδίκησις, avenge, punish, punishment, take *revenge*, take *vengeance*, vengeance, wrong
ἔκδικος, advocate, avenger, execute, vindicator
ἐκδιώκω, afflict, drive *out*
ἔκδοτον, give *over*
ἔκδοτος, deliver *up*
ἐκδοχή, prospect
ἐκδύω, strip, take *off*, unclothed
ἐκεῖ, contain, there, where, yonder
ἐκεῖθεν, away, place, there, where
ἐκεῖνος, any *one*, other, same, very, yonder
ἐκεῖσε, there
ἐκέκραγεν, crow
ἐκθαμβέω, amaze, frighten, *greatly* amaze, *greatly* distress
ἔκθαμβος, astound
ἐκθαυμάζω, admire, amaze, marvel
ἔκθεσις, expose
ἔκθεσμος, unlawfully
ἐκθλίβω, crowd *aside*
ἔκθυμος, excite, rage
ἐκζητέω, ask, compose, exact, investigation, require, search, seek, seek *out*, try, watch
ἐκζήτησις, speculation
ἐκζητητής, seeker
ἐκκαθαίρω, cleanse *out*, purify
ἐκκαίω, blaze, burn, consume, glow, kindle
ἐκκαύω, burn *up*
ἐκκενόω, dry
ἐκκεντέω, massacre, pierce
ἐκκλάω, break *off*
ἐκκλείω, exclude, shut *out*
ἐκκλησία, assembly, body, church, congregation, gather
ἔκκλητος, notorious
ἐκκλίνω, avoid, elude, falter, go *round*, pervert, shun, swerve, turn, turn *aside*, turn *away*, turn *away in flight*
ἐκκολυμβάω, swim *away*
ἐκκομιδή, removal
ἐκκομίζω, carry *out*
ἐκκόπτω, cut, cut *down*, cut *off*, destroy, eradicate, gouge *out*, undermine
ἐκκρεμάννυμι, hang *upon*
ἐκκύπτω, come *out*, emerge
ἐκλαλέω, say, tell
ἔκλαμπρος, brilliant
ἐκλάμπω, bright, shine, shine *forth*
ἔκλαμψις, flash
ἐκλανθάνομαι, forget
ἐκλέγομαι, choose, make *a choice*
ἐκλέγω, choice, pick
ἐκλείπω, abandon, cease, cease *to exist*, cease *to play*, come *to an end*, draw *one's last*, empty, end, exhaust, fail, faint, give *out*, grow *weak*, lack, leave *no one*, lose, run *out*, weak
ἐκλείπω ψυχή, die
ἐκλείχω, lick *up*, melt
ἐκλεκτός, choice, choose, chosen *one*, elect, eminent, pick, pure, *special* favor
ἐκλικμάω, ravage, winnow *away*
ἐκλογή, choose, elect, election
ἐκλογιστής, account
ἐκλογιστία, account
ἔκλυσις, faint
ἐκλύω, *become* faint, depart, disregard, exhaust, fail, faint, grow *weary*, lose *courage*, lose *heart*, relax, untie, withdraw
ἐκμαρτυρέω, bear *testimony*
ἐκμάσσω, polish, wipe, wipe *off*
ἐκμελετάω, train
ἐκμελίζω, disjoint *all members*, dislocate, dismember
ἐκμυκτηρίζω, mock, scoff
ἐκνεύω, incline, withdraw
ἐκνήφω, carry *off*, come *to mind*
ἑκουσιάζομαι, offer *willingly*
ἑκούσιος, arbitrarily, *free* will, freewill, *freewill* offering
ἑκουσίως, deliberately, wilfully, willingly
ἐκπαίζω, scoff
ἔκπαλαι, *long* ago, old
ἐκπειράζω, put *to the test*, tempt
ἐκπέμπω, send *away*, send *back*, send *out*
ἐκπερισσῶς, vehemently
ἐκπετάζω, hang *up*, open, spread *forth*, spread *out*
ἐκπετάννυμι, hold *out*
ἐκπέτομαι, fly *forth*
ἐκπηδάω, dash *out*, hurry *out*, rush *out*
ἐκπηρόω, fulfil
ἐκπίνω, drink
ἐκπίπτω, fail, fall, fall *away*, fall *off*, go, issue, lose, run
ἐκπλέω, sail, sail *away*
ἐκπληρόω, carry *out*, fulfillment, make *up*
ἐκπλήρωσις, fulfil, *full* measure
ἐκπλήσσω, amaze, astonish, strike
ἐκπνέω, breathe *one's last*
ἐκποιέω, enable, enough, give *power*
ἐκπολεμέω, attack, conquer, defeat, subdue
ἐκπολιτεύω, alter *a form of government*
ἐκπορεύομαι, come, come *forth*, come *out*, flow, go *abroad*, go *out*, issue, leave, pass, pour *out*, proceed, proceed *out*, sally *forth*, set *out*
ἐκπορεύω, come, go, out
ἐκπορθέω, ravage
ἐκπορνεύω, *act* immorally, fall *into idolatry*
ἐκπρεπής, magnificent
ἐκπρέπω, remarkably
ἐκπρίω, saw *down*
ἐκπτύω, despise
ἐκπυρόω, heat
ἐκρέω, slip *away*
ἐκριζόω, pluck *up*, raze, root *out*, root *up*, uproot
ἐκριζωτής, uproot
ἐκρίπτω, cast *out*, shower, throw *out*
ἐκσοβέω, scare
ἐκσπονδυλίζομαι, break *a back*
ἔκστασις, amazement, astonishment, trance
ἔκστασις μεγάλη, amazement
ἐκστρέφω, pervert
ἐκσυρίζω, hiss
ἐκταράσσω, appall, disturb, *greatly* trouble, terrify
ἐκτάσσω, drawn *up for battle*
ἐκτείνω, display, extend, lay, raise, reach *out*, set, spread *out*, stretch *forth*, stretch *out*
ἐκτελέω, finish, wholly, win
ἐκτέμνω, cut *out*
ἐκτένεια, concern, earnestly, fast, fervor zeal
ἐκτενῆ, eager
ἐκτενής, effort, unfailing
ἐκτενῶς, earnest, earnestly, fervently
ἐκτήκω, make *dim*, waste *away*
ἐκτίθημι, explain, expose, expound, lay *out*, make *a proposal*, post, stretch *out*
ἐκτίλλω, pluck *up*
ἐκτινάσσω, drive *out*, shake *off*, shake *out*, shoot
ἐκτοπίζω, get *away*
ἕκτος, sixth
ἐκτός, besides, except, free, out, outside, outsider
ἐκτὸς εἰ μή, unless
ἐκτὸς εἰ μή, except
ἐκτρέπω, avoid, put *out of joint*, stray, wander, wander *away*
ἐκτρέφω, bring *up*, nourish, rear
ἐκτρίβω, destroy, wear *out*, wipe *out*
ἔκτρωμα, bear *untimely*
ἐκτύπωμα, inscribe
ἐκυρεύω, *render* ineffective
ἐκφαίνω, betray, disclose, expound, gain, impart, make *evident*, *make* shine, *make* shine *forth*, *make* show, reveal
ἐκφαυλίζω, despise
ἐκφέρω, bear, bring, bring *out*, carry *away*, carry *out*, get, lead, take *out*
ἐκφεύγω, escape, flee, flee *out*, recover
ἐκφλέγω, rage *fiery*
ἐκφοβέω, fright, frighten, make *afraid*, spread *terror among*, terrify, terror
ἔκφοβος, *exceedingly* afraid, fear, fearful
ἐκφυγῆς, escape
ἐκφυσάω, breathe *out*, fan
ἐκφύω, put *forth*
ἐκχέω, abandon, circulate, give *up*, gush *out*, place, pour, pour *out*, rush *out*, shed, spill, waste
ἔκχυσις αἵματος, bloodshed
ἐκχωρέω, depart, withdraw
ἐκχωρίζω, set *apart*
ἐκψύχω, die
ἑκών, will
ἐλαία, olive, olive *tree*, *olive* wreath
ἔλαιον, oil
ἐλασσόω, fail, lack, little
ἐλάσσων, less, poor, young
ἐλατός, *hammered* work
ἔλαττον, inferior
ἐλαττονέω, lack
ἐλαττονόω, defeat, lessen, lose
ἐλαττόω, decrease, devoid, diminish, lack, lessen, limit, make *low*, oppress, shorten, suffer *loss*, take *away*, without
ἐλάττωμα, defeat, lack
ἐλάττων, few
ἐλάττωσις, diminish, loss
ἐλαύνω, drive, make *headway*, pursue, row
ἐλαφρός, light, slight
ἐλάχιστος, least, small *thing*, *very* least, *very* little, *very* small, *very* small *thing*
ἐλαχύς, least, little, lowly *man*, reduce, small, trivial, *very* little *thing*
ἐλεάω, convince, mercy, pity, *show* mercy
ἐλεγμός, inquiry, punishment, rebuke, reproach, reproof
ἔλεγξιν ἔχω, rebuke
ἔλεγχος, convict, conviction, punishment, rebuke, reproof
ἐλέγχω, ashamed, confute, convict, convince, correct, expose, prove, punish, question, rebuke, reprove, say, tell *a fault*
ἐλεεινός, pitiable, pity *most*

ἐλεέω, compassion, *do an act of* mercy, find *mercy*, merciful, mercy, mercy *upon*, obtain *mercy*, pity, receive *mercy*, *show* compassion, *show* mercy, *show* pity, *something* pitiable, take *pity*
ἐλεημοσύνη, act *of charity*, act *of mercy*, alms, almsgiving, charity, deed *of charity*, gift, kindness, mercy
ἐλεήμων, merciful
ἔλεον, object *of pity*
ἔλεος, compassion, kindness, loyal *deed*, merciful, mercy, pity
ἑλέπολις, *siege* engine
ἐλευθερία, freedom, liberty
ἐλεύθερος, free, free *man*, free *woman*, freedom
ἐλευθερόω, free, make *free*, *set* free
ἔλευσις, come
ἐλεφαντάρχης, command *of elephants*, *elephant* keeper, keeper *of elephants*
ἐλεφάντινος, ivory
ἐλέφας, elephant
ἑλίσσω, roll *up*
ἕλκος, sore, wound
ἑλκόω, full *of sores*
ἕλκω, bear, bring *forward*, drag, drag *along*, draw, haul, influence
ἐλλιπής, lack
ἐλλογέω, charge *to an account*, count
ἕλος, marsh
ἐλπίζω, expect, hope, put *hope*, put *trust*, set *one's hope*, *thing* hoped, trust
ἐλπίς, confidence, hope
ἐλύθη ὁ δεσμός, release
ἐμβαίνω, embark, get *into*, go *on board*
ἐμβάλλω, cast *into*, inject, lay, make, place, put, throw, throw *into*
ἐμβάπτω, dip
ἐμβατεύω, invade, occupy *ground*, take *a stand*
ἐμβιβάζω, put *on board*
ἐμβιόω, live
ἐμβίωσις, preserve *life*, way *of life*
ἐμβλέπω, consider, look, look *into*, look *upon*, see
ἐμβριμάομαι, move *deeply*, reproach, sternly, *sternly* charge
ἐμέω, spew
ἐμμαίνομαι, fury
ἐμμανής, frenzy
ἐμμελέτημα, fashion
ἐμμένω, abide, continue, keep, live, live *long*, persevere, true
ἔμμονος, chronic
ἔμπαιγμα, delusion
ἐμπαιγμονή, scoff
ἐμπαιγμός, insult, mock, mockery, sport
ἐμπαίζω, deride, make *sport*, mock, sport, trick, victim *of sport*
ἐμπαίκτης, scoffer
ἐμπαροχλέω, molest
ἐμπειράω, familiar
ἔμπειρος, acquaint
ἐμπεριπατέω, move *among*, strut, walk *among*
ἐμπηδάω, leap
ἐμπίμπλημι, eat *one's fill*, enjoy *company*, feed *upon*, fill, full, overflow, satisfy, take *one's fill*
ἐμπίμπρημι, burn, burn *up*, set *fire*
ἐμπίπτω, become, break *out*, encounter, fall, fall *among*, fall *into*, fall *into the hand*, incur, meet, push *forward*
ἐμπιστεύω, believe, entrust, faith, find *trustworthy*, put *confidence*, rely, trust
ἐμπλέκω, entangle, fight *hand to hand*, get *entangled*
ἐμπληθύνω, fill
ἐμπλοκή, braid
ἐμπνέω, breathe, inspire
ἔμπνους, alive, breathe
ἐμποδίζω, hinder, hold *back*, interrupt
ἐμποδιστικός, hinder, stand *in the way*
ἐμποιέω, assume
ἐμπονέω, vehement
ἐμπορεύομαι, exploit, trade
ἐμπορία, business
ἐμπόριον, trade
ἔμπορος, merchant, trader
ἐμπορπάομαι, gird
ἐμπορπόω, put
ἔμπροσθεν, against, ago, ahead, before, beforehand, former, forward, front, lie *ahead*, past, precede, presence
ἔμπροσθεν χρόνος, past
ἐμπρόσθιος, front
ἐμπτύω, spit, spit *upon*
ἐμπυρίζω, burn, burn *down*, burn *up*, char, set *fire*
ἐμπυριστής, fiery
ἐμφαίνω, disclose
ἐμφανής, clear, manifest, visible
ἐμφανὴς γίνομαι, show
ἐμφανίζω, appear, give *information*, give *notice*, inform, lay *a case*, make *clear*, make *known*, manifest, show, tell
ἐμφανισμός, disclosure
ἔμφασις, ostensibly
ἐμφέρω, attack
ἔμφοβος, alarm, frighten, God-fearing *man*, terrify, terror
ἐμφραγμός, stop
ἐμφράσσω, block *up*, seal *up*, stop
ἐμφυσάω, breathe, breathe *into*
ἐμφυσιόω, explain, inspire
ἔμφυτος, implant, inborn
ἔν τι, any
ἐν, about, accompaniment, according, across, after, against, along, among, attend, because, before, belong *still*, beneath, besides, charge, close, contain, depend, depend *upon*, deserve, do, down, during, handle, help, hold, if, incur, inspire, intact, involve, late, lead, long, means, more, near, open, out, over, part, possess, resident, *same* time, set, some, through, throughout, time, toward, under, upon, use, way, when, when *it is time*, where, while, within, withstand
ἐν ἀγαθοῖς, happy
ἐν αἰνίγματι, dimly
ἐν αἷς, when
ἐν αἰσθήσει, deeply
ἐν ἀποκρύφοις, conceal
ἐν αὐτοῖς, therein
ἐν βάρει, demand
ἐν γαστρί, child
ἐν γαστρί ἔχω, conceive
ἐν δυνάμει, mightily
ἐν ἐκλύσει, faint
ἐν ἐσθῆτι, clothe
ἐν εὐλογίαις, bless
ἐν ἡμέραις πολλαῖς, age
ἐν ἡμέραις, during, when
ἐν ἰσχύι, forcibly
ἐν λόγοις, speak
ἐν μηδενί, no
ἐν νηστείαις, *without* food
ἐν οἷς, include, where
ἐν ὁμοιώματι, resemble
ἐν οὐδενί, all
ἐν οὐδενὶ τίθημι, disdain
ἐν ὀφθαλμοῖς, seem
ἐν παντί, perfect
ἐν παραβάσει, transgressor
ἐν πᾶσιν, always
ἐν πένθει, mourn
ἐν πίστει, confidently, faithfully
ἐν πολλοῖς, often
ἐν πολλοῖς βρώμασιν, overeat
ἐν πρώτοις, first
ἐν σαρκί, physical
ἐν συνέσει, intelligently
ἐν συστέματι, organize
ἐν ταῖς ἡμέραις, while
ἐν ταῖς ἡμέραις ἐν αἷς, while
ἐν ταῖς ὁδοῖς, flee
ἐν ταῖς χερσίν, undertake
ἐν ταπεινώσει, depress
ἐν τάχει, quickly, shortly, soon, speedily
ἐν τίνι, about, how
ἐν τούτοις, meanwhile
ἐν χάριτι, gracious
ἐν χειρί, give *over*, singlehanded, through
ἐν χειρῶν νομαῖς, hand-to-hand
ἐν χερσὶν ἔχω, busy
ἐν ᾧ, thus
ἐναγκαλίζομαι, take *in one's arms*
ἐναγκάλισμα, embrace
ἐναγωνίζομαι, fight
ἐναθλέω, enter *the competition*
ἐνακούω, obey
ἐνάλιος, *sea* creature
ἐναλλαγή, perversion
ἐνάλλομαι, rush
ἔναντι, before, face, presence, sight
ἐναντία, face
ἐναντίον, against, before, contrary, eye, look *upon*, presence, sight, toward, turn
ἐναντιόομαι, adversary, contradiction *arise*, oppose
ἐναντίος, against, contrary, front, opponent, oppose, sight
ἐναντιόω, contrary, hostile
ἐναπερείδω, turn
ἐναποσφραγίζω, impress
ἐνάρετος, virtuous
ἐναρίθμιος, number
ἐναρμόζω, fitting, raise
ἐνάρχομαι, begin, *only* begin
ἐνάρχω, begin
ἐνατενίζω, look
ἔνατος, ninth
ἐνδεής, needy, poor *man*, suffer *want*
ἔνδεια, need, poverty, want
ἔνδειγμα, evidence
ἐνδείκνυμι, display, do, give, make *manifest*, reveal, show
ἐνδείκτης, inform
ἔνδειξις, *clear* omen, destruction, proof, prove, show
ἕνδεκα, eleven
ἑνδέκατος, eleventh
ἐνδελεχέω, often
ἐνδελεχής, continually, ever, perpetual
ἐνδελεχίζω, associate, continually, habitual, perpetual, persist, stay, stay *constantly*
ἐνδελεχισμός, continual, habit
ἐνδελεχῶς, continually, regularly
ἐνδέχομαι, possible
ἐνδεχομένως, best *possible*
ἐνδέω, *firmly* bond
ἐνδημέω, home
ἐνδιδύσκω, clothe
ἔνδικος, just
ἔνδοθεν, inner, within
ἔνδον, defender, within
ἐνδοξάζομαι, glorify
ἔνδοξος, complimentary, distinguish, eminent, famed, famous, glorious, glorious *thing*, gorgeously, *great* honor, hold *in honor*, honor, illustrious *man*, *most* honored, splendid, splendor
ἐνδόξως, gloriously, honor, magnificent, pay *honor*
ἔνδυμα, clothing, garment, raiment, robe
ἐνδυναμόω, give *strength*, grow *strong*, increase *in strength*, strengthen, strong
ἐνδύνω, make *one's way*, put
ἔνδυσις, train, wear
ἐνδύω, array, breastplate, clothe, don, endow, put, robe, wear
ἐνδώμησις, build
ἐνεδρεύω, ambush, lie *in ambush*, lie *in wait*
ἔνεδρον, ambush, *hidden* trap, man *in ambush*, wile
ἐνειλέω, wrap
ἐνειμί, exist
ἔνειμι, within
ἕνεκα, account, because, order, reason, sake
ἕνεκεν, because, decision
ἐνεξουσιάζομαι, usurp *the right*
ἐνεξουσιάζω, bring *into subjection*
ἐνεός, dumb *man*, speechless
ἐνεργάζομαι, do
ἐνέργεια, act, action, activity, energy, force, intervention, power, strong, work
ἐνεργέω, accomplish, active, effect, experience, go, inspire, work, work *through*
ἐνέργημα, work
ἐνεργής, active, effective *work*, promote
ἐνευλογέω, bless
ἐνεχυράζω, bind
ἐνέχω, *become* entangled, grudge, press, submit
ἐνῆλιξ, grow *up*
ἔνθα, there
ἔνθα καὶ ἔνθα, *both* sides
ἐνθάδε, here, there
ἔνθεν, here, hither
ἔνθεν καὶ ἔνθεν, *either* side, this *side and that*
ἔνθεσμος, lawful
ἐνθουσιάζω, devote
ἐνθρονίζομαι, enthrone
ἐνθρύπτω, break
ἐνθυμέομαι, conceive, consider, consider *seriously*, devise, discern, fix *one's thought*, ponder, think, thought
ἐνθυμέω, plan
ἐνθύμημα, device, imagination, mind, thought
ἐνθύμησις, imagination, thought
ἐνθυμόω, concern, dispose
ἐνιαυτὸν κατ' ἐνιαυτόν, *every* year
ἐνιαυτός, year
ἐνίημι, instill, send
ἔνιοι, some
ἐνίοτε, sometimes
ἐνίστημι, arise, arrive, bring, come, come *upon*, lodge, present, prevail, *thing* present
ἐνισχύω, *act* firmly, fortify, grow *strong*, hold *strongly*, strengthen
ἐννέα, nine
ἐννέμω, live *among*
ἐννεύω, make *a sign*
ἐννοέω, consider, intend, observe, ponder, reflect
ἐννόημα, thought
ἔννοια, intention, thought
ἐννοίας, plot
ἐννομέω, according *to the law*
ἔννομος, regular, *under the* law
ἐννόμως, according *to the law*
ἐννοσσοποιέομαι, nestling
ἔννυχον, *through the* night
ἔννυχος, while *before day*
ἐνοικέω, dwell, dwell *within*, inhabitant, live
ἐνοικίζω, receive *into one's home*
ἐνοπλίζω, bear *arms*
ἔνοπλος, arm, armed *man*
ἐνορκίζω, adjure
ἐνόρκως, oath
ἑνότης, unity
ἐνοχλέω, annoyance, *cause* trouble, trouble
ἔνοχος, conversant, deserve, guilty, liable, liable *to punishment*, subject
ἐνσείω, charge *against*, hurl, rush *upon*, strike
ἔνταλμα, precept
ἐνταῦθα, here, then, there, thereupon
ἐνταφιάζω, burial, prepare *for burial*
ἐνταφιασμός, burial, bury
ἐντέλλομαι, command, ordain
ἐντέλλω, command, give *a command*, give *a commandment*, give *charge*, give *commandment*, give *directions*, give *orders*, instruct, order
ἔντερον, eat, entrails
ἐντεῦθεν, away, hence, here, point
ἐντεῦθεν καὶ ἐντεῦθεν, *either* side
ἐντεῦθεν καὶ ἐκεῖθεν, *either* side
ἔντευξις, intercession, interview, prayer
ἐντήκω, excite

ἐντίθημι, implant, put
ἔντιμον ἔχω, honor
ἔντιμος, dear, honor, honored *one*, *more* eminent man, *most* valued, precious, worthy *of honor*
ἐντίμως, honor, splendor, worthily
ἐντιναγμός, shake *off*
ἐντινάσσω, hurl, throw
ἐντολή, authority, charge, command, commandment, instruction, order, requirement
ἐντολὴν λαμβάνω, command
ἐντόπιος, people *there*
ἐντός, inside, interior, midst
ἐντρέπω, ashamed, confound, deference, heed, make *ashamed*, mindful, put *to shame*, regard, respect, *show* deference, *show* respect, turn, turn *and flee*
ἐντρέφω, nourish
ἐντρεχής, industrious
ἔντρομος, tremble, tremble *with fear*, *trembling* fear
ἐντροπή, shame
ἐντρυφάω, enjoy, revel
ἐντυγχάνω, accuser, appeal, bring *a charge*, intercede, make *a complaint*, make *intercession*, petition, plead, pray, read, reader
ἐντυγχάνω κατά, accuse
ἐντυλίσσω, roll *up*, wrap
ἐντυπόω, carve
ἐντυχία, petition
ἐνυβρίζω, outrage
ἔνυδρος, fish, seafood, water
ἐνυπνιάζομαι, dream
ἐνύπνιον, dream
ἐνώπιον, against, among, before, *before the* eyes, between, *into the* presence, presence, see, sight
ἐνωτίζομαι, give *ear*, hearken
ἐνώτιον, earring
ἕξ, six
ἐξ ἀνάγκης, necessarily
ἐξ ἀναντίας, aloof
ἐξ ἀρχῆς, ancient
ἐξ ἐναντίας, against, before, face, face *to face*, opposite
ἐξ ἱκανῶν χρόνων, long
ἐξ ἰσχύος, mightily
ἐξ ὀνόματος, individually
ἐξ οὐρανοῦ, heavenly
ἐξ ὑστέρου, finally
ἐξαγγέλλω, declare, proclaim
ἐξαγείρω, arouse
ἐξαγοράζω, make *the most*, redeem
ἐξαγορεύω, make *confession*
ἐξάγω, banish, bring, bring *away*, bring *forth*, bring *out*, lead *out*, march *out*, take *out*
ἐξάδελφος, nephew
ἔξαιμος, drain *blood*
ἐξαιρέω, avoid, deliver, keep, pluck *out*, rescue, save
ἐξαίρω, abolish, blot *out*, cut *off*, deliver, destroy, do *away*, drive *out*, praise, put *out*, remove, slay, snatch *away*, take, take *away*, wipe *out*
ἐξαιτέω, demand
ἐξαίφνης, suddenly
ἐξακολουθέω, follow
ἐξαλείφω, blot *out*, cancel, wipe *away*
ἐξαλλάσσω, strange
ἐξαλλοιόω, make *a change*
ἐξάλλομαι, leap *out*, leap *up*
ἔξαλλος, strange, unusual
ἐξαλλοτριόω, *become* estranged
ἐξαμαρτάνω, *cause to* sin, sin
ἐξαναλίσκω, annihilate, consume
ἐξανάστασις, resurrection
ἐξανατέλλω, spring *up*
ἐξανίστημι, arise, emerge, get *up*, get *up again*, raise *up*, rise, rise *up*, rush
ἐξαπατάω, deceive
ἐξάπινα, suddenly
ἐξαπόλλυμι, perish
ἐξαπορέω, despair, drive *to despair*
ἐξαποστέλλω, send, send *a messenger*, send *away*, send *back*, send *forth*, send *off*, send *out*
ἐξαποστολής, expulsion
ἐξάπτω, kindle, light
ἔξαρθρος, dislocate
ἐξαρθρόω, disjoint
ἐξαριθμέω, apportion, count, measure
ἐξαρνέομαι, reject
ἐξαρπάζω, seize
ἐξαρτίζω, end, equip
ἐξάρχω, begin, raise, start
ἐξασκέω, train
ἐξαστράπτω, dazzle
ἐξαυτῆς, once, *very* moment
ἐξαφίημι, go
ἐξεγείρω, awake, leave, raise *up*, rise, rouse, wake *up*
ἔξειμι, depart, go *out*, make, opportunity, right
ἐξεκκλησιάζω, assemble, convene
ἐξελέγχω, rebuke
ἐξέλκω, drag *out*, lure
ἐξέραμα, vomit
ἐξεραυνάω, inquire
ἐξεργάζομαι, do
ἐξεργαστικός, exhaustive
ἐξερεύγομαι, spew *out*
ἐξερευνάω, consult, find *out*, search *out*
ἐξέρχομαι, come, come *forth*, come *forward*, come *out*, come *up*, depart, drive *out*, escape, evacuate, flee, flow, get *away*, get *out*, give *place*, go, go *ashore*, go *away*, go *forth*, go *off*, go *out*, go *outside*, God, issue, leave, march, march *out*, originate, out, proceed, rise, sally *out*, set *forth*, set *out*, spread, spread *abroad*, step *out*
ἐξέρχομαι ἐκ τῆς ὀσφύος, descend
ἐξέρχομαι καὶ εἰσέρχομαι, go
ἐξέρχομαι ὀπίσω, pursue
ἔξεστι, allow, lawful, permit, possible
ἐξετάζω, ask, consider, examine, examine *under torture*, find *out*, investigate, put *to the test*, search, search *out*
ἐξέτασις, examination, inquiry
ἐξετασμός, examine
ἐξευμενίζομαι, propitiate
ἐξεύρεσις, measure
ἐξευρίσκω, devise, find
ἐξηγέομαι, make *known*, relate, report, talk, tell
ἐξήγησις, narration
ἑξήκοντα, sixtyfold
ἐξημερόω, tame
ἑξῆς, fitting, next, *next* day, soon *afterward*, turn
ἐξηχέω, crash, sound *forth*
ἐξίημι, allow
ἐξιλάσκομαι, atone, make *atonement*, make *expiation*, propitiate
ἐξιλασμός, atonement, forgive, forgiveness, give, propitiation
ἕξις, constitution, practice, proficiency
ἐξισάζω, act *as an equal*
ἐξίστημι, amaze, astonish, astound, beside, change, overcome, ravish, shock
ἐξισχύω, power
ἐξιχνεύω, search *out*
ἐξιχνιάζω, fathom, search *out*, trace, trace *a course*, trace *out*
ἐξοβρέω, rain *down*
ἐξοδεύω, make *a raid*, march *out*, travel
ἔξοδος, come *forth*, come *out*, depart, departure, exodus, go *forth*, march *out*, spring
ἐξολέθρευσις, ruin
ἐξολεθρεύω, defeat, destroy, perish, *utterly* destroy
ἐξολλύω, perish
ἐξομβρέω, pour *out*
ἐξόμνυμι, renounce
ἐξομοιόω, imitate
ἐξομολογέω, acknowledge, confess, give *praise*, give *thanks*, make confess, praise, thank, thanks, thanksgiving, word *of praise*
ἐξομολόγησις, thanks, thanksgiving
ἐξόπισθεν, behind
ἐξοπλησία, parade *under arms*
ἐξοπλίζω, *fully* arm
ἐξορκίζω, adjure
ἐξορκιστής, exorcist
ἐξορμάω, march *out*, rush *off*, rush *out*
ἐξορύσσω, make *an opening*, pluck *out*
ἐξουδενέω, bring *into contempt*, contempt, despise, scorn, treat *with contempt*
ἐξουδενόω, annihilate, despise, disregard, worthless
ἐξουδένωσις, contempt
ἐξουθενέω, despise, *least* esteemed, *no* account, reject, scorn, treat *with contempt*
ἐξουσία, authority, charge, control, disposal, dominion, due *one's office*, except, government, jurisdiction, liberty, permission, power, prestige, right, *rightful* claim, rule
ἐξουσιάζω, assume *authority*, authority *over*, enslave, rule *over*
ἐξόχως, *extraordinary* degree
ἐξυβρίζω, insolent
ἐξυπνίζω, awake *out of sleep*
ἔξυπνος, wake
ἔξυπνος γίνομαι, awake
ἐξυπνόω, awaken
ἐξυψόω, exalt
ἔξω, away, foreign, forth, out, outer, outside
ἔξωθεν, about, external, outside, outsider, outward, outwardly, region, without
ἐξωθέω, bring *ashore*, thrust *out*
ἐξωμολογέω, agree
ἐξώτερος, outer
ἔοικα, like
ἑορτάζω, celebrate *the festival*
ἑόρτασμα, *festal* celebration
ἑορτή, feast, *feast* day, festival
ἐπ' ἀληθείας, certainly, truly
ἐπ' αὐταῖς, there
ἐπ' ἐλαττώσει, loss
ἐπ' ἐσχάτων, finally
ἐπ' εὐλογίαις, bountifully
ἐπαγγελία, declaration, promise
ἐπαγγέλλομαι, make *a promise*, profess, promise
ἐπάγγελμα, promise
ἐπάγω, bring, bring *against*, bring *upon*, fall, incur, *make* take, wage
ἐπαγωγή, affliction, attack, calamity
ἐπαγωγός, inducement
ἐπαγωνίζομαι, contend
ἐπαθροίζω, increase
ἐπαινέω, commend, praise
ἔπαινος, approval, commendation, famous, praise, worthy *of praise*
ἐπαίρω, carry *away*, elate, exalt, hoist, lift, lift *against*, lift *up*, lift *up against*, obstacle, put *on airs*, raise, rise *up*, rise *up against*, tower, transport
ἐπαισχύνομαι, ashamed
ἐπαιτέω, beg
ἐπαίτησις, beg, beggar
ἐπακολουθέω, appear *later*, attend, devote, follow, follow *wholly*, pursue
ἐπακουστός, obey
ἐπακούω, answer, hear, listen
ἐπακροάομαι, listen
ἐπαλγής, *more excruciatingly* painful
ἐπάλξις, battlement, parapet
ἐπαμύνω, defend, defend *against*
ἐπάν, when
ἐπάναγκες, necessary *thing*
ἐπανάγω, put *out*, return, take *out to sea*, turn *back*, way *back*
ἐπαναιρέω, kill, make *away*
ἐπαναπαύομαι, rely, rely *upon*, rest *upon*
ἐπανδρόω, awake *manliness*
ἐπανέρχομαι, come *back*, return
ἐπανήκω, come *back*, return
ἐπανιστάνω, assailant
ἐπανίστημι, *become* hostile, rise, rise *against*, rise *up against*
ἐπάνοδος, come *back*, renewal, return
ἐπανορθόω, restore
ἐπανόρθωσις, correction, restoration, support
ἐπάνω, above, all, beyond, more *than*, over, *right* over, thereon, up, upon, upper
ἐπαοιδός, charmer
ἐπαποστέλλω, send, send *out against*, send *upon*
ἐπάρατος, accursed
ἐπάρδω, water
ἐπαρήγω, protect
ἐπαρκέω, assist, grant *release*, relieve, supply
ἐπαρχεία, province
ἔπαρχος, captain, governor
ἐπάρχω, *become* ruler
ἐπασθμαίνω, gasp *for breath*
ἔπαυλις, build, habitation, town
ἐπαύξω, increase
ἐπαύριον, *following* day, morrow, next, *next* day
ἐπαφρίζω, cast *up foam*
ἐπεγγελάω, deride
ἐπεγείρω, adversary, *become* aroused, rise *against*, stir *up*
ἐπεί, because, otherwise, since, then, when, whereas
ἐπεὶ ἄρα, otherwise
ἐπείγω, need *more urgently*, press
ἐπειδή, after, because, since, time *when*, when
ἐπειδήπερ, inasmuch
ἐπεῖδον, look, look *upon*, see, watch *over*
ἐπειμί, fitting
ἔπειμι, follow, *following* day
ἐπεισαγωγή, introduce
ἐπεισέρχομαι, come *upon*, rush *in against*
ἔπειτα, after, then
ἐπέκεινα, beyond, henceforth, onward
ἐπεκτείνομαι, strain *forward*
ἐπεκχέω, rush *out upon*
ἐπενδύομαι, clothe *further*, put
ἐπενδύτης, clothes
ἐπεξέρχομαι, avenge, pursue
ἐπερείδω, lean
ἐπέρχομαι, approach, assail, beset, come, come *against*, come *over*, come *there*, come *upon*, follow, *forcibly* enter, visit
ἐπερωτάω, ask, ask *a question*, question
ἐπερώτημα, appeal
ἐπευθυμέω, rejoice
ἐπέχω, depend, fix *attention upon*, give *heed*, hold *fast*, *keep* watching, look, mark, pay *attention*, rely, set *one's heart*, stay, take *heed*, trust, try, wait
ἐπηρεάζω, abuse, revile
ἐπί, about, above, accept, account, add, addition, after, against, along, among, *at* hand, attack, because, before, beside, besides, case, charge, close, command, commander, concerning, condition, day, deal, depend, during, evidence, expense, face, gate, grip, hand, honor, hurt, if, insure, keeper, make, meet, observe, *only* wide *enough*, opposite, over, oversee, place, purpose, refer, respect, sake, sight, still, take, testimony, there, through, throughout, time, too, toward, under, upon, when, where, while
ἐπὶ πολύ, *long* time
ἐπὶ τὸ αὐτό, all
ἐπὶ γῆς, earthly
ἐπὶ δυσμάς, west
ἐπὶ κοιλίαν, prostrate
ἐπὶ μέρος εὔκαιρον, strategically
ἐπὶ μετεώρου, high
ἐπὶ πέρας ἄγω, complete
ἐπὶ πλεῖον, considerable, further, very
ἐπὶ πολύ, all *the more*, last, long
ἐπὶ πολὺ σφόδρα, greatly, utterly
ἐπὶ προσευχήν, pray
ἐπὶ σπουδῆς, rapidly
ἐπὶ τέλος, completely
ἐπὶ τὴν κοίτην, sick
ἐπὶ τὸ αὐτό, together

ἐπὶ τὸν αἰγιαλόν, ashore
ἐπὶ τόπον πλέω, seafaring *man*
ἐπὶ τοσοῦτον, enough
ἐπὶ τούτοις, moreover
ἐπὶ τῶν ἡνιῶν, authority
ἐπὶ χρόνον, while
ἐπιβάθρα, exact *a price for maintaining*
ἐπιβαίνω, come *into*, embark, enter *upon*, gain *mastery*, go, go *aboard*, go *up*, mount, put *to sea*, set *foot*, tread, walk *along*
ἐπίβαλημα, piece
ἐπιβάλλω, attack, beat, bestow, break *down*, *cause to* fall *upon*, come, connect, design, entitle, fall, fall *upon*, impose *upon*, incur, kill, lay, lay *upon*, put, put *upon*, throw
ἐπιβάλλω τάς χεῖρας, arrest
ἐπιβάλλω τὰς χεῖρας, pledge
ἐπιβαρέω, burden, put *too severely*
ἐπίβασις, come, walk
ἐπιβάτης, rider
ἐπιβιβάζω, ride, set, set *upon*
ἐπιβιόω, survive
ἐπιβλέπω, behold, gaze, look, look *favorably upon*, look *upon*, look *with greedy eye*, observe, pay *attention*, regard, see, *show* respect
ἐπίβλημα, piece
ἐπιβοάω, call *upon*, cry *out*
ἐπιβοηθέω, aid, help
ἐπιβολή, attack, tax
ἐπιβουλεύω, plot *against*
ἐπιβουλή, conspiracy, plan, plot, treachery
ἐπιβούλος, conspirator *against*, plotter *against*, traitor
ἐπιγαμβρεύω, *become a* son-in-law, *become* father-in-law, marry
ἐπίγειος, earth, earthly, earthly *thing*, terrestrial
ἐπιγελάω, laugh
ἐπιγίνομαι, come *after*, come *afterward*, spring *up*
ἐπιγινώσκω, acknowledge, acquaint, approve, ascertain, *become* aware, *come to* know, find *out*, give *recognition*, know, learn, notice, perceive, possess, realize, recognize, understand, understand *fully*, *well* known
ἐπίγνωσις, enlighten, know, knowledge, sense
ἐπιγραφή, inscription
ἐπιγράφω, inscribe, inscription, read, write
ἐπιδεής, needy
ἐπιδείκνυμι, demonstrate, demonstration, discuss, point *out*, prove, *set an* example, show
ἐπιδέομαι, need, needy
ἐπιδέχομαι, accept, accept *willingly*, acknowledge, agree, choose, enjoy, receive, undertake, welcome
ἐπίδηλος, clear
ἐπιδημέω, live, visitor
ἐπιδιατάσσομαι, add
ἐπιδίδωμι, apply, deliver, devote, give, give *way*, set
ἐπιδιορθόω, amend
ἐπιδιώκω, pursue
ἐπιδόξως, honor
ἐπιδύω, go *down*
ἐπιείκεια, clemency, forbearance, gentleness, *how* gentle, kindness, mildness
ἐπιεικής, forbearance, gentle, *more* equitable, reasonably
ἐπιεικῶς, moderation
ἐπιθανάτιος, man *sentenced to death*
ἐπίθεσις, assault, attack, gather, lay, lay *upon*
ἐπιθεωρέω, observe
ἐπιθυμέω, covet, desire, gladly, greedy, long, lustfully, set *one's desire*, wish
ἐπιθύμημα, delight, *desirable* goods
ἐπιθυμητής, desire
ἐπιθυμητός, costly, desirable, desire
ἐπιθυμία, *base* desire, covet, covetousness, crave, desire, earnestly, *evil* desire, impulse, liking, long, love, lust, lustful, passion
ἐπιθυμόω, crave
ἐπιθύω, sacrifice
ἐπιζάω, live *out*
ἐπιζεύγνυμι, add
ἐπιζητέω, require, seek
ἐπικάθημαι, rider, sit
ἐπικαθίζω, sit
ἐπικαινίζω, restore
ἐπίκαιρος, important, key, strategic
ἐπικαλέω, appeal, beseech, call, call *upon*, invoke, invoke *the aid*, *other* name, pray, surname
ἐπικάλυμμα, pretext
ἐπικαλύπτω, cover
ἐπικαρπολογέω, glean
ἐπικαταράομαι, curse
ἐπικατάρατος, accursed, curse
ἐπίκειμαι, impose, lay *upon*, lie, plan, press *hard upon*, press *upon*, press *urgently upon*, urgent
ἐπικέλλω, run *aground*
ἐπικερδής, hold *for profit*
ἐπικίνδυνον, dangerous
ἐπικινέω, move
ἐπίκλησις, call, invocation
ἐπικλύζω, overflow, overwhelm
ἐπικοινωνέω, make *known*, property
ἐπικουρία, aid, help
ἐπικουφίζω, lighten
ἐπικράτεια, dominance *over*, domination
ἐπικρατέω, *begin to* rule, gain *control*, governor, master, prevail, prevail *over*, rule *over*, sovereign, superior, take *possession*
ἐπικράτησις, kingdom
ἐπικρίνω, decree, give *sentence*, sentence
ἐπικροτέω, clap
ἐπίκτητος, reach
ἐπίκυφον, bend
ἐπιλαμβάνομαι, catch
ἐπιλαμβάνω, arrest, concern, give *help*, seize, take, take *hold*
ἐπιλάμπω, shine
ἐπιλανθάνομαι, forget, neglect
ἐπιλανθάνω, forget, forgetful, overlook
ἐπιλέγω, call, choose, pick, select
ἐπιλείπω, fail
ἐπιλείχω, lick
ἐπίλεκτος, pick
ἐπιλησμονή, forget
ἐπιλογίζομαι, consider, explain, take *account*
ἐπίλοιπος, other, remain, rest, survivor
ἐπιλυπέω, *cause* grief, grieve, trouble
ἐπίλυσις, interpretation
ἐπιλύω, explain, settle
ἐπιμαίνομαι, madden
ἐπιμαρτυρέω, call *to witness*, declare
ἐπιμέλεια, care, need
ἐπιμελέομαι, care, give *heed*, take *care*
ἐπιμελῶς, *all* diligence, carefully, diligently, portion, precisely, scrupulously, strictly, take *care*, *very great* care
ἐπιμένω, continue, hold, persist, remain, spend, stay
ἐπιμήκης, vast
ἐπιμίγνυμι, mix
ἐπίμικτος, mix
ἐπιμιμνήσκομαι, remember
ἐπιμίξ, *raging* riot
ἐπιμονή, diligent
ἐπίμοχθος, laboriously
ἐπινεύω, agree, assent, decline, give *orders*
ἐπινεφής, cloud *over*
ἐπινίκιος, honor *of victory*, victory
ἐπινοέω, contrive, plan
ἐπίνοια, design, idea, intent, thought
ἐπιξενόομαι, *become a* guest, *come to* stay
ἐπιορκέω, break *an oath*, swear *falsely*
ἐπιορκία, perjury
ἐπίορκος, perjurer
ἐπιούσιος, daily
ἐπιπέμπω, send *upon*, turn
ἐπιπίπτω, befall, bend *over*, come *over*, fall, fall *into*, fall *upon*, press *upon*
ἐπιπίπτω ἐπὶ τράχηλον, embrace
ἐπίπληξις, rebuke
ἐπιπληρόω, fill
ἐπιπλήσσω, rebuke
ἐπιποθέω, desire, long, yearn, yearn *over*
ἐπιπόθησις, long
ἐπιπόθητος, long
ἐπιποθίαν ἔχω, long
ἐπιπόλαιος, obvious
ἐπίπονος, grievous, toilsome
ἐπιπορεύομαι, arrive, come, go, go *over*
ἐπιπροσθέω, make *progress*
ἐπιράπτω, sew
ἐπιρίπτω, cast, throw
ἐπιρραίνω, sprinkle
ἐπιρριπτέω, inflict
ἐπιρρωνύω, strengthen
ἐπιρωγολογέομαι, gather *the last grape*
ἐπισάσσω, saddle
ἐπισείω, incite
ἐπισημαίνω, mark
ἐπίσημος, conspicuous, famous, man *of note*, notable, notorious
ἐπισιτισμός, food, provision
ἐπισκέπτομαι, care, consider
ἐπισκέπτομαι ἀνατολή, dawn *upon*
ἐπισκέπτομαι, deliver, examine, find *out*, look, look *after*, look *into*, make *a search*, marshal, pick *out*, punish, visit, watch *over*
ἐπισκέπτω, miss
ἐπισκευάζομαι, make *ready*
ἐπισκευάζω, repair
ἐπίσκεψις, consider, inspect, inspection, supervision
ἐπισκηνόω, rest
ἐπισκιάζω, overshadow, protect, shadow *fall*
ἐπισκοπέω, see
ἐπισκοπή, bishop, examine, office, protect, protection, providence, punishment, visitation, watch
ἐπίσκοπος, bishop, guardian
ἐπισκοπός, inspector, observer, overseer
ἔπισος, like
ἐπισπάομαι, remove *mark of circumcision*, take *aside*
ἐπισπάω, bring, drag, embrace, flay, reach, secure, seize
ἐπισπείρω, sow
ἐπισπεύδω, urge
επισπουδάζω, hastily
ἐπίσταμαι, expert, know, realize, understand
ἐπίστασιν ποιέω, stir *up*
ἐπίστασις, pressure
ἐπιστατέω, supervise
ἐπιστάτης, *chief* officer, governor, know, master, officer
ἐπιστέλλω, send *a letter*, write
ἐπιστήμη, knowledge, learn, skill, wise
ἐπιστήμων, competent, intelligent, man *of understanding*, understanding, wise
ἐπιστηρίζω, rest *upon*, strengthen
ἐπιστοιβάζω, heap
ἐπιστολή, letter
ἐπιστολή Φρουραι, *Letter of* Purim
ἐπιστομίζω, silence
ἐπιστοποιέω, confirm, make *credible*
ἐπιστρατεία, expedition
ἐπιστρατεύω, march, march *against*
ἐπιστράτηγος, commander-in-chief
ἐπιστρατοπεδεύω, camp
ἐπιστρέφω, bring, bring *back*, come, come *back*, come *home*, convene, repent, restore, return, turn, turn *about*, turn *again*, turn *back*, turn *round*, turn *toward*
ἐπιστροφή, conversion, convert, return
ἐπισυνάγω, appear *in a body*, assemble, bring, call, collect, converge *upon*, gather, gather *about*, gather *against*, gather *around*, gather *round*, gather *together*, gather *together against*, join, rally, *rebelliously* assemble
ἐπισυναγωγή, assemble, gather *together again*, meet
ἐπισυνέχω, come *together*
ἐπισυνίστημι, conspire *against*
ἐπισυντρέχω, *come* running *together*
ἐπισύστασις, uprising
ἐπισφαλής, dangerous
ἐπισφάλλω, likely *to fail*
ἐπισφαλῶς, insecurely
ἐπισχύω, grow *strong*, strengthen, urgent
ἐπισωρεύω, accumulate
ἐπιταγή, authority, command
ἐπίταγμα, order
ἐπιταράσσω, trouble
ἐπίτασις, intensify, onslaught
ἐπιτάσσω, command, detail, give *orders*, grant, issue *an order*, order
ἐπιτάφιον, tomb
ἐπιτείνω, exert, expand, spread *over*, strengthen, torment, torture
ἐπιτελέω, accomplish, bring *to completion*, carry *out*, complete, completion, end, erect, finish, fulfil, go *on with*, make *perfect*, perform, require, sure *to carry out*, take *action*, wipe *out*
ἐπιτέμνω, condense, cut *short*
ἐπιτερπής, delicious
ἐπιτήδειος, convenient, good, necessary, need, qualify, suitable, *thing* needed, worthy
ἐπιτήδευμα, plan, purpose, undertaking
ἐπιτηδεύω, practice, undertake
ἐπιτηρέω, wait
ἐπιτίθημι, add, attach, attack, bring, confer, gird, give *to carry*, inflict *upon*, lay, lay *upon*, load, place, put, put *on board*, put *upon*, set *upon*, sprinkle, touch
ἐπιτίθημι ἐπὶ τὰς ὀσφύας, gird
ἐπιτίθημι ὄνομα, surname
ἐπιτιμάω, charge, order, punish, rebuke, reprove
ἐπιτίμησις, rebuke, scold
ἐπιτιμία, punishment
ἐπιτίμιον, penalty
ἐπίτιμος, punishment
ἐπιτομή, abbreviate, condensation
ἐπιτρέπω, allow, appoint, confer *upon*, give *leave*, permission, permit
ἐπιτρέχω, run, run *to reach*
ἐπιτροπή, commission, decision
ἐπίτροπος, guardian, steward
ἐπιτυγχάνω, catch, obtain, receive
ἐπιτυχία, success
ἐπιφαίνω, appear, flash, give *light*, manifest, reveal
ἐπιφάνεια, apparition, appear, appearance, majesty, manifest, manifestation
ἐπιφανής, distinction, *majestically* adorn, manifest, splendid
ἐπιφαύσκω, give *light*
ἐπιφέρω, bear *down upon*, inflict, pronounce *upon*
ἐπιφέρω ῥῆμα, speak
ἐπιφημίζω, accuse
ἐπιφυτεύω, implant
ἐπιφύω, grow
ἐπιφωνέω, answer, respond, shout, shout *against*, shout *out*
ἐπιφώσκω, beginning, dawn
ἐπιχαίρω, please, rejoice, rejoice *over*
ἐπίχαρμα, laughingstock, *malicious* joy
ἐπιχειρέω, attempt, endeavor, seek, try, undertake
ἐπιχείρημα, intrigue
ἐπίχειρον, reward
ἐπιχέω, overwhelm, pour
ἐπιχορηγέω, nourish, provide, supplement, supply, support
ἐπιχορηγία, help, supply
ἐπιχρίω, anoint
ἐπιχωρέω, agree, give *permission*
ἐπιψάλλω, sing
ἐποικοδομέω, build, build *up*, build *upon*
ἕπομαι, follow
ἐπονείδιστος, treat *disgracefully*
ἐπονομάζω, call
ἐποξύνω, hasten

ἐποπτεύω, see
ἐπόπτης, *all* seeing, eyewitness, oversee, see, watch *over*
ἐποπτικός, watch *over*
ἐποργίζομαι, angry
ἔπος, verse
ἐποτρύνω, encourage, urge
ἐπουράνιος, celestial, heaven, heavenly, heavenly *place*, heavenly *thing*
ἑπτά, seven, seventh
ἑπτακαίδεκα, seventeen
ἑπτακαιδέκατος, seventeenth
ἑπτάκις, seven *times*
ἑπταμήτωρ, mother *of seven*
ἑπταπλάσιος, seven *times*, seven *times over*, sevenfold
ἑπταπλασίως, sevenfold
ἑπτάπυργος, seven-towered
ἐπωμίς, sidewall
ἐπώνυμος, commemorative
ἐραστής, enamor, lover
ἐραυνάω, inquire, search
ἐράω, love
εργαβ, stone *heap*
ἐργάζομαι, act, commit, cultivate, do, *do* work, doer, effect, effective, employ, enforce, labor, make, perform *work*, practice, produce, *render* service, serve, *set to* work, take *pains*, trade, utter, work, worker, wrought
ἐργάζομαι ἀνομίαν, evildoer
ἐργάζομαι ἐν, exploit
ἐργασία, business, effort, gain, labor, output, practice, service, task, work
ἐργατεία, craft
ἐργάτης, laborer, worker, workman
ἐργατὴς τῆς ἀνομίας, evildoer
ἐργολάβεια, gain
ἔργον, act, action, affair, art, conduct, deed, do, doing, effect, handiwork, labor, operation, power, product, require, service, structure, task, thing, undertaking, use, what, work, workmanship
ἔργω, exclude, hinder, keep
ἐρεθίζω, provoke, stir *up*
ἐρεθισμός, provocation
ἐρείδω, stick
ἐρεύγομαι, roar, utter
ἔρευνα, inquiry
ἐρευνάω, search, search *out*
ἐρημία, desert, desolation, wilderness
ἔρημος, alone, desert, *deserted* section, desolate, desolate *one*, desolation, empty, lonely, lonely *place*, ruins, undefended, uninhabited, wilderness, without
ἔρημος τόπος, country
ἐρημόω, *become* desolate, bereave, desolate, devastate, lay *waste*, leave *desolate*, make *desolate*
ἐρήμωσις, desolate, desolation
ἐριθεία, factious, partisanship, *selfish* ambition, selfishness
ἐριθεύομαι, earn *money*
ἐρίζω, argue, quarrel, wrangle
ἔριον, wool
ἔρις, dissension, quarrel, rivalry, strife
ἐρίφιον, goat, kid
ἔριφος, goat, kid, *young* goat
ἑρμηνεία, interpretation, translate
ἑρμηνεύω, mean, translate, translation
ἑρπετόν, creeping *thing*, reptile, serpent, worm
ἔρρω, fare *well*
ἐρρωμένος, turn *out*
ἔρρωσθε., farewell
ἐρυθαίνω, color *red*
ἐρυθρὰ θάλασσα, Red *Sea*
ἐρυθριάω, blush, radiant
ἐρυμνός, fortify
ἐρυμνότης, strength
ἔρχομαι, alight, appear, arrive, befall, bring, come, come *back*, come *up*, coming *one*, enter, fall, gather, go, God, grow, make *a visit*, next, pass, reach, return, serve, *thing to* come, way
ἔρχομαι εἰς, enter, invade, reach
ἔρχομαι ἐπὶ τὸ αὐτό, meet *again*
ἔρχομαι ἐπὶ τὴν κεφαλήν, overcome
ἔρχομαι πέραν, cross
ἔρχομαι πρός, join, visit
ἔρχομαι σύν, accompany
ἐρωτάω, ask, beg, beseech, pray, question
ἐρώτημα, inquiry
ἐσθής, apparel, clothing, mantle, robe, uniform, vestment
ἔσθησις, clothing
ἐσθίω, consume, devour, dine, do, earn, eat, enjoy, fitting, food, get, get *food*, take
ἔσοπτρον, mirror
ἑσπέρα, evening
ἐστέρημαι, deprive
ἔστι καὶ ὅτε, sometimes
ἐσχάρα, hearth
ἐσχατίζω, laggard
ἐσχατογήρος, *very* old
ἐσχατογήρως, aged *man*
ἔσχατος, end, end *of life*, finally, last, *last* end, last *one*, *last* state, last *thing*, latter, low, rear, turn *out*, uttermost *part*
ἐσχάτως, point *of death*
ἔσω, house, inmost, inner, inside, through
ἔσωθεν, inside, inwardly, within
ἐσώτερος, inner
ἐτάζω, investigate, test
ἑταίρα, harlot
ἑταιρίζω, loose
ἑταῖρος, companion, comrade, friend
ἐτασμός, affliction, search
ἑτερόγλωσσος, man *of a strange tongue*
ἑτεροδιδασκαλέω, teach *different doctrine*, teach *otherwise*
ἑτεροζυγέω, mismate
ἕτερον ἤ, except
ἕτερος, alter, another, another *man*, brother, different, else, foreigner, latter, more, neighbor, next, *next* day, one *another*, other, other *man*, playmate, second, some, *some one* else, unnatural
ἕτερος ἕκαστος, each
ἕτερος ἕτερος, *each* other
ἕτερος ἕτερον, one *another*
ἑτέρωθεν, opposite
ἑτέρως, otherwise
ἔτι, addition, again, already, *any* longer, *any* more, besides, continue, even, even *more*, *ever* again, further, just, keep, long, more, moreover, once *more*, other, still, well, yet, *yet* more
ἔτι ἅπαξ, another
ἔτι τε, moreover
ἔτι χρόνον, long
ἑτοιμάζω, array, destine, get *ready*, hold *ready*, make *preparation*, make *ready*, make *up*, prepare, ready
ἑτοιμασία, equipment, prepare
ἑτοιμάω, establish
ἕτοιμος, about, drawn *up*, here, prepare, readiness, ready, work *already done*
ἑτοίμως, ready
ἔτος, year
εὖ, good, kindness, well, *well* done
εὖ εἰμί, go *well*
εὖ μάλα, exceedingly, very
εὖ πράσσω, *good* wish f*or prosperity*
εὐαγγελίζω, announce, bring *good news*, *good* news *come*, preach, preach *a gospel*, preach *good news*, preach *the gospel*, proclaim, receive *the good news*, tell *the good news*
εὐαγγέλιον, gospel, term
εὐαγγελιστής, evangelist
εὐανδρία, courage, valor
εὐαπάντητος, gracious
εὐαρεστέω, please
εὐάρεστος, acceptable, give *satisfaction*, please
εὐάρμοστος, harmonious
εὖγε, *do* well
εὐγένεια, nobility, *noble* birth
εὐγενής, *more* noble, noble, *noble* birth, nobly, respect
εὐγενῶς, nobly
εὐγνωμοσύνη, *good* will
εὐδία, *fair* weather
εὔδιον, frost
εὐδοκέω, agree, approve, bestow *graciously*, choose, consent, content, decide, delight, enjoy, favor, *gladly* adopt, *good* pleasure, happy, please, please *well*, pleasure, rather, ready, take *pleasure*, *well* disposed, *well* pleased, willing
εὐδοκία, acceptable, approval, approve, choice, content, delight, desire, favor, *good* pleasure, *good* resolve, *good* will, *gracious* will, please, pleasure, purpose
εὐδοκιμέω, esteem, prove *good*
εὐδόκιμος, *good* repute
εὐδράνεια, strength
εὔελπις, *good* hope, *resolutely* hopeful
εὐεξία, soundness
εὐεργεσία, *do a good* deed, *kind* treatment, kindness, service
εὐεργετέω, benefactor, *do* good, receive *benefit*, receive *good*
εὐεργέτημα, benefit
εὐεργέτης, benefactor
εὐεργετικός, beneficent
εὐήθης, foolish
εὐήκοος, obedient
εὐημερέω, succeed, triumph, win *a victory*
εὐημερία, *good* fortune, prosperity, success
εὐθαρσής, encourage, *good* courage, morale
εὐθαρσῶς, courageously
εὔθετον, opportune
εὔθετος, fit, useful
εὐθέως, immediately, instantly, once, soon, then
εὐθής, right
εὐθίκτως, tell
εὔθραστος, fragile
εὐθυδρομέω, make *a direct voyage*, *straight* course
εὐθυμέω, cheerful, take *heart*
εὔθυμος, encourage, *good* cheer
εὐθύμως, cheerfully
εὐθύνω, call *to account*, direct, direct *aright*, make *straight*, pilot, punishment, *set* right
εὐθύς, immediately, once, right, soon, straight
εὐθύτης, integrity, righteous, straight, uprightness
εὔζωνος, nimble
εὐίλατος, *very* merciful
εὐιλατεύω, *show* mercy
εὐκαιρέω, leisure, opportunity, spend *time*
εὐκαιρία, opportunity
εὔκαιρος, *most* favorable, opportunity, time *of need*
εὐκαίρως, opportunity, promptly, season
εὐκατάλλακτος, reconcile *easily*
εὐκίνητος, easy *to handle*, mobile
εὐκλεής, renowned
εὔκλεια, honor, renown, reputation
εὐκοπία, make *easy*
εὔκοπος, easy
εὐκοσμέω, govern *well*
εὐκοσμία, *excellent* leadership, *splendid* vestment
εὔκυκλος, *well* drawn
εὐλάβεια, fear, *godly* fear, reverence
εὐλαβέομαι, afraid, cautious, fear, scruples, take *care*, take *heed*, timid, worry
εὐλαβέομαι ἀπὸ προσώπου, partial
εὐλαβής, devout
εὐλαβῶς, piety
εὔλαλος, gracious
εὐλογέω, bless, blessing, give *praise*, invoke *a blessing*, praise
εὐλογητός, bless
εὐλογία, blessing, *flattering* word, gift, praise, *willing* gift
εὐλογιστία, *right* reason, *right* reasoning
εὔλογος, blessing, praise
εὐμαθῶς, skilfully
εὐμεγέθης, great *in stature*
εὐμελής, melodious
εὐμένεια, *good* will
εὐμενής, *good* will, *well* disposed
εὐμενῶς, graciously
εὐμετάδοτος, liberal
εὐμορφία, beauty, *handsome* appearance
εὔμορφος, shapely
εὐνοέω, dispose *favorably*, friend, loyal
εὔνοια, affection, favor, *good* will, goodwill
εὐνομία, loyalty *to the law*, observance *of the law*
εὔνους, loyal
εὐνουχίζω, make *a eunuch*
εὐνοῦχος, eunuch
εὐοδία, *good* fortune, *prosperous* journey, success, ways *prosper*
εὔοδος γίνομαι, prosper
εὐοδόω, find *the way*, give *success*, go *well*, *good* success, grant *success*, guide, make *a success*, prosper, prosperous, succeed, success, successful, well
εὔοπτος, *widely* seen
εὐπάρεδρος, secure
εὐπείθεια, obedience, obey, persuade, *ready* obedience
εὐπειθής, open *to reason*
εὐπειθω, obey
εὐπερίστατος, cling *so closely*
εὐποιΐα, do, *do* good
εὐπορέω, ability, prosper
εὐπορία, wealth
εὐπραξία, good *deed*, *good* service
εὐπρέπεια, appearance, beauty, glorious
εὐπρεπής, beautiful, *more* beautiful
εὐπρεπῶς, please, *properly* array
εὐπρόσδεκτος, acceptable
εὐπροσήγορος, courtesy
εὐπροσωπέω, make *a good showing*
εὐρακύλων, northeaster
εὕρεμα, find, windfall
εὕρεσις, devise, invention
εὑρετής, contrive
εὑρίσκω, about, appreciate, burn *up*, catch, come *upon*, find, form, gain, get, meet, overtake, plumb, present, prove, receive, redound, secure, suffer, win
εὑρίσκω ἀνταπόδομα, repay
εὖρος, breadth, broad
εὔρυθμος, eloquent
εὐρύχωρος, easy, *open* square, square
εὔρωστος, robust
εὐρώστως, *main* strength, mightily, vigorous, vigorously
εὐσέβεια, devotion, devout, godliness, godly, piety, religion, religious, service
εὐσεβέω, devout, exercise *piety*, godly *man*, live *piously*, *religious* duty, revere, worship
εὐσεβής, devout, devout *man*, devout *one*, godly, godly *man*, pious, religious
εὐσεβῶς, godly
εὔσημος, intelligible
εὔσπλαγχνος, *great* compassion, *tender* heart, tenderhearted
εὐστάθεια, *good* order, stability, tranquillity
εὐσταθέω, *firmly* establish, live *quietly*, settle *down*
εὐσταθής, secure, steadfast
εὔστοχος, true *aim*, *true* aim
εὐσχημόνως, becomingly, decently, respect
εὐσχημοσύνη, gracefulness, modesty
εὐσχήμων, *good* order, *high* standing, *more* presentable *part*, respect
εὐτακτέω, pay *regularly*
εὐτάκτως, calm *dignity*
εὐταξία, *good* conduct, *good* order
εὐτεκνία, *good* child
εὐτελής, cheap, paltry, worthless
εὐτελῶς, *do* poorly

εὔτηκτος, melt *easily*
εὐτολμία, daring
εὔτονος, fierce, *utmost* vigor
εὐτόνως, powerfully, vehemently
εὐτραπελία, levity
εὐτρεπίζω, get *ready*
εὐφημέω, praise
εὐφημία, *good* repute
εὔφημος, gracious
εὔφθαρτος, perishable
εὐφορέω, bring *forth plentifully*
εὐφραίνω, cheer, delight, enjoy, exultation, feast, glad, gladden, *greatly* please, joy, make *glad*, make *merry*, *make* rejoice, make *rejoicing*, merry, rejoice, rejoicing, revel, take *pleasure*
εὐφροσύνη, celebrate, enjoyment, feast, festival, festivity, gay, glad, gladness, *great* festivity, happiness, joy, joyful, joyfulness, merry, merrymaking, mirth, pleasure, rejoicing
εὐφρόσυνος, festival, joyful, *joyous* festival
εὐφυής, skilled, suitable, *well* endowed *by nature*
εὔχαρις, charm
εὐχαριστέω, give *thanks*, thank, thankful
εὐχαριστία, give *thanks*, gratitude, thank, thankfulness, thanksgiving
εὐχάριστος, thankful
εὐχερής, easy, readily
εὐχερῶς, easily, easy
εὐχή, prayer, *votive* offering, vow
εὔχομαι, begin, make, make *a vow*, pray, proclaim, vow, will, wish
εὐχρηστία, *mutual* help
εὔχρηστος, useful, *very* useful
εὐψυχέω, cheer
εὐψυχία, courage, courageous, courageous *spirit*
εὔψυχος, stouthearted *man*
εὐψύχως, generously, *good* courage
εὐώδης, *very* fragrant
εὐωδία, aroma, fragrant, *pleasant* odor, *pleasing* odor, *sweet-smelling* sacrifice
εὐωδιάζω, send *forth fragrance*
εὐώνυμος, left
εὐωχέω, feast
εὐωχία, feast, festival, *good* cheer, revelry
ἐφ᾽ ἑαυτοῦ εἰμί, halt
ἐφ᾽ ἱκανόν, widely
ἐφ᾽ ὅ, why
ἐφ᾽ ὅσον, inasmuch, long
ἐφάλλομαι, leap
ἐφάπαξ, once *for all*, *one* time
ἐφάπτω, partake
ἐφαρμόζω, fitting
ἐφελκύω, lead *off*
ἐφέλκω, attract
ἐφέτειος, year
ἐφευρετής, inventor
ἐφηβεῖον, body *of youth*
ἔφηβος, young *man*
ἐφημερία, division, duty
ἐφήμερος, daily
ἐφικνέομαι, reach
ἐφικτός, good
ἔφιππος, horseback, horseman
ἐφίπταμαι, light
ἔφισος, compare
ἐφίστημι, appear, approach, arrive, assail, attack, begin, charge, come, come *up*, come *upon*, find, go, install, *make* stand *sure*, set, set *over*, stand, stand *overseeing*, store, urgent, watch
ἐφοδεύω, make *a tour of inspection*, visit
ἔφοδος, approach, arrival, attack, come, expedition, invasion
ἐφοράω, consider, look, see, watch *over*
ἐφορκέω, commit *perjury*
ἐφύβριστος, scornfully
ἐφφαθά, ephphatha
ἐχθές, yesterday
ἐχθὲς καὶ τρίτης ἡμέρας, before
ἔχθρα, enmity, hatred, hostility
ἐχθραίνω, detest, enmity, harass, hate
ἐχθρεύω, enemy
ἐχθρός, detestable, enemy, enmity, foe, hatred, hostile, *most* hateful
ἔχιδνα, viper
ἔχις, viper
ἐχολάω, *become* infuriated
ἐχομένως, next
ἔχω, able, after, away, bear, become, belong, booty, bring, can, catch *hold*, come, come *upon*, consider, content, deal, derive, endure, engage, enjoy, equip, express, feel, find, follow, get, hold, hold *fast*, incur, keep, live, maintain, make, meet, next, obtain, own, possess, read, reap, receive, recognize, show, stand, suffer, take, tolerate, treat, under, use, wear, wife
ἔχω ἀνάγκην, must
ἔχω ἄνδρα, marry
ἔχω διαφοράν, differ
ἔχω ἐλπίδα, hope
ἔχω ἐν ἐπιγνώσει, acknowledge
ἔχω ἐπίσημον, celebrate
ἔχω ἐπιτιμίαν, punish
ἔχω μέρος, share
ἔχω περίκειμαι, surround
ἔχω πιστά, believer
ἔχω πληγήν, wound
ἔχω πόνον, work
ἔχω στάσιν, stand
ἔχω ψυχήν, live
ἕψεμα, pottage
ἕψω, boil, cook
ἑωθινός, dawn, morning
ἕως, all *the way*, before, down, enough, even, far, far *away*, long, many, much, till, time, until, up, when, while
ἕως αἰῶνος, ever
ἕως ἄν, before, till, until
ἕως ἄρτι, hitherto, still
ἕως εἰς μακράν, afar
ἕως ἐσχάτου, utterly
ἕως ἔσω, right
ἕως ὅτου, till, while
ἕως οὗ, before, till, while
ἕως οὗ παρῆλθον, beyond
ἕως πότε, *how* long
ἕως πρός, far
ἕως τέλους, fully
ἕως τῆς νυκτός, *all* day
ἕως τοῦ αἰῶνος, ever
ἕως τοῦ ἐλθεῖν, even
ἕως τοῦ ἐλθεῖν εἰς, far
ἕως τοῦ νῦν, enough

ἤ, either, except, nor, rather, rather *than*, than, what, whether, without
ἡγεμονεύω, governor
ἡγεμονία, govern, *high* office, reign, rule, supremacy
ἡγεμών, authority, captain, commander, governor, guide, leader, *local* ruler, ruler
ἡγέομαι, account, chief, commander, consider, count, deem, esteem, governor, head, judge, lead, leader, leading *man*, look, master, principal *man*, put, regard, ruler, take *account*, think, *under the* leadership
ἤγησις, leadership
ἡδέως, glad, gladly, happily, merry, *most* gladly
ἤδη, about, already, even *now*, good, immediately, just, long, now, then, time, when
ἥδομαι, delight, rejoice
ἡδονή, joy, passion, pleasure
ἡδύνω, make *pleasant*
ἡδύοσμον, mint
ἡδυπάθεια, *sexual* desire
ἡδύς, delicious *thing*, good, *less* bitterly, *most* pleasant, pleasant, sweet
ἥδυσμα, perfume
ἠθολογέω, express
ἦθος, character, deal, disposition, habit, habitually, inclination, moral
ἥκω, come, come *forth*, go, occur
ἥκω εἰς τὸ αὐτό, meet
ἡλικία, age, figure, *long* life, point *in life*, ripe, span *of life*, stature, time *of life*, year, youth, youthful
ἡλικιώτης, equal
ἡλίκος, great, *how* greatly
ἥλιος, sun
ἧλος, nail
ἡμέρα, another, appoint, court, day, daytime, feast, life, tame, time, year
ἡμέρα αὕτη, today
ἡμέρα εὔκαιρος, opportunity
ἡμέρα μέση, midday
ἡμέρα τοῦ σαββάτου, sabbath
ἡμερόομαι, restrain
ἥμερος, kind, peaceable
ἥμερος φυτόν, *fruit* tree
ἡμέτερα φρονέω, loyal *to the government*
ἡμέτερος, after
ἡμιθανής, half *dead*
ἡμίθνητος, half *dead*
ἡμίονος, mule
ἥμισυς, half
ἡμίωρον, half *an hour*
ἡνίκα, *same* time, soon, when
ἡνίκα ἄν, whenever
ἡνίκα ἐάν, soon, when
ἧπαρ, liver
ἤπερ, rather *than*, than, than *even*
ἤπιος, gentle, kindly
ἠπιότης, kindness
ἤρεμος, quiet
ἡσσάομαι, defeat
ἥσσων, bad, less, weak
ἡσυχάζω, *become* quiet, cease, live *quietly*, quiet, rest, silence, silent, take *a rest*
ἡσυχία, leisure, peace, quiet, quietness, silence, silent
ἡσύχιος, peaceable, quiet
ἥσυχος, gentle, quiet
ἤτοι, either
ἡττάομαι, favor *little*, overcome, overpower
ἡττάω, lack
ἥττημα, defeat, failure
ἥττων γίνομαι, defeat
ἠχέω, echo, noisy, resound, send *forth*, sound
ἦχος, note, report, ring, roar, sound, tone
ἠχώ, echo, voice

θα, come
θάλαμος, chamber
θάλασσα, sea, seaside
θάλασσα ἐρυθρά, Red *Sea*
θαλάσσιος, sea
θαλλός, *olive* branch
θάλλω, flourish
θάλπω, cherish, take *care*
θαμβέομαι, astound
θαμβέω, alarm, amaze
θάμβος, amaze, astonish, wonder
θανάσιμος, deadly *thing*
θανατηφόρος, bear *death*, bring *death*, deadly, fatal
θάνατος, dead, death, *death* penalty, die, mortal, peril, pestilence
θανατόω, condemn *to death*, die, kill, put *to death*, slay, take *a life*
θάπτω, bury, give *a funeral*
θαρραλέως, boldly, courageously
θαρρέω, bold, brave, confidence, confidently, courage, *good* cheer, *good* courage, *show* boldness, take *courage*, take *heart*
θαρσαλέος, bravely, undaunted
θαρσέω, take *courage*, take *heart*
θάρσος, boldness, courage
θαρσύνω, give *courage*
θαῦμα, wonder
θαυμάζω, admire, amaze, astonish, flatter, honor, magnify, marvel, wonder, wonderful *thing*
θαυμάσιος, marvelous, *marvelous* work, *most* amazing, wonder, wonderful *thing*, wondrous, wondrous *deed*
θαυμάσιος σφόδρα, marvelously
θαυμασμός, admiration
θαυμαστός, admirable, amaze, illustrious, marvel, marvelous, marvelously, wonder, wonderful
θεά, goddess
θεάομαι, behold, look, look *upon*, see, witness
θεατρίζω, *publicly* expose
θέατρον, spectacle, theater
θεῖον, deity, sulphur
θεῖος, divine, God
θειότης, deity, divine
θειώδης, sulphur
θέλημα, desire, impulse, liking, please, will
θέλησις, desire, will
θελητής, devote
θέλω, accept, choose, decide, deliberately, desire, dispose, favor, glad, insist, intend, like, mean, will, willing
θέλω εἰμί, mean
θέμα, offering, treasure
θεμέλιον, foot
θεμέλιος, foundation
θεμελιόω, found, foundation, ground, lay *a foundation*, stable, strengthen
θέμις, right
θεμιτός, right
θεοδίδακτος, taught *by God*
θεόκτιστος, God-given
θεομαχέω, fight *against God*
θεομάχος, oppose *God*
θεόπνευστος, inspired *by God*
θεός, divine, father, god, God, goddess, godly, Lord
θεοσέβεια, godliness, religion, reverence, reverence *for God*
θεοσεβής, God-fearing, religious, worshiper *of God*
θεοστυγής, hater *of God*
θεότης, deity
θεραπεία, healing, household, servant, worship
θεραπεύω, cure, heal, healing, minister, repair, serve, service, take *care of health*
θεράπων, officer, servant
θερίζω, harvest, harvester, reap, reap *the harvest*, reaper
θερισμός, harvest
θεριστής, reaper
θερμαίνω, fervent, warm
θέρμη, heat, summer
θερμός, fresh, heat
θερμότης, heat
θέρος, summer
θέσις, constellation, put
θεσμόν, rite
θεσμός, custom, tradition
θεωρέω, behold, discern, face, gaze, look, observe, perceive, perception *comes*, see, sight, spectator, stare, watch
θεωρία, see, sight, spectacle
θεωρός, envoy
θήκη, sheath
θηλάζω, give *suck*, infant, nurse, suck, suckling
θῆλυς, female, woman
θημωνιά, harvest, heap
θήρ, beast, *wild* beast
θήρα, prey, trap
θηρευτής, decoy
θηρεύω, catch
θηριομαχέω, fight *with a beast*
θηρίον, beast, beast *of prey*, creature, elephant, *wild* animal, *wild* beast
θηριόομαι, rage
θηριώδης, *most savage* beast, savage
θηριωδῶς, furiously
θησαυρίζω, deposit, hoard *up*, lay *up*, lay *up treasure*, store *up*, treasure *up*
θησαυρός, store, storehouse, treasure, treasury

θίασος, *heathen* cult
θιγγάνω, touch
θίς, hill
θλάω, beat
θλίβω, afflict, crush, distress, hard, imminent, knead, oppress, oppressor, press, press *hard*, suffer *affliction*
θλῖψιν ἐγείρω, afflict
θλῖψις, afflict, affliction, anguish, burden, distress, persecution, suffer, tribulation, trouble
θνήσκω, dead, dead *man*, die
θνητός, mortal, *mortal* nature
θοῖνα, feast
θορυβάζω, trouble
θορυβέω, alarm, disturb, make *a tumult*, *set in an* uproar, trouble
θόρυβος, confusion, disturbance, riot, tumult, *tumultuous* noise, uproar
θράσος, audacity, boldness, daring, insolence, presumption, *rash* act
θρασύνω, arrogance, bold
θρασύς, audacious, audacity, bold, boldness, courageously, impudent, insolence, reckless
θραῦσις, plague
θραῦσμα, defeat, destruction
θραύω, break *in pieces*, break *in spirit*, crush, destroy, oppress, strike *down*
θρέμμα, cattle
θρηνέω, lament, make *lamentation*, mourn, wail
θρῆνος, dirge, *funeral* dirge, lament, lamentation
θρησκεία, religion, worship
θρησκεύω, worship
θρησκός, religious
θριαμβεύω, lead *in triumph*, triumph *over*
θρίξ, hair
θροέω, alarm, excite
θρόνος, throne
θροῦς, sound, *tumultuous* procession
θρυλέω, *common* talk, gossip
θυγάτηρ, another, daughter, village
θυγάτριον, *little* daughter
θύελλα, tempest
θύϊνος, scent
θυΐσκη, censer
θυλάκιον, *money* bag
θυμήρης, *great* delight
θυμίαμα, incense
θυμιατήριον, altar *of incense*, censer
θυμιάω, burn *for incense*, burn *incense*
θυμομαχέω, angry
θυμός, anger, courage, fierce, furious, fury, *hot* temper, passion, rage, temper, wrath
θυμόω, anger, angry, rage, stay *angry*
θυμώδης, given *to anger*, wrathful *man*
θύρα, door, entrance, gate
θυρεός, shield
θυρίς, window
θυρόω, furnish *with doors*
θύρσος, branch, *ivy* wreathed
θύρωμα, door
θυρωρός, doorkeeper, gatekeeper, keep *the door*, maid *who keeps the door*
θυσία, offering, sacrifice, sacrificial, *sacrificial* meal
θυσιάζω, offer *a sacrifice*, sacrifice
θυσιαστήριον, altar, altar *of sacrifice*, sacrifice, *sacrificial* offering
θύω, kill, offer, offer *a sacrifice*, sacrifice
θωρακίζω, arm, equip, fortify
θωρακισμός, armor
θώραξ, armor, breastplate, coat *of mail*, scale

ζάω, alive, bring *to life*, come *to life*, endure, get *a living*, life, lifelong, live, living *one*, man, spare
ζεστός, hot
ζευγίζω, join
ζεύγνυμι, hitch *up*
ζεῦγος, pair, yoke
ζευκτηρία, rope
ζέω, aglow, burn, fervent
ζηλεύω, zealous
ζῆλος, envy, fury, jealous, jealousy, zeal
ζηλόω, admire, burn *with zeal*, covet, earnestly *desire*, envy, feel, invite, jealous, make *much*, zeal, zealous
ζηλόω ζῆλον, *deeply* zealous
ζήλωσις, jealous
ζηλωτής, eager, zeal, zealot, Zealot, zealous
ζημία, loss, penalty
ζημιόω, fine, forfeit, suffer *loss*
ζῆν μεθίστημι, put *to death*
ζητέω, ask, attempt, desire, endeavor, find, inquire, inquiry, insist, look, look *after*, require, search, search *for*, seek, seek *after*, seek *out*, strive, try, try *to find*, wish
ζήτημα, controversy, point *of dispute*, question
ζήτησις, controversy, debate, discussion, investigate, seek
ζιζάνιον, weed
ζόφος, gloom, *nether* gloom
ζυγός, balance, bench, scale, yoke
ζύμη, leaven
ζυμόω, leaven
ζωγραφέω, decoration, paint
ζωγραφία, *lifelike* image
ζωγρέω, capture, catch
ζωγρία, alive
ζωή, alive, existence, flow, life, lifetime, live, survival
ζώνη, belt, girdle
ζώννυμι, dress, fasten, gird
ζῷον, live
ζώπυρον, bellows
ζωτικός, live

ἴαμα, healer, healing, slake
ἰάομαι, cure, heal, healing, satisfy
ἴασις, cure, heal, healing, perfect, remedy
ἴασπις, jasper
ἰατρός, physician
ἰδέα, appearance, kind
ἴδιος, act, affair, aside, course, due, family, fellow, friend, home, house, individually, man, native, normal, proper, purpose, relative
ἰδιότητα, characteristic
ἰδιώτης, common *man*, outsider, unskilled
ἰδιωτικός, private
ἰδού, behold, come, hark, here, herewith, how, indeed, lo, look, see, there, when
ἱδρόω, sweat
ἱδρύω, set
ἱδρῶν, bathe *in sweat*
ἱδρώς, sweat
ἱερατεία, priesthood, *priestly* office
ἱεράτευμα, priesthood
ἱερατεύω, *high* priest, serve *as priest*
ἱερατικός, priest, priestly
ἱερεύς, *high* priest, priest, priestly, temple
ἱερεὺς μέγας, *high* priest
ἱερόδουλος, servant, temple, *temple* servant
ἱερόθυτος, offer *in sacrifice*
ἱεροπρεπής, befit *holiness*, reverent, saintly
ἱερός, holy, *religious* rite, sacred, sanctuary, temple, *temple* service
ἱεροστάτης, *chief* officer *of the temple*
ἱεροσυλέω, rob *a temple*
ἱεροσύλημα, act *of sacrilege*
ἱεροσυλία, sacrilege
ἱερόσυλος, sacrilegious, *temple* robber
ἱερουργέω, *priestly* service
ἱερουργία, temple, *temple* service
ἱεροψάλτης, *temple* singer
ἱερόψυχος, holy-minded
ἱέρωμα, *sacred* token
ἱερωσύνη, *high* priest, priesthood
ἵημι, come, dawn, go, reach
ἱκανὸν ποιέω, satisfy
ἱκανός, able, ample, competence, competent, considerable, enough, great, large, long, many, mature, much, number, security, some, substantial, sufficient, sum, worthy
ἱκανόω, make *competent*, qualify, satisfy
ἱκανῶς, favor
ἱκετεία, prayer, supplication
ἱκετεύω, beg, beseech, entreat, implore
ἱκετήριος, supplication
ἱκέτης, servant, suppliant
ἰκμάς, moisture
ἱλαρός, cheerful, happy, joyous
ἱλαρότης, cheerfulness
ἱλαρόω, refresh, *show* cheerful
ἱλαρόω τὸ πρόσωπον, *show too* indulgent
ἱλαρύνω, gladden
ἱλάσκομαι, make *expiation*, merciful, mercy
ἱλασμός, expiation, offering *of atonement*
ἱλαστήριον, expiation, mercy *seat*
ἵλεως, far *be it*, gracious, merciful, mercy
ἵλεώς σοι, God *forbid*
ἴλη, troop
ἱμάντωσις, beam
ἱμάς, clothing, thong
ἱματίζω, clothe
ἱμάτιον, apparel, cloak, clothes, clothing, coat, *fine* clothes, garment, mantle, robe
ἱματισμός, apparel, attire, clothing, raiment, robe
ἵνα, how, lest, make, must, order, ready, see, since *one's aim*, tell, therefore, use, when
ἵνα μή, keep, lest, nor, prevent, rather *than*
ἵνα μήποτε, otherwise
ἵνα τί, why
ἴνδαλμα, specter
ἰοβόλος, venomous
ἰόομαι, rust
ἰός, poison, rust, venom
ἰουδαϊκῶς, *like a* Jew
ἰουδαΐζω, *live like a* Jew
ἱππεύς, cavalry, horseback, horseman
ἱππικός, cavalry
ἱππόδρομος, hippodrome
ἵπποι σὺν ἀναβάταις, cavalry
ἵππος, cavalry, horse, horseman
ἵππος εἰς ὀχείαν, stallion
ἶρις, rainbow
ἰσάγγελος, equal *to angel*
ἰσαστήρ, star-like
ἰσηγορέομαι, treat *as an equal*
ἰσοδυναμέω, *same* sense
ἰσοδύναμος, *equal* seriousness, equivalent
ἰσόθεος, equal *to God*
ἰσόμοιρος, *equal* share
ἰσονομέω, *act* impartially
ἰσόπεδον ποιέω, level *to the ground*
ἰσόπεδον τίθημι, level *to the ground*
ἰσόπεδος, level *to the ground*
ἰσοπολίτης, *equal* citizenship
ἰσοπολίτιδης, *same* ordeal
ἴσος, agree, common, equal, like, much, perhaps, same
ἰσότης, equality, fairly
ἰσότιμος, *equal* standing
ἰσόψυχος, like
ἵσταμαι, understand
ἵστημι, agree *to let*, appoint, arise, assure, bring *to an end*, build, bystander, cease, come *forward*, confirm, constitute, decide, decree, determine, do, erect, establish, fix, give *assurance*, God, hold *against*, institute, keep, make, make *a grant*, make *a treaty*, *make* stand, obtain, pay, pitch, place, pledge, present, preserve, put, put *forward*, put *up*, remain, *remain* valid, rest, set, set *up*, stand, stand *fast*, stand *firm*, stand *up*, station, stay, stop, sustain, swear, take, take *a stand*, uphold, wait, weigh, weigh *out*
ἵστημι καὶ ἵστημι, make *a binding agreement*
ἱστορέω, history, record, report, visit
ἱστορία, history, narrative, record
ἱστορία ἀρχηγέτης, *original* historian
ἱστός, support
ἰσχυρός, arduous, *beyond* power, great, heavy, loud, mighty, mighty *man*, powerful, strict, strong, strong *man*, *thing more* striking, warrior
ἰσχύς, authority, can, expert, might, mighty, power, resource, strength, strong, *strong* measure, violence
ἰσχύω, able, amass, avail, defeat, exert *pressure*, find *strength*, force, good, grow *strong*, man *of strength*, manage, overpower, power, prevail, provide, retain, *show* strength, strength, strong, strong *enough*, strong *man*, vigor, well
ἴσως, perhaps
ἰχθύδιον, *small* fish
ἰχθύς, fish
ἰχνευτής, hunter
ἰχνεύω, follow *steps*
ἴχνος, clue, example, footstep, mark, path, step, trace, track
ἰχώρων, gore
ἰῶτα, iota

καθ' ἅπαν, completely, ever
καθ' ἑαυτόν, privately
καθ' εἷς, individually
καθ' ἕν, every *one*
καθ' ἕνα, one *by one*, singly
καθ' ἡλικίαν προτέρου δεύτερος, *next* eldest
καθ' ἡμέραν, daily, day *after day*, day *by day*, *each* day, *every* day
καθ' ὅ, what
καθ' ὅλην, throughout
καθ' ὅσον, just
καθ' ὅσον ἄν, much
καθ' ὑπερβολήν, *beyond* measure, extreme, *more* excellent, utterly, violently
καθά, accordance, like
καθαγιάζω, consecrate, make *holy*
καθαίρεσις, destroy, destruction, tear *down*
καθαιρέω, cast *down*, cut *off*, depose, destroy, *part* demolished, pull *down*, put *down*, ruins, take *down*, tear *down*
καθαίρω, clean, prune
καθάπερ, case, just, like
καθάπτω, fasten
καθαρίζω, clean, cleanse, declare *clean*, make *clean*, purify
καθάριος, clear
καθαρισμός, cleanse, purification, purify, purity
καθαρός, clean, clear, fine, innocent, integrity, pure
καθαρότης, pureness, purification
καθάρσιος, purification
καθέδρα, seat, seat *of honor*
καθέζομαι, sit, sit *down*
καθεξῆς, come *afterwards*, order, orderly, place *to place*, soon *afterward*
καθεύδω, asleep, sleep, sleeper
καθηγεμών, leader
καθηγητής, master
καθήκω, appropriate, customary, due, duty, entitle, improper, inappropriate, necessary, ought, permit, proper, require, right
κάθημαι, business, dwell, enthrone, live, rider, seat, session, sit, sit *down*
καθημερινός, daily
κάθημι, dine
καθιδρύω, dedicate, found, set *up*
καθίημι, crown, lawful, let *down*
καθίζω, dwell, lay, *make* sit, remain, rest, seat, set, settle, sit, sit *down*, stay, take *a seat*
καθίπταμαι, fly *down*
καθίστημι, appoint, arise, become, build, come, conduct, continually, dwell, establish, keep, maintain, make, make *ruler*, place, place *in charge*, put, put *in a position*, real, remain, render, restore, set, set *over*, set *up*, settle, sovereign, stand, stand *before*, station, strengthen, suit, take *a stand*, take *one's place*, task
καθίστημι ἐν, among
καθό, because, far
καθὸ ἄν, whatever

κάθοδος, access
καθόλου, all
καθοπλίζω, arm, equip, put *on full armor*
καθοράω, behold, consider, look *down*, perceive
καθός, just
καθόσπερ, if, just, like, though
καθότι, because, just, since
καθυβρίζω, violate
καθύπερθε, under
καθυστερέω, destitute, frustrate
καθυφαίνω, weave
καθωπλίζω, *fully* arm
καθώς, accordance, according, equal, even, how, indeed, just, like, many, really, *same* term, same *way*, since, such, thus, well, what, whatever, when
καθώς καί, well
καθώσπερ, just
καί, after, against, along, also, although, besides, both, come, either, especially, even, even *so*, even *though*, exactly, hence, here, however, if, include, indeed, instead, mere, next, nor, now, once, only, perhaps, *same* time, still, then, therefore, though, thus, till, time, together, too, turn, until, upon, very, well, when, where, whether, while, yet
καί οὐ, nor, rather *than*
καί οὐ μή, nor
καὶ ἄν, even, even *if*, even *though*, if, if *even*, least, though
καὶ γάρ, indeed
καὶ γὰρ οὐ, neither
καὶ ἐιμί, then
καὶ ἔτι, even
καὶ ἰδού, now
καὶ μή, nor, than, without
καὶ νῦν, therefore
καὶ οὐ, without
καὶ οὕτως, just, nor
καὶ οὐχί, instead
καὶ πάλιν, again *and* again
καὶ τοῦτο, even
καινίζω, introduce, renew, restore
καινός, fresh, new
καινότης, new, newness
καινουργνός, inventor
καίπερ, although, even *though*, fact, spite, though
καιρός, age, *allotted* time, anniversary, *appointed* time, chance, condition, convenience, crisis, day, due *time*, event, hour, moment, occasion, *opportune* time, opportunity, period, plight, point, *proper* time, *right* moment, *right* time, season, space, time, when, while
καιρὸς ἡλικίας, age
καίτοι, although, even, fact, indeed, yet
καίτοιγε, although
καίω, blaze, burn, feed *fire*, kindle, light, *summer* heat
κἀκεῖ, there, too
κἀκεῖθεν, then, there
κἀκεῖνος, other, there
κακηγορέω, denounce
κακία, baseness, evil, iniquity, injury, malice, misdeed, treachery, trouble, vice, wicked, wickedness, wrong
κακίζω, reproach
κακοήθεια, *evil* nature, malice, *malicious* intent, malignity
κακοήθης, malevolent, malicious
κακολογέω, slander, speak *evil*
κακόμοχθος, *misspent* toil
κακὸν ποιέω, evildoer
κακοπαθεία, *severe* suffering
κακοπάθεια, suffer, toil, *uncomfortable* toil
κακοπαθέω, endure *suffering*, suffer
κακοποιέω, damage, *do* evil, *do* harm, *do* wrong, injure, wrongdoer
κακοποίησις, *do* ill
κακοποιός, wrongdoer
κακοπραγία, evil-doing
κακός, adversity, all, bad, bad *thing*, *base* means, basely, bitterly, calamity, crime, evil, evil *man*, evil *thing*, foul, harm, injure, miserable, misfortune, *more* intense, *most* cruel, trouble, wicked, wretch, wrong, wrongdoer
κακοτεχνέω, devise
κακότεχνος, deceitful, *evil* art, *maliciously* contrive
κακουργέω, scoundrel
κακουργία, *foul* play, treachery
κακοῦργος, criminal, evildoer, wicked
κακουχέω, ill-treat
κακόω, abuse, afflict, calamity *happen*, force, harm, hurt, ill-treat, injure, poison, violent
κακῶς, evil, miserable, severely, terribly, wicked, wickedly, wrong, wrongly
κακῶς ἔχω, sick, sick *people*
κάκωσις, affliction, *do* injury, ill-treatment, injure, misery
καλαμάομαι, glean
καλάμη, straw, stubble
κάλαμος, *measuring* rod, pen, reed, rod
καλέω, bring, call, call *forth*, give, give *a name*, host, invite, know, name, summon
καλέω τὸ ὄνομα, name
καλέω εἰς τὴν κλῆσιν, invite
καλλιέλαιος, *cultivated* olive *tree*
καλλίπαις, beautiful
καλλονή, beauty, excellence
κάλλος, beautiful, beauty, *good* looks
καλλωπίζω, make *beautiful*
καλοδιδάσκαλος, teach *what is good*
καλοκἀγαθία, nobility, nobility *and goodness*
καλοποιέω, well-doing
καλός, beautiful, beautiful *woman*, beauty, better, clear, excellent, fair, fine, fully, good, goodness, handsome, *high* value, honest, honorable, kindly, lovely, magnificently, *more* beautiful, *most* beautiful, *most* excellent, noble, right, seemly, splendid, truth, *very* well, welcome, well
καλούς λιμένας, Fair *Havens*
κάλπη, pitcher
κάλυμμα, armor, shield, veil
κάλυμνα, veil
καλύπτω, cover, hide, swamp, veil
καλύπτω τὸ πρόσωπον, spread *over*
καλῶς, fine *way*, good, honorably, *no good* purpose, please, properly, readily *enough*, right, rightly, true, *very* well, well
καλῶς ἔχω, recover
καλῶς ποιέω, kind, kind *enough*, please
κάμαξ, spear
κάμηλος, camel
κάμινος, furnace, kiln
καμμύω, close
κάμνω, die, exhaust, feeble, sick *man*
κάμπτω, bend, bow, make *pliable*, overcome, sap
κάμπτω τὰ γόνατα, kneel *down*
κάμπτω τὸν τράχηλον, make *obedient*
κανθός, corner
κανών, field, post, rule
καπηλεύω, peddler
κάπηλος, tradesman
καπνίζω, make *a smoke*, smoke
καπνός, smoke
καρδία, close, heart, mind, purpose, spirit, thought, understanding
καρδιογνώστης, know *the heart*
καρόω, swoon *away*
καρπός, crop, fruit, fruitful, grain, harvest, product, raise, return
καρπός τῆς ὀσφύος, descendant
καρποφορέω, bear *fruit*, bring *forth fruit*, produce
καρποφόρος, fruitful
καρπόω, make *an offering*, offer
κάρπωμα, sacrifice
κάρπωσις, offering *of fruit*
κάρταλλος, cage
καρτερέω, bear *up*, endure, keep, stand, steadfast, undergo
καρτερία, endurance, fortitude, steadfastness, stubbornness
καρτερός, bitter, endure, fierce, hard, staunch, stoutly, strong, violent
καρτεροψυχία, courageous *spirit*
κάρφος, speck
κασσίτερος, tin
κατ' ἀνδρολογίαν, collection *man by man*
κατ' ἐκλογήν, choose
κατ' ἐνιαυτόν, annually, *each* year, *every* year, year *after year*, yearly
κατ' ἐξοχήν, prominent
κατ' εὐθεῖαν, straight
κατ' εὐχάς, *votive* offering
κατ' ἰδίαν, apart, aside, private, privately
κατ' οἰκίαν εἰμί, rider
κατ' ὀλίγον, little *by little*
κατ' ὄνομα, every *one*
κατά, about, accord, accordance, according, after, *after the* likeness, against, all, along, along *the coast*, among, attack, authority, because, before, behind, belong, condition, correspond, crowd *one's way into*, deserve, direct, down, down *into*, due, each, every, example, favorable, fit, follow, follow *the course*, further, good, happen, harm, how, just, keep, lay *down*, like, live, much, near, off, opposite, over, point *of view*, prescribe, proportion, regard, reign, respect, rest, same, several, similar, since, subject, suit, take *place under*, term, through, throughout, toward, under, upon, use, various, very, view, virtue, way, weigh *down*, what, when, where
κατὰ ἀλήθειαν, rightly, truly
κατὰ ἀνάγκην, compel
κατὰ ἄνθρωπον, human *way*, man, speak *humanly*
κατὰ βάθους, extreme
κατὰ βραχύ, little *by little*
κατὰ γνῶσιν, considerately
κατὰ ἔχω, cover
κατὰ θεόν, godly
κατὰ κράτος, mightily
κατὰ λίβα, northeast
κατὰ μέλος, limb *by limb*
κατὰ μέρος, detail, piecemeal
κατὰ μῆνα, monthly
κατὰ μικρόν, little *by little*
κατὰ μόνας, alone, isolate
κατὰ οἰκίαν ὀροφοιτόω, build *on a housetop*
κατὰ πᾶν, completely, such, throughout
κατὰ πάντα, everywhere
κατὰ πόδας, close *behind*
κατὰ πόλιν, town *after town*
κατὰ πρόγνωσιν, destine
κατὰ πρόσωπον, against, along, before, edge, face, face *to face*, front, opposite
κατὰ σάρκα, earthly, people, worldly
κατὰ σπουδήν, quickly, speedily, zealous
κατὰ τὰ αὐτά, *same* effect
κατὰ τὰ ῥήματα, all
κατὰ τὰ ῥήματα ταῦτα, describe
κατὰ ταῦτα, accordingly
κατὰ τί, how
κατὰ τὸ αὐτό, together
κατὰ τὸ κρίμα, righteous
κατὰ τὸν λόγον, command
κατὰ τόπον, every *place*, wherever
κατὰ τοὺς οἴκους, house *after house*
κατὰ φύσιν, natural
κατὰ χεῖρας, near
κατὰ χῶρον, southeast
κατὰ ψυχήν, please
καταβαίνω, bring *down*, come *down*, descend, down, drop, fall, get *out*, go *down*, run *down*, step *down*
καταβάλλω, bring, cast *down*, disgrace, found, kill, lay, set *up*, shed, strike *down*, throw
καταβαρέω, burden
καταβαρύνω, *very* heavy
καταβάσιος, descend
κατάβασις, descent
καταβιβάζω, bring *down*
καταβιβρώσκω, consume, devour
καταβλάπτω, *do* harm
καταβοάω, cry *out*
καταβόησις, cry *out*
καταβολή, construction, foundation
καταβολὴ σπέρματος, conceive
καταβραβεύω, disqualify
κατάβρωμα, devour
κατάβρωσις, devour
καταγγελεύς, preacher
καταγγέλλω, advocate, proclaim
καταγέλαστος, ridiculous
καταγελάω, deride, laugh, laughing *stock*, mock, ridicule
κατάγελως, laughingstock
καταγινώσκω, condemn
κατάγνυμι, break
κατάγνωσις, condemnation
καταγογγύζω, murmur *against*
καταγορεύω, bring *a charge against*
καταγορεύω, bring *an accusation against*
καταγράφω, make *a record*, record, write
κατάγω, bring, bring *down*, bring *on board*, *cause to* fall, fall, land, lead *down*, lead *out*, *make* fall, put
καταγωνίζομαι, conquer
καταδαπανάομαι, consume
καταδεσμεύω, bind *up*, commit
καταδέω, bandage, bind *up*, fasten, lock *up*
κατάδηλος, evident
καταδικάζω, condemn, condemnation
καταδίκη, condemnation, sentence *against*
καταδιώκω, overtake, pursue, pursuer, run *after*
καταδουλόω, bring *into bondage*, enslave, make *a slave*
καταδρομή, counterattack
καταδυναστεύω, bring *into subjection*, hold *in power*, oppress
κατάθεμα, accursed
καταιγίς, storm, tempest
καταιδέομαι, respect
καταικίζω, buffet, maltreat, mangle, torture
καταίρω, tear *down*
καταισχύνω, *act* shamefully, ashamed, bring *shame*, burn *up*, disappoint, disgrace, dishonor, humiliate, put *to shame*, shame
κατακαίω, burn, burn *down*, burn *up*, consume
κατακαλύπτω, cover, veil, wear *a veil*
κατακάμπτω, twist, weight *down*
κατακαυχάομαι, boast, boast *over*, glory, triumph *over*
κατακαύω, burn
κατάκειμαι, lie, *lie* humbled, lie *humbled*, sit *at table*, table
κατάκειμαι ἐπὶ κραβάττου, bedridden
κατακεντέω, pierce *through*
κατακλάω, break
κατάκλειστος, enclose, imprison, keep *indoors*
κατακλείω, bind, put *in prison*, shut, shut *up*
κατακληροδοτέω, distribute
κατακληρονομέω, acquire, *cause to* inherit, give *an inheritance*, give *as an inheritance*, leave *for an inheritance*, obtain, receive *inheritance*
κατακλίνω, arrange *to sleep*, *make* sit *down*, recline, sit *down*, table, take *one's place at table*
κατακλύζω, deluge, drown, flood
κατακλυσμός, flood
κατακολουθέω, follow, follow *out*
κατακοντίζω, strike *down*
κατάκοπος, weary
κατακόπτω, bruise, cut *to pieces*, kill
κατακοσμέω, decorate
κατακρατέω, conquer, control, defeat, foil, gain *control*, get *control*, get *possession*, hold *control*, prevail *over*, rule *over*, subdue, take
κατακρημνίζω, overthrow, throw *down*, throw *down headlong*, throw *headlong from a height*
κατάκριμα, condemnation
κατακρίνω, condemn, judge

κατάκρισις, condemn, condemnation
κατακρύπτω, hide
κατακτείνω, murder
κατακύπτω, bend *down*
κατακυριεύω, conquer, domineer *over*, dominion *over*, lord *it over*, master
καταλαλέω, abuse, speak *against*, speak *evil*
καταλαλιά, slander
κατάλαλος, slanderer
καταλαμβάνω, against, attain, befall, capture, catch, comprehend, find, form, make *one's own*, obtain, occupy, overcome, overtake, perceive, remain, seize, surprise, take, take *possession*
καταλάμπω, illumine
καταλέγω, enrol, speak
κατάλειμμα, remnant
καταλείπω, abandon, against, bereave, desert, forsake, give *up*, keep, leave, leave *behind*, remain, rest, survive
καταλήγω, cease
καταλιθάζω, stone
καταλλαγή, *become* reconciled, reconciliation
καταλλάσσω, reconcile
καταλογίζομαι, number
κατάλοιπος, rest
καταλοχισμός, register
κατάλυμα, guest *room*, inn, lodging *place*
κατάλυσις, downfall, overthrow, rest
καταλύτης, guest
καταλύω, abandon, abolish, alight, break, destroy, disregard, dissolve, downfall, dwell, encamp, fail, fare, flock, guest, lodge, nullify, overthrow, paralyze, put *an end*, remove, stay, tear *down*, throw *down*
καταμανθάνω, consider, inspect, intent *upon*, look *intently*
καταμαρτυρέω, bear *witness against*, testify *against*
καταμένω, remain, stay
καταμερίζω, apportion
καταμεστόω, fill
καταμήνιος, menstruous
καταμηνύω, inform
καταμιμνήσκομαι, remind
καταμωκάομαι, deride
καταναγκάζω, enforce
καταναλίσκομαι, *utterly* consume
καταναλίσκω, consume, destroy, spend
καταναρκάω, burden
κατανεύω, beckon
κατανοέω, comprehend, consider, look, notice, observe, perceive, understand
κατανόησις, gaze
καταντάω, arrive, attain, come, proceed, reach, secure
καταντλέω, overwhelm
κατάνυξις, stupor
κατανύσσομαι, cut, feel *remorse*, grieve, sting, suffer
κατανύσσω, overwhelm *with passion*
κατανύω, complete
κατανωτίζομαι, refuse
καταξηραίνω, dry *up*
κατάξιος, deserve
καταξιόω, account *worthy*, beseech, claim, count *worthy*, deem *worthy*, make *worthy*
καταξύω, smooth
καταπαλαίω, overthrow
καταπάσσω, sprinkle, sprinkle *upon*
καταπατέω, oppress, spurn, trample, trample *down*, tread *under foot*, tread *upon*
κατάπαυμα, rest
κατάπαυσις, rest
καταπαύω, assign *a place*, *cause to* cease, cease, die *down*, end, extinguish, give *a resting place*, give *rest*, *make* rest, rest, restrain
καταπειράζω, try *attacking*
καταπέλτης, catapult
καταπέτασμα, curtain
καταπίνω, devour, drown, overwhelm, swallow, swallow *up*
καταπίπτω, downcast, fall, fall *down*
καταπλέω, arrive
καταπληγμός, terror
καταπλήσσω, astound, frighten, impress, panic-stricken, strike, strike *down*, terrify
καταποθέω, consume
καταπονέω, crush *with suffering*, *greatly* distress, oppressed *man*, suffer *grievously*
καταπονίνημι, hard
καταποντίζω, drown, sink
καταπορεύομαι, come *back*, go *home*
καταπραύνω, appease
καταπροδίδωμι, abandon
καταπτήσσω, cower
κατάπτωσις, downfall
κατάρα, accursed, curse
καταράομαι, accursed, call *down a curse upon*, curse
καταράσσω, hurl *down*
κατάρατος, accursed, accursed *man*
καταράω, curse
καταργέω, abolish, bring *to nothing*, destroy, discharge, doom *to pass away*, fade, fade *away*, give *up*, make *void*, nullify, overthrow, pass *away*, remove, sever, take *away*, use *up*, void
καταρέω, flow
καταριθμέω, number
καταρρήγνυμι, tear
καταρρίπτω, hurl *down*
κατάρρυτος, run *over*
καταρτίζω, bring, create, equip, make, mend, mend *one's ways*, prepare, restore, supply, teach *fully*, unite
κατάρτισις, improvement
καταρτισμός, equip
κατάρχω, launch, lead, raise
κατασβέννυμι, quench
κατασείω, harass, motion, sift
κατασκάπτω, demolish, destroy, ruins, tear *down*
κατασκευάζω, build, builder, cause, construct, equip, fashion, form, make, make *preparation*, prepare, render, vessel
κατασκεύασμα, furniture, *rich* setting
κατασκευή, construction, device, style
κατασκηνόω, dwell, make *a dwelling*, make *a nest*, settle *down*
κατασκήνωσις, dwell, habitation, nest
κατασκιάζω, overshadow
κατασκοπέω, spy *out*
κατάσκοπος, spy
κατασοφίζομαι, deal *craftily*, take *advantage*
κατασοφίζω, ensnare
κατασπάω, destroy
κατασπείρω, shed *abroad*
κατασπεύδω, eager, hasten, hasty, make *haste*, quickly, send *driving*, speed, urge, urgent
κατάστασις, plead
καταστέλλω, direct *to cease*, quiet, settle
κατάστεμα, state
καταστενάζω, groan
κατάστημα, behavior
καταστολή, apparel
καταστρατοπεδεύω, camp, march, spread *out*
καταστρέφω, alter, come *to an end*, destroy, overthrow, overturn
καταστρηνιάω, grow *wanton against*
καταστροφή, destruction, end, ruin
καταστρώννυμι, cut *down*, kill, lay *low*, overthrow, set *a table*, slay, strew *about*, strew *on the ground*
κατασύρω, drag
κατασφάζω, kill, slaughter, slay
κατασφαλίζομαι, take *precautions*
κατασφαλίζω, secure
κατασφραγίζω, seal, seal *up*
κατάσχεσις, dispossess, possess, possession
κατασχίζω, tear *to pieces*
κατατείνω, stretch *out*, stretch *tight*
κατατίθημι, bring *about*, do, expend, invoke *a curse*, keep, make
κατατίλλω, pull *out*
κατατιτρώσκω, cut *to pieces*
κατατολμάω, bold, dare
κατατομή, mutilate *the flesh*
κατατρέχω, pursuit, run *down*
καταυγάζω, gleam, illumine
καταφέρω, bring *against*, cast *against*, descend, overcome, sink, wield
καταφεύγω, flee, flee *for refuge*, take *refuge*
καταφθείρω, cause, corrupt, destroy
καταφθορά, annihilate, destruction
καταφιλέω, kiss
καταφλέγω, burn, consume, consume *with fire*
καταφράσσω, protect
καταφρονέω, contempt, despise, disrespectful, presume *upon*, treat *contemptuously*, treat *with contempt*, unconcerned
καταφρόνησις, contempt
καταφρονητής, scoffer
καταφυγή, reliance
καταφυτεύω, plant
καταχέω, pour, pour *over*, pour *upon*
καταχθόνιος, *under the* earth
καταχράομαι, deal, force, make *full use*, use
καταχράω, employ
κατάχρεος, enslave
καταχρίω, cover *with paint*, give *a coat*
καταχωρίζω, reduce
καταψεύδω, lie
καταψευσμός, *false* accusation
καταψύχω, cool
κατεγχειρέω, plot
κατείδωλος, full *of idols*
κατελεέω, take *pity*
κατέναντι, against, before, confront, front, opposite, presence, sight
κατενώπιον, before, *before the* presence
κατεξουσιάζω, exercise *authority over*
κατεπίθυμος, desire
κατεπικύπτω, collapse
κατεράω, curse
κατεργάζομαι, bring, commit, conquer, do, perform, prepare, produce, work, work *out*, wrought
κατέρχομαι, arrive, come, come *down*, fall, go *down*, land, return *home*
κατεσθίω, consume, devour, eat, prey *upon*
κατευθικτέω, exactly
κατευθύνω, bring, direct, direct *aright*, guide, intend, lead *aright*, prosperous, set
κατευλογέω, bless
κατευοδόω, prosper
κατευφημέω, applaud
κατεύχομαι, pray, *utter an* imprecation
κατεφίσταμαι, make
κατέχω, goods, hold, hold *captive*, hold *fast*, hold *firm*, keep, maintain, make, obtain, occupy, overcome, possess, restrain, stop, succeed, suppress, take
κατηγορέω, accusation, accuse, against, bring *a charge against*, bring *up against*, charge, charge *against*, charge *to bring against*, make *an accusation*
κατηγορία, accusation, charge
κατήγορος, accuser
κατήγωρ, accuser
κατήφεια, dejection
κατηφής, dismal
κατηχέω, inform, instruct, teach, tell
κατιόω, rust, tarnish
κατισχύω, able, against, oppressor, prevail, prevail *against*, strength, strengthen, strong
κατοικέω, dwell, dweller, inhabit, inhabitant, live, people, resident, settle
κατοίκησιν ἔχω, live
κατοίκησις, dwell
κατοικητήριον, dwelling, dwelling *place*
κατοικία, dwelling, habitation, settlement
κατοικίζω, *make* dwell, settle
κατοίκος, dwell, resident
κατοικτίρω, compassion, feel *strong compassion*
κατόπισθεν, after, behind
κατοπτεύω, see
κατοπτρίζω, behold
κατορθόω, erect, secure
κατόρθωσις, direct
κατορύσσω, bury
κάτω, below, beneath, bottom, down
κατώτατος, depth
κατώτερος, low
κατωτέρω, under
καῦμα, *burning* heat, heat, *scorching* heat, *very* hot
καυματίζω, scorch
καῦσις, burn
καυσόω, fire
καυστηριάζω, sear
καυστικός, burn, hot *enough*
καύσων, *burning* heat, heat, *scorching* heat
καύσωνος, *hot* wind
καυτηρίος, *hot* iron
καυχάομαι, boast, express *pride*, glory, rejoice
καύχημα, boast, *cause to* glory, exultation, glory, pride, prize, proud, reason *to boast*, *something to* boast *about*, superb
καύχησις, boast, boastful, pride, proud
καύχομαι, burn, pride
καψάκης, flask
κέδρινος, cedar
κέδρος, cedar
κεῖμαι, action, deposit, exist, lay, lay *down*, lay *up*, lie, lot, position, put, set, stand, there
κειρία, bandage
κείρω, cut, cut *off hair*, shearer, shorn
κέλευσμα, cry *of command*
κελεύω, bid, command, give *orders*, order
κενεών, *empty* space, side
κενοδοξέω, hold *a vain opinion*, take *hollow pride*
κενοδοξία, conceit, *vain* opinion, vainglory, vanity
κενόδοξος, self-conceit
κενός, empty, empty-handed, shallow, vain, vain *thing*, *without* result
κενοφωνία, chatter
κενόω, deprive, empty, null, prove *vain*
κέντρον, dart, goad, sting
κεντυρίων, centurion
κενῶς, vain
κεραία, dot
κεραμεύς, potter
κεραμικός, earthen
κεράμιον, jar
κέραμος, tile
κεράννυμι, mix, pour
κέρας, flank, horn, power, *upper* hand, wing
κεράτιον, pod
κεραυνός, thunder, thunderbolt
κερδαίνω, gain, get *gain*, incur, make, win
κέρδος, gain
κέρμα, coin
κερματιστής, money-changer
κεφάλαιον, point, sum
κεφαλαιόω, concisely, wound *in the head*
κεφαλή, hair, head
κεφαλῆς δορά, scalp
κεφαλίς, roll
κηδεία, funeral
κηδεμονία, service
κηδεμών, protector
κηλίς, blemish, disgrace
κημόω, muzzle
κῆνσος, tax, tribute
κῆπος, garden, orchard
κηπουρός, gardener
κηρογονία, make *a honeycomb*
κηρός, wax
κήρυγμα, message, preach, proclamation

κῆρυξ, herald, preacher

κηρύσσω, make *a proclamation*, preach, preacher, proclaim, proclamation, talk

κῆτος, *huge* creature *of the sea*, *huge sea* monster, whale

κίβδηλος, counterfeit *god*, *something* base

κιβωτός, ark, treasure *chest*

κίδαρις, turban

κιθάρα, harp

κιθαρίζω, play

κινδυνεύω, danger, peril

κίνδυνος, danger, peril

κινέω, arouse, attract, move, movement, remove, wag

κινέω στάσεις, agitator

κίνημα, impulse, tumult

κίνησις, beat, brandish, motion, shake

κινητικός, *more* mobile

κιννάμωμον, cassia, cinnamon

κινύρα, harp, lute, lyre

κισσός, wreath *of ivy*

κισσόφυλλον, ivy-leaf

κίχρημι, lend

κλάδος, bough, branch

κλαίω, cry, mourn, tear, weep

κλάσις, break

κλάσμα, basket, *broken* piece, fragment

κλαυθμός, lamentation, wail, weep

κλάω, break

κλεῖθρον, lock

κλείς, key

κλείω, close, confine, lock, lock *up*, shut, shut *up*

κλέμμα, theft

κλέος, credit

κλέπτης, thief

κλέπτω, secretly, steal, steal *away*, thief

κλεψιμαῖος, steal

κλῆμα, branch

κληματίς, brush

κληροδοσία, possession

κληροδοτέω, allot

κληρονομέω, heir, heritage, incur, inherit, inheritance, lot, obtain, possess, seize, take *possession*

κληρονομία, heritage, inherit, inheritance, territory

κληρονόμος, heir, inherit

κλῆρος, charge, inheritance, land, lot, place, share

κληρόω, appoint

κλῆσις, call, invitation, state

κλητέος, call, *must* call

κλητός, call, guest

κλίβανος, oven

κλίμα, region

κλίμαξ, ladder

κλινάριον, bed

κλίνη, bed, *marriage* vow, sickbed

κλινίδιον, bed

κλίνω, bend, bow, fall, *far* spent, incline, lay, put *to flight*, spend, tip *over*, wear *away*

κλισία, celebrant, company

κλοιός, collar

κλοπή, theft

κλύδων, billow, flood, rage, wave

κλυδωνίζομαι, toss *to and fro*

κλώθω, twist

κλών, branch

κλῶσμα, cord

κνήθω, itch

κνώδαλον, animal, beast

κοδράντης, penny

κοιλάς, valley

κοιλία, appetite, belly, birth, entrails, heart, stomach, womb

κοιλία μητρός, bear, birth

κοιλίας ὄρεξις, gluttony

κοιλότης, hollow

κοίλωμα, hollow

κοιμάω, adorn, asleep, camp *for the night*, die, fall *asleep*, go *to sleep*, lie, sleep, spend *the night*

κοίμησις, dead, sleep, take *rest*

κοινολογέομαι, confer, talk *together*

κοινολογία, conference

κοινὸν ἡγέομαι, profane

κοινός, apply *only to the people*, common, defile, embrace, general, public, *render* service, together, unclean, *unclean* food, whole

κοινόω, call *common*, defile, defiled *person*

κοινωνέω, associate, communicate, contribute, enter *into partnership*, fellowship, participate, share

κοινωνία, contribution, fellowship, participation, partnership, share, take *part*

κοινωνικός, generous

κοινωνός, associate, companion, partaker, partner, share, take *part*

κοινῶς, both

κοίτη, bed, debauchery, *marriage* bed, union

κοίτην ἔχω, conceive

κοιτών, bedchamber, bedroom, room

κόκκινος, scarlet

κόκκος, grain, kernel, scarlet

κολάζω, chastise, punish, punisher, *under* punishment

κολακεία, flattery

κολακεύω, flatter

κολάπτω, engrave

κολάπτω γραφήν, inscription

κόλασις, punish, punishment, vengeance

κολαφίζω, beat, buffet, harass, strike

κολλάω, associate, cleave, cling, consort, heap, hold *fast*, join, unite, yearn

κολλούριον, salve

κολλυβιστής, money-changer

κολοβόω, shorten

κόλπος, bay, bosom, breast, lap

κολυμβάω, swim

κολυμβήθρα, pool

κολωνία, colony

κομάω, *long* hair, wear *long hair*

κόμη, hair

κομιδῇ, entirely

κομίζω, bring, bring *forward*, get, get *back*, incur, meet, obtain, pay *back*, receive, receive *again*, receive *back*, recover, take

κόμμα, coinage

κόμπος, boast

κομψότερον ἔχω, *begin to* mend

κόνδυ, cup

κονιάω, whitewash

κονιορτός, dust

κόνις, ash, dust

κοπάζω, calm, cease, still

κοπετός, lamentation, mourn, wail

κοπή, labor, slaughter

κοπιάζω, toil

κοπιάω, difficulty, grow *tired*, grow *weary*, hard-working, labor, laborer, toil, wear *out*, weary, work, worker

κόπον παρέχω, bother

κόπος, labor, toil, trouble

κόπους παρέχω, trouble

κοπόω, weary

κοπρία, dunghill

κόπριον, dung, dunghill, manure, refuse

κόπτω, bewail, cut, cut *down*, make *lamentation*, mourn, wail, weary

κόραξ, raven

κοράσιον, girl, *little* girl, maid, maidservant

κορβανᾶς, treasury

κορέννυμι, enough, fill

κόρη, apple *of one's eye*, pupil

κόρος, cor, measure, prosperity

κόρυς, helmet

κορυφή, crown, top

κορυφὴ ὄρους, hilltop

κορώνη, crow

κόσκινον, sieve

κοσμέω, adorn, arrange, arrange *in an order*, array, deck *out*, decoration, equip, ordain, prepare, put *in order*, trim

κοσμικός, earthly, worldly

κόσμιος, dignify, seemly

κοσμοκράτωρ, *world* ruler

κοσμοπληθής, universal

κοσμοποιΐα, creation

κόσμος, adorn, adornment, array, beauty, creation, decoration, finery, order, ornament, setting, trappings, universe, *well* ordered, world, worldly

κοσμοφορέω, carry *the world*

κοῦμ, cumi

κουστωδία, guard, guard *of soldier*

κουφίζω, carry, lift *the burden*, lighten

κοῦφος, easy, light

κόφινος, basket, *broken* piece

κόχλαξ, pebble

κράβαττος, pallet

κραδαίνω, brandish, shake

κράζω, bleat, call, call *out*, cry, cry *out*, proclaim, shout

κραιπάλη, dissipation

κρανίον, skull

κράσπεδον, fringe

κραταιός, mighty, strong, sturdy

κραταιόω, *become* strong, defeat, give *strength*, stand *firm*, strengthen, strong

κραταίωσις, strength

κρατέω, arrest, capture, cling, come, conquer, control, establish, gain *control*, gain *full control*, get, govern, hold, hold *back*, hold *fast*, keep, lay *hold*, master, observe, obtain, occupy, overcome, possession, power, prevail, restrain, retain, rule, rule *over*, ruler, seize, steadfast, take, take *hold*, take *possession*

κράτησις, dominion

κράτιστος, *most* excellent

κράτος, cling, dominance, dominion, force, great, handle, hold *fast*, might, mighty, power, rule, strength

κρατύνω, grow *strong*

κραυγάζω, cry, cry *aloud*, cry *out*

κραυγή, *battle* cry, clamor, cry, *loud* cry, outcry, shout

κρέας, flesh, meat

κρέας ὕειον, pork

κρείσσων, mighty

κρείττων, better, good, good *thing*, *more* graciously, superior

κρεμάννυμι, depend, fasten, hang, leave *hanging*

κρεμάω, depend, hang, hang *up*

κρημνίζω, hurl *headlong*

κρημνός, *steep* bank

κρήνη, pool

κρηπίς, bank, step

κριθή, barley

κρίθινος, barley

κρίμα, condemn, condemnation, decision, decree, doom, judgment, justice, lawsuit, order, sentence, sentence *of condemnation*, verdict

κρίνον, consider, lily

κρίνω, approve, condemn, convince, deal, decide, decision, determine, discern, *do* justice, esteem, go *to law*, govern, judge, judgment, make *up one's mind*, pass *judgment*, pick, pronounce, pronounce *judgment*, quarrel, reach, *render* judgment, rule, ruler, *seem* good, *seem* wise, sue, suit *at law*, think, trial, try

κρίνω τό κρίμα, give *judgment*

κριός, *battering* ram, ram

κρίσιν εἰσφέρω, accuse

κρίσις, case, cause, charge, condemnation, decide, decision, discretion, honor, issue, judge, judgment, justice, law, lawsuit, punishment, right, sentence

κριτήριον, case, court, place *of judgment*

κριτής, decide, judge, magistrate

κριτικός, discern

κρουνηδόν, gush

κρούω, knock

κρύπτη, cellar, secret

κρυπτός, conceal, hidden *thing*, hide, private, secret, underhanded *way*

κρύπτω, conceal, cover *up*, guard, hidden *thing*, hide, keep *secret*, *remain* hidden, secret, secretly

κρυπτῶς, privately, secretly

κρυσταλλίζω, clear *as crystal*

κρυσταλλοειδής, crystalline

κρύσταλλος, crystal, ice

κρυφαῖος, secret

κρύφιος, secret

κρυφός, hide, hiding *place*

κρύψις, hide

κτάομαι, acquire, buy, gain, get, get *a possession*, make, obtain, owner, take

κτείνω, kill, stretch *forth*, stretch *out*

κτῆμα, piece *of property*, possession, property

κτῆνος, animal, beast, cattle, creature, mount

κτῆσις, acquire, get, possess

κτήτωρ, possessor

κτίζω, build, create, creator, make

κτίσις, creation, creature, institution

κτίσμα, create, created *thing*, creature, fabric

κτίσμα καλόν, beneficence

κτίστης, creator

κτύπος, crash

κυβεία, cunning

κυβερνάω, govern, guide, steer

κυβέρνησις, administrator

κυβερνήτης, captain, pilot, shipmaster

κυκλεύω, surround

κυκλόθεν, about, all *around*, around, circle, encircle, *every* side, round, round *about*

κύκλος, about, among, around, circle, circuit, cycle, environs, *every* side, neighbor, outside, round, round *about*, surround

κυκλόω, arc, around, circle *around*, encircle, gather *about*, gather *round*, go *about*, make *the circuit*, round *about*, stand *around*, surround

κύκνειος, swan

κυλικεῖον, sideboard

κυλισμός, wallow

κυλίω, roll *about*, roll *back*

κυλλός, maim

κῦμα, wave

κυμαίνω, billowy

κύμβαλον, cymbal

κύμινον, cummin

κυνάριον, dog

κυνήγιον, prey

κυοφορία, childbirth, pregnancy

κυπάρισσος, cypress

κυπόω, ratify

κύπτω, bend, bend *over*, bow *down*, stoop *down*

κυρέω, strengthen

κυρία, lady

κυριακός, Lord

κυριεία, dominion

κυριεύω, bind, capture, control, dominion *over*, exercise *lordship over*, gain *control*, gain *possession*, governor, lord, Lord, lord *over*, master, rule, rule *over*, take *possession*, take *precedence*

κύριος, charge, lord, LORD, Lord, man, master, owner, sir, sovereign, supreme, valid

κυριότης, authority, dominion

κυρόω, reaffirm

κύων, dog

κώδιον, *soft* fleece

κώδων, bell

κώθωνα, banquet

κωθωνίζομαι, feast

κωκυτός, wail

κῶλον, body

κωλυτικός, hinder, restrain

κωλύω, hinder, keep, keep *away*, prevent, refrain, restrain, stop, ward *off*, withhold, withstand

κωμή, town

κώμη, village

κωμόπολις, town
κῶμος, carouse, revel
κωνώπιον, canopy
κώνωψ, gnat
κωφός, deaf, dumb, dumb *man*, speechless *thing*

λάβρος πυρί, *intensely* hot
λαγχάνω, allot, attain, cast *lots*, fall *by lot*, fall *to one's lot*, obtain
λαγών, loin
λαθραῖος, secret
λαθραίως, secretly
λαῖλαψ, storm, tempest, whirlwind
λαιμαργία, gluttony
λάκκος, cistern, den, dungeon, pool, reservoir
λακτίζω, kick
λαλέω, address, bring, communicate, declare, impart, make, mean, preach, present, promise, pronounce, say, sound, speak, speaker, suggest, talk, teach, tell, *thing* spoken *later*, threaten, utter
λαλέω εἰρήνην, greet
λαλέω φωνάς, sound
λαλιά, accent, byword, gossip, rumor, say, speak, story, talk, talkative, word
λαλιὰν προΐημι, speak
λαμά, lama
λαμβάνω, accept, appoint, bring, capture, choose, collect, collector, experience, find, gain, gather, get, get *the better*, grant, grasp, incur, keep, make, marry, obtain, overtake, perceive, possess, procure, put, reach, receive, secure, seize, share, show, strike, take, take *up*, undergo
λαμβάνω γυναῖκα, marry
λαμβάνω διάδοχον, succeed
λαμβάνω καὶ μεταδίδωμι, exchange
λαμβάνω κρίμα, judge
λαμβάνω πρόσωπον, partiality
λαμβάνω σκῦλα, plunder
λαμβάνω τὰ σκῦλα, despoil
λαμβάνω τὸ τέλος, stop
λαμπάς, lamp, light, torch
λαμπρός, bright, brilliant, cheerful, fine, gorgeous, liberal, radiant, shine, splendor, sumptuous
λαμπρότης, bright, splendor
λαμπρῶς, sumptuously
λάμπω, give *light*, light *up*, shine
λάμψις, shine
λανθάνω, elude, escape *notice*, go *unnoticed*, hide, ignore, unawares, unobserved
λάξ τύπτω, kick
λαξευτός, rock-hewn
λαξεύω, hew
λαογραφία, registration *involving a poll tax*
λαός, army, company, man, people, soldier
λαός ἐπὶ τὴν συμμαχίαν, ally
λαὸς Μωαβ, Moabite
λαπιστής, braggart
λάρυγξ, throat, voice
λάσκω, burst *open*
λατομέω, hew
λατόμος, mason
λατρεία, religion, *ritual* duty, service, worship
λατρεία ἔργων, labor
λατρεύω, minister, offer *worship*, serve, worship, worshiper
λαφυρεύω, plunder
λάφυρον, booty, plunder
λάχανον, herb, shrub, vegetable
λέβης, caldron
λεβής, *iron* kettle
λεγιών, legion
λέγω πρός, address
λέγω, affirm, aloud, argument, ask, bid, call, charge, complain, cry, declare, designate, explain, express, follow, give, give *out*, hold, implore, inform, know, make *known*, mean, message, name, order, plead, pray, preach, pronounce, put, reply, say, saying, sing, so-called, speak, state, talk, tell, thought, word
λέγω μεθερμηνεύω, mean
λέγω ῥακά, insult
λέγω χαίρω, greet
λεηλατέω, seize
λεία, captive
λεῖμμα, remnant
λεῖος, smooth
λειποτακτέω, leave *one's post*
λείπω, beat, defective, incomplete, lack, omit, spare
λειτουργέω, minister, serve, service, worship
λειτουργία, ministry, offering, service, worship
λειτουργικός, minister
λειτουργός, minister, official, servant, service
λεληθότως, secretly
λέντιον, towel
λέξις, expression, phrase, utterance
λεοντηδόν, *like a* lion
λεπίζω, scale *away*, scale *off*, strip *off*
λεπίς, scale
λέπρα, leprosy
λεπρός, leper
λεπτός, copper, *copper* coin, light, *most* subtle, subtle
λευκαίνω, bleach, make *white*
λευκός, white
λευκότης, whiteness
λεχώ, childbirth
λέων, lion
λήγω, abate, cease, end, lose, stop
λήθη, forgetfulness
λήθη λαμβάνω, forget
λῆμψις, receive, take
ληνός, wine *press*
λῆρος, futile, *idle* tale
ληρώδης, foolish
λίαν, furious, great, greatly, intensely, strongly, very
λίαν ἐκ περισσοῦ, utterly
λιβανόομαι, mix *with frankincense*
λίβανος, frankincense, incense
λιβανωτός, censer, frankincense
λιβερτῖνος, freedman
λιθάζω, stone
λίθινος, stone
λιθοβολέω, stone
λιθοβόλος, stone
λίθος, another, flint, gem, jewel, stone
λίθος μυλικός, millstone
λίθος τίμιος, jewel
λίθος χαλάζης, hailstone
λιθόστρωτος, pavement
λιθούργος, jeweler
λιθώδεσις, *stony* ground
λικμάω, belch *forth*, crush, scatter, winnow
λιμήν, harbor, haven
λίμνη, lake, pit
λιμός, famine, hunger
λίνον, linen, wick
λινοῦς, gown
λιπαίνω, anoint, pour *oil*
λιπαρός, dainty
λίπασμα, fat
λιποθυμέω, expire
λιτανεία, entreaty, *solemn* supplication, supplication
λιτανεύω, pray
λίτρα, pound
λιχνεία, gluttony
λογεία, contribution
λογίζομαι, account, charge *against*, claim, compare, conclude, consider, count, decide, hold, hold *of account*, intend, plan, plot, reason, reckon, recognize, reflect, regard, suppose, suspect, think, think *about*, understand
λογίζομαι πάλιν, remind
λογίζομαι τὸ κακόν, resentful
λογικός, spiritual
λόγιον, command, oracle, word
λόγιος, eloquent
λογισμός, argument, conversation, counsel, decision, design, mind, plan, principle, rational *judgment*, reason, reasoning, resolve, thought, way *of thinking*, word
λογομαχέω, dispute *about a word*
λογομαχία, dispute *about a word*
λόγον ἔχω, worry
λόγος, account, act, appearance, argument, book, command, complaint, conversation, credit, decision, detail, do, doctrine, eloquent, encouragement, event, express, expression, ground, hear, income, justify, logic, matter, mean, message, news, notion, plan, preach, proposal, question, reason, report, request, retort, revenue, say, saying, secret, sentence, speak, speaker, speech, statement, story, subject, sue, tale, talk, teaching, tell, term, testimony, thing, utterance, what, word, work
λόγος κρύφιος, secret
λόγου ποιέω, account
λόγχη, lance, spear
λοιδορέω, rail, revile
λοιδορία, abuse, insult, reproach, revile
λοίδορος, reviler
λοιμός, pestilence, pestilent, pestilent *fellow*, pestilent *man*
λοιμότης, *pestilent* behavior
λοιπός, *all* other, beyond, continue, else, everything *else*, finally, future, henceforth, last, moreover, now, other, other *thing*, other *woman*, remain, rest, still, survivor, then
λουτρόν, wash
λούω, bathe, wash
λόχος, treacherously
λυθρώδης, defile *with blood*
λύκος, wolf
λυμαίνομαι, defile
λυμαίνω, mangle, ravage
λυμεών, destroyer
λυμεὼν φθορεύς, seducer
λυπέω, *cause* pain, distress, give *grief*, grief, grieve, hurt, injure, make *sorry*, pain, sorrowful, sorry, strike *with grief*, suffer
λύπη, grief, pain, painful, sorrow
λυπηρός, sorrowful
λύσις, free, solution
λυσιτέλεια, benefit
λυσιτελέω, better, profit
λυσιτελὴς μᾶλλον, preferable
λύτρον, ransom
λυτρόω, deliver, ransom, redeem
λύτρωσις, redemption
λυτρωτής, deliverer
λυχνία, lampstand, stand
λύχνος, lamp
λύω, *all* disheveled, break, break *down*, break *up*, destroy, dissolve, free, loose, open, pardon, relax, release, take *off*, tense, unbind, undo, untie
λωποδυτέω, plunder

μά, no
μαγεία, magic
μαγεύω, practice *magic*
μαγικός, magic
μάγος, magician, wise *man*
μαθητεύω, disciple, make *disciples*, train
μαθητής, disciple
μαθήτρια, disciple
μάζας, cake
μαίνομαι, display *madness*, give *way to insanity*, mad, rave
μακαρίζω, bless, call *blessed*, call *happy*, count *happy*, gladden, make *happy*
μακάριος, bless, fortunate, happy, happy *man*
μακαριότης, blessedness
μακαρισθήσομαι, happiness
μακαρισμός, blessing, satisfaction
μακαριστός, enviable
μάκελλον, *meat* market
μακράν, distance, far, far *off*
μακρὰν ἀπέχω, distance
μακρὰν ἀφίστημι, *too* far off
μακρόβιος, live *long*
μακροβίωσις, length *of days*
μακροημέρευσις, length *of days*, *long* life
μακρόθεν, afar, distance, far *off*, *long* way
μακροθυμέω, delay *long*, endure *patiently*, endure *with patience*, forbear, patience, patient
μακροθυμία, forbearance, patience
μακρόθυμος, long-suffering, patient, patient *man*, patiently, slow *to anger*
μακροθύμως, patiently
μακρός, far, long, many
μακρότης, length
μακροτονέω, continue
μακροχρόνιος, live *long*
μακρύνω, delay, far
μάλα, especially, very
μάλαγμα, poultice
μαλακία, infirmity
μαλακός, soft, *soft* raiment
μαλακοψυχάζω, cowardice
μάλιστα, *above* all, especially, extremely, greatly, most, most *of all*
μᾶλλον, all *the better*, all *the more*, better, especially, even *more*, far, good, instead, less, more, more *than ever*, moreover, much *the more*, must, prefer, rather, really
μᾶλλον δέ, yes
μάμμη, grandmother
μαμωνᾶς, mammon
μάνδρα, sheepfold
μάνδρα εἰς τὰ ποίμνια, sheepfold
μανθάνω, acquire, ask, gain, know, learn, listen, study, teach
μανία, insanity, mad, madness
μανιάκης, necklace
μανιώδης, madness
μάννα, *cereal* offering, manna
μαντεία, divination
μαντεύομαι, soothsaying
μαραίνω, consume, fade *away*, wither
μαργαρίτης, pearl
μάρμαρος, marble
μάρσιππος, purse
μαρτυρέω, attest, bear, bear *testimony*, bear *witness*, *good* repute, receive *approval*, receive *divine approval*, speak *well*, testify, testimony, warn, witness
μαρτυρία, testimony, thought, witness
μαρτύριον, bear *testimony*, evidence, proof, testify, testimony, witness
μαρτύρομαι, call *to witness*, charge, testify
μάρτυς, bear *witness*, martyr, testimony, witness
μασάομαι, gnaw
μαστιγόω, afflict, beat, chastise, flog, scourge, scourge *thoroughly*, *severely* afflict
μαστίζω, lash, scourge
μάστιξ, affliction, chastise, disease, lashing, plague, scourge, whip
μάστιξιν καταικίζω, scourge
μαστός, breast
ματαιολογία, *vain* discussion
ματαιολόγος, *empty* talker
μάταιος, all *in vain*, folly, foolish, futile, vain, vain *thing*, vanity
ματαιότης, folly, futility, vanity
ματαιόφρων, vain-minded
ματαιόω, *become* futile, vain
μάτην, vain
μάχαιρα, sword
μάχη, battle, fight, quarrel, strife
μάχομαι, dispute, fight, quarrel, quarrelsome
μέγα τι, greatly
μεγαλαυχέω, boastfully, make *a great boast*
μεγαλαυχία, arrogance
μεγαλεῖος, dignity, grandeur, great, great *thing*,

majestic, majesty, mighty, mighty *deed*, splendor
μεγαλειότης, magnificence, majesty
μεγάλη σφόδρα, fearful
μεγάλη φωνή, noise
μεγάλης τινὸς κοινωνέω, enhance
μεγαλόδοξος, *most* glorious
μεγαλοδόξως, *most* gloriously
μεγαλοκράτωρ, *great* power
μεγαλομερής, glorious
μεγαλομερῶς, lavishly, magnificently
μεγαλοπρέπεια, glorious
μεγαλοπρεπής, glorious, magnificent, majestic, majesty
μεγαλοπρεπῶς, magnificently, *proper* reverence
μεγαλορρημονέω, boastful, say *boastfully*
μεγαλοσθενής, *all* powerful
μεγαλοφρονέω, courageous
μεγαλόφρων, courageous
μεγαλόψυχος, magnanimous
μεγαλοψύχως, magnanimously
μεγαλύνω, enlarge, exalt, extol, great, hold *in high honor*, honor, long, magnify, make *great*, mean *more*
μεγάλως, great, greatly, specially, very
μεγαλωστί, loudly
μεγαλωσύνη, greatness, majestic, majesty
μεγαλωσύνην δίδωμι, exalt
μέγας, chief, completely, deep, deeply, elder, extreme, fierce, general, giant, grave, great, great *man*, great *thing*, greatly, haughty, heavy, high, large, large *one*, long, loud, might, mighty, more, *most* mighty, much, profound, rich, severe, strange, strong, supreme, tall, terribly, up, utter, vast, very, *very* great, wide
μέγας σφόδρα, famous
μέγεθος, greatly, greatness, might
μεγιστάν, courtier, great *man*, noble, nobleman, officer
μεγιστάνων, great
μεγιστάω, great, great *man*
μεθ' ἁγιότητος, hallow
μεθαρμόζω, change *places*
μεθερμηνεύω, mean, meaning, translation
μέθη, *drunken* stupor, drunkenness, excess
μεθίστημι, depose, deprive, go, put, put *aside*, remove, shift, transfer, turn *away*
μεθοδεία, wile
μέθοδος, craft, strategy
μεθύσκω, *become* drunk, drink *freely*, drunk, get *drunk*, satisfy
μέθυσος, drunkard, drunken
μεθύω, drench, drunk, drunken
μεῖγμα, compound
μείγνυμι, mingle, mix
μειδιάω, smile
μειόω, wane
μειράκιον, boy, young *fellow*, youth
μειρακίσκος, *mere* boy, *very* young
μεῖραξ, youth
μελανέω, blacken
μελανία, mourn
μέλας, black, ink
μέλει, care, concern, mind, pay *attention*
μέλεος, wretched
μέλεσιν ἀναπείρους ποιέω, disable
μελετάω, imagine, meditate, practice
μέλι, dirge, honey
μέλισσα, bee
μέλιτος κηρίον, honeycomb
μέλλω, about, almost, come, delay, destine, future, go, intend, *next* year, point, *thing to* come, wait
μέλος, limb, melody, member, organ, part, portion, tune, what
μέλος ποιέω, dismember
μέλω, distress, take *charge*
μεμβράνα, parchment
μέμφομαι, blame, find *fault*, rebuke
μεμψίμοιρος, malcontent
μέμψις, blame
μέν, all, although, *at* hand, hand, however, indeed, latter, nevertheless, now, one, only, surely, though, while
μὲν γάρ, now
μὲν οὖν, now
μενοῦν, rather
μενοῦνγε, indeed
μέντοι, really, yet
μένω, abide, alive, await, continue, dwell, endure, last, live, maintain, permanent, remain, rest, stay, still, survive, wait
μεριδάρχη, governor *of the province*
μεριδαρχία, group, grouping
μερίζω, allot, apportion, assign, bequeath, distribute, divide, give *some*, lot
μέριμνα, anxiety, care, purpose, worry
μεριμνάω, anxiety, anxious, anxious *about*, care, meditate
μερίς, allot, blessing, common, district, division, heritage, inheritance, part, party, portion, share
μερισμός, distribute, division
μεριστής, divider
μέρος, case, company, country, detachment, detail, district, flank, heavily, little, lot, measure, one, part, party, piece, place, portion, regard, share, side, *some* point, trade, turn, turn *of fortune*, wing
μέρος τι, partly
μεσάζω, half *gone*
μέση νύξ, midnight
μεσημβρία, noon, *noonday* sun, south
μεσημβρινός, midday
μεσιτεύω, interpose
μεσίτης, intermediary, mediate, mediator
μεσόγειος, country
μέσον ἡμέρας, noon
μέσον λαμβάνω, surround
μεσονύκτιον, midnight
μέσος, among, between, company, middle, midst, presence, two, way
μέσος τῆς νυκτός, midnight
μεσότης, middle
μεσότοιχον, divide
μεσουράνημα, midheaven
μεσόω, middle
μεσόω τῆς νυκτός, midnight
μεστάω, satiate
μεστός, full
μεστόω, fill
μετ' εἰρήνης, friendly, peaceable, *safe* conduct, safely
μετ' εὐφροσύνης, gladly, joyfully
μετ' ὀλίγον χρονίσκον, soon
μετ' ὀργῆς, angrily
μετ' οὐ, before
μετ' οὐ πολύ, soon
μετά, accompany, accordance, after, afterward, against, along, among, before, behind, between, bring, crown, fit, follow, help, join, late, later *than*, near, only, side, through, till, together, under, upon, utter, wear, when
μετὰ αἰδοῦς, modestly
μετὰ ἁπλότητος, liberally
μετὰ βίας, violently
μετὰ βλασφημίας, blasphemer
μετὰ βοῆς, loudly
μετὰ δακρύων, tearful
μετὰ δὲ τοῦτο, afterward
μετὰ δόλου, treacherous, treacherously
μετὰ δόξης, notable
μετὰ κόπων, painful
μετὰ νίκης, victorious
μετὰ παρρησίας, boldly, confidently, freely, openly, publicly
μετὰ πίστεως, confidently
μετὰ πολλῆς, earnestly
μετὰ σπουδῆς, eagerly, hastily, zealously
μετὰ ταῦτα, afterwards, future, late, still, subsequent, thereafter
μετὰ τοῦτο, afterward, hereafter, then
μετὰ ὕστερον, late
μετὰ χαρᾶς, joyful, joyfully
μετὰ χρόνον, afterward, late
μεταβαίνω, change *over*, depart, go, go *over*, leave, move, move *over*, pass, pass *out*
μεταβαίνω ἀπό, forsake
μεταβάλλω, change, change *attitude*, change *course*, change *one's mind*, transform
μεταβάλλω χρῶμα, turn *pale*
μεταβολή, bring *here*, change
μεταβολία, barter
μεταγενής, after
μεταγίνομαι, deport
μετάγω, bring, carry *away*, exile, guide, pass, remove, transfer, translate
μεταδιαιτέω, change *one's manner of living*
μεταδίδωμι, communicate, contribute, give, impart, share, tell
μεταδιώκω, strive
μετάθεσις, change, removal, take
μεταίρω, go *away*
μεταίτιος, *part* responsible
μετακαλέω, ask, call, call *back*, summon
μετακινέω, shift, sway
μετακιρνάομαι, change
μετακομίζω, bring *back*
μεταλαμβάνω, adopt, comprehend, exchange, get *word*, hear, learn, partake, receive, share, take
μεταλάσσω, deceased
μετάλημψις, receive
μεταλλάσσω, dead, death, die, exchange
μεταλλάσσω τὸν βίον, die
μεταλλεύω, change, pervert
μέταλλον, mine
μεταμέλεομαι, change *one's mind*, regret, repent
μετάμελος, regret
μεταμορφόω, change, transfigure, transform
μετανοέω, repent, repentance
μετάνοια, repent, repentance
μεταξύ, among, between, midst, next
μεταξὺ ἀλλήλων, conflict
μεταξὺ ἵστημι, intervene
μεταπαιδεύω, learn *a better way*
μεταπείθω, persuade *to change*
μεταπέμπω, bring, send, summon *to come*
μεταπίπτω, change
μεταστρέφω, avert *with vengeance*, change, pervert, turn
μετασχηματίζω, apply, change, disguise, transform
μετατίθημι, avert, carry *back*, change, correct, desert, induce *to change the mind*, pervert, take, take *up*, turn
μετατρέπω, pervert, turn, turn *aside*
μεταφέρω, bring
μετάφρασιν ποιέω, recast *a narrative*
μεταχέω, irrigate
μετέπειτα, afterward, follow, late
μετέρχομαι, overtake, proceed *against*, pursue, visit
μετέχω, after, belong, get, live, partake, place, share, take *part*
μετεωρίζομαι, *anxious* mind
μετεωρίζω, lift *up*
μετεωρισμός, elate, haughty, lustful
μετέωρος, high
μετοικεσία, deportation
μετοικίζω, carry *away*, remove
μετουσία, enjoyment
μετοχή, partnership
μέτοχος, comrade, partaker, participant, participate, partner, share
μετρέω, get *a measure*, give, give *a measure*, measure
μετρητάς δύο, twenty *gallons*
μετρητής, bath
μετριοπαθέω, deal *gently*
μέτριος, moderate
μετρίως, little, mediocre
μέτρον, limit, measure, moderation
μέτωπον, forehead
μετωρίζω, elate
μέχρι, about, even, even *unto*, far, nearly, point, throughout, till, until, unto, up, very, wear
μέχρι ἄν, until
μέχρι τίνος, *how* long
μέχρις, long
μέχρις οὗ, before
μή, against, avoid, cease, except, fail, fear, free, keep, lest, neither, never, no, no *more*, none, nor, nothing, nowhere, perhaps, prevent, refrain, refuse, stop, unable, without
μὴ ἀρέσκω, displease
μὴ βλέπω, unseen *thing*
μὴ γαμίζω, refrain *from marriage*
μή γε, even
μὴ γίγνομαι, God *forbid*
μὴ γίνομαι, *by no* means, far *be it*, never
μὴ δύναμαι, unable
μὴ ἐθέλω, refuse
μὴ εἷς, none
μή εἰς τὸν αἰῶνα, never
μὴ ἐσθίω, abstain
μὴ ἔτι, no *more*
μὴ ἔχω, devoid, escape, without
μὴ θέμις, unholy
μὴ θεωρέω, unseen
μὴ καθήκω, unfit *thing*
μὴ καλύω, forbid
μὴ λαμβάνω, gift
μὴ λογισμός, irrational
μὴ ὀκνέω δή, please
μὴ πάρειμι, lack
μὴ πᾶς, no
μὴ τηρέω, disobey
μή τις, no, no *one*, none, nothing
μὴ τίς, nothing
μὴ τὸ σύνολον, never
μὴ ὑπομένω, refuse
μηδαμόθεν, nowhere
μηδαμῶς, *at* all, never, no
μηδέ, either, even, neither, never, no, none, nor, nor *even*, refuse, without *even*
μηδέ τις, nothing
μηδὲ δύναμαι, unable *even*
μηδείς, any, any *one*, anything, least, no, no *anything*, no *man*, no *one*, *no* way, nobody, none, nothing, without, *without* anything
μηδέποτε, never
μηδέπω, yet
μηδέπω βλέπω, unseen
μηθέτερος, either
μηκέτι, again, *any* longer, any *more*, never *again*, no *again*, *no* longer, no *more*
μῆκος, length, long
μηκύνω, grow
μηλωτή, sheep
μήν, month, only, surely
μὴν ἡμερῶν, *whole* month
μηνίαμα, fury
μηνιάω, angry
μῆνις, anger, wrath
μηνίω, angry
μηνύω, betray, denounce, disclose, give *information*, inform, know, report, show
μήποτε, even, keep, lest, no *more*, perhaps, possible, prevent, whether *perhaps*
μήπω, yet
μήπως, lest
μηρός, thigh
μήτε, either, neither, no, nor, unable
μήτηρ, mother
μήτιγε, *how much* more
μήτρα, birth, womb
μηχανάομαι, arrange, devise, devise *a thing*, scheme *against*
μηχανή, engine *of war*, machine, machine *of war*, means, *special* harness
μηχανή ὀργανικός, engine *of war*

μηχάνημα, elaborate *setting*, *war* machine
μιαίνω, *become* defiled, corrupt, defile, pollute, stain
μιαιφονία, bloodthirstiness
μιαιφόνος, bloodthirsty, murderer
μιαρός, abominable, defile, *most* abominable, *most* defiled, pollute, vile
μιαροφαγέω, eat *defiling food*
μιαροφαγία, eat *defiling food*, profane
μίασμα, defile, defilement, pollution
μιασμός, defile, pollution
μίγμα, mixture
μικρολόγος, stingy
μικρός, brief, few, insignificant, least, little, little *one*, *little* while, long, petty, short, small, *small* number, small *thing*, tiny, weak, young
μικρύνω, *become* few, lessen
μικρῶς, small
μίλιον, mile
μίλτος, *red* paint
μιμέομαι, imitate
μίμημα, copy
μιμητής, imitator
μιμνήσκομαι, remember, remembrance
μιμνήσκω, call *to mind*, give *thought*, mindful, recall, take *notice*, think, thought
μισάνθρωπος, hater *of mankind*
μισάρετος, hater *of virtue*
μισέω, detest, hate, hateful, hatred
μισητός, detest, hate, hateful
μισθαποδοσία, retribution, reward
μισθαποδότης, reward
μίσθιος, employee, *hired* laborer, hired *man*, *hired* servant, man *whom one pays*
μισθός, gain, recompense, reward, wage
μισθόω, hire
μίσθωμα, expense
μισθωτός, hire *a laborer*, *hired* servant, hireling, mercenary
μισοξενία, hatred *of strangers*
μισοπονηρέω, *show* hatred *of crime*, *show* hatred *of evil*
μισοπονηρία, hatred *of wickedness*
μισοπόνηρος, evil-hating
μῖσος, hate
μίσυβρις, hate *insolence*
μίτρα, diadem, tiara
μνᾶ, mina, pound
μνεία, remember, remembrance, reminder
μνείαν ἔχω, remember
μνείαν ποιέω, mention, remember
μνῆμα, tomb
μνημεῖον, grave, monument, tomb
μνήμη, memory, remembrance
μνήμην ποιέω, recall
μνημονεύω, call *to remembrance*, make *mention*, remember, think
μνημόσυνον, memorial, *memorial* portion, memory, record, remembrance, reminder
μνηστεύομαι γυναῖκας, betroth
μνηστεύω, betroth
μογιλάλος, impediment *in speech*
μόγις, barely, hardly
μόδιος, bushel
μοιχαλίς, adulteress, adulterous, adultery, *unfaithful* creature
μοιχάω, commit *adultery*
μοιχεία, adultery
μοιχεύω, adultery, adultress, commit *adultery*
μοιχός, adulterer, adulterous
μολιβός, lead
μόλις, barely, difficulty, hardly, no *more than*, scarcely
μολόχη, mallow
μολύνω, defile, pollute, smear, soil, stain
μολυσμός, defilement, pollution
μομφή, complaint
μόναρχος, *only* ruler
μονή, room
μονογενής, only, *only* child, *only* son, unique
μονοήμερος, stay *but a day*
μόνον, even, nothing *except*
μόνος, alone, apart, home, live *long*, lonely, lonely *woman*, merely, one, only, *only* one, single-handed
μονοφαγία, *solitary* gormandizing
μονοφάγος, *solitary* gormandizer
μονόφθαλμος, *one* eye
μονόω, leave *all alone*
μόρα, mulberry
μόρος, death, doom, fate, means
μορφή, form, *good* appearance
μορφόω, form
μόρφωσις, embodiment, form
μόσχευμα, seedling
μοσχοποιέω, make *a calf*
μόσχος, calf, ox
μουσικός, minstrel, music, musical, *musical* instrument, musician
μοχθέω, toil
μοχθηρός, bad, grievous
μόχθος, hardship, labor, toil
μοχλός, bar, bolt
μυελός, marrow
μυέω, learn *the secret*, mystery
μυθολόγος, story-teller
μῦθος, myth, story
μυῖα, fly
μυκάομαι, roar
μυκτήρ, nostril
μυκτηρίζω, mock
μυκτηρισμός, scorn
μύλινος, millstone
μύλος, mill, millstone
μύλος ὀνικός, *great* millstone
μυρεψός, perfumer, pharmacist
μυριάς, innumerable, *many* thousands, myriad, ten *thousands*, tens *of thousands*, thousand
μυρίζω, anoint
μυρίος, countless
μύριοι, myriad
μυρισμός, ointment
μυροβρεχής, myrrh-perfumed
μύρον, myrrh, ointment, perfume
μύσος, defile, pollution
μυστήριον, mystery, secret, *secret* information, *secret* rite
μύστης, initiate
μυστικός, privately
μύστις, initiate
μυχός, *inner* chamber, recess
μυωπάζω, shortsighted
μωκός, mock
μώλωψ, bruise, stripe, welt, wound
μωμάομαι, accuse, blame, blemish, fault, find *fault*
μῶμος, blame, blemish, blot, reproach, stain
μωραίνω, *become a* fool, deem *a fool*, lose *taste*, make *foolish*
μωρία, folly
μωρολογία, *silly* talk
μωρός, fool, foolish, foolishly, foolishness, stupid

νάβλα, stringed *instrument*
ναί, even *so*, hear, indeed, surely, yea, yes
ναός, holy *of holies*, sanctuary, shrine, temple
νάρδος, nard
ναυαγέω, make *shipwreck*, shipwreck
ναύκληρος, owner *of the ship*
ναῦς, ship, vessel
ναύτης, sailor
νάφθα, naphtha
νεάζω, young
νεανίας, young *man*, youth
νεανικὴ ἡλικία, youth
νεᾶνις, daughter, maiden, young *woman*
νεανίσκος, young, young *man*, youth
νεκρός, corpse, dead, dead *man*, dead *thing*, death, enemy, man *who dies*
νεκρόω, dead, put *to death*
νέκρωσις, barrenness, death
νέμομαι, wander
νέμω, range
νεογνὸν βρέφος, baby
νεογνός, newborn
νεόκτιστος, *newly* created
νεομηνία, day *of the new moon*, *new* moon
νέος, boy, child, *first* fruit, new, young, young *man*, young *woman*
νεότης, young, youth
νεοττός, young
νεόφυτος, *recent* convert, young
νεῦμα, nod
νευρά, cord
νεῦρον, sinew
νεύω, beckon, motion
νεφέλη, cloud
νεφθαί, naphtha
νεφθαρ, nephthar
νέφος, cloud
νεφρός, heart, *inmost* feelings, mind
νεωκόρος, *temple* keeper
νεώς, sanctuary, temple
νεωστί, newly
νεωτερίζω, revolution
νεωτερικός, youthful
νή, protest
νήθω, spin
νηκτός, swim
νηπιάζω, babe
νηπιοκτόνος, slay *an infant*
νήπιος, babe, baby, child, childish, infant, young
νησίον, *small* island
νῆσος, island, isle
νηστεία, fast, hunger
νηστεύω, fast
νῆστις, hungry
νηφάλιος, temperate
νήφω, keep *sober*, sober, steady
νικάω, conquer, defeat, overcome, prevail, prevail *over*, victor, victorious, win, win *victory*
νίκη, victory
νῖκος, prize, victory
νιπτήρ, basin
νίπτω, wash
νιφετός, snow
νοερός, intelligent
νοέω, clearly, conclude, consider, judge, perceive, see, think, think *over*, understand, understanding
νόημα, design, mind, thought
νοήμων, sensible *man*
νοθεύω, adultery
νόθος, illegitimate, *illegitimate* child, insincerely
νομάς, nomad
νομή, district, fight, pasture
νομὴν ἔχω, eat *one's way*
νομίζω, consider, customary, hold, imagine, regard, suppose, think
νομικός, law, lawyer
νόμιμος, custom, law, law-abiding, lawful, lawfully, ordinance, religion
νομίμως, accordance *with law*, according *to the rules*, lawfully
νόμισμα, money
νομιστέον, *must* think, think
νομοδιδάσκαλος, teacher *of the law*
νομοθεσία, giving *of the law*, law, legislation
νομοθετέω, enact, give *law*, receive *the law*
νομοθέτης, lawgiver
νόμος, custom, district, law, legal, manner, principle
νομοφύλαξ, guardian *of the law*
νοσέω, *morbid* craving, sick
νόσος, disease, sickness
νοσσεύω, make
νοσσιά, brood, hive, home
νοσσίον, brood
νοσσός, young
νοσφίζω, keep *back*, pilfer, steal
νότος, south, *south* wind, southern
νουθεσία, admonish, instruction, warning
νουθετέω, admonish, God, heed *a warning*, instruct, warn
νουθέτησις, admonish
νουνεχῶς, wisely
νοῦς, attention, heart, mind, understanding
νυκτερίς, bat
νύκτωρ, night
νύμφη, bride, daughter-in-law
νυμφίος, bridegroom
νυμφών, *bridal* chamber, wedding, *wedding* hall
νῦν, even, henceforth, just, now, once, present, *present* case, rather, thus, time
νυνί, fact, now, present, then
νύξ, night
νὺξ οὗτος, tonight
νύσσω, nudge, pierce, prick
νυσταγμός, slumber
νυστάζω, asleep, drowsy *man*, grow *drowsy*, slumber
νυχθήμερον, night *and a day*
νωθρός, dull, slow, sluggish
νωθρότης ποδῶν, sluggish
νῶτον σκληρόν, stubbornness
νῶτος, back

ξένη γεῦσις, delicacy
ξενία, gift, gift *of welcome*, guest *room*, lodging, maintenance
ξένια, present
ξενίζω, barbarous, entertain, guest, lodge, play *the host*, strange, *strange* manner *of life*, strange *thing*, surprise
ξένιος, Friend *of Strangers*
ξενιτεία, wander
ξενοδοχέω, *show* hospitality
ξενολογέω, enlist *a mercenary*, recruit
ξένος, exile, foreign, foreigner, guest, host, mercenary, *something* strange, strange, *strange* land, stranger, unusual
ξένος γεῦσις τροφή, delicacy
ξενοτροφέω, maintain *a force of mercenaries*
ξέστης, pot
ξεστός, polish
ξηρά, dry, *dry* land
ξηραίνω, *become* rigid, cease, dry *up*, *fully* ripe, wither, wither *away*
ξηρός, dry, land, paralyze, wither
ξιφηφόρος, sword
ξίφος, sword
ξύλινος, make *of wood*, timber, tree, wood, wooden
ξύλον, beam, block, club, log, stick, stocks, timber, tree, wood
ξυράω, shave, shaven
ξυστός, colonnade, hew

ὁ, against, belong, brother, man, mother, people, son, what, whoever
ὁ ἀπό, serve
ὁ αὐτός, number
ὁ αὐτοῦ, *personal* affair
ὁ δέ, another, latter, other, partly, some
ὁ ἐκ, member
ὁ ἐκ τῆς οἰκίας, *household* servant
ὁ ἐκεῖ, bystander
ὁ ἐν, content, inhabitant
ὁ ἔξω, outsider
ὁ ἐπί, officer
ὁ ἐπὶ τοῖς κοιτῶνος, chamberlain
ὁ ἐπὶ τῶν χρειῶν, official
ὁ καθεῖς, one *by one*
ὁ κατά, opponent, story
ὁ μέν, other, partly, some
ὁ μετά, companion, company, man

ὁ παρά, army, companion, family *and friends*, man, officer, representative, say, soldier, supporter

ὁ πᾶς, universe

ὁ περί, army, associate, bodyguard, companion, company, court, household, how, man, neighborhood, offering, supporter

ὁ πιστός, faithful *one*

ὁ πρό, predecessor

ὁ πρός, relation, service

ὁ σύν, companion, follower, man

ὁ ὑπό, man

ὅ κατεργάζομαι, action

ὅ τι, what

ὃ δύναμαι, strength

ὀβελίσκος, spit

ὄγδοος, eighth, seven *other persons*

ὄγκος, weight

ὅδε, follow, such *and such*, thus

ὁδεύω, continue *on one's way*, journey

ὁδηγέω, guide, lead

ὁδηγός, guide

ὁδοιπορέω, journey, *traveling* companion

ὁδοιπορία, journey, march, *prosperous* journey

ὁδοιπόρος, wayfarer

ὁδός, conduct, course, go, highway, journey, passageway, path, road, roadside, route, street, toward, way, wayside

ὀδούς, open-mouthed, tooth

ὀδυνάω, able, anguish, anxiously, distress, grief, grieve, sorrow

ὀδύνη, agony, anguish, distress, pain, pang, sorrow

ὀδυρμός, lamentation, mourn

ὅθεν, consequently, hence, however, point, result, then, there, therefore, upon *this*, whence, where, wherefore

ὀθόνη, sheet

ὀθόνιον, *linen* cloth

ὄζος, knot

ὄζω, odor

οἱ αὐτοῦ, family

οἱ παρά, family

οἴαξ, rudder

οἶδα, regard

οἶδα, accustom, acquaint, aware, can, inform, know, know *how*, knowledge, perceive, respect, understand, understanding, witness

οἰκεῖος, belong, family, household, member *of the household*

οἰκειόω, *most* suitable

οἰκετεία, household

οἰκέτης, servant, slave

οἰκετικός, slave

οἰκέω, dwell, live

οἴκημα, cell, niche, place *of shelter*

οἴκησις, house, *where one* lives

οἰκητήριον, dwelling, home

οἰκητός, habitable, inhabit

οἰκήτωρ, dwell

οἰκία, home, house, house *to house*, household, live, lodging, temple

οἰκιακός, household

οἰκίδιον, *little* house

οἰκίζω, establish, grow

οἰκογενής, born *in one's house*

οἰκοδεσποτέω, rule *a household*

οἰκοδεσπότης, householder, master *of the house*

οἰκοδομέω, build, build *up*, builder, complete, construction, edify, encourage, erect, establish, form, fortify, house, make, raise, rebuild

οἰκοδομή, build, build *up*, edification, edify, house, structure, upbuild

οἰκοδομὴν λαμβάνω, edify

οἰκοδόμος, build, builder, house

οἰκονομέω, arrange, direct, steward

οἰκονομία, commission, office, plan, stewardship, train

οἰκονόμος, steward, treasurer, trustee

οἰκόπεδον, *ruined* house

οἶκος, house

οἶκος, dwell, family, habitation, home, house, household, palace, sanctuary, temple, treasury

οἶκος ἀντρώδης, cave

οἶκος καταπετάσματος, *inner* sanctuary

οἶκος, house

οἰκουμένη, world

οἰκουργός, domestic

οἰκτιρέω, compassion

οἰκτιρμός, compassion, mercy, sympathy

οἰκτίρμων, compassion, compassionate, merciful

οἰκτίρω, compassion, merciful, pity

οἴκτιστος, *most* pitiable

οἶκτος, lamentation, pity, wail

οἰκτρός, *most* pitiful, piteous, piteously

οἴμμοι, alas

οἰμωγή, mourn

οἰμώζω, wail

οἰνοπότης, drunkard

οἶνος, wine

οἶνος πολύς, drink

οἰνοφλυγία, drunkenness

οἰνοχόος, cupbearer

οἴομαι, conceive *an idea*, feel, imagine, suppose, think

οἷος, kind, like, such, what

οἷος τοιοῦτος, such

οἰστρηλασία, *frenzied* urge

οἶστρος, *frenzied* desire, frenzy

οἴχομαι, follow, go, go *away*, go *one's way*

οἰωνισμός, omen

οἰωνόβρωτος, bird *to pick*, food *for birds*

ὀκνέω, delay, hesitate, shrink, slow

ὀκνηρός, flag, idler, indolent, irksome, slothful

ὀκταήμερος, eighth *day*

ὀκτώ, eight

ὀκτωκαιδέκατος, eighteenth

ὄλβος, riches

ὀλεθρεύω, destroy, destroyer

ὀλέθριος, destruction, doom

ὄλεθρος, destroy, destruction, destructive, ruin

ὀλεθροφόρος, threaten *to destroy*

ὀλιγοπιστία, *little* faith

ὀλιγόπιστος, *little* faith, man *of little faith*

ὀλιγοποιέω, make *few in number*

ὀλίγος, few, few *in number*, few *men*, few *things*, light, little, *little* time, *little* while, moment, scant, short, shortly, small, *small* number, small *thing*, while

ὀλιγοστός, few, *small* company, *very* few *in number*

ὀλιγοχρόνιος, short-lived

ὀλιγόψυχος, fainthearted

ὀλιγοψυχω, fail, faint, fainthearted

ὀλιγωρέω, regard *lightly*

ὀλίγως, barely

ὀλισθαίνω, blunder, err

ὀλισθάνω, *cause to* slip, make *a slip*, plunge, slip

ὀλίσθημα, slip

ὁλκεῖον, bowl

ὁλκή, heavy, resource, weigh, weight, whole

ὀλοθρευτής, destroyer

ὀλοθρεύω, destroyer

ὁλοκαρπόομαι, burn *wholly*, offer *as a burnt offering*

ὁλοκάρπωμα, *burnt* offering

ὁλοκαύτωμα, *burnt* offering, *whole burnt* offering

ὁλοκαύτωσις, *burnt* offering

ὁλοκληρία, *perfect* health

ὁλόκληρος, complete, keep *sound*, *such* complete, unhewn

ὀλολύζω, howl

ὀλορρίζω, *utterly* destroy

ὅλος, all, all *over*, bottom, completely, full, throughout, utter, utterly, whole, wholly

ὁλοσφύρητος, hammer

ὁλοσχερῆ, full

ὁλοσχερῶς, completely

ὁλοτελής, wholly

ὀλοφύρομαι, mourn, wail

ὄλυνθος, *winter* fruit

ὅλως, actually, all

ὁμαλίζω, pave *smoothly*

ὁμαλισμός, make *level*

ὄμβρος, rain, shower, storm

ὁμείρομαι, *affectionately* desirous

ὅμηρα, hostage

ὅμηρος, hostage

ὁμιλέω, attend, converse, enjoy *company*, intimate, talk

ὁμιλία, company, party

ὁμίχλη, mist

ὄμμα, eye

ὄμνυμι, give *an oath*, promise *under oath*, swear, swear *an oath*, take *an oath*, vow

ὀμνύω, swear

ὁμοεθνεῖς, compatriot

ὁμοεθνῆ, *fellow* countryman

ὁμοεθνής, countryman, *fellow* countryman

ὁμοέθνος, *fellow* countryman

ὁμοθυμαδόν, *all* together, body, general, *one* accord, *one* impulse, one *man*, together, unison, unite

ὁμοζηλία, *common* zeal

ὁμοιοπαθέω, man *who has feelings like*

ὁμοιοπαθής, kindred, *like* nature

ὅμοιος, kind, like, likewise, look *like*, resemble, same, such

ὅμοιος τρόπος, likewise

ὁμοιότης, likeness

ὁμοιόω, *become* like, compare, like, liken, likeness, make *equal*, make *like*, paint

ὁμοίωμα, appearance, image, like, likeness, pattern

ὁμοίως, alike, equally, just, *like* manner, likewise, same *way*

ὁμοίωσις, likeness

ὁμολογέω, acknowledge, admit, agree, confess, declare, give *thanks*, grant, make *a confession*, profess, promise

ὁμολογία, acknowledge, confession

ὁμολογουμένως, admit, admittedly, confess, *most* certainly

ὁμονοέω, agree

ὁμόνοια, agreement, harmony, *one* accord

ὁμόσπονδος, loyal

ὁμότεχνος, *same* trade

ὁμοῦ, all, besides, *one* accord, *same* time, together, whole

ὁμόφρων, unity *of spirit*

ὁμόφυλος, compatriot, countryman

ὁμόψηφος, one

ὁμόψυχος, *same* mind

ὅμως, even, however, nevertheless, yet

ὃν τρόπον, how, just

ὄναγρος, wild *ass*

ὄναρ, dream

ὀνάριον, *young* ass

ὀνειδίζω, abusive, deride, rebuke, reproach, reproachful, revile, suffer *reproach*, upbraid

ὀνειδισμός, abuse, *abusive* word, desecrate, disgrace, insult, reproach, revile, shame

ὄνειδος, disgrace, reproach, shame, shameful

ὄνειρος, dream

ὀνικός, great

ὀνίνημι, benefit, profit

ὄνομα, call, fame, form, memorial, name, nature, person, renown, sake, say

ὄνομα ἔχω, call

ὀνομάζω, bear *the name*, call, name, pronounce, renowned, spread, utter *the name*

ὀνομασία, utter *the name*

ὀνομαστός, famous, notable, renowned

ὀνοματογραφία, list *of names*

ὄνος, ass, wild *ass*

ὄντως, certainly, indeed, real, really

ὄνυξ, hook, onycha

ὀξεῖα πορεία, march

ὀξέως, quickly, young

ὄξος, vinegar

ὀξύνω, sharpen

ὀξύς, intense, keen, severe, sharp, swift

ὀπή, cave, hole, opening

ὁπηνίκα, when

ὁπηνίκα ἄν, when

ὄπισθεν, after, back, behind, follow

ὀπίσω, after, against, back, behind, follow, lie *behind*, rear

ὀπίσω πορεύω, follow

ὁπλή, hoof

ὁπλίζω, arm

ὁπλοδοτέω, arm

ὁπλολογέω, collect *arms*

ὅπλον, arm, armed *man*, armor, instrument, shield, weapon

ὁπλοποιέω, arm

ὁποῖος, like, what, what *sort*

ὁπότε, when

ὅπου, above, here, since, there, when, where, whereas, wherever, while

ὅπου ἄν, wherever

ὅπου γε, since

ὅπου ἐάν, wherever

ὀπτάνομαι, appear

ὀπτασία, appear, appear *in public*, vision

ὀπτάω, roast

ὀπτός, broil

ὀπώρα, fruit

ὅπως, ask, how, make, order, purpose, tell

ὅραμα, sight, spectacle, vision

ὅρασις, appear, appearance, eye, look, see, seer, sight, vision

ὁρατός, visible

ὁράω, ah, appear, behold, consider, face, gaze, here, know, knowledge, look, must, must do, note, now, observe, perceive, see, seem, take *heed*, watch, witness

ὁράω τὸ πρόσωπον, meet

ὄργανον, harp, instrument, machine, organ, rim, *war* engine

ὀργή, anger, *overpowering* anger, rage, wrath

ὀργίζω, anger, angry, *become* angry, enrage, rage

ὀργίλος, anger, quick-tempered

ὀργυιά, fathom

ὀρέγω, aspire, crave, desire

ὀρεινή, hill, *hill* country, *mountain* district

ὀρεινός, *hill* country

ὄρεξις, appetite, desire, passion, yearn

ὀρθοποδέω, straightforward

ὀρθός, erect, sound, straight, upright

ὀρθοτομέω, *rightly* handle

ὀρθόω, straighten, upright

ὀρθρεύω, get *up early in the morning*

ὀρθρίζω, early, early *in the morning*, march, rise, rise *early*

ὀρθρινός, early *in the morning*, morning

ὄρθριος, early *in the morning*, *early* morning

ὄρθρος, dawn, daybreak, early, early *in the morning*, *early* morning, morning

ὀρθῶς, plainly, right, rightly, *very* well, well

ὁρίζω, appoint, definite, designate, determine, ordain, set, swear

ὅριον, border, coast, district, environs, frontier, land *on a border*, neighborhood, part, precinct, region, surrounding *part*, territory

ὁρισμός, ordain, *solemn* promise

ὁρκίζω, adjure, *make* swear, take *an oath*

ὁρκισμός, *appointed* time, oath

ὅρκος, oath, swear

ὁρκωμοσία, oath

ὁρμάω, hasten, rush, rush *off*

ὁρμή, attempt, *swift* pace, violence, will

ὅρμημα, attack, charge, *fierce* attack, *forced* march, violence

ὅρμος, *inner* basin

ὄρνεον, bird

ὄρνις, bird, fowl, hen

ὁροθεσία, boundary

ὅρος, see

ὄρος, height, hill, *hill* country, hillside, mount, mountain
ὄροφος, roof
ὁρόω, behold
ὀρτυγομήτρα, quail
ὀρύσσω, dig, dig *a grave*, pierce, tunnel
ὀρφανός, desolate, fatherless, orphan
ὀρχέομαι, dance
ὅς, answer, any, any *one*, because, case, how, if, moment, place, refer, same, situation, some, some *one*, state, such, there, what, whatever, when, where, wherever, whoever
ὃς ἄν, all, any, any *one*, whatever, whenever, whoever
ὃς δέ, another, another *man*, some
ὃς δ᾽ ἄν, whoever
ὃς δή ποτέ, whoever
ὃς ἐάν, everything, whatever, when, whichever, whoever
ὃς μέν, *one* case, one *man*, some
ὅς τε, namely
ὅς τις, something
ὅς τις ἄν, whatever
ὅς τις ἐάν, whatever
ὁσάκις, often
ὁσάκις ἐάν, often
ὅσιος, holy, holy *man*, holy *one*, holy *thing*, saint
ὁσιότης, holiness, integrity
ὁσιόω, make *holy*
ὅσιως, holiness
ὁσίως, holy
ὀσμή, aroma, fragrance, odor, offering, stench
ὀσμὴ εὐωδίας, fragrant
ὅσον οὐ, much *more than*
ὅσος, all, any, anything, consider, each *man*, even *to all*, ever, every, every *one*, everything, great *thing*, how, *how* many, *how* much, long, many, more, much, much *more*, only, same, what, whatever
ὅσος ἄν, whatever, wherever
ὅσος ἐάν, whatever, whoever
ὀστέον, bone, burial
ὅστις, any *one*, every *one*, since, such, whatever, whereas, whoever
ὅστις ἐάν, whoever
ὁστισοῦν, whatever
ὀστράκινος, earthen, earthenware
ὄστρακον, potsherd
ὀσφραίνομαι, smell
ὄσφρησις, sense *of smell*
ὀσφῦς, back, loin, waist
ὅταν, after, long, soon, when, whenever
ὅταν ἤδη, soon
ὅτε, long, since, when, while
ὅτι, after, because, fact, ground, how, if, mean, say, since, surely, though, why
ὅτι ἐάν, whenever
ὀτρύνω, urge
οὗ, where
οὗ ἄν, wherever
οὗ ἐάν, wherever
οὗ εἵνεκεν, because
οὗ χάριν, therefore
οὐ, before, beyond, cease, either, except, fail, instead, least, more *than*, neither, never, no, *no* longer, no *more*, no *one*, none, nor, nothing, refuse, stop, than, unable, without
οὐ ἀγνοέω, understand
οὐ ἅπαντες, none
οὐ βούλομαι, refuse, unwilling
οὐ γινώσκω ἀνήρ, *remain a* widow
οὐ δέχομαι, refuse
οὐ δοκέω, unexpected
οὐ δύναμαι, inability, unable
οὐ θέλω, unwilling
οὐ μετά, without
οὐ μετὰ εὐλογιστίας, irrational
οὐ μετατρέπω, unmoved
οὐ μή, able, all, *by no* means, certainly, never, no, no *ever*, nor, only
οὐ μή εἰς τὸν αἰῶνα, never
οὐ μὴ ἔτι, no *more*, never
οὐ μὴ πᾶς, nothing
οὐ μήποτε, never
οὐ μιμνήσκω, forget
οὐ μόνον δέ, more *than that*
οὐ πᾶν ῥῆμα, nothing
οὐ πᾶς, no, none
οὐ πᾶς λόγος, nothing
οὐ πειράω, inexperienced
οὐ πολύς, few
οὐ ποῦ, nowhere
οὐ τις, no, none, nothing, no *one*
οὐ τίς, none, nothing
οὐ τυγχάνω, extraordinary, unusual
οὐά, aha
οὐαί, alas, woe
οὐδαμός, no
οὐδαμῶς, *any* way, *by no* means, no *whatever*
οὐδέ, even, neither, never, no, no *even*, none, nor, nor *even*, without
οὐδὲ δύναμαι, cannot
οὐδὲ ἔτι, *no* longer *any*
οὐδὲ λόγος, none
οὐδὲ μή, never
οὐδείς, any, any *man*, any *one*, anything, *at* all, neither, no, no *any one*, no *anything*, no *at all*, *no* existence, no *man*, no *one*, *no* way, none, nothing
οὐδέν, anything
οὐδὲν βούλομαι, unwilling
οὐδὲν μετατρέπω, unmoved
οὐδὲν οὐδαμῶς, *no* way *whatever*
οὐδέποτε, never, no *ever*, nothing *ever*
οὐδέπω, ever, yet
οὐθείς, any, nothing
οὐθὲν ἕως τοῦ αἰῶνος, never
οὐκ ἀγαθός, evil
οὐκ ἀγνοέω, know
οὐκ αἰῶνα αἰῶνος, never *again*
οὐκ ἄξιος, unworthy
οὐκ ἀπό, without
οὐκ ἀργός, ineffective
οὐκ ἀφίημι, refuse
οὐκ ἐάω, keep
οὐκ ἐθέλω, refuse
οὐκ εἰς τὸν αἰῶνα, never
οὐκ ἐμπίμπλημι, insatiable
οὐκ ἔνι, no
οὐκ ἐσθίω, abstain
οὐκ ἔτι, *no* longer
οὐκ ἔχω, without
οὐκ ἦν ἀριθμός, innumerable
οὐκ ἦν ἴασις, incurable
οὐκ ἴδιος, foreign
οὐκ ἰσχύω, unable
οὐκ ὀρθῶς, unsoundly
οὐκέτι, again, any *after*, further, give *up*, never *again*, *no* longer, no *more*, now, refrain
οὖν, accordingly, hence, however, just, must, now, since, then, therefore, thus, when
οὔπερ, where
οὔπω, ever, ever *yet*, no, yet
οὐρά, tail
οὐραγέω, last
οὐράνιος, heaven, heavenly
οὐρανόθεν, heaven
οὐρανός, air, heaven, heavenly *thing*, sky
οὐρανὸς τοῦ οὐρανοῦ, *high* heaven
οὖς, ear, hear
οὐσία, property
οὔτε, any, either, neither, never, no, no *more*, none, nor, nothing, refuse, whether
οὔτε πώποτε, never
οὔτε τις, none
οὗτος, above, accordingly, another, dead, effect, even *so*, even *then*, ever, exactly, follow, following *thing*, here, incident, just, kind, like, likewise, match, matter, much, no *more*, only, other, present, same, same *way*, such, such *a one*, such *a thing*, then, there, thus, very, way, what, where
οὗτος καὶ οὗτος, *both* parties
οὕτω, thus
οὕτως, fashion, follow, how, just, like, likewise, such, such *an extent*, then, thus, way
οὕτως ἔχω, situation
οὕτως οὐδέ, neither
οὗτως, how
οὐχ ἕως αἰῶνος, never
οὐχ ἧττον, many
οὐχ ἱκανός, unfit
οὐχί, no
ὀφειλέτης, bind, debt, debtor, offender, owe, *under* obligation
ὀφειλή, debt, due, right
ὀφείλημα, debt, due
ὀφείλω, bind, bind *by oath*, debt, deserve, duty, incur, incur *a penalty*, indebted, need, ought, owe
ὄφελον, wish, would *that*
ὄφελος, gain, profit
ὀφθαλμοδουλία, eye-service, eyeservice
ὀφθαλμός, eye, sight
ὀφθαλμὸς πονηρός, begrudge, envy
ὀφιόδηκτος, bitten *by a serpent*
ὄφις, serpent, snake
ὄφλησις, punish
ὀφρῦς, brow
ὀχλέω, afflict, give *trouble*, trouble, tumult
ὀχλοποιέω, gather *a crowd*
ὄχλος, all *the people*, company, crowd, force, many, mob, multitude, number, people, throng, troop
ὄχλος πολύς, multitude
ὀχυρός, fortify, strong, strongly
ὀχυρόω, fortify, make *secure*, resolve
ὀχύρωμα, fortress, *strong* fortress, stronghold
ὀχυρωμάτιον, *little* stronghold
ὀχύρωσις, defense, fortification
ὀψάριον, fish
ὀψέ, after, evening
ὀψία, evening
ὀψίζω, night *finds*
ὄψιμος, late
ὄψιος, evening, late
ὄψις, appearance, eye, face, presence, see, sight
ὄψον, food, serving *of food*
ὀψοποίημα, food
ὀψώνιον, expense, pay, support, wage

παγγέωργος, *master* cultivator
παγετός, frost
παγιδεύω, entangle
παγίς, snare, trap
παγὶς θανάτου, deathtrap
παγκρατής, almighty
πάγος, ice
πάθημα, passion, suffer
παθητός, suffer
παθοκράτεια, self-control, sovereignty *over emotion*
παθοκρατέω, dominate *by emotion*
πάθος, birth-pang, emotion, passion, suffer
παιάν, *battle* song
παίγνιον, *idle* game, light
παιδαγωγός, custodian, guide
παιδάριον, boy, lad, servant, son, young *man*, *young* son
παιδεία, discipline, education, *good* manners, instruct, instruction, lesson, train
παιδείας οἶκος, school
παιδευτής, corrector, discipline, instructor, teacher, train
παιδεύω, *become* disciplined, chasten, chastise, correct, cultivate, discipline, educate, instruct, instruct *well*, learn, punish, teach, train, *well* disciplined
παιδιόθεν, childhood
παιδίον, child, daughter, lad, son
παιδίσκη, maid, maidservant, slave, slave *girl*, *woman* slave
παιδοποιέω, child
παιδοποιία, child
παίδων γόνος, child
παίζω, amuse, dance, make *merry*, play
παῖς, boy, child, childhood, lad, *male* child, *man* slave, manservant, officer, servant, slave, son
παίω, sting, strike
παλάθη, cake *of dried fruit*
πάλαι, *all* along, already, before, long, *long* ago, *long* before, old
παλαιός, *more* ancient, old, traditional
παλαιότης, old
παλαιόω, age, *become* obsolete, *become* old, grow *old*, *old* relic, treat *as obsolete*
παλαίστρα, *wrestling* arena
παλαίω, fight
πάλη, contend
παλιγγενεσία, *new* world, regeneration
πάλιν, again, another, back, fall *back*, further, likewise, now, once *more*, resume, then, turn, whereas, yet
πάλιν ἄνωθεν, anew, once *more*
πάλιν ἐξέρχομαι, return
πάλιν λέγω, repeat
παλλακή, concubine
παμβασιλεύς, king *of all*
παμμιαρός, *utterly* abominable
παμμιγής, all *sorts*, whole
παμπληθεί, *all* together
παμπληθής, tremendous
παμποίκιλος, various
παμπόνηρος, depraved *man*
πάμφυλος, *all* nations, open *to all*, people *of all nationalities*
πᾶν ῥῆμα, anything
πανάγιος, *most* holy, *most* holy *man*
πάνδεινος, *altogether* fearful, outrageous
πάνδημον, general
πανδοχεῖον, inn
πανδοχεύς, innkeeper
πανεθνί, *one* nation
πανεπίσκοπος, oversee *all*
πανήγυρις, *festal* gathering
πανηγυρισμός, festival
πανόδυρτος, lamentation
πανοικεί, *all the* household
πανοικία, *all the* household, family
πανοπλία, arm, armament, armor, armor *and weapons*, *full* armor, suit *of armor*, weapon, *whole* armor
πανοπούργευμα, crafty *device*
πανούργευμα, *clever* device
πανουργεύμα τῆς ψυχῆς, skill
πανουργία, cleverness, craftiness, cunning
πανοῦργος, clever, crafty, prudence, shrewd
πάνσοφος, *all* wise, *most* wise
πάντα παραπέμπω, take *heed of nothing*
πάντα τρόπον, thoroughly
πάντας αἰῶνας, ever
πανταχῇ, everywhere
πανταχόθεν, *every* side, everyone
πανταχοῦ, all, every, everywhere
παντελής, *all* time, full
παντελῶς, completely, quite, utterly, very, whole
παντεπόπτης, *all* seeing
παντευχία, fully
παντοδύναμος, *all* powerful
πάντοθεν, *all* sides, completely, *every* quarter, *every* side, everywhere, securely, total
παντοῖος, all *sorts*
παντοκράτωρ, almighty
πάντοτε, all, always, anybody, each, every
παντοτρόφος, *all* nourishing
παντοφαγία, *indiscriminate* eating
πάντως, all, *any* case, *by all* means, certainly, doubtless, entirely, least, *no* doubt

πάνυ, eminently, very
πανυπέρτατος, *most* high
πάππος, grandfather
παρ' ἕκαστα, *every* turn
παρ' οὐδέν, no
παρά, above, alone, along, alongside, among, *any* less, aside, because, befit, before, beside, better *than*, beyond, care, close, close *by*, contrary, deem, do, *just* outside, less, more, more *than*, next, opposition, part, past, possession, presence, provide, rather *than*, represent, send, sight, speak, spite, territory, than, throughout
παρὰ λόγον, irrational, unreasonable
παρὰ πόδας, now
παρὰ πόδας κεῖμαι, before
παρὰ ποταμόν, riverside
παρὰ φύσιν, unnatural
παραβαίνω, break, depart, disobey, transgress, transgressor, turn *aside*, unfaithful, violate
παραβάλλω, risk, touch
παραβασιλεύω, commit *treason*
παράβασις, break, transgress, transgression, violation
παραβάτης, break, transgressor
παραβιάζομαι, constrain, prevail *upon*
παραβλέπω, negligent
παραβολεύομαι, risk
παραβολή, byword, lesson, parable, proverb, saying, symbolic
παραγγελία, charge, instruction
παραγγέλλω, charge, command, give *a command*, give *charge*, give *orders*, instruction, issue *an order*, order, send *an order*
παραγίνομαι, appear, arrive, attack, come, come *before*, come *forward*, come *here*, come *out*, *come to* pass, enter, get, go, go *up*, invade, join, present, return, stand *ready*, take *a part*, visit
παράγω, arrive, bring, bring *before*, bring *forward*, lead, pass, pass *along*, pass *away*, passer-by
παράδειγμα, example
παραδειγματίζω, hold *up to contempt*, make *an example*
παραδειγματισμός, *obvious* spectacle, public *and shameful*
παράδεισος, garden, paradise, spacious *garden*
παραδέχομαι, accept, admit, receive, welcome
παραδίδωμι, arrest, betray, betrayer, bring *judgment upon*, commend, commit, consign, deal *out*, deliver, deliver *up*, entrust, give, give *over*, give *up*, hand, hand *over*, put *to death*, release, ripe, risk, surrender, trust, turn *over*
παραδοκέω, paradoxical, unbelievable, unexpected
παραδοξάζω, *act* marvelously, glorify
παράδοξος, incredible, *most* incredible, strange, strange *thing*, unexpected
παραδόξως, *beyond all* expectations
παράδοσις, tradition
παραδρομή, retinue
παραθαλάσσιος, sea, seacoast
παραθάρσυνω, encourage
παράθεσις, store, supply
παραθεωρέω, neglect
παραθήκη, entrust
παραζεύγνυμι, accompany
παραζηλόω, make *envious*, make *jealous*, provoke *to jealousy*
παραίνεσις, encouragement
παραινέω, advise, approve, bid, urge
παραιτέομαι, ask, entreat, excuse, nothing *more to do*, nothing *to do*, refuse, seek *to escape*
παραιτέω, beg *pardon*, forego, make *an excuse*
παραίτιος, help
παρακαθέζομαι, sit
παρακαθεύδω, companion
παρακαθίστημι, provide
παρακαλέω, apologize, appeal, ask, beg, beseech, call, comfort, compassion, conciliate, console, encourage, entreat, exhort, exhortation, give *encouragement*, give *instruction*, heed *an appeal*, invite, make *an appeal*, plead, urge
παρακάλυμμα, curtain
παρακαλύπτω, conceal
παρακαταθήκη, deposit
παρακατατίθημι, deposit, entrust
παράκειμαι, adjoin, along *the border*, lie, lie *about*, lie *close at hand*, lie *prostrate*, nearby, place, set *before*, urge
παρακελεύω, order
παρακλείω, put *out of the way*
παράκλησις, appeal, comfort, consolation, encouragement, exhortation, inspiration, preach
παράκλητος, advocate, counselor
παρακμάζω, marry
παρακοή, disobedience
παρακολουθέω, accompany, follow, observe, overtake
παρακομίζω, carrier, carry, take *home*
παρακούω, disobey, ignore, refuse *to listen*
παρακύπτω, look, peer, stoop *to look*
παραλαμβάνω, become, bring, imprison, learn, receive, seize *control*, succeed, take, take *along*, tradition
παραλέγομαι, coast *along*, sail *along*
παραλείπω, abandon, omit
παραλία, coastal, *coastal* country, coastland, seacoast
παράλιος, seacoast
παραλλαγή, variation
παραλλάσσω, change, perversely
παραλογίζομαι, beguile, deceive, delude
παραλογισμός, deceit, deception, trickery
παραλυτικός, paralytic, paralyze
παραλύω, paralyze, undo, weak
παραμένω, continue, endure, persevere, remain, stand, stay
παραμυθέομαι, console, encourage
παραμυθία, consolation, persuasion, relief
παραμύθιον, consolation, incentive
παραναγινώσκω, read, read *aloud*
παρανακλίνω, lay *beside*
παρανομέω, contrary *to the law*, transgress, transgress *the law*
παρανομία, break *the law*, lawlessness, transgression, violation *of the law*
παράνομος, contrary *to the law*, lawbreaker, lawless, transgression *of the law*, transgressor, unlawful, unusual, wicked *man*
παραπέμπω, disregard
παραπηδάω, leap *up*
παραπικραίνω, provoke, rebellious
παραπικρασμός, rebellion
παραπίπτω, commit *apostasy*, transgress, trespass
παραπλέω, sail *past*
παραπλήσιος, near
παραπλησίως, likewise
παράπλους, voyage
παραπομπή, escort
παραπορεύομαι, go, pass, passer-by
παραπορεύομαι διά, pass *through*
παράπτωμα, sinful, transgression, trespass
παραρρέω, drift *away*
παραρρίπτω, throw
παράσημος, figurehead, symbol
παρασκευάζω, get *ready*, prepare, provide, ready
παρασκευή, *day of* Preparation, preparation, provision, supply
παράστασις, magnificence
παράταξις, army, array, battle, *battle* array, division, force, line *of battle*
παράταξις ἰσχυρός, make *war*
παρατάσσω, fight, join *battle*, lead
παρατείνω, prolong, spread *out*
παρατηρέω, observe, watch
παρατήρησις, observe *a sign*
παρατίθημι, commend, commit, entrust, leave *in trust*, place *before*, prove, put *before*, serve *a meal*, set *before*, set *forth*, store, store *up*
παρατρέχω, pass, slip *by*
παρατυγχάνω, chance
παραυτίκα, momentary, once
παραφέρω, carry *along*, lead *away*, remove
παραφρονέω, madman
παραφρονία, madness
παράφρων, madman
παραφυάς, offshoot
παραχειμάζω, spend *the winter*, winter
παραχειμασία, winter
παραχρῆμα, direct, immediately, once, promptly, soon
παραχωρέω, hand *over*, leave
παρδάλεος, leopard-like
πάρδαλις, leopard
παρεδόξασεν, extraordinary
παρεδρεύω, serve
πάρεδρος, sit
πάρειμι, arrive, before, come, here, here *present*, moment, neglect, pass, power, present, resort, there
παρεισάγω, bring *secretly*
παρείσακτος, bring *secretly*
παρεισδύω, gain *admission secretly*
παρεισέρχομαι, come, slip
παρεισπορεύομαι, enter
παρεισφέρω, make
παρεκλείπω, exhaust
παρεκτός, except, other *thing*
παρέλκω, delay, *keep* waiting, *make* wait
παρέλκω χρόνον, delay
παρεμβάλλω, attack, begin, camp, cast *up*, encamp, enclose, fight *against*, interrupt, line *up*, muster
παρεμβάλλω ἐπί, besiege
παρεμβολή, army, barrack, camp, company, division, guard, host, post, troop
παρεμπίπτω, gain *entrance*
παρενοχλέω, annoy, trouble
πάρεξ, except
παρεπιδείκνυμι, point *out*
παρεπίδημος, exile
πάρεργος, little
παρέρχομαι, come, come *here*, disobey, disregard, escape, fail *to fulfill*, follow, go, neglect, occur, over, pass, pass *away*, past, turn *aside*, vanish
πάρεσις, pass *over*
παρέχω, bring, cause, craftsman, do, furnish, give, give *an opportunity*, grant, leave, make, offer, open, promote, provide, show, supply, take *care*, treat
παρηγορέω, console
παρηγορία, advice, comfort, exhortation
παρηκέω, disobey
παρθενία, virgin, virginity, youth
παρθένος, betroth, bride, chaste, girl, maiden, unmarried, virgin
παρίημι, droop, faint, go, overtake, remiss, slack, transgress
παρίστημι, arouse, arrive, attendant, bring *forth*, bring *into one's presence*, bystander, come, commend, fill, help, minister, present, prove, provide, send, serve, set *in array*, stand, stand *about*, stand *before*, stand *beside*, stand *near*, station, wait, yield
παροδεύω, pass
πάροδος, pass
παροικέω, live, live *among*, sojourn, stranger, visitor
παροίκησις, neighborhood
παροικία, community, exile, haunt, live *abroad*, neighbor, place *where lives*, sojourn, stay
πάροικος, alien, exile, neighbor, *resident* alien, sojourner
παροίκος, stranger
παροιμία, figure, maxim, proverb
παροιμιάζω, recount *a proverb*
πάροινος, drunkard
παροίχομαι, past
παρομοιάζω, like
παρόμοιος τοιοῦτος, such
παροξύνω, irritable, provoke
παροξυσμός, *sharp* contention, stir *up*
παρόρασις, disregard
παροράω, disregard, leave *to fate*, neglect, overlook, slight
παροργίζω, anger, angry, make *angry*, provoke *to anger*, provoke *wrath*
παροργισμός, anger
παρορμάω, arouse, influence
παροτρύνω, incite
παρουσία, arrival, before, come, presence
παροψίς, plate
παρρησία, bold, boldness, boldness *of speech*, confidence, courage, openly, outspoken, plainly
παρρησιάζομαι, bold, courage, declare *boldly*, freely, preach *boldly*, speak *boldly*, speak *out boldly*
παρωθέω, set *aside*
πᾶς, all, all *kinds*, *all* men, all *things*, always, any, any *one*, *any* other, any *part*, anything, complete, each, entire, every, every *one*, every *way*, *every* way, everyone, everything, everywhere, full, *full* payment, fully, general, great, man, *more* earnest, most, none, quite, rest, surely, total, unbroken, unfailing, utter, vast, very, well, whatever, whoever, whole
πᾶς καί, after
πᾶς ὁ, whatever, whoever
πᾶς ὅς, whatever, whoever
πᾶς ὅς τις ἐάν, whatever
πᾶς ὃς ἐάν, whatever
πᾶς ὅσος, whatever
πᾶς ὅσος ἄν, whatever
πᾶς οὐ, no *one*
πᾶς οὐδέ, no *one*
πᾶς οὗτος, such
πᾶσα σάρξ, anybody
πᾶσαι ἡμέραι, always
πάσας τὰς ἡμέρας, always, long
πάσσαλος, post, stake, *tent* peg
πάσσω, scatter
παστός, *bridal* chamber
παστοφόριον, chamber, chamber *for a priest*, chamber *of a priest*
πάσχα, *paschal* lamb, passover, *passover* lamb
πάσχω, do, endure *suffering*, experience, passion, suffer
πατάσσω, afflict, attack, batter, crush, deal, deal *a blow*, defeat, destroy, inflict, put *to death*, slay, smite, strike, strike *down*, subdue
πατέω, trample, tread, tread *down*
πατήρ, ancestor, father, *father's* house, forefather, parent, patriarch
πατριά, family, father, *father's* house, lineage
πατριάρχης, patriarch
πατρικός, father, *father's* house
πάτριος, ancestor, ancestral, family, father, native, ways *of fathers*
πατρίς, city *of one's fathers*, country, family, father, homeland, *native* land
πατροπαράδοτος, inherit *from father*
παῦλαν λαμβάνω, stop
παύω, cease, end, finish, hush, keep, *make* stop, stop
πάχνη, frost, hoarfrost
πάχος, block
παχύνω, grow *dull*
παχύς, precious, thick
πεδάω, shackle
πεδεινός, plain
πέδη, fetter, shackle
πεδήτης, prisoner
πεδινός, level
πεδίον, field, ground, land, plain
πεζεύω, go *by land*
πεζικός, infantry
πεζομαχία, *infantry* battle
πεζός, foot, foot *soldier*, infantry, man *on foot*, people *on foot*, troop *of infantry*
πειθαρχέω, listen, obedient, obey
πειθός, plausible
πείθω, confidence, confident, convince, do, feel *sure*, follow, *fully* believe, God, make

confident, obey, pay *attention*, persuade, plead, prove, put *confidence*, put *trust*, reason *for confidence*, reassure, rely, resort, satisfy, secure, seek *favor*, suffer, sure, take *advice*, trust, urge, win *over*, yield, yield *to persuasion*

πεινάω, hunger, hungry

πεῖρα, experience, test

πειράζω, attempt, examine, experience, make *trial*, put *to the test*, tempt, tempter, test, try

πεῖραν λαμβάνω, attempt, suffer

πειράομαι, try

πειρασμός, prove, temptation, test, trial

πειράω, attempt, endeavor, experience, test, try, undertake

πεισμονή, persuasion

πέλαγος, depth, sea

πελεκίζω, behead

πέλεκυς, axe

πέλμα, sole

πέλομαι, forget

πέμπτος, fifth

πέμπω, put, send

πέμπω ἀλλήλοις, exchange

πένης, poor, poor *man*

πενθερά, mother-in-law

πενθερός, father-in-law, father-in-law *and mother-in-law*

πενθέω, lament, mourn

πένθος, bereavement, grief, mourn, sorrow

πενιχρός, poor

πενταετηρικός, quadrennial

πεντάπολις, five *cities*

πέντε, five

πεντεκαιδέκατος, fifteenth

πεντήκοντα, fifty

πεντηκοντάρχος, charge *of fifties*

πεντηκοστή, Pentecost

πεποίθησις, confidence, reason *for confidence*, sure

περαιρέω, strip, strip *off*

περαιτέρω, further

πέραν, across, beyond, *other* side, over

περανθέντος,, conclude

περαντλέω, overwhelm

περάπτω, attach

πέρας, *all the* extent, end, final, finally

πέρδιξ, partridge

περί, about, account, against, around, behalf, case, celebrate, concern, concerning, deal, exchange, force, near, news, occupation, offering, out, over, regard, respect, round, sake, surround, under, upon

περὶ ἁμαρτίας, *sin* offering

περὶ γίνομαι, keep

περὶ πλημμελείας, *guilt* offering

περιαγκωνίζω, tie *one's arms*

περιάγω, accompany, go *about*, lead *about*, parade *about*, traverse

περιαιρέω, abandon, cast *off*, remove, take *away*

περιάπτω, kindle

περιάργυρος, overlay *with silver*, silver

περιαστράπτω, flash *about*, *lightning* flash, shine *about*

περιβάλλω, about, array, array *in attire*, clad, clothe, dress, encompass, involve, overcome, put, surround, wear, wrap, wrap *around*

περιβιόω, *remain* alive

περιβλέπω, look, look *around*, look *intently*, look *round*, see

περιβόητος, famous

περιβόλαιον, covering, mantle

περιβολή, about, court, dress, wear

περίβολος, area, enclosure, inside *the circuit of the city*, precinct, wall

περιγίνομαι, prevail

περίδειπνον, *funeral* feast

περιδέω, wrap

περιδιπλόω, wrap *up*

περιδύω, strip

περιεζωσμένον πρός, girdle *round*

περίειμι, alive, live

περιεκτικός, *most* comprehensive

περιελαύνω, take *away*

περιεργάζομαι, busybody, meddle

περιεργία, meddle

περίεργος, busybody, *magic* art

περιέρχομαι, gad *about*, go *about*, itinerant, make *a circuit*

περιέχω, confine, content, envelope, group *about*, include, overtake, possess, run, stand, surround

περίημι, go *about*

περίθεσις, decoration

περιζώννυμι, gird, put *upon*

περιΐστημι, avoid, stand, stand *about*, stand *around*

περικαθαίρω, weed

περικάθαρμα, refuse

περικάθημαι, besiege, continue lie *in wait*, siege

περικαθίζω, besiege,

περικαίω, inflame

περικαλύπτω, blindfold, cover

περικατάληπτος, surround

περίκειμαι, beset, bind, hang, hang *round*, wear

περικεφαλαία, helmet

περικλάω, break, break *off*

περικλύζω, wash

περικλύω, bathe

περικομπέω, ring *out around*

περικρατεῖς γίνομαι, secure

περικρατέω, control, *full* command, overcome

περικρύπτω, hide

περικυκλόω, about, gather *around*, surround

περιλακίζω, tear *all around*

περιλαμβάνω, embrace

περιλάμπω, shine *around*, shine *round*

περιλείπομαι, leave, leave *behind*

περιλείπω, remain, survive

περίλυπος, *exceedingly* sorry, grief, grief-stricken, sad, *very* sorrowful

περιλύω, abandon

περιμένω, wait

περίμετρον, circumference

πέριξ, around

περιξύω, strip *off*

περιοικέω, neighbor

περίοικος, neighbor

περιοχή, passage

περιπαθῶς, rage

περιπατέω, act, adherent, behave, command, conduct, do, follow, go, go *about*, lead *a life*, lead *the life*, live, observe, practice, prowl *around*, walk, walk *about*

περίπατον ποιέω, discuss *from every side*

περίπατος, go *about*

περιπείρω, pierce

περιπέτομαι, fly *around*

περιπίπτω, experience, fall *among*, meet, strike, suffer

περιπίπτω ἐπιτίμοις, punish

περιπλέκω, embrace, encircle, tie *up*

περιπλήσσω, smite

περιποιέω, acquire, gain, obtain, savior, spare, win

περιποίησις, keep, obtain, possession

περιπόλιον, suburb

περιρέω, fall *off*

περιρρήγνυμι, tear *off*

περισκελής, *linen* breeches

περισκυθίζω, scalp

περισπασμός, wheel *around*

περισπάω, distract

περισσεία, abundance, *rank* growth

περίσσευμα, abundance, leave *over*

περισσεύω, abound, abundance, abundantly, *act* immoderately, ample, *do* much, enough *and to spare*, exceed, excel, highly *man*, increase, lavish, leave, leave *over*, more, overflow, provide *in abundance*, surplus, well *off*

περισσός, abundantly, advantage, beyond, more, rest, superfluous

περισσότερος, excessive, great, hard, *more* convincingly, much *more*, *too* much, zealously

περισσοτέρως, abundant, all *the more*, close, extremely, far *greater*, far *more*, more, *more* earnestly, much *more*, still *more*

περισσοτέρως μᾶλλον, still *more*

περισσῶς, all *the more*, exceedingly, great, rage

περίστασις, disaster

περιστέλλω, lay *out*

περιστερά, dove, pigeon

περίστημι, hard-pressed, restore

περιστολή, robe

περιστροφή, gather *round*

περίστυλον, colonnade

περισύρω, tear *off*

περιτειχίζω, wall *all around*

περιτέμνω, circumcise, circumcision, receive *circumcision*, sever

περιτέμνω σάρκα ἀκροβυστίας, circumcise

περιτίθημι, about, bestow, erect *about*, invest, put, put *upon*, set *around*, wear

περιτομή, *after one* circumcises, circumcise, circumcision

περιτρέπω, overturn, turn

περιτρέχω, run *about*

περιφανῶς, conspicuously

περιφερής, run *around*

περιφέρω, bring, carry, carry *about*

περιφράσσω, enclose, fence, fortify, shut *on every side*

περιφρονέω, contemptuous, despise, disregard, scorn

περιφυτεύω, plant

περιχαίρω, *great* joy

περιχαλάω, flabby

περιχαρής, *great* joy

περιχέω, come *over*, overcome

περίχρυσος, gold, overlay *with gold*

περίχωρος, about, country *round about*, region, region *about*, *surrounding* country, *surrounding* region

περίψημα, offscouring, rubbish

περιψύχω, spoil

περκάζω, ripen

περπερεύομαι, boastful

πέρυσι, *last* year

πέτασος, Greek *hat*

πετεινόν, bird, *flying* creature

πέτομαι, fly

πέτρα, rock

πετροβόλος, catapult

πέτρος, stone

πετρώδης, *rocky* ground

πήγανον, rue

πηγή, fountain, hemorrhage, spring, well

πῆγμα, join

πήγνυμι, compact, drive *firmly*, fasten, freeze, pitch, set, set *up*, stick

πηδάλιον, rudder

πηδαλιουχέω, steer

πηλίκος, *how* great, large

πηλός, clay

πηλουργός, worker *in clay*

πῆξις ἀγκῶνος, *selfish* behavior

πήρα, bag

πηρόω, pierce

πῆχυς, cubit

πιάζω, arrest, capture, catch, seize, take

πιαίνω, put *fat*

πιέζω, drink, press *down*

πιθανολογία, *beguiling* speech

πικραίνω, bitter, embitter, harsh, lose *one's temper*, make *bitter*

πικρασμός, bitter

πικρία, bitterness, harsh

πικρός, bitter, bitterly, brackish, cruel, miserable, more, *more* bitter, *more* bitterly, *more* cruelly, sharp, violently

πικρῶς, bitterly

πικρῶς φέρω, enrage

πίμπλημι, come, cover, end, enough, fill, fulfil, fulness, heap, rejoice, take *one's fill*

πίμπρημι, swell *up*

πινακίς, *writing* tablet

πίναξ, dish, platter

πίνω, drink, serve

πιόνων, fat

πιπράσκω, give, sell

πίπτω, apply, *become* void, drink, end, fail, fall, fall *down*, falter, prostrate, strike, suffer, take

πίπτω ἀπό, give *up*

πίπτω βουλή, think

πίπτω ἐπὶ πρόσωπον, prostrate

πίσσα, pitch

πιστεύω, believe, believer, commit, entrust, faith, overconfident, put *trust*, trust

πιστικός, pure

πίστιν δίδωμι, pledge

πίστις, assurance, belief, confidence, confident, faith, faithfully, faithfulness, fidelity, loyalty, pledge, trust, truth

πιστός, believe, believer, believing *woman*, confidence, dependable, faith, faithful, faithful *man*, loyal *thing*, *more* faithful, promise, reliable *man*, sure, trustworthy, truthful

πιστόω, believe *firmly*, confirm, keep *faith*

πιστωθῆναι, convince

πίτυρον, bran

πλάγιος, side

πλανάω, beguile, deceive, deceiver, educate, err, go *astray*, go *on travels*, God, lead *astray*, misguide, mislead, stray, travel, wander, wander *about*, wayward, wrong

πλάνη, deceitful, delusion, error, fraud

πλανήτης, wander

πλάνος, deceitful, deceiver, impostor

πλάξ, table, tablet

πλάσμα, disposition, mold

πλάσσω, form, mold, molder, shape

πλάστιγξ, balance, scale

πλαστός, false

πλάτανος, plane *tree*

πλατεῖα, market, street, wide

πλάτος, breadth, broad, thick, wide

πλατύνω, extend, make *broad*, wide, widen

πλατύς, street

πλέγμα, braided *hair*

πλεῖον μέρος, most

πλείονα λογίζομαι, prefer

πλέκω, plait

πλεονάζω, abound, additional, extend, increase, lengthen, make *many*, over, rise, use *too many*

πλεονάκις, *many* times, often, oftentimes

πλεοναστός, *even larger* army

πλεονεκτέω, gain *an advantage over*, greedy *man*, take *advantage*, wrong

πλεονέκτης, covetous, greed, greedy

πλεονεξία, covet, covetous, covetousness, cupidity, exaction, greed, greedy

πλευρά, rib, side

πλέω, sail

πληγάς ἐπιτίθημι, beat

πληγή, beat, blow, calamity, damage, disaster, hit, plague, slaughter, strike, wound

πλῆθος, abundance, abundant, amount, army, assembly, body, brood, bundle, company, congregation, crowd, force, fulness, great, *great* army, greatness, horde, host, large, *large* troop, many, mass, mass *of people*, mob, multitude, number, number *of people*, people, populace, public, quantity, shoal, size, throng, troop, *vast* number

πληθύνω, abundance, abundant, acquire *much*, add, amass, *become* many, *cause* many, crowd, get *rich*, grant *in abundance*, grow, grow *up*, increase, increase *in number*, make *many*, many, much, multiply, prosper, put *forth all*, put *forth many*, throng

πληθύς, multitude

πλήκτης, violent

πλημμέλεια, fault, transgression, wrongdoing

πλημμέλειαν πλημμελέω, sin *greatly*

πλημμελέω, commit *an offense*, *do* wrong, make *a misstep*, offend, sin
πλημμελής, outrageous
πλήμμυρα, flood
πλήν, besides, except, however, indeed, instead, moreover, nevertheless, only, simply, than, yet
πλήρης, full
πλήρης θυμοῦ, enrage
πληροφορέω, accomplish, assure *fully*, fulfil, *fully* convince, proclaim *fully*
πληροφορία, assure, conviction, *full* assurance
πληρόω, accomplish, come *to fulness*, complete, cover, elapse, end, expire, fill, fill *up*, finish, fulfil, full, *fully* come, make *full*, make *fully known*, over, pass, perfect, preach *fully*, supply, throw
πληρόω τὰς χεῖρας, ordain
πλήρωμα, everything, fulfil, full, *full* inclusion, *full* number, fully, fulness, patch
πλήρωσις, fill
πλησιάζω, intercourse
πλησίον, before, near, nearby, neighbor, one *another*, woman *next*
πλησμονή, abundance, fill, *full* measure, indulgence, plenty
πλήσσω, sting, strike
πλίνθος, brick
πλοιάριον, boat
πλοῖον, boat, ship
πλοῖον πολεμικόν, warship
πλόκαμος, lock
πλόος, voyage
πλούσιος, rich, rich *man*, rich *one*, rich *people*
πλουσίως, richly
πλουτέω, *become* rich, bestow *riches*, enrich, gain *wealth*, grow *rich*, prosper, rich
πλουτιέω, make *rich*
πλουτίζω, *become* rich, enrich, make *rich*
πλοῦτος, abundant, rich, riches, wealth
πλύνω, wash
πλωτός, sail
πνεῦμα, air, breath, courage, life, manifestation *of the Spirit*, mind, spirit, spiritual, wind
πνευματικός, possess *a spirit*, spiritual, *spiritual* gift, *spiritual* good, *spiritual* host, spiritual *man*, *spiritual* truth, supernatural
πνευματικῶς, allegorically, spiritually
πνεύω, blow
πνέω, blow, breathe, wind
πνιγμός, choke
πνίγω, choke, drown, throat
πνικτός, strangle
πνοή, breath, wind
ποδάγρα, clamp
ποδήρης, long, *long* robe, robe
ποδὸς δάκτυλος, toe
ποθεινός, *more* desirable, *more* fervent
πόθεν, cause, how, what, whence, where, why
ποθέω, desire, long
ποιέω, about, accomplish, accord, act, adrift, appoint, attend, bear, beat, bring, bring *upon*, build, carry *out*, cause, celebrate, claim, commit, conduct, create, creator, deal, decide, defend, devise, divide, do, doer, effect, establish, exact, execute, exercise, fight, fill, follow, fulfil, fulfilment, gain, give, go, grant, guilty, hold, keep, level, live, live *according*, make, maker, mean, mint, obey, observe, offer, open, perform, pile, pitch, plan, practice, prepare, present, press, produce, provide, put, put *forth*, put *up*, raise, realize, see, set *out*, set *up*, show, spend, take, take *up*, task, treat, undertake, use, win, work, wrought, yield
ποιέω ἀκροβυστίαν, remove *mark of circumcision*
ποιέω ἀπαίτησιν, request *payment*
ποιέω ἐκδίκησιν, avenge, take *vengeance*, vindicate
ποιέω ἔκθετα, expose
ποιέω ἐκλεκτόν, choose
ποιέω κατά, obey
ποιέω μάχην, fight
ποιέω παράκλησιν, appeal
ποιέω πότον, celebrate
ποιέω σφαγάς, slaughter
ποιέω τὴν δέησιν, pray
ποιέω ὑγιῆ, heal
ποιέω φανερός, reveal
ποιέω ἀνομίαν, evildoer
ποιέω λύτρωσιν, redeem
ποιέω ὁμοῦ, join
ποίημα, create, make *a thing*, workmanship
ποίησις, fulfilment, make
ποίησις νόμου, conduct
ποιητής, doer, observe, poet
ποικιλία, *great* variety, kind, various
ποικίλος, diverse, ingenious, varied *ways*, various, vary
ποικιλτός, embroiderer
ποιμαίνω, care, govern, keep *sheep*, look *after*, rule, shepherd, tend
ποιμήν, pastor, shepherd
ποίμνη, flock
ποίμνιον, flock
ποῖος, do, execute, give, kind, way, what, what *sort*, what *thing*
πολεμέω, attack, battle, *cause to* make war, fight, fight *against*, make, make *war*, wage *war*, war
πολεμέω τὸν πόλεμον, fight
πολεμικός, military, valiant, war
πολέμιος, enemy, harmful
πολεμιστής, soldier, war, warrior
πόλεμος, attack, battle, campaign, fight, military, strife, use *in battle*, war
πολεμοτροφέω, keep *up a war*, war
πολιά, *gray* hair, *gray* haired *man*, old
πολιορκέω, besiege, besieger, cut *off supply*
πολιορκήσις, siege
πολιορκία, besiege, blockade, siege
πόλις, city, town
πόλις βασιλείας, capital
πολιτάρχης, *city* authority
πολιτεία, citizenship, commonwealth, *national* life, way *of life*, way *of living*
πολίτευμα, commonwealth, community
πολιτεύομαι, live, live *subject*, manner *of life*
πολιτεύω, adopt *a way of life*, conduct, govern, govern *a life*, observe *the law*
πολίτης, citizen, fellow, *fellow* citizen
πολλά, often
πολλαὶ μυριάδες, tens *of thousands*
πολλάκις, constant, frequent, many, *many* times, often, repeatedly
πολλαπλασίων, manifold *more*
πολλαχόθεν, many
πολλαχῶς, various *ways*
πολὺ πλέον, all *the more*, good
πολὺ σφόδρα, *huge* amount, *immense* amount, vast
πολυάνδριον, cemetery, , filled *with many spectators*
πολύγονος, give *birth to many*, prolific
πολύδακρυν, *most* tearful
πολυέλεος, *all* merciful, *very* merciful
πολυετής, prolong
πολύθρηνος, *many* sorrows
πολυκέφαλος, many-headed
πολυλογία, *many* words
πολυμερής, manifold
πολυμερῶς, *many* ways
πολύορκος, given *to swearing*, swear *many oaths*
πολυοχλία, *great* population
πολύπαις, many
πολυπειρία, *rich* experience, *wide* experience
πολύπειρος, experience, much *experience*
πολυπλάσιος, *many* times *over*
πολυπληθία, *great* multitude
πολύπλοκος, complex, ingenious, intricate
πολυποίκιλος, manifold
πολυπραγμονέω, take *trouble*
πολύς, abundance, abundant, all, ample, beyond, big, considerable, crowd, deep, eagerly, enough, especially, even *more*, exceed, excess, freely, full, fully, good, great, *great* amount, *great* body, *great* length, *great* number, greatly, hard, hearty, heavy, host, huge, large, *large* sum, late, liberally, long, loud, loudly, majority, many, many *in number*, many *men*, many *persons*, many *things*, more, *more* acceptable, more *and more people*, most, most *men*, much, much *more*, numerous, plentiful, plenty, quantity, quite, repeatedly, severe, some, strictly, strongly, terribly, than *ever*, thick, too, *too* great, utter, very, *very* great, *very great* number, *very* large, *very* many, *very* much, violent
πολὺς μᾶλλον, far
πολὺς χρόνος, long
πολύσπλαγχνος, compassionate
πολυτελής, costly, precious, *very* costly, *very* precious
πολύτιμος, costly, *great* value, *more* precious
πολυτρόπος, many *and various*, *more* diverse, *most* complex
πολυτρόπως, various *ways*
πολυφροντίς, thoughtful
πολυχρόνιος, endless, length *of time*, old, *very* long
πόμα, drink
πόμασιν, draught
πόματος, liquor
πομπεύω, march *in triumph*, walk *in procession*
πονέω, care, labor, oppress
πονηρεύω, evildoer, invent *wickedly*, rascal, *wickedly* plan
πονηρία, *act* wickedly, evil, malice, niggardliness, wicked, wicked *act*, wickedness
πονηρός, bad, base, evil, evil *one*, evil *thing*, greedy, ill, mean, miserable, *more* evil, *more* greedy, *most* wicked, niggardly, selfish, severe, sound, stingy *man*, ugly, vicious, wicked, wicked *man*, wicked *person*, wicked *thing*, wrong
πόνος, anguish, distress, labor, make, pain, suffer, toil, trouble
πόνος πονηρός, *great* misery
ποντόβροχος, drown *in the sea*
πορεία, course, go, journey, march, passage, pursuit, trample
πορείαν ποιέω, journey
πορεύομαι, come, depart, fly, follow, journey, way
πορευτός, travel, walk
πορεύω, continue *on one's way*, deal, go, go *away*, go *on a journey*, go *on one's way*, go *one's way*, go *out*, go *way*, indulge, leave, live, make *a journey*, march, proceed, return, ride *along*, rush, set, travel, walk
πορεύω ἀπό, leave
πορεύω ἐν, follow
πορεύω ὀπίσω, follow
πορεύω πρός, visit
πορεύω σύν, accompany
πορθέω, destroy, make *havoc*, plunder
πορίζω, get *money*
πορισμός, gain, means *of gain*, money-making
πορνεία, fornication, harlotry, immorality, impure, lust, unchastity
πορνεύω, commit *fornication*, immoral *man*, immorality, practice *immorality*
πόρνη, harlot, prostitute
πόρνος, commit *fornication*, fornicator, immoral, immoral *man*, immoral *person*, immorality
πόρπη, buckle
πόρρω, far, far-off, further, *great* way *off*, up
πόρρωθεν, afar, distance, far *away*
πορφύρα, purple, *purple* robe
πορφυρόπωλις, seller *of purple goods*
πορφυροῦς, purple
ποσάκις, *how many* times, *how* often
ποσαχῶς, *how much* more
πόσις, drink
πόσος, *how* great, *how* many, *how* many *things*, *how* much, measure, what
πόσος χρόνος, *how* long
ποταμός, flood, river, stream, torrent
ποταμοφόρητον ποιέω, sweep *away with the flood*
ποταπός, what, what *sort*, what *sort of person*, wonderful
ποτε καὶ ἄλλοτε, ever
ποτέ, again, *another* time, ever, former, formerly, just, last, length, never, once, *one* time, then
πότε, when
πότερος, whether
ποτήριον, cup
ποτίζω, drug, feed, give, give *drink*, give *to drink*, *make* drink, provide *drink*, water
ποτόν, drink
πότος, banquet, carouse
ποῦ, about, become, somewhere, what, where, whither
πούς, foot, hand, leg
πρᾶγμα, act, affair, business, debt, deed, do, fact, government, grievance, matter, policy, practice, *public* affair, reality, something, thing, trouble
πραγματεία, pursuit, treatment
πραγματεύομαι, trade
πραγματικός, employed *person*
πραιτώριον, *praetorian* guard, praetorium
πράκτωρ, officer
πρᾶξις, achievement, act, action, business, collection, deed, do, function, matter, plan, practice, undertaking
πρᾶος, gentle
πραότης, meekness
πρασιά, *garden* plot, group
πρᾶσις, buy, deal, sell
πράσσω, act, attempt, collect, commit, deed, do, exact, mind, obey, perform, practice, sell
πράσσω κακόν, harm
πράσσω καλῶς, prosper
πρατός, sale
πραϋπάθεια, gentleness
πραΰς, gentle, humble, lowly, meek
πραΰτης, gentleness, gently, humility, meekness, *perfect* courtesy
πρέπει, due
πρεπόντως, fittingly
πρέπω, appropriate, befit, fitting, proper
πρέρχομαι, come *out*
πρερῶ προσγράφω, *thing herein* written
πρεσβεία, embassy, mission
πρεσβεῖον, right
πρεσβευτής, envoy
πρεσβεύω, ambassador
πρέσβυς, age, ambassador, elder, envoy, old
πρεσβυτέριον, assembly *of the elders*, council *of elders*
πρεσβύτερος, age, elder, man *of old*, old, old *man*, old *woman*
πρεσβύτης, ambassador, elder, envoy, old *man*
πρεσβύτης πολυχρόνιος, age
πρεσβῦτις, elder, old *woman*
πρηνής, fall *headlong* ground, headlong
πρίζω, saw *in two*
πρίν, before, former, previously
πρὶν ἄν, before
πρὶν ἤ, before
πρῖνος, evergreen *oak*
πρίσκιλλα, Priscilla
πρίω, saw
πρίων, ridge
πρό, above, ago, before, front, precede, rather *than*, time *ago*
πρὸ ἱστορίας, preface
πρὸ καιροῦ, beforehand, *too* soon
πρὸ προσώπου, ahead, before
πρὸ τούτου, former
πρὸ τούτων τῶν ἡμερῶν, recently
πρὸ χρόνου, before
πρὸ χρόνων, ago
προάγω, advance, bring, bring *before*, bring *out*, carry *before*, come, come *forward*, former, front, go *ahead*, go *before*, lead, point, walk *ahead*
προαγωνίζομαι, *first* contestant
προαδικέω, *previously* wronged
προαίρεσις, policy

προαιρέω, choose, desire, make *up*, take
προαίρω, prefer
προαιτιάομαι, charge *already*
προακούω, hear *before*
προαλής, wilful
προαμαρτάνω, sin *before*
προαναμέλπω, sing
προαποδείκνυμι, mention *previously*
προασπίζω, protect
προαύλιον, gateway
προβαίνω, advance, go, go *further*, great, more *and more*, progress, push *ahead*
προβάλλω, come *out in leaf*, put *forward*, put *out*, tear *out*
προβασανίζω, *just* tortured
προβασκάνιον, scarecrow
προβατικός, Sheep *Gate*
πρόβατον, flock, sheep
προβιβάζω, prompt
προβλέπω, foresee
προβλής, jut *out*
προγίνομαι, former, formerly, prior
προγινώσκω, destine, foreknow, foreknowledge, know *a long time*, know *beforehand*, make *known*, make *known beforehand*
πρόγνωσις, foreknowledge
προγονικός, ancestral
πρόγονος, ancestor, father, forefather, parent
προγράφω, designate, enrol, *publicly* portray, write, write *in former days*
πρόδηλον ποιέω, exhibit
πρόδηλος, conspicuous, evident, plainly, show
πρόδηλος γίνομαι, show
προδηλόω, mention *before*
προδίδωμι, betray, give, give *up*
προδοσία, surrender
προδότης, betray, traitor, treacherous
πρόδρομος, forerunner
προεῖπον, aforementioned, aforesaid, forewarn, mention, mention *previously*, predict, say *already*, say *before*, speak *beforehand*, tell *beforehand*, utter, warn, word *already quoted*
προεῖπον ῥῆμα, prediction
προελπίζω, hope *first*
προενάρχομαι, *already* make a *beginning*, begin
προεξαποστέλλω, send *off*
προεπαγγέλλω, promise, promise *beforehand*
προέρχομαι, come *forward*, continue, get *there ahead*, go, go *ahead*, go *before*, go *far*, lead, pass, precede
προετοιμάζω, prepare, prepare *beforehand*
προευαγγελίζομαι, preach *the gospel beforehand*
προέχω, *any* better *off*
προηγέομαι, command, head, lead, leader, outdo, pre-eminent, principal *man*, take *the lead*, *under the* leadership
προηγορέω, speak
προήγορος, spokesman
προηκέω, advance
πρόθεσιν ποιέω, set *out*
πρόθεσις, aim *in life*, bread *of the presence*, God, presence, purpose, steadfast
προθεσμία, date *set*
προθυμέομαι, eager, eagerly, propose
προθυμία, eagerness, *good* will, readiness, ready
πρόθυμος, desire, eager, intent, *more* eager, willing, zealously
προθύμως, eagerly, earnest, *very* warmly, willingly
προίημι, give *over*, hurl *out*
πρόϊμος, early
προΐστημι, apply, give *aid*, manage, over, rule, set *over*, take *charge*
προΐδα, know *in advance*
προκαθηγέομαι, head
προκάθημαι, head, place *of honor*, principal *man*, rule
προκαθίζω, sit *in state*
προκακόω, afflict *previously*
προκαλέω, invite, provoke
προκαταγγέλλω, announce *beforehand*, foretell
προκαταλαμβάνω, capture, occupy, overtake, prevent, seize, seize *immediately*, seize *in advance*, take, take *by surprise*
προκαταρτίζω, arrange *in advance*
προκατασκευάζω, prepare
προκατασκιρρόομαι, inveterate
πρόκειμαι, hand, expose, open, precede, serve, set *before*, there
προκηρύσσω, preach
προκοπή, advance, progress
προκόπτω, advance, get *far*, go, go *far*, increase, lead
πρόκρημνος, *jutting* cliff
πρόκριμα, favor
προκρίνω, prefer
προκυρόω, *previously* ratified
προλαμβάνω, beforehand, go *ahead*, overtake, seize
προλέγω, tell *beforehand*, warn
προμαρτύρομαι, predict
προμαχέω, act *as a champion*
προμαχών, battlement
προμελετάω, meditate *beforehand*
προμεριμνάω, anxious *beforehand*
προμηνύω, forewarn
προνοέω, aim, attend, provide, take *care*, take *precautions*, take *thought*
πρόνοια, attention, providence, provision
προνομεύω, carry *away captive*, plunder, take *spoil*
προνομή, booty, plunder, prey
προνουμηνία, day *before the new moon*
προοδηγός, leader
προοράω, foresee, see *before*, see *previously*
προορίζω, decree, destine, predestine
προπάσχω, *already* suffered
προπάτωρ, *first* father, forefather
προπέμπω, bring, bring *on the way*, escort, give *escort*, provide, send, send *forth*, send *on one's way*, speed *on a journey*, speed *on the way*
προπετής, rash, reckless
προπίπτω, fall, lie *dead*, stretch *out*
προπομπή, escort
προπορεύομαι, go *ahead*, go *before*
προπράσσω, do *before*, *former* action
προπτύω, spit *out*
πρόπτωσις, lie *prostrate*, prostration
προράω, know *beforehand*
πρός, about, above, accordance, according, addition, against, along *toward*, among, answer, around, before, beside, besides, between, charge, check, compare, design, effect, face, give, long, make, match, meet, near, order, over, pertain, responsibility, round, suit, task, toward, unto, upon, visit, withstand
πρὸς ἀνατολάς, east
πρὸς ἑαυτούς, together
πρὸς ἐκδημίαν, out
πρὸς ἐπί, besides
πρὸς θάνατον, mortal
πρὸς κεῖμαι, near
πρὸς ὀλίγον, some
πρὸς τὰς χρείας, need
πρὸς ταῦτα, more, therefore
πρὸς τὴν ψυχὴν αὐτοῦ, congenial
πρὸς τί, why
πρὸς τὸ οὖς λαλέω, whisper
πρὸς τούτοις, moreover
πρὸς φθόνον, jealously
προσάββατον, day *before the sabbath*
προσαγγέλλω, give *information*, news *come*, report, tell, word *come*
προσαγορεύω, address, call, designate
προσάγω, advance, approach, bring, bring *before*, bring *forward*, bring *near*, bring *up*, come, go *near*, go *up*, near, offer, offering, present, provide, rally *about*, take, throw *against*, way
προσαγωγή, access
προσαίτης, beg, beggar
προσαναβαίνω, come *up*, go *up*
προσαναλέγω, tell
προσαναπαύω, find *rest*
προσαναπληρόω, fill *up*, supply
προσανατίθημι, add, confer
προσανατρέπω, even *push down*
προσαναφέρω, present, refer, tell
προσανοικοδομέω, credit
προσαξιόω, request
προσαπειλέω, threaten *further*
προσαπόλλυμι, put *to death*
προσαποστέλλω, send
προσαπωθέω, even *push away*
προσαρτίως, recently
προσβαίνω, come, reach, try *to enter*
προσβάλλω, attack, bring *upon*, join *battle*, storm
πρόσβασιν ποιέω, approach
πρόσβασις, approach, increase
προσβολή, attack, encounter
προσγελάω, smile
προσδαπανάω, spend *more*
προσδεκτός, acceptable
προσδέομαι, need
προσδέχομαι, accept, await, expect, get *back*, look, receive, reception, wait, welcome
προσδέω, add *an apology*, *become* impoverished, beggar, bind
προσδίδωμι, *also* give
προσδοκάω, cherish, expect, expectation, look, look *forward*, suspense, wait, wait *to see*
προσδοκία, anxiety, anxious, expect, expectation, forebode, suspense
προσεάω, allow *to go*
προσεγγίζω, approach
προσεδρείας, intentness
προσεδρεύω, *insistently* urge
προσεῖπον, say
προσεμβριμάομαι, add *reproach*
προσενέχω, involve
προσεξηγέομαι, relate
προσεπικατατείνω, tighten *further*
προσεπιτιμάω, even *reproach*, reproach
προσεργάζομαι, make *more*
προσέρχομαι, agree, approach, come, come *forward*, come *near*, come *up*, draw *near*, go, go *to see*, go *up*, take, visit
προσέτι, even, furthermore
προσευχή, pray, prayer
προσεύχομαι, ask *in prayer*, make *a prayer*, offer *a prayer*, pray, prayer
προσέχω, addict, attend, beware, careful, concern, devote, give *attention*, give *heed*, guard, heed, keep *watch*, listen, occupy, pay *attention*, pay *heed*, render, serve, take *care*, take *heed*, watch, watchful
προσηκέω, belong
προσηκόντως, properly
προσήκω, proper
προσηλόω, fasten, nail
προσήλυτος, convert, proselyte
προσημαίνω, aforementioned, appoint, mention *previously*
προσημειόω, sign *of approach*
πρόσθεμα, enlargement
προσθέω, addition, *do* much
προσίημι, approach, come, intruder
πρόσκαιρος, fleeting, temporal, temporary, time, transient, while
προσκαλέω, call, invite, summon
προσκαρτερέω, attend, constant, continue *steadfastly*, continue *with*, devote, frequently, ready, wait
προσκαρτέρησις, perseverance
προσκεφάλαιον, cushion, pillow
προσκήνιον, front *of tent*
προσκληρόω, join
πρόσκλησις, call
προσκλίνω, attach, join
πρόσκλισις, partiality
προσκολλάω, cleave, cling, join
πρόσκομμα, fall, injury, *make* stumble, obstacle, offense, stumble, *stumbling* block
προσκοπή, obstacle *in the way*
προσκόπτω, beat *against*, give *offense*, *make* stumble, offend, strike, stumble
προσκρούω, attack *again*, strike *against*
προσκυλίω, roll
προσκυνέω, bow *down*, bow *down in worship*, bow *in worship*, homage, honor, knee, kneel, make *obeisance*, worship, worshiper
προσκύνησις, worship
προσκυνητής, worshiper
προσκύπτω, lean *close*
προσκυρόω, adjoin
προσλαλέω, address, speak
προσλαμβάνω, eat, enlist, exaggerate, receive, take, welcome
πρόσλημψις, acceptance
προσλογίζομαι, count
προσμαρτυρέω, corroboration
προσμείγνυμι, close *at hand*
προσμειδιάω, smile
προσμένω, abide, continue, remain, *remain* faithful, stay, wait
προσνέμω, attribute
προσνοέω, catch *sight of*
πρόσοδος, access, revenue, source *of revenue*
προσοδύρομαι, lament
προσονομάζω, call
προσοράω, look
προσορμίζω, moor *to the shore*
προσοφείλω, owe
προσοχή, attention, care, diligence, give *heed*
προσοχθίζω, despise, fret, offend, provoke, vex
προσόχθισμα, offense, offensive
προσοχυρόω, strengthen *a fortification*
πρόσοψις προσώπου, presence
προσπαίζω, jest
προσπαρακαλέω, exhort
προσπάσσω, sprinkle
πρόσπεινος, hungry
προσπήγνυμι, crucify
προσπίπτω, arrive, beat *upon*, come, deliver, ensnare, fall, fall *down*, fall *down before*, message *come*, prostrate, reach, recorder, word *come*
προσποιέω, add, appear
προσπορεύομαι, approach, associate, come *forward*
προσπυρόω, inflame *still more*
προσρήσσω, break *against*
πρόσταγμα, command, commandment, commission, decree, law, order, ordinance, statute
προσταράσσω, add
προστάσσω, allot, assign, command, decree, give *command*, give *orders*, order
προστατέω, leader, protector
προστάτης, captain, governor
προστάτις, helper
προστίθημι, add, afflict, again, annex, another, bestow, continue, fully, further, gather, give *more*, give *still more*, God, heap, increase, join, lay, lengthen, make *an alliance*, more, proceed, prolong, well, yet
πρόστιμον, punishment
προστρέχω, run, run *to meet*, run *up*
προσυπομιμνήσκω, remind
προσυστέλλω, former *limited*
προσυψόω, build *still higher*
προσφάγιον, fish
πρόσφατος, new, new *one*
προσφάτως, lately, recently
προσφερής, offer
προσφέρω, apply, bring, bring *before*, declare, devote, eat, exert, get *near*, hold, make, make *an offering*, offer, offer *a sacrifice*, offer *up*, offering, present, take, treat, use
προσφιλής, beloved, lovely
προσφορά, oblation, offer *in sacrifice*, offering

προσφωνέω, address, call, make *a report*, send *directions*, speak

προσχράω, put *in execution*

πρόσχυσις, sprinkle

προσχωρέω, side

προσψαύω, touch

προσωθέω, push

προσωπεῖον, mask

προσωπολημπτέω, *show* partiality

προσωπολήμπτης, partiality

προσωποληψία, partiality

πρόσωπον, air, appeal, appearance, approach, before, countenance, expression, eye, face, face *to face*, favor, front, *full* view, look, *man's* position, partiality, people, person, position, presence, sight, sight, such, surface

πρόσωπον λαμβάνω, show

προτάσσω, ordain

προτείνω, extend, hold *up*, outstretched, stretch *forth*, stretch *out*, tie *up*

πρότερον, first, former, formerly, go, time *past*, while *before*

πρότερος, before, first, former, former *one*, go *before*, *one* time, past

προτίθημι, intend, place *before*, propose, put *forward*, set *forth*, set *out*

προτιμάω, honor *above other*, prefer

προτομή, head

προτρέπω, encourage, exhort, impel, urge

προτρέχω, run, run *ahead*

προτρέχω τάχιον, outrun

προϋπάρχω, before, previously

προϋποτάσσομαι, issue *previously*

προϋφίστημι, stand *before*

προφαίνομαι, appear

προφανής, openly

πρόφασις, cloak, excuse, pretense, pretext, *under* pretense

προφέρω, bring *out*, declare, maintain, produce, remonstrate

προφητεία, prophecy, prophesy, *prophetic* power, *prophetic* utterance

προφητεύω, prophecy, prophesy, prophet

προφήτης, prophet

προφητικός, prophetic

προφῆτις, prophetess

προφθάνω, *act* first, forestall, get *ahead*, speak *first*

προφυλακή, keep *watch*, outpost, patrol

προχαλάω, here

προχειρίζω, appoint, choose

προχειροτονέω, choose

πρύμνα, stern

πρύτανις, rule

πρωΐ, early, early *in the morning*, morning

πρωΐα, day *break*, daybreak, morning

πρωΐθεν, *early* morning, morning

πρωϊνός, morning

πρώϊος, *early* morning

πρωταγωνιστής, *chief* warrior, defender

πρώταρχος, chief

πρωτεύω, *high* position, lead, preeminent

πρωτογένημα, first, *first* fruit

πρωτόγονος, *first-born* son

πρωτοκαθεδρία, *good* seat

πρωτοκλισία, place *of honor*

πρωτοκλίσιον, coronation

πρωτοκουρά, *first* shearing

πρῶτον, begin, first

πρωτόπλαστος, *first* formed

πρῶτος, ahead, before, chief, chief *man*, early, first, first *man*, foremost, former, former *one*, former *thing*, good, lead, leader, leading *man*, once, outer, previously, principal *man*, superior

πρωτοστάτης, ringleader

πρωτοτόκια, birthright

πρωτότοκος, first-born

πρώτως, *first* time

πταίω, check, fail, fall, make *a mistake*, stumble

πτέρνα, heel

πτερύγιον, pinnacle

πτέρυξ, wing

πτηνόν, bird

πτηξάτω, cower *in fear*

πτήσσω, cower, terrify

πτοέω, afraid, startle, terrify, tremble

πτόη, terror

πτύον, *winnowing* fork

πτύρω, frighten

πτύσμα, spittle

πτύσσω, close

πτύω, spit

πτῶμα, body, catastrophe, corpse, *dead* body, fall, ruin

πτῶσις, destruction, downfall, fall, lie *prostrate*, ruin

πτωχεία, misery, poverty

πτωχεύω, *become* poor

πτωχός, beggar, beggarly, poor, poor *man*

πύθων, divination

πυκνός, continuous, frequent, frequently, intense, *more* frequent, *more* often, often, solid

πυκτεύω, box

πύλη, gate, power

πυλών, gate, gateway, porch

πυνθάνομαι, ask, demand *to know*, inquire, learn, tell

πῦρ, burn, fiery, fire, flame

πυρά, fire, flame

πυραμίς, pyramid

πύργος, fire, tower

πυρεῖον, censer

πυρέσσω, sick *with a fever*

πυρετός, fever

πυρίζω, burn

πύρινος, color *of fire* fire

πυριφλεγής, burn *with fire*, *flaming* fire

πυροβόλος, throw *fire*

πυρόπνους, fire-breathing

πυρός, wheat

πυρόω, aflame, burn, fire, flame, flush, heat *in the fire*, indignant, inflame, kindle, refine, strike *fire out*, try *with fire*

πύρπνοος, fiery

πυρπολέω, consume

πυρράζω, red

πυρρός, *bright* red, red

πυρώδης, fiery

πύρωσις, burn, *fiery* ordeal

πώγων, beard

πωλέω, dealer, sell

πῶλος, colt

πώποτε, ever, ever *yet*, never

πώποτε οὐκ, nothing *ever*

πωρόω, harden

πώρωσις, harden, hardness

πῶς, how, perhaps, possible, somehow, way, what, why

πῶς μᾶλλον, great

ῥαββί, master, rabbi

ῥαββουνί, master

ῥαβδίζω, beat *with a rod*

ῥάβδος, club, rod, scepter, staff, stick

ῥαβδοῦχος, police

ῥάκος, cloth, rag

ῥάμνος, *thorn* bush

ῥανίς, drop

ῥαντίζω, sprinkle

ῥαντισμός, sprinkle

ῥαπίζω, slap, strike

ῥάπισμα, blow

ῥάσσω, break

ῥαφίς, needle

ῥάχις, trunk

ῥέδη, chariot

ῥεμβασμός, rove

ῥέμβομαι, wander

ῥεῦμα, stream

ῥέω, current, flow

ῥῆγμα, ruin

ῥήγνυμι, attack, break *forth*, burst, dash, *make* burst, tear

ῥῆμα, ascription, charge, command, message, order, preach, report, say, saying, statement, take *place*, thing, word

ῥῆμα τοῦ στόματος, order

ῥήσσω, dash *down*

ῥήτωρ, spokesman

ῥητῶς, expressly

ῥίζα, foot, root, stock

ῥίζα καὶ πιότης, richness

ῥιζόω, root, take *root*

ῥιπή, twinkle

ῥιπίζω, toss

ῥίπτω, cast, cast *down*, cast *out*, fling, helpless, hurl, hurl *down*, let *out*, lie, lie *about*, lie *prostrate*, prostrate, put, throw, throw *away*, throw *down*, throw *out*, wave

ῥίπτω ἐμαυτόν, prostrate

ῥίς, nostril

ῥόδον, rose

ῥόδου κάλυξ, rosebud

ῥοδοφόρον, rose-bearing

ῥοΐσκος, pomegranate

ῥοιζηδόν, *loud* noise

ῥοῖζος, *rushing* flight, *rushing* sound

ῥομφαία, sword

ῥοπή, instant, moment, tip *the scale*

ῥύδη, furiously

ῥυθμός, rhythm

ῥύμη, lane, street

ῥύομαι, deliver, deliverer, flow *away*, rescue, rescuer, save

ῥυπαίνω, filthy

ῥυπαρία, filthiness

ῥυπαρός, filthy, shabby

ῥύπος, dirt

ῥύσις, deliverance, flow

ῥύστης, deliverer

ῥυτίς, wrinkle

ῥωμαλέος, stalwart

ῥώμη, strength, strong

ῥώννυμι, farewell, *good* health, well

σαβαχθανι, sabachthani

σαβαώθ, host

σαββατίζω, keep *sabbath*

σαββατισμός, *sabbath* rest

σάββατον, sabbath, *sabbatical* year, week

σαγήνη, net

σαθρός, *more* fragile

σαίνω, move

σάκκος, sackcloth

σαλεύω, chafe, move, shake, shake *together*, stir *up*, totter, tremble

σάλος, unrest, wave

σάλπιγξ, bugle, sound *of a trumpet*, trumpet, *trumpet* call

σαλπίζω, blow, blow *a trumpet*, sound *a trumpet*, sound *a trumpet call*, sound *on a trumpet*, trumpet *sound*

σαλπιστής, trumpeter

σανδάλιον, sandal

σανίδωμα, deck

σανίς, plank

σαπρία, decay

σαπρός, bad, evil

σάπφιρος, sapphire

σαργάνη, basket

σάρδιον, carnelian

σαρδόνυξ, onyx

σαρκικός, earthly, flesh, material, *material* benefit, worldly

σάρκινος, *bodily* descent, carnal, human, man *of the flesh*, mortal

σαρκοφαγέω, eat *meat*

σαρκοφαγία, eat *meat*

σάρξ, bodily, body, condition, earthly, *fellow* Jew, flesh, human, *human* being, *living* being, lust, mankind, meat, muscle, natural, race, sensuous, world, worldly, *worldly* fashion, worldly *man*, *worldly* standard, worldly *thing*

σαρόω, sweep

σατανᾶς, adversary

σάτον, measure

σατραπεία, province, satrapy

σατράπης, governor, satrap

σαφής, clear, clearly, distinct, fact, *more* clearly

σαφῶς, fully

σβέννυμι, extinguish, go *out*, put *out*, quench

σβεστικός, fire-quenching

σεαυτοῦ, self

σεβάζομαι, worship

σέβασμα, object *of worship*, object *one worships*, worship

σεβαστός, emperor

σέβω, devout, devout *person*, revere, worship, worshiper

σειρήνιος, siren

σεῖσμα, shake

σεισμός, earthquake, storm

σείω, quake, shake, stir, tremble

σελήνη, moon

σεληνιάζομαι, epileptic

σεμίδαλις, *cereal* offering, *fine* flour, flour

σεμνολογέω, praise

σεμνός, august, holy, honorable, *most* holy, revere, serious, venerable

σεμνότης, gravity, respectful, sanctity

σεμνῶς, reverently

σηκός, precinct

σημαίνω, command, foretell, indicate, make *known*, report, show, sound, tell

σημασία, *battle* call, signal

σημεῖον, mark, portent, sign

σημειόω, note

σήμερον, day, present, today, very

σήπη, decay

σήπω, decay, rot

σής, moth

σητόβρωτος, moth-eaten

σθένος, power

σθένω, strong *enough*

σιαγών, cheek

σιβύνη, *hunting* spear

σιγάω, finish *speaking*, keep *secret*, keep *silence*, keep *silent*, silent, still, stop *speaking*

σιγή, hush, silence

σιγηρός, silent

σιδηρόδεσμος, *iron* bond

σίδηρος, iron, sword

σιδηροῦς, iron

σικάριος, assassin

σίκερα, *strong* drink

σίκλος, shekel

σικυήρατον, *cucumber* bed

σιμικίνθιον, apron

σίναπι, mustard *seed*

σινδών, *linen* cloth, *linen* shroud

σινιάζω, sift

σιρικός, silk

σιρός, pit

σιτέομαι, live *on*

σιτευτός, fatted

σιτία, grain

σιτιστός, fat *calf*

σιτοβολών, storehouse

σιτομέτριον, portion *of food*

σῖτος, grain, wheat

σιωπάω, cease *speaking*, hold *one's tongue*, keep *silent*, mute, peace, silent

σιωπή, silence

σκανδαλίζω, cause *of falling*, *cause to* fall, *cause to* sin, fall *away*, give *offense*, *make* fall, offend, stumble, take *offense*, trip

σκάνδαλον, barricade, blot, cause *for stumbling*, cause *of sin*, difficulty, hindrance, hindrance *in the way*, *make* fall, *make* stumble, offense, pitfall, snare, *stumbling* block, temptation, temptation *to sin*, trap
σκάπτω, dig
σκάφη, boat, bowl
σκάφος, boat
σκέλος, leg
σκεπάζω, cover, find *protection*, protect, shelter
σκέπασμα, clothing
σκεπαστής, protector
σκέπη, help, protection, shade
σκέπης, aid, cover, shelter
σκευάζω, prepare
σκευή, armor, goods, pot, tackle
σκεῦος, anything, armor, article, bowl, dish, gear, goods, instrument, means, *military* equipment, object, sex, symbol, thing, utensil, vessel, wife
σκεῦος πολεμικόν, weapon
σκεῦός τις, something
σκηνή, booth, dwelling, habitation, tabernacle, tent
σκηνοπηγία, booth, feast *of booths*, tabernacle
σκηνοποιός, tentmaker
σκῆνος, tent
σκηνόω, dwell, shelter
σκήνωμα, body, dwelling *place*, feast *of booths*, habitation, tabernacle, tent, tent *to tent*
σκήνωσις, habitation
σκῆπτρον, scepter
σκιά, protection, shade, shadow
σκιαγράφος, painter
σκιάζω, overshadow, shade
σκιρτάω, leap, leap *for joy*
σκληροκαρδία, hardness *of heart*, stubbornness
σκληρός, cruel, cruel *thing*, hard, harsh *thing*, hurt, severely, strong, stubborn, terrible, *very* severely
σκληρότης, hard
σκληροτράχηλος, stiff-necked, stiff-necked *person*
σκληρύνω, *become* stubborn, harden, press *heavily*, stiffen, stubborn
σκνίψ, gnat
σκολιός, crooked, overbearing, perverse, writhe
σκόλοψ, thorn
σκοπεύω, watch
σκοπέω, careful, look, mark, see, take *note*
σκοπή, watchtower
σκοπιά, watch
σκοπός, goal, look, target, view, watchman
σκορακισμός, surliness
σκορπίδιον, machine *to shoot arrows*
σκορπίζω, absent, dismiss, disperse, drive *out*, scatter, scatter *abroad*
σκορπίος, scorpion
σκοτεινός, dark, darkness, full *of darkness*
σκοτία, dark, darkness
σκοτίζω, darken, darkness
σκότος, darkness
σκοτόω, darken, darkness
σκυβαλίζω, treat *contemptuously*
σκύβαλον, filth, refuse
σκυθρωπός, dismal, gloomy, look *sad*, sullenly
σκυλεία, plunder
σκυλεύω, despoil, plunder, sack, take *as booty*
σκυλεύω τὰ σκῦλα, plunder
σκύλλω, harass, trouble
σκυλμός, *harsh* treatment
σκῦλον, booty, goods, plunder, spoil
σκύμνος, lion *cub*
σκωληκόβρωτος, eaten *by worm*
σκώληξ, worm
σμαράγδινος, emerald
σμάραγδος, emerald
σμῆγμα, ointment
σμικρύνω, diminish, stint
σμύρνα, myrrh
σμυρνίζω, mingle *with myrrh*
σορός, bier
σουδάριον, cloth, handkerchief, napkin
σοφία, wisdom, wise
σοφίζω, *become* skilled, *become* wise, *cleverly* devise, display *cleverness*, display *wisdom*, instruct, make *a display of wisdom*, skilful, skilled *man*
σοφός, sage, skilled, wise, wise *man*, wisely
σπαίρω, scatter
σπανίζω, *almost* give *out*
σπάνις, lack
σπαράσσω, convulse, tear
σπάργανον, *swaddling* cloth
σπαργανόω, wrap *in swaddling cloths*
σπασμός, drawn
σπαταλάω, live *in pleasure*, reveler, self-indulgent
σπάω, breathe, draw, drawn
σπεῖρα, band *of soldiers*, battalion, cohort, company, division, sow, sower
σπειρηδόν, company, division
σπείρω, beget, sow, sower
σπεκουλάτωρ, soldier *of the guard*
σπένδω, pour *a libation*, pour *as a libation*, pour *out as an offering*, sacrifice
σπέρμα, child, descend, descendant, family, line, nature, offspring, posterity, race, seed, son
σπερμολόγος, babbler
σπεύδω, haste, hasten, hasty, hurry, make *haste*, once, press, promptly, quick, swift, take *quickly*, zealous
σπήλαιον, cave, den
σπιλάς, blemish
σπίλος, blot, spot
σπιλόω, spot, stain
σπινθήρ, spark, sparkling
σπλαγχνίζομαι, compassion, move *with pity*, *out of* pity, pity
σπλαγχνίζω, *make* partake *of a sacrifice*
σπλαγχνισμός, eat *of a sacrifice*, partake *of the sacrifice*, sacrifice
σπλάγχνον, affection, body, bowels, compassion, entrails, feel, heart, inmost *part*, tender, *very* heart
σπλάγχνον οἰκτιρμοῦ, compassion
σπλαγχνοφάγος, *sacrificial* feasting
σπόγγος, sponge
σποδός, ash
σποδόω, put *ashes*
σπονδεῖον, cup, cup *for drink offerings*
σπονδή, *drink* offering, libation
σπόνδυλος, vertebra
σπορά, grain, seed
σπόριμος, grainfield
σπόρος, grain, resource, seed
σπουδάζω, do *one's best*, eager, endeavor *eagerly*, hurry, quickly, see, strive, zealous
σπουδαῖος, earnest, full, *more* earnest, *very* earnest
σπουδαιότης, excellence
σπουδαίως, do *one's best*, eagerly, earnestly, *more* eager
σπουδή, *earnest* care, earnestness, effort, haste, heat, pain, zeal
σπουδὴν ποιέω, eager
σπυρίς, basket
σταγών, drop
στάδιοι δύο, quarter *of a mile*
στάδιοι ἐννέα, more *than a mile*
στάδιον, furlong, league, race, stadium
σταδίους εἴκοσι πέντε, three *miles*
σταδίους ἑξήκοντα, seven *miles*
σταδίων δεκαπέντε, two *miles*
σταθμίον, weight
σταθμός, balance, scale, weight
στακτή, stacte
σταλαγμός, drip
στάμνος, urn
στασιάζω, rebel, revolt, stir *up sedition*
στασιαστής, rebel
στάσιμος, stately
στάσις, agreement, dissension, insurrection, place, posture, riot, stand
στατήρ, shekel
σταυρός, cross, crucify
σταυρόω, crucify, hang
σταφυλή, grape
στάχυς, ear, head *of grain*
στέαρ, fat
στέγη, roof
στέγω, bear, endure, keep
στεῖρα, barren, barren *one*, barren *woman*
στειρόω, barren
στέλεχος, trunk
στέλλω, array, depress, go, intend, keep *away*, make, obtain, prepare
στέμμα, garland
στεναγμός, groan, sigh
στενάζω, groan, grumble, sadly, sigh
στενός, anguish, hem, narrow
στενότης, narrowness
στενοχωρέω, crush, gasp, restrict
στενοχωρία, anguish, calamity, difficulty, distress, tribulation, want
στέργω, love
στερεός, firm, solid
στερεόω, confirm, establish, fortify, heavily, keep *strict*, make *strong*, press, strengthen
στερέω, bereave, deprive, lack, withhold
στερέωμα, firmament, firmness, strength, stronghold
στερέωσις, obstinacy
στέρνον, heart
στεφανηφορέω, crown
στέφανος, crown, *crown* levy, *crown* tax, garland, wreath
στεφανόω, award, crown, give *a crown*
στέφος, garland
στέφω, crown
στῆθος, breast
στήκω, stand, stand *fast*, stand *firm*
στήλη, pillar, stone
στῆρ, fat
στήριγμα, strengthen, support
στηριγμός, stability, support
στηρίζω, *become* strong, convince, establish, *firmly* fix, *firmly* set, fix, keep *stable*, lean, set, stand *firm*, steadfast, steady, strengthen, support
στιβάς, *leafy* branch
στίγμα, mark
στιγμή, moment
στίλβω, ablaze, glisten, glitter, shine
στιππύον, tow
στοά, portico
στοιχεῖον, element, elemental *spirit*, principle
στοιχείωσις, element
στοιχέω, follow, hold *true*, live, walk
στολή, array, clothes, clothing, garment, *long* robe, mourn, robe
στολὴ ἔχω, clad
στολίζω, array *in one's garments*, division, dress, wear
στολισμός, attire
στόλος, fleet
στόμα, edge, evidence, face, lip, mouth, opinion, sight, speech, utterance, voice, word
στόμα λαλέω, loud-mouthed
στόμαχος, stomach
στοργή, affection, love
στοχάζομαι, aim, aim *to know*, investigate, regard
στραγγαλόομαι, strangle
στρατεία, battle, warfare
στράτευμα, army, soldier, strategy, troop
στρατεύω, carry *on a campaign*, carry *on war*, fight, march, serve *as soldier*, serve *in army*, soldier, soldier *on service*, wage *war*, wage *warfare*, war
στρατηγέω, commander, outwit
στρατήγημα, stratagem
στρατηγός, captain, commander, general, governor, magistrate, officer
στρατιά, army, force, host
στρατιώτης, soldier
στρατιῶτις, soldier
στρατολογέω, enlist
στρατοπεδεία, camp
στρατοπεδεύω, encamp, make *an expedition*
στρατόπεδον, army, camp
στρατός, army, *military* force
στρέβλη, perverse, rack, racking
στρεβλόω, torment, torture, torture *on wheel*, twist
στρεβλωτήριον, rack
στρεπτός, tangle
στρέφω, bring *back*, change, make *the circuit*, turn, turn *round*
στρηνιάω, play *the wanton*, wanton
στρῆνος, wantonness
στρουθίον, sparrow
στροφή, subtlety, turn
στρόφος, colic
στρωμνή, bed
στρώννυμι, spread
στρωννύω, furnish, make *a bed*, spread
στυγέω, abhorrence, hate
στυγητός, hated *by a man*
στυγνάζω, countenance *fall*, threaten
στυγνός, hateful
στῦλος, column, pillar, post
συγγελάω, laugh
συγγένεια, kindred, kinship
συγγενής, kin, kindred, kinsfolk, kinsman, officer, official, relative
συγγενίς, kinswoman
συγγίνομαι, embrace, possess
συγγινώσκω, *become* aware, excuse
συγγνώμη, concession, forbearance, indulgent
συγγνωμονέω, excuse
συγγνωστός, excuse, pardon
συγγραφεύς, compiler
συγγραφή, contract, document
συγγράφω, write
συγγυμνασία, experience
συγκάθημαι, sit
συγκαθίζω, begin *one's session*, *make* sit, sit, sit *down together*
συγκακοπαθέω, share *in suffering*
συγκακουχέομαι, ill-treatment
συγκαλέω, call *together*
συγκαλύπτω, cover *up*, hide
συγκάμπτω, bend, humble
συγκαταβαίνω, come *down*, descend, go *down*
συγκαταγηρασκω, grow *old together*
συγκατάθεσις, agreement, God
συγκατατίθημι, consent, give *consent*
συγκαταψηφίζομαι, enrol
συγκεῖμαι, hold *together*
συγκεντέω, put *to the sword*, stab
συγκεράννυμι, compose, meet, mix
συγκεραυνόω, strike *down*
συγκινέω, stir *up*
συγκλάω, crush
συγκλεισμός, siege
συγκλείω, close, consign, enclose, hem, keep *under restraint*, oblige, shut, shut *up*, store *up*, withstand *a siege*
συγκληρονομέω, share
συγκληρονόμος, *fellow* heir, heir, *joint* heirs
συγκλύζω, overwhelm
συγκοινωνέω, share, take *part*
συγκοινωνός, partaker, share
συγκολλάω, glue *together*
συγκομίζω, bury
συγκόπτω, put *to death*
σύγκριμα, concert, decision, decree
συγκρίνω, compare, interpret, judge, match *strength*

σύγκρισις, comparison

συγκρουσμός, clank

συγκρύπτω, bend *over*, go *into hiding*, hide

συγκτίζω, create

συγκύπτω, bow *down*, cringe

συγκυρία, chance

συγκυρόω, border

συγχαίρω, rejoice, rejoice *together*

συγχέω, bewilder, confound, confuse, confusion, dismay, perplex, stir *up*, trouble

συγχράομαι, deal

συγχρονίζω, stay *for some time*

σύγχυσις, confusion

συγχωρέω, agree, allow, grant

συγχωρητέον, allow

συζάω, live, live *together*

συζεύγνυμι, husband, join *together*

συζητέω, argue, discuss, discuss *together*, dispute, dispute *with one another*, question

συζητητής, debater

σύζυγος, yokefellow

συζώννυμι, gird

συζωοποιέω, make *alive together*

συκάμινος, sycamine *tree*

συκῆ, fig *tree*

συκομορέα, sycamore *tree*

σῦκον, fig

συκοφαντέω, defraud, *false* accusation

συλαγωγέω, make *a prey*

συλάω, plunder, rob

συλλαλέω, confer, say, talk

συλλαμβάνω, arrest, capture, conceive, help, seize, shut *up*, take, take *into custody*

συλλέγω, assemble, gather, gather *together*, sort

συλλογίζομαι, discuss

συλλογισμός, reckon *up*

συλλοχάω, muster

συλλυπέω, grieve

συλλύω, reach *an agreement*, settle

συμβαίνω, actually, befall, come, come *about*, happen, result, show, turn *out*

συμβάλλω, attack, bring *good*, compare, confer, encounter, help, join *battle*, meet, ponder

συμβασιλεύω, reign, share *the rule*

συμβιβάζω, conclude, instruct, knit *together*, prompt, prove

συμβιόω, live

συμβίωσις, life, live

συμβιωτής, companion

συμβολή, expense

συμβολοκοπέω, feast, revel

σύμβολον, sign, token

συμβουλευτής, counselor

συμβουλεύω, advise, consult, counsel, counselor, give *counsel*, plot, take *counsel together*

συμβουλία, advice, counsel, matter *of counsel*

συμβούλιον, consultation, council, counsel

σύμβουλος, advise, adviser, advocate, counsel, counselor

συμβραβεύω, serve *with as judge*

συμμαθητής, *fellow* disciple

συμμαρτυρέω, *also* bear witness, bear *witness*

συμμαχέω, act *as an ally*, ally, fight, fight *at one's side*, fight *on the side*, help, make *an alliance*, take *a part*

συμμαχία, alliance, alliance *in battle*, ally

συμμάχομαι, ally

σύμμαχος, ally, fight *on the side*

συμμείγνυμι, join, meet, meet *in battle*

συμμερίζω, share

συμμετέχω, share

συμμέτοχος, associate, partaker

συμμιαίνω, defile

σύμμικτος, *combined* forces

συμμιμητής, imitate

συμμίσγω, conference, engage *in battle*, join

συμμισοπονηρέω, share *hatred of crime*

συμμορφίζω, *become* like

σύμμορφος, conform, like

συμπάθεια, feel *emotion*, suffer, sympathy

συμπαθέω, compassion, *show* sympathy, sympathize

συμπαθής, *deep* sympathy, *more* sympathetic, sympathy

συμπαίζω, play

συμπαραγίνομαι, assemble

συμπαρακαλέω, *mutually* encourage

συμπαραλαμβάνω, bring, take, take *along*

συμπαραμένω, live

συμπάρειμι, present

σύμπας, whole

συμπάσχω, suffer, suffer *together*

συμπείθω, convince, persuade

συμπέμπω, send

συμπεριλαμβάνω, embrace

συμπεριφέρω, accommodate, live *in harmony*, treat

συμπίνω, drink

συμπίπτω, fall

συμπίπτω τὸ πρόσωπον, look *downcast*

συμπληρόω, come, draw *near*, fill

συμπλήρωσις, completion

συμπνίγω, choke, press *round*

συμποιέω, help

συμπολίτης, *fellow* citizen

συμπονέω, help

συμπορεύομαι, accompany, attend, gather, go

συμποσία, banquet, feast, festival

συμπόσιον, banquet, *banquet* hall, company, feast, guest, party

συμπότης, *drinking* companion

συμπραγματεύομαι, business *associate*

συμπρεσβύτερος, *fellow* elder

σύμπτωμα, trouble

συμφερόντως, advantage

συμφέρω, advantage, beneficial, better, bring *together*, *common* good, expedient, gain, good, helpful, profitable, use

συμφεύγω, flee, take *refuge*

σύμφημι, agree

συμφλογίζω, burn *together*

συμφορά, calamity, disaster, infliction, injury, misfortune

σύμφορος, advantage, benefit, welfare

συμφρονέω, conspire

συμφρύγω, inflame

συμφυλέτης, countryman

συμφύρω, *become* involved

σύμφυτος, innate, unite

συμφύω, full, grow

συμφωνέω, agree, agree *together*, harmony, match

συμφώνησις, accord

συμφωνία, concord, music

σύμφωνος, agreement, man *in harmony*

συμφώνως, harmony

συμψηφίζω, count

σύμψυχος, *full* accord

σύν, addition, along, among, beside, besides, together

σὺν εἰμί, accompany

σὺν ἐξέρχομαι, accompany

συναγελάζω, gather *together*

συνάγω, accumulate, assemble, associate, collect, come *together*, concerted, convene, gather, gather *together*, gather *up*, join, meet, raise, recruit, return, store, together, unite, welcome

συναγωγή, accumulate, assembly, company, congregation, group, pool, synagogue

συναγωνίζομαι, strive *together*

συναθλέω, labor *side by side*, strive *side by side*

συναθροίζω, assemble, collect, gather, gather *together*, join

συναινέω, give *approval*, grant *a request at once*

συναίρω, reckon, settle

συναιχμάλωτος, *fellow* prisoner

συνακολουθέω, follow

συναλγέω, sorrow

συναλίζω, stay

συνάλλαγμα, contract

συναλλάσσω εἰς εἰρήνην, reconcile

συναναβαίνω, come *up*, go *up*

συνανάκειμαι, guest, sit, sit *at table*, sit *down*, table

συναναμείγνυμι, associate, do

συναναπαύομαι, refresh

συναναστρέφω, frequent, live

συναναστροφή, association, companionship, fellowship, style *of life*

συναντάω, befall, encounter, go *to meet*, join, meet

συνάντησις, attack, encounter, meet

συναντιλαμβάνομαι, help

συναπάγω, associate, carry *away*

συναποκρύπτω, hide

συναπόλλυμι, perish

συναπολλύω, destroy

συναποστέλλω, send

συνάπτω, begin, engage, engage *in battle*, fight, join, join *battle*, meet, rage, reach

συναρμολογέω, join *together*

συναρπάζω, catch, drag, pick *up*, round *up*, seize, take *up*

συναρχία, unifying *of the kingdom*

συνασπίζω, protect

συναυξάνω, grow *together*

συναύξω, augment, intensify

συναφίστημι, join *in apostasy*

συνδάκνω, smart

σύνδειπνος, *dinner* companion

σύνδεσμος, bind *together*, bond, ligament

συνδέω, bind *together*, clog, prison

συνδιώκω, pursue

συνδοξάζω, glorify

σύνδουλος, *fellow* servant

συνδράω, counselor

συνδρομή, crowd, *great* excitement, run *together*

συνεγγίζω, approach, come *near*, draw *near*, reach

σύνεγγυς, near, *very* near

συνεγείρω, help *raise up*, lift *up*, raise, raise *up*

συνεδρεύω, sit, sit *among*

συνεδρία, council

συνέδριον, council, meeting *of the council*

συνεθίζω, accustom, habitually

συνείδησις, conscience, consciousness, mindful, scruples

συνείκω, yield

σύνειμι, come *together*, ride

συνεισέρχομαι, enter, enter *along*, penetrate

συνέκδημος, companion *in travel*, travel

συνεκκεντέω, put *to the sword*

συνεκλεκτός, choose *likewise*

συνεκπολεμέω, join *with to fight*

συνεκτρίβω, exterminate

συνεκτρόφος, bring *up*

συνελαύνω, drive, force *back*, put

συνεξέρχομαι, go *along*

συνεξορμάω, depart

συνεπιμαρτυρέω, *also* bear witness

συνεπισχύω, give *reinforcement*

συνεπιτίθημι, join *in a charge*

συνέπομαι, accompany, follow

συνεργέω, active *along with*, assist, favorable, *fellow* worker, work, work *together*

συνεργός, advantageous, *fellow* worker, further, servant, work

συνερίζω, encounter

συνέρχομαι, accompany, assemble, come, come *together*, gather, go, go *along*, join, meet, rally

συνεσθίω, eat

σύνεσις, cleverness, comprehension, *good* sense, insight, intelligence, intelligent, sensibly, skill, understand, understanding, wisdom, wise

συνέταιρος, associate

συνετός, clever, intelligence, intelligent, intelligent *man*, man *of understanding*, understand, understanding, understanding *man*

συνευδοκέω, adhere, approve, consent, give *consent*

συνευωχέομαι, carouse, carouse *together*

συνεφίστημι, join

συνέχω, afflict, constrain, control, detain, distress, endure, engage, hem, hold, hold *together*, ill, occupy, press *hard*, principal, seize, sick, stop, surround

συνήδομαι, delight

συνήθεια, accustom, acquaintance, companionship, custom, practice, relationship

συνήθης, friend

συνηλικιώτης, age

συνηχέω, resound

συνθάπτω, bury

σύνθεσις, blending

συνθήκη, agreement, covenant, terms *of peace*, treaty

σύνθημα, watchword

συνθλάω, break *to pieces*

συνθλίβω, crowd, press *around*, throng *about*

συνθρύπτω, break

συνίημι, know, understand, understanding

συνίστημι, arrange, associate, commend, convict, engage, erect, establish, fight, flock *together*, form, frame, hold *together*, join, organize, prepare, present, prove, reconvene, reside, serve *to show*, set, set *up*, show, stand, state *of affairs*, wage

συννοέω, realize

σύννους, anxiety

συνοδεύω, travel, travel *in company*

συνοδία, company

συνοδυνάομαι, sorrow

σύνοιδα, aware, knowledge

συνοικέω, dwell, live, marry

συνοικίζω, fill *with people*, give *in marriage*, marry

συνοικοδομέω, build, build *into*

συνολκή, draw

σύνολον, all, *any* way

σύνολος, *without* exception

συνομιλέω, talk

συνομολογέω, concede

συνομορέω, *next* door

συνοράω, *become* aware, consider, learn, look, notice, perceive, realize, recognize, see

συνουσιασμός, intercourse, lust

συνοχή, anguish, distress

σύνταξις, expense, point, troop, work

συνταράσσω, confound

συντάσσω, arrange, associate, declare, direct, give *orders*, marshal, order

συντέλεια, accomplish, close, complete, completion, consummation, end, final, finish, fulfilment, perfection, reach *the full*, sum

συντελέω, accomplish, bring *to fulfilment*, carry *out*, commit, complete, destroy, do, end, establish, expire, finish, fulfil, give *to*, happen, make, offer, over, perfectly, perpetrate, recount *fully*, rigor, take *place*, utterly

συντέμνω, dispatch, give *a brief summary*

συντηρέω, fulfil, harbor, keep, keep *safe*, keeper, maintain, observe, preserve, show, watch

συντίθημι, agree, engage, make, store

σύντομος, brevity, speedy, swift

συντόμως, briefly, once

συντρέφω, bring *up*, nourish, turn

συντρέχω, assemble, gather, join, run, run *together*, rush

συντριβή, destruction

συντρίβω, break, break *in pieces*, bruise, contrite, crush, defeat, overwhelm, shatter, subdue, wedge

σύντριμμα, affliction, destruction, ruin

συντροφία, *common* nurture, nurture *in common*

σύντροφος, courtier, member *of the court*

συντυγχάνω, meet, reach

συνυποκρίνομαι, *act* insincerely

συνυπουργέω, help

συνωδίνω, travail

συνωμοσία, conspiracy

σφηρίζω, whistle
συρισμός, hiss
σύρω, drag, drag *off*, sweep *down*
συσπαράσσω, convulse
συσσεισμός, earthquake
συσσείω, shake
σύσσημον, sign
συσσύρω, sweep *away*
σύσσωμος, member *of the same body*
σύστασις, *firm* foundation, structure
συστατικός, recommendation
συσταυρόω, crucify
συστέλλω, grow *very short*, humble, shrink *back*, waver, withdraw, wrap *up*
σύστεμα, community
συστενάζω, groan *together*
σύστημα, body
συστοιχέω, correspond
συστρατιώτης, *fellow* soldier
συστρέφω, *close* formation, conspire, gather
συστροφή, assembly, commotion, mass *of people*, plot
συστροφὴ πνεύματος, whirlwind
συσχηματίζω, conform
συχνός, many
σφαγή, slaughter
σφαγιάζω, sacrifice, slay
σφάγιον, *slain* beast
σφάζω, kill, murder, put *to death*, slay, wound
σφάλλω, failure, slip, stumble
σφενδόνη, catapult, sling
σφενδονήτης, slinger
σφήν, wedge
σφήξ, wasp
σφιγγία, self-denial
σφόδρα, badly, deeply, exceedingly, fill, firmly, great, greatly, hard, intensely, most, quite, strongly, utterly, very, violent
σφοδρός, heavily, mighty, *more* vehemently, strong, very
σφοδρῶς, violently
σφραγίζω, deliver, put *a seal upon*, seal, seal *up*, set *seal*
σφραγίς, seal, signet
σφυδρόν, ankle
σφῦρα, hammer
σχεδία, raft
σχεδιάζω, negligent
σχεδόν, almost, nearly, virtually
σχετλιάζω, complain *bitterly*, protest *indignantly*
σχέτλιος, abominable
σχῆμα, form
σχίζα, arrow
σχίζω, cut *in two*, divide, open, part, pierce, split, tear
σχῖνος, mastic *tree*
σχίσμα, discord, dissension, division, tear
σχοινίον, cord, rope
σχολάζω, devote, empty
σχολή, hall, leisure
σῴζω, make *well*, recover, rescue, save, well
σῶμα, bodily, body, chastity, corpse, people, person, slave, substance
σῶμα σαρκός, near *of kin*
σωματικός, bodily, body, physical
σωματικῶς, bodily
σωματοφύλαξ, bodyguard, guard
σῶος, safe, safely, safety
σωρεύω, burden, heap, pile
σωρηδόν, heap
σωρός, heap
σωτήρ, savior
σωτηρία, deliverance, preserve, recovery, rescue, safe, safety, salvation, save, savior, strength, welfare
σωτήριος, deliverance, *peace* offering, salvation, save, *saving* power, wholesome
σωφρονέω, control, keep *sane*, *right* mind, *sober* judgment
σωφρονίζω, train
σωφρονισμός, self-control
σωφρόνως, sober, wisely
σωφροσύνη, moderation, modesty, self-control, sensibly, sober, *sound* judgment
σώφρων, master, self-controlled, sensible, temperate

τὰ ἔνδον, internal
τὰ ἐντός, inwardly
τὰ κατά, case, episode
τὰ μετὰ ταῦτα, future
τὰ πρός, term
τάγμα, order
τακτός, appoint
ταλαιπωρέω, wretched
ταλαιπωρία, misery, misfortune
ταλαίπωρος, distress, doom, miserable, miserable *man*, pitiful, unfortunate *man*, wretched
ταλαντιαῖος, hundred-weight
τάλαντον, millions, talent
τάλας, miserable, miserably, wretch
ταλιθά, talitha
ταμεῖον, *inner* room, *private* room, room, storehouse
ταμιεῖον, chamber, room, treasury
ταμιεύω, lay *up*
τανύω, stretch *out*
τάξις, division, duty, force, form, *good* order, order, place, rank
ταπεινός, bow *low*, bring *low*, dejected, downcast, humble, humble *man*, *low* degree, lowly man *in humble circumstances*, oppress, plain
ταπεινότης, humility
ταπεινοφροσύνη, humility, lowliness, self-abasement
ταπεινόφρων, *humble* mind
ταπεινόω, abase, afflict, bring *low*, humble, humiliate, lower, make *low*, oppress
ταπείνωσις, *afflicted* soul, affliction, bring *low*, humble, *humble* circumstance, humiliation, *low* estate, lowly
ταράσσω, agitate, alarm, anxious, daunt, dismay, disturb, incite, shake, stir, stir *up*, terrify, trouble
ταραχή, commotion, confusion, disorder, disturbance, trouble, tumult
τάραχος, stir, tumult
ταραχώδης, disturb
ταριχεύω, preserve *with salt*
ταρσός, pinion
ταρταρόω, cast *into hell*
τάσσω, allot, appoint, authority, charge, command, deploy, devote, direct, drawn *up in formation*, furnish, get *ready*, institute, make, make *arrangement*, ordain, order, set
τάσσω ἐπί, charge
ταυρηδόν, boldly
ταῦρος, bull, ox
ταφή, burial, bury
τάφος, burial, grave, sepulchre, tomb
τάχα, perhaps
ταχέως, hasty, promptly, quickly, shortly, soon, speedily, swiftly, *without* delay
ταχινός, soon, swift, swiftly
τάχιον, quickly, soon
τάχος, quickly
ταχύνω, hasten, speed
ταχύς, hastily, hurry, once, quick, quickly, quickly *as possible*, readily, rush, soon, soon *after*, soon *as possible*, speedily, suddenly, swift, swiftly
τε, both, even, only, then, together, well, yes, yet
τέγος, brothel
τείνω, stretch
τειχίζω, fortify
τεῖχος, wall
τεκμήριον, evidence, indication, proof, sign
τεκνίον, *little* child
τεκνογονέω, bear *a child*
τεκνογονία, bear *a child*
τέκνον, child, son, young
τεκνοτροφέω, bring *up a child*
τεκνοφόνος, kill *a child*
τεκταίνω, devise, plan, scheme *to get*
τέκτων, carpenter, craftsman, skilled
τέλειος, full, mature, *more* perfect, perfect, perfectly
τελειότης, completeness, maturity, perfect
τελειόω, accomplish, complete, end, find *perfect*, finish, fulfil, make *perfect*, perfect, perfectly
τελείως, fully, wholly
τελείως ποιέω, accomplish
τελείωσις, accomplish, completion, fulfilment, make *perfect*, perfection
τελειωτής, perfecter
τέλεος, completion
τελεσφορέω, bring *to the light of day*, mature
τελετή, initiate, initiation, rite
τελευταῖος, last
τελευτάω, dead *man*, death, die, end *of life*
τελευτή, bind, come *to an end*, death, die, end, fulfil
τελέω, accomplish, complete, do, end, finish, fulfil, go *through all*, gratify, keep, make *perfect*, pay, perfect, perform, settle
τέλος, aim, conclusion, end, finally, fulfilment, height, last, outcome, purpose, result, revenue, tax, toll
τελωνέομαι, collect, collect *a tax*
τελώνης, *tax* collector
τελώνιον, *tax* office
τέμενος, *sacred* enclosure, sacred *place*, *sacred* precinct, temple
τέμνω, cut, cut *off*, divide
τένων, sinew
τέρας, monstrous, wonder
τερατεύομαι, take *as a sign*
τερατοποιός, work *a wonder*, worker *of wonders*
τερέμινθος, terebinth
τέρμα, utmost
τέρπω, delight
τέρψις, delight, joy
τέσσαρες, four
τεσσαρεσκαίδεκα, fourteenth
τεσσαρεσκαιδέκατος, fourteenth
τεταγμένως, *good* order
τεταρταῖος, four *days*
τέταρτος, four, fourth
τετράγωνος, foursquare
τετράδιον, squad
τετραμερής, four *parts*
τετράμηνος, four *months*
τετραπλοῦς, fourfold
τετράποδος, four-footed, square
τετράπους, animal
τετραρχέω, tetrarch
τετράρχης, tetrarch
τετράστιχος, four *rows*
τέφρα, ash
τεφρόω, turn *to ashes*
τεχνάομαι, workmanship
τέχνη, art, craft, skill, trade
τεχνίτης, builder, craftsman
τεχνῖτις, craftsman, fashioner
τηγανίζω, fry *in a pan*
τήγανον, brazier, pan
τηκτός, melt
τήκω, burn, consume, melt, pine *away*, sickly, waste *away*
τηλαυγῶς, clearly
τηλικοῦτος, deadly, great, such *a great*, *such* great
τηρέω, guard, hold, keep, keep *in custody*, keep *watch*, keep *watch over*, lay *up*, maintain, observe, preserve, prison, refrain, reserve, wait, watch
τήρησις, custody, guard, keep, keep *guard*, protection
τίθημι, appoint, arrange, believe, bring, contrive, dash, deposit, destine, drive, entrust, fix, give *orders*, God, grant, inscribe, issue, keep, lay, lay *aside*, lay *down*, lay *up*, make, place, provide, put, put *away*, put *up*, regard, resolve, seem, serve, set, set *down*, set *forth*, set *in place*, set *up*, settle, sink, station, store, suppose, take, turn, use, utter
τίθημι βουλήν, advise
τίθημι τὰ γόνατα, kneel *down*
τίθημι χεῖρας ἐπὶ χεῖρας, covenant
τιθηνέω, cherish, pamper
τιθηνία, nurture
τιθηνός, nurse
τίκτω, bear, bear *a child*, bring *forth*, deliver, delivery, divulge, give *birth*, mother, travail, *woman in* labor, woman *in travail*
τίλλω, pluck
τιμάω, honor, present, price *set*
τιμή, beauty, cost, distinction, esteem, gift, honor, money, noble, precious, price, proceeds, sum, tax, value
τίμιος, costly, hold *in honor*, honor, *most* precious, *most* rare, precious, value
τιμιότης, wealth
τιμωρέω, punish, take *vengeance*
τιμωρητής, punish
τιμωρία, hurt, penalty, punishment, *some other* punishment
τίνα τρόπον, how
τίνος ἕνεκα, why
τίνος ἕνεκεν, why
τίνος ἕνεκεν αἰτίας, why
τίνω, suffer
τις, any, any *one*, anything, artist, certain, certain *man*, certain *person*, else, every *one*, *how* much, little, man, other, person, piece, some, some *man*, some *one*, some *people*, some *person*, some *sort*, some *things*, somebody, someone, something, somewhat, sort, what, why
τις δέ, other
τίς, all, another, any, any *man*, any *one*, any *thing*, anything, each, how, *how* great, kind, man, matter, no *one*, only, other, several, such, then, what, what *about*, what *person*, whatever, whoever, why
τὶς δέ, other
τιτανες, Titan
τίτλος, title
τιτρώσκω, assail, wound
τὸ αὐτό, likewise
τὸ αὐτὸ λέγω, agree
τὸ αὐτὸ φρονέω, agree, agree *with one another*
τὸ κατά, affair
τὸ νῦν ἔχω, present
τοιγαροῦν, therefore
τοίνυν, accordingly, now, then, therefore, well
τοιόσδε, follow
τοιοῦτος, follow, kind, like, other, similar, such, such *a fellow*, such *a man*, such *a one*, such *a person*, such *a thing*, thus
τοιοῦτος οἷος, like
τοῖχος, offset, wall
τοκετός, birth
τόκος, interest
τόλμα, act *of daring*, boldness
τολμάω, bold, dare, presume, show, take *courage*, venture
τολμηρός, bold, foolhardy *fellow*, reckless, *very* boldly, *very* reckless
τόμος, scroll
τομός, sharp
τὸν ἅπαντα χρόνον, ever
τόνος, firm
τόξευμα, arrow
τόξον, bow, rainbow
τοξότης, archer
τοπάζιον, topaz
τοπαρχής, governor
τοπαρχία, district
τόπος, abode, approach, attention, chance, community, country, course, district, fortress, grave, land, locality, occasion, opportunity, part, place, port, position, region, room, room *for work*, site, territory, where
τόπος διθάλασσος, shoal

τοσοῦτο, *like* measure, long, more
τοσοῦτος, all, all *this*, enough, far, great, long, many, many *things*, much, such, *such* great, *without* meaning
τότε, accordingly, day, formerly, just, moment, now, *that* time, then, time, when
τοὐναντίον, contrary
τοῦτο δέ, sometimes
τοῦτο μέν, sometimes
τράγος, goat, *he* goat
τρανός, clear, speak *clearly*
τράπεζα, bank, food, table
τραπεζίτης, banker
τραῦμα, strike, wound
τραυματίας, wound
τραυματίας ποιέω, wound
τραυματίζω, wound
τραχηλίζω, lay *bare*
τράχηλος, arm, neck
τραχύς, harsh, rough, rough *way*
τραχὺς τόπος, rock
τραχύτης, disturbance
τρεῖς, three, three *things*, three *times*
τρεῖς ταβέρναι, Three *Taverns*
τρέμω, afraid, shiver, tremble
τρέπω, become, defeat, fill, give *way*, return, take, turn
τρέφω, bring *up*, depend *for food*, fatten, feed, give *suck*, nourish, nurture, rear, take *care*
τρέχω, charge, compete, exertion, run, runner, rush, speed
τρέχω ὀπίσω, pursue
τρῆμα, eye
τρϊετίζω, three-year-old
τριάκοντα, thirtyfold
τρίβολος, thistle
τρίβος, path, way
τρίβω, path
τριετής, three *years*
τριετία, three *years*
τριήρης, trireme
τρίζω, grind
τρικυμία, *mighty* wave
τρίμηνος, three *months*
τριπλασίος, three *times as much*
τρίς, three, three *times*
τρισάθλιος, unhappy
τρισαλιτήριος, thrice *accursed man*, thrice-accursed
τρισκαιδέκατος, thirteenth
τρίστεγον, *third* story
τρίτος, third, *third* time, three
τρίχωμα, hair
τρομέω, stir
τρόμος, dread, fear, terror, tremble
τρόπαιον, monument *of victory*, trophy *of victory*
τροπή, change, flight, rout, solstice, turn *away*
τρόπις, keel
τρόπον τοῦτον, follow
τρόπος, character, condition, detail, do, effect, evidence, fashion, kind, life, like, manner, respect, way, word
τροποφορέω, bear
τροπόω, conquer, put *to flight*, rout, turn *back*
τροφεία, nurture
τροφεύω, bring *up*
τροφή, eat, food, *food* supply, grow
τροφός, food, nurse
τροφοφορέω, take *care*
τροχαντήρ, hook
τροχιά, path
τροχιαῖος, wheel
τροχίζω, break *on the wheel*
τροχός, cycle, *torture* wheel, wheel
τρύβλιον, dish
τρυγάω, gather, pick
τρύγητος, *grape* gatherer, vintage
τρυγών, *grape* gatherer, turtledove
τρυμαλιά, eye
τρύπημα, eye
τρυφάω, live *in luxury*
τρυφερός, tender, *woman of great* refinement
τρυφή, food, luxury, revel
τρύφημα, dainty
τρύχω, consume, distress
τρώγω, eat
τυγχάνω, attain, burial, enjoy, find, get, happen, hope *of finding*, meet, obtain, ordinary, perhaps, reach, receive
τυγχάνω ἀναστάσεως, rise *again*
τυμπανίζω, torture
τύμπανον, drum, rack, tambourine
τύπος, effect, example, figure, form, mark, model, pattern, print, standard, type, warning
τυπόω, mould, shape
τύπτω, attack, beat, strike, wound
τυραννέω, master, oppressor, tyrannize
τυραννικός, tyrannical, *under* tyranny
τυραννίς, *royal* authority, sovereignty, tyranny
τύραννος, king, monarch, prince, ruler, tyrant
τυφλός, blind, blind *man*
τυφλόω, blind
τῦφος, conceit
τυφόω, puff *up with conceit*, swell *with conceit*
τύφω, smolder
τυφωνικός, tempestuous
τύχη, treat

ὕαινα, hyena
ὑακίνθινος, blue, purple, sapphire
ὑάκινθος, blue, cloth *dyed blue*, jacinth
ὑάλινος, glass
ὕαλος, glass
ὑβρίζω, molest, reproach, suffer *outrage*, treat *outrageously*, treat *shamefully*
ὕβρις, injury, insolence, insult, outrage, pride, violence
ὑβριστής, insolent, insult
ὑβριστός, insolent *fellow*
ὑγιαίνω, farewell, *good* health, *good* wish *for health*, health, safe *and sound*, sound, well
ὑγιαίνω ἔρχομαι, welcome
ὑγίεια, health, healthy, safety
ὑγιής, heal, safely, sound, well, whole
ὑγιὴς γίνομαι, heal
ὑγρός, green, water
ὑδραγωγός, *water* channel
ὑδρεύω, get *water*
ὑδρία, jar, *water* jar
ὑδροποτέω, drink *only water*
ὑδρωπικός, dropsy
ὕδωρ, flood, *fresh* water, liquid, water, *water* supply, wave
ὕειος, pork, swine
ὑετός, fall, rain, shower *of rain*
υἱοθεσία, adoption *as a son*, son, sonship
υἱός, child, descendant, foal, grandson, guest, man, other, people, son
υἱὸς Αμμων, Ammonite
υἱὸς Ασσουρ, Assyrian
υἱὸς Ισμαηλ, Ishmaelite
υἱὸς 'Ισραήλ, Israelite
υἱὸς Μαδιάμ, Midianite, Midianite
υἱὸς Μωαβ, Moabite, Moabite
υἱὸς Χανάαν, Canaanite
υἱὸς Χελεουδ, Chaldean
υἱὸς ἀλλογενής, alien
υἱὸς ἀνθρώπου, *human* being
υἱὸς δυνατός, valiant
υἱὸς τῆς αἰχμαλωσίας, captive
υἱὸς τοῦ βασιλέως, prince
υἱὸς τοῦ γένους, descendant
ὕλη, forest, fuel, jungle, material, matter
ὑλοτόμος, woodcutter
ὑμέναιος, *wedding* song
ὑμνέω, praise, sing, sing *a hymn*, sing *praise*, song
ὑμνητός, sing
ὑμνογράφος, psalmist
ὕμνος, hymn, song
ὑπαγορεύω, indicate
ὑπάγω, begone, get, go, go *away*, go *one's way*, move
ὕπαιθρος, *open* country
ὑπακοή, obedience, obedient, obey
ὑπακούω, answer, *become* obedient, give *answer*, obedient, obey
ὕπανδρος, another *man*, marry
ὑπαντάω, befall, *come to* meet, go *and meet*, go *to meet*, meet
ὑπάντησις, meet
ὕπαρ, vision
ὕπαρξις, estate, goods, possession, property
ὕπαρχος, possession
ὑπάρχω, belong, belongings, endure, goods, live, make, means, possess, possession, property, *thing* possessed, wealth
ὑπάρχω πρός, give
ὑπασπιστής, guard
ὕπατος, consul, prefect
ὑπείκω, submit, yield
ὑπεκρέω, slip *away*
ὑπεναντίος, adversary, against, enemy
ὑπέρ, about, above, account, assail, bear, because, behalf, better *off than*, better *than*, beyond, concerning, establish, excel, expiation, eye, favor, good, higher *than*, interest, many, more *than*, over, place, protect, regard, sake, show, superior, surpass, than, too, *where is* concerned, worse *than*, worth *more than*
ὑπὲρ ἄνθρωπον, superhuman
ὑπὲρ ἅπαν, chiefly
ὑπὲρ δύναμιν, unbearably
ὑπὲρ πάντα, far *more*
ὑπὲρ πάντας, most
ὑπὲρ σωτηρίου, *thank* offering
ὑπεράγαν, terribly
ὑπεραγόντως, especially
ὑπεράγω, excel, surpass, tall
ὑπεραινετός, *highly* praise
ὑπεραίρω, exalt, lord *over*, *too* elated, *too* hard
ὑπέρακμος, passion *be strong*
ὑπεραλόω, attain *eminence*
ὑπεράνω, above, far *above*, high, set *above*
ὑπερασπίζω, defend, protect, shield
ὑπερασπισμός, protection
ὑπερασπίστρια, champion
ὑπεραυξάνω, grow *abundantly*
ὑπερβαίνω, climb *over*, go *beyond*, go *outside*, surpass, transgress
ὑπερβαλλόντως, countless
ὑπερβάλλω, *exceedingly* great, extreme, immeasurable, outbid, postpone, surpass
ὑπερβολή, abundance, transcendent
ὑπερείδω, set *up*
ὑπερέκεινα, land *beyond*
ὑπερεκπερισσοῦ, abundantly, earnestly, *very* highly
ὑπερεκτείνω, overextend
ὑπερεκχύνω, run *over*
ὑπερένδοξος, *highly* glorify
ὑπερεντυγχάνω, intercede
ὑπερέχω, good, govern, high *place*, pass, supreme, surpass, *surpassing* worth
ὑπερηφανεύομαι, disdain
ὑπερηφανεύω, proud
ὑπερηφανέω, despise
ὑπερηφανία, arrogance, arrogant, arrogantly, insolence, man *of pride*, pride, proud, *proud* position
ὑπερήφανος, arrogant, costly, haughty, proud, proud *man*
ὑπερηφάνως, arrogance, arrogantly
ὑπερισχύω, strong, strongest *of all*
ὑπερκεράω, outflank
ὑπερλίαν, superlative
ὑπερμαχέω, fight
ὑπέρμαχος, defend, defender
ὑπερνικάω, more *than conqueror*
ὑπέρογκος, boaster, *loud* boast
ὑπεροράω, despise, disdain, disregard, forget, ignore, neglect, overlook
ὑπεροχή, authority, dignity, *high* position, lofty
ὑπεροχὴν ποιέω, notorious
ὑπερπερισσεύω, abound *all the more*, overjoyed
ὑπερπερισσῶς, *beyond* measure
ὑπερπλεονάζω, overflow
ὑπερρίπτω, throw *down*
ὑπερτήκω, consume
ὑπερτιμάω, *greatly* respect
ὑπερυμνητός, extol
ὑπερυψόω, *highly* exalt
ὑπερφέρω, mount *up*
ὑπερφρονέω, despise, think *highly*
ὑπερφωνέω, sing *loudly*
ὑπερχαίρω, overjoyed
ὑπέρχομαι, enter
ὑπετάγη, subject
ὑπευλαβέομαι, shrink
ὑπέχω, suffer, undergo
ὑπήκοος, obedient, obey
ὑπηρεσία, serve, service
ὑπηρετέω, attend *to needs*, comply, minister, serve
ὑπηρέτης, assist, attendant, guard, minister, officer, servant, serve
ὑπισχνέομαι, promise
ὕπνος, sleep, slumber, union
ὑπνόω, fall *asleep*, sleep
ὑπό, *at* hand, because, before, beneath, give, hand, under, wear
ὑπὸ καιρόν, within
ὑπὸ φόρον, pay *tribute*
ὑποβάλλω, instigate, lay *a foundation*
ὑποβλέπω, look *at suspiciously*
ὑπογραμμός, example, outline
ὑπογράφω, follow, indicate, inscribe *below*, sign, write *here*
ὑπόγυος, close *at hand*
ὑπόδειγμα, copy, example, sort
ὑποδείκνυμι, explain, indicate, inform, make *known*, point *out*, reveal, show, tell, warn
ὑποδείκνυμι λόγους, declare
ὑποδέχομαι, admit, receive, welcome
ὑποδέω, foot, put, shoe, wear
ὑπόδημα, pair *of shoes*, sandal, shoe
ὑπόδικος, accountable
ὑποδύω, get *under shelter*
ὑπόθεσις, *main* principle
ὑποζύγιον, ass
ὑποζώννυμι, gird, undergird
ὑποκαίω, roast *from underneath*
ὑποκάτω, below, low, under
ὑποκάτωθεν, low
ὑπόκειμαι, follow, show
ὑποκρίνομαι, pretend, pretense
ὑποκρίνω, feign, hypocrite, hypocritical
ὑπόκρισις, hypocrisy, insincerity, pretense, pretension
ὑποκριτής, hypocrite
ὑπολαμβάνω, accept, assume, determine, expect, reply, resume, support, suppose, take, think
ὑπόλειμμα, last, remnant
ὑπολείπω, leave, leave *alive*, remain
ὑπόλημψις, *hasty* judgment
ὑπολήνιον, pit *for the wine press*
ὑπολιμπάνω, leave
ὑπομάσθιος, infant
ὑπομένω, avail, await, bear, courage, endure, patient, remain, stand *firm*, stay *behind*, steadfast, submit, take *patiently*, wait, withstand
ὑπομιμνήσκω, appeal, remind
ὑπομνηματίζομαι, record
ὑπομνηματισμός, chronicle, memoir, record
ὑπόμνησιν λαμβάνω, remind
ὑπόμνησις, remind, reminder

ὑπομονή, endurance, endure, patience, *patient* endurance, perseverance, steadfastness

ὑπομονὴν ἔχω, endure *patiently*

ὑπομονόω, endurance

ὑπονοέω, expect, suppose, suspect

ὑπονόημα, thought

ὑπονοθεύω, obtain *by corruption*, supplant

ὑπόνοια, opinion, suspicion

ὑποπίπτω, fall, occur

ὑποπλέω, sail *under the lee*

ὑποπνέω, blow *gently*

ὑποπόδιον, foot, footstool, stool

ὑποπτεύω, worry

ὕποπτον ἔχω, suspect

ὕποπτος, fear

ὑποράπτω, repair

ὑποσημαίνω, send *word*

ὑπόστασις, assurance, confidence, confident, nature, sustenance

ὑποστέλλω, draw *back*, shrink, shrink *back*

ὑποστέλλω πρόσωπον, stand *in awe*

ὑποστολή, shrink *back*

ὑποστρέφω, come *back*, return, turn *back*

ὑποστρώννυμι, spread *under*, subject

ὑποστρωννύω, spread

ὑποσχάζω, trip

ὑπόσχεσις, promise

ὑποταγή, obedience, subject, submission, submissiveness

ὑποτάσσω, command, obedient, put *in subjection*, put *under*, subdue, subject, subjection, submissive, submit, subordinate, under, yield

ὑποτίθημι, fall *upon*, put *before*, put *under*, risk, stab *from beneath*, suggestion

ὑποτρέχω, run *under the lee*

ὑποτύπωσις, example, pattern

ὑποφαίνω, dawn

ὑποφέρω, bear, bear *up under*, endure, hold *firm*, patient, suffer

ὑπόφρικος, shudder

ὑποχείριος, control, dependent, hand, subjection

ὑποχωρέω, reserve, withdraw

ὑποψία, suspicion

ὑπωπιάζω, pommel, wear *out*

ὗς, sow

ὕσσωπος, hyssop

ὑστερέω, bad *off*, destitute, fail, fail *to obtain*, fail *to reach*, fall *short*, inferior, inferior *part*, lack, need, want

ὑστέρημα, absence, lack, need, poverty, want

ὑστέρησις, poverty, want

ὕστερον, afterward

ὕστερος, after, lack, last, late, then, want

ὑφαιρέω, *secretly* take

ὑφαντός, weave

ὑφάπτω, burn, set *fire*

ὑφίστημι, bear, resist, stand, withstand

ὑφοράω, suspect, suspicious

ὑψαυχενέω, arrogance, hold *head high in defiance*

ὑψηλὰ φρονέω, *become* proud, haughty

ὑψηλὸν ἀνατείνω, raise

ὑψηλός, exalt, exalt *above*, height, high, hilltop, outstretched, tall, uplift

ὑψηλοφρονέω, haughty

ὕψιστος, height, high, *most* high

ὕψος, barrier, exalt, exaltation, heaven, height, high, honor

ὕψος τῆς γῆς, *hill* country

ὑψόω, build *high*, erect, exalt, lift *up*, make *great*, make *high*, tower

ὕψωμα, exalt, exaltation, height, proud

φάγος, glutton

φαιδρός, cheerful, clear, conspicuous, disclose, know, light, manifest, see, visible

φαιλόνης, cloak

φαίνω, appear, become, *become* manifest, come *into being*, decision, evident, find, give *light*, obviously, prove, see, seem, *seem* good, shine, show

φάλαγξ, phalanx

φανερός, know, manifest, plain, recognize

φανερόω, appear, *become* visible, disclose, know, make *clear*, make *manifest*, make *plain*, manifest, open, *open* statement, plain, reveal, see, see *clearly*, show, spread

φανερῶς, clearly, openly, publicly

φανέρωσις, manifestation

φανός, lantern

φαντάζομαι, appear, fancy

φαντάζω, sight

φαντασία, apparition, pomp

φαντασιοκοπέω, faultfinder

φάντασμα, ghost, specter

φάραγξ, valley

φάραγχ, chasm

φαρέτρα, quiver

φαρμακεία, sorcery, *magic* art

φαρμακεύω, take *poison*

φάρμακον, medicine, sorcery

φαρμακός, elixir, poison

φάρμακος, sorcerer

φάρυγξ, palate

φάσις, word

φάσκω, affirm, allege, assert, claim, declare, state

φάσμα, phantom

φάτνη, manger

φατνόω, panel

φάτνωμα, ceiling

φαυλίζω, disregard, slight

φαῦλος, bad, evil, unkindly, vile

φαυλότης, wickedness

φαῦσις, light

φέγγος, light, radiance

φείδομαι, hesitate, keep, refrain, spare

φειδομένως, sparingly

φειδώ, forbearance, mercy

φειδωλός, greedy

φερνή, dowry

φέρω, bear, bestow, bring, bring *back*, buy, carry, carry *away*, come, drive, endure, establish, forth, go, lead, move, obtain, possess, pronounce, put, put *out*, regard, restrain, rush, stand, sweep, take, uphold, yield

φέρω πικρῶς, exasperate

φεύγω, escape, flee, flee *away*, flight, fly, give *up*, run *away*, shun, take *refuge*

φευκτός, avoid

φήμη, report, rumor

φημί, answer, charge, imply, mean, reply, say, sentence, speak, tell, utter, write

φθάνω, add, always, attain, come, early, excel, hasten, precede, rise *before*, succeed *in fulfilling*

φθαρτός, mortal, perishable, *perishable* nature, perishable *thing*

φθέγγομαι, speak, utter

φθέγγομαι ἀπόκρισιν, answer

φθέγμα, word

φθείρω, corrupt, destroy, lead *astray*, ruin

φθόγγος, note, voice

φθονερός, begrudge

φθονέω, begrudge, envy

φθόνος, envious, envy

φθορά, corruption, decay, destruction, kill, perishable

φιάλη, bowl

φιλάγαθος, love *the good*, lover *of goodness*

φιλαδελφία, *brotherly* affection, *brotherly* love, love *of the brother*

φιλάδελφος, brotherly-loving, love *a brother*, love *of the brother*

φίλανδρος, love *a husband*

φιλανθρωπέω, *show* generosity

φιλανθρωπία, benevolence, *good* will, kindly, kindness, *loving* kindness

φιλάνθρωπος, concession, gracious, humane, kind, kindly

φιλανθρώπως, benevolence, kindly, kindness

φιλαργυρέω, money-hungry

φιλαργυρία, covetousness, love *of money*

φιλάργυρος, lover *of money*

φιλαρχία, lust *for power*

φίλαυτος, lover *of self*

φιλελεήμων, merciful

φιλέω, fall *in love*, kiss, love

φιλήδονος, lover *of pleasure*

φιληκοΐα, attention

φίλημα, kiss

φιλία, friendship, love, passion

φιλιάζω, friend, friendly

φιλοδοξία, love *of glory*, thirst *for honor*

φιλόθεος, lover *of God*

φιλόκοσμος, love *an ornament*

φιλομαθέω, gain *learning*, love *learning*

φιλομήτωρ, love *a mother*

φιλονεικία, contentiousness, dispute, rivalry

φιλόνικος, contentious

φιλοξενία, hospitality, *show* hospitality to *a stranger*

φιλόξενος, hospitable, practice *hospitality*

φιλοπολίτης, love *a fellow citizen*

φιλοπονέω, *diligent* labor

φιλοπονία, labor

φιλοπρωτεύω, like *to put first*

φίλος, beloved, friend, friendly, love

φιλοσοφέω, follow *a philosophy*, philosopher, philosophize

φιλοσοφία, philosophy

φιλόσοφος, live *as a philosopher*, *most* philosophical, philosopher, philosophical

φιλοστοργία, *natural* love, *tender* love, tenderness

φιλόστοργος, love, yearn *toward*

φιλοστόργως, affection

φιλοτεκνία, love *for a child*, *parental* love

φιλότεκνος, love *a child*, love *a child more*, *more* devoted *to a child*

φιλοτιμέομαι, aspire, love, make *one's aim*, make *one's ambition*

φιλοτιμία, ambition

φιλότιμος, eagerly, glorious, zealous

φιλοτίμως, zealously

φιλοφρονέω, incline

φιλοφρόνως, hospitably, kindly, *kindly* manner

φιλόψυχος, love *the living*

φίλτρον, affection, affection *of love*

φιμός, muzzle

φιμόω, bridle, muzzle, put *to silence*, silence, silent, speechless, still

φλεγμονή, flame

φλέγω, blaze, burn

φλογίζω, blaze, burn, set *on fire*

φλοιός, bark

φλόξ, fiery, flame

φλυαρέω, prate *against*

φλύαρος, foolish, gossip

φοβέομαι, afraid, alarm

φοβεροειδής, *fearful* aspect

φοβερός, awe-inspiring, dread, fear, fearful, fearful *thing*, *frightening* mien, frightful, terrible, terrify

φοβέω, afraid, awe, *become* afraid, fear, fill *with fear*, frighten, respect, terrify

φοβέω πτόησιν, terrify

φοβέω σφόδρα, fill *with awe*

φοβέω φόβον μέγαν, fill *with awe*, fill *with fear*

φόβητρον, terror

φόβος, alarm, awe, fear, respect, reverence, terror

φόβον πλήρης, dreadful

φοῖνιξ, frond *of palm*, palm, palm *branch*, palm *tree*

φονεύς, murderer, slaughter

φονεύς γίνομαι, murder

φονεύω, kill, murder, put *to death*

φονοκτονία, deed *of murder*

φόνος, death, murder, slaughter, slay

φονώδης, murderous

φορά, tribute

φορεῖον, litter, stretcher

φορέω, bear, wear

φορολογέω, exact *tribute*

φορολογία, collector *of tribute*, tribute

φόρον, forum

φόρος, revenue, tax, tributary, tribute, *tribute* money

φορτίζω, *heavy* laden, load

φορτίον, burden, cargo, *heavy* burden, load

φραγέλλιον, whip

φραγελλόω, scourge

φραγμός, fence, hedge, wall

φράζω, explain

φράσσω, silence, stop

φρέαρ, cistern, pit, shaft, well

φρεναπατάω, deceive

φρεναπάτης, deceiver

φρενόομαι, elate

φρήν, mind, think

φρικασμός, tremble

φρικτός, dread

φρικτῶς, terribly

φρίσσω, shudder, tremble

φρονέω, *become* proud, concern, feel, live, mind, minded, observe, set *one's mind*, take *a view*, think, view

φρονέω τά, side, take *a side*

φρόνημα, arrogance, mind, spirit

φρόνησις, feel, *good* sense, insight, prudence, prudent, rational *judgment*, understanding, wisdom

φρόνιμος, discreet *man*, *more* shrewd, prudent, sensible, sensible *man*, wise, wise *man*

φρόνιμος παρ' ἑαυτόν, conceited

φρονίμως, shrewdness

φροντίζω, aim, attend, careful, concern, consider, regard, take *good care*, take *measures*, take *thought*, think

φροντίς, anxiety, care, concern, take *care*

φροντιστέον, concern

φρουρά, garrison, guard

φρουρέω, confine, guard, keep

φρούριον, fort, fortress, garrison

φρουρόω, station *a garrison*

φρύαγμα, arrogance

φρυάζω, puff *up*

φρυάσσω, rage

φρύγανον, stick

φυγαδευτήριον, place *of refuge*

φυγαδεύω, banish, *become a* fugitive, flee, put *to flight*, take *refuge*

φυγάς, exile, flee, fugitive

φυγὰς ἀπέρχομαι, flee

φυγὰς οἴχομαι, flee

φυγή, flight,

φῦκος, red

φύλαγμα, obligation

φυλακή, bulwark, guard, haunt, imprisonment, part *of the night*, prison, watch

φυλακίζω, imprison

φυλακτήριον, phylactery

φύλαξ, sentry

φυλάρχης, commander

φύλαρχος, leader, leader *of the tribe*

φυλάσσω, abstain, beware, give *good heed*, guard, keep, keep *guard over*, keep *under guard*, keep *watch*, maintain, observance, observe, preserve, wary, watch, watch *over*, watchman

φυλή, kindred, nation, tribe

φύλλον, leaf

φῦλον, nation, race

φύραμα, lump

φύρδην, *wild* confusion

φύρω, sprinkle

φυσάω, blow, breathe *out*, tend

φυσικός, instinct, natural

φυσικῶς, instinct

φυσιόω, arrogant, arrogant *people*, puff *up*

φύσις, birth, creature, innate, kind, nature, type
φύσις ἀνθρώπινος, humankind
φυσίωσις, conceit
φυτεία, plant
φυτεύω, implant, plant
φυτόν, bush, plant, tree
φύω, concerned *by nature*, grow, grow *up*, put *forth*, spring *up*
φωλεός, hole
φωνέω, call, call *out*, crow, cry, invite, shout, sing, sound, speak, voice
φωνή, aloud, blast, call, cry, language, noise, prayer, roar, say, shout, song, sound, speech, tone, tongue, utterance, voice
φωνὴ θρηνέω, lament
φωνὴ μεγάλη, loudly
φωνὴν δίδωμι, instrument
φῶς, fire, light
φῶς ἡμέρας, daylight
φωστήρ, light, luminary, radiance
φωσφόρος, *morning* star
φωταγωγέω, light *the way*
φωτεινός, bright, full *of light*, light
φωτίζω, bring *to light*, enlighten, give *light*, gleam, light, make *bright*, *make* see, *make* shine *forth*
φωτισμός, light

χαίρω, farewell, feel, glad, greeting, hail, joyfully, rejoice, rejoicing, send *greetings*
χάλαζα, hail, hailstone
χαλάω, let *down*, lower
χαλβάνη, galbanum
χαλεπαίνω, angry, grieve
χαλεπός, difficulty, fierce, grievous, harsh, heavy, *more* bitter, *more* grievous, *most* painful, serious, stress, *too* difficult
χαλιναγωγέω, bridle
χαλινός, bit, bridle
χαλκεῖον, brass, pot
χάλκειος, brass, bronze
χαλκεύς, coppersmith, smith
χαλκηδών, agate
χαλκίον, vessel *of bronze*
χαλκολίβανον, *burnished* bronze
χαλκοπλάστης, worker *in copper*
χαλκός, brass, copper, gong, money
χαλκοῦς, brass, bronze
χαμαί, ground
χαμαιπετής, lie *upon the ground*
χάρα, cart
χαρά, delight, gladness, joy, joyful, pleasant, rejoicing
χάραγμα, mark, representation
χαρακτήρ, character, *very* stamp, way *of life*
χάραξ, bank, fence, rampart
χαράσσω, brand, write
χαρίεις, accomplish
χαρίζομαι, bestow, *bestowed* gift, congratulate, favor, forgive, give, give *up*, grant, spare
χάριν, out
χάριν ἀποδίδωμι, thank
χάριν ἔχω, benefit, thank
χάριν τίνος, why
χάρις, account, approval, approve, avoid, because, blessing, charm, courtesy, credit, delight, enjoyment, favor, gain, gift, *good* luck, grace, graceful, gracious, *gracious* work, graciously, grateful, gratitude, kindly, kindness, loveliness, pardon, pleasure, reason, sake, thank, *thank* offering, thankfulness, thanks, why
χάρισμα, blessing, *free* gift, gift, grace, *special* gift, *spiritual* gift
χαριστήριος, reward
χαριτόομαι, gracious
χαριτόω, bestow *freely*, favor
χαρμονή, joy
χαρμόσυνος, day *of rejoicing*, gladness, joy
χαρτηρίαν, paper
χάρτης, paper
χάσκω, agape, open
χάσμα, chasm
χαῦνος, empty
χεῖλος, bank, lip, man, shore, speech, word
χεῖλος τῆς θαλάσσης, seashore
χειμάζω, storm-tossed
χειμάρρος, valley
χειμάρρους, brook, stream
χειμερινός, winter
χειμέριος, wintry
χειμών, *bad* weather, *burial* mound, stormy, tempest, winter, *wintry* storm
χείρ, arm, attack, band, care, claw, deed, direct, force, gauntlet, give, hand, power, skill, word
χειραγωγέω, lead *by the hand*
χειραγωγός, people *to lead by the hand*
χειράω, destroy
χειρίζω, administration
χειρίστως, bad
χειρόγραφον, bond, receipt
χειρονομία, action
χειροπέδη, hand, manacle
χειροποίητος, made *by man*, make *by hands*, make *with hands*, man-made
χειρὸς δάκτυλος, finger
χειροτονέω, appoint
χειρόω, kill
χείρων, bad, *far* worse *thing*
χελιδών, swallow
χελώνις, platform
χερούβ, cherub
χερουβείμ, cherub
χερουβίν, cherub
χερσαῖος, land
χέρσος, wasteland
χερσόω, leave *dry and barren*
χέω, pour
χήρα, widow
χήρευσις, widow, widowhood
χηρεύω, widow
χιλίαρχος, captain, captain *over thousands*, charge *of thousands*, general, *military* tribune, officer, tribune
χιλίας, thousand
χίμαρος, *he* goat
χιτών, clothes, coat, garment, shirt, tunic
χιών, snow
χλαμύς, cloak, robe
χλευάζω, deride, mock, mockingly, scoff
χλιαρός, lukewarm
χλιδῶν, anklet, bracelet
χλόη, *green* shoot, *tender* grass
χλοηφόρος, grassy
χλωρός, green, *green* growth, pale
χνοῦς, chaff
χοϊκός, dust
χοῖνιξ, quart
χοῖρος, swine
χολάω, angry
χολέρα, nausea
χολή, gall
χόλος, wrath
χορεία, dance
χορεύω, form *a chorus*, move *in choral dance*
χορηγέω, allow, allow *to take*, defray, furnish, provide, supply
χορηγία, abundance, proceedings, support
χορηγός, bountiful
χορός, choral *group*, chorus, dance
χορτάζω, eat *one's fill*, feed, fill, gorge, plenty, satisfy
χόρτασμα, fodder, food
χόρτος, blade, grass, hay, plant
χορτώδης, wild
χοῦς, dust
χόω, fill
χράομαι, avail *of the opportunity*, behave *toward*, deal, enjoy, live, make *use*, method, need, observe, take, treat, use
χράω, cause, do, employ, make *use*, practice
χρεία, action, affair, business, concern, crucial, duty, fit *the occasion*, government *official*, interest, necessary, necessity, need, needful, office, officer, position, *public* affair, rescue, service, use, usefulness
χρείαν ἔχω, dependent, need, require
χρεμετίζω, neigh
χρεοκοπέομαι, cancel
χρέος, lend
χρεοφειλέτης, debtor
χρή, ought
χρῆμα, bribe, fund, money, property, rich, riches, sum *of money*, treasure, wealth
χρηματίζω, call, direct, instruct, reveal, warn
χρηματισμός, communication, God's *reply*, oracle
χρηματιστήριον, *council* chamber
χρησιμεύω, use
χρήσιμος, *do* good, *more* profitable, profitable, right *man*, serve, useful
χρησίμος εἰμί, help
χρῆσις, relation, use
χρηστεύομαι, kind
χρηστοήθεια, kindness
χρηστολογία, *fair* word
χρηστός, easy, fine, good, kind, kindness, worthy
χρηστότης, good, goodness, kindliness, kindness
χρηστῶς, well
χρίσις, anoint
χρῖσμα, anoint, glazing
χρῖσμα ἔχω, anoint
χριστός, anoint
χρίω, anoint, commission
χρόα, color, surface
χρονίζω, delay, *long* delay, slow, tarry
χρόνος, age, day, delay, duration, during, lapse, long, old, period, time, while, year
χρονοτριβέω, spend *time*
χρυσίον, gold
χρυσοδακτύλιος, *gold* ring
χρυσοειδής, *like* gold
χρυσόλιθος, chrysolite
χρυσόπρασος, chrysoprase
χρυσός, gold, golden
χρυσουργός, worker *in gold*
χρυσοῦς, gold, golden
χρυσοφορέω, wear *gold*
χρυσοχάλινος, *gold* bridle, *golden* bridle
χρυσοχόος, goldsmith
χρυσόω, bedeck
χρύσωμα, gold, *gold* cup, *gold* plate, *gold* vessel, golden
χρῶμα, color
χρώς, body
χυλός, liquid
χύμα, flood
χύτρα, *clay* pot
χωλός, cripple, lame
χωνευτήριον, furnace
χωνεύω, cast
χώρα, country, countryside, field, land, local, neighborhood, province, realm, region, soil, vicinity, window
χωρέω, contain, find *a place*, hold, open *one's heart*, outcome, pass, penetrate, reach, receive, room, turn *out*
χωρίζω, away, depart, exclude, leave, part, put *asunder*, put *away*, remove, separate, set *apart*, set *off*, stranger
χωρίον, *city's* gate, field, land, place
χωρίς, apart, besides, beyond, deal, except, independent, out, separate, together, without
χωρίσμος, separateness

ψάλλω, make *melody*, sing, sing *praise*, *woman* singer
ψαλμός, hymn, psalm
ψαλτήριον, harp, lyre
ψάλτης, musician
ψάμμος, sand
ψαμμωτός, stucco
ψαύω, touch
ψέλιον, bracelet
ψευδάδελφος, *false* brother
ψευδαπόστολος, *false* apostle
ψευδής, deception, false, liar, lie, pretend, *something* false
ψευδοδιδάσκαλος, *false* teacher
ψευδολόγος, liar
ψεύδομαι, false, falsely, lie, prove *false*, tell *a lie*
ψευδομαρτυρέω, bear *false witness*
ψευδομαρτυρία, *false* testimony, *false* witness
ψευδόμαρτυς, *false* witness, misrepresent
ψευδοπροφήτης, *false* prophet
ψεῦδος, false, falsehood, lie
ψευδόχριστος, *false* Christ
ψεύδω, betray, break *a word*, deceive, liar, play *false*, *utter a* lie
ψευδώνυμος, call *falsely*
ψεῦσμα, falsehood
ψεύστης, false, liar
ψηλαφάω, feel *after*, handle, touch
ψηλάφησις, feel
ψηφίζω, count, reckon
ψήφισμα, decree, vote
ψηφολογέω, pave
ψῆφος, ballot, grain, stone, vote
ψιθυρίζω, whisperer
ψιθυρισμός, gossip
ψιθυριστής, gossip
ψίθυρος, slanderer, whisperer
ψιχίον, crumb
ψογίζω, throw *blame*
ψόγος, disgrace, reproach
ψυχαγωγία, please
ψυχή, advantage, being, breath, day, feel, heart, inclination, intend, inwardly, kind, life, live, *living* soul, mind, people, person, self, soul, spirit
ψυχὴ ἀνθρώπου, people
ψυχὴ ζωή, living *thing*
ψυχὴν αἴρω, keep *in suspense*
ψυχικός, mental, physical, unspiritual, worldly *people*
ψυχικῶς, heart, warmly
ψῦχος, cold, *winter* cold
ψυχουλκέομαι, *last* gasp
ψυχρός, cold
ψύχω, grow *cold*
ψωμίζω, eat, feed, give, give *away*
ψωμίον, morsel
ψώχω, rub

ὦ, alas
ὧδε, call, here, hither, place, there
ὠδίν, birth *pang*, birth-pang, pain, pang, travail
ὠδίνω, anguish, pang *of birth*, suffer *pangs*, travail, woman *in travail*
ὠμόλινον, burlap
ὠμός, cruel, *most* savage
ὦμος, arm, shoulder
ὠμότης, cruelty
ὠμότητα, savagery
ὠμόφρων, savage *of mind*
ὧν χάριν, result
ὠνέομαι, buy
ὥρα, day, *full* time, *good* time, hour, moment, short, time, while
ὥρα πολλή, late
ὡραῖος, attractive, attractive *thing*, beautiful, beautiful *thing*, fitting, lovely, timely, welcome
ὠρύομαι, howl, roar
ὡς, about, according, after, all, *any* way, appear, because, become, effect, equal, expect, how, *how* much, if, intend, just, like, pretend, purport, really, seem, since, soon, such, though, *under* pretext, way, well, what, when, where, while, yet
ὡς ἄν, however, when

ὡς ἂν ἐξαυτῆς, just *as soon*
ὡς ἐάν, like
ὡς εἰμί, seem
ὡς καί, just
ὡς ταχέως, soon *as possible*
ὡς τρυφερεύομαι, daintily
ὡσανεί, though
ὡσαύτως, like, *like* manner, likewise, same, same *way*
ὡσεί, about, like
ὡσεὶ περί, about
ὥσπερ, even, indeed, just, *just* like, like, though
ὥστε, even *to the thought of*, hence, make, point, purpose, result, such, then, therefore, thus
ὥστε καί, likewise
ὠτάριον, ear
ὠτίον, ear
ὠφέλεια, advantage, booty, profit, value
ὠφελέω, advantage, avail, benefit, do, *do* good, gain, good, help, profit, value
ὠφέλιμος, profitable, value

Latin

Aaron, Aaron
Abacuc, Habakkuk
Abdia, Obadiah
Abissei, Abishua
Abraham, Abraham
Achar, Achan
Achia, Ahijah
Acitob, Ahitub
Adam, Adam
Aegyptus, Egypt
Aggei, Haggai
Agyptius, Egyptian
Ameria, Amariah
Amos, Amos
Arabus, Arabia
Ardat, Ardat
Arna, Arna
Artaxerses, Artaxerxes
Arzar, Arzareth
Asia, Asia
Asihel, Asiel
Assur, Assyria
Assyrius, Assyrian
Azarei, Azariah
Aziei, Azariah

Babylon, Babylon
Babylonia, Babylon
Borith, Borith

Carmonius, Carmonian
Chananeus, Canaanite

Dabria, Dabria
Danihel, Daniel
David, David

Eleazar, Eleazar
Enoch, Behemoth
Esaia, Isaiah
Esau, Esau
Ethanus, Ethanus
Eufrates, Euphrates
Ezechias, Hezekiah
Ezra, Ezra

Ferezeus, Perizzite
Finees, Phinehas

Gerson, Gershom
Gomorra, Gomorrah

Helchia, Hilkiah
Heli, Eli
Helias, Elijah
Hieremia, Jeremiah
Hieremihel, Jeremiel
Hierusalem, Jerusalem
Horeb, Horeb

Iacob, Jacob
Iesus, Joshua
Iohel, Joel
Iona, Jonah
Ionatha, Jonathan
Iosiae, Hoshea
Isaac, Isaac
Israhel, Israel
Iuda, Judah

Levi, Levi
Leviathan, Leviathan
Levites, Levite
Libanus, Lebanon

Malachia, Malachi
Marimoth, Meraioth
Medus, Mede
Micha, Micah
Mnestheus, Menestheus
Moyses, Moses

Naum, Nahum
Noe, Noah

Osee, Hosea
Ozia, Uzzi

Perses, Persian
Phalthihel, Phaltiel
Pharao, Pharaoh
Philistheus, Philistine

Sadoch, Zadok
Salame, Shallum
Salathihel, Salathiel
Salmanassar, Shalmaneser
Salomon, Solomon
Samuhel, Samuel
Sarea, Sarea
Sarei, Seraiah
Selemia, Selemia
Sennacherib, Sennacherib
Sidon, Sidon
Sina, Sinai
Sion, Zion
Sodoma, Sodom
Sodomitae, *people of* Sodom
Sodomitus, Sodom
Sofonia, Zephaniah
Syria, Syria

Tyrus, Tyre

Urihel, Uriel

Zaccharia, Zechariah

ab, aside, because, before, concerning, through
abalieno, alienate, estrange
abeo, go
abnego, deny
abscido, cut *off*
abscondo, conceal, hidden *thing*, hide, keep *secret*
absconse, secret
absolutio, interpretation
absorbo, drink *one's fill*
abstinentia, self-control
abundantia, abundance, plentiful, plenty, wealth
abundo, abound, plentiful
abutor, abuse
abyssus, deep, depth
accedo, come, come *near*
accipio, consider, receive, take
accusator, accuser
accuso, accuse
acinus, grape
actus, course
acuo, sharp
ad, about, according, against, before, bring, near, upon
ad quis, why
adaequo, similar
adaperio, explain
adduco, bring, lead, lead *up*
adfero, bring
adfinis, relative
adhuc, again, *any* longer, besides, continue, further, just, more, moreover, still, yet
adhuc alius, more
adicio, *any* more, continue, tell *more*
adimpleo, reach *a limit*
adinventio, device, imagination
adiutorium, help, helper
adlevo, relieve
adlido, wreck
adligo, tread
admitto, commit
adnuntio, announce, declare, tell
adoro, adore
adpropinquo, hand, begin, come *near*, draw *near*
adquiro, get
adsimilo, like, liken, make *like*
adsto, stand *before*
adsum, hand, here
adtendo, consider, regard
adulor, defer
advena, stranger
advenio, assemble, come, come *here*, descendant
advento, appear
adversarius, enemy
adversum, against
adverto, against
advoco, call
adzelor, angry
aedificium, building
aedifico, build, build *a house*
aer, air
aeramentum, brass
aestas, summer
aestimo, consider, establish, judge
aestus, heat
aeternitas, everlasting, evermore
aeternus, everlasting
ager, field
agger, heap
ago, act, commit, do, give, pass *life*
agrestis, field, wild
agricola, farmer
ala, wing
alienigena, stranger
alieno, deprive
alienus, strange
aliqui, any, some
aliquis, another, other, some *things*
alius, another, any, different, else, following *one*, more, other, other *thing*, second
alius alio, one *another*
alligo, bind
altare, altar
alteruter, one *another*, other
altitudo, height
altus, deep, high, *most* high
amarico, bitter
amaritudo, bitter
amarus, bitter, embitter
amator, lover
ambulo, go, walk
amicus, friend
amitto, lose
amodo, henceforth, hereafter, immediately, once, then
amplector, embrace
amplius, long
amplus, great, long, more
ancilla, handmaid
angelus, angel, messenger
angustia, anguish, difficult
angustus, difficult, narrow, straits
anima, soul
animal, beast, *living* creature
animus, heart, mind, sincerely, spirit
anniculus, year *old*
annona, provision
annus, year
ante, about, ago, before, beforehand, old
ante facies, before
ante lucem, dawn
antepono, determine, set *before*
antequam, before
antiquitas, *former* state
antiquus, primeval
anxio, distress
aper, wild *boar*
aperio, open
apertus, open
apostata, faithless
appareo, appear, see
apparesco, appear
apprehendo, seize, understand
appropinquo, approach, symbolize
apud, before, between, lay *up*
aqua, water
aquila, eagle
arbor, tree
arca, ark
archangelus, archangel
arcus, bow
ardeo, flame
ardesco, melt
ardor, *burning* wrath, heat
area, *threshing* floor, time *of threshing*
arefacio, dry *up*
argentum, silver
arguo, denounce, reprove
aridus, wither
ascendo, ascend, come *up*, go *up*, light, well *up*
aspectus, look
aspicio, look, look *upon*
assatura, portion
assimilo, symbolize
assumo, take *up*
attamen, yet

audax, decisive
audeo, dare
audio, hear, listen, *surely* hear
aufero, take, take *away*
auris, ear
aurum, gold
aut, then
autem, moreover, nevertheless, now, only, yet
averto, turn, turn *back*

baiulo, burden
beatifico, bless
bellator, warrior
bellicosus, war
bello, make *war*
bellum, war, warfare
bene, rightly
beneficium, benefit
beo, bless
bestia, beast
bibo, drink
blasphemia, blasphemy
blasphemo, blaspheme
bonitas, goodness
bonus, good, good *thing*, virtuous
botrus, cluster, cluster *of grapes*
brachium, arm
buxum, *writing* tablet

cacumen, top
cado, fall, fall *down*
caecus, blind *man*
caelestis, heavenly
caelum, heaven
calcaneum, heel
calix, cup
camelus, camel
camera, arch
campester, plain
campus, field, *open* country, plain
candelabrum, lampstand
candidatus, people *clothed in white*
cano, sound
canticum, song
capax, possible
capio, able, comprehend, hold, make
capit vestigium, walk
captivitas, captivity
captivo, carry *away captive*, take *captive*
captivus, captive, captivity
caput, head
carbo, coal
caritas, love
carnalis, bodily
caro, flesh, meat
carta, paper
carus, dear, *most* dear
caste, pure
castigatio, punishment
castigo, punish
castrum, camp
casus, fall, fate, misfortune, over, trouble
celer, soon
celeritas, swiftness
celsus, great
cera, wax
certamen, contest
certe, even, surely
certo, strive, wage *a contest*
certus, indeed
cesso, cease
ceterus, other
chaus, chaos
christus, Messiah
cibo, feed
cilicium, haircloth
cinis, ash
circa, way
circueo, surround
circuitus, about
circum, about
circumcisio, circumcision
circumfero, embrace
circumteneo, seize *on every side*
circumventio, fraud
cito, swift
civis, neighbor
civitas, city
clamo, cry, cry *out*
claritas, brightness, brilliance, glory, splendor
claudo, close
claudus, lame *man*
clibanus, furnace
coadulesco, grow *up*
coepio, about, begin
coerceo, restrain
cogitamentum, meaning, thought
cogitatio, device, intrigue, plan, plot, thought
cogitatus, plan, thought
cogito, concern, consider, engage, intend, make, plan, think, wonder
cognatio, clan
cognosco, acknowledge, know, recognize, understand
cohero, cling
coinquino, defile
colligo, gather, gather *together*
collis, hill
colo, cultivate
color, color
columba, dove
columna, pillar
coma, hair
comedo, devour
commendo, commit, entrust
comminor, threaten
commisceo, associate, involve, mingle
committo, commit
commoneo, instruct, warn
commoror, dwell
commoveo, move, shake, trouble
commuto, change
compareo, see, visible
complector, embrace
complicatio, perplexity
conburo, burn
concido, fall
concipio, content
concludo, conclude, enclose
conculcatio, tread *under foot*
conculco, trample *upon*, tread *down*
concupiscentia, appeal
concupisco, desire, long
condemno, condemn
confero, bestow
confido, believe, confident, put *trust*, take *courage*
confirmo, establish, lay, strengthen
confiteor, confess
conforto, strengthen
confractio, plague
confringo, injure, ruin
confundo, confusion, put *to shame*
confusio, confusion
congrego, gather, gather *together*
conlaudo, praise
conlido, dash *against*
connumero, number *among*
conpareo, appear
complector, ally
compleo, complete, end, fulfil
conprehendo, comprehend
consentio, consent
consequor, obtain, receive
conservo, guard, keep, keep *in existence*, preserve, retain
considero, consider, look
consigno, seal
consilium, counsel, plan
consisto, stay
consolo, comfort, console
consolor, console
consors, share
conspectus, sight
conspicio, look
conspiro, combine
constabilitio, unrest
constanter, steadily
constituo, commandment, devise, place
constitutio, prescribed *order*, statute
consto, engage
constringo, choke
consuetudo, rule
consummatio, end
consummo, gain
consumo, burn, consume, destroy, kill
contamino, pollute
contemno, contemptuous, despise
contemptus, contempt
contentio, struggle
contero, break, wipe *out*
conterreo, shatter *utterly*
conticesco, silence
contingo, befall, come *upon*, go, happen, occur, overtake
contra, against, before, opposite, side
contradico, oppose, speak *against*
contrarius, oppose
contristo, grieve, sorrow
contritio, destruction
contumelia, abuse, insolence
conturbo, disturb, stir *up*, trouble
convalesco, grow *strong*
convenio, come
conventio, assemble
conversionem facio, turn *in repentance*
converso, lead *a life*, live
converto, convert, live, turn, turn *back*
converto pedes, turn
convivium, feast
convoco, call *together*
convolo, fly
copiosus, abundance, great, heavy, much
cor, heart, mind, understanding
coram, before, face, presence, sight
corona, circle, crown
corono, crown
corpus, body
corripio, admonish, reprove
corrumpo, *become* corrupt, destroy, ruin
corruptela, corruption
corruptibilis, corruptible, corruption, mortal, perish
corruptio, corruption
corruptus, corrupt, corruptible, mortal
corum, cor
coruscatio, lightning
corusco, flash *lightning*
coruscus, lightning
cotidie, daily
coturnix, quail
crastinum, *next* day, tomorrow
creata creatura, creation
creatio, create, product
creator, creator
creatura, created *thing*, creation, creature
credo, believe, entrust, trust
creo, bring *forth*, create, produce
cresco, grow, grow *up*, increase
cruciamentum, torment
cruciatus, torment
crucio, punish, torment, torture
cubile, bed
cultor, farmer
cultura, cultivation
cum, after, along, amid, among, because, see, since, when, while
cum sono, aloud
cupio fornicari, lust
curiosus, curious
curo, care, heal, respect
currus, chariot
custodio, keep, observe, protect

de, about, against, among, because, concern, concerning, out, some
de qua res, why
debello, make *war*, make *war against*, subdue
debeo, ought
debilis, weak
decem, ten
decet, becoming
declino, incline
decoris, beautiful, beauty
decurro, flow
deduco, bring, make
defatigatio, exhaustion
defendo, defend
deficio, fail, faint, miss
defleo, weep
deleo, blot *out*
delictum, sin, transgression
delinquo, sinner, transgress, wicked
demolio, destroy
demolior, demolish, throw *down*
demonstro, disclose, display, give *an explanation*, reveal, show
dens, tooth
deorsum, beneath
depono, lay, put *off*
deprecatio, prayer
deprecor, beseech, entreat, pray
deputo, repute
derelinquo, break *off*, forsake, leave, remain, transgress
derisus, derision
descendo, come *down*, go *down*
desero, lay *waste*
desertio, desolation, solitude
desertum, desert, wilderness
desertus, desolate
deservio, serve
desiderabilis, desirable
desidero, desire, love
desino, cease
desolatio, desolation
destrictio, harvest
destruo, destroy
detabesco, *utterly* waste *away*
deterior, bad
detineo, keep
deus, God
devasto, destroy, lay *waste*
devinco, conquer
devoratio, consume, eat
devoro, consume, devour
dexter, right, *right* hand
dico, answer, command, describe, dictate, direct, mention, oppose, promise, say, speak, speak *out*, talk, tell
dictum, utterance
die, day, daytime
difficile, hard
dignus, worthy
diligenter, carefully
diligentia, commandment
diligo, love
diluvium, flood
dimidium, half, half *as long*

dimidius, half
dimitto, dismiss, let *alone*, put *away*, return, send
directio, uprightness
direptio, ruin
dirigo, assure, prosper
diripio, plunder
discedo, depart, pass *away*
discindo, rend
disciplina, correction
discredo, disbelieve
discumbo, lie
disperdo, destroy
dispereo, perish
dispergo, die, scatter
dispono, devote, direct, guide, make, ordain, organize, set *in order*
dispositio, arrangement, command, covenant
dissipo, scatter
dissolvo, end
distinctio, meaning
dius, god
divido, divide, separate
divisio facio, separate
do, assign, bring, do, endow, form, give, give *over*, grant, *make* hear, produce, provide, send, utter
doceo, inform, teach
doleo, grief, grieve, lament, pity, sorrowful
dolor, affliction, mourn, pain, sorrow
dolus, deceit
dominatio, prevail
dominator, sovereign
dominor, dominate, domineer, gain *dominion over*, navigate, rule
dominus, lord, Lord, master
domus, house, household
donator, giver
donec, until
dono, give
dormio, asleep, sleep
draco, dragon
ducatus, leader
duco, lead
dulcis, sweet
dum, long, while
duo, two
duodecim, twelve
dux, chief, guide, leader, ruler

ebdomada, week
ecce, behold, here
educo, bring, bring *out*, bring *up*, come, lead *forth*, lead *out*
effero, exalt
efficio, affect
effugio, escape
effundo, pour *out*, shed
egens, needy
eicio, drive
Eleazar, Eleazar
electus, elect, precious
eligo, choose
eminens, height, lofty, tall
emitto, break *out*, send, send *forth*, shoot *forth*, sound, utter
emo, buy
enarro, declare, explain, tell
enim, because, haste, now, then, yet
enutrio, bring *up*
eo, go
epulum, *marriage* feast
equus, horse
ergo, then, therefore
erigo, rise *up*, set *up*
eripio, deliver
eructo, pour *forth*
erudio, discipline, instruct
esca, food, nourishment
esurio, hungry
et, both, even, even *so*, if, moreover, nevertheless, now, then, thus, well, when, where, while, yet
etiam valde, too
eurus, east
everto, overthrow, put *out*
evidens, hear
evigilo, awake, rouse *up*
ex, after, consequence, other, out, some
ex hoc, therefore
exalto, exalt, rise
exardesco, set *on fire*
exaudio, hear, listen
excedo, bewilder, fail, fail *utterly*, withdraw
excello, uplift
excelsus, high
excessus, bewilderment, disturb, perplexity
excessus mentis, bewilderment
excido, cleave
excipio, receive, suffer
excito, arouse, raise *from the dead*, rouse
excludo, shut *off*
excomedo, consume
excuso, intercede
excutio, pull *out*, shake *off*
exeo, come, come *out*, go *forth*, go *out*, issue
exerceo, practice
exercitus, army, host
exhibeo, make
exigo, take *away*
exilis, brief
existimo, consider
existo, amaze
exitus, exit, portal
exorno, adorn, deck *out*, trick *out*
exoro, pray
expando, spread
expavesco, terrify
expecto, await
expergefacio, awake
expono, explain
expugno, conquer, wage *war*
exquiro, require, search *out*
exsurgo, arise, rise, rise *up*
exsurrectio, insurrection
extendo, spread *out*
exteritio, destruction
exterminium, destruction
extermino, abolish, destroy
extero, break *down*, destroy, perish
extinguo, banish, extinguish, put *out*, quench
extollo, lift *up*
extritio, misery
extruo, raise
exubero, run *over*
exultatio, joy, rejoicing
exulto, exult, rejoice
exuo, divest

faceo, yet
facies, appear, appearance, before, countenance, face, presence
facilis, good
facinus, evil *deed*
facio, afford, become, befall, bring, bring *forth*, cause, come, commit, create, deed, do, fill, give, happen, lead *away*, make, maker, occur, perform, produce, publish, *really* yield, remove, set, show
facio conmigrationem, fly *away together*
facio sermonem, say
facio venire, bring
factum, deed, work
faenum, grass
fallo, deceive
false, wickedly
fames, famine, hunger
famula, servant
fastidio, scorn
fatigo, *become* weary, weary
femur, thigh
fero, bear, endure, spread
ferrum, iron
ferveo, burn *hotly*
festino, hasten, hasten *swiftly*, *make* haste, quick
festus, feast
fetus, child
fictilis, clay, earthenware
fidelis, trustworthy
fidem non habeo, unfaithful
fides, faith, faithfulness, trust
fiducia, boldness
fidus, friend
figmentum, creation, creature, workmanship
filia, daughter
filius, brood, child, son
fingo, form
finio, complete, end, finish
finis, border, end, goal
fio, become, come, come *into being*, *come to* pass, destine, do, flash, make, produce
firmamentum, firmament
fissura, cleft
flagellum, scourge
flamma, flame
flatus, wind
fleo, weep
floreo, flourish
flos, flower
fluctuo, churn *up*
fluctus, stream, wave
flumen, river, stream
fluo, flow
folium, leaf
fons, fountain, spring
fornax, furnace
fornicaria, harlot
fornicatio, harlotry
fortassis, perhaps, probably
forte, perhaps
fortis, almighty, mighty *one*, strong, strong *man*
fortiter, bravely, valiantly
fortitudo, strength
framea, spear
frater, brother
fraudo, deal *unfaithfully*
frequens, full
frequenter, often
frigus, cold
fructifero, bear *fruit*
fructifico, bear *fruit*, bring *forth fruit*
fructus, fruit, profit
fructus areae, harvest
frumentum, grain
fruniscor, enjoy
fugio, flee
fulcio, involve
fulgeo, shine
fumus, smoke
fundamentum, foundation
fundo, fix, found, pour *out*

gallina, hen
gaudeo, glad, joyful, rejoice
gaudium, joy
gehenna, Gehenna, hell
gelu, frost, ice
gemitus, groan, sorrow
gemo, great, groan
generatio, descendant, offspring, posterity
genero, bear, beget, produce
gens, Gentile, nation, people
genus, race
genus humanum, mankind
germino, bring *forth*, come *into being*
gero, act, do, wield
gigno, bear
gladius, sword
gleba, lump
gloria, glory, pride
glorifico, give *glory*, glorify, receive *glory*
glorior, glory
gloriosus, glorify
grando, hail
granum, grain
gratia, favor, grace, gratitude, thanks
gravis, weighty
gravo, burden, load
grex, flock
guberno, govern
gusto, eat, taste
gustus, taste
gutta, drop, drop *of water*, raindrop

habeo, deem, draw, grow, judge, live, maintain, practice
habeo longanimitatem, patient
habitaculum, habitation
habitatio, dwelling, residence
habito, dwell, inhabit, live
haesito, doubt
harena, sand
herba, plant
hereditas, inheritance
heredito, inherit
heres, heir
hic, here, such, thus
hiems, winter
hilaris, rejoice
hodie, day
homicidium, murder
homo, human, *human* being, man, mankind, people
honestas, wealth
honorifico, give *glory*
honos, glory
hora, hour, time
horreo, horror-stricken, shudder, terrify
horribilis, terrify
horridus, threaten
hostis, adversary
huc, here
humanus, man
humidus, watery
humilio, afflict, *great* affliction, humble, lay *low*
humilis, lowly
humilitas, humiliation, *low* estate
hymnus, song

iaceo, lie
iam, again, already, *any* longer, long, now
ibi, there
ideo, therefore
ideoque, therefore
idolum, idol
idoneus, respectable, worthy
ieiuno, fast
ignis, fire
ignoro, know
ignosco, pardon
ille, other
imago, image, picture
imitor, imitate
immaturus, premature
immensus, mighty
immitto, pour *down*, put, send, send *upon*, shoot
imperium, power
impero, command, rule *over*
impetus, assault, onrush, onrushing, violent
impetus pluviae, rainstorm
impie, wickedly
impietas, ungodliness, ungodly, ungodly *deed*, wickedness

impiger, swift
impius, godless, ungodly, ungodly *thing*
impleo, complete, fill, fulfil
impono, place
improperium, reproach
impropero, reproach
in, after, against, among, before, concerning, during, like, midst, over, regard, through, throughout, until, upon, when, within
in fugam, flee
in proximo, close *at hand*
in quibus, when
in quo, when
in sempiterno, never
inaestimabilis, *beyond* measure
incendium, burn
incendo, burn, kindle
inchoo, begin
incido, fall
incipio, about, begin, undertake
inclino, bend *down*
includo, shut *up*
inconpositus, waste
inconprehensibilis, *beyond* comprehension
inconstabilitio, indecision
inconstantia, waver
incontinentia, unrestraint
incorruptio, incorruption
incorruptus, unspoiled
incredulitas, unbelief
incredulus, unbeliever
incresco, grow *up*, increase
inde, there
indeficiens, unfailing
indignatio, indignation
indignor, angry
indignus, unworthy
indisciplinatus, rebellious
induco, bring, bring *upon*, lead
inebrio, drunk
infans, child, infant
infernus, Hades, hell
infero, *come to* pass
infirmitas, disease, illness, infirmity
infirmo, weaken
infirmus, weak
inflammo, arouse
infructuosus, unfruitful
infulcio, cast *up*
ingratus, ungrateful, unseemly
ingredior, enter, go, go *into*, pass *through*, reach
inhabitantes, inhabitant
inhabitatio, habitation
inhabito, dwell, inhabit, live
inimicus, enemy
inimitabilis, inimitable
inique, wicked
iniquitas, guilt, iniquity
iniquus, unrighteous
initio, beginning, first
initium, beginning, former
iniuste, harm, iniquity
iniustitia, iniquity, unrighteous *deed*, unrighteousness, wickedness
iniustus, unrighteous
inlumino, enlighten
inmensus, endless, vast
inmortalis, eternal, immortal, immortality
inmortalitas, immortality
innocuus, innocent
innoxius, innocent
innumerabilis, innumerable
inpedio, delay
inpetro, obtain
inproperium, contempt
inquiro, ask *a question*, inquire, require
inreligiose, impiously
inrito, anger
insanio, rage
insanus, mad *man*
insipiens, *without* wisdom
inspiratio, spirit
instituo, appoint
instruo, instruct
insuflo, blow, breathe
intellectus, meaning, understanding, wisdom
intellego, know, think, understand, wise
intemperantia, *sinful* indulgence
intendo, attend, give *heed*, pay *attention*
inter, among, between
interdie, during *the day*
intereo, die, perish
interficio, kill, slay
interitus, destruction, *no* effect
intermissio, cease
intermitto, pass
interpretatio, interpretation
interpretor, explain
interrogo, ask, inquire
intra, within
introeo, enter, go
introitus, entrance, passage
introrsus, far *in the interior*
invalidus, powerless, weak
invenio, discover, find
investigabilis, inexhaustible, inexpressible
investigo, reckon, search *out*
invicem, one *another*
invius, *where no* road
invoco, call, call *upon*
ipse, same, together, very
ira, wrath
iracundia, anger, wrath
irrideo, ridicule
irritus, void
ita, yes
item, example
iter, journey, set *out*, way
iterato, again, yet
iterum, again, fresh, hereafter, once *more*
iterum constituo, regain *power*
iubeo, command
iucunditas, delight, joy
iucundo, joyful, make *joyful*, rejoice
iudex, judge
iudicium, judgment, *judgment* seat
iudico, deem, judge, secure *justice*
iumentum, cattle
iussio, ordinance
iussum, command
iustifico, account *righteous*, acknowledge *to be just*, guard *a right*, justify
iustitia, righteous *deed*, righteousness
iustus, right, righteous, righteous *man*, righteous *one*
iuvenis, young, young *man*
iuventus, youth
iuxta, according

labia, lip
labor, care, effort, hardship, labor, laboriously, *much* care, oppression, travail, trouble
labore multo, oppressively
laboriosus, toilsome
laboro, labor, toil, trouble
lac, milk
lacus, pit, pool
laedo, injure
laetitia, gladness
laetor, glad
lanio, tear *in pieces*
lapis, stone
lapsus, fail
latibulum, hiding *place*
latitudo, broad *part*
laudo, give *praise*
lectus, bed
legislator, lawgiver
legitimus, statute
lego, read
leo, lion
levis, short
levo, lift, raise *up*
levus, left
lex, law
liber, book, free *man*
libero, deliver, free
libertas, freedom
lignum, tree, wood
lilium, lily
lingua, tongue
liquesco, melt
locus, expanse, opportunity, place
locusta, locust
longanimis, patient
longanimitas, patience
longe, far
loquor, declare, mention, say, speak, talk, tell
luceo, shine
lucerna, lamp
luctus, mourning
lugeo, lament, mourn, mourner, wail
lumen, lamp, light, ray
luna, moon
lupus, wolf
lux, light

maculo, defile
maeror, pain
maestitia, sadness
magis, best, more
magnifico, praise
magnitudo, vastness
magnus, great, great *thing*, huge, large, loud, more, profound
male, wickedly
malignitas, evil
malignus, cruel, evil, malicious
malus, adversity, affliction, bad, calamity, evil, grievous, *most* evil, *most* wicked, wicked
mamilla, breast
mancus, maim
mandatum, commandment
mando, command, command *strictly*, lay *a commandment upon*
manduco, eat
mane, morning
maneo, abide, await, remain
manifestus, manifest
manna, manna
mansuetus, meek
manus, hand, power
marcesco, wither
mare, sea
maritus, husband
mastigo a vulneribus, wound
mater, mother
matrix, womb
medella, healing
medietas, midst
medium, middle, midst
medius, half
megestanes, leader
mel, honey
membrum, member
memor, mindful, remember
memoria, memory, remembrance
memoro, recall, remember
mendacium, falsehood
mendax, liar
mens, mind
mensa, table
mensis, month
menstruo, menstruous
mensura, measure, quantity
mensuro, measure
merces, reward
mercor, *do* business
meridianus, south
meridies, noon
messem facio, reap
metior, measure *carefully*
meto, gather, measure, reap
metuo, afraid
militia, host
ministro, service
minoro, shorten
minutus, little
mirabilis, praiseworthy, wonder, wondrous, wondrous *thing*, wondrous *work*
miraculo, spellbind
miror, amaze, marvel
miser, miserable, unhappy
miserator, gracious
misereo, merciful, mercy, pity, *show* mercy
misereor, gracious, mercy, pity
miseria, misery
misericordia, compassion, mercy
misericors, merciful
mitto, give, give *up*, launch, send, send *forth*, shoot, throw
modicus, few, little, puny, short
modo, now
molestus, grievous, *most* grievous
momentum, turn
mons, mount, mountain
monstrum, monster
monumentum, tomb
morior, death, die, *must* die, perish
moror, delay
mors, death
mortalis, bring *death*, mortal
mortifico, take *away life*
mortuus, corpse, dead, lifeless
mos, way
motio locorum, earthquake
motus, movement
moveo, move, stir *up*
mox, once
mugio, roar
mulier, wife, woman
multiformis, vary
multiplico, abound, abundant, great, increase, *make* abound, multiply, multitude, produce
multitudo, abundance, great, many, multitude, overpower, *too* much
multo, still
multus, abundant, far, flood, great, heavy, long, many, many *things*, more, much, profound
multus magis, *very* much
multus plurimus, *very* many
mundus, world
munificus, bountiful
munitus, safe
murmuro, complain
murus, wall
muto, change
mutus, dumb
mysterium, secret

nam, however, now, yet
narro, declare
nascor, arise, bear, child, descend, grow, spring
natio, nation
nativitas, birth, origin
natura, nature
natus, descendant, man
navis, ship
ne, no

nec, even, neither, no, nor
nec quisquam, no *one*
necdum, yet
necessitas, distress, pang
neglego, disregard, give *heed*, neglect
nego, answer *no*, deny
negotior, conduct *business*
nemo, any *one*, no *one*
nempe, surely
neomenia, *new* moon
neque, even, neither, no, nor
nescio, know
niger, black
nihil, anything, nothing
nimbus, storm *cloud*
nisi, except, if *not*, only
nitor, flash, shine
noceo, *do* harm, doer *of iniquity*
nocivus, harmful
nolo, *against the* will, continue, nothing
nomen, name
nomino, call, honor, name
non, any, avoid, neither, never, no, without
non appareo, disappear, *surely* disappear
non calco, untrodden
non cognosco, ignore
non conpareo, disappear
non corruptus, incorruptible
non memoro, unmindful
non modicus, great
non nisi, only
non numerus, innumerable
non possum, cannot, unable
non semino, unsown
non sum, without
non umquam, never
nondum, yet
nonus, ninth
nosco, know
nota, character
notus, south
novem, nine
novus, last
nox, evening, night
nubes, cloud
nubo, marry
nudus, naked
numero, count, count *up*, number
numerus, number
numquam, never, no *ever*
numquid, any
nunc, day, now, recently, soon
nuntio, tell
nusquam, never, *no* longer
nutrio, bring *up*, nourish
nutrix, nurse

obaudio, obey
oblatio, oblation, offering
oblino, forget
obliviscor, forget
obmutesco, destroy
oboedio, obey
obscurus, dark
observo, keep, observe
obsideo, beset
obtego, overwhelm
occidens, west
occido, kill, sacrifice
occisio, slaughter
occulo, hide
occurro, attain
octavus, eighth
octo, eight
oculus, eye, sight
odi, hate, *really* hate
odibilis, hateful
odiosus, hateful
odor, fragrant, odor, smell
odoramentum, fragrance
offero, offer, offering
olim, before, formerly
oliva, olive
olivetum, *olive* orchard
omitto, leave *out*
omni tempore, always
omnipotens, almighty
omnis, all, *all* men, all *things*, any, every, every *one*, everything, whole
omnis qui, whoever
omnis unusquisque, every *one*
operatio, deed
operor, till
oportet, must
opprobrium, reproach
opto, desire
opus, deed, do, recompense, work
orabo, beseech
oraculum, *inner* sanctuary
oratio, pray, prayer
orbis, circle, earth, whole, world
orbis terrarum, earth
ordo, order
orfanus, orphan
oriens, east, *rising* sun
orientalis, east
orior, appear
orno, deck *out*
oro, pray
os, mouth
ostendo, disclose, explain, make *manifest*, manifest, reveal, show
ostensio, Urim
ovis, sheep

pacificus, peaceable
paene, almost
paenitentia, repentance
palam, openly, public, publicly
palma, palm
panis, bread
paradisus, garden, paradise
parco, spare
parens, parent
pareo, *become* manifest, manifest
pario, bear, bring *forth*, child, give *birth*, travail
paro, prepare, ready, supply, train
pars, part, portion, side
partus, birth, delivery
parvulus, child, little *one*
parvus, little, small
pastor, shepherd
pater, father
patior, allow, distress, endure, happen, suffer
paucus, few
paulatim, little *by little*
paululus, *little* while
paupera, wretched *woman*
paupertas, poverty
pausa, pause
paveo, frighten
pavor, fear
pax, peace
peccator, sinner
peccatum, sin
pecco, offend, sin, transgress
pectus, breast
pecus, cattle, flock
penes, midst
per, account, during, sake, through
per nomina, individual
per saeculum, ever
per tempus, one *after another*, time *to time*
percipio, give, receive
percontineo, gain *control*
percussio, clap
percutio, smite, strike *down*
perditio, destruction, perdition
perdo, destroy, lose
peregrinatio, pilgrimage
peregrinor, dwell *as an alien*
perennis, everlasting
pereo, perish
perfecte, perfectly
perficio, accomplish, establish, finish, perfect, perform
periclitor, danger, incur *peril*
periculum, danger, peril
permaneo, permanent, remain
permitto, grant, permit
perpetuus, eternal
perrogo, ask
persequor, pursue
perseveranter, continually
persevero, certain, remain
persona, person
persuadeo, assure, persuade
persuasum, obedient
pertranseo, end, experience, go, pass, pass *away*, pass *through*, past, travel *widely*
pervideo, look *upon*
pes, foot
pessime, miserably
pestis, pestilence
peto, ask, beg
petra, rock
piceus, pitch
pinguis, fertile
pinna, feathered, wing
pinnaculum, *little* wing, wing
piscis, fish
placeo, please, take *pleasure*
plaga, plague, scourge
plago, beat
planctus, lamentation
plango, wail
plantatio, plant, seedling
planto, form, plant
plasma, fashion
plasmatio, form, work
plasmo, fashion, form, make
platea, highway
plebs, people
plenissime, fully
plenitudo, abundance
plenus, full, full *thing*
ploro, weep
plumbum, lead
pluvia, rain
pomifer, fruitful
pondero, weigh
pondus, burden, weight
pono, lie, make, put, set
populus, people
porrigo, offer
porta, gate
portentum, wonder
portio, part, portion
porto, bear, bring, carry, support
portus, haven
possessio, possession
possibilis, possible
possido, inherit, possess
possum, able, can, mighty, strong
post, after, afterward, besides, then
postea, afterwards, again
postquam, after
potentatus, power, sway
potentia, might
potestas, power
potiono, give *to drink*
poto, water
potus, drink
prae, beyond, more *than*, than
praebeo, supply
praecedo, previous
praecingo, gird
praecipio, command, precept
praecipitium, precipitous *place*
praedico, aforesaid, foretell, predict, predicted *thing*, proclaim, promise, tell
praegnans, *woman with* child
praemium, reward
praeparo, prepare, provide
praepondero, pull *down*
praesens, alive, live, live *now*, now, *now* living, present, *thing* present
praesto, bestow, bring *upon*, furnish, provide
praesum, charge
praeter, besides
praetereo, go, pass, past, previous, transgress
pratum, meadow
precatio, petition
pressura, tribulation
pretiosus, *more* precious, precious
primogenitus, first-born
primus, first, former
princeps, chief, prince
principatus, power, rule
principium, beginning, first, source
prior, *all* others, ancestor, first, former, former *one*
prius, before
priusquam, before
pro, account, behalf, case, rather *than*, stead
probatio, *tested* quality
probo, approve, test
procedo, come *forth*, come *out*, go *forth*
procella, storm
proclamo, cry *out*
procreatio, child
procreo, bring *forth*
prodeo, come *forth*
prodigium, wonder
prodo, cast *out*
produco, bring *forth*
profano, profane
profero, bring *forth*
proficio, go, go *forth*, proceed
proficiscor, arise, depart, go, leave
profundus, depth
prohibeo, hinder, stop
proicio, cast *away*, cast *out*, drive *out*, hurl, reject
prolongo, go *far away*
promitto, promise
promptuarius, chamber, storehouse
propero, hasty
propheta, prophet
prophetia, prophecy
propono, propose, put *before*
propter, above, account, because, over, reason, sake, therefore, why
propter quod, why
propterea, because, therefore
prosum, good, profit
protego, defend
provideo, foreordain, observe, provide
provincia, province
proximus, kinsman, neighbor
psalmus, psalm
psalterium, harp
pudicitia, purity
puer, servant
pugna, battle, fight
pugno, fight
pulchritudo, loveliness
pulvis, dust
punctum, scale

pungo, moment
punio, punishment
punitio, punishment
pupillus, fatherless
pusillus, *little* while
puto, imagine, prune, think

quadrupes, four-footed
quaero, seek, strive, try
qualis, *how* great
quam, how, rather *than*, than
quamdiu, more
quando, when
quando adhuc, before
quanto, *how* much
quantum, far, *how* long, *how* much, much
quantus, *how* many
quapropter, therefore
quare, why
quartus, fourth
quasi, like, since, though
quattuor, four
quemadmodum, how, just
quercus, oak
qui, thing, what, whatever *thing*
quia, because, whereas
quid, why
quidam, certain, some, some *things*
quidem, *full* well, indeed
quiescentia, rest
quiesco, peaceable, quiet, *remain* quiet, rest, stop
quinque, five
quintus, fifth
quis, any *one*, how, what, why
quisquis, whatever
quo, where
quo tempore, when
quoadusque, until
quod, because
quomodo, how, just
quoniam, because, indeed, since, therefore
quotquot, many

racemus, cluster
radico, take *root*
radix, root
rapina, plunder
rapio, carry *off*, plunder
rarus, *more* rare, rare
recapitulo, sum *up*
recedo, leave, move, recede
receptio, receive
recipio, receive, receive *back*, take *again*, take *up*
recludo, dispel
recte, rightly
recumbo, lie
recutio, drive *away*, drive *off*, turn *back*
redditio, recompense
reddo, give *back*, give *up*, repay, yield *up*
refrigero, refresh
regio, country, haunt, land, region, territory
regno, reign, rule
regnum, king, kingdom, reign
rego, righteous
reicio, cast *up*
relevo, relieve
relinquo, leave, remain, survive
relucesco, shine *forth*
remaneo, leave, remain
renes, heart
renovo, renew
renuntio, declare, renounce, solve
repleo, fill
repono, lay, lay *up*, reserve
reprobo, reject
repromitto, promise
repropitio, merciful *again*
reptilis, creeping *thing*
repudio, reject
requies, rest
requiesco, enjoy *rest*, rest
requietio, relief, rest
requiro, require, seek
reservo, keep
residuus, henceforth, other, remnant
resigno, lose *the seal*
respicio, look, regard
respondeo, answer, give *answer*, reply
respuo, refuse
resto, come *short*
resumo, recover
resurrectio, resurrection
resuscito, raise *up*
retineo, keep
revelo, reveal
revereor, fear
reversio, repentance
reverto, return
revertor, return
revirido, *make* bloom *again*
revivesco, live *again*
revoco, call *back*
rex, king
rivus, river, stream
rogo, ask, beseech, entreat, pray, request
romphea, sword
ros, dew
rosa, rose
rubus, bush
ruina, destruction

saccus, sackcloth
sacerdos, priest
sacrifico, offer *a sacrifice*
saeculum, age, beginning, eternity, time, world
sagitta, arrow
sagittarius, archer
saliva, spittle
salsus, salt
salus, salvation
saluto, salvation
salvatio, salvation
salvator, savior
salvo, preserve *alive*, save
salvus, save
sancio, holy, holy *thing*
sanctificatio, sanctuary
sanctifico, consecrate, make *holy*, sanctify
sanguis, blood
sapientia, wisdom
sapio, understanding, wise
satago, anxious
satietas, abundance
saturitas, abundance, satisfy
scabillum, footstool
scientia, knowledge
scintilla, spark
scio, know, learn, understand
scirtor, dance
scribo, write
scrutino, explore, search *out*
scruto, search *out*
scrutor, search, *strictly* examine
sculpo, carve, carve *out*
secrete, secretly
secretum, secret
secundum, according
secundus, other, second
securitas, healthful, safe
securus, safe
sed, however, rather *than*, yet
sed tamen, yet
sedeo, sit, stay
sedes, seat
seduco, lead *astray*
segrego, set *apart*
semen, descendant, seed
semino, plant, sow
semita, path, way
semper, always, ever
sempiternus, always
senectus, *old* age
senesco, age, *become* old, grow *old*
senex, old
sensus, mind, power, reason, spirit, thought, understanding
sententia, decree
sentio, feel
separatio, divide
separo, exist, reject, separate, withdraw
septem, seven
septentriones, north
septimus, seventh
sepulchrum, grave
sequor, follow, next, *yet* again
sermo, direct, reflection, speech, teaching, thing, word
sero, sow
serus, evening
servio, bondage, enslave, serve
servitus, bondage
servo, keep, protect, reserve, save
servus, servant
sessio, place
sex, six
sextus, sixth
si, if, though, whether
si enim, yet
si non, unless
sibilatus, hiss
sic, cannot, well
sicco, dry *up*, wither
sicut, about, just, like, much
sidus, tempest
signaculum, seal
signator, seal
significo, show
signo, mark, seal, seal *up*
signum, sign
silentium, quiet, silence, silently
sileo, silence, silent
silva, forest, *thick* grove, underbrush
similis, like
similiter, before, *like* manner, likewise
similitudo, likeness, parable, problem
similo, compare, like, make *like*
simul, *same* time, together
sine, without
sine anima, lifeless
sine causa, vain
sine intermissione, continually
singillatim, one *after another*
singuli, each, every
sinister, left
sinus, bosom
sitio, thirsty
sitis, thirst
sol, sun
solummodo, one, only
solus, alone, only, *without* help
solvo, come *to an end*
somniator, dreamer
somnio, dream
somnium, dream
sonitus vocis, cry
sono, resound, sound
sonus, sound
sors, possession
spatiosus, broad, easy, spacious, wide
spatium habeo, last
species, beauty, form, glamour, like
sperno, despise, scorn, *show* scorn
spero, expect, hope, look
spes, hope
spica, head *of grain*
spina, thorn
spiramentum, breath, spirit
spiritus, breath, spirit, wind
spiro, blow
splendeo, shine
splendide, gloriously
splendidus, glorious
splendor, brightness, splendor
spolio, plunder
spondeo, bridegroom
sponsio, covenant, promise
spretio, *contemptuous* dealing
statera, balance
statim, immediately, once, suddenly
statuo, set, stop
statura, stature
status, stature
stella, star
stercus, dung
sterilis, barren, barren *woman*
stillicidium, drop
stillo, drip
stipula, straw
sto, place, stand, stand *firm*, stand *still*, stand *up*
stramen, straw, stubble
studium, endeavor
stultus, foolish
sub, during, under
subduco, hide
subeo, go *up*
subicio, subject
subito, immediately, suddenly
subremaneo, leave, survive
subsequor, follow
subsessor, enemy *in ambush*
substantia, goods, store
subverto, devastate, overthrow
succendo, burn *to death*, burn *up*, consume
successio, turn
sufficio, sufficient
suffrago, hock
sui ipse, one *another*
sum, about, alive, appoint, come, exist, future *thing*, give, go *before*, happen, hold, live, live *hereafter*, mean, *yet to* come
sumo, put, take *back*
super, about, above, addition, against, among, better *than*, beyond, greater *than*, more *than*, over, than, throughout, up *upon*, upon
super omnes, most
superabundo, far *greater*
superbia, pride
superdico, even *declare*
superelevo, prevail *over*
superfloresco, spring *up*
superinvalesco, prevail *over*
supernus, upper
supero, leave, remain, survive
superpono, spread
supersigno, place *a seal upon*
superus, above
supervalesco, *become still* stronger, grow *strong against*
suppleo, complete
supradico, mention
surgo, arise, attempt, get *up*, rise
sursum, upward
susceptor, *thing that* holds
suscipio, hear, put, receive
suscito, arouse, raise, raise *up*
suspendo, suspend

suspiro, lamentation
sustineo, endure, hold, sustain, tolerate, wait, withstand

tabernaculum, habitation
tabesco, melt *away*
taceo, silent
tamen, yet
tanto magis, more
tantum, more, only
tantus, great, many, *such* great
tarditas, slowness
tardo, delay
tego, cover, overwhelm
tempestas, storm
templum, temple
tempus, age, due *course*, due *season*, due *time*, long, season, time, turn
tendo, bend
tenebrae, darkness
teneo, continue, grasp, hold, hold *sway*, rule
teneo principatum, rule
terminus, border, decisive, decree
terra, clay, earth, ground, land, world
terraemotus, earthquake
terrenus, earth
terribilis, terrible
territorium, land
tertius, third
testamentum, covenant
testificor, bear *witness*
testimonium, covenant, witness
testis, witness
testor, call, call *to witness*
thalamus, *wedding* chamber
thesaurizo, store *up treasure*
thesaurus, treasure, treasury
thronus, throne
timeo, afraid, fear, terrify
timor, fear
timoratior, *more* terrifying
timoratus, anxious
timore plenus, fearful
tinctura, color
tollo, remove
tonitrus, thunder
tono, thunder
tormento, torment
tormentum, agony, torment
torqueo, suffer *agony*, torment
tot tempus, long
totidem, *same* number
toto corde, profoundly
totus, all
trado, deliver, give, give *over*, hand *over*, put
trado ad vindemiam, ripen
traduco, make *a public spectacle*
traicio, bring
traiicio, pass *over*
trans, across
transeo, go, go *along*, go *before*, go *over*, pass, pass *away*, pass *over*, pass *through*, past, walk
transfero, depart, take, take *across*, turn
transgredior, transgress
transmigratio, exile
transmigro, escape, roam *beyond*
tremesco, tremble
tremo, quake, tremble
tremor, terror, tremble
trepido, tremble
tres, three
tribulatio, distress, tribulation
tribulo, afflict
tribus, tribe
tristis, sad, sorrowful
tristitia, grief, sadness, sorrow
tristitia contristo, *deep* grief
tristor, sorrowful
triumpho, exult
tuba, trumpet
tueor, defend
tumultus, tumult
tunc, *that* time, then
tunica, clothing, garment
turba, multitude
turbatio, confusion, tumult
turbo, confusion, disorganize, throw *into confusion*, trouble
tutela, protection
tuto, protect

ubi, way, when, where, wherever
ubicumque, whenever
ulter, *more* distant
ululo, mourn
umbra, shadow
umquam, ever
ungo, Messiah
unguentum, perfume
unguis, talon
unicus, only
unigenitus, *only* begotten
unus, another, one, same, together
unusquisque, each, every, every *man*, every *one*
uredo, blight
usque, high, still, until
usque dum, until
usquequo, *how* long, until
ut, just, like, order, purpose, what, when
ut non, lest
ut quis, why
uterque, both, each
utique, course
uva, grape
uxor, wife

vaco, apply
vacuus, empty, empty *thing*
vado, depart, go
vae, alas, woe
vagor, wander, wander *about*
valde, deeply, exceedingly, great, greatly, just, much, very, violently
validus, mighty, *most* appropriate
vanitas, vain
vanum, vain
vanus, foolish, vain, worthless
vanus facio, fail
vapor, mist
varius, various
vas, body, bucket, dish, mind, weapon
vasto, devastate, ruin
vel, least
velocitas, haste
velociter, rapidly
velox, *more* quickly
vena, channel, spring, stream
vendo, sell
venio, approach, come, *come to* pass, enter, go
venter, belly, womb
ventilo, agitate
ventus, wind
vepres, brier
ver, spring
verbero, chastisement
verbum, word
vereor, fear
veritas, truth
vero, now
vertex, top
verum, truth
verus, sure, true
vestimentum, clothes
vestio, clothe
via, conduct, opportunity, road, way
vicinus, neighbor
video, appear, behold, gaze, look, look *upon*, please, see, understand
vidua, widow
viduitas, widowhood
viduus, widow
vigilo, awake, watch
vilis, *less* worth
vilitas, cheap
vim patior, ravish
vinco, condemn, defeat, overcome, victorious
vindemia, vineyard, vintage
vindemio, gather, gather *grapes*
vindico, *surely* avenge
vinea, vine, vineyard
vinum, wine
violatio, destruction
violo, drive *violently*
vir, husband, man
virgo, virgin
virtus, *mighty* work, power, strength
vis, violence
visio, sight, vision
visito, visit
viso, appear
visus, countenance, vision
vita, life
vivifico, *certainly* give *life*, give *life*, life, *make* live
vivo, alive, life, lifetime, live
vivus, alive, live
vix, difficulty
voco, call
volatile, bird
volo, desire, fly, hover, intend, want, will, wish
voluntas, will, willingly
vox, cry, rumble, voice
vultus, face

zelo, abhor, deal *violently*, envy